Peterson's Four-Year Colleges

2011

About Peterson's

To succeed on your lifelong educational journey, you will need accurate, dependable, and practical tools and resources. That is why Peterson's is everywhere education happens. Because whenever and however you need education content delivered, you can rely on Peterson's to provide the information, know-how, and guidance to help you reach your goals. Tools to match the right students with the right school. It's here. Personalized resources and expert guidance. It's here. Comprehensive and dependable education content—delivered whenever and however you need it. It's all here.

For more information, contact Peterson's, 2000 Lenox Drive, Lawrenceville, NJ 08648 or call 800-338-3282.

© 2010 Peterson's, a Nelnet company

Facebook® and Facebook logos are registered trademarks of Facebook, Inc. Twitter™ and Twitter logos are registered trademarks of Twitter, Inc. Neither Facebook, Inc. nor Twitter, Inc. were involved in the production of this book and make no endorsement of this product.

Previous editions published as *Peterson's Annual Guide to Undergraduate Study* © 1970, 1971, 1972, 1973, 1974, 1975, 1976, 1977, 1978, 1979, 1980, 1981, 1982 and as *Peterson's Four-Year Colleges* © 1983, 1984, 1985, 1986, 1987, 1988, 1989, 1990, 1991, 1992, 1993, 1994, 1995, 1996, 1997, 1998, 1999, 2000, 2001, 2002, 2003, 2004, 2005, 2006, 2007, 2008, 2009

Stephen Clemente, Managing Director, Publishing and Institutional Research; Bernadette Webster, Director of Publishing; Mark D. Snider, Editor; Ward Brigham, Research Project Manager; Cathleen Fee, Research Associate; Phyllis Johnson, Programmer; Ray Golaszewski, Manufacturing Manager; Linda M. Williams, Composition Manager; Karen Mount, Danielle Vreeland, Shannon White, Client Relations Representatives; Charlotte Thomas, Richard Woodland, Contributing Authors

Peterson's makes every reasonable effort to obtain accurate, complete, and timely data from reliable sources. Nevertheless, Peterson's and the third-party data suppliers make no representation or warranty, either expressed or implied, as to the accuracy, timeliness, or completeness of the data or the results to be obtained from using the data, including, but not limited to, its quality, performance, merchantability, or fitness for a particular purpose, non-infringement or otherwise.

Neither Peterson's nor the third-party data suppliers warrant, guarantee, or make any representations that the results from using the data will be successful or will satisfy users' requirements. The entire risk to the results and performance is assumed by the user.

ALL RIGHTS RESERVED. No part of this work covered by the copyright herein may be reproduced or used in any form or by any means—graphic, electronic, or mechanical, including photocopying, recording, taping, Web distribution, or information storage and retrieval systems—without the prior written permission of the publisher.

For permission to use material from this text or product, complete the Permission Request Form at http://www.petersons.com/permissions.

ISSN 1544-2330
ISBN-13: 978-0-7689-2834-1
ISBN-10: 0-7689-2834-6

Printed in the United States of America

10 9 8 7 6 5 4 3 2 1 12 11 10

Forty-first Edition

By producing this book on recycled paper (40% post-consumer waste) 1,152 trees were saved.

R03127 13361

Certified Chain of Custody

60% Certified Fiber Sourcing and
40% Post-Consumer Recycled

www.sfiprogram.org

*This label applies to the text stock.

Sustainability—Its Importance to Peterson's, a Nelnet company

What does sustainability mean to Peterson's? As a leading publisher, we are aware that our business has a direct impact on vital resources—most especially the trees that are used to make our books. Peterson's is proud that its products are certified by the Sustainable Forestry Initiative (SFI) and that all of its books are printed on paper that is 40 percent post-consumer waste.

Being a part of the Sustainable Forestry Initiative (SFI) means that all of our vendors—from paper suppliers to printers—have undergone rigorous audits to demonstrate that they are maintaining a sustainable environment.

Peterson's continually strives to find new ways to incorporate sustainability throughout all aspects of its business.

Contents

COLLEGES AT-A-GLANCE

COLLEGE CLOSE-UPS

INDEXES

A Note from the Peterson's Editors

For nearly forty years, Peterson's has given students and parents the most comprehensive, up-to-date information on undergraduate institutions in the United States and Canada. *Peterson's Four-Year Colleges 2011* features advice and tips on the college search and selection process, such as how to consider the factors that truly make a difference during your search, how to understand the application process, and how to get financial aid. Each year, Peterson's researches the data published in *Peterson's Four-Year Colleges*. The information is furnished by the colleges and is accurate at the time of publishing.

Opportunities abound for students, and this guide can help you find what you want in a number of ways:

- For application and admissions advice and guidance, just head to **THE ADVICE CENTER**. Within the **Search, Find, Select** section, the "College Admissions Countdown Calendar" outlines pertinent month-by-month milestones. "Choosing Your Top Ten Colleges" gets you started on putting together the most important top ten list you have ever made. "Surviving Standardized Tests" describes frequently used tests and what you need to know to succeed on them. Of course, part of the college selection process involves visiting the schools themselves, and "The Whys and Whats of College Visits" is just the planner you need to make those trips well worth your while. Next, "Applying 101" provides advice on how best to approach the application phase of the process. If you can't make sense out of the early decision/early action conundrum, "The Early Decision Decision" clarifies it for you. Finally, "What International Students Need to Know About Admission to U.S. Colleges and Universities" has tips on college admissions for non–U.S. citizens and can also be useful to U.S. citizens. Up next is the **Money, Money, Money** section, which provides all the essential information on how to meet your education expenses, starting with the "Financial Aid Countdown Calendar" and followed by articles covering "Who's Paying for This? Financial Aid Basics" and "Middle Income Families: Making the Financial Aid Process Work." And be sure to check out our **Options, Options, Options** section for some sneak peeks into specific institutions and programs that may be just right for you, including the latest on honors programs, public versus private colleges, women's colleges, and online learning. Make sure you take a look at the About the Peterson's Icon and Keyword Search section to find out which schools have chosen to provide expanded information to Peterson's. Finally, you'll want to read through the How to Use This Guide section which explains the information presented for each individual college, how we collect our data, and how we determine eligibility for inclusion in this guide.
- Next up is the **COLLEGES AT-A-GLANCE.** Here you'll find our unparalleled college descriptions, arranged alphabetically by state. They provide a complete picture of need-to-know information about accredited four-year colleges—including entrance difficulty, campus setting, total enrollment, student-faculty ratio, application deadlines, expenses, most frequently chosen baccalaureate fields, and academic programs. All the information you need to apply is placed together at the conclusion of each college description.
- And if you still thirst for even more information, 464 two-page narrative descriptions appear as **COLLEGE CLOSE-UPS**—descriptions written by admissions deans that provide great detail about each college. They are edited to provide a consistent format across entries for your ease of comparison.
- If you already have specifics in mind, such as a particular major or institution, turn to the **INDEXES** section. Here you can search for a school based on major, entrance difficulty, cost ranges, and geography. If you already have colleges in mind that pique your interest, you can use the "Alphabetical Listing of Colleges and Universities" to search for these schools. Page numbers referring to all information presented about a college are conveniently referenced.

Join the college conversation on Facebook® and Twitter™ at www.facebook.com/find.colleges and www.twitter.com/find_colleges and receive additional college search tips and advice. Peterson's resources are available to help you do your best in finding the right school!

Peterson's publishes a full line of books—college and grad guides, education exploration, financial aid, and career preparation. Peterson's publications can be found at high school guidance offices, college libraries and career centers, and your local bookstore and library. Peterson's books are now also available as eBooks.

We welcome any comments or suggestions you may have about this publication. Your feedback will help us make educational dreams possible for you—and others like you.

Colleges will be pleased to know that Peterson's helped you in your selection. Admissions staff members are more than happy to answer questions, address specific problems, and help in any way they can. The editors at Peterson's wish you great success in your college search!

The Advice Center

College Admissions Countdown Calendar

This practical month-by-month calendar is designed to help you stay on top of the process of applying to college. For most students, the process begins in September of the junior year of high school and ends in June of the senior year. You may want to begin considering financial aid options, reviewing your academic schedule, and attending college fairs before your junior year.

JUNIOR YEAR

September

- ❒ Check with your counselor to make sure your course credits will meet college requirements.
- ❒ Be sure you are involved in one or two extracurricular activities.
- ❒ Begin building your personal list of colleges at Petersons.com.

October

- ❒ Register for and take the PSAT.

November

- ❒ Strive to get the best grades you can. A serious effort will provide you with the most options during the application process.

December

- ❒ Get involved in a community service activity.
- ❒ Begin to read newspapers and a weekly news magazine.
- ❒ Buy *Peterson's Master the SAT, Peterson's Ultimate ACT Tool Kit*, or *The Real ACT Prep Guide* (published by Peterson's) and begin to study for the tests.

January

- ❒ With your school counselor, decide when to take the ACT, SAT, and SAT Subject Tests (and which Subject Tests to take). If English is not your primary language and you are planning on attending a college in North America, decide when to take the TOEFL.
- ❒ Keep your grades up!

February

- ❒ Plan a challenging schedule of classes for your senior year.
- ❒ Think about which teachers you will ask to write recommendations.
- ❒ Check http://www.nacacnet.org/EVENTSTRAINING/COLLEGEFAIRS/Pages/default.aspx for schedules and locations of college fairs.

March

- ❒ Register for the tests you will take in the spring (ACT, SAT, SAT Subject Tests, or the TOEFL).
- ❒ Meet with your school counselor to discuss college choices.
- ❒ Review your transcript and test scores with your counselor to determine how competitive your range of choices should be.
- ❒ Develop a preliminary list of fifteen to twenty colleges and universities.
- ❒ Start scheduling campus visits. The best time is when school is in session (but never during final exams). Summers are OK but will not show you what the college is really like. If possible, save your top college choices for the fall. Be aware, however, that fall is the busiest visit season, and you will need advance planning. Don't forget to write thank you letters to your interviewers.

April

- ❒ Take any standardized tests for which you have registered.
- ❒ Create a list of your potential college choices and begin to record personal and academic information that can be transferred later to your college applications.

May

- ❒ Plan college visits and make appointments.
- ❒ Structure your summer plans to include advanced academic work, travel, volunteer work, or a job.
- ❒ Confirm your academic schedule for the fall.

Summer

- ❒ Write to any colleges on your list that do not accept the Common Application to request application forms.
- ❒ Begin working on your application essays.

SENIOR YEAR

September

- ❒ Register for the ACT, SAT, SAT Subject Tests, or TOEFL, as necessary.
- ❒ Check with your school counselor for the fall visiting schedule of college reps.
- ❒ Ask appropriate teachers if they would write recommendations for you. Don't forget to write thank you letters when they accept.
- ❒ Meet with your counselor to compile your final list of colleges.

October

- ❒ Mail or send early applications electronically after carefully checking them to be sure they are completely filled out.
- ❒ Photocopy or print extra copies of your applications to use as a backup.
- ❒ Take the tests for which you have registered.
- ❒ Don't be late! Keep track of all deadlines for transcripts, recommendations, financial aid, etc.

November

- ❒ Be sure that you have requested your ACT and SAT scores be sent to your colleges of choice.
- ❒ Complete and submit all applications. Print or photocopy an extra copy for your records.

December

- ❒ Take any necessary tests: ACT, SAT, SAT Subject Tests, or TOEFL.
- ❒ Meet with your counselor to verify that all is in order and that transcripts are out to colleges.

January

- ❒ Prepare the Free Application for Federal Student Aid (FAFSA), available at www.fafsa.ed.gov or through your school counseling office. An estimated income tax statement (which can be corrected later) can be used. The sooner you apply for financial aid, the better your chances.

February

- ❒ Send in your FAFSA via the Web or U.S. mail.
- ❒ Be sure your midyear report has gone out to the colleges to which you've applied.
- ❒ Let colleges know of any new honors or accomplishments that were not in your original application.

March

- ❒ Register for any Advanced Placement (AP) tests you might take.
- ❒ Be sure you have received a FAFSA acknowledgment.

April

- ❒ Review the acceptances and financial aid offers you receive.
- ❒ Go back to visit one or two of your top-choice colleges.
- ❒ Notify your college of choice that you have accepted its offer (and send in a deposit by May 1).
- ❒ Notify the colleges you have chosen not to attend of your decision.

May

- ❒ Take AP tests.

June

- ❒ Graduate! Congratulations and best of luck.

Choosing Your Top Ten Colleges

By using all the information in the various sections of this guide, you will find colleges worthy of the most important top-ten list on the planet—yours.

The first thing you will need to do is decide what type of institution of higher learning you want to attend. Each of the thousands of four-year colleges and universities in the United States is as unique as the people applying to it. Although listening to the voices and media hype around you can make it sound as though there are only a few elite schools worth attending, this simply is not true. By considering some of the following criteria, you will soon find that the large pool of interesting colleges can be narrowed down to a more reasonable number.

SIZE AND CATEGORY

Schools come in all shapes and sizes, from tiny rural colleges of 400 students to massive state university systems serving 100,000 students or more. If you are coming from a small high school, a college with 3,500 students may seem large to you. If you are currently attending a high school with 3,000 students, selecting a college of a similar size may not feel like a new enough experience. Some students coming from very large impersonal high schools are looking for a place where they will be recognized from the beginning and offered a more personal approach. If you don't have a clue about what size might feel right to you, try visiting a couple of nearby colleges of varying sizes. You do not have to be seriously interested in them; just feel what impact the number of students on campus has on you.

Large Universities

Large universities offer a wide range of educational, athletic, and social experiences. Universities offer a full scope of undergraduate majors and award master's and doctoral degrees as well. Universities are usually composed of several smaller colleges. Depending on your interest in a major field or area of study, you would likely apply to a specific college within the university. Each college has the flexibility to set its own standards for admission, which may differ from the overall average of the university. The colleges within a university system also set their own course requirements for earning a degree.

Universities may be public or private. Some large private universities, such as Harvard, Yale, Princeton, University of Pennsylvania, New York University, Northwestern, and Stanford, are well-known for their high entrance standards, the excellence of their education, and the success rates of their graduates. These institutions place a great deal of emphasis on research and compete aggressively for grants from the federal government to fund these projects. Large public universities, such as the State University of New York (SUNY) System, University of Michigan, University of Texas, University of Illinois, University of Washington, and University of North Carolina, also support excellent educational programs, compete for and win research funding, and have successful graduates. Public universities usually offer substantially lower tuition rates to in-state students, although their tuition rates for out-of-state residents are often comparable to those of private institutions.

At many large universities, sports play a major role on campus. Athletics can dominate the calendar and set the tone year-round at some schools. Alumni travel from far and wide to attend their alma mater's football or basketball games, and the campus, and frequently the entire town, grinds to a halt when there is a home game. Athletes are heroes and dominate campus social life.

What are some other features of life on a university campus? Every kind of club imaginable, from literature to bioengineering and chorus to politics, can be found on most college campuses. You will be able to play the intramural version of almost every sport in which the university fields interscholastic teams and join fraternities, sororities, and groups dedicated to social action. You can become a member of a band, an orchestra, or perhaps a chamber music group or work on the newspaper, the literary magazine, or the Web site. The list can go on and on. You may want to try out a new interest or two or pursue what you have always been interested in and make like-minded friends along the way.

Take a look at the size of the classrooms in the larger universities and envision yourself sitting in that atmosphere. Would this offer a learning environment that would benefit you?

Liberal Arts Colleges

If you have considered large universities and come to the conclusion that all that action could be a distraction, a small liberal arts college might be right for you. Ideally tucked away on a picture-perfect campus, a liberal arts college generally has fewer than 5,000 students. The mission of most liberal arts schools is learning for the sake of learning, with a strong emphasis on creating lifelong learners who will be able to apply their education to any number of careers. This contrasts with objectives of the profession-based preparation of specialized colleges.

Liberal arts colleges cannot offer the breadth of courses provided by the large universities. As a result, liberal arts colleges try to create a niche for themselves. For instance, a college may place its emphasis on its humanities departments, whose professors are all well-known published authors and international presenters in their areas of expertise. A college may highlight its science departments by providing state-of-the-art facilities where undergraduates conduct research side by side with top-notch professors and copublish their findings in the most prestigious scientific journals in the country. The personal approach is very important at liberal arts colleges. Whether in advisement, course selection, athletic programs tailored to students' interests, or dinner with the department head at her home, liberal arts colleges emphasize that they get to know their students.

If they are so perfect, why doesn't everyone choose a liberal arts college? Well, the small size limits options. Fewer people may mean less diversity. The fact that many of these colleges encourage a study-abroad option (a student elects to spend a semester or a year studying in another country) reduces the number of students on campus even further. Some liberal arts colleges have a certain reputation that does not appeal to some students. You should ask yourself questions about the campus life that most appeals to you. Will you fit in with the campus culture? Will the small size mean that you go through your social options quickly? Check out the activities listed on the Student Center bulletin board. Does the student body look diverse enough for you? Will what is happening keep you busy and interested? Do the students have input into decision making? Do they create the social climate of the school?

Small Universities

Smaller universities often combine stringent admissions policies, handpicked faculty members, and attractive scholarship packages. These institutions generally have undergraduate enrollments of about 4,000 students. Some are more famous for their graduate and professional schools but have also established strong undergraduate colleges. Smaller universities balance the great majors options of large universities with a smaller campus community. They offer choices but not to the same extent as large universities. On the other hand, by limiting admissions and enrollment, they manage to cultivate some of the characteristics of a liberal arts college. Like a liberal arts college, a small university may emphasize a particular program and go out of its way to draw strong candidates in a specific area, such as premed, to its campus. Universities such as The Johns Hopkins University, University of Notre Dame, Vanderbilt University, Washington University in St. Louis, and Wesleyan University in Connecticut are a few examples of this category.

Technical or Specialized Colleges

Another alternative to the liberal arts college or large university is the technical or otherwise specialized college. Their goal is to offer a specialized and saturated experience in a particular field of study. Such an institution might limit its course offerings to engineering and science, the performing or fine arts, or business. Schools such as California Institute of Technology, Carnegie Mellon University, Massachusetts Institute of Technology, and Rensselaer Polytechnic Institute concentrate on attracting the finest math and science students in the country. At other schools, like Bentley College in Massachusetts or Bryant College in Rhode Island, students eat, sleep, and breathe business. These institutions are purists at heart and strong believers in the necessity of focused, specialized study to produce excellence in their graduates' achievements. If you are certain about your chosen path in life and want to immerse yourself in subjects such as math, music, or business, you will fit right in.

Religious Colleges

Many private colleges have religious origins, and many of these have become secular institutions with virtually no trace of their religious roots. Others remain dedicated to a religious way of education. What sets religious colleges apart is the way they combine faith, learning, and student life. Faculty members and administrators are hired with faith as a criterion as much as their academic credentials.

Single-Gender Colleges

There are strong arguments that being able to pursue one's education without the distraction, competition, and stress caused by the presence of the opposite sex helps a student evolve a stronger sense of her or his self-worth; achieve more academically; have a more fulfilling, less pressured social schedule; and achieve more later in life. For various historic, social, and psychological reasons, there are many more all-women than all-men colleges. A strict single-sex environment is rare. Even though the undergraduate day college adheres to an all-female or all-male admissions policy, coeducational evening classes or graduate programs and coordinate facilities and classes shared with nearby coed or opposite-sex institutions can result in a good number of students of the opposite sex being found on campus. If you want to concentrate on your studies and hone your leadership qualities, a single-gender school is an option.

LOCATION

Location and distance from home are two other important considerations. If you have always lived in the suburbs, choosing an urban campus can be an adventure, but after a week of the urban experience, will you long for a grassy campus and open space? On the other hand, if you choose a college in a rural area, will you run screaming into the Student Center some night looking for noise, lights, and people? The location—urban, rural, or suburban—can directly affect how easy or how difficult adjusting to college life will be for you.

Don't forget to factor in distance from home. Everyone going off to college wants to think he or she won't be homesick, but sometimes it's nice to get a home-cooked meal or to do the laundry in a place that does not require quarters. Even your kid sister may seem like less of a nuisance after a couple of months away.

Here are some questions you might ask yourself as you go through the selection process: In what part of the country do I want to be? How far away from home do I want to be? What is the cost of returning home? Do I need to be close to a city? How close? How large of a city? Would city life distract me? Would I concentrate better in a setting that is more rural or more suburban?

ENTRANCE DIFFICULTY

Many students will look at a college's entrance difficulty as an indicator of whether or not they will be admitted. For instance, if you have an excellent academic record, you might wish to primarily consider those colleges that are highly competitive. Although entrance difficulty does not translate directly to quality of education, it indicates which colleges are attracting large numbers of high-achieving students. A high-achieving student body usually translates into prestige for the college and its graduates. Prestige has some advantages but should definitely be viewed as a secondary factor that might tip the scales when all the other important factors are equal. Never base your decision on prestige alone!

The other principle to keep in mind when considering this factor is to not sell yourself short. If everything else tells you that a college might be right for you, but your numbers just miss that college's average range, apply there anyway. Your numbers—grades and test scores—are undeniably important in the admissions decision, but there are other considerations. First, lower grades in honors or AP courses will impress colleges more than top grades in regular-track courses because they demonstrate that you are the kind of student willing to accept challenges. Second, admissions directors are looking for different qualities in students that can be combined to create a multifaceted class. For example, if you did poorly in your freshman and sophomore years but made a great improvement in your grades in later years, this usually will impress a college. If you are likely to contribute to your class because of your special personal qualities, a strong sense of commitment and purpose, unusual and valuable experiences, or special interests and talents, these factors can outweigh numbers that are weaker than average. Nevertheless, be practical. Overreach yourself in a few applications, but put the bulk of your effort into gaining admission to colleges where you have a realistic chance for admission.

THE PRICE OF AN EDUCATION

The price tag for higher education continues to rise, and it has become an increasingly important factor for people. While it is necessary to consider your family's resources when choosing a list of colleges to which you might apply, never eliminate a college solely because of cost. There are many ways to pay for college, including loans, and a college education will never depreciate in value, unlike other purchases. It is an investment in yourself and will pay back the expense many times over in your lifetime.

Surviving Standardized Tests

WHAT ARE STANDARDIZED TESTS?

Colleges and universities in the United States use tests to help evaluate applicants' readiness for admission or to place them in appropriate courses. The tests that are most frequently used by colleges are the ACT of American College Testing, Inc., and the College Board's SAT. In addition, the Educational Testing Service (ETS) offers the TOEFL test, which evaluates the English-language proficiency of non-native speakers. The tests are offered at designated testing centers located at high schools and colleges throughout the United States and U.S. territories and at testing centers in various countries throughout the world.

Upon request, special accommodations for students with documented visual, hearing, physical, or learning disabilities are available. Examples of special accommodations include tests in Braille or large print and such aids as a reader, recorder, magnifying glass, or sign language interpreter. Additional testing time may be allowed in some instances. Contact the appropriate testing program or your guidance counselor for details on how to request special accommodations.

THE ACT

The ACT is a standardized college entrance examination that measures knowledge and skills in English, mathematics, reading, and science reasoning and the application of these skills to future academic tasks. The ACT consists of four multiple-choice tests.

Test 1: English
- 75 questions, 45 minutes
- Usage and mechanics
- Rhetorical skills

Test 2: Mathematics
- 60 questions, 60 minutes
- Pre-algebra
- Elementary algebra
- Intermediate algebra
- Coordinate geometry
- Plane geometry
- Trigonometry

Test 3: Reading
- 40 questions, 35 minutes
- Prose fiction
- Humanities
- Social studies
- Natural sciences

Test 4: Science
- 40 questions, 35 minutes
- Data representation
- Research summary
- Conflicting viewpoints

Each section is scored from 1 to 36 and is scaled for slight variations in difficulty. Students are not penalized for incorrect responses. The composite score is the average of the four scaled scores. The ACT Plus Writing includes the four multiple-choice tests and a writing test, which measures writing skills emphasized in high school English classes and in entry-level college composition courses.

To prepare for the ACT, ask your guidance counselor for a free guidebook called "Preparing for the ACT." Besides providing general test-preparation information and additional test-taking strategies, this guidebook describes the content and format of the four ACT subject area tests, summarizes test administration procedures followed at ACT test centers, and includes a practice test. Peterson's publishes *The Real ACT Prep Guide* that includes three official ACT tests.

THE SAT

The SAT measures developed critical reading and mathematical reasoning abilities as they relate to successful performance in college. It is intended to supplement the secondary school record and other information about the student in assessing readiness for college. There is one unscored, experimental section on the exam, which is used for equating and/or pretesting purposes and can cover either the mathematics or critical reading area.

Critical Reading
- 67 questions, 70 minutes
- Sentence completion
- Passage-based reading

DON'T FORGET TO . . .

- Take the SAT or ACT before application deadlines.
- Note that test registration deadlines precede test dates by about six weeks.
- Register to take the TOEFL test if English is not your native language and you are planning on studying at a North American college.
- Practice your test-taking skills with *Peterson's Master the SAT, Peterson's Ultimate ACT Tool Kit, The Real ACT Prep Guide* (published by Peterson's), *Peterson's Master TOEFL Reading Skills, Peterson's Master TOEFL Vocabulary,* and *Peterson's Master TOEFL Writing Skills.*
- Contact the College Board or American College Testing, Inc., in advance if you need special accommodations when taking tests.

Mathematics
- 54 questions, 70 minutes
- Multiple-choice
- Student-produced response (grid-ins)

Writing
- 49 questions plus essay, 60 minutes
- Identifying sentence errors
- Improving paragraphs
- Improving sentences
- Essay

Students receive one point for each correct response and lose a fraction of a point for each incorrect response (except for student-produced responses). These points are totaled to produce the raw scores, which are then scaled to equalize the scores for slight variations in difficulty for various editions of the test. The critical reading, writing, and mathematics scaled scores range from 200–800 per section. The total scaled score range is from 600–2400.

SAT SUBJECT TESTS

Subject Tests are required by some institutions for admission and/or placement in freshman-level courses. Each Subject Test measures one's knowledge of a specific subject and the ability to apply that knowledge. Students should check with each institution for its specific requirements. In general, students are required to take three Subject Tests (one English, one mathematics, and one of their choice).

Subject Tests are given in the following areas: biology, chemistry, Chinese, French, German, Italian, Japanese, Korean, Latin, literature, mathematics, modern Hebrew, physics, Spanish, U.S. history, and world history. These tests are 1 hour long and are primarily multiple-choice tests. Three Subject Tests may be taken on one test date.

Scored like the SAT, students gain a point for each correct answer and lose a fraction of a point for each incorrect answer. The raw scores are then converted to scaled scores that range from 200 to 800.

THE TOEFL INTERNET-BASED TEST (IBT)

The Test of English as a Foreign Language Internet-Based Test (TOEFL iBT) is designed to help assess a student's grasp of English if it is not the student's first language. Performance on the TOEFL test may help interpret scores on the critical reading sections of the SAT. The test consists of four integrated sections: speaking, listening, reading, and writing. The TOEFL iBT emphasizes integrated skills. The paper-based versions of the TOEFL will continue to be administered in certain countries where the Internet-based version has not yet been introduced. For further information, visit www.toefl.org.

WHAT OTHER TESTS SHOULD I KNOW ABOUT?

The AP Program

This program allows high school students to try college-level work and build valuable skills and study habits in the process. Subject matter is explored in more depth in AP courses than in other high school classes. A qualifying score on an AP test—which varies from school to school—can earn you college credit or advanced placement. Getting qualifying grades on enough exams can even earn you a full year's credit and sophomore standing at more than 1,500 higher-education institutions. There are more than thirty AP courses across multiple subject areas, including art history, biology, and computer science. Speak to your guidance counselor for information about your school's offerings.

College-Level Examination Program (CLEP)

The CLEP enables students to earn college credit for what they already know, whether it was learned in school, through independent study, or through other experiences outside of the classroom. More than 2,900 colleges and universities now award credit for qualifying scores on one or more of the 33 CLEP exams. The exams, which are 90 minutes in length and are primarily multiple choice, are administered at participating colleges and universities. For more information, check out the Web site at www.collegeboard.com/clep.

WHAT CAN I DO TO PREPARE FOR THESE TESTS?

Know what to expect. Get familiar with how the tests are structured, how much time is allowed, and the directions for each type of question. Get plenty of rest the night before the test and eat breakfast that morning.

There are a variety of products, from books to software to videos, available to help you prepare for most standardized tests. Find the learning style that suits you best. As for which products to buy, there are two major categories—those created by the test makers and those created by private companies. The best approach is to talk to someone who has been through the process and find out which product or products he or she recommends.

Some students report significant increases in scores after participating in coaching programs. Longer-term programs (40 hours) seem to raise scores more than short-term programs (20 hours), but beyond 40 hours, score gains are minor. Math scores appear to benefit more from coaching than critical reading scores.

Resources

There is a variety of ways to prepare for standardized tests—find a method that fits your schedule and your budget. But you should definitely prepare. Far too many students walk into these tests cold, either because they find standardized tests frightening or annoying or they just haven't found the time to study. The key is that these exams are standardized. That means these tests are largely the same from administration to administration; they always test the same concepts. They have to, or else you couldn't compare the scores of people who took the tests on different dates. The numbers or words may change, but the underlying content doesn't.

So how do you prepare? At the very least, you should review relevant material, such as math formulas and commonly used vocabulary words, and know the directions for

TOP 10 WAYS NOT TO TAKE THE TEST

10. Cramming the night before the test.
9. Not becoming familiar with the directions before you take the test.
8. Not becoming familiar with the format of the test before you take it.
7. Not knowing how the test is graded.
6. Spending too much time on any one question.
5. Not checking spelling, grammar, and sentence structure in essays.
4. Second-guessing yourself.
3. Forgetting to take a deep breath to keep from—
2. Losing It!
1. Writing a one-paragraph essay.

each question type or test section. You should take at least one practice test and review your mistakes so you don't make them again on the test day. Beyond that, you know best how much preparation you need. You'll also find lots of material in libraries or bookstores to help you: books and software from the test makers and from other publishers (including Peterson's) or live courses that range from national test-preparation companies to teachers at your high school who offer classes.

The Whys and Whats of College Visits

Dawn B. Sova, Ph.D.

The campus visit should not be a passive activity for you and your parents. Take the initiative and gather information beyond that provided in the official tour. You will see many important indicators during your visit that will tell you more about the true character of a college and its students than the tour guide will reveal. Know what to look for and how to assess the importance of such indicators.

WHAT SHOULD YOU ASK AND WHAT SHOULD YOU LOOK FOR?

Your first stop on a campus visit is the visitor center or admissions office, where you will probably have to wait to meet with a counselor. Colleges usually plan to greet visitors later than the appointed time in order to give them the opportunity to review some of the campus information that is liberally scattered throughout the visitor waiting room. Take advantage of the time to become even more familiar with the college by arriving 15 to 30 minutes before your appointment to observe the behavior of staff members and to browse through the yearbooks and student newspapers that will be available.

If you prepare in advance, you will have already reviewed the college catalog and map of the campus. These materials familiarize you with the academic offerings and the physical layout of the campus, but the true character of the college and its students emerges in other ways.

Begin your investigation with the visitor center staff members. As a student's first official contact with the college, they should make every effort to welcome prospective students and project a friendly image.

- How do they treat you and other prospective students who are waiting? Are they friendly and willing to speak with you, or do they try their hardest to avoid eye contact and conversation?
- Are they friendly with each other and with students who enter the office, or are they curt and unwilling to help?
- Does the waiting room have a friendly feeling or is it cold and sterile?

If the visitor center staff members seem indifferent to *prospective* students, there is little reason to believe that they will be warm and welcoming to current students. View such behavior as a warning to watch very carefully the interaction of others with you during the tour. An indifferent or unfriendly reception in the admissions office may be simply the first of many signs that attending this college will not be a pleasant experience.

Look through several yearbooks and see the types of activities that are actually photographed, as opposed to the activities that colleges promise in their promotional literature. Some questions are impossible to answer if the college is very large, but for small and moderately sized colleges the yearbook is a good indicator of campus activity.

- Has the number of clubs and organizations increased or decreased in the past five years?
- Do the same students appear repeatedly in activities?
- Do sororities and fraternities dominate campus activities?
- Are participants limited to one sex or one ethnic group, or is there diversity?
- Are all activities limited to the campus, or are students involved in activities in the community?

Use what you observe in the yearbooks as a means of forming a more complete understanding of the college, but don't base your entire impression on just one facet. If time permits, look through several copies of the school newspaper, which should reflect the major concerns and interests of the students. The paper is also a good way to learn about the campus social life.

- Does the paper contain a mix of national and local news?
- What products or services are advertised?
- How assertive are the editorials?
- With what topics are the columnists concerned?
- Are movies and concerts that meet your tastes advertised or reviewed?
- What types of ads appear in the classified section?

The newspaper should be a public forum for students, and, as such, should reflect the character of the campus and of the student body. A paper that deals only with seemingly safe and well-edited topics on the editorial page and in regular feature columns might indicate administrative censorship. A lack of ads for restaurants might indicate either a lack of good places to eat or that area restaurants do not welcome student business. A limited mention of movies, concerts, or other entertainment might reveal a severely limited campus social life. Even if ads and reviews are included, you should still balance how such activities reflect your tastes.

You will have only a limited amount of time to ask questions during your initial meeting with the admissions counselor, for very few schools include a formal interview in the initial campus visit or tour. Instead, this brief meeting is often just a nicety that allows the admissions office to begin a file for the student and to record some initial impressions. Save your questions for the tour guide and for students on campus you meet along the way.

HOW CAN YOU ASSESS THE TRUE CHARACTER OF A COLLEGE AND ITS STUDENTS?

Colleges do not train their tour guides to deceive prospective students, but they do caution guides to avoid unflattering topics and campus sites. Does this mean that you will see only a sugarcoated version of life on a particular college campus? Not at all, especially not if you are observant.

Most organized campus visits include such campus facilities as dormitories, dining halls, libraries, student activity and recreation centers, and the health and student services centers. Some may only be pointed out, while you will walk through others. Either way, you will find that many signs of the true character of the college emerge if you keep your eyes open.

Bulletin boards in dormitories and student centers contain a wealth of information about campus activities, student concerns, and campus groups. Read the posters, notices, and messages to learn what *really* interests students. Unlike ads in the school newspaper, posters put up by students advertise both on- and off-campus events, so they will give you an idea of what is also available in the surrounding community.

Review the notices, which may cover either campuswide events or events that concern only small groups of students. The catalog may not mention a performance group, but an individual dormitory with its own small theater may offer regular productions. Poetry readings, jam sessions, writers' groups, and other activities may be announced and show diversity of student interests.

Even the brief bulletin board messages offering objects for sale and noting objects that people want to purchase reveal a lot about a campus. Are most of the items computer related? Or do the messages specify CDs, audio equipment, or musical instruments? Are offers to trade goods or services posted? Don't ignore the "ride wanted" messages. Students who want to share rides home during a break may specify widely diverse geographical locations. If so, then you know that the student body is not limited to only the immediate area or one locale. Other messages can also enhance your knowledge of the true character of the campus and its students.

As you walk through various buildings, examine their condition carefully.

- Is the paint peeling, and do the exteriors look worn?
- Are the exteriors and interiors of the building clean?
- Is the equipment in the classrooms up-to-date or outdated?

Pay particular attention to the dormitories, especially to factors that might affect your safety. Observe the appearance of the structure, and ask about the security measures in and around the dormitories.

- Are the dormitories noisy or quiet?
- Do they seem crowded?
- How good is the lighting around each dormitory?
- Are the dormitories spread throughout the campus or are they clustered in one main area?
- Who has access to the dormitories in addition to students?
- How secure are the means by which students enter and leave the dormitory?

While you are on the subject of dormitory safety, you should also ask about campus safety. Don't expect that the guide will rattle off a list of crimes that have been committed in the past year. To obtain that information, access the recent year of issues of *The Chronicle of Higher Education* and locate its yearly report on campus crime. Also ask the guide about safety measures that the campus police take and those that students have initiated.

- Can students request escorts to their residences late at night?
- Do campus shuttle buses run at frequent intervals all night?
- Are "blue-light" telephones liberally placed throughout the campus for students to use to call for help?
- Do the campus police patrol the campus regularly?

If the guide does not answer your questions satisfactorily, wait until after the tour to contact the campus police or traffic office for answers.

Campus tours usually just point out the health services center without taking the time to walk through. Even if you don't see the inside of the building, you should take a close look at the location of the health services center and ask the guide questions about services.

- How far is the health center from the dormitories?
- Is a doctor always on call?
- Does the campus transport sick students from their dormitories or must they walk?
- What are the operating hours of the health center?
- Does the health center refer students to a nearby hospital?

If the guide can't answer your questions, visit the health center later and ask someone there.

Most campus tours take pride in showing students their activities centers, which may contain snack bars, game rooms, workout facilities, and other means of entertainment. Should you scrutinize this building as carefully as the rest? Of course. Outdated and poorly maintained activity equipment contributes to your total impression of the college. You should also ask about the hours, availability, and cost (no, the activities are usually *not* free) of using the bowling alleys, pool tables, air hockey tables, and other ammenities.

As you walk through campus with the tour, also look carefully at the appearance of the students who pass. The way in which both men and women groom themselves, the way they dress, and even their physical bearing communicate a lot more than any guidebook can. If everyone seems to conform to the same look, you might feel that you would be uncomfortable at the college, however nonconformist that look might be. On the other hand, you might not feel comfortable on a campus that stresses diversity of dress and behavior, and your observations now can save you discomfort later.

- Does every student seem to wear a sorority or fraternity t-shirt or jacket?
- Is everyone of your sex sporting the latest fad haircut?
- Do all of the men or the women seem to be wearing expensive name-brand clothes?
- Do most of the students seem to be working hard to look outrageous with regards to clothing, hair color, and body art?
- Would you feel uncomfortable in a room full of these students?

Is appearance important to you? If it is, then you should consider very seriously if you answer *yes* to any of the above questions. You don't have to be the same as everyone else on campus, but standing out too much may make you unhappy.

As you observe the physical appearance of the students, also listen to their conversations as you pass them. What are they talking about? How are they speaking? Are their voices and accents all the same, or do you hear diversity in their speech? Are you offended by their language? Think how you will feel if surrounded by the same speech habits and patterns for four years.

WHERE SHOULD YOU VISIT ON YOUR OWN?

Your campus visit is not over when the tour ends because you will probably have many questions yet to be answered and many places to still be seen. Where you go depends upon the extent to which the organized tour covers the campus. Your tour should take you to view residential halls, health and student services centers, the gymnasium or field house, dining halls, the library, and recreational centers. If any of the facilities on this list have been omitted, visit them on your own and ask questions of the students and staff members you meet. In addition, you should step off campus and gain an impression of the surrounding community. You will probably become bored with life on campus and spend at least some time off campus. Make certain that you know what the surrounding area is like.

The campus tour leaves little time to ask impromptu questions of current students, but you can do so after the tour. Eat lunch in one of the dining halls. Most will allow visitors to pay cash to experience a typical student meal. Food may not be important to you now while you are living at home and can simply take anything you want from the refrigerator at any time, but it will be when you are away at college with only a meal ticket to feed you.

- How clean is the dining hall? Consider serving tables, floors, and seating.
- What is the quality of the food?
- How big are the portions?
- How much variety do students have at each meal?
- How healthy are the food choices?

While you are eating, try to strike up a conversation with students and tell them that you are considering attending their college. Their reactions and advice can be eye-opening. Ask them questions about the academic atmosphere and the professors.

- Are the classes large or small?
- Do the majority of the professors only lecture or are tutorials and seminars common?
- Is the emphasis of the faculty career-oriented or abstract?
- Are the teaching methods innovative and stimulating or boring and dull?
- Is the academic atmosphere pressured, lax, or somewhere in between?
- Which are the strong majors? The weak majors?
- Is the emphasis on grades or social life or a mix of both at the college?
- How hard do students have to work to receive high grades?

Current students can also give you the inside line on the true nature of the college social life. You may gain some idea through looking in the yearbook, in the newspaper, and on the bulletin boards, but students will reveal the true highs and lows of campus life. Ask them about drug use, partying, dating, drinking, and anything else that may affect your life as a student.

- Which are the most popular club activities?
- What do students do on weekends? Do most go home?
- How frequently do concerts occur on campus? Who has recently performed?
- How can you become involved in specific activities (name them)?
- How strictly are campus rules enforced and how severe are penalties?
- What counseling services are available?
- Are academic tutoring services available?
- Do they feel that the faculty really cares about students, especially freshmen?

You will receive the most valuable information from current students, but you will only be able to speak with them after the tour is over. And you might have to risk rejection as you try to initiate conversations with students who might not want to reveal how they feel about the campus. Still, the value of this information is worth the chance.

If you have the time, you should also visit the library to see just how accessible research materials are and to observe the physical layout. The catalog usually specifies the days and hours of operation, as well as the number of volumes contained in the library and the number of periodicals to which it subscribes. A library also requires accessibility, good lighting, an adequate number of study carrels, and lounge areas for students. Many colleges have created 24-hour study lounges for students who find the residence halls too noisy for studying, although most colleges claim that they designate areas of the residences as "quiet study" areas. You may not be interested in any of this information, but when you are a student you will have to make frequent use of the campus library so you should know what is available. You should at least ask how extensive their holdings are in your proposed major area. If they have virtually nothing, you will have to spend a lot of time ordering items via interlibrary loan or making copies, which can become expensive. The ready answer of students that they will obtain their information from the Internet is unpleasantly countered by professors who demand journal articles with documentation.

Make a point of at least driving through the community surrounding the college because you will be spending time there shopping, dining, working in a part-time job, or attending events. Even the largest and best-stocked campus will not meet all of your social and personal needs. If you can spare the time, stop in several stores to see if they welcome college students.

- Is the surrounding community suburban, urban, or rural?
- Does the community offer stores of interest, such as bookstores, craft shops, and boutiques?
- Do the businesses employ college students?
- Does the community have a movie or stage theater?
- Are there several types of interesting restaurants?
- Do there seem to be any clubs that court a college clientele?
- Is the center of activity easy to walk to, or do you need other transportation?

You might feel that a day is not enough to answer all of your questions, but even answering some questions will provide you with a stronger basis for choosing a college. Many students visit a college campus several times before making their decision. Keep in mind that for the rest of your life you will be associated with the college that you attend. You will spend four years of your life at this college. The effort of spending several days to obtain the information to make your decision is worthwhile.

Dawn B. Sova, Ph.D., is a former newspaper reporter and columnist, as well as the author of more than eight books and numerous magazine articles. She teaches creative and research writing, as well as scientific and technical writing, newswriting, and journalism.

Applying 101

The words "applying yourself" have several important meanings in the college application process. One meaning refers to the fact that you need to keep focused during this important time in your life, keep your priorities straight, and know the dates that your applications are due so you can apply on time. The phrase might also refer to the person who is really responsible for your application—you.

You are the only person who should compile your college application. You need to take ownership of this process. The guidance counselor is not responsible for completing your applications, and neither are your parents. College applications must be completed in addition to your normal workload at school, college visits, and SAT, ACT, or TOEFL testing.

THE APPLICATION

The application is your way of introducing yourself to a college admissions office. As with any introduction, you want to make a good first impression. The first thing you should do in presenting your application is to find out what the college or university needs from you. Read the application carefully to find out the application fee and deadline, required standardized tests, number of essays, interview requirements, and anything else you can do or submit to help improve your chances for acceptance.

Completing college applications yourself helps you learn more about the schools to which you are applying. The information a college asks for in its application can tell you much about the school. State university applications often tell you how they are going to view their applicants. Usually, they select students based on GPAs and test scores. Colleges that request an interview, ask you to respond to a few open-ended questions, or require an essay are interested in a more personal approach to the application process and may be looking for different types of students than those sought by a state school.

In addition to submitting the actual application, there are several other items that are commonly required. You will be responsible for ensuring that your standardized test scores and your high school transcript arrive at the colleges to which you apply. Most colleges will ask that you submit teacher recommendations as well. Select teachers who know you and your abilities well and allow them plenty of time to complete the recommendations. When all portions of the application have been completed and sent in, whether electronically or by mail, make sure you follow up with the college to ensure their receipt.

FOLLOW THESE TIPS WHEN FILLING OUT YOUR APPLICATION

- **Follow the directions to the letter.** You don't want to be in a position to ask an admissions officer for exceptions due to your inattentiveness.
- **Proofread all parts of your application,** including your essay. Again, the final product indicates to the admissions staff how meticulous and careful you are in your work.
- **Submit your application as early as possible,** provided all of the pieces are available. If there is a problem with your application, this will allow you to work through it with the admissions staff in plenty of time. If you wait until the last minute, it not only takes away that cushion but also reflects poorly on your sense of priorities.
- **Keep a copy of the completed application,** whether it is a photocopy or a copy saved on your computer.

THE APPLICATION ESSAY

Whereas the other portions of your application—your transcript, test scores, and involvement in extracurricular activities—are a reflection of what you've accomplished up to this point, your application essay is an opportunity to present yourself in the here and now. The essay shows your originality and verbal skills and how you approach a topic or problem and express your opinion.

Some colleges may request one essay or a combination of essays and short-answer topics to learn more about who you are and how well you can communicate your thoughts. Common essay topics cover such simple themes as writing about yourself and your experiences or why you want to attend that particular school. Other colleges will ask that you show your imaginative or creative side by writing about a favorite author, for instance, or commenting on a hypothetical situation. In such cases, they will be looking at your thought processes and level of creativity.

Admissions officers, particularly those at small or mid-size colleges, use the essay to determine how you, as a student, will fit into life at that college. The essay, therefore, is a critical component of the application process. Here are some tips for writing a winning essay:

- Colleges are looking for an honest representation of who you are and what you think. Make sure that the tone of the essay reflects enthusiasm, maturity, creativity, the ability to communicate, talent, and your leadership skills.
- Be sure you set aside enough time to write the essay, revise it, and revise it *again*. Running "spell check" will

only detect a fraction of the errors you probably made on your first pass at writing it. Take a break and then come back to it and reread it. You will probably notice other style, content, and grammar problems—and ways that you can improve the essay overall.

- Always answer the question that is being asked, making sure that you are specific, clear, and true to your personality.
- Enlist the help of reviewers who know you well—friends, parents, teachers—since they are likely to be the most honest and will keep you on track in the presentation of your true self.

THE PERSONAL INTERVIEW

Although it is relatively rare that a personal interview is required, many colleges recommend that you take this opportunity for a face-to-face discussion with a member of the admissions staff. Read through the application materials to determine whether or not a college places great emphasis on the interview. If they strongly recommend that you have one, it may work against you to forego it.

In contrast to a group interview and some alumni interviews, which are intended to provide information about a college, the personal interview is viewed both as an information session and as further evaluation of your skills and strengths. You will meet with a member of the admissions staff who will be assessing your personal qualities, high school preparation, and your capacity to contribute to undergraduate life at the institution. On average, these meetings last about 45 minutes—a relatively short amount of time in which to gather information and leave the desired impression—so here are some suggestions on how to make the most of it.

Scheduling Your Visit

Generally, students choose to visit campuses in the summer or fall of their senior year. Both times have their advantages. A summer visit, when the campus is not in session, generally allows for a less hectic visit and interview. Visiting in the fall, on the other hand, provides the opportunity to see what campus life is like in full swing. If you choose the fall, consider arranging an overnight trip so that you can stay in one of the college dormitories. At the very least, you should make your way around campus to take part in classes, athletic events, and social activities. Always make an appointment and avoid scheduling more than two college interviews on any given day. Multiple interviews in a single day hinder your chances of making a good impression, and your impressions of the colleges will blur into each other as you hurriedly make your way from place to place.

Preparation

Know the basics about the college before going for your interview. Read the college catalog and Web site in addition to this guide. You will be better prepared to ask questions that are not answered in the literature and that will give you a better understanding of what the college has to offer. You should also spend some time thinking about your strengths and weaknesses and, in particular, what you are looking for in a college education. You will find that as you get a few interviews under your belt, they will get easier. You might consider starting with a college that is not a top contender on your list, so that the stakes are not as high.

Asking Questions

Inevitably, your interviewer will ask you, "Do you have any questions?" Not having one may suggest that you're unprepared or, even worse, not interested. When you do ask questions, make sure that they are ones that matter to you and that have a bearing on your decision about whether or not to attend that college. The questions that you ask will give the interviewer some insight into your personality and priorities. Avoid asking questions that are answered in the college literature—again, a sign of unpreparedness. Although the interviewer will undoubtedly pose questions to you, the interview should not be viewed merely as a question-and-answer session. If a conversation evolves out of a particular question, so much the better. Your interviewer can learn a great deal about you from how you sustain a conversation. Similarly, you will be able to learn a great deal about the college in a conversational format.

Separate the Interview from the Interviewer

Many students base their feelings about a college solely on their impressions of the interviewer. Try not to characterize a college based only on your personal reaction, however, since your impressions can be skewed by whether you and your interviewer hit it off. Pay lots of attention to everything else that you see, hear, and learn about a college. Once on campus, you may never see your interviewer again.

In the end, remember to relax and be yourself. Your interviewer will expect you to be somewhat nervous, which will relieve some of the pressure. Don't drink jitters-producing caffeinated beverages prior to the interview, and suppress nervous fidgets like leg-wagging, finger-drumming, or bracelet-jangling. Consider your interview an opportunity to put forth your best effort and to enhance everything that the college knows about you up to this point.

THE FINAL DECISION

Once you have received your acceptance letters, it is time to go back and look at the whole picture. Provided you received more than one acceptance, you are now in a position to compare your options. The best way to do this is to compare your original list of important college-ranking criteria with what you've discovered about each college along the way. In addition, you and your family will need to factor in the financial aid component. You will need to look beyond these cost issues and the quantifiable pros and cons of each college, however, and know that you have a good feeling about your final choice. Before sending off your acceptance letter, you need to feel confident that the college will feel like home for the next four years. Once the choice is made, the only hard part will be waiting for an entire summer before heading off to college!

The Early Decision Decision

Maybe a senior you knew last year didn't get into the college he wanted. He said it was because he didn't apply early decision. Maybe your friend's mom told your mom that unless students apply early decision, their chances of getting into top schools are slim to none, even though they have great grades and spectacular essays. Maybe you figure you'd better get in on the early decision action.

All of the above are true—well, sort of—because many students applying to college get the term "early decision" backwards. High school guidance and college counselors run into this kind of thinking all the time and suggest putting "decision" before "early"—as in making a wise decision about committing to a college before applying early. For some students, early decision is a great option. For others, early decision is loaded with pitfalls and dangers.

"When students come back in the fall of their senior year, I often hear 'I know I want to apply early. Can you help me choose the school?'" says Kathy Cleaver, Director of College Counseling at Durham Academy in Durham, North Carolina. She compares that to saying, "I know I want to get married, please help me pick the man." Continues Cleaver, "First you have to fall in love with the school and know it's your first choice and then join the circus for early decision." She's referring to the media hype flying around high school halls about early decision—it's easy to fall prey to the early decision madness. Hot competition to get into "top" schools creates early decision anxiety. Mickey Gilbert, Guidance Counselor at Passaic High School in Passaic, New Jersey, throws out some scary numbers that confirm that, yes, the competition for admittance to top schools is white-hot. There are about 30,000 high schools in the United States, and although the majority of high school seniors apply to institutions in their own states, there are still limited spaces in the "top" schools and the eight Ivy League schools. "No wonder kids think that early decision is the way to go," speculates Gilbert. Early decision panic sets in because students are convinced that if they get their applications in early, they have an edge. Sometimes early decision might make the difference, but there are many issues to consider before taking the early decision leap.

EARLY THIS, EARLY THAT

With all the buzz about early decision, do you really know what it means along with all the other early options, such as early action and early notification? And what about the variations of early decision? Each institution can have its own version of early decision, meaning that deadlines and criteria are different. There's the early decision that notifies students by December, there's the early decision round two, and then there is the early action/single choice.

Seeing the confusion, the National Association for College Admission Counseling (NACAC) developed a standard set of definitions. NACAC is an education association of secondary school counselors, college and university admissions and financial aid officers, counselors, and other individuals who work with students as they transition from high school to college. While each institution has its own variations of each early option, an understanding of the basic differences can help. The list that follows was adapted from the definitions found on the NACAC Web site.

Early Decision

- Early decision is the application process in which students make a commitment to a first-choice institution where, if admitted, they definitely will enroll. Should a student who applies for financial aid not be offered an award that makes attendance possible, the student may decline the offer of admission and be released from the early decision commitment.
- While pursuing admission under an early decision plan, students may apply to other institutions, but may have only one early decision application pending at any time.
- The institution must notify the applicant of the decision within a reasonable and clearly stated period of time after the early decision deadline. Usually, a nonrefundable deposit must be made well in advance of May 1.
- A student applying for financial aid must adhere to institutional early decision aid application deadlines.
- The institution will respond to an application for financial aid at or near the time of an offer of admission.
- The early decision application supercedes all other applications. Immediately upon acceptance of an offer of admission, a student must withdraw all other applications and make no subsequent applications.
- The application form will include a request for a parent and a counselor signature, in addition to the student's signature, indicating an understanding of the early decision commitment and agreement to abide by its terms.

Early Action

- Early action is the application process in which students make application to an institution of preference and receive a decision well in advance of the institution's regular response date. Students who are admitted under early action are not obligated to accept the institution's offer of admission or to submit a deposit until the regular reply date (not prior to May 1).
- A student may apply to other colleges without restriction.

- The institution must notify the applicant of the decision within a reasonable and clearly stated period of time after the early action deadline.
- A student applying for financial aid must adhere to institutional aid application deadlines.
- A student admitted under an early action plan may not be required to make a commitment prior to May 1, but may be encouraged to do so as soon as a final college choice is made. Colleges that solicit commitments to offers of early action admission and/or financial assistance prior to May 1 may do so provided those offers include a clear statement that written requests for extensions until May 1 will be granted, and that such requests will not jeopardize a student's status for admission or financial aid.

Regular Decision

- Regular decision is the application process in which a student submits an application to an institution by a specified date and receives a decision within a reasonable and clearly stated period of time, but not later than April 15.
- A student may apply to other colleges without restriction.
- The institution will state a deadline for completion of applications and will respond to completed applications by a specified date.
- A student applying for financial aid must adhere to institutional aid application deadlines.
- A student admitted under a regular decision plan may not be required to make a commitment prior to May 1, but may be encouraged to do so as soon as a final college choice is made. Colleges that solicit commitments to offers of admission and/or financial assistance prior to May 1 may do so provided those offers include a clear statement that written requests for extensions until May 1 will be granted, and that such requests will not jeopardize a student's status for admission or financial aid.

Rolling Admission

- Rolling admission is the application process in which an institution reviews applications as they are completed and renders admission decisions to students throughout the admission cycle.
- A student may apply to other colleges without restriction.
- The institution will respond to completed applications in a timely manner.
- A student applying for financial aid must adhere to institutional aid application deadlines.
- A student admitted under a rolling admission plan may not be required to make a commitment prior to May 1, but may be encouraged to do so as soon as a final college choice is made. Colleges that solicit commitments to offers of admission and/or financial assistance prior to May 1 may do so provided those offers include a clear statement that written requests for extensions until May 1 will be granted, and that such requests will not jeopardize a student's status for admission or financial aid.

Wait List

- Wait list is an admission decision option utilized by institutions to protect against shortfalls in enrollment. Wait lists are sometimes made necessary because of the uncertainty of the admission process, as students submit applications for admission to multiple institutions and may receive several offers of admission. By placing a student on the wait list, an institution does not initially offer or deny admission, but extends to a candidate the possibility of admission in the future before the institution's admission cycle is concluded.
- The institution will ensure that a wait list, if necessary, is of reasonable length and is maintained for a reasonable period of time, but never later than August 1.
- In the letter offering a wait list position, the institution should provide a past wait list history, which describes the number of students placed on the wait list(s), the number offered admission from the wait list, and the availability of financial aid. Students should be given an indication of when they can expect to be notified of a final admission decision.
- An institution must resolve final status and notify wait list candidates as soon after May 1 as possible.
- The institution will not require students to submit deposits to remain on a wait list or pressure students for a commitment to enroll prior to sending an official offer of admission in writing.

There is one more option, called early action/single choice (EASC), that some highly selective schools such as Harvard, Yale, and Stanford have begun using. Early action/single choice is a nonbinding early admission option for freshman applicants that replaces early decision. With this change, students learn about their admission decision in December without being required to reply until May 1. This option allows students to apply to as many colleges as they want under a regular admission time frame. The difference is that the early action/single choice option does not allow a candidate to apply to other schools under any type of early action, early decision, or early notification program. Students are asked to sign a statement in their application agreeing to file only one early application.

Each of these options has variations, depending on the institution using them. Some schools have a November 1 deadline for early decision round one. Smaller schools have a deadline of November 15, while others have a December 1 deadline. Then there's an early decision round two. To make matters even more complicated, some schools with early decision say that students can't apply to other institutions if they've sent in an early decision application to their admissions office. Others say it's okay to apply to other schools at the same time you're applying early decision to them, but if they send you an acceptance, you must withdraw the other applications.

Just because two institutions have an application process called early decision or early action doesn't mean that their policies are identical. "There is no common terminology, even among the colleges that have early

PARENTS, SOME ADVICE FOR YOU

Though guidance counselors stress that high school students should make the final decision about which college to attend, they also say that parents are a very important part of the decision equation. Parents can help as organizers of all the information and provide the support needed to make a good choice. "Little things like setting up file folders and keeping track of deadlines can keep a student on track," advises Gibson.

Along with their children, parents also need to understand the basics of early option terminology as it applies to each institution being considered. Five different colleges might have five different early decision criteria. Read the fine print, and make note of deadlines.

What really will help—you, your child, and your wallet—is to understand the basics about financial aid. Says Leftwich, "Have an in-depth discussion with the financial aid officer so that you are aware of the ramifications, restrictions, and implications of the financial aid offer."

If possible, make an appointment to visit with a financial aid officer at the college while your child is visiting the campus. Bring your tax forms and discuss the prospects of financial aid. "Financial aid people are straight shooters. It's not in their best interest to tell you one thing to get your foot in the door and then turn around and pull the rug out from under you," says McClintick. "Parents might not like the answer they get from the financial aid officer, but they will get a candid assessment of their eligibility for financial aid."

Leftwich suggests having an honest discussion with your child early in the college selection process. Talk about what you can realistically afford, what colleges will appropriately challenge him or her, if location is a factor, and what kind of environment best suits your child. Whichever option your child uses to apply, you both will know the decision is an informed one.

decision," says Christoph Guttentag, Dean of Undergraduate Admissions at Duke University in Durham, North Carolina. He also points out that just when you think you've got the definitions figured out, institutions change them. "Colleges are always balancing the needs of their institution and the needs of students," he comments.

EARLY DECISION: A MATCHMAKING TOOL OR A CLEVER STRATEGY?

Despite the differences in what actually constitutes early decision, it has become more of a strategy than a matchmaking tool, according to Bill McClintick, Director of College Counseling at Mercersburg Academy in Mercersburg, Pennsylvania. He also chairs the national steering committee on admissions standards for NACAC. The focus of early decision used to be on matching the student with the college and letting the admissions office know that that institution is where the student wants to be above all others. Today, early decision is misunderstood and misused. High school seniors think that they must use the early decision tactic to get an edge. The result, says McClintick is "at many of the top places, early decision applications have gone through the roof."

Though high school students may have exaggerated ideas of how much early decision can really help them, it is true that it does give a small segment of students applying at highly selective schools an advantage. Generally, the more selective the institution, the more small differences matter. "Even if it's a small increase, you need everything you can get," states John Latting, Dean of Undergraduate Admissions at The Johns Hopkins University in Baltimore, Maryland.

"Remember," cautions McClintick, "we're only talking about a small slice of kids in the grand scheme of things." He mentions 5 percent of high school seniors nationally who aspire to the "top" institutions. State colleges and universities fill a much lower percentage of their freshman class with early decision applications. "I don't believe that more kids are chasing the same number of spots," says Jon Reider, Director of College Counseling at San Francisco University High School in San Francisco, California. "Students are applying to more and more schools, even with the early decision option on the side. This is inflating the selectivity of some colleges beyond what it used to be." In reality, 90 percent of students apply regular admission. Interest in early decision comes from a relatively small segment of the college applicant pool.

THE BENEFITS OF EARLY DECISION

There are clear benefits for students who apply for early decision. Aside from the fact that early decision does play a role in acceptance rates for a relatively small percentage of students at a small number of schools, early decision is a good option. The caveat is that students must know, without a shred of doubt, that one institution, above all others, is the best match for their goals and their likes and dislikes, and that based on grades and test scores, they solidly match the institution's criteria for admission. The option to go early decision should be taken after extensive research, multiple visits to the campus, and talking to a lot of people. "Early decision is for those who can put their hearts and souls into one application," advises Cleaver.

There are other advantages. You have to make only one choice, and you will know by December if you've been accepted. You have to fill out only one application. You are not chewing your nails over your list of possibilities during the Christmas holiday. Instead, you know where you're going and can sit back and enjoy the rest of your senior year, while others in your class are madly filling out applications, writing essays, and agonizing over the thin envelopes that arrive in the mail. Says Guttentag, "The advantage of having that challenging process over with is not insignificant."

Early decision is helpful for admissions officers at selective colleges because it allows them to make decisions between well-qualified students and select those who really want to be at their institution. As Shawn Leftwich, Director of Undergraduate Admissions at Wheaton College in Illinois, points out, early decision is for the students who are strongly committed. "We like you. You like us. We know you're coming, and we can fill our freshman class." However, on the flip side, she adds that some students aren't so sure about which college they want to attend, and early decision only makes the process more stressful.

Before you decide to go with early decision, consider early action. Many high school counselors lean toward early action, which is another good option. With early action you're able to apply later in the process. This means you will be able to take the SATs again. Your first-semester grades and AP classes taken in the first semester of your senior year can be used to evaluate your eligibility. You have September and October to visit several campuses while they are in session and plenty of time to do the research to put more than one school on your list.

THE PITFALLS OF EARLY DECISION

Though early decision has benefits, before you jump into it, look at the ramifications of that option. Advises Gilbert, "Early decision might give you an edge, but the tradeoff is not so great."

Perhaps the most compelling reason why students should seriously examine early decision before jumping at it is because they are bound by an agreement to attend that school if accepted. Students sign a pledge to attend that institution and are required to withdraw applications from all other schools. They also are obligated to accept the financial aid award that the institution gives them. An early decision is a binding decision. "Regardless," advises David Gibson, College Advisor at St. Mary's Parish in Annapolis, Maryland, "students don't learn about their financial aid awards until March or April, and if the award funding is not at all acceptable because the family's financial need was not met, they need to decline the offer and begin searching for a new college. March or April is not a good time to start applying to new colleges."

How binding is binding? Though no school can force a student to attend if they've signed an early action agreement, students who decide not to attend that school hurt others with that decision. High school counselors have to sign the binding agreement, along with parents, and must state that they will not send out transcripts to other institutions. Many institutions will not accept the application of a student who applied early decision elsewhere and backed out of the agreement. Admissions officers may find out in May that an early decision student is not coming, so they'll call the counselor and ask if the student applied to another school. If so, often a phone call to the other institution is made and acceptance denied. Sometimes the counselor loses a good reputation with that institution, putting applicants who follow in subsequent years at a disadvantage.

After the consequences of signing a binding agreement, the financial aspect of early decision is the next biggest pitfall. "You can't compare financial aid offers," says Latting. "You have only one offer." Students won't know if they're eligible for Pell grants or merit scholarships. Government FAFSA forms are not submitted until January, and students might not find out how much aid they can get until March or April, long after the early decision agreement was signed and sealed. "This means that if they are accepted, they are then obligated to a college that might not fund them to the level of their financial need," says Gibson. Students who apply early action or regular decision are in a better position to negotiate financial aid packages.

QUESTIONS TO ASK YOURSELF BEFORE APPLYING EARLY DECISION

What if you don't get accepted early decision—then what? Speaking from the experience of seeing students deal with early decision rejection letters, Reider says, "Some of your friends are getting acceptance letters, and you get one thin envelope and the pain of rejection. You've given the early decision institution your best shot and you lost." Cleaver has seen kids in her high school end up thinking they won't get in anywhere. "This is the first time they've faced a big rejection and news they don't want to hear," she says, noting that because of the timetable of early decision, letters often come right around exam time in December.

When students apply regular decision, meaning they wait until well into their senior year and apply to several different institutions, it's "all or some," quips Latting. "With early decision, it's all or nothing." Many application deadlines for regular decision are in January. If you get that rejection letter from the school you were counting on, that doesn't give you much time to apply to other schools, much less visit them.

Are you ready to make such a drastic decision so early in your senior year? A lot can change in how you think about your future between the beginning of your senior year and graduation. With six or seven months behind you as a senior, you might be in a better position to compare colleges in April than you were back in September. Think about it—you're making the decision about where you want to spend the next four years of your life in early October of your senior year!

Have you given yourself enough time to pick one college above all others? If you want to apply early decision, you should start making plans to do so in your junior year. In order to apply early decision, you must have your ACTs or SATs taken, campus visits done, a final choice made, a dynamite essay written, a stellar application filled out, and teacher recommendation letters collected. That's a lot to cram into the end of your junior year and a few months into your senior year.

Have you given an admissions office enough information to make a decision about you? The more information the admissions office has about grades and classes you took and activities and leadership positions you held, the better they can decide if you're a good match for them. Do you really want decisions being made about you based on sophomore and junior grades and activities? What happens to that AP English class you finally felt ready to take the beginning of your senior year? What about that calculus class you kicked in the first semester of your senior year? Admissions won't be able to assess that on an early decision application.

EARLY DECISION REJECTION

In case you haven't heard, fat is good, thin is bad. Thin envelopes from college admissions offices usually mean a single-page letter saying good luck, we wish you the best, but you're not going to be attending our school next fall. However stated, it's hard to be rejected, especially when you've applied early decision, which states to the college and to yourself that this is the college you've decided is the only one you really, really want to attend above all others.

But thin envelopes don't mean the end of the world. Cleaver advises to not let early decision get control of you. "There are too many choices of colleges for you not to get into college. You might not get into Princeton, but there are many other wonderful schools if you do the research to look for a good match. Early decision is a tool to use to apply, but it is not always the best tool."

Objecting to the term "perfect match," Reider asks, "Does it really matter what kind of car you drive? There are twenty different colleges that can get you where you want to go. You'll be successful in most places."

HOW TO DO EARLY DECISION THE RIGHT WAY

Taking the early decision option requires more than gathering information, filling out an application, writing an essay, and waiting for an envelope to come in the mail. If you're going to be serious about early decision, the time to start is in your junior year.

Research the institutions at the top of your list. Think through what you want out of college—not just in terms of a future career, but also factors such as location, size, distance from home, sports, and other activities. Think about who you want to be. "It has to be a love connection," says Cleaver. Tune out all the early decision talk and do your homework about each college. Then ask yourself if one stands out above all the others you've researched. Is this the one to which you can commit to a binding agreement? Are you in the competition to be admitted? Will you have the funds to attend this college?

"Admissions can tell if your application is from the heart," Cleaver cautions. Students ask her how to make their applications "look like they want to go there." She replies that what they put on an application and in an essay has to pour out of their hearts. Students who visit the campus and sit in on a class or a campus organization have the edge if something really clicked with them. They will write a convincing application. Perhaps they'll tell about how exciting the professor they heard was or how wonderful it is that the college has a chess club. Cleaver observes that kids usually write about an institution's sports team or about the ivy-covered walls of the campus on their application essay instead of writing about some interesting aspect of the university that spoke to them, which takes research, time, and reflection. "Don't make the mistake of chasing a name and not being a good consumer," cautions McClintick. Part of being a good consumer is to make sure you are a reasonably competitive applicant. This means looking at the school's admission criteria and statistics. What percentage of the freshman class is filled with early decision and early action students? If it's a high percentage, then you might want to reconsider where that school falls on your wish list. How many students return for their sophomore year? If more than 10 percent leave after their freshman year, that should tell you something about student satisfaction—and ultimately yours.

One of the most important ways to choose the right school is to visit the campus, perhaps multiple times and preferably with students on campus. "Campus visits are a critical time to talk with undergraduates and to find out what the academic, social, and physical climate is like," advises Guttentag. If you're staying in a dorm on Tuesday night during a visit, you can tell how serious kids are about their work. What kinds of conversations are they having? "Are these the kind of kids you want to spend four years of your life with?" asks McClintick.

After you've thoroughly investigated all the aspects of a college and decided it's at the absolute top of your list, after you are familiar with the early decision requirements at that institution, after you've determined that you have a good chance of getting into that institution, then you can say early decision is for you. For those who are not so sure, fortunately, colleges and universities have plenty of other options for admission.

What International Students Need to Know About Admission to U.S. Colleges and Universities

Kitty M. Villa

There are two principles to remember about admission to a university in the United States. First, applying is almost never a one-time request for admission but an ongoing process that may involve several exchanges of information between applicant and institution. "Admission process" or "application process" means that a "yes" or "no" is usually not immediate, and requests for additional information are to be expected. To successfully manage this process, you must be prepared to send additional information when requested and then wait for replies. You need a thoughtful balance of persistence to communicate regularly and effectively with your selected universities and patience to endure what can be a very long process.

The second principle involves a marketplace analogy. The most successful applicants are alert to opportunities to create a positive impression that sets them apart from other applicants. They are able to market themselves to their target institution. Institutions are also trying to attract the highest-quality student that they can. The admissions process presents you with the opportunity to analyze your strengths and weaknesses as a student and to look for ways to present yourself in the most marketable manner.

FIRST STEP—SELECTING INSTITUTIONS

With thousands of institutions of higher education in the United States, how do you begin to narrow your choices down to the institutions that are best for you? There are many factors to consider, and you must ultimately decide which factors are most important to you.

Location

You may spend several years studying in the United States. Do you prefer an urban or rural campus? Large or small metropolitan area? If you need to live on campus, will you be unhappy at a university where most students commute from off-campus housing? How do you feel about extremely hot summers or cold winters? Eliminating institutions that do not match your preferences in terms of location will narrow your choices.

Recommendations from Friends, Professors, or Others

There are valid academic reasons to consider the recommendations of people who know you well and have firsthand knowledge about particular institutions. Friends and contacts may be able to provide you with "inside information" about the campus or its academic programs to which published sources have no access. You should carefully balance anecdotal information with your own research and your own impressions. However, current and former students, professors, and others may provide excellent information during the application process.

Your Own Academic and Career Goals

Consideration of your academic goals is more complex than it may seem at first glance. All institutions do not offer the same academic programs. The application form usually provides a definitive listing of the academic programs offered by an institution. A course catalog describes the degree program and all the courses offered. In addition to printed sources, there is a tremendous amount of institutional information available on the Web. Program descriptions, even course descriptions and course syllabi, are often available to peruse online.

You may be interested in the rankings of either the university or of a program of study. Keep in mind, however, that rankings usually assume that quality is quantifiable. Rankings are usually based on presumptions about how data relate to quality and are likely to be unproven. It is important to carefully consider the source and the criteria of any ranking information before believing and acting upon it.

Your Own Educational Background

You may be concerned about the interpretation of your educational credentials, since your country's degree nomenclature and the grading scale may differ from those in the United States. Universities use reference books about the educational systems of other countries to help them understand specific educational credentials. Generally, these credentials are interpreted by each institution; there is not a single interpretation that applies to every institution. The lack of uniformity is good news for most students, since it means that students from a wide variety of educational backgrounds can find a U.S. university that is appropriate to their needs.

To choose an appropriate institution, you can and should do an informal self-evaluation of your educational background. This self-analysis involves three important questions:

1. How Many Years of Study Have You Completed?
Completion of secondary school with at least twelve total years of education usually qualifies students to apply for undergraduate (bachelor's) degree programs. Completion of a university degree program that involves at least sixteen years of total education qualifies one to apply for admission to graduate (master's) degree programs in the United States.

2. Does the Education That You Have Completed in Your Country Provide Access to Further Study in the United States?
Consider the kind of institution where you completed your previous studies. If educational opportunities in your country are limited, it may be necessary to investigate many U.S. institutions and programs in order to find a match.

3. Are Your Previous Marks or Grades Excellent, Average, or Poor?
Your educational record influences your choice of U.S. institutions. If your grades are average or poor, it may be advisable to apply to several institutions with minimally difficult or noncompetitive entrance levels.

YOU are one of the best sources of information about the level and quality of your previous studies. Awareness of your educational assets and liabilities will serve you well throughout the application process.

SECOND STEP—PLANNING AND ASSEMBLING THE APPLICATION

Planning and assembling a university application can be compared to the construction of a building. First, you must start with a solid foundation, which is the application form itself. The application, often available online as well as in paper form, usually contains a wealth of useful information, such as deadlines, fees, and degree programs available at that institution. To build a solid application, it is best to begin well in advance of the application deadline.

How to Obtain the Application Form

Application forms and links to institutional Web sites may also be available at a U.S. educational advising center associated with the American Embassy or Consulate in your country. These centers are excellent resources for international students and provide information about standardized test administration, scholarships, and other matters to students who are interested in studying in the United States. Your local U.S. Embassy or Consulate can guide you to the nearest educational advising center.

What Are the Key Components of a Complete Application?

Institutional requirements vary, but the standard components of a complete application include the following:

- Transcript
- Required standardized examination scores
- Evidence of financial support
- Letters of recommendation
- Application fee

Transcript
A complete academic record or transcript includes all courses completed, grades earned, and degrees awarded. Most universities require an official transcript to be sent directly from the school or university. In many other countries, however, the practice is to issue official transcripts and degree certificates directly to the student. If you have only one official copy of your transcript, it may be a challenge to get additional certified copies that are acceptable to U.S. universities. Some institutions will issue additional official copies for application purposes.

If your institution does not provide this service, you may have to seek an alternate source of certification. As a last resort, you may send a photocopy of your official transcript, explain that you have only one original, and ask the university for advice on how to deal with this situation.

Required Standardized Examination Scores
Arranging to take standardized examinations and earning the required scores seem to cause the most anxiety for international students.

The university application form usually indicates which examinations are required. The standardized examination required most often for undergraduate admission is the Test of English as a Foreign Language (TOEFL). Institutions may also require the SAT of undergraduate applicants. These standardized examinations are administered by the Educational Testing Service (ETS).

These examinations are offered in almost every country of the world. It is advisable to begin planning for standardized examinations at least six months prior to the application deadline of your desired institutions. Test centers fill up quickly, so it is important to register as soon as possible. Information about the examinations is available at U.S. educational advising centers associated with embassies or consulates.

Most universities require that the original test scores, not a student copy, be sent directly by the testing service. When you register for the test, be sure to indicate that the testing service should send the test scores directly to the universities.

You should begin your application process before you receive your test scores. Delaying submission of your application until the test scores arrive may cause you to miss

FOR MORE INFORMATION

Questions about test formats, locations, dates, and registration may be addressed to:

ETS Corporate Headquarters
Rosedale Road
Princeton, New Jersey 08541
Web sites: http://www.ets.org
http://www.ets.org/toefl/
Phone: 609-921-9000
Fax: 609-734-5410

deadlines and negatively affect the outcome of your application. If you want to know your scores in order to assess your chances of admission to an institution with rigorous admission standards, you should take the tests early.

Many universities in the United States set minimum required scores on the TOEFL or other standardized examinations. Test scores are an important factor, but most institutions also look at a number of other factors in their consideration of a candidate for admission.

Evidence of Financial Support

Evidence of financial support is required to issue immigration documents to admitted students. This is part of a complete application package but usually plays no role in determining admission. Most institutions make admissions decisions without regard to the source and amount of financial support.

Letters of Recommendation

Most institutions require one or more letters of recommendation. The best letters are written by former professors, employers, or others who can comment on your academic achievements or professional potential.

Some universities provide a special form for the letters of recommendation. If possible, use the forms provided. If you are applying to a large number of universities, however, or if your recommenders are not available to complete several forms, it may be necessary for you to duplicate a general recommendation letter.

Application Fee

Most universities also require an application fee, ranging from $25 to $100, which must be paid to initiate consideration of the application.

Completing the Application Form

Whether sent by mail or electronically, the application form must be neat and thoroughly filled out. Although parts of the application may not seem to apply to you or your situation, do your best to answer all the questions.

Remember that this is a process. You provide information, and your proposed university then may request clarification and further information. If you have questions, it is better to initiate the entire process by submitting the application form rather than asking questions before you apply. The university will be better able to respond to you after it has your application. Always complete as much as you can. Do not permit uncertainty about the completion of the application form to cause unnecessary delays.

THIRD STEP—DISTINGUISH YOUR APPLICATION

To distinguish your application—to market yourself successfully—is ultimately the most important part of the application process. As you select your prospective universities, begin to analyze your strengths and weaknesses as a prospective student. As you complete your application, you should strive to create a positive impression and set yourself apart from other applicants, to highlight your assets and bring these qualities to the attention of the appropriate university administrators and professors. Applying early is a very easy way to distinguish your application.

Deadline or Guideline?

The application deadline is the last date that an application for a given semester will be accepted. Often, the application will specify that all required documents and information be submitted before the deadline date. To meet the deadlines, start the application process early. This also gives you more time to take—and perhaps retake and improve—the required standardized tests.

Admissions deliberations may take several weeks or months. In the meantime, most institutions accept additional information, including improved test scores, after the posted deadline.

Even if your application is initially rejected, you may be able to provide additional information to change the decision. You can request reconsideration based on additional information, such as improved test scores, strong letters of recommendation, or information about your class rank. Applying early allows more time to improve your application. Also, some students may decide not to accept their offers of admission, leaving room for offers to students on a waiting list. Reconsideration of the admission decisions can occur well beyond the application deadline.

Think of the deadline as a guideline rather than an impermeable barrier. Many factors—the strength of the application, your research interests, the number of spaces available at the proposed institution—can override the enforcement of an application deadline. So, if you lack a test score or transcript by the official deadline, you may still be able to apply and be accepted.

Statement of Purpose

The statement of purpose is your first and perhaps best opportunity to present yourself as an excellent candidate for admission. Whether or not a personal history essay or statement of purpose is required, always include a carefully written statement of purpose with your applications. A compelling statement of purpose does not have to be lengthy, but it should include some basic components:

- Part One—Introduce yourself and describe your educational background. This is your opportunity to describe any facet of your educational experience that you wish to emphasize. Perhaps you attended a highly ranked secondary school or university in your home country.

Mention the name and any noteworthy characteristics of the secondary school or university from which you graduated. Explain the grading scale used at your university. Do not forget to mention your rank in your graduating class and any honors you may have received. This is not the time to be modest.

- Part Two—Describe your current academic and career interests and goals. Think about how these will fit into those of the institution to which you are applying, and mention the reasons why you have selected that institution.
- Part Three—Describe your long-term goals. When you finish your program of study, what do you plan to do next? If you already have a job offer or a career plan, describe it. Give some thought to how you'll demonstrate that studying in the United States. will ultimately benefit others.

Use Personal Contacts When Possible

Appropriate and judicious use of your own network of contacts can be very helpful. Friends, former professors, former students of your selected institutions, and others may be willing to advise you during the application process and provide you with introductions to key administrators or professors. If suggested, you may wish to contact certain professors or administrators by mail, phone, or e-mail. A personal visit to discuss your interest in the institution may be appropriate. Whatever your choice of communication, try to make the encounter pleasant and personal. Your goal is to make a positive impression, not to rush the admission decision.

There is no single right way to be admitted to U.S. universities. The same characteristics that make the educational choice in the United States so difficult—the number of institutions and the variety of programs of study—are the same attributes that allow so many international students to find the institution that's right for them.

Kitty M. Villa is the former Assistant Director, International Office, at the University of Texas at Austin.

Financial Aid Countdown Calendar

JUNIOR YEAR

Fall

Now is the time to get serious about the colleges in which you are interested. Meet with your guidance counselor to help you narrow down your choices. Hopefully by the spring, your list will have five to ten solid choices. College visits are always a great idea—remember this will be the place you will call home for four years, so start your campus visits soon!

- ❒ Register for the PSAT.
- ❒ Check out local financial aid nights in the area. Be sure to attend these valuable sessions, especially if this is the first time your family is sending someone off to college. Try to become familiar with common financial aid terms. Start reviewing the literature available and begin to familiarize yourself with the various programs. A good booklet is published by the U.S. Department of Education, "Funding Education Beyond High School: The Guide to Federal Student Aid" and is available at any financial aid office or on the Web at http://studentaid.ed.gov/students/attachments/siteresources/Funding_Education_Beyond_HS_2010-11.pdf.
- ❒ In October, take the PSAT/NMSQT.
- ❒ Do some Web browsing! There are many free scholarship search engines, such as Petersons.com. Also, head to the bookstore or library and pick up a copy of *Peterson's Scholarships, Grants & Prizes*. It features details on billions of dollars of aid from private sources.
- ❒ Ask your parents to contact their employers, unions, and any church and fraternal organizations with which they have a connection to learn about possible scholarship opportunities.
- ❒ Check with your high school guidance counselor for the qualifications and deadlines of local scholarship awards. Many guidance counselors report that there are few applicants for these awards.

Winter

- ❒ Keep checking for scholarships! Remember that this is the one area over which you have control. The harder you work, the better your chances for success!
- ❒ Register and study for the SAT and SAT Subject Tests.

Spring

- ❒ Spring Break—a great time to visit colleges. Remember your top ten list? Time to start narrowing it down.
- ❒ Review the requirements for local scholarships. What can you do now and over the summer to improve your chances?
- ❒ Take the SATs. Good luck!
- ❒ Look for a summer job, especially one that ties in with your college plans. For example, if you want to major in premed, why not try to get a job at a hospital or with a laboratory?

Summer

- ❒ College visit time! Ask: Is this where I see myself getting my undergraduate degree? Can I adjust to the seasons, the town surrounding the campus, the distance from home, the college size? Does this school feel right for me?
- ❒ Why not get a jump on college (and maybe save some money!) and enroll for a college course at the local community college? Or, better yet, do some extra prep work for the SAT!

SENIOR YEAR

Fall

How's the college list coming? Can you get your list down to five or six choices? Your guidance counselor can help with this process. Once you have your top choices, make a list of what each college requires for admission and financial aid. Be sure your list includes all deadlines. Attend a financial aid night presentation with your parents. Some of these sessions offer help in completing forms; others offer a broader view of the process. Contact the presenter (usually a local college financial aid professional) to be sure you are getting the information you need.

❒ Do any of these colleges require the CSS/Financial Aid PROFILE® financial aid application? Many private colleges use this form for institutional aid. You need to file this comprehensive form in late September or early October. For more information or to find out which colleges use this supplemental form, go to http://profileonline.collegeboard.com/index.jsp. (Web site registration is free; however, PROFILE is a fee-based application).

❒ Don't falter now in your scholarship search. Get the applications filed by the published deadlines.

❒ Register now if you are planning to retake the SAT.

❒ Most important, start completing your college applications—the earlier, the better! If you are interested in early decision or early action, now is the time! Remember, accuracy and completeness are a must!

Winter

❒ Ensure all college applications are completed.

❒ Get the Free Application for Federal Student Aid (FAFSA). This is the key form for financial aid for every school across the country. Remember, watch your deadlines, but do not file until after January 1. Be sure to keep a copy of the form, whether you file electronically or with the paper application. Do you have some questions? Call the local financial aid office. Many states have special toll-free call-in programs in January and February, Financial Aid Awareness Month. Be sure that you have completed each school's required forms.

❒ As the letters of admission start to arrive, the financial aid award letters should be right behind them. Important question for parents: What is the bottom line? Remember, aid at a lower-cost state school will be less than a higher-cost private college. But what will you be required to pay? This can be confusing, so consider gift aid (scholarships and grants), student loans, and parent loans. The school with the lowest sticker price (tuition, fees, and room and board) might not be the best bargain when you look at the overall financial aid package.

Spring

❒ Still not sure where to go? The financial aid package at your top choice just not enough? Call the financial aid office and the admissions office. Talk it over. While schools don't like to bargain, they are usually willing to take a second look. Is there something unusual about your family's financial situation that might impact your parents' ability to pay?

❒ By May 1, you must make your final decision. Notify your chosen college and find out what you need to do next. Tell the other colleges you are not accepting their offers of admission and financial aid.

Summer

❒ Time to crunch the numbers. Parents, get information from the college on the total charges for the coming fall term. Deduct the aid package and then plan for how the balance will be paid. Contact the college financial aid office for the best parental loan program. If you want to arrange for a payment plan, contact the business office for further information. Most schools have deferred payment plans available for a nominal fee.

Congratulations! Remember that you need to reapply for aid every year!

Who's Paying for This? Financial Aid Basics

A college education can be expensive—costing more than $150,000 for four years at some of the higher priced private colleges and universities. Even at the lower cost state colleges and universities, the cost of a four-year education can approach $60,000. Determining how you and your family will come up with the necessary funds to pay for your education requires planning, perseverance, and learning as much as you can about the options that are available to you. But before you get discouraged, College Board statistics show that 53 percent of full-time students attend four-year public and private colleges with tuition and fees less than $9000, while 20 percent attend colleges that have tuition and fees more than $36,000. College costs tend to be less in the western states and higher in New England.

Paying for college should not be looked at as a four-year financial commitment. For many families, paying the total cost of a student's college education out of current income and savings is usually not realistic. For families that have planned ahead and have financial savings established for higher education, the burden is a lot easier. But for most, meeting the cost of college requires the pooling of current income and assets and investing in longer-term loan options. These family resources, together with financial assistance from state, federal, and institutional sources, enable millions of students each year to attend the institution of their choice.

FINANCIAL AID PROGRAMS

There are three types of financial aid:

1. Gift-aid—Scholarships and grants are funds that do not have to be repaid.
2. Loans—Loans must be repaid, usually after graduation; the amount you have to pay back is the total you've borrowed plus any accrued interest. This is considered a source of self-help aid.
3. Student employment—Student employment is a job arranged for you by the financial aid office. This is another source of self-help aid.

The federal government has four major grant programs—the Federal Pell Grant, the Federal Supplemental Educational Opportunity Grant, Academic Competitiveness Grants (ACG), and SMART grants. AGG and SMART grants are limited to students who qualify for a Pell grant and are awarded to a select group of students. Overall, these grants are targeted to low-to-moderate income families with significant financial need. The federal government also sponsors a student employment program called the Federal Work-Study Program, which offers jobs both on and off campus, and several loan programs, including those for students and for parents of undergraduate students.

There are two types of student loan programs: subsidized and unsubsidized. The subsidized Federal Direct Loan and the Federal Perkins Loan are need-based, government-subsidized loans. Students who borrow through these programs do not have to pay interest on the loan until after they graduate or leave school. The unsubsidized Federal Direct Loan and the Federal Direct PLUS Loan Program are not based on need, and borrowers are responsible for the interest while the student is in school. These loans are administered by different methods. Once you choose your college, the financial aid office will guide you through this process.

After you've submitted your financial aid application and you've been accepted for admission, each college will send you a letter describing your financial aid award. Most award letters show estimated college costs, how much you and your family are expected to contribute, and the amount and types of aid you have been awarded. Most students are awarded aid from a combination of sources and programs. Hence, your award is often called a financial aid "package."

SOURCES OF FINANCIAL AID

Millions of students and families apply for financial aid each year. Financial aid from all sources exceeds $143 billion per year. The largest single source of aid is the federal government, which will award more than $100 billion this year.

The next largest source of financial aid is found in the college and university community. Most of this aid is awarded to students who have a demonstrated need based on the Federal Methodology. Some institutions use a different formula, the Institutional Methodology (IM), to award their own funds in conjunction with other forms of aid. Institutional aid may be either need-based or non-need based. Aid that is not based on need is usually awarded for a student's academic performance (merit awards), specific talents or abilities, or to attract the type of students a college seeks to enroll.

Another source of financial aid is from state government. All states offer grant and/or scholarship aid, most of which is need-based. However, more and more states are offering substantial merit-based aid programs. Most state programs award aid only to students attending college in their home state.

Other sources of financial aid include:

- Private agencies
- Foundations
- Corporations
- Clubs
- Fraternal and service organizations
- Civic associations
- Unions
- Religious groups that award grants, scholarships, and low-interest loans
- Employers that provide tuition reimbursement benefits for employees and their children

More information about these different sources of aid is available from high school guidance offices, public libraries, college financial aid offices, directly from the sponsoring organizations, and on the Web at www.petersons.com and www.finaid.org.

HOW NEED-BASED FINANCIAL AID IS AWARDED

When you apply for aid, your family's financial situation is analyzed using a government-approved formula called the Federal Methodology. This formula looks at five items:

1. Demographic information of the family
2. Income of the parents
3. Assets of the parents
4. Income of the student
5. Assets of the student

This analysis determines the amount you and your family are expected to contribute toward your college expenses, called your Expected Family Contribution or EFC. If the EFC is equal to or more than the cost of attendance at a particular college, then you do not demonstrate financial need. However, even if you don't have financial need, you may still qualify for aid, as there are grants, scholarships, and loan programs that are not need-based.

If the cost of your education is greater than your EFC, then you do demonstrate financial need and qualify for assistance. The amount of your financial need that can be met varies from school to school. Some are able to meet your full need, while others can only cover a certain percentage of need. Here's the formula:

Cost of Attendance
− Expected Family Contribution

= Financial Need

The EFC remains constant, but your need will vary according to the costs of attendance at a particular college. In general, the higher the tuition and fees at a particular college, the higher the cost of attendance will be. Expenses for books and supplies, room and board, transportation, and other miscellaneous items are included in the overall cost of attendance. It is important to remember that you do not have to be "needy" to qualify for financial aid. Many middle and upper-middle income families qualify for need-based financial aid.

APPLYING FOR FINANCIAL AID

Every student must complete the Free Application for Federal Student Aid (FAFSA) to be considered for financial aid. The FAFSA is available from your high school guidance office, many public libraries, colleges in your area, or directly from the U.S. Department of Education.

Students are encouraged to apply for federal student aid on the Web. The electronic version of the FAFSA can be accessed at http://www.fafsa.ed.gov. Both the student and at least one parent must apply for a federal PIN at http://www.pin.ed.gov. The PIN serves as your electronic signature when applying for aid on the Web.

To award their own funds, some colleges require an additional application, the CSS/Financial Aid PROFILE® form. The PROFILE asks supplemental questions that some colleges and awarding agencies feel provide a more accurate assessment of the family's ability to pay for college. It is up to the college to decide whether it will use only the FAFSA or both the FAFSA and the PROFILE. PROFILE applications are available from the high school guidance office and on the Web. Both the paper application and the Web site list those colleges and programs that require the PROFILE application.

If Every College You're Applying to for Fall 2011 Requires the FAFSA

. . . then it's pretty simple: Complete the FAFSA after January 1, 2011, being certain to send it in before any college-imposed deadlines. (You are not permitted to send in the 2011–12 FAFSA before January 1, 2011.) Most college FAFSA application deadlines are in February or early March. It is easier if you have all your financial records for the previous year available, but if that is not possible, you are strongly encouraged to use estimated figures.

After you send in your FAFSA, either with the paper application or electronically, you'll receive a Student Aid Report (SAR) that includes all of the information you reported and shows your EFC. If you provided an e-mail address, the SAR is sent to you electronically; otherwise, you will receive a paper copy in the mail. Be sure to review the SAR, checking to see if the information you reported is accurately represented. If you used estimated numbers to complete the FAFSA, you may have to resubmit the SAR with any corrections to the data. The college(s) you have designated on the FAFSA will receive the information you reported and will use that data to make their decision. In many instances, the colleges to which you've applied will ask you to send copies of your and your parents' federal income tax returns for 2010, plus any other documents needed to verify the information you reported.

If a College Requires the PROFILE

Step 1: Register for the CSS/Financial Aid PROFILE in the fall of your senior year in high school. You can apply for the PROFILE online at http://profileonline.collegeboard.com/prf/index.jsp. Registration information, with a list of the colleges that require the PROFILE is available in most high school guidance offices. There is a fee for using the Financial Aid PROFILE application ($25 for the first college and $16 for each additional college). You must pay for the service by credit card when you register. If you do not have a credit card, you will be billed. A limited number of fee waivers are automatically granted to first-time applicants based on the financial information provided on the PROFILE.

Step 2: Fill out your customized CSS/Financial Aid PROFILE. Once you register, your application will be immediately available online and will have questions which all students must complete, questions which must be completed by the student's parents (unless the student is independent and the colleges or programs selected do not require parental information), and *may* have supplemental questions needed by one or more of your schools or programs. If required, those will be found in Section Q of the application.

In addition to the PROFILE application you complete online, you may also be required to complete a Business/Farm Supplement via traditional paper format. Completion of this form is not a part of the online process. If this form is required, instructions on how to download and print the supplemental form are provided. If your biological or adoptive parents are separated or divorced and your colleges and programs require it, your noncustodial parent may be asked to complete the Noncustodial PROFILE.

Once you complete and submit your PROFILE application, it will be processed and sent directly to your requested colleges and programs.

IF YOU DON'T QUALIFY FOR NEED-BASED AID

If you are not eligible for need-based aid, you can still find ways to lessen your burden.

Here are some suggestions:

- Search for merit scholarships. You can start at the initial stages of your application process. College merit awards are increasingly important as more and more colleges award these to students they especially want to attract. As a result, applying to a college at which your qualifications put you at the top of the entering class may give you a larger merit award. Another source of aid to look for is private scholarships that are given for special skills and talents. Additional information can be found at and at www.finaid.org.
- Seek employment during the summer and the academic year. The student employment office at your college can help you locate a school-year job. Many colleges and local businesses have vacancies remaining after they have hired students who are receiving Federal Work-Study Program financial aid.
- Borrow through the unsubsidized Federal Direct Loan program. This is generally available to all students. The terms and conditions are similar to the subsidized loans. The biggest difference is that the borrower is responsible for the interest while still in college, although the government permits students to delay paying the interest right away and add the accrued interest to the total amount owed. You must file the FAFSA to be considered.
- After you've secured what you can through scholarships, working, and borrowing, you and your parents will be expected to meet your share of the college bill (the Expected Family Contribution). Many colleges offer monthly payment plans that spread the cost over the academic year. If the monthly payments are too high, parents can borrow through the Federal Direct PLUS Loan Program, through one of the many private education loan programs available, or through home equity loans and lines of credit. Families seeking assistance in financing college expenses should inquire at the financial aid office about what programs are available at the college. Some families seek the advice of professional financial advisers and tax consultants.

Middle-Income Families: Making the Financial Aid Process Work

Richard Woodland

A report from the U.S. Department of Education's National Center for Education Statistics took a close look at how middle-income families finance a college education. The report, *Middle Income Undergraduates: Where They Enroll and How They Pay for Their Education,* was one of the first detailed studies of these families. Even though 31 percent of middle-income families have the entire cost of attendance covered by financial aid, there is widespread angst among middle-income families that, while they earn too much to qualify for grant assistance, they are financially unable to pay the spiraling costs of higher education.

First, we have to agree on what constitutes a "middle-income" family. For the purposes of the federal study, middle income is defined as those families with incomes between $35,000 and $70,000. The good news is that 52 percent of these families received grants, while the balance received loans. Other sources of aid, including work-study, also helped close the gap.

So how do these families do it? Is there a magic key that will open the door to significant amounts of grants and scholarships?

The report found some interesting trends. One way families can make college more affordable is by choosing a less expensive college. In fact, in this income group, 29 percent choose to enroll in low- to moderate-cost schools. These include schools where the total cost is less than $8,500 per year. In this sector, we find the community colleges and lower-priced state colleges and universities. But almost half of these middle-income families choose schools in the upper-level tier, with costs ranging from $8,500 to $16,000. The remaining 23 percent enrolled at the highest-tier schools, with costs above $16,000. Clearly, while cost is a factor, middle-income families are not limiting their choices based on costs alone.

The report shows that families pay these higher costs with a combination of family assets, current income, and long-term borrowing. This is often referred to as the "past-present-future" model of financing. In fact, just by looking at the Expected Family Contributions, it is clear that there is a significant gap in what families need and what the financial aid process can provide. Families are closing this gap by making the financial sacrifices necessary to pay the price at higher-cost schools, especially if they think their child is academically strong. The report concludes that parents are more likely to pay for a higher-priced education if their child scores high on the SAT.

The best place for middle-income families to start is with the high school guidance office. This office has information on financial aid and valuable leads on local scholarships. Most guidance officers report that there are far fewer applicants for these locally based scholarships than one would expect. So read the information they send home and check on the application process. A few of those $500–$1000 scholarships can add up!

Plan to attend a financial aid awareness program. If your school does not offer one, contact your local college financial aid office and see when and where they will be speaking. You can get a lot of "inside" information on how the financial aid process works.

Next, be sure to file the correct applications for aid. Remember, each school can have a different set of requirements. For example, many higher-cost private colleges will require the CSS/Financial Aid PROFILE® application, filed in September or October of the senior year. Other schools may have their own institutional aid application. All schools will require the Free Application for Federal Student Aid (FAFSA). Watch the deadlines! It is imperative that you meet the school's published application deadline. Generally, schools are not flexible about this, so be sure to double-check the due date of all applications.

Finally, become a smart educational consumer. Peterson's has a wide range of resources available to help you understand the process. Be sure to also check your local library, bookstore, and of course, the Internet. A great Web site to check is www.finaid.org.

Once admitted to the various colleges and universities, you will receive an award notice outlining the aid you are eligible to receive. If you feel the offer is not sufficient, or if you have some unique financial circumstances, call the school's financial aid office to see if you can have your application reviewed again. The financial aid office is your best source for putting the pieces together and finding financial solutions.

The financial aid office will help you determine the "net price." This is the actual out-of-pocket cost that you will need to cover. Through a combination of student and parent loans, most families are able to meet these expenses with other forms of financial aid and family resources.

Many students help meet their educational expenses by working while in school. While this works for many students, research shows that too many hours spent away from your studies will negatively impact your academic success. Most experts feel that working 10 to 15 hours a week is optimal.

An overlooked source of aid is the tax credits given to middle-income families. Rather than extending eligibility for traditional sources of grant assistance to middle-income families, the federal tax system has built in a number of significant tax benefits, known as the Hope Scholarship and Lifetime Learning tax credit, for middle-income families. While it may be seven or eight months before you see the tax credit, most families in this income group can count on this benefit, usually between $1500 to $2000 per student. This is real money in your pocket. You do not need to itemize your deductions to qualify for this tax credit.

A tool to help families get a handle on the ever-rising costs of college is to assume that you can pay one third of the "net charges" from savings, another third from available (non-retirement) assets, and the rest from parent borrowing. If any one of these "thirds" is not available, shift that amount to one of the other resources. However, if it looks like you will be financing most or all of the costs from future income (borrowing), it may be wise to consider a lower-cost college.

Millions of middle-income families send their children to colleges and universities every year. Only 8 percent attend the lowest-priced schools. By using the concept of past-present-future financing, institutional assistance, federal and state aid, meaningful targeted tax relief, and student earnings, you can afford even the highest-cost schools.

Richard Woodland is the former Director of Financial Aid at Rutgers University–Camden.

Honors Programs and Colleges: Smart Choices for an Undergraduate Education

Dr. Joan Digby

In general, students and their parents are guided toward a narrow selection of colleges and universities based on reputation, conversations with friends, or promotional material. Few people think to approach the college search focused on honors opportunities. As a result, students with extraordinary talents and interests miss out on a rich variety of untapped financial resources and exciting college experiences.

The smarter approach is to seek out a distinctive education that caters to students' great diversity of intellectual and creative strengths. If you are a strong student filled with ideas, longing for creative expression and ready to take on career-shaping challenges, then an honors education is just for you. Honors programs and colleges offer some of the finest undergraduate degrees available at U.S. colleges and do it with students in mind. The essence of honors is personal attention, top faculty, enlightening seminars, illuminating study-travel experiences, research options, and career-building internships—all designed to enhance a classic education and prepare you for life achievements. And here is an eye-opening bonus: Honors program and colleges may reward your past academic performance by giving you scholarships that will help you pay for your higher education!

Take your choice of institutions: community college, state or private, two- or four-year, college or large research university. There are honors opportunities in each. What they share is an unqualified commitment to academic excellence. Honors education teaches students to think and write clearly, be excited by ideas, and become independent, creative, self-confident learners. It prepares exceptional students for professional choices in every imaginable sphere of life: arts and sciences, engineering, business, health, education, medicine, theater, music, film, journalism, media, law, politics—invent your own professional goal and honors will guide you to it! Whichever honors program or college you choose, you can be sure to enjoy an extraordinarily fulfilling undergraduate education.

WHO ARE HONORS STUDENTS?

Who are you? Perhaps a high school junior filling out your first college application, a community college student seeking to transfer to a four-year college, or possibly a four-year college student doing better than you had expected. You might be an international student, a varsity athlete, captain of the debate team, or second violin in the orchestra. Whether you are the first person in your family to attend college or an adult with a grown family seeking a new career, honors might well be right for you. Honors programs admit students with every imaginable background and educational goal.

How does honors satisfy students and give them something special? Read what students in some honors programs and colleges say. Although they refer to particular honors colleges or programs, their experiences are typical of what students find exciting about honors education on hundreds of campuses around the country.

"Being an honors program student has been a life-changing experience for me. I have gained tremendously in knowledge, experience, and self-esteem. I have learned so much more in the program than any textbook could teach about the value of encouraging support and positive thinking."

—*Cheri Becker, Mount Wachusett Community College*

"I've been in a healing ceremony in Ecuador and have performed music on stage. I've guided my peers and Navajo children, hiked the Grand Canyon, and so much more. Sometimes, experience speaks for itself; always, it creates paths, opens eyes, and helps us find our places. Thanks to my honors program, I've experienced these wonders and accomplishments. Now I know that there are no greater lessons than how to learn and love discovery."

—*April Fisher, University of North Florida*

"The Honors College has been my home away from home. In the midst of a diverse, fairly large university, it has provided me with the intimacy that I needed . . . My freshman-year living situation on the honors floor . . . allowed me to find like-minded students early in my college career."

—*Brian Leech, Davidson Honors College, University of Montana*

"I was able to transition from an honors program at a two-year institution into an honors program at a four-year institution without any reservations or tribulations."

—*Rachel Jones Williams, Harrisburg Area Community College*

"Every single professor is in love with what they do and it shows in their research, their amazing teaching, and their interaction with students outside of the classroom. The undergraduate journey can be very difficult at times, but as an Honors College student, you're sure to have plenty of support every step of the way."

—*Walteria Tucker, Wilkes Honors College, Florida Atlantic University*

"The class size is perfect and I've been able to make some of my closest relationships with students and teachers through the program. The majority of honors faculty I have encountered have been overwhelmingly helpful . . . and my favorite courses have been honors classes."

—*Ellen Daschler, Eastern Illinois University*

"Our professor met us at a local restaurant the last evening of class and we shared a wonderful dinner. It had such a familiar feel to it because these are students I have known throughout my four years in the program."

—*Betsy Porter, University of La Verne*

"For the last two years, I have investigated new synthetic methods under the direction of a professor emeritus. Through the University Honors College, I am able to pursue this interest in chemistry and other academic endeavors . . . that have allowed me to develop my academic potential and contribute to the scientific body of knowledge."

—*Justin Chalker, University of Pittsburgh*

"The most rewarding part of being a member of the honors program is the joy of doing creative, meaningful projects with faculty I love."

—*Meleia Egger, Hartwick College*

"I would . . . like to add a word of praise for the way the curriculum is structured. It has deepened and enriched my thinking and helped me develop tools to negotiate the complex world we live in."

—*Monideepa Talukdar, Southeastern Louisiana University*

"We have a better time . . . our discussions get rather heated. In a lot of classes, only one or two students will speak up, but in the honors classes, it's a free-for-all."

—*Jonathan Post, Reinhardt College*

"My internship at a major international bank gave me an in-depth look into the world of investment and accounting. Funded by the Honors College, I was able to study business and culture in Shanghai, China, for a month. These valuable experiences are helping me to develop professionally, academically, and personally."

—*Jenny Lam, Honors College, The College of Staten Island, CUNY*

"The honors thesis was the key factor during the selection process at my future employer. . . . It helped me to get the job and have an advantage over others. It is a lot of work but, in the end, it is worth it."

—*Olgierd Hinz, Lee Honors College, Western Michigan University*

These portraits don't tell the whole story, but they should give you a sense of what it means to be part of an honors program or college. One of the great strengths of honors programs and colleges is that they are nurturing environments that encourage students to be well-rounded and help students make life choices.

WHAT IS AN HONORS PROGRAM?

An honors program is a sequence of courses designed specifically to encourage independent and creative learning. For more than half a century, honors education—given definition by the National Collegiate Honors Council—has been an institution on U.S. campuses. Although honors programs have many different designs, there are typical components. At two-year colleges, the programs often concentrate on special versions of general education courses and may have individual capstone projects that come out of students' special interests. At four-year colleges and universities, honors programs are generally designed for students of almost every major in every college on campus. In growing numbers, they are given additional prominence as honors colleges. Whether a program or a college, honors often includes a general education or "core" component followed by advanced courses (often called colloquia or seminars). Some programs have honors contracts that shape existing courses into honors components to suit the needs of individual students. Many have interdisciplinary or collaborative seminars that bring students of different majors together to discuss a complex topic with faculty members from different disciplines. A good number have final thesis, capstone, or creative projects, which may or may not be in the departmental major. Almost always, honors curriculum is incorporated within whatever number of credits is required of every student for graduation. Honors very rarely requires students to take additional credits. Students who complete an honors program or honors college curriculum frequently receive transcript and diploma notations as well as certificates, medallions, or other citations at graduation ceremonies.

In every case, catering to the student as an individual plays a central role in honors course design. Most honors classes are small (fewer than 20 students); most are discussion-oriented, giving students a chance to present their own interpretations of ideas and even teach a part of the course. Many classes are interdisciplinary, which means they are taught by faculty members from two or more departments, providing different perspectives on a subject. All honors classes help students develop and articulate their own perspectives by cultivating both verbal and written style. They help students mature intellectually, preparing them to engage in their own explorations and research. Some programs even extend the options for self-growth to study abroad and internships in science, government, the arts, or business related to the major. Other programs encourage or require community service as part of the honors experience. In every case, honors is an experiential education that deepens classroom learning and extends far beyond.

Despite their individual differences, all honors programs and honors colleges rely on faculty members who enjoy working with bright, independent students. The ideal honors faculty members are open-minded, encouraging master teachers. They want to see their students achieve at their highest capacity and are glad to spend time with students in discussions and laboratories, on field trips and at conferences, or online in e-mail. They often influence career decisions, are inspiring role models, and remain friends long after they have served as thesis advisers.

WHERE ARE HONORS PROGRAMS AND HONORS COLLEGES LOCATED?

Because honors programs and honors colleges include students from many different departments or colleges, they usually have their own offices and space on campus. Some have their own buildings. Most programs have honors centers or lounges, where students gather together for informal conversations, luncheons, discussions, lectures, and special projects.

Many honors students have cultivated strong personal interests that have nothing to do with classes. They may be multilingual; they may be fine artists or poets, musicians or racing car enthusiasts, mothers or fathers. Some volunteer in hospitals or do landscape gardening to pay for college. Many work in retail stores and catering. Some are avid sports enthusiasts, while others collect antiques. When they get together in honors lounges, there is always an interesting mixture of ideas!

In the honors center, you will also find the honors director or dean. The honors director often serves as a personal adviser to all of the students in the program. Many programs also have peer counselors and mentors who are upperclass honors students and know the ropes from a student's perspective and experience. Some have specially assigned honors advisers who guide honors students through their degrees, assist in registration, and answer every imaginable question. The honors office area usually is a good place to meet people, ask questions, and solve problems.

In general, honors provides an environment in which students feel free to talk about their passionate interests and ideas knowing that they will find good listeners and, sometimes, even arguers. There is no end to conversations among honors students. Like many students in honors, you may feel a great relief in finding a sympathetic group that respects your intelligence and creativity. In honors, you can be eccentric; you can be yourself! Some lifelong friendships, even marriages, are the result of social relationships developed in honors programs.

ARE YOU READY FOR HONORS?

Admission to honors programs and honors colleges is generally based on a combination of several factors: high school or previous college grades, experience taking AP or IB courses, SAT or ACT scores, personal essay, and extracurricular achievements. To stay in honors, students need to maintain a certain grade point average (GPA) and show progress toward the completion of the specific honors program or college requirements. Since you have probably exceeded admissions standards all along, maintaining your GPA will not be as big a problem as it sounds. Your professors and your honors director are there to help you succeed in the program. Most honors programs have very low attrition rates because students enjoy classes and do well.

Of course, you must be careful about how you budget your time for studying. Honors encourages well-rounded, diversified students, so you should play a sport, work at the radio station, join clubs of interest, or pledge a sorority or fraternity. You might find a job in the student center or library that will help you pay for your car expenses and that also is reasonable. But remember, each activity takes time, and you must strike the balance that leaves you enough time to do your homework, write papers, prepare for seminar discussions, do your research, and do well on exams. Choose the jobs and activities that attract you, but never let them overshadow your primary purpose—which is to be a student.

Sometimes even the very best students who apply for admission into an honors program or college are frightened by the thought of speaking in front of a group, giving seminar papers, or writing a thesis. But if you understand how the programs work, you will see that there is nothing to fear. The basis of honors is confidence in the student and building the student's self-confidence. Admittance to an honors program means you have already demonstrated your academic achievement in high school or college classes. Once in the honors environment, you learn how to formulate and structure ideas so that you can apply critical judgment to sets of facts and opinions. In small seminar classes, you practice discussion and arguments, so by the time you come to the senior thesis or project, the method is second nature. For most honors students, the senior thesis, performance, or portfolio presentation is the project that gives them the greatest fulfillment and pride. In many honors programs and colleges, students present their work either to other students or to faculty members in their major departments. Students often present their work at regional and national honors conferences. Some students even publish their work jointly with their faculty mentors. These are great achievements, and they come naturally with the training. There is nothing to fear. Honors will prepare you for life.

Dr. Joan Digby is Director of the Honors Program and Merit Fellowship at Long Island University, C.W. Post Campus. She was also President of the National Collegiate Honors Council from 1999 to 2000.

Public and Private Colleges and Universities—How to Choose

Debra Humphreys

As you survey the thousands of four-year colleges in the country and weigh the options before you, it is important to be aware of how colleges differ and what kind of educational experience each college offers you. In every state in the country, you will find both public and private colleges and universities. What are the differences between public and private colleges, and how should you approach the decision to attend one or the other? What are some common misconceptions regarding both public and private colleges that you should know about before you eliminate an entire category of institution from your list of prospective schools?

WHAT ARE THE BASIC CHARACTERISTICS OF PUBLIC AND PRIVATE INSTITUTIONS?

Over the course of the nation's history, what began as a small group of mostly church-affiliated colleges has grown in both size and complexity. Over the years, education in the United States became increasingly democratized, and more and more state-sponsored institutions and state systems of higher education emerged. These included small colleges, sometimes called "normal schools," designed to train school teachers for the expanding public school system; land-grant colleges and universities brought into existence with federal support in the mid-nineteenth century in order to prepare workers to expand the nation's agricultural and technological capacity; and large state systems that evolved in the twentieth century and now include two-year colleges, basic four-year institutions, and large research universities, all supported at least in part by state revenues.

While there are some clear distinctions to be made, even some of the core characteristics of public and private colleges vary from state to state. In general, a public institution receives at least part of its operating budget from state tax revenues, operates with a mandate and mission from the state where it is located, and is accountable to the elected officials of that state. Most private colleges and universities are independent, not-for-profit institutions. They operate with revenues from tuition, income from endowments, private gifts and bequests, and federal, private, or corporate foundation grants. These institutions are primarily accountable to a board of trustees, usually made up of local or national business and community leaders and esteemed alumni.

There are also a small but growing number of for-profit colleges whose operating revenues include tuition dollars but also might include investor financing. Some of these colleges are owned and operated by publicly traded corporations. Most of the following generalizations about private institutions however refer to the more familiar not-for-profit independent college previously described.

While the distinction between public and private institutions might seem clear at first, these two kinds of colleges and universities actually share many characteristics. All accredited colleges and universities in the country—whether public or private, for profit or not—are entitled to receive public funds from the federal government in the form of direct grants and loans for eligible students, support for student work-study programs, and competitive grants to support research or campus programs. In exchange for this federal support, all schools undergo a peer-reviewed accreditation process by a regional accreditor authorized by the federal government's Department of Education.

Whether a college is public or private, you should know if it is accredited and therefore an institution whose students are eligible for all available federal financial aid. Accreditation status also provides you with assurance that the school operates in a fiscally responsible manner and that its academic programs have been deemed sound by an outside group of educators from its peer institutions.

HOW ARE PUBLIC AND PRIVATE COLLEGES AND UNIVERSITIES RUN?

In many ways, your experience as a student will not differ significantly based on what type of governance system a college or university uses. However, some knowledge of this might be useful in making choices among the various options. Private colleges and universities tend to have more independence and autonomy in how they are run, with boards of trustees that oversee financial and other broad matters of governance. Academic and student services leaders determine the nature of the academic program and life on campus at these schools. Public colleges and universities often have more complex governing structures with boards of regents or other types of oversight committees made up of politically appointed or elected officials exercising more or less oversight and intrusion into their day-to-day operations. New York, for instance, has a board of regents that oversees the system's campuses and is more actively involved in reviewing and revising curricular requirements that apply to institutions throughout the system. Other states have multiple public colleges, each with its own board overseeing each campus' operations with more or less intrusion into day-to-day operations.

Whether an institution is public or private, you will want to ask lots of questions about campus climate and academic programs in order to help you determine if a school is right for you. Being aware of some facts about public and private institutions will help you frame these questions to get truly useful answers.

ARE ALL PUBLIC COLLEGES AND UNIVERSITIES BIG AND IMPERSONAL?

Like private institutions, public colleges come in all shapes and sizes. Some are large institutions offering multiple degrees and majors to both undergraduate and graduate students alike. These institutions offer students many curricular options as well as access to leading scholars and an environment where cutting-edge academic research is conducted. While an institution of this size and scope might seem intimidating at first, remember that there are large institutions that do take very seriously their undergraduate programs. While you may receive less customized attention at a larger institution, many large public and private research universities offer options such as smaller honors programs, academic learning communities with smaller cohorts of students, or theme residence halls that can minimize the potential that you will get lost in the crowd.

If you are considering a large research institution—whether it is public or private—you should ask questions about the undergraduate program. What is the student-faculty ratio for undergraduates? What is the average class size, especially for introductory first-year courses? How many courses are taught by graduate students, and what sort of teacher training do those students receive? Are there opportunities for undergraduate students to participate in research projects with university faculty members?

In addition to the large, public research universities, there are many other smaller, state-funded regional institutions that still offer a wide range of both liberal arts and sciences fields as well as professional fields of study. Many states also offer small, public liberal arts colleges that share many of the defining characteristics of traditional, private liberal arts colleges. In 1987, some of these institutions formed the Council of Public Liberal Arts Colleges (COPLAC). COPLAC schools pride themselves on providing students of high ability and from all backgrounds access to a quality liberal education. These colleges and universities have been nationally recognized as outstanding in many ways. They offer small classes, innovations in teaching, personal interactions with faculty members, opportunities for faculty-supervised research, and supportive atmospheres. Most of them are located on campuses in rural or small-town settings. In addition to offering rigorous and well-integrated undergraduate programs, these institutions often charge far less tuition than many private colleges do. More information can be found at http://www.coplac.org.

These public liberal arts colleges, along with more traditional private liberal arts institutions, do offer unique learning environments that research suggests often lead to higher levels of student achievement. Liberal arts colleges tend to offer a high degree of student-faculty interaction, high levels of student engagement with both in-class and out-of-class experiences, and lots of opportunities for collaborative and innovative learning practices. Businesses are also increasingly asking for exactly the set of skills and capacities that a liberal education provides, whether offered in a traditional liberal arts college setting or within a larger university that grants degrees in both liberal arts and other fields. Many public liberal arts and more comprehensive colleges and universities also now offer students a rigorous liberal education while integrating liberal learning into professional degree programs, for instance in health sciences, engineering, or education.

ARE PUBLIC COLLEGES CHEAPER THAN PRIVATE COLLEGES?

The cost of college is not easy to calculate and is not limited simply to the advertised price of tuition. It is absolutely not the case that attending a public college will always cost a student less money than attending a private institution. It is true that the basic tuition for in-state or out-of-state students attending public colleges is on average less expensive than the advertised tuition rate at private institutions. It is very important, however, to note that many private colleges and universities offer significant amounts of financial aid—often beyond the basic federal loans and grants available to all students. Many, but not all, private colleges have large endowments that allow them to effectively discount the standard, published tuition rates for a great number of their students. The National Association of College and University Business Officers sampled a small group of private colleges and discovered that only 10 percent of entering students were paying the full, advertised tuition. Ninety percent of their students received price discounts in the form of scholarships or financial aid. In other words, don't write off a college simply because its tuition looks extremely high relative to other institutions.

Both private and public institutions, however, have been fiscally stressed in recent years because of declining values of stock portfolios in endowments or because of declining state revenues resulting from the deteriorating economy. It is safe to say that for many students in the coming years, it will become increasingly difficult to get large amounts of financial aid. Many institutions, however, remain committed to widening access to more students from less economically privileged backgrounds. In addition, students demonstrating high levels of academic achievement are being rewarded at both private and public institutions—both in terms of admission and financial aid.

It is important to look carefully at the tuition and the financial aid requirements and availability at each school you are considering, private or public. In-state and out-of-state tuitions and the difference between them varies substantially from state to state. Out-of-state tuition also varies from state to state but still tends to be lower than average private tuition levels.

Policies vary as well for determining state residency status. In many states, the policy for dependent students requires that their parents must have lived in the state for at least twelve months prior to attendance in order to qualify for in-state tuition. For independent students, the requirement of twelve months residence prior to enrollment applies to the student. Independent status must be verified and generally entails proof that a student receives no support from parents or other relatives living in or out of the state in question. As budgets have increasingly tightened, states have over the past several years made it increasingly difficult to establish in-state residence after matriculating at a school. Exceptions are sometimes made, however, for students from migrant, refugee, or military families.

IS IT EASIER TO GAIN ADMISSION TO A PUBLIC INSTITUTION ESPECIALLY AS A STATE RESIDENT?

Few public colleges and universities automatically admit students who graduate from a public high school in their state. Many, however, give preference in admissions and financial assistance to in-state residents. Moreover, some states have implemented policies that guarantee admission to at least one of the state's public institutions for all students graduating in a top percentage of their high school classes.

There are, indeed, more highly selective private than public institutions. Many public colleges and universities, however, do admit very few applicants. These highly selective institutions might draw their students from a national pool of applicants and can be among the most selective in the country. However, the national universities and liberal arts colleges with the lowest acceptance rates in the country are mostly all private institutions.

While some public institutions offer virtually open admissions to state residents, it is important for all prospective students to realize that even an open-admission institution will require incoming students to meet certain academic standards before being admitted to credit-bearing courses. In most cases, public and private institutions give incoming students a series of placement exams that determines at what level the student can begin his or her course work. Depending on the results of these exams, a student may be required to take and pass one or more remedial courses before being admitted to courses that will actually count towards a degree.

Since each state's requirements are different and shift often, you should not assume that, regardless of your academic background, admission is automatic to your local state college. In the current climate—with costs rising and competition across systems tightening—admission rates are dropping at many public institutions.

IS THE CLIMATE ON A PUBLIC COLLEGE CAMPUS SIGNIFICANTLY DIFFERENT THAN THAT ON A PRIVATE COLLEGE CAMPUS?

The social and academic climate at colleges and universities varies substantially and public institutions do not necessarily offer a distinctively different climate than private institutions do. You can find, at some public institutions, the small, residential environment traditionally associated with private liberal arts colleges. You will also find the presence of fraternities and sororities at both public and private institutions. You should look carefully at whether a school in which you are interested has fraternities and sororities and how much influence the Greek system has on college life. At some institutions, fraternities and sororities dominate the entire social life of the campus.

One campus environment that can only be found at a private institution is a highly religious environment. Many early colleges and universities were founded by churches or religious orders. Some of these institutions no longer retain a strong affiliation with one church or denomination. Others do retain a strong affiliation, and church traditions can heavily influence the climate of these institutions. Usually, these campuses will admit a student from any religious background, but they may require students to attend chapel services and/or take religion or theology courses to graduate. In addition, some college missions and curricula are influenced by their religious affiliations. For instance, many Catholic institutions have a strong commitment to community service and social justice. Students may find, at these institutions, curricula related to social justice issues and requirements that they complete a community-service learning activity or course to graduate. Institutions with a strong mission are also often able to develop more coherent, cohesive, and innovative curricula for their students.

Finally, other important climate factors to consider include whether a college or university is in an urban or rural setting; what the diversity of the student body is in terms of geographic, religious, or racial/ethnic background; if most students live on campus or commute from home; and finally if the college dominates the life of the community in which it is located. Each of these options has advantages and disadvantages you will want to weigh in making your decisions.

ARE PRIVATE COLLEGES MORE ACADEMICALLY RIGOROUS THAN PUBLIC COLLEGES?

Private colleges and universities are not necessarily more academically rigorous than public institutions. You will find rigorous, intellectually challenging, and innovative academic programs at both private and public institutions. There is also a common misconception that schools that are more highly selective have the most effective or engaging academic

QUESTIONS TO ASK AS YOU EVALUATE PROSPECTIVE COLLEGES AND UNIVERSITIES

- Does the college offer a distinctive first-year experience?
- Does the college offer a small-size freshman seminar for all students?
- Are all students required to complete a senior project or assignment that allows them to integrate all that they have learned and demonstrate acquired skills and knowledge?
- Are students encouraged or required to complete internships and/or service learning courses?
- Are students encouraged to study abroad? Is support for study abroad provided to all students and are study abroad experiences integrated into a student's overall curricula?
- Does the college offer learning communities, especially in the student's early years?
- Are students required to complete rigorous writing courses not only in the freshman year but also across the curriculum in whatever major he or she chooses to pursue?
- Are there opportunities for students to pursue independent research or creative projects under the supervision of a senior faculty member?

programs. Research suggests that there is no connection between the selectivity of an institution and the presence of effective or innovative teaching and learning practices. There is, however, preliminary research that suggests that the academic quality of one's peers does seem to have an impact on the grade point averages of fellow students.

Nothing could be more important in your decision-making process than evaluating the nature of academic programs at prospective colleges or universities. Across both public and private institutions, there have been exciting and important changes in how colleges and universities are organizing undergraduate curricula. Many promising programs have been proven to result in higher levels of student retention, graduation, satisfaction, and academic achievement.

Many colleges and universities also now participate in the National Survey of Student Engagement. This survey asks students in both their first and last years about a series of effective educational practices and the degree to which they are engaged in the academic life of their school. Issues that are examined in the survey include the level of academic challenge, active and collaborative learning opportunities, the nature of student-faculty interactions, the number of enriching educational experiences available, and the supportive nature of the campus environment. Ask if the school you are considering participates in this survey and if you can see the results from recent classes of students.

THE PRIVATE/PUBLIC CHOICE

While there are distinct differences between public and private colleges and universities you should not limit your choice—whatever your background—to only one type of institution. There are wonderful opportunities at many different kinds of schools. The availability of many kinds of financial aid may bring private institutions with high-tuition levels within reach for you, whatever your financial background. Whether a school is highly selective or has open admissions, you should also be able to find a college or university that will challenge you academically and provide you with a supportive environment in which to live, learn, and pursue a college degree of lasting value.

Debra Humphreys is Vice President for Communications and Public Affairs for the Association of American Colleges and Universities.

Distance Education—It's Closer Than You Think

You may not realize it, but as an incoming college student, you are joining a revolution that is radically changing education. It's called distance learning. From kindergarten up to postgraduate degrees, distance learning is fast becoming an essential teaching tool. Most of the colleges and universities you are considering for a bachelor's degree offer distance learning in one form or another. Most likely you will be a distance learner at some point, whether during college or graduate school or throughout your career.

In case you're not familiar with distance learning—or asynchronous learning, online learning, or distance education—it means you don't sit in a classroom facing a teacher. You can be hundreds of miles or minutes from the teacher and other students. Most often you connect through the Internet to the teacher, fellow students, and study materials. However, increasingly sophisticated technologies, such as virtual laboratories, simulations, and interactive multimedia, are also used. You may run across the term "blended learning." Many institutions incorporate online learning into their face-to-face classes. In fact, a number of colleges require that a part of all classes is online.

FROM SNAIL-MAIL COURSES TO LEADING-EDGE TECHNOLOGY

Talk about change. Distance education began in the late 1800s, when schools mailed correspondence courses to farmers who wanted to learn how to grow better crops. Since technology came along, distance learning has become accessible and widespread. At first educators were skeptical, but as name-plate universities began to incorporate it into their teaching methodology, distance education became accepted.

When brick-and-mortar colleges and universities first considered distance education, the goal was to make it as good as face-to-face education. Now, says Ray Schroeder, Professor Emeritus of Communication and Director of the Center for Online Learning, Research, and Service (COLRS), at the University of Illinois at Springfield, "Field research shows that online learning technologies are better than face-to-face learning in a number of ways." Having taught online, he has seen firsthand how students participate more in discussions and learn from one another. Peg Miller, Ph.D., former Coordinator of Academic Support for Distributed Learning, University of Central Florida, cites a survey she conducted every other semester that compares face-to-face and distance learners at her institution. She has found that students from face-to-face and online classes were almost identical in the grades they earned and in their satisfaction with the classes.

ON THE UPSWING

Many reasons have caused the phenomenal growth of distance education. It's convenient and user-friendly, plus the scope of classes is stunning. Not that you'll likely begin your college years with classes in forensics or grading diamonds, but they are offered and indicate the enormous variety of courses. Along with many others in education, Michael P. Lambert, Secretary and Executive Director of the Distance Education Training Council, feels that online learning has transformed how people learn. "You no longer sit in a box with 35 other people where you might never raise your hand," he says. Adds Gerald Heeger, former President of the University of Maryland University College (UMUC), "Online learning gets rid of the limitations of geography and time. And as bandwidth increases, we will do more and more."

PROCEED WITH CAUTION

Now that you're convinced that distance education sounds great, sign me up, it's only fair to warn you that perhaps you shouldn't start your bachelor's degree totally online. Distance learning changes how you study, respond to your teachers, participate in class discussions, and take exams. If you're not prepared for the differences, you can easily fall behind and even fail. Though the age of online students continues to drop, most are older, have had some life experience since graduating from high school, and have the self-discipline, self-motivation, and maturity that distance education demands. The average age of distance students is in the mid-30s, and 95 percent of them work full-time. They know what they want from college and are willing to meet the rigors of online learning, which are considerable.

Of course, some students straight from high school do successfully start college as distance learners because they've already had some online learning experience. Some take online classes in high school or advanced-placement and college courses. At Stevens Institute of Technology's Web Campus, incoming freshmen brush up on math and precalculus online before their first fall semester. At first, Nathan Kahl, former instructor for the Euclid Program at Stevens Institute of Technology Web Campus, was skeptical that high school graduates could succeed in the online courses he taught, but he saw that "everyone quickly got into the swing of things." He admits that he underestimated the students' ability to learn online. Heeger agrees "There's no reason why a bright junior in high school who is ready to take college freshmen courses can't do it."

The University of Phoenix Online (parent company: Apollo Group, Inc.) has developed a bachelor's degree program specifically for incoming freshmen of any age—including those just out of high school. In today's job market, a college education is a necessity, yet many students have life situations that prevent them from attending. Notes Apollo Group, Inc., President Brian Muller about the accommodations their program makes for students who are new to higher education, "It is our experience that if you create an online classroom, it must have all the features that incoming students need, which are small, highly interactive, and collaborative classes." Their freshman classes average 15 and require that the instructor has consistent contact with the students. New freshmen also get a tremendous amount of support in writing, math, and online research skills and have the help of an academic counselor who closely tracks them for ten weeks into their first semester. "We think there are more students coming out of high school who must have jobs, so we took the model for working adults and created an environment for traditional students that combines education and work," says Muller.

However, not all educators have the same experience with incoming freshmen. Jimmy Reeves, Ph.D., Professor and Chair, Department of Chemistry and Biochemistry at the University of North Carolina at Wilmington, teaches both online and face-to-face classes and knows how students can react. Freshmen who fail his face-to-face class sometimes ask to take his class online. He says no because the discipline required is rare among 19-year-old students. "Junior and senior college students do well, but it has more to do with their level of maturity and the reasons why they're in college," he says, referring to the fact that many incoming college students want to experiment or come because their parents demand it. "Without any real desire to learn or sense of why they're in college, it's easy to get distracted in online classes," he notes. You can't hide in the back of a lecture hall half asleep on Monday morning and hope for the best on multiple-choice questions. In online classes, your active participation is noticed and taken into account for final grades.

Attending college isn't just about acquiring knowledge in a particular field in order to get a job. It's also about learning social skills and meeting people with different ideas from diverse backgrounds. "If you want to live in a dorm and have bull sessions on the meaning of life with the kids down the hall, then being a fully online freshman student isn't for you," advises Cynthia Davis, Associate Dean of Academic Affairs in the School of Undergraduate Studies at the University of Maryland University College (UMUC). She adds that sometimes students mistakenly think getting a bachelor's degree online will take less time than physically attending classes or won't require as much work. But as she points out, online classes demand the same amount of effort, if not more than face-to-face classes.

WHAT'S IT GOING TO BE LIKE?

Blended learning or mixed-mode classes, combining face-to-face and online instruction, are becoming a permanent fixture in higher education. Students might sit in a classroom on Monday but take the remaining two classes for that week online. Professors routinely post the syllabus, class calendar, or PowerPoint lectures. Reeves says that it's rare to see college classes without some Web-based materials. Davis comments that UMUC routinely Web-enhances all their face-to-face classes with companion Web classrooms. Students can have optional online discussions or print copies of class materials.

"We find more students use online technology to enhance their studies and get better grades," comments Schroeder. Educators see a trend of students enrolling in one university and taking courses from other institutions. For instance, say you're in an art class but want to study German cathedral architecture, which your university doesn't have but another one offers online. It's only a matter of time before this will be a standard option for college students.

LOTS TO LOOK FOR, LOTS TO AVOID, LOTS TO ASK

Though much of distance education depends on the Internet, you can't just type in "distance education" and see what comes up in a search for a college. You must seriously research and do background checks to make sure a diploma mill doesn't hand you a bachelor's degree that isn't credible. There are plenty of places to get information. Petersons.com offers a database of colleges and universities that have online courses, as well as totally online distance education providers. "You have to be a good consumer," recommends Heeger. "It's no different from getting a loan. You don't borrow money from people you never heard of. You shouldn't get degrees from people you never heard of." Schroeder suggests checking the course completion of online programs, their enrollment, and growth of programs. "Just as one checks with friends and colleagues about the quality of consumer services, such as computers and cars, one should check with students who are enrolled in online programs," he advises.

Is the Institution Accredited by a Valid Accrediting Body?

There are several kinds of accrediting organizations:

- The six regional accrediting agencies recognized by the U.S. Department of Education
- The Council for Higher Education Accreditation (www.chea.org)
- Other institutional accrediting agencies, such as the Accrediting Council for Independent Colleges and Schools and the Distance Education and Training Council
- Specialized accrediting agencies that cover schools offering everything from acupuncture to veterinary medicine
- Other discipline-based accrediting organizations, such as those for law and business schools

TEST-DRIVE AN ONLINE CLASS

Just like face-to-face instruction, online classes are different, depending on the course material and how each teacher chooses to structure the course, but here's a typical scenario of what it's like to be a distance learner.

Getting started. First you'll want to get to the general information page for the class, which you'll visit often. The professor's contact information, the class calendar, the syllabus, and announcements on quizzes and tests or links to other pages on which you'll find posted discussion questions may be found here. Some teachers will ask you to tell something about yourself to the other students in the class. Be sure to read the syllabus, which will outline the course and tell you when assignments are due and how grades are determined.

Responding to discussion questions. Those students who never raised their hands will get a shock in online courses. Responding with thoughtful answers to online discussion groups is mandatory. Usually the teacher will assign reading material and then post a discussion question. The material might be from your textbook or Web sites. You must respond to the question and possibly to the postings of other students in the class. Teachers will gauge your participation in the class and how well you learn the material.

Interacting with fellow students and your teacher. Ray Schroeder, Professor Emeritus of Communication and Director of the Center for Online Learning, Research, and Service (COLRS) at the University of Illinois at Springfield, gives talks about distance education. Often he'll ask his audience to recall their favorite class from elementary school up to college and what made it so memorable. Was it the textbook? The actual classroom? The view out the window? When he asks if it was the interaction among students and with the teacher, the audience realizes that's what made the class good. "Both in person and online, learning takes place in the interaction," says Schroeder. "Otherwise, we would do just as well to read a book or watch a video to learn." In online classes, interaction between you and the professor and other students is an enormous part of your success.

Nathan Kahl, former instructor for the Euclid Program at Stevens Institute of Technology Web Campus, explains, "Distance students expect that their teachers will be online at least as much as they are." The level of interaction expected from you will vary by school and course, but you should know that in online courses, you must be an active participant. On the flip side, teachers carefully monitor discussions to make sure the more talkative students don't dominate. Keith W. Miller, Professor of Computer Science at the University of Illinois at Springfield, interacts with his students in a variety of ways. "I make announcements to the whole class on the homepage. I send e-mails to the whole class. I enter into the electronic discussions on the bulletin board forums, and post daily reminders and assignments to the course calendar. The students interact with me using e-mail, notes in their assignments, and via the bulletin boards. Now and then someone calls me at my office on the phone, but that's rare." He likes to answer his e-mails at least once a day, which means that his students get much more feedback than they would if he were physically in a classroom with them.

As do most online teachers, Cynthia Davis, Associate Dean of Academic Affairs in the School of Undergraduate Studies at the University of Maryland University College, gets students to participate with a weekly discussion topic. "If we're reading a novel," she says, "I ask them to discuss the role of the narrator or analyze a passage. The students respond individually and then respond to other students' comments."

Attending virtual lectures. Some online courses allow you to hear and see the professor or other guest speakers who are also online. If you want to ask a question, there's a button to indicate you want to speak. Everyone else can hear you as if you all were in the same room. Other professors add voice to PowerPoint lectures, which you can view when you want to, not at some prearranged time.

Taking quizzes and tests. No more waiting weeks to get your tests back. Online technology in some courses instantly zaps back the corrected test and notes that you missed question six and need to study page 54 of the textbook. Just like in face-to-face classes, you have an allotted amount of time to take the quiz. Some online courses may have automated components, such as instant quizzes and animated and interactive practice sessions. Others have mandatory proctored exams at a nearby community college or learning center for students who are off campus.

Can You Transfer Credits Received Online from One Institution to Another?

Policies vary greatly among universities and colleges. Though distance education is widely accepted, there are so many places where students can take bogus online courses that institutions are justifiably cautious. If students do decide they want to get a bachelor's degree completely online, they need to be sure the campus-based program and distance education program offer the same degree. At most institutions both on-campus and online degrees are the same, but others do differentiate in the degrees conferred, and it will show up on your diploma.

What Kind of Refund Policy Does the University Have for Distance Learners?

It might become painfully apparent for students that online learning is not for them, and they want to drop out. Find out ahead of time about the refund policy for online classes. What happens if you're ill during an online class? How can you make up the work? Even before taking any classes, you should find out if you're suited for online learning. Many institutions offer self-assessment tests on their Web sites.

What Online Services Does the College Provide?

Is the dorm wired? Can you get an e-mail address from the university? What about browsers and computer compatibility? Ask how the Internet is part of face-to-face classes. To what extent is the library online, and is it available 24/7 for research? Ask about writing and math labs and help-desk support. Look for online tutorials that show students how to use the school's specific software. Is there a tech fee?

IF YOU'RE LEARNING ONLINE, YOU BETTER HAVE THESE

Since online learning is part of college, it's helpful to know what to expect ahead of time, rather than three weeks into the class, when you feel like throwing your laptop out the window and would happily settle for sitting in the back row of the nearest classroom. Here are the five skills and abilities that successful online students must have:

1. You must have the self-discipline to do things you don't want to do when you don't want to do them. If you're a procrastinator, you'll find the catch-up tactics that served you well in face-to-face classes won't work online. "Students get the idea they can whiz by without studying, or they came from high schools where they weren't pushed," cautions Heeger. "Maybe they never got Fs in high school, but they do here." That's because they don't realize they're responsible for learning the material on their own. The burden is on you to keep up with the homework. It doesn't take long to fall far behind in online classes.

Typically, students in face-to-face and online classes need 2 hours for work outside of class for every hour in class. But online students often forget to add that hour. For every hour they would have to sit in a traditional classroom, they should be listening, studying, thinking, writing, responding to discussions, and getting ready for tests, plus the 2 hours outside of class. Three classes a week—that's 9 to 10 hours for one class. Online teachers keep students on track with weekly quizzes and homework assignments. If students start lagging, they're likely to get an e-mail from the professor asking what's going on. Claudine SchWeber, Ph.D., Chair of the Doctor of Management Program at the University of Maryland University College, has taught online for years and states, "My classes are structured by weekly readings, activities, and discussions. Students can't decide to get around to doing the work when they feel like it. It must be done at the instructor's pace. The first shot of online can be a shock to their system."

2. You must have the ability to manage your time without anyone telling you do your homework NOW. In high school, students usually can put off studying until the weekend. "That doesn't work in college. You can't write complex papers the night before," says Karen L. Kirkendall, Ph.D., Associate Professor of Liberal and Integrative Studies and Director of the Capitol Scholars Honors Program at the University of Illinois at Springfield. She teaches both online and face-to-face classes and has seen first-time online students who have never failed before start to slip and suddenly realize they are in big trouble. "My online classes are extraordinarily structured so I pretty much know when students aren't engaged, which I monitor by seeing how much they participate in online discussions," she notes.

3. You must have the skills to communicate your thoughts in writing. "Online participation in class discussions isn't instant messaging. You are what you write in online classes," advises SchWeber. Most of the work in online

DISTANCE LEARNING MYTHS

As distance education becomes more accepted, people will readily discard some of the myths on this list. But for now, they persist.

Distance learning is for people on ranches 200 miles from the nearest freeway. Geography is not a factor. Many distance learners who are located across the campus or a few miles away just don't want to deal with the commute or have a work schedule that conflicts with being in a class at a certain time. They appreciate the flexibility that distance education gives them.

Distance learning is easier than face-to-face classes. Once you start an online class, you'll knock that myth off the list. Still, some students think it will be easier. When they realize they must not only respond to discussion questions but also comment on the responses from other students, they wonder why they ever thought distance education was going to be easy. Online teachers normally keep track of how their students progress with frequent monitoring and quizzes.

I'll get a better education in face-to-face classes. Much research has been conducted comparing the two and consistently, online learning is equivalent or better. Teachers of online courses now have plenty of precedents to follow, training and research to help them teach better, and technology to prepare for classes and keep up with their students' progress.

I'll talk to a computer all day. Yes, you are in front of a computer as a distance learner, but you also interact with professors and other students much more than you ever would in a core freshman class of 200. Teachers have sophisticated software to facilitate interaction. Even though you don't physically see your teachers, they put a great deal of effort into class preparation and reading e-mails. Some get as many as 3,000 e-mails in a ten-week class. Distance learners often get to know fellow students much more easily online than they would walking in and out of a class.

I need to be a computer geek. If you can handle the simplest maneuvers around a computer, such as attaching documents to e-mails or going to a specified Web address, you can be a distance learner. And you'll have tech support to help out if you run into problems.

Distance education is cheaper than face-to-face. Too bad this is a myth. It costs the same as a traditional college if you attend a recognized institution. Most students pay for distance education through student loans.

classes is written, whether it's participation in discussions, homework, quizzes, papers, or tests.

Since you'll communicate by e-mail and post your thoughts, netiquette is essential. You need to think differently online than when speaking on the phone or face-to-face. "You can't write a report that sounds like you are hanging out with friends," advises SchWeber. "When you are totally online, the only image people (including your professor) have of you is how you write." Kirkendall has reprimanded students who sent e-mails showing disrespect to the teacher because they were upset about something. Probably they would never respond that way if face-to-face. "Never hit the submit button when you're angry," Kirkendall cautions.

4. You must have the ability to research worthwhile information on the Web. You need to know what's junk and what's reliable. In addition, professors take plagiarism very seriously, especially because it's so easy to do.

5. You must have some computer skills and know some computer-speak. Those who design the software and set up how a distance learning class is taught are careful to make sure the technology doesn't get in the way of learning; however, you should know the basics. "In some classes, certain downloads are required, such as Adobe Acrobat, but in general, the skills are not beyond the abilities used daily by most elementary school children," says Schroeder, pointing out that if distance programs use expensive or exotic technology, they defeat the purpose. He reports that most computers that are five years old have the speed, memory, and capability to support online learning. Some classes might require a microphone. You should be familiar with some of the computer jargon so that if you're asked to post something or use a drop box, add an attachment, or take part in a threaded discussion, you'll know what what you need to do. Just about every distance learning provider has online tutorials to familiarize you with their particular online software. If you run into technical problems, help-desk support is available.

Why Not Women's Colleges?

Before we start talking about the many advantages that women's colleges offer, let's get some myths out of the way. It is almost certain that the minute you hear "women's colleges" in the same sentence with "choosing colleges" you immediately think: no boys, no fun, no way!

Maybe that is why some girls who visit Joan Jaffe's office at Mills College in San Francisco, California, rush in to tell her that they just saw some guys on the campus of this women's college. Jaffe, Associate Dean of Admission, frequently gets this reaction from the young women who visit the campus. That's because many think that if they go to a women's college they are never going to see a guy within 2 miles of the campus gates, which, by the way, will clang shut behind them, leaving them secluded inside a heavily guarded male-free zone.

KISS MYTH NUMBER ONE GOOD-BYE

Forget iron gates. The first myth to get rid of is the one that assumes attending a women's college means kissing your social life good-bye. In fact, as Patricia Gibbs, Vice President for Enrollment Services at Wesleyan College in Macon, Georgia, points out, "If you were a guy looking for a date, where would you go?" Not only that, the majority of women's colleges are near, if not next to, coed campuses. Most share activities with other colleges and universities, and many have reciprocal agreements so that guys can take classes at the women's college and vice versa.

When it comes to dating, women's colleges offer the best of both worlds. You can hang out with guys when you want to and then retreat to your own lovely environment (women's dorms usually are beautiful) and hang out with the girls. Julie Binder, who transferred from the University of Wisconsin to all-women's Barnard College in New York City, notes that there is open registration with Columbia University, which just happens to be right next door. "Campus life is shared. Sports are shared," she says.

As you dig deeper into this myth, you will find that attending a women's college is not about isolation, it's about options. You get to choose if you want to be in classes, clubs, and organizations only with women or mingle with the men.

SCRATCH MYTH NUMBER TWO

On to myth number two. Women's colleges are just a bunch of catty, competitive females waiting for the right moment to scratch each other's eyes out. Scratch that myth, too. Instead, women's colleges cultivate an environment of sisterhood-women looking out for each other and helping each other. Most women's colleges encourage women in the upper-level classes to help their younger classmates. Talking to their "big sisters," newcomers find out what classes to take, which professors are the best, and have sympathetic ears for the problems that most first-year college students face.

"The sense of community is very strong at women's colleges," observes Fran Samuels, former Director of College

THE RICH TRADITIONS IN WOMEN'S COLLEGES

Tradition plays an important part of the experience women have in women's colleges. They run the gamut from solemn ceremonies of passing along the bond of sisterhood to the fun of secret surprises. "Women's colleges have a strong sense of tradition," says Amy Shaver, former Academic Dean at Stephens College in Columbia, Missouri. It's also a wonderful way to help women from all social, economic, religious, and ethnic backgrounds to share a common experience and pass it on to the next generation of students. "Traditions bond women over the generations," says Jennifer Rickard, Chief Enrollment and Communications Officer at Bryn Mawr College, who notes that it's not unusual at all to have students today singing songs and participating in ceremonies that the class of 1945 did and which will be the same when today's students have their twenty-year reunion.

Here's a sampling of the many traditions you'll find on women's college campuses:

Lantern Night At Bryn Mawr's Lantern Night, women gather around a fountain on campus. Each woman is given a lantern as a symbol of knowledge and learning. Each class has a color, and as the lanterns are passed from the sophomores to the first-year students, songs are sung in Greek that are the same as the ones sung 100 years ago around the same fountain.

Senior Paint Night Mills College seniors get the okay to paint the campus in their class color. Along with brushes and cans of paint, they are given a few guidelines as to what can and cannot be painted, but the rest is up to them.

The Crossing of the Bridge As women students come to Stephens to begin their college education, they cross over a bridge on campus in a ceremony symbolizing their entrance into the world of academia. At graduation, they cross over another bridge on campus and are welcomed into the alumnae society.

Candlelight Induction Ceremony Spelman students dressed in white dresses and black shoes light candles and hear the charge to be the best they can be. While the candles are still lit, they sing the Spelman hymn.

Midnight Breakfast At Barnard, the night before finals, the president of the college, deans, and professors make breakfast for the students.

Counseling at The Master's School in Dobbs Ferry, New York. "The myth is that a women's college will be cliquish. In truth, the women are supportive of each other." The strong bonds of sisterhood that naturally develop connect students to their college, its history, and its students, past, present, and future. Many women's colleges designate a rotating color for each incoming class. For example, if the freshman class you enter is dubbed the golden hearts, by the time you graduate, you are connected to all the golden hearts who graduated ahead of you and all the golden hearts who will graduate after you.

TOSS MYTH NUMBER THREE

Another myth that should be tossed out is that women's colleges don't prepare you for the "real world." Well, try saying that to the 12 women members of Congress who graduated from women's colleges. Or to the 15 women on *Business Week*'s list of the rising stars in corporate America. Although you are not in a totally coed situation, on the other hand you are in an environment in which you can gain skills to think critically and learn to meet challenges. Becky Marsh, Director of Advancement at Whitfield School, in St. Louis, Missouri, points out that when you first ride a bike, training wheels allow you to learn how to balance. Once you are ready to race down the street, you take them off. Same with women's colleges. The focus is on your education and your strengths, and who you are. You graduate ready to take on the obstacles of the real world. "In high school, I had the feeling that boys were given more opportunities to share their knowledge. It was harder and more intimidating for me to share my opinions in a coed class," says Brittany Johnson, from Spelman College in Atlanta, Georgia. "Now I feel like I can do anything."

Graduates of women's colleges feel empowered and willing to confront any limits to their abilities. While in college, they have many opportunities to assume leadership roles and see women in leadership positions as professors and deans. "They don't doubt whether they can do anything. Instead, they ask, 'Why can't I do it now?'" reports Amy Shaver, former Academic Dean at Stephens College in Columbia, Missouri. Women can find their own voices and establish their own ways of approaching things that will ultimately make them successful in a male-dominated world. They learn from seeing other women students and professors engaged in the intellectual process.

THE ADVANTAGES

As more young women find out about the advantages that women's colleges offer them, they like what they see. Maybe that is why attendance at women's colleges is growing. Learning leadership skills tops the list of advantages. Says Shaver, "Women in a same-sex environment are more likely to take risks and speak up in class. They are more willing to stand up and voice an opinion." If you think about it, students get plenty of practice at a women's college because all the leadership roles go to women. From day one on a women's campus, you will see women leading the entire college or involved in interesting and significant research. You get more exposure to what leadership is and what to expect as a leader. "Leadership becomes ingrained," notes Jennifer Fondiller, Dean of Admissions at Barnard College in New York City.

You might not realize it, but women react differently in classrooms with all women. They tend to speak up with confidence and to test their ideas more readily when they are not competing with men. Researchers find that even as early as the fifth grade, girls are taught differently than boys. Teachers call on boys more frequently and don't ask girls the more thought-provoking questions or to critically analyze problems. In coed situations, the more aggressive and competitive guys take over, whereas in all-female classes, research indicates there is much more give-and-take and exchange of ideas.

Coming from a coed public school, Johnson realized that more attention was given to the guys in her classes, but at Spelman, she says, "Everyone is on the same path." Arlene Cash, Vice President for Enrollment Management at Spelman, notes that women don't have to vie for attention or retreat into the intellectual background in all-women classes. In a coed class, the environment becomes more adversarial. "Women feel they have to perform. In women's colleges they become more academically involved and interact with faculty members more frequently," says Debbie Greenberg, former College Counselor at Whitfield School. Speaking of the rich interaction that occurs in her classes at Barnard, Binder says, "The diversity of experience around the discussion table is unparalleled."

YOU CAN SUCCEED

Shaver characterizes the environment in women's colleges as one in which there is no fear of failing when the social pressures and dynamics of men and women are removed from the classroom. Women's colleges give women the opportunity to explore different avenues without the fear of failing. "We challenge them to become what they want to become," says Gibbs from Wesleyan. "No one says, 'You can't do that because you are a woman.'" At the same time, you are interacting with other women who have the same goals as you, which reinforces who you are. Or, as Jennifer Rickard, Chief Enrollment and Communications Officer at Bryn Mawr College, in Bryn Mawr, Pennsylvania, points out, women are not just sitting in classes to do well on exams and get good grades. They also are figuring out what they want to do with their education. "There's less expectation to conform to an external measure," she says.

Many women's colleges foster self-government and give their students responsibilities they might not find in a coed institution. At Bryn Mawr, for instance, students pay a self-government association fee as part of their tuition. This is put into a fund that is controlled by a student government that takes ownership of how the students want to govern themselves. "This isn't student government making only recommendations to the administration as to how to allocate the budget to the different student groups vying for funds," notes Rickard. "You have students dealing with real-world management issues, such as resource allocation."

Since women's colleges are smaller than big coed universities, women receive all the benefits that students get from a

WHAT MADE YOU CHOOSE A WOMEN'S COLLEGE?

When she got to the point of choosing which college to attend, Wisambi Loundu had plenty of options. Coming from San Diego, the California universities were a logical choice. Women's colleges were not on her list. In fact, she hardly knew they existed. Her first thought when someone suggested a women's college to her was, "I'm not going to a school full of girls minus boys." Her second thought was just as negative. "If it's all girls, they will always be fighting." The third and fourth thoughts assumed that a women's college wouldn't prepare her for the real world, plus she would be isolated.

But then her math teacher's daughter told her about Bryn Mawr, and as Wisambi started exploring the possibility, the advantages of a women's college started lining up. However, it wasn't until she visited Bryn Mawr that she really began to see herself there. "I fell in love with the campus," says Wisambi. "It was like nothing I'd ever seen before." Her stay in the dorm added to her steadily growing thoughts that Bryn Mawr might be it. "The girls I stayed with in the dorm were so friendly. At first I was suspicious, but I saw it was not a front. Plus, there were girls from all over the world."

But Wisambi didn't make her final decision just yet. She decided to look at other schools, like Wellesley and the University of California schools, as well as Stanford. Meanwhile, her friend told her more about Bryn Mawr. "She said I'd make lasting friends and she talked about how the academics would train me for the outside world even if there were no men on campus. Bryn Mawr would build my identity as a woman."

She still wasn't convinced and made a second visit, along with visits to Wellesley and Stanford, which she says were nice, but too big. It would be too hard to make friends there, she thought. When the time came to make her final selection, she chose Bryn Mawr.

Now at Bryn Mawr, how does Wisambi feel about her choice? The academics are more challenging than she anticipated but doable, and she is excited about the internships she will be able to access. She also finds that the staff and teachers at Bryn Mawr go out of their way to make her feel at home. "They match us up with a mentor and professor," she says.

How about dating? Since Bryn Mawr is part of a tri-college community, guys are around, though Wisambi says you have to make an effort to meet people on other campuses.

Talking to seniors who are getting ready to head out to the "real world," Wisambi can see that they are full of confidence and don't think for a minute that they won't do well. "And that's a positive," she says.

small liberal arts college in addition to the advantages that only a women's college offers. A big plus is interaction with professors and staff, which is hard to achieve when you are one of 200 students in a lecture hall taught by a graduate student. Women's colleges tend to foster seminar-style classes taught by full professors, many of them women. "You have an expert teaching you," says Gibbs. Faculty members get to know their students and can challenge them intellectually on an individual basis. "Within two days, all my teachers knew my name," recalls Johnson, who says she was given each professor's e-mail address, home phone number, and all the contact information she needed and was encouraged to reach out to them.

Women are encouraged to achieve their intellectual goals. Professors often will point out specific programs that they know suit the student's interests. Add to this the opportunities to conduct research with a professor, and in many cases actually present research findings to a professional society, and you can see why women graduate with a terrific resume before they even start their careers. Rickard mentions the opportunity that Bryn Mawr students have to work on funded projects with professors during the summer and then present the results along with them at conferences. "It's a window into the academic world and the world of the intellectual," she notes. It's no surprise that women in women's colleges major in math and science at a higher national average than women in coed institutions.

Paid and unpaid internships, too, are more available for women at women's colleges, mainly because of the network of women graduates in business and industry who want to help their "sisters" at their alma maters. "I'm getting my professional edge now," says Binder, who is interested in TV production and had a paid internship as a production assistant while a sophomore at Barnard. "You will have an amazing resume by the time you graduate," she says.

Peggy Hock, Ph.D., former College Counselor at Notre Dame High School in San Jose, California, points out that colleges naturally rely on their alumni to come forward with networking opportunities for students; however, the alumnae of women's colleges tend to be more loyal and willing to give of their time. This translates into many more opportunities for internships, mentoring, and job possibilities. At Barnard, for example, the career office has an alumna mentor network. Students can call, ask questions, and get advice about career choices. At alumnae events, current students mix with the graduates. Binder takes full advantage of the Web log of women who are working all over the world and willing to spend time online with Barnard students. She applied for a job at a public relations firm in New York after contacting a fellow Barnard graduate working there. She met with her and subsequently got a letter of recommendation.

HOW TO CHOOSE

Choosing a women's college isn't any different from choosing a coed college. You should definitely visit the campus and don't be afraid to ask lots of questions—even the ones that might make you uncomfortable. Because women's colleges are similar to small coed liberal arts colleges, make sure that you don't compare a women's campus to a big university.

Janet Ashley, former Interim Director for Admissions at Spelman College, advises high school women to ask what a women's college can give them academically. "Their choice depends on what their goals are," she says.

If you're worried about the dating scene, ask about the levels of interaction with guys and how close the relationships are with neighboring institutions.

"Look at the individuality of each women's college," suggests Rickard, "because each has its own personality."

Look at the school before looking at the fact that it's a women's college, and on the flip side, don't rule out a school just because it is a women's college. "So many students make quick decisions about where to apply," warns Fondiller, noting that sometimes the decision hinges on what schools a friend is applying to rather than if that institution really fits the student. Many women's colleges specialize in certain fields like science, math, or theater.

FAMOUS FIRSTS FROM WOMEN'S COLLEGES

Quick, from where did the first woman to be named Secretary of State graduate? Or the woman scientist who identified Hong Kong flu? Or the first woman executive vice president of the American Stock Exchange? Here's a big clue. They were all graduates of women's colleges.

SENATORS

- Hillary Rodham Clinton (NY)—Wellesley College
- Blanche Lambert Lincoln (AR)—Randolph-Macon Woman's College
- Barbara Mikulski (MD)—Mount Saint Agnes College

REPRESENTATIVES

- Tammy Baldwin (WI)—Smith College
- Donna Christian-Christensen (VI)—St. Mary's College
- Rosa DeLauro (CT)—Marymount College
- Jane Harman (CA)—Smith College
- Gabrielle Giffords (AZ)—Scripps College
- Eddie Bernice Johnson (TX)—Saint Mary's College
- Sue Kelly (NY)—Sarah Lawrence College
- Barbara Lee (CA)—Mills College
- Nita Lowey (NY)—Mount Holyoke College
- Betty McCollum (MN)—College of Saint Catherine
- Nancy Pelosi (CA), first woman elected as Speaker of the House of Representatives—Trinity College
- Allyson Schwartz (PA)—Simmons College

OTHER FAMOUS WOMEN FIRSTS

- Madeleine Albright, first woman to be named Secretary of State in the United States, appointed in 1997—Wellesley
- Jane Amsterdam, first woman editor, the *New York Post*—Cedar Crest
- Emily Green Balch, first woman to receive the Nobel Peace Prize in 1946—Bryn Mawr
- Catherine Brewer Benson, first woman to receive a college bachelor's degree—Wesleyan
- Earla Biekert, first scientist to identify the Hong Kong flu virus—Wesleyan
- Cathleen Black, first woman leader of the American Newspaper Publishers Association—Trinity, Washington, D.C.
- Sarah Porter Boehmler, first woman executive vice president of American Stock Exchange—Sweet Briar
- Jane Matilda Bolin, first African-American woman judge in the United States—Wellesley
- Dorothy L. Brown, first African-American woman general surgeon in the South—Bennett
- Pearl S. Buck, first American woman to win the Nobel Prize in Literature—Randolph-Macon Woman's College
- Ila Burdett, Georgia's first female Rhodes Scholar—Agnes Scott
- Dorothy Vredenburgh Bush, first woman secretary of the Democratic National Party—Mississippi University for Women
- Hon. Audrey J. S. Carrion, first Hispanic woman judge Circuit Court for Baltimore City—College of Notre Dame of Maryland
- Barbara Cassani, first female and CEO of a commercial airline—Mount Holyoke
- Elaine L. Chao, U.S. Secretary of Labor, 2001; First Asian-American woman appointed to a President's cabinet in U.S. history—Mount Holyoke

Adapted from the Web site of the Women's College Coalition at http://www.womenscolleges.org.

About the Peterson's Icon and Keyword Search

These schools have chosen to provide expanded information to users of this book. For instant access to the most current information on these schools, enter the Keywords at the end of the profile into the Quick College Search field at www.petersons.com. Peterson's does its very best to ensure that the following list is accurate at the time of publication; however, this list may change throughout the year. Depending on the status of a school's Web site service, the institution's online profile may not appear. In addition, new school profiles may be featured online that were not available at the time of publication. This Peterson's icon appears in each school's profile:

Adelphi University (NY)
Agnes Scott College (GA)
Albertus Magnus College (CT)
Alma College (MI)
Alvernia University (PA)
The American University of Paris (France)
Amridge University (AL)
Angelo State University (TX)
Antioch University Los Angeles (CA)
Aquinas College (MI)
Arcadia University (PA)
Argosy University, Atlanta (GA)
Argosy University, Chicago (IL)
Argosy University, Dallas (TX)
Argosy University, Denver (CO)
Argosy University, Hawai'i (HI)
Argosy University, Inland Empire (CA)
Argosy University, Los Angeles (CA)
Argosy University, Nashville (TN)
Argosy University, Orange County (CA)
Argosy University, Phoenix (AZ)
Argosy University, Salt Lake City (UT)
Argosy University, San Diego (CA)
Argosy University, San Francisco Bay Area (CA)
Argosy University, Sarasota (FL)
Argosy University, Schaumburg (IL)
Argosy University, Seattle (WA)
Argosy University, Tampa (FL)
Argosy University, Twin Cities (MN)
Argosy University, Washington DC (VA)
Art Center College of Design (CA)
The Art Institute of Atlanta (GA)
The Art Institute of Atlanta–Decatur (GA)
The Art Institute of Austin (TX)
The Art Institute of Boston at Lesley University (MA)
The Art Institute of California–Hollywood (CA)
The Art Institute of California–Inland Empire (CA)
The Art Institute of California–Los Angeles (CA)
The Art Institute of California–Orange County (CA)
The Art Institute of California–Sacramento (CA)
The Art Institute of California–San Diego (CA)
The Art Institute of California–San Francisco (CA)
The Art Institute of California–Sunnyvale (CA)
The Art Institute of Charleston (SC)
The Art Institute of Charlotte (NC)
The Art Institute of Colorado (CO)
The Art Institute of Dallas (TX)
The Art Institute of Fort Lauderdale (FL)
The Art Institute of Houston (TX)
The Art Institute of Houston–North (TX)
The Art Institute of Indianapolis (IN)
The Art Institute of Jacksonville (FL)
The Art Institute of Las Vegas (NV)
The Art Institute of Michigan (MI)
The Art Institute of Philadelphia (PA)
The Art Institute of Phoenix (AZ)
The Art Institute of Pittsburgh (PA)
The Art Institute of Portland (OR)
The Art Institute of Raleigh-Durham (NC)
The Art Institute of Salt Lake City (UT)
The Art Institute of Seattle (WA)
The Art Institute of Tampa (FL)
The Art Institute of Tennessee–Nashville (TN)
The Art Institute of Tucson (AZ)
The Art Institute of Washington (VA)
The Art Institutes International–Kansas City (KS)
The Art Institutes International Minnesota (MN)
Asbury University (KY)
Assumption College (MA)
Aurora University (IL)
Austin College (TX)
Averett University (VA)
Babson College (MA)
Baldwin-Wallace College (OH)
Bard College at Simon's Rock (MA)
Barnard College (NY)
Barry University (FL)
Barton College (NC)
Bastyr University (WA)
Baylor University (TX)
Bay State College (MA)
Belmont University (TN)
Beloit College (WI)
Benedictine University (IL)
Bentley University (MA)
Berkeley College–New York City Campus (NY)
Berklee College of Music (MA)
Bethel University (MN)
Birmingham-Southern College (AL)
Bishop's University (QC, Canada)
Bloomfield College (NJ)
Boston Architectural College (MA)
Boston College (MA)
The Boston Conservatory (MA)

Boston University (MA)
Bowie State University (MD)
Bradley University (IL)
Brevard College (NC)
Bridgewater State College (MA)
Brooklyn College of the City University of New York (NY)
Brown Mackie College–Boise (ID)
Brown Mackie College–Fort Wayne (IN)
Brown Mackie College–Indianapolis (IN)
Brown Mackie College–Merrillville (IN)
Brown Mackie College–Miami (FL)
Brown Mackie College–Michigan City (IN)
Brown Mackie College–Northern Kentucky (KY)
Brown Mackie College–Phoenix (AZ)
Brown Mackie College–South Bend (IN)
Brown Mackie College–Tucson (AZ)
Brown Mackie College–Tulsa (OK)
Bryant University (RI)
Bryn Mawr College (PA)
Bucknell University (PA)
Buffalo State College, State University of New York (NY)
Burlington College (VT)
Butler University (IN)
Cabrini College (PA)
Caldwell College (NJ)
California Institute of the Arts (CA)
California Lutheran University (CA)
California University of Pennsylvania (PA)
Calvin College (MI)
Campbell University (NC)
Canisius College (NY)
Capital University (OH)
Carleton College (MN)
Carlos Albizu University, Miami Campus (FL)
Carlow University (PA)
Carnegie Mellon University (PA)
Carroll College (MT)
Carroll University (WI)
Carson-Newman College (TN)
Case Western Reserve University (OH)
Castleton State College (VT)
Catawba College (NC)
Cedar Crest College (PA)
Central Connecticut State University (CT)
Chadron State College (NE)
Chapman University (CA)
Chatham University (PA)
Chestnut Hill College (PA)
Christopher Newport University (VA)
The Citadel, The Military College of South Carolina (SC)
City College of the City University of New York (NY)
Clarkson University (NY)
Clemson University (SC)
The Cleveland Institute of Art (OH)
Cleveland Institute of Music (OH)
The Colburn School Conservatory of Music (CA)
Colby-Sawyer College (NH)
College of Mount St. Joseph (OH)
College of Saint Elizabeth (NJ)
The College of Saint Rose (NY)
College of Staten Island of the City University of New York (NY)
The College of Wooster (OH)
Columbia College Chicago (IL)
Columbia University (NY)
Columbia University, School of General Studies (NY)
The Culinary Institute of America (NY)
Curry College (MA)
Daemen College (NY)
Dean College (MA)
Delaware Valley College (PA)
DePaul University (IL)
DeSales University (PA)
Dominican University of California (CA)
Drake University (IA)
Drexel University (PA)
Duke University (NC)
D'Youville College (NY)
Earlham College (IN)
Eastern Connecticut State University (CT)
Eastern Nazarene College (MA)
Elizabethtown College (PA)
Elmhurst College (IL)
Elmira College (NY)
Embry-Riddle Aeronautical University (AZ)
Embry-Riddle Aeronautical University (FL)
Emerson College (MA)
Emmanuel College (MA)
Emory & Henry College (VA)
Eugene Lang College The New School for Liberal Arts (NY)
Fairleigh Dickinson University, College at Florham (NJ)
Fairmont State University (WV)
Fashion Institute of Technology (NY)
Felician College (NJ)
FIDM/The Fashion Institute of Design & Merchandising, Los Angeles Campus (CA)
Fitchburg State College (MA)
Five Towns College (NY)
Florida Atlantic University (FL)
Florida Institute of Technology (FL)
Florida International University (FL)
Florida Southern College (FL)
Fordham University (NY)
Framingham State College (MA)
Franciscan University of Steubenville (OH)
Franklin College (IN)
Franklin College Switzerland (Switzerland)
Franklin Pierce University (NH)
Frostburg State University (MD)
Gannon University (PA)
Gardner-Webb University (NC)
George Fox University (OR)
The George Washington University (DC)
Georgian Court University (NJ)
Golden Gate University (CA)
Gonzaga University (WA)
Goucher College (MD)
Graceland University (IA)
Grand Canyon University (AZ)
Grand Valley State University (MI)
Grand View University (IA)
Greensboro College (NC)
Grinnell College (IA)
Grove City College (PA)
Gwynedd-Mercy College (PA)
Hamline University (MN)
Haverford College (PA)
Hawai'i Pacific University (HI)
Hesser College, Manchester (NH)
High Point University (NC)
Hilbert College (NY)
Hofstra University (NY)
Hollins University (VA)
Hope College (MI)
Hunter College of the City University of New York (NY)
The Illinois Institute of Art–Chicago (IL)
The Illinois Institute of Art–Schaumburg (IL)
Immaculata University (PA)
Indiana University of Pennsylvania (PA)
International Academy of Design & Technology (IL)
Iona College (NY)

John Cabot University (Italy)
John Carroll University (OH)
The Johns Hopkins University (MD)
Johnson & Wales University (RI)
Judson University (IL)
Keene State College (NH)
Keiser University (FL)
Kendall College (IL)
Kent State University (OH)
Kettering University (MI)
Keystone College (PA)
King's College (PA)
Kutztown University of Pennsylvania (PA)
Lafayette College (PA)
LaGrange College (GA)
Lawrence Technological University (MI)
Lehman College of the City University of New York (NY)
Le Moyne College (NY)
Lesley University (MA)
Lewis & Clark College (OR)
Lewis University (IL)
Liberty University (VA)
LIM College (NY)
Limestone College (SC)
Lindenwood University (MO)
Linfield College (OR)
Long Island University, Brooklyn Campus (NY)
Long Island University, C.W. Post Campus (NY)
Loyola Marymount University (CA)
Loyola University Chicago (IL)
Loyola University Maryland (MD)
Loyola University New Orleans (LA)
Luther College (IA)
Lynchburg College (VA)
Manchester College (IN)
Manhattan College (NY)
Manhattanville College (NY)
Mannes College The New School for Music (NY)
Marietta College (OH)
Marlboro College (VT)
Maryland Institute College of Art (MD)
Marymount Manhattan College (NY)
Marymount University (VA)
Marywood University (PA)
Massachusetts College of Pharmacy and Health Sciences (MA)
McNeese State University (LA)
Menlo College (CA)
Meredith College (NC)
Merrimack College (MA)
Messiah College (PA)
Miami International University of Art & Design (FL)
MidAmerica Nazarene University (KS)
Millersville University of Pennsylvania (PA)
Milligan College (TN)
Mills College (CA)
Milwaukee School of Engineering (WI)
Misericordia University (PA)
Molloy College (NY)
Monmouth University (NJ)
Montclair State University (NJ)
Moore College of Art & Design (PA)
Mountain State University (WV)
Mount Aloysius College (PA)
Mount Holyoke College (MA)
Mount Ida College (MA)
Mount Mary College (WI)
Muhlenberg College (PA)
Muskingum University (OH)
Naropa University (CO)
Neumann University (PA)
Newberry College (SC)
New College of Florida (FL)
New England College (NH)
The New England Institute of Art (MA)
New Hampshire Institute of Art (NH)
The New School for Jazz and Contemporary Music (NY)
New York College of Health Professions (NY)
New York School of Interior Design (NY)
New York University (NY)
Niagara University (NY)
Nichols College (MA)
North Central College (IL)
Northern Arizona University (AZ)
Northern Kentucky University (KY)
Norwich University (VT)
Notre Dame College (OH)
Oberlin College (OH)
Ohio Northern University (OH)
Ohio Wesleyan University (OH)
Olivet Nazarene University (IL)
Oregon State University (OR)
Pace University (NY)
Pacific University (OR)
Paier College of Art, Inc. (CT)
Palm Beach Atlantic University (FL)
Parsons The New School for Design (NY)
Penn State Erie, The Behrend College (PA)
Pennsylvania College of Technology (PA)
Philadelphia University (PA)
Pitzer College (CA)
Point Park University (PA)
Pratt Institute (NY)
Purchase College, State University of New York (NY)
Queens College of the City University of New York (NY)
Quinnipiac University (CT)
Radford University (VA)
Ramapo College of New Jersey (NJ)
Randolph College (VA)
Randolph-Macon College (VA)
Reed College (OR)
The Restaurant School at Walnut Hill College (PA)
The Richard Stockton College of New Jersey (NJ)
Richmond, The American International University in London (United Kingdom)
Rider University (NJ)
Ripon College (WI)
Rivier College (NH)
Robert Morris University (PA)
Roberts Wesleyan College (NY)
Rocky Mountain College of Art + Design (CO)
Roger Williams University (RI)
Roosevelt University (IL)
Rosemont College (PA)
Rowan University (NJ)
Rutgers, The State University of New Jersey, Camden (NJ)
Rutgers, The State University of New Jersey, New Brunswick (NJ)
Ryerson University (ON, Canada)
Sacred Heart University (CT)
Saint Anselm College (NH)
Saint Anthony College of Nursing (IL)
St. Bonaventure University (NY)
St. Edward's University (TX)
Saint Francis University (PA)
St. John Fisher College (NY)
St. John's College (MD)
Saint Joseph College (CT)
St. Joseph's College, New York (NY)
Saint Joseph's University (PA)
St. Lawrence University (NY)
Saint Leo University (FL)

St. Louis College of Pharmacy (MO)
Saint Louis University–Madrid Campus (Spain)
Saint Mary's College (IN)
St. Mary's College of Maryland (MD)
St. Mary's University (TX)
Saint Michael's College (VT)
St. Norbert College (WI)
Saint Peter's College (NJ)
St. Thomas Aquinas College (NY)
St. Thomas University (FL)
Saint Vincent College (PA)
Saint Xavier University (IL)
Salem College (NC)
Salem State College (MA)
Salisbury University (MD)
Samford University (AL)
Sam Houston State University (TX)
Sarah Lawrence College (NY)
School of the Art Institute of Chicago (IL)
School of the Museum of Fine Arts, Boston (MA)
Seattle Pacific University (WA)
Seattle University (WA)
Seton Hall University (NJ)
Seton Hill University (PA)
Shepherd University (WV)
Shippensburg University of Pennsylvania (PA)
Shorter University (GA)
Siena College (NY)
Simmons College (MA)
Simon Fraser University (BC, Canada)
Simpson College (IA)
Skidmore College (NY)
Smith College (MA)
Southern Connecticut State University (CT)
Southern New Hampshire University (NH)
South University (AL)
South University (FL)
South University (FL)
South University (GA)
South University (SC)
Springfield College (MA)
State University of New York at Oswego (NY)
State University of New York College of Environmental Science and Forestry (NY)
State University of New York Institute of Technology (NY)
Stephen F. Austin State University (TX)
Sterling College (VT)
Stevenson University (MD)
Stonehill College (MA)
Stratford University (VA)
Sullivan University (KY)
Susquehanna University (PA)
Sweet Briar College (VA)
Temple University (PA)
Tennessee State University (TN)
Texas Christian University (TX)
Texas Woman's University (TX)
Thomas Edison State College (NJ)
Thomas Jefferson University (PA)
Thomas More College (KY)
Tiffin University (OH)
Transylvania University (KY)
Trine University (IN)
Trinity College (CT)
Truman State University (MO)
Tulane University (LA)
Union College (NY)
Union University (TN)
United States Merchant Marine Academy (NY)
University at Albany, State University of New York (NY)
University of Advancing Technology (AZ)
The University of Alabama at Birmingham (AL)
The University of Alabama in Huntsville (AL)
University of Alaska Fairbanks (AK)
University of Charleston (WV)
University of Colorado at Boulder (CO)
University of Dallas (TX)
University of Denver (CO)
University of Dubuque (IA)
The University of Findlay (OH)
University of Great Falls (MT)
University of Hartford (CT)
University of Indianapolis (IN)
University of Maine (ME)
University of Maine at Fort Kent (ME)
University of Maine at Machias (ME)
University of Massachusetts Boston (MA)
University of Massachusetts Dartmouth (MA)
University of Massachusetts Lowell (MA)
University of Memphis (TN)
The University of Montana Western (MT)
University of New England (ME)
University of New Hampshire (NH)
University of New Haven (CT)
University of New Orleans (LA)
The University of North Carolina at Pembroke (NC)
University of Oregon (OR)
University of Pittsburgh at Bradford (PA)
University of Pittsburgh at Johnstown (PA)
University of Redlands (CA)
University of Richmond (VA)
University of Rochester (NY)
University of San Diego (CA)
University of San Francisco (CA)
University of South Carolina (SC)
The University of Tampa (FL)
The University of Texas at Dallas (TX)
The University of the Arts (PA)
University of the Cumberlands (KY)
University of the Incarnate Word (TX)
University of the Sciences in Philadelphia (PA)
University of Tulsa (OK)
University of Vermont (VT)
University of Windsor (ON, Canada)
University of Wyoming (WY)
Utica College (NY)
Valparaiso University (IN)
Vanderbilt University (TN)
Vaughn College of Aeronautics and Technology (NY)
Vermont Technical College (VT)
Villanova University (PA)
Virginia Military Institute (VA)
Wagner College (NY)
Walsh University (OH)
Warner Pacific College (OR)
Warren Wilson College (NC)
Washington College (MD)
Webber International University (FL)
Webb Institute (NY)
Wellesley College (MA)
Wells College (NY)
Wentworth Institute of Technology (MA)
Wesleyan College (GA)
West Chester University of Pennsylvania (PA)
Western Connecticut State University (CT)
Western Michigan University (MI)
Westminster College (UT)
Westmont College (CA)
West Virginia University Institute of Technology (WV)
Wheaton College (IL)

Wheaton College (MA)
Wheeling Jesuit University (WV)
Widener University (PA)
Wilkes University (PA)
William Paterson University of New Jersey (NJ)
Wittenberg University (OH)
Worcester Polytechnic Institute (MA)
York University (ON, Canada)

How to Use This Guide

COLLEGES AT-A-GLANCE AND SPECIAL MESSAGES

The **COLLEGES AT-A-GLANCE** contains basic data in capsule form for quick review and comparison. The following outline of the format shows the section headings and the items that each section covers. Any item that does not apply to a particular college or for which no information was supplied is omitted from that college's listing.

Category Overviews

General

The first category noted is *Institutional control*. Private institutions are designated as independent (nonprofit), proprietary (profit-making), or independent with a specific religious denomination or affiliation. Nondenominational or interdenominational religious orientation is possible and would be indicated. Public institutions are designated by the source of funding. Designations include federal, state, province, commonwealth (Puerto Rico), territory (U.S. territories), county, district (an educational administrative unit often having boundaries different from units of local government), city, state and local (local may refer to county, district, or city), or state-related (funded primarily by the state but administratively autonomous). *Religious affiliation* is then noted, followed by *Institutional type*. Each institution is classified as one of the following:

- Primarily two-year college: Awards baccalaureate degrees but the majority of students are enrolled in two-year programs.
- Four-year college: Awards baccalaureate degrees; may also award associate degrees; does not award graduate (postbaccalaureate) degrees.
- Five-year college: Awards a five-year baccalaureate in a professional field such as architecture or pharmacy; does not award graduate degrees.
- Upper-level institution: Awards baccalaureate degrees, but entering students must have at least two years of previous college-level credit; may also offer graduate degrees.
- Comprehensive institution: Awards baccalaureate degrees; may also award associate degrees; offers graduate degree programs, primarily at the master's, specialist's, or professional level, although one or two doctoral programs may be offered.
- University: Offers four years of undergraduate work, plus graduate degrees through the doctorate in more than two academic or professional fields.

The last category noted is *System or administrative affiliation*. Any coordinate institutions or system affiliations are indicated. An institution that has separate colleges or campuses for men and women but shares facilities and courses is termed a coordinate institution. A formal administrative grouping of institutions, either private or public, of which the college is a part, or the name of a single institution with which the college is administratively affiliated, is a system.

Entrance

The five levels of entrance difficulty *(most difficult, very difficult, moderately difficult, minimally difficult,* and *noncompetitive)* are based on the percentage of applicants who were accepted for fall 2009 freshman admission (or, in the case of upper-level schools, for entering-class admission) and on the high school class rank and standardized test scores of the accepted freshmen who actually enrolled in fall 2009. The colleges were asked to select the level that most closely corresponds to their entrance difficulty, according to these guidelines, to assist prospective students in assessing their chances for admission.

Setting

Designated as *urban* (located within a major city), *suburban* (a residential area within commuting distance of a major city), *small town* (a small but compactly settled area not within commuting distance of a major city), or *rural* (a remote and sparsely populated area).

Total enrollment

The number of undergraduate and (if applicable) graduate students, both full-time and part-time, as of fall 2009.

Student-faculty ratio

The school's estimate of the ratio of undergraduate students to faculty members teaching undergraduate courses.

Application deadline

Deadlines and dates for notification of acceptance or rejection are given either as specific dates or as rolling or continuous. *Rolling* means that applications are processed as they are received and qualified students are accepted as long as there are openings. *Continuous notification* means that applicants are notified of acceptance or rejection as applications are processed up until the date indicated or the actual beginning of classes.

Freshmen admission

Figures are given for the percentage of applicants who were accepted and for the average high school GPA.

Freshman test scores

The percentage of freshmen who took the SAT and received critical reading and math scores above 500 and 600, as well as the percentage of freshmen taking the ACT who received a composite score of 18 or higher and 24 or higher.

Housing
Indicates whether or not on-campus housing is available.

Expenses
The average basic tuition and fees for an academic year presented as a dollar amount. Room & Board is the average yearly room and board cost presented as a dollar amount. Comprehensive fee is a single charge combining tuition, fees, and room and board. For state supported and state-related schools figures are presented for the cost of state resident tuition and fees and nonresident tuition and fees.

Undergraduates
Percentages of undergraduates who are women, part-time students, 25 years or older, Native American (Indian, Eskimo, Polynesian), Hispanic, African American, and Asian American/ Pacific Islander are given.

Most frequently chosen baccalaureate fields
The most popular majors of the 2009 graduating class.

Academic program
The Academic program category includes the following offerings:

- English as a second language: A course of study designed specifically for students whose native language is not English.
- Advanced placement: Credit toward a degree awarded for acceptable scores on some or all College Board Advanced Placement tests.
- Accelerated degree program: Students may earn a bachelor's degree in three academic years.
- Student-designed majors: Students may design their own program of study based on individual interests.
- Honors program: Unusually challenging academic program for superior students.
- Summer session: Summer courses through which students may make up degree work or accelerate their program.
- Adult/continuing education programs: Courses offered for nontraditional students who are currently working or are returning to formal education.
- Internships: College-arranged work experience for which students earn academic credit.

Contact
The name, title, mailing address, and phone number of the person to contact for further information are given at the end of the profile. Toll-free phone numbers may also be included. The admission office fax number, e-mail address, and Web site may be provided.

Additional Information

Each school that has a **College Close-Up** in the guide will have a cross-reference referring you directly to that **College Close-Up.** For instant access to the most current information on these schools, enter the Keywords at the end of the profile into the Quick College Search field at www.petersons.com.

COLLEGE CLOSE-UPS

The 464 two-page narrative descriptions provide an inside look at colleges and universities, shifting the focus to a variety of other factors, some of them intangible, that should also be considered. The descriptions provide a wealth of statistics that are crucial components in the college decision-making equation—components such as tuition, financial aid, and major fields of study. Prepared exclusively by college officials, the descriptions are designed to help give students a better sense of the individuality of each institution, in terms that include campus environment, student activities, and lifestyle. Such quality-of-life intangibles can be the deciding factors in the college selection process. The absence of any college or university does not constitute an editorial decision on the part of Peterson's. In essence, these descriptions are an open forum for colleges and universities, on a voluntary basis, to communicate their particular message to prospective college students. The colleges included have paid a fee to Peterson's to provide this information. The **College Close-Ups** are edited to provide a consistent format across entries for your ease of comparison.

INDEXES

Here you'll find easy-to-use breakdowns of schools' majors, entrance difficulty, and cost ranges. For a quick look-up, we've also provided a "Geographical Listing of College Close-Ups" and an "Alphabetical Listing of Colleges and Universities."

Majors

This listing presents hundreds of undergraduate fields of study that are currently offered most widely, according to the colleges' responses on *Peterson's Annual Survey of Undergraduate Institutions*. The majors appear in alphabetical order, each followed by an alphabetical list of the schools that offer a bachelor's-level program in that field. Liberal Arts and Studies indicates a general program with no specified major.

The terms used for the majors are those of the U.S. Department of Education Classification of Instructional Programs (CIP). Many institutions, however, use different terms. Although the term "major" is used in this guide, some colleges may use other terms, such as "concentration," "program of study," or "field."

Entrance Difficulty

This listing groups colleges by their own assessment of their entrance difficulty level. The colleges were asked to select the level that most closely corresponds to their entrance difficulty. Institutions for which high school class rank and/or standardized test scores do not apply as admission criteria were asked to select the level that best indicates their entrance difficulty as compared to other institutions.

Cost Ranges

Colleges are grouped into thirteen price ranges, from under $2000 to $30,000 and over.

2010–11 CHANGES IN INSTITUTIONS

The following is an alphabetical listing of institutions that have closed, merged with other institutions, or changed their names or status since *Peterson's Four-Year Colleges 2010.* In the case of a name change, the former name appears first, followed by the new name.

Arkansas State University (State University, AR): name changed to Arkansas State University–Jonesboro.

Asbury College (Wilmore, KY): name changed to Asbury University.

Ashworth University (Norcross, GA): name changed to Ashworth College.

Atlantic Baptist University (Moncton, NB, Canada): name changed to Crandall University.

Ave Maria College (Ypsilanti, MI): closed.

Baltimore Hebrew University (Baltimore, MD): is now part of Towson University.

Belhaven College (Jackson, MS): name changed to Belhaven University.

Bellin College of Nursing (Green Bay, WI): name changed to Bellin College.

Beth Benjamin Academy of Connecticut (Stamford, CT): name changed to Bais Binyomin Academy.

Bethel College (McKenzie, TN): name changed to Bethel University.

British American College London (London, United Kingdom): name changed to Regent's American College London.

Charles R. Drew University of Medicine and Science (Los Angeles, CA): name changed to Charles Drew University of Medicine and Science.

Colegio Biblico Pentecostal (St. Just, PR): name changed to Universidad Teol&,ogica del Caribe.

Coleman College (San Diego, CA): name changed to Coleman University.

Columbia Union College (Takoma Park, MD): name changed to Washington Adventist University.

Corban College (Salem, OR): name changed to Corban University.

DeVry University (San Francisco, CA): closed.

DeVry University (Atlanta, GA): no longer offers undergraduate degrees.

DeVry University (Cleveland, OH): closed.

Electronic Data Processing College of Puerto Rico–San Sebastian (San Sebastian, PR): name changed to EDP College of Puerto Rico–San Sebastian.

George Meany Center for Labor Studies–The National Labor College (Silver Spring, MD): name changed to National Labor College.

Heidelberg College (Tiffin, OH): name changed to Heidelberg University.

Huron University USA in London (London, United Kingdom): name changed to Hult International Business School.

International Import-Export Institute (Phoenix, AZ): name changed to Dunlap-Stone University.

International University in Geneva (Geneva, Switzerland): withdrew from accreditation candidacy.

Jones College (Miami, FL): closed.

Kent State University, Stark Campus (Canton, OH): name changed to Kent State University at Stark.

Kwantlen University College (Surrey, BC, Canada): name changed to Kwantlen Polytechnic University.

Laboratory Institute of Merchandising (New York, NY): name changed to LIM College.

Lancaster Bible College (Lancaster, PA): name changed to Lancaster Bible College & Graduate School.

LES ROCHES, Swiss Hotel Association, School of Hotel Management (Bluche, Switzerland): name changed to Les Roches International School of Hotel Management.

Lewis University at Hickory Hills (Hickory Hills, IL): merged into a single entry for Lewis University (Romeoville, IL) by request from the institution.

Lewis University at Oak Brook (Oak Brook, IL): merged into a single entry for Lewis University (Romeoville, IL) by request from the institution.

Lewis University at Shorewood (Shorewood, IL): merged into a single entry for Lewis University (Romeoville, IL) by request from the institution.

Lewis University at Tinley Park (Tinley Park, IL): merged into a single entry for Lewis University (Romeoville, IL) by request from the institution.

Lincoln Christian College (Lincoln, IL): name changed to Lincoln Christian University.

Magnolia Bible College (Kosciusko, MS): closed.

Marian College (Indianapolis, IN): name changed to Marian University.

MedCentral College of Nursing (Mansfield, OH): is now part of Ashland University beginning July 1, 2010.

Midwestern University, Glendale Campus (Glendale, AZ): no longer accepting bachelor's students.

Mount Royal College (Calgary, AB, Canada): name changed to Mount Royal University.

Mount Union College (Alliance, OH): name changed to University of Mount Union.

Muskingum College (New Concord, OH): name changed to Muskingum University.

Neumann College (Aston, PA): name changed to Neumann University.

North Carolina School of the Arts (Winston-Salem, NC): name changed to University of North Carolina School of the Arts.

Otterbein College (Westerville, OH): name changed to Otterbein University.

Pacific Islands Bible College (Guam Main Facility, GU): name changed to Pacific Islands University.

Parsons Paris (Paris, France): name changed to Parsons Paris School of Art + Design.

Peabody Conservatory of Music of The Johns Hopkins University (Baltimore, MD): name changed to Peabody Conservatory of The Johns Hopkins University.

Roanoke Bible College (Elizabeth City, NC): name changed to Mid-Atlantic Christian University.

Robert Morris College (Chicago, IL): name changed to Robert Morris University Illinois.

Robert Morris College–DuPage (Aurora, IL): merged into a single entry for Robert Morris University Illinois (Chicago, IL) by request from the institution.

Robert Morris College–Orland Park (Orland Park, IL): merged into a single entry for Robert Morris University Illinois (Chicago, IL) by request from the institution.

St. Petersburg Theological Seminary (St. Petersburg, FL): no longer accredited by agency recognized by USDE or CHEA.

Samuel Merritt College (Oakland, CA): name changed to Samuel Merritt University.

Schiller International University, American College of Switzerland (Leysin, Switzerland): closed.

Shorter College (Rome, GA): name changed to Shorter University.

Southeastern University (Washington, DC): not accepting new students.

Taylor University College and Seminary (Edmonton, AB, Canada): name changed to Taylor College and Seminary.

Teikyo Loretto Heights University (Denver, CO): name changed to Colorado Heights University.

Trinity Life Bible College (Sacramento, CA): name changed to Epic Bible College.

The University of Maine at Augusta (Augusta, ME): name changed to University of Maine at Augusta.
University of Missouri–Columbia (Columbia, MO): name changed to University of Missouri.
University of Oklahoma–Tulsa (Tulsa, OK): will be included with main campus University of Oklahoma (Norman, OK) by request from the institution.
Valley Forge Christian College–Woodbridge Campus (Woodbridge, VA): name changed to Valley Forge Christian College Woodbridge Campus.
West Liberty State University (West Liberty, WV): name changed to West Liberty University.

DATA COLLECTION PROCEDURES

The data contained in the **COLLEGES AT-A-GLANCE** and **INDEXES** sections were researched between winter 2009 and spring 2010 through *Peterson's Annual Survey of Undergraduate Institutions*. Questionnaires were sent to the more than 2,700 colleges and universities that met the outlined inclusion criteria. All data included in this edition have been submitted by officials (usually admissions and financial aid officers, registrars, or institutional research personnel) at the colleges. In addition, some of the institutions that submitted data were contacted directly by the Peterson's research staff to verify unusual figures, resolve discrepancies, or obtain additional data. All usable information received in time for publication has been included. The omission of any particular item from the **COLLEGES AT-A-GLANCE** and **INDEXES** sections signifies that the information is either not applicable to that institution or not available. Because of Peterson's comprehensive editorial review and because all material comes directly from college officials, we believe that the information presented in this guide is accurate. You should check with a specific college or university at the time of application to verify such figures as tuition and fees, which may have changed since the publication of this volume.

CRITERIA FOR INCLUSION IN THIS BOOK

The term "four-year college" is the commonly used designation for institutions that grant the baccalaureate degree. Four years is the expected amount of time required to earn this degree, although some bachelor's degree programs may be completed in three years, others require five years, and part-time programs may take considerably longer. Upper-level institutions offer only the junior and senior years and accept only students with two years of college-level credit. Therefore, "four-year college" is a conventional term that accurately describes most of the institutions included in this guide, but should not be taken literally in all cases.

To be included in this guide, an institution must have full accreditation or be a candidate for accreditation (preaccreditation) status by an institutional or specialized accrediting body recognized by the U.S. Department of Education or the Council for Higher Education Accreditation (CHEA). Institutional accrediting bodies, which review each institution as a whole, include the six regional associations of schools and colleges (Middle States, New England, North Central, Northwest, Southern, and Western), each of which is responsible for a specified portion of the United States and its territories. Other institutional accrediting bodies are national in scope and accredit specific kinds of institutions (e.g., Bible colleges, independent colleges, and rabbinical and Talmudic schools). Program registration by the New York State Board of Regents is considered to be the equivalent of institutional accreditation, since the board requires that all programs offered by an institution meet its standards before recognition is granted. A Canadian institution must be chartered and authorized to grant degrees by the provincial government, affiliated with a chartered institution, or accredited by a recognized U.S. accrediting body. This guide also includes institutions outside the United States that are accredited by these U.S. accrediting bodies. There are recognized specialized or professional accrediting bodies in more than forty different fields, each of which is authorized to accredit institutions or specific programs in its particular field. For specialized institutions that offer programs in one field only, we designate this to be the equivalent of institutional accreditation. A full explanation of the accrediting process and complete information on recognized, institutional (regional and national) and specialized accrediting bodies can be found online at www.chea.org or at www.ed.gov/admins/finaid/accred/index.html.

Colleges At-a-Glance

U.S. AND U.S. TERRITORIES

ALABAMA

Alabama Agricultural and Mechanical University
Huntsville, Alabama

General State-supported, university, coed **Entrance** Minimally difficult **Setting** 2,001-acre suburban campus **Total enrollment** 5,327 **Student-faculty ratio** 14:1 **Application deadline** 6/15 (freshmen), rolling (transfer) **Freshman admission** 47% were admitted **Freshman test scores** ACT scores over 18: 46.79%; ACT scores over 24: 3.63% **Housing** Yes **Expenses** Tuition & Fees: state resident $3432, nonresident $6834; Room & Board $4770 **Undergraduates** 52% women, 8% part-time, 13% 25 or older, 0.2% Native American, 0.3% Hispanic American, 95% African American, 0.2% Asian American/Pacific Islander **The most frequently chosen baccalaureate fields are** biological/life sciences, business/marketing, education **Academic program** Advanced placement, honors program, summer session, adult/continuing education programs, internships **Contact** Dr. Evelyn Ellis, Interim Director of Admissions, Alabama Agricultural and Mechanical University, 4900 Meridian Street, Huntsville, AL 35811. *Phone:* 256-372-5245 or toll-free 800-553-0816. *Fax:* 256-851-9747. *Web site:* http://www.aamu.edu/.

Alabama State University
Montgomery, Alabama

General State-supported, comprehensive, coed **Entrance** Minimally difficult **Setting** 172-acre urban campus **Total enrollment** 5,564 **Student-faculty ratio** 16:1 **Application deadline** 7/31 (freshmen), 7/31 (transfer) **Freshman admission** 53% were admitted. Average high school GPA 2.91 **Freshman test scores** SAT critical reading scores over 500: 12.2%; SAT math scores over 500: 7.8%; ACT scores over 18: 33.4%; SAT critical reading scores over 600: 1.6%; SAT math scores over 600: .8%; ACT scores over 24: 2% **Housing** Yes **Expenses** Tuition & Fees: state resident $6468, nonresident $12,084; Room & Board $4600 **Undergraduates** 60% women, 9% part-time, 12% 25 or older, 0.04% Native American, 0.3% Hispanic American, 98% African American, 0.1% Asian American/Pacific Islander **The most frequently chosen baccalaureate fields are** business/marketing, education, security and protective services **Academic program** Advanced placement, self-designed majors, honors program, summer session, internships **Contact** Dr. Donta Truss, Director of Admissions and Recruitment, Alabama State University, 915 South Jackson Street, Montgomery, AL 36101-0271. *Phone:* 334-229-4291 or toll-free 800-253-5037. *Fax:* 334-229-4984. *E-mail:* dtruss@alasu.edu. *Web site:* http://www.alasu.edu/.

Amridge University
Montgomery, Alabama

General Independent, university, coed, affiliated with Church of Christ **Entrance** Minimally difficult **Setting** 9-acre urban campus **Total enrollment** 766 **Student-faculty ratio** 11:1 **Application deadline** Rolling (freshmen), rolling (transfer) **Housing** No **Expenses** Tuition & Fees $7700 **Undergraduates** 52% women, 37% part-time, 83% 25 or older, 0.3% Native American, 5% Hispanic American, 38% African American, 1% Asian American/Pacific Islander **The most frequently chosen baccalaureate fields are** liberal arts/general studies, business/marketing, theology and religious vocations **Academic program** Advanced placement, accelerated degree program, summer session, adult/continuing education programs, internships **Contact** Mrs. Ora Davis, Admissions Officer, Amridge University, 1200 Taylor Road, Montgomery, AL 36117. *Phone:* 334-387-3877 Ext. 7524 or toll-free 800-351-4040 Ext. 213. *Fax:* 334-387-3878. *E-mail:* oradavis@amridgeuniversity.edu. *Web site:* http://www.amridgeuniversity.edu/.

Visit Petersons.com and enter keyword Amridge

See page 474 for the College Close-Up.

Andrew Jackson University
Birmingham, Alabama

General Private, comprehensive, coed **Entrance** Noncompetitive **Setting** suburban campus **Total enrollment** 472 **Student-faculty ratio** 11:1 **Freshman admission** 87% were admitted **Housing** No **Expenses** Tuition & Fees $700 **Undergraduates** 31% women, 100% part-time, 95% 25 or older **Academic program** Advanced placement, accelerated degree program, summer session, adult/continuing education programs **Contact** Tammy J. Kassner, Director of Admissions, Andrew Jackson University, 2919 John Hawkins Parkway, Birmingham, AL 35244. *Phone:* 205-871-9288 Ext. 107. *Fax:* 800-871-9294. *E-mail:* admissions@aju.edu. *Web site:* http://www.aju.edu/.

Athens State University
Athens, Alabama

General State-supported, upper-level, coed **Entrance** Noncompetitive **Setting** 45-acre small-town campus **Total enrollment** 3,114 **Student-faculty ratio** 23:1 **Application deadline** Rolling (freshmen), rolling (transfer) **Housing** No **Expenses** Tuition & Fees: state resident $4350, nonresident $7950 **Undergraduates** 90% 25 or older, 3% Native American, 1% Hispanic American, 11% African American, 1% Asian American/Pacific Islander **The most frequently chosen baccalaureate fields are** business/marketing, engineering, library science **Academic program** Advanced placement, summer session, adult/continuing education programs, internships **Contact** Ms. Necedah Henderson, Coordinator of Admissions, Athens State University, 300 North Beaty Street, Athens, AL 35611. *Phone:* 256-233-8217 or toll-free 800-522-0272. *Fax:* 256-233-6565. *E-mail:* necedah.henderson@athens.edu. *Web site:* http://www.athens.edu/.

Auburn University
Auburn University, Alabama

General State-supported, university, coed **Entrance** Moderately difficult **Setting** 1,875-acre small-town campus **Total enrollment** 24,602 **Student-faculty ratio** 18:1 **Application deadline** Rolling (freshmen), rolling (transfer) **Freshman admission** 80% were admitted. Average high school GPA 3.69 **Freshman test scores** SAT critical reading scores over 500: 86.9%; SAT math scores over 500: 92.8%; ACT scores over 18: 99.7%; SAT critical reading scores over 600: 40.6%; SAT math scores over 600: 52.9%; ACT scores over 24: 74.1% **Housing** Yes **Expenses** Tuition & Fees: state resident $6972, nonresident $19,452; Room & Board $8972 **Undergraduates** 48% women, 8% part-time, 5% 25 or older, 1% Native American, 2% Hispanic American, 8% African American, 2% Asian American/Pacific Islander **The most frequently chosen baccalaureate fields are** business/marketing, education, engineering **Academic program** English as a second language, advanced placement, accelerated degree program, honors program, summer session, adult/continuing education programs, internships **Contact** Ms. Cindy Singley, Director, University Recruitment, Auburn University, Auburn University, AL 36849. *Phone:* 334-844-4080 or toll-free 800-AUBURN9. *E-mail:* admissions@auburn.edu. *Web site:* http://www.auburn.edu/.

Auburn University Montgomery
Montgomery, Alabama

General State-supported, comprehensive, coed **Entrance** Moderately difficult **Setting** 500-acre suburban campus **Total enrollment** 5,547

Auburn University Montgomery (continued)
Student-faculty ratio 18:1 **Application deadline** Rolling (freshmen), rolling (transfer) **Freshman admission** 95% were admitted. Average high school GPA 3.02 **Freshman test scores** ACT scores over 18: 83%; ACT scores over 24: 21% **Housing** Yes **Expenses** Tuition & Fees: state resident $6300, nonresident $17,580; Room only $3720 **Undergraduates** 62% women, 33% part-time, 29% 25 or older, 0.5% Native American, 1% Hispanic American, 32% African American, 2% Asian American/ Pacific Islander **The most frequently chosen baccalaureate fields are** business/marketing, education, health professions and related sciences **Academic program** English as a second language, advanced placement, honors program, summer session, adult/continuing education programs, internships **Contact** Mr. Ronnie McKinney, Director of Recruitment, Auburn University Montgomery, PO Box 244023, Montgomery, AL 36124-4023. *Phone:* 334-244-3615 or toll-free 800-227-2649. *Fax:* 334-244-3795. *E-mail:* rmckinne@aum.edu. *Web site:* http://www.aum.edu/.

Birmingham-Southern College
Birmingham, Alabama

General Independent Methodist, comprehensive, coed **Entrance** Moderately difficult **Setting** 196-acre urban campus **Total enrollment** 1,549 **Student-faculty ratio** 12:1 **Application deadline** Rolling (freshmen), rolling (transfer) **Freshman admission** 59% were admitted. Average high school GPA 3.43 **Freshman test scores** SAT critical reading scores over 500: 85.18%; SAT math scores over 500: 82.54%; ACT scores over 18: 99.97%; SAT critical reading scores over 600: 37.31%; SAT math scores over 600: 39.68%; ACT scores over 24: 71.44% **Housing** Yes **Expenses** Tuition & Fees $25,586; Room & Board $9105 **Undergraduates** 50% women, 2% part-time, 2% 25 or older, 1% Native American, 2% Hispanic American, 8% African American, 4% Asian American/Pacific Islander **The most frequently chosen baccalaureate fields are** biological/life sciences, business/marketing, visual and performing arts **Academic program** Advanced placement, self-designed majors, honors program, summer session, internships **Contact** Ms. Sheri E. Salmon, Dean of Enrollment Management, Birmingham-Southern College, Box 549008, Birmingham, AL 35254. *Phone:* 205-226-4696 or toll-free 800-523-5793. *Fax:* 205-226-3074. *E-mail:* admitme@bsc.edu. *Web site:* http://www.bsc.edu/.

Visit Petersons.com and enter keyword Birmingham-Southern

See page 602 for the College Close-Up.

Columbia Southern University
Orange Beach, Alabama

General Proprietary, comprehensive, coed **Entrance** Noncompetitive **Setting** small-town campus **Total enrollment** 22,557 **Application deadline** Rolling (freshmen), rolling (transfer) **Freshman admission** 100% were admitted **Housing** No **Expenses** Tuition & Fees $5895 **Undergraduates** 34% women, 93% 25 or older, 1% Native American, 4% Hispanic American, 13% African American, 2% Asian American/ Pacific Islander **Academic program** Adult/continuing education programs **Contact** Director of Admissions, Columbia Southern University, 21982 University Lane, Orange Beach, AL 36561. *Phone:* 251-981-3771 Ext. 521 or toll-free 800-977-8449. *Fax:* 251-224-0540. *E-mail:* admissions@columbiasouthern.edu. *Web site:* http://www.columbiasouthern.edu/.

Concordia College
Selma, Alabama

General Independent Lutheran, 4-year, coed **Entrance** Minimally difficult **Setting** 22-acre small-town campus **Total enrollment** 555 **Application deadline** 8/15 (freshmen), 8/15 (transfer) **Housing** Yes **Expenses** Tuition & Fees $7090; Room & Board $3500 **Undergraduates** 33% 25 or older **Academic program** Advanced placement, honors program, adult/continuing education programs, internships **Contact** Ms. Phyllis

Arrive... at Birmingham-Southern College and **become** whatever it is you imagine you can be.

- One of America's best liberal arts colleges, with three straight years of record freshman enrollments.
- One of 40 colleges and universities included in Loren Pope's *Colleges That Change Lives.*
- A Best Buy in the *Fiske Guide to Colleges.*
- One of America's Best 371 Colleges by *Princeton Review.*
- Quality academics, including new cutting-edge Media and Film Studies and Urban Environmental Studies majors.
- The highest ranked liberal arts college for safety preparedness by *Reader's Digest.*
- Three of Alabama's "Best Professors" in the past decade as determined by CASE and the Carnegie Foundation, including Physics Professor Dr. Duane Pontius in 2009.
- A new Urban Environmental Park on campus, complete with 1.5 acre lake.
- President's Higher Education Community Service Honor Roll.

But most importantly, Birmingham-Southern graduates are **difference-makers** in our world.

Find out more at:
www.gotobsc.com | admission@bsc.edu
800-523-5793, ext. 4696
900 Arkadelphia Road | Birmingham, AL 35254

Richardson, Director, STARS, Concordia College, 1804 Green Street, Selma, AL 36703. *Phone:* 334-874-5700 Ext. 102. *Fax:* 334-874-5755. *E-mail:* prichrdson@concordiaselma.edu. *Web site:* http://www.concordiaselma.edu/.

Faulkner University
Montgomery, Alabama

General Independent, comprehensive, coed, affiliated with Church of Christ **Entrance** Minimally difficult **Setting** 75-acre urban campus **Total enrollment** 3,349 **Student-faculty ratio** 12:1 **Application deadline** Rolling (freshmen), rolling (transfer) **Freshman admission** 58% were admitted. Average high school GPA 2.9 **Freshman test scores** SAT math scores over 500: 41%; ACT scores over 18: 81%; SAT math scores over 600: 14%; ACT scores over 24: 16% **Housing** Yes **Expenses** Tuition & Fees $14,810; Room & Board $6570 **Undergraduates** 63% women, 27% part-time, 54% 25 or older, 0.5% Native American, 1% Hispanic American, 50% African American, 0.4% Asian American/Pacific Islander **The most frequently chosen baccalaureate fields are** business/marketing, biological/life sciences, security and protective services **Academic program** English as a second language, advanced placement, accelerated degree program, honors program, summer session, adult/continuing education programs, internships **Contact** Mr. Keith Mock, Director of Admissions, Faulkner University, 5345 Atlanta Highway, Montgomery, AL 36109-3398. *Phone:* 334-386-7200 or toll-free 800-879-9816. *Fax:* 334-386-7137. *E-mail:* admissions@faulkner.edu. *Web site:* http://www.faulkner.edu/.

Heritage Christian University
Florence, Alabama

General Independent, comprehensive, coed, primarily men, affiliated with Church of Christ **Entrance** Noncompetitive **Setting** 43-acre small-town campus **Total enrollment** 119 **Application deadline** Rolling (freshmen), rolling (transfer) **Freshman admission** 62% were admitted **Housing** Yes **Expenses** Tuition & Fees $11,840; Room & Board $5425 **Undergraduates** 10% women, 44% part-time, 57% 25 or older, 1% Hispanic American, 11% African American **The most frequently chosen baccalaureate field is** philosophy and religious studies **Academic program** Accelerated degree program, summer session, adult/continuing education programs, internships **Contact** Mr. Cory Collins, Dean of Students, Heritage Christian University, PO Box HCU, Florence, AL 35630. *Phone:* 256-766-6610 or toll-free 800-367-3565. *Fax:* 256-766-9289. *E-mail:* ccollins@hcu.edu. *Web site:* http://www.hcu.edu/.

Herzing College
Birmingham, Alabama

General Proprietary, primarily 2-year, coed **Entrance** Minimally difficult **Setting** 4-acre urban campus **Total enrollment** 371 **Application deadline** Rolling (freshmen), rolling (transfer) **Housing** No **Undergraduates** 66% 25 or older **Academic program** Advanced placement, self-designed majors, summer session, adult/continuing education programs, internships **Contact** Ms. Tess Anderson, Admissions Coordinator, Herzing College, 280 West Valley Avenue, Birmingham, AL 35209. *Phone:* 205-916-2800. *E-mail:* admiss@bhm.herzing.edu. *Web site:* http://www.herzing.edu/birmingham/.

Huntingdon College
Montgomery, Alabama

General Independent United Methodist, 4-year, coed **Entrance** Moderately difficult **Setting** 71-acre suburban campus **Total enrollment** 1,075 **Student-faculty ratio** 13:1 **Application deadline** 8/15 (freshmen), 8/15 (transfer) **Freshman admission** 67% were admitted. Average high school GPA 3.31 **Freshman test scores** SAT critical reading scores over 500: 59%; SAT math scores over 500: 47%; ACT scores over 18: 99%; SAT critical reading scores over 600: 34%; SAT math scores over 600: 13%; ACT scores over 24: 27% **Housing** Yes **Expenses** Tuition & Fees $20,990; Room & Board $8000 **Undergraduates** 52% women, 20% part-time, 23% 25 or older, 0.3% Native American, 1% Hispanic American, 16% African American, 1% Asian American/Pacific Islander **The most frequently chosen baccalaureate fields are** biological/life sciences, business/marketing, parks and recreation **Academic program** Advanced placement, accelerated degree program, self-designed majors, honors program, summer session, adult/continuing education programs, internships **Contact** Office of Admission, Huntingdon College, 1500 East Fairview Avenue, Montgomery, AL 36106-2148. *Phone:* 334-833-4497 or toll-free 800-763-0313. *Fax:* 334-833-4347. *E-mail:* admiss@huntingdon.edu. *Web site:* http://www.huntingdon.edu/.

ITT Technical Institute
Bessemer, Alabama

General Proprietary, primarily 2-year, coed **Entrance** Minimally difficult **Setting** suburban campus **Housing** No **Contact** Director of Recruitment, ITT Technical Institute, 6270 Park South Drive, Bessemer, AL 35022. *Phone:* 205-497-5700 or toll-free 800-488-7033. *Web site:* http://www.itt-tech.edu/.

ITT Technical Institute
Madison, Alabama

General Proprietary, primarily 2-year, coed **Contact** Director of Recruitment, ITT Technical Institute, 9238 Madison Boulevard, Suite 500, Madison, AL 35758. *Phone:* 256-542-2900 or toll-free 877-210-4900. *Web site:* http://www.itt-tech.edu/.

ITT Technical Institute
Mobile, Alabama

General Proprietary, primarily 2-year, coed **Contact** Director of Recruitment, ITT Technical Institute, Office Mall South, 3100 Cottage Hill Road, Building 3, Mobile, AL 36606. *Phone:* 251-472-4760 or toll-free 877-327-1013. *Web site:* http://www.itt-tech.edu/.

Jacksonville State University
Jacksonville, Alabama

General State-supported, comprehensive, coed **Entrance** Minimally difficult **Setting** 459-acre small-town campus **Total enrollment** 9,351 **Student-faculty ratio** 20:1 **Application deadline** Rolling (freshmen), rolling (transfer) **Freshman admission** 88% were admitted. Average high school GPA 2.97 **Freshman test scores** SAT critical reading scores over 500: 27.8%; SAT math scores over 500: 29.46%; ACT scores over 18: 68.49%; SAT critical reading scores over 600: 2.9%; SAT math scores over 600: 4.56%; ACT scores over 24: 16.87% **Housing** Yes **Expenses** Tuition & Fees: state resident $6240, nonresident $12,480; Room & Board $5254 **Undergraduates** 58% women, 24% part-time, 23% 25 or older, 1% Native American, 1% Hispanic American, 29% African American, 1% Asian American/Pacific Islander **The most frequently chosen baccalaureate fields are** education, business/marketing, health professions and related sciences **Academic program** Advanced placement, accelerated degree program, honors program, summer session, adult/continuing education programs, internships **Contact** Ms. Martha Mitchell, Director of Admission, Jacksonville State University, 700 Pelham Road North, Jacksonville, AL 36265. *Phone:* 256-782-5363 or toll-free 800-231-5291. *Fax:* 256-782-5291. *E-mail:* info@jsu.edu. *Web site:* http://www.jsu.edu/.

Judson College
Marion, Alabama

General Independent Baptist, 4-year, women only **Entrance** Moderately difficult **Setting** 118-acre rural campus **Total enrollment** 313 **Student-faculty ratio** 9:1 **Application deadline** Rolling (freshmen),

Judson College (continued)
rolling (transfer) **Freshman admission** 82% were admitted. Average high school GPA 3.42 **Freshman test scores** SAT critical reading scores over 500: 40%; SAT math scores over 500: 40%; ACT scores over 18: 94%; SAT critical reading scores over 600: 20%; ACT scores over 24: 45% **Housing** Yes **Expenses** Tuition & Fees $13,535; Room & Board $8300 **Undergraduates** 21% part-time, 24% 25 or older, 1% Native American, 2% Hispanic American, 12% African American, 2% Asian American/Pacific Islander **The most frequently chosen baccalaureate fields are** history, psychology, social sciences **Academic program** Advanced placement, accelerated degree program, self-designed majors, honors program, summer session, adult/continuing education programs, internships **Contact** Mrs. Charlotte S. Clements, Vice President for Admissions and Financial Aid, Judson College, 302 Bibb Street, Marion, AL 36756. *Phone:* 334-683-5110 or toll-free 800-447-9472. *Fax:* 334-683-5282. *E-mail:* admissions@judson.edu. *Web site:* http://www.judson.edu/.

Miles College
Fairfield, Alabama

Contact Mr. Christopher Robertson, Director of Admissions and Recruitment, Miles College, 5500 Myron Massey Boulevard, Bell Building, Fairfield, AL 35064. *Phone:* 205-929-1657 or toll-free 800-445-0708. *Fax:* 205-929-1627. *E-mail:* admissions@miles.edu. *Web site:* http://www.miles.edu/.

Oakwood University
Huntsville, Alabama

General Independent Seventh-day Adventist, comprehensive, coed **Entrance** Minimally difficult **Setting** 1,200-acre campus **Total enrollment** 1,824 **Student-faculty ratio** 14:1 **Application deadline** Rolling (freshmen), rolling (transfer) **Freshman admission** 57% were admitted. Average high school GPA 2.99 **Freshman test scores** SAT critical reading scores over 500: 34%; SAT math scores over 500: 25%; ACT scores over 18: 53%; SAT critical reading scores over 600: 8%; SAT math scores over 600: 5%; ACT scores over 24: 12% **Housing** Yes **Expenses** Tuition & Fees $13,174; Room & Board $7458 **Undergraduates** 58% women, 6% part-time, 13% 25 or older, 0.1% Native American, 1% Hispanic American, 89% African American, 0.2% Asian American/Pacific Islander **The most frequently chosen baccalaureate fields are** biological/life sciences, business/marketing, psychology **Academic program** Advanced placement, honors program, internships **Contact** Mr. Jason McCracken, Director of Enrollment Management, Oakwood University, 7000 Adventist Boulevard, NW, Huntsville, AL 35896. *Phone:* 256-726-7354 or toll-free 800-358-3978. *Fax:* 256-726-7154. *E-mail:* admission@oakwood.edu. *Web site:* http://www.oakwood.edu/.

Remington College–Mobile Campus
Mobile, Alabama

Contact David Helveston, Director of Recruitment, Remington College–Mobile Campus, 828 Downtowner Loop West, Mobile, AL 36609-5404. *Phone:* 251-343-8200 or toll-free 800-866-0850. *Fax:* 251-343-0577. *E-mail:* david.helveston@remingtoncollege.edu. *Web site:* http://www.remingtoncollege.edu/.

Samford University
Birmingham, Alabama

General Independent Baptist, university, coed **Entrance** Moderately difficult **Setting** 180-acre suburban campus **Total enrollment** 4,658 **Student-faculty ratio** 12:1 **Application deadline** Rolling (freshmen), 8/15 (transfer) **Freshman admission** 84% were admitted. Average high school GPA 3.68 **Freshman test scores** SAT critical reading scores over 500: 85%; SAT math scores over 500: 81%; ACT scores over 18: 100%; SAT critical reading scores over 600: 43%; SAT math scores over 600: 43%; ACT scores over 24: 70% **Housing** Yes **Expenses** Tuition & Fees $20,420; Room & Board $6624 **Undergraduates** 64% women, 7% part-time, 6% 25 or older, 0.4% Native American, 1% Hispanic American, 7% African American, 1% Asian American/Pacific Islander **The most frequently chosen baccalaureate fields are** business/marketing, health professions and related sciences, visual and performing arts **Academic program** Advanced placement, accelerated degree program, honors program, summer session, adult/continuing education programs, internships **Contact** Mr. Jason J. Black, Director of Orientation and Visits, Samford University, 800 Lakeshore Drive, Samford Hall, Birmingham, AL 35229-0002. *Phone:* 205-726-3673 or toll-free 800-888-7218. *Fax:* 205-726-2171. *E-mail:* jjblack@samford.edu. *Web site:* http://www.samford.edu/.

Visit Petersons.com and enter keyword Samford

See page 1140 for the College Close-Up.

Southeastern Bible College
Birmingham, Alabama

General Independent nondenominational, 4-year, coed **Setting** 10-acre suburban campus **Total enrollment** 203 **Student-faculty ratio** 14:1 **Application deadline** 8/15 (freshmen), 8/15 (transfer) **Freshman admission** 100% were admitted. Average high school GPA 2.79 **Freshman test scores** ACT scores over 18: 59%; ACT scores over 24: 4% **Housing** Yes **Expenses** Tuition & Fees $11,150; Room only $2450 **Undergraduates** 37% women, 10% part-time, 45% 25 or older, 1% Hispanic American, 36% African American **The most frequently chosen baccalaureate field is** theology and religious vocations **Academic program** Advanced placement, summer session, adult/continuing education programs, internships **Contact** Mrs. Walker Harrison, Admissions Counselor, Southeastern Bible College, 2545 Valleydale Road, Birmingham, AL 35244. *Phone:* 205-970-9211 or toll-free 800-749-8878. *Fax:* 205-970-9207. *E-mail:* wharrison@sebc.edu. *Web site:* http://www.sebc.edu/.

South University
Montgomery, Alabama

General Proprietary, comprehensive, coed **Contact** Director of Admissions, South University, 5355 Vaughn Road, Montgomery, AL 36116-1120. *Phone:* 334-395-8800 or toll-free 866-629-2962. *Fax:* 334-395-8859. *Web site:* http://www.southuniversity.edu/montgomery/.

Visit Petersons.com and enter keywords South University

See page 1174 for the College Close-Up.

Spring Hill College
Mobile, Alabama

General Independent Roman Catholic (Jesuit), comprehensive, coed **Entrance** Moderately difficult **Setting** 450-acre suburban campus **Total enrollment** 1,521 **Student-faculty ratio** 13:1 **Application deadline** 7/15 (freshmen), rolling (transfer) **Freshman admission** 55% were admitted. Average high school GPA 3.49 **Freshman test scores** SAT critical reading scores over 500: 71%; SAT math scores over 500: 65%; ACT scores over 18: 99%; SAT critical reading scores over 600: 27%; SAT math scores over 600: 15%; ACT scores over 24: 53% **Housing** Yes **Expenses** Tuition & Fees $25,450; Room & Board $9730 **Undergraduates** 62% women, 10% part-time, 9% 25 or older, 1% Native American, 7% Hispanic American, 18% African American, 1% Asian American/Pacific Islander **The most frequently chosen baccalaureate fields are** biological/life sciences, business/marketing, social sciences **Academic program** Advanced placement, accelerated degree program, self-designed majors, honors program, summer session, adult/continuing education programs, internships **Contact** Ms. Ellen Richardson, Admissions Office, Spring Hill College, 4000 Dauphin Street, Mobile, AL 36608-1791. *Phone:* 251-380-3030 or toll-free 800-SHC-6704. *Fax:* 251-460-2186. *E-mail:* admit@shc.edu. *Web site:* http://www.shc.edu/.

• Samford has 138 majors, minors and concentrations.

• A community of 4,658 students from 44 states and 32 nations study in Samford's eight schools.

• Founded in 1841 as Howard College, Samford is the largest independently supported university in the state of Alabama.

• Samford is the only private university in the state ranked in the top tiers of national doctoral research universities by *U.S. News & World Report*.

• Three of Alabama's most recent Carnegie Professors of the Year teach at Samford.

• Samford students annually are involved in more than 200 university-related community service and global mission projects.

admission.samford.edu

1-800-888-7218 • 205-SAMFORD

Samford University is an Equal Opportunity Educational Institution/Employer.
Produced by Samford Office of Communication

Stillman College

Tuscaloosa, Alabama

General Independent, 4-year, coed, affiliated with Presbyterian Church (U.S.A.) **Entrance** Minimally difficult **Setting** 100-acre urban campus **Total enrollment** 1,048 **Student-faculty ratio** 18:1 **Application deadline** Rolling (freshmen), rolling (transfer) **Freshman admission** 45% were admitted. Average high school GPA 2.78 **Freshman test scores** SAT critical reading scores over 500: 11%; SAT math scores over 500: 17%; ACT scores over 18: 41%; SAT critical reading scores over 600: 2%; SAT math scores over 600: 2%; ACT scores over 24: 8% **Housing** Yes **Expenses** Tuition & Fees $13,462; Room & Board $6336 **Undergraduates** 54% women, 2% part-time, 7% 25 or older, 0.5% Hispanic American, 89% African American **The most frequently chosen baccalaureate fields are** business/marketing, history, parks and recreation **Academic program** Advanced placement, honors program, summer session, internships **Contact** Monica Finch, Director of Admissions, Stillman College, PO Drawer 1430, 3600 Stillman Boulevard, Tuscaloosa, AL 35403-9990. *Phone:* 205-366-8837 or toll-free 800-841-5722. *Fax:* 205-366-8941. *E-mail:* mfinch@stillman.edu. *Web site:* http://www.stillman.edu/.

Strayer University–Birmingham Campus

Birmingham, Alabama

General Proprietary, comprehensive, coed **Contact** Admissions Department, Strayer University–Birmingham Campus, 3570 Grandview Parkway, Suite 200, Birmingham, AL 35243. *Phone:* 205-453-6300. *Web site:* http://www.strayer.edu/birmingham.

Strayer University–Huntsville Campus

Huntsville, Alabama

General Proprietary, comprehensive, coed **Contact** Admissions Department, Strayer University–Huntsville Campus, 4955 Corporate Drive, NW, Suite 200, Huntsville, AL 35805. *Phone:* 256-665-9800. *Web site:* http://www.strayer.edu/huntsville.

Talladega College

Talladega, Alabama

General Independent, 4-year, coed **Entrance** Moderately difficult **Setting** 130-acre small-town campus **Total enrollment** 700 **Student-faculty ratio** 18:1 **Application deadline** Rolling (freshmen), rolling (transfer) **Freshman admission** 52% were admitted. Average high school GPA 2.7 **Housing** Yes **Expenses** Tuition & Fees $8528; Room & Board $4440 **Undergraduates** 60% women, 4% part-time, 16% 25 or older, 3% Hispanic American, 93% African American, 0.1% Asian American/Pacific Islander **The most frequently chosen baccalaureate fields are** biological/life sciences, business/marketing, visual and performing arts **Academic program** English as a second language, accelerated degree program, adult/continuing education programs, internships **Contact** Mrs. Floretta Dortch, Dean of Enrollment, Talladega College, 627 West Battle Street, Talladega, AL 35160-2354. *Phone:* 256-761-6415 or toll-free 800-762-2468 (in-state); 800-633-2440 (out-of-state). *Fax:* 256-362-0274. *E-mail:* fdortch@talladega.edu. *Web site:* http://www.talladega.edu/.

Troy University

Troy, Alabama

General State-supported, comprehensive, coed **Entrance** Moderately difficult **Setting** 877-acre small-town campus **Total enrollment** 29,327 **Student-faculty ratio** 21:1 **Application deadline** Rolling (freshmen), rolling (transfer) **Freshman admission** 66% were admitted. Average high school GPA 3.46 **Freshman test scores** ACT scores over 18: 78%;

Troy University (continued)
ACT scores over 24: 23% **Housing** Yes **Expenses** Tuition & Fees: state resident $7016, nonresident $13,182; Room & Board $6042 **Undergraduates** 60% women, 50% part-time, 58% 25 or older, 2% Native American, 3% Hispanic American, 42% African American, 1% Asian American/Pacific Islander **The most frequently chosen baccalaureate fields are** business/marketing, psychology, security and protective services **Academic program** English as a second language, advanced placement, accelerated degree program, honors program, summer session, internships **Contact** Mr. Buddy Starling, Dean of Enrollment Management, Troy University, University Avenue, Troy, AL 36082. *Phone:* 334-670-3243 or toll-free 800-551-9716. *Fax:* 334-670-3733. *E-mail:* bstar@troy.edu. *Web site:* http://www.troy.edu/.

Tuskegee University
Tuskegee, Alabama

General Independent, comprehensive, coed **Entrance** Moderately difficult **Setting** 4,390-acre small-town campus **Total enrollment** 2,931 **Student-faculty ratio** 11:1 **Application deadline** 4/15 (freshmen), 4/15 (transfer) **Freshman admission** 58% were admitted. Average high school GPA 3.2 **Freshman test scores** SAT critical reading scores over 500: 24%; SAT math scores over 500: 19.2%; ACT scores over 18: 64.6%; SAT critical reading scores over 600: 3%; SAT math scores over 600: 3.4%; ACT scores over 24: 8.8% **Housing** Yes **Expenses** Tuition & Fees $16,750; Room & Board $7570 **Undergraduates** 57% women, 2% part-time, 5% 25 or older, 0.1% Native American, 0.04% Hispanic American, 88% African American, 0.2% Asian American/Pacific Islander **The most frequently chosen baccalaureate fields are** business/marketing, biological/life sciences, engineering **Academic program** English as a second language, honors program, summer session, internships **Contact** Mr. Robert Laney Jr., Admissions, Tuskegee University, Tuskegee, AL 36088. *Phone:* 334-727-8500 or toll-free 800-622-6531. *Web site:* http://www.tuskegee.edu/.

United States Sports Academy
Daphne, Alabama

General Independent, upper-level, coed **Setting** 10-acre suburban campus **Total enrollment** 546 **Student-faculty ratio** 18:1 **Undergraduates** 78% 25 or older **Contact** Dean Craig T. Bogar, United States Sports Academy, One Academy Drive, Daphne, AL 36526-7055. *Phone:* toll-free 800-223-2668. *Web site:* http://www.ussa.edu/.

The University of Alabama
Tuscaloosa, Alabama

General State-supported, university, coed **Entrance** Moderately difficult **Setting** 1,000-acre suburban campus **Total enrollment** 28,699 **Student-faculty ratio** 20:1 **Application deadline** 2/1 (freshmen), 3/1 (transfer) **Freshman admission** 57% were admitted. Average high school GPA 3.5 **Freshman test scores** SAT critical reading scores over 500: 76%; SAT math scores over 500: 77%; ACT scores over 18: 99%; SAT critical reading scores over 600: 29%; SAT math scores over 600: 32%; ACT scores over 24: 54% **Housing** Yes **Expenses** Tuition & Fees: state resident $7000, nonresident $19,200; Room & Board $7796 **Undergraduates** 52% women, 8% part-time, 8% 25 or older, 1% Native American, 2% Hispanic American, 12% African American, 1% Asian American/Pacific Islander **The most frequently chosen baccalaureate fields are** business/marketing, communications/journalism, health professions and related sciences **Academic program** English as a second language, advanced placement, accelerated degree program, self-designed majors, honors program, summer session, adult/continuing education programs, internships **Contact** Ms. Mary K. Spiegel, Executive Director of Undergraduate Admissions, The University of Alabama, Box 870132, Tuscaloosa, AL 35487. *Phone:* 205-348-5666 or toll-free 800-933-BAMA. *Fax:* 205-348-9046. *E-mail:* admissions@ua.edu. *Web site:* http://www.ua.edu/.

The University of Alabama at Birmingham
Birmingham, Alabama

General State-supported, university, coed **Entrance** Moderately difficult **Setting** 183-acre urban campus **Total enrollment** 16,874 **Student-faculty ratio** 16:1 **Application deadline** Rolling (freshmen), 5/1 (transfer) **Freshman admission** 84% were admitted. Average high school GPA 3.5 **Freshman test scores** ACT scores over 18: 100%; ACT scores over 24: 54% **Housing** Yes **Expenses** Tuition & Fees: state resident $5096, nonresident $11,432; Room & Board $8142 **Undergraduates** 58% women, 25% part-time, 22% 25 or older, 0.5% Native American, 2% Hispanic American, 26% African American, 4% Asian American/Pacific Islander **Academic program** English as a second language, advanced placement, accelerated degree program, self-designed majors, honors program, summer session, adult/continuing education programs, internships **Contact** Ms. Chenise Ryan, Director of Undergraduate Admissions, The University of Alabama at Birmingham, 1530 3rd Avenue South, HUC 260, Birmingham, AL 35294-1150. *Phone:* 205-934-8221 or toll-free 800-421-8743. *Fax:* 205-975-7114. *E-mail:* undergradadmit@uab.edu. *Web site:* http://www.uab.edu/.

Visit Petersons.com and enter keywords Alabama at Birmingham

See page 1250 for the College Close-Up.

The University of Alabama in Huntsville
Huntsville, Alabama

General State-supported, university, coed **Entrance** Moderately difficult **Setting** 400-acre suburban campus **Total enrollment** 7,681 **Student-faculty ratio** 17:1 **Application deadline** 8/19 (freshmen), 8/19 (transfer) **Freshman admission** 72% were admitted. Average high school GPA 3.56 **Freshman test scores** SAT critical reading scores over 500: 75.44%; SAT math scores over 500: 81.87%; ACT scores over 18: 99.59%; SAT critical reading scores over 600: 36.84%; SAT math scores over 600: 45.03%; ACT scores over 24: 65% **Housing** Yes **Expenses** Tuition & Fees: state resident $6510, nonresident $15,628; Room & Board $7208 **Undergraduates** 47% women, 24% part-time, 24% 25 or older, 2% Native American, 2% Hispanic American, 15% African American, 3% Asian American/Pacific Islander **The most frequently chosen baccalaureate fields are** business/marketing, engineering, health professions and related sciences **Academic program** English as a second language, advanced placement, honors program, summer session, internships **Contact** Ms. Sandra Patterson, Director of Admissions, The University of Alabama in Huntsville, Enrollment Services, 301 Sparkman Drive, Huntsville, AL 35899. *Phone:* 256-824-6070 or toll-free 800-UAH-CALL. *Fax:* 256-824-6073. *E-mail:* admitme@email.uah.edu. *Web site:* http://www.uah.edu/.

Visit Petersons.com and enter keywords Alabama in Huntsville

See page 1252 for the College Close-Up.

University of Mobile
Mobile, Alabama

General Independent Southern Baptist, comprehensive, coed **Entrance** Moderately difficult **Setting** 830-acre suburban campus **Total enrollment** 1,572 **Student-faculty ratio** 12:1 **Application deadline** Rolling (freshmen), rolling (transfer) **Freshman admission** 78% were admitted. Average high school GPA 3.33 **Freshman test scores** SAT critical reading scores over 500: 70%; SAT math scores over 500: 42.11%; ACT scores over 18: 90.72%; SAT critical reading scores over 600: 16.67%; SAT math scores over 600: 15.79%; ACT scores over 24: 32.99% **Housing** Yes **Expenses** Tuition & Fees $14,850; Room & Board $7570 **Undergraduates** 66% women, 11% part-time, 30% 25 or older, 2% Native American, 1% Hispanic American, 22% African American, 0.4% Asian American/Pacific Islander **The most frequently chosen baccalaureate fields are** business/marketing, education, health professions and related sciences **Academic program** Advanced placement, accelerated degree program, honors program, summer session, adult/continuing education programs, internships **Contact** Mrs. Hali Givens, Assistant Director of Admissions, University of Mobile, 5735 College Parkway, Mobile, AL 36613-2842. *Phone:* 251-442-2221 or toll-free 800-946-7267. *Fax:* 251-442-2498. *E-mail:* halig@umobile.edu. *Web site:* http://www.umobile.edu/.

University of Montevallo
Montevallo, Alabama

General State-supported, comprehensive, coed **Entrance** Moderately difficult **Setting** 160-acre small-town campus **Total enrollment** 3,048 **Student-faculty ratio** 16:1 **Application deadline** 8/1 (freshmen), rolling (transfer) **Freshman admission** 72% were admitted **Freshman test scores** ACT scores over 18: 98%; ACT scores over 24: 41% **Housing** Yes **Expenses** Tuition & Fees: state resident $7010, nonresident $13,550; Room & Board $4650 **Undergraduates** 67% women, 12% part-time, 13% 25 or older, 1% Native American, 2% Hispanic American, 10% African American, 5% Asian American/Pacific Islander **The most frequently chosen baccalaureate fields are** business/marketing, family and consumer sciences, visual and performing arts **Academic program** Advanced placement, accelerated degree program, honors program, summer session, internships **Contact** Mr. Ira Lynn Gurganus, Director of Admissions, University of Montevallo, Office of Admissions, Station 6030, Montevallo, AL 35115-6030. *Phone:* 205-665-6030 or toll-free 800-292-4349. *Fax:* 205-665-6032. *E-mail:* admissions@montevallo.edu. *Web site:* http://www.montevallo.edu/.

University of North Alabama
Florence, Alabama

General State-supported, comprehensive, coed **Entrance** Minimally difficult **Setting** 200-acre urban campus **Total enrollment** 7,260 **Student-faculty ratio** 22:1 **Application deadline** Rolling (freshmen), rolling (transfer) **Freshman admission** 82% were admitted. Average high school GPA 2.89 **Freshman test scores** ACT scores over 18: 82%; ACT scores over 24: 27% **Housing** Yes **Expenses** Tuition & Fees: state resident $6042, nonresident $11,052; Room & Board $4784 **Undergraduates** 57% women, 19% part-time, 17% 25 or older, 1% Native American, 2% Hispanic American, 13% African American, 0.4% Asian American/Pacific Islander **The most frequently chosen baccalaureate fields are** business/marketing, education, health professions and related sciences **Academic program** English as a second language, advanced placement, accelerated degree program, self-designed majors, honors program, summer session, internships **Contact** Mrs. Kim O. Mauldin, Director of Admissions, University of North Alabama, One Harrison Plaza, Florence, AL 35632-0001. *Phone:* 256-765-4680 or toll-free 800-TALKUNA. *Fax:* 256-765-4329. *E-mail:* admissions@una.edu. *Web site:* http://www.una.edu/.

University of South Alabama
Mobile, Alabama

General State-supported, university, coed **Entrance** Moderately difficult **Setting** 1,225-acre suburban campus **Total enrollment** 14,522 **Student-faculty ratio** 14:1 **Application deadline** 7/15 (freshmen), 8/10 (transfer) **Freshman admission** 90% were admitted **Housing** Yes **Expenses** Tuition & Fees: state resident $5962, nonresident $11,302; Room & Board $5344 **Undergraduates** 57% women, 25% part-time, 29% 25 or older, 1% Native American, 2% Hispanic American, 19% African American, 3% Asian American/Pacific Islander **The most frequently chosen baccalaureate fields are** business/marketing, education, health professions and related sciences **Academic program** English as a second language, advanced placement, accelerated degree program, honors program, summer session, adult/continuing education programs **Contact** Mr. Christopher A. Lynch, Director, New Student Recruitment, University of South Alabama, 307 University Boulevard, Mobile, AL 36688-0002. *Phone:* 251-460-6141 or toll-free 800-872-5247. *Fax:* 251-460-7876. *E-mail:* admiss@usouthal.edu. *Web site:* http://www.southalabama.edu/.

The University of West Alabama
Livingston, Alabama

General State-supported, comprehensive, coed **Entrance** Minimally difficult **Setting** 595-acre small-town campus **Total enrollment** 5,157 **Student-faculty ratio** 19:1 **Application deadline** Rolling (freshmen), rolling (transfer) **Freshman admission** 61% were admitted **Freshman test scores** ACT scores over 18: 76%; ACT scores over 24: 14% **Housing** Yes **Expenses** Tuition & Fees: state resident $5420, nonresident $10,480; Room & Board $3748 **Undergraduates** 61% women, 21% part-time, 5% 25 or older, 0.4% Native American, 1% Hispanic American, 53% African American, 0.5% Asian American/Pacific Islander **The most frequently chosen baccalaureate fields are** business/marketing, education, social sciences **Academic program** Advanced placement, accelerated degree program, honors program, summer session, internships **Contact** Mr. Danny Buckalew, The University of West Alabama, Station 4, Livingston, AL 35470. *Phone:* 205-652-3581 or toll-free 800-621-7742 (in-state); 800-621-8044 (out-of-state). *Fax:* 205-652-3522. *E-mail:* db@uwa.edu. *Web site:* http://www.uwa.edu/.

Virginia College at Birmingham
Birmingham, Alabama

General Proprietary, comprehensive, coed **Entrance** Moderately difficult **Setting** 1-acre urban campus **Total enrollment** 3,826 **Application deadline** Rolling (freshmen) **Housing** No **Undergraduates** 71% 25 or older **Contact** Director of Admissions, Virginia College at Birmingham, 488 Palisades Boulevard, Birmingham, AL 35209. *Phone:* 205-802-1200. *Web site:* http://www.vc.edu/.

Virginia College at Huntsville
Huntsville, Alabama

Contact Director of Admission, Virginia College at Huntsville, 2800-A Bob Wallace Avenue, Huntsville, AL 35805. *Phone:* 256-533-7387. *Fax:* 256-533-7785. *Web site:* http://www.vc.edu/.

ALASKA

Alaska Bible College
Glennallen, Alaska

Contact Mrs. Carol C. Ridley, Director of Admissions, Alaska Bible College, Box 289, 200 College Road, Glennallen, AK 99588-0289. *Phone:* 907-822-3201 or toll-free 800-478-7884. *Fax:* 907-822-5027. *E-mail:* info@akbible.edu. *Web site:* http://www.akbible.edu/.

Alaska Pacific University
Anchorage, Alaska

General Independent, comprehensive, coed **Entrance** Moderately difficult **Setting** 170-acre urban campus **Total enrollment** 781 **Student-faculty ratio** 10:1 **Application deadline** 8/15 (freshmen), 8/15 (transfer) **Freshman admission** 10% were admitted. Average high school GPA 3.22 **Freshman test scores** SAT critical reading scores over 500: 69%; SAT math scores over 500: 54%; ACT scores over 18: 100%; SAT critical reading scores over 600: 28%; SAT math scores over 600: 18%; ACT scores over 24: 56% **Housing** Yes **Expenses** Tuition & Fees $26,360; Room & Board $9300 **Undergraduates** 67% women, 44% part-time, 48% 25 or older, 17% Native American, 5% Hispanic American, 4% African American, 2% Asian American/Pacific Islander **The most frequently chosen baccalaureate fields are** business/marketing, natural

Alaska Pacific University (continued)
resources/environmental science, parks and recreation **Academic program** Advanced placement, self-designed majors, summer session, adult/continuing education programs, internships **Contact** Ms. Jennifer Jensen, Director of Admissions, Alaska Pacific University, 4101 University Drive, Anchorage, AK 99508. *Phone:* 907-564-8248 or toll-free 800-252-7528. *Fax:* 907-564-8317. *E-mail:* admissions@alaskapacific.edu. *Web site:* http://www.alaskapacific.edu/.

Charter College
Anchorage, Alaska

General Proprietary, primarily 2-year, coed **Entrance** Noncompetitive **Setting** urban campus **Total enrollment** 516 **Student-faculty ratio** 15:1 **Application deadline** Rolling (freshmen), rolling (transfer) **Housing** No **Undergraduates** 69% 25 or older **Academic program** Summer session, adult/continuing education programs, internships **Contact** Ms. Lily Sirianni, Vice President, Charter College, 2221 East Northern Lights Boulevard, Suite 120, Anchorage, AK 99508. *Phone:* 907-277-1000 or toll-free 800-279-1008. *Web site:* http://www.chartercollege.edu/.

University of Alaska Anchorage
Anchorage, Alaska

General State-supported, comprehensive, coed **Entrance** Noncompetitive **Setting** 428-acre urban campus **Total enrollment** 17,825 **Application deadline** 7/1 (freshmen), rolling (transfer) **Freshman admission** 77% were admitted **Housing** Yes **Expenses** Tuition & Fees: state resident $4580, nonresident $14,000; Room & Board $7962 **Undergraduates** 59% women, 55% part-time, 46% 25 or older, 10% Native American, 5% Hispanic American, 3% African American, 8% Asian American/Pacific Islander **The most frequently chosen baccalaureate fields are** business/marketing, health professions and related sciences, psychology **Academic program** English as a second language, advanced placement, self-designed majors, honors program, summer session, adult/continuing education programs, internships **Contact** Enrollment Services, University of Alaska Anchorage, PO Box 141629, 3901 Old Seward Highway, Anchorage, AK 99508-8046. *Phone:* 907-786-1480. *Fax:* 907-786-4888. *E-mail:* enroll@uaa.alaska.edu. *Web site:* http://www.uaa.alaska.edu/.

University of Alaska Anchorage, Kenai Peninsula College
Soldotna, Alaska

General State-supported, primarily 2-year, coed **Entrance** Noncompetitive **Setting** 360-acre rural campus **Total enrollment** 2,230 **Application deadline** Rolling (freshmen), rolling (transfer) **Housing** No **Academic program** English as a second language, advanced placement, adult/continuing education programs **Contact** Ms. Shelly Love Blatchford, Admission and Registration Coordinator, University of Alaska Anchorage, Kenai Peninsula College, 156 College Road, Soldotna, AK 99669-9798. *Phone:* 907-262-0311 or toll-free 877-262-0330. *Web site:* http://www.kpc.alaska.edu/.

University of Alaska Fairbanks
Fairbanks, Alaska

General State-supported, university, coed **Entrance** Minimally difficult **Setting** 2,250-acre small-town campus **Total enrollment** 9,137 **Student-faculty ratio** 12:1 **Application deadline** 7/1 (freshmen), 7/1 (transfer) **Freshman admission** 74% were admitted. Average high school GPA 3.19 **Freshman test scores** SAT critical reading scores over 500: 59.95%; SAT math scores over 500: 53.24%; ACT scores over 18: 76.23%; SAT critical reading scores over 600: 25.95%; SAT math scores over 600: 24.02%; ACT scores over 24: 30.58% **Housing** Yes **Expenses** Tuition & Fees: state resident $5668, nonresident $16,258; Room & Board $6800 **Undergraduates** 60% women, 54% part-time, 34% 25 or older **The most frequently chosen baccalaureate fields are** business/marketing, engineering, psychology **Academic program** Advanced placement, accelerated degree program, self-designed majors, honors program, summer session, internships **Contact** Mike Earnest, Director of Admissions, University of Alaska Fairbanks, PO Box 757480, Fairbanks, AK 99775-7480. *Phone:* 907-474-7500 or toll-free 800-478-1823. *Fax:* 907-474-5379. *E-mail:* admissions@uaf.edu. *Web site:* http://www.uaf.edu/.
Visit Petersons.com and enter keyword Fairbanks

See page 1254 for the College Close-Up.

University of Alaska Southeast
Juneau, Alaska

General State-supported, comprehensive, coed **Entrance** Noncompetitive **Setting** 198-acre small-town campus **Total enrollment** 3,260 **Freshman admission** 92% were admitted **Freshman test scores** SAT critical reading scores over 500: 66.67%; SAT math scores over 500: 50%; SAT critical reading scores over 600: 16.67%; SAT math scores over 600: 16.67% **Housing** Yes **Expenses** Tuition & Fees: state resident $4903, nonresident $14,323; Room & Board $6260 **Undergraduates** 67% women, 73% part-time, 59% 25 or older, 20% Native American, 3% Hispanic American, 2% African American, 4% Asian American/Pacific Islander **The most frequently chosen baccalaureate fields are** business/marketing, biological/life sciences, liberal arts/general studies **Academic program** Advanced placement, self-designed majors, summer session, adult/continuing education programs, internships **Contact** Ms. Deema Ferguson, Admissions Clerk, University of Alaska Southeast, 11120 Glacier Highway, Juneau, AK 99801-8625. *Phone:* 907-796-6294 Ext. 6100 or toll-free 877-796-4827. *Fax:* 907-796-6365. *E-mail:* admissions@uas.alaska.edu. *Web site:* http://www.uas.alaska.edu/.

ARIZONA

American Indian College of the Assemblies of God, Inc.
Phoenix, Arizona

General Independent, 4-year, coed, affiliated with Assemblies of God **Entrance** Minimally difficult **Setting** 10-acre urban campus **Total enrollment** 68 **Application deadline** 8/15 (freshmen), 8/15 (transfer) **Housing** Yes **Expenses** Tuition & Fees $5854; Room & Board $5232 **Undergraduates** 28% 25 or older **Academic program** Internships **Contact** Sandra Gonzales, Director of Enrollment Management, American Indian College of the Assemblies of God, Inc., 10020 North Fifteenth Avenue, Phoenix, AZ 85021-2199. *Phone:* 602-944-3335 Ext. 226 or toll-free 800-933-3828. *E-mail:* sgonzales@aicag.edu. *Web site:* http://www.aicag.edu/.

Argosy University, Phoenix
Phoenix, Arizona

General Proprietary, university, coed **Setting** urban campus **Contact** Director of Admissions, Argosy University, Phoenix, 2233 West Dunlap Avenue, Phoenix, AZ 85021. *Phone:* 602-216-2600 or toll-free 866-216-2777. *Fax:* 602-216-3151. *Web site:* http://www.argosy.edu/phoenix/.
Visit Petersons.com and enter keywords Argosy University, Phoenix

See page 478 for the College Close-Up.

Arizona State University
Tempe, Arizona

General State-supported, university, coed **Entrance** Moderately difficult **Setting** 1,964-acre urban campus **Total enrollment** 68,064

Freshman admission 91% were admitted. Average high school GPA 3.38 **Freshman test scores** SAT critical reading scores over 500: 66%; SAT math scores over 500: 69.4%; ACT scores over 18: 91.6%; SAT critical reading scores over 600: 24.7%; SAT math scores over 600: 31.7%; ACT scores over 24: 49% **Housing** Yes **Expenses** Tuition & Fees: state resident $6334, nonresident $18,919; Room & Board $9210 **Undergraduates** 51% women, 16% part-time, 17% 25 or older, 2% Native American, 16% Hispanic American, 5% African American, 6% Asian American/Pacific Islander **The most frequently chosen baccalaureate fields are** business/marketing, education, interdisciplinary studies **Academic program** Advanced placement, accelerated degree program, honors program, summer session, adult/continuing education programs, internships **Contact** Kent Hopkins, Interim Dean, Arizona State University, PO Box 870112, Tempe, AZ 85287-0112. *Phone:* 480-965-7788. *Fax:* 480-965-3610. *E-mail:* ugradinq@asu.edu. *Web site:* http://www.asu.edu/.

The Art Center Design College
Tucson, Arizona

General Proprietary, 4-year, coed **Entrance** Moderately difficult **Setting** suburban campus **Total enrollment** 226 **Application deadline** Rolling (freshmen) **Housing** No **Expenses** Tuition & Fees $25,560 **Undergraduates** 53% women, 27% part-time **Academic program** Summer session **Contact** Sarah LaVetter, Director of Admissions, The Art Center Design College, 2525 North Country Club Road, Tucson, AZ 85716-2505. *Phone:* 520-325-0123 or toll-free 800-825-8753. *Fax:* 520-325-5535. *Web site:* http://www.theartcenter.edu/.

The Art Institute of Phoenix
Phoenix, Arizona

General Proprietary, 4-year, coed **Setting** suburban campus **Contact** Director of Admissions, The Art Institute of Phoenix, 2233 West Dunlap Avenue, Phoenix, AZ 85021-2859. *Phone:* 602-331-7500 or toll-free 800-474-2479. *Fax:* 602-331-5301. *Web site:* http://www.artinstitutes.edu/phoenix/.

Visit Petersons.com and enter keywords Art Institute of Phoenix

See page 532 for the College Close-Up.

The Art Institute of Tucson
Tucson, Arizona

General Proprietary, 4-year, coed **Contact** Director of Admissions, The Art Institute of Tucson, 5099 East Grant Road, Suite 100, Tucson, AZ 85712. *Phone:* 520-318-2700 or toll-free 866-690-8850. *Fax:* 520-881-4794. *Web site:* http://www.artinstitutes.edu/tucson/.

Visit Petersons.com and enter keywords Art Institute of Tucson

See page 550 for the College Close-Up.

Brookline College
Phoenix, Arizona

General Independent, 4-year, coed **Entrance** Noncompetitive **Setting** urban campus **Total enrollment** 1,186 **Student-faculty ratio** 17:1 **Application deadline** Rolling (freshmen), rolling (transfer) **Housing** No **Expenses** Tuition & Fees $14,000 **Undergraduates** 86% women, 55% 25 or older, 5% Native American, 34% Hispanic American, 24% African American, 1% Asian American/Pacific Islander **The most frequently chosen baccalaureate field is** business/marketing **Academic program** Accelerated degree program **Contact** Mr. Oleg Bortman, Campus Director, Brookline College, 2445 West Dunlap Avenue, Suite 100, Phoenix, AZ 85021. *Phone:* 602-242-6265 or toll-free 800-793-2428. *Fax:* 602-973-2572. *E-mail:* obortman@brooklinecollege.edu. *Web site:* http://brooklinecollege.edu/.

Brookline College
Tempe, Arizona

General Independent, 4-year, coed **Entrance** Noncompetitive **Setting** urban campus **Total enrollment** 301 **Student-faculty ratio** 14:1 **Application deadline** Rolling (freshmen), rolling (transfer) **Housing** No **Expenses** Tuition & Fees $14,000 **Undergraduates** 83% women, 50% 25 or older, 14% Native American, 28% Hispanic American, 15% African American, 0.3% Asian American/Pacific Islander **Academic program** Accelerated degree program **Contact** Ms. Cheryl Kindred, Campus Director, Brookline College, 1140-1150 South Priest Drive, Tempe, AZ 85281. *Phone:* 480-545-8755 or toll-free 888-886-2428. *Fax:* 480-926-1371. *E-mail:* ckindred@brooklinecollege.edu. *Web site:* http://brooklinecollege.edu/.

Brookline College
Tucson, Arizona

General Independent, 4-year, coed **Setting** urban campus **Total enrollment** 598 **Student-faculty ratio** 23:1 **Application deadline** Rolling (freshmen), rolling (transfer) **Housing** No **Expenses** Tuition & Fees $14,000 **Undergraduates** 75% women, 50% 25 or older, 5% Native American, 56% Hispanic American, 12% African American, 1% Asian American/Pacific Islander **Academic program** Accelerated degree program **Contact** Ms. Leigh Anne Pechota, Campus Director, Brookline College, 5441 East 22nd Street, Suite 125, Tucson, AZ 85711. *Phone:* 520-748-9799 or toll-free 888-292-2428. *Fax:* 520-748-9355. *E-mail:* lpechota@brooklinecollege.edu. *Web site:* http://brooklinecollege.edu/.

Brown Mackie College–Phoenix
Phoenix, Arizona

General Proprietary, primarily 2-year, coed **Contact** Director of Admissions, Brown Mackie College–Phoenix, 13430 North Black Canyon Highway, Suite 190, Phoenix, AZ 85029. *Phone:* 602-337-3044 or toll-free 866-824-4793. *Fax:* 480-375-2450. *Web site:* http://www.brownmackie.edu/Phoenix/.

Visit Petersons.com and enter keywords Brown Mackie College-Phoenix

See page 638 for the College Close-Up.

Brown Mackie College–Tucson
Tucson, Arizona

General Proprietary, primarily 2-year, coed **Setting** suburban campus **Contact** Director of Admissions, Brown Mackie College–Tucson, 4585 East Speedway, Suite 204, Tucson, AZ 85712. *Phone:* 520-319-3300. *Fax:* 520-325-0108. *Web site:* http://www.brownmackie.edu/tucson/.

Visit Petersons.com and enter keywords Brown Mackie College-Tucson

See page 644 for the College Close-Up.

College of the Humanities and Sciences, Harrison Middleton University
Tempe, Arizona

General Independent, comprehensive, coed **Setting** suburban campus **Application deadline** Rolling (freshmen), rolling (transfer) **Expenses** Tuition & Fees $27,200 **Academic program** Advanced placement, self-designed majors, summer session **Contact** College of the Humanities and Sciences, Harrison Middleton University, 1105 East Broadway, Tempe, AZ 85282. *Phone:* toll-free 877-248-6724. *Web site:* http://www.chumsci.edu/.

Collins College: A School of Design and Technology
Tempe, Arizona

General Proprietary, 4-year, coed **Setting** 3-acre urban campus **Total enrollment** 1,287 **Student-faculty ratio** 30:1 **Application deadline** Rolling (freshmen), rolling (transfer) **Undergraduates** 23% women, 26% 25 or older, 5% Native American, 9% Hispanic American, 6% African American, 2% Asian American/Pacific Islander **Contact** Admissions Department, Collins College: A School of Design and Technology, 1140 South Priest, Tempe, AZ 85281. *Phone:* 480-966-3000 or toll-free 800-876-7070. *Fax:* 480-966-2599. *E-mail:* contact@collinscollege.edu. *Web site:* http://www.collinscollege.edu/.

DeVry University
Mesa, Arizona

Contact DeVry University, 1201 South Alma School Road, Mesa, AZ 85210-2011. *Web site:* http://www.devry.edu/.

DeVry University
Phoenix, Arizona

General Proprietary, comprehensive, coed **Entrance** Minimally difficult **Setting** 18-acre urban campus **Total enrollment** 1,555 **Student-faculty ratio** 18:1 **Application deadline** Rolling (freshmen), rolling (transfer) **Housing** No **Expenses** Tuition & Fees $14,080 **Undergraduates** 27% women, 39% part-time, 49% 25 or older, 4% Native American, 27% Hispanic American, 8% African American, 4% Asian American/Pacific Islander **The most frequently chosen baccalaureate fields are** business/marketing, computer and information sciences, engineering technologies **Academic program** Advanced placement, accelerated degree program, summer session, adult/continuing education programs **Contact** Admissions Office, DeVry University, 2149 West Dunlap Avenue, Phoenix, AZ 85021-2995. *Web site:* http://www.devry.edu/.

Dunlap-Stone University
Phoenix, Arizona

General Proprietary, 4-year, coed **Setting** urban campus **Total enrollment** 500 **Student-faculty ratio** 15:1 **Application deadline** Rolling (freshmen), rolling (transfer) **Expenses** Tuition & Fees $7850 **Undergraduates** 75% 25 or older **Academic program** Advanced placement, accelerated degree program, internships **Contact** Dr. Donald N. Burton, Dunlap-Stone University, 11225 North 28th Drive, Suite B-201, Phoenix, AZ 85029. *Phone:* 602-648-5750 or toll-free 800-474-8013. *Fax:* 602-648-5755. *E-mail:* director@expandglobal.com. *Web site:* http://www.dunlap-stone.edu/.

Embry-Riddle Aeronautical University
Prescott, Arizona

General Independent, comprehensive, coed **Entrance** Moderately difficult **Setting** 547-acre small-town campus **Total enrollment** 1,672 **Student-faculty ratio** 16:1 **Application deadline** Rolling (freshmen), rolling (transfer) **Freshman admission** 85% were admitted. Average high school GPA 3.5 **Freshman test scores** SAT critical reading scores over 500: 71%; SAT math scores over 500: 83%; ACT scores over 18: 95%; SAT critical reading scores over 600: 28%; SAT math scores over 600: 41%; ACT scores over 24: 60% **Housing** Yes **Expenses** Tuition & Fees $29,380; Room & Board $8530 **Undergraduates** 19% women, 8% part-time, 9% 25 or older, 1% Native American, 8% Hispanic American, 2% African American, 6% Asian American/Pacific Islander **The most frequently chosen baccalaureate fields are** engineering, social sciences, transportation and materials moving **Academic program** English as a second language, advanced placement, accelerated degree program, self-designed majors, honors program, summer session, adult/continuing education programs, internships **Contact** Debra Cates-Foster, Interim Director of Admissions, Embry-Riddle Aeronautical University, 3700 Willow Creek Road, Prescott, AZ 86301-3720. *Phone:* 928-777-6600 or toll-free 800-888-3728. *Fax:* 928-777-6606. *E-mail:* pradmit@erau.edu. *Web site:* http://www.embryriddle.edu/.

Visit Petersons.com and enter keyword Embry-Riddle

Everest College
Phoenix, Arizona

Contact Mr. Jim Askins, Director of Admissions, Everest College, 10400 North 25th Avenue, Suite 190, Phoenix, AZ 85021. *Phone:* 602-942-4141. *Fax:* 602-943-0960. *E-mail:* jaskins@cci.edu. *Web site:* http://www.everest.edu/.

Everest Online
Tempe, Arizona

Contact Everest Online, 8150 South Hardy Drive #102, Tempe, AZ 85284-1117. *Web site:* http://www.everestonline.edu/.

Grand Canyon University
Phoenix, Arizona

Contact Enrollment, Grand Canyon University, 3300 West Camelback Road, PO Box 11097, Phoenix, AZ 86017-3030. *Phone:* 800-486-7085 or toll-free 800-800-9776. *E-mail:* admissionsonline@gcu.edu. *Web site:* http://www.gcu.edu/.

Visit Petersons.com and enter keyword Grand

See page 830 for the College Close-Up.

High-Tech Institute
Phoenix, Arizona

General Proprietary, primarily 2-year, coed **Entrance** Noncompetitive **Setting** 4-acre urban campus **Total enrollment** 5,742 **Application deadline** Rolling (freshmen), rolling (transfer) **Housing** No **Undergraduates** 70% 25 or older **Contact** Mr. Glen Husband, Vice President of Admissions, High-Tech Institute, 1515 East Indian School Road, Phoenix, AZ 85014-4901. *Phone:* 602-279-9700. *Fax:* 602-279-2999. *Web site:* http://www.high-techinstitute.com/.

International Baptist College
Chandler, Arizona

Contact Ms. Rebecca M. Stertzbach, Director of Recruitment, International Baptist College, 2211 West Germann Road, Chandler, AZ 85286. *Phone:* 480-245-7903 or toll-free 800-422-4858. *Web site:* http://www.ibconline.edu/ibc/.

ITT Technical Institute
Phoenix, Arizona

General Proprietary, primarily 2-year, coed **Entrance** Minimally difficult **Setting** urban campus **Housing** No **Contact** Director of Recruitment, ITT Technical Institute, 10220 North 25th Avenue, Suite 100, Phoenix, AZ 85021. *Phone:* 602-749-7900 or toll-free 877-221-1132. *Web site:* http://www.itt-tech.edu/.

ITT Technical Institute
Tempe, Arizona

General Proprietary, 4-year, coed **Contact** Director of Recruitment, ITT Technical Institute, 5005 S. Wendler Drive, Tempe, AZ 85282. *Phone:* 602-437-7500 or toll-free 800-879-4881. *Web site:* http://www.itt-tech.edu/.

ITT Technical Institute
Tucson, Arizona

General Proprietary, primarily 2-year, coed **Entrance** Minimally difficult **Setting** urban campus **Housing** No **Contact** Director of Recruitment, ITT Technical Institute, 1455 West River Road, Tucson, AZ 85704. *Phone:* 520-408-7488 or toll-free 800-870-9730. *Web site:* http://www.itt-tech.edu/.

National Paralegal College
Phoenix, Arizona

Contact National Paralegal College, 6516 N 7th Street, Suite 103, Phoenix, AZ 85014. *Phone:* toll-free 800-371-6105. *Web site:* http://nationalparalegal.edu/.

Northcentral University
Prescott Valley, Arizona

General Proprietary, comprehensive, coed **Entrance** Minimally difficult **Total enrollment** 8,384 **Student-faculty ratio** 18:1 **Application deadline** Rolling (freshmen), rolling (transfer) **Housing** No **Expenses** Tuition & Fees $8340 **Undergraduates** 55% women, 77% 25 or older **The most frequently chosen baccalaureate fields are** business/marketing, education, psychology **Academic program** Advanced placement, accelerated degree program, summer session **Contact** Mr. Eric Stoddard, Director of Admissions, Northcentral University, 10000 East University Drive, Prescott Valley, AZ 86314. *Phone:* 888-327-2877 Ext. 8083 or toll-free 888-327-2877. *Fax:* 928-759-6283. *E-mail:* info@ncu.edu. *Web site:* http://www.ncu.edu/.

Northern Arizona University
Flagstaff, Arizona

General State-supported, university, coed **Entrance** Moderately difficult **Setting** 730-acre small-town campus **Total enrollment** 23,600 **Student-faculty ratio** 19:1 **Application deadline** Rolling (freshmen), rolling (transfer) **Freshman admission** 73% were admitted. Average high school GPA 3.4 **Freshman test scores** SAT critical reading scores over 500: 65%; SAT math scores over 500: 64%; ACT scores over 18: 89%; SAT critical reading scores over 600: 20%; SAT math scores over 600: 21%; ACT scores over 24: 41% **Housing** Yes **Expenses** Tuition & Fees: state resident $6632, nonresident $17,858; Room & Board $7872 **Undergraduates** 59% women, 16% part-time, 23% 25 or older, 5% Native American, 14% Hispanic American, 3% African American, 3% Asian American/Pacific Islander **The most frequently chosen baccalaureate fields are** business/marketing, education, liberal arts/general studies **Academic program** English as a second language, advanced placement, accelerated degree program, honors program, summer session, internships **Contact** James E. Casebeer, Associate Director, Northern Arizona University, PO Box 4084, Flagstaff, AZ 86011. *Phone:* 928-523-6080 or toll-free 888-MORE-NAU. *Fax:* 928-523-1230. *E-mail:* undergraduate.admissions@nau.edu. *Web site:* http://www.nau.edu/.

Visit Petersons.com and enter keywords Northern Arizona

Northern Arizona University–Yuma
Yuma, Arizona

General State-supported, upper-level, coed **Total enrollment** 631 **Expenses** Tuition & Fees: state resident $5239, nonresident $15,843 **Undergraduates** 2% Native American, 60% Hispanic American, 2% African American, 2% Asian American/Pacific Islander **Contact** Eileen Knight, Associate Director of Admissions, Northern Arizona University–Yuma, 2020 South Avenue 8E, PO Box 6236, Yuma, AZ 85365. *Phone:* 928-317-6431 or toll-free 888-NAU-Yuma. *E-mail:* eileen.knight@nau.edu. *Web site:* http://www.yuma.nau.edu/.

Penn Foster College
Scottsdale, Arizona

Contact Penn Foster College, 14300 North Northsight Boulevard, Suite 111, Scottsdale, AZ 85260. *Phone:* toll-free 480-947-2680. *Web site:* http://www.pennfostercollege.edu/.

Prescott College
Prescott, Arizona

General Independent, comprehensive, coed **Entrance** Moderately difficult **Setting** 6-acre small-town campus **Total enrollment** 1,121 **Student-faculty ratio** 8:1 **Application deadline** 8/15 (freshmen), 8/15 (transfer) **Freshman admission** 81% were admitted. Average high school GPA 3.09 **Freshman test scores** SAT critical reading scores over 500: 81%; SAT math scores over 500: 67%; ACT scores over 18: 86%; SAT critical reading scores over 600: 59%; SAT math scores over 600: 19%; ACT scores over 24: 53% **Housing** Yes **Expenses** Tuition & Fees $23,643; Room only $3630 **Undergraduates** 58% women, 17% part-time, 42% 25 or older, 2% Native American, 7% Hispanic American, 2% African American, 1% Asian American/Pacific Islander **The most frequently chosen baccalaureate fields are** education, natural resources/environmental science, psychology **Academic program** Advanced placement, self-designed majors, summer session, adult/continuing education programs, internships **Contact** Nancy Simmons, Receptionist, Prescott College, 220 Grove Avenue, Prescott, AZ 86301. *Phone:* 928-350-2100 or toll-free 800-628-6364. *Fax:* 928-776-5242. *E-mail:* admissions@prescott.edu. *Web site:* http://www.prescott.edu/.

Scottsdale Culinary Institute
Scottsdale, Arizona

General Proprietary, primarily 2-year, coed **Total enrollment** 1,275 **Undergraduates** 40% 25 or older **Contact** Scottsdale Culinary Institute, 8100 East Camelback Road, Suite 1001, Scottsdale, AZ 85251-3940. *Phone:* toll-free 800-848-2433. *Web site:* http://www.scichefs.com/.

Southwestern College
Phoenix, Arizona

Contact Rebekah Dubina, Admissions Advisor, Southwestern College, 2625 East Cactus Road, Phoenix, AZ 85032. *Phone:* 602-386-4106 or toll-free 800-247-2697. *Fax:* 602-404-2159. *E-mail:* rebekah@swcaz.edu. *Web site:* http://www.swcaz.edu/.

University of Advancing Technology
Tempe, Arizona

General Proprietary, comprehensive, coed, primarily men **Setting** urban campus **Total enrollment** 1,147 **Student-faculty ratio** 19:1 **Application deadline** Rolling (freshmen) **Freshman admission** Average high school GPA 2.5 **Housing** Yes **Expenses** Tuition & Fees $18,900; Room & Board $11,034 **Undergraduates** 10% women, 1% Native American, 6% Hispanic American, 7% African American, 4% Asian American/Pacific Islander **Academic program** Summer session, internships **Contact** Admissions Office, University of Advancing Technology, 2625 West Baseline Road, Tempe, AZ 85283-1042. *Phone:* 602-383-8228 or toll-free 800-658-5744. *Fax:* 602-383-8222. *E-mail:* admissions@uat.edu. *Web site:* http://www.uat.edu/.

Visit Petersons.com and enter keyword Advancing

See page 1248 for the College Close-Up.

The University of Arizona
Tucson, Arizona

General State-supported, university, coed **Entrance** Moderately difficult **Setting** 362-acre urban campus **Total enrollment** 38,767 **Student-**

The University of Arizona (continued)
faculty ratio 20:1 **Application deadline** 5/1 (freshmen), rolling (transfer) **Freshman admission** 78% were admitted. Average high school GPA 3.37 **Freshman test scores** SAT critical reading scores over 500: 72%; SAT math scores over 500: 73%; ACT scores over 18: 92%; SAT critical reading scores over 600: 28%; SAT math scores over 600: 35%; ACT scores over 24: 51% **Housing** Yes **Expenses** Tuition & Fees: state resident $5542, nonresident $18,676; Room & Board $7812 **Undergraduates** 52% women, 11% part-time, 9% 25 or older, 3% Native American, 18% Hispanic American, 4% African American, 7% Asian American/Pacific Islander **The most frequently chosen baccalaureate fields are** business/marketing, biological/life sciences, social sciences **Academic program** English as a second language, advanced placement, accelerated degree program, honors program, summer session, adult/continuing education programs, internships **Contact** Paul Kohn, Dean of Admissions, The University of Arizona, Tucson, AZ 85721. *Phone:* 520-621-3705. *Fax:* 520-621-9799. *E-mail:* admissions@arizona.edu. *Web site:* http://www.arizona.edu/.

University of Phoenix
Phoenix, Arizona

General Proprietary, comprehensive, coed **Entrance** Noncompetitive **Total enrollment** 292,797 **Application deadline** Rolling (freshmen), rolling (transfer) **Housing** No **Expenses** Tuition & Fees $12,550 **Undergraduates** 69% women, 80% 25 or older, 1% Native American, 7% Hispanic American, 17% African American, 2% Asian American/Pacific Islander **The most frequently chosen baccalaureate fields are** business/marketing, computer and information sciences, health professions and related sciences **Academic program** Advanced placement, accelerated degree program, adult/continuing education programs **Contact** Ms. Audra McQuarie, Registrar/Executive Director, University of Phoenix, 4035 South Riverpoint Parkway, Mail Stop CF-L101, Phoenix, AZ 85040. *Phone:* 480-557-6151 or toll-free 800-776-4867 (in-state); 800-228-7240 (out-of-state). *Fax:* 480-643-3068. *E-mail:* audra.mcquarie@phoenix.edu. *Web site:* http://www.uopxonline.com/.

University of Phoenix–Phoenix Campus
Phoenix, Arizona

General Proprietary, comprehensive, coed **Entrance** Noncompetitive **Setting** urban campus **Total enrollment** 5,379 **Application deadline** Rolling (freshmen), rolling (transfer) **Housing** No **Expenses** Tuition & Fees $11,450 **Undergraduates** 59% women, 82% 25 or older, 2% Native American, 16% Hispanic American, 8% African American, 3% Asian American/Pacific Islander **The most frequently chosen baccalaureate fields are** business/marketing, computer and information sciences, health professions and related sciences **Academic program** Advanced placement, accelerated degree program, adult/continuing education programs **Contact** Ms. Audra McQuarie, Registrar/Executive Director, University of Phoenix–Phoenix Campus, 4035 South Riverpoint Parkway, Mail Stop CF-L101, Phoenix, AZ 85040. *Phone:* 480-557-6151 or toll-free 800-776-4867 (in-state); 800-228-7240 (out-of-state). *Fax:* 480-643-3068. *E-mail:* audra.mcquarie@phoenix.edu. *Web site:* http://www.phoenix.edu/.

University of Phoenix–Southern Arizona Campus
Tucson, Arizona

General Proprietary, comprehensive, coed **Entrance** Noncompetitive **Setting** urban campus **Total enrollment** 2,229 **Application deadline** Rolling (freshmen), rolling (transfer) **Housing** No **Expenses** Tuition & Fees $11,425 **Undergraduates** 63% women, 80% 25 or older, 2% Native American, 29% Hispanic American, 5% African American, 2% Asian American/Pacific Islander **The most frequently chosen baccalaureate fields are** business/marketing, computer and information sciences, public administration and social services **Academic program** Advanced placement, accelerated degree program, adult/continuing education programs **Contact** Ms. Audra McQuarie, Registrar/Executive Director, University of Phoenix–Southern Arizona Campus, 4035 South Riverpoint Parkway, Mail Stop CF-L101, Phoenix, AZ 85040-1958. *Phone:* 480-557-6151 or toll-free 800-776-4867 (in-state); 800-228-7240 (out-of-state). *Fax:* 480-643-3068. *E-mail:* audra.mcquarie@phoenix.edu. *Web site:* http://www.phoenix.edu/.

Western International University
Phoenix, Arizona

General Proprietary, comprehensive, coed **Entrance** Moderately difficult **Setting** 4-acre urban campus **Total enrollment** 3,021 **Student-faculty ratio** 10:1 **Application deadline** Rolling (freshmen), rolling (transfer) **Freshman admission** 78% were admitted **Housing** No **Expenses** Tuition & Fees $11,250 **Undergraduates** 63% women, 91% 25 or older, 1% Native American, 13% Hispanic American, 13% African American, 2% Asian American/Pacific Islander **The most frequently chosen baccalaureate fields are** business/marketing, computer and information sciences, liberal arts/general studies **Academic program** Advanced placement, accelerated degree program, honors program, summer session, adult/continuing education programs **Contact** Ms. Karen Janitell, Executive Director of Enrollment, Western International University, 9215 North Black Canyon Highway, Phoenix, AZ 85021-2718. *Phone:* 602-429-1063. *E-mail:* karen.janitell@west.edu. *Web site:* http://www.wintu.edu/.

ARKANSAS

Arkansas Baptist College
Little Rock, Arkansas

General Independent Baptist, 4-year, coed **Entrance** Minimally difficult **Setting** urban campus **Total enrollment** 626 **Student-faculty ratio** 22:1 **Application deadline** Rolling (freshmen) **Freshman admission** Average high school GPA 2.6 **Housing** Yes **Expenses** Tuition & Fees $7018; Room & Board $7606 **Undergraduates** 37% women, 21% part-time, 32% 25 or older, 98% African American **Academic program** Summer session, internships **Contact** Director of Enrollment Management, Arkansas Baptist College, 1621 Dr. Martin Luther King Jr. Drive, Little Rock, AR 72202-6067. *Phone:* 501-244-5104 Ext. 5124. *Web site:* http://www.arkansasbaptist.edu/.

Arkansas State University—Jonesboro
State University, Arkansas

General State-supported, university, coed **Entrance** Minimally difficult **Setting** 1,474-acre small-town campus **Total enrollment** 12,156 **Student-faculty ratio** 17:1 **Application deadline** Rolling (freshmen), rolling (transfer) **Freshman admission** 77% were admitted. Average high school GPA 3.15 **Freshman test scores** SAT critical reading scores over 500: 30.9%; SAT math scores over 500: 50%; ACT scores over 18: 80%; SAT critical reading scores over 600: 13.7%; SAT math scores over 600: 14.3%; ACT scores over 24: 31.7% **Housing** Yes **Expenses** Tuition & Fees: state resident $6370, nonresident $14,290; Room & Board $5856 **Undergraduates** 58% women, 23% part-time, 26% 25 or older, 1% Native American, 1% Hispanic American, 18% African American, 1% Asian American/Pacific Islander **The most frequently chosen baccalaureate fields are** business/marketing, education, health professions and related sciences **Academic program** English as a second language, advanced placement, accelerated degree program, honors program, summer session, internships **Contact** Ms. Tammy Fowler, Director of Admissions, Arkansas State University—Jonesboro, PO Box 1630, State

University, AR 72467. *Phone:* 870-972-3024 or toll-free 800-382-3030. *Fax:* 870-972-3406. *E-mail:* admissions@astate.edu. *Web site:* http://www.astate.edu/.

Arkansas Tech University

Russellville, Arkansas

General State-supported, comprehensive, coed **Entrance** Moderately difficult **Setting** 541-acre small-town campus **Total enrollment** 8,814 **Student-faculty ratio** 18:1 **Freshman admission** 94% were admitted. Average high school GPA 3.23 **Freshman test scores** SAT critical reading scores over 500: 36.36%; SAT math scores over 500: 54.54%; ACT scores over 18: 88.26%; SAT math scores over 600: 27.27%; ACT scores over 24: 47.36% **Housing** Yes **Expenses** Tuition & Fees: state resident $5610, nonresident $10,620; Room & Board $5156 **Undergraduates** 53% women, 23% part-time, 22% 25 or older, 2% Native American, 4% Hispanic American, 5% African American, 2% Asian American/Pacific Islander **The most frequently chosen baccalaureate fields are** education, business/marketing, health professions and related sciences **Academic program** Advanced placement, honors program, summer session, adult/continuing education programs, internships **Contact** Ms. Shauna Donnell, Director of Enrollment Management, Arkansas Tech University, L.L. "Doc" Bryan Student Services Building, Suite 141, Russellville, AR 72801-2222. *Phone:* 479-968-0343 or toll-free 800-582-6953. *Fax:* 479-964-0522. *E-mail:* tech.enroll@atu.edu. *Web site:* http://www.atu.edu/.

Central Baptist College

Conway, Arkansas

General Independent Baptist, 4-year, coed **Entrance** Minimally difficult **Setting** 11-acre small-town campus **Total enrollment** 625 **Student-faculty ratio** 21:1 **Application deadline** 8/15 (freshmen), 8/15 (transfer) **Freshman admission** 75% were admitted. Average high school GPA 3.15 **Housing** Yes **Expenses** Tuition & Fees $10,680; Room & Board $5800 **Undergraduates** 47% women, 16% part-time, 38% 25 or older, 1% Native American, 2% Hispanic American, 17% African American, 0.5% Asian American/Pacific Islander **The most frequently chosen baccalaureate fields are** business/marketing, computer and information sciences, theology and religious vocations **Academic program** Advanced placement, summer session, adult/continuing education programs, internships **Contact** Ms. Rachel Waymire, Admissions Counselor, Central Baptist College, 1501 College Avenue, Conway, AR 72034. *Phone:* 501-329-6872 Ext. 197 or toll-free 800-205-6872. *Fax:* 501-329-2941. *E-mail:* rwaymire@cbc.edu. *Web site:* http://www.cbc.edu/.

Ecclesia College

Springdale, Arkansas

General Independent religious, 4-year, coed **Entrance** Noncompetitive **Setting** 200-acre suburban campus **Total enrollment** 235 **Student-faculty ratio** 10:1 **Housing** Yes **Expenses** Tuition & Fees $14,250 **Academic program** Internships **Contact** Titus Hofer, Admissions Director, Ecclesia College, 9653 Nations Drive, Springdale, AR 72762. *Phone:* 479-248-7236 Ext. 223 or toll-free 800-735-9926. *Fax:* 479-248-1455. *E-mail:* myfuture@ecollege.edu.

Harding University

Searcy, Arkansas

General Independent, university, coed, affiliated with Church of Christ **Entrance** Moderately difficult **Setting** 275-acre small-town campus **Total enrollment** 6,484 **Student-faculty ratio** 17:1 **Application deadline** Rolling (freshmen), rolling (transfer) **Freshman admission** 73% were admitted. Average high school GPA 3.5 **Freshman test scores** SAT critical reading scores over 500: 74%; SAT math scores over 500: 73%; ACT scores over 18: 95%; SAT critical reading scores over 600: 33%; SAT math scores over 600: 37%; ACT scores over 24: 58% **Housing** Yes **Expenses** Tuition & Fees $13,580; Room & Board $5814 **Undergraduates** 53% women, 6% part-time, 6% 25 or older, 1% Native American, 2% Hispanic American, 4% African American, 1% Asian American/Pacific Islander **The most frequently chosen baccalaureate fields are** business/marketing, education, health professions and related sciences **Academic program** English as a second language, advanced placement, accelerated degree program, self-designed majors, honors program, summer session, adult/continuing education programs, internships **Contact** Mr. Glenn Dillard, Assistant Vice President for Enrollment Management, Harding University, Box 12255, Searcy, AR 72149-2255. *Phone:* 501-279-4407 or toll-free 800-477-4407. *Fax:* 501-279-4129. *E-mail:* admissions@harding.edu. *Web site:* http://www.harding.edu/.

Henderson State University

Arkadelphia, Arkansas

General State-supported, comprehensive, coed **Entrance** Moderately difficult **Setting** 151-acre small-town campus **Total enrollment** 3,578 **Student-faculty ratio** 18:1 **Application deadline** 7/15 (freshmen), rolling (transfer) **Freshman admission** 65% were admitted. Average high school GPA 3.19 **Freshman test scores** SAT math scores over 500: 66%; ACT scores over 18: 87%; SAT math scores over 600: 22%; ACT scores over 24: 42% **Housing** Yes **Expenses** Tuition & Fees: state resident $6204, nonresident $11,304; Room & Board $5034 **Undergraduates** 54% women, 11% part-time, 15% 25 or older, 0.2% Native American, 3% Hispanic American, 9% African American, 1% Asian American/Pacific Islander **The most frequently chosen baccalaureate fields are** business/marketing, education, health professions and related sciences **Academic program** Advanced placement, honors program, summer session, internships **Contact** Ms. Vikita Hardwrick, Director of University Relations/Admissions, Henderson State University, 1100 Henderson Street, PO Box 7560, Arkadelphia, AR 71999-0001. *Phone:* 870-230-5028 or toll-free 800-228-7333. *Fax:* 870-230-5066. *E-mail:* hardwrv@hsu.edu. *Web site:* http://www.hsu.edu/.

Hendrix College

Conway, Arkansas

General Independent United Methodist, comprehensive, coed **Entrance** Very difficult **Setting** 65-acre suburban campus **Total enrollment** 1,463 **Student-faculty ratio** 13:1 **Application deadline** 8/1 (freshmen), 8/1 (transfer) **Freshman admission** 80% were admitted. Average high school GPA 3.83 **Freshman test scores** SAT critical reading scores over 500: 94%; SAT math scores over 500: 91%; ACT scores over 18: 100%; SAT critical reading scores over 600: 69%; SAT math scores over 600: 54%; ACT scores over 24: 92% **Housing** Yes **Expenses** Tuition & Fees $30,270; Room & Board $8664 **Undergraduates** 56% women, 1% part-time, 1% Native American, 4% Hispanic American, 3% African American, 3% Asian American/Pacific Islander **The most frequently chosen baccalaureate fields are** biological/life sciences, psychology, social sciences **Academic program** Advanced placement, self-designed majors, honors program, internships **Contact** Ms. Laura E. Martin, Director of Admission, Hendrix College, 1600 Washington Avenue, Conway, AR 72032. *Phone:* 501-450-1362 or toll-free 800-277-9017. *Fax:* 501-450-3843. *E-mail:* martinl@hendrix.edu. *Web site:* http://www.hendrix.edu/.

ITT Technical Institute

Little Rock, Arkansas

General Proprietary, primarily 2-year, coed **Entrance** Minimally difficult **Setting** urban campus **Housing** No **Contact** Director of Recruitment, ITT Technical Institute, 4520 South University Avenue, Little Rock, AR 72204. *Phone:* 501-565-5550 or toll-free 800-359-4429. *Web site:* http://www.itt-tech.edu/.

John Brown University

Siloam Springs, Arkansas

General Independent interdenominational, comprehensive, coed **Entrance** Moderately difficult **Setting** 200-acre small-town campus

COLLEGES AT-A-GLANCE

John Brown University (continued)
Total enrollment 2,073 **Student-faculty ratio** 13:1 **Application deadline** Rolling (freshmen), rolling (transfer) **Freshman admission** 73% were admitted. Average high school GPA 3.58 **Freshman test scores** SAT critical reading scores over 500: 85%; SAT math scores over 500: 83%; ACT scores over 18: 97%; SAT critical reading scores over 600: 54%; SAT math scores over 600: 42%; ACT scores over 24: 62% **Housing** Yes **Expenses** Tuition & Fees $18,880; Room & Board $6876 **Undergraduates** 56% women, 20% part-time, 5% 25 or older, 2% Native American, 3% Hispanic American, 2% African American, 1% Asian American/Pacific Islander **The most frequently chosen baccalaureate fields are** business/marketing, education, theology and religious vocations **Academic program** English as a second language, accelerated degree program, honors program, adult/continuing education programs, internships **Contact** Mr. Don Crandall, Vice President for Enrollment Management, John Brown University, 2000 West University Street, Siloam Springs, AR 72761-2121. *Phone:* 479-524-7150 or toll-free 877-JBU-INFO. *Fax:* 479-524-4196. *E-mail:* dcrandal@jbu.edu. *Web site:* http://www.jbu.edu/.

Lyon College
Batesville, Arkansas

General Independent Presbyterian, 4-year, coed **Entrance** Moderately difficult **Setting** 136-acre small-town campus **Total enrollment** 614 **Student-faculty ratio** 12:1 **Application deadline** Rolling (freshmen), rolling (transfer) **Freshman admission** 67% were admitted. Average high school GPA 3.54 **Freshman test scores** SAT critical reading scores over 500: 70%; SAT math scores over 500: 66%; ACT scores over 18: 99%; SAT critical reading scores over 600: 45%; SAT math scores over 600: 22%; ACT scores over 24: 58% **Housing** Yes **Expenses** Tuition & Fees $19,968; Room & Board $7340 **Undergraduates** 55% women, 6% part-time, 5% 25 or older, 1% Native American, 2% Hispanic American, 4% African American, 1% Asian American/Pacific Islander **The most frequently chosen baccalaureate fields are** biological/life sciences, business/marketing, psychology **Academic program** Advanced placement, accelerated degree program, self-designed majors, summer session, internships **Contact** Office of Enrollment Services, Lyon College, 2300 Highland Road, Batesville, AR 72501. *Phone:* 870-307-7250 or toll-free 800-423-2542. *Fax:* 870-307-7542. *E-mail:* admissions@lyon.edu. *Web site:* http://www.lyon.edu/.

Ouachita Baptist University
Arkadelphia, Arkansas

General Independent Baptist, 4-year, coed **Entrance** Moderately difficult **Setting** 200-acre small-town campus **Total enrollment** 1,447 **Student-faculty ratio** 11:1 **Application deadline** 8/15 (freshmen), 8/15 (transfer) **Freshman admission** 67% were admitted. Average high school GPA 3.52 **Freshman test scores** SAT critical reading scores over 500: 65%; SAT math scores over 500: 69%; ACT scores over 18: 94%; SAT critical reading scores over 600: 26%; SAT math scores over 600: 33%; ACT scores over 24: 52% **Housing** Yes **Expenses** Tuition & Fees $19,820; Room & Board $5840 **Undergraduates** 53% women, 2% part-time, 3% 25 or older, 1% Native American, 2% Hispanic American, 7% African American, 1% Asian American/Pacific Islander **The most frequently chosen baccalaureate fields are** business/marketing, theology and religious vocations, visual and performing arts **Academic program** English as a second language, advanced placement, accelerated degree program, honors program, summer session, internships **Contact** Mrs. Lori Motl, Director of Admissions Counseling, Ouachita Baptist University, OBU Box 3776, Arkadelphia, AR 71998-0001. *Phone:* 870-245-5110 or toll-free 800-342-5628. *Fax:* 870-245-5500. *E-mail:* motll@obu.edu. *Web site:* http://www.obu.edu/.

Philander Smith College
Little Rock, Arkansas

Contact Mr. George Gray, Director of Recruitment and Admissions, Philander Smith College, 812 West 13th Street, Little Rock, AR 72202-3799. *Phone:* 501-370-5310 or toll-free 800-446-6772. *Fax:* 501-370-5225. *E-mail:* ggray@philander.edu. *Web site:* http://www.philander.edu/.

Southern Arkansas University–Magnolia
Magnolia, Arkansas

General State-supported, comprehensive, coed **Entrance** Moderately difficult **Setting** 781-acre small-town campus **Total enrollment** 3,226 **Student-faculty ratio** 15:1 **Application deadline** 8/27 (freshmen), 8/27 (transfer) **Freshman admission** 73% were admitted. Average high school GPA 3.09 **Freshman test scores** SAT critical reading scores over 500: 36%; SAT math scores over 500: 58%; ACT scores over 18: 76%; SAT critical reading scores over 600: 8%; SAT math scores over 600: 16%; ACT scores over 24: 27% **Housing** Yes **Expenses** Tuition & Fees: state resident $6066, nonresident $8706; Room & Board $4400 **Undergraduates** 59% women, 14% part-time, 22% 25 or older, 1% Native American, 2% Hispanic American, 30% African American, 1% Asian American/Pacific Islander **The most frequently chosen baccalaureate fields are** business/marketing, education, liberal arts/general studies **Academic program** Advanced placement, accelerated degree program, honors program, summer session, adult/continuing education programs, internships **Contact** Ms. Sarah Jennings, Dean of Enrollment Services, Southern Arkansas University–Magnolia, 100 East University, Magnolia, AR 71753. *Phone:* 870-235-4040 or toll-free 800-332-7286. *E-mail:* addanna@saumag.edu. *Web site:* http://www.saumag.edu/.

Strayer University–Little Rock Campus
Little Rock, Arkansas

General Proprietary, comprehensive, coed **Contact** Admissions Office, Strayer University–Little Rock Campus, 10825 Financial Centre Parkway, Suite 131, Little Rock, AR 72211. *Web site:* http://www.strayer.edu/little_rock.

University of Arkansas
Fayetteville, Arkansas

General State-supported, university, coed **Entrance** Moderately difficult **Setting** 410-acre suburban campus **Total enrollment** 19,849 **Student-faculty ratio** 17:1 **Application deadline** 8/1 (freshmen), 8/1 (transfer) **Freshman admission** 56% were admitted. Average high school GPA 3.55 **Freshman test scores** SAT critical reading scores over 500: 77.4%; SAT math scores over 500: 84%; ACT scores over 18: 99.7%; SAT critical reading scores over 600: 34.6%; SAT math scores over 600: 43.2%; ACT scores over 24: 67.9% **Housing** Yes **Expenses** Tuition & Fees: state resident $6400, nonresident $15,278; Room & Board $7422 **Undergraduates** 48% women, 13% part-time, 11% 25 or older, 2% Native American, 4% Hispanic American, 5% African American, 3% Asian American/Pacific Islander **The most frequently chosen baccalaureate fields are** business/marketing, education, engineering **Academic program** English as a second language, advanced placement, accelerated degree program, honors program, summer session, internships **Contact** Suzanne McCray, Vice Provost for Enrollment, University of Arkansas, 232 Silas H. Hunt Hall, Office of Admissions, Fayetteville, AR 72701-1201. *Phone:* 479-575-5346 or toll-free 800-377-5346 (in-state); 800-377-8632 (out-of-state). *Fax:* 479-575-7515. *E-mail:* uofa@uark.edu. *Web site:* http://www.uark.edu/.

University of Arkansas at Fort Smith
Fort Smith, Arkansas

General State and locally supported, 4-year, coed **Entrance** Minimally difficult **Setting** 120-acre suburban campus **Total enrollment** 7,335 **Student-faculty ratio** 20:1 **Application deadline** Rolling (freshmen), rolling (transfer) **Freshman admission** 61% were admitted. Average high school GPA 3.24 **Freshman test scores** ACT scores over 18: 81.9%; ACT scores over 24: 28.3% **Housing** Yes **Expenses** Tuition & Fees: state resident $4600, nonresident $10,000; Room only $4789 **Undergraduates** 58% women, 32% part-time, 34% 25 or older, 3% Native American, 6% Hispanic American, 4% African American, 4% Asian American/Pacific Islander **The most frequently chosen baccalaureate fields are** business/marketing, education, psychology **Academic program** Advanced placement, accelerated degree program, honors program, summer session, adult/continuing education programs, internships **Contact** Office of Admissions and School Relations, University of Arkansas at Fort Smith, 5210 Grand Avenue, PO Box 3649, Fort Smith, AR 72913-3649. *Phone:* 479-788-7120 or toll-free 888-512-5466. *Fax:* 479-788-7016. *E-mail:* information@uafortsmith.edu. *Web site:* http://www.uafortsmith.edu/.

University of Arkansas at Little Rock
Little Rock, Arkansas

General State-supported, university, coed **Entrance** Minimally difficult **Setting** 150-acre urban campus **Total enrollment** 13,132 **Student-faculty ratio** 16:1 **Application deadline** Rolling (freshmen), rolling (transfer) **Freshman admission** 99% were admitted **Freshman test scores** ACT scores over 18: 61.6%; ACT scores over 24: 17.7% **Housing** Yes **Expenses** Tuition & Fees: state resident $6083, nonresident $14,266; Room only $3100 **Undergraduates** 61% women, 44% part-time, 35% 25 or older, 1% Native American, 2% Hispanic American, 27% African American, 3% Asian American/Pacific Islander **Academic program** English as a second language, advanced placement, accelerated degree program, self-designed majors, honors program, summer session, adult/continuing education programs, internships **Contact** Ms. Tammy Harrison, Director of Admissions, University of Arkansas at Little Rock, 2801 South University Avenue, Little Rock, AR 72204-1099. *Phone:* 501-569-3127 or toll-free 800-482-8892. *Fax:* 501-569-8956. *E-mail:* twharrison@ualn.edu. *Web site:* http://www.ualr.edu/.

University of Arkansas at Monticello
Monticello, Arkansas

General State-supported, comprehensive, coed **Entrance** Noncompetitive **Setting** 1,600-acre small-town campus **Total enrollment** 3,479 **Student-faculty ratio** 15:1 **Application deadline** 8/1 (freshmen), 8/1 (transfer) **Freshman admission** 50% were admitted. Average high school GPA 2.77 **Freshman test scores** ACT scores over 18: 60%; ACT scores over 24: 17% **Housing** Yes **Expenses** Tuition & Fees: state resident $4740, nonresident $9000; Room & Board $3900 **Undergraduates** 59% women, 26% part-time, 28% 25 or older, 1% Native American, 1% Hispanic American, 31% African American, 0.3% Asian American/Pacific Islander **The most frequently chosen baccalaureate fields are** business/marketing, education, health professions and related sciences **Academic program** Advanced placement, accelerated degree program, summer session **Contact** Ms. Mary Whiting, Director of Admissions, University of Arkansas at Monticello, Monticello, AR 71656. *Phone:* 870-460-1026 or toll-free 800-844-1826. *Fax:* 870-460-1926. *E-mail:* admissions@uamont.edu. *Web site:* http://www.uamont.edu/.

University of Arkansas at Pine Bluff
Pine Bluff, Arkansas

General State-supported, comprehensive, coed **Setting** 327-acre urban campus **Total enrollment** 3,792 **Student-faculty ratio** 17:1 **Application deadline** Rolling (freshmen) **Freshman admission** 33% were admitted **Freshman test scores** SAT critical reading scores over 500: 24%; SAT math scores over 500: 23%; ACT scores over 18: 29%; SAT math scores over 600: 2%; ACT scores over 24: 2% **Housing** Yes **Expenses** Tuition & Fees: state resident $4796, nonresident $9476; Room & Board $6168 **Undergraduates** 58% women, 9% part-time, 20% 25 or older, 0.1% Native American, 0.4% Hispanic American, 95% African American, 0.1% Asian American/Pacific Islander **The most frequently chosen baccalaureate fields are** business/marketing, family and consumer sciences, security and protective services **Academic program** Advanced placement, accelerated degree program, honors program, summer session, adult/continuing education programs, internships **Contact** Mrs. Mary Jones, Director of Admissions and Academic Records, University of Arkansas at Pine Bluff, 1200 North University Drive, Pine Bluff, AR 71601-2799. *Phone:* 870-575-8461 or toll-free 800-264-6585. *Fax:* 870-575-4606. *E-mail:* jonesm@uapb.edu. *Web site:* http://www.uapb.edu/.

University of Arkansas for Medical Sciences
Little Rock, Arkansas

Contact Ms. Mona Stiles, Admissions Officer, University of Arkansas for Medical Sciences, 4301 West Markham, Little Rock, AR 72205-7199. *Phone:* 501-686-5730. *Web site:* http://www.uams.edu/.

University of Central Arkansas
Conway, Arkansas

General State-supported, university, coed **Entrance** Moderately difficult **Setting** 365-acre small-town campus **Total enrollment** 12,974 **Student-faculty ratio** 19:1 **Application deadline** Rolling (freshmen), rolling (transfer) **Freshman admission** 58% were admitted. Average high school GPA 3.3 **Freshman test scores** ACT scores over 18: 89.6%; ACT scores over 24: 46.4% **Housing** Yes **Expenses** Tuition & Fees: state resident $6699, nonresident $11,905; Room & Board $4880 **Undergraduates** 57% women, 18% part-time, 12% 25 or older **The most frequently chosen baccalaureate fields are** business/marketing, education, health professions and related sciences **Academic program** English as a second language, advanced placement, accelerated degree program, honors program, summer session, internships **Contact** Penny Hatfield, Interim Director of Admissions, University of Central Arkansas, 201 Donaghey Avenue, Bernard 100, Conway, AR 72035. *Phone:* 501-450-346 or toll-free 800-243-8245. *Fax:* 501-450-5228. *E-mail:* phatfield@uca.edu. *Web site:* http://www.uca.edu/.

University of Phoenix–Little Rock Campus
Little Rock, Arkansas

General Proprietary, comprehensive, coed **Entrance** Noncompetitive **Setting** urban campus **Total enrollment** 773 **Application deadline** Rolling (freshmen), rolling (transfer) **Housing** No **Expenses** Tuition & Fees $10,800 **Undergraduates** 68% women, 81% 25 or older, 1% Native American, 1% Hispanic American, 43% African American, 0.5% Asian American/Pacific Islander **The most frequently chosen baccalaureate fields are** business/marketing, computer and information sciences **Academic program** Advanced placement, accelerated degree program **Contact** Ms. Audra McQuarie, Registrar/Executive Director, University of Phoenix–Little Rock Campus, 4035 South Riverpoint Parkway, Mail Stop CF-L101, Phoenix, AZ 85040. *Phone:* 480-557-6151 or toll-free 800-776-4867 (in-state); 800-228-7240 (out-of-state). *Fax:* 480-643-3068. *E-mail:* audra.mcquarie@phoenix.edu. *Web site:* http://www.phoenix.edu/.

University of the Ozarks
Clarksville, Arkansas

General Independent Presbyterian, 4-year, coed **Entrance** Moderately difficult **Setting** 56-acre small-town campus **Total enrollment** 625 **Student-faculty ratio** 10:1 **Application deadline** Rolling (freshmen), rolling (transfer) **Freshman admission** 89% were admitted. Average high school GPA 3.35 **Freshman test scores** SAT critical reading scores over 500: 36.59%; SAT math scores over 500: 56.1%; ACT scores over 18: 84.55%; SAT critical reading scores over 600: 4.88%; SAT math

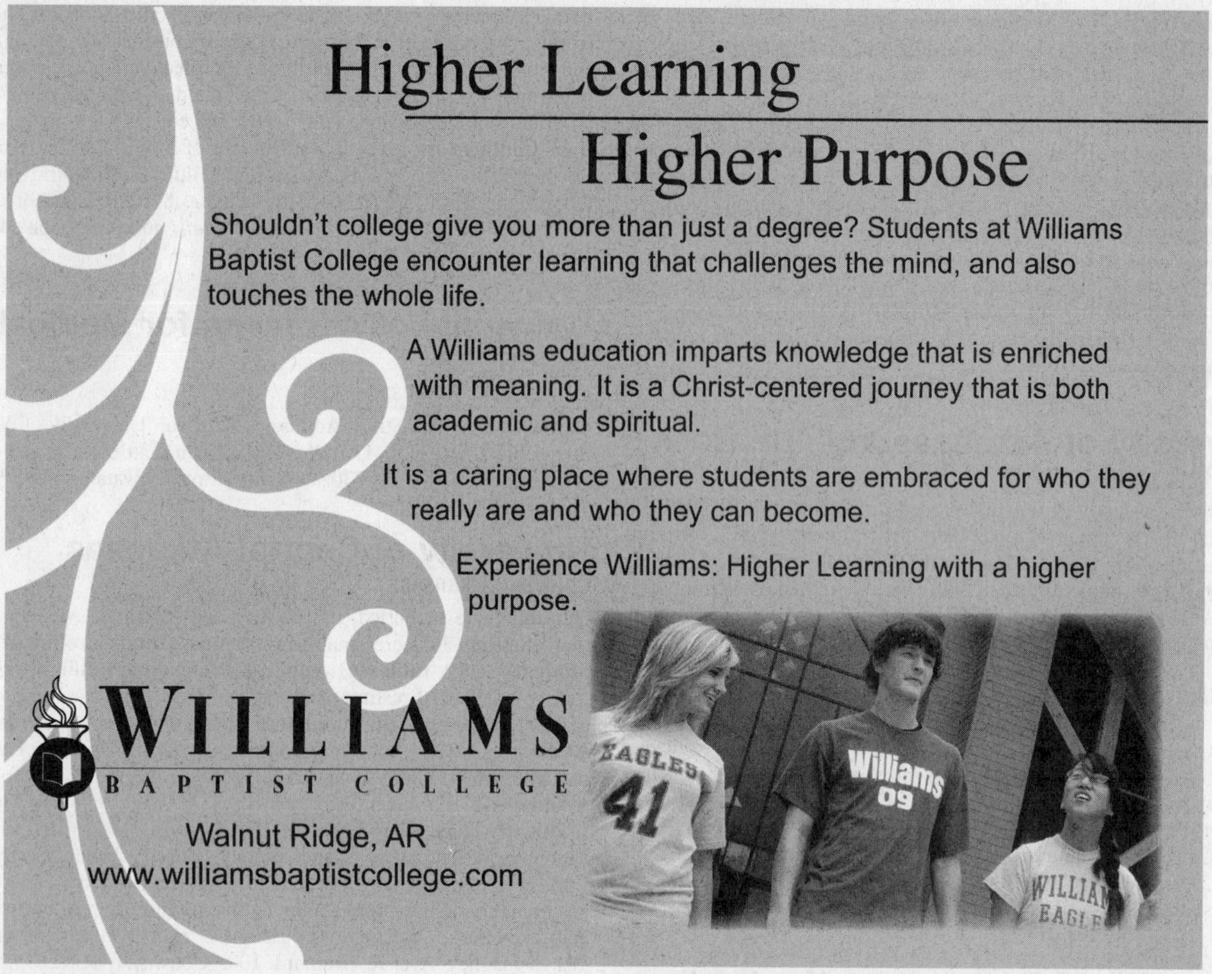

Higher Learning
Higher Purpose

Shouldn't college give you more than just a degree? Students at Williams Baptist College encounter learning that challenges the mind, and also touches the whole life.

A Williams education imparts knowledge that is enriched with meaning. It is a Christ-centered journey that is both academic and spiritual.

It is a caring place where students are embraced for who they really are and who they can become.

Experience Williams: Higher Learning with a higher purpose.

WILLIAMS
BAPTIST COLLEGE

Walnut Ridge, AR
www.williamsbaptistcollege.com

University of the Ozarks (continued)

scores over 600: 19.51%; ACT scores over 24: 32.52% **Housing** Yes **Expenses** Tuition & Fees $20,530; Room & Board $6300 **Undergraduates** 51% women, 6% part-time, 1% 25 or older, 2% Native American, 5% Hispanic American, 4% African American, 1% Asian American/Pacific Islander **The most frequently chosen baccalaureate fields are** business/marketing, education, social sciences **Academic program** English as a second language, advanced placement, summer session, internships **Contact** Ms. Kim Myrick, Vice President for Enrollment Management, University of the Ozarks, 415 North College Avenue, Clarksville, AR 72830-2880. *Phone:* 479-979-1227 or toll-free 800-264-8636. *Fax:* 479-979-1417. *E-mail:* admiss@ozarks.edu. *Web site:* http://www.ozarks.edu/.

Williams Baptist College
Walnut Ridge, Arkansas

Contact Mrs. Angela Flippo, Vice President for Enrollment, Williams Baptist College, 60 West Fulbright Avenue, Walnut Ridge, AR 72476. *Phone:* 870-759-4117 or toll-free 800-722-4434. *Fax:* 870-886-3924. *E-mail:* admissions@wbcoll.edu. *Web site:* http://www.wbcoll.edu/.
Visit Petersons.com and enter keywords Williams Baptist

CALIFORNIA

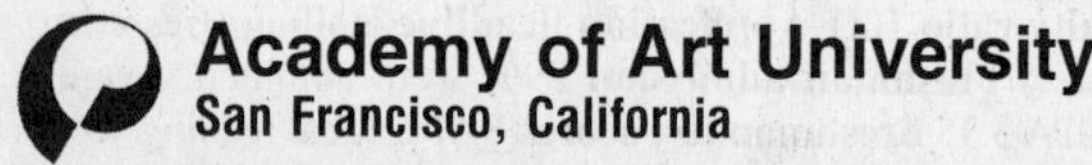

Academy of Art University
San Francisco, California

General Proprietary, comprehensive, coed **Entrance** Noncompetitive **Setting** 3-acre urban campus **Total enrollment** 15,791 **Student-faculty ratio** 20:1 **Application deadline** Rolling (freshmen), rolling (transfer) **Freshman admission** 100% were admitted **Housing** Yes **Expenses** Tuition & Fees $22,490; Room & Board $13,400 **Undergraduates** 56% women, 41% part-time, 39% 25 or older, 1% Native American, 8% Hispanic American, 5% African American, 10% Asian American/Pacific Islander **The most frequently chosen baccalaureate fields are** communication technologies, visual and performing arts **Academic program** English as a second language, summer session, adult/continuing education programs, internships **Contact** Admissions, Academy of Art University, 79 New Montgomery Street, San Francisco, CA 94105. *Phone:* toll-free 800-544-ARTS. *Fax:* 415-618-6287. *E-mail:* info@academyart.edu. *Web site:* http://www.academyart.edu/.

See page 462 for the College Close-Up.

Alliant International University
San Diego, California

General Independent, university, coed **Setting** 60-acre suburban campus **Total enrollment** 4,343 **Student-faculty ratio** 13:1 **Application deadline** Rolling (transfer) **Housing** Yes **Expenses** Tuition & Fees $15,220 **Undergraduates** 68% women, 33% part-time, 85% 25 or older, 1% Native American, 21% Hispanic American, 4% African American, 4% Asian American/Pacific Islander **Academic program** English as a second language, advanced placement, honors program, summer session, internships **Contact** Alliant International University, 10455 Pomerado Road, San Diego, CA 92131-1799. *Phone:* 858-635-4772 or toll-free 866-825-5426. *Fax:* 858-635-4739. *E-mail:* admissions@alliant.edu. *Web site:* http://www.alliant.edu/.

Allied American University

Laguna Hills, California

Contact Allied American University, 22952 Alcade Drive, Laguna Hills, CA 92653. *Web site:* http://allied.edu/.

American Jewish University

Bel Air, California

General Independent Jewish, comprehensive, coed **Entrance** Moderately difficult **Setting** 28-acre suburban campus **Total enrollment** 140 **Student-faculty ratio** 4:1 **Application deadline** 5/31 (freshmen), 5/31 (transfer) **Freshman admission** 96% were admitted. Average high school GPA 3.11 **Freshman test scores** SAT critical reading scores over 500: 45%; SAT math scores over 500: 33%; ACT scores over 18: 84%; SAT critical reading scores over 600: 17%; ACT scores over 24: 17% **Housing** Yes **Expenses** Tuition & Fees $22,352; Room & Board $11,216 **Undergraduates** 52% women, 4% part-time, 2% Native American, 6% Hispanic American, 4% African American, 1% Asian American/Pacific Islander **The most frequently chosen baccalaureate fields are** business/marketing, psychology, social sciences **Academic program** Advanced placement, self-designed majors, summer session, adult/continuing education programs, internships **Contact** Mr. Matt Spooner, Director of Undergraduate Admissions, American Jewish University, Familian Campus, 15600 Mulholland Drive, Los Angeles, CA 90077-1599. *Phone:* 310-440-1250 or toll-free 888-853-6763. *Fax:* 310-471-3657. *E-mail:* admissions@ajula.edu. *Web site:* http://www.ajula.edu/.

American Musical and Dramatic Academy, Los Angeles

Los Angeles, California

Contact Director of Admission, American Musical and Dramatic Academy, Los Angeles, 6305 Yucca Street, Los Angeles, CA 90028. *Phone:* 323-469-3300 or toll-free 866-374-5300. *E-mail:* info@amda.edu. *Web site:* http://www.amda.edu/.

Antioch University Los Angeles

Culver City, California

General Independent, upper-level, coed **Entrance** Moderately difficult **Setting** 1-acre urban campus **Total enrollment** 495 **Student-faculty ratio** 14:1 **Application deadline** 8/1 (transfer) **First-year students** 90% were admitted **Housing** No **Undergraduates** 68% women, 100% part-time, 97% 25 or older, 11% Hispanic American, 17% African American, 1% Asian American/Pacific Islander **Academic program** Advanced placement, accelerated degree program, self-designed majors, summer session, adult/continuing education programs, internships **Contact** Admissions, Antioch University Los Angeles, 400 Corporate Pointe, Culver City, CA 90230. *Phone:* 310-578-1080 Ext. 100 or toll-free 800-7ANTIOCH. *Fax:* 310-822-4824. *E-mail:* admissions@antiochla.edu. *Web site:* http://www.antiochla.edu/.

Visit Petersons.com and enter keyword Antioch

Antioch University Santa Barbara

Santa Barbara, California

General Independent, upper-level, coed **Setting** small-town campus **Total enrollment** 369 **Student-faculty ratio** 12:1 **Application deadline** Rolling (transfer) **Housing** No **Expenses** Tuition & Fees $15,948 **Undergraduates** 75% women, 65% part-time, 84% 25 or older, 2% Native American, 35% Hispanic American, 4% African American, 1% Asian American/Pacific Islander **The most frequently chosen baccalaureate field is** liberal arts/general studies **Academic program** Accelerated degree program, self-designed majors, summer session, internships **Contact** Steven Weir, Director of Marketing and Enrollment Management, Antioch University Santa Barbara, 801 Garden Street, Santa Barbara, CA 93101-1581. *Phone:* 805-962-8179 Ext. 152. *Fax:* 805-962-4786. *E-mail:* sweir@antiochsb.edu. *Web site:* http://www.antiochsb.edu/.

Argosy University, Inland Empire

San Bernardino, California

General Proprietary, university, coed **Contact** Director of Admissions, Argosy University, Inland Empire, 636 East Brier Drive, Suite 120, San Bernardino, CA 92408. *Phone:* 909-915-3800 or toll-free 866-217-9075. *Fax:* 909-915-3810. *Web site:* http://www.argosy.edu/inlandempire/.

Visit Petersons.com and enter keywords Argosy University, Inland Empire

See page 478 for the College Close-Up.

Argosy University, Los Angeles

Santa Monica, California

General Proprietary, university, coed **Contact** Director of Admissions, Argosy University, Los Angeles, 5230 Pacific Concourse, Suite 200, Santa Monica, CA 90045. *Phone:* 310-866-4000 or toll-free 866-505-0332. *Fax:* 310-452-8720. *Web site:* http://www.argosy.edu/santamonica/.

Visit Petersons.com and enter keywords Argosy University, Los Angeles

See page 478 for the College Close-Up.

Argosy University, Orange County

Orange, California

General Proprietary, university, coed **Setting** urban campus **Contact** Director of Admissions, Argosy University, Orange County, 601 South Lewis Street, Orange, CA 92868. *Phone:* 714-620-3700 or toll-free 800-716-9598. *Fax:* 714-620-3800. *Web site:* http://www.argosy.edu/orangecounty/.

Visit Petersons.com and enter keywords Argosy University, Orange County

See page 478 for the College Close-Up.

Argosy University, San Diego

San Diego, California

General Proprietary, university, coed **Contact** Director of Admissions, Argosy University, San Diego, 1615 Murray Canyon Road, Suite 100, San Diego, CA 92108. *Phone:* 619-321-3000 or toll-free 866-505-0333. *Fax:* 619-321-3005. *Web site:* http://www.argosy.edu/sandiego/.

Visit Petersons.com and enter keywords Argosy University, San Diego

See page 478 for the College Close-Up.

Argosy University, San Francisco Bay Area

Alameda, California

General Proprietary, university, coed **Contact** Director of Admissions, Argosy University, San Francisco Bay Area, 1005 Atlantic Avenue, Alameda, CA 94501. *Phone:* 510-217-4700 or toll-free 866-215-2777. *Fax:* 510-217-4806. *Web site:* http://www.argosy.edu/sanfrancisco/.

Visit Petersons.com and enter keywords Argosy University, San Francisco Bay Area

See page 478 for the College Close-Up.

Art Center College of Design

Pasadena, California

General Independent, comprehensive, coed **Entrance** Very difficult **Setting** 175-acre suburban campus **Student-faculty ratio** 8:1 **Application deadline** Rolling (freshmen), rolling (transfer) **Freshman admission** 66% were admitted. Average high school GPA 3.1 **Housing** No **Expenses** Tuition & Fees $31,326 **Undergraduates** 22% 25 or older,

Art Center College of Design (continued)
0.4% Native American, 11% Hispanic American, 2% African American, 35% Asian American/Pacific Islander **The most frequently chosen baccalaureate field is** visual and performing arts **Academic program** Advanced placement, accelerated degree program, summer session, internships **Contact** Ms. Kit Baron, Vice President, Admissions and Enrollment Management, Art Center College of Design, 1700 Lida Street, Pasadena, CA 91103. *Phone:* 626-396-2322. *Fax:* 626-795-0578. *E-mail:* kit.baron@artcenter.edu. *Web site:* http://www.artcenter.edu/.

Visit Petersons.com and enter keyword Art

The Art Institute of California–Hollywood

North Hollywood, California

General Proprietary, 4-year, coed **Setting** urban campus **Contact** Director of Admissions, The Art Institute of California–Hollywood, 5250 Lankershim Boulevard, North Hollywood, CA 91601. *Phone:* 213-251-3636 or toll-free 877-468-6232. *Fax:* 213-385-3545. *Web site:* http://www.artinstitutes.edu/hollywood.

Visit Petersons.com and enter keywords Art Institute of California-Hollywood

See page 488 for the College Close-Up.

The Art Institute of California–Inland Empire

San Bernardino, California

General Proprietary, 4-year, coed **Setting** suburban campus **Contact** Director of Admissions, The Art Institute of California–Inland Empire, 674 East Brier Drive, San Bernardino, CA 92408. *Phone:* 909-915-2100 or toll-free 800-353-0812. *Fax:* 909-915-2130. *Web site:* http://www.artinstitutes.edu/inlandempire/.

Visit Petersons.com and enter keywords Art Institute of California-Inland Empire

See page 490 for the College Close-Up.

The Art Institute of California–Los Angeles

Santa Monica, California

General Proprietary, 4-year, coed **Setting** urban campus **Contact** Director of Admissions, The Art Institute of California–Los Angeles, 2900 31st Street, Santa Monica, CA 90405-3035. *Phone:* 310-752-4700 or toll-free 888-646-4610. *Fax:* 310-752-4708. *Web site:* http://www.artinstitutes.edu/losangeles/.

Visit Petersons.com and enter keywords Art Institute of California-Los Angeles

See page 492 for the College Close-Up.

The Art Institute of California–Orange County

Santa Ana, California

General Proprietary, 4-year, coed **Setting** urban campus **Contact** Director of Admissions, The Art Institute of California–Orange County, 3601 West Sunflower Avenue, Santa Ana, CA 92704. *Phone:* 714-830-0200 or toll-free 888-549-3055. *Fax:* 714-556-1923. *Web site:* http://www.artinstitutes.edu/orangecounty/.

Visit Petersons.com and enter keywords Art Institute of California-Orange County

See page 494 for the College Close-Up.

The Art Institute of California–Sacramento

Sacramento, California

General Proprietary, 4-year, coed **Contact** Director of Admissions, The Art Institute of California–Sacramento, 2850 Gateway Oaks Drive, Suite 100, Sacramento, CA 95833. *Phone:* 916-830-6320 or toll-free 800-477-1957. *Fax:* 916-830-6344. *Web site:* http://www.artinstitutes.edu/sacramento/.

Visit Petersons.com and enter keywords Art Institute of California-Sacramento

See page 496 for the College Close-Up.

The Art Institute of California–San Diego

San Diego, California

General Proprietary, 4-year, coed **Setting** urban campus **Contact** Director of Admissions, The Art Institute of California–San Diego, 7650 Mission Valley Road, San Diego, CA 92108. *Phone:* 858-598-1200 or toll-free 866-275-2422. *Fax:* 619-291-3206. *Web site:* http://www.artinstitutes.edu/sandiego/.

Visit Petersons.com and enter keywords Art Institute of California-San Diego

See page 498 for the College Close-Up.

The Art Institute of California–San Francisco

San Francisco, California

General Proprietary, comprehensive, coed **Setting** urban campus **Contact** Director of Admissions, The Art Institute of California–San Francisco, 1170 Market Street, San Francisco, CA 94102. *Phone:* 415-865-0198 or toll-free 888-493-3261. *Fax:* 415-863-6344. *Web site:* http://www.artinstitutes.edu/sanfrancisco.

Visit Petersons.com and enter keywords Art Institute of California-San Francisco

See page 500 for the College Close-Up.

The Art Institute of California–Sunnyvale

Sunnyvale, California

General Proprietary, 4-year, coed **Contact** Director of Admissions, The Art Institute of California–Sunnyvale, 1120 Kifer Road, Sunnyvale, CA 94086. *Phone:* 408-962-6400 or toll-free 866-583-7961. *Fax:* 408-962-6498. *Web site:* http://www.artinstitutes.edu/sunnyvale/.

Visit Petersons.com and enter keywords Art Institute of California-Sunnyvale

See page 502 for the College Close-Up.

Azusa Pacific University

Azusa, California

General Independent nondenominational, university, coed **Entrance** Moderately difficult **Setting** 60-acre small-town campus **Total enrollment** 8,539 **Student-faculty ratio** 12:1 **Application deadline** 6/1 (freshmen), 6/1 (transfer) **Freshman admission** 59% were admitted. Average high school GPA 3.62 **Freshman test scores** SAT critical reading scores over 500: 73%; SAT math scores over 500: 66%; SAT critical reading scores over 600: 25%; SAT math scores over 600: 28% **Housing** Yes **Expenses** Tuition & Fees $27,750; Room & Board $8314 **Undergraduates** 14% 25 or older, 1% Native American, 15% Hispanic American, 5% African American, 8% Asian American/Pacific Islander **Academic program** English as a second language, advanced placement, accelerated degree program, honors program, summer session, adult/continuing education programs, internships **Contact** Ms. Lynnette Barnes, Processing Coordinator, Azusa Pacific University, 901 East Alosta Avenue, PO Box 7000, Undergraduate Admissions—7221, Azusa, CA 91702-7000. *Phone:* 626-815-6000 Ext. 3419 or toll-free 800-TALK-APU. *E-mail:* admissions@apu.edu. *Web site:* http://www.apu.edu/.

Bethany University
Scotts Valley, California

General Independent Assemblies of God, comprehensive, coed **Entrance** Minimally difficult **Setting** 40-acre small-town campus **Total enrollment** 502 **Student-faculty ratio** 12:1 **Application deadline** 7/31 (freshmen), 7/31 (transfer) **Freshman admission** 45% were admitted. Average high school GPA 2.5 **Housing** Yes **Expenses** Tuition & Fees $18,850; Room & Board $7450 **Undergraduates** 60% women, 18% part-time, 24% 25 or older, 1% Native American, 18% Hispanic American, 11% African American, 5% Asian American/Pacific Islander **The most frequently chosen baccalaureate fields are** business/marketing, psychology, theology and religious vocations **Academic program** Advanced placement, summer session, internships **Contact** Mr. Dan Mooney, Director of Admissions, Bethany University, 800 Bethany Drive, Scotts Valley, CA 95066-2820. *Phone:* 831-438-3800 Ext. 3900 or toll-free 800-843-9410. *Fax:* 831-438-4517. *E-mail:* info@bethany.edu. *Web site:* http://www.bethany.edu/.

Bethesda Christian University
Anaheim, California

General Independent, comprehensive, coed, affiliated with Full Gospel World Mission **Entrance** Minimally difficult **Setting** suburban campus **Total enrollment** 345 **Application deadline** 8/11 (freshmen) **Freshman admission** 95% were admitted **Undergraduates** 35% 25 or older **Academic program** English as a second language, accelerated degree program, summer session, adult/continuing education programs, internships **Contact** Jacquie Ha, Director of Admission, Bethesda Christian University, 730 North Euclid Street, Anaheim, CA 92801. *Phone:* 714-517-1945. *Fax:* 714-517-1948. *E-mail:* admission@bcu.edu. *Web site:* http://www.bcu.edu/.

Biola University
La Mirada, California

General Independent interdenominational, university, coed **Entrance** Moderately difficult **Setting** 95-acre suburban campus **Total enrollment** 5,893 **Student-faculty ratio** 16:1 **Application deadline** 3/1 (freshmen), 3/1 (transfer) **Freshman admission** 81% were admitted. Average high school GPA 3.51 **Freshman test scores** SAT critical reading scores over 500: 76%; SAT math scores over 500: 72%; ACT scores over 18: 93%; SAT critical reading scores over 600: 33%; SAT math scores over 600: 31%; ACT scores over 24: 54% **Housing** Yes **Expenses** Tuition & Fees $28,044; Room & Board $8367 **Undergraduates** 61% women, 9% part-time, 2% 25 or older, 1% Native American, 12% Hispanic American, 4% African American, 11% Asian American/Pacific Islander **Academic program** English as a second language, advanced placement, accelerated degree program, honors program, summer session, adult/continuing education programs, internships **Contact** Mr. Andre Stephens, Director of Enrollment Management, Biola University, 13800 Biola Avenue, La Mirada, CA 90639. *Phone:* 562-903-4752 or toll-free 800-652-4652. *Fax:* 562-903-4709. *E-mail:* admissions@biola.edu. *Web site:* http://www.biola.edu/.

Brooks Institute
Santa Barbara, California

Contact Admissions Office, Brooks Institute, 27 East Cota Street, Santa Barbara, CA 93101. *Phone:* 805-966-3888 or toll-free 888-276-4999. *Fax:* 805-565-1386. *E-mail:* admissions@brooks.edu. *Web site:* http://www.brooks.edu/.

California Baptist University
Riverside, California

General Independent Southern Baptist, comprehensive, coed **Entrance** Minimally difficult **Setting** 110-acre suburban campus **Total enrollment** 4,105 **Student-faculty ratio** 18:1 **Application deadline** Rolling (freshmen), rolling (transfer) **Freshman admission** 75% were admitted. Average high school GPA 3.4 **Freshman test scores** SAT critical reading scores over 500: 56.2%; SAT math scores over 500: 51.3%; ACT scores over 18: 85.9%; SAT critical reading scores over 600: 13.7%; SAT math scores over 600: 17.7%; ACT scores over 24: 26.9% **Housing** Yes **Expenses** Tuition & Fees $23,266; Room & Board $8170 **Undergraduates** 61% women, 14% part-time, 19% 25 or older, 1% Native American, 19% Hispanic American, 7% African American, 4% Asian American/Pacific Islander **The most frequently chosen baccalaureate fields are** business/marketing, health professions and related sciences, liberal arts/general studies **Academic program** English as a second language, advanced placement, accelerated degree program, honors program, summer session, adult/continuing education programs, internships **Contact** Mr. Allen Johnson, Director, Undergraduate Admissions, California Baptist University, 8432 Magnolia Avenue, Riverside, CA 92504-3297. *Phone:* 951-343-4212 or toll-free 877-228-8866. *Fax:* 951-343-4525. *E-mail:* admissions@calbaptist.edu. *Web site:* http://www.calbaptist.edu/.

California Christian College
Fresno, California

General Independent religious, 4-year, coed **Entrance** Noncompetitive **Setting** 5-acre urban campus **Total enrollment** 28 **Student-faculty ratio** 6:1 **Application deadline** Rolling (freshmen), rolling (transfer) **Freshman admission** Average high school GPA 2.50 **Housing** Yes **Expenses** Tuition & Fees $6840; Room & Board $3850 **Undergraduates** 36% women, 11% part-time, 28% 25 or older, 54% Hispanic American, 7% African American, 4% Asian American/Pacific Islander **The most frequently chosen baccalaureate field is** theology and religious vocations **Academic program** Accelerated degree program, summer session **Contact** Ms. Mallory Breshears, Director of Admissions and Recruitment, California Christian College, 4881 East University Avenue, Fresno, CA 93703-3533. *Phone:* 559-251-4215 Ext. 5571. *E-mail:* cccadmissions@calchristiancollege.org. *Web site:* http://www.calchristiancollege.org/.

California Coast University
Santa Ana, California

Contact Director of Admission, California Coast University, 700 North Main Street, Santa Ana, CA 92701. *Phone:* 888-CCU-UNIV or toll-free 888-CCU-UNIV. *Fax:* 714-547-5777. *E-mail:* admissions@calcoast.edu. *Web site:* http://www.calcoast.edu/.

California College
San Diego, California

Contact Director of Admission, California College, 2820 Camino del Rio South, Suite 300, San Diego, CA 92108. *Phone:* 619-295-5785 or toll-free 800-622-3188. *Web site:* http://www.cc-sd.edu.

California College of the Arts
San Francisco, California

General Independent, comprehensive, coed **Entrance** Moderately difficult **Setting** 4-acre urban campus **Total enrollment** 1,831 **Student-faculty ratio** 8:1 **Application deadline** 2/1 (freshmen), rolling (transfer) **Freshman admission** 75% were admitted. Average high school GPA 3.18 **Freshman test scores** SAT critical reading scores over 500: 67%; SAT math scores over 500: 70%; ACT scores over 18: 100%; SAT critical reading scores over 600: 32%; SAT math scores over 600: 30%; ACT scores over 24: 40% **Housing** Yes **Expenses** Tuition & Fees $33,264;

California College of the Arts (continued)

Room only $6600 **Undergraduates** 61% women, 8% part-time, 22% 25 or older, 1% Native American, 11% Hispanic American, 4% African American, 17% Asian American/Pacific Islander **The most frequently chosen baccalaureate fields are** architecture, English, visual and performing arts **Academic program** English as a second language, advanced placement, self-designed majors, honors program, summer session, internships **Contact** Ms. Robynne Royster, Director of Admissions, California College of the Arts, 1111 Eighth Street, San Francisco, CA 94107. *Phone:* 415-703-9523 Ext. 9532 or toll-free 800-447-1ART. *Fax:* 415-703-9539. *E-mail:* enroll@cca.edu. *Web site:* http://www.cca.edu/.

See page 662 for the College Close-Up.

California Institute of Integral Studies

San Francisco, California

Contact Admissions Department/Student Worker, California Institute of Integral Studies, 1453 Mission Street, San Francisco, CA 94103. *Phone:* 415-575-6156. *Fax:* 415-575-1268. *E-mail:* info@ciis.edu. *Web site:* http://www.ciis.edu/.

California Institute of Technology

Pasadena, California

General Independent, university, coed **Entrance** Most difficult **Setting** 124-acre suburban campus **Total enrollment** 2,130 **Student-faculty ratio** 3:1 **Application deadline** 1/1 (freshmen), 2/15 (transfer) **Freshman admission** 15% were admitted **Freshman test scores** SAT critical reading scores over 500: 100%; SAT math scores over 500: 100%; ACT scores over 18: 100%; SAT critical reading scores over 600: 98.37%; SAT math scores over 600: 100%; ACT scores over 24: 100% **Housing** Yes **Expenses** Tuition & Fees $34,437; Room & Board $10,146 **Undergraduates** 38% women, 7% Hispanic American, 1% African American, 40% Asian American/Pacific Islander **The most frequently chosen baccalaureate fields are** engineering, mathematics, physical sciences **Academic program** English as a second language, self-designed majors **Contact** Mr. Ray Prado, Acting Director of Admissions, California Institute of Technology, 355 South Holliston, MC 1-94, Pasadena, CA 91125. *Phone:* 626-395-6341. *Fax:* 626-683-3026. *E-mail:* ray@admissions.caltech.edu. *Web site:* http://www.caltech.edu/.

California Institute of the Arts

Valencia, California

General Independent, comprehensive, coed **Entrance** Very difficult **Setting** 60-acre suburban campus **Total enrollment** 1,392 **Student-faculty ratio** 7:1 **Application deadline** 1/5 (freshmen), 1/5 (transfer) **Freshman admission** 33% were admitted **Housing** Yes **Expenses** Tuition & Fees $36,742; Room & Board $9293 **Undergraduates** 49% women, 1% part-time, 10% 25 or older, 1% Native American, 12% Hispanic American, 8% African American, 12% Asian American/Pacific Islander **The most frequently chosen baccalaureate field is** visual and performing arts **Academic program** Advanced placement, self-designed majors, internships **Contact** Molly Ryan, Director of Admissions, California Institute of the Arts, 24700 McBean Parkway, Valencia, CA 91355-2340. *Phone:* 661-255-1050 or toll-free 800-545-2787. *Fax:* 661-253-7710. *E-mail:* admiss@calarts.edu. *Web site:* http://www.calarts.edu/.

Visit Petersons.com and enter keywords California Institute

California Intercontinental University

Diamond Bar, California

Contact Director of Admission, California Intercontinental University, 1470 Valley Vista Drive, Suite 150, Diamond Bar, CA 91765. *Phone:* 909-396-6090 or toll-free 866-687-2258. *E-mail:* info@caluniversity.com. *Web site:* http://caluniversity.edu/.

California Lutheran University

Thousand Oaks, California

General Independent Lutheran, comprehensive, coed **Entrance** Moderately difficult **Setting** 290-acre suburban campus **Total enrollment** 3,714 **Student-faculty ratio** 15:1 **Application deadline** 3/15 (freshmen) **Freshman admission** 62% were admitted. Average high school GPA 3.6 **Freshman test scores** SAT critical reading scores over 500: 73%; SAT math scores over 500: 79%; SAT critical reading scores over 600: 21%; SAT math scores over 600: 32% **Housing** Yes **Expenses** Tuition & Fees $31,000; Room & Board $10,580 **Undergraduates** 61% women, 3% part-time, 4% 25 or older, 1% Native American, 16% Hispanic American, 4% African American, 5% Asian American/Pacific Islander **The most frequently chosen baccalaureate fields are** business/marketing, communications/journalism, social sciences **Academic program** Advanced placement, accelerated degree program, self-designed majors, honors program, summer session, adult/continuing education programs, internships **Contact** Mr. Matthew Ward, Dean of Undergraduate Enrollment, California Lutheran University, Office of Admission, #1350, Thousand Oaks, CA 91360. *Phone:* 805-493-3135 or toll-free 877-258-3678. *Fax:* 805-493-3114. *E-mail:* cluadm@clunet.edu. *Web site:* http://www.callutheran.edu/.

Visit Petersons.com and enter keywords California Lutheran

See page 664 for the College Close-Up.

California Maritime Academy

Vallejo, California

General State-supported, 4-year, coed **Entrance** Moderately difficult **Setting** 64-acre suburban campus **Total enrollment** 823 **Student-faculty ratio** 22:1 **Freshman admission** 73% were admitted **Housing** Yes **Expenses** Tuition & Fees: state resident $4400, nonresident $14,570; Room & Board $9750 **Undergraduates** 14% women, 1% Native American, 8% Hispanic American, 2% African American, 10% Asian American/Pacific Islander **Academic program** Advanced placement, summer session, internships **Contact** Marc McGee, Director of Admission and Enrollment Services, California Maritime Academy, 200 Maritime Academy Drive, Vallejo, CA 94590. *Phone:* 707-654-1330 or toll-free 800-561-1945. *Fax:* 707-654-1336. *E-mail:* admission@csum.edu. *Web site:* http://www.csum.edu/.

California Miramar University

San Diego, California

Contact California Miramar University, 9750 Miramar Road, Suite 180, San Diego, CA 92126. *Phone:* toll-free 877-570-5678. *Web site:* http://www.calmu.edu/.

California National University for Advanced Studies

Northridge, California

Contact Ms. Stephanie Smith, Registrar, California National University for Advanced Studies, Admissions, 8550 Balboa Boulevard, Suite 210, Northridge, CA 91325. *Phone:* 818-830-2411 or toll-free 800-744-2822 (in-state); 800-782-2422 (out-of-state). *Fax:* 818-830-2418. *E-mail:* cnuadms@mail.cnuas.edu. *Web site:* http://www.cnuas.edu/.

California Polytechnic State University, San Luis Obispo

San Luis Obispo, California

General State-supported, comprehensive, coed **Entrance** Moderately difficult **Setting** 6,000-acre small-town campus **Total enrollment** 19,325 **Student-faculty ratio** 19:1 **Application deadline** 11/30 (freshmen), 11/30 (transfer) **Freshman admission** 37% were admitted. Average high school GPA 3.81 **Freshman test scores** SAT critical reading scores over 500: 87%; SAT math scores over 500: 95%; ACT scores over 18: 99%;

CALIFORNIA LUTHERAN UNIVERSITY

Learn local. Think global. CLU

California Lutheran University is a comprehensive institution offering undergraduate and graduate degrees in the liberal arts and sciences. Our mission is to educate leaders for a global society who are strong in character and judgment, confident in their identity and vocation, and committed to service and justice.

Undergraduate Majors
- 37 majors and 31 minors
- Academic programs completed in four years
- Among the best student housing in Southern California
- 95 percent success rate into graduate programs and professions
- Financial aid and scholarships available to qualified students
- CLU Guarantee – allows students who are admitted to one of four UC schools to attend CLU for the cost of attending a public university

Ranked by U.S. News & World Report as one of the top 20 western regional universities.

Office of Admission
60 W. Olsen Road #1350
Thousand Oaks, CA 91360
(805) 493-3135 • 1-877-CLU-FOR-U
Admissions@callutheran.edu

www.callutheran.edu/admission

SAT critical reading scores over 600: 42%; SAT math scores over 600: 65.5%; ACT scores over 24: 78.5% **Housing** Yes **Expenses** Tuition & Fees: state resident $6198, nonresident $17,358; Room & Board $9623 **Undergraduates** 44% women, 4% part-time, 4% 25 or older, 1% Native American, 12% Hispanic American, 1% African American, 11% Asian American/Pacific Islander **The most frequently chosen baccalaureate fields are** business/marketing, agriculture, engineering **Academic program** English as a second language, advanced placement, honors program, summer session, internships **Contact** Mr. James Maraviglia, Assistant Vice President of Admissions, Recruitment, and Financial Aid, California Polytechnic State University, San Luis Obispo, Admissions Office, 1 Grand Avenue, San Luis Obispo, CA 93407-0031. *Phone:* 805-756-2311. *Fax:* 805-756-5911. *E-mail:* admissions@calpoly.edu. *Web site:* http://www.calpoly.edu/.

California State Polytechnic University, Pomona

Pomona, California

General State-supported, comprehensive, coed **Entrance** Moderately difficult **Setting** 1,400-acre urban campus **Total enrollment** 22,273 **Student-faculty ratio** 25:1 **Application deadline** 11/30 (freshmen), 11/30 (transfer) **Freshman admission** 61% were admitted. Average high school GPA 3.36 **Freshman test scores** SAT critical reading scores over 500: 58.13%; SAT math scores over 500: 71.53%; ACT scores over 18: 90.32%; SAT critical reading scores over 600: 16.01%; SAT math scores over 600: 34.4%; ACT scores over 24: 45.23% **Housing** Yes **Expenses** Tuition & Fees: state resident $4551, nonresident $15,711; Room & Board $9570 **Undergraduates** 43% women, 17% part-time, 17% 25 or older, 0.3% Native American, 32% Hispanic American, 3% African American, 27% Asian American/Pacific Islander **The most frequently chosen baccalaureate fields are** business/marketing, biological/life sciences, engineering **Academic program** English as a second language, advanced placement, honors program, summer session, adult/continuing education programs, internships **Contact** Mr. Scott J. Duncan, Director, Admissions, California State Polytechnic University, Pomona, 3801 West Temple Avenue, Pomona, CA 91768-2557. *Phone:* 909-869-3258. *Fax:* 909-869-4529. *E-mail:* admissions@csupomona.edu. *Web site:* http://www.csupomona.edu/.

California State University, Bakersfield

Bakersfield, California

General State-supported, comprehensive, coed **Entrance** Moderately difficult **Setting** 575-acre urban campus **Total enrollment** 8,003 **Application deadline** 3/1 (freshmen), rolling (transfer) **Freshman admission** 70% were admitted. Average high school GPA 3.03 **Freshman test scores** SAT critical reading scores over 500: 26.5%; SAT math scores over 500: 30.4%; ACT scores over 18: 60%; SAT critical reading scores over 600: 4.7%; SAT math scores over 600: 7.9%; ACT scores over 24: 11.3% **Housing** Yes **Expenses** Tuition & Fees: state resident $4383, nonresident $14,553; Room & Board $7137 **Undergraduates** 65% women, 15% part-time, 23% 25 or older **The most frequently chosen baccalaureate fields are** business/marketing, health professions and related sciences, liberal arts/general studies **Academic program** English as a second language, advanced placement, accelerated degree program, self-designed majors, honors program, summer session, adult/continuing education programs, internships **Contact** Dr. Kendyl Magnuson, Associate Dean of Admissions and Records, California State University, Bakersfield, 9001 Stockdale Highway, Balersfield, CA 93311-1099. *Phone:* 661-664-3036 or toll-free 800-788-2782. *E-mail:* admissions@csub.edu. *Web site:* http://www.csub.edu/.

California State University Channel Islands

Camarillo, California

General State-supported, comprehensive, coed **Entrance** Noncompetitive **Setting** suburban campus **Total enrollment** 3,599 **Student-faculty ratio** 15:1 **Freshman admission** 53% were admitted. Average high school GPA 3.22 **Housing** Yes **Expenses** Tuition & Fees: state resident $3482, nonresident $13,652; Room & Board $10,200 **Undergraduates** 25% 25 or older, 1% Native American, 26% Hispanic American, 3% African American, 7% Asian American/Pacific Islander **The most frequently chosen baccalaureate fields are** liberal arts/ general studies, business/marketing, psychology **Academic program** Advanced placement **Contact** Ms. Ginger Reyes, California State University Channel Islands, One University Drive, Camarillo, CA 93012. *Phone:* 805-437-8520. *Fax:* 805-437-8519. *E-mail:* prospective.student@csuci.edu. *Web site:* http://www.csuci.edu/.

California State University, Chico

Chico, California

General State-supported, comprehensive, coed **Entrance** Moderately difficult **Setting** 119-acre small-town campus **Total enrollment** 17,095 **Student-faculty ratio** 23:1 **Application deadline** 11/30 (freshmen), 11/30 (transfer) **Freshman admission** 88% were admitted. Average high school GPA 3.12 **Freshman test scores** SAT critical reading scores over 500: 52%; SAT math scores over 500: 58%; ACT scores over 18: 85%; SAT critical reading scores over 600: 11%; SAT math scores over 600: 16%; ACT scores over 24: 28% **Housing** Yes **Expenses** Tuition & Fees: state resident $5336, nonresident $16,496; Room & Board $9404 **Undergraduates** 52% women, 9% part-time, 12% 25 or older, 1% Native American, 14% Hispanic American, 2% African American, 5% Asian American/Pacific Islander **The most frequently chosen baccalaureate fields are** business/marketing, social sciences, visual and performing arts **Academic program** English as a second language, advanced placement, self-designed majors, honors program, summer session, adult/continuing education programs, internships **Contact** Allan Bee, Director of Admissions, California State University, Chico, 400 West First Street, Chico, CA 95929-0722. *Phone:* 530-898-4428 or toll-free 800-542-4426. *Fax:* 530-898-6456. *E-mail:* info@csuchico.edu. *Web site:* http://www.csuchico.edu/.

California State University, Dominguez Hills

Carson, California

General State-supported, comprehensive, coed **Entrance** Moderately difficult **Setting** 350-acre urban campus **Total enrollment** 14,477 **Student-faculty ratio** 23:1 **Application deadline** Rolling (freshmen), rolling (transfer) **Freshman admission** 84% were admitted. Average high school GPA 2.9 **Freshman test scores** SAT critical reading scores over 500: 14.18%; SAT math scores over 500: 16.34%; ACT scores over 18: 39.2%; SAT critical reading scores over 600: .72%; SAT math scores over 600: 2.4%; ACT scores over 24: 3.3% **Housing** Yes **Expenses** Tuition & Fees: state resident $4645, nonresident $15,805; Room & Board $10,085 **Undergraduates** 66% women, 38% part-time, 39% 25 or older, 0.3% Native American, 40% Hispanic American, 27% African American, 9% Asian American/Pacific Islander **The most frequently chosen baccalaureate fields are** business/marketing, health professions and related sciences, liberal arts/general studies **Academic program** English as a second language, advanced placement, self-designed majors, honors program, summer session, adult/continuing education programs, internships **Contact** Information Center, California State University, Dominguez Hills, 1000 East Victoria Street, Carson, CA 90747-0001. *Phone:* 310-243-3696. *Fax:* 310-243-3609. *E-mail:* gball@csudh.edu. *Web site:* http://www.csudh.edu/.

California State University, East Bay

Hayward, California

General State-supported, comprehensive, coed **Entrance** Moderately difficult **Setting** 343-acre suburban campus **Total enrollment** 14,749 **Student-faculty ratio** 24:1 **Application deadline** 11/30 (freshmen), 11/11 (transfer) **Freshman admission** 73% were admitted. Average high school GPA 3 **Freshman test scores** SAT critical reading scores over 500: 30%; SAT math scores over 500: 35.1%; ACT scores over 18: 57.8%; SAT critical reading scores over 600: 6%; SAT math scores over 600: 8.5%; ACT scores over 24: 14.1% **Housing** Yes **Expenses** Tuition & Fees: state resident $4872, nonresident $18,672; Room & Board $10,029 **Undergraduates** 61% women, 17% part-time, 35% 25 or older, 0.5% Native American, 17% Hispanic American, 12% African American, 26% Asian American/Pacific Islander **The most frequently chosen baccalaureate fields are** business/marketing, health professions and related sciences, social sciences **Academic program** English as a second language, advanced placement, accelerated degree program, self-designed majors, honors program, summer session, adult/continuing education programs, internships **Contact** Dr. Colin Ormsby, Interim Executive Director of Undergraduate Admissions, California State University, East Bay, 25800 Carlos Bee Boulevard, Hayward, CA 94542-3000. *Phone:* 510-885-2784. *Fax:* 510-885-4059. *E-mail:* admissions@csueeastbay.edu. *Web site:* http://www.csueastbay.edu/.

California State University, Fresno

Fresno, California

General State-supported, comprehensive, coed **Entrance** Minimally difficult **Setting** 1,399-acre urban campus **Total enrollment** 21,500 **Student-faculty ratio** 20:1 **Application deadline** 11/30 (freshmen), 11/30 (transfer) **Freshman admission** 72% were admitted. Average high school GPA 3.28 **Freshman test scores** SAT critical reading scores over 500: 34.4%; SAT math scores over 500: 39.5%; ACT scores over 18: 67%; SAT critical reading scores over 600: 9.1%; SAT math scores over 600: 10.9%; ACT scores over 24: 18.4% **Housing** Yes **Expenses** Tuition & Fees: state resident $3687, nonresident $13,857; Room & Board $8590 **Undergraduates** 57% women, 15% part-time, 17% 25 or older, 1% Native American, 35% Hispanic American, 6% African American, 16% Asian American/Pacific Islander **The most frequently chosen baccalaureate fields are** business/marketing, health professions and related sciences, social sciences **Academic program** English as a second language, advanced placement, accelerated degree program, self-designed majors, honors program, summer session, adult/continuing education programs, internships **Contact** Mr. Andy Hernandez, Admissions Officer, California State University, Fresno, 5150 North Maple Avenue, M/S JA 57, Fresno, CA 93740-8026. *Phone:* 559-278-6115. *Fax:* 559-278-4812. *E-mail:* andyhe@csufresno.edu. *Web site:* http://www.csufresno.edu/.

California State University, Fullerton

Fullerton, California

General State-supported, comprehensive, coed **Entrance** Moderately difficult **Setting** 225-acre suburban campus **Total enrollment** 36,262 **Student-faculty ratio** 26:1 **Application deadline** 11/30 (freshmen), rolling (transfer) **Freshman admission** 55% were admitted. Average high school GPA 3.27 **Freshman test scores** SAT critical reading scores over 500: 46%; SAT math scores over 500: 53%; ACT scores over 18: 82%; SAT critical reading scores over 600: 10%; SAT math scores over 600: 16%; ACT scores over 24: 23% **Housing** Yes **Expenses** Tuition & Fees: state resident $4662, nonresident $20,484; Room & Board $9242 **Undergraduates** 58% women, 25% part-time, 24% 25 or older, 0.5% Native American, 31% Hispanic American, 3% African American, 22% Asian American/Pacific Islander **The most frequently chosen baccalaureate fields are** business/marketing, communications/journalism, education **Academic program** English as a second language, advanced placement, self-designed majors, honors program, summer session, adult/continuing education programs, internships **Contact** Ms. Nancy J.

Dority, Assistant Vice President of Enrollment Services, California State University, Fullerton, Office of Admissions and Records, PO Box 34080, Fullerton, CA 92834-9480. *Phone:* 657-278-2370. *Fax:* 657-278-2356. *E-mail:* admissions@fullerton.edu. *Web site:* http://www.fullerton.edu/.

California State University, Long Beach

Long Beach, California

General State-supported, comprehensive, coed **Entrance** Moderately difficult **Setting** 320-acre suburban campus **Total enrollment** 35,557 **Student-faculty ratio** 21:1 **Application deadline** 11/30 (freshmen), 11/30 (transfer) **Freshman admission** 32% were admitted. Average high school GPA 3.42 **Freshman test scores** SAT critical reading scores over 500: 52.99%; SAT math scores over 500: 60.54%; ACT scores over 18: 79.6%; SAT critical reading scores over 600: 13.3%; SAT math scores over 600: 24.24%; ACT scores over 24: 30.74% **Housing** Yes **Expenses** Tuition & Fees: state resident $4606, nonresident $15,766; Room & Board $11,038 **Undergraduates** 59% women, 19% part-time, 18% 25 or older, 1% Native American, 29% Hispanic American, 5% African American, 24% Asian American/Pacific Islander **The most frequently chosen baccalaureate fields are** business/marketing, English, visual and performing arts **Academic program** English as a second language, advanced placement, accelerated degree program, self-designed majors, honors program, summer session, adult/continuing education programs, internships **Contact** Mr. Thomas Enders, Director of Enrollment Services, California State University, Long Beach, Brotman Hall, 1250 Bellflower Boulevard, Long Beach, CA 90840. *Phone:* 562-985-4641. *Web site:* http://www.csulb.edu/.

California State University, Los Angeles

Los Angeles, California

General State-supported, comprehensive, coed **Entrance** Moderately difficult **Setting** 173-acre urban campus **Total enrollment** 20,619 **Student-faculty ratio** 21:1 **Application deadline** 6/15 (freshmen), 6/15 (transfer) **Freshman admission** 68% were admitted. Average high school GPA 3.1 **Freshman test scores** SAT critical reading scores over 500: 19.5%; SAT math scores over 500: 23.8%; ACT scores over 18: 46.3%; SAT critical reading scores over 600: 1.9%; SAT math scores over 600: 4.2%; ACT scores over 24: 8.9% **Housing** Yes **Expenses** Tuition & Fees: state resident $4640, nonresident $13,568; Room & Board $9105 **Undergraduates** 60% women, 25% part-time, 30% 25 or older, 0.1% Native American, 49% Hispanic American, 7% African American, 18% Asian American/Pacific Islander **The most frequently chosen baccalaureate fields are** business/marketing, public administration and social services, social sciences **Academic program** English as a second language, advanced placement, accelerated degree program, self-designed majors, honors program, summer session, adult/continuing education programs, internships **Contact** Mr. Vince Lopez, Director of Outreach and Recruitment, California State University, Los Angeles, 5151 State University Drive, Los Angeles, CA 90032-8530. *Phone:* 323-343-3839. *E-mail:* admission@calstatela.edu. *Web site:* http://www.calstatela.edu/.

California State University, Monterey Bay

Seaside, California

General State-supported, comprehensive, coed **Entrance** Moderately difficult **Setting** 1,387-acre small-town campus **Total enrollment** 4,688 **Student-faculty ratio** 27:1 **Application deadline** 11/30 (freshmen), 11/30 (transfer) **Freshman admission** 81% were admitted. Average high school GPA 3.11 **Freshman test scores** SAT critical reading scores over 500: 48%; SAT math scores over 500: 47%; ACT scores over 18: 77%; SAT critical reading scores over 600: 10%; SAT math scores over 600: 11%; ACT scores over 24: 24% **Housing** Yes **Expenses** Tuition & Fees: state resident $4517, nonresident $15,677; Room & Board $8290 **Undergraduates** 59% women, 8% part-time, 18% 25 or older, 1% Native American, 26% Hispanic American, 4% African American, 6% Asian American/Pacific Islander **The most frequently chosen baccalaureate fields are** business/marketing, liberal arts/general studies, social sciences **Academic program** Advanced placement, self-designed majors, summer session, adult/continuing education programs, internships **Contact** Mr. John Larsen, Assistant Director of Recruitment, California State University, Monterey Bay, 100 Campus Center, Seaside, CA 93955. *Phone:* 831-582-3738. *Fax:* 831-582-3783. *E-mail:* admissions@csumb.edu. *Web site:* http://www.csumb.edu/.

California State University, Northridge

Northridge, California

General State-supported, comprehensive, coed **Entrance** Moderately difficult **Setting** 356-acre urban campus **Total enrollment** 35,198 **Student-faculty ratio** 24:1 **Application deadline** 11/30 (freshmen), 11/30 (transfer) **Freshman admission** 73% were admitted. Average high school GPA 3.13 **Freshman test scores** SAT critical reading scores over 500: 37%; SAT math scores over 500: 38.1%; SAT critical reading scores over 600: 7.3%; SAT math scores over 600: 11.2% **Housing** Yes **Expenses** Tuition & Fees: state resident $3702, nonresident $13,872; Room & Board $10,152 **Undergraduates** 57% women, 26% part-time, 22% 25 or older, 0.3% Native American, 32% Hispanic American, 8% African American, 12% Asian American/Pacific Islander **Academic program** English as a second language, advanced placement, self-designed majors, summer session, adult/continuing education programs, internships **Contact** Ms. Mary Baxton, Associate Director of Admissions and Records, California State University, Northridge, 18111 Nordhoff Street, Northridge, CA 91330-8207. *Phone:* 818-677-3777. *Fax:* 818-677-3766. *E-mail:* admissions.records@csun.edu. *Web site:* http://www.csun.edu/.

California State University, Sacramento

Sacramento, California

General State-supported, comprehensive, coed **Entrance** Moderately difficult **Setting** 300-acre urban campus **Total enrollment** 29,241 **Student-faculty ratio** 26:1 **Freshman admission** 80% were admitted. Average high school GPA 3.19 **Freshman test scores** SAT critical reading scores over 500: 37.86%; SAT math scores over 500: 44.93%; ACT scores over 18: 71.84%; SAT critical reading scores over 600: 7.2%; SAT math scores over 600: 11.74%; ACT scores over 24: 19.83% **Housing** Yes **Expenses** Tuition & Fees: state resident $3048, nonresident $13,218; Room & Board $9428 **Undergraduates** 57% women, 19% part-time, 24% 25 or older, 1% Native American, 16% Hispanic American, 7% African American, 20% Asian American/Pacific Islander **The most frequently chosen baccalaureate fields are** business/marketing, security and protective services, social sciences **Academic program** English as a second language, advanced placement, accelerated degree program, self-designed majors, honors program, summer session, internships **Contact** Mr. Emiliano Diaz, Director of University Outreach Services, California State University, Sacramento, 6000 J Street, Lassen Hall, Sacramento, CA 95819-6048. *Phone:* 916-278-3901. *Fax:* 916-278-5603. *E-mail:* admissions@csus.edu. *Web site:* http://www.csus.edu/.

California State University, San Bernardino

San Bernardino, California

General State-supported, comprehensive, coed **Entrance** Moderately difficult **Setting** 430-acre suburban campus **Total enrollment** 17,842 **Student-faculty ratio** 21:1 **Application deadline** Rolling (freshmen), rolling (transfer) **Freshman admission** 70% were admitted. Average

California State University, San Bernardino (continued)

high school GPA 3.14 **Freshman test scores** SAT critical reading scores over 500: 27.4%; SAT math scores over 500: 28%; ACT scores over 18: 56.2%; SAT critical reading scores over 600: 3.7%; SAT math scores over 600: 5.2%; ACT scores over 24: 9.1% **Housing** Yes **Expenses** Tuition & Fees: state resident $5373, nonresident $16,818 **Undergraduates** 64% women, 15% part-time, 25% 25 or older, 1% Native American, 43% Hispanic American, 11% African American, 8% Asian American/Pacific Islander **The most frequently chosen baccalaureate fields are** business/marketing, liberal arts/general studies, social sciences **Academic program** Accelerated degree program, self-designed majors, honors program, summer session, internships **Contact** Ms. Julie Mellen, Assistant Director, California State University, San Bernardino, 5500 University Parkway, University Hall, Room 107, San Bernardino, CA 92407-2397. *Phone:* 909-537-5211. *Fax:* 909-537-7034. *E-mail:* moreinfo@mail.csusb.edu. *Web site:* http://www.csusb.edu/.

California State University, San Marcos

San Marcos, California

General State-supported, comprehensive, coed **Entrance** Moderately difficult **Setting** 304-acre suburban campus **Total enrollment** 9,745 **Student-faculty ratio** 25:1 **Application deadline** 11/30 (freshmen), 11/30 (transfer) **Freshman admission** 71% were admitted. Average high school GPA 3.15 **Freshman test scores** SAT critical reading scores over 500: 40.7%; SAT math scores over 500: 45.2%; SAT critical reading scores over 600: 7.2%; SAT math scores over 600: 10% **Housing** Yes **Expenses** Tuition & Fees: state resident $4650, nonresident $13,786; Room only $6250 **Undergraduates** 61% women, 30% part-time, 23% 25 or older **Academic program** English as a second language, advanced placement, self-designed majors, summer session, adult/continuing education programs, internships **Contact** Darren Bush, Director of Admissions, California State University, San Marcos, 333 South Twin Oaks Valley Road, San Marcos, CA 92096-0001. *Phone:* 760-750-4848. *Fax:* 760-750-3248. *E-mail:* apply@csusm.edu. *Web site:* http://www.csusm.edu/.

California State University, Stanislaus

Turlock, California

General State-supported, comprehensive, coed **Entrance** Moderately difficult **Setting** 228-acre small-town campus **Total enrollment** 8,586 **Student-faculty ratio** 21:1 **Application deadline** 3/1 (freshmen), rolling (transfer) **Freshman admission** 37% were admitted. Average high school GPA 3.3 **Freshman test scores** SAT critical reading scores over 500: 33.1%; SAT math scores over 500: 38.8%; ACT scores over 18: 70.4%; SAT critical reading scores over 600: 7.4%; SAT math scores over 600: 10.5%; ACT scores over 24: 16.3% **Housing** Yes **Expenses** Tuition & Fees: state resident $4840, nonresident $16,000; Room & Board $8880 **Undergraduates** 65% women, 31% part-time, 23% 25 or older, 1% Native American, 32% Hispanic American, 3% African American, 11% Asian American/Pacific Islander **The most frequently chosen baccalaureate fields are** business/marketing, liberal arts/general studies, social sciences **Academic program** English as a second language, advanced placement, self-designed majors, honors program, summer session, adult/continuing education programs, internships **Contact** Student Outreach, California State University, Stanislaus, One University Circle, Turlock, CA 95382. *Phone:* 209-667-3122 or toll-free 800-300-7420. *Fax:* 209-667-3788. *E-mail:* outreach_help_desk@csustan.edu. *Web site:* http://www.csustan.edu/.

Chapman University

Orange, California

General Independent, comprehensive, coed, affiliated with Christian Church (Disciples of Christ) **Entrance** Very difficult **Setting** 78-acre suburban campus **Total enrollment** 6,398 **Student-faculty ratio** 14:1 **Application deadline** 1/15 (freshmen), 3/1 (transfer) **Freshman admission** 56% were admitted. Average high school GPA 3.67 **Freshman test scores** SAT critical reading scores over 500: 97%; SAT math scores over 500: 96%; ACT scores over 18: 100%; SAT critical reading scores over 600: 50%; SAT math scores over 600: 52%; ACT scores over 24: 83% **Housing** Yes **Expenses** Tuition & Fees $38,524; Room & Board $12,957 **Undergraduates** 58% women, 5% part-time, 3% 25 or older, 1% Native American, 10% Hispanic American, 2% African American, 9% Asian American/Pacific Islander **The most frequently chosen baccalaureate fields are** business/marketing, communications/journalism, visual and performing arts **Academic program** English as a second language, advanced placement, self-designed majors, honors program, summer session, adult/continuing education programs, internships **Contact** Ms. Marcela Mejia-Martinez, Assistant Vice Chancellor and Chief Admission Officer, Chapman University, One University Drive, Orange, CA 92866. *Phone:* 714-997-6711 or toll-free 888-CUAPPLY. *Fax:* 714-997-6713. *E-mail:* admit@chapman.edu. *Web site:* http://www.chapman.edu/.

Visit Petersons.com and enter keyword Chapman

See page 698 for the College Close-Up.

Charles Drew University of Medicine and Science

Los Angeles, California

General Independent, comprehensive, coed **Entrance** Moderately difficult **Setting** urban campus **Total enrollment** 261 **Student-faculty ratio** 9:1 **Application deadline** 4/30 (freshmen), 4/30 (transfer) **Freshman admission** 21% were admitted **Housing** Yes **Expenses** Tuition & Fees $11,232; Room & Board $10,872 **Undergraduates** 62% women, 45% part-time, 1% Native American, 20% Hispanic American, 34% African American, 18% Asian American/Pacific Islander **The most frequently chosen baccalaureate field is** health professions and related sciences **Academic program** Internships **Contact** Ms. Yvette Lane, Associate Director, Student Service, Charles Drew University of Medicine and Science, 1731 East 120th Street, Los Angeles, CA 90059. *Phone:* 323-563-4922. *Fax:* 323-563-4923. *E-mail:* yvettelane@cdrewu.edu. *Web site:* http://www.cdrewu.edu/.

Claremont McKenna College

Claremont, California

General Independent, comprehensive, coed **Entrance** Most difficult **Setting** 50-acre small-town campus **Total enrollment** 1,237 **Student-faculty ratio** 9:1 **Application deadline** 1/2 (freshmen), 4/1 (transfer) **Freshman admission** 18% were admitted **Freshman test scores** SAT critical reading scores over 500: 100%; SAT math scores over 500: 100%; SAT critical reading scores over 600: 93.59%; SAT math scores over 600: 91.88% **Housing** Yes **Expenses** Tuition & Fees $38,745; Room & Board $12,525 **Undergraduates** 45% women, 0.1% part-time, 2% 25 or older, 0.2% Native American, 9% Hispanic American, 3% African American, 12% Asian American/Pacific Islander **The most frequently chosen baccalaureate fields are** psychology, interdisciplinary studies, social sciences **Academic program** English as a second language, advanced placement, self-designed majors, internships **Contact** Mr. Richard C. Vos, Vice President/Dean of Admission and Financial Aid, Claremont McKenna College, 890 Columbia Avenue, Claremont, CA91711. *Phone:* 909-621-8088. *Fax:* 909-621-8516. *E-mail:* admission@claremontmckenna.edu. *Web site:* http://www.claremontmckenna.edu/.

Cleveland Chiropractic College–Los Angeles Campus

Los Angeles, California

General Independent, comprehensive, coed **Entrance** Minimally difficult **Setting** urban campus **Total enrollment** 346 **Student-faculty ratio** 7:1 **Application deadline** 8/29 (freshmen), 8/29 (transfer) **Freshman admission** 67% were admitted. Average high school GPA 3.1

Housing No **Expenses** Tuition & Fees $6735 **Undergraduates** 42% women, 29% part-time, 62% 25 or older, 8% Hispanic American, 8% African American, 21% Asian American/Pacific Islander **The most frequently chosen baccalaureate field is** health professions and related sciences **Academic program** Advanced placement, accelerated degree program, summer session, adult/continuing education programs **Contact** Mr. Brian Kane, Director of Admissions, Cleveland Chiropractic College–Los Angeles Campus, 590 North Vermont, Los Angeles, CA 90004. *Phone:* 323-906-2162 or toll-free 800-446-CCLA. *Fax:* 323-906-2094. *E-mail:* la.admissions@cleveland.edu. *Web site:* http://www.clevelandchiropractic.edu/.

Cogswell Polytechnical College

Sunnyvale, California

General Independent, 4-year, coed, primarily men **Entrance** Moderately difficult **Setting** 2-acre suburban campus **Total enrollment** 199 **Student-faculty ratio** 6:1 **Application deadline** 3/1 (freshmen), 3/1 (transfer) **Freshman admission** 94% were admitted. Average high school GPA 3.04 **Freshman test scores** SAT critical reading scores over 500: 88%; SAT math scores over 500: 75%; SAT critical reading scores over 600: 38%; SAT math scores over 600: 38% **Housing** Yes **Expenses** Tuition & Fees $18,036; Room & Board $10,872 **Undergraduates** 16% women, 43% part-time, 20% 25 or older, 12% Hispanic American, 4% African American, 11% Asian American/Pacific Islander **The most frequently chosen baccalaureate fields are** security and protective services, visual and performing arts **Academic program** Advanced placement, summer session, internships **Contact** Mr. Brandace King, Assistant Director of Admissions, Cogswell Polytechnical College, 1175 Bordeaux Drive, Sunnyvale, CA 94089-1299. *Phone:* 408-541-0100 Ext. 147 or toll-free 800-264-7955. *Fax:* 408-747-0764. *E-mail:* bking@cogswell.edu. *Web site:* http://www.cogswell.edu/.

The Colburn School Conservatory of Music

Los Angeles, California

General Independent, 4-year, coed **Entrance** Most difficult **Setting** urban campus **Total enrollment** 114 **Student-faculty ratio** 4:1 **Application deadline** 1/15 (freshmen), 1/15 (transfer) **Freshman admission** 17% were admitted **Housing** Yes **Expenses** Tuition & Fees $0; Room & Board $0 **Undergraduates** 55% women **The most frequently chosen baccalaureate field is** visual and performing arts **Academic program** English as a second language **Contact** Ms. Kathleen Tesar, Associate Dean for Admissions and Records, The Colburn School Conservatory of Music, 200 South Grand Avenue, Los Angeles, CA 90012. *Phone:* 213-621-4534. *Fax:* 213-625-0371. *E-mail:* admissions@colburnschool.edu. *Web site:* http://www.colburnschool.edu/.

Visit Petersons.com and enter keyword Colburn

Coleman University

San Diego, California

General Independent, comprehensive, coed **Entrance** Moderately difficult **Setting** 3-acre suburban campus **Total enrollment** 488 **Application deadline** 8/1 (freshmen), rolling (transfer) **Freshman admission** 100% were admitted **Housing** No **Undergraduates** 64% 25 or older **Academic program** Accelerated degree program, summer session **Contact** Admissions Department, Coleman University, 7380 Parkway Drive, La Mesa, CA 91942-1532. *Phone:* 619-465-3990. *E-mail:* jschafer@cts.com. *Web site:* http://www.coleman.edu/.

Columbia College Hollywood

Tarzana, California

Contact Carmen Munoz, Admissions Director, Columbia College Hollywood, 18618 Oxnard Street, Tarzana, CA 91356. *Phone:* 818-345-8414 or toll-free 800-785-0585. *Fax:* 818-345-9053. *E-mail:* admissions@columbiacollege.edu. *Web site:* http://www.columbiacollege.edu/.

Concordia University

Irvine, California

General Independent, comprehensive, coed, affiliated with Lutheran Church–Missouri Synod **Entrance** Moderately difficult **Setting** 70-acre suburban campus **Total enrollment** 2,564 **Student-faculty ratio** 19:1 **Application deadline** Rolling (freshmen), rolling (transfer) **Freshman admission** 62% were admitted. Average high school GPA 3.5 **Freshman test scores** SAT critical reading scores over 500: 59.3%; SAT math scores over 500: 57.1%; ACT scores over 18: 93.8%; SAT critical reading scores over 600: 16.4%; SAT math scores over 600: 17.3%; ACT scores over 24: 36.3% **Housing** Yes **Expenses** Tuition & Fees $26,000; Room & Board $8380 **Undergraduates** 61% women, 5% part-time, 12% 25 or older, 1% Native American, 13% Hispanic American, 2% African American, 4% Asian American/Pacific Islander **The most frequently chosen baccalaureate fields are** business/marketing, education, liberal arts/general studies **Academic program** Advanced placement, accelerated degree program, honors program, summer session, adult/continuing education programs, internships **Contact** Mr. Scott Rhodes, Executive Director of Enrollment Services, Concordia University, 1530 Concordia West, Irvine, CA 92612-3299. *Phone:* 949-854-8002 Ext. 1118 or toll-free 800-229-1200. *Fax:* 949-854-6894. *E-mail:* admission@cui.edu. *Web site:* http://www.cui.edu/.

Design Institute of San Diego

San Diego, California

General Proprietary, 4-year, coed **Entrance** Noncompetitive **Setting** urban campus **Total enrollment** 457 **Application deadline** Rolling (freshmen), rolling (transfer) **Freshman admission** 54% were admitted **Housing** No **Undergraduates** 52% 25 or older **Academic program** Internships **Contact** Ms. Paula Parrish, Director of Admissions, Design Institute of San Diego, 8555 Commerce Avenue, San Diego, CA 92121-2685. *Phone:* 858-566-1200 or toll-free 800-619-4337. *Fax:* 858-566-2711. *E-mail:* admissions@disd.edu. *Web site:* http://www.disd.edu/.

DeVry University

Alhambra, California

Contact DeVry University, Unit 100, Building A-11, First Floor, 1000 South Fremont Avenue, Alhambra, CA 91803. *Web site:* http://www.devry.edu.

DeVry University

Anaheim, California

Contact DeVry University, 1900 South State College Boulevard, Suite 150, Anaheim, CA 92806-6136. *Web site:* http://www.devry.edu/.

DeVry University

Bakersfield, California

Contact DeVry University, 3000 Ming Avenue, Bakersfield, CA 93304-4136. *Web site:* http://www.devry.edu/.

DeVry University

Daly City, California

Contact DeVry University, 2001 Junipero Serra Boulevard, Suite 161, Daly City, CA 94014-3899. *Web site:* http://www.devry.edu/.

DeVry University

Elk Grove, California

Contact DeVry University, Sacramento Center, 2216 Kausen Drive, Elk Grove, CA 95758. *Phone:* toll-free 866-573-3879. *Web site:* http://www.devry.edu/.

DeVry University
Fremont, California

General Proprietary, comprehensive, coed **Entrance** Minimally difficult **Setting** 17-acre suburban campus **Total enrollment** 1,553 **Student-faculty ratio** 10:1 **Application deadline** Rolling (freshmen), rolling (transfer) **Housing** No **Expenses** Tuition & Fees $14,720 **Undergraduates** 31% women, 44% part-time, 49% 25 or older, 1% Native American, 22% Hispanic American, 10% African American, 22% Asian American/Pacific Islander **The most frequently chosen baccalaureate fields are** business/marketing, engineering, engineering technologies **Academic program** Advanced placement, accelerated degree program, summer session, adult/continuing education programs **Contact** Director of Admissions, DeVry University, 6600 Dumbarton Circle, Fremont, CA 94555. *Web site:* http://www.devry.edu/.

DeVry University
Irvine, California

Contact DeVry University, 430 Exchange, Suite 250, Irvine, CA 92602-1303. *Web site:* http://www.devry.edu/.

DeVry University
Long Beach, California

General Proprietary, comprehensive, coed **Entrance** Minimally difficult **Setting** 23-acre urban campus **Total enrollment** 1,172 **Student-faculty ratio** 14:1 **Application deadline** Rolling (freshmen), rolling (transfer) **Housing** No **Expenses** Tuition & Fees $14,080 **Undergraduates** 32% women, 56% part-time, 58% 25 or older, 0.3% Native American, 41% Hispanic American, 15% African American, 17% Asian American/Pacific Islander **The most frequently chosen baccalaureate fields are** business/marketing, computer and information sciences, engineering technologies **Academic program** Advanced placement, accelerated degree program, summer session, adult/continuing education programs **Contact** Admissions Office, DeVry University, 3880 Kilroy Airport Way, Long Beach, CA 90806. *Web site:* http://www.devry.edu/.

DeVry University
Oakland, California

Contact DeVry University, 505 14th Street, Oakland, CA 94612. *Web site:* http://www.devry.edu/.

DeVry University
Palmdale, California

Contact Admissions Office, DeVry University, One 39115 Trade Center Drive, Suite 100, Palmdale, CA 93551. *Phone:* toll-free 866-986-9388. *Web site:* http://www.devry.edu/.

DeVry University
Pomona, California

General Proprietary, comprehensive, coed **Entrance** Minimally difficult **Setting** 15-acre urban campus **Total enrollment** 2,323 **Student-faculty ratio** 20:1 **Application deadline** Rolling (freshmen), rolling (transfer) **Housing** No **Expenses** Tuition & Fees $14,080 **Undergraduates** 34% women, 56% part-time, 61% 25 or older, 1% Native American, 41% Hispanic American, 12% African American, 14% Asian American/Pacific Islander **The most frequently chosen baccalaureate fields are** business/marketing, computer and information sciences, engineering technologies **Academic program** Advanced placement, accelerated degree program, summer session, adult/continuing education programs **Contact** Admissions Office, DeVry University, 901 Corporate Center Drive, Pomona, CA 91768-2642. *Web site:* http://www.devry.edu/.

DeVry University
San Diego, California

Contact DeVry University, 2655 Camino Del Rio North, Suite 201, San Diego, CA 92108-1633. *Web site:* http://www.devry.edu/.

DeVry University
Sherman Oaks, California

General Proprietary, comprehensive, coed **Total enrollment** 931 **Student-faculty ratio** 23:1 **Application deadline** Rolling (freshmen), rolling (transfer) **Expenses** Tuition & Fees $14,080 **Undergraduates** 34% women, 37% part-time, 54% 25 or older, 0.4% Native American, 36% Hispanic American, 10% African American, 15% Asian American/Pacific Islander **The most frequently chosen baccalaureate fields are** business/marketing, computer and information sciences, engineering technologies **Academic program** Accelerated degree program **Contact** Admissions Office, DeVry University, 15301 Ventura Boulevard, D-100, Sherman Oaks, CA 91403. *Phone:* toll-free 888-610-0800. *Web site:* http://www.devry.edu/.

Dominican University of California
San Rafael, California

General Independent, comprehensive, coed, affiliated with Roman Catholic Church **Entrance** Moderately difficult **Setting** 85-acre suburban campus **Total enrollment** 2,094 **Student-faculty ratio** 11:1 **Application deadline** 2/1 (freshmen), 2/1 (transfer) **Freshman admission** 12% were admitted. Average high school GPA 3.39 **Freshman test scores** SAT critical reading scores over 500: 53.9%; ACT scores over 18: 90.3%; SAT critical reading scores over 600: 15%; ACT scores over 24: 32.2% **Housing** Yes **Expenses** Tuition & Fees $35,587; Room & Board $13,560 **Undergraduates** 74% women, 19% part-time, 26% 25 or older, 1% Native American, 16% Hispanic American, 6% African American, 23% Asian American/Pacific Islander **The most frequently chosen baccalaureate fields are** business/marketing, health professions and related sciences, liberal arts/general studies **Academic program** English as a second language, advanced placement, self-designed majors, honors program, summer session, adult/continuing education programs, internships **Contact** Ms. Rebecca Finn Kenney, Director of Undergraduate Admissions, Dominican University of California, 50 Acacia Avenue, San Rafael, CA 94901-2298. *Phone:* 415-485-3204 or toll-free 888-323-6763. *Fax:* 415-485-3214. *E-mail:* enroll@dominican.edu. *Web site:* http://www.dominican.edu/.

Visit Petersons.com and enter keyword Dominican

See page 758 for the College Close-Up.

Emmanuel Bible College
Pasadena, California

General Independent, 4-year, coed, affiliated with Church of the Nazarene **Total enrollment** 20 **Student-faculty ratio** 10:1 **Application deadline** 9/15 (freshmen) **Freshman admission** 100% were admitted **Undergraduates** 20% women, 70% part-time, 100% 25 or older **Academic program** Adult/continuing education programs, internships **Contact** Admissions, Emmanuel Bible College, 1605 East Elizabeth Street, Pasadena, CA 91104. *Phone:* 626-446-0300. *E-mail:* info@ebcministry.edu. *Web site:* http://www.emmanuelbiblecollege.edu/.

Epic Bible College
Sacramento, California

General Independent nondenominational, 4-year, coed **Total enrollment** 242 **Housing** No **Undergraduates** 61% 25 or older **Contact** Ms. Sheila Knoll, Assistant Director of Records, Epic Bible College, 5225 Hillsdale Boulevard, Sacramento, CA 95842. *Phone:* 916-348-4689. *E-mail:* kclarke@tlbc.edu. *Web site:* http://epic.edu/.

FIDM/The Fashion Institute of Design & Merchandising, Los Angeles Campus

Los Angeles, California

General Proprietary, primarily 2-year, coed, primarily women **Entrance** Moderately difficult **Setting** urban campus **Total enrollment** 4,562 **Student-faculty ratio** 17:1 **Application deadline** Rolling (freshmen), rolling (transfer) **Freshman admission** 71% were admitted. Average high school GPA 2.75 **Housing** No **Expenses** Room only $3250 **Undergraduates** 90% women, 12% part-time, 25% 25 or older, 1% Native American, 20% Hispanic American, 5% African American, 13% Asian American/Pacific Islander **The most frequently chosen baccalaureate field is** business/marketing **Academic program** English as a second language, advanced placement, summer session, adult/continuing education programs, internships **Contact** Ms. Susan Aronson, Director of Admissions, FIDM/The Fashion Institute of Design & Merchandising, Los Angeles Campus, 919 South Grand Avenue, Los Angeles, CA 90015. *Phone:* 213-624-1201 or toll-free 800-624-1200. *Fax:* 213-624-4799. *E-mail:* saronson@fidm.com. *Web site:* http://www.fidm.edu/.

Visit Petersons.com and enter keyword FIDM

Fresno Pacific University

Fresno, California

Contact Fresno Pacific University, 1717 South Chestnut Avenue, #2005, Fresno, CA 93727. *Phone:* 800-660-6089 or toll-free 800-660-6089. *Fax:* 559-453-2007. *E-mail:* ugadmis@fresno.edu. *Web site:* http://www.fresno.edu/.

Golden Gate University

San Francisco, California

General Independent, university, coed **Entrance** Moderately difficult **Setting** urban campus **Total enrollment** 3,528 **Student-faculty ratio** 16:1 **Application deadline** Rolling (freshmen), rolling (transfer) **Housing** No **Expenses** Tuition & Fees $15,120 **Undergraduates** 58% women, 84% part-time, 76% 25 or older, 1% Native American, 9% Hispanic American, 9% African American, 22% Asian American/Pacific Islander **The most frequently chosen baccalaureate fields are** business/marketing, computer and information sciences, liberal arts/general studies **Academic program** English as a second language, advanced placement, accelerated degree program, summer session, adult/continuing education programs, internships **Contact** Mr. Louis D. Riccardi Jr., Director of Enrollment Services, Golden Gate University, 536 Mission Street, San Francisco, CA 94105-2968. *Phone:* 415-442-7800 or toll-free 800-448-3381. *Fax:* 415-442-7807. *E-mail:* info@ggu.edu. *Web site:* http://www.ggu.edu/.

Visit Petersons.com and enter keyword Golden

Harvey Mudd College

Claremont, California

General Independent, 4-year, coed **Entrance** Most difficult **Setting** 33-acre suburban campus **Total enrollment** 757 **Student-faculty ratio** 8:1 **Application deadline** 1/2 (freshmen), 4/1 (transfer) **Freshman admission** 34% were admitted **Freshman test scores** SAT critical reading scores over 500: 100%; SAT math scores over 500: 100%; ACT scores over 18: 100%; SAT critical reading scores over 600: 99%; SAT math scores over 600: 100%; ACT scores over 24: 100% **Housing** Yes **Expenses** Tuition & Fees $40,390; Room & Board $13,198 **Undergraduates** 36% women, 0.1% part-time, 1% Native American, 7% Hispanic American, 1% African American, 20% Asian American/Pacific Islander **The most frequently chosen baccalaureate fields are** engineering, computer and information sciences, physical sciences **Academic program** Advanced placement, self-designed majors, internships **Contact** Mr. Peter Osgood, Director of Admissions, Harvey Mudd College, 301 Platt Boulevard, Claremont, CA 91711. *Phone:* 909-621-8011. *Fax:* 909-607-7046. *E-mail:* admission@hmc.edu. *Web site:* http://www.hmc.edu/.

Henley-Putnam University

San Jose, California

Contact Henley-Putnam University, 25 Metro Drive, Suite 500, San Jose, CA 95110. *Web site:* http://www.henley-putnam.edu/.

Holy Names University

Oakland, California

General Independent Roman Catholic, comprehensive, coed, primarily women **Entrance** Moderately difficult **Setting** 60-acre urban campus **Total enrollment** 1,135 **Student-faculty ratio** 16:1 **Application deadline** 8/15 (freshmen), 8/15 (transfer) **Freshman admission** 68% were admitted. Average high school GPA 3.09 **Housing** Yes **Expenses** Tuition & Fees $27,340; Room & Board $9320 **Undergraduates** 74% women, 23% part-time **The most frequently chosen baccalaureate fields are** business/marketing, health professions and related sciences, psychology **Academic program** English as a second language, advanced placement, accelerated degree program, self-designed majors, summer session, adult/continuing education programs, internships **Contact** Murad Dibbini, Dean of Enrollment Services, Holy Names University, 3500 Mountain Boulevard, Oakland, CA 94619-1699. *Phone:* 510-436-1430 or toll-free 800-430-1321. *Fax:* 510-436-1325. *E-mail:* admissions@hnu.edu. *Web site:* http://www.hnu.edu/.

Hope International University

Fullerton, California

General Independent, comprehensive, coed, affiliated with Christian Churches and Churches of Christ **Entrance** Moderately difficult **Setting** 16-acre suburban campus **Total enrollment** 1,059 **Student-faculty ratio** 10:1 **Application deadline** 5/1 (freshmen), 5/1 (transfer) **Freshman admission** 80% were admitted. Average high school GPA 3.2 **Freshman test scores** SAT critical reading scores over 500: 45.3%; SAT math scores over 500: 53.4%; ACT scores over 18: 77.3%; SAT critical reading scores over 600: 13.3%; SAT math scores over 600: 10.7%; ACT scores over 24: 27.3% **Housing** Yes **Expenses** Tuition & Fees $23,565; Room & Board $7400 **Undergraduates** 59% women, 25% part-time, 35% 25 or older, 1% Native American, 16% Hispanic American, 6% African American, 6% Asian American/Pacific Islander **The most frequently chosen baccalaureate fields are** business/marketing, family and consumer sciences, theology and religious vocations **Academic program** English as a second language, advanced placement, accelerated degree program, summer session, adult/continuing education programs, internships **Contact** Ms. Midge Madden, Office Manager, Hope International University, 2500 East Nutwood Avenue, Fullerton, CA 92831-3138. *Phone:* 714-879-3901 or toll-free 800-762-1294. *Fax:* 714-681-7423. *E-mail:* mfmadden@hiu.edu. *Web site:* http://www.hiu.edu/.

Humboldt State University

Arcata, California

General State-supported, comprehensive, coed **Entrance** Moderately difficult **Setting** 161-acre rural campus **Total enrollment** 7,954 **Student-faculty ratio** 22:1 **Application deadline** 11/30 (freshmen), 11/30 (transfer) **Freshman admission** 84% were admitted. Average high school GPA 3.17 **Freshman test scores** SAT critical reading scores over 500: 66%; SAT math scores over 500: 59%; ACT scores over 18: 78%; SAT critical reading scores over 600: 25%; SAT math scores over 600: 18%; ACT scores over 24: 37% **Housing** Yes **Expenses** Tuition & Fees: state resident $5166, nonresident $19,260; Room & Board $9510 **Undergraduates** 54% women, 9% part-time, 18% 25 or older, 2% Native American, 13% Hispanic American, 3% African American, 4% Asian American/Pacific Islander **The most frequently chosen baccalaureate fields are** natural resources/environmental science, social sciences, visual and performing arts **Academic program** English as a second language, advanced placement, self-designed majors, honors program, summer session, adult/continuing education programs, internships

Humboldt State University (continued)
Contact Ms. Rebecca Kalal, Associate Director of Admissions, Humboldt State University, 1 Harpst Street, Arcata, CA 95521. *Phone:* 707-826-4402. *Fax:* 707-826-6190. *E-mail:* hsuinfo@humboldt.edu. *Web site:* http://www.humboldt.edu/.

Humphreys College
Stockton, California

General Independent, comprehensive, coed **Entrance** Noncompetitive **Setting** 10-acre suburban campus **Total enrollment** 756 **Application deadline** Rolling (freshmen), rolling (transfer) **Housing** Yes **Expenses** Tuition & Fees $9180 **Undergraduates** 71% 25 or older **Academic program** Advanced placement, accelerated degree program, self-designed majors, summer session, adult/continuing education programs, internships **Contact** Director of Admission, Humphreys College, 6650 Inglewood Avenue, Stockton, CA 95207-3896. *Phone:* 209-235-2901. *E-mail:* ugadmission@humphreys.edu. *Web site:* http://www.humphreys.edu/.

Interior Designers Institute
Newport Beach, California

General Proprietary, comprehensive, coed **Setting** 1-acre suburban campus **Total enrollment** 468 **Undergraduates** 67% 25 or older **Contact** Admissions Office, Interior Designers Institute, 1061 Camelback Road, Newport Beach, CA 92660. *E-mail:* contact@idi.edu. *Web site:* http://www.idi.edu/.

International Technological University
Santa Clara, California

Contact Manisha Pai, Director of Admissions and Registrar, International Technological University, 1650 Warburton Avenue, Santa Clara, CA 95050. *Phone:* 408-331-1014. *Fax:* 408-331-1026. *E-mail:* mpai@itu.edu. *Web site:* http://www.itu.edu/.

ITT Technical Institute
Anaheim, California

General Proprietary, primarily 2-year, coed **Entrance** Minimally difficult **Setting** suburban campus **Housing** No **Contact** Director of Recruitment, ITT Technical Institute, 525 North Muller Avenue, Anaheim, CA 92801. *Phone:* 714-535-3700. *Fax:* 714-535-1802. *Web site:* http://www.itt-tech.edu/.

ITT Technical Institute
Clovis, California

General Proprietary, 4-year, coed **Contact** Director of Recruitment, ITT Technical Institute, 362 North Clovis Avenue, Clovis, CA 93612. *Phone:* 559-325-5400 or toll-free 800-564-9771. *Web site:* http://www.itt-tech.edu/.

ITT Technical Institute
Concord, California

General Proprietary, 4-year, coed **Contact** Director of Recruitment, ITT Technical Institute, 1140 Galaxy Way, Suite 400, Concord, CA 94520. *Phone:* 925-674-8200 or toll-free 800-211-7062. *Web site:* http://www.itt-tech.edu/.

ITT Technical Institute
Corona, California

General Proprietary, 4-year, coed **Contact** Director of Admissions, ITT Technical Institute, 4160 Temescal Canyon Road, Suite 100, Corona, CA 92883. *Phone:* 951-277-5400 or toll-free 877-764-9661. *Web site:* http://www.itt-tech.edu/.

ITT Technical Institute
Lathrop, California

General Proprietary, primarily 2-year, coed **Entrance** Minimally difficult **Housing** No **Contact** Director of Recruitment, ITT Technical Institute, 16916 South Harlan Road, Lathrop, CA 95330. *Phone:* 209-858-0077 or toll-free 800-346-1786. *Web site:* http://www.itt-tech.edu/.

ITT Technical Institute
Oxnard, California

General Proprietary, primarily 2-year, coed **Entrance** Minimally difficult **Setting** urban campus **Housing** No **Contact** Director of Recruitment, ITT Technical Institute, 2051 Solar Drive, Suite 150, Oxnard, CA 93036. *Phone:* 805-988-0143 or toll-free 800-530-1582. *Web site:* http://www.itt-tech.edu/.

ITT Technical Institute
Rancho Cordova, California

General Proprietary, primarily 2-year, coed **Entrance** Minimally difficult **Setting** urban campus **Housing** No **Contact** Director of Recruitment, ITT Technical Institute, 10863 Gold Center Drive, Rancho Cordova, CA 95670-6034. *Phone:* 916-851-3900 or toll-free 800-488-8466. *Web site:* http://www.itt-tech.edu/.

ITT Technical Institute
San Bernardino, California

General Proprietary, primarily 2-year, coed **Entrance** Minimally difficult **Setting** urban campus **Housing** No **Contact** Director of Recruitment, ITT Technical Institute, 670 East Carnegie Drive, San Bernardino, CA 92408. *Phone:* 909-806-4600 or toll-free 800-888-3801. *Web site:* http://www.itt-tech.edu/.

ITT Technical Institute
San Diego, California

General Proprietary, primarily 2-year, coed **Entrance** Minimally difficult **Setting** suburban campus **Housing** No **Contact** Director of Recruitment, ITT Technical Institute, 9680 Granite Ridge Drive, San Diego, CA 92123. *Phone:* 858-571-8500 or toll-free 800-883-0380. *Web site:* http://www.itt-tech.edu/.

ITT Technical Institute
San Dimas, California

General Proprietary, primarily 2-year, coed **Entrance** Minimally difficult **Setting** suburban campus **Housing** No **Contact** Director of Recruitment, ITT Technical Institute, 650 West Cienega Avenue, San Dimas, CA 91773. *Phone:* 909-971-2300 or toll-free 800-414-6522. *Web site:* http://www.itt-tech.edu/.

ITT Technical Institute
Sylmar, California

General Proprietary, primarily 2-year, coed **Entrance** Minimally difficult **Setting** urban campus **Housing** No **Contact** Director of Recruitment, ITT Technical Institute, 12669 Encinitas Avenue, Sylmar, CA 91342-3664. *Phone:* 818-364-5151 or toll-free 800-363-2086. *Web site:* http://www.itt-tech.edu/.

ITT Technical Institute
Torrance, California

General Proprietary, primarily 2-year, coed **Entrance** Minimally difficult **Setting** urban campus **Housing** No **Contact** Director of Recruitment,

ITT Technical Institute, 20050 South Vermont Avenue, Torrance, CA 90502. *Phone:* 310-380-1555. *Web site:* http://www.itt-tech.edu/.

John F. Kennedy University
Pleasant Hill, California

General Independent, upper-level, coed, primarily women **Entrance** Noncompetitive **Setting** 5-acre suburban campus **Total enrollment** 1,580 **Student-faculty ratio** 8:1 **Application deadline** Rolling (transfer) **Housing** No **Expenses** Tuition & Fees $13,161 **Undergraduates** 74% women, 81% part-time, 89% 25 or older **The most frequently chosen baccalaureate fields are** law/legal studies, business/marketing, psychology **Academic program** Advanced placement, self-designed majors, summer session, adult/continuing education programs **Contact** Ms. Jen Miller-Hogg, Director of Admissions, John F. Kennedy University, 100 Ellinwood Way, Pleasant Hill, CA 94523-4817. *Phone:* 925-969-3584 or toll-free 800-696-JFKU. *E-mail:* jmhogg@jfku.edu. *Web site:* http://www.jfku.edu/.

The King's College and Seminary
Van Nuys, California

General Independent, comprehensive, coed, affiliated with International Church of the Foursquare Gospel **Total enrollment** 531 **Housing** No **Expenses** Tuition & Fees $7395 **Undergraduates** 73% 25 or older **Contact** Mrs. Marilyn J. Chappell, Director of Admissions, The King's College and Seminary, 14800 Sherman Way, Van Nuys, CA 91405-8040. *Phone:* 818-779-8040 or toll-free 888-779-8040. *Fax:* 818-779-8429. *E-mail:* mchappell@kingscollege.edu. *Web site:* http://www.kingscollege.edu/.

LA College International
Los Angeles, California

Contact Director of Admissions, LA College International, 3200 Wilshire Boulevard, # 400, Los Angeles, CA 90010-1308. *Phone:* 213-381-3333 or toll-free 800-57 GO ICT. *Web site:* http://www.lac.edu/.

Laguna College of Art & Design
Laguna Beach, California

Contact Mike Rivas, Vice President of Enrollment, Laguna College of Art & Design, 2222 Laguna Canyon Road, Laguna Beach, CA 92651-1136. *Phone:* 949-376-6000 Ext. 232 or toll-free 800-255-0762. *Web site:* http://www.lagunacollege.edu/.

La Sierra University
Riverside, California

General Independent Seventh-day Adventist, comprehensive, coed **Entrance** Moderately difficult **Setting** 100-acre suburban campus **Total enrollment** 1,899 **Student-faculty ratio** 13:1 **Application deadline** Rolling (freshmen), rolling (transfer) **Freshman admission** 55% were admitted. Average high school GPA 3.37 **Freshman test scores** SAT critical reading scores over 500: 45%; SAT math scores over 500: 53%; ACT scores over 18: 78%; SAT critical reading scores over 600: 16%; SAT math scores over 600: 19%; ACT scores over 24: 20% **Housing** Yes **Expenses** Tuition & Fees $24,573; Room & Board $6990 **Undergraduates** 58% women, 12% part-time, 13% 25 or older, 1% Native American, 25% Hispanic American, 9% African American, 25% Asian American/Pacific Islander **The most frequently chosen baccalaureate fields are** biological/life sciences, business/marketing, liberal arts/general studies **Academic program** English as a second language, advanced placement, accelerated degree program, self-designed majors, honors program, summer session, adult/continuing education programs, internships **Contact** Faye Swayze, Director of Admissions and Registrar, La Sierra University, 4500 Riverwalk Parkway, Riverside, CA 92515. *Phone:* 951-785-2176 or toll-free 800-874-5587. *Fax:* 951-785-2477. *E-mail:* admissions@lasierra.edu. *Web site:* http://www.lasierra.edu/.

Life Pacific College
San Dimas, California

General Independent, 4-year, coed, affiliated with International Church of the Foursquare Gospel **Entrance** Minimally difficult **Setting** 9-acre suburban campus **Total enrollment** 514 **Student-faculty ratio** 16:1 **Application deadline** 5/1 (freshmen), 5/1 (transfer) **Freshman admission** 100% were admitted. Average high school GPA 2.91 **Freshman test scores** SAT critical reading scores over 500: 57%; SAT math scores over 500: 41%; ACT scores over 18: 67%; SAT critical reading scores over 600: 16%; SAT math scores over 600: 10%; ACT scores over 24: 25% **Housing** Yes **Expenses** Tuition & Fees $12,500; Room & Board $6000 **Undergraduates** 48% women, 37% part-time, 27% 25 or older, 1% Native American, 13% Hispanic American, 4% African American, 5% Asian American/Pacific Islander **The most frequently chosen baccalaureate field is** theology and religious vocations **Academic program** Advanced placement, accelerated degree program, summer session, adult/continuing education programs, internships **Contact** Ms. Dorienne Elston, Director of Admissions, Life Pacific College, 1100 Covina Boulevard, San Dimas, CA 91773-3298. *Phone:* 909-599-5433 Ext. 314 or toll-free 877-886-5433 Ext. 314. *Fax:* 909-706-3070. *E-mail:* adm@lifepacific.edu. *Web site:* http://www.lifepacific.edu/.

Lincoln University
Oakland, California

General Independent, comprehensive, coed **Entrance** Minimally difficult **Setting** 2-acre urban campus **Total enrollment** 624 **Student-faculty ratio** 14:1 **Application deadline** 8/22 (freshmen), 8/22 (transfer) **Freshman admission** 91% were admitted. Average high school GPA 2.5 **Expenses** Tuition & Fees $8630; Room & Board $8100 **Undergraduates** 48% women, 26% part-time, 20% 25 or older, 3% Hispanic American, 9% African American, 6% Asian American/Pacific Islander **The most frequently chosen baccalaureate field is** business/marketing **Academic program** English as a second language, advanced placement, summer session, internships **Contact** Ms. Reenu Shrestha, Admissions Officer, Lincoln University, 401 15th Street, Oakland, CA 94612. *Phone:* 510-628-8010 Ext. 8030. *Fax:* 510-628-8012. *E-mail:* admissions@lincolnuca.edu. *Web site:* http://www.lincolnuca.edu/.

Loma Linda University
Loma Linda, California

Contact Admissions Office, Loma Linda University, Loma Linda, CA 92350. *Phone:* 909-558-1000. *Web site:* http://www.llu.edu/.

Loyola Marymount University
Los Angeles, California

General Independent Roman Catholic, comprehensive, coed **Entrance** Very difficult **Setting** 150-acre suburban campus **Total enrollment** 9,010 **Student-faculty ratio** 11:1 **Application deadline** 1/15 (freshmen), 3/15 (transfer) **Freshman admission** 59% were admitted. Average high school GPA 3.66 **Freshman test scores** SAT critical reading scores over 500: 89.1%; SAT math scores over 500: 90.5%; ACT scores over 18: 99.4%; SAT critical reading scores over 600: 42.8%; SAT math scores over 600: 53.1%; ACT scores over 24: 75.8% **Housing** Yes **Expenses** Tuition & Fees $35,419; Room & Board $12,025 **Undergraduates** 57% women, 5% part-time, 3% 25 or older, 1% Native American, 19% Hispanic American, 8% African American, 13% Asian American/Pacific Islander **The most frequently chosen baccalaureate fields are** business/marketing, social sciences, visual and performing arts **Academic program** English as a second language, advanced placement, accelerated degree program, self-designed majors, honors program, summer session, internships **Contact** Mr. Matthew Fissinger, Director of Admissions, Loyola

Loyola Marymount University (continued)
Marymount University, One LMU Drive, Los Angeles, CA 90045-2659. *Phone:* 310-338-2750 or toll-free 800-LMU-INFO. *E-mail:* admissions@lmu.edu. *Web site:* http://www.lmu.edu/.
Visit Petersons.com and enter keyword Loyola

See page 924 for the College Close-Up.

Marymount College, Palos Verdes, California
Rancho Palos Verdes, California

General Independent Roman Catholic, 4-year, coed **Entrance** Minimally difficult **Setting** 26-acre suburban campus **Total enrollment** 561 **Student-faculty ratio** 15:1 **Application deadline** 7/1 (freshmen), 8/15 (transfer) **Freshman admission** 61% were admitted. Average high school GPA 2.69 **Freshman test scores** SAT critical reading scores over 500: 42.81%; SAT math scores over 500: 45.9%; SAT critical reading scores over 600: 11.61%; SAT math scores over 600: 10.4% **Housing** Yes **Expenses** Tuition & Fees $24,542; Room & Board $10,600 **Undergraduates** 51% women, 1% part-time, 1% 25 or older, 0.2% Native American, 20% Hispanic American, 7% African American, 7% Asian American/Pacific Islander **Academic program** English as a second language, advanced placement, honors program, summer session, adult/continuing education programs, internships **Contact** Ms. Paula Avery, Director of Admissions, Marymount College, Palos Verdes, California, 30800 Palos Verdes Drive East, Rancho Palos Verdes, CA 90275-6299. *Phone:* 310-377-5501 Ext. 211. *Fax:* 310-265-0962. *E-mail:* admissions@marymountpv.edu. *Web site:* http://www.marymountpv.edu/.

The Master's College and Seminary
Santa Clarita, California

General Independent nondenominational, comprehensive, coed **Entrance** Moderately difficult **Setting** 110-acre suburban campus **Total enrollment** 1,348 **Student-faculty ratio** 9:1 **Application deadline** 9/1 (freshmen), 9/1 (transfer) **Freshman admission** 83% were admitted. Average high school GPA 3.59 **Housing** Yes **Expenses** Tuition & Fees $24,650; Room & Board $8000 **Undergraduates** 48% women, 11% part-time, 14% 25 or older, 1% Native American, 9% Hispanic American, 3% African American, 5% Asian American/Pacific Islander **The most frequently chosen baccalaureate fields are** business/marketing, liberal arts/general studies, philosophy and religious studies **Academic program** Advanced placement, accelerated degree program, summer session, adult/continuing education programs, internships **Contact** Ms. Hollie Gorsh, Director of Admissions, The Master's College and Seminary, 21726 Placerita Canyon Road, Santa Clarita, CA 91321. *Phone:* 661-259-3540 Ext. 3369 or toll-free 800-568-6248. *Fax:* 661-288-1037. *E-mail:* admissions@masters.edu. *Web site:* http://www.masters.edu/.

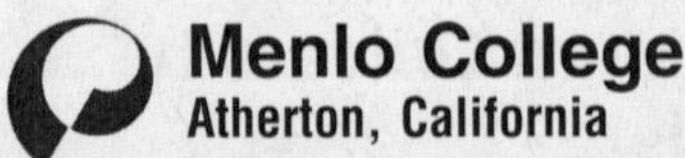

Menlo College
Atherton, California

General Independent, 4-year, coed **Entrance** Moderately difficult **Setting** 45-acre small-town campus **Total enrollment** 594 **Student-faculty ratio** 14:1 **Application deadline** Rolling (freshmen), rolling (transfer) **Freshman admission** 52% were admitted. Average high school GPA 3.13 **Freshman test scores** SAT critical reading scores over 500: 38.6%; SAT math scores over 500: 46.4%; ACT scores over 18: 75.5%; SAT critical reading scores over 600: 7.3%; SAT math scores over 600: 14.5%; ACT scores over 24: 26.4% **Housing** Yes **Expenses** Tuition & Fees $33,550; Room & Board $11,330 **Undergraduates** 36% women, 4% part-time, 6% 25 or older, 0.2% Native American, 14% Hispanic American, 4% African American, 12% Asian American/Pacific Islander **The most frequently chosen baccalaureate fields are** business/marketing, communications/journalism, liberal arts/general studies **Academic program** English as a second language, advanced placement, accelerated degree program, self-designed majors, summer session, adult/continuing education programs, internships **Contact** Cindy McGrew, Director, Enrollment Management Operations, Menlo College, 1000 El Camino Real, Atherton, CA 94027. *Phone:* 650-543-3940 or toll-free 800-556-3656. *Fax:* 650-543-4496. *E-mail:* admissions@menlo.edu. *Web site:* http://www.menlo.edu/.
Visit Petersons.com and enter keyword Menlo

See page 956 for the College Close-Up.

Mills College
Oakland, California

General Independent, comprehensive, undergraduate: women only; graduate: coed **Entrance** Moderately difficult **Setting** 135-acre urban campus **Total enrollment** 1,501 **Student-faculty ratio** 12:1 **Application deadline** 2/1 (freshmen), 3/1 (transfer) **Freshman admission** 57% were admitted. Average high school GPA 3.7 **Freshman test scores** SAT critical reading scores over 500: 89.3%; SAT math scores over 500: 76.4%; ACT scores over 18: 100%; SAT critical reading scores over 600: 50%; SAT math scores over 600: 27.2%; ACT scores over 24: 62.3% **Housing** Yes **Expenses** Tuition & Fees $37,605; Room & Board $11,644 **Undergraduates** 6% part-time, 20% 25 or older, 1% Native American, 14% Hispanic American, 9% African American, 7% Asian American/Pacific Islander **The most frequently chosen baccalaureate fields are** English, social sciences, visual and performing arts **Academic program** English as a second language, advanced placement, accelerated degree program, self-designed majors, honors program, adult/continuing education programs, internships **Contact** Ms. Giulietta Aquino, Vice President of Enrollment Management, Mills College, 5000 MacArthur Boulevard, Oakland, CA 94613-1301. *Phone:* 510-430-2135 or toll-free 800-87-MILLS. *Fax:* 510-430-3314. *E-mail:* admission@mills.edu. *Web site:* http://www.mills.edu/.
Visit Petersons.com and enter keyword Mills

See page 970 for the College Close-Up.

Mount St. Mary's College
Los Angeles, California

General Independent Roman Catholic, comprehensive, coed **Entrance** Moderately difficult **Setting** 71-acre suburban campus **Total enrollment** 2,482 **Student-faculty ratio** 11:1 **Application deadline** 2/15 (freshmen), 3/15 (transfer) **Freshman admission** 79% were admitted. Average high school GPA 3.13 **Freshman test scores** SAT critical reading scores over 500: 32%; SAT math scores over 500: 29%; ACT scores over 18: 63%; SAT critical reading scores over 600: 5%; SAT math scores over 600: 7%; ACT scores over 24: 14% **Housing** Yes **Expenses** Tuition & Fees $30,132; Room & Board $9830 **Undergraduates** 92% women, 25% part-time, 27% 25 or older, 0.4% Native American, 48% Hispanic American, 9% African American, 20% Asian American/Pacific Islander **The most frequently chosen baccalaureate fields are** health professions and related sciences, education, social sciences **Academic program** English as a second language, advanced placement, accelerated degree program, self-designed majors, honors program, summer session, internships **Contact** Yvonne Berumen, Director of Admissions, Mount St. Mary's College, 12001 Chalon Road, Los Angeles, CA 90049-1599. *Phone:* 310-954-4250 or toll-free 800-999-9893. *Fax:* 310-954-4259. *E-mail:* admissions@msmc.la.edu. *Web site:* http://www.msmc.la.edu/.

Mt. Sierra College
Monrovia, California

General Proprietary, 4-year, coed **Entrance** Moderately difficult **Setting** 5-acre suburban campus **Total enrollment** 511 **Application deadline** 10/8 (transfer) **Housing** No **Undergraduates** 45% 25 or older **Academic program** Accelerated degree program, summer session, adult/continuing education programs, internships **Contact** Enrollment Manager, Mt. Sierra College, 101 East Huntington Drive, Monrovia, CA 91016. *Phone:* 888-486-9818 or toll-free 888-828-8800. *E-mail:* enroll@mtsierra.edu. *Web site:* http://www.mtsierra.edu/.

Musicians Institute
Hollywood, California

General Proprietary, 4-year, coed **Entrance** Minimally difficult **Total enrollment** 1,252 **Application deadline** Rolling (freshmen) **Freshman admission** 100% were admitted **Housing** No **Undergraduates** 24% 25 or older **Contact** Mr. Steve Lunn, Director of Admissions, Musicians Institute, 1655 North McCadden Place, Hollywood, CA 90028. *Phone:* 323-462-1384 Ext. 156 or toll-free 800-255-PLAY. *Fax:* 323-462-6978. *E-mail:* admissions@mi.edu. *Web site:* http://www.mi.edu/.

The National Hispanic University
San Jose, California

General Independent, 4-year, coed **Entrance** Minimally difficult **Setting** 1-acre urban campus **Total enrollment** 551 **Application deadline** 8/15 (freshmen), 8/15 (transfer) **Housing** No **Undergraduates** 33% 25 or older **Academic program** English as a second language, advanced placement, accelerated degree program, summer session, adult/continuing education programs, internships **Contact** Ms. Pamela Bustillo, Director of Office of Admissions/Registrar, The National Hispanic University, 14271 Story Road, San Jose, CA 95127-3823. *Phone:* 408-273-2772. *E-mail:* chernandez@nhu.edu. *Web site:* http://www.nhu.edu/.

National University
La Jolla, California

General Independent, comprehensive, coed **Entrance** Minimally difficult **Setting** urban campus **Total enrollment** 17,041 **Student-faculty ratio** 19:1 **Application deadline** Rolling (freshmen), rolling (transfer) **Freshman admission** 100% were admitted **Housing** No **Expenses** Tuition & Fees $10,788 **Undergraduates** 72% women, 62% part-time, 82% 25 or older, 1% Native American, 18% Hispanic American, 11% African American, 9% Asian American/Pacific Islander **The most frequently chosen baccalaureate fields are** business/marketing, education, law/legal studies **Academic program** English as a second language, advanced placement, accelerated degree program, summer session, adult/continuing education programs, internships **Contact** Mr. Dominick Giovanniello, Associate Regional Dean, San Diego, National University, 11255 North Torrey Pines Road, La Jolla, CA 92037-1011. *Phone:* 858-628-8648 Ext. 7701 or toll-free 800-NAT-UNIV. *Fax:* 858-642-8709. *E-mail:* dgiovann@nu.edu. *Web site:* http://www.nu.edu/.

Newschool of Architecture & Design
San Diego, California

General Proprietary, comprehensive, coed, primarily men **Entrance** Moderately difficult **Setting** 1-acre urban campus **Total enrollment** 463 **Application deadline** Rolling (freshmen), 8/30 (transfer) **Freshman admission** 100% were admitted **Housing** No **Undergraduates** 36% 25 or older **Academic program** English as a second language, advanced placement, summer session, adult/continuing education programs, internships **Contact** Ms. Lexi Rogers, Director of Admissions, Newschool of Architecture & Design, 1249 F Street, San Diego, CA 92101-6634. *Phone:* 619-235-4100 Ext. 106. *E-mail:* admissions@newschoolarch.edu. *Web site:* http://www.newschoolarch.edu/.

Northwestern Polytechnic University
Fremont, California

General Independent, comprehensive, coed **Setting** 3-acre urban campus **Total enrollment** 927 **Student-faculty ratio** 16:1 **Application deadline** 8/2 (freshmen), 8/2 (transfer) **Freshman admission** 100% were admitted. Average high school GPA 2.72 **Housing** Yes **Expenses** Tuition & Fees $7340; Room only $4800 **Undergraduates** 40% women, 13% part-time, 45% 25 or older, 1% Hispanic American, 1% African American, 11% Asian American/Pacific Islander **Academic program** English as a second language, advanced placement, summer session, adult/continuing education programs **Contact** Mr. Michael Tang, Admission Officer, Northwestern Polytechnic University, 47671 Westinghouse Drive, Fremont, CA 94539. *Phone:* 510-592-9688 Ext. 15. *Fax:* 510-657-8975. *E-mail:* admission@npu.edu. *Web site:* http://www.npu.edu/.

Notre Dame de Namur University
Belmont, California

General Independent Roman Catholic, comprehensive, coed **Entrance** Minimally difficult **Setting** 50-acre suburban campus **Total enrollment** 1,613 **Student-faculty ratio** 11:1 **Application deadline** Rolling (freshmen), rolling (transfer) **Freshman admission** 79% were admitted. Average high school GPA 2.85 **Freshman test scores** SAT critical reading scores over 500: 40%; SAT math scores over 500: 33%; ACT scores over 18: 74%; SAT critical reading scores over 600: 4%; SAT math scores over 600: 9%; ACT scores over 24: 6% **Housing** Yes **Expenses** Tuition & Fees $28,500; Room & Board $11,600 **Undergraduates** 66% women, 40% part-time, 37% 25 or older, 1% Native American, 25% Hispanic American, 8% African American, 15% Asian American/Pacific Islander **The most frequently chosen baccalaureate fields are** business/marketing, liberal arts/general studies, public administration and social services **Academic program** English as a second language, advanced placement, accelerated degree program, self-designed majors, summer session, adult/continuing education programs, internships **Contact** Ms. Rejeetha Gort, Director of Admissions, Notre Dame de Namur University, 1500 Ralston Avenue, Belmont, CA 94002-1908. *Phone:* 650-508-3600 or toll-free 800-263-0545. *Fax:* 650-508-3426. *E-mail:* rgort@ndnu.edu. *Web site:* http://www.ndnu.edu/.

Occidental College
Los Angeles, California

General Independent, comprehensive, coed **Entrance** Very difficult **Setting** 120-acre urban campus **Total enrollment** 1,989 **Student-faculty ratio** 10:1 **Application deadline** 1/10 (freshmen), 3/15 (transfer) **Freshman admission** 44% were admitted. Average high school GPA 3.58 **Freshman test scores** SAT critical reading scores over 500: 97%; SAT math scores over 500: 99%; ACT scores over 18: 100%; SAT critical reading scores over 600: 79%; SAT math scores over 600: 78%; ACT scores over 24: 97% **Housing** Yes **Expenses** Tuition & Fees $40,903; Room & Board $11,360 **Undergraduates** 56% women, 1% part-time, 1% 25 or older, 1% Native American, 13% Hispanic American, 6% African American, 16% Asian American/Pacific Islander **The most frequently chosen baccalaureate fields are** biological/life sciences, physical sciences, social sciences **Academic program** Advanced placement, self-designed majors, honors program, summer session, internships **Contact** Mr. Vince Cuseo, Vice President of Admission and Financial Aid, Occidental College, 1600 Campus Road, Los Angeles, CA 90041. *Phone:* 323-259-2700 or toll-free 800-825-5262. *Fax:* 323-341-4875. *E-mail:* admission@oxy.edu. *Web site:* http://www.oxy.edu/.

Otis College of Art and Design
Los Angeles, California

General Independent, comprehensive, coed **Entrance** Moderately difficult **Setting** 5-acre urban campus **Total enrollment** 1,221 **Student-faculty ratio** 9:1 **Application deadline** Rolling (freshmen), rolling (transfer) **Freshman admission** 44% were admitted. Average high school GPA 3.1 **Freshman test scores** ACT scores over 18: 85.5%; ACT scores over 24: 40.5% **Housing** Yes **Expenses** Tuition & Fees $31,360 **Undergraduates** 68% women, 1% part-time, 18% 25 or older, 0.4% Native American, 13% Hispanic American, 3% African American, 32% Asian American/Pacific Islander **The most frequently chosen baccalaureate fields are** architecture, visual and performing arts **Academic program** Advanced placement, honors program, summer session, adult/continuing education programs, internships **Contact** Mr. Marc D. Meredith, Vice President of Enrollment Management and Dean of Admissions, Otis College of Art and Design, 9045 Lincoln Boulevard,

Otis College of Art and Design (continued)
Los Angeles, CA 90045-9785. *Phone:* 310-665-6820 or toll-free 800-527-OTIS. *E-mail:* admissions@otis.edu. *Web site:* http://www.otis.edu/.

Pacific Oaks College
Pasadena, California

Contact Ms. Augusta Pickens, Office of Admissions, Pacific Oaks College, 5 Westmoreland Place, Pasadena, CA 91103. *Phone:* 626-397-1349 or toll-free 800-684-0900. *Fax:* 626-666-1220. *E-mail:* admissions@pacificoaks.edu. *Web site:* http://www.pacificoaks.edu/.

Pacific States University
Los Angeles, California

General Independent, comprehensive, coed **Entrance** Minimally difficult **Setting** 1-acre urban campus **Total enrollment** 197 **Student-faculty ratio** 12:1 **Application deadline** Rolling (freshmen), rolling (transfer) **Freshman admission** 80% were admitted **Housing** Yes **Expenses** Tuition & Fees $14,680; Room only $9000 **Undergraduates** 50% women, 90% 25 or older, 17% Asian American/Pacific Islander **Academic program** English as a second language, accelerated degree program, summer session, adult/continuing education programs **Contact** Mr. Ryan Ray, Associate Director of Admission, Pacific States University, 1516 South Western Avenue, Los Angeles, CA 90006. *Phone:* 323-731-2383 Ext. 211 or toll-free 888-200-0383. *Fax:* 323-731-7276. *E-mail:* ryanray@psuca.edu. *Web site:* http://www.psuca.edu/.

Pacific Union College
Angwin, California

General Independent Seventh-day Adventist, comprehensive, coed **Entrance** Moderately difficult **Setting** 200-acre rural campus **Total enrollment** 1,528 **Student-faculty ratio** 15:1 **Application deadline** Rolling (freshmen), rolling (transfer) **Freshman admission** 71% were admitted. Average high school GPA 3.19 **Freshman test scores** SAT critical reading scores over 500: 60%; SAT math scores over 500: 58%; ACT scores over 18: 75%; SAT critical reading scores over 600: 24%; SAT math scores over 600: 24%; ACT scores over 24: 39% **Housing** Yes **Expenses** Tuition & Fees $23,979; Room & Board $6750 **Undergraduates** 56% women, 17% part-time, 18% 25 or older **The most frequently chosen baccalaureate fields are** biological/life sciences, business/marketing, education **Academic program** Advanced placement, honors program, summer session, adult/continuing education programs, internships **Contact** Mr. Darren Hagen, Director of Enrollment Services, Pacific Union College, Enrollment Services, One Angwin Avenue, Angwin, CA 94508. *Phone:* 707-965-6425 or toll-free 800-862-7080. *Fax:* 707-965-6432. *E-mail:* enroll@puc.edu. *Web site:* http://www.puc.edu/.

Patten University
Oakland, California

General Independent interdenominational, comprehensive, coed **Entrance** Noncompetitive **Setting** 5-acre urban campus **Total enrollment** 1,050 **Student-faculty ratio** 17:1 **Application deadline** Rolling (freshmen), rolling (transfer) **Freshman test scores** ACT scores over 18: 100% **Housing** Yes **Expenses** Tuition & Fees $13,440; Room & Board $7090 **Undergraduates** 44% women, 51% part-time, 59% 25 or older, 0.4% Native American, 6% Hispanic American, 12% African American, 9% Asian American/Pacific Islander **The most frequently chosen baccalaureate fields are** psychology, business/marketing, theology and religious vocations **Academic program** Advanced placement, accelerated degree program, honors program, summer session, internships **Contact** Ms. Kim Guerra, Director of Admissions, Patten University, 2433 Coolidge Avenue, Oakland, CA 94601-2699. *Phone:* 510-261-8500 Ext. 7763. *Fax:* 510-534-4344. *E-mail:* kim.guerra@patten.edu. *Web site:* http://www.patten.edu/.

Pepperdine University
Malibu, California

General Independent, university, coed, affiliated with Church of Christ **Entrance** Very difficult **Setting** 830-acre small-town campus **Total enrollment** 7,733 **Student-faculty ratio** 14:1 **Application deadline** 1/15 (freshmen), 1/15 (transfer) **Freshman admission** 41% were admitted. Average high school GPA 3.67 **Freshman test scores** SAT critical reading scores over 500: 92.4%; SAT math scores over 500: 93.3%; ACT scores over 18: 99.4%; SAT critical reading scores over 600: 54%; SAT math scores over 600: 65.6%; ACT scores over 24: 84.9% **Housing** Yes **Expenses** Tuition & Fees $37,850; Room & Board $10,900 **Undergraduates** 55% women, 11% part-time, 9% 25 or older, 1% Native American, 12% Hispanic American, 7% African American, 10% Asian American/Pacific Islander **The most frequently chosen baccalaureate fields are** business/marketing, communications/journalism, social sciences **Academic program** Advanced placement, self-designed majors, honors program, summer session, internships **Contact** Mrs. Kristin Paredes-Collins, Director of Admissions and Enrollment Management, Seaver College, Pepperdine University, 24255 Pacific Coast Highway, Malibu, CA 90263. *Phone:* 310-506-4392. *Fax:* 310-506-4861. *E-mail:* kristin.paredes@pepperdine.edu. *Web site:* http://www.pepperdine.edu/.

Perelandra College
La Mesa, California

Contact Perelandra College, 8697-C La Mesa Boulevard, PMB 21, La Mesa, CA 91941. *Web site:* http://perelandracollege.com/.

Pitzer College
Claremont, California

General Independent, 4-year, coed **Entrance** Moderately difficult **Setting** 35-acre suburban campus **Total enrollment** 1,043 **Student-faculty ratio** 11:1 **Application deadline** 1/1 (freshmen), 4/15 (transfer) **Freshman admission** 20% were admitted. Average high school GPA 3.84 **Freshman test scores** SAT critical reading scores over 500: 97%; SAT math scores over 500: 98%; ACT scores over 18: 100%; SAT critical reading scores over 600: 83%; SAT math scores over 600: 74%; ACT scores over 24: 94% **Housing** Yes **Expenses** Tuition & Fees $39,330; Room & Board $11,440 **Undergraduates** 59% women, 5% part-time, 7% 25 or older, 1% Native American, 15% Hispanic American, 6% African American, 8% Asian American/Pacific Islander **The most frequently chosen baccalaureate fields are** psychology, communications/journalism, social sciences **Academic program** English as a second language, advanced placement, self-designed majors, honors program, summer session, adult/continuing education programs, internships **Contact** Angel Perez, Director of Admission, Pitzer College, 1050 North Mills Avenue, Claremont, CA 91711-6101. *Phone:* 909-621-8129 or toll-free 800-748-9371. *Fax:* 909-621-8770. *E-mail:* admission@pitzer.edu. *Web site:* http://www.pitzer.edu/.
Visit Petersons.com and enter keyword Pitzer

See page 1052 for the College Close-Up.

Platt College
Huntington Beach, California

General Proprietary, primarily 2-year, coed **Entrance** Moderately difficult **Setting** urban campus **Total enrollment** 50 **Application deadline** Rolling (freshmen) **Housing** No **Undergraduates** 46% 25 or older **Academic program** Accelerated degree program, summer session, adult/continuing education programs **Contact** Ms. Lisa Rhodes, President, Platt College, 7755 Center Avenue, Suite 600, Huntington Beach, CA 92647. *Phone:* 949-833-2300 Ext. 222 or toll-free 888-866-6697 Ext. 230. *Web site:* http://www.plattcollege.edu/.

Platt College
Ontario, California

General Proprietary, primarily 2-year, coed **Entrance** Minimally difficult **Total enrollment** 604 **Application deadline** Rolling (freshmen), rolling (transfer) **Housing** No **Undergraduates** 39% 25 or older **Academic program** Accelerated degree program, honors program, summer session, internships **Contact** Ms. Jennifer Abandonato, Director of Admissions, Platt College, 3700 Inland Empire Boulevard, Suite 400, Ontario, CA 91764. *Phone:* 909-941-9410 or toll-free 888-866-6697. *Web site:* http://www.plattcollege.edu/.

Platt College San Diego

San Diego, California

General Proprietary, 4-year, coed **Setting** 1-acre suburban campus **Total enrollment** 292 **Student-faculty ratio** 21:1 **Application deadline** Rolling (freshmen), rolling (transfer) **Housing** No **Expenses** Tuition & Fees $25,040 **Undergraduates** 25% women, 44% 25 or older, 1% Native American, 22% Hispanic American, 5% African American, 10% Asian American/Pacific Islander **The most frequently chosen baccalaureate field is** visual and performing arts **Academic program** Accelerated degree program, adult/continuing education programs **Contact** Mr. Steve Gallup, Admissions Representative, Platt College San Diego, 6250 El Cajon Boulevard, San Diego, CA 92115-3919. *Phone:* 619-265-0107 or toll-free 866-752-8826. *Fax:* 619-265-8655. *E-mail:* sgallup@platt.edu. *Web site:* http://www.platt.edu/.

Point Loma Nazarene University

San Diego, California

General Independent Nazarene, comprehensive, coed **Entrance** Moderately difficult **Setting** 88-acre suburban campus **Total enrollment** 3,490 **Student-faculty ratio** 14:1 **Application deadline** 3/1 (freshmen), 3/1 (transfer) **Freshman admission** 78% were admitted. Average high school GPA 3.68 **Freshman test scores** SAT critical reading scores over 500: 80%; SAT math scores over 500: 82%; ACT scores over 18: 96%; SAT critical reading scores over 600: 31%; SAT math scores over 600: 35%; ACT scores over 24: 55% **Housing** Yes **Expenses** Tuition & Fees $25,840; Room & Board $8100 **Undergraduates** 61% women, 3% part-time, 2% 25 or older, 1% Native American, 11% Hispanic American, 2% African American, 6% Asian American/Pacific Islander **The most frequently chosen baccalaureate fields are** business/marketing, health professions and related sciences, psychology **Academic program** Advanced placement, honors program, summer session, internships **Contact** Eric Groves, Director of Admissions, Point Loma Nazarene University, 3900 Lomaland Drive, San Diego, CA 92106. *Phone:* 619-849-2273 or toll-free 800-733-7770. *Fax:* 619-849-2601. *E-mail:* admissions@pointloma.edu. *Web site:* http://www.pointloma.edu/.

Pomona College

Claremont, California

General Independent, 4-year, coed **Entrance** Most difficult **Setting** 140-acre suburban campus **Total enrollment** 1,550 **Student-faculty ratio** 7:1 **Application deadline** 1/2 (freshmen), 3/15 (transfer) **Freshman admission** 16% were admitted **Freshman test scores** SAT critical reading scores over 500: 100%; SAT math scores over 500: 100%; ACT scores over 18: 100%; SAT critical reading scores over 600: 96%; SAT math scores over 600: 97%; ACT scores over 24: 99% **Housing** Yes **Expenses** Tuition & Fees $38,394; Room & Board $12,936 **Undergraduates** 50% women, 1% part-time, 0.5% Native American, 11% Hispanic American, 9% African American, 14% Asian American/Pacific Islander **The most frequently chosen baccalaureate fields are** interdisciplinary studies, psychology, social sciences **Academic program** Advanced placement, self-designed majors, internships **Contact** Mr. Bruce Poch, Vice President and Dean of Admissions, Pomona College, 333 North College Way, Claremont, CA 91711. *Phone:* 909-621-8134. *Fax:* 909-621-8952. *E-mail:* admissions@pomona.edu. *Web site:* http://www.pomona.edu/.

Saint Mary's College of California

Moraga, California

General Independent Roman Catholic, comprehensive, coed **Entrance** Moderately difficult **Setting** 420-acre suburban campus **Total enrollment** 3,636 **Student-faculty ratio** 12:1 **Application deadline** 2/1 (freshmen), 7/1 (transfer) **Freshman admission** 79% were admitted. Average high school GPA 3.4 **Freshman test scores** SAT critical reading scores over 500: 73%; SAT math scores over 500: 71.7%; SAT critical reading scores over 600: 23.1%; SAT math scores over 600: 27.6% **Housing** Yes **Expenses** Tuition & Fees $33,910; Room & Board $11,940 **Undergraduates** 63% women, 10% part-time, 3% 25 or older, 1% Native American, 20% Hispanic American, 7% African American, 11% Asian American/Pacific Islander **The most frequently chosen baccalaureate fields are** business/marketing, liberal arts/general studies, social sciences **Academic program** Advanced placement, self-designed majors, honors program, summer session, adult/continuing education programs, internships **Contact** Mr. Michael McKeon, Dean of Admissions, Saint Mary's College of California, PO Box 4800, Moraga, CA 94575-4800. *Phone:* 925-631-4224 or toll-free 800-800-4SMC. *Fax:* 925-376-7193. *E-mail:* smcadmit@stmarys-ca.edu. *Web site:* http://www.stmarys-ca.edu/.

Samuel Merritt University

Oakland, California

General Independent, upper-level, coed, primarily women **Entrance** Moderately difficult **Setting** 1-acre urban campus **Total enrollment** 1,400 **Student-faculty ratio** 10:1 **Application deadline** 3/1 (transfer) **First-year students** 32% were admitted **Housing** No **Expenses** Tuition & Fees $34,148 **Undergraduates** 85% women, 12% part-time, 65% 25 or older, 1% Native American, 9% Hispanic American, 3% African American, 22% Asian American/Pacific Islander **The most frequently chosen baccalaureate field is** health professions and related sciences **Academic program** Advanced placement, accelerated degree program, summer session, internships **Contact** Ms. Anne Seed, Director of Admissions, Samuel Merritt University, 370 Hawthorne Avenue, Oakland, CA 94609-3108. *Phone:* 510-869-6610 or toll-free 800-607-MERRITT. *Fax:* 510-869-6525. *E-mail:* admission@samuelmerritt.edu. *Web site:* http://www.samuelmerritt.edu/.

San Diego Christian College

El Cajon, California

General Independent nondenominational, 4-year, coed **Entrance** Moderately difficult **Setting** 55-acre suburban campus **Total enrollment** 439 **Student-faculty ratio** 15:1 **Application deadline** 7/1 (freshmen), 7/1 (transfer) **Freshman admission** 60% were admitted. Average high school GPA 3.25 **Freshman test scores** SAT critical reading scores over 500: 48%; SAT math scores over 500: 30%; ACT scores over 18: 70%; SAT critical reading scores over 600: 10%; SAT math scores over 600: 8%; ACT scores over 24: 11% **Housing** Yes **Expenses** Tuition & Fees $22,692; Room & Board $8260 **Undergraduates** 47% women, 8% part-time, 50% 25 or older, 2% Native American, 16% Hispanic American, 10% African American, 6% Asian American/Pacific Islander **The most frequently chosen baccalaureate fields are** business/marketing, interdisciplinary studies, liberal arts/general studies **Academic program** English as a second language, advanced placement, accelerated degree program, self-designed majors, honors program, summer session, adult/continuing education programs, internships **Contact** Candice Del Giudice, Director of Admissions, San Diego Christian College, 2100 Greenfield Drive, El Cajon, CA 92019-1157. *Phone:* 619-588-7747 or toll-free 800-676-2242. *Fax:* 619-590-1739. *E-mail:* cdelgiudice@sdcc.edu. *Web site:* http://www.sdcc.edu/.

San Diego State University

San Diego, California

General State-supported, university, coed **Entrance** Moderately difficult **Setting** 300-acre urban campus **Total enrollment** 33,790 **Student-faculty ratio** 22:1 **Application deadline** 11/30 (freshmen), 11/30 (transfer) **Freshman admission** 36% were admitted. Average high school GPA 3.47 **Freshman test scores** SAT critical reading scores over

San Diego State University (continued)
500: 57%; SAT math scores over 500: 62.8%; ACT scores over 18: 86.7%; SAT critical reading scores over 600: 15.8%; SAT math scores over 600: 25.2%; ACT scores over 24: 40.1% **Housing** Yes **Expenses** Tuition & Fees: state resident $4902, nonresident $16,062; Room & Board $11,485 **Undergraduates** 57% women, 16% part-time, 14% 25 or older, 1% Native American, 26% Hispanic American, 4% African American, 15% Asian American/Pacific Islander **The most frequently chosen baccalaureate fields are** business/marketing, psychology, social sciences **Academic program** English as a second language, advanced placement, honors program, summer session, internships **Contact** Ms. Beverly Arata, Director of Admissions, San Diego State University, 5500 Campanile Drive, San Diego, CA 92182-0771. *Phone:* 619-594-6336. *E-mail:* admissions@sdsu.edu. *Web site:* http://www.sdsu.edu/.

San Diego State University–Imperial Valley Campus
Calexico, California

Contact Admissions Department, San Diego State University–Imperial Valley Campus, 720 Heber Avenue, Calexico, CA 92231. *Phone:* 760-768-5500. *Web site:* http://www.ivcampus.sdsu.edu/.

San Francisco Art Institute
San Francisco, California

General Independent, comprehensive, coed **Entrance** Moderately difficult **Setting** 3-acre urban campus **Total enrollment** 598 **Student-faculty ratio** 11:1 **Application deadline** Rolling (freshmen), rolling (transfer) **Freshman admission** 74% were admitted. Average high school GPA 3.02 **Freshman test scores** SAT critical reading scores over 500: 68%; SAT math scores over 500: 52%; ACT scores over 18: 100%; SAT critical reading scores over 600: 20%; SAT math scores over 600: 15%; ACT scores over 24: 63% **Housing** Yes **Expenses** Tuition & Fees $31,350; Room & Board $10,050 **Undergraduates** 53% women, 10% part-time, 29% 25 or older **The most frequently chosen baccalaureate field is** visual and performing arts **Academic program** English as a second language, advanced placement, summer session, adult/continuing education programs, internships **Contact** Office of Admissions, San Francisco Art Institute, 800 Chestnut Street, San Francisco, CA 94133. *Phone:* 415-749-4500 or toll-free 800-345-SFAI. *Fax:* 415-749-4592. *E-mail:* admissions@sfai.edu. *Web site:* http://www.sfai.edu/.

San Francisco Conservatory of Music
San Francisco, California

General Independent, comprehensive, coed **Entrance** Moderately difficult **Setting** 2-acre urban campus **Total enrollment** 415 **Student-faculty ratio** 7:1 **Application deadline** 12/1 (freshmen), 12/1 (transfer) **Freshman admission** 44% were admitted **Housing** Yes **Expenses** Tuition & Fees $35,180 **Undergraduates** 46% women, 3% part-time, 13% 25 or older, 1% Native American, 7% Hispanic American, 4% African American, 13% Asian American/Pacific Islander **The most frequently chosen baccalaureate field is** visual and performing arts **Academic program** Advanced placement, internships **Contact** Mr. Alexander Brose, San Francisco Conservatory of Music, 50 Oak Street, San Francisco, CA 94102. *Phone:* 800-899-7326. *Fax:* 415-503-6299. *E-mail:* admit@sfcm.edu. *Web site:* http://www.sfcm.edu/.

San Francisco State University
San Francisco, California

General State-supported, university, coed **Entrance** Moderately difficult **Setting** 142-acre urban campus **Total enrollment** 30,469 **Student-faculty ratio** 26:1 **Application deadline** 11/30 (freshmen) **Freshman admission** 73% were admitted. Average high school GPA 3.11 **Freshman test scores** SAT critical reading scores over 500: 54.1%; SAT math scores over 500: 53.4%; ACT scores over 18: 84.1%; SAT critical reading scores over 600: 14.2%; SAT math scores over 600: 16.1%; ACT scores over 24: 29.9% **Housing** Yes **Expenses** Tuition & Fees: state resident $4740, nonresident $15,900; Room & Board $10,904 **Undergraduates** 59% women, 20% part-time, 22% 25 or older, 0.5% Native American, 18% Hispanic American, 5% African American, 28% Asian American/Pacific Islander **Academic program** English as a second language, advanced placement, self-designed majors, honors program, summer session, adult/continuing education programs, internships **Contact** Admissions Officer, San Francisco State University, 1600 Holloway Avenue, San Francisco, CA 94132-1722. *Phone:* 415-338-1113. *Fax:* 415-338-7196. *E-mail:* ugadmit@sfsu.edu. *Web site:* http://www.sfsu.edu/.

San Jose State University
San Jose, California

General State-supported, comprehensive, coed **Setting** 104-acre urban campus **Total enrollment** 31,280 **Student-faculty ratio** 25:1 **Application deadline** 11/30 (freshmen), 11/30 (transfer) **Freshman admission** 74% were admitted. Average high school GPA 3.21 **Freshman test scores** SAT critical reading scores over 500: 46.2%; SAT math scores over 500: 58.9%; ACT scores over 18: 80.4%; SAT critical reading scores over 600: 8.4%; SAT math scores over 600: 20.5%; ACT scores over 24: 25.2% **Housing** Yes **Expenses** Tuition & Fees: state resident $3992, nonresident $14,162; Room & Board $8663 **Undergraduates** 52% women, 25% part-time, 24% 25 or older, 0.4% Native American, 19% Hispanic American, 5% African American, 34% Asian American/Pacific Islander **The most frequently chosen baccalaureate fields are** business/marketing, engineering, health professions and related sciences **Academic program** Advanced placement, self-designed majors, honors program, summer session, adult/continuing education programs, internships **Contact** San Jose State University, One Washington Square, San Jose, CA 95192-0001. *Phone:* 408-283-7500. *Fax:* 408-924-2050. *E-mail:* contact@sjsu.edu. *Web site:* http://www.sjsu.edu/.

Santa Clara University
Santa Clara, California

General Independent Roman Catholic (Jesuit), university, coed **Entrance** Moderately difficult **Setting** 106-acre suburban campus **Total enrollment** 8,846 **Student-faculty ratio** 13:1 **Application deadline** 1/7 (freshmen), 5/1 (transfer) **Freshman admission** 59% were admitted. Average high school GPA 3.55 **Freshman test scores** SAT critical reading scores over 500: 92%; SAT math scores over 500: 95%; ACT scores over 18: 99%; SAT critical reading scores over 600: 52%; SAT math scores over 600: 67%; ACT scores over 24: 85% **Housing** Yes **Expenses** Tuition & Fees $36,000; Room & Board $11,400 **Undergraduates** 53% women, 2% part-time, 3% 25 or older, 1% Native American, 15% Hispanic American, 4% African American, 17% Asian American/Pacific Islander **The most frequently chosen baccalaureate fields are** business/marketing, communications/journalism, social sciences **Academic program** Advanced placement, self-designed majors, honors program, summer session, internships **Contact** Ms. Sandra Hayes, Dean of Undergraduate Admissions, Santa Clara University, 500 El Camino Real, Santa Clara, CA 95053. *Phone:* 408-554-4700. *Fax:* 408-554-5255. *E-mail:* ugadmissions@scu.edu. *Web site:* http://www.scu.edu/.

School of Urban Missions
Oakland, California

General Independent interdenominational, primarily 2-year, coed **Total enrollment** 139 **Student-faculty ratio** 11:1 **Application deadline** Rolling (freshmen), rolling (transfer) **Freshman admission** 59% were admitted **Undergraduates** 43% women, 4% part-time, 22% Hispanic American, 32% African American, 16% Asian American/Pacific Islander **Contact** Admissions, School of Urban Missions, 735 105th Avenue, Oakland, CA 94603. *Phone:* 510-567-6174 or toll-free 800-385-6364. *Fax:* 510-568-1024. *Web site:* http://www.sum.edu/.

Scripps College
Claremont, California

General Independent, 4-year, women only **Entrance** Very difficult **Setting** 30-acre suburban campus **Total enrollment** 922 **Student-faculty ratio** 10:1 **Application deadline** 1/1 (freshmen), 4/1 (transfer) **Freshman admission** 33% were admitted. Average high school GPA 4.05 **Freshman test scores** SAT critical reading scores over 500: 100%; SAT math scores over 500: 98%; ACT scores over 18: 100%; SAT critical reading scores over 600: 87%; SAT math scores over 600: 81%; ACT scores over 24: 96% **Housing** Yes **Expenses** Tuition & Fees $39,060; Room & Board $11,850 **Undergraduates** 1% part-time, 1% Native American, 9% Hispanic American, 4% African American, 13% Asian American/Pacific Islander **The most frequently chosen baccalaureate fields are** area and ethnic studies, psychology, social sciences **Academic program** Advanced placement, accelerated degree program, self-designed majors, internships **Contact** Ms. Patricia F. Goldsmith, Vice President for Enrollment, Marketing, and Communications, Scripps College, 1030 Columbia Avenue, Claremont, CA 91711. *Phone:* 909-621-8149 or toll-free 800-770-1333. *Fax:* 909-607-7508. *E-mail:* admission@scrippscollege.edu. *Web site:* http://www.scrippscollege.edu/.

Shasta Bible College
Redding, California

General Independent nondenominational, comprehensive, coed **Entrance** Noncompetitive **Setting** 55-acre small-town campus **Total enrollment** 59 **Student-faculty ratio** 3:1 **Application deadline** Rolling (freshmen) **Freshman admission** 83% were admitted **Housing** Yes **Expenses** Tuition & Fees $9420; Room only $2400 **Undergraduates** 57% women, 27% part-time, 53% 25 or older **Academic program** Accelerated degree program, summer session, adult/continuing education programs **Contact** Connie Barton, Registrar, Shasta Bible College, 2951 Goodwater Avenue, Redding, CA 96002. *Phone:* 530-221-4275 Ext. 26 or toll-free 800-800-45BC (in-state); 800-800-6929 (out-of-state). *Fax:* 530-221-6929. *E-mail:* registrar@shasta.edu. *Web site:* http://www.shasta.edu/.

Silicon Valley University
San Jose, California

General Proprietary, comprehensive, coed **Setting** 1-acre suburban campus **Total enrollment** 1,090 **Student-faculty ratio** 24:1 **Housing** Yes **Undergraduates** 65% 25 or older, 2% Asian American/Pacific Islander **Academic program** English as a second language, accelerated degree program, honors program, summer session, internships **Contact** Admissions Office, Silicon Valley University, 2160 Lundy Avenue, Suite 110, San Jose, CA 95131. *Phone:* 408-435-8989 Ext. 109. *E-mail:* admission-office@svuca.edu. *Web site:* http://www.svuca.edu/.

Simpson University
Redding, California

General Independent, comprehensive, coed, affiliated with The Christian and Missionary Alliance **Entrance** Moderately difficult **Setting** 100-acre suburban campus **Total enrollment** 1,143 **Student-faculty ratio** 16:1 **Application deadline** Rolling (freshmen), rolling (transfer) **Freshman admission** 59% were admitted. Average high school GPA 3.38 **Freshman test scores** SAT critical reading scores over 500: 48%; SAT math scores over 500: 43%; ACT scores over 18: 79%; SAT critical reading scores over 600: 17%; SAT math scores over 600: 8%; ACT scores over 24: 31% **Housing** Yes **Expenses** Tuition & Fees $21,000; Room & Board $7000 **Undergraduates** 63% women, 3% part-time, 29% 25 or older, 1% Native American, 6% Hispanic American, 4% African American, 8% Asian American/Pacific Islander **The most frequently chosen baccalaureate fields are** business/marketing, liberal arts/general studies, psychology **Academic program** Advanced placement, accelerated degree program, self-designed majors, honors program, summer session, adult/continuing education programs, internships **Contact** Mrs. Kendell Kluttz, Director of Undergraduate Admissions, Simpson University, 2211 College View Drive, Redding, CA 96003-8606. *Phone:* 530-226-5600 or toll-free 800-598-2493. *Fax:* 530-226-4861. *E-mail:* admissions@simpsonu.edu. *Web site:* http://www.simpsonuniversity.edu/.

Soka University of America
Aliso Viejo, California

General Independent, comprehensive, coed **Entrance** Moderately difficult **Setting** 103-acre suburban campus **Total enrollment** 367 **Student-faculty ratio** 9:1 **Application deadline** 1/15 (freshmen) **Freshman admission** 26% were admitted. Average high school GPA 3.61 **Freshman test scores** SAT critical reading scores over 500: 53%; SAT math scores over 500: 95%; ACT scores over 18: 100%; SAT critical reading scores over 600: 27%; SAT math scores over 600: 75%; ACT scores over 24: 56% **Housing** Yes **Expenses** Tuition & Fees $26,110; Room & Board $9640 **Undergraduates** 63% women, 4% 25 or older **The most frequently chosen baccalaureate field is** liberal arts/general studies **Academic program** Internships **Contact** Ms. Marilyn Grove, Director of Student Recruitment Programs, Soka University of America, Enrollment Services, 1 University Drive, Aliso Viejo, CA 92656. *Phone:* 949-480-4131 or toll-free 888-600-SOKA. *Fax:* 949-480-4151. *E-mail:* admission@soka.edu. *Web site:* http://www.soka.edu/.

Sonoma State University
Rohnert Park, California

General State-supported, comprehensive, coed **Entrance** Moderately difficult **Setting** 280-acre small-town campus **Total enrollment** 8,921 **Student-faculty ratio** 23:1 **Application deadline** Rolling (freshmen), rolling (transfer) **Freshman admission** 77% were admitted. Average high school GPA 3.23 **Freshman test scores** SAT critical reading scores over 500: 59.5%; ACT scores over 18: 90%; SAT critical reading scores over 600: 14.5%; ACT scores over 24: 36% **Housing** Yes **Expenses** Tuition & Fees: state resident $5290, nonresident $15,637; Room & Board $10,086 **Undergraduates** 61% women, 11% part-time, 11% 25 or older, 1% Native American, 12% Hispanic American, 2% African American, 5% Asian American/Pacific Islander **The most frequently chosen baccalaureate fields are** business/marketing, liberal arts/general studies, psychology **Academic program** English as a second language, advanced placement, accelerated degree program, self-designed majors, honors program, summer session, adult/continuing education programs, internships **Contact** Mr. Gustavo Flores, Director of Admissions, Sonoma State University, 1801 East Cotati Avenue, Rohnert Park, CA 94928-3609. *Phone:* 707-664-2778. *E-mail:* gustavo.flores@sonoma.edu. *Web site:* http://www.sonoma.edu/.

Southern California Institute of Architecture
Los Angeles, California

General Independent, comprehensive, coed **Entrance** Moderately difficult **Setting** urban campus **Total enrollment** 466 **Student-faculty ratio** 15:1 **Application deadline** 2/1 (freshmen), 5/1 (transfer) **Freshman admission** 82% were admitted. Average high school GPA 3.1 **Freshman test scores** SAT critical reading scores over 500: 85%; SAT math scores over 500: 96%; ACT scores over 18: 100%; SAT critical reading scores over 600: 35%; SAT math scores over 600: 50% **Housing** No **Expenses** Tuition & Fees $27,750 **Undergraduates** 33% women, 82% 25 or older, 15% Hispanic American, 2% African American, 23% Asian American/Pacific Islander **The most frequently chosen baccalaureate field is** architecture **Academic program** English as a second language, advanced placement, summer session, internships **Contact** Mr. J.J. Jackman, Admissions Director, Southern California Institute of Architecture, 960 East Third Street, Los Angeles, CA 90013. *Phone:* 213-613-2200 Ext. 321 or toll-free 800-774-7242. *Fax:* 213-613-2260. *E-mail:* jj@sciarc.edu. *Web site:* http://www.sciarc.edu/.

Southern California Institute of Technology
Anaheim, California

General Proprietary, 4-year, coed **Setting** urban campus **Total enrollment** 600 **Undergraduates** 33% women, 83% 25 or older **Academic program** English as a second language, accelerated degree program **Contact** Director of Admissions, Southern California Institute of Technology, 222 Soouth Harbor Boulevard, Suite 200, Anaheim, CA 92805. *Phone:* 714-300-0300. *Fax:* 714-300-0311. *E-mail:* admissions@scitech.edu. *Web site:* http://www.scitcollege.com/.

Southern California Seminary
El Cajon, California

General Independent interdenominational, comprehensive, coed **Entrance** Moderately difficult **Total enrollment** 283 **Student-faculty ratio** 10:1 **Application deadline** 8/13 (freshmen) **Freshman admission** 88% were admitted **Housing** Yes **Expenses** Tuition & Fees $12,576; Room only $5110 **Undergraduates** 60% 25 or older **The most frequently chosen baccalaureate field is** theology and religious vocations **Contact** Thomas Pittman, Director of Admissions, Southern California Seminary, 2075 East Madison Avenue, El Cajon, CA 92019. *Phone:* 888-389-7244. *Fax:* 619-442-4510. *E-mail:* thpittman@socalsem.edu. *Web site:* http://www.socalsem.edu/.

Stanford University
Stanford, California

General Independent, university, coed **Entrance** Most difficult **Setting** 8,180-acre suburban campus **Total enrollment** 18,498 **Student-faculty ratio** 6:1 **Application deadline** 1/1 (freshmen), 3/15 (transfer) **Freshman admission** 8% were admitted **Freshman test scores** SAT critical reading scores over 500: 99.55%; SAT math scores over 500: 99.87%; SAT critical reading scores over 600: 93.25%; SAT math scores over 600: 95.7% **Housing** Yes **Expenses** Tuition & Fees $37,881; Room & Board $11,463 **Undergraduates** 49% women, 1% part-time, 1% 25 or older, 3% Native American, 13% Hispanic American, 10% African American, 23% Asian American/Pacific Islander **The most frequently chosen baccalaureate fields are** interdisciplinary studies, engineering, social sciences **Academic program** Advanced placement, self-designed majors, honors program, summer session, internships **Contact** Rick Shaw, Dean of Undergraduate Admission and Financial Aid, Stanford University, Montag Hall, 355 Galvez Street, Stanford, CA 94305-3020. *Phone:* 650-723-2091. *Fax:* 650-725-2846. *E-mail:* admission@stanford.edu. *Web site:* http://www.stanford.edu/.

Thomas Aquinas College
Santa Paula, California

General Independent Roman Catholic, 4-year, coed **Entrance** Very difficult **Setting** 170-acre rural campus **Total enrollment** 345 **Student-faculty ratio** 11:1 **Application deadline** Rolling (freshmen) **Freshman admission** 78% were admitted. Average high school GPA 3.74 **Freshman test scores** SAT critical reading scores over 500: 100%; SAT math scores over 500: 96%; ACT scores over 18: 97%; SAT critical reading scores over 600: 80%; SAT math scores over 600: 60%; ACT scores over 24: 85% **Housing** Yes **Expenses** Tuition & Fees $22,400; Room & Board $7400 **Undergraduates** 54% women, 2% 25 or older, 1% Native American, 8% Hispanic American, 2% Asian American/Pacific Islander **The most frequently chosen baccalaureate field is** liberal arts/general studies **Contact** Mr. Jonathan P. Daly, Director of Admissions, Thomas Aquinas College, 10000 North Ojai Road, Santa Paula, CA 93060-9621. *Phone:* 805-525-4417 Ext. 5901 or toll-free 800-634-9797. *Fax:* 805-421-5905. *E-mail:* admissions@thomasaqinas.edu. *Web site:* http://www.thomasaquinas.edu/.

TUI University
Cypress, California

General Independent, university, coed **Entrance** Minimally difficult **Setting** urban campus **Total enrollment** 8,046 **Student-faculty ratio** 18:1 **Application deadline** Rolling (freshmen) **Freshman admission** 72% were admitted **Housing** No **Expenses** Tuition & Fees $9440 **Undergraduates** 33% women, 51% part-time, 89% 25 or older, 0.5% Native American, 6% Hispanic American, 14% African American, 4% Asian American/Pacific Islander **Academic program** Honors program, summer session, adult/continuing education programs **Contact** Wei Ren, Registrar, TUI University, 5665 Plaza Drive, 3rd Floor, Cypress, CA 90630. *Phone:* 714-816-0366 Ext. 2015. *Fax:* 714-827-7407. *E-mail:* registration@tuiu.edu. *Web site:* http://www.tuiu.edu/.

United States University
National City, California

Contact United States University, 140 West 16th Street, National City, CA 91950. *Phone:* toll-free 888-422-3381. *Web site:* http://www.usuniversity.edu/.

University of California, Berkeley
Berkeley, California

General State-supported, university, coed **Entrance** Very difficult **Setting** 1,232-acre urban campus **Total enrollment** 35,843 **Application deadline** 11/30 (freshmen), 11/30 (transfer) **Freshman admission** 22% were admitted **Freshman test scores** SAT critical reading scores over 500: 95%; SAT math scores over 500: 96%; SAT critical reading scores over 600: 75%; SAT math scores over 600: 84% **Housing** Yes **Expenses** Tuition & Fees: state resident $9817, nonresident $32,486; Room & Board $15,308 **Undergraduates** 7% 25 or older, 1% Native American, 12% Hispanic American, 4% African American, 40% Asian American/Pacific Islander **Academic program** English as a second language, advanced placement, accelerated degree program, self-designed majors, honors program, summer session, adult/continuing education programs, internships **Contact** Mr. Walter Robinson, Director of Undergraduate Admissions, University of California, Berkeley, Berkeley, CA 94720-1500. *Phone:* 510-642-2316. *Web site:* http://www.berkeley.edu/.

University of California, Davis
Davis, California

General State-supported, university, coed **Entrance** Very difficult **Setting** 5,993-acre suburban campus **Total enrollment** 31,247 **Student-faculty ratio** 19:1 **Application deadline** 11/30 (freshmen), 11/30 (transfer) **Freshman admission** 47% were admitted. Average high school GPA 3.85 **Freshman test scores** SAT critical reading scores over 500: 81.01%; SAT math scores over 500: 88.23%; ACT scores over 18: 95.89%; SAT critical reading scores over 600: 41.94%; SAT math scores over 600: 62.38%; ACT scores over 24: 77.25% **Housing** Yes **Expenses** Tuition & Fees: state resident $9364, nonresident $31,385; Room & Board $12,361 **Undergraduates** 56% women, 1% part-time, 5% 25 or older, 1% Native American, 14% Hispanic American, 3% African American, 40% Asian American/Pacific Islander **The most frequently chosen baccalaureate fields are** biological/life sciences, psychology, social sciences **Academic program** English as a second language, advanced placement, self-designed majors, honors program, summer session, adult/continuing education programs, internships **Contact** Frank Wada, Interim Deputy Director of Undergraduate Admissions, University of California, Davis, Undergraduate Admission and Outreach Services, 178 Mrak Hall, Davis, CA 95616. *Phone:* 530-752-1011. *Fax:* 530-752-1280. *E-mail:* undergraduateadmissions@ucdavis.edu. *Web site:* http://www.ucdavis.edu/.

University of California, Irvine
Irvine, California

General State-supported, university, coed **Entrance** Very difficult **Setting** 1,477-acre suburban campus **Total enrollment** 27,142 **Student-faculty ratio** 19:1 **Application deadline** 11/30 (freshmen), 11/30 (transfer) **Freshman admission** 44% were admitted. Average high school GPA

3.85 **Freshman test scores** SAT critical reading scores over 500: 84%; SAT math scores over 500: 92%; SAT critical reading scores over 600: 42%; SAT math scores over 600: 66% **Housing** Yes **Expenses** Tuition & Fees: state resident $11,913, nonresident $34,792; Room & Board $10,655 **Undergraduates** 53% women, 2% part-time, 5% 25 or older, 0.4% Native American, 14% Hispanic American, 2% African American, 53% Asian American/Pacific Islander **The most frequently chosen baccalaureate fields are** biological/life sciences, psychology, social sciences **Academic program** English as a second language, advanced placement, accelerated degree program, honors program, summer session, internships **Contact** Brent W. Yunek, Director of Admissions and Relations with Schools, Acting, University of California, Irvine, Irvine, CA 92697. *Phone:* 949-824-6703. *Web site:* http://www.uci.edu/.

University of California, Los Angeles

Los Angeles, California

General State-supported, university, coed **Entrance** Very difficult **Setting** 419-acre urban campus **Total enrollment** 39,984 **Student-faculty ratio** 16:1 **Application deadline** 11/30 (freshmen), 11/30 (transfer) **Freshman admission** 22% were admitted. Average high school GPA 4.24 **Freshman test scores** SAT critical reading scores over 500: 92.19%; SAT math scores over 500: 93.53%; ACT scores over 18: 97.76%; SAT critical reading scores over 600: 64.48%; SAT math scores over 600: 76.45%; ACT scores over 24: 79.23% **Housing** Yes **Expenses** Tuition & Fees: state resident $9151, nonresident $31,172; Room & Board $13,314 **Undergraduates** 56% women, 3% part-time, 5% 25 or older, 0.5% Native American, 15% Hispanic American, 4% African American, 38% Asian American/Pacific Islander **The most frequently chosen baccalaureate fields are** biological/life sciences, psychology, social sciences **Academic program** Advanced placement, accelerated degree program, self-designed majors, honors program, summer session, adult/continuing education programs, internships **Contact** Dr. Vu T. Tran, Director of Undergraduate Admissions, University of California, Los Angeles, 405 Hilgard Avenue, Box 951436, Los Angeles, CA 90095-1436. *Phone:* 310-825-3101. *E-mail:* ugadm@saonet.ucla.edu. *Web site:* http://www.ucla.edu/.

University of California, Merced

Merced, California

General State-supported, university, coed **Entrance** Moderately difficult **Setting** 815-acre small-town campus **Total enrollment** 3,414 **Student-faculty ratio** 16:1 **Application deadline** 1/1 (freshmen), 1/31 (transfer) **Freshman admission** 91% were admitted. Average high school GPA 3.44 **Freshman test scores** SAT critical reading scores over 500: 53%; SAT math scores over 500: 62%; SAT critical reading scores over 600: 17%; SAT math scores over 600: 26% **Housing** Yes **Expenses** Tuition & Fees: state resident $4476, nonresident $14,486; Room & Board $10,550 **Undergraduates** 51% women, 1% part-time, 8% 25 or older, 1% Native American, 32% Hispanic American, 7% African American, 33% Asian American/Pacific Islander **The most frequently chosen baccalaureate fields are** biological/life sciences, engineering, psychology **Academic program** Advanced placement, summer session, internships **Contact** Susan Fauroat, Associate Director of Admissions and Outreach, University of California, Merced, 5200 North Lake Road, Merced, CA 95343. *Phone:* 209-228-4241. *E-mail:* eruiz@ucmerced.edu. *Web site:* http://www.ucmerced.edu/.

University of California, Riverside

Riverside, California

General State-supported, university, coed **Entrance** Very difficult **Setting** 1,200-acre urban campus **Total enrollment** 19,439 **Student-faculty ratio** 19:1 **Application deadline** 11/30 (freshmen), 11/30 (transfer) **Freshman admission** 80% were admitted. Average high school GPA 3.49 **Freshman test scores** SAT critical reading scores over 500: 57%; SAT math scores over 500: 68%; ACT scores over 18: 85%; SAT critical reading scores over 600: 16%; SAT math scores over 600: 32%; ACT scores over 24: 33% **Housing** Yes **Expenses** Tuition & Fees: state resident $8507, nonresident $31,178; Room & Board $10,900 **Undergraduates** 52% women, 3% part-time, 5% 25 or older, 0.4% Native American, 29% Hispanic American, 8% African American, 40% Asian American/Pacific Islander **The most frequently chosen baccalaureate fields are** business/marketing, biological/life sciences, social sciences **Academic program** English as a second language, advanced placement, accelerated degree program, honors program, summer session, adult/continuing education programs, internships **Contact** Emily Engelschall, Director, Undergraduate Recruitment, University of California, Riverside, 3221 Student Services, 900 University Avenue, Riverside, CA 92521. *Phone:* 951-827-3986. *Fax:* 951-827-6344. *E-mail:* discover@ucr.edu. *Web site:* http://www.ucr.edu/.

University of California, San Diego

La Jolla, California

General State-supported, university, coed **Entrance** Very difficult **Setting** 1,976-acre suburban campus **Total enrollment** 26,723 **Student-faculty ratio** 19:1 **Application deadline** 11/30 (freshmen), 11/30 (transfer) **Freshman admission** 42% were admitted. Average high school GPA 3.94 **Freshman test scores** SAT critical reading scores over 500: 89%; SAT math scores over 500: 97%; ACT scores over 18: 97%; SAT critical reading scores over 600: 56%; SAT math scores over 600: 78%; ACT scores over 24: 79% **Housing** Yes **Expenses** Tuition & Fees: state resident $9698, nonresident $32,367; Room & Board $11,057 **Undergraduates** 52% women, 1% part-time, 4% 25 or older, 0.4% Native American, 12% Hispanic American, 2% African American, 45% Asian American/Pacific Islander **The most frequently chosen baccalaureate fields are** biological/life sciences, engineering, social sciences **Academic program** English as a second language, advanced placement, accelerated degree program, self-designed majors, honors program, summer session, internships **Contact** Ms. Mae Brown, Assistant Vice Chancellor, Admissions and Relations with Schools, University of California, San Diego, 9500 Gilman Drive, 0021, La Jolla, CA 92093-0021. *Phone:* 858-534-4831. *E-mail:* admissionsreply@ucsd.edu. *Web site:* http://www.ucsd.edu/.

University of California, Santa Barbara

Santa Barbara, California

General State-supported, university, coed **Entrance** Very difficult **Setting** 989-acre suburban campus **Total enrollment** 22,850 **Student-faculty ratio** 17:1 **Application deadline** 11/30 (freshmen), 11/30 (transfer) **Freshman admission** 48% were admitted. Average high school GPA 3.85 **Freshman test scores** SAT critical reading scores over 500: 88%; SAT math scores over 500: 89%; ACT scores over 18: 97%; SAT critical reading scores over 600: 51%; SAT math scores over 600: 61%; ACT scores over 24: 76% **Housing** Yes **Expenses** Tuition & Fees: state resident $9055, nonresident $30,724; Room & Board $12,765 **Undergraduates** 54% women, 2% part-time, 3% 25 or older, 1% Native American, 22% Hispanic American, 3% African American, 17% Asian American/Pacific Islander **The most frequently chosen baccalaureate fields are** business/marketing, biological/life sciences, social sciences **Academic program** English as a second language, advanced placement, accelerated degree program, self-designed majors, honors program, summer session, internships **Contact** Office of Admissions, University of California, Santa Barbara, 1210 Cheadle Hall, Santa Barbara, CA 93106-2014. *Phone:* 805-893-2881. *Fax:* 805-893-2676. *E-mail:* admissions@sa.ucsb.edu. *Web site:* http://www.ucsb.edu/.

University of California, Santa Cruz

Santa Cruz, California

General State-supported, university, coed **Entrance** Very difficult **Setting** 2,000-acre small-town campus **Total enrollment** 16,775 **Student-**

University of California, Santa Cruz (continued)
faculty ratio 19:1 **Application deadline** 11/30 (freshmen), 11/30 (transfer) **Freshman admission** 64% were admitted. Average high school GPA 3.61 **Freshman test scores** SAT critical reading scores over 500: 81%; SAT math scores over 500: 83%; ACT scores over 18: 94%; SAT critical reading scores over 600: 41%; SAT math scores over 600: 46%; ACT scores over 24: 66% **Housing** Yes **Expenses** Tuition & Fees: state resident $10,095, nonresident $32,115; Room & Board $13,641 **Undergraduates** 4% 25 or older, 1% Native American, 18% Hispanic American, 3% African American, 22% Asian American/Pacific Islander **The most frequently chosen baccalaureate fields are** biological/life sciences, psychology, social sciences **Academic program** Advanced placement, accelerated degree program, self-designed majors, honors program, summer session, internships **Contact** Michelle Whittingham, Acting Director of Admissions and University Registrar, University of California, Santa Cruz, 1156 High Street, Santa Cruz, CA 95064. *Phone:* 831-459-1372. *Fax:* 831-459-4163. *E-mail:* admissions@ucsc.edu. *Web site:* http://www.ucsc.edu/.

University of La Verne
La Verne, California

General Independent, university, coed **Entrance** Moderately difficult **Setting** 38-acre suburban campus **Total enrollment** 4,060 **Student-faculty ratio** 12:1 **Application deadline** 2/1 (freshmen), 4/1 (transfer) **Freshman admission** 68% were admitted. Average high school GPA 3.32 **Freshman test scores** SAT critical reading scores over 500: 49%; SAT math scores over 500: 48%; ACT scores over 18: 75%; SAT critical reading scores over 600: 10%; SAT math scores over 600: 13%; ACT scores over 24: 23% **Housing** Yes **Expenses** Tuition & Fees $29,800; Room & Board $10,440 **Undergraduates** 59% women, 7% part-time, 5% 25 or older, 1% Native American, 39% Hispanic American, 7% African American, 4% Asian American/Pacific Islander **The most frequently chosen baccalaureate fields are** business/marketing, communications/journalism, social sciences **Academic program** English as a second language, advanced placement, accelerated degree program, self-designed majors, honors program, summer session, adult/continuing education programs, internships **Contact** Ms. Ana Liza V. Zell, Associate Dean of Undergraduate Admissions, University of La Verne, 1950 Third Street, La Verne, CA 91750. *Phone:* 909-593-3511 Ext. 4035 or toll-free 800-876-4858. *Fax:* 909-392-2714. *E-mail:* admissions@ulv.edu. *Web site:* http://www.laverne.edu/.

University of Phoenix–Bay Area Campus
Pleasanton, California

General Proprietary, comprehensive, coed **Entrance** Noncompetitive **Setting** urban campus **Total enrollment** 2,240 **Application deadline** Rolling (freshmen), rolling (transfer) **Housing** No **Expenses** Tuition & Fees $13,380 **Undergraduates** 64% women, 82% 25 or older, 1% Native American, 14% Hispanic American, 14% African American, 11% Asian American/Pacific Islander **Academic program** Advanced placement, accelerated degree program, adult/continuing education programs **Contact** Ms. Audra McQuarie, Registrar/Executive Director, University of Phoenix–Bay Area Campus, 4035 South Riverpoint Parkway, Mail Stop CF-L101, Phoenix, AZ 85040-1958. *Phone:* 480-557-6151 or toll-free 877-4-STUDENT. *Fax:* 480-643-3068. *E-mail:* audra.mcquarie@phoenix.edu. *Web site:* http://www.phoenix.edu/.

University of Phoenix–Central Valley Campus
Fresno, California

General Proprietary, comprehensive, coed **Entrance** Noncompetitive **Setting** urban campus **Total enrollment** 2,235 **Application deadline** Rolling (freshmen), rolling (transfer) **Housing** No **Expenses** Tuition & Fees $13,380 **Undergraduates** 71% women, 73% 25 or older, 1% Native American, 34% Hispanic American, 9% African American, 3% Asian American/Pacific Islander **The most frequently chosen baccalaureate fields are** business/marketing, public administration and social services, security and protective services **Academic program** Advanced placement, accelerated degree program **Contact** Ms. Audra McQuarie, Registrar/Executive Director, University of Phoenix–Central Valley Campus, 4035 South Riverpoint Parkway, Mail Stop CF-L101, Phoenix, AZ 85040. *Phone:* 480-557-6151 or toll-free 888-776-4867 (in-state); 888-228-7240 (out-of-state). *Fax:* 480-643-3068. *E-mail:* audra.mcquarie@phoenix.edu. *Web site:* http://phoenix.edu/.

University of Phoenix–Sacramento Valley Campus
Sacramento, California

General Proprietary, comprehensive, coed **Entrance** Noncompetitive **Setting** urban campus **Total enrollment** 3,842 **Application deadline** Rolling (freshmen), rolling (transfer) **Housing** No **Expenses** Tuition & Fees $13,380 **Undergraduates** 69% women, 81% 25 or older, 1% Native American, 14% Hispanic American, 15% African American, 8% Asian American/Pacific Islander **Academic program** Advanced placement, accelerated degree program, adult/continuing education programs **Contact** Ms. Audra McQuarie, Registrar/Executive Director, University of Phoenix–Sacramento Valley Campus, 4035 South Riverpoint Parkway, Mail Stop CF-L101, Phoenix, AZ 85040. *Phone:* 480-557-6151 or toll-free 800-776-4867 (in-state); 800-228-7240 (out-of-state). *Fax:* 480-643-3068. *E-mail:* audra.mcquarie@phoenix.edu. *Web site:* http://www.phoenix.edu/.

University of Phoenix–San Diego Campus
San Diego, California

General Proprietary, comprehensive, coed **Entrance** Noncompetitive **Setting** urban campus **Total enrollment** 3,212 **Application deadline** Rolling (freshmen), rolling (transfer) **Housing** No **Expenses** Tuition & Fees $13,200 **Undergraduates** 59% women, 79% 25 or older, 1% Native American, 24% Hispanic American, 8% African American, 7% Asian American/Pacific Islander **Academic program** Advanced placement, accelerated degree program, adult/continuing education programs **Contact** Ms. Audra McQuarie, Registrar/Executive Director, University of Phoenix–San Diego Campus, 4035 South Riverpoint Parkway, Mail Stop CF-L101, Phoenix, AZ 85040. *Phone:* 480-557-6151 or toll-free 888-776-4867 (in-state); 888-228-7240 (out-of-state). *Fax:* 480-643-3068. *E-mail:* audra.mcquarie@phoenix.edu. *Web site:* http://www.phoenix.edu/.

University of Phoenix–Southern California Campus
Costa Mesa, California

General Proprietary, comprehensive, coed **Entrance** Noncompetitive **Setting** urban campus **Total enrollment** 11,780 **Application deadline** Rolling (freshmen), rolling (transfer) **Housing** No **Expenses** Tuition & Fees $14,100 **Undergraduates** 67% women, 80% 25 or older, 1% Native American, 26% Hispanic American, 14% African American, 5% Asian American/Pacific Islander **The most frequently chosen baccalaureate fields are** business/marketing, computer and information sciences, public administration and social services **Academic program** Advanced placement, accelerated degree program, adult/continuing education programs **Contact** Ms. Audra McQuarie, Registrar/Executive Director, University of Phoenix–Southern California Campus, 4035 South Riverpoint Parkway, Mail Stop CF-L101, Phoenix, AZ 85040. *Phone:* 480-557-6151 or toll-free 800-776-4867 (in-state); 800-228-7240 (out-of-state). *Fax:* 480-643-3068. *E-mail:* audra.mcquarie@phoenix.edu. *Web site:* http://www.phoenix.edu/.

University of Redlands
Redlands, California

General Independent, comprehensive, coed **Entrance** Moderately difficult **Setting** 140-acre small-town campus **Total enrollment** 4,457 **Student-faculty ratio** 14:1 **Application deadline** 3/1 (freshmen), 3/1 (transfer) **Freshman admission** 70% were admitted. Average high school GPA 3.54 **Freshman test scores** SAT critical reading scores over 500: 85%; SAT math scores over 500: 85%; ACT scores over 18: 98%; SAT critical reading scores over 600: 34%; SAT math scores over 600: 44%; ACT scores over 24: 53% **Housing** Yes **Expenses** Tuition & Fees $33,894; Room & Board $10,472 **Undergraduates** 55% women, 23% part-time, 21% 25 or older, 1% Native American, 15% Hispanic American, 4% African American, 5% Asian American/Pacific Islander **The most frequently chosen baccalaureate fields are** business/marketing, health professions and related sciences, social sciences **Academic program** Advanced placement, self-designed majors, honors program, adult/continuing education programs, internships **Contact** Mr. Paul Driscoll, Dean of Admissions, University of Redlands, 1200 East Colton Avenue, PO Box 3080, Redlands, CA 92373-0999. *Phone:* 909-748-8159 or toll-free 800-455-5064. *Fax:* 909-335-4089. *E-mail:* admissions@redlands.edu. *Web site:* http://www.redlands.edu/.
Visit Petersons.com and enter keyword Redlands

See page 1300 for the College Close-Up.

University of San Diego
San Diego, California

General Independent Roman Catholic, university, coed **Entrance** Very difficult **Setting** 180-acre urban campus **Total enrollment** 7,868 **Student-faculty ratio** 15:1 **Application deadline** 1/15 (freshmen), 3/1 (transfer) **Freshman admission** 49% were admitted. Average high school GPA 3.84 **Freshman test scores** SAT critical reading scores over 500: 92%; SAT math scores over 500: 94%; ACT scores over 18: 100%; SAT critical reading scores over 600: 49%; SAT math scores over 600: 63%; ACT scores over 24: 88% **Housing** Yes **Expenses** Tuition & Fees $36,292; Room & Board $12,602 **Undergraduates** 57% women, 4% part-time, 4% 25 or older, 1% Native American, 15% Hispanic American, 3% African American, 10% Asian American/Pacific Islander **The most frequently chosen baccalaureate fields are** business/marketing, communications/journalism, social sciences **Academic program** English as a second language, advanced placement, honors program, summer session, internships **Contact** Mr. Stephen Pultz, Director of Admission, University of San Diego, 5998 Alcala Park, San Diego, CA 92110. *Phone:* 619-260-4506 or toll-free 800-248-4873. *Fax:* 619-260-6836. *E-mail:* admissions@sandiego.edu. *Web site:* http://www.sandiego.edu/.
Visit Petersons.com and enter keywords University of San Diego

University of San Francisco
San Francisco, California

General Independent Roman Catholic (Jesuit), university, coed **Entrance** Moderately difficult **Setting** 55-acre urban campus **Total enrollment** 9,012 **Student-faculty ratio** 15:1 **Application deadline** 1/15 (freshmen), rolling (transfer) **Freshman admission** 71% were admitted. Average high school GPA 3.5 **Freshman test scores** SAT critical reading scores over 500: 81%; SAT math scores over 500: 80%; ACT scores over 18: 99%; SAT critical reading scores over 600: 33%; SAT math scores over 600: 34%; ACT scores over 24: 56% **Housing** Yes **Expenses** Tuition & Fees $36,380; Room & Board $11,990 **Undergraduates** 63% women, 4% part-time, 5% 25 or older, 1% Native American, 14% Hispanic American, 5% African American, 21% Asian American/Pacific Islander **The most frequently chosen baccalaureate fields are** business/marketing, health professions and related sciences, public administration and social services **Academic program** English as a second language, advanced placement, self-designed majors, honors program, summer session, adult/continuing education programs, internships **Contact** Mr. Michael Hughes, Director, University of San Francisco, 2130 Fulton Street, San Francisco, CA 94117-1080. *Phone:* 415-422-6563 or toll-free 800-CALLUSF. *Fax:* 415-422-2217. *E-mail:* admissions@usfca.edu. *Web site:* http://www.usfca.edu/.
Visit Petersons.com and enter keywords University of San Francisco

See page 1308 for the College Close-Up.

University of Southern California
Los Angeles, California

General Independent, university, coed **Entrance** Most difficult **Setting** 155-acre rural campus **Total enrollment** 34,824 **Student-faculty ratio** 9:1 **Application deadline** 1/10 (freshmen), 2/1 (transfer) **Freshman admission** 24% were admitted. Average high school GPA 3.7 **Freshman test scores** SAT critical reading scores over 500: 99%; SAT math scores over 500: 99%; ACT scores over 18: 100%; SAT critical reading scores over 600: 83%; SAT math scores over 600: 90%; ACT scores over 24: 98% **Housing** Yes **Expenses** Tuition & Fees $39,184; Room & Board $11,458 **Undergraduates** 50% women, 4% part-time, 4% 25 or older, 1% Native American, 13% Hispanic American, 5% African American, 24% Asian American/Pacific Islander **The most frequently chosen baccalaureate fields are** business/marketing, social sciences, visual and performing arts **Academic program** English as a second language, advanced placement, accelerated degree program, self-designed majors, honors program, summer session, internships **Contact** Timothy Brunold, Associate Dean and Director of Undergraduate Admission, University of Southern California, University Park Campus, Los Angeles, CA 90089. *Phone:* 213-740-1111. *Fax:* 213-821-0200. *E-mail:* admitusc@usc.edu. *Web site:* http://www.usc.edu/.

University of the Pacific
Stockton, California

General Independent, university, coed **Entrance** Moderately difficult **Setting** 175-acre suburban campus **Total enrollment** 6,401 **Student-faculty ratio** 13:1 **Application deadline** 1/15 (freshmen), 6/1 (transfer) **Freshman admission** 42% were admitted. Average high school GPA 3.49 **Freshman test scores** SAT critical reading scores over 500: 81.8%; SAT math scores over 500: 89%; ACT scores over 18: 97.5%; SAT critical reading scores over 600: 43%; SAT math scores over 600: 57.7%; ACT scores over 24: 68.1% **Housing** Yes **Expenses** Tuition & Fees $32,230; Room & Board $10,616 **Undergraduates** 55% women, 3% part-time, 5% 25 or older, 1% Native American, 12% Hispanic American, 4% African American, 35% Asian American/Pacific Islander **The most frequently chosen baccalaureate fields are** biological/life sciences, business/marketing, engineering **Academic program** English as a second language, advanced placement, accelerated degree program, self-designed majors, honors program, summer session, internships **Contact** Mr. Rich Toledo, Director of Admissions, University of the Pacific, 3601 Pacific Avenue, Stockton, CA 95211-0197. *Phone:* 209-946-2211 or toll-free 800-959-2867. *Fax:* 209-946-2413. *E-mail:* admissions@pacific.edu. *Web site:* http://www.pacific.edu/.

University of the West
Rosemead, California

General Independent, comprehensive, coed **Setting** 10-acre suburban campus **Total enrollment** 255 **Student-faculty ratio** 8:1 **Application deadline** 6/1 (freshmen) **Freshman admission** 85% were admitted **Housing** Yes **Expenses** Tuition & Fees $8140; Room & Board $6182 **Undergraduates** 19% 25 or older, 6% Hispanic American, 8% Asian American/Pacific Islander **The most frequently chosen baccalaureate fields are** business/marketing, English, liberal arts/general studies **Academic program** English as a second language, accelerated degree program, summer session, internships **Contact** Ms. Grace Hsiao, Admissions Officer, University of the West, 1409 North Walnut Grove Avenue, Rosemead, CA 91770. *Phone:* 626-571-8811 Ext. 120. *Fax:* 626-571-4413. *E-mail:* graceh@uwest.edu. *Web site:* http://www.uwest.edu/.

See page 1318 for the College Close-Up.

Vanguard University of Southern California

Costa Mesa, California

General Independent, comprehensive, coed, affiliated with Assemblies of God **Entrance** Moderately difficult **Setting** 38-acre suburban campus **Total enrollment** 1,923 **Student-faculty ratio** 17:1 **Application deadline** 1/15 (freshmen), 12/1 (transfer) **Freshman admission** 79% were admitted. Average high school GPA 3.37 **Housing** Yes **Expenses** Tuition & Fees $26,342; Room & Board $8274 **Undergraduates** 62% women, 22% part-time, 9% 25 or older, 2% Native American, 18% Hispanic American, 4% African American, 5% Asian American/Pacific Islander **The most frequently chosen baccalaureate fields are** business/marketing, communications/journalism, psychology **Academic program** Advanced placement, accelerated degree program, summer session, adult/continuing education programs, internships **Contact** Kristi Pruett, Undergraduate Inquiry Data Coordinator, Vanguard University of Southern California, 55 Fair Drive, Costa Mesa, CA 92626. *Phone:* 800-722-6279 Ext. 4107 or toll-free 800-722-6279. *Fax:* 714-966-5471. *E-mail:* admissions@vanguard.edu. *Web site:* http://www.vanguard.edu/.

West Coast University

North Hollywood, California

Contact Mr. Roger A. Miller, Dean of Admissions and Registrar, West Coast University, 12215 Victory Boulevard, North Hollywood, CA 91606. *Phone:* 213-427-4400 or toll-free 866-508-2684. *E-mail:* info@katz.wcula.edu. *Web site:* http://www.westcoastuniversity.edu/.

Western Career College

Emeryville, California

Contact Admissions Office, Western Career College, 1400 65th Street, Suite 200, Emeryville, CA 94608. *Phone:* 510-601-0133 or toll-free 800-750-5627. *Fax:* 510-623-9822. *Web site:* http://www.westerncollege.edu/.

Western Career College

Fremont, California

Contact Mr. Anton Croos, Admissions Director, Western Career College, 41350 Christy Street, Fremont, CA 94538. *Phone:* 510-623-9966 Ext. 212 or toll-free 800-750-5627. *Web site:* http://www.westerncollege.edu/.

Westmont College

Santa Barbara, California

General Independent nondenominational, 4-year, coed **Entrance** Moderately difficult **Setting** 111-acre suburban campus **Total enrollment** 1,308 **Student-faculty ratio** 12:1 **Application deadline** 2/20 (freshmen), 3/1 (transfer) **Freshman admission** 80% were admitted. Average high school GPA 3.75 **Freshman test scores** SAT critical reading scores over 500: 86%; SAT math scores over 500: 85%; ACT scores over 18: 99%; SAT critical reading scores over 600: 46%; SAT math scores over 600: 48%; ACT scores over 24: 66% **Housing** Yes **Expenses** Tuition & Fees $34,460; Room & Board $10,960 **Undergraduates** 63% women, 1% part-time, 1% 25 or older, 2% Native American, 11% Hispanic American, 3% African American, 9% Asian American/Pacific Islander **The most frequently chosen baccalaureate fields are** business/marketing, English, visual and performing arts **Academic program** Advanced placement, accelerated degree program, self-designed majors, honors program, summer session, internships **Contact** Mrs. Joyce Luy, Dean of Admission, Westmont College, 955 La Paz Road, Santa Barbara, CA 93108. *Phone:* 805-565-6200 or toll-free 800-777-9011. *Fax:* 805-565-6234. *E-mail:* admissions@westmont.edu. *Web site:* http://www.westmont.edu/.

Visit Petersons.com and enter keyword Westmont

See page 1370 for the College Close-Up.

Westwood College–Anaheim

Anaheim, California

General Proprietary, 4-year, coed **Total enrollment** 1,206 **Contact** Director of Admissions, Westwood College–Anaheim, 1551 South Douglass Road, Anaheim, CA 92806. *Phone:* 714-704-2721 or toll-free 877-650-6050. *Fax:* 714-456-9971. *Web site:* http://www.westwood.edu/.

Westwood College–Inland Empire

Upland, California

General Proprietary, 4-year, coed **Total enrollment** 1,140 **Contact** Director of Admissions, Westwood College–Inland Empire, 20 West 7th Street, Upland, CA 91786. *Phone:* 909-931-7599 or toll-free 866-288-9488. *Fax:* 909-931-9195. *Web site:* http://www.westwood.edu/.

Westwood College–Los Angeles

Los Angeles, California

General Proprietary, 4-year, coed **Total enrollment** 948 **Contact** Director of Admissions, Westwood College–Los Angeles, 3250 Wilshire Boulevard, 4th Floor, Los Angeles, CA 90010. *Phone:* 213-382-2328 or toll-free 877-377-4600. *Fax:* 213-382-2468. *Web site:* http://www.westwood.edu/.

Westwood College–South Bay Campus

Torrance, California

General Proprietary, 4-year, coed **Total enrollment** 724 **Contact** Director of Admissions, Westwood College–South Bay Campus, 19700 South Vermont Avenue, Suite 100, Torrance, CA 90502. *Phone:* 310-965-0877 or toll-free 800-281-2978. *Fax:* 310-965-0881. *Web site:* http://www.westwood.edu/.

Whittier College

Whittier, California

General Independent, comprehensive, coed **Entrance** Moderately difficult **Setting** 95-acre suburban campus **Total enrollment** 2,009 **Student-faculty ratio** 13:1 **Application deadline** Rolling (freshmen), rolling (transfer) **Freshman admission** 72% were admitted. Average high school GPA 3.05 **Freshman test scores** SAT critical reading scores over 500: 62%; SAT math scores over 500: 65%; ACT scores over 18: 89%; SAT critical reading scores over 600: 20%; SAT math scores over 600: 24%; ACT scores over 24: 37% **Housing** Yes **Expenses** Tuition & Fees $34,388; Room & Board $9758 **Undergraduates** 53% women, 1% part-time, 3% 25 or older, 1% Native American, 30% Hispanic American, 6% African American, 9% Asian American/Pacific Islander **The most frequently chosen baccalaureate fields are** business/marketing, parks and recreation, social sciences **Academic program** Advanced placement, accelerated degree program, self-designed majors, summer session, adult/continuing education programs, internships **Contact** Mr. Kieron Miller, Director of Admission, Whittier College, Office of Admission, 13406 E. Philadelphia Street, Whittier, CA 90608-0634. *Phone:* 562-907-4238. *Fax:* 562-907-4870. *E-mail:* admission@whittier.edu. *Web site:* http://www.whittier.edu/.

William Jessup University

Rocklin, California

General Independent nondenominational, 4-year, coed **Entrance** Noncompetitive **Setting** 156-acre suburban campus **Total enrollment** 578 **Student-faculty ratio** 14:1 **Application deadline** 4/1 (freshmen), 4/1 (transfer) **Freshman admission** 76% were admitted. Average high school GPA 3.38 **Freshman test scores** SAT critical reading scores over 500: 61%; SAT math scores over 500: 61%; ACT scores over 18: 90%;

SAT critical reading scores over 600: 27%; SAT math scores over 600: 14%; ACT scores over 24: 35% **Housing** Yes **Expenses** Tuition & Fees $19,980; Room & Board $7840 **Undergraduates** 56% women, 26% part-time, 28% 25 or older, 2% Native American, 8% Hispanic American, 7% African American, 3% Asian American/Pacific Islander **Academic program** Advanced placement, summer session, adult/continuing education programs, internships **Contact** Mr. Vance Pascua, Director of Admission, William Jessup University, 333 Sunset Boulevard, Rocklin, CA 95765. *Phone:* 916-577-2222 or toll-free 800-355-7522. *Fax:* 916-577-2220. *E-mail:* admissions@jessup.edu. *Web site:* http://www.jessup.edu/.

Woodbury University

Burbank, California

General Independent, comprehensive, coed **Entrance** Moderately difficult **Setting** 22-acre suburban campus **Total enrollment** 1,614 **Student-faculty ratio** 11:1 **Application deadline** Rolling (freshmen), rolling (transfer) **Freshman admission** 41% were admitted **Freshman test scores** SAT critical reading scores over 500: 35.4%; SAT math scores over 500: 40.5%; ACT scores over 18: 69%; SAT critical reading scores over 600: 7.6%; SAT math scores over 600: 5.1%; ACT scores over 24: 23% **Housing** Yes **Expenses** Tuition & Fees $28,855; Room & Board $9293 **Undergraduates** 52% women, 17% part-time, 31% 25 or older, 0.1% Native American, 33% Hispanic American, 5% African American, 10% Asian American/Pacific Islander **The most frequently chosen baccalaureate fields are** architecture, business/marketing, visual and performing arts **Academic program** English as a second language, advanced placement, accelerated degree program, self-designed majors, summer session, adult/continuing education programs, internships **Contact** Ms. Sabrina Taylor, Woodbury University, 7500 Glenoaks Boulevard, Burbank, CA 91510-7846. *Phone:* 800-784-9663 or toll-free 800-784-WOOD. *Fax:* 818-767-0032. *E-mail:* admissions@woodbury.edu. *Web site:* http://www.woodbury.edu/.

Yeshiva Ohr Elchonon Chabad/West Coast Talmudical Seminary

Los Angeles, California

General Independent Jewish, 4-year, men only **Entrance** Moderately difficult **Setting** 4-acre urban campus **Total enrollment** 135 **Application deadline** Rolling (freshmen), rolling (transfer) **Freshman admission** 100% were admitted **Housing** Yes **Academic program** Honors program, summer session, adult/continuing education programs, internships **Contact** Rabbi Ezra Binyomin Schochet, Dean, Yeshiva Ohr Elchonon Chabad/West Coast Talmudical Seminary, 7215 Waring Avenue, Los Angeles, CA 90046-7660. *Phone:* 323-937-3763. *E-mail:* roshyeshiva@yoec.edu.

COLORADO

Adams State College

Alamosa, Colorado

General State-supported, comprehensive, coed **Entrance** Moderately difficult **Setting** 90-acre small-town campus **Total enrollment** 3,124 **Student-faculty ratio** 20:1 **Application deadline** 8/1 (freshmen), 8/1 (transfer) **Freshman admission** 57% were admitted. Average high school GPA 2.97 **Freshman test scores** SAT critical reading scores over 500: 45.78%; SAT math scores over 500: 43.37%; ACT scores over 18: 69.76%; SAT critical reading scores over 600: 10.84%; SAT math scores over 600: 13.25%; ACT scores over 24: 17.06% **Housing** Yes **Expenses** Tuition & Fees: state resident $4454, nonresident $13,598; Room & Board $7020 **Undergraduates** 56% women, 19% part-time, 26% 25 or older, 2% Native American, 29% Hispanic American, 5% African American, 2% Asian American/Pacific Islander **The most frequently chosen baccalaureate fields are** business/marketing, liberal arts/general studies, social sciences **Academic program** Advanced placement, accelerated degree program, self-designed majors, summer session, adult/continuing education programs, internships **Contact** Mr. Eric Carpio, Director of Admissions, Adams State College, 208 Edgemont Boulevard, Alamosa, CO 81102. *Phone:* 719-587-7712 or toll-free 800-824-6494. *Fax:* 719-587-7522. *E-mail:* ascadmit@adams.edu. *Web site:* http://www.adams.edu/.

American Sentinel University

Englewood, Colorado

Contact Director of Admission, American Sentinel University, 385 Inverness Parkway, Englewood, CO 80112. *Phone:* 800-729-2427 or toll-free 800-729-2427. *Fax:* 866-505-2450. *E-mail:* info@AmericanSentinel.edu. *Web site:* http://www.americansentinel.edu/.

Argosy University, Denver

Denver, Colorado

General Proprietary, university, coed **Contact** Director of Admissions, Argosy University, Denver, 1200 Lincoln Street, Denver, CO 80203. *Phone:* 303-248-2700 or toll-free 866-431-5981. *Fax:* 303-248-2715. *Web site:* http://www.argosy.edu/denver/.

Visit Petersons.com and enter keywords Argosy University, Denver

See page 478 for the College Close-Up.

The Art Institute of Colorado

Denver, Colorado

General Proprietary, 4-year, coed **Setting** urban campus **Contact** Director of Admissions, The Art Institute of Colorado, 1200 Lincoln Street, Denver, CO 80203. *Phone:* 303-837-0825 or toll-free 800-275-2420. *Fax:* 303-860-8520. *Web site:* http://www.artinstitutes.edu/denver/.

Visit Petersons.com and enter keywords Art Institute of Colorado

See page 508 for the College Close-Up.

Aspen University

Denver, Colorado

Contact Admissions, Aspen University, 501 South Cherry Street, Suite 350, Denver, CO 80246. *Phone:* 303-333-4224 or toll-free 800-441-4746. *Fax:* 303-336-1144. *E-mail:* admissions@aspen.edu. *Web site:* http://www.aspen.edu/.

CollegeAmerica–Colorado Springs

Colorado Springs, Colorado

Contact Admissions Office, CollegeAmerica–Colorado Springs, 3645 Citadel Drive South, Colorado Springs, CO 80909. *Web site:* http://www.collegeamerica.edu/.

CollegeAmerica–Denver

Denver, Colorado

Contact Admissions Office, CollegeAmerica–Denver, 1385 South Colorado Boulevard, Denver, CO 80222. *Phone:* 303-691-9756 or toll-free 800-97-SKILLS. *Fax:* 303-695-6059. *E-mail:* collegeamerica@aol.com. *Web site:* http://www.collegeamerica.com/.

CollegeAmerica–Fort Collins

Fort Collins, Colorado

General Proprietary, primarily 2-year, coed **Entrance** Noncompetitive **Setting** suburban campus **Total enrollment** 116 **Housing** No **Under-**

CollegeAmerica–Fort Collins (continued)
graduates 57% 25 or older **Academic program** Internships **Contact** Ms. Anna DiTorrice-Mull, Director of Admissions, CollegeAmerica–Fort Collins, 4601 South Mason Street, Fort Collins, CO 80525-3740. *Phone:* 970-223-6060 Ext. 8002 or toll-free 800-97-SKILLS. *Web site:* http://www.collegeamerica.edu/.

Colorado Christian University

Lakewood, Colorado

Contact Mr. Jeff Cazer, Associate, Colorado Christian University, 8787 W Alameda Avenue, Lakewood, CO 80226. *Phone:* 303-963-3200 or toll-free 800-44-FAITH. *Fax:* 303-963-3201. *E-mail:* admission@ccu.edu. *Web site:* http://www.ccu.edu/.

The Colorado College

Colorado Springs, Colorado

General Independent, comprehensive, coed **Entrance** Very difficult **Setting** 90-acre urban campus **Total enrollment** 2,032 **Student-faculty ratio** 10:1 **Application deadline** 1/15 (freshmen), 3/1 (transfer) **Freshman admission** 32% were admitted **Freshman test scores** SAT critical reading scores over 500: 98.99%; SAT math scores over 500: 98.65%; ACT scores over 18: 100%; SAT critical reading scores over 600: 84.41%; SAT math scores over 600: 84.07%; ACT scores over 24: 93.94% **Housing** Yes **Expenses** Tuition & Fees $37,478; Room & Board $9624 **Undergraduates** 53% women, 2% part-time, 1% 25 or older, 1% Native American, 6% Hispanic American, 2% African American, 6% Asian American/Pacific Islander **The most frequently chosen baccalaureate fields are** biological/life sciences, social sciences, visual and performing arts **Academic program** English as a second language, advanced placement, self-designed majors, summer session, internships **Contact** Mr. Matt Bonser, Associate Director of Admission, The Colorado College, 14 East Cache La Poudre, Colorado Springs, CO 80903-3294. *Phone:* 719-389-6344 or toll-free 800-542-7214. *Fax:* 719-389-6816. *E-mail:* admission@coloradocollege.edu. *Web site:* http://www.coloradocollege.edu/.

Colorado Heights University

Denver, Colorado

General Independent, 4-year, coed **Total enrollment** 504 **Freshman admission** 100% were admitted **Housing** Yes **Undergraduates** 58% 25 or older **Contact** Ashley Henderson, Admissions Coordinator, Colorado Heights University, 3001 South Federal Boulevard, Denver, CO 80236-2711. *Phone:* 303-937-4221. *E-mail:* admissions@tlhu.edu. *Web site:* http://www.chu.edu/.

Colorado School of Mines

Golden, Colorado

General State-supported, university, coed **Entrance** Very difficult **Setting** 373-acre small-town campus **Total enrollment** 4,849 **Student-faculty ratio** 15:1 **Application deadline** 5/1 (freshmen), 5/1 (transfer) **Freshman admission** 63% were admitted. Average high school GPA 3.7 **Freshman test scores** SAT critical reading scores over 500: 92%; SAT math scores over 500: 100%; ACT scores over 18: 100%; SAT critical reading scores over 600: 54%; SAT math scores over 600: 86%; ACT scores over 24: 92% **Housing** Yes **Expenses** Tuition & Fees: state resident $12,244, nonresident $26,404; Room & Board $8120 **Undergraduates** 25% women, 5% part-time, 5% 25 or older, 1% Native American, 6% Hispanic American, 1% African American, 5% Asian American/Pacific Islander **The most frequently chosen baccalaureate fields are** engineering, mathematics, physical sciences **Academic program** English as a second language, advanced placement, accelerated degree program, honors program, summer session, internships **Contact** Mrs. Joanne Lambert, Assistant Director of Enrollment Management, Colorado School of Mines, Student Center, 1600 Maple Street, Golden, CO 80401. *Phone:* 303-273-3220 or toll-free 800-446-9488 Ext. 3220. *Fax:* 303-273-3509. *E-mail:* admit@mines.edu. *Web site:* http://www.mines.edu/.

Colorado State University

Fort Collins, Colorado

General State-supported, university, coed **Entrance** Moderately difficult **Setting** 582-acre urban campus **Total enrollment** 28,547 **Student-faculty ratio** 17:1 **Application deadline** 2/1 (freshmen), 2/1 (transfer) **Freshman admission** 72% were admitted. Average high school GPA 3.56 **Freshman test scores** SAT critical reading scores over 500: 78.6%; SAT math scores over 500: 80.4%; ACT scores over 18: 98.7%; SAT critical reading scores over 600: 32.6%; SAT math scores over 600: 41.2%; ACT scores over 24: 60.3% **Housing** Yes **Expenses** Tuition & Fees: state resident $6318, nonresident $22,240; Room & Board $8378 **Undergraduates** 52% women, 10% part-time, 8% 25 or older, 2% Native American, 7% Hispanic American, 3% African American, 3% Asian American/Pacific Islander **The most frequently chosen baccalaureate fields are** biological/life sciences, business/marketing, family and consumer sciences **Academic program** English as a second language, advanced placement, accelerated degree program, honors program, summer session, internships **Contact** Mr. Jim Rawlins, Executive Director of Admissions, Colorado State University, Spruce Hall, Fort Collins, CO 80523-0015. *Phone:* 970-491-6909. *Fax:* 970-491-7799. *E-mail:* admissions@colostate.edu. *Web site:* http://www.colostate.edu/.

Colorado State University–Pueblo

Pueblo, Colorado

General State-supported, comprehensive, coed **Entrance** Moderately difficult **Setting** 275-acre small-town campus **Total enrollment** 7,210 **Student-faculty ratio** 16:1 **Application deadline** 8/1 (freshmen), 8/1 (transfer) **Freshman admission** 95% were admitted. Average high school GPA 3 **Freshman test scores** SAT critical reading scores over 500: 42%; SAT math scores over 500: 56%; ACT scores over 18: 79%; SAT critical reading scores over 600: 12%; SAT math scores over 600: 18%; ACT scores over 24: 20% **Housing** Yes **Expenses** Tuition & Fees: state resident $5210, nonresident $15,602; Room & Board $6750 **Undergraduates** 56% women, 30% part-time, 33% 25 or older, 2% Native American, 25% Hispanic American, 9% African American, 3% Asian American/Pacific Islander **The most frequently chosen baccalaureate fields are** business/marketing, health professions and related sciences, social sciences **Academic program** English as a second language, advanced placement, accelerated degree program, honors program, summer session, internships **Contact** Mrs. Dana Trujillo, Director of Admissions, Colorado State University–Pueblo, 2200 Bonforte Boulevard, Pueblo, CO 81001-4901. *Phone:* 719-549-2391. *Fax:* 719-549-2419. *E-mail:* dana.trujillo@colostate-pueblo.edu. *Web site:* http://www.colostate-pueblo.edu/.

Colorado Technical University Colorado Springs

Colorado Springs, Colorado

General Proprietary, university, coed **Entrance** Minimally difficult **Setting** 14-acre suburban campus **Total enrollment** 2,359 **Application deadline** Rolling (freshmen), rolling (transfer) **Undergraduates** 44% women, 64% part-time, 80% 25 or older, 0.5% Native American, 7% Hispanic American, 7% African American, 2% Asian American/Pacific Islander **The most frequently chosen baccalaureate fields are** business/marketing, computer and information sciences, security and protective services **Academic program** Advanced placement, accelerated degree program, summer session, adult/continuing education programs, internships **Contact** Beth Braaten, Vice President of Admissions, Colorado Technical University Colorado Springs, 4435 North Chestnut Street, Colorado Springs, CO 80907-3896. *Phone:* 888-404-7555. *E-mail:* bbraaten@coloradotech.edu. *Web site:* http://www.coloradotech.edu/.

Colorado Technical University Denver

Greenwood Village, Colorado

General Proprietary, comprehensive, coed **Setting** 1-acre urban campus **Total enrollment** 733 **Application deadline** Rolling (freshmen), rolling (transfer) **Housing** No **Undergraduates** 48% women, 60% part-time, 68% 25 or older, 1% Native American, 12% Hispanic American, 9% African American, 3% Asian American/Pacific Islander **The most frequently chosen baccalaureate fields are** business/marketing, computer and information sciences, security and protective services **Academic program** Advanced placement, accelerated degree program, summer session, adult/continuing education programs, internships **Contact** Rosaland Giboney, Associate Director of Admissions, Colorado Technical University Denver, 5775 Denver Tech Center Boulevard, Greenwood Village, CO 80111. *Phone:* 888-404-7555. *E-mail:* rgiboney@coloradotech.edu. *Web site:* http://www.coloradotech.edu/.

Colorado Technical University Online

Colorado Springs, Colorado

General Proprietary, comprehensive, coed **Entrance** Minimally difficult **Total enrollment** 25,797 **Application deadline** Rolling (freshmen), rolling (transfer) **Undergraduates** 65% women, 83% 25 or older, 2% Native American, 8% Hispanic American, 27% African American, 2% Asian American/Pacific Islander **The most frequently chosen baccalaureate fields are** business/marketing, computer and information sciences, security and protective services **Academic program** Advanced placement, accelerated degree program, adult/continuing education programs **Contact** William Beckley, Chief Admission Officer, Colorado Technical University Online, 4435 North Chestnut Street, Suite E, Colorado Springs, CO 80907. *Phone:* 888-404-7555. *Web site:* http://www.coloradotech.edu/.

DeVry University

Colorado Springs, Colorado

Contact Admissions Office, DeVry University, 1175 Kelly Johnson Boulevard, Colorado Springs, CO 80920. *Phone:* toll-free 866-338-7934. *Web site:* http://www.devry.edu/.

DeVry University

Westminster, Colorado

General Proprietary, comprehensive, coed **Entrance** Noncompetitive **Setting** 3-acre urban campus **Total enrollment** 941 **Student-faculty ratio** 13:1 **Application deadline** Rolling (freshmen), rolling (transfer) **Housing** No **Expenses** Tuition & Fees $14,080 **Undergraduates** 37% women, 63% part-time, 68% 25 or older, 1% Native American, 14% Hispanic American, 6% African American, 4% Asian American/Pacific Islander **The most frequently chosen baccalaureate fields are** business/marketing, computer and information sciences, engineering technologies **Academic program** Accelerated degree program, summer session, adult/continuing education programs **Contact** Admissions Office, DeVry University, 1870 West 122nd Avenue, Westminster, CO 80234-2010. *Web site:* http://www.devry.edu/.

Fort Lewis College

Durango, Colorado

General State-supported, 4-year, coed **Entrance** Moderately difficult **Setting** 350-acre small-town campus **Total enrollment** 3,685 **Student-faculty ratio** 17:1 **Application deadline** 8/1 (freshmen), rolling (transfer) **Freshman admission** 68% were admitted. Average high school GPA 3.1 **Freshman test scores** SAT critical reading scores over 500: 62%; SAT math scores over 500: 57%; ACT scores over 18: 93%; SAT critical reading scores over 600: 20%; SAT math scores over 600: 17%; ACT scores over 24: 34% **Housing** Yes **Expenses** Tuition & Fees: state resident $7632, nonresident $17,500; Room & Board $8304 **Undergraduates** 49% women, 8% part-time, 15% 25 or older, 21% Native American, 5% Hispanic American, 1% African American, 1% Asian American/Pacific Islander **The most frequently chosen baccalaureate fields are** business/marketing, liberal arts/general studies, social sciences **Academic program** English as a second language, advanced placement, accelerated degree program, self-designed majors, honors program, summer session, adult/continuing education programs, internships **Contact** Mr. Andrew Burns, Director of Admissions, Fort Lewis College, 1000 Rim Drive, Durango, CO 81301-3999. *Phone:* 970-247-7184. *Fax:* 970-247-7147. *E-mail:* burns_a@fortlewis.edu. *Web site:* http://www.fortlewis.edu/.

ITT Technical Institute

Aurora, Colorado

General Proprietary, primarily 2-year, coed **Contact** Director of Admissions, ITT Technical Institute, 12500 East Iliff Avenue, Suite 100, Aurora, CO 80014. *Phone:* 303-695-6317. *Web site:* http://www.itt-tech.edu/.

ITT Technical Institute

Thornton, Colorado

General Proprietary, primarily 2-year, coed **Entrance** Minimally difficult **Setting** suburban campus **Housing** No **Contact** Director of Recruitment, ITT Technical Institute, 500 East 84th Avenue, Suite B12, Thornton, CO 80229. *Phone:* 303-288-4488 or toll-free 800-395-4488. *Web site:* http://www.itt-tech.edu/.

Johnson & Wales University

Denver, Colorado

General Independent, 4-year, coed **Entrance** Minimally difficult **Setting** small-town campus **Total enrollment** 1,461 **Student-faculty ratio** 25:1 **Application deadline** Rolling (freshmen), rolling (transfer) **Freshman admission** 72% were admitted **Freshman test scores** SAT critical reading scores over 500: 52.9%; SAT math scores over 500: 53.8%; SAT critical reading scores over 600: 14.7%; SAT math scores over 600: 18.7% **Housing** Yes **Expenses** Tuition & Fees $24,141; Room & Board $8904 **Undergraduates** 55% women, 2% part-time, 9% 25 or older, 1% Native American, 7% Hispanic American, 4% African American, 3% Asian American/Pacific Islander **The most frequently chosen baccalaureate fields are** business/marketing, family and consumer sciences, personal and culinary services **Academic program** English as a second language, advanced placement, accelerated degree program, honors program, summer session, adult/continuing education programs, internships **Contact** Kim Ostrowski, Director of Admissions, Johnson & Wales University, 7150 Montview Boulevard, Denver, CO 80220. *Phone:* 303-256-9300 or toll-free 877-598-3368. *Fax:* 303-256-9333. *E-mail:* den.admissions@jwu.edu. *Web site:* http://www.jwu.edu/.

Jones International University

Centennial, Colorado

General Proprietary, university, coed **Entrance** Noncompetitive **Total enrollment** 3,861 **Student-faculty ratio** 8:1 **Application deadline** Rolling (freshmen), rolling (transfer) **Freshman admission** 52% were admitted **Expenses** Tuition & Fees $11,400 **Undergraduates** 60% women, 86% part-time, 85% 25 or older, 1% Native American, 4% Hispanic American, 26% African American, 2% Asian American/Pacific Islander **Academic program** Advanced placement, accelerated degree program, self-designed majors, summer session, adult/continuing education programs, internships **Contact** Enrollment Center, Jones International University, 9697 East Mineral Avenue, Centennial, CO 80112. *Phone:* 800-811-5663 Ext. 8247 or toll-free 800-811-5663. *Fax:* 303-799-0966. *E-mail:* admissions@international.edu. *Web site:* http://www.jiu.edu/.

Mesa State College

Grand Junction, Colorado

General State-supported, comprehensive, coed **Entrance** Minimally difficult **Setting** 42-acre small-town campus **Total enrollment** 6,261 **Student-faculty ratio** 18:1 **Application deadline** Rolling (freshmen), rolling (transfer) **Freshman admission** 81% were admitted. Average high school GPA 2.97 **Freshman test scores** SAT critical reading scores over 500: 55.9%; SAT math scores over 500: 49%; ACT scores over 18: 73.1%; SAT critical reading scores over 600: 13%; SAT math scores over 600: 17.7%; ACT scores over 24: 17.4% **Housing** Yes **Expenses** Tuition & Fees: state resident $4735, nonresident $13,508; Room & Board $7355 **Undergraduates** 59% women, 29% part-time, 28% 25 or older, 2% Native American, 10% Hispanic American, 2% African American, 3% Asian American/Pacific Islander **The most frequently chosen baccalaureate fields are** business/marketing, health professions and related sciences, visual and performing arts **Academic program** Advanced placement, accelerated degree program, honors program, summer session, adult/continuing education programs, internships **Contact** Mr. Rance Larsen, Director of Admission, Mesa State College, 1100 North Avenue, Grand Junction, CO 81501. *Phone:* 970-248-1802 or toll-free 800-982-MESA. *Fax:* 970-248-1973. *E-mail:* rlarsen@mesastate.edu. *Web site:* http://www.mesastate.edu/.

Metropolitan State College of Denver

Denver, Colorado

General State-supported, 4-year, coed **Entrance** Minimally difficult **Setting** 175-acre urban campus **Total enrollment** 22,837 **Student-faculty ratio** 22:1 **Application deadline** Rolling (transfer) **Freshman admission** 72% were admitted. Average high school GPA 3 **Freshman test scores** SAT critical reading scores over 500: 56%; SAT math scores over 500: 55%; ACT scores over 18: 85%; SAT critical reading scores over 600: 19%; SAT math scores over 600: 25%; ACT scores over 24: 23% **Housing** No **Expenses** Tuition & Fees: state resident $3639, nonresident $13,132 **Undergraduates** 55% women, 37% part-time, 41% 25 or older, 1% Native American, 14% Hispanic American, 6% African American, 4% Asian American/Pacific Islander **The most frequently chosen baccalaureate fields are** business/marketing, English, interdisciplinary studies **Academic program** Advanced placement, accelerated degree program, self-designed majors, honors program, summer session, adult/continuing education programs, internships **Contact** Ms. Michelle Brown, Associate Director of Admissions, Metropolitan State College of Denver, PO Box 173362, Denver, CO 80217-3362. *Phone:* 303-556-2615. *E-mail:* jbonacqui@mscd.edu. *Web site:* http://www.mscd.edu/.

Naropa University

Boulder, Colorado

General Independent, comprehensive, coed **Entrance** Moderately difficult **Setting** 12-acre urban campus **Total enrollment** 1,081 **Student-faculty ratio** 9:1 **Application deadline** 7/15 (freshmen), 7/15 (transfer) **Freshman admission** 75% were admitted. Average high school GPA 3.18 **Housing** Yes **Expenses** Tuition & Fees $23,520; Room & Board $8478 **Undergraduates** 61% women, 10% part-time, 34% 25 or older, 3% Native American, 4% Hispanic American, 2% African American, 3% Asian American/Pacific Islander **The most frequently chosen baccalaureate fields are** English, interdisciplinary studies, psychology **Academic program** Advanced placement, self-designed majors, summer session, internships **Contact** Ms. Amy Atkins, Associate Director of Admissions, Naropa University, 2130 Arapahoe Avenue, Boulder, CO 80302. *Phone:* 303-546-5285 or toll-free 800-772-0410. *Fax:* 303-546-3583. *E-mail:* admissions@naropa.edu. *Web site:* http://www.naropa.edu/.

Visit Petersons.com and enter keyword Naropa

See page 1002 for the College Close-Up.

National American University

Colorado Springs, Colorado

General Proprietary, 4-year, coed **Entrance** Noncompetitive **Setting** 1-acre suburban campus **Total enrollment** 285 **Application deadline** Rolling (freshmen), rolling (transfer) **Housing** No **Undergraduates** 88% 25 or older **Academic program** English as a second language, accelerated degree program, summer session, adult/continuing education programs, internships **Contact** Director of Admissions, National American University, 5125 North Academy Boulevard, Colorado Springs, CO 80918. *Phone:* 719-590-8300. *E-mail:* csadmissions@national.edu. *Web site:* http://www.national.edu/.

National American University

Denver, Colorado

Contact Jacklyn Haack, Director of Admissions, National American University, 1325 South Colorado Blvd, Suite 100, Denver, CO 80222. *Phone:* 303-876-7112. *Fax:* 303-876-7105. *E-mail:* jhaack@national.edu. *Web site:* http://www.national.edu/.

Nazarene Bible College

Colorado Springs, Colorado

General Independent, 4-year, coed, affiliated with Church of the Nazarene **Entrance** Noncompetitive **Setting** 64-acre urban campus **Total enrollment** 995 **Student-faculty ratio** 10:1 **Application deadline** 7/31 (freshmen), 7/31 (transfer) **Freshman admission** 20% were admitted **Housing** No **Expenses** Tuition & Fees $8640 **Undergraduates** 40% women, 79% part-time, 89% 25 or older **The most frequently chosen baccalaureate field is** theology and religious vocations **Academic program** Summer session, internships **Contact** Dr. Laurel Matson, Director of Admissions/Public Relations, Nazarene Bible College, 1111 Academy Park Loop, Colorado Springs, CO 80910-3704. *Phone:* 719-884-5061 or toll-free 800-873-3873. *Fax:* 719-884-5199. *Web site:* http://www.nbc.edu/.

Platt College

Aurora, Colorado

General Proprietary, primarily 2-year, coed **Entrance** Noncompetitive **Setting** suburban campus **Total enrollment** 134 **Application deadline** Rolling (freshmen), rolling (transfer) **Housing** No **Undergraduates** 64% 25 or older **Academic program** Advanced placement **Contact** Admissions Office, Platt College, 3100 South Parker Road, Suite 200, Aurora, CO 80014-3141. *Phone:* 303-369-5151. *Fax:* 303-745-1433. *Web site:* http://www.plattcolorado.edu/.

Regis University

Denver, Colorado

General Independent Roman Catholic (Jesuit), comprehensive, coed **Entrance** Moderately difficult **Setting** 90-acre suburban campus **Total enrollment** 11,038 **Student-faculty ratio** 14:1 **Application deadline** Rolling (freshmen), rolling (transfer) **Freshman admission** 74% were admitted. Average high school GPA 3.5 **Freshman test scores** SAT critical reading scores over 500: 67%; SAT math scores over 500: 68.4%; ACT scores over 18: 96.5%; SAT critical reading scores over 600: 25.5%; SAT math scores over 600: 28.3%; ACT scores over 24: 51.8% **Housing** Yes **Expenses** Tuition & Fees $28,700; Room & Board $8982 **Undergraduates** 64% women, 60% part-time, 73% 25 or older **The most frequently chosen baccalaureate fields are** business/marketing, interdisciplinary studies, social sciences **Academic program** Advanced placement, accelerated degree program, self-designed majors, honors program, summer session, adult/continuing education programs, internships **Contact** Mr. Vic Davolt, Director of Admission, Regis University, 3333 Regis Boulevard, Denver, CO 80221-1099. *Phone:* 303-458-4905 or toll-free 800-388-2366 Ext. 4900. *Fax:* 303-964-5534. *E-mail:* regisadm@regis.edu. *Web site:* http://www.regis.edu/.

Remington College–Colorado Springs Campus
Colorado Springs, Colorado

General Proprietary, primarily 2-year, coed **Setting** 3-acre urban campus **Housing** No **Contact** Mr. Larry Schafer, Director of Recruitment, Remington College–Colorado Springs Campus, 6050 Erin Park Drive, #250, Colorado Springs, CO 80918. *Phone:* 719-532-1234 Ext. 202. *Fax:* 719-264-1234. *E-mail:* larry.schafer@remingtoncollege.edu. *Web site:* http://www.remingtoncollege.edu/.

Rocky Mountain College of Art + Design
Lakewood, Colorado

General Proprietary, 4-year, coed **Entrance** Moderately difficult **Setting** 23-acre suburban campus **Total enrollment** 586 **Student-faculty ratio** 12:1 **Application deadline** Rolling (freshmen), rolling (transfer) **Freshman admission** 99% were admitted. Average high school GPA 3.13 **Freshman test scores** SAT critical reading scores over 500: 63%; SAT math scores over 500: 40%; ACT scores over 18: 87%; SAT critical reading scores over 600: 17%; SAT math scores over 600: 5%; ACT scores over 24: 26% **Housing** No **Expenses** Tuition & Fees $26,832 **Undergraduates** 63% women, 11% part-time, 9% 25 or older, 1% Native American, 10% Hispanic American, 2% African American, 3% Asian American/Pacific Islander **Academic program** Advanced placement, accelerated degree program, honors program, summer session, internships **Contact** Mr. John Meurer, Vice President of Admissions, Rocky Mountain College of Art + Design, 1600 Pierce Street, Lakewood, CO 80214. *Phone:* 303-225-8567 or toll-free 800-888-ARTS. *Fax:* 303-759-4970. *E-mail:* admit@rmcad.edu. *Web site:* http://www.rmcad.edu/.

Visit Petersons.com and enter keyword Rocky

See page 1090 for the College Close-Up.

United States Air Force Academy
USAF Academy, Colorado

General Federally supported, 4-year, coed, primarily men **Entrance** Most difficult **Setting** 18,000-acre suburban campus **Total enrollment** 4,620 **Student-faculty ratio** 9:1 **Application deadline** 1/31 (freshmen), 1/31 (transfer) **Freshman admission** 14% were admitted. Average high school GPA 3.86 **Freshman test scores** SAT critical reading scores over 500: 99%; SAT math scores over 500: 100%; SAT critical reading scores over 600: 76%; SAT math scores over 600: 89% **Housing** Yes **Expenses** Comprehensive Fee $0 **Undergraduates** 20% women, 1% 25 or older, 1% Native American, 8% Hispanic American, 5% African American, 8% Asian American/Pacific Islander **The most frequently chosen baccalaureate fields are** engineering, business/marketing, social sciences **Academic program** English as a second language, advanced placement, self-designed majors, honors program, summer session, internships **Contact** Selections Division Admission Counselor, United States Air Force Academy, HQ USAFA/RR, 2304 Cadet Drive, Suite 2400, USAF Academy, CO 80840-5025. *Phone:* 800-443-9266 or toll-free 800-443-9266. *Fax:* 719-333-3012. *Web site:* http://www.usafa.edu/.

See page 1242 for the College Close-Up.

University of Colorado at Boulder
Boulder, Colorado

General State-supported, university, coed **Entrance** Moderately difficult **Setting** 600-acre suburban campus **Total enrollment** 32,751 **Student-faculty ratio** 18:1 **Application deadline** 1/15 (freshmen), 4/1 (transfer) **Freshman admission** 84% were admitted. Average high school GPA 3.55 **Freshman test scores** SAT critical reading scores over 500: 85%; SAT math scores over 500: 90%; ACT scores over 18: 99%; SAT critical reading scores over 600: 41%; SAT math scores over 600: 53%; ACT scores over 24: 78% **Housing** Yes **Expenses** Tuition & Fees: state resident $7932, nonresident $28,186; Room & Board $10,378 **Undergraduates** 47% women, 8% part-time, 7% 25 or older, 1% Native American, 6% Hispanic American, 2% African American, 6% Asian American/Pacific Islander **The most frequently chosen baccalaureate fields are** business/marketing, biological/life sciences, social sciences **Academic program** English as a second language, advanced placement, accelerated degree program, self-designed majors, honors program, summer session, adult/continuing education programs, internships **Contact** Admissions Office, University of Colorado at Boulder, Regent Administrative Center 125, 552 UCB, Boulder, CO 80309. *Phone:* 303-492-6301. *Fax:* 303-492-7115. *E-mail:* apply@colorado.edu. *Web site:* http://www.colorado.edu/.

Visit Petersons.com and enter keyword Boulder

See page 1260 for the College Close-Up.

University of Colorado at Colorado Springs
Colorado Springs, Colorado

General State-supported, university, coed **Setting** 530-acre suburban campus **Total enrollment** 9,315 **Student-faculty ratio** 16:1 **Application deadline** 7/1 (freshmen), 7/1 (transfer) **Freshman admission** 62% were admitted. Average high school GPA 3.28 **Freshman test scores** SAT critical reading scores over 500: 73%; SAT math scores over 500: 73%; ACT scores over 18: 97%; SAT critical reading scores over 600: 24%; SAT math scores over 600: 28%; ACT scores over 24: 48% **Housing** Yes **Expenses** Tuition & Fees: state resident $5693, nonresident $16,613; Room & Board $7490 **Undergraduates** 55% women, 21% part-time, 26% 25 or older, 1% Native American, 10% Hispanic American, 4% African American, 5% Asian American/Pacific Islander **The most frequently chosen baccalaureate fields are** business/marketing, health professions and related sciences, social sciences **Academic program** English as a second language, advanced placement, accelerated degree program, self-designed majors, honors program, summer session, internships **Contact** Mr. John Salnaitis, Associate Director, University of Colorado at Colorado Springs, 1420 Austin Bluffs Parkway, Colorado Springs, CO 80918. *Phone:* 719-255-3795 or toll-free 800-990-8227 Ext. 3383. *Fax:* 719-255-3116. *E-mail:* john.salnaitis@uccs.edu. *Web site:* http://www.uccs.edu/.

University of Colorado Denver
Denver, Colorado

General State-supported, university, coed **Entrance** Moderately difficult **Setting** 171-acre urban campus **Total enrollment** 24,119 **Student-faculty ratio** 15:1 **Application deadline** 7/22 (freshmen), 7/22 (transfer) **Freshman admission** 61% were admitted. Average high school GPA 3.29 **Freshman test scores** SAT critical reading scores over 500: 69.76%; SAT math scores over 500: 70.97%; ACT scores over 18: 93.71%; SAT critical reading scores over 600: 26.61%; SAT math scores over 600: 31.45%; ACT scores over 24: 41.99% **Housing** Yes **Expenses** Tuition & Fees: state resident $6657, nonresident $19,689; Room & Board $11,374 **Undergraduates** 56% women, 45% part-time, 30% 25 or older **The most frequently chosen baccalaureate fields are** business/marketing, health professions and related sciences, visual and performing arts **Academic program** English as a second language, advanced placement, accelerated degree program, self-designed majors, honors program, summer session, adult/continuing education programs, internships **Contact** Ms. Barbara Edwards, Director of Admissions, University of Colorado Denver, PO Box 173354, Campus Box 167, Denver, CO 80217. *Phone:* 303-556-3287. *Fax:* 303-556-4838. *E-mail:* admissions@castle.cudenver.edu. *Web site:* http://www.ucdenver.edu/.

University of Denver
Denver, Colorado

General Independent, university, coed **Entrance** Moderately difficult **Setting** 125-acre urban campus **Total enrollment** 11,644 **Student-**

University of Denver (continued)
faculty ratio 9:1 **Application deadline** 1/15 (freshmen), rolling (transfer) **Freshman admission** 70% were admitted. Average high school GPA 3.68 **Freshman test scores** SAT critical reading scores over 500: 89.85%; SAT math scores over 500: 90.57%; ACT scores over 18: 99.89%; SAT critical reading scores over 600: 50.14%; SAT math scores over 600: 53.71%; ACT scores over 24: 80.34% **Housing** Yes **Expenses** Tuition & Fees $36,501; Room & Board $10,224 **Undergraduates** 56% women, 10% part-time, 13% 25 or older, 1% Native American, 8% Hispanic American, 4% African American, 5% Asian American/Pacific Islander **The most frequently chosen baccalaureate fields are** business/marketing, communications/journalism, social sciences **Academic program** English as a second language, advanced placement, accelerated degree program, self-designed majors, honors program, summer session, adult/continuing education programs, internships **Contact** Mr. Todd R. Rinehart, Assistant Vice Chancellor for Enrollment, University of Denver, 2197 South University Boulevard, Denver, CO 80208. *Phone:* 303-871-3125 or toll-free 800-525-9495. *Fax:* 303-871-3301. *E-mail:* admission@du.edu. *Web site:* http://www.du.edu/.

Visit Petersons.com and enter keywords University of Denver

See page 1264 for the College Close-Up.

University of Northern Colorado
Greeley, Colorado

General State-supported, university, coed **Entrance** Moderately difficult **Setting** 240-acre suburban campus **Total enrollment** 12,148 **Student-faculty ratio** 19:1 **Application deadline** 8/1 (freshmen), rolling (transfer) **Freshman admission** 92% were admitted. Average high school GPA 3.19 **Freshman test scores** SAT critical reading scores over 500: 67%; SAT math scores over 500: 66%; ACT scores over 18: 93%; SAT critical reading scores over 600: 21%; SAT math scores over 600: 23%; ACT scores over 24: 36% **Housing** Yes **Expenses** Tuition & Fees: state resident $5116, nonresident $15,364; Room & Board $8370 **Undergraduates** 61% women, 10% part-time, 9% 25 or older, 1% Native American, 10% Hispanic American, 4% African American, 2% Asian American/Pacific Islander **The most frequently chosen baccalaureate fields are** business/marketing, health professions and related sciences, interdisciplinary studies **Academic program** English as a second language, advanced placement, self-designed majors, honors program, summer session, adult/continuing education programs, internships **Contact** Randall Langston, Director of Admissions, University of Northern Colorado, Campus Box 10, Carter Hall 3006, Greeley, CO 80639. *Phone:* 970-351-2881 or toll-free 888-700-4UNC. *Fax:* 970-351-2984. *E-mail:* admissions.help@unco.edu. *Web site:* http://www.unco.edu/.

University of Phoenix–Denver Campus
Lone Tree, Colorado

General Proprietary, comprehensive, coed **Entrance** Noncompetitive **Setting** urban campus **Total enrollment** 2,264 **Application deadline** Rolling (freshmen), rolling (transfer) **Housing** No **Expenses** Tuition & Fees $11,000 **Undergraduates** 67% women, 88% 25 or older, 1% Native American, 12% Hispanic American, 7% African American, 2% Asian American/Pacific Islander **The most frequently chosen baccalaureate fields are** business/marketing, computer and information sciences, security and protective services **Academic program** Advanced placement, accelerated degree program, adult/continuing education programs **Contact** Ms. Audra McQuarie, Registrar/Executive Director, University of Phoenix–Denver Campus, 4035 South Riverpoint Parkway, Mail Stop CF-L101, Phoenix, AZ 85040. *Phone:* 480-557-6151 or toll-free 800-776-4867 (in-state); 800-228-7240 (out-of-state). *Fax:* 480-643-3068. *E-mail:* audra.mcquarie@phoenix.edu. *Web site:* http://www.phoenix.edu/.

University of Phoenix–Southern Colorado Campus
Colorado Springs, Colorado

General Proprietary, comprehensive, coed **Entrance** Noncompetitive **Setting** urban campus **Total enrollment** 560 **Application deadline** Rolling (freshmen), rolling (transfer) **Housing** No **Expenses** Tuition & Fees $11,000 **Undergraduates** 84% 25 or older, 2% Native American, 11% Hispanic American, 10% African American, 4% Asian American/Pacific Islander **The most frequently chosen baccalaureate fields are** business/marketing, computer and information sciences, interdisciplinary studies **Academic program** Advanced placement, accelerated degree program, adult/continuing education programs **Contact** Ms. Audra McQuarie, Registrar/Executive Director, University of Phoenix–Southern Colorado Campus, 4035 South Riverpoint Parkway, Mail Stop CF-L101, Phoenix, AZ 85040. *Phone:* 480-557-6151 or toll-free 800-776-4867 (in-state); 800-228-7240 (out-of-state). *Fax:* 480-643-3068. *E-mail:* audra.mcquarie@phoenix.edu. *Web site:* http://www.phoenix.edu/.

Western State College of Colorado
Gunnison, Colorado

General State-supported, comprehensive, coed **Entrance** Moderately difficult **Setting** 381-acre small-town campus **Total enrollment** 2,193 **Student-faculty ratio** 17:1 **Application deadline** 7/1 (freshmen), 7/1 (transfer) **Freshman admission** 72% were admitted. Average high school GPA 2.97 **Freshman test scores** SAT critical reading scores over 500: 47%; SAT math scores over 500: 44%; ACT scores over 18: 76%; SAT critical reading scores over 600: 17%; SAT math scores over 600: 12%; ACT scores over 24: 18% **Housing** Yes **Expenses** Tuition & Fees: state resident $4064, nonresident $13,260; Room & Board $8324 **Undergraduates** 39% women, 15% part-time, 11% 25 or older **The most frequently chosen baccalaureate fields are** business/marketing, parks and recreation, social sciences **Academic program** Advanced placement, honors program, summer session, adult/continuing education programs, internships **Contact** Mr. Timothy Albers, Director of Admissions, Western State College of Colorado, 600 North Adams Street, Gunnison, CO 81231. *Phone:* 970-943-2119 or toll-free 800-876-5309. *Fax:* 970-943-2212. *E-mail:* admissions@western.edu. *Web site:* http://www.western.edu/.

Westwood College–Denver North
Denver, Colorado

General Proprietary, 4-year, coed **Setting** suburban campus **Total enrollment** 829 **Contact** Director of Admissions, Westwood College–Denver North, 7350 North Broadway, Denver, CO 80221-3653. *Phone:* 303-426-7000 or toll-free 800-992-5050. *Fax:* 303-426-4647. *Web site:* http://www.westwood.edu/.

Westwood College–Denver South
Denver, Colorado

General Proprietary, 4-year, coed **Total enrollment** 445 **Contact** Director of Admissions, Westwood College–Denver South, 3150 South Sheridan Boulevard, Denver, CO 80227. *Phone:* 303-934-1122 or toll-free 800-281-2978. *Fax:* 303-934-2583. *Web site:* http://www.westwood.edu/.

Westwood College–Online Campus
Broomfield, Colorado

General Proprietary, comprehensive, coed **Total enrollment** 7,584 **Contact** Director of Admissions, Westwood College–Online Campus, 10249 Church Ranch Way, Broomfield, CO 80021. *Phone:* 720-887-8888 or toll-free 800-875-6050. *Web site:* http://www.westwood.edu/.

Yeshiva Toras Chaim Talmudical Seminary

Denver, Colorado

General Independent Jewish, comprehensive, men only **Entrance** Moderately difficult **Setting** urban campus **Total enrollment** 11 **Freshman admission** 100% were admitted **Housing** Yes **Academic program** Honors program, adult/continuing education programs **Contact** Rabbi Israel Kagan, Dean, Yeshiva Toras Chaim Talmudical Seminary, 1555 Stuart Street, Denver, CO 80204-1415. *Phone:* 303-629-8200. *Fax:* 303-623-5949.

Yorktown University

Denver, Colorado

Contact Yorktown University, 4340 East Kentucky Avenue, Suite 457, Denver, CO 80246. *Web site:* http://yorktownuniversity.edu/.

CONNECTICUT

Albertus Magnus College

New Haven, Connecticut

General Independent Roman Catholic, comprehensive, coed **Entrance** Moderately difficult **Setting** 55-acre suburban campus **Total enrollment** 2,023 **Student-faculty ratio** 15:1 **Application deadline** 8/20 (freshmen), rolling (transfer) **Freshman admission** 83% were admitted. Average high school GPA 2.61 **Freshman test scores** SAT critical reading scores over 500: 43%; SAT math scores over 500: 34%; SAT critical reading scores over 600: 13%; SAT math scores over 600: 10% **Housing** Yes **Expenses** Tuition & Fees $23,126; Room & Board $9914 **Undergraduates** 68% women, 7% part-time, 36% 25 or older, 0.3% Native American, 12% Hispanic American, 31% African American, 1% Asian American/Pacific Islander **The most frequently chosen baccalaureate fields are** business/marketing, psychology, social sciences **Academic program** English as a second language, advanced placement, accelerated degree program, self-designed majors, honors program, summer session, internships **Contact** Ms. Jessica Van Deren, Dean of Admissions, Albertus Magnus College, 700 Prospect Street, New Haven, CT 06511-1189. *Phone:* 203-773-8501 or toll-free 800-578-9160. *Fax:* 203-773-5248. *E-mail:* admissions@albertus.edu. *Web site:* http://www.albertus.edu/.

Visit Petersons.com and enter keyword Albertus

See page 466 for the College Close-Up.

Bais Binyomin Academy

Stamford, Connecticut

Contact Director of Admissions, Bais Binyomin Academy, 132 Prospect Street, Stamford, CT 06901-1202. *Phone:* 203-325-4351.

Central Connecticut State University

New Britain, Connecticut

General State-supported, comprehensive, coed **Entrance** Moderately difficult **Setting** 294-acre suburban campus **Total enrollment** 12,461 **Student-faculty ratio** 16:1 **Application deadline** 6/1 (freshmen), 6/1 (transfer) **Freshman admission** 54% were admitted **Freshman test scores** SAT critical reading scores over 500: 54%; SAT math scores over 500: 61%; SAT critical reading scores over 600: 10%; SAT math scores over 600: 12% **Housing** Yes **Expenses** Tuition & Fees: state resident $7414, nonresident $15,784; Room & Board $9122 **Undergraduates** 49% women, 21% part-time, 17% 25 or older, 0.4% Native American, 7% Hispanic American, 8% African American, 3% Asian American/Pacific Islander **The most frequently chosen baccalaureate fields are** business/marketing, education, social sciences **Academic program**

ALBERTUS MAGNUS COLLEGE

PERSONALIZED EDUCATION

DYNAMIC COMMUNITY

Call or Visit Us Online Today!
www.albertus.edu
800-578-9160

SIG·COLL·ALBERTI·MAGNI·NOV·PORT 1925

NEW HAVEN, CONNECTICUT

A CATHOLIC COLLEGE IN THE DOMINICAN TRADITION
www.albertus.edu

Central Connecticut State University (continued)
English as a second language, advanced placement, self-designed majors, honors program, summer session, adult/continuing education programs, internships **Contact** Mr. Larry Hall, Director, Recruitment and Admissions, Central Connecticut State University, 1615 Stanley Street, New Britain, CT 06050. *Phone:* 860-832-2285 or toll-free 888-733-2278. *Fax:* 860-832-2522. *E-mail:* admissions@ccsu.edu. *Web site:* http://www.ccsu.edu/.
Visit Petersons.com and enter keyword Central

Charter Oak State College
New Britain, Connecticut

General State-supported, 4-year, coed **Entrance** Noncompetitive **Setting** small-town campus **Total enrollment** 2,079 **Student-faculty ratio** 11:1 **Application deadline** Rolling (transfer) **Housing** No **Undergraduates** 63% women, 92% part-time, 90% 25 or older **The most frequently chosen baccalaureate field is** liberal arts/general studies **Academic program** Advanced placement, accelerated degree program, self-designed majors, summer session, adult/continuing education programs **Contact** Ms. Lori Pendleton, Director of Admissions, Charter Oak State College, 55 Paul J. Manafort Drive, New Britain, CT 06053-2150. *Phone:* 860-832-3858. *Fax:* 860-832-3999. *E-mail:* info@charteroak.edu. *Web site:* http://www.charteroak.edu/.

Connecticut College
New London, Connecticut

General Independent, comprehensive, coed **Entrance** Very difficult **Setting** 702-acre suburban campus **Total enrollment** 1,911 **Student-faculty ratio** 9:1 **Application deadline** 1/1 (freshmen), 4/1 (transfer) **Freshman admission** 37% were admitted **Freshman test scores** SAT critical reading scores over 500: 98%; SAT math scores over 500: 99%; ACT scores over 18: 100%; SAT critical reading scores over 600: 81%; SAT math scores over 600: 82%; ACT scores over 24: 85% **Housing** Yes **Expenses** Comprehensive Fee $51,115 **Undergraduates** 61% women, 4% part-time, 0.2% Native American, 6% Hispanic American, 4% African American, 5% Asian American/Pacific Islander **The most frequently chosen baccalaureate fields are** social sciences, biological/life sciences, visual and performing arts **Academic program** Advanced placement, self-designed majors, summer session, adult/continuing education programs, internships **Contact** Ms. Martha C. Merrill, Dean of Admissions and Financial Aid, Connecticut College, 270 Mohegan Avenue, New London, CT 06320-4196. *Phone:* 860-439-2200. *Fax:* 860-439-4301. *E-mail:* admission@conncoll.edu. *Web site:* http://www.conncoll.edu/.

Eastern Connecticut State University
Willimantic, Connecticut

General State-supported, comprehensive, coed **Entrance** Moderately difficult **Setting** 182-acre small-town campus **Total enrollment** 5,574 **Student-faculty ratio** 16:1 **Application deadline** Rolling (freshmen), rolling (transfer) **Freshman admission** 62% were admitted. Average high school GPA 3 **Freshman test scores** SAT critical reading scores over 500: 54%; SAT math scores over 500: 55%; SAT critical reading scores over 600: 10%; SAT math scores over 600: 10% **Housing** Yes **Expenses** Tuition & Fees: state resident $7643, nonresident $16,013; Room & Board $13,340 **Undergraduates** 54% women, 17% part-time, 6% 25 or older **The most frequently chosen baccalaureate fields are** business/marketing, liberal arts/general studies, psychology **Academic program** Advanced placement, self-designed majors, honors program, summer session, adult/continuing education programs, internships **Contact** Ms. Kimberly M. Crone, Director of Admissions and Enrollment Management, Eastern Connecticut State University, 83 Windham Street, Willimantic, CT 06226. *Phone:* 860-465-5286 or toll-free 877-353-3278. *Fax:* 860-465-5544. *E-mail:* admissions@easternct.edu. *Web site:* http://www.easternct.edu/.
Visit Petersons.com and enter keywords Eastern Connecticut

See page 766 for the College Close-Up.

Fairfield University
Fairfield, Connecticut

General Independent Roman Catholic (Jesuit), comprehensive, coed **Entrance** Moderately difficult **Setting** 200-acre suburban campus **Total enrollment** 5,074 **Student-faculty ratio** 13:1 **Application deadline** 1/15 (freshmen), 5/1 (transfer) **Freshman admission** 65% were admitted. Average high school GPA 3.4 **Freshman test scores** SAT critical reading scores over 500: 79%; SAT math scores over 500: 82%; SAT critical reading scores over 600: 30%; SAT math scores over 600: 40% **Housing** Yes **Expenses** Tuition & Fees $37,490; Room & Board $11,270 **Undergraduates** 58% women, 15% part-time, 4% 25 or older, 1% Native American, 8% Hispanic American, 4% African American, 3% Asian American/Pacific Islander **The most frequently chosen baccalaureate fields are** business/marketing, health professions and related sciences, social sciences **Academic program** Advanced placement, self-designed majors, honors program, summer session, adult/continuing education programs, internships **Contact** Ms. Karen Pellegrino, Director of Admission, Fairfield University, 1073 North Benson Road, Fairfield, CT 06824-5195. *Phone:* 203-254-4100. *Fax:* 203-254-4199. *E-mail:* admis@fairfield.edu. *Web site:* http://www.fairfield.edu/.

Goodwin College
East Hartford, Connecticut

General Proprietary, primarily 2-year, coed **Entrance** Minimally difficult **Setting** urban campus **Total enrollment** 2,083 **Student-faculty ratio** 12:1 **Application deadline** Rolling (freshmen), rolling (transfer) **Freshman admission** 100% were admitted **Housing** No **Expenses** Tuition & Fees $16,420 **Undergraduates** 85% women, 75% part-time, 62% 25 or older, 0.2% Native American, 18% Hispanic American, 27% African American, 2% Asian American/Pacific Islander **Academic program** English as a second language, advanced placement, summer session, adult/continuing education programs, internships **Contact** Mr. Nicholas Lantino, Director of High School Admissions, Goodwin College, 745 Burnside Avenue, East Hartford, CT 06108. *Phone:* 860-528-4111 Ext. 6765 or toll-free 800-889-3282. *Fax:* 860-291-8285. *E-mail:* nlantino@goodwin.edu. *Web site:* http://www.goodwin.edu/.

Holy Apostles College and Seminary
Cromwell, Connecticut

General Independent Roman Catholic, comprehensive, coed **Entrance** Noncompetitive **Setting** 17-acre suburban campus **Total enrollment** 317 **Application deadline** Rolling (freshmen), rolling (transfer) **Freshman admission** 100% were admitted **Housing** No **Expenses** Tuition & Fees $9360 **Undergraduates** 43% women, 43% part-time, 11% Hispanic American **The most frequently chosen baccalaureate fields are** philosophy and religious studies, social sciences **Academic program** English as a second language, summer session, adult/continuing education programs **Contact** Very Rev. Douglas Mosey CSB, Director of Admissions, Holy Apostles College and Seminary, 33 Prospect Hill Road, Cromwell, CT 06416-2005. *Phone:* 860-632-3010 or toll-free 800-330-7272. *Fax:* 860-632-3030. *E-mail:* admissions@holyapostles.edu. *Web site:* http://www.holyapostles.edu/.

Lincoln College of New England
Southington, Connecticut

General Proprietary, 4-year, coed **Entrance** Minimally difficult **Setting** 32-acre small-town campus **Total enrollment** 772 **Student-faculty ratio** 8:1 **Application deadline** Rolling (freshmen), rolling (transfer) **Freshman admission** 73% were admitted **Freshman test scores** SAT critical reading scores over 500: 16%; SAT math scores over 500: 19%; SAT critical reading scores over 600: 3%; SAT math scores over 600: 16% **Housing** Yes **Expenses** Tuition & Fees $19,000; Room only $4400 **Undergraduates** 78% women, 51% part-time, 38% 25 or older, 1% Native American, 13% Hispanic American, 19% African American, 1% Asian American/Pacific Islander **Academic program** English as a second language, advanced placement, accelerated degree program, summer session, adult/continuing education programs, internships **Contact** Anthony Reich, Vice President of Admissions, Lincoln College of New England, 2279 Mount Vernon Road, Southington, CT 06489. *Phone:* 860-628-4751 Ext. 40904 or toll-free 800-952-2444. *Fax:* 860-628-6444. *E-mail:* areich@lincolncollegene.edu. *Web site:* http://www.lincolncollegene.edu.

Lyme Academy College of Fine Arts
Old Lyme, Connecticut

General Independent, 4-year, coed **Entrance** Moderately difficult **Setting** 3-acre rural campus **Total enrollment** 97 **Application deadline** Rolling (freshmen), rolling (transfer) **Freshman admission** 93% were admitted. Average high school GPA 3.22 **Freshman test scores** SAT critical reading scores over 500: 82%; SAT math scores over 500: 54%; SAT critical reading scores over 600: 36%; SAT math scores over 600: 27% **Housing** Yes **Expenses** Tuition & Fees $24,860 **Undergraduates** 64% women, 29% part-time, 32% 25 or older, 2% Native American, 1% African American, 2% Asian American/Pacific Islander **The most frequently chosen baccalaureate field is** visual and performing arts **Academic program** Advanced placement, adult/continuing education programs **Contact** Miss Krissy Shaffer, Admissions Representative, Lyme Academy College of Fine Arts, 84 Lyme Street, Old Lyme, CT 06371. *Phone:* 860-434-3571 Ext. 127. *Fax:* 860-434-8725. *E-mail:* kshaffer@lymeacademy.edu. *Web site:* http://www.lymeacademy.edu/.

Mitchell College
New London, Connecticut

General Independent, 4-year, coed **Entrance** Moderately difficult **Setting** 67-acre suburban campus **Total enrollment** 961 **Student-faculty ratio** 15:1 **Application deadline** Rolling (freshmen), rolling (transfer) **Freshman admission** 83% were admitted. Average high school GPA 2.67 **Housing** Yes **Expenses** Tuition & Fees $25,627; Room & Board $11,548 **Undergraduates** 49% women, 15% part-time, 2% Native American, 8% Hispanic American, 12% African American, 2% Asian American/Pacific Islander **The most frequently chosen baccalaureate fields are** business/marketing, liberal arts/general studies, security and protective services **Academic program** Advanced placement, self-designed majors, summer session, internships **Contact** Ms. Kimberly Hodges, Director of Admissions, Mitchell College, 437 Pequot Avenue, New London, CT 06320. *Phone:* 860-701-5038 or toll-free 800-443-2811. *Fax:* 860-444-1209. *E-mail:* admissions@mitchell.edu. *Web site:* http://www.mitchell.edu/.

See page 976 for the College Close-Up.

Paier College of Art, Inc.
Hamden, Connecticut

Contact Ms. Lynn Pascale, Secretary to Admissions, Paier College of Art, Inc., 20 Gorham Avenue, Hamden, CT 06514-3902. *Phone:* 203-287-3031. *Fax:* 203-287-3021. *E-mail:* paier.admission@snet.net. *Web site:* http://www.paiercollegeofart.edu/.

Visit Petersons.com and enter keyword Paier

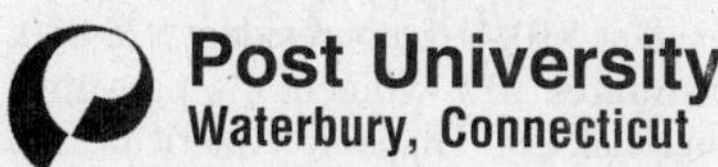

Post University
Waterbury, Connecticut

General Independent, comprehensive, coed **Entrance** Minimally difficult **Setting** 70-acre suburban campus **Total enrollment** 2,590 **Student-faculty ratio** 19:1 **Application deadline** Rolling (freshmen), rolling (transfer) **Freshman admission** 59% were admitted. Average high school GPA 2.4 **Freshman test scores** SAT critical reading scores over 500: 30%; SAT math scores over 500: 31%; ACT scores over 18: 50%; SAT critical reading scores over 600: 8%; SAT math scores over 600: 7%; ACT scores over 24: 17% **Housing** Yes **Expenses** Tuition & Fees $25,050; Room & Board $9700 **Undergraduates** 59% women, 44% part-time, 9% 25 or older, 0.3% Native American, 7% Hispanic American, 18% African American, 1% Asian American/Pacific Islander **The most frequently chosen baccalaureate fields are** business/marketing, law/legal studies, security and protective services **Academic program** English as a second language, advanced placement, accelerated degree program, summer session, adult/continuing education programs, internships **Contact** Mr. Jay Murray, Director of Admissions, Post University, PO Box 2540, Waterbury, CT 06723. *Phone:* 203-596-4500 or toll-free 800-345-2562. *Fax:* 203-756-5810. *E-mail:* admiss@post.edu. *Web site:* http://www.post.edu/.

See page 1056 for the College Close-Up.

Quinnipiac University
Hamden, Connecticut

General Independent, comprehensive, coed **Entrance** Moderately difficult **Setting** 640-acre suburban campus **Total enrollment** 7,758 **Student-faculty ratio** 12:1 **Application deadline** 2/1 (freshmen), 4/1 (transfer) **Freshman admission** 69% were admitted. Average high school GPA 3.4 **Freshman test scores** SAT critical reading scores over 500: 82%; SAT math scores over 500: 87%; ACT scores over 18: 100%; SAT critical reading scores over 600: 23%; SAT math scores over 600: 31%; ACT scores over 24: 80% **Housing** Yes **Expenses** Tuition & Fees $34,250; Room & Board $12,730 **Undergraduates** 62% women, 5% part-time, 5% 25 or older, 0.2% Native American, 5% Hispanic American, 3% African American, 3% Asian American/Pacific Islander **The most frequently chosen baccalaureate fields are** business/marketing, communications/journalism, health professions and related sciences **Academic program** Advanced placement, self-designed majors, honors program, summer session, adult/continuing education programs, internships **Contact** Ms. Joan Isaac Mohr, Vice President and Dean of Admissions, Quinnipiac University, 275 Mount Carmel Avenue, Hamden, CT 06518. *Phone:* 203-582-8600 or toll-free 800-462-1944. *Fax:* 203-582-8906. *E-mail:* admissions@quinnipiac.edu. *Web site:* http://www.quinnipiac.edu/.

Visit Petersons.com and enter keyword Quinnipiac

See page 1066 for the College Close-Up.

Sacred Heart University
Fairfield, Connecticut

General Independent Roman Catholic, comprehensive, coed **Entrance** Moderately difficult **Setting** 65-acre suburban campus **Total enrollment** 6,023 **Student-faculty ratio** 13:1 **Freshman admission** 66% were admitted. Average high school GPA 3.3 **Freshman test scores** SAT critical reading scores over 500: 63%; SAT math scores over 500: 71%; SAT critical reading scores over 600: 14%; SAT math scores over 600: 20% **Housing** Yes **Expenses** Tuition & Fees $30,298; Room & Board $11,684 **Undergraduates** 61% women, 16% part-time, 11% 25 or older, 0.2% Native American, 7% Hispanic American, 4% African American, 2% Asian American/Pacific Islander **The most frequently chosen baccalaureate fields are** business/marketing, health professions and related sciences, psychology **Academic program** English as a second language, advanced placement, accelerated degree program, honors program, summer session, adult/continuing education programs, internships **Contact** Ms. Karen N. Guastelle, Dean of Undergraduate Admissions, Sacred Heart University, 5151 Park Avenue, Fairfield, CT 06825-1000. *Phone:* 203-371-7880. *Fax:* 203-365-7607. *E-mail:* enroll@sacredheart.edu. *Web site:* http://www.sacredheart.edu/.

Visit Petersons.com and enter keyword Sacred

See page 1096 for the College Close-Up.

Saint Joseph College

West Hartford, Connecticut

General Independent Roman Catholic, comprehensive, undergraduate: women only; graduate: coed **Setting** 84-acre suburban campus **Total enrollment** 1,935 **Student-faculty ratio** 10:1 **Application deadline** Rolling (freshmen), rolling (transfer) **Freshman admission** 84% were admitted. Average high school GPA 3.2 **Freshman test scores** SAT critical reading scores over 500: 40%; SAT math scores over 500: 44%; SAT critical reading scores over 600: 8%; SAT math scores over 600: 6% **Housing** Yes **Expenses** Tuition & Fees $27,202; Room & Board $12,437 **Undergraduates** 20% part-time, 25% 25 or older, 0.1% Native American, 10% Hispanic American, 11% African American, 2% Asian American/Pacific Islander **The most frequently chosen baccalaureate fields are** health professions and related sciences, family and consumer sciences, psychology **Academic program** Advanced placement, accelerated degree program, self-designed majors, honors program, summer session, adult/continuing education programs, internships **Contact** Office of Admissions, Saint Joseph College, 1678 Asylum Avenue, West Hartford, CT 06117. *Phone:* 866-442-8752 or toll-free 866-442-8752. *Fax:* 860-231-5744. *E-mail:* admissions@sjc.edu. *Web site:* http://www.sjc.edu/.

Visit Petersons.com and enter keywords Joseph College

See page 1110 for the College Close-Up.

Southern Connecticut State University

New Haven, Connecticut

General State-supported, comprehensive, coed **Entrance** Moderately difficult **Setting** 168-acre suburban campus **Total enrollment** 11,815 **Student-faculty ratio** 16:1 **Application deadline** 4/1 (freshmen), 8/1 (transfer) **Freshman admission** 71% were admitted. Average high school GPA 2.94 **Freshman test scores** SAT critical reading scores over 500: 39.2%; SAT math scores over 500: 41.4%; SAT critical reading scores over 600: 6%; SAT math scores over 600: 6.3% **Housing** Yes **Expenses** Tuition & Fees: state resident $8050, nonresident $17,047; Room & Board $9983 **Undergraduates** 63% women, 14% part-time, 15% 25 or older, 0.3% Native American, 6% Hispanic American, 13% African American, 2% Asian American/Pacific Islander **The most frequently chosen baccalaureate fields are** business/marketing, education, psychology **Academic program** Advanced placement, accelerated degree program, self-designed majors, honors program, summer session, internships **Contact** Ms. Paula Kennedy, Associate Director of Admissions, Southern Connecticut State University, Admissions House, 131 Farnham Avenue, New Haven, CT 06515-1202. *Phone:* 203-392-5651. *Fax:* 203-392-5727. *E-mail:* joyners2@southernct.edu. *Web site:* http://www.southernct.edu/.

Visit Petersons.com and enter keywords Southern Connecticut

See page 1168 for the College Close-Up.

Trinity College

Hartford, Connecticut

General Independent, comprehensive, coed **Entrance** Most difficult **Setting** 100-acre urban campus **Total enrollment** 2,514 **Student-faculty ratio** 9:1 **Application deadline** 1/1 (freshmen), 4/1 (transfer) **Freshman admission** 41% were admitted **Freshman test scores** SAT critical reading scores over 500: 97.2%; SAT math scores over 500: 98.6%; ACT scores over 18: 99.4%; SAT critical reading scores over 600: 73.9%; SAT math scores over 600: 79.2%; ACT scores over 24: 91.3% **Housing** Yes **Expenses** Tuition & Fees $42,370; Room & Board $10,960 **Undergraduates** 50% women, 6% part-time, 0.2% Native American, 6% Hispanic American, 6% African American, 6% Asian American/Pacific Islander **The most frequently chosen baccalaureate fields are** area and ethnic studies, history, social sciences **Academic program** Advanced placement, accelerated degree program, self-designed majors, honors program, summer session, adult/continuing education programs, internships **Contact** Mr. Larry Dow, Dean of Admissions and Financial Aid, Trinity College, 300 Summit Street, Hartford, CT 06106-3100. *Phone:* 860-297-2180. *Fax:* 860-297-2287. *E-mail:* admissions.office@trincoll.edu. *Web site:* http://www.trincoll.edu/.

Visit Petersons.com and enter keyword Trinity

See page 1234 for the College Close-Up.

United States Coast Guard Academy

New London, Connecticut

General Federally supported, 4-year, coed **Entrance** Very difficult **Setting** 110-acre suburban campus **Total enrollment** 973 **Student-faculty ratio** 8:1 **Application deadline** 2/1 (freshmen), 2/1 (transfer) **Freshman admission** 25% were admitted. Average high school GPA 3.7 **Freshman test scores** SAT critical reading scores over 500: 93%; SAT math scores over 500: 98%; ACT scores over 18: 100%; SAT critical reading scores over 600: 56%; SAT math scores over 600: 73%; ACT scores over 24: 82% **Housing** Yes **Undergraduates** 27% women, 1% Native American, 7% Hispanic American, 3% African American, 4% Asian American/Pacific Islander **The most frequently chosen baccalaureate fields are** engineering, biological/life sciences, social sciences **Academic program** Honors program, summer session, internships **Contact** Capt. Susan Bibeau, Director of Admissions, United States Coast Guard Academy, 31 Mohegan Avenue, New London, CT 06320-4195. *Phone:* 860-444-8500 or toll-free 800-883-8724. *Fax:* 860-701-6700. *E-mail:* admissions@uscga.edu. *Web site:* http://www.uscga.edu/.

University of Bridgeport

Bridgeport, Connecticut

General Independent, comprehensive, coed **Entrance** Moderately difficult **Setting** 86-acre urban campus **Total enrollment** 5,103 **Student-faculty ratio** 12:1 **Application deadline** Rolling (freshmen), rolling (transfer) **Freshman admission** 55% were admitted. Average high school GPA 2.84 **Freshman test scores** SAT critical reading scores over 500: 22%; SAT math scores over 500: 26%; ACT scores over 18: 48%; SAT critical reading scores over 600: 2%; SAT math scores over 600: 4%; ACT scores over 24: 7% **Housing** Yes **Expenses** Tuition & Fees $25,465; Room & Board $11,080 **Undergraduates** 68% women, 33% part-time, 37% 25 or older, 0.3% Native American, 15% Hispanic American, 37% African American, 3% Asian American/Pacific Islander **The most frequently chosen baccalaureate fields are** business/marketing, health professions and related sciences, liberal arts/general studies **Academic program** English as a second language, advanced placement, accelerated degree program, self-designed majors, honors program, summer session, adult/continuing education programs, internships **Contact** Mr. Bryan Gross, Dean of Admissions, University of Bridgeport, 126 Park Avenue, Bridgeport, CT 06604. *Phone:* 203-576-4552 or toll-free 800-EXCEL-UB (in-state); 800-243-9496 (out-of-state). *Fax:* 203-576-4941. *E-mail:* admit@bridgeport.edu. *Web site:* http://www.bridgeport.edu/.

University of Connecticut

Storrs, Connecticut

General State-supported, university, coed **Entrance** Moderately difficult **Setting** 4,108-acre rural campus **Total enrollment** 25,029 **Student-faculty ratio** 18:1 **Application deadline** 2/1 (freshmen), 4/1 (transfer) **Freshman admission** 50% were admitted **Freshman test scores** SAT critical reading scores over 500: 91%; SAT math scores over 500: 95%; ACT scores over 18: 98%; SAT critical reading scores over 600: 49%; SAT math scores over 600: 65%; ACT scores over 24: 85% **Housing** Yes **Expenses** Tuition & Fees: state resident $10,416, nonresident $26,880; Room & Board $10,782 **Undergraduates** 50% women, 4% part-time, 3% 25 or older, 0.3% Native American, 5% Hispanic American, 5% African American, 8% Asian American/Pacific Islander **The most frequently chosen baccalaureate fields are** business/marketing, health professions and related sciences, social sciences **Academic program**

English as a second language, advanced placement, accelerated degree program, self-designed majors, honors program, summer session, adult/continuing education programs, internships **Contact** Mr. Brian Usher, Interim Director of Admissions, University of Connecticut, 2131 Hillside Road, U-88, Storrs, CT 06269. *Phone:* 860-486-3137. *Fax:* 860-486-1476. *E-mail:* beahusky@uconnvm.uconn.edu. *Web site:* http://www.uconn.edu/.

University of Hartford
West Hartford, Connecticut

General Independent, comprehensive, coed **Entrance** Moderately difficult **Setting** 320-acre suburban campus **Total enrollment** 7,212 **Student-faculty ratio** 12:1 **Application deadline** Rolling (freshmen), rolling (transfer) **Freshman admission** 69% were admitted **Freshman test scores** SAT critical reading scores over 500: 64%; SAT math scores over 500: 68%; ACT scores over 18: 92%; SAT critical reading scores over 600: 16%; SAT math scores over 600: 21%; ACT scores over 24: 24% **Housing** Yes **Expenses** Tuition & Fees $29,852; Room & Board $11,572 **Undergraduates** 53% women, 15% part-time, 1% 25 or older, 0.3% Native American, 7% Hispanic American, 12% African American, 3% Asian American/Pacific Islander **The most frequently chosen baccalaureate fields are** business/marketing, health professions and related sciences, visual and performing arts **Academic program** English as a second language, advanced placement, self-designed majors, honors program, summer session, adult/continuing education programs, internships **Contact** Mr. Richard Zeiser, Dean of Admissions, University of Hartford, 200 Bloomfield Avenue, West Hartford, CT 06117. *Phone:* 860-768-4296 or toll-free 800-947-4303. *Fax:* 860-768-4961. *E-mail:* admissions@hartford.edu. *Web site:* http://www.hartford.edu/.
Visit Petersons.com and enter keyword Hartford

See page 1274 for the College Close-Up.

University of New Haven
West Haven, Connecticut

General Independent, comprehensive, coed **Entrance** Moderately difficult **Setting** 78-acre suburban campus **Total enrollment** 5,770 **Student-faculty ratio** 15:1 **Application deadline** Rolling (freshmen), rolling (transfer) **Freshman admission** 61% were admitted. Average high school GPA 3.2 **Freshman test scores** SAT critical reading scores over 500: 50%; SAT math scores over 500: 56%; ACT scores over 18: 86%; SAT critical reading scores over 600: 12%; SAT math scores over 600: 16%; ACT scores over 24: 35% **Housing** Yes **Expenses** Tuition & Fees $29,470; Room & Board $12,204 **Undergraduates** 50% women, 12% part-time, 11% 25 or older, 0.3% Native American, 8% Hispanic American, 9% African American, 2% Asian American/Pacific Islander **The most frequently chosen baccalaureate fields are** business/marketing, security and protective services, visual and performing arts **Academic program** English as a second language, advanced placement, accelerated degree program, honors program, summer session, adult/continuing education programs, internships **Contact** Mr. Kevin Phillips, Associate Vice Presidents of Undergraduate Admissions, University of New Haven, Bayer Hall, 300 Boston Post Road, West Haven, CT 06516. *Phone:* 203-932-7318 or toll-free 800-DIAL-UNH. *Fax:* 203-931-6093. *E-mail:* adminfo@newhaven.edu. *Web site:* http://www.newhaven.edu/.
Visit Petersons.com and enter keywords New Haven

See page 1292 for the College Close-Up.

Wesleyan University
Middletown, Connecticut

General Independent, university, coed **Entrance** Most difficult **Setting** 240-acre small-town campus **Total enrollment** 3,148 **Student-faculty ratio** 9:1 **Application deadline** 1/1 (freshmen), 3/15 (transfer) **Freshman admission** 22% were admitted. Average high school GPA 3.82 **Freshman test scores** SAT critical reading scores over 500: 99.1%; SAT math scores over 500: 99.1%; ACT scores over 18: 100%; SAT critical reading scores over 600: 86.1%; SAT math scores over 600: 88.8%; ACT scores over 24: 98.44% **Housing** Yes **Expenses** Tuition & Fees $40,092; Room & Board $11,040 **Undergraduates** 51% women, 0.5% part-time, 1% Native American, 9% Hispanic American, 7% African American, 10% Asian American/Pacific Islander **The most frequently chosen baccalaureate fields are** area and ethnic studies, social sciences, visual and performing arts **Academic program** Advanced placement, self-designed majors, honors program, summer session, adult/continuing education programs **Contact** Ms. Nancy Meislahn, Dean of Admission and Financial Aid, Wesleyan University, Stewart M. Reid House, 70 Wyllys Avenue, Middletown, CT 06459-0265. *Phone:* 860-685-3000. *Fax:* 860-685-3001. *E-mail:* admissions@wesleyan.edu. *Web site:* http://www.wesleyan.edu/.

Western Connecticut State University
Danbury, Connecticut

General State-supported, comprehensive, coed **Entrance** Moderately difficult **Setting** 340-acre urban campus **Total enrollment** 6,617 **Student-faculty ratio** 15:1 **Application deadline** Rolling (transfer) **Freshman admission** 62% were admitted. Average high school GPA 2.76 **Freshman test scores** SAT critical reading scores over 500: 50%; SAT math scores over 500: 48%; SAT critical reading scores over 600: 9%; SAT math scores over 600: 10% **Housing** Yes **Expenses** Tuition & Fees: state resident $7909, nonresident $16,906; Room only $5858 **Undergraduates** 54% women, 19% part-time, 16% 25 or older, 0.3% Native American, 8% Hispanic American, 7% African American, 3% Asian American/Pacific Islander **The most frequently chosen baccalaureate fields are** business/marketing, education, health professions and related sciences **Academic program** Advanced placement, self-designed majors, honors program, summer session, internships **Contact** Office of University Admissions, Western Connecticut State University, 181 White Street, Danbury, CT 06810. *Phone:* 203-837-9000 or toll-free 877-837-WCSU. *E-mail:* admissions@wcsu.edu. *Web site:* http://www.wcsu.edu/.
Visit Petersons.com and enter keywords Western Connecticut

See page 1362 for the College Close-Up.

Yale University
New Haven, Connecticut

General Independent, university, coed **Entrance** Most difficult **Setting** 200-acre urban campus **Total enrollment** 11,593 **Student-faculty ratio** 6:1 **Application deadline** 12/31 (freshmen), 3/1 (transfer) **Freshman admission** 8% were admitted **Freshman test scores** SAT critical reading scores over 500: 100%; SAT math scores over 500: 100%; SAT critical reading scores over 600: 97%; SAT math scores over 600: 98% **Housing** Yes **Expenses** Tuition & Fees $36,500; Room & Board $11,000 **Undergraduates** 50% women, 0.3% part-time, 1% 25 or older, 1% Native American, 8% Hispanic American, 8% African American, 14% Asian American/Pacific Islander **The most frequently chosen baccalaureate fields are** history, interdisciplinary studies, social sciences **Academic program** English as a second language, advanced placement, accelerated degree program, self-designed majors, honors program, summer session, internships **Contact** Admissions Director, Yale University, PO Box 208234, New Haven, CT 06520. *Phone:* 203-432-9300. *E-mail:* student.questions@yale.edu. *Web site:* http://www.yale.edu/.

DELAWARE

Delaware State University
Dover, Delaware

General State-supported, university, coed **Entrance** Moderately difficult **Setting** 400-acre small-town campus **Total enrollment** 3,609

Delaware State University (continued)
Student-faculty ratio 16:1 **Freshman admission** 39% were admitted. Average high school GPA 2.78 **Freshman test scores** SAT critical reading scores over 500: 19%; SAT math scores over 500: 17%; ACT scores over 18: 49%; SAT critical reading scores over 600: 2%; SAT math scores over 600: 2%; ACT scores over 24: 7% **Housing** Yes **Expenses** Tuition & Fees: state resident $7261, nonresident $14,522; Room & Board $8752 **Undergraduates** 60% women, 13% part-time, 10% 25 or older, 0.1% Native American, 2% Hispanic American, 70% African American, 1% Asian American/Pacific Islander **The most frequently chosen baccalaureate fields are** business/marketing, communications/journalism, social sciences **Academic program** English as a second language, advanced placement, accelerated degree program, honors program, summer session, adult/continuing education programs, internships **Contact** Mrs. Lawita G. Scott-Cheatham, Executive Director for Admissions, Delaware State University, 1200 North DuPont Highway, Dover, DE 19901-2277. *Phone:* 302-857-6351 or toll-free 800-845-2544. *Fax:* 302-857-6352. *E-mail:* gcheatha@desu.edu. *Web site:* http://www.desu.edu/.

Goldey-Beacom College
Wilmington, Delaware

General Independent, comprehensive, coed **Entrance** Moderately difficult **Setting** 24-acre suburban campus **Total enrollment** 1,266 **Student-faculty ratio** 26:1 **Application deadline** Rolling (freshmen), rolling (transfer) **Freshman admission** 76% were admitted. Average high school GPA 2.92 **Freshman test scores** SAT critical reading scores over 500: 29%; SAT math scores over 500: 34%; ACT scores over 18: 50%; SAT critical reading scores over 600: 2%; SAT math scores over 600: 5% **Housing** Yes **Expenses** Tuition & Fees $18,660; Room only $5021 **Undergraduates** 56% women, 33% part-time, 30% 25 or older, 0.3% Native American, 7% Hispanic American, 20% African American, 7% Asian American/Pacific Islander **Academic program** Advanced placement, accelerated degree program, honors program, summer session, internships **Contact** Mr. Larry Eby, Director of Admissions, Goldey-Beacom College, 4701 Limestone Road, Wilmington, DE 19808. *Phone:* 302-225-6289 or toll-free 800-833-4877. *Fax:* 302-996-5408. *E-mail:* admissions@gbc.edu. *Web site:* http://www.gbc.edu/.

Strayer University–Christiana Campus
Newark, Delaware

General Proprietary, comprehensive, coed **Contact** Admissions Office, Strayer University–Christiana Campus, 240 Continental Drive, Suite 108, Newark, DE 19713. *Phone:* 302-292-6100. *Web site:* http://www.strayer.edu/christiana.

University of Delaware
Newark, Delaware

General State-related, university, coed **Entrance** Moderately difficult **Setting** 1,000-acre small-town campus **Total enrollment** 19,391 **Student-faculty ratio** 12:1 **Application deadline** 1/15 (freshmen), 5/1 (transfer) **Freshman admission** 57% were admitted. Average high school GPA 3.5 **Freshman test scores** SAT critical reading scores over 500: 89%; SAT math scores over 500: 92%; ACT scores over 18: 99%; SAT critical reading scores over 600: 46%; SAT math scores over 600: 58%; ACT scores over 24: 78% **Housing** Yes **Expenses** Tuition & Fees: state resident $9486, nonresident $23,186; Room & Board $9066 **Undergraduates** 4% 25 or older, 0.2% Native American, 6% Hispanic American, 5% African American, 5% Asian American/Pacific Islander **The most frequently chosen baccalaureate fields are** business/marketing, education, social sciences **Academic program** English as a second language, advanced placement, accelerated degree program, self-designed majors, honors program, summer session, adult/continuing education programs, internships **Contact** Mr. Lou Hirsh, Director of Admissions, University of Delaware, 116 Hullihen Hall, Newark, DE 19716. *Phone:* 302-831-8123. *Fax:* 302-831-6905. *E-mail:* admissions@udel.edu. *Web site:* http://www.udel.edu/.

Wesley College
Dover, Delaware

Contact Mr. Arthur Jacobs, Director of Undergraduate Admissions, Wesley College, 120 North State Street, Dover, DE 19901-3875. *Phone:* 302-736-2400 or toll-free 800-937-5398 Ext. 2400. *Fax:* 302-736-2382. *E-mail:* admissions@wesley.edu. *Web site:* http://www.wesley.edu/.

See page 1358 for the College Close-Up.

Wilmington University
New Castle, Delaware

General Independent, comprehensive, coed **Entrance** Noncompetitive **Setting** 17-acre suburban campus **Total enrollment** 9,658 **Student-faculty ratio** 17:1 **Application deadline** Rolling (freshmen), rolling (transfer) **Freshman admission** 97% were admitted **Housing** No **Expenses** Tuition & Fees $7274 **Undergraduates** 64% women, 46% part-time, 48% 25 or older, 0.3% Native American, 3% Hispanic American, 19% African American, 1% Asian American/Pacific Islander **The most frequently chosen baccalaureate fields are** business/marketing, education, liberal arts/general studies **Academic program** Accelerated degree program, summer session, adult/continuing education programs, internships **Contact** Mr. Christopher Ferguson, Director of Admissions, Wilmington University, 320 North DuPont Highway, New Castle, DE 19720-6491. *Phone:* 302-356-6745 or toll-free 877-967-5464. *Fax:* 302-328-5902. *E-mail:* inquire@wilmcoll.edu. *Web site:* http://www.wilmu.edu/.

DISTRICT OF COLUMBIA

American University
Washington, District of Columbia

General Independent Methodist, university, coed **Entrance** Very difficult **Setting** 84-acre suburban campus **Total enrollment** 6,648 **Student-faculty ratio** 13:1 **Application deadline** 1/15 (freshmen), 3/1 (transfer) **Freshman admission** 53% were admitted **Freshman test scores** SAT critical reading scores over 500: 97%; SAT math scores over 500: 95%; ACT scores over 18: 100%; SAT critical reading scores over 600: 73%; SAT math scores over 600: 67%; ACT scores over 24: 90% **Housing** Yes **Expenses** Tuition & Fees $36,697; Room & Board $13,468 **Undergraduates** 60% women, 4% part-time, 3% 25 or older, 0.5% Native American, 5% Hispanic American, 4% African American, 6% Asian American/Pacific Islander **The most frequently chosen baccalaureate fields are** business/marketing, communications/journalism, social sciences **Academic program** English as a second language, advanced placement, self-designed majors, honors program, summer session, internships **Contact** Greg Grauman, Director of Admissions, American University, 4400 Massachusetts Avenue, NW, Washington, DC 20016-8001. *E-mail:* admissions@american.edu. *Web site:* http://www.american.edu/.

See page 470 for the College Close-Up.

The Catholic University of America
Washington, District of Columbia

General Independent, university, coed, affiliated with Roman Catholic Church **Entrance** Moderately difficult **Setting** 193-acre urban campus **Total enrollment** 6,768 **Student-faculty ratio** 10:1 **Application deadline** 2/15 (freshmen), 7/15 (transfer) **Freshman admission** 86% were admitted. Average high school GPA 3.25 **Freshman test scores** SAT critical reading scores over 500: 80%; SAT math scores over 500: 79%; ACT scores over 18: 98%; SAT critical reading scores over 600: 31%; SAT math scores over 600: 29%; ACT scores over 24: 48% **Housing** Yes **Expenses** Tuition & Fees $31,890; Room & Board $12,134 **Undergraduates** 54% women, 7% part-time, 7% 25 or older, 0.3% Native American, 7% Hispanic American, 5% African American, 3% Asian American/Pacific Islander **The most frequently chosen baccalaureate fields are** architecture, social sciences, visual and performing arts **Academic program** English as a second language, advanced placement, accelerated degree program, honors program, summer session, adult/continuing education programs, internships **Contact** Ms. Christine Mica, Dean, University Admissions, The Catholic University of America, 102 McMahon Hall, 620 Michigan Avenue, NE, Washington, DC 20064. *Phone:* 202-319-5305 or toll-free 800-673-2772. *Fax:* 202-319-6533. *E-mail:* cua-admissions@cua.edu. *Web site:* http://www.cua.edu/.

Corcoran College of Art and Design

Washington, District of Columbia

General Independent, comprehensive, coed **Entrance** Moderately difficult **Setting** 7-acre urban campus **Total enrollment** 625 **Student-faculty ratio** 4:1 **Application deadline** Rolling (freshmen), rolling (transfer) **Freshman admission** 53% were admitted. Average high school GPA 3.37 **Freshman test scores** SAT critical reading scores over 500: 60%; SAT math scores over 500: 49%; ACT scores over 18: 92%; SAT critical reading scores over 600: 20%; SAT math scores over 600: 22%; ACT scores over 24: 38% **Housing** Yes **Expenses** Tuition & Fees $27,380; Room & Board $12,154 **Undergraduates** 67% women, 22% part-time, 7% 25 or older, 1% Native American, 10% Hispanic American, 8% African American, 7% Asian American/Pacific Islander **The most frequently chosen baccalaureate field is** visual and performing arts **Academic program** Advanced placement, summer session, adult/continuing education programs, internships **Contact** Ms. Elizabeth Smith Paladino, Director of Admissions, Corcoran College of Art and Design, 500 17th Street, NW, Washington, DC 20006-4804. *Phone:* 202-639-1814 or toll-free 888-CORCORAN. *Fax:* 202-639-1830. *E-mail:* admissions@corcoran.org. *Web site:* http://www.corcoran.edu/.

Gallaudet University

Washington, District of Columbia

General Independent, university, coed **Entrance** Moderately difficult **Setting** 99-acre urban campus **Total enrollment** 1,488 **Application deadline** Rolling (freshmen) **Freshman admission** 68% were admitted **Freshman test scores** ACT scores over 18: 42.5%; ACT scores over 24: 10% **Housing** Yes **Expenses** Tuition & Fees $11,226; Room & Board $9660 **Undergraduates** 54% women, 7% part-time, 24% 25 or older, 2% Native American, 9% Hispanic American, 11% African American, 4% Asian American/Pacific Islander **The most frequently chosen baccalaureate fields are** education, business/marketing, visual and performing arts **Academic program** English as a second language, advanced placement, accelerated degree program, self-designed majors, honors program, summer session, adult/continuing education programs, internships **Contact** Ms. Charity Reedy-Hines, Director of Admissions, Gallaudet University, 800 Florida Avenue, NE, Washington, DC 20002-3625. *Phone:* 202-651-5750 or toll-free 800-995-0550. *Fax:* 202-651-5744. *E-mail:* charity.reedy-hines@gallaudet.edu. *Web site:* http://www.gallaudet.edu/.

Georgetown University

Washington, District of Columbia

General Independent Roman Catholic (Jesuit), university, coed **Entrance** Most difficult **Setting** 110-acre urban campus **Total enrollment** 16,437 **Student-faculty ratio** 10:1 **Application deadline** 1/10 (freshmen), 3/1 (transfer) **Freshman admission** 20% were admitted **Freshman test scores** SAT critical reading scores over 500: 99.38%; SAT math scores over 500: 99.38%; SAT critical reading scores over 600: 89.22%; SAT math scores over 600: 91.83% **Housing** Yes **Expenses** Tuition & Fees $38,122; Room & Board $12,153 **Undergraduates** 55% women, 4% part-time, 5% 25 or older, 0.03% Native American, 6% Hispanic American, 6% African American, 9% Asian American/Pacific Islander **The most frequently chosen baccalaureate fields are** business/marketing, English, social sciences **Academic program** English as a second language, advanced placement, self-designed majors, honors program, summer session, adult/continuing education programs, internships **Contact** Mr. Charles A. Deacon, Dean of Undergraduate Admissions, Georgetown University, 37th and O Street, NW, Washington, DC 20057. *Phone:* 202-687-3600. *Fax:* 202-687-5084. *Web site:* http://www.georgetown.edu/.

The George Washington University

Washington, District of Columbia

General Independent, university, coed **Entrance** Very difficult **Setting** 36-acre urban campus **Total enrollment** 25,061 **Student-faculty ratio** 13:1 **Application deadline** 1/10 (freshmen), rolling (transfer) **Freshman admission** 37% were admitted **Freshman test scores** SAT critical reading scores over 500: 97%; SAT math scores over 500: 99%; ACT scores over 18: 100%; SAT critical reading scores over 600: 76%; SAT math scores over 600: 78%; ACT scores over 24: 94.39% **Housing** Yes **Expenses** Tuition & Fees $41,655; Room & Board $10,120 **Undergraduates** 55% women, 9% part-time, 6% 25 or older, 1% Native American, 7% Hispanic American, 7% African American, 11% Asian American/Pacific Islander **The most frequently chosen baccalaureate fields are** business/marketing, psychology, social sciences **Academic program** Advanced placement, accelerated degree program, self-designed majors, honors program, summer session, adult/continuing education programs, internships **Contact** Dr. Kathryn M. Napper, Director of Admission, The George Washington University, 2121 Eye Street, NW, Washington, DC 20052. *Phone:* 202-994-6040 or toll-free 800-447-3765. *Fax:* 202-994-0325. *E-mail:* gwadm@gwis2.circ.gwu.edu. *Web site:* http://www.gwu.edu/.

Visit Petersons.com and enter keywords George Washington

See page 820 for the College Close-Up.

Howard University

Washington, District of Columbia

General Independent, university, coed **Entrance** Moderately difficult **Setting** 256-acre urban campus **Total enrollment** 10,288 **Student-faculty ratio** 8:1 **Application deadline** 2/15 (freshmen), 4/1 (transfer) **Freshman admission** 49% were admitted. Average high school GPA 3.2 **Freshman test scores** SAT math scores over 500: 66%; SAT math scores over 600: 21% **Housing** Yes **Expenses** Tuition & Fees $16,075; Room & Board $7966 **Undergraduates** 67% women, 5% part-time, 9% 25 or older **The most frequently chosen baccalaureate fields are** business/marketing, communications/journalism, health professions and related sciences **Academic program** Advanced placement, accelerated degree program, self-designed majors, honors program, summer session, internships **Contact** Ms. Linda Sanders-Hawkins, Interim Director of Admissions, Howard University, 2400 Sixth Street, NW, Washington, DC 20059-0002. *Phone:* 202-806-2700 or toll-free 800-HOWARD-U. *Fax:* 202-806-4467. *E-mail:* lsanders-hawkins@howard.edu. *Web site:* http://www.howard.edu/.

Potomac College

Washington, District of Columbia

General Proprietary, 4-year, coed **Entrance** Noncompetitive **Setting** urban campus **Total enrollment** 398 **Student-faculty ratio** 15:1 **Application deadline** Rolling (freshmen), rolling (transfer) **Freshman admission** 76% were admitted **Housing** No **Undergraduates** 61% women, 78% part-time, 98% 25 or older, 3% Hispanic American, 76% African American, 1% Asian American/Pacific Islander **Academic program** Advanced placement, accelerated degree program, summer

COLLEGES AT-A-GLANCE

Potomac College (continued)

session, adult/continuing education programs, internships **Contact** Asha Ellison, Assistant to the President, Potomac College, 4000 Chesapeake Street, NW, Washington, DC 20016. *Phone:* 202-686-0876 Ext. 203 or toll-free 888-686-0876. *Fax:* 202-686-0818. *E-mail:* info@potomac.edu. *Web site:* http://www.potomac.edu/.

Strayer University–Takoma Park Campus

Washington, District of Columbia

General Proprietary, comprehensive, coed **Contact** Admissions Office, Strayer University–Takoma Park Campus, 6830 Laurel Street, NW, Washington, DC 20012. *Phone:* 202-722-8100. *Web site:* http://www.strayer.edu/takoma_park.

Strayer University–Washington Campus

Washington, District of Columbia

General Proprietary, comprehensive, coed **Contact** Admissions Office, Strayer University–Washington Campus, 1133 15th Street, NW, Washington, DC 200025. *Phone:* 202-408-2400. *Web site:* http://www.strayer.edu/washington_dc.

Trinity (Washington) University

Washington, District of Columbia

General Independent Roman Catholic, comprehensive, undergraduate: women only; graduate: coed **Entrance** Moderately difficult **Setting** 26-acre urban campus **Total enrollment** 1,630 **Application deadline** 3/1 (freshmen) **Housing** Yes **Expenses** Tuition & Fees $19,357; Room & Board $8450 **Undergraduates** 38% 25 or older **Academic program** English as a second language, advanced placement, accelerated degree program, self-designed majors, honors program, summer session, adult/continuing education programs, internships **Contact** Director of Admissions, Trinity (Washington) University, 125 Michigan Avenue, NE, Washington, DC 20017-1094. *Phone:* 800-492-6882 or toll-free 800-IWANTTC. *E-mail:* admissions@trinitydc.edu. *Web site:* http://www.trinitydc.edu/.

University of Phoenix–Washington D.C. Campus

Washington, District of Columbia

General Proprietary, comprehensive, coed **Total enrollment** 27 **Housing** No **Expenses** Tuition & Fees $13,200 **Undergraduates** 64% women, 71% 25 or older, 7% Hispanic American, 50% African American **The most frequently chosen baccalaureate field is** business/marketing **Contact** Ms. Audra McQuarie, Registrar/Executive Director, University of Phoenix–Washington D.C. Campus, 4035 South Riverpoint Parkway, Mail Stop CF-L101, Phoenix, AZ 85040. *Phone:* 480-557-6151. *Fax:* 480-643-3068. *E-mail:* audra.mcquarie@phoenix.edu. *Web site:* http://www.phoenix.edu/.

University of the District of Columbia

Washington, District of Columbia

General District-supported, comprehensive, coed **Entrance** Noncompetitive **Setting** 28-acre urban campus **Total enrollment** 4,960 **Student-faculty ratio** 13:1 **Application deadline** 8/1 (freshmen), 8/1 (transfer) **Freshman admission** 67% were admitted **Housing** No **Expenses** Tuition & Fees: state resident $5370, nonresident $12,300 **Undergraduates** 62% women, 54% part-time, 57% 25 or older, 0.1% Native American, 6% Hispanic American, 66% African American, 3% Asian American/Pacific Islander **The most frequently chosen baccalaureate fields are** business/marketing, health professions and related sciences, security and protective services **Academic program** English as a second language, accelerated degree program, honors program, summer session, adult/continuing education programs, internships **Contact** Ms. Ann Marie Waterman, Associate Vice President, University of the District of Columbia, 4200 Connecticut Avenue, NW, Washington, DC 20008-1175. *Phone:* 202-274-6110. *Fax:* 202-274-5553. *Web site:* http://www.udc.edu/.

FLORIDA

American InterContinental University South Florida

Weston, Florida

General Proprietary, comprehensive, coed **Setting** 3-acre suburban campus **Total enrollment** 887 **Application deadline** Rolling (freshmen), rolling (transfer) **Undergraduates** 61% women, 16% part-time, 48% 25 or older, 0.1% Native American, 32% Hispanic American, 35% African American, 1% Asian American/Pacific Islander **The most frequently chosen baccalaureate fields are** business/marketing, computer and information sciences, visual and performing arts **Academic program** Accelerated degree program, summer session, adult/continuing education programs **Contact** Piera Brum, Director of Admissions, American InterContinental University South Florida, 2250 North Commerce Parkway, Suite 100, Weston, FL 33326. *Phone:* 877-564-6248 or toll-free 888-603-4888. *Fax:* 877-564-6248. *Web site:* http://www.aiuniv.edu/.

Angley College

Deland, Florida

Contact Admissions Office, Angley College, 230 North Woodland Boulevard, Suite 310, Deland, FL 32720. *Phone:* 386-740-1215 Ext. 125 or toll-free 866-639-1215. *E-mail:* admissions@angley.edu. *Web site:* http://www.angley.edu/.

Argosy University, Sarasota

Sarasota, Florida

General Proprietary, university, coed **Contact** Director of Admissions, Argosy University, Sarasota, 5250 17th Street, Sarasota, FL 34235. *Phone:* 941-379-0404 or toll-free 800-331-5995. *Fax:* 941-379-5964. *Web site:* http://www.argosy.edu/sarasota/.

Visit Petersons.com and enter keywords Argosy University, Sarasota

See page 478 for the College Close-Up.

Argosy University, Tampa

Tampa, Florida

General Proprietary, university, coed **Setting** urban campus **Contact** Director of Admissions, Argosy University, Tampa, 1403 North Howard Avenue, Tampa, FL 33607. *Phone:* 813-393-5290 or toll-free 800-850-6488. *Fax:* 813-874-1989. *Web site:* http://www.argosy.edu/tampa/.

Visit Petersons.com and enter keywords Argosy University, Tampa

See page 478 for the College Close-Up.

The Art Institute of Fort Lauderdale

Fort Lauderdale, Florida

General Proprietary, 4-year, coed **Setting** urban campus **Contact** Director of Admissions, The Art Institute of Fort Lauderdale, 1799 Southeast 17th

Street, Fort Lauderdale, FL 33316. *Phone:* 954-463-3000 or toll-free 800-275-7603. *Fax:* 954-728-8637. *Web site:* http://www.artinstitutes.edu/fortlauderdale/.

Visit Petersons.com and enter keywords Art Institute of Fort Lauderdale

See page 512 for the College Close-Up.

The Art Institute of Jacksonville
Jacksonville, Florida

General Proprietary, 4-year, coed **Setting** suburban campus **Contact** Director of Admissions, The Art Institute of Jacksonville, 8775 Baypine Road, Jacksonville, FL 32256. *Phone:* 904-486-3000 or toll-free 800-924-1589. *Fax:* 904-732-9423. *Web site:* http://www.artinstitutes.edu/jacksonville/.

Visit Petersons.com and enter keywords Art Institute of Jacksonville

See page 522 for the College Close-Up.

The Art Institute of Tampa
Tampa, Florida

General Proprietary, 4-year, coed **Setting** suburban campus **Contact** Director of Admissions, The Art Institute of Tampa, Parkside at Tampa Bay Park, 4401 North Himes Avenue, Suite 150, Tampa, FL 33614. *Phone:* 813-873-2112 or toll-free 866-703-3277. *Fax:* 813-873-2171. *Web site:* http://www.artinstitutes.edu/tampa/.

Visit Petersons.com and enter keywords Art Institute of Tampa

See page 546 for the College Close-Up.

Ave Maria University
Ave Maria, Florida

General Independent Roman Catholic, comprehensive, coed **Entrance** Moderately difficult **Setting** suburban campus **Total enrollment** 672 **Student-faculty ratio** 10:1 **Application deadline** Rolling (freshmen), 12/1 (transfer) **Freshman admission** 56% were admitted. Average high school GPA 3.6 **Freshman test scores** SAT critical reading scores over 500: 97%; SAT math scores over 500: 86%; ACT scores over 18: 98%; SAT critical reading scores over 600: 73%; SAT math scores over 600: 51%; ACT scores over 24: 54% **Housing** Yes **Expenses** Tuition & Fees $17,745; Room & Board $7980 **Undergraduates** 54% women, 1% part-time, 1% 25 or older **The most frequently chosen baccalaureate fields are** philosophy and religious studies, biological/life sciences, theology and religious vocations **Academic program** Accelerated degree program, summer session, internships **Contact** Mr. Brett Ormandy, Director of Admissions, Ave Maria University, 5050 Ave Maria Boulevard, Ave Maria, FL 34142. *Phone:* 239-280-2487 or toll-free 877-283-8648. *Fax:* 239-280-2559. *E-mail:* brett.ormandy@avemaria.edu. *Web site:* http://www.avemaria.edu/.

The Baptist College of Florida
Graceville, Florida

General Independent Southern Baptist, 4-year, coed **Entrance** Noncompetitive **Setting** 165-acre small-town campus **Total enrollment** 588 **Student-faculty ratio** 13:1 **Application deadline** 8/11 (freshmen), 8/11 (transfer) **Housing** Yes **Expenses** Tuition & Fees $8500; Room & Board $4066 **Undergraduates** 38% women, 30% part-time, 39% 25 or older, 2% Hispanic American, 3% African American, 1% Asian American/Pacific Islander **The most frequently chosen baccalaureate fields are** education, theology and religious vocations **Academic program** Advanced placement, summer session, internships **Contact** Mrs. Sandra Richards, Director of Marketing, The Baptist College of Florida, 5400 College Drive, Graceville, FL 32440-1898. *Phone:* 850-263-3261 Ext. 460 or toll-free 800-328-2660 Ext. 460. *Fax:* 850-263-9026. *E-mail:* skrichards@baptistcollege.edu. *Web site:* http://www.baptistcollege.edu/.

Barry University
Miami Shores, Florida

General Independent Roman Catholic, university, coed **Entrance** Moderately difficult **Setting** 122-acre suburban campus **Total enrollment** 8,846 **Student-faculty ratio** 18:1 **Application deadline** Rolling (freshmen), rolling (transfer) **Freshman admission** 62% were admitted. Average high school GPA 2 **Freshman test scores** SAT critical reading scores over 500: 37%; SAT math scores over 500: 35%; ACT scores over 18: 77%; SAT critical reading scores over 600: 5%; SAT math scores over 600: 4%; ACT scores over 24: 8% **Housing** Yes **Expenses** Tuition & Fees $25,500; Room & Board $8486 **Undergraduates** 69% women, 18% part-time, 0.1% Native American, 25% Hispanic American, 20% African American, 1% Asian American/Pacific Islander **The most frequently chosen baccalaureate fields are** business/marketing, education, liberal arts/general studies **Academic program** English as a second language, advanced placement, accelerated degree program, honors program, summer session, adult/continuing education programs, internships **Contact** Ms. Magda Castineyra, Director of Undergraduate Admissions, Barry University, 11300 Northeast Second Avenue, Miami Shores, FL 33161-6695. *Phone:* 305-899-3100 or toll-free 800-695-2279. *Fax:* 305-899-2971. *E-mail:* admissions@mail.barry.edu. *Web site:* http://www.barry.edu/.

Visit Petersons.com and enter keyword Barry

See page 580 for the College Close-Up.

Beacon College
Leesburg, Florida

General Independent, 4-year, coed **Entrance** Minimally difficult **Setting** 5-acre small-town campus **Total enrollment** 128 **Student-faculty ratio** 6:1 **Application deadline** Rolling (freshmen), rolling (transfer) **Freshman admission** 85% were admitted. Average high school GPA 3.3 **Housing** Yes **Expenses** Tuition & Fees $28,710; Room & Board $8150 **Undergraduates** 38% women, 18% 25 or older, 3% Hispanic American, 9% African American, 2% Asian American/Pacific Islander **The most frequently chosen baccalaureate fields are** health professions and related sciences, computer and information sciences, liberal arts/general studies **Academic program** Summer session, adult/continuing education programs, internships **Contact** Ms. Celia Corrad, Coordinator of Admissions, Beacon College, 105 East Main Street, Leesburg, FL 34748. *Phone:* 352-787-7660. *Fax:* 352-787-0796. *E-mail:* ccorrad@beaconcollege.edu. *Web site:* http://www.beaconcollege.edu/.

See page 588 for the College Close-Up.

Belhaven College
Maitland, Florida

Contact Director of Admission, Belhaven College, Maitland 200 Suite 165, 2301 Maitland Center Parkway, Maitland, FL 32751. *Phone:* 407-804-1424 or toll-free 877-804-1424. *Fax:* 407-661-1732. *Web site:* http://www.belhaven.edu/.

Bethune-Cookman University
Daytona Beach, Florida

General Independent Methodist, comprehensive, coed **Entrance** Minimally difficult **Setting** 60-acre urban campus **Total enrollment** 3,614 **Student-faculty ratio** 16:1 **Application deadline** 6/30 (freshmen), 6/30 (transfer) **Freshman admission** 69% were admitted. Average high school GPA 2.9 **Freshman test scores** SAT critical reading scores over 500: 37.5%; SAT math scores over 500: 32%; ACT scores over 18: 25%; SAT critical reading scores over 600: 5%; SAT math scores over 600: 4%; ACT scores over 24: 1% **Housing** Yes **Expenses** Tuition & Fees

Bethune-Cookman University (continued)
$12,936; Room & Board $7672 **Undergraduates** 60% women, 4% part-time, 6% 25 or older, 0.2% Native American, 2% Hispanic American, 94% African American, 0.2% Asian American/Pacific Islander **The most frequently chosen baccalaureate fields are** business/marketing, education, health professions and related sciences **Academic program** Advanced placement, accelerated degree program, honors program, summer session, adult/continuing education programs, internships **Contact** Mrs. Aixa Melendez, Director of Admissions, Bethune-Cookman University, 640 Dr. Mary McLeod Bethune Boulevard, Daytona Beach, FL 32114-3099. *Phone:* 386-481-2600 or toll-free 800-448-0228. *Fax:* 386-481-2601. *E-mail:* admissions@cookman.edu. *Web site:* http://www.bethune.cookman.edu/.

Brown Mackie College–Miami
Miami, Florida

General Proprietary, primarily 2-year, coed **Contact** Director of Admissions, Brown Mackie College–Miami, One Herald Plaza, Miami, FL 33132. *Phone:* 305-341-6600 or toll-free 866-505-0335. *Fax:* 305-373-8814. *Web site:* http://www.brownmackie.edu/Miami/.

Visit Petersons.com and enter keywords Brown Mackie College-Miami

See page 632 for the College Close-Up.

Carlos Albizu University, Miami Campus
Miami, Florida

General Independent, comprehensive, coed, primarily women **Setting** 18-acre urban campus **Total enrollment** 1,081 **Student-faculty ratio** 9:1 **Application deadline** Rolling (freshmen), rolling (transfer) **Freshman admission** 88% were admitted. Average high school GPA 2.92 **Housing** No **Expenses** Tuition & Fees $11,724 **Undergraduates** 80% women, 54% part-time, 70% 25 or older, 88% Hispanic American, 4% African American **The most frequently chosen baccalaureate fields are** business/marketing, education, psychology **Academic program** English as a second language, advanced placement, accelerated degree program, summer session, adult/continuing education programs, internships **Contact** Ms. Mildred Triana, Admissions Officer, Carlos Albizu University, Miami Campus, 2173 N.W. 99th Avenue, Miami, FL 33172. *Phone:* 305-593-1223 Ext. 259 or toll-free 888-672-3246. *Fax:* 305-593-1854. *E-mail:* mtriana@albizu.edu. *Web site:* http://www.mia.albizu.edu/.

Visit Petersons.com and enter keyword Carlos

See page 678 for the College Close-Up.

Chipola College
Marianna, Florida

General State-supported, primarily 2-year, coed **Entrance** Noncompetitive **Setting** 105-acre rural campus **Total enrollment** 2,341 **Student-faculty ratio** 24:1 **Application deadline** Rolling (freshmen), rolling (transfer) **Freshman admission** 78% were admitted. Average high school GPA 2.5 **Freshman test scores** SAT critical reading scores over 500: 16%; SAT math scores over 500: 36%; ACT scores over 18: 81%; SAT critical reading scores over 600: 4%; SAT math scores over 600: 12%; ACT scores over 24: 25% **Housing** No **Expenses** Tuition & Fees: state resident $2550, nonresident $7314 **Undergraduates** 61% women, 52% part-time, 39% 25 or older, 1% Native American, 2% Hispanic American, 17% African American, 1% Asian American/Pacific Islander **Academic program** Advanced placement, honors program, summer session, adult/continuing education programs **Contact** Mrs. Kathy L. Rehberg, Registrar, Chipola College, 3094 Indian Circle, Marianna, FL 32446-3065. *Phone:* 850-718-2233. *Fax:* 850-718-2287. *E-mail:* rehbergk@chipola.edu. *Web site:* http://www.chipola.edu/.

City College
Casselberry, Florida

Contact Ms. Kimberly Bowden, Director of Admissions, City College, 853 Semoran Boulevard, Suite 200, Casselberry, FL 32707-5342. *Phone:* 352-335-4000. *Fax:* 352-335-4303. *E-mail:* kbowden@citycollege.edu. *Web site:* http://www.citycollegeorlando.edu/.

City College
Fort Lauderdale, Florida

Contact Admissions Office, City College, 2000 West Commercial Boulevard, Suite 200, Fort Lauderdale, FL 33309. *Phone:* 954-492-5353. *Web site:* http://www.citycollege.edu/.

City College
Gainesville, Florida

Contact Admissions Office, City College, 2400 Southwest 13th Street, Gainesville, FL 32608. *Web site:* http://www.citycollege.edu/.

City College
Miami, Florida

Contact Admissions Office, City College, 9300 South Dadeland Boulevard, Suite PH, Miami, FL 33156. *Phone:* 305-666-9242. *Fax:* 305-666-9243. *Web site:* http://www.citycollege.edu/.

Clearwater Christian College
Clearwater, Florida

General Independent nondenominational, comprehensive, coed **Entrance** Minimally difficult **Setting** 138-acre suburban campus **Total enrollment** 571 **Student-faculty ratio** 15:1 **Application deadline** Rolling (freshmen), rolling (transfer) **Freshman admission** 89% were admitted. Average high school GPA 3.32 **Freshman test scores** SAT critical reading scores over 500: 75%; SAT math scores over 500: 75%; ACT scores over 18: 100%; SAT critical reading scores over 600: 75%; ACT scores over 24: 75% **Housing** Yes **Expenses** Tuition & Fees $14,710; Room & Board $6740 **Undergraduates** 49% women, 3% part-time, 4% 25 or older, 0.2% Native American, 4% Hispanic American, 5% African American, 2% Asian American/Pacific Islander **The most frequently chosen baccalaureate fields are** business/marketing, education, liberal arts/general studies **Academic program** Advanced placement, summer session, internships **Contact** Dr. Keith Hutchison, Director of Admissions, Clearwater Christian College, 3400 Gulf-to-Bay Boulevard, Clearwater, FL 33759-4595. *Phone:* 727-726-1153 or toll-free 800-348-4463. *Fax:* 813-726-8597. *E-mail:* admissions@clearwater.edu. *Web site:* http://www.clearwater.edu/.

Daytona State College
Daytona Beach, Florida

General State-supported, primarily 2-year, coed **Entrance** Noncompetitive **Setting** 100-acre rural campus **Total enrollment** 17,779 **Student-faculty ratio** 19:1 **Application deadline** Rolling (freshmen), rolling (transfer) **Freshman admission** 100% were admitted **Housing** No **Expenses** Tuition & Fees: state resident $2313, nonresident $8158 **Undergraduates** 61% women, 55% part-time, 44% 25 or older, 0.5% Native American, 9% Hispanic American, 16% African American, 2% Asian American/Pacific Islander **Academic program** English as a second language, advanced placement, honors program, summer session, adult/continuing education programs, internships **Contact** Mrs. Karen Sanders, Director of Admissions and Recruitment, Daytona State College, 1200 International Speedway Boulevard, Daytona Beach, FL 32114. *Phone:* 386-506-3050. *E-mail:* sanderk@daytonastate.edu. *Web site:* http://www.daytonastate.edu/.

DeVry University
Jacksonville, Florida

Contact DeVry University, 5200 Belfort Road, Jacksonville, FL 32256-6040.

DeVry University
Miami, Florida

Contact DeVry University, 8700 West Flagler Street, Suite 100, Miami, FL 33174-2535. *Web site:* http://www.devry.edu/.

DeVry University
Miramar, Florida

General Proprietary, comprehensive, coed **Entrance** Minimally difficult **Total enrollment** 1,261 **Student-faculty ratio** 17:1 **Application deadline** Rolling (freshmen), rolling (transfer) **Housing** No **Expenses** Tuition & Fees $14,080 **Undergraduates** 40% women, 53% part-time, 59% 25 or older, 0.1% Native American, 43% Hispanic American, 30% African American, 1% Asian American/Pacific Islander **The most frequently chosen baccalaureate fields are** business/marketing, computer and information sciences, engineering technologies **Academic program** Advanced placement, accelerated degree program **Contact** Admissions Office, DeVry University, 2300 Southwest 145th Avenue, Miramar, FL 33027-4150. *Web site:* http://www.devry.edu/.

DeVry University
Orlando, Florida

General Proprietary, comprehensive, coed **Entrance** Minimally difficult **Setting** 10-acre urban campus **Total enrollment** 1,929 **Student-faculty ratio** 14:1 **Application deadline** Rolling (freshmen), rolling (transfer) **Housing** No **Expenses** Tuition & Fees $14,080 **Undergraduates** 36% women, 48% part-time, 61% 25 or older, 0.5% Native American, 24% Hispanic American, 22% African American, 3% Asian American/Pacific Islander **The most frequently chosen baccalaureate fields are** business/marketing, computer and information sciences, engineering technologies **Academic program** Advanced placement, accelerated degree program, summer session, adult/continuing education programs **Contact** Admissions Office, DeVry University, 4000 Millenia Boulevard, Orlando, FL 32839. *Web site:* http://www.devry.edu/.

DeVry University
Tampa, Florida

Contact DeVry University, 3030 North Rocky Point Drive West, Suite 100, Tampa, FL 33607-5901. *Web site:* http://www.devry.edu/.

Eckerd College
St. Petersburg, Florida

General Independent Presbyterian, 4-year, coed **Entrance** Moderately difficult **Setting** 188-acre suburban campus **Total enrollment** 1,863 **Student-faculty ratio** 14:1 **Application deadline** Rolling (freshmen), rolling (transfer) **Freshman admission** 72% were admitted. Average high school GPA 3.27 **Freshman test scores** SAT critical reading scores over 500: 83%; SAT math scores over 500: 77%; ACT scores over 18: 97%; SAT critical reading scores over 600: 42%; SAT math scores over 600: 34%; ACT scores over 24: 64% **Housing** Yes **Expenses** Tuition & Fees $33,228; Room & Board $9326 **Undergraduates** 58% women, 1% part-time, 1% 25 or older, 0.3% Native American, 4% Hispanic American, 4% African American, 2% Asian American/Pacific Islander **The most frequently chosen baccalaureate fields are** biological/life sciences, business/marketing, social sciences **Academic program** Advanced placement, accelerated degree program, self-designed majors, honors program, summer session, adult/continuing education programs, internships **Contact** Ms. Donna Grosso, Eckerd College, 4200 54th Avenue South, St. Petersburg, FL 33711. *Phone:* 727-864-8331 or toll-free 800-456-9009. *Fax:* 727-866-2304. *E-mail:* admissions@eckerd.edu. *Web site:* http://www.eckerd.edu/.

Edison State College
Fort Myers, Florida

General State and locally supported, primarily 2-year, coed **Entrance** Noncompetitive **Setting** 80-acre urban campus **Total enrollment** 13,007 **Application deadline** 8/18 (freshmen), 8/18 (transfer) **Housing** No **Expenses** Tuition & Fees: state resident $2397, nonresident $8880 **Undergraduates** 61% women, 65% part-time, 34% 25 or older, 0.3% Native American, 17% Hispanic American, 10% African American, 2% Asian American/Pacific Islander **The most frequently chosen baccalaureate field is** security and protective services **Academic program** English as a second language, advanced placement, accelerated degree program, honors program, summer session, adult/continuing education programs, internships **Contact** Ms. Pat Armstrong, Admissions Specialist, Edison State College, 8099 College Parkway, Fort Myers, FL 33919. *Phone:* 239-489-9360 Ext. 1360 or toll-free 800-749-2ECC. *E-mail:* registrar@edison.edu. *Web site:* http://www.edison.edu/.

Edward Waters College
Jacksonville, Florida

General Independent African Methodist Episcopal, 4-year, coed **Entrance** Noncompetitive **Setting** 44-acre urban campus **Total enrollment** 831 **Student-faculty ratio** 13:1 **Application deadline** Rolling (freshmen), rolling (transfer) **Freshman admission** 31% were admitted. Average high school GPA 2.64 **Housing** Yes **Expenses** Tuition & Fees $9990 **Undergraduates** 42% women, 2% part-time, 78% 25 or older, 1% Hispanic American, 90% African American **Academic program** Self-designed majors, honors program, summer session, adult/continuing education programs, internships **Contact** Mr. Lonnie Morris, Director of Admissions, Edward Waters College, 1658 Kings Road, Jacksonville, FL 32209-6199. *Phone:* 904-470-8202 or toll-free 888-898-3191. *E-mail:* Lmorris@ewc.edu. *Web site:* http://www.ewc.edu/.

Embry-Riddle Aeronautical University
Daytona Beach, Florida

General Independent, comprehensive, coed **Entrance** Moderately difficult **Setting** 178-acre suburban campus **Total enrollment** 4,935 **Student-faculty ratio** 16:1 **Application deadline** Rolling (freshmen), 5/1 (transfer) **Freshman admission** 81% were admitted. Average high school GPA 3.23 **Freshman test scores** SAT critical reading scores over 500: 63%; SAT math scores over 500: 74%; ACT scores over 18: 92%; SAT critical reading scores over 600: 22%; SAT math scores over 600: 40%; ACT scores over 24: 50% **Housing** Yes **Expenses** Tuition & Fees $29,724; Room & Board $8840 **Undergraduates** 17% women, 6% part-time, 9% 25 or older, 0.4% Native American, 8% Hispanic American, 6% African American, 6% Asian American/Pacific Islander **The most frequently chosen baccalaureate fields are** engineering, business/marketing, transportation and materials moving **Academic program** English as a second language, advanced placement, accelerated degree program, honors program, summer session, adult/continuing education programs, internships **Contact** Mr. Robert J. Adams, Director of Undergraduate Admissions, Embry-Riddle Aeronautical University, 600 South Clyde Morris Boulevard, Daytona Beach, FL 32114-3900. *Phone:* 386-226-6100 or toll-free 800-862-2416. *Fax:* 386-226-7070. *E-mail:* dbadmit@erau.edu. *Web site:* http://www.embryriddle.edu/.

Visit Petersons.com and enter keyword Embry-Riddle

See page 780 for the College Close-Up.

Embry-Riddle Aeronautical University Worldwide
Daytona Beach, Florida

General Independent, comprehensive, coed **Entrance** Minimally difficult **Total enrollment** 16,175 **Application deadline** Rolling (freshmen),

Embry-Riddle Aeronautical University Worldwide (continued)
rolling (transfer) **Housing** No **Expenses** Tuition & Fees $5520 **Undergraduates** 11% women, 82% part-time, 1% Native American, 10% Hispanic American, 10% African American, 4% Asian American/Pacific Islander **The most frequently chosen baccalaureate fields are** business/marketing, transportation and materials moving **Academic program** Advanced placement, adult/continuing education programs **Contact** Ms. Linda Dammer, Interim Director of Admissions, Embry-Riddle Aeronautical University Worldwide, 600 South Clyde Morris Boulevard, Daytona Beach, FL 32114-3900. *Phone:* 866-509-0743 or toll-free 800-522-6787. *Fax:* 386-226-6984. *E-mail:* ecinfo@erau.edu. *Web site:* http://www.embryriddle.edu/.

Everest University
Clearwater, Florida

General Proprietary, comprehensive, coed **Entrance** Minimally difficult **Setting** 3-acre urban campus **Total enrollment** 261 **Application deadline** Rolling (freshmen), rolling (transfer) **Housing** No **Undergraduates** 63% 25 or older **Academic program** Advanced placement, accelerated degree program, honors program, summer session, adult/continuing education programs, internships **Contact** Mr. Kevin Buskirk, Director of Admissions, Everest University, 2471 McMullen Road, Clearwater, FL 33759. *Phone:* 727-725-2688 or toll-free 800-353-FMUS. *Fax:* 727-796-3406. *E-mail:* kbuskirk@cci.edu. *Web site:* http://www.everest.edu/.

Everest University
Jacksonville, Florida

General Proprietary, comprehensive, coed **Entrance** Minimally difficult **Total enrollment** 409 **Undergraduates** 49% 25 or older **Contact** Mr. Robin Manning, Admissions Director, Everest University, 8226 Phillips Highway, Jacksonville, FL 32256. *Phone:* 904-731-4949 or toll-free 888-741-4270. *E-mail:* rmanning@cci.edu. *Web site:* http://www.everest.edu/.

Everest University
Lakeland, Florida

Contact Ms. Patricia Sabol, Director of Student Services, Everest University, 995 East Memorial Boulevard, Suite 110, Lakeland, FL 33801. *Phone:* 863-686-1444 or toll-free 877-225-0014. *Fax:* 863-688-9881. *E-mail:* psabol@cci.edu. *Web site:* http://www.everest.edu/.

Everest University
Melbourne, Florida

General Proprietary, comprehensive, coed **Entrance** Minimally difficult **Setting** 5-acre small-town campus **Total enrollment** 291 **Application deadline** Rolling (freshmen), rolling (transfer) **Housing** No **Undergraduates** 60% 25 or older **Academic program** Advanced placement, accelerated degree program, summer session, internships **Contact** Mr. Timothy Alexander, Director of Admissions, Everest University, 2401 North Harbor City Boulevard, Melbourne, FL 32935-6657. *Phone:* 321-253-2929 Ext. 121. *Web site:* http://www.everest.edu/.

Everest University
Orlando, Florida

General Proprietary, comprehensive, coed **Entrance** Minimally difficult **Setting** 1-acre urban campus **Total enrollment** 527 **Student-faculty ratio** 15:1 **Application deadline** Rolling (freshmen), rolling (transfer) **Housing** No **Undergraduates** 43% 25 or older **Academic program** Advanced placement, summer session, internships **Contact** Joann Derosa-Weber, Director of Admissions, Everest University, 5421 Diplomat Circle, Orlando, FL 32810-5674. *Phone:* 407-628-5870 or toll-free 800-628-5870. *Fax:* 407-628-1344. *Web site:* http://www.everest.edu/.

Everest University
Orlando, Florida

General Proprietary, comprehensive, coed **Entrance** Minimally difficult **Total enrollment** 823 **Application deadline** Rolling (freshmen) **Housing** No **Undergraduates** 48% 25 or older **Academic program** Accelerated degree program, adult/continuing education programs, internships **Contact** Ms. Annette Cloin, Director of Admissions, Everest University, 9200 South Park Center Loop, Orlando, FL 32819. *Phone:* 407-851-2525 Ext. 111 or toll-free 407-851-2525 (in-state); 888-471-4270 (out-of-state). *Fax:* 407-354-7946. *Web site:* http://www.everest.edu/.

Everest University
Pompano Beach, Florida

Contact Ms. Fran Heaston, Director of Admissions, Everest University, 225 North Federal Highway, Pompano Beach, FL 33062. *Phone:* 954-783-7339 or toll-free 800-468-0168. *Fax:* 954-783-7964. *E-mail:* fheaston@cci.edu. *Web site:* http://www.everest.edu/.

Everest University
Tampa, Florida

Contact Mr. Donnie Broughton, Director of Admissions, Everest University, 3319 West Hillsborough Avenue, Tampa, FL 33614-5899. *Phone:* 813-879-6000 Ext. 129. *Web site:* http://www.everest.edu/.

Everest University
Tampa, Florida

General Proprietary, comprehensive, coed **Entrance** Minimally difficult **Setting** 5-acre urban campus **Total enrollment** 5,984 **Student-faculty ratio** 17:1 **Application deadline** Rolling (freshmen), rolling (transfer) **Housing** No **Expenses** Tuition & Fees $17,040 **Undergraduates** 81% women, 79% part-time, 1% Native American, 9% Hispanic American, 32% African American, 1% Asian American/Pacific Islander **The most frequently chosen baccalaureate fields are** business/marketing, law/legal studies, security and protective services **Academic program** English as a second language, accelerated degree program, summer session, adult/continuing education programs **Contact** Ms. Shandretta Pointer, Director of Admissions, Everest University, 3924 Coconut Palm Drive, Tampa, FL 33619. *Phone:* 813-621-0041 Ext. 106 or toll-free 877-338-0068. *Fax:* 813-628-0919. *E-mail:* spointer@cci.edu. *Web site:* http://www.everest.edu/.

Everglades University
Altamonte Springs, Florida

Contact Admissions, Everglades University, 887 East Altamonte Drive, Altamonte Springs, FL 32701. *Phone:* 407-277-0311 or toll-free 866-289-1078. *Fax:* 407-482-9801. *Web site:* http://www.evergladesuniversity.edu/.

Everglades University
Boca Raton, Florida

Contact Ms. Jean Graham, Everglades University, 5002 T-Rex Avenue, Suite 100, Boca Raton, FL 33431. *Phone:* 561-912-1211 or toll-free 888-772-6077. *Fax:* 561-912-1191. *E-mail:* admissions-boca@evergladesuniversity.edu. *Web site:* http://www.evergladesuniversity.edu/.

Everglades University
Sarasota, Florida

Contact Kathleen Cornett, Campus President, Everglades University, 6151 Lake Osprey Drive, Sarasota, FL 34240. *Phone:* 941-907-2262 or toll-free 866-907-2262. *Fax:* 941-907-6634. *E-mail:* bbrewer@evergladesuniversity.edu. *Web site:* http://www.evergladesuniversity.edu/.

Flagler College
St. Augustine, Florida

General Independent, 4-year, coed **Entrance** Moderately difficult **Setting** 42-acre small-town campus **Total enrollment** 2,716 **Student-faculty ratio** 20:1 **Application deadline** 3/1 (freshmen), 3/1 (transfer) **Freshman admission** 44% were admitted. Average high school GPA 3.35 **Freshman test scores** SAT critical reading scores over 500: 87%; SAT math scores over 500: 85%; ACT scores over 18: 98%; SAT critical reading scores over 600: 24%; SAT math scores over 600: 21%; ACT scores over 24: 39% **Housing** Yes **Expenses** Tuition & Fees $13,330; Room & Board $7190 **Undergraduates** 60% women, 3% part-time, 4% 25 or older, 0.3% Native American, 4% Hispanic American, 2% African American, 0.4% Asian American/Pacific Islander **The most frequently chosen baccalaureate fields are** business/marketing, communications/journalism, visual and performing arts **Academic program** Advanced placement, summer session, internships **Contact** Mr. Marc Williar, Director of Admissions, Flagler College, 74 King Street, St. Augustine, FL 32085. *Phone:* 904-819-6220 or toll-free 800-304-4208. *Fax:* 904-819-6466. *E-mail:* admiss@flagler.edu. *Web site:* http://www.flagler.edu/.

Florida Agricultural and Mechanical University
Tallahassee, Florida

General State-supported, university, coed **Entrance** Moderately difficult **Setting** 419-acre urban campus **Total enrollment** 12,274 **Student-faculty ratio** 18:1 **Application deadline** 5/15 (freshmen), 5/15 (transfer) **Freshman admission** 61% were admitted. Average high school GPA 2.94 **Freshman test scores** SAT critical reading scores over 500: 28.8%; SAT math scores over 500: 28.4%; ACT scores over 18: 63.5%; SAT critical reading scores over 600: 6%; SAT math scores over 600: 6.3%; ACT scores over 24: 7.8% **Housing** Yes **Expenses** Tuition & Fees: state resident $4407, nonresident $16,347; Room & Board $6706 **Undergraduates** 59% women, 10% part-time, 10% 25 or older, 0.2% Native American, 1% Hispanic American, 94% African American, 1% Asian American/Pacific Islander **The most frequently chosen baccalaureate fields are** business/marketing, health professions and related sciences, security and protective services **Academic program** Advanced placement, accelerated degree program, honors program, summer session, adult/continuing education programs, internships **Contact** Barbara Cox, Director, Admissions, Florida Agricultural and Mechanical University, Office of Admissions, Tallahassee, FL 32307. *Phone:* 850-599-3796. *Fax:* 850-599-3069. *E-mail:* admission@famu.edu. *Web site:* http://www.famu.edu/.

Florida Atlantic University
Boca Raton, Florida

General State-supported, university, coed **Entrance** Moderately difficult **Setting** 850-acre suburban campus **Total enrollment** 27,700 **Student-faculty ratio** 20:1 **Application deadline** 6/1 (freshmen) **Freshman admission** 46% were admitted. Average high school GPA 3.4 **Freshman test scores** SAT critical reading scores over 500: 68.3%; SAT math scores over 500: 70.4%; ACT scores over 18: 98.3%; SAT critical reading scores over 600: 16.9%; SAT math scores over 600: 19.9%; ACT scores over 24: 38.2% **Housing** Yes **Expenses** Tuition & Fees: state resident $4187, nonresident $17,532; Room & Board $9582 **Undergraduates** 58% women, 41% part-time, 34% 25 or older, 0.4% Native American, 20% Hispanic American, 18% African American, 5% Asian American/Pacific Islander **The most frequently chosen baccalaureate fields are** business/marketing, education, social sciences **Academic program** English as a second language, advanced placement, accelerated degree program, honors program, summer session, adult/continuing education programs, internships **Contact** Assistant Director, Florida Atlantic University, 777 Glades Road, PO Box 3091, Boca Raton, FL 33431-0991. *Phone:* 561-297-3040 or toll-free 800-299-4FAU. *Fax:* 561-297-2758. *Web site:* http://www.fau.edu/.

Visit Petersons.com and enter keywords Florida Atlantic

See page 800 for the College Close-Up.

Florida Christian College
Kissimmee, Florida

General Independent, 4-year, coed, affiliated with Christian Churches and Churches of Christ **Entrance** Minimally difficult **Setting** 40-acre small-town campus **Total enrollment** 226 **Application deadline** 7/15 (freshmen), 7/15 (transfer) **Housing** Yes **Expenses** Tuition & Fees $8410; Room only $2400 **Undergraduates** 25% 25 or older **Academic program** Advanced placement, summer session, adult/continuing education programs, internships **Contact** Admissions Office, Florida Christian College, 1011 Bill Beck Boulevard, Kissimmee, FL 34744-5301. *Phone:* 407-569-1172 or toll-free 888-GO-TO-FCC. *E-mail:* admissionsforms@fcc.edu. *Web site:* http://www.fcc.edu/.

Florida College
Temple Terrace, Florida

General Independent, 4-year, coed **Entrance** Moderately difficult **Setting** 95-acre small-town campus **Total enrollment** 467 **Student-faculty ratio** 15:1 **Application deadline** 8/1 (freshmen), 8/1 (transfer) **Freshman admission** 61% were admitted **Freshman test scores** ACT scores over 18: 83%; ACT scores over 24: 40% **Housing** Yes **Expenses** Tuition & Fees $12,150; Room & Board $6440 **Undergraduates** 53% women, 3% part-time, 1% Native American, 6% Hispanic American, 4% African American, 1% Asian American/Pacific Islander **The most frequently chosen baccalaureate fields are** education, liberal arts/general studies, philosophy and religious studies **Academic program** Advanced placement, summer session **Contact** Mrs. Shay Angelo, Assistant Director of Admissions, Florida College, 119 North Glen Arven Avenue, Temple Terrace, FL 33617. *Phone:* 813-988-5131 Ext. 6716 or toll-free 800-326-7655. *Fax:* 813-899-6772. *E-mail:* admissions@floridacollege.edu. *Web site:* http://www.floridacollege.edu/.

Florida Culinary Institute
West Palm Beach, Florida

General Proprietary, 4-year, coed **Setting** 14-acre urban campus **Total enrollment** 600 **Undergraduates** 35% women **Contact** Mr. David Conway, Associate Director of Admissions, Florida Culinary Institute, 2400 Metrocenter Boulevard, West Palm Beach, FL 33407. *Phone:* 561-842-8324 Ext. 202 or toll-free 800-826-9986. *E-mail:* info@floridaculinary.com. *Web site:* http://www.floridaculinary.com/.

Florida Gulf Coast University
Fort Myers, Florida

General State-supported, comprehensive, coed **Entrance** Moderately difficult **Setting** 760-acre suburban campus **Total enrollment** 11,104 **Student-faculty ratio** 22:1 **Application deadline** 6/1 (freshmen), 7/1 (transfer) **Freshman admission** 66% were admitted. Average high school GPA 3.34 **Freshman test scores** SAT critical reading scores over 500: 57%; SAT math scores over 500: 62%; ACT scores over 18: 94%; SAT critical reading scores over 600: 9%; SAT math scores over 600: 14%; ACT scores over 24: 24% **Housing** Yes **Expenses** Tuition & Fees: state resident $5724, nonresident $20,983; Room & Board $7642 **Undergraduates** 56% women, 19% part-time, 15% 25 or older, 1% Native American, 14% Hispanic American, 5% African American, 2% Asian American/Pacific Islander **The most frequently chosen baccalaureate fields are** business/marketing, education, health professions and related sciences **Academic program** Advanced placement, accelerated degree

Florida Gulf Coast University (continued)

program, honors program, summer session, internships **Contact** Mr. Marc Laviolette, Director of Admissions, Florida Gulf Coast University, 10501 FGCU Boulevard South, Fort Myers, FL 33965-6565. *Phone:* 239-590-7878 or toll-free 888-889-1095. *Web site:* http://www.fgcu.edu/.

Florida Hospital College of Health Sciences
Orlando, Florida

General Independent, comprehensive, coed **Entrance** Minimally difficult **Setting** 9-acre urban campus **Total enrollment** 2,207 **Application deadline** 7/18 (freshmen), 7/18 (transfer) **Freshman test scores** ACT scores over 18: 68%; ACT scores over 24: 12% **Housing** Yes **Expenses** Tuition & Fees $8540 **Undergraduates** 63% 25 or older **Academic program** Advanced placement **Contact** Ms. Katie Shaw, Director of Enrollment Services, Florida Hospital College of Health Sciences, 671 Winyah Drive, Orlando, FL 32803. *Phone:* 407-303-7742 or toll-free 800-500-7747. *Fax:* 407-303-5671. *E-mail:* katie.shaw@fhchs.edu. *Web site:* http://www.fhchs.edu/.

Florida Institute of Technology
Melbourne, Florida

General Independent, university, coed **Entrance** Moderately difficult **Setting** 130-acre small-town campus **Total enrollment** 8,227 **Student-faculty ratio** 17:1 **Application deadline** Rolling (freshmen), rolling (transfer) **Freshman admission** 74% were admitted. Average high school GPA 3.5 **Freshman test scores** SAT critical reading scores over 500: 77%; SAT math scores over 500: 87%; ACT scores over 18: 98%; SAT critical reading scores over 600: 34%; SAT math scores over 600: 51%; ACT scores over 24: 67% **Housing** Yes **Expenses** Tuition & Fees $31,520; Room & Board $10,630 **Undergraduates** 46% women, 22% part-time, 8% 25 or older, 1% Native American, 7% Hispanic American, 14% African American, 2% Asian American/Pacific Islander **The most frequently chosen baccalaureate fields are** engineering, biological/life sciences, transportation and materials moving **Academic program** English as a second language, advanced placement, accelerated degree program, summer session, adult/continuing education programs, internships **Contact** Michael J. Perry, Director of Undergraduate Admission, Florida Institute of Technology, 150 West University Boulevard, Melbourne, FL 32901-6975. *Phone:* 321-674-8030 or toll-free 800-888-4348. *Fax:* 321-723-9468. *E-mail:* admission@fit.edu. *Web site:* http://www.fit.edu/.

Visit Petersons.com and enter keywords Florida Institute of Technology

See page 802 for the College Close-Up.

Florida International University
Miami, Florida

General State-supported, university, coed **Entrance** Moderately difficult **Setting** 573-acre urban campus **Total enrollment** 39,718 **Student-faculty ratio** 27:1 **Application deadline** Rolling (freshmen), rolling (transfer) **Freshman admission** 35% were admitted. Average high school GPA 3.7 **Freshman test scores** SAT critical reading scores over 500: 94.5%; SAT math scores over 500: 91.04%; ACT scores over 18: 99.81%; SAT critical reading scores over 600: 39.22%; SAT math scores over 600: 36.23%; ACT scores over 24: 77.34% **Housing** Yes **Expenses** Tuition & Fees: state resident $4580, nonresident $16,979; Room & Board $11,946 **Undergraduates** 56% women, 39% part-time, 23% 25 or older, 0.2% Native American, 64% Hispanic American, 12% African American, 3% Asian American/Pacific Islander **The most frequently chosen baccalaureate fields are** business/marketing, health professions and related sciences, psychology **Academic program** Advanced placement, accelerated degree program, honors program, summer session, adult/continuing education programs, internships **Contact** Ms. Valerire Peterson, Associate Director of Admissions, Florida International University, 11200 SW Eighth Street, PC 140, Miami, FL 33199. *Phone:* 305-348-3675. *Fax:* 305-348-3648. *E-mail:* admiss@fiu.edu. *Web site:* http://www.fiu.edu/.

Visit Petersons.com and enter keywords Florida International

Florida Memorial University
Miami-Dade, Florida

Contact Mrs. Peggy Murray Martin, Director of Admissions and International Student Advisor, Florida Memorial University, 15800 NW 42nd Avenue, Miami-Dade, FL 33054. *Phone:* 305-626-3147 or toll-free 800-822-1362. *Web site:* http://www.fmuniv.edu/.

Florida National College
Hialeah, Florida

General Proprietary, 4-year, coed **Entrance** Noncompetitive **Setting** urban campus **Total enrollment** 2,811 **Student-faculty ratio** 26:1 **Application deadline** Rolling (freshmen), rolling (transfer) **Freshman admission** 81% were admitted **Housing** No **Expenses** Tuition & Fees $13,170 **Undergraduates** 68% women, 27% part-time, 60% 25 or older, 0.3% Native American, 94% Hispanic American, 3% African American, 1% Asian American/Pacific Islander **Academic program** English as a second language, advanced placement, self-designed majors, summer session, adult/continuing education programs **Contact** Mr. Guillermo Araya, Admissions Coordinator, Florida National College, 4425 West 20th Avenue, Hialeah, FL 33012. *Phone:* 305-821-3333 Ext. 1015. *Fax:* 305-362-0595. *E-mail:* admissions@fnc.edu. *Web site:* http://www.fnc.edu/.

Florida Southern College
Lakeland, Florida

General Independent, comprehensive, coed, affiliated with United Methodist Church **Entrance** Moderately difficult **Setting** 100-acre suburban campus **Total enrollment** 2,059 **Student-faculty ratio** 13:1 **Application deadline** 3/1 (freshmen), rolling (transfer) **Freshman admission** 69% were admitted. Average high school GPA 3.4 **Freshman test scores** SAT critical reading scores over 500: 71%; SAT math scores over 500: 67%; ACT scores over 18: 100%; SAT critical reading scores over 600: 21%; SAT math scores over 600: 19%; ACT scores over 24: 39% **Housing** Yes **Expenses** Tuition & Fees $24,662; Room & Board $8310 **Undergraduates** 57% women, 4% part-time, 6% 25 or older, 1% Native American, 8% Hispanic American, 6% African American, 2% Asian American/Pacific Islander **The most frequently chosen baccalaureate fields are** business/marketing, education, social sciences **Academic program** Advanced placement, self-designed majors, honors program, summer session, internships **Contact** Mr. Bill C. Langston, Director of Admissions, Florida Southern College, 111 Lake Hollingsworth Drive, Lakeland, FL 33801-5698. *Phone:* 863-680-4131 or toll-free 800-274-4131. *Fax:* 863-680-4120. *E-mail:* fscadm@flsouthern.edu. *Web site:* http://www.flsouthern.edu/.

Visit Petersons.com and enter keywords Florida Southern

See page 804 for the College Close-Up.

Florida State College at Jacksonville
Jacksonville, Florida

General State-supported, primarily 2-year, coed **Entrance** Noncompetitive **Setting** 656-acre urban campus **Total enrollment** 25,903 **Student-faculty ratio** 22:1 **Application deadline** Rolling (freshmen), rolling (transfer) **Freshman admission** 49% were admitted **Freshman test scores** SAT critical reading scores over 500: 36.73%; SAT math scores over 500: 29.19%; ACT scores over 18: 39.96%; SAT critical reading scores over 600: 3.89%; SAT math scores over 600: 3.51%; ACT scores over 24: 6.01% **Housing** No **Expenses** Tuition & Fees: state resident $2569, nonresident $8322 **Undergraduates** 61% women, 69% part-time, 44% 25 or older **Academic program** English as a second language, advanced placement, accelerated degree program, honors program, summer session, adult/continuing education programs, internships **Contact** Mr. Peter Biegel, District Executive Director for Student Success and Services, Florida State College at Jacksonville, 501 West State Street, Jacksonville, FL 32202. *Phone:* 904-632-3131. *Fax:* 904-632-5105. *E-mail:* admissions@fccj.edu. *Web site:* http://www.fscj.edu/.

Florida State University
Tallahassee, Florida

General State-supported, university, coed **Entrance** Very difficult **Setting** 451-acre suburban campus **Total enrollment** 39,785 **Student-faculty ratio** 22:1 **Application deadline** 1/19 (freshmen), 7/1 (transfer) **Freshman admission** 61% were admitted. Average high school GPA 3.71 **Freshman test scores** SAT critical reading scores over 500: 97.5%; SAT math scores over 500: 96.4%; ACT scores over 18: 99.9%; SAT critical reading scores over 600: 46.6%; SAT math scores over 600: 53%; ACT scores over 24: 84.4% **Housing** Yes **Expenses** Tuition & Fees: state resident $4566, nonresident $18,804; Room & Board $8000 **Undergraduates** 55% women, 10% part-time, 7% 25 or older, 1% Native American, 13% Hispanic American, 10% African American, 4% Asian American/Pacific Islander **The most frequently chosen baccalaureate fields are** business/marketing, education, social sciences **Academic program** English as a second language, advanced placement, accelerated degree program, honors program, summer session, internships **Contact** Ms. Janice V. Finney, Director of Admissions, Florida State University, Tallahassee, FL 32306. *Phone:* 850-644-6200. *Fax:* 850-644-0197. *E-mail:* admissions@admin.fsu.edu. *Web site:* http://www.fsu.edu/.

Full Sail University
Winter Park, Florida

General Proprietary, comprehensive, coed, primarily men **Setting** 190-acre suburban campus **Total enrollment** 8,921 **Student-faculty ratio** 8:1 **Application deadline** Rolling (freshmen) **Housing** No **Academic program** Summer session, internships **Contact** Ms. Mary Beth Plank, Director of Admissions, Full Sail University, 3300 University Boulevard, Winter Park, FL 32792-7437. *Phone:* 407-679-6333 or toll-free 800-226-7625. *E-mail:* admissions@fullsail.com. *Web site:* http://www.fullsail.edu/.

Herzing College
Winter Park, Florida

General Proprietary, primarily 2-year, coed **Total enrollment** 209 **Housing** No **Undergraduates** 60% 25 or older **Contact** Tessie Uranga, Director of Admissions, Herzing College, 1595 South Semoran Boulevard, Suite 1501, Winter Park, FL 32792. *Phone:* 407-478-0500. *Fax:* 407-380-0269. *Web site:* http://www.herzing.edu/.

Hobe Sound Bible College
Hobe Sound, Florida

Contact Mrs. Ann French, Director of Admissions, Hobe Sound Bible College, PO Box 1065, Hobe Sound, FL 33475-1065. *Phone:* 772-546-5534 Ext. 1015 or toll-free 800-881-5534. *Fax:* 772-545-1422. *E-mail:* hsbcuwin@aol.com. *Web site:* http://www.hsbc.edu/.

Hodges University
Naples, Florida

General Independent, comprehensive, coed **Entrance** Minimally difficult **Setting** suburban campus **Total enrollment** 2,292 **Student-faculty ratio** 23:1 **Application deadline** Rolling (freshmen), rolling (transfer) **Freshman admission** 94% were admitted **Housing** No **Expenses** Tuition & Fees $16,940 **Undergraduates** 69% women, 22% part-time, 69% 25 or older, 0.3% Native American, 27% Hispanic American, 17% African American, 2% Asian American/Pacific Islander **The most frequently chosen baccalaureate fields are** business/marketing, health professions and related sciences, interdisciplinary studies **Academic program** English as a second language, advanced placement, accelerated degree program, summer session, adult/continuing education programs, internships **Contact** Ms. Rita Lampus, Vice President of Student Enrollment Management, Hodges University, 2655 Northbrooke Drive, Naples, FL 34119. *Phone:* 239-513-1122 Ext. 104 or toll-free 800-466-8017. *Fax:* 239-598-6254. *E-mail:* rlampus@hodges.edu. *Web site:* http://www.hodges.edu/.

Indian River State College
Fort Pierce, Florida

General State-supported, primarily 2-year, coed **Entrance** Noncompetitive **Setting** 133-acre small-town campus **Total enrollment** 17,110 **Student-faculty ratio** 24:1 **Application deadline** Rolling (freshmen), rolling (transfer) **Freshman admission** 100% were admitted. Average high school GPA 2.84 **Housing** No **Expenses** Tuition & Fees: state resident $1794, nonresident $6665 **Undergraduates** 61% women, 65% part-time, 45% 25 or older, 0.4% Native American, 12% Hispanic American, 16% African American, 2% Asian American/Pacific Islander **Academic program** English as a second language, advanced placement, summer session, adult/continuing education programs **Contact** Mr. Steven Payne, Dean of Educational Services, Indian River State College, 3209 Virginia Avenue, Fort Pierce, FL 34981-5596. *Phone:* 772-462-7805. *E-mail:* spayne@ircc.edu. *Web site:* http://www.ircc.edu/.

International Academy of Design & Technology
Tampa, Florida

General Proprietary, 4-year, coed **Entrance** Noncompetitive **Setting** 1-acre urban campus **Student-faculty ratio** 16:1 **Application deadline** Rolling (freshmen), rolling (transfer) **Housing** Yes **Expenses** Tuition & Fees $14,460; Room & Board $8547 **Academic program** Advanced placement, accelerated degree program, summer session, internships **Contact** Ms. Debbie Love/Mr. Jonathan Morris, Vice President of Admissions and Marketing, International Academy of Design & Technology, 5104 Eisenhower Boulevard, Tampa, FL 33634-7350. *Phone:* 813-881-0007- or toll-free 800-ACADEMY. *Fax:* 813-881-0008. *E-mail:* admissions@academy.edu. *Web site:* http://www.academy.edu/.

ITT Technical Institute
Fort Lauderdale, Florida

General Proprietary, primarily 2-year, coed **Entrance** Minimally difficult **Setting** suburban campus **Housing** No **Contact** Director of Recruitment, ITT Technical Institute, 3401 South University Drive, Fort Lauderdale, FL 33328-2021. *Phone:* 954-476-9300 or toll-free 800-488-7797. *Web site:* http://www.itt-tech.edu/.

ITT Technical Institute
Fort Myers, Florida

General Proprietary, primarily 2-year, coed **Contact** Director of Recruitment, ITT Technical Institute, 13500 Powers Court, Suite 100, Fort Myers, FL 33912. *Phone:* 239-603-8700 or toll-free 877-485-5313. *Web site:* http://www.itt-tech.edu/.

ITT Technical Institute
Jacksonville, Florida

General Proprietary, primarily 2-year, coed **Entrance** Minimally difficult **Setting** urban campus **Housing** No **Contact** Director of Recruitment, ITT Technical Institute, 7011 A.C. Skinner Parkway, Suite 140, Jackson-

ITT Technical Institute (continued)
ville, FL 32256. *Phone:* 904-573-9100 or toll-free 800-318-1264. *Web site:* http://www.itt-tech.edu/.

ITT Technical Institute
Lake Mary, Florida

General Proprietary, primarily 2-year, coed **Entrance** Minimally difficult **Setting** suburban campus **Housing** No **Contact** Director of Recruitment, ITT Technical Institute, 1400 South International Parkway, Lake Mary, FL 32746. *Phone:* 407-660-2900 or toll-free 866-489-8441. *Fax:* 407-660-2566. *Web site:* http://www.itt-tech.edu/.

ITT Technical Institute
Miami, Florida

General Proprietary, primarily 2-year, coed **Entrance** Minimally difficult **Housing** No **Contact** Director of Recruitment, ITT Technical Institute, 7955 NW 12th Street, Miami, FL 33126. *Phone:* 305-477-3080. *Web site:* http://www.itt-tech.edu/.

ITT Technical Institute
Pinellas Park, Florida

General Proprietary, primarily 2-year, coed **Contact** Director of Recruitment, ITT Technical Institute, 3491 Gandy Boulevard, Suite 101, Pinellas Park, FL 33781-2658. *Phone:* 727-209-4700 or toll-free 866-488-5084. *Web site:* http://www.itt-tech.edu/.

ITT Technical Institute
Tallahassee, Florida

General Proprietary, primarily 2-year, coed **Contact** Director of Recruitment, ITT Technical Institute, 2639 North Monroe Street, Tallahassee, FL 32303. *Phone:* 850-422-6300 or toll-free 877-230-3559. *Web site:* http://www.itt-tech.edu/.

ITT Technical Institute
Tampa, Florida

General Proprietary, primarily 2-year, coed **Entrance** Minimally difficult **Setting** suburban campus **Housing** No **Contact** Director of Recruitment, ITT Technical Institute, 4809 Memorial Highway, Tampa, FL 33634-7151. *Phone:* 813-885-2244 or toll-free 800-825-2831. *Web site:* http://www.itt-tech.edu/.

Jacksonville University
Jacksonville, Florida

General Independent, comprehensive, coed **Entrance** Moderately difficult **Setting** 198-acre suburban campus **Total enrollment** 3,554 **Student-faculty ratio** 14:1 **Application deadline** Rolling (freshmen), rolling (transfer) **Freshman admission** 54% were admitted. Average high school GPA 3.41 **Freshman test scores** SAT critical reading scores over 500: 59.3%; SAT math scores over 500: 58.9%; ACT scores over 18: 95.6%; SAT critical reading scores over 600: 14.7%; SAT math scores over 600: 13.9%; ACT scores over 24: 34% **Housing** Yes **Expenses** Tuition & Fees $25,300; Room & Board $9060 **Undergraduates** 60% women, 27% part-time, 35% 25 or older, 1% Native American, 6% Hispanic American, 19% African American, 3% Asian American/Pacific Islander **The most frequently chosen baccalaureate fields are** business/marketing, health professions and related sciences, social sciences **Academic program** Advanced placement, accelerated degree program, self-designed majors, honors program, summer session, adult/continuing education programs, internships **Contact** Ms. Lisa Hannasch, Director of First-Year Student Admission and Enrollment, Jacksonville University, 2800 University Boulevard North, Office of Admissions, Jacksonville, FL 32211. *Phone:* 904-256-7000 or toll-free 800-225-2027. *Fax:* 904-256-7012. *E-mail:* admissions@ju.edu. *Web site:* http://www.ju.edu/.

Johnson & Wales University
North Miami, Florida

General Independent, 4-year, coed **Entrance** Minimally difficult **Setting** 8-acre suburban campus **Total enrollment** 2,033 **Student-faculty ratio** 28:1 **Application deadline** Rolling (freshmen), rolling (transfer) **Freshman admission** 60% were admitted **Freshman test scores** SAT critical reading scores over 500: 29.1%; SAT math scores over 500: 29.7%; SAT critical reading scores over 600: 4.1%; SAT math scores over 600: 5.1% **Housing** Yes **Expenses** Tuition & Fees $24,429; Room & Board $8904 **Undergraduates** 55% women, 3% part-time, 9% 25 or older, 0.5% Native American, 17% Hispanic American, 22% African American, 1% Asian American/Pacific Islander **The most frequently chosen baccalaureate fields are** business/marketing, family and consumer sciences, parks and recreation **Academic program** English as a second language, advanced placement, accelerated degree program, honors program, summer session, internships **Contact** Mr. Jeff Greenip, Director of Admissions, Johnson & Wales University, 1701 Northeast 127th Street, North Miami, FL 33181. *Phone:* 305-892-7002 or toll-free 800-232-2433. *Fax:* 305-892-7020. *E-mail:* admissions.mia@jwu.edu. *Web site:* http://www.jwu.edu/northmiami/.

Jones College
Jacksonville, Florida

General Independent, 4-year, coed **Entrance** Noncompetitive **Setting** 5-acre urban campus **Total enrollment** 748 **Student-faculty ratio** 12:1 **Application deadline** Rolling (freshmen) **Freshman admission** 69% were admitted **Housing** No **Expenses** Tuition & Fees $6690 **Undergraduates** 81% women, 65% part-time, 78% 25 or older, 1% Native American, 9% Hispanic American, 65% African American, 1% Asian American/Pacific Islander **The most frequently chosen baccalaureate fields are** business/marketing, computer and information sciences, health professions and related sciences **Academic program** Advanced placement, accelerated degree program, self-designed majors, summer session, adult/continuing education programs, internships **Contact** Linda Vaughn, Director of Admissions, Jones College, 555 Arlington Expressway, Jacksonville, FL 32211-5588. *Phone:* 904-743-1122 Ext. 141. *E-mail:* lvaughn@jones.edu. *Web site:* http://www.jones.edu/.

Keiser University
Fort Lauderdale, Florida

General Proprietary, comprehensive, coed **Setting** urban campus **Student-faculty ratio** 11:1 **Application deadline** Rolling (freshmen), rolling (transfer) **Housing** No **Academic program** English as a second language, accelerated degree program, adult/continuing education programs **Contact** LaFrawn Mays, Admissions Director, Keiser University, 1500 NW 49th Street, Fort Lauderdale, FL 33309. *Phone:* 954-776-4456 or toll-free 888-KEISER-9. *E-mail:* admissions@keisercollege.edu. *Web site:* http://www.keiseruniversity.edu/.

Visit Petersons.com and enter keyword Keiser

See page 888 for the College Close-Up.

Lincoln College of Technology
West Palm Beach, Florida

General Proprietary, primarily 2-year, coed **Entrance** Noncompetitive **Setting** 7-acre urban campus **Total enrollment** 1,521 **Application deadline** Rolling (freshmen), rolling (transfer) **Housing** No **Undergraduates** 39% 25 or older **Academic program** Internships **Contact** Mr. Kevin Cassidy, Director of Admissions, Lincoln College of Technology, 2410 Metro Centre Boulevard, West Palm Beach, FL 33407.

Phone: 561-842-8324 Ext. 117 or toll-free 800-826-9986. *Fax:* 561-842-9503. *Web site:* http://www.lincolnedu.com/.

Lynn University
Boca Raton, Florida

General Independent, comprehensive, coed **Entrance** Moderately difficult **Setting** 123-acre suburban campus **Total enrollment** 2,224 **Student-faculty ratio** 16:1 **Application deadline** Rolling (freshmen), rolling (transfer) **Freshman admission** 72% were admitted. Average high school GPA 2.79 **Freshman test scores** SAT critical reading scores over 500: 37.46%; SAT math scores over 500: 40.72%; ACT scores over 18: 67.91%; SAT critical reading scores over 600: 6.18%; SAT math scores over 600: 9%; ACT scores over 24: 15.66% **Housing** Yes **Expenses** Tuition & Fees $30,100; Room & Board $10,900 **Undergraduates** 49% women, 12% part-time, 13% 25 or older, 0.2% Native American, 7% Hispanic American, 3% African American, 0.4% Asian American/Pacific Islander **The most frequently chosen baccalaureate fields are** business/marketing, communications/journalism, psychology **Academic program** English as a second language, advanced placement, accelerated degree program, honors program, summer session, adult/continuing education programs, internships **Contact** Juan Camilo Tamayo, Director of Undergraduate Admissions, Lynn University, 3601 North Military Trail, Boca Raton, FL 33431-5598. *Phone:* 561-237-7304 or toll-free 800-888-5966. *Fax:* 561-237-7100. *E-mail:* jtamayo@lynn.edu. *Web site:* http://www.lynn.edu/.

See page 934 for the College Close-Up.

Miami Dade College
Miami, Florida

General State and locally supported, primarily 2-year, coed **Entrance** Noncompetitive **Setting** urban campus **Total enrollment** 57,222 **Student-faculty ratio** 30:1 **Application deadline** Rolling (freshmen), rolling (transfer) **Freshman admission** 100% were admitted **Housing** No **Expenses** Tuition & Fees: state resident $2586, nonresident $8674 **Undergraduates** 60% women, 62% part-time, 32% 25 or older, 0.1% Native American, 67% Hispanic American, 18% African American, 1% Asian American/Pacific Islander **Academic program** English as a second language, advanced placement, honors program, summer session, adult/continuing education programs, internships **Contact** Ms. Dulce Beltran, College Registrar, Miami Dade College, 11011 SW 104th Street, Miami, FL 33176. *Phone:* 305-237-2103. *Fax:* 305-237-2964. *E-mail:* dbeltran@mdc.edu. *Web site:* http://www.mdc.edu/.

Miami International University of Art & Design
Miami, Florida

General Proprietary, comprehensive, coed **Setting** 4-acre urban campus **Contact** Director of Admissions, Miami International University of Art & Design, 1501 Biscayne Boulevard, Suite 100, Miami, FL 33132-1418. *Phone:* 305-428-5700 or toll-free 800-225-9023. *Fax:* 305-374-5933. *Web site:* http://www.artinstitutes.edu/miami.

Visit Petersons.com and enter keywords Miami International

See page 962 for the College Close-Up.

New College of Florida
Sarasota, Florida

General State-supported, 4-year, coed **Entrance** Very difficult **Setting** 119-acre suburban campus **Total enrollment** 825 **Student-faculty ratio** 10:1 **Application deadline** 4/15 (freshmen), 4/15 (transfer) **Freshman admission** 53% were admitted. Average high school GPA 4.02 **Freshman test scores** SAT critical reading scores over 500: 100%; SAT math scores over 500: 99%; ACT scores over 18: 100%; SAT critical reading scores over 600: 88%; SAT math scores over 600: 73%; ACT scores over 24: 92% **Housing** Yes **Expenses** Tuition & Fees: state resident $4784, nonresident $26,386; Room & Board $7783 **Undergraduates** 62% women, 2% 25 or older, 1% Native American, 11% Hispanic American, 2% African American, 3% Asian American/Pacific Islander **The most frequently chosen baccalaureate field is** liberal arts/general studies **Academic program** Self-designed majors, honors program, internships **Contact** Office of Admissions, New College of Florida, 5800 Bay Shore Road, Sarasota, FL 34243-2109. *Phone:* 941-487-5000. *Fax:* 941-487-5010. *E-mail:* admissions@ncf.edu. *Web site:* http://www.ncf.edu/.

Visit Petersons.com and enter keywords New College

See page 1008 for the College Close-Up.

New World School of the Arts
Miami, Florida

Contact Ms. Pamela Neumann, Recruitment and Admissions Coordinator, New World School of the Arts, 300 NE Second Avenue, Miami, FL 33132. *Phone:* 305-237-7007. *Fax:* 305-237-3794. *E-mail:* nwsaadm@mdc.edu. *Web site:* http://www.mdc.edu/nwsa.

Northwest Florida State College
Niceville, Florida

General State and locally supported, primarily 2-year, coed **Entrance** Noncompetitive **Setting** 264-acre small-town campus **Total enrollment** 10,317 **Student-faculty ratio** 15:1 **Application deadline** Rolling (freshmen), rolling (transfer) **Housing** No **Expenses** Tuition & Fees: state resident $2272, nonresident $9198 **Undergraduates** 43% 25 or older, 10% African American **Academic program** English as a second language, advanced placement, accelerated degree program, summer session, adult/continuing education programs **Contact** Ms. Christine Bishop, Registrar/Division Director Enrollment Services, Northwest Florida State College, 100 College Boulevard, Niceville, FL 32578. *Phone:* 850-729-5373. *Fax:* 850-729-5323. *E-mail:* registrar@nwfsc.edu. *Web site:* http://www.nwfstatecollege.edu/.

Northwood University, Florida Campus
West Palm Beach, Florida

General Independent, 4-year, coed **Entrance** Moderately difficult **Setting** 90-acre suburban campus **Total enrollment** 620 **Student-faculty ratio** 18:1 **Application deadline** Rolling (freshmen), rolling (transfer) **Freshman admission** 61% were admitted. Average high school GPA 2.93 **Freshman test scores** SAT critical reading scores over 500: 27%; SAT math scores over 500: 32.5%; ACT scores over 18: 68%; SAT critical reading scores over 600: 2%; SAT math scores over 600: 3% **Housing** Yes **Expenses** Tuition & Fees $18,408; Room & Board $8562 **Undergraduates** 40% women, 3% part-time, 6% 25 or older, 0.3% Native American, 11% Hispanic American, 10% African American, 2% Asian American/Pacific Islander **The most frequently chosen baccalaureate fields are** business/marketing, communications/journalism, parks and recreation **Academic program** Advanced placement, accelerated degree program, honors program, summer session, adult/continuing education programs, internships **Contact** Mr. John (Jack) M. Letvinchuck, Director of Admissions, Northwood University, Florida Campus, 2600 North Military Trail, West Palm Beach, FL 33409-2911. *Phone:* 561-478-5500 or toll-free 800-458-8325. *Fax:* 561-640-3328. *E-mail:* fladmit@northwood.edu. *Web site:* http://www.northwood.edu/.

Nova Southeastern University
Fort Lauderdale, Florida

General Independent, university, coed **Entrance** Moderately difficult **Setting** 300-acre suburban campus **Total enrollment** 29,154 **Application deadline** Rolling (freshmen), rolling (transfer) **Freshman admission** 45% were admitted **Freshman test scores** SAT critical reading scores over 500: 52%; SAT math scores over 500: 55%; ACT

Nova Southeastern University (continued)
scores over 18: 88%; SAT critical reading scores over 600: 12%; SAT math scores over 600: 13%; ACT scores over 24: 21% **Housing** Yes **Expenses** Tuition & Fees $21,100; Room & Board $8360 **Undergraduates** 72% women, 34% part-time **The most frequently chosen baccalaureate fields are** business/marketing, biological/life sciences, health professions and related sciences **Academic program** Advanced placement, honors program, summer session, adult/continuing education programs, internships **Contact** Ms. Maria Dillard, Director of Enrollment Management, Nova Southeastern University, Enrollment Processing Services, 3301 College Avenue, Ft. Lauderdale, FL 33329-9905. *Phone:* 954-262-8000 or toll-free 800-541-NOVA. *Fax:* 954-262-3811. *E-mail:* nsuinfo@nova.edu. *Web site:* http://www.nova.edu/.

See page 1028 for the College Close-Up.

Palm Beach Atlantic University
West Palm Beach, Florida

General Independent nondenominational, comprehensive, coed **Entrance** Moderately difficult **Setting** 25-acre urban campus **Total enrollment** 3,260 **Student-faculty ratio** 14:1 **Application deadline** Rolling (freshmen), rolling (transfer) **Freshman admission** 69% were admitted. Average high school GPA 3.5 **Freshman test scores** SAT critical reading scores over 500: 65.61%; SAT math scores over 500: 54.29%; ACT scores over 18: 91.04%; SAT critical reading scores over 600: 21.72%; SAT math scores over 600: 12.66%; ACT scores over 24: 36.32% **Housing** Yes **Expenses** Tuition & Fees $22,700; Room & Board $8220 **Undergraduates** 64% women, 8% part-time, 26% 25 or older, 0.5% Native American, 14% Hispanic American, 17% African American, 1% Asian American/Pacific Islander **The most frequently chosen baccalaureate fields are** business/marketing, communications/journalism, psychology **Academic program** Advanced placement, accelerated degree program, self-designed majors, honors program, summer session, adult/continuing education programs, internships **Contact** Mr. Joe Sharp, Dean of Admissions, Palm Beach Atlantic University, 901 South Flagler Drive, PO Box 24708, West Palm Beach, FL 33416-4708. *Phone:* 561-803-2102 or toll-free 800-238-3998. *Fax:* 561-803-2115. *E-mail:* admit@pba.edu. *Web site:* http://www.pba.edu/.

Visit Petersons.com and enter keywords Palm Beach Atlantic

Polk State College
Winter Haven, Florida

General State-supported, primarily 2-year, coed **Entrance** Noncompetitive **Setting** 98-acre suburban campus **Total enrollment** 9,437 **Student-faculty ratio** 19:1 **Application deadline** Rolling (freshmen), rolling (transfer) **Housing** No **Expenses** Tuition & Fees: state resident $2585, nonresident $9596 **Undergraduates** 63% women, 65% part-time, 35% 25 or older, 0.3% Native American, 13% Hispanic American, 16% African American, 3% Asian American/Pacific Islander **Academic program** English as a second language, advanced placement, accelerated degree program, self-designed majors, honors program, summer session, adult/continuing education programs **Contact** Kathy Bucklew, Registrar, Polk State College, 999 Avenue H, NE, Winter Haven, FL 33881-4299. *Phone:* 863-297-1010 Ext. 5016. *E-mail:* kbucklew@polk.edu. *Web site:* http://www.polk.edu/.

Polytechnic University of the Americas–Miami Campus
Miami, Florida

Contact Admissions Department, Polytechnic University of the Americas–Miami Campus, 8180 Northwest 36th Street, Suite 401, Miami, FL 33166. *Phone:* 305-418-4220 or toll-free 888-729-7659. *Fax:* 305-418-4325. *Web site:* http://www.pupr.edu/miami/.

Polytechnic University of the Americas–Orlando Campus
Winter Park, Florida

Contact Office of Admissions, Polytechnic University of the Americas–Orlando Campus, 4800 Howell Branch Road, Winter Park, FL 32792. *Phone:* 407-677-5661 or toll-free 888-729-7659. *Fax:* 407-677-5082. *Web site:* http://www.pupr.edu/orlando/.

Rasmussen College Fort Myers
Fort Myers, Florida

Contact Admissions Director, Rasmussen College Fort Myers, 9160 Forum Corporate Parkway, Suite 100, Fort Myers, FL 33905. *Phone:* 239-477-2100 or toll-free 866-344-0229. *Fax:* 239-477-2101. *Web site:* http://www.rasmussen.edu/.

Rasmussen College Ocala
Ocala, Florida

General Proprietary, primarily 2-year, coed, primarily women **Entrance** Noncompetitive **Setting** 3-acre suburban campus **Total enrollment** 507 **Application deadline** Rolling (freshmen), rolling (transfer) **Housing** No **Undergraduates** 59% 25 or older **Academic program** Summer session, adult/continuing education programs **Contact** Admissions Office, Rasmussen College Ocala, 2221 Southwest 19th Avenue Road, Ocala, FL 34471. *Phone:* 352-629-1941 or toll-free 877-593-2783. *Web site:* http://www.rasmussen.edu/.

Rasmussen College Pasco County
Holiday, Florida

General Proprietary, primarily 2-year, coed **Total enrollment** 453 **Application deadline** Rolling (freshmen), rolling (transfer) **Housing** No **Undergraduates** 69% 25 or older **Contact** Ms. Claire L. Walker, Senior Admissions Representative, Rasmussen College Pasco County, 2127 Grand Boulevard, Holiday, FL 34690. *Phone:* 727-942-0069 or toll-free 888-729-7247. *Web site:* http://www.rasmussen.edu/.

Remington College–Largo Campus
Largo, Florida

Contact Kathy McCabe, Director of Recruitment, Remington College–Largo Campus, 8550 Ulmerton Road, Largo, FL 33771. *Phone:* 727-532-1999 or toll-free 888-900-2343. *Fax:* 727-530-7710. *E-mail:* kathy.mccabe@remingtoncollege.edu. *Web site:* http://www.remingtoncollege.edu/.

Remington College–Tampa Campus
Tampa, Florida

Contact Raymond Johnson, Director of Recruitment, Remington College–Tampa Campus, 2410 East Busch Boulevard, Tampa, FL 33612-8410. *Phone:* 813-932-0701 or toll-free 800-992-4850. *Fax:* 813-935-7415. *E-mail:* raymond.johnson@remingtoncollege.edu. *Web site:* http://www.remingtoncollege.edu/.

Ringling College of Art and Design
Sarasota, Florida

General Independent, 4-year, coed **Entrance** Moderately difficult **Setting** 49-acre small-town campus **Total enrollment** 1,318 **Student-faculty ratio** 12:1 **Application deadline** Rolling (freshmen), rolling (transfer) **Freshman admission** 73% were admitted. Average high school GPA 3.17 **Housing** Yes **Expenses** Tuition & Fees $28,470; Room & Board $10,470 **Undergraduates** 57% women, 4% part-time, 9% 25 or older, 1% Native American, 12% Hispanic American, 4% African American, 7% Asian American/Pacific Islander **The most frequently chosen**

baccalaureate fields are communication technologies, visual and performing arts **Academic program** Advanced placement, internships **Contact** Ms. Tracy Stephanski, Associate Dean of Admissions, Ringling College of Art and Design, 2700 North Tamiami Trail, Sarasota, FL 34234-5895. *Phone:* 941-359-7526 or toll-free 800-255-7695. *Fax:* 941-359-7517. *E-mail:* admissions@ringling.edu. *Web site:* http://www.ringling.edu/.

Rollins College

Winter Park, Florida

General Independent, comprehensive, coed **Entrance** Very difficult **Setting** 70-acre suburban campus **Total enrollment** 2,486 **Student-faculty ratio** 10:1 **Application deadline** 2/15 (freshmen), 4/15 (transfer) **Freshman admission** 62% were admitted. Average high school GPA 3.25 **Freshman test scores** SAT critical reading scores over 500: 92.62%; SAT math scores over 500: 93.75%; ACT scores over 18: 99.55%; SAT critical reading scores over 600: 54.55%; SAT math scores over 600: 52.84%; ACT scores over 24: 80.97% **Housing** Yes **Expenses** Tuition & Fees $36,220; Room & Board $11,320 **Undergraduates** 58% women, 1% 25 or older, 1% Native American, 10% Hispanic American, 4% African American, 4% Asian American/Pacific Islander **The most frequently chosen baccalaureate fields are** psychology, business/marketing, social sciences **Academic program** Advanced placement, accelerated degree program, self-designed majors, honors program, adult/continuing education programs, internships **Contact** Mr. David Erdmann, Dean of Admission and Enrollment, Rollins College, 1000 Holt Avenue, Winter Park, FL 32789-4499. *Phone:* 407-646-2161. *Fax:* 407-646-1502. *E-mail:* admission@rollins.edu. *Web site:* http://www.rollins.edu/.

St. John Vianney College Seminary

Miami, Florida

General Independent Roman Catholic, 4-year, coed, primarily men **Entrance** Moderately difficult **Setting** 33-acre urban campus **Application deadline** Rolling (freshmen), rolling (transfer) **Freshman admission** 100% were admitted **Housing** Yes **Undergraduates** 24% 25 or older **Academic program** English as a second language, advanced placement, internships **Contact** Br. Edward Van Merrienboer, Academic Dean, St. John Vianney College Seminary, 2900 Southwest 87th Avenue, Miami, FL 33165-3244. *Phone:* 305-223-4561 Ext. 13. *Fax:* 305-223-0650. *E-mail:* carruthers@sjvcs.edu. *Web site:* http://www.sjvcs.edu/.

Saint Leo University

Saint Leo, Florida

General Independent Roman Catholic, comprehensive, coed **Entrance** Moderately difficult **Setting** 186-acre rural campus **Total enrollment** 4,127 **Student-faculty ratio** 15:1 **Application deadline** 8/15 (freshmen), 8/1 (transfer) **Freshman admission** 76% were admitted. Average high school GPA 3.3 **Freshman test scores** SAT critical reading scores over 500: 44%; SAT math scores over 500: 50%; ACT scores over 18: 98%; SAT critical reading scores over 600: 7%; SAT math scores over 600: 12%; ACT scores over 24: 27% **Housing** Yes **Expenses** Tuition & Fees $17,646; Room & Board $8724 **Undergraduates** 51% women, 6% part-time, 7% 25 or older, 0.3% Native American, 11% Hispanic American, 10% African American, 1% Asian American/Pacific Islander **The most frequently chosen baccalaureate fields are** business/marketing, psychology, security and protective services **Academic program** Advanced placement, honors program, summer session, adult/continuing education programs, internships **Contact** Ms. Christine O'Donnell, Associate Director for Enrollment, Saint Leo University, MC 2008, PO Box 6665, Saint Leo, FL 33574-6665. *Phone:* 352-588-8283 or toll-free 800-334-5532. *Fax:* 352-588-8257. *E-mail:* admissions@saintleo.edu. *Web site:* http://www.saintleo.edu/.

Visit Petersons.com and enter keyword Leo

See page 1118 for the College Close-Up.

St. Petersburg College

St. Petersburg, Florida

General State and locally supported, 4-year, coed **Entrance** Noncompetitive **Setting** 397-acre suburban campus **Total enrollment** 29,282 **Application deadline** Rolling (freshmen) **Housing** No **Undergraduates** 61% women, 67% part-time, 46% 25 or older **The most frequently chosen baccalaureate fields are** education, computer and information sciences, health professions and related sciences **Academic program** English as a second language, advanced placement, accelerated degree program, honors program, summer session, adult/continuing education programs, internships **Contact** Ms. Susan Fell, Director of Admissions and Records, St. Petersburg College, PO Box 13489, St. Petersburg, FL 33733-3489. *Phone:* 727-341-3166. *E-mail:* information@spcollege.edu. *Web site:* http://www.spjc.edu/.

St. Thomas University

Miami Gardens, Florida

General Independent Roman Catholic, comprehensive, coed **Entrance** Moderately difficult **Setting** 140-acre suburban campus **Total enrollment** 2,476 **Student-faculty ratio** 13:1 **Application deadline** Rolling (freshmen), rolling (transfer) **Freshman admission** 59% were admitted **Housing** Yes **Expenses** Tuition & Fees $21,690; Room & Board $6516 **Undergraduates** 56% women, 6% part-time, 26% 25 or older, 0.1% Native American, 48% Hispanic American, 25% African American, 1% Asian American/Pacific Islander **The most frequently chosen baccalaureate fields are** business/marketing, education, security and protective services **Academic program** Advanced placement, honors program, summer session, adult/continuing education programs, internships **Contact** Mr. Andre Lightbourne, Director of Admissions, St. Thomas University, 16401 Northwest 37th Avenue, Miami Gardens, FL 33054-6459. *Phone:* 305-628-6712 or toll-free 800-367-9010. *Fax:* 305-628-6591. *E-mail:* signup@stu.edu. *Web site:* http://www.stu.edu/.

Visit Petersons.com and enter keywords Thomas University

See page 1136 for the College Close-Up.

Santa Fe Community College

Gainesville, Florida

General State and locally supported, 4-year, coed **Entrance** Noncompetitive **Setting** 175-acre suburban campus **Total enrollment** 14,796 **Application deadline** Rolling (freshmen), rolling (transfer) **Expenses** Tuition & Fees: state resident $2031, nonresident $7620 **Undergraduates** 53% women, 54% part-time, 29% 25 or older, 0.5% Native American, 11% Hispanic American, 14% African American, 3% Asian American/Pacific Islander **Academic program** English as a second language, advanced placement, honors program, summer session, adult/continuing education programs, internships **Contact** Mr. Mike Hutley, Associate Registrar, Santa Fe Community College, 3000 Northwest 83rd Street, Gainesville, FL 32606. *Phone:* 352-395-4177. *Fax:* 352-395-4118. *E-mail:* michael.hutley@sfcollege.edu. *Web site:* http://www.sfcc.edu/.

Schiller International University

Largo, Florida

General Independent, comprehensive, coed **Entrance** Minimally difficult **Setting** 4-acre suburban campus **Total enrollment** 673 **Student-faculty ratio** 16:1 **Application deadline** Rolling (freshmen), rolling (transfer) **Housing** Yes **Expenses** Tuition & Fees $18,320 **Undergraduates** 40% women, 20% part-time **The most frequently chosen baccalaureate fields are** business/marketing, interdisciplinary studies, psychology **Academic program** English as a second language, advanced placement, accelerated degree program, self-designed majors, honors program, summer session, adult/continuing education programs, internships **Contact** Donald Trippe, Admissions Officer, Schiller International University, 300 East Bay Drive, Largo, FL 33770. *Phone:* 727-738-6365

Schiller International University (continued)
or toll-free 800-336-4133. *Fax:* 727-738-6376. *E-mail:* admissions@schiller.edu. *Web site:* http://www.schiller.edu/.

Southeastern University
Lakeland, Florida

General Independent, comprehensive, coed, affiliated with Assemblies of God **Entrance** Minimally difficult **Setting** 87-acre suburban campus **Total enrollment** 2,950 **Student-faculty ratio** 25:1 **Application deadline** 7/1 (freshmen), 7/1 (transfer) **Freshman admission** 76% were admitted. Average high school GPA 3.35 **Freshman test scores** SAT critical reading scores over 500: 53.99%; SAT math scores over 500: 39.37%; ACT scores over 18: 74.85%; SAT critical reading scores over 600: 14.87%; SAT math scores over 600: 10.91%; ACT scores over 24: 23.32% **Housing** Yes **Expenses** Tuition & Fees $15,000; Room & Board $7566 **Undergraduates** 58% women, 12% part-time, 18% 25 or older, 0.2% Native American, 12% Hispanic American, 9% African American, 1% Asian American/Pacific Islander **The most frequently chosen baccalaureate fields are** business/marketing, public administration and social services, theology and religious vocations **Academic program** Advanced placement, honors program, summer session, adult/continuing education programs, internships **Contact** Mr. Chris Diaz, Director, Admission, Southeastern University, 1000 Longfellow Boulevard, Lakeland, FL 33801-6099. *Phone:* 800-500-8760 or toll-free 800-500-8760. *Fax:* 863-667-5200. *E-mail:* admission@seuniversity.edu. *Web site:* http://www.seuniversity.edu/.

South University
Royal Palm Beach, Florida

General Proprietary, comprehensive, coed **Contact** Director of Admissions, South University, University Centre, 9801 Belvedere Road, Royal Palm Beach, FL 33411. *Phone:* 561-273-6500 or toll-free 866-629-2902. *Fax:* 561-273-6420. *Web site:* http://www.southuniversity.edu/west-palm-beach/.

Visit Petersons.com and enter keywords South University

See page 1178 for the College Close-Up.

South University
Tampa, Florida

General Proprietary, comprehensive, coed **Contact** Director of Admissions, South University, 4401 North Himes Avenue, Suite 175, Tampa, FL 33614. *Phone:* 813-393-3800 or toll-free 800-846-1472. *Fax:* 813-393-3814. *Web site:* http://www.southuniversity.edu/tampa/.

Visit Petersons.com and enter keywords South University

See page 1176 for the College Close-Up.

Southwest Florida College
Fort Myers, Florida

General Independent, 4-year, coed **Entrance** Noncompetitive **Setting** urban campus **Total enrollment** 1,263 **Application deadline** Rolling (freshmen), rolling (transfer) **Housing** No **Academic program** Advanced placement, accelerated degree program, internships **Contact** Mr. Ken Reynolds, Director of Admissions, Southwest Florida College, 1685 Medical Lane, Fort Myers, FL 33907. *Phone:* 239-939-4766 or toll-free 866-SWFC-NOW. *Fax:* 239-936-4040. *E-mail:* kreynolds@swfc.edu. *Web site:* http://www.swfc.edu/.

State College of Florida Manatee-Sarasota
Bradenton, Florida

General State-supported, primarily 2-year, coed **Entrance** Noncompetitive **Setting** 100-acre suburban campus **Total enrollment** 11,232 **Application deadline** 8/20 (freshmen), 8/20 (transfer) **Freshman admission** 100% were admitted **Freshman test scores** SAT critical reading scores over 500: 41.41%; SAT math scores over 500: 36.98%; ACT scores over 18: 54.48%; SAT critical reading scores over 600: 7.29%; SAT math scores over 600: 5.17%; ACT scores over 24: 16.96% **Housing** No **Expenses** Tuition & Fees: state resident $2676, nonresident $9982 **Undergraduates** 62% women, 52% part-time, 39% 25 or older, 0.4% Native American, 10% Hispanic American, 12% African American, 2% Asian American/Pacific Islander **Academic program** English as a second language, advanced placement, honors program, summer session **Contact** Ms. MariLynn Lewy, AVP, Student Services, State College of Florida Manatee-Sarasota, 5840 26th Street West, PO Box 1849, Bradenton, FL 34206. *Phone:* 941-752-5384. *Fax:* 941-727-6380. *E-mail:* lewym@scf.edu. *Web site:* http://www.scf.edu/.

Stetson University
DeLand, Florida

General Independent, comprehensive, coed **Entrance** Moderately difficult **Setting** 175-acre small-town campus **Total enrollment** 3,790 **Student-faculty ratio** 11:1 **Application deadline** 3/15 (freshmen), rolling (transfer) **Freshman admission** 53% were admitted. Average high school GPA 3.76 **Freshman test scores** SAT critical reading scores over 500: 76%; SAT math scores over 500: 73%; ACT scores over 18: 95%; SAT critical reading scores over 600: 28%; SAT math scores over 600: 27%; ACT scores over 24: 44% **Housing** Yes **Expenses** Tuition & Fees $33,424; Room & Board $9805 **Undergraduates** 57% women, 4% part-time, 6% 25 or older, 0.4% Native American, 11% Hispanic American, 6% African American, 2% Asian American/Pacific Islander **The most frequently chosen baccalaureate fields are** business/marketing, psychology, social sciences **Academic program** Advanced placement, accelerated degree program, self-designed majors, honors program, summer session, adult/continuing education programs, internships **Contact** Ms. Deborah Thompson, Vice President for Enrollment Management and Campus Life, Stetson University, Unit 8378, Griffith Hall, DeLand, FL 32723. *Phone:* 386-822-7100 or toll-free 800-688-0101. *Fax:* 386-822-7112. *E-mail:* admissions@stetson.edu. *Web site:* http://www.stetson.edu/.

Strayer University–Baymeadows Campus
Jacksonville, Florida

General Proprietary, comprehensive, coed **Contact** Admissions Office, Strayer University–Baymeadows Campus, 8375 Dix Ellis Trail, Suite 200, Jacksonville, FL 32256. *Phone:* 904-538-1000. *Web site:* http://www.strayer.edu/baymeadows.

Strayer University–Brickell Campus
Miami, Florida

General Proprietary, comprehensive, coed **Contact** Director of Admissions, Strayer University–Brickell Campus, 1201 Brickell Avenue, Suite 700, Miami, FL 33131. *Phone:* 305-507-5800. *Fax:* 305-416-2970. *E-mail:* brickell@strayer.edu. *Web site:* http://www.strayer.edu/brickell.

Strayer University–Coral Springs Campus
Coral Springs, Florida

General Proprietary, comprehensive, coed **Contact** Admissions Office, Strayer University–Coral Springs Campus, 5830 Coral Ridge Drive, Suite 300, Coral Springs, FL 33076. *Phone:* 954-369-0700. *Web site:* http://www.strayer.edu/coral_springs.

Strayer University–Doral Campus

Miami, Florida

General Proprietary, comprehensive, coed **Contact** Director of Admissions, Strayer University–Doral Campus, 11430 Northwest 20th Street, Suite 150, Miami, FL 33172. *Phone:* 305-507-5700. *Fax:* 305-470-3988. *E-mail:* doral@strayer.edu. *Web site:* http://www.strayer.edu/doral.

Strayer University–Fort Lauderdale Campus

Fort Lauderdale, Florida

General Proprietary, comprehensive, coed **Contact** Admissions Office, Strayer University–Fort Lauderdale Campus, 2307 West Broward Boulevard, Suite 100, Fort Lauderdale, FL 33312. *Phone:* 954-745-6960. *Web site:* http://www.strayer.edu/fort_lauderdale.

Strayer University–Maitland Campus

Maitland, Florida

General Proprietary, comprehensive, coed **Contact** Admissions Office, Strayer University–Maitland Campus, 850 Trafalgar Court, Suite 360, Maitland, FL 32751. *Phone:* 407-618-5900. *Web site:* http://www.strayer.edu/maitland.

Strayer University–Miramar Campus

Miramar, Florida

General Proprietary, comprehensive, coed **Contact** Admissions Office, Strayer University–Miramar Campus, 15620 Southwest 29th Street, Miramar, FL 33027. *Phone:* 954-378-2400. *Web site:* http://www.strayer.edu/miramar.

Strayer University–Orlando East Campus

Orlando, Florida

General Proprietary, comprehensive, coed **Contact** Admissions Office, Strayer University–Orlando East Campus, 2200 North Alafaya Trail, Suite 500, Orlando, FL 32826. *Phone:* 407-926-2000. *Web site:* http://www.strayer.edu/orlando_east.

Strayer University–Palm Beach Gardens Campus

Palm Beach Gardens, Florida

General Proprietary, comprehensive, coed **Contact** Admissions Office, Strayer University–Palm Beach Gardens Campus, 11025 RCA Center Drive, Suite 200, Palm Beach Gardens, FL 33410. *Phone:* 561-904-3000. *Web site:* http://www.strayer.edu/palm_beach_gardens.

Strayer University–Sand Lake Campus

Orlando, Florida

General Proprietary, comprehensive, coed **Contact** Admissions Office, Strayer University–Sand Lake Campus, 8541 South Park Circle, Building 900, Orlando, FL 32819. *Phone:* 407-264-9400. *Web site:* http://www.strayer.edu/sand_lake.

Strayer University–Tampa East Campus

Tampa, Florida

General Proprietary, comprehensive, coed **Contact** Admissions Office, Strayer University–Tampa East Campus, 6302 East Martin Luther King Boulevard, Suite 450, Tampa, FL 33619. *Phone:* 813-663-0100. *Web site:* http://www.strayer.edu/tampa_east.

Strayer University–Tampa Westshore Campus

Tampa, Florida

General Proprietary, comprehensive, coed **Contact** Admissions Office, Strayer University–Tampa Westshore Campus, 4902 Eisenhower Boulevard, Suite 100, Tampa, FL 33634. *Phone:* 813-882-0100. *Web site:* http://www.strayer.edu/tampa_westshore.

Talmudic College of Florida

Miami Beach, Florida

General Independent Jewish, comprehensive, men only **Entrance** Moderately difficult **Setting** urban campus **Total enrollment** 35 **Student-faculty ratio** 5:1 **Application deadline** Rolling (freshmen), rolling (transfer) **Freshman admission** 80% were admitted. Average high school GPA 3.5 **Housing** Yes **Undergraduates** 1% 25 or older, 17% Hispanic American **Academic program** English as a second language, honors program, summer session, adult/continuing education programs **Contact** Rabbi Yeshaya Greenberg, Dean of Students, Talmudic College of Florida, 1910 Alton Road, Miami Beach, FL 33139. *Phone:* 305-534-7050 or toll-free 888-825-6834. *Fax:* 305-534-8444. *E-mail:* yandtg@gmail.com. *Web site:* http://www.talmudicu.edu/.

Trinity Baptist College

Jacksonville, Florida

Contact Mr. Larry Appleby, Administrative Dean, Trinity Baptist College, 800 Hammond Boulevard, Jacksonville, FL 32221. *Phone:* 904-596-2538 or toll-free 800-786-2206. *Fax:* 904-596-2531. *E-mail:* trinity@tbc.edu. *Web site:* http://www.tbc.edu/.

Trinity College of Florida

New Port Richey, Florida

General Independent nondenominational, 4-year, coed **Entrance** Minimally difficult **Setting** 40-acre small-town campus **Total enrollment** 211 **Student-faculty ratio** 14:1 **Application deadline** 8/8 (freshmen), 8/8 (transfer) **Freshman admission** 85% were admitted. Average high school GPA 2.8 **Freshman test scores** SAT critical reading scores over 500: 59%; SAT math scores over 500: 17%; ACT scores over 18: 88%; SAT critical reading scores over 600: 18%; ACT scores over 24: 25% **Housing** Yes **Expenses** Tuition & Fees $11,824; Room & Board $6656 **Undergraduates** 39% women, 12% part-time, 35% 25 or older, 0.5% Native American, 16% Hispanic American, 18% African American, 0.5% Asian American/Pacific Islander **The most frequently chosen baccalaureate fields are** liberal arts/general studies, education, theology and religious vocations **Academic program** Advanced placement, accelerated degree program, self-designed majors, honors program, summer session, adult/continuing education programs, internships **Contact** Mark A. Sawyer, Director of Admissions, Trinity College of Florida, 24300 Welbilt Boulevard, Trinity, FL 34655. *Phone:* 727-376-6911 Ext. 309 or toll-free 800-388-0869. *Fax:* 727-569-1410. *E-mail:* msawyer@trinitycollege.edu. *Web site:* http://www.trinitycollege.edu/.

Universidad FLET

Miami, Florida

General Independent religious, comprehensive, coed **Setting** urban campus **Total enrollment** 902 **Student-faculty ratio** 33:1 **Housing** No **Expenses** Tuition & Fees $1820 **Undergraduates** 39% women, 100% part-time, 80% 25 or older **The most frequently chosen baccalaureate field is** theology and religious vocations **Academic program** Adult/continuing education programs **Contact** Dalia Sosa, Admissions Director, Universidad FLET, 14540 Southwest 136th Street, Suite 108, Miami, FL

Universidad FLET (continued)

33186. *Phone:* 305-378-8700 or toll-free 888-376-3538. *Fax:* 305-232-5832. *E-mail:* admissiones@flet.edu. *Web site:* http://www.flet.edu/.

University of Central Florida

Orlando, Florida

General State-supported, university, coed **Entrance** Moderately difficult **Setting** 1,415-acre suburban campus **Total enrollment** 53,537 **Student-faculty ratio** 31:1 **Application deadline** 3/1 (freshmen), 5/1 (transfer) **Freshman admission** 47% were admitted. Average high school GPA 3.71 **Freshman test scores** SAT critical reading scores over 500: 89.7%; SAT math scores over 500: 94.6%; ACT scores over 18: 99.8%; SAT critical reading scores over 600: 38.6%; SAT math scores over 600: 53.5%; ACT scores over 24: 74.9% **Housing** Yes **Expenses** Tuition & Fees: state resident $4526, nonresident $20,005; Room & Board $8540 **Undergraduates** 55% women, 25% part-time, 18% 25 or older, 0.4% Native American, 15% Hispanic American, 9% African American, 6% Asian American/Pacific Islander **The most frequently chosen baccalaureate fields are** business/marketing, education, health professions and related sciences **Academic program** English as a second language, advanced placement, accelerated degree program, honors program, summer session, adult/continuing education programs, internships **Contact** Dr. Gordon Chavis Jr., Associate Vice President, Undergraduate Admissions, Student Financial Assistance and Outreach Programs, University of Central Florida, PO Box 160111, Orlando, FL 32816-0111. *Phone:* 407-823-3000. *Fax:* 407-823-5625. *E-mail:* admission@mail.ucf.edu. *Web site:* http://www.ucf.edu/.

See page 1256 for the College Close-Up.

University of Florida

Gainesville, Florida

General State-supported, university, coed **Entrance** Very difficult **Setting** 2,000-acre suburban campus **Total enrollment** 50,691 **Student-faculty ratio** 20:1 **Application deadline** 11/1 (freshmen), rolling (transfer) **Freshman admission** 42% were admitted **Freshman test scores** SAT critical reading scores over 500: 99%; SAT math scores over 500: 94%; ACT scores over 18: 99%; SAT critical reading scores over 600: 61%; SAT math scores over 600: 71%; ACT scores over 24: 88% **Housing** Yes **Expenses** Tuition & Fees: state resident $4373, nonresident $23,744; Room & Board $7500 **Undergraduates** 55% women, 7% part-time, 5% 25 or older, 1% Native American, 15% Hispanic American, 10% African American, 9% Asian American/Pacific Islander **The most frequently chosen baccalaureate fields are** business/marketing, engineering, social sciences **Academic program** English as a second language, advanced placement, accelerated degree program, self-designed majors, honors program, summer session, adult/continuing education programs, internships **Contact** Office of Admissions, University of Florida, PO Box 114000, Gainesville, FL 32611-4000. *Phone:* 352-392-1365. *E-mail:* zevans@ufl.edu. *Web site:* http://www.ufl.edu/.

University of Miami

Coral Gables, Florida

General Independent, university, coed **Entrance** Very difficult **Setting** 230-acre suburban campus **Total enrollment** 15,629 **Student-faculty ratio** 11:1 **Application deadline** 1/15 (freshmen), 3/1 (transfer) **Freshman admission** 44% were admitted. Average high school GPA 4.2 **Freshman test scores** SAT critical reading scores over 500: 94%; SAT math scores over 500: 98%; ACT scores over 18: 100%; SAT critical reading scores over 600: 65%; SAT math scores over 600: 77%; ACT scores over 24: 93% **Housing** Yes **Expenses** Tuition & Fees $37,836; Room & Board $11,062 **Undergraduates** 52% women, 9% part-time, 6% 25 or older, 0.3% Native American, 24% Hispanic American, 8% African American, 5% Asian American/Pacific Islander **The most frequently chosen baccalaureate fields are** business/marketing, biological/life sciences, social sciences **Academic program** English as a second language, advanced placement, accelerated degree program, self-designed majors, honors program, summer session, adult/continuing education programs, internships **Contact** Mr. Edward Gillis, Assistant Vice President and Executive Director of Admission, University of Miami, University of Miami Branch, Coral Gables, FL 33124. *Phone:* 305-284-4323. *Fax:* 305-284-6605. *E-mail:* admission@miami.edu. *Web site:* http://www.miami.edu/.

University of North Florida

Jacksonville, Florida

General State-supported, comprehensive, coed **Entrance** Very difficult **Setting** 1,300-acre urban campus **Total enrollment** 16,477 **Student-faculty ratio** 23:1 **Application deadline** 6/11 (freshmen), 6/11 (transfer) **Freshman admission** 64% were admitted. Average high school GPA 3.49 **Freshman test scores** SAT critical reading scores over 500: 81%; SAT math scores over 500: 79%; ACT scores over 18: 98%; SAT critical reading scores over 600: 31%; SAT math scores over 600: 30%; ACT scores over 24: 27% **Housing** Yes **Expenses** Tuition & Fees: state resident $4193, nonresident $17,582; Room & Board $9982 **Undergraduates** 56% women, 28% part-time, 21% 25 or older, 0.4% Native American, 7% Hispanic American, 11% African American, 6% Asian American/Pacific Islander **The most frequently chosen baccalaureate fields are** business/marketing, education, health professions and related sciences **Academic program** English as a second language, advanced placement, accelerated degree program, self-designed majors, honors program, summer session, adult/continuing education programs, internships **Contact** Mr. John Yancey, Director of Admissions, University of North Florida, 1 UNF Drive, Jacksonville, FL 32224. *Phone:* 904-620-2624. *Fax:* 904-620-2014. *E-mail:* admissions@unf.edu. *Web site:* http://www.unf.edu/.

University of Phoenix–Central Florida Campus

Maitland, Florida

General Proprietary, comprehensive, coed **Entrance** Noncompetitive **Setting** urban campus **Total enrollment** 1,537 **Application deadline** Rolling (freshmen), rolling (transfer) **Housing** No **Expenses** Tuition & Fees $11,500 **Undergraduates** 66% women, 86% 25 or older, 0.3% Native American, 21% Hispanic American, 19% African American, 2% Asian American/Pacific Islander **The most frequently chosen baccalaureate fields are** business/marketing, computer and information sciences, health professions and related sciences **Academic program** Advanced placement, accelerated degree program, adult/continuing education programs **Contact** Ms. Audra McQuarie, Registrar/Executive Director, University of Phoenix–Central Florida Campus, 4035 South Riverpoint Parkway, Mail Stop CF-L101, Phoenix, AZ 85040. *Phone:* 480-557-6151 or toll-free 800-776-4867 (in-state); 800-228-7240 (out-of-state). *Fax:* 480-643-3068. *E-mail:* audra.mcquarie@phoenix.edu. *Web site:* http://www.phoenix.edu/.

University of Phoenix–North Florida Campus

Jacksonville, Florida

General Proprietary, comprehensive, coed **Entrance** Noncompetitive **Setting** urban campus **Total enrollment** 1,276 **Application deadline** Rolling (freshmen), rolling (transfer) **Housing** No **Expenses** Tuition & Fees $11,500 **Undergraduates** 63% women, 91% 25 or older, 0.5% Native American, 3% Hispanic American, 37% African American, 1% Asian American/Pacific Islander **The most frequently chosen baccalaureate fields are** business/marketing, computer and information sciences, health professions and related sciences **Academic program** Advanced placement, accelerated degree program **Contact** Ms. Audra McQuarie, Registrar/Executive Director, University of Phoenix–North Florida Campus, 4035 South Riverpoint Parkway, Mail Stop CF-L101, Phoenix, AZ 85040. *Phone:* 480-557-6151 or toll-free 800-776-4867 (in-state); 800-894-1758 (out-of-state). *Fax:* 480-643-3068. *E-mail:* audra.mcquarie@phoenix.edu. *Web site:* http://www.phoenix.edu/.

University of Phoenix–South Florida Campus

Fort Lauderdale, Florida

General Proprietary, comprehensive, coed **Entrance** Noncompetitive **Setting** urban campus **Total enrollment** 2,439 **Application deadline** Rolling (freshmen), rolling (transfer) **Housing** No **Expenses** Tuition & Fees $11,600 **Undergraduates** 73% women, 84% 25 or older, 0.2% Native American, 16% Hispanic American, 31% African American, 1% Asian American/Pacific Islander **The most frequently chosen baccalaureate fields are** business/marketing, computer and information sciences, health professions and related sciences **Academic program** Advanced placement, accelerated degree program, adult/continuing education programs **Contact** Ms. Audra McQuarie, Registrar/Executive Director, University of Phoenix–South Florida Campus, 4035 South Riverpoint Parkway, Mail Stop CF-L101, Phoenix, AZ 85040. *Phone:* 480-557-6151 or toll-free 800-228-7240. *Fax:* 480-643-3068. *E-mail:* audra.mcquarie@phoenix.edu. *Web site:* http://www.phoenix.edu/.

University of Phoenix–West Florida Campus

Temple Terrace, Florida

General Proprietary, comprehensive, coed **Entrance** Noncompetitive **Setting** urban campus **Total enrollment** 894 **Application deadline** Rolling (freshmen), rolling (transfer) **Freshman admission** 100% were admitted **Housing** No **Expenses** Tuition & Fees $11,500 **Undergraduates** 63% women, 90% 25 or older **The most frequently chosen baccalaureate fields are** business/marketing, computer and information sciences, health professions and related sciences **Academic program** Advanced placement, accelerated degree program, adult/continuing education programs **Contact** Ms. Evelyn Gaskin, Registrar/Executive Director, University of Phoenix–West Florida Campus, 4615 East Elwood Street, Mail Stop AA-K101, Phoenix, AZ 85040-1958. *Phone:* 480-557-3303 or toll-free 800-776-4867 (in-state); 800-228-7240 (out-of-state). *Fax:* 480-643-1020. *E-mail:* evelyn.gaskin@phoenix.edu. *Web site:* http://www.phoenix.edu/.

University of South Florida

Tampa, Florida

General State-supported, university, coed **Entrance** Moderately difficult **Setting** 1,797-acre urban campus **Total enrollment** 47,024 **Student-faculty ratio** 27:1 **Application deadline** 4/15 (freshmen), 4/15 (transfer) **Freshman admission** 43% were admitted. Average high school GPA 3.7 **Freshman test scores** SAT critical reading scores over 500: 85.3%; SAT math scores over 500: 86.56%; ACT scores over 18: 99.89%; SAT critical reading scores over 600: 35.4%; SAT math scores over 600: 40.86%; ACT scores over 24: 61.75% **Housing** Yes **Expenses** Tuition & Fees: state resident $4577, nonresident $15,386; Room & Board $8080 **Undergraduates** 57% women, 29% part-time, 25% 25 or older, 0.5% Native American, 14% Hispanic American, 12% African American, 6% Asian American/Pacific Islander **The most frequently chosen baccalaureate fields are** business/marketing, education, social sciences **Academic program** English as a second language, advanced placement, accelerated degree program, self-designed majors, honors program, summer session, adult/continuing education programs, internships **Contact** Ms. Alicia Kornowa, Undergraduate Admissions and Recruitment, University of South Florida, Office of Undergraduate Admissions, 4202 East Fowler Avenue, Tampa, FL 33620-9951. *Phone:* 813-974-3350. *Fax:* 813-974-9689. *E-mail:* bullseye@admin.usf.edu. *Web site:* http://www.usf.edu/.

The University of Tampa

Tampa, Florida

General Independent, comprehensive, coed **Entrance** Moderately difficult **Setting** 90-acre urban campus **Total enrollment** 6,306 **Student-faculty ratio** 17:1 **Application deadline** 5/1 (freshmen), rolling (transfer) **Freshman admission** 62% were admitted. Average high school GPA 3.24 **Freshman test scores** SAT critical reading scores over 500: 68%; SAT math scores over 500: 73%; ACT scores over 18: 97%; SAT critical reading scores over 600: 16%; SAT math scores over 600: 20%; ACT scores over 24: 39% **Housing** Yes **Expenses** Tuition & Fees $22,482; Room & Board $8296 **Undergraduates** 57% women, 7% part-time, 8% 25 or older, 0.3% Native American, 10% Hispanic American, 5% African American, 2% Asian American/Pacific Islander **The most frequently chosen baccalaureate fields are** business/marketing, communications/journalism, social sciences **Academic program** English as a second language, advanced placement, honors program, summer session, adult/continuing education programs, internships **Contact** Dennis Nostrand, Vice President for Enrollment, The University of Tampa, 401 West Kennedy Boulevard, Tampa, FL 33606-1480. *Phone:* 813-257-1808 or toll-free 888-646-2438 (in-state); 888-MINARET (out-of-state). *Fax:* 813-258-7398. *E-mail:* admissions@ut.edu. *Web site:* http://www.ut.edu/.

Visit Petersons.com and enter keywords University of Tampa

See page 1310 for the College Close-Up.

University of West Florida

Pensacola, Florida

General State-supported, comprehensive, coed **Entrance** Moderately difficult **Setting** 1,600-acre suburban campus **Total enrollment** 11,143 **Student-faculty ratio** 22:1 **Application deadline** 6/30 (freshmen), 6/30 (transfer) **Freshman admission** 70% were admitted. Average high school GPA 3.46 **Freshman test scores** SAT critical reading scores over 500: 70%; SAT math scores over 500: 64%; ACT scores over 18: 98%; SAT critical reading scores over 600: 22%; SAT math scores over 600: 15%; ACT scores over 24: 40% **Housing** Yes **Expenses** Tuition & Fees: state resident $4210, nonresident $16,478; Room & Board $6900 **Undergraduates** 59% women, 28% part-time, 33% 25 or older, 1% Native American, 6% Hispanic American, 10% African American, 5% Asian American/Pacific Islander **The most frequently chosen baccalaureate fields are** business/marketing, communications/journalism, education **Academic program** English as a second language, advanced placement, honors program, summer session, internships **Contact** Director of Admissions, University of West Florida, Admissions, 11000 University Parkway, Pensacola, FL 32514. *Phone:* 850-474-2230 or toll-free 800-263-1074. *Fax:* 850-474-3460. *E-mail:* admissions@uwf.edu. *Web site:* http://www.uwf.edu/.

Warner University

Lake Wales, Florida

Contact Mr. Jason Roe, Director of Admissions, Warner University, Warner Southern Center, 13895 Highway 27, Lake Wales, FL 33859. *Phone:* 863-638-7212 Ext. 7213 or toll-free 800-949-7248. *Fax:* 863-638-1472. *E-mail:* admissions@warner.edu. *Web site:* http://www.warner.edu/.

Webber International University

Babson Park, Florida

General Independent, comprehensive, coed **Entrance** Moderately difficult **Setting** 110-acre small-town campus **Total enrollment** 669 **Student-faculty ratio** 22:1 **Application deadline** 8/1 (freshmen), 8/1 (transfer) **Freshman admission** 53% were admitted. Average high school GPA 3.14 **Freshman test scores** SAT critical reading scores over 500: 32%; SAT math scores over 500: 43%; ACT scores over 18: 83%; SAT critical reading scores over 600: 2%; SAT math scores over 600: 10%; ACT scores over 24: 11% **Housing** Yes **Expenses** Tuition & Fees $17,850; Room & Board $6972 **Undergraduates** 35% women, 9%

Webber International University

1201 Scenic Highway, North, PO Box 96
Babson Park, FL 33827

E-mail: admissions@webber.edu
Phone: 863-638-2910

See our profile page for more information about our school.

Webber International University (continued)

part-time, 12% 25 or older, 0.2% Native American, 9% Hispanic American, 26% African American, 0.5% Asian American/Pacific Islander **The most frequently chosen baccalaureate fields are** business/marketing, computer and information sciences, parks and recreation **Academic program** English as a second language, advanced placement, accelerated degree program, summer session, adult/continuing education programs, internships **Contact** Mr. Mike Mattison, Director of Admissions, Webber International University, PO Box 96, 1200 North Scenic Highway, Babson Park, FL 33827-0096. *Phone:* 863-638-2910 or toll-free 800-741-1844. *Fax:* 863-638-1591. *E-mail:* admissions@webber.edu. *Web site:* http://www.webber.edu/.

Visit Petersons.com and enter keyword Webber

See page 1348 for the College Close-Up.

Yeshiva Gedolah Rabbinical College

Miami Beach, Florida

General Independent Jewish, comprehensive, men only **Total enrollment** 47 **Contact** Yeshiva Gedolah Rabbinical College, 1140 Alton Road, Miami Beach, FL 33139.

GEORGIA

Abraham Baldwin Agricultural College

Tifton, Georgia

General State-supported, 4-year, coed **Entrance** Noncompetitive **Setting** 421-acre small-town campus **Total enrollment** 3,600 **Student-faculty ratio** 26:1 **Freshman admission** 78% were admitted. Average high school GPA 2.86 **Housing** Yes **Expenses** Tuition & Fees: state resident $2285, nonresident $7628; Room & Board $6758 **Undergraduates** 54% women, 28% part-time, 20% 25 or older, 0.2% Native American, 3% Hispanic American, 20% African American, 1% Asian American/Pacific Islander **Academic program** Advanced placement, honors program, summer session, internships **Contact** Mrs. Donna Webb, Director of Enrollment Services, Abraham Baldwin Agricultural College, Box 4, 2802 Moore Highway, Tifton, GA 31793-2601. *Phone:* 229-391-5004 or toll-free 800-733-3653. *Fax:* 229-391-5002. *E-mail:* esaxon@abac.edu. *Web site:* http://www.abac.edu/.

Agnes Scott College

Decatur, Georgia

General Independent, comprehensive, undergraduate: women only; graduate: coed, affiliated with Presbyterian Church (U.S.A.) **Entrance** Very difficult **Setting** 100-acre urban campus **Total enrollment** 868 **Student-faculty ratio** 9:1 **Application deadline** 3/1 (freshmen), 3/1 (transfer) **Freshman admission** 46% were admitted. Average high school GPA 3.57 **Freshman test scores** SAT critical reading scores over 500: 84.7%; SAT math scores over 500: 72.96%; ACT scores over 18: 97.17%; SAT critical reading scores over 600: 46.94%; SAT math scores over 600: 31.12%; ACT scores over 24: 61.32% **Housing** Yes **Expenses** Tuition & Fees $31,283; Room & Board $9850 **Undergraduates** 4% part-time, 5% 25 or older, 0.1% Native American, 5% Hispanic American, 25% African American, 4% Asian American/Pacific Islander **The most frequently chosen baccalaureate fields are** psychology, history, social sciences **Academic program** Advanced placement, accelerated degree program, self-designed majors, summer session, adult/continuing education programs, internships **Contact** Ms. Alexa Gaeta, Director of Admission, Agnes Scott College, 141 East College Avenue, Decatur, GA

30030-3797. *Phone:* 404-471-6285 or toll-free 800-868-8602. *Fax:* 404-471-6414. *E-mail:* admission@agnesscott.edu. *Web site:* http://www.agnesscott.edu/.
Visit Petersons.com and enter keyword Agnes

Albany State University
Albany, Georgia

General State-supported, comprehensive, coed **Entrance** Minimally difficult **Setting** 232-acre urban campus **Total enrollment** 4,323 **Student-faculty ratio** 21:1 **Application deadline** 7/1 (freshmen), 7/1 (transfer) **Freshman admission** 42% were admitted. Average high school GPA 2.81 **Freshman test scores** SAT critical reading scores over 500: 18.3%; SAT math scores over 500: 16.1%; SAT critical reading scores over 600: .7%; SAT math scores over 600: .2% **Housing** Yes **Expenses** Tuition & Fees: state resident $4836, nonresident $16,450; Room & Board $5240 **Undergraduates** 67% women, 16% part-time, 34% 25 or older **Academic program** Advanced placement, honors program, summer session, internships **Contact** Office of Recruitment and Admissions, Albany State University, 504 College Drive, Albany, GA 31705-2717. *Phone:* 229-430-4646 or toll-free 800-822-RAMS. *Fax:* 229-430-4105. *E-mail:* admissions@asurams.edu. *Web site:* http://www.asurams.edu/.

American InterContinental University Buckhead Campus
Atlanta, Georgia

General Proprietary, comprehensive, coed **Setting** 3-acre urban campus **Total enrollment** 967 **Application deadline** Rolling (freshmen), rolling (transfer) **Undergraduates** 59% women, 65% part-time, 35% 25 or older, 0.2% Native American, 1% Hispanic American, 18% African American, 1% Asian American/Pacific Islander **The most frequently chosen baccalaureate fields are** business/marketing, security and protective services, visual and performing arts **Academic program** Accelerated degree program, summer session, adult/continuing education programs **Contact** Harold Saulsby, Vice President of Admissions, American InterContinental University Buckhead Campus, 3330 Peachtree Road, NE, Atlanta, GA 30326. *Phone:* 877-564-6248 or toll-free 888-591-7888. *Web site:* http://www.aiuniv.edu/.

American InterContinental University Dunwoody Campus
Atlanta, Georgia

General Proprietary, comprehensive, coed **Setting** 2-acre urban campus **Total enrollment** 585 **Application deadline** Rolling (freshmen), rolling (transfer) **Undergraduates** 59% women, 27% part-time, 47% 25 or older **The most frequently chosen baccalaureate fields are** business/marketing, computer and information sciences, security and protective services **Academic program** Accelerated degree program, adult/continuing education programs **Contact** Harold Saulsby, Vice President of Admissions, American InterContinental University Dunwoody Campus, 6600 Peachtree-Dunwoody Road, 500 Embassy Row, Atlanta, GA 30328. *Phone:* 877-564-6248 or toll-free 800-353-1744. *Fax:* 877-564-6248. *Web site:* http://www.aiuniv.edu/.

Argosy University, Atlanta
Atlanta, Georgia

General Proprietary, university, coed **Setting** suburban campus **Contact** Director of Admissions, Argosy University, Atlanta, 980 Hammond Drive, Suite 100, Atlanta, GA 30328. *Phone:* 770-671-1200 or toll-free 888-671-4777. *Fax:* 770-671-9055. *Web site:* http://www.argosy.edu/atlanta/.
Visit Petersons.com and enter keywords Argosy University, Atlanta

See page 478 for the College Close-Up.

Armstrong Atlantic State University
Savannah, Georgia

General State-supported, comprehensive, coed **Entrance** Minimally difficult **Setting** 250-acre suburban campus **Total enrollment** 7,507 **Student-faculty ratio** 17:1 **Application deadline** 8/1 (freshmen), 8/1 (transfer) **Freshman admission** 60% were admitted. Average high school GPA 3.09 **Freshman test scores** SAT critical reading scores over 500: 51.9%; SAT math scores over 500: 47.3%; ACT scores over 18: 88.4%; SAT critical reading scores over 600: 12.3%; SAT math scores over 600: 13.8%; ACT scores over 24: 24.2% **Housing** Yes **Expenses** Tuition & Fees: state resident $4048, nonresident $13,336; Room & Board $5398 **Undergraduates** 65% women, 30% part-time, 36% 25 or older, 1% Native American, 4% Hispanic American, 21% African American, 2% Asian American/Pacific Islander **The most frequently chosen baccalaureate fields are** education, health professions and related sciences, liberal arts/general studies **Academic program** Advanced placement, honors program, summer session, adult/continuing education programs, internships **Contact** Ms. Stephanie Whaley, Director of Admissions, Armstrong Atlantic State University, 11935 Abercorn Street, Savannah, GA 31419-1997. *Phone:* 912-344-2503 or toll-free 800-633-2349. *Fax:* 912-344-3417. *E-mail:* adm-info@mail.armstrong.edu. *Web site:* http://www.armstrong.edu/.

The Art Institute of Atlanta
Atlanta, Georgia

General Proprietary, 4-year, coed **Setting** 7-acre suburban campus **Contact** Director of Admissions, The Art Institute of Atlanta, 6600 Peachtree Dunwoody Road, NE, 100 Embassy Row, Atlanta, GA 30328. *Phone:* 770-394-8300 or toll-free 800-275-4242. *Fax:* 770-394-0008. *Web site:* http://www.artinstitutes.edu/atlanta.
Visit Petersons.com and enter keywords Art Institute of Atlanta

See page 480 for the College Close-Up.

The Art Institute of Atlanta–Decatur
Decatur, Georgia

General Proprietary, 4-year, coed **Contact** Director of Admissions, The Art Institute of Atlanta–Decatur, One West Court Square, Suite 110, Decatur, GA 30030. *Phone:* 404-942-1800 or toll-free 866-856-6203. *Fax:* 404-942-1818. *Web site:* http://www.artinstitutes.edu/decatur.
Visit Petersons.com and enter keywords Art Institute of Atlanta-Decatur

See page 482 for the College Close-Up.

Ashworth College
Norcross, Georgia

General Proprietary, comprehensive, coed **Entrance** Noncompetitive **Academic program** Advanced placement, accelerated degree program, summer session, adult/continuing education programs **Contact** Registrar, Ashworth College, 430 Technology Parkway, Norcross, GA 30092. *Phone:* toll-free 800-957-5412. *E-mail:* registrar@ashworthcollege.edu. *Web site:* http://www.ashworthuniversity.edu/.

Atlanta Christian College
East Point, Georgia

General Independent Christian, 4-year, coed **Entrance** Moderately difficult **Setting** 52-acre suburban campus **Total enrollment** 690 **Application deadline** 8/1 (freshmen), 8/1 (transfer) **Freshman admission** 57% were admitted **Housing** Yes **Expenses** Tuition & Fees $15,150; Room & Board $5500 **Undergraduates** 56% women, 4% part-time, 51% 25 or older, 0.1% Native American, 4% Hispanic American, 53% African American, 1% Asian American/Pacific Islander **The most fre-**

Atlanta Christian College (continued)

quently chosen baccalaureate fields are social sciences, education, theology and religious vocations **Academic program** Advanced placement, summer session, adult/continuing education programs, internships **Contact** Ms. Stacy Bartlett, Director of Admission, Atlanta Christian College, 2605 Ben Hill Road, East Point, GA 30344-1999. *Phone:* 404-669-4000 or toll-free 800-776-1ACC. *Fax:* 404-460-2451. *E-mail:* admissions@acc.edu. *Web site:* http://www.acc.edu/.

Augusta State University
Augusta, Georgia

General State-supported, comprehensive, coed **Entrance** Minimally difficult **Setting** 72-acre urban campus **Total enrollment** 6,689 **Student-faculty ratio** 18:1 **Application deadline** 7/21 (freshmen), rolling (transfer) **Freshman admission** 57% were admitted. Average high school GPA 2.93 **Freshman test scores** SAT critical reading scores over 500: 46.57%; SAT math scores over 500: 43.9%; ACT scores over 18: 74.09%; SAT critical reading scores over 600: 11.96%; SAT math scores over 600: 7.38%; ACT scores over 24: 10.36% **Housing** Yes **Expenses** Tuition & Fees: state resident $3730, nonresident $13,018; Room only $5250 **Undergraduates** 64% women, 29% part-time, 27% 25 or older, 0.2% Native American, 3% Hispanic American, 28% African American, 3% Asian American/Pacific Islander **The most frequently chosen baccalaureate fields are** business/marketing, education, social sciences **Academic program** English as a second language, advanced placement, honors program, summer session, internships **Contact** Ms. Jody Wilson, Coordinator of Publications and Marketing, Augusta State University, 2500 Walton Way, Augusta, GA 30904-2200. *Phone:* 706-737-1632 or toll-free 800-341-4373. *Fax:* 706-667-4355. *E-mail:* admissions@aug.edu. *Web site:* http://www.aug.edu/.

Bauder College
Atlanta, Georgia

General Proprietary, 4-year, coed **Setting** urban campus **Contact** Director of Admissions, Bauder College, 384 Northyards Boulevard NW, Suites 190 and 400, Atlanta, GA 30313. *Phone:* 404-237-7573 or toll-free 800-241-3797. *Web site:* http://www.bauder.edu/.

Berry College
Mount Berry, Georgia

General Independent interdenominational, comprehensive, coed **Entrance** Moderately difficult **Setting** 26,000-acre suburban campus **Total enrollment** 1,922 **Student-faculty ratio** 12:1 **Application deadline** 7/23 (freshmen), 7/23 (transfer) **Freshman admission** 67% were admitted. Average high school GPA 3.64 **Freshman test scores** SAT critical reading scores over 500: 90%; SAT math scores over 500: 80%; ACT scores over 18: 99%; SAT critical reading scores over 600: 42%; SAT math scores over 600: 31%; ACT scores over 24: 64% **Housing** Yes **Expenses** Tuition & Fees $23,360; Room & Board $8340 **Undergraduates** 69% women, 2% part-time, 1% 25 or older, 0.2% Native American, 3% Hispanic American, 5% African American, 2% Asian American/Pacific Islander **The most frequently chosen baccalaureate fields are** business/marketing, communications/journalism, education **Academic program** Advanced placement, self-designed majors, honors program, summer session, adult/continuing education programs, internships **Contact** Mr. Timothy Tarpley, Director of Operations, Enrollment Management, Berry College, PO Box 490159, 2277 Martha Berry Highway, NW, Mount Berry, GA 30149-0159. *Phone:* 706-236-2215 or toll-free 800-237-7942. *Fax:* 706-290-2178. *E-mail:* admissions@berry.edu. *Web site:* http://www.berry.edu/.

Beulah Heights University
Atlanta, Georgia

General Independent Pentecostal, comprehensive, coed **Entrance** Noncompetitive **Setting** 10-acre urban campus **Total enrollment** 901 **Student-faculty ratio** 12:1 **Application deadline** Rolling (freshmen), rolling (transfer) **Freshman admission** Average high school GPA 3 **Housing** Yes **Expenses** Tuition & Fees $7100; Room only $3200 **Undergraduates** 63% women, 62% part-time, 90% 25 or older, 1% Hispanic American, 80% African American, 11% Asian American/Pacific Islander **The most frequently chosen baccalaureate field is** theology and religious vocations **Academic program** Advanced placement, accelerated degree program, summer session, adult/continuing education programs, internships **Contact** Mr. John Dreher, Director of Admissions, Beulah Heights University, 892 Berne Street, SE, PO Box 18145, Atlanta, GA 30316. *Phone:* 404-627-2681 or toll-free 888-777-BHBC. *E-mail:* john.dreher@beulah.org. *Web site:* http://www.beulah.org/.

Brenau University
Gainesville, Georgia

General Independent, comprehensive, women only **Entrance** Moderately difficult **Setting** 57-acre small-town campus **Total enrollment** 891 **Student-faculty ratio** 8:1 **Application deadline** Rolling (freshmen), rolling (transfer) **Freshman admission** 38% were admitted **Freshman test scores** SAT critical reading scores over 500: 49%; SAT math scores over 500: 35%; SAT critical reading scores over 600: 12%; SAT math scores over 600: 7% **Housing** Yes **Expenses** Tuition & Fees $20,130; Room & Board $10,065 **Undergraduates** 8% part-time, 16% 25 or older, 0.4% Native American, 5% Hispanic American, 20% African American, 3% Asian American/Pacific Islander **The most frequently chosen baccalaureate fields are** education, health professions and related sciences, visual and performing arts **Academic program** English as a second language, advanced placement, accelerated degree program, self-designed majors, honors program, summer session, internships **Contact** Mr. Scott Briell, Senior Vice President, Enrollment Management and Student Services, Brenau University, Admissions, 500 Washington Street, SE, Gainesville, GA 30501. *Phone:* 770-538-4704 or toll-free 800-252-5119. *Fax:* 770-538-4701. *E-mail:* admissions@brenau.edu. *Web site:* http://www.brenau.edu/.

Brewton-Parker College
Mt. Vernon, Georgia

General Independent Southern Baptist, 4-year, coed **Entrance** Minimally difficult **Setting** 280-acre rural campus **Total enrollment** 1,017 **Student-faculty ratio** 9:1 **Application deadline** Rolling (freshmen), rolling (transfer) **Freshman admission** 96% were admitted **Freshman test scores** SAT critical reading scores over 500: 41%; SAT math scores over 500: 40%; ACT scores over 18: 49%; SAT critical reading scores over 600: 10%; SAT math scores over 600: 9%; ACT scores over 24: 13% **Housing** Yes **Expenses** Tuition & Fees $15,290; Room & Board $6253 **Undergraduates** 60% women, 28% part-time, 36% 25 or older, 0.2% Native American, 2% Hispanic American, 23% African American, 0.3% Asian American/Pacific Islander **The most frequently chosen baccalaureate fields are** business/marketing, education, psychology **Academic program** Advanced placement, accelerated degree program, honors program, summer session, adult/continuing education programs, internships **Contact** Mr. Ken Wuerzberger, Director of Admissions, Brewton-Parker College, PO Box 197, Mount Vernon, GA 30445. *Phone:* 912-583-3245 or toll-free 800-342-1087 Ext. 245. *Fax:* 912-583-3598. *E-mail:* kwuerzberger@bpc.edu. *Web site:* http://www.bpc.edu/.

Carver Bible College
Atlanta, Georgia

General Independent nondenominational, 4-year, coed **Entrance** Noncompetitive **Housing** Yes **Expenses** Tuition & Fees $5710; Room only $4800 **Academic program** Summer session, adult/continuing education programs, internships **Contact** Miss Bertha Mack, Vice President of Admissions Affairs and Dean of Admissions, Carver Bible College, 437 Nelson Street, Atlanta, GA 30313. *Phone:* 404-527-4520. *E-mail:* info@carver.edu. *Web site:* http://www.carver.edu/.

Clark Atlanta University
Atlanta, Georgia

General Independent United Methodist, university, coed **Entrance** Moderately difficult **Setting** 126-acre urban campus **Total enrollment** 3,873 **Student-faculty ratio** 17:1 **Application deadline** 6/1 (freshmen), 6/1 (transfer) **Freshman admission** 59% were admitted. Average high school GPA 3.02 **Freshman test scores** SAT critical reading scores over 500: 20%; SAT math scores over 500: 15%; ACT scores over 18: 85%; SAT critical reading scores over 600: 1%; SAT math scores over 600: 1%; ACT scores over 24: 4% **Housing** Yes **Expenses** Tuition & Fees $17,038; Room & Board $7620 **Undergraduates** 73% women, 4% part-time, 5% 25 or older, 0.1% Native American, 0.2% Hispanic American, 90% African American, 0.2% Asian American/Pacific Islander **The most frequently chosen baccalaureate fields are** business/marketing, communications/journalism, psychology **Academic program** Advanced placement, accelerated degree program, honors program, summer session, adult/continuing education programs, internships **Contact** Ms. Michelle Davis, Interim Director, Office of Admissions, Clark Atlanta University, 223 James P. Brawley Drive, SW, Atlanta, GA 30314. *Phone:* 404-880-8918 or toll-free 800-688-3228. *Fax:* 404-880-6174. *E-mail:* cauadmissions@cau.edu. *Web site:* http://www.cau.edu/.

Clayton State University
Morrow, Georgia

General State-supported, comprehensive, coed **Entrance** Minimally difficult **Setting** 163-acre suburban campus **Total enrollment** 6,586 **Student-faculty ratio** 19:1 **Application deadline** 7/17 (freshmen) **Freshman admission** 62% were admitted. Average high school GPA 3.07 **Freshman test scores** SAT critical reading scores over 500: 45.6%; SAT math scores over 500: 36.9%; SAT critical reading scores over 600: 6.6%; SAT math scores over 600: 5.4% **Housing** Yes **Expenses** Tuition & Fees: state resident $3852, nonresident $13,144; Room & Board $3900 **Undergraduates** 70% women, 43% part-time, 51% 25 or older, 0.3% Native American, 3% Hispanic American, 63% African American, 4% Asian American/Pacific Islander **The most frequently chosen baccalaureate fields are** business/marketing, health professions and related sciences, psychology **Academic program** English as a second language, advanced placement, self-designed majors, honors program, summer session, adult/continuing education programs, internships **Contact** Ms. Carol S. Montgomery, Admissions, Clayton State University, 2000 Clayton State Boulevard, Morrow, GA 30260-0285. *Phone:* 678-466-4115. *Fax:* 678-466-4149. *E-mail:* csc-info@clayton.edu. *Web site:* http://www.clayton.edu/.

See page 716 for the College Close-Up.

College of Coastal Georgia
Brunswick, Georgia

General State-supported, 4-year, coed **Entrance** Noncompetitive **Setting** 193-acre small-town campus **Total enrollment** 2,942 **Student-faculty ratio** 18:1 **Application deadline** 8/15 (freshmen), 8/15 (transfer) **Freshman admission** 66% were admitted **Housing** No **Expenses** Tuition & Fees: state resident $2154, nonresident $7656 **Undergraduates** 66% women, 63% part-time, 32% 25 or older, 1% Native American, 3% Hispanic American, 27% African American, 2% Asian American/Pacific Islander **Academic program** Advanced placement, summer session, adult/continuing education programs **Contact** Ms. Lisa Lessig, Director of Admissions/Registrar, College of Coastal Georgia, 3700 Altama Avenue, Brunswick, GA 31525. *Phone:* 912-264-7253 or toll-free 800-675-7235. *Fax:* 912-262-3072. *E-mail:* admiss@ccga.edu. *Web site:* http://www.ccga.edu/home.html.

Columbus State University
Columbus, Georgia

General State-supported, comprehensive, coed **Entrance** Minimally difficult **Setting** 132-acre suburban campus **Total enrollment** 8,179 **Student-faculty ratio** 18:1 **Application deadline** 7/1 (freshmen), 7/1 (transfer) **Freshman admission** 64% were admitted. Average high school GPA 3.01 **Freshman test scores** SAT critical reading scores over 500: 46.2%; SAT math scores over 500: 40.4%; ACT scores over 18: 70.4%; SAT critical reading scores over 600: 11%; SAT math scores over 600: 10.4%; ACT scores over 24: 12.3% **Housing** Yes **Expenses** Tuition & Fees: state resident $5024, nonresident $16,638; Room & Board $7090 **Undergraduates** 60% women, 30% part-time, 24% 25 or older, 1% Native American, 5% Hispanic American, 33% African American, 2% Asian American/Pacific Islander **The most frequently chosen baccalaureate fields are** business/marketing, education, health professions and related sciences **Academic program** English as a second language, advanced placement, honors program, summer session, adult/continuing education programs, internships **Contact** Ms. Susan Lovell, Director of Admissions, Columbus State University, 4225 University Avenue, Columbus, GA 31907-5645. *Phone:* 706-507-8806 or toll-free 866-264-2035. *Fax:* 706-568-5091. *E-mail:* lovell_susan@colstate.edu. *Web site:* http://www.colstate.edu/.

Covenant College
Lookout Mountain, Georgia

General Independent, comprehensive, coed, affiliated with Presbyterian Church in America **Entrance** Moderately difficult **Setting** 300-acre suburban campus **Total enrollment** 1,061 **Student-faculty ratio** 14:1 **Application deadline** Rolling (freshmen), rolling (transfer) **Freshman admission** 60% were admitted. Average high school GPA 3.7 **Freshman test scores** SAT critical reading scores over 500: 86.5%; SAT math scores over 500: 80.5%; ACT scores over 18: 98%; SAT critical reading scores over 600: 56.5%; SAT math scores over 600: 36.5%; ACT scores over 24: 66% **Housing** Yes **Expenses** Tuition & Fees $25,270; Room & Board $7170 **Undergraduates** 56% women, 3% part-time, 2% 25 or older, 0.3% Native American, 2% Hispanic American, 2% African American, 2% Asian American/Pacific Islander **The most frequently chosen baccalaureate fields are** interdisciplinary studies, social sciences, visual and performing arts **Academic program** Advanced placement, self-designed majors, summer session, adult/continuing education programs, internships **Contact** Mr. David Gambrell, Assistant Director of Admissions, Covenant College, 14049 Scenic Highway, Lookout Mountain, GA 30750. *Phone:* 706-419-1158 or toll-free 888-451-2683. *Fax:* 706-419-0893. *E-mail:* admissions@covenant.edu. *Web site:* http://www.covenant.edu/.

Dalton State College
Dalton, Georgia

General State-supported, 4-year, coed **Entrance** Noncompetitive **Setting** 141-acre small-town campus **Total enrollment** 5,722 **Student-faculty ratio** 25:1 **Application deadline** 7/15 (freshmen), 7/15 (transfer) **Freshman admission** 60% were admitted. Average high school GPA 2.99 **Freshman test scores** ACT scores over 18: 74%; ACT scores over 24: 21% **Housing** Yes **Expenses** Tuition & Fees: state resident $2292, nonresident $8268 **Undergraduates** 60% women, 40% part-time, 30% 25 or older, 0.4% Native American, 9% Hispanic American, 3% African American, 1% Asian American/Pacific Islander **The most frequently chosen baccalaureate fields are** business/marketing, education, public administration and social services **Academic program** English as a second language, advanced placement, summer session, adult/continuing education programs, internships **Contact** Dr. Angela Harris, Director of Admissions, Dalton State College, 650 College Drive, Dalton, GA 30720-3797. *Phone:* 706-272-4476 or toll-free 800-829-4436. *Fax:* 706-272-2530. *E-mail:* aharris@daltonstate.edu. *Web site:* http://www.daltonstate.edu/.

DeVry University
Alpharetta, Georgia

General Proprietary, comprehensive, coed **Entrance** Minimally difficult **Setting** 9-acre suburban campus **Total enrollment** 892 **Student-**

DeVry University (continued)
faculty ratio 14:1 **Application deadline** Rolling (freshmen), rolling (transfer) **Housing** No **Expenses** Tuition & Fees $14,080 **Undergraduates** 41% women, 52% part-time, 72% 25 or older, 1% Native American, 5% Hispanic American, 38% African American, 4% Asian American/Pacific Islander **The most frequently chosen baccalaureate fields are** business/marketing, computer and information sciences, engineering **Academic program** Advanced placement, accelerated degree program, summer session, adult/continuing education programs **Contact** Admissions Office, DeVry University, 2555 Northwinds Parkway, Alpharetta, GA 30009. *Phone:* toll-free 800-346-5420. *Web site:* http://www.devry.edu/.

DeVry University
Decatur, Georgia

General Proprietary, comprehensive, coed **Entrance** Minimally difficult **Setting** 21-acre suburban campus **Total enrollment** 3,157 **Student-faculty ratio** 22:1 **Application deadline** Rolling (freshmen), rolling (transfer) **Housing** No **Expenses** Tuition & Fees $14,080 **Undergraduates** 51% women, 53% part-time, 71% 25 or older, 0.2% Native American, 3% Hispanic American, 63% African American, 2% Asian American/Pacific Islander **The most frequently chosen baccalaureate fields are** business/marketing, computer and information sciences, engineering technologies **Academic program** Advanced placement, accelerated degree program, summer session, adult/continuing education programs **Contact** Admissions Department, DeVry University, 1 West Court Square, Decatur, GA 30030-2556. *Web site:* http://www.devry.edu/.

DeVry University
Duluth, Georgia

Contact DeVry University, 3505 Koger Boulevard, Suite 170, Duluth, GA 30096-7671. *Web site:* http://www.devry.edu/.

Emmanuel College
Franklin Springs, Georgia

General Independent, 4-year, coed, affiliated with Pentecostal Holiness Church **Entrance** Minimally difficult **Setting** 90-acre rural campus **Total enrollment** 732 **Student-faculty ratio** 15:1 **Application deadline** 8/1 (freshmen), 8/1 (transfer) **Freshman admission** 32% were admitted. Average high school GPA 3.09 **Housing** Yes **Expenses** Tuition & Fees $12,880; Room & Board $5520 **Undergraduates** 54% women, 10% part-time, 11% 25 or older, 0.3% Native American, 5% Hispanic American, 20% African American, 1% Asian American/Pacific Islander **The most frequently chosen baccalaureate fields are** business/marketing, education, theology and religious vocations **Academic program** Advanced placement, accelerated degree program, honors program, summer session, internships **Contact** Ms. Mariella Lora, Assistant Director of Admissions, Emmanuel College, PO Box 129, 181 Spring Street, Franklin Springs, GA 30639-0129. *Phone:* 706-245-7226 or toll-free 800-860-8800. *E-mail:* admissions@ec.edu. *Web site:* http://www.ec.edu/.

Emory University
Atlanta, Georgia

General Independent Methodist, university, coed **Entrance** Most difficult **Setting** 634-acre suburban campus **Total enrollment** 12,930 **Student-faculty ratio** 7:1 **Application deadline** 1/15 (freshmen), 6/1 (transfer) **Freshman admission** 30% were admitted. Average high school GPA 3.85 **Freshman test scores** SAT critical reading scores over 500: 100%; SAT math scores over 500: 100%; ACT scores over 18: 100%; SAT critical reading scores over 600: 89%; SAT math scores over 600: 94%; ACT scores over 24: 99% **Housing** Yes **Expenses** Tuition & Fees $38,600; Room & Board $12,300 **Undergraduates** 55% women, 1% part-time, 3% 25 or older, 0.3% Native American, 4% Hispanic American, 10% African American, 21% Asian American/Pacific Islander **The most frequently chosen baccalaureate fields are** business/marketing, psychology, social sciences **Academic program** English as a second language, advanced placement, honors program, summer session, internships **Contact** Ms. Jean Jordan, Dean of Admission, Emory University, 200 Dowman Drive, Boisfeuillet Jones Center, Atlanta, GA 30322-1100. *Phone:* 404-727-6036 or toll-free 800-727-6036. *Fax:* 404-727-4303. *E-mail:* admiss@emory.edu. *Web site:* http://www.emory.edu/.

Fort Valley State University
Fort Valley, Georgia

General State-supported, comprehensive, coed **Entrance** Moderately difficult **Setting** 1,365-acre small-town campus **Total enrollment** 3,571 **Student-faculty ratio** 19:1 **Application deadline** 7/19 (freshmen), rolling (transfer) **Freshman admission** 40% were admitted. Average high school GPA 2.8 **Housing** Yes **Expenses** Tuition & Fees: state resident $4478, nonresident $13,770; Room & Board $7540 **Undergraduates** 57% women, 12% part-time, 9% 25 or older, 0.4% Hispanic American, 97% African American, 0.03% Asian American/Pacific Islander **Academic program** Advanced placement, honors program, summer session, adult/continuing education programs, internships **Contact** Mr. Donald Moore, Director of Admissions and Recruitment, Fort Valley State University, 1005 State University Drive, Fort Valley, GA 31030. *Phone:* 478-825-6307 or toll-free 877-462-3878. *Fax:* 478-825-6169. *E-mail:* admissap@fvsu.edu. *Web site:* http://www.fvsu.edu/.

Gainesville State College
Gainesville, Georgia

General State-supported, primarily 2-year, coed **Entrance** Noncompetitive **Setting** 220-acre small-town campus **Total enrollment** 8,801 **Student-faculty ratio** 26:1 **Application deadline** 7/1 (freshmen), 7/1 (transfer) **Freshman admission** 83% were admitted. Average high school GPA 2.9 **Housing** No **Expenses** Tuition & Fees: state resident $2570, nonresident $8546 **Undergraduates** 54% women, 31% part-time, 16% 25 or older, 0.5% Native American, 8% Hispanic American, 5% African American, 3% Asian American/Pacific Islander **Academic program** English as a second language, advanced placement, honors program, summer session, adult/continuing education programs, internships **Contact** Mr. Mack Palmour, Director of Admissions, Gainesville State College, PO Box 1358, Gainesville, GA 30503. *Phone:* 678-717-3641. *Fax:* 678-717-3751. *E-mail:* admissions@gsc.edu. *Web site:* http://www.gsc.edu.

Georgia College & State University
Milledgeville, Georgia

General State-supported, comprehensive, coed **Entrance** Moderately difficult **Setting** 590-acre small-town campus **Total enrollment** 6,506 **Student-faculty ratio** 17:1 **Application deadline** 4/1 (freshmen), 7/1 (transfer) **Freshman admission** 59% were admitted. Average high school GPA 3.36 **Freshman test scores** SAT critical reading scores over 500: 84.8%; SAT math scores over 500: 86%; ACT scores over 18: 98%; SAT critical reading scores over 600: 26.4%; SAT math scores over 600: 26%; ACT scores over 24: 48% **Housing** Yes **Expenses** Tuition & Fees: state resident $6902, nonresident $23,940; Room & Board $8228 **Undergraduates** 59% women, 10% part-time, 3% 25 or older, 0.3% Native American, 3% Hispanic American, 6% African American, 1% Asian American/Pacific Islander **The most frequently chosen baccalaureate fields are** business/marketing, education, psychology **Academic program** English as a second language, advanced placement, accelerated degree program, self-designed majors, honors program, summer session, internships **Contact** Mr. Mike Augustine, Director of Admissions, Georgia College & State University, CPO Box 023, Milledgeville, GA 31061. *Phone:* 478-445-1283 or toll-free 800-342-0471. *Fax:* 478-445-3653. *E-mail:* info@gcsu.edu. *Web site:* http://www.gcsu.edu/.

Georgia Gwinnett College

Lawrenceville, Georgia

Contact Georgia Gwinnett College, 1000 Universit Center Lane, Lawrenceville, GA 60043. *Web site:* http://www.ggc.usg.edu/.

Georgia Institute of Technology

Atlanta, Georgia

General State-supported, university, coed, primarily men **Entrance** Very difficult **Setting** 450-acre urban campus **Total enrollment** 20,291 **Student-faculty ratio** 20:1 **Application deadline** 1/15 (freshmen), 2/1 (transfer) **Freshman admission** 59% were admitted. Average high school GPA 3.81 **Freshman test scores** SAT critical reading scores over 500: 96.59%; SAT math scores over 500: 99.27%; ACT scores over 18: 99.3%; SAT critical reading scores over 600: 70.36%; SAT math scores over 600: 93.18%; ACT scores over 24: 95.74% **Housing** Yes **Expenses** Tuition & Fees: state resident $7506, nonresident $25,916; Room & Board $8384 **Undergraduates** 30% women, 8% part-time, 4% 25 or older, 0.3% Native American, 4% Hispanic American, 6% African American, 17% Asian American/Pacific Islander **The most frequently chosen baccalaureate fields are** business/marketing, computer and information sciences, engineering **Academic program** English as a second language, advanced placement, accelerated degree program, self-designed majors, honors program, summer session, internships **Contact** Mr. Rick A. Clark Jr., Director of Undergraduate Admissions, Georgia Institute of Technology, Office of Undergraduate Admission, Atlanta, GA 30332-0320. *Phone:* 404-894-4154. *Fax:* 404-894-9511. *E-mail:* admission@gatech.edu. *Web site:* http://www.gatech.edu/.

Georgia Southern University

Statesboro, Georgia

General State-supported, university, coed **Entrance** Moderately difficult **Setting** 700-acre small-town campus **Total enrollment** 19,086 **Student-faculty ratio** 22:1 **Application deadline** 5/1 (freshmen), 8/1 (transfer) **Freshman admission** 56% were admitted. Average high school GPA 3.15 **Freshman test scores** SAT critical reading scores over 500: 83%; SAT math scores over 500: 85%; ACT scores over 18: 99%; SAT critical reading scores over 600: 20%; SAT math scores over 600: 25%; ACT scores over 24: 36% **Housing** Yes **Expenses** Tuition & Fees: state resident $5440, nonresident $17,416; Room & Board $7900 **Undergraduates** 48% women, 10% part-time, 8% 25 or older, 0.3% Native American, 3% Hispanic American, 22% African American, 1% Asian American/Pacific Islander **The most frequently chosen baccalaureate fields are** business/marketing, education, engineering technologies **Academic program** English as a second language, advanced placement, accelerated degree program, self-designed majors, honors program, summer session, adult/continuing education programs, internships **Contact** Mrs. Sarah Smith, Director, Georgia Southern University, PO Box 8024, Statesboro, GA 30460. *Phone:* 912-478-5391. *Fax:* 912-478-7240. *E-mail:* admissions@georgiasouthern.edu. *Web site:* http://www.georgiasouthern.edu/.

Georgia Southwestern State University

Americus, Georgia

General State-supported, comprehensive, coed **Entrance** Moderately difficult **Setting** 255-acre small-town campus **Total enrollment** 2,405 **Student-faculty ratio** 20:1 **Application deadline** 7/21 (freshmen), 7/21 (transfer) **Freshman admission** 79% were admitted. Average high school GPA 3.08 **Freshman test scores** SAT critical reading scores over 500: 46%; SAT math scores over 500: 40%; ACT scores over 18: 71%; SAT critical reading scores over 600: 12%; SAT math scores over 600: 7%; ACT scores over 24: 9% **Housing** Yes **Expenses** Tuition & Fees: state resident $3816, nonresident $13,108; Room & Board $5694 **Undergraduates** 65% women, 24% part-time, 29% 25 or older, 0.4% Native American, 1% Hispanic American, 31% African American, 1% Asian American/Pacific Islander **The most frequently chosen baccalaureate fields are** business/marketing, education, psychology **Academic program** English as a second language, advanced placement, honors program, summer session, internships **Contact** Mr. David Jenkins, Assistant Director of Admissions, Georgia Southwestern State University, 800 Wheatley Street, Americus, GA 31709. *Phone:* 229-928-1273 or toll-free 800-338-0082. *Fax:* 229-931-2983. *E-mail:* gswapps@canes.gsw.edu. *Web site:* http://www.gsw.edu/.

Georgia State University

Atlanta, Georgia

General State-supported, university, coed **Entrance** Moderately difficult **Setting** 48-acre urban campus **Total enrollment** 30,431 **Student-faculty ratio** 19:1 **Application deadline** 3/1 (freshmen), 6/1 (transfer) **Freshman admission** 41% were admitted. Average high school GPA 3.35 **Freshman test scores** SAT critical reading scores over 500: 73.16%; SAT math scores over 500: 69.24%; ACT scores over 18: 93.72%; SAT critical reading scores over 600: 23%; SAT math scores over 600: 22.02%; ACT scores over 24: 39.68% **Housing** Yes **Expenses** Tuition & Fees: state resident $7498, nonresident $25,708; Room & Board $10,140 **Undergraduates** 60% women, 24% part-time, 23% 25 or older, 0.3% Native American, 7% Hispanic American, 34% African American, 12% Asian American/Pacific Islander **The most frequently chosen baccalaureate fields are** business/marketing, psychology, social sciences **Academic program** English as a second language, advanced placement, accelerated degree program, self-designed majors, honors program, summer session, internships **Contact** Daniel Niccum, Associate Director of Admissions, Georgia State University, PO Box 4009, Atlanta, GA 30302-4009. *Phone:* 404-413-2500. *Fax:* 404-413-2002. *E-mail:* dniccum@gsu.edu. *Web site:* http://www.gsu.edu/.

Herzing University

Atlanta, Georgia

General Proprietary, 4-year, coed **Entrance** Moderately difficult **Setting** urban campus **Total enrollment** 609 **Student-faculty ratio** 8:1 **Application deadline** Rolling (freshmen), rolling (transfer) **Freshman admission** 75% were admitted **Housing** No **Expenses** Tuition & Fees $15,840 **Undergraduates** 67% women, 30% part-time, 56% 25 or older **Academic program** English as a second language, honors program, internships **Contact** Mrs. Rose White, Director of Admissions, Herzing University, 3393 Peachtree Road, Suite 1003, Atlanta, GA 30326. *Phone:* 404-816-4533 or toll-free 800-573-4533. *Fax:* 404-816-5576. *E-mail:* info@ath.herzing.edu. *Web site:* http://www.herzing.edu/atlanta/.

ITT Technical Institute

Atlanta, Georgia

General Proprietary, primarily 2-year, coed **Contact** Director of Recruitment, ITT Technical Institute, 485 Oak Place, Suite 800, Atlanta, GA 30349. *Phone:* 770-909-4606 or toll-free 877-488-6102. *Web site:* http://www.itt-tech.edu/.

ITT Technical Institute

Duluth, Georgia

General Proprietary, primarily 2-year, coed **Entrance** Minimally difficult **Housing** No **Contact** Director of Recruitment, ITT Technical Institute, 10700 Abbotts Bridge Road, Duluth, GA 30097. *Phone:* 678-957-8510 or toll-free 866-489-8818. *Web site:* http://www.itt-tech.edu/.

ITT Technical Institute

Kennesaw, Georgia

General Proprietary, primarily 2-year, coed **Contact** Director of Recruitment, ITT Technical Institute, 2065 ITT Tech Way, Kennesaw,

ITT Technical Institute (continued)
GA 30144. *Phone:* 770-426-2300 or toll-free 877-231-6415. *Web site:* http://www.itt-tech.edu/.

Kennesaw State University

Kennesaw, Georgia

General State-supported, comprehensive, coed **Entrance** Moderately difficult **Setting** 384-acre suburban campus **Total enrollment** 22,389 **Student-faculty ratio** 21:1 **Application deadline** 5/14 (freshmen), 6/25 (transfer) **Freshman admission** 64% were admitted. Average high school GPA 3.18 **Freshman test scores** SAT critical reading scores over 500: 77%; SAT math scores over 500: 74%; ACT scores over 18: 98%; SAT critical reading scores over 600: 18%; SAT math scores over 600: 17%; ACT scores over 24: 29% **Housing** Yes **Expenses** Tuition & Fees: state resident $5144, nonresident $17,120; Room & Board $6593 **Undergraduates** 59% women, 24% part-time, 35% 25 or older, 0.4% Native American, 5% Hispanic American, 13% African American, 3% Asian American/Pacific Islander **The most frequently chosen baccalaureate fields are** business/marketing, communications/journalism, education **Academic program** English as a second language, advanced placement, honors program, summer session, adult/continuing education programs, internships **Contact** Admissions Office, Kennesaw State University, 1000 Chastain Road, Campus Box #0115, Kennesaw, GA 30144-5591. *Phone:* 770-423-6300. *Fax:* 770-420-4435. *E-mail:* ksuadmit@kennesaw.edu. *Web site:* http://www.kennesaw.edu/.

LaGrange College

LaGrange, Georgia

General Independent United Methodist, comprehensive, coed **Entrance** Moderately difficult **Setting** 120-acre small-town campus **Total enrollment** 1,027 **Student-faculty ratio** 10:1 **Application deadline** Rolling (freshmen), rolling (transfer) **Freshman admission** 65% were admitted. Average high school GPA 3.47 **Freshman test scores** SAT critical reading scores over 500: 56.3%; SAT math scores over 500: 56.9%; ACT scores over 18: 100%; SAT critical reading scores over 600: 16.4%; SAT math scores over 600: 18.1%; ACT scores over 24: 36.8% **Housing** Yes **Expenses** Tuition & Fees $21,169; Room & Board $8576 **Undergraduates** 55% women, 10% part-time, 20% 25 or older, 0.3% Native American, 2% Hispanic American, 22% African American, 1% Asian American/Pacific Islander **The most frequently chosen baccalaureate fields are** business/marketing, biological/life sciences, health professions and related sciences **Academic program** Advanced placement, summer session, adult/continuing education programs, internships **Contact** Mr. Dana Paul, Vice President of Enrollment Management, LaGrange College, 601 Broad Street, LaGrange, GA 30240-2999. *Phone:* 706-880-8253 or toll-free 800-593-2885. *Fax:* 706-880-8010. *E-mail:* lgcadmis@lagrange.edu. *Web site:* http://www.lagrange.edu/.
Visit Petersons.com and enter keyword LaGrange

Life University

Marietta, Georgia

General Independent, comprehensive, coed **Entrance** Minimally difficult **Setting** 96-acre suburban campus **Total enrollment** 2,301 **Student-faculty ratio** 14:1 **Application deadline** 9/1 (freshmen) **Freshman admission** 82% were admitted. Average high school GPA 2.98 **Freshman test scores** SAT critical reading scores over 500: 22%; SAT math scores over 500: 34%; ACT scores over 18: 73%; SAT critical reading scores over 600: 7%; SAT math scores over 600: 13%; ACT scores over 24: 18% **Housing** Yes **Expenses** Tuition & Fees $8352; Room & Board $12,480 **Undergraduates** 48% women, 27% part-time, 52% 25 or older, 1% Native American, 6% Hispanic American, 30% African American, 4% Asian American/Pacific Islander **The most frequently chosen baccalaureate fields are** biological/life sciences, business/marketing, health professions and related sciences **Academic program** English as a second language, advanced placement, accelerated degree program, summer session, internships **Contact** Mr. Brian Gipson, Office of New Student Development, Life University, 1269 Barclay Circle, Marietta, GA 30060. *Phone:* 800-543-3202 or toll-free 800-543-3202. *Fax:* 770-426-2895. *E-mail:* admissions@life.edu. *Web site:* http://www.life.edu/.

Luther Rice University

Lithonia, Georgia

General Independent Baptist, comprehensive, coed **Entrance** Noncompetitive **Setting** 5-acre urban campus **Total enrollment** 1,047 **Application deadline** Rolling (freshmen), rolling (transfer) **Housing** No **Undergraduates** 90% 25 or older **Academic program** Advanced placement, adult/continuing education programs, internships **Contact** Mr. Steve Pray, Admissions Counselor, Luther Rice University, 3038 Evans Mill Road, Lithonia, GA 30038-2454. *Phone:* 770-484-1204 or toll-free 800-442-1577. *E-mail:* admissions@lru.edu. *Web site:* http://www.lru.edu/.

Macon State College

Macon, Georgia

Contact Mr. Ryan Tucker, Admissions Representative, Macon State College, 100 College Station Drive, Macon, GA 31206. *Phone:* 478-471-2800 or toll-free 800-272-7619 Ext. 2800. *Fax:* 478-471-5343. *E-mail:* mscinfo@mail.maconstate.edu. *Web site:* http://www.maconstate.edu/.

Medical College of Georgia

Augusta, Georgia

General State-supported, upper-level, coed **Entrance** Moderately difficult **Setting** 100-acre urban campus **Total enrollment** 2,515 **First-year students** 41% were admitted **Housing** Yes **Expenses** Tuition & Fees: state resident $6782, nonresident $24,992 **Undergraduates** 87% women, 6% part-time, 31% 25 or older, 0.4% Native American, 2% Hispanic American, 13% African American, 7% Asian American/Pacific Islander **The most frequently chosen baccalaureate field is** health professions and related sciences **Academic program** Summer session **Contact** Dr. Beverly Boggs, Executive Director, Academic Admissions and Student Financial Aid, Medical College of Georgia, 1120 15th Street, Augusta, GA 30912. *Phone:* 706-721-2725 or toll-free 800-519-3388. *Fax:* 706-721-7279. *E-mail:* underadm@mail.mcg.edu. *Web site:* http://www.mcg.edu/.

Mercer University

Macon, Georgia

General Independent Baptist, university, coed **Entrance** Moderately difficult **Setting** 150-acre suburban campus **Total enrollment** 5,849 **Student-faculty ratio** 14:1 **Application deadline** 7/1 (freshmen), rolling (transfer) **Freshman admission** 62% were admitted. Average high school GPA 3.65 **Freshman test scores** SAT critical reading scores over 500: 92%; SAT math scores over 500: 95%; ACT scores over 18: 100%; SAT critical reading scores over 600: 43%; SAT math scores over 600: 45%; ACT scores over 24: 83% **Housing** Yes **Expenses** Tuition & Fees $29,540; Room & Board $8788 **Undergraduates** 53% women, 2% part-time, 3% 25 or older, 0.3% Native American, 3% Hispanic American, 16% African American, 6% Asian American/Pacific Islander **The most frequently chosen baccalaureate fields are** business/marketing, communications/journalism, social sciences **Academic program** English as a second language, advanced placement, accelerated degree program, self-designed majors, honors program, summer session, adult/continuing education programs, internships **Contact** Mr. Emory Dunn, Director of Freshman Admissions, Mercer University, 1400 Coleman Avenue, Macon, GA 31207-0003. *Phone:* 478-301-2312 or toll-free 800-840-8577. *E-mail:* dunn_e@mercer.edu. *Web site:* http://www.mercer.edu/.

125 Years of Tradition, Innovation and Excellence

Middle Georgia College offers all the amenities of a larger college PLUS the individual attention to your education that only a smaller college can provide! With three campuses and over 40 majors including a **bachelor of science in aviation management** with specializations in flight, air traffic, business and logistics management and a **bachelor of science in education** with dual certification in early childhood and special education, MGC is sure to have the perfect program for you.

Call or visit our campuses today and discover MGC!

MIDDLE GEORGIA COLLEGE

WWW.MGC.EDU 478-934-3103

Middle Georgia College

Cochran, Georgia

General State-supported, primarily 2-year, coed **Entrance** Minimally difficult **Setting** 165-acre small-town campus **Total enrollment** 3,614 **Student-faculty ratio** 22:1 **Application deadline** Rolling (freshmen), rolling (transfer) **Freshman admission** 89% were admitted. Average high school GPA 2.68 **Freshman test scores** SAT critical reading scores over 500: 39%; SAT math scores over 500: 33%; ACT scores over 18: 42%; SAT critical reading scores over 600: 10%; SAT math scores over 600: 9%; ACT scores over 24: 9% **Housing** Yes **Expenses** Tuition & Fees: state resident $2968, nonresident $10,450; Room & Board $6800 **Undergraduates** 54% women, 28% part-time, 21% 25 or older, 0.3% Native American, 2% Hispanic American, 40% African American, 1% Asian American/Pacific Islander **Academic program** Advanced placement, accelerated degree program, self-designed majors, honors program, summer session, internships **Contact** Ms. Jennifer Brannon, Director of Admissions, Middle Georgia College, 1100 2nd Street, SE, Cochran, GA 31014. *Phone:* 478-934-3103. *Fax:* 478-934-3403. *E-mail:* admissions@mgc.edu. *Web site:* http://www.mgc.edu/.

Morehouse College

Atlanta, Georgia

General Independent, 4-year, men only **Entrance** Moderately difficult **Setting** 61-acre urban campus **Total enrollment** 2,689 **Application deadline** 2/15 (freshmen), 2/15 (transfer) **Freshman admission** 67% were admitted **Freshman test scores** SAT critical reading scores over 500: 61%; SAT math scores over 500: 65%; ACT scores over 18: 88%; SAT critical reading scores over 600: 17%; SAT math scores over 600: 23%; ACT scores over 24: 28% **Housing** Yes **Expenses** Tuition & Fees $21,376; Room & Board $10,946 **Undergraduates** 7% part-time, 4% 25 or older, 0.1% Native American, 0.4% Hispanic American, 95% African American, 0.04% Asian American/Pacific Islander **The most frequently chosen baccalaureate fields are** business/marketing, psychology, social sciences **Academic program** Advanced placement, honors program, summer session, internships **Contact** Mr. Terrance Dixon, Associate Dean for Admissions and Recruitment, Morehouse College, 830 Westview Drive, SW, Atlanta, GA 30314. *Phone:* 404-215-2632 or toll-free 800-851-1254. *Web site:* http://www.morehouse.edu/.

North Georgia College & State University

Dahlonega, Georgia

General State-supported, comprehensive, coed **Entrance** Moderately difficult **Setting** 140-acre small-town campus **Total enrollment** 5,652 **Student-faculty ratio** 20:1 **Application deadline** 7/1 (freshmen), rolling (transfer) **Freshman admission** 54% were admitted. Average high school GPA 3.44 **Freshman test scores** SAT critical reading scores over 500: 83%; SAT math scores over 500: 75%; ACT scores over 18: 97%; SAT critical reading scores over 600: 22%; SAT math scores over 600: 21%; ACT scores over 24: 39% **Housing** Yes **Expenses** Tuition & Fees: state resident $5036, nonresident $16,650; Room & Board $5248 **Undergraduates** 57% women, 18% part-time, 0.4% Native American, 4% Hispanic American, 2% African American, 1% Asian American/Pacific Islander **The most frequently chosen baccalaureate fields are** business/marketing, education, social sciences **Academic program** Advanced placement, honors program, summer session, adult/continuing education programs, internships **Contact** Jennifer Chadwick, Director of Admissions, North Georgia College & State University, Admissions Center, Dahlonega, GA 30533. *Phone:* 706-864-1800 or toll-free 800-498-9581. *Fax:* 706-864-1478. *E-mail:* admissions@northgeorgia.edu. *Web site:* http://www.northgeorgia.edu/.

Oglethorpe University
Atlanta, Georgia

General Independent, comprehensive, coed **Entrance** Very difficult **Setting** 102-acre suburban campus **Total enrollment** 1,099 **Student-faculty ratio** 16:1 **Application deadline** Rolling (freshmen), rolling (transfer) **Freshman admission** 42% were admitted. Average high school GPA 3.55 **Freshman test scores** SAT critical reading scores over 500: 91%; SAT math scores over 500: 82%; ACT scores over 18: 100%; SAT critical reading scores over 600: 46%; SAT math scores over 600: 37%; ACT scores over 24: 66% **Housing** Yes **Expenses** Tuition & Fees $26,700; Room & Board $9990 **Undergraduates** 60% women, 10% part-time, 11% 25 or older, 0.4% Native American, 5% Hispanic American, 23% African American, 4% Asian American/Pacific Islander **The most frequently chosen baccalaureate fields are** business/marketing, English, psychology **Academic program** Advanced placement, accelerated degree program, self-designed majors, honors program, summer session, adult/continuing education programs, internships **Contact** Ms. Lucy Leusch, Vice President for Enrollment and Financial Aid, Oglethorpe University, 4484 Peachtree Road, NE, Atlanta, GA 30319. *Phone:* 404-364-8307 or toll-free 800-428-4484. *Fax:* 404-364-8491. *E-mail:* admission@oglethorpe.edu. *Web site:* http://www.oglethorpe.edu/.

Paine College
Augusta, Georgia

General Independent Methodist, 4-year, coed **Entrance** Minimally difficult **Setting** 55-acre urban campus **Total enrollment** 908 **Student-faculty ratio** 13:1 **Application deadline** 8/1 (freshmen), 8/1 (transfer) **Freshman admission** 39% were admitted. Average high school GPA 2.7 **Freshman test scores** SAT critical reading scores over 500: 9%; SAT math scores over 500: 9%; ACT scores over 18: 22%; SAT critical reading scores over 600: 1%; SAT math scores over 600: 1%; ACT scores over 24: 1% **Housing** Yes **Expenses** Tuition & Fees $11,794; Room & Board $5748 **Undergraduates** 65% women, 6% part-time, 8% 25 or older, 1% Hispanic American, 96% African American, 0.1% Asian American/Pacific Islander **The most frequently chosen baccalaureate fields are** psychology, business/marketing, social sciences **Academic program** Advanced placement, accelerated degree program, honors program, summer session, internships **Contact** Mr. Joseph D. Tinsley, Director of Admissions, Paine College, 1235 15th Street, Augusta, GA 30901-3182. *Phone:* 706-821-8320 or toll-free 800-476-7703. *Fax:* 706-821-8691. *E-mail:* jtinsley@paine.edu. *Web site:* http://www.paine.edu/.

Piedmont College
Demorest, Georgia

General Independent, comprehensive, coed, affiliated with United Church of Christ **Entrance** Moderately difficult **Setting** 115-acre rural campus **Total enrollment** 2,775 **Application deadline** 7/1 (freshmen), 7/1 (transfer) **Freshman admission** 60% were admitted. Average high school GPA 3.38 **Freshman test scores** SAT critical reading scores over 500: 48.5%; SAT math scores over 500: 52.1%; ACT scores over 18: 84.3%; SAT critical reading scores over 600: 10.3%; SAT math scores over 600: 13.4%; ACT scores over 24: 22.5% **Housing** Yes **Expenses** Tuition & Fees $18,000 **Undergraduates** 70% women, 12% part-time, 36% 25 or older, 0.4% Native American, 2% Hispanic American, 10% African American, 1% Asian American/Pacific Islander **The most frequently chosen baccalaureate fields are** business/marketing, education, psychology **Academic program** Advanced placement, accelerated degree program, self-designed majors, honors program, summer session, adult/continuing education programs, internships **Contact** Ms. Cynthia L. Peterson, Director of Undergraduate Admissions, Piedmont College, PO Box 10, 165 Central Avenue, Demorest, GA 30535. *Phone:* 706-776-0103 Ext. 1188 or toll-free 800-277-7020. *Fax:* 706-776-6635. *E-mail:* cpeterson@piedmont.edu. *Web site:* http://www.piedmont.edu/.

Reinhardt College
Waleska, Georgia

General Independent, comprehensive, coed, affiliated with United Methodist Church **Entrance** Moderately difficult **Setting** 600-acre rural campus **Total enrollment** 1,123 **Student-faculty ratio** 12:1 **Application deadline** Rolling (freshmen), rolling (transfer) **Freshman admission** 68% were admitted. Average high school GPA 2.99 **Freshman test scores** SAT critical reading scores over 500: 40.1%; SAT math scores over 500: 37.2%; ACT scores over 18: 77.3%; SAT critical reading scores over 600: 11.9%; SAT math scores over 600: 6.7%; ACT scores over 24: 27.3% **Housing** Yes **Expenses** Tuition & Fees $16,670; Room & Board $6272 **Undergraduates** 61% women, 7% part-time, 23% 25 or older, 0.2% Native American, 4% Hispanic American, 8% African American, 1% Asian American/Pacific Islander **The most frequently chosen baccalaureate fields are** business/marketing, education, visual and performing arts **Academic program** Advanced placement, honors program, summer session, adult/continuing education programs, internships **Contact** Ms. Julie Fleming, Director of Admissions, Reinhardt College, 7300 Reinhardt College Circle, Waleska, GA 30183-0128. *Phone:* 770-720-5526. *Fax:* 770-720-5602. *E-mail:* admissions@mail.reinhardt.edu. *Web site:* http://www.reinhardt.edu/.

Savannah College of Art and Design
Savannah, Georgia

General Independent, comprehensive, coed **Entrance** Moderately difficult **Setting** urban campus **Total enrollment** 9,906 **Student-faculty ratio** 17:1 **Application deadline** Rolling (freshmen), rolling (transfer) **Freshman admission** 68% were admitted. Average high school GPA 3.4 **Freshman test scores** SAT critical reading scores over 500: 73%; SAT math scores over 500: 63%; ACT scores over 18: 94%; SAT critical reading scores over 600: 28%; SAT math scores over 600: 22%; ACT scores over 24: 47% **Housing** Yes **Expenses** Tuition & Fees $29,570; Room & Board $11,750 **Undergraduates** 60% women, 12% part-time, 8% 25 or older, 0.3% Native American, 3% Hispanic American, 4% African American, 1% Asian American/Pacific Islander **The most frequently chosen baccalaureate fields are** communication technologies, architecture, visual and performing arts **Academic program** English as a second language, advanced placement, summer session, internships **Contact** Ms. Ginger Hansen, Executive Director of Recruitment, Savannah College of Art and Design, 342 Bull Street, PO Box 3146, Savannah, GA 31402-3146. *Phone:* 912-525-5100 or toll-free 800-869-7223. *Fax:* 912-525-5983. *E-mail:* admission@scad.edu. *Web site:* http://www.scad.edu/.

Savannah State University
Savannah, Georgia

General State-supported, comprehensive, coed **Entrance** Minimally difficult **Setting** 173-acre suburban campus **Total enrollment** 3,820 **Student-faculty ratio** 21:1 **Application deadline** 7/15 (freshmen), 6/15 (transfer) **Freshman admission** 40% were admitted. Average high school GPA 2.74 **Freshman test scores** SAT critical reading scores over 500: 16%; SAT math scores over 500: 16%; ACT scores over 18: 57.65%; SAT critical reading scores over 600: 1%; SAT math scores over 600: 2%; ACT scores over 24: 1.91% **Housing** Yes **Expenses** Tuition & Fees: state resident $3726, nonresident $13,018; Room & Board $5644 **Undergraduates** 56% women, 14% part-time, 13% 25 or older, 0.1% Native American, 0.4% Hispanic American, 95% African American, 0.3% Asian American/Pacific Islander **The most frequently chosen baccalaureate fields are** biological/life sciences, business/marketing, communications/journalism **Academic program** Advanced placement, accelerated degree program, honors program, summer session, adult/continuing education programs, internships **Contact** Mrs. Carol Dolan, Assistant Director of Admissions for Operations, Savannah State University, PO Box 20209, Savannah, GA 31404. *Phone:* 912-356-2345 or toll-free 800-788-0478. *Fax:* 912-356-2256. *E-mail:* dolanc@savannahstate.edu. *Web site:* http://www.savannahstate.edu/.

Shorter University
Rome, Georgia

General Independent Baptist, comprehensive, coed **Entrance** Moderately difficult **Setting** 155-acre small-town campus **Total enrollment** 1,205 **Student-faculty ratio** 11:1 **Application deadline** 8/25 (freshmen), 8/25 (transfer) **Freshman admission** 65% were admitted. Average high school GPA 3.33 **Freshman test scores** SAT critical reading scores over 500: 60.5%; SAT math scores over 500: 48.4%; ACT scores over 18: 79.5%; SAT critical reading scores over 600: 20.9%; SAT math scores over 600: 12.6%; ACT scores over 24: 23.8% **Housing** Yes **Undergraduates** 50% women, 3% part-time, 6% 25 or older, 2% Hispanic American, 14% African American, 1% Asian American/Pacific Islander **The most frequently chosen baccalaureate fields are** business/marketing, education, visual and performing arts **Academic program** Advanced placement, self-designed majors, honors program, summer session, adult/continuing education programs, internships **Contact** Mr. John Head, Vice President for Enrollment Management, Shorter University, 315 Shorter Avenue, Rome, GA 30165. *Phone:* 706-233-7342 or toll-free 800-868-6980. *Fax:* 706-233-7224. *E-mail:* admissions@shorter.edu. *Web site:* http://www.shorter.edu/.

Visit Petersons.com and enter keyword Shorter

See page 1158 for the College Close-Up.

Southern Polytechnic State University
Marietta, Georgia

General State-supported, comprehensive, coed **Entrance** Moderately difficult **Setting** 203-acre suburban campus **Total enrollment** 5,186 **Student-faculty ratio** 18:1 **Application deadline** 7/1 (freshmen), 7/1 (transfer) **Freshman admission** 61% were admitted. Average high school GPA 3.21 **Freshman test scores** SAT critical reading scores over 500: 78%; SAT math scores over 500: 90%; ACT scores over 18: 98%; SAT critical reading scores over 600: 25%; SAT math scores over 600: 40%; ACT scores over 24: 38% **Housing** Yes **Expenses** Tuition & Fees: state resident $4498, nonresident $14,994; Room & Board $6350 **Undergraduates** 19% women, 27% part-time, 32% 25 or older, 0.2% Native American, 5% Hispanic American, 20% African American, 5% Asian American/Pacific Islander **The most frequently chosen baccalaureate fields are** business/marketing, computer and information sciences, engineering technologies **Academic program** Advanced placement, self-designed majors, honors program, summer session, internships **Contact** Mr. Gary Bush, Director of Admissions, Southern Polytechnic State University, 1100 South Marietta Parkway, Marietta, GA 30060-2896. *Phone:* 678-915-7468 or toll-free 800-635-3204. *Fax:* 678-915-7292. *E-mail:* gbush@spsu.edu. *Web site:* http://www.spsu.edu/.

South University
Savannah, Georgia

General Proprietary, comprehensive, coed **Contact** Director of Admissions, South University, 709 Mall Boulevard, Savannah, GA 31406. *Phone:* 912-201-8000 or toll-free 866-629-2901. *Fax:* 912-201-8070. *Web site:* http://www.southuniversity.edu/savannah/.

Visit Petersons.com and enter keywords South University

See page 1180 for the College Close-Up.

Spelman College
Atlanta, Georgia

General Independent, 4-year, women only **Entrance** Very difficult **Setting** 32-acre urban campus **Total enrollment** 2,229 **Student-faculty ratio** 11:1 **Application deadline** 2/1 (freshmen), 4/1 (transfer) **Freshman admission** 40% were admitted. Average high school GPA 3.53 **Freshman test scores** SAT math scores over 500: 57.91%; ACT scores over 18: 93.16%; SAT math scores over 600: 13.03%; ACT scores over 24: 28.27% **Housing** Yes **Expenses** Tuition & Fees $22,010; Room & Board $10,062 **Undergraduates** 5% part-time, 4% 25 or older, 0.1% Hispanic American, 92% African American, 0.1% Asian American/Pacific Islander **The most frequently chosen baccalaureate fields are** psychology, biological/life sciences, social sciences **Academic program** Advanced placement, self-designed majors, honors program, adult/continuing education programs, internships **Contact** Ms. Arlene Cash, Vice President for Admissions and Orientation, Spelman College, 350 Spelman Lane, SW, Atlanta, GA 30314-4399. *Phone:* 404-681-3643 or toll-free 800-982-2411. *Fax:* 404-270-5201. *E-mail:* admiss@spelman.edu. *Web site:* http://www.spelman.edu/.

Strayer University–Augusta Campus
Augusta, Georgia

General Proprietary, comprehensive, coed **Contact** Admissions Office, Strayer University–Augusta Campus, 1330 Augusta West Parkway, Augusta, GA 30909. *Phone:* 706-855-8233. *Web site:* http://www.strayer.edu/augusta.

Strayer University–Chamblee Campus
Atlanta, Georgia

General Proprietary, comprehensive, coed **Contact** Admissions Office, Strayer University–Chamblee Campus, 3355 Northeast Expressway, Suite 100, Atlanta, GA 30341. *Phone:* 770-454-9270. *Web site:* http://www.strayer.edu/chamblee.

Strayer University–Cobb County Campus
Atlanta, Georgia

General Proprietary, comprehensive, coed **Contact** Admissions Office, Strayer University–Cobb County Campus, 3101 Towercreek Parkway, SE, Suite 700, Atlanta, GA 30339-3256. *Phone:* 770-612-2170. *Web site:* http://www.strayer.edu/cobb_county.

Strayer University–Douglasville Campus
Douglasville, Georgia

General Proprietary, comprehensive, coed **Contact** Admissions Office, Strayer University–Douglasville Campus, 4655 Timber Ridge Drive, Douglasville, GA 30135. *Phone:* 678-715-2200. *Web site:* http://www.strayer.edu/douglasville.

Strayer University–Lithonia Campus
Lithonia, Georgia

General Proprietary, comprehensive, coed **Contact** Admissions Office, Strayer University–Lithonia Campus, 3120 Stonecrest Boulevard, Suite 200, Lithonia, GA 30038. *Phone:* 678-323-7700. *Web site:* http://www.strayer.edu/lithonia.

Strayer University–Morrow Campus
Morrow, Georgia

General Proprietary, comprehensive, coed **Contact** Admissions Office, Strayer University–Morrow Campus, 3000 Corporate Center Drive, Suite 100, Morrow, GA 30260. *Phone:* 678-422-4100. *Web site:* http://www.strayer.edu/morrow.

Strayer University–Roswell Campus
Roswell, Georgia

General Proprietary, comprehensive, coed **Contact** Admissions Office, Strayer University–Roswell Campus, 100 Mansell Court East, Suite 100, Roswell, GA 30076. *Phone:* 770-650-3000. *Web site:* http://www.strayer.edu/roswell.

Strayer University–Savannah Campus
Savannah, Georgia

General Proprietary, comprehensive, coed **Contact** Admissions Office, Strayer University–Savannah Campus, 20 Martin Court, Savannah, GA 31419. *Phone:* 912-921-2900. *Web site:* http://www.strayer.edu/savannah.

Thomas University
Thomasville, Georgia

Contact Thomas University Office of Admission, Thomas University, 1501 Millpond Road, Thomasville, GA 31792. *Phone:* 229-226-1621 Ext. 214 or toll-free 800-538-9784. *Fax:* 229-227-6919. *E-mail:* hmueller@thomasu.edu. *Web site:* http://www.thomasu.edu/.

Toccoa Falls College
Toccoa Falls, Georgia

General Independent interdenominational, 4-year, coed **Entrance** Moderately difficult **Setting** 500-acre small-town campus **Total enrollment** 859 **Student-faculty ratio** 14:1 **Application deadline** Rolling (freshmen), rolling (transfer) **Freshman admission** Average high school GPA 3.4 **Freshman test scores** SAT critical reading scores over 500: 55%; SAT math scores over 500: 48%; ACT scores over 18: 82%; SAT critical reading scores over 600: 18%; SAT math scores over 600: 14%; ACT scores over 24: 28% **Housing** Yes **Expenses** Tuition & Fees $15,575; Room & Board $5650 **Undergraduates** 55% women, 8% part-time, 14% 25 or older **The most frequently chosen baccalaureate fields are** area and ethnic studies, education, psychology **Academic program** Advanced placement, accelerated degree program, summer session, internships **Contact** Mike Davis, Director of Enrollment, Toccoa Falls College, 107 North Chapel Drive, Toccoa Falls, GA 30598. *Phone:* 888-785-5624. *Fax:* 706-282-6012. *E-mail:* admissions@tfc.edu. *Web site:* http://www.tfc.edu/.

See page 1228 for the College Close-Up.

Truett-McConnell College
Cleveland, Georgia

General Independent Baptist, 4-year, coed **Entrance** Minimally difficult **Setting** 310-acre rural campus **Total enrollment** 519 **Student-faculty ratio** 11:1 **Application deadline** 8/1 (freshmen), 8/1 (transfer) **Freshman admission** 62% were admitted. Average high school GPA 3.04 **Housing** Yes **Expenses** Tuition & Fees $14,000; Room & Board $5700 **Undergraduates** 53% women, 31% part-time, 7% 25 or older, 0.3% Native American, 3% Hispanic American, 9% African American, 0.3% Asian American/Pacific Islander **The most frequently chosen baccalaureate fields are** education, history, liberal arts/general studies **Academic program** Advanced placement, accelerated degree program, summer session **Contact** Mr. Andrew Gailey, Director of Admissions, Truett-McConnell College, 100 Alumni Drive, Cleveland, GA 30528. *Phone:* 706-865-2134 Ext. 210 or toll-free 800-226-8621. *Fax:* 706-865-3110. *E-mail:* agailey@truett.edu. *Web site:* http://www.truett.edu/.

University of Atlanta
Atlanta, Georgia

General Independent, comprehensive, coed **Entrance** Moderately difficult **Total enrollment** 1,410 **Student-faculty ratio** 6:1 **Application deadline** Rolling (freshmen) **Freshman admission** 48% were admitted. Average high school GPA 3.21 **Expenses** Tuition & Fees $3300 **Undergraduates** 46% women, 61% 25 or older **The most frequently chosen baccalaureate fields are** business/marketing, law/legal studies, social sciences **Academic program** Accelerated degree program, honors program, adult/continuing education programs, internships **Contact** Bill Kay, Vice President for Enrollment Management, University of Atlanta, 6685 Peachtree Industrial Boulevard, Atlanta, GA 30360. *Phone:* 404-424-8410 Ext. 5555 or toll-free 800-533-3378. *Fax:* 678-736-8042. *E-mail:* bkay@uofa.edu. *Web site:* http://www.uofa.edu/.

University of Georgia
Athens, Georgia

General State-supported, university, coed **Entrance** Moderately difficult **Setting** 1,289-acre suburban campus **Total enrollment** 34,885 **Student-faculty ratio** 18:1 **Application deadline** 1/15 (freshmen), 4/1 (transfer) **Freshman admission** 54% were admitted. Average high school GPA 3.83 **Freshman test scores** SAT math scores over 500: 95.92%; ACT scores over 18: 99.63%; SAT math scores over 600: 65.49%; ACT scores over 24: 86.82% **Housing** Yes **Expenses** Tuition & Fees: state resident $7530, nonresident $25,740; Room & Board $8046 **Undergraduates** 58% women, 6% part-time, 5% 25 or older, 0.2% Native American, 3% Hispanic American, 7% African American, 7% Asian American/Pacific Islander **The most frequently chosen baccalaureate fields are** business/marketing, education, social sciences **Academic program** Advanced placement, accelerated degree program, self-designed majors, honors program, summer session, adult/continuing education programs, internships **Contact** Mr. Charles Carabello, Associate Director for Enrollment Management, University of Georgia, Terrell Hall, Athens, GA 30602. *Phone:* 706-542-8776. *Fax:* 706-542-1466. *E-mail:* undergrad@admissions.uga.edu. *Web site:* http://www.uga.edu/.

University of Phoenix–Atlanta Campus
Sandy Springs, Georgia

General Proprietary, comprehensive, coed **Entrance** Noncompetitive **Setting** urban campus **Total enrollment** 1,573 **Application deadline** Rolling (freshmen), rolling (transfer) **Housing** No **Expenses** Tuition & Fees $12,090 **Undergraduates** 71% women, 89% 25 or older, 0.3% Native American, 3% Hispanic American, 53% African American, 1% Asian American/Pacific Islander **The most frequently chosen baccalaureate fields are** business/marketing, computer and information sciences, health professions and related sciences **Academic program** Advanced placement, accelerated degree program, adult/continuing education programs **Contact** Ms. Audra McQuarie, Registrar/Executive Director, University of Phoenix–Atlanta Campus, 4035 South Riverpoint Parkway, Mail Stop CF-L101, Phoenix, AZ 85040. *Phone:* 480-557-6151 or toll-free 800-776-4867 (in-state); 800-228-7240 (out-of-state). *Fax:* 480-643-3068. *E-mail:* audra.mcquarie@phoenix.edu. *Web site:* http://www.phoenix.edu/.

University of Phoenix–Columbus Georgia Campus
Columbus, Georgia

General Proprietary, comprehensive, coed **Entrance** Noncompetitive **Setting** urban campus **Total enrollment** 764 **Application deadline** Rolling (freshmen), rolling (transfer) **Housing** No **Expenses** Tuition & Fees $11,775 **Undergraduates** 75% women, 76% 25 or older, 0.3% Native American, 2% Hispanic American, 57% African American, 0.4% Asian American/Pacific Islander **The most frequently chosen baccalaureate fields are** business/marketing, health professions and related sciences, security and protective services **Academic program** Advanced placement, accelerated degree program **Contact** Ms. Audra McQuarie, Registrar/Executive Director, University of Phoenix–Columbus Georgia

Campus, 4035 South Riverpoint Parkway, Mail Stop CF-L101, Phoenix, AZ 85040. *Phone:* 480-557-6151 or toll-free 800-776-4867 (in-state); 800-228-7240 (out-of-state). *Fax:* 480-643-3068. *E-mail:* audra.mcquarie@phoenix.edu. *Web site:* http://www.phoenix.edu/.

University of West Georgia

Carrollton, Georgia

General State-supported, comprehensive, coed **Entrance** Minimally difficult **Setting** 645-acre small-town campus **Total enrollment** 11,500 **Student-faculty ratio** 20:1 **Application deadline** 6/1 (freshmen), 6/1 (transfer) **Freshman admission** 58% were admitted. Average high school GPA 2.93 **Freshman test scores** SAT critical reading scores over 500: 47.8%; SAT math scores over 500: 44.5%; ACT scores over 18: 84.1%; SAT critical reading scores over 600: 8.7%; SAT math scores over 600: 7.9%; ACT scores over 24: 11.3% **Housing** Yes **Expenses** Tuition & Fees: state resident $4582, nonresident $14,164; Room & Board $6254 **Undergraduates** 60% women, 16% part-time, 15% 25 or older, 0.3% Native American, 2% Hispanic American, 27% African American, 1% Asian American/Pacific Islander **The most frequently chosen baccalaureate fields are** business/marketing, education, social sciences **Academic program** Advanced placement, accelerated degree program, honors program, summer session, adult/continuing education programs, internships **Contact** Mr. Justin Barlow, Assistant Director of Admissions, University of West Georgia, 1601 Maple Street, Carrollton, GA 30118. *Phone:* 678-839-4000. *Fax:* 678-839-4747. *E-mail:* admiss@westga.edu. *Web site:* http://www.westga.edu/.

Valdosta State University

Valdosta, Georgia

General State-supported, university, coed **Entrance** Moderately difficult **Setting** 172-acre small-town campus **Total enrollment** 12,391 **Student-faculty ratio** 23:1 **Application deadline** 6/15 (freshmen), 6/15 (transfer) **Freshman admission** 71% were admitted. Average high school GPA 3.03 **Freshman test scores** SAT critical reading scores over 500: 48%; ACT scores over 18: 92%; SAT critical reading scores over 600: 8%; ACT scores over 24: 12% **Housing** Yes **Expenses** Tuition & Fees: state resident $4488, nonresident $13,417; Room & Board $6480 **Undergraduates** 58% women, 13% part-time, 16% 25 or older, 0.4% Native American, 1% Hispanic American, 31% African American, 1% Asian American/Pacific Islander **The most frequently chosen baccalaureate fields are** business/marketing, education, English **Academic program** English as a second language, advanced placement, accelerated degree program, honors program, summer session, internships **Contact** Mr. Walter Peacock, Director of Admissions, Valdosta State University, 1500 North Patterson Street, Valdosta, GA 31698. *Phone:* 229-333-5791 or toll-free 800-618-1878 Ext. 1. *Fax:* 229-333-5482. *E-mail:* wpeacock@valdosta.edu. *Web site:* http://www.valdosta.edu/.

Wesleyan College

Macon, Georgia

General Independent United Methodist, comprehensive, undergraduate: women only; graduate: coed **Entrance** Moderately difficult **Setting** 200-acre suburban campus **Total enrollment** 671 **Student-faculty ratio** 10:1 **Application deadline** Rolling (freshmen), rolling (transfer) **Freshman admission** 51% were admitted. Average high school GPA 3.5 **Freshman test scores** SAT critical reading scores over 500: 81%; SAT math scores over 500: 60%; ACT scores over 18: 97%; SAT critical reading scores over 600: 31%; SAT math scores over 600: 26%; ACT scores over 24: 67% **Housing** Yes **Expenses** Tuition & Fees $17,500; Room & Board $8000 **Undergraduates** 37% part-time, 39% 25 or older, 0.3% Native American, 3% Hispanic American, 37% African American, 2% Asian American/Pacific Islander **The most frequently chosen baccalaureate fields are** business/marketing, psychology, visual and performing arts **Academic program** Advanced placement, self-designed majors, honors program, summer session, adult/continuing education programs, internships **Contact** Mr. Stephen Farr, Vice President for Enrollment Services, Wesleyan College, 4760 Forsyth Road, Macon, GA 31210-4462. *Phone:* 478-757-3700 or toll-free 800-447-6610. *Fax:* 478-757-4030. *E-mail:* admissions@wesleyancollege.edu. *Web site:* http://www.wesleyancollege.edu/.

Visit Petersons.com and enter keywords Wesleyan College

See page 1356 for the College Close-Up.

Westwood College–Atlanta Midtown

Atlanta, Georgia

General Proprietary, 4-year, coed **Total enrollment** 675 **Contact** Director of Admissions, Westwood College–Atlanta Midtown, 1100 Spring Street, Atlanta, GA 30309. *Phone:* 404-745-9862. *Fax:* 404-892-7253. *Web site:* http://www.westwood.edu/.

Westwood College–Atlanta Northlake

Atlanta, Georgia

General Proprietary, 4-year, coed **Total enrollment** 490 **Contact** Director of Admission, Westwood College–Atlanta Northlake, 2309 Parklake Drive, NE, Building 10, Atlanta, GA 30345. *Phone:* 404-962-2998. *Fax:* 770-934-9539. *Web site:* http://www.westwood.edu/.

Young Harris College

Young Harris, Georgia

General Independent United Methodist, 4-year, coed **Entrance** Moderately difficult **Setting** 800-acre small-town campus **Total enrollment** 649 **Student-faculty ratio** 10:1 **Application deadline** Rolling (freshmen), rolling (transfer) **Freshman admission** 58% were admitted. Average high school GPA 3.13 **Freshman test scores** SAT critical reading scores over 500: 48.5%; SAT math scores over 500: 47%; ACT scores over 18: 86%; SAT critical reading scores over 600: 11%; SAT math scores over 600: 15%; ACT scores over 24: 21% **Housing** Yes **Expenses** Tuition & Fees $20,525; Room & Board $7084 **Undergraduates** 54% women, 4% part-time, 1% 25 or older, 0.3% Native American, 4% Hispanic American, 3% African American, 1% Asian American/Pacific Islander **Academic program** Advanced placement, honors program, summer session, internships **Contact** Mr. Clinton G. Hobbs, Vice President for Enrollment Management, Young Harris College, PO Box 116, Young Harris, GA 30582-0098. *Phone:* 706-379-3111 or toll-free 800-241-3754. *Fax:* 706-379-3108. *E-mail:* admissions@yhc.edu. *Web site:* http://www.yhc.edu/.

GUAM

Pacific Islands University

Guam Main Facility, Guam

Contact Ethel Laco, Admissions Office, Pacific Islands University, PO Box 22619, Guam Main Facility, GU 96921-2619. *Phone:* 671-734-1812. *Fax:* 671-734-1813. *E-mail:* guamcampus@pibc.edu. *Web site:* http://www.piu.edu/.

University of Guam

Mangilao, Guam

General Territory-supported, comprehensive, coed **Entrance** Noncompetitive **Setting** 100-acre suburban campus **Total enrollment** 3,550 **Student-faculty ratio** 14:1 **Application deadline** 6/1 (freshmen), 6/1 (transfer) **Freshman admission** 86% were admitted. Average high school GPA 2.9 **Housing** Yes **Expenses** Tuition & Fees: state resident $5770, nonresident $16,270; Room & Board $9102 **Undergraduates** 60% women, 23% part-time, 21% 25 or older, 0.2% Native American,

University of Guam (continued)
1% Hispanic American, 1% African American, 91% Asian American/Pacific Islander **The most frequently chosen baccalaureate fields are** business/marketing, education, security and protective services **Academic program** English as a second language, advanced placement, accelerated degree program, honors program, summer session, internships **Contact** Ms. Angelica Anthonio, Admissions Supervisor, University of Guam, Admissions and Records Office, UOG Station, Mangilao, GU 96923. *Phone:* 671-735-2201. *Fax:* 671-735-2203. *E-mail:* admitme@uguam.uog.edu. *Web site:* http://www.uog.edu/.

HAWAII

Argosy University, Hawai'i
Honolulu, Hawaii

General Proprietary, university, coed **Contact** Director of Admissions, Argosy University, Hawai'i, 400 ASBTower, 1001 Bishop Street, Honolulu, HI 96813. *Phone:* 808-536-5555 or toll-free 888-323-2777. *Fax:* 808-536-5505. *Web site:* http://www.argosy.edu/hawaii/.
Visit Petersons.com and enter keywords Argosy University, Hawaii

See page 478 for the College Close-Up.

Brigham Young University–Hawaii
Laie, Hawaii

General Independent Latter-day Saints, 4-year, coed **Entrance** Moderately difficult **Setting** 60-acre small-town campus **Total enrollment** 2,555 **Student-faculty ratio** 15:1 **Application deadline** 2/15 (freshmen), 3/15 (transfer) **Freshman admission** 58% were admitted **Freshman test scores** SAT critical reading scores over 500: 67%; SAT math scores over 500: 72%; ACT scores over 18: 97%; SAT critical reading scores over 600: 26%; SAT math scores over 600: 28%; ACT scores over 24: 54% **Housing** Yes **Expenses** Tuition & Fees $4330; Room & Board $4756 **Undergraduates** 54% women, 7% part-time, 26% 25 or older, 1% Native American, 3% Hispanic American, 1% African American, 22% Asian American/Pacific Islander **The most frequently chosen baccalaureate fields are** business/marketing, education, interdisciplinary studies **Academic program** English as a second language, advanced placement, accelerated degree program, honors program, summer session, adult/continuing education programs, internships **Contact** Mr. Arapata P. Meha, Brigham Young University–Hawaii, 55-220 Kulanui Street, Laie, HI 96762-1294. *Phone:* 808-675-3731. *Fax:* 808-675-3741. *E-mail:* admissions@byuh.edu. *Web site:* http://www.byuh.edu/.

Chaminade University of Honolulu
Honolulu, Hawaii

General Independent Roman Catholic, comprehensive, coed **Entrance** Moderately difficult **Setting** 62-acre urban campus **Total enrollment** 1,755 **Student-faculty ratio** 12:1 **Application deadline** Rolling (freshmen), rolling (transfer) **Freshman admission** 95% were admitted. Average high school GPA 3.17 **Freshman test scores** SAT critical reading scores over 500: 36%; SAT math scores over 500: 35%; ACT scores over 18: 77%; SAT critical reading scores over 600: 4%; SAT math scores over 600: 7%; ACT scores over 24: 10% **Housing** Yes **Expenses** Tuition & Fees $17,740; Room & Board $10,420 **Undergraduates** 66% women, 4% part-time, 11% 25 or older, 1% Native American, 7% Hispanic American, 3% African American, 68% Asian American/Pacific Islander **The most frequently chosen baccalaureate fields are** education, psychology, security and protective services **Academic program** Advanced placement, accelerated degree program, self-designed majors, summer session, adult/continuing education programs, internships **Contact** Mr. Martin Motooka, Assistant Director of Admissions, Chaminade University of Honolulu, 3140 Waialae Avenue, Honolulu, HI 96816-1578. *Phone:* 808-735-4735 or toll-free 800-735-3733. *Fax:* 808-739-4647. *E-mail:* admissions@chaminade.edu. *Web site:* http://www.chaminade.edu/.

Hawai'i Pacific University
Honolulu, Hawaii

General Independent, comprehensive, coed **Entrance** Moderately difficult **Setting** 140-acre urban campus **Total enrollment** 8,113 **Student-faculty ratio** 15:1 **Application deadline** Rolling (freshmen), rolling (transfer) **Freshman admission** 73% were admitted. Average high school GPA 3.29 **Freshman test scores** SAT critical reading scores over 500: 48%; SAT math scores over 500: 52.2%; ACT scores over 18: 81.2%; SAT critical reading scores over 600: 14.6%; SAT math scores over 600: 16.3%; ACT scores over 24: 27.1% **Housing** Yes **Expenses** Tuition & Fees $14,960; Room & Board $11,094 **Undergraduates** 58% women, 44% part-time, 41% 25 or older, 2% Native American, 9% Hispanic American, 7% African American, 37% Asian American/Pacific Islander **The most frequently chosen baccalaureate fields are** business/marketing, communications/journalism, health professions and related sciences **Academic program** English as a second language, advanced placement, accelerated degree program, self-designed majors, honors program, summer session, adult/continuing education programs, internships **Contact** Mr. Scott Stensrud, Vice President Enrollment Management, Hawai'i Pacific University, 1164 Bishop Street, Honolulu, HI 96813-2785. *Phone:* 808-544-0238 or toll-free 866-225-5478. *Fax:* 808-544-1136. *E-mail:* admissions@hpu.edu. *Web site:* http://www.hpu.edu/.
Visit Petersons.com and enter keywords Hawaii Pacific

See page 842 for the College Close-Up.

Remington College–Honolulu Campus
Honolulu, Hawaii

General Proprietary, primarily 2-year, coed **Contact** Louis LaMair, Director of Recruitment, Remington College–Honolulu Campus, 1111 Bishop Street, Suite 400, Honolulu, HI 96813. *Phone:* 808-942-1000. *Fax:* 808-533-3064. *E-mail:* louis.lamair@remingtoncollege.edu. *Web site:* http://www.remingtoncollege.edu/.

University of Hawaii at Hilo
Hilo, Hawaii

General State-supported, comprehensive, coed **Entrance** Moderately difficult **Setting** 115-acre small-town campus **Total enrollment** 3,974 **Student-faculty ratio** 14:1 **Application deadline** 7/1 (freshmen), 7/1 (transfer) **Freshman admission** 50% were admitted. Average high school GPA 3.5 **Freshman test scores** SAT critical reading scores over 500: 40%; SAT math scores over 500: 43%; ACT scores over 18: 81%; SAT critical reading scores over 600: 9%; SAT math scores over 600: 12%; ACT scores over 24: 27% **Housing** Yes **Expenses** Tuition & Fees: state resident $4360, nonresident $12,880; Room & Board $11,403 **Undergraduates** 59% women, 18% part-time, 23% 25 or older, 1% Native American, 3% Hispanic American, 1% African American, 50% Asian American/Pacific Islander **The most frequently chosen baccalaureate fields are** psychology, biological/life sciences, social sciences **Academic program** English as a second language, advanced placement, self-designed majors, honors program, summer session, internships **Contact** Mr. James Cromwell, Student Services Specialist/Director of Admissions, University of Hawaii at Hilo, 200 West Kawili Street, Hilo, HI 96720-4091. *Phone:* 808-974-7414 or toll-free 800-897-4456. *Fax:* 808-933-0861. *E-mail:* uhhao@hawaii.edu. *Web site:* http://www.uhh.hawaii.edu/.

University of Hawaii at Manoa
Honolulu, Hawaii

General State-supported, university, coed **Entrance** Moderately difficult **Setting** 300-acre urban campus **Total enrollment** 20,435 **Student-**

- **Ranked a "Best Buy" by Barron's** a high quality education at an affordable price
- **Choose from more than 50 programs** from International Business to Nursing to Marine Biology
- **Experience individual attention** in classes under 25; one-on-one interaction with professors
- **Get a global perspective** inside and outside the classroom with students from all 50 states and more than 100 countries

1-866-CALL-HPU
www.hpu.edu/petersons

faculty ratio 14:1 **Application deadline** 5/1 (freshmen), 5/1 (transfer) **Freshman admission** 67% were admitted. Average high school GPA 3.44 **Freshman test scores** SAT critical reading scores over 500: 68.6%; SAT math scores over 500: 80.6%; ACT scores over 18: 96%; SAT critical reading scores over 600: 19.9%; SAT math scores over 600: 34.4%; ACT scores over 24: 43.1% **Housing** Yes **Expenses** Tuition & Fees: state resident $7983, nonresident $21,423; Room & Board $8493 **Undergraduates** 54% women, 19% part-time, 16% 25 or older, 1% Native American, 3% Hispanic American, 1% African American, 67% Asian American/Pacific Islander **The most frequently chosen baccalaureate fields are** business/marketing, education, social sciences **Academic program** English as a second language, advanced placement, accelerated degree program, self-designed majors, honors program, summer session, internships **Contact** Ms. Lisa Buto, Student Services Specialist, University of Hawaii at Manoa, 2600 Campus Road, Room 001, Honolulu, HI 96822. *Phone:* 808-956-8975 or toll-free 800-823-9771. *Fax:* 808-956-4148. *E-mail:* ar-info@hawaii.edu. *Web site:* http://manoa.hawaii.edu/.

University of Hawaii–West Oahu

Pearl City, Hawaii

General State-supported, 4-year, coed **Entrance** Moderately difficult **Setting** small-town campus **Total enrollment** 1,293 **Student-faculty ratio** 13:1 **Application deadline** 4/1 (freshmen), 4/1 (transfer) **Freshman admission** 81% were admitted. Average high school GPA 3.17 **Housing** No **Expenses** Tuition & Fees: state resident $4666, nonresident $14,362 **Undergraduates** 71% women, 68% part-time, 58% 25 or older, 0.4% Native American, 2% Hispanic American, 2% African American, 64% Asian American/Pacific Islander **Academic program** Advanced placement, summer session **Contact** Robyn Oshiro, University of Hawaii–West Oahu, 96-129 Ala Ike Street, Pearl City, HI 96782. *Phone:* 808-454-4700 or toll-free 808-454-4700. *Fax:* 808-453-6075. *E-mail:* robyno@hawaii.edu. *Web site:* http://www.uhwo.hawaii.edu/.

University of Phoenix–Hawaii Campus

Honolulu, Hawaii

General Proprietary, comprehensive, coed **Entrance** Noncompetitive **Setting** urban campus **Total enrollment** 955 **Application deadline** Rolling (freshmen), rolling (transfer) **Housing** No **Expenses** Tuition & Fees $13,200 **Undergraduates** 71% women, 75% 25 or older, 0.3% Native American, 5% Hispanic American, 4% African American, 37% Asian American/Pacific Islander **The most frequently chosen baccalaureate fields are** business/marketing, computer and information sciences, health professions and related sciences **Academic program** Advanced placement, accelerated degree program, adult/continuing education programs **Contact** Ms. Audra McQuarie, Registrar/Executive Director, University of Phoenix–Hawaii Campus, 4035 South Riverpoint Parkway, Mail Stop CF-L101, Phoenix, AZ 85040. *Phone:* 480-557-6151 or toll-free 800-776-4867 (in-state); 800-228-7240 (out-of-state). *Fax:* 480-643-3068. *E-mail:* audra.mcquarie@phoenix.edu. *Web site:* http://www.phoenix.edu/.

IDAHO

Boise Bible College

Boise, Idaho

Contact Mr. Martin Flaherty, Director of Admissions, Boise Bible College, 8695 West Marigold Street, Boise, ID 83714-1220. *Phone:* 208-376-7731 or toll-free 800-893-7755. *Fax:* 208-376-7743. *E-mail:* martinf@boisebible.edu. *Web site:* http://www.boisebible.edu/.

Boise State University
Boise, Idaho

General State-supported, university, coed **Entrance** Moderately difficult **Setting** 175-acre urban campus **Total enrollment** 18,933 **Student-faculty ratio** 21:1 **Application deadline** 6/30 (freshmen), 6/30 (transfer) **Freshman admission** 87% were admitted. Average high school GPA 3.31 **Freshman test scores** SAT critical reading scores over 500: 60%; SAT math scores over 500: 62%; ACT scores over 18: 89%; SAT critical reading scores over 600: 17%; SAT math scores over 600: 22%; ACT scores over 24: 34% **Housing** Yes **Expenses** Tuition & Fees: state resident $4864, nonresident $13,868; Room & Board $5602 **Undergraduates** 54% women, 27% part-time, 38% 25 or older, 1% Native American, 7% Hispanic American, 2% African American, 3% Asian American/Pacific Islander **The most frequently chosen baccalaureate fields are** business/marketing, education, health professions and related sciences **Academic program** English as a second language, advanced placement, self-designed majors, honors program, summer session, adult/continuing education programs, internships **Contact** Ms. Jenny Cerda, Dean of Admissions, Boise State University, Enrollment Services, 1910 University Drive, Boise, ID 83725. *Phone:* 208-426-1177 or toll-free 800-632-6586 (in-state); 800-824-7017 (out-of-state). *E-mail:* bsuinfo@boisestate.edu. *Web site:* http://www.boisestate.edu/.

Brown Mackie College–Boise
Boise, Idaho

General Proprietary, primarily 2-year, coed **Contact** Director of Admissions, Brown Mackie College–Boise, 9050 West Overland Road, Suite 100, Boise, ID 83709. *Phone:* 208-321-8800. *Fax:* 208-375-3249. *Web site:* http://www.brownmackie.edu/boise/.

Visit Petersons.com and enter keywords Brown Mackie College-Boise

See page 620 for the College Close-Up.

The College of Idaho
Caldwell, Idaho

General Independent, comprehensive, coed **Entrance** Moderately difficult **Setting** 50-acre suburban campus **Total enrollment** 1,013 **Student-faculty ratio** 12:1 **Application deadline** 8/1 (freshmen), rolling (transfer) **Freshman admission** 62% were admitted. Average high school GPA 3.59 **Freshman test scores** SAT critical reading scores over 500: 57.2%; SAT math scores over 500: 59.4%; ACT scores over 18: 97.9%; SAT critical reading scores over 600: 23.1%; SAT math scores over 600: 25.3%; ACT scores over 24: 56.1% **Housing** Yes **Expenses** Tuition & Fees $21,050; Room & Board $7700 **Undergraduates** 58% women, 6% part-time, 4% 25 or older, 1% Native American, 8% Hispanic American, 1% African American, 2% Asian American/Pacific Islander **The most frequently chosen baccalaureate fields are** business/marketing, psychology, social sciences **Academic program** English as a second language, advanced placement, self-designed majors, honors program, internships **Contact** Brian Bava, Interim Dean of Enrollment Management, The College of Idaho, 2112 Cleveland Boulevard, Caldwell, ID 83605-4432. *Phone:* 208-459-5319 or toll-free 800-244-3246. *Fax:* 208-459-5757. *E-mail:* admission@collegeofidaho.edu. *Web site:* http://www.collegeofidaho.edu/.

Idaho State University
Pocatello, Idaho

General State-supported, university, coed **Entrance** Minimally difficult **Setting** 1,100-acre small-town campus **Total enrollment** 13,493 **Student-faculty ratio** 15:1 **Application deadline** 8/1 (freshmen), 8/1 (transfer) **Freshman admission** 73% were admitted. Average high school GPA 3.21 **Freshman test scores** SAT math scores over 500: 61%; ACT scores over 18: 83%; SAT math scores over 600: 20%; ACT scores over 24: 31% **Housing** Yes **Expenses** Tuition & Fees: state resident $4968, nonresident $14,770; Room & Board $5050 **Undergraduates** 55% women, 32% part-time, 43% 25 or older **The most frequently chosen baccalaureate fields are** business/marketing, education, health professions and related sciences **Academic program** English as a second language, advanced placement, self-designed majors, honors program, summer session, adult/continuing education programs, internships **Contact** Ms. Laura McKenzie, Director, Admissions and Registration, Idaho State University, 921 S. 7th, Stop 8270, Pocatello, ID 83209-8270. *Phone:* 208-282-2475. *Fax:* 208-282-4511. *E-mail:* info@isu.edu. *Web site:* http://www.isu.edu/.

ITT Technical Institute
Boise, Idaho

General Proprietary, primarily 2-year, coed **Entrance** Minimally difficult **Setting** urban campus **Housing** No **Contact** Director of Recruitment, ITT Technical Institute, 12302 West Explorer Drive, Boise, ID 83713. *Phone:* 208-322-8844 or toll-free 800-666-4888. *Fax:* 208-322-0173. *Web site:* http://www.itt-tech.edu/.

Lewis-Clark State College
Lewiston, Idaho

General State-supported, 4-year, coed **Entrance** Minimally difficult **Setting** 44-acre small-town campus **Total enrollment** 4,200 **Student-faculty ratio** 15:1 **Application deadline** Rolling (freshmen), rolling (transfer) **Freshman admission** 98% were admitted. Average high school GPA 2.98 **Freshman test scores** SAT critical reading scores over 500: 45.28%; SAT math scores over 500: 47.17%; ACT scores over 18: 62.09%; SAT critical reading scores over 600: 7.54%; SAT math scores over 600: 13.21%; ACT scores over 24: 18.95% **Housing** Yes **Expenses** Tuition & Fees: state resident $4296, nonresident $11,950; Room & Board $5400 **Undergraduates** 60% women, 40% part-time, 4% Native American, 4% Hispanic American, 1% African American, 2% Asian American/Pacific Islander **The most frequently chosen baccalaureate fields are** business/marketing, education, health professions and related sciences **Academic program** English as a second language, advanced placement, accelerated degree program, summer session, adult/continuing education programs, internships **Contact** Soo Lee Bruce-Smith, Coordinator of New Student Recruitment, Lewis-Clark State College, 500 Eighth Avenue, Lewiston, ID 83501-2698. *Phone:* 208-792-2210 or toll-free 800-933-5272. *Fax:* 208-792-2876. *E-mail:* admissions@lcsc.edu. *Web site:* http://www.lcsc.edu/.

New Saint Andrews College
Moscow, Idaho

General Proprietary, comprehensive, coed **Entrance** Moderately difficult **Setting** small-town campus **Total enrollment** 181 **Student-faculty ratio** 14:1 **Application deadline** 2/15 (freshmen), 2/15 (transfer) **Freshman admission** 69% were admitted **Freshman test scores** SAT critical reading scores over 500: 96%; SAT math scores over 500: 67%; ACT scores over 18: 92%; SAT critical reading scores over 600: 55%; SAT math scores over 600: 19%; ACT scores over 24: 61% **Housing** No **Expenses** Tuition & Fees $9890 **Undergraduates** 53% women, 10% part-time, 6% 25 or older, 1% Native American, 1% Hispanic American, 3% Asian American/Pacific Islander **The most frequently chosen baccalaureate field is** liberal arts/general studies **Academic program** Advanced placement, summer session **Contact** Lindsey Tollefson, Manager of New Student Services, New Saint Andrews College, PO Box 9025, Moscow, ID 83843. *Phone:* 208-882-1566 Ext. 100. *Fax:* 208-882-4293. *E-mail:* info@nsa.edu. *Web site:* http://www.nsa.edu/.

Northwest Nazarene University
Nampa, Idaho

General Independent, comprehensive, coed, affiliated with Church of the Nazarene **Entrance** Moderately difficult **Setting** 85-acre small-town campus **Total enrollment** 1,934 **Student-faculty ratio** 14:1 **Appli-**

cation deadline 8/15 (freshmen), 8/15 (transfer) **Freshman admission** 58% were admitted. Average high school GPA 3.43 **Freshman test scores** SAT critical reading scores over 500: 65%; SAT math scores over 500: 65%; ACT scores over 18: 88%; SAT critical reading scores over 600: 28%; SAT math scores over 600: 24%; ACT scores over 24: 40% **Housing** Yes **Expenses** Tuition & Fees $23,090; Room & Board $6020 **Undergraduates** 56% women, 10% part-time, 1% Native American, 4% Hispanic American, 1% African American, 2% Asian American/Pacific Islander **The most frequently chosen baccalaureate fields are** business/marketing, education, health professions and related sciences **Academic program** Advanced placement, accelerated degree program, self-designed majors, honors program, summer session, adult/continuing education programs, internships **Contact** Stacey Berggren, Director of Admissions, Northwest Nazarene University, 623 Holly Street, Nampa, ID 83686-5897. *Phone:* 208-467-8648 or toll-free 877-668-4968. *Fax:* 208-467-8645. *E-mail:* slberggren@nnu.edu. *Web site:* http://www.nnu.edu/.

Stevens-Henager College
Boise, Idaho

Contact Stevens-Henager College, 730 Americana Boulevard, Boise, ID 83702. *Web site:* http://www.stevenshenager.edu/.

University of Idaho
Moscow, Idaho

General State-supported, university, coed **Entrance** Moderately difficult **Setting** 1,450-acre small-town campus **Total enrollment** 11,957 **Student-faculty ratio** 17:1 **Application deadline** 8/1 (freshmen), rolling (transfer) **Freshman admission** 80% were admitted. Average high school GPA 3.38 **Freshman test scores** SAT critical reading scores over 500: 68.71%; SAT math scores over 500: 70.95%; ACT scores over 18: 93.13%; SAT critical reading scores over 600: 26.39%; SAT math scores over 600: 28.67%; ACT scores over 24: 45.06% **Housing** Yes **Expenses** Tuition & Fees: state resident $4932, nonresident $15,012; Room & Board $7242 **Undergraduates** 47% women, 11% part-time, 14% 25 or older, 1% Native American, 6% Hispanic American, 1% African American, 2% Asian American/Pacific Islander **The most frequently chosen baccalaureate fields are** agriculture, business/marketing, education **Academic program** English as a second language, advanced placement, accelerated degree program, self-designed majors, honors program, summer session, adult/continuing education programs, internships **Contact** Mr. Dan Davenport, Director of Admissions, University of Idaho, PO Box 444264, Moscow, ID 83844-4264. *Phone:* 208-885-6326 or toll-free 888-884-3246. *Fax:* 208-885-9119. *E-mail:* admissions@uidaho.edu. *Web site:* http://www.uidaho.edu/.

University of Phoenix–Idaho Campus
Meridian, Idaho

General Proprietary, comprehensive, coed **Entrance** Noncompetitive **Setting** urban campus **Total enrollment** 545 **Application deadline** Rolling (freshmen), rolling (transfer) **Housing** No **Expenses** Tuition & Fees $11,625 **Undergraduates** 59% women, 89% 25 or older, 0.4% Native American, 5% Hispanic American, 1% African American, 2% Asian American/Pacific Islander **The most frequently chosen baccalaureate fields are** business/marketing, computer and information sciences, health professions and related sciences **Academic program** Advanced placement, accelerated degree program, adult/continuing education programs **Contact** Ms. Audra McQuarie, Registrar/Executive Director, University of Phoenix–Idaho Campus, 4305 South Riverpoint Parkway, Mail Stop CF-L101, Phoenix, AZ 85040. *Phone:* 480-557-6151 or toll-free 800-776-4867 (in-state); 800-228-7240 (out-of-state). *Fax:* 480-643-3068. *E-mail:* audra.mcquarie@phoenix.edu. *Web site:* http://www.phoenix.edu/.

ILLINOIS

American Academy of Art
Chicago, Illinois

Contact Mr. Stuart Rosenbloom, Director of Admissions, American Academy of Art, 332 South Michigan Avenue, Suite 300, Chicago, IL 60604-4302. *Phone:* 312-461-0600 Ext. 159. *E-mail:* srosenbloom@aaart.edu. *Web site:* http://www.aaart.edu/.

American InterContinental University Online
Hoffman Estates, Illinois

General Proprietary, comprehensive, coed **Entrance** Minimally difficult **Setting** 1-acre suburban campus **Total enrollment** 22,424 **Application deadline** Rolling (freshmen), rolling (transfer) **Undergraduates** 67% women, 78% 25 or older, 1% Native American, 9% Hispanic American, 31% African American, 2% Asian American/Pacific Islander **The most frequently chosen baccalaureate fields are** business/marketing, computer and information sciences, security and protective services **Academic program** Advanced placement, accelerated degree program, adult/continuing education programs **Contact** Jennifer Ziegenmier, Senior Vice President of Admissions and Marketing, American InterContinental University Online, 5550 Prairie Stone Parkway, Suite 400, Hoffman Estates, IL 60192. *Phone:* 877-564-6248 or toll-free 877-701-3800. *E-mail:* jziegenmier@aiuonline.edu. *Web site:* http://www.aiuniv.edu/.

Argosy University, Chicago
Chicago, Illinois

General Proprietary, university, coed **Setting** urban campus **Contact** Director of Admissions, Argosy University, Chicago, 225 North Michigan Avenue, Suite 1300, Chicago, IL 60601. *Phone:* 312-777-7600 or toll-free 800-626-4123. *Fax:* 312-777-7748. *Web site:* http://www.argosy.edu/chicago/.

Visit Petersons.com and enter keywords Argosy University, Chicago

See page 478 for the College Close-Up.

Argosy University, Schaumburg
Schaumburg, Illinois

General Proprietary, university, coed **Contact** Director of Admissions, Argosy University, Schaumburg, 999 North Plaza Drive, Suite 111, Schaumburg, IL 60173-5403. *Phone:* 847-969-4900 or toll-free 866-290-2777. *Fax:* 847-969-4999. *Web site:* http://www.argosy.edu/schaumburg/.

Visit Petersons.com and enter keywords Argosy University, Schaumburg

See page 478 for the College Close-Up.

Augustana College
Rock Island, Illinois

General Independent, 4-year, coed, affiliated with Evangelical Lutheran Church in America **Entrance** Moderately difficult **Setting** 115-acre suburban campus **Total enrollment** 2,472 **Student-faculty ratio** 11:1 **Application deadline** Rolling (freshmen), rolling (transfer) **Freshman admission** 73% were admitted **Freshman test scores** ACT scores over 18: 99%; ACT scores over 24: 68% **Housing** Yes **Expenses** Tuition & Fees $31,326; Room & Board $7950 **Undergraduates** 57% women, 1% part-time, 1% 25 or older, 0.2% Native American, 3% Hispanic American, 2% African American, 2% Asian American/Pacific Islander **The most frequently chosen baccalaureate fields are** biological/life sciences, business/marketing, social sciences **Academic program** Advanced

Augustana College (continued)
placement, self-designed majors, honors program, summer session, internships **Contact** Megan Cooley, Director of Admissions, Augustana College, 639 38th Street, Rock Island, IL 61201-2296. *Phone:* 309-794-7341 or toll-free 800-798-8100. *Fax:* 309-794-7422. *E-mail:* admissions@augustana.edu. *Web site:* http://www.augustana.edu/.

Aurora University
Aurora, Illinois

General Independent, comprehensive, coed **Entrance** Moderately difficult **Setting** 32-acre suburban campus **Total enrollment** 4,355 **Student-faculty ratio** 14:1 **Application deadline** 5/1 (freshmen), rolling (transfer) **Freshman admission** 71% were admitted. Average high school GPA 3.34 **Freshman test scores** SAT critical reading scores over 500: 68%; SAT math scores over 500: 59%; ACT scores over 18: 98%; SAT critical reading scores over 600: 9%; SAT math scores over 600: 14%; ACT scores over 24: 32% **Housing** Yes **Expenses** Tuition & Fees $18,700; Room & Board $8800 **Undergraduates** 66% women, 14% part-time, 24% 25 or older, 0.5% Native American, 13% Hispanic American, 10% African American, 3% Asian American/Pacific Islander **The most frequently chosen baccalaureate fields are** business/marketing, education, health professions and related sciences **Academic program** Advanced placement, accelerated degree program, self-designed majors, honors program, summer session, adult/continuing education programs, internships **Contact** Mr. James Lancaster, Director, Freshman Admission, Aurora University, 347 South Gladstone Avenue, Aurora, IL 60506-4892. *Phone:* 630-844-5533 or toll-free 800-742-5281. *Fax:* 630-844-5535. *E-mail:* admission@aurora.edu. *Web site:* http://www.aurora.edu/. **Visit Petersons.com and enter keywords Aurora University**

See page 568 for the College Close-Up.

Benedictine University
Lisle, Illinois

General Independent Roman Catholic, comprehensive, coed **Entrance** Moderately difficult **Setting** 108-acre suburban campus **Total enrollment** 5,836 **Student-faculty ratio** 13:1 **Application deadline** Rolling (freshmen), rolling (transfer) **Freshman admission** 79% were admitted. Average high school GPA 3.29 **Freshman test scores** ACT scores over 18: 93%; ACT scores over 24: 40% **Housing** Yes **Expenses** Tuition & Fees $22,310; Room & Board $7360 **Undergraduates** 57% women, 33% part-time, 36% 25 or older, 0.2% Native American, 7% Hispanic American, 10% African American, 15% Asian American/Pacific Islander **The most frequently chosen baccalaureate fields are** business/marketing, education, health professions and related sciences **Academic program** English as a second language, advanced placement, accelerated degree program, honors program, summer session, adult/continuing education programs, internships **Contact** Ms. Kari Gibbons, Dean of Enrollment, Benedictine University, 5700 College Road, Lisle, IL 60532-0900. *Phone:* 630-829-6300 or toll-free 888-829-6363. *Fax:* 630-829-6301. *E-mail:* admissions@ben.edu. *Web site:* http://www.ben.edu/. **Visit Petersons.com and enter keyword Benedictine**

See page 594 for the College Close-Up.

Blackburn College
Carlinville, Illinois

General Independent Presbyterian, 4-year, coed **Entrance** Moderately difficult **Setting** 80-acre small-town campus **Total enrollment** 607 **Student-faculty ratio** 13:1 **Application deadline** Rolling (freshmen), rolling (transfer) **Freshman admission** 64% were admitted. Average high school GPA 3.4 **Freshman test scores** ACT scores over 18: 83%; ACT scores over 24: 30% **Housing** Yes **Expenses** Tuition & Fees $11,130; Room & Board $4363 **Undergraduates** 59% women, 4% part-time, 4% 25 or older, 0.5% Native American, 2% Hispanic American, 7% African American, 1% Asian American/Pacific Islander **Academic program** Advanced placement, self-designed majors, honors program, summer session, internships **Contact** John Malin, Director of Admission, Blackburn College, 700 College Avenue, Carlinville, IL 62626-1498. *Phone:* 217-854-3231 Ext. 4252 or toll-free 800-233-3550. *E-mail:* admit@mail.blackburn.edu. *Web site:* http://www.blackburn.edu/.

Blessing-Rieman College of Nursing
Quincy, Illinois

General Independent, comprehensive, coed, primarily women **Entrance** Moderately difficult **Setting** 1-acre small-town campus **Total enrollment** 219 **Student-faculty ratio** 12:1 **Application deadline** Rolling (freshmen), rolling (transfer) **Freshman admission** 77% were admitted. Average high school GPA 3.6 **Freshman test scores** ACT scores over 18: 100%; ACT scores over 24: 67% **Housing** Yes **Expenses** Tuition & Fees $22,290; Room & Board $7890 **Undergraduates** 92% women, 6% part-time, 41% 25 or older, 0.5% Native American, 1% Hispanic American, 4% African American, 3% Asian American/Pacific Islander **The most frequently chosen baccalaureate field is** health professions and related sciences **Academic program** Advanced placement, honors program, summer session, adult/continuing education programs, internships **Contact** Ms. Heather Mutter, Admissions Counselor, Blessing-Rieman College of Nursing, Broadway at 11th Street, POB 7005, Quincy, IL 62305-7005. *Phone:* 217-228-5520 Ext. 6979 or toll-free 800-877-9140 Ext. 6964. *Fax:* 217-223-4661. *E-mail:* admissions@brcn.edu. *Web site:* http://www.brcn.edu/.

Bradley University
Peoria, Illinois

General Independent, comprehensive, coed **Entrance** Minimally difficult **Setting** 85-acre suburban campus **Total enrollment** 5,800 **Student-faculty ratio** 13:1 **Application deadline** Rolling (freshmen), 8/1 (transfer) **Freshman admission** 73% were admitted. Average high school GPA 3.59 **Freshman test scores** SAT critical reading scores over 500: 73%; SAT math scores over 500: 80%; ACT scores over 18: 99%; SAT critical reading scores over 600: 29%; SAT math scores over 600: 42%; ACT scores over 24: 64% **Housing** Yes **Expenses** Tuition & Fees $24,224; Room & Board $7650 **Undergraduates** 54% women, 5% part-time, 11% 25 or older, 0.5% Native American, 4% Hispanic American, 8% African American, 4% Asian American/Pacific Islander **The most frequently chosen baccalaureate fields are** business/marketing, engineering, health professions and related sciences **Academic program** Advanced placement, self-designed majors, honors program, summer session, internships **Contact** Rodney San Jose, Director of Admissions, Bradley University, 1501 West Bradley Avenue, Peoria, IL 61625-0002. *Phone:* 309-677-1000 or toll-free 800-447-6460. *Fax:* 309-677-2797. *E-mail:* admissions@bradley.edu. *Web site:* http://www.bradley.edu/. **Visit Petersons.com and enter keywords Bradley University**

Chicago State University
Chicago, Illinois

Contact Ms. Addie Epps, Director of Admissions, Chicago State University, 95th Street at King Drive, ADM 200, Chicago, IL 60628. *Phone:* 773-995-2513. *Fax:* 773-995-3820. *E-mail:* ug-admissions@csu.edu. *Web site:* http://www.csu.edu/.

Christian Life College
Mount Prospect, Illinois

General Independent religious, 4-year, coed **Entrance** Noncompetitive **Setting** 5-acre suburban campus **Total enrollment** 44 **Student-faculty ratio** 10:1 **Application deadline** Rolling (freshmen), rolling (transfer) **Freshman admission** Average high school GPA 3.72 **Housing** Yes **Expenses** Tuition & Fees $10,070; Room only $3700 **Undergraduates** 50% women, 18% part-time, 38% 25 or older, 11% Hispanic American, 9% African American, 11% Asian American/Pacific Islander **The most frequently chosen baccalaureate field is** theology and religious vocations **Academic program** Adult/continuing education programs, internships **Contact** Director of Admissions, Christian Life College, 400 East Gregory Street, Mount Prospect, IL 60056. *Phone:* 847-259-1840. *E-mail:* mail@christianlifecollege.edu. *Web site:* http://www.christianlifecollege.edu/.

Columbia College Chicago
Chicago, Illinois

General Independent, comprehensive, coed **Entrance** Moderately difficult **Setting** urban campus **Total enrollment** 12,127 **Student-faculty ratio** 15:1 **Application deadline** Rolling (freshmen), rolling (transfer) **Freshman admission** 84% were admitted. Average high school GPA 2.95 **Freshman test scores** SAT critical reading scores over 500: 63%; SAT math scores over 500: 48%; ACT scores over 18: 81%; SAT critical reading scores over 600: 19%; SAT math scores over 600: 13%; ACT scores over 24: 31% **Housing** Yes **Expenses** Tuition & Fees $19,850; Room only $10,780 **Undergraduates** 52% women, 10% part-time, 12% 25 or older, 1% Native American, 10% Hispanic American, 16% African American, 3% Asian American/Pacific Islander **The most frequently chosen baccalaureate fields are** communications/journalism, business/marketing, visual and performing arts **Academic program** English as a second language, advanced placement, self-designed majors, honors program, summer session, adult/continuing education programs, internships **Contact** Mr. Murphy Monroe, Executive Director of Admissions, Columbia College Chicago, 600 South Michigan Avenue, Chicago, IL 60605-1996. *Phone:* 312-369-7133. *Fax:* 312-344-8024. *E-mail:* admissions@colum.edu. *Web site:* http://www.colum.edu/.
Visit Petersons.com and enter keyword Columbia

Concordia University Chicago
River Forest, Illinois

General Independent, comprehensive, coed, affiliated with Lutheran Church–Missouri Synod **Entrance** Moderately difficult **Setting** 40-acre suburban campus **Total enrollment** 5,049 **Student-faculty ratio** 17:1 **Application deadline** Rolling (freshmen), rolling (transfer) **Freshman admission** 83% were admitted. Average high school GPA 3.07 **Freshman test scores** ACT scores over 18: 91%; ACT scores over 24: 31% **Housing** Yes **Expenses** Tuition & Fees $24,581; Room & Board $8000 **Undergraduates** 57% women, 7% part-time, 11% 25 or older, 0.2% Native American, 13% Hispanic American, 12% African American, 2% Asian American/Pacific Islander **The most frequently chosen baccalaureate fields are** business/marketing, education, psychology **Academic program** Advanced placement, accelerated degree program, honors program, summer session, adult/continuing education programs, internships **Contact** Ms. Gwen Kanelos, Director of Admission, Concordia University Chicago, 7400 Augusta Street, River Forest, IL 60305. *Phone:* 708-209-3101 or toll-free 800-285-2668. *Fax:* 708-209-3473. *E-mail:* gwen.kanelos@cuchicago.edu. *Web site:* http://www.cuchicago.edu/.

DePaul University
Chicago, Illinois

General Independent Roman Catholic, university, coed **Entrance** Moderately difficult **Setting** 36-acre urban campus **Total enrollment** 25,072 **Student-faculty ratio** 16:1 **Application deadline** 2/1 (freshmen), rolling (transfer) **Freshman admission** 74% were admitted. Average high school GPA 3.36 **Freshman test scores** SAT critical reading scores over 500: 85.2%; SAT math scores over 500: 82%; ACT scores over 18: 98.4%; SAT critical reading scores over 600: 41.9%; SAT math scores over 600: 39.5%; ACT scores over 24: 59% **Housing** Yes **Expenses** Tuition & Fees $27,342; Room & Board $10,617 **Undergraduates** 55% women, 18% part-time, 20% 25 or older **The most frequently chosen baccalaureate fields are** business/marketing, communications/journalism, social sciences **Academic program** English as a second language, advanced placement, accelerated degree program, self-designed majors, honors program, summer session, adult/continuing education programs, internships **Contact** Carlene Klaas-Kennelly, Dean of Undergraduate Admissions, DePaul University, 1 East Jackson Boulevard, Suite 9000, Chicago, IL 60604. *Phone:* 312-362-8300. *E-mail:* admission@depaul.edu. *Web site:* http://www.depaul.edu/.
Visit Petersons.com and enter keyword DePaul

See page 754 for the College Close-Up.

DeVry University
Addison, Illinois

General Proprietary, 4-year, coed **Entrance** Minimally difficult **Setting** 14-acre suburban campus **Total enrollment** 1,508 **Student-faculty ratio** 14:1 **Application deadline** Rolling (freshmen), rolling (transfer) **Housing** No **Expenses** Tuition & Fees $14,080 **Undergraduates** 27% women, 39% part-time, 50% 25 or older, 1% Native American, 14% Hispanic American, 10% African American, 13% Asian American/Pacific Islander **The most frequently chosen baccalaureate fields are** business/marketing, computer and information sciences, engineering technologies **Academic program** Advanced placement, accelerated degree program, summer session, adult/continuing education programs **Contact** Admissions Office, DeVry University, 1221 North Swift Road, Addison, IL 60101-6106. *Phone:* toll-free 800-346-5420. *Web site:* http://www.devry.edu/.

DeVry University
Chicago, Illinois

General Proprietary, 4-year, coed **Entrance** Minimally difficult **Setting** 17-acre urban campus **Total enrollment** 2,075 **Student-faculty ratio** 16:1 **Application deadline** Rolling (freshmen), rolling (transfer) **Housing** No **Expenses** Tuition & Fees $14,080 **Undergraduates** 43% women, 44% part-time, 52% 25 or older, 0.4% Native American, 34% Hispanic American, 34% African American, 6% Asian American/Pacific Islander **The most frequently chosen baccalaureate fields are** business/marketing, computer and information sciences, engineering technologies **Academic program** Advanced placement, accelerated degree program, summer session, adult/continuing education programs **Contact** Admissions Office, DeVry University, 3300 North Campbell Avenue, Chicago, IL 60618-5994. *Web site:* http://www.devry.edu/.

DeVry University
Downers Grove, Illinois

Contact DeVry University, 3005 Highland Parkway, Downers Grove, IL 60515. *Web site:* http://www.devry.edu/.

DeVry University
Elgin, Illinois

Contact DeVry University, Randall Point, 2250 Point Boulevard, Suite 250, Elgin, IL 60123. *Web site:* http://www.devry.edu/.

DeVry University
Gurnee, Illinois

Contact DeVry University, 1075 Tri-State Parkway, Suite 800, Gurnee, IL 60031-9126. *Phone:* toll-free 866-563-3879. *Web site:* http://www.devry.edu/.

DeVry University
Naperville, Illinois

Contact Admissions Office, DeVry University, 2056 Westings Avenue, Suite 40, Naperville, IL 60563-2361. *Phone:* toll-free 877-496-9050. *Web site:* http://www.devry.edu/.

DeVry University
Tinley Park, Illinois

General Proprietary, comprehensive, coed **Entrance** Minimally difficult **Setting** 12-acre suburban campus **Total enrollment** 1,471 **Student-faculty ratio** 19:1 **Application deadline** Rolling (freshmen), rolling (transfer) **Housing** No **Expenses** Tuition & Fees $14,080 **Undergraduates** 34% women, 48% part-time, 54% 25 or older, 0.3% Native American, 9% Hispanic American, 36% African American, 2% Asian American/Pacific Islander **The most frequently chosen baccalaureate fields are** business/marketing, computer and information sciences, engineering technologies **Academic program** Advanced placement, accelerated degree program, summer session, adult/continuing education programs **Contact** Admissions Office, DeVry University, 18624 West Creek Drive, Tinley Park, IL 60477. *Web site:* http://www.devry.edu/.

DeVry University Online
Addison, Illinois

General Proprietary, comprehensive, coed **Total enrollment** 21,830 **Student-faculty ratio** 11:1 **Application deadline** Rolling (freshmen), rolling (transfer) **Expenses** Tuition & Fees $14,560 **Undergraduates** 54% women, 69% part-time, 80% 25 or older, 1% Native American, 8% Hispanic American, 23% African American, 2% Asian American/Pacific Islander **The most frequently chosen baccalaureate fields are** business/marketing, computer and information sciences, engineering **Academic program** Accelerated degree program **Contact** Admissions Office, DeVry University Online, 1221 North Swift Road, Addison, IL 60101-6106. *Web site:* http://www.devry.edu/.

Dominican University
River Forest, Illinois

General Independent Roman Catholic, comprehensive, coed **Entrance** Moderately difficult **Setting** 30-acre suburban campus **Total enrollment** 3,909 **Student-faculty ratio** 12:1 **Application deadline** Rolling (freshmen), rolling (transfer) **Freshman admission** 72% were admitted. Average high school GPA 3.36 **Freshman test scores** SAT critical reading scores over 500: 57%; SAT math scores over 500: 49%; ACT scores over 18: 96%; SAT critical reading scores over 600: 14%; SAT math scores over 600: 22%; ACT scores over 24: 33% **Housing** Yes **Expenses** Tuition & Fees $24,700; Room & Board $7620 **Undergraduates** 69% women, 10% part-time, 19% 25 or older, 0.2% Native American, 26% Hispanic American, 6% African American, 2% Asian American/Pacific Islander **The most frequently chosen baccalaureate fields are** business/marketing, interdisciplinary studies, social sciences **Academic program** English as a second language, advanced placement, accelerated degree program, self-designed majors, honors program, summer session, adult/continuing education programs, internships **Contact** Mr. Glenn Hamilton, Assistant Vice President, Enrollment Management, Dominican University, 7900 West Division Street, River Forest, IL 60305. *Phone:* 708-524-6800 or toll-free 800-828-8475. *Fax:* 708-524-6864. *E-mail:* domadmis@dom.edu. *Web site:* http://www.dom.edu/.

Eastern Illinois University
Charleston, Illinois

General State-supported, comprehensive, coed **Entrance** Moderately difficult **Setting** 320-acre small-town campus **Total enrollment** 11,966 **Student-faculty ratio** 16:1 **Application deadline** Rolling (freshmen), rolling (transfer) **Freshman admission** 68% were admitted. Average high school GPA 3.23 **Freshman test scores** ACT scores over 18: 90%; ACT scores over 24: 26% **Housing** Yes **Expenses** Tuition & Fees: state resident $9540, nonresident $23,880; Room & Board $8078 **Undergraduates** 58% women, 10% part-time, 12% 25 or older, 1% Native American, 3% Hispanic American, 12% African American, 1% Asian American/Pacific Islander **The most frequently chosen baccalaureate fields are** business/marketing, education, English **Academic program** Advanced placement, honors program, summer session, adult/continuing education programs, internships **Contact** Brenda Major, Director of Admissions, Eastern Illinois University, 600 Lincoln Avenue, Charleston, IL 61920-3099. *Phone:* 217-581-2223 or toll-free 800-252-5711. *Fax:* 217-581-7060. *E-mail:* admissions@eiu.edu. *Web site:* http://www.eiu.edu/.

East-West University
Chicago, Illinois

General Independent, 4-year, coed **Entrance** Minimally difficult **Setting** 1-acre urban campus **Total enrollment** 1,170 **Student-faculty ratio** 15:1 **Application deadline** Rolling (freshmen), rolling (transfer) **Freshman admission** 89% were admitted. Average high school GPA 2.67 **Freshman test scores** ACT scores over 18: 39%; ACT scores over 24: 4% **Housing** No **Expenses** Tuition & Fees $15,750 **Undergraduates** 63% women, 2% part-time, 31% 25 or older, 0.3% Native American, 12% Hispanic American, 68% African American, 3% Asian American/Pacific Islander **The most frequently chosen baccalaureate fields are** business/marketing, computer and information sciences, social sciences **Academic program** English as a second language, advanced placement, honors program, summer session, internships **Contact** Mr. Ho Chung, Director of Admissions, East-West University, 816 South Michigan Avenue, Chicago, IL 60605-2103. *Phone:* 312-939-0111 Ext. 1829. *Fax:* 312-939-0083. *E-mail:* ho@eastwest.edu. *Web site:* http://www.eastwest.edu/.

Ellis University
Chicago, Illinois

Contact Ellis University, 111 North Canal Street, Suite 380, Chicago, IL 60606-7204. *Phone:* toll-free 877-355-4762. *Web site:* http://www.ellis.edu/.

Elmhurst College
Elmhurst, Illinois

General Independent, comprehensive, coed, affiliated with United Church of Christ **Entrance** Moderately difficult **Setting** 38-acre suburban campus **Total enrollment** 3,363 **Student-faculty ratio** 14:1 **Application deadline** Rolling (freshmen), rolling (transfer) **Freshman admission** 70% were admitted. Average high school GPA 3.37 **Freshman test scores** SAT critical reading scores over 500: 61%; SAT math scores over 500: 66%; ACT scores over 18: 97%; SAT critical reading scores over 600: 12%; SAT math scores over 600: 26%; ACT scores over 24: 51% **Housing** Yes **Expenses** Tuition & Fees $28,660; Room & Board $8216 **Undergraduates** 62% women, 8% part-time, 13% 25 or older, 1% Native American, 8% Hispanic American, 4% African American, 4% Asian American/Pacific Islander **Academic program** Advanced placement, accelerated degree program, honors program, summer session, adult/continuing education programs, internships **Contact** Mrs. Stephanie Levenson, Director of Admission, Elmhurst College, Elmhurst College Admission Office, 190 South Prospect Avenue, Elmhurst, IL 60126-3296. *Phone:* 630-617-3400 or toll-free 800-697-1871. *Fax:* 630-617-5501. *E-mail:* admit@elmhurst.edu. *Web site:* http://www.elmhurst.edu/. **Visit Petersons.com and enter keyword Elmhurst**

See page 776 for the College Close-Up.

Eureka College
Eureka, Illinois

General Independent, 4-year, coed, affiliated with Christian Church (Disciples of Christ) **Entrance** Moderately difficult **Setting** 112-acre small-town campus **Total enrollment** 672 **Application deadline** 8/1 (freshmen), 8/15 (transfer) **Housing** Yes **Expenses** Tuition & Fees $16,255; Room & Board $7130 **Undergraduates** 16% 25 or older **Academic program** Advanced placement, self-designed majors, honors program, summer session, internships **Contact** Dr. Brian Sajko, Dean of

Admissions and Financial Aid, Eureka College, 300 East College Avenue, Eureka, IL 61530. *Phone:* 309-467-6350 or toll-free 888-4-EUREKA. *Fax:* 309-467-6576. *E-mail:* admissions@eureka.edu. *Web site:* http://www.eureka.edu/.

Governors State University
University Park, Illinois

General State-supported, upper-level, coed **Setting** 750-acre suburban campus **Total enrollment** 5,674 **Student-faculty ratio** 12:1 **Application deadline** Rolling (transfer) **Housing** No **Expenses** Tuition & Fees: state resident $4896, nonresident $14,688 **Undergraduates** 68% women, 63% part-time, 0.4% Native American, 9% Hispanic American, 36% African American, 2% Asian American/Pacific Islander **The most frequently chosen baccalaureate fields are** business/marketing, education, liberal arts/general studies **Academic program** Advanced placement, self-designed majors, honors program, summer session, adult/continuing education programs, internships **Contact** Ms. Sharon Evans, Director of Admissions, Governors State University, One University Parkway, University Park, IL 60466. *Phone:* 708-534-4490. *Fax:* 708-534-1640. *E-mail:* gsunow@govst.edu. *Web site:* http://www.govst.edu/.

Greenville College
Greenville, Illinois

General Independent Free Methodist, comprehensive, coed **Entrance** Moderately difficult **Setting** 12-acre small-town campus **Total enrollment** 1,576 **Student-faculty ratio** 16:1 **Application deadline** 8/1 (freshmen), 8/1 (transfer) **Freshman admission** 78% were admitted. Average high school GPA 3.32 **Freshman test scores** SAT critical reading scores over 500: 47%; SAT math scores over 500: 49%; ACT scores over 18: 88%; SAT critical reading scores over 600: 21%; SAT math scores over 600: 13%; ACT scores over 24: 47% **Housing** Yes **Expenses** Tuition & Fees $20,924; Room & Board $7034 **Undergraduates** 55% women, 4% part-time, 2% 25 or older, 1% Native American, 2% Hispanic American, 8% African American, 1% Asian American/Pacific Islander **The most frequently chosen baccalaureate fields are** business/marketing, education, visual and performing arts **Academic program** Advanced placement, accelerated degree program, self-designed majors, honors program, summer session, adult/continuing education programs, internships **Contact** Ms. Jen McMahon, Senior Admissions Counselor, Greenville College, 315 East College Avenue, Greenville, IL 62246. *Phone:* 618-664-7100 or toll-free 800-345-4440. *Fax:* 618-664-9841. *E-mail:* admissions@greenville.edu. *Web site:* http://www.greenville.edu/.

Harrington College of Design
Chicago, Illinois

General Proprietary, comprehensive, coed, primarily women **Entrance** Noncompetitive **Setting** urban campus **Total enrollment** 1,116 **Student-faculty ratio** 10:1 **Application deadline** Rolling (freshmen) **Housing** Yes **Expenses** Tuition & Fees $18,600 **Undergraduates** 79% women, 58% part-time, 52% 25 or older, 0.2% Native American, 11% Hispanic American, 10% African American, 6% Asian American/Pacific Islander **The most frequently chosen baccalaureate field is** visual and performing arts **Academic program** Internships **Contact** Ms. Rian Hacker, Director of Admissions (HS Team), Harrington College of Design, 200 West Madison, Chicago, IL 60606. *Phone:* 312-697-8022 or toll-free 877-939-4975. *E-mail:* rhacker@harringtoncollege.com. *Web site:* http://www.interiordesign.edu/.

Hebrew Theological College
Skokie, Illinois

General Independent Jewish, 4-year **Entrance** Moderately difficult **Setting** 13-acre suburban campus **Total enrollment** 422 **Application deadline** 8/15 (freshmen) **Housing** Yes **Undergraduates** 2% 25 or older **Academic program** Advanced placement, accelerated degree program, summer session, internships **Contact** Rabbi Berish Cardash, Hebrew Theological College, 7135 North Carpenter Road, Skokie, IL 60077-3263. *Phone:* 847-982-2500. *Web site:* http://www.htc.edu/.

Illinois College
Jacksonville, Illinois

General Independent interdenominational, 4-year, coed **Entrance** Moderately difficult **Setting** 62-acre small-town campus **Total enrollment** 894 **Student-faculty ratio** 11:1 **Application deadline** Rolling (freshmen), 8/1 (transfer) **Freshman admission** 55% were admitted. Average high school GPA 3.39 **Freshman test scores** ACT scores over 18: 95%; ACT scores over 24: 51% **Housing** Yes **Expenses** Tuition & Fees $21,300; Room & Board $7600 **Undergraduates** 3% 25 or older, 1% Native American, 2% Hispanic American, 5% African American, 1% Asian American/Pacific Islander **The most frequently chosen baccalaureate fields are** biological/life sciences, interdisciplinary studies, social sciences **Academic program** Advanced placement, self-designed majors, summer session, internships **Contact** Mr. Rick Bystry, Associate Director of Admission, Illinois College, 1101 West College, Jacksonville, IL 62650. *Phone:* 217-245-3030 or toll-free 866-464-5265. *Fax:* 217-245-3034. *E-mail:* admissions@ic.edu. *Web site:* http://www.ic.edu/.

The Illinois Institute of Art–Chicago
Chicago, Illinois

General Proprietary, 4-year, coed **Setting** urban campus **Contact** Director of Admissions, The Illinois Institute of Art–Chicago, 350 North Orleans Street, Chicago, IL 60654. *Phone:* 312-280-3500 or toll-free 800-351-3450. *Fax:* 312-280-8562. *Web site:* http://www.artinstitutes.edu/chicago.

Visit Petersons.com and enter keywords Illinois Institute of Art-Chicago

See page 862 for the College Close-Up.

The Illinois Institute of Art–Schaumburg
Schaumburg, Illinois

General Proprietary, 4-year, coed **Setting** suburban campus **Contact** Director of Admissions, The Illinois Institute of Art–Schaumburg, 1000 North Plaza Drive, Suite 100, Schaumburg, IL 60173. *Phone:* 847-619-3450 or toll-free 800-314-3450. *Fax:* 847-619-3064. *Web site:* http://www.artinstitutes.edu/schaumburg.

Visit Petersons.com and enter keywords Illinois Institute of Art-Schaumburg

See page 864 for the College Close-Up.

Illinois Institute of Technology
Chicago, Illinois

General Independent, university, coed **Entrance** Very difficult **Setting** 120-acre urban campus **Total enrollment** 7,707 **Student-faculty ratio** 10:1 **Application deadline** Rolling (freshmen), rolling (transfer) **Freshman admission** 60% were admitted. Average high school GPA 3.42 **Freshman test scores** SAT critical reading scores over 500: 86.42%; ACT scores over 18: 100%; SAT critical reading scores over 600: 53.81%; ACT scores over 24: 86.14% **Housing** Yes **Expenses** Tuition & Fees $32,443; Room & Board $10,094 **Undergraduates** 29% women, 7% part-time, 12% 25 or older, 1% Native American, 8% Hispanic American, 5% African American, 13% Asian American/Pacific Islander **The most frequently chosen baccalaureate fields are** architecture, computer and information sciences, engineering **Academic program** English as a second language, advanced placement, summer session, internships **Contact** Mr. Gerald Doyle, Vice Provost, Undergraduate Admissions and Financial Aid, Illinois Institute of Technology,

Illinois Institute of Technology (continued)
Office of Undergraduate Admission, Perlstein 101, 10 West 33rd Street, Chicago, IL 60616. *Phone:* 312-567-3025 or toll-free 800-448-2329. *Fax:* 312-567-6939. *E-mail:* admission@iit.edu. *Web site:* http://www.iit.edu/.

Illinois State University
Normal, Illinois

General State-supported, university, coed **Entrance** Moderately difficult **Setting** 850-acre urban campus **Total enrollment** 21,184 **Student-faculty ratio** 19:1 **Application deadline** 3/1 (freshmen), rolling (transfer) **Freshman admission** 62% were admitted. Average high school GPA 3.4 **Freshman test scores** ACT scores over 18: 98.5%; ACT scores over 24: 58.8% **Housing** Yes **Expenses** Tuition & Fees: state resident $10,471, nonresident $16,561; Room & Board $8093 **Undergraduates** 56% women, 6% part-time, 7% 25 or older, 0.4% Native American, 5% Hispanic American, 6% African American, 2% Asian American/Pacific Islander **The most frequently chosen baccalaureate fields are** business/marketing, education, health professions and related sciences **Academic program** English as a second language, advanced placement, accelerated degree program, self-designed majors, honors program, summer session, adult/continuing education programs, internships **Contact** Ms. Molly Arnold, Director of Admissions, Illinois State University, Campus Box 2200, Normal, IL 61790-2200. *Phone:* 309-438-2478 or toll-free 800-366-2478. *Fax:* 309-438-3932. *E-mail:* admissions@ilstu.edu. *Web site:* http://www.illinoisstate.edu/.

Illinois Wesleyan University
Bloomington, Illinois

General Independent, 4-year, coed **Entrance** Very difficult **Setting** 79-acre suburban campus **Total enrollment** 2,066 **Student-faculty ratio** 11:1 **Application deadline** Rolling (freshmen), 8/15 (transfer) **Freshman admission** 54% were admitted. Average high school GPA 3.91 **Freshman test scores** SAT critical reading scores over 500: 92%; SAT math scores over 500: 96%; ACT scores over 18: 100%; SAT critical reading scores over 600: 64%; SAT math scores over 600: 80%; ACT scores over 24: 92% **Housing** Yes **Expenses** Tuition & Fees $33,982; Room & Board $7776 **Undergraduates** 59% women, 0.4% part-time, 0.4% Native American, 3% Hispanic American, 5% African American, 5% Asian American/Pacific Islander **The most frequently chosen baccalaureate fields are** business/marketing, social sciences, visual and performing arts **Academic program** Advanced placement, self-designed majors, honors program, internships **Contact** Mr. Tony Bankston, Dean of Admissions, Illinois Wesleyan University, PO Box 2900, Bloomington, IL 61702-2900. *Phone:* 309-556-3031 or toll-free 800-332-2498. *Fax:* 309-556-3820. *E-mail:* iwuadmit@iwu.edu. *Web site:* http://www.iwu.edu/.

International Academy of Design & Technology
Chicago, Illinois

General Proprietary, 4-year, coed **Entrance** Minimally difficult **Setting** 1-acre urban campus **Total enrollment** 1,832 **Student-faculty ratio** 27:1 **Application deadline** Rolling (freshmen), rolling (transfer) **Freshman admission** 52% were admitted. Average high school GPA 2.1 **Housing** No **Expenses** Tuition & Fees $15,030 **Undergraduates** 61% women, 19% part-time, 39% 25 or older, 1% Native American, 19% Hispanic American, 42% African American, 4% Asian American/Pacific Islander **Academic program** Advanced placement, summer session, adult/continuing education programs, internships **Contact** Ms. Suzanne Reichart, Director of Student Management, International Academy of Design & Technology, One North State Street, Suite 500, Chicago, IL 60602. *Phone:* 312-980-9200 or toll-free 877-ACADEMY. *Fax:* 312-541-3929. *E-mail:* sreichart@iadtchicago.edu. *Web site:* http://www.iadtchicago.edu/.
Visit Petersons.com and enter keywords International Academy

See page 870 for the College Close-Up.

ITT Technical Institute
Burr Ridge, Illinois

General Proprietary, primarily 2-year, coed **Entrance** Minimally difficult **Housing** No **Contact** Director of Recruitment, ITT Technical Institute, 7040 High Grove Boulevard, Burr Ridge, IL 60527. *Phone:* 630-455-6470 or toll-free 877-488-0001. *Web site:* http://www.itt-tech.edu/.

ITT Technical Institute
Mount Prospect, Illinois

General Proprietary, primarily 2-year, coed **Entrance** Minimally difficult **Setting** suburban campus **Housing** No **Contact** Director of Recruitment, ITT Technical Institute, 1401 Feehanville Drive, Mount Prospect, IL 60056. *Phone:* 847-375-8800. *Web site:* http://www.itt-tech.edu/.

ITT Technical Institute
Orland Park, Illinois

General Proprietary, primarily 2-year, coed **Entrance** Minimally difficult **Setting** suburban campus **Housing** No **Contact** Director of Recruitment, ITT Technical Institute, 11551 184th Place, Orland Park, IL 60467. *Phone:* 708-326-3200. *Web site:* http://www.itt-tech.edu/.

Judson University
Elgin, Illinois

General Independent Baptist, comprehensive, coed **Entrance** Moderately difficult **Setting** 80-acre suburban campus **Total enrollment** 1,231 **Student-faculty ratio** 14:1 **Application deadline** Rolling (freshmen), rolling (transfer) **Freshman admission** 71% were admitted. Average high school GPA 3.2 **Freshman test scores** SAT critical reading scores over 500: 67%; SAT math scores over 500: 84%; ACT scores over 18: 97%; SAT critical reading scores over 600: 29%; SAT math scores over 600: 36%; ACT scores over 24: 37% **Housing** Yes **Expenses** Tuition & Fees $23,500; Room & Board $8200 **Undergraduates** 57% women, 23% part-time, 6% 25 or older **The most frequently chosen baccalaureate fields are** business/marketing, architecture, public administration and social services **Academic program** Advanced placement, accelerated degree program, honors program, internships **Contact** Mr. William W. Dean, Director of Enrollment Management, Judson University, 1151 North State Street, Elgin, IL 60123-1498. *Phone:* 847-695-2522 or toll-free 800-879-5376. *Fax:* 847-628-2526. *E-mail:* bdean@judsonu.edu. *Web site:* http://www.judsonu.edu/.
Visit Petersons.com and enter keyword Judson

Kendall College
Chicago, Illinois

General Independent United Methodist, 4-year, coed **Entrance** Moderately difficult **Setting** urban campus **Total enrollment** 2,389 **Student-faculty ratio** 19:1 **Application deadline** Rolling (freshmen), rolling (transfer) **Freshman admission** 99% were admitted **Housing** Yes **Expenses** Room & Board $13,200 **Undergraduates** 70% women, 41% part-time, 0.4% Native American, 13% Hispanic American, 18% African American, 4% Asian American/Pacific Islander **The most frequently chosen baccalaureate fields are** education, personal and culinary services **Academic program** Accelerated degree program, summer session, internships **Contact** Lisa Marrello, Director of Admissions, Kendall

College, 900 N North Branch Street, Chicago, IL 60642. *Phone:* 312-752-2020 or toll-free 866-667-3344 (in-state); 877-588-8860 (out-of-state). *Fax:* 312-752-2021. *E-mail:* admissions@kendall.edu. *Web site:* http://www.kendall.edu/.
Visit Petersons.com and enter keyword Kendall

See page 890 for the College Close-Up.

Knox College
Galesburg, Illinois

General Independent, 4-year, coed **Entrance** Very difficult **Setting** 82-acre small-town campus **Total enrollment** 1,407 **Student-faculty ratio** 12:1 **Application deadline** 2/1 (freshmen), 4/1 (transfer) **Freshman admission** 74% were admitted. Average high school GPA 3.32 **Freshman test scores** SAT critical reading scores over 500: 96%; SAT math scores over 500: 94%; ACT scores over 18: 100%; SAT critical reading scores over 600: 75%; SAT math scores over 600: 60%; ACT scores over 24: 93% **Housing** Yes **Expenses** Tuition & Fees $31,911; Room & Board $7164 **Undergraduates** 60% women, 2% part-time, 1% 25 or older, 1% Native American, 5% Hispanic American, 5% African American, 7% Asian American/Pacific Islander **The most frequently chosen baccalaureate fields are** English, foreign languages and literature, social sciences **Academic program** Advanced placement, self-designed majors, honors program, internships **Contact** Mr. Paul Steenis, Dean of Admissions, Knox College, 2 East South Street, Box K-148, Galesburg, IL 61401. *Phone:* 309-341-7100 or toll-free 800-678-KNOX. *Fax:* 309-341-7070. *E-mail:* admission@knox.edu. *Web site:* http://www.knox.edu/.

Lake Forest College
Lake Forest, Illinois

General Independent, comprehensive, coed **Entrance** Very difficult **Setting** 107-acre suburban campus **Total enrollment** 1,415 **Student-faculty ratio** 12:1 **Application deadline** Rolling (freshmen), rolling (transfer) **Freshman admission** 69% were admitted. Average high school GPA 3.48 **Housing** Yes **Expenses** Tuition & Fees $34,206; Room & Board $8006 **Undergraduates** 59% women, 1% part-time, 1% 25 or older, 0.4% Native American, 7% Hispanic American, 5% African American, 4% Asian American/Pacific Islander **The most frequently chosen baccalaureate fields are** communications/journalism, business/marketing, social sciences **Academic program** Advanced placement, accelerated degree program, self-designed majors, honors program, summer session, internships **Contact** Mr. William Motzer, Vice President for Admissions and Career Services, Lake Forest College, 555 North Sheridan Road, Lake Forest, IL 60045-2338. *Phone:* 847-735-5000 or toll-free 800-828-4751. *Fax:* 847-735-6271. *E-mail:* admissions@lakeforest.edu. *Web site:* http://www.lakeforest.edu/.

Lakeview College of Nursing
Danville, Illinois

General Independent, upper-level, coed **Entrance** Moderately difficult **Setting** 1-acre small-town campus **Total enrollment** 239 **Student-faculty ratio** 7:1 **Housing** No **Expenses** Tuition & Fees $12,800 **Undergraduates** 81% women, 31% 25 or older, 1% Native American, 2% Hispanic American, 13% African American, 8% Asian American/Pacific Islander **Academic program** Summer session **Contact** Admissions Office, Lakeview College of Nursing, 903 North Logan Avenue, Danville, IL 61832. *Phone:* 217-443-5238. *Fax:* 217-442-2279. *E-mail:* admission@lakeviewcol.edu. *Web site:* http://www.lakeviewcol.edu/.

Lewis University
Romeoville, Illinois

General Independent, comprehensive, coed, affiliated with Roman Catholic Church **Entrance** Moderately difficult **Setting** 375-acre suburban campus **Total enrollment** 5,847 **Student-faculty ratio** 14:1 **Application deadline** 8/1 (freshmen), rolling (transfer) **Freshman admission** 74% were admitted. Average high school GPA 3.19 **Freshman test scores** SAT critical reading scores over 500: 47.37%; SAT math scores over 500: 73.68%; ACT scores over 18: 95.22%; SAT critical reading scores over 600: 5.26%; SAT math scores over 600: 21.05%; ACT scores over 24: 33.76% **Housing** Yes **Expenses** Tuition & Fees $22,990; Room & Board $8350 **Undergraduates** 58% women, 20% part-time, 25% 25 or older, 0.1% Native American, 11% Hispanic American, 9% African American, 4% Asian American/Pacific Islander **The most frequently chosen baccalaureate fields are** business/marketing, health professions and related sciences, security and protective services **Academic program** English as a second language, advanced placement, accelerated degree program, self-designed majors, honors program, summer session, adult/continuing education programs, internships **Contact** Mr. Ryan Cockerill, Director of Freshman Admission, Lewis University, Box 297, One University Parkway, Romeoville, IL 60446. *Phone:* 815-838-0500 Ext. 5237 or toll-free 800-897-9000. *Fax:* 815-836-5002. *E-mail:* admissions@lewisu.edu. *Web site:* http://www.lewisu.edu/.
Visit Petersons.com and enter keywords Lewis University

See page 914 for the College Close-Up.

Lexington College
Chicago, Illinois

General Independent, 4-year, women only **Entrance** Noncompetitive **Setting** urban campus **Total enrollment** 54 **Student-faculty ratio** 6:1 **Application deadline** Rolling (freshmen), rolling (transfer) **Freshman admission** 47% were admitted. Average high school GPA 3.15 **Housing** No **Expenses** Tuition & Fees $23,800 **Undergraduates** 4% part-time, 35% 25 or older, 2% Native American, 28% Hispanic American, 30% African American, 6% Asian American/Pacific Islander **Academic program** Advanced placement, internships **Contact** Mrs. Carmen Larios, Admissions Director, Lexington College, 310 South Peoria Street, Suite 512, Chicago, IL 60607-3534. *Phone:* 312-226-6294 Ext. 226. *Fax:* 312-226-6405. *E-mail:* admissions@lexingtoncollege.edu. *Web site:* http://www.lexingtoncollege.edu/.

Lincoln Christian University
Lincoln, Illinois

General Independent, 4-year, coed, affiliated with Christian Churches and Churches of Christ **Entrance** Moderately difficult **Setting** 227-acre small-town campus **Total enrollment** 643 **Student-faculty ratio** 13:1 **Application deadline** Rolling (freshmen), rolling (transfer) **Freshman admission** 78% were admitted. Average high school GPA 3.3 **Freshman test scores** ACT scores over 18: 86%; ACT scores over 24: 27% **Housing** Yes **Expenses** Tuition & Fees $13,020; Room & Board $5783 **Undergraduates** 49% women, 16% part-time, 23% 25 or older, 0.5% Native American, 3% Hispanic American, 5% African American, 0.3% Asian American/Pacific Islander **The most frequently chosen baccalaureate fields are** business/marketing, theology and religious vocations **Academic program** English as a second language, advanced placement, honors program, summer session, adult/continuing education programs, internships **Contact** Mrs. Mary K. Davis, Assistant Director of Admissions, Lincoln Christian University, 100 Campus View Drive, Lincoln, IL 62656. *Phone:* 217-732-3168 Ext. 2251 or toll-free 888-522-5228. *Fax:* 217-732-4199. *E-mail:* coladmis@lincolnchristian.edu. *Web site:* http://www.lincolnchristian.edu/.

Lincoln College–Normal
Normal, Illinois

General Independent, 4-year, coed **Entrance** Minimally difficult **Setting** 10-acre suburban campus **Total enrollment** 527 **Student-faculty ratio** 14:1 **Application deadline** 9/1 (freshmen), 9/1 (transfer) **Freshman admission** 72% were admitted. Average high school GPA 2.3 **Housing** Yes **Expenses** Tuition & Fees $21,000; Room only $3500 **Under-**

VALUES ARE KEY AT LEWIS UNIVERSITY

At Lewis University we value you as an individual. Lewis engages its students in intellectual growth and social development with an emphasis on values. Lewis offers academic choices, career preparation based on a strong liberal arts foundation, social opportunities and the chance to make lifelong friendships.

Small, interactive classes, nearly 80 undergraduate majors and programs of study, 22 graduate programs, service and internship opportunities, dedicated faculty, an active campus life, a sense of community, and an ideal location all combine to offer you the kind of quality, values-based educational experience that will help you succeed in life.

PRACTICAL. FOCUSED. RELEVANT.

Romeoville (Main Campus)
Chicago | Hickory Hills | Oak Brook
Shorewood | Tinley Park

graduates 52% women, 45% part-time, 39% 25 or older, 0.4% Native American, 2% Hispanic American, 32% African American, 1% Asian American/Pacific Islander **The most frequently chosen baccalaureate fields are** business/marketing, liberal arts/general studies, security and protective services **Academic program** Accelerated degree program, honors program, summer session, adult/continuing education programs, internships **Contact** Mr. Steve Puck, Director of Admissions, Lincoln College–Normal, 715 West Raab Road, Normal, IL 61761. *Phone:* 309-268-4314 or toll-free 800-569-0558. *Fax:* 309-862-3352. *E-mail:* spuck@lincolncollege.edu. *Web site:* http://www.lincolncollege.edu/normal/.

Loyola University Chicago
Chicago, Illinois

General Independent Roman Catholic (Jesuit), university, coed **Entrance** Moderately difficult **Setting** 105-acre urban campus **Total enrollment** 15,879 **Student-faculty ratio** 15:1 **Application deadline** 4/1 (freshmen), 7/1 (transfer) **Freshman admission** 78% were admitted. Average high school GPA 3.7 **Freshman test scores** SAT critical reading scores over 500: 90.1%; SAT math scores over 500: 86.5%; ACT scores over 18: 100%; SAT critical reading scores over 600: 50.3%; SAT math scores over 600: 47.1%; ACT scores over 24: 80.6% **Housing** Yes **Expenses** Tuition & Fees $32,114; Room & Board $11,220 **Undergraduates** 65% women, 7% part-time, 9% 25 or older, 0.2% Native American, 10% Hispanic American, 5% African American, 12% Asian American/Pacific Islander **The most frequently chosen baccalaureate fields are** business/marketing, psychology, social sciences **Academic program** English as a second language, advanced placement, accelerated degree program, honors program, summer session, adult/continuing education programs, internships **Contact** Ms. Lori Greene, Director of Undergraduate Admissions, Loyola University Chicago, 1032 West Sheridan Road, Chicago, IL 60660. *Phone:* 773-508-3079 or toll-free 800-262-2373. *E-mail:* admission@luc.edu. *Web site:* http://www.luc.edu/.
Visit Petersons.com and enter keywords Loyola University

MacMurray College
Jacksonville, Illinois

General Independent United Methodist, 4-year, coed **Entrance** Moderately difficult **Setting** 60-acre small-town campus **Total enrollment** 602 **Student-faculty ratio** 14:1 **Application deadline** Rolling (freshmen), rolling (transfer) **Freshman admission** 60% were admitted. Average high school GPA 2.77 **Freshman test scores** SAT critical reading scores over 500: 14%; ACT scores over 18: 46%; ACT scores over 24: 13% **Housing** Yes **Expenses** Tuition & Fees $18,165; Room & Board $7538 **Undergraduates** 66% women, 10% part-time, 15% 25 or older, 3% Hispanic American, 12% African American, 1% Asian American/Pacific Islander **The most frequently chosen baccalaureate fields are** personal and culinary services, psychology, social sciences **Academic program** Advanced placement, self-designed majors, summer session, internships **Contact** Ms. Alicia Zeone, Senior Admission Counselor, MacMurray College, 447 East College Avenue, Jacksonville, IL 62650. *Phone:* 217-479-7059 or toll-free 800-252-7485. *Fax:* 217-291-0702. *E-mail:* alicia.zeone@mac.edu. *Web site:* http://www.mac.edu/.

McKendree University
Lebanon, Illinois

General Independent, comprehensive, coed, affiliated with United Methodist Church **Entrance** Moderately difficult **Setting** 80-acre small-town campus **Total enrollment** 3,307 **Student-faculty ratio** 13:1 **Application deadline** Rolling (freshmen), rolling (transfer) **Freshman admission** 71% were admitted. Average high school GPA 3.5 **Freshman test scores** SAT critical reading scores over 500: 41.1%; SAT math scores over 500: 70.5%; SAT critical reading scores over 600: 17.6%; SAT math scores over 600: 5.8% **Housing** Yes **Expenses** Tuition & Fees $22,070; Room & Board $7850 **Undergraduates** 34% 25 or older, 1%

Native American, 2% Hispanic American, 13% African American, 1% Asian American/Pacific Islander **The most frequently chosen baccalaureate fields are** business/marketing, education, health professions and related sciences **Academic program** Advanced placement, accelerated degree program, self-designed majors, honors program, summer session, internships **Contact** Chris Hall, Vice President for Admissions and Financial Aid, McKendree University, 701 College Road, Lebanon, IL 62254. *Phone:* 618-537-6833 or toll-free 800-232-7228 Ext. 6831. *Fax:* 618-537-6496. *E-mail:* inquiry@mckendree.edu. *Web site:* http://www.mckendree.edu/.

Midstate College

Peoria, Illinois

General Proprietary, 4-year, coed, primarily women **Entrance** Moderately difficult **Setting** 1-acre urban campus **Total enrollment** 641 **Application deadline** Rolling (freshmen), rolling (transfer) **Housing** No **Expenses** Tuition & Fees $11,985 **Undergraduates** 82% 25 or older **Academic program** Honors program, summer session, internships **Contact** Ms. Jessica Hancock, Director of Admissions, Midstate College, 411 West Northmoor Road, Peoria, IL 61614. *Phone:* 309-692-4092. *Fax:* 309-692-3893. *E-mail:* jhancock2@midstate.edu. *Web site:* http://www.midstate.edu/.

Millikin University

Decatur, Illinois

General Independent, comprehensive, coed, affiliated with Presbyterian Church (U.S.A.) **Entrance** Moderately difficult **Setting** 75-acre suburban campus **Total enrollment** 2,314 **Student-faculty ratio** 11:1 **Application deadline** Rolling (freshmen), rolling (transfer) **Freshman admission** 60% were admitted. Average high school GPA 3.34 **Freshman test scores** SAT critical reading scores over 500: 68%; SAT math scores over 500: 59%; ACT scores over 18: 96%; SAT critical reading scores over 600: 28%; SAT math scores over 600: 19%; ACT scores over 24: 46% **Housing** Yes **Expenses** Tuition & Fees $26,345; Room & Board $7866 **Undergraduates** 60% women, 5% part-time, 13% 25 or older, 0.3% Native American, 3% Hispanic American, 10% African American, 1% Asian American/Pacific Islander **The most frequently chosen baccalaureate fields are** business/marketing, education, visual and performing arts **Academic program** Advanced placement, accelerated degree program, self-designed majors, honors program, summer session, adult/continuing education programs, internships **Contact** Mr. Joe Havis, Assistant Director of Admission, Millikin University, 1184 West Main Street, Decatur, IL 62522-2084. *Phone:* 217-424-6210 or toll-free 800-373-7733. *Fax:* 217-425-4669. *E-mail:* admis@millikin.edu. *Web site:* http://www.millikin.edu/.

Monmouth College

Monmouth, Illinois

General Independent, 4-year, coed, affiliated with Presbyterian Church **Entrance** Moderately difficult **Setting** 80-acre small-town campus **Total enrollment** 1,379 **Student-faculty ratio** 14:1 **Application deadline** Rolling (freshmen), rolling (transfer) **Freshman admission** 70% were admitted. Average high school GPA 3.2 **Freshman test scores** ACT scores over 18: 95%; ACT scores over 24: 36% **Housing** Yes **Expenses** Tuition & Fees $24,950; Room & Board $7300 **Undergraduates** 52% women, 1% part-time, 1% Native American, 5% Hispanic American, 6% African American, 1% Asian American/Pacific Islander **The most frequently chosen baccalaureate fields are** business/marketing, education, English **Academic program** English as a second language, advanced placement, self-designed majors, honors program, internships **Contact** Ms. Christine Johnston, Dean of Admission, Monmouth College, 700 East Broadway, Monmouth, IL 61462-1988. *Phone:* 309-457-2210 or toll-free 800-747-2687. *Fax:* 309-457-2141. *E-mail:* admit@monm.edu. *Web site:* http://www.monm.edu/.

Moody Bible Institute

Chicago, Illinois

General Independent nondenominational, comprehensive, coed **Entrance** Moderately difficult **Setting** 25-acre urban campus **Total enrollment** 3,031 **Student-faculty ratio** 15:1 **Application deadline** 3/1 (freshmen), 3/1 (transfer) **Freshman admission** 75% were admitted. Average high school GPA 3.35 **Housing** Yes **Expenses** Tuition & Fees $1275; Room & Board $8240 **Undergraduates** 44% women, 25% part-time, 0.3% Native American, 3% Hispanic American, 4% African American, 3% Asian American/Pacific Islander **The most frequently chosen baccalaureate fields are** education, communications/journalism, theology and religious vocations **Academic program** English as a second language, advanced placement, summer session, adult/continuing education programs, internships **Contact** Ms. Jacqueline Holman, Admissions Office, Moody Bible Institute, 820 North LaSalle Boulevard, Chicago, IL 60610. *Phone:* 312-329-4307 or toll-free 800-967-4MBI. *Fax:* 312-329-8987. *E-mail:* admissions@moody.edu. *Web site:* http://www.moody.edu/.

National-Louis University

Chicago, Illinois

General Independent, university, coed **Entrance** Minimally difficult **Setting** 12-acre urban campus **Total enrollment** 7,056 **Student-faculty ratio** 9:1 **Application deadline** Rolling (freshmen), rolling (transfer) **Housing** No **Expenses** Tuition & Fees $19,155 **Undergraduates** 77% women, 30% part-time, 91% 25 or older, 0.2% Native American, 15% Hispanic American, 35% African American, 2% Asian American/Pacific Islander **The most frequently chosen baccalaureate fields are** business/marketing, interdisciplinary studies, liberal arts/general studies **Academic program** English as a second language, advanced placement, accelerated degree program, honors program, summer session, adult/continuing education programs, internships **Contact** Dr. Larry Poselli, Vice President of Enrollment and Student Services, National-Louis University, 1000 Capitol Drive, Wheeling, IL 60090. *Phone:* 888-NLU-TODAY or toll-free 888-NLU-TODAY (in-state); 800-443-5522 (out-of-state). *Web site:* http://www.nl.edu/.

North Central College

Naperville, Illinois

General Independent United Methodist, comprehensive, coed **Entrance** Moderately difficult **Setting** 59-acre suburban campus **Total enrollment** 2,798 **Student-faculty ratio** 16:1 **Application deadline** Rolling (freshmen), rolling (transfer) **Freshman admission** 67% were admitted. Average high school GPA 3.5 **Freshman test scores** ACT scores over 18: 98.5%; ACT scores over 24: 57.8% **Housing** Yes **Expenses** Tuition & Fees $26,916; Room & Board $8565 **Undergraduates** 57% women, 7% part-time, 7% 25 or older, 0.2% Native American, 6% Hispanic American, 4% African American, 3% Asian American/Pacific Islander **The most frequently chosen baccalaureate fields are** business/marketing, education, social sciences **Academic program** English as a second language, advanced placement, accelerated degree program, self-designed majors, honors program, summer session, internships **Contact** Ms. Martha Stolze, Director of Freshman Admission, North Central College, 30 North Brainard Street, PO Box 3063, Naperville, IL 60566-7063. *Phone:* 630-637-5800 or toll-free 800-411-1861. *Fax:* 630-637-5819. *E-mail:* admissions@noctrl.edu. *Web site:* http://www.noctrl.edu/.

Visit Petersons.com and enter keywords North Central

Northeastern Illinois University

Chicago, Illinois

General State-supported, comprehensive, coed **Entrance** Minimally difficult **Setting** 67-acre urban campus **Total enrollment** 11,631 **Student-faculty ratio** 15:1 **Application deadline** 7/1 (freshmen), 7/1 (transfer) **Freshman admission** 74% were admitted. Average high school GPA 2.86 **Freshman test scores** ACT scores over 18: 63.9%; ACT scores over

Northeastern Illinois University (continued)
24: 12.1% **Housing** No **Expenses** Tuition & Fees: state resident $8508, nonresident $15,858 **Undergraduates** 58% women, 42% part-time, 38% 25 or older, 0.3% Native American, 30% Hispanic American, 10% African American, 10% Asian American/Pacific Islander **The most frequently chosen baccalaureate fields are** business/marketing, education, social sciences **Academic program** English as a second language, advanced placement, honors program, summer session, adult/continuing education programs, internships **Contact** Ms. Zarrin Kerwell, Admissions Counselor, Northeastern Illinois University, 5500 North St. Louis Avenue, Chicago, IL 60625. *Phone:* 773-442-4026. *Fax:* 773-794-6243. *E-mail:* admrec@neiu.edu. *Web site:* http://www.neiu.edu/.

Northern Illinois University
De Kalb, Illinois

Contact Dr. Robert Burk, Director of Admissions, Northern Illinois University, Office of Admissions, DeKalb, IL 60115-2857. *Phone:* 815-753-0446 or toll-free 800-892-3050. *E-mail:* admission-info@niu.edu. *Web site:* http://www.niu.edu/.

North Park University
Chicago, Illinois

General Independent, comprehensive, coed, affiliated with Evangelical Covenant Church **Entrance** Moderately difficult **Setting** 30-acre urban campus **Total enrollment** 2,181 **Application deadline** Rolling (freshmen), rolling (transfer) **Housing** Yes **Expenses** Tuition & Fees $18,800; Room & Board $7580 **Undergraduates** 62% women, 20% part-time, 22% 25 or older **Academic program** English as a second language, advanced placement, accelerated degree program, self-designed majors, honors program, summer session, adult/continuing education programs, internships **Contact** Office of Admissions, North Park University, 3225 West Foster Avenue, Chicago, IL 60625-4895. *Phone:* 773-244-5500 or toll-free 800-888-NPC8. *Fax:* 773-583-0858. *E-mail:* afao@northpark.edu. *Web site:* http://www.northpark.edu/.

Northwestern University
Evanston, Illinois

General Independent, university, coed **Entrance** Most difficult **Setting** 250-acre suburban campus **Total enrollment** 18,431 **Student-faculty ratio** 7:1 **Application deadline** 1/1 (freshmen), 5/1 (transfer) **Freshman admission** 26% were admitted **Freshman test scores** SAT critical reading scores over 500: 100%; SAT math scores over 500: 99%; ACT scores over 18: 100%; SAT critical reading scores over 600: 95%; SAT math scores over 600: 96%; ACT scores over 24: 97% **Housing** Yes **Expenses** Tuition & Fees $38,461; Room & Board $11,703 **Undergraduates** 52% women, 2% part-time, 1% 25 or older, 0.1% Native American, 7% Hispanic American, 5% African American, 18% Asian American/Pacific Islander **The most frequently chosen baccalaureate fields are** communications/journalism, engineering, social sciences **Academic program** Advanced placement, accelerated degree program, self-designed majors, honors program, summer session, adult/continuing education programs, internships **Contact** Mr. Christopher Watson, Dean of Undergraduate Admission, Northwestern University, PO Box 3060, Evanston, IL 60204-3060. *Phone:* 847-491-7271. *E-mail:* ug-admission@northwestern.edu. *Web site:* http://www.northwestern.edu/.

Olivet Nazarene University
Bourbonnais, Illinois

General Independent, comprehensive, coed, affiliated with Church of the Nazarene **Entrance** Minimally difficult **Setting** 200-acre small-town campus **Total enrollment** 4,636 **Application deadline** Rolling (freshmen), rolling (transfer) **Housing** Yes **Expenses** Tuition & Fees $21,590; Room & Board $6400 **Undergraduates** 20% 25 or older **Academic program** Advanced placement, summer session, adult/continuing education programs, internships **Contact** Susan Wolfe, Director of Admissions, Olivet Nazarene University, One University Avenue, Bourbonnais, IL 60914. *Phone:* 815-939-5203 or toll-free 800-648-1463. *E-mail:* swolfe@olivet.edu. *Web site:* http://www.olivet.edu/.
Visit Petersons.com and enter keyword Olivet

See page 1036 for the College Close-Up.

Principia College
Elsah, Illinois

General Independent Christian Science, 4-year, coed **Entrance** Moderately difficult **Setting** 2,600-acre rural campus **Total enrollment** 542 **Student-faculty ratio** 8:1 **Application deadline** Rolling (freshmen), rolling (transfer) **Freshman admission** Average high school GPA 3.4 **Freshman test scores** SAT critical reading scores over 500: 81.2%; SAT math scores over 500: 72.94%; ACT scores over 18: 92%; SAT critical reading scores over 600: 50.6%; SAT math scores over 600: 32.94%; ACT scores over 24: 62% **Housing** Yes **Expenses** Tuition & Fees $23,625; Room & Board $9000 **Undergraduates** 52% women, 1% part-time, 2% 25 or older, 1% Hispanic American, 1% African American, 1% Asian American/Pacific Islander **The most frequently chosen baccalaureate fields are** social sciences, business/marketing, visual and performing arts **Academic program** English as a second language, advanced placement, accelerated degree program, self-designed majors, honors program, internships **Contact** Mr. Brian McCauley, Dean of Enrollment Management, Principia College, One Maybeck Place, Elsah, IL 62028-9799. *Phone:* 618-374-5180 or toll-free 800-277-4648 Ext. 2802. *Fax:* 618-374-4000. *E-mail:* collegeadmissions@prin.edu. *Web site:* http://www.prin.edu/college/.

Quincy University
Quincy, Illinois

General Independent Roman Catholic, comprehensive, coed **Entrance** Moderately difficult **Setting** 70-acre small-town campus **Total enrollment** 1,845 **Student-faculty ratio** 14:1 **Application deadline** Rolling (freshmen), rolling (transfer) **Freshman admission** 90% were admitted. Average high school GPA 3.19 **Freshman test scores** SAT critical reading scores over 500: 21%; SAT math scores over 500: 48%; ACT scores over 18: 88%; SAT math scores over 600: 16%; ACT scores over 24: 25% **Housing** Yes **Expenses** Tuition & Fees $22,030; Room & Board $8380 **Undergraduates** 56% women, 12% part-time, 9% 25 or older, 0.3% Native American, 4% Hispanic American, 10% African American, 1% Asian American/Pacific Islander **The most frequently chosen baccalaureate fields are** business/marketing, education, health professions and related sciences **Academic program** Advanced placement, accelerated degree program, self-designed majors, honors program, summer session, adult/continuing education programs, internships **Contact** Mrs. Syndi Peck, Director of Admissions, Quincy University, Admissions Office, 1800 College Avenue, Quincy, IL 62301-2699. *Phone:* 217-228-5210 or toll-free 800-688-4295. *E-mail:* admissions@quincy.edu. *Web site:* http://www.quincy.edu/.

Robert Morris University Illinois
Chicago, Illinois

General Independent, comprehensive, coed **Entrance** Minimally difficult **Setting** urban campus **Total enrollment** 4,619 **Student-faculty ratio** 23:1 **Application deadline** Rolling (freshmen), rolling (transfer) **Freshman admission** 81% were admitted. Average high school GPA 2.65 **Freshman test scores** ACT scores over 18: 51.35%; ACT scores over 24: 11.18% **Housing** Yes **Expenses** Tuition & Fees $20,100; Room & Board $9945 **Undergraduates** 62% women, 5% part-time, 32% 25 or older, 0.4% Native American, 23% Hispanic American, 35% African American, 2% Asian American/Pacific Islander **The most frequently chosen baccalaureate fields are** business/marketing, computer and information sciences, visual and performing arts **Academic program**

Advanced placement, accelerated degree program, honors program, summer session, adult/continuing education programs, internships **Contact** Ms. Connie Esparza, Vice President of Marketing, Robert Morris University Illinois, 401 South State Street, Chicago, IL 60605. *Phone:* 312-935-4141 or toll-free 800-RMC-5960. *Fax:* 312-935-4440. *E-mail:* enroll@robertmorris.edu. *Web site:* http://www.robertmorris.edu/.

Rockford College
Rockford, Illinois

General Independent, comprehensive, coed **Entrance** Moderately difficult **Setting** 130-acre suburban campus **Total enrollment** 1,340 **Student-faculty ratio** 9:1 **Application deadline** 8/15 (freshmen), 8/15 (transfer) **Freshman admission** 41% were admitted. Average high school GPA 3.07 **Freshman test scores** ACT scores over 18: 92.13%; ACT scores over 24: 31.46% **Housing** Yes **Expenses** Tuition & Fees $24,750; Room & Board $6950 **Undergraduates** 60% women, 13% part-time, 28% 25 or older, 6% Hispanic American, 8% African American, 2% Asian American/Pacific Islander **The most frequently chosen baccalaureate fields are** business/marketing, education, health professions and related sciences **Academic program** English as a second language, advanced placement, accelerated degree program, honors program, summer session, adult/continuing education programs, internships **Contact** Rebecca Miziniak, Assistant Director of Admission, Rockford College, 5050 East State Street, Rockford, IL 61108-2393. *Phone:* 815-226-4050 or toll-free 800-892-2984. *Fax:* 815-226-2822. *E-mail:* rcadmissions@rockford.edu. *Web site:* http://www.rockford.edu/.

Roosevelt University
Chicago, Illinois

General Independent, comprehensive, coed **Entrance** Moderately difficult **Setting** urban campus **Total enrollment** 7,306 **Application deadline** 8/1 (freshmen), rolling (transfer) **Freshman admission** 50% were admitted. Average high school GPA 3.09 **Freshman test scores** SAT critical reading scores over 500: 87.5%; SAT math scores over 500: 63.5%; ACT scores over 18: 99%; SAT critical reading scores over 600: 50%; SAT math scores over 600: 14.5%; ACT scores over 24: 33% **Housing** Yes **Expenses** Tuition & Fees $23,000; Room & Board $11,200 **Undergraduates** 66% women, 32% part-time, 45% 25 or older, 0.2% Native American, 15% Hispanic American, 21% African American, 5% Asian American/Pacific Islander **The most frequently chosen baccalaureate fields are** business/marketing, psychology, visual and performing arts **Academic program** English as a second language, advanced placement, accelerated degree program, self-designed majors, honors program, summer session, adult/continuing education programs, internships **Contact** Ms. Beth Gierach, Assistant Vice President for Admission, Roosevelt University, 430 South Michigan Avenue, Chicago, IL 60605. *Phone:* 312-341-6733 or toll-free 877-APPLYRU. *Fax:* 312-341-3523. *E-mail:* bgierach@roosevelt.edu. *Web site:* http://www.roosevelt.edu/.
Visit Petersons.com and enter keyword Roosevelt

Rush University
Chicago, Illinois

General Independent, upper-level, coed **Entrance** Moderately difficult **Setting** 35-acre urban campus **Total enrollment** 1,566 **Student-faculty ratio** 8:1 **Application deadline** Rolling (transfer) **First-year students** 37% were admitted **Housing** Yes **Expenses** Tuition & Fees $20,352; Room & Board $9960 **Undergraduates** 87% women, 4% part-time, 60% 25 or older, 7% Hispanic American, 5% African American, 12% Asian American/Pacific Islander **The most frequently chosen baccalaureate field is** health professions and related sciences **Contact** Ms. Hicela Castruita Woods, Director of College Admission Services, Rush University, 600 South Paulina, Chicago, IL 60612-3832. *Phone:* 312-942-7100. *Fax:* 312-942-2219. *E-mail:* hicela_castruita@rush.edu. *Web site:* http://www.rushu.rush.edu/.

Saint Anthony College of Nursing
Rockford, Illinois

Contact Ms. Nancy Sanders, Assistant Dean for Admissions and Student Affairs, Saint Anthony College of Nursing, 5658 East State Street, Rockford, IL 61108-2468. *Phone:* 815-395-5100. *Fax:* 815-395-2275. *E-mail:* info@sacn.edu. *Web site:* http://www.sacn.edu/.
Visit Petersons.com and enter keyword Anthony

St. Augustine College
Chicago, Illinois

General Independent, 4-year, coed **Entrance** Noncompetitive **Setting** 4-acre urban campus **Total enrollment** 1,430 **Student-faculty ratio** 20:1 **Application deadline** Rolling (freshmen), rolling (transfer) **Freshman admission** 60% were admitted **Housing** No **Expenses** Tuition & Fees $8400 **Undergraduates** 75% women, 15% part-time, 69% 25 or older, 0.2% Native American, 85% Hispanic American, 4% African American, 8% Asian American/Pacific Islander **Academic program** English as a second language, summer session, adult/continuing education programs, internships **Contact** Ms. Gloria Quiroz, Director of Admissions, St. Augustine College, 1333-1345 West Argyle, Chicago, IL 60640-3501. *Phone:* 773-878-3256. *Fax:* 773-878-0937. *E-mail:* info@staugustine.edu. *Web site:* http://www.staugustine.edu/.

Saint Francis Medical Center College of Nursing
Peoria, Illinois

General Independent Roman Catholic, upper-level, coed, primarily women **Setting** urban campus **Total enrollment** 499 **First-year students** 67% were admitted **Housing** Yes **Expenses** Tuition & Fees $15,436; Room only $2400 **Undergraduates** 88% women, 22% part-time, 61% 25 or older, 1% Native American, 3% Hispanic American, 7% African American, 2% Asian American/Pacific Islander **The most frequently chosen baccalaureate field is** health professions and related sciences **Academic program** Advanced placement, summer session **Contact** Mrs. Janice Farquharson, Director of Admissions and Registrar, Saint Francis Medical Center College of Nursing, 511 Northeast Greenleaf Street, Peoria, IL 61603-3783. *Phone:* 309-624-8980. *E-mail:* janice.farquharson@osfhealthcare.org. *Web site:* http://www.sfmccon.edu/.

St. John's College
Springfield, Illinois

Contact Admissions Office, St. John's College, 729 East Carpenter Street, Springfield, IL 62702. *Phone:* 217-525-5628. *E-mail:* college@st-johns.org. *Web site:* http://www.st-johns.org/education/schools/nursing/.

Saint Xavier University
Chicago, Illinois

General Independent Roman Catholic, comprehensive, coed **Entrance** Moderately difficult **Setting** 70-acre urban campus **Total enrollment** 5,048 **Student-faculty ratio** 15:1 **Application deadline** Rolling (freshmen), rolling (transfer) **Freshman admission** 87% were admitted. Average high school GPA 3.2 **Freshman test scores** SAT critical reading scores over 500: 77.3%; ACT scores over 18: 93.2%; SAT critical reading scores over 600: 22.8%; ACT scores over 24: 33.6% **Housing** Yes **Expenses** Tuition & Fees $24,340; Room & Board $8408 **Undergraduates** 70% women, 19% part-time, 23% 25 or older, 0.4% Native American, 14% Hispanic American, 17% African American, 3% Asian American/Pacific Islander **The most frequently chosen baccalaureate fields are** business/marketing, education, health professions and related sciences **Academic program** English as a second language, advanced placement, accelerated degree program, self-designed majors, honors program, summer session, adult/continuing education programs, intern-

Saint Xavier University (continued)
ships **Contact** Dr. Kathleen Carlson, Vice President, Saint Xavier University, 3700 West 103rd Street, Chicago, IL 60655-3105. *Phone:* 773-298-3305 or toll-free 800-462-9288. *E-mail:* carlson@sxu.edu. *Web site:* http://www.sxu.edu/.
Visit Petersons.com and enter keyword Xavier

School of the Art Institute of Chicago
Chicago, Illinois

General Independent, comprehensive, coed **Entrance** Very difficult **Setting** 1-acre urban campus **Total enrollment** 3,170 **Student-faculty ratio** 8:1 **Application deadline** 6/1 (freshmen), 8/15 (transfer) **Freshman admission** 81% were admitted **Housing** Yes **Expenses** Tuition & Fees $35,950; Room only $9800 **Undergraduates** 66% women, 9% part-time, 15% 25 or older, 1% Native American, 9% Hispanic American, 4% African American, 12% Asian American/Pacific Islander **The most frequently chosen baccalaureate field is** visual and performing arts **Academic program** English as a second language, advanced placement, self-designed majors, summer session, internships **Contact** Mr. Scott Ramon, Director, Undergraduate Admissions, School of the Art Institute of Chicago, 36 South Wabash, Chicago, IL 60603. *Phone:* 312-629-6100 or toll-free 800-232-SAIC. *Fax:* 312-629-6101. *E-mail:* ugadmiss@saic.edu. *Web site:* http://www.saic.edu/.
Visit Petersons.com and enter keywords Art Institute of Chicago

See page 1144 for the College Close-Up.

Shimer College
Chicago, Illinois

General Independent, 4-year, coed **Entrance** Moderately difficult **Setting** 3-acre urban campus **Total enrollment** 100 **Student-faculty ratio** 8:1 **Application deadline** 7/31 (freshmen), rolling (transfer) **Freshman admission** 90% were admitted. Average high school GPA 3.29 **Freshman test scores** SAT critical reading scores over 500: 100%; SAT math scores over 500: 91%; ACT scores over 18: 100%; SAT critical reading scores over 600: 91%; SAT math scores over 600: 36%; ACT scores over 24: 100% **Housing** Yes **Expenses** Tuition & Fees $25,960; Room & Board $10,415 **Undergraduates** 52% women, 22% part-time, 15% 25 or older, 1% Native American, 3% Hispanic American, 5% African American, 4% Asian American/Pacific Islander **The most frequently chosen baccalaureate fields are** liberal arts/general studies, biological/life sciences, social sciences **Academic program** Self-designed majors, summer session, adult/continuing education programs, internships **Contact** Ms. Elaine Vincent, Director of Admission, Shimer College, 3424 South State Street, Chicago, IL 60616. *Phone:* 312-235-3504 or toll-free 800-215-7173. *E-mail:* e.vincent@shimer.edu. *Web site:* http://www.shimer.edu/.

Southern Illinois University Carbondale
Carbondale, Illinois

General State-supported, university, coed **Entrance** Moderately difficult **Setting** 1,136-acre rural campus **Total enrollment** 20,350 **Student-faculty ratio** 16:1 **Application deadline** Rolling (freshmen), 7/1 (transfer) **Freshman admission** 69% were admitted **Freshman test scores** SAT math scores over 500: 40%; ACT scores over 18: 85%; SAT math scores over 600: 17%; ACT scores over 24: 30% **Housing** Yes **Expenses** Tuition & Fees: state resident $10,411, nonresident $21,346; Room & Board $7673 **Undergraduates** 44% women, 12% part-time, 23% 25 or older, 0.4% Native American, 5% Hispanic American, 19% African American, 2% Asian American/Pacific Islander **The most frequently chosen baccalaureate fields are** business/marketing, education, engineering technologies **Academic program** English as a second language, advanced placement, self-designed majors, honors program, summer session, adult/continuing education programs, internships **Contact** Patsy Reynolds, Director, Undergraduate Admissions, Southern Illinois University Carbondale, Carbondale, IL 62901-4701. *Phone:* 618-536-4405. *Fax:* 618-453-4609. *E-mail:* pradmit@siu.edu. *Web site:* http://www.siuc.edu.

See page 1170 for the College Close-Up.

Southern Illinois University Edwardsville
Edwardsville, Illinois

General State-supported, comprehensive, coed **Entrance** Moderately difficult **Setting** 2,660-acre suburban campus **Total enrollment** 13,940 **Student-faculty ratio** 17:1 **Application deadline** 5/1 (freshmen), 7/24 (transfer) **Freshman admission** 87% were admitted **Freshman test scores** ACT scores over 18: 95.2%; ACT scores over 24: 40.3% **Housing** Yes **Expenses** Tuition & Fees: state resident $8336, nonresident $17,638; Room & Board $7461 **Undergraduates** 54% women, 15% part-time, 16% 25 or older, 0.2% Native American, 2% Hispanic American, 11% African American, 2% Asian American/Pacific Islander **The most frequently chosen baccalaureate fields are** business/marketing, education, health professions and related sciences **Academic program** English as a second language, advanced placement, accelerated degree program, self-designed majors, honors program, summer session, internships **Contact** Mr. Todd Burrell, Director of Admissions, Southern Illinois University Edwardsville, Campus Box 1600, Rendleman Hall, Edwardsville, IL 62026-1600. *Phone:* 618-650-3705 or toll-free 800-447-SIUE. *Fax:* 618-650-5013. *E-mail:* admissions@siue.edu. *Web site:* http://www.siue.edu/.

Telshe Yeshiva–Chicago
Chicago, Illinois

General Independent Jewish, comprehensive, men only **Total enrollment** 77 **Freshman admission** 100% were admitted **Housing** No **Academic program** Summer session **Contact** Rosh Hayeshiva, Telshe Yeshiva–Chicago, 3535 West Foster Avenue, Chicago, IL 60625-5598. *Phone:* 773-463-7738.

Trinity Christian College
Palos Heights, Illinois

General Independent Christian Reformed, 4-year, coed **Entrance** Moderately difficult **Setting** 53-acre suburban campus **Total enrollment** 1,450 **Student-faculty ratio** 12:1 **Application deadline** Rolling (freshmen) **Freshman admission** 86% were admitted. Average high school GPA 3.37 **Freshman test scores** SAT critical reading scores over 500: 76%; SAT math scores over 500: 80%; ACT scores over 18: 78%; SAT critical reading scores over 600: 28%; SAT math scores over 600: 42%; ACT scores over 24: 42% **Housing** Yes **Expenses** Tuition & Fees $21,335; Room & Board $8125 **Undergraduates** 67% women, 25% part-time, 29% 25 or older, 0.3% Native American, 7% Hispanic American, 8% African American, 2% Asian American/Pacific Islander **The most frequently chosen baccalaureate fields are** business/marketing, education, health professions and related sciences **Academic program** Advanced placement, honors program, adult/continuing education programs, internships **Contact** Mr. Jeremy Klyn, Director of Admissions, Trinity Christian College, 6601 West College Drive, Palos Heights, IL 60463. *Phone:* 708-239-4708 or toll-free 800-748-0085. *Fax:* 708-239-4826. *E-mail:* admissions@trnty.edu. *Web site:* http://www.trnty.edu/.

Trinity College of Nursing and Health Sciences
Rock Island, Illinois

Contact Ms. Barbara Kimpe, Admissions Representative, Trinity College of Nursing and Health Sciences, 2122 25th Avenue, Rock Island, IL

61201. *Phone:* 309-779-7812. *E-mail:* kimpeb@trintyqc.com. *Web site:* http://www.trinitycollegeqc.edu/.

Trinity International University

Deerfield, Illinois

General Independent, university, coed, affiliated with Evangelical Free Church of America **Entrance** Moderately difficult **Setting** 108-acre suburban campus **Total enrollment** 2,671 **Student-faculty ratio** 12:1 **Application deadline** Rolling (freshmen), rolling (transfer) **Freshman admission** 63% were admitted. Average high school GPA 3.26 **Freshman test scores** SAT critical reading scores over 500: 46%; SAT math scores over 500: 64%; ACT scores over 18: 92%; SAT critical reading scores over 600: 25%; SAT math scores over 600: 25%; ACT scores over 24: 42% **Housing** Yes **Expenses** Tuition & Fees $21,980; Room & Board $7430 **Undergraduates** 57% women, 13% part-time, 2% 25 or older, 0.3% Native American, 4% Hispanic American, 16% African American, 5% Asian American/Pacific Islander **The most frequently chosen baccalaureate fields are** business/marketing, education, theology and religious vocations **Academic program** Advanced placement, honors program, adult/continuing education programs, internships **Contact** Mr. Aaron Mahl, Director of Undergraduate Admissions, Trinity International University, 2065 Half Day Road, Deerfield, IL 60015-1284. *Phone:* 847-317-7000 or toll-free 800-822-3225. *Fax:* 847-317-8097. *E-mail:* tcadmissions@tiu.edu. *Web site:* http://www.tiu.edu/.

University of Chicago

Chicago, Illinois

General Independent, university, coed **Entrance** Most difficult **Setting** 211-acre urban campus **Total enrollment** 12,332 **Student-faculty ratio** 6:1 **Application deadline** 1/2 (freshmen), 3/1 (transfer) **Freshman admission** 27% were admitted **Freshman test scores** SAT critical reading scores over 500: 100%; SAT math scores over 500: 99%; ACT scores over 18: 100%; SAT critical reading scores over 600: 93%; SAT math scores over 600: 96%; ACT scores over 24: 95% **Housing** Yes **Expenses** Tuition & Fees $39,432; Room & Board $11,697 **Undergraduates** 49% women, 1% part-time, 0.3% Native American, 9% Hispanic American, 6% African American, 15% Asian American/Pacific Islander **The most frequently chosen baccalaureate fields are** biological/life sciences, foreign languages and literature, social sciences **Academic program** Advanced placement, accelerated degree program, self-designed majors, summer session, adult/continuing education programs, internships **Contact** Mr. James G. Nondorf, Vice President, Dean of College Admissions and Financial Aid, University of Chicago, Rosenwald Hall, 1101 East 58th Street, Suite 105, Chicago, IL 60637. *Phone:* 773-702-8650. *Fax:* 773-702-4199. *E-mail:* collegeadmissions@uchicago.edu. *Web site:* http://www.uchicago.edu/.

University of Illinois at Chicago

Chicago, Illinois

General State-supported, university, coed **Entrance** Moderately difficult **Setting** 240-acre urban campus **Total enrollment** 26,840 **Student-faculty ratio** 18:1 **Application deadline** 1/15 (freshmen), 3/31 (transfer) **Freshman admission** 63% were admitted **Freshman test scores** ACT scores over 18: 97.8%; ACT scores over 24: 50.9% **Housing** Yes **Expenses** Tuition & Fees: state resident $12,034, nonresident $24,424; Room & Board $9435 **Undergraduates** 52% women, 7% part-time, 11% 25 or older, 0.2% Native American, 18% Hispanic American, 8% African American, 22% Asian American/Pacific Islander **The most frequently chosen baccalaureate fields are** business/marketing, biological/life sciences, psychology **Academic program** English as a second language, advanced placement, accelerated degree program, self-designed majors, honors program, summer session, internships **Contact** Mr. Thomas Glenn, Executive Director of Admissions, University of Illinois at Chicago, 1100 SSB, m/c 018, Chicago, IL 60607-7128. *Phone:* 312-996-5133. *Fax:* 312-996-2953. *E-mail:* uic.admit@uic.edu. *Web site:* http://www.uic.edu/.

University of Illinois at Springfield

Springfield, Illinois

General State-supported, comprehensive, coed **Entrance** Moderately difficult **Setting** 746-acre suburban campus **Total enrollment** 4,961 **Student-faculty ratio** 13:1 **Application deadline** Rolling (freshmen), rolling (transfer) **Freshman admission** 58% were admitted. Average high school GPA 3.24 **Freshman test scores** ACT scores over 18: 91.6%; ACT scores over 24: 44.4% **Housing** Yes **Expenses** Tuition & Fees: state resident $9532, nonresident $18,682; Room & Board $9200 **Undergraduates** 55% women, 35% part-time, 42% 25 or older, 1% Native American, 3% Hispanic American, 13% African American, 3% Asian American/Pacific Islander **The most frequently chosen baccalaureate fields are** business/marketing, liberal arts/general studies, psychology **Academic program** English as a second language, advanced placement, self-designed majors, honors program, summer session, internships **Contact** Dr. Lori Giordano, Interim Director of Student Services/ Admissions, University of Illinois at Springfield, One University Plaza, Springfield, IL 62703. *Phone:* 217-206-4847 or toll-free 888-977-4847. *E-mail:* admissions@uis.edu. *Web site:* http://www.uis.edu/.

University of Illinois at Urbana–Champaign

Champaign, Illinois

General State-supported, university, coed **Entrance** Very difficult **Setting** 1,470-acre urban campus **Total enrollment** 43,881 **Student-faculty ratio** 16:1 **Application deadline** 1/2 (freshmen), 3/1 (transfer) **Freshman admission** 65% were admitted **Freshman test scores** SAT critical reading scores over 500: 86.9%; SAT math scores over 500: 97.16%; ACT scores over 18: 98.99%; SAT critical reading scores over 600: 51.68%; SAT math scores over 600: 88.53%; ACT scores over 24: 89.13% **Housing** Yes **Expenses** Tuition & Fees: state resident $12,660, nonresident $26,802; Room & Board $9284 **Undergraduates** 46% women, 3% part-time, 2% 25 or older, 0.3% Native American, 7% Hispanic American, 7% African American, 13% Asian American/Pacific Islander **The most frequently chosen baccalaureate fields are** business/marketing, engineering, social sciences **Academic program** English as a second language, advanced placement, accelerated degree program, self-designed majors, honors program, summer session, internships **Contact** Mrs. Stacey Kostell, Director of Admissions, University of Illinois at Urbana–Champaign, 901 West Illinois, Urbana, IL 61801. *Phone:* 217-333-0302. *Fax:* 217-244-4614. *E-mail:* ugradadmissions@uiuc.edu. *Web site:* http://www.illinois.edu/.

University of Phoenix–Chicago Campus

Schaumburg, Illinois

General Proprietary, comprehensive, coed **Entrance** Noncompetitive **Setting** urban campus **Total enrollment** 1,178 **Application deadline** Rolling (freshmen), rolling (transfer) **Housing** No **Expenses** Tuition & Fees $12,225 **Undergraduates** 64% women, 78% 25 or older, 0.3% Native American, 7% Hispanic American, 37% African American, 2% Asian American/Pacific Islander **The most frequently chosen baccalaureate fields are** business/marketing, computer and information sciences, health professions and related sciences **Academic program** Advanced placement, accelerated degree program, adult/continuing education programs **Contact** Ms. Audra McQuarie, Registrar/Executive Director, University of Phoenix–Chicago Campus, 4035 South Riverpoint Parkway, Mail Stop CF-L101, Phoenix, AZ 85040-1958. *Phone:* 480-557-6151 or toll-free 800-776-4867 (in-state); 800-228-7240 (out-of-state). *Fax:* 480-643-3068. *E-mail:* audra.mcquarie@phoenix.edu. *Web site:* http://www.phoenix.edu/.

University of St. Francis

Joliet, Illinois

General Independent Roman Catholic, comprehensive, coed **Entrance** Moderately difficult **Setting** 22-acre suburban campus **Total enrollment**

University of St. Francis (continued)
2,157 **Student-faculty ratio** 12:1 **Application deadline** 8/1 (freshmen) **Freshman admission** 50% were admitted. Average high school GPA 3.3 **Freshman test scores** ACT scores over 18: 98%; ACT scores over 24: 45% **Housing** Yes **Expenses** Tuition & Fees $22,698; Room & Board $7938 **Undergraduates** 67% women, 5% part-time, 16% 25 or older, 0.1% Native American, 12% Hispanic American, 7% African American, 4% Asian American/Pacific Islander **The most frequently chosen baccalaureate fields are** education, business/marketing, health professions and related sciences **Academic program** Advanced placement, accelerated degree program, self-designed majors, honors program, summer session, adult/continuing education programs, internships **Contact** Ms. Julie Marlatt, Director of Undergraduate Admissions, University of St. Francis, 500 North Wilcox Street, Joliet, IL 60435-6188. *Phone:* 800-735-7500 or toll-free 800-735-3500 (in-state); 800-735-7500 (out-of-state). *Fax:* 815-740-5032. *E-mail:* jmarlatt@stfrancis.edu. *Web site:* http://www.stfrancis.edu/.

VanderCook College of Music
Chicago, Illinois

General Independent, comprehensive, coed **Entrance** Moderately difficult **Setting** 1-acre urban campus **Total enrollment** 403 **Student-faculty ratio** 8:1 **Application deadline** Rolling (freshmen), rolling (transfer) **Freshman admission** 98% were admitted. Average high school GPA 3.32 **Freshman test scores** SAT math scores over 500: 83.4%; ACT scores over 18: 88%; SAT math scores over 600: 33.4%; ACT scores over 24: 32% **Housing** Yes **Expenses** Tuition & Fees $22,020; Room & Board $10,094 **Undergraduates** 42% women, 23% part-time, 8% 25 or older, 11% Hispanic American, 14% African American, 4% Asian American/Pacific Islander **The most frequently chosen baccalaureate field is** education **Academic program** Advanced placement, internships **Contact** Ms. Amy Lenting, Director of Admissions, VanderCook College of Music, 3140 South Federal Street, Chicago, IL 60616. *Phone:* 312-225-6288 Ext. 230 or toll-free 800-448-2655. *Fax:* 312-225-5211. *E-mail:* admissions@vandercook.edu. *Web site:* http://www.vandercook.edu/.

Western Illinois University
Macomb, Illinois

General State-supported, comprehensive, coed **Entrance** Moderately difficult **Setting** 1,050-acre small-town campus **Total enrollment** 12,679 **Student-faculty ratio** 16:1 **Application deadline** 5/15 (freshmen), rolling (transfer) **Freshman admission** 64% were admitted. Average high school GPA 3.01 **Freshman test scores** ACT scores over 18: 89%; ACT scores over 24: 23% **Housing** Yes **Expenses** Tuition & Fees: state resident $8958, nonresident $12,347; Room & Board $7642 **Undergraduates** 47% women, 9% part-time, 23% 25 or older, 0.2% Native American, 5% Hispanic American, 9% African American, 1% Asian American/Pacific Islander **The most frequently chosen baccalaureate fields are** business/marketing, liberal arts/general studies, security and protective services **Academic program** English as a second language, advanced placement, self-designed majors, honors program, summer session, adult/continuing education programs, internships **Contact** Mr. Eric Campbell, Director of Admissions, Western Illinois University, 1 University Circle, Macomb, IL 61455-1390. *Phone:* 309-298-3157 or toll-free 877-742-5948. *Fax:* 309-298-3111. *E-mail:* e-campbell@wiu.edu. *Web site:* http://www.wiu.edu/.

West Suburban College of Nursing
Oak Park, Illinois

General Independent, upper-level, coed, primarily women **Entrance** Moderately difficult **Setting** 10-acre suburban campus **Total enrollment** 252 **Student-faculty ratio** 10:1 **Application deadline** 4/1 (transfer) **Housing** No **Expenses** Tuition & Fees $21,536 **Undergraduates** 86% women, 20% part-time, 69% 25 or older, 13% Hispanic American, 10% African American, 24% Asian American/Pacific Islander **The most frequently chosen baccalaureate field is** health professions and related sciences **Academic program** Advanced placement, accelerated degree program, summer session **Contact** Ms. Cynthia Valdez, Director of Enrollment Management, West Suburban College of Nursing, 3 Erie Court, Oak Park, IL 60302. *Phone:* 708-763-6530. *Fax:* 708-763-1531. *Web site:* http://www.wscn.edu/.

Westwood College–Chicago Du Page
Woodridge, Illinois

General Proprietary, 4-year, coed **Total enrollment** 582 **Contact** Director of Admissions, Westwood College–Chicago Du Page, 7155 Janes Avenue, Woodridge, IL 60517. *Phone:* 630-434-8250 or toll-free 888-721-7646. *Fax:* 630-434-8255. *Web site:* http://www.westwood.edu/.

Westwood College–Chicago Loop Campus
Chicago, Illinois

General Proprietary, 4-year, coed **Total enrollment** 885 **Contact** Director of Admissions, Westwood College–Chicago Loop Campus, 17 North State Street, Suite 300, Chicago, IL 60602. *Phone:* 312-739-0890. *Fax:* 312-739-1004. *Web site:* http://www.westwood.edu/.

Westwood College–Chicago O'Hare Airport
Chicago, Illinois

General Proprietary, 4-year, coed **Total enrollment** 888 **Contact** Director of Admissions, Westwood College–Chicago O'Hare Airport, 8501 West Higgins Road, Suite 100, Chicago, IL 60631. *Phone:* 773-380-6801 or toll-free 877-877-8857. *Fax:* 773-714-0828. *Web site:* http://www.westwood.edu/.

Westwood College–Chicago River Oaks
Calumet City, Illinois

General Proprietary, 4-year, coed **Total enrollment** 722 **Contact** Director of Admissions, Westwood College–Chicago River Oaks, 80 River Oaks Drive, Suite D-49, Calumet City, IL 60409. *Phone:* 708-832-9760 or toll-free 888-549-6873. *Fax:* 708-832-9623. *Web site:* http://www.westwood.edu/.

Wheaton College
Wheaton, Illinois

General Independent nondenominational, comprehensive, coed **Entrance** Very difficult **Setting** 80-acre suburban campus **Total enrollment** 2,920 **Student-faculty ratio** 11:1 **Application deadline** 1/10 (freshmen), 3/1 (transfer) **Freshman admission** 71% were admitted. Average high school GPA 3.7 **Freshman test scores** SAT critical reading scores over 500: 98.1%; SAT math scores over 500: 97.9%; ACT scores over 18: 100%; SAT critical reading scores over 600: 76.3%; SAT math scores over 600: 76.6%; ACT scores over 24: 92.2% **Housing** Yes **Expenses** Tuition & Fees $27,580; Room & Board $8050 **Undergraduates** 50% women, 3% part-time, 0.2% Native American, 4% Hispanic American, 4% African American, 8% Asian American/Pacific Islander **The most frequently chosen baccalaureate fields are** social sciences, business/marketing, theology and religious vocations **Academic program** Advanced placement, self-designed majors, summer session, internships **Contact** Ms. Shawn Leftwich, Director of Admissions, Wheaton College, 501 College Avenue, Wheaton, IL 60187-5593. *Phone:* 630-752-5011 or toll-free 800-222-2419. *Fax:* 630-752-5285. *E-mail:* admissions@wheaton.edu. *Web site:* http://www.wheaton.edu/.

Visit Petersons.com and enter keyword Wheaton

See page 1374 for the College Close-Up.

INDIANA

Anderson University

Anderson, Indiana

General Independent, comprehensive, coed, affiliated with Church of God **Entrance** Moderately difficult **Setting** 143-acre suburban campus **Total enrollment** 2,691 **Student-faculty ratio** 12:1 **Application deadline** 7/1 (freshmen), rolling (transfer) **Freshman admission** 60% were admitted. Average high school GPA 3.37 **Freshman test scores** SAT critical reading scores over 500: 60%; SAT math scores over 500: 61%; ACT scores over 18: 91%; SAT critical reading scores over 600: 17%; SAT math scores over 600: 19%; ACT scores over 24: 47% **Housing** Yes **Expenses** Tuition & Fees $23,970; Room & Board $8350 **Undergraduates** 57% women, 10% part-time, 6% 25 or older, 0.3% Native American, 1% Hispanic American, 6% African American, 1% Asian American/Pacific Islander **The most frequently chosen baccalaureate fields are** business/marketing, education, visual and performing arts **Academic program** Advanced placement, accelerated degree program, self-designed majors, honors program, summer session, adult/continuing education programs, internships **Contact** Mr. Jim King, Director of Admissions, Anderson University, 1100 East 5th Street, Anderson, IN 46012-3495. *Phone:* 765-641-4080 or toll-free 800-421-3014 (in-state); 800-428-6414 (out-of-state). *Fax:* 765-641-3851. *E-mail:* info@anderson.edu. *Web site:* http://www.anderson.edu/.

The Art Institute of Indianapolis

Indianapolis, Indiana

General Proprietary, 4-year, coed **Setting** suburban campus **Contact** Director of Admissions, The Art Institute of Indianapolis, 3500 Depauw Boulevard, Suite 1010, Indianapolis, IN 46268. *Phone:* 317-613-4800. *Fax:* 317-613-4808. *Web site:* http://www.artinstitutes.edu/indianapolis/.

Visit Petersons.com and enter keywords Art Institute of Indianapolis

See page 520 for the College Close-Up.

Ball State University

Muncie, Indiana

General State-supported, university, coed **Entrance** Moderately difficult **Setting** 1,035-acre suburban campus **Total enrollment** 21,401 **Student-faculty ratio** 18:1 **Application deadline** 8/15 (freshmen), rolling (transfer) **Freshman admission** 74% were admitted. Average high school GPA 3.28 **Freshman test scores** SAT critical reading scores over 500: 61%; SAT math scores over 500: 63%; ACT scores over 18: 94%; SAT critical reading scores over 600: 17%; SAT math scores over 600: 20%; ACT scores over 24: 29% **Housing** Yes **Expenses** Tuition & Fees: state resident $7830, nonresident $20,398; Room & Board $7932 **Undergraduates** 52% women, 7% part-time, 5% 25 or older, 0.3% Native American, 2% Hispanic American, 7% African American, 1% Asian American/Pacific Islander **The most frequently chosen baccalaureate fields are** business/marketing, education, liberal arts/general studies **Academic program** English as a second language, advanced placement, accelerated degree program, self-designed majors, honors program, summer session, adult/continuing education programs, internships **Contact** Mr. Christopher T. Munchel, Director of Admissions and Orientation, Ball State University, 2000 West University Avenue, Muncie, IN 47306-1099. *Phone:* 765-285-8300 or toll-free 800-482-4BSU. *E-mail:* askus@bsu.edu. *Web site:* http://www.bsu.edu/.

Bethel College

Mishawaka, Indiana

General Independent, comprehensive, coed, affiliated with Missionary Church **Entrance** Minimally difficult **Setting** 80-acre suburban campus **Total enrollment** 2,163 **Student-faculty ratio** 13:1 **Application deadline** 8/15 (freshmen), 8/15 (transfer) **Freshman admission** 78% were admitted. Average high school GPA 3.37 **Freshman test scores** SAT critical reading scores over 500: 59%; SAT math scores over 500: 62%; ACT scores over 18: 89%; SAT critical reading scores over 600: 16%; SAT math scores over 600: 21%; ACT scores over 24: 41% **Housing** Yes **Expenses** Tuition & Fees $20,978; Room & Board $6250 **Undergraduates** 67% women, 23% part-time, 37% 25 or older, 1% Native American, 3% Hispanic American, 13% African American, 1% Asian American/Pacific Islander **The most frequently chosen baccalaureate fields are** business/marketing, health professions and related sciences, liberal arts/general studies **Academic program** Advanced placement, accelerated degree program, self-designed majors, summer session, adult/continuing education programs, internships **Contact** Ms. Krista Wong, Director of Admission, Bethel College, 1001 Bethel Circle, Mishwawaka, IN 46545. *Phone:* 574-807-7600 or toll-free 800-422-4101. *Fax:* 574-807-7650. *E-mail:* admissions@bethelcollege.edu. *Web site:* http://www.bethelcollege.edu.

Brown Mackie College–Fort Wayne

Fort Wayne, Indiana

General Proprietary, primarily 2-year, coed **Contact** Director of Admissions, Brown Mackie College–Fort Wayne, 3000 East Coliseum Boulevard, Fort Wayne, IN 46805. *Phone:* 260-484-4400 or toll-free 866-433-2289. *Fax:* 260-484-2678. *Web site:* http://www.brownmackie.edu/fortwayne.

Visit Petersons.com and enter keywords Brown Mackie College-Fort Wayne

See page 622 for the College Close-Up.

Brown Mackie College–Indianapolis

Indianapolis, Indiana

General Proprietary, primarily 2-year, coed **Contact** Director of Admissions, Brown Mackie College–Indianapolis, 1200 North Meridian Street, Suite 100, Indianapolis, IN 46204. *Phone:* 317-554-8301 or toll-free 866-255-0279. *Fax:* 317-632-4557. *Web site:* http://www.brownmackie.edu/Indianapolis/.

Visit Petersons.com and enter keywords Brown Mackie College-Indianapolis

See page 626 for the College Close-Up.

Brown Mackie College–Merrillville

Merrillville, Indiana

General Proprietary, primarily 2-year, coed **Setting** small-town campus **Contact** Director of Admissions, Brown Mackie College–Merrillville, 1000 East 80th Place, Suite 205S, Merrillville, IN 46410. *Phone:* 219-769-3321 or toll-free 800-258-3321. *Fax:* 219-738-1076. *Web site:* http://www.brownmackie.edu/Merrillville.

Visit Petersons.com and enter keywords Brown Mackie College-Merrillville

See page 630 for the College Close-Up.

Brown Mackie College–Michigan City

Michigan City, Indiana

General Proprietary, primarily 2-year, coed **Setting** rural campus **Contact** Director of Admissions, Brown Mackie College–Michigan City, 325 East US Highway 20, Michigan City, IN 46360. *Phone:* 219-877-3100 or

Brown Mackie College–Michigan City (continued)
toll-free 800-519-2416. *Fax:* 219-877-3110. *Web site:* http://www.brownmackie.edu/MichiganCity.
Visit Petersons.com and enter keywords Brown Mackie College-Michigan City

See page 634 for the College Close-Up.

Brown Mackie College–South Bend
South Bend, Indiana

General Proprietary, primarily 2-year, coed **Setting** urban campus **Contact** Director of Admissions, Brown Mackie College–South Bend, 3454 Douglas Road, South Bend, IN 46635. *Phone:* 574-237-0774 or toll-free 800-743-2447. *Fax:* 574-237-3585. *Web site:* http://www.brownmackie.edu/SouthBend.
Visit Petersons.com and enter keywords Brown Mackie College-South Bend

See page 642 for the College Close-Up.

Butler University
Indianapolis, Indiana

General Independent, comprehensive, coed **Entrance** Moderately difficult **Setting** 290-acre urban campus **Total enrollment** 4,505 **Student-faculty ratio** 11:1 **Application deadline** Rolling (freshmen), 8/15 (transfer) **Freshman admission** 79% were admitted. Average high school GPA 3.75 **Freshman test scores** SAT critical reading scores over 500: 85.2%; SAT math scores over 500: 88.4%; ACT scores over 18: 100%; SAT critical reading scores over 600: 39.1%; SAT math scores over 600: 50.6%; ACT scores over 24: 85.4% **Housing** Yes **Expenses** Tuition & Fees $29,246; Room & Board $9740 **Undergraduates** 60% women, 2% part-time, 2% 25 or older, 0.2% Native American, 2% Hispanic American, 4% African American, 2% Asian American/Pacific Islander **The most frequently chosen baccalaureate fields are** business/marketing, education, health professions and related sciences **Academic program** Advanced placement, self-designed majors, honors program, summer session, adult/continuing education programs, internships **Contact** Mr. Scott Ham, Director of Admissions, Butler University, 4600 Sunset Avenue, Indianapolis, IN 46208-3485. *Phone:* 317-940-8100 or toll-free 888-940-8100. *Fax:* 317-940-8150. *E-mail:* admission@butler.edu. *Web site:* http://www.butler.edu/.
Visit Petersons.com and enter keyword Butler

See page 656 for the College Close-Up.

Calumet College of Saint Joseph
Whiting, Indiana

General Independent Roman Catholic, comprehensive, coed **Entrance** Noncompetitive **Setting** 25-acre urban campus **Total enrollment** 1,292 **Student-faculty ratio** 12:1 **Application deadline** Rolling (freshmen), rolling (transfer) **Freshman admission** 51% were admitted. Average high school GPA 2.49 **Freshman test scores** SAT critical reading scores over 500: 8%; SAT math scores over 500: 19%; ACT scores over 18: 50%; SAT critical reading scores over 600: 1%; SAT math scores over 600: 1%; ACT scores over 24: 3% **Housing** No **Expenses** Tuition & Fees $13,220 **Undergraduates** 48% women, 50% part-time, 70% 25 or older, 0.4% Native American, 25% Hispanic American, 28% African American, 1% Asian American/Pacific Islander **The most frequently chosen baccalaureate fields are** business/marketing, education, law/legal studies **Academic program** Advanced placement, accelerated degree program, summer session, adult/continuing education programs, internships **Contact** Miss Rebecca Leevey, Assistant Director of Admissions, Calumet College of Saint Joseph, 2400 New York Avenue, Whiting, IN 46394. *Phone:* 219-473-4215 Ext. 218 or toll-free 877-700-9100. *Fax:* 219-473-4259. *E-mail:* admissions@ccsj.edu. *Web site:* http://www.ccsj.edu/.

Crossroads Bible College
Indianapolis, Indiana

General Independent Baptist, 4-year, coed **Entrance** Noncompetitive **Setting** 6-acre urban campus **Total enrollment** 228 **Application deadline** 8/8 (freshmen), 8/8 (transfer) **Housing** Yes **Expenses** Tuition & Fees $9850; Room only $3000 **Undergraduates** 68% 25 or older **Academic program** Accelerated degree program, summer session, adult/continuing education programs, internships **Contact** Michael Garrison, Admissions Counselor, Crossroads Bible College, 601 North Shortridge Road, Indianapolis, IN 46219. *Phone:* 317-3528736 Ext. 232 or toll-free 800-273-2224 Ext. 230. *Fax:* 317-352-2441. *E-mail:* admissions@crossroads.edu. *Web site:* http://www.crossroads.edu/.

DePauw University
Greencastle, Indiana

General Independent, 4-year, coed, affiliated with United Methodist Church **Entrance** Moderately difficult **Setting** 655-acre small-town campus **Total enrollment** 2,396 **Student-faculty ratio** 10:1 **Application deadline** 2/1 (freshmen), 3/1 (transfer) **Freshman admission** 66% were admitted. Average high school GPA 3.6 **Freshman test scores** SAT critical reading scores over 500: 85.4%; SAT math scores over 500: 92%; ACT scores over 18: 99.8%; SAT critical reading scores over 600: 45.2%; SAT math scores over 600: 55.5%; ACT scores over 24: 80.5% **Housing** Yes **Expenses** Tuition & Fees $33,250; Room & Board $8740 **Undergraduates** 57% women, 1% part-time, 5% 25 or older, 0.2% Native American, 4% Hispanic American, 6% African American, 3% Asian American/Pacific Islander **The most frequently chosen baccalaureate fields are** communications/journalism, English, social sciences **Academic program** Advanced placement, self-designed majors, honors program, internships **Contact** Brett Kennedy, Senior Associate Director of Admission, DePauw University, 313 South Locust Street, Greencastle, IN 46135. *Phone:* 765-658-4006 or toll-free 800-447-2495. *Fax:* 765-658-4007. *E-mail:* admission@depauw.edu. *Web site:* http://www.depauw.edu/.

DeVry University
Indianapolis, Indiana

General Proprietary, comprehensive, coed **Entrance** Minimally difficult **Total enrollment** 365 **Student-faculty ratio** 18:1 **Application deadline** Rolling (freshmen), rolling (transfer) **Housing** No **Expenses** Tuition & Fees $14,080 **Undergraduates** 44% women, 57% part-time, 81% 25 or older, 2% Hispanic American, 30% African American, 2% Asian American/Pacific Islander **The most frequently chosen baccalaureate fields are** business/marketing, computer and information sciences **Academic program** Advanced placement, accelerated degree program, summer session, adult/continuing education programs **Contact** Admissions Office, DeVry University, 9100 Keystone Crossing, Suite 350, Indianapolis, IN 46240-2158. *Web site:* http://www.devry.edu/.

DeVry University
Merrillville, Indiana

Contact DeVry University, Twin Towers, 1000 East 80th Place, Suite 222 Mall, Merrillville, IN 46410-5673. *Web site:* http://www.devry.edu/.

Earlham College
Richmond, Indiana

General Independent, comprehensive, coed, affiliated with Society of Friends **Entrance** Very difficult **Setting** 800-acre small-town campus **Total enrollment** 1,308 **Student-faculty ratio** 12:1 **Application deadline** 2/15 (freshmen), 4/1 (transfer) **Freshman admission** 75% were admitted. Average high school GPA 3.5 **Freshman test scores** SAT critical reading scores over 500: 87%; SAT math scores over 500: 85%; ACT scores over 18: 96%; SAT critical reading scores over 600: 59%; SAT math scores over 600: 50%; ACT scores over 24: 75% **Housing** Yes **Expenses** Tuition & Fees $36,494; Room & Board $7400 **Undergraduates** 56% women, 1% part-time, 2% 25 or older, 0.3% Native American, 3% Hispanic American, 6% African American, 3% Asian American/Pacific Islander **The most frequently chosen baccalaureate fields are** biological/life sciences, interdisciplinary studies, social sciences **Academic program** English as a second language, advanced placement, accelerated degree program, self-designed majors, internships **Contact** Mr. Jeff Rickey, Dean of Admissions and Financial Aid, Earlham College, 801 National Road West, Richmond, IN 47374. *Phone:* 765-983-1600 or toll-free 800-327-5426. *Fax:* 765-983-1560. *E-mail:* admission@earlham.edu. *Web site:* http://www.earlham.edu/.

Visit Petersons.com and enter keyword Earlham

Franklin College
Franklin, Indiana

General Independent, 4-year, coed, affiliated with American Baptist Churches in the U.S.A. **Entrance** Moderately difficult **Setting** 74-acre small-town campus **Total enrollment** 1,153 **Student-faculty ratio** 12:1 **Application deadline** Rolling (freshmen) **Freshman admission** 67% were admitted. Average high school GPA 3.42 **Freshman test scores** SAT critical reading scores over 500: 50%; SAT math scores over 500: 60%; ACT scores over 18: 91%; SAT critical reading scores over 600: 12%; SAT math scores over 600: 16%; ACT scores over 24: 30% **Housing** Yes **Expenses** Tuition & Fees $23,275; Room & Board $6885 **Undergraduates** 50% women, 12% part-time, 3% 25 or older, 0.2% Native American, 1% Hispanic American, 3% African American, 1% Asian American/Pacific Islander **The most frequently chosen baccalaureate fields are** business/marketing, communications/journalism, education **Academic program** Advanced placement, summer session, internships **Contact** Ms. Jacqueline Acosta, Director of Admissions, Franklin College, 101 Branigin Boulevard, Franklin, IN 46131-2623. *Phone:* 317-738-8062 or toll-free 800-852-0232. *Fax:* 317-738-8274. *E-mail:* jacosta@franklincollege.edu. *Web site:* http://www.franklincollege.edu/.

Visit Petersons.com and enter keyword Franklin

See page 810 for the College Close-Up.

Goshen College
Goshen, Indiana

General Independent Mennonite, comprehensive, coed **Entrance** Moderately difficult **Setting** 135-acre small-town campus **Total enrollment** 1,017 **Student-faculty ratio** 11:1 **Application deadline** 8/15 (freshmen), 8/15 (transfer) **Freshman admission** 68% were admitted. Average high school GPA 3.58 **Freshman test scores** SAT critical reading scores over 500: 63%; SAT math scores over 500: 70%; ACT scores over 18: 95%; SAT critical reading scores over 600: 35%; SAT math scores over 600: 37%; ACT scores over 24: 62% **Housing** Yes **Expenses** Tuition & Fees $23,400; Room & Board $7900 **Undergraduates** 61% women, 7% part-time, 6% 25 or older, 0.2% Native American, 7% Hispanic American, 4% African American, 2% Asian American/Pacific Islander **The most frequently chosen baccalaureate fields are** business/marketing, health professions and related sciences, visual and performing arts **Academic program** Advanced placement, accelerated degree program, self-designed majors, honors program, summer session, internships **Contact** Ms. Lynn Jackson, Vice President for Enrollment Management, Goshen College, 1700 South Main Street, Goshen, IN 46526-4794. *Phone:* 574-535-7535 or toll-free 800-348-7422. *Fax:* 574-535-7609. *E-mail:* lynnj@goshen.edu. *Web site:* http://www.goshen.edu/.

Grace College
Winona Lake, Indiana

General Independent, comprehensive, coed, affiliated with Fellowship of Grace Brethren Churches **Entrance** Moderately difficult **Setting** 160-acre small-town campus **Total enrollment** 1,641 **Student-faculty ratio** 18:1 **Application deadline** 8/1 (freshmen), 8/1 (transfer) **Freshman admission** 97% were admitted. Average high school GPA 3.48 **Freshman test scores** SAT critical reading scores over 500: 62.1%; SAT math scores over 500: 69.2%; ACT scores over 18: 95%; SAT critical reading scores over 600: 24.8%; SAT math scores over 600: 23.3%; ACT scores over 24: 59.5% **Housing** Yes **Expenses** Tuition & Fees $21,100; Room & Board $6880 **Undergraduates** 48% women, 12% part-time, 8% 25 or older, 1% Native American, 2% Hispanic American, 11% African American, 1% Asian American/Pacific Islander **The most frequently chosen baccalaureate fields are** business/marketing, education, psychology **Academic program** Advanced placement, accelerated degree program, honors program, summer session, adult/continuing education programs, internships **Contact** Mrs. Jessica Hauck, Admissions Office, Grace College, 200 Seminary Drive, Winona Lake, IN 46590. *Phone:* 574-372-5100 Ext. 6008 or toll-free 800-54-GRACE Ext. 6412 (in-state); 800-54 GRACE Ext. 6412 (out-of-state). *Fax:* 574-372-5120. *E-mail:* enroll@grace.edu. *Web site:* http://www.grace.edu/.

Hanover College
Hanover, Indiana

General Independent Presbyterian, 4-year, coed **Entrance** Moderately difficult **Setting** 630-acre rural campus **Total enrollment** 938 **Student-faculty ratio** 10:1 **Application deadline** 3/1 (freshmen), rolling (transfer) **Freshman admission** 61% were admitted. Average high school GPA 3.63 **Freshman test scores** SAT critical reading scores over 500: 74%; SAT math scores over 500: 77%; ACT scores over 18: 98%; SAT critical reading scores over 600: 30%; SAT math scores over 600: 34%; ACT scores over 24: 55% **Housing** Yes **Expenses** Tuition & Fees $26,350; Room & Board $7900 **Undergraduates** 54% women, 1% part-time, 1% 25 or older, 0.3% Native American, 2% Hispanic American, 2% African American, 1% Asian American/Pacific Islander **The most frequently chosen baccalaureate fields are** psychology, communications/journalism, social sciences **Academic program** Advanced placement, self-designed majors, internships **Contact** Mr. Christopher Gage, Director of Admission, Hanover College, PO Box 108, Hanover, IN 47243-0108. *Phone:* 812-866-7021 or toll-free 800-213-2178. *Fax:* 812-866-7098. *E-mail:* admission@hanover.edu. *Web site:* http://www.hanover.edu/.

Harrison College
Elkhart, Indiana

General Proprietary, primarily 2-year, coed **Entrance** Moderately difficult **Total enrollment** 192 **Student-faculty ratio** 25:1 **Application deadline** Rolling (freshmen), rolling (transfer) **Contact** Matt Brady, Director of Admissions, Harrison College, 56075 Parkway Avenue, Elkhart, IN 46516. *Phone:* 574-522-0397 or toll-free 888-544-4422. *E-mail:* matt.brady@harrison.edu. *Web site:* http://www.harrison.edu/.

Harrison College
Evansville, Indiana

General Proprietary, primarily 2-year, coed **Entrance** Moderately difficult **Setting** urban campus **Total enrollment** 212 **Student-faculty ratio** 15:1 **Application deadline** Rolling (freshmen), rolling (transfer) **Academic program** Adult/continuing education programs, internships **Contact** Mr. Bryan Barber, Harrison College, 4601 Theater Drive, Evansville, IN 47715. *Phone:* 812-476-6000 or toll-free 888-544-4422. *Fax:* 812-471-8576. *E-mail:* bryan.barber@harrison.edu. *Web site:* http://www.harrison.edu/.

Harrison College
Fort Wayne, Indiana

General Proprietary, primarily 2-year, coed **Entrance** Moderately difficult **Setting** urban campus **Total enrollment** 561 **Student-faculty ratio** 15:1 **Application deadline** Rolling (freshmen), rolling (transfer) **Housing** No **Academic program** Adult/continuing education programs, internships **Contact** Mr. Matt Wallace, Associate Director of Admis-

Harrison College (continued)

sions, Harrison College, 6413 North Clinton Street, Fort Wayne, IN 46825. *Phone:* 260-471-7667 or toll-free 888-544-4422. *Fax:* 260-471-6918. *E-mail:* matt.wallace@harrison.edu. *Web site:* http://www.harrison.edu/.

Harrison College
Indianapolis, Indiana

General Proprietary, primarily 2-year, coed **Entrance** Moderately difficult **Setting** 1-acre urban campus **Total enrollment** 1,889 **Student-faculty ratio** 16:1 **Application deadline** Rolling (freshmen), rolling (transfer) **Housing** No **Academic program** Summer session, adult/continuing education programs, internships **Contact** Mr. Ted Lukomski, Director of Admissions, Harrison College, 550 East Washington Street, Indianapolis, IN 46204. *Phone:* 317-264-5656 or toll-free 888-544-4422. *Fax:* 317-264-5650. *E-mail:* ted.lukomski@ibcschools.edu. *Web site:* http://www.harrison.edu/.

Harrison College
Lafayette, Indiana

General Proprietary, primarily 2-year, coed **Entrance** Moderately difficult **Setting** small-town campus **Total enrollment** 272 **Student-faculty ratio** 15:1 **Application deadline** Rolling (freshmen), rolling (transfer) **Housing** No **Academic program** Adult/continuing education programs, internships **Contact** Ms. Stacy Golleher, Associate Director of Admissions, Harrison College, 4705 Meijer Court, Lafayette, IN 47905. *Phone:* 765-447-9550 or toll-free 888-544-4422. *Fax:* 765-447-0868. *E-mail:* stacy.golleher@harrison.edu. *Web site:* http://www.harrison.edu/.

Harrison College
Muncie, Indiana

General Proprietary, primarily 2-year, coed **Entrance** Moderately difficult **Setting** small-town campus **Total enrollment** 201 **Student-faculty ratio** 16:1 **Application deadline** Rolling (freshmen), rolling (transfer) **Housing** No **Academic program** Adult/continuing education programs **Contact** Mr. Jeremy Linder, Associate Director of Admissions, Harrison College, 411 West Riggin Road, Muncie, IN 47303. *Phone:* 765-288-8681 or toll-free 888-544-4422. *Fax:* 765-288-8797. *E-mail:* Jeremy.linder@harrison.edu. *Web site:* http://www.harrison.edu/.

Harrison College
Terre Haute, Indiana

General Proprietary, primarily 2-year, coed **Entrance** Moderately difficult **Setting** small-town campus **Total enrollment** 257 **Student-faculty ratio** 15:1 **Application deadline** Rolling (freshmen), rolling (transfer) **Academic program** Adult/continuing education programs, internships **Contact** Sarah Stultz, Associate Director of Admissions, Harrison College, 1378 South State Road 46, Terre Haute, IN 47803. *Phone:* 812-877-2100 or toll-free 888-544-4422. *Fax:* 812-877-4440. *E-mail:* sarah.stultz@harrison.edu. *Web site:* http://www.harrison.edu/.

Holy Cross College
Notre Dame, Indiana

Contact Office of Admissions, Holy Cross College, PO Box 308, 54515 State Road 933 North, Notre Dame, IN 46556. *Phone:* 574-239-8400. *Fax:* 574-239-8323. *E-mail:* vduke@hcc-nd.edu. *Web site:* http://www.hcc-nd.edu/.

Huntington University
Huntington, Indiana

General Independent, comprehensive, coed, affiliated with Church of the United Brethren in Christ **Entrance** Moderately difficult **Setting** 170-acre small-town campus **Total enrollment** 1,297 **Student-faculty ratio** 13:1 **Application deadline** 8/1 (freshmen), rolling (transfer) **Freshman admission** 89% were admitted. Average high school GPA 3.39 **Freshman test scores** SAT critical reading scores over 500: 59%; SAT math scores over 500: 60%; ACT scores over 18: 97%; SAT critical reading scores over 600: 20%; SAT math scores over 600: 19%; ACT scores over 24: 48% **Housing** Yes **Expenses** Tuition & Fees $22,330; Room & Board $7430 **Undergraduates** 56% women, 12% part-time, 2% 25 or older, 0.2% Native American, 2% Hispanic American, 1% African American, 0.5% Asian American/Pacific Islander **The most frequently chosen baccalaureate fields are** business/marketing, education, theology and religious vocations **Academic program** Advanced placement, accelerated degree program, summer session, adult/continuing education programs, internships **Contact** Mr. Jeff Berggren, Vice President of Enrollment Management and Marketing, Huntington University, 2303 College Avenue, Huntington, IN 46750-1299. *Phone:* 260-356-6000 Ext. 4016 or toll-free 800-642-6493. *Fax:* 260-356-9448. *E-mail:* jberggren@huntington.edu. *Web site:* http://www.huntington.edu/.

Indiana State University
Terre Haute, Indiana

General State-supported, university, coed **Entrance** Moderately difficult **Setting** 91-acre small-town campus **Total enrollment** 10,534 **Student-faculty ratio** 18:1 **Application deadline** 8/15 (freshmen) **Freshman admission** 68% were admitted. Average high school GPA 3 **Freshman test scores** SAT critical reading scores over 500: 33.2%; SAT math scores over 500: 34%; ACT scores over 18: 64.8%; SAT critical reading scores over 600: 5.7%; SAT math scores over 600: 7.6%; ACT scores over 24: 17.1% **Housing** Yes **Expenses** Tuition & Fees: state resident $7426, nonresident $16,002; Room & Board $7463 **Undergraduates** 51% women, 14% part-time, 23% 25 or older, 0.4% Native American, 2% Hispanic American, 15% African American, 1% Asian American/Pacific Islander **The most frequently chosen baccalaureate fields are** business/marketing, education, social sciences **Academic program** English as a second language, advanced placement, accelerated degree program, honors program, summer session, adult/continuing education programs, internships **Contact** Mr. Richard Toomey, Executive Director of Admissions, Indiana State University, 218 North Sixth Street, Erickson Hall, Terre Haute, IN 47809-9989. *Phone:* 812-237-2121 or toll-free 800-742-0891. *Fax:* 812-237-8023. *E-mail:* admisu@isugw.indstate.edu. *Web site:* http://www.indstate.edu/.

Indiana Tech
Fort Wayne, Indiana

General Independent, comprehensive, coed **Entrance** Moderately difficult **Setting** 42-acre urban campus **Total enrollment** 4,022 **Freshman admission** 74% were admitted **Freshman test scores** SAT critical reading scores over 500: 35%; SAT math scores over 500: 48%; ACT scores over 18: 71%; SAT critical reading scores over 600: 6%; SAT math scores over 600: 14%; ACT scores over 24: 15% **Housing** Yes **Expenses** Tuition & Fees $21,400; Room & Board $8040 **Undergraduates** 56% women, 34% part-time, 64% 25 or older, 1% Native American, 3% Hispanic American, 23% African American, 1% Asian American/Pacific Islander **The most frequently chosen baccalaureate fields are** business/marketing, computer and information sciences, engineering **Academic program** Advanced placement, accelerated degree program, self-designed majors, summer session, adult/continuing education programs, internships **Contact** Ms. Monica Chamberlain, Associate Vice President of Enrollment Management, Indiana Tech, 1600 East Washington Boulevard, Fort Wayne, IN 46803. *Phone:* 260-422-5561 Ext. 2348 or toll-free 800-937-2448 (in-state); 888-666-TECH (out-of-state). *Fax:* 260-422-7696. *E-mail:* admissions@indianatech.edu. *Web site:* http://www.indianatech.edu.

Indiana University Bloomington
Bloomington, Indiana

General State-supported, university, coed **Entrance** Moderately difficult **Setting** 1,933-acre small-town campus **Total enrollment** 42,347

Student-faculty ratio 19:1 **Application deadline** Rolling (freshmen), rolling (transfer) **Freshman admission** 73% were admitted. Average high school GPA 3.6 **Freshman test scores** SAT critical reading scores over 500: 85.2%; SAT math scores over 500: 90%; ACT scores over 18: 98.3%; SAT critical reading scores over 600: 39.8%; SAT math scores over 600: 52.3%; ACT scores over 24: 81.7% **Housing** Yes **Expenses** Tuition & Fees: state resident $8613, nonresident $26,160; Room & Board $7546 **Undergraduates** 50% women, 4% part-time, 3% 25 or older, 0.3% Native American, 3% Hispanic American, 5% African American, 4% Asian American/Pacific Islander **The most frequently chosen baccalaureate fields are** business/marketing, communications/journalism, education **Academic program** English as a second language, advanced placement, accelerated degree program, self-designed majors, honors program, summer session, adult/continuing education programs, internships **Contact** Ms. Mary Ellen Anderson, Director of Admissions, Indiana University Bloomington, 300 North Jordan Avenue, Bloomington, IN 47405-1106. *Phone:* 812-855-0661. *Fax:* 812-855-5102. *E-mail:* iuadmit@indiana.edu. *Web site:* http://www.iub.edu/.

Indiana University East

Richmond, Indiana

General State-supported, comprehensive, coed **Entrance** Moderately difficult **Setting** 182-acre small-town campus **Total enrollment** 2,924 **Student-faculty ratio** 16:1 **Application deadline** Rolling (freshmen), rolling (transfer) **Freshman admission** 74% were admitted. Average high school GPA 2.99 **Freshman test scores** SAT critical reading scores over 500: 30.2%; SAT math scores over 500: 30.6%; ACT scores over 18: 71.1%; SAT critical reading scores over 600: 5.3%; SAT math scores over 600: 4.4%; ACT scores over 24: 16.3% **Housing** No **Expenses** Tuition & Fees: state resident $5801, nonresident $14,957 **Undergraduates** 67% women, 46% part-time, 49% 25 or older, 0.3% Native American, 1% Hispanic American, 4% African American, 1% Asian American/Pacific Islander **The most frequently chosen baccalaureate fields are** business/marketing, health professions and related sciences, liberal arts/general studies **Academic program** Advanced placement, summer session, adult/continuing education programs, internships **Contact** Ms. Molly Vanderpool, Admissions Counselor, Indiana University East, 2325 Chester Boulevard, WZ 116, Richmond, IN 47374-1289. *Phone:* 765-973-8415 or toll-free 800-959-EAST. *Fax:* 765-973-8288. *E-mail:* moberry@iue.edu. *Web site:* http://www.iue.edu/.

Indiana University Kokomo

Kokomo, Indiana

General State-supported, comprehensive, coed **Entrance** Minimally difficult **Setting** 51-acre small-town campus **Total enrollment** 2,992 **Student-faculty ratio** 17:1 **Application deadline** Rolling (freshmen) **Freshman admission** 81% were admitted. Average high school GPA 2.93 **Freshman test scores** SAT critical reading scores over 500: 35.7%; SAT math scores over 500: 38%; ACT scores over 18: 67.4%; SAT critical reading scores over 600: 5.1%; SAT math scores over 600: 8%; ACT scores over 24: 12.7% **Housing** No **Expenses** Tuition & Fees: state resident $5838, nonresident $14,527 **Undergraduates** 65% women, 46% part-time, 43% 25 or older, 0.5% Native American, 2% Hispanic American, 5% African American, 1% Asian American/Pacific Islander **The most frequently chosen baccalaureate fields are** health professions and related sciences, business/marketing, liberal arts/general studies **Academic program** Advanced placement, accelerated degree program, honors program, summer session, adult/continuing education programs, internships **Contact** Ms. Reeta Piirala-Skoglund, Associate Director of Admissions, Indiana University Kokomo, Kelley Student Center, Room 230, 2300 S. Washington Street, Kokomo, IN 46904-9003. *Phone:* 765-455-9217 or toll-free 888-875-4485. *Fax:* 765-455-9537. *E-mail:* iuadmis@iuk.edu. *Web site:* http://www.iuk.edu/.

Indiana University Northwest

Gary, Indiana

General State-supported, comprehensive, coed **Entrance** Minimally difficult **Setting** 38-acre urban campus **Total enrollment** 5,560 **Student-faculty ratio** 16:1 **Application deadline** Rolling (freshmen), rolling (transfer) **Freshman admission** 79% were admitted. Average high school GPA 2.62 **Freshman test scores** SAT critical reading scores over 500: 27.5%; SAT math scores over 500: 26.2%; ACT scores over 18: 60.3%; SAT critical reading scores over 600: 5%; SAT math scores over 600: 4.1%; ACT scores over 24: 14.9% **Housing** No **Expenses** Tuition & Fees: state resident $5919, nonresident $15,024 **Undergraduates** 68% women, 37% part-time, 39% 25 or older, 0.4% Native American, 13% Hispanic American, 21% African American, 2% Asian American/Pacific Islander **The most frequently chosen baccalaureate fields are** health professions and related sciences, business/marketing, liberal arts/general studies **Academic program** Advanced placement, accelerated degree program, self-designed majors, honors program, summer session, adult/continuing education programs, internships **Contact** Dr. Linda B. Templeton, Director of Admissions, Indiana University Northwest, Hawthorn Hall 100, 3400 Broadway, Gary, IN 46408-1197. *Phone:* 219-980-6991 or toll-free 800-968-7486. *Fax:* 219-981-4219. *E-mail:* admit@iun.edu. *Web site:* http://www.iun.edu/.

Indiana University–Purdue University Fort Wayne

Fort Wayne, Indiana

General State-supported, comprehensive, coed **Entrance** Minimally difficult **Setting** 682-acre urban campus **Total enrollment** 13,675 **Student-faculty ratio** 18:1 **Application deadline** 8/1 (freshmen), 8/1 (transfer) **Freshman admission** 96% were admitted. Average high school GPA 3.02 **Freshman test scores** SAT critical reading scores over 500: 40.9%; SAT math scores over 500: 46.4%; ACT scores over 18: 81.7%; SAT critical reading scores over 600: 9.2%; SAT math scores over 600: 11.4%; ACT scores over 24: 28.6% **Housing** Yes **Expenses** Tuition & Fees: state resident $6233, nonresident $14,829; Room only $5620 **Undergraduates** 55% women, 35% part-time, 32% 25 or older, 0.4% Native American, 3% Hispanic American, 7% African American, 2% Asian American/Pacific Islander **The most frequently chosen baccalaureate fields are** business/marketing, education, liberal arts/general studies **Academic program** English as a second language, advanced placement, accelerated degree program, self-designed majors, honors program, summer session, adult/continuing education programs, internships **Contact** Angela Morren, Undergraduate Applications Coordinator, Indiana University–Purdue University Fort Wayne, 2101 East Coliseum Boulevard, Fort Wayne, IN 46805-1499. *Phone:* 260-481-6142 or toll-free 800-324-4739. *Fax:* 260-481-6880. *E-mail:* morrena@ipfw.edu. *Web site:* http://www.ipfw.edu/.

Indiana University–Purdue University Indianapolis

Indianapolis, Indiana

General State-supported, university, coed **Entrance** Moderately difficult **Setting** 509-acre urban campus **Total enrollment** 30,383 **Student-faculty ratio** 16:1 **Application deadline** 6/1 (freshmen), rolling (transfer) **Freshman admission** 67% were admitted. Average high school GPA 3.27 **Freshman test scores** SAT critical reading scores over 500: 48.5%; SAT math scores over 500: 53.6%; ACT scores over 18: 84%; SAT critical reading scores over 600: 12%; SAT math scores over 600: 16.1%; ACT scores over 24: 29.3% **Housing** Yes **Expenses** Tuition & Fees: state resident $7523, nonresident $22,420; Room only $3370 **Undergraduates** 58% women, 29% part-time, 34% 25 or older, 0.2% Native American, 3% Hispanic American, 10% African American, 3% Asian American/Pacific Islander **The most frequently chosen baccalaureate fields are** business/marketing, health professions and related sciences, liberal arts/general studies **Academic program** English as a second language, advanced placement, accelerated degree program, self-designed majors, honors program, summer session, adult/continuing education programs, internships **Contact** Mr. Chris J. Foley, Director of Admissions, Indiana University–Purdue University Indianapolis, Cavanaugh Hall 129, 425

Indiana University–Purdue University Indianapolis (continued)
University Boulevard, Indianapolis, IN 46202-5143. *Phone:* 317-274-4591. *Fax:* 317-278-1862. *E-mail:* apply@iupui.edu. *Web site:* http://www.iupui.edu/.

Indiana University South Bend
South Bend, Indiana

General State-supported, comprehensive, coed **Entrance** Moderately difficult **Setting** 102-acre suburban campus **Total enrollment** 8,394 **Student-faculty ratio** 15:1 **Application deadline** Rolling (freshmen), rolling (transfer) **Freshman admission** 80% were admitted. Average high school GPA 2.84 **Freshman test scores** SAT critical reading scores over 500: 36.2%; SAT math scores over 500: 40.4%; ACT scores over 18: 71.7%; SAT critical reading scores over 600: 6.5%; SAT math scores over 600: 8%; ACT scores over 24: 21.4% **Housing** No **Expenses** Tuition & Fees: state resident $6015, nonresident $15,712 **Undergraduates** 61% women, 42% part-time, 36% 25 or older, 0.4% Native American, 5% Hispanic American, 8% African American, 1% Asian American/Pacific Islander **The most frequently chosen baccalaureate fields are** education, business/marketing, liberal arts/general studies **Academic program** English as a second language, accelerated degree program, honors program, summer session, adult/continuing education programs, internships **Contact** Mr. Michael Renfrow, Associate Director of Admissions, Indiana University South Bend, 1700 Mishawaka Avenue, PO Box 7111, South Bend, IN 46634-7111. *Phone:* 574-520-4839 or toll-free 877-GO-2-IUSB. *Fax:* 574-520-4834. *E-mail:* admissio@iusb.edu. *Web site:* http://www.iusb.edu/.

Indiana University Southeast
New Albany, Indiana

General State-supported, comprehensive, coed **Entrance** Minimally difficult **Setting** 177-acre suburban campus **Total enrollment** 6,840 **Student-faculty ratio** 17:1 **Application deadline** Rolling (freshmen), rolling (transfer) **Freshman admission** 85% were admitted. Average high school GPA 2.95 **Freshman test scores** SAT critical reading scores over 500: 32.7%; SAT math scores over 500: 37.7%; ACT scores over 18: 70.9%; SAT critical reading scores over 600: 6.9%; SAT math scores over 600: 5.1%; ACT scores over 24: 15.6% **Housing** Yes **Expenses** Tuition & Fees: state resident $5890, nonresident $14,578; Room only $5630 **Undergraduates** 60% women, 34% part-time, 34% 25 or older, 0.5% Native American, 2% Hispanic American, 6% African American, 2% Asian American/Pacific Islander **The most frequently chosen baccalaureate fields are** business/marketing, education, liberal arts/general studies **Academic program** Advanced placement, accelerated degree program, self-designed majors, summer session, adult/continuing education programs, internships **Contact** Ms. Anne Skuce, Director of Admissions/Assistant Vice Chancellor for Enrollment Management, Indiana University Southeast, University Center Building, Room 100, 4201 Grant Line Road, New Albany, IN 47150. *Phone:* 812-941-2212 or toll-free 800-852-8835. *Fax:* 812-941-2595. *E-mail:* admissions@ius.edu. *Web site:* http://www.ius.edu/.

Indiana Wesleyan University
Marion, Indiana

General Independent Wesleyan, comprehensive, coed **Entrance** Moderately difficult **Setting** 220-acre small-town campus **Total enrollment** 3,245 **Student-faculty ratio** 15:1 **Application deadline** Rolling (freshmen), rolling (transfer) **Freshman admission** 76% were admitted. Average high school GPA 3.65 **Freshman test scores** SAT critical reading scores over 500: 69%; SAT math scores over 500: 69%; ACT scores over 18: 94%; SAT critical reading scores over 600: 26%; SAT math scores over 600: 26%; ACT scores over 24: 56% **Housing** Yes **Expenses** Tuition & Fees $21,213; Room & Board $7008 **Undergraduates** 63% women, 8% part-time, 3% 25 or older, 0.1% Native American, 2% Hispanic American, 1% African American, 1% Asian American/Pacific Islander **The most frequently chosen baccalaureate fields are** education, business/marketing, health professions and related sciences **Academic program** Advanced placement, accelerated degree program, self-designed majors, honors program, summer session, adult/continuing education programs, internships **Contact** Mr. Daniel Solms, Director of Admissions, Indiana Wesleyan University, 4201 South Washington Street, Marion, IN 46953-4974. *Phone:* 866-468-6498 Ext. 2138 or toll-free 800-332-6901. *Fax:* 765-677-2333. *E-mail:* admissions@indwes.edu. *Web site:* http://www.indwes.edu/.

International Business College
Fort Wayne, Indiana

Contact Admissions Office, International Business College, 5699 Coventry Lane, Fort Wayne, IN 46804. *Phone:* 260-459-4500 or toll-free 800-589-6363. *Web site:* http://www.ibcfortwayne.edu/.

ITT Technical Institute
Fort Wayne, Indiana

General Proprietary, primarily 2-year, coed **Entrance** Minimally difficult **Housing** No **Contact** Director of Recruitment, ITT Technical Institute, 2810 Dupont Commerce Court, Fort Wayne, IN 46825. *Phone:* 260-497-6200 or toll-free 800-866-4488. *Fax:* 260-497-6299. *Web site:* http://www.itt-tech.edu/.

ITT Technical Institute
Indianapolis, Indiana

General Proprietary, primarily 2-year, coed **Entrance** Minimally difficult **Setting** suburban campus **Housing** No **Contact** Director of Recruitment, ITT Technical Institute, 9511 Angola Court, Indianapolis, IN 46268-1119. *Phone:* 317-875-8640 or toll-free 800-937-4488. *Web site:* http://www.itt-tech.edu/.

ITT Technical Institute
Merrillville, Indiana

General Proprietary, primarily 2-year, coed **Contact** Director of Recruitment, ITT Technical Institute, 8488 Georgia Street, Merrillville, IN 46410. *Phone:* 219-738-6100 or toll-free 877-418-8134. *Web site:* http://www.itt-tech.edu/.

ITT Technical Institute
Newburgh, Indiana

General Proprietary, primarily 2-year, coed **Entrance** Minimally difficult **Housing** No **Contact** Director of Recruitment, ITT Technical Institute, 10999 Stahl Road, Newburgh, IN 47630-7430. *Phone:* 812-858-1600 or toll-free 800-832-4488. *Web site:* http://www.itt-tech.edu/.

ITT Technical Institute
South Bend, Indiana

General Proprietary, 4-year, coed **Contact** Director of Recruitment, ITT Technical Institute, 17390 Dugdale Drive, Suite 100, South Bend, IN 46635. *Phone:* 574-247-8300 or toll-free 877-474-1926. *Web site:* http://www.itt-tech.edu/.

Manchester College
North Manchester, Indiana

General Independent, 4-year, coed, affiliated with Church of the Brethren **Entrance** Moderately difficult **Setting** 125-acre small-town campus **Total enrollment** 1,223 **Student-faculty ratio** 16:1 **Application deadline** Rolling (freshmen), rolling (transfer) **Freshman admission** 77% were admitted. Average high school GPA 3.25 **Freshman test scores** SAT critical reading scores over 500: 54%; SAT math scores over 500: 61%; ACT scores over 18: 88%; SAT critical reading scores over 600: 13%; SAT math scores over 600: 19%; ACT scores over 24: 39% **Housing** Yes **Expenses** Tuition & Fees $23,790; Room & Board $8550 **Undergraduates** 51% women, 3% part-time, 2% 25 or older **The most frequently chosen baccalaureate fields are** business/marketing, education, health professions and related sciences **Academic program** Advanced placement, accelerated degree program, self-designed majors, honors program, summer session, adult/continuing education programs, internships **Contact** Mr. Adam Hohman, Assistant Director of Admissions, Manchester College, 604 East College Avenue, North Manchester, IN 46962-1225. *Phone:* 260-982-5055 or toll-free 800-852-3648. *Fax:* 260-982-5239. *E-mail:* admitinfo@manchester.edu. *Web site:* http://www.manchester.edu/.

Visit Petersons.com and enter keywords Manchester College

See page 936 for the College Close-Up.

Marian University
Indianapolis, Indiana

General Independent Roman Catholic, comprehensive, coed **Entrance** Moderately difficult **Setting** 114-acre suburban campus **Total enrollment** 2,287 **Student-faculty ratio** 14:1 **Application deadline** 8/1 (freshmen), 8/1 (transfer) **Freshman admission** 54% were admitted. Average high school GPA 3.24 **Freshman test scores** SAT critical reading scores over 500: 46%; SAT math scores over 500: 52%; ACT scores over 18: 82%; SAT critical reading scores over 600: 10%; SAT math scores over 600: 12%; ACT scores over 24: 12% **Housing** Yes **Expenses** Tuition & Fees $24,960; Room & Board $7810 **Undergraduates** 64% women, 27% part-time, 38% 25 or older, 0.2% Native American, 3% Hispanic American, 18% African American, 1% Asian American/Pacific Islander **The most frequently chosen baccalaureate fields are** business/marketing, education, health professions and related sciences **Academic program** Advanced placement, accelerated degree program, self-designed majors, honors program, summer session, adult/continuing education programs, internships **Contact** Ms. Luann Brames, Director of Enrollment, Marian University, 3200 Cold Spring Road, Indianapolis, IN 46222-1997. *Phone:* 317-955-6300 or toll-free 800-772-7264. *Fax:* 317-955-6401. *E-mail:* admissions@marian.edu. *Web site:* http://www.marian.edu/.

Martin University
Indianapolis, Indiana

General Independent, comprehensive, coed **Entrance** Noncompetitive **Setting** 5-acre urban campus **Total enrollment** 1,236 **Student-faculty ratio** 21:1 **Application deadline** Rolling (freshmen), rolling (transfer) **Freshman admission** 96% were admitted **Housing** No **Expenses** Tuition & Fees $13,520 **Undergraduates** 68% women, 69% part-time, 93% 25 or older, 0.3% Native American, 1% Hispanic American, 93% African American **The most frequently chosen baccalaureate fields are** liberal arts/general studies, business/marketing, psychology **Academic program** Advanced placement, accelerated degree program, self-designed majors, honors program, summer session, adult/continuing education programs, internships **Contact** Ms. Brenda Shaheed, Director of Enrollment Management, Martin University, 2171 Avondale Place, PO Box 18567, Indianapolis, IN 46218-3867. *Phone:* 317-543-3237. *Fax:* 317-543-4790. *E-mail:* bshaheed@martin.edu. *Web site:* http://www.martin.edu/.

Mid-America College of Funeral Service
Jeffersonville, Indiana

Contact Mr. Richard Nelson, Dean of Students, Mid-America College of Funeral Service, 3111 Hamburg Pike, Jeffersonville, IN 47130-9630. *Phone:* 812-288-8878 or toll-free 800-221-6158. *Fax:* 812-288-5942. *E-mail:* macfs@mindspring.com. *Web site:* http://www.mid-america.edu/.

Oakland City University
Oakland City, Indiana

General Independent General Baptist, comprehensive, coed **Entrance** Minimally difficult **Setting** 20-acre rural campus **Total enrollment** 2,550 **Student-faculty ratio** 14:1 **Application deadline** Rolling (freshmen), rolling (transfer) **Freshman admission** 44% were admitted. Average high school GPA 3.15 **Freshman test scores** SAT critical reading scores over 500: 32%; SAT math scores over 500: 38%; ACT scores over 18: 72%; SAT critical reading scores over 600: 7%; SAT math scores over 600: 7%; ACT scores over 24: 19% **Housing** Yes **Expenses** Tuition & Fees $16,000; Room & Board $6700 **Undergraduates** 55% women, 48% part-time, 59% 25 or older, 0.4% Native American, 2% Hispanic American, 12% African American, 0.4% Asian American/Pacific Islander **Academic program** Advanced placement, accelerated degree program, summer session, adult/continuing education programs **Contact** Ms. Kim Heldt, Director of Admissions, Oakland City University, 138 North Lucretia Street, Oakland City, IN 47660. *Phone:* 812-749-1222 or toll-free 800-737-5125. *Web site:* http://www.oak.edu/.

Purdue University
West Lafayette, Indiana

General State-supported, university, coed **Entrance** Moderately difficult **Setting** 2,552-acre suburban campus **Total enrollment** 39,697 **Student-faculty ratio** 14:1 **Application deadline** 3/1 (freshmen), rolling (transfer) **Freshman admission** 73% were admitted. Average high school GPA 3.5 **Freshman test scores** SAT critical reading scores over 500: 76%; SAT math scores over 500: 89%; ACT scores over 18: 99%; SAT critical reading scores over 600: 31%; SAT math scores over 600: 56%; ACT scores over 24: 72% **Housing** Yes **Expenses** Tuition & Fees: state resident $8638, nonresident $25,118; Room & Board $8710 **Undergraduates** 42% women, 5% part-time, 4% 25 or older, 0.5% Native American, 3% Hispanic American, 3% African American, 5% Asian American/Pacific Islander **The most frequently chosen baccalaureate fields are** business/marketing, engineering, engineering technologies **Academic program** English as a second language, advanced placement, accelerated degree program, honors program, summer session, adult/continuing education programs, internships **Contact** Ms. Pamela T. Horne, Assistant Vice President for Enrollment Management and Dean of Admissions, Purdue University, 475 Stadium Mall Drive, Schleman Hall, West Lafayette, IN 47907-2050. *Phone:* 765-494-1776. *Fax:* 765-494-0544. *E-mail:* admissions@purdue.edu. *Web site:* http://www.purdue.edu/.

Purdue University Calumet
Hammond, Indiana

General State-supported, comprehensive, coed **Entrance** Moderately difficult **Setting** 167-acre urban campus **Total enrollment** 10,133 **Student-faculty ratio** 21:1 **Application deadline** Rolling (freshmen), rolling (transfer) **Freshman admission** 69% were admitted. Average high school GPA 2.58 **Freshman test scores** SAT critical reading scores over 500: 35.1%; SAT math scores over 500: 40.1%; ACT scores over 18: 80.24%; SAT critical reading scores over 600: 5.1%; SAT math scores over 600: 8.1%; ACT scores over 24: 23.26% **Housing** Yes **Expenses** Tuition & Fees: state resident $6337, nonresident $13,624; Room & Board $6653 **Undergraduates** 55% women, 35% part-time, 34% 25 or older, 0.4% Native American, 15% Hispanic American, 19% African American, 1% Asian American/Pacific Islander **Academic program** English as a second language, advanced placement, accelerated degree program, honors program, summer session, adult/continuing education programs, internships **Contact** Mr. Paul McGuinness, Director of Admissions, Purdue University Calumet, 2200 169th Street, Hammond, IN 46323-2094. *Phone:* 219-989-2213 or toll-free 800-447-8738. *E-mail:* mcguinn@calumet.purdue.edu. *Web site:* http://www.calumet.purdue.edu/.

Purdue University North Central
Westville, Indiana

General State-supported, comprehensive, coed **Entrance** Minimally difficult **Setting** 305-acre rural campus **Total enrollment** 4,463 **Student-faculty ratio** 18:1 **Application deadline** 8/15 (freshmen), 8/15 (transfer) **Freshman admission** 86% were admitted. Average high school GPA 2.75 **Freshman test scores** SAT critical reading scores over 500: 36.4%; SAT math scores over 500: 40.22%; ACT scores over 18: 75.54%; SAT critical reading scores over 600: 6.29%; SAT math scores over 600: 8.76%; ACT scores over 24: 19.15% **Housing** No **Expenses** Tuition & Fees: state resident $6704, nonresident $15,960 **Undergraduates** 57% women, 37% part-time, 38% 25 or older, 1% Native American, 5% Hispanic American, 7% African American, 1% Asian American/Pacific Islander **The most frequently chosen baccalaureate fields are** business/marketing, education, liberal arts/general studies **Academic program** Advanced placement, summer session, internships **Contact** Mr. Anthony Cardenas, Assistant Dean of Enrollment and Outreach Recruitment, Purdue University North Central, 1401 South U.S. Highway 421, Westville, IN 46391. *Phone:* 219-785-5283 or toll-free 800-872-1231. *Fax:* 219-785-5538. *E-mail:* acardenas@pnc.edu. *Web site:* http://www.pnc.edu/.

Rose-Hulman Institute of Technology
Terre Haute, Indiana

General Independent, comprehensive, coed, primarily men **Entrance** Very difficult **Setting** 200-acre suburban campus **Total enrollment** 1,964 **Student-faculty ratio** 12:1 **Application deadline** 3/1 (freshmen) **Freshman admission** 70% were admitted **Freshman test scores** SAT critical reading scores over 500: 92.2%; SAT math scores over 500: 100%; ACT scores over 18: 100%; SAT critical reading scores over 600: 54.8%; SAT math scores over 600: 89.7%; ACT scores over 24: 91.6% **Housing** Yes **Expenses** Tuition & Fees $34,560; Room & Board $9441 **Undergraduates** 20% women, 0.5% part-time, 1% 25 or older, 0.3% Native American, 2% Hispanic American, 3% African American, 5% Asian American/Pacific Islander **The most frequently chosen baccalaureate fields are** computer and information sciences, engineering, mathematics **Academic program** Advanced placement, accelerated degree program, summer session, adult/continuing education programs, internships **Contact** Mr. James Goecker, Vice President for Enrollment Management, Rose-Hulman Institute of Technology, 5500 Wabash Avenue, CM 1, Terre Haute, IN 47803-3920. *Phone:* 812-877-8894 or toll-free 800-248-7448. *Fax:* 812-877-8941. *E-mail:* admissions@rose-hulman.edu. *Web site:* http://www.rose-hulman.edu/.

Saint Joseph's College
Rensselaer, Indiana

General Independent Roman Catholic, comprehensive, coed **Entrance** Moderately difficult **Setting** 180-acre small-town campus **Total enrollment** 1,076 **Student-faculty ratio** 15:1 **Application deadline** Rolling (freshmen), rolling (transfer) **Freshman admission** 74% were admitted. Average high school GPA 3.00 **Freshman test scores** SAT critical reading scores over 500: 38%; SAT math scores over 500: 43.5%; ACT scores over 18: 86%; SAT critical reading scores over 600: 5%; SAT math scores over 600: 11%; ACT scores over 24: 27% **Housing** Yes **Expenses** Tuition & Fees $24,530; Room & Board $7420 **Undergraduates** 57% women, 5% part-time, 14% 25 or older, 0.1% Native American, 4% Hispanic American, 8% African American, 1% Asian American/Pacific Islander **The most frequently chosen baccalaureate fields are** business/marketing, education, health professions and related sciences **Academic program** Advanced placement, accelerated degree program, self-designed majors, honors program, summer session, internships **Contact** Ms. Karen Raftus, Director of Admissions, Saint Joseph's College, PO Box 815, Rensselaer, IN 47978-0850. *Phone:* 219-866-6170 or toll-free 800-447-8781. *Fax:* 219-866-6122. *E-mail:* admissions@saintjoe.edu. *Web site:* http://www.saintjoe.edu/.

Saint Mary-of-the-Woods College
Saint Mary-of-the-Woods, Indiana

General Independent Roman Catholic, comprehensive, coed, primarily women **Entrance** Moderately difficult **Setting** 67-acre rural campus **Total enrollment** 1,677 **Student-faculty ratio** 8:1 **Application deadline** 8/1 (freshmen), 8/1 (transfer) **Freshman admission** 67% were admitted. Average high school GPA 3.2 **Freshman test scores** SAT critical reading scores over 500: 56%; SAT math scores over 500: 32%; ACT scores over 18: 84%; SAT critical reading scores over 600: 11%; SAT math scores over 600: 6%; ACT scores over 24: 49% **Housing** Yes **Expenses** Tuition & Fees $23,060; Room & Board $8450 **Undergraduates** 95% women, 60% part-time, 78% 25 or older, 1% Native American, 1% Hispanic American, 3% African American, 1% Asian American/Pacific Islander **Academic program** Advanced placement, accelerated degree program, self-designed majors, honors program, summer session, adult/continuing education programs, internships **Contact** Mr. Aaron Kelley, Director of Admission, Saint Mary-of-the-Woods College, Rooney Library, SMWC, Saint Mary-of-the-Woods, IN 47876. *Phone:* 812-535-5107 or toll-free 800-926-SMWC. *Fax:* 812-535-5010. *E-mail:* smwcadms@smwc.edu. *Web site:* http://www.smwc.edu/.

Saint Mary's College
Notre Dame, Indiana

General Independent Roman Catholic, 4-year, women only **Entrance** Moderately difficult **Setting** 275-acre suburban campus **Total enrollment** 1,664 **Student-faculty ratio** 11:1 **Application deadline** 2/15 (freshmen), 4/15 (transfer) **Freshman admission** 86% were admitted. Average high school GPA 3.71 **Freshman test scores** SAT critical reading scores over 500: 81.65%; SAT math scores over 500: 80.16%; ACT scores over 18: 98.73%; SAT critical reading scores over 600: 33.71%; SAT math scores over 600: 29.97%; ACT scores over 24: 66.88% **Housing** Yes **Expenses** Tuition & Fees $29,616; Room & Board $9206 **Undergraduates** 1% part-time, 1% 25 or older, 0.2% Native American, 7% Hispanic American, 1% African American, 1% Asian American/Pacific Islander **The most frequently chosen baccalaureate fields are** business/marketing, communications/journalism, health professions and related sciences **Academic program** Advanced placement, accelerated degree program, self-designed majors, summer session, internships **Contact** Mona Bowe, Director of Admission, Saint Mary's College, Notre Dame, IN 46556. *Phone:* 574-284-4587 or toll-free 800-551-7621. *Fax:* 574-284-4841. *E-mail:* admission@saintmarys.edu. *Web site:* http://www.saintmarys.edu/.

Visit Petersons.com and enter keywords Saint Mary's College

See page 1124 for the College Close-Up.

Taylor University
Upland, Indiana

General Independent interdenominational, comprehensive, coed **Entrance** Moderately difficult **Setting** 950-acre rural campus **Total enrollment** 2,560 **Student-faculty ratio** 12:1 **Application deadline** Rolling (freshmen), rolling (transfer) **Freshman admission** 83% were admitted. Average high school GPA 3.61 **Freshman test scores** SAT critical reading scores over 500: 78%; SAT math scores over 500: 79%; ACT scores over 18: 99%; SAT critical reading scores over 600: 45%; SAT math scores over 600: 42%; ACT scores over 24: 78% **Housing** Yes **Expenses** Tuition & Fees $25,396; Room & Board $6708 **Undergraduates** 55% women, 22% part-time, 2% 25 or older, 0.3% Native American, 2% Hispanic American, 2% African American, 3% Asian American/Pacific Islander **The most frequently chosen baccalaureate fields are** business/marketing, education, psychology **Academic program** English as a second language, advanced placement, self-designed majors, honors program, summer session, internships **Contact** Ms. Amy Barnett, Visit Coordinator, Taylor University, 236 West Reade Avenue, Upland, IN 46989-1001. *Phone:* 765-998-5565 or toll-free 800-882-3456. *Fax:* 765-998-4925. *E-mail:* admissions@taylor.edu. *Web site:* http://www.taylor.edu/.

Trine University
Angola, Indiana

General Independent, comprehensive, coed **Entrance** Moderately difficult **Setting** 400-acre small-town campus **Total enrollment** 1,616 **Student-faculty ratio** 15:1 **Application deadline** 8/1 (freshmen), 8/1 (transfer) **Freshman admission** 75% were admitted. Average high school GPA 3.38 **Freshman test scores** SAT critical reading scores over 500: 45%; SAT math scores over 500: 72%; ACT scores over 18: 92%; SAT critical reading scores over 600: 12%; SAT math scores over 600: 33%; ACT scores over 24: 39% **Housing** Yes **Expenses** Tuition & Fees $25,400; Room & Board $8500 **Undergraduates** 35% women, 8% part-time, 3% 25 or older, 0.5% Native American, 2% Hispanic American, 4% African American, 1% Asian American/Pacific Islander **Academic program** Advanced placement, self-designed majors, honors program, summer session, adult/continuing education programs, internships **Contact** Mr. Scott Goplin, Dean of Admission, Trine University, 1 University Avenue, Angola, IN 46703. *Phone:* 260-665-4365 or toll-free 800-347-4TSU. *Fax:* 260-665-4578. *E-mail:* admit@trine.edu. *Web site:* http://www.trine.edu/.

Visit Petersons.com and enter keyword Trine

See page 1232 for the College Close-Up.

University of Evansville
Evansville, Indiana

General Independent, comprehensive, coed, affiliated with United Methodist Church **Entrance** Moderately difficult **Setting** 75-acre urban campus **Total enrollment** 2,884 **Student-faculty ratio** 14:1 **Application deadline** 2/1 (freshmen), rolling (transfer) **Freshman admission** 86% were admitted. Average high school GPA 3.67 **Freshman test scores** SAT critical reading scores over 500: 78%; SAT math scores over 500: 79%; ACT scores over 18: 97%; SAT critical reading scores over 600: 32%; SAT math scores over 600: 40%; ACT scores over 24: 66% **Housing** Yes **Expenses** Tuition & Fees $26,756; Room & Board $8670 **Undergraduates** 60% women, 9% part-time, 4% 25 or older, 0.3% Native American, 2% Hispanic American, 2% African American, 1% Asian American/Pacific Islander **The most frequently chosen baccalaureate fields are** business/marketing, education, visual and performing arts **Academic program** English as a second language, advanced placement, accelerated degree program, self-designed majors, honors program, summer session, adult/continuing education programs, internships **Contact** Don Vos, Dean of Admission, University of Evansville, 1800 Lincoln Avenue, Evansville, IN 47722. *Phone:* 812-488-2468 or toll-free 800-423-8633 Ext. 2468. *Fax:* 812-488-4076. *E-mail:* admission@evansville.edu. *Web site:* http://www.evansville.edu/.

University of Indianapolis
Indianapolis, Indiana

General Independent, comprehensive, coed, affiliated with United Methodist Church **Entrance** Moderately difficult **Setting** 65-acre urban campus **Total enrollment** 4,989 **Student-faculty ratio** 13:1 **Application deadline** Rolling (freshmen), rolling (transfer) **Freshman admission** 80% were admitted. Average high school GPA 3.36 **Freshman test scores** SAT critical reading scores over 500: 50%; SAT math scores over 500: 58%; ACT scores over 18: 84%; SAT critical reading scores over 600: 13%; SAT math scores over 600: 17%; ACT scores over 24: 37% **Housing** Yes **Expenses** Tuition & Fees $21,170; Room & Board $8040 **Undergraduates** 67% women, 24% part-time, 23% 25 or older, 0.2% Native American, 2% Hispanic American, 11% African American, 1% Asian American/Pacific Islander **The most frequently chosen baccalaureate fields are** business/marketing, education, health professions and related sciences **Academic program** English as a second language, advanced placement, accelerated degree program, self-designed majors, honors program, summer session, adult/continuing education programs, internships **Contact** Mr. Ronald Wilks, Director of Admissions, University of Indianapolis, 1400 East Hanna Avenue, Indianapolis, IN 46227-3697. *Phone:* 317-788-3216 or toll-free 800-232-8634 Ext. 3216. *Fax:* 317-788-3300. *E-mail:* admissions@uindy.edu. *Web site:* http://www.uindy.edu/.

Visit Petersons.com and enter keywords University of Indianapolis

See page 1276 for the College Close-Up.

University of Notre Dame
Notre Dame, Indiana

General Independent Roman Catholic, university, coed **Entrance** Most difficult **Setting** 1,250-acre suburban campus **Total enrollment** 11,816 **Student-faculty ratio** 12:1 **Application deadline** 12/31 (freshmen), 4/15 (transfer) **Freshman admission** 29% were admitted **Housing** Yes **Expenses** Tuition & Fees $38,477; Room & Board $10,368 **Undergraduates** 46% women, 0.2% part-time, 1% Native American, 10% Hispanic American, 4% African American, 7% Asian American/Pacific Islander **The most frequently chosen baccalaureate fields are** business/marketing, engineering, social sciences **Academic program** Advanced placement, self-designed majors, honors program, summer session, internships **Contact** Office of Undergraduate Admissions, University of Notre Dame, 220 Main Building, Notre Dame, IN 46556-5612. *Phone:* 574-631-7505. *Fax:* 574-631-8865. *E-mail:* admissions@nd.edu. *Web site:* http://www.nd.edu/.

University of Phoenix–Indianapolis Campus
Indianapolis, Indiana

General Proprietary, comprehensive, coed **Entrance** Noncompetitive **Setting** urban campus **Total enrollment** 339 **Application deadline** Rolling (freshmen), rolling (transfer) **Freshman admission** 100% were admitted **Housing** No **Expenses** Tuition & Fees $11,438 **Undergraduates** 73% women, 85% 25 or older, 1% Native American, 1% Hispanic American, 38% African American, 1% Asian American/Pacific Islander **The most frequently chosen baccalaureate fields are** business/marketing, health professions and related sciences **Academic program** Advanced placement, accelerated degree program **Contact** Ms. Audra McQuarie, Registrar/Executive Director, University of Phoenix–Indianapolis Campus, 4035 South Riverpoint Parkway, Mail Stop CF-L101, Phoenix, AZ 85040. *Phone:* 480-557-6151 or toll-free 800-776-4867 (in-state); 800-228-7240 (out-of-state). *Fax:* 480-643-3068. *E-mail:* audra.mcquarie@phoenix.edu. *Web site:* http://www.phoenix.edu/.

University of Saint Francis
Fort Wayne, Indiana

General Independent Roman Catholic, comprehensive, coed **Entrance** Moderately difficult **Setting** 74-acre suburban campus **Total enrollment** 2,112 **Student-faculty ratio** 12:1 **Application deadline** Rolling (freshmen), rolling (transfer) **Freshman admission** 47% were admitted. Average high school GPA 3.16 **Freshman test scores** SAT critical reading scores over 500: 47%; SAT math scores over 500: 51%; ACT scores over 18: 85%; SAT critical reading scores over 600: 11%; SAT math scores over 600: 11%; ACT scores over 24: 24% **Housing** Yes **Expenses** Tuition & Fees $21,760; Room & Board $6750 **Undergraduates** 68% women, 19% part-time, 22% 25 or older, 0.3% Native American, 2% Hispanic American, 5% African American, 1% Asian American/Pacific Islander **The most frequently chosen baccalaureate fields are** education, business/marketing, health professions and related sciences **Academic program** Advanced placement, honors program, summer session, internships **Contact** Mr. Ron Schumacher, Vice President for Enrollment Management, University of Saint Francis, 2701 Spring Street, Fort Wayne, IN 46808. *Phone:* 260-434-3279 or toll-free 800-729-4732. *Fax:* 260-434-7590. *E-mail:* admis@sf.edu. *Web site:* http://www.sf.edu/.

University of Southern Indiana
Evansville, Indiana

General State-supported, comprehensive, coed **Entrance** Moderately difficult **Setting** 330-acre suburban campus **Total enrollment** 10,516

University of Southern Indiana (continued)

Student-faculty ratio 18:1 **Application deadline** 8/15 (freshmen) **Freshman admission** 88% were admitted. Average high school GPA 3.02 **Freshman test scores** SAT critical reading scores over 500: 38.35%; SAT math scores over 500: 42.63%; ACT scores over 18: 77.79%; SAT critical reading scores over 600: 7.53%; SAT math scores over 600: 11.17%; ACT scores over 24: 20.41% **Housing** Yes **Expenses** Tuition & Fees: state resident $5474, nonresident $12,755; Room & Board $6700 **Undergraduates** 59% women, 17% part-time, 18% 25 or older, 0.4% Native American, 1% Hispanic American, 5% African American, 1% Asian American/Pacific Islander **The most frequently chosen baccalaureate fields are** business/marketing, education, health professions and related sciences **Academic program** English as a second language, advanced placement, honors program, summer session, adult/continuing education programs, internships **Contact** Mr. Eric Otto, Director of Admission, University of Southern Indiana, 8600 University Boulevard, Evansville, IN 47712-3590. *Phone:* 812-464-1765 or toll-free 800-467-1965. *Fax:* 812-465-7154. *E-mail:* enroll@usi.edu. *Web site:* http://www.usi.edu/.

Valparaiso University
Valparaiso, Indiana

General Independent, university, coed, affiliated with Lutheran Church **Entrance** Moderately difficult **Setting** 320-acre small-town campus **Total enrollment** 4,065 **Student-faculty ratio** 14:1 **Application deadline** 8/15 (freshmen) **Freshman admission** 91% were admitted. Average high school GPA 3.48 **Freshman test scores** SAT critical reading scores over 500: 71%; SAT math scores over 500: 78%; ACT scores over 18: 97%; SAT critical reading scores over 600: 32%; SAT math scores over 600: 37%; ACT scores over 24: 64% **Housing** Yes **Expenses** Tuition & Fees $28,320; Room & Board $7960 **Undergraduates** 52% women, 5% part-time, 5% 25 or older, 1% Native American, 5% Hispanic American, 6% African American, 2% Asian American/Pacific Islander **The most frequently chosen baccalaureate fields are** business/marketing, health professions and related sciences, social sciences **Academic program** English as a second language, advanced placement, accelerated degree program, self-designed majors, honors program, summer session, adult/continuing education programs, internships **Contact** Office of Admission, Valparaiso University, Kretzmann Hall, 1700 Chapel Drive, Valparaiso, IN 46383-6493. *Phone:* 219-464-5011 or toll-free 888-GO-VALPO. *Fax:* 219-464-6898. *E-mail:* Undergrad.Admissions@valpo.edu. *Web site:* http://www.valpo.edu/.

Visit Petersons.com and enter keyword Valparaiso

See page 1328 for the College Close-Up.

Vincennes University
Vincennes, Indiana

Contact Christian Blome, Director of Admissions, Vincennes University, 1002 North First Street, Vincennes, IN 47591-5202. *Phone:* 800-742-9198 or toll-free 800-742-9198. *E-mail:* cblome@vinu.edu. *Web site:* http://www.vinu.edu/.

Vincennes University Jasper Campus
Jasper, Indiana

General State-supported, primarily 2-year, coed **Entrance** Noncompetitive **Setting** 120-acre small-town campus **Total enrollment** 915 **Student-faculty ratio** 16:1 **Application deadline** Rolling (freshmen), rolling (transfer) **Housing** No **Undergraduates** 50% 25 or older, 0.3% Native American, 3% Hispanic American, 1% African American, 0.4% Asian American/Pacific Islander **Academic program** Advanced placement, summer session, adult/continuing education programs **Contact** Ms. Louann Gilbert, Director, Vincennes University Jasper Campus, 850 College Avenue, Jasper, IN 47546-9393. *Phone:* 812-482-3030 or toll-free 800-809-VUJC. *Fax:* 812-481-5960. *E-mail:* lagilbert@vinu.edu. *Web site:* http://vujc.vinu.edu/.

Wabash College
Crawfordsville, Indiana

General Independent, 4-year, men only **Entrance** Moderately difficult **Setting** 60-acre small-town campus **Total enrollment** 883 **Student-faculty ratio** 10:1 **Application deadline** Rolling (freshmen), 3/15 (transfer) **Freshman admission** 49% were admitted. Average high school GPA 3.52 **Freshman test scores** SAT critical reading scores over 500: 76%; SAT math scores over 500: 88%; ACT scores over 18: 96%; SAT critical reading scores over 600: 29%; SAT math scores over 600: 53%; ACT scores over 24: 59% **Housing** Yes **Expenses** Tuition & Fees $29,750; Room & Board $7600 **Undergraduates** 1% part-time, 1% Native American, 5% Hispanic American, 6% African American, 2% Asian American/Pacific Islander **The most frequently chosen baccalaureate fields are** philosophy and religious studies, English, social sciences **Academic program** Advanced placement, internships **Contact** Mr. Steven J. Klein, Dean of Admissions, Wabash College, PO Box 362, Crawfordsville, IN 47933-0352. *Phone:* 765-361-6225 or toll-free 800-345-5385. *Fax:* 765-361-6437. *E-mail:* admissions@wabash.edu. *Web site:* http://www.wabash.edu/.

IOWA

AIB College of Business
Des Moines, Iowa

General Independent, 4-year, coed **Entrance** Minimally difficult **Setting** 20-acre urban campus **Total enrollment** 969 **Student-faculty ratio** 18:1 **Application deadline** Rolling (freshmen), rolling (transfer) **Freshman admission** 70% were admitted. Average high school GPA 3.11 **Housing** Yes **Expenses** Tuition & Fees $13,140; Room only $4311 **Undergraduates** 70% women, 39% part-time, 35% 25 or older, 1% Native American, 2% Hispanic American, 3% African American, 3% Asian American/Pacific Islander **The most frequently chosen baccalaureate field is** business/marketing **Academic program** Summer session, adult/continuing education programs, internships **Contact** Mr. Mark Thompson, Director of Admissions, AIB College of Business, 2500 Fleur Drive, Des Moines, IA 50321-1799. *Phone:* 515-244-4221 or toll-free 800-444-1921. *Fax:* 515-244-6773. *E-mail:* thompsonm@aib.edu. *Web site:* http://www.aib.edu/.

Allen College
Waterloo, Iowa

General Independent, comprehensive, coed, primarily women **Entrance** Moderately difficult **Setting** 20-acre suburban campus **Total enrollment** 454 **Student-faculty ratio** 12:1 **Application deadline** 7/1 (freshmen), 7/1 (transfer) **Freshman admission** 40% were admitted. Average high school GPA 3.54 **Freshman test scores** ACT scores over 18: 100%; ACT scores over 24: 66.67% **Housing** Yes **Expenses** Tuition & Fees $14,995 **Undergraduates** 93% women, 21% part-time, 30% 25 or older, 1% Native American, 0.3% Hispanic American, 2% African American, 0.3% Asian American/Pacific Islander **The most frequently chosen baccalaureate field is** health professions and related sciences **Academic program** Advanced placement, accelerated degree program, honors program, internships **Contact** Dina Dowden, Education Secretary, Student Services, Allen College, Barrett Forum, 1825 Logan Avenue, Waterloo, IA 50703. *Phone:* 319-226-2000. *Fax:* 319-226-2051. *E-mail:* allencollegeadmissions@ihs.org. *Web site:* http://www.allencollege.edu/.

Ashford University
Clinton, Iowa

Contact Ms. Waunita M. Sullivan, Director of Enrollment, Ashford University, 400 North Bluff Boulevard, PO Box 2967, Clinton, IA

52733-2967. *Phone:* 563-242-4023 Ext. 3401 or toll-free 800-242-4153. *E-mail:* admissns@tfu.edu. *Web site:* http://www.ashford.edu/.

Briar Cliff University
Sioux City, Iowa

General Independent Roman Catholic, comprehensive, coed **Entrance** Moderately difficult **Setting** 75-acre suburban campus **Total enrollment** 1,158 **Student-faculty ratio** 13:1 **Application deadline** Rolling (freshmen), rolling (transfer) **Freshman admission** 62% were admitted. Average high school GPA 3.19 **Housing** Yes **Expenses** Tuition & Fees $22,536; Room & Board $6978 **Undergraduates** 56% women, 17% part-time, 21% 25 or older, 2% Native American, 7% Hispanic American, 6% African American, 3% Asian American/Pacific Islander **The most frequently chosen baccalaureate fields are** business/marketing, education, health professions and related sciences **Academic program** Advanced placement, accelerated degree program, self-designed majors, honors program, summer session, adult/continuing education programs, internships **Contact** Admissions Office, Briar Cliff University, 3303 Rebecca Street, Sioux City, IA 51104-0100. *Phone:* 712-279-5200 or toll-free 800-662-3303 Ext. 5200. *Fax:* 712-279-1632. *E-mail:* admissions@briarcliff.edu. *Web site:* http://www.briarcliff.edu/.

Buena Vista University
Storm Lake, Iowa

General Independent, comprehensive, coed, affiliated with Presbyterian Church (U.S.A.) **Entrance** Moderately difficult **Setting** 60-acre small-town campus **Total enrollment** 1,014 **Student-faculty ratio** 10:1 **Freshman admission** 72% were admitted. Average high school GPA 3.26 **Freshman test scores** ACT scores over 18: 86%; ACT scores over 24: 30% **Housing** Yes **Expenses** Tuition & Fees $25,540; Room & Board $7292 **Undergraduates** 51% women, 1% part-time, 5% 25 or older, 0.4% Native American, 5% Hispanic American, 5% African American, 2% Asian American/Pacific Islander **The most frequently chosen baccalaureate fields are** business/marketing, education, interdisciplinary studies **Academic program** English as a second language, advanced placement, self-designed majors, honors program, summer session, adult/continuing education programs, internships **Contact** Marcia Nance, Vice President for Enrollment Management, Buena Vista University, 610 West Fourth Street, Storm Lake, IA 50588. *Phone:* 712-749-2235 or toll-free 800-383-9600. *E-mail:* admissions@bvu.edu. *Web site:* http://www.bvu.edu/.

Central College
Pella, Iowa

General Independent, 4-year, coed, affiliated with Reformed Church in America **Entrance** Moderately difficult **Setting** 169-acre small-town campus **Total enrollment** 1,636 **Student-faculty ratio** 13:1 **Application deadline** Rolling (freshmen), rolling (transfer) **Freshman admission** 74% were admitted. Average high school GPA 3.51 **Freshman test scores** SAT critical reading scores over 500: 67%; ACT scores over 18: 97%; SAT critical reading scores over 600: 54%; ACT scores over 24: 54% **Housing** Yes **Expenses** Tuition & Fees $25,010; Room & Board $8368 **Undergraduates** 53% women, 2% part-time, 2% 25 or older, 0.3% Native American, 2% Hispanic American, 2% African American, 2% Asian American/Pacific Islander **The most frequently chosen baccalaureate fields are** business/marketing, foreign languages and literature, parks and recreation **Academic program** Self-designed majors, honors program, summer session, internships **Contact** Ms. Carol Williamson, Dean of Admission and Student Enrollment Services, Central College, 812 University Street, Pella, IA 50219. *Phone:* 641-628-7600 or toll-free 877-462-3687 (in-state); 877-462-3689 (out-of-state). *Fax:* 641-628-5316. *E-mail:* admissions@central.edu. *Web site:* http://www.central.edu/.

Clarke College
Dubuque, Iowa

General Independent Roman Catholic, comprehensive, coed **Entrance** Moderately difficult **Setting** 55-acre urban campus **Total enrollment**

Clarke College (continued)

1,202 **Student-faculty ratio** 11:1 **Application deadline** Rolling (freshmen), rolling (transfer) **Freshman admission** 77% were admitted. Average high school GPA 3.34 **Freshman test scores** ACT scores over 18: 95%; ACT scores over 24: 48% **Housing** Yes **Expenses** Tuition & Fees $23,520; Room & Board $6840 **Undergraduates** 68% women, 18% part-time, 22% 25 or older, 2% Hispanic American, 1% African American, 1% Asian American/Pacific Islander **The most frequently chosen baccalaureate fields are** education, business/marketing, health professions and related sciences **Academic program** English as a second language, advanced placement, accelerated degree program, self-designed majors, honors program, summer session, adult/continuing education programs, internships **Contact** Ms. Emily Kruse, Director of Admissions, Clarke College, 1550 Clarke Drive, Dubuque, IA 52001-3198. *Phone:* 563-588-6436 or toll-free 800-383-2345. *E-mail:* admissions@clarke.edu. *Web site:* http://www.clarke.edu/.

Coe College
Cedar Rapids, Iowa

General Independent, comprehensive, coed, affiliated with Presbyterian Church **Entrance** Moderately difficult **Setting** 53-acre urban campus **Total enrollment** 1,326 **Student-faculty ratio** 11:1 **Application deadline** 3/1 (freshmen), rolling (transfer) **Freshman admission** Average high school GPA 3.66 **Freshman test scores** SAT critical reading scores over 500: 94%; SAT math scores over 500: 87%; ACT scores over 18: 100%; SAT critical reading scores over 600: 62%; SAT math scores over 600: 45%; ACT scores over 24: 71% **Housing** Yes **Expenses** Tuition & Fees $29,270; Room & Board $7150 **Undergraduates** 55% women, 5% part-time, 4% 25 or older, 0.2% Native American, 2% Hispanic American, 2% African American, 1% Asian American/Pacific Islander **The most frequently chosen baccalaureate fields are** business/marketing, social sciences, visual and performing arts **Academic program** English as a second language, advanced placement, accelerated degree program, self-designed majors, honors program, summer session, internships **Contact** Mr. John Grundig, Dean of Admission, Coe College, 1220 1st Avenue, NE, Cedar Rapids, IA 52402-5070. *Phone:* 319-399-8500 or toll-free 877-225-5263. *Fax:* 319-399-8816. *E-mail:* admission@coe.edu. *Web site:* http://www.coe.edu/.

Cornell College
Mount Vernon, Iowa

General Independent Methodist, 4-year, coed **Entrance** Moderately difficult **Setting** 129-acre small-town campus **Total enrollment** 1,141 **Student-faculty ratio** 12:1 **Application deadline** 2/1 (freshmen), 3/1 (transfer) **Freshman admission** 44% were admitted. Average high school GPA 3.5 **Freshman test scores** SAT critical reading scores over 500: 93%; SAT math scores over 500: 93%; ACT scores over 18: 99%; SAT critical reading scores over 600: 57%; SAT math scores over 600: 58%; ACT scores over 24: 77% **Housing** Yes **Expenses** Tuition & Fees $29,400; Room & Board $7500 **Undergraduates** 52% women, 1% part-time, 1% 25 or older, 1% Native American, 4% Hispanic American, 3% African American, 3% Asian American/Pacific Islander **The most frequently chosen baccalaureate fields are** biological/life sciences, psychology, social sciences **Academic program** English as a second language, advanced placement, self-designed majors, internships **Contact** Todd White, Director of Admission, Cornell College, 600 First Street SW, Mount Vernon, IA 52314-1098. *Phone:* 319-895-4167 or toll-free 800-747-1112. *Fax:* 319-895-4451. *E-mail:* twhite@cornellcollege.edu. *Web site:* http://www.cornellcollege.edu/.

Divine Word College
Epworth, Iowa

General Independent Roman Catholic, 4-year, coed, primarily men **Entrance** Minimally difficult **Setting** 28-acre rural campus **Total enrollment** 59 **Application deadline** 7/15 (freshmen), 7/15 (transfer) **Housing** Yes **Expenses** Tuition & Fees $10,900; Room & Board $2850 **Undergraduates** 47% 25 or older **Academic program** English as a second language, advanced placement **Contact** Mr. Len Uhal, Vice President of Recruitment/Director of Admissions, Divine Word College, 102 Jacoby Drive SW, Epworth, IA 52045-0380. *Phone:* 563-876-3353 or toll-free 800-553-3321. *Fax:* 563-876-5515. *E-mail:* luhal@dwci.edu. *Web site:* http://www.dwci.edu/.

Dordt College
Sioux Center, Iowa

General Independent Christian Reformed, comprehensive, coed **Entrance** Moderately difficult **Setting** 110-acre small-town campus **Total enrollment** 1,331 **Student-faculty ratio** 15:1 **Application deadline** 8/1 (freshmen), 8/1 (transfer) **Freshman admission** 84% were admitted. Average high school GPA 3.5 **Freshman test scores** SAT critical reading scores over 500: 65.2%; ACT scores over 18: 97.5%; SAT critical reading scores over 600: 28.2%; ACT scores over 24: 59.7% **Housing** Yes **Expenses** Tuition & Fees $22,080; Room & Board $6010 **Undergraduates** 51% women, 2% part-time, 5% 25 or older, 0.2% Native American, 1% Hispanic American, 0.3% African American, 1% Asian American/Pacific Islander **Academic program** English as a second language, advanced placement, self-designed majors, honors program, internships **Contact** Mr. Quentin Van Essen, Executive Director of Admissions, Dordt College, 498 4th Avenue, NE, Sioux Center, IA 51250-1697. *Phone:* 712-722-6080 or toll-free 800-343-6738. *Fax:* 712-722-6035. *E-mail:* admissions@dordt.edu. *Web site:* http://www.dordt.edu/.

Drake University
Des Moines, Iowa

General Independent, university, coed **Entrance** Moderately difficult **Setting** 120-acre suburban campus **Total enrollment** 5,653 **Student-faculty ratio** 13:1 **Application deadline** 3/1 (freshmen), rolling (transfer) **Freshman admission** 74% were admitted. Average high school GPA 3.63 **Freshman test scores** SAT critical reading scores over 500: 76%; SAT math scores over 500: 81%; ACT scores over 18: 100%; SAT critical reading scores over 600: 49%; SAT math scores over 600: 55%; ACT scores over 24: 80% **Housing** Yes **Expenses** Tuition & Fees $25,622; Room & Board $7800 **Undergraduates** 58% women, 6% part-time, 6% 25 or older, 0.1% Native American, 2% Hispanic American, 3% African American, 3% Asian American/Pacific Islander **The most frequently chosen baccalaureate fields are** business/marketing, biological/life sciences, communications/journalism **Academic program** English as a second language, advanced placement, accelerated degree program, self-designed majors, honors program, summer session, internships **Contact** Ms. Laura Linn, Director of Admission, Drake University, 2507 University Avenue, Des Moines, IA 50311. *Phone:* 515-271-3181 Ext. 3182 or toll-free 800-44DRAKE Ext. 3181. *Fax:* 515-271-2831. *E-mail:* admission@drake.edu. *Web site:* http://www.drake.edu/.

Visit Petersons.com and enter keyword Drake

Emmaus Bible College
Dubuque, Iowa

General Independent nondenominational, 4-year, coed **Entrance** Noncompetitive **Setting** 22-acre small-town campus **Total enrollment** 244 **Application deadline** 6/1 (freshmen), 8/1 (transfer) **Housing** Yes **Expenses** Tuition & Fees $11,578; Room & Board $5396 **Undergraduates** 9% 25 or older **Academic program** Advanced placement, internships **Contact** Israel Chavez, Enrollment Services Director, Emmaus Bible College, 2570 Asbury Road, Dubuque, IA 52001-3097. *Phone:* 563-588-8000 Ext. 1310 or toll-free 800-397-2425. *E-mail:* ichavez@emmaus.edu. *Web site:* http://www.emmaus.edu/.

Faith Baptist Bible College and Theological Seminary

Ankeny, Iowa

General Independent, comprehensive, coed, affiliated with General Association of Regular Baptist Churches **Entrance** Minimally difficult **Setting** 52-acre small-town campus **Total enrollment** 417 **Student-faculty ratio** 12:1 **Application deadline** 8/1 (freshmen), 8/1 (transfer) **Freshman admission** 94% were admitted. Average high school GPA 3.38 **Freshman test scores** SAT critical reading scores over 500: 100%; SAT math scores over 500: 83.34%; ACT scores over 18: 92%; SAT critical reading scores over 600: 33.33%; SAT math scores over 600: 16.67%; ACT scores over 24: 40% **Housing** Yes **Expenses** Tuition & Fees $13,260; Room & Board $5510 **Undergraduates** 60% women, 13% part-time, 7% 25 or older, 1% Native American, 2% Hispanic American, 1% African American, 1% Asian American/Pacific Islander **The most frequently chosen baccalaureate fields are** education, philosophy and religious studies, theology and religious vocations **Academic program** Advanced placement, summer session, adult/continuing education programs, internships **Contact** Miss Carrie Johnson, Admissions Secretary, Faith Baptist Bible College and Theological Seminary, 1900 NW 4th Street, Ankeny, IA 50023. *Phone:* 515-964-0601 or toll-free 888-FAITH 4U. *Fax:* 515-964-1638. *E-mail:* admissions@faith.edu. *Web site:* http://www.faith.edu/.

Graceland University

Lamoni, Iowa

General Independent Community of Christ, comprehensive, coed **Entrance** Moderately difficult **Setting** 170-acre rural campus **Total enrollment** 2,355 **Student-faculty ratio** 16:1 **Application deadline** Rolling (freshmen), rolling (transfer) **Freshman admission** 88% were admitted. Average high school GPA 3.13 **Freshman test scores** SAT critical reading scores over 500: 40%; SAT math scores over 500: 39%; ACT scores over 18: 79%; SAT critical reading scores over 600: 5%; SAT math scores over 600: 16%; ACT scores over 24: 25% **Housing** Yes **Expenses** Tuition & Fees $20,980; Room & Board $7040 **Undergraduates** 61% women, 23% part-time, 1% Native American, 3% Hispanic American, 9% African American, 2% Asian American/Pacific Islander **The most frequently chosen baccalaureate fields are** engineering, business/marketing, health professions and related sciences **Academic program** English as a second language, advanced placement, accelerated degree program, self-designed majors, honors program, summer session, adult/continuing education programs, internships **Contact** Mr. Greg Sutherland, Vice President of Enrollment and Dean of Admissions, Graceland University, 1 University Place, Lamoni, IA 50140. *Phone:* 641-784-5110 or toll-free 866-GRACELAND. *Fax:* 641-784-5480. *E-mail:* sutherla@graceland.edu. *Web site:* http://www.graceland.edu/.

Visit Petersons.com and enter keyword Graceland

See page 828 for the College Close-Up.

Grand View University

Des Moines, Iowa

General Independent, comprehensive, coed, affiliated with Evangelical Lutheran Church in America **Entrance** Minimally difficult **Setting** 25-acre urban campus **Total enrollment** 2,039 **Student-faculty ratio** 14:1 **Application deadline** 8/15 (freshmen), 8/15 (transfer) **Freshman admission** 95% were admitted. Average high school GPA 3.22 **Freshman test scores** SAT critical reading scores over 500: 29%; SAT math scores over 500: 25%; ACT scores over 18: 89%; SAT critical reading scores over 600: 4%; SAT math scores over 600: 4%; ACT scores over 24: 20% **Housing** Yes **Expenses** Tuition & Fees $19,324; Room & Board $6442 **Undergraduates** 62% women, 19% part-time, 3% 25 or older, 0.2% Native American, 3% Hispanic American, 7% African American, 3% Asian American/Pacific Islander **The most frequently chosen baccalaureate fields are** business/marketing, education, health professions and related sciences **Academic program** Advanced placement, accelerated degree program, self-designed majors, honors program, summer session, adult/continuing education programs, internships **Contact** Ms. Diane Schaefer, Director of Admissions, Grand View University, 1200 Grandview Avenue, Des Moines, IA 50316-1599. *Phone:* 515-263-2810 or toll-free 800-444-6083 Ext. 2810. *Fax:* 515-263-2974. *E-mail:* admissions@grandview.edu. *Web site:* http://www.grandview.edu/.

Visit Petersons.com and enter keywords Grand View

See page 832 for the College Close-Up.

Grinnell College

Grinnell, Iowa

General Independent, 4-year, coed **Entrance** Very difficult **Setting** 120-acre small-town campus **Total enrollment** 1,688 **Student-faculty ratio** 9:1 **Application deadline** 1/2 (freshmen), 5/1 (transfer) **Freshman admission** 34% were admitted **Freshman test scores** SAT critical reading scores over 500: 92.4%; SAT math scores over 500: 95.2%; ACT scores over 18: 100%; SAT critical reading scores over 600: 77.6%; SAT math scores over 600: 80.4%; ACT scores over 24: 96.4% **Housing** Yes **Expenses** Tuition & Fees $36,476; Room & Board $8536 **Undergraduates** 53% women, 3% part-time, 1% Native American, 7% Hispanic American, 6% African American, 8% Asian American/Pacific Islander **The most frequently chosen baccalaureate fields are** biological/life sciences, foreign languages and literature, social sciences **Academic program** Advanced placement, accelerated degree program, self-designed majors, internships **Contact** Mr. Seth Allen, Dean for Admission and Financial Aid, Grinnell College, 1103 Park Street, Grinnell, IA 50112. *Phone:* 641-269-3600 or toll-free 800-247-0113. *Fax:* 641-269-4800. *E-mail:* askgrin@grinnell.edu. *Web site:* http://www.grinnell.edu/.

Visit Petersons.com and enter keyword Grinnell

Hamilton Technical College

Davenport, Iowa

General Proprietary, 4-year, coed **Entrance** Noncompetitive **Setting** urban campus **Student-faculty ratio** 20:1 **Application deadline** Rolling (freshmen), rolling (transfer) **Housing** No **Expenses** Tuition & Fees $8926 **Undergraduates** 4% Hispanic American, 10% African American **The most frequently chosen baccalaureate field is** engineering technologies **Contact** Mr. Scott Ervin, Director of Admissions, Hamilton Technical College, 1011 East 53rd Street, Davenport, IA 52807-2653. *Phone:* 563-386-3570. *Fax:* 563-386-6756. *E-mail:* servin@hamiltontechcollege.com. *Web site:* http://www.hamiltontechcollege.com/.

INSTE Bible College

Ankeny, Iowa

Contact INSTE Bible College, 2302 SW 3rd Street, Ankeny, IA 50023. *Web site:* http://www.inste.edu/.

Iowa State University of Science and Technology

Ames, Iowa

General State-supported, university, coed **Entrance** Moderately difficult **Setting** 1,794-acre suburban campus **Total enrollment** 27,945 **Student-faculty ratio** 16:1 **Application deadline** 7/1 (freshmen), 7/1 (transfer) **Freshman admission** 85% were admitted. Average high school GPA 3.53 **Freshman test scores** SAT critical reading scores over 500: 74%; SAT math scores over 500: 86%; ACT scores over 18: 98%; SAT critical reading scores over 600: 38%; SAT math scores over 600: 59%; ACT scores over 24: 60.5% **Housing** Yes **Expenses** Tuition & Fees: state resident $6997, nonresident $18,563 **Undergraduates** 43% women, 5% part-time, 9% 25 or older, 0.2% Native American, 3% Hispanic American, 3% African American, 3% Asian American/Pacific

Iowa State University of Science and Technology (continued)
Islander **The most frequently chosen baccalaureate fields are** business/marketing, agriculture, engineering **Academic program** English as a second language, advanced placement, accelerated degree program, self-designed majors, honors program, summer session, adult/continuing education programs, internships **Contact** Mr. Phil Caffrey, Associate Director for Freshman Admissions, Iowa State University of Science and Technology, 100 Enrollment Services Center, Ames, IA 50011-2010. *Phone:* 515-294-5836 or toll-free 800-262-3810. *Fax:* 515-294-2592. *E-mail:* admissions@iastate.edu. *Web site:* http://www.iastate.edu/.

Iowa Wesleyan College
Mount Pleasant, Iowa

General Independent United Methodist, 4-year, coed **Entrance** Moderately difficult **Setting** 60-acre small-town campus **Total enrollment** 858 **Student-faculty ratio** 14:1 **Application deadline** 8/15 (freshmen), 8/15 (transfer) **Freshman admission** 68% were admitted. Average high school GPA 2.82 **Freshman test scores** SAT critical reading scores over 500: 20%; SAT math scores over 500: 23%; ACT scores over 18: 68%; SAT math scores over 600: 10%; ACT scores over 24: 15% **Housing** Yes **Expenses** Tuition & Fees $21,000; Room & Board $6654 **Undergraduates** 60% women, 23% part-time, 30% 25 or older, 1% Native American, 8% Hispanic American, 13% African American, 3% Asian American/Pacific Islander **The most frequently chosen baccalaureate fields are** business/marketing, education, parks and recreation **Academic program** Advanced placement, self-designed majors, summer session, adult/continuing education programs, internships **Contact** Mr. Mark T. Petty, Dean of Admissions, Iowa Wesleyan College, 601 N Main Street, Mount Pleasant, IA 52641. *Phone:* 319-385-6231 or toll-free 800-582-2383 Ext. 6231. *Fax:* 319-385-6240. *E-mail:* mpetty@iwc.edu. *Web site:* http://www.iwc.edu/.

ITT Technical Institute
Cedar Rapids, Iowa

General Proprietary, primarily 2-year, coed **Contact** Director of Admissions, ITT Technical Institute, 3735 Queen Court SW, Cedar Rapids, IA 52404. *Phone:* 319-297-3400 or toll-free 877-320-4625. *Web site:* http://www.itt-tech.edu/.

ITT Technical Institute
Clive, Iowa

General Proprietary, primarily 2-year, coed **Contact** Director of Recruitment, ITT Technical Institute, 1860 Northwest 118th Street, Suite 110, Clive, IA 50325. *Phone:* 515-327-5500 or toll-free 877-526-7312. *Web site:* http://www.itt-tech.edu/.

Kaplan University, Cedar Falls
Cedar Falls, Iowa

General Proprietary, primarily 2-year, coed **Application deadline** Rolling (freshmen) **Contact** Director of Admissions, Kaplan University, Cedar Falls, 7009 Nordic Drive, Cedar Falls, IA 50613. *Phone:* 319-277-0220 or toll-free 800-728-1220. *Web site:* http://www.cedarfalls.kaplanuniversity.edu.

Kaplan University, Cedar Rapids
Cedar Rapids, Iowa

General Proprietary, primarily 2-year, coed **Setting** suburban campus **Contact** Director of Admissions, Kaplan University, Cedar Rapids, 3165 Edgewood Parkway, SW, Cedar Rapids, IA 52404. *Phone:* 319-363-0481 or toll-free 800-728-0481. *Web site:* http://www.cedarrapids.kaplanuniversity.edu.

Kaplan University, Council Bluffs
Council Bluffs, Iowa

General Proprietary, primarily 2-year, coed **Housing** No **Contact** Director of Admissions, Kaplan University, Council Bluffs, 1751 Madison Avenue, Council Bluffs, IA 51503. *Phone:* 712-328-4212 or toll-free 800-518-4212. *Web site:* http://www.councilbluffs.kaplanuniversity.edu.

Kaplan University, Davenport Campus
Davenport, Iowa

General Proprietary, comprehensive, coed **Setting** suburban campus **Contact** Director of Admissions, Kaplan University, Davenport Campus, 1801 East Kimberly Road, Suite 1, Davenport, IA 52807-2095. *Phone:* 563-355-3500 or toll-free 800-747-1035. *Web site:* http://www.ku-davenport.edu.

Kaplan University, Des Moines
Urbandale, Iowa

General Proprietary, primarily 2-year, coed **Contact** Director of Admissions, Kaplan University, Des Moines, 4655 121st Street, Urbandale, IA 50323. *Phone:* 515-727-2100. *Web site:* http://www.desmoines.kaplanuniversity.edu.

Kaplan University, Mason City Campus
Mason City, Iowa

General Proprietary, 4-year, coed **Contact** Director of Admissions, Kaplan University, Mason City Campus, 2570 4th Street, SW, Mason City, IA 50401. *Phone:* 641-423-2530.

Loras College
Dubuque, Iowa

General Independent Roman Catholic, comprehensive, coed **Entrance** Moderately difficult **Setting** 60-acre suburban campus **Total enrollment** 1,568 **Student-faculty ratio** 12:1 **Application deadline** Rolling (freshmen), rolling (transfer) **Freshman admission** 61% were admitted. Average high school GPA 3.32 **Freshman test scores** ACT scores over 18: 96%; ACT scores over 24: 40% **Housing** Yes **Expenses** Tuition & Fees $26,234; Room & Board $7271 **Undergraduates** 49% women, 3% part-time, 4% 25 or older, 0.3% Native American, 3% Hispanic American, 1% African American, 0.4% Asian American/Pacific Islander **The most frequently chosen baccalaureate fields are** business/marketing, education, social sciences **Academic program** Advanced placement, self-designed majors, honors program, summer session, internships **Contact** Ms. Sharon Lyons, Director of Admissions, Loras College, 1450 Alta Vista, Dubuque, IA 52004-0178. *Phone:* 563-588-7829 or toll-free 800-245-6727. *Fax:* 563-588-7119. *E-mail:* adms@loras.edu. *Web site:* http://www.loras.edu/.

Luther College
Decorah, Iowa

General Independent, 4-year, coed, affiliated with Evangelical Lutheran Church in America **Entrance** Moderately difficult **Setting** 200-acre small-town campus **Total enrollment** 2,519 **Student-faculty ratio** 12:1 **Freshman admission** 70% were admitted. Average high school GPA 3.64 **Freshman test scores** SAT critical reading scores over 500: 75.2%; SAT math scores over 500: 85.4%; ACT scores over 18: 98.9%; SAT critical reading scores over 600: 40.4%; SAT math scores over 600: 45%; ACT scores over 24: 73.6% **Housing** Yes **Expenses** Tuition & Fees $33,480; Room & Board $5800 **Undergraduates** 58% women, 2% part-time, 1% 25 or older, 0.1% Native American, 2% Hispanic American, 1% African American, 2% Asian American/Pacific Islander **The most frequently chosen baccalaureate fields are** business/marketing, biological/life

sciences, visual and performing arts **Academic program** Advanced placement, self-designed majors, honors program, summer session, internships **Contact** Kirk Neubauer, Director of Recruiting Services, Luther College, 700 College Drive, Decorah, IA 52101. *Phone:* 563-387-1287 or toll-free 800-458-8437. *Fax:* 563-387-2159. *E-mail:* admissions@luther.edu. *Web site:* http://www.luther.edu/.
Visit Petersons.com and enter keywords Luther College

See page 930 for the College Close-Up.

Maharishi University of Management
Fairfield, Iowa

General Independent, university, coed **Entrance** Moderately difficult **Setting** 272-acre small-town campus **Total enrollment** 1,207 **Student-faculty ratio** 16:1 **Application deadline** 8/1 (freshmen), 8/1 (transfer) **Freshman admission** Average high school GPA 3.1 **Housing** Yes **Expenses** Tuition & Fees $24,000; Room & Board $6000 **Undergraduates** 43% women, 8% part-time, 32% 25 or older **The most frequently chosen baccalaureate fields are** liberal arts/general studies, natural resources/environmental science, visual and performing arts **Academic program** Advanced placement, self-designed majors, honors program, adult/continuing education programs, internships **Contact** Mother Supr. Michelle Paton, Associate Dean of Admissions, Maharishi University of Management, Office of Admissions, Fairfield, IA 52557. *Phone:* 641-472-1110 or toll-free 800-369-6480. *Fax:* 641-472-1179. *E-mail:* admissions@mum.edu. *Web site:* http://www.mum.edu/.

Mercy College of Health Sciences
Des Moines, Iowa

General Independent, 4-year, coed, primarily women, affiliated with Roman Catholic Church **Setting** 5-acre urban campus **Total enrollment** 778 **Student-faculty ratio** 12:1 **Application deadline** Rolling (freshmen), rolling (transfer) **Housing** No **Expenses** Tuition & Fees $13,000 **Undergraduates** 82% women, 41% part-time, 1% Native American, 3% Hispanic American, 3% African American, 2% Asian American/Pacific Islander **The most frequently chosen baccalaureate field is** health professions and related sciences **Academic program** Advanced placement, accelerated degree program, summer session **Contact** Kara Scholten, Admissions Manager, Mercy College of Health Sciences, 928 Sixth Avenue, Des Moines, IA 50309-1239. *Phone:* 515-643-3180 or toll-free 800-637-2994. *Fax:* 515-643-6698. *E-mail:* kscholten@mercydesmoines.org. *Web site:* http://www.mchs.edu/.

Morningside College
Sioux City, Iowa

General Independent, comprehensive, coed, affiliated with United Methodist Church **Entrance** Moderately difficult **Setting** 68-acre suburban campus **Total enrollment** 2,036 **Student-faculty ratio** 14:1 **Application deadline** Rolling (freshmen), rolling (transfer) **Freshman admission** 71% were admitted. Average high school GPA 3.39 **Freshman test scores** ACT scores over 18: 96%; ACT scores over 24: 38% **Housing** Yes **Expenses** Tuition & Fees $22,980; Room & Board $7040 **Undergraduates** 54% women, 3% part-time, 5% 25 or older, 1% Native American, 2% Hispanic American, 1% African American, 1% Asian American/Pacific Islander **The most frequently chosen baccalaureate fields are** business/marketing, education, health professions and related sciences **Academic program** English as a second language, advanced placement, self-designed majors, honors program, summer session, adult/continuing education programs, internships **Contact** Ms. Amy Williams, Co-Director of Admissions, Morningside College, 1501 Morningside Avenue, Sioux City, IA 51106. *Phone:* 712-274-5111 or toll-free 800-831-0806 Ext. 5111. *Fax:* 712-274-5101. *E-mail:* mscadm@morningside.edu. *Web site:* http://www.morningside.edu/.

See page 986 for the College Close-Up.

Sioux City, Iowa
(800) 831-0806, ext 5111
www.morningside.edu

The Morningside College experience cultivates a passion for life-long learning and a dedication to ethical leadership and civic responsibility.

Mount Mercy College
Cedar Rapids, Iowa

General Independent Roman Catholic, comprehensive, coed **Entrance** Moderately difficult **Setting** 40-acre suburban campus **Total enrollment** 1,666 **Student-faculty ratio** 13:1 **Application deadline** 8/15 (freshmen), 8/15 (transfer) **Freshman admission** 78% were admitted. Average high school GPA 3.42 **Freshman test scores** ACT scores over 18: 98.6%; ACT scores over 24: 35.8% **Housing** Yes **Expenses** Tuition & Fees $22,100; Room & Board $6984 **Undergraduates** 70% women, 37% part-time, 39% 25 or older, 0.1% Native American, 3% Hispanic American, 2% African American, 1% Asian American/Pacific Islander **The most frequently chosen baccalaureate fields are** business/marketing, education, health professions and related sciences **Academic program** Advanced placement, accelerated degree program, honors program, summer session, adult/continuing education programs, internships **Contact** Ms. Liz Metz, Assistant Director of Admissions, Mount Mercy College, 1330 Elmhurst Drive, NE, Cedar Rapids, IA 52402. *Phone:* 319-368-6460 or toll-free 800-248-4504. *Fax:* 319-363-5270. *E-mail:* emetz@mtmercy.edu. *Web site:* http://www.mtmercy.edu/.

Northwestern College
Orange City, Iowa

General Independent, 4-year, coed, affiliated with Reformed Church in America **Entrance** Moderately difficult **Setting** 45-acre rural campus **Total enrollment** 1,206 **Student-faculty ratio** 14:1 **Application deadline** Rolling (freshmen), rolling (transfer) **Freshman admission** 75% were admitted. Average high school GPA 3.52 **Freshman test scores** ACT scores over 18: 98.5%; ACT scores over 24: 61% **Housing** Yes **Expenses** Tuition & Fees $22,240; Room & Board $6756 **Undergraduates** 59% women, 3% part-time, 3% 25 or older, 0.2% Native American, 2% Hispanic American, 1% African American, 1% Asian American/Pacific Islander **The most frequently chosen baccalaureate fields are** business/marketing, education, psychology **Academic program** English as a second language, advanced placement, self-designed majors, honors program, summer session, internships **Contact** Mr. Mark Bloemendaal, Director of Admissions, Northwestern College, 101 7th Street SW, Orange City, IA 51041-1996. *Phone:* 712-737-7130 or toll-free 800-747-4757. *Fax:* 712-707-7164. *E-mail:* admissions@nwciowa.edu. *Web site:* http://www.nwciowa.edu/.

Palmer College of Chiropractic
Davenport, Iowa

General Independent, comprehensive, coed **Entrance** Noncompetitive **Setting** urban campus **Total enrollment** 2,116 **Application deadline** Rolling (freshmen) **Freshman admission** 67% were admitted **Housing** Yes **Expenses** Tuition & Fees $6975 **Undergraduates** 53% women, 4% part-time **The most frequently chosen baccalaureate field is** biological/life sciences **Academic program** Summer session, internships **Contact** Lisa Gisel, Undergraduate Admissions Representative, Palmer College of Chiropractic, 1000 Brady Street, Davenport, IA 52803-5287. *Phone:* 563-884-5743 or toll-free 800-722-3648. *Fax:* 563-884-5226. *E-mail:* lisa.gisel@palmer.edu. *Web site:* http://www.palmer.edu/.

St. Ambrose University
Davenport, Iowa

General Independent Roman Catholic, comprehensive, coed **Entrance** Moderately difficult **Setting** 118-acre urban campus **Total enrollment** 3,729 **Student-faculty ratio** 11:1 **Application deadline** Rolling (freshmen), rolling (transfer) **Freshman admission** 82% were admitted. Average high school GPA 3.12 **Freshman test scores** ACT scores over 18: 97.49%; ACT scores over 24: 36.31% **Housing** Yes **Expenses** Tuition & Fees $23,910; Room & Board $8585 **Undergraduates** 61% women, 16% part-time, 19% 25 or older, 0.5% Native American, 4% Hispanic American, 3% African American, 1% Asian American/Pacific Islander **The most frequently chosen baccalaureate fields are** business/marketing, education, health professions and related sciences **Academic program** Advanced placement, accelerated degree program, self-designed majors, summer session, adult/continuing education programs, internships **Contact** Ms. Meg Halligan, Director of Admissions, St. Ambrose University, 518 West Locust Street, Davenport, IA 52803-2898. *Phone:* 563-333-6300 Ext. 6311 or toll-free 800-383-2627. *Fax:* 563-333-6297. *E-mail:* higginsmegf@sau.edu. *Web site:* http://www.sau.edu/.

Simpson College
Indianola, Iowa

General Independent United Methodist, comprehensive, coed **Entrance** Moderately difficult **Setting** 85-acre suburban campus **Total enrollment** 2,023 **Student-faculty ratio** 14:1 **Application deadline** 8/15 (freshmen), 8/15 (transfer) **Freshman admission** 89% were admitted **Freshman test scores** ACT scores over 18: 99.2%; ACT scores over 24: 53.9% **Housing** Yes **Expenses** Tuition & Fees $25,733; Room & Board $7261 **Undergraduates** 57% women, 26% part-time, 20% 25 or older, 0.4% Native American, 2% Hispanic American, 2% African American, 2% Asian American/Pacific Islander **The most frequently chosen baccalaureate fields are** business/marketing, education, social sciences **Academic program** Advanced placement, accelerated degree program, self-designed majors, honors program, summer session, adult/continuing education programs, internships **Contact** Deborah Tierney, Vice President for Enrollment, Simpson College, 701 North C Street, Indianola, IA 50125. *Phone:* 515-961-1624 or toll-free 800-362-2454 (in-state); 800-362-2454 Ext. 1624 (out-of-state). *Fax:* 515-961-1870. *E-mail:* admiss@simpson.edu. *Web site:* http://www.simpson.edu/.

Visit Petersons.com and enter keyword Simpson

See page 1164 for the College Close-Up.

University of Dubuque
Dubuque, Iowa

General Independent Presbyterian, comprehensive, coed **Entrance** Moderately difficult **Setting** 56-acre suburban campus **Total enrollment** 1,718 **Student-faculty ratio** 14:1 **Application deadline** Rolling (freshmen), rolling (transfer) **Freshman admission** 75% were admitted. Average high school GPA 3 **Freshman test scores** SAT critical reading scores over 500: 40%; SAT math scores over 500: 45%; ACT scores over 18: 78%; SAT critical reading scores over 600: 4%; SAT math scores over 600: 12%; ACT scores over 24: 22% **Housing** Yes **Expenses** Tuition & Fees $21,590; Room & Board $7370 **Undergraduates** 45% women, 6% part-time, 12% 25 or older, 1% Native American, 4% Hispanic American, 12% African American, 2% Asian American/Pacific Islander **The most frequently chosen baccalaureate fields are** business/marketing, health professions and related sciences, transportation and materials moving **Academic program** English as a second language, advanced placement, accelerated degree program, self-designed majors, summer session, adult/continuing education programs, internships **Contact** Mr. Jesse James, Director of Admissions, University of Dubuque, 2000 University Avenue, Dubuque, IA 52001-5099. *Phone:* 563-589-3214 or toll-free 800-722-5583. *Fax:* 563-589-3690. *E-mail:* admissns@dbq.edu. *Web site:* http://www.dbq.edu/.

Visit Petersons.com and enter keyword Dubuque

See page 1266 for the College Close-Up.

The University of Iowa
Iowa City, Iowa

General State-supported, university, coed **Entrance** Moderately difficult **Setting** 1,900-acre small-town campus **Total enrollment** 28,987 **Student-faculty ratio** 15:1 **Application deadline** 4/1 (freshmen), 4/1 (transfer) **Freshman admission** 83% were admitted. Average high school GPA 3.57 **Freshman test scores** SAT critical reading scores over 500: 78%; SAT math scores over 500: 89%; ACT scores over 18: 99%; SAT critical reading scores over 600: 43%; SAT math scores over 600:

This is
SIMPSON

- Simpson College offers more than 50 majors, minors and pre-professional programs and is recognized for quality and value by national publications
- Located just miles from Iowa's capital city
- Combines an energetic academic environment with personal attention; 14:1 student/faculty ratio
- Student organizations and activities include award-winnig fine arts programs and nationally-ranked athletic teams
- Outstanding internship and study abroad opportunities
- Over 98 percent of Simpson students receive financial assistance

Indianola, Iowa
800-362-2454 | www.simpson.edu

62%; ACT scores over 24: 70% **Housing** Yes **Expenses** Tuition & Fees: state resident $7417, nonresident $23,713; Room & Board $8331 **Undergraduates** 52% women, 10% part-time, 9% 25 or older, 1% Native American, 3% Hispanic American, 2% African American, 4% Asian American/Pacific Islander **The most frequently chosen baccalaureate fields are** business/marketing, communications/journalism, social sciences **Academic program** English as a second language, advanced placement, accelerated degree program, self-designed majors, honors program, summer session, adult/continuing education programs, internships **Contact** Mr. Michael Barron, Assistant Provost for Enrollment Services and Director of Admissions, The University of Iowa, 107 Calvin Hall, Iowa City, IA 52242. *Phone:* 319-335-3847 or toll-free 800-553-4692. *Fax:* 319-335-1535. *E-mail:* admissions@uiowa.edu. *Web site:* http://www.uiowa.edu/.

University of Northern Iowa

Cedar Falls, Iowa

General State-supported, comprehensive, coed **Entrance** Moderately difficult **Setting** 916-acre small-town campus **Total enrollment** 13,303 **Student-faculty ratio** 17:1 **Application deadline** 8/15 (freshmen), 8/15 (transfer) **Freshman admission** 85% were admitted. Average high school GPA 3.41 **Freshman test scores** ACT scores over 18: 96.16%; ACT scores over 24: 42.21% **Housing** Yes **Expenses** Tuition & Fees: state resident $7008, nonresident $15,348; Room & Board $7189 **Undergraduates** 57% women, 10% part-time, 10% 25 or older, 0.2% Native American, 2% Hispanic American, 3% African American, 1% Asian American/Pacific Islander **The most frequently chosen baccalaureate fields are** business/marketing, communications/journalism, education **Academic program** English as a second language, advanced placement, accelerated degree program, self-designed majors, honors program, summer session, adult/continuing education programs, internships **Contact** Ms. Christie Kangas, Director of Admissions, University of Northern Iowa, 1227 West 27th Street, Cedar Falls, IA 50614. *Phone:* 319-273-2281 or toll-free 800-772-2037. *Fax:* 319-273-2885. *E-mail:* admissions@uni.edu. *Web site:* http://www.uni.edu/.

Upper Iowa University

Fayette, Iowa

General Independent, comprehensive, coed **Entrance** Moderately difficult **Setting** 80-acre rural campus **Total enrollment** 6,605 **Student-faculty ratio** 24:1 **Application deadline** Rolling (freshmen), rolling (transfer) **Freshman admission** 42% were admitted. Average high school GPA 2.94 **Housing** Yes **Expenses** Tuition & Fees $22,350; Room & Board $6870 **Undergraduates** 61% women, 49% part-time, 1% 25 or older, 0.2% Native American, 2% Hispanic American, 14% African American, 1% Asian American/Pacific Islander **Academic program** English as a second language, advanced placement, accelerated degree program, self-designed majors, summer session, adult/continuing education programs, internships **Contact** Renee Lape, Director for Admissions, Upper Iowa University, 605 Washington Street, Parker Fox Hall, Fayette, IA 52142. *Phone:* 800-553-4150 or toll-free 800-553-4150 Ext. 2. *E-mail:* admission@uiu.edu. *Web site:* http://www.uiu.edu/.

Vatterott College

Des Moines, Iowa

Contact Mr. Henry Franken, Co-Director, Vatterott College, 6100 Thornton Avenue, Suite 290, Des Moines, IA 50321. *Phone:* 515-309-9000 or toll-free 800-353-7264. *Fax:* 515-309-0366. *Web site:* http://www.vatterott-college.edu/.

Waldorf College

Forest City, Iowa

General Independent Lutheran, 4-year, coed **Entrance** Moderately difficult **Setting** 51-acre rural campus **Total enrollment** 558 **Student-**

Waldorf College (continued)
faculty ratio 14:1 **Application deadline** Rolling (freshmen), rolling (transfer) **Freshman admission** 59% were admitted. Average high school GPA 3.01 **Freshman test scores** ACT scores over 18: 79%; ACT scores over 24: 15% **Housing** Yes **Expenses** Tuition & Fees $18,760; Room & Board $5954 **Undergraduates** 45% women, 12% part-time, 7% 25 or older, 0.4% Native American, 5% Hispanic American, 9% African American, 1% Asian American/Pacific Islander **The most frequently chosen baccalaureate fields are** business/marketing, communications/journalism, education **Academic program** Advanced placement, accelerated degree program, self-designed majors, honors program, summer session, adult/continuing education programs, internships **Contact** Carl Childs, Director for Admission, Waldorf College, 106 South 6th Street, Forest City, IA 50436-1713. *Phone:* 641-585-8112 or toll-free 800-292-1903. *Fax:* 641-585-8125. *E-mail:* admissions@waldorf.edu. *Web site:* http://www.waldorf.edu/.

Wartburg College
Waverly, Iowa

General Independent Lutheran, 4-year, coed **Entrance** Moderately difficult **Setting** 118-acre small-town campus **Total enrollment** 1,800 **Student-faculty ratio** 12:1 **Application deadline** Rolling (freshmen), rolling (transfer) **Freshman admission** 73% were admitted. Average high school GPA 3.48 **Freshman test scores** SAT critical reading scores over 500: 52%; SAT math scores over 500: 66%; ACT scores over 18: 95%; SAT critical reading scores over 600: 29%; SAT math scores over 600: 32%; ACT scores over 24: 52% **Housing** Yes **Expenses** Tuition & Fees $29,020; Room & Board $7975 **Undergraduates** 52% women, 4% part-time, 1% 25 or older, 0.2% Native American, 2% Hispanic American, 5% African American, 2% Asian American/Pacific Islander **The most frequently chosen baccalaureate fields are** biological/life sciences, business/marketing, education **Academic program** Advanced placement, accelerated degree program, self-designed majors, honors program, summer session, internships **Contact** Mr. Todd Coleman, Assistant Vice President for Admissions, Wartburg College, 100 Wartburg Boulevard, PO Box 1003, Waverly, IA 50677-0903. *Phone:* 319-352-8264 or toll-free 800-772-2085. *Fax:* 319-352-8579. *E-mail:* admissions@wartburg.edu. *Web site:* http://www.wartburg.edu/.

William Penn University
Oskaloosa, Iowa

General Independent, comprehensive, coed, affiliated with Society of Friends **Entrance** Moderately difficult **Setting** 60-acre rural campus **Total enrollment** 1,861 **Student-faculty ratio** 15:1 **Freshman admission** 55% were admitted. Average high school GPA 2.88 **Freshman test scores** ACT scores over 18: 69%; ACT scores over 24: 11% **Housing** Yes **Expenses** Tuition & Fees $20,234; Room & Board $5392 **Undergraduates** 53% women, 2% part-time, 31% 25 or older, 1% Native American, 6% Hispanic American, 11% African American, 2% Asian American/Pacific Islander **The most frequently chosen baccalaureate fields are** business/marketing, education, social sciences **Academic program** English as a second language, advanced placement, self-designed majors, summer session, adult/continuing education programs, internships **Contact** John Ottosson, Vice President for Enrollment Management, William Penn University, 201 Trueblood Avenue, Oskaloosa, IA 52577-1799. *Phone:* 641-673-1012 or toll-free 800-779-7366. *Fax:* 641-673-2113. *E-mail:* admissions@wmpenn.edu. *Web site:* http://www.wmpenn.edu/.

KANSAS

The Art Institutes International–Kansas City
Lenexa, Kansas

General Proprietary, 4-year, coed **Contact** Admissions Office, The Art Institutes International–Kansas City, 8208 Melrose Drive, Lenexa, KS 66214. *Phone:* 913-217-4600 or toll-free 866-530-8508. *Fax:* 913-217-4690. *Web site:* http://www.artinstitutes.edu/kansascity/.
Visit Petersons.com and enter keywords Art Institutes International-Kansas City

See page 560 for the College Close-Up.

Baker University
Baldwin City, Kansas

General Independent United Methodist, comprehensive, coed **Entrance** Moderately difficult **Setting** 26-acre small-town campus **Total enrollment** 992 **Student-faculty ratio** 12:1 **Application deadline** Rolling (freshmen), rolling (transfer) **Freshman admission** 56% were admitted. Average high school GPA 3.48 **Freshman test scores** ACT scores over 18: 98%; ACT scores over 24: 47% **Housing** Yes **Expenses** Tuition & Fees $21,050; Room & Board $6800 **Undergraduates** 53% women, 9% part-time, 3% 25 or older, 1% Native American, 1% Hispanic American, 8% African American, 1% Asian American/Pacific Islander **The most frequently chosen baccalaureate fields are** business/marketing, education, parks and recreation **Academic program** Advanced placement, self-designed majors, honors program, summer session, internships **Contact** Mr. Daniel McKinney, Director of Admissions, Baker University, PO Box 65, Baldwin City, KS 66006-0065. *Phone:* 785-594-8307 or toll-free 800-873-4282. *Fax:* 785-594-8372. *E-mail:* admissions@bakeru.edu. *Web site:* http://www.bakeru.edu/.

Barclay College
Haviland, Kansas

General Independent, 4-year, coed, affiliated with Society of Friends **Entrance** Minimally difficult **Setting** 13-acre rural campus **Total enrollment** 194 **Student-faculty ratio** 12:1 **Application deadline** 9/1 (freshmen), 9/1 (transfer) **Freshman admission** 73% were admitted **Freshman test scores** ACT scores over 18: 82%; ACT scores over 24: 14% **Housing** Yes **Expenses** Tuition & Fees $13,690; Room & Board $6600 **Undergraduates** 49% women, 12% part-time, 24% 25 or older, 1% Native American, 5% Hispanic American, 5% African American, 2% Asian American/Pacific Islander **The most frequently chosen baccalaureate fields are** psychology, business/marketing, theology and religious vocations **Academic program** Advanced placement, adult/continuing education programs, internships **Contact** Mr. Justin Kendall, Admissions Recruiter, Barclay College, 607 North Kingman, Haviland, KS 67059. *Phone:* 620-862-5252 Ext. 21 or toll-free 800-862-0226. *Fax:* 620-862-5242. *E-mail:* jkendall@barclaycollege.edu. *Web site:* http://www.barclaycollege.edu/.

Benedictine College
Atchison, Kansas

General Independent Roman Catholic, comprehensive, coed **Entrance** Moderately difficult **Setting** 225-acre small-town campus **Total enrollment** 1,874 **Student-faculty ratio** 15:1 **Freshman admission** 61% were admitted. Average high school GPA 3.34 **Freshman test scores** ACT scores over 18: 96%; ACT scores over 24: 52% **Housing** Yes **Expenses** Tuition & Fees $19,500; Room & Board $6575 **Undergraduates** 53% women, 19% part-time, 3% 25 or older, 0.3% Native American, 5% Hispanic American, 4% African American, 0.4% Asian American/Pacific Islander **The most frequently chosen baccalaureate fields are** business/marketing, education, visual and performing arts

Academic program English as a second language, advanced placement, self-designed majors, summer session, internships **Contact** Mr. Pete Helgesen, Dean of Enrollment Management, Benedictine College, 1020 North 2nd Street, Atchison, KS 66002-1499. *Phone:* 913-367-5340 Ext. 2476 or toll-free 800-467-5340. *E-mail:* phelgesen@benedictine.edu. *Web site:* http://www.benedictine.edu/.

Bethany College
Lindsborg, Kansas

General Independent Lutheran, 4-year, coed **Entrance** Moderately difficult **Setting** 80-acre small-town campus **Total enrollment** 587 **Student-faculty ratio** 9:1 **Application deadline** Rolling (freshmen), rolling (transfer) **Freshman admission** 65% were admitted. Average high school GPA 3.33 **Freshman test scores** SAT critical reading scores over 500: 26%; SAT math scores over 500: 50%; ACT scores over 18: 86%; SAT critical reading scores over 600: 3%; SAT math scores over 600: 10%; ACT scores over 24: 34% **Housing** Yes **Expenses** Tuition & Fees $20,026; Room & Board $6174 **Undergraduates** 49% women, 5% part-time, 4% 25 or older, 1% Native American, 7% Hispanic American, 11% African American, 1% Asian American/Pacific Islander **The most frequently chosen baccalaureate fields are** biological/life sciences, business/marketing, education **Academic program** Advanced placement, accelerated degree program, self-designed majors, honors program, summer session, internships **Contact** Mrs. Tricia Hawk, Dean of Admissions and Financial Aid, Bethany College, 335 East Swensson Street, Lindsborg, KS 67456-1897. *Phone:* 785-227-3311 Ext. 8344 or toll-free 800-826-2281. *Fax:* 785-227-8993. *E-mail:* admissions@bethanylb.edu. *Web site:* http://www.bethanylb.edu/.

Bethel College
North Newton, Kansas

General Independent, 4-year, coed, affiliated with Mennonite Church USA **Entrance** Moderately difficult **Setting** 60-acre small-town campus **Total enrollment** 437 **Student-faculty ratio** 9:1 **Application deadline** Rolling (freshmen), rolling (transfer) **Freshman admission** 75% were admitted. Average high school GPA 3.6 **Freshman test scores** SAT critical reading scores over 500: 50%; SAT math scores over 500: 70%; ACT scores over 18: 90%; SAT critical reading scores over 600: 30%; SAT math scores over 600: 30%; ACT scores over 24: 60% **Housing** Yes **Expenses** Tuition & Fees $19,990; Room & Board $6770 **Undergraduates** 49% women, 5% part-time, 7% 25 or older, 1% Native American, 7% Hispanic American, 5% African American, 2% Asian American/Pacific Islander **The most frequently chosen baccalaureate fields are** business/marketing, biological/life sciences, health professions and related sciences **Academic program** Advanced placement, internships **Contact** Mr. Todd H. Moore, Vice President for Admissions, Bethel College, 300 East 27th Street, North Newton, KS 67117-0531. *Phone:* 316-284-5230 or toll-free 800-522-1887 Ext. 230. *Fax:* 316-284-5870. *E-mail:* admissions@bethelks.edu. *Web site:* http://www.bethelks.edu/.

Central Christian College of Kansas
McPherson, Kansas

General Independent Free Methodist, 4-year, coed **Entrance** Minimally difficult **Setting** 16-acre small-town campus **Total enrollment** 466 **Student-faculty ratio** 14:1 **Application deadline** Rolling (freshmen), rolling (transfer) **Freshman admission** 99% were admitted. Average high school GPA 3.27 **Freshman test scores** ACT scores over 18: 80%; ACT scores over 24: 27% **Housing** Yes **Expenses** Tuition & Fees $18,000; Room & Board $5900 **Undergraduates** 49% women, 30% part-time, 5% 25 or older, 2% Native American, 4% Hispanic American, 15% African American, 0.3% Asian American/Pacific Islander **The most frequently chosen baccalaureate fields are** business/marketing, liberal arts/general studies, theology and religious vocations **Academic program** Advanced placement, self-designed majors, adult/continuing education programs, internships **Contact** Mr. Rick Wyatt, Director of Admissions, Central Christian College of Kansas, 1200 South Main, PO Box 1403, McPherson, KS 67460-5799. *Phone:* 620-241-0723 Ext. 380 or toll-free 800-835-0078 Ext. 337. *Fax:* 620-241-6032. *E-mail:* rick.wyatt@centralchristian.edu. *Web site:* http://www.centralchristian.edu/.

Cleveland Chiropractic College–Kansas City Campus
Overland Park, Kansas

Contact Ms. Melissa Denton, Director of Admissions, Cleveland Chiropractic College–Kansas City Campus, 10850 Lowell Avenue, Overland Park, KS 66210. *Phone:* 913-234-0750 or toll-free 800-467-2252. *Fax:* 913-234-0912. *E-mail:* kc.admissions@cleveland.edu. *Web site:* http://www.cleveland.edu/.

Donnelly College
Kansas City, Kansas

General Independent Roman Catholic, primarily 2-year, coed **Entrance** Noncompetitive **Setting** 4-acre urban campus **Total enrollment** 661 **Student-faculty ratio** 16:1 **Application deadline** Rolling (freshmen), rolling (transfer) **Housing** Yes **Undergraduates** 75% women, 56% part-time, 65% 25 or older, 1% Native American, 26% Hispanic American, 48% African American, 5% Asian American/Pacific Islander **The most frequently chosen baccalaureate field is** public administration and social services **Academic program** English as a second language, advanced placement, summer session, internships **Contact** Mr. Edward Marquez, Director of Admissions, Donnelly College, 608 N. 18th Street, Kansas City, KS 66102. *Phone:* 913-621-8713. *Fax:* 913-621-8719. *E-mail:* admissions@donnelly.edu. *Web site:* http://www.donnelly.edu/.

Emporia State University
Emporia, Kansas

General State-supported, comprehensive, coed **Entrance** Noncompetitive **Setting** 207-acre small-town campus **Total enrollment** 6,314 **Student-faculty ratio** 18:1 **Application deadline** Rolling (freshmen), rolling (transfer) **Freshman admission** 88% were admitted. Average high school GPA 3.24 **Freshman test scores** ACT scores over 18: 85%; ACT scores over 24: 36% **Housing** Yes **Expenses** Tuition & Fees: state resident $4374, nonresident $13,578; Room & Board $6146 **Undergraduates** 60% women, 11% part-time, 18% 25 or older, 1% Native American, 5% Hispanic American, 6% African American, 1% Asian American/Pacific Islander **The most frequently chosen baccalaureate fields are** business/marketing, education, social sciences **Academic program** English as a second language, advanced placement, accelerated degree program, honors program, summer session, adult/continuing education programs, internships **Contact** Ms. Laura Eddy, Director of Admissions, Emporia State University, 1200 Commercial Street, Campus Box 4034, Emporia, KS 66801-5087. *Phone:* 620-341-5465 or toll-free 877-GOTOESU (in-state); 877-468-6378 (out-of-state). *Fax:* 620-341-5599. *E-mail:* go2esu@emporia.edu. *Web site:* http://www.emporia.edu/.

Fort Hays State University
Hays, Kansas

General State-supported, comprehensive, coed **Entrance** Noncompetitive **Setting** 200-acre small-town campus **Total enrollment** 11,537 **Student-faculty ratio** 17:1 **Application deadline** Rolling (freshmen) **Expenses** Tuition & Fees: state resident $3762, nonresident $11,915; Room & Board $6370 **Academic program** Summer session, internships **Contact** Tricia Cline, Director, Admissions, Fort Hays State University, 600 Park Street, Hays, KS 67601-4099. *Phone:* 785-628-4091 or toll-free 800-628-FHSU. *E-mail:* tcline@fhsu.edu. *Web site:* http://www.fhsu.edu/.

Friends University
Wichita, Kansas

General Independent, comprehensive, coed **Entrance** Moderately difficult **Setting** 45-acre urban campus **Total enrollment** 2,853 **Student-faculty ratio** 13:1 **Application deadline** Rolling (freshmen), rolling (transfer) **Freshman admission** 66% were admitted. Average high school GPA 3.21 **Freshman test scores** ACT scores over 18: 76.8%; ACT scores over 24: 35.6% **Housing** Yes **Expenses** Tuition & Fees $20,040; Room & Board $5790 **Undergraduates** 59% women, 19% part-time, 50% 25 or older, 1% Native American, 5% Hispanic American, 9% African American, 1% Asian American/Pacific Islander **The most frequently chosen baccalaureate fields are** business/marketing, computer and information sciences, education **Academic program** Advanced placement, accelerated degree program, summer session, adult/continuing education programs, internships **Contact** Erin Haneberg, Director of Admissions, Friends University, 2100 W University Avenue, Wichita, KS 67213. *Phone:* 316-794-6945 or toll-free 800-577-2233. *Fax:* 316-295-5101. *E-mail:* haneberg@friends.edu. *Web site:* http://www.friends.edu/.

Haskell Indian Nations University
Lawrence, Kansas

General Federally supported, 4-year, coed **Entrance** Minimally difficult **Setting** 320-acre suburban campus **Total enrollment** 894 **Application deadline** 7/30 (freshmen), 7/30 (transfer) **Housing** Yes **Undergraduates** 24% 25 or older, 100% Native American **Academic program** Advanced placement, self-designed majors, summer session, internships **Contact** Ms. Patty Grant, Recruitment Officer, Haskell Indian Nations University, 155 Indian Avenue, #5031, Lawrence, KS 66046-4800. *Phone:* 785-749-8437 Ext. 437. *E-mail:* admissions@haskell.edu. *Web site:* http://www.haskell.edu/.

ITT Technical Institute
Wichita, Kansas

General Proprietary, 4-year, coed **Contact** Director of Recruitment, ITT Technical Institute, One Brittany Place, Suite 100, 2024 North Woodlawn, Wichita, KS 67208. *Phone:* 316-681-8400 or toll-free 877-207-1047. *Web site:* http://www.itt-tech.edu/.

Kansas State University
Manhattan, Kansas

General State-supported, university, coed **Entrance** Noncompetitive **Setting** 668-acre suburban campus **Total enrollment** 23,581 **Student-faculty ratio** 20:1 **Application deadline** Rolling (freshmen), rolling (transfer) **Freshman admission** 55% were admitted. Average high school GPA 3.4 **Freshman test scores** ACT scores over 18: 94%; ACT scores over 24: 54.8% **Housing** Yes **Expenses** Tuition & Fees: state resident $6870, nonresident $17,577; Room & Board $6752 **Undergraduates** 48% women, 12% part-time, 10% 25 or older, 1% Native American, 4% Hispanic American, 4% African American, 1% Asian American/Pacific Islander **The most frequently chosen baccalaureate fields are** business/marketing, agriculture, social sciences **Academic program** English as a second language, advanced placement, accelerated degree program, honors program, summer session, adult/continuing education programs, internships **Contact** Ms. Molly McGaughey, Associate Director of Admissions, Kansas State University, 119 Anderson Hall, Manhattan, KS 66506. *Phone:* 785-532-6250 or toll-free 800-432-8270. *Fax:* 785-532-6393. *E-mail:* k-state@k-state.edu. *Web site:* http://www.k-state.edu/.

Kansas Wesleyan University
Salina, Kansas

General Independent United Methodist, comprehensive, coed **Entrance** Moderately difficult **Setting** 28-acre urban campus **Total enrollment** 879 **Student-faculty ratio** 14:1 **Application deadline** Rolling (freshmen), rolling (transfer) **Freshman admission** 63% were admitted. Average high school GPA 3.20 **Freshman test scores** ACT scores over 18: 100%; ACT scores over 24: 30% **Housing** Yes **Expenses** Tuition & Fees $19,200; Room & Board $6600 **Undergraduates** 17% 25 or older **The most frequently chosen baccalaureate fields are** business/marketing, health professions and related sciences, parks and recreation **Academic program** English as a second language, advanced placement, self-designed majors, summer session, adult/continuing education programs, internships **Contact** Mr. Jim Allen, Director of Admissions, Kansas Wesleyan University, 100 East Claflin Avenue, Salina, KS 67401-6196. *Phone:* 785-827-5541 Ext. 1283 or toll-free 800-874-1154 Ext. 1285. *E-mail:* jallen@kwu.edu. *Web site:* http://www.kwu.edu/.

Manhattan Christian College
Manhattan, Kansas

General Independent, 4-year, coed, affiliated with Christian Churches and Churches of Christ **Entrance** Minimally difficult **Setting** 10-acre small-town campus **Total enrollment** 388 **Application deadline** 8/1 (freshmen), 8/1 (transfer) **Housing** Yes **Expenses** Tuition & Fees $11,374; Room & Board $6720 **Undergraduates** 21% 25 or older **Academic program** Advanced placement, summer session, adult/continuing education programs, internships **Contact** Eric Ingmire, Director of Admissions, Manhattan Christian College, 1415 Anderson Avenue, Manhattan, KS 66502-4081. *Phone:* 785-539-3571 Ext. 324 or toll-free 877-246-4622. *E-mail:* admit@mccks.edu. *Web site:* http://www.mccks.edu/.

McPherson College
McPherson, Kansas

General Independent, 4-year, coed, affiliated with Church of the Brethren **Entrance** Moderately difficult **Setting** 26-acre small-town campus **Total enrollment** 629 **Student-faculty ratio** 15:1 **Application deadline** Rolling (freshmen), rolling (transfer) **Freshman admission** 87% were admitted. Average high school GPA 3.16 **Freshman test scores** SAT critical reading scores over 500: 45%; SAT math scores over 500: 60%; ACT scores over 18: 96.58%; SAT critical reading scores over 600: 20%; SAT math scores over 600: 10%; ACT scores over 24: 31.62% **Housing** Yes **Expenses** Tuition & Fees $18,400; Room & Board $6910 **Undergraduates** 44% women, 14% part-time **The most frequently chosen baccalaureate fields are** business/marketing, engineering technologies, visual and performing arts **Academic program** Advanced placement, self-designed majors, summer session, adult/continuing education programs, internships **Contact** Mr. Matt Pfannenstiel, Director of Admissions, McPherson College, 1600 E Euclid, McPherson, KS 67460. *Phone:* 800-365-7402 or toll-free 800-365-7402. *E-mail:* admiss@mcpherson.edu. *Web site:* http://www.mcpherson.edu/.

MidAmerica Nazarene University
Olathe, Kansas

General Independent, comprehensive, coed, affiliated with Church of the Nazarene **Entrance** Moderately difficult **Setting** 105-acre suburban campus **Total enrollment** 1,778 **Student-faculty ratio** 8:1 **Application deadline** 8/1 (freshmen), 8/1 (transfer) **Freshman admission** 74% were admitted. Average high school GPA 3.4 **Freshman test scores** SAT critical reading scores over 500: 58%; SAT math scores over 500: 54%; ACT scores over 18: 91%; SAT critical reading scores over 600: 21%; SAT math scores over 600: 17%; ACT scores over 24: 43% **Housing** Yes **Expenses** Tuition & Fees $20,250; Room & Board $6750 **Undergraduates** 58% women, 22% part-time, 33% 25 or older, 0.5% Native American, 4% Hispanic American, 11% African American, 1% Asian American/Pacific Islander **The most frequently chosen baccalaureate fields are** business/marketing, education, health professions and related sciences **Academic program** Advanced placement, accelerated degree program, self-designed majors, summer session, adult/continuing education programs, internships **Contact** Mr. Dennis Miller, Associate

Director of Admissions, MidAmerica Nazarene University, 2030 East College Way, Olathe, KS 66062-1899. *Phone:* 913-971-3380 or toll-free 800-800-8887. *Fax:* 913-971-3481. *E-mail:* admissions@mnu.edu. *Web site:* http://www.mnu.edu/.

Visit Petersons.com and enter keyword MidAmerica

Newman University
Wichita, Kansas

General Independent Roman Catholic, comprehensive, coed **Entrance** Minimally difficult **Setting** 61-acre urban campus **Total enrollment** 2,557 **Student-faculty ratio** 14:1 **Application deadline** Rolling (freshmen), rolling (transfer) **Freshman admission** 42% were admitted. Average high school GPA 3.4 **Freshman test scores** SAT critical reading scores over 500: 39%; SAT math scores over 500: 52%; ACT scores over 18: 95%; SAT critical reading scores over 600: 18%; SAT math scores over 600: 18%; ACT scores over 24: 42% **Housing** Yes **Expenses** Tuition & Fees $20,712; Room & Board $6938 **Undergraduates** 66% women, 47% part-time, 36% 25 or older, 2% Native American, 10% Hispanic American, 6% African American, 4% Asian American/Pacific Islander **The most frequently chosen baccalaureate fields are** education, business/marketing, health professions and related sciences **Academic program** Advanced placement, accelerated degree program, self-designed majors, honors program, summer session, adult/continuing education programs, internships **Contact** Jann Reusser, Admissions Coordinator, Newman University, 3100 McCormick Avenue, Wichita, KS 67213. *Phone:* 316-942-1291 Ext. 2144 or toll-free 877-NEWMANU Ext. 2144. *Fax:* 316-942-4483. *E-mail:* reusserj@newmanu.edu. *Web site:* http://www.newmanu.edu/.

Ottawa University
Ottawa, Kansas

General Independent American Baptist Churches in the USA, 4-year, coed **Entrance** Moderately difficult **Setting** 64-acre small-town campus **Total enrollment** 531 **Student-faculty ratio** 18:1 **Application deadline** Rolling (freshmen), rolling (transfer) **Freshman admission** 70% were admitted. Average high school GPA 3.28 **Freshman test scores** SAT critical reading scores over 500: 30%; SAT math scores over 500: 43%; ACT scores over 18: 84%; SAT critical reading scores over 600: 15%; ACT scores over 24: 23% **Housing** Yes **Expenses** Tuition & Fees $20,400; Room & Board $7014 **Undergraduates** 48% women, 4% part-time, 15% 25 or older, 3% Native American, 4% Hispanic American, 15% African American, 1% Asian American/Pacific Islander **The most frequently chosen baccalaureate fields are** business/marketing, communications/journalism, parks and recreation **Academic program** Advanced placement, self-designed majors, summer session, internships **Contact** Ms. June Unrein, Dean of Enrollment Management, Ottawa University, 1001 South Cedar, Ottawa, KS 66067-3399. *Phone:* 785-229-1051 or toll-free 800-755-5200 Ext. 5559. *E-mail:* june.unrein@ottawa.edu. *Web site:* http://www.ottawa.edu/.

Pittsburg State University
Pittsburg, Kansas

General State-supported, comprehensive, coed **Entrance** Minimally difficult **Setting** 443-acre small-town campus **Total enrollment** 7,277 **Student-faculty ratio** 19:1 **Application deadline** Rolling (freshmen), rolling (transfer) **Freshman admission** 80% were admitted. Average high school GPA 3.3 **Freshman test scores** ACT scores over 18: 89%; ACT scores over 24: 32% **Housing** Yes **Expenses** Tuition & Fees: state resident $4592, nonresident $13,116; Room & Board $5744 **Undergraduates** 46% women, 5% part-time, 16% 25 or older, 2% Native American, 3% Hispanic American, 3% African American, 1% Asian American/Pacific Islander **The most frequently chosen baccalaureate fields are** business/marketing, education, engineering technologies **Academic program** English as a second language, advanced placement, self-designed majors, honors program, summer session, adult/continuing education programs, internships **Contact** Director of Admission, Pittsburg State University, 1701 South Broadway, Pittsburg, KS 66762. *Phone:* 620-235-4251 or toll-free 800-854-7488 Ext. 1. *Fax:* 620-235-6003. *E-mail:* psuadmit@pittstate.edu. *Web site:* http://www.pittstate.edu/.

Southwestern College
Winfield, Kansas

General Independent United Methodist, comprehensive, coed **Entrance** Moderately difficult **Setting** 70-acre small-town campus **Total enrollment** 1,810 **Student-faculty ratio** 12:1 **Application deadline** 8/25 (freshmen), 8/25 (transfer) **Freshman admission** 90% were admitted. Average high school GPA 3.33 **Freshman test scores** SAT critical reading scores over 500: 40%; SAT math scores over 500: 64%; ACT scores over 18: 81%; SAT critical reading scores over 600: 12%; SAT math scores over 600: 12%; ACT scores over 24: 33% **Housing** Yes **Expenses** Tuition & Fees $19,630; Room & Board $5750 **Undergraduates** 48% women, 62% part-time, 7% 25 or older, 2% Native American, 6% Hispanic American, 8% African American, 2% Asian American/Pacific Islander **The most frequently chosen baccalaureate fields are** business/marketing, computer and information sciences, security and protective services **Academic program** Advanced placement, accelerated degree program, self-designed majors, honors program, summer session, adult/continuing education programs, internships **Contact** Mrs. Marla Sexson, Director of Admission, Southwestern College, 100 College Street, Winfield, KS 67156-2499. *Phone:* 620-229-6364 or toll-free 800-846-1543. *E-mail:* scadmit@sckans.edu. *Web site:* http://www.sckans.edu/.

Sterling College
Sterling, Kansas

General Independent Presbyterian, 4-year, coed **Entrance** Minimally difficult **Setting** 46-acre rural campus **Total enrollment** 722 **Student-faculty ratio** 14:1 **Application deadline** 7/15 (freshmen), rolling (transfer) **Freshman admission** 55% were admitted. Average high school GPA 3.2 **Freshman test scores** SAT critical reading scores over 500: 36%; SAT math scores over 500: 47%; ACT scores over 18: 87%; SAT critical reading scores over 600: 4%; SAT math scores over 600: 4%; ACT scores over 24: 28% **Housing** Yes **Expenses** Tuition & Fees $19,000; Room & Board $6830 **Undergraduates** 49% women, 17% part-time, 7% 25 or older, 2% Native American, 7% Hispanic American, 7% African American, 1% Asian American/Pacific Islander **The most frequently chosen baccalaureate fields are** business/marketing, parks and recreation, theology and religious vocations **Academic program** Advanced placement, self-designed majors, internships **Contact** Marge Jones, Admissions Office Manager, Sterling College, 125 West Cooper, Sterling, KS 67579. *Phone:* 620-278-4275 or toll-free 800-346-1017. *Fax:* 620-278-4416. *E-mail:* admissions@sterling.edu. *Web site:* http://www.sterling.edu/.

Tabor College
Hillsboro, Kansas

General Independent Mennonite Brethren, comprehensive, coed **Entrance** Moderately difficult **Setting** 26-acre small-town campus **Total enrollment** 640 **Student-faculty ratio** 12:1 **Application deadline** 8/1 (freshmen), 8/1 (transfer) **Freshman admission** 94% were admitted. Average high school GPA 3.31 **Freshman test scores** ACT scores over 18: 85%; ACT scores over 24: 35% **Housing** Yes **Expenses** Tuition & Fees $19,660; Room & Board $6870 **Undergraduates** 50% women, 17% part-time, 4% 25 or older, 1% Native American, 7% Hispanic American, 7% African American, 1% Asian American/Pacific Islander **The most frequently chosen baccalaureate fields are** business/marketing, education, health professions and related sciences **Academic program** Advanced placement, accelerated degree program, self-designed majors, honors program, adult/continuing education programs, internships **Contact** Dr. Linda Cantwell, Vice President of Enrollment Management, Tabor College, 400 South Jefferson, Hillsboro, KS 67063.

Tabor College (continued)
Phone: 620-947-3121 Ext. 1727 or toll-free 800-822-6799. *Fax:* 620-947-6276. *E-mail:* lindac@tabor.edu. *Web site:* http://www.tabor.edu/.

The University of Kansas
Lawrence, Kansas

General State-supported, university, coed **Entrance** Moderately difficult **Setting** 1,100-acre suburban campus **Total enrollment** 29,242 **Student-faculty ratio** 20:1 **Application deadline** 4/1 (freshmen), 5/1 (transfer) **Freshman admission** 91% were admitted. Average high school GPA 3.4 **Freshman test scores** ACT scores over 18: 98%; ACT scores over 24: 60% **Housing** Yes **Expenses** Tuition & Fees: state resident $8206, nonresident $20,174; Room & Board $6802 **Undergraduates** 50% women, 10% part-time, 8% 25 or older, 1% Native American, 4% Hispanic American, 4% African American, 4% Asian American/Pacific Islander **The most frequently chosen baccalaureate fields are** business/marketing, health professions and related sciences, social sciences **Academic program** English as a second language, advanced placement, accelerated degree program, honors program, summer session, internships **Contact** Ms. Lisa Pinamonti Kress, Director of Admissions and Scholarships, The University of Kansas, KU Visitor Center, 1502 Iowa Street, Lawrence, KS 66045-7576. *Phone:* 785-864-3911 or toll-free 888-686-7323. *Fax:* 785-864-5006. *E-mail:* adm@ku.edu. *Web site:* http://www.ku.edu.

University of Phoenix–Wichita Campus
Wichita, Kansas

General Proprietary, comprehensive, coed **Entrance** Noncompetitive **Setting** urban campus **Total enrollment** 135 **Application deadline** Rolling (freshmen), rolling (transfer) **Housing** No **Expenses** Tuition & Fees $11,775 **Undergraduates** 57% women, 82% 25 or older, 2% Native American, 4% Hispanic American, 14% African American, 2% Asian American/Pacific Islander **The most frequently chosen baccalaureate fields are** business/marketing, computer and information sciences, health professions and related sciences **Academic program** Advanced placement, accelerated degree program **Contact** Ms. Audra McQuarie, Registrar/Executive Director, University of Phoenix–Wichita Campus, 4035 South Riverpoint Parkway, Mail Stop CF-L101, Phoenix, AZ 85040. *Phone:* 480-557-6151 or toll-free 800-776-4867 (in-state); 800-228-7240 (out-of-state). *Fax:* 480-643-3068. *E-mail:* audra.mcquarie@phoenix.edu. *Web site:* http://www.phoenix.edu/.

University of Saint Mary
Leavenworth, Kansas

General Independent Roman Catholic, comprehensive, coed **Entrance** Moderately difficult **Setting** 240-acre small-town campus **Total enrollment** 1,072 **Student-faculty ratio** 11:1 **Application deadline** Rolling (freshmen), rolling (transfer) **Freshman admission** 70% were admitted **Freshman test scores** SAT critical reading scores over 500: 39%; SAT math scores over 500: 53%; ACT scores over 18: 82%; SAT critical reading scores over 600: 8%; SAT math scores over 600: 15%; ACT scores over 24: 27% **Housing** Yes **Expenses** Tuition & Fees $19,960; Room & Board $6350 **Undergraduates** 64% women, 34% part-time, 19% 25 or older, 1% Native American, 8% Hispanic American, 12% African American, 1% Asian American/Pacific Islander **The most frequently chosen baccalaureate fields are** business/marketing, health professions and related sciences, psychology **Academic program** Advanced placement, self-designed majors, honors program, summer session, adult/continuing education programs, internships **Contact** Mr. Brandon Johnson, Director of Admissions, University of Saint Mary, 4100 South Fourth Street, Leavenworth, KS 66048. *Phone:* 913-758-6118 or toll-free 800-752-7043. *Fax:* 913-758-6140. *E-mail:* admiss@stmary.edu. *Web site:* http://www.stmary.edu/.

Washburn University
Topeka, Kansas

General City-supported, comprehensive, coed **Entrance** Noncompetitive **Setting** 160-acre urban campus **Total enrollment** 6,652 **Student-faculty ratio** 16:1 **Application deadline** 7/31 (freshmen), 7/31 (transfer) **Freshman admission** 100% were admitted. Average high school GPA 3.2 **Freshman test scores** ACT scores over 18: 83%; ACT scores over 24: 31% **Housing** Yes **Expenses** Tuition & Fees: state resident $6116, nonresident $13,766; Room & Board $5792 **Undergraduates** 61% women, 32% part-time, 34% 25 or older **The most frequently chosen baccalaureate fields are** business/marketing, education, health professions and related sciences **Academic program** English as a second language, advanced placement, self-designed majors, honors program, summer session, adult/continuing education programs, internships **Contact** Director of Admission, Washburn University, 1700 SW College, MO 114, Topeka, KS 66621. *Phone:* 785-670-1030 or toll-free 800-332-0291. *Fax:* 785-670-1113. *E-mail:* admissions@washburn.edu. *Web site:* http://www.washburn.edu/.

Wichita State University
Wichita, Kansas

General State-supported, university, coed **Entrance** Noncompetitive **Setting** 335-acre urban campus **Total enrollment** 14,823 **Student-faculty ratio** 20:1 **Application deadline** Rolling (freshmen), rolling (transfer) **Freshman admission** 89% were admitted. Average high school GPA 3.31 **Freshman test scores** SAT critical reading scores over 500: 63%; SAT math scores over 500: 78%; ACT scores over 18: 92%; SAT critical reading scores over 600: 26%; SAT math scores over 600: 39%; ACT scores over 24: 44% **Housing** Yes **Expenses** Tuition & Fees: state resident $5450, nonresident $13,484; Room & Board $6700 **Undergraduates** 54% women, 30% part-time, 30% 25 or older, 1% Native American, 5% Hispanic American, 6% African American, 6% Asian American/Pacific Islander **The most frequently chosen baccalaureate fields are** business/marketing, education, health professions and related sciences **Academic program** English as a second language, advanced placement, accelerated degree program, honors program, summer session, internships **Contact** Mr. Bobby Gandu, Director of Admissions, Wichita State University, 1845 North Fairmount, Wichita, KS 67260. *Phone:* 316-978-3085 or toll-free 800-362-2594. *Fax:* 316-978-3174. *E-mail:* bobby.gandu@wichita.edu. *Web site:* http://www.wichita.edu/.

KENTUCKY

Alice Lloyd College
Pippa Passes, Kentucky

General Independent, 4-year, coed **Entrance** Moderately difficult **Setting** 175-acre rural campus **Total enrollment** 609 **Student-faculty ratio** 18:1 **Application deadline** Rolling (freshmen), rolling (transfer) **Freshman admission** 10% were admitted. Average high school GPA 3.30 **Freshman test scores** SAT critical reading scores over 500: 50%; SAT math scores over 500: 33%; SAT critical reading scores over 600: 8%; SAT math scores over 600: 8% **Housing** Yes **Expenses** Tuition & Fees $1400; Room & Board $4450 **Undergraduates** 53% women, 4% part-time, 2% 25 or older, 0.2% Native American, 1% Hispanic American, 1% African American, 1% Asian American/Pacific Islander **The most frequently chosen baccalaureate fields are** biological/life sciences, business/marketing, education **Academic program** Advanced placement, self-designed majors, internships **Contact** Mr. Ronnie Collins, Director of Admissions, Alice Lloyd College, 100 Purpose Road, Pippa Passes, KY 41844. *Phone:* 606-368-6036. *Fax:* 606-368-6215. *E-mail:* ronniecollins@alc.edu. *Web site:* http://www.alc.edu/.

Asbury University
Wilmore, Kentucky

General Independent nondenominational, comprehensive, coed **Entrance** Moderately difficult **Setting** 400-acre small-town campus **Total enrollment** 1,608 **Student-faculty ratio** 15:1 **Application deadline** Rolling (freshmen), rolling (transfer) **Freshman admission** 57% were admitted. Average high school GPA 3.62 **Freshman test scores** SAT critical reading scores over 500: 83.96%; SAT math scores over 500: 73.59%; ACT scores over 18: 96.76%; SAT critical reading scores over 600: 46.22%; SAT math scores over 600: 33.97%; ACT scores over 24: 56.02% **Housing** Yes **Expenses** Tuition & Fees $23,303; Room & Board $5566 **Undergraduates** 63% women, 6% part-time, 3% 25 or older, 1% Native American, 2% Hispanic American, 2% African American, 1% Asian American/Pacific Islander **The most frequently chosen baccalaureate fields are** business/marketing, communication technologies, visual and performing arts **Academic program** Advanced placement, summer session, adult/continuing education programs **Contact** Mrs. Lisa D. Harper, Director of Admissions, Asbury University, One Macklem Drive, Wilmore, KY 40390. *Phone:* 800-888-1818 or toll-free 800-888-1818. *E-mail:* admissions@asbury.edu. *Web site:* http://www.asbury.edu/.
Visit Petersons.com and enter keyword Asbury

See page 564 for the College Close-Up.

Beckfield College
Florence, Kentucky

General Proprietary, primarily 2-year, coed **Setting** suburban campus **Total enrollment** 605 **Housing** No **Undergraduates** 69% 25 or older **Contact** Mrs. Leah Boerger, Director of Admissions, Beckfield College, 16 Spiral Drive, Florence, KY 41042. *Phone:* 859-371-9393. *E-mail:* lboerger@beckfield.edu. *Web site:* http://www.beckfield.edu/.

Bellarmine University
Louisville, Kentucky

General Independent Roman Catholic, comprehensive, coed **Entrance** Moderately difficult **Setting** 144-acre suburban campus **Total enrollment** 3,090 **Student-faculty ratio** 12:1 **Application deadline** 8/15 (freshmen), 8/15 (transfer) **Freshman admission** 53% were admitted. Average high school GPA 3.48 **Freshman test scores** SAT critical reading scores over 500: 70%; SAT math scores over 500: 78%; ACT scores over 18: 100%; SAT critical reading scores over 600: 26%; SAT math scores over 600: 31%; ACT scores over 24: 61% **Housing** Yes **Expenses** Tuition & Fees $30,310; Room & Board $8550 **Undergraduates** 65% women, 15% part-time, 7% 25 or older, 0.2% Native American, 2% Hispanic American, 3% African American, 3% Asian American/Pacific Islander **The most frequently chosen baccalaureate fields are** business/marketing, health professions and related sciences, psychology **Academic program** Advanced placement, accelerated degree program, self-designed majors, honors program, summer session, adult/continuing education programs, internships **Contact** Mr. Timothy A. Sturgeon, Dean of Admission, Bellarmine University, 2001 Newburg Road, Louisville, KY 40205-0671. *Phone:* 502-452-8131 or toll-free 800-274-4723 Ext. 8131. *Fax:* 502-452-8002. *E-mail:* admissions@bellarmine.edu. *Web site:* http://www.bellarmine.edu/.

Berea College
Berea, Kentucky

General Independent, 4-year, coed **Entrance** Very difficult **Setting** 140-acre small-town campus **Total enrollment** 1,548 **Student-faculty ratio** 10:1 **Application deadline** 4/30 (freshmen), rolling (transfer) **Freshman admission** 14% were admitted. Average high school GPA 3.37 **Freshman test scores** SAT critical reading scores over 500: 77.8%; SAT math scores over 500: 66.6%; ACT scores over 18: 95.7%; SAT critical reading scores over 600: 34.9%; SAT math scores over 600: 20.6%; ACT scores over 24: 50.2% **Housing** Yes **Expenses** Tuition & Fees $876; Room & Board $5768 **Undergraduates** 59% women, 3% part-time, 6% 25 or older, 1% Native American, 3% Hispanic American, 18% African American, 1% Asian American/Pacific Islander **The most frequently chosen baccalaureate fields are** business/marketing, engineering technologies, visual and performing arts **Academic program** English as a second language, advanced placement, self-designed majors, honors program, summer session, internships **Contact** Mr. Luke Hodson, Director of Admissions/Operations, Berea College, CPO 2220, Berea, KY 40404. *Phone:* 859-985-3500 or toll-free 800-326-5948. *Fax:* 859-985-3512. *E-mail:* admissions@berea.edu. *Web site:* http://www.berea.edu/.

Brescia University
Owensboro, Kentucky

General Independent Roman Catholic, comprehensive, coed **Entrance** Moderately difficult **Setting** 9-acre urban campus **Total enrollment** 725 **Student-faculty ratio** 11:1 **Application deadline** Rolling (freshmen), rolling (transfer) **Freshman admission** 67% were admitted. Average high school GPA 3.27 **Freshman test scores** ACT scores over 18: 82%; ACT scores over 24: 29% **Housing** Yes **Expenses** Tuition & Fees $17,390; Room & Board $8000 **Undergraduates** 60% women, 27% part-time, 33% 25 or older **The most frequently chosen baccalaureate fields are** business/marketing, education, public administration and social services **Academic program** Advanced placement, self-designed majors, honors program, summer session, adult/continuing education programs, internships **Contact** Chris Houk, Dean of Enrollment, Brescia University, 717 Frederica Street, Owensboro, KY 42301-3023. *Phone:* 270-686-4241 Ext. 241 or toll-free 877-273-7242. *E-mail:* admissions@brescia.edu. *Web site:* http://www.brescia.edu/.

Brown Mackie College–Louisville
Louisville, Kentucky

General Proprietary, primarily 2-year, coed **Setting** suburban campus **Contact** Director of Admissions, Brown Mackie College–Louisville, 3605 Fern Valley Road, Louisville, KY 40219. *Phone:* 502-968-7191 or toll-free 800-999-7387. *Fax:* 502-357-9956. *Web site:* http://www.brownmackie.edu/Louisville/.

See page 628 for the College Close-Up.

Brown Mackie College–Northern Kentucky
Fort Mitchell, Kentucky

General Proprietary, 2-year, coed **Setting** suburban campus **Contact** Director of Admissions, Brown Mackie College–Northern Kentucky, 309 Buttermilk Pike, Fort Mitchell, KY 41017-2191. *Phone:* 859-341-5627 or toll-free 800-888-1445. *Fax:* 859-341-6483. *Web site:* http://www.brownmackie.edu/NorthernKentucky/.
Visit Petersons.com and enter keywords Brown Mackie College-Northern Kentucky

See page 636 for the College Close-Up.

Campbellsville University
Campbellsville, Kentucky

General Independent, comprehensive, coed, affiliated with Kentucky Baptist Convention **Entrance** Moderately difficult **Setting** 90-acre small-town campus **Total enrollment** 3,178 **Student-faculty ratio** 13:1 **Application deadline** Rolling (freshmen), rolling (transfer) **Freshman admission** 67% were admitted. Average high school GPA 3.18 **Freshman test scores** SAT critical reading scores over 500: 39%; SAT math scores over 500: 58%; ACT scores over 18: 77%; SAT critical reading scores over 600: 8%; SAT math scores over 600: 23%; ACT scores over 24: 22% **Housing** Yes **Expenses** Tuition & Fees $19,710; Room & Board $6740 **Undergraduates** 57% women, 37% part-time, 17% 25 or older

Campbellsville University (continued)

The most frequently chosen baccalaureate fields are business/marketing, communications/journalism, education **Academic program** English as a second language, advanced placement, accelerated degree program, honors program, summer session, adult/continuing education programs, internships **Contact** Mr. David Walters, Vice President for Admissions and Student Services, Campbellsville University, 1 University Drive, Campbellsville, KY 42718-2799. *Phone:* 270-789-5220 Ext. 5007 or toll-free 800-264-6014. *Fax:* 270-789-5071. *E-mail:* admissions@campbellsville.edu. *Web site:* http://www.campbellsville.edu/.

Centre College
Danville, Kentucky

General Independent, 4-year, coed, affiliated with Presbyterian Church (U.S.A.) **Entrance** Very difficult **Setting** 100-acre small-town campus **Total enrollment** 1,197 **Student-faculty ratio** 11:1 **Application deadline** 2/1 (freshmen), 6/1 (transfer) **Freshman admission** 63% were admitted. Average high school GPA 3.54 **Freshman test scores** SAT critical reading scores over 500: 93%; SAT math scores over 500: 94%; ACT scores over 18: 100%; SAT critical reading scores over 600: 61%; SAT math scores over 600: 63%; ACT scores over 24: 92% **Housing** Yes **Expenses** Comprehensive Fee $37,000 **Undergraduates** 54% women, 0.1% part-time, 0.2% Native American, 2% Hispanic American, 4% African American, 2% Asian American/Pacific Islander **The most frequently chosen baccalaureate fields are** biological/life sciences, English, social sciences **Academic program** Advanced placement, self-designed majors, internships **Contact** Mr. Bob Nesmith, Director of Admission, Centre College, 600 West Walnut Street, Danville, KY 40422-1394. *Phone:* 859-238-5350 or toll-free 800-423-6236. *Fax:* 859-238-5373. *E-mail:* admission@centre.edu. *Web site:* http://www.centre.edu/.

Clear Creek Baptist Bible College
Pineville, Kentucky

General Independent Southern Baptist, 4-year, coed, primarily men **Entrance** Noncompetitive **Setting** 700-acre rural campus **Total enrollment** 175 **Student-faculty ratio** 13:1 **Application deadline** 7/15 (freshmen), 7/15 (transfer) **Housing** Yes **Expenses** Tuition & Fees $8700 **Undergraduates** 18% women, 33% part-time, 84% 25 or older **Academic program** Summer session **Contact** Mr. Billy Howell, Director of Admissions, Clear Creek Baptist Bible College, 300 Clear Creek Road, Pineville, KY 40977. *Phone:* 606-337-3196. *Fax:* 606-337-1631. *E-mail:* bhowell@ccbbc.edu. *Web site:* http://www.ccbbc.edu/.

DeVry University
Louisville, Kentucky

General Proprietary, 4-year, coed **Total enrollment** 89 **Student-faculty ratio** 9:1 **Application deadline** Rolling (freshmen), rolling (transfer) **Expenses** Tuition & Fees $14,080 **Undergraduates** 43% women, 45% part-time, 74% 25 or older, 1% Native American, 2% Hispanic American, 24% African American **Academic program** Accelerated degree program **Contact** Admissions Office, DeVry University, 10172 Linn Station Road, Suite 300, Louisville, KY 40223. *Phone:* toll-free 866-906-9388. *Web site:* http://www.devry.edu/.

Eastern Kentucky University
Richmond, Kentucky

Contact Mr. Stephen Byrn, Director of Admissions, Eastern Kentucky University, SSB CPO 54, 521 Lancaster Avenue, Richmond, KY 40475-3102. *Phone:* 859-622-2106 or toll-free 800-465-9191. *Fax:* 859-622-8024. *E-mail:* admissions@eku.edu. *Web site:* http://www.eku.edu/.

Georgetown College
Georgetown, Kentucky

General Independent, comprehensive, coed, affiliated with Baptist Church **Entrance** Moderately difficult **Setting** 110-acre suburban campus **Total enrollment** 1,882 **Student-faculty ratio** 11:1 **Application deadline** 8/1 (freshmen), rolling (transfer) **Freshman admission** 79% were admitted. Average high school GPA 3.48 **Freshman test scores** SAT critical reading scores over 500: 61%; SAT math scores over 500: 64%; ACT scores over 18: 97%; SAT critical reading scores over 600: 18%; SAT math scores over 600: 21%; ACT scores over 24: 47% **Housing** Yes **Expenses** Tuition & Fees $26,080; Room & Board $7030 **Undergraduates** 56% women, 4% part-time, 2% 25 or older, 1% Hispanic American, 7% African American, 0.3% Asian American/Pacific Islander **The most frequently chosen baccalaureate fields are** business/marketing, communications/journalism, psychology **Academic program** Advanced placement, self-designed majors, honors program, summer session, internships **Contact** Mr. Garvel Kindrick, Vice President for Enrollment Management, Georgetown College, 400 East College Street, Georgetown, KY 40324. *Phone:* 502-863-8015 or toll-free 800-788-9985. *Fax:* 502-868-7733. *E-mail:* admissions@georgetowncollege.edu. *Web site:* http://www.georgetowncollege.edu/.

ITT Technical Institute
Lexington, Kentucky

General Proprietary, 4-year, coed **Contact** Director of Recruitment, ITT Technical Institute, 2473 Fortune Drive, Suite 180, Lexington, KY 40509. *Phone:* 859-246-3300 or toll-free 800-519-8151. *Web site:* http://www.itt-tech.edu/.

ITT Technical Institute
Louisville, Kentucky

General Proprietary, primarily 2-year, coed **Entrance** Minimally difficult **Setting** suburban campus **Housing** No **Contact** Director of Recruitment, ITT Technical Institute, 9500 Ormsby Station Road, Louisville, KY 40223. *Phone:* 502-327-7424 or toll-free 888-790-7427. *Web site:* http://www.itt-tech.edu/.

Kentucky Christian University
Grayson, Kentucky

General Independent, comprehensive, coed, affiliated with Christian Churches and Churches of Christ **Entrance** Moderately difficult **Setting** 124-acre rural campus **Total enrollment** 663 **Student-faculty ratio** 14:1 **Application deadline** Rolling (freshmen), rolling (transfer) **Freshman admission** 71% were admitted. Average high school GPA 3.03 **Freshman test scores** SAT critical reading scores over 500: 33%; SAT math scores over 500: 29%; ACT scores over 18: 72%; SAT critical reading scores over 600: 10%; SAT math scores over 600: 10%; ACT scores over 24: 17% **Housing** Yes **Expenses** Tuition & Fees $14,088; Room & Board $5800 **Undergraduates** 50% women, 10% part-time, 9% 25 or older, 0.5% Native American, 1% Hispanic American, 7% African American, 0.2% Asian American/Pacific Islander **The most frequently chosen baccalaureate fields are** education, health professions and related sciences, theology and religious vocations **Academic program** Advanced placement, summer session, internships **Contact** Ms. Kara Bomer, Director of Admissions, Kentucky Christian University, 100 Academic Parkway, Grayson, KY 41143. *Phone:* 606-474-3266 or toll-free 800-522-3181. *Fax:* 606-474-3155. *E-mail:* kbomer@kcu.edu. *Web site:* http://www.kcu.edu/.

Kentucky Mountain Bible College
Vancleve, Kentucky

General Independent interdenominational, 4-year, coed **Setting** 400-acre rural campus **Total enrollment** 89 **Student-faculty ratio** 6:1 **Application deadline** Rolling (freshmen), rolling (transfer) **Expenses** Tuition & Fees $5920; Room & Board $3700 **Undergraduates** 31% 25 or older, 1% Hispanic American, 3% African American **The most frequently chosen baccalaureate field is** theology and religious vocations **Academic program** Internships **Contact** Mr. David Lorimer, Director of

Recruiting, Kentucky Mountain Bible College, PO Box 10, Vancleve, KY 41385. *Phone:* 606-693-5000 Ext. 138 or toll-free 800-879-KMBC Ext. 130 (in-state); 800-879-KMBC Ext. 136 (out-of-state). *Fax:* 606-693-4884. *E-mail:* kmbc@kmbc.edu. *Web site:* http://www.kmbc.edu/.

Kentucky State University
Frankfort, Kentucky

General State-related, comprehensive, coed **Entrance** Minimally difficult **Setting** 915-acre small-town campus **Total enrollment** 2,834 **Student-faculty ratio** 15:1 **Application deadline** Rolling (freshmen), rolling (transfer) **Freshman admission** 24% were admitted. Average high school GPA 2.58 **Freshman test scores** SAT critical reading scores over 500: 15%; SAT math scores over 500: 18%; ACT scores over 18: 43%; SAT critical reading scores over 600: 2%; SAT math scores over 600: 3%; ACT scores over 24: 6% **Housing** Yes **Expenses** Tuition & Fees: state resident $5920, nonresident $14,208; Room & Board $6480 **Undergraduates** 58% women, 20% part-time, 24% 25 or older **The most frequently chosen baccalaureate fields are** business/marketing, biological/life sciences, liberal arts/general studies **Academic program** English as a second language, advanced placement, self-designed majors, honors program, summer session, adult/continuing education programs, internships **Contact** Mr. James Burrell, Director of Admission, Kentucky State University, 400 East Main Street, Frankfort, KY 40601. *Phone:* 502-597-6813 or toll-free 800-633-9415 (in-state); 800-325-1716 (out-of-state). *Fax:* 502-597-5814. *E-mail:* james.burrell@kysu.edu. *Web site:* http://www.kysu.edu/.

Kentucky Wesleyan College
Owensboro, Kentucky

General Independent Methodist, 4-year, coed **Entrance** Moderately difficult **Setting** 52-acre suburban campus **Total enrollment** 876 **Student-faculty ratio** 15:1 **Freshman admission** 67% were admitted. Average high school GPA 3.18 **Freshman test scores** SAT critical reading scores over 500: 45%; SAT math scores over 500: 65%; ACT scores over 18: 85%; SAT critical reading scores over 600: 10%; SAT math scores over 600: 15%; ACT scores over 24: 28% **Housing** Yes **Expenses** Tuition & Fees $16,870; Room & Board $6440 **Undergraduates** 47% women, 5% part-time, 8% 25 or older, 0.2% Native American, 1% Hispanic American, 9% African American, 0.3% Asian American/Pacific Islander **The most frequently chosen baccalaureate fields are** business/marketing, biological/life sciences, education **Academic program** Advanced placement, self-designed majors, honors program, summer session, adult/continuing education programs, internships **Contact** Mr. Scott Kramer, Vice President of Student Affairs, Kentucky Wesleyan College, 3000 Frederica Street, Owensboro, KY 42301. *Phone:* 270-852-3120 or toll-free 800-999-0592 (in-state); 800-990-0592 (out-of-state). *Fax:* 270-852-3133. *E-mail:* admitme@kwc.edu. *Web site:* http://www.kwc.edu/.

Lindsey Wilson College
Columbia, Kentucky

General Independent United Methodist, comprehensive, coed **Entrance** Minimally difficult **Setting** 225-acre rural campus **Total enrollment** 2,349 **Student-faculty ratio** 16:1 **Application deadline** Rolling (freshmen), rolling (transfer) **Freshman admission** 78% were admitted. Average high school GPA 2.96 **Freshman test scores** ACT scores over 18: 63.8%; ACT scores over 24: 15.5% **Housing** Yes **Expenses** Tuition & Fees $18,950; Room & Board $7645 **Undergraduates** 61% women, 5% part-time, 28% 25 or older, 1% Native American, 1% Hispanic American, 8% African American, 0.3% Asian American/Pacific Islander **The most frequently chosen baccalaureate fields are** education, communications/journalism, interdisciplinary studies **Academic program** English as a second language, advanced placement, accelerated degree program, self-designed majors, summer session, adult/continuing education programs, internships **Contact** Mrs. Charity Ferguson, Assistant Director of Admissions, Lindsey Wilson College, 210 Lindsey Wilson Street, Columbia, KY 42728-1298. *Phone:* 270-384-8100 or toll-free 800-264-0138. *Fax:* 270-384-8591. *E-mail:* poolert@lindsey.edu. *Web site:* http://www.lindsey.edu/.

Mid-Continent University
Mayfield, Kentucky

General Independent Southern Baptist, comprehensive, coed **Entrance** Minimally difficult **Setting** 60-acre small-town campus **Total enrollment** 1,823 **Student-faculty ratio** 16:1 **Application deadline** Rolling (freshmen), rolling (transfer) **Freshman admission** 57% were admitted. Average high school GPA 2.94 **Freshman test scores** ACT scores over 18: 77%; ACT scores over 24: 13% **Housing** Yes **Expenses** Tuition & Fees $13,700; Room & Board $6500 **Undergraduates** 64% women, 14% part-time, 82% 25 or older, 0.4% Native American, 1% Hispanic American, 13% African American, 0.2% Asian American/Pacific Islander **The most frequently chosen baccalaureate fields are** business/marketing, psychology, theology and religious vocations **Academic program** English as a second language, advanced placement, accelerated degree program, self-designed majors, summer session **Contact** Mrs. Debbie Smith, Acting Director of Admissions, Mid-Continent University, 99 Powell Road East, Mayfield, KY 42066-9007. *Phone:* 270-247-8521. *Fax:* 270-247-3115. *E-mail:* admissions@midcontinent.edu. *Web site:* http://www.midcontinent.edu/.

Midway College
Midway, Kentucky

General Independent, comprehensive, coed, primarily women, affiliated with Christian Church (Disciples of Christ) **Entrance** Minimally difficult **Setting** 110-acre small-town campus **Student-faculty ratio** 15:1 **Application deadline** Rolling (freshmen), rolling (transfer) **Freshman admission** 71% were admitted. Average high school GPA 3.19 **Freshman test scores** SAT critical reading scores over 500: 50%; SAT math scores over 500: 38%; ACT scores over 18: 72%; SAT critical reading scores over 600: 13%; SAT math scores over 600: 13%; ACT scores over 24: 20% **Housing** Yes **Expenses** Tuition & Fees $18,000; Room & Board $6940 **Undergraduates** 36% 25 or older **The most frequently chosen baccalaureate fields are** business/marketing, agriculture, education **Academic program** Advanced placement, honors program, summer session, adult/continuing education programs, internships **Contact** Dr. Jim Wombles, Vice President of Admissions, Chief Enrollment Officer, Midway College, 512 East Stephens Street, Midway, KY 40347-1120. *Phone:* 859-846-5799 or toll-free 800-755-0031. *Web site:* http://www.midway.edu/.

Morehead State University
Morehead, Kentucky

General State-supported, comprehensive, coed **Entrance** Minimally difficult **Setting** 1,016-acre small-town campus **Total enrollment** 9,046 **Student-faculty ratio** 17:1 **Application deadline** Rolling (freshmen), rolling (transfer) **Freshman admission** 80% were admitted. Average high school GPA 3.31 **Freshman test scores** SAT critical reading scores over 500: 47%; SAT math scores over 500: 47%; ACT scores over 18: 87%; SAT critical reading scores over 600: 15%; SAT math scores over 600: 19%; ACT scores over 24: 26% **Housing** Yes **Expenses** Tuition & Fees: state resident $6036, nonresident $15,096; Room & Board $6192 **Undergraduates** 61% women, 26% part-time, 24% 25 or older, 0.4% Native American, 1% Hispanic American, 3% African American, 0.3% Asian American/Pacific Islander **The most frequently chosen baccalaureate fields are** education, business/marketing, liberal arts/general studies **Academic program** Advanced placement, accelerated degree program, self-designed majors, honors program, summer session, adult/continuing education programs, internships **Contact** Mr. Jeffrey Liles, Associate Vice President for Enrollment Services, Morehead State University, 100 Admissions Center, Morehead, KY 40351. *Phone:* 606-783-2000 or toll-free 800-585-6781. *Fax:* 606-783-5038. *E-mail:* admissions@moreheadstate.edu. *Web site:* http://www.moreheadstate.edu/.

Murray State University
Murray, Kentucky

General State-supported, comprehensive, coed **Entrance** Moderately difficult **Setting** 238-acre small-town campus **Total enrollment** 10,071 **Student-faculty ratio** 16:1 **Freshman admission** 73% were admitted. Average high school GPA 3.31 **Freshman test scores** ACT scores over 18: 98%; ACT scores over 24: 43% **Housing** Yes **Expenses** Tuition & Fees: state resident $5976, nonresident $8852; Room & Board $6562 **Undergraduates** 59% women, 17% part-time, 19% 25 or older, 0.3% Native American, 1% Hispanic American, 6% African American, 1% Asian American/Pacific Islander **The most frequently chosen baccalaureate fields are** business/marketing, education, health professions and related sciences **Academic program** English as a second language, advanced placement, honors program, summer session, adult/continuing education programs, internships **Contact** Ms. Stacy Bell, Undergraduate Admissions Specialist, Murray State University, 113 Sparks Hall, Murray, KY 42701-0009. *Phone:* 270-809-3035 or toll-free 800-272-4678. *Fax:* 270-809-3050. *E-mail:* admissions@murraystate.edu. *Web site:* http://www.murraystate.edu/.

National College
Lexington, Kentucky

Contact Kim Thomasson, Campus Director, National College, 2376 Sir Barton Way, Lexington, KY 40509. *Phone:* 859-253-0621 or toll-free 800-664-1886. *Web site:* http://www.national-college.edu/.

National College
Louisville, Kentucky

Contact Vincent C. Tinebra, Campus Director, National College, 3950 Dixie Highway, Louisville, KY 40216. *Phone:* 502-447-7634 or toll-free 800-664-1886. *Web site:* http://www.national-college.edu/.

Northern Kentucky University
Highland Heights, Kentucky

General State-supported, comprehensive, coed **Entrance** Minimally difficult **Setting** 398-acre suburban campus **Total enrollment** 15,372 **Student-faculty ratio** 17:1 **Application deadline** 8/1 (freshmen), 8/1 (transfer) **Freshman admission** 69% were admitted. Average high school GPA 3.12 **Freshman test scores** SAT critical reading scores over 500: 46.66%; SAT math scores over 500: 42.66%; ACT scores over 18: 88.03%; SAT critical reading scores over 600: 10.13%; SAT math scores over 600: 13.86%; ACT scores over 24: 26.4% **Housing** Yes **Expenses** Tuition & Fees: state resident $6792, nonresident $12,792 **Undergraduates** 56% women, 24% part-time, 27% 25 or older, 0.2% Native American, 1% Hispanic American, 6% African American, 1% Asian American/Pacific Islander **The most frequently chosen baccalaureate fields are** business/marketing, education, health professions and related sciences **Academic program** English as a second language, advanced placement, accelerated degree program, honors program, summer session, adult/continuing education programs, internships **Contact** Ms. Melissa Gorbandt, Director of Admissions and Outreach, Northern Kentucky University, Louie B Nunn Drive, Highland Heights, KY 41099. *Phone:* 859-572-5220 Ext. 5744 or toll-free 800-637-9948. *Fax:* 859-572-6665. *E-mail:* admitnku@nku.edu. *Web site:* http://www.nku.edu/.

Visit Petersons.com and enter keywords Northern Kentucky University

See page 1022 for the College Close-Up.

Pikeville College
Pikeville, Kentucky

General Independent, comprehensive, coed, affiliated with Presbyterian Church (U.S.A.) **Entrance** Noncompetitive **Setting** 25-acre small-town campus **Total enrollment** 1,005 **Student-faculty ratio** 11:1 **Application deadline** 8/15 (freshmen), 8/15 (transfer) **Freshman admission** 100% were admitted. Average high school GPA 3.23 **Freshman test scores** ACT scores over 18: 74%; ACT scores over 24: 19% **Housing** Yes **Expenses** Tuition & Fees $14,535; Room & Board $6000 **Undergraduates** 50% women, 11% part-time, 12% 25 or older, 0.1% Native American, 1% Hispanic American, 9% African American, 1% Asian American/Pacific Islander **The most frequently chosen baccalaureate fields are** biological/life sciences, business/marketing, psychology **Academic program** Advanced placement, self-designed majors, summer session, internships **Contact** Ms. Amanda Slone, Assistant Dean for Admissions, Pikeville College, 147 Sycamore Street, Pikeville, KY 41501. *Phone:* 606-218-5251 or toll-free 866-232-7700. *Fax:* 606-218-5255. *E-mail:* wewantyou@pc.edu. *Web site:* http://www.pc.edu/.

Southern Baptist Theological Seminary
Louisville, Kentucky

Contact Dr. Daniel DeWitt, Southern Baptist Theological Seminary, 2825 Lexington Road, Louisville, KY 40280-0004. *Phone:* 502-897-4011 Ext. 4617. *Web site:* http://www.sbts.edu/.

Spalding University
Louisville, Kentucky

General Independent, comprehensive, coed, affiliated with Roman Catholic Church **Entrance** Moderately difficult **Setting** 5-acre urban campus **Total enrollment** 2,069 **Student-faculty ratio** 17:1 **Application deadline** Rolling (freshmen), rolling (transfer) **Freshman admission** 49% were admitted. Average high school GPA 2.79 **Freshman test scores** SAT critical reading scores over 500: 12.5%; SAT math scores over 500: 25% **Housing** Yes **Expenses** Tuition & Fees $17,550; Room & Board $4560 **Undergraduates** 74% women, 29% part-time, 58% 25 or older, 0.1% Native American, 2% Hispanic American, 31% African American, 1% Asian American/Pacific Islander **The most frequently chosen baccalaureate fields are** business/marketing, health professions and related sciences, psychology **Academic program** Advanced placement, accelerated degree program, summer session, adult/continuing education programs, internships **Contact** Mr. Matt Elder, Assistant Director of Admissions, Spalding University, 851 South Fourth Street, Louisville, KY 40203. *Phone:* 502-585-9911 Ext. 2220 or toll-free 800-896-8941 Ext. 2111. *Fax:* 502-992-2418. *E-mail:* admissions@spalding.edu. *Web site:* http://www.spalding.edu/.

Strayer University–Florence Campus
Florence, Kentucky

General Proprietary, comprehensive, coed **Contact** Admissions Office, Strayer University–Florence Campus, 7300 Turfway Road, Suite 250, Florence, KY 41042. *Phone:* 859-692-2800. *Web site:* http://strayer.edu/florence.

Strayer University–Lexington Campus
Lexington, Kentucky

General Proprietary, comprehensive, coed **Contact** Admissions Office, Strayer University–Lexington Campus, 220 Lexington Green Circle, Suite 550, Lexington, KY 40503. *Phone:* 859-971-4400. *Web site:* http://www.strayer.edu/lexington.

Strayer University–Louisville Campus
Louisville, Kentucky

General Proprietary, comprehensive, coed **Contact** Admissions Office, Strayer University–Louisville Campus, 2650 Eastpoint Parkway, Suite

100, Louisville, KY 40223. *Phone:* 502-253-5000. *Web site:* http://www.strayer.edu/louisville.

Sullivan College of Technology and Design
Louisville, Kentucky

General Proprietary, primarily 2-year, coed **Entrance** Moderately difficult **Setting** 10-acre suburban campus **Total enrollment** 662 **Student-faculty ratio** 14:1 **Application deadline** Rolling (freshmen), rolling (transfer) **Freshman admission** 65% were admitted **Housing** Yes **Expenses** Tuition & Fees $16,110; Room only $4950 **Undergraduates** 34% women, 38% part-time, 44% 25 or older, 0.5% Native American, 0.2% Hispanic American, 17% African American, 1% Asian American/Pacific Islander **The most frequently chosen baccalaureate field is** visual and performing arts **Academic program** Accelerated degree program, summer session, adult/continuing education programs, internships **Contact** Mr. Aamer Z. Chauhdri, Director of Admissions, Sullivan College of Technology and Design, 3901 Atkinson Square Drive, Louisville, KY 40218. *Phone:* 502-456-6509 Ext. 8220 or toll-free 800-884-6528. *Fax:* 502-456-2341. *E-mail:* achauhdri@sctd.edu. *Web site:* http://www.louisvilletech.com/.

Sullivan University
Louisville, Kentucky

General Proprietary, comprehensive, coed **Entrance** Minimally difficult **Setting** 10-acre suburban campus **Total enrollment** 4,538 **Student-faculty ratio** 20:1 **Application deadline** Rolling (freshmen), rolling (transfer) **Housing** Yes **Expenses** Tuition & Fees $14,940; Room only $4320 **Undergraduates** 53% women, 15% part-time, 68% 25 or older **Academic program** Advanced placement, accelerated degree program, summer session, adult/continuing education programs **Contact** Ms. Terri Thomas, Director of Admissions, Sullivan University, 3101 Bardstown Road, Louisville, KY 40205. *Phone:* 502-456-6505 Ext. 370 or toll-free 800-844-1354. *Fax:* 502-456-0040. *E-mail:* admissions@sullivan.edu. *Web site:* http://www.sullivan.edu/.

Visit Petersons.com and enter keywords Sullivan University

Thomas More College
Crestview Hills, Kentucky

General Independent Roman Catholic, comprehensive, coed **Entrance** Moderately difficult **Setting** 100-acre suburban campus **Total enrollment** 1,858 **Student-faculty ratio** 18:1 **Application deadline** 8/1 (freshmen), 8/1 (transfer) **Freshman admission** 93% were admitted. Average high school GPA 3.3 **Freshman test scores** SAT critical reading scores over 500: 46%; SAT math scores over 500: 49%; ACT scores over 18: 99%; SAT critical reading scores over 600: 14%; SAT math scores over 600: 13%; ACT scores over 24: 36% **Housing** Yes **Expenses** Tuition & Fees $24,720; Room & Board $6530 **Undergraduates** 53% women, 22% part-time, 35% 25 or older, 1% Native American, 1% Hispanic American, 5% African American, 1% Asian American/Pacific Islander **The most frequently chosen baccalaureate fields are** business/marketing, health professions and related sciences, liberal arts/general studies **Academic program** Advanced placement, accelerated degree program, self-designed majors, honors program, summer session, adult/continuing education programs, internships **Contact** Mr. Billy Sarge, Associate Director of Admissions, Thomas More College, 333 Thomas More Parkway, Crestview Hills, KY 41017-3495. *Phone:* 859-344-3332 or toll-free 800-825-4557. *Fax:* 859-344-3444. *E-mail:* admissions@thomasmore.edu. *Web site:* http://www.thomasmore.edu/.

Visit Petersons.com and enter keywords Thomas More

See page 1226 for the College Close-Up.

Transylvania University
Lexington, Kentucky

General Independent, 4-year, coed, affiliated with Christian Church (Disciples of Christ) **Entrance** Very difficult **Setting** 40-acre urban campus **Total enrollment** 1,092 **Student-faculty ratio** 13:1 **Application deadline** 2/1 (freshmen), rolling (transfer) **Freshman admission** 80% were admitted. Average high school GPA 3.73 **Freshman test scores** SAT critical reading scores over 500: 83%; SAT math scores over 500: 86%; ACT scores over 18: 100%; SAT critical reading scores over 600: 47%; SAT math scores over 600: 46%; ACT scores over 24: 76% **Housing** Yes **Expenses** Tuition & Fees $25,280; Room & Board $7770 **Undergraduates** 59% women, 1% part-time, 1% 25 or older, 0.3% Native American, 1% Hispanic American, 4% African American, 1% Asian American/Pacific Islander **The most frequently chosen baccalaureate fields are** business/marketing, biological/life sciences, social sciences **Academic program** Advanced placement, self-designed majors, summer session, internships **Contact** Mr. Bradley Goan, Director of Admissions, Transylvania University, 300 North Broadway, Lexington, KY 40508-1797. *Phone:* 859-233-4242 or toll-free 800-872-6798. *Fax:* 859-281-3649. *E-mail:* admissions@transy.edu. *Web site:* http://www.transy.edu/.

Visit Petersons.com and enter keyword Transylvania

See page 1230 for the College Close-Up.

Union College
Barbourville, Kentucky

General Independent United Methodist, comprehensive, coed **Entrance** Moderately difficult **Setting** 100-acre small-town campus **Total enrollment** 1,421 **Student-faculty ratio** 12:1 **Freshman admission** 28% were admitted. Average high school GPA 2.9 **Freshman test scores** SAT critical reading scores over 500: 17%; SAT math scores over 500: 42%; ACT scores over 18: 65.8%; ACT scores over 24: 13.56% **Housing** Yes **Expenses** Tuition & Fees $18,860; Room & Board $5950 **Undergraduates** 46% women, 7% part-time, 15% 25 or older, 0.4% Native American, 1% Hispanic American, 12% African American, 0.4% Asian American/Pacific Islander **The most frequently chosen baccalaureate fields are** business/marketing, education, psychology **Academic program** Advanced placement, accelerated degree program, self-designed majors, honors program, summer session, internships **Contact** Mr. Jerry Jackson, Dean for Enrollment Management, Union College, 310 College Street, Barbourville, KY 40906. *Phone:* 606-546-1222 or toll-free 800-489-8646. *Fax:* 606-546-1667. *E-mail:* enroll@unionky.edu. *Web site:* http://www.unionky.edu/.

University of Kentucky
Lexington, Kentucky

General State-supported, university, coed **Entrance** Moderately difficult **Setting** 685-acre urban campus **Total enrollment** 26,295 **Student-faculty ratio** 18:1 **Application deadline** 2/15 (freshmen), 8/1 (transfer) **Freshman admission** 74% were admitted. Average high school GPA 3.4 **Freshman test scores** SAT critical reading scores over 500: 72.54%; SAT math scores over 500: 74.89%; ACT scores over 18: 98.05%; SAT critical reading scores over 600: 30.9%; SAT math scores over 600: 40.16%; ACT scores over 24: 57.42% **Housing** Yes **Expenses** Tuition & Fees: state resident $8123, nonresident $16,678; Room & Board $9125 **Undergraduates** 50% women, 8% part-time, 10% 25 or older, 0.2% Native American, 2% Hispanic American, 7% African American, 2% Asian American/Pacific Islander **The most frequently chosen baccalaureate fields are** business/marketing, communications/journalism, social sciences **Academic program** English as a second language, advanced placement, accelerated degree program, honors program, summer session, adult/continuing education programs, internships **Contact** Ms. Michelle Nordin, Associate Director of Admissions, University of Kentucky, 100 W.D. Funkhouser Building, Lexington, KY 40506-0054. *Phone:* 859-257-2000 or toll-free 800-432-0967. *E-mail:* admissio@uky.edu. *Web site:* http://www.uky.edu/.

University of Louisville
Louisville, Kentucky

General State-supported, university, coed **Entrance** Moderately difficult **Setting** 274-acre urban campus **Total enrollment** 21,016 **Student-**

University of Louisville (continued)
faculty ratio 18:1 **Application deadline** 2/15 (freshmen), 7/1 (transfer) **Freshman admission** 73% were admitted. Average high school GPA 3.46 **Freshman test scores** SAT critical reading scores over 500: 75.21%; SAT math scores over 500: 79.31%; ACT scores over 18: 99.41%; SAT critical reading scores over 600: 34.53%; SAT math scores over 600: 42.22%; ACT scores over 24: 55.66% **Housing** Yes **Expenses** Tuition & Fees: state resident $7944, nonresident $19,272; Room & Board $5437 **Undergraduates** 51% women, 23% part-time, 21% 25 or older, 0.3% Native American, 2% Hispanic American, 13% African American, 3% Asian American/Pacific Islander **The most frequently chosen baccalaureate fields are** business/marketing, communication technologies, engineering **Academic program** English as a second language, advanced placement, accelerated degree program, self-designed majors, honors program, summer session, adult/continuing education programs, internships **Contact** Ms. Jenny L. Sawyer, Executive Director for Admissions, University of Louisville, 2301 South Third Street, Louisville, KY 40292-0001. *Phone:* 502-852-6531 or toll-free 800-334-8635. *Fax:* 502-852-4776. *E-mail:* admitme@louisville.edu. *Web site:* http://www.louisville.edu/.

University of the Cumberlands
Williamsburg, Kentucky

General Independent Kentucky Baptist, comprehensive, coed **Entrance** Moderately difficult **Setting** 60-acre rural campus **Total enrollment** 2,955 **Student-faculty ratio** 19:1 **Application deadline** Rolling (freshmen) **Freshman admission** 73% were admitted. Average high school GPA 3.3 **Freshman test scores** SAT critical reading scores over 500: 51%; SAT math scores over 500: 55%; ACT scores over 18: 99%; SAT critical reading scores over 600: 17%; SAT math scores over 600: 15%; ACT scores over 24: 32% **Housing** Yes **Expenses** Tuition & Fees $17,000; Room & Board $6826 **Undergraduates** 51% women, 19% part-time, 7% 25 or older **The most frequently chosen baccalaureate fields are** business/marketing, biological/life sciences, education **Academic program** English as a second language, advanced placement, accelerated degree program, self-designed majors, honors program, summer session, adult/continuing education programs, internships **Contact** Mrs. Erica Harris, Director of Admissions, University of the Cumberlands, 6178 College Station Drive, Williamsburg, KY 40769. *Phone:* 606-539-4241 or toll-free 800-343-1609. *Fax:* 606-539-4303. *E-mail:* admiss@ucumberlands.edu. *Web site:* http://www.ucumberlands.edu/. **Visit Petersons.com and enter keyword Cumberlands**

Western Kentucky University
Bowling Green, Kentucky

General State-supported, comprehensive, coed **Entrance** Minimally difficult **Setting** 235-acre suburban campus **Total enrollment** 20,712 **Student-faculty ratio** 19:1 **Application deadline** 8/1 (freshmen), 8/1 (transfer) **Freshman admission** 95% were admitted. Average high school GPA 3.15 **Freshman test scores** SAT critical reading scores over 500: 52%; SAT math scores over 500: 47%; ACT scores over 18: 79%; SAT critical reading scores over 600: 11%; SAT math scores over 600: 12%; ACT scores over 24: 30% **Housing** Yes **Expenses** Tuition & Fees: state resident $7200, nonresident $17,784; Room & Board $6351 **Undergraduates** 57% women, 21% part-time, 20% 25 or older, 0.3% Native American, 1% Hispanic American, 11% African American, 1% Asian American/Pacific Islander **The most frequently chosen baccalaureate fields are** business/marketing, communications/journalism, education **Academic program** English as a second language, advanced placement, accelerated degree program, self-designed majors, honors program, summer session, adult/continuing education programs, internships **Contact** Mr. Scott S. Gordon, Director of Admissions and Academic Services, Western Kentucky University, 1906 College Heights Boulevard, Bowling Green, KY 42101. *Phone:* 270-745-2551 or toll-free 800-495-8463. *Fax:* 270-745-6133. *E-mail:* admission@wku.edu. *Web site:* http://www.wku.edu/.

LOUISIANA

Centenary College of Louisiana
Shreveport, Louisiana

General Independent United Methodist, comprehensive, coed **Entrance** Moderately difficult **Setting** 65-acre suburban campus **Total enrollment** 974 **Student-faculty ratio** 12:1 **Application deadline** 8/1 (freshmen), 8/15 (transfer) **Freshman admission** 54% were admitted **Freshman test scores** SAT critical reading scores over 500: 78.2%; SAT math scores over 500: 78.2%; ACT scores over 18: 100%; SAT critical reading scores over 600: 32.7%; SAT math scores over 600: 30%; ACT scores over 24: 61.5% **Housing** Yes **Expenses** Tuition & Fees $23,280; Room & Board $7940 **Undergraduates** 56% women, 1% part-time, 2% 25 or older, 0.1% Native American, 3% Hispanic American, 10% African American, 3% Asian American/Pacific Islander **The most frequently chosen baccalaureate fields are** biological/life sciences, business/marketing, communications/journalism **Academic program** Advanced placement, self-designed majors, honors program, summer session, adult/continuing education programs, internships **Contact** Mr. David Voskuil, Vice President of Enrollment Services, Centenary College of Louisiana, Office of Admissions, 2911 Centenary Boulevard, PO Box 41188, Shreveport, LA 71134-1188. *Phone:* 318-869-5134 or toll-free 800-234-4448. *Fax:* 318-869-5005. *E-mail:* dvoskuil@centenary.edu. *Web site:* http://www.centenary.edu/.

Dillard University
New Orleans, Louisiana

General Independent interdenominational, 4-year, coed **Entrance** Moderately difficult **Setting** 55-acre urban campus **Total enrollment** 1,011 **Student-faculty ratio** 10:1 **Application deadline** Rolling (freshmen), rolling (transfer) **Freshman admission** 48% were admitted. Average high school GPA 2.8 **Freshman test scores** SAT critical reading scores over 500: 21%; SAT math scores over 500: 10%; ACT scores over 18: 53%; SAT critical reading scores over 600: 2%; SAT math scores over 600: 2%; ACT scores over 24: 7% **Housing** Yes **Expenses** Tuition & Fees $13,880; Room & Board $8386 **Undergraduates** 73% women, 6% part-time, 8% 25 or older, 1% Hispanic American, 95% African American, 0.1% Asian American/Pacific Islander **The most frequently chosen baccalaureate fields are** health professions and related sciences, business/marketing, social sciences **Academic program** Advanced placement, honors program, summer session, internships **Contact** Ms. Meredith Reed, Director of Admissions, Dillard University, 2601 Gentilly Boulevard, New Orleans, LA 70122-3097. *Phone:* 504-816-4670 or toll-free 800-716-8353 (in-state); 800-216-6637 (out-of-state). *Fax:* 504-816-4895. *E-mail:* mreed@dillard.edu. *Web site:* http://www.dillard.edu/.

Grambling State University
Grambling, Louisiana

General State-supported, university, coed **Entrance** Noncompetitive **Setting** 383-acre small-town campus **Total enrollment** 4,992 **Student-faculty ratio** 19:1 **Application deadline** 6/30 (freshmen), 6/30 (transfer) **Freshman admission** 33% were admitted. Average high school GPA 2.8 **Freshman test scores** SAT critical reading scores over 500: 16%; SAT math scores over 500: 17%; ACT scores over 18: 46%; SAT critical reading scores over 600: 1%; SAT math scores over 600: 2%; ACT scores over 24: 3% **Housing** Yes **Expenses** Tuition & Fees: state resident $4016, nonresident $9902; Room & Board $7168 **Undergraduates** 61% women, 7% part-time, 12% 25 or older, 0.2% Native American, 0.3% Hispanic American, 88% African American, 0.3% Asian American/Pacific Islander **The most frequently chosen baccalaureate fields are** business/marketing, health professions and related sciences, security and protective services **Academic program** Advanced placement, honors program, summer session, adult/continuing education programs, internships **Contact** Ms. Annie L. Moss, Director of Admissions and

Recruitment, Grambling State University, GSU Box 4200, Grambling, LA 71270. *Phone:* 318-274-6183. *Fax:* 318-274-3292. *E-mail:* mossa@gram.edu. *Web site:* http://www.gram.edu/.

Herzing College

Kenner, Louisiana

General Proprietary, primarily 2-year, coed **Entrance** Moderately difficult **Total enrollment** 166 **Freshman admission** 100% were admitted **Undergraduates** 63% 25 or older **Contact** Genny Bordelon, Director of Admissions, Herzing College, 2500 Williams Boulevard, Kenner, LA 70062. *Phone:* 504-733-0074. *Fax:* 504-733-0020. *Web site:* http://www.herzing.edu/.

ITT Technical Institute

St. Rose, Louisiana

General Proprietary, primarily 2-year, coed **Entrance** Minimally difficult **Housing** No **Contact** Director of Recruitment, ITT Technical Institute, 140 James Drive East, St. Rose, LA 70087. *Phone:* 504-463-0338 or toll-free 866-463-0338. *Web site:* http://www.itt-tech.edu/.

Louisiana College

Pineville, Louisiana

General Independent Southern Baptist, comprehensive, coed **Entrance** Moderately difficult **Setting** 81-acre small-town campus **Total enrollment** 1,461 **Student-faculty ratio** 23:1 **Application deadline** 8/15 (freshmen) **Freshman admission** 51% were admitted. Average high school GPA 3.12 **Housing** Yes **Expenses** Tuition & Fees $12,480; Room & Board $4316 **Undergraduates** 49% women, 7% part-time, 37% 25 or older **Academic program** Advanced placement, accelerated degree program, self-designed majors, honors program, summer session, adult/continuing education programs, internships **Contact** Mr. Byron McGee, Director of Enrollment Management, Louisiana College, LC Box 566, Pineville, LA 71359. *Phone:* 318-487-7439 or toll-free 800-487-1906. *Fax:* 318-487-7550. *E-mail:* admissions@lacollege.edu. *Web site:* http://www.lacollege.edu/.

Louisiana State University and Agricultural and Mechanical College

Baton Rouge, Louisiana

General State-supported, university, coed **Entrance** Moderately difficult **Setting** 2,000-acre urban campus **Total enrollment** 28,643 **Student-faculty ratio** 20:1 **Application deadline** 4/15 (freshmen), 4/15 (transfer) **Freshman admission** 69% were admitted. Average high school GPA 3.49 **Freshman test scores** SAT critical reading scores over 500: 80.46%; SAT math scores over 500: 89.46%; ACT scores over 18: 99.78%; SAT critical reading scores over 600: 39.22%; SAT math scores over 600: 48.37%; ACT scores over 24: 68.72% **Housing** Yes **Expenses** Tuition & Fees: state resident $5233, nonresident $14,383; Room & Board $7738 **Undergraduates** 51% women, 6% part-time, 6% 25 or older, 0.5% Native American, 3% Hispanic American, 9% African American, 3% Asian American/Pacific Islander **The most frequently chosen baccalaureate fields are** business/marketing, biological/life sciences, social sciences **Academic program** English as a second language, advanced placement, accelerated degree program, self-designed majors, honors program, summer session, adult/continuing education programs, internships **Contact** Ms. Mary G. Parker, Executive Director of Undergraduate Admissions and Student Aid, Louisiana State University and Agricultural and Mechanical College, Baton Rouge, LA 70803. *Phone:* 225-578-3113. *E-mail:* admissions@lsu.edu. *Web site:* http://www.lsu.edu/.

Louisiana State University at Alexandria

Alexandria, Louisiana

Contact Ms. Shelly Kieffer, Recruiter/Admissions Counselor, Louisiana State University at Alexandria, 8100 Highway 71 South, Alexandria, LA 71302-9121. *Phone:* 318-473-6508 or toll-free 888-473-6417. *Fax:* 318-473-6418. *E-mail:* skieffer@isua.edu. *Web site:* http://www.lsua.edu/.

Louisiana State University Health Sciences Center

New Orleans, Louisiana

General State-supported, university, coed **Setting** 80-acre urban campus **Total enrollment** 2,644 **Application deadline** 3/1 (transfer) **Housing** Yes **Expenses** Tuition & Fees: state resident $4196, nonresident $6538; Room only $6396 **Undergraduates** 83% women, 22% part-time, 28% 25 or older, 0.1% Native American, 5% Hispanic American, 9% African American, 7% Asian American/Pacific Islander **The most frequently chosen baccalaureate field is** health professions and related sciences **Academic program** Advanced placement, accelerated degree program, summer session, internships **Contact** Mr. William Bryant Faust IV, University Registrar, Louisiana State University Health Sciences Center, 433 Bolivar Street, New Orleans, LA 70112-2223. *Phone:* 504-568-4829. *Fax:* 504-568-5545. *Web site:* http://www.lsuhsc.edu/.

Louisiana State University in Shreveport

Shreveport, Louisiana

General State-supported, comprehensive, coed **Entrance** Moderately difficult **Setting** 200-acre urban campus **Total enrollment** 4,667 **Application deadline** 8/1 (freshmen) **Freshman admission** Average high school GPA 3.16 **Freshman test scores** ACT scores over 18: 94.1%; ACT scores over 24: 30.8% **Housing** Yes **Expenses** Tuition & Fees: state resident $3925, nonresident $8695 **Undergraduates** 62% women, 40% part-time, 37% 25 or older **The most frequently chosen baccalaureate fields are** business/marketing, education, liberal arts/general studies **Academic program** Advanced placement, accelerated degree program, self-designed majors, honors program, summer session, adult/continuing education programs, internships **Contact** Mr. Mickey Diez, Dean of Enrollment Services and Registrar, Louisiana State University in Shreveport, 1 University Place, Shreveport, LA 71115-2399. *Phone:* 318-797-5063 or toll-free 800-229-5957. *Fax:* 318-797-5286. *E-mail:* admissions@pilot.lsus.edu. *Web site:* http://www.lsus.edu/.

Louisiana Tech University

Ruston, Louisiana

General State-supported, university, coed **Entrance** Moderately difficult **Setting** 247-acre small-town campus **Total enrollment** 11,264 **Student-faculty ratio** 21:1 **Application deadline** 7/31 (freshmen), rolling (transfer) **Freshman admission** 63% were admitted. Average high school GPA 3.33 **Freshman test scores** ACT scores over 18: 96%; ACT scores over 24: 45% **Housing** Yes **Expenses** Tuition & Fees: state resident $5220, nonresident $10,617; Room & Board $5055 **Undergraduates** 48% women, 26% part-time, 20% 25 or older, 0.4% Native American, 2% Hispanic American, 14% African American, 1% Asian American/Pacific Islander **The most frequently chosen baccalaureate fields are** business/marketing, engineering, liberal arts/general studies **Academic program** Advanced placement, honors program, summer session, adult/continuing education programs, internships **Contact** Mrs. Jan B. Albritton, Director of Admissions, Louisiana Tech University, PO Box 3168, Ruston, LA 71272. *Phone:* 318-257-3036 or toll-free 800-528-3241. *Fax:* 318-257-2499. *E-mail:* bulldog@latech.edu. *Web site:* http://www.latech.edu/.

Loyola University New Orleans

New Orleans, Louisiana

General Independent Roman Catholic (Jesuit), comprehensive, coed **Entrance** Moderately difficult **Setting** 26-acre suburban campus **Total enrollment** 4,714 **Student-faculty ratio** 11:1 **Application deadline**

Loyola University New Orleans (continued)

Rolling (freshmen), rolling (transfer) **Freshman admission** 58% were admitted. Average high school GPA 3.72 **Freshman test scores** SAT critical reading scores over 500: 97.9%; SAT math scores over 500: 94.5%; ACT scores over 18: 100%; SAT critical reading scores over 600: 66.9%; SAT math scores over 600: 55.7%; ACT scores over 24: 77.8% **Housing** Yes **Expenses** Tuition & Fees $31,504; Room & Board $10,388 **Undergraduates** 57% women, 11% part-time, 2% 25 or older, 1% Native American, 11% Hispanic American, 14% African American, 5% Asian American/Pacific Islander **The most frequently chosen baccalaureate fields are** business/marketing, social sciences, visual and performing arts **Academic program** English as a second language, advanced placement, accelerated degree program, self-designed majors, honors program, summer session, adult/continuing education programs, internships **Contact** Mr. Keith E. Gramling, Director, Admissions, Loyola University New Orleans, 6363 St. Charles Avenue, Campus Box 18, New Orleans, LA 70118. *Phone:* 504-865-3240 or toll-free 800-4-LOYOLA. *Fax:* 504-865-3383. *E-mail:* admit@loyno.edu. *Web site:* http://www.loyno.edu/.

Visit Petersons.com and enter keywords Loyola University New Orleans

See page 928 for the College Close-Up.

McNeese State University

Lake Charles, Louisiana

General State-supported, comprehensive, coed **Entrance** Moderately difficult **Setting** 766-acre suburban campus **Total enrollment** 8,645 **Student-faculty ratio** 21:1 **Application deadline** Rolling (freshmen), rolling (transfer) **Freshman admission** 67% were admitted. Average high school GPA 3.21 **Freshman test scores** ACT scores over 18: 89%; ACT scores over 24: 24% **Housing** Yes **Expenses** Tuition & Fees: state resident $3422, nonresident $9488; Room & Board $4050 **Undergraduates** 61% women, 21% part-time, 23% 25 or older, 1% Native American, 1% Hispanic American, 19% African American, 1% Asian American/Pacific Islander **The most frequently chosen baccalaureate fields are** health professions and related sciences, business/marketing, liberal arts/general studies **Academic program** English as a second language, advanced placement, accelerated degree program, honors program, summer session, internships **Contact** Ms. Kara Smith, Director of Admissions, McNeese State University, Box 91740, Lake Charles, LA 70609. *Phone:* 337-475-5504 or toll-free 800-622-3352. *Fax:* 337-475-5978. *E-mail:* ksmith2@mcneese.edu. *Web site:* http://www.mcneese.edu/.

Visit Petersons.com and enter keyword McNeese

New Orleans Baptist Theological Seminary

New Orleans, Louisiana

General Independent Southern Baptist, comprehensive, coed, primarily men **Entrance** Minimally difficult **Setting** 81-acre suburban campus **Total enrollment** 2,036 **Application deadline** 8/9 (freshmen) **Housing** Yes **Academic program** English as a second language, summer session, adult/continuing education programs, internships **Contact** Dr. Paul E. Gregoire Jr., Registrar/Director of Admissions, New Orleans Baptist Theological Seminary, 3939 Gentilly Boulevard, New Orleans, LA 70126-4858. *Phone:* 504-282-4455 Ext. 3337 or toll-free 800-662-8701. *Web site:* http://www.nobts.edu/.

Nicholls State University

Thibodaux, Louisiana

General State-supported, comprehensive, coed **Entrance** Noncompetitive **Setting** 210-acre small-town campus **Total enrollment** 7,181 **Student-faculty ratio** 22:1 **Application deadline** Rolling (freshmen), rolling (transfer) **Freshman admission** 78% were admitted. Average high school GPA 3.15 **Freshman test scores** ACT scores over 18: 91%; ACT scores over 24: 24% **Housing** Yes **Expenses** Tuition & Fees: state resident $3965, nonresident $10,433; Room & Board $7310 **Undergraduates** 62% women, 21% part-time, 18% 25 or older, 2% Native American, 2% Hispanic American, 18% African American, 1% Asian American/Pacific Islander **The most frequently chosen baccalaureate fields are** business/marketing, health professions and related sciences, liberal arts/general studies **Academic program** English as a second language, advanced placement, accelerated degree program, honors program, summer session, adult/continuing education programs, internships **Contact** Mrs. Becky L. Durocher, Director of Admissions, Nicholls State University, PO Box 2004-NSU, Thibodaux, LA 70310. *Phone:* 985-448-4507 or toll-free 877-NICHOLLS. *Fax:* 985-448-4929. *E-mail:* nicholls@nicholls.edu. *Web site:* http://www.nicholls.edu.

Northwestern State University of Louisiana

Natchitoches, Louisiana

General State-supported, comprehensive, coed **Entrance** Moderately difficult **Setting** 916-acre small-town campus **Total enrollment** 9,247 **Student-faculty ratio** 18:1 **Application deadline** 7/6 (freshmen), 7/6 (transfer) **Freshman admission** 81% were admitted. Average high school GPA 3.11 **Freshman test scores** SAT critical reading scores over 500: 38.68%; SAT math scores over 500: 55.67%; ACT scores over 18: 81.77%; SAT critical reading scores over 600: 6.6%; SAT math scores over 600: 12.27%; ACT scores over 24: 19.85% **Housing** Yes **Expenses** Tuition & Fees: state resident $3786, nonresident $10,472; Room & Board $6682 **Undergraduates** 67% women, 34% part-time, 33% 25 or older, 2% Native American, 2% Hispanic American, 30% African American, 1% Asian American/Pacific Islander **The most frequently chosen baccalaureate fields are** health professions and related sciences, business/marketing, liberal arts/general studies **Academic program** Advanced placement, honors program, summer session, adult/continuing education programs, internships **Contact** Ms. Jana Lucky, Director of University Recruiting, Northwestern State University of Louisiana, South Hall, Natchitoches, LA 71497. *Phone:* 318-357-4503 or toll-free 800-327-1903. *Fax:* 318-357-5567. *E-mail:* recruiting@nsula.edu. *Web site:* http://www.nsula.edu/.

Our Lady of Holy Cross College

New Orleans, Louisiana

General Independent Roman Catholic, comprehensive, coed **Entrance** Minimally difficult **Setting** 40-acre suburban campus **Total enrollment** 1,298 **Application deadline** 7/20 (freshmen), rolling (transfer) **Housing** No **Expenses** Tuition & Fees $4035 **Undergraduates** 42% 25 or older **Academic program** Advanced placement, summer session, adult/continuing education programs, internships **Contact** Donna Kennedy, Director of Admissions and Financial Aid, Our Lady of Holy Cross College, 4123 Woodland Drive, New Orleans, LA 70131-7399. *Phone:* 504-398-2175 or toll-free 800-259-7744 Ext. 175. *E-mail:* dkennedy@olhcc.edu. *Web site:* http://www.olhcc.edu/.

Our Lady of the Lake College

Baton Rouge, Louisiana

General Independent Roman Catholic, comprehensive, coed, primarily women **Entrance** Minimally difficult **Setting** 5-acre suburban campus **Total enrollment** 1,872 **Student-faculty ratio** 20:1 **Application deadline** 8/15 (freshmen), rolling (transfer) **Freshman admission** 88% were admitted **Freshman test scores** ACT scores over 18: 92.4%; ACT scores over 24: 10.1% **Housing** No **Expenses** Tuition & Fees $6920 **Undergraduates** 84% women, 34% part-time, 0.4% Native American, 2% Hispanic American, 23% African American, 3% Asian American/Pacific Islander **The most frequently chosen baccalaureate fields are** biological/life sciences, health professions and related sciences, security and protective services **Academic program** Advanced placement, accelerated degree program, summer session **Contact** Director of Admissions, Our Lady of the Lake College, 7434 Perkins Road, Baton Rouge,

LA 70808. *Phone:* 225-768-1718 or toll-free 877-242-3509. *E-mail:* admissions@ololcollege.edu. *Web site:* http://www.ololcollege.edu/.

Saint Joseph Seminary College

Saint Benedict, Louisiana

General Independent Roman Catholic, 4-year, men only **Entrance** Minimally difficult **Setting** 1,300-acre rural campus **Total enrollment** 121 **Application deadline** Rolling (freshmen), rolling (transfer) **Freshman admission** Average high school GPA 3.25 **Freshman test scores** ACT scores over 18: 55%; ACT scores over 24: 22% **Housing** Yes **Expenses** Tuition & Fees $12,882; Room & Board $11,168 **Undergraduates** 31% part-time, 24% 25 or older, 1% Native American, 27% Hispanic American, 4% African American, 4% Asian American/Pacific Islander **The most frequently chosen baccalaureate field is** philosophy and religious studies **Academic program** English as a second language, advanced placement, adult/continuing education programs **Contact** Registrar, Saint Joseph Seminary College, 75376 River Road, St. Benedict, LA 70457. *Phone:* 985-867-2225. *Fax:* 985-327-1085. *E-mail:* acdean@sjasc.edu. *Web site:* http://www.sjasc.edu/.

Southeastern Louisiana University

Hammond, Louisiana

General State-supported, comprehensive, coed **Entrance** Moderately difficult **Setting** 375-acre small-town campus **Total enrollment** 15,160 **Student-faculty ratio** 25:1 **Application deadline** 8/1 (freshmen), 8/1 (transfer) **Freshman admission** 93% were admitted. Average high school GPA 3.12 **Freshman test scores** ACT scores over 18: 93.6%; ACT scores over 24: 27.7% **Housing** Yes **Expenses** Tuition & Fees: state resident $3932, nonresident $11,188; Room & Board $6450 **Undergraduates** 61% women, 19% part-time, 17% 25 or older, 0.5% Native American, 2% Hispanic American, 18% African American, 1% Asian American/Pacific Islander **The most frequently chosen baccalaureate fields are** business/marketing, education, liberal arts/general studies **Academic program** English as a second language, advanced placement, honors program, summer session, adult/continuing education programs, internships **Contact** Dr. Jeff Rhodes, Dean of Enrollment Management, Southeastern Louisiana University, SLU 10752, Hammond, LA 70402. *Phone:* 985-549-5067 or toll-free 800-222-7358. *Fax:* 985-549-5272. *E-mail:* admissions@selu.edu. *Web site:* http://www.selu.edu/.

Southern University and Agricultural and Mechanical College

Baton Rouge, Louisiana

General State-supported, university, coed **Entrance** Moderately difficult **Setting** 964-acre suburban campus **Total enrollment** 7,699 **Student-faculty ratio** 16:1 **Application deadline** 7/1 (freshmen), 7/1 (transfer) **Freshman admission** 57% were admitted. Average high school GPA 2.9 **Freshman test scores** SAT math scores over 500: 27.2%; ACT scores over 18: 64.2%; SAT math scores over 600: 6.8%; ACT scores over 24: 10.5% **Housing** Yes **Expenses** Tuition & Fees: state resident $4100, nonresident $9892; Room & Board $5666 **Undergraduates** 61% women, 11% part-time, 20% 25 or older, 0.05% Native American, 0.1% Hispanic American, 95% African American, 0.4% Asian American/Pacific Islander **The most frequently chosen baccalaureate fields are** business/marketing, health professions and related sciences, security and protective services **Academic program** Advanced placement, honors program, summer session, adult/continuing education programs, internships **Contact** Ms. Velva Thomas, Director of Admissions, Southern University and Agricultural and Mechanical College, PO Box 9901, Baton Rouge, LA 70813. *Phone:* 225-771-2430 or toll-free 800-256-1531. *Fax:* 225-771-2500. *E-mail:* velva_thomas@subr.edu. *Web site:* http://www.subr.edu/.

Southern University at New Orleans

New Orleans, Louisiana

General State-supported, comprehensive, coed, primarily women **Entrance** Noncompetitive **Setting** 66-acre urban campus **Total enrollment** 3,141 **Student-faculty ratio** 31:1 **Application deadline** 7/1 (freshmen), 7/1 (transfer) **Freshman admission** 79% were admitted. Average high school GPA 2.4 **Housing** No **Expenses** Tuition & Fees: state resident $3072, nonresident $4772 **Undergraduates** 70% women, 21% part-time, 49% 25 or older, 0.1% Native American, 0.4% Hispanic American, 97% African American, 1% Asian American/Pacific Islander **The most frequently chosen baccalaureate fields are** business/marketing, liberal arts/general studies, security and protective services **Academic program** Self-designed majors, summer session, adult/continuing education programs, internships **Contact** Ms. Leatrice D. Latimore, Interim Director of Admissions, Recruitment and Retention, Southern University at New Orleans, 6400 Press Drive, New Orleans, LA 70126-1009. *Phone:* 504-286-5033. *Fax:* 504-284-5481. *E-mail:* llatimor@suno.edu. *Web site:* http://www.suno.edu/.

Southwest University

Kenner, Louisiana

Contact Southwest University, 2200 Veterans Memorial Boulevard, Kenner, LA 70062. *Phone:* toll-free 800-433-5923. *Web site:* http://www.southwest.edu/.

Strayer University–Metairie Campus

Metairie, Louisiana

General Proprietary, comprehensive, coed **Contact** Director of Admissions, Strayer University–Metairie Campus, 111 Veterans Memorial Boulevard, Suite 420, Metairie, LA 70005. *Phone:* 504-799-1700. *Fax:* 504-849-9980. *E-mail:* metairie@strayer.edu. *Web site:* http://www.strayer.edu/metairie.

Tulane University

New Orleans, Louisiana

General Independent, university, coed **Entrance** Very difficult **Setting** 110-acre urban campus **Total enrollment** 11,911 **Student-faculty ratio** 8:1 **Application deadline** 1/15 (freshmen), 6/1 (transfer) **Freshman admission** 26% were admitted. Average high school GPA 3.49 **Freshman test scores** SAT critical reading scores over 500: 96.2%; SAT math scores over 500: 96.13%; ACT scores over 18: 99.46%; SAT critical reading scores over 600: 87%; SAT math scores over 600: 71.2%; ACT scores over 24: 94.89% **Housing** Yes **Expenses** Tuition & Fees $40,584; Room & Board $9606 **Undergraduates** 55% women, 24% part-time, 2% Native American, 4% Hispanic American, 10% African American, 4% Asian American/Pacific Islander **The most frequently chosen baccalaureate fields are** business/marketing, architecture, social sciences **Academic program** English as a second language, advanced placement, accelerated degree program, self-designed majors, honors program, summer session, adult/continuing education programs, internships **Contact** Mr. Earl Retif, Vice President for Enrollment Management and University Registrar, Tulane University, Office of Admissions, 210 Gibson Hall, New Orleans, LA 70118. *Phone:* 504-865-5731 or toll-free 800-873-9283. *Fax:* 504-862-8715. *E-mail:* undergrad.admission@tulane.edu. *Web site:* http://www.tulane.edu/.

Visit Petersons.com and enter keyword Tulane

University of Louisiana at Lafayette

Lafayette, Louisiana

Contact Mr. Leroy Broussard Jr., Admissions Director, University of Louisiana at Lafayette, PO Drawer 41210, Lafayette, LA 70504. *Phone:* 337-482-6473 or toll-free 800-752-6553. *Fax:* 337-482-1317. *E-mail:* admissions@louisiana.edu. *Web site:* http://www.louisiana.edu/.

University of Louisiana at Monroe

Monroe, Louisiana

General State-supported, university, coed **Entrance** Minimally difficult **Setting** 238-acre urban campus **Total enrollment** 9,004 **Student-**

University of Louisiana at Monroe (continued)
faculty ratio 18:1 **Application deadline** Rolling (freshmen), rolling (transfer) **Freshman admission** 74% were admitted. Average high school GPA 3.23 **Freshman test scores** SAT critical reading scores over 500: 32%; SAT math scores over 500: 56%; ACT scores over 18: 92%; SAT critical reading scores over 600: 10%; SAT math scores over 600: 17%; ACT scores over 24: 24% **Housing** Yes **Expenses** Tuition & Fees: state resident $3791, nonresident $10,125; Room & Board $3370 **Undergraduates** 63% women, 23% part-time, 20% 25 or older, 0.4% Native American, 1% Hispanic American, 28% African American, 2% Asian American/Pacific Islander **The most frequently chosen baccalaureate fields are** business/marketing, health professions and related sciences, liberal arts/general studies **Academic program** English as a second language, advanced placement, accelerated degree program, honors program, summer session, internships **Contact** Ms. Frances Self, Assistant Director of Admissions, University of Louisiana at Monroe, Office of Recruitment and Admissions, Sandel Hall, 4020 Northeast Drive, Monroe, LA 71209. *Phone:* 318-342-5430 or toll-free 800-372-5272 (in-state); 800-372-5127 (out-of-state). *Fax:* 318-342-1915. *E-mail:* admissions@ulm.edu. *Web site:* http://www.ulm.edu/.

University of New Orleans
New Orleans, Louisiana

General State-supported, university, coed **Entrance** Moderately difficult **Setting** 345-acre urban campus **Total enrollment** 11,724 **Student-faculty ratio** 18:1 **Application deadline** 7/1 (freshmen), 7/1 (transfer) **Freshman admission** 57% were admitted. Average high school GPA 3.08 **Freshman test scores** SAT critical reading scores over 500: 65.43%; SAT math scores over 500: 71.8%; ACT scores over 18: 94.94%; SAT critical reading scores over 600: 27.13%; SAT math scores over 600: 31.91%; ACT scores over 24: 32.2% **Housing** Yes **Expenses** Tuition & Fees: state resident $4372, nonresident $12,528; Room & Board $6700 **Undergraduates** 51% women, 23% part-time, 29% 25 or older, 1% Native American, 7% Hispanic American, 18% African American, 6% Asian American/Pacific Islander **The most frequently chosen baccalaureate fields are** business/marketing, liberal arts/general studies, psychology **Academic program** English as a second language, advanced placement, self-designed majors, honors program, summer session, adult/continuing education programs, internships **Contact** Mr. Andy Benoit, Director of Admissions, University of New Orleans, 2000 Lakeshore Drive, New Orleans, LA 70148. *Phone:* 504-280-7013 or toll-free 800-256-5866. *Fax:* 504-280-5522. *E-mail:* admissions@uno.edu. *Web site:* http://www.uno.edu/.

Visit Petersons.com and enter keywords University of New Orleans

University of Phoenix–Louisiana Campus
Metairie, Louisiana

General Proprietary, comprehensive, coed **Entrance** Noncompetitive **Setting** urban campus **Total enrollment** 1,919 **Application deadline** Rolling (freshmen), rolling (transfer) **Housing** No **Expenses** Tuition & Fees $11,025 **Undergraduates** 75% women, 83% 25 or older, 1% Native American, 1% Hispanic American, 48% African American, 1% Asian American/Pacific Islander **The most frequently chosen baccalaureate fields are** business/marketing, computer and information sciences, security and protective services **Academic program** Advanced placement, accelerated degree program, adult/continuing education programs **Contact** Ms. Audra McQuarie, Registrar/Executive Director, University of Phoenix–Louisiana Campus, 4035 South Riverpoint Parkway, Mail Stop CF-L101, Phoenix, AZ 85040. *Phone:* 480-557-6151 or toll-free 800-776-4867 (in-state); 800-228-7240 (out-of-state). *Fax:* 480-643-3068. *E-mail:* audra.mcquarie@phoenix.edu. *Web site:* http://www.phoenix.edu/.

Xavier University of Louisiana
New Orleans, Louisiana

General Independent Roman Catholic, comprehensive, coed **Entrance** Moderately difficult **Setting** 23-acre urban campus **Total enrollment** 3,338 **Student-faculty ratio** 13:1 **Application deadline** 7/1 (freshmen), 6/1 (transfer) **Freshman admission** 67% were admitted. Average high school GPA 3.16 **Freshman test scores** SAT critical reading scores over 500: 40%; SAT math scores over 500: 41%; ACT scores over 18: 81%; SAT critical reading scores over 600: 9%; SAT math scores over 600: 9%; ACT scores over 24: 25% **Housing** Yes **Expenses** Tuition & Fees $15,300; Room & Board $7000 **Undergraduates** 72% women, 4% part-time, 2% 25 or older, 0.1% Native American, 1% Hispanic American, 74% African American, 10% Asian American/Pacific Islander **The most frequently chosen baccalaureate fields are** biological/life sciences, physical sciences, psychology **Academic program** Advanced placement, accelerated degree program, honors program, summer session, adult/continuing education programs, internships **Contact** Mr. Winston Brown, Dean of Admissions, Xavier University of Louisiana, 7325 Palmetto Street, New Orleans, LA 70125. *Phone:* 504-520-7388 or toll-free 877-XAVIERU. *Fax:* 504-520-7941. *E-mail:* apply@xula.edu. *Web site:* http://www.xula.edu/.

MAINE

Bates College
Lewiston, Maine

General Independent, 4-year, coed **Entrance** Most difficult **Setting** 109-acre small-town campus **Total enrollment** 1,738 **Student-faculty ratio** 10:1 **Application deadline** 1/1 (freshmen), 3/1 (transfer) **Freshman admission** 27% were admitted **Freshman test scores** SAT critical reading scores over 500: 98.76%; SAT math scores over 500: 98.34%; ACT scores over 18: 100%; SAT critical reading scores over 600: 83.06%; SAT math scores over 600: 90.08%; ACT scores over 24: 100% **Housing** Yes **Expenses** Comprehensive Fee $51,300 **Undergraduates** 53% women, 1% Native American, 4% Hispanic American, 5% African American, 7% Asian American/Pacific Islander **The most frequently chosen baccalaureate fields are** psychology, history, social sciences **Academic program** Advanced placement, accelerated degree program, self-designed majors, honors program, internships **Contact** Mr. Wylie Mitchell, Dean of Admissions, Bates College, 2 Andrews Road, Bates College, Lewiston, ME 04240-6028. *Phone:* 207-786-6000. *Fax:* 207-786-6025. *E-mail:* admissions@bates.edu. *Web site:* http://www.bates.edu/.

Bowdoin College
Brunswick, Maine

General Independent, 4-year, coed **Entrance** Most difficult **Setting** 205-acre small-town campus **Total enrollment** 1,777 **Student-faculty ratio** 9:1 **Application deadline** 1/1 (freshmen), 3/1 (transfer) **Freshman admission** 19% were admitted **Freshman test scores** SAT critical reading scores over 500: 100%; SAT math scores over 500: 100%; ACT scores over 18: 100%; SAT critical reading scores over 600: 91%; SAT math scores over 600: 93%; ACT scores over 24: 97% **Housing** Yes **Expenses** Tuition & Fees $40,020; Room & Board $10,880 **Undergraduates** 51% women, 0.3% part-time, 1% Native American, 10% Hispanic American, 6% African American, 12% Asian American/Pacific Islander **The most frequently chosen baccalaureate fields are** foreign languages and literature, biological/life sciences, social sciences **Academic program** Advanced placement, accelerated degree program, self-designed majors **Contact** Peter T. Wiley, Associate Dean of Admissions, Bowdoin College, 5000 College Station, Brunswick, ME 04011-8411. *Phone:* 207-725-3190. *Fax:* 207-725-3101. *E-mail:* admissions@bowdoin.edu. *Web site:* http://www.bowdoin.edu/.

Colby College

Waterville, Maine

General Independent, 4-year, coed **Entrance** Most difficult **Setting** 714-acre small-town campus **Total enrollment** 1,838 **Student-faculty ratio** 10:1 **Application deadline** 1/1 (freshmen), 3/1 (transfer) **Freshman admission** 34% were admitted **Freshman test scores** SAT critical reading scores over 500: 96%; SAT math scores over 500: 99%; ACT scores over 18: 100%; SAT critical reading scores over 600: 84%; SAT math scores over 600: 85%; ACT scores over 24: 98% **Housing** Yes **Expenses** Comprehensive Fee $50,320 **Undergraduates** 54% women, 1% 25 or older, 1% Native American, 3% Hispanic American, 3% African American, 8% Asian American/Pacific Islander **The most frequently chosen baccalaureate fields are** area and ethnic studies, biological/life sciences, social sciences **Academic program** Advanced placement, self-designed majors, honors program, internships **Contact** Mr. Steve Thomas, Director of Admissions, Colby College, Mayflower Hill, Waterville, ME 04901-8840. *Phone:* 207-859-4800 or toll-free 800-723-3032. *Fax:* 207-859-4828. *E-mail:* admissions@colby.edu. *Web site:* http://www.colby.edu/.

College of the Atlantic

Bar Harbor, Maine

General Independent, comprehensive, coed **Entrance** Very difficult **Setting** 35-acre small-town campus **Total enrollment** 341 **Student-faculty ratio** 11:1 **Application deadline** 2/15 (freshmen), 4/1 (transfer) **Freshman admission** 75% were admitted. Average high school GPA 3.52 **Freshman test scores** SAT critical reading scores over 500: 95%; SAT math scores over 500: 78%; ACT scores over 18: 100%; SAT critical reading scores over 600: 80%; SAT math scores over 600: 39%; ACT scores over 24: 70% **Housing** Yes **Expenses** Tuition & Fees $34,380; Room & Board $8250 **Undergraduates** 68% women, 7% part-time, 4% 25 or older, 1% Native American, 1% Hispanic American, 1% African American, 1% Asian American/Pacific Islander **The most frequently chosen baccalaureate field is** liberal arts/general studies **Academic program** Advanced placement, accelerated degree program, self-designed majors, internships **Contact** Ms. Sarah Baker, Dean of Admission, College of the Atlantic, 105 Eden Street, Bar Harbor, ME 04609-1198. *Phone:* 207-801-5640 or toll-free 800-528-0025. *Fax:* 207-288-4126. *E-mail:* inquiry@coa.edu. *Web site:* http://www.coa.edu/.

See page 736 for the College Close-Up.

Husson University

Bangor, Maine

General Independent, comprehensive, coed **Entrance** Moderately difficult **Setting** 170-acre suburban campus **Total enrollment** 2,976 **Student-faculty ratio** 19:1 **Application deadline** 8/1 (freshmen), 8/1 (transfer) **Freshman admission** 87% were admitted. Average high school GPA 3.12 **Freshman test scores** SAT critical reading scores over 500: 33%; SAT math scores over 500: 33%; ACT scores over 18: 67%; SAT critical reading scores over 600: 4%; SAT math scores over 600: 4%; ACT scores over 24: 15% **Housing** Yes **Expenses** Tuition & Fees $13,450; Room & Board $7239 **Undergraduates** 59% women, 23% part-time, 12% 25 or older, 0.3% Native American, 1% Hispanic American, 5% African American, 1% Asian American/Pacific Islander **The most frequently chosen baccalaureate fields are** business/marketing, health professions and related sciences, psychology **Academic program** Advanced placement, self-designed majors, summer session, adult/continuing education programs, internships **Contact** Ms. Carlena Bean, Director of Admissions, Husson University, One College Circle, Bangor, ME 04401-2999. *Phone:* 207-941-7067 or toll-free 800-4-HUSSON. *Fax:* 207-941-7935. *E-mail:* beanc@husson.edu. *Web site:* http://www.husson.edu/.

Maine College of Art

Portland, Maine

General Independent, comprehensive, coed **Entrance** Moderately difficult **Setting** urban campus **Total enrollment** 325 **Student-faculty ratio** 10:1 **Application deadline** Rolling (freshmen), rolling (transfer) **Freshman admission** 77% were admitted. Average high school GPA 3.05 **Freshman test scores** SAT critical reading scores over 500: 60%; SAT math scores over 500: 50%; ACT scores over 18: 100%; SAT critical reading scores over 600: 23%; SAT math scores over 600: 17%; ACT scores over 24: 42% **Housing** Yes **Expenses** Tuition & Fees $30,115; Room & Board $9800 **Undergraduates** 69% women, 3% part-time, 3% 25 or older, 1% Native American, 1% Hispanic American, 1% African American, 2% Asian American/Pacific Islander **The most frequently chosen baccalaureate field is** visual and performing arts **Academic program** Advanced placement, internships **Contact** Ms. Blaise Maccarrone, Admissions Operations Coordinator, Maine College of Art, 522 Congress Street, Portland, ME 04101-3987. *Phone:* 207-699-5026 or toll-free 800-639-4808. *Fax:* 207-699-5080. *E-mail:* admissions@meca.edu. *Web site:* http://www.meca.edu/.

Maine Maritime Academy

Castine, Maine

General State-supported, comprehensive, coed, primarily men **Entrance** Moderately difficult **Setting** 35-acre small-town campus **Total enrollment** 860 **Student-faculty ratio** 12:1 **Application deadline** 7/1 (freshmen), 7/1 (transfer) **Freshman admission** 67% were admitted. Average high school GPA 2.8 **Housing** Yes **Expenses** Tuition & Fees: state resident $10,105, nonresident $17,805; Room & Board $8450 **Undergraduates** 16% women, 2% part-time, 18% 25 or older, 1% Native American, 1% Hispanic American, 0.5% African American, 0.3% Asian American/Pacific Islander **The most frequently chosen baccalaureate fields are** engineering, engineering technologies, transportation and materials moving **Academic program** Advanced placement, self-designed majors, adult/continuing education programs, internships **Contact** Mr. Jeffrey C. Wright, Director of Admissions, Maine Maritime Academy, Castine, ME 04420. *Phone:* 207-326-2215 or toll-free 800-464-6565 (in-state); 800-227-8465 (out-of-state). *E-mail:* jeff.wright@mma.edu. *Web site:* http://www.mainemaritime.edu/.

New England School of Communications

Bangor, Maine

General Independent, 4-year, coed, primarily men **Entrance** Minimally difficult **Setting** 200-acre small-town campus **Total enrollment** 499 **Student-faculty ratio** 14:1 **Application deadline** Rolling (freshmen), rolling (transfer) **Freshman admission** 64% were admitted. Average high school GPA 2.6 **Housing** Yes **Expenses** Tuition & Fees $11,500; Room & Board $6994 **Undergraduates** 27% women, 6% part-time, 3% 25 or older, 0.2% Native American, 2% Hispanic American, 2% African American, 1% Asian American/Pacific Islander **The most frequently chosen baccalaureate fields are** communication technologies, communications/journalism **Academic program** Advanced placement, self-designed majors, summer session, adult/continuing education programs, internships **Contact** Ms. Louise Grant, Director of Admissions, New England School of Communications, 1 College Circle, Bangor, ME 04401. *Phone:* 207-941-7176 Ext. 1093 or toll-free 888-877-1876. *Fax:* 207-947-3987. *E-mail:* info@nescom.edu. *Web site:* http://www.nescom.edu/.

Saint Joseph's College of Maine

Standish, Maine

Contact Mr. Vincent J. Kloskowski, Dean of Admission, Saint Joseph's College of Maine, 278 Whites Bridge Road, Standish, ME 04084-5263. *Phone:* 207-893-7746 or toll-free 800-338-7057. *Fax:* 207-893-7862. *E-mail:* admission@sjcme.edu. *Web site:* http://www.sjcme.edu/.

Thomas College

Waterville, Maine

Contact Mr. James Love, Dean of Admissions, Thomas College, 180 West River Road, Waterville, ME 04901. *Phone:* 207-859-1101 or

Thomas College (continued)
toll-free 800-339-7001. *Fax:* 207-859-1114. *E-mail:* admiss@thomas.edu. *Web site:* http://www.thomas.edu/.

Unity College
Unity, Maine

Contact Mr. Gary Zane, Dean of Students, Unity College, 90 Quaker Hill Road, Unity, ME 04988. *Phone:* 207-948-3131. *Fax:* 207-948-6277. *E-mail:* gzane@unity.edu. *Web site:* http://www.unity.edu/.

University of Maine
Orono, Maine

General State-supported, university, coed **Entrance** Moderately difficult **Setting** 3,300-acre small-town campus **Total enrollment** 11,867 **Student-faculty ratio** 15:1 **Application deadline** Rolling (freshmen), rolling (transfer) **Freshman admission** 80% were admitted. Average high school GPA 3.18 **Freshman test scores** SAT critical reading scores over 500: 66%; SAT math scores over 500: 68%; ACT scores over 18: 91%; SAT critical reading scores over 600: 20%; SAT math scores over 600: 25%; ACT scores over 24: 40% **Housing** Yes **Expenses** Tuition & Fees: state resident $9626, nonresident $23,876; Room & Board $8008 **Undergraduates** 49% women, 16% part-time, 9% 25 or older, 2% Native American, 1% Hispanic American, 1% African American, 1% Asian American/Pacific Islander **The most frequently chosen baccalaureate fields are** business/marketing, education, engineering **Academic program** English as a second language, advanced placement, accelerated degree program, self-designed majors, honors program, summer session, internships **Contact** Ms. Sharon Oliver, Director of Admissions, University of Maine, 5713 Chadbourne Hall, Orono, ME 04469-5713. *Phone:* 207-581-1561 or toll-free 877-486-2364. *Fax:* 207-581-1213. *E-mail:* um-admit@maine.edu. *Web site:* http://www.umaine.edu/.

Visit Petersons.com and enter keyword Maine

See page 1278 for the College Close-Up.

University of Maine at Augusta
Augusta, Maine

General State-supported, 4-year, coed **Entrance** Noncompetitive **Setting** 159-acre small-town campus **Total enrollment** 5,054 **Student-faculty ratio** 18:1 **Application deadline** 8/31 (freshmen), rolling (transfer) **Freshman admission** 93% were admitted **Housing** No **Expenses** Tuition & Fees: state resident $6855, nonresident $15,375 **Undergraduates** 73% women, 66% part-time, 3% Native American, 1% Hispanic American, 1% African American, 0.5% Asian American/Pacific Islander **The most frequently chosen baccalaureate fields are** business/marketing, health professions and related sciences, liberal arts/general studies **Academic program** Advanced placement, self-designed majors, honors program, summer session, adult/continuing education programs, internships **Contact** Jonathan Henry, Director of Admissions/Dean of Enrollment, University of Maine at Augusta, 46 University Drive, Robinson Hall, Augusta, ME 04330. *Phone:* 207-621-3465 or toll-free 877-862-1234 Ext. 3185. *Fax:* 207-621-3333. *E-mail:* umaadm@maine.edu. *Web site:* http://www.uma.maine.edu/.

University of Maine at Farmington
Farmington, Maine

General State-supported, comprehensive, coed **Entrance** Moderately difficult **Setting** 50-acre small-town campus **Total enrollment** 2,238 **Student-faculty ratio** 14:1 **Application deadline** Rolling (freshmen) **Freshman admission** 80% were admitted **Freshman test scores** SAT critical reading scores over 500: 56%; SAT math scores over 500: 49.2%; SAT critical reading scores over 600: 16%; SAT math scores over 600: 9.2% **Housing** Yes **Expenses** Tuition & Fees: state resident $8710, nonresident $17,094; Room & Board $7552 **Undergraduates** 65% women, 10% part-time, 14% 25 or older, 1% Native American, 1% Hispanic American, 1% African American, 1% Asian American/Pacific Islander **The most frequently chosen baccalaureate fields are** education, health professions and related sciences, psychology **Academic program** Advanced placement, accelerated degree program, self-designed majors, honors program, summer session, internships **Contact** Mr. James G. Collins, Associate Director of Admissions, University of Maine at Farmington, 246 Main Street, Farmington, ME 04938-1994. *Phone:* 207-778-7050. *Fax:* 207-778-8182. *E-mail:* umfadmit@maine.edu. *Web site:* http://www.umf.maine.edu/.

University of Maine at Fort Kent
Fort Kent, Maine

General State-supported, 4-year, coed **Entrance** Minimally difficult **Setting** 52-acre rural campus **Total enrollment** 1,126 **Student-faculty ratio** 15:1 **Application deadline** Rolling (freshmen), rolling (transfer) **Freshman admission** 78% were admitted. Average high school GPA 2.64 **Freshman test scores** SAT critical reading scores over 500: 28%; SAT math scores over 500: 36%; SAT critical reading scores over 600: 6%; SAT math scores over 600: 3% **Housing** Yes **Expenses** Tuition & Fees: state resident $6803, nonresident $15,953; Room & Board $7080 **Undergraduates** 67% women, 49% part-time, 48% 25 or older, 2% Native American, 1% Hispanic American, 2% African American, 0.5% Asian American/Pacific Islander **The most frequently chosen baccalaureate fields are** education, business/marketing, health professions and related sciences **Academic program** English as a second language, advanced placement, accelerated degree program, self-designed majors, honors program, summer session, internships **Contact** Ms. Jill Cairns, Acting Director of Admissions, University of Maine at Fort Kent, 23 University Drive, Fort Kent, ME 04743-1292. *Phone:* 207-834-7600 or toll-free 888-TRY-UMFK. *E-mail:* jillb@maine.edu. *Web site:* http://www.umfk.maine.edu/.

Visit Petersons.com and enter keywords Fort Kent

University of Maine at Machias
Machias, Maine

General State-supported, 4-year, coed **Entrance** Moderately difficult **Setting** 42-acre rural campus **Total enrollment** 964 **Student-faculty ratio** 14:1 **Application deadline** 8/15 (freshmen), rolling (transfer) **Freshman admission** 74% were admitted **Freshman test scores** SAT critical reading scores over 500: 39.1%; SAT math scores over 500: 23%; ACT scores over 18: 56.5%; SAT critical reading scores over 600: 6.9%; SAT math scores over 600: 4.6%; ACT scores over 24: 17.4% **Housing** Yes **Expenses** Tuition & Fees: state resident $6871, nonresident $17,011; Room & Board $6574 **Undergraduates** 70% women, 53% part-time, 27% 25 or older, 4% Native American, 2% Hispanic American, 3% African American, 1% Asian American/Pacific Islander **The most frequently chosen baccalaureate fields are** biological/life sciences, interdisciplinary studies, parks and recreation **Academic program** Advanced placement, self-designed majors, summer session, internships **Contact** Mr. David Dollins, Director of Admissions, University of Maine at Machias, 9 O'Brien Avenue, Machias, ME 04654. *Phone:* 207-255-1318 or toll-free 888-GOTOUMM (in-state); 888-468-6866 (out-of-state). *Fax:* 207-255-1363. *E-mail:* ummadmissions@maine.edu. *Web site:* http://umm.maine.edu/.

Visit Petersons.com and enter keyword Machias

See page 1280 for the College Close-Up.

University of Maine at Presque Isle
Presque Isle, Maine

General State-supported, 4-year, coed **Entrance** Minimally difficult **Setting** 150-acre small-town campus **Total enrollment** 1,412 **Student-faculty ratio** 20:1 **Application deadline** Rolling (freshmen) **Freshman admission** 87% were admitted. Average high school GPA 3 **Freshman test scores** SAT critical reading scores over 500: 35%; SAT math scores

At the University of Southern Maine you'll find a learning environment where you won't get lost; respected professors, whose priority is providing the individualized attention you need to succeed; and classmates whose varied experiences and cultures enrich each discussion.

Add to that our location in Portland, Maine, voted America's most liveable city by Forbes.com, and our expansive array of areas of study to choose from...

USM...where you'll gain not just knowledge, but wisdom; not just practice, but experience.

www.usm.maine.edu/admit

over 500: 31%; SAT critical reading scores over 600: 8%; SAT math scores over 600: 2% **Housing** Yes **Expenses** Tuition & Fees: state resident $6875, nonresident $16,025; Room & Board $7300 **Undergraduates** 65% women, 35% part-time, 42% 25 or older, 4% Native American, 1% Hispanic American, 1% African American, 1% Asian American/Pacific Islander **Academic program** Advanced placement, accelerated degree program, self-designed majors, honors program, summer session, adult/continuing education programs, internships **Contact** Ms. Erin V. Benson, Director of University Relations and Student Enrollment Services, University of Maine at Presque Isle, 181 Main Street, Presque Isle, ME 04769-2888. *Phone:* 207-768-9453. *Fax:* 207-768-9608. *E-mail:* erin.benson@umpi.edu. *Web site:* http://www.umpi.edu/.

University of New England
Biddeford, Maine

General Independent, comprehensive, coed **Entrance** Moderately difficult **Setting** 540-acre small-town campus **Total enrollment** 4,493 **Student-faculty ratio** 13:1 **Application deadline** 2/15 (freshmen), rolling (transfer) **Freshman admission** 80% were admitted. Average high school GPA 3.2 **Freshman test scores** SAT critical reading scores over 500: 66.78%; SAT math scores over 500: 70.76%; ACT scores over 18: 97.87%; SAT critical reading scores over 600: 16.96%; SAT math scores over 600: 23.65%; ACT scores over 24: 53.19% **Housing** Yes **Expenses** Tuition & Fees $27,920; Room & Board $10,870 **Undergraduates** 69% women, 16% part-time, 6% 25 or older, 0.3% Native American, 1% Hispanic American, 1% African American, 2% Asian American/Pacific Islander **The most frequently chosen baccalaureate fields are** biological/life sciences, health professions and related sciences, psychology **Academic program** Advanced placement, accelerated degree program, summer session, internships **Contact** Mr. Robert J. Pecchia, Associate Dean of Admissions, University of New England, Hills Beach Road, Biddeford, ME 04005-9526. *Phone:* 207-283-0170 Ext. 2297 or toll-free 800-477-4UNE. *Fax:* 207-602-5900. *E-mail:* admissions@une.edu. *Web site:* http://www.une.edu/.

Visit Petersons.com and enter keywords University of New England

See page 1288 for the College Close-Up.

University of Southern Maine
Portland, Maine

General State-supported, comprehensive, coed **Entrance** Moderately difficult **Setting** 144-acre suburban campus **Total enrollment** 9,655 **Student-faculty ratio** 13:1 **Application deadline** 2/15 (freshmen), 2/15 (transfer) **Freshman admission** 84% were admitted. Average high school GPA 3.03 **Freshman test scores** SAT critical reading scores over 500: 53%; SAT math scores over 500: 50%; ACT scores over 18: 80%; SAT critical reading scores over 600: 14%; SAT math scores over 600: 10%; ACT scores over 24: 23% **Housing** Yes **Expenses** Tuition & Fees: state resident $7467, nonresident $18,987; Room & Board $8344 **Undergraduates** 57% women, 37% part-time, 30% 25 or older **The most frequently chosen baccalaureate fields are** health professions and related sciences, business/marketing, social sciences **Academic program** English as a second language, advanced placement, accelerated degree program, self-designed majors, honors program, summer session, adult/continuing education programs, internships **Contact** Mr. Jonathan Barker, Director of Technology for Enrollment Management, University of Southern Maine, 96 Falmouth Street, PO Box 9300, Portland, ME 04104-9300. *Phone:* 207-780-5724 or toll-free 800-800-4USM Ext. 5670. *Fax:* 207-780-5640. *E-mail:* usmadm@usm.maine.edu. *Web site:* http://www.usm.maine.edu/.

MARYLAND

Baltimore International College
Baltimore, Maryland

Contact Ms. Kristin Ciarlo, Director of Admissions, Baltimore International College, Commerce Exchange, 17 Commerce Street, Baltimore, MD 21202-3230. *Phone:* 410-752-4710 Ext. 239 or toll-free 800-624-9926 Ext. 120. *Fax:* 410-752-3730. *E-mail:* admissions@bic.edu. *Web site:* http://www.bic.edu/.

Bowie State University
Bowie, Maryland

General State-supported, comprehensive, coed **Entrance** Minimally difficult **Setting** 295-acre small-town campus **Total enrollment** 5,617 **Student-faculty ratio** 16:1 **Application deadline** 4/1 (freshmen), 4/1 (transfer) **Freshman admission** 48% were admitted. Average high school GPA 2.73 **Freshman test scores** SAT critical reading scores over 500: 21%; SAT math scores over 500: 17.7%; SAT critical reading scores over 600: 2.7%; SAT math scores over 600: 2.2% **Housing** Yes **Expenses** Tuition & Fees: state resident $6040, nonresident $16,479; Room & Board $7536 **Undergraduates** 63% women, 16% part-time, 18% 25 or older, 0.4% Native American, 2% Hispanic American, 90% African American, 2% Asian American/Pacific Islander **The most frequently chosen baccalaureate fields are** business/marketing, communications/journalism, social sciences **Academic program** Advanced placement, honors program, summer session, adult/continuing education programs, internships **Contact** Don Kiah, Director of Admissions, Bowie State University, Administration Building, 1st Floor, Bowie, MD 20715-9465. *Phone:* 301-860-3415 or toll-free 877-772-6943. *Fax:* 301-860-3438. *E-mail:* sholt@bowiestate.edu. *Web site:* http://www.bowiestate.edu/. **Visit Petersons.com and enter keyword Bowie**

See page 612 for the College Close-Up.

Capitol College
Laurel, Maryland

General Independent, comprehensive, coed **Entrance** Minimally difficult **Setting** 52-acre suburban campus **Total enrollment** 699 **Student-faculty ratio** 12:1 **Application deadline** Rolling (freshmen), rolling (transfer) **Housing** Yes **Undergraduates** 41% 25 or older **Academic program** English as a second language, advanced placement, accelerated degree program, summer session, adult/continuing education programs **Contact** Mr. George Walls, Director of Recruiting and Admissions, Capitol College, 11301 Springfield Road, Laurel, MD 20708-9759. *Phone:* 301-953-3200 Ext. 3033 or toll-free 800-950-1992. *E-mail:* ghwalls@capitol-college.edu. *Web site:* http://www.capitol-college.edu/.

College of Notre Dame of Maryland
Baltimore, Maryland

General Independent Roman Catholic, comprehensive, undergraduate: women only; graduate: coed **Entrance** Moderately difficult **Setting** 58-acre urban campus **Total enrollment** 2,971 **Student-faculty ratio** 12:1 **Application deadline** 2/15 (freshmen), 2/15 (transfer) **Freshman admission** 65% were admitted. Average high school GPA 3.46 **Housing** Yes **Expenses** Tuition & Fees $28,350; Room & Board $9500 **Undergraduates** 61% part-time, 11% 25 or older, 0.2% Native American, 2% Hispanic American, 29% African American, 3% Asian American/Pacific Islander **The most frequently chosen baccalaureate fields are** business/marketing, communications/journalism, social sciences **Academic program** English as a second language, advanced placement, accelerated degree program, self-designed majors, honors program, summer session, adult/continuing education programs, internships **Contact** Sharon Bogdan, Associate Vice President for Enrollment, College of Notre Dame of Maryland, 4701 North Charles Street, Baltimore, MD 21210-2476. *Phone:* 410-532-5332 or toll-free 800-435-0200 (in-state); 800-435-0300 (out-of-state). *E-mail:* sbogdon@ndm.edu. *Web site:* http://www.ndm.edu/.

See page 728 for the College Close-Up.

Coppin State University
Baltimore, Maryland

General State-supported, comprehensive, coed **Entrance** Moderately difficult **Setting** 33-acre urban campus **Total enrollment** 3,801 **Student-faculty ratio** 16:1 **Application deadline** 7/15 (freshmen), 7/15 (transfer) **Freshman admission** 50% were admitted. Average high school GPA 2.71 **Freshman test scores** SAT critical reading scores over 500: 19%; SAT math scores over 500: 13%; SAT critical reading scores over 600: 2%; SAT math scores over 600: 1% **Housing** Yes **Expenses** Tuition & Fees: state resident $5276, nonresident $13,971; Room & Board $7496 **Undergraduates** 76% women, 22% part-time, 40% 25 or older, 0.1% Native American, 0.5% Hispanic American, 88% African American, 0.2% Asian American/Pacific Islander **The most frequently chosen baccalaureate fields are** health professions and related sciences, liberal arts/general studies, psychology **Academic program** English as a second language, advanced placement, honors program, summer session, adult/continuing education programs, internships **Contact** Ms. Michelle Gross, Director of Admissions, Coppin State University, 2500 West North Avenue, Baltimore, MD 21216-3698. *Phone:* 410-951-3600 or toll-free 800-635-3674. *Fax:* 410-523-7351. *E-mail:* mgross@coppin.edu. *Web site:* http://www.coppin.edu/.

DeVry University
Bethesda, Maryland

General Proprietary, comprehensive, coed **Entrance** Minimally difficult **Total enrollment** 142 **Student-faculty ratio** 10:1 **Application deadline** Rolling (freshmen), rolling (transfer) **Housing** No **Expenses** Tuition & Fees $14,080 **Undergraduates** 51% women, 57% part-time, 74% 25 or older, 21% Hispanic American, 47% African American, 3% Asian American/Pacific Islander **The most frequently chosen baccalaureate field is** business/marketing **Academic program** Advanced placement, accelerated degree program, summer session, adult/continuing education programs **Contact** Admissions Office, DeVry University, 4550 Montgomery Avenue. Suite 100 North, Bethesda, MD 20814-3304. *Web site:* http://www.devry.edu/.

Faith Theological Seminary
Baltimore, Maryland

Contact Faith Theological Seminary, 529 Walker Avenue, Baltimore, MD 21212. *Web site:* http://www.faiththeological.org/.

Frostburg State University
Frostburg, Maryland

General State-supported, comprehensive, coed **Entrance** Moderately difficult **Setting** 260-acre small-town campus **Total enrollment** 5,385 **Student-faculty ratio** 17:1 **Application deadline** 2/15 (freshmen), 6/1 (transfer) **Freshman admission** 59% were admitted. Average high school GPA 3.11 **Freshman test scores** SAT critical reading scores over 500: 39%; SAT math scores over 500: 38%; ACT scores over 18: 60%; SAT critical reading scores over 600: 7.5%; SAT math scores over 600: 8%; ACT scores over 24: 7% **Housing** Yes **Expenses** Tuition & Fees: state resident $6684, nonresident $16,880; Room & Board $7304 **Undergraduates** 49% women, 7% part-time, 7% 25 or older, 0.4% Native American, 3% Hispanic American, 24% African American, 2% Asian American/Pacific Islander **The most frequently chosen baccalaureate fields are** business/marketing, education, social sciences **Academic program** Advanced placement, honors program, summer session, adult/

continuing education programs, internships **Contact** Ms. Trish Gregory, Director for Admissions, Frostburg State University, 101 Braddock Road, Frostburg, MD 21532-1099. *Phone:* 301-687-4201. *E-mail:* fsuadmissions@frostburg.edu. *Web site:* http://www.frostburg.edu/.
Visit Petersons.com and enter keyword Frostburg

Goucher College
Baltimore, Maryland

General Independent, comprehensive, coed **Entrance** Moderately difficult **Setting** 287-acre suburban campus **Total enrollment** 2,279 **Student-faculty ratio** 9:1 **Application deadline** 2/1 (freshmen), 5/1 (transfer) **Freshman admission** 73% were admitted. Average high school GPA 3.17 **Freshman test scores** SAT critical reading scores over 500: 88.93%; ACT scores over 18: 95.88%; SAT critical reading scores over 600: 54.73%; ACT scores over 24: 74.23% **Housing** Yes **Expenses** Tuition & Fees $35,142; Room & Board $10,756 **Undergraduates** 68% women, 2% part-time, 3% 25 or older, 1% Native American, 5% Hispanic American, 8% African American, 3% Asian American/Pacific Islander **The most frequently chosen baccalaureate fields are** psychology, social sciences, visual and performing arts **Academic program** Advanced placement, self-designed majors, adult/continuing education programs, internships **Contact** Mr. Carlton E. Surbeck III, Director of Admissions, Goucher College, 1021 Dulaney Valley Road, Baltimore, MD 21204-2794. *Phone:* 410-337-6100 or toll-free 800-468-2437. *E-mail:* admissions@goucher.edu. *Web site:* http://www.goucher.edu/.
Visit Petersons.com and enter keyword Goucher

See page 826 for the College Close-Up.

Griggs University
Silver Spring, Maryland

General Independent Seventh-day Adventist, 4-year, coed **Entrance** Minimally difficult **Setting** suburban campus **Total enrollment** 865 **Application deadline** Rolling (freshmen), rolling (transfer) **Freshman admission** 100% were admitted **Housing** No **Expenses** Tuition & Fees $7960 **Undergraduates** 58% women, 81% part-time **Academic program** Advanced placement, accelerated degree program, summer session, adult/continuing education programs **Contact** Ms. Linda Lundberg, Enrollment Officer, Griggs University, PO Box 4437, Silver Spring, MD 20914-4437. *Phone:* 301-680-6590 or toll-free 800-782-4769. *Fax:* 301-680-6577. *E-mail:* LLundberg@griggs.edu. *Web site:* http://www.griggs.edu/.

Hood College
Frederick, Maryland

General Independent, comprehensive, coed **Entrance** Moderately difficult **Setting** 50-acre suburban campus **Total enrollment** 2,493 **Student-faculty ratio** 12:1 **Application deadline** Rolling (freshmen), rolling (transfer) **Freshman admission** 72% were admitted. Average high school GPA 3.52 **Freshman test scores** SAT critical reading scores over 500: 71%; SAT math scores over 500: 62%; ACT scores over 18: 94%; SAT critical reading scores over 600: 30%; SAT math scores over 600: 23%; ACT scores over 24: 38% **Housing** Yes **Expenses** Tuition & Fees $29,860; Room & Board $9901 **Undergraduates** 68% women, 12% part-time, 15% 25 or older, 4% Hispanic American, 11% African American, 2% Asian American/Pacific Islander **The most frequently chosen baccalaureate fields are** education, business/marketing, psychology **Academic program** Advanced placement, self-designed majors, honors program, summer session, internships **Contact** Mr. David Adams, Director of Admissions, Hood College, 401 Rosemont Avenue, Frederick, MD 21701. *Phone:* 301-696-3400 or toll-free 800-922-1599. *Fax:* 301-696-3819. *E-mail:* admissions@hood.edu. *Web site:* http://www.hood.edu/.

ITT Technical Institute
Owings Mills, Maryland

General Proprietary, primarily 2-year, coed **Contact** Director of Recruitment, ITT Technical Institute, 11301 Red Run Boulevard, Owings Mills, MD 21117. *Phone:* 443-394-7115 or toll-free 877-411-6782. *Web site:* http://www.itt-tech.edu/.

The Johns Hopkins University
Baltimore, Maryland

General Independent, university, coed **Entrance** Most difficult **Setting** 140-acre urban campus **Total enrollment** 6,782 **Student-faculty ratio** 12:1 **Application deadline** 1/1 (freshmen), 3/15 (transfer) **Freshman admission** 27% were admitted. Average high school GPA 3.68 **Freshman test scores** SAT critical reading scores over 500: 99.12%; SAT math scores over 500: 99.6%; ACT scores over 18: 99.79%; SAT critical reading scores over 600: 88.14%; SAT math scores over 600: 95.38%; ACT scores over 24: 97.72% **Housing** Yes **Expenses** Tuition & Fees $39,150; Room & Board $12,040 **Undergraduates** 47% women, 1% part-time, 1% 25 or older, 0.4% Native American, 7% Hispanic American, 7% African American, 23% Asian American/Pacific Islander **The most frequently chosen baccalaureate fields are** engineering, biological/life sciences, health professions and related sciences **Academic program** Advanced placement, self-designed majors, honors program, summer session, adult/continuing education programs, internships **Contact** Dr. John Latting, Dean of Undergraduate Admissions, The Johns Hopkins University, Mason Hall, 3400 North Charles Street, Baltimore, MD 21218-2699. *Phone:* 410-516-8341. *Fax:* 410-516-6025. *E-mail:* gotojhu@jhu.edu. *Web site:* http://www.jhu.edu/.
Visit Petersons.com and enter keyword Johns

See pages 878 and 880 for the College Close-Ups.

Kaplan University, Hagerstown Campus
Hagerstown, Maryland

General Proprietary, primarily 2-year, coed **Setting** 8-acre small-town campus **Contact** Shinham, Director of Admissions, Kaplan University, Hagerstown Campus, 18618 Crestwood Drive, Hagerstown, MD 21742-2797. *Phone:* 301-739-2680 Ext. 217 or toll-free 800-422-2670. *Web site:* http://www.ku-hagerstown.com.

Loyola University Maryland
Baltimore, Maryland

General Independent Roman Catholic (Jesuit), university, coed **Entrance** Moderately difficult **Setting** 89-acre urban campus **Total enrollment** 6,067 **Student-faculty ratio** 12:1 **Application deadline** 1/15 (freshmen), 7/15 (transfer) **Freshman admission** 66% were admitted. Average high school GPA 3.41 **Freshman test scores** SAT critical reading scores over 500: 91%; SAT math scores over 500: 91%; ACT scores over 18: 99%; SAT critical reading scores over 600: 42%; SAT math scores over 600: 48%; ACT scores over 24: 76% **Housing** Yes **Expenses** Tuition & Fees $37,610; Room & Board $11,280 **Undergraduates** 59% women, 1% part-time, 1% 25 or older **The most frequently chosen baccalaureate fields are** business/marketing, biological/life sciences, communications/journalism **Academic program** Advanced placement, accelerated degree program, honors program, summer session, internships **Contact** Ms. Elena Hicks, Director of Undergraduate Admissions, Loyola University Maryland, 4501 North Charles Street, Baltimore, MD 21210-2699. *Phone:* 410-617-2251 or toll-free 800-221-9107 Ext. 2252. *Fax:* 410-617-5413. *Web site:* http://www.loyola.edu/.
Visit Petersons.com and enter keywords Loyola University Maryland

See page 926 for the College Close-Up.

Maple Springs Baptist Bible College and Seminary
Capitol Heights, Maryland

General Independent Baptist, comprehensive, coed **Entrance** Minimally difficult **Setting** 1-acre suburban campus **Total enrollment** 167

JOHNS HOPKINS
UNIVERSITY

Undergraduate studies in Liberal Arts and Engineering

Visit apply.jhu.edu

Maple Springs Baptist Bible College and Seminary (continued)

Application deadline Rolling (freshmen), rolling (transfer) **Housing** No **Undergraduates** 98% 25 or older **Academic program** Accelerated degree program, adult/continuing education programs, internships **Contact** Ms. Jeannie Bowman, Assistant Director of Admissions and Records, Maple Springs Baptist Bible College and Seminary, 4130 Belt Road, Capitol Heights, MD 20743. *Phone:* 301-736-3631. *Fax:* 301-735-6507. *E-mail:* esther.birch@msbbcs.edu. *Web site:* http://www.msbbcs.edu/.

Maryland Institute College of Art
Baltimore, Maryland

General Independent, comprehensive, coed **Entrance** Very difficult **Setting** 15-acre urban campus **Total enrollment** 1,919 **Student-faculty ratio** 10:1 **Application deadline** 2/13 (freshmen), 3/2 (transfer) **Freshman admission** 47% were admitted. Average high school GPA 3.5 **Freshman test scores** SAT critical reading scores over 500: 87%; SAT math scores over 500: 78%; SAT critical reading scores over 600: 49%; SAT math scores over 600: 34% **Housing** Yes **Expenses** Tuition & Fees $34,090; Room & Board $9450 **Undergraduates** 70% women, 1% part-time, 3% 25 or older, 0.2% Native American, 4% Hispanic American, 4% African American, 11% Asian American/Pacific Islander **The most frequently chosen baccalaureate fields are** education, visual and performing arts **Academic program** English as a second language, advanced placement, accelerated degree program, self-designed majors, summer session, adult/continuing education programs, internships **Contact** Ms. Christine Seese, Director of Undergraduate Admission, Maryland Institute College of Art, 1300 Mount Royal Avenue, Baltimore, MD 21217. *Phone:* 410-225-2222. *Fax:* 410-225-2337. *E-mail:* cgyland@mica.edu. *Web site:* http://www.mica.edu/.

Visit Petersons.com and enter keywords Maryland Institute

See page 948 for the College Close-Up.

McDaniel College
Westminster, Maryland

General Independent, comprehensive, coed **Entrance** Moderately difficult **Setting** 160-acre suburban campus **Total enrollment** 3,623 **Student-faculty ratio** 12:1 **Application deadline** 2/15 (freshmen), 4/1 (transfer) **Freshman admission** 79% were admitted. Average high school GPA 3.41 **Freshman test scores** SAT critical reading scores over 500: 77%; SAT math scores over 500: 76%; SAT critical reading scores over 600: 34%; SAT math scores over 600: 32% **Housing** Yes **Expenses** Tuition & Fees $32,000; Room & Board $6820 **Undergraduates** 54% women, 3% part-time, 2% 25 or older, 0.5% Native American, 3% Hispanic American, 6% African American, 4% Asian American/Pacific Islander **The most frequently chosen baccalaureate fields are** business/marketing, psychology, social sciences **Academic program** Advanced placement, self-designed majors, honors program, summer session, adult/continuing education programs, internships **Contact** Ms. Florence Hines, Vice President for Enrollment Management and Dean of Admissions, McDaniel College, 2 College Hill, Westminster, MD 21157-4390. *Phone:* 410-857-2230 or toll-free 800-638-5005. *Fax:* 410-857-2757. *E-mail:* admissions@mcdaniel.edu. *Web site:* http://www.mcdaniel.edu/.

Morgan State University
Baltimore, Maryland

General State-supported, university, coed **Entrance** Moderately difficult **Setting** 143-acre urban campus **Total enrollment** 7,005 **Student-**

faculty ratio 13:1 **Application deadline** 4/15 (freshmen), rolling (transfer) **Freshman admission** 43% were admitted. Average high school GPA 3.0 **Housing** Yes **Expenses** Tuition & Fees: state resident $6438, nonresident $14,928; Room & Board $8030 **Undergraduates** 55% women, 11% part-time, 12% 25 or older, 0.1% Native American, 1% Hispanic American, 92% African American, 1% Asian American/Pacific Islander **The most frequently chosen baccalaureate fields are** business/marketing, communications/journalism, family and consumer sciences **Academic program** Advanced placement, accelerated degree program, honors program, summer session, internships **Contact** Ms. Shonda Gray, Acting Director of Admissions and Recruitment, Morgan State University, 1700 East Cold Spring Lane, Baltimore, MD 21251. *Phone:* 443-885-3000 or toll-free 800-332-6674. *E-mail:* shantell.saunders@morgan.edu. *Web site:* http://www.morgan.edu/.

Mount St. Mary's University
Emmitsburg, Maryland

General Independent Roman Catholic, comprehensive, coed **Entrance** Moderately difficult **Setting** 1,400-acre rural campus **Total enrollment** 2,080 **Student-faculty ratio** 13:1 **Application deadline** Rolling (freshmen), 6/1 (transfer) **Freshman admission** 84% were admitted. Average high school GPA 3.11 **Freshman test scores** SAT critical reading scores over 500: 67%; SAT math scores over 500: 62%; ACT scores over 18: 87%; SAT critical reading scores over 600: 18%; SAT math scores over 600: 22%; ACT scores over 24: 37% **Housing** Yes **Expenses** Tuition & Fees $30,350; Room & Board $10,308 **Undergraduates** 58% women, 7% part-time, 2% 25 or older, 1% Native American, 6% Hispanic American, 8% African American, 3% Asian American/Pacific Islander **The most frequently chosen baccalaureate fields are** business/marketing, education, social sciences **Academic program** Advanced placement, accelerated degree program, self-designed majors, honors program, summer session, adult/continuing education programs, internships **Contact** Mr. Michael Post, Dean of Admissions and Enrollment Management, Mount St. Mary's University, 16300 Old Emmitsburg Road, Emmitsburg, MD 21727. *Phone:* 301-447-5214 or toll-free 800-448-4347. *Fax:* 301-447-5860. *E-mail:* admissions@msmary.edu. *Web site:* http://www.msmary.edu/.

National Labor College
Silver Spring, Maryland

Contact Karen Banks, Director of Admissions, National Labor College, 10000 New Hampshire Avenue, Silver Spring, MD 20903. *Phone:* 301-431-5422 or toll-free 800-GMC-4CDP. *E-mail:* kbanks@nlc.edu. *Web site:* http://www.nlc.edu/.

Ner Israel Rabbinical College
Baltimore, Maryland

General Independent Jewish, comprehensive, men only **Entrance** Moderately difficult **Setting** 54-acre suburban campus **Total enrollment** 574 **Application deadline** Rolling (freshmen), rolling (transfer) **Housing** Yes **Undergraduates** 7% 25 or older **Academic program** English as a second language, honors program, summer session **Contact** Dean of Admissions, Ner Israel Rabbinical College, 400 Mount Wilson Lane, Baltimore, MD 21208. *Phone:* 410-484-7200.

Peabody Conservatory of The Johns Hopkins University
Baltimore, Maryland

General Independent, comprehensive, coed **Entrance** Very difficult **Setting** 1-acre urban campus **Total enrollment** 682 **Student-faculty ratio** 4:1 **Application deadline** 12/1 (freshmen), 12/1 (transfer) **Freshman admission** 53% were admitted **Housing** Yes **Expenses** Tuition & Fees $34,675; Room & Board $11,100 **Undergraduates** 45% women, 3% part-time, 2% 25 or older, 0.3% Native American, 6% Hispanic American, 3% African American, 14% Asian American/Pacific Islander **The most frequently chosen baccalaureate field is** visual and performing arts **Academic program** English as a second language, advanced placement, accelerated degree program, honors program, internships **Contact** Mr. David Lane, Director of Admissions, Peabody Conservatory of The Johns Hopkins University, Peabody Conservatory Admissions Office, One East Mount Vernon Place, Baltimore, MD 21202-2397. *Phone:* 410-659-8110 or toll-free 800-368-2521. *Web site:* http://www.peabody.jhu.edu/.

St. John's College
Annapolis, Maryland

General Independent, comprehensive, coed **Entrance** Moderately difficult **Setting** 36-acre small-town campus **Total enrollment** 562 **Student-faculty ratio** 8:1 **Application deadline** Rolling (freshmen), rolling (transfer) **Freshman admission** 81% were admitted **Freshman test scores** SAT critical reading scores over 500: 98%; SAT math scores over 500: 97%; ACT scores over 18: 100%; SAT critical reading scores over 600: 88%; SAT math scores over 600: 66%; ACT scores over 24: 96% **Housing** Yes **Expenses** Tuition & Fees $42,192; Room & Board $9984 **Undergraduates** 47% women, 3% 25 or older, 0.2% Native American, 5% Hispanic American, 1% African American, 2% Asian American/Pacific Islander **The most frequently chosen baccalaureate field is** liberal arts/general studies **Academic program** Internships **Contact** Mr. John Christensen, Director of Admissions, St. John's College, PO Box 2800, 60 College Avenue, Annapolis, MD 21404. *Phone:* 410-626-2522 or toll-free 800-727-9238. *Fax:* 410-269-7916. *E-mail:* admissions@sjca.edu. *Web site:* http://www.stjohnscollege.edu/.

Visit Petersons.com and enter keywords St. John's

See page 1108 for the College Close-Up.

St. Mary's College of Maryland
St. Mary's City, Maryland

General State-supported, comprehensive, coed **Entrance** Very difficult **Setting** 319-acre rural campus **Total enrollment** 2,060 **Student-faculty ratio** 12:1 **Application deadline** 1/1 (freshmen), 2/1 (transfer) **Freshman admission** 58% were admitted. Average high school GPA 3.78 **Freshman test scores** SAT critical reading scores over 500: 92.81%; SAT math scores over 500: 88.02%; ACT scores over 18: 99%; SAT critical reading scores over 600: 68.41%; SAT math scores over 600: 57.95%; ACT scores over 24: 77% **Housing** Yes **Expenses** Tuition & Fees: state resident $13,630, nonresident $25,023; Room & Board $10,245 **Undergraduates** 58% women, 3% part-time, 1% 25 or older, 1% Native American, 4% Hispanic American, 8% African American, 4% Asian American/Pacific Islander **The most frequently chosen baccalaureate fields are** psychology, English, social sciences **Academic program** Advanced placement, self-designed majors, honors program, summer session, internships **Contact** Mr. Richard J. Edgar, Director of Admissions, St. Mary's College of Maryland, 18952 East Fisher Road, St. Mary's City, MD 20686-3001. *Phone:* 240-895-5000 or toll-free 800-492-7181. *Fax:* 240-895-5001. *E-mail:* admissions@smcm.edu. *Web site:* http://www.smcm.edu/.

Visit Petersons.com and enter keywords College of Maryland

See page 1126 for the College Close-Up.

Salisbury University
Salisbury, Maryland

General State-supported, comprehensive, coed **Entrance** Moderately difficult **Setting** 154-acre small-town campus **Total enrollment** 8,204 **Student-faculty ratio** 17:1 **Application deadline** 1/15 (freshmen), rolling (transfer) **Freshman admission** 54% were admitted. Average high school GPA 3.59 **Freshman test scores** SAT critical reading scores over 500: 86.5%; SAT math scores over 500: 88.5%; ACT scores over 18: 97.5%; SAT critical reading scores over 600: 35.9%; SAT math scores over 600: 26.3%; ACT scores over 24: 48.8% **Housing** Yes

THE PUBLIC HONORS COLLEGE

St. Mary's College of Maryland
at Historic St. Mary's City

Public

Prepare for the real world at a public honors college. Immerse yourself in a real diversity of backgrounds and perspectives and a true commitment to democratic ideals and social responsibility.

"A liberal arts education teaches students to look at the world with new eyes. By teaching them to think critically and solve challenges creatively, we're preparing them for jobs that don't yet exist–the careers they'll invent in a world we can't even imagine."

~ Alan Dillingham, Professor of Economics

Honors

St. Mary's is an entire honors college, not just an honors program within a larger college or university. We believe all students should have access to challenging academic programs and individual attention from faculty.

Discover the exceptional value of the public honors college.

www.SMCM.edu

Expenses Tuition & Fees: state resident $6618, nonresident $15,114; Room & Board $8070 **Undergraduates** 55% women, 8% part-time, 7% 25 or older, 1% Native American, 3% Hispanic American, 11% African American, 3% Asian American/Pacific Islander **The most frequently chosen baccalaureate fields are** business/marketing, communications/journalism, education **Academic program** English as a second language, advanced placement, self-designed majors, honors program, summer session, adult/continuing education programs, internships **Contact** Aaron Basko, Director of Admissions, Salisbury University, Admissions House, 1101 Camden Avenue, Salisbury, MD 21801. *Phone:* 410-543-6161 or toll-free 888-543-0148. *Fax:* 410-546-6016. *E-mail:* admissions@salisbury.edu. *Web site:* http://www.salisbury.edu/.

Visit Petersons.com and enter keyword Salisbury

See page 1138 for the College Close-Up.

Sojourner-Douglass College
Baltimore, Maryland

General Independent, comprehensive, coed, primarily women **Entrance** Noncompetitive **Setting** 15-acre urban campus **Total enrollment** 1,151 **Application deadline** Rolling (freshmen), rolling (transfer) **Housing** No **Expenses** Tuition & Fees $7478 **Undergraduates** 86% 25 or older **Academic program** Accelerated degree program, self-designed majors, honors program, summer session, adult/continuing education programs, internships **Contact** Ms. Diana Samuels, Director, Office of Admissions, Sojourner-Douglass College, 500 North Caroline Street, Baltimore, MD 21205-1814. *Phone:* 410-276-0306 Ext. 251. *E-mail:* dsamuels@host.sdc.edu. *Web site:* http://sdc.edu/.

Stevenson University
Stevenson, Maryland

General Independent, comprehensive, coed **Entrance** Moderately difficult **Setting** 150-acre suburban campus **Total enrollment** 3,432 **Student-faculty ratio** 15:1 **Application deadline** Rolling (freshmen), rolling (transfer) **Freshman admission** 57% were admitted. Average high school GPA 3.42 **Freshman test scores** SAT critical reading scores over 500: 53.2%; SAT math scores over 500: 55.14%; ACT scores over 18: 79.72%; SAT critical reading scores over 600: 13.98%; SAT math scores over 600: 14.56%; ACT scores over 24: 18.91% **Housing** Yes **Expenses** Tuition & Fees $20,644; Room & Board $10,296 **Undergraduates** 70% women, 18% part-time, 17% 25 or older, 1% Native American, 2% Hispanic American, 17% African American, 3% Asian American/Pacific Islander **The most frequently chosen baccalaureate fields are** business/marketing, health professions and related sciences, visual and performing arts **Academic program** Advanced placement, accelerated degree program, self-designed majors, honors program, summer session, adult/continuing education programs, internships **Contact** Mr. Mark Hergan, Vice President, Enrollment Management, Stevenson University, 1525 Greenspring Valley Road, Stevenson, MD 21153. *Phone:* 410-486-7001 or toll-free 877-468-6852 (in-state); 877-468-3852 (out-of-state). *Fax:* 410-352-4440. *E-mail:* admissions@stevenson.edu. *Web site:* http://www.stevenson.edu/.

Visit Petersons.com and enter keyword Stevenson

See page 1202 for the College Close-Up.

Strayer University–Anne Arundel Campus
Millersville, Maryland

General Proprietary, comprehensive, coed **Contact** Admissions Office, Strayer University–Anne Arundel Campus, 1520 Jabez Run, Millersville, MD 21108. *Phone:* 410-923-4500. *Web site:* http://www.strayer.edu/anne_arundel.

Strayer University–Owings Mills Campus
Owings Mills, Maryland

General Proprietary, comprehensive, coed **Contact** Admissions Office, Strayer University–Owings Mills Campus, 500 Redland Court, Suite

Top 5 Reasons Salisbury University Is A Great Value

1 Excellence At The Right Price: Named one of the nation's Top 100 and Top 50 "Best Value" public colleges by *Kiplinger's Personal Finance* and *The Princeton Review*, respectively, SU provides a quality education with a reasonable price tag. Students get to know their professors—many of whom have earned state and national teaching honors.

2 Private School Feel: A creative curriculum, undergraduate research and private endowments allow SU to be one of those rare public universities where individual talents are celebrated while big ideas are encouraged and developed.

3 National Distinction: SU consistently ranks among the nation's top colleges and universities in *U.S. News & World Report* and *The Princeton Review's The Best Colleges.*

To find out how Salisbury University is the right—and affordable—fit for you visit **www.salisbury.edu**

4 Formidable Facilities: SU is building for a better tomorrow with its state-of-the-art science hall and new Teacher Education and Technology Center. Other buildings on SU's horizon are a new residence hall and business school.

5 Alumni Network: With over 30,000 alumni worldwide, SU grads are taking the lead in the boardroom, the lab, the classroom, the legislature and even on Broadway. For many, the SU diploma is a passport to greatness.

A Maryland University of National Distinction

100, Owings Mills, MD 21117. *Phone:* 443-394-3339. *Web site:* http://www.strayer.edu/owings_mills.

Strayer University–Prince George's Campus

Suitland, Maryland

General Proprietary, comprehensive, coed **Contact** Admissions Office, Strayer University–Prince George's Campus, 4710 Auth Place, First Floor, Suitland, MD 20746. *Phone:* 301-423-3600. *Web site:* http://www.strayer.edu/prince_georges.

Strayer University–Rockville Campus

Rockville, Maryland

General Proprietary, comprehensive, coed **Contact** Admissions Office, Strayer University–Rockville Campus, 4 Research Place, Suite 100, Rockville, MD 20850. *Phone:* 301-548-5500. *Web site:* http://www.strayer.edu/rockville.

Strayer University–White Marsh Campus

Baltimore, Maryland

General Proprietary, comprehensive, coed **Contact** Admissions Office, Strayer University–White Marsh Campus, 9920 Franklin Square Drive, Suite 200, Baltimore, MD 21236. *Phone:* 410-238-9000. *Web site:* http://www.strayer.edu/white_marsh.

Towson University

Towson, Maryland

General State-supported, university, coed **Entrance** Moderately difficult **Setting** 321-acre suburban campus **Total enrollment** 21,177 **Student-faculty ratio** 17:1 **Application deadline** 2/15 (freshmen), 2/15 (transfer) **Freshman admission** 63% were admitted. Average high school GPA 3.55 **Freshman test scores** SAT critical reading scores over 500: 72.9%; SAT math scores over 500: 74.9%; ACT scores over 18: 96%; SAT critical reading scores over 600: 17.8%; SAT math scores over 600: 24.2%; ACT scores over 24: 34% **Housing** Yes **Expenses** Tuition & Fees: state resident $7418, nonresident $18,232; Room & Board $8670 **Undergraduates** 60% women, 11% part-time, 11% 25 or older, 0.4% Native American, 3% Hispanic American, 12% African American, 4% Asian American/Pacific Islander **The most frequently chosen baccalaureate fields are** business/marketing, education, social sciences **Academic program** English as a second language, advanced placement, accelerated degree program, self-designed majors, honors program, summer session, adult/continuing education programs, internships **Contact** Ms. Louise Shulack, Director of Admissions, Towson University, 8000 York Road, Towson, MD 21252. *Phone:* 410-704-2113 or toll-free 888-4TOWSON. *Fax:* 410-704-3030. *E-mail:* admissions@towson.edu. *Web site:* http://www.towson.edu/.

United States Naval Academy

Annapolis, Maryland

General Federally supported, 4-year, coed, primarily men **Entrance** Very difficult **Setting** 329-acre small-town campus **Total enrollment** 4,552 **Student-faculty ratio** 9:1 **Application deadline** 1/31 (freshmen) **Freshman admission** 8% were admitted **Freshman test scores** SAT critical reading scores over 500: 92%; SAT math scores over 500: 95%; SAT critical reading scores over 600: 57%; SAT math scores over 600: 70% **Housing** Yes **Undergraduates** 20% women, 2% 25 or older, 0.4% Native American, 12% Hispanic American, 5% African American, 4% Asian American/Pacific Islander **The most frequently chosen baccalaureate fields are** engineering, physical sciences, social sciences **Academic program** Advanced placement, honors program, summer session

United States Naval Academy (continued)
Contact Capt. Pat L. Williams, United States Naval Academy, 117 Decatur Road, Annapolis, MD 21402. *Phone:* 410-293-4361. *Fax:* 410-293-4348. *E-mail:* webmail@usna.edu. *Web site:* http://www.usna.edu/.

University of Baltimore
Baltimore, Maryland

General State-supported, comprehensive, coed **Entrance** Minimally difficult **Setting** 49-acre urban campus **Total enrollment** 6,265 **Student-faculty ratio** 20:1 **Application deadline** Rolling (freshmen), 6/1 (transfer) **Freshman admission** Average high school GPA 3.04 **Housing** Yes **Expenses** Tuition & Fees: state resident $7330, nonresident $16,846 **Undergraduates** 58% women, 41% part-time, 50% 25 or older, 1% Native American, 2% Hispanic American, 38% African American, 4% Asian American/Pacific Islander **Academic program** Advanced placement, accelerated degree program, self-designed majors, honors program, summer session, adult/continuing education programs, internships **Contact** Dr. Valarie J. Trimarchi, University of Baltimore, 1420 North Charles Street, Baltimore, MD 21201. *Phone:* 410-837-4777 or toll-free 877-APPLYUB. *Fax:* 410-837-4793. *E-mail:* admissions@ubalt.edu. *Web site:* http://www.ubalt.edu/.

University of Maryland, Baltimore County
Baltimore, Maryland

General State-supported, university, coed **Entrance** Moderately difficult **Setting** 530-acre suburban campus **Total enrollment** 12,870 **Student-faculty ratio** 19:1 **Application deadline** 2/1 (freshmen), 5/31 (transfer) **Freshman admission** 69% were admitted. Average high school GPA 3.61 **Freshman test scores** SAT critical reading scores over 500: 87%; SAT math scores over 500: 91.3%; ACT scores over 18: 100%; SAT critical reading scores over 600: 39.6%; SAT math scores over 600: 52.5%; ACT scores over 24: 64.5% **Housing** Yes **Expenses** Tuition & Fees: state resident $8872, nonresident $18,213; Room & Board $9303 **Undergraduates** 46% women, 13% part-time, 14% 25 or older, 1% Native American, 4% Hispanic American, 17% African American, 21% Asian American/Pacific Islander **The most frequently chosen baccalaureate fields are** psychology, biological/life sciences, social sciences **Academic program** English as a second language, advanced placement, self-designed majors, honors program, summer session, adult/continuing education programs, internships **Contact** Mr. Dale Bittinger, Director of Admissions, University of Maryland, Baltimore County, 1000 Hilltop Circle, Baltimore, MD 21250. *Phone:* 410-455-2291 or toll-free 800-UMBC-4U2 (in-state); 800-862-2402 (out-of-state). *Fax:* 410-455-1094. *E-mail:* admissions@umbc.edu. *Web site:* http://www.umbc.edu/.

University of Maryland, College Park
College Park, Maryland

General State-supported, university, coed **Entrance** Moderately difficult **Setting** 1,500-acre suburban campus **Total enrollment** 37,146 **Student-faculty ratio** 18:1 **Application deadline** 1/20 (freshmen), 6/1 (transfer) **Freshman admission** 42% were admitted. Average high school GPA 3.93 **Freshman test scores** SAT critical reading scores over 500: 95.5%; SAT math scores over 500: 96.6%; SAT critical reading scores over 600: 66.9%; SAT math scores over 600: 81.8% **Housing** Yes **Expenses** Tuition & Fees: state resident $8053, nonresident $23,989; Room & Board $9377 **Undergraduates** 47% women, 7% part-time, 6% 25 or older, 0.3% Native American, 6% Hispanic American, 12% African American, 15% Asian American/Pacific Islander **The most frequently chosen baccalaureate fields are** business/marketing, engineering, social sciences **Academic program** English as a second language, advanced placement, accelerated degree program, self-designed majors, honors program, summer session, adult/continuing education programs, internships **Contact** Ms. Barbara Gill, Director of Undergraduate Admissions, University of Maryland, College Park, College Park, MD 20742. *Phone:* 301-314-8385 or toll-free 800-422-5867. *Fax:* 301-314-9693. *Web site:* http://www.maryland.edu/.

University of Maryland Eastern Shore
Princess Anne, Maryland

General State-supported, university, coed **Entrance** Moderately difficult **Setting** 700-acre rural campus **Total enrollment** 3,762 **Student-faculty ratio** 20:1 **Application deadline** 7/15 (freshmen), rolling (transfer) **Freshman admission** 58% were admitted. Average high school GPA 2.8 **Freshman test scores** SAT critical reading scores over 500: 19%; SAT math scores over 500: 17.3%; ACT scores over 18: 2.8%; SAT critical reading scores over 600: 2.6%; SAT math scores over 600: 2.8% **Housing** Yes **Expenses** Tuition & Fees: state resident $6082, nonresident $13,306; Room & Board $7230 **Undergraduates** 59% women, 13% part-time, 13% 25 or older, 0.4% Native American, 1% Hispanic American, 76% African American, 2% Asian American/Pacific Islander **Academic program** Advanced placement, accelerated degree program, self-designed majors, honors program, summer session, internships **Contact** Tyrone Young, Director of Admissions, University of Maryland Eastern Shore, Princess Anne, MD 21853-1299. *Phone:* 410-651-6410. *Web site:* http://www.umes.edu/.

University of Maryland University College
Adelphi, Maryland

General State-supported, comprehensive, coed **Entrance** Noncompetitive **Setting** suburban campus **Total enrollment** 37,347 **Student-faculty ratio** 19:1 **Application deadline** Rolling (freshmen), rolling (transfer) **Freshman admission** 100% were admitted **Housing** No **Expenses** Tuition & Fees: state resident $5760, nonresident $12,216 **Undergraduates** 56% women, 86% part-time, 83% 25 or older, 1% Native American, 6% Hispanic American, 32% African American, 4% Asian American/Pacific Islander **The most frequently chosen baccalaureate fields are** business/marketing, computer and information sciences, interdisciplinary studies **Academic program** Advanced placement, accelerated degree program, summer session **Contact** Ms. Jessica Sadaka, Director of Admissions, University of Maryland University College, 3501 University Boulevard East, Adelphi, MD 20783. *Phone:* 800-888-UMUC (8682) or toll-free 800-888-8682. *E-mail:* enroll@umuc.edu. *Web site:* http://www.umuc.edu/.

University of Phoenix–Maryland Campus
Columbia, Maryland

General Proprietary, comprehensive, coed **Entrance** Noncompetitive **Setting** urban campus **Total enrollment** 755 **Application deadline** Rolling (freshmen), rolling (transfer) **Housing** No **Expenses** Tuition & Fees $12,250 **Undergraduates** 62% women, 92% 25 or older, 0.5% Native American, 3% Hispanic American, 44% African American, 1% Asian American/Pacific Islander **The most frequently chosen baccalaureate fields are** business/marketing, computer and information sciences, security and protective services **Academic program** Advanced placement, accelerated degree program, adult/continuing education programs **Contact** Ms. Audra McQuarie, Registrar/Executive Director, University of Phoenix–Maryland Campus, 4035 South Riverpoint Parkway, Mail Stop CF-L101, Phoenix, AZ 85040. *Phone:* 480-557-6151 or toll-free 800-776-4867 (in-state); 800-228-7240 (out-of-state). *Fax:* 480-643-3068. *E-mail:* audra.mcquarie@phoenix.edu. *Web site:* http://www.phoenix.edu/.

Washington Adventist University
Takoma Park, Maryland

General Independent Seventh-day Adventist, comprehensive, coed **Entrance** Moderately difficult **Setting** 19-acre suburban campus **Total**

Washington College
www.washcoll.edu
800.422.1782

A premier liberal arts college located on Maryland's Eastern Shore.

enrollment 1,183 **Student-faculty ratio** 14:1 **Application deadline** 8/1 (freshmen), 8/1 (transfer) **Freshman admission** 41% were admitted **Housing** Yes **Expenses** Tuition & Fees $19,480; Room & Board $7200 **Undergraduates** 66% women, 25% part-time, 39% 25 or older, 0.1% Native American, 11% Hispanic American, 52% African American, 6% Asian American/Pacific Islander **The most frequently chosen baccalaureate fields are** health professions and related sciences, business/ marketing, psychology **Academic program** English as a second language, advanced placement, accelerated degree program, self-designed majors, honors program, summer session, adult/continuing education programs, internships **Contact** Elaine Oliver, Associate Vice President, Enrollment Services, Washington Adventist University, 7600 Flower Avenue, Takoma Park, MD 20912. *Phone:* 301-891-4502 or toll-free 800-835-4212. *Fax:* 301-971-4230. *E-mail:* enroll@cuc.edu. *Web site:* http://www.wau.edu/.

Washington Bible College
Lanham, Maryland

General Independent nondenominational, comprehensive, coed **Entrance** Moderately difficult **Setting** 63-acre suburban campus **Total enrollment** 616 **Student-faculty ratio** 13:1 **Application deadline** 1/9 (freshmen), rolling (transfer) **Freshman admission** 65% were admitted. Average high school GPA 2.8 **Housing** Yes **Expenses** Tuition & Fees $10,200; Room & Board $6770 **Undergraduates** 46% women, 50% part-time, 57% 25 or older, 1% Native American, 3% Hispanic American, 44% African American, 7% Asian American/Pacific Islander **The most frequently chosen baccalaureate field is** theology and religious vocations **Academic program** English as a second language, advanced placement, accelerated degree program, summer session, internships **Contact** Mr. Mark D. Johnson, Director of Admissions, Washington Bible College, 6511 Princess Garden Parkway, Lanham, MD 20706-3599. *Phone:* 877-793-7227 or toll-free 877-793-7227 Ext. 1212. *Fax:* 301-552-2775. *E-mail:* admissions@bible.edu. *Web site:* http://www.bible.edu/.

Washington College
Chestertown, Maryland

General Independent, comprehensive, coed **Entrance** Moderately difficult **Setting** 140-acre small-town campus **Total enrollment** 1,372 **Student-faculty ratio** 12:1 **Application deadline** 3/1 (freshmen), 7/15 (transfer) **Freshman admission** 72% were admitted. Average high school GPA 3.44 **Freshman test scores** SAT critical reading scores over 500: 88%; SAT math scores over 500: 86%; ACT scores over 18: 98%; SAT critical reading scores over 600: 35%; SAT math scores over 600: 34%; ACT scores over 24: 62% **Housing** Yes **Expenses** Tuition & Fees $35,350; Room & Board $7460 **Undergraduates** 59% women, 2% part-time, 1% 25 or older, 0.5% Native American, 1% Hispanic American, 5% African American, 2% Asian American/Pacific Islander **The most frequently chosen baccalaureate fields are** business/marketing, English, social sciences **Academic program** English as a second language, advanced placement, self-designed majors, honors program, internships **Contact** Mr. Kevin Coveney, Vice President for Admissions and Enrollment Management, Washington College, 300 Washington Avenue, Chesterton, MD 21620. *Phone:* 410-778-7700 or toll-free 800-422-1782. *Fax:* 410-778-7287. *E-mail:* admissions_office@washcoll.edu. *Web site:* http://www.washcoll.edu/.

Visit Petersons.com and enter keywords Washington College

See page 1346 for the College Close-Up.

Yeshiva College of the Nation's Capital
Silver Spring, Maryland

General Independent Jewish, 4-year, men only **Total enrollment** 43 **Housing** Yes **Undergraduates** 30% 25 or older **Contact** Yeshiva College of the Nation's Capital, 1216 Arcola Avenue, Silver Spring, MD 20902. *Web site:* http://www.yeshiva.edu/default.shtml.

MASSACHUSETTS

American International College
Springfield, Massachusetts

General Independent, comprehensive, coed **Entrance** Moderately difficult **Setting** 58-acre urban campus **Total enrollment** 3,401 **Student-faculty ratio** 15:1 **Application deadline** Rolling (freshmen), rolling (transfer) **Freshman admission** 79% were admitted. Average high school GPA 2.5 **Freshman test scores** SAT critical reading scores over 500: 32%; SAT math scores over 500: 37%; ACT scores over 18: 59%; SAT critical reading scores over 600: 4%; SAT math scores over 600: 11%; ACT scores over 24: 10% **Housing** Yes **Expenses** Tuition & Fees $24,100; Room & Board $10,150 **Undergraduates** 58% women, 9% part-time, 23% 25 or older, 1% Native American, 9% Hispanic American, 27% African American, 3% Asian American/Pacific Islander **The most frequently chosen baccalaureate fields are** business/marketing, health professions and related sciences, security and protective services **Academic program** English as a second language, advanced placement, accelerated degree program, honors program, summer session, adult/continuing education programs, internships **Contact** Miss Kim LaBlanc, Director of Freshman Admissions, American International College, 1000 State Street, Springfield, MA 01109-3189. *Phone:* 413-205-3275. *Fax:* 413-205-3051. *E-mail:* kim.lablanc@aic.edu. *Web site:* http://www.aic.edu/.

Amherst College
Amherst, Massachusetts

General Independent, 4-year, coed **Entrance** Most difficult **Setting** 1,020-acre small-town campus **Total enrollment** 1,744 **Student-faculty ratio** 8:1 **Application deadline** 1/1 (freshmen), 2/1 (transfer) **Freshman admission** 16% were admitted **Freshman test scores** SAT critical reading scores over 500: 99%; SAT math scores over 500: 97%; ACT scores over 18: 101%; SAT critical reading scores over 600: 90%; SAT math scores over 600: 89%; ACT scores over 24: 100% **Housing** Yes **Expenses** Tuition & Fees $38,928; Room & Board $10,150 **Undergraduates** 50% women, 1% 25 or older, 0.1% Native American, 11% Hispanic American, 11% African American, 10% Asian American/Pacific Islander **The most frequently chosen baccalaureate fields are** English, foreign languages and literature, social sciences **Academic program** Self-designed majors, honors program **Contact** Mr. Thomas H. Parker, Dean of Admission and Financial Aid, Amherst College, PO Box 5000, Amherst, MA 01002-5000. *Phone:* 413-542-2328. *Fax:* 413-542-2040. *E-mail:* admission@amherst.edu. *Web site:* http://www.amherst.edu/.

Anna Maria College
Paxton, Massachusetts

General Independent Roman Catholic, comprehensive, coed **Entrance** Minimally difficult **Setting** 180-acre rural campus **Total enrollment** 1,333 **Student-faculty ratio** 10:1 **Application deadline** Rolling (freshmen), rolling (transfer) **Freshman admission** 89% were admitted. Average high school GPA 2.62 **Freshman test scores** SAT critical reading scores over 500: 22%; SAT math scores over 500: 21%; SAT critical reading scores over 600: 5%; SAT math scores over 600: 4% **Housing** Yes **Expenses** Tuition & Fees $26,620; Room & Board $9630 **Undergraduates** 56% women, 21% part-time, 20% 25 or older, 0.4% Native American, 5% Hispanic American, 6% African American, 1% Asian American/Pacific Islander **The most frequently chosen baccalaureate fields are** health professions and related sciences, business/marketing, security and protective services **Academic program** Advanced placement, accelerated degree program, self-designed majors, honors program, summer session, adult/continuing education programs, internships **Contact** Ms. Jenna Noel, Admissions Coordinator, Anna Maria College, Box O, Sunset Lane, Paxton, MA 01612. *Phone:* 508-849-3360 or toll-free 800-344-4586 Ext. 360. *Fax:* 508-849-3362. *E-mail:* admissions@annamaria.edu. *Web site:* http://www.annamaria.edu/.

The Art Institute of Boston at Lesley University
Boston, Massachusetts

General Independent, comprehensive, coed **Setting** 1-acre urban campus **Total enrollment** 5,564 **Student-faculty ratio** 10:1 **Application deadline** Rolling (freshmen), rolling (transfer) **Freshman admission** 67% were admitted. Average high school GPA 2.9 **Freshman test scores** SAT critical reading scores over 500: 68%; SAT math scores over 500: 61%; ACT scores over 18: 94%; SAT critical reading scores over 600: 26%; SAT math scores over 600: 20%; ACT scores over 24: 41% **Housing** Yes **Expenses** Tuition & Fees $27,600; Room & Board $12,800 **Undergraduates** 76% women, 4% part-time, 5% 25 or older, 1% Native American, 5% Hispanic American, 4% African American, 3% Asian American/Pacific Islander **The most frequently chosen baccalaureate fields are** liberal arts/general studies, psychology, visual and performing arts **Academic program** English as a second language, advanced placement, accelerated degree program, self-designed majors, honors program, summer session, adult/continuing education programs, internships **Contact** Bob Gielow, Director of Admission, The Art Institute of Boston at Lesley University, 700 Beacon Street, Boston, MA 02215-2598. *Phone:* 617-585-6710 or toll-free 800-773-0494. *Fax:* 617-585-6720. *E-mail:* admissions@aiboston.edu. *Web site:* http://www.aiboston.edu/.
Visit Petersons.com and enter keywords Art Institute of Boston at Lesley

See page 486 for the College Close-Up.

Assumption College
Worcester, Massachusetts

General Independent Roman Catholic, comprehensive, coed **Entrance** Moderately difficult **Setting** 180-acre suburban campus **Total enrollment** 2,601 **Student-faculty ratio** 12:1 **Application deadline** 2/15 (freshmen), 7/1 (transfer) **Freshman admission** 79% were admitted. Average high school GPA 3.42 **Freshman test scores** SAT critical reading scores over 500: 71.5%; SAT math scores over 500: 72.5%; ACT scores over 18: 88.2%; SAT critical reading scores over 600: 18.4%; SAT math scores over 600: 22.2%; ACT scores over 24: 36.9% **Housing** Yes **Expenses** Tuition & Fees $30,171; Room & Board $6340 **Undergraduates** 58% women, 0.1% part-time, 0.3% 25 or older, 0.05% Native American, 3% Hispanic American, 2% African American, 1% Asian American/Pacific Islander **The most frequently chosen baccalaureate fields are** business/marketing, psychology, social sciences **Academic program** Advanced placement, self-designed majors, honors program, summer session, internships **Contact** Ms. Kathleen Murphy, Dean of Enrollment, Assumption College, 500 Salisbury Street, Worcester, MA 01609-1296. *Phone:* 508-767-7110 or toll-free 888-882-7786. *Fax:* 508-799-4412. *E-mail:* admiss@assumption.edu. *Web site:* http://www.assumption.edu/.
Visit Petersons.com and enter keyword Assumption

See page 566 for the College Close-Up.

Atlantic Union College
South Lancaster, Massachusetts

General Independent Seventh-day Adventist, comprehensive, coed **Entrance** Moderately difficult **Setting** 314-acre small-town campus **Total enrollment** 461 **Student-faculty ratio** 10:1 **Application deadline** 8/1 (freshmen), 8/1 (transfer) **Freshman admission** 59% were admitted. Average high school GPA 2.92 **Housing** Yes **Expenses** Tuition & Fees $17,066; Room & Board $5150 **Undergraduates** 67% women, 20% part-time, 19% Hispanic American, 53% African American, 4% Asian American/Pacific Islander **Academic program** English as a second language, advanced placement, self-designed majors, honors program, summer session, adult/continuing education programs, internships

Contact Dr. Bordes Henry-Saturne, Director for Admissions, Atlantic Union College, PO Box 1000, South Lancaster, MA 01561-1000. *Phone:* 978-368-2239 or toll-free 800-282-2030. *Fax:* 978-368-2015. *E-mail:* bordes.henry-saturne@auc.edu. *Web site:* http://www.auc.edu/.

Babson College
Babson Park, Massachusetts

General Independent, comprehensive, coed **Entrance** Very difficult **Setting** 370-acre suburban campus **Total enrollment** 3,445 **Student-faculty ratio** 13:1 **Application deadline** 1/15 (freshmen), 4/1 (transfer) **Freshman admission** 40% were admitted. Average high school GPA 3.53 **Freshman test scores** SAT critical reading scores over 500: 95%; SAT math scores over 500: 98%; ACT scores over 18: 97%; SAT critical reading scores over 600: 55%; SAT math scores over 600: 80%; ACT scores over 24: 88% **Housing** Yes **Expenses** Tuition & Fees $37,824; Room & Board $13,500 **Undergraduates** 43% women, 1% 25 or older, 0.4% Native American, 8% Hispanic American, 5% African American, 13% Asian American/Pacific Islander **The most frequently chosen baccalaureate field is** business/marketing **Academic program** Advanced placement, self-designed majors, honors program, summer session, internships **Contact** Ms. Adrienne Ramsey, Senior Assistant Director of Undergraduate Admission, Babson College, Lunder Undergraduate Admission Center, Babson Park, MA 02457-0310. *Phone:* 781-239-5522 or toll-free 800-488-3696. *Fax:* 781-239-4135. *E-mail:* ugradadmission@babson.edu. *Web site:* http://www.babson.edu/.

Visit Petersons.com and enter keyword Babson

See page 572 for the College Close-Up.

Bard College at Simon's Rock
Great Barrington, Massachusetts

General Independent, 4-year, coed **Entrance** Very difficult **Setting** 275-acre rural campus **Total enrollment** 431 **Student-faculty ratio** 8:1 **Application deadline** 5/31 (freshmen), 7/15 (transfer) **Freshman admission** 84% were admitted **Housing** Yes **Expenses** Tuition & Fees $40,170; Room & Board $10,960 **Undergraduates** 59% women, 2% part-time, 0.5% Native American, 4% Hispanic American, 6% African American, 5% Asian American/Pacific Islander **The most frequently chosen baccalaureate fields are** biological/life sciences, area and ethnic studies, visual and performing arts **Academic program** Self-designed majors, internships **Contact** Steven Coleman, Director of Admissions, Bard College at Simon's Rock, 84 Alford Road, Great Barrington, MA 01230-9702. *Phone:* 413-528-7312 or toll-free 800-235-7186. *Fax:* 413-528-7334. *E-mail:* admit@simons-rock.edu. *Web site:* http://www.simons-rock.edu/.

Visit Petersons.com and enter keyword Simon's

See page 576 for the College Close-Up.

Bay Path College
Longmeadow, Massachusetts

General Independent, comprehensive, undergraduate: women only; graduate: coed **Entrance** Moderately difficult **Setting** 48-acre suburban campus **Total enrollment** 2,034 **Student-faculty ratio** 15:1 **Application deadline** Rolling (freshmen), rolling (transfer) **Freshman admission** 83% were admitted. Average high school GPA 3.16 **Freshman test scores** SAT critical reading scores over 500: 42%; SAT math scores over 500: 39%; ACT scores over 18: 88%; SAT critical reading scores over 600: 10%; SAT math scores over 600: 10%; ACT scores over 24: 25% **Housing** Yes **Expenses** Tuition & Fees $24,530; Room & Board $10,035 **Undergraduates** 19% part-time, 0.3% Native American, 11% Hispanic American, 11% African American, 2% Asian American/Pacific Islander **The most frequently chosen baccalaureate fields are** business/marketing, liberal arts/general studies, psychology **Academic program** English as a second language, advanced placement, accelerated degree program, self-designed majors, honors program, summer session, adult/continuing education programs, internships **Contact** Diane Ranaldi, Dean of Enrollment Management, Bay Path College, 588 Longmeadow Street, Longmeadow, MA 01106-2292. *Phone:* 413-565-1000 Ext. 1331 or toll-free 800-782-7284 Ext. 1331. *Fax:* 413-565-1105. *E-mail:* admiss@baypath.edu. *Web site:* http://www.baypath.edu/.

Bay State College
Boston, Massachusetts

Contact Kim Olds, Director of Admissions, Bay State College, 122 Commonwealth Avenue, Boston, MA 02116. *Phone:* 617-217-9115 or toll-free 800-81-LEARN. *Fax:* 617-536-1735. *E-mail:* admissions@baystate.edu. *Web site:* http://www.baystate.edu/.

Visit Petersons.com and enter keywords Bay State

See page 586 for the College Close-Up.

Becker College
Worcester, Massachusetts

General Independent, 4-year, coed **Entrance** Minimally difficult **Setting** 100-acre rural campus **Total enrollment** 1,752 **Student-faculty ratio** 16:1 **Application deadline** Rolling (freshmen), rolling (transfer) **Freshman admission** 72% were admitted. Average high school GPA 2.60 **Freshman test scores** SAT critical reading scores over 500: 22%; SAT math scores over 500: 25%; ACT scores over 18: 54%; SAT critical reading scores over 600: 4%; SAT math scores over 600: 4%; ACT scores over 24: 13% **Housing** Yes **Expenses** Tuition & Fees $27,748; Room & Board $9760 **Undergraduates** 67% women, 23% part-time, 30% 25 or older, 1% Native American, 4% Hispanic American, 6% African American, 1% Asian American/Pacific Islander **The most frequently chosen baccalaureate fields are** business/marketing, science technologies, visual and performing arts **Academic program** Advanced placement, accelerated degree program, summer session, adult/continuing education programs, internships **Contact** Admissions Receptionist, Becker College, 61 Sever Street, Worcester, MA 01609. *Phone:* 508-373-9400 or toll-free 877-5BECKER Ext. 245. *Fax:* 508-890-1500. *E-mail:* admissions@beckercollege.edu. *Web site:* http://www.becker.edu/.

Benjamin Franklin Institute of Technology
Boston, Massachusetts

General Independent, primarily 2-year, coed **Entrance** Minimally difficult **Setting** 3-acre urban campus **Total enrollment** 536 **Student-faculty ratio** 12:1 **Application deadline** 8/15 (freshmen), rolling (transfer) **Freshman admission** 66% were admitted. Average high school GPA 2.7 **Housing** Yes **Expenses** Tuition & Fees $14,284; Room & Board $9600 **Undergraduates** 11% women, 22% part-time, 19% 25 or older, 1% Native American, 7% Hispanic American, 18% African American, 8% Asian American/Pacific Islander **Academic program** English as a second language, advanced placement, summer session, adult/continuing education programs, internships **Contact** Ms. Brittainy Johnson, Associate Director of Admissions, Benjamin Franklin Institute of Technology, 41 Berkeley Street, Boston, MA 02116-6296. *Phone:* 617-423-4630 Ext. 122. *Fax:* 617-482-3706. *E-mail:* bjohnson@bfit.edu. *Web site:* http://www.bfit.edu/.

Bentley University
Waltham, Massachusetts

General Independent, comprehensive, coed **Entrance** Very difficult **Setting** 163-acre suburban campus **Total enrollment** 5,616 **Student-faculty ratio** 14:1 **Application deadline** 1/15 (freshmen) **Freshman admission** 43% were admitted **Freshman test scores** SAT critical reading scores over 500: 92%; SAT math scores over 500: 97%; ACT scores over 18: 100%; SAT critical reading scores over 600: 45%; SAT math scores over 600: 79%; ACT scores over 24: 86% **Housing** Yes **Expenses** Tuition & Fees $35,828; Room & Board $11,740 **Undergraduates** 40% women, 5% part-time, 3% 25 or older, 0.1% Native

Bentley University (continued)
American, 5% Hispanic American, 3% African American, 7% Asian American/Pacific Islander **The most frequently chosen baccalaureate fields are** business/marketing, communication technologies, interdisciplinary studies **Academic program** Advanced placement, accelerated degree program, self-designed majors, honors program, summer session, adult/continuing education programs, internships **Contact** Admissions Office, Bentley University, 175 Forest Street, Waltham, MA 02452. *Phone:* 781-891-2244 or toll-free 800-523-2354. *Fax:* 781-891-3414. *E-mail:* ugadmission@bentley.edu. *Web site:* http://www.bentley.edu.
Visit Petersons.com and enter keyword Bentley

See page 596 for the College Close-Up.

Berklee College of Music
Boston, Massachusetts

General Independent, 4-year, coed **Entrance** Moderately difficult **Setting** urban campus **Total enrollment** 4,145 **Student-faculty ratio** 12:1 **Application deadline** 1/15 (freshmen), 1/15 (transfer) **Freshman admission** 42% were admitted **Housing** Yes **Expenses** Tuition & Fees $30,650; Room & Board $15,080 **Undergraduates** 29% women, 8% part-time, 0.4% Native American, 8% Hispanic American, 8% African American, 4% Asian American/Pacific Islander **The most frequently chosen baccalaureate fields are** business/marketing, engineering, visual and performing arts **Academic program** English as a second language, advanced placement, self-designed majors, summer session, internships **Contact** Mr. Damien Bracken, Director of Admissions, Berklee College of Music, 1140 Boyleston Street, Boston, MA 02215-3693. *Phone:* 617-747-2222 or toll-free 800-BERKLEE. *Fax:* 617-747-2047. *E-mail:* admissions@berklee.edu. *Web site:* http://www.berklee.edu/.
Visit Petersons.com and enter keyword Berklee

See page 598 for the College Close-Up.

Boston Architectural College
Boston, Massachusetts

General Independent, comprehensive, coed **Entrance** Noncompetitive **Setting** 1-acre urban campus **Total enrollment** 1,146 **Student-faculty ratio** 4:1 **Application deadline** Rolling (freshmen), rolling (transfer) **Freshman admission** 71% were admitted. Average high school GPA 2.7 **Housing** No **Expenses** Tuition & Fees $11,468 **Undergraduates** 32% women, 2% part-time, 37% 25 or older, 0.2% Native American, 12% Hispanic American, 7% African American, 6% Asian American/Pacific Islander **The most frequently chosen baccalaureate field is** architecture **Academic program** Advanced placement, summer session, adult/continuing education programs, internships **Contact** Richard Moyer, Director of Admission, Boston Architectural College, 320 Newbury Street, Boston, MA 02115-2795. *Phone:* 617-585-0256 or toll-free 877-585-0100. *Fax:* 617-585-0121. *E-mail:* admissions@the-bac.edu. *Web site:* http://www.the-bac.edu/.
Visit Petersons.com and enter keywords Boston Architectural

Boston Baptist College
Boston, Massachusetts

General Independent Baptist, 4-year, coed **Entrance** Moderately difficult **Setting** 8-acre suburban campus **Total enrollment** 148 **Student-faculty ratio** 8:1 **Application deadline** Rolling (freshmen), rolling (transfer) **Freshman admission** 47% were admitted. Average high school GPA 2.68 **Housing** Yes **Expenses** Tuition & Fees $10,829; Room & Board $7666 **Undergraduates** 51% women, 27% part-time, 11% 25 or older, 2% Hispanic American, 3% African American, 1% Asian American/Pacific Islander **The most frequently chosen baccalaureate field is** theology and religious vocations **Academic program** Advanced placement, honors program, summer session, adult/continuing education programs **Contact** Mrs. Karen Fox, Director of Admissions, Boston Baptist College, 950 Metropolitan Avenue, Boston, MA 02136. *Phone:* 617-364-3510 Ext. 217 or toll-free 888-235-2014. *E-mail:* kfox@boston.edu. *Web site:* http://www.boston.edu/.

Boston College
Chestnut Hill, Massachusetts

General Independent Roman Catholic (Jesuit), university, coed **Entrance** Very difficult **Setting** 386-acre suburban campus **Total enrollment** 14,131 **Student-faculty ratio** 13:1 **Application deadline** 1/1 (freshmen), 4/1 (transfer) **Freshman admission** 30% were admitted **Freshman test scores** SAT critical reading scores over 500: 96.8%; SAT math scores over 500: 98.4%; ACT scores over 18: 99.9%; SAT critical reading scores over 600: 82.2%; SAT math scores over 600: 87.3%; ACT scores over 24: 96.4% **Housing** Yes **Expenses** Tuition & Fees $39,130; Room & Board $12,909 **Undergraduates** 52% women, 0.3% Native American, 8% Hispanic American, 5% African American, 10% Asian American/Pacific Islander **The most frequently chosen baccalaureate fields are** business/marketing, communications/journalism, social sciences **Academic program** Advanced placement, accelerated degree program, self-designed majors, honors program, summer session, internships **Contact** Office of Undergraduate Admissions, Boston College, 140 Commonwealth Avenue, Devlin 208, Chestnut Hill, MA 02467-3809. *Phone:* 617-552-3100 or toll-free 800-360-2522. *Fax:* 617-552-0798. *Web site:* http://www.bc.edu/.
Visit Petersons.com and enter keywords Boston College

See page 608 for the College Close-Up.

The Boston Conservatory
Boston, Massachusetts

General Independent, comprehensive, coed **Entrance** Moderately difficult **Setting** urban campus **Total enrollment** 676 **Student-faculty ratio** 4:1 **Application deadline** 12/1 (freshmen), 12/1 (transfer) **Freshman admission** 34% were admitted **Housing** Yes **Expenses** Tuition & Fees $33,700; Room & Board $15,880 **Undergraduates** 58% women, 0.4% part-time **The most frequently chosen baccalaureate field is** visual and performing arts **Academic program** English as a second language, advanced placement, summer session, internships **Contact** Ms. Halley Shefler, Dean of Enrollment, The Boston Conservatory, 8 The Fenway, Boston, MA 02215. *Phone:* 617-912-9153. *E-mail:* hshefler@bostonconservatory.edu. *Web site:* http://www.bostonconservatory.edu/.
Visit Petersons.com and enter keywords Boston Conservatory

Boston University
Boston, Massachusetts

General Independent, university, coed **Entrance** Very difficult **Setting** 132-acre urban campus **Total enrollment** 31,960 **Student-faculty ratio** 13:1 **Application deadline** 1/1 (freshmen), 4/1 (transfer) **Freshman admission** 58% were admitted. Average high school GPA 3.49 **Freshman test scores** SAT critical reading scores over 500: 96%; SAT math scores over 500: 99%; ACT scores over 18: 100%; SAT critical reading scores over 600: 63%; SAT math scores over 600: 77%; ACT scores over 24: 93% **Housing** Yes **Expenses** Tuition & Fees $39,864; Room & Board $12,260 **Undergraduates** 60% women, 8% part-time, 5% 25 or older, 0.4% Native American, 7% Hispanic American, 3% African American, 14% Asian American/Pacific Islander **The most frequently chosen baccalaureate fields are** business/marketing, communications/journalism, social sciences **Academic program** English as a second language, advanced placement, accelerated degree program, self-designed majors, honors program, summer session, adult/continuing education programs, internships **Contact** Ms. Kelly Walter, Director of Undergraduate Admissions, Boston University, 121 Bay State Road, Boston, MA 02215. *Phone:* 617-353-2300. *Fax:* 617-353-9695. *E-mail:* admissions@bu.edu. *Web site:* http://www.bu.edu/.
Visit Petersons.com and enter keywords Boston University

See page 610 for the College Close-Up.

Brandeis University
Waltham, Massachusetts

General Independent, university, coed **Entrance** Most difficult **Setting** 235-acre suburban campus **Total enrollment** 5,598 **Student-faculty ratio** 9:1 **Application deadline** 1/15 (freshmen), 4/1 (transfer) **Freshman admission** 40% were admitted. Average high school GPA 3.77 **Freshman test scores** SAT critical reading scores over 500: 98.7%; SAT math scores over 500: 99.3%; ACT scores over 18: 100%; SAT critical reading scores over 600: 87.3%; SAT math scores over 600: 91.1%; ACT scores over 24: 97.4% **Housing** Yes **Expenses** Tuition & Fees $38,762; Room & Board $10,792 **Undergraduates** 56% women, 1% part-time, 0.4% Native American, 5% Hispanic American, 5% African American, 11% Asian American/Pacific Islander **The most frequently chosen baccalaureate fields are** area and ethnic studies, biological/life sciences, social sciences **Academic program** English as a second language, advanced placement, self-designed majors, honors program, summer session, adult/continuing education programs, internships **Contact** Ms. Jean C. Eddy, Senior Vice President for Students and Enrollment, Brandeis University, 415 South Street, Waltham, MA 02254-9110. *Phone:* 781-736-3500 or toll-free 800-622-0622. *Fax:* 781-736-3536. *E-mail:* admissions@brandeis.edu. *Web site:* http://www.brandeis.edu/.

Bridgewater State College
Bridgewater, Massachusetts

General State-supported, comprehensive, coed **Entrance** Moderately difficult **Setting** 235-acre suburban campus **Total enrollment** 10,774 **Student-faculty ratio** 23:1 **Application deadline** 2/15 (freshmen), 6/1 (transfer) **Freshman admission** 61% were admitted. Average high school GPA 3.1 **Freshman test scores** SAT critical reading scores over 500: 57.9%; SAT math scores over 500: 60.2%; ACT scores over 18: 98.1%; SAT critical reading scores over 600: 12.4%; SAT math scores over 600: 14.2%; ACT scores over 24: 24.5% **Housing** Yes **Expenses** Tuition & Fees: state resident $6604, nonresident $12,744; Room & Board $9670 **Undergraduates** 60% women, 16% part-time, 13% 25 or older, 0.3% Native American, 3% Hispanic American, 6% African American, 2% Asian American/Pacific Islander **The most frequently chosen baccalaureate fields are** business/marketing, education, psychology **Academic program** English as a second language, advanced placement, accelerated degree program, honors program, summer session, adult/continuing education programs, internships **Contact** Mr. Gregg Meyer, Director of Admissions, Bridgewater State College, Bridgewater, MA 02325-0001. *Phone:* 508-531-1237. *E-mail:* admission@bridgew.edu. *Web site:* http://www.bridgew.edu/.

Visit Petersons.com and enter keyword Bridgewater

See page 614 for the College Close-Up.

Cambridge College
Cambridge, Massachusetts

General Independent, comprehensive, coed **Entrance** Noncompetitive **Setting** urban campus **Total enrollment** 4,961 **Student-faculty ratio** 16:1 **Application deadline** Rolling (freshmen), rolling (transfer) **Freshman admission** 100% were admitted **Housing** No **Expenses** Tuition & Fees $10,950 **Undergraduates** 76% 25 or older, 0.5% Native American, 19% Hispanic American, 29% African American, 3% Asian American/Pacific Islander **The most frequently chosen baccalaureate fields are** business/marketing, liberal arts/general studies, psychology **Academic program** Advanced placement, accelerated degree program, summer session, adult/continuing education programs, internships **Contact** Mr. Stephen Lyons, Director of Undergraduate and Graduate Admissions, Cambridge College, 1000 Massachusetts Avenue, Cambridge, MA 02138-5304. *Phone:* 617-873-0167 or toll-free 800-877-4723. *Fax:* 617-349-3561. *E-mail:* stephen.lyons@cambridgecollege.edu. *Web site:* http://www.cambridgecollege.edu/.

Clark University
Worcester, Massachusetts

General Independent, university, coed **Entrance** Moderately difficult **Setting** 50-acre urban campus **Total enrollment** 3,416 **Student-faculty ratio** 10:1 **Application deadline** 1/15 (freshmen), 4/15 (transfer) **Freshman admission** 64% were admitted. Average high school GPA 3.46 **Freshman test scores** SAT critical reading scores over 500: 89%; SAT math scores over 500: 88%; ACT scores over 18: 99%; SAT critical reading scores over 600: 52%; SAT math scores over 600: 46%; ACT scores over 24: 78% **Housing** Yes **Expenses** Tuition & Fees $36,420; Room & Board $6950 **Undergraduates** 61% women, 5% part-time, 1% 25 or older, 0.4% Native American, 2% Hispanic American, 2% African American, 4% Asian American/Pacific Islander **The most frequently chosen baccalaureate fields are** psychology, biological/life sciences, social sciences **Academic program** English as a second language, advanced placement, accelerated degree program, self-designed majors, honors program, summer session, adult/continuing education programs, internships **Contact** Mr. Donald Honeman, Dean of Admissions, Clark University, Admissions House, 950 Main Street, Worcester, MA 01610. *Phone:* 508-793-7431 or toll-free 800-GO-CLARK. *Fax:* 508-793-8821. *E-mail:* admissions@clarku.edu. *Web site:* http://www.clarku.edu/.

See page 714 for the College Close-Up.

College of the Holy Cross
Worcester, Massachusetts

General Independent Roman Catholic (Jesuit), 4-year, coed **Entrance** Very difficult **Setting** 174-acre suburban campus **Total enrollment** 2,933 **Student-faculty ratio** 11:1 **Application deadline** 1/15 (freshmen), 4/1 (transfer) **Freshman admission** 36% were admitted. Average high school GPA 3.79 **Freshman test scores** SAT critical reading scores over 500: 97%; SAT math scores over 500: 97%; ACT scores over 18: 99%; SAT critical reading scores over 600: 76%; SAT math scores over 600: 81%; ACT scores over 24: 87% **Housing** Yes **Expenses** Tuition & Fees $39,892; Room & Board $10,940 **Undergraduates** 54% women, 1% part-time, 0.4% Native American, 8% Hispanic American, 4% African American, 6% Asian American/Pacific Islander **The most frequently chosen baccalaureate fields are** English, psychology, social sciences **Academic program** Advanced placement, accelerated degree program, self-designed majors, honors program, internships **Contact** Ms. Ann McDermott, Director of Admissions, College of the Holy Cross, 1 College Street, Worcester, MA 01610-2395. *Phone:* 508-793-2443 or toll-free 800-442-2421. *Fax:* 508-793-3888. *E-mail:* admissions@holycross.edu. *Web site:* http://www.holycross.edu/.

Curry College
Milton, Massachusetts

General Independent, comprehensive, coed **Entrance** Moderately difficult **Setting** 131-acre suburban campus **Total enrollment** 3,125 **Student-faculty ratio** 10:1 **Application deadline** 4/1 (freshmen), 7/1 (transfer) **Freshman admission** 75% were admitted. Average high school GPA 2.7 **Freshman test scores** SAT critical reading scores over 500: 28%; SAT math scores over 500: 31%; ACT scores over 18: 77%; SAT critical reading scores over 600: 4%; SAT math scores over 600: 4%; ACT scores over 24: 11% **Housing** Yes **Undergraduates** 57% women, 29% part-time, 25% 25 or older, 0.2% Native American, 3% Hispanic American, 8% African American, 1% Asian American/Pacific Islander **The most frequently chosen baccalaureate fields are** health professions and related sciences, business/marketing, security and protective services **Academic program** Advanced placement, accelerated degree program, self-designed majors, honors program, summer session, adult/continuing education programs, internships **Contact** Ms. Jane P. Fidler, Dean of Admission, Curry College, 1071 Blue Hill Avenue, Milton, MA 02186. *Phone:* 617-333-2210 or toll-free 800-669-0686. *Fax:* 617-333-2114. *E-mail:* curryadm@curry.edu. *Web site:* http://www.curry.edu/.

Visit Petersons.com and enter keyword Curry

See page 746 for the College Close-Up.

Dean College
Franklin, Massachusetts

Contact Mr. Paul Vaccaro, Assistant Vice President for Enrollment Services and Dean of Admission, Dean College, 99 Main Street, Franklin, MA 02038. *Phone:* 508-541-1508 or toll-free 877-TRY-DEAN. *Fax:* 508-541-8726. *E-mail:* admission@dean.edu. *Web site:* http://www.dean.edu/.

Visit Petersons.com and enter keyword Dean

Eastern Nazarene College
Quincy, Massachusetts

General Independent, comprehensive, coed, affiliated with Church of the Nazarene **Entrance** Moderately difficult **Setting** 17-acre urban campus **Total enrollment** 1,075 **Student-faculty ratio** 13:1 **Application deadline** Rolling (freshmen), rolling (transfer) **Freshman admission** 61% were admitted. Average high school GPA 3.1 **Freshman test scores** SAT critical reading scores over 500: 53%; SAT math scores over 500: 53%; ACT scores over 18: 84%; SAT critical reading scores over 600: 17%; SAT math scores over 600: 19%; ACT scores over 24: 44% **Housing** Yes **Expenses** Tuition & Fees $23,772; Room & Board $8000 **Undergraduates** 59% women, 3% part-time, 3% 25 or older, 1% Native American, 5% Hispanic American, 16% African American, 2% Asian American/Pacific Islander **The most frequently chosen baccalaureate fields are** business/marketing, liberal arts/general studies, psychology **Academic program** Advanced placement, accelerated degree program, honors program, summer session, adult/continuing education programs, internships **Contact** Mr. Andrew R. Wright, Director of Admissions, Eastern Nazarene College, 23 East Elm Avenue, Quincy, MA 02170. *Phone:* 617-745-3864 or toll-free 800-88-ENC88. *Fax:* 617-745-3992. *E-mail:* andrew.wright@enc.edu. *Web site:* http://www.enc.edu/.

Visit Petersons.com and enter keywords Eastern Nazarene

See page 768 for the College Close-Up.

Elms College
Chicopee, Massachusetts

Contact Mr. Joseph Wagner, Director of Admissions, Elms College, 291 Springfield Street, Chicopee, MA 01013-2839. *Phone:* 413-592-3189 Ext. 350 or toll-free 800-255-ELMS. *Fax:* 413-594-2781. *E-mail:* admissions@elms.edu. *Web site:* http://www.elms.edu/.

Emerson College
Boston, Massachusetts

General Independent, comprehensive, coed **Entrance** Very difficult **Setting** urban campus **Total enrollment** 4,546 **Student-faculty ratio** 13:1 **Application deadline** 1/5 (freshmen), 3/1 (transfer) **Freshman admission** 42% were admitted. Average high school GPA 3.59 **Freshman test scores** SAT critical reading scores over 500: 96%; SAT math scores over 500: 93%; ACT scores over 18: 99%; SAT critical reading scores over 600: 65%; SAT math scores over 600: 49%; ACT scores over 24: 79% **Housing** Yes **Expenses** Tuition & Fees $29,918; Room & Board $12,280 **Undergraduates** 60% women, 7% part-time, 1% 25 or older, 0.5% Native American, 8% Hispanic American, 3% African American, 5% Asian American/Pacific Islander **The most frequently chosen baccalaureate fields are** communications/journalism, English, visual and performing arts **Academic program** Advanced placement, self-designed majors, honors program, summer session, adult/continuing education programs, internships **Contact** Ms. Sara S. Ramirez, Director of Undergraduate Admission, Emerson College, 120 Boylston Street, Boston, MA 02116-4624. *Phone:* 617-824-8600. *Fax:* 617-824-8609. *E-mail:* admission@emerson.edu. *Web site:* http://www.emerson.edu/.

Visit Petersons.com and enter keyword Emerson

See page 782 for the College Close-Up.

Emmanuel College
Boston, Massachusetts

General Independent Roman Catholic, comprehensive, coed **Entrance** Moderately difficult **Setting** 17-acre urban campus **Total enrollment** 2,286 **Student-faculty ratio** 16:1 **Application deadline** 3/1 (freshmen), 4/1 (transfer) **Freshman admission** 56% were admitted. Average high school GPA 3.44 **Freshman test scores** SAT critical reading scores over 500: 82%; SAT math scores over 500: 69%; ACT scores over 18: 94%; SAT critical reading scores over 600: 24%; SAT math scores over 600: 17%; ACT scores over 24: 30% **Housing** Yes **Expenses** Tuition & Fees $29,365; Room & Board $11,950 **Undergraduates** 74% women, 18% part-time, 0.2% Native American, 5% Hispanic American, 7% African American, 3% Asian American/Pacific Islander **The most frequently chosen baccalaureate fields are** business/marketing, communications/journalism, psychology **Academic program** Advanced placement, accelerated degree program, self-designed majors, honors program, summer session, adult/continuing education programs, internships **Contact** Ms. Sandra Robbins, Dean for Enrollment, Emmanuel College, Admissions Office, 400 The Fenway, Boston, MA 02115. *Phone:* 617-735-9715. *Fax:* 617-735-9801. *E-mail:* enroll@emmanuel.edu. *Web site:* http://www.emmanuel.edu/.

Visit Petersons.com and enter keyword Emmanuel

Endicott College
Beverly, Massachusetts

General Independent, comprehensive, coed **Entrance** Moderately difficult **Setting** 231-acre suburban campus **Total enrollment** 4,144 **Student-faculty ratio** 16:1 **Application deadline** 2/15 (freshmen), 3/15 (transfer) **Freshman admission** 53% were admitted **Freshman test scores** SAT critical reading scores over 500: 72%; SAT math scores over 500: 79%; ACT scores over 18: 97%; SAT critical reading scores over 600: 16%; SAT math scores over 600: 23%; ACT scores over 24: 39% **Housing** Yes **Expenses** Tuition & Fees $25,376; Room & Board $11,836 **Undergraduates** 58% women, 8% part-time, 1% 25 or older, 0.3% Native American, 2% Hispanic American, 1% African American, 1% Asian American/Pacific Islander **The most frequently chosen baccalaureate fields are** business/marketing, communications/journalism, parks and recreation **Academic program** Advanced placement, accelerated degree program, self-designed majors, honors program, summer session, adult/continuing education programs, internships **Contact** Mr. Thomas J. Redman, Vice President of Admission and Financial Aid, Endicott College, 376 Hale Street, Beverly, MA 01915. *Phone:* 978-921-1000 or toll-free 800-325-1114. *Fax:* 978-232-2520. *E-mail:* admissio@endicott.edu. *Web site:* http://www.endicott.edu/.

Fisher College
Boston, Massachusetts

General Independent, 4-year, coed **Entrance** Minimally difficult **Setting** urban campus **Total enrollment** 1,310 **Student-faculty ratio** 23:1 **Application deadline** Rolling (freshmen), rolling (transfer) **Freshman admission** 60% were admitted. Average high school GPA 2.14 **Freshman test scores** SAT critical reading scores over 500: 21%; SAT math scores over 500: 20%; ACT scores over 18: 42%; SAT critical reading scores over 600: 1%; SAT math scores over 600: 3%; ACT scores over 24: 4% **Housing** Yes **Expenses** Tuition & Fees $24,575; Room & Board $12,600 **Undergraduates** 70% women, 32% part-time, 45% 25 or older **Academic program** English as a second language, advanced placement, honors program, summer session, adult/continuing education programs, internships **Contact** Mr. Robert Melaragni, Dean of Admissions, Fisher College, 118 Beacon Street, Boston, MA 02116. *Phone:* 617-236-8818 or toll-free 800-821-3050 (in-state); 800-446-1226 (out-of-state). *Fax:* 617-236-5473. *E-mail:* admissions@fisher.edu. *Web site:* http://www.fisher.edu/.

MAJORS
Art History
Art Studio
Biology
Business Administration
Business and Information Technology
Chemistry
Communication Arts
Computer Science
Early Childhood Education
Economics
Elementary Education
English
Environmental Science
Fashion Design and Retailing
Food and Nutrition
Food Science
Geography
Health and Consumer Sciences
History
Mathematics
Modern Languages
Nursing (RNs only)
Politics
Pre-Engineering
Psychology
Sociology
PRE-PROFESSIONAL PROGRAMS
Pre-Dental, Pre-Law, Pre-Medicine, and Pre-Veterinary

www.framingham.edu/admissions
508-626-4500

★ Just 20 miles from Boston
★ Close to many major corporations offering internships to FSC students
★ More than 60 clubs and organizations
★ NCAA Division III Athletics

1839
Framingham
STATE COLLEGE

Discover. Achieve. Succeed.

Fitchburg State College

Fitchburg, Massachusetts

General State-supported, comprehensive, coed **Entrance** Moderately difficult **Setting** 78-acre suburban campus **Total enrollment** 7,043 **Student-faculty ratio** 17:1 **Application deadline** Rolling (freshmen), rolling (transfer) **Freshman admission** 64% were admitted. Average high school GPA 3.03 **Freshman test scores** SAT critical reading scores over 500: 56%; SAT math scores over 500: 57%; ACT scores over 18: 83%; SAT critical reading scores over 600: 12%; SAT math scores over 600: 13%; ACT scores over 24: 19% **Housing** Yes **Expenses** Tuition & Fees: state resident $6900, nonresident $12,980; Room & Board $7632 **Undergraduates** 53% women, 17% part-time, 14% 25 or older, 0.2% Native American, 4% Hispanic American, 4% African American, 2% Asian American/Pacific Islander **The most frequently chosen baccalaureate fields are** business/marketing, liberal arts/general studies, visual and performing arts **Academic program** Advanced placement, accelerated degree program, self-designed majors, honors program, summer session, adult/continuing education programs, internships **Contact** Pamela McCafferty, Director of Admissions, Fitchburg State College, 160 Pearl Street, Fitchburg, MA 01420-2697. *Phone:* 978-665-3140 or toll-free 800-705-9692. *Fax:* 978-665-4540. *E-mail:* admissions@fsc.edu. *Web site:* http://www.fsc.edu/.

Visit Petersons.com and enter keyword Fitchburg

See page 796 for the College Close-Up.

Framingham State College

Framingham, Massachusetts

General State-supported, comprehensive, coed **Entrance** Moderately difficult **Setting** 50-acre suburban campus **Total enrollment** 5,989 **Student-faculty ratio** 17:1 **Application deadline** 5/15 (freshmen), 5/1 (transfer) **Freshman admission** 63% were admitted. Average high school GPA 3.18 **Freshman test scores** SAT critical reading scores over 500: 59%; SAT math scores over 500: 60%; ACT scores over 18: 89%; SAT critical reading scores over 600: 13%; SAT math scores over 600: 12%; ACT scores over 24: 11% **Housing** Yes **Expenses** Tuition & Fees: state resident $6540, nonresident $12,620; Room & Board $8148 **Undergraduates** 65% women, 19% part-time, 15% 25 or older, 0.4% Native American, 4% Hispanic American, 5% African American, 2% Asian American/Pacific Islander **The most frequently chosen baccalaureate fields are** business/marketing, family and consumer sciences, psychology **Academic program** English as a second language, advanced placement, honors program, summer session, internships **Contact** Ms. Shayna Bailey, Assistant Dean of Admissions, Framingham State College, 100 State Street, PO Box 9101, Framingham, MA 01701-9101. *Phone:* 508-626-4500. *Fax:* 508-626-4017. *E-mail:* admiss@framingham.edu. *Web site:* http://www.framingham.edu/.

Visit Petersons.com and enter keyword Framingham

See page 808 for the College Close-Up.

Franklin W. Olin College of Engineering

Needham, Massachusetts

General Independent, 4-year, coed **Entrance** Most difficult **Setting** 75-acre suburban campus **Total enrollment** 337 **Student-faculty ratio** 9:1 **Application deadline** 1/1 (freshmen) **Freshman admission** 18% were admitted. Average high school GPA 4 **Freshman test scores** SAT critical reading scores over 500: 100%; SAT math scores over 500: 100%; ACT scores over 18: 100%; SAT critical reading scores over 600: 99%; SAT math scores over 600: 99%; ACT scores over 24: 100% **Housing** Yes **Expenses** Tuition & Fees $38,045; Room & Board $13,230 **Undergraduates** 44% women, 0.3% Native American, 3% Hispanic American, 1% African American, 12% Asian American/Pacific Islander

Franklin W. Olin College of Engineering (continued)
The most frequently chosen baccalaureate field is engineering **Academic program** Self-designed majors, internships **Contact** Dr. Charles Nolan, Vice President for External Relations and Dean of Admission, Franklin W. Olin College of Engineering, Olin Way, Needham, MA 02492-1200. *Phone:* 781-292-2250. *Fax:* 781-292-2310. *E-mail:* info@olin.edu. *Web site:* http://www.olin.edu/.

Gordon College
Wenham, Massachusetts

General Independent nondenominational, comprehensive, coed **Entrance** Moderately difficult **Setting** 500-acre suburban campus **Total enrollment** 1,681 **Student-faculty ratio** 14:1 **Application deadline** Rolling (freshmen), rolling (transfer) **Freshman admission** 66% were admitted. Average high school GPA 3.53 **Freshman test scores** SAT critical reading scores over 500: 85%; SAT math scores over 500: 77%; SAT critical reading scores over 600: 47%; SAT math scores over 600: 41% **Housing** Yes **Expenses** Tuition & Fees $29,458; Room & Board $8100 **Undergraduates** 63% women, 2% part-time, 2% 25 or older, 0.2% Native American, 3% Hispanic American, 2% African American, 2% Asian American/Pacific Islander **The most frequently chosen baccalaureate fields are** business/marketing, communications/journalism, social sciences **Academic program** Advanced placement, self-designed majors, honors program, internships **Contact** Mr. Brook Berry, Vice President for Enrollment and Marketing, Gordon College, 255 Grapevine Road, Wenham, MA 01984. *Phone:* 978-867-4217 or toll-free 866-464-6736. *Fax:* 978-867-4682. *E-mail:* admissions@gordon.edu. *Web site:* http://www.gordon.edu/.

Hampshire College
Amherst, Massachusetts

General Independent, 4-year, coed **Entrance** Moderately difficult **Setting** 800-acre small-town campus **Total enrollment** 1,463 **Student-faculty ratio** 12:1 **Application deadline** 1/1 (freshmen), 3/1 (transfer) **Freshman admission** 63% were admitted. Average high school GPA 3.49 **Freshman test scores** SAT critical reading scores over 500: 96%; SAT math scores over 500: 89%; ACT scores over 18: 99%; SAT critical reading scores over 600: 77%; SAT math scores over 600: 54%; ACT scores over 24: 83% **Housing** Yes **Expenses** Tuition & Fees $39,912; Room & Board $10,433 **Undergraduates** 60% women, 1% Native American, 8% Hispanic American, 5% African American, 4% Asian American/Pacific Islander **The most frequently chosen baccalaureate fields are** English, social sciences, visual and performing arts **Academic program** Self-designed majors, internships **Contact** Ms. Karen S. Parker, Director of Admissions, Hampshire College, 893 West Street, Amherst, MA 01002. *Phone:* 413-559-5471 or toll-free 877-937-4267. *Fax:* 413-559-5631. *E-mail:* admissions@hampshire.edu. *Web site:* http://www.hampshire.edu/.

Harvard University
Cambridge, Massachusetts

General Independent, university, coed **Entrance** Most difficult **Setting** 380-acre urban campus **Total enrollment** 10,393 **Student-faculty ratio** 7:1 **Application deadline** 1/1 (freshmen) **Freshman admission** 7% were admitted **Housing** Yes **Expenses** Tuition & Fees $36,828; Room & Board $11,856 **Undergraduates** 51% women, 0.1% part-time, 1% 25 or older, 1% Native American, 7% Hispanic American, 8% African American, 17% Asian American/Pacific Islander **The most frequently chosen baccalaureate fields are** biological/life sciences, history, social sciences **Academic program** Advanced placement, accelerated degree program, self-designed majors, honors program, summer session, internships **Contact** Dr. William R. Fitzsimmons, Dean of Admissions and Financial Aid, Harvard University, Cambridge, MA 02138. *Phone:* 617-495-1551. *E-mail:* college@harvard.edu. *Web site:* http://www.harvard.edu/.

Hebrew College
Newton Centre, Massachusetts

General Independent Jewish, comprehensive, coed **Entrance** Minimally difficult **Setting** 3-acre suburban campus **Total enrollment** 8 **Application deadline** Rolling (freshmen), 4/15 (transfer) **Housing** No **Undergraduates** 75% women, 50% part-time, 99% 25 or older **Academic program** Summer session, internships **Contact** Kristin Card, Director of Enrollment Management, Hebrew College, 160 Herreck Road, Newton Centre, MA 02459. *Phone:* 617-559-8610 or toll-free 800-866-4814 Ext. 8619. *Fax:* 617-559-8601. *E-mail:* admissions@lhebrewcollege.edu. *Web site:* http://www.hebrewcollege.edu/.

Hellenic College
Brookline, Massachusetts

General Independent Greek Orthodox, comprehensive, coed **Entrance** Minimally difficult **Setting** 59-acre suburban campus **Total enrollment** 212 **Student-faculty ratio** 9:1 **Application deadline** Rolling (freshmen), rolling (transfer) **Freshman admission** 57% were admitted. Average high school GPA 3 **Freshman test scores** SAT critical reading scores over 500: 50%; SAT math scores over 500: 50%; SAT critical reading scores over 600: 25%; SAT math scores over 600: 10% **Housing** Yes **Expenses** Tuition & Fees $18,850; Room & Board $11,780 **Undergraduates** 41% women, 10% 25 or older **The most frequently chosen baccalaureate field is** liberal arts/general studies **Academic program** Advanced placement, summer session, internships **Contact** Mr. Gregory Floor, Director of Admissions, Hellenic College, 50 Goddard Avenue, Brookline, MA 02445-7496. *Phone:* 617-850-1285 or toll-free 866-424-2338. *Fax:* 617-850-1460. *E-mail:* admissions@hchc.edu. *Web site:* http://www.hchc.edu/.

ITT Technical Institute
Norwood, Massachusetts

General Proprietary, primarily 2-year, coed **Entrance** Minimally difficult **Setting** suburban campus **Housing** No **Contact** Director of Recruitment, ITT Technical Institute, 333 Providence Highway, Route 1, Norwood, MA 02062. *Phone:* 781-278-7200 or toll-free 800-879-8324. *Web site:* http://www.itt-tech.edu/.

ITT Technical Institute
Woburn, Massachusetts

General Proprietary, primarily 2-year, coed **Entrance** Minimally difficult **Housing** No **Contact** Director of Recruitment, ITT Technical Institute, 10 Forbes Road, Woburn, MA 01801. *Phone:* 781-937-8324 or toll-free 800-430-5097. *Web site:* http://www.itt-tech.edu/.

Lasell College
Newton, Massachusetts

General Independent, comprehensive, coed **Entrance** Moderately difficult **Setting** 50-acre suburban campus **Total enrollment** 1,672 **Student-faculty ratio** 14:1 **Application deadline** Rolling (freshmen), rolling (transfer) **Freshman admission** 64% were admitted. Average high school GPA 2.8 **Freshman test scores** SAT critical reading scores over 500: 45.97%; SAT math scores over 500: 47.28%; ACT scores over 18: 89.59%; SAT critical reading scores over 600: 7.41%; SAT math scores over 600: 8.5%; ACT scores over 24: 16.67% **Housing** Yes **Expenses** Tuition & Fees $25,300; Room & Board $10,500 **Undergraduates** 67% women, 2% part-time, 2% 25 or older, 0.3% Native American, 4% Hispanic American, 6% African American, 3% Asian American/Pacific Islander **The most frequently chosen baccalaureate fields are** business/marketing, parks and recreation, visual and performing arts **Academic program** English as a second language, advanced placement, self-designed majors, honors program, internships **Contact** Mr. James Tweed, Dean of Undergraduate Admission, Lasell College, 1844 Commonwealth Avenue, Newton, MA 02466-2709. *Phone:* 617-243-2225 or toll-free 888-LASELL-4. *E-mail:* info@lasell.edu. *Web site:* http://www.lasell.edu/.

Lesley University
Cambridge, Massachusetts

General Independent, comprehensive, coed **Setting** urban campus **Total enrollment** 5,564 **Student-faculty ratio** 10:1 **Application deadline** Rolling (freshmen), rolling (transfer) **Freshman admission** 67% were admitted. Average high school GPA 2.9 **Freshman test scores** SAT critical reading scores over 500: 68%; SAT math scores over 500: 61%; ACT scores over 18: 94%; SAT critical reading scores over 600: 26%; SAT math scores over 600: 20%; ACT scores over 24: 41% **Housing** Yes **Expenses** Tuition & Fees $29,400; Room & Board $12,800 **Undergraduates** 76% women, 4% part-time, 5% 25 or older, 1% Native American, 5% Hispanic American, 4% African American, 3% Asian American/Pacific Islander **The most frequently chosen baccalaureate fields are** liberal arts/general studies, psychology, visual and performing arts **Academic program** Advanced placement, accelerated degree program, self-designed majors, honors program, summer session, adult/continuing education programs, internships **Contact** Ms. Deborah Kocar, Director of Admissions, Lesley University, 29 Everett Street, Cambridge, MA 02138-2790. *Phone:* 617-349-8800 or toll-free 800-999-1959 Ext. 8800. *Fax:* 617-349-8810. *E-mail:* lcadmissions@lesley.edu. *Web site:* http://www.lesley.edu/.

Visit Petersons.com and enter keywords Lesley University

See page 910 for the College Close-Up.

Massachusetts College of Art and Design
Boston, Massachusetts

General State-supported, comprehensive, coed **Entrance** Very difficult **Setting** 5-acre urban campus **Total enrollment** 2,405 **Student-faculty ratio** 13:1 **Application deadline** 2/1 (freshmen), 2/1 (transfer) **Freshman admission** 51% were admitted. Average high school GPA 3.31 **Freshman test scores** SAT critical reading scores over 500: 82%; SAT math scores over 500: 74%; SAT critical reading scores over 600: 35%; SAT math scores over 600: 25% **Housing** Yes **Expenses** Tuition & Fees: state resident $8400, nonresident $24,400; Room & Board $11,288 **Undergraduates** 67% women, 29% part-time, 15% 25 or older, 1% Native American, 5% Hispanic American, 3% African American, 6% Asian American/Pacific Islander **The most frequently chosen baccalaureate fields are** education, visual and performing arts **Academic program** Self-designed majors, summer session, internships **Contact** Karen Townsend, Director of Admissions, Massachusetts College of Art and Design, 621 Huntington Avenue, Boston, MA 02115. *Phone:* 617-879-7230. *Fax:* 617-879-7250. *E-mail:* admissions@massart.edu. *Web site:* http://www.massart.edu/.

Massachusetts College of Liberal Arts
North Adams, Massachusetts

General State-supported, comprehensive, coed **Entrance** Moderately difficult **Setting** 105-acre small-town campus **Total enrollment** 1,962 **Student-faculty ratio** 14:1 **Application deadline** Rolling (freshmen), rolling (transfer) **Freshman admission** 70% were admitted. Average high school GPA 3 **Freshman test scores** SAT critical reading scores over 500: 63%; SAT math scores over 500: 56%; SAT critical reading scores over 600: 24%; SAT math scores over 600: 13% **Housing** Yes **Expenses** Tuition & Fees: state resident $6875, nonresident $15,820; Room & Board $7868 **Undergraduates** 60% women, 12% part-time, 17% 25 or older, 0.3% Native American, 5% Hispanic American, 6% African American, 1% Asian American/Pacific Islander **The most frequently chosen baccalaureate fields are** business/marketing, English, social sciences **Academic program** Advanced placement, accelerated degree program, self-designed majors, honors program, summer session, internships **Contact** Mr. Joshua Mendal, Associate Director of Admission, Massachusetts College of Liberal Arts, 375 Church Street, North Adams, MA 01247. *Phone:* 413-662-5410 or toll-free 800-292-6632. *Fax:* 413-662-5179. *E-mail:* j.mendel@mcla.edu. *Web site:* http://www.mcla.edu/.

Massachusetts College of Pharmacy and Health Sciences
Boston, Massachusetts

General Independent, university, coed **Entrance** Moderately difficult **Setting** 3-acre urban campus **Total enrollment** 4,278 **Student-faculty ratio** 18:1 **Application deadline** 2/1 (freshmen), 2/1 (transfer) **Freshman admission** 55% were admitted. Average high school GPA 3.46 **Freshman test scores** SAT critical reading scores over 500: 69%; SAT math scores over 500: 84.1%; ACT scores over 18: 96.2%; SAT critical reading scores over 600: 14%; SAT math scores over 600: 37.3%; ACT scores over 24: 51.2% **Housing** Yes **Expenses** Tuition & Fees $24,550; Room & Board $11,900 **Undergraduates** 68% women, 5% part-time, 12% 25 or older, 0.3% Native American, 3% Hispanic American, 5% African American, 27% Asian American/Pacific Islander **The most frequently chosen baccalaureate fields are** health professions and related sciences, physical sciences, psychology **Academic program** Advanced placement, accelerated degree program, summer session, adult/continuing education programs, internships **Contact** Sandra Hernandez, Visit Concierge, Massachusetts College of Pharmacy and Health Sciences, 179 Longwood Avenue, Boston, MA 02115. *Phone:* 617-732-2850 or toll-free 800-225-5506. *Fax:* 617-732-2118. *E-mail:* admissions@mcphs.edu. *Web site:* http://www.mcphs.edu/.

Visit Petersons.com and enter keyword Pharmacy

See page 954 for the College Close-Up.

Massachusetts Institute of Technology
Cambridge, Massachusetts

General Independent, university, coed **Entrance** Most difficult **Setting** 168-acre urban campus **Total enrollment** 10,384 **Student-faculty ratio** 7:1 **Application deadline** 1/1 (freshmen), 3/15 (transfer) **Freshman admission** 11% were admitted **Freshman test scores** SAT critical reading scores over 500: 98.9%; SAT math scores over 500: 100%; ACT scores over 18: 100%; SAT critical reading scores over 600: 91.7%; SAT math scores over 600: 100%; ACT scores over 24: 100% **Housing** Yes **Expenses** Tuition & Fees $37,782; Room & Board $11,360 **Undergraduates** 45% women, 1% part-time, 1% 25 or older, 1% Native American, 13% Hispanic American, 8% African American, 26% Asian American/Pacific Islander **The most frequently chosen baccalaureate fields are** computer and information sciences, engineering, physical sciences **Academic program** English as a second language, advanced placement, internships **Contact** Admissions Counselors, Massachusetts Institute of Technology, 77 Massachusetts Avenue, Building 3-108, Cambridge, MA 02139-4307. *Phone:* 617-253-3400. *Fax:* 617-258-8304. *E-mail:* admissions@mit.edu. *Web site:* http://web.mit.edu/.

Massachusetts Maritime Academy
Buzzards Bay, Massachusetts

General State-supported, comprehensive, coed, primarily men **Entrance** Moderately difficult **Setting** 55-acre small-town campus **Total enrollment** 1,288 **Student-faculty ratio** 15:1 **Application deadline** Rolling (freshmen), rolling (transfer) **Freshman admission** 61% were admitted. Average high school GPA 2.97 **Freshman test scores** SAT critical reading scores over 500: 63%; SAT math scores over 500: 75%; ACT scores over 18: 95%; SAT critical reading scores over 600: 12%; SAT math scores over 600: 26%; ACT scores over 24: 38% **Housing** Yes **Expenses** Tuition & Fees: state resident $6509, nonresident $19,148; Room & Board $8917 **Undergraduates** 9% women, 5% part-time, 5% 25 or older, 0.3% Native American, 2% Hispanic American, 1% African

Massachusetts Maritime Academy (continued)
American, 1% Asian American/Pacific Islander **The most frequently chosen baccalaureate fields are** engineering, natural resources/ environmental science, transportation and materials moving **Academic program** Advanced placement, summer session, adult/continuing education programs, internships **Contact** Roy Fulgueras, Director of Admissions, Massachusetts Maritime Academy, 101 Academy Drive, Blinn Hall, Buzzards Bay, MA 02532. *Phone:* 508-830-5031 or toll-free 800-544-3411. *Fax:* 508-830-5077. *E-mail:* fuji@maritime.edu. *Web site:* http://www.maritime.edu/.

Merrimack College
North Andover, Massachusetts

General Independent Roman Catholic, comprehensive, coed **Entrance** Moderately difficult **Setting** 220-acre suburban campus **Total enrollment** 2,090 **Student-faculty ratio** 13:1 **Application deadline** 2/1 (freshmen), 12/30 (transfer) **Freshman admission** 79% were admitted **Housing** Yes **Expenses** Tuition & Fees $29,810; Room & Board $10,190 **Undergraduates** 48% women, 7% part-time, 7% 25 or older, 0.1% Native American, 3% Hispanic American, 2% African American, 2% Asian American/Pacific Islander **The most frequently chosen baccalaureate fields are** business/marketing, psychology, social sciences **Academic program** English as a second language, advanced placement, self-designed majors, honors program, summer session, adult/continuing education programs, internships **Contact** Director of Admissions, Merrimack College, Austin Hall, A22, North Andover, MA 01845. *Phone:* 978-837-5100. *Fax:* 978-837-5133. *E-mail:* admission@merrimack.edu. *Web site:* http://www.merrimack.edu/.
Visit Petersons.com and enter keyword Merrimack

Montserrat College of Art
Beverly, Massachusetts

Contact Mr. Brian Bicknell, Dean of Students, Montserrat College of Art, 23 Essex Street, PO Box 26, Beverly, MA 01915. *Phone:* 978-921-4242 Ext. 1153 or toll-free 800-836-0487. *Fax:* 978-921-4241. *E-mail:* bbicknell@montserrat.edu. *Web site:* http://www.montserrat.edu/.

Mount Holyoke College
South Hadley, Massachusetts

General Independent, comprehensive, women only **Entrance** Very difficult **Setting** 800-acre small-town campus **Total enrollment** 2,304 **Student-faculty ratio** 9:1 **Application deadline** 1/15 (freshmen), 5/15 (transfer) **Freshman admission** 58% were admitted. Average high school GPA 3.66 **Freshman test scores** SAT critical reading scores over 500: 99.47%; SAT math scores over 500: 95.82%; ACT scores over 18: 100%; SAT critical reading scores over 600: 82.5%; SAT math scores over 600: 78.07%; ACT scores over 24: 96.46% **Housing** Yes **Expenses** Tuition & Fees $39,126; Room & Board $11,450 **Undergraduates** 3% part-time, 6% 25 or older, 0.3% Native American, 6% Hispanic American, 7% African American, 10% Asian American/Pacific Islander **The most frequently chosen baccalaureate fields are** biological/life sciences, social sciences, visual and performing arts **Academic program** Advanced placement, self-designed majors, adult/continuing education programs, internships **Contact** Ms. Diane Anci, Dean of Admission, Mount Holyoke College, 50 College Street, South Hadley, MA 01075. *Phone:* 413-538-2023. *Fax:* 413-538-2409. *E-mail:* admission@mtholyoke.edu. *Web site:* http://www.mtholyoke.edu/.
Visit Petersons.com and enter keyword Holyoke

See page 992 for the College Close-Up.

Mount Ida College
Newton, Massachusetts

General Independent, comprehensive, coed **Entrance** Moderately difficult **Setting** 72-acre suburban campus **Total enrollment** 1,501 **Student-faculty ratio** 13:1 **Application deadline** Rolling (freshmen), rolling (transfer) **Freshman admission** 74% were admitted. Average high school GPA 2.7 **Freshman test scores** SAT critical reading scores over 500: 23%; SAT math scores over 500: 21%; ACT scores over 18: 56%; SAT critical reading scores over 600: 2%; SAT math scores over 600: 3%; ACT scores over 24: 10% **Housing** Yes **Expenses** Tuition & Fees $24,500; Room & Board $12,000 **Undergraduates** 65% women, 6% part-time, 9% 25 or older, 0.4% Native American, 6% Hispanic American, 12% African American, 2% Asian American/Pacific Islander **The most frequently chosen baccalaureate fields are** business/marketing, health professions and related sciences, visual and performing arts **Academic program** English as a second language, advanced placement, accelerated degree program, self-designed majors, honors program, summer session, internships **Contact** Jay Titus, Dean of Admissions, Mount Ida College, 777 Dedham Street, Newton, MA 02459-3310. *Phone:* 617-928-4553. *Fax:* 617-928-4507. *E-mail:* admissions@mountida.edu. *Web site:* http://www.mountida.edu/.
Visit Petersons.com and enter keywords Mount Ida

Newbury College
Brookline, Massachusetts

General Independent, 4-year, coed **Entrance** Minimally difficult **Setting** 10-acre suburban campus **Total enrollment** 994 **Student-faculty ratio** 16:1 **Application deadline** 9/1 (freshmen), rolling (transfer) **Freshman admission** 66% were admitted. Average high school GPA 2.54 **Housing** Yes **Expenses** Tuition & Fees $23,500; Room & Board $11,230 **Undergraduates** 58% women, 13% part-time, 10% 25 or older, 12% Hispanic American, 27% African American, 7% Asian American/Pacific Islander **Academic program** Advanced placement, accelerated degree program, self-designed majors, honors program, summer session, adult/continuing education programs, internships **Contact** Mr. Joseph Chillo, Vice President for Enrollment and Dean of Admission, Newbury College, 129 Fisher Avenue, Brookline, MA 02445-5796. *Phone:* 617-730-7007 or toll-free 800-NEWBURY. *Fax:* 617-731-9618. *E-mail:* info@newbury.edu. *Web site:* http://www.newbury.edu/.

New England Conservatory of Music
Boston, Massachusetts

General Independent, comprehensive, coed **Entrance** Very difficult **Setting** 2-acre urban campus **Total enrollment** 785 **Student-faculty ratio** 6:1 **Application deadline** 12/1 (freshmen), 12/1 (transfer) **Freshman admission** 33% were admitted **Housing** Yes **Expenses** Tuition & Fees $34,950; Room & Board $12,100 **Undergraduates** 46% women, 8% part-time, 3% 25 or older, 6% Hispanic American, 4% African American, 9% Asian American/Pacific Islander **The most frequently chosen baccalaureate field is** visual and performing arts **Academic program** English as a second language, advanced placement, summer session, internships **Contact** Ms. Christina Daly, Director of Admissions, New England Conservatory of Music, 290 Huntington Avenue, Boston, MA 02115-5000. *Phone:* 617-585-1103. *Fax:* 617-585-1115. *E-mail:* christina.daly@necmusic.edu. *Web site:* http://necmusic.edu/.

The New England Institute of Art
Brookline, Massachusetts

General Proprietary, 4-year, coed **Setting** urban campus **Contact** Director of Admissions, The New England Institute of Art, 10 Brookline Place West, Brookline, MA 02445. *Phone:* 617-739-1700 or toll-free 800-903-4425. *Fax:* 617-582-4500. *Web site:* http://www.artinstitutes.edu/boston.
Visit Petersons.com and enter keywords New England Institute of Art

See page 1012 for the College Close-Up.

Nichols College
Dudley, Massachusetts

General Independent, comprehensive, coed **Entrance** Moderately difficult **Setting** 210-acre suburban campus **Total enrollment** 1,547 **Student-**

faculty ratio 18:1 **Application deadline** Rolling (freshmen), rolling (transfer) **Freshman admission** 74% were admitted. Average high school GPA 2.58 **Freshman test scores** SAT critical reading scores over 500: 27%; SAT math scores over 500: 36%; ACT scores over 18: 72%; SAT critical reading scores over 600: 3%; SAT math scores over 600: 9%; ACT scores over 24: 16% **Housing** Yes **Expenses** Tuition & Fees $28,870; Room & Board $9330 **Undergraduates** 41% women, 13% part-time, 1% Native American, 4% Hispanic American, 5% African American, 2% Asian American/Pacific Islander **The most frequently chosen baccalaureate fields are** business/marketing, English, psychology **Academic program** Advanced placement, accelerated degree program, honors program, summer session, adult/continuing education programs, internships **Contact** Ms. Marie Keegan, Admissions Assistant, Nichols College, 124 Center Road, Dudley, MA 01571. *Phone:* 508-213-2203 or toll-free 800-470-3379. *Fax:* 508-943-9885. *E-mail:* admissions@nichols.edu. *Web site:* http://www.nichols.edu/.
Visit Petersons.com and enter keyword Nichols

Northeastern University
Boston, Massachusetts

General Independent, university, coed **Entrance** Very difficult **Setting** 73-acre urban campus **Total enrollment** 22,091 **Student-faculty ratio** 15:1 **Application deadline** 1/15 (freshmen), 5/1 (transfer) **Freshman admission** 41% were admitted **Freshman test scores** SAT critical reading scores over 500: 95%; SAT math scores over 500: 98%; ACT scores over 18: 99%; SAT critical reading scores over 600: 68%; SAT math scores over 600: 84%; ACT scores over 24: 93% **Housing** Yes **Expenses** Tuition & Fees $35,362; Room & Board $12,350 **Undergraduates** 51% women, 4% 25 or older, 0.3% Native American, 5% Hispanic American, 4% African American, 9% Asian American/Pacific Islander **The most frequently chosen baccalaureate fields are** business/marketing, engineering, health professions and related sciences **Academic program** English as a second language, advanced placement, accelerated degree program, self-designed majors, honors program, summer session, adult/continuing education programs, internships **Contact** Ronne Turner, Director of Admissions, Northeastern University, 360 Huntington Avenue, 150 Richards Hall, Boston, MA 02115. *Phone:* 617-373-2200. *Fax:* 617-373-8780. *E-mail:* admissions@neu.edu. *Web site:* http://www.northeastern.edu/.

See color display following page 234.

Pine Manor College
Chestnut Hill, Massachusetts

Contact Mr. Robin Engel, Dean of Admissions and Financial Aid, Pine Manor College, 400 Heath Street, Chestnut Hill, MA 02467-2332. *Phone:* 617-731-7104 or toll-free 800-762-1357. *Fax:* 617-731-7102. *E-mail:* admisson@pmc.edu. *Web site:* http://www.pmc.edu/.

Regis College
Weston, Massachusetts

General Independent Roman Catholic, comprehensive, coed **Entrance** Moderately difficult **Setting** 131-acre small-town campus **Total enrollment** 1,586 **Student-faculty ratio** 13:1 **Application deadline** Rolling (freshmen), rolling (transfer) **Freshman admission** 73% were admitted. Average high school GPA 2.84 **Freshman test scores** SAT critical reading scores over 500: 33.05%; SAT math scores over 500: 30%; ACT scores over 18: 71.43%; SAT critical reading scores over 600: 4.35%; SAT math scores over 600: 6.09%; ACT scores over 24: 7.14% **Housing** Yes **Expenses** Tuition & Fees $28,900; Room & Board $12,190 **Undergraduates** 82% women, 23% part-time, 10% 25 or older, 1% Native American, 9% Hispanic American, 22% African American, 5% Asian American/Pacific Islander **The most frequently chosen baccalaureate fields are** health professions and related sciences, communications/journalism, social sciences **Academic program** English as a second language, advanced placement, accelerated degree program, self-designed majors, honors program, summer session, adult/continuing education programs, internships **Contact** Ms. Wanda Suriel, Director of Admission, Regis College, 235 Wellesley Street, Weston, MA 02493. *Phone:* 781-768-7100 or toll-free 866-438-7344. *Fax:* 781-768-7071. *E-mail:* admission@regiscollege.edu. *Web site:* http://www.regiscollege.edu/.

Salem State College
Salem, Massachusetts

General State-supported, comprehensive, coed **Entrance** Minimally difficult **Setting** 62-acre suburban campus **Total enrollment** 10,125 **Student-faculty ratio** 14:1 **Application deadline** Rolling (freshmen), rolling (transfer) **Freshman admission** 54% were admitted. Average high school GPA 2.94 **Freshman test scores** SAT critical reading scores over 500: 57%; SAT math scores over 500: 48%; SAT critical reading scores over 600: 10%; SAT math scores over 600: 9% **Housing** Yes **Expenses** Tuition & Fees: state resident $6790, nonresident $12,930; Room only $6625 **Undergraduates** 62% women, 24% part-time, 21% 25 or older, 0.4% Native American, 7% Hispanic American, 9% African American, 3% Asian American/Pacific Islander **The most frequently chosen baccalaureate fields are** business/marketing, education, health professions and related sciences **Academic program** English as a second language, advanced placement, honors program, summer session, adult/continuing education programs, internships **Contact** Ms. Mary Dunn, Assistant Dean for Undergraduate Admissions, Salem State College, 352 Lafayette Street, Salem, MA 01970. *Phone:* 978-542-6202. *Fax:* 978-542-6893. *E-mail:* admissions@salemstate.edu. *Web site:* http://www.salemstate.edu/.
Visit Petersons.com and enter keyword Salem

School of the Museum of Fine Arts, Boston
Boston, Massachusetts

General Independent, comprehensive, coed **Entrance** Moderately difficult **Setting** 14-acre urban campus **Total enrollment** 755 **Student-faculty ratio** 10:1 **Application deadline** 2/1 (freshmen), 3/1 (transfer) **Freshman admission** 81% were admitted **Freshman test scores** SAT critical reading scores over 500: 79.8%; SAT math scores over 500: 60.6%; ACT scores over 18: 88%; SAT critical reading scores over 600: 40.5%; SAT math scores over 600: 24.4%; ACT scores over 24: 52% **Housing** Yes **Expenses** Tuition & Fees $30,660; Room only $13,046 **Undergraduates** 68% women, 12% part-time, 13% 25 or older, 0.2% Native American, 6% Hispanic American, 2% African American, 5% Asian American/Pacific Islander **The most frequently chosen baccalaureate fields are** education, visual and performing arts **Academic program** English as a second language, self-designed majors, summer session, adult/continuing education programs, internships **Contact** Jesse Tarantino, Assistant Dean of Admissions, School of the Museum of Fine Arts, Boston, 230 The Fenway, Boston, MA 02115. *Phone:* 617-369-3626 or toll-free 800-643-6078. *Fax:* 617-369-4264. *E-mail:* admissions@smfa.edu. *Web site:* http://www.smfa.edu/.
Visit Petersons.com and enter keywords Arts Boston

See page 1146 for the College Close-Up.

Simmons College
Boston, Massachusetts

General Independent, university, undergraduate: women only; graduate: coed **Entrance** Moderately difficult **Setting** 12-acre urban campus **Total enrollment** 5,003 **Student-faculty ratio** 13:1 **Application deadline** 2/1 (freshmen), 4/1 (transfer) **Freshman admission** 57% were admitted. Average high school GPA 3.15 **Freshman test scores** SAT critical reading scores over 500: 74%; SAT math scores over 500: 73%; ACT scores over 18: 99%; SAT critical reading scores over 600: 24%; SAT math scores over 600: 26%; ACT scores over 24: 50% **Housing** Yes **Expenses** Tuition & Fees $31,450; Room & Board $12,050 **Undergraduates** 11% part-time, 12% 25 or older, 0.1% Native American, 4%

Simmons College (continued)
Hispanic American, 6% African American, 7% Asian American/Pacific Islander **The most frequently chosen baccalaureate fields are** health professions and related sciences, psychology, social sciences **Academic program** Advanced placement, accelerated degree program, self-designed majors, honors program, summer session, adult/continuing education programs, internships **Contact** Catherine Capolupo, Director of Undergraduate Admissions, Simmons College, 300 The Fenway, Boston, MA 02115. *Phone:* 617-521-2057 or toll-free 800-345-8468. *Fax:* 617-521-3190. *E-mail:* ugadm@simmons.edu. *Web site:* http://www.simmons.edu/.
Visit Petersons.com and enter keyword Simmons

See page 1162 for the College Close-Up.

Smith College
Northampton, Massachusetts

General Independent, comprehensive, women only **Entrance** Very difficult **Setting** 147-acre small-town campus **Total enrollment** 3,121 **Student-faculty ratio** 9:1 **Application deadline** 1/15 (freshmen), 5/15 (transfer) **Freshman admission** 47% were admitted. Average high school GPA 3.9 **Freshman test scores** SAT critical reading scores over 500: 98.41%; SAT math scores over 500: 96.37%; ACT scores over 18: 100%; SAT critical reading scores over 600: 78.64%; SAT math scores over 600: 72.73%; ACT scores over 24: 90.86% **Housing** Yes **Expenses** Tuition & Fees $37,758; Room & Board $12,622 **Undergraduates** 1% part-time, 6% 25 or older **The most frequently chosen baccalaureate fields are** psychology, area and ethnic studies, social sciences **Academic program** Advanced placement, accelerated degree program, self-designed majors, honors program, adult/continuing education programs, internships **Contact** Ms. Debra Shaver, Director of Admissions, Smith College, 7 College Lane, Northampton, MA 01063. *Phone:* 413-585-2500 or toll-free 800-383-3232. *Fax:* 413-585-2527. *E-mail:* admission@smith.edu. *Web site:* http://www.smith.edu/.
Visit Petersons.com and enter keyword Smith

Springfield College
Springfield, Massachusetts

Contact Ms. Mary DeAngelo, Director of Undergraduate Admissions, Springfield College, 263 Alden Street, Box M, Springfield, MA 01109. *Phone:* 413-748-3136 or toll-free 800-343-1257. *Fax:* 413-748-3694. *E-mail:* admissions@spfldcol.edu. *Web site:* http://www.spfldcol.edu/.
Visit Petersons.com and enter keyword Springfield

See page 1188 for the College Close-Up.

Stonehill College
Easton, Massachusetts

General Independent Roman Catholic, 4-year, coed **Entrance** Very difficult **Setting** 375-acre suburban campus **Total enrollment** 2,468 **Student-faculty ratio** 13:1 **Application deadline** 1/15 (freshmen), 4/1 (transfer) **Freshman admission** 56% were admitted. Average high school GPA 3.49 **Freshman test scores** SAT critical reading scores over 500: 96%; SAT math scores over 500: 96%; ACT scores over 18: 100%; SAT critical reading scores over 600: 51%; SAT math scores over 600: 64%; ACT scores over 24: 86% **Housing** Yes **Expenses** Tuition & Fees $31,210; Room & Board $12,240 **Undergraduates** 60% women, 2% part-time, 1% 25 or older, 0.1% Native American, 4% Hispanic American, 3% African American, 1% Asian American/Pacific Islander **The most frequently chosen baccalaureate fields are** business/marketing, psychology, social sciences **Academic program** Advanced placement, self-designed majors, honors program, summer session, internships **Contact** Stonehill College, 320 Washington Street, Easton, MA 02357-5610. *Phone:* 508-565-1373. *Fax:* 508-565-1545. *E-mail:* admissions@stonehill.edu. *Web site:* http://www.stonehill.edu/.
Visit Petersons.com and enter keyword Stonehill

See page 1204 for the College Close-Up.

Suffolk University
Boston, Massachusetts

General Independent, comprehensive, coed **Entrance** Moderately difficult **Setting** 2-acre urban campus **Total enrollment** 9,457 **Student-faculty ratio** 13:1 **Application deadline** 3/1 (freshmen), 3/30 (transfer) **Freshman admission** 85% were admitted. Average high school GPA 3.02 **Freshman test scores** ACT scores over 18: 89%; ACT scores over 24: 30.1% **Housing** Yes **Expenses** Tuition & Fees $27,208; Room & Board $14,544 **Undergraduates** 56% women, 8% part-time, 5% 25 or older, 0.3% Native American, 7% Hispanic American, 4% African American, 7% Asian American/Pacific Islander **The most frequently chosen baccalaureate fields are** business/marketing, communications/journalism, social sciences **Academic program** English as a second language, advanced placement, accelerated degree program, honors program, summer session, adult/continuing education programs, internships **Contact** Mr. John Hamel, Vice President Undergraduate Admissions, Suffolk University, 8 Ashburton Place, Boston, MA 02108. *Phone:* 617-573-8460 or toll-free 800-6-SUFFOLK. *Fax:* 617-742-4291. *E-mail:* admission@suffolk.edu. *Web site:* http://www.suffolk.edu/.

Tufts University
Medford, Massachusetts

General Independent, university, coed **Entrance** Most difficult **Setting** 150-acre suburban campus **Total enrollment** 10,030 **Student-faculty ratio** 9:1 **Application deadline** 1/1 (freshmen), 3/1 (transfer) **Freshman admission** 27% were admitted **Freshman test scores** SAT critical reading scores over 500: 100%; SAT math scores over 500: 99%; ACT scores over 18: 100%; SAT critical reading scores over 600: 96%; SAT math scores over 600: 96%; ACT scores over 24: 99% **Housing** Yes **Expenses** Tuition & Fees $40,342; Room & Board $10,746 **Undergraduates** 51% women, 1% part-time, 0.1% 25 or older, 0.3% Native American, 6% Hispanic American, 5% African American, 13% Asian American/Pacific Islander **The most frequently chosen baccalaureate fields are** engineering, social sciences, visual and performing arts **Academic program** Advanced placement, self-designed majors, honors program, summer session, adult/continuing education programs, internships **Contact** Mr. Lee Coffin, Office of Undergraduate Admissions, Tufts University, Bendetson Hall, Medford, MA 02155. *Phone:* 617-627-3170. *Fax:* 617-627-3860. *E-mail:* admissions.inquiry@ase.tufts.edu. *Web site:* http://www.tufts.edu/.

University of Massachusetts Amherst
Amherst, Massachusetts

General State-supported, university, coed **Entrance** Moderately difficult **Setting** 1,463-acre small-town campus **Total enrollment** 27,016 **Student-faculty ratio** 18:1 **Application deadline** 1/15 (freshmen), 4/15 (transfer) **Freshman admission** 67% were admitted. Average high school GPA 3.6 **Freshman test scores** SAT critical reading scores over 500: 86%; SAT math scores over 500: 90.4%; ACT scores over 18: 98.5%; SAT critical reading scores over 600: 38.4%; SAT math scores over 600: 49.5%; ACT scores over 24: 69.8% **Housing** Yes **Expenses** Tuition & Fees: state resident $11,917, nonresident $20,140; Room & Board $8276 **Undergraduates** 50% women, 7% part-time, 7% 25 or older, 0.4% Native American, 4% Hispanic American, 5% African American, 8% Asian American/Pacific Islander **The most frequently chosen baccalaureate fields are** business/marketing, psychology, social sciences **Academic program** English as a second language, advanced placement, self-designed majors, honors program, summer session, adult/continuing education programs, internships **Contact** Mr. Kevin Kelly, Director, Undergraduate Admissions, University of Massachusetts Amherst, 37 Mather Drive, Amherst, MA 01003. *Phone:* 413-545-0222. *Fax:* 413-545-4312. *E-mail:* mail@admissions.umass.edu. *Web site:* http://www.umass.edu/.

University of Massachusetts Boston

Boston, Massachusetts

General State-supported, university, coed **Entrance** Moderately difficult **Setting** 177-acre urban campus **Total enrollment** 14,912 **Student-faculty ratio** 16:1 **Application deadline** 6/1 (freshmen), 7/1 (transfer) **Freshman admission** 61% were admitted. Average high school GPA 3 **Freshman test scores** SAT critical reading scores over 500: 58%; SAT math scores over 500: 68%; SAT critical reading scores over 600: 15%; SAT math scores over 600: 21% **Housing** No **Expenses** Tuition & Fees: state resident $10,611, nonresident $18,655 **Undergraduates** 57% women, 30% part-time, 33% 25 or older, 0.4% Native American, 9% Hispanic American, 16% African American, 13% Asian American/Pacific Islander **The most frequently chosen baccalaureate fields are** business/marketing, health professions and related sciences, social sciences **Academic program** English as a second language, advanced placement, accelerated degree program, self-designed majors, honors program, summer session, adult/continuing education programs, internships **Contact** Mrs. Liliana Mickle, Director of Undergraduate Admissions, University of Massachusetts Boston, 100 Morrissey Boulevard, Boston, MA 02125-3393. *Phone:* 617-287-6000. *Fax:* 617-287-5999. *E-mail:* enrollment.info@umb.edu. *Web site:* http://www.umb.edu/.

Visit Petersons.com and enter keywords Massachusetts Boston

See page 1282 for the College Close-Up.

University of Massachusetts Dartmouth

North Dartmouth, Massachusetts

General State-supported, university, coed **Entrance** Moderately difficult **Setting** 710-acre suburban campus **Total enrollment** 9,302 **Student-faculty ratio** 18:1 **Application deadline** Rolling (freshmen), rolling (transfer) **Freshman admission** 68% were admitted. Average high school GPA 3.08 **Freshman test scores** SAT critical reading scores over 500: 63%; SAT math scores over 500: 72%; ACT scores over 18: 96%; SAT critical reading scores over 600: 15%; SAT math scores over 600: 23%; ACT scores over 24: 38% **Housing** Yes **Expenses** Tuition & Fees: state resident $10,358, nonresident $17,040; Room & Board $8950 **Undergraduates** 48% women, 11% part-time, 8% 25 or older, 1% Native American, 3% Hispanic American, 8% African American, 3% Asian American/Pacific Islander **The most frequently chosen baccalaureate fields are** business/marketing, health professions and related sciences, social sciences **Academic program** Advanced placement, self-designed majors, honors program, summer session, internships **Contact** Interim Director of Admissions, University of Massachusetts Dartmouth, 285 Old Westport Road, North Dartmouth, MA 02747-2300. *Phone:* 508-999-8605. *Fax:* 508-999-8755. *E-mail:* admissions@umassd.edu. *Web site:* http://www.umassd.edu/.

Visit Petersons.com and enter keyword Dartmouth

University of Massachusetts Lowell

Lowell, Massachusetts

General State-supported, university, coed **Entrance** Moderately difficult **Setting** 100-acre urban campus **Total enrollment** 13,602 **Student-faculty ratio** 15:1 **Application deadline** Rolling (freshmen), rolling (transfer) **Freshman admission** 73% were admitted. Average high school GPA 3.25 **Freshman test scores** SAT critical reading scores over 500: 66.26%; SAT math scores over 500: 77.55%; SAT critical reading scores over 600: 17.81%; SAT math scores over 600: 30.1% **Housing** Yes **Expenses** Tuition & Fees: state resident $10,681, nonresident $22,701; Room & Board $8635 **Undergraduates** 40% women, 28% part-time, 29% 25 or older, 0.2% Native American, 6% Hispanic American, 5% African American, 8% Asian American/Pacific Islander **The most frequently chosen baccalaureate fields are** business/marketing, engineering, security and protective services **Academic program** Advanced placement, accelerated degree program, honors program, summer session, adult/continuing education programs, internships **Contact** Admissions Office, University of Massachusetts Lowell, 883 Broadway Street, Room 110, Lowell, MA 01854-5104. *Phone:* 978-934-3944 or toll-free 800-410-4607. *Fax:* 978-934-3086. *E-mail:* admissions@umi.edu. *Web site:* http://www.uml.edu/.

Visit Petersons.com and enter keyword Lowell

University of Phoenix–Boston Campus

Braintree, Massachusetts

General Proprietary, comprehensive, coed **Entrance** Noncompetitive **Setting** urban campus **Total enrollment** 361 **Application deadline** Rolling (freshmen), rolling (transfer) **Housing** No **Expenses** Tuition & Fees $13,875 **Undergraduates** 54% women, 79% 25 or older, 2% Native American, 8% Hispanic American, 19% African American, 4% Asian American/Pacific Islander **The most frequently chosen baccalaureate fields are** business/marketing, computer and information sciences **Academic program** Advanced placement, accelerated degree program, adult/continuing education programs **Contact** Ms. Audra McQuarie, Registrar/Executive Director, University of Phoenix–Boston Campus, 4035 South Riverpoint Parkway, Mail Stop CF-L101, Phoenix, AZ 85040. *Phone:* 480-557-6151 or toll-free 800-228-7240. *Fax:* 480-643-3068. *E-mail:* audra.mcquarie@phoenix.edu. *Web site:* http://www.phoenix.edu/.

University of Phoenix–Central Massachusetts Campus

Westborough, Massachusetts

General Proprietary, comprehensive, coed **Entrance** Noncompetitive **Setting** urban campus **Total enrollment** 148 **Application deadline** Rolling (freshmen), rolling (transfer) **Housing** No **Expenses** Tuition & Fees $13,875 **Undergraduates** 52% women, 83% 25 or older, 1% Native American, 11% Hispanic American, 6% African American **The most frequently chosen baccalaureate fields are** business/marketing, computer and information sciences **Academic program** Advanced placement, accelerated degree program **Contact** Ms. Audra McQuarie, Registrar/Executive Director, University of Phoenix–Central Massachusetts Campus, 4035 South Riverpoint Parkway, Mail Stop CF-L101, Phoenix, AZ 85040. *Phone:* 480-557-6151 or toll-free 800-776-4867 (in-state); 800-228-7240 (out-of-state). *Fax:* 480-643-3068. *E-mail:* audra.mcquarie@phoenix.edu. *Web site:* http://www.phoenix.edu/.

Wellesley College

Wellesley, Massachusetts

General Independent, 4-year, women only **Entrance** Most difficult **Setting** 500-acre suburban campus **Total enrollment** 2,324 **Student-faculty ratio** 8:1 **Application deadline** 1/15 (freshmen), 3/1 (transfer) **Freshman admission** 35% were admitted **Freshman test scores** SAT critical reading scores over 500: 99.6%; SAT math scores over 500: 99.6%; ACT scores over 18: 100%; SAT critical reading scores over 600: 90.2%; SAT math scores over 600: 88.8%; ACT scores over 24: 98.6% **Housing** Yes **Expenses** Tuition & Fees $38,062; Room & Board $11,732 **Undergraduates** 6% part-time, 3% 25 or older, 0.5% Native American, 7% Hispanic American, 6% African American, 25% Asian American/Pacific Islander **The most frequently chosen baccalaureate fields are** foreign languages and literature, social sciences, visual and performing arts **Academic program** Advanced placement, self-designed majors, honors program, summer session, adult/continuing education programs, internships **Contact** Director of Admission, Wellesley College, 106 Central Street, Wellesley, MA 02481. *Phone:* 781-283-2270. *Fax:* 781-283-3678. *E-mail:* admission@wellesley.edu. *Web site:* http://www.wellesley.edu/.

Visit Petersons.com and enter keyword Wellesley

UMass Lowell at a Glance

Experiential Learning transforms knowledge into experience through co-ops and internships, service learning, and real-world research.

Interdisciplinary Programs broaden your perspective.

Learning Communities help you connect with the campus, your professors and your classmates.

Bachelor's to Master's Programs: Enter the job market with two degrees.

A Lively Community: It's a great time to be at UMass Lowell! Enjoy River Hawks Div. I Hockey, which plays in Hockey East, exciting housing options, 125 student clubs, a packed schedule of activities and a Rec Center where you can work out or hang out.

UMass Lowell Numbers

7,300: Undergraduate students
2,900: Students living in University housing
10: University Residence Halls
75: Percent of Freshmen living in University housing
75: Undergraduate majors
423: Average number of internships per semester
14:1: Student to Faculty ratio
50: Percent of classes with fewer than 20 students
406: Full time faculty
93: Percent of Faculty with the highest degree in their field
25: Miles from Boston
925: Average number of students who use the Rec. Center daily
4,300: Average number of attendees at each UMass Lowell hockey game
15: Varsity Sports
63: Recreational Sports

To catch up with UMass Lowell tweets and blogs, go to www.uml.edu/social-media

Office of Undergraduate Admissions
UMass Lowell, 883 Broadway, Suite 110, Lowell, MA 01854
www.uml.edu/admissions

Wentworth Institute of Technology
Boston, Massachusetts

General Independent, comprehensive, coed **Entrance** Moderately difficult **Setting** 35-acre urban campus **Total enrollment** 3,892 **Student-faculty ratio** 15:1 **Application deadline** Rolling (freshmen), rolling (transfer) **Freshman admission** 67% were admitted. Average high school GPA 3 **Freshman test scores** SAT critical reading scores over 500: 58%; SAT math scores over 500: 79%; ACT scores over 18: 95%; SAT critical reading scores over 600: 15%; SAT math scores over 600: 32%; ACT scores over 24: 41% **Housing** Yes **Expenses** Tuition & Fees $21,800; Room & Board $10,500 **Undergraduates** 19% women, 11% part-time, 11% 25 or older, 0.1% Native American, 4% Hispanic American, 4% African American, 5% Asian American/Pacific Islander **The most frequently chosen baccalaureate fields are** architecture, engineering technologies, visual and performing arts **Academic program** Advanced placement, summer session, internships **Contact** Ms. Amy Dufour, Associate Director of Admissions, Wentworth Institute of Technology, 550 Huntington Avenue, Boston, MA 02115. *Phone:* 617-989-4116 or toll-free 800-556-0610. *Fax:* 617-989-4010. *E-mail:* dufoura@wit.edu. *Web site:* http://www.wit.edu/.

Visit Petersons.com and enter keyword Wentworth

See page 1354 for the College Close-Up.

Western New England College
Springfield, Massachusetts

General Independent, comprehensive, coed **Entrance** Moderately difficult **Setting** 215-acre suburban campus **Total enrollment** 3,710 **Student-faculty ratio** 15:1 **Application deadline** Rolling (freshmen), rolling (transfer) **Freshman admission** 81% were admitted. Average high school GPA 3.16 **Freshman test scores** SAT critical reading scores over 500: 63%; SAT math scores over 500: 71%; ACT scores over 18: 94%; SAT critical reading scores over 600: 15%; SAT math scores over 600: 28%; ACT scores over 24: 38% **Housing** Yes **Expenses** Tuition & Fees $28,816; Room & Board $10,980 **Undergraduates** 40% women, 10% part-time, 0.3% Native American, 4% Hispanic American, 4% African American, 2% Asian American/Pacific Islander **The most frequently chosen baccalaureate fields are** business/marketing, psychology, security and protective services **Academic program** Advanced placement, accelerated degree program, self-designed majors, honors program, summer session, adult/continuing education programs, internships **Contact** Dr. Charles R. Pollock, Vice President of Enrollment Management, Western New England College, 1215 Wilbraham Road, Springfield, MA 01119. *Phone:* 413-782-1321 or toll-free 800-325-1122 Ext. 1321. *Fax:* 413-782-1777. *E-mail:* ugradmis@wnec.edu. *Web site:* http://www.wnec.edu/.

Westfield State College
Westfield, Massachusetts

General State-supported, comprehensive, coed **Entrance** Moderately difficult **Setting** 227-acre small-town campus **Total enrollment** 5,675 **Student-faculty ratio** 17:1 **Application deadline** 3/1 (freshmen), 3/1 (transfer) **Freshman admission** 58% were admitted. Average high school GPA 3.04 **Freshman test scores** SAT critical reading scores over 500: 56.4%; SAT math scores over 500: 62.6%; ACT scores over 18: 84%; SAT critical reading scores over 600: 9.4%; SAT math scores over 600: 13.6%; ACT scores over 24: 21% **Housing** Yes **Expenses** Tuition & Fees: state resident $7016, nonresident $13,096; Room & Board $7728 **Undergraduates** 52% women, 10% part-time, 8% 25 or older, 0.3% Native American, 4% Hispanic American, 4% African American, 1% Asian American/Pacific Islander **The most frequently chosen baccalaureate fields are** liberal arts/general studies, business/marketing, security and protective services **Academic program** Advanced placement, self-designed majors, honors program, summer session, adult/continuing education programs, internships **Contact** Ms. Emily Gibbings, Associate Director of Admissions, Westfield State College, 333 Western Avenue, Westfield, MA 01002. *Phone:* 413-572-5218 or toll-free 800-322-8401. *Fax:* 413-572-0520. *E-mail:* admission@wsc.ma.edu. *Web site:* http://www.wsc.ma.edu/.

Wheaton College
Norton, Massachusetts

General Independent, 4-year, coed **Entrance** Very difficult **Setting** 400-acre suburban campus **Total enrollment** 1,632 **Student-faculty ratio** 11:1 **Application deadline** 1/15 (freshmen), 3/1 (transfer) **Freshman admission** 59% were admitted. Average high school GPA 3.5 **Housing** Yes **Expenses** Tuition & Fees $41,084; Room & Board $10,180 **Undergraduates** 62% women, 0.3% part-time, 1% 25 or older, 0.2% Native American, 4% Hispanic American, 5% African American, 2% Asian American/Pacific Islander **The most frequently chosen baccalaureate fields are** psychology, social sciences, visual and performing arts **Academic program** Advanced placement, accelerated degree program, self-designed majors, honors program, internships **Contact** Gail Berson, Vice President For Enrollment and Dean of Admission and Student Aid, Wheaton College, 26 East Main Street, Norton, MA 02766. *Phone:* 508-286-8251 or toll-free 800-394-6003. *Fax:* 508-286-8271. *E-mail:* admission@wheatoncollege.edu. *Web site:* http://www.wheatoncollege.edu/.

Visit Petersons.com and enter keyword Wheaton

See page 1376 for the College Close-Up.

Wheelock College
Boston, Massachusetts

General Independent, comprehensive, coed, primarily women **Entrance** Minimally difficult **Setting** urban campus **Total enrollment** 1,055 **Student-faculty ratio** 10:1 **Application deadline** 3/1 (freshmen), 6/1 (transfer) **Freshman admission** 75% were admitted. Average high school GPA 3 **Freshman test scores** SAT critical reading scores over 500: 48%; SAT math scores over 500: 39%; ACT scores over 18: 79%; SAT critical reading scores over 600: 10%; SAT math scores over 600: 9%; ACT scores over 24: 24% **Housing** Yes **Expenses** Tuition & Fees $28,160; Room & Board $11,200 **Undergraduates** 91% women, 4% part-time, 1% Native American, 8% Hispanic American, 9% African American, 2% Asian American/Pacific Islander **The most frequently chosen baccalaureate fields are** education, family and consumer sciences, public administration and social services **Academic program** Advanced placement, honors program, summer session, internships **Contact** Ms. Kristen Harrington, Director of Undergraduate Admissions, Wheelock College, 200 The Riverway, Boston, MA 02215. *Phone:* 617-879-2206 or toll-free 800-734-5212. *Fax:* 617-879-2449. *E-mail:* kharrington@wheelock.edu. *Web site:* http://www.wheelock.edu/.

See page 1378 for the College Close-Up.

Williams College
Williamstown, Massachusetts

General Independent, comprehensive, coed **Entrance** Most difficult **Setting** 450-acre small-town campus **Total enrollment** 2,123 **Student-faculty ratio** 7:1 **Application deadline** 1/1 (freshmen), 3/15 (transfer) **Freshman admission** 20% were admitted **Freshman test scores** SAT critical reading scores over 500: 100%; SAT math scores over 500: 100%; ACT scores over 18: 100%; SAT critical reading scores over 600: 92%; SAT math scores over 600: 91%; ACT scores over 24: 99% **Housing** Yes **Expenses** Tuition & Fees $39,490; Room & Board $10,390 **Undergraduates** 52% women, 2% part-time, 1% 25 or older, 0.4% Native American, 10% Hispanic American, 10% African American, 12% Asian American/Pacific Islander **The most frequently chosen baccalaureate fields are** social sciences, English, visual and performing arts **Academic program** Advanced placement, self-designed majors, internships **Contact** Mr. Richard L. Nesbitt, Director of Admission, Williams College, 33 Stetson Court, Williamstown, MA 01267. *Phone:* 413-597-

Williams College (continued)
2211. *Fax:* 413-597-4052. *E-mail:* admission@williams.edu. *Web site:* http://www.williams.edu/.

Worcester Polytechnic Institute
Worcester, Massachusetts

General Independent, university, coed **Entrance** Very difficult **Setting** 80-acre suburban campus **Total enrollment** 4,978 **Student-faculty ratio** 14:1 **Application deadline** 2/1 (freshmen), 4/15 (transfer) **Freshman admission** 63% were admitted. Average high school GPA 3.8 **Freshman test scores** SAT critical reading scores over 500: 92%; SAT math scores over 500: 100%; ACT scores over 18: 100%; SAT critical reading scores over 600: 57%; SAT math scores over 600: 88%; ACT scores over 24: 89% **Housing** Yes **Expenses** Tuition & Fees $38,920; Room & Board $11,610 **Undergraduates** 28% women, 4% part-time, 2% 25 or older, 0.5% Native American, 6% Hispanic American, 3% African American, 6% Asian American/Pacific Islander **The most frequently chosen baccalaureate fields are** biological/life sciences, computer and information sciences, engineering **Academic program** English as a second language, advanced placement, accelerated degree program, self-designed majors, summer session, internships **Contact** Mr. Edward J. Connor, Director of Admissions, Worcester Polytechnic Institute, 100 Institute Road, Worcester, MA 01609-2280. *Phone:* 508-831-5286. *Fax:* 508-831-5875. *E-mail:* admissions@wpi.edu. *Web site:* http://www.wpi.edu/.

Visit Petersons.com and enter keyword Worcester

See page 1386 for the College Close-Up.

Worcester State College
Worcester, Massachusetts

General State-supported, comprehensive, coed **Entrance** Moderately difficult **Setting** 58-acre urban campus **Total enrollment** 5,473 **Student-faculty ratio** 17:1 **Application deadline** 2/1 (freshmen), 5/1 (transfer) **Freshman admission** 59% were admitted. Average high school GPA 3.06 **Freshman test scores** SAT critical reading scores over 500: 56.14%; SAT math scores over 500: 60.83%; ACT scores over 18: 93.75%; SAT critical reading scores over 600: 8.59%; SAT math scores over 600: 12.9%; ACT scores over 24: 25% **Housing** Yes **Expenses** Tuition & Fees: state resident $6605, nonresident $12,685; Room & Board $9067 **Undergraduates** 60% women, 26% part-time, 18% 25 or older, 1% Native American, 6% Hispanic American, 6% African American, 3% Asian American/Pacific Islander **The most frequently chosen baccalaureate fields are** business/marketing, health professions and related sciences, psychology **Academic program** English as a second language, advanced placement, accelerated degree program, honors program, summer session, adult/continuing education programs, internships **Contact** Ms. Kim Albro, Clerk of Admissions, Worcester State College, 486 Chandler Street, Administration Building, Worcester, MA 01602-2597. *Phone:* 508-929-8040 or toll-free 866-WSC-CALL. *Fax:* 508-929-8183. *E-mail:* admissions@worcester.edu. *Web site:* http://www.worcester.edu/.

Zion Bible College
Haverhill, Massachusetts

General Independent, 4-year, coed, affiliated with Assembly of God Church **Total enrollment** 265 **Housing** Yes **Expenses** Tuition & Fees $7640; Room & Board $5700 **Undergraduates** 35% 25 or older **Contact** Helen Brouillette, Admissions Director, Zion Bible College, 320 South Main Street, Haverhill, MA 01835. *Phone:* 800-356-4014 or toll-free 800-356-4014. *E-mail:* admissions@zbc.edu. *Web site:* http://www.zbc.edu/.

MICHIGAN

Adrian College
Adrian, Michigan

General Independent, 4-year, coed, affiliated with United Methodist Church **Entrance** Moderately difficult **Setting** 100-acre small-town campus **Total enrollment** 1,469 **Student-faculty ratio** 13:1 **Application deadline** 3/15 (freshmen), 3/15 (transfer) **Freshman admission** 58% were admitted. Average high school GPA 3.38 **Freshman test scores** ACT scores over 18: 98%; ACT scores over 24: 42% **Housing** Yes **Expenses** Tuition & Fees $24,440; Room & Board $7460 **Undergraduates** 47% women, 3% part-time, 2% 25 or older, 0.1% Native American, 2% Hispanic American, 4% African American, 0.5% Asian American/Pacific Islander **The most frequently chosen baccalaureate fields are** business/marketing, parks and recreation, visual and performing arts **Academic program** English as a second language, advanced placement, self-designed majors, honors program, summer session, adult/continuing education programs, internships **Contact** Ms. Carolyn Quinlan, Director of Admissions, Adrian College, 110 South Madison Street, Adrian, MI 49221. *Phone:* 800-877-2246 or toll-free 800-877-2246. *Fax:* 517-264-3331. *E-mail:* admissions@adrian.edu. *Web site:* http://www.adrian.edu/.

Albion College
Albion, Michigan

General Independent Methodist, 4-year, coed **Entrance** Moderately difficult **Setting** 565-acre small-town campus **Total enrollment** 1,860 **Student-faculty ratio** 12:1 **Application deadline** 5/1 (freshmen), 6/1 (transfer) **Freshman admission** 83% were admitted. Average high school GPA 3.55 **Freshman test scores** SAT critical reading scores over 500: 82%; SAT math scores over 500: 82%; ACT scores over 18: 97%; SAT critical reading scores over 600: 49%; SAT math scores over 600: 45%; ACT scores over 24: 69% **Housing** Yes **Expenses** Tuition & Fees $30,002; Room & Board $8510 **Undergraduates** 54% women, 1% part-time, 1% 25 or older, 0.4% Native American, 1% Hispanic American, 3% African American, 2% Asian American/Pacific Islander **The most frequently chosen baccalaureate fields are** biological/life sciences, psychology, social sciences **Academic program** Advanced placement, self-designed majors, honors program, summer session, internships **Contact** Mr. Doug Kellar, Associate Vice President for Enrollment, Albion College, 611 East Porter Street, Albion, MI 49224-1831. *Phone:* 517-629-0600 or toll-free 800-858-6770. *E-mail:* admissions@albion.edu. *Web site:* http://www.albion.edu/.

Alma College
Alma, Michigan

General Independent Presbyterian, 4-year, coed **Entrance** Moderately difficult **Setting** 125-acre small-town campus **Total enrollment** 1,444 **Student-faculty ratio** 14:1 **Application deadline** Rolling (freshmen), rolling (transfer) **Freshman admission** 75% were admitted. Average high school GPA 3.48 **Freshman test scores** SAT critical reading scores over 500: 63.64%; SAT math scores over 500: 68.18%; ACT scores over 18: 97.44%; SAT critical reading scores over 600: 50%; SAT math scores over 600: 40.91%; ACT scores over 24: 54.36% **Housing** Yes **Expenses** Tuition & Fees $26,068; Room & Board $8518 **Undergraduates** 56% women, 5% part-time, 2% 25 or older, 1% Native American, 3% Hispanic American, 2% African American, 2% Asian American/Pacific Islander **The most frequently chosen baccalaureate fields are** biological/life sciences, business/marketing, social sciences **Academic program** Advanced placement, self-designed majors, honors program, summer session, internships **Contact** Mr. Bob Garcia, Director of Admissions, Alma College, Admissions Office, Alma, MI 48801-1599. *Phone:* 800-321-2562 or toll-free 800-321-ALMA. *Fax:* 989-463-7057. *E-mail:* admissions@alma.edu. *Web site:* http://www.alma.edu/.

Visit Petersons.com and enter keyword Alma

Andrews University
Berrien Springs, Michigan

General Independent Seventh-day Adventist, university, coed **Entrance** Moderately difficult **Setting** 1,650-acre small-town campus **Total enrollment** 3,589 **Student-faculty ratio** 13:1 **Application deadline** Rolling (freshmen), rolling (transfer) **Freshman admission** 49% were admitted. Average high school GPA 3.36 **Freshman test scores** SAT critical reading scores over 500: 58%; SAT math scores over 500: 54%; ACT scores over 18: 65%; SAT critical reading scores over 600: 15%; SAT math scores over 600: 21%; ACT scores over 24: 24% **Housing** Yes **Expenses** Tuition & Fees $21,170; Room & Board $6860 **Undergraduates** 55% women, 13% part-time, 14% 25 or older, 1% Native American, 12% Hispanic American, 25% African American, 10% Asian American/Pacific Islander **The most frequently chosen baccalaureate fields are** business/marketing, biological/life sciences, health professions and related sciences **Academic program** English as a second language, advanced placement, accelerated degree program, self-designed majors, honors program, summer session, adult/continuing education programs, internships **Contact** Shanna Leak, Undergraduate Admissions Coordinator, Andrews University, Berrien Springs, MI 49104. *Phone:* 800-253-2874 or toll-free 800-253-2874. *Fax:* 269-471-3228. *E-mail:* enroll@andrews.edu. *Web site:* http://www.andrews.edu/.

Aquinas College
Grand Rapids, Michigan

General Independent Roman Catholic, comprehensive, coed **Entrance** Moderately difficult **Setting** 107-acre suburban campus **Total enrollment** 2,145 **Student-faculty ratio** 13:1 **Application deadline** Rolling (freshmen), rolling (transfer) **Freshman admission** 80% were admitted. Average high school GPA 3.4 **Freshman test scores** ACT scores over 18: 95%; ACT scores over 24: 42% **Housing** Yes **Expenses** Tuition & Fees $22,314; Room & Board $7014 **Undergraduates** 64% women, 14% part-time, 15% 25 or older, 1% Native American, 4% Hispanic American, 4% African American, 2% Asian American/Pacific Islander **The most frequently chosen baccalaureate fields are** business/marketing, education, social sciences **Academic program** Advanced placement, accelerated degree program, self-designed majors, honors program, summer session, adult/continuing education programs, internships **Contact** Ms. Vicki Bassett, Admissions Office Manager, Aquinas College, 1607 Robinson Road, SE, Grand Rapids, MI 49506-1799. *Phone:* 616-632-2851 or toll-free 800-678-9593. *Fax:* 616-732-4469. *E-mail:* admissions@aquinas.edu. *Web site:* http://www.aquinas.edu/.
Visit Petersons.com and enter keyword Aquinas

The Art Institute of Michigan
Novi, Michigan

General Proprietary, 4-year, coed **Contact** Director of Admissions, The Art Institute of Michigan, 28125 Cabot Drive, Suite 120, Novi, MI 48377. *Phone:* 248-675-3800 or toll-free 800-479-0087. *Fax:* 248-675-3830. *Web site:* http://www.artinstitutes.edu/detroit/.
Visit Petersons.com and enter keywords Art Institute of Michigan

See page 526 for the College Close-Up.

Baker College of Allen Park
Allen Park, Michigan

General Independent, 4-year, coed, primarily women **Entrance** Minimally difficult **Setting** 13-acre suburban campus **Total enrollment** 3,384 **Student-faculty ratio** 34:1 **Application deadline** 9/24 (freshmen) **Freshman admission** 100% were admitted **Housing** No **Expenses** Tuition & Fees $7380 **Undergraduates** 72% women, 40% part-time, 1% Native American, 5% Hispanic American, 33% African American, 1% Asian American/Pacific Islander **Academic program** Advanced placement, accelerated degree program, summer session, internships **Contact** Mr. Steve Peterson, Vice President of Admissions, Baker College of Allen Park, 4500 Enterprise Drive, Allen Park, MI 48101. *Phone:* 313-425-3700 or toll-free 800-767-4120. *E-mail:* steve.peterson@baker.edu. *Web site:* http://www.baker.edu/.

Baker College of Auburn Hills
Auburn Hills, Michigan

General Independent, 4-year, coed **Entrance** Minimally difficult **Setting** 8-acre urban campus **Total enrollment** 4,285 **Student-faculty ratio** 41:1 **Application deadline** Rolling (freshmen), rolling (transfer) **Freshman admission** 100% were admitted **Housing** No **Expenses** Tuition & Fees $7380 **Undergraduates** 72% women, 47% part-time, 41% 25 or older, 1% Native American, 4% Hispanic American, 21% African American, 2% Asian American/Pacific Islander **Academic program** Advanced placement, accelerated degree program, summer session, internships **Contact** Ms. Jan Bohlen, Vice President for Admissions, Baker College of Auburn Hills, 1500 University Drive, Auburn Hills, MI 48326-1586. *Phone:* 248-340-0600 or toll-free 888-429-0410. *Fax:* 248-340-0608. *E-mail:* jan.bohlen@baker.edu. *Web site:* http://www.baker.edu/.

Baker College of Cadillac
Cadillac, Michigan

General Independent, 4-year, coed **Entrance** Minimally difficult **Setting** 40-acre small-town campus **Total enrollment** 2,070 **Student-faculty ratio** 42:1 **Application deadline** 9/24 (freshmen), rolling (transfer) **Freshman admission** 100% were admitted **Housing** No **Expenses** Tuition & Fees $7380 **Undergraduates** 73% women, 40% part-time, 56% 25 or older, 0.1% Hispanic American, 0.3% African American, 0.1% Asian American/Pacific Islander **Academic program** Advanced placement, summer session, internships **Contact** Mr. Mike Tisdale, Director of Admissions, Baker College of Cadillac, 9600 East 13th Street, Cadillac, MI 49601. *Phone:* 231-876-3100 or toll-free 888-313-3463. *Fax:* 231-775-8505. *E-mail:* mike.tisdale@baker.edu. *Web site:* http://www.baker.edu/.

Baker College of Clinton Township
Clinton Township, Michigan

General Independent, 4-year, coed **Entrance** Minimally difficult **Setting** 27-acre urban campus **Total enrollment** 6,455 **Student-faculty ratio** 45:1 **Application deadline** Rolling (freshmen), rolling (transfer) **Freshman admission** 100% were admitted **Housing** No **Expenses** Tuition & Fees $7380 **Undergraduates** 71% women, 42% part-time, 42% 25 or older, 1% Native American, 2% Hispanic American, 22% African American, 2% Asian American/Pacific Islander **Academic program** Advanced placement, summer session, internships **Contact** Ms. Annette Looser, Vice President for Admissions, Baker College of Clinton Township, 34401 South Gratiot Avenue, Clinton Township, MI 48035. *Phone:* 586-790-3000 or toll-free 888-272-2842. *Fax:* 586-791-6811. *E-mail:* annette.looser@baker.edu. *Web site:* http://www.baker.edu/.

Baker College of Flint
Flint, Michigan

General Independent, 4-year, coed **Entrance** Minimally difficult **Setting** 42-acre urban campus **Total enrollment** 7,305 **Student-faculty ratio** 31:1 **Application deadline** 9/20 (freshmen), 9/20 (transfer) **Freshman admission** 100% were admitted **Housing** Yes **Expenses** Tuition & Fees $7380; Room only $3000 **Undergraduates** 67% women, 39% part-time, 1% Native American, 2% Hispanic American, 23% African American, 0.3% Asian American/Pacific Islander **Academic program** Advanced placement, accelerated degree program, summer session, internships **Contact** Ms. Jodi Cunez, Director of Admissions, Baker College of Flint, 1050 West Bristol Road, Flint, MI 48507-5508. *Phone:* 810-766-4008 or toll-free 800-964-4299. *Fax:* 810-766-4049. *Web site:* http://www.baker.edu/.

Baker College of Jackson
Jackson, Michigan

General Independent, 4-year, coed **Entrance** Minimally difficult **Setting** 42-acre suburban campus **Total enrollment** 2,432 **Student-faculty ratio** 36:1 **Application deadline** 9/19 (freshmen), rolling (transfer) **Freshman admission** 100% were admitted **Housing** No **Expenses** Tuition & Fees $7400 **Undergraduates** 75% women, 43% part-time, 56% 25 or older, 0.3% Native American, 2% Hispanic American, 8% African American, 1% Asian American/Pacific Islander **Academic program** Advanced placement, accelerated degree program, summer session, internships **Contact** Mr. Kevin Pnacek, Vice President for Admissions, Baker College of Jackson, 2800 Springport Road, Jackson, MI 49202. *Phone:* 517-788-7800 or toll-free 888-343-3683. *Fax:* 517-789-7331. *E-mail:* kevin.pnacek@baker.edu. *Web site:* http://www.baker.edu/.

Baker College of Muskegon
Muskegon, Michigan

General Independent, 4-year, coed **Entrance** Minimally difficult **Setting** 45-acre suburban campus **Total enrollment** 6,133 **Student-faculty ratio** 55:1 **Application deadline** 9/24 (freshmen), rolling (transfer) **Freshman admission** 100% were admitted **Housing** Yes **Expenses** Tuition & Fees $7400; Room only $3000 **Undergraduates** 69% women, 37% part-time, 45% 25 or older, 1% Native American, 5% Hispanic American, 14% African American, 1% Asian American/Pacific Islander **Academic program** Advanced placement, accelerated degree program, summer session, adult/continuing education programs, internships **Contact** Ms. Kathy Jacobson, Vice President of Admissions, Baker College of Muskegon, 1903 Marquette Avenue, Muskegon, MI 49442-3497. *Phone:* 231-777-5207 or toll-free 800-937-0337. *Fax:* 231-777-5201. *E-mail:* kathy.jacobson@baker.edu. *Web site:* http://www.baker.edu/.

Baker College of Owosso
Owosso, Michigan

General Independent, 4-year, coed **Entrance** Minimally difficult **Setting** 36-acre small-town campus **Total enrollment** 3,637 **Student-faculty ratio** 40:1 **Application deadline** Rolling (freshmen), rolling (transfer) **Freshman admission** 100% were admitted **Housing** Yes **Expenses** Tuition & Fees $7400; Room only $2700 **Undergraduates** 63% women, 32% part-time, 41% 25 or older, 1% Native American, 2% Hispanic American, 4% African American, 0.4% Asian American/Pacific Islander **Academic program** Advanced placement, accelerated degree program, summer session, adult/continuing education programs, internships **Contact** Mr. Michael Konopacke, Vice President for Admissions, Baker College of Owosso, 1020 South Washington Street, Owosso, MI 48867-4400. *Phone:* 989-729-3350 or toll-free 800-879-3797. *Fax:* 989-729-3441. *E-mail:* mike.konopacke@baker.edu. *Web site:* http://www.baker.edu/.

Baker College of Port Huron
Port Huron, Michigan

General Independent, 4-year, coed **Entrance** Minimally difficult **Setting** 10-acre urban campus **Total enrollment** 1,984 **Student-faculty ratio** 28:1 **Application deadline** 9/24 (freshmen), rolling (transfer) **Freshman admission** 100% were admitted **Housing** No **Expenses** Tuition & Fees $7380 **Undergraduates** 70% women, 31% part-time, 51% 25 or older, 1% Native American, 2% Hispanic American, 4% African American, 0.2% Asian American/Pacific Islander **Academic program** Advanced placement, accelerated degree program, summer session, internships **Contact** Mr. Daniel Kenny, Vice President for Admissions, Baker College of Port Huron, 3403 Lapeer Road, Port Huron, MI 48060-2597. *Phone:* 810-985-7000 or toll-free 888-262-2442. *Fax:* 810-985-7066. *E-mail:* kenny_d@porthuron.baker.edu. *Web site:* http://www.baker.edu/.

Calvin College
Grand Rapids, Michigan

General Independent Christian Reformed, comprehensive, coed **Entrance** Moderately difficult **Setting** 370-acre suburban campus **Total enrollment** 4,092 **Student-faculty ratio** 11:1 **Application deadline** 8/15 (freshmen), rolling (transfer) **Freshman admission** 93% were admitted. Average high school GPA 3.6 **Freshman test scores** SAT critical reading scores over 500: 82.6%; SAT math scores over 500: 89%; ACT scores over 18: 98.9%; SAT critical reading scores over 600: 50.7%; SAT math scores over 600: 55.4%; ACT scores over 24: 70.3% **Housing** Yes **Expenses** Tuition & Fees $24,035; Room & Board $8275 **Undergraduates** 54% women, 3% part-time, 1% 25 or older, 0.3% Native American, 2% Hispanic American, 2% African American, 3% Asian American/Pacific Islander **The most frequently chosen baccalaureate fields are** business/marketing, social sciences, visual and performing arts **Academic program** Advanced placement, accelerated degree program, self-designed majors, honors program, summer session, adult/continuing education programs, internships **Contact** Mr. Dale Kuiper, Director of Admissions and Financial Aid, Calvin College, 3201 Burton Street, SE, Grand Rapids, MI 49546. *Phone:* 616-526-6106 or toll-free 800-688-0122. *Fax:* 616-526-6777. *E-mail:* admissions@calvin.edu. *Web site:* http://www.calvin.edu/.

Visit Petersons.com and enter keyword Calvin

See page 668 for the College Close-Up.

Central Michigan University
Mount Pleasant, Michigan

General State-supported, university, coed **Entrance** Moderately difficult **Setting** 854-acre small-town campus **Total enrollment** 27,246 **Student-faculty ratio** 21:1 **Application deadline** Rolling (freshmen), rolling (transfer) **Freshman admission** 73% were admitted. Average high school GPA 3.3 **Freshman test scores** SAT critical reading scores over 500: 48.7%; SAT math scores over 500: 52.7%; ACT scores over 18: 94.8%; SAT critical reading scores over 600: 14.9%; SAT math scores over 600: 20.3%; ACT scores over 24: 33.8% **Housing** Yes **Expenses** Tuition & Fees: state resident $10,170, nonresident $23,670; Room & Board $7896 **Undergraduates** 55% women, 11% part-time, 6% 25 or older, 1% Native American, 2% Hispanic American, 6% African American, 1% Asian American/Pacific Islander **The most frequently chosen baccalaureate fields are** business/marketing, education, parks and recreation **Academic program** English as a second language, advanced placement, accelerated degree program, self-designed majors, honors program, summer session, adult/continuing education programs, internships **Contact** Ms. Betty J. Wagner, Director of Admissions, Central Michigan University, Mount Pleasant, MI 48859. *Phone:* 989-774-3076 or toll-free 888-292-5366. *Fax:* 989-774-7267. *Web site:* http://www.cmich.edu/.

Cleary University
Ann Arbor, Michigan

General Independent, comprehensive, coed **Entrance** Moderately difficult **Setting** 32-acre suburban campus **Total enrollment** 774 **Student-faculty ratio** 10:1 **Application deadline** 8/15 (freshmen), 8/15 (transfer) **Freshman admission** 85% were admitted. Average high school GPA 2.72 **Freshman test scores** ACT scores over 18: 77%; ACT scores over 24: 27% **Housing** No **Expenses** Tuition & Fees $15,600 **Undergraduates** 58% women, 37% part-time, 71% 25 or older, 0.5% Native American, 2% Hispanic American, 8% African American, 1% Asian American/Pacific Islander **The most frequently chosen baccalaureate field is** business/marketing **Academic program** Advanced placement, accelerated degree program, summer session, internships **Contact** Ms. Charlotte Paquette, Admissions Representative, Cleary University, 3601 Plymouth Road, Ann Arbor, MI 48105-2659. *Phone:* 517-338-3330 Ext. 2249 or toll-free 888-5-CLEARY Ext. 2249. *Fax:* 517-338-3336. *E-mail:* admissions@cleary.edu. *Web site:* http://www.cleary.edu/.

College for Creative Studies

Detroit, Michigan

General Independent, comprehensive, coed **Entrance** Moderately difficult **Setting** 11-acre urban campus **Total enrollment** 1,400 **Student-faculty ratio** 11:1 **Application deadline** 8/1 (freshmen), rolling (transfer) **Freshman admission** 39% were admitted. Average high school GPA 3.18 **Freshman test scores** ACT scores over 18: 79%; ACT scores over 24: 26% **Housing** Yes **Expenses** Tuition & Fees $31,275; Room & Board $8500 **Undergraduates** 1% Native American, 5% Hispanic American, 7% African American, 4% Asian American/Pacific Islander **The most frequently chosen baccalaureate field is** visual and performing arts **Academic program** English as a second language, advanced placement, summer session, internships **Contact** Office of Admissions, College for Creative Studies, 201 East Kirby, Detroit, MI 48202-4034. *Phone:* 800-952-2787 or toll-free 800-872-2739. *Fax:* 313-872-2739. *E-mail:* admissions@ccscad.edu. *Web site:* http://www.collegeforcreativestudies.edu/.

Concordia University

Ann Arbor, Michigan

General Independent, comprehensive, coed, affiliated with Lutheran Church–Missouri Synod **Entrance** Moderately difficult **Setting** 187-acre suburban campus **Total enrollment** 1,075 **Student-faculty ratio** 17:1 **Application deadline** Rolling (freshmen), rolling (transfer) **Freshman admission** 66% were admitted. Average high school GPA 3.22 **Freshman test scores** SAT critical reading scores over 500: 63%; SAT math scores over 500: 72%; ACT scores over 18: 92%; SAT critical reading scores over 600: 42%; SAT math scores over 600: 29%; ACT scores over 24: 44% **Housing** Yes **Expenses** Tuition & Fees $20,390; Room & Board $7606 **Undergraduates** 54% women, 18% part-time, 17% 25 or older, 2% Native American, 2% Hispanic American, 8% African American, 2% Asian American/Pacific Islander **The most frequently chosen baccalaureate fields are** business/marketing, communications/journalism, education **Academic program** Advanced placement, accelerated degree program, self-designed majors, summer session, internships **Contact** Amy Becher, Executive Director of Enrollment Services, Concordia University, 4090 Geddes Road, Ann Arbor, MI 48105-2797. *Phone:* 734-995-7450 or toll-free 800-253-0680. *Fax:* 734-995-4610. *E-mail:* admissions@cuaa.edu. *Web site:* http://www.cuaa.edu/.

Cornerstone University

Grand Rapids, Michigan

General Independent nondenominational, comprehensive, coed **Entrance** Minimally difficult **Setting** 132-acre suburban campus **Total enrollment** 2,606 **Student-faculty ratio** 20:1 **Application deadline** Rolling (freshmen), rolling (transfer) **Freshman admission** 79% were admitted. Average high school GPA 3.45 **Freshman test scores** SAT critical reading scores over 500: 72%; SAT math scores over 500: 64%; ACT scores over 18: 96%; SAT critical reading scores over 600: 20%; SAT math scores over 600: 13%; ACT scores over 24: 44% **Housing** Yes **Expenses** Tuition & Fees $20,520; Room & Board $6510 **Undergraduates** 59% women, 25% part-time, 5% 25 or older, 0.4% Native American, 3% Hispanic American, 9% African American, 1% Asian American/Pacific Islander **The most frequently chosen baccalaureate fields are** business/marketing, education, theology and religious vocations **Academic program** English as a second language, advanced placement, accelerated degree program, honors program, summer session, adult/continuing education programs, internships **Contact** Office of Admissions, Cornerstone University, 1001 East Beltline Avenue, NE, Grand Rapids, MI 49525. *Phone:* 616-222-1426 or toll-free 800-787-9778. *Fax:* 616-222-1400. *E-mail:* admissions@cornerstone.edu. *Web site:* http://www.cornerstone.edu/.

Davenport University
Grand Rapids, Michigan

General Independent, comprehensive, coed **Entrance** Minimally difficult **Setting** suburban campus **Total enrollment** 11,506 **Student-faculty ratio** 14:1 **Application deadline** Rolling (freshmen), rolling (transfer) **Freshman admission** Average high school GPA 2.91 **Housing** Yes **Expenses** Tuition & Fees $11,241; Room & Board $9500 **Undergraduates** 67% women, 67% part-time, 66% 25 or older, 0.4% Native American, 3% Hispanic American, 19% African American, 2% Asian American/Pacific Islander **Academic program** English as a second language, advanced placement, accelerated degree program, summer session, adult/continuing education programs, internships **Contact** Ms. Heather Knechtel, Director of Admissions, Davenport University, 415 East Fulton, Grand Rapids, MI 49503. *Phone:* 616-451-3511 or toll-free 800-632-9569. *E-mail:* heather.knechtel@davenport.edu. *Web site:* http://www.davenport.edu/.

DeVry University
Southfield, Michigan

General Proprietary, 4-year, coed **Total enrollment** 88 **Student-faculty ratio** 10:1 **Application deadline** Rolling (freshmen), rolling (transfer) **Housing** No **Expenses** Tuition & Fees $14,080 **Undergraduates** 43% women, 68% part-time, 70% 25 or older, 1% Native American, 60% African American, 1% Asian American/Pacific Islander **The most frequently chosen baccalaureate field is** business/marketing **Academic program** Accelerated degree program **Contact** Admissions Office, DeVry University, 26999 Central Park Boulevard, Suite 125, Southfield, MI 48076. *Web site:* http://www.devry.edu/.

Eastern Michigan University
Ypsilanti, Michigan

General State-supported, comprehensive, coed **Entrance** Moderately difficult **Setting** 460-acre suburban campus **Total enrollment** 22,859 **Student-faculty ratio** 18:1 **Application deadline** Rolling (freshmen), rolling (transfer) **Freshman admission** 71% were admitted. Average high school GPA 3.08 **Freshman test scores** SAT critical reading scores over 500: 52.05%; SAT math scores over 500: 63.01%; ACT scores over 18: 80.5%; SAT critical reading scores over 600: 20.09%; SAT math scores over 600: 21.46%; ACT scores over 24: 26.26% **Housing** Yes **Expenses** Tuition & Fees: state resident $8378, nonresident $22,283; Room & Board $7785 **Undergraduates** 57% women, 28% part-time, 28% 25 or older, 1% Native American, 3% Hispanic American, 21% African American, 2% Asian American/Pacific Islander **The most frequently chosen baccalaureate fields are** business/marketing, education, health professions and related sciences **Academic program** English as a second language, advanced placement, accelerated degree program, self-designed majors, honors program, summer session, internships **Contact** Kathy Orscheln, Director of Admissions, Eastern Michigan University, Ypsilanti, MI 48197. *Phone:* 734-487-3060 or toll-free 800-GO TO EMU. *Web site:* http://www.emich.edu/.

Ferris State University
Big Rapids, Michigan

General State-supported, comprehensive, coed **Entrance** Minimally difficult **Setting** 880-acre small-town campus **Total enrollment** 13,865 **Student-faculty ratio** 16:1 **Application deadline** 8/1 (freshmen), 7/1 (transfer) **Freshman admission** 55% were admitted. Average high school GPA 3.21 **Freshman test scores** ACT scores over 18: 81.25%; ACT scores over 24: 27.72% **Housing** Yes **Expenses** Tuition & Fees: state resident $9162, nonresident $16,062; Room & Board $7944 **Undergraduates** 49% women, 27% part-time, 24% 25 or older, 1% Native American, 2% Hispanic American, 7% African American, 2% Asian American/Pacific Islander **The most frequently chosen baccalaureate fields are** business/marketing, engineering technologies, health professions and related sciences **Academic program** Advanced placement, accelerated degree program, self-designed majors, honors program, summer session, internships **Contact** Troy Tissue, Associate Director of Admissions, Ferris State University, 1201 South State Street, CSS201, Big Rapids, MI 49307-2742. *Phone:* 231-591-2000 or toll-free 800-433-7747. *Fax:* 231-591-3944. *E-mail:* admissions@ferris.edu. *Web site:* http://www.ferris.edu/.

Finlandia University
Hancock, Michigan

Contact Martin Kinard, Finlandia University, 601 Quincy Street, Hancock, MI 49930. *Phone:* 906-487-7352 or toll-free 877-202-5491. *Fax:* 906-487-7383. *E-mail:* admissions@finlandia.edu. *Web site:* http://www.finlandia.edu/.

Grace Bible College
Grand Rapids, Michigan

General Independent, 4-year, coed, affiliated with Grace Gospel Fellowship **Entrance** Minimally difficult **Setting** 16-acre suburban campus **Total enrollment** 194 **Student-faculty ratio** 19:1 **Application deadline** 7/15 (freshmen) **Freshman admission** 61% were admitted. Average high school GPA 3.29 **Freshman test scores** SAT critical reading scores over 500: 67%; SAT math scores over 500: 67%; ACT scores over 18: 84%; ACT scores over 24: 26% **Housing** Yes **Expenses** Tuition & Fees $11,400; Room & Board $6250 **Undergraduates** 45% women, 7% part-time, 11% 25 or older, 1% Hispanic American, 3% African American, 1% Asian American/Pacific Islander **The most frequently chosen baccalaureate fields are** education, interdisciplinary studies, theology and religious vocations **Academic program** English as a second language, advanced placement, internships **Contact** Mr. Kevin Gilliam, Director of Enrollment, Grace Bible College, 1101 Aldon Street, SW, PO Box 910, Grand Rapids, MI 49509. *Phone:* 616-538-2330 Ext. 239 or toll-free 800-968-1887. *Fax:* 616-538-0599. *E-mail:* gbc@gbcol.edu. *Web site:* http://www.gbcol.edu/.

Grand Valley State University
Allendale, Michigan

General State-supported, comprehensive, coed **Entrance** Moderately difficult **Setting** 900-acre small-town campus **Total enrollment** 24,408 **Student-faculty ratio** 17:1 **Application deadline** 5/1 (freshmen), 7/24 (transfer) **Freshman admission** 81% were admitted. Average high school GPA 3.53 **Freshman test scores** SAT critical reading scores over 500: 72.4%; SAT math scores over 500: 80.71%; ACT scores over 18: 98.15%; SAT critical reading scores over 600: 29.17%; SAT math scores over 600: 39.09%; ACT scores over 24: 52.92% **Housing** Yes **Expenses** Tuition & Fees: state resident $8630, nonresident $12,944; Room & Board $7478 **Undergraduates** 59% women, 12% part-time, 11% 25 or older, 1% Native American, 3% Hispanic American, 5% African American, 3% Asian American/Pacific Islander **The most frequently chosen baccalaureate fields are** business/marketing, biological/life sciences, health professions and related sciences **Academic program** English as a second language, advanced placement, accelerated degree program, honors program, summer session, adult/continuing education programs, internships **Contact** Ms. Jodi Chycinski, Director of Admissions, Grand Valley State University, 1 Campus Drive, Allendale, MI 49401. *Phone:* 616-331-2025 or toll-free 800-748-0246. *Fax:* 616-331-2000. *E-mail:* go2gvsu@gvsu.edu. *Web site:* http://www.gvsu.edu/.
Visit Petersons.com and enter keywords Grand Valley

Great Lakes Christian College
Lansing, Michigan

General Independent, 4-year, coed, affiliated with Christian Churches and Churches of Christ **Entrance** Moderately difficult **Setting** 47-acre suburban campus **Total enrollment** 241 **Student-faculty ratio** 13:1 **Application deadline** 8/1 (freshmen), 8/1 (transfer) **Freshman test**

scores ACT scores over 18: 79%; ACT scores over 24: 19% **Housing** Yes **Expenses** Tuition & Fees $12,600; Room & Board $7000 **Undergraduates** 44% women, 28% part-time, 0.4% Native American, 0.4% Hispanic American, 11% African American **The most frequently chosen baccalaureate field is** theology and religious vocations **Academic program** Advanced placement, internships **Contact** Mr. Lloyd Scharer, Director of Admissions and College Relations, Great Lakes Christian College, 6211 West Willow Highway, Lansing, MI 48917-1299. *Phone:* 517-321-0242 or toll-free 800-YES-GLCC. *Fax:* 517-321-5902. *E-mail:* lscharer@glcc.edu. *Web site:* http://www.glcc.edu/.

Hillsdale College
Hillsdale, Michigan

General Independent, 4-year, coed **Entrance** Very difficult **Setting** 200-acre small-town campus **Total enrollment** 1,316 **Student-faculty ratio** 10:1 **Application deadline** 2/15 (freshmen), 2/15 (transfer) **Freshman admission** 62% were admitted. Average high school GPA 3.72 **Freshman test scores** SAT critical reading scores over 500: 100%; SAT math scores over 500: 96%; ACT scores over 18: 100%; SAT critical reading scores over 600: 85%; SAT math scores over 600: 65%; ACT scores over 24: 90% **Housing** Yes **Expenses** Tuition & Fees $20,500; Room & Board $7990 **Undergraduates** 53% women, 3% part-time, 1% 25 or older **Academic program** Advanced placement, accelerated degree program, honors program, summer session, internships **Contact** Mr. Jeffrey S. Lantis, Director of Admissions, Hillsdale College, 33 East College Street, Hillsdale, MI 49242-1298. *Phone:* 517-607-2327. *Fax:* 517-607-2223. *E-mail:* admissions@hillsdale.edu. *Web site:* http://www.hillsdale.edu/.

See page 850 for the College Close-Up.

Hope College
Holland, Michigan

General Independent, 4-year, coed, affiliated with Reformed Church in America **Entrance** Moderately difficult **Setting** 45-acre suburban campus **Total enrollment** 3,230 **Student-faculty ratio** 12:1 **Application deadline** Rolling (freshmen), rolling (transfer) **Freshman admission** 84% were admitted. Average high school GPA 3.72 **Freshman test scores** SAT critical reading scores over 500: 83.1%; SAT math scores over 500: 85.9%; ACT scores over 18: 99.6%; SAT critical reading scores over 600: 51.4%; SAT math scores over 600: 52.1%; ACT scores over 24: 69.7% **Housing** Yes **Expenses** Tuition & Fees $26,510; Room & Board $8110 **Undergraduates** 60% women, 4% part-time, 1% 25 or older, 0.3% Native American, 4% Hispanic American, 2% African American, 2% Asian American/Pacific Islander **The most frequently chosen baccalaureate fields are** business/marketing, education, psychology **Academic program** English as a second language, advanced placement, self-designed majors, summer session, internships **Contact** Admissions Office, Hope College, 69 East 10th Street, P.O. Box 9000, Holland, MI 49422-9000. *Phone:* 616-395-7850 or toll-free 800-968-7850. *E-mail:* admissions@hope.edu. *Web site:* http://www.hope.edu/.

Visit Petersons.com and enter keyword Hope

See page 858 for the College Close-Up.

ITT Technical Institute
Canton, Michigan

General Proprietary, primarily 2-year, coed **Entrance** Minimally difficult **Housing** No **Contact** Director of Recruitment, ITT Technical Institute, 1905 South Haggerty Road, Canton, MI 48188-2025. *Phone:* 784-397-7800 or toll-free 800-247-4477. *Web site:* http://www.itt-tech.edu/.

ITT Technical Institute
Troy, Michigan

General Proprietary, primarily 2-year, coed **Entrance** Minimally difficult **Housing** No **Contact** Director of Recruitment, ITT Technical Institute, 1522 East Big Beaver Road, Troy, MI 48083-1905. *Phone:* 248-524-1800 or toll-free 800-832-6817. *Fax:* 248-524-1965. *Web site:* http://www.itt-tech.edu/.

ITT Technical Institute
Wyoming, Michigan

General Proprietary, primarily 2-year, coed **Entrance** Minimally difficult **Housing** No **Contact** Director of Recruitment, ITT Technical Institute, 1980 Metro Court SW, Wyoming, MI 49519. *Phone:* 616-406-1200 or toll-free 800-632-4676. *Web site:* http://www.itt-tech.edu/.

Kalamazoo College
Kalamazoo, Michigan

General Independent, 4-year, coed, affiliated with American Baptist Churches in the U.S.A. **Entrance** Very difficult **Setting** 60-acre suburban campus **Total enrollment** 1,384 **Student-faculty ratio** 14:1 **Application deadline** 2/1 (freshmen), 5/1 (transfer) **Freshman admission** 73% were admitted. Average high school GPA 3.6 **Freshman test scores** SAT critical reading scores over 500: 89%; SAT math scores over 500: 90%; ACT scores over 18: 100%; SAT critical reading scores over 600: 66%; SAT math scores over 600: 67%; ACT scores over 24: 89% **Housing** Yes **Expenses** Tuition & Fees $32,643; Room & Board $7776 **Undergraduates** 57% women, 1% 25 or older, 0.5% Native American, 4% Hispanic American, 4% African American, 5% Asian American/Pacific Islander **The most frequently chosen baccalaureate fields are** biological/life sciences, psychology, social sciences **Academic program** Advanced placement, self-designed majors, internships **Contact** Mrs. Linda Wirgau, Records Manager, Kalamazoo College, Mandelle Hall, 1200 Academy Street, Kalamazoo, MI 49006-3295. *Phone:* 269-337-7166 or toll-free 800-253-3602. *Fax:* 269-337-7390. *E-mail:* admission@kzoo.edu. *Web site:* http://www.kzoo.edu/.

Kettering University
Flint, Michigan

General Independent, comprehensive, coed, primarily men **Entrance** Very difficult **Setting** 85-acre urban campus **Total enrollment** 2,410 **Student-faculty ratio** 16:1 **Application deadline** Rolling (freshmen), rolling (transfer) **Freshman admission** 64% were admitted. Average high school GPA 3.8 **Freshman test scores** SAT critical reading scores over 500: 85.49%; SAT math scores over 500: 96.77%; ACT scores over 18: 99.74%; SAT critical reading scores over 600: 51.62%; SAT math scores over 600: 77.42%; ACT scores over 24: 87.5% **Housing** Yes **Expenses** Tuition & Fees $29,120; Room & Board $6390 **Undergraduates** 17% women, 2% part-time, 4% 25 or older **The most frequently chosen baccalaureate fields are** business/marketing, computer and information sciences, engineering **Academic program** Advanced placement, accelerated degree program, summer session, internships **Contact** Mrs. Shari Luck, Director of Admissions, Kettering University, 1700 University Avenue, Flint, MI 48504-6214. *Phone:* 810-762-7865 or toll-free 800-955-4464 Ext. 7865 (in-state); 800-955-4464 (out-of-state). *Fax:* 810-762-9837. *E-mail:* admissions@kettering.edu. *Web site:* http://www.kettering.edu/.

Visit Petersons.com and enter keyword Kettering

See page 894 for the College Close-Up.

Kuyper College
Grand Rapids, Michigan

General Independent religious, 4-year, coed **Entrance** Moderately difficult **Setting** 34-acre suburban campus **Total enrollment** 348 **Student-faculty ratio** 15:1 **Application deadline** Rolling (freshmen), rolling (transfer) **Freshman admission** 88% were admitted. Average high school GPA 3.21 **Freshman test scores** SAT critical reading scores over 500: 100%; SAT math scores over 500: 84%; SAT critical reading scores over 600: 40%; SAT math scores over 600: 16% **Housing** Yes **Expenses**

Kuyper College (continued)
Tuition & Fees $16,416; Room & Board $6280 **Undergraduates** 50% women, 13% part-time, 16% 25 or older, 0.3% Native American, 2% Hispanic American, 4% African American, 2% Asian American/Pacific Islander **The most frequently chosen baccalaureate fields are** liberal arts/general studies, public administration and social services, theology and religious vocations **Academic program** English as a second language, advanced placement, self-designed majors, summer session, internships **Contact** Admissions Office, Kuyper College, 3333 East Beltline Avenue, NE, Grand Rapids, MI 49525. *Phone:* 616-222-3000 Ext. 632 or toll-free 800-511-3749. *Fax:* 616-222-3045. *E-mail:* admissions@kuyper.edu. *Web site:* http://www.kuyper.edu/.

Lake Superior State University
Sault Sainte Marie, Michigan

General State-supported, comprehensive, coed **Entrance** Moderately difficult **Setting** 115-acre small-town campus **Total enrollment** 2,588 **Student-faculty ratio** 16:1 **Application deadline** Rolling (freshmen), rolling (transfer) **Freshman admission** 29% were admitted. Average high school GPA 3 **Freshman test scores** ACT scores over 18: 83%; ACT scores over 24: 30% **Housing** Yes **Expenses** Tuition & Fees: state resident $8384, nonresident $16,568; Room & Board $7994 **Undergraduates** 51% women, 18% part-time, 20% 25 or older, 9% Native American, 1% Hispanic American, 1% African American, 0.5% Asian American/Pacific Islander **The most frequently chosen baccalaureate fields are** business/marketing, health professions and related sciences, security and protective services **Academic program** Advanced placement, self-designed majors, honors program, summer session, internships **Contact** Ms. Susan Camp, Director of Admissions, Lake Superior State University, 650 West Easterday Avenue, Sault Sainte Marie, MI 49783. *Phone:* 906-635-2231 or toll-free 888-800-LSSU Ext. 2231. *Fax:* 906-635-6696. *E-mail:* admissions@lssu.edu. *Web site:* http://www.lssu.edu/.

Lawrence Technological University
Southfield, Michigan

General Independent, university, coed **Entrance** Moderately difficult **Setting** 102-acre suburban campus **Total enrollment** 4,518 **Student-faculty ratio** 11:1 **Application deadline** 8/15 (freshmen), 8/15 (transfer) **Freshman admission** 50% were admitted. Average high school GPA 3.34 **Freshman test scores** ACT scores over 18: 92%; ACT scores over 24: 54% **Housing** Yes **Expenses** Tuition & Fees $23,008; Room & Board $9353 **Undergraduates** 23% women, 49% part-time, 22% 25 or older, 0.3% Native American, 1% Hispanic American, 9% African American, 22% Asian American/Pacific Islander **The most frequently chosen baccalaureate fields are** architecture, engineering, engineering technologies **Academic program** English as a second language, advanced placement, honors program, summer session, adult/continuing education programs, internships **Contact** Jane Rohrback, Director of Admissions, Lawrence Technological University, 21000 West Ten Mile Road, Southfield, MI 48075. *Phone:* 248-204-3160 or toll-free 800-225-5588. *Fax:* 248-204-2228. *E-mail:* admissions@ltu.edu. *Web site:* http://www.ltu.edu/.
Visit Petersons.com and enter keyword Lawrence

See page 904 for the College Close-Up.

Madonna University
Livonia, Michigan

General Independent Roman Catholic, comprehensive, coed **Entrance** Moderately difficult **Setting** 49-acre suburban campus **Total enrollment** 4,467 **Student-faculty ratio** 11:1 **Application deadline** Rolling (freshmen), rolling (transfer) **Freshman admission** 74% were admitted. Average high school GPA 3.18 **Freshman test scores** SAT critical reading scores over 500: 60%; ACT scores over 18: 90%; SAT critical reading scores over 600: 40%; ACT scores over 24: 36% **Housing** Yes **Expenses** Tuition & Fees $13,150; Room & Board $6808 **Undergraduates** 74% women, 47% part-time, 49% 25 or older, 0.4% Native American, 3% Hispanic American, 13% African American, 2% Asian American/Pacific Islander **The most frequently chosen baccalaureate fields are** business/marketing, health professions and related sciences, security and protective services **Academic program** English as a second language, advanced placement, accelerated degree program, self-designed majors, summer session, adult/continuing education programs, internships **Contact** Mr. Mike Quattro, Director of Enrollment Management, Madonna University, 36600 Schoolcraft Road, Livonia, MI 48150-1173. *Phone:* 734-432-5341 or toll-free 800-852-4951. *Fax:* 734-432-5393. *E-mail:* muinfo@madonna.edu. *Web site:* http://www.madonna.edu/.

Marygrove College
Detroit, Michigan

Contact Mr. John Ambrose, Director of Undergraduate Admissions, Marygrove College, Admissions Office, Detroit, MI 48221-2599. *Phone:* 313-927-1236 or toll-free 866-313-1297. *Fax:* 313-927-1345. *E-mail:* info@marygrove.edu. *Web site:* http://www.marygrove.edu/.

Michigan Jewish Institute
Oak Park, Michigan

Contact Mr. Dov Stein, Michigan Jewish Institute, 25401 Coolidge Highway, Oak Park, MI 48237. *Phone:* 248-414-6900 Ext. 103. *Fax:* 248-414-6907. *E-mail:* dstein@mji.edu. *Web site:* http://www.mji.edu/.

Michigan State University
East Lansing, Michigan

General State-supported, university, coed **Entrance** Moderately difficult **Setting** 5,192-acre suburban campus **Total enrollment** 47,278 **Student-faculty ratio** 17:1 **Application deadline** Rolling (freshmen), rolling (transfer) **Freshman admission** 73% were admitted. Average high school GPA 3.6 **Freshman test scores** SAT critical reading scores over 500: 68.1%; SAT math scores over 500: 85.9%; ACT scores over 18: 96.5%; SAT critical reading scores over 600: 30.6%; SAT math scores over 600: 53.9%; ACT scores over 24: 69% **Housing** Yes **Expenses** Tuition & Fees: state resident $10,880, nonresident $27,343; Room & Board $7394 **Undergraduates** 52% women, 8% part-time, 4% 25 or older, 1% Native American, 3% Hispanic American, 8% African American, 5% Asian American/Pacific Islander **The most frequently chosen baccalaureate fields are** business/marketing, communications/journalism, social sciences **Academic program** English as a second language, advanced placement, accelerated degree program, self-designed majors, honors program, summer session, adult/continuing education programs, internships **Contact** James Cotter, Director of Admissions, Michigan State University, 250 Administration Building, East Lansing, MI 48824. *Phone:* 517-355-8332. *Fax:* 517-353-1647. *E-mail:* admis@msu.edu. *Web site:* http://www.msu.edu/.

Michigan Technological University
Houghton, Michigan

General State-supported, university, coed **Entrance** Moderately difficult **Setting** 925-acre small-town campus **Total enrollment** 7,148 **Student-faculty ratio** 15:1 **Application deadline** Rolling (freshmen), rolling (transfer) **Freshman admission** 73% were admitted. Average high school GPA 3.56 **Freshman test scores** SAT critical reading scores over 500: 80.8%; SAT math scores over 500: 94.8%; ACT scores over 18: 100%; SAT critical reading scores over 600: 50.4%; SAT math scores over 600: 75.7%; ACT scores over 24: 73.3% **Housing** Yes **Expenses** Tuition & Fees: state resident $11,348, nonresident $23,618; Room & Board $8121 **Undergraduates** 25% women, 6% part-time, 4% 25 or older, 1% Native American, 2% Hispanic American, 2% African

American, 1% Asian American/Pacific Islander **The most frequently chosen baccalaureate fields are** business/marketing, computer and information sciences, engineering **Academic program** English as a second language, advanced placement, honors program, summer session, internships **Contact** Ms. Allison Carter, Director of Admissions, Michigan Technological University, 1400 Townsend Drive, Houghton, MI 49931-1295. *Phone:* 906-487-2335 or toll-free 888-MTU-1885. *Fax:* 906-487-2125. *E-mail:* mtu4u@mtu.edu. *Web site:* http://www.mtu.edu/.

See page 964 for the College Close-Up.

Northern Michigan University
Marquette, Michigan

General State-supported, comprehensive, coed **Entrance** Minimally difficult **Setting** 300-acre small-town campus **Total enrollment** 9,258 **Student-faculty ratio** 23:1 **Application deadline** Rolling (freshmen), rolling (transfer) **Freshman admission** 73% were admitted. Average high school GPA 2.9 **Freshman test scores** ACT scores over 18: 95%; ACT scores over 24: 38% **Housing** Yes **Expenses** Tuition & Fees: state resident $7454, nonresident $11,828; Room & Board $7846 **Undergraduates** 53% women, 9% part-time, 16% 25 or older, 3% Native American, 1% Hispanic American, 2% African American, 1% Asian American/Pacific Islander **The most frequently chosen baccalaureate fields are** business/marketing, education, health professions and related sciences **Academic program** Advanced placement, self-designed majors, honors program, summer session, adult/continuing education programs, internships **Contact** Ms. Gerri Daniels, Director of Admissions, Northern Michigan University, 1401 Preque Isle Avenue, Marquette, MI 49855. *Phone:* 906-227-2650 or toll-free 800-682-9797. *Fax:* 906-227-1747. *E-mail:* admiss@nmu.edu. *Web site:* http://www.nmu.edu/.

Northwood University
Midland, Michigan

General Independent, comprehensive, coed **Entrance** Moderately difficult **Setting** 434-acre small-town campus **Total enrollment** 2,269 **Student-faculty ratio** 26:1 **Application deadline** Rolling (freshmen), rolling (transfer) **Freshman admission** 75% were admitted. Average high school GPA 3.03 **Freshman test scores** SAT critical reading scores over 500: 39%; SAT math scores over 500: 55%; ACT scores over 18: 87%; SAT critical reading scores over 600: 6%; SAT math scores over 600: 11%; ACT scores over 24: 22% **Housing** Yes **Expenses** Tuition & Fees $18,408 **Undergraduates** 38% women, 3% part-time, 4% 25 or older, 0.4% Native American, 2% Hispanic American, 12% African American, 1% Asian American/Pacific Islander **The most frequently chosen baccalaureate fields are** business/marketing, communications/journalism, parks and recreation **Academic program** English as a second language, advanced placement, accelerated degree program, honors program, summer session, adult/continuing education programs, internships **Contact** Mr. Daniel F. Toland, Dean of Admission, Northwood University, 4000 Whiting Drive, Midland, MI 48640. *Phone:* 989-837-4273 or toll-free 800-457-7878. *Fax:* 989-837-4490. *E-mail:* miadmit@northwood.edu. *Web site:* http://www.northwood.edu/.

Oakland University
Rochester, Michigan

General State-supported, university, coed **Entrance** Moderately difficult **Setting** 1,444-acre suburban campus **Total enrollment** 18,920 **Student-faculty ratio** 21:1 **Application deadline** Rolling (freshmen), rolling (transfer) **Freshman admission** 69% were admitted. Average high school GPA 3.27 **Freshman test scores** ACT scores over 18: 86.8%; ACT scores over 24: 36.2% **Housing** Yes **Expenses** Tuition & Fees: state resident $8783, nonresident $20,498; Room & Board $7350 **Undergraduates** 61% women, 26% part-time, 21% 25 or older, 0.4% Native American, 2% Hispanic American, 9% African American, 4% Asian American/Pacific Islander **The most frequently chosen baccalaureate fields are** business/marketing, communications/journalism, health professions and related sciences **Academic program** English as a second language, advanced placement, accelerated degree program, self-designed majors, honors program, summer session, internships **Contact** Ms. Eleanor Reynolds, Interim Assistant Vice President, Student Affairs, Oakland University, Rochester, MI 48309-4401. *Phone:* 248-370-3364 or toll-free 800-OAK-UNIV. *Fax:* 248-370-4462. *E-mail:* ouinfo@oakland.edu. *Web site:* http://www.oakland.edu/.

Olivet College
Olivet, Michigan

General Independent, comprehensive, coed, affiliated with Congregational Christian Church **Entrance** Minimally difficult **Setting** 92-acre small-town campus **Total enrollment** 1,049 **Application deadline** Rolling (freshmen), rolling (transfer) **Housing** Yes **Expenses** Tuition & Fees $19,928; Room & Board $6872 **Undergraduates** 9% 25 or older **Academic program** Advanced placement, accelerated degree program, self-designed majors, honors program, summer session, internships **Contact** Mr. Larry Vallar, Vice President for Enrollment Management, Olivet College, 320 South Main Street, Olivet, MI 49076-9701. *Phone:* 269-749-7635 or toll-free 800-456-7189. *Fax:* 269-749-6617. *E-mail:* lvallar@olivetcollege.edu. *Web site:* http://www.olivetcollege.edu/.

Rochester College
Rochester Hills, Michigan

General Independent, comprehensive, coed, affiliated with Church of Christ **Entrance** Minimally difficult **Setting** 83-acre suburban campus **Total enrollment** 980 **Student-faculty ratio** 6:1 **Application deadline** Rolling (freshmen), rolling (transfer) **Freshman admission** 80% were admitted. Average high school GPA 3 **Freshman test scores** SAT critical reading scores over 500: 61%; SAT math scores over 500: 50%; ACT scores over 18: 86%; SAT critical reading scores over 600: 28%; SAT math scores over 600: 11%; ACT scores over 24: 36% **Housing** Yes **Expenses** Tuition & Fees $17,362; Room & Board $5496 **Undergraduates** 62% women, 34% part-time, 47% 25 or older, 1% Native American, 2% Hispanic American, 20% African American, 1% Asian American/Pacific Islander **The most frequently chosen baccalaureate fields are** business/marketing, family and consumer sciences, psychology **Academic program** Advanced placement, accelerated degree program, summer session, adult/continuing education programs, internships **Contact** Mr. Larry Norman, Dean of Admissions, Rochester College, 800 West Avon Road, Rochester Hills, MI 48307-2764. *Phone:* 248-218-2190 or toll-free 800-521-6010. *Fax:* 248-218-2035. *E-mail:* admissions@rc.edu. *Web site:* http://www.rc.edu/.

Sacred Heart Major Seminary
Detroit, Michigan

General Independent Roman Catholic, comprehensive, coed **Entrance** Moderately difficult **Setting** 24-acre urban campus **Total enrollment** 410 **Student-faculty ratio** 5:1 **Application deadline** 8/15 (freshmen), 8/15 (transfer) **Freshman admission** 100% were admitted. Average high school GPA 3.78 **Freshman test scores** ACT scores over 18: 100%; ACT scores over 24: 60% **Housing** Yes **Expenses** Tuition & Fees $14,390; Room & Board $7800 **Undergraduates** 38% women, 79% part-time, 83% 25 or older, 5% Hispanic American, 2% African American **The most frequently chosen baccalaureate fields are** liberal arts/general studies, philosophy and religious studies **Academic program** English as a second language, advanced placement **Contact** Fr. Michael Byrnes, Vice Rector, Sacred Heart Major Seminary, 2701 Chicago Boulevard, Detroit, MI 48206. *Phone:* 313-883-8552. *Fax:* 313-868-6400. *Web site:* http://www.shms.edu/.

Saginaw Valley State University
University Center, Michigan

General State-supported, comprehensive, coed **Entrance** Moderately difficult **Setting** 782-acre small-town campus **Total enrollment** 10,498

Saginaw Valley State University (continued)
Student-faculty ratio 22:1 **Application deadline** Rolling (freshmen), rolling (transfer) **Freshman admission** 86% were admitted. Average high school GPA 3.21 **Freshman test scores** ACT scores over 18: 77.9%; ACT scores over 24: 29.5% **Housing** Yes **Expenses** Tuition & Fees: state resident $6890, nonresident $16,200; Room & Board $7270 **Undergraduates** 58% women, 16% part-time, 20% 25 or older, 0.5% Native American, 3% Hispanic American, 9% African American, 1% Asian American/Pacific Islander **The most frequently chosen baccalaureate fields are** business/marketing, education, health professions and related sciences **Academic program** English as a second language, advanced placement, accelerated degree program, self-designed majors, honors program, summer session, adult/continuing education programs, internships **Contact** Jennifer Pahl, Director of Admissions, Saginaw Valley State University, 7400 Bay Road, University Center, MI 48710-0001. *Phone:* 989-964-4200 or toll-free 800-968-9500. *Fax:* 989-790-0180. *E-mail:* admissions@svsu.edu. *Web site:* http://www.svsu.edu/.

Siena Heights University
Adrian, Michigan

General Independent Roman Catholic, comprehensive, coed **Entrance** Moderately difficult **Setting** 140-acre small-town campus **Total enrollment** 2,351 **Student-faculty ratio** 12:1 **Application deadline** Rolling (freshmen), rolling (transfer) **Freshman admission** 69% were admitted. Average high school GPA 3.01 **Freshman test scores** ACT scores over 18: 71%; ACT scores over 24: 15% **Housing** Yes **Expenses** Tuition & Fees $19,210; Room & Board $7070 **Undergraduates** 58% women, 51% part-time, 50% 25 or older, 0.3% Native American, 4% Hispanic American, 11% African American, 1% Asian American/Pacific Islander **The most frequently chosen baccalaureate fields are** business/marketing, engineering technologies, health professions and related sciences **Academic program** English as a second language, advanced placement, accelerated degree program, self-designed majors, summer session, adult/continuing education programs, internships **Contact** Ms. Sara Johnson, Director of Admissions, Siena Heights University, 1247 East Siena Heights Drive, Adrian, MI 49221. *Phone:* 517-264-7185 or toll-free 800-521-0009. *Fax:* 517-264-7745. *E-mail:* sjohnson@sienaheights.edu. *Web site:* http://www.sienaheights.edu/.

Spring Arbor University
Spring Arbor, Michigan

General Independent Free Methodist, comprehensive, coed **Entrance** Moderately difficult **Setting** 120-acre rural campus **Total enrollment** 4,120 **Student-faculty ratio** 15:1 **Application deadline** 8/1 (freshmen), rolling (transfer) **Freshman admission** 78% were admitted. Average high school GPA 3.4 **Freshman test scores** SAT critical reading scores over 500: 69%; SAT math scores over 500: 62%; ACT scores over 18: 89%; SAT critical reading scores over 600: 24.5%; SAT math scores over 600: 24%; ACT scores over 24: 37% **Housing** Yes **Expenses** Tuition & Fees $19,790; Room & Board $6950 **Undergraduates** 68% women, 31% part-time, 9% 25 or older, 1% Native American, 2% Hispanic American, 11% African American, 1% Asian American/Pacific Islander **The most frequently chosen baccalaureate fields are** business/marketing, education, family and consumer sciences **Academic program** Advanced placement, accelerated degree program, self-designed majors, honors program, summer session, adult/continuing education programs, internships **Contact** Mr. Randy Comfort, Executive Director of Admissions, Spring Arbor University, 106 East Main Street, Spring Arbor, MI 49283-9799. *Phone:* 517-750-1200 Ext. 1468 or toll-free 800-968-0011. *Fax:* 517-750-6620. *E-mail:* admissions@arbor.edu. *Web site:* http://www.arbor.edu/.

University of Detroit Mercy
Detroit, Michigan

Contact Office of Admissions, University of Detroit Mercy, 4001 West McNichols Road, Detroit, MI 48221-3038. *Phone:* 313-993-1245 or toll-free 800-635-5020. *Fax:* 313-993-3326. *E-mail:* admissions@udmercy.edu. *Web site:* http://www.udmercy.edu/.

University of Michigan
Ann Arbor, Michigan

General State-supported, university, coed **Entrance** Very difficult **Setting** 3,070-acre small-town campus **Total enrollment** 41,674 **Student-faculty ratio** 15:1 **Application deadline** 2/1 (freshmen), 2/1 (transfer) **Freshman admission** 50% were admitted. Average high school GPA 3.75 **Freshman test scores** SAT critical reading scores over 500: 97%; SAT math scores over 500: 98%; ACT scores over 18: 100%; SAT critical reading scores over 600: 73%; SAT math scores over 600: 88%; ACT scores over 24: 94% **Housing** Yes **Expenses** Tuition & Fees: state resident $12,589, nonresident $36,352; Room & Board $8924 **Undergraduates** 49% women, 3% part-time, 2% 25 or older, 1% Native American, 4% Hispanic American, 6% African American, 12% Asian American/Pacific Islander **The most frequently chosen baccalaureate fields are** engineering, psychology, social sciences **Academic program** Advanced placement, accelerated degree program, self-designed majors, honors program, summer session, adult/continuing education programs, internships **Contact** Mr. Theodore Spencer, Director, Undergraduate Admissions, University of Michigan, Ann Arbor, MI 48109. *Phone:* 734-764-7433. *Fax:* 734-936-0740. *Web site:* http://www.umich.edu/.

University of Michigan–Dearborn
Dearborn, Michigan

General State-supported, comprehensive, coed **Entrance** Moderately difficult **Setting** 210-acre suburban campus **Total enrollment** 8,343 **Student-faculty ratio** 17:1 **Application deadline** Rolling (freshmen), rolling (transfer) **Freshman admission** 67% were admitted. Average high school GPA 3.49 **Freshman test scores** ACT scores over 18: 100.2%; ACT scores over 24: 53.1% **Housing** No **Expenses** Tuition & Fees: state resident $9100, nonresident $19,883 **Undergraduates** 52% women, 30% part-time, 0.5% Native American, 3% Hispanic American, 11% African American, 6% Asian American/Pacific Islander **The most frequently chosen baccalaureate fields are** business/marketing, education, engineering **Academic program** Advanced placement, self-designed majors, honors program, summer session, adult/continuing education programs, internships **Contact** Mr. Christopher Tremblay, Director of Admissions and Orientation, University of Michigan–Dearborn, 4901 Evergreen Road, Room 1145 UC, Dearborn, MI 48128-1491. *Phone:* 313-593-5100. *Fax:* 313-436-9167. *E-mail:* admissions@umd.umich.edu. *Web site:* http://www.umd.umich.edu/.

University of Michigan–Flint
Flint, Michigan

General State-supported, comprehensive, coed **Entrance** Moderately difficult **Setting** 72-acre urban campus **Total enrollment** 7,773 **Student-faculty ratio** 15:1 **Application deadline** 8/19 (transfer) **Freshman admission** 82% were admitted. Average high school GPA 3.19 **Freshman test scores** SAT math scores over 500: 62.5%; ACT scores over 18: 79.78%; SAT math scores over 600: 25%; ACT scores over 24: 30.75% **Housing** Yes **Expenses** Tuition & Fees: state resident $8279, nonresident $15,793; Room & Board $6874 **Undergraduates** 61% women, 34% part-time, 38% 25 or older, 1% Native American, 3% Hispanic American, 14% African American, 2% Asian American/Pacific Islander **The most frequently chosen baccalaureate fields are** business/marketing, education, health professions and related sciences **Academic program** English as a second language, advanced placement, accelerated degree program, self-designed majors, honors program, summer session, adult/continuing education programs, internships **Contact** Ms. Kimberley Buster-Williams, Director of Admissions, University of Michigan–Flint, 303 East Kearsley Street, Flint, MI 48502-1950. *Phone:* 810-762-3300 or toll-free 800-942-5636. *Fax:* 810-762-3272. *E-mail:* admissions@umflint.edu. *Web site:* http://www.umflint.edu/.

University of Phoenix–Detroit Campus

Southfield, Michigan

Contact University of Phoenix–Detroit Campus, 26999 Central Park Boulevard, Suite 100, Southfield, MI 48076. *Web site:* http://www.phoenix.edu/.

University of Phoenix–Metro Detroit Campus

Troy, Michigan

General Proprietary, comprehensive, coed **Entrance** Noncompetitive **Setting** urban campus **Total enrollment** 2,547 **Application deadline** Rolling (freshmen), rolling (transfer) **Housing** No **Expenses** Tuition & Fees $13,200 **Undergraduates** 67% women, 83% 25 or older, 1% Native American, 0.4% Hispanic American, 46% African American, 1% Asian American/Pacific Islander **The most frequently chosen baccalaureate fields are** business/marketing, computer and information sciences, security and protective services **Academic program** Advanced placement, accelerated degree program, adult/continuing education programs **Contact** Ms. Audra McQuarie, Registrar/Executive Director, University of Phoenix–Metro Detroit Campus, 4035 South Riverpoint Parkway, Mail Stop CF-L101, Phoenix, AZ 85040. *Phone:* 480-557-6151 or toll-free 800-776-4867 (in-state); 800-228-7240 (out-of-state). *Fax:* 480-643-3068. *E-mail:* audra.mcquarie@phoenix.edu. *Web site:* http://www.phoenix.edu/.

University of Phoenix–West Michigan Campus

Walker, Michigan

General Proprietary, comprehensive, coed **Entrance** Noncompetitive **Setting** urban campus **Total enrollment** 524 **Application deadline** Rolling (freshmen), rolling (transfer) **Housing** No **Expenses** Tuition & Fees $12,525 **Undergraduates** 65% women, 85% 25 or older, 0.2% Native American, 3% Hispanic American, 14% African American, 0.2% Asian American/Pacific Islander **The most frequently chosen baccalaureate fields are** business/marketing, computer and information sciences, public administration and social services **Academic program** Advanced placement, accelerated degree program, adult/continuing education programs **Contact** Ms. Audra McQuarie, Registrar/Executive Director, University of Phoenix–West Michigan Campus, 4035 South Riverpoint Parkway, Mail Stop CF-L101, Phoenix, AZ 85040. *Phone:* 480-557-6151 or toll-free 800-776-4867 (in-state); 800-228-7240 (out-of-state). *Fax:* 480-643-3068. *E-mail:* audra.mcquarie@phoenix.edu. *Web site:* http://www.phoenix.edu/.

Walsh College of Accountancy and Business Administration

Troy, Michigan

General Independent, upper-level, coed **Entrance** Noncompetitive **Setting** 29-acre suburban campus **Total enrollment** 3,106 **Student-faculty ratio** 17:1 **Application deadline** Rolling (transfer) **Housing** No **Expenses** Tuition & Fees $10,959 **Undergraduates** 55% women, 85% part-time, 67% 25 or older, 0.3% Native American, 1% Hispanic American, 5% African American, 3% Asian American/Pacific Islander **The most frequently chosen baccalaureate fields are** business/marketing, computer and information sciences **Academic program** Advanced placement, summer session, adult/continuing education programs, internships **Contact** Mr. Jeremy Guc, Director of Admissions and Advising, Walsh College of Accountancy and Business Administration, 3838 Livernois Road, PO Box 7006, Troy, MI 48007-7006. *Phone:* 248-823-1344 or toll-free 800-925-7401. *Fax:* 248-823-1611. *E-mail:* jguc@walshcollege.edu. *Web site:* http://www.walshcollege.edu/.

Wayne State University

Detroit, Michigan

General State-supported, university, coed **Entrance** Moderately difficult **Setting** 210-acre urban campus **Total enrollment** 31,786 **Student-faculty ratio** 16:1 **Application deadline** 8/1 (freshmen), 8/1 (transfer) **Freshman admission** 75% were admitted. Average high school GPA 3.12 **Freshman test scores** ACT scores over 18: 70%; ACT scores over 24: 25% **Housing** Yes **Expenses** Tuition & Fees: state resident $8643, nonresident $18,412; Room & Board $7210 **Undergraduates** 58% women, 36% part-time, 31% 25 or older, 1% Native American, 3% Hispanic American, 32% African American, 7% Asian American/Pacific Islander **The most frequently chosen baccalaureate fields are** business/marketing, education, health professions and related sciences **Academic program** English as a second language, advanced placement, accelerated degree program, honors program, summer session, adult/continuing education programs, internships **Contact** Ms. Judy Benfield Tatam, Director, Undergraduate Admissions, Wayne State University, 656 West Kirby Street, Detroit, MI 48202. *Phone:* 313-577-3577 or toll-free 877-WSU-INFO. *Fax:* 313-577-7536. *E-mail:* admissions@wayne.edu. *Web site:* http://www.wayne.edu/.

Western Michigan University

Kalamazoo, Michigan

General State-supported, university, coed **Entrance** Moderately difficult **Setting** 1,200-acre urban campus **Total enrollment** 24,576 **Student-faculty ratio** 19:1 **Application deadline** Rolling (freshmen), 8/1 (transfer) **Freshman admission** 83% were admitted. Average high school GPA 3.24 **Freshman test scores** ACT scores over 18: 90.51%; ACT scores over 24: 32.54% **Housing** Yes **Expenses** Tuition & Fees: state resident $8382, nonresident $19,502; Room & Board $7784 **Undergraduates** 49% women, 13% part-time, 12% 25 or older, 1% Native American, 3% Hispanic American, 8% African American, 2% Asian American/Pacific Islander **The most frequently chosen baccalaureate fields are** business/marketing, education, health professions and related sciences **Academic program** English as a second language, advanced placement, accelerated degree program, self-designed majors, honors program, summer session, adult/continuing education programs, internships **Contact** Mrs. Penny Bundy, Director, Office of Admissions and Orientation, Western Michigan University, 1903 West Michigan Avenue, Kalamazoo, MI 49008. *Phone:* 269-387-2000. *Fax:* 269-387-2096. *E-mail:* ask-wmu@wmich.edu. *Web site:* http://www.wmich.edu/.

Visit Petersons.com and enter keywords Western Michigan

See page 1364 for the College Close-Up.

Yeshiva Gedolah of Greater Detroit

Oak Park, Michigan

General Independent Jewish, comprehensive, men only **Setting** 1-acre campus **Total enrollment** 64 **Freshman admission** 100% were admitted **Housing** Yes **Undergraduates** 2% 25 or older **Contact** Rabbi P. Rushnawitz, Director, Yeshiva Gedolah of Greater Detroit, 24600 Greenfield, Oak Park, MI 48237-1544.

MINNESOTA

Academy College

Minneapolis, Minnesota

Contact Ms. Tracey Schantz, Director, Academy College, 1101 East 78th Street, Suite 100, Bloomington, MN 55420. *Phone:* 952-851-0066 or toll-free 800-292-9149. *Fax:* 952-851-0094. *E-mail:* admissions@academycollege.edu. *Web site:* http://www.academycollege.edu/.

Argosy University, Twin Cities
Eagan, Minnesota

General Proprietary, university, coed **Setting** suburban campus **Contact** Admissions Director, Argosy University, Twin Cities, 1515 Central Parkway, Eagan, MN 55121. *Phone:* 651-846-2882 or toll-free 888-844-2004. *Fax:* 651-994-7956. *Web site:* http://www.argosy.edu/twincities.
Visit Petersons.com and enter keywords Argosy University, Twin Cities

See page 478 for the College Close-Up.

The Art Institutes International Minnesota
Minneapolis, Minnesota

General Proprietary, 4-year, coed **Setting** urban campus **Contact** Director of Admissions, The Art Institutes International Minnesota, 15 South 9th Street, Minneapolis, MN 55402. *Phone:* 612-332-3361 or toll-free 800-777-3643. *Fax:* 612-332-3934. *Web site:* http://www.artinstitutes.edu/minneapolis/.
Visit Petersons.com and enter keywords Art Institutes International Minnesota

See page 562 for the College Close-Up.

Augsburg College
Minneapolis, Minnesota

General Independent Lutheran, comprehensive, coed **Entrance** Moderately difficult **Setting** 23-acre urban campus **Total enrollment** 3,993 **Student-faculty ratio** 13:1 **Application deadline** 8/15 (freshmen), 8/15 (transfer) **Freshman admission** 52% were admitted. Average high school GPA 3.08 **Freshman test scores** SAT critical reading scores over 500: 82.9%; SAT math scores over 500: 80%; ACT scores over 18: 89%; SAT critical reading scores over 600: 37.2%; SAT math scores over 600: 42.9%; ACT scores over 24: 39.7% **Housing** Yes **Expenses** Tuition & Fees $28,864; Room & Board $7760 **Undergraduates** 54% women, 18% part-time, 34% 25 or older, 2% Native American, 3% Hispanic American, 8% African American, 6% Asian American/Pacific Islander **The most frequently chosen baccalaureate fields are** business/marketing, education, health professions and related sciences **Academic program** English as a second language, advanced placement, self-designed majors, honors program, summer session, adult/continuing education programs, internships **Contact** Ms. Carrie Carroll, Assistant Vice President for Admissions, Augsburg College, 2211 Riverside Avenue, Minneapolis, MN 55454-1351. *Phone:* 612-330-1001 or toll-free 800-788-5678. *Fax:* 612-330-1590. *E-mail:* admissions@augsburg.edu. *Web site:* http://www.augsburg.edu/.

Bemidji State University
Bemidji, Minnesota

General State-supported, comprehensive, coed **Entrance** Moderately difficult **Setting** 89-acre small-town campus **Total enrollment** 5,175 **Student-faculty ratio** 21:1 **Application deadline** Rolling (freshmen), rolling (transfer) **Freshman admission** 81% were admitted **Freshman test scores** ACT scores over 18: 89%; ACT scores over 24: 25% **Housing** Yes **Expenses** Tuition & Fees: state resident $7510, nonresident $7510; Room & Board $6425 **Undergraduates** 53% women, 24% part-time, 21% 25 or older, 4% Native American, 1% Hispanic American, 1% African American, 1% Asian American/Pacific Islander **The most frequently chosen baccalaureate fields are** business/marketing, education, engineering technologies **Academic program** English as a second language, advanced placement, honors program, summer session, adult/continuing education programs, internships **Contact** Mr. Russ Kreager, Director of Admissions, Bemidji State University, 1500 Birchmont Drive, NE, Bemidji, MN 56601-2699. *Phone:* 218-755-2040 or toll-free 800-475-2001 (in-state); 800-652-9747 (out-of-state). *E-mail:* admissions@bemidjistate.edu. *Web site:* http://www.bemidjistate.edu/.

Bethany Lutheran College
Mankato, Minnesota

General Independent Lutheran, 4-year, coed **Entrance** Moderately difficult **Setting** 50-acre small-town campus **Total enrollment** 646 **Student-faculty ratio** 12:1 **Application deadline** 7/1 (freshmen) **Freshman admission** 83% were admitted. Average high school GPA 3.3 **Freshman test scores** ACT scores over 18: 88%; ACT scores over 24: 35% **Housing** Yes **Expenses** Tuition & Fees $20,650; Room & Board $6500 **Undergraduates** 0.4% Native American, 0.4% Hispanic American, 2% African American, 2% Asian American/Pacific Islander **The most frequently chosen baccalaureate fields are** business/marketing, communications/journalism, psychology **Academic program** Advanced placement, internships **Contact** Mr. Donald Westphal, Dean of Admissions, Bethany Lutheran College, 700 Luther Drive, Mankato, MN 56001. *Phone:* 507-344-7320 or toll-free 800-944-3066 Ext. 331. *Fax:* 507-344-7376. *E-mail:* dwestpha@blc.edu. *Web site:* http://www.blc.edu/.

Bethel University
St. Paul, Minnesota

General Independent, comprehensive, coed, affiliated with Baptist General Conference **Entrance** Moderately difficult **Setting** 247-acre suburban campus **Total enrollment** 5,438 **Student-faculty ratio** 12:1 **Application deadline** Rolling (freshmen), rolling (transfer) **Freshman admission** 80% were admitted. Average high school GPA 3.5 **Freshman test scores** SAT critical reading scores over 500: 79.73%; SAT math scores over 500: 81.08%; ACT scores over 18: 96.91%; SAT critical reading scores over 600: 48.65%; SAT math scores over 600: 41.89%; ACT scores over 24: 60.35% **Housing** Yes **Expenses** Tuition & Fees $28,080; Room & Board $8220 **Undergraduates** 61% women, 19% part-time, 3% 25 or older, 0.3% Native American, 1% Hispanic American, 4% African American, 2% Asian American/Pacific Islander **The most frequently chosen baccalaureate fields are** business/marketing, education, health professions and related sciences **Academic program** Advanced placement, accelerated degree program, self-designed majors, honors program, summer session, adult/continuing education programs, internships **Contact** Admissions Office, Bethel University, 3900 Bethel Drive, St. Paul, MN 55112. *Phone:* 651-638-6242 or toll-free 800-255-8706 Ext. 6242. *Fax:* 651-635-1490. *E-mail:* buadmissions-cas@bethel.edu. *Web site:* http://www.bethel.edu/.
Visit Petersons.com and enter keyword Bethel

See page 600 for the College Close-Up.

Brown College
Mendota Heights, Minnesota

Contact Mr. Mark Fredrichs, Registrar, Brown College, 1440 Northland Drive, Mendota Heights, MN 55120. *Phone:* 651-905-3400 or toll-free 800-6BROWN6. *Fax:* 651-905-3550. *E-mail:* RHubbard@browncollege.edu. *Web site:* http://www.browncollege.edu/.

Capella University
Minneapolis, Minnesota

General Proprietary, upper-level, coed **Entrance** Minimally difficult **Setting** urban campus **Total enrollment** 31,998 **Application deadline** Rolling (freshmen), rolling (transfer) **Expenses** Tuition & Fees $10,620 **Undergraduates** 57% women, 84% part-time, 1% Native American, 4% Hispanic American, 21% African American, 2% Asian American/Pacific Islander **The most frequently chosen baccalaureate fields are** business/marketing, computer and information sciences **Academic program** Advanced placement, accelerated degree program, summer session, adult/continuing education programs, internships **Contact** Learner Support, Capella University, 225 South Sixth Street, Capella Tower, 9th Floor, Minneapolis, MN 55402. *Phone:* 888-277-3552 or toll-free 888-CAPELLA. *Fax:* 612-977-5060. *E-mail:* info@capella.edu. *Web site:* http://www.capella.edu/.

Carleton College
Northfield, Minnesota

General Independent, 4-year, coed **Entrance** Very difficult **Setting** 955-acre small-town campus **Total enrollment** 2,009 **Student-faculty ratio** 9:1 **Application deadline** 1/15 (freshmen), 3/31 (transfer) **Freshman admission** 30% were admitted **Freshman test scores** SAT critical reading scores over 500: 99.73%; SAT math scores over 500: 99.46%; ACT scores over 18: 100%; SAT critical reading scores over 600: 92.94%; SAT math scores over 600: 95.38%; ACT scores over 24: 95.47% **Housing** Yes **Expenses** Tuition & Fees $41,304; Room & Board $10,806 **Undergraduates** 52% women, 1% part-time, 1% Native American, 6% Hispanic American, 5% African American, 10% Asian American/Pacific Islander **The most frequently chosen baccalaureate fields are** physical sciences, biological/life sciences, social sciences **Academic program** Advanced placement, accelerated degree program, self-designed majors, internships **Contact** Paul Thiboutot, Vice President and Dean of Admissions and Financial Aid, Carleton College, One North College Street, Northfield, MN 55057-4001. *Phone:* 507-222-4190 or toll-free 800-995-2275. *E-mail:* admissions@carleton.edu. *Web site:* http://www.carleton.edu/.
Visit Petersons.com and enter keyword Carleton

See page 676 for the College Close-Up.

College of Saint Benedict
Saint Joseph, Minnesota

General Independent Roman Catholic, 4-year, coed, primarily women **Entrance** Moderately difficult **Setting** 800-acre small-town campus **Total enrollment** 2,106 **Student-faculty ratio** 12:1 **Application deadline** Rolling (freshmen), rolling (transfer) **Freshman admission** 85% were admitted. Average high school GPA 3.72 **Freshman test scores** SAT critical reading scores over 500: 81%; SAT math scores over 500: 78%; ACT scores over 18: 98%; SAT critical reading scores over 600: 42%; SAT math scores over 600: 42%; ACT scores over 24: 72% **Housing** Yes **Expenses** Tuition & Fees $30,186; Room & Board $8358 **Undergraduates** 100% women, 2% part-time, 2% 25 or older, 0.4% Native American, 2% Hispanic American, 1% African American, 4% Asian American/Pacific Islander **The most frequently chosen baccalaureate fields are** business/marketing, biological/life sciences, English **Academic program** English as a second language, advanced placement, self-designed majors, honors program, internships **Contact** Ms. Karen Backes, Dean of Admissions, College of Saint Benedict, 37 South College Avenue, St. Joseph, MN 56374. *Phone:* 320-363-2196 or toll-free 800-544-1489. *Fax:* 320-363-2750. *E-mail:* admissions@csbsju.edu. *Web site:* http://www.csbsju.edu/.

The College of St. Scholastica
Duluth, Minnesota

General Independent, comprehensive, coed, affiliated with Roman Catholic Church **Entrance** Moderately difficult **Setting** 186-acre suburban campus **Total enrollment** 3,746 **Student-faculty ratio** 14:1 **Application deadline** Rolling (freshmen), rolling (transfer) **Freshman admission** 85% were admitted. Average high school GPA 3.49 **Freshman test scores** SAT critical reading scores over 500: 72%; ACT scores over 18: 95%; SAT critical reading scores over 600: 28%; ACT scores over 24: 48% **Housing** Yes **Expenses** Tuition & Fees $28,370; Room & Board $7498 **Undergraduates** 69% women, 9% part-time, 24% 25 or older, 3% Native American, 1% Hispanic American, 2% African American, 1% Asian American/Pacific Islander **The most frequently chosen baccalaureate fields are** business/marketing, biological/life sciences, health professions and related sciences **Academic program** Advanced placement, accelerated degree program, self-designed majors, honors program, summer session, adult/continuing education programs, internships **Contact** Mr. Eric Berg, Vice President for Enrollment Management, The College of St. Scholastica, 1200 Kenwood Avenue, Duluth, MN 55811-4199. *Phone:* 218-723-6053 or toll-free 800-249-6412. *E-mail:* admissions@css.edu. *Web site:* http://www.css.edu/.

College of Visual Arts
St. Paul, Minnesota

General Independent, 4-year, coed **Entrance** Moderately difficult **Setting** 2-acre urban campus **Total enrollment** 186 **Student-faculty ratio** 9:1 **Application deadline** Rolling (freshmen), rolling (transfer) **Freshman admission** 72% were admitted **Freshman test scores** ACT scores over 18: 85.4%; ACT scores over 24: 7.3% **Housing** No **Expenses** Tuition & Fees $23,988 **Undergraduates** 66% women, 3% part-time, 12% 25 or older, 2% Hispanic American, 2% African American, 4% Asian American/Pacific Islander **The most frequently chosen baccalaureate field is** visual and performing arts **Academic program** Advanced placement, honors program, summer session, internships **Contact** Anne White, Director for Student Life, College of Visual Arts, 344 Summit Avenue, St. Paul, MN 55102-2124. *Phone:* 651-757-4049 or toll-free 800-224-1536. *Fax:* 651-757-4010. *E-mail:* awhite@cva.edu. *Web site:* http://www.cva.edu/.

Concordia College
Moorhead, Minnesota

General Independent, comprehensive, coed, affiliated with Evangelical Lutheran Church in America **Entrance** Moderately difficult **Setting** 113-acre suburban campus **Total enrollment** 2,811 **Student-faculty ratio** 13:1 **Application deadline** Rolling (freshmen), rolling (transfer) **Freshman admission** 79% were admitted. Average high school GPA 3.61 **Freshman test scores** SAT critical reading scores over 500: 82%; SAT math scores over 500: 79%; ACT scores over 18: 99%; SAT critical reading scores over 600: 46%; SAT math scores over 600: 46%; ACT scores over 24: 64% **Housing** Yes **Expenses** Tuition & Fees $27,160; Room & Board $6510 **Undergraduates** 61% women, 2% part-time, 1% 25 or older, 0.2% Native American, 1% Hispanic American, 1% African American, 1% Asian American/Pacific Islander **The most frequently chosen baccalaureate fields are** business/marketing, communications/journalism, education **Academic program** Advanced placement, self-designed majors, honors program, summer session, adult/continuing education programs, internships **Contact** Mr. Scott D. Ellingson, Director of Admissions, Concordia College, 901 8th Street South, Moorhead, MN 56562. *Phone:* 218-299-3004 or toll-free 800-699-9897. *Fax:* 218-299-4720. *E-mail:* admissions@cord.edu. *Web site:* http://www.concordiacollege.edu/.

Concordia University, St. Paul
St. Paul, Minnesota

General Independent, comprehensive, coed, affiliated with Lutheran Church–Missouri Synod **Entrance** Minimally difficult **Setting** 37-acre urban campus **Total enrollment** 2,816 **Student-faculty ratio** 17:1 **Application deadline** 8/1 (freshmen), 8/1 (transfer) **Freshman admission** 56% were admitted. Average high school GPA 3.06 **Freshman test scores** ACT scores over 18: 77%; ACT scores over 24: 26% **Housing** Yes **Expenses** Tuition & Fees $27,400; Room & Board $7500 **Undergraduates** 58% women, 21% part-time, 43% 25 or older, 1% Native American, 2% Hispanic American, 10% African American, 7% Asian American/Pacific Islander **The most frequently chosen baccalaureate fields are** business/marketing, family and consumer sciences, security and protective services **Academic program** Advanced placement, accelerated degree program, self-designed majors, honors program, summer session, adult/continuing education programs, internships **Contact** Kristin Schoon, Director of Undergraduate Admission, Concordia University, St. Paul, 275 Syndicate North, St. Paul, MN 55104-5494. *Phone:* 651-641-8230 or toll-free 800-333-4705. *Fax:* 651-603-6320. *E-mail:* admission@csp.edu. *Web site:* http://www.csp.edu/.

Crossroads College
Rochester, Minnesota

General Independent, 4-year, coed, affiliated with Christian Churches and Churches of Christ **Entrance** Noncompetitive **Setting** 40-acre urban

Crossroads College (continued)
campus **Total enrollment** 160 **Student-faculty ratio** 9:1 **Application deadline** 8/15 (freshmen), 8/15 (transfer) **Freshman admission** Average high school GPA 3.15 **Freshman test scores** SAT critical reading scores over 500: 50%; SAT math scores over 500: 100%; ACT scores over 18: 76%; SAT math scores over 600: 100%; ACT scores over 24: 23% **Housing** Yes **Expenses** Tuition & Fees $13,210; Room only $3900 **Undergraduates** 47% women, 16% part-time, 32% 25 or older, 1% Native American, 3% Hispanic American, 9% African American, 2% Asian American/Pacific Islander **The most frequently chosen baccalaureate field is** theology and religious vocations **Academic program** Advanced placement, self-designed majors, adult/continuing education programs, internships **Contact** Mr. Scott Klaehn, Director of Admissions, Crossroads College, 920 Mayowood Road, SW, Rochester, MN 55902-2382. *Phone:* 507-288-4563 Ext. 304 or toll-free 800-456-7651. *Fax:* 507-288-9046. *E-mail:* admissions@crossroadscollege.edu. *Web site:* http://www.crossroadscollege.edu/.

Crown College

St. Bonifacius, Minnesota

General Independent, comprehensive, coed, affiliated with The Christian and Missionary Alliance **Entrance** Minimally difficult **Setting** 215-acre small-town campus **Total enrollment** 1,221 **Student-faculty ratio** 14:1 **Application deadline** Rolling (freshmen), rolling (transfer) **Freshman admission** 66% were admitted. Average high school GPA 3.23 **Freshman test scores** SAT critical reading scores over 500: 76%; SAT math scores over 500: 57%; ACT scores over 18: 93%; SAT critical reading scores over 600: 38%; SAT math scores over 600: 33%; ACT scores over 24: 34% **Expenses** Tuition & Fees $20,870; Room & Board $7580 **Undergraduates** 59% women, 23% part-time, 7% 25 or older **Academic program** English as a second language, advanced placement, accelerated degree program, honors program, summer session, adult/continuing education programs, internships **Contact** Mr. Bret Hyder, Assistant Director of Admissions, Crown College, 8700 College View Drive, St. Bonifacius, MN 55375-9001. *Phone:* 952-446-4144 or toll-free 800-68-CROWN. *Fax:* 952-446-4149. *E-mail:* info@crown.edu. *Web site:* http://www.crown.edu/.

DeVry University

Edina, Minnesota

General Proprietary, comprehensive, coed **Total enrollment** 207 **Application deadline** Rolling (freshmen), rolling (transfer) **Expenses** Tuition & Fees $14,080 **Undergraduates** 40% women, 56% part-time, 77% 25 or older, 5% Hispanic American, 6% African American, 4% Asian American/Pacific Islander **The most frequently chosen baccalaureate fields are** business/marketing, computer and information sciences **Academic program** Accelerated degree program **Contact** Admissions Office, DeVry University, 7700 France Avenue South, Suite 575, Edina, MN 55435. *Web site:* http://www.devry.edu/.

Dunwoody College of Technology

Minneapolis, Minnesota

Contact Shaun Manning, Director of Admissions, Dunwoody College of Technology, 818 Dunwoody Boulevard, Minneapolis, MN 55403. *Phone:* 612-374-5800 Ext. 8110 or toll-free 800-292-4625. *E-mail:* smanning@dunwoody.edu. *Web site:* http://www.dunwoody.edu/.

Globe University

Woodbury, Minnesota

Contact Ms. Christina Hilipipre, Director of Admissions, Globe University, 8089 Globe Drive, Woodbury, MN 55125. *Phone:* 651-730-5100. *Fax:* 651-730-5151. *Web site:* http://www.globeuniversity.edu/.

Gustavus Adolphus College

St. Peter, Minnesota

General Independent, 4-year, coed, affiliated with Evangelical Lutheran Church in America **Entrance** Very difficult **Setting** 340-acre small-town campus **Total enrollment** 2,475 **Student-faculty ratio** 11:1 **Application deadline** 4/1 (freshmen), rolling (transfer) **Freshman admission** 74% were admitted. Average high school GPA 3.61 **Freshman test scores** ACT scores over 18: 100%; ACT scores over 24: 81% **Housing** Yes **Expenses** Tuition & Fees $33,400; Room & Board $8400 **Undergraduates** 58% women, 1% part-time, 0.2% 25 or older, 0.4% Native American, 2% Hispanic American, 3% African American, 6% Asian American/Pacific Islander **The most frequently chosen baccalaureate fields are** business/marketing, psychology, social sciences **Academic program** Advanced placement, accelerated degree program, self-designed majors, honors program, summer session, internships **Contact** Mr. Mark Anderson, Vice President for Admission and Student Financial Aid, Gustavus Adolphus College, 800 West College Avenue, St. Peter, MN 56082-1498. *Phone:* 507-933-7676 or toll-free 800-GUSTAVU (S). *Fax:* 507-933-7474. *E-mail:* admission@gac.edu. *Web site:* http://www.gustavus.edu/.

Hamline University

St. Paul, Minnesota

General Independent, comprehensive, coed, affiliated with United Methodist Church **Entrance** Moderately difficult **Setting** 50-acre urban campus **Total enrollment** 5,166 **Student-faculty ratio** 12:1 **Application deadline** Rolling (freshmen), rolling (transfer) **Freshman admission** 75% were admitted. Average high school GPA 3.4 **Freshman test scores** SAT critical reading scores over 500: 80%; SAT math scores over 500: 73%; ACT scores over 18: 93%; SAT critical reading scores over 600: 36%; SAT math scores over 600: 20%; ACT scores over 24: 56% **Housing** Yes **Expenses** Tuition & Fees $30,503; Room & Board $8396 **Undergraduates** 56% women, 6% part-time, 6% 25 or older, 1% Native American, 3% Hispanic American, 7% African American, 5% Asian American/Pacific Islander **The most frequently chosen baccalaureate fields are** psychology, business/marketing, social sciences **Academic program** English as a second language, advanced placement, self-designed majors, honors program, summer session, internships **Contact** Mr. Milyon Trulove, Director of Admission, Hamline University, 1536 Hewitt Avenue, C1930, St. Paul, MN 55104. *Phone:* 651-523-2207 or toll-free 800-753-9753. *Fax:* 651-523-2458. *E-mail:* admission@hamline.edu. *Web site:* http://www.hamline.edu/.
Visit Petersons.com and enter keyword Hamline

Herzing College

Minneapolis, Minnesota

Contact Ms. Shelly Larson, Director of Admissions, Herzing College, 5700 West Broadway, Minneapolis, MN 55428. *Phone:* 763-231-3155 or toll-free 800-878-DRAW. *Fax:* 763-535-9205. *E-mail:* info@mpls.herzing.edu. *Web site:* http://www.herzing.edu/.

ITT Technical Institute

Eden Prairie, Minnesota

General Proprietary, primarily 2-year, coed **Contact** Director of Recruitment, ITT Technical Institute, 8911 Columbine Road, Eden Prairie, MN 55347. *Phone:* 952-914-5300 or toll-free 888-488-9646. *Web site:* http://www.itt-tech.edu/.

Macalester College

St. Paul, Minnesota

General Independent Presbyterian, 4-year, coed **Entrance** Very difficult **Setting** 53-acre urban campus **Total enrollment** 1,996 **Student-faculty ratio** 11:1 **Application deadline** 1/15 (freshmen), 4/15 (transfer) **Freshman admission** 46% were admitted **Freshman test scores** SAT critical reading scores over 500: 98.8%; SAT math scores over 500: 98.5%; ACT scores over 18: 100%; SAT critical reading scores over 600: 91.6%; SAT math scores over 600: 85.4%; ACT scores over 24: 98.1% **Housing** Yes **Expenses** Tuition & Fees $40,046; Room & Board $9078 **Undergraduates** 58% women, 2% part-time, 0.2% 25 or older, 1% Native American, 4% Hispanic American, 4% African American, 9% Asian American/Pacific Islander **Academic program** Self-designed majors, honors program, internships **Contact** Mr. Lorne T. Robinson, Dean of Admissions and Financial Aid, Macalester College, 1600 Grand Avenue, St. Paul, MN 55105-1899. *Phone:* 651-696-6357 or toll-free 800-231-7974. *Fax:* 651-696-6724. *E-mail:* admissions@macalester.edu. *Web site:* http://www.macalester.edu/.

Martin Luther College

New Ulm, Minnesota

General Independent, comprehensive, coed, affiliated with Wisconsin Evangelical Lutheran Synod **Entrance** Moderately difficult **Setting** 50-acre small-town campus **Total enrollment** 826 **Student-faculty ratio** 12:1 **Application deadline** 4/15 (freshmen), 4/15 (transfer) **Freshman admission** 98% were admitted. Average high school GPA 3.44 **Freshman test scores** ACT scores over 18: 99%; ACT scores over 24: 61% **Housing** Yes **Expenses** Tuition & Fees $10,990; Room & Board $4260 **Undergraduates** 51% women, 7% part-time, 3% 25 or older, 0.3% Native American, 0.4% Hispanic American, 1% African American, 1% Asian American/Pacific Islander **Academic program** Advanced placement, summer session **Contact** Prof. Ronald B. Brutlag, Associate Director of Admissions, Martin Luther College, 1995 Luther Court, New Ulm, MN 56073. *Phone:* 507-354-8221 Ext. 280. *E-mail:* brutlaro@mlc-wels.edu. *Web site:* http://www.mlc-wels.edu/.

McNally Smith College of Music

Saint Paul, Minnesota

General Proprietary, 4-year, coed **Entrance** Moderately difficult **Setting** 1-acre urban campus **Total enrollment** 680 **Student-faculty ratio** 9:1 **Application deadline** 8/1 (freshmen) **Housing** No **Expenses** Tuition & Fees $23,770 **Undergraduates** 21% women, 10% part-time, 15% 25 or older, 1% Native American, 5% Hispanic American, 9% African American, 3% Asian American/Pacific Islander **The most frequently chosen baccalaureate fields are** business/marketing, visual and performing arts **Academic program** Advanced placement, summer session, internships **Contact** Mrs. Kathy Hawks, Director of Admissions, McNally Smith College of Music, 19 Exchange Street East, St. Paul, MN 55101. *Phone:* 651-361-3450 or toll-free 800-594-9500. *Fax:* 651-291-0366. *E-mail:* kathy.hawks@mcnallysmith.edu. *Web site:* http://www.mcnallysmith.edu/.

Metropolitan State University

St. Paul, Minnesota

Contact Ms. Monir Johnson, Director, Metropolitan State University, 700 East 7th Street, St. Paul, MN 55106. *Phone:* 651-793-1303. *Fax:* 651-793-1310. *E-mail:* monir.johnson@metrostate.edu. *Web site:* http://www.metrostate.edu/.

Minneapolis College of Art and Design

Minneapolis, Minnesota

General Independent, comprehensive, coed **Entrance** Moderately difficult **Setting** 7-acre urban campus **Total enrollment** 733 **Student-faculty ratio** 13:1 **Application deadline** 5/1 (freshmen), 5/1 (transfer) **Freshman admission** 66% were admitted. Average high school GPA 3.2 **Freshman test scores** SAT critical reading scores over 500: 86%; SAT math scores over 500: 60%; ACT scores over 18: 97%; SAT critical reading scores over 600: 50%; SAT math scores over 600: 28%; ACT scores over 24: 44% **Housing** Yes **Expenses** Tuition & Fees $29,700 **Undergraduates** 58% women, 9% part-time, 5% 25 or older, 1% Native American, 5% Hispanic American, 2% African American, 4% Asian American/Pacific Islander **The most frequently chosen baccalaureate field is** visual and performing arts **Academic program** Advanced placement, summer session, adult/continuing education programs, internships **Contact** Mr. William Mullen, Director of Admissions, Minneapolis College of Art and Design, 2501 Stevens Avenue, Minneapolis, MN 55404-4347. *Phone:* 612-874-3762 or toll-free 800-874-6223. *E-mail:* admissions@mn.mcad.edu. *Web site:* http://www.mcad.edu/.

Minnesota School of Business–Blaine

Blaine, Minnesota

General Proprietary, 4-year, coed, primarily women **Entrance** Moderately difficult **Total enrollment** 751 **Student-faculty ratio** 22:1 **Application deadline** 10/5 (freshmen), 10/5 (transfer) **Freshman admission** 100% were admitted **Housing** No **Expenses** Tuition & Fees $21,020 **Undergraduates** 75% women, 71% part-time, 46% 25 or older, 1% Native American, 1% Hispanic American, 1% African American, 3% Asian American/Pacific Islander **Academic program** Advanced placement, adult/continuing education programs, internships **Contact** Ms. Kristen Swanson, Director of Admissions, Minnesota School of Business–Blaine, 3680 Pheasant Ridge Drive NE, Blaine, MN 55449. *Phone:* 763-225-8003. *Fax:* 763-225-8001. *E-mail:* kswanson@msbcollege.edu. *Web site:* http://www.msbcollege.edu/oncampus/blaine/.

Minnesota School of Business–Brooklyn Center

Brooklyn Center, Minnesota

Contact Mr. Bruce Christman, Director of Admissions, Minnesota School of Business–Brooklyn Center, 5910 Shingle Creek Parkway, Brooklyn Center, MN 55430. *Phone:* 763-585-7777. *Fax:* 763-566-7030. *Web site:* http://www.msbcollege.edu/.

Minnesota School of Business–Plymouth

Minneapolis, Minnesota

Contact Director of Admissions, Minnesota School of Business–Plymouth, 1455 Country Road 101 North, Plymouth, MN 55447. *Phone:* 763-476-2000. *Fax:* 763-476-1000. *Web site:* http://www.msbcollege.edu/.

Minnesota School of Business–Richfield

Richfield, Minnesota

Contact Ms. Patricia Murray, Director of Admissions, Minnesota School of Business–Richfield, 1401 West 76th Street, Suite 500, Richfield, MN 55430. *Phone:* 612-861-2000 Ext. 720 or toll-free 800-752-4223. *Fax:* 612-861-5548. *E-mail:* pmurray@msbcollege.com. *Web site:* http://www.msbcollege.edu/.

Minnesota School of Business–Rochester

Rochester, Minnesota

Contact Mr. Shan Pollitt, Director of Admissions, Minnesota School of Business–Rochester, 2521 Pennington Drive NW, Rochester, MN 55901. *Phone:* 507-536-9500 or toll-free 888-662-8772. *Fax:* 507-535-8011. *E-mail:* spollitt@msbcollege.edu. *Web site:* http://www.msbcollege.edu/.

Minnesota School of Business–St. Cloud

Waite Park, Minnesota

Contact Ms. Candi Janssen, Director of Admissions, Minnesota School of Business–St. Cloud, 1201 2nd Street South, Waite Park, MN 56387.

Minnesota School of Business–St. Cloud (continued)
Phone: 320-257-2000 or toll-free 866-403-3333. *Fax:* 320-257-0131. *E-mail:* cjanssen@msbcollege.edu. *Web site:* http://www.msbcollege.edu/.

Minnesota School of Business–Shakopee

Shakopee, Minnesota

Contact Ms. Gretchen Seifert, Director of Admissions, Minnesota School of Business–Shakopee, 1200 Shakopee Town Square, Shakopee, MN 55379. *Phone:* 952-516-7015 or toll-free 866-766-1200. *Fax:* 952-345-1201. *Web site:* http://www.msbcollege.edu/.

Minnesota State University Mankato

Mankato, Minnesota

General State-supported, university, coed **Entrance** Moderately difficult **Setting** 303-acre small-town campus **Total enrollment** 14,621 **Student-faculty ratio** 22:1 **Application deadline** Rolling (freshmen), rolling (transfer) **Freshman admission** 88% were admitted **Freshman test scores** ACT scores over 18: 91%; ACT scores over 24: 30% **Housing** Yes **Expenses** Tuition & Fees: state resident $6429, nonresident $12,861; Room & Board $6019 **Undergraduates** 51% women, 10% part-time, 11% 25 or older, 0.5% Native American, 1% Hispanic American, 4% African American, 2% Asian American/Pacific Islander **The most frequently chosen baccalaureate fields are** business/marketing, education, health professions and related sciences **Academic program** English as a second language, advanced placement, accelerated degree program, self-designed majors, honors program, summer session, adult/continuing education programs, internships **Contact** Office of Admissions, Minnesota State University Mankato, 122 Taylor Center, Mankato, MN 56001. *Phone:* 507-389-1822 or toll-free 800-722-0544. *Fax:* 507-389-1511. *E-mail:* admissions@mnsu.edu. *Web site:* http://www.mnsu.edu/.

Minnesota State University Moorhead

Moorhead, Minnesota

General State-supported, comprehensive, coed **Entrance** Moderately difficult **Setting** 119-acre urban campus **Total enrollment** 7,510 **Student-faculty ratio** 19:1 **Application deadline** 8/1 (freshmen), 8/1 (transfer) **Freshman admission** 77% were admitted **Freshman test scores** ACT scores over 18: 90.3%; ACT scores over 24: 31.9% **Housing** Yes **Expenses** Tuition & Fees: state resident $6918, nonresident $6918; Room & Board $6468 **Undergraduates** 57% women, 17% part-time, 21% 25 or older, 1% Native American, 1% Hispanic American, 3% African American, 1% Asian American/Pacific Islander **The most frequently chosen baccalaureate fields are** business/marketing, education, health professions and related sciences **Academic program** Advanced placement, self-designed majors, honors program, summer session, adult/continuing education programs, internships **Contact** Mr. Jeremy Johnson, Interim Director of Admissions, Minnesota State University Moorhead, Owens Hall, Moorhead, MN 56563-0002. *Phone:* 218-477-2161 or toll-free 800-593-7246. *Fax:* 218-477-4374. *E-mail:* dragon@mnstate.edu. *Web site:* http://www.mnstate.edu/.

National American University

Roseville, Minnesota

Contact Mr. Steve Grunlan, Director of Admissions, National American University, 1500 West Highway 36, Roseville, MN 55113. *Phone:* 651-644-1265. *Web site:* http://www.national.edu/.

North Central University

Minneapolis, Minnesota

General Independent, 4-year, coed, affiliated with Assemblies of God **Entrance** Noncompetitive **Setting** 9-acre urban campus **Total enrollment** 1,125 **Student-faculty ratio** 19:1 **Application deadline** 6/1 (freshmen), 6/1 (transfer) **Housing** Yes **Expenses** Tuition & Fees $15,701; Room & Board $5500 **Undergraduates** 57% women, 10% 25 or older **Academic program** Advanced placement, self-designed majors, summer session, internships **Contact** Ms. Sigi Shawa, Assistant Director, North Central University, 910 Elliot Avenue, Minneapolis, MN 55404-1322. *Phone:* 612-343-4460 or toll-free 800-289-6222. *Fax:* 612-343-4146. *E-mail:* admissions@northcentral.edu. *Web site:* http://www.northcentral.edu/.

Northwestern College

St. Paul, Minnesota

General Independent nondenominational, comprehensive, coed **Entrance** Moderately difficult **Setting** 107-acre suburban campus **Total enrollment** 1,947 **Student-faculty ratio** 14:1 **Application deadline** 8/1 (freshmen), 8/1 (transfer) **Freshman admission** 98% were admitted. Average high school GPA 3.48 **Freshman test scores** SAT critical reading scores over 500: 83%; SAT math scores over 500: 63%; ACT scores over 18: 97%; SAT critical reading scores over 600: 44%; SAT math scores over 600: 31%; ACT scores over 24: 55% **Housing** Yes **Expenses** Tuition & Fees $24,570; Room & Board $7720 **Undergraduates** 57% women, 3% part-time, 3% 25 or older, 0.3% Native American, 2% Hispanic American, 2% African American, 4% Asian American/Pacific Islander **The most frequently chosen baccalaureate fields are** education, business/marketing, theology and religious vocations **Academic program** Advanced placement, self-designed majors, honors program, summer session, adult/continuing education programs, internships **Contact** Mr. Kenneth K. Faffler, Director of Admissions, Northwestern College, Officer of Admissions, 3003 Snelling Avenue North, 212 Nazareth Hall, St. Paul, MN 55113-1598. *Phone:* 651-631-5111 or toll-free 800-827-6827. *Fax:* 651-631-5680. *E-mail:* admissions@nwc.edu. *Web site:* http://www.nwc.edu/.

Oak Hills Christian College

Bemidji, Minnesota

General Independent interdenominational, 4-year, coed **Entrance** Minimally difficult **Setting** 180-acre rural campus **Total enrollment** 149 **Student-faculty ratio** 14:1 **Application deadline** Rolling (freshmen), rolling (transfer) **Freshman admission** 67% were admitted. Average high school GPA 2.91 **Freshman test scores** ACT scores over 18: 68%; ACT scores over 24: 15% **Housing** Yes **Expenses** Tuition & Fees $13,480; Room & Board $4840 **Undergraduates** 52% women, 17% part-time, 19% 25 or older, 1% Native American, 1% Hispanic American, 1% African American, 2% Asian American/Pacific Islander **The most frequently chosen baccalaureate fields are** liberal arts/general studies, theology and religious vocations **Academic program** Advanced placement, internships **Contact** Shelly Fast, Assistant Director of Admissions, Oak Hills Christian College, 1600 Oak Hills Road SW, Bemidji, MN 56601. *Phone:* 218-751-8670 Ext. 1285 or toll-free 888-751-8670 Ext. 285. *Fax:* 218-751-8825. *E-mail:* admissions@oakhills.edu. *Web site:* http://www.oakhills.edu/.

Rasmussen College Eagan

Eagan, Minnesota

General Proprietary, primarily 2-year, coed, primarily women **Entrance** Moderately difficult **Setting** 10-acre suburban campus **Total enrollment** 537 **Student-faculty ratio** 12:1 **Application deadline** Rolling (freshmen), rolling (transfer) **Housing** No **Undergraduates** 65% 25 or older **Academic program** Adult/continuing education programs, internships **Contact** Ms. Jacinda Miller, Admissions Coordinator, Rasmussen College Eagan, 3500 Federal Drive, Eagan, MN 55122-1346. *Phone:* 651-687-9000 or toll-free 800-852-6367. *Web site:* http://www.rasmussen.edu/.

Rasmussen College Mankato

Mankato, Minnesota

Contact Ms. Kathy Clifford, Director of Admissions, Rasmussen College Mankato, 501 Holly Lane, Mankato, MN 56001-6803. *Phone:* 507-

Northeastern offers the world's most powerful learning experience

- Classroom study integrated with opportunities for professional work, research, and civic engagement in the United States and more than 50 other countries around the globe
- The flexibility to pursue the education that best matches up with your goals
- Experience that will inspire you to ask new questions and pursue new challenges, and open you to a more sophisticated worldview

At Northeastern, you will make an impact on the world—and the world will make an impact on you—before you graduate, enabling you to discover your passion and find your path.

www.northeastern.edu/admissions

Northeastern University

BRINGING BOOKS BACK TO LIFE.

From algebra to American government to biology, HippoCampus and Peterson's bring subjects to life by embedding multimedia lessons and course materials into our academic test prep titles. Students now have the ability to navigate from the book to a HippoCampus lesson—and back again.

HippoCampus and Peterson's originally partnered in 2008 to offer a greater number of students access to the finest educational content—and to leverage the academic playing field for high school students across the country. This venture is just another example of the innovative ways that Peterson's brings its educational resources to students, teachers, and parents.

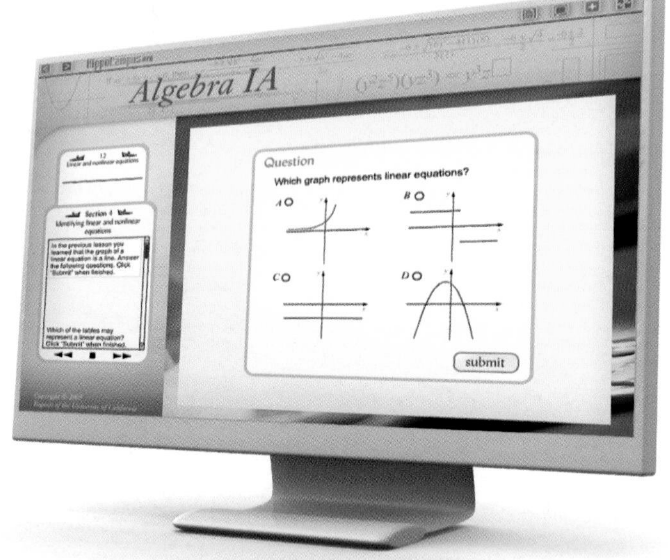

ABOUT HIPPOCAMPUS

HippoCampus is a project of the Monterey Institute for Technology and Education and is based in Marina, California. A nonprofit organization, HippoCampus is supported by The William and Flora Hewlett Foundation and was designed as part of the Open Education Resource Project, which works to improve access to high-quality education for individuals throughout the world. All the content on HippoCampus was created by colleges and universities worldwide and continues to grow.

625-6556 or toll-free 800-657-6767. *Fax:* 507-625-6557. *E-mail:* rascoll@ic.mankato.mn.us. *Web site:* http://www.rasmussen.edu/.

Rasmussen College Moorhead
Moorhead, Minnesota

Contact Rasmussen College Moorhead, 1250 29th Avenue South, Moorhead, MN 56560. *Phone:* toll-free 866-562-2758. *Web site:* http://www.rasmussen.edu/.

Rasmussen College St. Cloud
St. Cloud, Minnesota

General Proprietary, primarily 2-year, coed, primarily women **Entrance** Minimally difficult **Setting** urban campus **Total enrollment** 743 **Application deadline** Rolling (freshmen), rolling (transfer) **Housing** No **Undergraduates** 58% 25 or older **Academic program** Summer session, adult/continuing education programs, internships **Contact** Ms. Andrea Peters, Director of Admissions, Rasmussen College St. Cloud, 226 Park Avenue South, St. Cloud, MN 56301-3713. *Phone:* 320-251-5600 or toll-free 800-852-0460. *Fax:* 320-251-3702. *E-mail:* admstc@rasmussen.edu. *Web site:* http://www.rasmussen.edu/.

Rochester Community and Technical College
Rochester, Minnesota

General State-supported, primarily 2-year, coed **Entrance** Noncompetitive **Setting** 460-acre small-town campus **Total enrollment** 5,898 **Application deadline** 8/24 (freshmen), 8/24 (transfer) **Housing** No **Expenses** Tuition & Fees: state resident $4151, nonresident $4151 **Undergraduates** 34% 25 or older **Academic program** English as a second language, advanced placement, honors program, summer session, internships **Contact** Mr. Troy Tynsky, Director of Admissions, Rochester Community and Technical College, 851 30th Avenue, SE, Rochester, MN 55904-4999. *Phone:* 507-280-3509. *Web site:* http://www.rctc.edu/.

St. Catherine University
St. Paul, Minnesota

General Independent Roman Catholic, comprehensive, undergraduate: women only; graduate: coed **Entrance** Moderately difficult **Setting** 110-acre urban campus **Total enrollment** 5,277 **Student-faculty ratio** 12:1 **Application deadline** Rolling (freshmen), rolling (transfer) **Freshman admission** 67% were admitted. Average high school GPA 3.56 **Freshman test scores** ACT scores over 18: 98%; ACT scores over 24: 48% **Housing** Yes **Expenses** Tuition & Fees $28,758; Room & Board $7330 **Undergraduates** 35% part-time, 13% 25 or older, 1% Native American, 3% Hispanic American, 11% African American, 10% Asian American/Pacific Islander **The most frequently chosen baccalaureate fields are** business/marketing, English, health professions and related sciences **Academic program** Advanced placement, self-designed majors, honors program, summer session, adult/continuing education programs, internships **Contact** Ms. Cory Piper-Hauswirth, Associate Director of Admission and Financial Aid, St. Catherine University, 2004 Randolph Avenue, St. Paul, MN 55105. *Phone:* 651-690-6047 or toll-free 800-656-5283. *E-mail:* stkate@stkate.edu. *Web site:* http://www.stkate.edu/.

St. Cloud State University
St. Cloud, Minnesota

General State-supported, comprehensive, coed **Entrance** Moderately difficult **Setting** 922-acre suburban campus **Total enrollment** 17,785 **Student-faculty ratio** 19:1 **Application deadline** 6/1 (freshmen), 8/15 (transfer) **Freshman admission** 87% were admitted **Freshman test scores** ACT scores over 18: 88.23%; ACT scores over 24: 26.48% **Housing** Yes **Expenses** Tuition & Fees: state resident $6300, nonresident $13,814; Room & Board $5984 **Undergraduates** 52% women, 22% part-time, 12% 25 or older, 1% Native American, 1% Hispanic American, 4% African American, 3% Asian American/Pacific Islander **The most frequently chosen baccalaureate fields are** business/marketing, communications/journalism, education **Academic program** English as a second language, advanced placement, accelerated degree program, self-designed majors, honors program, summer session, adult/continuing education programs, internships **Contact** Mr. Richard Shearer, Director of Admissions, St. Cloud State University, 115 AS Building, 720 4th Avenue South, St. Cloud, MN 56301-4498. *Phone:* 320-308-2244 or toll-free 877-654-7278. *Fax:* 320-308-2243. *E-mail:* scsu4u@stcloudstate.edu. *Web site:* http://www.stcloudstate.edu/.

Saint John's University
Collegeville, Minnesota

General Independent Roman Catholic, comprehensive, coed, primarily men **Entrance** Moderately difficult **Setting** 2,500-acre rural campus **Total enrollment** 2,020 **Student-faculty ratio** 12:1 **Application deadline** Rolling (freshmen), rolling (transfer) **Freshman admission** 84% were admitted. Average high school GPA 3.53 **Freshman test scores** SAT critical reading scores over 500: 75%; SAT math scores over 500: 80%; ACT scores over 18: 99%; SAT critical reading scores over 600: 48%; SAT math scores over 600: 51%; ACT scores over 24: 72% **Housing** Yes **Expenses** Tuition & Fees $29,936; Room & Board $7714 **Undergraduates** 3% part-time, 1% 25 or older, 0.4% Native American, 2% Hispanic American, 2% African American, 3% Asian American/Pacific Islander **The most frequently chosen baccalaureate fields are** business/marketing, English, social sciences **Academic program** English as a second language, advanced placement, self-designed majors, honors program, internships **Contact** Mr. Matt Beirne, Director of Admission, Saint John's University, PO Box 7155, Collegeville, MN 56321-7155. *Phone:* 320-363-2196 or toll-free 800-544-1489. *Fax:* 320-363-2750. *E-mail:* admissions@csbsju.edu. *Web site:* http://www.csbsju.edu/.

Saint Mary's University of Minnesota
Winona, Minnesota

General Independent Roman Catholic, comprehensive, coed **Entrance** Moderately difficult **Setting** 350-acre small-town campus **Total enrollment** 5,565 **Student-faculty ratio** 12:1 **Application deadline** 5/1 (freshmen), rolling (transfer) **Freshman admission** 72% were admitted. Average high school GPA 3.16 **Freshman test scores** SAT critical reading scores over 500: 81%; SAT math scores over 500: 62%; ACT scores over 18: 91%; SAT critical reading scores over 600: 16%; SAT math scores over 600: 27%; ACT scores over 24: 43% **Housing** Yes **Expenses** Tuition & Fees $26,090; Room & Board $6940 **Undergraduates** 52% women, 31% part-time, 2% 25 or older, 0.3% Native American, 3% Hispanic American, 3% African American, 2% Asian American/Pacific Islander **The most frequently chosen baccalaureate fields are** business/marketing, security and protective services, visual and performing arts **Academic program** English as a second language, advanced placement, accelerated degree program, self-designed majors, honors program, summer session, adult/continuing education programs, internships **Contact** Mr. Anthony M. Piscitiello, Vice President for Admission, Saint Mary's University of Minnesota, 700 Terrace Heights, Winona, MN 55987-1399. *Phone:* 507-457-1700 or toll-free 800-635-5987. *Fax:* 507-457-1722. *E-mail:* admission@smumn.edu. *Web site:* http://www.smumn.edu/.

St. Olaf College
Northfield, Minnesota

General Independent Lutheran, 4-year, coed **Entrance** Very difficult **Setting** 300-acre small-town campus **Total enrollment** 3,099 **Student-faculty ratio** 12:1 **Application deadline** 1/15 (freshmen), 3/1 (transfer) **Freshman admission** 57% were admitted. Average high school GPA 3.63 **Freshman test scores** SAT critical reading scores over 500: 92%;

St. Olaf College (continued)

SAT math scores over 500: 95%; ACT scores over 18: 99%; SAT critical reading scores over 600: 73%; SAT math scores over 600: 72%; ACT scores over 24: 88% **Housing** Yes **Expenses** Tuition & Fees $35,500; Room & Board $8200 **Undergraduates** 55% women, 2% part-time, 1% 25 or older, 0.2% Native American, 2% Hispanic American, 2% African American, 5% Asian American/Pacific Islander **The most frequently chosen baccalaureate fields are** social sciences, biological/life sciences, visual and performing arts **Academic program** Advanced placement, self-designed majors, summer session, internships **Contact** Derek Gueldenzoph, Dean of Admissions, St. Olaf College, 1520 St. Olaf Avenue, Northfield, MN 55057. *Phone:* 507-786-3025 or toll-free 800-800-3025. *Fax:* 507-786-3832. *E-mail:* admissions@stolaf.edu. *Web site:* http://www.stolaf.edu/.

Southwest Minnesota State University
Marshall, Minnesota

General State-supported, comprehensive, coed **Entrance** Minimally difficult **Setting** 216-acre small-town campus **Total enrollment** 6,740 **Student-faculty ratio** 20:1 **Application deadline** 8/13 (freshmen), 8/13 (transfer) **Freshman admission** 65% were admitted. Average high school GPA 3.3 **Freshman test scores** ACT scores over 18: 86%; ACT scores over 24: 24% **Housing** Yes **Expenses** Tuition & Fees: state resident $7229, nonresident $7229; Room & Board $6846 **Undergraduates** 58% women, 62% part-time, 18% 25 or older, 0.5% Native American, 2% Hispanic American, 3% African American, 3% Asian American/Pacific Islander **The most frequently chosen baccalaureate fields are** business/marketing, education, parks and recreation **Academic program** English as a second language, advanced placement, accelerated degree program, self-designed majors, honors program, summer session, adult/continuing education programs, internships **Contact** Ms. LeAnn Thooft, Director of Admissions (Interim), Southwest Minnesota State University, Southwest Minnesota State University, 1501 State Street, Marshall, MN 56258, Marshall, MN 56258. *Phone:* 507-537-6286 or toll-free 800-642-0684. *Fax:* 507-537-7145. *E-mail:* leann.thooft@smsu.edu. *Web site:* http://www.smsu.edu/.

University of Minnesota, Crookston
Crookston, Minnesota

General State-supported, 4-year, coed **Entrance** Moderately difficult **Setting** 237-acre rural campus **Total enrollment** 2,279 **Student-faculty ratio** 17:1 **Application deadline** Rolling (freshmen), rolling (transfer) **Freshman admission** 83% were admitted. Average high school GPA 3.12 **Freshman test scores** SAT critical reading scores over 500: 48%; SAT math scores over 500: 49%; ACT scores over 18: 91%; SAT critical reading scores over 600: 15%; SAT math scores over 600: 19%; ACT scores over 24: 28% **Housing** Yes **Expenses** Tuition & Fees: state resident $10,647, nonresident $10,647; Room & Board $6563 **Undergraduates** 50% women, 49% part-time, 25% 25 or older **The most frequently chosen baccalaureate fields are** agriculture, business/marketing, natural resources/environmental science **Academic program** English as a second language, advanced placement, self-designed majors, honors program, summer session, internships **Contact** Ms. Amber Evans-Dailey, Director of Admissions, University of Minnesota, Crookston, 2900 University Avenue, Crookston, MN 56716-5001. *Phone:* 218-281-8569 or toll-free 800-862-6466. *Fax:* 218-281-8575. *E-mail:* umcinfo@umn.edu. *Web site:* http://www.umcrookston.edu/.

University of Minnesota, Duluth
Duluth, Minnesota

General State-supported, comprehensive, coed **Entrance** Moderately difficult **Setting** 250-acre suburban campus **Total enrollment** 11,664 **Student-faculty ratio** 21:1 **Application deadline** 12/15 (freshmen), 8/1 (transfer) **Freshman admission** 71% were admitted **Freshman test scores** SAT critical reading scores over 500: 65%; SAT math scores over 500: 70%; ACT scores over 18: 99%; SAT critical reading scores over 600: 25%; SAT math scores over 600: 29%; ACT scores over 24: 50% **Housing** Yes **Expenses** Tuition & Fees: state resident $11,004, nonresident $13,004; Room & Board $6176 **Undergraduates** 46% women, 12% part-time, 11% 25 or older **The most frequently chosen baccalaureate fields are** business/marketing, education, social sciences **Academic program** Advanced placement, self-designed majors, honors program, summer session, adult/continuing education programs, internships **Contact** Admissions, University of Minnesota, Duluth, 23 Solon Campus Center, 1117 University Drive, Duluth, MN 55812-3000. *Phone:* 218-726-7171 or toll-free 800-232-1339. *Fax:* 218-726-7040. *E-mail:* umdadmis@d.umn.edu. *Web site:* http://www.d.umn.edu/.

University of Minnesota, Morris
Morris, Minnesota

General State-supported, 4-year, coed **Entrance** Moderately difficult **Setting** 130-acre small-town campus **Total enrollment** 1,607 **Student-faculty ratio** 13:1 **Application deadline** 3/15 (freshmen), 5/1 (transfer) **Freshman admission** 71% were admitted **Freshman test scores** SAT critical reading scores over 500: 83%; SAT math scores over 500: 89%; ACT scores over 18: 96%; SAT critical reading scores over 600: 66%; SAT math scores over 600: 66%; ACT scores over 24: 56% **Housing** Yes **Expenses** Tuition & Fees: state resident $10,716, nonresident $10,716; Room & Board $7050 **Undergraduates** 58% women, 7% part-time, 5% 25 or older **The most frequently chosen baccalaureate fields are** English, biological/life sciences, social sciences **Academic program** English as a second language, advanced placement, accelerated degree program, self-designed majors, honors program, summer session, internships **Contact** Bryan Herrmann, Director of Admissions, University of Minnesota, Morris, 600 East 4th Street, Morris, MN 56267-2134. *Phone:* 320-539-6035 or toll-free 800-992-8863. *Fax:* 320-589-1673. *E-mail:* admissions@morris.umn.edu. *Web site:* http://www.mrs.umn.edu/.

University of Minnesota, Twin Cities Campus
Minneapolis, Minnesota

General State-supported, university, coed **Entrance** Moderately difficult **Setting** 2,000-acre urban campus **Total enrollment** 51,659 **Application deadline** Rolling (freshmen), rolling (transfer) **Freshman admission** 50% were admitted **Freshman test scores** SAT critical reading scores over 500: 82.48%; SAT math scores over 500: 94.12%; ACT scores over 18: 98.28%; SAT critical reading scores over 600: 52.33%; SAT math scores over 600: 76.23%; ACT scores over 24: 79.67% **Housing** Yes **Expenses** Tuition & Fees: state resident $11,017, nonresident $15,017; Room & Board $7534 **Undergraduates** 52% women, 14% part-time, 11% 25 or older, 1% Native American, 2% Hispanic American, 5% African American, 10% Asian American/Pacific Islander **The most frequently chosen baccalaureate fields are** engineering, business/marketing, social sciences **Academic program** English as a second language, advanced placement, accelerated degree program, self-designed majors, honors program, summer session, adult/continuing education programs, internships **Contact** Rachelle Hernandez, Associate Director of Admissions, University of Minnesota, Twin Cities Campus, 240 Williamson, Minneapolis, MN 55455-0213. *Phone:* 612-625-2008 or toll-free 800-752-1000. *Fax:* 612-626-1693. *E-mail:* admissions@tc.umn.edu. *Web site:* http://www.umn.edu/tc/.

University of St. Thomas
St. Paul, Minnesota

General Independent Roman Catholic, university, coed **Entrance** Moderately difficult **Setting** 78-acre urban campus **Total enrollment** 10,851 **Student-faculty ratio** 15:1 **Application deadline** Rolling (freshmen), rolling (transfer) **Freshman admission** 87% were admitted. Average high school GPA 3.52 **Freshman test scores** SAT critical reading scores over 500: 84%; SAT math scores over 500: 84%; ACT scores over 18:

100%; SAT critical reading scores over 600: 38%; SAT math scores over 600: 47%; ACT scores over 24: 71% **Housing** Yes **Expenses** Tuition & Fees $29,467; Room & Board $8042 **Undergraduates** 46% women, 6% part-time, 4% 25 or older, 0.2% Native American, 4% Hispanic American, 3% African American, 5% Asian American/Pacific Islander **The most frequently chosen baccalaureate fields are** business/marketing, communications/journalism, social sciences **Academic program** English as a second language, advanced placement, self-designed majors, honors program, summer session, internships **Contact** Ms. Marla Friederichs, Associate Vice President of Enrollment Management, University of St. Thomas, 2115 Summit Avenue, St. Paul, MN 55105-1096. *Phone:* 651-962-6150 or toll-free 800-328-6819 Ext. 26150. *E-mail:* admissions@stthomas.edu. *Web site:* http://www.stthomas.edu/.

See page 1306 for the College Close-Up.

Walden University
Minneapolis, Minnesota

General Proprietary, upper-level, coed **Total enrollment** 40,714 **Application deadline** Rolling (freshmen), rolling (transfer) **First-year students** 30% were admitted **Expenses** Tuition & Fees $9105 **Undergraduates** 73% women, 88% part-time, 82% 25 or older, 1% Native American, 13% Hispanic American, 34% African American, 1% Asian American/Pacific Islander **The most frequently chosen baccalaureate field is** business/marketing **Academic program** Advanced placement, self-designed majors, internships **Contact** Director of Admissions, Walden University, 155 Fifth Avenue South, Minneapolis, MN 55401. *Phone:* 800-925-3368 or toll-free 866-492-5336. *Fax:* 410-843-8780. *E-mail:* request@waldenu.edu. *Web site:* http://www.waldenu.edu/.

Winona State University
Winona, Minnesota

General State-supported, comprehensive, coed **Entrance** Moderately difficult **Setting** 40-acre small-town campus **Total enrollment** 8,606 **Student-faculty ratio** 21:1 **Application deadline** 3/5 (freshmen), 7/15 (transfer) **Freshman admission** 71% were admitted. Average high school GPA 3.3 **Freshman test scores** SAT critical reading scores over 500: 68%; SAT math scores over 500: 80%; ACT scores over 18: 99%; SAT critical reading scores over 600: 28%; SAT math scores over 600: 40%; ACT scores over 24: 36% **Housing** Yes **Expenses** Tuition & Fees: state resident $7916, nonresident $12,750; Room & Board $6556 **Undergraduates** 60% women, 7% part-time, 13% 25 or older, 0.4% Native American, 1% Hispanic American, 1% African American, 2% Asian American/Pacific Islander **The most frequently chosen baccalaureate fields are** business/marketing, education, health professions and related sciences **Academic program** English as a second language, advanced placement, accelerated degree program, self-designed majors, honors program, summer session, adult/continuing education programs, internships **Contact** Carl Stange, Director of Admissions, Winona State University, 170 West Sanborn, PO Box 5838, Winona, MN 55987-5838. *Phone:* 507-457-5100 or toll-free 800-DIAL WSU. *Fax:* 507-457-5620. *E-mail:* admissions@winona.edu. *Web site:* http://www.winona.edu/.

MISSISSIPPI

Alcorn State University
Alcorn State, Mississippi

General State-supported, comprehensive, coed **Entrance** Moderately difficult **Setting** 1,756-acre rural campus **Total enrollment** 3,334 **Student-faculty ratio** 15:1 **Application deadline** Rolling (freshmen), rolling (transfer) **Freshman admission** 40% were admitted. Average high school GPA 2.76 **Freshman test scores** SAT critical reading scores over 500: 12%; SAT math scores over 500: 20%; ACT scores over 18: 47%; ACT scores over 24: 6% **Housing** Yes **Expenses** Tuition & Fees: state resident $4488, nonresident $11,054; Room & Board $5384 **Undergraduates** 67% women, 10% part-time, 26% 25 or older, 1% Hispanic American, 93% African American, 0.2% Asian American/Pacific Islander **The most frequently chosen baccalaureate fields are** biological/life sciences, health professions and related sciences, liberal arts/general studies **Academic program** Advanced placement, accelerated degree program, honors program, summer session, adult/continuing education programs, internships **Contact** Mr. Emanuel Barnes, Director of Admissions, Alcorn State University, 1000 ASU Drive #300, Alcorn State, MS 39096-7500. *Phone:* 601-877-6147 or toll-free 800-222-6790. *Fax:* 601-877-6347. *E-mail:* ebarnes@alcorn.edu. *Web site:* http://www.alcorn.edu/.

Belhaven University
Jackson, Mississippi

General Independent Presbyterian, comprehensive, coed **Entrance** Moderately difficult **Setting** 42-acre urban campus **Total enrollment** 2,883 **Student-faculty ratio** 10:1 **Application deadline** Rolling (freshmen), rolling (transfer) **Freshman admission** 52% were admitted. Average high school GPA 3.3 **Freshman test scores** SAT critical reading scores over 500: 74%; SAT math scores over 500: 65%; ACT scores over 18: 92%; SAT critical reading scores over 600: 31%; SAT math scores over 600: 18%; ACT scores over 24: 26% **Housing** Yes **Expenses** Tuition & Fees $17,700; Room & Board $6500 **Undergraduates** 65% women, 6% part-time, 2% 25 or older **The most frequently chosen baccalaureate fields are** business/marketing, parks and recreation, visual and performing arts **Academic program** English as a second language, advanced placement, accelerated degree program, self-designed majors, honors program, summer session, adult/continuing education programs, internships **Contact** Ms. Suzanne T. Sullivan, Director of Admission, Belhaven University, 1500 Peachtree Street, Jackson, MS 39202. *Phone:* 601-968-5940 or toll-free 800-960-5940. *Fax:* 601-968-8946. *E-mail:* admission@belhaven.edu. *Web site:* http://www.belhaven.edu/.

Blue Mountain College
Blue Mountain, Mississippi

General Independent Southern Baptist, comprehensive, coed **Entrance** Minimally difficult **Setting** 44-acre rural campus **Total enrollment** 505 **Student-faculty ratio** 14:1 **Application deadline** Rolling (freshmen), rolling (transfer) **Freshman admission** 44% were admitted. Average high school GPA 3.37 **Freshman test scores** ACT scores over 18: 81%; ACT scores over 24: 30% **Housing** Yes **Expenses** Tuition & Fees $8570; Room & Board $3850 **Undergraduates** 68% women, 15% part-time, 34% 25 or older, 1% Hispanic American, 15% African American, 0.4% Asian American/Pacific Islander **The most frequently chosen baccalaureate fields are** education, psychology, theology and religious vocations **Academic program** Advanced placement, accelerated degree program, honors program, summer session, internships **Contact** Ms. Maria Teel, Director of Admissions, Blue Mountain College, PO Box 160, Blue Mountain, MS 38610-0160. *Phone:* 662-685-4771 Ext. 176 or toll-free 800-235-0136. *Fax:* 662-685-4776. *E-mail:* mteel@bmc.edu. *Web site:* http://www.bmc.edu/.

Delta State University
Cleveland, Mississippi

General State-supported, comprehensive, coed **Entrance** Noncompetitive **Setting** 332-acre small-town campus **Total enrollment** 4,031 **Student-faculty ratio** 15:1 **Application deadline** Rolling (freshmen), rolling (transfer) **Freshman admission** 24% were admitted. Average high school GPA 3.15 **Freshman test scores** ACT scores over 18: 75.07%; ACT scores over 24: 15.56% **Housing** Yes **Expenses** Tuition & Fees: state resident $4450, nonresident $11,520; Room & Board $5714 **Undergraduates** 61% women, 20% part-time, 37% 25 or older, 0.2% Native American, 1% Hispanic American, 39% African American, 1% Asian American/Pacific Islander **The most frequently chosen bacca-**

Delta State University (continued)
laureate fields are business/marketing, education, health professions and related sciences **Academic program** Advanced placement, honors program, summer session, adult/continuing education programs, internships **Contact** Dr. Debbie Heslep, Dean of Enrollment Services, Delta State University, Highway 8 West, Cleveland, MS 38733-0001. *Phone:* 662-846-4655 or toll-free 800-468-6378. *Fax:* 662-846-4684. *E-mail:* dheslep@deltastate.edu. *Web site:* http://www.deltastate.edu/.

ITT Technical Institute
Madison, Mississippi

General Proprietary, 4-year, coed **Contact** Director of Recruitment, ITT Technical Institute, 382 Galleria Parkway, Suite 100, Madison, MS 39110. *Phone:* 601-607-4500 or toll-free 800-209-2521. *Web site:* http://www.itt-tech.edu/.

Jackson State University
Jackson, Mississippi

General State-supported, university, coed **Entrance** Minimally difficult **Setting** 250-acre urban campus **Total enrollment** 8,783 **Student-faculty ratio** 16:1 **Application deadline** 8/1 (freshmen), rolling (transfer) **Freshman admission** 54% were admitted. Average high school GPA 2.88 **Freshman test scores** ACT scores over 18: 60%; ACT scores over 24: 9% **Housing** Yes **Expenses** Tuition & Fees: state resident $4634, nonresident $10,978; Room & Board $5810 **Undergraduates** 62% women, 14% part-time, 33% 25 or older, 0.1% Native American, 0.4% Hispanic American, 95% African American, 0.2% Asian American/Pacific Islander **The most frequently chosen baccalaureate fields are** business/marketing, education, interdisciplinary studies **Academic program** English as a second language, advanced placement, honors program, summer session, adult/continuing education programs, internships **Contact** Mrs. Linda Rush, Director, Marketing and Recruitment, Jackson State University, PO Box 17330, 1400 John R. Lynch Street, Jackson, MS 39217. *Phone:* 601-979-2911 or toll-free 800-682-5390 (in-state); 800-848-6817 (out-of-state). *E-mail:* schatman@ccaix.jsums.edu. *Web site:* http://www.jsums.edu/.

Millsaps College
Jackson, Mississippi

General Independent United Methodist, comprehensive, coed **Entrance** Moderately difficult **Setting** 100-acre urban campus **Total enrollment** 1,117 **Student-faculty ratio** 10:1 **Application deadline** Rolling (freshmen), 7/1 (transfer) **Freshman admission** 74% were admitted. Average high school GPA 3.51 **Freshman test scores** SAT critical reading scores over 500: 79.81%; SAT math scores over 500: 84.62%; ACT scores over 18: 100%; SAT critical reading scores over 600: 37.5%; SAT math scores over 600: 42.31%; ACT scores over 24: 64.17% **Housing** Yes **Expenses** Tuition & Fees $26,240; Room & Board $9252 **Undergraduates** 50% women, 2% part-time, 4% 25 or older, 0.3% Native American, 2% Hispanic American, 11% African American, 4% Asian American/Pacific Islander **The most frequently chosen baccalaureate fields are** business/marketing, psychology, social sciences **Academic program** Advanced placement, accelerated degree program, self-designed majors, honors program, summer session, adult/continuing education programs, internships **Contact** Mr. Michael Thorp, Dean of Enrollment, Millsaps College, 1701 North State Street, Jackson, MS 39210-0001. *Phone:* 601-974-1050 or toll-free 800-352-1050. *Fax:* 601-974-1059. *E-mail:* admissions@millsaps.edu. *Web site:* http://www.millsaps.edu/.

Mississippi College
Clinton, Mississippi

General Independent Southern Baptist, comprehensive, coed **Entrance** Moderately difficult **Setting** 320-acre suburban campus **Total enrollment** 4,772 **Student-faculty ratio** 16:1 **Application deadline** Rolling (freshmen), rolling (transfer) **Freshman admission** 61% were admitted. Average high school GPA 3.36 **Freshman test scores** SAT critical reading scores over 500: 58%; SAT math scores over 500: 59%; ACT scores over 18: 95%; SAT critical reading scores over 600: 28%; SAT math scores over 600: 26%; ACT scores over 24: 47% **Housing** Yes **Expenses** Tuition & Fees $13,550; Room & Board $6150 **Undergraduates** 60% women, 13% part-time, 23% 25 or older, 0.4% Native American, 1% Hispanic American, 25% African American, 1% Asian American/Pacific Islander **The most frequently chosen baccalaureate fields are** business/marketing, education, health professions and related sciences **Academic program** English as a second language, advanced placement, accelerated degree program, honors program, summer session, adult/continuing education programs, internships **Contact** Mr. Chad Phillips, Director of Admissions, Mississippi College, PO Box 4026, 200 South Capitol Street, Clinton, MS 39058. *Phone:* 601-925-3800 or toll-free 800-738-1236. *Fax:* 601-925-3804. *E-mail:* enrollment-services@mc.edu. *Web site:* http://www.mc.edu/.

Mississippi State University
Mississippi State, Mississippi

General State-supported, university, coed **Entrance** Moderately difficult **Setting** 4,200-acre small-town campus **Total enrollment** 18,601 **Student-faculty ratio** 18:1 **Application deadline** 8/1 (freshmen), 8/1 (transfer) **Freshman admission** 65% were admitted. Average high school GPA 3.17 **Freshman test scores** SAT critical reading scores over 500: 67.01%; SAT math scores over 500: 71.95%; ACT scores over 18: 93.51%; SAT critical reading scores over 600: 32.46%; SAT math scores over 600: 41.3%; ACT scores over 24: 49.94% **Housing** Yes **Expenses** Tuition & Fees: state resident $5151, nonresident $13,021; Room & Board $7520 **Undergraduates** 48% women, 10% part-time, 14% 25 or older, 1% Native American, 1% Hispanic American, 20% African American, 1% Asian American/Pacific Islander **The most frequently chosen baccalaureate fields are** business/marketing, education, engineering **Academic program** English as a second language, advanced placement, accelerated degree program, self-designed majors, honors program, summer session, adult/continuing education programs, internships **Contact** Ms. Cheryl Dill, Associate Director of Admissions and Scholarships, Mississippi State University, PO Box 6334, Mississippi State, MS 39762. *Phone:* 662-325-2224. *Fax:* 662-325-1MSU. *E-mail:* admit@msstate.edu. *Web site:* http://www.msstate.edu/.

Mississippi University for Women
Columbus, Mississippi

General State-supported, comprehensive, coed, primarily women **Entrance** Moderately difficult **Setting** 110-acre small-town campus **Total enrollment** 2,476 **Student-faculty ratio** 13:1 **Application deadline** Rolling (freshmen), rolling (transfer) **Freshman admission** 42% were admitted. Average high school GPA 3.29 **Freshman test scores** ACT scores over 18: 82%; ACT scores over 24: 27% **Housing** Yes **Expenses** Tuition & Fees: state resident $4423, nonresident $12,051; Room & Board $5164 **Undergraduates** 81% women, 23% part-time, 34% 25 or older, 0.5% Native American, 1% Hispanic American, 38% African American, 2% Asian American/Pacific Islander **The most frequently chosen baccalaureate fields are** education, business/marketing, health professions and related sciences **Academic program** Advanced placement, honors program, summer session, adult/continuing education programs, internships **Contact** Ms. Cassie Derden, Director of Admissions, Mississippi University for Women, 1100 College Street, MUW-1600, Columbus, MS 39701-9998. *Phone:* 601-329-7106 or toll-free 877-GO 2 THE W. *E-mail:* cderden@admissions.muw.edu. *Web site:* http://www.muw.edu/.

Mississippi Valley State University
Itta Bena, Mississippi

General State-supported, comprehensive, coed **Entrance** Minimally difficult **Setting** 450-acre small-town campus **Total enrollment** 2,850

Student-faculty ratio 16:1 **Application deadline** Rolling (freshmen), rolling (transfer) **Freshman admission** 30% were admitted. Average high school GPA 2.45 **Freshman test scores** ACT scores over 18: 40%; ACT scores over 24: 4% **Housing** Yes **Undergraduates** 63% women, 10% part-time, 34% 25 or older, 0.2% Native American, 1% Hispanic American, 93% African American, 0.2% Asian American/Pacific Islander **The most frequently chosen baccalaureate fields are** education, business/marketing, public administration and social services **Academic program** Honors program, summer session, internships **Contact** Ms. Nora Taylor, Director of Admissions and Recruitment, Mississippi Valley State University, 14000 Highway 82 West, Itta Bena, MS 38941-1400. *Phone:* 662-254-3344 or toll-free 800-844-6885. *Fax:* 662-254-7900. *E-mail:* nbtaylor@mvsu.edu. *Web site:* http://www.mvsu.edu/.

Rust College
Holly Springs, Mississippi

Contact Mr. Johnny McDonald, Director of Enrollment Services, Rust College, 150 Rust Avenue, Holly Springs, MS 38635-2328. *Phone:* 601-252-8000 or toll-free 888-886-8492 Ext. 4065. *Fax:* 662-252-8895. *E-mail:* admissions@rustcollege.edu. *Web site:* http://www.rustcollege.edu/.

Southeastern Baptist College
Laurel, Mississippi

Contact Mrs. Emma Bond, Director of Admissions, Southeastern Baptist College, 4229 Highway 15 North, Laurel, MS 39440-1096. *Phone:* 601-426-6346.

Tougaloo College
Tougaloo, Mississippi

Contact Ms. Juno Jacobs, Director of Admissions, Tougaloo College, 500 West County Line Road, Tougaloo, MS 39174. *Phone:* 601-977-7765 or toll-free 888-42GALOO. *Fax:* 601-977-4501. *E-mail:* jjacobs@tougaloo.edu. *Web site:* http://www.tougaloo.edu/.

University of Mississippi
University, Mississippi

General State-supported, university, coed **Entrance** Moderately difficult **Setting** 2,500-acre small-town campus **Total enrollment** 15,932 **Student-faculty ratio** 17:1 **Application deadline** Rolling (freshmen), rolling (transfer) **Freshman admission** 79% were admitted. Average high school GPA 3.17 **Freshman test scores** SAT critical reading scores over 500: 62%; SAT math scores over 500: 62%; ACT scores over 18: 94%; SAT critical reading scores over 600: 23%; SAT math scores over 600: 25%; ACT scores over 24: 44% **Housing** Yes **Expenses** Tuition & Fees: state resident $5106, nonresident $12,468; Room & Board $7778 **Undergraduates** 53% women, 8% part-time, 13% 25 or older, 0.4% Native American, 1% Hispanic American, 15% African American, 2% Asian American/Pacific Islander **The most frequently chosen baccalaureate fields are** business/marketing, education, psychology **Academic program** English as a second language, advanced placement, accelerated degree program, honors program, summer session, adult/continuing education programs, internships **Contact** Mr. Jody Lowe, Associate Director of Enrollment Services, University of Mississippi, 145 Martindale Student Services Center, University, MS 38677. *Phone:* 662-915-7226 or toll-free 800-653-6477. *Fax:* 662-915-5869. *E-mail:* admissions@olemiss.edu. *Web site:* http://www.olemiss.edu/.

University of Mississippi Medical Center
Jackson, Mississippi

Contact Ms. Barbara Westerfield, Director of Student Records and Registrar, University of Mississippi Medical Center, 2500 North State Street, Jackson, MS 39216-4505. *Phone:* 601-984-1080. *Fax:* 601-984-1079. *Web site:* http://www.umc.edu/.

University of Southern Mississippi
Hattiesburg, Mississippi

General State-supported, university, coed **Entrance** Moderately difficult **Setting** 1,090-acre suburban campus **Total enrollment** 15,293 **Student-faculty ratio** 16:1 **Application deadline** 7/1 (freshmen), 7/1 (transfer) **Freshman admission** 68% were admitted. Average high school GPA 3.06 **Freshman test scores** SAT critical reading scores over 500: 55%; SAT math scores over 500: 49%; ACT scores over 18: 86%; SAT critical reading scores over 600: 21%; SAT math scores over 600: 22%; ACT scores over 24: 31% **Housing** Yes **Expenses** Tuition & Fees: state resident $5096, nonresident $12,746; Room & Board $6200 **Undergraduates** 61% women, 14% part-time, 24% 25 or older, 0.4% Native American, 2% Hispanic American, 30% African American, 1% Asian American/Pacific Islander **The most frequently chosen baccalaureate fields are** business/marketing, education, health professions and related sciences **Academic program** English as a second language, advanced placement, accelerated degree program, honors program, summer session, internships **Contact** Mr. Jason Beverly, Senior Admissions Counselor, University of Southern Mississippi, 118 College Drive, #5166, Hattiesburg, MS 39406-1000. *Phone:* 601-266-5000. *Fax:* 601-266-5148. *E-mail:* admissions@usm.edu. *Web site:* http://www.usm.edu/.

Wesley College
Florence, Mississippi

Contact Mr. Chris Garcia, Director of Admissions, Wesley College, PO Box 1070, 111 Wesley Circle, Florence, MS 39073. *Phone:* 601-845-2265 Ext. 21 or toll-free 800-748-9972. *Fax:* 601-845-2266. *E-mail:* cgarcia@admin.wesleycollege.edu. *Web site:* http://www.wesleycollege.com/.

William Carey University
Hattiesburg, Mississippi

Contact Mr. William N. Curry, Dean of Enrollment Management, William Carey University, 498 Tuscan Avenue, Hattiesburg, MS 39401-5499. *Phone:* 601-318-6051 or toll-free 800-962-5991. *Fax:* 601-318-6154. *E-mail:* admissions@wmcarey.edu. *Web site:* http://www.wmcarey.edu/.

MISSOURI

Avila University
Kansas City, Missouri

General Independent Roman Catholic, comprehensive, coed **Entrance** Minimally difficult **Setting** 50-acre suburban campus **Total enrollment** 1,893 **Student-faculty ratio** 14:1 **Application deadline** 8/15 (freshmen), 8/15 (transfer) **Freshman admission** 43% were admitted. Average high school GPA 3.36 **Freshman test scores** SAT critical reading scores over 500: 100%; SAT math scores over 500: 50%; ACT scores over 18: 94%; SAT math scores over 600: 25%; ACT scores over 24: 39% **Housing** Yes **Expenses** Tuition & Fees $21,800; Room & Board $6350 **Undergraduates** 66% women, 17% part-time, 36% 25 or older, 1% Native American, 5% Hispanic American, 15% African American, 1% Asian American/Pacific Islander **The most frequently chosen baccalaureate fields are** business/marketing, health professions and related sciences, visual and performing arts **Academic program** English as a second language, advanced placement, accelerated degree program, summer session, adult/continuing education programs, internships **Contact** Ms. Patricia Harper, Director of Admission, Avila University, 11901 Wornall Road, Kansas City, MO 64145. *Phone:* 816-501-2400 or toll-free 800-

Avila University (continued)
GO-AVILA. *Fax:* 816-501-2453. *E-mail:* patti.harper@avila.edu. *Web site:* http://www.avila.edu/.

Baptist Bible College
Springfield, Missouri

Contact Mr. Terry Allcorn, Director of Admissions, Baptist Bible College, 628 East Kearney Street, Springfield, MO 65803-3498. *Phone:* 417-268-6000. *Fax:* 417-268-6694. *Web site:* http://www.gobbc.edu/.

Brown Mackie College–St. Louis
Fenton, Missouri

General Proprietary, primarily 2-year, coed **Contact** Director of Admissions, Brown Mackie College–St. Louis, #2 Soccer Park Road, Fenton, MO 63026. *Phone:* 636-651-3290. *Fax:* 636-651-3349.

See page 640 for the College Close-Up.

Calvary Bible College and Theological Seminary
Kansas City, Missouri

General Independent nondenominational, comprehensive, coed **Entrance** Minimally difficult **Setting** 55-acre suburban campus **Total enrollment** 276 **Student-faculty ratio** 10:1 **Application deadline** 7/15 (freshmen), 7/15 (transfer) **Freshman admission** 80% were admitted **Freshman test scores** SAT critical reading scores over 500: 100%; SAT math scores over 500: 100%; ACT scores over 18: 96%; SAT critical reading scores over 600: 100%; ACT scores over 24: 32% **Housing** Yes **Expenses** Tuition & Fees $8328; Room & Board $4400 **Undergraduates** 46% women, 33% part-time, 2% Native American, 2% Hispanic American, 8% African American, 1% Asian American/Pacific Islander **The most frequently chosen baccalaureate fields are** business/marketing, education, theology and religious vocations **Academic program** Advanced placement, self-designed majors, summer session, adult/continuing education programs, internships **Contact** Bob Crank, Director of Admissions, Calvary Bible College and Theological Seminary, 15800 Calvary Road, Kansas City, MO 64147-1341. *Phone:* 816-322-0110 Ext. 1326 or toll-free 800-326-3960. *Fax:* 816-331-4474. *E-mail:* admissions@calvary.edu. *Web site:* http://www.calvary.edu/.

Central Bible College
Springfield, Missouri

General Independent Assemblies of God, 4-year, coed **Entrance** Moderately difficult **Setting** 108-acre suburban campus **Total enrollment** 673 **Application deadline** Rolling (freshmen), rolling (transfer) **Housing** Yes **Expenses** Tuition & Fees $10,630; Room & Board $5032 **Undergraduates** 19% 25 or older **Academic program** Advanced placement, summer session, internships **Contact** James Bell, Executive Director for Enrollment Services, Central Bible College, 3000 North Grant Avenue, Springfield, MO 65803-1096. *Phone:* 417-833-2551 Ext. 1290 or toll-free 800-831-4222 Ext. 1184. *E-mail:* jbell@cbcag.edu. *Web site:* http://www.cbcag.edu/.

Central Christian College of the Bible
Moberly, Missouri

Contact Mr. Jason Rodenbeck, Director of Admissions, Central Christian College of the Bible, 911 Urbandale Drive East, Moberly, MO 65270-1997. *Phone:* 660-263-3900 or toll-free 888-263-3900. *Fax:* 660-263-3936. *E-mail:* iwant2be@cccb.edu. *Web site:* http://www.cccb.edu/.

Central Methodist University
Fayette, Missouri

General Independent Methodist, comprehensive, coed **Entrance** Moderately difficult **Setting** 80-acre small-town campus **Total enrollment** 1,031 **Student-faculty ratio** 14:1 **Application deadline** Rolling (freshmen), rolling (transfer) **Freshman admission** 66% were admitted. Average high school GPA 3.35 **Freshman test scores** ACT scores over 18: 93.13%; ACT scores over 24: 25.43% **Housing** Yes **Expenses** Tuition & Fees $18,670; Room & Board $6240 **Undergraduates** 51% women, 3% part-time, 10% 25 or older, 1% Native American, 2% Hispanic American, 9% African American, 0.4% Asian American/Pacific Islander **The most frequently chosen baccalaureate fields are** education, business/marketing, health professions and related sciences **Academic program** Accelerated degree program, honors program, internships **Contact** Mr. Larry Anderson, Director of Admissions, Central Methodist University, 411 Central Methodist Square, Fayette, MO 65248-1198. *Phone:* 660-248-6247 or toll-free 888-CMU-1854. *Fax:* 660-248-1872. *E-mail:* admissions@centralmethodist.edu. *Web site:* http://www.centralmethodist.edu/.

Chamberlain College of Nursing
St. Louis, Missouri

General Proprietary, 4-year, coed **Entrance** Moderately difficult **Setting** 15-acre urban campus **Total enrollment** 1,452 **Application deadline** Rolling (freshmen), rolling (transfer) **Freshman admission** Average high school GPA 3.04 **Housing** Yes **Undergraduates** 77% 25 or older **Academic program** English as a second language, advanced placement, summer session **Contact** Larry Veeneman, National Director of Admissions, Chamberlain College of Nursing, 6150 Oakland Avenue, St. Louis, MO 63139-3215. *Phone:* 630-953-3690 or toll-free 800-942-4310. *Fax:* 630-628-1051. *E-mail:* info@chamberlain.edu. *Web site:* http://www.chamberlain.edu/.

City Vision College
Kansas City, Missouri

Contact City Vision College, PO Box 413188, Kansas City, MO 64141-3188. *Web site:* http://www.cityvision.edu/.

College of the Ozarks
Point Lookout, Missouri

General Independent Presbyterian, 4-year, coed **Entrance** Moderately difficult **Setting** 1,000-acre small-town campus **Total enrollment** 1,356 **Student-faculty ratio** 13:1 **Application deadline** 2/15 (freshmen), 2/15 (transfer) **Freshman admission** 9% were admitted. Average high school GPA 3.53 **Freshman test scores** ACT scores over 18: 96%; ACT scores over 24: 32% **Housing** Yes **Expenses** Tuition & Fees $410; Room & Board $5300 **Undergraduates** 57% women, 2% part-time, 3% 25 or older **The most frequently chosen baccalaureate fields are** business/marketing, education, visual and performing arts **Academic program** Advanced placement, accelerated degree program, self-designed majors, internships **Contact** Mrs. Gayle Groves, Admissions Secretary, College of the Ozarks, PO Box 17, Point Lookout, MO 65726. *Phone:* 417-690-2637 or toll-free 800-222-0525. *Fax:* 417-335-2618. *E-mail:* admiss4@cofo.edu. *Web site:* http://www.cofo.edu/.

Colorado Technical University North Kansas City
North Kansas City, Missouri

General Proprietary, 4-year, coed **Entrance** Minimally difficult **Setting** suburban campus **Total enrollment** 679 **Application deadline** Rolling (freshmen), rolling (transfer) **Undergraduates** 78% women, 50% part-time, 30% 25 or older, 0.3% Native American, 1% Hispanic American, 10% African American, 1% Asian American/Pacific Islander **The most frequently chosen baccalaureate fields are** business/marketing, health professions and related sciences, security and protective services **Academic program** Advanced placement, accelerated degree program, adult/continuing education programs, internships **Contact** Angela Vietti, Director of Admissions, Colorado Technical University North Kansas

City, 520 East 19th Avenue, North Kansas City, MO 64116. *Phone:* 888-404-7555. *E-mail:* avietti@kc.coloradotech.edu. *Web site:* http://kc.coloradotech.edu/.

Columbia College
Columbia, Missouri

General Independent, comprehensive, coed, affiliated with Christian Church (Disciples of Christ) **Entrance** Moderately difficult **Setting** 33-acre urban campus **Total enrollment** 1,342 **Student-faculty ratio** 14:1 **Application deadline** 8/14 (freshmen), 8/14 (transfer) **Freshman admission** 47% were admitted. Average high school GPA 3.38 **Freshman test scores** SAT critical reading scores over 500: 60%; SAT math scores over 500: 87%; ACT scores over 18: 91%; SAT critical reading scores over 600: 13%; SAT math scores over 600: 47%; ACT scores over 24: 48% **Housing** Yes **Expenses** Tuition & Fees $15,596; Room & Board $6074 **Undergraduates** 59% women, 22% part-time, 17% 25 or older, 1% Native American, 2% Hispanic American, 6% African American, 1% Asian American/Pacific Islander **The most frequently chosen baccalaureate fields are** biological/life sciences, business/marketing, security and protective services **Academic program** English as a second language, advanced placement, self-designed majors, honors program, summer session, adult/continuing education programs, internships **Contact** Daniel Kruse, Admissions Counselor, Columbia College, 1001 Rogers Street, Columbia, MO 65216. *Phone:* 573-875-7358 or toll-free 800-231-2391 Ext. 7366. *Fax:* 573-875-7506. *E-mail:* admissions@ccis.edu. *Web site:* http://www.ccis.edu/.

Conception Seminary College
Conception, Missouri

Contact Fr. Pachomius Meade OSB, Director of Recruitment and Admissions, Conception Seminary College, PO Box 502, Conception, MO 64433-0502. *Phone:* 660-944-2886. *Fax:* 660-944-2829. *E-mail:* vocations@conception.edu. *Web site:* http://www.conceptionabbey.org/.

Cox College of Nursing and Health Sciences
Springfield, Missouri

Contact Ms. Stacy Danaher, Admission Coordinator, Cox College of Nursing and Health Sciences, 1423 North Jefferson, Springfield, MO 65802. *Phone:* 417-269-3038 or toll-free 866-898-5355. *Fax:* 417-269-3581. *E-mail:* admissions@coxcollege.edu. *Web site:* http://www.coxcollege.edu/.

Culver-Stockton College
Canton, Missouri

General Independent, 4-year, coed, affiliated with Christian Church (Disciples of Christ) **Entrance** Moderately difficult **Setting** 143-acre rural campus **Total enrollment** 754 **Student-faculty ratio** 13:1 **Application deadline** Rolling (freshmen), rolling (transfer) **Freshman admission** 60% were admitted. Average high school GPA 3.27 **Freshman test scores** SAT critical reading scores over 500: 62.5%; SAT math scores over 500: 75%; ACT scores over 18: 93%; SAT critical reading scores over 600: 37.5%; SAT math scores over 600: 62.5%; ACT scores over 24: 27% **Housing** Yes **Expenses** Tuition & Fees $22,550; Room & Board $7400 **Undergraduates** 55% women, 7% part-time, 3% 25 or older, 1% Native American, 2% Hispanic American, 9% African American, 1% Asian American/Pacific Islander **The most frequently chosen baccalaureate fields are** business/marketing, education, health professions and related sciences **Academic program** Advanced placement, self-designed majors, honors program, summer session, internships **Contact** Mr. Richard (Dick) Tabb, Interim Director of Admissions, Culver-Stockton College, One College Hill, Canton, MO 63435-1299. *Phone:* 573-288-6456 or toll-free 800-537-1883. *Fax:* 573-288-6618. *E-mail:* dtabb@culver.edu. *Web site:* http://www.culver.edu/.

DeVry University
Kansas City, Missouri

General Proprietary, comprehensive, coed **Entrance** Minimally difficult **Setting** 12-acre urban campus **Total enrollment** 1,269 **Student-faculty ratio** 18:1 **Application deadline** Rolling (freshmen), rolling (transfer) **Housing** No **Expenses** Tuition & Fees $14,080 **Undergraduates** 32% women, 46% part-time, 56% 25 or older, 1% Native American, 4% Hispanic American, 18% African American, 3% Asian American/Pacific Islander **The most frequently chosen baccalaureate fields are** business/marketing, computer and information sciences, engineering technologies **Academic program** Advanced placement, accelerated degree program, summer session, adult/continuing education programs **Contact** Admissions Office, DeVry University, 11224 Holmes Road, Kansas City, MO 64131. *Web site:* http://www.devry.edu/.

DeVry University
Kansas City, Missouri

Contact DeVry University, City Center Square, 1100 Main Street, Suite 118, Kansas City, MO 64105-2112. *Web site:* http://www.devry.edu/.

DeVry University
St. Louis, Missouri

Contact DeVry University, 1801 Park 270 Drive, Suite 260, St. Louis, MO 63146-4020. *Web site:* http://www.devry.edu/.

Drury University
Springfield, Missouri

General Independent, comprehensive, coed **Entrance** Moderately difficult **Setting** 80-acre urban campus **Total enrollment** 2,076 **Student-faculty ratio** 12:1 **Application deadline** 8/1 (freshmen), rolling (transfer) **Freshman admission** 70% were admitted. Average high school GPA 3.74 **Freshman test scores** ACT scores over 18: 100%; ACT scores over 24: 60% **Housing** Yes **Expenses** Tuition & Fees $19,854; Room & Board $6971 **Undergraduates** 53% women, 2% part-time, 4% 25 or older, 0.5% Native American, 2% Hispanic American, 3% African American, 2% Asian American/Pacific Islander **The most frequently chosen baccalaureate fields are** business/marketing, psychology, security and protective services **Academic program** English as a second language, advanced placement, accelerated degree program, self-designed majors, honors program, summer session, adult/continuing education programs, internships **Contact** Mr. Chip Parker, Director of Admission, Drury University, 900 North Benton, Springfield, MO 65802. *Phone:* 417-873-7205 or toll-free 800-922-2274. *Fax:* 417-866-3873. *E-mail:* druryad@drury.edu. *Web site:* http://www.drury.edu/.

Evangel University
Springfield, Missouri

General Independent, comprehensive, coed, affiliated with Assemblies of God **Entrance** Moderately difficult **Setting** 80-acre urban campus **Total enrollment** 1,955 **Student-faculty ratio** 18:1 **Application deadline** Rolling (freshmen) **Freshman admission** 74% were admitted **Freshman test scores** SAT math scores over 500: 66%; ACT scores over 18: 92%; SAT math scores over 600: 18%; ACT scores over 24: 40% **Housing** Yes **Expenses** Tuition & Fees $15,950; Room & Board $6000 **Undergraduates** 56% women, 6% part-time, 2% 25 or older, 1% Native American, 4% Hispanic American, 4% African American, 1% Asian American/Pacific Islander **The most frequently chosen baccalaureate fields are** business/marketing, communications/journalism, education **Academic program** Advanced placement, accelerated degree program, summer session, internships **Contact** Mr. Jeff Burnett, Director of

Evangel University (continued)
Admissions, Evangel University, 1111 North Glenstone, Springfield, MO 65802. *Phone:* 417-865-2811 Ext. 7205 or toll-free 800-382-6435. *Fax:* 417-865-9599. *E-mail:* admissions@evangel.edu. *Web site:* http://www.evangel.edu/.

Everest College
Springfield, Missouri

Contact Admissions Office, Everest College, 1010 West Sunshine, Springfield, MO 65807-2488. *Phone:* 417-864-7220. *Fax:* 417-864-5697. *Web site:* http://www.everest.edu/campus/springfield.

Fontbonne University
St. Louis, Missouri

General Independent Roman Catholic, comprehensive, coed, primarily women **Entrance** Moderately difficult **Setting** 13-acre suburban campus **Total enrollment** 3,002 **Student-faculty ratio** 13:1 **Application deadline** Rolling (freshmen), rolling (transfer) **Freshman admission** 85% were admitted **Housing** Yes **Expenses** Tuition & Fees $20,380; Room & Board $7800 **Undergraduates** 70% women, 29% part-time, 53% 25 or older, 0.3% Native American, 2% Hispanic American, 33% African American, 1% Asian American/Pacific Islander **The most frequently chosen baccalaureate fields are** business/marketing, communications/journalism, education **Academic program** English as a second language, advanced placement, accelerated degree program, self-designed majors, honors program, summer session, adult/continuing education programs, internships **Contact** Ms. Peggy Musen, Vice President for Enrollment Management, Fontbonne University, 6800 Wydown Boulevard, St. Louis, MO 63105. *Phone:* 314-889-1400. *Fax:* 314-889-1451. *E-mail:* pmusen@fontbonne.edu. *Web site:* http://www.fontbonne.edu/.

Global University
Springfield, Missouri

General Independent, comprehensive, coed, affiliated with Assemblies of God **Entrance** Noncompetitive **Setting** small-town campus **Total enrollment** 4,551 **Student-faculty ratio** 11:1 **Application deadline** Rolling (freshmen), rolling (transfer) **Expenses** Tuition & Fees $3168 **Undergraduates** 34% women, 91% part-time, 91% 25 or older **The most frequently chosen baccalaureate field is** theology and religious vocations **Academic program** Honors program, adult/continuing education programs, internships **Contact** Rev. Todd Waggoner, Enrollment and International Student Services Director, Global University, 1211 South Glenstone Avenue, Springfield, MO 65804. *Phone:* 417-862-9533 Ext. 2335 or toll-free 800-443-1083. *Fax:* 417-863-9621. *E-mail:* twaggoner@globaluniversity.edu. *Web site:* http://www.globaluniversity.edu/.

Goldfarb School of Nursing at Barnes-Jewish College
St. Louis, Missouri

General Independent, comprehensive, coed **Setting** urban campus **Total enrollment** 634 **Student-faculty ratio** 11:1 **Application deadline** Rolling (transfer) **Housing** No **Expenses** Tuition & Fees $17,020 **Undergraduates** 88% women, 29% part-time, 68% 25 or older, 0.4% Native American, 1% Hispanic American, 11% African American, 4% Asian American/Pacific Islander **The most frequently chosen baccalaureate field is** health professions and related sciences **Academic program** Advanced placement, accelerated degree program, summer session **Contact** Dr. Michael D. Ward, Associate Dean for Student Programs, Goldfarb School of Nursing at Barnes-Jewish College, 4483 Duncan Avenue, St. Louis, MO 63110. *Phone:* 314-362-9155 or toll-free 800-832-9009. *E-mail:* mward@bjc.org. *Web site:* http://www.barnesjewishcollege.edu/.

Graceland University
Independence, Missouri

General Independent Community of Christ, comprehensive, coed **Contact** Admissions, Graceland University, 1401 West Truman Road, Independence, MO 64050-3434. *Phone:* 816-833-0524. *E-mail:* gic@graceland.edu. *Web site:* http://www.graceland.edu/.

Grantham University
Kansas City, Missouri

General Proprietary, comprehensive, coed **Entrance** Noncompetitive **Setting** urban campus **Total enrollment** 6,214 **Application deadline** Rolling (freshmen), rolling (transfer) **Housing** No **Expenses** Tuition & Fees $7950 **Undergraduates** 1% Native American, 6% Hispanic American, 16% African American, 2% Asian American/Pacific Islander **Academic program** Advanced placement, accelerated degree program, self-designed majors, adult/continuing education programs **Contact** Mr. Matthew Hawes, Vice President of Enrollment Management, Grantham University, 7200 NW 86th Street, Kansas City, MO 64153. *Phone:* 800-955-2527 or toll-free 800-955-2527. *Fax:* 816-595-5757. *E-mail:* admissions@grantham.edu. *Web site:* http://www.grantham.edu/.

Hannibal-LaGrange College
Hannibal, Missouri

General Independent Southern Baptist, comprehensive, coed **Entrance** Moderately difficult **Setting** 110-acre small-town campus **Total enrollment** 977 **Student-faculty ratio** 14:1 **Application deadline** 9/10 (freshmen), rolling (transfer) **Freshman admission** 94% were admitted **Housing** Yes **Expenses** Tuition & Fees $15,380; Room & Board $6000 **Undergraduates** 63% women, 12% part-time, 19% 25 or older, 0.4% Native American, 2% Hispanic American, 3% African American, 1% Asian American/Pacific Islander **Academic program** English as a second language, advanced placement, accelerated degree program, self-designed majors, honors program, summer session, adult/continuing education programs, internships **Contact** Dr. Raymond Carty, Vice President for Enrollment Management, Hannibal-LaGrange College, 2800 Palmyra Road, Hannibal, MO 63401-1999. *Phone:* 573-629-2278 or toll-free 800-HLG-1119. *E-mail:* admissio@hlg.edu. *Web site:* http://www.hlg.edu/.

Harris-Stowe State University
St. Louis, Missouri

General State-supported, 4-year, coed **Entrance** Noncompetitive **Setting** 22-acre urban campus **Total enrollment** 1,886 **Student-faculty ratio** 30:1 **Application deadline** Rolling (freshmen), rolling (transfer) **Freshman admission** 94% were admitted **Freshman test scores** ACT scores over 18: 25%; ACT scores over 24: 1% **Housing** Yes **Expenses** Tuition & Fees: state resident $5320, nonresident $10,092; Room & Board $7861 **Undergraduates** 67% women, 25% part-time, 39% 25 or older, 0.1% Native American, 1% Hispanic American, 91% African American, 0.1% Asian American/Pacific Islander **The most frequently chosen baccalaureate fields are** business/marketing, education, security and protective services **Academic program** Advanced placement, self-designed majors, summer session, internships **Contact** Meghan Sprung, Assistant Director of Admissions, Harris-Stowe State University, 3026 Laclede Avenue, St. Louis, MO 63103. *Phone:* 314-340-3300. *Fax:* 314-340-3555. *E-mail:* admissions@hssu.edu. *Web site:* http://www.hssu.edu/.

Hickey College
St. Louis, Missouri

General Private, 4-year, coed **Setting** 9-acre suburban campus **Total enrollment** 359 **Freshman admission** 74% were admitted **Housing** Yes **Undergraduates** 77% women, 30% 25 or older, 1% Hispanic American, 17% African American, 1% Asian American/Pacific Islander **Academic**

program Accelerated degree program, internships **Contact** Admissions Office, Hickey College, 940 West Port Plaza, Suite 101, St. Louis, MO 63146. *Phone:* 314-434-2212 or toll-free 800-777-1544. *Web site:* http://www.hickeycollege.edu/.

ITT Technical Institute
Arnold, Missouri

General Proprietary, primarily 2-year, coed **Entrance** Minimally difficult **Housing** No **Contact** Director of Recruitment, ITT Technical Institute, 1930 Meyer Drury Drive, Arnold, MO 63010. *Phone:* 636-464-6600 or toll-free 888-488-1082. *Web site:* http://www.itt-tech.edu/.

ITT Technical Institute
Earth City, Missouri

General Proprietary, primarily 2-year, coed **Entrance** Minimally difficult **Setting** suburban campus **Housing** No **Contact** Director of Recruitment, ITT Technical Institute, 3640 Corporate Trail Drive, Earth City, MO 63045. *Phone:* 314-298-7800 or toll-free 800-235-5488. *Web site:* http://www.itt-tech.edu/.

ITT Technical Institute
Kansas City, Missouri

General Proprietary, primarily 2-year, coed **Contact** Director of Recruitment, ITT Technical Institute, 9150 East 41st Terrace, Kansas City, MO 64133. *Phone:* 816-276-1400 or toll-free 877-488-1442. *Web site:* http://www.itt-tech.edu/.

ITT Technical Institute
Springfield, Missouri

General Proprietary, 4-year, coed **Contact** Director of Recruitment, ITT Technical Institute, 3216 South National Avenue, Springfield, MO 65807. *Phone:* 417-877-4800 or toll-free 877-219-4387. *Web site:* http://www.itt-tech.edu/.

Kansas City Art Institute
Kansas City, Missouri

General Independent, 4-year, coed **Entrance** Moderately difficult **Setting** 18-acre urban campus **Total enrollment** 676 **Student-faculty ratio** 12:1 **Application deadline** Rolling (freshmen), rolling (transfer) **Freshman admission** 63% were admitted. Average high school GPA 3.19 **Freshman test scores** SAT critical reading scores over 500: 78%; SAT math scores over 500: 71%; ACT scores over 18: 96%; SAT critical reading scores over 600: 39%; SAT math scores over 600: 32%; ACT scores over 24: 45% **Housing** Yes **Expenses** Tuition & Fees $28,580; Room & Board $8710 **Undergraduates** 55% women, 1% part-time, 12% 25 or older, 1% Native American, 5% Hispanic American, 3% African American, 4% Asian American/Pacific Islander **The most frequently chosen baccalaureate field is** visual and performing arts **Academic program** English as a second language, advanced placement, summer session, internships **Contact** Mr. Gerald Valet, Director of Admission Technology, Kansas City Art Institute, 4415 Warwick Boulevard, Kansas City, MO 64111-1874. *Phone:* 816-474-5224 or toll-free 800-522-5224. *Fax:* 816-802-3309. *E-mail:* admiss@kcai.edu. *Web site:* http://www.kcai.edu/.

Lincoln University
Jefferson City, Missouri

General State-supported, comprehensive, coed **Entrance** Noncompetitive **Setting** 165-acre small-town campus **Total enrollment** 3,314 **Student-faculty ratio** 15:1 **Application deadline** 7/15 (freshmen), 7/15 (transfer) **Freshman admission** 68% were admitted. Average high school GPA 2.6 **Freshman test scores** ACT scores over 18: 41.9%; ACT scores over 24: 6.22% **Housing** Yes **Expenses** Tuition & Fees: state resident $5685, nonresident $10,395 **Undergraduates** 60% women, 32% part-time, 27% 25 or older, 0.4% Native American, 2% Hispanic American, 46% African American, 1% Asian American/Pacific Islander **The most frequently chosen baccalaureate fields are** business/marketing, education, security and protective services **Academic program** Advanced placement, accelerated degree program, honors program, summer session, adult/continuing education programs, internships **Contact** Mr. Mike Kosher, Director of Admissions, Lincoln University, Office of Admissions, 820 Chestnut Street, B-7 Young Hall, Jefferson City, MO 65102-0029. *Phone:* 573-681-5599 or toll-free 800-521-5052. *Fax:* 573-681-5889. *E-mail:* enroll@lincolnu.edu. *Web site:* http://www.lincolnu.edu/.

Lindenwood University
St. Charles, Missouri

General Independent Presbyterian, comprehensive, coed **Entrance** Moderately difficult **Setting** 500-acre suburban campus **Total enrollment** 10,413 **Student-faculty ratio** 20:1 **Application deadline** Rolling (freshmen), rolling (transfer) **Freshman admission** 57% were admitted. Average high school GPA 3.08 **Freshman test scores** SAT critical reading scores over 500: 56%; SAT math scores over 500: 57%; ACT scores over 18: 98%; SAT critical reading scores over 600: 18%; SAT math scores over 600: 22%; ACT scores over 24: 29% **Housing** Yes **Expenses** Tuition & Fees $13,600; Room & Board $7210 **Undergraduates** 56% women, 9% part-time, 30% 25 or older, 0.2% Native American, 3% Hispanic American, 9% African American, 1% Asian American/Pacific Islander **The most frequently chosen baccalaureate fields are** business/marketing, education, social sciences **Academic program** English as a second language, advanced placement, accelerated degree program, self-designed majors, honors program, summer session, adult/continuing education programs, internships **Contact** Mr. Joseph Parisi, Dean of Undergraduate Day Admissions, Lindenwood University, 209 South Kingshighway, St. Charles, MO 63301-1695. *Phone:* 636-949-4949. *Fax:* 636-949-4989. *E-mail:* jparisi@lindenwood.edu. *Web site:* http://www.lindenwood.edu/.

Visit Petersons.com and enter keyword Lindenwood

See page 920 for the College Close-Up.

Logan University–College of Chiropractic
Chesterfield, Missouri

General Independent, upper-level, coed **Entrance** Moderately difficult **Setting** 111-acre suburban campus **Total enrollment** 1,054 **Application deadline** Rolling (transfer) **Housing** No **Expenses** Tuition & Fees $5730 **Undergraduates** 43% women, 37% part-time, 42% 25 or older, 3% Native American, 1% Hispanic American, 4% African American, 3% Asian American/Pacific Islander **The most frequently chosen baccalaureate field is** biological/life sciences **Academic program** Advanced placement, adult/continuing education programs, internships **Contact** Dr. Tom Huebner, Vice President of Enrollment, Logan University–College of Chiropractic, 1851 Schoettler Road, Chesterfield, MO 63006-1065. *Phone:* 636-227-2100 or toll-free 800-533-9210. *Fax:* 636-207-2425. *E-mail:* loganadm@logan.edu. *Web site:* http://www.logan.edu/.

Maryville University of Saint Louis
St. Louis, Missouri

General Independent, comprehensive, coed **Entrance** Moderately difficult **Setting** 130-acre suburban campus **Total enrollment** 3,534 **Student-faculty ratio** 12:1 **Application deadline** 8/15 (freshmen), rolling (transfer) **Freshman admission** 66% were admitted. Average high school GPA 3.53 **Freshman test scores** ACT scores over 18: 98%; ACT scores over 24: 57% **Housing** Yes **Expenses** Tuition & Fees $20,994; Room & Board $8210 **Undergraduates** 76% women, 43% part-time, 40% 25 or older, 1% Native American, 2% Hispanic American, 7% African American, 2% Asian American/Pacific Islander **The most fre-**

Maryville University of Saint Louis (continued)

quently chosen baccalaureate fields are business/marketing, health professions and related sciences, psychology **Academic program** Advanced placement, accelerated degree program, honors program, summer session, adult/continuing education programs, internships **Contact** Ms. Shani Lenore-Jenkins, Assistant Vice President of Enrollment, Maryville University of Saint Louis, 650 Maryville University Drive, St. Louis, MO 63141-7299. *Phone:* 314-529-9350 or toll-free 800-627-9855. *Fax:* 314-529-9927. *E-mail:* admissions@maryville.edu. *Web site:* http://www.maryville.edu/.

Messenger College

Joplin, Missouri

General Independent Pentecostal, 4-year, coed **Entrance** Moderately difficult **Setting** 16-acre suburban campus **Total enrollment** 70 **Application deadline** 8/14 (freshmen), 8/14 (transfer) **Freshman admission** 77% were admitted **Freshman test scores** ACT scores over 18: 57%; ACT scores over 24: 21% **Housing** Yes **Expenses** Tuition & Fees $7495; Room & Board $4000 **Undergraduates** 50% women, 17% part-time, 23% 25 or older, 3% Native American, 9% Hispanic American, 7% African American, 1% Asian American/Pacific Islander **Academic program** Honors program, internships **Contact** Ron Cannon, Vice President of Academic Affairs, Messenger College, 300 East 50th Street, Joplin, MO 64804. *Phone:* 417-624-7070 Ext. 108 or toll-free 800-385-8940. *Fax:* 417-624-5070. *E-mail:* info@messengercollege.edu. *Web site:* http://www.messengercollege.edu/.

Metro Business College

Cape Girardeau, Missouri

General Proprietary, primarily 2-year, coed **Entrance** Minimally difficult **Total enrollment** 396 **Housing** No **Undergraduates** 57% 25 or older **Contact** Ms. Kyla Evans, Admissions Director, Metro Business College, 1732 North Kingshighway, Cape Girardeau, MO 63701. *Phone:* 573-334-9181. *Fax:* 573-334-0617. *Web site:* http://www.metrobusinesscollege.edu/.

Midwest University

Wentzville, Missouri

Contact Jeoung H. Ham, Registrar/Director of Admissions, Midwest University, PO Box 365, 851 Parr Road, Wentzville, MO 63385. *Phone:* 636-327-4645. *E-mail:* usa@midwest.edu. *Web site:* http://www.midwest.edu/.

Missouri Baptist University

St. Louis, Missouri

General Independent Southern Baptist, comprehensive, coed **Entrance** Moderately difficult **Setting** 65-acre suburban campus **Total enrollment** 4,836 **Student-faculty ratio** 18:1 **Application deadline** Rolling (freshmen), rolling (transfer) **Freshman admission** 59% were admitted **Housing** Yes **Expenses** Tuition & Fees $17,860; Room & Board $7090 **Undergraduates** 61% women, 62% part-time, 28% 25 or older, 1% Native American, 3% Hispanic American, 11% African American, 1% Asian American/Pacific Islander **The most frequently chosen baccalaureate fields are** business/marketing, education, psychology **Academic program** Advanced placement, accelerated degree program, self-designed majors, summer session, adult/continuing education programs, internships **Contact** Mr. Terry Dale Cruse, Director of Admissions, Missouri Baptist University, One College Park Drive, St. Louis, MO 63141-8660. *Phone:* 877-434-1115 or toll-free 877-434-1115 Ext. 2290. *Fax:* 314-434-7596. *E-mail:* admissions@mobap.edu. *Web site:* http://www.mobap.edu/.

Missouri College

St. Louis, Missouri

General Proprietary, primarily 2-year, coed, primarily women **Total enrollment** 508 **Application deadline** Rolling (freshmen) **Housing** No **Undergraduates** 43% 25 or older **Contact** Mr. Doug Brinker, Admissions Director, Missouri College, 10121 Manchester Road, St. Louis, MO 63122-1583. *Phone:* 314-821-7700. *Fax:* 314-821-0891. *Web site:* http://www.mocollege.com/.

Missouri Southern State University

Joplin, Missouri

General State-supported, comprehensive, coed **Entrance** Moderately difficult **Setting** 350-acre small-town campus **Total enrollment** 5,701 **Student-faculty ratio** 19:1 **Application deadline** 8/1 (freshmen), 8/1 (transfer) **Freshman admission** 95% were admitted **Freshman test scores** ACT scores over 18: 83.1%; ACT scores over 24: 28.5% **Housing** Yes **Expenses** Tuition & Fees: state resident $4290, nonresident $8580; Room & Board $5500 **Undergraduates** 58% women, 27% part-time, 36% 25 or older, 3% Native American, 3% Hispanic American, 4% African American, 1% Asian American/Pacific Islander **The most frequently chosen baccalaureate fields are** business/marketing, engineering technologies, security and protective services **Academic program** English as a second language, advanced placement, accelerated degree program, honors program, summer session, adult/continuing education programs, internships **Contact** Mr. Derek Skaggs, Director of Enrollment Services, Missouri Southern State University, 3950 East Newman Road, Joplin, MO 64801-1595. *Phone:* 417-625-9537 or toll-free 866-818-MSSU. *Fax:* 417-659-4429. *E-mail:* admissions@mssu.edu. *Web site:* http://www.mssu.edu/.

Missouri State University

Springfield, Missouri

General State-supported, comprehensive, coed **Entrance** Moderately difficult **Setting** 225-acre suburban campus **Total enrollment** 20,371 **Student-faculty ratio** 21:1 **Application deadline** 7/20 (freshmen), 7/20 (transfer) **Freshman admission** 83% were admitted. Average high school GPA 3.52 **Freshman test scores** ACT scores over 18: 97.08%; ACT scores over 24: 49.24% **Housing** Yes **Expenses** Tuition & Fees: state resident $6972, nonresident $12,252; Room & Board $5925 **Undergraduates** 56% women, 22% part-time, 15% 25 or older, 1% Native American, 2% Hispanic American, 4% African American, 2% Asian American/Pacific Islander **The most frequently chosen baccalaureate fields are** business/marketing, education, social sciences **Academic program** English as a second language, advanced placement, accelerated degree program, self-designed majors, honors program, summer session, internships **Contact** Ms. Jill Duncan, Associate Director of Admissions and Recruitment, Missouri State University, 901 S National Avenue, Springfield, MO 65897. *Phone:* 417-836-5517 or toll-free 800-492-7900. *Fax:* 417-836-6334. *E-mail:* info@missouristate.edu. *Web site:* http://www.missouristate.edu/.

Missouri Tech

St. Louis, Missouri

General Proprietary, 4-year, coed, primarily men **Entrance** Moderately difficult **Setting** suburban campus **Total enrollment** 114 **Application deadline** Rolling (freshmen) **Housing** Yes **Expenses** Tuition & Fees $12,790 **Undergraduates** 63% 25 or older **Academic program** Advanced placement, accelerated degree program, summer session, adult/continuing education programs, internships **Contact** Mr. Bob Honaker, Director of Admissions, Missouri Tech, 1167 Corporate Lake Drive, St. Louis, MO 63132. *Phone:* 314-569-3600. *Fax:* 314-569-1167. *Web site:* http://www.motech.edu/.

Missouri University of Science and Technology

Rolla, Missouri

General State-supported, university, coed, primarily men **Entrance** Very difficult **Setting** 284-acre small-town campus **Total enrollment**

6,815 **Student-faculty ratio** 16:1 **Application deadline** 7/1 (freshmen), 7/1 (transfer) **Freshman admission** 93% were admitted. Average high school GPA 3.6 **Freshman test scores** SAT critical reading scores over 500: 84.62%; SAT math scores over 500: 95.39%; ACT scores over 18: 99.91%; SAT critical reading scores over 600: 60%; SAT math scores over 600: 76.93%; ACT scores over 24: 87.08% **Housing** Yes **Expenses** Tuition & Fees: state resident $8488, nonresident $19,579; Room & Board $7595 **Undergraduates** 22% women, 6% part-time, 6% 25 or older, 1% Native American, 2% Hispanic American, 5% African American, 2% Asian American/Pacific Islander **The most frequently chosen baccalaureate fields are** computer and information sciences, biological/life sciences, engineering **Academic program** English as a second language, advanced placement, accelerated degree program, honors program, summer session, adult/continuing education programs, internships **Contact** Admissions Office, Missouri University of Science and Technology, 300 West 13th Street, 106 Parker Hall, Rolla, MO 65401. *Phone:* 573-341-4165 or toll-free 800-522-0938. *Fax:* 573-341-4082. *E-mail:* admissions@mst.edu. *Web site:* http://www.mst.edu/.

Missouri Valley College

Marshall, Missouri

Contact Ms. Debi Bultmann, Admissions Office Manager, Missouri Valley College, 500 East College, Marshall, MO 65340-3197. *Phone:* 660-831-4125. *Fax:* 660-831-4233. *E-mail:* admissions@moval.edu. *Web site:* http://www.moval.edu/.

Missouri Western State University

St. Joseph, Missouri

General State-supported, comprehensive, coed **Entrance** Noncompetitive **Setting** 744-acre suburban campus **Total enrollment** 5,703 **Student-faculty ratio** 19:1 **Application deadline** 5/1 (freshmen), 6/1 (transfer) **Freshman admission** 100% were admitted **Freshman test scores** ACT scores over 18: 70%; ACT scores over 24: 23% **Housing** Yes **Expenses** Tuition & Fees: state resident $5560, nonresident $9688; Room & Board $6600 **Undergraduates** 58% women, 28% part-time, 23% 25 or older, 1% Native American, 2% Hispanic American, 11% African American, 1% Asian American/Pacific Islander **The most frequently chosen baccalaureate fields are** business/marketing, education, health professions and related sciences **Academic program** Advanced placement, accelerated degree program, honors program, summer session, internships **Contact** Mr. Howard McCauley, Director of Admissions, Missouri Western State University, 4525 Downs Drive, St. Joseph, MO 64507-2294. *Phone:* 816-271-4267 or toll-free 800-662-7041 Ext. 60. *Fax:* 816-271-5833. *E-mail:* admission@missouriwestern.edu. *Web site:* http://www.missouriwestern.edu/.

National American University

Kansas City, Missouri

General Proprietary, 4-year, coed **Entrance** Noncompetitive **Setting** 1-acre urban campus **Total enrollment** 315 **Application deadline** Rolling (freshmen) **Housing** No **Undergraduates** 77% 25 or older **Academic program** Summer session **Contact** Admissions Office, National American University, 7490 Northwest 87th Street, Kansas City, MO 64153. *Phone:* 816-412-5500. *E-mail:* zradmissions@national.edu. *Web site:* http://www.national.edu/.

Northwest Missouri State University

Maryville, Missouri

General State-supported, comprehensive, coed **Entrance** Moderately difficult **Setting** 240-acre small-town campus **Total enrollment** 7,076 **Student-faculty ratio** 21:1 **Application deadline** Rolling (freshmen), rolling (transfer) **Freshman admission** 70% were admitted. Average high school GPA 3.3 **Freshman test scores** SAT critical reading scores over 500: 44.83%; SAT math scores over 500: 72.41%; SAT critical reading scores over 600: 3.45%; SAT math scores over 600: 17.24% **Housing** Yes **Expenses** Tuition & Fees: state resident $7032, nonresident $11,753; Room & Board $7408 **Undergraduates** 55% women, 10% part-time, 5% 25 or older, 0.3% Native American, 2% Hispanic American, 5% African American, 1% Asian American/Pacific Islander **The most frequently chosen baccalaureate fields are** business/marketing, education, psychology **Academic program** English as a second language, advanced placement, honors program, summer session, internships **Contact** Ms. Tammi Grow, Associate Director of Admission, Northwest Missouri State University, 800 University Drive, Maryville, MO 64468-6001. *Phone:* 660-562-1146 or toll-free 800-633-1175. *Fax:* 660-562-1146. *E-mail:* admissions@nwmissouri.edu. *Web site:* http://www.nwmissouri.edu/.

Ozark Christian College

Joplin, Missouri

Contact Mr. Troy B. Nelson, Executive Director of Admissions, Ozark Christian College, 1111 North Main Street, Joplin, MO 64801-4804. *Phone:* 417-624-2518 or toll-free 800-299-4622. *Fax:* 417-624-0090. *E-mail:* occadmin@occ.edu. *Web site:* http://www.occ.edu/.

Park University

Parkville, Missouri

General Independent, comprehensive, coed **Entrance** Moderately difficult **Setting** 800-acre suburban campus **Total enrollment** 12,775 **Student-faculty ratio** 12:1 **Application deadline** 8/1 (freshmen), 8/1 (transfer) **Freshman admission** 70% were admitted. Average high school GPA 3 **Freshman test scores** ACT scores over 18: 90%; ACT scores over 24: 42% **Housing** Yes **Expenses** Tuition & Fees $8898; Room & Board $7580 **Undergraduates** 52% women, 89% part-time, 78% 25 or older, 1% Native American, 15% Hispanic American, 22% African American, 2% Asian American/Pacific Islander **The most frequently chosen baccalaureate fields are** business/marketing, psychology, security and protective services **Academic program** English as a second language, advanced placement, self-designed majors, honors program, summer session, adult/continuing education programs, internships **Contact** Cathy Colapietro, Director of Admissions and Student Financial Services, Park University, 8700 NW River Park Drive, Campus Box 1, Parkville, MO 64152. *Phone:* 816-584-6728 or toll-free 800-745-7275. *Fax:* 816-741-4462. *E-mail:* admissions@mail.park.edu. *Web site:* http://www.park.edu/.

Patricia Stevens College

St. Louis, Missouri

General Proprietary, 4-year, coed **Entrance** Moderately difficult **Setting** urban campus **Total enrollment** 200 **Student-faculty ratio** 10:1 **Application deadline** Rolling (freshmen), rolling (transfer) **Freshman admission** 75% were admitted. Average high school GPA 2.8 **Housing** No **Expenses** Tuition & Fees $15,120 **Undergraduates** 90% women, 33% part-time, 45% 25 or older, 1% Hispanic American, 57% African American **Academic program** Advanced placement, accelerated degree program, honors program, summer session, adult/continuing education programs, internships **Contact** Mr. John Willmon, Director of Admissions, Patricia Stevens College, 330 North Fourth Street, Suite 306, St. Louis, MO 63102. *Phone:* 314-421-0949 or toll-free 800-871-0949. *Fax:* 314-421-0304. *E-mail:* admission@patriciastevenscollege.com. *Web site:* http://www.patriciastevenscollege.edu/.

Ranken Technical College

St. Louis, Missouri

General Independent, primarily 2-year, coed, primarily men **Entrance** Moderately difficult **Setting** 10-acre urban campus **Total enrollment** 1,743 **Application deadline** Rolling (freshmen) **Housing** Yes **Expenses** Tuition & Fees $12,918; Room & Board $7500 **Undergraduates** 34%

Ranken Technical College (continued)
25 or older **Academic program** Advanced placement, summer session, adult/continuing education programs, internships **Contact** Ms. Elizabeth Keserauskis, Director of Admissions, Ranken Technical College, 4431 Finney Avenue, St. Louis, MO 63113. *Phone:* 314-371-0233 Ext. 4811 or toll-free 866-4RANKEN. *Web site:* http://www.ranken.edu/.

Research College of Nursing
Kansas City, Missouri

General Independent, comprehensive, coed, primarily women **Entrance** Moderately difficult **Setting** 66-acre urban campus **Total enrollment** 382 **Student-faculty ratio** 7:1 **Application deadline** 6/30 (freshmen), 2/15 (transfer) **Freshman admission** 68% were admitted. Average high school GPA 3.46 **Housing** Yes **Expenses** Tuition & Fees $25,700; Room & Board $7280 **Undergraduates** 94% women, 1% part-time, 30% 25 or older **The most frequently chosen baccalaureate field is** health professions and related sciences **Academic program** Advanced placement, accelerated degree program, honors program, summer session **Contact** Mrs. Leslie A. Mendenhall, Director of Transfer and Graduate Recruitment, Research College of Nursing, 2252 East Meyer Boulevard, Kansas City, MO 64132. *Phone:* 816-995-2820 or toll-free 800-842-6776. *Fax:* 816-995-2813. *E-mail:* leslie.mendenhall@researchcollege.edu. *Web site:* http://www.researchcollege.edu/.

Rockhurst University
Kansas City, Missouri

General Independent Roman Catholic (Jesuit), comprehensive, coed **Entrance** Moderately difficult **Setting** 35-acre urban campus **Total enrollment** 3,029 **Student-faculty ratio** 10:1 **Application deadline** 6/30 (freshmen), rolling (transfer) **Freshman admission** 76% were admitted. Average high school GPA 3.48 **Freshman test scores** SAT critical reading scores over 500: 83%; SAT math scores over 500: 83%; ACT scores over 18: 98%; SAT critical reading scores over 600: 50%; SAT math scores over 600: 50%; ACT scores over 24: 59% **Housing** Yes **Expenses** Tuition & Fees $25,890; Room & Board $7080 **Undergraduates** 61% women, 34% part-time, 9% 25 or older, 0.4% Native American, 6% Hispanic American, 6% African American, 3% Asian American/Pacific Islander **The most frequently chosen baccalaureate fields are** business/marketing, health professions and related sciences, psychology **Academic program** Advanced placement, accelerated degree program, honors program, summer session, internships **Contact** Lane Ramey, Director of Freshman Admissions, Rockhurst University, 1100 Rockhurst Road, Kansas City, MO 64110-2561. *Phone:* 816-501-4100 or toll-free 800-842-6776. *Fax:* 816-501-4142. *E-mail:* admission@rockhurst.edu. *Web site:* http://www.rockhurst.edu/.

St. Louis Christian College
Florissant, Missouri

General Independent Christian, 4-year, coed **Entrance** Minimally difficult **Setting** 20-acre suburban campus **Total enrollment** 336 **Student-faculty ratio** 15:1 **Application deadline** 8/7 (freshmen), 8/7 (transfer) **Freshman admission** 43% were admitted. Average high school GPA 2.99 **Freshman test scores** ACT scores over 18: 74%; ACT scores over 24: 28% **Housing** Yes **Expenses** Tuition & Fees $11,000; Room & Board $3600 **Undergraduates** 42% women, 13% part-time, 42% 25 or older, 3% Hispanic American, 23% African American, 1% Asian American/Pacific Islander **The most frequently chosen baccalaureate field is** theology and religious vocations **Academic program** English as a second language, advanced placement, accelerated degree program, summer session, adult/continuing education programs, internships **Contact** Carrie Chapman, Admissions Director, St. Louis Christian College, 1360 Grandview Drive, Florissant, MO 63033. *Phone:* 314-837-6777 Ext. 1500 or toll-free 800-887-SLCC. *E-mail:* cchapman@slcconline.edu. *Web site:* http://www.slcconline.edu/.

St. Louis College of Pharmacy
St. Louis, Missouri

General Independent, comprehensive, coed **Entrance** Moderately difficult **Setting** 5-acre urban campus **Total enrollment** 1,233 **Student-faculty ratio** 20:1 **Application deadline** 2/1 (freshmen), 2/1 (transfer) **Freshman admission** 45% were admitted. Average high school GPA 3.77 **Freshman test scores** ACT scores over 18: 100%; ACT scores over 24: 100% **Housing** Yes **Expenses** Tuition & Fees $23,010; Room & Board $8560 **Undergraduates** 57% women, 0.2% part-time, 0.2% Native American, 1% Hispanic American, 2% African American, 20% Asian American/Pacific Islander **Academic program** Advanced placement, summer session, internships **Contact** Connie Horrall, Administrative Assistant, St. Louis College of Pharmacy, 4588 Parkview Place, St. Louis, MO 63110-1088. *Phone:* 314-446-8328 or toll-free 800-278-5267. *Fax:* 314-446-8310. *E-mail:* chorrall@stlcop.edu. *Web site:* http://www.stlcop.edu/.

Visit Petersons.com and enter keywords Louis College

See page 1120 for the College Close-Up.

Saint Louis University
St. Louis, Missouri

General Independent Roman Catholic (Jesuit), university, coed **Entrance** Moderately difficult **Setting** 235-acre urban campus **Total enrollment** 13,313 **Student-faculty ratio** 13:1 **Application deadline** 8/1 (freshmen), rolling (transfer) **Freshman admission** 71% were admitted. Average high school GPA 3.71 **Freshman test scores** SAT critical reading scores over 500: 89.32%; SAT math scores over 500: 89.11%; ACT scores over 18: 99.72%; SAT critical reading scores over 600: 51.63%; SAT math scores over 600: 56.86%; ACT scores over 24: 82.55% **Housing** Yes **Expenses** Tuition & Fees $31,342; Room & Board $8900 **Undergraduates** 59% women, 10% part-time, 6% 25 or older, 0.3% Native American, 3% Hispanic American, 8% African American, 6% Asian American/Pacific Islander **The most frequently chosen baccalaureate fields are** business/marketing, biological/life sciences, health professions and related sciences **Academic program** English as a second language, advanced placement, accelerated degree program, self-designed majors, honors program, summer session, adult/continuing education programs, internships **Contact** Director, Saint Louis University, 221 North Grand Boulevard, DuBourg Hall, Room 100, St. Louis, MO 63103-2097. *Phone:* 314-977-2500 or toll-free 800-758-3678. *Fax:* 314-977-7136. *E-mail:* admitme@slu.edu. *Web site:* http://www.slu.edu/.

Saint Luke's College
Kansas City, Missouri

Contact Assistant Director of Admissions, Saint Luke's College, 8320 Ward Parkway, Suite 300, Kansas City, MO 64114. *Phone:* 816-932-3372. *Fax:* 816-932-9064. *E-mail:* jmrichards@saint-lukes.org. *Web site:* http://www.saintlukescollege.edu/.

Sanford-Brown College
Fenton, Missouri

General Proprietary, primarily 2-year, coed **Entrance** Minimally difficult **Setting** 6-acre suburban campus **Total enrollment** 659 **Housing** No **Undergraduates** 55% 25 or older **Academic program** Adult/continuing education programs, internships **Contact** Ms. Judy Wilga, Director of Admissions, Sanford-Brown College, 1203 Smizer Mill Road, Fenton, MO 63026. *Phone:* 636-349-4900 Ext. 102 or toll-free 800-456-7222. *Fax:* 636-349-9170. *Web site:* http://www.sanford-brown.edu/.

Southeast Missouri State University
Cape Girardeau, Missouri

General State-supported, comprehensive, coed **Entrance** Moderately difficult **Setting** 400-acre small-town campus **Total enrollment** 10,859

Student-faculty ratio 18:1 **Application deadline** 7/1 (freshmen), 8/1 (transfer) **Freshman admission** 92% were admitted. Average high school GPA 3.27 **Freshman test scores** SAT critical reading scores over 500: 52.94%; SAT math scores over 500: 60.79%; ACT scores over 18: 95.53%; SAT critical reading scores over 600: 19.61%; SAT math scores over 600: 17.65%; ACT scores over 24: 39.7% **Housing** Yes **Expenses** Tuition & Fees: state resident $6255, nonresident $10,890; Room & Board $6358 **Undergraduates** 59% women, 24% part-time, 21% 25 or older, 0.4% Native American, 1% Hispanic American, 8% African American, 1% Asian American/Pacific Islander **The most frequently chosen baccalaureate fields are** business/marketing, education, liberal arts/general studies **Academic program** English as a second language, advanced placement, accelerated degree program, self-designed majors, honors program, summer session, adult/continuing education programs, internships **Contact** Dr. Deborah Below, Assistant Vice President for Enrollment Management & Director of Admissions, Southeast Missouri State University, One University Plaza, Cape Girardeau, MO 63701-4799. *Phone:* 573-651-2590. *Fax:* 573-651-5936. *E-mail:* dbelow@semo.edu. *Web site:* http://www.semo.edu/.

Southwest Baptist University
Bolivar, Missouri

General Independent Southern Baptist, comprehensive, coed **Entrance** Moderately difficult **Setting** 152-acre small-town campus **Total enrollment** 3,716 **Student-faculty ratio** 13:1 **Application deadline** Rolling (freshmen), rolling (transfer) **Freshman admission** 92% were admitted. Average high school GPA 3.47 **Freshman test scores** SAT critical reading scores over 500: 48%; SAT math scores over 500: 65%; SAT critical reading scores over 600: 13%; SAT math scores over 600: 25% **Housing** Yes **Expenses** Tuition & Fees $17,280; Room & Board $5720 **Undergraduates** 65% women, 31% part-time, 4% 25 or older, 1% Native American, 1% Hispanic American, 4% African American, 1% Asian American/Pacific Islander **The most frequently chosen baccalaureate fields are** business/marketing, education, health professions and related sciences **Academic program** Advanced placement, self-designed majors, honors program, summer session, internships **Contact** Mr. Darren Crowder, Director of Admissions, Southwest Baptist University, 1600 University Avenue, Bolivar, MO 65613-2597. *Phone:* 417-328-1817 or toll-free 800-526-5859. *Fax:* 417-328-1808. *E-mail:* dcrowder@sbuniv.edu. *Web site:* http://www.sbuniv.edu/.

Stephens College
Columbia, Missouri

General Independent, comprehensive, undergraduate: women only; graduate: coed **Entrance** Moderately difficult **Setting** 86-acre urban campus **Total enrollment** 1,238 **Student-faculty ratio** 12:1 **Freshman admission** 72% were admitted. Average high school GPA 3.31 **Freshman test scores** SAT critical reading scores over 500: 81%; SAT math scores over 500: 53%; SAT critical reading scores over 600: 28%; SAT math scores over 600: 15% **Housing** Yes **Expenses** Tuition & Fees $25,400; Room & Board $7170 **Undergraduates** 20% part-time, 20% 25 or older, 1% Native American, 3% Hispanic American, 13% African American, 1% Asian American/Pacific Islander **Academic program** Advanced placement, self-designed majors, summer session, adult/continuing education programs, internships **Contact** Mr. Chris Collier, Interim Dean of Enrollment Management, Stephens College, 1200 East Broadway, Box 2121, Columbia, MO 65215-0002. *Phone:* 573-876-7207 or toll-free 800-876-7207. *Fax:* 573-876-7237. *E-mail:* apply@stephens.edu. *Web site:* http://www.stephens.edu/.

See page 1200 for the College Close-Up.

Truman State University
Kirksville, Missouri

General State-supported, comprehensive, coed **Entrance** Moderately difficult **Setting** 180-acre small-town campus **Total enrollment** 5,747 **Student-faculty ratio** 16:1 **Application deadline** Rolling (freshmen), rolling (transfer) **Freshman admission** 72% were admitted. Average high school GPA 3.74 **Freshman test scores** SAT critical reading scores over 500: 87.86%; SAT math scores over 500: 87.86%; ACT scores over 18: 99.85%; SAT critical reading scores over 600: 47.86%; SAT math scores over 600: 60%; ACT scores over 24: 83.31% **Housing** Yes **Expenses** Tuition & Fees: state resident $6692, nonresident $11,543; Room & Board $6854 **Undergraduates** 58% women, 2% part-time, 1% 25 or older, 1% Native American, 2% Hispanic American, 4% African American, 2% Asian American/Pacific Islander **The most frequently chosen baccalaureate fields are** business/marketing, biological/life sciences, English **Academic program** Advanced placement, self-designed majors, honors program, summer session, internships **Contact** Melody Chambers, Director of Admissions, Truman State University, 205 McClain Hall, 100 East Normal Street, Kirksville, MO 63501-4221. *Phone:* 660-785-4114 or toll-free 800-892-7792. *Fax:* 660-785-7456. *E-mail:* admissions@truman.edu. *Web site:* http://www.truman.edu/. **Visit Petersons.com and enter keyword Truman**

See page 1236 for the College Close-Up.

University of Central Missouri
Warrensburg, Missouri

General State-supported, comprehensive, coed **Entrance** Moderately difficult **Setting** 1,561-acre small-town campus **Total enrollment** 11,191 **Student-faculty ratio** 17:1 **Application deadline** Rolling (freshmen), rolling (transfer) **Freshman admission** 85% were admitted. Average high school GPA 3.26 **Freshman test scores** ACT scores over 18: 90.9%; ACT scores over 24: 31.5% **Housing** Yes **Expenses** Tuition & Fees: state resident $7311, nonresident $13,170; Room & Board $6320 **Undergraduates** 55% women, 17% part-time, 17% 25 or older **The most frequently chosen baccalaureate fields are** business/marketing, education, engineering technologies **Academic program** English as a second language, advanced placement, self-designed majors, honors program, summer session, adult/continuing education programs, internships **Contact** Ms. Ann Nordyke, Director of Admissions, University of Central Missouri, 1400 Ward Edwards, Warrensburg, MO 64093. *Phone:* 660-543-4170 or toll-free 800-729-8266. *Fax:* 660-543-8517. *E-mail:* admit@ucmo.edu. *Web site:* http://www.ucmo.edu/.

University of Missouri
Columbia, Missouri

General State-supported, university, coed **Entrance** Moderately difficult **Setting** 1,374-acre suburban campus **Total enrollment** 31,314 **Student-faculty ratio** 19:1 **Application deadline** Rolling (freshmen), rolling (transfer) **Freshman admission** 83% were admitted **Freshman test scores** SAT critical reading scores over 500: 86.92%; SAT math scores over 500: 89.48%; ACT scores over 18: 99.47%; SAT critical reading scores over 600: 48.96%; SAT math scores over 600: 49.29%; ACT scores over 24: 69.48% **Housing** Yes **Expenses** Tuition & Fees: state resident $8501, nonresident $19,592; Room & Board $8100 **Undergraduates** 52% women, 6% part-time, 4% 25 or older, 1% Native American, 2% Hispanic American, 7% African American, 2% Asian American/Pacific Islander **The most frequently chosen baccalaureate fields are** business/marketing, communications/journalism, social sciences **Academic program** English as a second language, advanced placement, accelerated degree program, self-designed majors, honors program, summer session, adult/continuing education programs, internships **Contact** Ms. Barbara Rupp, Director of Admissions, University of Missouri, 230 Jesse Hall, Columbia, MO 65211. *Phone:* 573-882-7786 or toll-free 800-225-6075. *Fax:* 573-882-7887. *E-mail:* mu4u@missouri.edu. *Web site:* http://www.missouri.edu/.

University of Missouri–Kansas City
Kansas City, Missouri

General State-supported, university, coed **Entrance** Moderately difficult **Setting** 191-acre urban campus **Total enrollment** 14,818 **Student-**

University of Missouri–Kansas City (continued)
faculty ratio 13:1 **Application deadline** Rolling (freshmen), rolling (transfer) **Freshman admission** 62% were admitted. Average high school GPA 3.31 **Freshman test scores** SAT critical reading scores over 500: 79%; SAT math scores over 500: 90%; ACT scores over 18: 93%; SAT critical reading scores over 600: 51%; SAT math scores over 600: 54%; ACT scores over 24: 53% **Housing** Yes **Expenses** Tuition & Fees: state resident $8273, nonresident $19,364; Room & Board $10,467 **Undergraduates** 58% women, 33% part-time, 29% 25 or older, 1% Native American, 5% Hispanic American, 15% African American, 6% Asian American/Pacific Islander **The most frequently chosen baccalaureate fields are** business/marketing, education, liberal arts/general studies **Academic program** English as a second language, advanced placement, accelerated degree program, self-designed majors, honors program, summer session, adult/continuing education programs, internships **Contact** Ms. Tammy Cloutier, Associate Director of Recruitment, University of Missouri–Kansas City, Office of Admissions, 5100 Rockhill Road, Kansas City, MO 64110-2499. *Phone:* 816-235-1111 or toll-free 800-775-8652. *Fax:* 816-235-5544. *E-mail:* admit@umkc.edu. *Web site:* http://www.umkc.edu/.

University of Missouri–St. Louis
St. Louis, Missouri

General State-supported, university, coed **Entrance** Moderately difficult **Setting** 350-acre suburban campus **Total enrollment** 16,548 **Student-faculty ratio** 17:1 **Application deadline** 8/23 (freshmen), rolling (transfer) **Freshman admission** 79% were admitted **Freshman test scores** SAT math scores over 500: 74%; ACT scores over 18: 90%; SAT math scores over 600: 35%; ACT scores over 24: 41% **Housing** Yes **Expenses** Tuition & Fees: state resident $8595, nonresident $19,686; Room & Board $8164 **Undergraduates** 61% women, 54% part-time, 39% 25 or older, 0.3% Native American, 2% Hispanic American, 21% African American, 3% Asian American/Pacific Islander **The most frequently chosen baccalaureate fields are** business/marketing, education, health professions and related sciences **Academic program** English as a second language, advanced placement, accelerated degree program, self-designed majors, honors program, summer session, adult/continuing education programs, internships **Contact** Mr. Andrew L. Griffin, Associate Director of Admissions, University of Missouri–St. Louis, 351 Millennium Student Center, One University Boulevard, St. Louis, MO 63121-4400. *Phone:* 314-516-6941 or toll-free 888-GO2-UMSL. *Fax:* 314-516-5310. *E-mail:* askdrew@umsl.edu. *Web site:* http://www.umsl.edu/.

University of Phoenix–Kansas City Campus
Kansas City, Missouri

General Proprietary, comprehensive, coed **Entrance** Noncompetitive **Setting** urban campus **Total enrollment** 770 **Application deadline** Rolling (freshmen), rolling (transfer) **Housing** No **Expenses** Tuition & Fees $12,525 **Undergraduates** 65% women, 82% 25 or older **The most frequently chosen baccalaureate fields are** business/marketing, computer and information sciences, security and protective services **Academic program** Advanced placement, accelerated degree program, adult/continuing education programs **Contact** Ms. Audra McQuarie, Registrar/Executive Director, University of Phoenix–Kansas City Campus, 4035 South Riverpoint Parkway, Mail Stop CF-L101, Phoenix, AZ 85040. *Phone:* 480-557-6151 or toll-free 800-776-4867 (in-state); 800-228-7240 (out-of-state). *Fax:* 480-643-3068. *E-mail:* audra.mcquarie@phoenix.edu. *Web site:* http://www.phoenix.edu/.

University of Phoenix–St. Louis Campus
St. Louis, Missouri

General Proprietary, comprehensive, coed **Entrance** Noncompetitive **Setting** urban campus **Total enrollment** 445 **Application deadline** Rolling (freshmen), rolling (transfer) **Housing** No **Expenses** Tuition & Fees $13,200 **Undergraduates** 65% women, 80% 25 or older, 1% Hispanic American, 34% African American, 1% Asian American/Pacific Islander **The most frequently chosen baccalaureate fields are** business/marketing, computer and information sciences, security and protective services **Academic program** Advanced placement, accelerated degree program, adult/continuing education programs **Contact** Ms. Audra McQuarie, Registrar/Executive Director, University of Phoenix–St. Louis Campus, 4035 South Riverpoint Parkway, Mail Stop CF-L101, Phoenix, AZ 85040. *Phone:* 480-557-6151 or toll-free 800-776-4867 (in-state); 800-228-7240 (out-of-state). *Fax:* 480-643-3068. *E-mail:* audra.mcquarie@phoenix.edu. *Web site:* http://www.phoenix.edu/.

University of Phoenix–Springfield Campus
Springfield, Missouri

General Proprietary, comprehensive, coed **Entrance** Noncompetitive **Setting** urban campus **Total enrollment** 119 **Student-faculty ratio** 9:1 **Application deadline** Rolling (freshmen), rolling (transfer) **Housing** No **Expenses** Tuition & Fees $11,025 **Undergraduates** 60% women, 76% 25 or older, 1% Hispanic American, 3% African American, 1% Asian American/Pacific Islander **The most frequently chosen baccalaureate fields are** business/marketing, computer and information sciences, security and protective services **Academic program** Advanced placement, accelerated degree program **Contact** Ms. Audra McQuarie, Registrar/Executive Director, University of Phoenix–Springfield Campus, 4035 South Riverpoint Parkway, Mail Stop CF-L101, Phoenix, AZ 85040. *Phone:* 480-557-6151 or toll-free 800-776-4867 (in-state); 800-228-7240 (out-of-state). *Fax:* 480-643-3068. *E-mail:* audra.mcquarie@phoenix.edu. *Web site:* http://www.phoenix.edu/.

Vatterott College
St. Ann, Missouri

Contact Ann Farajallah, Director of Admissions, Vatterott College, 3925 Industrial Drive, St. Ann, MO 63074-1807. *Phone:* 314-264-1020 or toll-free 866-314-6454. *Web site:* http://www.vatterott-college.edu/.

Vatterott College
St. Louis, Missouri

Contact Director of Admission, Vatterott College, 12970 Maurer Industrial Drive, St. Louis, MO 63127. *Phone:* 314-843-4200. *Fax:* 314-843-1709. *Web site:* http://www.vatterott-college.edu/.

Washington University in St. Louis
St. Louis, Missouri

General Independent, university, coed **Entrance** Most difficult **Setting** 169-acre suburban campus **Total enrollment** 13,575 **Student-faculty ratio** 7:1 **Application deadline** 1/15 (freshmen), 4/15 (transfer) **Freshman admission** 22% were admitted **Freshman test scores** SAT critical reading scores over 500: 100%; SAT math scores over 500: 100%; ACT scores over 18: 100%; SAT critical reading scores over 600: 98%; SAT math scores over 600: 100%; ACT scores over 24: 100% **Housing** Yes **Expenses** Tuition & Fees $40,374; Room & Board $12,941 **Undergraduates** 51% women, 13% part-time, 4% 25 or older, 0.1% Native American, 3% Hispanic American, 9% African American, 14% Asian American/Pacific Islander **The most frequently chosen baccalaureate fields are** engineering, business/marketing, social sciences **Academic program** English as a second language, advanced placement, accelerated degree program, self-designed majors, summer session, adult/continuing education programs, internships **Contact** Ms. Julie Shimabukuro, Director of Admissions, Washington University in St. Louis, Campus Box 1089, One Brookings Drive, St. Louis, MO 63130-4899. *Phone:* 314-935-6000 or toll-free 800-638-0700. *Fax:* 314-935-4290. *E-mail:* admissions@wustl.edu. *Web site:* http://www.wustl.edu/.

Webster University
St. Louis, Missouri

General Independent, comprehensive, coed **Entrance** Moderately difficult **Setting** 47-acre suburban campus **Total enrollment** 8,241 **Student-faculty ratio** 12:1 **Application deadline** 6/1 (freshmen), 8/1 (transfer) **Freshman admission** 52% were admitted. Average high school GPA 3.45 **Freshman test scores** ACT scores over 18: 94%; ACT scores over 24: 54% **Housing** Yes **Expenses** Tuition & Fees $21,056; Room & Board $9070 **Undergraduates** 59% women, 26% part-time, 29% 25 or older, 1% Native American, 3% Hispanic American, 13% African American, 2% Asian American/Pacific Islander **The most frequently chosen baccalaureate fields are** business/marketing, communications/ journalism, visual and performing arts **Academic program** English as a second language, advanced placement, accelerated degree program, self-designed majors, summer session, adult/continuing education programs, internships **Contact** Mr. Andrew Laue, Associate Director of Undergraduate Admission, Webster University, 470 East Lockwood Avenue, St. Louis, MO 63119-3194. *Phone:* 314-961-2660 or toll-free 800-75-ENROL. *Fax:* 314-968-7115. *E-mail:* admit@webster.edu. *Web site:* http://www.webster.edu/.

Westminster College
Fulton, Missouri

General Independent, 4-year, coed, affiliated with Presbyterian Church **Entrance** Moderately difficult **Setting** 80-acre small-town campus **Total enrollment** 1,087 **Student-faculty ratio** 15:1 **Freshman admission** 78% were admitted. Average high school GPA 3.44 **Freshman test scores** SAT critical reading scores over 500: 56%; SAT math scores over 500: 64%; ACT scores over 18: 99%; SAT critical reading scores over 600: 30%; SAT math scores over 600: 30%; ACT scores over 24: 56% **Housing** Yes **Expenses** Tuition & Fees $17,990; Room & Board $7120 **Undergraduates** 45% women, 1% part-time, 3% 25 or older, 2% Native American, 2% Hispanic American, 6% African American, 1% Asian American/Pacific Islander **The most frequently chosen baccalaureate fields are** biological/life sciences, business/marketing, education **Academic program** English as a second language, advanced placement, self-designed majors, honors program, summer session, internships **Contact** Mr. George Wolf, Vice President and Dean of Enrollment Services, Westminster College, 501 Westminster Avenue, Fulton, MO 65251-1299. *Phone:* 573-592-5251 or toll-free 800-475-3361. *Fax:* 573-592-5255. *E-mail:* admissions@westminster-mo.edu. *Web site:* http://www.westminster-mo.edu/.

William Jewell College
Liberty, Missouri

General Independent Baptist, 4-year, coed **Entrance** Moderately difficult **Setting** 200-acre small-town campus **Total enrollment** 1,083 **Student-faculty ratio** 11:1 **Application deadline** 8/15 (freshmen), rolling (transfer) **Freshman admission** 55% were admitted. Average high school GPA 3.68 **Freshman test scores** SAT critical reading scores over 500: 76%; SAT math scores over 500: 84%; ACT scores over 18: 99%; SAT critical reading scores over 600: 46%; SAT math scores over 600: 50%; ACT scores over 24: 69% **Housing** Yes **Expenses** Tuition & Fees $28,750; Room & Board $7200 **Undergraduates** 60% women, 5% part-time, 1% Native American, 3% Hispanic American, 4% African American, 2% Asian American/Pacific Islander **The most frequently chosen baccalaureate fields are** business/marketing, health professions and related sciences, psychology **Academic program** Advanced placement, self-designed majors, honors program, summer session, internships **Contact** Ms. Bridget Gramling, Dean of Admission, William Jewell College, 500 College Hill, Liberty, MO 64068-1843. *Phone:* 816-415-7511 or toll-free 888-2JEWELL. *E-mail:* gramblingb@william.jewell.edu. *Web site:* http://www.jewell.edu/.

William Woods University
Fulton, Missouri

Contact Ms. Sharon Horn, Admissions Data Analyst, William Woods University, One University Avenue, Fulton, MO 65251. *Phone:* 573-592-4221 or toll-free 800-995-3159 Ext. 4221. *Fax:* 573-592-1146. *E-mail:* admissions@williamwoods.edu. *Web site:* http://www.williamwoods.edu/.

MONTANA

Carroll College
Helena, Montana

General Independent Roman Catholic, 4-year, coed **Entrance** Moderately difficult **Setting** 64-acre small-town campus **Total enrollment** 1,409 **Application deadline** 6/1 (freshmen), 6/1 (transfer) **Freshman admission** 76% were admitted. Average high school GPA 3.47 **Freshman test scores** SAT critical reading scores over 500: 74%; SAT math scores over 500: 76%; ACT scores over 18: 97%; SAT critical reading scores over 600: 27%; SAT math scores over 600: 32%; ACT scores over 24: 52% **Housing** Yes **Expenses** Tuition & Fees $22,592; Room & Board $7118 **Undergraduates** 56% women, 13% part-time, 9% 25 or older, 1% Native American, 2% Hispanic American, 0.5% African American, 1% Asian American/Pacific Islander **The most frequently chosen baccalaureate fields are** business/marketing, biological/life sciences, health professions and related sciences **Academic program** English as a second language, advanced placement, accelerated degree program, self-designed majors, honors program, summer session, adult/continuing education programs, internships **Contact** Ms. Cynthia Thornquist, Director of Admissions and Enrollment Operations, Carroll College, 1601 North Benton Avenue, Helena, MT 59625-0002. *Phone:* toll-free 800-992-3648. *Web site:* http://www.carroll.edu/.

Visit Petersons.com and enter keyword Carroll

See page 684 for the College Close-Up.

Montana State University
Bozeman, Montana

General State-supported, university, coed **Entrance** Moderately difficult **Setting** 1,781-acre small-town campus **Total enrollment** 12,764 **Student-faculty ratio** 16:1 **Application deadline** Rolling (freshmen), rolling (transfer) **Freshman admission** 64% were admitted. Average high school GPA 3.28 **Freshman test scores** SAT critical reading scores over 500: 76%; SAT math scores over 500: 77%; ACT scores over 18: 94%; SAT critical reading scores over 600: 33%; SAT math scores over 600: 40%; ACT scores over 24: 52% **Housing** Yes **Expenses** Tuition & Fees: state resident $5988, nonresident $17,651 **Undergraduates** 45% women, 17% part-time, 17% 25 or older, 3% Native American, 2% Hispanic American, 1% African American, 2% Asian American/Pacific Islander **The most frequently chosen baccalaureate fields are** business/ marketing, engineering, health professions and related sciences **Academic program** English as a second language, advanced placement, self-designed majors, honors program, summer session, adult/continuing education programs, internships **Contact** Ms. Ronda Russell, Director of New Student Services, Montana State University, PO Box 172190, Bozeman, MT 59717-2190. *Phone:* 406-994-2452 or toll-free 888-MSU-CATS. *Fax:* 406-994-1923. *E-mail:* admissions@montana.edu. *Web site:* http://www.montana.edu/.

Montana State University Billings
Billings, Montana

General State-supported, comprehensive, coed **Entrance** Moderately difficult **Setting** 92-acre urban campus **Total enrollment** 4,912 **Student-faculty ratio** 20:1 **Application deadline** 7/1 (freshmen), rolling (transfer)

Montana State University Billings (continued)

Freshman admission 100% were admitted. Average high school GPA 3.1 **Freshman test scores** SAT critical reading scores over 500: 60%; SAT math scores over 500: 62%; SAT critical reading scores over 600: 22%; SAT math scores over 600: 24% **Housing** Yes **Expenses** Tuition & Fees: state resident $5207, nonresident $15,867; Room & Board $5460 **Undergraduates** 62% women, 29% part-time, 37% 25 or older, 6% Native American, 4% Hispanic American, 1% African American, 1% Asian American/Pacific Islander **The most frequently chosen baccalaureate fields are** business/marketing, education, liberal arts/general studies **Academic program** English as a second language, advanced placement, accelerated degree program, honors program, summer session, adult/continuing education programs, internships **Contact** Ms. Shelly Andersen, Associate Director of Admissions, Montana State University Billings, 1500 University Drive, Billings, MT 59101. *Phone:* 406-657-2158 or toll-free 800-565-6782. *Fax:* 406-657-2302. *E-mail:* sandersen@msubillings.edu. *Web site:* http://www.msubillings.edu/.

Montana State University–Northern

Havre, Montana

General State-supported, comprehensive, coed **Entrance** Moderately difficult **Setting** 105-acre small-town campus **Total enrollment** 1,215 **Application deadline** Rolling (freshmen), rolling (transfer) **Freshman admission** 100% were admitted **Housing** Yes **Expenses** Tuition & Fees: state resident $5573, nonresident $16,314; Room & Board $5928 **Undergraduates** 32% 25 or older **Academic program** English as a second language, advanced placement, honors program, summer session, adult/continuing education programs, internships **Contact** Ms. Rosalie Spinler, Director of Admissions, Montana State University–Northern, PO Box 7751, Havre, MT 59501-7751. *Phone:* 406-265-3704 or toll-free 800-662-6132. *Web site:* http://www.msun.edu/.

Montana Tech of The University of Montana

Butte, Montana

General State-supported, comprehensive, coed **Entrance** Moderately difficult **Setting** 56-acre small-town campus **Total enrollment** 2,694 **Student-faculty ratio** 15:1 **Application deadline** Rolling (freshmen), rolling (transfer) **Freshman admission** 91% were admitted. Average high school GPA 3.35 **Freshman test scores** SAT critical reading scores over 500: 53%; SAT math scores over 500: 74%; ACT scores over 18: 94%; SAT critical reading scores over 600: 23%; SAT math scores over 600: 37%; ACT scores over 24: 44% **Housing** Yes **Expenses** Tuition & Fees: state resident $6007, nonresident $16,821; Room & Board $6602 **Undergraduates** 39% women, 15% part-time, 24% 25 or older, 2% Native American, 2% Hispanic American, 1% African American, 1% Asian American/Pacific Islander **The most frequently chosen baccalaureate fields are** business/marketing, engineering, health professions and related sciences **Academic program** Advanced placement, self-designed majors, honors program, summer session, adult/continuing education programs, internships **Contact** Mr. Tony Campeau, Director of Enrollment Management, Montana Tech of The University of Montana, 1300 West Park Street, Butte, MT 59701-8997. *Phone:* 406-496-4256 or toll-free 800-445-TECH Ext. 1. *Fax:* 406-496-4710. *E-mail:* tcampeau@mtech.edu. *Web site:* http://www.mtech.edu/.

Rocky Mountain College

Billings, Montana

General Independent interdenominational, comprehensive, coed **Entrance** Moderately difficult **Setting** 60-acre urban campus **Total enrollment** 880 **Student-faculty ratio** 10:1 **Application deadline** Rolling (freshmen), rolling (transfer) **Freshman admission** 63% were admitted. Average high school GPA 3.36 **Freshman test scores** SAT critical reading scores over 500: 50%; SAT math scores over 500: 47%; ACT scores over 18: 91%; SAT critical reading scores over 600: 7%; SAT math scores over 600: 9%; ACT scores over 24: 38% **Housing** Yes **Expenses** Tuition & Fees $21,100; Room & Board $6580 **Undergraduates** 50% women, 4% part-time, 9% 25 or older, 4% Native American, 3% Hispanic American, 2% African American, 1% Asian American/Pacific Islander **The most frequently chosen baccalaureate fields are** business/marketing, education, transportation and materials moving **Academic program** English as a second language, advanced placement, accelerated degree program, self-designed majors, honors program, summer session, adult/continuing education programs, internships **Contact** Mrs. Kelly Edwards, Director of Admissions, Rocky Mountain College, 1511 Poly Drive, Billings, MT 59102. *Phone:* 406-657-1026 or toll-free 800-877-6259. *Fax:* 406-259-9751. *E-mail:* admissions@rocky.edu. *Web site:* http://www.rocky.edu/.

Salish Kootenai College

Pablo, Montana

Contact Ms. Jackie Moran, Admissions Officer, Salish Kootenai College, 52000 Highway 93, PO Box 70, Pablo, MT 59855-0117. *Phone:* 406-275-4866. *Fax:* 406-275-4810. *E-mail:* jackie_moran@skc.edu. *Web site:* http://www.skc.edu/.

University of Great Falls

Great Falls, Montana

Contact April Clutter, Director of Admissions, University of Great Falls, 1301 20th Street South, Great Falls, MT 59405. *Phone:* 406-791-5200 or toll-free 800-856-9544. *Fax:* 406-791-5209. *E-mail:* enroll@ugf.edu. *Web site:* http://www.ugf.edu/.

Visit Petersons.com and enter keywords Great Falls

See page 1270 for the College Close-Up.

The University of Montana

Missoula, Montana

General State-supported, university, coed **Entrance** Moderately difficult **Setting** 220-acre urban campus **Total enrollment** 14,207 **Student-faculty ratio** 19:1 **Application deadline** Rolling (freshmen), rolling (transfer) **Freshman admission** 96% were admitted. Average high school GPA 3.22 **Freshman test scores** SAT critical reading scores over 500: 70%; SAT math scores over 500: 69.5%; ACT scores over 18: 94%; SAT critical reading scores over 600: 28%; SAT math scores over 600: 23%; ACT scores over 24: 44% **Housing** Yes **Expenses** Tuition & Fees: state resident $5533, nonresident $18,373; Room & Board $6611 **Undergraduates** 53% women, 17% part-time, 19% 25 or older, 4% Native American, 2% Hispanic American, 1% African American, 2% Asian American/Pacific Islander **The most frequently chosen baccalaureate fields are** business/marketing, natural resources/environmental science, social sciences **Academic program** English as a second language, advanced placement, honors program, summer session, internships **Contact** Ms. Juana Alcala, Manager, Enrollment Services, The University of Montana, Missoula, MT 59812-0002. *Phone:* 406-243-6266 or toll-free 800-462-8636. *Fax:* 406-243-5711. *E-mail:* admiss@umontana.edu. *Web site:* http://www.umt.edu/.

The University of Montana Western

Dillon, Montana

General State-supported, 4-year, coed **Entrance** Minimally difficult **Setting** 36-acre small-town campus **Total enrollment** 1,255 **Student-faculty ratio** 14:1 **Application deadline** Rolling (freshmen), rolling (transfer) **Freshman admission** 70% were admitted. Average high school GPA 2.96 **Freshman test scores** SAT critical reading scores over 500: 32%; SAT math scores over 500: 38%; ACT scores over 18: 73%; SAT critical reading scores over 600: 12%; SAT math scores over 600: 8%; ACT scores over 24: 15% **Housing** Yes **Expenses** Tuition & Fees: state resident $4279, nonresident $12,959; Room & Board $6420 **Undergraduates** 55% women, 17% part-time, 23% 25 or older, 2% Native

American, 2% Hispanic American, 1% African American, 3% Asian American/Pacific Islander **The most frequently chosen baccalaureate fields are** education, business/marketing, liberal arts/general studies **Academic program** Advanced placement, accelerated degree program, self-designed majors, honors program, summer session, adult/continuing education programs, internships **Contact** Office of Admissions, The University of Montana Western, 710 South Atlantic, Dillon, MT 59725. *Phone:* 406-683-7331 or toll-free 866-869-6668 (in-state); 877-683-7493 (out-of-state). *Fax:* 406-683-7493. *E-mail:* admissions@umwestern.edu. *Web site:* http://www.umwestern.edu/.
Visit Petersons.com and enter keyword Montana

NEBRASKA

Bellevue University
Bellevue, Nebraska

Contact Michelle Eppler, Dean of Students/Dean of Academic Services, Bellevue University, 1000 Galvin Road South, Bellevue, NE 68005-3098. *Phone:* 402-557-7010 or toll-free 800-756-7920. *Fax:* 402-557-5404. *E-mail:* michelle.eppler@bellevue.edu. *Web site:* http://www.bellevue.edu/.

Chadron State College
Chadron, Nebraska

Contact Ms. Tena Cook Gould, Director of Admissions, Chadron State College, 1000 Main Street, Chadron, NE 69337-2690. *Phone:* 308-432-6263 or toll-free 800-242-3766. *Fax:* 308-432-6229. *E-mail:* inquire@csc1.csc.edu. *Web site:* http://www.csc.edu/.
Visit Petersons.com and enter keyword Chadron

See page 696 for the College Close-Up.

Clarkson College
Omaha, Nebraska

General Independent, comprehensive, coed, primarily women **Entrance** Moderately difficult **Setting** 3-acre urban campus **Total enrollment** 820 **Student-faculty ratio** 8:1 **Application deadline** Rolling (freshmen), rolling (transfer) **Freshman admission** 55% were admitted **Freshman test scores** ACT scores over 18: 91%; ACT scores over 24: 30% **Housing** Yes **Expenses** Tuition & Fees $11,310; Room only $6200 **Undergraduates** 90% women, 42% 25 or older, 0.5% Native American, 4% Hispanic American, 4% African American, 2% Asian American/Pacific Islander **The most frequently chosen baccalaureate field is** health professions and related sciences **Academic program** Advanced placement, accelerated degree program, summer session, adult/continuing education programs, internships **Contact** Ms. Denise Work, Director of Admissions, Clarkson College, 101 South 42nd Street, Omaha, NE 68131-2739. *Phone:* 402-552-3100 or toll-free 800-647-5500. *E-mail:* workdenise@clarksoncollege.edu. *Web site:* http://www.clarksoncollege.edu/.

College of Saint Mary
Omaha, Nebraska

General Independent Roman Catholic, comprehensive, women only **Entrance** Minimally difficult **Setting** 25-acre urban campus **Total enrollment** 1,120 **Student-faculty ratio** 14:1 **Application deadline** Rolling (freshmen), rolling (transfer) **Freshman admission** 42% were admitted. Average high school GPA 3.41 **Freshman test scores** ACT scores over 18: 89%; ACT scores over 24: 17% **Housing** Yes **Expenses** Tuition & Fees $23,130; Room & Board $6400 **Undergraduates** 20% part-time, 45% 25 or older, 1% Native American, 9% Hispanic American, 12% African American, 1% Asian American/Pacific Islander **The most frequently chosen baccalaureate fields are** business/marketing, health professions and related sciences, psychology **Academic program** Advanced placement, accelerated degree program, honors program, summer session, internships **Contact** Ms. Erika Pritchard, Admissions Officer, College of Saint Mary, 7000 Mercy Road, Omaha, NE 68106. *Phone:* 402-399-2406 or toll-free 800-926-5534. *Fax:* 402-399-2412. *E-mail:* enroll@csm.edu. *Web site:* http://www.csm.edu/.

Concordia University, Nebraska
Seward, Nebraska

General Independent, comprehensive, coed, affiliated with Lutheran Church–Missouri Synod **Entrance** Moderately difficult **Setting** 120-acre small-town campus **Total enrollment** 1,344 **Student-faculty ratio** 14:1 **Application deadline** 8/1 (freshmen), 8/1 (transfer) **Freshman admission** 68% were admitted. Average high school GPA 3.49 **Freshman test scores** SAT critical reading scores over 500: 60%; SAT math scores over 500: 67%; ACT scores over 18: 97%; SAT critical reading scores over 600: 25%; SAT math scores over 600: 15%; ACT scores over 24: 50% **Housing** Yes **Expenses** Tuition & Fees $21,250; Room & Board $5520 **Undergraduates** 52% women, 7% part-time, 2% 25 or older, 0.2% Native American, 1% Hispanic American, 2% African American, 1% Asian American/Pacific Islander **The most frequently chosen baccalaureate fields are** business/marketing, education, theology and religious vocations **Academic program** English as a second language, advanced placement, accelerated degree program, summer session, adult/continuing education programs, internships **Contact** Mr. Aaron Roberts, Director of Undergraduate Recruitment, Concordia University, Nebraska, 800 North Columbia Avenue, Seward, NE 68434-1599. *Phone:* 800-535-5494 Ext. 7233 or toll-free 800-535-5494. *Fax:* 402-643-4073. *E-mail:* admiss@cune.edu. *Web site:* http://www.cune.edu/.

Creative Center
Omaha, Nebraska

General Proprietary, primarily 2-year, coed **Setting** 1-acre urban campus **Student-faculty ratio** 26:1 **Housing** No **Contact** Admissions and Placement Coordinator, Creative Center, 10850 Emmet Street, Omaha, NE 68164. *Phone:* 402-898-1000 or toll-free 888-898-1789. *Fax:* 402-898-1301. *E-mail:* admission@creativecenter.edu. *Web site:* http://www.creativecenter.edu/.

Creighton University
Omaha, Nebraska

General Independent Roman Catholic (Jesuit), university, coed **Entrance** Moderately difficult **Setting** 110-acre urban campus **Total enrollment** 7,385 **Student-faculty ratio** 11:1 **Application deadline** 2/15 (freshmen), 8/1 (transfer) **Freshman admission** 82% were admitted. Average high school GPA 3.75 **Freshman test scores** SAT critical reading scores over 500: 81.6%; SAT math scores over 500: 86.6%; ACT scores over 18: 98.9%; SAT critical reading scores over 600: 44%; SAT math scores over 600: 50.4%; ACT scores over 24: 77.7% **Housing** Yes **Expenses** Tuition & Fees $22,118; Room & Board $8814 **Undergraduates** 59% women, 6% part-time, 1% 25 or older, 1% Native American, 4% Hispanic American, 3% African American, 10% Asian American/Pacific Islander **The most frequently chosen baccalaureate fields are** business/marketing, biological/life sciences, health professions and related sciences **Academic program** English as a second language, advanced placement, accelerated degree program, self-designed majors, honors program, summer session, adult/continuing education programs, internships **Contact** Ms. Mary Chase, Assistant Vice President for Enrollment Management and Director of Admissions and Scholarships, Creighton University, 2500 California Plaza, Omaha, NE 68178-0001. *Phone:* 402-280-3105 or toll-free 800-282-5835. *Fax:* 402-280-2685. *E-mail:* admissions@creighton.edu. *Web site:* http://www.creighton.edu/.

Dana College
Blair, Nebraska

General Independent, 4-year, coed, affiliated with Evangelical Lutheran Church in America **Entrance** Moderately difficult **Setting** 150-acre

Dana College (continued)
small-town campus **Total enrollment** 596 **Student-faculty ratio** 14:1 **Application deadline** Rolling (freshmen), rolling (transfer) **Freshman admission** 66% were admitted. Average high school GPA 3.26 **Freshman test scores** SAT critical reading scores over 500: 18.75%; SAT math scores over 500: 50%; ACT scores over 18: 94.55%; SAT math scores over 600: 12.5%; ACT scores over 24: 30.91% **Housing** Yes **Expenses** Tuition & Fees $21,100; Room & Board $6220 **Undergraduates** 46% women, 3% part-time, 7% 25 or older, 1% Native American, 5% Hispanic American, 6% African American, 2% Asian American/Pacific Islander **The most frequently chosen baccalaureate fields are** business/marketing, education, parks and recreation **Academic program** Advanced placement, accelerated degree program, self-designed majors, honors program, summer session, adult/continuing education programs, internships **Contact** Tina Blair, Director of Admissions, Dana College, 2848 College Drive, Blair, NE 68008-1099. *Phone:* 402-426-7220 or toll-free 800-444-3262. *E-mail:* admissions@dana.edu. *Web site:* http://www.dana.edu/.

Doane College
Crete, Nebraska

General Independent, comprehensive, coed, affiliated with United Church of Christ **Entrance** Moderately difficult **Setting** 300-acre small-town campus **Total enrollment** 969 **Student-faculty ratio** 11:1 **Application deadline** Rolling (freshmen), rolling (transfer) **Freshman admission** 76% were admitted. Average high school GPA 3.44 **Freshman test scores** ACT scores over 18: 93%; ACT scores over 24: 43% **Housing** Yes **Expenses** Tuition & Fees $21,040; Room & Board $5970 **Undergraduates** 50% women, 1% part-time, 1% 25 or older, 1% Native American, 4% Hispanic American, 3% African American, 1% Asian American/Pacific Islander **The most frequently chosen baccalaureate fields are** business/marketing, education, social sciences **Academic program** English as a second language, advanced placement, self-designed majors, honors program, summer session, internships **Contact** Mr. Joel M. Weyand, Vice President for Admission, Doane College, 1014 Boswell Avenue, Crete, NE 68333-2430. *Phone:* 800-333-6263 or toll-free 800-333-6263. *E-mail:* joel.weyand@doane.edu. *Web site:* http://www.doane.edu/.

Grace University
Omaha, Nebraska

General Independent interdenominational, comprehensive, coed **Entrance** Moderately difficult **Setting** 15-acre urban campus **Total enrollment** 434 **Student-faculty ratio** 18:1 **Application deadline** Rolling (freshmen), rolling (transfer) **Freshman admission** 64% were admitted. Average high school GPA 3.26 **Housing** Yes **Expenses** Tuition & Fees $14,290; Room & Board $5740 **Undergraduates** 57% women, 22% part-time, 34% 25 or older, 0.3% Native American, 3% Hispanic American, 5% African American, 2% Asian American/Pacific Islander **The most frequently chosen baccalaureate fields are** psychology, business/marketing, theology and religious vocations **Academic program** Advanced placement, accelerated degree program, self-designed majors, summer session, adult/continuing education programs, internships **Contact** Angela Wayman, Director of Admissions, Grace University, 1311 South Ninth Street, Omaha, NE 68108. *Phone:* 402-449-2831 or toll-free 800-383-1422. *Fax:* 402-341-9587. *E-mail:* admissions@graceuniversity.com. *Web site:* http://www.graceuniversity.edu/.

Hastings College
Hastings, Nebraska

Contact Ms. Mary Molliconi, Director of Admissions, Hastings College, 710 North Turner Avenue, Hastings, NE 68901-7621. *Phone:* 402-461-7320 or toll-free 800-532-7642. *Fax:* 402-461-7490. *E-mail:* mmolliconi@hastings.edu. *Web site:* http://www.hastings.edu/.

ITT Technical Institute
Omaha, Nebraska

General Proprietary, primarily 2-year, coed **Entrance** Minimally difficult **Setting** urban campus **Housing** No **Contact** Director of Recruitment, ITT Technical Institute, 9814 M Street, Omaha, NE 68127-2056. *Phone:* 402-331-2900 or toll-free 800-677-9260. *Web site:* http://www.itt-tech.edu/.

Kaplan University, Lincoln
Lincoln, Nebraska

General Proprietary, primarily 2-year, coed **Setting** urban campus **Contact** Office of Admissions, Kaplan University, Lincoln, 1821 K Street, Lincoln, NE 68501-2826. *Phone:* 402-474-5315. *Web site:* http://www.lincoln.kaplanuniversity.edu.

Kaplan University, Omaha
Omaha, Nebraska

General Proprietary, primarily 2-year, coed **Setting** urban campus **Contact** Director of Admissions, Kaplan University, Omaha, 5425 North 103rd Street, Omaha, NE 68134. *Phone:* 402-572-8500 or toll-free 800-642-1456. *Web site:* http://www.omaha.kaplanuniversity.edu.

Midland Lutheran College
Fremont, Nebraska

Contact Mr. Todd Hansen, Associate Director of Admissions, Midland Lutheran College, 900 North Clarkson Street, Fremont, NE 68025-4200. *Phone:* 402-941-6504 or toll-free 800-642-8382 Ext. 6501. *Fax:* 402-941-6513. *E-mail:* admissions@mlc.edu. *Web site:* http://www.mlc.edu/.

Nebraska Christian College
Papillion, Nebraska

Contact Ms. Alisha Livengood, Associate Director of Admissions, Nebraska Christian College, 12550 South 114th Steet, Papillion, NE 68046. *Phone:* 402-935-9407. *Web site:* http://www.nechristian.edu/.

Nebraska Methodist College
Omaha, Nebraska

General Independent, comprehensive, coed, primarily women, affiliated with United Methodist Church **Entrance** Moderately difficult **Setting** 5-acre urban campus **Total enrollment** 672 **Student-faculty ratio** 9:1 **Application deadline** Rolling (freshmen), rolling (transfer) **Freshman admission** 38% were admitted. Average high school GPA 3.41 **Freshman test scores** ACT scores over 18: 93%; ACT scores over 24: 39% **Housing** Yes **Expenses** Tuition & Fees $12,740; Room only $5770 **Undergraduates** 91% women, 27% part-time, 25% 25 or older, 1% Native American, 1% Hispanic American, 3% African American, 3% Asian American/Pacific Islander **The most frequently chosen baccalaureate field is** health professions and related sciences **Academic program** Advanced placement, accelerated degree program, summer session, adult/continuing education programs, internships **Contact** Sara Bonney, Director of Enrollment Services, Nebraska Methodist College, 720 North 87th Street, Omaha, NE 68114. *Phone:* 402-354-7111 or toll-free 800-335-5510. *Fax:* 402-354-7020. *E-mail:* sara.bonney@methodistcollege.edu. *Web site:* http://www.methodistcollege.edu/.

Nebraska Wesleyan University
Lincoln, Nebraska

General Independent United Methodist, comprehensive, coed **Entrance** Moderately difficult **Setting** 50-acre suburban campus **Total enrollment** 2,093 **Student-faculty ratio** 13:1 **Application deadline** 8/15 (freshmen),

8/15 (transfer) **Freshman admission** 82% were admitted **Freshman test scores** ACT scores over 18: 100%; ACT scores over 24: 66% **Housing** Yes **Expenses** Tuition & Fees $22,432; Room & Board $6230 **Undergraduates** 58% women, 12% part-time, 2% 25 or older, 0.2% Native American, 1% Hispanic American, 2% African American, 2% Asian American/Pacific Islander **The most frequently chosen baccalaureate fields are** biological/life sciences, business/marketing, health professions and related sciences **Academic program** Advanced placement, accelerated degree program, summer session, adult/continuing education programs, internships **Contact** David Duzik, Director of Admissions, Nebraska Wesleyan University, 5000 Saint Paul Avenue, Lincoln, NE 68504. *Phone:* 402-465-2144 or toll-free 800-541-3818. *Fax:* 402-465-2177. *E-mail:* admissions@nebrwesleyan.edu. *Web site:* http://www.nebrwesleyan.edu/.

Peru State College
Peru, Nebraska

General State-supported, comprehensive, coed **Entrance** Noncompetitive **Setting** 104-acre rural campus **Total enrollment** 2,492 **Student-faculty ratio** 20:1 **Application deadline** Rolling (freshmen), rolling (transfer) **Freshman admission** 48% were admitted. Average high school GPA 3.01 **Freshman test scores** ACT scores over 18: 72%; ACT scores over 24: 24% **Housing** Yes **Expenses** Tuition & Fees: state resident $4763; Room & Board $4962 **Undergraduates** 58% women, 42% part-time, 32% 25 or older, 1% Native American, 2% Hispanic American, 3% African American, 1% Asian American/Pacific Islander **The most frequently chosen baccalaureate fields are** business/marketing, education, psychology **Academic program** Advanced placement, accelerated degree program, honors program, summer session, adult/continuing education programs, internships **Contact** Ms. Micki Willis, Vice President for Enrollment Management & Student Affairs, Peru State College, PO Box 10, Peru, NE 68421. *Phone:* 402-872-2221 or toll-free 800-742-4412. *Fax:* 402-872-2296. *E-mail:* mwillis@peru.edu. *Web site:* http://www.peru.edu/.

St. Gregory the Great Seminary
Seward, Nebraska

Contact St. Gregory the Great Seminary, 800 Fletcher Road, Seward, NE 67434. *Web site:* http://www.stgregoryseminary.edu/.

Union College
Lincoln, Nebraska

General Independent Seventh-day Adventist, comprehensive, coed **Entrance** Moderately difficult **Setting** 26-acre suburban campus **Total enrollment** 883 **Student-faculty ratio** 13:1 **Application deadline** Rolling (freshmen), rolling (transfer) **Freshman admission** 41% were admitted. Average high school GPA 3.43 **Freshman test scores** ACT scores over 18: 90%; ACT scores over 24: 41% **Housing** Yes **Expenses** Tuition & Fees $18,150; Room & Board $5900 **Undergraduates** 59% women, 18% part-time, 10% 25 or older, 1% Native American, 8% Hispanic American, 3% African American, 3% Asian American/Pacific Islander **The most frequently chosen baccalaureate fields are** business/marketing, education, health professions and related sciences **Academic program** English as a second language, advanced placement, accelerated degree program, self-designed majors, honors program, summer session, adult/continuing education programs, internships **Contact** Jennifer Enos, Admissions Assistant Director, Union College, 3800 South 48th Street, Lincoln, NE 68506. *Phone:* 402-486-2600 Ext. 2052 or toll-free 800-228-4600. *Fax:* 402-486-2895. *E-mail:* ucenroll@ucollege.edu. *Web site:* http://www.ucollege.edu/.

University of Nebraska at Kearney
Kearney, Nebraska

General State-supported, comprehensive, coed **Entrance** Moderately difficult **Setting** 235-acre small-town campus **Total enrollment** 6,650 **Student-faculty ratio** 16:1 **Application deadline** Rolling (freshmen), rolling (transfer) **Freshman admission** 77% were admitted. Average high school GPA 3.3 **Freshman test scores** ACT scores over 18: 93%; ACT scores over 24: 40% **Housing** Yes **Expenses** Tuition & Fees: state resident $5634, nonresident $10,397; Room & Board $6830 **Undergraduates** 52% women, 10% part-time, 10% 25 or older, 0.3% Native American, 5% Hispanic American, 1% African American, 1% Asian American/Pacific Islander **The most frequently chosen baccalaureate fields are** business/marketing, education, parks and recreation **Academic program** English as a second language, advanced placement, honors program, summer session, internships **Contact** Mr. Dusty Newton, Director of Admissions, University of Nebraska at Kearney, 905 West 25th Street, Kearney, NE 68849-0001. *Phone:* 308-865-8702 or toll-free 800-532-7639. *Fax:* 308-865-8987. *E-mail:* admissionsug@unk.edu. *Web site:* http://www.unk.edu/.

University of Nebraska at Omaha
Omaha, Nebraska

General State-supported, university, coed **Entrance** Minimally difficult **Setting** 503-acre urban campus **Total enrollment** 14,620 **Student-faculty ratio** 19:1 **Application deadline** 8/1 (freshmen), 8/1 (transfer) **Freshman admission** 80% were admitted. Average high school GPA 3.3 **Freshman test scores** ACT scores over 18: 91%; ACT scores over 24: 41% **Housing** Yes **Expenses** Tuition & Fees: state resident $6229, nonresident $16,189; Room & Board $7230 **Undergraduates** 51% women, 22% part-time, 20% 25 or older, 1% Native American, 4% Hispanic American, 6% African American, 3% Asian American/Pacific Islander **The most frequently chosen baccalaureate fields are** business/marketing, education, security and protective services **Academic program** English as a second language, advanced placement, self-designed majors, honors program, summer session, adult/continuing education programs, internships **Contact** Ms. Jolene Adams, Associate Director of Admissions, University of Nebraska at Omaha, 6001 Dodge Street, Omaha, NE 68182. *Phone:* 402-554-2416 or toll-free 800-858-8648. *Fax:* 402-554-3472. *E-mail:* jadams@mail.unomaha.edu. *Web site:* http://www.unomaha.edu/.

University of Nebraska–Lincoln
Lincoln, Nebraska

General State-supported, university, coed **Entrance** Moderately difficult **Setting** 624-acre urban campus **Total enrollment** 24,100 **Student-faculty ratio** 20:1 **Application deadline** 5/1 (freshmen), 5/1 (transfer) **Freshman admission** 63% were admitted **Freshman test scores** SAT critical reading scores over 500: 80%; SAT math scores over 500: 86%; ACT scores over 18: 99%; SAT critical reading scores over 600: 52%; SAT math scores over 600: 58%; ACT scores over 24: 64% **Housing** Yes **Expenses** Tuition & Fees: state resident $6857, nonresident $17,897; Room & Board $7260 **Undergraduates** 46% women, 6% part-time, 6% 25 or older, 1% Native American, 4% Hispanic American, 3% African American, 3% Asian American/Pacific Islander **The most frequently chosen baccalaureate fields are** business/marketing, education, engineering **Academic program** English as a second language, advanced placement, accelerated degree program, self-designed majors, honors program, summer session, adult/continuing education programs, internships **Contact** Pat McBride, Director, New Student Enrollment, University of Nebraska–Lincoln, 1410 Q Street, Lincoln, NE 68588-0417. *Phone:* 402-472-2023 or toll-free 800-742-8800. *Fax:* 402-472-0670. *E-mail:* admissions@unl.edu. *Web site:* http://www.unl.edu/.

University of Nebraska Medical Center
Omaha, Nebraska

General State-supported, upper-level, coed **Setting** 51-acre urban campus **Total enrollment** 3,237 **Application deadline** Rolling (transfer) **Housing** No **Expenses** Tuition & Fees: state resident $5800, nonresident $16,420

University of Nebraska Medical Center (continued)
Undergraduates 91% women, 11% part-time, 3% 25 or older, 0.5% Native American, 4% Hispanic American, 2% African American, 2% Asian American/Pacific Islander **The most frequently chosen baccalaureate field is** health professions and related sciences **Academic program** Accelerated degree program, honors program, summer session **Contact** Ms. Tymaree Tonjes, Administrative Technician, University of Nebraska Medical Center, Nebraska Medical Center, Omaha, NE 68198. *Phone:* 402-559-6468 or toll-free 800-626-8431 Ext. 6468. *Fax:* 402-559-6796. *E-mail:* ttonjes@unmc.edu. *Web site:* http://www.unmc.edu/.

Wayne State College
Wayne, Nebraska

General State-supported, comprehensive, coed **Entrance** Noncompetitive **Setting** 128-acre small-town campus **Total enrollment** 3,631 **Student-faculty ratio** 20:1 **Application deadline** Rolling (freshmen), rolling (transfer) **Freshman admission** 100% were admitted. Average high school GPA 3.21 **Freshman test scores** ACT scores over 18: 80%; ACT scores over 24: 29% **Housing** Yes **Expenses** Tuition & Fees: state resident $4805, nonresident $8480; Room & Board $5280 **Undergraduates** 54% women, 8% part-time, 12% 25 or older, 1% Native American, 2% Hispanic American, 3% African American, 1% Asian American/Pacific Islander **The most frequently chosen baccalaureate fields are** business/marketing, education, parks and recreation **Academic program** Advanced placement, self-designed majors, honors program, summer session, adult/continuing education programs, internships **Contact** Ms. Tammy Young, Director of Admissions, Wayne State College, 1111 Main Street, Wayne, NE 68787. *Phone:* 402-375-7234 or toll-free 800-228-9972. *Fax:* 402-375-7204. *E-mail:* admit1@wsc.edu. *Web site:* http://www.wsc.edu/.

York College
York, Nebraska

General Independent, 4-year, coed, affiliated with Church of Christ **Entrance** Moderately difficult **Setting** 44-acre small-town campus **Total enrollment** 430 **Student-faculty ratio** 11:1 **Application deadline** Rolling (freshmen), rolling (transfer) **Freshman admission** 60% were admitted. Average high school GPA 3.02 **Freshman test scores** SAT critical reading scores over 500: 50%; SAT math scores over 500: 50%; ACT scores over 18: 74%; SAT critical reading scores over 600: 10%; SAT math scores over 600: 10%; ACT scores over 24: 34% **Housing** Yes **Expenses** Tuition & Fees $14,998; Room & Board $5680 **Undergraduates** 44% women, 3% part-time, 5% 25 or older, 1% Native American, 5% Hispanic American, 9% African American, 1% Asian American/Pacific Islander **The most frequently chosen baccalaureate fields are** business/marketing, education, psychology **Academic program** Advanced placement, honors program, summer session, internships **Contact** Ms. Janae Parsons, York College, 1125 East 8th Street, York, NE 68467-2699. *Phone:* 402-363-5627 or toll-free 800-950-9675. *Fax:* 402-363-5623. *E-mail:* enroll@york.edu. *Web site:* http://www.york.edu/.

NEVADA

The Art Institute of Las Vegas
Henderson, Nevada

General Proprietary, 4-year, coed **Setting** suburban campus **Contact** Director of Admissions, The Art Institute of Las Vegas, 2350 Corporate Circle Drive, Henderson, NV 89074. *Phone:* 702-369-9944. *Fax:* 702-992-8458. *Web site:* http://www.artinstitutes.edu/lasvegas.
Visit Petersons.com and enter keywords Art Institute of Las Vegas

See page 524 for the College Close-Up.

DeVry University
Henderson, Nevada

General Proprietary, comprehensive, coed **Entrance** Minimally difficult **Total enrollment** 373 **Student-faculty ratio** 20:1 **Application deadline** Rolling (freshmen), rolling (transfer) **Housing** No **Expenses** Tuition & Fees $14,080 **Undergraduates** 42% women, 51% part-time, 70% 25 or older, 0.4% Native American, 19% Hispanic American, 20% African American, 11% Asian American/Pacific Islander **The most frequently chosen baccalaureate field is** business/marketing **Academic program** Advanced placement, accelerated degree program, summer session, adult/continuing education programs **Contact** Admissions Office, DeVry University, 2490 Paseo Verde Parkway, Henderson, NV 89074-7120. *Web site:* http://www.devry.edu/.

Great Basin College
Elko, Nevada

Contact Ms. Julie Byrnes, Director of Enrollment Management, Great Basin College, 1500 College Parkway, Elko, NV 89801-3348. *Phone:* 775-753-2271. *Fax:* 775-753-2311. *E-mail:* stdsvc@gbcnv.edu. *Web site:* http://www.gbcnv.edu/.

ITT Technical Institute
Henderson, Nevada

General Proprietary, primarily 2-year, coed **Entrance** Minimally difficult **Housing** No **Contact** Director of Recruitment, ITT Technical Institute, 168 North Gibson Road, Henderson, NV 89014. *Phone:* 702-558-5404 or toll-free 800-488-8459. *Web site:* http://www.itt-tech.edu/.

Morrison University
Reno, Nevada

Contact Mr. Charles Timinsky, Director of Enrollment, Morrison University, 10315 Professional Circle, Suite 201, Reno, NV 89521. *Phone:* 775-850-0700 Ext. 101 or toll-free 800-369-6144. *Fax:* 775-850-0711. *E-mail:* ctiminsky@morrison.neumont.edu. *Web site:* http://www.morrison.neumont.edu/.

Nevada State College at Henderson
Henderson, Nevada

General State-supported, 4-year, coed **Entrance** Minimally difficult **Setting** 520-acre suburban campus **Total enrollment** 2,516 **Student-faculty ratio** 20:1 **Application deadline** 8/20 (freshmen), 8/20 (transfer) **Freshman admission** 72% were admitted. Average high school GPA 2.82 **Freshman test scores** SAT critical reading scores over 500: 20.45%; SAT math scores over 500: 25%; ACT scores over 18: 70.27%; SAT math scores over 600: 2.27%; ACT scores over 24: 24.32% **Housing** No **Expenses** Tuition & Fees: state resident $3248, nonresident $12,512 **Undergraduates** 75% women, 60% part-time, 49% 25 or older, 1% Native American, 16% Hispanic American, 10% African American, 14% Asian American/Pacific Islander **The most frequently chosen baccalaureate fields are** business/marketing, education, health professions and related sciences **Academic program** English as a second language, advanced placement, accelerated degree program, self-designed majors, summer session, adult/continuing education programs, internships **Contact** Ms. Patricia Ring, Registrar, Nevada State College at Henderson, Office of Admissions and Records, 1125 Nevada State Drive, Henderson, NV 89002. *Phone:* 702-992-2114. *Fax:* 702-992-2111. *E-mail:* admissions@nsc.nevada.edu. *Web site:* http://www.nsc.nevada.edu/.

Sierra Nevada College
Incline Village, Nevada

Contact Matt Delekta, James McMaster, Dean of Enrollment Services and Registrar, Sierra Nevada College, 999 Tahoe Boulevard, Incline

Village, NV 89451. *Phone:* 866-412-4636. *Fax:* 775-831-6223. *E-mail:* admissions@sierranevada.edu. *Web site:* http://www.sierranevada.edu/.

University of Nevada, Las Vegas
Las Vegas, Nevada

General State-supported, university, coed **Entrance** Moderately difficult **Setting** 358-acre urban campus **Total enrollment** 29,086 **Student-faculty ratio** 21:1 **Application deadline** Rolling (freshmen), rolling (transfer) **Freshman admission** 78% were admitted. Average high school GPA 3.26 **Freshman test scores** SAT critical reading scores over 500: 52.6%; SAT math scores over 500: 57.2%; ACT scores over 18: 86.3%; SAT critical reading scores over 600: 12.8%; SAT math scores over 600: 19.5%; ACT scores over 24: 31.5% **Housing** Yes **Expenses** Tuition & Fees: state resident $5525, nonresident $18,815; Room & Board $10,454 **Undergraduates** 55% women, 28% part-time, 27% 25 or older, 1% Native American, 18% Hispanic American, 9% African American, 18% Asian American/Pacific Islander **The most frequently chosen baccalaureate fields are** business/marketing, education, psychology **Academic program** English as a second language, advanced placement, accelerated degree program, self-designed majors, honors program, summer session, adult/continuing education programs, internships **Contact** Carrie Trentham, Assistant Director of Admissions, University of Nevada, Las Vegas, 4505 Maryland Parkway, Box 451021, Las Vegas, NV 89154-1021. *Phone:* 702-774-8010. *Fax:* 702-774-8008. *E-mail:* admissions@unlv.edu. *Web site:* http://www.unlv.edu/.

University of Nevada, Reno
Reno, Nevada

General State-supported, university, coed **Entrance** Moderately difficult **Setting** 200-acre urban campus **Total enrollment** 16,862 **Student-faculty ratio** 23:1 **Application deadline** Rolling (freshmen), rolling (transfer) **Freshman admission** 88% were admitted. Average high school GPA 3.35 **Freshman test scores** SAT critical reading scores over 500: 64%; SAT math scores over 500: 67%; ACT scores over 18: 90%; SAT critical reading scores over 600: 21%; SAT math scores over 600: 27%; ACT scores over 24: 43% **Housing** Yes **Expenses** Tuition & Fees: state resident $5051, nonresident $17,391; Room & Board $10,595 **Undergraduates** 17% 25 or older, 1% Native American, 10% Hispanic American, 3% African American, 7% Asian American/Pacific Islander **The most frequently chosen baccalaureate fields are** business/marketing, health professions and related sciences, social sciences **Academic program** English as a second language, advanced placement, honors program, summer session, adult/continuing education programs, internships **Contact** Dr. Steve Maples, Director of Undergraduate Admissions, University of Nevada, Reno, Mail Stop 120, Reno, NV 89557. *Phone:* 775-784-4700 or toll-free 866-263-8232. *Fax:* 775-784-4283. *E-mail:* asknevada@unr.edu. *Web site:* http://www.unr.edu/.

University of Phoenix–Las Vegas Campus
Las Vegas, Nevada

General Proprietary, comprehensive, coed **Entrance** Noncompetitive **Setting** urban campus **Total enrollment** 3,162 **Application deadline** Rolling (freshmen), rolling (transfer) **Housing** No **Expenses** Tuition & Fees $11,438 **Undergraduates** 67% women, 83% 25 or older, 1% Native American, 14% Hispanic American, 17% African American, 5% Asian American/Pacific Islander **The most frequently chosen baccalaureate fields are** business/marketing, computer and information sciences, security and protective services **Academic program** Advanced placement, accelerated degree program, adult/continuing education programs **Contact** Ms. Audra McQuarie, Registrar/Executive Director, University of Phoenix–Las Vegas Campus, 4305 South Riverpoint Parkway, Mail Stop CF-L101, Phoenix, AZ 85040. *Phone:* 480-557-6151 or toll-free 800-776-4867 (in-state); 800-228-7240 (out-of-state). *Fax:* 480-643-3068. *E-mail:* audra.mcquarie@phoenix.edu. *Web site:* http://www.phoenix.edu/.

University of Phoenix–Northern Nevada Campus
Reno, Nevada

General Proprietary, comprehensive, coed **Entrance** Noncompetitive **Total enrollment** 605 **Housing** No **Expenses** Tuition & Fees $11,438 **Undergraduates** 63% women, 87% 25 or older, 2% Native American, 7% Hispanic American, 2% African American, 3% Asian American/Pacific Islander **The most frequently chosen baccalaureate fields are** business/marketing, computer and information sciences, interdisciplinary studies **Contact** Ms. Audra McQuarie, Registrar/Executive Director, University of Phoenix–Northern Nevada Campus, 4035 South Riverpoint Parkway, Mail Stop CF-L101, Phoenix, AZ 85040. *Phone:* 480-557-6151. *Fax:* 480-643-3068. *E-mail:* audra.mcquarie@phoenix.edu. *Web site:* http://www.phoenix.edu/.

NEW HAMPSHIRE

Chester College of New England
Chester, New Hampshire

Contact Ms. Sarah Vogell, Director of Admissions, Chester College of New England, 40 Chester Street, Chester, NH 03036. *Phone:* 603-887-7400 or toll-free 800-974-6372. *Fax:* 603-887-1777. *E-mail:* admissions@chestercollege.edu. *Web site:* http://www.chestercollege.edu/.

Colby-Sawyer College
New London, New Hampshire

Contact Director of Admissions and Financial Aid, Colby-Sawyer College, 541 Main Street, New London, NH 03257-4648. *Phone:* 603-526-3700 or toll-free 800-272-1015. *Fax:* 603-526-3452. *E-mail:* admissions@colby-sawyer.edu. *Web site:* http://www.colby-sawyer.edu/.
Visit Petersons.com and enter keyword Colby-Sawyer

See page 722 for the College Close-Up.

Daniel Webster College
Nashua, New Hampshire

General Independent, comprehensive, coed **Entrance** Moderately difficult **Setting** 50-acre suburban campus **Total enrollment** 1,007 **Student-faculty ratio** 14:1 **Application deadline** Rolling (freshmen), rolling (transfer) **Freshman admission** 74% were admitted. Average high school GPA 3.2 **Freshman test scores** SAT critical reading scores over 500: 60%; SAT math scores over 500: 62%; ACT scores over 18: 78%; SAT critical reading scores over 600: 25%; SAT math scores over 600: 26%; ACT scores over 24: 21% **Housing** Yes **Expenses** Tuition & Fees $28,864; Room & Board $9698 **Undergraduates** 26% women, 10% part-time **Academic program** Advanced placement, accelerated degree program, summer session, adult/continuing education programs, internships **Contact** Mr. Daniel Monahan, Dean of Admissions and Financial Assistance, Daniel Webster College, 20 University Drive, Nashua, NH 03063-1300. *Phone:* 603-577-6600 or toll-free 800-325-6876. *Fax:* 603-577-6001. *E-mail:* monahan@dwc.edu. *Web site:* http://www.dwc.edu/.

Daniel Webster College–Portsmouth Campus
Portsmouth, New Hampshire

Contact Daniel Webster College–Portsmouth Campus, 119 International Drive, Pease International Tradeport, Portsmouth, NH 03801. *Phone:* toll-free 800-794-6188. *Web site:* http://www.dwc.edu/gcde/portsmouth/.

Dartmouth College
Hanover, New Hampshire

General Independent, university, coed **Entrance** Most difficult **Setting** 265-acre small-town campus **Total enrollment** 5,987 **Student-faculty ratio** 8:1 **Application deadline** 1/1 (freshmen), 3/1 (transfer) **Freshman admission** 13% were admitted **Freshman test scores** SAT critical reading scores over 500: 99%; SAT math scores over 500: 99%; SAT critical reading scores over 600: 93%; SAT math scores over 600: 93% **Housing** Yes **Expenses** Tuition & Fees $38,679; Room & Board $11,295 **Undergraduates** 49% women, 1% part-time, 4% Native American, 7% Hispanic American, 8% African American, 14% Asian American/Pacific Islander **The most frequently chosen baccalaureate fields are** biological/life sciences, area and ethnic studies, social sciences **Academic program** Advanced placement, self-designed majors, honors program, summer session, internships **Contact** Maria Laskaris, Dean of Admissions and Financial Aid, Dartmouth College, 6016 McNutt Hall, Hanover, NH 03755. *Phone:* 603-646-2875. *E-mail:* admissions.office@dartmouth.edu. *Web site:* http://www.dartmouth.edu/.

Franklin Pierce University
Rindge, New Hampshire

General Independent, university, coed **Entrance** Moderately difficult **Setting** 1,000-acre rural campus **Total enrollment** 2,437 **Student-faculty ratio** 14:1 **Application deadline** Rolling (freshmen) **Freshman admission** 81% were admitted. Average high school GPA 2.83 **Freshman test scores** SAT critical reading scores over 500: 46.2%; SAT math scores over 500: 42%; ACT scores over 18: 76.9%; SAT critical reading scores over 600: 8.8%; SAT math scores over 600: 7.8%; ACT scores over 24: 12.8% **Housing** Yes **Expenses** Tuition & Fees $28,700; Room & Board $9800 **Undergraduates** 54% women, 15% part-time, 0.4% Native American, 3% Hispanic American, 3% African American, 1% Asian American/Pacific Islander **The most frequently chosen baccalaureate fields are** business/marketing, security and protective services, visual and performing arts **Academic program** English as a second language, advanced placement, accelerated degree program, self-designed majors, honors program, summer session, adult/continuing education programs, internships **Contact** Office of Admissions, Franklin Pierce University, 40 University Drive, Rindge, NH 03461. *Phone:* 603-899-4050 or toll-free 800-437-0048. *Fax:* 603-899-4394. *E-mail:* admissions@fpc.edu. *Web site:* http://www.franklinpierce.edu/.

Visit Petersons.com and enter keywords Franklin Pierce

See page 814 for the College Close-Up.

Granite State College
Concord, New Hampshire

General State and locally supported, 4-year, coed, primarily women **Entrance** Noncompetitive **Setting** suburban campus **Total enrollment** 1,734 **Student-faculty ratio** 10:1 **Application deadline** Rolling (freshmen), rolling (transfer) **Freshman admission** 100% were admitted **Housing** No **Expenses** Tuition & Fees: state resident $6195, nonresident $6555 **Undergraduates** 73% women, 55% part-time, 80% 25 or older, 1% Native American, 1% Hispanic American, 1% African American, 1% Asian American/Pacific Islander **The most frequently chosen baccalaureate fields are** interdisciplinary studies, business/marketing, liberal arts/general studies **Academic program** Advanced placement, accelerated degree program, self-designed majors, summer session, adult/continuing education programs, internships **Contact** Ms. Tessa McDonnell, Dean of Learner Services, Granite State College, 8 Old Suncook Road, Concord, NH 03301. *Phone:* 603-513-1308 or toll-free 800-582-7248 Ext. 313. *Fax:* 603-513-1386. *E-mail:* tessa.mcdonnell@granite.edu. *Web site:* http://www.granite.edu/.

Hesser College, Concord
Concord, New Hampshire

General Proprietary, primarily 2-year, coed **Contact** Director of Admissions, Hesser College, Concord, 25 Hall Street, Suite 104, Concord, NH 03301. *Phone:* 603-225-9200. *Web site:* http://www.concord.hesser.edu/.

Hesser College, Manchester
Manchester, New Hampshire

General Proprietary, primarily 2-year, coed **Setting** urban campus **Contact** Director of Admissions, Hesser College, Manchester, 3 Sundial Avenue, Manchester, NH 03103. *Phone:* 603-668-6660. *Web site:* http://www.manchester.hesser.edu/.

Visit Petersons.com and enter keyword Hesser

See page 844 for the College Close-Up.

Hesser College, Nashua
Nashua, New Hampshire

General Proprietary, primarily 2-year, coed **Contact** Director of Admissions, Hesser College, Nashua, 410 Amherst Street, Nashua, NH 03063. *Phone:* 603-883-0404. *Web site:* http://www.nashua.hesser.edu/.

Hesser College, Portsmouth
Portsmouth, New Hampshire

General Proprietary, primarily 2-year, coed **Contact** Director of Admissions, Hesser College, Portsmouth, 170 Commerce Way, Portsmouth, NH03801. *Phone:* 603-436-5300. *Web site:* http://www.portsmouth.hesser.edu/.

Hesser College, Salem
Salem, New Hampshire

General Proprietary, primarily 2-year, coed **Contact** Director of Admissions, Hesser College, Salem, 11 Manor Parkway, Salem, NH 03079. *Phone:* 603-898-3480. *Web site:* http://www.salem.hesser.edu/.

Keene State College
Keene, New Hampshire

General State-supported, comprehensive, coed **Entrance** Moderately difficult **Setting** 160-acre small-town campus **Total enrollment** 5,356 **Student-faculty ratio** 18:1 **Application deadline** 4/1 (freshmen), rolling (transfer) **Freshman admission** 71% were admitted. Average high school GPA 3.03 **Freshman test scores** SAT critical reading scores over 500: 49.5%; SAT math scores over 500: 50.4%; SAT critical reading scores over 600: 11.1%; SAT math scores over 600: 9.6% **Housing** Yes **Expenses** Tuition & Fees: state resident $9334, nonresident $17,504; Room & Board $8444 **Undergraduates** 56% women, 7% part-time, 4% 25 or older, 0.2% Native American, 1% Hispanic American, 0.4% African American, 0.5% Asian American/Pacific Islander **The most frequently chosen baccalaureate fields are** education, psychology, social sciences **Academic program** English as a second language, advanced placement, self-designed majors, honors program, summer session, internships **Contact** Ms. Margaret Richmond, Director of Admissions, Keene State College, 229 Main Street, Keene, NH 03435-2604. *Phone:* 603-358-2273 or toll-free 800-KSC-1909. *Fax:* 603-358-2767. *E-mail:* admissions@keene.edu. *Web site:* http://www.keene.edu/.

Visit Petersons.com and enter keyword Keene

See page 886 for the College Close-Up.

Magdalen College
Warner, New Hampshire

Contact Mr. Justin Fout, Admissions Counselor, Magdalen College, 511 Kearsarge Mountain Road, Warner, NH 03278. *Phone:* 603-456-2656

Get to the heart of a liberal arts education, and graduate with the ability to connect, interpret, and apply your knowledge and experience.

Find your best self. Here.

Nate Rowe '10
"It's how college life should be – challenging academics, great friends, and a beautiful campus to enjoy it all."

Renee Staudinger '09
"My favorite class was Philosophy of Law. My career goal is to work for a nonprofit organization focusing on civil rights."

Chris Langille '03
"My internship was a diesel particulate study. I'm now a research associate at Keene State, working to bring a biodiesel refinery to the area."

Keene State College ▪ Keene, New Hampshire ▪ www.keene.edu

Ext. 12 or toll-free 877-498-1723. *Fax:* 603-456-2660. *E-mail:* admissions@magdalen.edu. *Web site:* http://www.magdalen.edu/.

New England College
Henniker, New Hampshire

General Independent, comprehensive, coed **Entrance** Minimally difficult **Setting** 225-acre small-town campus **Total enrollment** 1,916 **Student-faculty ratio** 12:1 **Application deadline** 9/7 (freshmen), 8/7 (transfer) **Freshman admission** 81% were admitted. Average high school GPA 2.72 **Freshman test scores** SAT critical reading scores over 500: 26.22%; SAT math scores over 500: 27.71%; ACT scores over 18: 54.55%; SAT critical reading scores over 600: 2.43%; SAT math scores over 600: 1.82%; ACT scores over 24: 13.64% **Housing** Yes **Expenses** Tuition & Fees $27,450; Room & Board $9626 **Undergraduates** 50% women, 7% part-time, 6% 25 or older **The most frequently chosen baccalaureate fields are** business/marketing, education, parks and recreation **Academic program** English as a second language, advanced placement, accelerated degree program, self-designed majors, honors program, summer session, adult/continuing education programs, internships **Contact** Diane Raymond, Director of Admission, New England College, 15 Main Street, Henniker, NH 03242-3293. *Phone:* 603-428-2223 or toll-free 800-521-7642. *Fax:* 603-428-7230. *E-mail:* admission@nec.edu. *Web site:* http://www.nec.edu/.

Visit Petersons.com and enter keywords New England College

See page 1010 for the College Close-Up.

New Hampshire Institute of Art
Manchester, New Hampshire

General Proprietary, 4-year, coed **Entrance** Moderately difficult **Setting** urban campus **Total enrollment** 445 **Student-faculty ratio** 11:1 **Application deadline** Rolling (freshmen), rolling (transfer) **Freshman admission** 54% were admitted. Average high school GPA 2.97 **Freshman test scores** SAT critical reading scores over 500: 47%; SAT math scores over 500: 43%; SAT critical reading scores over 600: 14%; SAT math scores over 600: 5% **Housing** Yes **Expenses** Tuition & Fees $19,560; Room only $7000 **Undergraduates** 69% women, 13% part-time, 4% 25 or older, 0.5% Native American, 3% Hispanic American, 1% African American, 2% Asian American/Pacific Islander **The most frequently chosen baccalaureate field is** visual and performing arts **Academic program** Advanced placement, summer session, adult/continuing education programs **Contact** Ms. Amanda Abbott, Assistant Director of Enrollment, New Hampshire Institute of Art, 148 Concord Street, Manchester, NH 03104-4158. *Phone:* 866-241-4918 Ext. 576 or toll-free 866-241-4918. *Fax:* 603-647-0658. *E-mail:* aabbott@nhia.edu. *Web site:* http://www.nhia.edu/.

Visit Petersons.com and enter keywords New Hampshire

Plymouth State University
Plymouth, New Hampshire

General State-supported, comprehensive, coed **Entrance** Moderately difficult **Setting** 170-acre small-town campus **Total enrollment** 6,245 **Student-faculty ratio** 16:1 **Application deadline** 4/1 (freshmen), 4/1 (transfer) **Freshman admission** 70% were admitted. Average high school GPA 2.88 **Freshman test scores** SAT critical reading scores over 500: 42%; SAT math scores over 500: 44%; ACT scores over 18: 77%; SAT critical reading scores over 600: 8%; SAT math scores over 600: 8%; ACT scores over 24: 13% **Housing** Yes **Expenses** Tuition & Fees: state resident $8944, nonresident $17,114; Room & Board $8594 **Undergraduates** 46% women, 6% part-time, 3% 25 or older, 0.4% Native American, 1% Hispanic American, 0.4% African American, 1% Asian American/Pacific Islander **The most frequently chosen baccalaureate fields are** business/marketing, education, visual and performing arts

Learn more at www.rivier.edu

YOUR FUTURE STARTS AT

Rivier College

Nashua, NH • 1-800-447-4843

Small classes, great facilities and a convenient location—Rivier College has everything you need to meet your personal and professional goals.

▶ More than 30 majors to choose from, including education, nursing, and business.

▶ Over $6 million in financial aid awarded annually.

▶ Hands-on programs that give you a head start in your career.

Check us out online!

Plymouth State University (continued)

Academic program Advanced placement, accelerated degree program, self-designed majors, honors program, summer session, internships **Contact** Mr. Eugene Fahey, Senior Associate Director of Admission, Plymouth State University, 17 High Street, MSC #52, Plymouth, NH 03264-1595. *Phone:* toll-free 800-842-6900. *Fax:* 603-535-2714. *E-mail:* plymouthadmit@plymouth.edu. *Web site:* http://www.plymouth.edu/.

Rivier College
Nashua, New Hampshire

General Independent Roman Catholic, comprehensive, coed **Entrance** Moderately difficult **Setting** 68-acre suburban campus **Total enrollment** 2,256 **Student-faculty ratio** 15:1 **Application deadline** Rolling (freshmen), rolling (transfer) **Freshman admission** 81% were admitted. Average high school GPA 3.31 **Freshman test scores** SAT critical reading scores over 500: 34.7%; SAT critical reading scores over 600: 5.6% **Housing** Yes **Expenses** Tuition & Fees $25,050; Room & Board $9428 **Undergraduates** 82% women, 35% part-time, 33% 25 or older, 1% Native American, 4% Hispanic American, 2% African American, 2% Asian American/Pacific Islander **The most frequently chosen baccalaureate fields are** business/marketing, education, health professions and related sciences **Academic program** English as a second language, advanced placement, accelerated degree program, honors program, internships **Contact** David Boisvert, Vice President of Enrollment, Rivier College, 420 South Main Street, Nashua, NH 03060. *Phone:* 603-897-8507 or toll-free 800-44RIVIER. *Fax:* 603-891-1799. *E-mail:* rivadmit@rivier.edu. *Web site:* http://www.rivier.edu/.

Visit Petersons.com and enter keyword Rivier

See page 1082 for the College Close-Up.

Saint Anselm College
Manchester, New Hampshire

General Independent Roman Catholic, 4-year, coed **Entrance** Moderately difficult **Setting** 450-acre suburban campus **Total enrollment** 1,915 **Student-faculty ratio** 11:1 **Application deadline** 3/1 (freshmen), rolling (transfer) **Freshman admission** 77% were admitted. Average high school GPA 3.13 **Freshman test scores** SAT critical reading scores over 500: 73%; SAT math scores over 500: 78%; ACT scores over 18: 95%; SAT critical reading scores over 600: 22%; SAT math scores over 600: 26%; ACT scores over 24: 43% **Housing** Yes **Expenses** Tuition & Fees $30,515; Room & Board $11,550 **Undergraduates** 57% women, 2% part-time, 1% 25 or older, 1% Native American, 2% Hispanic American, 1% African American, 1% Asian American/Pacific Islander **The most frequently chosen baccalaureate fields are** business/marketing, health professions and related sciences, social sciences **Academic program** Advanced placement, honors program, summer session, internships **Contact** Ms. Nancy Davis Griffin, Director of Admission, Saint Anselm College, 100 Saint Anselm Drive, Manchester, NH 03102-1310. *Phone:* 603-641-7500 or toll-free 888-4ANSELM. *E-mail:* admission@anselm.edu. *Web site:* http://www.anselm.edu/.

Visit Petersons.com and enter keyword Anselm

See page 1098 for the College Close-Up.

Southern New Hampshire University
Manchester, New Hampshire

General Independent, comprehensive, coed **Entrance** Moderately difficult **Setting** 288-acre suburban campus **Total enrollment** 4,211 **Student-faculty ratio** 16:1 **Application deadline** Rolling (freshmen), rolling (transfer) **Freshman admission** 86% were admitted. Average high school GPA 2.94 **Freshman test scores** SAT critical reading scores over

Go-getters go here.

At Southern New Hampshire University, we believe there are no limits to what you can do, what you can be or what you can achieve.

We're dedicated to helping you make the most of your potential. Wherever you're going, we can help you get there.

Best M.B.A. and Best Online Degree Program
– NHBR Best of Business Awards voters

Southern New Hampshire University

snhu.edu

on campus. on location. online.

1.800.642.4968 | admission@snhu.edu
www.snhu.edu/Petersons

500: 38.4%; SAT math scores over 500: 47.29%; ACT scores over 18: 77.42%; SAT critical reading scores over 600: 7.24%; SAT math scores over 600: 9.79%; ACT scores over 24: 12.9% **Housing** Yes **Expenses** Tuition & Fees $26,442; Room & Board $10,176 **Undergraduates** 54% women, 2% part-time, 2% 25 or older, 0.5% Native American, 2% Hispanic American, 1% African American, 1% Asian American/Pacific Islander **The most frequently chosen baccalaureate fields are** business/marketing, education, psychology **Academic program** English as a second language, advanced placement, accelerated degree program, honors program, summer session, adult/continuing education programs, internships **Contact** Mr. Steve Soba, Director of Admission, Southern New Hampshire University, 2500 North River Road, Manchester, NH 03106-1045. *Phone:* 603-645-9611 or toll-free 800-642-4968. *Fax:* 603-645-9693. *E-mail:* admission@snhu.edu. *Web site:* http://www.snhu.edu/.

Visit Petersons.com and enter keywords Southern New

See page 1172 for the College Close-Up.

Thomas More College of Liberal Arts

Merrimack, New Hampshire

General Independent, 4-year, coed, affiliated with Roman Catholic Church **Entrance** Moderately difficult **Setting** 14-acre small-town campus **Total enrollment** 99 **Student-faculty ratio** 14:1 **Application deadline** Rolling (freshmen), rolling (transfer) **Freshman admission** Average high school GPA 3.33 **Freshman test scores** SAT critical reading scores over 500: 95.45%; SAT math scores over 500: 72.72%; ACT scores over 18: 100%; SAT critical reading scores over 600: 63.65%; SAT math scores over 600: 27.27%; ACT scores over 24: 100% **Housing** Yes **Expenses** Tuition & Fees $13,200; Room & Board $8800 **Undergraduates** 49% women, 3% 25 or older **The most frequently chosen baccalaureate fields are** English, philosophy and religious studies, social sciences **Contact** Teddy Sifert, Director of Admissions, Thomas More College of Liberal Arts, 6 Manchester Street, Merrimack, NH 03054-4818. *Phone:* toll-free 800-880-8308. *Fax:* 603-880-9280. *E-mail:* admissions@thomasmorecollege.edu. *Web site:* http://www.thomasmorecollege.edu/.

University of New Hampshire

Durham, New Hampshire

General State-supported, university, coed **Entrance** Moderately difficult **Setting** 2,600-acre small-town campus **Total enrollment** 15,311 **Student-faculty ratio** 19:1 **Application deadline** 2/1 (freshmen), 3/1 (transfer) **Freshman admission** 72% were admitted **Freshman test scores** SAT critical reading scores over 500: 79%; SAT math scores over 500: 84%; ACT scores over 18: 98%; SAT critical reading scores over 600: 28%; SAT math scores over 600: 38%; ACT scores over 24: 60% **Housing** Yes **Expenses** Tuition & Fees: state resident $12,743, nonresident $26,713; Room & Board $8874 **Undergraduates** 55% women, 4% part-time, 3% 25 or older, 0.4% Native American, 2% Hispanic American, 2% African American, 2% Asian American/Pacific Islander **The most frequently chosen baccalaureate fields are** business/marketing, health professions and related sciences, social sciences **Academic program** English as a second language, advanced placement, accelerated degree program, self-designed majors, honors program, summer session, internships **Contact** Admissions Office, University of New Hampshire, 4 Garrison Avenue, Durham, NH 03824. *Phone:* 603-862-0077. *Fax:* 603-862-0077. *E-mail:* admissions@unh.edu. *Web site:* http://www.unh.edu/.

Visit Petersons.com and enter keywords University of New Hampshire

See page 1290 for the College Close-Up.

University of New Hampshire at Manchester

Manchester, New Hampshire

General State-supported, comprehensive, coed **Entrance** Moderately difficult **Setting** urban campus **Total enrollment** 845 **Student-faculty ratio** 12:1 **Application deadline** 6/15 (freshmen), 6/15 (transfer) **Freshman admission** 80% were admitted **Housing** No **Expenses** Tuition & Fees: state resident $11,126, nonresident $25,396 **Undergraduates** 54% women, 19% part-time, 1% Native American, 16% Hispanic American, 5% African American, 15% Asian American/Pacific Islander **The most frequently chosen baccalaureate fields are** business/marketing, communications/journalism, engineering technologies **Academic program** Advanced placement, self-designed majors, summer session, adult/continuing education programs, internships **Contact** Ms. Donna Lukasiak, Senior Assistant Director Admissions, University of New Hampshire at Manchester, 400 Commercial Street, Manchester, NH 03101. *Phone:* 603-641-4150. *Fax:* 603-641-4342. *E-mail:* unhm@unh.edu. *Web site:* http://www.unhm.unh.edu/.

NEW JERSEY

Berkeley College

West Paterson, New Jersey

Contact Mr. David Bertone, Senior Director of Enrollment, Berkeley College, 44 Rifle Camp Road, West Paterson, NJ 07424-3353. *Phone:* 973-278-5400 or toll-free 800-446-5400. *Fax:* 973-328-9141. *E-mail:* info@berkeleycollege.edu. *Web site:* http://www.berkeleycollege.edu/.

Beth Medrash Govoha

Lakewood, New Jersey

Contact Director of Admissions, Beth Medrash Govoha, 617 Sixth Street, Lakewood, NJ 08701-2797. *Phone:* 908-367-1060 Ext. 4224.

Bloomfield College

Bloomfield, New Jersey

General Independent, 4-year, coed, affiliated with Presbyterian Church (U.S.A.) **Entrance** Moderately difficult **Setting** 12-acre suburban campus **Total enrollment** 2,142 **Student-faculty ratio** 15:1 **Application deadline** 8/1 (freshmen), 8/1 (transfer) **Freshman admission** 52% were admitted. Average high school GPA 2.56 **Freshman test scores** SAT critical reading scores over 500: 11%; SAT math scores over 500: 10%; SAT critical reading scores over 600: 2%; SAT math scores over 600: 1% **Housing** Yes **Expenses** Tuition & Fees $21,000; Room & Board $10,300 **Undergraduates** 65% women, 19% part-time, 26% 25 or older, 0.05% Native American, 19% Hispanic American, 50% African American, 3% Asian American/Pacific Islander **The most frequently chosen baccalaureate fields are** business/marketing, psychology, social sciences **Academic program** English as a second language, advanced placement, accelerated degree program, self-designed majors, honors program, summer session, adult/continuing education programs, internships **Contact** Mr. Adam Castro, Director of Admissions, Bloomfield College, Office of Enrollment Management and Admission, Bloomfield, NJ 07003-9981. *Phone:* 973-748-9000 Ext. 219 or toll-free 800-848-4555 Ext. 230. *Fax:* 973-748-0916. *E-mail:* admission@bloomfield.edu. *Web site:* http://www.bloomfield.edu/.

Visit Petersons.com and enter keyword Bloomfield

See page 606 for the College Close-Up.

Caldwell College

Caldwell, New Jersey

Contact Ms. Kathryn Reilly, Director of Admissions, Caldwell College, 9 Ryerson Avenue, Caldwell, NJ 07006. *Phone:* 973-618-3226 or toll-free

- Ranked New Jersey's best small institution by *Forbes Magazine*
- Scholarships and financial aid for most students
- More than 60 majors available including:

Video Game Design/Development
3D Animation & Graphic Design
Business Administration
Nursing & Health Technologies
Education
Music Technology

For more information visit:
bloomfield.edu/petersons

888-864-9516. *Fax:* 973-618-3600. *E-mail:* admissions@caldwell.edu. *Web site:* http://www.caldwell.edu/.
Visit Petersons.com and enter keyword Caldwell

See page 660 for the College Close-Up.

Centenary College
Hackettstown, New Jersey

General Independent, comprehensive, coed, affiliated with United Methodist Church **Entrance** Moderately difficult **Setting** suburban campus **Total enrollment** 2,939 **Student-faculty ratio** 16:1 **Application deadline** Rolling (freshmen), rolling (transfer) **Freshman admission** 89% were admitted. Average high school GPA 2.72 **Freshman test scores** SAT critical reading scores over 500: 29%; SAT math scores over 500: 28%; ACT scores over 18: 58%; SAT critical reading scores over 600: 4%; SAT math scores over 600: 4%; ACT scores over 24: 21% **Housing** Yes **Undergraduates** 63% women, 8% part-time, 27% 25 or older, 0.1% Native American, 5% Hispanic American, 6% African American, 6% Asian American/Pacific Islander **The most frequently chosen baccalaureate fields are** business/marketing, English, social sciences **Academic program** English as a second language, advanced placement, accelerated degree program, self-designed majors, honors program, summer session, adult/continuing education programs, internships **Contact** Ms. Diane Finnan, Vice President for Enrollment Management and Strategic Branding, Centenary College, 400 Jefferson Street, Hackettstown, NJ 07840-2100. *Phone:* 908-852-1400 or toll-free 800-236-8679. *Web site:* http://www.centenarycollege.edu/.

The College of New Jersey
Ewing, New Jersey

General State-supported, comprehensive, coed **Entrance** Very difficult **Setting** 255-acre suburban campus **Total enrollment** 6,980 **Student-faculty ratio** 13:1 **Application deadline** 1/15 (freshmen), 2/15 (transfer) **Freshman admission** 46% were admitted **Freshman test scores** SAT critical reading scores over 500: 99%; SAT math scores over 500: 100%; SAT critical reading scores over 600: 68%; SAT math scores over 600: 84% **Housing** Yes **Expenses** Tuition & Fees: state resident $12,722, nonresident $21,408; Room & Board $9996 **Undergraduates** 59% women, 3% part-time, 2% 25 or older, 0.1% Native American, 9% Hispanic American, 6% African American, 6% Asian American/Pacific Islander **The most frequently chosen baccalaureate fields are** business/marketing, education, English **Academic program** Advanced placement, accelerated degree program, self-designed majors, honors program, summer session, internships **Contact** Ms. Lisa Angeloni, Dean of Admissions, The College of New Jersey, PO Box 7718, Ewing, NJ 08628. *Phone:* 609-771-2131 or toll-free 800-624-0967. *Fax:* 609-637-5174. *E-mail:* admiss@tcnj.edu. *Web site:* http://www.tcnj.edu/.

See page 726 for the College Close-Up.

College of Saint Elizabeth
Morristown, New Jersey

General Independent Roman Catholic, comprehensive, undergraduate: women only; graduate: coed **Entrance** Moderately difficult **Setting** 188-acre suburban campus **Total enrollment** 2,157 **Student-faculty ratio** 11:1 **Application deadline** 8/15 (freshmen), rolling (transfer) **Freshman admission** 83% were admitted **Freshman test scores** SAT critical reading scores over 500: 27%; SAT math scores over 500: 25%; SAT critical reading scores over 600: 5%; SAT math scores over 600: 5% **Housing** Yes **Expenses** Tuition & Fees $25,058; Room & Board $10,904 **Undergraduates** 47% part-time, 1% 25 or older, 0.2% Native American, 16% Hispanic American, 18% African American, 4% Asian American/Pacific Islander **The most frequently chosen baccalaureate fields are** business/marketing, communications/journalism, health professions and related sciences **Academic program** English as a second language, advanced placement, accelerated degree program, self-designed majors, honors program, summer session, internships **Contact** Ms. Donna Tatarka, Dean of Admissions, College of Saint Elizabeth, 2 Convent Road, Morristown, NJ 07960-6989. *Phone:* 973-290-4700 or toll-free 800-210-7900. *Fax:* 973-290-4710. *E-mail:* apply@csa.edu. *Web site:* http://www.cse.edu/.
Visit Petersons.com and enter keyword Elizabeth

See page 730 for the College Close-Up.

DeVry University
North Brunswick, New Jersey

General Proprietary, comprehensive, coed **Entrance** Minimally difficult **Setting** 10-acre urban campus **Total enrollment** 1,440 **Student-faculty ratio** 14:1 **Application deadline** Rolling (freshmen), rolling (transfer) **Housing** No **Expenses** Tuition & Fees $14,720 **Undergraduates** 28% women, 42% part-time, 47% 25 or older, 1% Native American, 21% Hispanic American, 24% African American, 8% Asian American/Pacific Islander **The most frequently chosen baccalaureate fields are** business/marketing, computer and information sciences, engineering technologies **Academic program** Advanced placement, accelerated degree program, summer session, adult/continuing education programs **Contact** Admissions Office, DeVry University, 630 US Highway 1, North Brunswick, NJ 08902-3362. *Web site:* http://www.devry.edu/.

DeVry University
Paramus, New Jersey

Contact DeVry University, 35 Plaza, 81 East State Route 4, Suite 102, Paramus, NJ 07652. *Web site:* http://www.devry.edu/.

Drew University
Madison, New Jersey

General Independent, university, coed, affiliated with United Methodist Church **Entrance** Moderately difficult **Setting** 186-acre suburban campus **Total enrollment** 2,667 **Student-faculty ratio** 11:1 **Application deadline** 2/15 (freshmen), 8/1 (transfer) **Freshman admission** 74% were admitted. Average high school GPA 3.27 **Freshman test scores** SAT critical reading scores over 500: 80.05%; SAT math scores over 500: 78.79%; ACT scores over 18: 94.87%; SAT critical reading scores over 600: 40.4%; SAT math scores over 600: 33.84%; ACT scores over 24: 57.69% **Housing** Yes **Expenses** Tuition & Fees $38,017; Room & Board $10,368 **Undergraduates** 60% women, 3% part-time, 2% 25 or older, 1% Native American, 9% Hispanic American, 9% African American, 6% Asian American/Pacific Islander **The most frequently chosen baccalaureate fields are** social sciences, psychology, visual and performing arts **Academic program** Advanced placement, accelerated degree program, self-designed majors, honors program, summer session, internships **Contact** Ms. Alyssa McCloud, Vice President for Enrolment Management, Drew University, 36 Madison Avenue, Madison, NJ 07940-1493. *Phone:* 973-408-3250. *Fax:* 973-408-3068. *E-mail:* cadm@drew.edu. *Web site:* http://www.drew.edu/.

Fairleigh Dickinson University, College at Florham
Madison, New Jersey

General Independent, comprehensive, coed **Entrance** Moderately difficult **Setting** 178-acre suburban campus **Total enrollment** 3,509 **Application deadline** Rolling (freshmen) **Freshman admission** 67% were admitted. Average high school GPA 3.17 **Freshman test scores** SAT critical reading scores over 500: 55.3%; SAT math scores over 500: 59.3%; SAT critical reading scores over 600: 11%; SAT math scores over 600: 16.1% **Housing** Yes **Expenses** Tuition & Fees $31,264; Room & Board $11,058 **Undergraduates** 53% women, 8% part-time, 7% 25 or older, 0.5% Native American, 8% Hispanic American, 8% African American, 3% Asian American/Pacific Islander **The most frequently chosen baccalaureate fields are** business/marketing, psychology, visual

Fairleigh Dickinson University, College at Florham (continued)

and performing arts **Academic program** Advanced placement, accelerated degree program, honors program, summer session, adult/continuing education programs, internships **Contact** Mr. Jonathan Wexler, Associate Vice President of Enrollment Management, Fairleigh Dickinson University, College at Florham, 285 Madison Avenue, Madison, NJ 07940-1099. *Phone:* toll-free 800-338-8803. *E-mail:* globaleducation@fdu.edu. *Web site:* http://www.fdu.edu/.

Visit Petersons.com and enter keyword Florham

See page 788 for the College Close-Up.

Fairleigh Dickinson University, Metropolitan Campus

Teaneck, New Jersey

General Independent, comprehensive, coed **Entrance** Moderately difficult **Setting** 88-acre suburban campus **Total enrollment** 8,804 **Application deadline** Rolling (freshmen) **Freshman admission** 57% were admitted. Average high school GPA 3.05 **Freshman test scores** SAT critical reading scores over 500: 41.6%; SAT math scores over 500: 50%; SAT critical reading scores over 600: 7.8%; SAT math scores over 600: 12.8% **Housing** Yes **Expenses** Tuition & Fees $29,066; Room & Board $11,368 **Undergraduates** 58% women, 59% part-time, 37% 25 or older, 0.1% Native American, 26% Hispanic American, 14% African American, 6% Asian American/Pacific Islander **The most frequently chosen baccalaureate fields are** health professions and related sciences, business/marketing, liberal arts/general studies **Academic program** English as a second language, advanced placement, accelerated degree program, self-designed majors, honors program, summer session, adult/continuing education programs, internships **Contact** Mr. Jonathan Wexler, Associate Vice President of Enrollment Management, Fairleigh Dickinson University, Metropolitan Campus, 1000 River Road, Teaneck, NJ 07666-1914. *Phone:* toll-free 800-338-8803. *E-mail:* globaleducation@fdu.edu. *Web site:* http://www.fdu.edu/.

See page 788 for the College Close-Up.

Felician College

Lodi, New Jersey

General Independent Roman Catholic, comprehensive, coed **Entrance** Moderately difficult **Setting** 37-acre suburban campus **Total enrollment** 2,088 **Student-faculty ratio** 12:1 **Application deadline** Rolling (freshmen), rolling (transfer) **Freshman admission** 84% were admitted. Average high school GPA 2.98 **Freshman test scores** SAT critical reading scores over 500: 21.4%; SAT math scores over 500: 23%; SAT critical reading scores over 600: 5.9%; SAT math scores over 600: 7.5% **Housing** Yes **Expenses** Tuition & Fees $25,050; Room & Board $9700 **Undergraduates** 77% women, 23% part-time, 39% 25 or older, 0.3% Native American, 18% Hispanic American, 12% African American, 8% Asian American/Pacific Islander **The most frequently chosen baccalaureate fields are** business/marketing, education, health professions and related sciences **Academic program** English as a second language, advanced placement, accelerated degree program, self-designed majors, honors program, summer session, adult/continuing education programs, internships **Contact** College Admissions Office, Felician College, 262 South Main Street, Lodi, NJ 07644-2117. *Phone:* 201-559-6131. *Fax:* 201-559-6138. *E-mail:* admissions@felician.edu. *Web site:* http://www.felician.edu/.

Visit Petersons.com and enter keyword Felician

See page 794 for the College Close-Up.

Georgian Court University
Lakewood, New Jersey
Start here, go anywhere

An **affordable,** values-based private education

Significant **financial aid** available

New, state-of-the-art **Wellness Center**

Renowned **Women's College** provides opportunities to learn & lead

Coed University College offers undergraduate, graduate & certificate programs

NEW! Four new bachelor's degree programs: Exercise Science, Hospitality, Nursing & Dance

GEORGIAN COURT UNIVERSITY

Call **800.458.8422, ext. 2700**
Click **www.georgian.edu**

Georgian Court University
Lakewood, New Jersey

General Independent Roman Catholic, comprehensive, coed, primarily women **Entrance** Moderately difficult **Setting** 156-acre suburban campus **Total enrollment** 3,023 **Student-faculty ratio** 15:1 **Application deadline** 8/1 (freshmen), 8/1 (transfer) **Freshman admission** 62% were admitted. Average high school GPA 3.1 **Housing** Yes **Expenses** Tuition & Fees $24,490; Room & Board $9386 **Undergraduates** 91% women, 23% part-time, 26% 25 or older, 0.2% Native American, 8% Hispanic American, 11% African American, 2% Asian American/Pacific Islander **The most frequently chosen baccalaureate fields are** education, business/marketing, psychology **Academic program** English as a second language, advanced placement, accelerated degree program, honors program, summer session, adult/continuing education programs, internships **Contact** Ms. Kathie Gallant, Director of Admissions, Georgian Court University, 900 Lakewood Avenue, Lakewood, NJ 08701-2697. *Phone:* 732-987-2760 or toll-free 800-458-8422. *Fax:* 732-987-2000. *E-mail:* admissions@georgian.edu. *Web site:* http://www.georgian.edu/. **Visit Petersons.com and enter keyword Georgian**

See page 822 for the College Close-Up.

Kean University
Union, New Jersey

General State-supported, comprehensive, coed **Entrance** Moderately difficult **Setting** 186-acre suburban campus **Total enrollment** 15,051 **Student-faculty ratio** 17:1 **Application deadline** 5/31 (freshmen), 7/6 (transfer) **Freshman admission** 62% were admitted. Average high school GPA 2.96 **Freshman test scores** SAT critical reading scores over 500: 28.3%; SAT math scores over 500: 33.6%; SAT critical reading scores over 600: 2.9%; SAT math scores over 600: 6.2% **Housing** Yes **Expenses** Tuition & Fees: state resident $9446, nonresident $14,081; Room & Board $12,264 **Undergraduates** 62% women, 23% part-time, 26% 25 or older, 0.3% Native American, 21% Hispanic American, 19% African American, 7% Asian American/Pacific Islander **The most frequently chosen baccalaureate fields are** business/marketing, education, psychology **Academic program** English as a second language, advanced placement, accelerated degree program, honors program, summer session, adult/continuing education programs, internships **Contact** Ms. Valerie Winslow, Director of Undergraduate Admissions, Kean University, 1000 Morris Avenue, Union, NJ 07083. *Phone:* 908-737-7100. *Fax:* 908-737-7105. *E-mail:* admitme@kean.edu. *Web site:* http://www.kean.edu/.

Monmouth University
West Long Branch, New Jersey

General Independent, comprehensive, coed **Entrance** Moderately difficult **Setting** 156-acre suburban campus **Total enrollment** 6,499 **Student-faculty ratio** 15:1 **Application deadline** 3/1 (freshmen), 7/15 (transfer) **Freshman admission** 62% were admitted. Average high school GPA 3.31 **Freshman test scores** SAT critical reading scores over 500: 72%; SAT math scores over 500: 81%; ACT scores over 18: 100%; SAT critical reading scores over 600: 15%; SAT math scores over 600: 26%; ACT scores over 24: 46% **Housing** Yes **Expenses** Tuition & Fees $25,013; Room & Board $9554 **Undergraduates** 58% women, 8% part-time, 9% 25 or older, 0.2% Native American, 6% Hispanic American, 4% African American, 2% Asian American/Pacific Islander **The most frequently chosen baccalaureate fields are** business/marketing, communications/journalism, education **Academic program** Advanced placement, accelerated degree program, self-designed majors, honors program, summer session, internships **Contact** Ms. Victoria Bobik, Director of Undergraduate Admission, Monmouth University, 400 Cedar Avenue, West Long Branch, NJ 07764-1898. *Phone:* 732-571-3456 or toll-free 800-

Monmouth University (continued)
543-9671. *Fax:* 732-263-5166. *E-mail:* admission@monmouth.edu. *Web site:* http://www.monmouth.edu/.
Visit Petersons.com and enter keyword Monmouth

See page 980 for the College Close-Up.

Montclair State University
Montclair, New Jersey

General State-supported, comprehensive, coed **Entrance** Moderately difficult **Setting** 275-acre suburban campus **Total enrollment** 18,171 **Student-faculty ratio** 17:1 **Application deadline** 3/1 (freshmen), 6/15 (transfer) **Freshman admission** 47% were admitted **Freshman test scores** SAT critical reading scores over 500: 45.94%; SAT math scores over 500: 53%; SAT critical reading scores over 600: 9.94%; SAT math scores over 600: 11% **Housing** Yes **Expenses** Tuition & Fees: state resident $7042 **Undergraduates** 61% women, 14% part-time, 16% 25 or older, 0.2% Native American, 19% Hispanic American, 9% African American, 6% Asian American/Pacific Islander **Academic program** English as a second language, advanced placement, accelerated degree program, honors program, summer session, adult/continuing education programs, internships **Contact** Jason Langdon, Director of Admissions, Montclair State University, One Normal Avenue, Montclair, NJ 07043-1624. *Phone:* 973-655-5116 or toll-free 800-331-9205. *Fax:* 973-655-7700. *E-mail:* undergraduate.admissions@montclair.edu. *Web site:* http://www.montclair.edu/.
Visit Petersons.com and enter keyword Montclair

See page 982 for the College Close-Up.

New Jersey City University
Jersey City, New Jersey

General State-supported, comprehensive, coed **Entrance** Moderately difficult **Setting** 51-acre urban campus **Total enrollment** 8,399 **Student-faculty ratio** 13:1 **Application deadline** 4/1 (freshmen), rolling (transfer) **Freshman admission** 35% were admitted **Freshman test scores** SAT critical reading scores over 500: 27%; SAT math scores over 500: 35%; SAT critical reading scores over 600: 4%; SAT math scores over 600: 5% **Housing** Yes **Expenses** Tuition & Fees: state resident $8988, nonresident $16,266; Room & Board $9043 **Undergraduates** 61% women, 26% part-time, 34% 25 or older, 0.1% Native American, 35% Hispanic American, 20% African American, 7% Asian American/Pacific Islander **The most frequently chosen baccalaureate fields are** business/marketing, health professions and related sciences, security and protective services **Academic program** English as a second language, advanced placement, accelerated degree program, honors program, summer session, adult/continuing education programs, internships **Contact** Mr. Jose Balda, Director of Admissions, New Jersey City University, 2039 Kennedy Loulevard, Jersey City, NJ 07305. *Phone:* 201-200-3234 or toll-free 888-441-NJCU. *E-mail:* admissions@nicu.edu. *Web site:* http://www.njcu.edu/.

New Jersey Institute of Technology
Newark, New Jersey

General State-supported, university, coed **Entrance** Moderately difficult **Setting** 48-acre urban campus **Total enrollment** 8,840 **Student-faculty ratio** 15:1 **Application deadline** 4/1 (freshmen), 6/1 (transfer) **Freshman admission** 67% were admitted **Freshman test scores** SAT critical reading scores over 500: 71.65%; SAT math scores over 500: 93.53%; SAT critical reading scores over 600: 22.43%; SAT math scores over 600: 52.79% **Housing** Yes **Expenses** Tuition & Fees: state resident $12,856, nonresident $22,600; Room & Board $9806 **Undergraduates** 21% women, 19% part-time, 19% 25 or older, 1% Native American, 19% Hispanic American, 10% African American, 21% Asian American/Pacific Islander **The most frequently chosen baccalaureate fields are** computer and information sciences, engineering, engineering technologies **Academic program** English as a second language, advanced placement, accelerated degree program, honors program, summer session, adult/continuing education programs, internships **Contact** Mr. Stephen M. Eck, Director of University Admissions, New Jersey Institute of Technology, University Heights, Newark, NJ 07102. *Phone:* 973-596-3306 or toll-free 800-925-NJIT. *Fax:* 973-596-3461. *E-mail:* admissions@njit.edu. *Web site:* http://www.njit.edu/.

Princeton University
Princeton, New Jersey

General Independent, university, coed **Entrance** Most difficult **Setting** 600-acre suburban campus **Total enrollment** 7,592 **Student-faculty ratio** 6:1 **Application deadline** 1/1 (freshmen) **Freshman admission** 10% were admitted. Average high school GPA 3.88 **Freshman test scores** SAT critical reading scores over 500: 100%; SAT math scores over 500: 100%; ACT scores over 18: 100%; SAT critical reading scores over 600: 96%; SAT math scores over 600: 98%; ACT scores over 24: 100% **Housing** Yes **Expenses** Tuition & Fees $36,640; Room & Board $11,940 **Undergraduates** 49% women, 1% part-time, 0.5% Native American, 8% Hispanic American, 8% African American, 16% Asian American/Pacific Islander **The most frequently chosen baccalaureate fields are** engineering, biological/life sciences, social sciences **Academic program** Advanced placement, self-designed majors, adult/continuing education programs **Contact** Ms. Janet Rapelye, Dean of Admission, Princeton University, PO Box 430, Princeton, NJ 08542-0430. *Phone:* 609-258-3060. *Fax:* 609-258-6743. *E-mail:* uaoffice@princeton.edu. *Web site:* http://www.princeton.edu/.

Rabbi Jacob Joseph School
Edison, New Jersey

General Independent Jewish, 4-year, men only **Total enrollment** 41 **Freshman admission** 100% were admitted **Housing** Yes **Contact** Rabbi Jacob Joseph School, One Plainfield Ave, Edison, NJ 08817.

Rabbinical College of America
Morristown, New Jersey

Contact Sharon Miller, Registrar, Rabbinical College of America, 226 Sussex Avenue, PO Box 1996, Morristown, NJ 07962-1996. *Phone:* 973-267-9404. *E-mail:* rca079@aol.com.

Ramapo College of New Jersey
Mahwah, New Jersey

General State-supported, comprehensive, coed **Entrance** Moderately difficult **Setting** 300-acre suburban campus **Total enrollment** 6,026 **Student-faculty ratio** 18:1 **Application deadline** 3/1 (freshmen), 5/1 (transfer) **Freshman admission** 51% were admitted. Average high school GPA 3.4 **Freshman test scores** SAT critical reading scores over 500: 90%; SAT math scores over 500: 96%; SAT critical reading scores over 600: 27%; SAT math scores over 600: 45% **Housing** Yes **Expenses** Tuition & Fees: state resident $11,416, nonresident $19,099; Room & Board $11,290 **Undergraduates** 58% women, 10% part-time, 11% 25 or older, 0.4% Native American, 9% Hispanic American, 5% African American, 5% Asian American/Pacific Islander **The most frequently chosen baccalaureate fields are** business/marketing, communications/journalism, psychology **Academic program** Advanced placement, accelerated degree program, self-designed majors, honors program, summer session, adult/continuing education programs, internships **Contact** Michael DiBartolomeo, Associate Director for Freshmen Admissions, Ramapo College of New Jersey, Office of Admissions, 505 Ramapo Valley Road, Mahwah, NJ 07430-1680. *Phone:* 201-684-7300 or toll-free 800-9RAMAPO. *Fax:* 201-684-7964. *E-mail:* admissions@ramapo.edu. *Web site:* http://www.ramapo.edu/.
Visit Petersons.com and enter keyword Ramapo

See page 1068 for the College Close-Up.

The Richard Stockton College of New Jersey
Pomona, New Jersey

General State-supported, comprehensive, coed **Entrance** Very difficult **Setting** 1,600-acre suburban campus **Total enrollment** 7,559 **Student-faculty ratio** 19:1 **Application deadline** 5/1 (freshmen), 6/1 (transfer) **Freshman admission** 61% were admitted **Freshman test scores** SAT critical reading scores over 500: 68%; SAT math scores over 500: 76%; ACT scores over 18: 92%; SAT critical reading scores over 600: 18%; SAT math scores over 600: 27%; ACT scores over 24: 21% **Housing** Yes **Expenses** Tuition & Fees: state resident $11,041, nonresident $16,724; Room & Board $10,189 **Undergraduates** 57% women, 11% part-time, 14% 25 or older, 1% Native American, 6% Hispanic American, 8% African American, 5% Asian American/Pacific Islander **The most frequently chosen baccalaureate fields are** business/marketing, biological/life sciences, social sciences **Academic program** Advanced placement, accelerated degree program, honors program, summer session, adult/continuing education programs, internships **Contact** Mr. John Iacovelli, Dean of Enrollment Management, The Richard Stockton College of New Jersey, PO Box 195, Jimmie Leeds Road, Pomona, NJ 08240-0195. *Phone:* 609-652-4261. *E-mail:* admissions@stockton.edu. *Web site:* http://www.stockton.edu/.
Visit Petersons.com and enter keywords Richard Stockton

See page 1074 for the College Close-Up.

Rider University
Lawrenceville, New Jersey

General Independent, comprehensive, coed **Entrance** Moderately difficult **Setting** 280-acre suburban campus **Total enrollment** 6,073 **Student-faculty ratio** 13:1 **Application deadline** Rolling (freshmen), rolling (transfer) **Freshman admission** 75% were admitted. Average high school GPA 3.27 **Freshman test scores** SAT critical reading scores over 500: 60%; SAT math scores over 500: 64%; ACT scores over 18: 91%; SAT critical reading scores over 600: 15%; SAT math scores over 600: 19%; ACT scores over 24: 31% **Housing** Yes **Expenses** Tuition & Fees $29,060; Room & Board $10,720 **Undergraduates** 60% women, 17% part-time, 14% 25 or older, 0.4% Native American, 6% Hispanic American, 10% African American, 3% Asian American/Pacific Islander **The most frequently chosen baccalaureate fields are** business/marketing, education, English **Academic program** English as a second language, advanced placement, honors program, summer session, adult/continuing education programs, internships **Contact** Mr. William Larrousse, Director of Admissions, Rider University, 2083 Lawrenceville Road, Lawrenceville, NJ 08648. *Phone:* 609-896-5177 or toll-free 800-257-9026. *Fax:* 609-895-6645. *E-mail:* wlarrousse@rider.edu. *Web site:* http://www.rider.edu/.
Visit Petersons.com and enter keyword Rider

See page 1078 for the College Close-Up.

Rowan University
Glassboro, New Jersey

General State-supported, comprehensive, coed **Entrance** Moderately difficult **Setting** 800-acre suburban campus **Total enrollment** 11,006 **Student-faculty ratio** 15:1 **Application deadline** 3/1 (freshmen), 3/1 (transfer) **Freshman admission** 68% were admitted. Average high school GPA 3.35 **Freshman test scores** SAT critical reading scores over 500: 66.39%; SAT math scores over 500: 74.08%; SAT critical reading scores over 600: 16.94%; SAT math scores over 600: 28.25% **Housing** Yes **Expenses** Tuition & Fees: state resident $11,234, nonresident $18,308; Room & Board $9958 **Undergraduates** 53% women, 14% part-time, 10% 25 or older, 0.2% Native American, 7% Hispanic American, 9% African American, 4% Asian American/Pacific Islander **The most frequently chosen baccalaureate fields are** business/marketing, communications/journalism, education **Academic program** English as a second language, advanced placement, honors program, summer session, adult/continuing education programs, internships **Contact** Mr. Albert Betts, Director of Admissions, Rowan University, 201 Mullica Hill Road, Glassboro, NJ 08028. *Phone:* 856-256-4200 or toll-free 800-447-1165. *Fax:* 856-256-4430. *E-mail:* admissions@rowan.edu. *Web site:* http://www.rowan.edu/.
Visit Petersons.com and enter keyword Rowan

Rutgers, The State University of New Jersey, Camden
Camden, New Jersey

General State-supported, university, coed **Entrance** Moderately difficult **Setting** 34-acre urban campus **Total enrollment** 5,781 **Student-faculty ratio** 12:1 **Application deadline** 12/1 (freshmen), 1/15 (transfer) **Freshman admission** 49% were admitted **Freshman test scores** SAT critical reading scores over 500: 74.1%; SAT math scores over 500: 82.8%; SAT critical reading scores over 600: 26.2%; SAT math scores over 600: 27.5% **Housing** Yes **Expenses** Tuition & Fees: state resident $11,698, nonresident $22,330; Room & Board $9788 **Undergraduates** 55% women, 19% part-time, 40% 25 or older, 0.2% Native American, 9% Hispanic American, 16% African American, 8% Asian American/Pacific Islander **The most frequently chosen baccalaureate fields are** business/marketing, psychology, social sciences **Academic program** English as a second language, advanced placement, accelerated degree program, self-designed majors, honors program, summer session, internships **Contact** Dr. Deborah Bowles, Associate Chancellor, Enrollment Management, Rutgers, The State University of New Jersey, Camden, 406 Penn Street, Camden, NJ 08102-1401. *Phone:* 856-225-6104. *Fax:* 856-225-6498. *E-mail:* bowles@ugadm.rutgers.edu. *Web site:* http://www.rutgers.edu/.
Visit Petersons.com and enter keywords Jersey Camden

Rutgers, The State University of New Jersey, Newark
Newark, New Jersey

General State-supported, university, coed **Entrance** Moderately difficult **Setting** 38-acre urban campus **Total enrollment** 11,500 **Student-faculty ratio** 12:1 **Application deadline** 12/1 (freshmen), 1/15 (transfer) **Freshman admission** 60% were admitted **Freshman test scores** SAT critical reading scores over 500: 62.6%; SAT math scores over 500: 80.1%; SAT critical reading scores over 600: 17.2%; SAT math scores over 600: 34.7% **Housing** Yes **Expenses** Tuition & Fees: state resident $11,414, nonresident $22,046; Room & Board $11,155 **Undergraduates** 53% women, 21% part-time, 0.1% Native American, 20% Hispanic American, 18% African American, 24% Asian American/Pacific Islander **The most frequently chosen baccalaureate fields are** business/marketing, biological/life sciences, health professions and related sciences **Academic program** English as a second language, advanced placement, accelerated degree program, self-designed majors, honors program, summer session, adult/continuing education programs, internships **Contact** Mr. Jason Hand, Director of Admissions, Rutgers, The State University of New Jersey, Newark, 249 University Avenue, Newark, NJ 07102. *Phone:* 973-353-5205. *Fax:* 973-353-1440. *E-mail:* admissions@ugadm.rutgers.edu. *Web site:* http://www.rutgers.edu/.

Rutgers, The State University of New Jersey, New Brunswick
Piscataway, New Jersey

General State-supported, university, coed **Entrance** Moderately difficult **Setting** 2,683-acre urban campus **Total enrollment** 37,364 **Student-faculty ratio** 14:1 **Application deadline** 12/1 (freshmen), 1/15 (transfer) **Freshman admission** 61% were admitted **Freshman test scores** SAT critical reading scores over 500: 89%; SAT math scores over 500: 93.8%; SAT critical reading scores over 600: 40.1%; SAT math scores over 600: 60.6% **Housing** Yes **Expenses** Tuition & Fees: state resident $11,886, nonresident $22,518; Room & Board $10,676 **Undergraduates** 48%

Rutgers, The State University of New Jersey, New Brunswick (continued)
women, 5% part-time, 11% 25 or older, 0.1% Native American, 10% Hispanic American, 8% African American, 25% Asian American/Pacific Islander **The most frequently chosen baccalaureate fields are** psychology, biological/life sciences, social sciences **Academic program** English as a second language, advanced placement, accelerated degree program, self-designed majors, honors program, internships **Contact** Ms. Diane Williams Harris, Associate Director of University Undergraduate Admissions, Rutgers, The State University of New Jersey, New Brunswick, 65 Davidson Road, Room 202, Piscataway, NJ 08854-8097. *Phone:* 732-445-4636. *Web site:* http://www.rutgers.edu/.
Visit Petersons.com and enter keywords Jersey, New Brunswick

Saint Peter's College
Jersey City, New Jersey

Contact Mr. Joe Giglio, Director of Admissions, Saint Peter's College, 2641 Kennedy Boulevard, Jersey City, NJ 07306-5997. *Phone:* 201-761-7106 or toll-free 888-SPC-9933. *Fax:* 201-761-7105. *E-mail:* admissions@spc.edu. *Web site:* http://www.spc.edu/.
Visit Petersons.com and enter keyword Peter's

See page 1132 for the College Close-Up.

Seton Hall University
South Orange, New Jersey

General Independent Roman Catholic, university, coed **Entrance** Moderately difficult **Setting** 58-acre suburban campus **Total enrollment** 9,616 **Student-faculty ratio** 14:1 **Application deadline** Rolling (freshmen), rolling (transfer) **Freshman admission** 79% were admitted. Average high school GPA 3.13 **Freshman test scores** SAT critical reading scores over 500: 63%; SAT math scores over 500: 62%; ACT scores over 18: 92%; SAT critical reading scores over 600: 16%; SAT math scores over 600: 20%; ACT scores over 24: 42% **Housing** Yes **Expenses** Tuition & Fees $31,890; Room & Board $12,050 **Undergraduates** 58% women, 10% part-time, 7% 25 or older, 0.3% Native American, 12% Hispanic American, 14% African American, 7% Asian American/Pacific Islander **The most frequently chosen baccalaureate fields are** business/marketing, health professions and related sciences, social sciences **Academic program** English as a second language, advanced placement, accelerated degree program, honors program, summer session, internships **Contact** Mr. Peter Nacy, Assistant Vice President for Admissions, Seton Hall University, Enrollment Management, South Orange, NJ 07079-2697. *Phone:* 973-275-2498 or toll-free 800-THE HALL. *Fax:* 973-275-2040. *E-mail:* thehall@shu.edu. *Web site:* http://www.shu.edu/.
Visit Petersons.com and enter keyword Seton

See page 1152 for the College Close-Up.

Somerset Christian College
Zarephath, New Jersey

General Independent Pillar of Fire International, 4-year, coed **Entrance** Minimally difficult **Setting** rural campus **Total enrollment** 240 **Student-faculty ratio** 15:1 **Application deadline** Rolling (freshmen), 9/1 (transfer) **Freshman admission** 48% were admitted **Housing** No **Expenses** Tuition & Fees $11,294 **Undergraduates** 57% women, 28% part-time, 75% 25 or older, 19% Hispanic American, 40% African American, 2% Asian American/Pacific Islander **Academic program** Advanced placement, accelerated degree program, summer session, adult/continuing education programs, internships **Contact** Ms. Linda Aarni, Senior Admissions Counselor, Somerset Christian College, 10 College Way, PO Box 9035, Zarephath, NJ 08890-9035. *Phone:* 732-356-1595 or toll-free 800-234-9305. *Fax:* 732-356-4846. *E-mail:* info@somerset.edu. *Web site:* http://www.somerset.edu/.

Stevens Institute of Technology
Hoboken, New Jersey

General Independent, university, coed **Entrance** Very difficult **Setting** 55-acre urban campus **Total enrollment** 5,862 **Student-faculty ratio** 7:1 **Application deadline** 2/1 (freshmen), 7/1 (transfer) **Freshman admission** 51% were admitted. Average high school GPA 3.7 **Freshman test scores** SAT critical reading scores over 500: 91%; SAT math scores over 500: 100%; ACT scores over 18: 100%; SAT critical reading scores over 600: 50%; SAT math scores over 600: 86%; ACT scores over 24: 82% **Housing** Yes **Expenses** Tuition & Fees $37,980; Room & Board $12,150 **Undergraduates** 26% women, 0.04% part-time, 0.2% Native American, 10% Hispanic American, 3% African American, 11% Asian American/Pacific Islander **The most frequently chosen baccalaureate fields are** business/marketing, biological/life sciences, engineering **Academic program** Advanced placement, accelerated degree program, honors program, summer session, internships **Contact** Mr. Daniel Gallagher, Dean of University Admissions, Stevens Institute of Technology, Castle Point on Hudson, Hoboken, NJ 07030. *Phone:* 201-216-5197 or toll-free 800-458-5323. *E-mail:* admissions@stevens.edu. *Web site:* http://www.stevens.edu/.

Strayer University–Cherry Hill Campus
Cherry Hill, New Jersey

General Proprietary, comprehensive, coed **Contact** Admissions Office, Strayer University–Cherry Hill Campus, 2201 Route 38, Suite 100, Cherry Hill, NJ 08002. *Phone:* 856-482-4200. *Web site:* http://www.strayer.edu/cherry_hill.

Strayer University–Lawrenceville Campus
Lawrenceville, New Jersey

General Proprietary, comprehensive, coed **Contact** Admissions Office, Strayer University–Lawrenceville Campus, 3150 Brunswick Pike, Suite 100, Lawrenceville, NJ 08648. *Web site:* http://www.strayer.edu/lawrenceville.

Strayer University–New Brunswick Campus
Piscataway, New Jersey

General Proprietary, comprehensive, coed **Contact** Admissions Office, Strayer University–New Brunswick Campus, 242 Old New Brunswick Road, Suite 110, Piscataway, NJ 08854. *Web site:* http://www.strayer.edu/new_brunswick.

Strayer University–Willingboro Campus
Willingboro, New Jersey

General Proprietary, comprehensive, coed **Contact** Admissions Office, Strayer University–Willingboro Campus, 300 Willingboro Parkway, Willingboro Town Center, Suite 125, Willingboro, NJ 08046. *Phone:* 609-835-6000. *Web site:* http://www.strayer.edu/willingboro.

Talmudical Academy of New Jersey
Adelphia, New Jersey

General Independent Jewish, comprehensive, men only **Setting** small-town campus **Total enrollment** 48 **Freshman admission** 100% were admitted **Housing** Yes **Undergraduates** 8% 25 or older **Contact** Director of Admissions, Talmudical Academy of New Jersey, 868 Route 524, Adelphia, NJ 07710. *Phone:* 201-431-1600.

WILLIAM PATERSON UNIVERSITY
wpunj.edu/undergraduate

Connie Kocur
Major: Art

Zhiyuan Cong,
Professor, Art, College of the Arts and Communication

Your next mentor.

LEARN FROM EXPERIENCE
AT WILLIAM PATERSON UNIVERSITY.

At William Paterson University, enterprising students and expert faculty have one big thing in common: a belief that we're all in this together. Just ask Connie. Her trip to China with Professor Zhiyuan Cong transformed her creative process—and the way she sees the world.

Become inspired. Apply online at
wpunj.edu/applynow

Thomas Edison State College

Trenton, New Jersey

General State-supported, comprehensive, coed **Entrance** Noncompetitive **Setting** 2-acre urban campus **Total enrollment** 18,206 **Application deadline** Rolling (freshmen), rolling (transfer) **Housing** No **Expenses** Tuition & Fees: state resident $4695, nonresident $6720 **Undergraduates** 38% women, 100% part-time, 88% 25 or older, 1% Native American, 8% Hispanic American, 16% African American, 3% Asian American/Pacific Islander **The most frequently chosen baccalaureate fields are** engineering technologies, business/marketing, liberal arts/general studies **Academic program** Advanced placement, self-designed majors, summer session, adult/continuing education programs **Contact** Mr. David Hoftiezer, Director of Admissions, Thomas Edison State College, 101 W. State Street, Trenton, NJ 08608. *Phone:* 888-442-8372 or toll-free 888-442-8372. *Fax:* 609-984-8447. *E-mail:* admissions@tesc.edu. *Web site:* http://www.tesc.edu/.

Visit Petersons.com and enter keyword Edison

See page 1222 for the College Close-Up.

William Paterson University of New Jersey

Wayne, New Jersey

General State-supported, comprehensive, coed **Entrance** Moderately difficult **Setting** 370-acre suburban campus **Total enrollment** 10,819 **Student-faculty ratio** 15:1 **Application deadline** 5/1 (freshmen), 6/1 (transfer) **Freshman admission** 65% were admitted **Freshman test scores** SAT critical reading scores over 500: 43.5%; SAT math scores over 500: 50%; SAT critical reading scores over 600: 7.6%; SAT math scores over 600: 10.4% **Housing** Yes **Expenses** Tuition & Fees: state resident $10,838, nonresident $17,592; Room & Board $10,280 **Undergraduates** 55% women, 15% part-time, 19% 25 or older **The most frequently chosen baccalaureate fields are** business/marketing, communications/journalism, education **Academic program** English as a second language, advanced placement, accelerated degree program, honors program, summer session, adult/continuing education programs, internships **Contact** Mr. Anthony Leckey, Associate Director of Admissions, William Paterson University of New Jersey, 300 Pompton Road, Wayne, NJ 07470-8420. *Phone:* 973-720-2903 or toll-free 877-WPU-EXCEL. *Fax:* 973-720-2910. *E-mail:* admissions@wpunj.edu. *Web site:* http://www.wpunj.edu/.

Visit Petersons.com and enter keyword Paterson

See page 1382 for the College Close-Up.

NEW MEXICO

Brookline College

Albuquerque, New Mexico

General Independent, 4-year, coed **Entrance** Noncompetitive **Setting** urban campus **Total enrollment** 472 **Student-faculty ratio** 17:1 **Application deadline** Rolling (freshmen), rolling (transfer) **Housing** No **Expenses** Tuition & Fees $14,000 **Undergraduates** 78% women, 50% 25 or older, 13% Native American, 67% Hispanic American, 5% African American **Academic program** Accelerated degree program **Contact** Mr. Andrew Webb, Campus Director, Brookline College, 4201 Central Avenue NW, Suite J, Albuquerque, NM 87105. *Phone:* 505-880-2877 or toll-free 888-660-2428. *Fax:* 505-352-0199. *E-mail:* awebb@brooklinecollege.edu. *Web site:* http://brooklinecollege.edu/.

Brown Mackie College–Albuquerque
Albuquerque, New Mexico

General Proprietary, primarily 2-year, coed **Contact** Director of Admissions, Brown Mackie College–Albuquerque, 10500 Cooper Avenue NE, Albuquerque, NM 87123. *Phone:* 505-559-5200 or toll-free 877-271-3488. *Fax:* 505-559-5222. *Web site:* http://www.brownmackie.edu/.

See page 618 for the College Close-Up.

College of Santa Fe
Santa Fe, New Mexico

General Independent, comprehensive, coed **Entrance** Moderately difficult **Setting** 100-acre suburban campus **Total enrollment** 672 **Student-faculty ratio** 12:1 **Application deadline** Rolling (freshmen), rolling (transfer) **Freshman admission** 83% were admitted. Average high school GPA 3.2 **Freshman test scores** SAT critical reading scores over 500: 82%; SAT math scores over 500: 68%; ACT scores over 18: 97%; SAT critical reading scores over 600: 44%; SAT math scores over 600: 23%; ACT scores over 24: 54% **Housing** Yes **Expenses** Tuition & Fees $28,504; Room & Board $8094 **Undergraduates** 49% women, 9% part-time, 14% 25 or older, 1% Native American, 12% Hispanic American, 2% African American, 3% Asian American/Pacific Islander **The most frequently chosen baccalaureate fields are** business/marketing, psychology, visual and performing arts **Academic program** Advanced placement, accelerated degree program, self-designed majors, summer session, adult/continuing education programs, internships **Contact** Ms. Jackie Donohoe, College of Santa Fe, 1600 Saint Michael's Drive, Santa Fe, NM 87505-7634. *Phone:* 505-473-6133 or toll-free 800-456-2673. *Fax:* 505-473-6129. *E-mail:* admissions@csf.edu. *Web site:* http://www.csf.edu.

Eastern New Mexico University
Portales, New Mexico

General State-supported, comprehensive, coed **Entrance** Minimally difficult **Setting** 400-acre rural campus **Total enrollment** 4,679 **Student-faculty ratio** 17:1 **Application deadline** Rolling (freshmen), rolling (transfer) **Freshman admission** 65% were admitted. Average high school GPA 3.22 **Freshman test scores** SAT critical reading scores over 500: 41%; SAT math scores over 500: 42%; ACT scores over 18: 72%; SAT critical reading scores over 600: 7%; SAT math scores over 600: 8%; ACT scores over 24: 19% **Housing** Yes **Expenses** Tuition & Fees: state resident $3552, nonresident $9102; Room & Board $5374 **Undergraduates** 55% women, 34% part-time, 33% 25 or older, 3% Native American, 29% Hispanic American, 7% African American, 1% Asian American/Pacific Islander **The most frequently chosen baccalaureate fields are** education, business/marketing, liberal arts/general studies **Academic program** English as a second language, advanced placement, accelerated degree program, self-designed majors, summer session, adult/continuing education programs, internships **Contact** Ms. Donna Kittrell, Director, Enrollment Services, Eastern New Mexico University, Station #7 ENMU, Portales, NM 88130. *Phone:* 575-562-2178 or toll-free 800-367-3668. *Fax:* 575-562-2118. *E-mail:* donna.kittrell@enmu.edu. *Web site:* http://www.enmu.edu/.

Institute of American Indian Arts
Santa Fe, New Mexico

General Federally supported, primarily 2-year, coed **Entrance** Minimally difficult **Setting** 120-acre urban campus **Total enrollment** 231 **Application deadline** 4/15 (freshmen), 4/15 (transfer) **Housing** Yes **Expenses** Tuition & Fees: state resident $2500, nonresident $2500; Room & Board $4900 **Undergraduates** 53% 25 or older **Academic program** Internships **Contact** Myra Garro, Manager of Enrollment and Admissions, Institute of American Indian Arts, 83 Avan Nu Po Road, Santa Fe, NM 87508. *Phone:* 505-424-2328. *Web site:* http://www.iaia.edu/.

ITT Technical Institute
Albuquerque, New Mexico

General Proprietary, primarily 2-year, coed **Entrance** Minimally difficult **Housing** No **Contact** Director of Recruitment, ITT Technical Institute, 5100 Masthead Street, NE, Albuquerque, NM 87109. *Phone:* 505-828-1114 or toll-free 800-636-1114. *Web site:* http://www.itt-tech.edu/.

National American University
Albuquerque, New Mexico

General Proprietary, 4-year, coed **Entrance** Noncompetitive **Setting** 5-acre suburban campus **Total enrollment** 336 **Application deadline** Rolling (freshmen), rolling (transfer) **Housing** No **Undergraduates** 90% 25 or older **Academic program** Accelerated degree program, summer session, adult/continuing education programs, internships **Contact** Director of Admissions, National American University, 4775 Indian School, NE, Suite 200, Albuquerque, NM 87110. *Phone:* 505-265-7517 or toll-free 800-843-8892. *E-mail:* albadmissions@national.edu. *Web site:* http://www.national.edu/.

National College of Midwifery
Taos, New Mexico

General Independent, comprehensive, women only **Housing** No **Contact** Ms. Beth Enson, Dean of Students, National College of Midwifery, 209 State Road 240, Taos, NM 87571. *Phone:* 505-758-8914. *E-mail:* info@midwiferycollege.org. *Web site:* http://www.midwiferycollege.org/.

New Mexico Highlands University
Las Vegas, New Mexico

General State-supported, comprehensive, coed **Entrance** Minimally difficult **Setting** small-town campus **Total enrollment** 3,784 **Student-faculty ratio** 15:1 **Application deadline** Rolling (freshmen), rolling (transfer) **Freshman admission** 56% were admitted. Average high school GPA 2.97 **Freshman test scores** ACT scores over 18: 52%; ACT scores over 24: 5% **Housing** Yes **Expenses** Tuition & Fees: state resident $2741, nonresident $4308; Room & Board $5967 **Undergraduates** 59% women, 28% part-time, 38% 25 or older, 8% Native American, 56% Hispanic American, 7% African American, 1% Asian American/Pacific Islander **The most frequently chosen baccalaureate fields are** business/marketing, education, social sciences **Academic program** Advanced placement, accelerated degree program, honors program, summer session, internships **Contact** Ms. Judy Cordova, Vice President for Student Affairs, New Mexico Highlands University, Box 9000, Las Vegas, NM 87701. *Phone:* 505-454-3566 or toll-free 800-338-6648. *Fax:* 505-454-3552. *E-mail:* judycordova@nmhu.edu. *Web site:* http://www.nmhu.edu/.

New Mexico Institute of Mining and Technology
Socorro, New Mexico

General State-supported, university, coed **Entrance** Moderately difficult **Setting** 320-acre small-town campus **Total enrollment** 1,897 **Student-faculty ratio** 11:1 **Application deadline** 8/1 (freshmen), 8/1 (transfer) **Freshman admission** 79% were admitted. Average high school GPA 3.6 **Freshman test scores** SAT critical reading scores over 500: 93%; SAT math scores over 500: 93%; ACT scores over 18: 100%; SAT critical reading scores over 600: 41%; SAT math scores over 600: 54%; ACT scores over 24: 68% **Housing** Yes **Expenses** Tuition & Fees: state resident $4607, nonresident $13,568; Room & Board $5702 **Undergraduates** 34% women, 17% part-time, 12% 25 or older, 3% Native American, 25% Hispanic American, 1% African American, 3% Asian American/Pacific Islander **The most frequently chosen baccalaureate fields are** computer and information sciences, engineering, physical sciences **Academic program** Advanced placement, accelerated degree program, self-designed majors, summer session, internships **Contact** Mr. Mike Kloeppel, Director of Admissions, New Mexico Institute of Mining and Technology, 801 Leroy Place, Socorro, NM 87801. *Phone:* 575-835-5424 or toll-free 800-428-TECH. *Fax:* 575-835-5989. *E-mail:* admission@admin.nmt.edu. *Web site:* http://www.nmt.edu/.

New Mexico State University

Las Cruces, New Mexico

General State-supported, university, coed **Entrance** Moderately difficult **Setting** 900-acre suburban campus **Total enrollment** 18,497 **Student-faculty ratio** 20:1 **Application deadline** 8/19 (freshmen), 8/14 (transfer) **Freshman admission** 96% were admitted. Average high school GPA 3.29 **Freshman test scores** SAT critical reading scores over 500: 45%; SAT math scores over 500: 45%; ACT scores over 18: 75%; SAT critical reading scores over 600: 14%; SAT math scores over 600: 13%; ACT scores over 24: 24% **Housing** Yes **Expenses** Tuition & Fees: state resident $4998, nonresident $15,150; Room & Board $6338 **Undergraduates** 55% women, 14% part-time, 24% 25 or older, 4% Native American, 44% Hispanic American, 3% African American, 1% Asian American/Pacific Islander **The most frequently chosen baccalaureate fields are** business/marketing, education, health professions and related sciences **Academic program** Advanced placement, accelerated degree program, self-designed majors, honors program, summer session, adult/continuing education programs, internships **Contact** Valerie Pickett, Director of Admissions, New Mexico State University, Box 30001, MSC 3A, Las Cruces, NM 88003-8001. *Phone:* 575-646-3121 or toll-free 800-662-6678. *Fax:* 575-646-6330. *E-mail:* admssions@nmsu.edu. *Web site:* http://www.nmsu.edu/.

Northern New Mexico College

Española, New Mexico

General State-supported, primarily 2-year, coed **Entrance** Noncompetitive **Setting** 35-acre rural campus **Total enrollment** 2,272 **Application deadline** Rolling (freshmen), rolling (transfer) **Freshman admission** 100% were admitted. Average high school GPA 2.63 **Housing** Yes **Undergraduates** 60% 25 or older **Academic program** Advanced placement, summer session **Contact** Mr. Mike L. Costello, Registrar, Northern New Mexico College, 921 Paseo de Oñate, Española, NM 87532. *Phone:* 505-747-2193. *Fax:* 505-747-2191. *E-mail:* dms@nnmc.edu. *Web site:* http://www.nnmc.edu/.

St. John's College

Santa Fe, New Mexico

General Independent, comprehensive, coed **Entrance** Very difficult **Setting** 250-acre suburban campus **Total enrollment** 511 **Student-faculty ratio** 7:1 **Application deadline** Rolling (freshmen), rolling (transfer) **Freshman admission** 81% were admitted **Freshman test scores** SAT critical reading scores over 500: 97%; SAT math scores over 500: 94%; ACT scores over 18: 100%; SAT critical reading scores over 600: 86%; SAT math scores over 600: 74%; ACT scores over 24: 80% **Housing** Yes **Expenses** Tuition & Fees $40,392; Room & Board $9562 **Undergraduates** 39% women, 1% part-time, 5% 25 or older, 1% Native American, 5% Hispanic American, 0.5% African American, 3% Asian American/Pacific Islander **The most frequently chosen baccalaureate field is** liberal arts/general studies **Academic program** Summer session, internships **Contact** Mr. Larry Clendenin, Director of Admissions, St. John's College, 1160 Camino Cruz Blanca, Santa Fe, NM 87505. *Phone:* 505-984-6060 or toll-free 800-331-5232. *Fax:* 505-984-6162. *E-mail:* admissions@sjcsf.edu. *Web site:* http://www.stjohnscollege.edu/.

University of New Mexico

Albuquerque, New Mexico

General State-supported, university, coed **Entrance** Moderately difficult **Setting** 769-acre urban campus **Total enrollment** 27,241 **Student-faculty ratio** 19:1 **Application deadline** Rolling (freshmen), rolling (transfer) **Freshman admission** 62% were admitted. Average high school GPA 3.28 **Freshman test scores** SAT critical reading scores over 500: 71%; SAT math scores over 500: 68%; ACT scores over 18: 86%; SAT critical reading scores over 600: 33%; SAT math scores over 600: 32%; ACT scores over 24: 35% **Housing** Yes **Expenses** Tuition & Fees: state resident $5101, nonresident $17,253; Room & Board $7778 **Undergraduates** 56% women, 25% part-time, 24% 25 or older, 7% Native American, 37% Hispanic American, 3% African American, 4% Asian American/Pacific Islander **The most frequently chosen baccalaureate fields are** business/marketing, education, social sciences **Academic program** English as a second language, advanced placement, accelerated degree program, self-designed majors, honors program, summer session, adult/continuing education programs, internships **Contact** Ms. Kathleen Roberts, Coordinator of Freshmen Admissions, University of New Mexico, Office of Admissions, PO Box 4895, Albuquerque, NM 87196-4895. *Phone:* 505-277-8900 or toll-free 800-CALLUNM. *Fax:* 505-277-6686. *E-mail:* apply@unm.edu. *Web site:* http://www.unm.edu/.

University of New Mexico–Gallup

Gallup, New Mexico

Contact Ms. Pearl A. Morris, Admissions Representative, University of New Mexico–Gallup, 200 College Road, Gallup, NM 87301-5603. *Phone:* 505-863-7576. *Web site:* http://www.gallup.unm.edu/.

University of Phoenix–New Mexico Campus

Albuquerque, New Mexico

General Proprietary, comprehensive, coed **Entrance** Noncompetitive **Setting** urban campus **Total enrollment** 4,170 **Application deadline** Rolling (freshmen), rolling (transfer) **Housing** No **Expenses** Tuition & Fees $10,950 **Undergraduates** 64% women, 80% 25 or older, 1% Native American, 55% Hispanic American, 2% African American, 1% Asian American/Pacific Islander **The most frequently chosen baccalaureate fields are** business/marketing, computer and information sciences, public administration and social services **Academic program** Advanced placement, accelerated degree program, adult/continuing education programs **Contact** Ms. Audra McQuarie, Registrar/Executive Director, University of Phoenix–New Mexico Campus, 4035 South Riverpoint Parkway, Mail Stop CF-L101, Phoenix, AZ 85040. *Phone:* 480-557-6151 or toll-free 800-776-4867 (in-state); 800-228-7240 (out-of-state). *Fax:* 480-643-3068. *E-mail:* audra.mcquarie@phoenix.edu. *Web site:* http://www.phoenix.edu/.

University of the Southwest

Hobbs, New Mexico

General Independent, comprehensive, coed **Entrance** Moderately difficult **Setting** 162-acre small-town campus **Total enrollment** 528 **Student-faculty ratio** 10:1 **Application deadline** Rolling (freshmen), rolling (transfer) **Freshman admission** 91% were admitted. Average high school GPA 3.13 **Freshman test scores** SAT critical reading scores over 500: 27%; SAT math scores over 500: 43%; ACT scores over 18: 63%; SAT critical reading scores over 600: 1%; SAT math scores over 600: 9%; ACT scores over 24: 9% **Housing** Yes **Expenses** Tuition & Fees $12,964; Room & Board $9385 **Undergraduates** 49% women, 16% part-time, 49% 25 or older, 0.3% Native American, 45% Hispanic American, 4% African American, 1% Asian American/Pacific Islander **Academic program** Advanced placement, summer session, internships **Contact** Ashley Taylor, Admissions Coordinator, University of the Southwest, 6610 Lovington Highway, Hobbs, NM 88240-9129. *Phone:* 575-392-6563 Ext. 1048 or toll-free 800-530-4400. *Fax:* 575-392-6006. *E-mail:* ataylor@usw.edu. *Web site:* http://www.usw.edu/.

Western New Mexico University
Silver City, New Mexico

Contact Mr. Dan Tressler, Director of Admissions, Western New Mexico University, PO Box 680, Silver City, NM 88062-0680. *Phone:* 505-538-6106 or toll-free 800-872-WNMU. *Fax:* 505-538-6127. *E-mail:* tresslerd@wnmu.edu. *Web site:* http://www.wnmu.edu/.

NEW YORK

Adelphi University
Garden City, New York

General Independent, university, coed **Entrance** Moderately difficult **Setting** 75-acre suburban campus **Total enrollment** 7,951 **Student-faculty ratio** 9:1 **Application deadline** Rolling (freshmen), rolling (transfer) **Freshman admission** 70% were admitted. Average high school GPA 3.37 **Freshman test scores** SAT critical reading scores over 500: 68.94%; SAT math scores over 500: 76.1%; ACT scores over 18: 97.36%; SAT critical reading scores over 600: 20.63%; SAT math scores over 600: 25.6%; ACT scores over 24: 43.72% **Housing** Yes **Undergraduates** 71% women, 13% part-time, 17% 25 or older, 0.3% Native American, 7% Hispanic American, 11% African American, 6% Asian American/Pacific Islander **The most frequently chosen baccalaureate fields are** business/marketing, health professions and related sciences, social sciences **Academic program** English as a second language, advanced placement, accelerated degree program, self-designed majors, honors program, summer session, internships **Contact** Ms. Christine Murphy, Director of Admissions, Adelphi University, Levermore Hall 110, 1 South Avenue, PO Box 701, Garden City, NY 11530-0701. *Phone:* 516-877-3050 or toll-free 800-ADELPHI. *Fax:* 516-877-3039. *E-mail:* admissions@adelphi.edu. *Web site:* http://www.adelphi.edu/.
Visit Petersons.com and enter keyword Adelphi

See page 464 for the College Close-Up.

Albany College of Pharmacy and Health Sciences
Albany, New York

General Independent, comprehensive, coed **Entrance** Very difficult **Setting** 20-acre urban campus **Total enrollment** 1,566 **Student-faculty ratio** 15:1 **Application deadline** 2/1 (freshmen), 2/1 (transfer) **Freshman admission** 66% were admitted. Average high school GPA 3.7 **Freshman test scores** SAT critical reading scores over 500: 85%; SAT math scores over 500: 97%; ACT scores over 18: 100%; SAT critical reading scores over 600: 33%; SAT math scores over 600: 67%; ACT scores over 24: 88% **Housing** Yes **Expenses** Tuition & Fees $23,860; Room & Board $8300 **Undergraduates** 60% women, 2% part-time, 7% 25 or older, 0.4% Native American, 2% Hispanic American, 3% African American, 14% Asian American/Pacific Islander **The most frequently chosen baccalaureate field is** health professions and related sciences **Academic program** Advanced placement, summer session **Contact** Mr. Matthew Stever, Director of Admissions, Albany College of Pharmacy and Health Sciences, 106 New Scotland Avenue, Albany, NY 12208. *Phone:* 518-694-7221 or toll-free 888-203-8010. *Fax:* 518-694-7322. *E-mail:* admissions@acphs.edu. *Web site:* http://www.acphs.edu/.

Alfred University
Alfred, New York

General Independent, university, coed **Entrance** Moderately difficult **Setting** 232-acre rural campus **Total enrollment** 2,319 **Student-faculty ratio** 12:1 **Application deadline** 2/1 (freshmen), 8/1 (transfer) **Freshman admission** 70% were admitted. Average high school GPA 3.19 **Freshman test scores** SAT critical reading scores over 500: 74%; SAT math scores over 500: 79.8%; ACT scores over 18: 99.2%; SAT critical reading scores over 600: 27.8%; SAT math scores over 600: 30.9%; ACT scores over 24: 56.7% **Housing** Yes **Expenses** Tuition & Fees $25,976; Room & Board $11,364 **Undergraduates** 51% women, 4% part-time, 5% 25 or older, 0.3% Native American, 3% Hispanic American, 5% African American, 2% Asian American/Pacific Islander **The most frequently chosen baccalaureate fields are** business/marketing, engineering, visual and performing arts **Academic program** Advanced placement, accelerated degree program, self-designed majors, honors program, summer session, internships **Contact** Mr. Jeremy C. Spencer, Director of Admissions, Alfred University, Alumni Hall, Alfred, NY 14802-1205. *Phone:* 607-871-2115 or toll-free 800-541-9229. *Fax:* 607-871-2198. *E-mail:* admissions@alfred.edu. *Web site:* http://www.alfred.edu/.

Bard College
Annandale-on-Hudson, New York

General Independent, comprehensive, coed **Entrance** Very difficult **Setting** 600-acre rural campus **Total enrollment** 2,234 **Student-faculty ratio** 10:1 **Application deadline** 1/15 (freshmen), 3/15 (transfer) **Freshman admission** 33% were admitted. Average high school GPA 3.5 **Freshman test scores** SAT math scores over 500: 100%; SAT math scores over 600: 73% **Housing** Yes **Expenses** Tuition & Fees $39,880; Room & Board $11,300 **Undergraduates** 57% women, 4% part-time, 1% 25 or older, 1% Native American, 3% Hispanic American, 2% African American, 3% Asian American/Pacific Islander **The most frequently chosen baccalaureate fields are** social sciences, English, visual and performing arts **Academic program** Advanced placement, self-designed majors, adult/continuing education programs, internships **Contact** Ms. Mary Backlund, Director of Admissions, Bard College, PO Box 5000, 51 Ravine Road, Annandale-on-Hudson, NY 12504-5000. *Phone:* 845-758-7472. *Fax:* 845-758-5208. *E-mail:* admission@bard.edu. *Web site:* http://www.bard.edu/.

Barnard College
New York, New York

General Independent, 4-year, women only **Entrance** Most difficult **Setting** 4-acre urban campus **Total enrollment** 2,417 **Student-faculty ratio** 9:1 **Application deadline** 1/1 (freshmen), 4/1 (transfer) **Freshman admission** 31% were admitted. Average high school GPA 3.84 **Freshman test scores** SAT critical reading scores over 500: 99%; SAT math scores over 500: 99%; ACT scores over 18: 100%; SAT critical reading scores over 600: 89%; SAT math scores over 600: 86%; ACT scores over 24: 96% **Housing** Yes **Expenses** Tuition & Fees $38,650; Room & Board $12,319 **Undergraduates** 3% part-time, 0.2% 25 or older, 0.2% Native American, 9% Hispanic American, 4% African American, 16% Asian American/Pacific Islander **The most frequently chosen baccalaureate fields are** social sciences, English, visual and performing arts **Academic program** Advanced placement, accelerated degree program, self-designed majors, internships **Contact** Ms. Jennifer Gill Fondiller, Dean of Admissions, Barnard College, 3009 Broadway, New York, NY 10027-6598. *Phone:* 212-854-2014. *Fax:* 212-854-6220. *E-mail:* admissions@barnard.edu. *Web site:* http://www.barnard.edu/.
Visit Petersons.com and enter keyword Barnard

See page 578 for the College Close-Up.

Beis Medrash Heichal Dovid
Far Rockaway, New York

General Proprietary, comprehensive, men only **Total enrollment** 111 **Housing** Yes **Contact** Beis Medrash Heichal Dovid, 257 Beach 17th Street, Far Rockaway, NY 11691.

Berkeley College–New York City Campus
New York, New York

Contact Ms. Linda Pinsky, Associate Vice President, Enrollment, Berkeley College–New York City Campus, 3 East 43rd Street, New

York, NY 10017. *Phone:* 212-986-4343 Ext. 4117 or toll-free 800-446-5400. *Fax:* 212-818-1079. *E-mail:* info@berkeleycollege.edu. *Web site:* http://www.berkeleycollege.edu/.

Visit Petersons.com and enter keyword Berkeley

Berkeley College–Westchester Campus
White Plains, New York

Contact Mr. John Wool, Assistant Director of Admissions, Berkeley College–Westchester Campus, 99 Church Street, White Plains, NY 10601. *Phone:* 914-694-1122 Ext. 3110 or toll-free 800-446-5400. *Fax:* 914-328-9469. *E-mail:* info@berkeleycollege.edu. *Web site:* http://www.berkeleycollege.edu/.

Bernard M. Baruch College of the City University of New York
New York, New York

General State and locally supported, comprehensive, coed **Entrance** Very difficult **Setting** urban campus **Total enrollment** 16,195 **Student-faculty ratio** 17:1 **Application deadline** 2/1 (freshmen), 3/1 (transfer) **Freshman admission** 23% were admitted. Average high school GPA 3.13 **Freshman test scores** SAT critical reading scores over 500: 77%; SAT math scores over 500: 95%; SAT critical reading scores over 600: 26%; SAT math scores over 600: 62% **Housing** No **Expenses** Tuition & Fees: state resident $4600, nonresident $12,450 **Undergraduates** 51% women, 23% part-time, 25% 25 or older, 0.1% Native American, 16% Hispanic American, 10% African American, 32% Asian American/Pacific Islander **The most frequently chosen baccalaureate fields are** business/marketing, communications/journalism, psychology **Academic program** English as a second language, advanced placement, accelerated degree program, self-designed majors, honors program, summer session, adult/continuing education programs, internships **Contact** Mr. Jimmy Jung, Assistant Vice President for Undergraduate Admissions and Financial Aid, Bernard M. Baruch College of the City University of New York, 1 Bernard Baruch Way, New York, NY 10010-5585. *Phone:* 646-312-1400. *Fax:* 646-312-1363. *E-mail:* jimmy.jung@baruch.cuny.edu. *Web site:* http://www.baruch.cuny.edu/.

Beth HaMedrash Shaarei Yosher Institute
Brooklyn, New York

General Independent Jewish, comprehensive, men only **Total enrollment** 82 **Freshman admission** 100% were admitted **Housing** Yes **Contact** Director of Admissions, Beth HaMedrash Shaarei Yosher Institute, 4102-10 Sixteenth Avenue, Brooklyn, NY 11204. *Phone:* 718-854-2290.

Beth Hatalmud Rabbinical College
Brooklyn, New York

General Independent Jewish, comprehensive, men only **Total enrollment** 75 **Freshman admission** 100% were admitted **Housing** No **Contact** Rabbi Osina, Director of Admissions, Beth Hatalmud Rabbinical College, 2127 Eighty-second Street, Brooklyn, NY 11214. *Phone:* 718-259-2525.

Boricua College
New York, New York

Contact Mrs. Miriam Pfeffer, Director of Student Services, Boricua College, 186 North 6th Street, Brooklyn, NY 11211. *Phone:* 718-782-2200. *Fax:* 718-782-2025. *E-mail:* mpfeffer@boricuacollege.edu. *Web site:* http://www.boricuacollege.edu/.

Briarcliffe College
Bethpage, New York

Contact Ms. Theresa Donohue, Vice President of Marketing and Admissions, Briarcliffe College, 1055 Stewart Avenue, Bethpage, NY 11714. *Phone:* 516-918-3705 or toll-free 888-333-1150. *Fax:* 516-470-6020. *E-mail:* info@bcl.edu. *Web site:* http://www.bcl.edu/.

Brooklyn College of the City University of New York
Brooklyn, New York

General State and locally supported, comprehensive, coed **Entrance** Moderately difficult **Setting** 26-acre urban campus **Total enrollment** 17,094 **Student-faculty ratio** 15:1 **Application deadline** 2/1 (freshmen), 2/1 (transfer) **Freshman admission** 28% were admitted. Average high school GPA 3.4 **Freshman test scores** SAT critical reading scores over 500: 66.6%; SAT math scores over 500: 83.4%; SAT critical reading scores over 600: 20%; SAT math scores over 600: 32.8% **Housing** Yes **Expenses** Tuition & Fees: state resident $5051, nonresident $12,901 **Undergraduates** 60% women, 29% part-time, 29% 25 or older, 0.1% Native American, 12% Hispanic American, 25% African American, 16% Asian American/Pacific Islander **The most frequently chosen baccalaureate fields are** business/marketing, education, psychology **Academic program** English as a second language, advanced placement, honors program, summer session, adult/continuing education programs, internships **Contact** Mr. Duane Lee, Admissions Office, Brooklyn College of the City University of New York, 2900 Bedford Avenue, West Quad Building, Room 222, Brooklyn, NY 11210-2889. *Phone:* 718-951-5001. *Fax:* 718-951-4506. *E-mail:* adminqry@brooklyn.cuny.edu. *Web site:* http://www.brooklyn.cuny.edu/.

Visit Petersons.com and enter keyword Brooklyn

See page 616 for the College Close-Up.

Bryant & Stratton College—Amherst Campus
Amherst, New York

General Proprietary, primarily 2-year, coed **Setting** 5-acre suburban campus **Total enrollment** 474 **Application deadline** Rolling (freshmen), rolling (transfer) **Housing** No **Undergraduates** 75% women, 42% part-time, 56% 25 or older, 1% Native American, 3% Hispanic American, 19% African American, 1% Asian American/Pacific Islander **Academic program** Advanced placement, summer session, adult/continuing education programs, internships **Contact** Mr. Brian K. Dioguardi, Director of Admissions, Bryant & Stratton College—Amherst Campus, Audubon Business Center, 40 Hazelwood Drive, Amherst, NY 14228. *Phone:* 716-691-0012. *Fax:* 716-691-0012. *E-mail:* bkdioguardi@bryantstratton.edu. *Web site:* http://www.bryantstratton.edu/.

Bryant & Stratton College—Buffalo Campus
Buffalo, New York

General Proprietary, primarily 2-year, coed **Setting** urban campus **Total enrollment** 693 **Application deadline** Rolling (freshmen), rolling (transfer) **Freshman admission** 75% were admitted **Housing** No **Undergraduates** 76% women, 32% part-time, 46% 25 or older, 1% Native American, 9% Hispanic American, 56% African American **Academic program** Advanced placement, summer session, adult/continuing education programs, internships **Contact** Mr. Philip J. Struebel, Director of Admissions, Bryant & Stratton College—Buffalo Campus, 465 Main Street—Suite 400, Buffalo, NY 14203. *Phone:* 716-884-9120. *Fax:* 716-884-0091. *E-mail:* pjstruebel@bryantstratton.edu. *Web site:* http://www.bryantstratton.edu/.

Bryant & Stratton College—Southtowns Campus

Orchard Park, New York

General Proprietary, primarily 2-year, coed **Setting** suburban campus **Total enrollment** 1,206 **Application deadline** Rolling (freshmen), rolling (transfer) **Housing** No **Undergraduates** 79% women, 45% part-time, 49% 25 or older, 0.5% Native American, 3% Hispanic American, 20% African American, 1% Asian American/Pacific Islander **Academic program** Advanced placement, summer session, adult/continuing education programs, internships **Contact** Ms. Tracy Dominiak, Associate Director of Admissions, Bryant & Stratton College—Southtowns Campus, 200 Redtail, Orchard Park, NY 14127. *Phone:* 716-677-9500. *Fax:* 716-677-9599. *E-mail:* tdominiak@bryantstratton.edu. *Web site:* http://www.bryantstratton.edu/.

Buffalo State College, State University of New York

Buffalo, New York

General State-supported, comprehensive, coed **Entrance** Moderately difficult **Setting** 115-acre urban campus **Total enrollment** 11,714 **Student-faculty ratio** 17:1 **Application deadline** Rolling (freshmen), rolling (transfer) **Freshman admission** 43% were admitted. Average high school GPA 3.15 **Freshman test scores** SAT critical reading scores over 500: 43.4%; SAT math scores over 500: 48.57%; SAT critical reading scores over 600: 7.4%; SAT math scores over 600: 7.77% **Housing** Yes **Expenses** Tuition & Fees: state resident $6007, nonresident $13,907; Room & Board $9748 **Undergraduates** 59% women, 11% part-time, 18% 25 or older **The most frequently chosen baccalaureate fields are** business/marketing, education, social sciences **Academic program** English as a second language, advanced placement, honors program, summer session, adult/continuing education programs, internships **Contact** Ms. Carmella Thompson, Director of Admissions, Buffalo State College, State University of New York, 110 Moot Hall, Buffalo, NY 14222. *Phone:* 716-878-4017. *Fax:* 716-878-6100. *E-mail:* admissions@buffalostate.edu. *Web site:* http://www.buffalostate.edu/.
Visit Petersons.com and enter keyword Buffalo

See page 654 for the College Close-Up.

Canisius College

Buffalo, New York

General Independent Roman Catholic (Jesuit), comprehensive, coed **Entrance** Moderately difficult **Setting** 36-acre urban campus **Total enrollment** 4,774 **Student-faculty ratio** 11:1 **Application deadline** 5/1 (freshmen), rolling (transfer) **Freshman admission** 77% were admitted. Average high school GPA 3.5 **Freshman test scores** SAT critical reading scores over 500: 76%; SAT math scores over 500: 81.1%; ACT scores over 18: 98.4%; SAT critical reading scores over 600: 28.2%; SAT math scores over 600: 38.1%; ACT scores over 24: 75.2% **Housing** Yes **Expenses** Tuition & Fees $29,512; Room & Board $10,556 **Undergraduates** 52% women, 5% part-time, 4% 25 or older, 0.4% Native American, 2% Hispanic American, 6% African American, 1% Asian American/Pacific Islander **The most frequently chosen baccalaureate fields are** business/marketing, communications/journalism, education **Academic program** English as a second language, advanced placement, honors program, summer session, adult/continuing education programs, internships **Contact** Ms. Ann Marie Moscovic, Director of Admissions, Canisius College, 2001 Main Street, Buffalo, NY 14208-1098. *Phone:* 716-888-2200 or toll-free 800-843-1517. *Fax:* 716-888-3230. *E-mail:* admissions@canisius.edu. *Web site:* http://www.canisius.edu/.
Visit Petersons.com and enter keyword Canisius

See page 672 for the College Close-Up.

Cazenovia College

Cazenovia, New York

General Independent, 4-year, coed **Entrance** Minimally difficult **Setting** 40-acre small-town campus **Total enrollment** 1,119 **Student-faculty ratio** 12:1 **Application deadline** Rolling (freshmen), rolling (transfer) **Freshman admission** 74% were admitted. Average high school GPA 3.2 **Freshman test scores** SAT critical reading scores over 500: 47%; SAT math scores over 500: 52%; ACT scores over 18: 74%; SAT critical reading scores over 600: 14%; SAT math scores over 600: 11%; ACT scores over 24: 29% **Housing** Yes **Expenses** Tuition & Fees $24,152; Room & Board $10,222 **Undergraduates** 73% women, 14% part-time, 2% 25 or older, 0.4% Native American, 3% Hispanic American, 4% African American, 0.3% Asian American/Pacific Islander **The most frequently chosen baccalaureate fields are** business/marketing, security and protective services, visual and performing arts **Academic program** Advanced placement, accelerated degree program, honors program, summer session, adult/continuing education programs, internships **Contact** Office of Admission and Enrollment Services, Cazenovia College, 3 Sullivan Street, Cazenovia, NY 13035. *Phone:* 315-655-7208 or toll-free 800-654-3210. *Fax:* 315-655-4860. *E-mail:* admission@cazenovia.edu. *Web site:* http://www.cazenovia.edu/.

Central Yeshiva Tomchei Tmimim-Lubavitch

Brooklyn, New York

General Independent Jewish, comprehensive, men only **Total enrollment** 664 **Freshman admission** 100% were admitted **Housing** Yes **Undergraduates** 2% 25 or older **Contact** Director of Admissions, Central Yeshiva Tomchei Tmimim-Lubavitch, 841-853 Ocean Parkway, Brooklyn, NY 11230. *Phone:* 718-859-7600.

City College of the City University of New York

New York, New York

General State and locally supported, comprehensive, coed **Entrance** Moderately difficult **Setting** 35-acre urban campus **Total enrollment** 16,308 **Student-faculty ratio** 13:1 **Application deadline** 2/1 (freshmen), 2/1 (transfer) **Freshman admission** 38% were admitted. Average high school GPA 2.81 **Freshman test scores** SAT critical reading scores over 500: 47%; SAT math scores over 500: 65%; SAT critical reading scores over 600: 13%; SAT math scores over 600: 27% **Housing** Yes **Expenses** Tuition & Fees: state resident $4929, nonresident $10,289 **Undergraduates** 51% women, 26% part-time, 29% 25 or older **The most frequently chosen baccalaureate fields are** engineering, psychology, visual and performing arts **Academic program** English as a second language, advanced placement, accelerated degree program, self-designed majors, honors program, summer session, adult/continuing education programs, internships **Contact** Joseph Fantozzi, Director of Admissions, City College of the City University of New York, 160 Convent Avenue, New York, NY 10031-9198. *Phone:* 212-650-6977. *E-mail:* admissions@ccny.cuny.edu. *Web site:* http://www.ccny.cuny.edu/.
Visit Petersons.com and enter keywords City College

See page 710 for the College Close-Up.

Clarkson University

Potsdam, New York

General Independent, university, coed **Entrance** Very difficult **Setting** 640-acre small-town campus **Total enrollment** 3,187 **Student-faculty ratio** 15:1 **Application deadline** 1/15 (freshmen) **Freshman admission** 73% were admitted. Average high school GPA 3.49 **Freshman test scores** SAT critical reading scores over 500: 78%; SAT math scores over 500: 93%; ACT scores over 18: 99%; SAT critical reading scores over 600: 31%; SAT math scores over 600: 59%; ACT scores over 24: 67% **Housing** Yes **Expenses** Tuition & Fees $34,760; Room & Board $11,564 **Undergraduates** 28% women, 0.4% part-time, 2% 25 or older, 1% Native American, 3% Hispanic American, 3% African American, 4% Asian American/Pacific Islander **The most frequently chosen baccalaureate fields are** business/marketing, engineering, engineering technologies **Academic program** English as a second language, advanced placement, accelerated degree program, self-designed majors, honors program, summer session, internships **Contact** Mr. Brian T. Grant, Dean of Admissions, Clarkson University, Holcroft House, PO Box 5605, Potsdam, NY 13699-5605. *Phone:* 315-268-6480 or toll-free 800-527-6577. *Fax:* 315-268-7647. *E-mail:* admission@clarkson.edu. *Web site:* http://www.clarkson.edu/.

Visit Petersons.com and enter keyword Clarkson

See page 712 for the College Close-Up.

Colgate University
Hamilton, New York

General Independent, comprehensive, coed **Entrance** Most difficult **Setting** 515-acre rural campus **Total enrollment** 2,837 **Student-faculty ratio** 10:1 **Application deadline** 1/15 (freshmen), 3/15 (transfer) **Freshman admission** 32% were admitted. Average high school GPA 3.62 **Freshman test scores** SAT critical reading scores over 500: 96%; SAT math scores over 500: 98%; ACT scores over 18: 100%; SAT critical reading scores over 600: 84%; SAT math scores over 600: 87%; ACT scores over 24: 97% **Housing** Yes **Expenses** Tuition & Fees $40,970; Room & Board $9970 **Undergraduates** 53% women, 1% part-time, 1% Native American, 6% Hispanic American, 6% African American, 5% Asian American/Pacific Islander **The most frequently chosen baccalaureate fields are** foreign languages and literature, history, social sciences **Academic program** Advanced placement, self-designed majors, honors program, internships **Contact** Mr. Gary L. Ross, Dean of Admission, Colgate University, 13 Oak Drive, Hamilton, NY 13346-1383. *Phone:* 315-228-7401. *Fax:* 315-228-7544. *E-mail:* admission@mail.colgate.edu. *Web site:* http://www.colgate.edu/.

The College at Brockport, State University of New York
Brockport, New York

General State-supported, comprehensive, coed **Entrance** Moderately difficult **Setting** 454-acre small-town campus **Total enrollment** 8,490 **Student-faculty ratio** 18:1 **Application deadline** Rolling (freshmen), 8/1 (transfer) **Freshman admission** 45% were admitted. Average high school GPA 3.5 **Freshman test scores** SAT critical reading scores over 500: 64.9%; SAT math scores over 500: 76%; ACT scores over 18: 95.7%; SAT critical reading scores over 600: 13.6%; SAT math scores over 600: 24.5%; ACT scores over 24: 44.1% **Housing** Yes **Expenses** Tuition & Fees: state resident $6108, nonresident $14,008; Room & Board $9200 **Undergraduates** 57% women, 9% part-time, 16% 25 or older, 0.5% Native American, 3% Hispanic American, 6% African American, 2% Asian American/Pacific Islander **The most frequently chosen baccalaureate fields are** business/marketing, education, health professions and related sciences **Academic program** Advanced placement, accelerated degree program, self-designed majors, honors program, summer session, internships **Contact** Mr. Bernard Valento, Director of Undergraduate Admissions, The College at Brockport, State University of New York, 350 New Campus Drive, Brockport, NY 14420-2997. *Phone:* 585-395-2751. *Fax:* 585-395-5452. *E-mail:* admit@brockport.edu. *Web site:* http://www.brockport.edu/.

College of Mount Saint Vincent
Riverdale, New York

General Independent, comprehensive, coed **Entrance** Moderately difficult **Setting** 70-acre suburban campus **Total enrollment** 1,896 **Student-faculty ratio** 12:1 **Application deadline** Rolling (freshmen), rolling (transfer) **Freshman admission** 72% were admitted. Average high school GPA 2.8 **Freshman test scores** SAT critical reading scores over 500: 35%; SAT math scores over 500: 30%; SAT critical reading scores over 600: 7%; SAT math scores over 600: 7% **Housing** Yes **Expenses** Tuition & Fees $26,910; Room & Board $10,380 **Undergraduates** 75% women, 13% part-time, 11% 25 or older, 30% Hispanic American, 12% African American, 10% Asian American/Pacific Islander **The most frequently chosen baccalaureate fields are** business/marketing, communications/journalism, health professions and related sciences **Academic program** Advanced placement, accelerated degree program, self-designed majors, honors program, summer session, adult/continuing education programs, internships **Contact** Mr. Roland Pinzon, Director of Admissions, College of Mount Saint Vincent, 6301 Riverdale Avenue, Riverdale, NY 10471-1093. *Phone:* 718-405-3268 or toll-free 800-665-CMSV. *Fax:* 718-549-7945. *E-mail:* roland.pinzon@mountsaintvincent.edu. *Web site:* http://www.mountsaintvincent.edu/.

The College of New Rochelle
New Rochelle, New York

General Independent, comprehensive, coed, primarily women **Entrance** Moderately difficult **Setting** 20-acre suburban campus **Total enrollment** 1,820 **Student-faculty ratio** 11:1 **Application deadline** Rolling (freshmen), rolling (transfer) **Freshman admission** 30% were admitted. Average high school GPA 3.25 **Freshman test scores** SAT critical reading scores over 500: 43.8%; SAT math scores over 500: 49.5%; SAT critical reading scores over 600: 8.6%; SAT math scores over 600: 6.7% **Housing** Yes **Expenses** Tuition & Fees $26,426; Room & Board $9600 **Undergraduates** 93% women, 35% part-time, 37% 25 or older, 0.5% Native American, 15% Hispanic American, 34% African American, 6% Asian American/Pacific Islander **The most frequently chosen baccalaureate fields are** health professions and related sciences, communications/journalism, psychology **Academic program** Advanced placement, accelerated degree program, self-designed majors, honors program, summer session, adult/continuing education programs, internships **Contact** Ms. Bridget Kennedy, Assistant Director, Enrollment Management, The College of New Rochelle, 29 Castle Place, New Rochelle, NY 10805-2339. *Phone:* 914-654-5452 or toll-free 800-933-5923. *Fax:* 914-654-5464. *E-mail:* admission@cnr.edu. *Web site:* http://www.cnr.edu/.

The College of Saint Rose
Albany, New York

General Independent, comprehensive, coed **Entrance** Moderately difficult **Setting** 35-acre urban campus **Total enrollment** 5,158 **Student-faculty ratio** 14:1 **Application deadline** 5/1 (freshmen), 5/1 (transfer) **Freshman admission** 72% were admitted. Average high school GPA 3.31 **Freshman test scores** SAT critical reading scores over 500: 57%; SAT math scores over 500: 60%; ACT scores over 18: 90%; SAT critical reading scores over 600: 17%; SAT math scores over 600: 18%; ACT scores over 24: 32% **Housing** Yes **Expenses** Tuition & Fees $24,135; Room & Board $9880 **Undergraduates** 69% women, 6% part-time, 8% 25 or older, 0.3% Native American, 5% Hispanic American, 4% African American, 2% Asian American/Pacific Islander **The most frequently chosen baccalaureate fields are** business/marketing, education, visual and performing arts **Academic program** Advanced placement, accelerated degree program, self-designed majors, summer session, internships **Contact** Mr. Jeremy Bogan, Assistant Vice President of Undergraduate Admissions, The College of Saint Rose, 1001 Madison Avenue, Albany, NY 12203. *Phone:* 518-454-5154 or toll-free 800-637-8556. *Fax:* 518-454-2013. *E-mail:* admit@strose.edu. *Web site:* http://www.strose.edu/.

Visit Petersons.com and enter keyword Rose

See page 732 for the College Close-Up.

College of Staten Island of the City University of New York
Staten Island, New York

General State and locally supported, comprehensive, coed **Entrance** Moderately difficult **Setting** 204-acre urban campus **Total enrollment** 13,858 **Student-faculty ratio** 18:1 **Application deadline** Rolling (freshmen), rolling (transfer) **Freshman admission** 100% were admitted. Average high school GPA 2.96 **Freshman test scores** SAT critical reading scores over 500: 40.74%; SAT math scores over 500: 53.19%;

College of Staten Island of the City University of New York (continued)
SAT critical reading scores over 600: 10.67%; SAT math scores over 600: 12.3% **Housing** No **Expenses** Tuition & Fees: state resident $4978, nonresident $10,338 **Undergraduates** 58% women, 28% part-time, 24% 25 or older, 0.1% Native American, 8% Hispanic American, 6% African American, 6% Asian American/Pacific Islander **The most frequently chosen baccalaureate fields are** business/marketing, psychology, social sciences **Academic program** English as a second language, advanced placement, self-designed majors, honors program, summer session, adult/continuing education programs, internships **Contact** Mr. Emmanuel Esperance Jr., Interim Director of Recruitment and Admissions, College of Staten Island of the City University of New York, 2800 Victory Boulevard, Building 2A Room 103, Staten Island, NY 10314. *Phone:* 718-982-2010. *Fax:* 718-982-2500. *E-mail:* admissions@mail.cuny.csi.edu. *Web site:* http://www.csi.cuny.edu/.
Visit Petersons.com and enter keyword Staten

See page 734 for the College Close-Up.

Columbia University
New York, New York

General Independent, university, coed **Entrance** Most difficult **Setting** urban campus **Total enrollment** 5,766 **Student-faculty ratio** 6:1 **Application deadline** 1/2 (freshmen), 3/15 (transfer) **Freshman admission** 10% were admitted **Freshman test scores** SAT critical reading scores over 500: 100%; SAT math scores over 500: 100%; SAT critical reading scores over 600: 96.97%; SAT math scores over 600: 97.6% **Housing** Yes **Expenses** Tuition & Fees $39,296; Room & Board $10,228 **Undergraduates** 48% women, 1% Native American, 13% Hispanic American, 11% African American, 18% Asian American/Pacific Islander **The most frequently chosen baccalaureate fields are** engineering, history, social sciences **Academic program** Advanced placement, accelerated degree program, self-designed majors, internships **Contact** Ms. Jessica Marinaccio, Dean of Undergraduate Admissions, Columbia University, 116th Street and Broadway, New York, NY 10027. *Phone:* 212-854-1222. *Web site:* http://www.columbia.edu/.
Visit Petersons.com and enter keywords Columbia University

See page 740 for the College Close-Up.

Columbia University, School of General Studies
New York, New York

General Independent, 4-year, coed **Entrance** Most difficult **Setting** 36-acre urban campus **Total enrollment** 1,351 **Student-faculty ratio** 7:1 **Application deadline** 6/1 (freshmen), 6/1 (transfer) **Freshman admission** 37% were admitted **Housing** Yes **Expenses** Tuition & Fees $39,910; Room & Board $12,020 **Undergraduates** 50% women, 40% part-time, 65% 25 or older, 0.3% Native American, 10% Hispanic American, 7% African American, 13% Asian American/Pacific Islander **The most frequently chosen baccalaureate fields are** English, history, social sciences **Academic program** Advanced placement, self-designed majors, summer session, adult/continuing education programs, internships **Contact** Mr. Curtis M. Rodgers, Dean of Enrollment Management, Columbia University, School of General Studies, 2970 Broadway, 408 Lewisohn Hall, MC 4101, New York, NY 10027-6939. *Phone:* 212-854-2772 or toll-free 800-895-1169. *E-mail:* gs-admit@columbia.edu. *Web site:* http://www.gs.columbia.edu/.
Visit Petersons.com and enter keyword General

See page 742 for the College Close-Up.

Concordia College–New York
Bronxville, New York

Contact Ms. Donna J. Hoyt, Dean of Enrollment, Concordia College–New York, 171 White Plains Road, Bronxville, NY 10708. *Phone:* 914-337-9300 Ext. 2149 or toll-free 800-YES-COLLEGE. *Fax:* 914-395-4636. *E-mail:* admission@concordia-ny.edu. *Web site:* http://www.concordia-ny.edu/.

Cooper Union for the Advancement of Science and Art
New York, New York

General Independent, comprehensive, coed **Entrance** Most difficult **Setting** urban campus **Total enrollment** 990 **Student-faculty ratio** 9:1 **Application deadline** 1/1 (freshmen), 1/1 (transfer) **Freshman admission** 7% were admitted. Average high school GPA 3.6 **Freshman test scores** SAT critical reading scores over 500: 96%; SAT math scores over 500: 93%; SAT critical reading scores over 600: 74%; SAT math scores over 600: 76% **Housing** Yes **Expenses** Tuition & Fees $36,650; Room & Board $13,700 **Undergraduates** 37% women, 0.2% part-time, 10% 25 or older, 1% Native American, 7% Hispanic American, 5% African American, 19% Asian American/Pacific Islander **The most frequently chosen baccalaureate fields are** engineering, architecture, visual and performing arts **Academic program** Advanced placement, self-designed majors, honors program, summer session, internships **Contact** Mr. Mitchell L. Lipton, Dean of Admissions and Records and Registrar, Cooper Union for the Advancement of Science and Art, 30 Cooper Square, New York, NY 10003. *Phone:* 212-353-4120. *Fax:* 212-353-4342. *E-mail:* admissions@cooper.edu. *Web site:* http://www.cooper.edu/.

Cornell University
Ithaca, New York

General Independent, university, coed **Entrance** Most difficult **Setting** 745-acre small-town campus **Total enrollment** 20,633 **Student-faculty ratio** 9:1 **Application deadline** 1/2 (freshmen), 3/15 (transfer) **Freshman admission** 19% were admitted **Freshman test scores** SAT critical reading scores over 500: 99%; SAT math scores over 500: 99%; ACT scores over 18: 100%; SAT critical reading scores over 600: 86%; SAT math scores over 600: 93%; ACT scores over 24: 98% **Housing** Yes **Expenses** Tuition & Fees $37,954; Room & Board $12,160 **Undergraduates** 49% women, 1% 25 or older, 0.4% Native American, 6% Hispanic American, 5% African American, 17% Asian American/Pacific Islander **The most frequently chosen baccalaureate fields are** business/marketing, agriculture, engineering **Academic program** English as a second language, advanced placement, accelerated degree program, self-designed majors, honors program, summer session, internships **Contact** Mr. Jason Locke, Director of Undergraduate Admissions, Cornell University, Ithaca, NY 14853-0001. *Phone:* 607-255-1446. *Fax:* 607-255-0659. *E-mail:* admissions@cornell.edu. *Web site:* http://www.cornell.edu/.

The Culinary Institute of America
Hyde Park, New York

General Independent, 4-year, coed **Entrance** Moderately difficult **Setting** 170-acre suburban campus **Total enrollment** 2,914 **Student-faculty ratio** 18:1 **Application deadline** Rolling (freshmen) **Freshman admission** 82% were admitted. Average high school GPA 3.1 **Housing** Yes **Expenses** Tuition & Fees $24,550; Room & Board $8110 **Undergraduates** 45% women, 23% 25 or older, 0.4% Native American, 7% Hispanic American, 4% African American, 5% Asian American/Pacific Islander **Academic program** Internships **Contact** Ms. Rachel Birchwood, Director of Admissions, The Culinary Institute of America, 1946 Campus Drive, Hudson Hall, Hyde Park, NY 12538. *Phone:* 845-451-1459 or toll-free 800-CULINARY. *Fax:* 845-451-1068. *E-mail:* admissions@culinary.edu. *Web site:* http://www.ciachef.edu/.
Visit Petersons.com and enter keywords Culinary Institute of America

See page 744 for the College Close-Up.

Daemen College
Amherst, New York

General Independent, comprehensive, coed **Entrance** Moderately difficult **Setting** 35-acre suburban campus **Total enrollment** 2,921 **Student-faculty ratio** 15:1 **Application deadline** Rolling (freshmen), rolling (transfer) **Freshman admission** 62% were admitted. Average high school GPA 3.57 **Freshman test scores** SAT critical reading scores over 500: 49.8%; SAT math scores over 500: 59%; ACT scores over 18: 90.7%; SAT critical reading scores over 600: 9.4%; SAT math scores over 600: 20.6%; ACT scores over 24: 39.5% **Housing** Yes **Expenses** Tuition & Fees $20,720; Room & Board $9450 **Undergraduates** 75% women, 26% part-time, 18% 25 or older, 0.3% Native American, 3% Hispanic American, 10% African American, 1% Asian American/Pacific Islander **The most frequently chosen baccalaureate fields are** biological/life sciences, education, health professions and related sciences **Academic program** Advanced placement, accelerated degree program, self-designed majors, honors program, summer session, adult/continuing education programs, internships **Contact** Mr. Frank Williams, Director of Undergraduate Admissions, Daemen College, 4380 Main Street, Amherst, NY 14226-3592. *Phone:* 716-839-8225 or toll-free 800-462-7652. *Fax:* 716-839-8229. *E-mail:* admissions@daemen.edu. *Web site:* http://www.daemen.edu/.

Visit Petersons.com and enter keyword Daemen

See page 748 for the College Close-Up.

Darkei Noam Rabbinical College
Brooklyn, New York

General Independent Jewish, comprehensive, men only **Entrance** Minimally difficult **Setting** urban campus **Total enrollment** 16 **Freshman admission** 100% were admitted **Housing** No **Contact** Rabbi Pinchas Horowitz, Director of Admissions, Darkei Noam Rabbinical College, 2822 Avenue J, Brooklyn, NY 11210. *Phone:* 718-338-6464.

Davis College
Johnson City, New York

General Independent nondenominational, 4-year, coed **Entrance** Minimally difficult **Setting** 22-acre suburban campus **Total enrollment** 323 **Student-faculty ratio** 14:1 **Application deadline** Rolling (freshmen), rolling (transfer) **Freshman admission** 68% were admitted. Average high school GPA 3.18 **Freshman test scores** ACT scores over 18: 62%; ACT scores over 24: 26% **Housing** Yes **Expenses** Tuition & Fees $12,600; Room & Board $6000 **Undergraduates** 54% women, 37% part-time, 29% 25 or older, 0.3% Native American, 2% Hispanic American, 6% African American, 2% Asian American/Pacific Islander **The most frequently chosen baccalaureate field is** theology and religious vocations **Academic program** English as a second language, advanced placement, summer session, adult/continuing education programs, internships **Contact** Admissions Coordinator, Davis College, 400 Riverside Drive, Johnson City, NY 13790. *Phone:* 607-729-1581 Ext. 406 or toll-free 800-331-4137 Ext. 406. *Fax:* 607-798-7754. *E-mail:* admissions@davisny.edu. *Web site:* http://www.davisny.edu/.

DeVry College of New York
Long Island City, New York

General Proprietary, comprehensive, coed **Entrance** Minimally difficult **Setting** 4-acre urban campus **Total enrollment** 1,390 **Student-faculty ratio** 17:1 **Application deadline** Rolling (freshmen), rolling (transfer) **Housing** No **Expenses** Tuition & Fees $14,720 **Undergraduates** 28% women, 22% part-time, 54% 25 or older, 0.3% Native American, 32% Hispanic American, 36% African American, 10% Asian American/Pacific Islander **The most frequently chosen baccalaureate fields are** business/marketing, computer and information sciences, engineering technologies **Academic program** Advanced placement, accelerated degree program, summer session, adult/continuing education programs **Contact** Admissions Office, DeVry College of New York, 30-20 Thomson Avenue, Long Island City, NY 11101. *Web site:* http://www.devry.edu/.

Dominican College
Orangeburg, New York

General Independent, comprehensive, coed **Entrance** Noncompetitive **Setting** 70-acre suburban campus **Total enrollment** 2,005 **Student-faculty ratio** 15:1 **Application deadline** Rolling (freshmen), rolling (transfer) **Freshman admission** 73% were admitted. Average high school GPA 2.66 **Freshman test scores** SAT critical reading scores over 500: 23%; SAT math scores over 500: 25%; ACT scores over 18: 68%; SAT critical reading scores over 600: 3%; SAT math scores over 600: 4%; ACT scores over 24: 10% **Housing** Yes **Expenses** Tuition & Fees $21,120; Room & Board $10,150 **Undergraduates** 68% women, 19% part-time, 28% 25 or older, 0.1% Native American, 21% Hispanic American, 11% African American, 10% Asian American/Pacific Islander **The most frequently chosen baccalaureate fields are** business/marketing, health professions and related sciences, social sciences **Academic program** Advanced placement, accelerated degree program, honors program, summer session, adult/continuing education programs, internships **Contact** Ms. Joyce Elbe, Director of Admissions, Dominican College, 470 Western Highway, Orangeburg, NY 10962-1210. *Phone:* 845-359-7900 or toll-free 866-432-4636. *Fax:* 845-365-3150. *E-mail:* admissions@dc.edu. *Web site:* http://www.dc.edu/.

Dowling College
Oakdale, New York

General Independent, comprehensive, coed **Entrance** Moderately difficult **Setting** 157-acre suburban campus **Total enrollment** 5,532 **Student-faculty ratio** 16:1 **Application deadline** Rolling (freshmen), rolling (transfer) **Freshman admission** 86% were admitted. Average high school GPA 3 **Freshman test scores** SAT critical reading scores over 500: 24.8%; SAT math scores over 500: 29%; SAT critical reading scores over 600: 4.2%; SAT math scores over 600: 5% **Housing** Yes **Expenses** Tuition & Fees $22,850; Room & Board $10,200 **Undergraduates** 55% women, 37% part-time, 21% 25 or older **The most frequently chosen baccalaureate fields are** business/marketing, education, psychology **Academic program** English as a second language, advanced placement, accelerated degree program, self-designed majors, honors program, summer session, internships **Contact** Mr. Glenn S. Berman, Assistant Vice President for Enrollment Services/Dean of Admissions, Dowling College, 150 Idle Hour Boulevard, Oakdale, NY 11769. *Phone:* 631-244-3357 or toll-free 800-DOWLING. *Fax:* 631-244-1059. *E-mail:* admissions@dowling.edu. *Web site:* http://www.dowling.edu/.

D'Youville College
Buffalo, New York

General Independent, comprehensive, coed **Entrance** Moderately difficult **Setting** 7-acre urban campus **Total enrollment** 2,971 **Student-faculty ratio** 12:1 **Application deadline** Rolling (freshmen), rolling (transfer) **Freshman admission** 83% were admitted **Freshman test scores** SAT critical reading scores over 500: 64%; SAT math scores over 500: 68%; ACT scores over 18: 98%; SAT critical reading scores over 600: 14%; SAT math scores over 600: 18%; ACT scores over 24: 43% **Housing** Yes **Expenses** Tuition & Fees $20,030; Room & Board $9800 **Undergraduates** 74% women, 21% part-time, 25% 25 or older, 1% Native American, 4% Hispanic American, 11% African American, 2% Asian American/Pacific Islander **The most frequently chosen baccalaureate fields are** business/marketing, health professions and related sciences, interdisciplinary studies **Academic program** Accelerated degree program, summer session, adult/continuing education programs, internships **Contact** Dr. Steve Smith, Director of Undergraduate Admissions, D'Youville College, 320 Porter Avenue, Buffalo, NY 14201-1084. *Phone:* 716-829-7600 or toll-free 800-777-3921. *Web site:* http://www.dyc.edu/.

Visit Petersons.com and enter keyword D'Youville

See page 764 for the College Close-Up.

"My program at D'Youville College has opened so many doors for me. The instructors are focused on helping me succeed and they're always there for me every step of the way. They really prepare you to head out into the working world with more confidence than you've ever had. I've had more real world experience than most people my age by doing internships and meeting professionals."

– Kristin, class of 2010

www.dyc.edu
1.800.777.3921

www.dyc.edu
For a Full List of Our Degree Programs

Affordable...
Merit-Based Scholarships
D'Youville offers significant merit-based scholarships to qualifying students including transfer students.

Accelerated...
Spend Less Time Earning a Higher Degree.
D'Youville offers combined degrees that take less time to complete than it would at other schools.

Earning Power...
Graduate with More Potential
D'Youville offers dual and sequential degree programs in high-demand career fields. We are a global leader in education & health care programs with a strong, respected reputation.

Merit-Based Scholarships worth up to $64,000

EDUCATING FOR LIFE

320 Porter Avenue ■ Buffalo, New York 14201

Elmira College
Elmira, New York

General Independent, comprehensive, coed **Entrance** Moderately difficult **Setting** 42-acre suburban campus **Total enrollment** 1,657 **Student-faculty ratio** 12:1 **Application deadline** 3/31 (freshmen), rolling (transfer) **Freshman admission** 79% were admitted. Average high school GPA 3.35 **Freshman test scores** SAT critical reading scores over 500: 63%; ACT scores over 18: 100%; SAT critical reading scores over 600: 21%; ACT scores over 24: 40% **Housing** Yes **Expenses** Tuition & Fees $34,800; Room & Board $10,800 **Undergraduates** 72% women, 17% part-time, 4% 25 or older, 0.3% Native American, 2% Hispanic American, 3% African American, 1% Asian American/Pacific Islander **The most frequently chosen baccalaureate fields are** business/marketing, education, social sciences **Academic program** English as a second language, advanced placement, accelerated degree program, self-designed majors, summer session, adult/continuing education programs, internships **Contact** Mr. Brett Moore, Director of Admissions, Elmira College, One Park Place, Elmira, NY 14901. *Phone:* 607-735-1724 or toll-free 800-935-6472. *Fax:* 607-735-1718. *E-mail:* admissions@elmira.edu. *Web site:* http://www.elmira.edu/.

Visit Petersons.com and enter keyword Elmira

See page 778 for the College Close-Up.

Eugene Lang College The New School for Liberal Arts
New York, New York

General Independent, 4-year, coed **Entrance** Very difficult **Setting** 5-acre urban campus **Total enrollment** 1,439 **Student-faculty ratio** 15:1 **Application deadline** 2/1 (freshmen), 5/15 (transfer) **Freshman admission** 68% were admitted. Average high school GPA 3.2 **Freshman test scores** SAT critical reading scores over 500: 87%; SAT math scores over 500: 66%; ACT scores over 18: 97%; SAT critical reading scores over 600: 49%; SAT math scores over 600: 19%; ACT scores over 24: 58% **Housing** Yes **Expenses** Tuition & Fees $34,550; Room & Board $15,260 **Undergraduates** 67% women, 6% part-time, 3% 25 or older, 0.5% Native American, 9% Hispanic American, 5% African American, 5% Asian American/Pacific Islander **The most frequently chosen baccalaureate field is** liberal arts/general studies **Academic program** English as a second language, advanced placement, accelerated degree program, self-designed majors, summer session, internships **Contact** Karen Williams, Director of Admissions, Eugene Lang College The New School for Liberal Arts, 65 West 11th Street, New York, NY 10011-8601. *Phone:* 212-229-5665 or toll-free 877-528-3321. *Fax:* 212-229-5355. *E-mail:* lang@newschool.edu. *Web site:* http://www.lang.edu/.

Visit Petersons.com and enter keyword Eugene

See page 786 for the College Close-Up.

Excelsior College
Albany, New York

General Independent, comprehensive, coed **Entrance** Noncompetitive **Setting** suburban campus **Total enrollment** 31,924 **Student-faculty ratio** 79:1 **Application deadline** Rolling (freshmen), rolling (transfer) **Housing** No **Undergraduates** 56% women, 100% part-time, 97% 25 or older, 1% Native American, 7% Hispanic American, 20% African American, 5% Asian American/Pacific Islander **The most frequently chosen baccalaureate fields are** business/marketing, engineering technologies, liberal arts/general studies **Academic program** Advanced placement, accelerated degree program, self-designed majors, honors program, adult/continuing education programs **Contact** Admissions, Excelsior College, 7 Columbia Circle, Albany, NY 12203-5159. *Phone:* 518-464-8500 or toll-free 888-647-2388. *Fax:* 518-464-8777. *E-mail:* admissions@excelsior.edu. *Web site:* http://www.excelsior.edu/.

FIVE TOWNS COLLEGE

When You're Serious About Music, Media, Education & The Performing Arts

- AUDIO RECORDING TECHNOLOGY
- BROADCASTING
- BUSINESS
- ELEMENTARY TEACHER EDUCATION
- FILM/VIDEO
- JOURNALISM
- MASS COMMUNICATION
- MUSIC TEACHER EDUCATION
- MUSIC BUSINESS
- MUSIC PERFORMANCE
- THEATRE ARTS

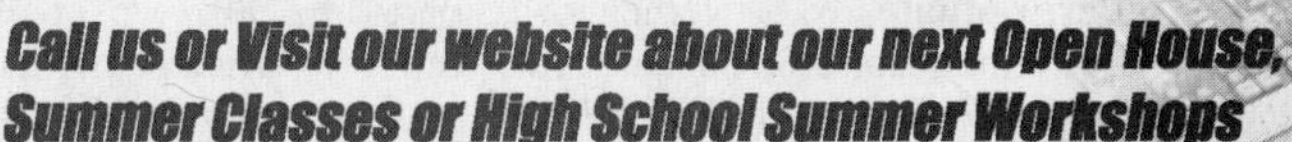

Call us or Visit our website about our next Open House, Summer Classes or High School Summer Workshops

305 N. Service Road Dix Hills, New York 11746 www.ftc.edu 631.656.2110

Farmingdale State College
Farmingdale, New York

General State-supported, 4-year, coed **Entrance** Moderately difficult **Setting** 380-acre small-town campus **Total enrollment** 6,988 **Student-faculty ratio** 18:1 **Application deadline** Rolling (freshmen), rolling (transfer) **Freshman admission** 40% were admitted. Average high school GPA 3.21 **Freshman test scores** SAT critical reading scores over 500: 36%; SAT math scores over 500: 53%; SAT critical reading scores over 600: 4%; SAT math scores over 600: 10% **Housing** Yes **Expenses** Tuition & Fees: state resident $6000, nonresident $13,900; Room & Board $11,618 **Undergraduates** 43% women, 28% part-time, 24% 25 or older, 0.2% Native American, 8% Hispanic American, 7% African American, 3% Asian American/Pacific Islander **The most frequently chosen baccalaureate fields are** business/marketing, biological/life sciences, engineering technologies **Academic program** Advanced placement, summer session, internships **Contact** Mr. Jim Hall, Director of Admissions, Farmingdale State College, 2350 Broadhollow Road, Farmingdale, NY 11735. *Phone:* 631-420-2457 or toll-free 877-4-FARMINGDALE. *Web site:* http://www.farmingdale.edu/.

Fashion Institute of Technology
New York, New York

General State and locally supported, comprehensive, coed, primarily women **Entrance** Moderately difficult **Setting** 5-acre urban campus **Total enrollment** 10,413 **Student-faculty ratio** 17:1 **Application deadline** 1/15 (freshmen), 1/15 (transfer) **Freshman admission** 40% were admitted. Average high school GPA 3.3 **Housing** Yes **Expenses** Tuition & Fees: state resident $5618, nonresident $13,054; Room & Board $11,248 **Undergraduates** 84% women, 30% part-time, 26% 25 or older, 0.1% Native American, 9% Hispanic American, 6% African American, 7% Asian American/Pacific Islander **The most frequently chosen baccalaureate fields are** business/marketing, communications/journalism, visual and performing arts **Academic program** English as a second language, advanced placement, honors program, summer session, adult/continuing education programs, internships **Contact** Ms. Yamiley Saintvil, Director of Admissions, Fashion Institute of Technology, Seventh Avenue at 27th Street, New York, NY 10001-5992. *Phone:* 212-217-3760 or toll-free 800-GOTOFIT. *Fax:* 212-217-3761. *E-mail:* fitinfo@fitnyc.edu. *Web site:* http://www.fitnyc.edu/.

Visit Petersons.com and enter keyword Fashion

See page 792 for the College Close-Up.

Five Towns College
Dix Hills, New York

General Independent, comprehensive, coed **Entrance** Moderately difficult **Setting** 40-acre suburban campus **Total enrollment** 1,447 **Student-faculty ratio** 13:1 **Application deadline** Rolling (freshmen), rolling (transfer) **Freshman admission** 53% were admitted **Housing** Yes **Expenses** Tuition & Fees $17,750; Room & Board $12,300 **Undergraduates** 36% women, 3% part-time, 2% 25 or older **Academic program** Advanced placement, summer session, adult/continuing education programs, internships **Contact** Mr. Jerry Cohen, Dean of Enrollment, Five Towns College, 305 North Service Road, Dix Hills, NY 11746-6055. *Phone:* 631-424-7000 Ext. 2110. *Fax:* 631-656-3199. *E-mail:* jcohen@ftc.edu. *Web site:* http://www.ftc.edu/.

Visit Petersons.com and enter keyword Five

See page 798 for the College Close-Up.

Fordham University
New York, New York

General Independent Roman Catholic (Jesuit), university, coed **Entrance** Very difficult **Setting** 85-acre urban campus **Total enrollment** 14,544

Fordham University (continued)
Student-faculty ratio 13:1 **Application deadline** 1/15 (freshmen), 6/1 (transfer) **Freshman admission** 50% were admitted. Average high school GPA 3.54 **Freshman test scores** SAT critical reading scores over 500: 93.91%; SAT math scores over 500: 94.89%; ACT scores over 18: 99.81%; SAT critical reading scores over 600: 63.5%; SAT math scores over 600: 66.85%; ACT scores over 24: 89.49% **Housing** Yes **Expenses** Tuition & Fees $35,257; Room & Board $12,980 **Undergraduates** 53% women, 7% part-time, 8% 25 or older, 0.4% Native American, 13% Hispanic American, 5% African American, 8% Asian American/Pacific Islander **Academic program** English as a second language, advanced placement, accelerated degree program, self-designed majors, honors program, summer session, adult/continuing education programs, internships **Contact** Mr. Peter Farrell, Director of Admission, Fordham University, 441 East Fordham Road, New York, NY 10458. *Phone:* 718-817-4000 or toll-free 800-FORDHAM. *Fax:* 718-367-9404. *E-mail:* enroll@fordham.edu. *Web site:* http://www.fordham.edu/.
Visit Petersons.com and enter keyword Fordham

See page 806 for the College Close-Up.

Global College of Long Island University
Brooklyn, New York

Contact Amy Greenstein, Director of Admissions, Global College of Long Island University, 9 Hanover Place, 4th Floor, Brooklyn, NY 11201. *Phone:* 718-780-4320. *Fax:* 718-780-4325. *E-mail:* amy.greenstein@liu.edu. *Web site:* http://www.liu.edu/globalcollege/.

Globe Institute of Technology
New York, New York

General Proprietary, 4-year, coed **Entrance** Minimally difficult **Setting** urban campus **Application deadline** Rolling (freshmen) **Freshman admission** Average high school GPA 3 **Housing** Yes **Undergraduates** 63% 25 or older **Academic program** English as a second language, advanced placement, accelerated degree program, summer session, internships **Contact** Mr. Michael Scalice, Admissions Director, Globe Institute of Technology, 500 7th Avenue, New York, NY 10018. *Phone:* 212-349-4330 Ext. 1624 or toll-free 877-394-5623. *Fax:* 212-227-5920. *E-mail:* admissions@globe.edu. *Web site:* http://www.globe.edu/.

Hamilton College
Clinton, New York

General Independent, 4-year, coed **Entrance** Very difficult **Setting** 1,300-acre small-town campus **Total enrollment** 1,882 **Student-faculty ratio** 10:1 **Application deadline** 1/1 (freshmen), 4/15 (transfer) **Freshman admission** 30% were admitted **Freshman test scores** SAT critical reading scores over 500: 97.48%; SAT math scores over 500: 98.2%; ACT scores over 18: 100%; SAT critical reading scores over 600: 89.93%; SAT math scores over 600: 90.29%; ACT scores over 24: 93.55% **Housing** Yes **Expenses** Tuition & Fees $39,760; Room & Board $10,100 **Undergraduates** 53% women, 2% part-time, 1% 25 or older, 1% Native American, 5% Hispanic American, 4% African American, 8% Asian American/Pacific Islander **The most frequently chosen baccalaureate fields are** foreign languages and literature, psychology, social sciences **Academic program** English as a second language, advanced placement, accelerated degree program, self-designed majors, adult/continuing education programs, internships **Contact** Ms. Monica Inzer, Vice President and Dean of Admission and Financial Aid, Hamilton College, 198 College Hill Road, Clinton, NY 13323. *Phone:* 800-843-2655 or toll-free 800-843-2655. *Fax:* 315-859-4457. *E-mail:* admission@hamilton.edu. *Web site:* http://www.hamilton.edu/.

Hartwick College
Oneonta, New York

General Independent, 4-year, coed **Entrance** Moderately difficult **Setting** 425-acre small-town campus **Total enrollment** 1,473 **Student-faculty ratio** 11:1 **Application deadline** 2/15 (freshmen), 8/1 (transfer) **Freshman admission** 91% were admitted. Average high school GPA 3.1 **Freshman test scores** SAT critical reading scores over 500: 70%; SAT math scores over 500: 73%; ACT scores over 18: 99%; SAT critical reading scores over 600: 25%; SAT math scores over 600: 30%; ACT scores over 24: 57% **Housing** Yes **Expenses** Tuition & Fees $33,330; Room & Board $9075 **Undergraduates** 59% women, 3% part-time, 14% 25 or older, 0.3% Native American, 4% Hispanic American, 4% African American, 2% Asian American/Pacific Islander **The most frequently chosen baccalaureate fields are** business/marketing, social sciences, visual and performing arts **Academic program** Advanced placement, accelerated degree program, self-designed majors, honors program, internships **Contact** Director of Admissions, Hartwick College, PO Box 4022, Oneonta, NY 13820-4022. *Phone:* 607-431-4150 or toll-free 888-HARTWICK. *Fax:* 607-431-4102. *E-mail:* admissions@hartwick.edu. *Web site:* http://www.hartwick.edu/.

Hilbert College
Hamburg, New York

General Independent, 4-year, coed **Entrance** Minimally difficult **Setting** 40-acre small-town campus **Total enrollment** 1,046 **Student-faculty ratio** 12:1 **Application deadline** 9/1 (freshmen), 8/1 (transfer) **Freshman admission** 85% were admitted. Average high school GPA 3.2 **Freshman test scores** SAT critical reading scores over 500: 27%; SAT math scores over 500: 41%; ACT scores over 18: 71%; SAT critical reading scores over 600: 6%; SAT math scores over 600: 8%; ACT scores over 24: 18% **Housing** Yes **Expenses** Tuition & Fees $18,490; Room & Board $7990 **Undergraduates** 61% women, 24% part-time, 30% 25 or older, 2% Native American, 2% Hispanic American, 6% African American, 0.1% Asian American/Pacific Islander **The most frequently chosen baccalaureate fields are** business/marketing, liberal arts/general studies, security and protective services **Academic program** Advanced placement, honors program, summer session, internships **Contact** Mr. Timothy Lee, Director of Admissions, Hilbert College, 5200 South Park Avenue, Hamburg, NY 14075-1597. *Phone:* 716-649-7900. *Fax:* 716-649-0702. *E-mail:* tlee@hilbert.edu. *Web site:* http://www.hilbert.edu/.
Visit Petersons.com and enter keyword Hilbert

See page 848 for the College Close-Up.

Hobart and William Smith Colleges
Geneva, New York

Contact Don W. Emmons, Dean of Admissions and Vice President of Enrollment, Hobart and William Smith Colleges, Geneva, NY 14456-3397. *Phone:* 315-781-3622 or toll-free 800-245-0100. *Fax:* 315-781-3914. *E-mail:* emmons@hws.edu. *Web site:* http://www.hws.edu/.

See page 852 for the College Close-Up.

Hofstra University
Hempstead, New York

General Independent, university, coed **Entrance** Moderately difficult **Setting** 240-acre suburban campus **Total enrollment** 12,068 **Student-faculty ratio** 14:1 **Application deadline** Rolling (freshmen) **Freshman admission** 57% were admitted. Average high school GPA 3.4 **Freshman test scores** SAT critical reading scores over 500: 93%; SAT math scores over 500: 96%; ACT scores over 18: 100%; SAT critical reading scores over 600: 43%; SAT math scores over 600: 52%; ACT scores over 24: 77% **Housing** Yes **Expenses** Tuition & Fees $30,130; Room & Board $11,330 **Undergraduates** 52% women, 7% part-time, 6% 25 or older, 0.4% Native American, 9% Hispanic American, 9% African American, 5% Asian American/Pacific Islander **The most frequently chosen baccalaureate fields are** business/marketing, communications/journalism, social sciences **Academic program** English as a second language, advanced placement, accelerated degree program, self-

designed majors, honors program, summer session, internships **Contact** Mr. Sunil Samuel, Director of Admissions, Hofstra University, 100 Hofstra University, Hempstead, NY 11549. *Phone:* 516-463-6700 or toll-free 800-HOFSTRA. *Fax:* 516-463-5100. *E-mail:* admission@hofstra.edu. *Web site:* http://www.hofstra.edu/.
Visit Petersons.com and enter keyword Hofstra

See page 854 for the College Close-Up.

Holy Trinity Orthodox Seminary
Jordanville, New York

Contact Fr. Vladimir Tsurikov, Assistant Dean, Holy Trinity Orthodox Seminary, PO Box 36, Jordanville, NY 13361. *Phone:* 315-858-0945. *Fax:* 315-858-0945. *E-mail:* info@hts.edu. *Web site:* http://www.hts.edu/.

Houghton College
Houghton, New York

General Independent Wesleyan, comprehensive, coed **Entrance** Moderately difficult **Setting** 1,300-acre rural campus **Total enrollment** 1,336 **Student-faculty ratio** 12:1 **Application deadline** Rolling (freshmen), rolling (transfer) **Freshman admission** 82% were admitted. Average high school GPA 3.56 **Freshman test scores** SAT critical reading scores over 500: 85%; SAT math scores over 500: 82%; ACT scores over 18: 100%; SAT critical reading scores over 600: 48%; SAT math scores over 600: 40%; ACT scores over 24: 64% **Housing** Yes **Expenses** Tuition & Fees $24,440; Room & Board $7000 **Undergraduates** 65% women, 5% part-time, 8% 25 or older, 0.4% Native American, 1% Hispanic American, 2% African American, 2% Asian American/Pacific Islander **The most frequently chosen baccalaureate fields are** business/marketing, education, visual and performing arts **Academic program** Advanced placement, honors program, summer session, adult/continuing education programs, internships **Contact** Mr. Matthew Reitnour, Director of Admission, Houghton College, PO Box 128, Houghton, NY 14744. *Phone:* 585-567-9353 or toll-free 800-777-2556. *Fax:* 585-567-9522. *E-mail:* admission@houghton.edu. *Web site:* http://www.houghton.edu/.

Hunter College of the City University of New York
New York, New York

General State and locally supported, comprehensive, coed **Entrance** Moderately difficult **Setting** urban campus **Total enrollment** 22,168 **Student-faculty ratio** 15:1 **Application deadline** 3/15 (freshmen), 3/15 (transfer) **Freshman admission** 26% were admitted. Average high school GPA 3 **Freshman test scores** SAT critical reading scores over 500: 84%; SAT math scores over 500: 89%; SAT critical reading scores over 600: 30%; SAT math scores over 600: 37% **Housing** Yes **Expenses** Tuition & Fees: state resident $4999, nonresident $12,849; Room only $5500 **Undergraduates** 67% women, 30% part-time, 26% 25 or older, 0.2% Native American, 19% Hispanic American, 12% African American, 21% Asian American/Pacific Islander **The most frequently chosen baccalaureate fields are** English, psychology, social sciences **Academic program** English as a second language, advanced placement, self-designed majors, honors program, summer session, internships **Contact** Mr. William Zlata, Director of Admissions, Hunter College of the City University of New York, 695 Park Avenue, New York, NY 10021-5085. *Phone:* 212-772-4490. *Fax:* 212-650-3472. *E-mail:* bill.zlata@hunter.cuny.edu. *Web site:* http://www.hunter.cuny.edu/.
Visit Petersons.com and enter keyword Hunter

See page 860 for the College Close-Up.

Iona College
New Rochelle, New York

General Independent, comprehensive, coed, affiliated with Roman Catholic Church **Entrance** Moderately difficult **Setting** 35-acre suburban campus **Total enrollment** 4,248 **Student-faculty ratio** 13:1 **Application deadline** 2/15 (freshmen), 8/15 (transfer) **Freshman admission** 58% were admitted. Average high school GPA 3.5 **Freshman test scores** SAT critical reading scores over 500: 65%; SAT math scores over 500: 68%; SAT critical reading scores over 600: 17%; SAT math scores over 600: 18% **Housing** Yes **Expenses** Tuition & Fees $28,850; Room & Board $11,800 **Undergraduates** 56% women, 3% part-time, 3% 25 or older, 0.2% Native American, 12% Hispanic American, 5% African American, 2% Asian American/Pacific Islander **The most frequently chosen baccalaureate fields are** business/marketing, communications/journalism, psychology **Academic program** Advanced placement, accelerated degree program, honors program, summer session, adult/continuing education programs, internships **Contact** Mr. Kevin Cavanagh, Assistant Vice President for College Admissions, Iona College, Admissions, 715 North Avenue, New Rochelle, NY 10801. *Phone:* 914-633-2502 or toll-free 800-231-IONA. *Fax:* 914-637-2778. *E-mail:* icad@iona.edu. *Web site:* http://www.iona.edu/.
Visit Petersons.com and enter keywords Iona College

See page 872 for the College Close-Up.

Ithaca College
Ithaca, New York

General Independent, comprehensive, coed **Entrance** Moderately difficult **Setting** 650-acre small-town campus **Total enrollment** 6,894 **Student-faculty ratio** 12:1 **Application deadline** 2/1 (freshmen), 3/1 (transfer) **Freshman admission** 79% were admitted **Freshman test scores** SAT critical reading scores over 500: 86.3%; SAT math scores over 500: 86.3%; SAT critical reading scores over 600: 40.4%; SAT math scores over 600: 44.6% **Housing** Yes **Expenses** Tuition & Fees $32,060; Room & Board $11,780 **Undergraduates** 57% women, 1% part-time, 1% 25 or older, 1% Native American, 4% Hispanic American, 3% African American, 4% Asian American/Pacific Islander **The most frequently chosen baccalaureate fields are** communications/journalism, health professions and related sciences, visual and performing arts **Academic program** Advanced placement, accelerated degree program, self-designed majors, honors program, summer session, adult/continuing education programs, internships **Contact** Gerard Turbide, Director of Admission, Ithaca College, 953 Danby Road, Ithaca, NY 14850-7000. *Phone:* 607-274-3124 or toll-free 800-429-4274. *Fax:* 607-274-1900. *E-mail:* admission@ithaca.edu. *Web site:* http://www.ithaca.edu/.

Jamestown Business College
Jamestown, New York

General Proprietary, primarily 2-year, coed **Entrance** Minimally difficult **Setting** 1-acre small-town campus **Total enrollment** 329 **Student-faculty ratio** 25:1 **Application deadline** Rolling (freshmen), rolling (transfer) **Freshman admission** 91% were admitted **Housing** No **Expenses** Tuition & Fees $11,100 **Undergraduates** 74% women, 5% part-time, 53% 25 or older, 2% Native American, 5% Hispanic American, 2% African American, 1% Asian American/Pacific Islander **Academic program** Advanced placement, summer session, internships **Contact** Mrs. Brenda Salemme, Director of Admissions and Placement, Jamestown Business College, 7 Fairmount Avenue, Box 429, Jamestown, NY 14702-0429. *Phone:* 716-664-5100. *Fax:* 716-664-3144. *E-mail:* admissions@jbcny.org. *Web site:* http://www.jbcny.org/.

John Jay College of Criminal Justice of the City University of New York
New York, New York

General State and locally supported, comprehensive, coed **Entrance** Moderately difficult **Setting** urban campus **Total enrollment** 15,330 **Student-faculty ratio** 19:1 **Application deadline** 5/31 (freshmen), rolling (transfer) **Freshman admission** 63% were admitted. Average high school GPA 2.55 **Freshman test scores** SAT critical reading scores over 500: 25.3%; SAT math scores over 500: 31%; SAT critical reading

John Jay College of Criminal Justice of the City University of New York (continued)

scores over 600: 3.3%; SAT math scores over 600: 5% **Housing** No **Expenses** Tuition & Fees: state resident $4600, nonresident $12,450 **Undergraduates** 57% women, 22% part-time, 18% 25 or older, 0.3% Native American, 41% Hispanic American, 23% African American, 8% Asian American/Pacific Islander **The most frequently chosen baccalaureate fields are** psychology, security and protective services, social sciences **Academic program** English as a second language, advanced placement, self-designed majors, honors program, summer session, internships **Contact** Sandra Palleja, Director of Admissions, John Jay College of Criminal Justice of the City University of New York, 899 Tenth Avenue, New York, NY 10019-1093. *Phone:* 212-237-8878 or toll-free 877-JOHNJAY. *E-mail:* spalleja@jjay.cuny.edu. *Web site:* http://www.jjay.cuny.edu/.

The Juilliard School
New York, New York

General Independent, comprehensive, coed **Entrance** Most difficult **Setting** urban campus **Total enrollment** 833 **Student-faculty ratio** 3:1 **Application deadline** 12/1 (freshmen), 12/1 (transfer) **Freshman admission** 7% were admitted **Housing** Yes **Expenses** Tuition & Fees $30,500; Room & Board $11,810 **Undergraduates** 48% women, 1% 25 or older, 4% Hispanic American, 5% African American, 15% Asian American/Pacific Islander **The most frequently chosen baccalaureate field is** visual and performing arts **Academic program** Adult/continuing education programs **Contact** Ms. Lee Cioppa, Associate Dean for Admissions, The Juilliard School, 60 Lincoln Center Plaza, New York, NY 10023-6588. *Phone:* 212-799-5000. *Fax:* 212-724-0263. *E-mail:* admissions@julliard.edu. *Web site:* http://www.juilliard.edu/.

Kehilath Yakov Rabbinical Seminary
Ossining, New York

General Independent Jewish, comprehensive, men only **Total enrollment** 88 **Housing** Yes **Contact** Admissions Officer, Kehilath Yakov Rabbinical Seminary, 340 Illington Road, Ossining, NY 10562. *Phone:* 718-963-1212.

Keuka College
Keuka Park, New York

General Independent, comprehensive, coed, affiliated with American Baptist Churches in the U.S.A. **Entrance** Moderately difficult **Setting** 173-acre rural campus **Total enrollment** 1,676 **Student-faculty ratio** 14:1 **Application deadline** Rolling (freshmen), rolling (transfer) **Freshman admission** 77% were admitted. Average high school GPA 3.12 **Freshman test scores** SAT critical reading scores over 500: 31%; SAT math scores over 500: 40%; ACT scores over 18: 72%; SAT critical reading scores over 600: 6%; SAT math scores over 600: 7%; ACT scores over 24: 24% **Housing** Yes **Expenses** Tuition & Fees $22,680; Room & Board $9160 **Undergraduates** 75% women, 20% part-time, 34% 25 or older, 2% Native American, 3% Hispanic American, 7% African American, 2% Asian American/Pacific Islander **The most frequently chosen baccalaureate fields are** business/marketing, education, health professions and related sciences **Academic program** Advanced placement, accelerated degree program, self-designed majors, summer session, adult/continuing education programs, internships **Contact** Fred Hoyle, Associate Vice President of Admissions, Keuka College, Wagner House, Keuka Park, NY 14478. *Phone:* 315-279-5254 or toll-free 800-33-KEUKA. *Fax:* 315-279-5386. *E-mail:* admissions@mail.keuka.edu. *Web site:* http://www.keuka.edu/.

The King's College
New York, New York

General Independent nondenominational, 4-year, coed **Entrance** Very difficult **Setting** urban campus **Total enrollment** 302 **Student-faculty ratio** 14:1 **Application deadline** Rolling (freshmen), rolling (transfer) **Freshman admission** 74% were admitted. Average high school GPA 3.62 **Freshman test scores** SAT critical reading scores over 500: 98.5%; SAT math scores over 500: 91.5%; ACT scores over 18: 100%; SAT critical reading scores over 600: 79.5%; SAT math scores over 600: 45.5%; ACT scores over 24: 81.8% **Housing** Yes **Expenses** Tuition & Fees $27,350; Room only $10,500 **Undergraduates** 62% women, 4% part-time, 3% 25 or older, 6% Hispanic American, 2% African American, 3% Asian American/Pacific Islander **The most frequently chosen baccalaureate fields are** business/marketing, interdisciplinary studies **Academic program** Advanced placement, summer session, internships **Contact** Mr. Brian Parker, Vice President for Admissions, The King's College, 350 Fifth Avenue, 15th Floor Empire State Building, New York, NY 10118. *Phone:* 212-659-7217 or toll-free 888-969-7200 Ext. 3610. *Fax:* 212-659-7210. *E-mail:* bparker@tkc.edu. *Web site:* http://www.tkc.edu/.

Kol Yaakov Torah Center
Monsey, New York

General Independent Jewish, comprehensive, men only **Entrance** Minimally difficult **Setting** 3-acre small-town campus **Total enrollment** 23 **Application deadline** Rolling (freshmen), rolling (transfer) **Freshman admission** 100% were admitted **Housing** Yes **Undergraduates** 18% 25 or older **Academic program** English as a second language, self-designed majors, honors program, summer session, adult/continuing education programs **Contact** Assistant Director of Admissions, Kol Yaakov Torah Center, 29 West Maple Avenue, Monsey, NY 10952-2954. *Phone:* 914-425-3871. *E-mail:* horizonss@aol.com. *Web site:* http://horizons.edu/.

Lehman College of the City University of New York
Bronx, New York

General State and locally supported, comprehensive, coed **Entrance** Moderately difficult **Setting** 37-acre urban campus **Total enrollment** 12,188 **Student-faculty ratio** 14:1 **Application deadline** Rolling (freshmen), rolling (transfer) **Freshman admission** 26% were admitted **Freshman test scores** SAT critical reading scores over 500: 40%; SAT math scores over 500: 49%; SAT critical reading scores over 600: 7%; SAT math scores over 600: 7% **Housing** Yes **Expenses** Tuition & Fees: state resident $4770, nonresident $10,130; Room & Board $12,569 **Undergraduates** 70% women, 38% part-time, 3% 25 or older **The most frequently chosen baccalaureate fields are** education, business/marketing, health professions and related sciences **Academic program** English as a second language, advanced placement, self-designed majors, honors program, summer session, adult/continuing education programs, internships **Contact** Mr. Clarence Wilkes, Director of Admissions, Lehman College of the City University of New York, 250 Bedford Park Boulevard West, Bronx, NY 10468. *Phone:* 718-960-8713 or toll-free 877-Lehman1. *Fax:* 718-960-8712. *E-mail:* enroll@lehman.cuny.edu. *Web site:* http://www.lehman.cuny.edu/.

Visit Petersons.com and enter keyword Lehman

Le Moyne College
Syracuse, New York

General Independent Roman Catholic (Jesuit), comprehensive, coed **Entrance** Moderately difficult **Setting** 161-acre suburban campus **Total enrollment** 3,524 **Student-faculty ratio** 13:1 **Application deadline** 2/1 (freshmen), 6/1 (transfer) **Freshman admission** 67% were admitted. Average high school GPA 3.34 **Freshman test scores** SAT critical reading scores over 500: 71%; SAT math scores over 500: 79%; ACT scores over 18: 96%; SAT critical reading scores over 600: 21%; SAT math scores over 600: 30%; ACT scores over 24: 41% **Housing** Yes **Expenses** Tuition & Fees $25,830; Room & Board $9990 **Undergraduates** 63% women, 16% part-time, 8% 25 or older, 1% Native

American, 5% Hispanic American, 4% African American, 2% Asian American/Pacific Islander **The most frequently chosen baccalaureate fields are** business/marketing, psychology, social sciences **Academic program** Advanced placement, accelerated degree program, honors program, summer session, adult/continuing education programs, internships **Contact** Mr. Dennis J. Nicholson, Director of Admission, Le Moyne College, 1419 Salt Springs Road, Syracuse, NY 13214-1301. *Phone:* 315-445-4300 or toll-free 800-333-4733. *Fax:* 315-445-4711. *E-mail:* admission@lemoyne.edu. *Web site:* http://www.lemoyne.edu/.
Visit Petersons.com and enter keywords Le Moyne

See page 908 for the College Close-Up.

LIM College
New York, New York

General Proprietary, comprehensive, coed, primarily women **Entrance** Moderately difficult **Setting** urban campus **Total enrollment** 1,388 **Student-faculty ratio** 18:1 **Application deadline** Rolling (freshmen), rolling (transfer) **Freshman admission** 65% were admitted. Average high school GPA 2.9 **Freshman test scores** SAT critical reading scores over 500: 37%; SAT math scores over 500: 33%; SAT critical reading scores over 600: 3%; SAT math scores over 600: 4% **Housing** Yes **Expenses** Tuition & Fees $21,450; Room & Board $19,875 **Undergraduates** 94% women, 5% part-time, 1% 25 or older, 0.3% Native American, 14% Hispanic American, 12% African American, 5% Asian American/Pacific Islander **The most frequently chosen baccalaureate fields are** business/marketing, family and consumer sciences, visual and performing arts **Academic program** Advanced placement, accelerated degree program, honors program, summer session, internships **Contact** Ms. Kristina Ortiz, Assistant Dean of Admissions, LIM College, 12 East 53rd Street, New York, NY 10022. *Phone:* 212-752-1530 Ext. 217 or toll-free 800-677-1323. *Fax:* 212-317-8602. *E-mail:* admissions@limcollege.edu. *Web site:* http://www.limcollege.edu/.
Visit Petersons.com and enter keyword LIM

See page 916 for the College Close-Up.

List College, The Jewish Theological Seminary
New York, New York

General Independent Jewish, university, coed **Entrance** Very difficult **Setting** 1-acre urban campus **Total enrollment** 566 **Student-faculty ratio** 5:1 **Application deadline** 2/15 (freshmen), 5/1 (transfer) **Freshman admission** 60% were admitted. Average high school GPA 3.7 **Freshman test scores** SAT critical reading scores over 500: 100%; SAT math scores over 500: 97%; ACT scores over 18: 100%; SAT critical reading scores over 600: 95%; SAT math scores over 600: 89%; ACT scores over 24: 100% **Housing** Yes **Expenses** Tuition & Fees $15,000; Room only $9200 **Undergraduates** 57% women, 4% part-time, 1% Hispanic American **Academic program** Advanced placement, self-designed majors, honors program, summer session, adult/continuing education programs, internships **Contact** Mr. Sergio Lineberge, List College Admissions Coordinator, List College, The Jewish Theological Seminary, 3080 Broadway, New York, NY 10027. *Phone:* 212-678-8820. *E-mail:* lcadmissions@jtsa.edu. *Web site:* http://www.jtsa.edu/.

Long Island University, Brentwood Campus
Brentwood, New York

Contact Mr. John P. Metcalfe, Director of Admissions, Long Island University, Brentwood Campus, 100 Second Avenue, Brentwood, NY 11717. *Phone:* 631-273-5112 Ext. 202. *Web site:* http://www.liu.edu/.

Long Island University, Brooklyn Campus
Brooklyn, New York

General Independent, university, coed **Entrance** Minimally difficult **Setting** 10-acre urban campus **Total enrollment** 8,051 **Student-faculty**

Study where Judaism is lived as well as learned, surrounded by the excitement and opportunities of New York City. **The Albert A. List College of Jewish Studies** offers students an opportunity to receive two degrees in four years. Through our Dual Degree programs with Columbia University and Barnard College, students receive a liberal arts or sciences degree from an Ivy League institution and a second bachelor's degree in Jewish Studies from The Jewish Theological Seminary.

Look into it.

List College

3080 BROADWAY,
NEW YORK, NY 10027
(212) 678-8000 • www.jtsa.edu/list

Long Island University, Brooklyn Campus (continued)
ratio 14:1 **Application deadline** Rolling (freshmen), rolling (transfer) **Freshman admission** 80% were admitted. Average high school GPA 2.8 **Freshman test scores** SAT critical reading scores over 500: 30%; SAT math scores over 500: 43%; ACT scores over 18: 61%; SAT critical reading scores over 600: 5%; SAT math scores over 600: 14%; ACT scores over 24: 15% **Housing** Yes **Expenses** Tuition & Fees $27,358; Room & Board $10,140 **Undergraduates** 73% women, 20% part-time, 26% 25 or older, 0.4% Native American, 14% Hispanic American, 36% African American, 12% Asian American/Pacific Islander **The most frequently chosen baccalaureate fields are** business/marketing, health professions and related sciences, psychology **Academic program** English as a second language, advanced placement, accelerated degree program, self-designed majors, honors program, summer session, internships **Contact** Elizabeth Storinge, Dean of Admissions, Long Island University, Brooklyn Campus, 1 University Plaza, Brooklyn, NY 11201. *Phone:* 718-488-1011 or toll-free 800-LIU-PLAN. *E-mail:* admissions@brooklyn.liu.edu. *Web site:* http://www.liu.edu/.
Visit Petersons.com and enter keyword Brooklyn

Long Island University, C.W. Post Campus
Brookville, New York

General Independent, comprehensive, coed **Entrance** Moderately difficult **Setting** 308-acre suburban campus **Total enrollment** 11,749 **Student-faculty ratio** 13:1 **Application deadline** Rolling (freshmen), rolling (transfer) **Freshman admission** 82% were admitted. Average high school GPA 2.9 **Freshman test scores** SAT critical reading scores over 500: 43%; SAT math scores over 500: 50%; ACT scores over 18: 85%; SAT critical reading scores over 600: 5%; SAT math scores over 600: 13%; ACT scores over 24: 25% **Housing** Yes **Expenses** Tuition & Fees $27,400; Room & Board $10,140 **Undergraduates** 71% women, 51% part-time, 14% 25 or older **The most frequently chosen baccalaureate fields are** business/marketing, education, visual and performing arts **Academic program** English as a second language, advanced placement, accelerated degree program, self-designed majors, honors program, summer session, internships **Contact** Ms. Joanne Graziano, Executive Director of Admissions and Recruitment, Long Island University, C.W. Post Campus, 720 Northern Boulevard, Brookville, NY 11548-1300. *Phone:* 516-299-2900 or toll-free 800-LIU-PLAN. *Fax:* 516-299-2137. *E-mail:* enroll@cwpost.liu.edu. *Web site:* http://www.liu.edu/.
Visit Petersons.com and enter keyword C.W.

Machzikei Hadath Rabbinical College
Brooklyn, New York

General Independent Jewish, comprehensive, men only **Entrance** Moderately difficult **Total enrollment** 112 **Application deadline** Rolling (freshmen) **Housing** No **Undergraduates** 2% 25 or older **Contact** Rabbi Abraham M. Lezerowitz, Director of Admissions, Machzikei Hadath Rabbinical College, 5407 Sixteenth Avenue, Brooklyn, NY 11204-1805. *Phone:* 718-854-8777.

Manhattan College
Riverdale, New York

General Independent, comprehensive, coed, affiliated with Roman Catholic Church **Entrance** Moderately difficult **Setting** 31-acre urban campus **Total enrollment** 3,461 **Student-faculty ratio** 12:1 **Application deadline** 4/15 (freshmen), 7/1 (transfer) **Freshman admission** 65% were admitted. Average high school GPA 3.37 **Freshman test scores** SAT critical reading scores over 500: 71%; SAT math scores over 500: 77%; SAT critical reading scores over 600: 20%; SAT math scores over 600: 34% **Housing** Yes **Expenses** Tuition & Fees $27,455; Room & Board $10,670 **Undergraduates** 47% women, 3% part-time, 2% 25 or older, 0.1% Native American, 12% Hispanic American, 3% African American, 3% Asian American/Pacific Islander **The most frequently chosen baccalaureate fields are** education, business/marketing, engineering **Academic program** English as a second language, advanced placement, accelerated degree program, honors program, summer session, adult/continuing education programs, internships **Contact** Mr. William Bisset, Assistant Vice President for Enrollment Management, Manhattan College, 4513 Manhattan College Parkway, Riverdale, NY 10471. *Phone:* 718-862-7200 or toll-free 800-622-9235. *Fax:* 718-862-8019. *E-mail:* admit@manhattan.edu. *Web site:* http://www.manhattan.edu/.
Visit Petersons.com and enter keyword Manhattan

See page 938 for the College Close-Up.

Manhattan School of Music
New York, New York

General Independent, comprehensive, coed **Entrance** Very difficult **Setting** 1-acre urban campus **Total enrollment** 930 **Student-faculty ratio** 6:1 **Application deadline** 12/1 (freshmen), 12/1 (transfer) **Freshman admission** 35% were admitted. Average high school GPA 3.55 **Housing** Yes **Expenses** Tuition & Fees $34,800; Room & Board $14,650 **Undergraduates** 48% women, 1% part-time, 4% 25 or older, 0.3% Native American, 5% Hispanic American, 3% African American, 10% Asian American/Pacific Islander **The most frequently chosen baccalaureate field is** visual and performing arts **Academic program** English as a second language, advanced placement **Contact** Amy Anderson, Associate Dean for Enrollment Management, Manhattan School of Music, 120 Claremont Avenue, New York, NY 10027-4698. *Phone:* 917-493-4501. *Fax:* 212-749-3025. *E-mail:* admission@msmnyc.edu. *Web site:* http://www.msmnyc.edu/.

Manhattanville College
Purchase, New York

General Independent, comprehensive, coed **Entrance** Moderately difficult **Setting** 100-acre suburban campus **Total enrollment** 2,890 **Student-faculty ratio** 13:1 **Application deadline** 3/1 (freshmen), 3/1 (transfer) **Freshman admission** 53% were admitted. Average high school GPA 3 **Housing** Yes **Expenses** Tuition & Fees $34,350; Room & Board $13,920 **Undergraduates** 65% women, 6% part-time, 1% 25 or older, 0.3% Native American, 16% Hispanic American, 8% African American, 2% Asian American/Pacific Islander **The most frequently chosen baccalaureate fields are** business/marketing, social sciences, visual and performing arts **Academic program** English as a second language, advanced placement, accelerated degree program, self-designed majors, honors program, summer session, adult/continuing education programs, internships **Contact** Ms. Erica Padilla, Director of Admissions, Manhattanville College, 2900 Purchase Street, Purchase, NY 10577. *Phone:* 914-323-5129 or toll-free 800-328-4553. *Fax:* 914-694-1732. *E-mail:* admissions@mville.edu. *Web site:* http://www.manhattanville.edu/.
Visit Petersons.com and enter keyword Manhattanville

See page 940 for the College Close-Up.

Mannes College The New School for Music
New York, New York

General Independent, comprehensive, coed **Entrance** Very difficult **Setting** urban campus **Total enrollment** 384 **Student-faculty ratio** 7:1 **Application deadline** 12/1 (freshmen), 4/1 (transfer) **Freshman admission** 35% were admitted. Average high school GPA 3.4 **Housing** Yes **Expenses** Tuition & Fees $33,600; Room & Board $15,260 **Undergraduates** 57% women, 10% part-time, 18% 25 or older, 3% Hispanic American, 4% African American, 11% Asian American/Pacific Islander **The most frequently chosen baccalaureate field is** visual and performing arts **Academic program** English as a second language, advanced placement, summer session, internships **Contact** Ms. Georgia Schmitt, Director of Admissions, Mannes College The New School for Music,

150 West 85th Street, New York, NY 10024-4402. *Phone:* 212-580-0210 Ext. 4862 or toll-free 800-292-3040. *Fax:* 212-580-1738. *E-mail:* mannesadmissions@newschool.edu. *Web site:* http://www.mannes.edu/.
Visit Petersons.com and enter keyword Mannes

See page 942 for the College Close-Up.

Maria College
Albany, New York

General Independent, 4-year, coed **Entrance** Minimally difficult **Setting** 9-acre urban campus **Total enrollment** 851 **Student-faculty ratio** 14:1 **Application deadline** 8/25 (freshmen), 8/25 (transfer) **Freshman admission** 46% were admitted **Housing** No **Expenses** Tuition & Fees $9320 **Undergraduates** 88% women, 71% part-time, 1% Native American, 3% Hispanic American, 19% African American, 4% Asian American/Pacific Islander **Academic program** Advanced placement, summer session, adult/continuing education programs **Contact** Ms. Laurie A. Gilmore, Director of Admissions, Maria College, 700 New Scotland Avenue, Albany, NY 12208-1798. *Phone:* 518-438-3111. *Fax:* 518-453-1366. *E-mail:* admissions@mariacollege.edu. *Web site:* http://www.mariacollege.edu/.

Marist College
Poughkeepsie, New York

General Independent, comprehensive, coed **Entrance** Very difficult **Setting** 180-acre suburban campus **Total enrollment** 6,179 **Student-faculty ratio** 15:1 **Application deadline** 2/15 (freshmen), 6/1 (transfer) **Freshman admission** 36% were admitted. Average high school GPA 3.2 **Freshman test scores** SAT critical reading scores over 500: 88.1%; SAT math scores over 500: 91.2%; ACT scores over 18: 99.1%; SAT critical reading scores over 600: 37.3%; SAT math scores over 600: 47.1%; ACT scores over 24: 72.7% **Housing** Yes **Expenses** Tuition & Fees $26,604; Room & Board $11,225 **Undergraduates** 56% women, 15% part-time, 7% 25 or older, 0.2% Native American, 6% Hispanic American, 3% African American, 2% Asian American/Pacific Islander **The most frequently chosen baccalaureate fields are** business/marketing, communications/journalism, education **Academic program** English as a second language, advanced placement, accelerated degree program, honors program, summer session, adult/continuing education programs, internships **Contact** Mr. Kenton Rinehart, Dean of Undergraduate Admissions, Marist College, 3399 North Road, Poughkeepsie, NY 12601. *Phone:* 845-575-3226 or toll-free 800-436-5483. *Fax:* 845-575-3215. *E-mail:* admission@marist.edu. *Web site:* http://www.marist.edu/.

Marymount Manhattan College
New York, New York

General Independent, 4-year, coed **Entrance** Moderately difficult **Setting** 3-acre urban campus **Total enrollment** 2,040 **Student-faculty ratio** 11:1 **Application deadline** Rolling (freshmen), rolling (transfer) **Freshman admission** 70% were admitted. Average high school GPA 3.15 **Freshman test scores** SAT critical reading scores over 500: 73%; SAT math scores over 500: 57%; ACT scores over 18: 100%; SAT critical reading scores over 600: 27%; SAT math scores over 600: 14%; ACT scores over 24: 50% **Housing** Yes **Expenses** Tuition & Fees $22,656; Room & Board $12,874 **Undergraduates** 76% women, 14% part-time, 12% 25 or older, 0.3% Native American, 14% Hispanic American, 12% African American, 3% Asian American/Pacific Islander **Academic program** Advanced placement, accelerated degree program, summer session, adult/continuing education programs, internships **Contact** Mr. James Rogers, Dean of Admissions, Marymount Manhattan College, 221 East 71st Street, New York, NY 10021. *Phone:* 212-517-0430 or toll-free 800-MARYMOUNT. *Fax:* 212-517-0448. *E-mail:* admissions@mmm.edu. *Web site:* http://www.mmm.edu/.
Visit Petersons.com and enter keywords Marymount Manhattan

See page 950 for the College Close-Up.

Medaille College
Buffalo, New York

General Independent, comprehensive, coed **Entrance** Moderately difficult **Setting** 13-acre urban campus **Total enrollment** 2,923 **Student-faculty ratio** 17:1 **Application deadline** 8/1 (freshmen), rolling (transfer) **Freshman admission** 72% were admitted **Freshman test scores** SAT critical reading scores over 500: 27%; SAT math scores over 500: 36%; SAT critical reading scores over 600: 4%; SAT math scores over 600: 5% **Housing** Yes **Expenses** Tuition & Fees $19,590; Room & Board $9288 **Undergraduates** 64% women, 6% part-time, 8% 25 or older, 0.3% Native American, 2% Hispanic American, 12% African American, 0.4% Asian American/Pacific Islander **The most frequently chosen baccalaureate fields are** business/marketing, education, parks and recreation **Academic program** Advanced placement, accelerated degree program, self-designed majors, honors program, summer session, adult/continuing education programs, internships **Contact** Mr. Greg Florczak, Director of Undergraduate Admissions, Medaille College, Office of Admissions, Buffalo, NY 14214. *Phone:* 716-880-2200 or toll-free 800-292-1582. *Fax:* 716-880-2007. *E-mail:* admissionsug@medaille.edu. *Web site:* http://www.medaille.edu/.

Medgar Evers College of the City University of New York
Brooklyn, New York

General State and locally supported, 4-year, coed **Entrance** Noncompetitive **Setting** 8-acre urban campus **Total enrollment** 7,081 **Student-faculty ratio** 19:1 **Application deadline** Rolling (freshmen), rolling (transfer) **Freshman admission** 100% were admitted **Housing** No **Expenses** Tuition & Fees: state resident $4902, nonresident $10,262 **Undergraduates** 75% women, 34% part-time, 51% 25 or older, 0.1% Native American, 6% Hispanic American, 89% African American, 1% Asian American/Pacific Islander **The most frequently chosen baccalaureate fields are** business/marketing, biological/life sciences, psychology **Academic program** English as a second language, advanced placement, honors program, summer session, adult/continuing education programs, internships **Contact** Ms. Julie M. Augustin, Director of Admissions, Medgar Evers College of the City University of New York, 1650 Bedford Avenue, Brooklyn, NY 11225. *Phone:* 718-270-6021. *Fax:* 718-270-6411. *E-mail:* jaugustin@mec.cuny.edu. *Web site:* http://www.mec.cuny.edu/.

Mercy College
Dobbs Ferry, New York

General Independent, comprehensive, coed **Entrance** Moderately difficult **Setting** 45-acre suburban campus **Total enrollment** 9,673 **Student-faculty ratio** 17:1 **Application deadline** Rolling (freshmen), rolling (transfer) **Freshman admission** 59% were admitted **Housing** Yes **Expenses** Tuition & Fees $17,010 **Undergraduates** 67% women, 31% part-time, 40% 25 or older, 0.4% Native American, 29% Hispanic American, 26% African American, 3% Asian American/Pacific Islander **The most frequently chosen baccalaureate fields are** business/marketing, health professions and related sciences, social sciences **Academic program** Advanced placement, accelerated degree program, honors program, summer session, adult/continuing education programs, internships **Contact** Mrs. Tara Fay-Reilly, Senior Director of Admissions, Mercy College, 555 Broadway, Dobbs Ferry, NY 10522-1189. *Phone:* 914-674-7762 Ext. 7762 or toll-free 800-MERCY-NY. *Fax:* 914-674-7608. *E-mail:* admissions@mercy.edu. *Web site:* http://www.mercy.edu/.

Mesivta of Eastern Parkway–Yeshiva Zichron Meilech
Brooklyn, New York

General Independent Jewish, comprehensive, men only **Entrance** Moderately difficult **Setting** 1-acre campus **Total enrollment** 40 **Appli-**

Mesivta of Eastern Parkway–Yeshiva Zichron Meilech (continued)

cation deadline Rolling (freshmen), rolling (transfer) **Freshman admission** 100% were admitted **Housing** Yes **Academic program** Honors program **Contact** Rabbi Joseph Halberstadt, Dean, Mesivta of Eastern Parkway–Yeshiva Zichron Meilech, 510 Dahill Road, Brooklyn, NY 11218-5559. *Phone:* 718-438-1002.

Mesivta Tifereth Jerusalem of America

New York, New York

General Independent Jewish, comprehensive, men only **Total enrollment** 72 **Freshman admission** 100% were admitted **Housing** Yes **Contact** Rabbi Fishellis, Director of Admissions, Mesivta Tifereth Jerusalem of America, 145 East Broadway, New York, NY 10002-6301. *Phone:* 212-964-2830.

Mesivta Torah Vodaath Rabbinical Seminary

Brooklyn, New York

General Independent Jewish, comprehensive, men only **Entrance** Moderately difficult **Total enrollment** 354 **Application deadline** Rolling (freshmen), rolling (transfer) **Housing** Yes **Undergraduates** 35% 25 or older **Academic program** Summer session **Contact** Rabbi Issac Braun, Administrator, Mesivta Torah Vodaath Rabbinical Seminary, 425 East Ninth Street, Brooklyn, NY 11218-5299. *Phone:* 718-941-8000.

Metropolitan College of New York

New York, New York

General Independent, comprehensive, coed, primarily women **Entrance** Moderately difficult **Setting** urban campus **Total enrollment** 1,084 **Student-faculty ratio** 11:1 **Application deadline** 8/15 (freshmen), 8/15 (transfer) **Freshman admission** 51% were admitted **Housing** No **Expenses** Tuition & Fees $16,750 **Undergraduates** 71% women, 7% part-time, 76% 25 or older, 1% Native American, 19% Hispanic American, 63% African American, 1% Asian American/Pacific Islander **The most frequently chosen baccalaureate fields are** business/marketing, liberal arts/general studies **Academic program** English as a second language, accelerated degree program, honors program, summer session, adult/continuing education programs, internships **Contact** Mr. Steven Lenhart, Dean of Enrollment Services, Metropolitan College of New York, 431 Canal Street, New York, NY 10013. *Phone:* 212-343-1234 Ext. 2700 or toll-free 800-33-THINK Ext. 5001. *Fax:* 212-343-8470. *Web site:* http://www.metropolitan.edu/.

Mirrer Yeshiva

Brooklyn, New York

General Independent Jewish, comprehensive, men only **Total enrollment** 307 **Freshman admission** 100% were admitted **Housing** Yes **Undergraduates** 4% 25 or older **Contact** Director of Admissions, Mirrer Yeshiva, 1795 Ocean Parkway, Brooklyn, NY 11223-2010. *Phone:* 718-645-0536.

Molloy College

Rockville Centre, New York

General Independent, comprehensive, coed **Entrance** Moderately difficult **Setting** 30-acre suburban campus **Total enrollment** 4,025 **Student-faculty ratio** 10:1 **Application deadline** Rolling (freshmen), rolling (transfer) **Freshman admission** 59% were admitted. Average high school GPA 2.9 **Freshman test scores** SAT critical reading scores over 500: 58%; SAT math scores over 500: 64%; ACT scores over 18: 99%; SAT critical reading scores over 600: 14%; SAT math scores over 600: 19%; ACT scores over 24: 66% **Housing** No **Expenses** Tuition & Fees $20,960 **Undergraduates** 78% women, 24% part-time, 25% 25 or older, 0.4% Native American, 11% Hispanic American, 15% African American, 7% Asian American/Pacific Islander **The most frequently chosen baccalaureate fields are** education, business/marketing, health professions and related sciences **Academic program** English as a second language, advanced placement, honors program, summer session, adult/continuing education programs, internships **Contact** Ms. Marguerite Lane, Director of Admissions, Molloy College, 1000 Hempstead Avenue, PO Box 5002, Rockville Centre, NY 11571-5002. *Phone:* 516-678-5000 Ext. 6240 or toll-free 888-4MOLLOY. *Fax:* 516-256-2247. *E-mail:* admissions@molloy.edu. *Web site:* http://www.molloy.edu/.

Visit Petersons.com and enter keyword Molloy

See page 978 for the College Close-Up.

Monroe College

Bronx, New York

General Proprietary, comprehensive, coed **Entrance** Moderately difficult **Setting** urban campus **Total enrollment** 5,068 **Student-faculty ratio** 32:1 **Application deadline** 8/26 (freshmen), 8/26 (transfer) **Freshman admission** 61% were admitted **Housing** Yes **Expenses** Tuition & Fees $12,544; Room & Board $7940 **Undergraduates** 73% women, 28% part-time, 56% 25 or older, 0.1% Native American, 50% Hispanic American, 42% African American, 1% Asian American/Pacific Islander **The most frequently chosen baccalaureate fields are** business/marketing, health professions and related sciences, security and protective services **Academic program** English as a second language, summer session, adult/continuing education programs, internships **Contact** Mr. Evan Jerome, Director of Admissions, Monroe College, Monroe College Way, Bronx, NY 10468-5407. *Phone:* 718-933-6700 Ext. 8246 or toll-free 800-55MONROE. *Web site:* http://www.monroecoll.edu/.

Monroe College

New Rochelle, New York

General Proprietary, comprehensive, coed **Entrance** Moderately difficult **Setting** suburban campus **Total enrollment** 2,222 **Student-faculty ratio** 38:1 **Application deadline** 8/26 (freshmen), 8/26 (transfer) **Freshman admission** 60% were admitted **Housing** Yes **Expenses** Tuition & Fees $11,744; Room & Board $7940 **Undergraduates** 64% women, 15% part-time, 31% 25 or older, 0.05% Native American, 23% Hispanic American, 56% African American, 0.4% Asian American/Pacific Islander **The most frequently chosen baccalaureate fields are** business/marketing, computer and information sciences, security and protective services **Academic program** English as a second language, summer session, adult/continuing education programs, internships **Contact** Ms. Lisa Scorca, High School Admissions, Monroe College, 434 Main Street, New Rochelle, NY 10801. *Phone:* 914-654-3200 or toll-free 800-55MONROE. *E-mail:* lscorca@monroecollege.edu. *Web site:* http://www.monroecollege.edu/.

Mount Saint Mary College

Newburgh, New York

General Independent, comprehensive, coed **Entrance** Moderately difficult **Setting** 72-acre suburban campus **Total enrollment** 2,717 **Student-faculty ratio** 17:1 **Application deadline** 8/15 (freshmen), rolling (transfer) **Freshman admission** 72% were admitted. Average high school GPA 3.2 **Freshman test scores** SAT critical reading scores over 500: 47%; SAT math scores over 500: 55%; ACT scores over 18: 86%; SAT critical reading scores over 600: 8%; SAT math scores over 600: 14%; ACT scores over 24: 21% **Housing** Yes **Expenses** Tuition & Fees $23,300; Room & Board $11,900 **Undergraduates** 75% women, 17% part-time, 19% 25 or older, 0.3% Native American, 10% Hispanic American, 7% African American, 2% Asian American/Pacific Islander **The most frequently chosen baccalaureate fields are** business/

marketing, health professions and related sciences, history **Academic program** Advanced placement, accelerated degree program, self-designed majors, honors program, summer session, adult/continuing education programs, internships **Contact** Mr. Rodney Morrison, Director of Admissions, Mount Saint Mary College, 330 Powell Avenue, Newburgh, NY 12550-3494. *Phone:* 845-569-3248 or toll-free 888-937-6762. *Fax:* 845-562-6762. *E-mail:* admissions@msmc.edu. *Web site:* http://www.msmc.edu/.

Nazareth College of Rochester

Rochester, New York

General Independent, comprehensive, coed **Entrance** Moderately difficult **Setting** 150-acre suburban campus **Total enrollment** 3,307 **Student-faculty ratio** 12:1 **Application deadline** 2/15 (freshmen), 5/15 (transfer) **Freshman admission** 77% were admitted. Average high school GPA 3.37 **Freshman test scores** SAT critical reading scores over 500: 83%; SAT math scores over 500: 85%; SAT critical reading scores over 600: 33%; SAT math scores over 600: 40% **Housing** Yes **Expenses** Tuition & Fees $26,140; Room & Board $10,716 **Undergraduates** 76% women, 7% part-time, 9% 25 or older, 0.4% Native American, 4% Hispanic American, 4% African American, 2% Asian American/Pacific Islander **The most frequently chosen baccalaureate fields are** business/marketing, health professions and related sciences, visual and performing arts **Academic program** English as a second language, advanced placement, honors program, summer session, adult/continuing education programs, internships **Contact** Mr. Thomas DaRin, Vice President for Enrollment Management, Nazareth College of Rochester, 4245 East Avenue, Rochester, NY 14618-3790. *Phone:* 585-389-2860 or toll-free 800-462-3944. *Fax:* 585-389-2826. *E-mail:* admissions@naz.edu. *Web site:* http://www.naz.edu/.

See page 1004 for the College Close-Up.

The New School for General Studies

New York, New York

General Independent, upper-level, coed **Entrance** Moderately difficult **Setting** urban campus **Total enrollment** 1,871 **Student-faculty ratio** 9:1 **Application deadline** 6/1 (freshmen), 6/1 (transfer) **First-year students** 56% were admitted **Housing** Yes **Expenses** Tuition & Fees $24,288; Room & Board $15,260 **Undergraduates** 66% women, 52% part-time, 67% 25 or older, 1% Native American, 8% Hispanic American, 10% African American, 3% Asian American/Pacific Islander **The most frequently chosen baccalaureate fields are** liberal arts/general studies, visual and performing arts **Academic program** English as a second language, advanced placement, self-designed majors, summer session, adult/continuing education programs, internships **Contact** Ms. Cory Meyers, Assistant Director of Admissions, The New School for General Studies, 72 Fifth Avenue, Room 304, New York, NY 10011. *Phone:* 212-229-5630 or toll-free 800-862-5039. *Fax:* 212-989-3887. *E-mail:* nsadmissions@newschool.edu. *Web site:* http://www.newschool.edu/generalstudies/.

The New School for Jazz and Contemporary Music

New York, New York

General Independent, 4-year, coed **Entrance** Very difficult **Setting** urban campus **Total enrollment** 253 **Student-faculty ratio** 11:1 **Application deadline** 1/1 (freshmen), 1/1 (transfer) **Freshman admission** 71% were admitted. Average high school GPA 3.2 **Housing** Yes **Expenses** Tuition & Fees $33,600; Room & Board $15,260 **Undergraduates** 18% women, 6% part-time, 19% 25 or older, 6% Hispanic American, 6% African American, 2% Asian American/Pacific Islander **The most frequently chosen baccalaureate field is** visual and performing arts **Academic program** English as a second language, advanced placement, internships **Contact** Ms. Terri Lucas, Jazz Admissions, The New School for Jazz and Contemporary Music, 66 West 12th Street, New York, NY 10011. *Phone:* 212-229-5896. *Fax:* 212-229-8936. *E-mail:* jazzadm@newschool.edu. *Web site:* http://www.jazz.newschool.edu.
Visit Petersons.com and enter keyword Jazz

See page 1014 for the College Close-Up.

New York City College of Technology of the City University of New York

Brooklyn, New York

General State and locally supported, 4-year, coed **Entrance** Noncompetitive **Setting** urban campus **Total enrollment** 15,404 **Student-faculty ratio** 17:1 **Application deadline** 3/15 (freshmen), 3/15 (transfer) **Freshman admission** 84% were admitted **Expenses** Tuition & Fees: state resident $4939, nonresident $12,789; Room & Board $1500 **Undergraduates** 48% women, 41% part-time, 31% 25 or older, 0.3% Native American, 26% Hispanic American, 38% African American, 16% Asian American/Pacific Islander **The most frequently chosen baccalaureate fields are** business/marketing, computer and information sciences, visual and performing arts **Academic program** English as a second language, advanced placement, accelerated degree program, self-designed majors, honors program, summer session, adult/continuing education programs, internships **Contact** Alexis Chaconis, Director of Admissions, New York City College of Technology of the City University of New York, 300 Jay Street, Brooklyn, NY 11201-2983. *Phone:* 718-260-5500. *E-mail:* achaconis@citytech.cuny.edu. *Web site:* http://www.citytech.cuny.edu/.

New York College of Health Professions

Syosset, New York

Contact Ms. Mary Rodas, Associate Director of Admissions, New York College of Health Professions, 6801 Jericho Turnpike, Syosset, NY 11791-4413. *Phone:* toll-free 800-922-7337 Ext. 351. *E-mail:* rdodas@nycollege.edu. *Web site:* http://www.nycollege.edu/.
Visit Petersons.com and enter keyword Professions

New York Institute of Technology

Old Westbury, New York

General Independent, university, coed **Entrance** Moderately difficult **Setting** 1,050-acre suburban campus **Total enrollment** 11,695 **Student-faculty ratio** 14:1 **Application deadline** Rolling (freshmen), rolling (transfer) **Freshman admission** 74% were admitted. Average high school GPA 3.1 **Freshman test scores** SAT critical reading scores over 500: 61%; SAT math scores over 500: 91%; ACT scores over 18: 98%; SAT critical reading scores over 600: 14%; SAT math scores over 600: 45%; ACT scores over 24: 40% **Housing** Yes **Expenses** Tuition & Fees $24,140; Room & Board $10,520 **Undergraduates** 37% women, 20% part-time, 15% 25 or older, 0.2% Native American, 7% Hispanic American, 7% African American, 9% Asian American/Pacific Islander **The most frequently chosen baccalaureate fields are** business/marketing, architecture, interdisciplinary studies **Academic program** English as a second language, advanced placement, accelerated degree program, self-designed majors, honors program, summer session, adult/continuing education programs, internships **Contact** Ms. Doreen Meyer, Director of Financial Aid, New York Institute of Technology, PO Box 8000, Old Westbury, NY 11568. *Phone:* 516-686-1083 or toll-free 800-345-NYIT. *Fax:* 516-686-7613. *E-mail:* admissions@nyit.edu. *Web site:* http://www.nyit.edu/.

New York School of Interior Design

New York, New York

General Independent, comprehensive, coed, primarily women **Entrance** Moderately difficult **Setting** 1-acre urban campus **Total enrollment** 714

New York School of Interior Design (continued)
Student-faculty ratio 9:1 **Application deadline** 3/1 (freshmen), 3/1 (transfer) **Freshman admission** 52% were admitted. Average high school GPA 3.49 **Freshman test scores** SAT critical reading scores over 500: 21%; SAT math scores over 500: 52%; SAT critical reading scores over 600: 9%; SAT math scores over 600: 11% **Housing** Yes **Expenses** Tuition & Fees $22,895; Room only $15,600 **Undergraduates** 90% women, 70% part-time, 65% 25 or older, 0.2% Native American, 9% Hispanic American, 5% African American, 13% Asian American/Pacific Islander **Academic program** English as a second language, advanced placement, summer session, adult/continuing education programs, internships **Contact** Cassandra Ramirez, Admissions Associate, New York School of Interior Design, 170 East 70th Street, New York, NY 10021-5110. *Phone:* 212-472-1500 Ext. 204 or toll-free 800-336-9743 Ext. 204. *Fax:* 212-472-1867. *E-mail:* admissions@nysid.edu. *Web site:* http://www.nysid.edu/.
Visit Petersons.com and enter keyword Interior

See page 1016 for the College Close-Up.

New York University
New York, New York

General Independent, university, coed **Entrance** Most difficult **Setting** urban campus **Total enrollment** 43,404 **Student-faculty ratio** 11:1 **Application deadline** 1/1 (freshmen), 4/1 (transfer) **Freshman admission** 38% were admitted. Average high school GPA 3.6 **Freshman test scores** SAT critical reading scores over 500: 99%; SAT math scores over 500: 100%; ACT scores over 18: 100%; SAT critical reading scores over 600: 82%; SAT math scores over 600: 86%; ACT scores over 24: 98% **Housing** Yes **Expenses** Tuition & Fees $38,765; Room & Board $13,228 **Undergraduates** 61% women, 6% part-time, 8% 25 or older, 0.3% Native American, 8% Hispanic American, 4% African American, 20% Asian American/Pacific Islander **The most frequently chosen baccalaureate fields are** business/marketing, social sciences, visual and performing arts **Academic program** English as a second language, advanced placement, self-designed majors, honors program, summer session, adult/continuing education programs, internships **Contact** Undergraduate Admissions Processing Center, New York University, 665 Broadway, 11th Floor, New York, NY 10011. *Phone:* 212-998-4500. *Fax:* 212-995-4902. *E-mail:* nyuadmit@uccvm.nyu.edu. *Web site:* http://www.nyu.edu/.
Visit Petersons.com and enter keywords New York University

See page 1018 for the College Close-Up.

Niagara University
Niagara University, New York

General Independent, comprehensive, coed, affiliated with Roman Catholic Church **Entrance** Moderately difficult **Setting** 160-acre suburban campus **Total enrollment** 4,255 **Student-faculty ratio** 14:1 **Application deadline** 8/1 (freshmen), 8/15 (transfer) **Freshman admission** 74% were admitted. Average high school GPA 3.3 **Freshman test scores** SAT critical reading scores over 500: 57%; SAT math scores over 500: 65%; ACT scores over 18: 91%; SAT critical reading scores over 600: 12%; SAT math scores over 600: 17%; ACT scores over 24: 30% **Housing** Yes **Expenses** Tuition & Fees $24,700; Room & Board $10,250 **Undergraduates** 62% women, 9% part-time, 10% 25 or older, 1% Native American, 2% Hispanic American, 4% African American, 1% Asian American/Pacific Islander **The most frequently chosen baccalaureate fields are** business/marketing, education, security and protective services **Academic program** English as a second language, advanced placement, accelerated degree program, honors program, summer session, internships **Contact** Ms. Christine M. McDermott, Associate Director of Admissions, Niagara University, Niagara University, NY 14109. *Phone:* 716-286-8700 Ext. 8715 or toll-free 800-462-2111. *Fax:* 716-286-8733. *E-mail:* admissions@niagara.edu. *Web site:* http://www.niagara.edu/.
Visit Petersons.com and enter keyword Niagara

See page 1020 for the College Close-Up.

Nyack College
Nyack, New York

General Independent, comprehensive, coed, affiliated with The Christian and Missionary Alliance **Entrance** Moderately difficult **Setting** 125-acre suburban campus **Total enrollment** 3,151 **Student-faculty ratio** 20:1 **Application deadline** Rolling (freshmen), rolling (transfer) **Freshman admission** 99% were admitted **Freshman test scores** SAT critical reading scores over 500: 38%; ACT scores over 18: 79%; SAT critical reading scores over 600: 11%; ACT scores over 24: 35% **Housing** Yes **Expenses** Tuition & Fees $20,500; Room & Board $8200 **Undergraduates** 58% women, 19% part-time, 0.5% Native American, 23% Hispanic American, 36% African American, 7% Asian American/Pacific Islander **The most frequently chosen baccalaureate fields are** business/marketing, interdisciplinary studies, theology and religious vocations **Academic program** English as a second language, advanced placement, accelerated degree program, honors program, summer session, adult/continuing education programs, internships **Contact** Ms. Andrea Hennessey JD, Vice President of Enrollment and Marketing, Nyack College, 1 South Boulevard, Nyack, NY 10960-3698. *Phone:* 845-675-4414 or toll-free 800-33-NYACK. *Fax:* 845-353-1297. *E-mail:* admissions@nyack.edu. *Web site:* http://www.nyack.edu.

Ohr Hameir Theological Seminary
Cortlandt Manor, New York

General Independent Jewish, comprehensive, men only **Total enrollment** 86 **Freshman admission** 100% were admitted **Housing** Yes **Contact** Director of Admissions, Ohr Hameir Theological Seminary, 141 Furnace Woods Road, Cortlandt Manor, NY 10567. *Phone:* 914-736-1500.

Ohr Somayach/Joseph Tanenbaum Educational Center
Monsey, New York

General Independent Jewish, comprehensive, men only **Entrance** Moderately difficult **Setting** 7-acre small-town campus **Total enrollment** 89 **Application deadline** Rolling (freshmen), rolling (transfer) **Freshman admission** 65% were admitted **Housing** Yes **Undergraduates** 1% part-time, 75% 25 or older **Academic program** Honors program, summer session, adult/continuing education programs, internships **Contact** Rabbi Avrohom Braun, Dean of Students, Ohr Somayach/Joseph Tanenbaum Educational Center, PO Box 334, 244 Route 306, Monsey, NY 10952-0334. *Phone:* 845-425-1370 Ext. 22. *E-mail:* ohr@os.edu. *Web site:* http://www.ohrsomayach.edu/.

Pace University
New York, New York

General Independent, university, coed **Entrance** Moderately difficult **Setting** urban campus **Total enrollment** 12,706 **Student-faculty ratio** 15:1 **Application deadline** 2/15 (freshmen), rolling (transfer) **Freshman admission** 78% were admitted. Average high school GPA 3.2 **Freshman test scores** SAT math scores over 500: 75%; ACT scores over 18: 100%; SAT math scores over 600: 24%; ACT scores over 24: 63% **Housing** Yes **Expenses** Tuition & Fees $33,542; Room & Board $12,240 **Undergraduates** 60% women, 18% part-time, 16% 25 or older, 0.3% Native American, 12% Hispanic American, 10% African American, 8% Asian American/Pacific Islander **The most frequently chosen baccalaureate fields are** business/marketing, communications/journalism, health professions and related sciences **Academic program** English as a second language, advanced placement, accelerated degree program, honors program, summer session, adult/continuing education programs, internships **Contact** Ms. Donna J. Hoyt, Dean of Admissions, Pace University, One Pace Plaza, 163 William Street, New York, NY 10038. *Phone:* 212-346-1794 or toll-free 800-874-7223. *Fax:* 212-346-1821. *E-mail:* dhoyt@pace.edu. *Web site:* http://www.pace.edu/.
Visit Petersons.com and enter keyword Pace

See page 1040 for the College Close-Up.

Parsons The New School for Design

New York, New York

General Independent, comprehensive, coed **Entrance** Very difficult **Setting** 2-acre urban campus **Total enrollment** 4,598 **Student-faculty ratio** 9:1 **Application deadline** 2/1 (freshmen), 2/1 (transfer) **Freshman admission** 62% were admitted. Average high school GPA 3.3 **Freshman test scores** SAT critical reading scores over 500: 66%; SAT math scores over 500: 72%; ACT scores over 18: 96%; SAT critical reading scores over 600: 27%; SAT math scores over 600: 31%; ACT scores over 24: 51% **Housing** Yes **Expenses** Tuition & Fees $36,010; Room & Board $15,260 **Undergraduates** 78% women, 10% part-time, 22% 25 or older, 0.5% Native American, 8% Hispanic American, 4% African American, 16% Asian American/Pacific Islander **The most frequently chosen baccalaureate fields are** architecture, visual and performing arts **Academic program** English as a second language, advanced placement, self-designed majors, summer session, internships **Contact** Director of Admissions, Parsons The New School for Design, 65 Fifth Avenue, New York, NY 10011-8878. *Phone:* 212-229-8989 or toll-free 877-528-3321. *Fax:* 212-229-8975. *E-mail:* parsadm@newschool.edu. *Web site:* http://www.parsons.edu/.

Visit Petersons.com and enter keyword Parsons

See page 1044 for the College Close-Up.

Paul Smith's College

Paul Smiths, New York

Contact Admissions Office, Paul Smith's College, Routes 86 and 30, PO Box 265, Paul Smiths, NY 12970. *Phone:* 518-327-6227 or toll-free 800-421-2605. *Fax:* 518-327-6016. *E-mail:* admissions@paulsmiths.edu. *Web site:* http://www.paulsmiths.edu/.

Plaza College

Jackson Heights, New York

General Proprietary, primarily 2-year, coed **Entrance** Moderately difficult **Setting** urban campus **Total enrollment** 776 **Application deadline** Rolling (freshmen), rolling (transfer) **Housing** No **Expenses** Tuition & Fees $11,350 **Undergraduates** 56% 25 or older **Academic program** English as a second language, summer session, internships **Contact** Dean Rose Ann Black, Dean of Administration, Plaza College, 74-09 37th Avenue, Jackson Heights, NY 11372. *Phone:* 718-779-1430 or toll-free 877-752-9233. *E-mail:* info@plazacollege.edu. *Web site:* http://www.plazacollege.edu/.

Polytechnic Institute of NYU

Brooklyn, New York

General Independent, university, coed **Entrance** Very difficult **Setting** 3-acre urban campus **Total enrollment** 4,514 **Student-faculty ratio** 15:1 **Application deadline** 2/1 (freshmen), rolling (transfer) **Freshman admission** 55% were admitted. Average high school GPA 3.4 **Freshman test scores** SAT critical reading scores over 500: 96%; SAT math scores over 500: 99%; SAT critical reading scores over 600: 53%; SAT math scores over 600: 85% **Housing** Yes **Expenses** Tuition & Fees $34,420; Room & Board $9000 **Undergraduates** 20% women, 4% part-time, 7% 25 or older, 0.1% Native American, 11% Hispanic American, 10% African American, 28% Asian American/Pacific Islander **The most frequently chosen baccalaureate fields are** computer and information sciences, business/marketing, engineering **Academic program** English as a second language, advanced placement, accelerated degree program, honors program, summer session, internships **Contact** Joy Colelli, Dean of Admissions and New Students, Polytechnic Institute of NYU, Six Metrotech Center, Brooklyn, NY 11201-2990. *Phone:* 718-260-5917 or toll-free 800-POLYTECH. *Fax:* 718-260-3446. *E-mail:* uadmit@poly.edu. *Web site:* http://www.poly.edu/.

See page 1054 for the College Close-Up.

Pratt Institute

Brooklyn, New York

General Independent, comprehensive, coed **Entrance** Very difficult **Setting** 25-acre urban campus **Total enrollment** 4,707 **Student-faculty ratio** 11:1 **Application deadline** 1/5 (freshmen), 2/1 (transfer) **Freshman admission** 41% were admitted. Average high school GPA 3.5 **Freshman test scores** SAT critical reading scores over 500: 86%; SAT math scores over 500: 84%; ACT scores over 18: 99%; SAT critical reading scores over 600: 48%; SAT math scores over 600: 49%; ACT scores over 24: 69% **Housing** Yes **Expenses** Tuition & Fees $34,880; Room & Board $9756 **Undergraduates** 62% women, 5% part-time, 10% 25 or older, 0.2% Native American, 9% Hispanic American, 5% African American, 15% Asian American/Pacific Islander **The most frequently chosen baccalaureate fields are** architecture, liberal arts/general studies, visual and performing arts **Academic program** English as a second language, advanced placement, summer session, internships **Contact** Ms. Olga Burger, Visit Coordinator, Pratt Institute, 200 Willoughby Avenue, DeKalb Hall, Brooklyn, NY 11205. *Phone:* 718-636-3779 or toll-free 800-331-0834. *Fax:* 718-636-3670. *E-mail:* visit@pratt.edu. *Web site:* http://www.pratt.edu/.

Visit Petersons.com and enter keyword Pratt

See page 1058 for the College Close-Up.

Purchase College, State University of New York

Purchase, New York

General State-supported, comprehensive, coed **Entrance** Moderately difficult **Setting** 500-acre small-town campus **Total enrollment** 4,204 **Student-faculty ratio** 16:1 **Application deadline** 7/15 (freshmen), rolling (transfer) **Freshman admission** 27% were admitted. Average high school GPA 3.2 **Freshman test scores** SAT critical reading scores over 500: 83%; SAT math scores over 500: 70%; ACT scores over 18: 99%; SAT critical reading scores over 600: 37%; SAT math scores over 600: 21%; ACT scores over 24: 47% **Housing** Yes **Expenses** Tuition & Fees: state resident $6431, nonresident $14,331; Room & Board $9908 **Undergraduates** 56% women, 9% part-time, 10% 25 or older, 0.5% Native American, 12% Hispanic American, 7% African American, 3% Asian American/Pacific Islander **The most frequently chosen baccalaureate fields are** liberal arts/general studies, social sciences, visual and performing arts **Academic program** English as a second language, advanced placement, self-designed majors, summer session, adult/continuing education programs, internships **Contact** Stephanie McCaine, Director of Admissions, Purchase College, State University of New York, 735 Anderson Hill Road, Purchase, NY 10577-1400. *Phone:* 914-251-6300. *Fax:* 914-251-6314. *E-mail:* admission@purchase.edu. *Web site:* http://www.purchase.edu/.

Visit Petersons.com and enter keyword Purchase

See page 1062 for the College Close-Up.

Queens College of the City University of New York

Flushing, New York

General State and locally supported, comprehensive, coed **Entrance** Very difficult **Setting** 77-acre urban campus **Total enrollment** 20,711 **Student-faculty ratio** 16:1 **Application deadline** 5/15 (freshmen) **Freshman admission** 33% were admitted. Average high school GPA 3.5 **Freshman test scores** SAT critical reading scores over 500: 68%; SAT math scores over 500: 85%; SAT critical reading scores over 600: 20%; SAT math scores over 600: 29% **Housing** Yes **Expenses** Tuition & Fees: state resident $5047, nonresident $10,407; Room & Board $11,125 **Undergraduates** 59% women, 27% part-time, 25% 25 or older, 0.1% Native American, 18% Hispanic American, 9% African American, 22% Asian American/Pacific Islander **The most frequently chosen baccalaureate fields are** business/marketing, psychology, social sciences **Academic program** English as a second language, advanced placement,

Queens College of the City University of New York (continued) accelerated degree program, self-designed majors, honors program, summer session, adult/continuing education programs, internships **Contact** Mr. Vincent Angrisani, Executive Director of Enrollment Management and Admissions, Queens College of the City University of New York, 65-30 Kissena Boulevard, Flushing, NY 11367-1597. *Phone:* 718-997-5600. *Fax:* 718-997-5617. *E-mail:* vincent.angrisani@qc.cuny.edu. *Web site:* http://www.qc.cuny.edu/.
Visit Petersons.com and enter keyword Queens

See page 1064 for the College Close-Up.

Rabbinical Academy Mesivta Rabbi Chaim Berlin

Brooklyn, New York

General Independent Jewish, comprehensive, men only **Entrance** Moderately difficult **Total enrollment** 243 **Freshman admission** 100% were admitted **Housing** Yes **Undergraduates** 10% 25 or older **Contact** Executive Administrator, Rabbinical Academy Mesivta Rabbi Chaim Berlin, 1605 Coney Island Avenue, Brooklyn, NY 11230-4715. *Phone:* 718-377-0777. *Fax:* 718-338-5578.

Rabbinical College Beth Shraga

Monsey, New York

General Independent Jewish, comprehensive, men only **Setting** small-town campus **Total enrollment** 42 **Freshman admission** 100% were admitted **Contact** Rabbi Sydney Schiff, Director of Admissions, Rabbinical College Beth Shraga, 28 Saddle River Road, Monsey, NY 10952-3035.

Rabbinical College Bobover Yeshiva B'nei Zion

Brooklyn, New York

General Independent Jewish, comprehensive, men only **Entrance** Moderately difficult **Total enrollment** 235 **Housing** Yes **Contact** Director of Admissions, Rabbinical College Bobover Yeshiva B'nei Zion, 1577 Forty-eighth Street, Brooklyn, NY 11219. *Phone:* 718-438-2018.

Rabbinical College Ch'san Sofer

Brooklyn, New York

General Independent Jewish, comprehensive, men only **Total enrollment** 56 **Housing** Yes **Contact** Director of Admissions, Rabbinical College Ch'san Sofer, 1876 Fiftieth Street, Brooklyn, NY 11204. *Phone:* 718-236-1171.

Rabbinical College of Long Island

Long Beach, New York

General Independent Jewish, comprehensive, men only **Setting** small-town campus **Total enrollment** 145 **Freshman admission** 100% were admitted **Housing** Yes **Contact** Director of Admissions, Rabbinical College of Long Island, 205 West Beech Street, Long Beach, NY 11561-3305. *Phone:* 516-431-7414.

Rabbinical College of Ohr Shimon Yisroel

Brooklyn, New York

General Independent Jewish, 4-year, men only **Total enrollment** 186 **Housing** Yes **Undergraduates** 6% 25 or older **Contact** Rabbinical College of Ohr Shimon Yisroel, 215-217 Hewes Street, Brooklyn, NY 11211.

Rabbinical Seminary Adas Yereim

Brooklyn, New York

General Independent religious, comprehensive, men only **Total enrollment** 58 **Housing** No **Contact** Director of Admissions, Rabbinical Seminary Adas Yereim, 185 Wilson Street, Brooklyn, NY 11211-7206. *Phone:* 718-388-1751.

Rabbinical Seminary M'kor Chaim

Brooklyn, New York

General Independent Jewish, 4-year, men only **Total enrollment** 53 **Freshman admission** 100% were admitted **Housing** Yes **Contact** Director of Admissions, Rabbinical Seminary M'kor Chaim, 1571 Fifty-fifth Street, Brooklyn, NY 11219. *Phone:* 718-851-0183.

Rabbinical Seminary of America

Flushing, New York

General Independent Jewish, comprehensive, men only **Entrance** Very difficult **Setting** urban campus **Total enrollment** 516 **Application deadline** 12/1 (freshmen) **Housing** Yes **Undergraduates** 3% 25 or older **Academic program** Honors program, adult/continuing education programs **Contact** Rabbi Abraham Semmel, Director of Admissions, Rabbinical Seminary of America, 76-01 147th Street, Flushing, NY 11367. *Phone:* 718-268-4700.

Rensselaer Polytechnic Institute

Troy, New York

General Independent, university, coed **Entrance** Very difficult **Setting** 284-acre suburban campus **Total enrollment** 7,656 **Student-faculty ratio** 16:1 **Application deadline** 1/15 (freshmen) **Freshman admission** 43% were admitted. Average high school GPA 3.67 **Freshman test scores** SAT critical reading scores over 500: 100%; SAT math scores over 500: 100%; ACT scores over 18: 99%; SAT critical reading scores over 600: 81%; SAT math scores over 600: 95%; ACT scores over 24: 86% **Housing** Yes **Expenses** Tuition & Fees $39,165; Room & Board $11,145 **Undergraduates** 28% women, 1% part-time, 2% 25 or older, 1% Native American, 6% Hispanic American, 3% African American, 11% Asian American/Pacific Islander **The most frequently chosen baccalaureate fields are** business/marketing, computer and information sciences, engineering **Academic program** English as a second language, advanced placement, accelerated degree program, self-designed majors, honors program, summer session, adult/continuing education programs, internships **Contact** Mr. Paul Marthers, Vice President for Enrollment, Rensselaer Polytechnic Institute, 110 8th Street, Troy, NY 12180. *Phone:* 518-276-6216 or toll-free 800-448-6562. *Fax:* 518-276-4072. *E-mail:* admissions@rpi.edu. *Web site:* http://www.rpi.edu/.

Roberts Wesleyan College

Rochester, New York

General Independent, comprehensive, coed, affiliated with Free Methodist Church of North America **Entrance** Moderately difficult **Setting** 75-acre suburban campus **Total enrollment** 1,928 **Student-faculty ratio** 11:1 **Application deadline** 2/1 (freshmen), rolling (transfer) **Freshman admission** 65% were admitted. Average high school GPA 3.3 **Freshman test scores** SAT critical reading scores over 500: 64%; SAT math scores over 500: 66%; ACT scores over 18: 92%; SAT critical reading scores over 600: 22%; SAT math scores over 600: 31%; ACT scores over 24: 42% **Housing** Yes **Expenses** Tuition & Fees $23,780; Room & Board $8520 **Undergraduates** 69% women, 9% part-time, 26% 25 or older, 0.3% Native American, 4% Hispanic American, 9% African American, 1% Asian American/Pacific Islander **The most frequently chosen baccalaureate fields are** business/marketing, education, health professions and related sciences **Academic program** English as a second language, advanced placement, accelerated degree program, self-designed majors, honors program, summer session, internships **Contact** Ms. Linda Kurtz Hoffman, Admissions and Marketing Specialist, Roberts Wesleyan College, 2301 Westside Drive, Rochester, NY 14624-1997. *Phone:* 585-594-6400 or toll-free 800-777-4RWC. *Fax:* 585-594-6371. *E-mail:* admissions@roberts.edu. *Web site:* http://www.roberts.edu/.

Visit Petersons.com and enter keyword Roberts

See page 1086 for the College Close-Up.

Rochester Institute of Technology
Rochester, New York

General Independent, comprehensive, coed **Entrance** Moderately difficult **Setting** 1,300-acre suburban campus **Total enrollment** 16,773 **Student-faculty ratio** 13:1 **Application deadline** 2/1 (freshmen) **Freshman admission** 61% were admitted. Average high school GPA 3.7 **Freshman test scores** SAT critical reading scores over 500: 88%; SAT math scores over 500: 94%; ACT scores over 18: 100%; SAT critical reading scores over 600: 45%; SAT math scores over 600: 61%; ACT scores over 24: 82% **Housing** Yes **Expenses** Tuition & Fees $29,283; Room & Board $9642 **Undergraduates** 33% women, 12% part-time, 9% 25 or older, 0.4% Native American, 4% Hispanic American, 5% African American, 5% Asian American/Pacific Islander **The most frequently chosen baccalaureate fields are** computer and information sciences, engineering, visual and performing arts **Academic program** English as a second language, advanced placement, accelerated degree program, self-designed majors, honors program, summer session, adult/continuing education programs, internships **Contact** Dr. Daniel Shelley, Assistant Vice President, Rochester Institute of Technology, 60 Lomb Memorial Drive, Rochester, NY 14623-5604. *Phone:* 585-475-6631. *Fax:* 585-475-7424. *E-mail:* admissions@rit.edu. *Web site:* http://www.rit.edu/.

See page 1088 for the College Close-Up.

Russell Sage College
Troy, New York

General Independent, 4-year, women only **Entrance** Moderately difficult **Setting** 8-acre urban campus **Total enrollment** 749 **Student-faculty ratio** 11:1 **Application deadline** Rolling (freshmen), rolling (transfer) **Freshman admission** 76% were admitted. Average high school GPA 3.33 **Freshman test scores** SAT critical reading scores over 500: 74%; SAT math scores over 500: 74%; ACT scores over 18: 94%; SAT critical reading scores over 600: 22%; SAT math scores over 600: 20%; ACT scores over 24: 58% **Housing** Yes **Expenses** Tuition & Fees $27,790; Room & Board $9670 **Undergraduates** 8% part-time, 16% 25 or older, 0.3% Native American, 3% Hispanic American, 7% African American, 3% Asian American/Pacific Islander **The most frequently chosen baccalaureate fields are** education, health professions and related sciences, liberal arts/general studies **Academic program** Advanced placement, accelerated degree program, self-designed majors, honors program, summer session, internships **Contact** Ms. Kathy Rusch, Director of Admission, Russell Sage College, 45 Ferry Street, Troy, NY 12180. *Phone:* 518-244-2444 or toll-free 888-VERY-SAGE (in-state); 888-VERY SAGE (out-of-state). *Fax:* 518-244-6880. *E-mail:* ruschk@sage.edu. *Web site:* http://www.sage.edu/rsc/index.php.

Sage College of Albany
Albany, New York

General Independent, 4-year, coed **Entrance** Minimally difficult **Setting** 15-acre urban campus **Total enrollment** 848 **Student-faculty ratio** 12:1 **Application deadline** Rolling (freshmen), 8/1 (transfer) **Freshman admission** 65% were admitted. Average high school GPA 2.83 **Freshman test scores** SAT critical reading scores over 500: 28%; SAT math scores over 500: 42%; SAT critical reading scores over 600: 6%; SAT math scores over 600: 10% **Housing** Yes **Expenses** Tuition & Fees $27,790; Room & Board $9830 **Undergraduates** 66% women, 34% part-time, 41% 25 or older, 0.1% Native American, 4% Hispanic American, 14% African American, 2% Asian American/Pacific Islander **The most frequently chosen baccalaureate fields are** business/marketing, liberal arts/general studies, visual and performing arts **Academic program** Advanced placement, self-designed majors, honors program, summer session, adult/continuing education programs, internships **Contact** Andrew Palumbo, Director of Undergraduate Admission, Sage College of Albany, 140 New Scotland Avenue, Albany, NY 12208. *Phone:* 518-292-1730 or toll-free 888-VERY-SAGE. *Fax:* 518-292-1912. *E-mail:* scaadm@sage.edu. *Web site:* http://www.sage.edu/sca/index.php.

St. Bonaventure University
St. Bonaventure, New York

General Independent, comprehensive, coed, affiliated with Roman Catholic Church **Entrance** Moderately difficult **Setting** 600-acre small-town campus **Total enrollment** 2,472 **Student-faculty ratio** 14:1 **Application deadline** 7/15 (freshmen), 8/15 (transfer) **Freshman admission** 84% were admitted. Average high school GPA 3.2 **Freshman test scores** SAT critical reading scores over 500: 55%; SAT math scores over 500: 62%; ACT scores over 18: 90%; SAT critical reading scores over 600: 16%; SAT math scores over 600: 17%; ACT scores over 24: 37% **Housing** Yes **Expenses** Tuition & Fees $26,895; Room & Board $9071 **Undergraduates** 52% women, 5% part-time, 2% 25 or older, 0.4% Native American, 3% Hispanic American, 4% African American, 2% Asian American/Pacific Islander **The most frequently chosen baccalaureate fields are** business/marketing, communications/journalism, education **Academic program** Advanced placement, self-designed majors, honors program, summer session, internships **Contact** Monica Emery, Acting Director of Admissions, St. Bonaventure University, PO Box D, St. Bonaventure, NY 14778. *Phone:* 716-375-2400 or toll-free 800-462-5050. *Fax:* 716-375-4005. *E-mail:* memery@sbu.edu. *Web site:* http://www.sbu.edu/.

Visit Petersons.com and enter keyword Bonaventure

See page 1100 for the College Close-Up.

St. Francis College
Brooklyn Heights, New York

General Independent Roman Catholic, comprehensive, coed **Entrance** Moderately difficult **Setting** 1-acre urban campus **Total enrollment** 2,511 **Student-faculty ratio** 18:1 **Application deadline** Rolling (freshmen), rolling (transfer) **Freshman admission** 78% were admitted **Freshman test scores** SAT critical reading scores over 500: 33%; SAT math scores over 500: 35%; SAT critical reading scores over 600: 5%; SAT math scores over 600: 5% **Housing** Yes **Expenses** Tuition & Fees $17,000; Room & Board $14,350 **Undergraduates** 55% women, 11% part-time, 15% 25 or older, 0.2% Native American, 15% Hispanic American, 15% African American, 4% Asian American/Pacific Islander **Academic program** English as a second language, advanced placement, accelerated degree program, self-designed majors, honors program, summer session, internships **Contact** Ms. Monica Michalski, Assistant Dean of Freshman Studies and Academic Enhancement, St. Francis College, 180 Remsen Street, Brooklyn Heights, NY 11201-4398. *Phone:* 718-489-5226. *Fax:* 718-522-1274. *E-mail:* mmichalski@stfranciscollege.edu. *Web site:* http://www.stfranciscollege.edu/.

St. John Fisher College
Rochester, New York

General Independent, comprehensive, coed, affiliated with Roman Catholic Church **Entrance** Moderately difficult **Setting** 154-acre suburban campus **Total enrollment** 3,913 **Student-faculty ratio** 14:1 **Application deadline** Rolling (freshmen), rolling (transfer) **Freshman admission** 65% were admitted. Average high school GPA 3.5 **Freshman test scores** SAT critical reading scores over 500: 70%; SAT math scores over 500: 82%; ACT scores over 18: 100%; SAT critical reading scores

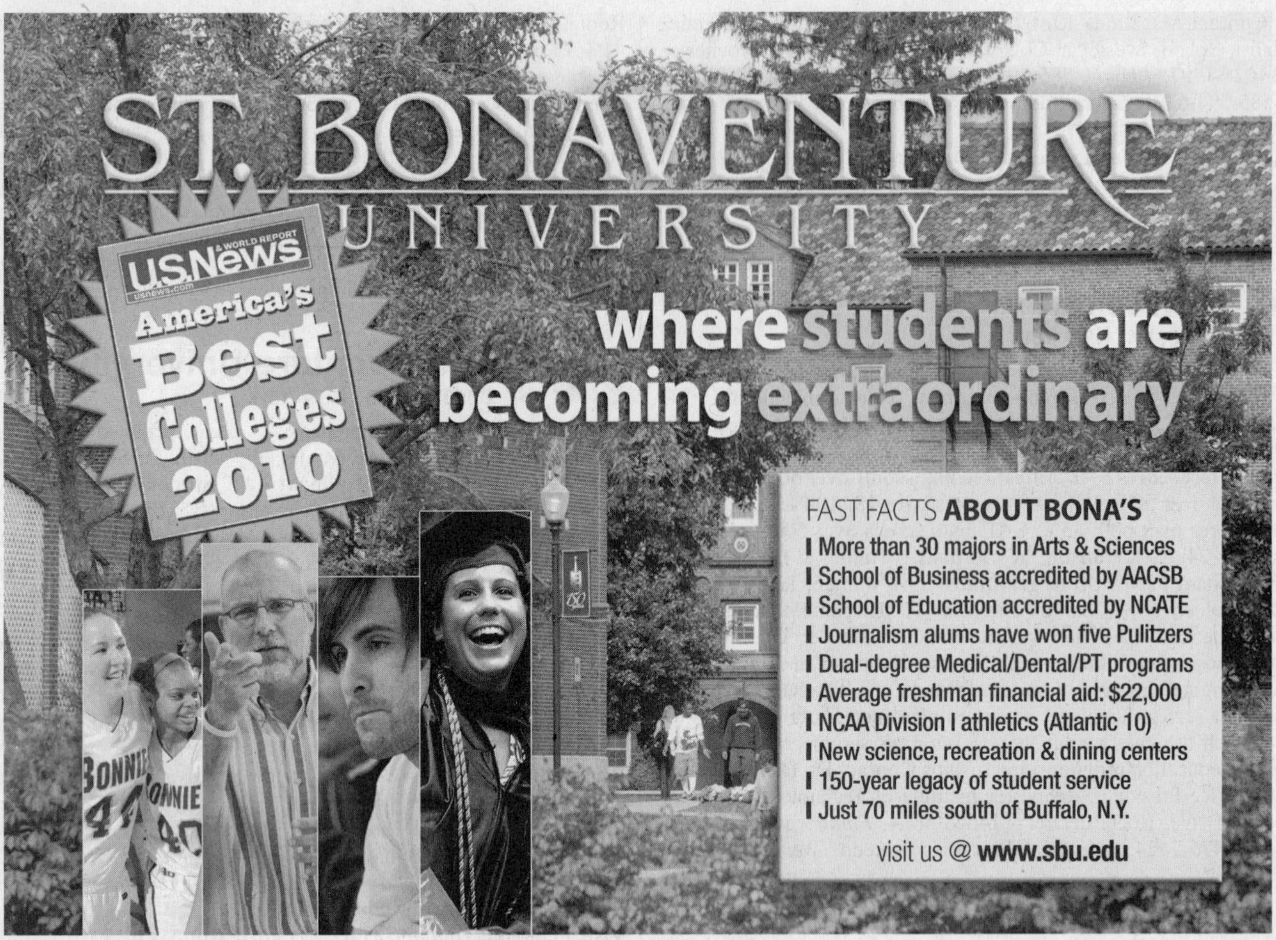

ST. BONAVENTURE
UNIVERSITY
U.S.News & WORLD REPORT
America's Best Colleges 2010
where students are becoming extraordinary
FAST FACTS ABOUT BONA'S
- More than 30 majors in Arts & Sciences
- School of Business accredited by AACSB
- School of Education accredited by NCATE
- Journalism alums have won five Pulitzers
- Dual-degree Medical/Dental/PT programs
- Average freshman financial aid: $22,000
- NCAA Division I athletics (Atlantic 10)
- New science, recreation & dining centers
- 150-year legacy of student service
- Just 70 miles south of Buffalo, N.Y.

visit us @ **www.sbu.edu**

St. John Fisher College (continued)

over 600: 17%; SAT math scores over 600: 30%; ACT scores over 24: 52% **Housing** Yes **Expenses** Tuition & Fees $24,320; Room & Board $10,090 **Undergraduates** 58% women, 7% part-time, 8% 25 or older, 0.4% Native American, 3% Hispanic American, 5% African American, 2% Asian American/Pacific Islander **The most frequently chosen baccalaureate fields are** business/marketing, education, health professions and related sciences **Academic program** Advanced placement, accelerated degree program, self-designed majors, honors program, summer session, adult/continuing education programs, internships **Contact** Mrs. Stacy A. Ledermann, Director of Freshmen Admissions, St. John Fisher College, 3690 East Avenue, Rochester, NY 14618. *Phone:* 585-385-8064 or toll-free 800-444-4640. *Fax:* 585-385-8386. *E-mail:* admissions@sjfc.edu. *Web site:* http://www.sjfc.edu/.

Visit Petersons.com and enter keyword Fisher

See page 1106 for the College Close-Up.

St. John's University

Queens, New York

General Independent, university, coed, affiliated with Roman Catholic Church **Entrance** Moderately difficult **Setting** 98-acre urban campus **Total enrollment** 20,352 **Student-faculty ratio** 19:1 **Application deadline** Rolling (freshmen), rolling (transfer) **Freshman admission** 43% were admitted. Average high school GPA 3.3 **Freshman test scores** SAT critical reading scores over 500: 67%; SAT math scores over 500: 72%; SAT critical reading scores over 600: 23%; SAT math scores over 600: 31% **Housing** Yes **Expenses** Tuition & Fees $30,040; Room & Board $13,140 **Undergraduates** 55% women, 20% part-time, 5% 25 or older, 0.2% Native American, 15% Hispanic American, 18% African American, 18% Asian American/Pacific Islander **The most frequently chosen baccalaureate fields are** business/marketing, communications/journalism, security and protective services **Academic program** English as a second language, advanced placement, accelerated degree program, honors program, summer session, adult/continuing education programs, internships **Contact** Mrs. Karen Vahey, Admission Director, St. John's University, 8000 Utopia Parkway, Queens, NY 11439. *Phone:* 718-990-2000 or toll-free 888-9STJOHNS. *Fax:* 718-990-2096. *E-mail:* admhelp@stjohns.edu. *Web site:* http://www.stjohns.edu/.

St. Joseph's College, Long Island Campus

Patchogue, New York

General Independent, comprehensive, coed **Entrance** Moderately difficult **Setting** 28-acre small-town campus **Total enrollment** 4,358 **Student-faculty ratio** 17:1 **Application deadline** 8/15 (freshmen), 8/15 (transfer) **Freshman admission** 74% were admitted **Freshman test scores** SAT critical reading scores over 500: 76%; SAT math scores over 500: 75%; SAT critical reading scores over 600: 23%; SAT math scores over 600: 15% **Housing** No **Expenses** Tuition & Fees $16,765 **Undergraduates** 72% women, 20% part-time, 25% 25 or older, 0.2% Native American, 8% Hispanic American, 4% African American, 1% Asian American/Pacific Islander **The most frequently chosen baccalaureate fields are** business/marketing, English, family and consumer sciences **Academic program** Advanced placement, honors program, summer session, adult/continuing education programs, internships **Contact** Ms. Gigi Lamens, Director of Admissions, St. Joseph's College, Long Island Campus, 155 West Roe Boulevard, Patchogue, NY 11772-2399. *Phone:* 631-447-3216 or toll-free 866-AT ST JOE. *E-mail:* glamens@sjcny.edu. *Web site:* http://www.sjcny.edu/.

St. Joseph's College, New York

Brooklyn, New York

General Independent, comprehensive, coed **Entrance** Moderately difficult **Setting** urban campus **Total enrollment** 1,358 **Student-faculty**

ratio 13:1 **Application deadline** 8/15 (freshmen), 8/15 (transfer) **Freshman admission** 73% were admitted **Freshman test scores** SAT critical reading scores over 500: 45%; SAT math scores over 500: 55%; SAT critical reading scores over 600: 9%; SAT math scores over 600: 10% **Housing** No **Expenses** Tuition & Fees $16,765 **Undergraduates** 75% women, 28% part-time, 25% 25 or older, 0.3% Native American, 16% Hispanic American, 35% African American, 6% Asian American/Pacific Islander **The most frequently chosen baccalaureate fields are** business/marketing, family and consumer sciences, health professions and related sciences **Academic program** Advanced placement, honors program, summer session, adult/continuing education programs, internships **Contact** Ms. Theresa LaRocca Meyer, Director of Admissions, St. Joseph's College, New York, 245 Clinton Avenue, Brooklyn, NY 11205-3688. *Phone:* 718-636-6868. *E-mail:* asinfob@sjcny.edu. *Web site:* http://www.sjcny.edu/.

Visit Petersons.com and enter keyword Joseph's

See page 1112 for the College Close-Up.

St. Lawrence University

Canton, New York

General Independent, comprehensive, coed **Entrance** Very difficult **Setting** 1,000-acre small-town campus **Total enrollment** 2,401 **Student-faculty ratio** 11:1 **Application deadline** 2/1 (freshmen), 4/1 (transfer) **Freshman admission** 39% were admitted. Average high school GPA 3.46 **Freshman test scores** SAT critical reading scores over 500: 93.5%; SAT math scores over 500: 95.3%; ACT scores over 18: 98.4%; SAT critical reading scores over 600: 58.1%; SAT math scores over 600: 63%; ACT scores over 24: 91.9% **Housing** Yes **Expenses** Tuition & Fees $39,765; Room & Board $10,160 **Undergraduates** 55% women, 1% part-time, 1% Native American, 4% Hispanic American, 3% African American, 2% Asian American/Pacific Islander **The most frequently chosen baccalaureate fields are** psychology, social sciences, visual and performing arts **Academic program** Advanced placement, self-designed majors, summer session, internships **Contact** Ms. Terry Cowdrey, Vice President and Dean of Admissions and Financial Aid, St. Lawrence University, 23 Romoda Drive, Canton, NY 13617-1455. *Phone:* 315-229-5261 or toll-free 800-285-1856. *Fax:* 315-229-5818. *E-mail:* tcowdrey@stlawu.edu. *Web site:* http://www.stlawu.edu/.

Visit Petersons.com and enter keywords St. Lawrence

See page 1116 for the College Close-Up.

St. Thomas Aquinas College

Sparkill, New York

General Independent, comprehensive, coed **Entrance** Moderately difficult **Setting** 46-acre suburban campus **Total enrollment** 2,132 **Student-faculty ratio** 16:1 **Application deadline** Rolling (freshmen), rolling (transfer) **Freshman admission** 84% were admitted. Average high school GPA 2.73 **Freshman test scores** SAT critical reading scores over 500: 33%; SAT math scores over 500: 42%; SAT critical reading scores over 600: 8%; SAT math scores over 600: 11% **Housing** Yes **Expenses** Tuition & Fees $22,410; Room & Board $10,300 **Undergraduates** 55% women, 30% part-time, 4% 25 or older, 0.3% Native American, 16% Hispanic American, 6% African American, 3% Asian American/Pacific Islander **The most frequently chosen baccalaureate fields are** business/marketing, education, social sciences **Academic program** Advanced placement, accelerated degree program, honors program, summer session, adult/continuing education programs, internships **Contact** Danielle Mac Kay, Director of Admissions, St. Thomas Aquinas College, 125 Route 340, Sparkill, NY 10976. *Phone:* 845-398-4100 or toll-free 800-999-STAC. *Fax:* 845-398-4114. *E-mail:* dmackay@stac.edu. *Web site:* http://www.stac.edu/.

Visit Petersons.com and enter keywords Thomas Aquinas

See page 1134 for the College Close-Up.

Sarah Lawrence College

Bronxville, New York

General Independent, comprehensive, coed **Entrance** Very difficult **Setting** 44-acre suburban campus **Total enrollment** 1,701 **Student-faculty ratio** 9:1 **Application deadline** 1/1 (freshmen), 3/1 (transfer) **Freshman admission** 59% were admitted. Average high school GPA 3.6 **Housing** Yes **Expenses** Tuition & Fees $40,350; Room & Board $13,104 **Undergraduates** 73% women, 4% part-time, 3% 25 or older, 0.1% Native American, 5% Hispanic American, 3% African American, 5% Asian American/Pacific Islander **The most frequently chosen baccalaureate field is** liberal arts/general studies **Academic program** Advanced placement, self-designed majors, adult/continuing education programs, internships **Contact** Mr. Stephen M. Schierloh, Acting Dean of Admission, Sarah Lawrence College, 1 Mead Way, Bronxville, NY 10708-5999. *Phone:* 914-395-2510 or toll-free 800-888-2858. *Fax:* 914-395-2515. *E-mail:* slcadmit@sarahlawrence.edu. *Web site:* http://www.sarahlawrence.edu/.

Visit Petersons.com and enter keywords Sarah Lawrence

See page 1142 for the College Close-Up.

School of Visual Arts

New York, New York

General Proprietary, comprehensive, coed **Entrance** Moderately difficult **Setting** 1-acre urban campus **Total enrollment** 4,051 **Student-faculty ratio** 9:1 **Application deadline** Rolling (freshmen), rolling (transfer) **Freshman admission** 69% were admitted. Average high school GPA 3.11 **Freshman test scores** SAT critical reading scores over 500: 64%; SAT math scores over 500: 56%; ACT scores over 18: 87%; SAT critical reading scores over 600: 22%; SAT math scores over 600: 21%; ACT scores over 24: 36% **Housing** Yes **Undergraduates** 11% 25 or older, 0.3% Native American, 10% Hispanic American, 3% African American, 13% Asian American/Pacific Islander **The most frequently chosen baccalaureate fields are** computer and information sciences, communication technologies, visual and performing arts **Academic program** English as a second language, advanced placement, honors program, summer session, adult/continuing education programs, internships **Contact** Admissions Office, School of Visual Arts, 209 East 23rd Street, New York, NY 10010. *Phone:* 212-592-2100 or toll-free 800-436-4204. *Fax:* 212-592-2116. *E-mail:* admissions@sva.edu. *Web site:* http://www.sva.edu/.

Sh'or Yoshuv Rabbinical College

Lawrence, New York

General Independent Jewish, comprehensive, men only **Entrance** Noncompetitive **Total enrollment** 257 **Student-faculty ratio** 15:1 **Application deadline** 9/20 (freshmen) **Housing** Yes **Expenses** Tuition & Fees $16,060; Room & Board $6000 **Undergraduates** 13% 25 or older **Academic program** Self-designed majors, summer session, adult/continuing education programs, internships **Contact** Rabbi Moshe Rubin, Registrar, Sh'or Yoshuv Rabbinical College, 1 Cedarlawn Avenue, Lawrence, NY 11559-1714. *Phone:* 516-239-9002 Ext. 124. *Fax:* 516-977-1282. *E-mail:* mrubin@shoryoshuv.org. *Web site:* http://www.shoryoshuv.org/.

Siena College

Loudonville, New York

General Independent Roman Catholic, comprehensive, coed **Entrance** Moderately difficult **Setting** 164-acre suburban campus **Total enrollment** 3,305 **Student-faculty ratio** 13:1 **Application deadline** 3/1 (freshmen), 8/15 (transfer) **Freshman admission** 53% were admitted **Freshman test scores** SAT critical reading scores over 500: 79.1%; SAT math scores over 500: 87.2%; ACT scores over 18: 97.1%; SAT critical reading scores over 600: 31.1%; SAT math scores over 600: 43.1%; ACT scores over 24: 67.7% **Housing** Yes **Expenses** Tuition & Fees $25,285; Room & Board $9930 **Undergraduates** 54% women, 6% part-time, 4% 25 or older, 0.1% Native American, 4% Hispanic American, 2% African

Siena College (continued)

American, 3% Asian American/Pacific Islander **The most frequently chosen baccalaureate fields are** business/marketing, psychology, social sciences **Academic program** Advanced placement, accelerated degree program, honors program, summer session, internships **Contact** Ms. Heather Renault, Director of Admissions, Siena College, 515 Loudon Road, Loudonville, NY 12211-1462. *Phone:* 518-783-2426 or toll-free 888-AT-SIENA. *Fax:* 518-783-2436. *E-mail:* admit@siena.edu. *Web site:* http://www.siena.edu/.

Visit Petersons.com and enter keyword Siena

See page 1160 for the College Close-Up.

Skidmore College
Saratoga Springs, New York

General Independent, comprehensive, coed **Entrance** Very difficult **Setting** 800-acre small-town campus **Total enrollment** 2,720 **Student-faculty ratio** 9:1 **Application deadline** 1/15 (freshmen), 4/1 (transfer) **Freshman admission** 42% were admitted. Average high school GPA 3.36 **Freshman test scores** SAT critical reading scores over 500: 94%; SAT math scores over 500: 95.6%; ACT scores over 18: 100.1%; SAT critical reading scores over 600: 64.7%; SAT math scores over 600: 69.8%; ACT scores over 24: 92.3% **Housing** Yes **Expenses** Tuition & Fees $40,420; Room & Board $10,776 **Undergraduates** 60% women, 3% part-time, 0.3% 25 or older, 1% Native American, 5% Hispanic American, 4% African American, 9% Asian American/Pacific Islander **The most frequently chosen baccalaureate fields are** social sciences, business/marketing, visual and performing arts **Academic program** Advanced placement, accelerated degree program, self-designed majors, honors program, summer session, adult/continuing education programs, internships **Contact** Ms. Mary Lou Bates, Dean of Admissions and Financial Aid, Skidmore College, 815 North Broadway, Saratoga Springs, NY 12866-1632. *Phone:* 518-580-5570 or toll-free 800-867-6007. *Fax:* 518-580-5584. *E-mail:* admissions@skidmore.edu. *Web site:* http://www.skidmore.edu/.

Visit Petersons.com and enter keyword Skidmore

See page 1166 for the College Close-Up.

State University of New York at Binghamton
Binghamton, New York

General State-supported, university, coed **Entrance** Very difficult **Setting** 930-acre suburban campus **Total enrollment** 14,711 **Student-faculty ratio** 20:1 **Application deadline** 1/15 (freshmen), rolling (transfer) **Freshman admission** 33% were admitted. Average high school GPA 3.6 **Freshman test scores** SAT critical reading scores over 500: 96.7%; SAT math scores over 500: 99.6%; ACT scores over 18: 100%; SAT critical reading scores over 600: 67.2%; SAT math scores over 600: 84.8%; ACT scores over 24: 93.9% **Housing** Yes **Expenses** Tuition & Fees: state resident $6761, nonresident $14,661; Room & Board $10,614 **Undergraduates** 47% women, 4% part-time, 3% 25 or older, 0.2% Native American, 7% Hispanic American, 5% African American, 12% Asian American/Pacific Islander **The most frequently chosen baccalaureate fields are** business/marketing, English, social sciences **Academic program** English as a second language, advanced placement, accelerated degree program, self-designed majors, honors program, summer session, adult/continuing education programs, internships **Contact** Ms. Cheryl S. Brown, Director of Admissions, State University of New York at Binghamton, PO Box 6000, Binghamton, NY 13902-6000. *Phone:* 607-777-2171. *Fax:* 607-777-4445. *E-mail:* admit@binghamton.edu. *Web site:* http://www.binghamton.edu/.

State University of New York at Fredonia
Fredonia, New York

General State-supported, comprehensive, coed **Entrance** Moderately difficult **Setting** 249-acre small-town campus **Total enrollment** 5,776 **Student-faculty ratio** 16:1 **Application deadline** Rolling (freshmen), rolling (transfer) **Freshman admission** 49% were admitted. Average high school GPA 3.4 **Freshman test scores** SAT critical reading scores over 500: 79%; SAT math scores over 500: 85%; ACT scores over 18: 94%; SAT critical reading scores over 600: 23%; SAT math scores over 600: 28%; ACT scores over 24: 48% **Housing** Yes **Expenses** Tuition & Fees: state resident $6308, nonresident $14,208; Room & Board $9330 **Undergraduates** 56% women, 3% part-time, 6% 25 or older, 1% Native American, 3% Hispanic American, 3% African American, 1% Asian American/Pacific Islander **The most frequently chosen baccalaureate fields are** business/marketing, education, visual and performing arts **Academic program** Advanced placement, accelerated degree program, self-designed majors, honors program, summer session, adult/continuing education programs, internships **Contact** Office of Admissions, State University of New York at Fredonia, 178 Central Avenue, Fredonia, NY 14063. *Phone:* 716-673-3251 or toll-free 800-252-1212. *Fax:* 716-673-3249. *E-mail:* admissions@fredonia.edu. *Web site:* http://www.fredonia.edu/.

State University of New York at New Paltz
New Paltz, New York

General State-supported, comprehensive, coed **Entrance** Very difficult **Setting** 216-acre small-town campus **Total enrollment** 7,957 **Student-faculty ratio** 16:1 **Application deadline** 4/1 (freshmen), 4/1 (transfer) **Freshman admission** 34% were admitted. Average high school GPA 3.5 **Freshman test scores** SAT critical reading scores over 500: 84%; SAT math scores over 500: 86%; ACT scores over 18: 99%; SAT critical reading scores over 600: 34%; SAT math scores over 600: 36%; ACT scores over 24: 68% **Housing** Yes **Expenses** Tuition & Fees: state resident $6081, nonresident $13,981; Room & Board $9202 **Undergraduates** 66% women, 9% part-time, 11% 25 or older, 1% Native American, 10% Hispanic American, 5% African American, 4% Asian American/Pacific Islander **The most frequently chosen baccalaureate fields are** business/marketing, education, visual and performing arts **Academic program** English as a second language, advanced placement, self-designed majors, honors program, summer session, adult/continuing education programs, internships **Contact** Ms. Kimberly A. Strano, Director of Freshman Admissions, State University of New York at New Paltz, 1 Hawk Drive, New Paltz, NY 12561-2499. *Phone:* 845-257-3200. *Fax:* 845-257-3209. *E-mail:* admissions@newpaltz.edu. *Web site:* http://www.newpaltz.edu/.

State University of New York at Oswego
Oswego, New York

General State-supported, comprehensive, coed **Entrance** Moderately difficult **Setting** 696-acre small-town campus **Total enrollment** 8,119 **Student-faculty ratio** 18:1 **Application deadline** Rolling (freshmen), rolling (transfer) **Freshman admission** 47% were admitted. Average high school GPA 3.3 **Freshman test scores** SAT critical reading scores over 500: 78%; SAT math scores over 500: 83%; ACT scores over 18: 100%; SAT critical reading scores over 600: 19%; SAT math scores over 600: 20%; ACT scores over 24: 42% **Housing** Yes **Expenses** Tuition & Fees: state resident $6256, nonresident $14,156; Room & Board $10,870 **Undergraduates** 52% women, 6% part-time, 10% 25 or older, 0.4% Native American, 5% Hispanic American, 4% African American, 2% Asian American/Pacific Islander **The most frequently chosen baccalaureate fields are** business/marketing, communications/journalism, education **Academic program** English as a second language, advanced placement, accelerated degree program, self-designed majors, honors program, summer session, adult/continuing education programs, internships **Contact** Dr. Joseph Grant, Vice President for Student Affairs and Enrollment, State University of New York at Oswego, 7060 State Route 104, Oswego, NY 13126. *Phone:* 315-312-2250. *Fax:* 315-312-3260. *E-mail:* admiss@oswego.edu. *Web site:* http://www.oswego.edu/.

Visit Petersons.com and enter keyword Oswego

See page 1190 for the College Close-Up.

State University of New York at Plattsburgh

Plattsburgh, New York

General State-supported, comprehensive, coed **Entrance** Moderately difficult **Setting** 265-acre small-town campus **Total enrollment** 6,453 **Student-faculty ratio** 17:1 **Application deadline** Rolling (transfer) **Freshman admission** 48% were admitted. Average high school GPA 3.14 **Freshman test scores** SAT critical reading scores over 500: 68%; SAT math scores over 500: 76.4%; ACT scores over 18: 98.6%; SAT critical reading scores over 600: 16.2%; SAT math scores over 600: 18.9%; ACT scores over 24: 30.8% **Housing** Yes **Expenses** Tuition & Fees: state resident $6100, nonresident $14,000; Room & Board $8600 **Undergraduates** 55% women, 6% part-time, 9% 25 or older, 1% Native American, 5% Hispanic American, 5% African American, 2% Asian American/Pacific Islander **The most frequently chosen baccalaureate fields are** business/marketing, communications/journalism, education **Academic program** English as a second language, advanced placement, accelerated degree program, self-designed majors, honors program, summer session, adult/continuing education programs, internships **Contact** Mrs. Carrie Woodward, Assistant Director for Freshman Admissions, State University of New York at Plattsburgh, 101 Broad Street, Plattsburgh, NY 12901. *Phone:* 888-673-0012 or toll-free 888-673-0012. *Fax:* 518-564-2045. *E-mail:* carrie.woodward@plattsburgh.edu. *Web site:* http://www.plattsburgh.edu/.

State University of New York College at Cortland

Cortland, New York

General State-supported, comprehensive, coed **Entrance** Moderately difficult **Setting** 191-acre small-town campus **Total enrollment** 7,322 **Student-faculty ratio** 16:1 **Application deadline** Rolling (freshmen), rolling (transfer) **Freshman admission** 39% were admitted. Average high school GPA 3.41 **Freshman test scores** SAT critical reading scores over 500: 83%; SAT math scores over 500: 69%; SAT critical reading scores over 600: 23%; SAT math scores over 600: 11% **Housing** Yes **Expenses** Tuition & Fees: state resident $6145, nonresident $14,045; Room & Board $9790 **Undergraduates** 57% women, 3% part-time, 6% 25 or older, 1% Native American, 6% Hispanic American, 3% African American, 2% Asian American/Pacific Islander **The most frequently chosen baccalaureate fields are** education, parks and recreation, social sciences **Academic program** Advanced placement, self-designed majors, honors program, summer session, adult/continuing education programs, internships **Contact** Mr. Mark Yacavone, Director of Admission, State University of New York College at Cortland, PO Box 2000, Cortland, NY 13045. *Phone:* 607-753-4711. *Fax:* 607-753-5998. *E-mail:* admissions@cortland.edu. *Web site:* http://www.cortland.edu/.

State University of New York College at Geneseo

Geneseo, New York

General State-supported, comprehensive, coed **Entrance** Very difficult **Setting** 220-acre small-town campus **Total enrollment** 5,660 **Student-faculty ratio** 19:1 **Application deadline** 1/1 (freshmen), 2/15 (transfer) **Freshman admission** 35% were admitted. Average high school GPA 3.75 **Freshman test scores** SAT critical reading scores over 500: 94.6%; SAT math scores over 500: 96.7%; ACT scores over 18: 98.9%; SAT critical reading scores over 600: 80.4%; SAT math scores over 600: 87.3%; ACT scores over 24: 96% **Housing** Yes **Expenses** Tuition & Fees: state resident $6326, nonresident $14,226; Room & Board $9550 **Undergraduates** 57% women, 2% part-time, 3% 25 or older, 1% Native American, 2% Hispanic American, 3% African American, 8% Asian American/Pacific Islander **The most frequently chosen baccalaureate fields are** education, business/marketing, social sciences **Academic program** English as a second language, advanced placement, honors program, summer session, internships **Contact** Kris Shay, Director of Admissions, State University of New York College at Geneseo, 1 College Circle, Geneseo, NY 14454-1401. *Phone:* 585-245-5571 or toll-free 866-245-5211. *Fax:* 585-245-5550. *E-mail:* admissions@geneseo.edu. *Web site:* http://www.geneseo.edu/.

State University of New York College at Old Westbury

Old Westbury, New York

General State-supported, comprehensive, coed **Entrance** Moderately difficult **Setting** 604-acre suburban campus **Total enrollment** 3,897 **Student-faculty ratio** 20:1 **Application deadline** Rolling (freshmen), 12/15 (transfer) **Freshman admission** 51% were admitted. Average high school GPA 2.86 **Freshman test scores** SAT critical reading scores over 500: 45%; SAT math scores over 500: 59%; ACT scores over 18: 94%; SAT critical reading scores over 600: 6%; SAT math scores over 600: 9%; ACT scores over 24: 12% **Housing** Yes **Expenses** Tuition & Fees: state resident $5797, nonresident $13,697; Room & Board $9390 **Undergraduates** 59% women, 16% part-time, 26% 25 or older, 1% Native American, 18% Hispanic American, 32% African American, 8% Asian American/Pacific Islander **The most frequently chosen baccalaureate fields are** business/marketing, education, social sciences **Academic program** English as a second language, advanced placement, honors program, summer session, internships **Contact** Ms. Mary Marquez Bell, Vice President Enrollment Services, State University of New York College at Old Westbury, PO Box 307, Old Westbury, NY 11568. *Phone:* 516-876-3073. *Fax:* 516-876-3307. *E-mail:* enroll@oldwestbury.edu. *Web site:* http://www.oldwestbury.edu/.

State University of New York College at Oneonta

Oneonta, New York

General State-supported, comprehensive, coed **Entrance** Very difficult **Setting** 250-acre small-town campus **Total enrollment** 5,893 **Student-faculty ratio** 17:1 **Application deadline** Rolling (freshmen), rolling (transfer) **Freshman admission** 39% were admitted. Average high school GPA 3.5 **Freshman test scores** SAT critical reading scores over 500: 87%; SAT math scores over 500: 95%; ACT scores over 18: 100%; SAT critical reading scores over 600: 21%; SAT math scores over 600: 39%; ACT scores over 24: 71% **Housing** Yes **Expenses** Tuition & Fees: state resident $6185, nonresident $14,085; Room & Board $8900 **Undergraduates** 57% women, 2% part-time, 5% 25 or older, 0.3% Native American, 5% Hispanic American, 3% African American, 2% Asian American/Pacific Islander **The most frequently chosen baccalaureate fields are** education, communications/journalism, visual and performing arts **Academic program** English as a second language, advanced placement, honors program, summer session, adult/continuing education programs, internships **Contact** Ms. Karen Brown, Director of Admissions, State University of New York College at Oneonta, Alumni Hall 116, Oneonta, NY 13820-4015. *Phone:* 607-436-2524 or toll-free 800-SUNY-123. *Fax:* 607-436-3074. *E-mail:* admissions@oneonta.edu. *Web site:* http://www.oneonta.edu/.

State University of New York College at Potsdam

Potsdam, New York

General State-supported, comprehensive, coed **Entrance** Moderately difficult **Setting** 240-acre small-town campus **Total enrollment** 4,298 **Student-faculty ratio** 13:1 **Application deadline** Rolling (freshmen), rolling (transfer) **Freshman admission** 66% were admitted. Average high school GPA 3.2 **Freshman test scores** SAT critical reading scores over 500: 60%; SAT math scores over 500: 61%; ACT scores over 18: 93%; SAT critical reading scores over 600: 17%; SAT math scores over 600: 18%; ACT scores over 24: 35% **Housing** Yes **Expenses** Tuition & Fees: state resident $6124, nonresident $14,024; Room & Board $9270 **Undergraduates** 57% women, 3% part-time, 8% 25 or older, 2% Native

State University of New York College at Potsdam (continued)
American, 3% Hispanic American, 3% African American, 1% Asian American/Pacific Islander **The most frequently chosen baccalaureate fields are** education, social sciences, visual and performing arts **Academic program** Advanced placement, self-designed majors, honors program, summer session, internships **Contact** Mr. Thomas Nesbitt, Director of Admissions, State University of New York College at Potsdam, 44 Pierrepont Avenue, Potsdam, NY 13676. *Phone:* 315-267-2180 or toll-free 877-POTSDAM. *Fax:* 315-267-2163. *E-mail:* admissions@potsdam.edu. *Web site:* http://www.potsdam.edu/.

State University of New York College of Agriculture and Technology at Cobleskill

Cobleskill, New York

General State-supported, 4-year, coed **Entrance** Minimally difficult **Setting** 750-acre rural campus **Total enrollment** 2,619 **Student-faculty ratio** 17:1 **Application deadline** Rolling (freshmen), rolling (transfer) **Freshman admission** 79% were admitted. Average high school GPA 2.4 **Freshman test scores** ACT scores over 18: 64.4%; ACT scores over 24: 8.8% **Housing** Yes **Expenses** Tuition & Fees: state resident $6311, nonresident $14,211; Room & Board $9460 **Undergraduates** 49% women, 5% part-time, 9% 25 or older, 0.5% Native American, 5% Hispanic American, 8% African American, 1% Asian American/Pacific Islander **The most frequently chosen baccalaureate fields are** agriculture, business/marketing, natural resources/environmental science **Academic program** English as a second language, advanced placement, honors program, summer session, adult/continuing education programs, internships **Contact** Christopher Tacea, Interim Director of Admissions, State University of New York College of Agriculture and Technology at Cobleskill, Cobleskill, NY 12043. *Phone:* 518-255-5525 or toll-free 800-295-8988. *E-mail:* admissions@cobleskill.edu. *Web site:* http://www.cobleskill.edu/.

State University of New York College of Agriculture and Technology at Morrisville

Morrisville, New York

Contact Mr. Thomas VerDow, Director of Admissions, State University of New York College of Agriculture and Technology at Morrisville, PO Box 901, Morrisville, NY 13408-0901. *Phone:* 800-258-0111 or toll-free 800-258-0111. *Fax:* 315-684-6427. *E-mail:* admissions@morrisville.edu. *Web site:* http://www.morrisville.edu/.

State University of New York College of Environmental Science and Forestry

Syracuse, New York

General State-supported, university, coed **Entrance** Moderately difficult **Setting** 12-acre urban campus **Total enrollment** 2,199 **Student-faculty ratio** 12:1 **Application deadline** Rolling (freshmen), rolling (transfer) **Freshman admission** 43% were admitted. Average high school GPA 3.75 **Freshman test scores** SAT math scores over 500: 95%; ACT scores over 18: 100%; SAT math scores over 600: 51%; ACT scores over 24: 80% **Housing** Yes **Expenses** Tuition & Fees: state resident $5891, nonresident $13,791; Room & Board $12,460 **Undergraduates** 40% women, 3% part-time, 9% 25 or older, 1% Native American, 3% Hispanic American, 1% African American, 4% Asian American/Pacific Islander **The most frequently chosen baccalaureate fields are** biological/life sciences, engineering, natural resources/environmental science **Academic program** English as a second language, advanced placement, accelerated degree program, honors program, adult/continuing education programs, internships **Contact** Ms. Susan Sanford, Director of Admissions, State University of New York College of Environmental Science and Forestry, Office of Undergraduate Admissions, 106 Bray Hall, 1 Forestry Lane, Syracuse, NY 13210-2779. *Phone:* 315-470-6600 or toll-free 800-777-7373. *Fax:* 315-470-6933. *E-mail:* esfinfo@esf.edu. *Web site:* http://www.esf.edu/.

Visit Petersons.com and enter keyword Environmental

See page 1192 for the College Close-Up.

State University of New York College of Technology at Alfred

Alfred, New York

General State-supported, primarily 2-year, coed **Entrance** Moderately difficult **Setting** 1,084-acre rural campus **Total enrollment** 3,539 **Student-faculty ratio** 18:1 **Application deadline** Rolling (freshmen), rolling (transfer) **Freshman admission** 61% were admitted. Average high school GPA 2.8 **Housing** Yes **Expenses** Tuition & Fees: state resident $6162, nonresident $9942; Room & Board $9190 **Undergraduates** 38% women, 10% part-time, 14% 25 or older, 0.2% Native American, 4% Hispanic American, 9% African American, 3% Asian American/Pacific Islander **The most frequently chosen baccalaureate fields are** computer and information sciences, business/marketing, engineering technologies **Academic program** English as a second language, advanced placement, self-designed majors, honors program, summer session, adult/continuing education programs, internships **Contact** Mrs. Deborah Goodrich, Associate Vice President for Enrollment Management, State University of New York College of Technology at Alfred, Huntington Administration Building, 10 Upper College Drive, Alfred, NY 14802. *Phone:* 607-587-4215 or toll-free 800-4-ALFRED. *Fax:* 607-587-4299. *E-mail:* admissions@alfredstate.edu. *Web site:* http://www.alfredstate.edu/.

State University of New York College of Technology at Canton

Canton, New York

General State-supported, 4-year, coed **Entrance** Minimally difficult **Setting** 555-acre small-town campus **Total enrollment** 3,320 **Student-faculty ratio** 19:1 **Application deadline** Rolling (freshmen), rolling (transfer) **Freshman admission** 87% were admitted **Freshman test scores** SAT critical reading scores over 500: 32%; SAT math scores over 500: 23%; ACT scores over 18: 64%; SAT critical reading scores over 600: 6%; SAT math scores over 600: 4%; ACT scores over 24: 11% **Housing** Yes **Expenses** Tuition & Fees: state resident $6279, nonresident $10,059; Room & Board $9320 **Undergraduates** 51% women, 23% part-time, 23% 25 or older, 2% Native American, 5% Hispanic American, 11% African American, 1% Asian American/Pacific Islander **The most frequently chosen baccalaureate fields are** business/marketing, health professions and related sciences, security and protective services **Academic program** Advanced placement, self-designed majors, summer session, internships **Contact** Mr. Randy B. Sieminski, Assistant Vice President for Advancement, State University of New York College of Technology at Canton, Cornell Drive, Canton, NY 13617. *Phone:* 315-386-7123 or toll-free 800-388-7123. *Fax:* 315-386-7929. *E-mail:* admissions@canton.edu. *Web site:* http://www.canton.edu/.

State University of New York College of Technology at Delhi

Delhi, New York

General State-supported, 4-year, coed **Entrance** Moderately difficult **Setting** 405-acre rural campus **Total enrollment** 2,971 **Student-faculty ratio** 16:1 **Application deadline** Rolling (freshmen), rolling (transfer) **Freshman admission** 52% were admitted **Housing** Yes **Expenses** Tuition & Fees: state resident $6360, nonresident $14,260; Room & Board $9300 **Undergraduates** 47% women, 16% part-time, 16% 25 or older **The most frequently chosen baccalaureate fields are** architecture, business/marketing, computer and information sciences **Aca-**

demic program English as a second language, advanced placement, self-designed majors, honors program, summer session, internships **Contact** Mr. Craig Wesley, Dean of Enrollment, State University of New York College of Technology at Delhi, Main Street, Delhi, NY 13753. *Phone:* 607-746-4550 Ext. 4556 or toll-free 800-96-DELHI. *E-mail:* wesleycs@delhi.edu. *Web site:* http://www.delhi.edu/.

State University of New York Downstate Medical Center

Brooklyn, New York

General State-supported, upper-level, coed **Entrance** Moderately difficult **Setting** urban campus **Total enrollment** 1,660 **Application deadline** 5/1 (transfer) **First-year students** 14% were admitted **Housing** Yes **Expenses** Tuition & Fees: state resident $7453, nonresident $15,473; Room & Board $11,898 **Undergraduates** 84% women, 43% part-time, 0.3% Native American, 6% Hispanic American, 39% African American, 10% Asian American/Pacific Islander **The most frequently chosen baccalaureate field is** health professions and related sciences **Academic program** Advanced placement, accelerated degree program, summer session, internships **Contact** Admissions Office, State University of New York Downstate Medical Center, 450 Clarkson Avenue, Brooklyn, NY 11203-2446. *Phone:* 718-270-2446. *Fax:* 718-270-7592. *E-mail:* admissions@downstate.edu. *Web site:* http://www.downstate.edu/.

State University of New York Empire State College

Saratoga Springs, New York

General State-supported, comprehensive, coed **Entrance** Minimally difficult **Setting** small-town campus **Total enrollment** 14,325 **Student-faculty ratio** 10:1 **Application deadline** Rolling (freshmen), rolling (transfer) **Freshman admission** 78% were admitted **Housing** No **Expenses** Tuition & Fees: state resident $5195, nonresident $13,095 **Undergraduates** 60% women, 64% part-time, 84% 25 or older, 1% Native American, 8% Hispanic American, 14% African American, 2% Asian American/Pacific Islander **The most frequently chosen baccalaureate fields are** business/marketing, physical sciences, public administration and social services **Academic program** Advanced placement, self-designed majors, adult/continuing education programs **Contact** Ms. Jennifer D'Agostino, Director of Admissions, State University of New York Empire State College, Two Union Avenue, Saratoga Springs, NY 12866. *Phone:* 518-587-2100 Ext. 2214 or toll-free 800-847-3000. *Fax:* 518-587-9759. *E-mail:* jennifer.d'agostino@esc.edu. *Web site:* http://www.esc.edu/.

State University of New York Institute of Technology

Utica, New York

Contact Amy Stokes, State University of New York Institute of Technology, PO Box 3050, Utica, NY 13504-3050. *Phone:* 315-792-7500 or toll-free 800-SUNYTEC. *Fax:* 315-792-7837. *E-mail:* admissions@sunyit.edu. *Web site:* http://www.sunyit.edu/.

Visit Petersons.com and enter keywords University of New York Institute

See page 1194 for the College Close-Up.

State University of New York Maritime College

Throggs Neck, New York

General State-supported, comprehensive, coed, primarily men **Entrance** Very difficult **Setting** 56-acre suburban campus **Total enrollment** 1,757 **Student-faculty ratio** 17:1 **Application deadline** Rolling (freshmen), rolling (transfer) **Freshman admission** 63% were admitted. Average high school GPA 2.95 **Freshman test scores** SAT critical reading scores over 500: 57%; SAT math scores over 500: 79%; ACT scores over 18: 96%; SAT critical reading scores over 600: 12%; SAT math scores over 600: 28%; ACT scores over 24: 25% **Housing** Yes **Expenses** Tuition & Fees: state resident $6090, nonresident $13,990; Room & Board $9930 **Undergraduates** 10% women, 7% part-time, 9% 25 or older, 0.4% Native American, 9% Hispanic American, 6% African American, 4% Asian American/Pacific Islander **The most frequently chosen baccalaureate fields are** business/marketing, engineering, physical sciences **Academic program** English as a second language, advanced placement, accelerated degree program, honors program, summer session, adult/continuing education programs, internships **Contact** Mr. Jonathan White, Dean of Admissions, State University of New York Maritime College, 6 Pennyfield Avenue, Throggs Neck, NY 10465. *Phone:* 718-409-7222 or toll-free 800-654-1874 (in-state); 800-642-1874 (out-of-state). *Fax:* 718-409-7465. *E-mail:* jwhite@sunymaritime.edu. *Web site:* http://www.sunymaritime.edu/.

See page 1196 for the College Close-Up.

State University of New York Upstate Medical University

Syracuse, New York

General State-supported, upper-level, coed **Entrance** Moderately difficult **Setting** 25-acre urban campus **Total enrollment** 1,443 **Application deadline** Rolling (transfer) **First-year students** 31% were admitted **Housing** Yes **Expenses** Tuition & Fees: state resident $5550, nonresident $13,450; Room & Board $10,422 **Undergraduates** 76% women, 50% part-time, 57% 25 or older, 0.4% Native American, 1% Hispanic American, 10% African American, 4% Asian American/Pacific Islander **The most frequently chosen baccalaureate field is** health professions and related sciences **Academic program** Summer session, internships **Contact** Mrs. Donna L. Vavonese, Associate Director of Admissions, State University of New York Upstate Medical University, Weiskotten Hall, 766 Irving Avenue, Syracuse, NY 13210. *Phone:* 315-464-4570 or toll-free 800-736-2171. *Fax:* 315-464-8867. *E-mail:* admiss@upstate.edu. *Web site:* http://www.upstate.edu/.

Stony Brook University, State University of New York

Stony Brook, New York

General State-supported, university, coed **Entrance** Very difficult **Setting** 1,450-acre small-town campus **Total enrollment** 24,692 **Student-faculty ratio** 19:1 **Application deadline** 3/1 (freshmen), 4/15 (transfer) **Freshman admission** 40% were admitted. Average high school GPA 3.6 **Freshman test scores** SAT critical reading scores over 500: 85%; SAT math scores over 500: 94%; ACT scores over 18: 99%; SAT critical reading scores over 600: 38%; SAT math scores over 600: 67%; ACT scores over 24: 80% **Housing** Yes **Expenses** Tuition & Fees: state resident $6489, nonresident $14,389; Room & Board $9590 **Undergraduates** 48% women, 8% part-time, 10% 25 or older, 0.2% Native American, 9% Hispanic American, 7% African American, 23% Asian American/Pacific Islander **The most frequently chosen baccalaureate fields are** health professions and related sciences, psychology, social sciences **Academic program** English as a second language, advanced placement, self-designed majors, honors program, summer session, adult/continuing education programs, internships **Contact** Ms. Judith Burke-Berhanan, Stony Brook University, State University of New York, Admissions Office, 118 Administration Bldg, Stony Brook, NY 11794-1901. *Phone:* 631-632-6868 or toll-free 800-872-7869. *Fax:* 631-632-9898. *E-mail:* enroll@stonybrook.edu. *Web site:* http://www.sunysb.edu/.

Swedish Institute, College of Health Sciences

New York, New York

Contact Admissions Advisor, Swedish Institute, College of Health Sciences, 226 West 26th Street, New York, NY 10001. *Phone:* 212-

Swedish Institute, College of Health Sciences (continued)
914-5900 Ext. 125. *E-mail:* admissions@swedishinstitute.edu. *Web site:* http://www.swedishinstitute.org/.

Syracuse University
Syracuse, New York

General Independent, university, coed **Entrance** Moderately difficult **Setting** 200-acre urban campus **Total enrollment** 19,638 **Student-faculty ratio** 15:1 **Application deadline** 1/1 (freshmen), 1/1 (transfer) **Freshman admission** 60% were admitted. Average high school GPA 3.6 **Freshman test scores** SAT critical reading scores over 500: 80.5%; SAT math scores over 500: 88.3%; ACT scores over 18: 99%; SAT critical reading scores over 600: 34%; SAT math scores over 600: 50.9%; ACT scores over 24: 72% **Housing** Yes **Expenses** Tuition & Fees $34,926; Room & Board $12,374 **Undergraduates** 57% women, 5% part-time, 4% 25 or older, 1% Native American, 7% Hispanic American, 8% African American, 9% Asian American/Pacific Islander **The most frequently chosen baccalaureate fields are** business/marketing, social sciences, visual and performing arts **Academic program** English as a second language, advanced placement, accelerated degree program, self-designed majors, honors program, summer session, adult/continuing education programs, internships **Contact** Office of Admissions, Syracuse University, 100 Crouse-Hinds Hall, 900 South Crouse Avenue, Syracuse, NY 13244-2130. *Phone:* 315-443-3611. *E-mail:* orange@syr.edu. *Web site:* http://www.syracuse.edu/.

See page 1212 for the College Close-Up.

Talmudical Institute of Upstate New York
Rochester, New York

General Independent Jewish, 5-year, men only **Entrance** Noncompetitive **Setting** 1-acre urban campus **Total enrollment** 26 **Application deadline** Rolling (freshmen), rolling (transfer) **Freshman admission** 100% were admitted **Housing** Yes **Academic program** Self-designed majors **Contact** Rabbi Menachem Davidowitz, Director of Admissions, Talmudical Institute of Upstate New York, 769 Park Avenue, Rochester, NY 14607-3046. *Phone:* 716-473-2810. *E-mail:* yeshiva@tiuny.org. *Web site:* http://www.tiuny.org/.

Talmudical Seminary Oholei Torah
Brooklyn, New York

General Independent religious, 4-year, men only **Setting** urban campus **Total enrollment** 337 **Application deadline** 9/1 (freshmen) **Freshman admission** 100% were admitted **Housing** Yes **Academic program** Honors program **Contact** Rabbi Yisroel Friedman, Director of Academic Affairs, Talmudical Seminary Oholei Torah, 667 Eastern Parkway, Brooklyn, NY 11213-3310. *Phone:* 718-363-2034. *E-mail:* info@oholeitorah.com.

Torah Temimah Talmudical Seminary
Brooklyn, New York

General Independent Jewish, 4-year, men only **Total enrollment** 170 **Freshman admission** 100% were admitted **Housing** Yes **Contact** Principal, Torah Temimah Talmudical Seminary, 507 Ocean Parkway, Brooklyn, NY 11218-5913. *Phone:* 718-853-8500.

Touro College
New York, New York

General Independent, comprehensive, coed **Entrance** Moderately difficult **Setting** urban campus **Total enrollment** 17,129 **Application deadline** Rolling (freshmen), rolling (transfer) **Housing** Yes **Expenses** Tuition & Fees $15,300; Room only $6600 **Undergraduates** 46% 25 or older **Academic program** English as a second language, advanced placement, accelerated degree program, self-designed majors, honors program, summer session, internships **Contact** Mr. Andre Baron, Director of Admissions, Touro College, 27-33 West 23rd Street, New York, NY 10010. *Phone:* 212-463-0400 Ext. 665. *Web site:* http://www.touro.edu/.

Union College
Schenectady, New York

General Independent, 4-year, coed **Entrance** Very difficult **Setting** 100-acre urban campus **Total enrollment** 2,194 **Student-faculty ratio** 10:1 **Application deadline** 1/15 (freshmen), 5/1 (transfer) **Freshman admission** 41% were admitted. Average high school GPA 3.56 **Freshman test scores** SAT critical reading scores over 500: 98.19%; SAT math scores over 500: 99.64%; ACT scores over 18: 100%; SAT critical reading scores over 600: 71.38%; SAT math scores over 600: 82.97%; ACT scores over 24: 93.8% **Housing** Yes **Expenses** Comprehensive Fee $50,439 **Undergraduates** 49% women, 2% part-time, 0.3% Native American, 5% Hispanic American, 5% African American, 7% Asian American/Pacific Islander **The most frequently chosen baccalaureate fields are** biological/life sciences, engineering, social sciences **Academic program** Advanced placement, accelerated degree program, self-designed majors, honors program, summer session, internships **Contact** Dean of Admissions, Union College, Grant Hall, Schenectady, NY 02308. *Phone:* 518-388-6112 or toll-free 888-843-6688. *Fax:* 518-388-6986. *E-mail:* admissions@union.edu. *Web site:* http://www.union.edu/.

Visit Petersons.com and enter keyword Union

See page 1238 for the College Close-Up.

United States Merchant Marine Academy
Kings Point, New York

General Federally supported, comprehensive, coed **Entrance** Very difficult **Setting** 82-acre suburban campus **Total enrollment** 1,003 **Student-faculty ratio** 11:1 **Application deadline** 3/1 (freshmen), 3/1 (transfer) **Freshman admission** 18% were admitted. Average high school GPA 3.6 **Freshman test scores** SAT critical reading scores over 500: 100%; SAT math scores over 500: 100%; ACT scores over 18: 100%; SAT critical reading scores over 600: 43%; SAT math scores over 600: 72%; ACT scores over 24: 98% **Housing** Yes **Expenses** Comprehensive Fee $0 **Undergraduates** 12% women, 1% Native American, 5% Hispanic American, 3% African American, 5% Asian American/Pacific Islander **The most frequently chosen baccalaureate fields are** engineering, transportation and materials moving **Academic program** Honors program, internships **Contact** Capt. Robert E. Johnson, Director of Admissions and Financial Aid, United States Merchant Marine Academy, 300 Steamboat Road, Kings Point, NY 11024-1699. *Phone:* 516-773-5391 or toll-free 866-546-4778. *Fax:* 516-773-5390. *E-mail:* admissions@usmma.edu. *Web site:* http://www.usmma.edu/.

Visit Petersons.com and enter keyword Merchant

See page 1244 for the College Close-Up.

United States Military Academy
West Point, New York

General Federally supported, 4-year, coed **Entrance** Most difficult **Setting** 16,080-acre small-town campus **Total enrollment** 4,621 **Student-faculty ratio** 7:1 **Application deadline** 2/28 (freshmen) **Freshman admission** 14% were admitted **Freshman test scores** SAT critical reading scores over 500: 94%; SAT math scores over 500: 97%; ACT scores over 18: 99%; SAT critical reading scores over 600: 61%; SAT math scores over 600: 70%; ACT scores over 24: 86% **Housing** Yes **Expenses** Comprehensive Fee $0 **Undergraduates** 15% women, 1% Native American, 9% Hispanic American, 6% African American, 7%

Asian American/Pacific Islander **The most frequently chosen baccalaureate fields are** engineering, foreign languages and literature, social sciences **Academic program** Advanced placement, honors program, summer session **Contact** Col. Deborah J. McDonald, Director of Admissions, United States Military Academy, 600 Thayer Road, West Point, NY 10996. *Phone:* 845-938-4041. *E-mail:* 8dad@sunams.usma.army.mil. *Web site:* http://www.usma.edu/.

United Talmudical Seminary

Brooklyn, New York

General Independent Jewish, comprehensive, men only **Total enrollment** 1,500 **Housing** Yes **Undergraduates** 4% 25 or older **Contact** Director of Admissions, United Talmudical Seminary, 191 Rodney Street, Brooklyn, NY 11211. *Phone:* 718-963-9770.

University at Albany, State University of New York

Albany, New York

General State-supported, university, coed **Entrance** Very difficult **Setting** 560-acre suburban campus **Total enrollment** 18,020 **Student-faculty ratio** 19:1 **Application deadline** 3/1 (freshmen), 8/1 (transfer) **Freshman admission** 47% were admitted. Average high school GPA 3.4 **Freshman test scores** SAT critical reading scores over 500: 90%; SAT math scores over 500: 96%; ACT scores over 18: 100%; SAT critical reading scores over 600: 30%; SAT math scores over 600: 45%; ACT scores over 24: 69% **Housing** Yes **Expenses** Tuition & Fees: state resident $6748, nonresident $14,648; Room & Board $10,238 **Undergraduates** 48% women, 6% part-time, 7% 25 or older, 0.3% Native American, 9% Hispanic American, 10% African American, 6% Asian American/Pacific Islander **The most frequently chosen baccalaureate fields are** business/marketing, psychology, social sciences **Academic program** English as a second language, advanced placement, accelerated degree program, self-designed majors, honors program, summer session, internships **Contact** Mr. Robert Andrea, Director of Undergraduate Admissions, University at Albany, State University of New York, 1400 Washington Avenue, Albany, NY 12222-0001. *Phone:* 518-442-5435 or toll-free 800-293-7869. *Fax:* 518-442-5383. *E-mail:* ugadmissions@albany.edu. *Web site:* http://www.albany.edu/.

Visit Petersons.com and enter keywords Albany State University of New York

University at Buffalo, the State University of New York

Buffalo, New York

General State-supported, university, coed **Entrance** Moderately difficult **Setting** 1,350-acre suburban campus **Total enrollment** 28,881 **Student-faculty ratio** 16:1 **Freshman admission** 52% were admitted. Average high school GPA 3.3 **Freshman test scores** SAT critical reading scores over 500: 91%; SAT math scores over 500: 98%; ACT scores over 18: 99%; SAT critical reading scores over 600: 35%; SAT math scores over 600: 63%; ACT scores over 24: 70% **Housing** Yes **Expenses** Tuition & Fees: state resident $7013, nonresident $14,913; Room & Board $9648 **Undergraduates** 46% women, 7% part-time, 5% 25 or older, 0.4% Native American, 3% Hispanic American, 7% African American, 10% Asian American/Pacific Islander **The most frequently chosen baccalaureate fields are** business/marketing, engineering, social sciences **Academic program** English as a second language, advanced placement, accelerated degree program, self-designed majors, honors program, summer session, internships **Contact** Ms. Patricia Armstrong, Director of Admissions, University at Buffalo, the State University of New York, 12 Capen Hall, North Campus, Buffalo, NY 14260-1660. *Phone:* 716-645-6900 or toll-free 888-UB-ADMIT. *Fax:* 716-645-6411. *E-mail:* ub-admissions@buffalo.edu. *Web site:* http://www.buffalo.edu/.

See page 1246 for the College Close-Up.

University of Rochester

Rochester, New York

General Independent, university, coed **Entrance** Very difficult **Setting** 655-acre suburban campus **Total enrollment** 9,976 **Student-faculty ratio** 9:1 **Application deadline** 1/1 (freshmen), 6/1 (transfer) **Freshman admission** 39% were admitted. Average high school GPA 3.8 **Freshman test scores** SAT critical reading scores over 500: 96%; SAT math scores over 500: 98%; ACT scores over 18: 100%; SAT critical reading scores over 600: 70%; SAT math scores over 600: 85%; ACT scores over 24: 96% **Housing** Yes **Expenses** Tuition & Fees $38,690; Room & Board $11,200 **Undergraduates** 52% women, 5% part-time, 2% 25 or older, 0.2% Native American, 4% Hispanic American, 4% African American, 10% Asian American/Pacific Islander **The most frequently chosen baccalaureate fields are** biological/life sciences, psychology, social sciences **Academic program** English as a second language, advanced placement, accelerated degree program, self-designed majors, honors program, summer session, internships **Contact** Office of Admissions, University of Rochester, PO Box 270251, 300 Wilson Boulevard, Rochester, NY 14627-0251. *Phone:* 585-275-3221 or toll-free 888-822-2256. *Fax:* 585-461-4595. *E-mail:* admit@admissions.rochester.edu. *Web site:* http://www.rochester.edu/.

Visit Petersons.com and enter keywords University of Rochester

See page 1304 for the College Close-Up.

U.T.A. Mesivta of Kiryas Joel

Monroe, New York

General Independent Jewish, 4-year, men only **Total enrollment** 989 **Housing** Yes **Undergraduates** 1% 25 or older **Contact** U.T.A. Mesivta of Kiryas Joel, 9 Nickelsburg Road, Unit 312, Monroe, NY 10950.

Utica College

Utica, New York

General Independent, comprehensive, coed **Entrance** Moderately difficult **Setting** 128-acre suburban campus **Total enrollment** 3,273 **Student-faculty ratio** 11:1 **Application deadline** Rolling (freshmen), rolling (transfer) **Freshman admission** 78% were admitted. Average high school GPA 2.91 **Freshman test scores** SAT critical reading scores over 500: 29.96%; SAT math scores over 500: 35.87%; ACT scores over 18: 75.9%; SAT critical reading scores over 600: 5.49%; SAT math scores over 600: 8.86%; ACT scores over 24: 24% **Housing** Yes **Expenses** Tuition & Fees $27,284; Room & Board $10,850 **Undergraduates** 57% women, 19% part-time, 22% 25 or older, 1% Native American, 4% Hispanic American, 11% African American, 2% Asian American/Pacific Islander **The most frequently chosen baccalaureate fields are** health professions and related sciences, business/marketing, security and protective services **Academic program** Advanced placement, accelerated degree program, honors program, summer session, adult/continuing education programs, internships **Contact** Mr. Patrick Quinn, Vice President for Enrollment Management, Utica College, 1600 Burrstone Road, Utica, NY 13502-4892. *Phone:* 315-792-3006 or toll-free 800-782-8884. *Web site:* http://www.utica.edu/.

Visit Petersons.com and enter keywords Utica College

See page 1326 for the College Close-Up.

Vassar College

Poughkeepsie, New York

General Independent, comprehensive, coed **Entrance** Very difficult **Setting** 1,000-acre suburban campus **Total enrollment** 2,453 **Student-faculty ratio** 8:1 **Application deadline** 1/1 (freshmen), 4/1 (transfer) **Freshman admission** 25% were admitted. Average high school GPA 3.77 **Freshman test scores** SAT critical reading scores over 500: 100%; SAT math scores over 500: 100%; ACT scores over 18: 100%; SAT critical reading scores over 600: 95%; SAT math scores over 600: 94%;

UTICA COLLEGE
TRADITION. OPPORTUNITY. TRANSFORMATION.®

Learn to Make a Difference … Right Here.

Since its founding, Utica College has built a tradition of helping people pursue their goals, discover their talents, and achieve success, with programs that include:

- 37 Undergraduate Majors
- 22 Graduate Programs
- Many options for part-time study
- Innovative online programs … and more

UC's excellent academic programs, outstanding faculty, and high degree of personal attention offer students from diverse backgrounds the opportunity to realize their full potential … so that they can make a difference as individuals, professionals, and members of their communities.

Learn more about the UC experience.

Contact us today.

Office of Admissions
(800) 782-8884 • admiss@utica.edu
www.utica.edu

ACT scores over 24: 100% **Housing** Yes **Expenses** Tuition & Fees $41,930; Room & Board $9370 **Undergraduates** 59% women, 2% part-time, 1% 25 or older, 0.3% Native American, 7% Hispanic American, 6% African American, 11% Asian American/Pacific Islander **The most frequently chosen baccalaureate fields are** social sciences, foreign languages and literature, visual and performing arts **Academic program** Advanced placement, self-designed majors, internships **Contact** Dr. David M. Borus, Dean of Admission and Financial Aid, Vassar College, 124 Raymond Avenue, Poughkeepsie, NY 12604. *Phone:* 845-437-7300 or toll-free 800-827-7270. *Fax:* 845-437-7063. *E-mail:* admissions@vassar.edu. *Web site:* http://www.vassar.edu/.

Vaughn College of Aeronautics and Technology

Flushing, New York

General Independent, comprehensive, coed, primarily men **Entrance** Minimally difficult **Setting** 6-acre urban campus **Total enrollment** 1,294 **Student-faculty ratio** 14:1 **Application deadline** Rolling (freshmen), rolling (transfer) **Expenses** Tuition & Fees $16,700; Room & Board $11,280 **Undergraduates** 12% women, 28% part-time, 1% Native American, 37% Hispanic American, 21% African American, 12% Asian American/Pacific Islander **The most frequently chosen baccalaureate fields are** business/marketing, engineering technologies, transportation and materials moving **Academic program** Honors program, summer session, internships **Contact** Mr. Ernie Shepelsky, Vice President, Enrollment Management and Public Affairs, Vaughn College of Aeronautics and Technology, 86-01 23rd Avenue, Flushing, NY 11369. *Phone:* 718-429-6600 Ext. 141 or toll-free 800-776-2376 Ext. 145. *Fax:* 718-779-2231. *E-mail:* ernie.shepelsky@vaughn.edu. *Web site:* http://www.vaughn.edu/.

Visit Petersons.com and enter keyword Vaughn

See page 1332 for the College Close-Up.

Villa Maria College of Buffalo

Buffalo, New York

General Independent, 4-year, coed, affiliated with Roman Catholic Church **Entrance** Minimally difficult **Setting** 9-acre suburban campus **Total enrollment** 503 **Student-faculty ratio** 10:1 **Application deadline** Rolling (freshmen), rolling (transfer) **Freshman admission** 71% were admitted. Average high school GPA 2.65 **Freshman test scores** SAT math scores over 500: 26%; ACT scores over 18: 84%; SAT math scores over 600: 5%; ACT scores over 24: 17% **Housing** Yes **Expenses** Tuition & Fees $14,380 **Undergraduates** 64% women, 17% part-time, 23% 25 or older, 1% Native American, 3% Hispanic American, 22% African American, 1% Asian American/Pacific Islander **Academic program** Advanced placement, summer session, internships **Contact** Mr. Kevin Donovan, Director of Admissions, Villa Maria College of Buffalo, 240 Pine Ridge Road, Buffalo, NY 14211. *Phone:* 716-896-0700 Ext. 1802. *Fax:* 716-896-0705. *E-mail:* admissions@villa.edu. *Web site:* http://www.villa.edu/.

Wagner College

Staten Island, New York

General Independent, comprehensive, coed **Entrance** Moderately difficult **Setting** 105-acre urban campus **Total enrollment** 2,265 **Student-faculty ratio** 13:1 **Application deadline** 2/15 (freshmen), 5/1 (transfer) **Freshman admission** 70% were admitted. Average high school GPA 3.56 **Freshman test scores** SAT critical reading scores over 500: 89%; SAT math scores over 500: 93%; ACT scores over 18: 99%; SAT critical reading scores over 600: 47%; SAT math scores over 600: 50%; ACT scores over 24: 89% **Housing** Yes **Expenses** Tuition & Fees $32,580; Room & Board $9700 **Undergraduates** 63% women, 4% part-time, 5% 25 or older, 0.2% Native American, 6% Hispanic American, 5% African American, 2% Asian American/Pacific Islander **The most frequently chosen baccalaureate fields are** business/marketing, health professions

and related sciences, visual and performing arts **Academic program** Self-designed majors, honors program, summer session, adult/continuing education programs, internships **Contact** Ms. Leigh-Ann Nowicki, Dean of Admissions, Wagner College, 1 Campus Road, Staten Island, NY 10301-4495. *Phone:* 718-420-4242 or toll-free 800-221-1010. *Fax:* 718-390-3105. *E-mail:* leigh-ann.nowicki@wagner.edu. *Web site:* http://www.wagner.edu/.
Visit Petersons.com and enter keyword Wagner

See page 1338 for the College Close-Up.

Webb Institute
Glen Cove, New York

General Independent, 4-year, coed **Entrance** Most difficult **Setting** 26-acre suburban campus **Total enrollment** 89 **Student-faculty ratio** 7:1 **Application deadline** 2/15 (freshmen), 2/15 (transfer) **Freshman admission** 35% were admitted. Average high school GPA 3.8 **Freshman test scores** SAT critical reading scores over 500: 100%; SAT math scores over 500: 100%; SAT critical reading scores over 600: 84%; SAT math scores over 600: 100% **Housing** Yes **Expenses** Tuition & Fees $0; Room & Board $10,200 **Undergraduates** 13% women, 1% 25 or older, 4% Hispanic American, 8% Asian American/Pacific Islander **The most frequently chosen baccalaureate field is** engineering **Academic program** Internships **Contact** Mr. William Murray, Director of Enrollment Management, Webb Institute, Crescent Beach Road, Glen Cove, NY 11542-1398. *Phone:* 516-671-2213. *Fax:* 516-674-9838. *E-mail:* admissions@webb-institute.edu. *Web site:* http://www.webb-institute.edu/.
Visit Petersons.com and enter keywords Webb Institute

See page 1350 for the College Close-Up.

Wells College
Aurora, New York

General Independent, 4-year, coed, primarily women **Entrance** Moderately difficult **Setting** 365-acre rural campus **Total enrollment** 568 **Student-faculty ratio** 9:1 **Application deadline** 3/1 (freshmen), rolling (transfer) **Freshman admission** 64% were admitted. Average high school GPA 3.5 **Freshman test scores** SAT critical reading scores over 500: 77%; SAT math scores over 500: 71%; ACT scores over 18: 95%; SAT critical reading scores over 600: 33%; SAT math scores over 600: 27%; ACT scores over 24: 54% **Housing** Yes **Expenses** Tuition & Fees $29,680; Room & Board $9000 **Undergraduates** 71% women, 2% part-time, 8% 25 or older, 1% Native American, 4% Hispanic American, 6% African American, 2% Asian American/Pacific Islander **The most frequently chosen baccalaureate fields are** psychology, English, social sciences **Academic program** English as a second language, advanced placement, accelerated degree program, self-designed majors, adult/continuing education programs, internships **Contact** Ms. Susan Raith Sloan, Director of Admission, Wells College, 170 Main Street, Aurora, NY 13026. *Phone:* 315-364-3264 or toll-free 800-952-9355. *Fax:* 315-364-3227. *E-mail:* admissions@wells.edu. *Web site:* http://www.wells.edu/.
Visit Petersons.com and enter keywords Wells College

See page 1352 for the College Close-Up.

Yeshiva and Kolel Bais Medrash Elyon
Monsey, New York

General Independent Jewish, 4-year, men only **Total enrollment** 24 **Freshman admission** 100% were admitted **Housing** Yes **Contact** Yeshiva and Kolel Bais Medrash Elyon, 73 Main Street, Monsey, NY 10952.

Yeshiva and Kollel Harbotzas Torah
Brooklyn, New York

General Independent Jewish, 4-year, men only **Total enrollment** 31 **Contact** Yeshiva and Kollel Harbotzas Torah, 1049 East 15th Street, Brooklyn, NY 11230.

Yeshiva Derech Chaim
Brooklyn, New York

General Independent Jewish, comprehensive, men only **Total enrollment** 162 **Freshman admission** 100% were admitted **Housing** Yes **Undergraduates** 3% 25 or older **Contact** Administrator, Yeshiva Derech Chaim, 1573 39th Street, Brooklyn, NY 11218. *Phone:* 718-438-5476.

Yeshiva D'Monsey Rabbinical College
Monsey, New York

General Independent Jewish, 4-year, men only **Total enrollment** 72 **Freshman admission** 100% were admitted **Housing** Yes **Contact** Yeshiva D'Monsey Rabbinical College, 2 Roman Boulevard, Monsey, NY 10952.

Yeshiva Gedolah Imrei Yosef D'Spinka
Brooklyn, New York

General Independent Jewish, 4-year, men only **Total enrollment** 153 **Housing** No **Undergraduates** 5% 25 or older **Contact** Yeshiva Gedolah Imrei Yosef D'Spinka, 1466 56th Street, Brooklyn, NY 11219.

Yeshiva Karlin Stolin Rabbinical Institute
Brooklyn, New York

General Independent Jewish, comprehensive, men only **Entrance** Very difficult **Setting** urban campus **Total enrollment** 69 **Application deadline** Rolling (freshmen), rolling (transfer) **Freshman admission** 100% were admitted **Housing** Yes **Undergraduates** 7% 25 or older **Contact** Director of Admissions, Yeshiva Karlin Stolin Rabbinical Institute, 1818 Fifty-fourth Street, Brooklyn, NY 11204. *Phone:* 718-232-7800 Ext. 26.

Yeshiva of Nitra Rabbinical College
Mount Kisco, New York

General Independent Jewish, comprehensive, men only **Setting** small-town campus **Total enrollment** 214 **Housing** Yes **Contact** Administrator, Yeshiva of Nitra Rabbinical College, Pines Bridge Road, Mount Kisco, NY 10549. *Phone:* 718-384-5460. *Fax:* 718-387-9400.

Yeshiva of the Telshe Alumni
Riverdale, New York

General Independent Jewish, 4-year, men only **Total enrollment** 112 **Freshman admission** 100% were admitted **Housing** Yes **Contact** Yeshiva of the Telshe Alumni, 4904 Independence Avenue, Riverdale, NY 10471.

Yeshiva Shaarei Torah of Rockland
Suffern, New York

General Independent Jewish, 4-year, men only **Total enrollment** 46 **Housing** Yes **Contact** Yeshiva Shaarei Torah of Rockland, 91 West Carlton Road, Suffern, NY 10901.

Yeshiva Shaar Hatorah Talmudic Research Institute
Kew Gardens, New York

General Independent Jewish, comprehensive, men only **Total enrollment** 141 **Housing** Yes **Contact** Assistant Dean, Yeshiva Shaar Hatorah Talmudic Research Institute, 117-06 84th Avenue, Kew Gardens, NY 11418-1469. *Phone:* 718-846-1940.

Yeshivas Novominsk
Brooklyn, New York

General Independent Jewish, 4-year, men only **Total enrollment** 100 **Freshman admission** 100% were admitted **Housing** Yes **Contact** Yeshivas Novominsk, 1569 47th Street, Brooklyn, NY 11219.

Yeshivath Viznitz
Monsey, New York

General Independent Jewish, comprehensive, men only **Setting** small-town campus **Total enrollment** 420 **Freshman admission** 100% were admitted **Housing** Yes **Contact** Registrar, Yeshivath Viznitz, 25 Phyllis Terrace, Monsey, NY 10952. *Phone:* 914-356-1010.

Yeshivath Zichron Moshe
South Fallsburg, New York

General Independent Jewish, comprehensive, men only **Setting** 70-acre small-town campus **Total enrollment** 222 **Freshman admission** 100% were admitted **Housing** Yes **Contact** Rabbi Abba Gorelick, Dean, Yeshivath Zichron Moshe, Laurel Park Road, South Fallsburg, NY 12779. *Phone:* 914-434-5240.

Yeshivat Mikdash Melech
Brooklyn, New York

General Independent Jewish, 4-year, men only **Total enrollment** 87 **Application deadline** Rolling (freshmen) **Freshman admission** 100% were admitted **Housing** Yes **Undergraduates** 17% 25 or older **Contact** Rabbi S. Beyda, Director of Admissions, Yeshivat Mikdash Melech, 1326 Ocean Parkway, Brooklyn, NY 11230-5601. *Phone:* 718-339-1090. *E-mail:* mikdashmelech@verizon.net.

Yeshiva University
New York, New York

General Independent, university, coed **Entrance** Moderately difficult **Setting** urban campus **Total enrollment** 6,246 **Student-faculty ratio** 7:1 **Application deadline** 2/1 (freshmen), rolling (transfer) **Freshman admission** 63% were admitted. Average high school GPA 3.46 **Freshman test scores** SAT critical reading scores over 500: 89.42%; SAT math scores over 500: 89.22%; ACT scores over 18: 98.01%; SAT critical reading scores over 600: 56.9%; SAT math scores over 600: 60.16%; ACT scores over 24: 62.37% **Housing** Yes **Expenses** Tuition & Fees $32,094; Room & Board $10,380 **Undergraduates** 46% women, 3% part-time, 1% 25 or older, 0.1% Native American, 2% Hispanic American, 0.03% African American, 0.1% Asian American/Pacific Islander **The most frequently chosen baccalaureate fields are** business/marketing, biological/life sciences, psychology **Academic program** Advanced placement, self-designed majors, honors program, summer session, internships **Contact** Mr. Michael Kranzler, Director of Undergraduate Admissions, Yeshiva University, 500 West 185th Street, New York, NY 10033-3201. *Phone:* 212-960-5277. *Web site:* http://www.yu.edu/.

York College of the City University of New York
Jamaica, New York

General State and locally supported, comprehensive, coed **Entrance** Moderately difficult **Setting** 50-acre urban campus **Total enrollment** 7,780 **Student-faculty ratio** 17:1 **Application deadline** Rolling (freshmen), rolling (transfer) **Freshman test scores** SAT critical reading scores over 500: 14.8%; SAT math scores over 500: 29.4%; SAT critical reading scores over 600: 1.5%; SAT math scores over 600: 4.2% **Housing** No **Expenses** Tuition & Fees: state resident $4912, nonresident $10,272 **Undergraduates** 66% women, 37% part-time, 32% 25 or older, 0.3% Native American, 14% Hispanic American, 35% African American, 9% Asian American/Pacific Islander **The most frequently chosen baccalaureate fields are** business/marketing, health professions and related sciences, psychology **Academic program** English as a second language, advanced placement, honors program, summer session, adult/continuing education programs, internships **Contact** Ms. Diane Warmsley, Director of Admissions, York College of the City University of New York, 94-20 Guy R. Brewer Boulevard, Jamaica, NY 11451. *Phone:* 718-262-2188. *Fax:* 718-262-2601. *E-mail:* warmsley@york.cuny.edu. *Web site:* http://www.york.cuny.edu/.

NORTH CAROLINA

Apex School of Theology
Durham, North Carolina

General Independent interdenominational, comprehensive, coed **Setting** suburban campus **Total enrollment** 294 **Freshman admission** 100% were admitted **Housing** No **Expenses** Tuition & Fees $4800 **Undergraduates** 55% women, 11% part-time, 100% 25 or older **Contact** Dr. Henry D. Wells Jr., Registrar, Apex School of Theology, 2945 South Miami Boulevard, Suite 114, Durham, NC 27703. *Phone:* 919-572-1625. *Fax:* 919-572-1762. *E-mail:* registrar@apexsot.edu. *Web site:* http://www.apexsot.edu/.

Appalachian State University
Boone, North Carolina

General State-supported, comprehensive, coed **Entrance** Moderately difficult **Setting** 411-acre small-town campus **Total enrollment** 16,968 **Student-faculty ratio** 17:1 **Freshman admission** 63% were admitted. Average high school GPA 3.92 **Freshman test scores** SAT critical reading scores over 500: 88.43%; SAT math scores over 500: 92.37%; ACT scores over 18: 96.78%; SAT critical reading scores over 600: 38.02%; SAT math scores over 600: 43.31%; ACT scores over 24: 55.72% **Housing** Yes **Expenses** Tuition & Fees: state resident $4425, nonresident $15,046; Room & Board $6400 **Undergraduates** 52% women, 5% part-time, 7% 25 or older, 0.4% Native American, 3% Hispanic American, 3% African American, 1% Asian American/Pacific Islander **The most frequently chosen baccalaureate fields are** business/marketing, communications/journalism, education **Academic program** English as a second language, advanced placement, self-designed majors, honors program, summer session, adult/continuing education programs, internships **Contact** Ms. Misti Reese, Interim Director of Admissions, Appalachian State University, Boone, NC 28608. *Phone:* 828-262-2120. *Fax:* 828-262-3296. *E-mail:* admissions@appstate.edu. *Web site:* http://www.appstate.edu/.

The Art Institute of Charlotte
Charlotte, North Carolina

General Proprietary, 4-year, coed **Setting** suburban campus **Academic program** Summer session **Contact** Director of Admissions, The Art Institute of Charlotte, Three LakePointe Plaza, 2110 Water Ridge Parkway, Charlotte, NC 28217. *Phone:* 704-357-8020 or toll-free 800-872-4417. *Fax:* 704-357-1133. *Web site:* http://www.artinstitutes.edu/charlotte/. **Visit Petersons.com and enter keywords Art Institute of Charlotte**

See page 506 for the College Close-Up.

The Art Institute of Raleigh-Durham
Durham, North Carolina

General Proprietary, 4-year, coed **Contact** Director of Admissions, The Art Institute of Raleigh-Durham, 410 Blackwell Street, Suite 200,

Durham, NC 27701. *Phone:* 919-317-3050 or toll-free 888-245-9593. *Fax:* 919-317-3231. *Web site:* http://www.artinstitutes.edu/raleigh-durham.
Visit Petersons.com and enter keywords Art Institute of Raleigh-Durham

See page 538 for the College Close-Up.

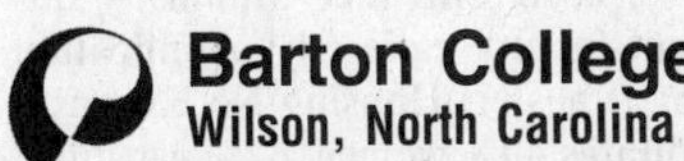

Barton College
Wilson, North Carolina

General Independent, 4-year, coed, affiliated with Christian Church (Disciples of Christ) **Entrance** Minimally difficult **Setting** 76-acre small-town campus **Total enrollment** 1,150 **Student-faculty ratio** 12:1 **Application deadline** Rolling (freshmen), rolling (transfer) **Freshman admission** 51% were admitted. Average high school GPA 3 **Freshman test scores** SAT critical reading scores over 500: 26%; SAT math scores over 500: 33%; ACT scores over 18: 66%; SAT critical reading scores over 600: 5%; SAT math scores over 600: 9%; ACT scores over 24: 6% **Housing** Yes **Expenses** Tuition & Fees $20,648; Room & Board $7012 **Undergraduates** 72% women, 24% part-time, 29% 25 or older, 1% Native American, 2% Hispanic American, 26% African American, 2% Asian American/Pacific Islander **The most frequently chosen baccalaureate fields are** business/marketing, education, health professions and related sciences **Academic program** English as a second language, advanced placement, honors program, summer session, adult/continuing education programs, internships **Contact** Mrs. Amanda Metts, Director of Admissions, Barton College, PO Box 5000, Wilson, NC 27893-7000. *Phone:* 800-345-4973 or toll-free 800-345-4973. *Fax:* 252-399-6572. *E-mail:* ahmetts@barton.edu. *Web site:* http://www.barton.edu/.
Visit Petersons.com and enter keyword Barton

See page 582 for the College Close-Up.

Belmont Abbey College
Belmont, North Carolina

General Independent Roman Catholic, 4-year, coed **Entrance** Moderately difficult **Setting** 650-acre small-town campus **Total enrollment** 1,638 **Student-faculty ratio** 18:1 **Application deadline** 8/1 (freshmen), 8/15 (transfer) **Freshman admission** 63% were admitted. Average high school GPA 3.06 **Freshman test scores** SAT critical reading scores over 500: 55%; SAT math scores over 500: 61%; SAT critical reading scores over 600: 16%; SAT math scores over 600: 14% **Housing** Yes **Expenses** Tuition & Fees $21,506; Room & Board $9948 **Undergraduates** 63% women, 7% part-time, 44% 25 or older, 0.5% Native American, 5% Hispanic American, 27% African American, 2% Asian American/Pacific Islander **The most frequently chosen baccalaureate fields are** business/marketing, education, psychology **Academic program** Advanced placement, accelerated degree program, honors program, summer session, adult/continuing education programs, internships **Contact** Danielle Blanchard, Assistant Director of Admission, Belmont Abbey College, 100 Belmont-Mt. Holly Road, Belmont, NC 28012-1802. *Phone:* 704-461-6668 or toll-free 888-BAC-0110. *Fax:* 704-461-6220. *E-mail:* danielleblanchard@bac.edu. *Web site:* http://www.belmontabbeycollege.edu/.

Bennett College for Women
Greensboro, North Carolina

General Independent United Methodist, 4-year, women only **Entrance** Moderately difficult **Setting** 55-acre urban campus **Total enrollment** 766 **Student-faculty ratio** 11:1 **Application deadline** Rolling (freshmen), rolling (transfer) **Freshman admission** 54% were admitted. Average high school GPA 2.61 **Freshman test scores** SAT critical reading scores over 500: 9%; SAT math scores over 500: 8% **Housing** Yes **Expenses** Tuition & Fees $14,648; Room & Board $6478 **Undergraduates** 7% part-time, 3% 25 or older, 1% Hispanic American, 97% African American, 0.1% Asian American/Pacific Islander **The most frequently chosen baccalaureate fields are** psychology, communications/journalism, public administration and social services **Academic program** Advanced placement, honors program, summer session, adult/continuing education programs, internships **Contact** Ms. Jocelyn Biggs, Director of Admissions, Bennett College for Women, 900 East Washington Street, Campus Box H, Greensboro, NC 27401. *Phone:* 336-517-2167. *E-mail:* jbiggs@bennett.edu. *Web site:* http://www.bennett.edu/.

Brevard College
Brevard, North Carolina

General Independent United Methodist, 4-year, coed **Entrance** Minimally difficult **Setting** 120-acre small-town campus **Total enrollment** 658 **Student-faculty ratio** 10:1 **Application deadline** Rolling (freshmen), rolling (transfer) **Freshman admission** 54% were admitted. Average high school GPA 2.86 **Freshman test scores** SAT critical reading scores over 500: 44%; SAT math scores over 500: 41%; ACT scores over 18: 70%; SAT critical reading scores over 600: 10%; SAT math scores over 600: 6%; ACT scores over 24: 10% **Housing** Yes **Expenses** Tuition & Fees $20,900; Room & Board $7850 **Undergraduates** 43% women, 2% part-time, 5% 25 or older, 1% Native American, 2% Hispanic American, 11% African American, 0.3% Asian American/Pacific Islander **The most frequently chosen baccalaureate fields are** business/marketing, interdisciplinary studies, parks and recreation **Academic program** Advanced placement, self-designed majors, honors program, internships **Contact** Karen Atkins, Associate Director of Admissions, Brevard College, One Brevard College Drive, Brevard, NC 28712. *Phone:* 828-884-8378 or toll-free 800-527-9090. *Fax:* 828-884-3790. *E-mail:* admissions@brevard.edu. *Web site:* http://www.brevard.edu/.
Visit Petersons.com and enter keyword Brevard

Cabarrus College of Health Sciences
Concord, North Carolina

General Independent, 4-year, coed **Entrance** Moderately difficult **Setting** 5-acre suburban campus **Total enrollment** 372 **Student-faculty ratio** 7:1 **Application deadline** 3/1 (freshmen), 3/1 (transfer) **Freshman admission** 43% were admitted. Average high school GPA 3.34 **Freshman test scores** SAT critical reading scores over 500: 44%; SAT math scores over 500: 54%; ACT scores over 18: 91%; SAT critical reading scores over 600: 10%; SAT math scores over 600: 11%; ACT scores over 24: 21% **Housing** No **Expenses** Tuition & Fees $9950 **Undergraduates** 90% women, 39% part-time, 42% 25 or older, 1% Native American, 2% Hispanic American, 6% African American, 2% Asian American/Pacific Islander **The most frequently chosen baccalaureate field is** health professions and related sciences **Academic program** Advanced placement **Contact** Mr. Mark Ellison, Director of Admissions, Cabarrus College of Health Sciences, 401 Medical Park Drive, Concord, NC 28025-2077. *Phone:* 704-403-1616. *Fax:* 704-403-2077. *E-mail:* mellison@cabarruscollege.edu. *Web site:* http://www.cabarruscollege.edu/.

Campbell University
Buies Creek, North Carolina

Contact Ms. Peggy Mason, Director of Admissions, Campbell University, PO Box 546, 450 Leslie Campbell Avenue, Buies Creek, NC 27506. *Phone:* 910-893-1290 or toll-free 800-334-4111. *Fax:* 910-893-1288. *E-mail:* adm@mailcenter.campbell.edu. *Web site:* http://www.campbell.edu/.
Visit Petersons.com and enter keyword Campbell

See page 670 for the College Close-Up.

Carolina Christian College
Winston-Salem, North Carolina

General Independent nondenominational, 4-year, coed **Entrance** Noncompetitive **Setting** 2-acre small-town campus **Total enrollment** 23 **Student-faculty ratio** 40:1 **Application deadline** Rolling (freshmen), rolling (transfer) **Freshman admission** Average high school GPA 3.2

COLLEGES AT-A-GLANCE

Carolina Christian College (continued)
Expenses Tuition & Fees $6200; Room & Board $12,108 **Undergraduates** 43% women, 13% part-time, 80% 25 or older **The most frequently chosen baccalaureate field is** philosophy and religious studies **Academic program** Accelerated degree program, adult/continuing education programs **Contact** Admissions Office, Carolina Christian College, 4209 Indiana Avenue, PO Box 777, Winston-Salem, NC 27102-0777. *Phone:* 336-744-0900. *E-mail:* info@wsbc.edu. *Web site:* http://www.carolina.edu/.

Catawba College
Salisbury, North Carolina

General Independent, comprehensive, coed, affiliated with United Church of Christ **Entrance** Moderately difficult **Setting** 210-acre small-town campus **Total enrollment** 1,358 **Student-faculty ratio** 16:1 **Application deadline** Rolling (freshmen), rolling (transfer) **Freshman admission** 70% were admitted. Average high school GPA 3.48 **Freshman test scores** SAT critical reading scores over 500: 50%; SAT math scores over 500: 60%; ACT scores over 18: 80%; SAT critical reading scores over 600: 14%; SAT math scores over 600: 17%; ACT scores over 24: 38% **Housing** Yes **Expenses** Tuition & Fees $23,740; Room & Board $8200 **Undergraduates** 52% women, 4% part-time, 25% 25 or older, 0.4% Native American, 1% Hispanic American, 18% African American, 1% Asian American/Pacific Islander **The most frequently chosen baccalaureate fields are** business/marketing, education, visual and performing arts **Academic program** Advanced placement, self-designed majors, honors program, summer session, internships **Contact** Mrs. Lois Williams, Vice President for Enrollment Services, Catawba College, 2300 West Innes Street, Salisbury, NC 28144-2488. *Phone:* 704-637-4414 or toll-free 800-CATAWBA. *E-mail:* admissions@catawba.edu. *Web site:* http://www.catawba.edu/.
Visit Petersons.com and enter keyword Catawba

Chowan University
Murfreesboro, North Carolina

General Independent Baptist, 4-year, coed **Entrance** Minimally difficult **Setting** 300-acre rural campus **Total enrollment** 1,080 **Student-faculty ratio** 16:1 **Application deadline** Rolling (freshmen), rolling (transfer) **Freshman admission** 53% were admitted. Average high school GPA 2.7 **Housing** Yes **Expenses** Tuition & Fees $18,850; Room & Board $7310 **Undergraduates** 47% women, 7% 25 or older **Academic program** Advanced placement, self-designed majors, honors program, summer session, internships **Contact** Chad Holt, Vice President of Enrollment Management/Dean of Admissions, Chowan University, One University Place, Murfreesboro, NC 27855. *Phone:* 252-398-6298 or toll-free 888-4-Chowan. *Fax:* 252-398-1190. *E-mail:* holtc@chowan.edu. *Web site:* http://www.chowan.edu.

Davidson College
Davidson, North Carolina

General Independent Presbyterian, 4-year, coed **Entrance** Very difficult **Setting** 556-acre small-town campus **Total enrollment** 1,743 **Student-faculty ratio** 11:1 **Application deadline** 1/2 (freshmen), 3/15 (transfer) **Freshman admission** 26% were admitted. Average high school GPA 4 **Freshman test scores** SAT critical reading scores over 500: 99%; SAT math scores over 500: 99%; ACT scores over 18: 100%; SAT critical reading scores over 600: 88%; SAT math scores over 600: 89%; ACT scores over 24: 98% **Housing** Yes **Expenses** Tuition & Fees $35,124; Room & Board $9906 **Undergraduates** 51% women, 1% Native American, 5% Hispanic American, 7% African American, 5% Asian American/Pacific Islander **The most frequently chosen baccalaureate fields are** history, English, social sciences **Academic program** Advanced placement, self-designed majors, honors program **Contact** Mr. Christopher J. Gruber, Vice President and Dean of Admission and Financial Aid, Davidson College, Box 7156, Davidson, NC 28035-7156. *Phone:* 704-894-2230 or toll-free 800-768-0380. *Fax:* 704-894-2016. *E-mail:* admission@davidson.edu. *Web site:* http://www.davidson.edu/.

DeVry University
Charlotte, North Carolina

General Proprietary, comprehensive, coed **Entrance** Minimally difficult **Total enrollment** 393 **Student-faculty ratio** 64:1 **Application deadline** Rolling (freshmen), rolling (transfer) **Housing** No **Expenses** Tuition & Fees $14,080 **Undergraduates** 49% women, 42% part-time, 76% 25 or older, 0.4% Native American, 6% Hispanic American, 64% African American, 1% Asian American/Pacific Islander **The most frequently chosen baccalaureate fields are** business/marketing, computer and information sciences **Academic program** Advanced placement, accelerated degree program, summer session, adult/continuing education programs **Contact** Admissions Office, DeVry University, 2015 Ayrsley Town Boulevard, Suite 109, Charlotte, NC 28273-4068. *Web site:* http://www.devry.edu/.

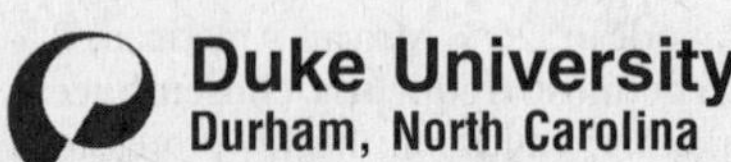

Duke University
Durham, North Carolina

General Independent, university, coed, affiliated with United Methodist Church **Entrance** Most difficult **Setting** 8,500-acre suburban campus **Total enrollment** 14,350 **Student-faculty ratio** 8:1 **Application deadline** 1/2 (freshmen), 3/15 (transfer) **Freshman admission** 19% were admitted **Freshman test scores** SAT critical reading scores over 500: 99%; SAT math scores over 500: 100%; ACT scores over 18: 100%; SAT critical reading scores over 600: 92%; SAT math scores over 600: 95%; ACT scores over 24: 98% **Housing** Yes **Expenses** Tuition & Fees $40,243; Room & Board $11,622 **Undergraduates** 49% women, 0.4% part-time, 0.4% Native American, 7% Hispanic American, 10% African American, 22% Asian American/Pacific Islander **The most frequently chosen baccalaureate fields are** engineering, psychology, social sciences **Academic program** English as a second language, advanced placement, accelerated degree program, self-designed majors, honors program, summer session, adult/continuing education programs, internships **Contact** Mr. Christoph Guttentag, Director of Admissions, Duke University, Durham, NC 27708-0586. *Phone:* 919-684-3214. *E-mail:* askduke@admiss.duke.edu. *Web site:* http://www.duke.edu/.
Visit Petersons.com and enter keyword Duke

See page 762 for the College Close-Up.

East Carolina University
Greenville, North Carolina

General State-supported, university, coed **Entrance** Moderately difficult **Setting** 1,377-acre urban campus **Total enrollment** 27,654 **Student-faculty ratio** 18:1 **Application deadline** 3/15 (freshmen), rolling (transfer) **Freshman admission** 67% were admitted. Average high school GPA 3.44 **Freshman test scores** SAT critical reading scores over 500: 50.16%; SAT math scores over 500: 66.4%; ACT scores over 18: 92.32%; SAT critical reading scores over 600: 7.68%; SAT math scores over 600: 12.9%; ACT scores over 24: 19.96% **Housing** Yes **Expenses** Tuition & Fees: state resident $4477, nonresident $15,311; Room & Board $7480 **Undergraduates** 59% women, 14% part-time, 18% 25 or older, 1% Native American, 2% Hispanic American, 14% African American, 2% Asian American/Pacific Islander **The most frequently chosen baccalaureate fields are** business/marketing, education, health professions and related sciences **Academic program** Advanced placement, accelerated degree program, self-designed majors, honors program, summer session, adult/continuing education programs, internships **Contact** Anthony C. Britt, Director of Admissions, East Carolina University, Undergraduate Admission, Whichard Building 106, Greenville, NC 27858-4353. *Phone:* 252-328-6131. *E-mail:* admis@ecu.edu. *Web site:* http://www.ecu.edu/.

Elizabeth City State University
Elizabeth City, North Carolina

General State-supported, comprehensive, coed **Entrance** Moderately difficult **Setting** 125-acre small-town campus **Total enrollment** 3,264 **Student-faculty ratio** 20:1 **Application deadline** 5/8 (freshmen), 5/8 (transfer) **Freshman admission** 47% were admitted. Average high school GPA 2.79 **Freshman test scores** SAT critical reading scores over 500: 10.82%; SAT math scores over 500: 11.97%; ACT scores over 18: 26.37%; SAT critical reading scores over 600: 1.15%; SAT math scores over 600: 1.31%; ACT scores over 24: 5.49% **Housing** Yes **Expenses** Tuition & Fees: state resident $1681, nonresident $10,730; Room & Board $6828 **Undergraduates** 61% women, 11% part-time, 19% 25 or older, 0.2% Native American, 1% Hispanic American, 80% African American, 0.4% Asian American/Pacific Islander **The most frequently chosen baccalaureate fields are** business/marketing, education, security and protective services **Academic program** Advanced placement, honors program, summer session, adult/continuing education programs, internships **Contact** Mr. Harold Murrill, Director of Admissions, Elizabeth City State University, 1704 Weeksville Road, Elizabeth City, NC 27909-7806. *Phone:* 252-335-3307 or toll-free 800-347-3278. *Web site:* http://www.ecsu.edu/.

Elon University
Elon, North Carolina

General Independent, comprehensive, coed, affiliated with United Church of Christ **Entrance** Moderately difficult **Setting** 580-acre suburban campus **Total enrollment** 5,666 **Student-faculty ratio** 13:1 **Application deadline** 1/10 (freshmen), rolling (transfer) **Freshman admission** 48% were admitted. Average high school GPA 4 **Freshman test scores** SAT critical reading scores over 500: 94%; SAT math scores over 500: 94%; ACT scores over 18: 99%; SAT critical reading scores over 600: 59%; SAT math scores over 600: 63%; ACT scores over 24: 83% **Housing** Yes **Expenses** Tuition & Fees $25,489; Room & Board $8236 **Undergraduates** 59% women, 2% part-time, 1% 25 or older, 0.2% Native American, 2% Hispanic American, 6% African American, 1% Asian American/Pacific Islander **The most frequently chosen baccalaureate fields are** business/marketing, communications/journalism, social sciences **Academic program** English as a second language, advanced placement, accelerated degree program, self-designed majors, honors program, summer session, internships **Contact** Ms. Melinda Wood, Associate Director of Admissions and Director of Applications, Elon University, 100 Campus Box, Elon, NC 27244. *Phone:* 336-278-3566 or toll-free 800-334-8448. *Fax:* 336-278-7699. *E-mail:* admissions@elon.edu. *Web site:* http://www.elon.edu/.

Fayetteville State University
Fayetteville, North Carolina

General State-supported, comprehensive, coed **Entrance** Minimally difficult **Setting** 156-acre urban campus **Total enrollment** 6,283 **Student-faculty ratio** 20:1 **Application deadline** 6/30 (freshmen), 6/30 (transfer) **Freshman admission** 69% were admitted. Average high school GPA 2.76 **Housing** Yes **Expenses** Tuition & Fees: state resident $3301, nonresident $13,483; Room & Board $5010 **Undergraduates** 67% women, 24% part-time, 33% 25 or older, 1% Native American, 4% Hispanic American, 74% African American, 1% Asian American/Pacific Islander **The most frequently chosen baccalaureate fields are** business/marketing, psychology, security and protective services **Academic program** Advanced placement, accelerated degree program, honors program, summer session, adult/continuing education programs, internships **Contact** Ulisa E. Bowles, Director of Admissions, Fayetteville State University, 1200 Murchison Road, Fayetteville, NC 28301-4298. *Phone:* 910-672-1371 or toll-free 800-222-2594. *Fax:* 910-672-1414. *E-mail:* admissions@uncfsu.edu. *Web site:* http://www.uncfsu.edu/.

Gardner-Webb University
Boiling Springs, North Carolina

General Independent Baptist, comprehensive, coed **Entrance** Moderately difficult **Setting** 250-acre small-town campus **Total enrollment** 3,855 **Student-faculty ratio** 13:1 **Application deadline** Rolling (freshmen), rolling (transfer) **Freshman admission** 62% were admitted. Average high school GPA 3.48 **Freshman test scores** SAT critical reading scores over 500: 46%; SAT math scores over 500: 43%; SAT critical reading scores over 600: 17%; SAT math scores over 600: 12% **Housing** Yes **Expenses** Tuition & Fees $22,440; Room & Board $6810 **Undergraduates** 65% women, 15% part-time, 53% 25 or older, 1% Native American, 2% Hispanic American, 19% African American, 0.4% Asian American/Pacific Islander **The most frequently chosen baccalaureate fields are** business/marketing, health professions and related sciences, social sciences **Academic program** English as a second language, advanced placement, accelerated degree program, honors program, summer session, adult/continuing education programs, internships **Contact** Mr. Nathan Alexander, Assistant Vice President of Admissions, Gardner-Webb University, PO Box 817, 110 South Main Street, Boiling Springs, NC 28017. *Phone:* 704-406-4491 or toll-free 800-253-6472. *Fax:* 704-406-4488. *E-mail:* admissions@gardner-webb.edu. *Web site:* http://www.gardner-webb.edu/.

Visit Petersons.com and enter keyword Gardner-Webb

See page 818 for the College Close-Up.

Greensboro College
Greensboro, North Carolina

General Independent United Methodist, comprehensive, coed **Entrance** Moderately difficult **Setting** 75-acre urban campus **Total enrollment** 1,264 **Student-faculty ratio** 11:1 **Application deadline** Rolling (freshmen), rolling (transfer) **Freshman admission** 55% were admitted. Average high school GPA 3.2 **Freshman test scores** SAT critical reading scores over 500: 44%; SAT math scores over 500: 46%; ACT scores over 18: 63%; SAT critical reading scores over 600: 16%; SAT math scores over 600: 23%; ACT scores over 24: 17% **Housing** Yes **Expenses** Tuition & Fees $23,616; Room & Board $8721 **Undergraduates** 55% women, 25% part-time, 33% 25 or older, 0.1% Native American, 2% Hispanic American, 21% African American, 0.2% Asian American/Pacific Islander **The most frequently chosen baccalaureate fields are** education, social sciences, visual and performing arts **Academic program** English as a second language, advanced placement, accelerated degree program, self-designed majors, honors program, summer session, adult/continuing education programs, internships **Contact** Mr. Timothy L. Jackson, Dean of Enrollment Management, Greensboro College, 815 West Market Street, Greensboro, NC 27401-1875. *Phone:* 336-272-7102 or toll-free 800-346-8226. *Fax:* 336-378-0154. *E-mail:* admissions@greensborocollege.edu. *Web site:* http://www.greensborocollege.edu/.

Visit Petersons.com and enter keyword Greensboro

See page 834 for the College Close-Up.

Guilford College
Greensboro, North Carolina

General Independent, 4-year, coed, affiliated with Society of Friends **Entrance** Moderately difficult **Setting** 340-acre suburban campus **Total enrollment** 2,833 **Student-faculty ratio** 15:1 **Application deadline** 2/15 (freshmen), 4/1 (transfer) **Freshman admission** 62% were admitted. Average high school GPA 3.12 **Freshman test scores** SAT critical reading scores over 500: 65%; SAT math scores over 500: 62%; ACT scores over 18: 91%; SAT critical reading scores over 600: 28%; SAT math scores over 600: 24%; ACT scores over 24: 45% **Housing** Yes **Expenses** Tuition & Fees $27,450; Room & Board $7560 **Undergraduates** 59% women, 18% part-time, 41% 25 or older, 1% Native American, 3% Hispanic American, 24% African American, 2% Asian American/Pacific Islander **The most frequently chosen baccalaureate fields are** business/marketing, security and protective services, social

Guilford College (continued)

sciences **Academic program** English as a second language, advanced placement, accelerated degree program, self-designed majors, honors program, summer session, adult/continuing education programs, internships **Contact** Ms. Tania Johnson, Associate Director of Admissions, Guilford College, 5800 West Friendly Avenue, Greensboro, NC 27410. *Phone:* 336-316-2100 or toll-free 800-992-7759. *Fax:* 336-316-2954. *E-mail:* admission@guilford.edu. *Web site:* http://www.guilford.edu/.

See page 838 for the College Close-Up.

Heritage Bible College
Dunn, North Carolina

General Independent Pentecostal Free Will Baptist, 4-year, coed **Entrance** Minimally difficult **Setting** 82-acre small-town campus **Total enrollment** 69 **Student-faculty ratio** 20:1 **Application deadline** Rolling (freshmen), rolling (transfer) **Freshman admission** 50% were admitted **Housing** Yes **Expenses** Tuition & Fees $6840; Room & Board $2800 **Undergraduates** 46% women, 51% part-time, 77% 25 or older, 1% Hispanic American, 32% African American **The most frequently chosen baccalaureate field is** theology and religious vocations **Academic program** Summer session, adult/continuing education programs, internships **Contact** Mrs. Traci Newton, Director of Recruitment & Marketing, Heritage Bible College, PO Box 1628, Dunn, NC 28335-1628. *Phone:* 910-892-3178 Ext. 239 or toll-free 800-297-6351 Ext. 230. *Fax:* 910-891-1660. *E-mail:* tnewton@heritagebiblecollege.edu. *Web site:* http://www.heritagebiblecollege.edu/.

High Point University
High Point, North Carolina

General Independent United Methodist, comprehensive, coed **Entrance** Moderately difficult **Setting** 200-acre suburban campus **Total enrollment** 3,603 **Student-faculty ratio** 16:1 **Application deadline** 8/15 (freshmen), 8/15 (transfer) **Freshman admission** 71% were admitted. Average high school GPA 3.06 **Freshman test scores** SAT critical reading scores over 500: 65%; SAT math scores over 500: 69%; ACT scores over 18: 95%; SAT critical reading scores over 600: 15%; SAT math scores over 600: 19%; ACT scores over 24: 36% **Housing** Yes **Expenses** Comprehensive Fee $35,900 **Undergraduates** 63% women, 4% part-time, 3% 25 or older, 0.4% Native American, 2% Hispanic American, 13% African American, 1% Asian American/Pacific Islander **The most frequently chosen baccalaureate fields are** business/marketing, education, public administration and social services **Academic program** English as a second language, advanced placement, accelerated degree program, self-designed majors, honors program, summer session, adult/continuing education programs, internships **Contact** Ms. Beth McCarthy, Director of Admissions, High Point University, University Station, Montlieu Avenue, High Point, NC 27262-3598. *Phone:* 336-841-9148 or toll-free 800-345-6993. *Fax:* 336-888-6382. *E-mail:* jmcilrat@highpoint.edu. *Web site:* http://www.highpoint.edu/.

Visit Petersons.com and enter keyword High

See page 846 for the College Close-Up.

ITT Technical Institute
Charlotte, North Carolina

General Proprietary, 4-year, coed **Contact** Director of Recruitment, ITT Technical Institute, 10926 David Taylor Drive, Suite 100, Charlotte, NC 28262. *Phone:* 704-548-2300 or toll-free 877-243-7685. *Web site:* http://www.itt-tech.edu/.

ITT Technical Institute
Charlotte, North Carolina

General Proprietary, primarily 2-year, coed **Contact** Director of Recruitment, ITT Technical Institute, 4135 Southstream Boulevard, Suite 200, Charlotte, NC 28217. *Phone:* 704-423-3100 or toll-free 800-488-0173. *Web site:* http://www.itt-tech.edu/.

ITT Technical Institute
High Point, North Carolina

General Proprietary, primarily 2-year, coed **Contact** Director of Recruitment, ITT Technical Institute, 4050 Piedmont Parkway, Suite 110, High Point, NC 27265. *Phone:* 336-819-5900 or toll-free 877-536-5231. *Web site:* http://www.itt-tech.edu/.

ITT Technical Institute
Morrisville, North Carolina

General Proprietary, primarily 2-year, coed **Contact** Director of Recruitment, ITT Technical Institute, 3200 Gateway Centre Boulevard, Suite 105, Morrisville, NC 27560. *Phone:* 919-463-5800 or toll-free 877-203-5533. *Web site:* http://www.itt-tech.edu/.

Johnson & Wales University—Charlotte Campus
Charlotte, North Carolina

General Independent, 4-year, coed **Entrance** Minimally difficult **Total enrollment** 2,452 **Student-faculty ratio** 27:1 **Application deadline** Rolling (freshmen), rolling (transfer) **Freshman admission** 62% were admitted **Freshman test scores** SAT critical reading scores over 500: 38.9%; SAT math scores over 500: 40.3%; SAT critical reading scores over 600: 7.6%; SAT math scores over 600: 11.9% **Housing** Yes **Expenses** Tuition & Fees $24,429; Room & Board $9918 **Undergraduates** 58% women, 1% part-time, 9% 25 or older, 1% Native American, 3% Hispanic American, 24% African American, 2% Asian American/Pacific Islander **The most frequently chosen baccalaureate fields are** business/marketing, family and consumer sciences, parks and recreation **Academic program** English as a second language, advanced placement, accelerated degree program, honors program, internships **Contact** Director of Admissions, Johnson & Wales University—Charlotte Campus, 801 West Trade Street, Charlotte, NC 28202. *Phone:* 866-598-2427 or toll-free 866-598-2427. *Fax:* 980-598-1111. *E-mail:* admissions.clt@jwu.edu. *Web site:* http://www.jwu.edu/charlotte/.

Johnson C. Smith University
Charlotte, North Carolina

General Independent, 4-year, coed **Entrance** Moderately difficult **Setting** 100-acre urban campus **Total enrollment** 1,571 **Student-faculty ratio** 13:1 **Application deadline** 3/15 (freshmen), 5/15 (transfer) **Freshman admission** 30% were admitted. Average high school GPA 2.89 **Freshman test scores** SAT critical reading scores over 500: 9.5%; SAT math scores over 500: 17%; ACT scores over 18: 41%; SAT critical reading scores over 600: 1.5%; SAT math scores over 600: 2%; ACT scores over 24: 2% **Housing** Yes **Expenses** Tuition & Fees $15,754; Room & Board $6132 **Undergraduates** 60% women, 2% part-time, 4% 25 or older, 0.1% Native American, 0.2% Hispanic American, 99% African American **The most frequently chosen baccalaureate fields are** business/marketing, communications/journalism, computer and information sciences **Academic program** Advanced placement, honors program, summer session, adult/continuing education programs, internships **Contact** Dr. Kevin Williams, Director of Admissions, Johnson C. Smith University, 100 Beatties Ford Road, Charlotte, NC 28216. *Phone:* 704-378-3500 or toll-free 800-782-7303. *Fax:* 704-378-1242. *E-mail:* kwilliams@jcsu.edu. *Web site:* http://www.jcsu.edu/.

John Wesley College
High Point, North Carolina

General Independent interdenominational, 4-year, coed **Entrance** Minimally difficult **Setting** 24-acre urban campus **Total enrollment** 95

Student-faculty ratio 7:1 **Application deadline** 8/1 (freshmen), 8/1 (transfer) **Freshman admission** 68% were admitted. Average high school GPA 3.28 **Housing** Yes **Expenses** Tuition & Fees $10,730; Room only $2344 **Undergraduates** 45% women, 29% part-time, 66% 25 or older, 1% Native American, 2% Hispanic American, 35% African American **The most frequently chosen baccalaureate fields are** business/marketing, theology and religious vocations **Academic program** Advanced placement, summer session, adult/continuing education programs, internships **Contact** Jeremy Reese, Admissions Officer, John Wesley College, 2314 North Centennial Street, High Point, NC 27265-3197. *Phone:* 336-889-2262 Ext. 127. *Fax:* 336-889-2261. *E-mail:* admissions@johnwesley.edu. *Web site:* http://www.johnwesley.edu/.

Lees-McRae College

Banner Elk, North Carolina

General Independent, 4-year, coed, affiliated with Presbyterian Church (U.S.A.) **Entrance** Minimally difficult **Setting** 400-acre rural campus **Total enrollment** 906 **Student-faculty ratio** 16:1 **Application deadline** Rolling (freshmen), rolling (transfer) **Freshman admission** 53% were admitted. Average high school GPA 3.05 **Freshman test scores** SAT critical reading scores over 500: 52%; SAT math scores over 500: 49%; ACT scores over 18: 63%; SAT critical reading scores over 600: 13%; SAT math scores over 600: 10%; ACT scores over 24: 16% **Housing** Yes **Expenses** Tuition & Fees $20,500; Room & Board $7000 **Undergraduates** 62% women, 1% part-time, 24% 25 or older, 0.1% Native American, 3% Hispanic American, 8% African American, 0.3% Asian American/Pacific Islander **The most frequently chosen baccalaureate fields are** education, business/marketing, social sciences **Academic program** English as a second language, advanced placement, accelerated degree program, self-designed majors, honors program, summer session, adult/continuing education programs, internships **Contact** Mr. Bill Sliwa, Lees-McRae College, PO Box 128, Banner Elk, NC 28604-0128. *Phone:* 828-898-8723 or toll-free 800-280-4562. *Fax:* 828-898-8707. *E-mail:* admissions@lmc.edu. *Web site:* http://www.lmc.edu/.

Lenoir-Rhyne University

Hickory, North Carolina

General Independent Lutheran, comprehensive, coed **Entrance** Moderately difficult **Setting** 100-acre small-town campus **Total enrollment** 1,562 **Student-faculty ratio** 13:1 **Application deadline** 8/15 (freshmen), 8/15 (transfer) **Freshman admission** 81% were admitted. Average high school GPA 3.59 **Freshman test scores** SAT critical reading scores over 500: 47.8%; SAT math scores over 500: 59%; SAT critical reading scores over 600: 12.1%; SAT math scores over 600: 19.2% **Housing** Yes **Expenses** Tuition & Fees $23,070; Room & Board $8150 **Undergraduates** 64% women, 8% part-time, 10% 25 or older, 0.4% Native American, 2% Hispanic American, 9% African American, 3% Asian American/Pacific Islander **The most frequently chosen baccalaureate fields are** education, business/marketing, health professions and related sciences **Academic program** English as a second language, advanced placement, accelerated degree program, self-designed majors, honors program, summer session, adult/continuing education programs, internships **Contact** Karen Feezor, Lenoir-Rhyne University, 625 7th Avenue NE, Hickory, NC 28601. *Phone:* 828-328-7300 or toll-free 800-277-5721. *Fax:* 828-328-7378. *E-mail:* admission@lr.edu. *Web site:* http://www.lr.edu/.

Livingstone College

Salisbury, North Carolina

Contact Ms. Nicole Daniels, Director of Admissions, Livingstone College, 701 West Monroe Street, Salifbury, NC 28144. *Phone:* 704-216-6001 or toll-free 800-835-3435. *Fax:* 704-216-6215. *E-mail:* admissions@livingstone.edu. *Web site:* http://www.livingstone.edu/.

Mars Hill College

Mars Hill, North Carolina

General Independent Baptist, 4-year, coed **Entrance** Moderately difficult **Setting** 194-acre small-town campus **Total enrollment** 1,237 **Student-faculty ratio** 12:1 **Application deadline** Rolling (freshmen), rolling (transfer) **Freshman admission** 57% were admitted. Average high school GPA 3.17 **Freshman test scores** SAT critical reading scores over 500: 35%; SAT math scores over 500: 44%; ACT scores over 18: 69%; SAT critical reading scores over 600: 11%; SAT math scores over 600: 11%; ACT scores over 24: 27% **Housing** Yes **Expenses** Tuition & Fees $20,849; Room & Board $7285 **Undergraduates** 52% women, 7% part-time, 19% 25 or older, 1% Native American, 3% Hispanic American, 15% African American, 2% Asian American/Pacific Islander **The most frequently chosen baccalaureate fields are** business/marketing, biological/life sciences, education **Academic program** English as a second language, advanced placement, accelerated degree program, self-designed majors, honors program, summer session, adult/continuing education programs, internships **Contact** Ed Hoffmeyer, Dean of Admissions and Financial Aid, Mars Hill College, PO Box 370, Mars Hill, NC 28754. *Phone:* 828-689-1201 or toll-free 866-MHC-4-YOU. *Fax:* 828-689-1473. *E-mail:* ehoffmeyer@mhc.edu. *Web site:* http://www.mhc.edu/.

Meredith College

Raleigh, North Carolina

General Independent, comprehensive, undergraduate: women only; graduate: coed **Entrance** Moderately difficult **Setting** 225-acre urban campus **Total enrollment** 2,262 **Student-faculty ratio** 10:1 **Application deadline** 2/15 (freshmen), 2/15 (transfer) **Freshman admission** 65% were admitted. Average high school GPA 3.27 **Freshman test scores** SAT critical reading scores over 500: 58%; SAT math scores over 500: 61%; ACT scores over 18: 77%; SAT critical reading scores over 600: 17%; SAT math scores over 600: 18%; ACT scores over 24: 29% **Housing** Yes **Expenses** Tuition & Fees $23,550; Room & Board $6740 **Undergraduates** 10% part-time, 12% 25 or older, 1% Native American, 3% Hispanic American, 11% African American, 3% Asian American/Pacific Islander **The most frequently chosen baccalaureate fields are** business/marketing, psychology, visual and performing arts **Academic program** Advanced placement, accelerated degree program, self-designed majors, honors program, summer session, internships **Contact** Ms. Christan Trahey Harris, Director of Admissions, Meredith College, 3800 Hillsborough Street, Raleigh, NC 27807-5298. *Phone:* 919-760-8581 or toll-free 800-MEREDITH. *Fax:* 919-760-2348. *E-mail:* admissions@meredith.edu. *Web site:* http://www.meredith.edu/.

Visit Petersons.com and enter keyword Meredith

See page 958 for the College Close-Up.

Methodist University

Fayetteville, North Carolina

General Independent United Methodist, comprehensive, coed **Entrance** Moderately difficult **Setting** 600-acre suburban campus **Total enrollment** 2,183 **Student-faculty ratio** 12:1 **Application deadline** Rolling (freshmen), rolling (transfer) **Freshman admission** 63% were admitted. Average high school GPA 3.28 **Freshman test scores** SAT critical reading scores over 500: 45%; SAT math scores over 500: 55%; ACT scores over 18: 80%; SAT critical reading scores over 600: 10%; SAT math scores over 600: 16%; ACT scores over 24: 18% **Housing** Yes **Expenses** Tuition & Fees $24,220; Room & Board $8400 **Undergraduates** 45% women, 14% part-time, 24% 25 or older, 1% Native American, 5% Hispanic American, 18% African American, 1% Asian American/Pacific Islander **The most frequently chosen baccalaureate fields are** business/marketing, parks and recreation, social sciences **Academic program** English as a second language, advanced placement, accelerated degree program, honors program, summer session, adult/continuing education programs, internships **Contact** Mr. Jamie Legg, Director of Admissions, Methodist University, 5400 Ramset Street, Fayetteville, NC 28311-1496. *Phone:* 910-630-7027 or toll-free 800-488-7110 Ext. 7027. *Fax:* 910-630-7285. *E-mail:* admissions@methodist.edu. *Web site:* http://www.methodist.edu/.

Mid-Atlantic Christian University
Elizabeth City, North Carolina

General Independent Christian, 4-year, coed **Entrance** Minimally difficult **Setting** 19-acre small-town campus **Total enrollment** 165 **Student-faculty ratio** 12:1 **Application deadline** 8/1 (freshmen), 8/1 (transfer) **Freshman admission** 40% were admitted. Average high school GPA 2.85 **Freshman test scores** SAT critical reading scores over 500: 71%; SAT math scores over 500: 43%; ACT scores over 18: 71%; SAT critical reading scores over 600: 19%; SAT math scores over 600: 19%; ACT scores over 24: 14% **Housing** Yes **Expenses** Tuition & Fees $10,320; Room & Board $6790 **Undergraduates** 42% women, 21% part-time, 28% 25 or older, 2% Hispanic American, 16% African American **The most frequently chosen baccalaureate fields are** business/marketing, foreign languages and literature, theology and religious vocations **Academic program** Advanced placement, internships **Contact** Mrs. Julie A. Fields, Mid-Atlantic Christian University, 715 North Poindexter Street, Elizabeth City, NC 27909-4054. *Phone:* 252-334-2028 or toll-free 800-RBC-8980. *Fax:* 252-334-2064. *E-mail:* julie.fields@macuniversity.edu. *Web site:* http://www.macuniversity.edu/.

Montreat College
Montreat, North Carolina

Contact Kate Rogers, Director of Admissions, Montreat College, PO Box 1267, Montreat, NC 28757-1267. *Phone:* 828-669-8012 or toll-free 800-622-6968. *Fax:* 828-669-0120. *E-mail:* admissions@montreat.edu. *Web site:* http://www.montreat.edu/.

Mount Olive College
Mount Olive, North Carolina

General Independent Free Will Baptist, 4-year, coed **Entrance** Minimally difficult **Setting** 123-acre small-town campus **Total enrollment** 3,569 **Student-faculty ratio** 26:1 **Application deadline** 8/18 (freshmen), rolling (transfer) **Freshman admission** 50% were admitted. Average high school GPA 3.05 **Freshman test scores** SAT critical reading scores over 500: 23.71%; SAT critical reading scores over 600: 3.09% **Housing** Yes **Expenses** Tuition & Fees $13,776; Room & Board $5540 **Undergraduates** 67% women, 21% part-time, 69% 25 or older, 0.5% Native American, 3% Hispanic American, 36% African American, 1% Asian American/Pacific Islander **The most frequently chosen baccalaureate fields are** business/marketing, education, health professions and related sciences **Academic program** Advanced placement, accelerated degree program, honors program, summer session, adult/continuing education programs, internships **Contact** Mr. Tim Woodard, Director of Admissions, Mount Olive College, 634 Henderson Street, Mount Olive, NC 28365. *Phone:* 919-658-2502 Ext. 3009 or toll-free 800-653-0854. *Fax:* 919-658-9816. *E-mail:* admissions@moc.edu. *Web site:* http://www.moc.edu/.

New Life Theological Seminary
Charlotte, North Carolina

Contact Mrs. Paula Emrich, Director of Admission, New Life Theological Seminary, PO Box 790106, Charlotte, NC 28206-7901. *Phone:* 704-334-6882 Ext. 108. *Fax:* 704-334-6885. *E-mail:* pemrich@nlts.edu. *Web site:* http://www.nlts.org/.

North Carolina Agricultural and Technical State University
Greensboro, North Carolina

Contact Mr. Lee Young, Director of Admissions, North Carolina Agricultural and Technical State University, 1601 East Market Street, Greensboro, NC 27411. *Phone:* 336-334-7946 or toll-free 800-443-8964. *Fax:* 336-334-7478. *E-mail:* uadmit@ncat.edu. *Web site:* http://www.ncat.edu/.

North Carolina Central University
Durham, North Carolina

General State-supported, comprehensive, coed **Entrance** Minimally difficult **Setting** 115-acre urban campus **Total enrollment** 8,587 **Student-faculty ratio** 15:1 **Application deadline** 7/1 (freshmen), 7/1 (transfer) **Freshman admission** 81% were admitted. Average high school GPA 2.85 **Freshman test scores** SAT math scores over 500: 14%; ACT scores over 18: 30%; SAT math scores over 600: 3%; ACT scores over 24: 2% **Housing** Yes **Expenses** Tuition & Fees: state resident $3670, nonresident $13,414; Room & Board $6015 **Undergraduates** 66% women, 17% part-time, 23% 25 or older, 0.4% Native American, 1% Hispanic American, 87% African American, 1% Asian American/Pacific Islander **The most frequently chosen baccalaureate fields are** business/marketing, health professions and related sciences, security and protective services **Academic program** English as a second language, advanced placement, honors program, summer session, adult/continuing education programs, internships **Contact** Mr. Anthony Brooks, Undergraduate Director of Admissions, North Carolina Central University, 1801 Fayetteville Street, McDougald House, Durham, NC 27707. *Phone:* 919-530-6298 or toll-free 877-667-7533. *Fax:* 919-530-7625. *E-mail:* admissions@nccu.edu. *Web site:* http://www.nccu.edu/.

North Carolina State University
Raleigh, North Carolina

General State-supported, university, coed **Entrance** Very difficult **Setting** 2,110-acre urban campus **Total enrollment** 33,819 **Student-faculty ratio** 17:1 **Application deadline** 2/1 (freshmen), 4/1 (transfer) **Freshman admission** 55% were admitted. Average high school GPA 4.19 **Freshman test scores** SAT critical reading scores over 500: 85%; SAT math scores over 500: 94%; ACT scores over 18: 99%; SAT critical reading scores over 600: 36%; SAT math scores over 600: 59%; ACT scores over 24: 69% **Housing** Yes **Expenses** Tuition & Fees: state resident $5474, nonresident $17,959; Room & Board $7966 **Undergraduates** 44% women, 13% part-time, 7% 25 or older, 1% Native American, 3% Hispanic American, 8% African American, 5% Asian American/Pacific Islander **The most frequently chosen baccalaureate fields are** business/marketing, biological/life sciences, engineering **Academic program** Advanced placement, accelerated degree program, self-designed majors, honors program, summer session, adult/continuing education programs, internships **Contact** Mr. Thomas Griffin, Director of Undergraduate Admissions, North Carolina State University, Box 7103, Raleigh, NC 27695. *Phone:* 919-515-2434. *Fax:* 919-515-5039. *E-mail:* undergrad_admissions@ncsu.edu. *Web site:* http://www.ncsu.edu/.

North Carolina Wesleyan College
Rocky Mount, North Carolina

Contact Ms. Cecelia Summers, Associate Director of Admissions, North Carolina Wesleyan College, 3400 North Wesleyan Boulevard, Rocky Mount, NC 27804. *Phone:* 252-985-5200 or toll-free 800-488-6292. *Fax:* 252-985-5295. *E-mail:* adm@ncwc.edu. *Web site:* http://www.ncwc.edu/.

Peace College
Raleigh, North Carolina

General Independent, 4-year, women only, affiliated with Presbyterian Church (U.S.A.) **Entrance** Moderately difficult **Setting** 19-acre urban campus **Total enrollment** 693 **Student-faculty ratio** 14:1 **Application deadline** Rolling (freshmen), rolling (transfer) **Freshman admission** 64% were admitted. Average high school GPA 3.3 **Freshman test scores** SAT critical reading scores over 500: 34.4%; SAT math scores over 500: 27%; ACT scores over 18: 46%; SAT critical reading scores over 600: 6.4%; SAT math scores over 600: 6%; ACT scores over 24: 6% **Housing** Yes **Expenses** Tuition & Fees $24,308; Room & Board $8250 **Undergraduates** 5% part-time, 17% 25 or older, 2% Native American, 5% Hispanic American, 19% African American, 2% Asian American/Pacific

Islander **The most frequently chosen baccalaureate fields are** communications/journalism, psychology, social sciences **Academic program** Accelerated degree program, honors program, summer session, adult/continuing education programs, internships **Contact** Mr. Matt Green, Dean of Enrollment, Peace College, 15 East Peace Street, Raleigh, NC 27604-1194. *Phone:* 919-509-2000 Ext. 2016 or toll-free 800-PEACE-47. *Fax:* 919-508-2326. *E-mail:* mtgreen@peace.edu. *Web site:* http://www.peace.edu/.

Pfeiffer University
Misenheimer, North Carolina

General Independent United Methodist, comprehensive, coed **Entrance** Moderately difficult **Setting** 300-acre rural campus **Total enrollment** 2,019 **Student-faculty ratio** 14:1 **Application deadline** Rolling (freshmen), rolling (transfer) **Freshman admission** 71% were admitted. Average high school GPA 3.20 **Freshman test scores** SAT critical reading scores over 500: 35%; SAT math scores over 500: 48%; SAT critical reading scores over 600: 9%; SAT math scores over 600: 14% **Housing** Yes **Expenses** Tuition & Fees $19,040; Room & Board $7798 **Undergraduates** 35% 25 or older, 1% Native American, 3% Hispanic American, 20% African American, 1% Asian American/Pacific Islander **The most frequently chosen baccalaureate fields are** business/marketing, education, security and protective services **Academic program** English as a second language, advanced placement, accelerated degree program, honors program, summer session, internships **Contact** Ms. Diane Martin, Associate Director of Admissions, Pfeiffer University, PO Box 960, Highway 52 North, Misenheimer, NC 28109. *Phone:* 704-463-3052 or toll-free 800-338-2060. *Fax:* 704-463-1363. *E-mail:* admiss@pfeiffer.edu. *Web site:* http://www.pfeiffer.edu/.

Piedmont Baptist College and Graduate School
Winston-Salem, North Carolina

General Independent Baptist, comprehensive, coed **Entrance** Noncompetitive **Setting** 12-acre urban campus **Total enrollment** 373 **Application deadline** Rolling (freshmen), rolling (transfer) **Freshman admission** 48% were admitted **Housing** Yes **Expenses** Tuition & Fees $11,170; Room & Board $5760 **Undergraduates** 32% 25 or older, 2% Hispanic American, 3% African American **Academic program** Advanced placement, summer session, adult/continuing education programs, internships **Contact** Ms. Angela Hoover, Director of Admissions, Piedmont Baptist College and Graduate School, 420 South Broad Street, Winston-Salem, NC 27101-5197. *Phone:* 336-725-8344 Ext. 2322 or toll-free 800-937-5097. *Fax:* 336-725-5522. *E-mail:* admissions@pbc.edu. *Web site:* http://www.pbc.edu/.

Queens University of Charlotte
Charlotte, North Carolina

General Independent Presbyterian, comprehensive, coed **Entrance** Moderately difficult **Setting** 30-acre suburban campus **Total enrollment** 2,568 **Student-faculty ratio** 12:1 **Application deadline** Rolling (freshmen), rolling (transfer) **Freshman admission** 76% were admitted. Average high school GPA 3.6 **Freshman test scores** SAT critical reading scores over 500: 61.9%; SAT math scores over 500: 60%; ACT scores over 18: 92.5%; SAT critical reading scores over 600: 19.6%; SAT math scores over 600: 20%; ACT scores over 24: 38.7% **Housing** Yes **Expenses** Tuition & Fees $22,730; Room & Board $8236 **Undergraduates** 77% women, 31% part-time, 0.5% Native American, 5% Hispanic American, 17% African American, 2% Asian American/Pacific Islander **The most frequently chosen baccalaureate fields are** business/marketing, communications/journalism, health professions and related sciences **Academic program** Advanced placement, honors program, summer session, adult/continuing education programs, internships **Contact** Mr. William Lee, Director of Admissions—Traditional Undergraduate, Queens University of Charlotte, 1900 Selwyn Avenue, Harris Welcome Center, Charlotte, NC 28274. *Phone:* 704-337-2212 or toll-free 800-849-0202. *Fax:* 704-337-2403. *E-mail:* admissions@queens.edu. *Web site:* http://www.queens.edu/.

St. Andrews Presbyterian College
Laurinburg, North Carolina

General Independent Presbyterian, 4-year, coed **Entrance** Moderately difficult **Setting** 600-acre small-town campus **Total enrollment** 600 **Student-faculty ratio** 10:1 **Application deadline** Rolling (freshmen), rolling (transfer) **Freshman admission** 76% were admitted. Average high school GPA 3.04 **Freshman test scores** SAT critical reading scores over 500: 43%; SAT math scores over 500: 47%; ACT scores over 18: 71%; SAT critical reading scores over 600: 9%; SAT math scores over 600: 12%; ACT scores over 24: 15% **Housing** Yes **Expenses** Tuition & Fees $21,190; Room & Board $8672 **Undergraduates** 58% women, 7% part-time, 10% 25 or older, 1% Native American, 3% Hispanic American, 10% African American, 1% Asian American/Pacific Islander **The most frequently chosen baccalaureate fields are** business/marketing, education, psychology **Academic program** Advanced placement, accelerated degree program, self-designed majors, honors program, summer session, adult/continuing education programs, internships **Contact** Kristen Simmons, Director of Admissions, St. Andrews Presbyterian College, 1700 Dogwood Mile, Laurinburg, NC 28352. *Phone:* 910-277-5555 or toll-free 800-763-0198. *Fax:* 910-277-5087. *E-mail:* admission@sapc.edu. *Web site:* http://www.sapc.edu/.

Saint Augustine's College
Raleigh, North Carolina

General Independent Episcopal, 4-year, coed **Entrance** Moderately difficult **Setting** 105-acre urban campus **Total enrollment** 1,529 **Student-faculty ratio** 16:1 **Application deadline** Rolling (freshmen), rolling (transfer) **Freshman admission** 98% were admitted. Average high school GPA 2.4 **Housing** Yes **Expenses** Tuition & Fees $17,160; Room & Board $7126 **Undergraduates** 49% women, 3% part-time, 13% 25 or older, 0.1% Native American, 0.5% Hispanic American, 97% African American, 0.1% Asian American/Pacific Islander **The most frequently chosen baccalaureate fields are** business/marketing, health professions and related sciences, social sciences **Academic program** Advanced placement, accelerated degree program, honors program, summer session, adult/continuing education programs, internships **Contact** Mr. Jorge E. Sousa, Director of Admissions, Saint Augustine's College, 1315 Oakwood Avenue, Raleigh, NC 27610-2298. *Phone:* 919-516-4012 or toll-free 800-948-1126. *Fax:* 919-516-5805. *E-mail:* jesousa@st-aug.edu. *Web site:* http://www.st-aug.edu/.

Salem College
Winston-Salem, North Carolina

General Independent religious, comprehensive, undergraduate: women only; graduate: coed **Entrance** Moderately difficult **Setting** 67-acre urban campus **Total enrollment** 985 **Student-faculty ratio** 11:1 **Application deadline** Rolling (freshmen), rolling (transfer) **Freshman admission** 60% were admitted. Average high school GPA 3.7 **Freshman test scores** SAT critical reading scores over 500: 60%; SAT math scores over 500: 66%; ACT scores over 18: 100%; SAT critical reading scores over 600: 26%; SAT math scores over 600: 21%; ACT scores over 24: 66% **Housing** Yes **Expenses** Tuition & Fees $21,965; Room & Board $11,520 **Undergraduates** 20% part-time, 39% 25 or older, 0.3% Native American, 5% Hispanic American, 18% African American, 1% Asian American/Pacific Islander **Academic program** Advanced placement, self-designed majors, honors program, summer session, adult/continuing education programs, internships **Contact** Dean Katherine Knapp Watts, Dean of Admissions and Financial Aid, Salem College, Single Sisters House, 601 South Church Street, Winston-Salem, NC 27101. *Phone:* 336-721-2621 or toll-free 800-327-2536. *Fax:* 336-917-5572. *E-mail:* admissions@salem.edu. *Web site:* http://www.salem.edu/.

Visit Petersons.com and enter keywords Salem College

Shaw University
Raleigh, North Carolina

General Independent Baptist, comprehensive, coed **Entrance** Minimally difficult **Setting** 30-acre urban campus **Total enrollment** 2,538 **Student-faculty ratio** 16:1 **Application deadline** 7/30 (freshmen) **Freshman admission** 44% were admitted. Average high school GPA 2.35 **Freshman test scores** SAT critical reading scores over 500: 7%; SAT math scores over 500: 8%; ACT scores over 18: 18%; SAT math scores over 600: 1%; ACT scores over 24: 1% **Housing** Yes **Expenses** Tuition & Fees $11,696; Room & Board $7200 **Undergraduates** 63% women, 9% part-time, 39% 25 or older, 0.2% Native American, 0.4% Hispanic American, 86% African American **The most frequently chosen baccalaureate fields are** business/marketing, public administration and social services, security and protective services **Academic program** Advanced placement, accelerated degree program, self-designed majors, honors program, summer session, adult/continuing education programs, internships **Contact** Ms. Sandy Clifton, Interim Director of Admissions and Recruitment, Shaw University, 118 East South Street, Raleigh, NC 27601-2399. *Phone:* 919-546-8275 or toll-free 800-214-6683. *Fax:* 919-546-8271. *E-mail:* sclifton@shawu.edu. *Web site:* http://www.shawu.edu/.

South College–Asheville
Asheville, North Carolina

Contact Director of Admissions, South College–Asheville, 1567 Patton Avenue, Asheville, NC 28806. *Phone:* 828-277-5521. *Fax:* 828-277-6151. *Web site:* http://www.southcollegenc.com/.

Southeastern Baptist Theological Seminary
Wake Forest, North Carolina

General Independent Southern Baptist, comprehensive, coed, primarily men **Setting** 450-acre small-town campus **Total enrollment** 391 **Student-faculty ratio** 17:1 **Application deadline** 7/20 (freshmen), 7/20 (transfer) **Housing** Yes **Undergraduates** 30% women, 42% part-time, 1% Native American, 2% Hispanic American, 2% African American, 2% Asian American/Pacific Islander **The most frequently chosen baccalaureate field is** philosophy and religious studies **Academic program** Summer session, adult/continuing education programs, internships **Contact** Ms. Penny Keathley, Admissions Counselor, Southeastern Baptist Theological Seminary, PO Box 1889, Wake Forest, NC 27588-1889. *Phone:* 800-284-6317 or toll-free 800-284-6317. *E-mail:* admissions@sebts.edu. *Web site:* http://www.sebts.edu/.

Strayer University–Garner Campus
Raleigh, North Carolina

General Proprietary, comprehensive, coed **Contact** Admissions Office, Strayer University–Garner Campus, 1812 Garner Station Boulevard, Raleigh, NC 27603. *Phone:* 919-890-7500. *Web site:* http://www.strayer.edu/garner.

Strayer University–Greensboro Campus
Greensboro, North Carolina

General Proprietary, comprehensive, coed **Contact** Admissions Office, Strayer University–Greensboro Campus, 4900 Koger Boulevard, Suite 400, Greensboro, NC 27407. *Phone:* 336-315-7800. *Web site:* http://www.strayer.edu/greensboro.

Strayer University–Huntersville Campus
Huntersville, North Carolina

General Proprietary, comprehensive, coed **Contact** Admissions Office, Strayer University–Huntersville Campus, 13620 Reese Boulevard, Suite 130, Huntersville, NC 28078. *Phone:* 704-379-6800. *Web site:* http://www.strayer.edu/huntersville.

Strayer University–North Charlotte Campus
Charlotte, North Carolina

General Proprietary, comprehensive, coed **Contact** Admissions Office, Strayer University–North Charlotte Campus, 8335 IBM Drive, Suite 150, Charlotte, NC 28262. *Phone:* 704-717-4000. *Web site:* http://www.strayer.edu/north_charlotte.

Strayer University–North Raleigh Campus
Raleigh, North Carolina

General Proprietary, comprehensive, coed **Contact** Admissions Office, Strayer University–North Raleigh Campus, 3200 Spring Forest Road, Suite 214, Raleigh, NC 27616. *Phone:* 919-878-9900. *Web site:* http://www.strayer.edu/north_raleigh.

Strayer University–RTP Campus
Morrisville, North Carolina

General Proprietary, comprehensive, coed **Contact** Admissions Office, Strayer University–RTP Campus, 4 Copley Parkway, Morrisville, NC 27560. *Phone:* 919-466-4400. *Web site:* http://www.strayer.edu/rtp_campus.

Strayer University–South Charlotte Campus
Charlotte, North Carolina

General Proprietary, comprehensive, coed **Contact** Admissions Office, Strayer University–South Charlotte Campus, 9101 Kings Parade Boulevard, Suite 200, Charlotte, NC 28273. *Phone:* 704-499-9200. *Web site:* http://www.strayer.edu/south_charlotte.

The University of North Carolina at Asheville
Asheville, North Carolina

General State-supported, comprehensive, coed **Entrance** Moderately difficult **Setting** 265-acre suburban campus **Total enrollment** 3,897 **Student-faculty ratio** 14:1 **Application deadline** 2/15 (freshmen), 3/15 (transfer) **Freshman admission** 77% were admitted. Average high school GPA 3.91 **Freshman test scores** SAT critical reading scores over 500: 88.4%; SAT math scores over 500: 88.5%; ACT scores over 18: 100%; SAT critical reading scores over 600: 49.9%; SAT math scores over 600: 44.3%; ACT scores over 24: 64.2% **Housing** Yes **Expenses** Tuition & Fees: state resident $4411, nonresident $16,128; Room & Board $6890 **Undergraduates** 57% women, 19% part-time, 15% 25 or older **The most frequently chosen baccalaureate fields are** psychology, social sciences, visual and performing arts **Academic program** Advanced placement, self-designed majors, honors program, summer session, adult/continuing education programs, internships **Contact** Ms. Leigh McBride, Associate Director of Admissions, The University of North Carolina at Asheville, University Dining Hall, CPO # 1320, Asheville, NC 28804-8510. *Phone:* 828-251-6481 or toll-free 800-531-9842. *Fax:* 828-251-6482. *E-mail:* admissions@unca.edu. *Web site:* http://www.unca.edu/.

The University of North Carolina at Chapel Hill
Chapel Hill, North Carolina

General State-supported, university, coed **Entrance** Very difficult **Setting** 729-acre suburban campus **Total enrollment** 28,916 **Student-faculty**

ratio 14:1 **Application deadline** 1/15 (freshmen), 3/1 (transfer) **Freshman admission** 32% were admitted. Average high school GPA 4.47 **Freshman test scores** SAT critical reading scores over 500: 96.63%; SAT math scores over 500: 97.96%; ACT scores over 18: 99.53%; SAT critical reading scores over 600: 73.06%; SAT math scores over 600: 83.2%; ACT scores over 24: 90.38% **Housing** Yes **Expenses** Tuition & Fees: state resident $5626, nonresident $23,514; Room & Board $8670 **Undergraduates** 59% women, 4% part-time, 4% 25 or older, 1% Native American, 5% Hispanic American, 11% African American, 7% Asian American/Pacific Islander **The most frequently chosen baccalaureate fields are** communications/journalism, psychology, social sciences **Academic program** Advanced placement, self-designed majors, honors program, summer session, internships **Contact** Mr. Stephen Farmer, Assistant Provost and Director of Undergraduate Admissions, The University of North Carolina at Chapel Hill, Chapel Hill, NC 27599. *Phone:* 919-966-3621. *Fax:* 919-962-3045. *E-mail:* uadm@email.unc.edu. *Web site:* http://www.unc.edu/.

The University of North Carolina at Charlotte

Charlotte, North Carolina

General State-supported, university, coed **Entrance** Moderately difficult **Setting** 1,000-acre suburban campus **Total enrollment** 24,701 **Student-faculty ratio** 19:1 **Application deadline** 7/1 (freshmen), 7/1 (transfer) **Freshman admission** 76% were admitted. Average high school GPA 3.54 **Freshman test scores** SAT critical reading scores over 500: 59%; SAT math scores over 500: 73%; ACT scores over 18: 92%; SAT critical reading scores over 600: 12%; SAT math scores over 600: 24%; ACT scores over 24: 28% **Housing** Yes **Expenses** Tuition & Fees: state resident $4427, nonresident $15,039; Room & Board $6796 **Undergraduates** 51% women, 15% part-time, 20% 25 or older, 0.4% Native American, 5% Hispanic American, 16% African American, 5% Asian American/Pacific Islander **The most frequently chosen baccalaureate fields are** business/marketing, education, psychology **Academic program** English as a second language, advanced placement, accelerated degree program, honors program, summer session, adult/continuing education programs, internships **Contact** Tina McEntire, Director of Admissions, The University of North Carolina at Charlotte, 9201 University City Boulevard, 1st Floor, Cato Hall, Charlotte, NC 28223-0001. *Phone:* 704-687-2213. *Fax:* 704-687-6483. *E-mail:* unccadm@uncc.edu. *Web site:* http://www.uncc.edu/.

The University of North Carolina at Greensboro

Greensboro, North Carolina

General State-supported, university, coed **Entrance** Moderately difficult **Setting** 357-acre urban campus **Total enrollment** 18,433 **Student-faculty ratio** 17:1 **Application deadline** 3/1 (freshmen), 8/1 (transfer) **Freshman admission** 73% were admitted. Average high school GPA 3.58 **Freshman test scores** SAT critical reading scores over 500: 53.96%; SAT math scores over 500: 59.29%; SAT critical reading scores over 600: 14.64%; SAT math scores over 600: 15.34% **Housing** Yes **Expenses** Tuition & Fees: state resident $4234, nonresident $15,995; Room & Board $6506 **Undergraduates** 67% women, 12% part-time, 17% 25 or older, 0.4% Native American, 2% Hispanic American, 22% African American, 4% Asian American/Pacific Islander **The most frequently chosen baccalaureate fields are** business/marketing, education, health professions and related sciences **Academic program** Advanced placement, accelerated degree program, honors program, summer session, adult/continuing education programs, internships **Contact** Ms. Lise Keller, Director of Admissions, The University of North Carolina at Greensboro, Armfield-Preyer Admissions and Visitor Center, 1400 Spring Garden Street, Greensboro, NC 27412. *Phone:* 336-334-5243. *Fax:* 336-334-4180. *E-mail:* admissions@uncg.edu. *Web site:* http://www.uncg.edu/.

The University of North Carolina at Pembroke

Pembroke, North Carolina

General State-supported, comprehensive, coed **Entrance** Moderately difficult **Setting** 161-acre rural campus **Total enrollment** 6,661 **Student-faculty ratio** 15:1 **Application deadline** Rolling (freshmen), rolling (transfer) **Freshman admission** 79% were admitted. Average high school GPA 3.07 **Housing** Yes **Expenses** Tuition & Fees: state resident $3890, nonresident $13,097; Room & Board $5990 **Undergraduates** 61% women, 20% part-time, 36% 25 or older **The most frequently chosen baccalaureate fields are** education, biological/life sciences, social sciences **Academic program** English as a second language, advanced placement, accelerated degree program, honors program, summer session, adult/continuing education programs, internships **Contact** Ms. Jennifer McNeil, Associate Director of Admissions, The University of North Carolina at Pembroke, PO Box 1510, Pembroke, NC 28372-1510. *Phone:* 910-521-6507 or toll-free 800-949-UNCP. *Fax:* 910-521-6497. *E-mail:* jennifer.mcneill@uncp.edu. *Web site:* http://www.uncp.edu/.

Visit Petersons.com and enter keyword Pembroke

See page 1294 for the College Close-Up.

University of North Carolina School of the Arts

Winston-Salem, North Carolina

General State-supported, comprehensive, coed **Entrance** Very difficult **Setting** 57-acre urban campus **Total enrollment** 873 **Student-faculty ratio** 8:1 **Application deadline** 3/1 (freshmen), rolling (transfer) **Freshman admission** 45% were admitted **Housing** Yes **Expenses** Tuition & Fees: state resident $5299, nonresident $17,245; Room & Board $7256 **Undergraduates** 40% women, 1% part-time, 1% 25 or older **The most frequently chosen baccalaureate field is** visual and performing arts **Academic program** English as a second language, advanced placement, internships **Contact** Ms. Sheeler Lawson, Director of Admissions, University of North Carolina School of the Arts, 1533 South Main Street, PO Box 12189, Winston-Salem, NC 27127-2188. *Phone:* 336-770-3290. *E-mail:* admissions@uncsa.edu. *Web site:* http://www.ncarts.edu/.

The University of North Carolina Wilmington

Wilmington, North Carolina

General State-supported, comprehensive, coed **Entrance** Moderately difficult **Setting** 656-acre urban campus **Total enrollment** 12,413 **Student-faculty ratio** 17:1 **Application deadline** 2/1 (freshmen), 3/1 (transfer) **Freshman admission** 58% were admitted. Average high school GPA 3.78 **Freshman test scores** SAT critical reading scores over 500: 88%; SAT math scores over 500: 92%; ACT scores over 18: 99%; SAT critical reading scores over 600: 31%; SAT math scores over 600: 39%; ACT scores over 24: 60% **Housing** Yes **Expenses** Tuition & Fees: state resident $4873, nonresident $15,755; Room & Board $7798 **Undergraduates** 58% women, 9% part-time, 19% 25 or older, 1% Native American, 4% Hispanic American, 4% African American, 2% Asian American/Pacific Islander **The most frequently chosen baccalaureate fields are** business/marketing, education, psychology **Academic program** English as a second language, advanced placement, accelerated degree program, honors program, summer session, internships **Contact** Dr. Terrence M. Curran, Associate Provost, The University of North Carolina Wilmington, 601 South College Road, Wilmington, NC 28403-3297. *Phone:* 910-962-3876 or toll-free 800-228-5571. *Fax:* 910-962-3922. *E-mail:* admissions@uncw.edu. *Web site:* http://www.uncw.edu/.

COLLEGES AT-A-GLANCE

University of Phoenix–Charlotte Campus
Charlotte, North Carolina

General Proprietary, comprehensive, coed **Entrance** Noncompetitive **Setting** urban campus **Total enrollment** 1,149 **Application deadline** Rolling (freshmen), rolling (transfer) **Housing** No **Expenses** Tuition & Fees $11,300 **Undergraduates** 67% women, 88% 25 or older, 0.5% Native American, 4% Hispanic American, 47% African American, 1% Asian American/Pacific Islander **The most frequently chosen baccalaureate fields are** business/marketing, computer and information sciences **Academic program** Advanced placement, accelerated degree program **Contact** Ms. Audra McQuarie, Registrar/Executive Director, University of Phoenix–Charlotte Campus, 4035 South Riverpoint Parkway, Mail Stop CF-L101, Phoenix, AZ 85040. *Phone:* 480-557-6151 or toll-free 800-776-4867 (in-state); 800-228-7240 (out-of-state). *Fax:* 480-643-3068. *E-mail:* audra.mcquarie@phoenix.edu. *Web site:* http://www.phoenix.edu/.

University of Phoenix–Raleigh Campus
Raleigh, North Carolina

General Proprietary, comprehensive, coed **Entrance** Noncompetitive **Setting** urban campus **Total enrollment** 500 **Application deadline** Rolling (freshmen), rolling (transfer) **Housing** No **Expenses** Tuition & Fees $11,775 **Undergraduates** 58% women, 88% 25 or older, 0.3% Native American, 1% Hispanic American, 37% African American, 1% Asian American/Pacific Islander **The most frequently chosen baccalaureate fields are** business/marketing, computer and information sciences, security and protective services **Academic program** Advanced placement, accelerated degree program **Contact** Ms. Audra McQuarie, Registrar/Executive Director, University of Phoenix–Raleigh Campus, 4035 South Riverpoint Parkway, Mail Stop CF-L101, Phoenix, AZ 85040. *Phone:* 480-557-6151 or toll-free 800-776-4867 (in-state); 800-228-7240 (out-of-state). *Fax:* 480-643-3068. *E-mail:* audra.mcquarie@phoenix.edu. *Web site:* http://www.phoenix.edu/.

Wake Forest University
Winston-Salem, North Carolina

General Independent, university, coed **Entrance** Very difficult **Setting** 340-acre suburban campus **Total enrollment** 7,079 **Student-faculty ratio** 11:1 **Application deadline** 1/1 (freshmen) **Freshman admission** 38% were admitted **Freshman test scores** SAT critical reading scores over 500: 93.7%; SAT math scores over 500: 95.5%; ACT scores over 18: 99.8%; SAT critical reading scores over 600: 71.4%; SAT math scores over 600: 79.2%; ACT scores over 24: 90.9% **Housing** Yes **Expenses** Tuition & Fees $39,970; Room & Board $11,010 **Undergraduates** 51% women, 1% part-time, 0.5% Native American, 4% Hispanic American, 7% African American, 6% Asian American/Pacific Islander **The most frequently chosen baccalaureate fields are** business/marketing, history, social sciences **Academic program** Advanced placement, honors program, summer session, internships **Contact** Ms. Martha Allman, Director of Admissions, Wake Forest University, PO Box 7373, Reynolda Station, Winston-Salem, NC 27109. *Phone:* 336-758-5201. *Web site:* http://www.wfu.edu/.

Warren Wilson College
Asheville, North Carolina

General Independent, comprehensive, coed, affiliated with Presbyterian Church (U.S.A.) **Entrance** Moderately difficult **Setting** 1,135-acre small-town campus **Total enrollment** 1,002 **Student-faculty ratio** 13:1 **Application deadline** 3/15 (freshmen), 3/15 (transfer) **Freshman admission** 76% were admitted. Average high school GPA 3.2 **Freshman test scores** SAT critical reading scores over 500: 89%; SAT math scores over 500: 69%; ACT scores over 18: 98%; SAT critical reading scores over 600: 52%; SAT math scores over 600: 23%; ACT scores over 24: 74% **Housing** Yes **Expenses** Tuition & Fees $24,196; Room & Board $7770 **Undergraduates** 60% women, 1% part-time, 2% 25 or older, 0.4% Native American, 2% Hispanic American, 1% African American, 1% Asian American/Pacific Islander **The most frequently chosen baccalaureate fields are** natural resources/environmental science, interdisciplinary studies, social sciences **Academic program** English as a second language, advanced placement, self-designed majors, honors program, internships **Contact** Mr. Richard Blomgren, Dean of Admission, Warren Wilson College, PO Box 9000, Asheville, NC 28815-9000. *Phone:* 828-771-2073 or toll-free 800-934-3536. *Fax:* 828-298-1440. *E-mail:* admit@warren-wilson.edu. *Web site:* http://www.warren-wilson.edu/.

Visit Petersons.com and enter keyword Warren

See page 1344 for the College Close-Up.

Western Carolina University
Cullowhee, North Carolina

General State-supported, comprehensive, coed **Entrance** Moderately difficult **Setting** 682-acre rural campus **Total enrollment** 9,429 **Student-faculty ratio** 15:1 **Application deadline** 3/1 (freshmen), 6/1 (transfer) **Freshman admission** 19% were admitted. Average high school GPA 3.49 **Freshman test scores** SAT critical reading scores over 500: 53%; SAT math scores over 500: 62%; ACT scores over 18: 85%; SAT critical reading scores over 600: 13%; SAT math scores over 600: 15%; ACT scores over 24: 20% **Housing** Yes **Expenses** Tuition & Fees: state resident $4330, nonresident $13,927; Room & Board $5912 **Undergraduates** 54% women, 17% part-time, 19% 25 or older, 1% Native American, 2% Hispanic American, 6% African American, 1% Asian American/Pacific Islander **The most frequently chosen baccalaureate fields are** business/marketing, education, health professions and related sciences **Academic program** English as a second language, advanced placement, self-designed majors, honors program, summer session, internships **Contact** Mr. Chris Parrish, Senior Assistant Director of Admissions, Western Carolina University, 102 Cordelia Camp Building, Cullowhee, NC 28723. *Phone:* 828-227-7317 or toll-free 877-WCU4YOU. *E-mail:* admiss@email.wcu.edu. *Web site:* http://www.wcu.edu/.

Wingate University
Wingate, North Carolina

General Independent Baptist, comprehensive, coed **Entrance** Moderately difficult **Setting** 330-acre small-town campus **Total enrollment** 2,159 **Student-faculty ratio** 13:1 **Application deadline** Rolling (freshmen), rolling (transfer) **Freshman admission** 52% were admitted. Average high school GPA 3.61 **Freshman test scores** SAT critical reading scores over 500: 46%; SAT math scores over 500: 61%; ACT scores over 18: 86%; SAT critical reading scores over 600: 11%; SAT math scores over 600: 20%; ACT scores over 24: 34% **Housing** Yes **Expenses** Tuition & Fees $21,140; Room & Board $8350 **Undergraduates** 54% women, 3% part-time, 6% 25 or older, 1% Native American, 3% Hispanic American, 10% African American, 2% Asian American/Pacific Islander **The most frequently chosen baccalaureate fields are** business/marketing, biological/life sciences, communications/journalism **Academic program** Advanced placement, honors program, summer session, internships **Contact** Ms. Lindsay Kreis, Director of Student Recruitment, Wingate University, PO Box 159, Wingate, NC 28174. *Phone:* 704-233-8000 or toll-free 800-755-5550. *Fax:* 704-233-8110. *E-mail:* admit@wingate.edu. *Web site:* http://www.wingate.edu/.

Winston-Salem State University
Winston-Salem, North Carolina

General State-supported, comprehensive, coed **Entrance** Minimally difficult **Setting** 94-acre urban campus **Total enrollment** 6,427 **Student-faculty ratio** 19:1 **Application deadline** 2/15 (freshmen), rolling (transfer) **Freshman admission** 57% were admitted. Average high school GPA 3.01 **Freshman test scores** SAT critical reading scores over 500: 14%; SAT math scores over 500: 15%; ACT scores over 18: 42.76%; SAT critical reading scores over 600: 2%; SAT math scores over 600: 2%; ACT scores over 24: 3.14% **Housing** Yes **Expenses** Tuition & Fees: state resident $3522, nonresident $12,508; Room & Board $6954 **Undergraduates** 70% women, 11% part-time, 31% 25 or older, 0.4% Native American, 1% Hispanic American, 81% African American, 1% Asian American/Pacific Islander **The most frequently chosen baccalaureate fields are** business/marketing, health professions and related sciences, social sciences **Academic program** Advanced placement, accelerated degree program, honors program, summer session, internships **Contact** Ms. Tomikia LeGrande, Assistant Vice Chancellor for Enrollment Services, Winston-Salem State University, 601 Martin Luther King Jr. Drive, Thompson Center, Winston-Salem, NC 27110. *Phone:* 336-750-2070 or toll-free 800-257-4052. *Fax:* 336-750-2079. *E-mail:* Legrandet@wssu.edu. *Web site:* http://www.wssu.edu/.

NORTH DAKOTA

Dickinson State University

Dickinson, North Dakota

General State-supported, 4-year, coed **Entrance** Minimally difficult **Setting** 132-acre small-town campus **Total enrollment** 2,767 **Student-faculty ratio** 15:1 **Application deadline** Rolling (freshmen), rolling (transfer) **Freshman admission** 96% were admitted. Average high school GPA 3.22 **Freshman test scores** SAT critical reading scores over 500: 46%; ACT scores over 18: 78%; SAT critical reading scores over 600: 9%; ACT scores over 24: 21% **Housing** Yes **Expenses** Tuition & Fees: state resident $5249, nonresident $12,195; Room & Board $4262 **Undergraduates** 62% women, 35% part-time, 20% 25 or older, 2% Native American, 2% Hispanic American, 1% African American, 1% Asian American/Pacific Islander **The most frequently chosen baccalaureate fields are** business/marketing, communications/journalism, education **Academic program** Advanced placement, accelerated degree program, self-designed majors, honors program, summer session, adult/continuing education programs, internships **Contact** Mr. Norman Coley, Director of Enrollment Services, Dickinson State University, Campus Box 169, Dickinson, ND 58601. *Phone:* 701-483-2175 or toll-free 800-279-4295. *Fax:* 701-483-2409. *E-mail:* dsu.hawks@dsu.nodak.edu. *Web site:* http://www.dsu.nodak.edu/.

Jamestown College

Jamestown, North Dakota

General Independent Presbyterian, 4-year, coed **Entrance** Minimally difficult **Setting** 110-acre small-town campus **Total enrollment** 1,004 **Student-faculty ratio** 15:1 **Application deadline** Rolling (freshmen), rolling (transfer) **Freshman admission** 67% were admitted. Average high school GPA 3.34 **Freshman test scores** ACT scores over 18: 94%; ACT scores over 24: 38% **Housing** Yes **Expenses** Tuition & Fees $16,780; Room & Board $5536 **Undergraduates** 54% women, 7% part-time, 8% 25 or older, 1% Native American, 2% Hispanic American, 1% African American, 1% Asian American/Pacific Islander **The most frequently chosen baccalaureate fields are** business/marketing, education, health professions and related sciences **Academic program** Advanced placement, self-designed majors, honors program, summer session, internships **Contact** Ms. Tena Lawrence, Dean of Enrollment Management, Jamestown College, 6000 College Lane, Jamestown, ND 58405. *Phone:* 701-252-3467 Ext. 5512 or toll-free 800-336-2554. *E-mail:* admissions@jc.edu. *Web site:* http://www.jc.edu/.

Mayville State University

Mayville, North Dakota

General State-supported, 4-year, coed **Entrance** Noncompetitive **Setting** 60-acre rural campus **Total enrollment** 887 **Student-faculty ratio** 14:1 **Application deadline** Rolling (freshmen), rolling (transfer) **Freshman admission** 57% were admitted. Average high school GPA 2.93 **Freshman test scores** ACT scores over 18: 62%; ACT scores over 24: 15% **Housing** Yes **Expenses** Tuition & Fees: state resident $5793, nonresident $7849; Room & Board $4488 **Undergraduates** 57% women, 39% part-time, 6% 25 or older, 2% Native American, 4% Hispanic American, 6% African American, 1% Asian American/Pacific Islander **The most frequently chosen baccalaureate fields are** business/marketing, education, parks and recreation **Academic program** Advanced placement, accelerated degree program, self-designed majors, summer session, adult/continuing education programs, internships **Contact** Jim Morowski, Director of Freshmen Enrollment Services, Mayville State University, 330 3rd Street, NE, Mayville, ND 58257-1299. *Phone:* 701-788-4842 or toll-free 800-437-4104. *Fax:* 701-788-4748. *E-mail:* james.morowski@mayvillestate.edu. *Web site:* http://www.mayvillestate.edu/.

Medcenter One College of Nursing

Bismarck, North Dakota

General Independent, upper-level, coed, primarily women **Entrance** Moderately difficult **Setting** 15-acre small-town campus **Total enrollment** 89 **Student-faculty ratio** 8:1 **Application deadline** 11/7 (transfer) **First-year students** 58% were admitted **Housing** No **Expenses** Tuition & Fees $10,012 **Undergraduates** 93% women, 36% 25 or older, 2% Native American, 2% African American **The most frequently chosen baccalaureate field is** health professions and related sciences **Academic program** Internships **Contact** Ms. Mary Smith, Director of Student Services, Medcenter One College of Nursing, 512 North 7th Street, Bismarck, ND 58501-4494. *Phone:* 701-323-6271. *Fax:* 701-323-6289. *E-mail:* msmith@mohs.org. *Web site:* http://www.medcenterone.com/collegeofnursing/index.asp.

Minot State University

Minot, North Dakota

General State-supported, comprehensive, coed **Entrance** Minimally difficult **Setting** 103-acre small-town campus **Total enrollment** 3,649 **Student-faculty ratio** 13:1 **Application deadline** Rolling (freshmen), rolling (transfer) **Freshman admission** 82% were admitted. Average high school GPA 2.01 **Housing** Yes **Expenses** Tuition & Fees: state resident $5389, nonresident $5389; Room & Board $4602 **Undergraduates** 62% women, 31% part-time, 30% 25 or older, 4% Native American, 2% Hispanic American, 3% African American, 1% Asian American/Pacific Islander **The most frequently chosen baccalaureate fields are** business/marketing, education, health professions and related sciences **Academic program** Advanced placement, accelerated degree program, self-designed majors, honors program, summer session, adult/continuing education programs, internships **Contact** Kevin Harmon, Dean of Enrollment Services, Minot State University, 500 University Avenue West, Minot, ND 58707-0002. *Phone:* 701-858-3126 or toll-free 800-777-0750 Ext. 3350. *Fax:* 701-858-3825. *E-mail:* askmsu@minotstateu.edu. *Web site:* http://www.minotstateu.edu/.

North Dakota State University

Fargo, North Dakota

General State-supported, university, coed **Entrance** Moderately difficult **Setting** 2,100-acre urban campus **Total enrollment** 14,189 **Student-faculty ratio** 18:1 **Application deadline** 8/15 (freshmen), 8/15 (transfer) **Freshman admission** 79% were admitted. Average high school GPA 3.37 **Freshman test scores** SAT critical reading scores over 500: 64.4%; SAT math scores over 500: 75.9%; ACT scores over 18: 95.1%; SAT critical reading scores over 600: 31.5%; SAT math scores over 600: 43%; ACT scores over 24: 46% **Housing** Yes **Expenses** Tuition & Fees: state resident $6410, nonresident $15,509; Room & Board $6568 **Undergraduates** 43% women, 9% part-time, 9% 25 or older, 1% Native American, 1% Hispanic American, 2% African American, 1% Asian American/Pacific Islander **The most frequently chosen baccalaureate**

North Dakota State University (continued)
fields are business/marketing, engineering, health professions and related sciences **Academic program** English as a second language, advanced placement, self-designed majors, honors program, summer session, internships **Contact** Jobey Lichtblau, Director of Admission, North Dakota State University, PO Box 5454, Fargo, ND 58105-5454. *Phone:* 701-231-8643 or toll-free 800-488-NDSU. *Fax:* 701-231-8802. *E-mail:* ndsu.admission@ndsu.edu. *Web site:* http://www.ndsu.edu/.

Rasmussen College Fargo

Fargo, North Dakota

Contact Ms. Elizabeth Largent, Director, Rasmussen College Fargo, 4012 19th Avenue, SW, Fargo, ND 58103. *Phone:* 701-277-3889 or toll-free 800-817-0009. *Fax:* 701-277-5604. *E-mail:* blargent@aakers.edu. *Web site:* http://www.rasmussen.edu/.

Trinity Bible College

Ellendale, North Dakota

General Independent Assemblies of God, 4-year, coed **Entrance** Noncompetitive **Setting** 28-acre rural campus **Total enrollment** 292 **Application deadline** Rolling (freshmen), rolling (transfer) **Housing** Yes **Expenses** Tuition & Fees $12,940; Room & Board $4590 **Undergraduates** 14% 25 or older **Academic program** Advanced placement, accelerated degree program, summer session, internships **Contact** Rev. Steve Tvedt, Vice President of College Relations, Trinity Bible College, 50 South 6th Avenue, Ellendale, ND 58436-7150. *Phone:* 701-349-3621 Ext. 2045 or toll-free 888-TBC-2DAY. *Web site:* http://www.trinitybiblecollege.edu/.

University of Mary

Bismarck, North Dakota

General Independent Roman Catholic, comprehensive, coed **Entrance** Minimally difficult **Setting** 107-acre rural campus **Total enrollment** 2,849 **Student-faculty ratio** 15:1 **Application deadline** Rolling (freshmen), rolling (transfer) **Freshman admission** 78% were admitted. Average high school GPA 3.43 **Housing** Yes **Expenses** Tuition & Fees $13,126; Room & Board $5150 **Undergraduates** 62% women, 21% part-time, 28% 25 or older, 4% Native American, 2% Hispanic American, 2% African American, 1% Asian American/Pacific Islander **The most frequently chosen baccalaureate fields are** business/marketing, education, health professions and related sciences **Academic program** Advanced placement, accelerated degree program, honors program, summer session, adult/continuing education programs, internships **Contact** Pam Helm, University of Mary, 7500 University Drive, Bismarck, ND 58504-9652. *Phone:* 701-355-8390 or toll-free 800-288-6279. *Fax:* 701-255-7687. *E-mail:* phelm@umary.edu. *Web site:* http://www.umary.edu/.

University of North Dakota

Grand Forks, North Dakota

General State-supported, university, coed **Entrance** Minimally difficult **Setting** 550-acre urban campus **Total enrollment** 13,172 **Student-faculty ratio** 18:1 **Application deadline** Rolling (transfer) **Freshman admission** 73% were admitted. Average high school GPA 3.38 **Freshman test scores** ACT scores over 18: 96%; ACT scores over 24: 46% **Housing** Yes **Expenses** Tuition & Fees: state resident $6727, nonresident $15,846; Room & Board $5702 **Undergraduates** 45% women, 16% part-time, 15% 25 or older, 3% Native American, 1% Hispanic American, 1% African American, 1% Asian American/Pacific Islander **The most frequently chosen baccalaureate fields are** business/marketing, health professions and related sciences, transportation and materials moving **Academic program** English as a second language, advanced placement, accelerated degree program, self-designed majors, honors program, summer session, adult/continuing education programs, internships **Contact** Deborah Melby, Director of Admissions, University of North Dakota, Stop 8357, 205 Twamley Hall, 264 Centennial Drive, Grand Forks, ND 58202. *Phone:* 701-777-3821 or toll-free 800-CALLUND. *Fax:* 701-777-2721. *E-mail:* enrollmentservices@mail.und.nodak.edu. *Web site:* http://www.und.nodak.edu/.

Valley City State University

Valley City, North Dakota

General State-supported, comprehensive, coed **Entrance** Noncompetitive **Setting** 55-acre small-town campus **Total enrollment** 1,083 **Student-faculty ratio** 12:1 **Application deadline** Rolling (freshmen), rolling (transfer) **Freshman admission** 90% were admitted. Average high school GPA 3.08 **Freshman test scores** SAT critical reading scores over 500: 39%; SAT math scores over 500: 16%; ACT scores over 18: 77%; SAT critical reading scores over 600: 8%; SAT math scores over 600: 8%; ACT scores over 24: 21% **Housing** Yes **Expenses** Tuition & Fees: state resident $6075, nonresident $13,477; Room & Board $4528 **Undergraduates** 53% women, 28% part-time, 24% 25 or older, 2% Native American, 2% Hispanic American, 4% African American, 1% Asian American/Pacific Islander **The most frequently chosen baccalaureate fields are** business/marketing, education, natural resources/environmental science **Academic program** Self-designed majors, summer session, internships **Contact** Ms. Alison Kasowski, Admission Counselor, Valley City State University, 101 College Street Southwest, Valley City, ND 58072. *Phone:* 701-845-7204 or toll-free 800-532-8641 Ext. 37101. *Fax:* 701-845-7299. *E-mail:* alison.kasowski@vcsu.edu. *Web site:* http://www.vcsu.edu/.

NORTHERN MARIANA ISLANDS

Northern Marianas College

Saipan, Northern Mariana Islands

Contact Ms. Leilani M. Basa-Alam, Admission Specialist, Northern Marianas College, PO Box 501250, Saipan, MP 96950-1250. *Phone:* 670-234-3690 Ext. 1539. *Fax:* 670-235-4967. *E-mail:* leilanib@nmcnet.edu. *Web site:* http://www.nmcnet.edu/.

OHIO

Allegheny Wesleyan College

Salem, Ohio

General Independent religious, 4-year, coed **Total enrollment** 54 **Expenses** Tuition & Fees $4480 **Undergraduates** 17% 25 or older **Contact** Admissions Office, Allegheny Wesleyan College, 2161 Woodsdale Road, Salem, OH 44460. *Phone:* 330-337-6403 or toll-free 800-292-3153. *E-mail:* college@awc.edu. *Web site:* http://www.awc.edu/.

Antioch University McGregor

Yellow Springs, Ohio

General Independent, upper-level, coed **Entrance** Noncompetitive **Setting** 100-acre small-town campus **Total enrollment** 698 **Student-faculty ratio** 10:1 **Application deadline** Rolling (transfer) **Housing** No **Expenses** Tuition & Fees $20,760 **Undergraduates** 77% women, 50% part-time, 95% 25 or older **The most frequently chosen baccalaureate fields are** business/marketing, liberal arts/general studies, psychology **Academic program** Advanced placement, accelerated degree program, summer session, adult/continuing education programs, internships **Contact** Mr. Oscar Robinson, Director of Admissions, Antioch University McGregor, 900 Dayton Street, Yellow Springs, OH 45387-1609.

Phone: 937-769-1823. *Fax:* 937-769-1804. *E-mail:* orobinson@antioch.edu. *Web site:* http://www.mcgregor.edu/.

Art Academy of Cincinnati
Cincinnati, Ohio

General Independent, comprehensive, coed **Entrance** Moderately difficult **Setting** 184-acre urban campus **Total enrollment** 165 **Student-faculty ratio** 10:1 **Application deadline** 6/30 (freshmen), 6/30 (transfer) **Freshman admission** 21% were admitted. Average high school GPA 3.1 **Freshman test scores** SAT critical reading scores over 500: 75%; SAT math scores over 500: 57%; ACT scores over 18: 84%; SAT critical reading scores over 600: 25%; SAT math scores over 600: 14%; ACT scores over 24: 26% **Housing** Yes **Expenses** Tuition & Fees $21,880; Room only $6000 **Undergraduates** 63% women, 7% part-time, 8% 25 or older, 1% Hispanic American, 4% African American, 1% Asian American/Pacific Islander **The most frequently chosen baccalaureate field is** visual and performing arts **Academic program** Advanced placement, self-designed majors, honors program, summer session, adult/continuing education programs, internships **Contact** Mr. John J. Wadell, Director of Admissions, Art Academy of Cincinnati, 1212 Jackson Street, Cincinnati, OH 45202-7106. *Phone:* 513-562-8744 or toll-free 800-323-5692. *Fax:* 513-562-8778. *E-mail:* admissions@artacademy.edu. *Web site:* http://www.artacademy.edu/.

The Art Institute of Ohio–Cincinnati
Cincinnati, Ohio

General Proprietary, primarily 2-year, coed **Setting** urban campus **Contact** Director of Admissions, The Art Institute of Ohio–Cincinnati, 8845 Governors Hill Drive, Cincinnati, OH 45249-3317. *Phone:* 513-833-2400 or toll-free 866-613-5184. *Fax:* 877-477-8486. *Web site:* http://www.artinstitutes.edu/cincinnati/.

See page 528 for the College Close-Up.

Ashland University
Ashland, Ohio

General Independent, comprehensive, coed, affiliated with Brethren Church **Entrance** Moderately difficult **Setting** 98-acre small-town campus **Total enrollment** 6,475 **Student-faculty ratio** 16:1 **Application deadline** Rolling (freshmen), rolling (transfer) **Freshman admission** 82% were admitted. Average high school GPA 3.35 **Freshman test scores** SAT critical reading scores over 500: 55%; SAT math scores over 500: 59%; ACT scores over 18: 90%; SAT critical reading scores over 600: 17%; SAT math scores over 600: 14%; ACT scores over 24: 33% **Housing** Yes **Expenses** Tuition & Fees $25,640; Room & Board $9352 **Undergraduates** 52% women, 11% part-time, 22% 25 or older, 0.3% Native American, 3% Hispanic American, 10% African American, 1% Asian American/Pacific Islander **The most frequently chosen baccalaureate fields are** business/marketing, education, visual and performing arts **Academic program** English as a second language, advanced placement, self-designed majors, honors program, summer session, adult/continuing education programs, internships **Contact** Mr. Thomas Mansperger, Director of Admission, Ashland University, 401 College Avenue, Ashland, OH 44805. *Phone:* 419-289-5052 or toll-free 800-882-1548. *Fax:* 419-289-5999. *E-mail:* enrollme@ashland.edu. *Web site:* http://www.exploreashland.com/.

Baldwin-Wallace College
Berea, Ohio

General Independent Methodist, comprehensive, coed **Entrance** Moderately difficult **Setting** 100-acre suburban campus **Total enrollment** 4,397 **Student-faculty ratio** 15:1 **Application deadline** 3/1 (freshmen), 8/1 (transfer) **Freshman admission** 67% were admitted. Average high school GPA 3.5 **Freshman test scores** SAT critical reading scores over 500: 71.07%; SAT math scores over 500: 71.19%; ACT scores over 18: 93.96%; SAT critical reading scores over 600: 30.17%; SAT math scores over 600: 31.29%; ACT scores over 24: 52.16% **Housing** Yes **Expenses** Tuition & Fees $24,230; Room & Board $7960 **Undergraduates** 58% women, 14% part-time, 2% 25 or older, 0.1% Native American, 3% Hispanic American, 7% African American, 1% Asian American/Pacific Islander **The most frequently chosen baccalaureate fields are** business/marketing, education, visual and performing arts **Academic program** English as a second language, advanced placement, accelerated degree program, self-designed majors, honors program, summer session, adult/continuing education programs, internships **Contact** Patricia Skrha, Director of Undergraduate Admission, Baldwin-Wallace College, Bonds Administration Building, 275 Eastland Road, Berea, OH 44017. *Phone:* 440-826-2222 or toll-free 877-BWAPPLY. *Fax:* 440-826-3830. *E-mail:* admission@bw.edu. *Web site:* http://www.bw.edu/.

Visit Petersons.com and enter keyword Baldwin-Wallace

See page 574 for the College Close-Up.

Bluffton University
Bluffton, Ohio

General Independent Mennonite, comprehensive, coed **Entrance** Moderately difficult **Setting** 65-acre small-town campus **Total enrollment** 1,127 **Student-faculty ratio** 13:1 **Application deadline** 8/15 (freshmen), rolling (transfer) **Freshman admission** 66% were admitted. Average high school GPA 3.18 **Freshman test scores** SAT critical reading scores over 500: 51%; SAT math scores over 500: 55%; ACT scores over 18: 86%; SAT critical reading scores over 600: 18%; SAT math scores over 600: 24%; ACT scores over 24: 30% **Housing** Yes **Expenses** Tuition & Fees $24,930; Room & Board $8348 **Undergraduates** 51% women, 9% part-time, 11% 25 or older, 0.2% Native American, 2% Hispanic American, 6% African American, 1% Asian American/Pacific Islander **The most frequently chosen baccalaureate fields are** business/marketing, education, parks and recreation **Academic program** Advanced placement, accelerated degree program, self-designed majors, honors program, summer session, adult/continuing education programs, internships **Contact** Mr. Chris Jebsen, Director of Admissions, Bluffton University, 1 University Drive, Bluffton, OH 45817. *Phone:* 419-358-3254 or toll-free 800-488-3257. *Fax:* 419-358-3081. *E-mail:* admissions@bluffton.edu. *Web site:* http://www.bluffton.edu/.

Bowling Green State University
Bowling Green, Ohio

General State-supported, university, coed **Entrance** Moderately difficult **Setting** 1,230-acre small-town campus **Total enrollment** 17,309 **Student-faculty ratio** 18:1 **Application deadline** 7/15 (freshmen), 7/15 (transfer) **Freshman admission** 89% were admitted. Average high school GPA 3.2 **Freshman test scores** SAT critical reading scores over 500: 58%; SAT math scores over 500: 53%; ACT scores over 18: 90%; SAT critical reading scores over 600: 21%; SAT math scores over 600: 16%; ACT scores over 24: 33% **Housing** Yes **Expenses** Tuition & Fees: state resident $9060, nonresident $16,368; Room & Board $7670 **Undergraduates** 54% women, 8% part-time, 8% 25 or older, 1% Native American, 3% Hispanic American, 11% African American, 1% Asian American/Pacific Islander **The most frequently chosen baccalaureate fields are** business/marketing, education, visual and performing arts **Academic program** English as a second language, advanced placement, accelerated degree program, self-designed majors, honors program, summer session, adult/continuing education programs, internships **Contact** Mr. Gary Swegan, Assistant Vice President/Director of Admissions, Bowling Green State University, 110 McFall, Bowling Green, OH 43403. *Phone:* 419-372-BGSU. *Fax:* 419-372-6955. *E-mail:* choosebgsu@bgsu.edu. *Web site:* http://www.bgsu.edu/.

Bowling Green State University–Firelands College
Huron, Ohio

General State-supported, primarily 2-year, coed **Entrance** Noncompetitive **Setting** 216-acre rural campus **Total enrollment** 2,455 **Student-faculty ratio** 18:1 **Application deadline** 8/6 (freshmen), 8/6 (transfer) **Housing** No **Expenses** Tuition & Fees: state resident $4228, nonresident $11,506 **Undergraduates** 65% women, 45% part-time, 1% Native American, 4% Hispanic American, 10% African American, 0.3% Asian American/Pacific Islander **Academic program** Advanced placement, self-designed majors, summer session, adult/continuing education programs, internships **Contact** Debralee Divers, Director of Admissions and Financial Aid, Bowling Green State University–Firelands College, One University Drive, Huron, OH 44839-9791. *Phone:* 419-433-5560 or toll-free 800-322-4787. *Fax:* 419-372-0604. *E-mail:* divers@bgsu.edu. *Web site:* http://www.firelands.bgsu.edu/.

Bryant & Stratton College
Cleveland, Ohio

General Proprietary, 4-year, coed **Entrance** Minimally difficult **Setting** urban campus **Total enrollment** 524 **Student-faculty ratio** 10:1 **Application deadline** Rolling (freshmen), rolling (transfer) **Housing** Yes **Expenses** Tuition & Fees $14,430 **Undergraduates** 63% women, 28% part-time, 59% 25 or older, 0.2% Native American, 2% Hispanic American, 90% African American **The most frequently chosen baccalaureate field is** business/marketing **Academic program** Summer session, adult/continuing education programs, internships **Contact** Mr. John Girard, Campus Director, Bryant & Stratton College, 1700 East 13th Street, Cleveland, OH 44114-3203. *Phone:* 216-771-1700. *Fax:* 216-771-7787. *Web site:* http://www.bryantstratton.edu/.

Bryant & Stratton College
Eastlake, Ohio

General Proprietary, primarily 2-year, coed **Entrance** Minimally difficult **Setting** suburban campus **Total enrollment** 762 **Student-faculty ratio** 12:1 **Application deadline** Rolling (freshmen), rolling (transfer) **Housing** No **Expenses** Tuition & Fees $14,430 **Undergraduates** 88% women, 36% part-time, 63% 25 or older, 0.3% Native American, 2% Hispanic American, 58% African American **Academic program** Advanced placement, summer session, internships **Contact** Ms. Melanie Pettit, Director of Admissions, Bryant & Stratton College, 35350 Curtis Boulevard, Eastlake, OH 44095. *Phone:* 440-510-1112. *E-mail:* mejohnson@bryantstratton.edu. *Web site:* http://www.bryantstratton.edu/.

Bryant & Stratton College
Parma, Ohio

General Proprietary, primarily 2-year, coed **Entrance** Minimally difficult **Setting** 4-acre suburban campus **Total enrollment** 528 **Student-faculty ratio** 12:1 **Application deadline** Rolling (freshmen), rolling (transfer) **Housing** No **Expenses** Tuition & Fees $14,430 **Undergraduates** 81% women, 45% part-time, 34% 25 or older, 1% Native American, 16% Hispanic American, 24% African American, 1% Asian American/Pacific Islander **Academic program** Summer session, internships **Contact** Ms. Andrea Inman, Associate Director of Admissions, Bryant & Stratton College, 12955 Snow Road, Parma, OH 44130-1013. *Phone:* 216-265-3151 or toll-free 800-327-3151. *E-mail:* atinman@bryantstratton.edu. *Web site:* http://www.bryantstratton.edu/.

Capital University
Columbus, Ohio

General Independent, comprehensive, coed, affiliated with Evangelical Lutheran Church in America **Entrance** Moderately difficult **Setting** 48-acre suburban campus **Total enrollment** 3,540 **Student-faculty ratio** 11:1 **Application deadline** 5/1 (freshmen), rolling (transfer)

Will you?

Play hard

Help others

Work hard, too

Make an impact

Realize that's different than making money.

We're a bridge between who you are now, and who you'll become.

At Capital University, our students have goals large and small – and they work hard toward achieving them. Our students choose from diverse majors and equally divergent career possibilities. But there's one thing we all share – determination.

To learn more, go to capital.edu. or give us a call at 1-866-544-6175.

Capital University

Ask. Think. Lead.

Freshman admission 75% were admitted. Average high school GPA 3.45 **Freshman test scores** SAT critical reading scores over 500: 72%; SAT math scores over 500: 70%; ACT scores over 18: 96%; SAT critical reading scores over 600: 25%; SAT math scores over 600: 28%; ACT scores over 24: 51% **Housing** Yes **Expenses** Tuition & Fees $28,480; Room & Board $7510 **Undergraduates** 59% women, 10% part-time, 12% 25 or older, 0.3% Native American, 2% Hispanic American, 9% African American, 2% Asian American/Pacific Islander **The most frequently chosen baccalaureate fields are** education, business/marketing, health professions and related sciences **Academic program** English as a second language, advanced placement, accelerated degree program, self-designed majors, honors program, summer session, adult/continuing education programs, internships **Contact** Ms. Amanda Steiner, Director of Admission, Capital University, 1 College and Main, Columbus, OH 43209. *Phone:* 614-236-6574 or toll-free 800-289-6289. *Fax:* 614-236-6926. *E-mail:* asteiner@capital.edu. *Web site:* http://www.capital.edu/.
Visit Petersons.com and enter keyword Capital

See page 674 for the College Close-Up.

Case Western Reserve University
Cleveland, Ohio

General Independent, university, coed **Entrance** Very difficult **Setting** 155-acre urban campus **Total enrollment** 9,738 **Student-faculty ratio** 9:1 **Application deadline** 1/15 (freshmen), 5/15 (transfer) **Freshman admission** 70% were admitted **Freshman test scores** SAT critical reading scores over 500: 95.1%; SAT math scores over 500: 98.8%; ACT scores over 18: 100%; SAT critical reading scores over 600: 74.5%; SAT math scores over 600: 91.5%; ACT scores over 24: 97.5% **Housing** Yes **Expenses** Tuition & Fees $36,238; Room & Board $10,890 **Undergraduates** 44% women, 3% part-time, 2% 25 or older, 0.2% Native American, 3% Hispanic American, 5% African American, 16% Asian American/Pacific Islander **The most frequently chosen baccalaureate fields are** biological/life sciences, engineering, social sciences **Academic program** English as a second language, advanced placement, accelerated degree program, self-designed majors, honors program, summer session, adult/continuing education programs, internships **Contact** Mr. Robert McCullough, Director of Undergraduate Admission, Case Western Reserve University, 10900 Euclid Avenue, Cleveland, OH 44106. *Phone:* 216-368-4450. *Fax:* 216-368-5111. *E-mail:* admission@case.edu. *Web site:* http://www.case.edu/.
Visit Petersons.com and enter keyword Case

See page 690 for the College Close-Up.

Cedarville University
Cedarville, Ohio

General Independent Baptist, comprehensive, coed **Entrance** Moderately difficult **Setting** 400-acre rural campus **Total enrollment** 3,094 **Student-faculty ratio** 15:1 **Application deadline** Rolling (freshmen), rolling (transfer) **Freshman admission** 76% were admitted. Average high school GPA 3.61 **Freshman test scores** SAT critical reading scores over 500: 88%; SAT math scores over 500: 86%; ACT scores over 18: 99%; SAT critical reading scores over 600: 48%; SAT math scores over 600: 45%; ACT scores over 24: 71% **Housing** Yes **Expenses** Tuition & Fees $23,500; Room & Board $5086 **Undergraduates** 54% women, 6% part-time, 2% 25 or older, 0.3% Native American, 3% Hispanic American, 1% African American, 1% Asian American/Pacific Islander **The most frequently chosen baccalaureate fields are** education, business/marketing, health professions and related sciences **Academic program** Advanced placement, accelerated degree program, honors program, summer session, internships **Contact** Mr. Mark Weinstein, Director of Admissions, Cedarville University, 251 North Main Street, Cedarville, OH 45314-0601. *Phone:* 937-766-7700 or toll-free 800-CEDARVILLE. *Fax:* 937-766-7575. *E-mail:* admiss@cedarville.edu. *Web site:* http://www.cedarville.edu/.

Central State University
Wilberforce, Ohio

General State-supported, comprehensive, coed **Entrance** Minimally difficult **Setting** 60-acre rural campus **Total enrollment** 2,436 **Student-faculty ratio** 16:1 **Application deadline** 6/15 (freshmen), 6/15 (transfer) **Freshman admission** 39% were admitted. Average high school GPA 2.4 **Freshman test scores** SAT critical reading scores over 500: 7%; SAT math scores over 500: 7%; ACT scores over 18: 21%; ACT scores over 24: 1% **Housing** Yes **Expenses** Tuition & Fees: state resident $5294, nonresident $11,806; Room & Board $7920 **Undergraduates** 49% women, 7% part-time, 13% 25 or older, 0.1% Native American, 1% Hispanic American, 96% African American, 0.1% Asian American/Pacific Islander **The most frequently chosen baccalaureate fields are** business/marketing, communications/journalism, education **Academic program** Honors program, summer session, adult/continuing education programs, internships **Contact** Ms. Robin Rucker, Director, Admissions, Central State University, PO Box 1004, 1400 Blush Row Road, Wilberforce, OH 45384. *Phone:* 937-376-6580 or toll-free 800-388-CSU1. *Fax:* 937-376-6648. *E-mail:* admissions@centralstate.edu. *Web site:* http://www.centralstate.edu/.

Chancellor University
Cleveland, Ohio

General Independent, comprehensive, coed **Entrance** Minimally difficult **Setting** 1-acre urban campus **Total enrollment** 570 **Application deadline** Rolling (freshmen), rolling (transfer) **Housing** No **Expenses** Tuition & Fees $10,900 **Undergraduates** 85% 25 or older **Academic program** Advanced placement, accelerated degree program, self-designed majors, summer session, adult/continuing education programs, internships **Contact** Vice President for Enrollment Management, Chancellor University, 3921 Chester Avenue, Cleveland, OH 44114-4624. *Phone:* 216-523-3806 Ext. 805 or toll-free 877-366-9377. *E-mail:* admissions@myers.edu. *Web site:* http://www.myers.edu/.

Cincinnati Christian University
Cincinnati, Ohio

General Independent, comprehensive, coed, affiliated with Church of Christ **Entrance** Minimally difficult **Setting** 40-acre urban campus **Total enrollment** 1,020 **Student-faculty ratio** 20:1 **Application deadline** 7/1 (freshmen), rolling (transfer) **Freshman admission** 99% were admitted. Average high school GPA 2.93 **Freshman test scores** SAT critical reading scores over 500: 58.1%; SAT math scores over 500: 58%; ACT scores over 18: 75.79%; SAT critical reading scores over 600: 19.4%; SAT math scores over 600: 16.1%; ACT scores over 24: 21.05% **Housing** Yes **Expenses** Tuition & Fees $12,580; Room & Board $6470 **Undergraduates** 43% women, 12% part-time, 33% 25 or older, 1% Hispanic American, 13% African American, 0.1% Asian American/Pacific Islander **The most frequently chosen baccalaureate fields are** business/marketing, education, theology and religious vocations **Academic program** Advanced placement, honors program, summer session, adult/continuing education programs, internships **Contact** Paul Presta, Director of Undergraduate Admissions, Cincinnati Christian University, 2700 Glenway Avenue, PO Box 04320, Cincinnati, OH 45204-3200. *Phone:* toll-free 800-949-4228. *Web site:* http://www.ccuniversity.edu/.

Cincinnati College of Mortuary Science
Cincinnati, Ohio

General Independent, 4-year, coed **Entrance** Moderately difficult **Setting** 10-acre urban campus **Total enrollment** 117 **Student-faculty ratio** 5:1 **Application deadline** Rolling (freshmen), rolling (transfer) **Freshman admission** 100% were admitted **Housing** No **Expenses** Tuition & Fees $20,250 **Undergraduates** 43% women, 25% 25 or older, 1% Hispanic American, 12% African American **Academic program** Summer session, adult/continuing education programs **Contact** Ms. Pat Sullivan, Executive

Cincinnati College of Mortuary Science (continued)
Director, Enrollment Management, Cincinnati College of Mortuary Science, 645 West North Bend Road, Cincinnati, OH 45224-1462. *Phone:* 513-761-2020. *Fax:* 513-761-3333. *E-mail:* psullivan@ccms.edu. *Web site:* http://www.ccms.edu/.

The Cleveland Institute of Art

Cleveland, Ohio

General Independent, 4-year, coed **Entrance** Moderately difficult **Setting** 488-acre urban campus **Total enrollment** 507 **Student-faculty ratio** 8:1 **Application deadline** Rolling (freshmen), rolling (transfer) **Freshman admission** 79% were admitted. Average high school GPA 3.17 **Freshman test scores** SAT critical reading scores over 500: 72%; SAT math scores over 500: 56%; ACT scores over 18: 89%; SAT critical reading scores over 600: 29%; SAT math scores over 600: 17%; ACT scores over 24: 43% **Housing** Yes **Expenses** Tuition & Fees $31,904; Room & Board $10,536 **Undergraduates** 52% women, 3% part-time, 12% 25 or older, 0.2% Native American, 5% Hispanic American, 6% African American, 5% Asian American/Pacific Islander **The most frequently chosen baccalaureate field is** visual and performing arts **Academic program** Advanced placement, honors program, internships **Contact** Office of Admissions, The Cleveland Institute of Art, 11141 East Boulevard, Cleveland, OH 44106-1700. *Phone:* 216-421-7418 or toll-free 800-223-4700. *Fax:* 216-754-3634. *E-mail:* admissions@cia.edu. *Web site:* http://www.cia.edu/.

Visit Petersons.com and enter keyword Cleveland

Cleveland Institute of Music

Cleveland, Ohio

Contact Mr. William Fay, Director of Admission, Cleveland Institute of Music, 11021 East Boulevard, Cleveland, OH 44106-1776. *Phone:* 216-795-3107. *Fax:* 216-791-1530. *E-mail:* cimadmission@po.cwru.edu. *Web site:* http://www.cim.edu/.

Visit Petersons.com and enter keywords Cleveland Institute of Music

See page 720 for the College Close-Up.

Cleveland State University

Cleveland, Ohio

General State-supported, university, coed **Entrance** Moderately difficult **Setting** 82-acre urban campus **Total enrollment** 16,131 **Student-faculty ratio** 18:1 **Application deadline** Rolling (freshmen), 7/15 (transfer) **Freshman admission** 64% were admitted. Average high school GPA 3.09 **Freshman test scores** SAT critical reading scores over 500: 43.85%; SAT math scores over 500: 45.39%; ACT scores over 18: 76.34%; SAT critical reading scores over 600: 11.28%; SAT math scores over 600: 15.9%; ACT scores over 24: 22.91% **Housing** Yes **Expenses** Tuition & Fees: state resident $8196, nonresident $11,026; Room & Board $10,250 **Undergraduates** 55% women, 27% part-time, 38% 25 or older, 0.3% Native American, 4% Hispanic American, 21% African American, 3% Asian American/Pacific Islander **The most frequently chosen baccalaureate fields are** business/marketing, health professions and related sciences, social sciences **Academic program** English as a second language, advanced placement, accelerated degree program, self-designed majors, honors program, summer session, adult/continuing education programs, internships **Contact** Undergraduate Admissions Office, Cleveland State University, 2121 Euclid Avenue, RW 204, Cleveland, OH 44115. *Phone:* 216-687-2100 or toll-free 888-CSU-OHIO. *E-mail:* admissions@csuohio.edu. *Web site:* http://www.csuohio.edu/.

College of Mount St. Joseph

Cincinnati, Ohio

General Independent Roman Catholic, comprehensive, coed **Entrance** Moderately difficult **Setting** 92-acre suburban campus **Total enrollment** 2,324 **Student-faculty ratio** 12:1 **Application deadline** 8/15 (freshmen), 8/1 (transfer) **Freshman admission** 70% were admitted. Average high school GPA 3.19 **Freshman test scores** SAT critical reading scores over 500: 44%; SAT math scores over 500: 43%; ACT scores over 18: 90%; SAT critical reading scores over 600: 4%; SAT math scores over 600: 6%; ACT scores over 24: 31% **Housing** Yes **Expenses** Tuition & Fees $22,800; Room & Board $7000 **Undergraduates** 64% women, 29% part-time, 29% 25 or older, 0.3% Native American, 1% Hispanic American, 10% African American, 0.3% Asian American/Pacific Islander **The most frequently chosen baccalaureate fields are** business/marketing, health professions and related sciences, visual and performing arts **Academic program** Advanced placement, accelerated degree program, honors program, summer session, internships **Contact** Peggy Minnich, Director of Admission, College of Mount St. Joseph, 5701 Delhi Road, Cincinnati, OH 45233-1670. *Phone:* 513-244-4531 or toll-free 800-654-9314. *Fax:* 513-244-4629. *E-mail:* admissions@mail.msj.edu. *Web site:* http://www.msj.edu/.

Visit Petersons.com and enter keyword Mount

See page 724 for the College Close-Up.

The College of Wooster

Wooster, Ohio

General Independent, 4-year, coed, affiliated with Presbyterian Church (U.S.A.) **Entrance** Moderately difficult **Setting** 240-acre small-town campus **Total enrollment** 1,854 **Student-faculty ratio** 11:1 **Application deadline** 2/15 (freshmen), 6/1 (transfer) **Freshman admission** 59% were admitted. Average high school GPA 3.6 **Freshman test scores** SAT critical reading scores over 500: 89%; SAT math scores over 500: 86%; ACT scores over 18: 99%; SAT critical reading scores over 600: 61%; SAT math scores over 600: 49%; ACT scores over 24: 76% **Housing** Yes **Expenses** Tuition & Fees $36,598; Room & Board $9070 **Undergraduates** 54% women, 3% part-time, 0.2% 25 or older, 0.4% Native American, 2% Hispanic American, 6% African American, 3% Asian American/Pacific Islander **The most frequently chosen baccalaureate fields are** English, history, social sciences **Academic program** Advanced placement, self-designed majors, internships **Contact** Ms. Mary Karen Vellines, Vice President for Enrollment, The College of Wooster, 1189 Beall Avenue, Wooster, OH 44691-2363. *Phone:* 330-263-2270 or toll-free 800-877-9905. *Fax:* 330-263-2621. *E-mail:* admissions@wooster.edu. *Web site:* http://www.wooster.edu/.

Visit Petersons.com and enter keyword Wooster

See page 738 for the College Close-Up.

Columbus College of Art & Design

Columbus, Ohio

General Independent, 4-year, coed **Entrance** Moderately difficult **Setting** 10-acre urban campus **Total enrollment** 1,493 **Student-faculty ratio** 12:1 **Application deadline** Rolling (freshmen), rolling (transfer) **Freshman admission** 72% were admitted. Average high school GPA 3.07 **Freshman test scores** SAT critical reading scores over 500: 58%; SAT math scores over 500: 43%; ACT scores over 18: 83%; SAT critical reading scores over 600: 23%; SAT math scores over 600: 11%; ACT scores over 24: 24% **Housing** Yes **Expenses** Tuition & Fees $24,648; Room & Board $8630 **Undergraduates** 61% women, 17% part-time, 9% 25 or older, 0.2% Native American, 4% Hispanic American, 7% African American, 4% Asian American/Pacific Islander **The most frequently chosen baccalaureate field is** visual and performing arts **Academic program** English as a second language, advanced placement, honors program, summer session, internships **Contact** Mr. Thomas E. Green, Director of Admissions, Columbus College of Art & Design, 60 Cleveland Avenue, Columbus, OH 43215-1758. *Phone:* 614-224-9101 or toll-free 877-997-2223. *Fax:* 614-232-8344. *E-mail:* admissions@ccad.edu. *Web site:* http://www.ccad.edu/.

Defiance College
Defiance, Ohio

General Independent, comprehensive, coed, affiliated with United Church of Christ **Entrance** Moderately difficult **Setting** 150-acre small-town campus **Total enrollment** 1,070 **Student-faculty ratio** 13:1 **Application deadline** 8/15 (freshmen), 8/15 (transfer) **Freshman admission** 74% were admitted. Average high school GPA 3.09 **Freshman test scores** SAT critical reading scores over 500: 40%; ACT scores over 18: 88%; SAT critical reading scores over 600: 8%; ACT scores over 24: 30% **Housing** Yes **Expenses** Tuition & Fees $24,330; Room & Board $8120 **Undergraduates** 52% women, 21% part-time, 5% 25 or older, 1% Native American, 4% Hispanic American, 7% African American, 1% Asian American/Pacific Islander **The most frequently chosen baccalaureate fields are** business/marketing, education, security and protective services **Academic program** Advanced placement, self-designed majors, honors program, summer session, adult/continuing education programs, internships **Contact** Mr. Brad Harsha, Director of Admissions, Defiance College, 701 North Clinton Street, Defiance, OH 43512. *Phone:* 419-783-2365 or toll-free 800-520-4632 Ext. 2359. *Fax:* 419-783-2468. *E-mail:* bharsha@defiance.edu. *Web site:* http://www.defiance.edu/.

Denison University
Granville, Ohio

General Independent, 4-year, coed **Entrance** Very difficult **Setting** 800-acre small-town campus **Total enrollment** 2,267 **Student-faculty ratio** 10:1 **Application deadline** 1/15 (freshmen), 6/1 (transfer) **Freshman admission** 50% were admitted. Average high school GPA 3.5 **Freshman test scores** SAT critical reading scores over 500: 99%; SAT math scores over 500: 100%; ACT scores over 18: 100%; SAT critical reading scores over 600: 78%; SAT math scores over 600: 77%; ACT scores over 24: 98% **Housing** Yes **Expenses** Tuition & Fees $36,560; Room & Board $8930 **Undergraduates** 56% women, 1% part-time, 1% 25 or older, 0.4% Native American, 3% Hispanic American, 6% African American, 2% Asian American/Pacific Islander **The most frequently chosen baccalaureate fields are** communications/journalism, social sciences, visual and performing arts **Academic program** Advanced placement, self-designed majors, honors program, internships **Contact** Mr. Perry Robinson, Director of Admissions, Denison University, Granville, OH 43023. *Phone:* 740-587-6276 or toll-free 800-DENISON. *E-mail:* admissions@denison.edu. *Web site:* http://www.denison.edu/.

See page 752 for the College Close-Up.

DeVry University
Columbus, Ohio

General Proprietary, comprehensive, coed **Entrance** Minimally difficult **Setting** 21-acre urban campus **Total enrollment** 3,011 **Student-faculty ratio** 18:1 **Application deadline** Rolling (freshmen), rolling (transfer) **Housing** No **Expenses** Tuition & Fees $14,080 **Undergraduates** 42% women, 47% part-time, 63% 25 or older, 0.3% Native American, 2% Hispanic American, 23% African American, 2% Asian American/Pacific Islander **The most frequently chosen baccalaureate fields are** business/marketing, computer and information sciences, engineering technologies **Academic program** Advanced placement, accelerated degree program, summer session, adult/continuing education programs **Contact** Admissions Office, DeVry University, 1350 Alum Creek Drive, Columbus, OH 43209-2705. *Web site:* http://www.devry.edu/.

DeVry University
Columbus, Ohio

Contact DeVry University, 8800 Lyra Drive, Columbus, OH 43240. *Web site:* http://www.devry.edu/.

DeVry University
Seven Hills, Ohio

Contact DeVry University, The Genesis Building, 6000 Lombardo Center, Suite 200, Seven Hills, OH 44131. *Phone:* toll-free 866-453-3879. *Web site:* http://www.devry.edu/.

Franciscan University of Steubenville
Steubenville, Ohio

General Independent Roman Catholic, comprehensive, coed **Entrance** Moderately difficult **Setting** 242-acre suburban campus **Total enrollment** 2,725 **Student-faculty ratio** 15:1 **Application deadline** Rolling (freshmen), rolling (transfer) **Freshman admission** 72% were admitted. Average high school GPA 3.66 **Freshman test scores** SAT critical reading scores over 500: 89.92%; SAT math scores over 500: 80.62%; ACT scores over 18: 100%; SAT critical reading scores over 600: 48.83%; SAT math scores over 600: 36.05%; ACT scores over 24: 66.5% **Housing** Yes **Expenses** Tuition & Fees $20,320; Room & Board $6900 **Undergraduates** 61% women, 6% part-time, 5% 25 or older, 0.4% Native American, 6% Hispanic American, 0.3% African American, 2% Asian American/Pacific Islander **The most frequently chosen baccalaureate fields are** health professions and related sciences, business/marketing, theology and religious vocations **Academic program** Advanced placement, accelerated degree program, honors program, summer session, adult/continuing education programs, internships **Contact** Mrs. Margaret Weber, Director of Admissions, Franciscan University of Steubenville, 1235 University Boulevard, Steubenville, OH 43952-1763. *Phone:* 740-283-6226 or toll-free 800-783-6220. *Fax:* 740-284-5456. *E-mail:* admissions@franciscan.edu. *Web site:* http://www.franciscan.edu/.

Visit Petersons.com and enter keyword Steubenville

Franklin University
Columbus, Ohio

General Independent, comprehensive, coed **Entrance** Noncompetitive **Setting** 14-acre urban campus **Total enrollment** 7,942 **Student-faculty ratio** 12:1 **Application deadline** Rolling (freshmen), rolling (transfer) **Housing** No **Expenses** Tuition & Fees $10,728 **Undergraduates** 59% women, 63% part-time, 81% 25 or older **The most frequently chosen baccalaureate fields are** business/marketing, computer and information sciences, health professions and related sciences **Academic program** English as a second language, advanced placement, accelerated degree program, self-designed majors, summer session, adult/continuing education programs, internships **Contact** Franklin University, 201 South Grant Avenue, Columbus, OH 43215-5399. *Phone:* toll-free 877-341-6300. *Web site:* http://www.franklin.edu/.

God's Bible School and College
Cincinnati, Ohio

Contact Mrs. Lisa Profitt, Director of Admissions, God's Bible School and College, 1810 Young Street, Cincinnati, OH 45202-6838. *Phone:* 513-721-7944 Ext. 205 or toll-free 800-486-4637. *Fax:* 513-721-3971. *E-mail:* lprofitt@gbs.edu. *Web site:* http://www.gbs.edu/.

Heidelberg University
Tiffin, Ohio

General Independent, comprehensive, coed, affiliated with United Church of Christ **Entrance** Moderately difficult **Setting** 115-acre small-town campus **Total enrollment** 1,656 **Student-faculty ratio** 13:1 **Application deadline** 8/15 (freshmen), 8/15 (transfer) **Freshman admission** 69% were admitted. Average high school GPA 3.12 **Freshman test scores** SAT critical reading scores over 500: 48.9%; ACT scores over 18: 85.4%; SAT critical reading scores over 600: 13.8%; ACT scores over 24: 27.5% **Housing** Yes **Expenses** Tuition & Fees $22,962; Room & Board $8635 **Undergraduates** 50% women, 16% part-time, 10% 25 or

Heidelberg University (continued)
older, 3% Hispanic American, 10% African American, 1% Asian American/Pacific Islander **The most frequently chosen baccalaureate fields are** business/marketing, education, parks and recreation **Academic program** English as a second language, advanced placement, accelerated degree program, honors program, summer session, adult/continuing education programs, internships **Contact** Ms. Lindsay Sooy, Director of Admission, Heidelberg University, 310 East Market Street, Tiffin, OH 44883. *Phone:* 419-448-2330 or toll-free 800-434-3352. *Fax:* 419-448-2334. *E-mail:* adminfo@heidelberg.edu. *Web site:* http://www.heidelberg.edu/.

Hiram College
Hiram, Ohio

General Independent, comprehensive, coed, affiliated with Christian Church (Disciples of Christ) **Entrance** Moderately difficult **Setting** 110-acre rural campus **Total enrollment** 1,395 **Student-faculty ratio** 13:1 **Application deadline** 4/1 (freshmen), 7/15 (transfer) **Freshman admission** 88% were admitted. Average high school GPA 3.29 **Freshman test scores** SAT critical reading scores over 500: 60%; SAT math scores over 500: 60%; ACT scores over 18: 95%; SAT critical reading scores over 600: 25%; SAT math scores over 600: 24%; ACT scores over 24: 40% **Housing** Yes **Expenses** Tuition & Fees $27,135; Room & Board $9010 **Undergraduates** 55% women, 13% part-time, 0.4% Native American, 2% Hispanic American, 10% African American, 1% Asian American/Pacific Islander **Academic program** English as a second language, advanced placement, accelerated degree program, self-designed majors, summer session, adult/continuing education programs, internships **Contact** Mr. Sherman C. Dean II, Director of Admission, Hiram College, PO Box 96, Hiram, OH 44234. *Phone:* 330-569-5169 or toll-free 800-362-5280. *Fax:* 330-569-5944. *E-mail:* admission@hiram.edu. *Web site:* http://www.hiram.edu/.

John Carroll University
University Heights, Ohio

General Independent Roman Catholic (Jesuit), comprehensive, coed **Entrance** Moderately difficult **Setting** 60-acre suburban campus **Total enrollment** 3,714 **Student-faculty ratio** 15:1 **Application deadline** 2/1 (freshmen), rolling (transfer) **Freshman admission** 81% were admitted. Average high school GPA 3.36 **Freshman test scores** SAT critical reading scores over 500: 69.9%; SAT math scores over 500: 64.6%; ACT scores over 18: 95.4%; SAT critical reading scores over 600: 18.7%; SAT math scores over 600: 26.4%; ACT scores over 24: 45.4% **Housing** Yes **Expenses** Tuition & Fees $30,250; Room & Board $8750 **Undergraduates** 51% women, 3% part-time, 2% 25 or older, 0.3% Native American, 3% Hispanic American, 6% African American, 2% Asian American/Pacific Islander **The most frequently chosen baccalaureate fields are** business/marketing, biological/life sciences, communications/journalism **Academic program** Advanced placement, self-designed majors, honors program, summer session, internships **Contact** Mr. Steven P. Vitatoe, Executive Director of Enrollment, John Carroll University, 20700 North Park Boulevard, University Heights, OH 44118. *Phone:* 216-397-4294. *Fax:* 216-397-4981. *E-mail:* svitatoe@jcu.edu. *Web site:* http://www.jcu.edu/.

Visit Petersons.com and enter keywords John Carroll

See page 876 for the College Close-Up.

Kent State University
Kent, Ohio

General State-supported, university, coed **Entrance** Moderately difficult **Setting** 1,347-acre suburban campus **Total enrollment** 24,930 **Student-faculty ratio** 20:1 **Application deadline** Rolling (freshmen), rolling (transfer) **Freshman admission** 72% were admitted. Average high school GPA 3.19 **Freshman test scores** SAT critical reading scores over 500: 57%; SAT math scores over 500: 58%; ACT scores over 18: 93%; SAT critical reading scores over 600: 17%; SAT math scores over 600: 20%; ACT scores over 24: 34% **Housing** Yes **Expenses** Tuition & Fees: state resident $8726, nonresident $16,418; Room & Board $7940 **Undergraduates** 58% women, 11% part-time, 13% 25 or older, 1% Native American, 2% Hispanic American, 9% African American, 2% Asian American/Pacific Islander **The most frequently chosen baccalaureate fields are** business/marketing, education, health professions and related sciences **Academic program** English as a second language, advanced placement, accelerated degree program, self-designed majors, honors program, summer session, adult/continuing education programs, internships **Contact** Mr. Christopher Buttenschon, Assistant Director of Admissions, Kent State University, 161 Michael Schwartz Center, Kent, OH 44242-0001. *Phone:* 330-672-2444 or toll-free 800-988-KENT. *Fax:* 330-672-2499. *E-mail:* admissions@kent.edu. *Web site:* http://www.kent.edu/.

Visit Petersons.com and enter keywords Kent State

See page 892 for the College Close-Up.

Kent State University at Ashtabula
Ashtabula, Ohio

General State-supported, primarily 2-year, coed **Entrance** Noncompetitive **Setting** 120-acre small-town campus **Total enrollment** 2,192 **Student-faculty ratio** 22:1 **Application deadline** 8/1 (freshmen), 7/15 (transfer) **Freshman admission** 79% were admitted. Average high school GPA 2.55 **Freshman test scores** SAT critical reading scores over 500: 50%; SAT math scores over 500: 33.34%; ACT scores over 18: 66.91%; SAT critical reading scores over 600: 16.67%; SAT math scores over 600: 16.67%; ACT scores over 24: 14.71% **Housing** No **Expenses** Tuition & Fees: state resident $4938, nonresident $12,630 **Undergraduates** 64% women, 47% part-time, 55% 25 or older, 0.4% Native American, 3% Hispanic American, 9% African American, 1% Asian American/Pacific Islander **Academic program** Advanced placement, self-designed majors, honors program, summer session, internships **Contact** Ms. Kelly Sanford, Director, Enrollment Management and Student Services, Kent State University at Ashtabula, 3300 Lake Road West, Ashtabula, OH 44004-2299. *Phone:* 440-964-4217. *E-mail:* sanford@ashtabula.kent.edu. *Web site:* http://www.ashtabula.kent.edu/.

Kent State University at Salem
Salem, Ohio

General State-supported, primarily 2-year, coed **Entrance** Noncompetitive **Setting** 98-acre rural campus **Total enrollment** 1,580 **Student-faculty ratio** 21:1 **Application deadline** Rolling (freshmen), rolling (transfer) **Freshman admission** 62% were admitted. Average high school GPA 2.71 **Freshman test scores** SAT critical reading scores over 500: 100%; ACT scores over 18: 67.44%; SAT critical reading scores over 600: 50%; ACT scores over 24: 10.85% **Housing** No **Expenses** Tuition & Fees: state resident $4770, nonresident $12,202 **Undergraduates** 69% women, 28% part-time, 41% 25 or older, 1% Native American, 1% Hispanic American, 2% African American, 1% Asian American/Pacific Islander **The most frequently chosen baccalaureate field is** health professions and related sciences **Academic program** Advanced placement, honors program, summer session, adult/continuing education programs, internships **Contact** Mrs. Judy Heisler, Admissions Secretary, Kent State University at Salem, 2491 State Route 45 South, Salem, OH 44460-9412. *Phone:* 330-332-0361 Ext. 74201. *E-mail:* ask-us@salem.kent.edu. *Web site:* http://www.salem.kent.edu/.

Kent State University at Stark
Canton, Ohio

General State-supported, comprehensive, coed **Entrance** Noncompetitive **Setting** 200-acre suburban campus **Total enrollment** 4,363 **Student-faculty ratio** 25:1 **Application deadline** Rolling (freshmen), rolling (transfer) **Freshman admission** 73% were admitted. Average high school GPA 2.82 **Freshman test scores** SAT critical reading scores over 500: 60%; SAT math scores over 500: 45%; ACT scores over 18: 74%; SAT critical reading scores over 600: 23%; SAT math scores over 600: 14%; ACT scores over 24: 16% **Housing** No **Expenses** Tuition & Fees: state resident $4938, nonresident $12,630 **Undergraduates** 62% women, 32% part-time, 33% 25 or older, 1% Native American, 1% Hispanic American, 7% African American, 1% Asian American/Pacific Islander **Academic program** English as a second language, advanced placement, accelerated degree program, self-designed majors, honors program, summer session, adult/continuing education programs, internships **Contact** Ms. Deborah Ann Speck, Director of Admissions, Kent State University at Stark, 6000 Frank Avenue, NW, Canton, OH 44720-7599. *Phone:* 330-499-9600 Ext. 53259. *E-mail:* admit@stark.kent.edu. *Web site:* http://www.stark.kent.edu/.

Kent State University at Trumbull
Warren, Ohio

General State-supported, primarily 2-year, coed **Entrance** Noncompetitive **Setting** 200-acre suburban campus **Total enrollment** 2,612 **Student-faculty ratio** 25:1 **Application deadline** Rolling (freshmen), rolling (transfer) **Freshman admission** 79% were admitted. Average high school GPA 2.66 **Freshman test scores** SAT critical reading scores over 500: 57.14%; SAT math scores over 500: 28.58%; ACT scores over 18: 63.81%; SAT critical reading scores over 600: 14.29%; SAT math scores over 600: 14.29%; ACT scores over 24: 10.48% **Housing** No **Expenses** Tuition & Fees: state resident $4770, nonresident $12,202 **Undergraduates** 45% 25 or older, 1% Native American, 1% Hispanic American, 13% African American, 1% Asian American/Pacific Islander **Academic program** Advanced placement, self-designed majors, honors program, summer session, adult/continuing education programs, internships **Contact** Linda Petrilla, Director of Enrollment Management and Student Services, Kent State University at Trumbull, 4314 Mahoning Avenue, NW, Warren, OH 44483-1998. *Phone:* 330-675-8935. *Fax:* 330-675-8855. *E-mail:* lppetril@kent.edu. *Web site:* http://www.trumbull.kent.edu/.

Kent State University at Tuscarawas
New Philadelphia, Ohio

General State-supported, primarily 2-year, coed **Entrance** Noncompetitive **Setting** 172-acre small-town campus **Total enrollment** 2,384 **Student-faculty ratio** 24:1 **Application deadline** 9/1 (freshmen), 9/1 (transfer) **Freshman admission** 82% were admitted. Average high school GPA 2.7 **Freshman test scores** SAT critical reading scores over 500: 50%; SAT math scores over 500: 16.66%; ACT scores over 18: 78.91%; SAT math scores over 600: 16.66%; ACT scores over 24: 14.77% **Housing** No **Expenses** Tuition & Fees: state resident $4938, nonresident $12,630 **Undergraduates** 61% women, 40% part-time, 44% 25 or older, 0.4% Native American, 1% Hispanic American, 2% African American, 1% Asian American/Pacific Islander **Academic program** Advanced placement, accelerated degree program, self-designed majors, honors program, summer session, adult/continuing education programs, internships **Contact** Mrs. Laurie R. Donley, Director of Enrollment Management and Student Services, Kent State University at Tuscarawas, Kent State University at Tuscarawas, 330 University Drive NE, New Philadelphia, OH 44663-9403. *Phone:* 330-339-3391 Ext. 47425. *Fax:* 330-339-3321. *E-mail:* ldonley@kent.edu. *Web site:* http://www.tusc.kent.edu/.

Kenyon College
Gambier, Ohio

General Independent, 4-year, coed **Entrance** Very difficult **Setting** 1,200-acre rural campus **Total enrollment** 1,633 **Student-faculty ratio** 10:1 **Application deadline** 1/15 (freshmen), 4/5 (transfer) **Freshman admission** 39% were admitted. Average high school GPA 3.82 **Freshman test scores** SAT critical reading scores over 500: 99.5%; SAT math scores over 500: 98.8%; ACT scores over 18: 100%; SAT critical reading scores over 600: 86.5%; SAT math scores over 600: 79.8%; ACT scores over 24: 95.7% **Housing** Yes **Expenses** Tuition & Fees $40,900; Room & Board $9500 **Undergraduates** 52% women, 1% part-time, 1% Native American, 3% Hispanic American, 4% African American, 6% Asian American/Pacific Islander **The most frequently chosen baccalaureate fields are** English, social sciences, visual and performing arts **Academic program** Advanced placement, accelerated degree program, self-designed majors, honors program **Contact** Ms. Jennifer Delahunty, Dean of Admissions, Kenyon College, Ransom Hall, Gambier, OH 43022. *Phone:* 740-427-5776 or toll-free 800-848-2468. *Fax:* 740-427-5770. *E-mail:* admissions@kenyon.edu. *Web site:* http://www.kenyon.edu/.

Kettering College of Medical Arts
Kettering, Ohio

Contact Mrs. Becky McDonald, Director of Enrollment Services, Kettering College of Medical Arts, 3737 Southern Boulevard, Kettering, OH 45429-1299. *Phone:* 937-395-8628 or toll-free 800-433-5262. *Fax:* 937-296-4238. *Web site:* http://www.kcma.edu/.

Lake Erie College
Painesville, Ohio

General Independent, comprehensive, coed **Entrance** Moderately difficult **Setting** 57-acre small-town campus **Total enrollment** 1,131 **Student-faculty ratio** 15:1 **Application deadline** 8/1 (freshmen), 8/1 (transfer) **Freshman admission** 56% were admitted. Average high school GPA 3.07 **Freshman test scores** SAT critical reading scores over 500: 44.5%; SAT math scores over 500: 51%; ACT scores over 18: 77%; SAT critical reading scores over 600: 10.5%; SAT math scores over 600: 14%; ACT scores over 24: 20% **Housing** Yes **Expenses** Tuition & Fees $25,674; Room & Board $8192 **Undergraduates** 53% women, 5% part-time, 9% 25 or older, 0.4% Native American, 2% Hispanic American, 9% African American, 1% Asian American/Pacific Islander **The most frequently chosen baccalaureate fields are** agriculture, business/marketing, education **Academic program** Advanced placement, accelerated degree program, self-designed majors, honors program, summer session, adult/continuing education programs, internships **Contact** Mr. Eric Felver, Dean of Admissions and Financial Aid, Lake Erie College, 391 West Washington Street, Painesville, OH 44077-3389. *Phone:* 440-375-7050 or toll-free 800-916-0904. *Fax:* 440-375-7005. *E-mail:* admissions@lec.edu. *Web site:* http://www.lec.edu/.

Laura and Alvin Siegal College of Judaic Studies
Beachwood, Ohio

General Independent, comprehensive, coed **Entrance** Noncompetitive **Setting** 2-acre suburban campus **Total enrollment** 105 **Application deadline** Rolling (freshmen), rolling (transfer) **Housing** No **Expenses** Tuition & Fees $12,600 **Undergraduates** 75% women, 100% part-time, 100% 25 or older **Academic program** Summer session, adult/continuing education programs, internships **Contact** Ms. Ruth Kronick, Director of Student Services, Laura and Alvin Siegal College of Judaic Studies, 26500 Shaker Boulevard, Beachwood, OH 44122. *Phone:* 216-464-4050 Ext. 101 or toll-free 888-336-2257. *Fax:* 216-464-5827. *E-mail:* admissions@siegalcollege.edu. *Web site:* http://www.siegalcollege.edu/.

Lourdes College
Sylvania, Ohio

General Independent Roman Catholic, comprehensive, coed **Entrance** Minimally difficult **Setting** 89-acre suburban campus **Total enrollment** 2,220 **Student-faculty ratio** 11:1 **Application deadline** Rolling (freshmen), rolling (transfer) **Freshman admission** 80% were admitted. Average high school GPA 2.91 **Freshman test scores** SAT critical reading scores

Lourdes College (continued)
over 500: 33%; ACT scores over 18: 67%; ACT scores over 24: 13% **Housing** No **Expenses** Tuition & Fees $15,300 **Undergraduates** 80% women, 48% part-time, 57% 25 or older, 0.3% Native American, 4% Hispanic American, 15% African American, 1% Asian American/Pacific Islander **The most frequently chosen baccalaureate fields are** business/marketing, education, health professions and related sciences **Academic program** Advanced placement, self-designed majors, summer session, adult/continuing education programs, internships **Contact** Ms. Amy Mergen, Office of Admissions, Lourdes College, 6832 Convent Boulevard, Sylvania, OH 43560-2898. *Phone:* 419-885-5291 or toll-free 800-878-3210 Ext. 1299. *Fax:* 419-882-3987. *E-mail:* lcadmits@lourdes.edu. *Web site:* http://www.lourdes.edu/.

Malone University
Canton, Ohio

General Independent, comprehensive, coed, affiliated with Evangelical Friends Church–Eastern Region **Entrance** Moderately difficult **Setting** 87-acre suburban campus **Total enrollment** 2,620 **Student-faculty ratio** 15:1 **Application deadline** 7/1 (freshmen), 7/1 (transfer) **Freshman admission** 71% were admitted. Average high school GPA 3.34 **Freshman test scores** SAT critical reading scores over 500: 65.2%; SAT math scores over 500: 64.2%; ACT scores over 18: 94.1%; SAT critical reading scores over 600: 25%; SAT math scores over 600: 24%; ACT scores over 24: 42.6% **Housing** Yes **Expenses** Tuition & Fees $22,444; Room & Board $7548 **Undergraduates** 59% women, 15% part-time, 23% 25 or older, 0.4% Native American, 1% Hispanic American, 8% African American, 1% Asian American/Pacific Islander **The most frequently chosen baccalaureate fields are** business/marketing, education, health professions and related sciences **Academic program** Advanced placement, accelerated degree program, self-designed majors, honors program, summer session, adult/continuing education programs, internships **Contact** Dr. Brock C. Schroeder, Vice President for Enrollment, Malone University, 2600 Cleveland Avenue NW, Canton, OH 44709-3897. *Phone:* 330-471-8145 or toll-free 800-521-1146. *Fax:* 330-471-8149. *E-mail:* admissions@malone.edu. *Web site:* http://www3.malone.edu/.

Marietta College
Marietta, Ohio

General Independent, comprehensive, coed **Entrance** Moderately difficult **Setting** 90-acre small-town campus **Total enrollment** 1,588 **Student-faculty ratio** 12:1 **Application deadline** 5/1 (freshmen), rolling (transfer) **Freshman admission** 76% were admitted. Average high school GPA 3.45 **Freshman test scores** SAT critical reading scores over 500: 68%; SAT math scores over 500: 73%; ACT scores over 18: 97%; SAT critical reading scores over 600: 25%; SAT math scores over 600: 29%; ACT scores over 24: 50% **Housing** Yes **Expenses** Tuition & Fees $27,066; Room & Board $8046 **Undergraduates** 49% women, 5% part-time, 0.3% Native American, 1% Hispanic American, 4% African American, 1% Asian American/Pacific Islander **The most frequently chosen baccalaureate fields are** business/marketing, communications/journalism, visual and performing arts **Academic program** English as a second language, advanced placement, accelerated degree program, self-designed majors, honors program, summer session, adult/continuing education programs, internships **Contact** Mr. Jason Turley, Director of Admission, Marietta College, 215 Fifth Street, Marietta, OH 45750. *Phone:* 740-376-4600 or toll-free 800-331-7896. *Fax:* 740-376-8888. *E-mail:* admit@marietta.edu. *Web site:* http://www.marietta.edu/.
Visit Petersons.com and enter keyword Marietta

See page 944 for the College Close-Up.

Mercy College of Northwest Ohio
Toledo, Ohio

General Independent, 4-year, coed, primarily women, affiliated with Roman Catholic Church **Entrance** Moderately difficult **Setting** urban campus **Total enrollment** 1,048 **Student-faculty ratio** 11:1 **Application deadline** Rolling (freshmen), rolling (transfer) **Housing** Yes **Expenses** Tuition & Fees $10,090 **Undergraduates** 85% women, 48% part-time, 44% 25 or older, 0.5% Native American, 2% Hispanic American, 8% African American, 1% Asian American/Pacific Islander **The most frequently chosen baccalaureate field is** health professions and related sciences **Academic program** Advanced placement, summer session, internships **Contact** Admissions Counselor, Mercy College of Northwest Ohio, 2221 Madison Avenue, Toledo, OH 43604. *Phone:* 419-251-1313 or toll-free 888-80-Mercy. *Fax:* 419-251-1462. *E-mail:* admissions@mercycollege.edu. *Web site:* http://www.mercycollege.edu/.

Miami University
Oxford, Ohio

General State-related, university, coed **Entrance** Moderately difficult **Setting** 2,000-acre small-town campus **Total enrollment** 16,884 **Student-faculty ratio** 17:1 **Application deadline** 2/1 (freshmen), 5/1 (transfer) **Freshman admission** 79% were admitted. Average high school GPA 3.65 **Freshman test scores** SAT critical reading scores over 500: 88%; SAT math scores over 500: 95%; ACT scores over 18: 99%; SAT critical reading scores over 600: 41%; SAT math scores over 600: 59%; ACT scores over 24: 76% **Housing** Yes **Expenses** Tuition & Fees: state resident $11,910, nonresident $26,670; Room & Board $9458 **Undergraduates** 53% women, 1% part-time, 2% 25 or older, 1% Native American, 2% Hispanic American, 4% African American, 3% Asian American/Pacific Islander **The most frequently chosen baccalaureate fields are** business/marketing, education, social sciences **Academic program** Advanced placement, self-designed majors, honors program, summer session, adult/continuing education programs, internships **Contact** Office of Admissions, Miami University, 301 South Campus Avenue, Oxford, OH 45056. *Phone:* 513-529-2531. *Fax:* 513-529-1550. *E-mail:* admission@muohio.edu. *Web site:* http://www.muohio.edu/.

Miami University Hamilton
Hamilton, Ohio

General State-supported, comprehensive, coed **Entrance** Noncompetitive **Setting** 78-acre suburban campus **Total enrollment** 4,194 **Student-faculty ratio** 21:1 **Application deadline** Rolling (freshmen), rolling (transfer) **Housing** No **Expenses** Tuition & Fees: state resident $4350, nonresident $12,402 **Undergraduates** 55% women, 22% part-time, 24% 25 or older, 1% Native American, 2% Hispanic American, 8% African American, 2% Asian American/Pacific Islander **Academic program** English as a second language, advanced placement, self-designed majors, honors program, summer session, adult/continuing education programs, internships **Contact** Mr. Archie Nelson, Director of Admission and Financial Aid, Miami University Hamilton, 1601 Peck Boulevard, Hamilton, OH 45011-3399. *Phone:* 513-785-3111. *Fax:* 513-785-1807. *E-mail:* nelsona3@muohio.edu. *Web site:* http://www.ham.muohio.edu/.

Miami University–Middletown Campus
Middletown, Ohio

Contact Diane Cantonwine, Assistant Director of Admission and Financial Aid, Miami University–Middletown Campus, 4200 East University Boulevard, Middletown, OH 45042-3497. *Phone:* 513-727-3346 or toll-free 866-426-4643. *Fax:* 513-727-3223. *E-mail:* cantondm@muohio.edu. *Web site:* http://www.mid.muohio.edu/.

Mount Carmel College of Nursing
Columbus, Ohio

General Independent, comprehensive, coed, primarily women **Entrance** Moderately difficult **Setting** urban campus **Total enrollment** 782 **Application deadline** 4/1 (freshmen) **Freshman admission** 86% were admitted.

Average high school GPA 3.44 **Freshman test scores** ACT scores over 18: 98.02%; ACT scores over 24: 23.76% **Housing** Yes **Expenses** Tuition & Fees $15,061; Room only $4500 **Undergraduates** 89% women, 18% part-time, 29% 25 or older, 0.3% Native American, 2% Hispanic American, 6% African American, 2% Asian American/Pacific Islander **The most frequently chosen baccalaureate field is** health professions and related sciences **Academic program** Accelerated degree program, honors program **Contact** Kim Campbell, Director, Admissions and Recruitment, Mount Carmel College of Nursing, 127 South Davis Avenue, Columbus, OH 43222. *Phone:* 614-234-1085. *Fax:* 614-234-5427. *E-mail:* mccnadmissions@mchs.com. *Web site:* http://www.mccn.edu/.

Mount Vernon Nazarene University
Mount Vernon, Ohio

General Independent Nazarene, comprehensive, coed **Entrance** Moderately difficult **Setting** 401-acre small-town campus **Total enrollment** 2,622 **Student-faculty ratio** 14:1 **Application deadline** 7/15 (freshmen) **Freshman admission** 72% were admitted. Average high school GPA 3.27 **Freshman test scores** SAT critical reading scores over 500: 65%; SAT math scores over 500: 60%; ACT scores over 18: 89%; SAT critical reading scores over 600: 19%; SAT math scores over 600: 21%; ACT scores over 24: 36% **Housing** Yes **Expenses** Tuition & Fees $21,330; Room & Board $6180 **Undergraduates** 60% women, 16% part-time, 31% 25 or older, 0.4% Native American, 2% Hispanic American, 5% African American, 1% Asian American/Pacific Islander **The most frequently chosen baccalaureate fields are** business/marketing, communications/journalism, education **Academic program** Advanced placement, honors program, summer session, adult/continuing education programs, internships **Contact** James Smith, Director of Admissions and Student Recruitment, Mount Vernon Nazarene University, 800 Martinsburg Road, Mount Vernon, OH 43050. *Phone:* 740-392-6868 Ext. 4516 or toll-free 866-462-6868. *Fax:* 740-393-0511. *E-mail:* admissions@mvnu.edu. *Web site:* http://www.mvnu.edu/.

Muskingum University
New Concord, Ohio

General Independent, comprehensive, coed, affiliated with Presbyterian Church (U.S.A.) **Entrance** Moderately difficult **Setting** 215-acre small-town campus **Total enrollment** 2,099 **Application deadline** 6/1 (freshmen), 8/1 (transfer) **Housing** Yes **Expenses** Tuition & Fees $18,910; Room & Board $7350 **Undergraduates** 6% 25 or older **Academic program** English as a second language, advanced placement, accelerated degree program, self-designed majors, summer session, internships **Contact** Mrs. Beth DaLonzo, Director of Admission, Muskingum University, 163 Stormont Street, New Concord, OH 43762. *Phone:* 740-826-8137 or toll-free 800-752-6082. *Fax:* 740-826-8100. *E-mail:* adminfo@muskingum.edu. *Web site:* http://www.muskingum.edu/.
Visit Petersons.com and enter keyword Muskingum

See page 1000 for the College Close-Up.

Notre Dame College
South Euclid, Ohio

Contact Mr. David Armstrong, Dean of Admissions, Notre Dame College, 4545 College Road, South Euclid, OH 44121-4293. *Phone:* 216-373-5214 or toll-free 800-632-1680. *Fax:* 216-381-3802. *E-mail:* admissinos@ndc.edu. *Web site:* http://www.notredamecollege.edu/.
Visit Petersons.com and enter keywords Notre Dame

See page 1026 for the College Close-Up.

Oberlin College
Oberlin, Ohio

General Independent, comprehensive, coed **Entrance** Very difficult **Setting** 440-acre small-town campus **Total enrollment** 2,919 **Student-**

Experience the Excitement!

- Over 30 career-focused academic programs including Nursing, International Business, and Sports Management
- 23 Intercollegiate sports for men and women NEW 2010: Waterpolo
- Marching Band, Choir, Theater, and Cheerleading Scholarships available
- New apartment-style residence halls

MIDWESTERN

Notre Dame College is one of the best colleges and universities in the Midwest according to The Princeton Review.

APPLY NOW at *www.NotreDameCollege.edu*
or contact us for more details at 877.NDC.OHIO
or *admissions@ndc.edu.*

4545 College Road
Cleveland, OH 44121
1.877.NDC.OHIO
www.NotreDameCollege.edu

Changing the World… One Student at a Time.

Oberlin College (continued)
faculty ratio 9:1 **Application deadline** 1/15 (freshmen), 3/15 (transfer) **Freshman admission** 34% were admitted. Average high school GPA 3.6 **Freshman test scores** SAT critical reading scores over 500: 98%; SAT math scores over 500: 98%; ACT scores over 18: 100%; SAT critical reading scores over 600: 90%; SAT math scores over 600: 85%; ACT scores over 24: 94% **Housing** Yes **Expenses** Tuition & Fees $40,004; Room & Board $10,480 **Undergraduates** 55% women, 2% part-time, 1% 25 or older, 1% Native American, 5% Hispanic American, 7% African American, 7% Asian American/Pacific Islander **Academic program** English as a second language, advanced placement, self-designed majors, honors program, internships **Contact** Ms. Debra Chermonte, Dean of Admissions and Financial Aid, Oberlin College, Admissions Office, Carnegie Building, Oberlin, OH 44074-1090. *Phone:* 440-775-8411 or toll-free 800-622-OBIE. *Fax:* 440-775-6905. *E-mail:* college.admissions@oberlin.edu. *Web site:* http://www.oberlin.edu/.
Visit Petersons.com and enter keyword Oberlin

See page 1030 for the College Close-Up.

Ohio Christian University
Circleville, Ohio

General Independent, 4-year, coed, affiliated with Churches of Christ in Christian Union **Entrance** Minimally difficult **Setting** 40-acre small-town campus **Total enrollment** 636 **Application deadline** Rolling (freshmen), rolling (transfer) **Housing** Yes **Expenses** Tuition & Fees $13,960; Room & Board $5990 **Undergraduates** 54% 25 or older **Academic program** Advanced placement, self-designed majors, honors program, summer session, adult/continuing education programs, internships **Contact** Mike Egenreider, Associate Vice President for Enrollment, Ohio Christian University, 1476 Lancaster Pike, PO Box 458, Circleville, OH 43113-9487. *Phone:* 740-477-7741 or toll-free 800-701-0222. *E-mail:* enroll@ohiochristian.edu. *Web site:* http://www.ohiochristian.edu/.

Ohio Dominican University
Columbus, Ohio

General Independent Roman Catholic, comprehensive, coed **Entrance** Moderately difficult **Setting** 71-acre urban campus **Total enrollment** 3,052 **Student-faculty ratio** 14:1 **Application deadline** Rolling (freshmen), rolling (transfer) **Freshman admission** 59% were admitted. Average high school GPA 3.04 **Freshman test scores** ACT scores over 18: 92%; ACT scores over 24: 25% **Housing** Yes **Expenses** Tuition & Fees $24,616; Room & Board $8100 **Undergraduates** 60% women, 32% part-time, 37% 25 or older, 0.4% Native American, 2% Hispanic American, 21% African American, 1% Asian American/Pacific Islander **The most frequently chosen baccalaureate fields are** business/marketing, education, social sciences **Academic program** Advanced placement, self-designed majors, honors program, summer session, internships **Contact** Ms. Nicole A. Evans, Director of Admissions, Ohio Dominican University, 1216 Sunbury Road, Columbus, OH 43219. *Phone:* 614-251-4500 or toll-free 800-854-2670. *Fax:* 614-251-0156. *E-mail:* admissions@ohiodominican.edu. *Web site:* http://www.ohiodominican.edu/.

Ohio Northern University
Ada, Ohio

General Independent, comprehensive, coed, affiliated with United Methodist Church **Entrance** Moderately difficult **Setting** 300-acre small-town campus **Total enrollment** 3,651 **Student-faculty ratio** 12:1 **Application deadline** 8/15 (freshmen), 9/1 (transfer) **Freshman admission** 89% were admitted. Average high school GPA 3.64 **Freshman test scores** SAT critical reading scores over 500: 78%; SAT math scores over 500: 92%; ACT scores over 18: 99%; SAT critical reading scores over 600: 40%; SAT math scores over 600: 57%; ACT scores over 24: 73% **Housing** Yes **Expenses** Tuition & Fees $31,866; Room & Board $8280 **Undergraduates** 46% women, 10% part-time, 3% 25 or older, 0.5% Native American, 2% Hispanic American, 4% African American, 2% Asian American/Pacific Islander **The most frequently chosen baccalaureate fields are** business/marketing, biological/life sciences, engineering **Academic program** English as a second language, advanced placement, honors program, summer session, internships **Contact** Ms. Deborah Miller, Director of Admission, Ohio Northern University, 525 South Main Street, Ada, OH 45810-1599. *Phone:* 419-772-2260 Ext. 2464 or toll-free 888-408-4ONU. *Fax:* 419-772-2821. *E-mail:* admissions-ug@onu.edu. *Web site:* http://www.onu.edu/.
Visit Petersons.com and enter keywords Ohio Northern

See page 1032 for the College Close-Up.

The Ohio State University
Columbus, Ohio

General State-supported, university, coed **Entrance** Moderately difficult **Setting** 3,469-acre urban campus **Total enrollment** 55,014 **Student-faculty ratio** 12:1 **Application deadline** 2/1 (freshmen), 2/1 (transfer) **Freshman admission** 76% were admitted **Freshman test scores** SAT critical reading scores over 500: 90%; SAT math scores over 500: 96%; ACT scores over 18: 100%; SAT critical reading scores over 600: 51%; SAT math scores over 600: 70%; ACT scores over 24: 91% **Housing** Yes **Expenses** Tuition & Fees: state resident $8706, nonresident $22,278; Room & Board $8409 **Undergraduates** 46% women, 8% part-time, 8% 25 or older **The most frequently chosen baccalaureate fields are** business/marketing, family and consumer sciences, social sciences **Academic program** English as a second language, advanced placement, accelerated degree program, self-designed majors, honors program, summer session, adult/continuing education programs, internships **Contact** Dr. Mabel Freeman, Assistant Vice President for Undergraduate Admissions and First Year Experience, The Ohio State University, 110 Enarson Hall, 154 West 12th Avenue, Columbus, OH 43210. *Phone:* 614-292-3980. *Fax:* 614-292-4818. *E-mail:* askabuckeye@osu.edu. *Web site:* http://www.osu.edu/.

The Ohio State University at Lima
Lima, Ohio

General State-supported, comprehensive, coed **Entrance** Noncompetitive **Setting** 565-acre suburban campus **Total enrollment** 1,508 **Student-faculty ratio** 17:1 **Application deadline** 7/1 (freshmen) **Freshman admission** 98% were admitted **Freshman test scores** SAT critical reading scores over 500: 60%; SAT math scores over 500: 75%; ACT scores over 18: 90%; SAT critical reading scores over 600: 20%; SAT math scores over 600: 30%; ACT scores over 24: 28% **Housing** No **Expenses** Tuition & Fees: state resident $5661, nonresident $19,233 **Undergraduates** 53% women, 14% part-time, 19% 25 or older, 0.5% Native American, 2% Hispanic American, 4% African American, 2% Asian American/Pacific Islander **Academic program** English as a second language, advanced placement, accelerated degree program, self-designed majors, honors program, summer session, adult/continuing education programs, internships **Contact** Ms. Garlene Smithson, Director of Admissions, The Ohio State University at Lima, 4240 Campus Drive, Lima, OH 45804. *Phone:* 419-995-8434. *Fax:* 419-995-8483. *E-mail:* admissions@lima.ohio-state.edu. *Web site:* http://www.lima.ohio-state.edu/.

The Ohio State University at Marion
Marion, Ohio

General State-supported, comprehensive, coed **Entrance** Noncompetitive **Setting** 188-acre small-town campus **Total enrollment** 1,828 **Student-faculty ratio** 16:1 **Application deadline** 7/1 (freshmen) **Freshman admission** 98% were admitted **Freshman test scores** SAT critical reading scores over 500: 46%; SAT math scores over 500: 65%; ACT scores over 18: 87%; SAT critical reading scores over 600: 11%; SAT math scores over 600: 23%; ACT scores over 24: 28% **Housing** No **Expenses** Tuition & Fees: state resident $5661, nonresident $19,233

Undergraduates 54% women, 15% part-time, 17% 25 or older, 1% Native American, 2% Hispanic American, 8% African American, 5% Asian American/Pacific Islander **Academic program** English as a second language, advanced placement, accelerated degree program, self-designed majors, honors program, summer session, adult/continuing education programs, internships **Contact** Mr. Matthew Moreau, Admissions and Financial Aid Coordinator, The Ohio State University at Marion, 1465 Mount Vernon Avenue, Marion, OH 43302. *Phone:* 740-725-6337. *Fax:* 740-386-2439. *E-mail:* moreau.1@osu.edu. *Web site:* http://www.marion.ohio-state.edu/.

The Ohio State University–Mansfield Campus

Mansfield, Ohio

General State-supported, comprehensive, coed **Entrance** Noncompetitive **Setting** 640-acre suburban campus **Total enrollment** 1,647 **Student-faculty ratio** 12:1 **Application deadline** 7/1 (freshmen) **Freshman admission** 99% were admitted **Freshman test scores** SAT critical reading scores over 500: 58%; SAT math scores over 500: 53%; ACT scores over 18: 91%; SAT critical reading scores over 600: 17%; SAT math scores over 600: 18%; ACT scores over 24: 35% **Housing** Yes **Expenses** Tuition & Fees: state resident $5661, nonresident $19,233; Room only $5205 **Undergraduates** 59% women, 27% part-time, 20% 25 or older **Academic program** English as a second language, advanced placement, accelerated degree program, self-designed majors, honors program, summer session, adult/continuing education programs, internships **Contact** Mr. Henry D. Thomas, Coordinator of Admissions and Financial Aid, The Ohio State University–Mansfield Campus, 1760 University Drive, Mansfield, OH 44906. *Phone:* 419-755-4225. *Fax:* 419-755-4241. *E-mail:* admissions@mansfield.ohio-state.edu. *Web site:* http://www.mansfield.osu.edu/.

The Ohio State University–Newark Campus

Newark, Ohio

General State-supported, comprehensive, coed **Entrance** Noncompetitive **Setting** 106-acre suburban campus **Total enrollment** 2,515 **Student-faculty ratio** 19:1 **Application deadline** 7/1 (freshmen) **Freshman admission** 99% were admitted **Freshman test scores** SAT critical reading scores over 500: 46%; SAT math scores over 500: 50%; ACT scores over 18: 85%; SAT critical reading scores over 600: 12%; SAT math scores over 600: 12%; ACT scores over 24: 24% **Housing** Yes **Expenses** Tuition & Fees: state resident $5661, nonresident $19,233 **Undergraduates** 51% women, 14% part-time, 17% 25 or older, 0.5% Native American, 2% Hispanic American, 10% African American, 3% Asian American/Pacific Islander **Academic program** English as a second language, advanced placement, accelerated degree program, self-designed majors, honors program, summer session, adult/continuing education programs, internships **Contact** Ms. Ann Donahue, Director of Enrollment, The Ohio State University–Newark Campus, 1179 University Drive, Newark, OH 43055. *Phone:* 740-366-9333. *Fax:* 740-364-9645. *E-mail:* barclay.3@osu.edu. *Web site:* http://www.newark.osu.edu/.

Ohio University

Athens, Ohio

General State-supported, university, coed **Entrance** Moderately difficult **Setting** 1,762-acre small-town campus **Total enrollment** 22,647 **Student-faculty ratio** 19:1 **Application deadline** 2/1 (freshmen), 6/15 (transfer) **Freshman admission** 82% were admitted. Average high school GPA 3.36 **Freshman test scores** SAT critical reading scores over 500: 69%; SAT math scores over 500: 70%; ACT scores over 18: 98%; SAT critical reading scores over 600: 26%; SAT math scores over 600: 27%; ACT scores over 24: 48% **Housing** Yes **Expenses** Tuition & Fees: state resident $8973, nonresident $17,937; Room & Board $9408 **Undergraduates** 52% women, 11% part-time, 4% 25 or older, 0.3% Native American, 2% Hispanic American, 5% African American, 1% Asian American/Pacific Islander **The most frequently chosen baccalaureate fields are** business/marketing, communications/journalism, education **Academic program** English as a second language, advanced placement, accelerated degree program, self-designed majors, honors program, summer session, adult/continuing education programs, internships **Contact** Undergraduate Admissions, Ohio University, Athens, OH 45701-2979. *Phone:* 740-593-4100. *Fax:* 740-593-0560. *E-mail:* admissions@ohio.edu. *Web site:* http://www.ohio.edu/.

Ohio University–Chillicothe

Chillicothe, Ohio

General State-supported, comprehensive, coed **Entrance** Noncompetitive **Setting** 124-acre small-town campus **Total enrollment** 1,836 **Application deadline** 9/1 (freshmen), 9/1 (transfer) **Housing** No **Expenses** Tuition & Fees: state resident $4581, nonresident $8904 **Undergraduates** 47% 25 or older **Academic program** Advanced placement, accelerated degree program, self-designed majors, summer session, adult/continuing education programs, internships **Contact** TJ Eveland, Coordinator of Student Enrollment, Ohio University–Chillicothe, 101 University Drive, Chillicothe, OH 45601. *Phone:* 740-774-7200 Ext. 242 or toll-free 877-462-6824. *Fax:* 740-774-7295. *E-mail:* evelandt@ohio.edu. *Web site:* http://www.chillicothe.ohiou.edu/.

Ohio University–Eastern

St. Clairsville, Ohio

General State-supported, comprehensive, coed **Entrance** Noncompetitive **Setting** 300-acre rural campus **Total enrollment** 751 **Application deadline** Rolling (freshmen), rolling (transfer) **Housing** No **Expenses** Tuition & Fees: state resident $4395, nonresident $5715 **Undergraduates** 26% 25 or older **Academic program** Advanced placement, accelerated degree program, self-designed majors, summer session, adult/continuing education programs **Contact** N. Kip Howard, Assistant Vice President for Enrollment Services/Director of Admissions, Ohio University–Eastern, 45425 National Road, St. Clairsville, OH 43950-9724. *Phone:* 740-593-4120 or toll-free 800-648-3331. *E-mail:* howardn@ohio.edu. *Web site:* http://www.eastern.ohiou.edu/.

Ohio University–Lancaster

Lancaster, Ohio

General State-supported, comprehensive, coed **Entrance** Noncompetitive **Setting** 360-acre small-town campus **Total enrollment** 1,728 **Application deadline** Rolling (freshmen), rolling (transfer) **Housing** No **Expenses** Tuition & Fees: state resident $4581, nonresident $8904 **Undergraduates** 31% 25 or older **Academic program** Advanced placement, accelerated degree program, self-designed majors, summer session, adult/continuing education programs, internships **Contact** Pat Fox, Enrollment Manager, Ohio University–Lancaster, 1570 Granville Pike, Lancaster, OH 43130-1097. *Phone:* 740-654-6711 Ext. 215 or toll-free 888-446-4468 Ext. 215. *E-mail:* fox@ohio.edu. *Web site:* http://www.ohiou.edu/lancaster/.

Ohio University–Southern Campus

Ironton, Ohio

General State-supported, comprehensive, coed **Entrance** Noncompetitive **Setting** 9-acre small-town campus **Total enrollment** 1,836 **Application deadline** Rolling (freshmen), rolling (transfer) **Freshman admission** 100% were admitted **Housing** No **Expenses** Tuition & Fees: state resident $4395, nonresident $5715 **Undergraduates** 51% women, 50% part-time, 51% 25 or older **Academic program** Self-designed majors, summer session, adult/continuing education programs **Contact** Linda Harlow, Admission, Registration and Records Coordinator, Ohio University–Southern Campus, 1804 Liberty Avenue, Ironton, OH 45638-

Ohio University–Southern Campus (continued)
2214. *Phone:* 740-533-4584 or toll-free 800-626-0513. *E-mail:* harlow@ohio.edu. *Web site:* http://www.ohiou.edu/.

Ohio University–Zanesville
Zanesville, Ohio

General State-supported, comprehensive, coed **Entrance** Noncompetitive **Setting** 179-acre rural campus **Total enrollment** 1,985 **Student-faculty ratio** 23:1 **Application deadline** Rolling (freshmen), rolling (transfer) **Freshman admission** 91% were admitted **Freshman test scores** ACT scores over 18: 74%; ACT scores over 24: 21% **Expenses** Tuition & Fees: state resident $4662, nonresident $8985 **Undergraduates** 70% women, 41% part-time, 43% 25 or older, 1% Hispanic American, 4% African American, 0.3% Asian American/Pacific Islander **Academic program** Advanced placement, self-designed majors, summer session, adult/continuing education programs **Contact** Mrs. Karen Ragsdale, Student Services Secretary, Ohio University–Zanesville, Office of Student Services, 1425 Newark Road, Zanesville, OH 43701. *Phone:* 740-588-1440. *Fax:* 740-588-1444. *E-mail:* ouzservices@ohio.edu. *Web site:* http://www.zanesville.ohiou.edu/.

Ohio Wesleyan University
Delaware, Ohio

General Independent United Methodist, 4-year, coed **Entrance** Very difficult **Setting** 200-acre small-town campus **Total enrollment** 1,893 **Student-faculty ratio** 11:1 **Application deadline** 3/1 (freshmen), 6/1 (transfer) **Freshman admission** 64% were admitted. Average high school GPA 3.46 **Freshman test scores** SAT critical reading scores over 500: 85.66%; SAT math scores over 500: 83.03%; ACT scores over 18: 98.2%; SAT critical reading scores over 600: 48.29%; SAT math scores over 600: 50.91%; ACT scores over 24: 68.98% **Housing** Yes **Expenses** Tuition & Fees $35,030; Room & Board $9224 **Undergraduates** 54% women, 1% part-time, 1% 25 or older, 1% Native American, 2% Hispanic American, 5% African American, 2% Asian American/Pacific Islander **The most frequently chosen baccalaureate fields are** biological/life sciences, psychology, social sciences **Academic program** Advanced placement, self-designed majors, honors program, summer session, internships **Contact** Ms. Carol DelPropost, Assistant Vice President of Admission and Financial Aid, Ohio Wesleyan University, 61 South Sandusky Street, Delaware, OH 43015. *Phone:* 740-368-3059 or toll-free 800-922-8953. *Fax:* 740-368-3314. *E-mail:* cjdelpro@owu.edu. *Web site:* http://www.owu.edu/.

Visit Petersons.com and enter keywords Ohio Wesleyan

See page 1034 for the College Close-Up.

Otterbein University
Westerville, Ohio

General Independent United Methodist, comprehensive, coed **Entrance** Moderately difficult **Setting** 142-acre suburban campus **Total enrollment** 3,131 **Student-faculty ratio** 12:1 **Application deadline** 3/1 (freshmen), rolling (transfer) **Freshman admission** 82% were admitted. Average high school GPA 3.39 **Freshman test scores** SAT critical reading scores over 500: 65%; SAT math scores over 500: 67%; ACT scores over 18: 94%; SAT critical reading scores over 600: 24%; SAT math scores over 600: 24%; ACT scores over 24: 45% **Housing** Yes **Expenses** Tuition & Fees $26,319; Room & Board $7461 **Undergraduates** 63% women, 15% part-time, 1% 25 or older **The most frequently chosen baccalaureate fields are** business/marketing, education, visual and performing arts **Academic program** Advanced placement, self-designed majors, honors program, summer session, adult/continuing education programs, internships **Contact** Dr. Cass Johnson, Director of Admissions, Otterbein University, One Otterbein College, Westerville, OH 43081-9924. *Phone:* 614-823-1500 or toll-free 800-488-8144. *Fax:* 614-823-1200. *E-mail:* uotterb@otterbein.edu. *Web site:* http://www.otterbein.edu/.

Ohio Wesleyan?
Who Says?

Forbes Magazine
Lists Ohio Wesleyan in the **top third of the nation's best** public and private colleges and universities.

Colleges That Change Lives
Selected OWU as **one of its 40 schools.**

The Daily Beast
Picks Ohio Wesleyan as **one of the decade's hottest colleges.**

Phi Beta Kappa
Has had a **chapter at OWU for more than a century.**

The John Templeton Foundation
Cites Ohio Wesleyan's **"exemplary programs" in character development and service learning.**

- Our Nobel Prize laureates.
- Our Oscar® and Emmy winners.
- Our top-echelon business leaders, scientists, artists and writers.
- And our students.

That's who.

Ohio Wesleyan University

www.owu.edu

Pontifical College Josephinum
Columbus, Ohio

General Independent Roman Catholic, comprehensive, men only **Entrance** Minimally difficult **Setting** 100-acre suburban campus **Total enrollment** 119 **Application deadline** 7/31 (freshmen), rolling (transfer) **Freshman admission** 75% were admitted **Freshman test scores** ACT scores over 18: 75%; ACT scores over 24: 25% **Housing** Yes **Expenses** Tuition & Fees $15,697 **Undergraduates** 30% 25 or older, 1% Native American, 12% Hispanic American, 1% Asian American/Pacific Islander **The most frequently chosen baccalaureate fields are** history, English, philosophy and religious studies **Academic program** English as a second language, advanced placement, honors program, internships **Contact** Mrs. Arminda Crawford, Secretary for Admissions, Pontifical College Josephinum, 7825 North High Street, Columbus, OH 43235. *Phone:* 614-985-2241 or toll-free 888-252-5812. *Fax:* 614-885-2307. *E-mail:* acrawford@pcj.edu. *Web site:* http://www.pcj.edu/.

Rabbinical College of Telshe
Wickliffe, Ohio

Contact Admissions Office, Rabbinical College of Telshe, 28400 Euclid Avenue, Wickliffe, OH 44092-2523. *Phone:* 440-943-5300.

Shawnee State University
Portsmouth, Ohio

General State-supported, comprehensive, coed **Entrance** Noncompetitive **Setting** 52-acre small-town campus **Total enrollment** 4,300 **Student-faculty ratio** 18:1 **Application deadline** Rolling (freshmen), rolling (transfer) **Freshman admission** 84% were admitted **Freshman test scores** ACT scores over 18: 63%; ACT scores over 24: 21% **Housing** Yes **Expenses** Tuition & Fees: state resident $6132, nonresident $10,476; Room & Board $7944 **Undergraduates** 58% women, 16% part-time, 24% 25 or older, 1% Native American, 0.4% Hispanic American, 4% African American, 0.3% Asian American/Pacific Islander **The most frequently chosen baccalaureate fields are** business/marketing, health professions and related sciences, social sciences **Academic program** Advanced placement, accelerated degree program, self-designed majors, honors program, summer session, adult/continuing education programs, internships **Contact** Mr. Bob Trusz, Director of Admission, Shawnee State University, 940 Second Street, Portsmouth, OH 45662-4344. *Phone:* 740-351-3610 Ext. 610 or toll-free 800-959-2SSU. *Fax:* 740-351-3111. *E-mail:* admsn@shawnee.edu. *Web site:* http://www.shawnee.edu/.

Strayer University–Akron Campus
Akron, Ohio

General Proprietary, comprehensive, coed **Contact** Admissions Office, Strayer University–Akron Campus, 51 Park West Boulevard, Akron, OH 44320. *Phone:* 330-734-6700. *Web site:* http://strayer.edu/akron.

Strayer University–Columbus Campus
Columbus, Ohio

General Proprietary, comprehensive, coed **Contact** Admissions Office, Strayer University–Columbus Campus, 8425 Pulsar Place, Suite 400, Columbus, OH 43240. *Phone:* 614-310-6700. *Web site:* http://www.strayer.edu/columbus.

Strayer University–Fairview Park Campus
Fairview Park, Ohio

General Proprietary, comprehensive, coed **Contact** Admissions Office, Strayer University–Fairview Park Campus, 22730 Fairview Center Drive, Suite 150, Fairview Park, OH 44126-3616. *Phone:* 440-471-6400. *Web site:* http://strayer.edu/fairview_park.

Strayer University–Mason Campus
Mason, Ohio

General Proprietary, comprehensive, coed **Contact** Admissions Office, Strayer University–Mason Campus, 4605 Duke Drive, Suite 700, Mason, OH 45040. *Phone:* 513-234-6450. *Web site:* http://www.strayer.edu/mason.

Temple Baptist College
Cincinnati, Ohio

General Independent religious, 4-year, coed **Total enrollment** 60 **Housing** No **Expenses** Tuition & Fees $8670 **Undergraduates** 60% 25 or older **Contact** Temple Baptist College, 11965 Kenn Road, Cincinnati, OH 45240. *Web site:* http://www.templebaptistcollege.com/.

Tiffin University
Tiffin, Ohio

General Independent, comprehensive, coed **Entrance** Moderately difficult **Setting** 110-acre small-town campus **Total enrollment** 3,429 **Student-faculty ratio** 19:1 **Application deadline** Rolling (freshmen) **Freshman admission** 60% were admitted. Average high school GPA 3.05 **Freshman test scores** SAT critical reading scores over 500: 41.9%; SAT math scores over 500: 37.9%; ACT scores over 18: 84%; SAT critical reading scores over 600: 6.8%; SAT math scores over 600: 10.9%; ACT scores over 24: 22.6% **Housing** Yes **Expenses** Tuition & Fees $18,390; Room & Board $8340 **Undergraduates** 56% women, 22% part-time, 33% 25 or older, 0.3% Native American, 3% Hispanic American, 18% African American, 1% Asian American/Pacific Islander **The most frequently chosen baccalaureate fields are** business/marketing, psychology, security and protective services **Academic program** English as a second language, advanced placement, accelerated degree program, honors program, summer session, adult/continuing education programs, internships **Contact** Mr. Jeremy Marinis, Director of Undergraduate Admissions, Tiffin University, 155 Miami Street, Tiffin, OH 44883. *Phone:* 419-448-3301 or toll-free 800-968-6446. *Fax:* 419-443-5006. *E-mail:* marinisjj@tiffin.edu. *Web site:* http://www.tiffin.edu/.

Visit Petersons.com and enter keyword Tiffin

Tri-State Bible College
South Point, Ohio

General Independent nondenominational, 4-year, coed **Setting** 4-acre suburban campus **Total enrollment** 65 **Expenses** Tuition & Fees $6190 **Undergraduates** 86% 25 or older **Contact** Admissions Director, Tri-State Bible College, 506 Margaret Street, PO Box 445, South Point, OH 45680-8402. *Phone:* 740-377-2520. *Fax:* 740-377-0001. *E-mail:* recruitment@tsbc.edu. *Web site:* http://www.tsbc.edu/.

Union Institute & University
Cincinnati, Ohio

General Independent, university, coed **Entrance** Minimally difficult **Setting** 5-acre urban campus **Total enrollment** 1,523 **Application deadline** Rolling (freshmen), rolling (transfer) **Housing** No **Expenses** Tuition & Fees $10,528 **Undergraduates** 60% women, 32% part-time, 93% 25 or older, 1% Native American, 13% Hispanic American, 30% African American, 2% Asian American/Pacific Islander **The most frequently chosen baccalaureate fields are** liberal arts/general studies, education, security and protective services **Academic program** Advanced placement, accelerated degree program, self-designed majors, summer session, internships **Contact** Dr. Gregory Stewart, Vice President,

Union Institute & University (continued)
Enrollment Management, Union Institute & University, 440 East McMillan Street, Cincinnati, OH 45206-1925. *Phone:* 513-487-1173 or toll-free 800-486-3116. *Web site:* http://www.tui.edu/.

The University of Akron
Akron, Ohio

General State-supported, university, coed **Entrance** Moderately difficult **Setting** 223-acre urban campus **Total enrollment** 25,959 **Student-faculty ratio** 21:1 **Application deadline** 8/11 (freshmen), rolling (transfer) **Freshman admission** 76% were admitted. Average high school GPA 3.02 **Freshman test scores** SAT critical reading scores over 500: 50%; SAT math scores over 500: 52.1%; ACT scores over 18: 76.1%; SAT critical reading scores over 600: 16.1%; SAT math scores over 600: 21.8%; ACT scores over 24: 28% **Housing** Yes **Expenses** Tuition & Fees: state resident $8752, nonresident $18,000; Room & Board $8697 **Undergraduates** 49% women, 22% part-time, 22% 25 or older, 0.2% Native American, 1% Hispanic American, 15% African American, 2% Asian American/Pacific Islander **The most frequently chosen baccalaureate fields are** business/marketing, education, health professions and related sciences **Academic program** English as a second language, advanced placement, accelerated degree program, self-designed majors, honors program, summer session, adult/continuing education programs, internships **Contact** Ms. Diane Raybuck, Director of Admissions, The University of Akron, 302 Buchtel Common, Akron, OH 44325. *Phone:* 330-972-7100 or toll-free 800-655-4884. *Fax:* 330-972-7022. *E-mail:* admissions@uakron.edu. *Web site:* http://www.uakron.edu/.

University of Cincinnati
Cincinnati, Ohio

General State-supported, university, coed **Entrance** Moderately difficult **Setting** 137-acre urban campus **Total enrollment** 31,134 **Student-faculty ratio** 16:1 **Application deadline** 9/1 (freshmen) **Freshman admission** 67% were admitted. Average high school GPA 3.42 **Freshman test scores** SAT critical reading scores over 500: 73.92%; SAT math scores over 500: 82.46%; ACT scores over 18: 99.69%; SAT critical reading scores over 600: 30.57%; SAT math scores over 600: 41.18%; ACT scores over 24: 59.51% **Housing** Yes **Expenses** Tuition & Fees: state resident $9399, nonresident $25,425; Room & Board $9702 **Undergraduates** 50% women, 17% part-time, 19% 25 or older, 0.2% Native American, 2% Hispanic American, 10% African American, 3% Asian American/Pacific Islander **The most frequently chosen baccalaureate fields are** business/marketing, health professions and related sciences, visual and performing arts **Academic program** English as a second language, advanced placement, accelerated degree program, honors program, summer session, adult/continuing education programs, internships **Contact** Mr. Thomas Canepa, Associate Vice President, Admissions, University of Cincinnati, Office of Admissions, PO Box210091, Cincinnati, OH 45221-0091. *Phone:* 513-556-1100. *Fax:* 513-556-1105. *E-mail:* admissions@uc.edu. *Web site:* http://www.uc.edu/.

University of Dayton
Dayton, Ohio

General Independent Roman Catholic, university, coed **Entrance** Moderately difficult **Setting** 373-acre suburban campus **Total enrollment** 10,908 **Student-faculty ratio** 15:1 **Application deadline** Rolling (freshmen), 6/15 (transfer) **Freshman admission** 73% were admitted. Average high school GPA 3.6 **Freshman test scores** SAT critical reading scores over 500: 82.34%; SAT math scores over 500: 83.72%; ACT scores over 18: 99.93%; SAT critical reading scores over 600: 34.68%; SAT math scores over 600: 44.36%; ACT scores over 24: 75.2% **Housing** Yes **Expenses** Tuition & Fees $29,930; Room & Board $9400 **Undergraduates** 49% women, 7% part-time, 4% 25 or older, 0.3% Native American, 2% Hispanic American, 3% African American, 1% Asian American/Pacific Islander **The most frequently chosen baccalaureate fields are** business/marketing, communications/journalism, education **Academic program** English as a second language, advanced placement, accelerated degree program, self-designed majors, honors program, summer session, adult/continuing education programs, internships **Contact** Mr. Robert Durkle, Assistant Vice President and Dean of Admission, University of Dayton, 300 College Park, Dayton, OH 45469-1300. *Phone:* 937-229-4411 or toll-free 800-837-7433. *Fax:* 937-229-4729. *E-mail:* admission@udayton.edu. *Web site:* http://www.udayton.edu/.

The University of Findlay
Findlay, Ohio

General Independent, comprehensive, coed, affiliated with Church of God **Entrance** Moderately difficult **Setting** 390-acre small-town campus **Total enrollment** 4,278 **Student-faculty ratio** 17:1 **Application deadline** Rolling (freshmen), rolling (transfer) **Freshman admission** 68% were admitted. Average high school GPA 3.4 **Freshman test scores** SAT critical reading scores over 500: 67.9%; SAT math scores over 500: 65.7%; SAT critical reading scores over 600: 22.9%; SAT math scores over 600: 22.1% **Housing** Yes **Expenses** Tuition & Fees $25,774; Room & Board $8554 **Undergraduates** 64% women, 13% part-time, 18% 25 or older, 0.3% Native American, 1% Hispanic American, 3% African American, 1% Asian American/Pacific Islander **The most frequently chosen baccalaureate fields are** business/marketing, education, health professions and related sciences **Academic program** English as a second language, advanced placement, accelerated degree program, self-designed majors, honors program, summer session, adult/continuing education programs, internships **Contact** Mr. Donna Gruber, Director of Undergraduate Admissions, The University of Findlay, 1000 North Main Street, Findlay, OH 45840-3653. *Phone:* 419-434-4540 or toll-free 800-548-0932. *Fax:* 419-434-4898. *E-mail:* admissions@findlay.edu. *Web site:* http://www.findlay.edu/.

Visit Petersons.com and enter keywords University of Findlay

See page 1268 for the College Close-Up.

University of Mount Union
Alliance, Ohio

General Independent United Methodist, comprehensive, coed **Entrance** Moderately difficult **Setting** 115-acre suburban campus **Total enrollment** 2,212 **Student-faculty ratio** 14:1 **Application deadline** Rolling (freshmen), rolling (transfer) **Freshman admission** 75% were admitted. Average high school GPA 3.19 **Freshman test scores** SAT critical reading scores over 500: 47%; SAT math scores over 500: 55%; ACT scores over 18: 91%; SAT critical reading scores over 600: 12%; SAT math scores over 600: 24%; ACT scores over 24: 34% **Housing** Yes **Expenses** Tuition & Fees $23,880; Room & Board $7420 **Undergraduates** 50% women, 2% part-time, 2% 25 or older, 0.1% Native American, 2% Hispanic American, 5% African American, 1% Asian American/Pacific Islander **The most frequently chosen baccalaureate fields are** business/marketing, education, parks and recreation **Academic program** English as a second language, advanced placement, accelerated degree program, self-designed majors, honors program, summer session, adult/continuing education programs, internships **Contact** Mr. Vincent Heslop, Director of Enrollment Technology, University of Mount Union, 1972 Clark Avenue, Alliance, OH 44601. *Phone:* 330-823-2590 or toll-free 800-334-6682 (in-state); 800-992-6682 (out-of-state). *Fax:* 330-823-5097. *E-mail:* admission@muc.edu. *Web site:* http://www.mountunion.edu/.

See page 1286 for the College Close-Up.

University of Northwestern Ohio
Lima, Ohio

Contact Mr. Dan Klopp, Vice President for Enrollment Management, University of Northwestern Ohio, 1441 North Cable Road, Lima, OH

45805-1498. *Phone:* 419-227-3141. *Fax:* 419-229-6926. *E-mail:* klopp_d@unoh.edu. *Web site:* http://www.unoh.edu/.

University of Phoenix–Cincinnati Campus

West Chester, Ohio

General Proprietary, comprehensive, coed **Entrance** Noncompetitive **Setting** urban campus **Total enrollment** 143 **Application deadline** Rolling (freshmen), rolling (transfer) **Housing** No **Expenses** Tuition & Fees $11,925 **Undergraduates** 60% women, 93% 25 or older, 16% African American, 1% Asian American/Pacific Islander **The most frequently chosen baccalaureate fields are** business/marketing, computer and information sciences **Academic program** Advanced placement, accelerated degree program **Contact** Ms. Audra McQuarie, Registrar/Executive Director, University of Phoenix–Cincinnati Campus, 4035 South Riverpoint Parkway, Mail Stop CF-L101, Phoenix, AZ 85040. *Phone:* 480-557-6151 or toll-free 800-776-4867 (in-state); 800-228-7240 (out-of-state). *Fax:* 480-643-3068. *E-mail:* audra.mcquarie@phoenix.edu. *Web site:* http://www.phoenix.edu/.

University of Phoenix–Cleveland Campus

Independence, Ohio

General Proprietary, comprehensive, coed **Entrance** Noncompetitive **Setting** urban campus **Total enrollment** 664 **Application deadline** Rolling (freshmen), rolling (transfer) **Housing** No **Expenses** Tuition & Fees $13,200 **Undergraduates** 73% women, 91% 25 or older, 0.3% Native American, 2% Hispanic American, 39% African American, 1% Asian American/Pacific Islander **The most frequently chosen baccalaureate fields are** business/marketing, computer and information sciences, health professions and related sciences **Academic program** Advanced placement, accelerated degree program, adult/continuing education programs **Contact** Ms. Audra McQuarie, Registrar/Executive Director, University of Phoenix–Cleveland Campus, 4035 South Riverpoint Parkway, Mail Stop CF-L101, Phoenix, AZ 85040. *Phone:* 480-557-6151 or toll-free 800-776-4867 (in-state); 800-228-7240 (out-of-state). *Fax:* 480-643-3068. *E-mail:* audra.mcquarie@phoenix.edu. *Web site:* http://www.phoenix.edu/.

University of Phoenix–Columbus Ohio Campus

Columbus, Ohio

General Proprietary, comprehensive, coed **Entrance** Noncompetitive **Setting** urban campus **Total enrollment** 208 **Application deadline** Rolling (freshmen), rolling (transfer) **Housing** No **Expenses** Tuition & Fees $13,200 **Undergraduates** 56% women, 81% 25 or older, 1% Native American, 2% Hispanic American, 29% African American **The most frequently chosen baccalaureate field is** business/marketing **Academic program** Advanced placement, accelerated degree program **Contact** Ms. Audra McQuarie, Registrar/Executive Director, University of Phoenix–Columbus Ohio Campus, 4035 South Riverpoint Parkway, Mall Stop CF-L101, Phoenix, AZ 85040. *Phone:* 480-557-6151 or toll-free 800-776-4867 (in-state); 800-228-7240 (out-of-state). *Fax:* 480-643-3068. *E-mail:* audra.mcquarie@phoenix.edu. *Web site:* http://www.phoenix.edu/.

University of Rio Grande

Rio Grande, Ohio

General Independent, comprehensive, coed **Entrance** Noncompetitive **Setting** 170-acre rural campus **Total enrollment** 2,142 **Student-faculty ratio** 15:1 **Application deadline** Rolling (freshmen), rolling (transfer) **Freshman admission** 76% were admitted. Average high school GPA 3.06 **Freshman test scores** ACT scores over 18: 68%; ACT scores over 24: 11% **Housing** Yes **Expenses** Tuition & Fees $18,760; Room & Board $7600 **Undergraduates** 60% women, 21% part-time, 9% 25 or older, 0.4% Native American, 1% Hispanic American, 3% African American, 0.4% Asian American/Pacific Islander **The most frequently chosen baccalaureate fields are** business/marketing, education, natural resources/environmental science **Academic program** English as a second language, advanced placement, accelerated degree program, self-designed majors, honors program, summer session, adult/continuing education programs, internships **Contact** Ms. Rebecca Long, Director of Admissions, University of Rio Grande, PO Box 500, Rio Grande, OH 45674. *Phone:* 740-245-7425 or toll-free 800-282-7201. *Fax:* 740-245-7260. *E-mail:* admissions@rio.edu. *Web site:* http://www.rio.edu/.

The University of Toledo

Toledo, Ohio

General State-supported, university, coed **Entrance** Noncompetitive **Setting** 813-acre suburban campus **Total enrollment** 23,064 **Student-faculty ratio** 19:1 **Application deadline** Rolling (freshmen), rolling (transfer) **Freshman admission** 90% were admitted. Average high school GPA 3.06 **Freshman test scores** ACT scores over 18: 79.2%; ACT scores over 24: 29.82% **Housing** Yes **Expenses** Tuition & Fees: state resident $8066, nonresident $16,877; Room & Board $9478 **Undergraduates** 50% women, 17% part-time, 17% 25 or older, 0.3% Native American, 3% Hispanic American, 16% African American, 2% Asian American/Pacific Islander **The most frequently chosen baccalaureate fields are** business/marketing, engineering, health professions and related sciences **Academic program** English as a second language, advanced placement, self-designed majors, honors program, summer session, adult/continuing education programs, internships **Contact** William Pierce, Director of Undergraduate Admissions, The University of Toledo, 2801 West Bancroft, Toledo, OH 43606-3390. *Phone:* 419-530-5705 or toll-free 800-5TOLEDO. *Fax:* 419-530-5713. *E-mail:* william.pierce@utoledo.edu. *Web site:* http://www.utoledo.edu/.

Urbana University

Urbana, Ohio

Contact Ms. Paula Brown, Director of Admissions, Urbana University, 579 College Way, Urbana, OH 43078. *Phone:* 937-484-1356 or toll-free 800-7-URBANA. *Fax:* 937-652-6871. *E-mail:* admiss@urbana.edu. *Web site:* http://www.urbana.edu/.

Ursuline College

Pepper Pike, Ohio

General Independent Roman Catholic, comprehensive, coed, primarily women **Entrance** Minimally difficult **Setting** 112-acre suburban campus **Total enrollment** 1,515 **Student-faculty ratio** 9:1 **Application deadline** Rolling (freshmen), rolling (transfer) **Freshman admission** 90% were admitted. Average high school GPA 3.09 **Freshman test scores** SAT critical reading scores over 500: 39%; SAT math scores over 500: 36%; ACT scores over 18: 91%; SAT critical reading scores over 600: 7%; SAT math scores over 600: 7%; ACT scores over 24: 18% **Housing** Yes **Expenses** Tuition & Fees $23,000; Room & Board $7664 **Undergraduates** 91% women, 36% part-time, 46% 25 or older, 0.4% Native American, 2% Hispanic American, 26% African American, 1% Asian American/Pacific Islander **The most frequently chosen baccalaureate fields are** business/marketing, health professions and related sciences, visual and performing arts **Academic program** Advanced placement, accelerated degree program, summer session, adult/continuing education programs, internships **Contact** Ms. Kimberly Shepherd, Director, Graduate and Undergraduate Admission, Ursuline College, 2550 Lander Road, Pepper Pike, OH 44124-4398. *Phone:* 440-449-4203 or toll-free 888-URSULINE. *Fax:* 440-684-6138. *E-mail:* admission@ursuline.edu. *Web site:* http://www.ursuline.edu/.

Walsh University

North Canton, Ohio

General Independent Roman Catholic, comprehensive, coed **Entrance** Moderately difficult **Setting** 134-acre small-town campus **Total**

Walsh University (continued)
enrollment 2,760 **Student-faculty ratio** 14:1 **Application deadline** Rolling (freshmen), rolling (transfer) **Freshman admission** 81% were admitted. Average high school GPA 3.31 **Freshman test scores** SAT critical reading scores over 500: 47%; SAT math scores over 500: 54%; ACT scores over 18: 93%; SAT critical reading scores over 600: 7%; SAT math scores over 600: 14%; ACT scores over 24: 32% **Housing** Yes **Expenses** Tuition & Fees $22,280; Room & Board $8360 **Undergraduates** 63% women, 18% part-time, 25% 25 or older, 0.3% Native American, 1% Hispanic American, 4% African American, 1% Asian American/Pacific Islander **The most frequently chosen baccalaureate fields are** business/marketing, education, health professions and related sciences **Academic program** English as a second language, advanced placement, accelerated degree program, honors program, summer session, adult/continuing education programs, internships **Contact** Mr. Brett Freshour, Vice President for Enrollment Management, Walsh University, 2020 East Maple, North Canton, OH 44720. *Phone:* 330-490-7171 or toll-free 800-362-9846 (in-state); 800-362-8846 (out-of-state). *Fax:* 330-490-7165. *E-mail:* admissions@walsh.edu. *Web site:* http://www.walsh.edu/.
Visit Petersons.com and enter keywords Walsh University

See page 1340 for the College Close-Up.

Wilberforce University
Wilberforce, Ohio

General Independent, comprehensive, coed, affiliated with African Methodist Episcopal Church **Entrance** Minimally difficult **Setting** 125-acre rural campus **Total enrollment** 834 **Application deadline** 7/1 (freshmen), 7/1 (transfer) **Housing** Yes **Expenses** Tuition & Fees $11,560; Room & Board $5320 **Undergraduates** 18% 25 or older **Academic program** Advanced placement, honors program **Contact** Ms. Kenya LeNoir Messer, Vice President for Student Development and Enrollment Management/Dean of Admissions, Wilberforce University, 1055 North Bickett Road, Wilberforce, OH 45384. *Phone:* 937-708-5789 or toll-free 800-367-8568. *Fax:* 937-376-4751. *E-mail:* kmesser@wilberforce.edu. *Web site:* http://www.wilberforce.edu/.

Wilmington College
Wilmington, Ohio

General Independent Friends, comprehensive, coed **Entrance** Moderately difficult **Setting** 1,465-acre small-town campus **Total enrollment** 1,603 **Application deadline** 8/1 (freshmen), rolling (transfer) **Freshman admission** 93% were admitted. Average high school GPA 3.2 **Freshman test scores** SAT critical reading scores over 500: 39.79%; SAT math scores over 500: 51.62%; ACT scores over 18: 74.22%; SAT critical reading scores over 600: 12.91%; SAT math scores over 600: 15.06%; ACT scores over 24: 19.83% **Housing** Yes **Expenses** Tuition & Fees $24,286; Room & Board $8272 **Undergraduates** 54% women, 19% part-time, 1% Native American, 1% Hispanic American, 9% African American, 0.2% Asian American/Pacific Islander **Academic program** Advanced placement, self-designed majors, honors program, summer session, adult/continuing education programs, internships **Contact** Ms. Tina Garland, Director of Admission and Financial Aid, Wilmington College, 1870 Quaker Way, Wilmington, OH 45177. *Phone:* 937-382-6661 Ext. 426 or toll-free 800-341-9318. *Fax:* 937-383-8542. *E-mail:* admissions@wilmington.edu. *Web site:* http://www.wilmington.edu/.

Wittenberg University
Springfield, Ohio

General Independent, comprehensive, coed, affiliated with Evangelical Lutheran Church **Entrance** Moderately difficult **Setting** 71-acre suburban campus **Total enrollment** 1,934 **Student-faculty ratio** 12:1 **Application deadline** Rolling (transfer) **Freshman admission** 72% were admitted. Average high school GPA 3.44 **Freshman test scores** SAT critical reading scores over 500: 79%; SAT math scores over 500: 76%; ACT scores over 18: 97%; SAT critical reading scores over 600: 33%; SAT math scores over 600: 35%; ACT scores over 24: 65% **Housing** Yes **Expenses** Tuition & Fees $34,190; Room & Board $8772 **Undergraduates** 58% women, 5% part-time, 5% 25 or older, 0.2% Native American, 1% Hispanic American, 5% African American, 1% Asian American/Pacific Islander **The most frequently chosen baccalaureate fields are** business/marketing, biological/life sciences, social sciences **Academic program** English as a second language, advanced placement, self-designed majors, honors program, summer session, adult/continuing education programs, internships **Contact** Ms. Karen Hunt, Director of Admission, Wittenberg University, PO Box 720, Springfield, OH 45501-0720. *Phone:* 877-206-0332 Ext. 6377 or toll-free 800-677-7558 Ext. 6314. *Fax:* 937-327-6379. *E-mail:* admission@wittenberg.edu. *Web site:* http://www.wittenberg.edu/.
Visit Petersons.com and enter keyword Wittenberg

See page 1384 for the College Close-Up.

Wright State University
Dayton, Ohio

General State-supported, university, coed **Entrance** Minimally difficult **Setting** 557-acre suburban campus **Total enrollment** 17,558 **Student-faculty ratio** 17:1 **Application deadline** Rolling (freshmen), rolling (transfer) **Freshman admission** 84% were admitted. Average high school GPA 3.06 **Freshman test scores** SAT critical reading scores over 500: 54%; SAT math scores over 500: 57%; ACT scores over 18: 80%; SAT critical reading scores over 600: 18%; SAT math scores over 600: 21%; ACT scores over 24: 28% **Housing** Yes **Expenses** Tuition & Fees: state resident $7533, nonresident $14,595; Room & Board $7829 **Undergraduates** 55% women, 16% part-time, 17% 25 or older, 0.4% Native American, 2% Hispanic American, 16% African American, 3% Asian American/Pacific Islander **The most frequently chosen baccalaureate fields are** business/marketing, education, health professions and related sciences **Academic program** English as a second language, advanced placement, self-designed majors, honors program, summer session, adult/continuing education programs, internships **Contact** Ms. Cathy Davis, Director of Undergraduate Admissions, Wright State University, 3640 Colonel Glenn Highway, Dayton, OH 45435. *Phone:* 937-775-5700 or toll-free 800-247-1770. *Fax:* 937-775-5795. *E-mail:* admissions@wright.edu. *Web site:* http://www.wright.edu/.

Xavier University
Cincinnati, Ohio

General Independent Roman Catholic, comprehensive, coed **Entrance** Moderately difficult **Setting** 148-acre urban campus **Total enrollment** 6,966 **Student-faculty ratio** 13:1 **Application deadline** 2/1 (freshmen), rolling (transfer) **Freshman admission** 73% were admitted. Average high school GPA 3.54 **Freshman test scores** SAT critical reading scores over 500: 81%; SAT math scores over 500: 80%; ACT scores over 18: 99%; SAT critical reading scores over 600: 33%; SAT math scores over 600: 35%; ACT scores over 24: 64% **Housing** Yes **Expenses** Tuition & Fees $28,570; Room & Board $9530 **Undergraduates** 55% women, 12% part-time, 12% 25 or older, 0.3% Native American, 3% Hispanic American, 11% African American, 2% Asian American/Pacific Islander **The most frequently chosen baccalaureate fields are** business/marketing, liberal arts/general studies, social sciences **Academic program** English as a second language, advanced placement, honors program, summer session, adult/continuing education programs, internships **Contact** Mr. Aaron J. Meis, Dean of Undergraduate Admissions, Xavier University, 3800 Victory Parkway, Cincinnati, OH 45207-5311. *Phone:* 513-745-2941 or toll-free 800-344-4698. *Fax:* 513-745-4319. *E-mail:* xuadmit@xavier.edu. *Web site:* http://www.xu.edu/.

Youngstown State University
Youngstown, Ohio

General State-supported, comprehensive, coed **Entrance** Noncompetitive **Setting** 200-acre urban campus **Total enrollment** 14,672 **Student-**

faculty ratio 19:1 **Application deadline** 8/15 (freshmen), 8/15 (transfer) **Freshman admission** 89% were admitted. Average high school GPA 2.82 **Freshman test scores** SAT critical reading scores over 500: 35%; SAT math scores over 500: 38%; ACT scores over 18: 71%; SAT critical reading scores over 600: 9%; SAT math scores over 600: 11%; ACT scores over 24: 19% **Housing** Yes **Expenses** Tuition & Fees: state resident $6956, nonresident $12,629; Room & Board $7400 **Undergraduates** 53% women, 22% part-time, 28% 25 or older, 0.3% Native American, 2% Hispanic American, 16% African American, 1% Asian American/Pacific Islander **The most frequently chosen baccalaureate fields are** business/marketing, education, health professions and related sciences **Academic program** English as a second language, advanced placement, accelerated degree program, self-designed majors, honors program, summer session, internships **Contact** Ms. Sue Davis, Director of Undergraduate Admissions, Youngstown State University, One University Plaza, Youngstown, OH 44555-0001. *Phone:* 330-941-2000 or toll-free 877-468-6978. *Fax:* 330-941-3674. *E-mail:* enroll@ysu.edu. *Web site:* http://www.ysu.edu/.

OKLAHOMA

Bacone College
Muskogee, Oklahoma

General Independent, 4-year, coed, affiliated with American Baptist Churches in the U.S.A. **Entrance** Minimally difficult **Setting** 220-acre small-town campus **Total enrollment** 884 **Application deadline** Rolling (freshmen), rolling (transfer) **Housing** Yes **Undergraduates** 34% 25 or older **Academic program** Advanced placement, accelerated degree program, self-designed majors, summer session, adult/continuing education programs, internships **Contact** Admissions and Enrollment Management, Bacone College, 2299 Old Bacone Road, Muskogee, OK 74403-1597. *Phone:* 918-781-7342 or toll-free 888-682-5514 Ext. 7340. *Fax:* 918-682-5514. *Web site:* http://www.bacone.edu/.

Brown Mackie College–Tulsa
Tulsa, Oklahoma

General Proprietary, primarily 2-year, coed **Contact** Director of Admissions, Brown Mackie College–Tulsa, 4608 South Garnett, Suite 110, Tulsa, OK 74146. *Phone:* 918-628-3700 or toll-free 888-794-8411. *Fax:* 918-828-9083. *Web site:* http://www.brownmackie.edu/Tulsa.

Visit Petersons.com and enter keywords Brown Mackie College-Tulsa

See page 646 for the College Close-Up.

Cameron University
Lawton, Oklahoma

General State-supported, comprehensive, coed **Entrance** Minimally difficult **Setting** 160-acre small-town campus **Total enrollment** 6,131 **Student-faculty ratio** 20:1 **Application deadline** Rolling (freshmen), rolling (transfer) **Freshman admission** 100% were admitted. Average high school GPA 3.19 **Freshman test scores** ACT scores over 18: 67.2%; ACT scores over 24: 17.3% **Housing** Yes **Expenses** Tuition & Fees: state resident $5415, nonresident $11,279; Room & Board $3589 **Undergraduates** 59% women, 33% part-time, 41% 25 or older, 8% Native American, 8% Hispanic American, 15% African American, 3% Asian American/Pacific Islander **The most frequently chosen baccalaureate fields are** business/marketing, education, security and protective services **Academic program** English as a second language, advanced placement, accelerated degree program, honors program, summer session, adult/continuing education programs, internships **Contact** Mr. Frank Myers, Admissions Counselor Coordinator, Cameron University, Admissions, 2800 West Gore Boulevard, Lawton, OK 73505-6377. *Phone:* 580-581-5496 or toll-free 888-454-7600. *Fax:* 580-581-5514. *E-mail:* admissions@cameron.edu. *Web site:* http://www.cameron.edu/.

DeVry University
Oklahoma City, Oklahoma

General Proprietary, comprehensive, coed **Total enrollment** 155 **Student-faculty ratio** 27:1 **Application deadline** Rolling (freshmen), rolling (transfer) **Expenses** Tuition & Fees $14,080 **Undergraduates** 41% women, 52% part-time, 67% 25 or older, 7% Native American, 7% Hispanic American, 20% African American, 2% Asian American/Pacific Islander **The most frequently chosen baccalaureate fields are** business/marketing, computer and information sciences **Academic program** Accelerated degree program **Contact** Admissions Office, DeVry University, Lakepointe Towers, 4013 Northwest Expressway Street, Suite 100, Oklahoma City, OK 73116. *Web site:* http://www.devry.edu/.

East Central University
Ada, Oklahoma

General State-supported, comprehensive, coed **Entrance** Minimally difficult **Setting** 140-acre small-town campus **Total enrollment** 4,612 **Student-faculty ratio** 18:1 **Freshman admission** 93% were admitted. Average high school GPA 3.28 **Freshman test scores** SAT critical reading scores over 500: 36%; ACT scores over 18: 79%; SAT critical reading scores over 600: 10%; ACT scores over 24: 24% **Housing** Yes **Expenses** Tuition & Fees: state resident $3436, nonresident $8248; Room & Board $4100 **Undergraduates** 58% women, 19% part-time, 40% 25 or older, 21% Native American, 6% Hispanic American, 4% African American, 1% Asian American/Pacific Islander **Academic program** Advanced placement, honors program, summer session, adult/continuing education programs, internships **Contact** Ms. Pam Denny, Freshman Admissions Officer, East Central University, PMBJ8, 1100 East 14th Street, Ada, OK 74820-6999. *Phone:* 580-310-5233 Ext. 233. *Fax:* 580-310-5432. *E-mail:* pdenny@ecok.edu. *Web site:* http://www.ecok.edu/.

Hillsdale Free Will Baptist College
Moore, Oklahoma

General Independent Free Will Baptist, comprehensive, coed **Entrance** Noncompetitive **Setting** 41-acre suburban campus **Total enrollment** 241 **Freshman test scores** ACT scores over 18: 65%; ACT scores over 24: 11.2% **Housing** Yes **Expenses** Tuition & Fees $9650; Room & Board $5200 **Undergraduates** 39% women, 9% part-time, 10% Native American, 2% Hispanic American, 12% African American **Academic program** English as a second language, advanced placement, accelerated degree program, summer session, adult/continuing education programs, internships **Contact** Lyndsey Barentine, Admission Officer, Hillsdale Free Will Baptist College, PO Box 7208, Moore, OK 73160. *Phone:* 405-912-9007. *Fax:* 405-912-9050. *E-mail:* recruitment@hc.edu. *Web site:* http://www.hc.edu/.

ITT Technical Institute
Oklahoma City, Oklahoma

General Proprietary, 4-year, coed **Contact** Director of Recruitment, ITT Technical Institute, 50 Penn Place Office Tower, 1900 Northwest Expressway, Suite 305R, Oklahoma City, OK 73118. *Phone:* 405-810-4100 or toll-free 800-518-1612. *Web site:* http://www.itt-tech.edu/.

ITT Technical Institute
Tulsa, Oklahoma

General Proprietary, primarily 2-year, coed **Contact** Director of Recruitment, ITT Technical Institute, 8421 East 61st Street, Suite U,

ITT Technical Institute (continued)
Tulsa, OK 74133. *Phone:* 918-615-3900 or toll-free 800-514-6535. *Web site:* http://www.itt-tech.edu/.

Langston University
Langston, Oklahoma

Contact Maurice Osborne, Assistant Director of Admission, Langston University, PO Box 667, Langston, OK 73050. *Phone:* 405-466-2984. *Web site:* http://www.lunet.edu/.

Mid-America Christian University
Oklahoma City, Oklahoma

General Independent, comprehensive, coed, affiliated with Church of God **Entrance** Noncompetitive **Setting** 145-acre suburban campus **Total enrollment** 869 **Application deadline** Rolling (freshmen), rolling (transfer) **Housing** Yes **Expenses** Tuition & Fees $12,955; Room & Board $5560 **Undergraduates** 53% 25 or older **Academic program** Advanced placement, accelerated degree program, summer session, adult/continuing education programs, internships **Contact** Jason Duda, Director of Admissions, Mid-America Christian University, 3500 Southwest 119th Street, Oklahoma City, OK 73170-4504. *Phone:* 405-392-3180. *Fax:* 405-692-3165. *E-mail:* info@macu.edu. *Web site:* http://www.macu.edu/.

Northeastern State University
Tahlequah, Oklahoma

General State-supported, comprehensive, coed **Entrance** Moderately difficult **Setting** 160-acre small-town campus **Total enrollment** 9,318 **Student-faculty ratio** 22:1 **Application deadline** 8/1 (freshmen), 8/1 (transfer) **Freshman admission** 72% were admitted. Average high school GPA 3.18 **Freshman test scores** ACT scores over 18: 76.7%; ACT scores over 24: 19.7% **Housing** Yes **Expenses** Tuition & Fees: state resident $4155, nonresident $10,245; Room & Board $4826 **Undergraduates** 60% women, 27% part-time, 38% 25 or older, 30% Native American, 2% Hispanic American, 6% African American, 1% Asian American/Pacific Islander **The most frequently chosen baccalaureate fields are** business/marketing, education, security and protective services **Academic program** Advanced placement, self-designed majors, honors program, summer session, adult/continuing education programs, internships **Contact** Ms. Dawn Cain, Director of Admissions, Northeastern State University, 600 North Grand Avenue, Tahlequah, OK 74464. *Phone:* 918-444-2211 or toll-free 800-722-9614. *Fax:* 918-458-2342. *E-mail:* cain@nsuok.edu. *Web site:* http://www.nsuok.edu/.

Northwestern Oklahoma State University
Alva, Oklahoma

General State-supported, comprehensive, coed **Entrance** Moderately difficult **Setting** 70-acre small-town campus **Total enrollment** 2,232 **Student-faculty ratio** 16:1 **Application deadline** Rolling (freshmen), rolling (transfer) **Freshman admission** 100% were admitted. Average high school GPA 3.21 **Freshman test scores** ACT scores over 18: 64%; ACT scores over 24: 22% **Housing** Yes **Expenses** Tuition & Fees: state resident $4111, nonresident $10,141; Room & Board $3430 **Undergraduates** 56% women, 31% part-time, 20% 25 or older, 6% Native American, 4% Hispanic American, 5% African American, 1% Asian American/Pacific Islander **The most frequently chosen baccalaureate fields are** business/marketing, education, psychology **Academic program** Advanced placement, honors program, summer session, adult/continuing education programs, internships **Contact** Mr. Matt Adair, Director of Recruitment, Northwestern Oklahoma State University, 709 Oklahoma Boulevard, Alva, OK 73717-2799. *Phone:* 580-327-8545. *Fax:* 580-327-8699. *E-mail:* wmadair@nwosu.edu. *Web site:* http://www.nwosu.edu/.

Oklahoma Baptist University
Shawnee, Oklahoma

General Independent Southern Baptist, comprehensive, coed **Entrance** Moderately difficult **Setting** 125-acre small-town campus **Total enrollment** 1,764 **Student-faculty ratio** 11:1 **Application deadline** Rolling (freshmen), 8/1 (transfer) **Freshman admission** 66% were admitted. Average high school GPA 3.62 **Freshman test scores** SAT critical reading scores over 500: 69%; SAT math scores over 500: 64%; ACT scores over 18: 94%; SAT critical reading scores over 600: 24%; SAT math scores over 600: 33%; ACT scores over 24: 46% **Housing** Yes **Expenses** Tuition & Fees $18,670; Room & Board $5630 **Undergraduates** 57% women, 16% part-time, 20% 25 or older, 7% Native American, 4% Hispanic American, 6% African American, 1% Asian American/Pacific Islander **The most frequently chosen baccalaureate fields are** education, health professions and related sciences, theology and religious vocations **Academic program** Advanced placement, self-designed majors, honors program, summer session, internships **Contact** Mr. Bruce Perkins, Director of Admissions, Oklahoma Baptist University, 500 West University, Shawnee, OK 74804. *Phone:* 405-878-2033 or toll-free 800-654-3285. *Fax:* 405-878-2046. *E-mail:* admissions@mail.okbu.edu. *Web site:* http://www.okbu.edu/.

Oklahoma Christian University
Oklahoma City, Oklahoma

General Independent, comprehensive, coed, affiliated with Church of Christ **Entrance** Noncompetitive **Setting** 200-acre suburban campus **Total enrollment** 2,172 **Student-faculty ratio** 15:1 **Application deadline** Rolling (freshmen), rolling (transfer) **Freshman admission** 56% were admitted. Average high school GPA 3.43 **Freshman test scores** SAT critical reading scores over 500: 68%; SAT math scores over 500: 70%; ACT scores over 18: 85%; SAT critical reading scores over 600: 35%; SAT math scores over 600: 35%; ACT scores over 24: 51% **Housing** Yes **Expenses** Tuition & Fees $17,456; Room & Board $5850 **Undergraduates** 48% women, 3% part-time, 5% Native American, 3% Hispanic American, 4% African American, 1% Asian American/Pacific Islander **The most frequently chosen baccalaureate fields are** business/marketing, communications/journalism, education **Academic program** English as a second language, advanced placement, accelerated degree program, honors program, summer session, internships **Contact** Ms. Risa Forrester, Vice President for Enrollment Management, Oklahoma Christian University, Box 11000, Oklahoma City, OK 73136-1100. *Phone:* 405-425-5050 or toll-free 800-877-5010. *Fax:* 405-425-5208. *E-mail:* info@oc.edu. *Web site:* http://www.oc.edu/.

Oklahoma City University
Oklahoma City, Oklahoma

General Independent United Methodist, comprehensive, coed **Entrance** Moderately difficult **Setting** 75-acre urban campus **Total enrollment** 3,810 **Student-faculty ratio** 11:1 **Application deadline** 8/21 (freshmen), rolling (transfer) **Freshman admission** 79% were admitted. Average high school GPA 3.51 **Freshman test scores** SAT critical reading scores over 500: 80%; SAT math scores over 500: 79%; ACT scores over 18: 98%; SAT critical reading scores over 600: 35%; SAT math scores over 600: 37%; ACT scores over 24: 68% **Housing** Yes **Expenses** Tuition & Fees $22,250; Room & Board $8350 **Undergraduates** 60% women, 17% part-time, 17% 25 or older, 4% Native American, 6% Hispanic American, 8% African American, 3% Asian American/Pacific Islander **The most frequently chosen baccalaureate fields are** health professions and related sciences, liberal arts/general studies, visual and performing arts **Academic program** English as a second language, advanced placement, accelerated degree program, self-designed majors, honors program, summer session, adult/continuing education programs, internships **Contact** Ms. Michelle Lockhart, Director, Admissions, Oklahoma City University, 2501 North Blackwelder, Oklahoma City, OK 73106. *Phone:* 405-208-5340 or toll-free 800-633-7242. *Fax:* 405-208-5916. *E-mail:* mlockhart@okcu.edu. *Web site:* http://www.okcu.edu/.

Oklahoma Panhandle State University

Goodwell, Oklahoma

General State-supported, 4-year, coed **Entrance** Noncompetitive **Setting** 40-acre rural campus **Total enrollment** 1,268 **Student-faculty ratio** 12:1 **Application deadline** Rolling (freshmen), rolling (transfer) **Freshman admission** 100% were admitted. Average high school GPA 3.13 **Freshman test scores** SAT critical reading scores over 500: 9%; SAT math scores over 500: 19%; ACT scores over 18: 63%; SAT math scores over 600: 3%; ACT scores over 24: 14% **Housing** Yes **Expenses** Tuition & Fees: state resident $4242, nonresident $9581; Room & Board $3320 **Undergraduates** 48% women, 18% part-time, 23% 25 or older, 4% Native American, 14% Hispanic American, 7% African American, 1% Asian American/Pacific Islander **The most frequently chosen baccalaureate fields are** agriculture, biological/life sciences, parks and recreation **Academic program** English as a second language, advanced placement, summer session **Contact** Mr. Bobby Jenkins, Registrar and Director of Admissions, Oklahoma Panhandle State University, PO Box 430, 323 Eagle Boulevard, Goodwell, OK 73939-0430. *Phone:* 580-349-1376 or toll-free 800-664-6778. *Fax:* 580-349-1371. *E-mail:* opsu@opsu.edu. *Web site:* http://www.opsu.edu/.

Oklahoma State University

Stillwater, Oklahoma

General State-supported, university, coed **Entrance** Moderately difficult **Setting** 840-acre small-town campus **Total enrollment** 22,845 **Student-faculty ratio** 18:1 **Application deadline** Rolling (freshmen), rolling (transfer) **Freshman admission** 86% were admitted. Average high school GPA 3.52 **Freshman test scores** SAT critical reading scores over 500: 70.82%; SAT math scores over 500: 76.83%; ACT scores over 18: 97.64%; SAT critical reading scores over 600: 27.41%; SAT math scores over 600: 39.42%; ACT scores over 24: 60.17% **Housing** Yes **Expenses** Tuition & Fees: state resident $6202, nonresident $16,556; Room & Board $6402 **Undergraduates** 49% women, 14% part-time, 13% 25 or older, 9% Native American, 3% Hispanic American, 4% African American, 2% Asian American/Pacific Islander **The most frequently chosen baccalaureate fields are** business/marketing, agriculture, family and consumer sciences **Academic program** English as a second language, advanced placement, accelerated degree program, self-designed majors, honors program, summer session, internships **Contact** Christine Crenshaw, Director of Undergraduate Admissions, Oklahoma State University, Stillwater, OK 74078. *Phone:* 405-744-3087 or toll-free 800-233-5019 Ext. 1 (in-state); 800-852-1255 (out-of-state). *Fax:* 405-744-7092. *E-mail:* christine.crenshaw@okstate.edu. *Web site:* http://www.okstate.edu/.

Oklahoma State University, Oklahoma City

Oklahoma City, Oklahoma

General State-supported, primarily 2-year, coed **Entrance** Noncompetitive **Setting** 80-acre urban campus **Total enrollment** 7,179 **Student-faculty ratio** 20:1 **Application deadline** Rolling (freshmen), rolling (transfer) **Freshman admission** 100% were admitted **Housing** No **Expenses** Tuition & Fees: state resident $2919, nonresident $7779 **Undergraduates** 51% 25 or older, 5% Native American, 7% Hispanic American, 14% African American, 3% Asian American/Pacific Islander **Academic program** Advanced placement, honors program, summer session **Contact** Kyle Williams, Director, Enrollment Management, Oklahoma State University, Oklahoma City, 900 North Portland, AD202, Oklahoma City, OK 73107. *Phone:* 405-945-9152. *E-mail:* wilkylw@osuokc.edu. *Web site:* http://www.osuokc.edu/.

Oklahoma Wesleyan University

Bartlesville, Oklahoma

General Independent, comprehensive, coed, affiliated with Wesleyan Church **Entrance** Minimally difficult **Setting** 127-acre small-town campus **Total enrollment** 1,100 **Student-faculty ratio** 14:1 **Application deadline** Rolling (freshmen), rolling (transfer) **Freshman admission** 14% were admitted. Average high school GPA 3.26 **Freshman test scores** ACT scores over 18: 92%; ACT scores over 24: 34% **Housing** Yes **Expenses** Tuition & Fees $17,970; Room & Board $6288 **Undergraduates** 62% women, 56% part-time, 8% 25 or older, 10% Native American, 3% Hispanic American, 9% African American, 1% Asian American/Pacific Islander **Academic program** Advanced placement, accelerated degree program, self-designed majors, summer session, adult/continuing education programs, internships **Contact** Jennifer Weaver, Enrollment Counselor, Oklahoma Wesleyan University, 2201 Silver Lake Drive, Bartlesville, OK 74006. *Phone:* 866-222-8226 or toll-free 866-222-8226. *Fax:* 918-335-6229. *E-mail:* admissions@okwu.edu. *Web site:* http://www.okwu.edu/.

Oral Roberts University

Tulsa, Oklahoma

General Independent interdenominational, comprehensive, coed **Entrance** Moderately difficult **Setting** 263-acre urban campus **Total enrollment** 3,067 **Student-faculty ratio** 12:1 **Application deadline** Rolling (freshmen), rolling (transfer) **Freshman admission** 74% were admitted. Average high school GPA 3.36 **Freshman test scores** SAT critical reading scores over 500: 64.93%; SAT math scores over 500: 56.28%; ACT scores over 18: 92.43%; SAT critical reading scores over 600: 22.94%; SAT math scores over 600: 18.18%; ACT scores over 24: 41.52% **Housing** Yes **Expenses** Tuition & Fees $18,916; Room & Board $7916 **Undergraduates** 58% women, 9% part-time, 12% 25 or older, 3% Native American, 6% Hispanic American, 16% African American, 2% Asian American/Pacific Islander **The most frequently chosen baccalaureate fields are** business/marketing, communications/journalism, theology and religious vocations **Academic program** English as a second language, advanced placement, accelerated degree program, self-designed majors, honors program, summer session, adult/continuing education programs, internships **Contact** Director of Admissions, Oral Roberts University, 7777 South Lewis Avenue, Tulsa, OK 74171. *Phone:* 918-495-6529 or toll-free 800-678-8876. *Fax:* 918-495-6222495-6222. *E-mail:* admissions@oru.edu. *Web site:* http://www.oru.edu/.

Rogers State University

Claremore, Oklahoma

General State-supported, 4-year, coed **Entrance** Noncompetitive **Setting** 40-acre small-town campus **Total enrollment** 4,154 **Student-faculty ratio** 21:1 **Application deadline** Rolling (freshmen), rolling (transfer) **Freshman admission** 58% were admitted. Average high school GPA 3.07 **Freshman test scores** ACT scores over 18: 75%; ACT scores over 24: 18% **Housing** Yes **Expenses** Tuition & Fees: state resident $4277, nonresident $9734; Room only $4505 **Undergraduates** 63% women, 37% part-time, 36% 25 or older, 30% Native American, 2% Hispanic American, 3% African American, 2% Asian American/Pacific Islander **The most frequently chosen baccalaureate fields are** business/marketing, engineering technologies, social sciences **Academic program** Advanced placement, honors program, summer session, adult/continuing education programs, internships **Contact** Ms. Julie Rampey, Director of Admissions, Rogers State University, 1701 West Will Rogers Boulevard, Claremore, OK 74017. *Phone:* 918-343-7545 or toll-free 800-256-7511. *Fax:* 918-343-7595. *E-mail:* info@rsu.edu. *Web site:* http://www.rsu.edu/.

St. Gregory's University

Shawnee, Oklahoma

General Independent Roman Catholic, comprehensive, coed **Entrance** Minimally difficult **Setting** 640-acre small-town campus **Total enrollment** 743 **Student-faculty ratio** 9:1 **Application deadline** Rolling (freshmen), rolling (transfer) **Freshman admission** 97% were admitted. Average high school GPA 3.23 **Freshman test scores** SAT critical

St. Gregory's University (continued)
reading scores over 500: 50%; SAT math scores over 500: 40%; ACT scores over 18: 75%; SAT critical reading scores over 600: 10%; ACT scores over 24: 12% **Housing** Yes **Expenses** Tuition & Fees $16,294; Room & Board $6196 **Undergraduates** 63% women, 58% part-time, 57% 25 or older, 9% Native American, 8% Hispanic American, 6% African American, 1% Asian American/Pacific Islander **Academic program** English as a second language, advanced placement, accelerated degree program, self-designed majors, honors program, summer session, adult/continuing education programs, internships **Contact** Director of Admissions, St. Gregory's University, 1900 West MacArthur Drive, Shawnee, OK 74804. *Phone:* 405-878-5447 or toll-free 888-STGREGS. *Fax:* 405-878-5198. *E-mail:* admissions@stgregorys.edu. *Web site:* http://www.stgregorys.edu/.

Southeastern Oklahoma State University
Durant, Oklahoma

General State-supported, comprehensive, coed **Entrance** Moderately difficult **Setting** 177-acre small-town campus **Total enrollment** 4,228 **Student-faculty ratio** 18:1 **Application deadline** Rolling (freshmen), rolling (transfer) **Freshman admission** 97% were admitted. Average high school GPA 3.26 **Freshman test scores** ACT scores over 18: 80%; ACT scores over 24: 15.7% **Housing** Yes **Expenses** Tuition & Fees: state resident $4316, nonresident $10,686; Room & Board $4290 **Undergraduates** 55% women, 22% part-time, 25% 25 or older, 30% Native American, 3% Hispanic American, 6% African American, 1% Asian American/Pacific Islander **The most frequently chosen baccalaureate fields are** education, engineering technologies, liberal arts/general studies **Academic program** Advanced placement, accelerated degree program, honors program, summer session, adult/continuing education programs, internships **Contact** Ms. Kristie Luke, Associate Dean of Admissions and Records/Registrar, Southeastern Oklahoma State University, 1405 North 4th Avenue, Durant, OK 74701-0609. *Phone:* 580-745-2060 or toll-free 800-435-1327. *Fax:* 580-745-7502. *E-mail:* kluke@se.edu. *Web site:* http://www.se.edu/.

Southern Nazarene University
Bethany, Oklahoma

General Independent Nazarene, comprehensive, coed **Entrance** Noncompetitive **Setting** 40-acre suburban campus **Total enrollment** 2,069 **Student-faculty ratio** 15:1 **Application deadline** 8/15 (freshmen), 8/15 (transfer) **Freshman admission** 100% were admitted. Average high school GPA 3.4 **Freshman test scores** ACT scores over 18: 81%; ACT scores over 24: 41% **Housing** Yes **Expenses** Tuition & Fees $17,664; Room & Board $6490 **Undergraduates** 53% women, 4% part-time, 8% 25 or older, 5% Native American, 6% Hispanic American, 11% African American, 4% Asian American/Pacific Islander **The most frequently chosen baccalaureate fields are** business/marketing, family and consumer sciences, health professions and related sciences **Academic program** Advanced placement, accelerated degree program, self-designed majors, honors program, summer session, adult/continuing education programs, internships **Contact** Mr. Warren W. Rogers III, Director of Admissions, Southern Nazarene University, 6729 Northwest 39th Expressway, Bethany, OK 73008. *Phone:* 405-491-6324 or toll-free 800-648-9899. *Fax:* 405-491-6320. *E-mail:* admiss@snu.edu. *Web site:* http://www.snu.edu/.

Southwestern Christian University
Bethany, Oklahoma

General Independent, comprehensive, coed, affiliated with Pentecostal Holiness Church **Entrance** Minimally difficult **Setting** 7-acre suburban campus **Total enrollment** 264 **Application deadline** Rolling (freshmen), rolling (transfer) **Housing** Yes **Expenses** Tuition & Fees $9800; Room & Board $4600 **Undergraduates** 34% 25 or older **Academic program** Advanced placement, summer session, internships **Contact** Jason Vaughn, Director of Admissions, Southwestern Christian University, PO Box 340, Bethany, OK 73008-0340. *Phone:* 405-789-7661. *Fax:* 405-495-0078. *E-mail:* admissions@swcu.edu. *Web site:* http://www.swcu.edu/.

Southwestern Oklahoma State University
Weatherford, Oklahoma

General State-supported, comprehensive, coed **Entrance** Minimally difficult **Setting** 73-acre small-town campus **Total enrollment** 5,046 **Student-faculty ratio** 20:1 **Application deadline** Rolling (freshmen), rolling (transfer) **Freshman admission** 92% were admitted. Average high school GPA 3.34 **Freshman test scores** ACT scores over 18: 80%; ACT scores over 24: 27% **Housing** Yes **Expenses** Tuition & Fees: state resident $4110, nonresident $9450; Room & Board $3900 **Undergraduates** 57% women, 16% part-time, 18% 25 or older, 9% Native American, 5% Hispanic American, 5% African American, 2% Asian American/Pacific Islander **The most frequently chosen baccalaureate fields are** business/marketing, education, health professions and related sciences **Academic program** Advanced placement, accelerated degree program, self-designed majors, summer session, adult/continuing education programs, internships **Contact** Ms. Connie Phillips, Admission Counselor, Southwestern Oklahoma State University, 100 Campus Drive, Weatherford, OK 73096-3098. *Phone:* 580-774-3009. *Fax:* 580-774-3795. *E-mail:* ropers@swosu.edu. *Web site:* http://www.swosu.edu/.

Spartan College of Aeronautics and Technology
Tulsa, Oklahoma

General Proprietary, primarily 2-year, coed, primarily men **Entrance** Noncompetitive **Setting** 26-acre urban campus **Total enrollment** 1,438 **Student-faculty ratio** 14:1 **Application deadline** Rolling (freshmen), rolling (transfer) **Housing** Yes **Undergraduates** 30% 25 or older, 3% Native American, 10% Hispanic American, 8% African American **Academic program** Honors program **Contact** Mr. Mark Fowler, Vice President of Student Records and Finance, Spartan College of Aeronautics and Technology, 8820 East Pine Street, PO Box 582833, Tulsa, OK 74158-2833. *Phone:* 918-836-6886 or toll-free 800-331-1204 (in-state); 800-331-124 (out-of-state). *Web site:* http://www.spartan.edu/.

University of Central Oklahoma
Edmond, Oklahoma

General State-supported, comprehensive, coed **Entrance** Minimally difficult **Setting** 200-acre suburban campus **Total enrollment** 16,092 **Student-faculty ratio** 19:1 **Application deadline** Rolling (freshmen), rolling (transfer) **Freshman admission** 75% were admitted. Average high school GPA 3.26 **Freshman test scores** ACT scores over 18: 87.75%; ACT scores over 24: 25.04% **Housing** Yes **Expenses** Tuition & Fees: state resident $4223, nonresident $10,652; Room & Board $7776 **Undergraduates** 58% women, 31% part-time, 26% 25 or older, 6% Native American, 4% Hispanic American, 10% African American, 4% Asian American/Pacific Islander **The most frequently chosen baccalaureate fields are** business/marketing, education, liberal arts/general studies **Academic program** English as a second language, advanced placement, accelerated degree program, honors program, summer session, internships **Contact** Ms. Linda Lofton, Director, Admissions and Records Processing, University of Central Oklahoma, Office of Enrollment Services, 100 North University Drive, Box 151, Edmond, OK 73034-5209. *Phone:* 405-974-2338 Ext. 2338 or toll-free 800-254-4215. *Fax:* 405-341-4964. *E-mail:* admituco@uco.edu. *Web site:* http://www.uco.edu/.

University of Oklahoma
Norman, Oklahoma

General State-supported, university, coed **Entrance** Moderately difficult **Setting** 3,754-acre suburban campus **Total enrollment** 26,638

Student-faculty ratio 19:1 **Application deadline** 4/1 (freshmen), 4/1 (transfer) **Freshman admission** 93% were admitted. Average high school GPA 3.59 **Freshman test scores** SAT critical reading scores over 500: 80.15%; SAT math scores over 500: 85.96%; ACT scores over 18: 98.51%; SAT critical reading scores over 600: 39.89%; SAT math scores over 600: 47.76%; ACT scores over 24: 73.04% **Housing** Yes **Expenses** Tuition & Fees: state resident $5245, nonresident $13,229; Room & Board $7598 **Undergraduates** 51% women, 14% part-time, 13% 25 or older, 7% Native American, 5% Hispanic American, 6% African American, 6% Asian American/Pacific Islander **The most frequently chosen baccalaureate fields are** business/marketing, communications/ journalism, social sciences **Academic program** English as a second language, advanced placement, accelerated degree program, self-designed majors, honors program, summer session, adult/continuing education programs, internships **Contact** Mr. Craig Hayes, Executive Director of Recruitment Services, University of Oklahoma, 550 Parrington Oval, L-1, Norman, OK 73019-3032. *Phone:* 405-325-2151 or toll-free 800-234-6868. *Fax:* 405-325-7478. *E-mail:* ou-pss@ou.edu. *Web site:* http://www.ou.edu/.

University of Oklahoma Health Sciences Center
Oklahoma City, Oklahoma

General State-supported, upper-level, coed **Setting** 200-acre urban campus **Total enrollment** 3,964 **Student-faculty ratio** 9:1 **Application deadline** Rolling (transfer) **First-year students** 36% were admitted **Housing** No **Expenses** Tuition & Fees: state resident $5557, nonresident $15,538 **Undergraduates** 86% women, 7% part-time, 48% 25 or older, 8% Native American, 5% Hispanic American, 5% African American, 9% Asian American/Pacific Islander **The most frequently chosen baccalaureate fields are** health professions and related sciences, interdisciplinary studies **Academic program** Advanced placement, honors program, summer session, internships **Contact** Mr. Scott Boeh, Assistant Vice Provost for Academic Affairs, University of Oklahoma Health Sciences Center, PO Box 26901, Oklahoma City, OK 73190. *Phone:* 405-271-2359 Ext. 48916. *Fax:* 405-271-2480. *E-mail:* scott-boeh@ ouhsc.edu. *Web site:* http://www.ouhsc.edu/.

University of Phoenix–Oklahoma City Campus
Oklahoma City, Oklahoma

General Proprietary, comprehensive, coed **Entrance** Noncompetitive **Setting** urban campus **Total enrollment** 801 **Student-faculty ratio** 13:1 **Application deadline** Rolling (freshmen), rolling (transfer) **Freshman admission** 100% were admitted **Housing** No **Expenses** Tuition & Fees $11,025 **Undergraduates** 69% women, 80% 25 or older, 3% Native American, 4% Hispanic American, 26% African American, 2% Asian American/Pacific Islander **The most frequently chosen baccalaureate fields are** business/marketing, computer and information sciences, security and protective services **Academic program** Advanced placement, accelerated degree program, adult/continuing education programs **Contact** Ms. Audra McQuarie, Registrar/Executive Director, University of Phoenix–Oklahoma City Campus, 4035 South Riverpoint Parkway, Mail Stop CF-L101, Phoenix, AZ 85040-1958. *Phone:* 480-557-3303 or toll-free 800-776-4867 (in-state); 800-228-7240 (out-of-state). *Fax:* 480-643-1020. *E-mail:* audra.mcquarie@phoenix.edu. *Web site:* http:// www.phoenix.edu/.

University of Phoenix–Tulsa Campus
Tulsa, Oklahoma

General Proprietary, comprehensive, coed **Entrance** Noncompetitive **Setting** urban campus **Total enrollment** 785 **Application deadline** Rolling (freshmen), rolling (transfer) **Housing** No **Expenses** Tuition & Fees $11,025 **Undergraduates** 66% women, 81% 25 or older, 7% Native American, 4% Hispanic American, 15% African American, 1% Asian American/Pacific Islander **The most frequently chosen baccalaureate fields are** business/marketing, computer and information sciences, security and protective services **Academic program** Advanced placement, accelerated degree program, adult/continuing education programs **Contact** Ms. Evelyn Gaskin, Registrar/Executive Director, University of Phoenix–Tulsa Campus, 4615 East Elwood Street, Mail Stop AA-K101, Phoenix, AZ 85040-1958. *Phone:* 480-557-3303 or toll-free 800-776-4867 (in-state); 800-228-7240 (out-of-state). *Fax:* 480-643-1020. *E-mail:* evelyn.gaskin@phoenix.edu. *Web site:* http:// www.phoenix.edu/.

University of Science and Arts of Oklahoma
Chickasha, Oklahoma

General State-supported, 4-year, coed **Entrance** Moderately difficult **Setting** 75-acre small-town campus **Total enrollment** 1,087 **Student-faculty ratio** 15:1 **Application deadline** 9/1 (freshmen), 9/1 (transfer) **Freshman admission** 74% were admitted. Average high school GPA 3.42 **Freshman test scores** ACT scores over 18: 90.2%; ACT scores over 24: 41.8% **Housing** Yes **Expenses** Tuition & Fees: state resident $4440, nonresident $10,560; Room & Board $4850 **Undergraduates** 65% women, 15% part-time, 20% 25 or older, 11% Native American, 5% Hispanic American, 5% African American, 1% Asian American/Pacific Islander **The most frequently chosen baccalaureate fields are** business/ marketing, education, psychology **Academic program** Advanced placement, accelerated degree program, self-designed majors, summer session, internships **Contact** Ms. Kellee Johnson, Director of Admissions, University of Science and Arts of Oklahoma, 1727 West Alabama, Chickasha, OK 73018-5322. *Phone:* 405-574-1357 or toll-free 800-933-8726 Ext. 1212. *Fax:* 405-574-1220. *E-mail:* usao-admissions@ usao.edu. *Web site:* http://www.usao.edu/.

University of Tulsa
Tulsa, Oklahoma

General Independent, university, coed, affiliated with Presbyterian Church (U.S.A.) **Entrance** Very difficult **Setting** 2,090-acre urban campus **Total enrollment** 4,192 **Student-faculty ratio** 10:1 **Application deadline** Rolling (freshmen), rolling (transfer) **Freshman admission** 46% were admitted. Average high school GPA 3.75 **Freshman test scores** SAT critical reading scores over 500: 89%; SAT math scores over 500: 90%; ACT scores over 18: 100%; SAT critical reading scores over 600: 59%; SAT math scores over 600: 63%; ACT scores over 24: 82% **Housing** Yes **Expenses** Tuition & Fees $25,144; Room & Board $8544 **Undergraduates** 48% women, 6% part-time, 7% 25 or older, 4% Native American, 4% Hispanic American, 6% African American, 3% Asian American/Pacific Islander **The most frequently chosen baccalaureate fields are** business/marketing, engineering, visual and performing arts **Academic program** English as a second language, advanced placement, accelerated degree program, self-designed majors, honors program, summer session, adult/continuing education programs, internships **Contact** Mr. Earl Johnson, Dean of Admission, University of Tulsa, 600 South College Avenue, Tulsa, OK 74104. *Phone:* 918-631-2307 or toll-free 800-331-3050. *Fax:* 918-631-5003. *E-mail:* admission@utulsa.edu. *Web site:* http://www.utulsa.edu/.

Visit Petersons.com and enter keywords University of Tulsa

See page 1320 for the College Close-Up.

OREGON

The Art Institute of Portland
Portland, Oregon

General Proprietary, 4-year, coed **Setting** urban campus **Contact** Director of Admissions, The Art Institute of Portland, 1122 NW Davis Street,

The Art Institute of Portland (continued)
Portland, OR 97209. *Phone:* 503-228-6528 or toll-free 888-228-6528. *Fax:* 503-227-1945. *Web site:* http://www.artinstitutes.edu/portland/. **Visit Petersons.com and enter keywords Art Institute of Portland**

See page 536 for the College Close-Up.

Birthingway College of Midwifery
Portland, Oregon

Contact Director of Admission, Birthingway College of Midwifery, 12113 SE Foster Road, Portland, OR 97299. *Phone:* 503-760-3131. *E-mail:* info@birthingway.edu. *Web site:* http://www.birthingway.edu/.

Concordia University
Portland, Oregon

General Independent, comprehensive, coed, affiliated with Lutheran Church–Missouri Synod **Entrance** Moderately difficult **Setting** 13-acre urban campus **Total enrollment** 1,709 **Student-faculty ratio** 16:1 **Application deadline** Rolling (freshmen), rolling (transfer) **Freshman admission** 60% were admitted. Average high school GPA 3.3 **Freshman test scores** SAT critical reading scores over 500: 56.6%; SAT math scores over 500: 60.4%; SAT critical reading scores over 600: 23.3%; SAT math scores over 600: 21.8% **Housing** Yes **Expenses** Tuition & Fees $23,400; Room & Board $6800 **Undergraduates** 65% women, 17% part-time, 32% 25 or older, 1% Native American, 5% Hispanic American, 7% African American, 5% Asian American/Pacific Islander **The most frequently chosen baccalaureate fields are** business/marketing, education, health professions and related sciences **Academic program** English as a second language, advanced placement, accelerated degree program, self-designed majors, summer session, adult/continuing education programs, internships **Contact** Ms. Bobi Swan, Dean of Admission, Concordia University, 2811 Northeast Holman, Portland, OR 97211-6099. *Phone:* 503-493-6526 or toll-free 800-321-9371. *Fax:* 503-280-8531. *E-mail:* admissions@cu-portland.edu. *Web site:* http://www.cu-portland.edu/.

Corban University
Salem, Oregon

General Independent religious, comprehensive, coed **Entrance** Moderately difficult **Setting** 145-acre suburban campus **Total enrollment** 1,100 **Student-faculty ratio** 14:1 **Application deadline** 8/1 (freshmen), 8/1 (transfer) **Freshman admission** 57% were admitted. Average high school GPA 3.58 **Freshman test scores** SAT critical reading scores over 500: 76.5%; SAT math scores over 500: 75.5%; ACT scores over 18: 92.5%; SAT critical reading scores over 600: 35%; SAT math scores over 600: 31%; ACT scores over 24: 49% **Housing** Yes **Expenses** Tuition & Fees $24,230; Room & Board $7642 **Undergraduates** 60% women, 15% part-time, 9% 25 or older, 1% Native American, 3% Hispanic American, 2% African American, 4% Asian American/Pacific Islander **The most frequently chosen baccalaureate fields are** business/marketing, education, psychology **Academic program** Advanced placement, accelerated degree program, self-designed majors, honors program, summer session, adult/continuing education programs, internships **Contact** Ms. Heidi Stowman, Director of Admissions, Corban University, 5000 Deer Park Drive, SE, Salem, OR 97301-9392. *Phone:* 503-375-7115 or toll-free 800-845-3005. *Fax:* 503-585-4316. *E-mail:* admissions@corban.edu. *Web site:* http://www.corban.edu/.

DeVry University
Portland, Oregon

General Proprietary, comprehensive, coed **Entrance** Minimally difficult **Total enrollment** 218 **Student-faculty ratio** 11:1 **Application deadline** Rolling (freshmen), rolling (transfer) **Housing** No **Expenses** Tuition & Fees $14,080 **Undergraduates** 39% women, 50% part-time, 72% 25 or older, 2% Native American, 8% Hispanic American, 9% African American, 2% Asian American/Pacific Islander **The most frequently chosen baccalaureate fields are** business/marketing, computer and information sciences **Academic program** Advanced placement, accelerated degree program, summer session, adult/continuing education programs **Contact** Admissions Office, DeVry University, 9755 Southwest Barnes Road, Suite 150, Portland, OR 97225-6651. *Web site:* http://www.devry.edu/.

Eastern Oregon University
La Grande, Oregon

General State-supported, comprehensive, coed **Entrance** Moderately difficult **Setting** 121-acre rural campus **Total enrollment** 3,666 **Student-faculty ratio** 23:1 **Application deadline** 9/1 (freshmen) **Freshman admission** 39% were admitted. Average high school GPA 3.15 **Freshman test scores** SAT critical reading scores over 500: 35.22%; SAT math scores over 500: 34.35%; ACT scores over 18: 71.62%; SAT critical reading scores over 600: 10.87%; SAT math scores over 600: 6.52%; ACT scores over 24: 17.57% **Housing** Yes **Expenses** Tuition & Fees: state resident $6456, nonresident $6456; Room & Board $7870 **Undergraduates** 62% women, 43% part-time, 54% 25 or older **The most frequently chosen baccalaureate fields are** business/marketing, education, liberal arts/general studies **Academic program** Advanced placement, self-designed majors, honors program, summer session, adult/continuing education programs, internships **Contact** Mr. Tyler Dubsky, Assistant Director of Admissions, Eastern Oregon University, One University Boulevard, Zabel Hall, Room 116, La Grande, OR 97850-2899. *Phone:* 541-962-3085 or toll-free 800-452-8639 (in-state); 800-452-3393 (out-of-state). *Fax:* 541-962-3418. *E-mail:* admissions@eou.edu. *Web site:* http://www.eou.edu/.

Eugene Bible College
Eugene, Oregon

General Independent, 4-year, coed, affiliated with Open Bible Standard Churches **Entrance** Minimally difficult **Setting** 40-acre suburban campus **Total enrollment** 101 **Student-faculty ratio** 7:1 **Application deadline** 8/1 (freshmen), rolling (transfer) **Freshman admission** 100% were admitted **Housing** Yes **Expenses** Tuition & Fees $12,430; Room & Board $6010 **Undergraduates** 47% women, 12% part-time, 33% 25 or older, 5% Native American, 2% Hispanic American, 2% African American **Academic program** Advanced placement, summer session, internships **Contact** Sarah Maestas, Director of Admissions, Eugene Bible College, 2155 Bailey Hill Road, Eugene, OR 97405. *Phone:* 541-485-1780 Ext. 3115 or toll-free 800-322-2638. *Fax:* 541-343-5801. *E-mail:* admissions@ebc.edu. *Web site:* http://www.ebc.edu/.

George Fox University
Newberg, Oregon

General Independent Friends, university, coed **Entrance** Moderately difficult **Setting** 85-acre small-town campus **Total enrollment** 3,388 **Student-faculty ratio** 11:1 **Application deadline** Rolling (freshmen), 6/1 (transfer) **Freshman admission** 69% were admitted. Average high school GPA 3.65 **Freshman test scores** SAT critical reading scores over 500: 73.29%; SAT math scores over 500: 66.87%; ACT scores over 18: 94.78%; SAT critical reading scores over 600: 29.67%; SAT math scores over 600: 29.59%; ACT scores over 24: 41.05% **Housing** Yes **Expenses** Tuition & Fees $26,180; Room & Board $8320 **Undergraduates** 60% women, 15% part-time, 16% 25 or older, 2% Native American, 5% Hispanic American, 2% African American, 5% Asian American/Pacific Islander **The most frequently chosen baccalaureate fields are** business/marketing, interdisciplinary studies, visual and performing arts **Academic program** English as a second language, advanced placement, accelerated degree program, self-designed majors, honors program, summer session, adult/continuing education programs, internships **Contact** Mr. Ryan Dougherty, Director of Undergraduate Admissions,

George Fox University, 414 North Meridian Street, Newberg, OR 97132. *Phone:* 503-554-2240 or toll-free 800-765-4369. *Fax:* 503-554-3110. *E-mail:* admissions@georgefox.edu. *Web site:* http://www.georgefox.edu/.
Visit Petersons.com and enter keywords George Fox University

Gutenberg College
Eugene, Oregon

General Independent religious, 4-year, coed **Entrance** Moderately difficult **Setting** urban campus **Total enrollment** 38 **Student-faculty ratio** 6:1 **Application deadline** 3/1 (freshmen) **Freshman admission** 64% were admitted **Freshman test scores** SAT critical reading scores over 500: 100%; SAT math scores over 500: 43%; SAT critical reading scores over 600: 57%; SAT math scores over 600: 14% **Housing** Yes **Expenses** Tuition & Fees $11,852; Room & Board $5000 **Undergraduates** 39% women, 10% 25 or older, 5% Hispanic American **The most frequently chosen baccalaureate field is** liberal arts/general studies **Contact** Mr. Terry Stollar, Director of Admissions and Development, Gutenberg College, 1883 University Street, Eugene, OR 97403. *Phone:* 541-736-9071. *Fax:* 541-683-6997. *E-mail:* tstollar@gutenberg.edu. *Web site:* http://www.gutenberg.edu/.

ITT Technical Institute
Portland, Oregon

General Proprietary, primarily 2-year, coed **Entrance** Minimally difficult **Setting** urban campus **Housing** No **Contact** Director of Recruitment, ITT Technical Institute, 9500 Northeast Cascades Parkway, Portland, OR 97220. *Phone:* 503-255-6500 or toll-free 800-234-5488. *Web site:* http://www.itt-tech.edu/.

Lewis & Clark College
Portland, Oregon

General Independent, comprehensive, coed **Entrance** Very difficult **Setting** 137-acre suburban campus **Total enrollment** 3,523 **Student-faculty ratio** 12:1 **Application deadline** 2/1 (freshmen), 7/1 (transfer) **Freshman admission** 65% were admitted. Average high school GPA 3.69 **Freshman test scores** SAT critical reading scores over 500: 97.7%; SAT math scores over 500: 98.5%; ACT scores over 18: 100%; SAT critical reading scores over 600: 84.4%; SAT math scores over 600: 80.1%; ACT scores over 24: 95% **Housing** Yes **Expenses** Tuition & Fees $35,233; Room & Board $9006 **Undergraduates** 60% women, 1% part-time, 1% 25 or older, 1% Native American, 5% Hispanic American, 2% African American, 7% Asian American/Pacific Islander **The most frequently chosen baccalaureate fields are** psychology, social sciences, visual and performing arts **Academic program** English as a second language, advanced placement, accelerated degree program, self-designed majors, honors program, summer session, internships **Contact** Ms. Erica Johnson, Interim Dean of Admissions, Lewis & Clark College, 0615 SW Palatine Hill Road, Portland, OR 97219. *Phone:* 503-768-7040 or toll-free 800-444-4111. *Fax:* 503-768-7055. *E-mail:* admissions@lclark.edu. *Web site:* http://www.lclark.edu/.
Visit Petersons.com and enter keyword Lewis

See page 912 for the College Close-Up.

Linfield College
McMinnville, Oregon

General Independent American Baptist Churches in the USA, 4-year, coed **Entrance** Moderately difficult **Setting** 193-acre small-town campus **Total enrollment** 1,677 **Student-faculty ratio** 12:1 **Application deadline** 2/15 (freshmen), 4/15 (transfer) **Freshman admission** 82% were admitted. Average high school GPA 3.55 **Freshman test scores** SAT critical reading scores over 500: 70%; SAT math scores over 500: 71%; ACT scores over 18: 93%; SAT critical reading scores over 600: 30%; SAT math scores over 600: 27%; ACT scores over 24: 50% **Housing** Yes **Expenses** Tuition & Fees $29,034; Room & Board $8280 **Undergraduates** 57% women, 3% part-time, 2% 25 or older, 2% Native American, 5% Hispanic American, 2% African American, 9% Asian American/Pacific Islander **The most frequently chosen baccalaureate fields are** business/marketing, education, social sciences **Academic program** English as a second language, advanced placement, accelerated degree program, self-designed majors, summer session, adult/continuing education programs, internships **Contact** Ms. Lisa Knodle-Bragiel, Director of Admission, Linfield College, 900 SE Baker Street, McMinnville, OR 97128. *Phone:* 503-883-2213 or toll-free 800-640-2287. *Fax:* 503-883-2472. *E-mail:* admission@linfield.edu. *Web site:* http://www.linfield.edu/.
Visit Petersons.com and enter keyword Linfield

See page 922 for the College Close-Up.

Marylhurst University
Marylhurst, Oregon

General Independent Roman Catholic, comprehensive, coed, primarily women **Entrance** Noncompetitive **Setting** 73-acre suburban campus **Total enrollment** 1,902 **Student-faculty ratio** 6:1 **Application deadline** Rolling (freshmen), rolling (transfer) **Freshman admission** 61% were admitted **Housing** No **Expenses** Tuition & Fees $16,920 **Undergraduates** 70% women, 71% part-time, 79% 25 or older, 0.3% Native American, 3% Hispanic American, 5% African American, 1% Asian American/Pacific Islander **The most frequently chosen baccalaureate fields are** business/marketing, interdisciplinary studies, visual and performing arts **Academic program** English as a second language, advanced placement, accelerated degree program, self-designed majors, summer session, adult/continuing education programs, internships **Contact** Gretchen Potter, Director of Admissions, Marylhurst University, 17600 Pacific Highway, PO Box 261, Marylhurst, OR 97036-0261. *Phone:* 503-636-8141 or toll-free 800-634-9982. *Fax:* 503-635-6585. *E-mail:* admissions@marylhurst.edu. *Web site:* http://www.marylhurst.edu/.

Mount Angel Seminary
Saint Benedict, Oregon

General Independent Roman Catholic, comprehensive, undergraduate: men only; graduate: coed **Entrance** Moderately difficult **Setting** 75-acre rural campus **Total enrollment** 181 **Application deadline** 7/15 (freshmen), 7/15 (transfer) **Freshman admission** 100% were admitted **Housing** Yes **Undergraduates** 51% 25 or older **Academic program** English as a second language, advanced placement, adult/continuing education programs **Contact** Registrar/Admissions Officer, Mount Angel Seminary, Saint Benedict, OR 97373. *Phone:* 503-845-3951 Ext. 14. *E-mail:* seminary@mountangelabbey.org. *Web site:* http://www.mountangelabbey.org/seminary/.

Multnomah University
Portland, Oregon

General Independent interdenominational, comprehensive, coed **Entrance** Moderately difficult **Setting** 22-acre urban campus **Total enrollment** 841 **Student-faculty ratio** 13:1 **Application deadline** 7/15 (freshmen), 7/15 (transfer) **Freshman admission** 87% were admitted. Average high school GPA 3.2 **Freshman test scores** SAT critical reading scores over 500: 85.8%; SAT math scores over 500: 57.2%; ACT scores over 18: 93.4%; SAT critical reading scores over 600: 42.9%; SAT math scores over 600: 21.5%; ACT scores over 24: 60% **Housing** Yes **Undergraduates** 42% women, 17% part-time, 19% 25 or older, 1% Native American, 3% Hispanic American, 1% African American, 2% Asian American/Pacific Islander **The most frequently chosen baccalaureate field is** theology and religious vocations **Academic program** Advanced placement, summer session, adult/continuing education programs, internships **Contact** Ms. Nancy Gerecz, Admissions Assistant, Multnomah University, 8435 Northeast Glisan Street, Portland, OR

Multnomah University (continued)

97220-5898. *Phone:* 503-255-0332 Ext. 5373 or toll-free 800-275-4672. *Fax:* 503-254-1268. *E-mail:* admiss@multnomah.edu. *Web site:* http://www.multnomah.edu/.

See page 998 for the College Close-Up.

Northwest Christian University
Eugene, Oregon

General Independent Christian, comprehensive, coed **Entrance** Moderately difficult **Setting** 8-acre urban campus **Total enrollment** 557 **Student-faculty ratio** 21:1 **Application deadline** Rolling (freshmen), rolling (transfer) **Freshman admission** 95% were admitted. Average high school GPA 3.4 **Freshman test scores** SAT critical reading scores over 500: 41%; SAT critical reading scores over 600: 11% **Housing** Yes **Expenses** Tuition & Fees $22,900; Room & Board $6800 **Undergraduates** 59% women, 18% part-time, 37% 25 or older, 2% Native American, 4% Hispanic American, 2% African American, 3% Asian American/Pacific Islander **The most frequently chosen baccalaureate fields are** business/marketing, education, health professions and related sciences **Academic program** Advanced placement, accelerated degree program, self-designed majors, summer session, adult/continuing education programs, internships **Contact** Jennifer Samples, Director of Admissions, Northwest Christian University, 828 East 11th Avenue, Eugene, OR 97401-3745. *Phone:* 541-684-7201 or toll-free 877-463-6622. *Fax:* 541-684-7317. *E-mail:* admissions@northwestchristian.edu. *Web site:* http://www.northwestchristian.edu/.

Oregon College of Art & Craft
Portland, Oregon

General Independent, 4-year, coed **Entrance** Minimally difficult **Setting** 10-acre urban campus **Total enrollment** 169 **Student-faculty ratio** 9:1 **Application deadline** Rolling (freshmen), rolling (transfer) **Freshman admission** 88% were admitted. Average high school GPA 3 **Freshman test scores** SAT math scores over 500: 74%; ACT scores over 18: 100%; SAT math scores over 600: 63%; ACT scores over 24: 40% **Housing** Yes **Expenses** Tuition & Fees $22,608; Room & Board $6210 **Undergraduates** 70% women, 35% part-time, 60% 25 or older, 3% Native American, 1% Hispanic American, 1% Asian American/Pacific Islander **The most frequently chosen baccalaureate field is** visual and performing arts **Academic program** Advanced placement, adult/continuing education programs, internships **Contact** Ms. Devon Simpson, Assistant Director of Admissions, Oregon College of Art & Craft, 8245 Southwest Barnes Road, Portland, OR 97225-6349. *Phone:* 503-297-5544 Ext. 141 or toll-free 800-390-0632 Ext. 129. *Fax:* 503-297-9651. *E-mail:* admissions@ocac.edu. *Web site:* http://www.ocac.edu/.

Oregon Health & Science University
Portland, Oregon

General State-related, upper-level, coed **Setting** 116-acre urban campus **Total enrollment** 2,583 **Application deadline** 2/1 (transfer) **Housing** No **Expenses** Tuition & Fees: state resident $16,051, nonresident $25,051 **Undergraduates** 83% women, 75% part-time, 68% 25 or older, 2% Native American, 5% Hispanic American, 1% African American, 4% Asian American/Pacific Islander **The most frequently chosen baccalaureate field is** health professions and related sciences **Academic program** Advanced placement, summer session **Contact** Jennifer Anderson, Director of Admissions, Oregon Health & Science University, 3181 Southwest Sam Jackson Park Road, Mail Code: 337A/SNADM, Portland, OR 97201-3098. *Phone:* 503-494-0647. *Fax:* 503-494-4350. *E-mail:* andersje@ohsu.edu. *Web site:* http://www.ohsu.edu/.

Oregon Institute of Technology
Klamath Falls, Oregon

General State-supported, comprehensive, coed **Entrance** Moderately difficult **Setting** 173-acre small-town campus **Total enrollment** 3,915 **Student-faculty ratio** 20:1 **Application deadline** 10/1 (freshmen), rolling (transfer) **Freshman admission** 93% were admitted. Average high school GPA 3.41 **Freshman test scores** SAT critical reading scores over 500: 56.34%; SAT math scores over 500: 61.34%; ACT scores over 18: 85.54%; SAT critical reading scores over 600: 15.34%; SAT math scores over 600: 25%; ACT scores over 24: 42.17% **Housing** Yes **Expenses** Tuition & Fees: state resident $6765, nonresident $18,195; Room & Board $8615 **Undergraduates** 49% women, 47% part-time, 2% Native American, 5% Hispanic American, 1% African American, 6% Asian American/Pacific Islander **The most frequently chosen baccalaureate fields are** engineering technologies, engineering, health professions and related sciences **Academic program** Advanced placement, summer session, internships **Contact** Ginny Garner, Assistant Director of Admissions, Oregon Institute of Technology, 3201 Campus Drive, Klamath Falls, OR 97601-8801. *Phone:* 541-885-1151 or toll-free 800-422-2017 (in-state); 800-343-6653 (out-of-state). *E-mail:* oit@oit.edu. *Web site:* http://www.oit.edu/.

Oregon State University
Corvallis, Oregon

General State-supported, university, coed **Entrance** Moderately difficult **Setting** 422-acre small-town campus **Total enrollment** 21,969 **Student-faculty ratio** 20:1 **Application deadline** 9/1 (freshmen), 5/1 (transfer) **Freshman admission** 83% were admitted. Average high school GPA 3.47 **Freshman test scores** SAT critical reading scores over 500: 63%; SAT math scores over 500: 70%; ACT scores over 18: 93%; SAT critical reading scores over 600: 21%; SAT math scores over 600: 30%; ACT scores over 24: 49% **Housing** Yes **Expenses** Tuition & Fees: state resident $6727, nonresident $19,651; Room & Board $8352 **Undergraduates** 47% women, 16% part-time, 12% 25 or older, 1% Native American, 5% Hispanic American, 1% African American, 9% Asian American/Pacific Islander **The most frequently chosen baccalaureate fields are** business/marketing, engineering, family and consumer sciences **Academic program** English as a second language, advanced placement, accelerated degree program, self-designed majors, honors program, summer session, internships **Contact** Ms. Michele Sandlin, Director of Admissions, Oregon State University, Corvallis, OR 97331. *Phone:* 541-737-4411 or toll-free 800-291-4192. *E-mail:* osuadmit@ccmail.orst.edu. *Web site:* http://www.oregonstate.edu/.

Visit Petersons.com and enter keywords Oregon State

See page 1038 for the College Close-Up.

Oregon State University–Cascades
Bend, Oregon

General State-supported, comprehensive, coed **Setting** 193-acre small-town campus **Total enrollment** 611 **Student-faculty ratio** 15:1 **Application deadline** Rolling (freshmen), rolling (transfer) **Housing** Yes **Expenses** Tuition & Fees: state resident $5796, nonresident $18,900 **Undergraduates** 44% 25 or older, 3% Native American, 4% Hispanic American, 1% African American, 1% Asian American/Pacific Islander **Academic program** Advanced placement, summer session, internships **Contact** Admissions Department, Oregon State University–Cascades, 2600 Northwest College Way, Bend, OR 97701. *Phone:* 541-322-3150. *E-mail:* cascadeadmit@osucascades.edu. *Web site:* http://www.osucascades.edu/.

Pacific Northwest College of Art
Portland, Oregon

General Independent, comprehensive, coed **Entrance** Moderately difficult **Setting** 2-acre urban campus **Total enrollment** 507 **Student-faculty ratio** 9:1 **Freshman admission** 51% were admitted. Average high school GPA 2.79 **Housing** Yes **Expenses** Tuition & Fees $23,284; Room & Board $8004 **Undergraduates** 65% women, 8% part-time, 25% 25 or older, 1% Native American, 6% Hispanic American, 2% African American, 3% Asian American/Pacific Islander **The most frequently chosen baccalaureate field is** visual and performing arts **Academic program** Advanced placement, self-designed majors, internships **Contact** Mr. Chris Sweet Jr., Director of Admissions, Pacific Northwest College of Art, 1241 NW Johnson Street, Portland, OR 97209. *Phone:* 503-821-8972. *Fax:* 503-821-8978. *E-mail:* admissions@pnca.edu. *Web site:* http://www.pnca.edu/.

Pacific University
Forest Grove, Oregon

General Independent, comprehensive, coed **Entrance** Moderately difficult **Setting** 60-acre small-town campus **Total enrollment** 3,167 **Student-faculty ratio** 11:1 **Application deadline** 8/15 (freshmen), rolling (transfer) **Freshman admission** 78% were admitted. Average high school GPA 3.61 **Freshman test scores** SAT critical reading scores over 500: 71%; SAT math scores over 500: 74%; ACT scores over 18: 96%; SAT critical reading scores over 600: 25%; SAT math scores over 600: 25%; ACT scores over 24: 54% **Housing** Yes **Expenses** Tuition & Fees $29,966; Room & Board $8118 **Undergraduates** 64% women, 5% part-time, 9% 25 or older, 1% Native American, 5% Hispanic American, 1% African American, 23% Asian American/Pacific Islander **The most frequently chosen baccalaureate fields are** business/marketing, parks and recreation, social sciences **Academic program** English as a second language, advanced placement, summer session, internships **Contact** Ms. Karen Dunston, Executive Director, Pacific University, 2043 College Way, Forest Grove, OR 97116-1797. *Phone:* 503-352-2218 or toll-free 877-722-8648. *Fax:* 503-352-2975. *E-mail:* admissions@pacificu.edu. *Web site:* http://www.pacificu.edu/.

Visit Petersons.com and enter keywords Pacific University

See page 1042 for the College Close-Up.

Pioneer Pacific College
Clackamas, Oregon

General Proprietary, 4-year, coed **Setting** urban campus **Contact** Admissions Office, Pioneer Pacific College, 8800 SE Sunnyside Road, Clackamas, OR 97015. *Phone:* 503-654-8000 or toll-free 866-772-4636. *E-mail:* inquiries@pioneerpacific.edu. *Web site:* http://www.pioneerpacific.edu/.

Pioneer Pacific College
Wilsonville, Oregon

General Proprietary, 4-year, coed **Entrance** Noncompetitive **Setting** suburban campus **Student-faculty ratio** 15:1 **Application deadline** Rolling (freshmen) **Housing** No **Academic program** Accelerated degree program, honors program, internships **Contact** Ms. Kristin Lynn, Director of Admissions, Pioneer Pacific College, 27501 Southwest Parkway Avenue, Wilsonville, OR 97070. *Phone:* 866-772-4636 or toll-free 866-PPC-INFO. *Fax:* 503-682-1514. *E-mail:* inquiries@pioneerpacific.edu. *Web site:* http://www.pioneerpacific.edu/.

Pioneer Pacific College–Eugene/Springfield Branch
Springfield, Oregon

General Proprietary, 4-year, coed **Setting** urban campus **Contact** Admissions Office, Pioneer Pacific College–Eugene/Springfield Branch, 3800 Sports Way, Springfield, OR 97477. *Phone:* 541-684-4644 or toll-free 866-772-4636. *E-mail:* inquiries@pioneerpacific.edu. *Web site:* http://www.pioneerpacific.edu.

Portland State University
Portland, Oregon

General State-supported, university, coed **Entrance** Moderately difficult **Setting** 49-acre urban campus **Total enrollment** 26,382 **Student-faculty ratio** 20:1 **Application deadline** Rolling (freshmen), rolling (transfer) **Freshman admission** 90% were admitted. Average high school GPA 3.25 **Freshman test scores** SAT critical reading scores over 500: 62%; SAT math scores over 500: 60%; ACT scores over 18: 82%; SAT critical reading scores over 600: 23%; SAT math scores over 600: 18%; ACT scores over 24: 33% **Housing** Yes **Expenses** Tuition & Fees: state resident $6764, nonresident $21,198; Room & Board $9774 **Undergraduates** 53% women, 37% part-time, 38% 25 or older, 1% Native American, 6% Hispanic American, 3% African American, 10% Asian American/Pacific Islander **The most frequently chosen baccalaureate fields are** business/marketing, liberal arts/general studies, social sciences **Academic program** English as a second language, advanced placement, accelerated degree program, honors program, summer session, adult/continuing education programs, internships **Contact** Ms. Agnes A. Hoffman, Associate Vice Provost for Enrollment Management and Student Affairs, Portland State University, PO Box 751, Portland, OR 97207-0751. *Phone:* 503-725-5502 or toll-free 800-547-8887. *Fax:* 503-725-5525. *E-mail:* askadm@ofa.pdx.edu. *Web site:* http://www.pdx.edu/.

Reed College
Portland, Oregon

General Independent, comprehensive, coed **Entrance** Most difficult **Setting** 116-acre urban campus **Total enrollment** 1,481 **Student-faculty ratio** 10:1 **Application deadline** 1/15 (freshmen), 3/1 (transfer) **Freshman admission** 41% were admitted. Average high school GPA 3.9 **Freshman test scores** SAT critical reading scores over 500: 100%; SAT math scores over 500: 100%; ACT scores over 18: 100%; SAT critical reading scores over 600: 94%; SAT math scores over 600: 86%; ACT scores over 24: 98% **Housing** Yes **Expenses** Tuition & Fees $39,700; Room & Board $10,250 **Undergraduates** 55% women, 3% part-time, 2% 25 or older, 1% Native American, 7% Hispanic American, 3% African American, 9% Asian American/Pacific Islander **The most frequently chosen baccalaureate fields are** English, foreign languages and literature, social sciences **Academic program** Advanced placement, internships **Contact** Mr. Keith Todd, Dean of Admission, Reed College, 3203 Southeast Woodstock Boulevard, Portland, OR 97202-8199. *Phone:* 503-777-7511 or toll-free 800-547-4750. *Fax:* 503-777-7553. *E-mail:* admission@reed.edu. *Web site:* http://www.reed.edu/.

Visit Petersons.com and enter keyword Reed

See page 1070 for the College Close-Up.

Southern Oregon University
Ashland, Oregon

General State-supported, comprehensive, coed **Entrance** Moderately difficult **Setting** 175-acre small-town campus **Total enrollment** 5,103 **Student-faculty ratio** 18:1 **Application deadline** Rolling (freshmen), rolling (transfer) **Freshman admission** 89% were admitted. Average high school GPA 3.2 **Freshman test scores** SAT critical reading scores over 500: 57.8%; SAT math scores over 500: 53.1%; ACT scores over 18: 83.3%; SAT critical reading scores over 600: 21.3%; SAT math scores over 600: 13.3%; ACT scores over 24: 32.5% **Housing** Yes **Expenses** Tuition & Fees: state resident $5718, nonresident $18,264; Room & Board $8250 **Undergraduates** 57% women, 24% part-time, 21% 25 or older, 2% Native American, 5% Hispanic American, 2% African American, 4% Asian American/Pacific Islander **The most frequently chosen baccalaureate fields are** business/marketing, psychology, visual and performing arts **Academic program** English as a second language, advanced placement, accelerated degree program, self-designed majors, honors program, summer session, adult/continuing education programs, internships **Contact** Mr. Mark Bottorff, Director of Admissions, Southern Oregon University, 1250 Siskiyou Boulevard, Ashland, OR 97520. *Phone:* 541-552-6411 or toll-free 800-482-7672. *Fax:* 541-552-6614. *E-mail:* admissions@sou.edu. *Web site:* http://www.sou.edu/.

University of Oregon
Eugene, Oregon

General State-supported, university, coed **Entrance** Moderately difficult **Setting** 295-acre urban campus **Total enrollment** 22,335 **Student-faculty ratio** 20:1 **Application deadline** 1/15 (freshmen), 5/15 (transfer) **Freshman admission** 80% were admitted. Average high school GPA 3.54 **Freshman test scores** SAT critical reading scores over 500: 75%; SAT math scores over 500: 75%; SAT critical reading scores over 600: 31%; SAT math scores over 600: 33% **Housing** Yes **Expenses** Tuition & Fees: state resident $7428, nonresident $23,718; Room & Board $8620 **Undergraduates** 50% women, 8% part-time, 9% 25 or older, 1% Native American, 4% Hispanic American, 2% African American, 6% Asian American/Pacific Islander **The most frequently chosen baccalaureate fields are** business/marketing, communications/journalism, social sciences **Academic program** English as a second language, advanced placement, self-designed majors, honors program, summer session, adult/continuing education programs, internships **Contact** Brian Henley, Director of Admissions, University of Oregon, Eugene, OR 97403. *Phone:* 541-346-3201 or toll-free 800-232-3825. *Fax:* 541-346-5815. *E-mail:* uoadmit@uoregon.edu. *Web site:* http://www.uoregon.edu/.

Visit Petersons.com and enter keywords University of Oregon

See page 1296 for the College Close-Up.

University of Phoenix–Oregon Campus
Tigard, Oregon

General Proprietary, comprehensive, coed **Entrance** Noncompetitive **Setting** urban campus **Total enrollment** 1,265 **Application deadline** Rolling (freshmen), rolling (transfer) **Housing** No **Expenses** Tuition & Fees $12,225 **Undergraduates** 57% women, 87% 25 or older **The most frequently chosen baccalaureate fields are** business/marketing, computer and information sciences, public administration and social services **Academic program** Advanced placement, accelerated degree program, adult/continuing education programs **Contact** Ms. Audra McQuarie, Registrar/Executive Director, University of Phoenix–Oregon Campus, 4035 South Riverpoint Parkway, Mail Stop CF-L101, Phoenix, AZ 85040. *Phone:* 480-557-6151 or toll-free 800-776-4867 (in-state); 800-228-7240 (out-of-state). *Fax:* 480-643-3068. *E-mail:* audra.mcquarie@phoenix.edu. *Web site:* http://www.phoenix.edu/.

University of Portland
Portland, Oregon

General Independent Roman Catholic, comprehensive, coed **Entrance** Moderately difficult **Setting** 125-acre urban campus **Total enrollment** 3,706 **Student-faculty ratio** 13:1 **Application deadline** 6/1 (freshmen), 6/1 (transfer) **Freshman admission** 56% were admitted. Average high school GPA 3.63 **Freshman test scores** SAT math scores over 500: 91%; SAT math scores over 600: 53% **Housing** Yes **Expenses** Tuition & Fees $31,996; Room & Board $9135 **Undergraduates** 61% women, 2% part-time, 3% 25 or older, 1% Native American, 5% Hispanic American, 1% African American, 12% Asian American/Pacific Islander **The most frequently chosen baccalaureate fields are** business/marketing, biological/life sciences, health professions and related sciences **Academic program** Advanced placement, honors program, summer session, adult/continuing education programs, internships **Contact** Mr. Jason McDonald, Dean of Admissions, University of Portland, 5000 North Willamette Boulevard, Portland, OR 97203-5798. *Phone:* 503-943-7147 or toll-free 888-627-5601. *Fax:* 503-943-7315. *E-mail:* admissions@up.edu. *Web site:* http://www.up.edu/.

Warner Pacific College
Portland, Oregon

General Independent, comprehensive, coed, affiliated with Church of God **Entrance** Moderately difficult **Setting** 15-acre urban campus **Total enrollment** 1,333 **Student-faculty ratio** 22:1 **Application deadline** Rolling (freshmen), rolling (transfer) **Freshman admission** 61% were admitted. Average high school GPA 3.1 **Freshman test scores** SAT critical reading scores over 500: 61.4%; SAT math scores over 500: 62.7%; ACT scores over 18: 76.9%; SAT critical reading scores over 600: 18.9%; SAT math scores over 600: 14.2%; ACT scores over 24: 23.3% **Housing** Yes **Expenses** Tuition & Fees $17,110; Room & Board $6646 **Undergraduates** 62% women, 1% part-time, 60% 25 or older, 0.3% Native American, 4% Hispanic American, 4% African American, 3% Asian American/Pacific Islander **The most frequently chosen baccalaureate fields are** business/marketing, social sciences, theology and religious vocations **Academic program** Advanced placement, accelerated degree program, self-designed majors, honors program, summer session, adult/continuing education programs, internships **Contact** Mrs. Shannon Mackey, Executive Director of Enrollment Management, Warner Pacific College, 2219 Southeast 68th Avenue, Portland, OR 97215. *Phone:* 503-517-1020 or toll-free 800-804-1510. *Fax:* 503-517-1540. *E-mail:* admiss@warnerpacific.edu. *Web site:* http://www.warnerpacific.edu/. **Visit Petersons.com and enter keyword Warner**

See page 1342 for the College Close-Up.

Western Oregon University
Monmouth, Oregon

General State-supported, comprehensive, coed **Entrance** Moderately difficult **Setting** 157-acre rural campus **Total enrollment** 5,654 **Student-faculty ratio** 25:1 **Application deadline** Rolling (freshmen), rolling (transfer) **Freshman admission** 89% were admitted. Average high school GPA 3.24 **Freshman test scores** SAT critical reading scores over 500: 40%; SAT math scores over 500: 44%; ACT scores over 18: 72%; SAT critical reading scores over 600: 9%; SAT math scores over 600: 11%; ACT scores over 24: 17% **Housing** Yes **Expenses** Tuition & Fees: state resident $7458, nonresident $18,549; Room & Board $8208 **Undergraduates** 57% women, 12% part-time, 16% 25 or older, 2% Native American, 9% Hispanic American, 3% African American, 4% Asian American/Pacific Islander **The most frequently chosen baccalaureate fields are** business/marketing, education, interdisciplinary studies **Academic program** English as a second language, advanced placement, self-designed majors, honors program, summer session, internships **Contact** Mr. Rob Findtner, Assistant Director of Admissions, Western Oregon University, 345 North Monmouth Avenue, Monmouth, OR 97361. *Phone:* 503-838-8211 or toll-free 877-877-1593. *Fax:* 503-838-8067. *E-mail:* wolfgram@wou.edu. *Web site:* http://www.wou.edu/.

Willamette University
Salem, Oregon

General Independent United Methodist, comprehensive, coed **Entrance** Very difficult **Setting** 72-acre urban campus **Total enrollment** 2,886 **Student-faculty ratio** 10:1 **Application deadline** 2/1 (freshmen), 2/1 (transfer) **Freshman admission** 60% were admitted. Average high school GPA 3.72 **Freshman test scores** SAT critical reading scores over 500: 95%; SAT math scores over 500: 94%; ACT scores over 18: 100%; SAT critical reading scores over 600: 59%; SAT math scores over 600: 59%; ACT scores over 24: 90% **Housing** Yes **Expenses** Tuition & Fees $35,610; Room & Board $8350 **Undergraduates** 56% women, 7% part-time, 2% 25 or older, 1% Native American, 6% Hispanic American, 2% African American, 7% Asian American/Pacific Islander **The most frequently chosen baccalaureate fields are** English, foreign languages and literature, social sciences **Academic program** Advanced placement, accelerated degree program, self-designed majors, internships **Contact** Susan Rauch, Vice President for Admission and Financial Aid, Willamette University, 900 State Street, Salem, OR 97301. *Phone:* 877-542-2787 or toll-free 877-542-2787. *Fax:* 503-375-5363. *E-mail:* libarts@williamette.edu. *Web site:* http://www.willamette.edu/.

PENNSYLVANIA

Albright College
Reading, Pennsylvania

General Independent, comprehensive, coed, affiliated with United Methodist Church **Entrance** Moderately difficult **Setting** 118-acre suburban campus **Total enrollment** 2,358 **Student-faculty ratio** 13:1 **Application deadline** Rolling (freshmen), rolling (transfer) **Freshman admission** 56% were admitted. Average high school GPA 3.29 **Freshman test scores** SAT critical reading scores over 500: 64%; SAT math scores over 500: 64%; SAT critical reading scores over 600: 19%; SAT math scores over 600: 17% **Housing** Yes **Expenses** Tuition & Fees $32,740; Room & Board $8858 **Undergraduates** 59% women, 1% part-time, 1% 25 or older, 0.4% Native American, 6% Hispanic American, 11% African American, 1% Asian American/Pacific Islander **The most frequently chosen baccalaureate fields are** business/marketing, psychology, social sciences **Academic program** English as a second language, advanced placement, accelerated degree program, self-designed majors, honors program, summer session, internships **Contact** Mr. Gregory Eichhorn, Vice President for Enrollment Management, Albright College, PO Box 15234, 13th and Bern Streets, Reading, PA 19612-5234. *Phone:* 610-921-7260 or toll-free 800-252-1856. *Fax:* 610-921-7294. *E-mail:* admission@albright.edu. *Web site:* http://www.albright.edu/.

Allegheny College
Meadville, Pennsylvania

General Independent, 4-year, coed **Entrance** Very difficult **Setting** 565-acre suburban campus **Total enrollment** 2,132 **Student-faculty ratio** 13:1 **Application deadline** 2/15 (freshmen), 7/1 (transfer) **Freshman admission** 66% were admitted. Average high school GPA 3.75 **Freshman test scores** SAT critical reading scores over 500: 90%; SAT math scores over 500: 91%; ACT scores over 18: 100%; SAT critical reading scores over 600: 58%; SAT math scores over 600: 57%; ACT scores over 24: 69% **Housing** Yes **Expenses** Tuition & Fees $34,810; Room & Board $8790 **Undergraduates** 55% women, 2% part-time, 1% 25 or older, 0.2% Native American, 3% Hispanic American, 4% African American, 3% Asian American/Pacific Islander **The most frequently chosen baccalaureate fields are** psychology, biological/life sciences, social sciences **Academic program** English as a second language, advanced placement, self-designed majors, internships **Contact** Ms. Jennifer Winge, Director of Admissions, Allegheny College, 520 North Main Street, Box 5, Meadville, PA 16335. *Phone:* 814-332-4351 or toll-free 800-521-5293. *Fax:* 814-337-0431. *E-mail:* admissions@allegheny.edu. *Web site:* http://www.allegheny.edu/.

Alvernia University
Reading, Pennsylvania

General Independent Roman Catholic, comprehensive, coed **Entrance** Moderately difficult **Setting** 121-acre suburban campus **Total enrollment** 2,856 **Student-faculty ratio** 14:1 **Application deadline** Rolling (freshmen), rolling (transfer) **Freshman admission** 78% were admitted. Average high school GPA 3.1 **Freshman test scores** SAT critical reading scores over 500: 43%; SAT math scores over 500: 44%; ACT scores over 18: 74%; SAT critical reading scores over 600: 7%; SAT math scores over 600: 8%; ACT scores over 24: 14% **Housing** Yes **Expenses** Tuition & Fees $24,350; Room & Board $9212 **Undergraduates** 68% women, 22% part-time, 12% 25 or older, 0.5% Native American, 6% Hispanic American, 11% African American, 1% Asian American/Pacific Islander **The most frequently chosen baccalaureate fields are** business/marketing, health professions and related sciences, security and protective services **Academic program** English as a second language, advanced placement, accelerated degree program, self-designed majors, honors program, summer session, adult/continuing education programs, internships **Contact** Mr. Jeff Dittman, Vice President for Enrollment

Alvernia University (continued)
Management, Alvernia University, 400 Saint Bernardine Street, Reading, PA 19607-1799. *Phone:* 610-796-8269 or toll-free 888-ALVERNIA. *Fax:* 610-796-2873. *E-mail:* admissions@alvernia.edu. *Web site:* http://www.alvernia.edu/.
Visit Petersons.com and enter keyword Alvernia

See page 468 for the College Close-Up.

Arcadia University
Glenside, Pennsylvania

General Independent, comprehensive, coed, affiliated with Presbyterian Church (U.S.A.) **Entrance** Moderately difficult **Setting** 71-acre suburban campus **Total enrollment** 4,021 **Student-faculty ratio** 15:1 **Application deadline** 3/1 (freshmen), 6/15 (transfer) **Freshman admission** 61% were admitted. Average high school GPA 3.55 **Freshman test scores** SAT critical reading scores over 500: 81%; SAT math scores over 500: 74%; ACT scores over 18: 96%; SAT critical reading scores over 600: 30%; SAT math scores over 600: 25%; ACT scores over 24: 47% **Housing** Yes **Expenses** Tuition & Fees $31,260; Room & Board $10,680 **Undergraduates** 73% women, 10% part-time, 17% 25 or older, 0.3% Native American, 4% Hispanic American, 8% African American, 3% Asian American/Pacific Islander **The most frequently chosen baccalaureate fields are** business/marketing, psychology, visual and performing arts **Academic program** English as a second language, advanced placement, self-designed majors, honors program, summer session, internships **Contact** Mr. Mark Lapreziosa, Assistant Vice President of Enrollment Management, Arcadia University, 450 South Easton Road, Glenside, PA 19038. *Phone:* 215-572-2910 or toll-free 877-ARCADIA. *Fax:* 215-572-4049. *E-mail:* admiss@arcadia.edu. *Web site:* http://www.arcadia.edu/.
Visit Petersons.com and enter keyword Arcadia

See page 476 for the College Close-Up.

The Art Institute of Philadelphia
Philadelphia, Pennsylvania

General Proprietary, 4-year, coed **Setting** urban campus **Contact** Director of Admissions, The Art Institute of Philadelphia, 1622 Chestnut Street, Philadelphia, PA 19103. *Phone:* 215-567-7080 or toll-free 800-275-2474. *Fax:* 215-405-6399. *Web site:* http://www.artinstitutes.edu/philadelphia/.
Visit Petersons.com and enter keywords Art Institute of Philadelphia

See page 530 for the College Close-Up.

The Art Institute of Pittsburgh
Pittsburgh, Pennsylvania

General Proprietary, 4-year, coed **Setting** urban campus **Contact** Director of Admissions, The Art Institute of Pittsburgh, 420 Boulevard of the Allies, Pittsburgh, PA 15219. *Phone:* 412-263-6600 or toll-free 800-275-2470. *Fax:* 412-263-6667. *Web site:* http://www.artinstitutes.edu/pittsburgh/.
Visit Petersons.com and enter keywords Art Institute of Pittsburgh

See page 534 for the College Close-Up.

The Art Institute of York–Pennsylvania
York, Pennsylvania

General Proprietary, primarily 2-year, coed **Setting** suburban campus **Contact** Director of Admissions, The Art Institute of York–Pennsylvania, 1409 Williams Road, York, PA 17402-9012. *Phone:* 717-755-2300 or toll-free 800-864-7725. *Fax:* 717-840-1951. *Web site:* http://www.artinstitutes.edu/york/.

See page 558 for the College Close-Up.

Baptist Bible College of Pennsylvania
Clarks Summit, Pennsylvania

General Independent Baptist, comprehensive, coed **Entrance** Minimally difficult **Setting** 124-acre suburban campus **Total enrollment** 999 **Student-faculty ratio** 14:1 **Application deadline** 8/15 (freshmen), rolling (transfer) **Freshman admission** 64% were admitted. Average high school GPA 3.31 **Freshman test scores** SAT critical reading scores over 500: 63%; SAT math scores over 500: 44%; ACT scores over 18: 85%; SAT critical reading scores over 600: 24%; SAT math scores over 600: 14%; ACT scores over 24: 35% **Housing** Yes **Expenses** Tuition & Fees $17,340; Room & Board $6350 **Undergraduates** 59% women, 8% part-time, 3% 25 or older, 0.4% Native American, 2% Hispanic American, 2% African American, 1% Asian American/Pacific Islander **The most frequently chosen baccalaureate field is** theology and religious vocations **Academic program** Advanced placement, self-designed majors, summer session, adult/continuing education programs, internships **Contact** Ms. Summer Kinder, Admissions Counselor, Baptist Bible College of Pennsylvania, 538 Venard Road, Clarks Summit, PA 18411-1297. *Phone:* 800-451-7664 or toll-free 800-451-7664. *Fax:* 570-585-9299. *E-mail:* admissions@bbc.edu. *Web site:* http://www.bbc.edu/.

Bloomsburg University of Pennsylvania
Bloomsburg, Pennsylvania

General State-supported, comprehensive, coed **Entrance** Moderately difficult **Setting** 282-acre small-town campus **Total enrollment** 9,512 **Student-faculty ratio** 21:1 **Application deadline** Rolling (freshmen), rolling (transfer) **Freshman admission** 64% were admitted. Average high school GPA 3.4 **Freshman test scores** SAT critical reading scores over 500: 50.9%; SAT math scores over 500: 59.6%; SAT critical reading scores over 600: 8.5%; SAT math scores over 600: 13.8% **Housing** Yes **Expenses** Tuition & Fees: state resident $7110, nonresident $15,442; Room & Board $6488 **Undergraduates** 58% women, 6% part-time, 5% 25 or older, 0.3% Native American, 3% Hispanic American, 7% African American, 1% Asian American/Pacific Islander **The most frequently chosen baccalaureate fields are** business/marketing, education, health professions and related sciences **Academic program** English as a second language, advanced placement, honors program, summer session, adult/continuing education programs, internships **Contact** Mr. Christopher Keller, Director of Admissions, Bloomsburg University of Pennsylvania, 104 Student Services Center, Bloomsburg, PA 17815-1905. *Phone:* 570-389-4316. *Fax:* 570-389-4741. *E-mail:* buadmiss@bloomu.edu. *Web site:* http://www.bloomu.edu/.

Bryn Athyn College of the New Church
Bryn Athyn, Pennsylvania

General Independent, comprehensive, coed, affiliated with Church of the New Jerusalem **Entrance** Minimally difficult **Setting** 130-acre suburban campus **Total enrollment** 211 **Student-faculty ratio** 6:1 **Application deadline** 7/1 (freshmen), 7/1 (transfer) **Freshman admission** 92% were admitted. Average high school GPA 3.36 **Freshman test scores** SAT critical reading scores over 500: 72%; SAT math scores over 500: 62%; ACT scores over 18: 92%; SAT critical reading scores over 600: 36%; SAT math scores over 600: 27%; ACT scores over 24: 15% **Housing** Yes **Expenses** Tuition & Fees $15,000; Room & Board $8541 **Undergraduates** 50% women, 4% part-time, 12% 25 or older, 7% African American, 2% Asian American/Pacific Islander **The most frequently chosen baccalaureate fields are** history, education, interdisciplinary studies **Academic program** English as a second language, advanced placement, accelerated degree program, self-designed majors, internships **Contact** Admissions Office, Bryn Athyn College of the New Church, 2945 College Drive, Box 462, Bryn Athyn, PA 19009. *Phone:* 267-502-6000. *Fax:* 267-502-2593. *E-mail:* admissions@brynathyn.edu. *Web site:* http://www.brynathyn.edu/.

Bryn Mawr College
Bryn Mawr, Pennsylvania

General Independent, university, undergraduate: women only; graduate: coed **Entrance** Most difficult **Setting** 135-acre suburban campus **Total enrollment** 1,771 **Student-faculty ratio** 8:1 **Application deadline** 1/15 (freshmen), 3/15 (transfer) **Freshman admission** 49% were admitted **Freshman test scores** SAT critical reading scores over 500: 97.54%; SAT math scores over 500: 97.53%; ACT scores over 18: 100%; SAT critical reading scores over 600: 78.71%; SAT math scores over 600: 68.83%; ACT scores over 24: 95.04% **Housing** Yes **Expenses** Tuition & Fees $38,034; Room & Board $12,000 **Undergraduates** 2% part-time, 1% 25 or older, 5% Hispanic American, 7% African American, 12% Asian American/Pacific Islander **The most frequently chosen baccalaureate fields are** English, psychology, social sciences **Academic program** Advanced placement, accelerated degree program, self-designed majors, summer session, internships **Contact** Ms. Marjorie Torchon, Director of Admissions, Bryn Mawr College, 101 North Merion Avenue, Bryn Mawr, PA 19010. *Phone:* 610-526-5152 or toll-free 800-BMC-1885. *Fax:* 610-526-7471. *E-mail:* admissions@brynmawr.edu. *Web site:* http://www.brynmawr.edu/.
Visit Petersons.com and enter keyword Bryn

See page 650 for the College Close-Up.

Bucknell University
Lewisburg, Pennsylvania

General Independent, comprehensive, coed **Entrance** Most difficult **Setting** 445-acre small-town campus **Total enrollment** 3,673 **Student-faculty ratio** 10:1 **Application deadline** 1/15 (freshmen), 3/15 (transfer) **Freshman admission** 30% were admitted. Average high school GPA 3.49 **Freshman test scores** SAT critical reading scores over 500: 98%; SAT math scores over 500: 98%; ACT scores over 18: 100%; SAT critical reading scores over 600: 77%; SAT math scores over 600: 88%; ACT scores over 24: 95% **Housing** Yes **Expenses** Tuition & Fees $42,342; Room & Board $9938 **Undergraduates** 51% women, 1% part-time, 1% 25 or older, 0.2% Native American, 3% Hispanic American, 3% African American, 4% Asian American/Pacific Islander **The most frequently chosen baccalaureate fields are** engineering, business/marketing, social sciences **Academic program** Advanced placement, self-designed majors, honors program, summer session, internships **Contact** Dean Robert Springall, Dean of Admissions, Bucknell University, 701 Moore Avenue, Lewisburg, PA 17837. *Phone:* 570-577-1101. *Fax:* 570-577-3538. *E-mail:* admissions@bucknell.edu. *Web site:* http://www.bucknell.edu/.
Visit Petersons.com and enter keyword Bucknell

See page 652 for the College Close-Up.

Cabrini College
Radnor, Pennsylvania

General Independent Roman Catholic, comprehensive, coed **Entrance** Moderately difficult **Setting** 112-acre suburban campus **Total enrollment** 3,514 **Student-faculty ratio** 14:1 **Application deadline** Rolling (freshmen), rolling (transfer) **Freshman admission** 75% were admitted. Average high school GPA 3 **Freshman test scores** SAT critical reading scores over 500: 37%; SAT math scores over 500: 35%; SAT critical reading scores over 600: 5%; SAT math scores over 600: 5% **Housing** Yes **Expenses** Tuition & Fees $31,030; Room & Board $11,400 **Undergraduates** 64% women, 7% part-time, 7% 25 or older, 0.1% Native American, 1% Hispanic American, 6% African American, 1% Asian American/Pacific Islander **The most frequently chosen baccalaureate fields are** business/marketing, communications/journalism, education **Academic program** Advanced placement, self-designed majors, honors program, summer session, adult/continuing education programs, internships **Contact** Mr. Stephen Colfer, Senior Associate Director of Admissions, Cabrini College, 610 King of Prussia Road, Radnor, PA 19087-3698. *Phone:* 610-902-8557 or toll-free 800-848-1003. *Fax:* 610-902-8508. *E-mail:* admit@cabrini.edu. *Web site:* http://www.cabrini.edu/.
Visit Petersons.com and enter keyword Cabrini

See page 658 for the College Close-Up.

California University of Pennsylvania
California, Pennsylvania

Contact Mr. William Edmonds, Dean of Enrollment Management and Academic Services, California University of Pennsylvania, 250 University Avenue, California, PA 15419. *Phone:* 724-938-4404. *Fax:* 724-938-4564. *E-mail:* inquiry@cup.edu. *Web site:* http://www.cup.edu/.
Visit Petersons.com and enter keywords California University

See page 666 for the College Close-Up.

Carlow University
Pittsburgh, Pennsylvania

General Independent Roman Catholic, comprehensive, coed, primarily women **Entrance** Moderately difficult **Setting** 14-acre urban campus **Total enrollment** 2,533 **Student-faculty ratio** 10:1 **Application deadline** Rolling (freshmen), rolling (transfer) **Freshman admission** 70% were admitted. Average high school GPA 3.3 **Freshman test scores** SAT critical reading scores over 500: 41.5%; SAT math scores over 500: 34.6%; ACT scores over 18: 81.2%; SAT critical reading scores over 600: 9.4%; SAT math scores over 600: 2.9%; ACT scores over 24: 21.7% **Housing** Yes **Expenses** Tuition & Fees $21,720; Room & Board $8552 **Undergraduates** 89% women, 39% part-time, 34% 25 or older, 1% Native American, 1% Hispanic American, 17% African American, 1% Asian American/Pacific Islander **The most frequently chosen baccalaureate fields are** business/marketing, education, health professions and related sciences **Academic program** Advanced placement, accelerated degree program, self-designed majors, honors program, summer session, adult/continuing education programs, internships **Contact** Ms. Susan Winstel, Director of Admissions, Carlow University, 3333 Fifth Avenue, Pittsburgh, PA 15213. *Phone:* 412-578-6059 or toll-free 800-333-CARLOW. *Fax:* 412-578-6668. *E-mail:* admissions@carlow.edu. *Web site:* http://www.carlow.edu/.
Visit Petersons.com and enter keyword Carlow

See page 680 for the College Close-Up.

Carnegie Mellon University
Pittsburgh, Pennsylvania

General Independent, university, coed **Entrance** Most difficult **Setting** 144-acre urban campus **Total enrollment** 11,443 **Student-faculty ratio** 12:1 **Application deadline** 1/1 (freshmen), 3/1 (transfer) **Freshman admission** 36% were admitted. Average high school GPA 3.62 **Freshman test scores** SAT critical reading scores over 500: 99%; SAT math scores over 500: 99%; ACT scores over 18: 100%; SAT critical reading scores over 600: 85%; SAT math scores over 600: 94%; ACT scores over 24: 98% **Housing** Yes **Expenses** Tuition & Fees $40,728; Room & Board $10,840 **Undergraduates** 42% women, 3% part-time, 1% 25 or older, 1% Native American, 5% Hispanic American, 5% African American, 24% Asian American/Pacific Islander **The most frequently chosen baccalaureate fields are** business/marketing, computer and information sciences, engineering **Academic program** Advanced placement, self-designed majors, summer session, internships **Contact** Mr. Michael Steidel, Director of Admissions, Carnegie Mellon University, 5000 Forbes Avenue, Pittsburgh, PA 15213. *Phone:* 412-268-2082. *Fax:* 412-268-7838. *E-mail:* undergraduate-admissions@andrew.cmu.edu. *Web site:* http://www.cmu.edu/.
Visit Petersons.com and enter keyword Carnegie

See page 682 for the College Close-Up.

Big thinking for a big world.

chatham UNIVERSITY

CHATHAM COLLEGE FOR WOMEN COLLEGE FOR GRADUATE STUDIES COLLEGE FOR CONTINUING & PROFESSIONAL STUDIES

The world is yours – to protect, improve, explore, and enjoy. And every student at Chatham knows it. We deliver a unique learning experience that allows you to define what you want out of your education – whether you're an undergraduate, graduate, or continuing education student. With small class sizes, a dedicated faculty, distinctive programs, and unusual opportunities, Chatham encourages you to get involved, get ready, and get what you want out of life. **Think of the possibilities.**

Woodland Road . . . Pittsburgh, PA 15232

800-837-1290 . . . admissions@chatham.edu

chatham.edu

Cedar Crest College
Allentown, Pennsylvania

General Independent, comprehensive, women only, affiliated with United Church of Christ **Entrance** Moderately difficult **Setting** 84-acre suburban campus **Total enrollment** 1,887 **Student-faculty ratio** 11:1 **Application deadline** Rolling (freshmen), rolling (transfer) **Freshman admission** 63% were admitted. Average high school GPA 3.18 **Freshman test scores** SAT math scores over 500: 63%; ACT scores over 18: 100%; SAT math scores over 600: 13%; ACT scores over 24: 53% **Housing** Yes **Expenses** Tuition & Fees $28,135; Room & Board $9321 **Undergraduates** 43% part-time, 42% 25 or older, 0.2% Native American, 7% Hispanic American, 7% African American, 3% Asian American/Pacific Islander **The most frequently chosen baccalaureate fields are** biological/life sciences, business/marketing, health professions and related sciences **Academic program** Advanced placement, self-designed majors, honors program, summer session, internships **Contact** Andrea Stewart, Associate Director of Admissions, Cedar Crest College, 100 College Drive, Allentown, PA 18104. *Phone:* 610-606-4666 or toll-free 800-360-1222. *E-mail:* astewart@cedarcrest.edu. *Web site:* http://www.cedarcrest.edu/. **Visit Petersons.com and enter keywords Cedar Crest**

See page 694 for the College Close-Up.

Central Pennsylvania College
Summerdale, Pennsylvania

General Proprietary, 4-year, coed **Entrance** Minimally difficult **Setting** 35-acre small-town campus **Total enrollment** 1,216 **Student-faculty ratio** 15:1 **Application deadline** Rolling (freshmen), rolling (transfer) **Freshman admission** 51% were admitted **Housing** Yes **Expenses** Tuition & Fees $13,845; Room & Board $6285 **Undergraduates** 64% women, 45% part-time, 44% 25 or older, 1% Native American, 6% Hispanic American, 23% African American, 2% Asian American/Pacific Islander **The most frequently chosen baccalaureate fields are** business/marketing, computer and information sciences, security and protective services **Academic program** Advanced placement, honors program, summer session, adult/continuing education programs, internships **Contact** Ms. Stacy Scott, Director of Admissions, Central Pennsylvania College, College Hill and Valley Roads, Mechanicsburg, PA 17093. *Phone:* 717-728-2531 or toll-free 800-759-2727 Ext. 2201. *Fax:* 717-728-2505. *E-mail:* stacyscott@centralpenn.edu. *Web site:* http://www.centralpenn.edu/.

Chatham University
Pittsburgh, Pennsylvania

General Independent, university, undergraduate: women only; graduate: coed **Entrance** Moderately difficult **Setting** 32-acre urban campus **Total enrollment** 2,219 **Student-faculty ratio** 10:1 **Application deadline** 8/1 (freshmen), rolling (transfer) **Freshman admission** 68% were admitted. Average high school GPA 3.35 **Freshman test scores** SAT critical reading scores over 500: 69.4%; SAT math scores over 500: 58.1%; ACT scores over 18: 83.3%; SAT critical reading scores over 600: 28.6%; SAT math scores over 600: 19.3%; ACT scores over 24: 58.3% **Housing** Yes **Undergraduates** 37% part-time, 11% 25 or older **The most frequently chosen baccalaureate fields are** biological/life sciences, health professions and related sciences, psychology **Academic program** English as a second language, advanced placement, accelerated degree program, self-designed majors, honors program, summer session, adult/continuing education programs, internships **Contact** Ms. Lisa D. Meyers, Director of Admissions, Chatham University, Woodland Road, Pittsburgh, PA 15232. *Phone:* 412-365-1672 or toll-free 800-837-1290. *Fax:* 412-365-1609. *E-mail:* lmeyers@chatham.edu. *Web site:* http://www.chatham.edu/. **Visit Petersons.com and enter keyword Chatham**

See page 700 for the College Close-Up.

Chestnut Hill College
Philadelphia, Pennsylvania

General Independent Roman Catholic, comprehensive, coed **Entrance** Moderately difficult **Setting** 75-acre suburban campus **Total enrollment** 2,085 **Student-faculty ratio** 10:1 **Application deadline** Rolling (freshmen), rolling (transfer) **Freshman admission** 72% were admitted. Average high school GPA 3.02 **Freshman test scores** SAT critical reading scores over 500: 50.5%; SAT math scores over 500: 44%; ACT scores over 18: 100%; SAT critical reading scores over 600: 10%; SAT math scores over 600: 11%; ACT scores over 24: 14% **Housing** Yes **Expenses** Tuition & Fees $27,100; Room & Board $8800 **Undergraduates** 70% women, 23% part-time, 5% 25 or older, 0.4% Native American, 5% Hispanic American, 37% African American, 2% Asian American/Pacific Islander **The most frequently chosen baccalaureate fields are** business/marketing, education, public administration and social services **Academic program** English as a second language, advanced placement, self-designed majors, honors program, summer session, adult/continuing education programs, internships **Contact** Director of Admissions, Chestnut Hill College, 9601 Germantown Avenue, Philadelphia, PA 19118-2693. *Phone:* 215-248-7001 or toll-free 800-248-0052. *Fax:* 215-248-7082. *Web site:* http://www.chc.edu/.

Visit Petersons.com and enter keyword Chestnut

See page 702 for the College Close-Up.

Cheyney University of Pennsylvania
Cheyney, Pennsylvania

General State-supported, comprehensive, coed **Entrance** Minimally difficult **Setting** 275-acre suburban campus **Total enrollment** 1,488 **Student-faculty ratio** 15:1 **Application deadline** 3/31 (freshmen) **Freshman admission** 50% were admitted. Average high school GPA 2.4 **Freshman test scores** SAT critical reading scores over 500: 7%; SAT math scores over 500: 7%; ACT scores over 18: 42%; SAT critical reading scores over 600: 1%; SAT math scores over 600: 1% **Housing** Yes **Expenses** Tuition & Fees: state resident $7360, nonresident $15,692; Room & Board $7746 **Undergraduates** 54% women, 10% part-time, 12% 25 or older, 0.2% Native American, 1% Hispanic American, 92% African American, 0.1% Asian American/Pacific Islander **The most frequently chosen baccalaureate fields are** business/marketing, psychology, social sciences **Academic program** Honors program, summer session, adult/continuing education programs, internships **Contact** Ms. Angela Brown, Director of Admissions, Cheyney University of Pennsylvania, 1837 University Circle, PO Box 200, Cheyney, PA 19319. *Phone:* 610-399-2275 or toll-free 800-CHEYNEY. *Fax:* 610-399-2099. *E-mail:* abrown@cheyney.edu. *Web site:* http://www.cheyney.edu/.

Clarion University of Pennsylvania
Clarion, Pennsylvania

General State-supported, comprehensive, coed **Entrance** Minimally difficult **Setting** 100-acre rural campus **Total enrollment** 7,346 **Student-faculty ratio** 19:1 **Application deadline** Rolling (freshmen), rolling (transfer) **Freshman admission** 68% were admitted. Average high school GPA 3.2 **Freshman test scores** SAT critical reading scores over 500: 34.3%; SAT math scores over 500: 38.3%; SAT critical reading scores over 600: 7.4%; SAT math scores over 600: 8.5% **Housing** Yes **Expenses** Tuition & Fees: state resident $7381, nonresident $12,935; Room & Board $6884 **Undergraduates** 61% women, 16% part-time, 15% 25 or older, 0.3% Native American, 1% Hispanic American, 6% African American, 1% Asian American/Pacific Islander **The most frequently chosen baccalaureate fields are** business/marketing, education, health professions and related sciences **Academic program** Advanced placement, accelerated degree program, honors program, summer session, adult/continuing education programs, internships **Contact** Mr. William Bailey, Dean of Enrollment Management, Clarion University of Pennsylvania, 890 Wood Street, Clarion, PA 16214. *Phone:* 814-393-2306 or toll-free 800-672-7171. *Fax:* 814-393-2030. *E-mail:* wbailey@clarion.edu. *Web site:* http://www.clarion.edu/.

Curtis Institute of Music
Philadelphia, Pennsylvania

General Independent, comprehensive, coed **Entrance** Most difficult **Setting** urban campus **Total enrollment** 164 **Application deadline** 12/11 (freshmen), 12/11 (transfer) **Housing** Yes **Expenses** Tuition & Fees $2290 **Undergraduates** 1% 25 or older **Academic program** English as a second language, advanced placement, accelerated degree program **Contact** Mr. Christopher Hodges, Admissions Officer, Curtis Institute of Music, 1726 Locust Street, Philadelphia, PA 19103-6107. *Phone:* 215-893-5262. *E-mail:* chris.hodges@curtis.edu. *Web site:* http://www.curtis.edu/.

Delaware Valley College
Doylestown, Pennsylvania

General Independent, comprehensive, coed **Entrance** Moderately difficult **Setting** 600-acre suburban campus **Total enrollment** 2,253 **Student-faculty ratio** 15:1 **Application deadline** 5/1 (freshmen) **Freshman admission** 72% were admitted. Average high school GPA 3.47 **Freshman test scores** SAT critical reading scores over 500: 51.84%; SAT math scores over 500: 54.11%; ACT scores over 18: 97.92%; SAT critical reading scores over 600: 11.61%; SAT math scores over 600: 13.88%; ACT scores over 24: 43.75% **Housing** Yes **Expenses** Tuition & Fees $27,742; Room & Board $9836 **Undergraduates** 57% women, 17% part-time, 11% 25 or older, 0.2% Native American, 2% Hispanic American, 4% African American, 1% Asian American/Pacific Islander **The most frequently chosen baccalaureate fields are** agriculture, biological/life sciences, business/marketing **Academic program** Advanced placement, accelerated degree program, honors program, summer session, adult/continuing education programs, internships **Contact** Mr. Stephen Zenko, Director of Admissions, Delaware Valley College, 700 East Butler Avenue, Doylestown, PA 18901-2697. *Phone:* 215-489-2211 or toll-free 800-2DELVAL. *Fax:* 215-230-2968. *E-mail:* admitme@devalcol.edu. *Web site:* http://www.delval.edu/.

Visit Petersons.com and enter keyword Delaware

See page 750 for the College Close-Up.

DeSales University
Center Valley, Pennsylvania

General Independent Roman Catholic, comprehensive, coed **Entrance** Moderately difficult **Setting** 580-acre suburban campus **Total enrollment** 3,150 **Student-faculty ratio** 12:1 **Application deadline** 8/1 (freshmen), 8/1 (transfer) **Freshman admission** 73% were admitted **Freshman test scores** SAT critical reading scores over 500: 70%; SAT math scores over 500: 70%; ACT scores over 18: 94%; SAT critical reading scores over 600: 26%; SAT math scores over 600: 27%; ACT scores over 24: 25% **Housing** Yes **Expenses** Tuition & Fees $27,200; Room & Board $9750 **Undergraduates** 59% women, 26% part-time, 11% 25 or older **The most frequently chosen baccalaureate fields are** business/marketing, health professions and related sciences, visual and performing arts **Academic program** Advanced placement, accelerated degree program, honors program, summer session, internships **Contact** Mr. Derrick Wetzell, Director of Admissions, DeSales University, 2755 Station Avenue, Center Valley, PA 18034-9568. *Phone:* 610-282-1100 Ext. 1711 or toll-free 877-4DESALES. *Fax:* 610-282-0131. *E-mail:* derrick.wetzell@desales.edu. *Web site:* http://www.desales.edu.

Visit Petersons.com and enter keyword DeSales

See page 756 for the College Close-Up.

DeVry University
Fort Washington, Pennsylvania

General Proprietary, comprehensive, coed **Entrance** Minimally difficult **Total enrollment** 1,049 **Student-faculty ratio** 10:1 **Application deadline** Rolling (freshmen), rolling (transfer) **Housing** No **Expenses** Tuition & Fees $14,720 **Undergraduates** 32% women, 51% part-time,

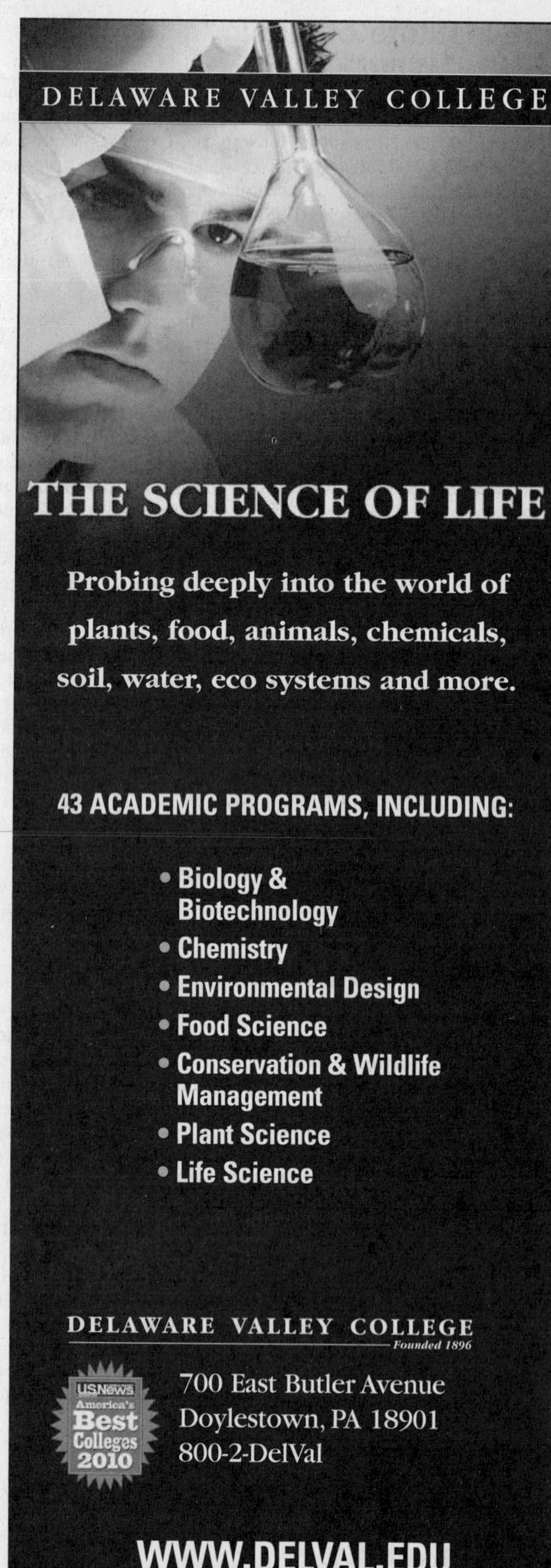

51% 25 or older, 1% Native American, 8% Hispanic American, 33% African American, 4% Asian American/Pacific Islander **The most frequently chosen baccalaureate fields are** business/marketing, computer and information sciences, engineering technologies **Academic program** Advanced placement, accelerated degree program, summer session, adult/continuing education programs **Contact** Admissions Office, DeVry University, 1140 Virginia Drive, Fort Washington, PA 19034. *Web site:* http://www.devry.edu/.

DeVry University
King of Prussia, Pennsylvania

Contact DeVry University, 150 Allendale Road, Buillding 3, Suite 3201, King of Prussia, PA 19406-2926. *Web site:* http://www.devry.edu/.

DeVry University
Philadelphia, Pennsylvania

Contact DeVry University, Philadelphia Downtown Center, 1800 JFK Boulevard, Suite 104, Philadelphia, PA 19103-7421. *Web site:* http://www.devry.edu/.

DeVry University
Pittsburgh, Pennsylvania

Contact DeVry University, FreeMarkets Center, 210 Sixth Avenue, Suite 200, Pittsburgh, PA 15222-2606. *Phone:* toll-free 866-77DEVRY. *Web site:* http://www.devry.edu/.

Dickinson College
Carlisle, Pennsylvania

General Independent, 4-year, coed **Entrance** Very difficult **Setting** 120-acre suburban campus **Total enrollment** 2,376 **Student-faculty ratio** 10:1 **Application deadline** 2/1 (freshmen), 4/1 (transfer) **Freshman admission** 49% were admitted **Freshman test scores** SAT critical reading scores over 500: 97.3%; SAT math scores over 500: 95.8%; ACT scores over 18: 100%; SAT critical reading scores over 600: 75.5%; SAT math scores over 600: 72.8%; ACT scores over 24: 94.6% **Housing** Yes **Expenses** Tuition & Fees $40,114; Room & Board $10,080 **Undergraduates** 56% women, 2% part-time, 1% 25 or older, 0.3% Native American, 5% Hispanic American, 4% African American, 4% Asian American/Pacific Islander **The most frequently chosen baccalaureate fields are** business/marketing, foreign languages and literature, social sciences **Academic program** English as a second language, advanced placement, accelerated degree program, self-designed majors, summer session, adult/continuing education programs, internships **Contact** Stephanie Balmer, Vice President for Enrollment and Communications/Dean of Admissions, Dickinson College, PO Box 1773, Admission's Office, Carlisle, PA 17013-2896. *Phone:* 717-245-1231 or toll-free 800-644-1773. *Fax:* 717-245-1442. *E-mail:* admit@dickinson.edu. *Web site:* http://www.dickinson.edu/.

Drexel University
Philadelphia, Pennsylvania

General Independent, university, coed **Entrance** Moderately difficult **Setting** 96-acre urban campus **Total enrollment** 22,493 **Student-faculty ratio** 9:1 **Application deadline** 3/1 (freshmen), 8/15 (transfer) **Freshman admission** 55% were admitted. Average high school GPA 3.5 **Freshman test scores** SAT critical reading scores over 500: 91%; SAT math scores over 500: 97%; SAT critical reading scores over 600: 44%; SAT math scores over 600: 66% **Housing** Yes **Expenses** Tuition & Fees $33,005; Room & Board $13,125 **Undergraduates** 45% women, 20% part-time, 20% 25 or older, 0.4% Native American, 3% Hispanic American, 9% African American, 12% Asian American/Pacific Islander **The most frequently chosen baccalaureate fields are** business/marketing, engineering, health professions and related sciences **Aca-**

demic program English as a second language, advanced placement, accelerated degree program, honors program, summer session, adult/continuing education programs, internships **Contact** Ms. Margaret Sparzani, Director of Freshman Admissions, Drexel University, 3141 Chestnut Street, Philadelphia, PA 19104-2875. *Phone:* 215-895-2400 or toll-free 800-2-DREXEL. *Fax:* 215-895-5939. *E-mail:* enroll@drexel.edu. *Web site:* http://www.drexel.edu/.

Visit Petersons.com and enter keyword Drexel

See page 760 for the College Close-Up.

Duquesne University
Pittsburgh, Pennsylvania

General Independent Roman Catholic, university, coed **Entrance** Moderately difficult **Setting** 49-acre urban campus **Total enrollment** 10,270 **Student-faculty ratio** 14:1 **Application deadline** 7/1 (freshmen), 7/1 (transfer) **Freshman admission** 76% were admitted. Average high school GPA 3.57 **Freshman test scores** SAT critical reading scores over 500: 84%; SAT math scores over 500: 86%; ACT scores over 18: 100%; SAT critical reading scores over 600: 28%; SAT math scores over 600: 36%; ACT scores over 24: 71% **Housing** Yes **Expenses** Tuition & Fees $26,468; Room & Board $9200 **Undergraduates** 57% women, 4% part-time, 4% 25 or older, 0.2% Native American, 2% Hispanic American, 4% African American, 2% Asian American/Pacific Islander **The most frequently chosen baccalaureate fields are** business/marketing, education, health professions and related sciences **Academic program** English as a second language, advanced placement, accelerated degree program, self-designed majors, honors program, summer session, adult/continuing education programs, internships **Contact** Mr. Paul-James Cukanna, Associate Provost/Associate Vice President for Enrollment Management and Director of Admissions, Duquesne University, 1st Floor Administration Building, 600 Forbes Avenue, Pittsburgh, PA 15282-0201. *Phone:* 412-396-5002 or toll-free 800-456-0590. *Fax:* 412-396-6223. *E-mail:* admissions@duq.edu. *Web site:* http://www.duq.edu/.

Eastern University
St. Davids, Pennsylvania

Contact Mr. Michael Dziedziak, Director of Undergraduate Admissions, Eastern University, 1300 Eagle Road, St. Davids, PA 19087-3696. *Phone:* 610-341-5967 or toll-free 800-452-0996. *Fax:* 610-341-1723. *E-mail:* ugadm@eastern.edu. *Web site:* http://www.eastern.edu/.

See page 770 for the College Close-Up.

East Stroudsburg University of Pennsylvania
East Stroudsburg, Pennsylvania

General State-supported, comprehensive, coed **Entrance** Moderately difficult **Setting** 213-acre small-town campus **Total enrollment** 7,576 **Student-faculty ratio** 18:1 **Application deadline** 4/1 (freshmen), 5/1 (transfer) **Freshman admission** 69% were admitted **Freshman test scores** SAT critical reading scores over 500: 39.01%; SAT math scores over 500: 47.7%; SAT critical reading scores over 600: 4.71%; SAT math scores over 600: 9.2% **Housing** Yes **Expenses** Tuition & Fees: state resident $7394, nonresident $15,726; Room & Board $6418 **Undergraduates** 54% women, 9% part-time, 9% 25 or older, 0.3% Native American, 6% Hispanic American, 6% African American, 2% Asian American/Pacific Islander **The most frequently chosen baccalaureate fields are** business/marketing, education, social sciences **Academic program** Advanced placement, accelerated degree program, self-designed majors, honors program, summer session, adult/continuing education programs, internships **Contact** Mr. Jeff Jones, Director of Admissions, East Stroudsburg University of Pennsylvania, 200 Prospect Street, East Stroudsburg, PA 18301. *Phone:* 570-422-3542 or toll-free 877-230-5547. *Fax:* 570-422-3933. *E-mail:* undergrads@po-box.esu.edu. *Web site:* http://www4.esu.edu/.

Edinboro University of Pennsylvania
Edinboro, Pennsylvania

General State-supported, comprehensive, coed **Entrance** Moderately difficult **Setting** 585-acre small-town campus **Total enrollment** 8,286 **Application deadline** Rolling (transfer) **Freshman admission** 73% were admitted. Average high school GPA 3.15 **Freshman test scores** SAT critical reading scores over 500: 36.3%; SAT math scores over 500: 35.3%; ACT scores over 18: 69%; SAT critical reading scores over 600: 7.1%; SAT math scores over 600: 7.3%; ACT scores over 24: 15% **Housing** Yes **Expenses** Tuition & Fees: state resident $7316, nonresident $10,094; Room & Board $7430 **Undergraduates** 56% women, 11% part-time, 19% 25 or older, 0.3% Native American, 2% Hispanic American, 9% African American, 1% Asian American/Pacific Islander **The most frequently chosen baccalaureate fields are** education, health professions and related sciences, visual and performing arts **Academic program** Advanced placement, self-designed majors, honors program, summer session, adult/continuing education programs, internships **Contact** Mr. J. P. Cooney, Director of Undergraduate Admissions, Edinboro University of Pennsylvania, Academy Hall, Edinboro, PA 16444. *Phone:* 814-732-2761 or toll-free 888-846-2676 (in-state); 800-626-2203 (out-of-state). *Fax:* 814-732-2420. *E-mail:* eup_admissions@edinboro.edu. *Web site:* http://www.edinboro.edu/.

See page 772 for the College Close-Up.

Elizabethtown College
Elizabethtown, Pennsylvania

General Independent, comprehensive, coed, affiliated with Church of the Brethren **Entrance** Moderately difficult **Setting** 201-acre small-town campus **Total enrollment** 2,367 **Student-faculty ratio** 12:1 **Application deadline** 3/1 (freshmen), 8/1 (transfer) **Freshman admission** 75% were admitted **Freshman test scores** SAT critical reading scores over 500: 78%; SAT math scores over 500: 80%; ACT scores over 18: 92%; SAT critical reading scores over 600: 26%; SAT math scores over 600: 38%; ACT scores over 24: 50% **Housing** Yes **Expenses** Tuition & Fees $33,250; Room & Board $8500 **Undergraduates** 64% women, 19% part-time, 17% 25 or older, 0.4% Native American, 2% Hispanic American, 3% African American, 2% Asian American/Pacific Islander **The most frequently chosen baccalaureate fields are** business/marketing, communications/journalism, education **Academic program** English as a second language, advanced placement, honors program, summer session, adult/continuing education programs, internships **Contact** Ms. Debra Murray, Director of Admissions, Elizabethtown College, One Alpha Drive, Elizabethtown, PA 17022. *Phone:* 717-361-1400. *Fax:* 717-361-1365. *E-mail:* admissions@etown.edu. *Web site:* http://www.etown.edu/.

Visit Petersons.com and enter keyword Elizabethtown

See page 774 for the College Close-Up.

Franklin & Marshall College
Lancaster, Pennsylvania

General Independent, 4-year, coed **Entrance** Very difficult **Setting** 180-acre suburban campus **Total enrollment** 2,179 **Student-faculty ratio** 10:1 **Application deadline** 2/1 (freshmen), 5/15 (transfer) **Freshman admission** 48% were admitted **Freshman test scores** SAT critical reading scores over 500: 96%; SAT math scores over 500: 99%; ACT scores over 18: 100%; SAT critical reading scores over 600: 76%; SAT math scores over 600: 89%; ACT scores over 24: 98.6% **Housing** Yes **Expenses** Tuition & Fees $39,990; Room & Board $10,430 **Undergraduates** 52% women, 2% part-time, 1% 25 or older, 1% Native American, 5% Hispanic American, 4% African American, 4% Asian American/Pacific Islander **The most frequently chosen baccalaureate fields are** business/marketing, interdisciplinary studies, social sciences **Academic program** Advanced placement, accelerated degree program, self-designed majors, summer session, internships **Contact** Sara Shapiro

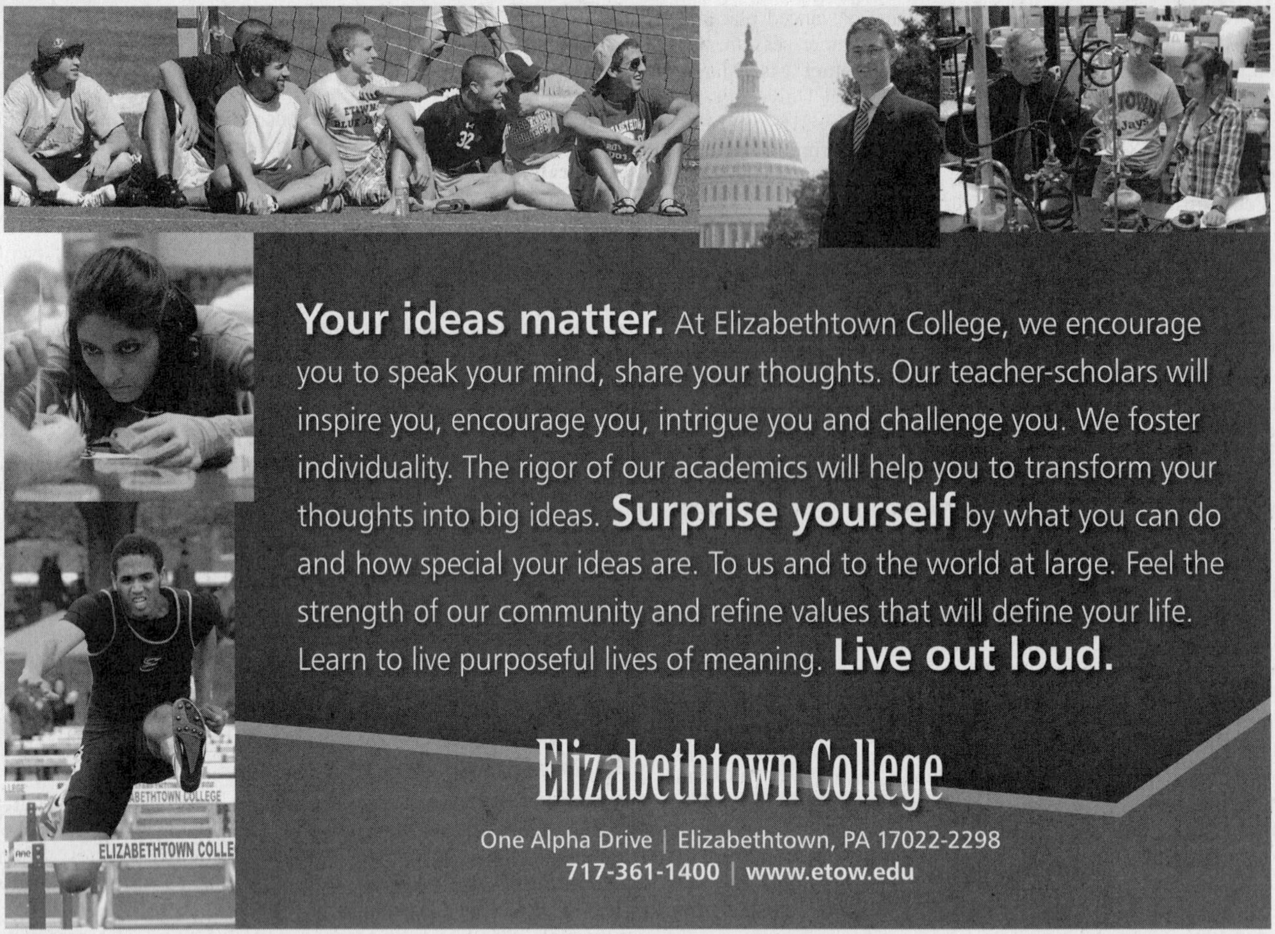

Your ideas matter. At Elizabethtown College, we encourage you to speak your mind, share your thoughts. Our teacher-scholars will inspire you, encourage you, intrigue you and challenge you. We foster individuality. The rigor of our academics will help you to transform your thoughts into big ideas. **Surprise yourself** by what you can do and how special your ideas are. To us and to the world at large. Feel the strength of our community and refine values that will define your life. Learn to live purposeful lives of meaning. **Live out loud.**

Elizabethtown College

One Alpha Drive | Elizabethtown, PA 17022-2298

717-361-1400 | www.etow.edu

Franklin & Marshall College (continued)

Harberson, Vice President for Enrollment Management, Franklin & Marshall College, PO Box 3003, Lancaster, PA 17604-3003. *Phone:* 717-291-3953. *Fax:* 717-291-4389. *E-mail:* sara.harbersob@fandm.edu. *Web site:* http://www.fandm.edu/.

Gannon University
Erie, Pennsylvania

General Independent Roman Catholic, university, coed **Entrance** Moderately difficult **Setting** 13-acre urban campus **Total enrollment** 4,238 **Student-faculty ratio** 13:1 **Application deadline** Rolling (freshmen), rolling (transfer) **Freshman admission** 84% were admitted. Average high school GPA 3.42 **Freshman test scores** SAT critical reading scores over 500: 52.4%; SAT math scores over 500: 59.8%; ACT scores over 18: 84.5%; SAT critical reading scores over 600: 12.7%; SAT math scores over 600: 22.7%; ACT scores over 24: 42.5% **Housing** Yes **Expenses** Tuition & Fees $23,574; Room & Board $9330 **Undergraduates** 59% women, 18% part-time, 10% 25 or older, 0.3% Native American, 2% Hispanic American, 6% African American, 2% Asian American/Pacific Islander **The most frequently chosen baccalaureate fields are** business/marketing, biological/life sciences, health professions and related sciences **Academic program** English as a second language, advanced placement, accelerated degree program, honors program, summer session, adult/continuing education programs, internships **Contact** Office of Admissions, Gannon University, 109 University Square, Erie, PA 16541. *Phone:* 814-871-7240 or toll-free 800-GANNONU. *Fax:* 814-871-5803. *E-mail:* admissions@gannon.edu. *Web site:* http://www.gannon.edu/.

Visit Petersons.com and enter keyword Gannon

See page 816 for the College Close-Up.

Geneva College
Beaver Falls, Pennsylvania

General Independent, comprehensive, coed, affiliated with Reformed Presbyterian Church of North America **Entrance** Moderately difficult **Setting** 55-acre small-town campus **Total enrollment** 1,580 **Student-faculty ratio** 13:1 **Application deadline** Rolling (freshmen), rolling (transfer) **Freshman admission** 80% were admitted. Average high school GPA 3.43 **Freshman test scores** SAT critical reading scores over 500: 66%; SAT math scores over 500: 63%; ACT scores over 18: 93%; SAT critical reading scores over 600: 27%; SAT math scores over 600: 26%; ACT scores over 24: 39% **Housing** Yes **Expenses** Tuition & Fees $22,236; Room & Board $8000 **Undergraduates** 49% women, 2% part-time, 3% 25 or older, 0.1% Native American, 1% Hispanic American, 4% African American, 1% Asian American/Pacific Islander **The most frequently chosen baccalaureate fields are** business/marketing, education, theology and religious vocations **Academic program** English as a second language, advanced placement, accelerated degree program, self-designed majors, honors program, summer session, adult/continuing education programs, internships **Contact** Mr. David Layton, Dean for Undergraduate Enrollment, Geneva College, 3200 College Avenue, Beaver Falls, PA 15010-3599. *Phone:* 724-847-6500 or toll-free 800-847-8255. *Fax:* 724-847-6776. *E-mail:* admissions@geneva.edu. *Web site:* http://www.geneva.edu/.

Gettysburg College
Gettysburg, Pennsylvania

General Independent, 4-year, coed, affiliated with Evangelical Lutheran Church in America **Entrance** Most difficult **Setting** 200-acre small-town campus **Total enrollment** 2,516 **Student-faculty ratio** 11:1 **Application deadline** 2/1 (freshmen), rolling (transfer) **Freshman admission** 40% were admitted **Freshman test scores** SAT critical reading scores over 500: 100%; SAT math scores over 500: 100%; SAT critical reading

GANNON UNIVERSITY

diverse ideas in a global environment

Gannon University students come from all over the country and the world to study at our vibrant downtown campus near the Lake Erie bayfront in Erie, Pennsylvania. Representing 24 countries and 28 states, students benefit from exposure to an array of ethnic, religious and cultural backgrounds. That diversity extends into the classroom, where nearly 100 exceptional academic programs are taught by dynamic faculty in a personal, interactive setting.

Whether you come from Pittsburgh, Punjab or somewhere in between, you are welcome at Gannon.

For more information or to schedule a visit, call **800-GANNON-U** or visit us online at **www.gannon.edu** today!

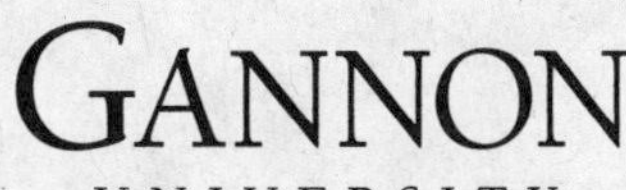

Believe in the possibilities.

800-GANNON-U | WWW.GANNON.EDU

scores over 600: 84%; SAT math scores over 600: 80% **Housing** Yes **Expenses** Tuition & Fees $37,600; Room & Board $9100 **Undergraduates** 51% women, 1% part-time, 1% 25 or older, 0.1% Native American, 3% Hispanic American, 5% African American, 1% Asian American/Pacific Islander **The most frequently chosen baccalaureate fields are** biological/life sciences, business/marketing, social sciences **Academic program** Advanced placement, self-designed majors, adult/continuing education programs, internships **Contact** Ms. Gail Sweezey, Director of Admissions, Gettysburg College, 300 North Washington Street, Gettysburg, PA 17325. *Phone:* 717-337-6100 or toll-free 800-431-0803. *Fax:* 717-337-6145. *E-mail:* admiss@gettysburg.edu. *Web site:* http://www.gettysburg.edu/.

Gratz College
Melrose Park, Pennsylvania

Contact Ms. Ruthann Crosby, Director of Student Life, Gratz College, 7605 Old York Road, Melrose Park, PA 19027. *Phone:* 215-635-7300 or toll-free 800-475-4635 Ext. 140. *Fax:* 215-635-7399. *E-mail:* admissions@gratz.edu. *Web site:* http://www.gratzcollege.edu/.

Grove City College
Grove City, Pennsylvania

General Independent Presbyterian, 4-year, coed **Entrance** Most difficult **Setting** 150-acre small-town campus **Total enrollment** 2,530 **Student-faculty ratio** 16:1 **Application deadline** 2/1 (freshmen), 8/15 (transfer) **Freshman admission** 64% were admitted. Average high school GPA 3.8 **Freshman test scores** SAT critical reading scores over 500: 99%; SAT math scores over 500: 98%; ACT scores over 18: 100%; SAT critical reading scores over 600: 72%; SAT math scores over 600: 71%; ACT scores over 24: 89% **Housing** Yes **Expenses** Tuition & Fees $12,590; Room & Board $6824 **Undergraduates** 50% women, 1% part-time, 0.1% Native American, 2% Hispanic American, 1% African American, 2% Asian American/Pacific Islander **The most frequently chosen baccalaureate fields are** business/marketing, biological/life sciences, education **Academic program** Advanced placement, self-designed majors, internships **Contact** Mr. Jeffrey Mincey, Director of Admissions, Grove City College, 100 Campus Drive, Grove City, PA 16127-2104. *Phone:* 724-458-2100. *Fax:* 724-458-3395. *E-mail:* admissions@gcc.edu. *Web site:* http://www.gcc.edu/.

Visit Petersons.com and enter keywords Grove City

See page 836 for the College Close-Up.

Gwynedd-Mercy College
Gwynedd Valley, Pennsylvania

General Independent Roman Catholic, comprehensive, coed **Entrance** Moderately difficult **Setting** 170-acre suburban campus **Total enrollment** 2,636 **Student-faculty ratio** 13:1 **Application deadline** Rolling (freshmen), 8/20 (transfer) **Freshman admission** 67% were admitted **Freshman test scores** SAT critical reading scores over 500: 44%; SAT math scores over 500: 39%; SAT critical reading scores over 600: 7%; SAT math scores over 600: 8% **Housing** Yes **Expenses** Tuition & Fees $25,610; Room & Board $9760 **Undergraduates** 74% women, 32% part-time, 40% 25 or older, 0.3% Native American, 1% Hispanic American, 21% African American, 2% Asian American/Pacific Islander **The most frequently chosen baccalaureate fields are** business/marketing, education, health professions and related sciences **Academic program** English as a second language, advanced placement, accelerated degree program, honors program, summer session, adult/continuing education programs, internships **Contact** Ms. Michelle Diehl, Director of Admissions, Gwynedd-Mercy College, 1325 Sumneytown Pike, Gwynedd Valley, PA 19437-0901. *Phone:* 215-646-7300 or toll-free

COLLEGES AT-A-GLANCE

Gwynedd-Mercy College (continued)
800-DIAL-GMC. *Fax:* 215-641-5556. *E-mail:* admissions@gmc.edu. *Web site:* http://www.gmc.edu/.
Visit Petersons.com and enter keyword Gwynedd-Mercy

See page 840 for the College Close-Up.

Harrisburg University of Science and Technology
Harrisburg, Pennsylvania

General Independent, comprehensive, coed **Entrance** Minimally difficult **Setting** urban campus **Total enrollment** 244 **Student-faculty ratio** 5:1 **Application deadline** Rolling (freshmen) **Freshman admission** 55% were admitted. Average high school GPA 2.79 **Housing** No **Expenses** Tuition & Fees $19,500 **Undergraduates** 20% 25 or older, 12% Hispanic American, 30% African American, 5% Asian American/Pacific Islander **The most frequently chosen baccalaureate fields are** computer and information sciences, physical sciences **Academic program** Advanced placement, self-designed majors, summer session, adult/continuing education programs, internships **Contact** Mr. Timothy Dawson, Director of Admissions and Enrollment Systems, Harrisburg University of Science and Technology, 326 Market Street, Harrisburg, PA 17101. *Phone:* 717-901-5158 or toll-free 866-HBG-UNIV. *Fax:* 717-901-3158. *E-mail:* tdawson@harrisburgu.edu. *Web site:* http://www.HarrisburgU.edu/.

Haverford College
Haverford, Pennsylvania

General Independent, 4-year, coed **Entrance** Most difficult **Setting** 200-acre suburban campus **Total enrollment** 1,190 **Student-faculty ratio** 8:1 **Application deadline** 1/15 (freshmen), 3/31 (transfer) **Freshman admission** 25% were admitted **Freshman test scores** SAT critical reading scores over 500: 99%; SAT math scores over 500: 99%; SAT critical reading scores over 600: 93%; SAT math scores over 600: 88% **Housing** Yes **Expenses** Tuition & Fees $39,085; Room & Board $11,890 **Undergraduates** 55% women, 0.2% Native American, 8% Hispanic American, 8% African American, 9% Asian American/Pacific Islander **The most frequently chosen baccalaureate fields are** biological/life sciences, English, social sciences **Academic program** Advanced placement, self-designed majors, internships **Contact** Mr. Jess Lord, Dean of Admissions and Financial Aid, Haverford College, 370 Lancaster Avenue, Haverford, PA 19041-1392. *Phone:* 610-896-1350. *Fax:* 610-896-1338. *E-mail:* admitme@haverford.edu. *Web site:* http://www.haverford.edu/.
Visit Petersons.com and enter keyword Haverford

Holy Family University
Philadelphia, Pennsylvania

General Independent Roman Catholic, comprehensive, coed, primarily women **Entrance** Moderately difficult **Setting** 47-acre suburban campus **Total enrollment** 3,345 **Student-faculty ratio** 12:1 **Application deadline** Rolling (freshmen), rolling (transfer) **Freshman admission** 74% were admitted. Average high school GPA 3.05 **Freshman test scores** SAT critical reading scores over 500: 34.35%; SAT math scores over 500: 28.4%; SAT critical reading scores over 600: 4.6%; SAT math scores over 600: 3.8% **Housing** Yes **Expenses** Tuition & Fees $23,520; Room & Board $10,400 **Undergraduates** 72% women, 31% part-time, 27% 25 or older, 0.5% Native American, 5% Hispanic American, 6% African American, 5% Asian American/Pacific Islander **The most frequently chosen baccalaureate fields are** education, business/marketing, health professions and related sciences **Academic program** Advanced placement, accelerated degree program, honors program, summer session, adult/continuing education programs, internships **Contact** Ms. Lauren

Immaculata University

PO Box 642
Immaculata, PA 19345-0642

E-mail: admiss@immaculata.edu
Phone: 610-647-4400

See our profile page for more information about our school.

McDermott-Campbell, Director of Admissions, Holy Family University, 9801 Frankford Avenue, Philadelphia, PA 19114-2009. *Phone:* 215-637-3050 or toll-free 800-637-1191. *Fax:* 215-281-1022. *E-mail:* admissions@holyfamily.edu. *Web site:* http://www.holyfamily.edu/.

Immaculata University
Immaculata, Pennsylvania

General Independent Roman Catholic, comprehensive, coed, primarily women **Entrance** Moderately difficult **Setting** 400-acre suburban campus **Total enrollment** 4,302 **Student-faculty ratio** 11:1 **Application deadline** Rolling (freshmen), rolling (transfer) **Freshman admission** 80% were admitted. Average high school GPA 3.02 **Freshman test scores** SAT critical reading scores over 500: 37.18%; SAT math scores over 500: 33.7%; ACT scores over 18: 71%; SAT critical reading scores over 600: 4.28%; SAT math scores over 600: 7.4%; ACT scores over 24: 13% **Housing** Yes **Expenses** Tuition & Fees $27,870; Room & Board $11,460 **Undergraduates** 78% women, 65% part-time, 2% 25 or older, 1% Native American, 2% Hispanic American, 13% African American, 2% Asian American/Pacific Islander **The most frequently chosen baccalaureate fields are** business/marketing, health professions and related sciences, psychology **Academic program** Advanced placement, accelerated degree program, honors program, summer session, adult/continuing education programs, internships **Contact** Ms. Rebecca Bowlby, Director of Admissions, Immaculata University, PO Box 642, Immaculata, PA 19345-0702. *Phone:* 610-647-4400 Ext. 3046 or toll-free 877-428-6329. *Fax:* 610-640-0836. *E-mail:* admiss@immaculata.edu. *Web site:* http://www.immaculata.edu/.

Visit Petersons.com and enter keyword Immaculata

See page 866 for the College Close-Up.

Indiana University of Pennsylvania
Indiana, Pennsylvania

General State-supported, university, coed **Entrance** Moderately difficult **Setting** 374-acre small-town campus **Total enrollment** 14,638 **Student-faculty ratio** 18:1 **Application deadline** Rolling (freshmen), rolling (transfer) **Freshman admission** 60% were admitted **Freshman test scores** SAT critical reading scores over 500: 44.1%; SAT math scores over 500: 46.8%; SAT critical reading scores over 600: 7.6%; SAT math scores over 600: 8.4% **Housing** Yes **Expenses** Tuition & Fees: state resident $7209, nonresident $15,541; Room & Board $8558 **Undergraduates** 56% women, 8% part-time, 7% 25 or older, 0.2% Native American, 2% Hispanic American, 11% African American, 1% Asian American/Pacific Islander **The most frequently chosen baccalaureate fields are** business/marketing, health professions and related sciences, social sciences **Academic program** English as a second language, advanced placement, accelerated degree program, honors program, summer session, adult/continuing education programs, internships **Contact** Office of Admissions, Indiana University of Pennsylvania, 1011 South Drive, Sutton Hall 214, Indiana, PA 15705. *Phone:* 724-357-2230 or toll-free 800-442-6830. *Fax:* 724-357-6281. *E-mail:* admissions-inquiry@iup.edu. *Web site:* http://www.iup.edu/.

Visit Petersons.com and enter keywords Indiana University

See page 868 for the College Close-Up.

Juniata College
Huntingdon, Pennsylvania

General Independent, 4-year, coed, affiliated with Church of the Brethren **Entrance** Moderately difficult **Setting** 110-acre small-town campus **Total enrollment** 1,468 **Student-faculty ratio** 12:1 **Application deadline** 3/15 (freshmen), 6/15 (transfer) **Freshman admission** 72% were admitted. Average high school GPA 3.75 **Freshman test scores** SAT critical

Juniata College (continued)

reading scores over 500: 90.9%; SAT math scores over 500: 92.8%; SAT critical reading scores over 600: 47.2%; SAT math scores over 600: 52.9% **Housing** Yes **Expenses** Tuition & Fees $32,820; Room & Board $8980 **Undergraduates** 56% women, 5% part-time, 2% 25 or older, 0.1% Native American, 2% Hispanic American, 2% African American, 2% Asian American/Pacific Islander **The most frequently chosen baccalaureate fields are** biological/life sciences, business/marketing, psychology **Academic program** English as a second language, advanced placement, accelerated degree program, self-designed majors, honors program, summer session, internships **Contact** Terry Bollman-Dalansky, Director of Admissions, Juniata College, 1700 Moore Street, Huntingdon, PA 16652-2119. *Phone:* 814-641-3424 or toll-free 877-JUNIATA. *Fax:* 814-641-3100. *E-mail:* admissions@juniata.edu. *Web site:* http://www.juniata.edu/.

Visit Petersons.com and enter keyword Juniata

See page 884 for the College Close-Up.

Keystone College
La Plume, Pennsylvania

General Independent, 4-year, coed **Entrance** Minimally difficult **Setting** 270-acre rural campus **Total enrollment** 1,691 **Student-faculty ratio** 10:1 **Application deadline** 7/15 (freshmen), 8/1 (transfer) **Freshman admission** 95% were admitted. Average high school GPA 2.82 **Freshman test scores** SAT critical reading scores over 500: 20.5%; SAT math scores over 500: 21.5%; ACT scores over 18: 50%; SAT critical reading scores over 600: 2%; SAT math scores over 600: 4%; ACT scores over 24: 8% **Housing** Yes **Expenses** Tuition & Fees $19,120; Room & Board $9250 **Undergraduates** 60% women, 22% part-time, 26% 25 or older **The most frequently chosen baccalaureate fields are** business/marketing, education, security and protective services **Academic program** Advanced placement, honors program, summer session, adult/continuing education programs, internships **Contact** Jessica Lopez, Senior Administrative Assistant, Keystone College, One College Green, La Plume, PA 18440-1099. *Phone:* 570-945-8111 or toll-free 877-4COLLEGE Ext. 1. *Fax:* 570-945-7916. *E-mail:* admissions@keystone.edu. *Web site:* http://www.keystone.edu/.

Visit Petersons.com and enter keyword Keystone

See page 896 for the College Close-Up.

King's College
Wilkes-Barre, Pennsylvania

General Independent Roman Catholic, comprehensive, coed **Entrance** Moderately difficult **Setting** 48-acre urban campus **Total enrollment** 2,645 **Student-faculty ratio** 13:1 **Application deadline** Rolling (freshmen), rolling (transfer) **Freshman admission** 75% were admitted. Average high school GPA 3.3 **Freshman test scores** SAT critical reading scores over 500: 43%; SAT math scores over 500: 41%; SAT critical reading scores over 600: 3%; SAT math scores over 600: 4% **Housing** Yes **Expenses** Tuition & Fees $25,644; Room & Board $9838 **Undergraduates** 50% women, 14% part-time, 0.02% 25 or older, 0.3% Native American, 4% Hispanic American, 2% African American, 1% Asian American/Pacific Islander **The most frequently chosen baccalaureate fields are** business/marketing, education, health professions and related sciences **Academic program** English as a second language, advanced placement, accelerated degree program, self-designed majors, honors program, summer session, adult/continuing education programs, internships **Contact** Ms. Michelle Lawrence-Schmude, Director of Admissions, King's College, 133 North River Street, Wilkes-Barre, PA 18711-0801. *Phone:* 570-208-5858 or toll-free 888-KINGSPA. *Fax:* 570-208-5971. *E-mail:* admissions@kings.edu. *Web site:* http://www.kings.edu/.

Visit Petersons.com and enter keyword King's

See page 898 for the College Close-Up.

Graduate in 4 years or less. Guaranteed.
JUNIATA
COLLEGE
photo by: Sacha Potter '09
www.juniata.edu

Kutztown University of Pennsylvania
Kutztown, Pennsylvania

General State-supported, comprehensive, coed **Entrance** Moderately difficult **Setting** 326-acre rural campus **Total enrollment** 10,634 **Student-faculty ratio** 19:1 **Application deadline** Rolling (freshmen), rolling (transfer) **Freshman admission** 66% were admitted. Average high school GPA 3.03 **Freshman test scores** SAT critical reading scores over 500: 41%; SAT math scores over 500: 42.5%; ACT scores over 18: 72.1%; SAT critical reading scores over 600: 7.1%; SAT math scores over 600: 8.3%; ACT scores over 24: 12% **Housing** Yes **Expenses** Tuition & Fees: state resident $7397, nonresident $15,729; Room & Board $7698 **Undergraduates** 58% women, 9% part-time, 7% 25 or older, 0.3% Native American, 5% Hispanic American, 6% African American, 1% Asian American/Pacific Islander **The most frequently chosen baccalaureate fields are** business/marketing, education, visual and performing arts **Academic program** Advanced placement, accelerated degree program, self-designed majors, honors program, summer session, adult/continuing education programs, internships **Contact** Dr. William Stahler, Director of Admissions, Kutztown University of Pennsylvania, 15200 Kutztown Road, Kutztown, PA 19530-0730. *Phone:* 610-683-4060 or toll-free 877-628-1915. *Fax:* 610-683-1375. *E-mail:* admission@kutztown.edu. *Web site:* http://www.kutztown.edu/.
Visit Petersons.com and enter keyword Kutztown

See page 900 for the College Close-Up.

Lafayette College
Easton, Pennsylvania

General Independent, 4-year, coed, affiliated with Presbyterian Church (U.S.A.) **Entrance** Most difficult **Setting** 340-acre suburban campus **Total enrollment** 2,406 **Student-faculty ratio** 11:1 **Application deadline** 1/1 (freshmen), 6/1 (transfer) **Freshman admission** 42% were admitted. Average high school GPA 3.46 **Freshman test scores** SAT critical reading scores over 500: 96%; SAT math scores over 500: 99%; ACT scores over 18: 99.5%; SAT critical reading scores over 600: 63%; SAT math scores over 600: 79%; ACT scores over 24: 91.04% **Housing** Yes **Expenses** Tuition & Fees $37,815; Room & Board $11,799 **Undergraduates** 47% women, 2% part-time, 0.1% Native American, 5% Hispanic American, 5% African American, 4% Asian American/Pacific Islander **The most frequently chosen baccalaureate fields are** engineering, psychology, social sciences **Academic program** Advanced placement, accelerated degree program, self-designed majors, honors program, summer session, internships **Contact** Ms. Carol Rowlands, Director of Admissions, Lafayette College, Easton, PA 18042-1798. *Phone:* 610-330-5100. *Fax:* 610-330-5355. *E-mail:* admissions@lafayette.edu. *Web site:* http://www.lafayette.edu/.
Visit Petersons.com and enter keyword Lafayette

See page 902 for the College Close-Up.

Lancaster Bible College & Graduate School
Lancaster, Pennsylvania

Contact Mrs. Joanne M. Roper, Associate Vice President for Admissions, Lancaster Bible College & Graduate School, PO Box 83403, Lancaster, PA 17608. *Phone:* 717-560-8271 or toll-free 866-LBC4YOU. *Fax:* 717-560-8213. *E-mail:* admissions@lbc.edu. *Web site:* http://www.lbc.edu/.

La Roche College
Pittsburgh, Pennsylvania

General Independent, comprehensive, coed, affiliated with Roman Catholic Church **Entrance** Minimally difficult **Setting** 43-acre suburban campus **Total enrollment** 1,356 **Student-faculty ratio** 12:1 **Application deadline** Rolling (freshmen), rolling (transfer) **Freshman admission** 68% were admitted. Average high school GPA 3.08 **Freshman test scores** SAT critical reading scores over 500: 25%; SAT math scores over 500: 26%; ACT scores over 18: 70%; SAT critical reading scores over 600: 4%; SAT math scores over 600: 5%; ACT scores over 24: 15% **Housing** Yes **Expenses** Tuition & Fees $21,638; Room & Board $8756 **Undergraduates** 64% women, 20% part-time, 20% 25 or older, 0.3% Native American, 1% Hispanic American, 6% African American, 1% Asian American/Pacific Islander **The most frequently chosen baccalaureate fields are** architecture, business/marketing, psychology **Academic program** English as a second language, advanced placement, accelerated degree program, self-designed majors, honors program, summer session, adult/continuing education programs, internships **Contact** Mr. David McFarland, Director of Admissions, La Roche College, 9000 Babcock Boulevard, Pittsburgh, PA 15237. *Phone:* 412-536-1275 or toll-free 800-838-4LRC. *Fax:* 412-536-1048. *E-mail:* admissions@laroche.edu. *Web site:* http://www.laroche.edu/.

La Salle University
Philadelphia, Pennsylvania

General Independent Roman Catholic, comprehensive, coed **Entrance** Moderately difficult **Setting** 130-acre urban campus **Total enrollment** 6,470 **Student-faculty ratio** 13:1 **Application deadline** 8/15 (transfer) **Freshman admission** 66% were admitted. Average high school GPA 3.34 **Freshman test scores** SAT critical reading scores over 500: 50%; SAT math scores over 500: 53%; SAT critical reading scores over 600: 15%; SAT math scores over 600: 13% **Housing** Yes **Expenses** Tuition & Fees $33,700; Room & Board $11,230 **Undergraduates** 64% women, 25% part-time, 4% 25 or older, 0.2% Native American, 9% Hispanic American, 17% African American, 4% Asian American/Pacific Islander **The most frequently chosen baccalaureate fields are** business/marketing, communications/journalism, health professions and related sciences **Academic program** Advanced placement, accelerated degree program, self-designed majors, honors program, summer session, adult/continuing education programs, internships **Contact** Mr. James Plunkett, Executive Director of Undergraduate Admission, La Salle University, 1900 West Olney Avenue, Philadelphia, PA 19141-1199. *Phone:* 215-951-1500 or toll-free 800-328-1910. *Fax:* 215-951-1656. *E-mail:* admiss@lasalle.edu. *Web site:* http://www.lasalle.edu/.

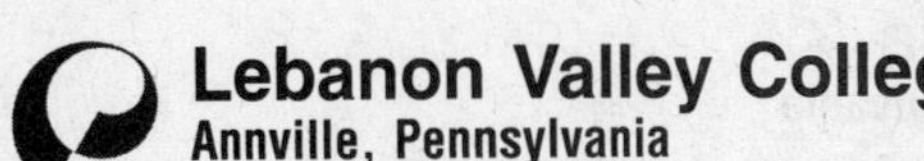

Lebanon Valley College
Annville, Pennsylvania

General Independent United Methodist, comprehensive, coed **Entrance** Moderately difficult **Setting** 340-acre small-town campus **Total enrollment** 2,045 **Student-faculty ratio** 13:1 **Application deadline** Rolling (freshmen), rolling (transfer) **Freshman admission** 81% were admitted **Freshman test scores** SAT critical reading scores over 500: 69.1%; SAT math scores over 500: 76.1%; ACT scores over 18: 92.2%; SAT critical reading scores over 600: 21%; SAT math scores over 600: 35.6%; ACT scores over 24: 41.2% **Housing** Yes **Expenses** Tuition & Fees $30,490; Room & Board $8080 **Undergraduates** 56% women, 9% part-time, 4% 25 or older, 0.2% Native American, 2% Hispanic American, 2% African American, 2% Asian American/Pacific Islander **The most frequently chosen baccalaureate fields are** business/marketing, education, social sciences **Academic program** Advanced placement, self-designed majors, summer session, adult/continuing education programs, internships **Contact** Ms. Susan Jones, Director of Admission, Lebanon Valley College, 101 North College Avenue, Annville, PA 17003. *Phone:* 717-867-6181 or toll-free 866-LVC-4ADM. *Fax:* 717-867-6026. *E-mail:* admission@lvc.edu. *Web site:* http://www.lvc.edu/.

See page 906 for the College Close-Up.

Lehigh University
Bethlehem, Pennsylvania

General Independent, university, coed **Entrance** Most difficult **Setting** 1,600-acre suburban campus **Total enrollment** 6,996 **Student-faculty**

Lehigh University (continued)

ratio 10:1 **Application deadline** 1/1 (freshmen), 4/1 (transfer) **Freshman admission** 33% were admitted **Freshman test scores** SAT critical reading scores over 500: 96%; SAT math scores over 500: 99%; SAT critical reading scores over 600: 71%; SAT math scores over 600: 87% **Housing** Yes **Expenses** Tuition & Fees $38,630; Room & Board $10,200 **Undergraduates** 41% women, 1% part-time, 0.04% Native American, 6% Hispanic American, 4% African American, 6% Asian American/Pacific Islander **The most frequently chosen baccalaureate fields are** business/marketing, engineering, social sciences **Academic program** English as a second language, advanced placement, accelerated degree program, honors program, summer session, internships **Contact** J. Bruce Gardiner, Director of Admissions, Lehigh University, 27 Memorial Drive West, Bethlehem, PA 18015. *Phone:* 610-758-3100. *Fax:* 610-758-4361. *E-mail:* admissions@lehigh.edu. *Web site:* http://www.lehigh.edu/.

Lincoln University

Lincoln University, Pennsylvania

General State-related, comprehensive, coed **Entrance** Moderately difficult **Setting** 422-acre rural campus **Total enrollment** 2,649 **Student-faculty ratio** 19:1 **Application deadline** Rolling (freshmen), rolling (transfer) **Freshman admission** 31% were admitted. Average high school GPA 2.7 **Freshman test scores** SAT critical reading scores over 500: 10%; SAT math scores over 500: 11%; ACT scores over 18: 42%; SAT critical reading scores over 600: 1%; SAT math scores over 600: 1%; ACT scores over 24: 7% **Housing** Yes **Expenses** Tuition & Fees: state resident $8222, nonresident $12,336; Room & Board $7770 **Undergraduates** 58% women, 2% part-time, 3% 25 or older, 0.05% Native American, 0.5% Hispanic American, 79% African American **The most frequently chosen baccalaureate fields are** business/marketing, communications/journalism, social sciences **Academic program** Advanced placement, accelerated degree program, self-designed majors, honors program, summer session, internships **Contact** Ms. Germel Eaton-Clarke, Interim Director of Admissions, Lincoln University, PO Box 179, Lincoln University, PA 19352. *Phone:* 484-365-7218 or toll-free 800-790-0191. *Fax:* 484-365-8109. *E-mail:* admiss@lincoln.edu. *Web site:* http://www.lincoln.edu/.

Lock Haven University of Pennsylvania

Lock Haven, Pennsylvania

General State-supported, comprehensive, coed **Entrance** Moderately difficult **Setting** 165-acre rural campus **Total enrollment** 5,329 **Student-faculty ratio** 21:1 **Application deadline** Rolling (freshmen), rolling (transfer) **Freshman admission** 76% were admitted. Average high school GPA 3.25 **Freshman test scores** SAT critical reading scores over 500: 31.95%; SAT math scores over 500: 36.01%; ACT scores over 18: 62.7%; SAT critical reading scores over 600: 6.05%; SAT math scores over 600: 7.18%; ACT scores over 24: 9.53% **Housing** Yes **Expenses** Tuition & Fees: state resident $7201, nonresident $13,533; Room & Board $6736 **Undergraduates** 57% women, 7% part-time, 9% 25 or older, 0.1% Native American, 2% Hispanic American, 7% African American, 1% Asian American/Pacific Islander **The most frequently chosen baccalaureate fields are** education, business/marketing, parks and recreation **Academic program** English as a second language, advanced placement, self-designed majors, honors program, summer session, adult/continuing education programs, internships **Contact** Mr. Steven Lee, Director of Admissions, Lock Haven University of Pennsylvania, Office of Admission, Akeley Hall, Lock Haven, PA 17745. *Phone:* 570-484-2027 or toll-free 800-332-8900 (in-state); 800-233-8978 (out-of-state). *Fax:* 570-484-2201. *E-mail:* admissions@lhup.edu. *Web site:* http://www.lhup.edu/.

Lycoming College

Williamsport, Pennsylvania

General Independent United Methodist, 4-year, coed **Entrance** Moderately difficult **Setting** 35-acre small-town campus **Total enrollment** 1,373 **Student-faculty ratio** 13:1 **Application deadline** 5/1 (freshmen), rolling (transfer) **Freshman admission** 68% were admitted **Freshman test scores** SAT critical reading scores over 500: 64%; SAT math scores over 500: 63%; ACT scores over 18: 93%; SAT critical reading scores over 600: 22%; SAT math scores over 600: 19%; ACT scores over 24: 52% **Housing** Yes **Expenses** Tuition & Fees $29,894; Room & Board $8134 **Undergraduates** 53% women, 2% part-time, 3% 25 or older, 1% Native American, 2% Hispanic American, 3% African American, 1% Asian American/Pacific Islander **The most frequently chosen baccalaureate fields are** business/marketing, psychology, social sciences **Academic program** Advanced placement, accelerated degree program, self-designed majors, honors program, summer session, internships **Contact** Mr. James Spencer, Vice President of Admissions and Financial Aid, Lycoming College, 700 College Place, Williamsport, PA 17701. *Phone:* 570-321-4026 or toll-free 800-345-3920 Ext. 4026. *Fax:* 570-321-4317. *E-mail:* admissions@lycoming.edu. *Web site:* http://www.lycoming.edu/.

Mansfield University of Pennsylvania

Mansfield, Pennsylvania

General State-supported, comprehensive, coed **Entrance** Moderately difficult **Setting** 174-acre small-town campus **Total enrollment** 3,569 **Student-faculty ratio** 16:1 **Application deadline** Rolling (freshmen), rolling (transfer) **Freshman admission** 75% were admitted. Average high school GPA 3.27 **Freshman test scores** SAT critical reading scores over 500: 40.7%; SAT math scores over 500: 38.7%; SAT critical reading scores over 600: 8.8%; SAT math scores over 600: 8.4% **Housing** Yes **Expenses** Tuition & Fees: state resident $7358, nonresident $15,396; Room & Board $6672 **Undergraduates** 60% women, 7% part-time, 14% 25 or older, 1% Native American, 2% Hispanic American, 7% African American, 1% Asian American/Pacific Islander **The most frequently chosen baccalaureate fields are** education, security and protective services, visual and performing arts **Academic program** Advanced placement, accelerated degree program, self-designed majors, honors program, summer session, adult/continuing education programs, internships **Contact** Mr. Brian Barden, Director of Admissions, Mansfield University of Pennsylvania, Academy Street, Mansfield, PA 16933. *Phone:* 570-662-4813 or toll-free 800-577-6826. *E-mail:* admissions@mnsfld.edu. *Web site:* http://www.mansfield.edu/.

Marywood University

Scranton, Pennsylvania

General Independent Roman Catholic, comprehensive, coed **Entrance** Moderately difficult **Setting** 115-acre suburban campus **Total enrollment** 3,471 **Student-faculty ratio** 13:1 **Application deadline** Rolling (freshmen), rolling (transfer) **Freshman admission** 72% were admitted. Average high school GPA 3.19 **Freshman test scores** SAT critical reading scores over 500: 65%; SAT math scores over 500: 62.9%; SAT critical reading scores over 600: 16.8%; SAT math scores over 600: 15.7% **Housing** Yes **Expenses** Tuition & Fees $26,270; Room & Board $11,498 **Undergraduates** 70% women, 6% part-time, 9% 25 or older, 0.3% Native American, 3% Hispanic American, 1% African American, 2% Asian American/Pacific Islander **The most frequently chosen baccalaureate fields are** education, health professions and related sciences, visual and performing arts **Academic program** English as a second language, advanced placement, self-designed majors, honors program, summer session, adult/continuing education programs, internships **Contact** Mr. Christian DiGregorio, Director of University Admissions, Marywood University, 2300 Adams Avenue, Scranton, PA 18509. *Phone:* 570-348-6234 or toll-free 866-279-9663. *Fax:* 570-961-4763. *E-mail:* yourfuture@marywood.edu. *Web site:* http://www.marywood.edu/. **Visit Petersons.com and enter keyword Marywood**

See page 952 for the College Close-Up.

Mercyhurst College

Erie, Pennsylvania

General Independent Roman Catholic, comprehensive, coed **Entrance** Moderately difficult **Setting** 88-acre suburban campus **Total enrollment**

We believe you can ***dream big***...and ***achieve*** those dreams.

Believe. It begins with a community that stands behind and beside you.

Prepare. It builds with academic excellence in programs that stretch your mind.

Connect. It expands with intellectual, personal, and professional bonds that are lifelong.

Serve. It inspires you to move, in your own way, from worthy dreams to deeds that change lives.

MARYWOOD

Marywood UNIVERSITY

Lead On. *The world awaits.*

For more information: **1-866-279-9663 • www.MyMarywood.com**
Scranton, Pennsylvania

3,217 **Student-faculty ratio** 16:1 **Application deadline** Rolling (freshmen), rolling (transfer) **Freshman admission** 74% were admitted. Average high school GPA 3.4 **Freshman test scores** SAT critical reading scores over 500: 62%; SAT math scores over 500: 63%; ACT scores over 18: 94%; SAT critical reading scores over 600: 17%; SAT math scores over 600: 19%; ACT scores over 24: 41% **Housing** Yes **Expenses** Tuition & Fees $26,346; Room & Board $9195 **Undergraduates** 58% women, 7% part-time, 9% 25 or older, 0.2% Native American, 2% Hispanic American, 4% African American, 1% Asian American/Pacific Islander **The most frequently chosen baccalaureate fields are** business/marketing, education, interdisciplinary studies **Academic program** Advanced placement, accelerated degree program, self-designed majors, honors program, summer session, adult/continuing education programs, internships **Contact** Christopher Coons, Director of Undergraduate Admissions, Mercyhurst College, 501 East 38th Street, Erie, PA 16546-0001. *Phone:* 814-824-2202 or toll-free 800-825-1926 Ext. 2202. *Fax:* 814-824-2071. *E-mail:* ccoons@mercyhurst.edu. *Web site:* http://www.mercyhurst.edu/.

Messiah College
Grantham, Pennsylvania

General Independent interdenominational, comprehensive, coed **Entrance** Moderately difficult **Setting** 485-acre small-town campus **Total enrollment** 2,801 **Student-faculty ratio** 13:1 **Application deadline** Rolling (freshmen), rolling (transfer) **Freshman admission** 69% were admitted. Average high school GPA 3.71 **Freshman test scores** SAT critical reading scores over 500: 82.59%; SAT math scores over 500: 81.68%; ACT scores over 18: 95.98%; SAT critical reading scores over 600: 35.44%; SAT math scores over 600: 41.74%; ACT scores over 24: 69.13% **Housing** Yes **Expenses** Tuition & Fees $27,480; Room & Board $8160 **Undergraduates** 63% women, 2% part-time, 2% 25 or older, 0.2% Native American, 2% Hispanic American, 2% African American, 2% Asian American/Pacific Islander **The most frequently chosen baccalaureate fields are** business/marketing, education, health professions and related sciences **Academic program** English as a second language, advanced placement, accelerated degree program, self-designed majors, honors program, summer session, adult/continuing education programs, internships **Contact** Mr. John Chopka, Vice President for Enrollment Management, Messiah College, PO Box 3005, One College Avenue, Grantham, PA 17027. *Phone:* 717-691-6000 or toll-free 800-233-4220. *Fax:* 717-791-2307. *E-mail:* admiss@messiah.edu. *Web site:* http://www.messiah.edu/.

Visit Petersons.com and enter keyword Messiah

See page 960 for the College Close-Up.

Millersville University of Pennsylvania
Millersville, Pennsylvania

General State-supported, comprehensive, coed **Entrance** Moderately difficult **Setting** 250-acre small-town campus **Total enrollment** 8,427 **Student-faculty ratio** 21:1 **Application deadline** Rolling (freshmen), rolling (transfer) **Freshman admission** 53% were admitted **Freshman test scores** SAT critical reading scores over 500: 67.01%; SAT math scores over 500: 71.82%; ACT scores over 18: 87.1%; SAT critical reading scores over 600: 17.68%; SAT math scores over 600: 22.81%; ACT scores over 24: 27.1% **Housing** Yes **Expenses** Tuition & Fees: state resident $7147, nonresident $15,479; Room & Board $7766 **Undergraduates** 56% women, 9% part-time, 9% 25 or older, 0.2% Native American, 4% Hispanic American, 7% African American, 1% Asian American/Pacific Islander **The most frequently chosen baccalaureate fields are** business/marketing, education, social sciences **Academic**

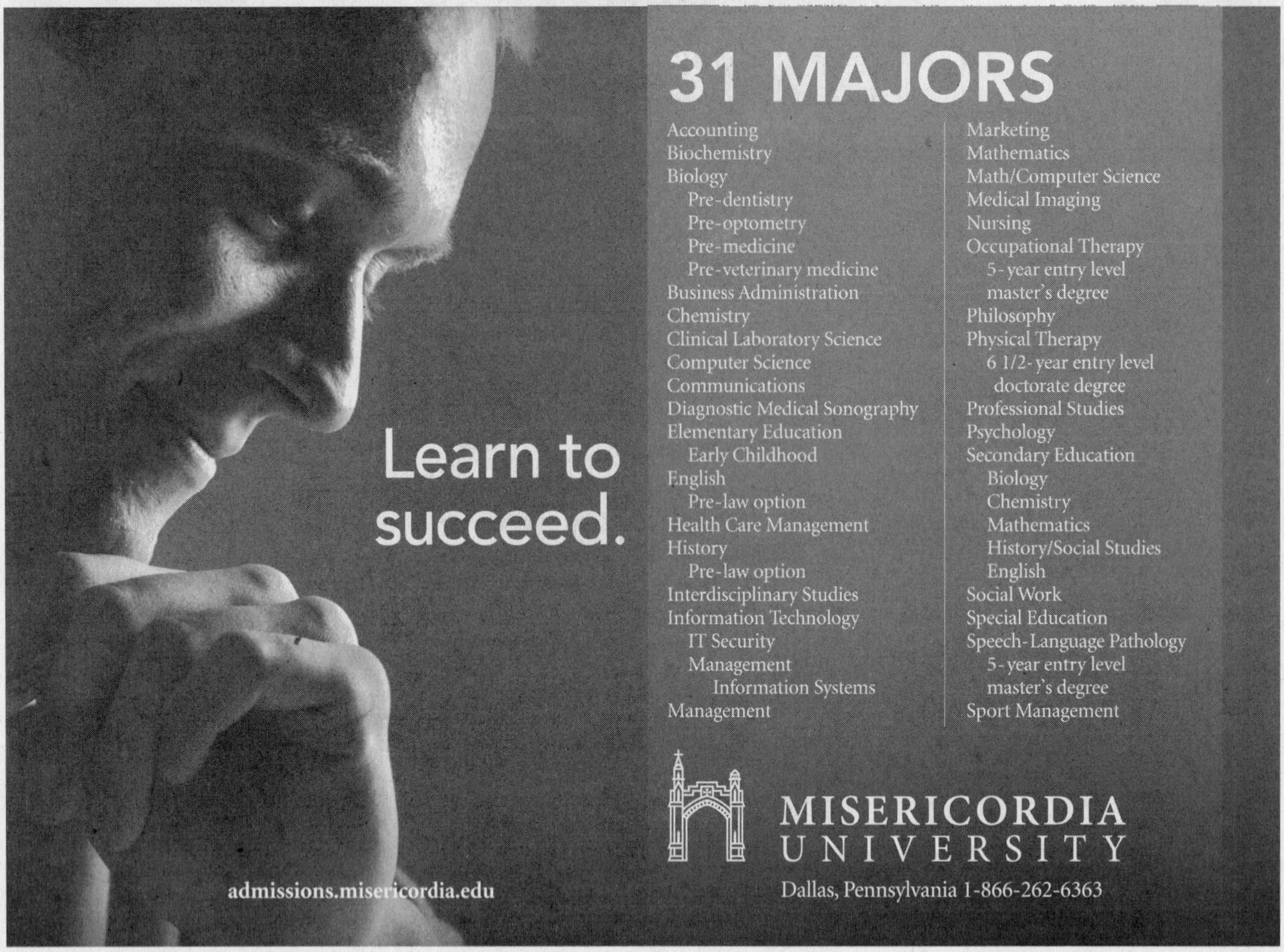

31 MAJORS

Accounting
Biochemistry
Biology
Pre-dentistry
Pre-optometry
Pre-medicine
Pre-veterinary medicine
Business Administration
Chemistry
Clinical Laboratory Science
Computer Science
Communications
Diagnostic Medical Sonography
Elementary Education
Early Childhood
English
Pre-law option
Health Care Management
History
Pre-law option
Interdisciplinary Studies
Information Technology
IT Security
Management
Information Systems
Management
Marketing
Mathematics
Math/Computer Science
Medical Imaging
Nursing
Occupational Therapy
5-year entry level
master's degree
Philosophy
Physical Therapy
6 1/2-year entry level
doctorate degree
Professional Studies
Psychology
Secondary Education
Biology
Chemistry
Mathematics
History/Social Studies
English
Social Work
Special Education
Speech-Language Pathology
5-year entry level
master's degree
Sport Management

Learn to succeed.

MISERICORDIA UNIVERSITY
Dallas, Pennsylvania 1-866-262-6363

admissions.misericordia.edu

Millersville University of Pennsylvania (continued)

program Advanced placement, accelerated degree program, honors program, summer session, adult/continuing education programs, internships **Contact** Dr. Douglas Zander, Director of Admissions, Millersville University of Pennsylvania, PO Box 1002, Millersville, PA 17551-0302. *Phone:* 717-872-3371 or toll-free 800-MU-ADMIT. *Fax:* 717-871-2147. *E-mail:* admissions@millersville.edu. *Web site:* http://www.millersville.edu/.

Visit Petersons.com and enter keyword Millersville

See page 966 for the College Close-Up.

Misericordia University
Dallas, Pennsylvania

General Independent Roman Catholic, comprehensive, coed, primarily women **Entrance** Moderately difficult **Setting** 100-acre small-town campus **Total enrollment** 2,736 **Student-faculty ratio** 13:1 **Application deadline** Rolling (freshmen), rolling (transfer) **Freshman admission** 69% were admitted. Average high school GPA 3.2 **Freshman test scores** SAT critical reading scores over 500: 58%; SAT math scores over 500: 61%; ACT scores over 18: 93%; SAT critical reading scores over 600: 10%; SAT math scores over 600: 17%; ACT scores over 24: 40% **Housing** Yes **Expenses** Tuition & Fees $24,050; Room & Board $10,050 **Undergraduates** 71% women, 30% part-time, 27% 25 or older, 0.2% Native American, 2% Hispanic American, 1% African American, 1% Asian American/Pacific Islander **The most frequently chosen baccalaureate fields are** business/marketing, education, health professions and related sciences **Academic program** Advanced placement, accelerated degree program, self-designed majors, honors program, summer session, adult/continuing education programs, internships **Contact** Mr. Glenn Bozinski, Director of Admissions, Misericordia University, 301 Lake Street, Dallas, PA 18612-1098. *Phone:* 570-675-6264 or toll-free 866-262-6363. *Fax:* 570-674-6232. *E-mail:* admiss@misericordia.edu. *Web site:* http://www.misericordia.edu/.

Visit Petersons.com and enter keyword Misericordia

See page 974 for the College Close-Up.

Moore College of Art & Design
Philadelphia, Pennsylvania

General Independent, comprehensive, women only **Entrance** Moderately difficult **Setting** 3-acre urban campus **Total enrollment** 582 **Student-faculty ratio** 9:1 **Application deadline** 8/15 (freshmen), rolling (transfer) **Freshman admission** 64% were admitted. Average high school GPA 3.11 **Freshman test scores** SAT critical reading scores over 500: 55%; SAT math scores over 500: 41%; ACT scores over 18: 92%; SAT critical reading scores over 600: 17%; SAT math scores over 600: 8%; ACT scores over 24: 42% **Housing** Yes **Expenses** Tuition & Fees $30,409; Room & Board $11,367 **Undergraduates** 6% part-time, 12% 25 or older, 0.2% Native American, 6% Hispanic American, 12% African American, 2% Asian American/Pacific Islander **The most frequently chosen baccalaureate fields are** education, visual and performing arts **Academic program** Advanced placement, summer session, internships **Contact** Ms. Heesung Lee, Director of Admissions, Moore College of Art & Design, 20th and The Parkway, Philadelphia, PA 19103. *Phone:*

215-965-4014 or toll-free 800-523-2025. *Fax:* 215-965-8544. *E-mail:* enroll@moore.edu. *Web site:* http://www.moore.edu/.
Visit Petersons.com and enter keyword Moore

See page 984 for the College Close-Up.

Moravian College
Bethlehem, Pennsylvania

General Independent, comprehensive, coed, affiliated with Moravian Church **Entrance** Moderately difficult **Setting** 60-acre suburban campus **Total enrollment** 2,057 **Student-faculty ratio** 10:1 **Application deadline** 3/1 (freshmen), 3/1 (transfer) **Freshman admission** 75% were admitted **Freshman test scores** SAT critical reading scores over 500: 73%; SAT math scores over 500: 74%; SAT critical reading scores over 600: 25%; SAT math scores over 600: 29% **Housing** Yes **Expenses** Tuition & Fees $32,177; Room & Board $9164 **Undergraduates** 60% women, 13% part-time, 3% 25 or older, 0.1% Native American, 5% Hispanic American, 3% African American, 2% Asian American/Pacific Islander **The most frequently chosen baccalaureate fields are** business/marketing, social sciences, visual and performing arts **Academic program** Advanced placement, self-designed majors, honors program, summer session, adult/continuing education programs, internships **Contact** Mr. James Mackin, Director of Admission, Moravian College, 1200 Main Street, Bethlehem, PA 18018. *Phone:* 610-861-1320 or toll-free 800-441-3191. *Fax:* 610-625-7930. *E-mail:* admissions@moravian.edu. *Web site:* http://www.moravian.edu/.

Mount Aloysius College
Cresson, Pennsylvania

General Independent Roman Catholic, comprehensive, coed **Entrance** Minimally difficult **Setting** small-town campus **Total enrollment** 1,604 **Student-faculty ratio** 14:1 **Application deadline** Rolling (freshmen), rolling (transfer) **Freshman admission** 80% were admitted. Average high school GPA 3.2 **Freshman test scores** SAT critical reading scores over 500: 32%; SAT math scores over 500: 30%; ACT scores over 18: 64%; SAT critical reading scores over 600: 4%; SAT math scores over 600: 4%; ACT scores over 24: 7% **Housing** Yes **Expenses** Tuition & Fees $17,280; Room & Board $7300 **Undergraduates** 73% women, 26% part-time, 31% 25 or older, 0.3% Native American, 1% Hispanic American, 3% African American, 0.2% Asian American/Pacific Islander **The most frequently chosen baccalaureate fields are** business/marketing, health professions and related sciences, liberal arts/general studies **Academic program** Advanced placement, accelerated degree program, self-designed majors, honors program, summer session, internships **Contact** Mr. Frank C. Crouse Jr., Vice President for Enrollment Management/Dean of Admissions, Mount Aloysius College, 7373 Admiral Peary Highway, Cresson, PA 16630-1999. *Phone:* 814-886-6383 or toll-free 888-823-2220. *Fax:* 814-886-6441. *E-mail:* admissions@mtaloy.edu. *Web site:* http://www.mtaloy.edu/.
Visit Petersons.com and enter keyword Aloysius

See page 990 for the College Close-Up.

Muhlenberg College
Allentown, Pennsylvania

General Independent, 4-year, coed, affiliated with Lutheran Church **Entrance** Very difficult **Setting** 75-acre suburban campus **Total enrollment** 2,517 **Student-faculty ratio** 12:1 **Application deadline** 2/15 (freshmen), 6/15 (transfer) **Freshman admission** 45% were admitted. Average high school GPA 3.27 **Freshman test scores** SAT critical reading scores over 500: 91.4%; SAT math scores over 500: 92.1%; ACT scores over 18: 100%; SAT critical reading scores over 600: 57.8%; SAT math scores over 600: 57.5%; ACT scores over 24: 89.7% **Housing** Yes **Expenses** Tuition & Fees $36,990; Room & Board $8440 **Undergraduates** 57% women, 7% part-time, 4% 25 or older, 0.04% Native American, 3% Hispanic American, 2% African American, 2% Asian American/Pacific Islander **The most frequently chosen baccalaureate fields are** business/marketing, social sciences, visual and performing arts **Academic program** Advanced placement, accelerated degree program, self-designed majors, honors program, summer session, adult/continuing education programs, internships **Contact** Mr. Christopher Hooker-Haring, Director of Undergraduate Admissions, Muhlenberg College, 2400 Chew Street, Allentown, PA 18104. *Phone:* 484-664-3245. *Fax:* 484-664-3234. *E-mail:* adm@muhlenberg.edu. *Web site:* http://www.muhlenberg.edu/.
Visit Petersons.com and enter keyword Muhlenberg

See page 996 for the College Close-Up.

Neumann University
Aston, Pennsylvania

General Independent Roman Catholic, comprehensive, coed **Entrance** Moderately difficult **Setting** 50-acre suburban campus **Total enrollment** 3,099 **Student-faculty ratio** 14:1 **Application deadline** 4/1 (freshmen), rolling (transfer) **Freshman admission** 94% were admitted. Average high school GPA 3.25 **Freshman test scores** SAT critical reading scores over 500: 22%; SAT math scores over 500: 23%; SAT critical reading scores over 600: 3%; SAT math scores over 600: 2% **Housing** Yes **Expenses** Tuition & Fees $21,360; Room & Board $9718 **Undergraduates** 65% women, 20% part-time, 26% 25 or older, 0.1% Native American, 3% Hispanic American, 13% African American, 1% Asian American/Pacific Islander **The most frequently chosen baccalaureate fields are** health professions and related sciences, education, liberal arts/general studies **Academic program** Advanced placement, accelerated degree program, self-designed majors, honors program, summer session, adult/continuing education programs, internships **Contact** Mr. Dennis J. Murphy, Vice President for Enrollment Management, Neumann University, One Neumann Drive, Aston, PA 19014-1298. *Phone:* 610-361-2448 or toll-free 800-963-8626. *Fax:* 610-558-5652. *E-mail:* neumann@neumann.edu. *Web site:* http://www.neumann.edu/.
Visit Petersons.com and enter keyword Neumann

See page 1006 for the College Close-Up.

Peirce College
Philadelphia, Pennsylvania

General Independent, 4-year, coed **Entrance** Noncompetitive **Setting** 1-acre urban campus **Total enrollment** 2,083 **Student-faculty ratio** 17:1 **Application deadline** Rolling (freshmen), rolling (transfer) **Housing** No **Expenses** Tuition & Fees $14,850 **Undergraduates** 72% women, 60% part-time, 82% 25 or older, 0.4% Native American, 5% Hispanic American, 59% African American, 1% Asian American/Pacific Islander **The most frequently chosen baccalaureate fields are** business/marketing, computer and information sciences, law/legal studies **Academic program** Advanced placement, accelerated degree program, summer session, adult/continuing education programs **Contact** Mr. Paul Ballentine, Supervisor, Admissions, Peirce College, 1420 Pine Street, Philadelphia, PA 19102. *Phone:* 215-670-9214 or toll-free 888-467-3472. *Fax:* 215-670-9366. *E-mail:* info@peirce.edu. *Web site:* http://www.peirce.edu/.

Penn State Abington
Abington, Pennsylvania

General State-related, 4-year, coed **Entrance** Very difficult **Setting** 45-acre small-town campus **Total enrollment** 3,397 **Student-faculty ratio** 20:1 **Application deadline** Rolling (freshmen), rolling (transfer) **Freshman admission** 84% were admitted. Average high school GPA 2.98 **Freshman test scores** SAT critical reading scores over 500: 34.93%; SAT math scores over 500: 46.4%; SAT critical reading scores over 600: 7.69%; SAT math scores over 600: 13.99% **Housing** No **Expenses** Tuition & Fees: state resident $12,250, nonresident $18,268 **Undergraduates** 49% women, 21% part-time, 11% 25 or older, 0.2% Native American, 7% Hispanic American, 13% African American, 15% Asian American/Pacific Islander **The most frequently chosen bacca-**

Penn State Abington (continued)
laureate fields are business/marketing, psychology, security and protective services **Academic program** English as a second language, advanced placement, accelerated degree program, self-designed majors, honors program, summer session, adult/continuing education programs, internships **Contact** Anne L. Rohrbach, Executive Director for Undergraduate Admissions, Penn State Abington, 201 Shields Building, Box 3000, University Park, PA 16804-3000. *Phone:* 814-865-4700. *Fax:* 814-863-7590. *E-mail:* admissions@psu.edu. *Web site:* http://www.abington.psu.edu/.

Penn State Altoona

Altoona, Pennsylvania

General State-related, 4-year, coed **Entrance** Very difficult **Setting** 150-acre suburban campus **Total enrollment** 4,147 **Student-faculty ratio** 17:1 **Application deadline** Rolling (freshmen), rolling (transfer) **Freshman admission** 87% were admitted. Average high school GPA 3.04 **Freshman test scores** SAT critical reading scores over 500: 48.96%; SAT math scores over 500: 59.09%; SAT critical reading scores over 600: 8.05%; SAT math scores over 600: 17.17% **Housing** Yes **Expenses** Tuition & Fees: state resident $12,750, nonresident $19,078; Room & Board $8170 **Undergraduates** 47% women, 5% part-time, 9% 25 or older, 0.1% Native American, 3% Hispanic American, 6% African American, 2% Asian American/Pacific Islander **The most frequently chosen baccalaureate fields are** business/marketing, education, security and protective services **Academic program** English as a second language, advanced placement, accelerated degree program, self-designed majors, honors program, summer session, adult/continuing education programs, internships **Contact** Anne L. Rohrbach, Executive Director for Undergraduate Admissions, Penn State Altoona, 201 Shields Building, Box 3000, University Park, PA 16804-3000. *Phone:* 814-865-4700 or toll-free 800-848-9843. *Fax:* 814-863-7590. *E-mail:* admissions@psu.edu. *Web site:* http://www.aa.psu.edu/.

Penn State Beaver

Monaca, Pennsylvania

General State-related, primarily 2-year, coed **Entrance** Moderately difficult **Setting** 91-acre small-town campus **Total enrollment** 855 **Student-faculty ratio** 18:1 **Application deadline** Rolling (freshmen), rolling (transfer) **Freshman admission** 93% were admitted. Average high school GPA 2.91 **Freshman test scores** SAT critical reading scores over 500: 38.19%; SAT math scores over 500: 49.36%; SAT critical reading scores over 600: 3.86%; SAT math scores over 600: 12.02% **Housing** Yes **Expenses** Tuition & Fees: state resident $12,250, nonresident $18,268; Room & Board $8170 **Undergraduates** 45% women, 23% part-time, 9% 25 or older, 3% Hispanic American, 8% African American, 3% Asian American/Pacific Islander **The most frequently chosen baccalaureate fields are** business/marketing, computer and information sciences, psychology **Academic program** English as a second language, advanced placement, honors program, summer session, adult/continuing education programs, internships **Contact** Mr. Randall C. Deike, Assistant Vice President for Enrollment Management, Penn State Beaver, 100 University Drive, Monaca, PA 15061. *Phone:* 814-865-5471. *E-mail:* br-admissions@psu.edu. *Web site:* http://www.br.psu.edu/.

Penn State Berks

Reading, Pennsylvania

General State-related, 4-year, coed **Entrance** Very difficult **Setting** 258-acre suburban campus **Total enrollment** 2,647 **Student-faculty ratio** 18:1 **Application deadline** Rolling (freshmen), rolling (transfer) **Freshman admission** 83% were admitted. Average high school GPA 2.97 **Freshman test scores** SAT critical reading scores over 500: 47.8%; SAT math scores over 500: 56.04%; SAT critical reading scores over 600: 8.1%; SAT math scores over 600: 16.34% **Housing** Yes **Expenses** Tuition & Fees: state resident $12,750, nonresident $19,078; Room & Board $8940 **Undergraduates** 43% women, 11% part-time, 10% 25 or older, 0.2% Native American, 6% Hispanic American, 7% African American, 4% Asian American/Pacific Islander **The most frequently chosen baccalaureate fields are** business/marketing, education, interdisciplinary studies **Academic program** English as a second language, advanced placement, accelerated degree program, honors program, summer session, adult/continuing education programs, internships **Contact** Anne L. Rohrbach, Executive Director for Undergraduate Admissions, Penn State Berks, 201 Shields Building, Box 3000, University Park, PA 16804-3000. *Phone:* 814-865-4700. *Fax:* 814-863-7590. *E-mail:* admissions@psu.edu. *Web site:* http://www.bk.psu.edu/.

Penn State Brandywine

Media, Pennsylvania

General State-related, primarily 2-year, coed **Entrance** Moderately difficult **Setting** 87-acre small-town campus **Total enrollment** 1,608 **Student-faculty ratio** 17:1 **Application deadline** Rolling (freshmen), rolling (transfer) **Freshman admission** 85% were admitted. Average high school GPA 2.96 **Freshman test scores** SAT critical reading scores over 500: 37.57%; SAT math scores over 500: 43.12%; SAT critical reading scores over 600: 10.32%; SAT math scores over 600: 12.17% **Housing** No **Expenses** Tuition & Fees: state resident $12,150, nonresident $18,168 **Undergraduates** 42% women, 14% part-time, 11% 25 or older, 0.1% Native American, 3% Hispanic American, 12% African American, 7% Asian American/Pacific Islander **The most frequently chosen baccalaureate fields are** business/marketing, communications/journalism, family and consumer sciences **Academic program** English as a second language, advanced placement, honors program, summer session, adult/continuing education programs, internships **Contact** Mr. Randall C. Deike, Assistant Vice President for Enrollment Management, Penn State Brandywine, 25 Yearsley Mill Road, Media, PA 19063-5596. *Phone:* 814-865-5471. *E-mail:* bwadmissions@psu.edu. *Web site:* http://www.brandywine.psu.edu/.

Penn State DuBois

DuBois, Pennsylvania

General State-related, primarily 2-year, coed **Entrance** Moderately difficult **Setting** 20-acre small-town campus **Total enrollment** 938 **Student-faculty ratio** 13:1 **Application deadline** Rolling (freshmen), rolling (transfer) **Freshman admission** 92% were admitted. Average high school GPA 2.83 **Freshman test scores** SAT critical reading scores over 500: 27.57%; SAT math scores over 500: 36.76%; SAT critical reading scores over 600: 2.16%; SAT math scores over 600: 9.73% **Housing** No **Expenses** Tuition & Fees: state resident $12,130, nonresident $18,148 **Undergraduates** 49% women, 19% part-time, 30% 25 or older, 0.4% Native American, 2% Hispanic American, 1% African American, 1% Asian American/Pacific Islander **The most frequently chosen baccalaureate fields are** business/marketing, family and consumer sciences, liberal arts/general studies **Academic program** Advanced placement, accelerated degree program, self-designed majors, honors program, summer session, adult/continuing education programs, internships **Contact** Mr. Randall C. Deike, Assistant Vice President for Enrollment Management, Penn State DuBois, College Place, DuBois, PA 15801-3199. *Phone:* 814-865-5471 or toll-free 800-346-7627. *E-mail:* duboisinfo@psu.edu. *Web site:* http://www.ds.psu.edu/.

Penn State Erie, The Behrend College

Erie, Pennsylvania

General State-related, comprehensive, coed **Entrance** Very difficult **Setting** 725-acre suburban campus **Total enrollment** 4,400 **Student-faculty ratio** 17:1 **Application deadline** Rolling (freshmen), rolling (transfer) **Freshman admission** 87% were admitted. Average high school GPA 3.21 **Freshman test scores** SAT critical reading scores over

500: 55.18%; SAT math scores over 500: 68.49%; SAT critical reading scores over 600: 9.62%; SAT math scores over 600: 25.26% **Housing** Yes **Expenses** Tuition & Fees: state resident $12,750, nonresident $19,078; Room & Board $8170 **Undergraduates** 37% women, 7% part-time, 8% 25 or older, 0.1% Native American, 2% Hispanic American, 3% African American, 2% Asian American/Pacific Islander **The most frequently chosen baccalaureate fields are** business/marketing, engineering, engineering technologies **Academic program** Advanced placement, accelerated degree program, honors program, summer session, adult/continuing education programs, internships **Contact** Anne L. Rohrbach, Executive Director for Undergraduate Admissions, Penn State Erie, The Behrend College, 201 Shields Building, Box 3000, University Park, PA 16804-3000. *Phone:* 814-865-4700 or toll-free 866-374-3378. *Fax:* 814-863-7590. *E-mail:* admissions@psu.edu. *Web site:* http://www.pserie.psu.edu/.

Visit Petersons.com and enter keyword Behrand

See page 1046 for the College Close-Up.

Penn State Fayette, The Eberly Campus

Uniontown, Pennsylvania

General State-related, primarily 2-year, coed **Entrance** Moderately difficult **Setting** 92-acre small-town campus **Total enrollment** 1,095 **Student-faculty ratio** 13:1 **Application deadline** Rolling (freshmen), rolling (transfer) **Freshman admission** 93% were admitted. Average high school GPA 3 **Freshman test scores** SAT critical reading scores over 500: 27.89%; SAT math scores over 500: 40.86%; SAT critical reading scores over 600: 4.33%; SAT math scores over 600: 10.09% **Housing** No **Expenses** Tuition & Fees: state resident $12,150, nonresident $18,168 **Undergraduates** 55% women, 26% part-time, 31% 25 or older, 0.3% Native American, 1% Hispanic American, 5% African American, 0.3% Asian American/Pacific Islander **The most frequently chosen baccalaureate fields are** family and consumer sciences, business/marketing, security and protective services **Academic program** Advanced placement, accelerated degree program, self-designed majors, honors program, summer session, adult/continuing education programs, internships **Contact** Mr. Randall C. Deike, Assistant Vice President for Enrollment Management, Penn State Fayette, The Eberly Campus, 1 University Drive, PO Box 519, Uniontown, PA 15401-0519. *Phone:* 814-865-5471 or toll-free 877-568-4130. *E-mail:* feadm@psu.edu. *Web site:* http://www.fe.psu.edu/.

Penn State Greater Allegheny

McKeesport, Pennsylvania

General State-related, primarily 2-year, coed **Entrance** Moderately difficult **Setting** 40-acre small-town campus **Total enrollment** 750 **Student-faculty ratio** 15:1 **Application deadline** Rolling (freshmen), rolling (transfer) **Freshman admission** 86% were admitted. Average high school GPA 2.85 **Freshman test scores** SAT critical reading scores over 500: 34.44%; SAT math scores over 500: 40.24%; SAT critical reading scores over 600: 7.05%; SAT math scores over 600: 12.44% **Housing** Yes **Expenses** Tuition & Fees: state resident $12,250, nonresident $18,268; Room & Board $8170 **Undergraduates** 44% women, 14% part-time, 7% 25 or older, 0.3% Native American, 3% Hispanic American, 25% African American, 4% Asian American/Pacific Islander **The most frequently chosen baccalaureate fields are** business/marketing, communications/journalism, psychology **Academic program** English as a second language, advanced placement, self-designed majors, honors program, summer session, adult/continuing education programs, internships **Contact** Mr. Randall C. Deike, Assistant Vice President for Enrollment Management, Penn State Greater Allegheny, 4000 University Drive, McKeesport, PA 15132-7698. *Phone:* 814-865-5471. *E-mail:* psumk@psu.edu. *Web site:* http://www.mk.psu.edu/.

Penn State Harrisburg

Middletown, Pennsylvania

General State-related, comprehensive, coed **Entrance** Very difficult **Setting** 218-acre small-town campus **Total enrollment** 4,012 **Student-faculty ratio** 13:1 **Application deadline** Rolling (freshmen), rolling (transfer) **Freshman admission** 86% were admitted. Average high school GPA 3.08 **Freshman test scores** SAT critical reading scores over 500: 53.05%; SAT math scores over 500: 65.26%; SAT critical reading scores over 600: 10.33%; SAT math scores over 600: 24.18% **Housing** Yes **Expenses** Tuition & Fees: state resident $12,750, nonresident $19,078; Room & Board $9350 **Undergraduates** 46% women, 18% part-time, 21% 25 or older, 0.2% Native American, 4% Hispanic American, 8% African American, 7% Asian American/Pacific Islander **The most frequently chosen baccalaureate fields are** business/marketing, education, engineering **Academic program** Advanced placement, self-designed majors, honors program, summer session, adult/continuing education programs, internships **Contact** Anne L. Rohrbach, Executive Director for Undergraduate Admissions, Penn State Harrisburg, 201 Shields Building, Box 3000, University Park, PA 16804-3000. *Phone:* 814-865-4700 or toll-free 800-222-2056. *Fax:* 814-863-7590. *E-mail:* admissions@psu.edu. *Web site:* http://www.hbg.psu.edu/.

Penn State Hazleton

Hazleton, Pennsylvania

General State-related, primarily 2-year, coed **Entrance** Moderately difficult **Setting** 98-acre small-town campus **Total enrollment** 1,245 **Student-faculty ratio** 19:1 **Application deadline** Rolling (freshmen), rolling (transfer) **Freshman admission** 92% were admitted. Average high school GPA 2.81 **Freshman test scores** SAT critical reading scores over 500: 33.59%; SAT math scores over 500: 38.46%; SAT critical reading scores over 600: 4.32%; SAT math scores over 600: 11.07% **Housing** Yes **Expenses** Tuition & Fees: state resident $12,200, nonresident $18,218; Room & Board $8170 **Undergraduates** 43% women, 4% part-time, 5% 25 or older, 0.1% Native American, 13% Hispanic American, 11% African American, 4% Asian American/Pacific Islander **The most frequently chosen baccalaureate fields are** business/marketing, computer and information sciences, liberal arts/general studies **Academic program** English as a second language, advanced placement, accelerated degree program, self-designed majors, honors program, summer session, adult/continuing education programs, internships **Contact** Mr. Randall C. Deike, Assistant Vice President for Enrollment Management, Penn State Hazleton, Hazleton, PA 18202-1291. *Phone:* 814-865-5471 or toll-free 800-279-8495. *E-mail:* admissions-hn@psu.edu. *Web site:* http://www.hn.psu.edu/.

Penn State Lehigh Valley

Fogelsville, Pennsylvania

General State-related, primarily 2-year, coed **Entrance** Moderately difficult **Setting** 42-acre small-town campus **Total enrollment** 840 **Student-faculty ratio** 13:1 **Application deadline** Rolling (freshmen), rolling (transfer) **Freshman admission** 94% were admitted. Average high school GPA 2.81 **Freshman test scores** SAT critical reading scores over 500: 37.44%; SAT math scores over 500: 40.18%; SAT critical reading scores over 600: 10.04%; SAT math scores over 600: 11.41% **Housing** No **Expenses** Tuition & Fees: state resident $12,250, nonresident $18,268 **Undergraduates** 44% women, 26% part-time, 13% 25 or older, 0.2% Native American, 12% Hispanic American, 3% African American, 9% Asian American/Pacific Islander **The most frequently chosen baccalaureate fields are** business/marketing, education, psychology **Academic program** Advanced placement, accelerated degree program, honors program, summer session, adult/continuing education programs, internships **Contact** Mr. Randall C. Deike, Assistant Vice President for Enrollment Management, Penn State Lehigh Valley, 8380 Mohr Lane, Fogelsville, PA 18051-9999. *Phone:* 814-865-5471. *E-mail:* admissions-lv@psu.edu. *Web site:* http://www.lv.psu.edu/.

It's Your Time at Penn State Harrisburg

Personal attention. Award-winning faculty. The resources of a world class research university.

PENNSTATE

Harrisburg

717-948-6250 • hbg.psu.edu

hbgadmit@psu.edu

Penn State Harrisburg • 777 West Harrisburg Pike, Middletown, PA 17057

Penn State Mont Alto

Mont Alto, Pennsylvania

General State-related, primarily 2-year, coed **Entrance** Moderately difficult **Setting** 64-acre small-town campus **Total enrollment** 1,182 **Student-faculty ratio** 13:1 **Application deadline** Rolling (freshmen), rolling (transfer) **Freshman admission** 90% were admitted. Average high school GPA 2.93 **Freshman test scores** SAT critical reading scores over 500: 36.34%; SAT math scores over 500: 45.1%; SAT critical reading scores over 600: 7.43%; SAT math scores over 600: 13% **Housing** Yes **Expenses** Tuition & Fees: state resident $12,250, nonresident $18,268; Room & Board $8170 **Undergraduates** 57% women, 25% part-time, 21% 25 or older, 0.4% Native American, 4% Hispanic American, 13% African American, 3% Asian American/Pacific Islander **The most frequently chosen baccalaureate fields are** business/marketing, English, family and consumer sciences **Academic program** Advanced placement, accelerated degree program, honors program, summer session, adult/continuing education programs, internships **Contact** Mr. Randall C. Deike, Assistant Vice President for Enrollment Management, Penn State Mont Alto, 1 Campus Drive, Mont Alto, PA 17237-9703. *Phone:* 814-865-5471 or toll-free 800-392-6173. *E-mail:* psuma@psu.edu. *Web site:* http://www.ma.psu.edu/.

Penn State New Kensington

New Kensington, Pennsylvania

General State-related, primarily 2-year, coed **Entrance** Moderately difficult **Setting** 71-acre small-town campus **Total enrollment** 820 **Student-faculty ratio** 14:1 **Application deadline** Rolling (freshmen), rolling (transfer) **Freshman admission** 89% were admitted. Average high school GPA 2.87 **Freshman test scores** SAT critical reading scores over 500: 35.72%; SAT math scores over 500: 50.6%; SAT critical reading scores over 600: 2.98%; SAT math scores over 600: 8.93% **Housing** No **Expenses** Tuition & Fees: state resident $12,200, nonresident $18,218 **Undergraduates** 40% women, 25% part-time, 23% 25 or older, 0.1% Native American, 1% Hispanic American, 2% African American, 1% Asian American/Pacific Islander **The most frequently chosen baccalaureate fields are** business/marketing, computer and information sciences, psychology **Academic program** Advanced placement, honors program, summer session, adult/continuing education programs, internships **Contact** Mr. Randall C. Deike, Assistant Vice President for Enrollment Management, Penn State New Kensington, 3550 7th Street Road, RT 780, New Kensington, PA 15068. *Phone:* 814-865-5471 or toll-free 888-968-7297. *E-mail:* nkadmissions@psu.edu. *Web site:* http://www.nk.psu.edu/.

Penn State Schuylkill

Schuylkill Haven, Pennsylvania

General State-related, primarily 2-year, coed **Entrance** Moderately difficult **Setting** 42-acre small-town campus **Total enrollment** 1,010 **Student-faculty ratio** 17:1 **Application deadline** Rolling (freshmen), rolling (transfer) **Freshman admission** 86% were admitted. Average high school GPA 2.74 **Freshman test scores** SAT critical reading scores over 500: 19.81%; SAT math scores over 500: 20.75%; SAT critical reading scores over 600: 4.4%; SAT math scores over 600: 2.83% **Housing** Yes **Expenses** Tuition & Fees: state resident $12,150, nonresident $18,168 **Undergraduates** 55% women, 15% part-time, 12% 25 or older, 0.2% Native American, 5% Hispanic American, 29% African American, 2% Asian American/Pacific Islander **The most frequently chosen baccalaureate fields are** business/marketing, psychology, security and protective services **Academic program** Advanced placement, accelerated degree program, self-designed majors, honors program, summer session, adult/continuing education programs, internships **Contact** Mr. Randall C. Deike, Assistant Vice President for Enrollment Management, Penn State Schuylkill, 200 University Drive, Schuylkill Haven, PA 17972-2208. *Phone:* 814-865-5471. *E-mail:* sl-admissions@psu.edu. *Web site:* http://www.sl.psu.edu/.

Penn State Shenango

Sharon, Pennsylvania

General State-related, primarily 2-year, coed **Entrance** Moderately difficult **Setting** 14-acre small-town campus **Total enrollment** 816 **Student-faculty ratio** 13:1 **Application deadline** Rolling (freshmen), rolling (transfer) **Freshman admission** 77% were admitted. Average high school GPA 2.86 **Freshman test scores** SAT critical reading scores over 500: 38.2%; SAT math scores over 500: 37.08%; SAT critical reading scores over 600: 4.49%; SAT math scores over 600: 6.74% **Housing** No **Expenses** Tuition & Fees: state resident $12,050, nonresident $18,068 **Undergraduates** 69% women, 40% part-time, 49% 25 or older, 0.2% Native American, 2% Hispanic American, 7% African American, 1% Asian American/Pacific Islander **The most frequently chosen baccalaureate fields are** family and consumer sciences, business/marketing, health professions and related sciences **Academic program** Advanced placement, accelerated degree program, self-designed majors, honors program, summer session, adult/continuing education programs, internships **Contact** Mr. Randall C. Deike, Assistant Vice President for Enrollment Management, Penn State Shenango, 147 Shenango Avenue, Sharon, PA 16146-1537. *Phone:* 814-865-5471. *E-mail:* psushenango@psu.edu. *Web site:* http://www.shenango.psu.edu/.

Penn State University Park

University Park, Pennsylvania

General State-related, university, coed **Entrance** Very difficult **Setting** 7,264-acre small-town campus **Total enrollment** 45,185 **Student-faculty ratio** 17:1 **Application deadline** Rolling (freshmen), rolling (transfer) **Freshman admission** 52% were admitted. Average high school GPA 3.55 **Freshman test scores** SAT critical reading scores over 500: 86.9%; SAT math scores over 500: 91.88%; SAT critical reading scores over 600: 42.77%; SAT math scores over 600: 62.42% **Housing** Yes **Expenses** Tuition & Fees: state resident $14,416, nonresident $25,946; Room & Board $8170 **Undergraduates** 45% women, 3% part-time, 2% 25 or older **The most frequently chosen baccalaureate fields are** business/marketing, communications/journalism, engineering **Academic program** English as a second language, advanced placement, accelerated degree program, self-designed majors, honors program, summer session, adult/continuing education programs, internships **Contact** Anne L. Rohrbach, Director for Undergraduate Admissions, Penn State University Park, 201 Shields Building, Box 3000, University Park, PA 16804-3000. *Phone:* 814-865-4700. *Fax:* 814-863-7590. *E-mail:* admissions@psu.edu. *Web site:* http://www.psu.edu/.

Penn State Wilkes-Barre

Lehman, Pennsylvania

General State-related, primarily 2-year, coed **Entrance** Moderately difficult **Setting** 156-acre rural campus **Total enrollment** 711 **Student-faculty ratio** 15:1 **Application deadline** Rolling (freshmen), rolling (transfer) **Freshman admission** 91% were admitted. Average high school GPA 2.95 **Freshman test scores** SAT critical reading scores over 500: 39.79%; SAT math scores over 500: 47.64%; SAT critical reading scores over 600: 5.24%; SAT math scores over 600: 14.66% **Housing** No **Expenses** Tuition & Fees: state resident $12,150, nonresident $18,168 **Undergraduates** 31% women, 14% part-time, 12% 25 or older, 0.3% Native American, 2% Hispanic American, 3% African American, 2% Asian American/Pacific Islander **The most frequently chosen baccalaureate fields are** business/marketing, English, security and protective services **Academic program** Advanced placement, accelerated degree program, self-designed majors, honors program, summer session, adult/continuing education programs, internships **Contact** Mr. Randall C. Deike, Assistant Vice President for Enrollment Management, Penn State Wilkes-Barre, PO PSU, Lehman, PA 18627-0217. *Phone:* 814-865-5471 or toll-free 800-966-6613. *E-mail:* wbadmissions@psu.edu. *Web site:* http://www.wb.psu.edu/.

Penn State Worthington Scranton

Dunmore, Pennsylvania

General State-related, primarily 2-year, coed **Entrance** Moderately difficult **Setting** 43-acre small-town campus **Total enrollment** 1,388 **Student-faculty ratio** 16:1 **Application deadline** Rolling (freshmen), rolling (transfer) **Freshman admission** 89% were admitted. Average high school GPA 2.83 **Freshman test scores** SAT critical reading scores over 500: 30.75%; SAT math scores over 500: 30.43%; SAT critical reading scores over 600: 4.66%; SAT math scores over 600: 6.21% **Housing** No **Expenses** Tuition & Fees: state resident $12,110, nonresident $18,128 **Undergraduates** 51% women, 22% part-time, 21% 25 or older, 0.4% Native American, 3% Hispanic American, 1% African American, 2% Asian American/Pacific Islander **The most frequently chosen baccalaureate fields are** business/marketing, computer and information sciences, family and consumer sciences **Academic program** Advanced placement, accelerated degree program, honors program, summer session, adult/continuing education programs, internships **Contact** Mr. Randall C. Deike, Assistant Vice President for Enrollment Management, Penn State Worthington Scranton, 120 Ridge View Drive, Dunmore, PA 18512-1699. *Phone:* 814-865-5471. *E-mail:* wsadmissions@psu.edu. *Web site:* http://www.sn.psu.edu/.

Penn State York

York, Pennsylvania

General State-related, primarily 2-year, coed **Entrance** Moderately difficult **Setting** 53-acre suburban campus **Total enrollment** 1,505 **Student-faculty ratio** 15:1 **Application deadline** Rolling (freshmen), rolling (transfer) **Freshman admission** 87% were admitted. Average high school GPA 2.91 **Freshman test scores** SAT critical reading scores over 500: 38.97%; SAT math scores over 500: 48.53%; SAT critical reading scores over 600: 8.09%; SAT math scores over 600: 14.71% **Housing** No **Expenses** Tuition & Fees: state resident $12,110, nonresident $18,128 **Undergraduates** 46% women, 32% part-time, 25% 25 or older, 0.1% Native American, 5% Hispanic American, 6% African American, 5% Asian American/Pacific Islander **The most frequently chosen baccalaureate fields are** business/marketing, computer and information sciences, family and consumer sciences **Academic program** English as a second language, advanced placement, accelerated degree program, self-designed majors, honors program, summer session, adult/continuing education programs, internships **Contact** Mr. Randall C. Deike, Assistant Vice President for Enrollment Management, Penn State York, 1031 Edgecomb Avenue, York, PA 17403-3398. *Phone:* 814-865-5471 or toll-free 800-778-6227. *E-mail:* ykadmission@psu.edu. *Web site:* http://www.yk.psu.edu/.

Pennsylvania College of Art & Design

Lancaster, Pennsylvania

General Independent, 4-year, coed **Entrance** Moderately difficult **Setting** urban campus **Total enrollment** 278 **Student-faculty ratio** 9:1 **Application deadline** Rolling (freshmen), rolling (transfer) **Freshman admission** 42% were admitted. Average high school GPA 3.02 **Housing** No **Expenses** Tuition & Fees $17,280 **Undergraduates** 65% women, 9% part-time, 6% 25 or older, 1% Native American, 4% Hispanic American, 4% African American, 3% Asian American/Pacific Islander **The most frequently chosen baccalaureate field is** visual and performing arts **Academic program** Advanced placement, internships **Contact** Director of Admissions, Marketing & Recruitment, Pennsylvania College of Art & Design, 204 North Prince Street, PO Box 59, Lancaster, PA 17608. *Phone:* 717-396-7833. *Fax:* 717-396-1339. *E-mail:* admissions@pcad.edu. *Web site:* http://www.pcad.edu/.

Pennsylvania College of Technology

Williamsport, Pennsylvania

General State-related, 4-year, coed **Entrance** Noncompetitive **Setting** 996-acre small-town campus **Total enrollment** 6,409 **Student-faculty**

Pennsylvania College of Technology (continued)
ratio 18:1 **Application deadline** 7/1 (freshmen), rolling (transfer) **Freshman admission** 88% were admitted **Housing** Yes **Expenses** Tuition & Fees: state resident $12,480, nonresident $15,630; Room & Board $8350 **Undergraduates** 35% women, 15% part-time, 18% 25 or older, 0.4% Native American, 2% Hispanic American, 3% African American, 1% Asian American/Pacific Islander **The most frequently chosen baccalaureate fields are** business/marketing, computer and information sciences, engineering technologies **Academic program** English as a second language, advanced placement, self-designed majors, summer session, internships **Contact** Mr. Dennis Correll, Associate Dean for Admissions/Financial Aid, Pennsylvania College of Technology, One College Avenue, DIF #119, Williamsport, PA 17701. *Phone:* 570-327-4761 Ext. 7337 or toll-free 800-367-9222. *Fax:* 570-321-5551. *E-mail:* dcorrell@pct.edu. *Web site:* http://www.pct.edu/.
Visit Petersons.com and enter keywords Pennsylvania College of Technology

See page 1048 for the College Close-Up.

Philadelphia Biblical University
Langhorne, Pennsylvania

General Independent nondenominational, comprehensive, coed **Entrance** Moderately difficult **Setting** 105-acre suburban campus **Total enrollment** 1,373 **Student-faculty ratio** 14:1 **Application deadline** Rolling (freshmen), rolling (transfer) **Freshman admission** 156% were admitted. Average high school GPA 3.29 **Freshman test scores** SAT critical reading scores over 500: 67.5%; SAT math scores over 500: 57.1%; ACT scores over 18: 88%; SAT critical reading scores over 600: 16.2%; SAT math scores over 600: 12.9%; ACT scores over 24: 38% **Housing** Yes **Expenses** Tuition & Fees $19,997; Room & Board $8050 **Undergraduates** 55% women, 7% part-time, 16% 25 or older, 3% Hispanic American, 12% African American, 4% Asian American/Pacific Islander **The most frequently chosen baccalaureate fields are** education, philosophy and religious studies, public administration and social services **Academic program** Advanced placement, accelerated degree program, honors program, summer session, adult/continuing education programs, internships **Contact** Ms. Lisa Yoder, Director of Undergraduate Admissions, Philadelphia Biblical University, 200 Manor Avenue, Langhorne, PA 19047. *Phone:* 215-702-4550 or toll-free 800-366-0049. *Fax:* 215-702-4248. *E-mail:* admissions@pbu.edu. *Web site:* http://www.pbu.edu/.

Philadelphia University
Philadelphia, Pennsylvania

General Independent, comprehensive, coed **Entrance** Moderately difficult **Setting** 100-acre suburban campus **Total enrollment** 3,497 **Student-faculty ratio** 15:1 **Application deadline** Rolling (freshmen), rolling (transfer) **Freshman admission** 71% were admitted. Average high school GPA 3.4 **Freshman test scores** SAT critical reading scores over 500: 71.6%; SAT math scores over 500: 74.3%; SAT critical reading scores over 600: 16.7%; SAT math scores over 600: 25.4% **Housing** Yes **Expenses** Tuition & Fees $27,498; Room & Board $9182 **Undergraduates** 67% women, 8% part-time, 9% 25 or older, 0.2% Native American, 6% Hispanic American, 10% African American, 4% Asian American/Pacific Islander **The most frequently chosen baccalaureate fields are** business/marketing, architecture, visual and performing arts **Academic program** Advanced placement, accelerated degree program, honors program, summer session, adult/continuing education programs, internships **Contact** Ms. Christine Greb, Director of Admissions, Philadelphia University, School House Lane and Henry Avenue, Philadelphia, PA 19144-5497. *Phone:* 215-951-2800. *Fax:* 215-951-2907. *E-mail:* admissions@philau.edu. *Web site:* http://www.philau.edu/.
Visit Petersons.com and enter keywords Philadelphia University

See page 1050 for the College Close-Up.

Point Park University
Pittsburgh, Pennsylvania

General Independent, comprehensive, coed **Entrance** Moderately difficult **Setting** urban campus **Total enrollment** 3,986 **Student-faculty ratio** 14:1 **Application deadline** Rolling (freshmen), rolling (transfer) **Freshman admission** 72% were admitted. Average high school GPA 3.24 **Freshman test scores** SAT critical reading scores over 500: 63%; SAT math scores over 500: 52%; ACT scores over 18: 90%; SAT critical reading scores over 600: 16%; SAT math scores over 600: 15%; ACT scores over 24: 31% **Housing** Yes **Expenses** Tuition & Fees $21,334; Room & Board $9020 **Undergraduates** 60% women, 24% part-time, 31% 25 or older, 0.3% Native American, 2% Hispanic American, 20% African American, 1% Asian American/Pacific Islander **The most frequently chosen baccalaureate fields are** business/marketing, security and protective services, visual and performing arts **Academic program** English as a second language, advanced placement, accelerated degree program, self-designed majors, honors program, summer session, adult/continuing education programs, internships **Contact** Ms. Joell Minford, Director, Full-Time Admissions, Point Park University, 201 Wood Street, Pittsburgh, PA 15222-1984. *Phone:* 412-392-3430 or toll-free 800-321-0129. *Fax:* 412-392-3902. *E-mail:* enroll@pointpark.edu. *Web site:* http://www.pointpark.edu/.
Visit Petersons.com and enter keywords Point Park

The Restaurant School at Walnut Hill College
Philadelphia, Pennsylvania

General Proprietary, primarily 2-year, coed **Setting** 2-acre urban campus **Total enrollment** 509 **Student-faculty ratio** 29:1 **Application deadline** Rolling (freshmen) **Housing** Yes **Undergraduates** 13% 25 or older **Academic program** Internships **Contact** Mr. Karl D. Becker, Director of Admissions, The Restaurant School at Walnut Hill College, 4207 Walnut Street, Philadelphia, PA 19104-3518. *Phone:* 267-295-2373 or toll-free 877-925-6884 Ext. 3011. *Fax:* 215-222-4219. *E-mail:* kbecker@walnuthillcollege.edu. *Web site:* http://www.walnuthillcollege.edu/.
Visit Petersons.com and enter keyword Walnut

See page 1072 for the College Close-Up.

Robert Morris University
Moon Township, Pennsylvania

General Independent, university, coed **Entrance** Minimally difficult **Setting** 230-acre suburban campus **Total enrollment** 4,783 **Student-faculty ratio** 15:1 **Application deadline** 7/1 (freshmen), 7/1 (transfer) **Freshman admission** 92% were admitted. Average high school GPA 3.26 **Freshman test scores** SAT critical reading scores over 500: 50.1%; SAT math scores over 500: 57.7%; ACT scores over 18: 90.3%; SAT critical reading scores over 600: 10.4%; SAT math scores over 600: 21.6%; ACT scores over 24: 40.8% **Housing** Yes **Expenses** Tuition & Fees $20,560; Room & Board $10,370 **Undergraduates** 45% women, 15% part-time, 18% 25 or older, 0.1% Native American, 1% Hispanic American, 8% African American, 1% Asian American/Pacific Islander **The most frequently chosen baccalaureate fields are** business/marketing, communications/journalism, parks and recreation **Academic program** Advanced placement, accelerated degree program, honors program, summer session, adult/continuing education programs, internships **Contact** Enrollment Services Department, Robert Morris University, 6001 University Boulevard, Moon Township, PA 15108-1189. *Phone:* 412-397-5200 or toll-free 800-762-0097. *Fax:* 412-397-2425. *E-mail:* admissionsoffice@rmu.edu. *Web site:* http://www.rmu.edu/.
Visit Petersons.com and enter keywords Robert Morris

See page 1084 for the College Close-Up.

Rosemont College
Rosemont, Pennsylvania

General Independent Roman Catholic, comprehensive, coed **Entrance** Moderately difficult **Setting** 56-acre suburban campus **Total enrollment**

940 **Student-faculty ratio** 9:1 **Application deadline** Rolling (freshmen), rolling (transfer) **Freshman admission** 54% were admitted. Average high school GPA 3.4 **Freshman test scores** SAT critical reading scores over 500: 29%; SAT math scores over 500: 23%; ACT scores over 18: 100%; SAT critical reading scores over 600: 8%; SAT math scores over 600: 5% **Housing** Yes **Expenses** Tuition & Fees $26,250; Room & Board $10,580 **Undergraduates** 80% women, 22% part-time, 25% 25 or older, 7% Hispanic American, 46% African American, 4% Asian American/Pacific Islander **The most frequently chosen baccalaureate fields are** business/marketing, social sciences, visual and performing arts **Academic program** English as a second language, advanced placement, accelerated degree program, self-designed majors, honors program, summer session, adult/continuing education programs, internships **Contact** Mr. Chuck Walz, Vice President for Enrollment Management, Rosemont College, 1400 Montgomery Avenue, Main Building, Rosemont, PA 19010. *Phone:* 610-527-0200 Ext. 2905 or toll-free 800-331-0708. *Fax:* 610-520-4399. *E-mail:* admissions@rosemont.edu. *Web site:* http://www.rosemont.edu/.

Visit Petersons.com and enter keyword Rosemont

See page 1092 for the College Close-Up.

St. Charles Borromeo Seminary, Overbrook

Wynnewood, Pennsylvania

General Independent Roman Catholic, comprehensive, undergraduate: men only; graduate: coed **Entrance** Moderately difficult **Setting** 77-acre suburban campus **Total enrollment** 245 **Student-faculty ratio** 8:1 **Application deadline** 7/15 (freshmen), 7/15 (transfer) **Freshman admission** 100% were admitted **Housing** Yes **Expenses** Tuition & Fees $15,190; Room & Board $9560 **Undergraduates** 36% part-time, 13% 25 or older, 7% Hispanic American, 2% African American, 4% Asian American/Pacific Islander **The most frequently chosen baccalaureate field is** philosophy and religious studies **Academic program** English as a second language, advanced placement, accelerated degree program, summer session, adult/continuing education programs **Contact** Rev. Msgr. David E. Diamond, Vice Rector, St. Charles Borromeo Seminary, Overbrook, 100 East Wynnewood Road, Wynnewood, PA 19096. *Phone:* 610-785-6271. *Fax:* 610-617-9267. *E-mail:* cao@adphila.org. *Web site:* http://www.scs.edu/.

Saint Francis University

Loretto, Pennsylvania

General Independent Roman Catholic, comprehensive, coed **Entrance** Moderately difficult **Setting** 600-acre rural campus **Total enrollment** 2,300 **Student-faculty ratio** 14:1 **Application deadline** Rolling (freshmen), rolling (transfer) **Freshman admission** 77% were admitted. Average high school GPA 3.47 **Freshman test scores** SAT critical reading scores over 500: 66%; SAT math scores over 500: 68%; ACT scores over 18: 92%; SAT critical reading scores over 600: 17%; SAT math scores over 600: 24%; ACT scores over 24: 60% **Housing** Yes **Expenses** Tuition & Fees $25,554; Room & Board $8716 **Undergraduates** 60% women, 7% part-time, 3% 25 or older, 0.1% Native American, 1% Hispanic American, 5% African American, 1% Asian American/Pacific Islander **The most frequently chosen baccalaureate fields are** business/marketing, education, health professions and related sciences **Academic program** Advanced placement, accelerated degree program, self-designed majors, honors program, summer session, adult/continuing education programs, internships **Contact** Robert Beener, Associate Dean for Enrollment Management, Saint Francis University, PO Box 600, 117 Evergreen Drive, Loretto, PA 15940-0600. *Phone:* 814-472-3100 or toll-free 800-342-5732. *Fax:* 814-472-3335. *E-mail:* rbeener@francis.edu. *Web site:* http://www.francis.edu/.

Visit Petersons.com and enter keywords Saint Francis

See page 1104 for the College Close-Up.

Saint Joseph's University

Philadelphia, Pennsylvania

General Independent Roman Catholic (Jesuit), comprehensive, coed **Entrance** Moderately difficult **Setting** 103-acre suburban campus **Total enrollment** 8,337 **Student-faculty ratio** 14:1 **Application deadline** 2/1 (freshmen), 3/1 (transfer) **Freshman admission** 82% were admitted. Average high school GPA 3.39 **Freshman test scores** SAT critical reading scores over 500: 80%; SAT math scores over 500: 83%; ACT scores over 18: 98%; SAT critical reading scores over 600: 27%; SAT math scores over 600: 35%; ACT scores over 24: 49% **Housing** Yes **Expenses** Tuition & Fees $34,090; Room & Board $11,575 **Undergraduates** 52% women, 16% part-time, 10% 25 or older, 0.1% Native American, 4% Hispanic American, 8% African American, 2% Asian American/Pacific Islander **The most frequently chosen baccalaureate fields are** business/marketing, education, social sciences **Academic program** English as a second language, advanced placement, accelerated degree program, self-designed majors, honors program, summer session, adult/continuing education programs, internships **Contact** Admissions Department, Saint Joseph's University, 5600 City Avenue, Philadelphia, PA 19131-1395. *Phone:* 610-660-1300 or toll-free 888-BEAHAWK. *Fax:* 610-660-1314. *E-mail:* admit@sju.edu. *Web site:* http://www.sju.edu/.

Visit Petersons.com and enter keywords Joseph's University

See page 1114 for the College Close-Up.

Saint Vincent College

Latrobe, Pennsylvania

General Independent Roman Catholic, comprehensive, coed **Entrance** Moderately difficult **Setting** 200-acre suburban campus **Total enrollment** 1,984 **Student-faculty ratio** 13:1 **Application deadline** 4/1 (freshmen), 7/1 (transfer) **Freshman admission** 67% were admitted. Average high school GPA 3.5 **Freshman test scores** SAT critical reading scores over 500: 64.7%; SAT math scores over 500: 70.7%; SAT critical reading scores over 600: 21.1%; SAT math scores over 600: 26.4% **Housing** Yes **Expenses** Tuition & Fees $27,190; Room & Board $9048 **Undergraduates** 47% women, 6% part-time, 5% 25 or older, 0.2% Native American, 2% Hispanic American, 6% African American, 1% Asian American/Pacific Islander **The most frequently chosen baccalaureate fields are** biological/life sciences, business/marketing, psychology **Academic program** Advanced placement, accelerated degree program, honors program, summer session, internships **Contact** Mr. David Collins, Assistant Vice President of Admission and Financial Aid, Saint Vincent College, 300 Fraser Purchase Road, Latrobe, PA 15650-2690. *Phone:* 800-782-5549 or toll-free 800-782-5549. *Fax:* 724-532-5069. *E-mail:* admission@stvincent.edu. *Web site:* http://www.stvincent.edu/.

Visit Petersons.com and enter keyword Vincent

Seton Hill University

Greensburg, Pennsylvania

General Independent Roman Catholic, comprehensive, coed **Entrance** Moderately difficult **Setting** 200-acre small-town campus **Total enrollment** 2,145 **Student-faculty ratio** 15:1 **Application deadline** 8/15 (freshmen), rolling (transfer) **Freshman admission** 66% were admitted. Average high school GPA 3.24 **Housing** Yes **Expenses** Tuition & Fees $26,622; Room & Board $8810 **Undergraduates** 63% women, 21% part-time, 6% 25 or older **The most frequently chosen baccalaureate fields are** business/marketing, public administration and social services, visual and performing arts **Academic program** English as a second language, advanced placement, accelerated degree program, self-designed majors, honors program, summer session, adult/continuing education programs, internships **Contact** Ms. Sherri Bett, Director of Admissions, Seton Hill University, Seton Hill Drive, Greensburg, PA 15601. *Phone:* 724-838-4255 or toll-free 800-826-6234. *Fax:* 724-830-1294. *E-mail:* admit@setonhill.edu. *Web site:* http://www.setonhill.edu/.

Visit Petersons.com and enter keywords Seton Hill

See page 1154 for the College Close-Up.

SAINT FRANCIS UNIVERSITY • P.O. BOX 600 • LORETTO, PA 15940 • 866-DIAL SFU (866-342-5738) • www.francis.edu

Shippensburg University of Pennsylvania

Shippensburg, Pennsylvania

General State-supported, comprehensive, coed **Entrance** Moderately difficult **Setting** 200-acre rural campus **Total enrollment** 8,253 **Student-faculty ratio** 20:1 **Application deadline** Rolling (freshmen), rolling (transfer) **Freshman admission** 72% were admitted. Average high school GPA 3.2 **Freshman test scores** SAT critical reading scores over 500: 50.3%; SAT math scores over 500: 56.2%; ACT scores over 18: 81.5%; SAT critical reading scores over 600: 10.5%; SAT math scores over 600: 13.7%; ACT scores over 24: 16.8% **Housing** Yes **Expenses** Tuition & Fees: state resident $7444, nonresident $15,776; Room & Board $7086 **Undergraduates** 53% women, 4% part-time, 6% 25 or older, 0.2% Native American, 2% Hispanic American, 7% African American, 1% Asian American/Pacific Islander **The most frequently chosen baccalaureate fields are** business/marketing, education, psychology **Academic program** Advanced placement, accelerated degree program, honors program, summer session, internships **Contact** Dr. Thomas Speakman, Dean of Enrollment Services, Shippensburg University of Pennsylvania, 1871 Old Main Drive, Shippensburg, PA 17257-2299. *Phone:* 717-477-1231 or toll-free 800-822-8028. *Fax:* 717-477-4016. *E-mail:* admiss@ship.edu. *Web site:* http://www.ship.edu/.
Visit Petersons.com and enter keyword Shippensburg

See page 1156 for the College Close-Up.

Slippery Rock University of Pennsylvania

Slippery Rock, Pennsylvania

General State-supported, comprehensive, coed **Entrance** Moderately difficult **Setting** 650-acre rural campus **Total enrollment** 8,648 **Student-faculty ratio** 20:1 **Freshman admission** 63% were admitted. Average high school GPA 3.39 **Freshman test scores** SAT critical reading scores over 500: 54.87%; SAT math scores over 500: 61.03%; ACT scores over 18: 91.25%; SAT critical reading scores over 600: 8.69%; SAT math scores over 600: 13.89%; ACT scores over 24: 26.79% **Housing** Yes **Expenses** Tuition & Fees: state resident $7235, nonresident $10,012; Room & Board $8454 **Undergraduates** 56% women, 7% part-time, 9% 25 or older, 0.3% Native American, 1% Hispanic American, 5% African American, 1% Asian American/Pacific Islander **The most frequently chosen baccalaureate fields are** business/marketing, education, health professions and related sciences **Academic program** Advanced placement, self-designed majors, honors program, summer session, adult/continuing education programs, internships **Contact** Ms. Mimi Campbell, Director of Admissions, Slippery Rock University of Pennsylvania, 1 Morrow Way, Slippery Rock, PA 16057-1383. *Phone:* 724-738-2015 or toll-free 800-SRU-9111. *Fax:* 724-738-2913. *E-mail:* asktherock@sru.edu. *Web site:* http://www.sru.edu/.

Strayer University–Allentown Campus

Center Valley, Pennsylvania

General Proprietary, comprehensive, coed **Contact** Admissions Office, Strayer University–Allentown Campus, 3800 Sierra Circle, Suite 300, Center Valley, PA 18034. *Phone:* 484-809-7770. *Web site:* http://www.strayer.edu/allentown.

Strayer University–Center City Campus

Philadelphia, Pennsylvania

General Proprietary, comprehensive, coed **Contact** Admissions Office, Strayer University–Center City Campus, 1601 Cherry Street, Suite 100,

Philadelphia, PA 19102. *Phone:* 267-256-0200. *Web site:* http://www.strayer.edu/center_city.

Strayer University–Cranberry Woods Campus

Cranberry Township, Pennsylvania

General Proprietary, comprehensive, coed **Contact** Admissions Office, Strayer University–Cranberry Woods Campus, Regional Learning Alliance, 850 Cranberry Woods Drive, Suite 2241, Cranberry Township, PA 16066. *Phone:* 724-741-1064. *Web site:* http://www.strayer.edu/cranberry_woods.

Strayer University–Delaware County Campus

Springfield, Pennsylvania

General Proprietary, comprehensive, coed **Contact** Admissions Office, Strayer University–Delaware County Campus, 760 West Sproul Road, Suite 200, Springfield, PA 19064-1215. *Phone:* 610-604-7700. *Web site:* http://www.strayer.edu/delaware_county.

Strayer University–King of Prussia Campus

King of Prussia, Pennsylvania

General Proprietary, comprehensive, coed **Contact** Admissions Office, Strayer University–King of Prussia Campus, 234 Mall Boulevard, Suite G-50, King of Prussia, PA 19406. *Phone:* 610-992-1700. *Web site:* http://www.strayer.edu/king_of_prussia.

Strayer University–Lower Bucks County Campus

Trevose, Pennsylvania

General Proprietary, comprehensive, coed **Contact** Admissions Office, Strayer University–Lower Bucks County Campus, 3600 Horizon Boulevard, Suite 100, Trevose, PA 19053. *Phone:* 215-953-5999. *Web site:* http://www.strayer.edu/lower_bucks_county.

Strayer University–Penn Center West Campus

Pittsburgh, Pennsylvania

General Proprietary, comprehensive, coed **Contact** Admissions Office, Strayer University–Penn Center West Campus, One Penn Center West, Suite 320, Pittsburgh, PA 15276. *Phone:* 412-747-7800. *Web site:* http://www.strayer.edu/penn_center_west.

Susquehanna University

Selinsgrove, Pennsylvania

General Independent, 4-year, coed, affiliated with Evangelical Lutheran Church in America **Entrance** Moderately difficult **Setting** 306-acre small-town campus **Total enrollment** 2,231 **Student-faculty ratio** 13:1 **Application deadline** 3/1 (freshmen), 7/1 (transfer) **Freshman admission** 75% were admitted. Average high school GPA 3.24 **Freshman test scores** SAT critical reading scores over 500: 78.6%; SAT math scores over 500: 80.4%; ACT scores over 18: 100%; SAT critical reading scores over 600: 27.2%; SAT math scores over 600: 29.9%; ACT scores over 24: 67.8% **Housing** Yes **Expenses** Tuition & Fees $32,850; Room & Board $8800 **Undergraduates** 53% women, 2% part-time, 2% 25 or older, 0.1% Native American, 3% Hispanic American, 3% African American, 2% Asian American/Pacific Islander **The most frequently chosen baccalaureate fields are** business/marketing, communications/journalism, English **Academic program** Advanced placement, accelerated degree program, self-designed majors, honors program, summer session, internships **Contact** Mr. Chris Markle, Director of Admissions, Susquehanna University, 514 University Avenue, Selinsgrove, PA 17870. *Phone:* 570-372-4260 or toll-free 800-326-9672. *Fax:* 570-372-2722. *E-mail:* suadmiss@susqu.edu. *Web site:* http://www.susqu.edu/.
Visit Petersons.com and enter keyword Susquehanna

See page 1208 for the College Close-Up.

Swarthmore College

Swarthmore, Pennsylvania

General Independent, 4-year, coed **Entrance** Most difficult **Setting** 357-acre suburban campus **Total enrollment** 1,525 **Student-faculty ratio** 8:1 **Application deadline** 1/2 (freshmen), 4/1 (transfer) **Freshman admission** 17% were admitted **Freshman test scores** SAT critical reading scores over 500: 99.5%; SAT math scores over 500: 99.7%; ACT scores over 18: 100%; SAT critical reading scores over 600: 92%; SAT math scores over 600: 94.4%; ACT scores over 24: 98.4% **Housing** Yes **Expenses** Tuition & Fees $37,860; Room & Board $11,740 **Undergraduates** 52% women, 1% part-time, 1% Native American, 11% Hispanic American, 10% African American, 16% Asian American/Pacific Islander **The most frequently chosen baccalaureate fields are** biological/life sciences, social sciences, visual and performing arts **Academic program** Advanced placement, accelerated degree program, self-designed majors, honors program, internships **Contact** Mr. Jim Bock, Dean of Admissions and Financial Aid, Swarthmore College, 500 College Avenue, Swarthmore, PA 19081. *Phone:* 610-328-8300 or toll-free 800-667-3110. *Fax:* 610-328-8580. *E-mail:* admissions@swarthmore.edu. *Web site:* http://www.swarthmore.edu/.

Talmudical Yeshiva of Philadelphia

Philadelphia, Pennsylvania

General Independent Jewish, 4-year, men only **Entrance** Moderately difficult **Setting** 3-acre urban campus **Total enrollment** 112 **Application deadline** 7/15 (freshmen), 7/15 (transfer) **Housing** Yes **Academic program** Honors program, internships **Contact** Rabbi Shmuel Kamenetsky, Co-Dean, Talmudical Yeshiva of Philadelphia, 6063 Drexel Road, Philadelphia, PA 19131-1296. *Phone:* 215-473-1212.

Temple University

Philadelphia, Pennsylvania

General State-related, university, coed **Entrance** Moderately difficult **Setting** 115-acre urban campus **Total enrollment** 36,505 **Student-faculty ratio** 17:1 **Application deadline** 3/1 (freshmen), 6/1 (transfer) **Freshman admission** 61% were admitted. Average high school GPA 3.41 **Freshman test scores** SAT critical reading scores over 500: 74%; SAT math scores over 500: 80%; ACT scores over 18: 92%; SAT critical reading scores over 600: 27%; SAT math scores over 600: 32%; ACT scores over 24: 47% **Housing** Yes **Expenses** Tuition & Fees: state resident $11,764, nonresident $21,044; Room & Board $9198 **Undergraduates** 53% women, 11% part-time, 13% 25 or older, 0.3% Native American, 4% Hispanic American, 16% African American, 10% Asian American/Pacific Islander **The most frequently chosen baccalaureate fields are** business/marketing, communications/journalism, visual and performing arts **Academic program** English as a second language, advanced placement, self-designed majors, honors program, summer session, adult/continuing education programs, internships **Contact** Ms. Karin Mormando, Director, Undergraduate Admissions, Temple University, 1801 North Broad Street, Philadelphia, PA 19122-6096. *Phone:* 215-204-7200 or toll-free 888-340-2222. *E-mail:* tuadm@temple.edu. *Web site:* http://www.temple.edu/.
Visit Petersons.com and enter keyword Temple

See page 1214 for the College Close-Up.

Thiel College

Greenville, Pennsylvania

General Independent, 4-year, coed, affiliated with Evangelical Lutheran Church in America **Setting** 135-acre rural campus **Total enrollment** 999

Thiel College (continued)

Student-faculty ratio 13:1 **Application deadline** Rolling (freshmen), rolling (transfer) **Freshman admission** 72% were admitted. Average high school GPA 3 **Freshman test scores** SAT critical reading scores over 500: 29.9%; SAT math scores over 500: 33.4%; ACT scores over 18: 72.8%; SAT critical reading scores over 600: 4.5%; SAT math scores over 600: 4.6%; ACT scores over 24: 19.1% **Housing** Yes **Expenses** Tuition & Fees $20,998; Room & Board $8790 **Undergraduates** 47% women, 6% part-time, 5% 25 or older, 0.3% Native American, 1% Hispanic American, 4% African American, 0.4% Asian American/Pacific Islander **The most frequently chosen baccalaureate fields are** business/marketing, psychology, security and protective services **Academic program** Advanced placement, honors program, summer session, adult/continuing education programs, internships **Contact** Ms. Amy Becker, Chief Admissions Officer, Thiel College, 75 College Avenue, Greenville, PA 16125. *Phone:* 724-589-2182 or toll-free 800-248-4435. *Fax:* 724-589-2013. *E-mail:* admissions@thiel.edu. *Web site:* http://www.thiel.edu/.

Thomas Jefferson University
Philadelphia, Pennsylvania

Contact Ms. Karen Jacobs, Director of Admissions, Thomas Jefferson University, Edison Building, 130 South Ninth Street, Philadelphia, PA 19107. *Phone:* 215-503-8890 or toll-free 877-533-3247. *Fax:* 215-503-7241. *E-mail:* chpadmissions@mail.tju.edu. *Web site:* http://www.jefferson.edu/.

Visit Petersons.com and enter keyword Jefferson

See page 1224 for the College Close-Up.

University of Pennsylvania
Philadelphia, Pennsylvania

General Independent, university, coed **Entrance** Most difficult **Setting** 279-acre urban campus **Total enrollment** 19,311 **Student-faculty ratio** 6:1 **Application deadline** 1/1 (freshmen), 3/15 (transfer) **Freshman admission** 18% were admitted. Average high school GPA 3.86 **Freshman test scores** SAT critical reading scores over 500: 100%; SAT math scores over 500: 101%; ACT scores over 18: 99%; SAT critical reading scores over 600: 94%; SAT math scores over 600: 98%; ACT scores over 24: 99% **Housing** Yes **Expenses** Tuition & Fees $40,514; Room & Board $11,430 **Undergraduates** 51% women, 3% part-time, 1% 25 or older, 0.5% Native American, 6% Hispanic American, 8% African American, 19% Asian American/Pacific Islander **The most frequently chosen baccalaureate fields are** business/marketing, engineering, social sciences **Academic program** English as a second language, advanced placement, accelerated degree program, self-designed majors, honors program, summer session, adult/continuing education programs, internships **Contact** Eric J. Furda, Dean of Admissions, University of Pennsylvania, 1 College Hall, Levy Park, Philadelphia, PA 19104. *Phone:* 215-898-7507. *E-mail:* info@admissions.ugao.upenn.edu. *Web site:* http://www.upenn.edu/.

University of Phoenix–Philadelphia Campus
Wayne, Pennsylvania

General Proprietary, comprehensive, coed **Entrance** Noncompetitive **Setting** urban campus **Total enrollment** 883 **Application deadline** Rolling (freshmen), rolling (transfer) **Housing** No **Expenses** Tuition & Fees $13,875 **Undergraduates** 72% women, 80% 25 or older, 0.3% Native American, 4% Hispanic American, 47% African American, 1% Asian American/Pacific Islander **The most frequently chosen baccalaureate fields are** business/marketing, computer and information sciences, security and protective services **Academic program** Advanced placement, accelerated degree program, adult/continuing education programs **Contact** Ms. Audra McQuarie, Registrar/Executive Director, University of Phoenix–Philadelphia Campus, 4035 South Riverpoint Parkway, Mail Stop CF-L101, Phoenix, AZ 85040. *Phone:* 480-557-6151 or toll-free 800-776-4867 (in-state); 800-228-7240 (out-of-state). *Fax:* 480-643-3068. *E-mail:* audra.mcquarie@phoenix.edu. *Web site:* http://www.phoenix.edu/.

University of Phoenix–Pittsburgh Campus
Pittsburgh, Pennsylvania

General Proprietary, comprehensive, coed **Entrance** Noncompetitive **Setting** urban campus **Total enrollment** 101 **Application deadline** Rolling (freshmen), rolling (transfer) **Freshman admission** 100% were admitted **Housing** No **Expenses** Tuition & Fees $13,875 **Undergraduates** 49% women, 95% 25 or older, 1% Native American, 22% African American **The most frequently chosen baccalaureate fields are** business/marketing, computer and information sciences, security and protective services **Academic program** Advanced placement, accelerated degree program, adult/continuing education programs **Contact** Ms. Audra McQuarie, Registrar/Executive Director, University of Phoenix–Pittsburgh Campus, 4035 South Riverpoint Parkway, Mail Stop CF-L101, Phoenix, AZ 85040. *Phone:* 480-557-6151 or toll-free 800-776-4867 (in-state); 800-228-7240 (out-of-state). *Fax:* 480-643-3068. *E-mail:* audra.mcquarie@phoenix.edu. *Web site:* http://www.phoenix.edu/.

University of Pittsburgh
Pittsburgh, Pennsylvania

General State-related, university, coed **Entrance** Moderately difficult **Setting** 132-acre urban campus **Total enrollment** 28,328 **Student-faculty ratio** 15:1 **Application deadline** Rolling (freshmen), rolling (transfer) **Freshman admission** 59% were admitted. Average high school GPA 3.87 **Freshman test scores** SAT critical reading scores over 500: 97%; SAT math scores over 500: 98%; ACT scores over 18: 99%; SAT critical reading scores over 600: 61%; SAT math scores over 600: 74%; ACT scores over 24: 87% **Housing** Yes **Expenses** Tuition & Fees: state resident $14,154, nonresident $23,852; Room & Board $8900 **Undergraduates** 51% women, 7% part-time, 8% 25 or older, 0.1% Native American, 1% Hispanic American, 8% African American, 5% Asian American/Pacific Islander **The most frequently chosen baccalaureate fields are** business/marketing, English, social sciences **Academic program** English as a second language, advanced placement, accelerated degree program, self-designed majors, honors program, summer session, adult/continuing education programs, internships **Contact** Dr. Betsy A. Porter, Director of Office of Admissions and Financial Aid, University of Pittsburgh, 4227 Fifth Avenue, First Floor, Alumni Hall, Pittsburgh, PA 15260. *Phone:* 412-624-7488. *Fax:* 412-648-8815. *E-mail:* oafa@pitt.edu. *Web site:* http://www.pitt.edu/.

University of Pittsburgh at Bradford
Bradford, Pennsylvania

General State-related, 4-year, coed **Entrance** Minimally difficult **Setting** 317-acre small-town campus **Total enrollment** 1,652 **Student-faculty ratio** 18:1 **Application deadline** Rolling (freshmen), rolling (transfer) **Freshman admission** 48% were admitted. Average high school GPA 3.11 **Freshman test scores** SAT critical reading scores over 500: 45.5%; SAT math scores over 500: 48.41%; ACT scores over 18: 95%; SAT critical reading scores over 600: 6.35%; SAT math scores over 600: 11.9%; ACT scores over 24: 21.67% **Housing** Yes **Expenses** Tuition & Fees: state resident $11,722, nonresident $21,282; Room & Board $7480 **Undergraduates** 55% women, 12% part-time, 19% 25 or older, 1% Native American, 1% Hispanic American, 6% African American, 2% Asian American/Pacific Islander **The most frequently chosen baccalaureate fields are** business/marketing, health professions and related sciences, social sciences **Academic program** Advanced placement, accelerated degree program, summer session, adult/continuing education programs, internships **Contact** Ms. Vicky Pingie, Associate Director of Admissions, University of Pittsburgh at Bradford, 300 Campus Drive, Bradford, PA 16701. *Phone:* 814-362-7552 or toll-free 800-872-1787. *Fax:* 814-362-5150. *E-mail:* monti@pitt.edu. *Web site:* http://www.upb.pitt.edu/.

Visit Petersons.com and enter keywords Pittsburgh at Bradford

See page 1298 for the College Close-Up.

University of Pittsburgh at Greensburg

Greensburg, Pennsylvania

General State-related, 4-year, coed **Entrance** Moderately difficult **Setting** 219-acre small-town campus **Total enrollment** 1,808 **Student-faculty ratio** 18:1 **Application deadline** 8/1 (freshmen), 8/1 (transfer) **Freshman admission** 74% were admitted. Average high school GPA 3.37 **Freshman test scores** SAT critical reading scores over 500: 56.35%; SAT math scores over 500: 58.28%; ACT scores over 18: 91.67%; SAT critical reading scores over 600: 9.59%; SAT math scores over 600: 15.35%; ACT scores over 24: 20% **Housing** Yes **Expenses** Tuition & Fees: state resident $11,852, nonresident $21,412; Room & Board $7840 **Undergraduates** 49% women, 7% part-time, 8% 25 or older, 0.2% Native American, 2% Hispanic American, 5% African American, 2% Asian American/Pacific Islander **The most frequently chosen baccalaureate fields are** business/marketing, English, psychology **Academic program** Advanced placement, accelerated degree program, self-designed majors, summer session, adult/continuing education programs, internships **Contact** Ms. Heather Kabala, Director of Admissions, University of Pittsburgh at Greensburg, 150 Finoli Drive, Greensburg, PA 15601. *Phone:* 724-836-9880. *Fax:* 724-836-7471. *E-mail:* upgadmit@pitt.edu. *Web site:* http://www.greensburg.pitt.edu/.

University of Pittsburgh at Johnstown

Johnstown, Pennsylvania

General State-related, 4-year, coed **Entrance** Moderately difficult **Setting** 650-acre suburban campus **Total enrollment** 3,057 **Student-faculty ratio** 18:1 **Application deadline** Rolling (freshmen), rolling (transfer) **Freshman admission** 85% were admitted. Average high school GPA 3.36 **Freshman test scores** SAT critical reading scores over 500: 49.62%; SAT math scores over 500: 58.36%; ACT scores over 18: 84.03%; SAT critical reading scores over 600: 8.73%; SAT math scores over 600: 15.7%; ACT scores over 24: 23.53% **Housing** Yes **Expenses** Tuition & Fees: state resident $11,754, nonresident $21,314; Room & Board $7290 **Undergraduates** 46% women, 4% part-time, 7% 25 or older, 0.1% Native American, 1% Hispanic American, 2% African American, 2% Asian American/Pacific Islander **The most frequently chosen baccalaureate fields are** business/marketing, education, engineering technologies **Academic program** Advanced placement, accelerated degree program, self-designed majors, summer session, adult/continuing education programs, internships **Contact** Office of Admissions, University of Pittsburgh at Johnstown, 157 Blackington Hall, Johnstown, PA 15904. *Phone:* 814-269-7050 or toll-free 800-765-4875. *Fax:* 814-269-7044. *E-mail:* upjadmit@pitt.edu. *Web site:* http://www.upj.pitt.edu/.

Visit Petersons.com and enter keyword Johnstown

University of Pittsburgh at Titusville

Titusville, Pennsylvania

General State-related, primarily 2-year, coed **Entrance** Minimally difficult **Setting** 10-acre small-town campus **Total enrollment** 544 **Application deadline** Rolling (freshmen), rolling (transfer) **Freshman admission** 84% were admitted. Average high school GPA 2.94 **Freshman test scores** SAT critical reading scores over 500: 19.3%; SAT math scores over 500: 22.8%; ACT scores over 18: 58.62%; SAT critical reading scores over 600: 2.34%; SAT math scores over 600: 1.75%; ACT scores over 24: 10.34% **Housing** Yes **Expenses** Tuition & Fees: state resident $10,500, nonresident $19,120; Room & Board $8156 **Undergraduates** 65% women, 14% part-time, 15% 25 or older, 1% Native American, 2% Hispanic American, 20% African American, 2% Asian American/Pacific Islander **Academic program** Advanced placement, summer session, internships **Contact** Mr. John R. Mumford, Executive Director of Enrollment Management, University of Pittsburgh at Titusville, University of Pittsburgh at Titusville, PO Box 287, Titusville, PA 16354. *Phone:* 814-827-4409 or toll-free 888-878-0462. *Fax:* 814-827-4519. *E-mail:* uptadm@pitt.edu. *Web site:* http://www.upt.pitt.edu/.

The University of Scranton

Scranton, Pennsylvania

General Independent Roman Catholic (Jesuit), comprehensive, coed **Entrance** Moderately difficult **Setting** 50-acre urban campus **Total enrollment** 5,811 **Student-faculty ratio** 12:1 **Application deadline** 3/1 (freshmen), rolling (transfer) **Freshman admission** 70% were admitted. Average high school GPA 3.35 **Freshman test scores** SAT critical reading scores over 500: 82%; SAT math scores over 500: 86.3%; SAT critical reading scores over 600: 25.5%; SAT math scores over 600: 35.4% **Housing** Yes **Expenses** Tuition & Fees $34,536; Room & Board $11,862 **Undergraduates** 56% women, 5% part-time, 4% 25 or older, 0.3% Native American, 4% Hispanic American, 1% African American, 3% Asian American/Pacific Islander **The most frequently chosen baccalaureate fields are** business/marketing, education, health professions and related sciences **Academic program** Advanced placement, accelerated degree program, self-designed majors, honors program, summer session, adult/continuing education programs, internships **Contact** Mr. Joseph Roback, Associate Vice President, Undergraduate Admissions and Enrollment, The University of Scranton, 800 Linden Street, The Estate Room 208, Scranton, PA 18510-4501. *Phone:* 570-941-7540 or toll-free 888-SCRANTON. *Fax:* 570-941-5928. *E-mail:* admissions@scranton.edu. *Web site:* http://www.scranton.edu/.

The University of the Arts

Philadelphia, Pennsylvania

General Independent, comprehensive, coed **Entrance** Moderately difficult **Setting** 18-acre urban campus **Total enrollment** 2,401 **Student-faculty ratio** 10:1 **Application deadline** Rolling (freshmen), rolling (transfer) **Freshman admission** 52% were admitted. Average high school GPA 2.90 **Freshman test scores** SAT critical reading scores over 500: 67.5%; SAT math scores over 500: 56%; ACT scores over 18: 88%; SAT critical reading scores over 600: 23%; SAT math scores over 600: 13.5%; ACT scores over 24: 39% **Housing** Yes **Expenses** Tuition & Fees $31,000; Room only $7200 **Undergraduates** 57% women, 2% part-time, 4% 25 or older, 1% Native American, 5% Hispanic American, 10% African American, 3% Asian American/Pacific Islander **The most frequently chosen baccalaureate fields are** communications/journalism, education, visual and performing arts **Academic program** English as a second language, advanced placement, internships **Contact** Ms. Susan Gandy, Director of Admission, The University of the Arts, 320 South Broad Street, Philadelphia, PA 19102-4944. *Phone:* 215-717-6030 or toll-free 800-616-ARTS. *Fax:* 215-717-6045. *E-mail:* admissions@uarts.edu. *Web site:* http://www.uarts.edu/.

Visit Petersons.com and enter keywords University of the Arts

See page 1314 for the College Close-Up.

University of the Sciences in Philadelphia

Philadelphia, Pennsylvania

General Independent, university, coed **Entrance** Moderately difficult **Setting** 35-acre urban campus **Total enrollment** 2,984 **Student-faculty ratio** 14:1 **Application deadline** Rolling (freshmen) **Freshman admission** 62% were admitted. Average high school GPA 3.6 **Freshman test scores** SAT critical reading scores over 500: 85%; SAT math scores over 500: 97%; ACT scores over 18: 99%; SAT critical reading scores

The University of the Arts

320 South Broad Street
Philadelphia, PA 19102-4944

E-mail: admissions@uarts.edu
Phone: 215-717-6030

See our profile page for more information about our school.

University of the Sciences in Philadelphia (continued)

over 600: 26%; SAT math scores over 600: 56%; ACT scores over 24: 70% **Housing** Yes **Expenses** Tuition & Fees $29,630; Room & Board $11,582 **Undergraduates** 60% women, 2% part-time, 4% 25 or older, 0.2% Native American, 2% Hispanic American, 4% African American, 38% Asian American/Pacific Islander **The most frequently chosen baccalaureate fields are** biological/life sciences, health professions and related sciences, physical sciences **Academic program** English as a second language, advanced placement, honors program, summer session, adult/continuing education programs, internships **Contact** Ms. Dianna Collins, Executive Director of Admission and Enrollment Services, University of the Sciences in Philadelphia, 600 South 43rd Street, Philadelphia, PA 19104-4495. *Phone:* 215-596-8815 or toll-free 888-996-8747. *Fax:* 215-596-8821. *E-mail:* admit@usp.edu. *Web site:* http://www.usip.edu/.

Visit Petersons.com and enter keywords Sciences in Philadelphia

See page 1316 for the College Close-Up.

Ursinus College
Collegeville, Pennsylvania

General Independent, 4-year, coed **Entrance** Very difficult **Setting** 168-acre suburban campus **Total enrollment** 1,742 **Student-faculty ratio** 12:1 **Application deadline** 2/15 (freshmen), 8/15 (transfer) **Freshman admission** 57% were admitted. Average high school GPA 3.63 **Freshman test scores** SAT critical reading scores over 500: 96%; SAT math scores over 500: 96%; ACT scores over 18: 100%; SAT critical reading scores over 600: 65%; SAT math scores over 600: 62%; ACT scores over 24: 81% **Housing** Yes **Expenses** Tuition & Fees $40,120; Room & Board $9750 **Undergraduates** 54% women, 1% part-time, 0.2% Native American, 3% Hispanic American, 6% African American, 4% Asian American/Pacific Islander **The most frequently chosen baccalaureate fields are** biological/life sciences, parks and recreation, social sciences **Academic program** English as a second language, advanced placement, self-designed majors, honors program, internships **Contact** Mr. Richard Floyd, Dean of Admission, Ursinus College, PO Box 1000, Main Street, Collegeville, PA 19426. *Phone:* 610-409-3200. *Fax:* 610-409-3197. *E-mail:* admissions@ursinus.edu. *Web site:* http://www.ursinus.edu/.

Valley Forge Christian College
Phoenixville, Pennsylvania

General Independent Assemblies of God, comprehensive, coed **Entrance** Minimally difficult **Setting** 106-acre small-town campus **Total enrollment** 1,204 **Student-faculty ratio** 19:1 **Application deadline** 8/1 (freshmen), 8/1 (transfer) **Freshman admission** 73% were admitted. Average high school GPA 3.71 **Freshman test scores** SAT critical reading scores over 500: 57.5%; SAT math scores over 500: 39.5%; ACT scores over 18: 71.9%; SAT critical reading scores over 600: 14.2%; SAT math scores over 600: 9.9%; ACT scores over 24: 28.1% **Housing** Yes **Expenses** Tuition & Fees $16,250; Room & Board $7556 **Undergraduates** 52% women, 27% part-time, 13% 25 or older **The most frequently chosen baccalaureate fields are** education, psychology, theology and religious vocations **Academic program** English as a second language, advanced placement, honors program, summer session, adult/continuing education programs, internships **Contact** Rev. William Chenco, Director of Admissions, Valley Forge Christian College, 1401 Charlestown Road, Phoenixville, PA 19460. *Phone:* 610-935-0450 Ext. 1430 or toll-free 800-432-8322. *Fax:* 610-917-2069. *E-mail:* admissions@vfcc.edu. *Web site:* http://www.vfcc.edu/.

Villanova University
Villanova, Pennsylvania

General Independent Roman Catholic, comprehensive, coed **Entrance** Very difficult **Setting** 254-acre suburban campus **Total enrollment**

10,375 **Student-faculty ratio** 11:1 **Application deadline** 1/7 (freshmen), 6/1 (transfer) **Freshman admission** 46% were admitted. Average high school GPA 3.76 **Freshman test scores** SAT critical reading scores over 500: 96%; SAT math scores over 500: 97%; ACT scores over 18: 100%; SAT critical reading scores over 600: 69%; SAT math scores over 600: 82%; ACT scores over 24: 96% **Housing** Yes **Expenses** Tuition & Fees $38,305; Room & Board $10,320 **Undergraduates** 50% women, 8% part-time, 9% 25 or older, 0.1% Native American, 7% Hispanic American, 5% African American, 7% Asian American/Pacific Islander **The most frequently chosen baccalaureate fields are** business/marketing, engineering, health professions and related sciences **Academic program** English as a second language, advanced placement, accelerated degree program, honors program, summer session, adult/continuing education programs, internships **Contact** Mr. Michael Gaynor, Director of University Admission, Villanova University, 800 Lancaster Avenue, Villanova, PA 19085-1672. *Phone:* 610-519-4000. *Fax:* 610-519-6450. *E-mail:* gotovu@villanova.edu. *Web site:* http://www.villanova.edu/.

Visit Petersons.com and enter keyword Villanova

See page 1334 for the College Close-Up.

Washington & Jefferson College
Washington, Pennsylvania

General Independent, 4-year, coed **Entrance** Very difficult **Setting** 60-acre small-town campus **Total enrollment** 1,514 **Student-faculty ratio** 12:1 **Application deadline** 3/1 (freshmen), rolling (transfer) **Freshman admission** 42% were admitted. Average high school GPA 3.34 **Freshman test scores** SAT critical reading scores over 500: 80%; SAT math scores over 500: 87%; ACT scores over 18: 100%; SAT critical reading scores over 600: 31%; SAT math scores over 600: 39%; ACT scores over 24: 63% **Housing** Yes **Expenses** Tuition & Fees $32,895; Room & Board $8925 **Undergraduates** 48% women, 1% part-time, 1% 25 or older, 0.5% Native American, 1% Hispanic American, 3% African American, 1% Asian American/Pacific Islander **The most frequently chosen baccalaureate fields are** business/marketing, psychology, social sciences **Academic program** Advanced placement, accelerated degree program, self-designed majors, honors program, summer session, internships **Contact** Mr. Alton E. Newell, Vice President for Enrollment, Washington & Jefferson College, 60 South Lincoln Street, Washington, PA 15301. *Phone:* 724-223-6025 or toll-free 888-WANDJAY. *Fax:* 724-223-6534. *E-mail:* admission@washjeff.edu. *Web site:* http://www.washjeff.edu/.

Waynesburg University
Waynesburg, Pennsylvania

General Independent, comprehensive, coed, affiliated with Presbyterian Church (U.S.A.) **Entrance** Moderately difficult **Setting** 30-acre small-town campus **Total enrollment** 2,515 **Student-faculty ratio** 15:1 **Application deadline** Rolling (freshmen), rolling (transfer) **Freshman admission** 71% were admitted. Average high school GPA 3.43 **Housing** Yes **Expenses** Tuition & Fees $17,760; Room & Board $7370 **Undergraduates** 62% women, 10% part-time, 18% 25 or older, 0.3% Native American, 1% Hispanic American, 3% African American, 0.4% Asian American/Pacific Islander **The most frequently chosen baccalaureate fields are** business/marketing, education, health professions and related sciences **Academic program** Advanced placement, accelerated degree program, honors program, adult/continuing education programs, internships **Contact** Ms. Robin L. King, Dean of Admissions, Waynesburg University, 51 West College Street, Waynesburg, PA 15370. *Phone:* 724-852-3333 or toll-free 800-225-7393. *Fax:* 724-627-8124. *E-mail:* admissions@waynesburg.edu. *Web site:* http://www.waynesburg.edu/.

West Chester University of Pennsylvania
West Chester, Pennsylvania

General State-supported, comprehensive, coed **Entrance** Moderately difficult **Setting** 403-acre suburban campus **Total enrollment** 14,211 **Student-faculty ratio** 17:1 **Application deadline** Rolling (freshmen), rolling (transfer) **Freshman admission** 49% were admitted. Average high school GPA 3.32 **Freshman test scores** SAT critical reading scores over 500: 67.8%; SAT math scores over 500: 73.4%; SAT critical reading scores over 600: 13.9%; SAT math scores over 600: 18.8% **Housing** Yes **Expenses** Tuition & Fees: state resident $7211, nonresident $15,543; Room & Board $7032 **Undergraduates** 60% women, 9% part-time, 10% 25 or older, 0.3% Native American, 3% Hispanic American, 9% African American, 2% Asian American/Pacific Islander **The most frequently chosen baccalaureate fields are** business/marketing, education, health professions and related sciences **Academic program** English as a second language, advanced placement, self-designed majors, honors program, summer session, adult/continuing education programs, internships **Contact** Ms. Marsha Haug, Vice President of Enrollment Services and Admissions, West Chester University of Pennsylvania, University Avenue and High Street, West Chester, PA 19383. *Phone:* 610-436-3414 or toll-free 877-315-2165. *Fax:* 610-436-2907. *E-mail:* ugadmiss@wcupa.edu. *Web site:* http://www.wcupa.edu/.

Visit Petersons.com and enter keywords West Chester

See page 1360 for the College Close-Up.

Westminster College
New Wilmington, Pennsylvania

Contact Bradley Tokar, Director of Admissions, Westminster College, 319 South Market Street, New Wilmington, PA 16172-0001. *Phone:* 724-946-7100 or toll-free 800-942-8033. *Fax:* 724-946-7171. *E-mail:* tokarbp@westminster.edu. *Web site:* http://www.westminster.edu/.

Widener University
Chester, Pennsylvania

General Independent, comprehensive, coed **Entrance** Moderately difficult **Setting** 110-acre suburban campus **Total enrollment** 6,549 **Student-faculty ratio** 12:1 **Application deadline** Rolling (freshmen), rolling (transfer) **Freshman admission** 70% were admitted. Average high school GPA 3.3 **Freshman test scores** SAT critical reading scores over 500: 47%; SAT math scores over 500: 58%; SAT critical reading scores over 600: 10%; SAT math scores over 600: 18% **Housing** Yes **Expenses** Tuition & Fees $31,840; Room & Board $11,270 **Undergraduates** 56% women, 20% part-time, 18% 25 or older, 0.3% Native American, 3% Hispanic American, 14% African American, 3% Asian American/Pacific Islander **The most frequently chosen baccalaureate fields are** business/marketing, health professions and related sciences, psychology **Academic program** English as a second language, advanced placement, accelerated degree program, self-designed majors, honors program, summer session, adult/continuing education programs, internships **Contact** Office of Admissions, Widener University, One University Place, Chester, PA 19013. *Phone:* 610-499-4126 or toll-free 888-WIDENER. *Fax:* 610-499-4676. *E-mail:* admissions.office@widener.edu. *Web site:* http://www.widener.edu/.

Visit Petersons.com and enter keyword Widener

Wilkes University
Wilkes-Barre, Pennsylvania

General Independent, comprehensive, coed **Entrance** Moderately difficult **Setting** 25-acre urban campus **Total enrollment** 6,239 **Student-faculty ratio** 15:1 **Application deadline** Rolling (freshmen), rolling (transfer) **Freshman admission** 76% were admitted **Freshman test scores** SAT critical reading scores over 500: 61%; SAT math scores over 500: 69%; SAT critical reading scores over 600: 20%; SAT math scores over 600: 28% **Housing** Yes **Expenses** Tuition & Fees $26,010; Room & Board $11,100 **Undergraduates** 49% women, 10% part-time, 4% 25 or older, 0.2% Native American, 2% Hispanic American, 3% African American, 2% Asian American/Pacific Islander **The most frequently chosen baccalaureate fields are** business/marketing, health professions and related sciences, liberal arts/general studies **Academic program**

Wilkes University (continued)
English as a second language, advanced placement, accelerated degree program, self-designed majors, honors program, summer session, adult/continuing education programs, internships **Contact** Ms. Melanie Mickelson, Vice President of Enrollment Services, Wilkes University, 84 West South Street, Wilkes-Barre, PA 18766. *Phone:* 570-408-4400 or toll-free 800-945-5378 Ext. 4400. *Fax:* 570-408-4904. *E-mail:* admissions@wilkes.edu. *Web site:* http://www.wilkes.edu/.

Visit Petersons.com and enter keyword Wilkes

See page 1380 for the College Close-Up.

Wilson College
Chambersburg, Pennsylvania

General Independent, comprehensive, coed, primarily women, affiliated with Presbyterian Church (U.S.A.) **Entrance** Moderately difficult **Setting** 300-acre small-town campus **Total enrollment** 838 **Student-faculty ratio** 10:1 **Application deadline** Rolling (freshmen), rolling (transfer) **Freshman admission** 70% were admitted. Average high school GPA 3.23 **Freshman test scores** SAT critical reading scores over 500: 51%; SAT math scores over 500: 44%; ACT scores over 18: 65%; SAT critical reading scores over 600: 8%; SAT math scores over 600: 13%; ACT scores over 24: 20% **Housing** Yes **Expenses** Tuition & Fees $28,220; Room & Board $9430 **Undergraduates** 84% women, 54% part-time, 38% 25 or older **The most frequently chosen baccalaureate fields are** education, agriculture, health professions and related sciences **Academic program** English as a second language, advanced placement, self-designed majors, honors program, summer session, adult/continuing education programs, internships **Contact** Deborah Arthur, Admissions Administrator, Wilson College, 1015 Philadelphia Avenue, Chambersburg, PA 17201. *Phone:* 717-262-2002 or toll-free 800-421-8402. *Fax:* 717-262-2546. *E-mail:* admissions@wilson.edu. *Web site:* http://www.wilson.edu/.

Yeshiva Beth Moshe
Scranton, Pennsylvania

General Independent Jewish, comprehensive, men only **Total enrollment** 54 **Housing** Yes **Contact** Dean, Yeshiva Beth Moshe, 930 Hickory Street, PO Box 1141, Scranton, PA 18505-2124. *Phone:* 717-346-1747.

York College of Pennsylvania
York, Pennsylvania

General Independent, comprehensive, coed **Entrance** Moderately difficult **Setting** 190-acre suburban campus **Total enrollment** 5,564 **Student-faculty ratio** 17:1 **Application deadline** 8/15 (freshmen), rolling (transfer) **Freshman admission** 56% were admitted. Average high school GPA 3.51 **Freshman test scores** SAT critical reading scores over 500: 80.73%; SAT math scores over 500: 71.49%; ACT scores over 18: 94.2%; SAT critical reading scores over 600: 28.04%; SAT math scores over 600: 16.35%; ACT scores over 24: 36.31% **Housing** Yes **Expenses** Tuition & Fees $15,140; Room & Board $8530 **Undergraduates** 55% women, 13% part-time, 11% 25 or older, 0.2% Native American, 1% Hispanic American, 3% African American, 1% Asian American/Pacific Islander **The most frequently chosen baccalaureate fields are** business/marketing, education, health professions and related sciences **Academic program** Advanced placement, self-designed majors, honors program, summer session, internships **Contact** Mrs. Nancy L. Spataro, Director of Admissions, York College of Pennsylvania, York, PA 17405-7199. *Phone:* 717-849-1600 or toll-free 800-455-8018. *Fax:* 717-849-1607. *E-mail:* admissions@ycp.edu. *Web site:* http://www.ycp.edu/.

PUERTO RICO

American University of Puerto Rico
Bayamón, Puerto Rico

General Independent, comprehensive, coed **Entrance** Noncompetitive **Setting** 21-acre urban campus **Total enrollment** 1,747 **Housing** No **Expenses** Tuition & Fees $4435 **Undergraduates** 30% 25 or older, 100% Hispanic American **Academic program** English as a second language, advanced placement, honors program, summer session, adult/continuing education programs, internships **Contact** Ms. Margarita Cruz Santiago, Director of Admissions, American University of Puerto Rico, PO Box 2037, Bayamón, PR 00960-2037. *Phone:* 787-740-6410. *Fax:* 787-785-7377. *E-mail:* oficinaadmisiones@aupr.edu. *Web site:* http://www.aupr.edu/.

Atlantic College
Guaynabo, Puerto Rico

General Independent, comprehensive, coed **Total enrollment** 1,186 **Housing** No **Expenses** Tuition & Fees $5495 **Undergraduates** 11% 25 or older, 100% Hispanic American **Academic program** Internships **Contact** Ms. Zaida Perez, Admission's Officer, Atlantic College, PO Box 3918, Guaynabo, PR 00970. *Phone:* 787-720-1022 Ext. 13. *E-mail:* admisiones@atlanticcollege.edu. *Web site:* http://www.atlanticcollege.edu/.

Bayamón Central University
Bayamón, Puerto Rico

General Independent Roman Catholic, comprehensive, coed **Entrance** Moderately difficult **Setting** 55-acre suburban campus **Total enrollment** 2,382 **Freshman admission** 20% were admitted **Expenses** Tuition & Fees $4340 **Undergraduates** 43% 25 or older, 100% Hispanic American **Academic program** English as a second language, advanced placement, accelerated degree program, self-designed majors, honors program, summer session, adult/continuing education programs, internships **Contact** Sra. Christine M. Hernandez, Director of Admissions, Bayamón Central University, PO Box 1725, Bayamón, PR 00960-1725. *Phone:* 787-786-3030 Ext. 2102. *Web site:* http://www.ucb.edu.pr/.

Caribbean University
Bayamón, Puerto Rico

General Independent, comprehensive, coed **Entrance** Minimally difficult **Setting** 16-acre campus **Total enrollment** 2,009 **Application deadline** Rolling (freshmen) **Housing** No **Expenses** Tuition & Fees $4100 **Undergraduates** 38% 25 or older, 100% Hispanic American **Academic program** English as a second language, accelerated degree program, summer session, adult/continuing education programs **Contact** Mr. Hector Gracia, Director of Admissions, Caribbean University, Box 493, Bayamón, PR 00960-0493. *Phone:* 787-780-0070 Ext. 226. *Web site:* http://www.caribbean.edu/.

Carlos Albizu University
San Juan, Puerto Rico

General Independent, university, coed, primarily women **Entrance** Noncompetitive **Setting** urban campus **Total enrollment** 898 **Student-faculty ratio** 33:1 **Application deadline** 7/16 (freshmen), 7/17 (transfer) **Freshman admission** 88% were admitted **Housing** No **Expenses** Tuition & Fees $6739 **Undergraduates** 96% women, 43% part-time, 38% 25 or older, 72% Hispanic American **The most frequently chosen baccalaureate fields are** health professions and related sciences, psychology **Contact** Mr. Carlos Rodriguez, Admissions Department, Carlos Albizu University, 151 Tanca Street, San Juan, PR 00901. *Phone:* 787-725-6500

Ext. 1521. *Fax:* 787-721-7187. *E-mail:* crodriguez@albizu.edu. *Web site:* http://www.albizu.edu/.

Colegio Pentecostal Mizpa

Río Piedras, Puerto Rico

Contact Admissions Department, Colegio Pentecostal Mizpa, Bo Caimito Road 199, Apartado 20966, Río Piedras, PR 00928-0966.

Colegio Universitario de San Juan

San Juan, Puerto Rico

Contact Mrs. Nilsa E. Rivera-Almenas, Director of Enrollment Management, Colegio Universitario de San Juan, Jose R. Oliver Street, Hato Rey, PR 00918. *Phone:* 787-250-7111. *Fax:* 787-250-7395. *Web site:* http://www.cunisanjuan.edu/.

Columbia College

Caguas, Puerto Rico

General Proprietary, comprehensive, coed **Entrance** Noncompetitive **Setting** 6-acre rural campus **Total enrollment** 1,344 **Student-faculty ratio** 21:1 **Application deadline** Rolling (freshmen) **Freshman admission** Average high school GPA 2 **Housing** No **Expenses** Tuition & Fees $9100 **Undergraduates** 70% women, 44% part-time, 48% 25 or older, 100% Hispanic American **The most frequently chosen baccalaureate fields are** business/marketing, health professions and related sciences **Academic program** Accelerated degree program **Contact** Mrs. Xiomara Sanchez, Admission Coordinator, Columbia College, PO Box 8517, Caguas, PR 00726. *Phone:* 787-743-4041 Ext. 239 or toll-free 800-981-4877 Ext. 239. *Fax:* 787-744-7031. *E-mail:* xsanchez@columbianco.edu. *Web site:* http://www.columbiaco.edu/.

Columbia College

Yauco, Puerto Rico

General Proprietary, 4-year, coed **Setting** urban campus **Total enrollment** 566 **Student-faculty ratio** 9:1 **Application deadline** Rolling (freshmen) **Freshman admission** 79% were admitted. Average high school GPA 2 **Expenses** Tuition & Fees $7440 **Undergraduates** 76% women, 45% part-time, 100% Hispanic American **The most frequently chosen baccalaureate fields are** business/marketing, health professions and related sciences **Contact** Ms. Rosario Padilla, Admissions, Columbia College, Box 3062, Yauco, PR 00698. *Phone:* 787-856-0845 Ext. 11. *Fax:* 787-267-2335. *E-mail:* rpadilla@columbiaco.edu. *Web site:* http://www.columbiaco.edu/.

Conservatorio de Musica

San Juan, Puerto Rico

Contact Eutimia Santiago, Admissions Department, Conservatorio de Musica, Calle Rafael Lamar #350, Esquina F. D. Roosevelt, San Juan, PR 00918-2199. *Phone:* 787-751-0160 Ext. 275. *Fax:* 787-754-6284. *E-mail:* esantiago@cmpr.gobierno.pr. *Web site:* http://www.cmpr.edu/.

Conservatory of Music of Puerto Rico

San Juan, Puerto Rico

General Commonwealth-supported, comprehensive, coed **Entrance** Moderately difficult **Setting** 6-acre urban campus **Total enrollment** 386 **Application deadline** 3/6 (freshmen), 3/6 (transfer) **Housing** No **Undergraduates** 19% 25 or older **Academic program** Advanced placement, summer session **Contact** Eutimia Santiago, Admissions Coordinator, Conservatory of Music of Puerto Rico, 350 Rafael Lamar St at FDR Ave, San Juan, PR 00918. *Phone:* 787-751-0160 Ext. 275. *Fax:* 787-767-4331. *E-mail:* admisiones@cmpr.edu. *Web site:* http://www.cmpr.edu/.

EDP College of Puerto Rico, Inc.

Hato Rey, Puerto Rico

General Proprietary, comprehensive, coed **Entrance** Minimally difficult **Setting** 1-acre urban campus **Total enrollment** 1,016 **Student-faculty ratio** 19:1 **Application deadline** Rolling (freshmen), rolling (transfer) **Freshman admission** 86% were admitted. Average high school GPA 2 **Housing** No **Expenses** Tuition & Fees $6120 **Undergraduates** 59% women, 34% part-time, 100% Hispanic American **The most frequently chosen baccalaureate fields are** business/marketing, communication technologies **Academic program** English as a second language, accelerated degree program, summer session, adult/continuing education programs, internships **Contact** Ms. Leila M. Andino, Student Affairs Dean, EDP College of Puerto Rico, Inc., Avenue Ponce de Leon #560, Hato Rey, PR 00918. *Phone:* 787-765-3560 Ext. 262. *Fax:* 787-777-0024. *E-mail:* landino@edpcollege.edu. *Web site:* http://www.edpcollege.edu/.

EDP College of Puerto Rico–San Sebastian

San Sebastian, Puerto Rico

General Proprietary, 4-year, coed **Entrance** Minimally difficult **Setting** rural campus **Total enrollment** 858 **Application deadline** Rolling (freshmen) **Expenses** Tuition & Fees $6120 **Undergraduates** 100% Hispanic American **Contact** Mr. Zenaida Olavarria Rodriguez, Admissions Department, EDP College of Puerto Rico–San Sebastian, Avenue Betances #49, San Sebastian, PR 00685. *Phone:* 787-896-2252 Ext. 300. *Fax:* 787-896-0066. *E-mail:* zolavarria@edpcollege.edu. *Web site:* http://www.edpcollege.edu/.

Escuela de Artes Plasticas de Puerto Rico

San Juan, Puerto Rico

General Commonwealth-supported, 4-year, coed **Entrance** Moderately difficult **Setting** urban campus **Total enrollment** 530 **Student-faculty ratio** 13:1 **Application deadline** 3/6 (freshmen), 3/6 (transfer) **Freshman admission** 50% were admitted. Average high school GPA 3.25 **Housing** No **Expenses** Tuition & Fees: state resident $2728 **Undergraduates** 57% women, 31% part-time, 26% 25 or older, 99% Hispanic American, 0.2% Asian American/Pacific Islander **The most frequently chosen baccalaureate fields are** education, visual and performing arts **Academic program** Adult/continuing education programs, internships **Contact** Mrs. Liza Layer, Admission Assistant, Escuela de Artes Plasticas de Puerto Rico, PO Box 902112, San Juan, PR 00902-1112. *Phone:* 787-725-8120 Ext. 319. *Fax:* 787-721-3798. *E-mail:* nadjac_eap@yahoo.com. *Web site:* http://www.eap.edu/.

Inter American University of Puerto Rico, Aguadilla Campus

Aguadilla, Puerto Rico

General Independent, comprehensive, coed **Entrance** Moderately difficult **Setting** 50-acre small-town campus **Total enrollment** 4,502 **Student-faculty ratio** 29:1 **Application deadline** Rolling (freshmen), rolling (transfer) **Freshman admission** 59% were admitted. Average high school GPA 2.62 **Housing** No **Expenses** Tuition & Fees $5495 **Undergraduates** 54% women, 17% part-time, 32% 25 or older, 100% Hispanic American **The most frequently chosen baccalaureate fields are** business/marketing, education, security and protective services **Academic program** Advanced placement, honors program, summer session, adult/continuing education programs, internships **Contact** Mrs. Doris Perez, Admissions Director, Inter American University of Puerto Rico, Aguadilla Campus, PO Box 20,000, Road 459 Intersection 463, Aguadilla, PR 00605. *Phone:* 787-891-0925 Ext. 2101. *Fax:* 787-882-3020. *Web site:* http://www.aguadilla.inter.edu/.

Inter American University of Puerto Rico, Arecibo Campus

Arecibo, Puerto Rico

General Independent, comprehensive, coed **Entrance** Moderately difficult **Setting** 20-acre urban campus **Total enrollment** 4,878 **Student-faculty ratio** 24:1 **Application deadline** Rolling (freshmen), rolling (transfer) **Housing** No **Expenses** Tuition & Fees $4212 **Undergraduates** 61% women, 17% part-time, 27% 25 or older, 100% Hispanic American **The most frequently chosen baccalaureate fields are** business/marketing, education, public administration and social services **Academic program** Advanced placement, honors program, summer session, adult/continuing education programs, internships **Contact** Ms. Provi Montalvo, Admission Director, Inter American University of Puerto Rico, Arecibo Campus, PO Box 4050, Arecibo, PR 00614-4050. *Phone:* 787-878-5475. *Fax:* 787-880-1624. *E-mail:* pmontalvo@arecibo.inter.edu. *Web site:* http://www.arecibo.inter.edu/.

Inter American University of Puerto Rico, Barranquitas Campus

Barranquitas, Puerto Rico

General Independent, comprehensive, coed **Entrance** Moderately difficult **Setting** small-town campus **Total enrollment** 2,329 **Student-faculty ratio** 29:1 **Application deadline** 5/15 (freshmen), 5/15 (transfer) **Freshman admission** 34% were admitted. Average high school GPA 2.75 **Housing** No **Undergraduates** 67% women, 19% part-time, 14% 25 or older, 100% Hispanic American **Academic program** English as a second language, advanced placement, summer session, adult/continuing education programs **Contact** Mrs. Aramilda Cartagena, Dean of Students, Inter American University of Puerto Rico, Barranquitas Campus, PO Box 517, Barranquitas, PR 00794. *Phone:* 787-857-3600 Ext. 2009. *Fax:* 787-857-2125. *E-mail:* acartagena@br.inter.edu. *Web site:* http://www.br.inter.edu/.

Inter American University of Puerto Rico, Bayamón Campus

Bayamón, Puerto Rico

General Independent, comprehensive, coed **Setting** 51-acre urban campus **Total enrollment** 5,162 **Student-faculty ratio** 23:1 **Application deadline** 7/30 (freshmen) **Freshman admission** Average high school GPA 3 **Housing** No **Expenses** Tuition & Fees $5136 **Undergraduates** 44% women, 14% part-time, 19% 25 or older, 100% Hispanic American **Academic program** English as a second language, advanced placement, accelerated degree program, honors program, summer session, adult/continuing education programs, internships **Contact** Mr. Carlos Alicea, Director of Admissions, Inter American University of Puerto Rico, Bayamón Campus, 500 Road 830, Bayamón, PR 00957. *Phone:* 787-279-1912 Ext. 2017. *Fax:* 787-279-2205. *E-mail:* calicea@bc.inter.edu. *Web site:* http://www.bc.inter.edu/.

Inter American University of Puerto Rico, Fajardo Campus

Fajardo, Puerto Rico

General Independent, comprehensive, coed **Entrance** Moderately difficult **Setting** 11-acre small-town campus **Total enrollment** 2,239 **Student-faculty ratio** 11:1 **Application deadline** Rolling (freshmen), rolling (transfer) **Freshman admission** 39% were admitted. Average high school GPA 2 **Housing** No **Undergraduates** 63% women, 23% part-time, 36% 25 or older **Academic program** English as a second language, advanced placement, honors program, summer session, adult/continuing education programs, internships **Contact** Ms. Jackeline Melèndez, Administrative Assistant II, Inter American University of Puerto Rico, Fajardo Campus, Call Box 70003, Fajardo, PR 00738-7003, Puerto Rico. *Phone:* 787-863-2390 Ext. 2210. *Fax:* 787-860-3470. *E-mail:* jackeline.melendez@fajardo.inter.edu. *Web site:* http://www.fajardo.inter.edu/.

Inter American University of Puerto Rico, Guayama Campus

Guayama, Puerto Rico

General Independent, comprehensive, coed **Entrance** Moderately difficult **Setting** 50-acre small-town campus **Total enrollment** 2,356 **Student-faculty ratio** 25:1 **Application deadline** 8/1 (freshmen), 8/1 (transfer) **Freshman admission** 39% were admitted **Housing** No **Expenses** Tuition & Fees $5368 **Undergraduates** 67% women, 18% part-time, 40% 25 or older, 100% Hispanic American **The most frequently chosen baccalaureate fields are** business/marketing, education, security and protective services **Academic program** English as a second language, honors program, summer session, adult/continuing education programs **Contact** Mrs. Laura E. Ferrer, Director of Admissions, Inter American University of Puerto Rico, Guayama Campus, Call Box 10004, Guayama, PR 00785. *Phone:* 787-864-2222 Ext. 220 or toll-free 787-864-2222 Ext. 2243. *Fax:* 787-864-8232. *E-mail:* lferrer@inter.edu. *Web site:* http://www.guayama.inter.edu/.

Inter American University of Puerto Rico, Metropolitan Campus

San Juan, Puerto Rico

General Independent, comprehensive, coed **Entrance** Moderately difficult **Total enrollment** 10,613 **Freshman admission** 27% were admitted **Housing** No **Expenses** Tuition & Fees $4212 **Undergraduates** 40% 25 or older, 100% Hispanic American **Academic program** English as a second language, accelerated degree program, honors program, summer session, adult/continuing education programs, internships **Contact** Ms. Ida G. Betancourt, Official Admission, Inter American University of Puerto Rico, Metropolitan Campus, PO Box 191293, San Juan, PR 00919-1293. *Phone:* 787-250-1912 Ext. 2188. *Fax:* 787-250-1025. *E-mail:* jbetancourt@metro.inter.edu. *Web site:* http://metro.inter.edu/.

Inter American University of Puerto Rico, Ponce Campus

Mercedita, Puerto Rico

General Independent, comprehensive, coed **Entrance** Moderately difficult **Setting** 50-acre urban campus **Total enrollment** 5,997 **Application deadline** 5/15 (freshmen), 5/15 (transfer) **Freshman admission** 97% were admitted **Housing** No **Expenses** Tuition & Fees $4428 **Undergraduates** 59% women, 14% part-time, 31% 25 or older, 100% Hispanic American **The most frequently chosen baccalaureate fields are** business/marketing, education, law/legal studies **Academic program** English as a second language, honors program, summer session, adult/continuing education programs, internships **Contact** Mr. Franco Diaz, Admissions Officer, Inter American University of Puerto Rico, Ponce Campus, Ponce Campus, 104 Turpo Industrial Park Road #1, Mercedita, PR 00715-1602. *Phone:* 787-284-1912 Ext. 2025. *Fax:* 787-841-0103. *E-mail:* fidiaz@ponce.inter.edu. *Web site:* http://www.ponce.inter.edu/.

Inter American University of Puerto Rico, San Germán Campus

San Germán, Puerto Rico

General Independent, university, coed **Entrance** Moderately difficult **Setting** 260-acre small-town campus **Total enrollment** 5,716 **Student-faculty ratio** 27:1 **Application deadline** 5/15 (freshmen), 5/15 (transfer) **Freshman admission** 84% were admitted. Average high school GPA 2.9 **Housing** Yes **Expenses** Tuition & Fees $5616 **Undergraduates** 53% women, 14% part-time, 2% 25 or older, 100% Hispanic American **The most frequently chosen baccalaureate fields are** business/marketing, biological/life sciences, education **Academic program** English as a second language, advanced placement, accelerated degree program, honors program, summer session, adult/continuing education programs, internships **Contact** Prof. Mildred Camacho, Director of Admissions, Inter American University of Puerto Rico, San Germán Campus, PO Box

5100, San German, PR 00683-5008. *Phone:* 787-264-1912 Ext. 7283. *Fax:* 787-892-7020. *E-mail:* milcama@sg.inter.edu. *Web site:* http://www.sg.inter.edu/.

National College

Bayamón, Puerto Rico

Contact Admissions, National College, PO Box 2036, National College Plaza Building, Bayamón, PR 00960. *Phone:* 787-780-5134 or toll-free 800-780-5134. *Fax:* 787-779-4909. *E-mail:* infobayamon@nationalcollegepr.edu. *Web site:* http://www.nationalcollegepr.edu/.

Polytechnic University of Puerto Rico

Hato Rey, Puerto Rico

General Independent, comprehensive, coed, primarily men **Entrance** Minimally difficult **Setting** 10-acre urban campus **Total enrollment** 5,520 **Student-faculty ratio** 20:1 **Application deadline** 8/15 (freshmen) **Freshman admission** 94% were admitted. Average high school GPA 2.45 **Expenses** Tuition & Fees $6837; Room & Board $11,704 **Undergraduates** 23% women, 47% part-time, 25% 25 or older, 100% Hispanic American **The most frequently chosen baccalaureate fields are** business/marketing, architecture, engineering **Academic program** English as a second language, self-designed majors, summer session **Contact** Ms. Teresa Cardona, Director of Admissions, Polytechnic University of Puerto Rico, PO Box 192017, San Juan, PR 00919-2017. *Phone:* 787-754-8000 Ext. 240. *Fax:* 787-764-8712. *E-mail:* tcardona@pupr.edu. *Web site:* http://www.pupr.edu/.

Pontifical Catholic University of Puerto Rico

Ponce, Puerto Rico

General Independent Roman Catholic, university, coed **Entrance** Moderately difficult **Setting** 120-acre urban campus **Total enrollment** 7,682 **Student-faculty ratio** 23:1 **Freshman admission** 83% were admitted. Average high school GPA 3.14 **Housing** Yes **Expenses** Tuition & Fees $5478; Room & Board $2990 **Undergraduates** 63% women, 10% part-time, 13% 25 or older, 98% Hispanic American **Academic program** English as a second language, advanced placement, honors program, summer session, adult/continuing education programs **Contact** Sra. Ana O. Bonilla, Director of Admissions, Pontifical Catholic University of Puerto Rico, 2250 Avenida Las Americas Avenue, Suite 584, Ponce, PR 00717-9777. *Phone:* 787-841-2000 Ext. 1004 or toll-free 800-981-5040. *Fax:* 787-840-4295. *E-mail:* admissions@email.pucpr.edu. *Web site:* http://www.pucpr.edu/.

Universidad Adventista de las Antillas

Mayagüez, Puerto Rico

General Independent Seventh-day Adventist, comprehensive, coed **Entrance** Minimally difficult **Setting** 284-acre rural campus **Total enrollment** 1,019 **Student-faculty ratio** 17:1 **Freshman admission** 44% were admitted **Housing** Yes **Expenses** Tuition & Fees $6170; Room & Board $2900 **Undergraduates** 57% women, 7% part-time **Academic program** English as a second language, advanced placement, summer session, internships **Contact** Ms. Evelyn del Valle, Director of Admissions, Universidad Adventista de las Antillas, Oficina de Admisiones, PO Box 118, Mayaguez, PR 00681-0118. *Phone:* 787-834-9595 Ext. 2208. *Fax:* 787-834-9597. *E-mail:* admissions@uaa.edu. *Web site:* http://www.uaa.edu/.

Universidad del Este

Carolina, Puerto Rico

Contact Clotilde Santiago, Director of Admissions, Universidad del Este, PO Box 2010, Carolina, PR 00984. *Phone:* 787-257-7373 Ext. 3401. *E-mail:* ue_csantiago@suagm.edu. *Web site:* http://www.suagm.edu/une/.

Universidad del Turabo

Gurabo, Puerto Rico

Contact Carmen Rivera, Director of Admissions and Financial Aid, Universidad del Turabo, PO Box 3030, Gurabo, PR 00778-3030. *Phone:* 787-743-7979 Ext. 4352. *E-mail:* ut_crivera@suagm.edu. *Web site:* http://www.suagm.edu/ut/.

Universidad Metropolitana

San Juan, Puerto Rico

General Independent, comprehensive, coed **Entrance** Moderately difficult **Setting** small-town campus **Total enrollment** 12,389 **Application deadline** 7/30 (freshmen), 7/30 (transfer) **Freshman admission** 62% were admitted. Average high school GPA 2.77 **Housing** No **Undergraduates** 67% women, 20% part-time, 26% 25 or older, 100% Hispanic American **The most frequently chosen baccalaureate fields are** business/marketing, education, public administration and social services **Academic program** Advanced placement, honors program, summer session, adult/continuing education programs **Contact** Mr. Julio Rodriguez Soiza, Director of Admissions, Universidad Metropolitana, Box 21150, San Juan, PR 00928-1150. *Phone:* 787-766-1717 Ext. 6587 or toll-free 800-747-8362. *Fax:* 787-751-0992. *E-mail:* um_frivera@suagm1.suagm.edu. *Web site:* http://www.suagm.edu/umet/.

Universidad Teológica del Caribe

St. Just, Puerto Rico

General Independent Pentecostal, 4-year, coed **Setting** 4-acre suburban campus **Total enrollment** 251 **Student-faculty ratio** 15:1 **Freshman admission** 82% were admitted **Housing** Yes **Expenses** Tuition & Fees $3520; Room & Board $2400 **Undergraduates** 45% women, 64% part-time, 86% 25 or older, 100% Hispanic American **The most frequently chosen baccalaureate field is** theology and religious vocations **Academic program** Honors program, summer session, internships **Contact** Ms. Carolyn Figueroa, Registrar, Universidad Teológica del Caribe, PO Box 901, St. Just, PR 00978-0901. *Phone:* 787-761-0640 Ext. 231. *Fax:* 787-748-9220. *E-mail:* registraduriautc@yahoo.com. *Web site:* http://www.cbp.edu/.

University of Phoenix–Puerto Rico Campus

Guaynabo, Puerto Rico

General Proprietary, comprehensive, coed **Entrance** Noncompetitive **Setting** urban campus **Total enrollment** 2,815 **Application deadline** Rolling (freshmen), rolling (transfer) **Freshman admission** 100% were admitted **Housing** No **Expenses** Tuition & Fees $6750 **Undergraduates** 55% women, 89% 25 or older, 0.3% Native American, 53% Hispanic American, 1% African American, 0.2% Asian American/Pacific Islander **The most frequently chosen baccalaureate field is** business/marketing **Academic program** Advanced placement, accelerated degree program, adult/continuing education programs **Contact** Ms. Audra McQuarie, Registrar/Executive Director, University of Phoenix–Puerto Rico Campus, 4035 South Riverpoint Parkway, Mail Stop CF-L101, Phoenix, AZ 85040. *Phone:* 480-557-6151 or toll-free 800-776-4867 (in-state); 800-228-7240 (out-of-state). *Fax:* 480-643-3068. *E-mail:* audra.mcquarie@phoenix.edu. *Web site:* http://www.phoenix.edu/.

University of Puerto Rico, Aguadilla University College

Aguadilla, Puerto Rico

General Commonwealth-supported, 4-year, coed **Entrance** Moderately difficult **Setting** 32-acre suburban campus **Total enrollment** 3,036 **Freshman admission** 85% were admitted **Housing** No **Expenses** Tuition & Fees: state resident $1747, nonresident $3884 **Undergraduates** 12% 25 or older **Academic program** English as a second language, advanced

University of Puerto Rico, Aguadilla University College (continued)

placement, honors program, summer session, adult/continuing education programs **Contact** Ms. Melba Serrano Lugo, Admissions Officer, University of Puerto Rico, Aguadilla University College, PO Box 6150, Aguadilla, PR 00604. *Phone:* 787-890-2681 Ext. 280. *Web site:* http://www.uprag.edu/.

University of Puerto Rico at Arecibo

Arecibo, Puerto Rico

General Commonwealth-supported, 4-year, coed **Entrance** Very difficult **Setting** 44-acre urban campus **Total enrollment** 4,094 **Freshman admission** 46% were admitted **Expenses** Tuition & Fees: state resident $1872, nonresident $3938 **Undergraduates** 8% 25 or older **Academic program** English as a second language, advanced placement, honors program, summer session, adult/continuing education programs **Contact** Delma Barrios Colon, Director of Admissions, University of Puerto Rico at Arecibo, PO Box 4010, Arecibo, PR 00613. *Phone:* 787-878-2830 Ext. 4101. *E-mail:* dbarrios@upra.edu. *Web site:* http://www.upra.edu/.

University of Puerto Rico at Bayamón

Bayamón, Puerto Rico

General Commonwealth-supported, 4-year, coed **Entrance** Very difficult **Setting** 78-acre urban campus **Total enrollment** 5,184 **Student-faculty ratio** 20:1 **Application deadline** 12/15 (freshmen), 2/15 (transfer) **Freshman admission** 22% were admitted. Average high school GPA 3.51 **Housing** No **Expenses** Tuition & Fees: state resident $2076, nonresident $4381 **Undergraduates** 53% women, 15% part-time, 11% 25 or older, 100% Hispanic American **Academic program** Advanced placement, honors program, summer session, adult/continuing education programs, internships **Contact** Ms. Carmen I. Montes, Admissions Director, University of Puerto Rico at Bayamón, OPEI Office, Street 174 #170 Minillas Industrial Park, Bayamon, PR 00959, Puerto Rico. *Phone:* 787-993-8952. *Fax:* 787-993-8929. *E-mail:* cmontes@upr.edu. *Web site:* http://www.uprb.edu/.

University of Puerto Rico at Carolina

Carolina, Puerto Rico

Contact Ms. Celia Mendez, Admissions Officer, University of Puerto Rico at Carolina, PO Box 4800, Carolina, PR 00984-4800. *Phone:* 787-757-1485. *Web site:* http://uprc.edu/.

University of Puerto Rico at Humacao

Humacao, Puerto Rico

General Commonwealth-supported, 4-year, coed **Entrance** Moderately difficult **Setting** 62-acre suburban campus **Total enrollment** 4,676 **Student-faculty ratio** 15:1 **Application deadline** 1/9 (freshmen), 3/9 (transfer) **Freshman admission** 37% were admitted. Average high school GPA 3.6 **Housing** No **Expenses** Tuition & Fees: state resident $2013, nonresident $3943 **Undergraduates** 67% women, 11% part-time, 8% 25 or older, 99% Hispanic American, 0.1% Asian American/Pacific Islander **The most frequently chosen baccalaureate fields are** business/marketing, biological/life sciences, education **Academic program** English as a second language, advanced placement, honors program, summer session, internships **Contact** Mrs. Elizabeth Gerena, Acting Director of Admissions, University of Puerto Rico at Humacao, HUC Station 100, Road 908, Humacao, PR 00791, Puerto Rico. *Phone:* 787-850-9301. *Fax:* 787-850-9428. *E-mail:* elizabeth.gerena@upr.edu. *Web site:* http://www.uprh.edu/.

University of Puerto Rico at Ponce

Ponce, Puerto Rico

General Commonwealth-supported, 4-year, coed **Entrance** Moderately difficult **Setting** 86-acre urban campus **Total enrollment** 3,232 **Student-faculty ratio** 16:1 **Application deadline** 11/15 (freshmen), 2/23 (transfer) **Freshman admission** 37% were admitted **Freshman test scores** SAT critical reading scores over 500: 67.6%; SAT math scores over 500: 70%; SAT critical reading scores over 600: 19.2%; SAT math scores over 600: 28% **Housing** No **Expenses** Tuition & Fees: state resident $1747, nonresident $3341 **Undergraduates** 61% women, 12% part-time, 8% 25 or older, 100% Hispanic American **The most frequently chosen baccalaureate fields are** business/marketing, health professions and related sciences, personal and culinary services **Academic program** English as a second language, advanced placement, accelerated degree program, honors program, summer session, internships **Contact** Acmin Velazquez Rivera, Admissions Director, University of Puerto Rico at Ponce, PO Box 7186, Ponce, PR 00732-7186. *Phone:* 787-844-8181 Ext. 2533. *E-mail:* avelazquez@uprp.edu. *Web site:* http://upr-ponce.upr.edu/.

University of Puerto Rico at Utuado

Utuado, Puerto Rico

General Commonwealth-supported, 4-year, coed **Entrance** Moderately difficult **Setting** 180-acre small-town campus **Total enrollment** 1,623 **Student-faculty ratio** 18:1 **Application deadline** Rolling (freshmen), rolling (transfer) **Freshman admission** 45% were admitted. Average high school GPA 2.5 **Housing** No **Expenses** Tuition & Fees: state resident $1940, nonresident $4077 **Undergraduates** 57% women, 11% part-time, 8% 25 or older, 100% Hispanic American **The most frequently chosen baccalaureate fields are** business/marketing, education **Academic program** Honors program, summer session **Contact** Mrs. Maria Robles Serrano, Admissions Officer, University of Puerto Rico at Utuado, PO Box 2500, Utuado, PR 00641-2500. *Phone:* 787-894-2828 Ext. 2240. *Fax:* 787-894-2316. *Web site:* http://upr-utuado.upr.clu.edu/.

University of Puerto Rico, Cayey University College

Cayey, Puerto Rico

General Commonwealth-supported, 4-year, coed **Entrance** Moderately difficult **Setting** 177-acre urban campus **Total enrollment** 3,830 **Student-faculty ratio** 21:1 **Freshman admission** 78% were admitted. Average high school GPA 3.67 **Expenses** Tuition & Fees: state resident $1973, nonresident $4387; Room & Board $8180 **Undergraduates** 71% women, 10% part-time, 0.1% 25 or older, 100% Hispanic American **The most frequently chosen baccalaureate fields are** business/marketing, education, interdisciplinary studies **Academic program** Advanced placement, accelerated degree program, honors program, summer session **Contact** Mr. Wilfredo Lopez, Admissions Director, University of Puerto Rico, Cayey University College, 205 Avenue Antonio R. Barcelo, Cayey, PR 00736. *Phone:* 787-738-2161 Ext. 2233. *Fax:* 878-738-5633. *E-mail:* wilfredo.lopez3@upr.edu. *Web site:* http://www.cayey.upr.edu/.

University of Puerto Rico, Mayagüez Campus

Mayagüez, Puerto Rico

Contact Ms. Sheila Marty-Rodriquez, Director, Admissions Office, University of Puerto Rico, Mayagüez Campus, PO Box 9000, Mayagüez, PR 00681-9000. *Phone:* 787-265-5465. *Fax:* 787-265-5465. *E-mail:* smarty@uprm.edu. *Web site:* http://www.uprm.edu.

University of Puerto Rico, Medical Sciences Campus

San Juan, Puerto Rico

Contact Margarita Rivera Rosario, Director of Admissions, University of Puerto Rico, Medical Sciences Campus, PO Box 365067, San Juan, PR 00936-5067. *Phone:* 787-758-2525 Ext. 5214. *E-mail:* margarita.rivera4@upr.edu. *Web site:* http://www.rcm.upr.edu/.

University of Puerto Rico, Río Piedras
San Juan, Puerto Rico

General Commonwealth-supported, university, coed **Entrance** Very difficult **Setting** 281-acre urban campus **Total enrollment** 18,966 **Student-faculty ratio** 16:1 **Application deadline** 12/15 (freshmen), 9/21 (transfer) **Freshman admission** 36% were admitted. Average high school GPA 3.6 **Housing** Yes **Expenses** Tuition & Fees: state resident $1320, nonresident $4027; Room & Board $8280 **Undergraduates** 7% 25 or older, 0.01% Native American, 97% Hispanic American, 0.04% African American, 0.1% Asian American/Pacific Islander **The most frequently chosen baccalaureate fields are** business/marketing, education, interdisciplinary studies **Academic program** Advanced placement, self-designed majors, honors program, summer session, adult/continuing education programs, internships **Contact** Mrs. Cruz B. Valentìn, Director of Admissions, University of Puerto Rico, Río Piedras, PO Box 23300, San Juan, PR 00931-3300. *Phone:* 787-764-0000 Ext. 85700. *Web site:* http://www.uprrp.edu/.

University of the Sacred Heart
San Juan, Puerto Rico

General Independent Roman Catholic, comprehensive, coed **Entrance** Moderately difficult **Setting** 33-acre urban campus **Total enrollment** 5,666 **Student-faculty ratio** 20:1 **Application deadline** 6/30 (freshmen), 6/30 (transfer) **Freshman admission** 35% were admitted. Average high school GPA 2.99 **Housing** Yes **Expenses** Tuition & Fees $5870; Room only $2500 **Undergraduates** 61% women, 19% part-time, 20% 25 or older, 100% Hispanic American **The most frequently chosen baccalaureate fields are** business/marketing, communications/journalism, psychology **Academic program** Advanced placement, accelerated degree program, honors program, summer session, internships **Contact** Mr. Luis Heviquez, Director of Admissions, University of the Sacred Heart, PO Box 12383, San Juan, PR 00914-0383. *Phone:* 787-728-1515 Ext. 3237. *Web site:* http://www.sagrado.edu/.

RHODE ISLAND

Brown University
Providence, Rhode Island

General Independent, university, coed **Entrance** Most difficult **Setting** 140-acre urban campus **Total enrollment** 6,095 **Student-faculty ratio** 9:1 **Application deadline** 1/1 (freshmen), 3/1 (transfer) **Freshman admission** 14% were admitted **Freshman test scores** SAT critical reading scores over 500: 99%; SAT math scores over 500: 100%; ACT scores over 18: 100%; SAT critical reading scores over 600: 89.8%; SAT math scores over 600: 93%; ACT scores over 24: 96% **Housing** Yes **Expenses** Tuition & Fees $37,718; Room & Board $10,022 **Undergraduates** 52% women, 4% part-time, 1% 25 or older, 1% Native American, 8% Hispanic American, 7% African American, 16% Asian American/Pacific Islander **The most frequently chosen baccalaureate fields are** biological/life sciences, physical sciences, social sciences **Academic program** Advanced placement, accelerated degree program, self-designed majors, honors program, summer session, adult/continuing education programs, internships **Contact** Mr. James Miller, Dean of Admission, Brown University, Box 1876, Providence, RI 02912. *Phone:* 401-863-2378. *Fax:* 401-863-9300. *E-mail:* admission_undergraduate@brown.edu. *Web site:* http://www.brown.edu/.

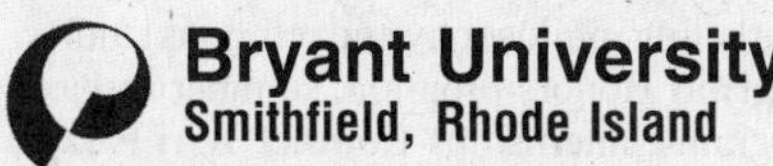

Bryant University
Smithfield, Rhode Island

General Independent, comprehensive, coed **Entrance** Moderately difficult **Setting** 420-acre suburban campus **Total enrollment** 3,632 **Student-faculty ratio** 18:1 **Application deadline** 2/1 (freshmen), rolling (transfer) **Freshman admission** 53% were admitted. Average high school GPA 3.35 **Freshman test scores** SAT critical reading scores over 500: 83.18%; SAT math scores over 500: 92.73%; ACT scores over 18: 100%; SAT critical reading scores over 600: 22.48%; SAT math scores over 600: 47.64%; ACT scores over 24: 65.03% **Housing** Yes **Expenses** Tuition & Fees $32,106; Room & Board $11,757 **Undergraduates** 43% women, 4% part-time, 3% 25 or older, 0.1% Native American, 4% Hispanic American, 4% African American, 3% Asian American/Pacific Islander **The most frequently chosen baccalaureate fields are** business/marketing, communications/journalism, mathematics **Academic program** English as a second language, advanced placement, honors program, summer session, adult/continuing education programs, internships **Contact** Ms. Michelle Beauregard, Director of Admission, Bryant University, 1150 Douglas Pike, Smithfield, RI 02917. *Phone:* 401-232-6100 or toll-free 800-622-7001. *Fax:* 401-232-6741. *E-mail:* admission@bryant.edu. *Web site:* http://www.bryant.edu/.

Visit Petersons.com and enter keyword Bryant

See page 648 for the College Close-Up.

Johnson & Wales University
Providence, Rhode Island

General Independent, comprehensive, coed **Entrance** Minimally difficult **Setting** 47-acre urban campus **Total enrollment** 10,709 **Student-faculty ratio** 31:1 **Application deadline** Rolling (freshmen), rolling (transfer) **Freshman admission** 72% were admitted **Freshman test scores** SAT critical reading scores over 500: 38.1%; SAT math scores over 500: 42.7%; SAT critical reading scores over 600: 7.7%; SAT math scores over 600: 8.7% **Housing** Yes **Expenses** Tuition & Fees $24,141 **Undergraduates** 54% women, 8% part-time, 11% 25 or older, 0.2% Native American, 6% Hispanic American, 7% African American, 2% Asian American/Pacific Islander **The most frequently chosen baccalaureate fields are** business/marketing, family and consumer sciences, personal and culinary services **Academic program** English as a second language, advanced placement, accelerated degree program, honors program, summer session, adult/continuing education programs, internships **Contact** Ms. Maureen Dumas, Dean of Admissions, Johnson & Wales University, 8 Abbott Park Place, Providence, RI 02903-3703. *Phone:* 401-598-2310 or toll-free 800-598-1000 (in-state); 800-342-5598 (out-of-state). *Fax:* 401-598-2948. *E-mail:* admissions.pvd@jwu.edu. *Web site:* http://www.jwu.edu/.

Visit Petersons.com and enter keyword Johnson

See page 882 for the College Close-Up.

Mater Ecclesiae College
Greenville, Rhode Island

Contact Mater Ecclesiae College, 60 Austin Avenue, Greenville, RI 02828. *Web site:* http://www.materecclesiae.net/.

New England Institute of Technology
Warwick, Rhode Island

Contact Mr. Michael Kwiatkowski, Director of Admissions, New England Institute of Technology, 2500 Post Road, Warwick, RI 02886-2244. *Phone:* 401-739-5000. *Fax:* 401-738-5122. *E-mail:* neit@ids.net. *Web site:* http://www.neit.edu/.

Providence College
Providence, Rhode Island

General Independent Roman Catholic, comprehensive, coed **Entrance** Very difficult **Setting** 105-acre suburban campus **Total enrollment** 4,500 **Student-faculty ratio** 13:1 **Application deadline** 1/15 (freshmen), 4/1 (transfer) **Freshman admission** 60% were admitted. Average high school GPA 3.49 **Freshman test scores** SAT critical reading scores over 500: 86%; SAT math scores over 500: 88%; ACT scores over 18: 98%; SAT critical reading scores over 600: 41%; SAT math scores over 600: 49%; ACT scores over 24: 71% **Housing** Yes **Expenses** Tuition & Fees

Providence College (continued)
$39,435; Room & Board $11,690 **Undergraduates** 57% women, 0.2% part-time, 0.3% Native American, 4% Hispanic American, 3% African American, 2% Asian American/Pacific Islander **The most frequently chosen baccalaureate fields are** business/marketing, education, social sciences **Academic program** Advanced placement, self-designed majors, honors program, summer session, adult/continuing education programs, internships **Contact** Mr. Christopher Lydon, Associate Vice President for Admission and Enrollment Planning, Providence College, 1 Cunningham Square, Providence, RI 02918. *Phone:* 401-865-2535 or toll-free 800-721-6444. *Fax:* 401-865-2826. *E-mail:* pcadmiss@providence.edu. *Web site:* http://www.providence.edu/.

See page 1060 for the College Close-Up.

Rhode Island College
Providence, Rhode Island

General State-supported, comprehensive, coed **Entrance** Moderately difficult **Setting** 180-acre suburban campus **Total enrollment** 9,260 **Student-faculty ratio** 16:1 **Application deadline** 3/15 (freshmen), 6/1 (transfer) **Freshman admission** 77% were admitted **Freshman test scores** SAT critical reading scores over 500: 36.8%; SAT math scores over 500: 33.6%; ACT scores over 18: 62.8%; SAT critical reading scores over 600: 7%; SAT math scores over 600: 5%; ACT scores over 24: 11.5% **Housing** Yes **Expenses** Tuition & Fees: state resident $6976, nonresident $16,868; Room & Board $9270 **Undergraduates** 67% women, 26% part-time, 22% 25 or older, 0.3% Native American, 5% Hispanic American, 4% African American, 2% Asian American/Pacific Islander **The most frequently chosen baccalaureate fields are** business/marketing, education, psychology **Academic program** English as a second language, advanced placement, self-designed majors, honors program, summer session, adult/continuing education programs, internships **Contact** Deborah Johnson, Interim Director of Admissions, Rhode Island College, 600 Mount Pleasant Avenue, Providence, RI 02908-1927. *Phone:* 401-456-8234 or toll-free 800-669-5760. *Fax:* 401-456-8817. *E-mail:* admissions@ric.edu. *Web site:* http://www.ric.edu/.

Rhode Island School of Design
Providence, Rhode Island

Contact Mr. Edward Newhall, Director of Admissions, Rhode Island School of Design, 2 College Street, Providence, RI 02905-2791. *Phone:* 401-454-6307 or toll-free 800-364-7473. *Fax:* 401-454-6309. *E-mail:* admissions@risd.edu. *Web site:* http://www.risd.edu/.

Roger Williams University
Bristol, Rhode Island

General Independent, comprehensive, coed **Entrance** Moderately difficult **Setting** 140-acre small-town campus **Total enrollment** 5,159 **Student-faculty ratio** 12:1 **Application deadline** 2/1 (freshmen), rolling (transfer) **Freshman admission** 61% were admitted. Average high school GPA 3.21 **Freshman test scores** SAT critical reading scores over 500: 77.1%; SAT math scores over 500: 84.53%; ACT scores over 18: 98.5%; SAT critical reading scores over 600: 23.1%; SAT math scores over 600: 28.1%; ACT scores over 24: 43.9% **Housing** Yes **Expenses** Tuition & Fees $27,718; Room & Board $11,880 **Undergraduates** 48% women, 13% part-time, 11% 25 or older, 0.3% Native American, 2% Hispanic American, 2% African American, 1% Asian American/Pacific Islander **The most frequently chosen baccalaureate fields are** business/marketing, psychology, security and protective services **Academic program** English as a second language, advanced placement, self-designed majors, honors program, summer session, adult/continuing education programs, internships **Contact** Mr. Didier Bouvet, Dean of Undergraduate Admission, Roger Williams University, 1 Old Ferry Road, Bristol, RI 02809. *Phone:* 401-254-3500 or toll-free 800-458-7144. *Fax:* 401-254-3557. *E-mail:* admit@rwu.edu. *Web site:* http://www.rwu.edu/.

Visit Petersons.com and enter keyword Roger

Salve Regina University
Newport, Rhode Island

General Independent Roman Catholic, comprehensive, coed **Entrance** Moderately difficult **Setting** 75-acre suburban campus **Total enrollment** 2,578 **Student-faculty ratio** 14:1 **Application deadline** 2/1 (freshmen), rolling (transfer) **Freshman admission** 64% were admitted. Average high school GPA 3.38 **Freshman test scores** SAT critical reading scores over 500: 79%; SAT math scores over 500: 78%; ACT scores over 18: 100%; SAT critical reading scores over 600: 21%; SAT math scores over 600: 23%; ACT scores over 24: 59% **Housing** Yes **Expenses** Tuition & Fees $30,000; Room & Board $10,950 **Undergraduates** 69% women, 5% part-time, 5% 25 or older, 1% Native American, 3% Hispanic American, 2% African American, 1% Asian American/Pacific Islander **The most frequently chosen baccalaureate fields are** business/marketing, education, health professions and related sciences **Academic program** English as a second language, advanced placement, accelerated degree program, honors program, summer session, adult/continuing education programs, internships **Contact** Ms. Colleen Emerson, Dean of Undergraduate Admissions, Salve Regina University, 100 Ochre Point Avenue, Newport, RI 02840-4192. *Phone:* 401-341-2908 or toll-free 888-GO SALVE. *Fax:* 401-848-2823. *E-mail:* sruadmis@salve.edu. *Web site:* http://www.salve.edu/.

University of Rhode Island
Kingston, Rhode Island

General State-supported, university, coed **Entrance** Moderately difficult **Setting** 1,200-acre small-town campus **Total enrollment** 16,392 **Student-faculty ratio** 15:1 **Application deadline** 2/1 (freshmen), 6/1 (transfer) **Freshman admission** 84% were admitted. Average high school GPA 3.21 **Freshman test scores** SAT critical reading scores over 500: 67.95%; SAT math scores over 500: 73.11%; ACT scores over 18: 95.67%; SAT critical reading scores over 600: 17.25%; SAT math scores over 600: 25.73%; ACT scores over 24: 45.05% **Housing** Yes **Expenses** Tuition & Fees: state resident $9528, nonresident $26,026; Room & Board $9892 **Undergraduates** 55% women, 11% part-time, 4% 25 or older, 0.4% Native American, 6% Hispanic American, 5% African American, 3% Asian American/Pacific Islander **The most frequently chosen baccalaureate fields are** business/marketing, communications/journalism, health professions and related sciences **Academic program** Advanced placement, honors program, summer session, adult/continuing education programs, internships **Contact** Ms. Joanne Lynch, Assistant Dean of Admissions, University of Rhode Island, Undergraduate Admission Office, Newman Hall, 14 Upper College Road, Kingston, RI 02881. *Phone:* 401-874-7110. *Fax:* 401-874-5523. *E-mail:* lynch@uri.edu. *Web site:* http://www.uri.edu.

See page 1302 for the College Close-Up.

SOUTH CAROLINA

Allen University
Columbia, South Carolina

General Independent African Methodist Episcopal, 4-year, coed **Entrance** Minimally difficult **Setting** suburban campus **Total enrollment** 827 **Application deadline** 7/31 (freshmen) **Freshman admission** 72% were admitted **Housing** Yes **Expenses** Tuition & Fees $10,881 **Undergraduates** 56% women, 3% part-time, 30% 25 or older, 0.2% Hispanic American, 99% African American **The most frequently chosen baccalaureate fields are** business/marketing, philosophy and religious studies, social sciences **Academic program** Honors program, summer session, adult/continuing education programs, internships **Contact** Terri Parker, Director of Admission, Allen University, 1530 Harden Street, Columbia, SC 29204. *Phone:* 803-376-5733 or toll-free 877-625-5368. *E-mail:* tparker@allenuniversity.edu. *Web site:* http://www.allenuniversity.edu/.

Anderson University
Anderson, South Carolina

General Independent Baptist, comprehensive, coed **Entrance** Minimally difficult **Setting** 44-acre suburban campus **Total enrollment** 2,064 **Student-faculty ratio** 17:1 **Application deadline** 7/1 (freshmen) **Freshman admission** 78% were admitted. Average high school GPA 3.33 **Freshman test scores** SAT critical reading scores over 500: 56%; SAT math scores over 500: 54%; ACT scores over 18: 80%; SAT critical reading scores over 600: 18%; SAT math scores over 600: 14%; ACT scores over 24: 25% **Housing** Yes **Expenses** Tuition & Fees $19,212; Room & Board $7250 **Undergraduates** 66% women, 24% part-time, 22% 25 or older, 0.2% Native American, 2% Hispanic American, 11% African American, 1% Asian American/Pacific Islander **The most frequently chosen baccalaureate fields are** business/marketing, education, visual and performing arts **Academic program** Advanced placement, accelerated degree program, honors program, summer session, adult/continuing education programs, internships **Contact** Ms. Pam Bryant, Director of Admissions, Anderson University, 316 Boulevard, Anderson, SC 29621-4035. *Phone:* 864-231-2030 or toll-free 800-542-3594. *Fax:* 864-233-3033. *E-mail:* admissions@andersonuniversity.edu. *Web site:* http://www.andersonuniversity.edu/.

The Art Institute of Charleston
Charleston, South Carolina

General Proprietary, 4-year, coed **Setting** urban campus **Contact** Director of Admissions, The Art Institute of Charleston, 24 North Market Street, Charleston, SC 29401. *Phone:* 843-727-3500 or toll-free 866-211-0107. *Fax:* 843-727-3440. *Web site:* http://www.artinstitutes.edu/charleston/. **Visit Petersons.com and enter keywords Art Institute of Charleston**

See page 504 for the College Close-Up.

Benedict College
Columbia, South Carolina

General Independent Baptist, 4-year, coed **Entrance** Minimally difficult **Setting** 20-acre urban campus **Total enrollment** 2,641 **Application deadline** Rolling (freshmen), rolling (transfer) **Housing** Yes **Expenses** Tuition & Fees $14,570; Room & Board $6702 **Undergraduates** 10% 25 or older **Academic program** Advanced placement, honors program, summer session, adult/continuing education programs, internships **Contact** Phyllis Thompson, Director of Admissions and Student Marketing, Benedict College, 1600 Harden Street, Columbia, SC 29204. *Phone:* 803-705-4491 or toll-free 800-868-6598. *Fax:* 803-253-5167. *E-mail:* thompsop@benedict.edu. *Web site:* http://www.benedict.edu/.

Bob Jones University
Greenville, South Carolina

General Independent religious, university, coed **Entrance** Minimally difficult **Setting** 225-acre urban campus **Total enrollment** 3,956 **Student-faculty ratio** 13:1 **Application deadline** 8/1 (freshmen), 8/1 (transfer) **Freshman admission** 75% were admitted. Average high school GPA 3.42 **Freshman test scores** ACT scores over 18: 92.26%; ACT scores over 24: 51.79% **Housing** Yes **Expenses** Tuition & Fees $11,920; Room & Board $5100 **Undergraduates** 55% women, 3% part-time, 5% 25 or older, 0.2% Native American, 3% Hispanic American, 1% African American, 5% Asian American/Pacific Islander **The most frequently chosen baccalaureate fields are** education, business/marketing, theology and religious vocations **Academic program** English as a second language, advanced placement, accelerated degree program, summer session, adult/continuing education programs, internships **Contact** Mr. Gary Deedrick, Director of Admissions, Bob Jones University, 1700 Wade Hampton Boulevard, Greenville, SC 29614. *Phone:* 864-242-5100 or toll-free 800-BJANDME. *Fax:* 800-232-9258. *E-mail:* admissions@bju.edu. *Web site:* http://www.bju.edu/.

Brown Mackie College–Greenville
Greenville, South Carolina

General Proprietary, primarily 2-year, coed **Contact** Director of Admissions, Brown Mackie College–Greenville, Two Liberty Square, 75 Beattie Place, Suite 100, Greenville, SC 29601. *Phone:* 864-239-5300 or toll-free 877-479-8465. *Fax:* 864-232-4094. *Web site:* http://www.brownmackie.edu/Greenville.

See page 624 for the College Close-Up.

Charleston Southern University
Charleston, South Carolina

Contact Mr. Jim Rhoden, Director of Enrollment Management, Charleston Southern University, PO Box 118087, Charleston, SC 29423-8087. *Phone:* 843-863-7050 or toll-free 800-947-7474. *E-mail:* enroll@csuniv.edu. *Web site:* http://www.charlestonsouthern.edu/.

The Citadel, The Military College of South Carolina
Charleston, South Carolina

General State-supported, comprehensive, coed **Entrance** Moderately difficult **Setting** 300-acre suburban campus **Total enrollment** 3,339 **Student-faculty ratio** 16:1 **Application deadline** Rolling (freshmen), rolling (transfer) **Freshman admission** 79% were admitted. Average high school GPA 3.37 **Freshman test scores** SAT critical reading scores over 500: 70%; SAT math scores over 500: 81%; ACT scores over 18: 100%; SAT critical reading scores over 600: 21%; SAT math scores over 600: 29%; ACT scores over 24: 24% **Housing** Yes **Expenses** Tuition & Fees: state resident $9824, nonresident $23,634; Room & Board $5965 **Undergraduates** 8% women, 5% part-time, 5% 25 or older, 0.3% Native American, 5% Hispanic American, 7% African American, 3% Asian American/Pacific Islander **The most frequently chosen baccalaureate fields are** business/marketing, engineering, security and protective services **Academic program** English as a second language, advanced placement, honors program, summer session, internships **Contact** Lt. Col. John W. Powell Jr., Director of Admissions, The Citadel, The Military College of South Carolina, 171 Moultrie Street, Charleston, SC 29409. *Phone:* 843-953-5230 or toll-free 800-868-1842. *Fax:* 843-953-7036. *E-mail:* john.powell@citadel.edu. *Web site:* http://www.citadel.edu.

Visit Petersons.com and enter keyword Citadel

See page 708 for the College Close-Up.

Claflin University
Orangeburg, South Carolina

General Independent United Methodist, comprehensive, coed **Entrance** Minimally difficult **Setting** 43-acre small-town campus **Total enrollment** 1,860 **Student-faculty ratio** 14:1 **Application deadline** Rolling (freshmen), rolling (transfer) **Freshman admission** 35% were admitted. Average high school GPA 3 **Freshman test scores** SAT critical reading scores over 500: 32%; SAT math scores over 500: 24%; SAT critical reading scores over 600: 6%; SAT math scores over 600: 4% **Housing** Yes **Expenses** Tuition & Fees $12,666; Room & Board $6806 **Undergraduates** 66% women, 4% part-time, 17% 25 or older, 0.2% Native American, 0.4% Hispanic American, 95% African American, 0.1% Asian American/Pacific Islander **The most frequently chosen baccalaureate fields are** business/marketing, security and protective services, social sciences **Academic program** Advanced placement, honors program, summer session, adult/continuing education programs, internships **Contact** Claflin University, 400 Magnolia Street, Orangeburg, SC 29115. *Phone:* toll-free 800-922-1276. *Web site:* http://www.claflin.edu/.

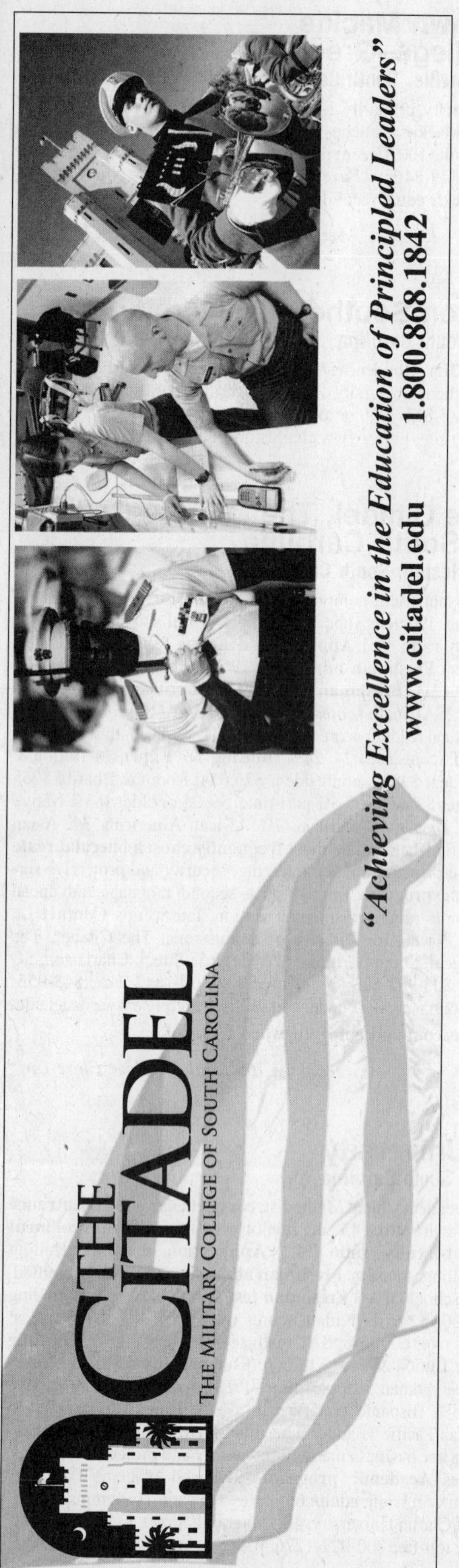

Clemson University
Clemson, South Carolina

General State-supported, university, coed **Entrance** Moderately difficult **Setting** 1,400-acre small-town campus **Total enrollment** 18,317 **Student-faculty ratio** 14:1 **Application deadline** 5/1 (freshmen), 7/1 (transfer) **Freshman admission** 63% were admitted. Average high school GPA 3.89 **Freshman test scores** SAT critical reading scores over 500: 92%; SAT math scores over 500: 96%; ACT scores over 18: 99%; SAT critical reading scores over 600: 51%; SAT math scores over 600: 71%; ACT scores over 24: 86% **Housing** Yes **Expenses** Tuition & Fees: state resident $11,609, nonresident $25,910; Room & Board $6774 **Undergraduates** 46% women, 6% part-time, 4% 25 or older, 0.3% Native American, 1% Hispanic American, 7% African American, 2% Asian American/Pacific Islander **The most frequently chosen baccalaureate fields are** business/marketing, education, engineering **Academic program** Advanced placement, honors program, summer session, internships **Contact** Ms. Audrey R. Bodell, Associate Director of Admissions, Clemson University, PO Box 345124, 105 Sikes Hall, Clemson, SC 29634. *Phone:* 864-656-2287. *Fax:* 864-656-2464. *E-mail:* cuadmissions@clemson.edu. *Web site:* http://www.clemson.edu/.

Visit Petersons.com and enter keyword Clemson

See page 718 for the College Close-Up.

Coastal Carolina University
Conway, South Carolina

General State-supported, comprehensive, coed **Entrance** Moderately difficult **Setting** 307-acre suburban campus **Total enrollment** 8,360 **Student-faculty ratio** 18:1 **Application deadline** 8/15 (freshmen), 8/15 (transfer) **Freshman admission** 74% were admitted. Average high school GPA 3.31 **Freshman test scores** SAT critical reading scores over 500: 52.65%; SAT math scores over 500: 61.82%; ACT scores over 18: 92.6%; SAT critical reading scores over 600: 10.81%; SAT math scores over 600: 14.79%; ACT scores over 24: 13.12% **Housing** Yes **Expenses** Tuition & Fees: state resident $8950, nonresident $18,770; Room & Board $7200 **Undergraduates** 53% women, 10% part-time, 9% 25 or older, 1% Native American, 3% Hispanic American, 15% African American, 1% Asian American/Pacific Islander **The most frequently chosen baccalaureate fields are** biological/life sciences, business/marketing, education **Academic program** Advanced placement, accelerated degree program, self-designed majors, honors program, summer session, adult/continuing education programs, internships **Contact** Dr. Judy Vogt, Vice President, Enrollment Services, Coastal Carolina University, PO Box 261954, Conway, SC 29528-6054. *Phone:* 843-349-2037 or toll-free 800-277-7000. *Fax:* 843-349-2127. *E-mail:* admissions@coastal.edu. *Web site:* http://www.coastal.edu/.

Coker College
Hartsville, South Carolina

General Independent, 4-year, coed **Entrance** Moderately difficult **Setting** 30-acre small-town campus **Total enrollment** 658 **Student-faculty ratio** 10:1 **Application deadline** 8/1 (freshmen), rolling (transfer) **Freshman admission** 56% were admitted. Average high school GPA 3.36 **Freshman test scores** SAT critical reading scores over 500: 51%; SAT math scores over 500: 50%; ACT scores over 18: 100%; SAT critical reading scores over 600: 15%; SAT math scores over 600: 7%; ACT scores over 24: 80% **Housing** Yes **Expenses** Tuition & Fees $19,858; Room & Board $6240 **Undergraduates** 62% women, 2% part-time, 4% 25 or older, 1% Native American, 2% Hispanic American, 25% African American, 0.5% Asian American/Pacific Islander **The most frequently chosen baccalaureate fields are** business/marketing, psychology, visual and performing arts **Academic program** Honors program, summer session **Contact** Mrs. Perry Wilson, Director of Admissions, Coker College, 300 East College Avenue, Hartsville, SC 29550. *Phone:* 843-383-8050 or toll-free 800-950-1908. *Fax:* 843-383-8056. *E-mail:* admissions@coker.edu. *Web site:* http://www.coker.edu/.

College of Charleston

Charleston, South Carolina

General State-supported, comprehensive, coed **Entrance** Moderately difficult **Setting** 52-acre urban campus **Total enrollment** 11,772 **Student-faculty ratio** 16:1 **Application deadline** 4/1 (freshmen), 4/1 (transfer) **Freshman admission** 70% were admitted. Average high school GPA 3.89 **Freshman test scores** SAT critical reading scores over 500: 97.8%; SAT math scores over 500: 97.6%; ACT scores over 18: 99.8%; SAT critical reading scores over 600: 53.8%; SAT math scores over 600: 57.7%; ACT scores over 24: 65.3% **Housing** Yes **Expenses** Tuition & Fees: state resident $8988, nonresident $21,846; Room & Board $9411 **Undergraduates** 64% women, 8% part-time, 7% 25 or older, 0.4% Native American, 2% Hispanic American, 5% African American, 2% Asian American/Pacific Islander **The most frequently chosen baccalaureate fields are** business/marketing, communications/journalism, social sciences **Academic program** English as a second language, advanced placement, accelerated degree program, honors program, summer session, adult/continuing education programs, internships **Contact** Ms. Suzette Stille, Director of Undergraduate Admissions, College of Charleston, 66 George Street, Charleston, SC 29424-0001. *Phone:* 843-953-5670 or toll-free 843-953-5670. *Fax:* 843-953-6322. *E-mail:* admissions@cofc.edu. *Web site:* http://www.cofc.edu/.

Columbia College

Columbia, South Carolina

General Independent United Methodist, comprehensive, undergraduate: women only; graduate: coed **Entrance** Moderately difficult **Setting** 33-acre suburban campus **Total enrollment** 1,445 **Student-faculty ratio** 10:1 **Application deadline** 8/1 (freshmen), 8/1 (transfer) **Freshman admission** 74% were admitted. Average high school GPA 3.5 **Freshman test scores** SAT critical reading scores over 500: 52%; SAT math scores over 500: 42%; SAT critical reading scores over 600: 18%; SAT math scores over 600: 13% **Housing** Yes **Expenses** Tuition & Fees $23,480; Room & Board $6450 **Undergraduates** 19% part-time, 30% 25 or older, 1% Native American, 2% Hispanic American, 42% African American, 2% Asian American/Pacific Islander **The most frequently chosen baccalaureate fields are** business/marketing, education, public administration and social services **Academic program** Advanced placement, self-designed majors, honors program, summer session, adult/continuing education programs, internships **Contact** Ms. Julie King, Director of Admissions, Columbia College, 1301 Columbia College Drive, Columbia, SC 29203. *Phone:* 803-786-3765 or toll-free 800-277-1301. *Fax:* 803-786-3674. *E-mail:* admissions@colacoll.edu. *Web site:* http://www.columbiacollegesc.edu/.

Columbia International University

Columbia, South Carolina

General Independent nondenominational, university, coed **Entrance** Minimally difficult **Setting** 450-acre suburban campus **Total enrollment** 1,139 **Student-faculty ratio** 20:1 **Application deadline** Rolling (freshmen), rolling (transfer) **Freshman admission** 82% were admitted. Average high school GPA 3.52 **Freshman test scores** SAT critical reading scores over 500: 82%; SAT math scores over 500: 71%; ACT scores over 18: 96%; SAT critical reading scores over 600: 41%; SAT math scores over 600: 15%; ACT scores over 24: 39% **Housing** Yes **Expenses** Tuition & Fees $17,395; Room & Board $6410 **Undergraduates** 52% women, 15% part-time, 23% 25 or older **The most frequently chosen baccalaureate fields are** psychology, education, theology and religious vocations **Academic program** Advanced placement, accelerated degree program, summer session, internships **Contact** Mr. Dan Griffin, Director of Admissions and Student Financial Services, Columbia International University, PO Box 3122, Columbia, SC 29230-3122. *Phone:* 803-807-5024 or toll-free 800-777-2227 Ext. 3024. *Fax:* 803-786-4041. *E-mail:* yesciu@ciu.edu. *Web site:* http://www.ciu.edu/.

Converse College

Spartanburg, South Carolina

General Independent, comprehensive, undergraduate: women only; graduate: coed **Entrance** Moderately difficult **Setting** 70-acre urban campus **Total enrollment** 1,720 **Student-faculty ratio** 9:1 **Application deadline** Rolling (freshmen), 7/1 (transfer) **Freshman admission** 68% were admitted. Average high school GPA 3.86 **Freshman test scores** SAT critical reading scores over 500: 70%; SAT math scores over 500: 67%; ACT scores over 18: 93%; SAT critical reading scores over 600: 23%; SAT math scores over 600: 17%; ACT scores over 24: 42% **Housing** Yes **Expenses** Tuition & Fees $26,138; Room & Board $8032 **Undergraduates** 15% part-time, 13% 25 or older, 1% Native American, 3% Hispanic American, 15% African American, 1% Asian American/Pacific Islander **The most frequently chosen baccalaureate fields are** education, psychology, visual and performing arts **Academic program** English as a second language, advanced placement, self-designed majors, honors program, summer session, adult/continuing education programs, internships **Contact** Ms. April Lewis, Director of Admissions, Converse College, 580 East Main Street, Spartanburg, SC 29302. *Phone:* 864-596-9040 Ext. 9746 or toll-free 800-766-1125. *Fax:* 864-596-9225. *E-mail:* admissions@converse.edu. *Web site:* http://www.converse.edu/.

Erskine College

Due West, South Carolina

General Independent, comprehensive, coed, affiliated with Associate Reformed Presbyterian Church **Entrance** Moderately difficult **Setting** 93-acre rural campus **Total enrollment** 874 **Student-faculty ratio** 11:1 **Application deadline** Rolling (freshmen), rolling (transfer) **Freshman admission** 70% were admitted. Average high school GPA 3.83 **Freshman test scores** SAT critical reading scores over 500: 67%; SAT math scores over 500: 70%; ACT scores over 18: 98%; SAT critical reading scores over 600: 22%; SAT math scores over 600: 31%; ACT scores over 24: 67% **Housing** Yes **Expenses** Tuition & Fees $24,645; Room & Board $8325 **Undergraduates** 55% women, 3% part-time, 1% Hispanic American, 7% African American, 1% Asian American/Pacific Islander **The most frequently chosen baccalaureate fields are** biological/life sciences, business/marketing, education **Academic program** Advanced placement, summer session, internships **Contact** Mr. Woody O'Cain, Vice President for Enrollment, Erskine College, 2 Washington Street, PO Box 338, Due West, SC 29639. *Phone:* 864-379-8838 or toll-free 800-241-8721. *Fax:* 864-379-2167. *E-mail:* ocain@erskine.edu. *Web site:* http://www.erskine.edu/.

Francis Marion University

Florence, South Carolina

General State-supported, comprehensive, coed **Entrance** Moderately difficult **Setting** 400-acre rural campus **Total enrollment** 3,957 **Student-faculty ratio** 15:1 **Application deadline** Rolling (freshmen), rolling (transfer) **Freshman admission** 56% were admitted. Average high school GPA 3.56 **Freshman test scores** SAT critical reading scores over 500: 40.2%; SAT math scores over 500: 42.5%; ACT scores over 18: 79.1%; SAT critical reading scores over 600: 8.4%; SAT math scores over 600: 8.2%; ACT scores over 24: 14.1% **Housing** Yes **Expenses** Tuition & Fees: state resident $7960, nonresident $15,585; Room & Board $6024 **Undergraduates** 68% women, 9% part-time, 9% 25 or older, 1% Native American, 1% Hispanic American, 48% African American, 1% Asian American/Pacific Islander **The most frequently chosen baccalaureate fields are** biological/life sciences, business/marketing, social sciences **Academic program** Advanced placement, accelerated degree program, honors program, summer session, adult/continuing education programs, internships **Contact** Mr. James Schlimmer, Director of Admissions, Francis Marion University, PO Box 100547, Florence, SC 29502-0547. *Phone:* 843-661-1231 or toll-free 800-368-7551. *Fax:* 843-661-4635. *E-mail:* admission@fmarion.edu. *Web site:* http://www.fmarion.edu/.

Furman University

Greenville, South Carolina

General Independent, comprehensive, coed **Entrance** Very difficult **Setting** 800-acre suburban campus **Total enrollment** 2,964 **Student-faculty ratio** 11:1 **Application deadline** 1/15 (freshmen), 6/1 (transfer) **Freshman admission** 68% were admitted. Average high school GPA 3.83 **Freshman test scores** SAT critical reading scores over 500: 96.9%; SAT math scores over 500: 95.2%; ACT scores over 18: 99.8%; SAT critical reading scores over 600: 71.6%; SAT math scores over 600: 75.2%; ACT scores over 24: 88.3% **Housing** Yes **Expenses** Tuition & Fees $36,656; Room & Board $9170 **Undergraduates** 57% women, 5% part-time, 0.1% Native American, 2% Hispanic American, 7% African American, 2% Asian American/Pacific Islander **The most frequently chosen baccalaureate fields are** business/marketing, history, social sciences **Academic program** Advanced placement, accelerated degree program, self-designed majors, summer session, adult/continuing education programs, internships **Contact** Mr. Brad Pochard, Director of Admissions, Furman University, 3300 Poinsett Highway, Greenville, SC 29613. *Phone:* 864-294-2034. *Fax:* 864-294-2018. *E-mail:* admissions@furman.edu. *Web site:* http://www.furman.edu/.

ITT Technical Institute

Columbia, South Carolina

General Proprietary, primarily 2-year, coed **Contact** Director of Recruitment, ITT Technical Institute, 720 Gracern Road, Suite 120, Columbia, SC 29210. *Phone:* 803-216-6000 or toll-free 800-242-5158. *Web site:* http://www.itt-tech.edu/.

ITT Technical Institute

Greenville, South Carolina

General Proprietary, primarily 2-year, coed **Entrance** Minimally difficult **Housing** No **Contact** Director of Recruitment, ITT Technical Institute, 6 Independence Pointe, Greenville, SC 29615. *Phone:* 864-288-0777 or toll-free 800-932-4488. *Web site:* http://www.itt-tech.edu/.

Lander University

Greenwood, South Carolina

General State-supported, comprehensive, coed **Entrance** Moderately difficult **Setting** 100-acre small-town campus **Total enrollment** 2,614 **Student-faculty ratio** 14:1 **Application deadline** 8/1 (freshmen), rolling (transfer) **Freshman admission** 47% were admitted. Average high school GPA 3.56 **Freshman test scores** SAT critical reading scores over 500: 37.6%; SAT math scores over 500: 46.8%; ACT scores over 18: 76.5%; SAT critical reading scores over 600: 10.4%; SAT math scores over 600: 12.4%; ACT scores over 24: 14% **Housing** Yes **Expenses** Tuition & Fees: state resident $9540, nonresident $17,340; Room & Board $6400 **Undergraduates** 65% women, 11% part-time, 19% 25 or older, 1% Native American, 1% Hispanic American, 27% African American, 1% Asian American/Pacific Islander **The most frequently chosen baccalaureate fields are** business/marketing, education, social sciences **Academic program** Advanced placement, accelerated degree program, self-designed majors, honors program, summer session, adult/continuing education programs, internships **Contact** Dr. Bettie R. Horne, Director of Admissions, Lander University, 320 Stanley Avenue, Greenwood, SC 29649. *Phone:* 864-388-8307 or toll-free 888-452-6337. *Fax:* 864-388-8125. *E-mail:* admissions@lander.edu. *Web site:* http://www.lander.edu/.

Limestone College

Gaffney, South Carolina

General Independent, 4-year, coed **Entrance** Minimally difficult **Setting** 115-acre suburban campus **Total enrollment** 808 **Student-faculty ratio** 12:1 **Application deadline** Rolling (freshmen), rolling (transfer) **Freshman admission** 71% were admitted. Average high school GPA 3.09 **Freshman test scores** SAT critical reading scores over 500: 23%; SAT math scores over 500: 41%; ACT scores over 18: 66%; SAT critical reading scores over 600: 4%; SAT math scores over 600: 10%; ACT scores over 24: 27% **Housing** Yes **Expenses** Tuition & Fees $19,200; Room & Board $7000 **Undergraduates** 42% women, 2% part-time, 6% 25 or older, 0.4% Native American, 3% Hispanic American, 20% African American, 0.5% Asian American/Pacific Islander **The most frequently chosen baccalaureate fields are** business/marketing, education, parks and recreation **Academic program** Advanced placement, accelerated degree program, self-designed majors, honors program, summer session, adult/continuing education programs, internships **Contact** Ms. Sharon Chery, Admissions Office Manager, Limestone College, 1115 College Drive, Gaffney, SC 29340-3799. *Phone:* 864-488-4554 or toll-free 800-795-7151 Ext. 554. *Fax:* 864-487-8706. *E-mail:* cphenicie@limestone.edu. *Web site:* http://www.limestone.edu/.

Visit Petersons.com and enter keyword Limestone

See page 918 for the College Close-Up.

Medical University of South Carolina

Charleston, South Carolina

General State-supported, upper-level, coed **Entrance** Very difficult **Setting** 80-acre urban campus **Total enrollment** 2,514 **Student-faculty ratio** 8:1 **Housing** No **Expenses** Tuition & Fees: state resident $13,768, nonresident $23,376 **Undergraduates** 83% women, 18% part-time, 59% 25 or older, 1% Native American, 1% Hispanic American, 10% African American, 5% Asian American/Pacific Islander **The most frequently chosen baccalaureate field is** health professions and related sciences **Academic program** Advanced placement, internships **Contact** Lyla E. Hudson, Director of Admissions, Medical University of South Carolina, 41 Bee Street MSC203, Charleston, SC 29425-2030. *Phone:* 843-792-7408. *E-mail:* hudsonly@musc.edu. *Web site:* http://www.musc.edu/.

Morris College

Sumter, South Carolina

General Independent, 4-year, coed, affiliated with Baptist Educational and Missionary Convention of South Carolina **Entrance** Noncompetitive **Setting** 34-acre small-town campus **Total enrollment** 966 **Student-faculty ratio** 18:1 **Application deadline** Rolling (freshmen), rolling (transfer) **Freshman admission** 91% were admitted. Average high school GPA 2.51 **Housing** Yes **Expenses** Tuition & Fees $9901; Room & Board $4386 **Undergraduates** 58% women, 1% part-time, 11% 25 or older, 0.1% Hispanic American, 99% African American **The most frequently chosen baccalaureate fields are** business/marketing, health professions and related sciences, social sciences **Academic program** Advanced placement, accelerated degree program, honors program, summer session, adult/continuing education programs, internships **Contact** Ms. Deborah C. Calhoun, Director of Admissions and Records, Morris College, 100 West College Street, Sumter, SC 29150-3599. *Phone:* 803-934-3225 or toll-free 866-853-1345. *Fax:* 803-773-8241. *E-mail:* dcalhoun@morris.edu. *Web site:* http://www.morris.edu/.

Newberry College

Newberry, South Carolina

General Independent Evangelical Lutheran, 4-year, coed **Entrance** Moderately difficult **Setting** 60-acre small-town campus **Total enrollment** 1,103 **Student-faculty ratio** 17:1 **Application deadline** Rolling (freshmen), rolling (transfer) **Freshman admission** 69% were admitted. Average high school GPA 3.3 **Housing** Yes **Expenses** Tuition & Fees $22,470; Room & Board $7750 **Undergraduates** 45% women, 2% part-time, 3% 25 or older, 2% Hispanic American, 27% African American, 1% Asian American/Pacific Islander **The most frequently chosen baccalaureate fields are** business/marketing, education, parks and recreation **Academic program** Advanced placement, self-designed

LIMESTONE COLLEGE

Small Enough to Know You
Big Enough for Success

Our small student population cultivates a family-like atmosphere where students, faculty, and staff get to know each other. Students will experience excellent academics, award winning academic interest groups, active student service groups, and nationally ranked athletic teams, Success Begins Here...

Limestone College
Gaffney, South Carolina

Traditional Day Program Admissions
864-488-4554 or 1-800-795-7151

www.LIMESTONE.edu

majors, honors program, summer session, adult/continuing education programs, internships **Contact** Mrs. Amanda Richardson, Director of Admissions, Newberry College, 2100 College Street, Holland Hall, Newberry, SC 29108. *Phone:* 803-321-5129 or toll-free 800-845-4955 Ext. 5127. *Fax:* 803-321-5138. *E-mail:* admissions@newberry.edu. *Web site:* http://www.newberry.edu/.

Visit Petersons.com and enter keyword Newberry

North Greenville University
Tigerville, South Carolina

General Independent Southern Baptist, comprehensive, coed **Entrance** Minimally difficult **Setting** 330-acre rural campus **Total enrollment** 2,260 **Student-faculty ratio** 15:1 **Application deadline** 8/18 (freshmen), 8/21 (transfer) **Freshman admission** 55% were admitted. Average high school GPA 3.72 **Freshman test scores** SAT critical reading scores over 500: 55%; SAT math scores over 500: 54%; ACT scores over 18: 80%; SAT critical reading scores over 600: 20%; SAT math scores over 600: 15%; ACT scores over 24: 27% **Housing** Yes **Expenses** Tuition & Fees $12,264; Room & Board $7056 **Undergraduates** 51% women, 11% part-time, 5% 25 or older, 0.04% Native American, 1% Hispanic American, 8% African American, 0.3% Asian American/Pacific Islander **The most frequently chosen baccalaureate fields are** business/marketing, education, theology and religious vocations **Academic program** English as a second language, advanced placement, accelerated degree program, self-designed majors, honors program, summer session, internships **Contact** Ms. Keli Sewell, Vice President of Admissions and Financial Aid, North Greenville University, PO Box 1892, Tigerville, SC 29688-1892. *Phone:* 864-977-7052 or toll-free 800-468-6642 Ext. 7001. *E-mail:* ksewell@ngu.edu. *Web site:* http://www.ngu.edu/.

Presbyterian College
Clinton, South Carolina

General Independent, 4-year, coed, affiliated with Presbyterian Church (U.S.A.) **Entrance** Very difficult **Setting** 240-acre small-town campus **Total enrollment** 1,221 **Student-faculty ratio** 12:1 **Application deadline** 2/1 (freshmen), 7/1 (transfer) **Freshman admission** 70% were admitted. Average high school GPA 3.43 **Freshman test scores** SAT critical reading scores over 500: 71%; SAT math scores over 500: 80%; ACT scores over 18: 96%; SAT critical reading scores over 600: 31%; SAT math scores over 600: 42%; ACT scores over 24: 55% **Housing** Yes **Expenses** Tuition & Fees $28,880; Room & Board $8345 **Undergraduates** 51% women, 2% part-time, 0.2% Native American, 1% Hispanic American, 8% African American, 1% Asian American/Pacific Islander **The most frequently chosen baccalaureate fields are** business/marketing, psychology, social sciences **Academic program** Advanced placement, honors program, summer session, internships **Contact** Mrs. Leni N. Patterson, Dean of Admissions and Financial Aid, Presbyterian College, 503 South Broad Street, Clinton, SC 29325. *Phone:* 864-833-8229 or toll-free 800-476-7272. *Fax:* 864-833-8481. *E-mail:* lpatters@presby.edu. *Web site:* http://www.presby.edu/.

South Carolina State University
Orangeburg, South Carolina

General State-supported, comprehensive, coed **Entrance** Minimally difficult **Setting** 160-acre small-town campus **Total enrollment** 4,538 **Student-faculty ratio** 16:1 **Application deadline** 7/31 (freshmen), 7/31 (transfer) **Freshman admission** 78% were admitted. Average high school GPA 2.84 **Freshman test scores** SAT critical reading scores over 500: 18%; SAT math scores over 500: 19%; ACT scores over 18: 37%; SAT critical reading scores over 600: 3%; SAT math scores over 600: 7%; ACT scores over 24: 6% **Housing** Yes **Expenses** Tuition & Fees: state resident $8462, nonresident $16,626; Room & Board $8862 **Undergraduates** 54% women, 8% part-time, 10% 25 or older, 0.1% Native

South Carolina State University (continued)
American, 1% Hispanic American, 96% African American, 0.2% Asian American/Pacific Islander **The most frequently chosen baccalaureate fields are** business/marketing, biological/life sciences, family and consumer sciences **Academic program** Advanced placement, honors program, summer session, adult/continuing education programs, internships **Contact** Mr. Antonio Boyle, Assistant Vice President of Enrollment Management, South Carolina State University, 300 College Street Northeast, Orangeburg, SC 29117-0001. *Phone:* 803-536-7186 or toll-free 800-260-5956. *Fax:* 803-536-8990. *E-mail:* admissions@scsu.edu. *Web site:* http://www.scsu.edu/.

Southern Methodist College
Orangeburg, South Carolina

General Independent religious, 4-year, coed **Entrance** Minimally difficult **Total enrollment** 26 **Application deadline** 7/15 (freshmen), 7/15 (transfer) **Freshman admission** 100% were admitted **Housing** Yes **Expenses** Tuition & Fees $7432; Room & Board $4640 **Undergraduates** 81% 25 or older **Academic program** Advanced placement, accelerated degree program, honors program, summer session, adult/continuing education programs, internships **Contact** Ms. Juanta Webb, Recruitment Officer, Southern Methodist College, PO Box 1027, Orangeburg, SC 29116-7827. *Phone:* 803-268-1322 or toll-free 800-360-1503. *Fax:* 803-534-7827. *E-mail:* jwebb@smcollege.edu. *Web site:* http://www.smcollege.edu/.

Southern Wesleyan University
Central, South Carolina

General Independent, comprehensive, coed, affiliated with Wesleyan Church **Entrance** Minimally difficult **Setting** 350-acre small-town campus **Total enrollment** 2,382 **Student-faculty ratio** 23:1 **Application deadline** 8/1 (freshmen), 8/1 (transfer) **Freshman admission** 95% were admitted. Average high school GPA 3.6 **Freshman test scores** SAT critical reading scores over 500: 46%; SAT math scores over 500: 46%; ACT scores over 18: 80%; SAT critical reading scores over 600: 7%; SAT math scores over 600: 13%; ACT scores over 24: 21% **Housing** Yes **Expenses** Tuition & Fees $19,500; Room & Board $7200 **Undergraduates** 63% women, 2% part-time, 60% 25 or older, 1% Native American, 2% Hispanic American, 29% African American, 0.2% Asian American/Pacific Islander **The most frequently chosen baccalaureate fields are** business/marketing, education, psychology **Academic program** Advanced placement, accelerated degree program, self-designed majors, honors program, summer session, adult/continuing education programs, internships **Contact** Mrs. Beth Roe, Director of First Year Experience, Southern Wesleyan University, PO Box 1020, 907 Wesleyan Drive, Central, SC 29630-1020. *Phone:* 864-644-5149 or toll-free 800-289-1292 Ext. 5550. *Fax:* 864-644-5901. *E-mail:* broe@swu.edu. *Web site:* http://www.swu.edu/.

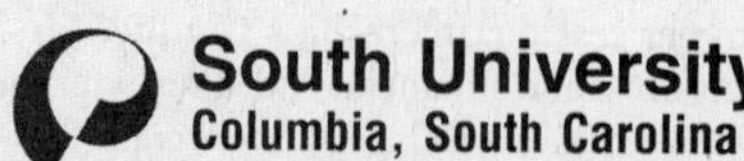

South University
Columbia, South Carolina

General Proprietary, comprehensive, coed **Contact** Director of Admissions, South University, 9 Science Court, Columbia, SC 29203. *Phone:* 803-799-9082 or toll-free 866-629-3031. *Fax:* 803-935-4382. *Web site:* http://www.southuniversity.edu/columbia/.

Visit Petersons.com and enter keywords South University

See page 1182 for the College Close-Up.

Strayer University–Charleston Campus
North Charleston, South Carolina

General Proprietary, comprehensive, coed **Contact** Admissions Office, Strayer University–Charleston Campus, 5010 Wetland Crossing, North Charleston, SC 29418. *Phone:* 843-746-5100. *Web site:* http://www.strayer.edu/charleston.

Strayer University–Columbia Campus
Columbia, South Carolina

General Proprietary, comprehensive, coed **Contact** Admissions Office, Strayer University–Columbia Campus, 200 Center Point Circle, Suite 300, Columbia, SC 29210. *Phone:* 803-750-2500. *Web site:* http://www.strayer.edu/columbia.

Strayer University–Greenville Campus
Greenville, South Carolina

General Proprietary, comprehensive, coed **Contact** Admissions Office, Strayer University–Greenville Campus, 555 North Pleasantburg Drive, Suite 300, Greenville, SC 29607. *Phone:* 864-250-7000. *Web site:* http://www.strayer.edu/greenville.

University of South Carolina
Columbia, South Carolina

General State-supported, university, coed **Entrance** Moderately difficult **Setting** 315-acre urban campus **Total enrollment** 28,481 **Student-faculty ratio** 18:1 **Application deadline** 12/1 (freshmen), 6/1 (transfer) **Freshman admission** 64% were admitted. Average high school GPA 3.86 **Freshman test scores** SAT critical reading scores over 500: 90.87%; SAT math scores over 500: 95.05%; ACT scores over 18: 99.73%; SAT critical reading scores over 600: 44.26%; SAT math scores over 600: 55.48%; ACT scores over 24: 77.89% **Housing** Yes **Expenses** Tuition & Fees: state resident $9156, nonresident $23,732; Room & Board $7328 **Undergraduates** 54% women, 7% part-time, 8% 25 or older, 0.3% Native American, 3% Hispanic American, 11% African American **The most frequently chosen baccalaureate fields are** business/marketing, parks and recreation, social sciences **Academic program** English as a second language, advanced placement, accelerated degree program, self-designed majors, honors program, summer session, adult/continuing education programs, internships **Contact** Dr. Mary Wagner, Senior Associate Director, Undergraduate Admissions, University of South Carolina, Columbia, SC 29208. *Phone:* 803-777-7700 or toll-free 800-868-5872. *Fax:* 803-777-0101. *E-mail:* admissions-ugrad@sc.edu. *Web site:* http://www.sc.edu/.

Visit Petersons.com and enter keywords University of South Carolina

University of South Carolina Aiken
Aiken, South Carolina

General State-supported, comprehensive, coed **Entrance** Moderately difficult **Setting** 453-acre suburban campus **Total enrollment** 3,269 **Student-faculty ratio** 15:1 **Application deadline** 8/1 (freshmen), 8/1 (transfer) **Freshman admission** 38% were admitted. Average high school GPA 3.58 **Freshman test scores** SAT critical reading scores over 500: 44%; SAT math scores over 500: 52%; ACT scores over 18: 84%; SAT critical reading scores over 600: 9%; SAT math scores over 600: 12%; ACT scores over 24: 20% **Housing** Yes **Expenses** Tuition & Fees: state resident $7582, nonresident $14,946; Room & Board $6620 **Undergraduates** 66% women, 23% part-time, 15% 25 or older **The most frequently chosen baccalaureate fields are** business/marketing, education, health professions and related sciences **Academic program** English as a second language, advanced placement, accelerated degree program, self-designed majors, honors program, summer session, adult/continuing education programs, internships **Contact** Mr. Andrew Hendrix, Director of Admissions, University of South Carolina Aiken, 471 University Parkway, Aiken, SC 29801-6309. *Phone:* 803-648-6851 Ext. 3366 or toll-free 888-WOW-USCA. *Fax:* 803-641-3727. *E-mail:* admit@usca.edu. *Web site:* http://www.usca.edu/.

University of South Carolina Beaufort
Bluffton, South Carolina

General State-supported, 4-year, coed **Entrance** Minimally difficult **Setting** 200-acre small-town campus **Total enrollment** 1,684 **Application deadline** Rolling (freshmen), rolling (transfer) **Freshman admission** 73% were admitted **Housing** Yes **Expenses** Tuition & Fees: state resident $7330, nonresident $15,180; Room & Board $6100 **Undergraduates** 60% women, 25% part-time **The most frequently chosen baccalaureate fields are** business/marketing, psychology, social sciences **Academic program** Advanced placement, summer session, adult/continuing education programs, internships **Contact** Ms. Monica Williams, University of South Carolina Beaufort, 1 University Boulevard, Bluffton, SC 29909. *Phone:* 843-208-8112. *Fax:* 843-208-8015. *E-mail:* mrwilli5@uscb.edu. *Web site:* http://www.uscb.edu/.

University of South Carolina Upstate
Spartanburg, South Carolina

General State-supported, comprehensive, coed **Entrance** Moderately difficult **Setting** 300-acre urban campus **Total enrollment** 5,403 **Student-faculty ratio** 17:1 **Freshman admission** 78% were admitted. Average high school GPA 3.53 **Freshman test scores** SAT critical reading scores over 500: 40.32%; SAT math scores over 500: 42.05%; ACT scores over 18: 81.6%; SAT critical reading scores over 600: 8.21%; SAT math scores over 600: 7.16%; ACT scores over 24: 15.52% **Housing** Yes **Expenses** Tuition & Fees: state resident $8862, nonresident $17,504; Room & Board $6300 **Undergraduates** 64% women, 21% part-time, 21% 25 or older, 0.3% Native American, 4% Hispanic American, 25% African American, 2% Asian American/Pacific Islander **The most frequently chosen baccalaureate fields are** business/marketing, education, health professions and related sciences **Academic program** English as a second language, advanced placement, accelerated degree program, self-designed majors, honors program, summer session, adult/continuing education programs, internships **Contact** Ms. Donette Stewart, Assistant Vice Chancellor for Enrollment Services, University of South Carolina Upstate, 800 University Way, Spartanburg, SC 29303. *Phone:* 864-503-5280 or toll-free 800-277-8727. *Fax:* 864-503-5727. *E-mail:* dstewart@uscupstate.edu. *Web site:* http://www.uscupstate.edu/.

Voorhees College
Denmark, South Carolina

General Independent Episcopal, 4-year, coed **Entrance** Moderately difficult **Setting** 350-acre rural campus **Total enrollment** 701 **Student-faculty ratio** 16:1 **Application deadline** Rolling (freshmen), rolling (transfer) **Freshman admission** 70% were admitted. Average high school GPA 2 **Housing** Yes **Expenses** Tuition & Fees $10,164; Room & Board $6314 **Undergraduates** 55% women, 4% part-time, 19% 25 or older, 0.3% Native American, 0.1% Hispanic American, 95% African American **Academic program** Advanced placement, honors program, summer session, adult/continuing education programs, internships **Contact** Dr. Willie Jefferson, Dean of Enrollment Management, Voorhees College, PO Box 678, Denmark, SC 29042. *Phone:* 803-703-1049 or toll-free 866-685-9904. *Fax:* 803-780-1038. *E-mail:* williej@voorhees.edu. *Web site:* http://www.voorhees.edu/.

Winthrop University
Rock Hill, South Carolina

General State-supported, comprehensive, coed **Entrance** Moderately difficult **Setting** 418-acre suburban campus **Total enrollment** 6,241 **Student-faculty ratio** 15:1 **Application deadline** 5/1 (freshmen) **Freshman admission** 65% were admitted. Average high school GPA 3.68 **Freshman test scores** SAT critical reading scores over 500: 63%; SAT math scores over 500: 66%; ACT scores over 18: 100%; SAT critical reading scores over 600: 19%; SAT math scores over 600: 19%; ACT scores over 24: 37% **Housing** Yes **Expenses** Tuition & Fees: state resident $11,606, nonresident $21,596; Room & Board $6530 **Undergraduates** 68% women, 12% part-time, 10% 25 or older, 0.5% Native American, 2% Hispanic American, 27% African American, 2% Asian American/Pacific Islander **The most frequently chosen baccalaureate fields are** business/marketing, education, visual and performing arts **Academic program** Advanced placement, honors program, summer session, internships **Contact** Ms. Deborah Barber, Director of Admissions, Winthrop University, 701 Oakland Avenue, Rock Hill, SC 29733. *Phone:* 803-323-2191 or toll-free 800-763-0230. *Fax:* 803-323-2137. *E-mail:* admissions@winthrop.edu. *Web site:* http://www.winthrop.edu/.

Wofford College
Spartanburg, South Carolina

General Independent, 4-year, coed, affiliated with United Methodist Church **Entrance** Very difficult **Setting** 170-acre urban campus **Total enrollment** 1,439 **Student-faculty ratio** 11:1 **Application deadline** 2/1 (freshmen), rolling (transfer) **Freshman admission** 58% were admitted. Average high school GPA 3.5 **Freshman test scores** SAT critical reading scores over 500: 91%; SAT math scores over 500: 96%; ACT scores over 18: 99%; SAT critical reading scores over 600: 64%; SAT math scores over 600: 69%; ACT scores over 24: 66% **Housing** Yes **Expenses** Tuition & Fees $30,280; Room & Board $8480 **Undergraduates** 50% women, 1% part-time, 0.2% Native American, 2% Hispanic American, 7% African American, 3% Asian American/Pacific Islander **The most frequently chosen baccalaureate fields are** biological/life sciences, business/marketing, social sciences **Academic program** Advanced placement, accelerated degree program, self-designed majors, summer session, internships **Contact** Mr. S. Wells Shepard, Director of Admission, Wofford College, 429 North Church Street, Spartanburg, SC 29303-3663. *Phone:* 864-597-4130. *Fax:* 864-597-4147. *E-mail:* admission@wofford.edu. *Web site:* http://www.wofford.edu/.

SOUTH DAKOTA

Augustana College
Sioux Falls, South Dakota

General Independent, comprehensive, coed, affiliated with Evangelical Lutheran Church in America **Entrance** Moderately difficult **Setting** 100-acre urban campus **Total enrollment** 1,793 **Student-faculty ratio** 12:1 **Application deadline** 8/1 (freshmen), rolling (transfer) **Freshman admission** 81% were admitted. Average high school GPA 3.6 **Freshman test scores** ACT scores over 18: 98.09%; ACT scores over 24: 65.31% **Housing** Yes **Expenses** Tuition & Fees $23,550; Room & Board $6188 **Undergraduates** 63% women, 6% part-time, 5% 25 or older, 0.4% Native American, 0.2% Hispanic American, 1% African American, 1% Asian American/Pacific Islander **The most frequently chosen baccalaureate fields are** education, business/marketing, health professions and related sciences **Academic program** Advanced placement, accelerated degree program, self-designed majors, honors program, summer session, internships **Contact** Ms. Nancy Davidson, Vice President for Enrollment, Augustana College, 2001 South Summit Avenue, Sioux Falls, SD 57197. *Phone:* 605-274-5516 or toll-free 800-727-2844 Ext. 5516 (in-state); 800-727-2844 (out-of-state). *Fax:* 605-274-5518. *E-mail:* admission@augie.edu. *Web site:* http://www.augie.edu/.

Black Hills State University
Spearfish, South Dakota

General State-supported, comprehensive, coed **Entrance** Minimally difficult **Setting** 123-acre small-town campus **Total enrollment** 4,076 **Student-faculty ratio** 19:1 **Application deadline** 7/18 (freshmen), 7/18 (transfer) **Freshman admission** 93% were admitted. Average high school GPA 3.02 **Freshman test scores** ACT scores over 18: 86.4%; ACT scores over 24: 23.1% **Housing** Yes **Expenses** Tuition & Fees: state

Black Hills State University (continued)
resident $6227, nonresident $7600; Room & Board $5523 **Undergraduates** 62% women, 32% part-time, 27% 25 or older, 4% Native American, 2% Hispanic American, 1% African American, 1% Asian American/Pacific Islander **The most frequently chosen baccalaureate fields are** business/marketing, education, social sciences **Academic program** Advanced placement, accelerated degree program, honors program, summer session, internships **Contact** Ms. Beth Oaks, Director of Admissions, Black Hills State University, 1200 University ST USB 9502, Spearfish, SD 57799-9502. *Phone:* 605-642-6343 or toll-free 800-255-2478. *Fax:* 605-642-6254. *E-mail:* admissions@bhsu.edu. *Web site:* http://www.bhsu.edu/.

Colorado Technical University Sioux Falls

Sioux Falls, South Dakota

General Proprietary, comprehensive, coed **Entrance** Minimally difficult **Setting** 3-acre urban campus **Total enrollment** 912 **Application deadline** Rolling (freshmen), rolling (transfer) **Housing** No **Undergraduates** 64% women, 40% part-time, 17% 25 or older, 1% Native American, 1% Hispanic American, 2% African American, 1% Asian American/Pacific Islander **The most frequently chosen baccalaureate fields are** business/marketing, computer and information sciences, security and protective services **Academic program** Advanced placement, accelerated degree program, summer session, adult/continuing education programs, internships **Contact** Catherine Taplett Allen, Vice President of Admissions, Colorado Technical University Sioux Falls, 3901 West 59th Street, Sioux Falls, SD 57108. *Phone:* 605-361-0200. *E-mail:* callen@sf.coloradotech.edu. *Web site:* http://www.ctu-siouxfalls.com/.

Dakota State University

Madison, South Dakota

General State-supported, comprehensive, coed **Entrance** Minimally difficult **Setting** 40-acre rural campus **Total enrollment** 2,827 **Student-faculty ratio** 17:1 **Application deadline** Rolling (freshmen), rolling (transfer) **Freshman admission** 94% were admitted. Average high school GPA 3.06 **Freshman test scores** ACT scores over 18: 85.92%; ACT scores over 24: 32.96% **Housing** Yes **Expenses** Tuition & Fees: state resident $6872, nonresident $8245; Room & Board $4818 **Undergraduates** 55% women, 56% part-time, 22% 25 or older **The most frequently chosen baccalaureate fields are** business/marketing, computer and information sciences, education **Academic program** English as a second language, advanced placement, honors program, summer session, adult/continuing education programs, internships **Contact** Ms. Dana Hoff, Admissions Secretary, Dakota State University, 820 North Washington, Madison, SD 57042-1799. *Phone:* 605-256-5139 or toll-free 888-DSU-9988. *Fax:* 605-256-5020. *E-mail:* yourfuture@dsu.edu. *Web site:* http://www.dsu.edu/.

Dakota Wesleyan University

Mitchell, South Dakota

General Independent United Methodist, comprehensive, coed **Entrance** Moderately difficult **Setting** 50-acre small-town campus **Total enrollment** 764 **Student-faculty ratio** 13:1 **Application deadline** 8/27 (freshmen), 8/27 (transfer) **Freshman admission** 81% were admitted. Average high school GPA 3.08 **Freshman test scores** SAT critical reading scores over 500: 46%; ACT scores over 18: 92%; SAT critical reading scores over 600: 23%; ACT scores over 24: 25% **Housing** Yes **Expenses** Tuition & Fees $19,850 **Undergraduates** 59% women, 8% part-time, 17% 25 or older, 2% Native American, 4% Hispanic American, 2% African American, 1% Asian American/Pacific Islander **The most frequently chosen baccalaureate fields are** business/marketing, education, security and protective services **Academic program** Advanced placement, self-designed majors, honors program, summer session, internships **Contact** Mrs. Melissa Herr-Valburg, Director of Admissions, Dakota Wesleyan University, 1200 West University Avenue, Mitchell, SD 57301-4398. *Phone:* 605-995-2600 Ext. 2652 or toll-free 800-333-8506. *Fax:* 605-995-2699. *E-mail:* admissions@dwu.edu. *Web site:* http://www.dwu.edu/.

Globe University

Sioux Falls, South Dakota

Contact Globe University, 5101 South Broadband Lane, Sioux Falls, SD 57108-2208. *Phone:* toll-free 866-437-0705. *Web site:* http://www.globeuniversity.edu/.

Mount Marty College

Yankton, South Dakota

General Independent Roman Catholic, comprehensive, coed **Entrance** Minimally difficult **Setting** 80-acre small-town campus **Total enrollment** 1,214 **Student-faculty ratio** 13:1 **Application deadline** Rolling (freshmen), rolling (transfer) **Freshman admission** 78% were admitted. Average high school GPA 3.32 **Freshman test scores** ACT scores over 18: 93%; ACT scores over 24: 33% **Housing** Yes **Expenses** Tuition & Fees $18,908; Room & Board $5366 **Undergraduates** 63% women, 46% part-time, 32% 25 or older **The most frequently chosen baccalaureate fields are** education, business/marketing, health professions and related sciences **Academic program** Advanced placement, accelerated degree program, self-designed majors, honors program, summer session, adult/continuing education programs, internships **Contact** Ms. Brandi DeFries, Vice President for Enrollment Management, Mount Marty College, 1105 West 8th Street, Yankton, SD 57078. *Phone:* 605-668-1545 or toll-free 800-658-4552. *E-mail:* brandi.defries@mtmc.edu. *Web site:* http://www.mtmc.edu/.

National American University

Rapid City, South Dakota

Contact Ms. Angela Beck, Director of Enrollment Management, National American University, 321 Kansas City Street, Rapid City, SD 57701. *Phone:* 605-394-4902 or toll-free 800-843-8892. *Fax:* 605-394-4871. *E-mail:* abeck@national.edu. *Web site:* http://www.rapid.national.edu/.

National American University–Sioux Falls Branch

Sioux Falls, South Dakota

Contact Ms. Lisa Houtsma, Director of Admissions, National American University–Sioux Falls Branch, 2801 South Kiwanis Avenue, Suite 100, Sioux Falls, SD 57105-4293. *Phone:* 605-336-4600 or toll-free 800-388-5430. *Fax:* 605-336-4605. *E-mail:* lhoutsma@national.edu. *Web site:* http://www.national.edu/.

Northern State University

Aberdeen, South Dakota

General State-supported, comprehensive, coed **Entrance** Minimally difficult **Setting** 72-acre small-town campus **Total enrollment** 2,625 **Student-faculty ratio** 17:1 **Freshman admission** 93% were admitted. Average high school GPA 3.2 **Freshman test scores** ACT scores over 18: 88.79%; ACT scores over 24: 33.64% **Housing** Yes **Expenses** Tuition & Fees: state resident $6063, nonresident $12,139; Room & Board $4874 **Undergraduates** 61% women, 33% part-time, 20% 25 or older **The most frequently chosen baccalaureate fields are** business/marketing, education, social sciences **Academic program** English as a second language, advanced placement, accelerated degree program, self-designed majors, honors program, summer session, adult/continuing education programs, internships **Contact** Mr. Allan Vogel, Director of Admissions, Northern State University, 1200 South Jay Street, Aberdeen, SD 57401. *Phone:* 605-626-2544 or toll-free 800-678-5330. *Fax:* 605-626-2587.. *E-mail:* admission2@northern.edu. *Web site:* http://www.northern.edu/.

Oglala Lakota College
Kyle, South Dakota

General State and locally supported, comprehensive, coed **Setting** rural campus **Total enrollment** 1,000 **Housing** No **Undergraduates** 70% 25 or older **Academic program** Accelerated degree program, summer session, adult/continuing education programs, internships **Contact** Director of Admissions, Oglala Lakota College, 490 Piya Wiconi Road, Kyle, SD 57752-0490. *Phone:* 605-455-2321 Ext. 236. *E-mail:* lmeseteth@olc.edu. *Web site:* http://www.olc.edu/.

Presentation College
Aberdeen, South Dakota

General Independent Roman Catholic, 4-year, coed, primarily women **Entrance** Noncompetitive **Setting** 100-acre small-town campus **Total enrollment** 700 **Student-faculty ratio** 10:1 **Application deadline** Rolling (freshmen), rolling (transfer) **Freshman admission** 76% were admitted. Average high school GPA 3 **Freshman test scores** ACT scores over 18: 82%; ACT scores over 24: 23% **Housing** Yes **Expenses** Tuition & Fees $14,250; Room & Board $5500 **Undergraduates** 82% women, 37% part-time, 41% 25 or older, 8% Native American, 1% Hispanic American, 2% African American, 0.5% Asian American/Pacific Islander **The most frequently chosen baccalaureate fields are** health professions and related sciences, business/marketing, public administration and social services **Academic program** Advanced placement, accelerated degree program, summer session, adult/continuing education programs, internships **Contact** Ms. Jo Ellen Lindner, Vice President for Enrollment and Student Retention Services, Presentation College, 1500 North Main Street, Aberdeen, SD 57401. *Phone:* 605-229-8492 or toll-free 800-437-6060. *Fax:* 605-229-8425. *E-mail:* admit@presentation.edu. *Web site:* http://www.presentation.edu/.

Sinte Gleska University
Mission, South Dakota

General Independent, comprehensive, coed **Entrance** Noncompetitive **Setting** 52-acre rural campus **Total enrollment** 971 **Application deadline** 8/20 (freshmen), 8/20 (transfer) **Housing** No **Undergraduates** 70% 25 or older **Academic program** Honors program, summer session, adult/continuing education programs, internships **Contact** Mr. Jack Herman, Registrar and Director of Admissions, Sinte Gleska University, 101 Antelope Lake Circle, PO Box 105, Mission, SD 57555. *Phone:* 605-856-8100 Ext. 8479. *Web site:* http://www.sintegleska.edu/.

South Dakota School of Mines and Technology
Rapid City, South Dakota

General State-supported, university, coed **Entrance** Moderately difficult **Setting** 120-acre suburban campus **Total enrollment** 2,177 **Student-faculty ratio** 14:1 **Application deadline** Rolling (freshmen), rolling (transfer) **Freshman admission** 82% were admitted. Average high school GPA 3.51 **Freshman test scores** SAT critical reading scores over 500: 76.5%; SAT math scores over 500: 96.5%; ACT scores over 18: 99.4%; SAT critical reading scores over 600: 44.5%; SAT math scores over 600: 57.5%; ACT scores over 24: 78.6% **Housing** Yes **Expenses** Tuition & Fees: state resident $6830, nonresident $8210; Room & Board $5080 **Undergraduates** 29% women, 21% part-time, 14% 25 or older, 3% Native American, 1% Hispanic American, 0.4% African American, 1% Asian American/Pacific Islander **The most frequently chosen baccalaureate fields are** engineering, interdisciplinary studies, physical sciences **Academic program** English as a second language, advanced placement, summer session, adult/continuing education programs, internships **Contact** Genene Sigler, Applications Processor, South Dakota School of Mines and Technology, 501 East Saint Joseph, Rapid City, SD 57701-3995. *Phone:* 605-394-2414 Ext. 5209 or toll-free 800-544-8162 Ext. 2414. *Fax:* 605-394-1979. *E-mail:* admissions@sdsmt.edu. *Web site:* http://www.sdsmt.edu/.

South Dakota State University
Brookings, South Dakota

General State-supported, university, coed **Entrance** Minimally difficult **Setting** 272-acre small-town campus **Total enrollment** 12,376 **Student-faculty ratio** 18:1 **Application deadline** Rolling (freshmen), rolling (transfer) **Freshman admission** 93% were admitted. Average high school GPA 3.34 **Freshman test scores** ACT scores over 18: 94%; ACT scores over 24: 47% **Housing** Yes **Expenses** Tuition & Fees: state resident $6155, nonresident $7528; Room & Board $5668 **Undergraduates** 52% women, 21% part-time, 13% 25 or older **The most frequently chosen baccalaureate fields are** health professions and related sciences, agriculture, social sciences **Academic program** English as a second language, advanced placement, accelerated degree program, honors program, summer session, adult/continuing education programs, internships **Contact** Ms. Michelle Kuebler, Assistant Director of Admissions, South Dakota State University, PO Box 2201, Brookings, SD 57007. *Phone:* 605-688-4121 or toll-free 800-952-3541. *Fax:* 605-688-6891. *E-mail:* sdsu.admissions@sdstate.edu. *Web site:* http://www.sdstate.edu/.

University of Sioux Falls
Sioux Falls, South Dakota

General Independent American Baptist Churches in the USA, comprehensive, coed **Entrance** Moderately difficult **Setting** 22-acre suburban campus **Total enrollment** 1,564 **Student-faculty ratio** 15:1 **Application deadline** Rolling (freshmen), rolling (transfer) **Freshman admission** 97% were admitted. Average high school GPA 3.3 **Freshman test scores** SAT critical reading scores over 500: 56%; SAT math scores over 500: 45%; ACT scores over 18: 92%; SAT critical reading scores over 600: 22%; SAT math scores over 600: 11%; ACT scores over 24: 41% **Housing** Yes **Expenses** Tuition & Fees $20,270; Room & Board $5920 **Undergraduates** 53% women, 19% part-time, 15% 25 or older, 0.3% Native American, 1% Hispanic American, 2% African American, 0.5% Asian American/Pacific Islander **The most frequently chosen baccalaureate fields are** business/marketing, biological/life sciences, health professions and related sciences **Academic program** Advanced placement, accelerated degree program, self-designed majors, honors program, summer session, adult/continuing education programs, internships **Contact** Ms. Amanda Anderson, Director of Admissions and Academic Advising, University of Sioux Falls, 1101 West 22nd Street, Sioux Falls, SD 57105. *Phone:* 605-331-6600 Ext. 6743 or toll-free 800-888-1047. *Fax:* 605-331-6615. *E-mail:* admissions@usiouxfalls.edu. *Web site:* http://www.usiouxfalls.edu/.

The University of South Dakota
Vermillion, South Dakota

General State-supported, university, coed **Entrance** Moderately difficult **Setting** 216-acre small-town campus **Total enrollment** 9,617 **Student-faculty ratio** 15:1 **Application deadline** Rolling (freshmen), rolling (transfer) **Freshman admission** 87% were admitted. Average high school GPA 3.31 **Freshman test scores** SAT critical reading scores over 500: 56%; SAT math scores over 500: 63%; ACT scores over 18: 92%; SAT critical reading scores over 600: 38%; SAT math scores over 600: 32%; ACT scores over 24: 42% **Housing** Yes **Expenses** Tuition & Fees: state resident $6468, nonresident $7841; Room & Board $5787 **Undergraduates** 62% women, 38% part-time, 18% 25 or older **The most frequently chosen baccalaureate fields are** business/marketing, education, health professions and related sciences **Academic program** English as a second language, advanced placement, accelerated degree program, self-designed majors, honors program, summer session, adult/continuing education programs, internships **Contact** Ms. Stephanie Moser, Director of Admissions, The University of South Dakota, 414 East Clark Street, Vermillion, SD 57069-2390. *Phone:* 605-677-5434 or toll-free 877-269-6837. *Fax:* 605-677-6753. *E-mail:* admiss@usd.edu. *Web site:* http://www.usd.edu/.

TENNESSEE

American Baptist College of American Baptist Theological Seminary
Nashville, Tennessee

General Independent Baptist, 4-year, coed **Entrance** Noncompetitive **Setting** 52-acre urban campus **Total enrollment** 84 **Student-faculty ratio** 14:1 **Application deadline** 7/12 (freshmen), 7/12 (transfer) **Freshman admission** 77% were admitted. Average high school GPA 2.7 **Housing** Yes **Expenses** Tuition & Fees $4800; Room & Board $2600 **Undergraduates** 23% women, 33% part-time, 90% 25 or older, 95% African American **The most frequently chosen baccalaureate field is** theology and religious vocations **Academic program** Summer session, adult/continuing education programs **Contact** Ms. Marcella Lockhart, Director of Enrollment Management, American Baptist College of American Baptist Theological Seminary, 1800 Baptist World Center Drive, Nashville, TN 37207. *Phone:* 615-687-6896. *Fax:* 615-226-7855. *E-mail:* mlockhart@abcnash.edu. *Web site:* http://www.abcnash.edu/.

Aquinas College
Nashville, Tennessee

General Independent Roman Catholic, 4-year, coed **Entrance** Minimally difficult **Setting** 92-acre urban campus **Total enrollment** 858 **Student-faculty ratio** 14:1 **Application deadline** Rolling (freshmen), rolling (transfer) **Freshman admission** 16% were admitted. Average high school GPA 3.03 **Housing** No **Expenses** Tuition & Fees $17,180 **Undergraduates** 2% Hispanic American, 14% African American, 3% Asian American/Pacific Islander **The most frequently chosen baccalaureate fields are** business/marketing, computer and information sciences, health professions and related sciences **Academic program** Advanced placement, accelerated degree program, summer session, internships **Contact** Ms. Connie Hansom, Director of Admission, Aquinas College, 4210 Harding Road, Nashville, TN 37205-2005. *Phone:* 615-297-7545 Ext. 411 or toll-free 800-649-9956. *Fax:* 615-279-3893. *E-mail:* hansomc@aquinascollege.edu. *Web site:* http://www.aquinascollege.edu/.

Argosy University, Nashville
Nashville, Tennessee

General Proprietary, university, coed **Contact** Director of Admissions, Argosy University, Nashville, 100 Centerview Drive, Suite 225, Nashville, TN 37214. *Phone:* 615-525-2800 or toll-free 866-833-6598. *Fax:* 615-525-2900. *Web site:* http://www.argosy.edu/nashville/.

Visit Petersons.com and enter keywords Argosy University, Nashville

See page 478 for the College Close-Up.

The Art Institute of Tennessee–Nashville
Nashville, Tennessee

General Proprietary, 4-year, coed **Setting** urban campus **Contact** Director of Admissions, The Art Institute of Tennessee–Nashville, 100 Centerview Drive, Suite 250, Nashville, TN 37214. *Phone:* 615-874-1067 or toll-free 866-747-5770. *Fax:* 615-874-3530. *Web site:* http://www.artinstitutes.edu/nashville/.

Visit Petersons.com and enter keywords Art Institute of Tennessee-Nashville

See page 548 for the College Close-Up.

Austin Peay State University
Clarksville, Tennessee

General State-supported, comprehensive, coed **Entrance** Moderately difficult **Setting** 200-acre suburban campus **Total enrollment** 10,188 **Student-faculty ratio** 21:1 **Application deadline** 7/25 (freshmen), rolling (transfer) **Freshman admission** 90% were admitted. Average high school GPA 3.11 **Freshman test scores** SAT critical reading scores over 500: 51%; SAT math scores over 500: 51%; ACT scores over 18: 89%; SAT critical reading scores over 600: 14%; SAT math scores over 600: 11%; ACT scores over 24: 25% **Housing** Yes **Expenses** Tuition & Fees: state resident $5808, nonresident $17,736; Room & Board $6120 **Undergraduates** 61% women, 25% part-time, 40% 25 or older **The most frequently chosen baccalaureate fields are** business/marketing, health professions and related sciences, liberal arts/general studies **Academic program** English as a second language, advanced placement, accelerated degree program, honors program, summer session, adult/continuing education programs, internships **Contact** Mr. Ryan Forsythe, Director of Admissions, Austin Peay State University, 601 College Street, Clarksville, TN 37044. *Phone:* 931-221-7661 or toll-free 800-844-2778. *Fax:* 931-221-6168. *E-mail:* admissions@apsu.edu. *Web site:* http://www.apsu.edu/.

Baptist College of Health Sciences
Memphis, Tennessee

General Independent Southern Baptist, 4-year, coed, primarily women **Entrance** Moderately difficult **Setting** urban campus **Total enrollment** 1,021 **Student-faculty ratio** 14:1 **Application deadline** 5/1 (freshmen), 5/1 (transfer) **Freshman admission** 15% were admitted **Freshman test scores** ACT scores over 18: 100%; ACT scores over 24: 15% **Housing** Yes **Expenses** Tuition & Fees $9730 **Undergraduates** 87% women, 46% part-time, 0.3% Native American, 2% Hispanic American, 33% African American, 2% Asian American/Pacific Islander **The most frequently chosen baccalaureate field is** health professions and related sciences **Academic program** Advanced placement, accelerated degree program, summer session **Contact** Ms. Lissa Morgan, Manager of Admissions/Retention, Baptist College of Health Sciences, 1003 Monroe Avenue, Memphis, TN 38104. *Phone:* 901-572-2441 or toll-free 866-575-2247. *E-mail:* Lissa.Morgan@bchs.edu. *Web site:* http://www.bchs.edu/.

Belhaven College
Memphis, Tennessee

Contact Director of Admission, Belhaven College, 5100 Poplar Avenue, Suite 200, Memphis, TN 38137. *Phone:* 901-888-3343. *Fax:* 901-888-0771. *E-mail:* memphisadmission@belhaven.edu. *Web site:* http://www.belhaven.edu/.

Belmont University
Nashville, Tennessee

General Independent Christian, comprehensive, coed **Entrance** Moderately difficult **Setting** 46-acre urban campus **Total enrollment** 5,424 **Student-faculty ratio** 12:1 **Application deadline** 8/1 (freshmen), 8/1 (transfer) **Freshman admission** 77% were admitted. Average high school GPA 3.53 **Freshman test scores** SAT critical reading scores over 500: 92%; SAT math scores over 500: 88%; ACT scores over 18: 100%; SAT critical reading scores over 600: 42%; SAT math scores over 600: 41%; ACT scores over 24: 86.7% **Housing** Yes **Expenses** Tuition & Fees $22,360; Room & Board $10,000 **Undergraduates** 57% women, 8% part-time, 12% 25 or older, 0.5% Native American, 2% Hispanic American, 4% African American, 3% Asian American/Pacific Islander **The most frequently chosen baccalaureate fields are** business/marketing, health professions and related sciences, visual and performing arts **Academic program** English as a second language, advanced placement, accelerated degree program, self-designed majors, honors program, summer session, adult/continuing education programs, internships **Contact** Dean of Enrollment Services, Belmont University, 1900 Belmont Boulevard, Nashville, TN 37212-3757. *Phone:* 615-460-6785 or toll-free 800-56E-NROL. *Fax:* 615-460-5434. *E-mail:* buadmission@belmont.edu. *Web site:* http://www.belmont.edu/.

Visit Petersons.com and enter keyword Belmont

See page 590 for the College Close-Up.

Bethel University
McKenzie, Tennessee

General Independent Cumberland Presbyterian, comprehensive, coed **Entrance** Minimally difficult **Setting** 100-acre small-town campus **Total enrollment** 3,141 **Student-faculty ratio** 19:1 **Application deadline** Rolling (freshmen), rolling (transfer) **Freshman admission** 54% were admitted. Average high school GPA 3.05 **Housing** Yes **Expenses** Tuition & Fees $12,242; Room & Board $6926 **Undergraduates** 59% women, 1% part-time, 55% 25 or older, 0.1% Native American, 1% Hispanic American, 37% African American, 0.4% Asian American/Pacific Islander **The most frequently chosen baccalaureate fields are** business/marketing, education, health professions and related sciences **Academic program** Advanced placement, accelerated degree program, self-designed majors, honors program, summer session, adult/continuing education programs, internships **Contact** Tina Hodges, Enrollment Director of Admissions & Financial Aid, Bethel University, 325 Cherry Avenue, McKenzie, TN 38201. *Phone:* 731-352-4030. *Fax:* 731-352-4069. *E-mail:* hodgest@bethelu.edu. *Web site:* http://www.bethel-college.edu/.

Bryan College
Dayton, Tennessee

General Independent interdenominational, comprehensive, coed **Entrance** Moderately difficult **Setting** 100-acre small-town campus **Total enrollment** 1,160 **Student-faculty ratio** 17:1 **Application deadline** Rolling (freshmen), rolling (transfer) **Freshman admission** 75% were admitted. Average high school GPA 3.62 **Freshman test scores** SAT critical reading scores over 500: 82%; SAT math scores over 500: 71%; ACT scores over 18: 94%; SAT critical reading scores over 600: 55%; SAT math scores over 600: 32%; ACT scores over 24: 61% **Housing** Yes **Expenses** Tuition & Fees $18,740; Room & Board $5454 **Undergraduates** 54% women, 11% part-time, 2% 25 or older, 0.5% Native American, 2% Hispanic American, 5% African American, 1% Asian American/Pacific Islander **The most frequently chosen baccalaureate fields are** business/marketing, communications/journalism, education **Academic program** Advanced placement, honors program, summer session, adult/continuing education programs, internships **Contact** Michael Sapienza, Vice President for Enrollment Management, Bryan College, PO Box 7000, Dayton, TN 37321-7000. *Phone:* 423-775-2041 or toll-free 800-277-9522. *Fax:* 423-775-7199. *E-mail:* admissions@bryan.edu. *Web site:* http://www.bryan.edu/.

Carson-Newman College
Jefferson City, Tennessee

General Independent Southern Baptist, comprehensive, coed **Entrance** Moderately difficult **Setting** 90-acre small-town campus **Total enrollment** 2,148 **Student-faculty ratio** 12:1 **Application deadline** 8/1 (freshmen), 8/1 (transfer) **Freshman admission** 74% were admitted. Average high school GPA 3.38 **Freshman test scores** ACT scores over 18: 96%; ACT scores over 24: 38% **Housing** Yes **Expenses** Tuition & Fees $20,562; Room & Board $5918 **Undergraduates** 58% women, 7% part-time, 10% 25 or older, 0.3% Native American, 1% Hispanic American, 8% African American, 1% Asian American/Pacific Islander **The most frequently chosen baccalaureate fields are** education, business/marketing, health professions and related sciences **Academic program** English as a second language, advanced placement, accelerated degree program, self-designed majors, honors program, summer session, adult/continuing education programs, internships **Contact** Melanie Redding, Director of Admissions, Carson-Newman College, 1646 Russell Avenue, PO Box 557, Jefferson City, TN 37760. *Phone:* 865-471-3223 or toll-free 800-678-9061. *Fax:* 865-471-3502. *E-mail:* cnadmiss@cn.edu. *Web site:* http://www.cn.edu/.

Visit Petersons.com and enter keyword Carson-Newman

See page 688 for the College Close-Up.

Christian Brothers University
Memphis, Tennessee

General Independent Roman Catholic, comprehensive, coed **Entrance** Moderately difficult **Setting** 75-acre urban campus **Total enrollment** 1,926 **Student-faculty ratio** 13:1 **Application deadline** 8/1 (freshmen), 8/23 (transfer) **Freshman admission** 49% were admitted. Average high school GPA 3.56 **Freshman test scores** ACT scores over 18: 100%; ACT scores over 24: 50% **Housing** Yes **Expenses** Tuition & Fees $23,730; Room & Board $6140 **Undergraduates** 56% women, 12% part-time, 22% 25 or older **The most frequently chosen baccalaureate fields are** business/marketing, biological/life sciences, psychology **Academic program** Advanced placement, accelerated degree program, honors program, summer session, adult/continuing education programs, internships **Contact** Dr. Anne Kenworthy, Interim Dean of Admissions, Christian Brothers University, 650 East Parkway South, Memphis, TN 38104. *Phone:* 901-321-3205 or toll-free 800-288-7576. *Fax:* 901-321-3202. *E-mail:* admissions@cbu.edu. *Web site:* http://www.cbu.edu/.

See page 704 for the College Close-Up.

Crichton College
Memphis, Tennessee

General Independent, 4-year, coed **Entrance** Minimally difficult **Setting** 7-acre urban campus **Total enrollment** 717 **Student-faculty ratio** 18:1 **Application deadline** Rolling (freshmen), rolling (transfer) **Freshman admission** Average high school GPA 2.24 **Freshman test scores** ACT scores over 18: 33.33% **Housing** No **Expenses** Tuition & Fees $10,320 **Undergraduates** 75% women, 28% part-time, 77% 25 or older, 1% Hispanic American, 79% African American, 1% Asian American/Pacific Islander **The most frequently chosen baccalaureate fields are** business/marketing, psychology, theology and religious vocations **Academic program** Advanced placement, accelerated degree program, self-designed majors, summer session, adult/continuing education programs, internships **Contact** Ms. Shelley Dunn, Director of Admissions, Crichton College, 255 North Highland, Memphis, TN 38111-1375. *Phone:* 901-320-9777 or toll-free 800-960-9777. *Fax:* 901-320-9791. *E-mail:* admissions@crichton.edu. *Web site:* http://www.crichton.edu/.

Cumberland University
Lebanon, Tennessee

General Independent, comprehensive, coed **Entrance** Moderately difficult **Setting** 44-acre small-town campus **Total enrollment** 1,355 **Student-faculty ratio** 16:1 **Application deadline** Rolling (freshmen), rolling (transfer) **Freshman admission** 57% were admitted. Average high school GPA 3.3 **Freshman test scores** SAT critical reading scores over 500: 43%; ACT scores over 18: 90%; SAT critical reading scores over 600: 15%; ACT scores over 24: 24% **Housing** Yes **Expenses** Tuition & Fees $18,256; Room & Board $6760 **Undergraduates** 55% women, 13% part-time, 19% 25 or older, 0.4% Native American, 2% Hispanic American, 11% African American, 1% Asian American/Pacific Islander **The most frequently chosen baccalaureate fields are** education, business/marketing, health professions and related sciences **Academic program** Advanced placement, accelerated degree program, honors program, summer session, adult/continuing education programs, internships **Contact** Ms. Beatrice LaChance, Director of Enrollment Services, Cumberland University, One Cumberland Square, Lebanon, TN 37087. *Phone:* 615-547-1244 or toll-free 800-467-0562. *Fax:* 615-444-2569. *E-mail:* admissions@cumberland.edu. *Web site:* http://www.cumberland.edu/.

Daymar Institute
Clarksville, Tennessee

General Proprietary, 4-year, coed **Entrance** Noncompetitive **Setting** small-town campus **Total enrollment** 532 **Student-faculty ratio** 7:1 **Application deadline** Rolling (freshmen), rolling (transfer) **Housing** No **Expenses** Tuition & Fees $14,400 **Undergraduates** 79% women, 28%

Daymar Institute (continued)
part-time, 62% 25 or older, 0.2% Native American, 6% Hispanic American, 31% African American, 1% Asian American/Pacific Islander **Academic program** Honors program, internships **Contact** Alphonse Prather, Admissions Office, Daymar Institute, 1860 Wilma Rudolph Boulevard, Clarksville, TN 37040. *Phone:* 931-552-7600 Ext. 204. *E-mail:* aprather@daymarinstitute.edu. *Web site:* http://www.daymarinstitute.edu/.

DeVry University
Memphis, Tennessee

General Proprietary, comprehensive, coed **Total enrollment** 172 **Application deadline** Rolling (freshmen), rolling (transfer) **Expenses** Tuition & Fees $14,080 **Undergraduates** 66% women, 49% part-time, 75% 25 or older, 1% Hispanic American, 75% African American **The most frequently chosen baccalaureate field is** business/marketing **Academic program** Accelerated degree program **Contact** DeVry University, 6401 Poplar Avenue, Suite 600, Memphis, TN 38119. *Phone:* toll-free 888-563-3879. *Web site:* http://www.devry.edu/.

DeVry University
Nashville, Tennessee

Contact DeVry University, 3343 Perimeter Hill Drive, Suite 200, Nashville, TN 37211-4147. *Web site:* http://www.devry.edu/.

East Tennessee State University
Johnson City, Tennessee

General State-supported, university, coed **Entrance** Moderately difficult **Setting** 366-acre small-town campus **Total enrollment** 14,421 **Student-faculty ratio** 19:1 **Application deadline** Rolling (freshmen), rolling (transfer) **Freshman admission** 85% were admitted. Average high school GPA 3.22 **Freshman test scores** SAT critical reading scores over 500: 42.36%; SAT math scores over 500: 47.45%; ACT scores over 18: 89.37%; SAT critical reading scores over 600: 12.95%; SAT math scores over 600: 13.33%; ACT scores over 24: 36.1% **Housing** Yes **Expenses** Tuition & Fees: state resident $5533, nonresident $17,461; Room & Board $5500 **Undergraduates** 56% women, 15% part-time, 24% 25 or older, 1% Native American, 2% Hispanic American, 5% African American, 2% Asian American/Pacific Islander **The most frequently chosen baccalaureate fields are** business/marketing, health professions and related sciences, liberal arts/general studies **Academic program** Advanced placement, self-designed majors, honors program, summer session, adult/continuing education programs, internships **Contact** Mr. Mike Pitts, Director of Admissions, East Tennessee State University, PO Box 70731, Johnson City, TN 37614-0734. *Phone:* 423-439-4213 or toll-free 800-462-3878. *Fax:* 423-439-4630. *E-mail:* go2etsu@etsu.edu. *Web site:* http://www.etsu.edu/.

Fisk University
Nashville, Tennessee

General Independent, comprehensive, coed, affiliated with United Church of Christ **Entrance** Moderately difficult **Setting** 40-acre urban campus **Total enrollment** 635 **Student-faculty ratio** 9:1 **Application deadline** 3/1 (freshmen) **Freshman admission** 65% were admitted. Average high school GPA 2.87 **Housing** Yes **Expenses** Tuition & Fees $18,345; Room & Board $8585 **Undergraduates** 66% women, 6% part-time, 5% 25 or older, 85% African American, 1% Asian American/Pacific Islander **The most frequently chosen baccalaureate fields are** psychology, English, social sciences **Academic program** Advanced placement, self-designed majors, honors program, internships **Contact** Keith Chandler, Dean of Admission, Fisk University, 1000 17th Avenue North, Nashville, TN 37208-3051. *Phone:* 615-329-8665 or toll-free 800-443-FISK. *Fax:* 615-329-8774. *E-mail:* admit@fisk.edu. *Web site:* http://www.fisk.edu/.

Fountainhead College of Technology
Knoxville, Tennessee

Contact Mr. Todd Hill, Director of Administration, Fountainhead College of Technology, 3203 Tazewell Pike, Knoxville, TN 37918-2530. *Phone:* 865-688-9422 or toll-free 888-218-7335. *Fax:* 865-688-2419. *Web site:* http://www.fountainheadcollege.edu/.

Freed-Hardeman University
Henderson, Tennessee

General Independent, comprehensive, coed, affiliated with Church of Christ **Entrance** Moderately difficult **Setting** 96-acre small-town campus **Total enrollment** 2,061 **Student-faculty ratio** 14:1 **Application deadline** Rolling (freshmen), rolling (transfer) **Freshman admission** 56% were admitted. Average high school GPA 3.37 **Freshman test scores** SAT critical reading scores over 500: 78%; SAT math scores over 500: 73%; ACT scores over 18: 91%; SAT critical reading scores over 600: 31%; SAT math scores over 600: 24%; ACT scores over 24: 46% **Housing** Yes **Expenses** Tuition & Fees $14,998; Room & Board $7090 **Undergraduates** 55% women, 8% part-time, 4% 25 or older, 1% Native American, 1% Hispanic American, 4% African American, 0.1% Asian American/Pacific Islander **The most frequently chosen baccalaureate fields are** business/marketing, education, theology and religious vocations **Academic program** Advanced placement, accelerated degree program, self-designed majors, honors program, summer session, internships **Contact** Dr. Belinda Anderson, Director of Admissions, Freed-Hardeman University, 158 East Main Street, Henderson, TN 38340-2399. *Phone:* 731-989-6651 or toll-free 800-630-3480. *Fax:* 731-989-6047. *E-mail:* admissions@fhu.edu. *Web site:* http://www.fhu.edu/.

Free Will Baptist Bible College
Nashville, Tennessee

General Independent Free Will Baptist, 4-year, coed **Entrance** Noncompetitive **Setting** 10-acre urban campus **Total enrollment** 303 **Student-faculty ratio** 11:1 **Application deadline** Rolling (freshmen) **Freshman admission** 75% were admitted. Average high school GPA 3.01 **Freshman test scores** ACT scores over 18: 76%; ACT scores over 24: 28% **Housing** Yes **Expenses** Tuition & Fees $13,534; Room & Board $5700 **Undergraduates** 45% women, 24% part-time, 25% 25 or older **The most frequently chosen baccalaureate fields are** education, business/marketing, theology and religious vocations **Academic program** Advanced placement, self-designed majors, summer session, internships **Contact** Mr. Heath Hubbard, Director of Recruitment, Free Will Baptist Bible College, 3606 West End Avenue, Nashville, TN 37205. *Phone:* 615-844-5197 or toll-free 800-763-9222. *Fax:* 615-269-6028. *E-mail:* hhubbard@fwbbc.edu. *Web site:* http://www.fwbbc.edu/.

Huntington College of Health Sciences
Knoxville, Tennessee

General Proprietary, comprehensive, coed **Entrance** Noncompetitive **Setting** suburban campus **Total enrollment** 460 **Student-faculty ratio** 29:1 **Application deadline** Rolling (freshmen), rolling (transfer) **Freshman admission** 100% were admitted **Undergraduates** 64% women, 90% 25 or older **Academic program** Self-designed majors, summer session, adult/continuing education programs **Contact** Ms. Cheryl Freeman, Director/Registrar, Huntington College of Health Sciences, 1204 Kenesaw Avenue, Suite D, Knoxville, TN 37919. *Phone:* 800-290-4226 or toll-free 800-290-4226. *Fax:* 865-524-8339. *E-mail:* cfreeman@hchs.edu. *Web site:* http://www.hchs.edu/.

ITT Technical Institute
Chattanooga, Tennessee

General Proprietary, primarily 2-year, coed **Contact** Director of Recruitment, ITT Technical Institute, 5600 Brainerd Road, Suite G-1,

Chattanooga, TN 37411. *Phone:* 423-510-6800 or toll-free 877-474-8312. *Web site:* http://www.itt-tech.edu/.

ITT Technical Institute
Cordova, Tennessee

General Proprietary, primarily 2-year, coed **Entrance** Minimally difficult **Setting** suburban campus **Housing** No **Contact** Director of Recruitment, ITT Technical Institute, 7260 Goodlett Farms Parkway, Cordova, TN 38016. *Phone:* 901-381-0200 or toll-free 866-444-5141. *Web site:* http://www.itt-tech.edu/.

ITT Technical Institute
Johnson City, Tennessee

General Proprietary, primarily 2-year, coed **Contact** Director of Admissions, ITT Technical Institute, 4721 Lake Park Drive, Suite 100, Johnson City, TN 37615. *Phone:* 423-952-4400 or toll-free 877-301-9691. *Web site:* http://www.itt-tech.edu/.

ITT Technical Institute
Knoxville, Tennessee

General Proprietary, primarily 2-year, coed **Entrance** Minimally difficult **Setting** suburban campus **Housing** No **Contact** Director of Recruitment, ITT Technical Institute, 10208 Technology Drive, Knoxville, TN 37932. *Phone:* 865-671-2800 or toll-free 800-671-2801. *Web site:* http://www.itt-tech.edu/.

ITT Technical Institute
Nashville, Tennessee

General Proprietary, primarily 2-year, coed **Entrance** Minimally difficult **Setting** urban campus **Housing** No **Contact** Director of Recruitment, ITT Technical Institute, 2845 Elm Hill Pike, Nashville, TN 37214. *Phone:* 615-889-8700 or toll-free 800-331-8386. *Web site:* http://www.itt-tech.edu/.

Johnson Bible College
Knoxville, Tennessee

General Independent, comprehensive, coed, affiliated with Christian Churches and Churches of Christ **Entrance** Moderately difficult **Setting** 75-acre rural campus **Total enrollment** 779 **Student-faculty ratio** 15:1 **Application deadline** 7/1 (freshmen), 7/1 (transfer) **Freshman admission** 72% were admitted. Average high school GPA 3 **Freshman test scores** SAT critical reading scores over 500: 68.6%; SAT math scores over 500: 60.5%; ACT scores over 18: 86.8%; SAT critical reading scores over 600: 26.2%; SAT math scores over 600: 10.5%; ACT scores over 24: 42.1% **Housing** Yes **Expenses** Tuition & Fees $9100; Room & Board $5100 **Undergraduates** 47% women, 5% part-time, 8% 25 or older, 1% Native American, 3% Hispanic American, 2% African American, 1% Asian American/Pacific Islander **The most frequently chosen baccalaureate fields are** education, family and consumer sciences, philosophy and religious studies **Academic program** English as a second language, advanced placement, accelerated degree program, honors program, summer session, adult/continuing education programs, internships **Contact** Mr. Tim Wingfield, Director of Admissions, Johnson Bible College, 7900 Johnson Drive, Knoxville, TN 37998-1001. *Phone:* 865-251-2346 or toll-free 800-827-2122. *Fax:* 865-251-2336. *E-mail:* twingfield@jbc.edu. *Web site:* http://www.jbc.edu/.

King College
Bristol, Tennessee

General Independent, comprehensive, coed, affiliated with Presbyterian Church (U.S.A.) **Entrance** Moderately difficult **Setting** 135-acre suburban campus **Total enrollment** 1,804 **Student-faculty ratio** 14:1 **Application deadline** Rolling (freshmen), rolling (transfer) **Freshman admission** 62% were admitted. Average high school GPA 3.32 **Freshman test scores** SAT critical reading scores over 500: 49.04%; SAT math scores over 500: 48.07%; ACT scores over 18: 92.74%; SAT critical reading scores over 600: 14.42%; SAT math scores over 600: 16.34%; ACT scores over 24: 35.75% **Housing** Yes **Expenses** Tuition & Fees $21,880; Room & Board $7418 **Undergraduates** 64% women, 12% part-time, 37% 25 or older, 0.5% Native American, 2% Hispanic American, 3% African American, 0.4% Asian American/Pacific Islander **The most frequently chosen baccalaureate fields are** business/marketing, biological/life sciences, health professions and related sciences **Academic program** Advanced placement, self-designed majors, honors program, summer session, adult/continuing education programs, internships **Contact** Mr. Greg King, Director of Recruitment, King College, 1350 King College Road, Bristol, TN 37620-2699. *Phone:* 423-652-4861 or toll-free 800-362-0014. *Fax:* 423-652-4727. *E-mail:* admissions@king.edu. *Web site:* http://www.king.edu/.

Lambuth University
Jackson, Tennessee

General Independent United Methodist, 4-year, coed **Entrance** Moderately difficult **Setting** 50-acre urban campus **Total enrollment** 815 **Student-faculty ratio** 12:1 **Application deadline** Rolling (freshmen), rolling (transfer) **Freshman admission** 62% were admitted. Average high school GPA 3.30 **Freshman test scores** SAT critical reading scores over 500: 46%; SAT math scores over 500: 52%; ACT scores over 18: 94%; SAT critical reading scores over 600: 18%; SAT math scores over 600: 24%; ACT scores over 24: 39% **Housing** Yes **Expenses** Tuition & Fees $18,570; Room & Board $8015 **Undergraduates** 47% women, 8% part-time, 8% 25 or older, 0.1% Native American, 2% Hispanic American, 20% African American, 2% Asian American/Pacific Islander **The most frequently chosen baccalaureate fields are** business/marketing, parks and recreation, social sciences **Academic program** English as a second language, advanced placement, accelerated degree program, self-designed majors, honors program, summer session, adult/continuing education programs, internships **Contact** Ms. Karen Myers, Director of Financial Aid, Lambuth University, 705 Lambuth Boulevard, Jackson, TN 38301. *Phone:* 731-425-3332 or toll-free 800-526-2884. *Fax:* 731-425-3496. *E-mail:* myers-k@lambuth.edu. *Web site:* http://www.lambuth.edu/.

Lane College
Jackson, Tennessee

General Independent, 4-year, coed, affiliated with Christian Methodist Episcopal Church **Entrance** Minimally difficult **Setting** 25-acre suburban campus **Total enrollment** 2,146 **Student-faculty ratio** 21:1 **Application deadline** Rolling (freshmen), rolling (transfer) **Freshman admission** 37% were admitted. Average high school GPA 2.8 **Freshman test scores** ACT scores over 18: 18%; ACT scores over 24: 1% **Housing** Yes **Expenses** Tuition & Fees $8000; Room & Board $5520 **Undergraduates** 53% women, 1% part-time, 10% 25 or older, 0.1% Native American, 0.1% Hispanic American, 99% African American **The most frequently chosen baccalaureate fields are** business/marketing, interdisciplinary studies, security and protective services **Academic program** Advanced placement, accelerated degree program, honors program, summer session, adult/continuing education programs, internships **Contact** Ms. Kelly Boyd, Director of Enrollment Management, Lane College, 545 Lane Avenue, Jackson, TN 38301. *Phone:* 731-426-7533 or toll-free 800-960-7533. *Fax:* 731-426-7559. *E-mail:* kboyd@lanecollege.edu. *Web site:* http://www.lanecollege.edu/.

Lee University
Cleveland, Tennessee

General Independent, comprehensive, coed, affiliated with Church of God **Entrance** Minimally difficult **Setting** 115-acre small-town campus

Lee University (continued)
Total enrollment 4,262 **Student-faculty ratio** 18:1 **Application deadline** 9/1 (freshmen), 9/1 (transfer) **Freshman admission** 65% were admitted. Average high school GPA 3.42 **Freshman test scores** SAT critical reading scores over 500: 70.39%; SAT math scores over 500: 59.36%; ACT scores over 18: 87.38%; SAT critical reading scores over 600: 32.49%; SAT math scores over 600: 26.66%; ACT scores over 24: 52.28% **Housing** Yes **Expenses** Tuition & Fees $11,610; Room & Board $5650 **Undergraduates** 56% women, 12% part-time, 10% 25 or older, 0.3% Native American, 3% Hispanic American, 4% African American, 1% Asian American/Pacific Islander **The most frequently chosen baccalaureate fields are** education, psychology, theology and religious vocations **Academic program** English as a second language, advanced placement, honors program, summer session, adult/continuing education programs, internships **Contact** Mr. Phillip Cook, Assistant Vice President for Enrollment, Lee University, PO Box 3450, Cleveland, TN 37320-3450. *Phone:* 423-614-8500 or toll-free 800-533-9930. *Fax:* 423-614-8533. *E-mail:* admissions@leeuniversity.edu. *Web site:* http://www.leeuniversity.edu/.

LeMoyne-Owen College
Memphis, Tennessee

General Independent, 4-year, coed, affiliated with United Church of Christ **Entrance** Minimally difficult **Setting** 15-acre urban campus **Total enrollment** 592 **Student-faculty ratio** 10:1 **Application deadline** 4/1 (freshmen), rolling (transfer) **Freshman admission** 51% were admitted. Average high school GPA 2.5 **Freshman test scores** ACT scores over 18: 15%; ACT scores over 24: 3% **Housing** Yes **Expenses** Tuition & Fees $10,318; Room & Board $4852 **Undergraduates** 65% women, 15% part-time, 40% 25 or older, 0.2% Hispanic American, 98% African American **The most frequently chosen baccalaureate fields are** business/marketing, education, security and protective services **Academic program** Advanced placement, accelerated degree program, honors program, summer session, internships **Contact** Samuel King, Interim Director of Admissions and Recruitment, LeMoyne-Owen College, 807 Walker Avenue, Memphis, TN 38126-6595. *Phone:* 901-435-1500. *Fax:* 901-435-1524. *E-mail:* samuel_king@loc.edu. *Web site:* http://www.loc.edu/.

Lincoln Memorial University
Harrogate, Tennessee

General Independent, comprehensive, coed **Entrance** Moderately difficult **Setting** 1,000-acre small-town campus **Total enrollment** 3,948 **Student-faculty ratio** 12:1 **Application deadline** Rolling (freshmen), rolling (transfer) **Freshman admission** 76% were admitted. Average high school GPA 3.35 **Freshman test scores** SAT critical reading scores over 500: 44%; SAT math scores over 500: 42%; ACT scores over 18: 86.7%; SAT critical reading scores over 600: 10%; SAT math scores over 600: 18%; ACT scores over 24: 22.5% **Housing** Yes **Expenses** Tuition & Fees $15,700; Room & Board $5680 **Undergraduates** 71% women, 18% part-time, 29% 25 or older, 0.1% Native American, 1% Hispanic American, 5% African American, 1% Asian American/Pacific Islander **Academic program** English as a second language, advanced placement, accelerated degree program, honors program, summer session, adult/continuing education programs, internships **Contact** Miss Cindy Skaruppa, Dean of Admissions and Recruitment, Lincoln Memorial University, 6965 Cumberland Gap Parkway, Harrogate, TN 37752-1901. *Phone:* 423-869-6280 or toll-free 800-325-0900. *Fax:* 423-869-6444. *E-mail:* admissions@lmunet.edu. *Web site:* http://www.lmunet.edu/.

Lipscomb University
Nashville, Tennessee

General Independent, comprehensive, coed, affiliated with Church of Christ **Entrance** Moderately difficult **Setting** 65-acre suburban campus **Total enrollment** 3,418 **Student-faculty ratio** 16:1 **Application deadline** Rolling (freshmen), rolling (transfer) **Freshman admission** 66% were admitted. Average high school GPA 3.47 **Freshman test scores** SAT critical reading scores over 500: 77.71%; SAT math scores over 500: 72.62%; ACT scores over 18: 97.47%; SAT critical reading scores over 600: 31.21%; SAT math scores over 600: 36.31%; ACT scores over 24: 50.9% **Housing** Yes **Expenses** Tuition & Fees $20,390; Room & Board $7850 **Undergraduates** 58% women, 8% part-time, 10% 25 or older, 0.4% Native American, 2% Hispanic American, 5% African American, 2% Asian American/Pacific Islander **The most frequently chosen baccalaureate fields are** biological/life sciences, business/marketing, education **Academic program** Advanced placement, accelerated degree program, honors program, summer session, adult/continuing education programs, internships **Contact** Office of Admissions, Lipscomb University, One University Park Drive, Nashville, TN 37204-3951. *Phone:* 615-966-1776 or toll-free 877-582-4766. *Fax:* 615-966-1804. *E-mail:* admissions@lipscomb.edu. *Web site:* http://www.lipscomb.edu/.

Martin Methodist College
Pulaski, Tennessee

General Independent United Methodist, 4-year, coed **Entrance** Minimally difficult **Setting** 6-acre small-town campus **Total enrollment** 924 **Application deadline** 8/26 (freshmen), 8/30 (transfer) **Housing** Yes **Expenses** Tuition & Fees $17,626; Room & Board $6100 **Undergraduates** 22% 25 or older **Academic program** English as a second language, advanced placement, honors program, summer session, adult/continuing education programs, internships **Contact** Lisa Smith, Director of Admissions, Martin Methodist College, 433 West Madison Street, Pulaski, TN 38478-2716. *Phone:* 931-363-9868 or toll-free 800-467-1273. *Fax:* 931-363-9818. *E-mail:* admit@martinmethodist.edu. *Web site:* http://www.martinmethodist.edu/.

Maryville College
Maryville, Tennessee

General Independent Presbyterian, 4-year, coed **Entrance** Moderately difficult **Setting** 350-acre suburban campus **Total enrollment** 1,103 **Student-faculty ratio** 11:1 **Application deadline** 3/1 (freshmen), rolling (transfer) **Freshman admission** 73% were admitted. Average high school GPA 3.51 **Freshman test scores** SAT critical reading scores over 500: 66%; SAT math scores over 500: 68%; ACT scores over 18: 100%; SAT critical reading scores over 600: 27%; SAT math scores over 600: 24%; ACT scores over 24: 60% **Housing** Yes **Expenses** Tuition & Fees $29,473; Room & Board $9032 **Undergraduates** 55% women, 1% part-time, 5% 25 or older, 0.5% Native American, 2% Hispanic American, 6% African American, 1% Asian American/Pacific Islander **The most frequently chosen baccalaureate fields are** business/marketing, education, psychology **Academic program** English as a second language, advanced placement, self-designed majors, honors program, summer session, adult/continuing education programs, internships **Contact** Ms. Linda L. Moore, Administrative Assistant of Admissions, Maryville College, 502 East Lamar Alexander Parkway, Maryville, TN 37804-5907. *Phone:* 865-981-8092 or toll-free 800-597-2687. *Fax:* 865-981-8005. *E-mail:* admissions@maryvillecollege.edu. *Web site:* http://www.maryvillecollege.edu/.

Memphis College of Art
Memphis, Tennessee

General Independent, comprehensive, coed **Entrance** Moderately difficult **Setting** 340-acre urban campus **Total enrollment** 449 **Student-faculty ratio** 10:1 **Application deadline** Rolling (freshmen), rolling (transfer) **Freshman admission** 47% were admitted. Average high school GPA 3.19 **Freshman test scores** ACT scores over 18: 91%; ACT scores over 24: 42% **Housing** Yes **Expenses** Tuition & Fees $23,950; Room & Board $8000 **Undergraduates** 60% women, 6% part-time, 9% 25 or older, 4% Hispanic American, 18% African American, 2% Asian American/Pacific Islander **The most frequently chosen baccalaureate**

field is visual and performing arts **Academic program** Advanced placement, summer session, adult/continuing education programs, internships **Contact** Ms. Annette Moore, Dean of Admissions, Memphis College of Art, Overton Park, 1930 Poplar Avenue, Memphis, TN 38104-2764. *Phone:* 901-272-5153 or toll-free 800-727-1088. *Fax:* 901-272-5158. *E-mail:* amoore@mca.edu. *Web site:* http://www.mca.edu/.

Middle Tennessee State University
Murfreesboro, Tennessee

General State-supported, university, coed **Entrance** Moderately difficult **Setting** 500-acre urban campus **Total enrollment** 25,188 **Freshman admission** 70% were admitted **Freshman test scores** SAT critical reading scores over 500: 63%; SAT math scores over 500: 64%; ACT scores over 18: 92%; SAT critical reading scores over 600: 18%; SAT math scores over 600: 12%; ACT scores over 24: 33% **Housing** Yes **Expenses** Tuition & Fees: state resident $5988, nonresident $17,916; Room & Board $6514 **Undergraduates** 52% women, 15% part-time, 30% 25 or older, 0.5% Native American, 3% Hispanic American, 16% African American, 3% Asian American/Pacific Islander **The most frequently chosen baccalaureate fields are** business/marketing, communications/journalism, visual and performing arts **Academic program** Advanced placement, honors program, summer session, adult/continuing education programs, internships **Contact** Ms. Lynn Palmer, Director of Admissions, Middle Tennessee State University, 1301 East Main Street, Murfreesboro, TN 37132. *Phone:* 615-898-2111. *Fax:* 615-898-5478. *E-mail:* admissions@mtsu.edu. *Web site:* http://www.mtsu.edu/.

Milligan College
Milligan College, Tennessee

General Independent Christian, comprehensive, coed **Entrance** Moderately difficult **Setting** 181-acre suburban campus **Total enrollment** 1,100 **Student-faculty ratio** 13:1 **Application deadline** 8/1 (freshmen), rolling (transfer) **Freshman admission** 68% were admitted. Average high school GPA 3.58 **Freshman test scores** SAT critical reading scores over 500: 66%; SAT math scores over 500: 61%; ACT scores over 18: 94%; SAT critical reading scores over 600: 21%; SAT math scores over 600: 18%; ACT scores over 24: 44% **Housing** Yes **Expenses** Tuition & Fees $23,460; Room & Board $5650 **Undergraduates** 59% women, 10% part-time, 16% 25 or older, 0.4% Native American, 3% Hispanic American, 7% African American, 0.4% Asian American/Pacific Islander **The most frequently chosen baccalaureate fields are** business/marketing, education, health professions and related sciences **Academic program** Advanced placement, summer session, adult/continuing education programs, internships **Contact** Ms. Tracy Brinn, Director of Enrollment Management, Milligan College, PO Box 210, Milligan College, TN 37682. *Phone:* 423-461-8730 or toll-free 800-262-8337. *Fax:* 423-461-8982. *E-mail:* admissions@milligan.edu. *Web site:* http://www.milligan.edu/.

Visit Petersons.com and enter keyword Milligan

See page 968 for the College Close-Up.

National College
Bristol, Tennessee

Contact Patrick DeMesa, Campus Director, National College, 1328 Highway 11 West, Bristol, TN 37620. *Phone:* 423-878-4440. *Web site:* http://www.national-college.edu/.

O'More College of Design
Franklin, Tennessee

General Independent, 4-year, coed, primarily women **Entrance** Moderately difficult **Setting** 6-acre small-town campus **Total enrollment** 222 **Student-faculty ratio** 8:1 **Application deadline** 8/1 (freshmen), 8/1 (transfer) **Freshman admission** 81% were admitted. Average high

Bachelor of Fine Arts

Animation | Graphic Design | Printmaking
Digital Cinema | Illustration | Sculpture
Digital Media | Painting | Sequential Narrative
Drawing | Photography

Master of Fine Arts | Master of Arts in Art Education
Master of Arts in Teaching

1.800.727.1088
info@mca.edu | www.mca.edu

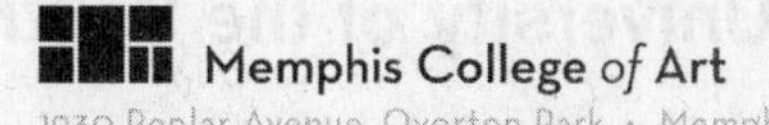

1930 Poplar Avenue, Overton Park • Memphis, TN 38104

O'More College of Design (continued)

school GPA 3.2 **Freshman test scores** ACT scores over 18: 95.7%; ACT scores over 24: 30.5% **Housing** No **Expenses** Tuition & Fees $17,690 **Undergraduates** 91% women, 14% part-time, 24% 25 or older, 1% Native American, 4% Hispanic American, 5% African American, 5% Asian American/Pacific Islander **The most frequently chosen baccalaureate field is** visual and performing arts **Academic program** Advanced placement, summer session, internships **Contact** Mr. Chris Lee, Vice President of Enrollment, O'More College of Design, 423 South Margin Street, Franklin, TN 37064-2816. *Phone:* 615-794-4254 Ext. 232. *Fax:* 615-790-1662. *E-mail:* clee@omorecollege.edu. *Web site:* http://www.omorecollege.edu/.

Remington College–Memphis Campus
Memphis, Tennessee

Contact Randal Hayes, Director of Recruitment, Remington College–Memphis Campus, 2731 Nonconnah Boulevard, Memphis, TN 38132-2131. *Phone:* 901-345-1000. *Fax:* 901-396-8310. *E-mail:* randal.hayes@remingtoncollege.edu. *Web site:* http://www.remingtoncollege.edu/.

Rhodes College
Memphis, Tennessee

General Independent Presbyterian, comprehensive, coed **Entrance** Very difficult **Setting** 100-acre suburban campus **Total enrollment** 1,685 **Student-faculty ratio** 10:1 **Application deadline** 1/15 (freshmen), 1/15 (transfer) **Freshman admission** 42% were admitted. Average high school GPA 3.81 **Freshman test scores** SAT critical reading scores over 500: 95.57%; SAT math scores over 500: 96.59%; ACT scores over 18: 100%; SAT critical reading scores over 600: 65.19%; SAT math scores over 600: 69.63%; ACT scores over 24: 94.95% **Housing** Yes **Expenses** Tuition & Fees $33,710; Room & Board $8314 **Undergraduates** 57% women, 1% part-time, 1% Native American, 2% Hispanic American, 7% African American, 5% Asian American/Pacific Islander **The most frequently chosen baccalaureate fields are** biological/life sciences, history, social sciences **Academic program** Advanced placement, self-designed majors, honors program, internships **Contact** Mr. David J. Wottle, Dean of Admissions and Financial Aid, Rhodes College, 2000 North Parkway, Memphis, TN 38112-1690. *Phone:* 901-843-3700 or toll-free 800-844-5969. *Fax:* 901-843-3631. *E-mail:* adminfo@rhodes.edu. *Web site:* http://www.rhodes.edu/.

Sewanee: The University of the South
Sewanee, Tennessee

General Independent Episcopal, comprehensive, coed **Entrance** Very difficult **Setting** 13,000-acre small-town campus **Total enrollment** 1,543 **Student-faculty ratio** 11:1 **Application deadline** 2/1 (freshmen), 4/1 (transfer) **Freshman admission** 68% were admitted. Average high school GPA 3.6 **Freshman test scores** SAT critical reading scores over 500: 93.4%; SAT math scores over 500: 95.6%; ACT scores over 18: 100%; SAT critical reading scores over 600: 65.6%; SAT math scores over 600: 65.6%; ACT scores over 24: 90.6% **Housing** Yes **Expenses** Tuition & Fees $35,862; Room & Board $10,250 **Undergraduates** 51% women, 1% part-time, 1% Native American, 3% Hispanic American, 5% African American, 3% Asian American/Pacific Islander **The most frequently chosen baccalaureate fields are** English, history, social sciences **Academic program** Advanced placement, self-designed majors, summer session, internships **Contact** Mr. Jay Fisher, Acting Dean of Admission and Financial Aid, Sewanee: The University of the South, 735 University Avenue, Sewanee, TN 37383-1000. *Phone:* 931-598-1238 or toll-free 800-522-2234. *Fax:* 931-598-3248. *E-mail:* admiss@sewanee.edu. *Web site:* http://www.sewanee.edu/.

South College
Knoxville, Tennessee

Contact Mr. Walter Hosea, Director of Admissions, South College, 720 North Fifth Avenue, Knoxville, TN 37917. *Phone:* 865-524-3043 Ext. 1825. *E-mail:* whosea@southcollegetn.edu. *Web site:* http://www.southcollegetn.edu/.

Southern Adventist University
Collegedale, Tennessee

General Independent Seventh-day Adventist, comprehensive, coed **Entrance** Moderately difficult **Setting** 1,000-acre small-town campus **Total enrollment** 2,891 **Student-faculty ratio** 15:1 **Application deadline** Rolling (freshmen), rolling (transfer) **Freshman admission** 71% were admitted. Average high school GPA 3.39 **Freshman test scores** SAT critical reading scores over 500: 56%; SAT math scores over 500: 49%; ACT scores over 18: 91%; SAT critical reading scores over 600: 19%; SAT math scores over 600: 15%; ACT scores over 24: 40% **Housing** Yes **Expenses** Tuition & Fees $17,712; Room & Board $5174 **Undergraduates** 56% women, 17% part-time, 10% 25 or older, 0.5% Native American, 13% Hispanic American, 11% African American, 5% Asian American/Pacific Islander **The most frequently chosen baccalaureate fields are** business/marketing, biological/life sciences, health professions and related sciences **Academic program** English as a second language, advanced placement, honors program, summer session, internships **Contact** Mr. Marc Grundy, Associate Vice President, Marketing and Enrollment Services, Southern Adventist University, PO Box 370, Collegedale, TN 37315-0370. *Phone:* 423-236-2844 or toll-free 800-768-8437. *Fax:* 423-236-1844. *E-mail:* admissions@southern.edu. *Web site:* http://www.southern.edu/.

Strayer University–Knoxville Campus
Knoxville, Tennessee

General Proprietary, comprehensive, coed **Contact** Admissions Office, Strayer University–Knoxville Campus, 10118 Parkside Drive, Suite 200, Knoxville, TN 37922. *Phone:* 865-288-6000. *Web site:* http://www.strayer.edu/knoxville.

Strayer University–Nashville Campus
Nashville, Tennessee

General Proprietary, comprehensive, coed **Contact** Admissions Office, Strayer University–Nashville Campus, 1809 Dabbs Avenue, Nashville, TN 37210. *Phone:* 615-871-2260. *Web site:* http://www.strayer.edu/nashville.

Strayer University–Shelby Oaks Campus
Memphis, Tennessee

General Proprietary, comprehensive, coed **Contact** Admissions Office, Strayer University–Shelby Oaks Campus, 6211 Shelby Oaks Drive, Suite 100, Memphis, TN 38134. *Phone:* 901-383-6750. *Web site:* http://www.strayer.edu/shelby_oaks.

Strayer University–Thousand Oaks Campus
Memphis, Tennessee

General Proprietary, comprehensive, coed **Contact** Admissions Office, Strayer University–Thousand Oaks Campus, 2620 Thousand Oaks Boulevard, Suite 1100, Memphis, TN 38118. *Phone:* 901-369-0835. *Web site:* http://www.strayer.edu/thousand_oaks_campus.

Tennessee State University
Nashville, Tennessee

General State-supported, comprehensive, coed **Entrance** Minimally difficult **Setting** 450-acre urban campus **Total enrollment** 8,254 **Student-**

faculty ratio 15:1 **Application deadline** 8/1 (freshmen), 8/1 (transfer) **Freshman admission** 91% were admitted. Average high school GPA 2.93 **Housing** Yes **Expenses** Tuition & Fees: state resident $5132, nonresident $16,024; Room & Board $5462 **Undergraduates** 64% women, 20% part-time, 26% 25 or older, 0.1% Native American, 1% Hispanic American, 80% African American, 1% Asian American/Pacific Islander **The most frequently chosen baccalaureate fields are** health professions and related sciences, business/marketing, liberal arts/general studies **Academic program** Accelerated degree program, honors program, summer session, adult/continuing education programs, internships **Contact** Ms. Vernella Smith, Admissions Coordinator, Tennessee State University, 3500 John A Merritt Boulevard, Nashville, TN 37209-1561. *Phone:* 615-963-5104. *Fax:* 615-963-5108. *E-mail:* vsmith@tnstate.edu. *Web site:* http://www.tnstate.edu/.

Visit Petersons.com and enter keywords Tennessee State

See page 1216 for the College Close-Up.

Tennessee Technological University
Cookeville, Tennessee

General State-supported, university, coed **Entrance** Moderately difficult **Setting** 235-acre small-town campus **Total enrollment** 10,847 **Student-faculty ratio** 19:1 **Application deadline** 8/1 (freshmen), 8/1 (transfer) **Freshman admission** 84% were admitted. Average high school GPA 3.4 **Freshman test scores** SAT critical reading scores over 500: 66%; SAT math scores over 500: 72%; ACT scores over 18: 98%; SAT critical reading scores over 600: 31%; SAT math scores over 600: 39%; ACT scores over 24: 43% **Housing** Yes **Expenses** Tuition & Fees: state resident $5498, nonresident $17,454; Room & Board $7124 **Undergraduates** 47% women, 10% part-time, 15% 25 or older, 0.3% Native American, 2% Hispanic American, 4% African American, 1% Asian American/Pacific Islander **The most frequently chosen baccalaureate fields are** business/marketing, engineering, interdisciplinary studies **Academic program** English as a second language, advanced placement, accelerated degree program, honors program, summer session, adult/continuing education programs, internships **Contact** Ms. Vanessa Palmer, Director of Admissions, Tennessee Technological University, PO Box 5006, Cookeville, TN 38505. *Phone:* 931-372-3888 or toll-free 800-255-8881. *Fax:* 931-372-6250. *E-mail:* admissions@tntech.edu. *Web site:* http://www.tntech.edu/.

Tennessee Temple University
Chattanooga, Tennessee

General Independent Baptist, comprehensive, coed **Entrance** Minimally difficult **Setting** 55-acre urban campus **Total enrollment** 623 **Application deadline** 8/20 (freshmen), 8/15 (transfer) **Housing** Yes **Expenses** Tuition & Fees $10,950; Room & Board $6030 **Undergraduates** 27% 25 or older **Academic program** Advanced placement, summer session, internships **Contact** Eric Lovett, Director of Recruitment, Tennessee Temple University, 1815 Union Avenue, Chattanooga, TN 37404-3587. *Phone:* 423-493-4371 or toll-free 800-553-4050. *E-mail:* eric.lovett@tntemple.edu. *Web site:* http://www.tntemple.edu/.

Tennessee Wesleyan College
Athens, Tennessee

General Independent United Methodist, 4-year, coed **Entrance** Minimally difficult **Setting** 40-acre small-town campus **Total enrollment** 1,070 **Student-faculty ratio** 15:1 **Freshman admission** 84% were admitted. Average high school GPA 3.33 **Freshman test scores** SAT critical reading scores over 500: 39%; SAT math scores over 500: 28%; ACT scores over 18: 88%; SAT critical reading scores over 600: 14%; SAT math scores over 600: 6%; ACT scores over 24: 29% **Housing** Yes **Expenses** Tuition & Fees $18,600; Room & Board $6100 **Undergraduates** 64% women, 13% part-time, 22% 25 or older, 1% Hispanic American, 4% African American, 1% Asian American/Pacific Islander **The most frequently chosen baccalaureate fields are** business/marketing, education, health professions and related sciences **Academic program** Advanced placement, accelerated degree program, self-designed majors, honors program, summer session, adult/continuing education programs, internships **Contact** Stan Harrison, Vice President of Enrollment Services and Director of Athletics, Tennessee Wesleyan College, 204 East College Street, Athens, TN 37303. *Phone:* 423-746-7504 Ext. 5310 or toll-free 800-PICK-TWC. *Fax:* 423-745-9335. *E-mail:* sharrison@twcnet.edu. *Web site:* http://www.twcnet.edu/.

Trevecca Nazarene University
Nashville, Tennessee

General Independent Nazarene, comprehensive, coed **Entrance** Moderately difficult **Setting** 65-acre urban campus **Total enrollment** 2,476 **Student-faculty ratio** 12:1 **Application deadline** 8/1 (freshmen), rolling (transfer) **Freshman admission** 69% were admitted. Average high school GPA 3.17 **Freshman test scores** SAT critical reading scores over 500: 55%; SAT math scores over 500: 60%; ACT scores over 18: 87%; SAT critical reading scores over 600: 20%; SAT math scores over 600: 19%; ACT scores over 24: 36% **Housing** Yes **Expenses** Tuition & Fees $18,318; Room & Board $7734 **Undergraduates** 56% women, 11% part-time, 25% 25 or older, 0.5% Native American, 3% Hispanic American, 8% African American, 1% Asian American/Pacific Islander **The most frequently chosen baccalaureate fields are** business/marketing, education, philosophy and religious studies **Academic program** Advanced placement, summer session, adult/continuing education programs, internships **Contact** Dr. Michael Cantrell, Director of Undergraduate Admissions, Trevecca Nazarene University, 333 Murfreesboro Road, Nashville, TN 37210-2834. *Phone:* 615-248-1320 or toll-free 888-210-4TNU. *Fax:* 615-248-7406. *E-mail:* admissions_und@trevecca.edu. *Web site:* http://www.trevecca.edu/.

Tusculum College
Greeneville, Tennessee

General Independent Presbyterian, comprehensive, coed **Entrance** Moderately difficult **Setting** 140-acre small-town campus **Total enrollment** 2,203 **Student-faculty ratio** 16:1 **Application deadline** Rolling (freshmen), rolling (transfer) **Freshman admission** 75% were admitted. Average high school GPA 3.1 **Freshman test scores** SAT critical reading scores over 500: 32%; SAT math scores over 500: 44%; ACT scores over 18: 89%; SAT critical reading scores over 600: 7%; SAT math scores over 600: 6%; ACT scores over 24: 28% **Housing** Yes **Expenses** Tuition & Fees $19,530; Room & Board $7735 **Undergraduates** 60% women, 3% part-time, 6% 25 or older, 0.3% Native American, 1% Hispanic American, 11% African American, 0.5% Asian American/Pacific Islander **The most frequently chosen baccalaureate fields are** business/marketing, education, parks and recreation **Academic program** English as a second language, advanced placement, self-designed majors, honors program, summer session, adult/continuing education programs, internships **Contact** Ms. Melissa Ripley, Director of Operations, Tusculum College, PO Box 5047, Greeneville, TN 37743-9997. *Phone:* 423-636-7300 Ext. 5374 or toll-free 800-729-0256. *Fax:* 423-798-1622. *E-mail:* admissions@tusculum.edu. *Web site:* http://www.tusculum.edu/.

Union University
Jackson, Tennessee

General Independent Southern Baptist, comprehensive, coed **Entrance** Moderately difficult **Setting** 360-acre small-town campus **Total enrollment** 3,922 **Student-faculty ratio** 12:1 **Application deadline** Rolling (freshmen), rolling (transfer) **Freshman admission** 84% were admitted. Average high school GPA 3.52 **Freshman test scores** SAT critical reading scores over 500: 80%; SAT math scores over 500: 80%; ACT scores over 18: 98%; SAT critical reading scores over 600: 47%; SAT math scores over 600: 39%; ACT scores over 24: 64% **Housing** Yes **Expenses** Tuition & Fees $20,940; Room & Board $6930 **Under-**

Union University (continued)

graduates 59% women, 21% part-time, 26% 25 or older, 0.1% Native American, 1% Hispanic American, 12% African American, 1% Asian American/Pacific Islander **The most frequently chosen baccalaureate fields are** health professions and related sciences, business/marketing, interdisciplinary studies **Academic program** English as a second language, advanced placement, accelerated degree program, honors program, summer session, adult/continuing education programs, internships **Contact** Mr. Robbie Graves, Director of Enrollment Services, Union University, 1050 Union University Drive, Jackson, TN 38305-3697. *Phone:* 731-661-5590 or toll-free 800-33-UNION. *Fax:* 731-661-5017. *E-mail:* rgraves@uu.edu. *Web site:* http://www.uu.edu/.

Visit Petersons.com and enter keywords Union University

See page 1240 for the College Close-Up.

University of Memphis

Memphis, Tennessee

General State-supported, university, coed **Entrance** Moderately difficult **Setting** 1,160-acre urban campus **Total enrollment** 21,424 **Student-faculty ratio** 15:1 **Application deadline** 7/1 (freshmen), 7/1 (transfer) **Freshman admission** 67% were admitted. Average high school GPA 3.23 **Freshman test scores** ACT scores over 18: 84.5%; ACT scores over 24: 30.5% **Housing** Yes **Expenses** Tuition & Fees: state resident $7058, nonresident $19,778; Room & Board $5950 **Undergraduates** 61% women, 25% part-time, 34% 25 or older, 0.3% Native American, 2% Hispanic American, 39% African American, 3% Asian American/Pacific Islander **The most frequently chosen baccalaureate fields are** business/marketing, education, interdisciplinary studies **Academic program** English as a second language, advanced placement, accelerated degree program, self-designed majors, honors program, summer session, adult/continuing education programs, internships **Contact** Dr. Brian Meredith, Director of Admissions, University of Memphis, Memphis, TN 38152. *Phone:* 901-678-2111 or toll-free 800-669-2678. *Fax:* 901-678-5318. *E-mail:* bmeredith@memphis.edu. *Web site:* http://www.memphis.edu/.

Visit Petersons.com and enter keywords University of Memphis

See page 1284 for the College Close-Up.

University of Phoenix–Nashville Campus

Nashville, Tennessee

General Proprietary, comprehensive, coed **Entrance** Noncompetitive **Setting** urban campus **Total enrollment** 917 **Application deadline** Rolling (freshmen), rolling (transfer) **Expenses** Tuition & Fees $11,421 **Undergraduates** 64% women, 84% 25 or older, 1% Native American, 2% Hispanic American, 28% African American, 1% Asian American/Pacific Islander **The most frequently chosen baccalaureate fields are** business/marketing, computer and information sciences, health professions and related sciences **Academic program** Advanced placement, accelerated degree program **Contact** Ms. Audra McQuarie, Registrar/Executive Director, University of Phoenix–Nashville Campus, 4035 South Riverpoint Parkway, Mail Stop CF-L101, Phoenix, AZ 85040. *Phone:* 480-557-6151 or toll-free 800-776-4867 (in-state); 800-228-7240 (out-of-state). *Fax:* 480-643-3068. *E-mail:* audra.mcquarie@phoenix.edu. *Web site:* http://www.phoenix.edu/.

The University of Tennessee

Knoxville, Tennessee

General State-supported, university, coed **Entrance** Moderately difficult **Setting** 550-acre urban campus **Total enrollment** 29,934 **Student-faculty ratio** 16:1 **Application deadline** 12/1 (freshmen), 6/1 (transfer) **Freshman admission** 73% were admitted. Average high school GPA 3.78 **Freshman test scores** SAT critical reading scores over 500: 83.06%; SAT math scores over 500: 85.25%; ACT scores over 18: 99.45%; SAT critical reading scores over 600: 40.87%; SAT math scores over 600: 46.08%; ACT scores over 24: 79.95% **Housing** Yes **Expenses** Tuition & Fees: state resident $6850, nonresident $20,946; Room & Board $7254 **Undergraduates** 49% women, 7% part-time, 9% 25 or older, 1% Native American, 2% Hispanic American, 8% African American, 3% Asian American/Pacific Islander **The most frequently chosen baccalaureate fields are** business/marketing, communications/journalism, psychology **Academic program** English as a second language, advanced placement, accelerated degree program, self-designed majors, honors program, summer session, internships **Contact** Ms. Norma Harrington, Assistant Provost and Director, The University of Tennessee, 320 Student Services Building, 1331 Circle Park, Knoxville, TN 37996-0230. *Phone:* 865-974-2184 or toll-free 800-221-8657. *Fax:* 865-974-6341. *E-mail:* admissions@tennessee.edu. *Web site:* http://www.tennessee.edu/.

The University of Tennessee at Chattanooga

Chattanooga, Tennessee

General State-supported, comprehensive, coed **Entrance** Moderately difficult **Setting** 120-acre urban campus **Total enrollment** 10,526 **Student-faculty ratio** 18:1 **Application deadline** 8/1 (freshmen), 8/1 (transfer) **Freshman admission** 79% were admitted. Average high school GPA 3.26 **Housing** Yes **Expenses** Tuition & Fees: state resident $5656, nonresident $16,954; Room & Board $8056 **Undergraduates** 56% women, 11% part-time, 14% 25 or older, 1% Native American, 2% Hispanic American, 16% African American, 2% Asian American/Pacific Islander **The most frequently chosen baccalaureate fields are** business/marketing, education, social sciences **Academic program** English as a second language, advanced placement, honors program, summer session, adult/continuing education programs, internships **Contact** Mr. Yancy Freeman, Director, Admissions and Recruitment, The University of Tennessee at Chattanooga, 715 Oak Street, Dept. 5105, Guerry Hall, Chattanooga, TN 37403. *Phone:* 423-425-4662 or toll-free 800-UTC-MOCS. *Fax:* 423-425-4157. *E-mail:* yancy-freeman@utc.edu. *Web site:* http://www.utc.edu/.

The University of Tennessee at Martin

Martin, Tennessee

General State-supported, comprehensive, coed **Entrance** Moderately difficult **Setting** 250-acre small-town campus **Total enrollment** 8,101 **Student-faculty ratio** 19:1 **Application deadline** Rolling (freshmen), rolling (transfer) **Freshman admission** 75% were admitted. Average high school GPA 3.39 **Freshman test scores** ACT scores over 18: 95.87%; ACT scores over 24: 32.2% **Housing** Yes **Expenses** Tuition & Fees: state resident $5769, nonresident $17,155; Room & Board $4914 **Undergraduates** 57% women, 23% part-time, 20% 25 or older, 0.2% Native American, 1% Hispanic American, 16% African American, 1% Asian American/Pacific Islander **The most frequently chosen baccalaureate fields are** business/marketing, biological/life sciences, interdisciplinary studies **Academic program** English as a second language, advanced placement, accelerated degree program, self-designed majors, honors program, summer session, adult/continuing education programs, internships **Contact** Ms. Judy Rayburn, Director of Admissions, The University of Tennessee at Martin, 200 Hall-Moody Administration Building, Martin, TN 38238. *Phone:* 731-881-7032 or toll-free 800-829-8861. *Fax:* 731-881-7029. *E-mail:* jrayburn@utm.edu. *Web site:* http://www.utm.edu/.

Vanderbilt University

Nashville, Tennessee

General Independent, university, coed **Entrance** Very difficult **Setting** 330-acre urban campus **Total enrollment** 12,506 **Student-faculty ratio** 8:1 **Application deadline** 1/3 (freshmen), 3/1 (transfer) **Freshman admission** 20% were admitted. Average high school GPA 3.7 **Freshman**

test scores SAT critical reading scores over 500: 98.9%; SAT math scores over 500: 99.8%; ACT scores over 18: 100%; SAT critical reading scores over 600: 93.4%; SAT math scores over 600: 96.1%; ACT scores over 24: 99% **Housing** Yes **Expenses** Tuition & Fees $38,578; Room & Board $12,650 **Undergraduates** 52% women, 1% part-time, 1% Native American, 6% Hispanic American, 9% African American, 8% Asian American/Pacific Islander **The most frequently chosen baccalaureate fields are** engineering, interdisciplinary studies, social sciences **Academic program** English as a second language, advanced placement, accelerated degree program, self-designed majors, honors program, summer session, internships **Contact** John O. Gaines, Director of Admissions, Vanderbilt University, 2305 West End Avenue, Nashville, TN 37203. *Phone:* 615-936-2811 or toll-free 800-288-0432. *Fax:* 615-343-8326. *E-mail:* admissions@vanderbilt.edu. *Web site:* http://www.vanderbilt.edu/.

Visit Petersons.com and enter keyword Vanderbilt

See page 1330 for the College Close-Up.

Watkins College of Art, Design, & Film
Nashville, Tennessee

General Independent, 4-year, coed **Entrance** Moderately difficult **Setting** 13-acre urban campus **Total enrollment** 379 **Student-faculty ratio** 8:1 **Application deadline** 7/15 (freshmen), 7/15 (transfer) **Freshman admission** 75% were admitted. Average high school GPA 3.01 **Housing** Yes **Expenses** Tuition & Fees $18,600; Room only $6000 **Undergraduates** 53% women, 31% part-time, 29% 25 or older, 0.3% Native American, 2% Hispanic American, 5% African American, 1% Asian American/Pacific Islander **The most frequently chosen baccalaureate field is** visual and performing arts **Academic program** Advanced placement, summer session, internships **Contact** Ms. Linda E. Schwab, Director of Admissions, Watkins College of Art, Design, & Film, 2298 Rosa L. Parks Boulevard, Nashville, TN 37228. *Phone:* 615-383-4848 Ext. 7458. *Fax:* 615-383-4849. *E-mail:* admissions@watkins.edu. *Web site:* http://www.watkins.edu/.

Williamson Christian College
Franklin, Tennessee

Contact Ms. Mary Newby, Recruiter, Williamson Christian College, 200 Seaboard Lane, Franklin, TN 37067. *Phone:* 615-771-7821. *Fax:* 615-771-7810. *E-mail:* mary@williamsoncc.edu. *Web site:* http://www.williamsoncc.edu/.

TEXAS

Abilene Christian University
Abilene, Texas

General Independent, comprehensive, coed, affiliated with Church of Christ **Entrance** Moderately difficult **Setting** 208-acre urban campus **Total enrollment** 4,813 **Student-faculty ratio** 15:1 **Application deadline** 2/15 (freshmen), rolling (transfer) **Freshman admission** 49% were admitted. Average high school GPA 3.49 **Freshman test scores** SAT critical reading scores over 500: 67.73%; SAT math scores over 500: 74.1%; ACT scores over 18: 97.32%; SAT critical reading scores over 600: 29.08%; SAT math scores over 600: 34.14%; ACT scores over 24: 53.47% **Housing** Yes **Expenses** Tuition & Fees $20,290; Room & Board $7510 **Undergraduates** 54% women, 8% part-time, 5% 25 or older, 1% Native American, 8% Hispanic American, 8% African American, 1% Asian American/Pacific Islander **The most frequently chosen baccalaureate fields are** business/marketing, education, interdisciplinary studies **Academic program** English as a second language, advanced placement, self-designed majors, honors program, summer session, adult/continuing education programs, internships **Contact** Mark Lavender, Director of Admissions, Abilene Christian University, ACU Box 29000, Abilene, TX 79699-9000. *Phone:* 325-674-2650. *Fax:* 325-674-2130. *E-mail:* info@admissions.acu.edu. *Web site:* http://www.acu.edu/.

Amberton University
Garland, Texas

General Independent nondenominational, upper-level, coed **Entrance** Minimally difficult **Setting** 5-acre suburban campus **Total enrollment** 1,533 **Student-faculty ratio** 25:1 **Application deadline** Rolling (transfer) **Housing** No **Expenses** Tuition & Fees $5400 **Undergraduates** 60% women, 43% part-time, 98% 25 or older, 6% Hispanic American, 27% African American, 3% Asian American/Pacific Islander **The most frequently chosen baccalaureate fields are** business/marketing, interdisciplinary studies **Academic program** Self-designed majors, summer session, adult/continuing education programs, internships **Contact** Dr. Don Hebbard, Academic Dean, Amberton University, 1700 Eastgate Drive, Garland, TX 75041-5595. *Phone:* 972-279-6511. *Fax:* 972-279-9773. *E-mail:* advisor@amberton.edu. *Web site:* http://www.amberton.edu/.

American InterContinental University
Houston, Texas

General Proprietary, comprehensive, coed **Total enrollment** 474 **Application deadline** Rolling (freshmen), rolling (transfer) **Undergraduates** 54% women, 20% part-time, 53% 25 or older, 0.2% Native American, 26% Hispanic American, 38% African American, 4% Asian American/Pacific Islander **The most frequently chosen baccalaureate fields are** business/marketing, computer and information sciences, visual and performing arts **Academic program** Accelerated degree program, adult/continuing education programs **Contact** Ashia Kayzer, Director of Admissions, American InterContinental University, 9999 Richmond Avenue, Houston, TX 77042. *Phone:* 877-564-6248 or toll-free 888-607-9888. *Web site:* http://www.aiuniv.edu/.

Angelo State University
San Angelo, Texas

General State-supported, comprehensive, coed **Entrance** Moderately difficult **Setting** 268-acre urban campus **Total enrollment** 6,387 **Student-faculty ratio** 19:1 **Application deadline** Rolling (freshmen), rolling (transfer) **Freshman admission** 92% were admitted **Freshman test scores** SAT critical reading scores over 500: 32.83%; SAT math scores over 500: 44.24%; ACT scores over 18: 77.78%; SAT critical reading scores over 600: 7.22%; SAT math scores over 600: 8.5%; ACT scores over 24: 21.03% **Housing** Yes **Expenses** Tuition & Fees: state resident $6138, nonresident $14,568; Room & Board $6612 **Undergraduates** 55% women, 16% part-time, 21% 25 or older **The most frequently chosen baccalaureate fields are** business/marketing, interdisciplinary studies, parks and recreation **Academic program** Advanced placement, honors program, summer session, internships **Contact** Ms. Megan Wheeler, Coordinator of Recruiting, Angelo State University, 2601 West Avenue N, San Angelo, TX 76909. *Phone:* 325-942-2259 Ext. 233 or toll-free 800-946-8627. *Fax:* 325-942-2128. *E-mail:* admissions@angelo.edu. *Web site:* http://www.angelo.edu/.

Visit Petersons.com and enter keyword Angelo

Argosy University, Dallas
Farmers Branch, Texas

General Proprietary, university, coed **Setting** urban campus **Contact** Director of Admissions, Argosy University, Dallas, 5001 Lyndon B. Johnson Freeway, Heritage Square, Farmers Branch, TX 75244. *Phone:* 214-890-9900 or toll-free 866-954-9900. *Fax:* 214-378-8555. *Web site:* http://www.argosy.edu/dallas/.

Visit Petersons.com and enter keywords Argosy University, Dallas

See page 478 for the College Close-Up.

Arlington Baptist College
Arlington, Texas

General Independent Baptist, 4-year, coed **Entrance** Noncompetitive **Setting** 32-acre urban campus **Total enrollment** 138 **Student-faculty ratio** 7:1 **Application deadline** Rolling (freshmen), rolling (transfer) **Freshman admission** 100% were admitted **Housing** Yes **Expenses** Tuition & Fees $6740; Room & Board $4200 **Undergraduates** 53% women, 22% part-time, 42% 25 or older **The most frequently chosen baccalaureate fields are** education, theology and religious vocations **Academic program** Advanced placement, summer session, internships **Contact** Ms. Janie Taylor, Registrar/Admissions, Arlington Baptist College, 3001 West Division, Arlington, TX 76012-3425. *Phone:* 817-461-8741 Ext. 105. *Fax:* 817-274-1138. *E-mail:* jhall@abconline.org. *Web site:* http://www.abconline.edu/.

The Art Institute of Austin
Austin, Texas

General Proprietary, 4-year, coed **Contact** Director of Admissions, The Art Institute of Austin, 101 W. Louis Henna Boulevard, Suite 100, Austin, TX 78728. *Phone:* 512-691-1707 or toll-free 866-583-7952. *Fax:* 512-691-1790. *Web site:* http://www.artinstitutes.edu/austin.
Visit Petersons.com and enter keywords Art Institute of Austin

See page 484 for the College Close-Up.

The Art Institute of Dallas
Dallas, Texas

General Proprietary, 4-year, coed **Setting** 2-acre urban campus **Contact** Director of Admissions, The Art Institute of Dallas, 8080 Park Lane, Suite 100, Dallas, TX 75231-5993. *Phone:* 214-692-8080 or toll-free 800-275-4243. *Fax:* 214-750-9460. *Web site:* http://www.artinstitutes.edu/dallas.
Visit Petersons.com and enter keywords Art Institute of Dallas

See page 510 for the College Close-Up.

The Art Institute of Fort Worth
Fort Worth, Texas

General Proprietary, 4-year, coed **Contact** Director of Admissions, The Art Institute of Fort Worth, 7000 Calmont Avenue, Suite 150, Fort Worth, TX 76116. *Phone:* 817-210-0808 or toll-free 888-422-9686. *Fax:* 817-210-0901. *Web site:* http://www.artinstitutes.edu/fort-worth/.

See page 514 for the College Close-Up.

The Art Institute of Houston
Houston, Texas

General Proprietary, 4-year, coed **Setting** urban campus **Contact** Director of Admissions, The Art Institute of Houston, 1900 Yorktown Street, Houston, TX 77056. *Phone:* 713-623-2040 or toll-free 800-275-4244. *Fax:* 713-966-2797. *Web site:* http://www.artinstitutes.edu/houston.
Visit Petersons.com and enter keywords Art Institute of Houston

See page 516 for the College Close-Up.

The Art Institute of Houston—North
Houston, Texas

General Proprietary, 4-year, coed **Contact** Director of Admissions, The Art Institute of Houston—North, 10740 North Gessner Drive, Suite 190, Houston, TX 77064. *Phone:* 281-671-3381 or toll-free 866-830-4450. *Fax:* 281-671-3550. *Web site:* http://www.artinstitutes.edu/houston-north.
Visit Petersons.com and enter keywords Art Institute of Houston-North

See page 518 for the College Close-Up.

The Art Institute of San Antonio
San Antonio, Texas

General Proprietary, 4-year, coed **Contact** Director of Admissions, The Art Institute of San Antonio, 1000 IH-10 West, Suite 200, San Antonio, TX 78230. *Phone:* 210-338-7320 or toll-free 888-222-0040. *Web site:* http://www.artinstitutes.edu/san-antonio/.

See page 542 for the College Close-Up.

Austin College
Sherman, Texas

General Independent Presbyterian, comprehensive, coed **Entrance** Very difficult **Setting** 60-acre small-town campus **Total enrollment** 1,364 **Student-faculty ratio** 14:1 **Application deadline** 5/1 (freshmen), 5/1 (transfer) **Freshman admission** 80% were admitted. Average high school GPA 3.56 **Freshman test scores** SAT critical reading scores over 500: 90.1%; SAT math scores over 500: 94.38%; ACT scores over 18: 99.5%; SAT critical reading scores over 600: 54.2%; SAT math scores over 600: 64.43%; ACT scores over 24: 75.2% **Housing** Yes **Expenses** Tuition & Fees $29,235; Room & Board $9549 **Undergraduates** 54% women, 1% part-time, 1% 25 or older, 1% Native American, 10% Hispanic American, 3% African American, 15% Asian American/Pacific Islander **The most frequently chosen baccalaureate fields are** psychology, business/marketing, social sciences **Academic program** Advanced placement, self-designed majors, honors program, summer session, adult/continuing education programs, internships **Contact** Ms. Nan Davis, Vice President for Institutional Enrollment, Austin College, 900 North Grand Avenue, Suite 6N, Sherman, TX 75090-4400. *Phone:* 903-813-3000 or toll-free 800-442-5363. *Fax:* 903-813-3198. *E-mail:* admission@austincollege.edu. *Web site:* http://www.austincollege.edu/.
Visit Petersons.com and enter keywords Austin College

See page 570 for the College Close-Up.

Austin Graduate School of Theology
Austin, Texas

General Independent, upper-level, coed, affiliated with Church of Christ **Entrance** Minimally difficult **Setting** 2-acre urban campus **Total enrollment** 60 **Application deadline** Rolling (transfer) **First-year students** 100% were admitted **Housing** No **Expenses** Tuition & Fees $7100 **Undergraduates** 37% women, 80% part-time, 83% 25 or older, 20% Hispanic American, 28% African American, 4% Asian American/Pacific Islander **The most frequently chosen baccalaureate field is** philosophy and religious studies **Academic program** Summer session, adult/continuing education programs **Contact** Mrs. Celeste Scarbrough, Director of Admissions, Austin Graduate School of Theology, 7640 Guadalupe Street, Austin, TX 78752. *Phone:* 512-476-2772 or toll-free 866-AUS-GRAD. *Fax:* 512-476-3919. *E-mail:* registrar@austingrad.edu. *Web site:* http://www.austingrad.edu/.

Baptist Missionary Association Theological Seminary
Jacksonville, Texas

General Independent Baptist, comprehensive, coed, primarily men **Entrance** Noncompetitive **Setting** 17-acre small-town campus **Total enrollment** 128 **Application deadline** 7/25 (freshmen), 8/1 (transfer) **Housing** Yes **Undergraduates** 82% 25 or older **Academic program** Summer session, adult/continuing education programs, internships **Contact** Dr. Philip Attebery, Dean and Registrar, Baptist Missionary Association Theological Seminary, 1530 East Pine Street, Jacksonville, TX 75766-5407. *Phone:* 903-586-2501 Ext. 229. *E-mail:* attebery@bmats.edu. *Web site:* http://www.bmats.edu/.

Baptist University of the Americas
San Antonio, Texas

Contact Abraham Garcia, Student Council President, Baptist University of the Americas, 8019 South Pan Am Expressway, San Antonio, TX

78224. *Phone:* 210-924-4338 or toll-free 800-721-1396. *Fax:* 210-924-2701. *E-mail:* agarcia@bua.edu. *Web site:* http://www.bua.edu/.

Baylor University
Waco, Texas

General Independent Baptist, university, coed **Entrance** Moderately difficult **Setting** 508-acre urban campus **Total enrollment** 14,614 **Student-faculty ratio** 15:1 **Application deadline** 2/1 (freshmen), rolling (transfer) **Freshman admission** 50% were admitted **Freshman test scores** SAT critical reading scores over 500: 88%; SAT math scores over 500: 95%; ACT scores over 18: 99%; SAT critical reading scores over 600: 43%; SAT math scores over 600: 54%; ACT scores over 24: 71% **Housing** Yes **Expenses** Tuition & Fees $29,754; Room & Board $8331 **Undergraduates** 59% women, 2% part-time, 2% 25 or older, 1% Native American, 11% Hispanic American, 8% African American, 7% Asian American/Pacific Islander **The most frequently chosen baccalaureate fields are** biological/life sciences, business/marketing, communications/journalism **Academic program** Advanced placement, accelerated degree program, self-designed majors, honors program, summer session, internships **Contact** Ms. Jessica King Gereghty, Director of Admissions, Baylor University, PO Box 97056, Waco, TX 76798. *Phone:* 254-710-3435 or toll-free 800-BAYLORU. *Fax:* 254-710-3436. *E-mail:* admissions@baylor.edu. *Web site:* http://www.baylor.edu/.
Visit Petersons.com and enter keyword Baylor

College of Biblical Studies–Houston
Houston, Texas

General Independent nondenominational, 4-year, coed **Entrance** Noncompetitive **Setting** 12-acre urban campus **Total enrollment** 643 **Housing** No **Expenses** Tuition & Fees $4560 **Undergraduates** 28% Hispanic American, 45% African American, 2% Asian American/Pacific Islander **The most frequently chosen baccalaureate field is** philosophy and religious studies **Academic program** English as a second language, accelerated degree program, honors program, summer session, adult/continuing education programs **Contact** Admissions, College of Biblical Studies–Houston, 7000 Regency Square Boulevard, Houston, TX 77036. *Phone:* 832-252-3377. *Fax:* 713-532-8150. *E-mail:* admissions@cbshouston.edu. *Web site:* http://www.cbshouston.edu/.

The College of Saint Thomas More
Fort Worth, Texas

Contact Dr. James A. Patrick, The College of Saint Thomas More, 3020 Lubbock Avenue, Fort Worth, TX 76109-2323. *Phone:* 817-928-8459 or toll-free 800-583-6489. *Fax:* 817-924-3206. *E-mail:* more-info@cstm.edu. *Web site:* http://www.cstm.edu/.

Concordia University Texas
Austin, Texas

General Independent, comprehensive, coed, affiliated with Lutheran Church–Missouri Synod **Entrance** Moderately difficult **Setting** 20-acre urban campus **Total enrollment** 2,185 **Student-faculty ratio** 10:1 **Application deadline** Rolling (freshmen), rolling (transfer) **Freshman admission** 53% were admitted. Average high school GPA 3.37 **Freshman test scores** SAT critical reading scores over 500: 46.4%; SAT math scores over 500: 59.43%; ACT scores over 18: 85.99%; SAT critical reading scores over 600: 12.7%; SAT math scores over 600: 21.87%; ACT scores over 24: 28.99% **Housing** Yes **Expenses** Tuition & Fees $21,200; Room & Board $8000 **Undergraduates** 58% women, 22% part-time, 1% Native American, 18% Hispanic American, 11% African American, 2% Asian American/Pacific Islander **The most frequently chosen baccalaureate fields are** business/marketing, education, social sciences **Academic program** Advanced placement, accelerated degree program, summer session, adult/continuing education programs **Contact** Kristi Kirk, Director of Enrollment Services, Concordia University Texas, 11400 Concordia University Drive, Austin, TX 78726. *Phone:* 512-486-2000 Ext. 1156 or toll-free 800-865-4282. *Fax:* 512-459-8517. *E-mail:* ctxadmis@crf.cuis.edu. *Web site:* http://www.concordia.edu/.

The Criswell College
Dallas, Texas

Contact Admissions, The Criswell College, 4010 Gaston Avenue, Dallas, TX 75246-1537. *Phone:* 214-821-5433 or toll-free 800-899-0012. *Fax:* 214-818-1310. *Web site:* http://www.criswell.edu/.

Dallas Baptist University
Dallas, Texas

General Independent, comprehensive, coed, affiliated with Baptist General Convention of Texas **Entrance** Moderately difficult **Setting** 293-acre urban campus **Total enrollment** 5,400 **Student-faculty ratio** 14:1 **Application deadline** Rolling (freshmen), rolling (transfer) **Freshman admission** 46% were admitted. Average high school GPA 3.54 **Freshman test scores** SAT critical reading scores over 500: 80%; SAT math scores over 500: 80%; ACT scores over 18: 97%; SAT critical reading scores over 600: 33%; SAT math scores over 600: 33%; ACT scores over 24: 25% **Housing** Yes **Expenses** Tuition & Fees $17,490; Room & Board $5636 **Undergraduates** 59% women, 37% part-time, 43% 25 or older, 1% Native American, 9% Hispanic American, 19% African American, 2% Asian American/Pacific Islander **Academic program** English as a second language, advanced placement, accelerated degree program, honors program, summer session, adult/continuing education programs, internships **Contact** Ms. Erin Dennis, Director of Recruitment/Undergraduate Admissions, Dallas Baptist University, 3000 Mountain Creek Parkway, Dallas, TX 75211-9299. *Phone:* 214-333-5360 or toll-free 800-460-1328. *Fax:* 214-333-5447. *E-mail:* admiss@dbu.edu. *Web site:* http://www.dbu.edu/.

Dallas Christian College
Dallas, Texas

General Independent, 4-year, coed, affiliated with Christian Churches and Churches of Christ **Entrance** Minimally difficult **Setting** 22-acre urban campus **Total enrollment** 315 **Student-faculty ratio** 16:1 **Application deadline** Rolling (freshmen), rolling (transfer) **Freshman admission** 18% were admitted. Average high school GPA 3.14 **Housing** Yes **Expenses** Tuition & Fees $10,770; Room & Board $6500 **Undergraduates** 47% women, 36% part-time, 40% 25 or older, 3% Native American, 11% Hispanic American, 17% African American, 1% Asian American/Pacific Islander **The most frequently chosen baccalaureate fields are** business/marketing, education, theology and religious vocations **Academic program** Advanced placement, accelerated degree program, summer session, internships **Contact** Ms. Kristi Boggs, Director of Admissions, Dallas Christian College, 2700 Christian Parkway, Dallas, TX 75234-7299. *Phone:* 972-241-3371 Ext. 161. *Fax:* 972-241-8021. *E-mail:* kboggs@dallas.edu. *Web site:* http://www.dallas.edu/.

DeVry University
Houston, Texas

General Proprietary, comprehensive, coed **Total enrollment** 1,694 **Student-faculty ratio** 15:1 **Application deadline** Rolling (freshmen), rolling (transfer) **Expenses** Tuition & Fees $14,080 **Undergraduates** 51% women, 45% part-time, 61% 25 or older, 0.4% Native American, 34% Hispanic American, 33% African American, 5% Asian American/Pacific Islander **The most frequently chosen baccalaureate fields are** business/marketing, computer and information sciences, engineering technologies **Academic program** Advanced placement, accelerated degree program, summer session **Contact** Admissions Office, DeVry University, 11125 Equity Drive, Houston, TX 77041. *Phone:* toll-free 866-703-3879. *Web site:* http://www.devry.edu/.

DeVry University
Irving, Texas

General Proprietary, comprehensive, coed **Entrance** Minimally difficult **Setting** 13-acre suburban campus **Total enrollment** 2,019 **Student-faculty ratio** 16:1 **Application deadline** Rolling (freshmen), rolling (transfer) **Housing** No **Expenses** Tuition & Fees $14,080 **Undergraduates** 31% women, 52% part-time, 57% 25 or older, 1% Native American, 23% Hispanic American, 30% African American, 3% Asian American/Pacific Islander **The most frequently chosen baccalaureate fields are** business/marketing, computer and information sciences, engineering technologies **Academic program** Advanced placement, accelerated degree program, summer session, adult/continuing education programs **Contact** Admissions Office, DeVry University, 4800 Regent Boulevard, Irving, TX 75063-2439. *Web site:* http://www.devry.edu/.

DeVry University
Richardson, Texas

Contact DeVry University, Richardson Center, 2201 North Central Expressway, Richardson, TX 75080. *Web site:* http://www.devry.edu/.

East Texas Baptist University
Marshall, Texas

General Independent Baptist, 4-year, coed **Entrance** Moderately difficult **Setting** 200-acre small-town campus **Total enrollment** 1,179 **Student-faculty ratio** 15:1 **Application deadline** 8/16 (freshmen), 8/16 (transfer) **Freshman admission** 53% were admitted. Average high school GPA 3.34 **Freshman test scores** SAT critical reading scores over 500: 36%; SAT math scores over 500: 49%; ACT scores over 18: 88%; SAT critical reading scores over 600: 6%; SAT math scores over 600: 10%; ACT scores over 24: 24% **Housing** Yes **Expenses** Tuition & Fees $19,550; Room & Board $5436 **Undergraduates** 51% women, 8% part-time, 8% 25 or older, 2% Native American, 8% Hispanic American, 15% African American, 1% Asian American/Pacific Islander **The most frequently chosen baccalaureate fields are** education, business/marketing, interdisciplinary studies **Academic program** Advanced placement, honors program, summer session, adult/continuing education programs, internships **Contact** Ms. Melissa Fitts, Director of Admissions, East Texas Baptist University, 1209 North Grove, Marshall, TX 75670-1498. *Phone:* 903-923-2000 or toll-free 800-804-ETBU. *Fax:* 903-923-2001. *E-mail:* admissions@etbu.edu. *Web site:* http://www.etbu.edu/.

Hallmark College of Technology
San Antonio, Texas

General Proprietary, primarily 2-year, coed **Entrance** Moderately difficult **Setting** 3-acre suburban campus **Total enrollment** 294 **Student-faculty ratio** 10:1 **Application deadline** Rolling (freshmen), rolling (transfer) **Housing** No **Undergraduates** 51% women, 50% 25 or older, 0.3% Native American, 59% Hispanic American, 9% African American, 3% Asian American/Pacific Islander **Academic program** Accelerated degree program, internships **Contact** Ms. Sonia Ross, Vice President of Marketing, Director of Admissions, Hallmark College of Technology, 10401 IH 10 West, San Antonio, TX 78230. *Phone:* 210-690-9000 Ext. 212 or toll-free 800-880-6600. *Fax:* 210-697-8225. *E-mail:* sross@hallmarkcollege.edu. *Web site:* http://www.hallmarkcollege.edu/.

Hardin-Simmons University
Abilene, Texas

General Independent Baptist, comprehensive, coed **Entrance** Moderately difficult **Setting** 120-acre urban campus **Total enrollment** 2,305 **Student-faculty ratio** 13:1 **Application deadline** Rolling (freshmen), rolling (transfer) **Freshman admission** 38% were admitted. Average high school GPA 3.56 **Freshman test scores** SAT critical reading scores over 500: 56.12%; SAT math scores over 500: 68.06%; ACT scores over 18: 93.82%; SAT critical reading scores over 600: 17.09%; SAT math scores over 600: 27.74%; ACT scores over 24: 36.43% **Housing** Yes **Expenses** Tuition & Fees $20,990; Room & Board $6282 **Undergraduates** 56% women, 9% part-time, 7% 25 or older, 1% Native American, 10% Hispanic American, 6% African American, 1% Asian American/Pacific Islander **The most frequently chosen baccalaureate fields are** business/marketing, education, health professions and related sciences **Academic program** Advanced placement, accelerated degree program, honors program, summer session, adult/continuing education programs, internships **Contact** Ms. Brynn Reynolds, Visitor Coordinator, Hardin-Simmons University, Box 16050, Abilene, TX 79698-0001. *Phone:* 325-670-5890 or toll-free 877-464-7889. *Fax:* 325-671-2115. *E-mail:* breynolds@hsutx.edu. *Web site:* http://www.hsutx.edu/.

Houston Baptist University
Houston, Texas

General Independent Baptist, comprehensive, coed **Entrance** Moderately difficult **Setting** 100-acre urban campus **Total enrollment** 2,710 **Student-faculty ratio** 15:1 **Application deadline** Rolling (freshmen), rolling (transfer) **Freshman admission** 42% were admitted **Freshman test scores** SAT critical reading scores over 500: 51.5%; SAT math scores over 500: 63.1%; ACT scores over 18: 98.9%; SAT critical reading scores over 600: 17.5%; SAT math scores over 600: 22.7%; ACT scores over 24: 32.6% **Housing** Yes **Expenses** Tuition & Fees $23,180; Room & Board $6975 **Undergraduates** 65% women, 14% part-time, 16% 25 or older, 0.3% Native American, 25% Hispanic American, 20% African American, 14% Asian American/Pacific Islander **The most frequently chosen baccalaureate fields are** biological/life sciences, business/marketing, education **Academic program** Advanced placement, accelerated degree program, honors program, summer session, adult/continuing education programs, internships **Contact** Eduardo Borges, Director of Admissions, Houston Baptist University, 7502 Fondren Road, Houston, TX 77074-3298. *Phone:* 281-649-3299 or toll-free 800-696-3210. *Fax:* 281-649-3217. *E-mail:* eborges@hbu.edu. *Web site:* http://www.hbu.edu/.

Howard Payne University
Brownwood, Texas

General Independent, comprehensive, coed, affiliated with Baptist General Convention of Texas **Entrance** Moderately difficult **Setting** 30-acre small-town campus **Total enrollment** 1,232 **Student-faculty ratio** 10:1 **Application deadline** Rolling (freshmen), rolling (transfer) **Freshman admission** 59% were admitted. Average high school GPA 3.37 **Freshman test scores** SAT critical reading scores over 500: 55%; SAT math scores over 500: 51%; ACT scores over 18: 77%; SAT critical reading scores over 600: 18%; SAT math scores over 600: 16%; ACT scores over 24: 30% **Housing** Yes **Expenses** Tuition & Fees $19,950; Room & Board $5694 **Undergraduates** 48% women, 23% part-time, 18% 25 or older, 1% Native American, 17% Hispanic American, 6% African American, 0.5% Asian American/Pacific Islander **The most frequently chosen baccalaureate fields are** business/marketing, education, theology and religious vocations **Academic program** English as a second language, advanced placement, honors program, summer session, internships **Contact** Ms. Cheryl Mangrum, Associate Director of Admission, Howard Payne University, 1000 Fisk Street, Brownwood, TX 76801. *Phone:* 325-649-8027 or toll-free 800-880-4478. *Fax:* 325-649-8901. *E-mail:* enroll@hputx.edu. *Web site:* http://www.hputx.edu/.

Huston-Tillotson University
Austin, Texas

General Independent interdenominational, 4-year, coed **Entrance** Moderately difficult **Setting** 23-acre urban campus **Total enrollment** 882 **Student-faculty ratio** 16:1 **Application deadline** 7/1 (freshmen), 7/1 (transfer) **Freshman admission** 48% were admitted. Average high school GPA 2.83 **Freshman test scores** SAT critical reading scores over

500: 13%; SAT math scores over 500: 12%; ACT scores over 18: 31%; SAT critical reading scores over 600: 1%; SAT math scores over 600: 2%; ACT scores over 24: 3% **Housing** Yes **Expenses** Tuition & Fees $11,434; Room & Board $6690 **Undergraduates** 52% women, 4% part-time, 20% 25 or older, 0.1% Native American, 13% Hispanic American, 76% African American, 0.1% Asian American/Pacific Islander **The most frequently chosen baccalaureate fields are** business/marketing, interdisciplinary studies, social sciences **Academic program** Advanced placement, accelerated degree program, honors program, summer session, internships **Contact** Mrs. Shakitha Stinson, Director of Admission, Huston-Tillotson University, 900 Chicon Street, Austin, TX 78702. *Phone:* 512-505-3029. *Fax:* 512-505-3192. *E-mail:* slstinson@htu.edu. *Web site:* http://www.htu.edu/.

ITT Technical Institute
Arlington, Texas

General Proprietary, primarily 2-year, coed **Entrance** Minimally difficult **Setting** suburban campus **Housing** No **Contact** Director of Recruitment, ITT Technical Institute, 551 Ryan Plaza Drive, Arlington, TX 76011. *Phone:* 817-794-5100 or toll-free 888-288-4950. *Fax:* 817-275-8446. *Web site:* http://www.itt-tech.edu/.

ITT Technical Institute
Austin, Texas

General Proprietary, primarily 2-year, coed **Entrance** Minimally difficult **Setting** urban campus **Housing** No **Contact** Director of Recruitment, ITT Technical Institute, 6330 Highway 290 East, Austin, TX 78723. *Phone:* 512-467-6800 or toll-free 800-431-0677. *Fax:* 512-467-6677. *Web site:* http://www.itt-tech.edu/.

ITT Technical Institute
DeSoto, Texas

General Proprietary, primarily 2-year, coed **Contact** Director of Admissions, ITT Technical Institute, 921 West Belt Line Road, Suite 181, DeSoto, TX 75115. *Phone:* 972-274-8600 or toll-free 877-854-5728. *Web site:* http://www.itt-tech.edu/.

ITT Technical Institute
Houston, Texas

General Proprietary, primarily 2-year, coed **Entrance** Minimally difficult **Setting** suburban campus **Housing** No **Contact** Director of Recruitment, ITT Technical Institute, 15621 North Freeway, Houston, TX 77090. *Phone:* 281-873-0512 or toll-free 800-879-6486. *Web site:* http://www.itt-tech.edu/.

ITT Technical Institute
Houston, Texas

General Proprietary, primarily 2-year, coed **Entrance** Minimally difficult **Setting** urban campus **Housing** No **Contact** Director of Recruitment, ITT Technical Institute, 2950 South Gessner, Houston, TX 77063-3751. *Phone:* 713-952-2294 or toll-free 800-235-4787. *Web site:* http://www.itt-tech.edu/.

ITT Technical Institute
Webster, Texas

General Proprietary, primarily 2-year, coed **Entrance** Minimally difficult **Housing** No **Contact** Director of Recruitment, ITT Technical Institute, 1001 Magnolia Avenue, Webster, TX 77598. *Phone:* 281-316-4700 or toll-free 888-488-9347. *Web site:* http://www.itt-tech.edu/.

Jarvis Christian College
Hawkins, Texas

General Independent, 4-year, coed, affiliated with Christian Church (Disciples of Christ) **Entrance** Minimally difficult **Setting** 465-acre rural campus **Total enrollment** 628 **Student-faculty ratio** 13:1 **Application deadline** 8/1 (freshmen), rolling (transfer) **Freshman admission** 23% were admitted. Average high school GPA 2.5 **Freshman test scores** SAT critical reading scores over 500: 3%; ACT scores over 18: 13% **Housing** Yes **Expenses** Tuition & Fees $9600; Room & Board $6715 **Undergraduates** 55% women, 2% part-time, 8% 25 or older, 0.2% Native American, 3% Hispanic American, 94% African American **The most frequently chosen baccalaureate fields are** education, business/marketing, interdisciplinary studies **Academic program** English as a second language, advanced placement, honors program, summer session, adult/continuing education programs, internships **Contact** Mr. Robert Harper, Admissions Counselor, Jarvis Christian College, PO Box 1470, Hawkins, TX 75765-9989. *Phone:* 903-769-5734. *Fax:* 903-769-4842. *E-mail:* robert.harper@jarvis.edu. *Web site:* http://www.jarvis.edu/.

Lamar University
Beaumont, Texas

General State-supported, university, coed **Entrance** Minimally difficult **Setting** 200-acre suburban campus **Total enrollment** 13,992 **Student-faculty ratio** 20:1 **Application deadline** 8/1 (freshmen), 8/1 (transfer) **Freshman admission** 59% were admitted **Freshman test scores** SAT critical reading scores over 500: 30.39%; SAT math scores over 500: 34.72%; ACT scores over 18: 62.16%; SAT critical reading scores over 600: 6.3%; SAT math scores over 600: 7.79%; ACT scores over 24: 12.48% **Housing** Yes **Expenses** Tuition & Fees: state resident $6944, nonresident $16,244; Room & Board $6900 **Undergraduates** 60% women, 29% part-time, 26% 25 or older, 0.5% Native American, 8% Hispanic American, 32% African American, 4% Asian American/Pacific Islander **The most frequently chosen baccalaureate fields are** business/marketing, interdisciplinary studies, liberal arts/general studies **Academic program** English as a second language, advanced placement, accelerated degree program, self-designed majors, honors program, summer session, internships **Contact** Ms. Melissa Chesser, Director of Recruitment, Lamar University, PO Box 10009, Beaumont, TX 77710. *Phone:* 409-880-8888. *Fax:* 409-880-8463. *E-mail:* admissions@lamar.edu. *Web site:* http://www.lamar.edu/.

LeTourneau University
Longview, Texas

General Independent nondenominational, comprehensive, coed **Setting** 162-acre suburban campus **Total enrollment** 3,386 **Student-faculty ratio** 23:1 **Application deadline** Rolling (freshmen), rolling (transfer) **Freshman admission** 70% were admitted. Average high school GPA 3.6 **Freshman test scores** SAT critical reading scores over 500: 83.77%; SAT math scores over 500: 89.47%; ACT scores over 18: 95.56%; SAT critical reading scores over 600: 45.17%; SAT math scores over 600: 53.94%; ACT scores over 24: 65.56% **Housing** Yes **Expenses** Tuition & Fees $21,980; Room & Board $8390 **Undergraduates** 55% women, 6% part-time, 8% 25 or older, 0.4% Native American, 7% Hispanic American, 20% African American, 1% Asian American/Pacific Islander **The most frequently chosen baccalaureate fields are** engineering, business/marketing, transportation and materials moving **Academic program** Advanced placement, accelerated degree program, honors program, summer session, adult/continuing education programs, internships **Contact** Mr. James Townsend, Director of Admissions, LeTourneau University, PO Box 7001, Longview, TX 75607-7001. *Phone:* 903-233-3400 or toll-free 800-759-8811. *Fax:* 903-233-3411. *E-mail:* admissions@letu.edu. *Web site:* http://www.letu.edu/.

Lubbock Christian University
Lubbock, Texas

General Independent, comprehensive, coed, affiliated with Church of Christ **Entrance** Moderately difficult **Setting** 120-acre suburban campus **Total enrollment** 1,906 **Student-faculty ratio** 12:1 **Application deadline** 8/1 (freshmen), rolling (transfer) **Freshman admission** 66% were

Lubbock Christian University (continued)

admitted. Average high school GPA 3.47 **Freshman test scores** SAT critical reading scores over 500: 46.22%; ACT scores over 18: 83.61%; SAT critical reading scores over 600: 11.37%; ACT scores over 24: 28.97% **Housing** Yes **Expenses** Tuition & Fees $15,120; Room & Board $6182 **Undergraduates** 59% women, 17% part-time, 24% 25 or older, 0.5% Native American, 17% Hispanic American, 6% African American, 1% Asian American/Pacific Islander **The most frequently chosen baccalaureate fields are** business/marketing, education, health professions and related sciences **Academic program** English as a second language, advanced placement, self-designed majors, honors program, summer session, adult/continuing education programs, internships **Contact** Mr. Charles Webb, Director of Admissions, Lubbock Christian University, 5601 19th Street, Lubbock, TX 79407. *Phone:* 806-720-7156 or toll-free 800-933-7601. *Fax:* 806-720-7162. *E-mail:* admissions@lcu.edu. *Web site:* http://www.lcu.edu/.

McMurry University
Abilene, Texas

General Independent United Methodist, 4-year, coed **Entrance** Moderately difficult **Setting** 43-acre suburban campus **Total enrollment** 1,509 **Student-faculty ratio** 14:1 **Application deadline** 8/15 (freshmen), 8/15 (transfer) **Freshman admission** 57% were admitted. Average high school GPA 3.31 **Freshman test scores** SAT critical reading scores over 500: 39%; SAT math scores over 500: 51%; ACT scores over 18: 73%; SAT critical reading scores over 600: 11%; SAT math scores over 600: 13%; ACT scores over 24: 27% **Housing** Yes **Expenses** Tuition & Fees $19,205; Room & Board $6757 **Undergraduates** 51% women, 19% part-time, 20% 25 or older, 1% Native American, 15% Hispanic American, 16% African American, 1% Asian American/Pacific Islander **The most frequently chosen baccalaureate fields are** business/marketing, education, health professions and related sciences **Academic program** Advanced placement, accelerated degree program, self-designed majors, honors program, summer session, adult/continuing education programs, internships **Contact** Ms. Trudy Mohre, Dean of Admission, McMurry University, McMurry Station 278, Abilene, TX 79697. *Phone:* 325-793-4700 or toll-free 800-477-0077. *Fax:* 325-793-4701. *E-mail:* admissions@mcm.edu. *Web site:* http://www.mcm.edu/.

Midland College
Midland, Texas

General State and locally supported, 4-year, coed **Entrance** Noncompetitive **Setting** 163-acre suburban campus **Total enrollment** 5,739 **Student-faculty ratio** 18:1 **Application deadline** Rolling (freshmen), rolling (transfer) **Housing** Yes **Expenses** Tuition & Fees: area resident $2192, state resident $2852, nonresident $3842; Room & Board $3900 **Undergraduates** 60% women, 69% part-time, 16% 25 or older **Academic program** Advanced placement, honors program, adult/continuing education programs **Contact** Mr. Ryan Gibbs, Director of Admissions, Midland College, 3600 North Garfield, Midland, TX 79705-6399. *Phone:* 432-685-5502. *Fax:* 432-685-6401. *E-mail:* rgibbs@midland.edu. *Web site:* http://www.midland.edu/.

Midwestern State University
Wichita Falls, Texas

General State-supported, comprehensive, coed **Entrance** Minimally difficult **Setting** 255-acre urban campus **Total enrollment** 6,341 **Student-faculty ratio** 18:1 **Application deadline** 8/7 (freshmen), 8/7 (transfer) **Freshman admission** 88% were admitted. Average high school GPA 3.49 **Freshman test scores** SAT critical reading scores over 500: 50.82%; SAT math scores over 500: 56.42%; ACT scores over 18: 86.73%; SAT critical reading scores over 600: 12.48%; SAT math scores over 600: 14.65%; ACT scores over 24: 24.57% **Housing** Yes **Expenses** Tuition & Fees: state resident $6226, nonresident $7126; Room & Board $5560 **Undergraduates** 58% women, 26% part-time, 28% 25 or older, 1% Native American, 11% Hispanic American, 13% African American, 4% Asian American/Pacific Islander **The most frequently chosen baccalaureate fields are** business/marketing, health professions and related sciences, interdisciplinary studies **Academic program** English as a second language, advanced placement, honors program, summer session, adult/continuing education programs, internships **Contact** Ms. Barbara Merkle, Director of Admissions, Midwestern State University, 3410 Taft Boulevard, Wichita Falls, TX 76308. *Phone:* 940-397-4334 or toll-free 800-842-1922. *Fax:* 940-397-4672. *E-mail:* admissions@mwsu.edu. *Web site:* http://www.mwsu.edu/.

Northwood University, Texas Campus
Cedar Hill, Texas

General Independent, 4-year, coed **Entrance** Moderately difficult **Setting** 360-acre small-town campus **Total enrollment** 461 **Student-faculty ratio** 15:1 **Application deadline** Rolling (freshmen), rolling (transfer) **Freshman admission** 55% were admitted. Average high school GPA 3.29 **Freshman test scores** SAT critical reading scores over 500: 41%; SAT math scores over 500: 42%; ACT scores over 18: 77%; SAT critical reading scores over 600: 2%; SAT math scores over 600: 6%; ACT scores over 24: 15% **Housing** Yes **Expenses** Tuition & Fees $18,408; Room & Board $7590 **Undergraduates** 46% women, 5% part-time, 3% 25 or older, 2% Native American, 30% Hispanic American, 15% African American, 4% Asian American/Pacific Islander **The most frequently chosen baccalaureate fields are** business/marketing, communications/journalism, parks and recreation **Academic program** Advanced placement, accelerated degree program, honors program, summer session, adult/continuing education programs, internships **Contact** Ms. Sylvia Correa, Director of Admissions, Northwood University, Texas Campus, 1114 West FM 1382, Cedar Hill, TX 75104. *Phone:* 972-293-5400 or toll-free 800-927-9663. *Fax:* 972-291-3824. *E-mail:* txadmit@northwood.edu. *Web site:* http://www.northwood.edu/.

Our Lady of the Lake University of San Antonio
San Antonio, Texas

General Independent Roman Catholic, comprehensive, coed **Entrance** Moderately difficult **Setting** 75-acre urban campus **Total enrollment** 2,660 **Student-faculty ratio** 11:1 **Application deadline** Rolling (freshmen), rolling (transfer) **Freshman admission** 63% were admitted. Average high school GPA 3.15 **Freshman test scores** SAT critical reading scores over 500: 26%; SAT critical reading scores over 600: 5% **Housing** Yes **Expenses** Tuition & Fees $21,900; Room & Board $6838 **Undergraduates** 72% women, 26% part-time, 40% 25 or older, 0.3% Native American, 71% Hispanic American, 8% African American, 1% Asian American/Pacific Islander **The most frequently chosen baccalaureate fields are** business/marketing, education, public administration and social services **Academic program** Advanced placement, accelerated degree program, honors program, summer session, adult/continuing education programs, internships **Contact** Gilberto Becerra, Assistant Director of Undergraduate Admissions, Our Lady of the Lake University of San Antonio, 411 Southwest 24th Street, San Antonio, TX 78207-4689. *Phone:* 210-434-6711 Ext. 4129 or toll-free 800-436-6558. *Fax:* 210-431-4036. *E-mail:* admission@lake.ollusa.edu. *Web site:* http://www.ollusa.edu/.

Paul Quinn College
Dallas, Texas

Contact Ms. Nena Taylor-Richey, Director of Admissions and Recruitment, Paul Quinn College, 3837 Simpson-Stuart Road, Dallas, TX 75241-4331. *Phone:* 214-302-3575 or toll-free 800-237-2648. *Web site:* http://www.pqc.edu/.

Prairie View A&M University
Prairie View, Texas

General State-supported, university, coed **Entrance** Moderately difficult **Setting** 1,502-acre small-town campus **Total enrollment** 8,608

Student-faculty ratio 18:1 **Application deadline** 6/1 (freshmen), 6/1 (transfer) **Freshman admission** 86% were admitted. Average high school GPA 2.61 **Freshman test scores** SAT critical reading scores over 500: 14%; SAT math scores over 500: 19%; ACT scores over 18: 41%; SAT critical reading scores over 600: 2%; SAT math scores over 600: 3%; ACT scores over 24: 4% **Housing** Yes **Expenses** Tuition & Fees: state resident $6664, nonresident $14,974; Room & Board $6738 **Undergraduates** 58% women, 10% part-time, 0.1% Native American, 4% Hispanic American, 88% African American, 2% Asian American/Pacific Islander **The most frequently chosen baccalaureate fields are** engineering, business/marketing, health professions and related sciences **Academic program** English as a second language, advanced placement, accelerated degree program, honors program, summer session, internships **Contact** Ms. Mary Gooch, Director of Admissions, Prairie View A&M University, PO Box 519, MS #1009, Prairie View, TX 77446-0188. *Phone:* 936-261-1066. *E-mail:* megooch@pvamu.edu. *Web site:* http://www.pvamu.edu/.

Rice University
Houston, Texas

General Independent, university, coed **Entrance** Most difficult **Setting** 300-acre urban campus **Total enrollment** 5,663 **Student-faculty ratio** 5:1 **Application deadline** 1/2 (freshmen), 3/15 (transfer) **Freshman admission** 22% were admitted **Freshman test scores** SAT critical reading scores over 500: 97.9%; SAT math scores over 500: 99.7%; ACT scores over 18: 99.9%; SAT critical reading scores over 600: 88.3%; SAT math scores over 600: 92.9%; ACT scores over 24: 96.6% **Housing** Yes **Expenses** Tuition & Fees $32,105; Room & Board $11,230 **Undergraduates** 48% women, 2% part-time, 1% 25 or older, 0.4% Native American, 12% Hispanic American, 7% African American, 21% Asian American/Pacific Islander **The most frequently chosen baccalaureate fields are** engineering, biological/life sciences, social sciences **Academic program** English as a second language, advanced placement, accelerated degree program, self-designed majors, honors program, summer session, internships **Contact** Office of Admission, Rice University, Office of Admission, PO Box 1892, MS 17, Houston, TX 77251-1892. *Phone:* 713-348-RICE or toll-free 800-527-OWLS. *E-mail:* admi@rice.edu. *Web site:* http://www.rice.edu/.

Rio Grande Bible Institute
Edinburg, Texas

Contact Rio Grande Bible Institute, 4300 S US Hwy 281, Edinburg, TX 78539. *Web site:* http://www.riogrande.edu/.

St. Edward's University
Austin, Texas

General Independent Roman Catholic, comprehensive, coed **Entrance** Moderately difficult **Setting** 160-acre urban campus **Total enrollment** 5,293 **Student-faculty ratio** 15:1 **Application deadline** 5/1 (freshmen), 7/1 (transfer) **Freshman admission** 66% were admitted **Freshman test scores** SAT critical reading scores over 500: 83%; SAT math scores over 500: 83%; ACT scores over 18: 99%; SAT critical reading scores over 600: 36%; SAT math scores over 600: 32%; ACT scores over 24: 60% **Housing** Yes **Expenses** Tuition & Fees $26,484; Room & Board $9036 **Undergraduates** 59% women, 21% part-time, 5% 25 or older, 1% Native American, 30% Hispanic American, 5% African American, 3% Asian American/Pacific Islander **The most frequently chosen baccalaureate fields are** business/marketing, communications/journalism, psychology **Academic program** Advanced placement, honors program, summer session, adult/continuing education programs, internships **Contact** Ms. Karen Gregg, Inquiry Coordinator, St. Edward's University, 3001 South Congress Avenue, Austin, TX 78704. *Phone:* 512-448-8580 or toll-free 800-555-0164. *Fax:* 512-464-8877. *E-mail:* seu.admit@stedwards.edu. *Web site:* http://www.gotostedwards.com/.
Visit Petersons.com and enter keyword Edward's

See page 1102 for the College Close-Up.

St. Mary's University
San Antonio, Texas

General Independent Roman Catholic, comprehensive, coed **Entrance** Moderately difficult **Setting** 135-acre urban campus **Total enrollment** 3,893 **Student-faculty ratio** 13:1 **Application deadline** Rolling (freshmen), rolling (transfer) **Freshman admission** 76% were admitted. Average high school GPA 3.42 **Freshman test scores** SAT critical reading scores over 500: 60.71%; SAT math scores over 500: 62.92%; ACT scores over 18: 94.58%; SAT critical reading scores over 600: 16.56%; SAT math scores over 600: 22.08%; ACT scores over 24: 34.48% **Housing** Yes **Expenses** Tuition & Fees $22,556; Room & Board $7550 **Undergraduates** 60% women, 7% part-time, 10% 25 or older, 0.3% Native American, 69% Hispanic American, 4% African American, 3% Asian American/Pacific Islander **The most frequently chosen baccalaureate fields are** business/marketing, biological/life sciences, social sciences **Academic program** English as a second language, advanced placement, honors program, summer session, adult/continuing education programs, internships **Contact** Mr. Chadd J. Bridwell, Director of Undergraduate Admission, St. Mary's University, One Camino Santa Maria, San Antonio, TX 78228. *Phone:* 210-436-3126 or toll-free 800-FOR-STMU. *Fax:* 210-431-6742. *E-mail:* uadm@stmarytx.edu. *Web site:* http://www.stmarytx.edu/.
Visit Petersons.com and enter keywords St. Mary's University

Sam Houston State University
Huntsville, Texas

General State-supported, university, coed **Entrance** Moderately difficult **Setting** 1,256-acre small-town campus **Total enrollment** 16,772 **Student-faculty ratio** 30:1 **Application deadline** 8/1 (freshmen), rolling (transfer) **Freshman admission** 72% were admitted **Freshman test scores** SAT critical reading scores over 500: 44.9%; SAT math scores over 500: 51.2%; ACT scores over 18: 81.9%; SAT critical reading scores over 600: 8.5%; SAT math scores over 600: 11.7%; ACT scores over 24: 15.9% **Housing** Yes **Expenses** Tuition & Fees: state resident $7000, nonresident $16,300; Room & Board $7022 **Undergraduates** 56% women, 16% part-time, 15% 25 or older, 1% Native American, 14% Hispanic American, 16% African American, 2% Asian American/Pacific Islander **The most frequently chosen baccalaureate fields are** business/marketing, interdisciplinary studies, security and protective services **Academic program** English as a second language, advanced placement, honors program, summer session, internships **Contact** Mr. Trevor B. Thorn, Director of Admissions and Recruitment, Sam Houston State University, PO Box 2418, Huntsville, TX 77341. *Phone:* 936-294-1828 or toll-free 866-232-7528 Ext. 1828. *Fax:* 936-294-3758. *E-mail:* admissions@shsu.edu. *Web site:* http://www.shsu.edu/.
Visit Petersons.com and enter keywords Sam Houston

Schreiner University
Kerrville, Texas

General Independent Presbyterian, comprehensive, coed **Entrance** Moderately difficult **Setting** 175-acre small-town campus **Total enrollment** 1,049 **Student-faculty ratio** 14:1 **Application deadline** 5/1 (freshmen), 5/1 (transfer) **Freshman admission** 62% were admitted. Average high school GPA 3.54 **Freshman test scores** SAT critical reading scores over 500: 47.17%; SAT critical reading scores over 600: 11.69% **Housing** Yes **Expenses** Tuition & Fees $18,731; Room & Board $8726 **Undergraduates** 56% women, 5% part-time, 10% 25 or older, 2% Native American, 22% Hispanic American, 4% African American **The most frequently chosen baccalaureate fields are** business/marketing, biological/life sciences, parks and recreation **Academic program** Advanced placement, accelerated degree program, self-designed majors, honors program, summer session, internships **Contact** Ms. Sandy Speed, Dean of Admission and Financial Aid, Schreiner University, 2100 Memorial Boulevard, Kerrville, TX 78028. *Phone:* 830-792-7217 or toll-free 800-343-4919. *Fax:* 830-792-7226. *E-mail:* admissions@schreiner.edu. *Web site:* http://www.schreiner.edu/.

Southern Methodist University
Dallas, Texas

General Independent, university, coed, affiliated with United Methodist Church **Entrance** Moderately difficult **Setting** 231-acre suburban campus **Total enrollment** 10,891 **Student-faculty ratio** 12:1 **Application deadline** 1/15 (freshmen), 7/1 (transfer) **Freshman admission** 50% were admitted. Average high school GPA 3.57 **Freshman test scores** SAT critical reading scores over 500: 94.81%; SAT math scores over 500: 96.38%; ACT scores over 18: 99.31%; SAT critical reading scores over 600: 57.82%; SAT math scores over 600: 71.3%; ACT scores over 24: 87.5% **Housing** Yes **Expenses** Tuition & Fees $35,160; Room & Board $12,445 **Undergraduates** 53% women, 5% part-time, 4% 25 or older, 1% Native American, 8% Hispanic American, 5% African American, 6% Asian American/Pacific Islander **The most frequently chosen baccalaureate fields are** business/marketing, communications/journalism, social sciences **Academic program** English as a second language, advanced placement, accelerated degree program, self-designed majors, honors program, summer session, adult/continuing education programs, internships **Contact** Dr. Ron W. Moss, Director of Admission and Enrollment Management, Southern Methodist University, PO Box 750181, Dallas, TX 75275-0181. *Phone:* 214-768-2058 or toll-free 800-323-0672. *Fax:* 214-768-0202. *E-mail:* ugadmission@smu.edu. *Web site:* http://www.smu.edu/.

South Texas College
McAllen, Texas

Contact Mr. Matthew Hebbard, Director of Enrollment Services and Registrar, South Texas College, 3201 West Pecan, McAllen, TX 78501. *Phone:* 956-872-2147 or toll-free 800-742-7822. *E-mail:* mshebbar@southtexascollege.edu. *Web site:* http://www.southtexascollege.edu/.

Southwestern Adventist University
Keene, Texas

General Independent Seventh-day Adventist, comprehensive, coed **Entrance** Minimally difficult **Setting** 150-acre small-town campus **Total enrollment** 815 **Student-faculty ratio** 12:1 **Application deadline** 8/31 (freshmen), 8/31 (transfer) **Freshman admission** 56% were admitted **Freshman test scores** SAT critical reading scores over 500: 43%; SAT math scores over 500: 28%; ACT scores over 18: 79%; SAT critical reading scores over 600: 9%; SAT math scores over 600: 3%; ACT scores over 24: 18% **Housing** Yes **Expenses** Tuition & Fees $16,216; Room & Board $7148 **Undergraduates** 57% women, 14% part-time, 35% 25 or older, 1% Native American, 26% Hispanic American, 10% African American, 4% Asian American/Pacific Islander **Academic program** English as a second language, advanced placement, accelerated degree program, self-designed majors, honors program, summer session, adult/continuing education programs, internships **Contact** Ms. Diem Dennis, Associate Director of Admissions and Records, Southwestern Adventist University, 100 West Hillcrest, Keene, TX 76059. *Phone:* 817-202-6252 or toll-free 800-433-2240. *E-mail:* ddennis@swau.edu. *Web site:* http://www.swau.edu/.

Southwestern Assemblies of God University
Waxahachie, Texas

General Independent, comprehensive, coed, affiliated with Assemblies of God **Entrance** Noncompetitive **Setting** 70-acre small-town campus **Total enrollment** 2,018 **Student-faculty ratio** 16:1 **Application deadline** Rolling (freshmen), rolling (transfer) **Freshman admission** 43% were admitted **Housing** Yes **Expenses** Tuition & Fees $13,780; Room & Board $5112 **Undergraduates** 50% women, 18% part-time, 23% 25 or older, 1% Native American, 16% Hispanic American, 9% African American, 2% Asian American/Pacific Islander **Academic program** Advanced placement, summer session, adult/continuing education programs, internships **Contact** Mr. Eddie M. Davis, Vice President for Enrollment and Recruitment, Southwestern Assemblies of God University, 1200 Sycamore Street, Waxahachie, TX 75165. *Phone:* 972-825-4686 or toll-free 888-937-7248. *Fax:* 972-923-8131. *E-mail:* edavis@sagu.edu. *Web site:* http://www.sagu.edu/.

Southwestern Christian College
Terrell, Texas

General Independent, 4-year, coed, affiliated with Church of Christ **Entrance** Noncompetitive **Setting** 25-acre small-town campus **Application deadline** 8/1 (freshmen), 8/1 (transfer) **Housing** Yes **Expenses** Tuition & Fees $5694; Room & Board $4132 **Contact** Admissions Department, Southwestern Christian College, Box 10, 200 Bowser Street, Terrell, TX 75160. *Phone:* 214-524-3341. *Fax:* 972-563-7133. *E-mail:* swccadmissions@yahoo.com. *Web site:* http://www.swcc.edu/.

Southwestern University
Georgetown, Texas

General Independent Methodist, 4-year, coed **Entrance** Very difficult **Setting** 700-acre suburban campus **Total enrollment** 1,301 **Student-faculty ratio** 10:1 **Application deadline** Rolling (freshmen), 4/1 (transfer) **Freshman admission** 63% were admitted **Freshman test scores** SAT critical reading scores over 500: 93.25%; SAT math scores over 500: 94.43%; ACT scores over 18: 99.54%; SAT critical reading scores over 600: 65.1%; SAT math scores over 600: 60.71%; ACT scores over 24: 82.87% **Housing** Yes **Expenses** Tuition & Fees $30,220; Room & Board $9130 **Undergraduates** 62% women, 2% part-time, 2% 25 or older, 1% Native American, 15% Hispanic American, 3% African American, 4% Asian American/Pacific Islander **The most frequently chosen baccalaureate fields are** business/marketing, biological/life sciences, social sciences **Academic program** Advanced placement, self-designed majors, honors program, summer session, internships **Contact** Mr. Tom Oliver, Vice President for Enrollment Services, Southwestern University, 1001 East University Avenue, Georgetown, TX 78626. *Phone:* 512-863-1200 or toll-free 800-252-3166. *Fax:* 512-863-9601. *E-mail:* admission@southwestern.edu. *Web site:* http://www.southwestern.edu/.

Stephen F. Austin State University
Nacogdoches, Texas

General State-supported, comprehensive, coed **Entrance** Moderately difficult **Setting** 400-acre small-town campus **Total enrollment** 12,845 **Student-faculty ratio** 21:1 **Application deadline** Rolling (freshmen) **Freshman admission** 73% were admitted **Freshman test scores** SAT critical reading scores over 500: 39.62%; SAT math scores over 500: 45.08%; ACT scores over 18: 77.2%; SAT critical reading scores over 600: 9.05%; SAT math scores over 600: 9.15%; ACT scores over 24: 20.18% **Housing** Yes **Expenses** Tuition & Fees: state resident $6732, nonresident $15,042; Room & Board $7377 **Undergraduates** 61% women, 13% part-time, 12% 25 or older, 1% Native American, 10% Hispanic American, 23% African American, 1% Asian American/Pacific Islander **The most frequently chosen baccalaureate fields are** business/marketing, health professions and related sciences, interdisciplinary studies **Academic program** Advanced placement, accelerated degree program, self-designed majors, honors program, summer session, adult/continuing education programs, internships **Contact** Ms. Beth Smith, Associate Director of Admissions, Stephen F. Austin State University, PO Box 13051, SFA Station, Nacogdoches, TX 75962. *Phone:* 936-468-2504 or toll-free 800-731-2902. *Fax:* 936-468-3849. *E-mail:* admissions@sfasu.edu. *Web site:* http://www.sfasu.edu/.

Visit Petersons.com and enter keywords Austin State

See page 1198 for the College Close-Up.

Strayer University–Central Austin Campus
Austin, Texas

General Proprietary, comprehensive, coed **Contact** Director of Admissions, Strayer University–Central Austin Campus, 8501 North Mopac

Expressway, Suite 100, Austin, TX 78759. *Phone:* 512-568-3300. *Fax:* 512-340-9130. *E-mail:* centralaustin@strayer.edu. *Web site:* http://www.strayer.edu/central_austin.

Sul Ross State University

Alpine, Texas

General State-supported, comprehensive, coed **Entrance** Noncompetitive **Setting** 640-acre small-town campus **Total enrollment** 2,778 **Student-faculty ratio** 14:1 **Application deadline** Rolling (freshmen), rolling (transfer) **Freshman admission** 73% were admitted **Freshman test scores** SAT critical reading scores over 500: 19%; SAT math scores over 500: 19%; ACT scores over 18: 43%; SAT critical reading scores over 600: 3%; SAT math scores over 600: 3%; ACT scores over 24: 6% **Housing** Yes **Expenses** Tuition & Fees: state resident $2928, nonresident $9576; Room & Board $6370 **Undergraduates** 57% women, 35% part-time, 23% 25 or older, 1% Native American, 62% Hispanic American, 5% African American, 1% Asian American/Pacific Islander **The most frequently chosen baccalaureate fields are** business/marketing, English, interdisciplinary studies **Academic program** Advanced placement, honors program, summer session, internships **Contact** Mr. Gregory Schwab, Associate Vice President for Enrollment Management, Sul Ross State University, East Highway 90, Alpine, TX 79832. *Phone:* 432-837-8432 or toll-free 888-722-7778. *Fax:* 432-837-8028. *E-mail:* gschwab@sulross.edu. *Web site:* http://www.sulross.edu/.

Tarleton State University

Stephenville, Texas

General State-supported, comprehensive, coed **Entrance** Moderately difficult **Setting** 125-acre small-town campus **Total enrollment** 10,424 **Student-faculty ratio** 18:1 **Application deadline** 8/1 (freshmen), 7/1 (transfer) **Freshman admission** 56% were admitted **Freshman test scores** SAT critical reading scores over 500: 39.5%; SAT math scores over 500: 51.65%; ACT scores over 18: 83.15%; SAT critical reading scores over 600: 8.43%; SAT math scores over 600: 11.06%; ACT scores over 24: 18.92% **Housing** Yes **Expenses** Tuition & Fees: state resident $7150, nonresident $15,580; Room & Board $6591 **Undergraduates** 57% women, 27% part-time, 21% 25 or older, 1% Native American, 10% Hispanic American, 9% African American, 1% Asian American/Pacific Islander **The most frequently chosen baccalaureate fields are** business/marketing, agriculture, interdisciplinary studies **Academic program** Advanced placement, accelerated degree program, honors program, summer session, adult/continuing education programs, internships **Contact** Ms. Cindy Hess, Director of Undergraduate Admissions, Tarleton State University, Box T-0030, Tarleton Station, Stephenville, TX 76402. *Phone:* 254-968-9123 or toll-free 800-687-8236. *Fax:* 254-968-9951. *E-mail:* uadm@tarleton.edu. *Web site:* http://www.tarleton.edu/.

Texas A&M Health Science Center

College Station, Texas

General State-supported, upper-level, coed **Setting** urban campus **Total enrollment** 544 **Application deadline** Rolling (transfer) **Housing** No **Expenses** Tuition & Fees: state resident $1750, nonresident $11,585 **Undergraduates** 97% women, 19% 25 or older, 17% Hispanic American, 18% Asian American/Pacific Islander **The most frequently chosen baccalaureate field is** health professions and related sciences **Contact** Dr. Jack L. Long, Associate Dean for Student Services, Texas A&M Health Science Center, PO Box 660677, 3302 Gaston Avenue, Dallas, TX 75266-0677. *Phone:* 214-828-8232. *Fax:* 214-874-4567. *Web site:* http://www.tamhsc.edu/.

Texas A&M International University

Laredo, Texas

General State-supported, comprehensive, coed **Entrance** Moderately difficult **Setting** 300-acre urban campus **Total enrollment** 6,419 **Student-faculty ratio** 20:1 **Application deadline** 7/1 (freshmen), 7/1 (transfer) **Freshman admission** 53% were admitted. Average high school GPA 3.6 **Freshman test scores** SAT critical reading scores over 500: 21.52%; SAT math scores over 500: 29.8%; ACT scores over 18: 52.98%; SAT critical reading scores over 600: 2.81%; SAT math scores over 600: 3.81%; ACT scores over 24: 7.46% **Housing** Yes **Expenses** Tuition & Fees: state resident $5717, nonresident $14,027; Room & Board $6918 **Undergraduates** 60% women, 37% part-time, 21% 25 or older, 0.02% Native American, 93% Hispanic American, 1% African American, 1% Asian American/Pacific Islander **The most frequently chosen baccalaureate fields are** business/marketing, interdisciplinary studies, security and protective services **Academic program** English as a second language, advanced placement, honors program, summer session, internships **Contact** Ms. Rosa Dickinson, Director of Admissions, Texas A&M International University, 5201 University Boulevard, Laredo, TX 78041-1900. *Phone:* 956-326-2200 or toll-free 888-489-2648. *Fax:* 956-326-2199. *E-mail:* adms@tamiu.edu. *Web site:* http://www.tamiu.edu/.

Texas A&M University

College Station, Texas

General State-supported, university, coed **Entrance** Moderately difficult **Setting** 5,200-acre suburban campus **Total enrollment** 48,703 **Student-faculty ratio** 19:1 **Application deadline** 1/15 (freshmen), 3/15 (transfer) **Freshman admission** 67% were admitted **Freshman test scores** SAT critical reading scores over 500: 84%; SAT math scores over 500: 92%; ACT scores over 18: 99%; SAT critical reading scores over 600: 44%; SAT math scores over 600: 63%; ACT scores over 24: 79% **Housing** Yes **Expenses** Tuition & Fees: state resident $8176, nonresident $22,606; Room & Board $8039 **Undergraduates** 48% women, 9% part-time, 3% 25 or older, 1% Native American, 14% Hispanic American, 3% African American, 5% Asian American/Pacific Islander **The most frequently chosen baccalaureate fields are** agriculture, business/marketing, engineering **Academic program** English as a second language, advanced placement, accelerated degree program, honors program, summer session, internships **Contact** Mr. Scott McDonald, Director of Admissions, Texas A&M University, 217 John J. Koldus Building, College Station, TX 77843-1265. *Phone:* 979-845-3741. *Fax:* 979-845-8737. *E-mail:* admissions@tamu.edu. *Web site:* http://www.tamu.edu/.

Texas A&M University at Galveston

Galveston, Texas

General State-supported, comprehensive, coed **Entrance** Moderately difficult **Setting** 122-acre suburban campus **Total enrollment** 1,774 **Student-faculty ratio** 12:1 **Application deadline** Rolling (freshmen), rolling (transfer) **Freshman admission** 77% were admitted **Freshman test scores** SAT critical reading scores over 500: 74%; SAT math scores over 500: 79%; ACT scores over 18: 94%; SAT critical reading scores over 600: 29%; SAT math scores over 600: 30%; ACT scores over 24: 40% **Housing** Yes **Expenses** Tuition & Fees: state resident $6818, nonresident $15,128; Room & Board $5676 **Undergraduates** 39% women, 7% part-time, 5% 25 or older, 1% Native American, 13% Hispanic American, 3% African American, 2% Asian American/Pacific Islander **The most frequently chosen baccalaureate fields are** biological/life sciences, business/marketing, engineering **Academic program** English as a second language, advanced placement, accelerated degree program, summer session, internships **Contact** Ms. Sarah Trombley, Associate Director of Admissions and Records, Texas A&M University at Galveston, PO Box 1675, Galveston, TX 77553-1675. *Phone:* 409-740-4448. *Fax:* 409-740-4731. *E-mail:* seaaggie@tamug.edu. *Web site:* http://www.tamug.edu/.

Texas A&M University–Commerce

Commerce, Texas

General State-supported, university, coed **Entrance** Moderately difficult **Setting** 1,883-acre small-town campus **Total enrollment** 9,170

Texas A&M University–Commerce (continued)

Student-faculty ratio 17:1 **Application deadline** 8/11 (freshmen), rolling (transfer) **Freshman admission** 70% were admitted **Freshman test scores** SAT critical reading scores over 500: 48.77%; SAT math scores over 500: 51.7%; SAT critical reading scores over 600: 14.42%; SAT math scores over 600: 14.57% **Housing** Yes **Expenses** Tuition & Fees: state resident $5500, nonresident $13,840; Room & Board $7090 **Undergraduates** 62% women, 23% part-time, 37% 25 or older, 1% Native American, 10% Hispanic American, 18% African American, 2% Asian American/Pacific Islander **The most frequently chosen baccalaureate fields are** business/marketing, interdisciplinary studies, parks and recreation **Academic program** Advanced placement, honors program, summer session, adult/continuing education programs, internships **Contact** Hope Young, Director of Admissions, Texas A&M University–Commerce, PO Box 3011, Commerce, TX 75429. *Phone:* 903-886-5103 or toll-free 800-331-3878. *Fax:* 903-886-5888. *E-mail:* admissions@tamu-commerce.edu. *Web site:* http://www.tamu-commerce.edu/.

Texas A&M University–Corpus Christi

Corpus Christi, Texas

General State-supported, university, coed **Entrance** Moderately difficult **Setting** 240-acre suburban campus **Total enrollment** 9,468 **Student-faculty ratio** 19:1 **Application deadline** 7/1 (freshmen), 7/1 (transfer) **Freshman admission** 85% were admitted. Average high school GPA 3.3 **Freshman test scores** SAT critical reading scores over 500: 40.96%; SAT math scores over 500: 48.75%; ACT scores over 18: 73.9%; SAT critical reading scores over 600: 8.14%; SAT math scores over 600: 9.93%; ACT scores over 24: 15.34% **Housing** Yes **Expenses** Tuition & Fees: state resident $6221, nonresident $14,781; Room & Board $9528 **Undergraduates** 59% women, 23% part-time, 23% 25 or older **The most frequently chosen baccalaureate fields are** business/marketing, health professions and related sciences, interdisciplinary studies **Academic program** English as a second language, advanced placement, honors program, summer session, internships **Contact** Mrs. Monica Martinez, Assistant Director of Admissions, Texas A&M University–Corpus Christi, SSC 107, 6300 Ocean Drive, Unit 5774, Corpus Christi, TX 78412-5774. *Phone:* 361-825-2624 or toll-free 800-482-6822. *Fax:* 361-825-5887. *E-mail:* monica.martinez@tamucc.edu. *Web site:* http://www.tamucc.edu/.

Texas A&M University–Kingsville

Kingsville, Texas

General State-supported, university, coed **Entrance** Moderately difficult **Setting** 255-acre small-town campus **Total enrollment** 7,133 **Student-faculty ratio** 15:1 **Application deadline** Rolling (freshmen), rolling (transfer) **Freshman admission** 91% were admitted **Housing** Yes **Expenses** Tuition & Fees: state resident $5882, nonresident $14,192; Room & Board $5020 **Undergraduates** 30% 25 or older **Academic program** English as a second language, advanced placement, honors program, summer session, internships **Contact** William Carter, Director of Admissions, Texas A&M University–Kingsville, West Santa Gertrudis, Kingsville, TX 78363. *Phone:* 361-593-2315 or toll-free 800-687-6000. *Web site:* http://www.tamuk.edu/.

Texas A&M University–San Antonio

San Antonio, Texas

Contact Texas A&M University–San Antonio, 1450 Gillette Boulevard, San Antonio, TX 78224. *Web site:* http://www.tamuk.edu/sanantonio/.

Texas A&M University–Texarkana

Texarkana, Texas

Contact Mrs. Patricia Black, Director of Admissions and Registrar, Texas A&M University–Texarkana, PO Box 5518, Texarkana, TX 75505-5518. *Phone:* 903-223-3068. *Fax:* 903-223-3140. *E-mail:* admissions@tamut.edu. *Web site:* http://www.tamut.edu/.

Texas Christian University

Fort Worth, Texas

General Independent, university, coed, affiliated with Christian Church (Disciples of Christ) **Entrance** Moderately difficult **Setting** 272-acre suburban campus **Total enrollment** 8,853 **Student-faculty ratio** 13:1 **Application deadline** 2/15 (freshmen), 4/15 (transfer) **Freshman admission** 59% were admitted **Housing** Yes **Expenses** Tuition & Fees $30,048; Room & Board $10,112 **Undergraduates** 59% women, 4% part-time, 5% 25 or older, 1% Native American, 9% Hispanic American, 5% African American, 3% Asian American/Pacific Islander **The most frequently chosen baccalaureate fields are** business/marketing, communications/journalism, health professions and related sciences **Academic program** English as a second language, advanced placement, accelerated degree program, honors program, summer session, adult/continuing education programs, internships **Contact** Mr. Wes Waggoner, Director of Freshman Admissions, Texas Christian University, 2800 South University Drive, Fort Worth, TX 76129-0002. *Phone:* 817-257-7490 or toll-free 800-828-3764. *Fax:* 817-257-7268. *E-mail:* frogmail@tcu.edu. *Web site:* http://www.tcu.edu/.

Visit Petersons.com and enter keywords Texas Christian

See page 1218 for the College Close-Up.

Texas College

Tyler, Texas

General Independent, 4-year, coed, affiliated with Christian Methodist Episcopal Church **Entrance** Noncompetitive **Setting** 25-acre urban campus **Total enrollment** 964 **Student-faculty ratio** 24:1 **Application deadline** Rolling (freshmen), rolling (transfer) **Freshman admission** Average high school GPA 2.86 **Housing** Yes **Expenses** Tuition & Fees $9490; Room & Board $6600 **Undergraduates** 45% women, 3% part-time, 16% 25 or older, 12% Hispanic American, 83% African American **The most frequently chosen baccalaureate fields are** business/marketing, biological/life sciences, health professions and related sciences **Academic program** Advanced placement, accelerated degree program, honors program, summer session, adult/continuing education programs **Contact** Mr. John Roberts, Director of Admissions, Texas College, 2404 North Grand Avenue, Tyler, TX 75702. *Phone:* 903-593-8311 Ext. 2297 or toll-free 800-306-6299. *Fax:* 903-596-0001. *E-mail:* jroberts@texascollege.edu. *Web site:* http://www.texascollege.edu/.

Texas Lutheran University

Seguin, Texas

General Independent, 4-year, coed, affiliated with Evangelical Lutheran Church **Entrance** Moderately difficult **Setting** 196-acre suburban campus **Total enrollment** 1,387 **Student-faculty ratio** 15:1 **Application deadline** Rolling (freshmen), rolling (transfer) **Freshman admission** 66% were admitted. Average high school GPA 3.52 **Freshman test scores** SAT critical reading scores over 500: 46.71%; SAT math scores over 500: 59.2%; ACT scores over 18: 83.02%; SAT critical reading scores over 600: 16.78%; SAT math scores over 600: 19.4%; ACT scores over 24: 23.63% **Housing** Yes **Expenses** Tuition & Fees $21,910; Room & Board $6400 **Undergraduates** 52% women, 6% part-time, 6% 25 or older, 0.4% Native American, 23% Hispanic American, 10% African American, 1% Asian American/Pacific Islander **The most frequently chosen baccalaureate fields are** business/marketing, biological/life sciences, parks and recreation **Academic program** Advanced placement, honors program, summer session, adult/continuing education programs, internships **Contact** Mr. Norm Jones, Vice President for Enrollment Services, Texas Lutheran University, 1000 West Court Street, Seguin, TX 78155-5999. *Phone:* 830-372-8053 or toll-free 800-771-8521. *Fax:* 830-372-8096. *E-mail:* njones@tlu.edu. *Web site:* http://www.tlu.edu/.

Texas Southern University

Houston, Texas

General State-supported, university, coed **Entrance** Noncompetitive **Setting** 147-acre urban campus **Total enrollment** 9,394 **Student-**

faculty ratio 19:1 **Application deadline** 8/15 (freshmen), 8/13 (transfer) **Freshman admission** 26% were admitted. Average high school GPA 2.6 **Freshman test scores** SAT critical reading scores over 500: 9%; SAT math scores over 500: 12%; ACT scores over 18: 35%; SAT critical reading scores over 600: 1%; SAT math scores over 600: 1%; ACT scores over 24: 3% **Housing** Yes **Expenses** Tuition & Fees: state resident $7080, nonresident $15,390; Room & Board $11,620 **Undergraduates** 57% women, 19% part-time, 28% 25 or older, 0.1% Native American, 4% Hispanic American, 89% African American, 2% Asian American/Pacific Islander **The most frequently chosen baccalaureate fields are** business/marketing, biological/life sciences, health professions and related sciences **Academic program** English as a second language, accelerated degree program, honors program, summer session, adult/continuing education programs, internships **Contact** Enrollment Services Customer Service Center, Texas Southern University, 3100 Cleburne Street, Houston, TX 77004-4598. *Phone:* 713-313-7071. *Fax:* 713-313-7851. *E-mail:* eservices@em.tsu.edu. *Web site:* http://www.tsu.edu/.

Texas State University–San Marcos
San Marcos, Texas

General State-supported, university, coed **Entrance** Moderately difficult **Setting** 423-acre suburban campus **Total enrollment** 30,803 **Student-faculty ratio** 22:1 **Application deadline** 5/1 (freshmen), 7/1 (transfer) **Freshman admission** 76% were admitted **Freshman test scores** SAT critical reading scores over 500: 65%; SAT math scores over 500: 73.4%; ACT scores over 18: 97.7%; SAT critical reading scores over 600: 16.6%; SAT math scores over 600: 21.3%; ACT scores over 24: 41.1% **Housing** Yes **Expenses** Tuition & Fees: state resident $7482, nonresident $15,792; Room & Board $6392 **Undergraduates** 55% women, 18% part-time, 18% 25 or older, 1% Native American, 24% Hispanic American, 6% African American, 2% Asian American/Pacific Islander **The most frequently chosen baccalaureate fields are** business/marketing, interdisciplinary studies, visual and performing arts **Academic program** English as a second language, advanced placement, accelerated degree program, honors program, summer session, adult/continuing education programs, internships **Contact** Mrs. Stephanie Anderson, Director of Admissions, Texas State University–San Marcos, 601 University Drive, San Marcos, TX 78666. *Phone:* 512-245-2364 Ext. 2803. *Fax:* 512-245-8044. *E-mail:* admissions@txstate.edu. *Web site:* http://www.txstate.edu/.

Texas Tech University
Lubbock, Texas

General State-supported, university, coed **Entrance** Moderately difficult **Setting** 1,839-acre urban campus **Total enrollment** 30,049 **Student-faculty ratio** 22:1 **Application deadline** 5/1 (freshmen), rolling (transfer) **Freshman admission** 68% were admitted **Freshman test scores** SAT critical reading scores over 500: 69.2%; SAT math scores over 500: 82.8%; ACT scores over 18: 97.3%; SAT critical reading scores over 600: 20.5%; SAT math scores over 600: 33.3%; ACT scores over 24: 48.4% **Housing** Yes **Expenses** Tuition & Fees: state resident $7485, nonresident $15,795; Room & Board $7527 **Undergraduates** 44% women, 9% part-time, 8% 25 or older, 1% Native American, 14% Hispanic American, 5% African American, 3% Asian American/Pacific Islander **The most frequently chosen baccalaureate fields are** business/marketing, engineering, family and consumer sciences **Academic program** English as a second language, advanced placement, accelerated degree program, self-designed majors, honors program, summer session, internships **Contact** Ethan Logan, Director, Office of Admissions, Texas Tech University, Lubbock, TX 79409. *Phone:* 806-742-1480. *Fax:* 806-742-0062. *Web site:* http://www.ttu.edu/.

Texas Wesleyan University
Fort Worth, Texas

General Independent United Methodist, comprehensive, coed **Entrance** Moderately difficult **Setting** 74-acre urban campus **Total enrollment** 3,333 **Student-faculty ratio** 12:1 **Application deadline** Rolling (freshmen), rolling (transfer) **Freshman admission** 61% were admitted. Average high school GPA 3.27 **Freshman test scores** SAT critical reading scores over 500: 35%; SAT math scores over 500: 41%; ACT scores over 18: 79%; SAT critical reading scores over 600: 4%; SAT math scores over 600: 10%; ACT scores over 24: 19% **Housing** Yes **Expenses** Tuition & Fees $17,760; Room & Board $6656 **Undergraduates** 65% women, 35% part-time, 32% 25 or older, 1% Native American, 19% Hispanic American, 17% African American, 2% Asian American/Pacific Islander **The most frequently chosen baccalaureate fields are** business/marketing, education, interdisciplinary studies **Academic program** English as a second language, advanced placement, accelerated degree program, summer session, internships **Contact** Holly Kiser, Director of Admissions, Texas Wesleyan University, 1201 Wesleyan Street, Fort Worth, TX 76105-1536. *Phone:* 817-531-4422 or toll-free 800-580-8980. *Fax:* 817-531-7515. *E-mail:* admission@txwes.edu. *Web site:* http://www.txwes.edu/.

Texas Woman's University
Denton, Texas

General State-supported, university, coed, primarily women **Entrance** Minimally difficult **Setting** 270-acre suburban campus **Total enrollment** 13,237 **Student-faculty ratio** 17:1 **Application deadline** 7/1 (freshmen), 7/15 (transfer) **Freshman admission** 84% were admitted **Freshman test scores** SAT critical reading scores over 500: 51%; SAT math scores over 500: 53%; ACT scores over 18: 81%; SAT critical reading scores over 600: 13%; SAT math scores over 600: 15%; ACT scores over 24: 32% **Housing** Yes **Expenses** Tuition & Fees: state resident $6660, nonresident $15,000; Room & Board $5967 **Undergraduates** 92% women, 31% part-time, 38% 25 or older, 1% Native American, 19% Hispanic American, 21% African American, 8% Asian American/Pacific Islander **The most frequently chosen baccalaureate fields are** health professions and related sciences, interdisciplinary studies, liberal arts/general studies **Academic program** Advanced placement, accelerated degree program, honors program, summer session, adult/continuing education programs, internships **Contact** Ms. Erma Nieto-Brecht, Director of Admissions, Texas Woman's University, 304 Administration Drive, Denton, TX 76201. *Phone:* 940-898-3188 or toll-free 888-948-9984. *Fax:* 940-898-3081. *E-mail:* admissions@twu.edu. *Web site:* http://www.twu.edu/.

Visit Petersons.com and enter keywords Texas Woman's

See page 1220 for the College Close-Up.

Trinity University
San Antonio, Texas

General Independent, comprehensive, coed, affiliated with Presbyterian Church **Entrance** Very difficult **Setting** 113-acre urban campus **Total enrollment** 2,693 **Student-faculty ratio** 9:1 **Application deadline** 2/1 (freshmen), 3/1 (transfer) **Freshman admission** 59% were admitted. Average high school GPA 3.56 **Freshman test scores** SAT critical reading scores over 500: 98.2%; SAT math scores over 500: 99.6%; ACT scores over 18: 100%; SAT critical reading scores over 600: 74.5%; SAT math scores over 600: 81.3%; ACT scores over 24: 99% **Housing** Yes **Expenses** Tuition & Fees $29,317; Room & Board $8895 **Undergraduates** 54% women, 2% part-time, 1% 25 or older, 1% Native American, 11% Hispanic American, 4% African American, 7% Asian American/Pacific Islander **The most frequently chosen baccalaureate fields are** business/marketing, communications/journalism, social sciences **Academic program** Advanced placement, accelerated degree program, honors program, summer session, internships **Contact** Mr. Christopher Ellertson, Dean of Admissions and Financial Aid, Trinity University, One Trinity Place, San Antonio, TX 78212-7200. *Phone:* 210-999-7207 or toll-free 800-TRINITY. *Fax:* 210-999-8164. *E-mail:* admissions@trinity.edu. *Web site:* http://www.trinity.edu/.

Texas Woman's University

PO Box 425589
Denton, TX 76204-5589

E-mail: admissions@twu.edu
Phone: 940-898-3188

See our profile page for more information about our school.

University of Dallas
Irving, Texas

General Independent Roman Catholic, university, coed **Entrance** Moderately difficult **Setting** 215-acre suburban campus **Total enrollment** 2,883 **Student-faculty ratio** 13:1 **Application deadline** 8/1 (freshmen), 7/1 (transfer) **Freshman admission** 92% were admitted. Average high school GPA 3.7 **Freshman test scores** SAT critical reading scores over 500: 91.9%; SAT math scores over 500: 85.84%; ACT scores over 18: 98.77%; SAT critical reading scores over 600: 61.54%; SAT math scores over 600: 46.97%; ACT scores over 24: 70.55% **Housing** Yes **Expenses** Tuition & Fees $27,815; Room & Board $8650 **Undergraduates** 51% women, 2% part-time, 3% 25 or older, 0.3% Native American, 15% Hispanic American, 1% African American, 5% Asian American/Pacific Islander **The most frequently chosen baccalaureate fields are** biological/life sciences, English, social sciences **Academic program** Advanced placement, self-designed majors, summer session, internships **Contact** Ms. Amanda Lively, University of Dallas, 1845 East Northgate Drive, Irving, TX 75062-4736. *Phone:* 972-721-5266 or toll-free 800-628-6999. *Fax:* 972-721-5017. *E-mail:* ugadmis@udallas.edu. *Web site:* http://www.udallas.edu/.

Visit Petersons.com and enter keywords University of Dallas

See page 1262 for the College Close-Up.

University of Houston
Houston, Texas

General State-supported, university, coed **Entrance** Moderately difficult **Setting** 667-acre urban campus **Total enrollment** 37,000 **Student-faculty ratio** 22:1 **Application deadline** 4/1 (freshmen), 5/1 (transfer) **Freshman admission** 70% were admitted **Freshman test scores** SAT critical reading scores over 500: 62%; SAT math scores over 500: 78%; ACT scores over 18: 90%; SAT critical reading scores over 600: 19%; SAT math scores over 600: 34%; ACT scores over 24: 36% **Housing** Yes **Expenses** Tuition & Fees: state resident $8496, nonresident $16,806; Room & Board $7164 **Undergraduates** 50% women, 28% part-time, 20% 25 or older, 0.4% Native American, 24% Hispanic American, 15% African American, 22% Asian American/Pacific Islander **The most frequently chosen baccalaureate fields are** business/marketing, psychology, social sciences **Academic program** English as a second language, advanced placement, honors program, summer session, adult/continuing education programs, internships **Contact** Jeff Fuller, Director, Student Recruitment, University of Houston, Welcome Center, 4400 University Boulevard, Houston, TX 77204-2023. *Phone:* 713-743-1010. *Fax:* 713-743-9633. *E-mail:* jdfuller@central.uh.edu. *Web site:* http://www.uh.edu/.

University of Houston–Clear Lake
Houston, Texas

General State-supported, upper-level, coed **Entrance** Minimally difficult **Setting** 487-acre suburban campus **Total enrollment** 7,662 **Student-faculty ratio** 10:1 **Application deadline** Rolling (transfer) **Housing** Yes **Expenses** Tuition & Fees: state resident $5708, nonresident $14,918; Room only $7896 **Undergraduates** 69% women, 52% part-time, 41% 25 or older, 1% Native American, 25% Hispanic American, 8% African American, 6% Asian American/Pacific Islander **The most frequently chosen baccalaureate fields are** business/marketing, interdisciplinary studies, psychology **Academic program** English as a second language, accelerated degree program, self-designed majors, summer session, internships **Contact** Ms. Rauchelle Jones, Executive Director of Admissions, University of Houston–Clear Lake, 2700 Bay Area Boulevard, Box 13, Houston, TX 77058-1098. *Phone:* 281-283-2518. *Fax:* 281-283-2530. *E-mail:* admissions@uhcl.edu. *Web site:* http://www.uhcl.edu/.

University of Houston–Downtown

Houston, Texas

General State-supported, comprehensive, coed **Entrance** Noncompetitive **Setting** 24-acre urban campus **Total enrollment** 12,742 **Student-faculty ratio** 20:1 **Application deadline** 6/1 (freshmen), 8/1 (transfer) **Freshman admission** 100% were admitted **Housing** No **Expenses** Tuition & Fees: state resident $5232, nonresident $13,542 **Undergraduates** 62% women, 52% part-time, 49% 25 or older, 0.3% Native American, 37% Hispanic American, 29% African American, 10% Asian American/Pacific Islander **The most frequently chosen baccalaureate fields are** business/marketing, interdisciplinary studies, liberal arts/general studies **Academic program** English as a second language, advanced placement, honors program, summer session, internships **Contact** Ms. Patricia Santos, Assistant Director of Admissions-Freshman Admissions, University of Houston–Downtown, One Main Street, Suite 350-S, Houston, TX 77002. *Phone:* 713-221-8522. *Fax:* 713-221-8157. *E-mail:* uhdadmit@uhd.edu. *Web site:* http://www.uhd.edu/.

University of Houston–Victoria

Victoria, Texas

General State-supported, upper-level, coed **Entrance** Minimally difficult **Setting** 20-acre small-town campus **Total enrollment** 3,655 **Student-faculty ratio** 16:1 **Application deadline** Rolling (freshmen), rolling (transfer) **Housing** No **Expenses** Tuition & Fees: state resident $5400, nonresident $13,710 **Undergraduates** 70% women, 62% part-time, 65% 25 or older, 1% Native American, 21% Hispanic American, 12% African American, 7% Asian American/Pacific Islander **Academic program** Summer session, adult/continuing education programs, internships **Contact** Mrs. Trudy Wortham, Registrar, University of Houston–Victoria, 3007 North Ben Wilson Street, Victoria, TX 77901-4450. *Phone:* 361-570-4290 or toll-free 877-970-4848 Ext. 110. *E-mail:* worthamt@uhv.edu. *Web site:* http://www.uhv.edu/.

University of Mary Hardin-Baylor

Belton, Texas

General Independent Southern Baptist, comprehensive, coed **Entrance** Moderately difficult **Setting** 100-acre small-town campus **Total enrollment** 2,768 **Student-faculty ratio** 14:1 **Application deadline** Rolling (freshmen), rolling (transfer) **Freshman admission** 42% were admitted **Freshman test scores** SAT critical reading scores over 500: 64%; SAT math scores over 500: 66%; ACT scores over 18: 97%; SAT critical reading scores over 600: 22%; SAT math scores over 600: 23%; ACT scores over 24: 45% **Housing** Yes **Expenses** Tuition & Fees $20,650; Room & Board $5350 **Undergraduates** 61% women, 10% part-time, 18% 25 or older, 0.4% Native American, 14% Hispanic American, 13% African American, 2% Asian American/Pacific Islander **The most frequently chosen baccalaureate fields are** business/marketing, education, health professions and related sciences **Academic program** English as a second language, advanced placement, accelerated degree program, self-designed majors, honors program, summer session, internships **Contact** Mr. Brent Burks, Director of Admissions, University of Mary Hardin-Baylor, UMHB Station Box 8004, 900 College Street, Belton, TX 76513-2599. *Phone:* 254-295-4520 or toll-free 800-727-8642. *Fax:* 254-295-5049. *E-mail:* admission@umhb.edu. *Web site:* http://www.umhb.edu/.

University of North Texas

Denton, Texas

General State-supported, university, coed **Setting** 875-acre suburban campus **Total enrollment** 36,123 **Student-faculty ratio** 23:1 **Application deadline** 8/1 (freshmen), rolling (transfer) **Freshman admission** 64% were admitted **Freshman test scores** SAT critical reading scores over 500: 69.36%; SAT math scores over 500: 73.67%; ACT scores over 18: 92.7%; SAT critical reading scores over 600: 24.76%; SAT math scores over 600: 28.28%; ACT scores over 24: 40.3% **Housing** Yes **Expenses** Tuition & Fees: state resident $7301, nonresident $15,611; Room & Board $6534 **Undergraduates** 54% women, 22% part-time, 15% 25 or older, 1% Native American, 14% Hispanic American, 14% African American, 6% Asian American/Pacific Islander **The most frequently chosen baccalaureate fields are** business/marketing, interdisciplinary studies, social sciences **Academic program** English as a second language, advanced placement, accelerated degree program, honors program, summer session, adult/continuing education programs, internships **Contact** Dr. Rebecca Lothringer, Director of Admissions and School Relations, University of North Texas, 1155 Union Circle #311425, Denton, TX 76203. *Phone:* 940-565-3921 or toll-free 800-868-8211. *E-mail:* undergradadm@unt.edu. *Web site:* http://www.unt.edu/.

University of Phoenix–Dallas Campus

Dallas, Texas

General Proprietary, comprehensive, coed **Entrance** Noncompetitive **Setting** urban campus **Total enrollment** 1,371 **Application deadline** Rolling (freshmen), rolling (transfer) **Housing** No **Expenses** Tuition & Fees $12,525 **Undergraduates** 64% women, 90% 25 or older, 1% Native American, 11% Hispanic American, 32% African American, 2% Asian American/Pacific Islander **The most frequently chosen baccalaureate fields are** business/marketing, public administration and social services **Academic program** Advanced placement, accelerated degree program, adult/continuing education programs **Contact** Ms. Audra McQuarie, Registrar/Executive Director, University of Phoenix–Dallas Campus, 4035 South Riverpoint Parkway, Mail Stop CF-L101, Phoenix, AZ 85040. *Phone:* 480-557-6151 or toll-free 800-776-4867 (in-state); 800-228-7240 (out-of-state). *Fax:* 480-643-3068. *E-mail:* audra.mcquarie@phoenix.edu. *Web site:* http://www.phoenix.edu/.

University of Phoenix–Houston Campus

Houston, Texas

General Proprietary, comprehensive, coed **Entrance** Noncompetitive **Setting** urban campus **Total enrollment** 2,748 **Application deadline** Rolling (freshmen), rolling (transfer) **Housing** No **Expenses** Tuition & Fees $12,525 **Undergraduates** 68% women, 89% 25 or older, 0.2% Native American, 13% Hispanic American, 39% African American, 2% Asian American/Pacific Islander **The most frequently chosen baccalaureate fields are** business/marketing, health professions and related sciences **Academic program** Advanced placement, accelerated degree program, adult/continuing education programs **Contact** Ms. Audra McQuarie, Registrar/Executive Director, University of Phoenix–Houston Campus, 4305 South Riverpoint Parkway, Mail Stop CF-L101, Phoenix, AZ 85040. *Phone:* 480-557-6151 or toll-free 800-776-4867 (in-state); 800-228-7240 (out-of-state). *Fax:* 480-643-3068. *E-mail:* audra.mcquarie@phoenix.edu. *Web site:* http://www.phoenix.edu/.

University of St. Thomas

Houston, Texas

General Independent Roman Catholic, comprehensive, coed **Entrance** Moderately difficult **Setting** 20-acre urban campus **Total enrollment** 3,234 **Student-faculty ratio** 12:1 **Application deadline** 5/1 (freshmen), rolling (transfer) **Freshman admission** 80% were admitted. Average high school GPA 3.44 **Freshman test scores** SAT critical reading scores over 500: 82.63%; SAT math scores over 500: 80.75%; ACT scores over 18: 100%; SAT critical reading scores over 600: 30.99%; SAT math scores over 600: 35.68%; ACT scores over 24: 63.64% **Housing** Yes **Expenses** Tuition & Fees $21,830; Room & Board $7400 **Undergraduates** 60% women, 27% part-time, 25% 25 or older, 1% Native American, 32% Hispanic American, 5% African American, 12% Asian American/Pacific Islander **The most frequently chosen baccalaureate fields are** business/marketing, biological/life sciences, liberal arts/general studies **Academic program** Advanced placement, accelerated

University of St. Thomas (continued)

degree program, self-designed majors, honors program, summer session, adult/continuing education programs, internships **Contact** Lee Holm, Director of Admissions, University of St. Thomas, 3800 Montrose Boulevard, Houston, TX 77006-4696. *Phone:* 713-525-3500 or toll-free 800-856-8565. *Fax:* 713-525-3558. *E-mail:* admissions@stthom.edu. *Web site:* http://www.stthom.edu/.

The University of Texas at Arlington

Arlington, Texas

General State-supported, university, coed **Entrance** Moderately difficult **Setting** 395-acre urban campus **Total enrollment** 28,085 **Student-faculty ratio** 23:1 **Application deadline** 6/1 (freshmen), rolling (transfer) **Freshman admission** 69% were admitted **Freshman test scores** SAT critical reading scores over 500: 61%; SAT math scores over 500: 72%; ACT scores over 18: 88%; SAT critical reading scores over 600: 19%; SAT math scores over 600: 30%; ACT scores over 24: 39% **Housing** Yes **Expenses** Tuition & Fees: state resident $8186, nonresident $16,496; Room & Board $6658 **Undergraduates** 54% women, 33% part-time, 33% 25 or older, 1% Native American, 19% Hispanic American, 16% African American, 12% Asian American/Pacific Islander **The most frequently chosen baccalaureate fields are** business/marketing, biological/life sciences, interdisciplinary studies **Academic program** English as a second language, advanced placement, self-designed majors, honors program, summer session, adult/continuing education programs, internships **Contact** Dr. Hans Gatterdam, Executive Director of Admissions and Records, The University of Texas at Arlington, UTA Box 19088, 701 South Nedderman Drive, Arlington, TX 76019-0088. *Phone:* 817-272-6287. *Fax:* 817-272-3435. *E-mail:* admissions@uta.edu. *Web site:* http://www.uta.edu/.

The University of Texas at Austin

Austin, Texas

General State-supported, university, coed **Entrance** Very difficult **Setting** 350-acre urban campus **Total enrollment** 50,995 **Student-faculty ratio** 17:1 **Application deadline** 12/1 (freshmen), 3/1 (transfer) **Freshman admission** 45% were admitted **Freshman test scores** SAT critical reading scores over 500: 85.7%; SAT math scores over 500: 92.4%; ACT scores over 18: 97.6%; SAT critical reading scores over 600: 52.2%; SAT math scores over 600: 68.2%; ACT scores over 24: 78.6% **Housing** Yes **Expenses** Tuition & Fees: state resident $8930, nonresident $30,006; Room & Board $9602 **Undergraduates** 51% women, 7% part-time, 6% 25 or older, 0.5% Native American, 18% Hispanic American, 5% African American, 18% Asian American/Pacific Islander **The most frequently chosen baccalaureate fields are** communications/journalism, business/marketing, social sciences **Academic program** English as a second language, advanced placement, accelerated degree program, self-designed majors, honors program, summer session, internships **Contact** Kedra Ishop, Vice Provost and Director of Admissions, The University of Texas at Austin, Office of Admissions, Freshman Admissions Center, PO Box 8058, Austin, TX 78713-8058. *Phone:* 512-475-7440. *Fax:* 512-475-7475. *Web site:* http://www.utexas.edu/.

The University of Texas at Brownsville

Brownsville, Texas

General State-supported, comprehensive, coed **Entrance** Noncompetitive **Setting** 380-acre urban campus **Total enrollment** 17,189 **Student-faculty ratio** 21:1 **Application deadline** 7/1 (freshmen), 8/1 (transfer) **Freshman admission** 100% were admitted. Average high school GPA 2.61 **Housing** Yes **Expenses** Tuition & Fees: state resident $4547, nonresident $11,195; Room & Board $5742 **Undergraduates** 60% women, 65% part-time, 36% 25 or older, 0.1% Native American, 90% Hispanic American, 0.4% African American, 0.4% Asian American/Pacific Islander **The most frequently chosen baccalaureate fields are** business/marketing, interdisciplinary studies, security and protective services **Academic program** English as a second language, advanced placement, summer session, internships **Contact** Carlo Tamayo, New Student Relations Coordinator, The University of Texas at Brownsville, 80 Fort Brown, Brownsville, TX 78520-4991. *Phone:* 956-882-8860 or toll-free 800-850-0160. *Fax:* 956-882-8959. *E-mail:* admissions@utb.edu. *Web site:* http://www.utb.edu/.

The University of Texas at Dallas

Richardson, Texas

General State-supported, university, coed **Entrance** Very difficult **Setting** 500-acre suburban campus **Total enrollment** 15,783 **Student-faculty ratio** 20:1 **Application deadline** 7/1 (freshmen) **Freshman admission** 52% were admitted. Average high school GPA 3.58 **Freshman test scores** SAT critical reading scores over 500: 83%; SAT math scores over 500: 92%; ACT scores over 18: 98%; SAT critical reading scores over 600: 47%; SAT math scores over 600: 65%; ACT scores over 24: 77% **Housing** Yes **Expenses** Tuition & Fees: state resident $10,340, nonresident $23,730; Room & Board $7733 **Undergraduates** 45% women, 25% part-time, 27% 25 or older, 1% Native American, 12% Hispanic American, 7% African American, 22% Asian American/Pacific Islander **The most frequently chosen baccalaureate fields are** business/marketing, interdisciplinary studies, psychology **Academic program** Advanced placement, accelerated degree program, self-designed majors, honors program, summer session, adult/continuing education programs, internships **Contact** Enrollment Services, The University of Texas at Dallas, 800 West Campbell Road, Mail Station HH10, Richardson, TX 75083-0688. *Phone:* 972-883-2270 or toll-free 800-889-2443. *Fax:* 972-883-2599. *E-mail:* interest@utdallas.edu. *Web site:* http://www.utdallas.edu/.

Visit Petersons.com and enter keywords Texas at Dallas

See page 1312 for the College Close-Up.

The University of Texas at El Paso

El Paso, Texas

General State-supported, university, coed **Entrance** Minimally difficult **Setting** 360-acre urban campus **Total enrollment** 21,011 **Student-faculty ratio** 20:1 **Application deadline** 7/31 (freshmen), 7/31 (transfer) **Freshman admission** 99% were admitted. Average high school GPA 3.13 **Freshman test scores** SAT critical reading scores over 500: 26.2%; SAT math scores over 500: 34.7%; ACT scores over 18: 54.1%; SAT critical reading scores over 600: 4.6%; SAT math scores over 600: 7.5%; ACT scores over 24: 11.8% **Housing** Yes **Expenses** Tuition & Fees: state resident $5925, nonresident $14,355 **Undergraduates** 55% women, 34% part-time, 28% 25 or older, 0.2% Native American, 80% Hispanic American, 3% African American, 1% Asian American/Pacific Islander **The most frequently chosen baccalaureate fields are** business/marketing, education, health professions and related sciences **Academic program** English as a second language, advanced placement, accelerated degree program, honors program, summer session, adult/continuing education programs, internships **Contact** Director of Admissions, The University of Texas at El Paso, 500 West University Avenue, El Paso, TX 79968-0001. *Phone:* 915-747-5588 or toll-free 877-746-4636. *Fax:* 915-747-8893. *E-mail:* futureminer@utep.edu. *Web site:* http://www.utep.edu/.

The University of Texas at San Antonio

San Antonio, Texas

General State-supported, university, coed **Entrance** Moderately difficult **Setting** 600-acre suburban campus **Total enrollment** 28,955 **Student-faculty ratio** 23:1 **Application deadline** 7/1 (freshmen), 7/1 (transfer) **Freshman admission** 87% were admitted **Freshman test scores** SAT critical reading scores over 500: 53.34%; SAT math scores over 500: 63.89%; ACT scores over 18: 87.56%; SAT critical reading scores over 600: 13.21%; SAT math scores over 600: 21.65%; ACT scores over 24: 31.77% **Housing** Yes **Expenses** Tuition & Fees: state resident $7527, nonresident $15,837; Room & Board $8937 **Undergraduates** 50% women, 21% part-time, 23% 25 or older, 0.4% Native American, 44% Hispanic American, 9% African American, 7% Asian American/Pacific Islander **The most frequently chosen baccalaureate fields are** business/marketing, biological/life sciences, interdisciplinary studies **Academic program** English as a second language, advanced placement, honors program, summer session, adult/continuing education programs, internships **Contact** Ms. Jennifer Ehlers, Director of Admissions, The University of Texas at San Antonio, 6900 North Loop 1604 West, San Antonio, TX 78249-0617. *Phone:* 210-458-4536 or toll-free 800-669-0919. *Fax:* 210-458-2001. *E-mail:* prospects@utsa.edu. *Web site:* http://www.utsa.edu/.

The University of Texas at Tyler

Tyler, Texas

General State-supported, comprehensive, coed **Entrance** Moderately difficult **Setting** 200-acre urban campus **Total enrollment** 6,163 **Student-faculty ratio** 16:1 **Application deadline** Rolling (freshmen), rolling (transfer) **Freshman admission** 86% were admitted. Average high school GPA 3.37 **Freshman test scores** SAT critical reading scores over 500: 59.83%; SAT math scores over 500: 71.06%; ACT scores over 18: 97.02%; SAT critical reading scores over 600: 21.17%; SAT math scores over 600: 24.19%; ACT scores over 24: 38.21% **Housing** Yes **Expenses** Tuition & Fees: state resident $6042, nonresident $14,472; Room & Board $8016 **Undergraduates** 58% women, 24% part-time, 25% 25 or older, 1% Native American, 8% Hispanic American, 10% African American, 2% Asian American/Pacific Islander **The most frequently chosen baccalaureate fields are** business/marketing, health professions and related sciences, interdisciplinary studies **Academic program** Advanced placement, self-designed majors, honors program, summer session, adult/continuing education programs, internships **Contact** Ms. Sarah Bowdin, Director of Admissions, The University of Texas at Tyler, 3900 University Boulevard, Tyler, TX 75799-0001. *Phone:* 903-566-7057 or toll-free 800-UTTYLER. *Fax:* 903-566-7068. *E-mail:* admissions@uttyler.edu. *Web site:* http://www.uttyler.edu/.

The University of Texas Health Science Center at Houston

Houston, Texas

General State-supported, upper-level, coed **Entrance** Moderately difficult **Setting** urban campus **Total enrollment** 3,969 **Student-faculty ratio** 11:1 **Application deadline** 9/1 (transfer) **First-year students** 35% were admitted **Undergraduates** 87% women, 26% part-time, 52% 25 or older, 0.2% Native American, 16% Hispanic American, 10% African American, 18% Asian American/Pacific Islander **Academic program** Accelerated degree program, summer session, internships **Contact** Mr. Robert L. Jenkins, Registrar, The University of Texas Health Science Center at Houston, PO Box 20036, Houston, TX 77225-0036. *Phone:* 713-500-3361. *Fax:* 713-500-3356. *E-mail:* registrar@uth.tmc.edu. *Web site:* http://www.uth.tmc.edu/.

The University of Texas Health Science Center at San Antonio

San Antonio, Texas

Contact Associate Registrar, The University of Texas Health Science Center at San Antonio, 7703 Floyd Curl Drive, San Antonio, TX 78229-3900. *Phone:* 210-567-2659. *Fax:* 210-567-2685. *Web site:* http://www.uthscsa.edu/.

The University of Texas Medical Branch

Galveston, Texas

General State-supported, comprehensive, coed **Entrance** Very difficult **Setting** 85-acre small-town campus **Total enrollment** 2,430 **Housing** Yes **Expenses** Tuition & Fees: state resident $5502, nonresident $13,932; Room only $4620 **Undergraduates** 80% women, 36% part-time, 65% 25 or older, 1% Native American, 14% Hispanic American, 18% African American, 18% Asian American/Pacific Islander **The most frequently chosen baccalaureate field is** health professions and related sciences **Academic program** Advanced placement, accelerated degree program, summer session, internships **Contact** Ms. Vicki L. Brewer, Registrar, The University of Texas Medical Branch, 301 University Boulevard, Galveston, TX 77555. *Phone:* 409-772-1215. *Fax:* 409-772-4466. *E-mail:* enrollment.services@utmb.edu. *Web site:* http://www.utmb.edu/.

The University of Texas of the Permian Basin

Odessa, Texas

General State-supported, comprehensive, coed **Entrance** Moderately difficult **Setting** 600-acre urban campus **Total enrollment** 3,546 **Student-faculty ratio** 17:1 **Application deadline** 7/15 (freshmen), rolling (transfer) **Freshman admission** 85% were admitted **Freshman test scores** SAT critical reading scores over 500: 47.6%; SAT math scores over 500: 57.2%; ACT scores over 18: 90.2%; SAT critical reading scores over 600: 11.7%; SAT math scores over 600: 11.7%; ACT scores over 24: 21.9% **Housing** Yes **Expenses** Tuition & Fees: state resident $5378, nonresident $13,688; Room & Board $6445 **Undergraduates** 59% women, 30% part-time, 32% 25 or older, 1% Native American, 43% Hispanic American, 5% African American, 1% Asian American/Pacific Islander **The most frequently chosen baccalaureate fields are** business/marketing, family and consumer sciences, psychology **Academic program** English as a second language, advanced placement, honors program, summer session, internships **Contact** Scott Smiley, Director of Admissions, The University of Texas of the Permian Basin, 4901 East University Boulevard, Odessa, TX 79762-0001. *Phone:* 432-552-2605 or toll-free 866-552-UTPB. *Fax:* 432-552-3605. *E-mail:* admissions@utpb.edu. *Web site:* http://www.utpb.edu/.

The University of Texas–Pan American

Edinburg, Texas

General State-supported, comprehensive, coed **Entrance** Noncompetitive **Setting** 289-acre small-town campus **Total enrollment** 18,337 **Student-faculty ratio** 21:1 **Application deadline** 8/11 (freshmen), 8/11 (transfer) **Freshman admission** 68% were admitted **Freshman test scores** SAT critical reading scores over 500: 31%; SAT math scores over 500: 41%; ACT scores over 18: 64%; SAT critical reading scores over 600: 7%; SAT math scores over 600: 9%; ACT scores over 24: 7% **Housing** Yes **Expenses** Tuition & Fees: state resident $4304, nonresident $11,048; Room & Board $5294 **Undergraduates** 57% women, 26% part-time, 19% 25 or older, 0.1% Native American, 90% Hispanic American, 1% African American, 1% Asian American/Pacific Islander **The most frequently chosen baccalaureate fields are** business/marketing, health professions and related sciences, interdisciplinary studies **Academic program** English as a second language, advanced placement, accelerated degree program, honors program, summer session, adult/continuing education programs, internships **Contact** Dr. Magdalena Hinojosa, Dean of Admissions and Enrollment Services, The University of Texas–Pan American, Office of Admissions and Records, 1201 West University Drive, Edinburg, TX 78539. *Phone:* 956-381-2481. *Fax:* 956-381-2321. *E-mail:* recruitment@utpa.edu. *Web site:* http://www.utpa.edu/.

The University of Texas Southwestern Medical Center at Dallas

Dallas, Texas

General State-supported, upper-level, coed **Entrance** Moderately difficult **Setting** 98-acre urban campus **Total enrollment** 2,445 **Application deadline** Rolling (transfer) **First-year students** 28% were admitted

The University of Texas Southwestern Medical Center at Dallas (continued)

Housing Yes **Expenses** Tuition & Fees: state resident $4878, nonresident $13,589; Room & Board $11,353 **Undergraduates** 78% women, 14% part-time, 69% 25 or older, 13% Hispanic American, 21% African American, 8% Asian American/Pacific Islander **The most frequently chosen baccalaureate field is** health professions and related sciences **Academic program** Advanced placement, internships **Contact** Anne Mclane, Associate Director of Admissions, The University of Texas Southwestern Medical Center at Dallas, 5323 Harry Hines Boulevard, Dallas, TX 75390. *Phone:* 214-648-5617. *Fax:* 214-648-3289. *E-mail:* admissions@utsouthwestern.edu. *Web site:* http://www.utsouthwestern.edu/.

University of the Incarnate Word

San Antonio, Texas

General Independent Roman Catholic, comprehensive, coed **Entrance** Moderately difficult **Setting** 200-acre urban campus **Total enrollment** 6,756 **Student-faculty ratio** 15:1 **Application deadline** Rolling (freshmen), rolling (transfer) **Freshman admission** 66% were admitted. Average high school GPA 3.5 **Freshman test scores** SAT critical reading scores over 500: 46.41%; SAT math scores over 500: 49.77%; ACT scores over 18: 77.7%; SAT critical reading scores over 600: 10.42%; SAT math scores over 600: 15.47%; ACT scores over 24: 22.3% **Housing** Yes **Expenses** Tuition & Fees $21,890; Room & Board $9220 **Undergraduates** 65% women, 35% part-time, 40% 25 or older, 0.3% Native American, 57% Hispanic American, 7% African American, 3% Asian American/Pacific Islander **The most frequently chosen baccalaureate fields are** business/marketing, education, health professions and related sciences **Academic program** English as a second language, advanced placement, accelerated degree program, self-designed majors, honors program, summer session, adult/continuing education programs, internships **Contact** Ms. Andrea Cyterski-Acosta, Dean of Enrollment, University of the Incarnate Word, 4301 Broadway, San Antonio, TX 78209-6397. *Phone:* 210-829-6005 or toll-free 800-749-WORD. *Fax:* 210-829-3921. *E-mail:* admis@uiwtx.edu. *Web site:* http://www.uiw.edu/.

Visit Petersons.com and enter keyword Incarnate

Wayland Baptist University

Plainview, Texas

General Independent Baptist, comprehensive, coed **Entrance** Minimally difficult **Setting** 80-acre small-town campus **Total enrollment** 1,260 **Student-faculty ratio** 10:1 **Application deadline** 8/1 (freshmen), rolling (transfer) **Freshman admission** 99% were admitted. Average high school GPA 3.55 **Freshman test scores** SAT critical reading scores over 500: 47%; SAT math scores over 500: 48%; ACT scores over 18: 77%; SAT critical reading scores over 600: 11%; SAT math scores over 600: 16%; ACT scores over 24: 24% **Housing** Yes **Expenses** Tuition & Fees $12,470; Room & Board $3864 **Undergraduates** 53% women, 23% part-time, 16% 25 or older **The most frequently chosen baccalaureate fields are** business/marketing, biological/life sciences, education **Academic program** Advanced placement, accelerated degree program, honors program, summer session, adult/continuing education programs **Contact** Ms. Debbie Stennett, Director of Student Admissions, Wayland Baptist University, 1900 West 7th Street, CMB 712, Plainview, TX 79072. *Phone:* 806-291-3500 or toll-free 800-588-1928. *Fax:* 806-291-1973. *E-mail:* admityou@wbu.edu. *Web site:* http://www.wbu.edu/.

West Texas A&M University

Canyon, Texas

General State-supported, comprehensive, coed **Entrance** Moderately difficult **Setting** 128-acre small-town campus **Total enrollment** 7,535 **Student-faculty ratio** 18:1 **Application deadline** Rolling (freshmen), rolling (transfer) **Freshman admission** 66% were admitted **Freshman test scores** SAT critical reading scores over 500: 48%; SAT math scores over 500: 54%; ACT scores over 18: 79.8%; SAT critical reading scores over 600: 12.7%; SAT math scores over 600: 15.1%; ACT scores over 24: 19.2% **Housing** Yes **Expenses** Tuition & Fees: state resident $5382, nonresident $13,812; Room & Board $5627 **Undergraduates** 55% women, 23% part-time, 27% 25 or older, 1% Native American, 19% Hispanic American, 5% African American, 2% Asian American/Pacific Islander **The most frequently chosen baccalaureate fields are** interdisciplinary studies, business/marketing, liberal arts/general studies **Academic program** English as a second language, advanced placement, honors program, summer session, adult/continuing education programs, internships **Contact** Mr. Shawn Thomas, Director of Admissions, West Texas A&M University, WT Box 60907, Canyon, TX 79016-0001. *Phone:* 806-651-2020 or toll-free 800-99-WTAMU. *Fax:* 806-651-5285. *E-mail:* sthomas@mail.wtamu.edu. *Web site:* http://www.wtamu.edu/.

Westwood College–Dallas

Dallas, Texas

General Proprietary, 4-year, coed **Total enrollment** 629 **Contact** Director of Admissions, Westwood College–Dallas, 8390 LBJ Freeway, Executive Center 1, Suite 100, Dallas, TX 75243. *Phone:* 214-570-9100 or toll-free 800-281-2978. *Fax:* 214-570-8502. *Web site:* http://www.westwood.edu/.

Westwood College–Fort Worth

Fort Worth, Texas

General Proprietary, 4-year, coed **Total enrollment** 367 **Contact** Director of Admissions, Westwood College–Fort Worth, 4232 North Freeway, Fort Worth, TX 76137. *Phone:* 817-547-9601 or toll-free 866-533-9997. *Fax:* 817-547-9602. *Web site:* http://www.westwood.edu/.

Westwood College–Houston South Campus

Houston, Texas

General Proprietary, primarily 2-year, coed **Total enrollment** 478 **Contact** Director of Admissions, Westwood College–Houston South Campus, 7322 Southwest Freeway #110, Houston, TX 77074. *Phone:* 713-777-4779 or toll-free 800-281-2978. *Fax:* 713-219-2088. *Web site:* http://www.westwood.edu/.

Wiley College

Marshall, Texas

Contact Ms. Alvena Jones, Interim Director of Admissions/Recruitment, Wiley College, 711 Wiley Avenue, Marshall, TX 75670-5199. *Phone:* 903-927-3222 or toll-free 800-658-6889. *Fax:* 903-923-8878. *E-mail:* ajones@wileyc.edu. *Web site:* http://www.wileyc.edu/.

UTAH

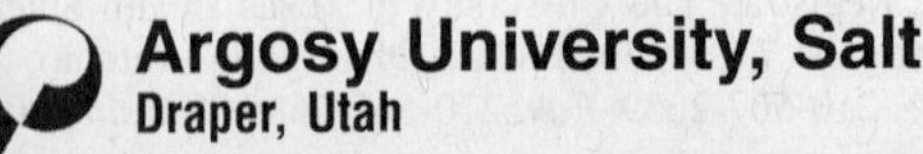

Argosy University, Salt Lake City

Draper, Utah

General Proprietary, university, coed **Contact** Director of Admissions, Argosy University, Salt Lake City, 121 West Election Road, Suite 300, Draper, UT 84020. *Phone:* 801-601-5000 or toll-free 888-639-4756. *Fax:* 801-601-4990. *Web site:* http://www.argosy.edu/saltlakecity/.

Visit Petersons.com and enter keywords Argosy University, Salt Lake City

See page 478 for the College Close-Up.

The Art Institute of Salt Lake City
Draper, Utah

General Proprietary, 4-year, coed **Contact** Director of Admissions, The Art Institute of Salt Lake City, 121 West Election Road, Suite 100, Draper, UT 84020-9492. *Phone:* 801-601-4700 or toll-free 800-978-0096. *Fax:* 801-601-4724. *Web site:* http://www.artinstitutes.edu/SaltLakeCity/.

Visit Petersons.com and enter keywords Art Institute of Salt Lake City

See page 540 for the College Close-Up.

Brigham Young University
Provo, Utah

General Independent, university, coed, affiliated with The Church of Jesus Christ of Latter-day Saints **Entrance** Moderately difficult **Setting** 557-acre suburban campus **Total enrollment** 34,130 **Student-faculty ratio** 21:1 **Application deadline** 2/1 (freshmen), 3/1 (transfer) **Freshman admission** 69% were admitted. Average high school GPA 3.76 **Freshman test scores** SAT critical reading scores over 500: 93%; SAT math scores over 500: 94%; ACT scores over 18: 100%; SAT critical reading scores over 600: 58%; SAT math scores over 600: 66%; ACT scores over 24: 90% **Housing** Yes **Expenses** Tuition & Fees $4420; Room & Board $7120 **Undergraduates** 49% women, 9% part-time, 14% 25 or older, 0.5% Native American, 4% Hispanic American, 0.5% African American, 4% Asian American/Pacific Islander **The most frequently chosen baccalaureate fields are** biological/life sciences, business/marketing, social sciences **Academic program** English as a second language, advanced placement, accelerated degree program, honors program, summer session, adult/continuing education programs, internships **Contact** Mr. Tom Gourley, Dean of Admissions and Records, Brigham Young University, A-153 Abraham Smoot Building, Provo, UT 84602. *Phone:* 801-422-2507. *Fax:* 801-422-0005. *E-mail:* admissions@byu.edu. *Web site:* http://www.byu.edu/.

DeVry University
Sandy, Utah

General Proprietary, comprehensive, coed **Total enrollment** 147 **Student-faculty ratio** 13:1 **Application deadline** Rolling (freshmen), rolling (transfer) **Expenses** Tuition & Fees $14,080 **Undergraduates** 34% women, 54% part-time, 80% 25 or older, 5% Hispanic American, 1% African American, 4% Asian American/Pacific Islander **The most frequently chosen baccalaureate field is** business/marketing **Academic program** Accelerated degree program **Contact** Admissions Office, DeVry University, 9350 South 150 E, Suite 420, Sandy, UT 84070. *Web site:* http://www.devry.edu/.

Dixie State College of Utah
St. George, Utah

General State-supported, 4-year, coed **Entrance** Noncompetitive **Setting** 117-acre small-town campus **Total enrollment** 7,708 **Student-faculty ratio** 21:1 **Application deadline** Rolling (freshmen), rolling (transfer) **Freshman admission** 66% were admitted. Average high school GPA 3.14 **Freshman test scores** SAT critical reading scores over 500: 28%; ACT scores over 18: 77.58%; SAT critical reading scores over 600: 1.33%; ACT scores over 24: 21.66% **Housing** Yes **Expenses** Tuition & Fees: state resident $3146, nonresident $10,898; Room & Board $3948 **Undergraduates** 51% women, 41% part-time, 33% 25 or older, 1% Native American, 5% Hispanic American, 2% African American, 3% Asian American/Pacific Islander **The most frequently chosen baccalaureate fields are** business/marketing, communications/journalism, education **Academic program** English as a second language, advanced placement, accelerated degree program, self-designed majors, honors program, summer session, adult/continuing education programs, internships **Contact** Brandon Boulter, Director of Admissions, Dixie State College of Utah, 225 South 700 East, St. George, UT 84770-3876. *Phone:* 435-652-7591 or toll-free 888-GO2DIXIE. *E-mail:* bboulter@dixie.edu. *Web site:* http://www.dixie.edu/.

Independence University
Salt Lake City, Utah

General Proprietary, comprehensive, coed **Entrance** Noncompetitive **Setting** 2-acre urban campus **Application deadline** Rolling (freshmen), rolling (transfer) **Housing** No **Contact** Ms. Deborah Hopkins, Enrollment Manager, Independence University, 5295 South Commerce Drive, Salt Lake City, UT 84107. *Phone:* toll-free 800-791-7353. *E-mail:* info@independence.edu. *Web site:* http://www.independence.edu/.

ITT Technical Institute
Murray, Utah

General Proprietary, primarily 2-year, coed **Entrance** Minimally difficult **Setting** suburban campus **Housing** No **Contact** Director of Recruitment, ITT Technical Institute, 920 West Levoy Drive, Murray, UT 84123-2500. *Phone:* 801-263-3313 or toll-free 800-365-2136. *Web site:* http://www.itt-tech.edu/.

Midwives College of Utah
Salt Lake City, Utah

General Independent, comprehensive, women only **Entrance** Noncompetitive **Setting** suburban campus **Total enrollment** 130 **Application deadline** 7/29 (freshmen) **Freshman admission** Average high school GPA 3.2 **Housing** No **Undergraduates** 100% part-time **The most frequently chosen baccalaureate field is** health professions and related sciences **Contact** Kristi Ridd-Young, President, Midwives College of Utah, 1174 East 2700 South, Suite 2, Salt Lake City, UT 84106. *Phone:* 801-649-5230 or toll-free 866-764-9068. *Fax:* 866-207-2024. *E-mail:* office@midwifery.edu. *Web site:* http://www.midwifery.edu/.

Neumont University
South Jordan, Utah

General Proprietary, comprehensive, coed, primarily men **Entrance** Moderately difficult **Setting** suburban campus **Total enrollment** 240 **Student-faculty ratio** 13:1 **Application deadline** Rolling (freshmen), rolling (transfer) **Freshman admission** 94% were admitted **Freshman test scores** ACT scores over 18: 93%; ACT scores over 24: 48% **Housing** Yes **Expenses** Tuition & Fees $28,800; Room only $5700 **Undergraduates** 6% women **The most frequently chosen baccalaureate field is** computer and information sciences **Academic program** Accelerated degree program **Contact** Charlie Parker, Dean of Admissions, Neumont University, 10701 South River Front Parkway Suite 200, South Jordan, UT 84095. *Phone:* 801-302-2856 or toll-free 866-622-3448. *Fax:* 801-302-2811. *E-mail:* charlie.parker@neumont.edu. *Web site:* http://www.neumont.edu/.

Southern Utah University
Cedar City, Utah

General State-supported, comprehensive, coed **Entrance** Moderately difficult **Setting** 113-acre small-town campus **Total enrollment** 8,066 **Student-faculty ratio** 26:1 **Application deadline** 8/1 (freshmen), rolling (transfer) **Freshman admission** 81% were admitted. Average high school GPA 3.42 **Freshman test scores** SAT critical reading scores over 500: 52.9%; SAT math scores over 500: 50.59%; ACT scores over 18: 84.67%; SAT critical reading scores over 600: 18.6%; SAT math scores over 600: 14.54%; ACT scores over 24: 33.62% **Housing** Yes **Expenses** Tuition & Fees: state resident $4269, nonresident $12,847; Room only $1950 **Undergraduates** 58% women, 24% part-time, 17% 25 or older, 2% Native American, 4% Hispanic American, 1% African American, 2%

Southern Utah University (continued)
Asian American/Pacific Islander **The most frequently chosen baccalaureate fields are** business/marketing, education, health professions and related sciences **Academic program** English as a second language, advanced placement, honors program, summer session, adult/continuing education programs, internships **Contact** Mr. Stephen Allen, Director of Admissions, Southern Utah University, 351 West University Boulevard, Cedar City, UT 84720-2498. *Phone:* 435-586-7740. *E-mail:* admininfo@suu.edu. *Web site:* http://www.suu.edu/.

Stevens-Henager College
West Haven, Utah

Contact Admissions Office, Stevens-Henager College, 1890 South 1350 West, West Haven, UT 84401. *Phone:* 801-394-7791 or toll-free 800-622-2640. *Web site:* http://www.stevenshenager.edu/.

Strayer University–Salt Lake Campus
Sandy, Utah

General Proprietary, comprehensive, coed **Contact** Admissions Office, Strayer University–Salt Lake Campus, 9815 South Monroe Street, Suite 200, Sandy, UT 84070. *Phone:* 801-432-5000. *Web site:* http://www.strayer.edu/salt_lake.

University of Phoenix–Utah Campus
Salt Lake City, Utah

General Proprietary, comprehensive, coed **Entrance** Noncompetitive **Setting** urban campus **Total enrollment** 3,169 **Application deadline** Rolling (freshmen), rolling (transfer) **Freshman admission** 100% were admitted **Housing** No **Expenses** Tuition & Fees $11,500 **Undergraduates** 45% women, 90% 25 or older, 1% Native American, 4% Hispanic American, 1% African American, 2% Asian American/Pacific Islander **The most frequently chosen baccalaureate fields are** business/marketing, computer and information sciences, health professions and related sciences **Academic program** Advanced placement, accelerated degree program, adult/continuing education programs **Contact** Ms. Evelyn Gaskin, Registrar/Executive Director, University of Phoenix–Utah Campus, 4615 East Elwood Street, Mail Stop AA-K101, Phoenix, AZ 85040-1958. *Phone:* 480-557-3303 or toll-free 800-776-4867 (in-state); 800-228-7240 (out-of-state). *Fax:* 480-643-1020. *E-mail:* evelyn.gaskin@phoenix.edu. *Web site:* http://www.phoenix.edu/.

University of Utah
Salt Lake City, Utah

General State-supported, university, coed **Entrance** Moderately difficult **Setting** 1,535-acre urban campus **Total enrollment** 29,284 **Student-faculty ratio** 15:1 **Application deadline** 4/1 (freshmen), 4/1 (transfer) **Freshman admission** 80% were admitted. Average high school GPA 3.52 **Freshman test scores** SAT critical reading scores over 500: 75%; SAT math scores over 500: 78%; ACT scores over 18: 96%; SAT critical reading scores over 600: 35%; SAT math scores over 600: 39%; ACT scores over 24: 52% **Housing** Yes **Expenses** Tuition & Fees: state resident $5746, nonresident $18,136; Room & Board $6240 **Undergraduates** 45% women, 31% part-time, 32% 25 or older, 1% Native American, 6% Hispanic American, 1% African American, 5% Asian American/Pacific Islander **The most frequently chosen baccalaureate fields are** business/marketing, communications/journalism, social sciences **Academic program** English as a second language, advanced placement, accelerated degree program, self-designed majors, honors program, summer session, internships **Contact** Mateo Remsburg, Director of High School Services, University of Utah, 201 Presidents Circle Room 206, Salt Lake City, UT 84112. *Phone:* 801-581-8761 or toll-free 800-444-8638. *Fax:* 801-585-3257. *E-mail:* mremsburg@sa.utah.edu. *Web site:* http://www.utah.edu/.

Utah Career College
West Jordan, Utah

Contact Ms. Karma Cooper, Director of Admissions, Utah Career College, 1902 West 7800 South, West Jordan, UT 84088. *Phone:* 801-304-4224 Ext. 158 or toll-free 866-304-4224. *Fax:* 801-304-4229. *E-mail:* kcooper@utahcollege.edu. *Web site:* http://www.utahcollege.edu/.

Utah Career College–Layton Campus
Layton, Utah

Contact Utah Career College–Layton Campus, 869 West Hill Field Road, Layton, UT 84041. *Web site:* http://www.utahcollege.edu/.

Utah State University
Logan, Utah

General State-supported, university, coed **Entrance** Moderately difficult **Setting** 456-acre urban campus **Total enrollment** 15,612 **Student-faculty ratio** 18:1 **Application deadline** Rolling (freshmen), rolling (transfer) **Freshman admission** 98% were admitted. Average high school GPA 3.54 **Freshman test scores** SAT critical reading scores over 500: 66.2%; SAT math scores over 500: 66.7%; ACT scores over 18: 96%; SAT critical reading scores over 600: 32.9%; SAT math scores over 600: 33.4%; ACT scores over 24: 50.7% **Housing** Yes **Expenses** Tuition & Fees: state resident $4828, nonresident $13,802; Room & Board $4900 **Undergraduates** 49% women, 16% part-time, 17% 25 or older, 1% Native American, 3% Hispanic American, 1% African American, 2% Asian American/Pacific Islander **The most frequently chosen baccalaureate fields are** business/marketing, education, engineering **Academic program** English as a second language, advanced placement, accelerated degree program, self-designed majors, honors program, summer session, adult/continuing education programs, internships **Contact** Ms. Jenn Putnam, Director, Admissions Office, Utah State University, 0160 Old Main Hill, Logan, UT 84322-0160. *Phone:* 435-797-1079 or toll-free 800-488-8108. *Fax:* 435-797-3708. *E-mail:* admit@usu.edu. *Web site:* http://www.usu.edu/.

Utah Valley University
Orem, Utah

General State-supported, comprehensive, coed, affiliated with Advent Christian Church **Entrance** Noncompetitive **Setting** 228-acre suburban campus **Total enrollment** 28,765 **Student-faculty ratio** 24:1 **Application deadline** Rolling (freshmen), rolling (transfer) **Freshman admission** 100% were admitted. Average high school GPA 3.24 **Freshman test scores** SAT critical reading scores over 500: 45.81%; SAT math scores over 500: 47.7%; ACT scores over 18: 67.88%; SAT critical reading scores over 600: 10.97%; SAT math scores over 600: 14.94%; ACT scores over 24: 26.05% **Expenses** Tuition & Fees: state resident $4258, nonresident $11,888; Room & Board $8670 **Undergraduates** 43% women, 48% part-time, 38% 25 or older **Academic program** English as a second language, advanced placement, self-designed majors, honors program, summer session, internships **Contact** Mrs. Liz Childs, Senior Director of Admissions, Utah Valley University, 800 West University Parkway, Orem, UT 84058-5999. *Phone:* 801-863-8460. *Fax:* 801-225-4677. *E-mail:* info@uvsc.edu. *Web site:* http://www.uvu.edu/.

Weber State University
Ogden, Utah

General State-supported, comprehensive, coed **Entrance** Noncompetitive **Setting** 526-acre urban campus **Total enrollment** 23,001 **Student-**

faculty ratio 22:1 **Application deadline** 8/22 (freshmen), rolling (transfer) **Freshman admission** 100% were admitted. Average high school GPA 3.3 **Freshman test scores** ACT scores over 18: 83%; ACT scores over 24: 30% **Housing** Yes **Undergraduates** 52% women, 53% part-time, 44% 25 or older **The most frequently chosen baccalaureate fields are** business/marketing, education, health professions and related sciences **Academic program** English as a second language, advanced placement, accelerated degree program, self-designed majors, honors program, summer session, adult/continuing education programs, internships **Contact** Mr. Mark Simpson, Admissions Advisor, Weber State University, 1137 University Circle, Ogden, UT 84408-1137. *Phone:* 801-626-6047 or toll-free 800-634-6568 (in-state); 800-848-7770 (out-of-state). *Fax:* 801-626-6744. *E-mail:* admissions@weber.edu. *Web site:* http://www.weber.edu/.

Western Governors University
Salt Lake City, Utah

General Independent, comprehensive, coed **Entrance** Minimally difficult **Total enrollment** 9,022 **Housing** No **Undergraduates** 92% 25 or older **Academic program** Accelerated degree program, adult/continuing education programs **Contact** Director of Enrollment, Western Governors University, 4001 South 700 East, Suite 700, Salt Lake City, UT 84107. *Phone:* 801-274-3280 Ext. 336 or toll-free 877-435-7948. *E-mail:* admissions@wgu.edu. *Web site:* http://www.wgu.edu/.

Westminster College
Salt Lake City, Utah

General Independent, comprehensive, coed **Entrance** Moderately difficult **Setting** 27-acre suburban campus **Total enrollment** 3,037 **Student-faculty ratio** 10:1 **Application deadline** Rolling (freshmen), rolling (transfer) **Freshman admission** 82% were admitted. Average high school GPA 3.5 **Freshman test scores** SAT critical reading scores over 500: 80%; SAT math scores over 500: 76%; ACT scores over 18: 97%; SAT critical reading scores over 600: 36%; SAT math scores over 600: 38%; ACT scores over 24: 61% **Housing** Yes **Expenses** Tuition & Fees $24,996; Room & Board $7006 **Undergraduates** 55% women, 6% part-time, 19% 25 or older, 1% Native American, 6% Hispanic American, 1% African American, 3% Asian American/Pacific Islander **The most frequently chosen baccalaureate fields are** business/marketing, health professions and related sciences, social sciences **Academic program** English as a second language, advanced placement, accelerated degree program, self-designed majors, honors program, summer session, internships **Contact** Louis Levy, Interim Director of Undergraduate Admissions, Westminster College, 1840 South 1300 East, Salt Lake City, UT 84105-3697. *Phone:* 801-832-2200 or toll-free 800-748-4753. *Fax:* 801-832-3101. *E-mail:* admission@westminstercollege.edu. *Web site:* http://www.westminstercollege.edu/.
Visit Petersons.com and enter keyword Westminster

See page 1368 for the College Close-Up.

VERMONT

Bennington College
Bennington, Vermont

General Independent, comprehensive, coed **Entrance** Very difficult **Setting** 470-acre small-town campus **Total enrollment** 808 **Student-faculty ratio** 9:1 **Application deadline** 1/3 (freshmen), 3/15 (transfer) **Freshman admission** 66% were admitted. Average high school GPA 3.45 **Freshman test scores** SAT critical reading scores over 500: 98.75%; SAT math scores over 500: 90%; ACT scores over 18: 99.99%; SAT critical reading scores over 600: 83.75%; SAT math scores over 600: 52.5%; ACT scores over 24: 96.66% **Housing** Yes **Expenses** Tuition & Fees $39,760; Room & Board $11,100 **Undergraduates** 67% women, 1% part-time, 1% 25 or older, 0.5% Native American, 2% Hispanic American, 2% African American, 2% Asian American/Pacific Islander **The most frequently chosen baccalaureate fields are** English, social sciences, visual and performing arts **Academic program** English as a second language, accelerated degree program, self-designed majors, internships **Contact** Mr. Ken Himmelman, Dean of Admissions and Financial Aid, Bennington College, One College Drive, Bennington, VT 05201-6003. *Phone:* 802-440-4312 or toll-free 800-833-6845. *Fax:* 802-440-4320. *E-mail:* admissions@bennington.edu. *Web site:* http://www.bennington.edu/.

Burlington College
Burlington, Vermont

General Independent, 4-year, coed **Entrance** Moderately difficult **Setting** 1-acre urban campus **Total enrollment** 175 **Student-faculty ratio** 6:1 **Application deadline** 8/15 (freshmen), 8/15 (transfer) **Freshman admission** 83% were admitted. Average high school GPA 2.72 **Housing** Yes **Expenses** Tuition & Fees $20,424; Room only $6750 **Undergraduates** 45% women, 31% part-time, 36% 25 or older, 2% Hispanic American, 2% African American, 2% Asian American/Pacific Islander **The most frequently chosen baccalaureate fields are** interdisciplinary studies, psychology, visual and performing arts **Academic program** Advanced placement, self-designed majors, summer session, internships **Contact** Ms. Gillian Homsted, Admissions Director, Burlington College, 95 North Avenue, Burlington, VT 05401-2998. *Phone:* 802-862-9616 Ext. 104 or toll-free 800-862-9616. *Fax:* 802-660-4331. *E-mail:* admissions@burlington.edu. *Web site:* http://www.burlington.edu/.
Visit Petersons.com and enter keyword Burlington

Castleton State College
Castleton, Vermont

General State-supported, comprehensive, coed **Entrance** Moderately difficult **Setting** 165-acre rural campus **Total enrollment** 2,191 **Student-faculty ratio** 14:1 **Application deadline** Rolling (freshmen), rolling (transfer) **Freshman admission** 71% were admitted. Average high school GPA 2.9 **Freshman test scores** SAT critical reading scores over 500: 40%; SAT math scores over 500: 44%; ACT scores over 18: 73%; SAT critical reading scores over 600: 8%; SAT math scores over 600: 10%; ACT scores over 24: 11% **Housing** Yes **Expenses** Tuition & Fees: state resident $9096, nonresident $19,656; Room & Board $8120 **Undergraduates** 54% women, 11% part-time, 6% 25 or older, 1% Native American, 2% Hispanic American, 1% African American, 1% Asian American/Pacific Islander **The most frequently chosen baccalaureate fields are** business/marketing, interdisciplinary studies, parks and recreation **Academic program** Advanced placement, self-designed majors, honors program, summer session, internships **Contact** Mr. Maurice Ouimet, Admissions Director, Castleton State College, Castleton, VT 05735. *Phone:* 802-468-1213 or toll-free 800-639-8521. *Fax:* 802-468-1476. *E-mail:* info@castleton.edu. *Web site:* http://www.castleton.edu/.
Visit Petersons.com and enter keyword Castleton

See page 692 for the College Close-Up.

Champlain College
Burlington, Vermont

General Independent, comprehensive, coed **Entrance** Moderately difficult **Setting** 21-acre suburban campus **Total enrollment** 2,268 **Student-faculty ratio** 14:1 **Application deadline** 1/31 (freshmen), rolling (transfer) **Freshman admission** 78% were admitted **Freshman test scores** SAT critical reading scores over 500: 81%; SAT math scores over 500: 79%; ACT scores over 18: 100%; SAT critical reading scores over 600: 32%; SAT math scores over 600: 30%; ACT scores over 24: 47% **Housing** Yes **Expenses** Tuition & Fees $25,950; Room & Board $11,670 **Undergraduates** 40% women, 3% part-time, 26% 25 or older **The most frequently chosen baccalaureate fields are** business/marketing, computer and information sciences, visual and performing arts **Academic**

Champlain College (continued)

program Advanced placement, honors program, summer session, internships **Contact** Ian Mortimer, Director of Admissions, Champlain College, 163 South Willard Street, Burlington, VT 05401. *Phone:* 802-860-2727 or toll-free 800-570-5858. *Fax:* 802-860-2767. *E-mail:* admission@champlain.edu. *Web site:* http://www.champlain.edu/.

College of St. Joseph
Rutland, Vermont

General Independent Roman Catholic, comprehensive, coed **Entrance** Minimally difficult **Setting** 117-acre small-town campus **Total enrollment** 422 **Student-faculty ratio** 10:1 **Application deadline** Rolling (freshmen), rolling (transfer) **Freshman admission** 35% were admitted. Average high school GPA 2.8 **Freshman test scores** SAT critical reading scores over 500: 17.2%; SAT math scores over 500: 17.2%; ACT scores over 18: 60%; SAT critical reading scores over 600: 2.6% **Housing** Yes **Expenses** Tuition & Fees $18,300; Room & Board $8600 **Undergraduates** 63% women, 28% part-time, 33% 25 or older, 1% Native American, 1% Hispanic American, 6% African American, 0.5% Asian American/Pacific Islander **The most frequently chosen baccalaureate fields are** business/marketing, education, psychology **Academic program** Advanced placement, accelerated degree program, summer session, adult/continuing education programs, internships **Contact** Susan Englese, Dean of Admissions, College of St. Joseph, 71 Clement Road, Rutland, VT 05701-3899. *Phone:* 802-773-5900 Ext. 3227 or toll-free 877-270-9998. *Fax:* 802-776-5258. *E-mail:* admissions@csj.edu. *Web site:* http://www.csj.edu/.

Goddard College
Plainfield, Vermont

General Independent, comprehensive, coed **Entrance** Moderately difficult **Setting** 250-acre rural campus **Total enrollment** 768 **Student-faculty ratio** 12:1 **Application deadline** Rolling (freshmen), rolling (transfer) **Freshman admission** 83% were admitted **Housing** Yes **Expenses** Tuition & Fees $13,022; Room & Board $1152 **Undergraduates** 63% women, 60% 25 or older, 1% Native American, 6% Hispanic American, 5% African American, 1% Asian American/Pacific Islander **Academic program** Advanced placement, self-designed majors, adult/continuing education programs, internships **Contact** Erin Johnson, Admissions Counselor, Goddard College, 123 Pitkin Road, Plainfield, VT 05667-9432. *Phone:* 800-906-8312 Ext. 262 or toll-free 800-906-8312 Ext. 243. *Fax:* 802-454-1029. *E-mail:* admissions@goddard.edu. *Web site:* http://www.goddard.edu/.

Green Mountain College
Poultney, Vermont

General Independent, comprehensive, coed **Entrance** Moderately difficult **Setting** 155-acre small-town campus **Total enrollment** 858 **Student-faculty ratio** 14:1 **Application deadline** Rolling (freshmen), rolling (transfer) **Freshman admission** 72% were admitted. Average high school GPA 3 **Housing** Yes **Expenses** Tuition & Fees $26,910; Room & Board $9670 **Undergraduates** 55% women, 3% part-time, 4% 25 or older, 1% Native American, 3% Hispanic American, 3% African American, 1% Asian American/Pacific Islander **The most frequently chosen baccalaureate fields are** business/marketing, natural resources/environmental science, psychology **Academic program** English as a second language, advanced placement, accelerated degree program, self-designed majors, honors program, summer session, adult/continuing education programs, internships **Contact** Dr. Sandra Bartholomew, Dean of Enrollment, Green Mountain College, One Brennan Circle, Poultney, VT 05764. *Phone:* 802-287-8207 or toll-free 800-776-6675. *Fax:* 802-287-8099. *E-mail:* admiss@greenmtn.edu. *Web site:* http://www.greenmtn.edu/.

Johnson State College
Johnson, Vermont

General State-supported, comprehensive, coed **Entrance** Moderately difficult **Setting** 350-acre rural campus **Total enrollment** 1,989 **Student-faculty ratio** 17:1 **Application deadline** Rolling (freshmen), rolling (transfer) **Freshman admission** 82% were admitted. Average high school GPA 3.32 **Freshman test scores** SAT critical reading scores over 500: 45%; SAT math scores over 500: 36%; SAT critical reading scores over 600: 11%; SAT math scores over 600: 6% **Housing** Yes **Expenses** Tuition & Fees: state resident $8913, nonresident $18,153; Room & Board $7808 **Undergraduates** 61% women, 29% part-time, 33% 25 or older, 1% Native American, 2% Hispanic American, 2% African American, 1% Asian American/Pacific Islander **The most frequently chosen baccalaureate fields are** business/marketing, liberal arts/general studies, psychology **Academic program** English as a second language, advanced placement, accelerated degree program, honors program, summer session, internships **Contact** Bethany Harrington, Admissions Specialist, Johnson State College, 337 College Hill, Johnson, VT 05656. *Phone:* 802-635-1219 or toll-free 800-635-2356. *Fax:* 802-635-1230. *E-mail:* jscadmissions@jsc.edu. *Web site:* http://www.jsc.edu/.

Lyndon State College
Lyndonville, Vermont

General State-supported, comprehensive, coed **Entrance** Moderately difficult **Setting** 175-acre rural campus **Total enrollment** 1,385 **Student-faculty ratio** 15:1 **Application deadline** Rolling (freshmen), rolling (transfer) **Freshman admission** Average high school GPA 2.5 **Freshman test scores** SAT critical reading scores over 500: 33.8%; SAT math scores over 500: 29.3%; SAT critical reading scores over 600: 6.6%; SAT math scores over 600: 3.3% **Housing** Yes **Expenses** Tuition & Fees: state resident $7684, nonresident $16,348; Room & Board $7509 **Undergraduates** 16% 25 or older **The most frequently chosen baccalaureate fields are** business/marketing, health professions and related sciences, psychology **Academic program** Advanced placement, accelerated degree program, self-designed majors, honors program, summer session, adult/continuing education programs, internships **Contact** Ms. Donna "Dee" Gile, Admissions Assistant, Lyndon State College, 1001 College Road, PO Box 919, Lyndonville, VT 05851. *Phone:* 802-626-6413 or toll-free 800-225-1998. *Fax:* 802-626-6335. *E-mail:* admissions@lyndonstate.edu. *Web site:* http://www.lyndonstate.edu/.

Marlboro College
Marlboro, Vermont

General Independent, comprehensive, coed **Entrance** Moderately difficult **Setting** 350-acre rural campus **Total enrollment** 313 **Student-faculty ratio** 8:1 **Application deadline** 3/1 (freshmen), 4/1 (transfer) **Freshman admission** 71% were admitted. Average high school GPA 3.2 **Freshman test scores** SAT critical reading scores over 500: 96%; SAT math scores over 500: 77%; ACT scores over 18: 100%; SAT critical reading scores over 600: 72%; SAT math scores over 600: 43%; ACT scores over 24: 77% **Housing** Yes **Expenses** Tuition & Fees $33,660; Room & Board $9220 **Undergraduates** 48% women, 2% part-time, 1% 25 or older, 1% Native American, 4% Hispanic American, 1% African American, 4% Asian American/Pacific Islander **The most frequently chosen baccalaureate fields are** English, social sciences, visual and performing arts **Academic program** Advanced placement, accelerated degree program, self-designed majors, internships **Contact** Mr. Mark Crowther, Associate Director of Admission, Marlboro College, PO Box A, South Road, Marlboro, VT 05344-0300. *Phone:* toll-free 800-343-0049. *Fax:* 800-451-7555. *E-mail:* admissions@marlboro.edu. *Web site:* http://www.marlboro.edu/.

Visit Petersons.com and enter keyword Marlboro

See page 946 for the College Close-Up.

Middlebury College
Middlebury, Vermont

General Independent, comprehensive, coed **Entrance** Most difficult **Setting** 350-acre small-town campus **Total enrollment** 2,482 **Student-faculty ratio** 9:1 **Application deadline** 1/1 (freshmen), 3/1 (transfer) **Freshman admission** 20% were admitted **Freshman test scores** SAT critical reading scores over 500: 98%; SAT math scores over 500: 99%; ACT scores over 18: 100%; SAT critical reading scores over 600: 86%; SAT math scores over 600: 91%; ACT scores over 24: 98% **Housing** Yes **Expenses** Comprehensive Fee $50,780 **Undergraduates** 51% women, 1% part-time, 0.5% Native American, 5% Hispanic American, 4% African American, 9% Asian American/Pacific Islander **The most frequently chosen baccalaureate fields are** area and ethnic studies, foreign languages and literature, social sciences **Academic program** Advanced placement, accelerated degree program, self-designed majors, honors program, summer session, internships **Contact** Mr. Robert Clagett, Dean of Admissions, Middlebury College, Emma Willard House, Middlebury, VT 05753-6002. *Phone:* 802-443-3000. *Fax:* 802-443-2056. *E-mail:* admissions@middlebury.edu. *Web site:* http://www.middlebury.edu/.

New England Culinary Institute
Montpelier, Vermont

Contact Jan Knutsen, Vice President of Enrollment, New England Culinary Institute, 56 College Street, Montpelier, VT 05602-3115. *Phone:* toll-free 877-223-6324. *Fax:* 802-225-3280. *E-mail:* janknutsen@neci.edu. *Web site:* http://www.neci.edu/.

New England Culinary Institute at Essex
Essex Junction, Vermont

Contact Sherri Gilmore, Director of Admissions, New England Culinary Institute at Essex, 56 College Street, Montpelier, VT 05602. *Phone:* 802-223-6324. *Fax:* 802-225-3280. *E-mail:* sherrigilmore@neci.edu. *Web site:* http://www.neci.edu/.

Norwich University
Northfield, Vermont

Contact Ms. Shelby Wallace, Director of Admissions, Norwich University, 158 Harmon Drive, Northfield, VT 05663. *Phone:* 802-485-2658 or toll-free 800-468-6679. *E-mail:* nuadm@norwich.edu. *Web site:* http://www.norwich.edu/.

Visit Petersons.com and enter keyword Norwich

See page 1024 for the College Close-Up.

Saint Michael's College
Colchester, Vermont

General Independent Roman Catholic, comprehensive, coed **Entrance** Moderately difficult **Setting** 440-acre suburban campus **Total enrollment** 2,466 **Student-faculty ratio** 13:1 **Application deadline** 2/1 (freshmen), 3/15 (transfer) **Freshman admission** 81% were admitted. Average high school GPA 3.4 **Freshman test scores** SAT critical reading scores over 500: 84%; SAT math scores over 500: 84%; SAT critical reading scores over 600: 38%; SAT math scores over 600: 37% **Housing** Yes **Expenses** Tuition & Fees $34,845; Room & Board $8685 **Undergraduates** 52% women, 3% part-time, 1% 25 or older, 0.4% Native American, 2% Hispanic American, 1% African American, 1% Asian American/Pacific Islander **The most frequently chosen baccalaureate fields are** business/marketing, psychology, social sciences **Academic program** English as a second language, advanced placement, self-designed majors, honors program, summer session, internships **Contact** Ms. Jacqueline Murphy, Director of Admission, Saint Michael's College, One Winooski Park, Colchester, VT 05452. *Phone:* 802-654-3000 or toll-free 800-762-8000. *Fax:* 802-654-2906. *E-mail:* admission@smcvt.edu. *Web site:* http://www.smcvt.edu/.

Visit Petersons.com and enter keyword Michael's

See page 1128 for the College Close-Up.

Southern Vermont College
Bennington, Vermont

General Independent, 4-year, coed **Entrance** Minimally difficult **Setting** 371-acre small-town campus **Total enrollment** 486 **Student-faculty ratio** 17:1 **Application deadline** Rolling (freshmen), rolling (transfer) **Freshman admission** 85% were admitted. Average high school GPA 2.7 **Freshman test scores** SAT critical reading scores over 500: 31.87%; SAT math scores over 500: 18.69%; ACT scores over 18: 45.45%; SAT critical reading scores over 600: 8.79%; SAT math scores over 600: 4.4% **Housing** Yes **Undergraduates** 64% women, 12% part-time, 0.2% Native American, 2% Hispanic American, 6% African American, 2% Asian American/Pacific Islander **The most frequently chosen baccalaureate fields are** business/marketing, health professions and related sciences, science technologies **Academic program** Advanced placement, accelerated degree program, self-designed majors, honors program, summer session, adult/continuing education programs, internships **Contact** Mr. Grant Thatcher, Director of Admissions, Southern Vermont College, 982 Mansion Drive, Bennington, VT 05201. *Phone:* 802-447-6331 or toll-free 800-378-2782. *Fax:* 802-447-4695. *E-mail:* admis@svc.edu. *Web site:* http://www.svc.edu/.

Sterling College
Craftsbury Common, Vermont

General Independent, 4-year, coed **Entrance** Moderately difficult **Setting** 430-acre rural campus **Total enrollment** 108 **Application deadline** 2/15 (freshmen), rolling (transfer) **Freshman admission** 79% were admitted **Housing** Yes **Expenses** Tuition & Fees $23,621; Room & Board $7554 **Undergraduates** 46% women, 7% part-time, 11% 25 or older, 2% Hispanic American, 1% Asian American/Pacific Islander **The most frequently chosen baccalaureate fields are** biological/life sciences, agriculture, parks and recreation **Academic program** Advanced placement, self-designed majors, summer session, internships **Contact** Lynne A. Birdsall, Director of Admissions, Sterling College, PO Box 72, Craftsbury Common, VT 05827. *Phone:* 802-586-7711 Ext. 135 or toll-free 800-648-3591 Ext. 100. *Fax:* 802-586-2596. *E-mail:* lbirdsall@sterlingcollege.edu. *Web site:* http://www.sterlingcollege.edu/.

Visit Petersons.com and enter keyword Sterling

University of Vermont
Burlington, Vermont

General State-supported, university, coed **Entrance** Moderately difficult **Setting** 459-acre suburban campus **Total enrollment** 13,391 **Student-faculty ratio** 17:1 **Application deadline** 1/15 (freshmen), 4/15 (transfer) **Freshman admission** 71% were admitted **Freshman test scores** SAT critical reading scores over 500: 89%; SAT math scores over 500: 92%; ACT scores over 18: 99%; SAT critical reading scores over 600: 47%; SAT math scores over 600: 52%; ACT scores over 24: 77% **Housing** Yes **Expenses** Tuition & Fees: state resident $13,524, nonresident $31,380; Room & Board $9026 **Undergraduates** 56% women, 10% part-time, 3% 25 or older, 0.2% Native American, 2% Hispanic American, 1% African American, 2% Asian American/Pacific Islander **Academic program** English as a second language, advanced placement, self-designed majors, honors program, summer session, internships **Contact** Beth A. Wiser PhD, Director of Admissions, University of Vermont, Office of Admissions, 194 South Prospect Street, Burlington, VT 05401-3596. *Phone:* 802-656-3370. *Fax:* 802-656-8611. *E-mail:* admissions@uvm.edu. *Web site:* http://www.uvm.edu/.

Visit Petersons.com and enter keyword Vermont

Vermont Technical College

Randolph Center, Vermont

General State-supported, 4-year, coed **Entrance** Moderately difficult **Setting** 544-acre rural campus **Total enrollment** 1,663 **Student-faculty ratio** 10:1 **Application deadline** Rolling (freshmen), rolling (transfer) **Freshman admission** 63% were admitted. Average high school GPA 3 **Freshman test scores** SAT critical reading scores over 500: 42%; SAT math scores over 500: 47%; ACT scores over 18: 82%; SAT critical reading scores over 600: 9%; SAT math scores over 600: 8%; ACT scores over 24: 15% **Housing** Yes **Expenses** Tuition & Fees: state resident $10,892, nonresident $19,940; Room & Board $7808 **Undergraduates** 43% women, 24% part-time, 36% 25 or older, 0.4% Native American, 1% Hispanic American, 1% African American, 1% Asian American/Pacific Islander **The most frequently chosen baccalaureate fields are** business/marketing, computer and information sciences, engineering technologies **Academic program** English as a second language, advanced placement, accelerated degree program, honors program, summer session, internships **Contact** Mr. Dwight A. Cross, Assistant Dean of Enrollment, Vermont Technical College, PO Box 500, Randolph Center, VT 05061. *Phone:* 802-728-1244 or toll-free 800-442-VTC1. *Fax:* 802-728-1390. *E-mail:* admissions@vtc.edu. *Web site:* http://www.vtc.edu/.

Visit Petersons.com and enter keywords Vermont Technical

VIRGIN ISLANDS

University of the Virgin Islands

Saint Thomas, Virgin Islands

General Territory-supported, comprehensive, coed **Entrance** Minimally difficult **Setting** 518-acre small-town campus **Total enrollment** 2,602 **Student-faculty ratio** 16:1 **Application deadline** 4/30 (freshmen), 4/30 (transfer) **Freshman admission** 70% were admitted. Average high school GPA 2.68 **Freshman test scores** SAT critical reading scores over 500: 12%; SAT math scores over 500: 6%; ACT scores over 18: 32%; SAT critical reading scores over 600: 1%; SAT math scores over 600: 1%; ACT scores over 24: 4% **Housing** Yes **Expenses** Tuition & Fees: state resident $4150, nonresident $11,350; Room & Board $8570 **Undergraduates** 73% women, 37% part-time, 33% 25 or older, 0.1% Native American, 7% Hispanic American, 76% African American, 0.3% Asian American/Pacific Islander **The most frequently chosen baccalaureate fields are** biological/life sciences, business/marketing, psychology **Academic program** Advanced placement, summer session, adult/continuing education programs, internships **Contact** Dr. Judith Edwin, Vice Provost for Access and Enrollment Managment, University of the Virgin Islands, 2 John Brewers Bay, St. Thomas, VI 00802. *Phone:* 340-693-1152. *Fax:* 340-693-1167. *E-mail:* jedwin@uvi.edu. *Web site:* http://www.uvi.edu/.

VIRGINIA

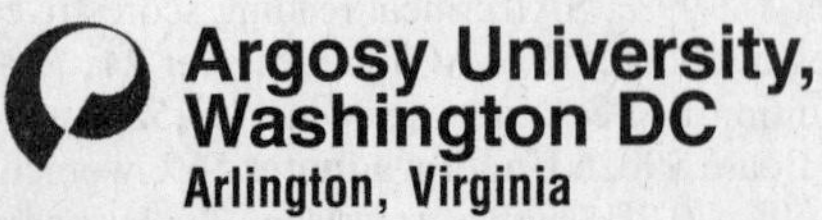

Argosy University, Washington DC

Arlington, Virginia

General Proprietary, university, coed **Setting** urban campus **Contact** Director of Admissions, Argosy University, Washington DC, 1550 Wilson Boulevard, Suite 600, Arlington, VA 22209. *Phone:* 703-526-5800 or toll-free 866-703-2777. *Fax:* 703-526-5850. *Web site:* http://www.argosy.edu/washingtondc/.

Visit Petersons.com and enter keywords Argosy University, Washington DC

See page 478 for the College Close-Up.

The Art Institute of Vriginia Beach

Virginia Beach, Virginia

General Proprietary, 4-year, coed **Contact** Director of Admissions, The Art Institute of Vriginia Beach, Two Columbus Center, 4500 Main Street, Suite 100, Virginia Beach, VA 23462. *Phone:* 757-493-6700 or toll-free 877-437-4428. *Fax:* 757-493-6800. *Web site:* http://www.artinstitutes.edu/virginia-beach/.

See page 552 for the College Close-Up.

The Art Institute of Washington

Arlington, Virginia

General Proprietary, 4-year, coed **Setting** urban campus **Contact** Director of Admissions, The Art Institute of Washington, 1820 North Fort Meyer Drive, Arlington, VA 22209. *Phone:* 703-358-9550 or toll-free 877-303-3771. *Fax:* 703-358-9759. *Web site:* http://www.artinstitutes.edu/arlington/.

Visit Petersons.com and enter keywords Art Institute of Washington

See page 554 for the College Close-Up.

The Art Institute of Washington–Northern Virginia

Sterling, Virginia

General Proprietary, 4-year, coed **Contact** Director of Admissions, The Art Institute of Washington–Northern Virginia, The Corporate Office Park at Dulles Town Center, 21000 Atlantic Boulevard, Suite 100, Sterling, VA 20166. *Phone:* 571-449-4400 or toll-free 888-627-5008. *Fax:* 571-449-4500. *Web site:* http://www.artinstitutes.edu/northern-virginia/.

See page 556 for the College Close-Up.

Averett University

Danville, Virginia

General Independent, comprehensive, coed, affiliated with Baptist General Association of Virginia **Entrance** Moderately difficult **Setting** 19-acre small-town campus **Total enrollment** 828 **Student-faculty ratio** 12:1 **Application deadline** 7/15 (freshmen), 8/15 (transfer) **Freshman admission** 91% were admitted. Average high school GPA 3.03 **Freshman test scores** SAT critical reading scores over 500: 33.5%; SAT math scores over 500: 36.5%; ACT scores over 18: 61.88%; SAT critical reading scores over 600: 6.5%; SAT math scores over 600: 6.5%; ACT scores over 24: 14.61% **Housing** Yes **Expenses** Tuition & Fees $22,112; Room & Board $7800 **Undergraduates** 48% women, 9% part-time, 11% 25 or older **The most frequently chosen baccalaureate fields are** business/marketing, education, parks and recreation **Academic program** Advanced placement, accelerated degree program, self-designed majors, honors program, summer session, internships **Contact** Mr. Joel Nester, Director of Admissions, Averett University, 420 West Main Street, Danville, VA 24541-3692. *Phone:* 434-791-5663 or toll-free 800-AVERETT. *Fax:* 434-797-2784. *E-mail:* joel.nester@averett.edu. *Web site:* http://www.averett.edu/.

Visit Petersons.com and enter keyword Averett

Bluefield College

Bluefield, Virginia

General Independent Southern Baptist, 4-year, coed **Entrance** Minimally difficult **Setting** 85-acre small-town campus **Total enrollment** 738 **Student-faculty ratio** 11:1 **Application deadline** Rolling (freshmen), rolling (transfer) **Freshman admission** 47% were admitted. Average high school GPA 3.1 **Freshman test scores** SAT critical reading scores over 500: 33%; SAT math scores over 500: 40%; ACT scores over 18:

62%; SAT critical reading scores over 600: 6%; SAT math scores over 600: 6%; ACT scores over 24: 10% **Housing** Yes **Expenses** Tuition & Fees $18,800; Room & Board $7350 **Undergraduates** 59% women, 13% part-time, 43% 25 or older, 0.3% Native American, 2% Hispanic American, 20% African American, 1% Asian American/Pacific Islander **The most frequently chosen baccalaureate fields are** business/marketing, psychology, security and protective services **Academic program** Advanced placement, accelerated degree program, honors program, summer session, adult/continuing education programs, internships **Contact** Mr. Mark Hipes, Bluefield College, 3000 College Drive, Bluefield, VA 24605-1799. *Phone:* 276-326-4340 or toll-free 800-872-0175. *Fax:* 276-326-4395. *E-mail:* mhipes@bluefield.edu. *Web site:* http://www.bluefield.edu/.

Bridgewater College
Bridgewater, Virginia

General Independent, 4-year, coed, affiliated with Church of the Brethren **Entrance** Moderately difficult **Setting** 300-acre small-town campus **Total enrollment** 1,590 **Student-faculty ratio** 14:1 **Application deadline** Rolling (freshmen), rolling (transfer) **Freshman admission** 86% were admitted. Average high school GPA 3.4 **Freshman test scores** SAT critical reading scores over 500: 50.8%; SAT math scores over 500: 57.4%; ACT scores over 18: 80.8%; SAT critical reading scores over 600: 12.9%; SAT math scores over 600: 12.7%; ACT scores over 24: 23.3% **Housing** Yes **Expenses** Tuition & Fees $25,500; Room & Board $10,350 **Undergraduates** 59% women, 1% part-time, 1% 25 or older, 0.3% Native American, 2% Hispanic American, 7% African American, 1% Asian American/Pacific Islander **The most frequently chosen baccalaureate fields are** biological/life sciences, business/marketing, social sciences **Academic program** Advanced placement, honors program, summer session, adult/continuing education programs, internships **Contact** Ms. Linda Stout, Director of Enrollment Operations, Bridgewater College, 402 East College Street, Bridgewater, VA 22812-1599. *Phone:* 540-828-5375 or toll-free 800-759-8328. *Fax:* 540-828-5481. *E-mail:* admissions@bridgewater.edu. *Web site:* http://www.bridgewater.edu/.

Bryant & Stratton College—Richmond Campus
Richmond, Virginia

General Proprietary, primarily 2-year, coed, primarily women **Entrance** Minimally difficult **Setting** suburban campus **Total enrollment** 572 **Student-faculty ratio** 10:1 **Application deadline** Rolling (freshmen), rolling (transfer) **Housing** No **Expenses** Tuition & Fees $14,430 **Undergraduates** 82% women, 51% part-time, 84% 25 or older, 0.2% Native American, 2% Hispanic American, 85% African American, 1% Asian American/Pacific Islander **The most frequently chosen baccalaureate field is** business/marketing **Academic program** Advanced placement, summer session, adult/continuing education programs, internships **Contact** Mr. David K. Mayle, Director of Admissions, Bryant & Stratton College—Richmond Campus, 8141 Hull Street Road, Richmond, VA 23235-6411. *Phone:* 804-745-2444. *Fax:* 804-745-6884. *E-mail:* tlawson@bryanstratton.edu. *Web site:* http://www.bryantstratton.edu/.

Bryant & Stratton College—Virginia Beach
Virginia Beach, Virginia

General Proprietary, primarily 2-year, coed, primarily women **Entrance** Minimally difficult **Setting** suburban campus **Total enrollment** 595 **Student-faculty ratio** 12:1 **Application deadline** Rolling (freshmen), rolling (transfer) **Freshman admission** 88% were admitted **Housing** No **Expenses** Tuition & Fees $14,670 **Undergraduates** 77% women, 55% part-time, 64% 25 or older, 1% Native American, 6% Hispanic American, 63% African American, 2% Asian American/Pacific Islander **The most frequently chosen baccalaureate field is** business/marketing **Academic program** Advanced placement, summer session, adult/continuing education programs, internships **Contact** Mrs. Deana M. Southerland, Director of Admissions, Bryant & Stratton College—Virginia Beach, 301 Centre Pointe Drive, Virginia Beach, VA 23462-4417. *Phone:* 757-499-7900 Ext. 173. *Fax:* 757-499-9977. *E-mail:* dmsoutherland@bryantstratton.edu. *Web site:* http://www.bryantstratton.edu/.

Christendom College
Front Royal, Virginia

General Independent Roman Catholic, comprehensive, coed **Entrance** Very difficult **Setting** 100-acre rural campus **Total enrollment** 450 **Student-faculty ratio** 14:1 **Application deadline** 3/1 (freshmen), 3/1 (transfer) **Freshman admission** 86% were admitted. Average high school GPA 3.6 **Freshman test scores** SAT critical reading scores over 500: 95%; SAT math scores over 500: 79%; SAT critical reading scores over 600: 63%; SAT math scores over 600: 45% **Housing** Yes **Expenses** Tuition & Fees $19,668; Room & Board $7506 **Undergraduates** 52% women, 1% part-time, 3% 25 or older **The most frequently chosen baccalaureate fields are** history, philosophy and religious studies, theology and religious vocations **Academic program** Advanced placement, accelerated degree program, summer session, internships **Contact** Mr. Tom McFadden, Director of Admissions, Christendom College, 134 Christendom Drive, Front Royal, VA 22630-5103. *Phone:* 540-636-2900 Ext. 290 or toll-free 800-877-5456 Ext. 290. *E-mail:* tmcfadden@christendom.edu. *Web site:* http://www.christendom.edu/.

Christopher Newport University
Newport News, Virginia

General State-supported, comprehensive, coed **Setting** 260-acre suburban campus **Total enrollment** 4,952 **Student-faculty ratio** 18:1 **Application deadline** 3/1 (freshmen), 3/1 (transfer) **Freshman admission** 60% were admitted. Average high school GPA 3.62 **Freshman test scores** SAT critical reading scores over 500: 96%; SAT math scores over 500: 95%; ACT scores over 18: 98%; SAT critical reading scores over 600: 55%; SAT math scores over 600: 49%; ACT scores over 24: 63% **Housing** Yes **Expenses** Tuition & Fees: state resident $11,720, nonresident $19,662; Room & Board $9240 **Undergraduates** 56% women, 3% part-time, 3% 25 or older, 1% Native American, 3% Hispanic American, 8% African American, 3% Asian American/Pacific Islander **The most frequently chosen baccalaureate fields are** business/marketing, biological/life sciences, social sciences **Academic program** Advanced placement, accelerated degree program, self-designed majors, honors program, summer session, internships **Contact** Mr. Curtis Davidson, Senior Associate Director of Admissions, Christopher Newport University, 1 University Place, Newport News, VA 23606-2998. *Phone:* 757-594-7015 or toll-free 800-333-4268. *Fax:* 757-594-7333. *E-mail:* admit@cnu.edu. *Web site:* http://www.cnu.edu/.

Visit Petersons.com and enter keyword Christopher

See page 706 for the College Close-Up.

The College of William and Mary
Williamsburg, Virginia

General State-supported, university, coed **Entrance** Most difficult **Setting** 1,200-acre small-town campus **Total enrollment** 7,874 **Student-faculty ratio** 11:1 **Application deadline** 1/1 (freshmen), 3/1 (transfer) **Freshman admission** 34% were admitted. Average high school GPA 4 **Freshman test scores** SAT critical reading scores over 500: 98%; SAT math scores over 500: 98.2%; ACT scores over 18: 100%; SAT critical reading scores over 600: 82.6%; SAT math scores over 600: 84.6%; ACT scores over 24: 93.8% **Housing** Yes **Expenses** Tuition & Fees: state resident $10,800, nonresident $30,592; Room & Board $8382 **Undergraduates** 54% women, 1% part-time, 2% 25 or older, 1% Native American, 7% Hispanic American, 7% African American, 8% Asian American/Pacific Islander **The most frequently chosen baccalaureate fields are** business/marketing, interdisciplinary studies, social sciences **Academic program**

The College of William and Mary (continued)
Advanced placement, accelerated degree program, self-designed majors, honors program, summer session, internships **Contact** Henry Broaddus, Dean of Admissions, The College of William and Mary, PO Box 8795, Williamsburg, VA 23187-8795. *Phone:* 757-221-4223. *Fax:* 757-221-1242. *E-mail:* admission@wm.edu. *Web site:* http://www.wm.edu/.

Culinary Institute of Virginia
Norfolk, Virginia

General Proprietary, 4-year, coed **Entrance** Minimally difficult **Setting** urban campus **Application deadline** Rolling (freshmen), rolling (transfer) **Housing** Yes **Academic program** Advanced placement, internships **Contact** Director of Admissions, Culinary Institute of Virginia, 2428 Almeda Avenue, Suite 316, Norfolk, VA 23513. *Phone:* 757-858-2433 or toll-free 866-619-CHEF. *Fax:* 757-213-5299. *E-mail:* hsadmissions@chefva.com. *Web site:* http://www.jwu.edu/.

DeVry University
Arlington, Virginia

General Proprietary, comprehensive, coed **Entrance** Minimally difficult **Total enrollment** 833 **Student-faculty ratio** 10:1 **Application deadline** Rolling (freshmen), rolling (transfer) **Housing** No **Expenses** Tuition & Fees $14,080 **Undergraduates** 27% women, 41% part-time, 51% 25 or older, 0.3% Native American, 12% Hispanic American, 51% African American, 4% Asian American/Pacific Islander **The most frequently chosen baccalaureate fields are** business/marketing, computer and information sciences, engineering technologies **Academic program** Advanced placement, accelerated degree program, summer session, adult/continuing education programs **Contact** Admissions Office, DeVry University, 2450 Crystal Drive, Arlington, VA 22202. *Web site:* http://www.devry.edu/.

DeVry University
Chesapeake, Virginia

Contact DeVry University, 1317 Executive Boulevard, Suite 100, Chesapeake, VA 23320-3671. *Web site:* http://www.devry.edu/.

DeVry University
Manassas, Virginia

Contact DeVry University, 10432 Balls Ford Road, Suite 130, Manassas, VA 20109-3173. *Web site:* http://www.devry.edu/.

Eastern Mennonite University
Harrisonburg, Virginia

General Independent Mennonite, comprehensive, coed **Entrance** Moderately difficult **Setting** 93-acre small-town campus **Total enrollment** 1,525 **Student-faculty ratio** 7:1 **Application deadline** Rolling (freshmen), rolling (transfer) **Freshman admission** 41% were admitted. Average high school GPA 3.5 **Freshman test scores** SAT math scores over 500: 64.07%; ACT scores over 18: 92.65%; SAT math scores over 600: 31.73%; ACT scores over 24: 60.3% **Housing** Yes **Expenses** Tuition & Fees $24,120; Room & Board $7650 **Undergraduates** 63% women, 21% part-time, 21% 25 or older, 0.5% Native American, 4% Hispanic American, 7% African American, 1% Asian American/Pacific Islander **The most frequently chosen baccalaureate fields are** business/marketing, education, health professions and related sciences **Academic program** English as a second language, advanced placement, honors program, summer session, adult/continuing education programs, internships **Contact** Mrs. Stephanie C. Shafer, Director of Admissions, Eastern Mennonite University, 1200 Park Road, Harrisonburg, VA 22802-2462. *Phone:* 540-432-4118 or toll-free 800-368-2665. *Fax:* 540-432-4444. *E-mail:* admiss@emu.edu. *Web site:* http://www.emu.edu/.

ECPI College of Technology
Virginia Beach, Virginia

General Proprietary, 4-year, coed **Entrance** Moderately difficult **Setting** 8-acre suburban campus **Total enrollment** 12,669 **Student-faculty ratio** 16:1 **Freshman admission** 80% were admitted **Housing** Yes **Undergraduates** 61% women, 47% 25 or older, 0.5% Native American, 5% Hispanic American, 42% African American, 3% Asian American/Pacific Islander **Academic program** Advanced placement, accelerated degree program, honors program, summer session, adult/continuing education programs, internships **Contact** Mr. Ronald Ballance, Vice President, ECPI College of Technology, 5555 Greenwich Road, Suite 100, Virginia Beach, VA 23462. *Phone:* 757-671-7171 or toll-free 800-986-1200. *Fax:* 757-671-8661. *E-mail:* rballance@ecpi.edu. *Web site:* http://www.ecpi.edu/.

ECPI Technical College
Richmond, Virginia

Contact Director, ECPI Technical College, 800 Moorefield Park Drive, Richmond, VA 23236. *Phone:* 804-330-5533 or toll-free 800-986-1200. *Fax:* 804-330-5577. *E-mail:* agerard@ecpi.edu. *Web site:* http://www.ecpitech.edu/.

ECPI Technical College
Roanoke, Virginia

General Proprietary, 4-year, coed **Entrance** Moderately difficult **Setting** 3-acre suburban campus **Total enrollment** 461 **Student-faculty ratio** 13:1 **Application deadline** Rolling (freshmen), rolling (transfer) **Freshman admission** 80% were admitted **Housing** No **Undergraduates** 62% women, 48% 25 or older, 2% Hispanic American, 30% African American, 0.4% Asian American/Pacific Islander **Academic program** Advanced placement, accelerated degree program, honors program, summer session, adult/continuing education programs, internships **Contact** Dr. Walter Merchant, Campus Provost—Interim, ECPI Technical College, 5234 Airport Road, Roanoke, VA 24012. *Phone:* 540-563-8080 or toll-free 800-986-1200. *Fax:* 540-362-5400. *E-mail:* wmerchant@ecpi.edu. *Web site:* http://www.ecpi.net/.

Emory & Henry College
Emory, Virginia

General Independent United Methodist, comprehensive, coed **Entrance** Moderately difficult **Setting** 331-acre rural campus **Total enrollment** 1,002 **Student-faculty ratio** 10:1 **Application deadline** Rolling (freshmen), rolling (transfer) **Freshman admission** 70% were admitted. Average high school GPA 3.43 **Freshman test scores** SAT critical reading scores over 500: 58.14%; SAT math scores over 500: 63.26%; ACT scores over 18: 82%; SAT critical reading scores over 600: 17.68%; SAT math scores over 600: 16.28%; ACT scores over 24: 33% **Housing** Yes **Expenses** Tuition & Fees $24,880; Room & Board $8300 **Undergraduates** 48% women, 8% part-time, 1% Native American, 1% Hispanic American, 8% African American, 0.4% Asian American/Pacific Islander **The most frequently chosen baccalaureate fields are** business/marketing, biological/life sciences, social sciences **Academic program** Advanced placement, self-designed majors, honors program, summer session, internships **Contact** Mr. David Hawsey, Vice President of Enrollment Management, Emory & Henry College, PO Box 947, Emory, VA 24327-0947. *Phone:* 276-944-6133 or toll-free 800-848-5493. *E-mail:* ehadmiss@ehc.edu. *Web site:* http://www.ehc.edu/.
Visit Petersons.com and enter keyword Emory

See page 784 for the College Close-Up.

Ferrum College
Ferrum, Virginia

General Independent United Methodist, 4-year, coed **Entrance** Minimally difficult **Setting** 720-acre rural campus **Total enrollment** 1,426

Student-faculty ratio 16:1 **Application deadline** Rolling (freshmen) **Freshman admission** 80% were admitted. Average high school GPA 2.8 **Freshman test scores** SAT critical reading scores over 500: 27%; SAT math scores over 500: 25%; SAT critical reading scores over 600: 6%; SAT math scores over 600: 3% **Housing** Yes **Expenses** Tuition & Fees $23,565; Room & Board $7630 **Undergraduates** 49% women, 3% part-time, 1% Native American, 3% Hispanic American, 31% African American, 1% Asian American/Pacific Islander **The most frequently chosen baccalaureate fields are** business/marketing, health professions and related sciences, liberal arts/general studies **Academic program** Advanced placement, self-designed majors, honors program, summer session, adult/continuing education programs, internships **Contact** Ms. Gilda Q. Woods, Director of Admissions, Ferrum College, Spilman-Daniel House, PO Box 1000, Ferrum, VA 24088-9001. *Phone:* 540-365-4290 or toll-free 800-868-9797. *Fax:* 540-365-4266. *E-mail:* admissions@ferrum.edu. *Web site:* http://www.ferrum.edu/.

George Mason University
Fairfax, Virginia

General State-supported, university, coed **Entrance** Moderately difficult **Setting** 806-acre suburban campus **Total enrollment** 32,067 **Student-faculty ratio** 16:1 **Application deadline** 1/15 (freshmen), 4/1 (transfer) **Freshman admission** 63% were admitted. Average high school GPA 3.55 **Freshman test scores** SAT critical reading scores over 500: 85%; SAT math scores over 500: 88%; ACT scores over 18: 100%; SAT critical reading scores over 600: 33%; SAT math scores over 600: 39%; ACT scores over 24: 67% **Housing** Yes **Expenses** Tuition & Fees: state resident $8024, nonresident $24,008; Room & Board $7700 **Undergraduates** 53% women, 23% part-time, 23% 25 or older, 0.2% Native American, 9% Hispanic American, 8% African American, 16% Asian American/Pacific Islander **The most frequently chosen baccalaureate fields are** business/marketing, English, social sciences **Academic program** English as a second language, advanced placement, accelerated degree program, self-designed majors, honors program, summer session, adult/continuing education programs, internships **Contact** Mr. Eddie Tallent, Assistant Dean, Executive Director of Undergraduate Admissions, George Mason University, 4400 University Drive, Fairfax, VA 22030. *Phone:* 703-993-2398. *E-mail:* etallent@gmu.edu. *Web site:* http://www.gmu.edu/.

Hampden-Sydney College
Hampden-Sydney, Virginia

General Independent, 4-year, men only, affiliated with Presbyterian Church (U.S.A.) **Entrance** Moderately difficult **Setting** 1,340-acre rural campus **Total enrollment** 1,068 **Student-faculty ratio** 9:1 **Application deadline** 3/1 (freshmen), 7/1 (transfer) **Freshman admission** 56% were admitted. Average high school GPA 3.2 **Freshman test scores** SAT critical reading scores over 500: 77.28%; SAT math scores over 500: 78.64%; SAT critical reading scores over 600: 28.81%; SAT math scores over 600: 29.83% **Housing** Yes **Expenses** Tuition & Fees $32,364; Room & Board $10,126 **Undergraduates** 1% 25 or older, 0.3% Native American, 1% Hispanic American, 5% African American, 1% Asian American/Pacific Islander **The most frequently chosen baccalaureate fields are** history, business/marketing, social sciences **Academic program** Advanced placement, accelerated degree program, honors program, summer session, internships **Contact** Ms. Anita Garland, Dean of Admissions, Hampden-Sydney College, PO Box 667, Hampden-Sydney, VA 23943-0667. *Phone:* 434-223-6120 or toll-free 800-755-0733. *Fax:* 434-223-6346. *E-mail:* hsapp@hsc.edu. *Web site:* http://www.hsc.edu/.

Hampton University
Hampton, Virginia

General Independent, comprehensive, coed **Entrance** Moderately difficult **Setting** 210-acre urban campus **Total enrollment** 5,401 **Student-faculty ratio** 13:1 **Application deadline** 3/1 (freshmen) **Freshman admission** 56% were admitted. Average high school GPA 3.3 **Freshman test scores** SAT critical reading scores over 500: 86.1%; SAT math scores over 500: 82.1%; ACT scores over 18: 77%; SAT critical reading scores over 600: 17.3%; SAT math scores over 600: 40.2%; ACT scores over 24: 22% **Housing** Yes **Expenses** Tuition & Fees $17,212; Room & Board $7664 **Undergraduates** 64% women, 7% part-time, 9% 25 or older, 0.3% Native American, 1% Hispanic American, 95% African American, 1% Asian American/Pacific Islander **The most frequently chosen baccalaureate fields are** business/marketing, health professions and related sciences, psychology **Academic program** Advanced placement, accelerated degree program, honors program, summer session, adult/continuing education programs, internships **Contact** Ms. Patra Johnson, Director, Freshman Studies, Hampton University, 200 Student Center, Hampton University, Hampton, VA 23668. *Phone:* 757-727-5901 or toll-free 800-624-3328. *Fax:* 757-727-5095. *E-mail:* patra.johnson@hamptonu.edu. *Web site:* http://www.hamptonu.edu/.

Hollins University
Roanoke, Virginia

General Independent, comprehensive, undergraduate: women only; graduate: coed **Entrance** Moderately difficult **Setting** 475-acre suburban campus **Total enrollment** 1,057 **Student-faculty ratio** 11:1 **Application deadline** Rolling (freshmen) **Freshman admission** 90% were admitted. Average high school GPA 3.5 **Freshman test scores** SAT critical reading scores over 500: 80.4%; SAT math scores over 500: 57.5%; ACT scores over 18: 100%; SAT critical reading scores over 600: 43.8%; SAT math scores over 600: 21.5%; ACT scores over 24: 64.3% **Housing** Yes **Expenses** Tuition & Fees $28,115; Room & Board $10,040 **Undergraduates** 4% part-time, 12% 25 or older, 1% Native American, 4% Hispanic American, 8% African American, 2% Asian American/Pacific Islander **The most frequently chosen baccalaureate fields are** English, social sciences, visual and performing arts **Academic program** Advanced placement, accelerated degree program, self-designed majors, adult/continuing education programs, internships **Contact** Ms. Rebecca Eckstein, Dean of Admissions, Hollins University, PO Box 9707, Roanoke, VA 24020-1707. *Phone:* 540-362-6401 or toll-free 800-456-9595. *Fax:* 540-362-6218. *E-mail:* huadm@hollins.edu. *Web site:* http://www.hollins.edu/.

Visit Petersons.com and enter keyword Hollins

See page 856 for the College Close-Up.

ITT Technical Institute
Chantilly, Virginia

General Proprietary, primarily 2-year, coed **Entrance** Minimally difficult **Housing** No **Contact** Director of Recruitment, ITT Technical Institute, 14420 Abermarle Point Place, Chantilly, VA 20151. *Phone:* 703-263-2541 or toll-free 888-895-8324. *Web site:* http://www.itt-tech.edu/.

ITT Technical Institute
Norfolk, Virginia

General Proprietary, primarily 2-year, coed **Entrance** Minimally difficult **Setting** suburban campus **Housing** No **Contact** Director of Recruitment, ITT Technical Institute, 863 Glenrock Road, Suite 100, Norfolk, VA 23502-3701. *Phone:* 757-466-1260 or toll-free 888-253-8324. *Web site:* http://www.itt-tech.edu/.

ITT Technical Institute
Richmond, Virginia

General Proprietary, primarily 2-year, coed **Entrance** Minimally difficult **Housing** No **Contact** Director of Recruitment, ITT Technical Institute, 300 Gateway Centre Parkway, Richmond, VA 23235. *Phone:* 804-330-4992 or toll-free 888-330-4888. *Web site:* http://www.itt-tech.edu/.

ITT Technical Institute
Salem, Virginia

General Proprietary, primarily 2-year, coed **Contact** Director of Recruitment, ITT Technical Institute, 2159 Apperson Drive, Salem, VA 24153. *Phone:* 540-989-2500 or toll-free 877-208-6132. *Web site:* http://www.itt-tech.edu/.

ITT Technical Institute
Springfield, Virginia

General Proprietary, primarily 2-year, coed **Entrance** Minimally difficult **Housing** No **Contact** Director of Recruitment, ITT Technical Institute, 7300 Boston Boulevard, Springfield, VA 22153. *Phone:* 703-440-9535 or toll-free 866-817-8324. *Web site:* http://www.itt-tech.edu/.

James Madison University
Harrisonburg, Virginia

General State-supported, comprehensive, coed **Entrance** Very difficult **Setting** 712-acre small-town campus **Total enrollment** 18,971 **Student-faculty ratio** 16:1 **Application deadline** 1/15 (freshmen), 3/1 (transfer) **Freshman admission** 61% were admitted. Average high school GPA 3.8 **Freshman test scores** SAT critical reading scores over 500: 81.8%; SAT math scores over 500: 85.9%; ACT scores over 18: 98%; SAT critical reading scores over 600: 26.8%; SAT math scores over 600: 35.4%; ACT scores over 24: 62% **Housing** Yes **Expenses** Tuition & Fees: state resident $7244, nonresident $19,376; Room & Board $7690 **Undergraduates** 60% women, 5% part-time, 2% 25 or older, 0.3% Native American, 3% Hispanic American, 4% African American, 5% Asian American/Pacific Islander **The most frequently chosen baccalaureate fields are** business/marketing, communications/journalism, health professions and related sciences **Academic program** English as a second language, advanced placement, accelerated degree program, honors program, summer session, adult/continuing education programs, internships **Contact** Mr. Michael D. Walsh, Director of Admissions, James Madison University, 800 South Main Street, Harrisonburg, VA 22807. *Phone:* 540-568-5681. *Fax:* 540-568-3332. *E-mail:* admissions@jmu.edu. *Web site:* http://www.jmu.edu/.

Jefferson College of Health Sciences
Roanoke, Virginia

General Independent, comprehensive, coed **Entrance** Moderately difficult **Setting** 1-acre urban campus **Total enrollment** 1,041 **Student-faculty ratio** 10:1 **Application deadline** Rolling (freshmen) **Freshman admission** 44% were admitted. Average high school GPA 3.3 **Freshman test scores** SAT critical reading scores over 500: 41%; SAT math scores over 500: 35%; ACT scores over 18: 58%; SAT critical reading scores over 600: 3%; SAT math scores over 600: 2%; ACT scores over 24: 5% **Housing** Yes **Expenses** Tuition & Fees $17,740; Room & Board $7010 **Undergraduates** 85% women, 30% part-time, 49% 25 or older, 0.1% Native American, 1% Hispanic American, 11% African American, 1% Asian American/Pacific Islander **The most frequently chosen baccalaureate fields are** biological/life sciences, health professions and related sciences **Academic program** English as a second language, advanced placement, accelerated degree program, summer session, adult/continuing education programs, internships **Contact** Ms. Judith McKeon, Director of Admissions, Jefferson College of Health Sciences, PO Box 13186, Roanoke, VA 24031-3186. *Phone:* 540-985-9083 or toll-free 888-985-8483. *E-mail:* cijom1@jchs.edu. *Web site:* http://www.jchs.edu/.

Liberty University
Lynchburg, Virginia

General Independent nondenominational, comprehensive, coed **Entrance** Minimally difficult **Setting** 4,400-acre suburban campus **Total enrollment** 46,126 **Student-faculty ratio** 45:1 **Application deadline** 6/30 (freshmen) **Freshman admission** 20% were admitted. Average high school GPA 3.23 **Freshman test scores** SAT critical reading scores over 500: 53.45%; SAT math scores over 500: 47.15%; ACT scores over 18: 82.78%; SAT critical reading scores over 600: 16.97%; SAT math scores over 600: 13.97%; ACT scores over 24: 30.39% **Housing** Yes **Expenses** Tuition & Fees $17,202; Room & Board $5996 **Undergraduates** 54% women, 35% part-time, 41% 25 or older, 0.5% Native American, 3% Hispanic American, 14% African American, 1% Asian American/Pacific Islander **The most frequently chosen baccalaureate fields are** interdisciplinary studies, business/marketing, philosophy and religious studies **Academic program** English as a second language, advanced placement, accelerated degree program, self-designed majors, honors program, summer session, internships **Contact** Mr. Tim Rees, Director of Admissions, Liberty University, 1971 University Boulevard, Lynchburg, VA 24502. *Phone:* 434-592-3054 or toll-free 800-543-5317. *Fax:* 800-542-2311. *E-mail:* admissions@liberty.edu. *Web site:* http://www.liberty.edu/.

Visit Petersons.com and enter keyword Liberty

Longwood University
Farmville, Virginia

General State-supported, comprehensive, coed **Entrance** Moderately difficult **Setting** 160-acre small-town campus **Total enrollment** 4,832 **Student-faculty ratio** 18:1 **Application deadline** 3/1 (freshmen), 3/1 (transfer) **Freshman admission** 69% were admitted. Average high school GPA 3.36 **Freshman test scores** SAT critical reading scores over 500: 66.97%; SAT math scores over 500: 62.3%; ACT scores over 18: 99.24%; SAT critical reading scores over 600: 13.89%; SAT math scores over 600: 11.27%; ACT scores over 24: 27.27% **Housing** Yes **Expenses** Tuition & Fees: state resident $8925, nonresident $17,835; Room & Board $7596 **Undergraduates** 65% women, 5% part-time, 2% 25 or older, 1% Native American, 2% Hispanic American, 6% African American, 1% Asian American/Pacific Islander **The most frequently chosen baccalaureate fields are** business/marketing, liberal arts/general studies, social sciences **Academic program** Advanced placement, accelerated degree program, honors program, summer session, internships **Contact** Mr. Robert J. Chonko, Dean of Admissions, Longwood University, 201 High Street, Farmville, VA 23909. *Phone:* 434-395-2060 or toll-free 800-281-4677. *Fax:* 434-395-2332. *E-mail:* admissions@longwood.edu. *Web site:* http://www.longwood.edu/.

Lynchburg College
Lynchburg, Virginia

General Independent, comprehensive, coed, affiliated with Christian Church (Disciples of Christ) **Entrance** Moderately difficult **Setting** 214-acre suburban campus **Total enrollment** 2,589 **Student-faculty ratio** 12:1 **Application deadline** Rolling (freshmen), rolling (transfer) **Freshman admission** 66% were admitted. Average high school GPA 3.16 **Freshman test scores** SAT critical reading scores over 500: 59%; SAT math scores over 500: 54%; ACT scores over 18: 84%; SAT critical reading scores over 600: 15%; SAT math scores over 600: 16%; ACT scores over 24: 28% **Housing** Yes **Expenses** Tuition & Fees $28,925; Room & Board $6970 **Undergraduates** 60% women, 4% part-time, 6% 25 or older, 1% Native American, 2% Hispanic American, 8% African American, 1% Asian American/Pacific Islander **The most frequently chosen baccalaureate fields are** education, communications/journalism, health professions and related sciences **Academic program** Advanced placement, accelerated degree program, honors program, summer session, adult/continuing education programs, internships **Contact** Ms. Sharon Walters-Bower, Director of Admissions, Lynchburg College, 1501 Lakeside Drive, Lynchburg, VA 24501-3199. *Phone:* 434-544-8300 or toll-free 800-426-8101. *Fax:* 434-544-8653. *E-mail:* admissions@lynchburg.edu. *Web site:* http://www.lynchburg.edu/.

Visit Petersons.com and enter keyword Lynchburg

See page 932 for the College Close-Up.

Mary Baldwin College
Staunton, Virginia

General Independent, comprehensive, coed, primarily women **Entrance** Moderately difficult **Setting** 54-acre small-town campus **Total enrollment** 1,783 **Student-faculty ratio** 10:1 **Application deadline** Rolling (freshmen), rolling (transfer) **Freshman admission** 62% were admitted. Average high school GPA 3.19 **Freshman test scores** SAT critical reading scores over 500: 56%; SAT math scores over 500: 49%; ACT scores over 18: 77%; SAT critical reading scores over 600: 25%; SAT math scores over 600: 13%; ACT scores over 24: 22% **Housing** Yes **Expenses** Tuition & Fees $24,585; Room & Board $7070 **Undergraduates** 91% women, 30% part-time, 2% 25 or older, 0.5% Native American, 4% Hispanic American, 17% African American, 2% Asian American/Pacific Islander **The most frequently chosen baccalaureate fields are** history, social sciences, visual and performing arts **Academic program** English as a second language, advanced placement, accelerated degree program, self-designed majors, honors program, adult/continuing education programs, internships **Contact** Ms. Roberta Palmer, Director of Admissions, Mary Baldwin College, Frederick and New Streets, Staunton, VA 24401. *Phone:* 540-887-7260 or toll-free 800-468-2262. *Fax:* 540-887-7229. *E-mail:* rpalmer@mbc.edu. *Web site:* http://www.mbc.edu/.

Marymount University
Arlington, Virginia

General Independent, comprehensive, coed, affiliated with Roman Catholic Church **Entrance** Moderately difficult **Setting** 21-acre suburban campus **Total enrollment** 3,480 **Student-faculty ratio** 14:1 **Application deadline** Rolling (freshmen), rolling (transfer) **Freshman admission** 83% were admitted. Average high school GPA 3.06 **Freshman test scores** SAT critical reading scores over 500: 44%; SAT math scores over 500: 40%; ACT scores over 18: 81%; SAT critical reading scores over 600: 14%; SAT math scores over 600: 12%; ACT scores over 24: 18% **Housing** Yes **Expenses** Tuition & Fees $22,620; Room & Board $9745 **Undergraduates** 72% women, 15% part-time, 20% 25 or older, 0.2% Native American, 13% Hispanic American, 15% African American, 8% Asian American/Pacific Islander **The most frequently chosen baccalaureate fields are** business/marketing, health professions and related sciences, visual and performing arts **Academic program** English as a second language, advanced placement, accelerated degree program, self-designed majors, honors program, summer session, internships **Contact** Mr. Mike Canfield, Director of Undergraduate Admissions, Marymount University, 2807 North Glebe Road, Arlington, VA 22207-4299. *Phone:* 703-284-1500 or toll-free 800-548-7638. *Fax:* 703-522-0349. *E-mail:* admissions@marymount.edu. *Web site:* http://www.marymount.edu/.

Visit Petersons.com and enter keywords Marymount University

National College
Danville, Virginia

Contact Admissions Office, National College, 734 Main Street, Danville, VA 24541-1819. *Phone:* 434-793-6822 or toll-free 800-664-1886. *Web site:* http://www.national-college.edu/.

National College
Harrisonburg, Virginia

Contact Jack Evey, Campus Director, National College, 51 B Burgess Road, Harrisonburg, VA 22801-9709. *Phone:* 540-432-0943 or toll-free 800-664-1886. *Web site:* http://www.national-college.edu/.

National College
Lynchburg, Virginia

Contact Admissions Representative, National College, 104 Candlewood Court, Lynchburg, VA 24502-2653. *Phone:* 804-239-3500 or toll-free 800-664-1886. *Web site:* http://www.national-college.edu/.

National College
Salem, Virginia

Contact Director of Admissions, National College, 1813 East Main Street, Salem, VA 24153. *Phone:* 540-986-1800 or toll-free 800-664-1886. *Fax:* 540-444-4198. *Web site:* http://www.national-college.edu/.

Norfolk State University
Norfolk, Virginia

General State-supported, comprehensive, coed **Setting** 134-acre urban campus **Total enrollment** 6,993 **Application deadline** Rolling (transfer) **Freshman admission** 68% were admitted. Average high school GPA 2.73 **Freshman test scores** SAT critical reading scores over 500: 17.6%; SAT math scores over 500: 17.4%; SAT critical reading scores over 600: 1.9%; SAT math scores over 600: 1.3% **Housing** Yes **Expenses** Tuition & Fees: state resident $5138, nonresident $16,897 **Undergraduates** 63% women, 16% part-time, 59% 25 or older, 0.2% Native American, 1% Hispanic American, 88% African American, 1% Asian American/Pacific Islander **Academic program** English as a second language, advanced placement, honors program **Contact** Mr. Kevin M. Holmes, Director of Recruitment and Admissions, Norfolk State University, 700 Park Avenue, Norfolk, VA 23504. *Phone:* 757-823-9222. *Fax:* 757-823-2078. *E-mail:* admissions@nsu.edu. *Web site:* http://www.nsu.edu/.

Old Dominion University
Norfolk, Virginia

General State-supported, university, coed **Entrance** Moderately difficult **Setting** 188-acre urban campus **Total enrollment** 24,013 **Student-faculty ratio** 18:1 **Application deadline** 2/1 (freshmen), 5/1 (transfer) **Freshman admission** 72% were admitted. Average high school GPA 3.29 **Freshman test scores** SAT critical reading scores over 500: 65%; SAT math scores over 500: 68%; ACT scores over 18: 86%; SAT critical reading scores over 600: 17%; SAT math scores over 600: 20%; ACT scores over 24: 20% **Housing** Yes **Expenses** Tuition & Fees: state resident $7318, nonresident $19,768; Room & Board $7868 **Undergraduates** 55% women, 25% part-time, 26% 25 or older, 1% Native American, 4% Hispanic American, 24% African American, 5% Asian American/Pacific Islander **The most frequently chosen baccalaureate fields are** business/marketing, health professions and related sciences, social sciences **Academic program** English as a second language, advanced placement, accelerated degree program, self-designed majors, honors program, summer session, adult/continuing education programs, internships **Contact** Ms. Barbara Boyce, Administrative Assistant to the Director of Admissions, Old Dominion University, 108 Rollins Hall, 5215 Hampton Boulevard, Norfolk, VA 23529. *Phone:* 757-683-3648 or toll-free 800-348-7926. *Fax:* 757-683-3255. *E-mail:* admit@odu.edu. *Web site:* http://www.odu.edu/.

Patrick Henry College
Purcellville, Virginia

General Independent nondenominational, 4-year, coed **Entrance** Very difficult **Setting** 106-acre small-town campus **Total enrollment** 404 **Student-faculty ratio** 11:1 **Application deadline** 6/15 (freshmen) **Freshman admission** Average high school GPA 3.73 **Freshman test scores** SAT critical reading scores over 500: 100%; SAT math scores over 500: 90%; ACT scores over 18: 100%; SAT critical reading scores over 600: 90%; SAT math scores over 600: 54%; ACT scores over 24: 93% **Housing** Yes **Expenses** Tuition & Fees $21,770; Room & Board $8530 **Undergraduates** 48% women, 25% part-time **Academic program** Internships **Contact** Director of Admissions, Patrick Henry College, Ten Patrick Henry Circle, Purcellville, VA 20132. *Phone:* 540-338-1776. *Fax:* 540-338-9808. *E-mail:* admissions@phc.edu. *Web site:* http://www.phc.edu/.

Potomac College
Herndon, Virginia

Contact Admissions Office, Potomac College, 1029 Herndon Parkway, Herndon, VA 20170. *Phone:* 703-709-5875. *Fax:* 703-709-8972. *E-mail:* admissions@potomac.edu. *Web site:* http://www.potomac.edu/.

Radford University
Radford, Virginia

General State-supported, comprehensive, coed **Entrance** Moderately difficult **Setting** 191-acre small-town campus **Total enrollment** 8,878 **Student-faculty ratio** 19:1 **Application deadline** 2/1 (freshmen), 6/1 (transfer) **Freshman admission** 71% were admitted. Average high school GPA 3.19 **Freshman test scores** SAT critical reading scores over 500: 55%; SAT math scores over 500: 56%; ACT scores over 18: 98%; SAT critical reading scores over 600: 12%; SAT math scores over 600: 12%; ACT scores over 24: 19% **Housing** Yes **Expenses** Tuition & Fees: state resident $6904, nonresident $16,568; Room & Board $6970 **Undergraduates** 57% women, 4% part-time, 6% 25 or older, 0.4% Native American, 3% Hispanic American, 6% African American, 2% Asian American/Pacific Islander **The most frequently chosen baccalaureate fields are** business/marketing, communications/journalism, interdisciplinary studies **Academic program** Advanced placement, accelerated degree program, self-designed majors, honors program, summer session, internships **Contact** Dr. Steven Nape, Radford University, PO Box 6903, Radford, VA 24142. *Phone:* 540-831-5460 or toll-free 800-890-4265. *Fax:* 540-831-5142. *E-mail:* ruadmiss@radford.edu. *Web site:* http://www.radford.edu/.
Visit Petersons.com and enter keywords Radford University

Randolph College
Lynchburg, Virginia

General Independent Methodist, comprehensive, coed **Entrance** Moderately difficult **Setting** 100-acre suburban campus **Total enrollment** 574 **Student-faculty ratio** 8:1 **Application deadline** 4/1 (freshmen), 7/1 (transfer) **Freshman admission** 81% were admitted. Average high school GPA 3.4 **Freshman test scores** SAT critical reading scores over 500: 76%; SAT math scores over 500: 77%; ACT scores over 18: 91%; SAT critical reading scores over 600: 34%; SAT math scores over 600: 27%; ACT scores over 24: 50% **Housing** Yes **Expenses** Tuition & Fees $29,254; Room & Board $9995 **Undergraduates** 82% women, 2% part-time, 6% 25 or older, 1% Native American, 7% Hispanic American, 9% African American, 3% Asian American/Pacific Islander **The most frequently chosen baccalaureate fields are** social sciences, biological/life sciences, visual and performing arts **Academic program** Advanced placement, accelerated degree program, self-designed majors, honors program, adult/continuing education programs, internships **Contact** Ms. Margaret Blount, Director of Recruitment, Randolph College, 2500 Rivermont Avenue, Lynchburg, VA 24503-1555. *Phone:* 434-947-8100 or toll-free 800-745-7692. *Fax:* 434-947-8996. *E-mail:* admissions@randolphcollege.edu. *Web site:* http://www.randolphcollege.edu/.
Visit Petersons.com and enter keyword Randolph

Randolph-Macon College
Ashland, Virginia

General Independent United Methodist, 4-year, coed **Entrance** Moderately difficult **Setting** 120-acre suburban campus **Total enrollment** 1,246 **Student-faculty ratio** 11:1 **Application deadline** 3/1 (freshmen), 4/1 (transfer) **Freshman admission** 58% were admitted. Average high school GPA 3.3 **Freshman test scores** SAT critical reading scores over 500: 73%; SAT critical reading scores over 600: 20% **Housing** Yes **Expenses** Tuition & Fees $29,182; Room & Board $8891 **Undergraduates** 53% women, 2% part-time, 2% 25 or older, 1% Native American, 2% Hispanic American, 11% African American, 2% Asian American/Pacific Islander **The most frequently chosen baccalaureate fields are** history, business/marketing, social sciences **Academic program** Advanced placement, accelerated degree program, honors program, summer session, internships **Contact** Anthony Ambrogi, Director of Admissions and Enrollment Research, Randolph-Macon College, PO Box 5005, Ashland, VA 23005-5505. *Phone:* 804-752-7305 or toll-free 800-888-1762. *Fax:* 804-752-4707. *E-mail:* admissions@rmc.edu. *Web site:* http://www.rmc.edu/.
Visit Petersons.com and enter keywords Randolph-Macon College

Regent University
Virginia Beach, Virginia

General Independent, comprehensive, coed **Entrance** Minimally difficult **Setting** 70-acre suburban campus **Total enrollment** 4,886 **Student-faculty ratio** 16:1 **Application deadline** 8/1 (freshmen), 8/1 (transfer) **Freshman admission** 64% were admitted. Average high school GPA 3 **Freshman test scores** SAT critical reading scores over 500: 67%; SAT math scores over 500: 46%; ACT scores over 18: 72%; SAT critical reading scores over 600: 27%; SAT math scores over 600: 18%; ACT scores over 24: 10% **Housing** Yes **Expenses** Tuition & Fees $14,200; Room only $5175 **Undergraduates** 66% women, 45% part-time, 63% 25 or older, 1% Native American, 6% Hispanic American, 26% African American, 2% Asian American/Pacific Islander **The most frequently chosen baccalaureate fields are** business/marketing, communications/journalism, psychology **Academic program** Advanced placement, summer session, adult/continuing education programs, internships **Contact** Mr. Ken Baker, Director of Admissions, Regent University, 1000 Regent University Drive, SC 218, Virginia Beach, VA 23464. *Phone:* 757-352-4845 or toll-free 800-373-5504. *Fax:* 757-352-4509. *E-mail:* kbaker@regent.edu. *Web site:* http://www.regent.edu/.

Roanoke College
Salem, Virginia

General Independent, 4-year, coed, affiliated with Evangelical Lutheran Church in America **Entrance** Moderately difficult **Setting** 68-acre suburban campus **Total enrollment** 2,044 **Student-faculty ratio** 13:1 **Application deadline** 3/15 (freshmen), 8/1 (transfer) **Freshman admission** 68% were admitted. Average high school GPA 3.33 **Freshman test scores** SAT critical reading scores over 500: 78%; SAT math scores over 500: 73%; SAT critical reading scores over 600: 28%; SAT math scores over 600: 25% **Housing** Yes **Expenses** Tuition & Fees $31,214; Room & Board $10,308 **Undergraduates** 56% women, 5% part-time, 4% 25 or older, 1% Native American, 3% Hispanic American, 4% African American, 1% Asian American/Pacific Islander **The most frequently chosen baccalaureate fields are** business/marketing, psychology, social sciences **Academic program** English as a second language, advanced placement, accelerated degree program, honors program, summer session, adult/continuing education programs, internships **Contact** Ms. Brenda Poggendorf, Vice President of Enrollment, Roanoke College, 221 College Lane, Salem, VA 24153. *Phone:* 540-375-2270 or toll-free 800-388-2276. *Fax:* 540-375-2267. *E-mail:* admissions@roanoke.edu. *Web site:* http://www.roanoke.edu/.

Saint Paul's College
Lawrenceville, Virginia

General Independent Episcopal, 4-year, coed **Entrance** Minimally difficult **Setting** 75-acre small-town campus **Total enrollment** 584 **Student-faculty ratio** 17:1 **Application deadline** Rolling (freshmen), rolling (transfer) **Freshman admission** 99% were admitted. Average high school GPA 2.17 **Freshman test scores** ACT scores over 18: 4%; ACT scores over 24: 3% **Housing** Yes **Expenses** Tuition & Fees $13,210; Room & Board $6640 **Undergraduates** 50% women, 3% part-time, 23% 25 or older, 1% Hispanic American, 97% African American, 0.3% Asian American/Pacific Islander **The most frequently chosen baccalaureate fields are** business/marketing, security and protective services, social sciences **Academic program** Accelerated degree program, honors program, summer session, adult/continuing education programs, internships **Contact** Mrs. Rosemary Lewis, Vice President for Student Affairs, Saint Paul's College, 115 College Drive, Lawrenceville, VA 23868-1202. *Phone:* 434-848-6493 or toll-free 800-678-7071. *Fax:* 434-848-0229. *E-mail:* rlewis@saintpauls.edu. *Web site:* http://www.saintpauls.edu/.

Shenandoah University
Winchester, Virginia

General Independent United Methodist, comprehensive, coed **Entrance** Moderately difficult **Setting** 100-acre small-town campus **Total enrollment** 3,619 **Student-faculty ratio** 9:1 **Application deadline** Rolling (freshmen), rolling (transfer) **Freshman admission** 84% were admitted. Average high school GPA 3.28 **Freshman test scores** SAT critical reading scores over 500: 53.35%; SAT math scores over 500: 51.91%; ACT scores over 18: 80%; SAT critical reading scores over 600: 17.95%; SAT math scores over 600: 15.3%; ACT scores over 24: 21% **Housing** Yes **Expenses** Tuition & Fees $25,080; Room & Board $8870 **Undergraduates** 57% women, 5% part-time, 18% 25 or older, 0.4% Native American, 3% Hispanic American, 12% African American, 2% Asian American/Pacific Islander **The most frequently chosen baccalaureate fields are** health professions and related sciences, business/marketing, visual and performing arts **Academic program** English as a second language, advanced placement, accelerated degree program, self-designed majors, summer session, adult/continuing education programs, internships **Contact** Mr. David Anthony, Dean of Admissions, Shenandoah University, 1460 University Drive, Winchester, VA 22601-5195. *Phone:* 540-665-4581 or toll-free 800-432-2266. *Fax:* 540-665-4627. *E-mail:* admit@su.edu. *Web site:* http://www.su.edu/.

Southern Virginia University
Buena Vista, Virginia

Contact Mr. Tony Caputo, Dean of Admissions, Southern Virginia University, One University Hill Drive, Buena Vista, VA 24416. *Phone:* 540-261-2756 or toll-free 800-229-8420. *Fax:* 540-261-8559. *E-mail:* admissions@southernvirginia.edu. *Web site:* http://www.svu.edu/.

South University
Glen Allen, Virginia

General Proprietary, comprehensive, coed **Contact** Director of Admissions, South University, 2151 Old Brick Road, Glen Allen, VA 23060. *Phone:* 804-727-6800 or toll-free 888-422-5076. *Fax:* 804-727-6790. *Web site:* http://www.southuniversity.edu/richmond.

See page 1184 for the College Close-Up.

South University
Virginia Beach, Virginia

General Proprietary, comprehensive, coed **Contact** Director of Admissions, South University, 301 Bendix Road, Suite 100, Virginia Beach, VA 23452. *Phone:* 757-493-6900 or toll-free 877-206-1845. *Fax:* 757-493-6990. *Web site:* http://www.southuniversity.edu/virginia-beach.

See page 1186 for the College Close-Up.

Stratford University
Falls Church, Virginia

Contact Kelly Martin, Director of High School Program, Stratford University, 7777 Leesburg Pike, Falls Church, VA 22043. *Phone:* 703-821-8570 or toll-free 800-444-0804. *Fax:* 703-734-5339. *E-mail:* kmartin@stratford.edu. *Web site:* http://www.stratford.edu/.

Visit Petersons.com and enter keyword Stratford

See page 1206 for the College Close-Up.

Stratford University
Woodbridge, Virginia

General Proprietary, comprehensive, coed **Application deadline** Rolling (freshmen), rolling (transfer) **Academic program** Advanced placement, accelerated degree program, summer session, adult/continuing education programs, internships **Contact** Director of Admissions, Stratford University, 14349 Gideon Drive, Woodbridge, VA 22192. *Phone:* 703-897-1982 or toll-free 888-546-1250. *E-mail:* admissions@stratford.edu. *Web site:* http://www.stratford.edu/.

Strayer University–Alexandria Campus
Alexandria, Virginia

General Proprietary, comprehensive, coed **Contact** Admissions Office, Strayer University–Alexandria Campus, 2730 Eisenhower Avenue, Alexandria, VA 22314. *Phone:* 703-317-2626. *Web site:* http://www.strayer.edu/alexandria.

Strayer University–Arlington Campus
Arlington, Virginia

General Proprietary, comprehensive, coed **Contact** Admissions Office, Strayer University–Arlington Campus, 2121 15th Street North, Arlington, VA 22201. *Phone:* 703-892-5100. *Web site:* http://www.strayer.edu/arlington.

Strayer University–Chesapeake Campus
Chesapeake, Virginia

General Proprietary, comprehensive, coed **Contact** Admissions Office, Strayer University–Chesapeake Campus, 700 Independent Parkway, Suite 400, Chesapeake, VA 23320. *Phone:* 757-382-9900. *Web site:* http://www.strayer.edu/chesapeake.

Strayer University–Chesterfield Campus
Midlothian, Virginia

General Proprietary, comprehensive, coed **Contact** Admissions Office, Strayer University–Chesterfield Campus, 2820 Waterford Lake Drive, Suite 100, Midlothian, VA 23112. *Phone:* 804-763-6300. *Web site:* http://www.strayer.edu/chesterfield.

Strayer University–Fredericksburg Campus
Fredericksburg, Virginia

General Proprietary, comprehensive, coed **Contact** Admissions Office, Strayer University–Fredericksburg Campus, 150 Riverside Parkway, Suite 100, Fredericksburg, VA 22406. *Phone:* 540-374-4300. *Web site:* http://www.strayer.edu/fredericksburg.

Strayer University–Henrico Campus
Glen Allen, Virginia

General Proprietary, comprehensive, coed **Contact** Admissions Office, Strayer University–Henrico Campus, 11501 Nuckols Road, Glen Allen, VA 23059. *Phone:* 804-527-1000. *Web site:* http://www.strayer.edu/henrico.

Strayer University–Loudoun Campus

Ashburn, Virginia

General Proprietary, comprehensive, coed **Contact** Admissions Office, Strayer University–Loudoun Campus, 45150 Russell Branch Parkway, Suite 200, Ashburn, VA 20147. *Phone:* 703-729-8800. *Web site:* http://www.strayer.edu/loudoun.

Strayer University–Manassas Campus

Manassas, Virginia

General Proprietary, comprehensive, coed **Contact** Admissions Office, Strayer University–Manassas Campus, 9990 Battleview Parkway, Manassas, VA 20109. *Phone:* 703-330-8400. *Web site:* http://www.strayer.edu/manassas.

Strayer University–Newport News Campus

Newport News, Virginia

General Proprietary, comprehensive, coed **Contact** Admissions Office, Strayer University–Newport News Campus, 813 Diligence Drive, Suite 100, Newport News, VA 23606. *Phone:* 757-873-3100. *Web site:* http://www.strayer.edu/newport_news.

Strayer University–Virginia Beach Campus

Virginia Beach, Virginia

General Proprietary, comprehensive, coed **Contact** Admissions Office, Strayer University–Virginia Beach Campus, 249 Central Park Avenue, Suite 350, Virginia Beach, VA 23462. *Phone:* 757-493-6000. *Web site:* http://www.strayer.edu/virginia_beach.

Strayer University–Woodbridge Campus

Woodbridge, Virginia

General Proprietary, comprehensive, coed **Contact** Admissions Office, Strayer University–Woodbridge Campus, 13385 Minnieville Road, Woodbridge, VA 22192. *Phone:* 703-878-2800. *Web site:* http://www.strayer.edu/woodbridge.

Sweet Briar College

Sweet Briar, Virginia

General Independent, comprehensive, women only **Entrance** Moderately difficult **Setting** 3,250-acre rural campus **Total enrollment** 756 **Student-faculty ratio** 8:1 **Application deadline** 2/1 (freshmen), 5/1 (transfer) **Freshman admission** 82% were admitted. Average high school GPA 3.37 **Freshman test scores** SAT critical reading scores over 500: 70.92%; SAT math scores over 500: 58.87%; ACT scores over 18: 94.23%; SAT critical reading scores over 600: 34.04%; SAT math scores over 600: 24.83%; ACT scores over 24: 44.23% **Housing** Yes **Expenses** Tuition & Fees $30,195; Room & Board $10,780 **Undergraduates** 5% part-time, 2% 25 or older **Academic program** Advanced placement, accelerated degree program, self-designed majors, honors program, summer session, adult/continuing education programs, internships **Contact** Mr. Ken Huus, Director of Admissions, Sweet Briar College, PO Box B, Sweet Briar, VA 24595. *Phone:* 434-381-6142 or toll-free 800-381-6142. *Fax:* 434-381-6152. *E-mail:* admissions@sbc.edu. *Web site:* http://www.sbc.edu/.

Visit Petersons.com and enter keyword Sweet

See page 1210 for the College Close-Up.

University of Management and Technology

Arlington, Virginia

Contact Vice President, University of Management and Technology, Suite 700, 1901 North Fort Meyers Drive, Arlington, VA 22209. *Phone:* 703-516-0035 or toll-free 800-924-4885. *Fax:* 703-516-0985. *E-mail:* admissions@umtweb.edu. *Web site:* http://www.umtweb.edu/.

University of Mary Washington

Fredericksburg, Virginia

General State-supported, comprehensive, coed **Entrance** Very difficult **Setting** 176-acre small-town campus **Total enrollment** 5,084 **Student-faculty ratio** 15:1 **Application deadline** 2/1 (freshmen), 3/1 (transfer) **Freshman admission** 71% were admitted. Average high school GPA 3.59 **Freshman test scores** SAT critical reading scores over 500: 92%; SAT math scores over 500: 90%; ACT scores over 18: 100%; SAT critical reading scores over 600: 55%; SAT math scores over 600: 40%; ACT scores over 24: 82% **Housing** Yes **Expenses** Tuition & Fees: state resident $3900, nonresident $16,810; Room & Board $8200 **Undergraduates** 66% women, 15% part-time, 10% 25 or older, 0.5% Native American, 4% Hispanic American, 4% African American, 4% Asian American/Pacific Islander **The most frequently chosen baccalaureate fields are** business/marketing, English, social sciences **Academic program** Advanced placement, accelerated degree program, self-designed majors, summer session, adult/continuing education programs, internships **Contact** Ms. Kimberly Johnston, Vice President for Enrollment and Communications, University of Mary Washington, 1301 College Avenue, Fredericksburg, VA 22401-5358. *Phone:* 540-654-2000 or toll-free 800-468-5614. *Fax:* 540-654-1857. *E-mail:* admit@umw.edu. *Web site:* http://www.umw.edu/.

University of Phoenix–Northern Virginia Campus

Reston, Virginia

General Proprietary, comprehensive, coed **Entrance** Noncompetitive **Setting** urban campus **Total enrollment** 419 **Application deadline** Rolling (freshmen), rolling (transfer) **Housing** No **Expenses** Tuition & Fees $12,250 **Undergraduates** 46% women, 87% 25 or older, 1% Native American, 9% Hispanic American, 25% African American, 4% Asian American/Pacific Islander **The most frequently chosen baccalaureate fields are** business/marketing, computer and information sciences, public administration and social services **Academic program** Advanced placement, accelerated degree program **Contact** Ms. Audra McQuarie, Registrar/Executive Director, University of Phoenix–Northern Virginia Campus, 4035 South Riverpoint Parkway, Mail Stop CF-L101, Phoenix, AZ 85040. *Phone:* 480-557-6151 or toll-free 800-776-4867 (in-state); 800-228-7240 (out-of-state). *Fax:* 480-643-3068. *E-mail:* audra.mcquarie@phoenix.edu. *Web site:* http://www.phoenix.edu/.

University of Phoenix–Richmond Campus

Richmond, Virginia

General Proprietary, comprehensive, coed **Entrance** Noncompetitive **Setting** urban campus **Total enrollment** 129 **Application deadline** Rolling (freshmen), rolling (transfer) **Housing** No **Expenses** Tuition & Fees $13,200 **Undergraduates** 67% women, 89% 25 or older, 2% Hispanic American, 40% African American **The most frequently chosen baccalaureate fields are** computer and information sciences, history **Academic program** Advanced placement, accelerated degree program **Contact** Ms. Audra McQuarie, Registrar/Executive Director, University of Phoenix–Richmond Campus, 4035 South Riverpoint Parkway, Mail Stop CF-L101, Phoenix, AZ 85040. *Phone:* 480-557-6151 or toll-free 800-776-4867 (in-state); 800-228-7240 (out-of-state). *Fax:* 480-643-3068. *E-mail:* audra.mcquarie@phoenix.edu. *Web site:* http://www.phoenix.edu/.

University of Richmond

University of Richmond, Virginia

General Independent, comprehensive, coed **Entrance** Very difficult **Setting** 350-acre suburban campus **Total enrollment** 3,513 **Student-faculty ratio** 8:1 **Application deadline** 1/15 (freshmen), 2/15 (transfer) **Freshman admission** 39% were admitted **Freshman test scores** SAT critical reading scores over 500: 93.08%; SAT math scores over 500: 96.86%; ACT scores over 18: 99.7%; SAT critical reading scores over 600: 67.58%; SAT math scores over 600: 73.49%; ACT scores over 24: 90.3% **Housing** Yes **Expenses** Tuition & Fees $41,610; Room & Board $8810 **Undergraduates** 53% women, 2% part-time, 0.3% Native American, 4% Hispanic American, 7% African American, 5% Asian American/Pacific Islander **The most frequently chosen baccalaureate fields are** business/marketing, English, social sciences **Academic program** English as a second language, advanced placement, self-designed majors, summer session, adult/continuing education programs, internships **Contact** Ms. Pamela Spence, Dean of Admission, University of Richmond, 28 Westhampton Way, University of Richmond, VA 23173. *Phone:* 804-289-8640 or toll-free 800-700-1662. *Fax:* 804-287-6003. *E-mail:* admissions@richmond.edu. *Web site:* http://www.richmond.edu/. **Visit Petersons.com and enter keywords University of Richmond**

University of Virginia

Charlottesville, Virginia

General State-supported, university, coed **Entrance** Very difficult **Setting** 1,167-acre suburban campus **Total enrollment** 24,262 **Student-faculty ratio** 16:1 **Application deadline** 1/1 (freshmen), 3/1 (transfer) **Freshman admission** 32% were admitted. Average high school GPA 4.11 **Freshman test scores** SAT critical reading scores over 500: 97%; SAT math scores over 500: 97%; ACT scores over 18: 100%; SAT critical reading scores over 600: 78%; SAT math scores over 600: 84%; ACT scores over 24: 94% **Housing** Yes **Expenses** Tuition & Fees: state resident $9672, nonresident $31,230; Room & Board $8290 **Undergraduates** 56% women, 5% part-time, 3% 25 or older, 0.3% Native American, 5% Hispanic American, 8% African American, 12% Asian American/Pacific Islander **The most frequently chosen baccalaureate fields are** engineering, business/marketing, social sciences **Academic program** English as a second language, advanced placement, accelerated degree program, self-designed majors, honors program, summer session, adult/continuing education programs, internships **Contact** Mr. Gregory W. Roberts, Dean of Admission, University of Virginia, PO Box 400160, Charlottesville, VA 22904-4727. *Phone:* 434-982-3200. *Fax:* 434-924-3587. *E-mail:* undergrad-admission@virginia.edu. *Web site:* http://www.virginia.edu/.

The University of Virginia's College at Wise

Wise, Virginia

General State-supported, 4-year, coed **Entrance** Moderately difficult **Setting** 396-acre small-town campus **Total enrollment** 2,015 **Student-faculty ratio** 14:1 **Application deadline** 8/1 (freshmen), 8/15 (transfer) **Freshman admission** 89% were admitted. Average high school GPA 3.2 **Freshman test scores** SAT critical reading scores over 500: 39%; SAT math scores over 500: 37%; ACT scores over 18: 64%; SAT critical reading scores over 600: 8%; SAT math scores over 600: 8%; ACT scores over 24: 12% **Housing** Yes **Expenses** Tuition & Fees: state resident $6748, nonresident $18,876; Room & Board $7323 **Undergraduates** 53% women, 26% part-time, 10% 25 or older, 0.3% Native American, 2% Hispanic American, 9% African American, 1% Asian American/Pacific Islander **The most frequently chosen baccalaureate fields are** business/marketing, liberal arts/general studies, social sciences **Academic program** Advanced placement, accelerated degree program, self-designed majors, honors program, summer session, adult/continuing education programs, internships **Contact** Mr. Russell D. Necessary, Vice Chancellor for Enrollment Management, The University of Virginia's College at Wise, 1 College Avenue, Wise, VA 24293. *Phone:* 276-328-0322 or toll-free 888-282-9324. *Fax:* 276-328-0251. *E-mail:* admissions@uvawise.edu. *Web site:* http://www.uvawise.edu/.

Valley Forge Christian College Woodbridge Campus

Woodbridge, Virginia

General Independent Assemblies of God, 4-year, coed **Entrance** Minimally difficult **Setting** suburban campus **Total enrollment** 136 **Expenses** Tuition & Fees $7150 **Contact** Admissions Office, Valley Forge Christian College Woodbridge Campus, 13909 Smoketown Road, Woodbridge, VA 22192. *Phone:* 703-580-4810 or toll-free 800-432-8322. *Web site:* http://www.vfcc.edu/woodbridge/.

Virginia Commonwealth University

Richmond, Virginia

General State-supported, university, coed **Setting** 143-acre urban campus **Total enrollment** 32,436 **Student-faculty ratio** 18:1 **Freshman admission** 59% were admitted. Average high school GPA 3.43 **Freshman test scores** SAT critical reading scores over 500: 73%; SAT math scores over 500: 70%; ACT scores over 18: 93%; SAT critical reading scores over 600: 27%; SAT math scores over 600: 25%; ACT scores over 24: 38% **Housing** Yes **Expenses** Tuition & Fees: state resident $7117, nonresident $20,341; Room & Board $8335 **Undergraduates** 57% women, 17% part-time, 14% 25 or older, 1% Native American, 4% Hispanic American, 20% African American, 12% Asian American/Pacific Islander **The most frequently chosen baccalaureate fields are** business/marketing, health professions and related sciences, visual and performing arts **Academic program** English as a second language, advanced placement, accelerated degree program, self-designed majors, honors program, summer session, adult/continuing education programs, internships **Contact** Ms. Sybil Halloran, Director of Undergraduate Admissions, Virginia Commonwealth University, 821 West Franklin Street, Box 842526, Richmond, VA 23284-2526. *Phone:* 804-828-6125 or toll-free 800-841-3638. *Fax:* 804-828-1899. *E-mail:* schallor@vcu.edu. *Web site:* http://www.vcu.edu/.

Virginia Intermont College

Bristol, Virginia

General Independent, 4-year, coed, affiliated with Baptist Church **Entrance** Minimally difficult **Setting** 13-acre small-town campus **Total enrollment** 589 **Student-faculty ratio** 9:1 **Application deadline** Rolling (freshmen), rolling (transfer) **Freshman admission** 46% were admitted. Average high school GPA 3.07 **Freshman test scores** SAT critical reading scores over 500: 35%; SAT math scores over 500: 43%; SAT critical reading scores over 600: 5%; SAT math scores over 600: 5% **Housing** Yes **Expenses** Tuition & Fees $23,373; Room & Board $7324 **Undergraduates** 67% women, 16% part-time, 33% 25 or older, 0.2% Native American, 2% Hispanic American, 7% African American, 1% Asian American/Pacific Islander **The most frequently chosen baccalaureate fields are** business/marketing, education, visual and performing arts **Academic program** English as a second language, advanced placement, accelerated degree program, honors program, summer session, adult/continuing education programs, internships **Contact** Mr. Con Sauls, Director of Enrollment, Virginia Intermont College, 1013 Moore Street, Campus Box D-460, Bristol, VA 24201. *Phone:* 276-466-7856 or toll-free 800-451-1842. *Fax:* 276-466-7885. *E-mail:* viadmit@vic.edu. *Web site:* http://www.vic.edu/.

Virginia International University

Fairfax, Virginia

Contact Admissions Department, Virginia International University, 11200 Waples Mill Road, Fairfax, VA 22030. *Phone:* 703-591-7042 Ext. 313 or

Virginia International University (continued)
toll-free 800-514 6848. *Fax:* 703-591-7048. *E-mail:* admissions@viu.edu. *Web site:* http://www.viu.edu/.

Virginia Military Institute
Lexington, Virginia

General State-supported, 4-year, coed, primarily men **Entrance** Moderately difficult **Setting** 134-acre small-town campus **Total enrollment** 1,500 **Student-faculty ratio** 11:1 **Application deadline** 2/1 (freshmen), 2/1 (transfer) **Freshman admission** 56% were admitted. Average high school GPA 3.41 **Freshman test scores** SAT critical reading scores over 500: 85.7%; SAT math scores over 500: 87%; ACT scores over 18: 96.1%; SAT critical reading scores over 600: 30%; SAT math scores over 600: 32.8%; ACT scores over 24: 61.5% **Housing** Yes **Expenses** Tuition & Fees: state resident $11,190, nonresident $28,738; Room & Board $6792 **Undergraduates** 8% women, 0.4% Native American, 4% Hispanic American, 6% African American, 4% Asian American/Pacific Islander **The most frequently chosen baccalaureate fields are** engineering, history, social sciences **Academic program** Advanced placement, honors program, summer session, internships **Contact** Lt. Col. Tom Mortenson, Associate Director of Admissions, Virginia Military Institute, Admissions Office, Lexington, VA 24450. *Phone:* 540-464-7211 or toll-free 800-767-4207. *Fax:* 540-464-7746. *E-mail:* admissions@vmi.edu. *Web site:* http://www.vmi.edu/.

Visit Petersons.com and enter keywords Virginia Military

See page 1336 for the College Close-Up.

Virginia Polytechnic Institute and State University
Blacksburg, Virginia

General State-supported, university, coed **Entrance** Moderately difficult **Setting** 2,600-acre small-town campus **Total enrollment** 30,870 **Student-faculty ratio** 16:1 **Application deadline** 1/15 (freshmen), 2/15 (transfer) **Freshman admission** 61% were admitted. Average high school GPA 3.91 **Freshman test scores** SAT critical reading scores over 500: 72%; SAT math scores over 500: 83%; SAT critical reading scores over 600: 29%; SAT math scores over 600: 44% **Housing** Yes **Expenses** Tuition & Fees: state resident $8198, nonresident $20,655; Room & Board $5476 **Undergraduates** 43% women, 2% part-time, 2% 25 or older, 0.5% Native American, 3% Hispanic American, 4% African American, 8% Asian American/Pacific Islander **The most frequently chosen baccalaureate fields are** business/marketing, engineering, social sciences **Academic program** English as a second language, advanced placement, accelerated degree program, honors program, summer session, adult/continuing education programs, internships **Contact** Mrs. Mildred R. Johnson, Director of Undergraduate Admissions, Virginia Polytechnic Institute and State University, Blacksburg, VA 24061. *Phone:* 540-231-6267. *Fax:* 540-231-3242. *E-mail:* vtadmiss@vt.edu. *Web site:* http://www.vt.edu/.

Virginia State University
Petersburg, Virginia

General State-supported, comprehensive, coed **Entrance** Minimally difficult **Setting** 236-acre suburban campus **Total enrollment** 5,366 **Student-faculty ratio** 17:1 **Application deadline** 5/1 (freshmen), 5/1 (transfer) **Freshman admission** 67% were admitted. Average high school GPA 2.9 **Freshman test scores** SAT critical reading scores over 500: 15%; SAT math scores over 500: 14%; SAT math scores over 600: 1% **Housing** Yes **Expenses** Tuition & Fees: state resident $6174, nonresident $14,236; Room & Board $8050 **Undergraduates** 62% women, 7% part-time, 12% 25 or older, 0.1% Native American, 1% Hispanic American, 93% African American, 0.1% Asian American/Pacific Islander **The most frequently chosen baccalaureate fields are** business/marketing, education, security and protective services **Academic program** Advanced placement, self-designed majors, honors program, summer session, adult/continuing education programs, internships **Contact** Mrs. Irene Logan, Director of Admissions, Virginia State University, Office of Admissions, Petersburg, VA 23806-2096. *Phone:* 804-524-5902 or toll-free 800-871-7611. *Fax:* 804-524-5055. *E-mail:* ilogan@vsu.edu. *Web site:* http://www.vsu.edu/.

Virginia Union University
Richmond, Virginia

General Independent Baptist, comprehensive, coed **Entrance** Moderately difficult **Setting** 72-acre urban campus **Total enrollment** 1,700 **Student-faculty ratio** 15:1 **Application deadline** Rolling (freshmen), rolling (transfer) **Freshman admission** 81% were admitted. Average high school GPA 2.39 **Freshman test scores** SAT critical reading scores over 500: 6.13%; SAT math scores over 500: 6.14%; SAT critical reading scores over 600: .92%; SAT math scores over 600: 1.54% **Housing** Yes **Expenses** Tuition & Fees $14,630; Room & Board $6830 **Undergraduates** 58% women, 3% part-time, 6% 25 or older, 1% Hispanic American, 96% African American, 0.3% Asian American/Pacific Islander **The most frequently chosen baccalaureate fields are** business/marketing, law/legal studies, social sciences **Academic program** English as a second language, advanced placement, honors program, summer session, adult/continuing education programs, internships **Contact** Mr. Gil Powell, Director of Admissions, Virginia Union University, 1500 North Lombardy Street, Richmond, VA 23220-1170. *Phone:* 804-257-5881 or toll-free 800-368-3227. *Fax:* 804-329-8477. *E-mail:* gpowell@vuu.edu. *Web site:* http://www.vuu.edu/.

Virginia University of Lynchburg
Lynchburg, Virginia

General Independent religious, comprehensive, coed **Entrance** Noncompetitive **Setting** urban campus **Total enrollment** 327 **Student-faculty ratio** 9:1 **Application deadline** Rolling (freshmen), rolling (transfer) **Housing** Yes **Expenses** Tuition & Fees $5300; Room & Board $3600 **Undergraduates** 53% women, 41% part-time, 61% 25 or older, 98% African American **The most frequently chosen baccalaureate fields are** business/marketing, philosophy and religious studies, social sciences **Academic program** Advanced placement, summer session, adult/continuing education programs **Contact** Ms. Cheryl Glass, Director of Admissions, Virginia University of Lynchburg, 2058 Garfield Avenue, Lynchburg, VA 24501. *Phone:* 434-528-5276 Ext. 106. *Fax:* 434-528-4275. *E-mail:* cglass@vul.edu. *Web site:* http://www.vul.edu/.

Virginia Wesleyan College
Norfolk, Virginia

General Independent United Methodist, 4-year, coed **Entrance** Moderately difficult **Setting** 300-acre urban campus **Total enrollment** 1,336 **Student-faculty ratio** 11:1 **Application deadline** Rolling (freshmen), rolling (transfer) **Freshman admission** 75% were admitted. Average high school GPA 3.1 **Freshman test scores** SAT critical reading scores over 500: 44.3%; SAT math scores over 500: 44.7%; ACT scores over 18: 85.5%; SAT critical reading scores over 600: 6.4%; SAT math scores over 600: 8%; ACT scores over 24: 23.6% **Housing** Yes **Expenses** Tuition & Fees $27,476; Room & Board $7384 **Undergraduates** 63% women, 14% part-time, 15% 25 or older, 0.2% Native American, 4% Hispanic American, 21% African American, 2% Asian American/Pacific Islander **The most frequently chosen baccalaureate fields are** business/marketing, security and protective services, social sciences **Academic program** Advanced placement, self-designed majors, honors program, summer session, adult/continuing education programs, internships **Contact** Mrs. Sara Gastler, Director of Admissions, Virginia Wesleyan College, 1584 Wesleyan Drive, Norfolk, VA 23502-5599. *Phone:* 757-455-3208 or toll-free 800-737-8684. *Fax:* 757-461-5238. *E-mail:* admissions@vwc.edu. *Web site:* http://www.vwc.edu/.

Washington and Lee University
Lexington, Virginia

General Independent, comprehensive, coed **Entrance** Most difficult **Setting** 322-acre small-town campus **Total enrollment** 2,153 **Student-**

faculty ratio 9:1 **Application deadline** 1/15 (freshmen), 4/1 (transfer) **Freshman admission** 19% were admitted **Freshman test scores** SAT critical reading scores over 500: 100%; SAT math scores over 500: 100%; ACT scores over 18: 100%; SAT critical reading scores over 600: 96%; SAT math scores over 600: 97%; ACT scores over 24: 100% **Housing** Yes **Expenses** Tuition & Fees $38,877; Room & Board $8410 **Undergraduates** 50% women, 0.1% part-time, 0.4% Native American, 2% Hispanic American, 4% African American, 4% Asian American/Pacific Islander **The most frequently chosen baccalaureate fields are** business/marketing, foreign languages and literature, social sciences **Academic program** Advanced placement, self-designed majors, honors program, internships **Contact** Mr. William M. Hartog, Dean of Admissions and Financial Aid, Washington and Lee University, 204 West Washington Street, Lexington, VA 24450-2116. *Phone:* 540-458-8710. *Fax:* 540-458-8062. *E-mail:* admissions@wlu.edu. *Web site:* http://www.wlu.edu/.

Westwood College–Annandale Campus
Annandale, Virginia

General Proprietary, 4-year, coed **Total enrollment** 473 **Contact** Director of Admissions, Westwood College–Annandale Campus, 7611 Little River Turnpike, 5th Floor, Annandale, VA 22003. *Phone:* 703-642-3633 or toll-free 800-281-2978. *Fax:* 703-642-3772. *Web site:* http://www.westwood.edu/.

Westwood College–Arlington Ballston Campus
Arlington, Virginia

General Proprietary, 4-year, coed **Total enrollment** 473 **Contact** Director of Admissions, Westwood College–Arlington Ballston Campus, 4300 Wilson Boulevard, Suite 200, Arlington, VA 22203. *Phone:* 703-243-1662. *Fax:* 703-243-3992. *Web site:* http://www.westwood.edu/.

World College
Virginia Beach, Virginia

General Proprietary, 4-year, coed **Entrance** Noncompetitive **Setting** suburban campus **Total enrollment** 465 **Application deadline** Rolling (freshmen) **Housing** No **Undergraduates** 94% 25 or older **The most frequently chosen baccalaureate fields are** computer and information sciences, engineering technologies **Academic program** Accelerated degree program, adult/continuing education programs **Contact** Mrs. Audre Piratsky, Admissions Counselor, World College, 5193 Shore Drive, Suite 105, Virginia Beach, VA 23455. *Phone:* 757-464-4600 or toll-free 800-696-7532. *Fax:* 757-464-3687. *E-mail:* instruct@cie-wc.edu. *Web site:* http://www.worldcollege.edu/.

WASHINGTON

Antioch University Seattle
Seattle, Washington

General Independent, university, coed **Entrance** Noncompetitive **Setting** urban campus **Total enrollment** 848 **Student-faculty ratio** 8:1 **Housing** No **Expenses** Tuition & Fees $12,030 **Undergraduates** 75% women, 83% part-time, 91% 25 or older **Academic program** Summer session **Contact** Admissions Office, Antioch University Seattle, 2326 Sixth Avenue, Seattle, WA 98121-1814. *Phone:* 206-268-4202. *E-mail:* admissions@antiochseattle.edu. *Web site:* http://www.antiochsea.edu/.

Argosy University, Seattle
Seattle, Washington

General Proprietary, university, coed **Setting** urban campus **Contact** Director of Admissions, Argosy University, Seattle, 2601-A Elliott Avenue, Seattle, WA 98121. *Phone:* 206-283-4500 or toll-free 866-283-2777. *Fax:* 206-393-3592. *Web site:* http://www.argosy.edu/seattle/.
Visit Petersons.com and enter keywords Argosy University, Seattle

See page 478 for the College Close-Up.

The Art Institute of Seattle
Seattle, Washington

General Proprietary, primarily 2-year, coed **Setting** urban campus **Contact** Director of Admissions, The Art Institute of Seattle, 2323 Elliott Avenue, Seattle, WA 98121-1642. *Phone:* 206-448-6600 or toll-free 800-275-2471. *Fax:* 206-269-0275. *Web site:* http://www.artinstitutes.edu/seattle/.
Visit Petersons.com and enter keywords Art Institute of Seattle

See page 544 for the College Close-Up.

Bastyr University
Kenmore, Washington

General Independent, upper-level, coed **Setting** 51-acre suburban campus **Total enrollment** 928 **Student-faculty ratio** 9:1 **Application deadline** 3/15 (transfer) **Housing** Yes **Expenses** Tuition & Fees $19,050 **Undergraduates** 84% women, 25% part-time, 63% 25 or older **The most frequently chosen baccalaureate field is** health professions and related sciences **Academic program** Summer session, internships **Contact** Mr. Ted Olsen, Director of Admissions, Bastyr University, 14500 Juanita Drive NE, Kenmore, WA 98028-4966. *Phone:* 425-602-3101. *Fax:* 425-602-3090. *E-mail:* admissions@bastyr.edu. *Web site:* http://www.bastyr.edu/.
Visit Petersons.com and enter keyword Bastyr

See page 584 for the College Close-Up.

Bellevue College
Bellevue, Washington

General State-supported, primarily 2-year, coed **Entrance** Noncompetitive **Setting** 96-acre suburban campus **Total enrollment** 12,305 **Application deadline** Rolling (freshmen), rolling (transfer) **Housing** No **Expenses** Tuition & Fees: state resident $2940, nonresident $8154 **Undergraduates** 37% 25 or older **Academic program** English as a second language, advanced placement, honors program, summer session, internships **Contact** Morenika Jacobs, Associate Dean of Enrollment Services, Bellevue College, 3000 Landerholm Circle, SE, Bellevue, WA 98007-6484. *Phone:* 425-564-2205. *Fax:* 425-564-4065. *Web site:* http://www.bcc.ctc.edu/.

Central Washington University
Ellensburg, Washington

General State-supported, comprehensive, coed **Entrance** Moderately difficult **Setting** 380-acre small-town campus **Total enrollment** 10,662 **Student-faculty ratio** 20:1 **Application deadline** 4/1 (freshmen), 4/1 (transfer) **Freshman admission** 79% were admitted. Average high school GPA 3.2 **Freshman test scores** SAT critical reading scores over 500: 46.1%; SAT math scores over 500: 50.2%; ACT scores over 18: 78.5%; SAT critical reading scores over 600: 11.4%; SAT math scores over 600: 10.1%; ACT scores over 24: 23.5% **Housing** Yes **Expenses** Tuition & Fees: state resident $6399, nonresident $17,742; Room & Board $8460 **Undergraduates** 52% women, 14% part-time, 18% 25 or older, 2% Native American, 7% Hispanic American, 3% African American, 6% Asian American/Pacific Islander **The most frequently chosen baccalaureate fields are** business/marketing, education, social

Central Washington University (continued)

sciences **Academic program** English as a second language, advanced placement, self-designed majors, honors program, summer session, internships **Contact** Ms. Lisa Garcia-Hanson, Director of Admissions, Central Washington University, 400 East University Way, Ellensburg, WA 98926-7463. *Phone:* 509-963-1211 or toll-free 866-298-4968. *Fax:* 509-963-3022. *E-mail:* cwuadmis@cwu.edu. *Web site:* http://www.cwu.edu/.

City University of Seattle

Bellevue, Washington

General Independent, comprehensive, coed **Entrance** Noncompetitive **Setting** suburban campus **Total enrollment** 2,885 **Student-faculty ratio** 13:1 **Application deadline** Rolling (freshmen), rolling (transfer) **Housing** No **Expenses** Tuition & Fees $15,615 **Undergraduates** 58% women, 44% part-time, 78% 25 or older, 1% Native American, 2% Hispanic American, 5% African American, 4% Asian American/Pacific Islander **The most frequently chosen baccalaureate fields are** business/marketing, computer and information sciences, education **Academic program** English as a second language, advanced placement, accelerated degree program, self-designed majors, summer session, adult/continuing education programs, internships **Contact** Student Services Center, City University of Seattle, 11900 NE First Street, Bellvue, WA 98005. *Phone:* 888-422-4898 or toll-free 888-42-CITYU. *Fax:* 425-709-5361. *E-mail:* info@cityu.edu. *Web site:* http://www.cityu.edu/.

Cornish College of the Arts

Seattle, Washington

General Independent, 4-year, coed **Entrance** Moderately difficult **Setting** 4-acre urban campus **Total enrollment** 794 **Student-faculty ratio** 8:1 **Application deadline** 8/15 (freshmen), 8/15 (transfer) **Freshman admission** 67% were admitted. Average high school GPA 3.13 **Housing** Yes **Expenses** Tuition & Fees $28,297; Room & Board $8500 **Undergraduates** 63% women, 2% part-time, 15% 25 or older, 1% Native American, 4% Hispanic American, 3% African American, 6% Asian American/Pacific Islander **The most frequently chosen baccalaureate field is** visual and performing arts **Academic program** Advanced placement, summer session, internships **Contact** Ms. Sharron Starling, Director of Admissions, Cornish College of the Arts, 1000 Lenora Street, Seattle, WA 98121. *Phone:* 206-726-5017 or toll-free 800-726-ARTS. *Fax:* 206-720-1011. *E-mail:* admissions@cornish.edu. *Web site:* http://www.cornish.edu/.

DeVry University

Bellevue, Washington

Contact DeVry University, 600 108th Avenue NE, Suite 230, Bellevue, WA 98004-5110. *Web site:* http://www.devry.edu/.

DeVry University

Federal Way, Washington

General Proprietary, comprehensive, coed **Entrance** Minimally difficult **Setting** 12-acre suburban campus **Total enrollment** 827 **Student-faculty ratio** 15:1 **Application deadline** Rolling (freshmen), rolling (transfer) **Housing** No **Expenses** Tuition & Fees $14,720 **Undergraduates** 29% women, 37% part-time, 58% 25 or older, 1% Native American, 9% Hispanic American, 11% African American, 8% Asian American/Pacific Islander **The most frequently chosen baccalaureate fields are** business/marketing, computer and information sciences, engineering **Academic program** Advanced placement, accelerated degree program, summer session, adult/continuing education programs **Contact** Admissions Department, DeVry University, 3600 South 344th Way, Federal Way, WA 98001. *Web site:* http://www.devry.edu/.

DigiPen Institute of Technology

Redmond, Washington

General Proprietary, comprehensive, coed **Entrance** Minimally difficult **Setting** 1-acre suburban campus **Total enrollment** 890 **Student-faculty ratio** 12:1 **Application deadline** Rolling (freshmen), rolling (transfer) **Freshman admission** 33% were admitted **Housing** No **Expenses** Tuition & Fees $20,760 **Undergraduates** 19% 25 or older, 0.3% Native American, 7% Hispanic American, 0.4% African American, 8% Asian American/Pacific Islander **Academic program** Advanced placement, summer session, internships **Contact** Ms. Angela Kugler, Admissions Director, DigiPen Institute of Technology, 5001 150th Avenue NE, Redmond, WA 98052. *Phone:* 425-895-4438. *Fax:* 425-558-0378. *E-mail:* admissions@digipen.edu. *Web site:* http://www.digipen.edu/.

Eastern Washington University

Cheney, Washington

General State-supported, comprehensive, coed **Entrance** Moderately difficult **Setting** 335-acre small-town campus **Total enrollment** 11,302 **Student-faculty ratio** 21:1 **Application deadline** 8/15 (freshmen), rolling (transfer) **Freshman admission** 82% were admitted. Average high school GPA 3.18 **Freshman test scores** SAT critical reading scores over 500: 39.77%; SAT math scores over 500: 43.77%; ACT scores over 18: 73.24%; SAT critical reading scores over 600: 9.62%; SAT math scores over 600: 10.63%; ACT scores over 24: 20% **Housing** Yes **Expenses** Tuition & Fees: state resident $5872, nonresident $14,590; Room & Board $7080 **Undergraduates** 55% women, 13% part-time, 23% 25 or older, 2% Native American, 9% Hispanic American, 4% African American, 4% Asian American/Pacific Islander **The most frequently chosen baccalaureate fields are** business/marketing, education, social sciences **Academic program** English as a second language, advanced placement, self-designed majors, honors program, summer session, internships **Contact** Ms. Shannon Carr, Director of Admissions, Eastern Washington University, 526 Fifth Street, Suite 101, Cheney, WA 99004-2447. *Phone:* 509-359-6582. *Fax:* 509-359-6692. *E-mail:* admissions@mail.ewu.edu. *Web site:* http://www.ewu.edu/.

The Evergreen State College

Olympia, Washington

General State-supported, comprehensive, coed **Entrance** Moderately difficult **Setting** 1,000-acre rural campus **Total enrollment** 4,891 **Student-faculty ratio** 23:1 **Application deadline** Rolling (freshmen), rolling (transfer) **Freshman admission** 95% were admitted. Average high school GPA 3.01 **Freshman test scores** SAT critical reading scores over 500: 80%; SAT math scores over 500: 64%; ACT scores over 18: 88%; SAT critical reading scores over 600: 42%; SAT math scores over 600: 24%; ACT scores over 24: 51% **Housing** Yes **Expenses** Tuition & Fees: state resident $5959, nonresident $16,987; Room & Board $8052 **Undergraduates** 54% women, 9% part-time, 31% 25 or older, 4% Native American, 5% Hispanic American, 5% African American, 5% Asian American/Pacific Islander **The most frequently chosen baccalaureate fields are** interdisciplinary studies, liberal arts/general studies **Academic program** Advanced placement, accelerated degree program, self-designed majors, summer session, internships **Contact** Mr. Doug P. Scrima, Director of Admissions, The Evergreen State College, 2700 Evergreen Parkway, NW, Olympia, WA 98505. *Phone:* 360-867-6170. *Fax:* 360-867-5114. *E-mail:* admissions@evergreen.edu. *Web site:* http://www.evergreen.edu/.

Gonzaga University

Spokane, Washington

General Independent Roman Catholic, comprehensive, coed **Entrance** Moderately difficult **Setting** 130-acre urban campus **Total enrollment** 7,637 **Student-faculty ratio** 10:1 **Application deadline** 2/1 (freshmen), 6/1 (transfer) **Freshman admission** 78% were admitted. Average high

LOOKING FOR INSPIRATION?

110,000+ hours volunteered by students for social justice and service projects.

40% of students study abroad through Gonzaga-in-Florence and other programs

32 retreats and liturgies offered for GU students

For more information visit: www.gonzaga.edu

school GPA 3.66 **Freshman test scores** SAT critical reading scores over 500: 91.97%; SAT math scores over 500: 91.6%; ACT scores over 18: 100%; SAT critical reading scores over 600: 45.45%; SAT math scores over 600: 52.27%; ACT scores over 24: 84.65% **Housing** Yes **Expenses** Tuition & Fees $28,262; Room & Board $7860 **Undergraduates** 53% women, 3% part-time, 4% 25 or older, 1% Native American, 5% Hispanic American, 1% African American, 5% Asian American/Pacific Islander **The most frequently chosen baccalaureate fields are** business/marketing, communications/journalism, social sciences **Academic program** English as a second language, advanced placement, accelerated degree program, honors program, summer session, adult/continuing education programs, internships **Contact** Ms. Julie McCulloh, Dean of Admission, Gonzaga University, 502 East Boone Avenue, Spokane, WA 99258-0102. *Phone:* 509-313-6591 or toll-free 800-322-2584 Ext. 6572. *Fax:* 509-313-5780. *E-mail:* admissions@gonzaga.edu. *Web site:* http://www.gonzaga.edu/.

Visit Petersons.com and enter keyword Gonzaga

See page 824 for the College Close-Up.

Heritage University
Toppenish, Washington

Contact Ms. Leticia Garcia, Director of Admissions and Recruitment, Heritage University, 3240 Fort Road, Toppenish, WA 98948-9599. *Phone:* 509-865-8508 or toll-free 888-272-6190. *Fax:* 509-865-4469. *E-mail:* garcia_l@heritage.edu. *Web site:* http://www.heritage.edu/.

ITT Technical Institute
Everett, Washington

General Proprietary, primarily 2-year, coed **Contact** Director of Recruitment, ITT Technical Institute, 1615 75th Street SW, Everett, WA 98203. *Phone:* 425-583-0200 or toll-free 800-272-3791. *Web site:* http://www.itt-tech.edu/.

ITT Technical Institute
Seattle, Washington

General Proprietary, primarily 2-year, coed **Entrance** Minimally difficult **Setting** urban campus **Housing** No **Contact** Director of Recruitment, ITT Technical Institute, 12720 Gateway Drive, Suite 100, Seattle, WA 98168-3333. *Phone:* 206-244-3300 or toll-free 800-422-2029. *Web site:* http://www.itt-tech.edu/.

ITT Technical Institute
Spokane Valley, Washington

General Proprietary, primarily 2-year, coed **Entrance** Minimally difficult **Setting** suburban campus **Housing** No **Contact** Director of Recruitment, ITT Technical Institute, 13518 East Indiana Avenue, Spokane Valley, WA 99212-2682. *Phone:* 509-926-2900 or toll-free 800-777-8324. *Web site:* http://www.itt-tech.edu/.

Northwest College of Art
Poulsbo, Washington

Contact Mr. Mark Stoddard, Admissions, Northwest College of Art, 16301 Creative Drive, NE, Poulsbo, WA 98370. *Phone:* 360-779-9993 or toll-free 800-769-ARTS. *E-mail:* mstoddard@nca.edu. *Web site:* http://www.nca.edu/.

Northwest University
Kirkland, Washington

General Independent, comprehensive, coed, affiliated with Assemblies of God **Entrance** Moderately difficult **Setting** 56-acre suburban campus **Total enrollment** 1,383 **Student-faculty ratio** 17:1 **Application deadline** 7/15 (freshmen), 7/15 (transfer) **Freshman admission** 74% were admitted.

Northwest University (continued)
Average high school GPA 3.34 **Freshman test scores** SAT critical reading scores over 500: 62.5%; SAT math scores over 500: 47.5%; ACT scores over 18: 74%; SAT critical reading scores over 600: 20%; SAT math scores over 600: 14%; ACT scores over 24: 29% **Housing** Yes **Expenses** Tuition & Fees $22,650; Room & Board $6724 **Undergraduates** 60% women, 15% part-time, 24% 25 or older **The most frequently chosen baccalaureate fields are** business/marketing, health professions and related sciences, theology and religious vocations **Academic program** English as a second language, advanced placement, accelerated degree program, summer session, adult/continuing education programs, internships **Contact** Mr. Ben Thomas, Director of Admissions, Northwest University, PO Box 579, Kirkland, WA 98083-0579. *Phone:* 425-889-5212 or toll-free 800-669-3781. *Fax:* 425-889-5224. *E-mail:* admissions@northwestu.edu. *Web site:* http://www.northwestu.edu/.

Olympic College
Bremerton, Washington

Contact Ms. Jennifer Fyllingness, Director of Admissions and Outreach, Olympic College, 1600 Chester Avenue, Bremerton, WA 98337-1699. *Phone:* 360-475-7126 or toll-free 800-259-6718. *Fax:* 360-475-7202. *E-mail:* jfyllingness@olympic.edu. *Web site:* http://www.olympic.edu/.

Pacific Lutheran University
Tacoma, Washington

General Independent, comprehensive, coed, affiliated with Evangelical Lutheran Church in America **Entrance** Moderately difficult **Setting** 126-acre suburban campus **Total enrollment** 3,581 **Student-faculty ratio** 14:1 **Application deadline** Rolling (freshmen), rolling (transfer) **Freshman admission** 78% were admitted. Average high school GPA 3.62 **Freshman test scores** SAT critical reading scores over 500: 71.12%; SAT math scores over 500: 76.12%; ACT scores over 18: 95.63%; SAT critical reading scores over 600: 29.83%; SAT math scores over 600: 34.25%; ACT scores over 24: 69.38% **Housing** Yes **Expenses** Tuition & Fees $28,100; Room & Board $8600 **Undergraduates** 62% women, 5% part-time, 9% 25 or older, 1% Native American, 3% Hispanic American, 3% African American, 6% Asian American/Pacific Islander **The most frequently chosen baccalaureate fields are** business/marketing, health professions and related sciences, social sciences **Academic program** English as a second language, advanced placement, self-designed majors, summer session, internships **Contact** Mr. Karl Stumo, Vice President for Admission and Enrollment Services, Pacific Lutheran University, Tacoma, WA 98447. *Phone:* 253-535-7151 or toll-free 800-274-6758. *Fax:* 253-536-5136. *E-mail:* admission@plu.edu. *Web site:* http://www.plu.edu/.

Peninsula College
Port Angeles, Washington

General State-supported, primarily 2-year, coed **Entrance** Noncompetitive **Setting** 75-acre small-town campus **Total enrollment** 3,776 **Student-faculty ratio** 18:1 **Application deadline** Rolling (freshmen), rolling (transfer) **Housing** No **Expenses** Tuition & Fees: state resident $3099, nonresident $3489 **Undergraduates** 53% women, 51% part-time, 3% Native American, 5% Hispanic American, 1% African American, 2% Asian American/Pacific Islander **Academic program** English as a second language, advanced placement, honors program, summer session, adult/continuing education programs, internships **Contact** Ms. Pauline Marvin, Peninsula College, 1502 East Lauridsen Boulevard, Port Angeles, WA 98362. *Phone:* 360-417-6596. *Fax:* 360-457-8100. *E-mail:* admissions@pcadmin.ctc.edu. *Web site:* http://www.pc.ctc.edu/.

Saint Martin's University
Lacey, Washington

General Independent Roman Catholic, comprehensive, coed **Entrance** Moderately difficult **Setting** 380-acre suburban campus **Total enrollment** 1,687 **Student-faculty ratio** 12:1 **Application deadline** 8/1 (transfer) **Freshman admission** 78% were admitted. Average high school GPA 3.27 **Freshman test scores** SAT critical reading scores over 500: 53%; SAT math scores over 500: 54%; ACT scores over 18: 54%; SAT critical reading scores over 600: 10%; SAT math scores over 600: 15%; ACT scores over 24: 24% **Housing** Yes **Expenses** Tuition & Fees $26,402; Room & Board $8660 **Undergraduates** 55% women, 23% part-time, 30% 25 or older, 2% Native American, 9% Hispanic American, 8% African American, 10% Asian American/Pacific Islander **The most frequently chosen baccalaureate fields are** business/marketing, education, psychology **Academic program** English as a second language, advanced placement, accelerated degree program, summer session, adult/continuing education programs, internships **Contact** Mr. Matt Gruhler, Assistant Director of Admissions, Saint Martin's University, 5300 Pacific Avenue SE, Lacey, WA 98503-7500. *Phone:* 360-438-4596 or toll-free 800-368-8803. *Fax:* 360-412-6189. *E-mail:* admissions@stmartin.edu. *Web site:* http://www.stmartin.edu/.

Seattle Pacific University
Seattle, Washington

General Independent Free Methodist, comprehensive, coed **Entrance** Moderately difficult **Setting** 35-acre urban campus **Total enrollment** 4,000 **Student-faculty ratio** 14:1 **Application deadline** 2/1 (freshmen), 8/1 (transfer) **Freshman admission** 93% were admitted. Average high school GPA 3.56 **Freshman test scores** SAT critical reading scores over 500: 78.77%; SAT math scores over 500: 72.29%; ACT scores over 18: 95.08%; SAT critical reading scores over 600: 35.33%; SAT math scores over 600: 35.01%; ACT scores over 24: 62.45% **Housing** Yes **Expenses** Tuition & Fees $27,810; Room & Board $8544 **Undergraduates** 67% women, 4% part-time, 6% 25 or older, 1% Native American, 4% Hispanic American, 3% African American, 9% Asian American/Pacific Islander **The most frequently chosen baccalaureate fields are** business/marketing, health professions and related sciences, social sciences **Academic program** Advanced placement, self-designed majors, honors program, summer session, adult/continuing education programs, internships **Contact** Mr. Jobe Korb-Nice, Director of Admissions, Seattle Pacific University, 3307 3rd Avenue, W, Seattle, WA 98119-1997. *Phone:* 206-281-2021 or toll-free 800-366-3344. *Fax:* 206-281-2669. *E-mail:* admissions@spu.edu. *Web site:* http://www.spu.edu/.
Visit Petersons.com and enter keywords Seattle Pacific

See page 1148 for the College Close-Up.

Seattle University
Seattle, Washington

General Independent Roman Catholic, comprehensive, coed **Entrance** Moderately difficult **Setting** 50-acre urban campus **Total enrollment** 7,751 **Student-faculty ratio** 13:1 **Application deadline** Rolling (freshmen), 8/15 (transfer) **Freshman admission** 66% were admitted. Average high school GPA 3.59 **Freshman test scores** SAT critical reading scores over 500: 81.6%; SAT math scores over 500: 86.8%; ACT scores over 18: 99%; SAT critical reading scores over 600: 43.4%; SAT math scores over 600: 44.5%; ACT scores over 24: 71.5% **Housing** Yes **Expenses** Tuition & Fees $29,340; Room & Board $8805 **Undergraduates** 60% women, 6% part-time, 9% 25 or older, 1% Native American, 7% Hispanic American, 5% African American, 19% Asian American/Pacific Islander **The most frequently chosen baccalaureate fields are** business/marketing, health professions and related sciences, social sciences **Academic program** English as a second language, advanced placement, accelerated degree program, self-designed majors, honors program, summer session, adult/continuing education programs, internships **Contact** Melore Nielsen, Acting Dean of Admissions, Seattle University, 901 12th Avenue, PO Box 222000, Seattle, WA 98122-1090. *Phone:* 206-296-2000 or toll-free 800-542-0833 (in-state); 800-426-7123 (out-of-state). *Fax:* 206-296-5656. *E-mail:* admissions@seattleu.edu. *Web site:* http://www.seattleu.edu/.
Visit Petersons.com and enter keywords Seattle University

See page 1150 for the College Close-Up.

A FREE Magazine all about University Life!

etc IS MORE THAN THE NAME OF OUR MAGAZINE — IT'S OUR VISION — TO ENGAGE THE CULTURE AND CHANGE THE WORLD WITH THE GOSPEL OF JESUS CHRIST. AT SEATTLE PACIFIC UNIVERSITY, STUDENTS STUDY BIG IDEAS, EXPERIENCE CHRISTIAN COMMUNITY, LIVE OUT URBAN ADVENTURES — AND LEARN HOW TO MAKE THE WORLD A BETTER PLACE.

BE A PART OF IT!

Subscribe at
spu.edu/freemagazine
OR 800-366-3344

Seattle Pacific UNIVERSITY

Engaging the culture, changing the world

Trinity Lutheran College
Issaquah, Washington

Contact Ms. Pamela Renn, Director of Admissions, Trinity Lutheran College, 4221 228th Avenue, SE, Issaquah, WA 98029-9299. *Phone:* 425-961-5512 or toll-free 800-843-5659. *Fax:* 425-392-0404. *E-mail:* admissn@lbi.edu. *Web site:* http://www.tlc.edu/.

University of Phoenix–Eastern Washington Campus
Spokane Valley, Washington

General Proprietary, comprehensive, coed **Entrance** Noncompetitive **Setting** urban campus **Total enrollment** 44 **Student-faculty ratio** 9:1 **Application deadline** Rolling (freshmen), rolling (transfer) **Housing** No **Expenses** Tuition & Fees $11,625 **Undergraduates** 54% women, 92% 25 or older, 3% Hispanic American, 3% Asian American/Pacific Islander **The most frequently chosen baccalaureate fields are** business/marketing, computer and information sciences, security and protective services **Academic program** Advanced placement, accelerated degree program **Contact** Ms. Audra McQuarie, Registrar/Executive Director, University of Phoenix–Eastern Washington Campus, 4035 South Riverpoint Parkway, Mail Stop CF-L101, Phoenix, AZ 85040. *Phone:* 480-557-6151 or toll-free 800-697-8223 (in-state); 800-228-7240 (out-of-state). *Fax:* 480-643-3068. *E-mail:* audra.mcquarie@phoenix.edu. *Web site:* http://www.phoenix.edu/.

University of Phoenix–Washington Campus
Seattle, Washington

General Proprietary, comprehensive, coed **Entrance** Noncompetitive **Setting** urban campus **Total enrollment** 749 **Application deadline** Rolling (freshmen), rolling (transfer) **Housing** No **Expenses** Tuition & Fees $12,525 **Undergraduates** 56% women, 90% 25 or older, 2% Native American, 4% Hispanic American, 16% African American, 10% Asian American/Pacific Islander **The most frequently chosen baccalaureate fields are** business/marketing, computer and information sciences, interdisciplinary studies **Academic program** Advanced placement, accelerated degree program, adult/continuing education programs **Contact** Ms. Evelyn Gaskin, Registrar/Executive Director, University of Phoenix–Washington Campus, 4615 East Elwood Street, Mail Stop AA-K101, Phoenix, AZ 85040-1958. *Phone:* 480-557-3303 or toll-free 800-776-4867 (in-state); 800-228-7240 (out-of-state). *Fax:* 480-643-1020. *E-mail:* evelyn.gaskin@phoenix.edu. *Web site:* http://www.phoenix.edu/.

University of Puget Sound
Tacoma, Washington

General Independent, comprehensive, coed **Entrance** Very difficult **Setting** 97-acre suburban campus **Total enrollment** 2,901 **Student-faculty ratio** 12:1 **Application deadline** 1/15 (freshmen), 7/1 (transfer) **Freshman admission** 63% were admitted. Average high school GPA 3.5 **Freshman test scores** SAT critical reading scores over 500: 93.21%; SAT math scores over 500: 91.06%; ACT scores over 18: 99.46%; SAT critical reading scores over 600: 63.74%; SAT math scores over 600: 53.48%; ACT scores over 24: 86.83% **Housing** Yes **Expenses** Tuition & Fees $37,225; Room & Board $9650 **Undergraduates** 59% women, 1% part-time, 2% 25 or older, 2% Native American, 4% Hispanic American, 3% African American, 10% Asian American/Pacific Islander **The most frequently chosen baccalaureate fields are** business/marketing, biological/life sciences, social sciences **Academic program** Advanced placement, self-designed majors, honors program, summer session, internships **Contact** Dr. George Mills, Vice President for Enrollment, University of Puget Sound, 1500 North Warner Street, Tacoma, WA 98416. *Phone:* 253-879-3211 or toll-free 800-396-7191. *Fax:* 253-879-3993. *E-mail:* admission@ups.edu. *Web site:* http://www.ups.edu/.

University of Washington
Seattle, Washington

General State-supported, university, coed **Entrance** Moderately difficult **Setting** 703-acre urban campus **Total enrollment** 45,943 **Application deadline** 1/15 (freshmen), 2/15 (transfer) **Freshman admission** 58% were admitted **Freshman test scores** SAT critical reading scores over 500: 85%; SAT math scores over 500: 93%; ACT scores over 18: 98%; SAT critical reading scores over 600: 48%; SAT math scores over 600: 67%; ACT scores over 24: 79% **Housing** Yes **Expenses** Tuition & Fees: state resident $7692, nonresident $24,367; Room & Board $7800 **Undergraduates** 50% women, 14% part-time, 12% 25 or older **The most frequently chosen baccalaureate fields are** business/marketing, biological/life sciences, social sciences **Academic program** English as a second language, advanced placement, self-designed majors, honors program, summer session, adult/continuing education programs, internships **Contact** Emily Leggio, Senior Associate Director of Admissions, University of Washington, Seattle, WA 98195. *Phone:* 206-543-9686. *Fax:* 206-685-3655. *Web site:* http://www.washington.edu/.

University of Washington, Bothell
Bothell, Washington

General State-supported, comprehensive, coed **Entrance** Moderately difficult **Setting** 128-acre suburban campus **Total enrollment** 2,820 **Student-faculty ratio** 19:1 **Application deadline** 1/15 (freshmen) **Freshman admission** 77% were admitted. Average high school GPA 3.2 **Freshman test scores** SAT critical reading scores over 500: 50%; SAT math scores over 500: 64%; ACT scores over 18: 78%; SAT critical reading scores over 600: 15%; SAT math scores over 600: 26%; ACT scores over 24: 24% **Housing** Yes **Expenses** Tuition & Fees: state resident $7575, nonresident $24,250 **Undergraduates** 54% women, 34% part-time, 38% 25 or older, 1% Native American, 6% Hispanic American, 4% African American, 24% Asian American/Pacific Islander **The most frequently chosen baccalaureate fields are** business/marketing, health professions and related sciences, interdisciplinary studies **Academic program** Advanced placement, self-designed majors, honors program, summer session, adult/continuing education programs, internships **Contact** Lindsey Wille, Assistant Director of Admissions, University of Washington, Bothell, 18115 Campus Way NE, Bothell, WA 98011-8246. *Phone:* 425-352-5000. *Fax:* 425-352-5455. *E-mail:* freshmen@uwb.edu. *Web site:* http://www.uwb.edu.

University of Washington, Tacoma
Tacoma, Washington

General State-supported, comprehensive, coed **Entrance** Minimally difficult **Setting** 46-acre urban campus **Total enrollment** 3,111 **Student-faculty ratio** 16:1 **Application deadline** 3/1 (freshmen), 4/15 (transfer) **Freshman admission** 31% were admitted. Average high school GPA 3.3 **Freshman test scores** SAT critical reading scores over 500: 51.7%; SAT math scores over 500: 57.8%; ACT scores over 18: 84.6%; SAT critical reading scores over 600: 12%; SAT math scores over 600: 18.6%; ACT scores over 24: 25.6% **Housing** Yes **Expenses** Tuition & Fees: state resident $7653, nonresident $24,328; Room only $8949 **Undergraduates** 57% women, 22% part-time, 39% 25 or older, 1% Native American, 7% Hispanic American, 8% African American, 17% Asian American/Pacific Islander **The most frequently chosen baccalaureate fields are** business/marketing, health professions and related sciences, interdisciplinary studies **Academic program** Advanced placement, accelerated degree program, self-designed majors, honors program, summer session, internships **Contact** Ms. Fiona Johnson, Admissions Advising and Outreach, University of Washington, Tacoma, 1900 Commerce Street, Tacoma, WA 98402-3100. *Phone:* 253-692-4742 or toll-free 800-736-7750. *Fax:* 253-692-4788. *E-mail:* fionaj@u.washington.edu. *Web site:* http://www.tacoma.washington.edu/.

Walla Walla University
College Place, Washington

General Independent Seventh-day Adventist, comprehensive, coed **Entrance** Moderately difficult **Setting** 77-acre small-town campus **Total enrollment** 1,800 **Student-faculty ratio** 13:1 **Application deadline** Rolling (freshmen), rolling (transfer) **Freshman admission** 98% were admitted. Average high school GPA 3.41 **Housing** Yes **Expenses** Tuition & Fees $21,936; Room & Board $4320 **Undergraduates** 48% women, 6% part-time, 10% 25 or older, 1% Native American, 10% Hispanic American, 3% African American, 6% Asian American/Pacific Islander **The most frequently chosen baccalaureate fields are** business/marketing, engineering, health professions and related sciences **Academic program** Advanced placement, honors program, summer session, internships **Contact** Mr. Dallas Weis, Director for Admissions, Walla Walla University, 204 South College Avenue, College Place, WA 99324-1198. *Phone:* 509-527-2327 or toll-free 800-541-8900. *Fax:* 509-527-2397. *E-mail:* dallas@wallawalla.edu. *Web site:* http://www.wallawalla.edu/.

Washington State University
Pullman, Washington

General State-supported, university, coed **Entrance** Moderately difficult **Setting** 620-acre small-town campus **Total enrollment** 26,101 **Student-faculty ratio** 15:1 **Application deadline** 1/31 (freshmen), 1/31 (transfer) **Freshman admission** 76% were admitted. Average high school GPA 3.42 **Freshman test scores** SAT critical reading scores over 500: 66.7%; SAT math scores over 500: 73.9%; ACT scores over 18: 93.4%; SAT critical reading scores over 600: 22.2%; SAT math scores over 600: 30%; ACT scores over 24: 46.9% **Housing** Yes **Expenses** Tuition & Fees: state resident $8489, nonresident $19,565; Room & Board $8886 **Undergraduates** 52% women, 14% part-time, 7% 25 or older, 1% Native American, 7% Hispanic American, 2% African American, 6% Asian American/Pacific Islander **The most frequently chosen baccalaureate fields are** business/marketing, health professions and related sciences, social sciences **Academic program** English as a second language, advanced placement, accelerated degree program, self-designed majors, honors program, summer session, adult/continuing education programs, internships **Contact** Ms. Wendy Peterson, Director of Admissions, Washington State University, PO Box 641067, Pullman, WA 99164-1067. *Phone:* 888-468-6978 or toll-free 888-468-6978. *Fax:* 509-335-4902. *E-mail:* admiss2@wsu.edu. *Web site:* http://www.wsu.edu/.

Western Washington University
Bellingham, Washington

General State-supported, comprehensive, coed **Entrance** Moderately difficult **Setting** 223-acre small-town campus **Total enrollment** 14,575 **Student-faculty ratio** 19:1 **Application deadline** 3/1 (freshmen), 4/1 (transfer) **Freshman admission** 73% were admitted. Average high school GPA 3.5 **Freshman test scores** SAT critical reading scores over 500: 78.38%; SAT math scores over 500: 79.42%; ACT scores over 18: 95.85%; SAT critical reading scores over 600: 35.23%; SAT math scores over 600: 32.42%; ACT scores over 24: 57.04% **Housing** Yes **Expenses** Tuition & Fees: state resident $6159, nonresident $17,190; Room & Board $8393 **Undergraduates** 55% women, 8% part-time, 11% 25 or older, 2% Native American, 5% Hispanic American, 3% African American, 9% Asian American/Pacific Islander **The most frequently chosen baccalaureate fields are** business/marketing, social sciences, visual and performing arts **Academic program** English as a second language, advanced placement, accelerated degree program, self-designed majors, honors program, summer session, internships **Contact** Ms. Karen Copetas, Director of Admissions, Western Washington University, 516 High Street, Bellingham, WA 98225-9009. *Phone:* 360-650-3440. *Fax:* 360-650-7369. *E-mail:* admit@wwu.edu. *Web site:* http://www.wwu.edu/.

See page 1366 for the College Close-Up.

Whitman College

Walla Walla, Washington

General Independent, 4-year, coed **Entrance** Very difficult **Setting** 117-acre small-town campus **Total enrollment** 1,515 **Student-faculty ratio** 10:1 **Application deadline** 1/15 (freshmen), 3/1 (transfer) **Freshman admission** 44% were admitted. Average high school GPA 3.78 **Freshman test scores** SAT critical reading scores over 500: 98.98%; SAT math scores over 500: 97.63%; ACT scores over 18: 100%; SAT critical reading scores over 600: 83.39%; SAT math scores over 600: 83.05%; ACT scores over 24: 98.02% **Housing** Yes **Expenses** Tuition & Fees $38,770; Room & Board $9720 **Undergraduates** 58% women, 2% part-time, 1% 25 or older, 1% Native American, 6% Hispanic American, 2% African American, 11% Asian American/Pacific Islander **The most frequently chosen baccalaureate fields are** biological/life sciences, social sciences, visual and performing arts **Academic program** Advanced placement, accelerated degree program, self-designed majors, honors program **Contact** Mr. Tony Cabasco, Dean of Admission and Financial Aid, Whitman College, 515 Boyer Avenue, Walla Walla, WA 99362-2083. *Phone:* 509-527-5176 or toll-free 877-462-9448. *Fax:* 509-527-4967. *E-mail:* admission@whitman.edu. *Web site:* http://www.whitman.edu/.

Whitworth University

Spokane, Washington

Contact Ms. Marianne Hansen, Director of Admission, Whitworth University, 300 West, Hawthorne Road, Spokane, WA 99251. *Phone:* 509-777-4348 or toll-free 800-533-4668. *Fax:* 509-777-3758. *E-mail:* admission@whitworth.edu. *Web site:* http://www.whitworth.edu/.

WEST VIRGINIA

Alderson-Broaddus College

Philippi, West Virginia

General Independent, comprehensive, coed, affiliated with American Baptist Churches in the U.S.A. **Entrance** Moderately difficult **Setting** 170-acre rural campus **Total enrollment** 711 **Student-faculty ratio** 10:1 **Application deadline** Rolling (freshmen), rolling (transfer) **Freshman admission** 74% were admitted. Average high school GPA 3.3 **Freshman test scores** SAT critical reading scores over 500: 43%; SAT math scores over 500: 39%; ACT scores over 18: 81%; SAT critical reading scores over 600: 5%; SAT math scores over 600: 7%; ACT scores over 24: 24% **Housing** Yes **Expenses** Tuition & Fees $21,654; Room & Board $7002 **Undergraduates** 66% women, 4% part-time, 10% 25 or older, 0.3% Native American, 2% Hispanic American, 4% African American, 1% Asian American/Pacific Islander **The most frequently chosen baccalaureate fields are** business/marketing, education, health professions and related sciences **Academic program** Advanced placement, honors program, summer session, internships **Contact** Ms. Kimberly N. Klaus, Director of Admissions, Alderson-Broaddus College, 101 College Hill Drive, Campus Box 2003, Philippi, WV 26416. *Phone:* 304-457-1700 or toll-free 800-263-1549. *Fax:* 304-457-6239. *E-mail:* admissions@ab.edu. *Web site:* http://www.ab.edu/.

American Public University System

Charles Town, West Virginia

General Proprietary, comprehensive, coed **Entrance** Noncompetitive **Setting** rural campus **Total enrollment** 31,331 **Student-faculty ratio** 28:1 **Application deadline** Rolling (freshmen), rolling (transfer) **Freshman admission** 100% were admitted **Housing** No **Expenses** Tuition & Fees $6000 **Undergraduates** 32% women, 80% part-time, 79% 25 or older, 1% Native American, 12% Hispanic American, 15% African American, 3% Asian American/Pacific Islander **The most frequently chosen baccalaureate fields are** business/marketing, interdisciplinary studies, security and protective services **Academic program** Adult/continuing education programs **Contact** Ms. Terry Grant, Associate Vice President, Enrollment Management, American Public University System, 111 West Congress Street, Charles Town, WV 25414. *Phone:* 877-468-6268. *Fax:* 304-724-3788. *E-mail:* info@apus.edu. *Web site:* http://www.apus.edu/.

Appalachian Bible College

Bradley, West Virginia

General Independent nondenominational, comprehensive, coed **Entrance** Noncompetitive **Setting** 110-acre small-town campus **Total enrollment** 283 **Student-faculty ratio** 17:1 **Application deadline** Rolling (freshmen), rolling (transfer) **Freshman admission** 62% were admitted **Freshman test scores** SAT critical reading scores over 500: 63%; SAT math scores over 500: 46%; ACT scores over 18: 86%; SAT critical reading scores over 600: 25%; SAT math scores over 600: 21%; ACT scores over 24: 40% **Housing** Yes **Expenses** Tuition & Fees $10,290; Room & Board $5400 **Undergraduates** 47% women, 19% part-time **The most frequently chosen baccalaureate field is** theology and religious vocations **Academic program** Advanced placement, honors program, summer session, adult/continuing education programs, internships **Contact** Miss Ashley Siders, Admissions Assistant, Appalachian Bible College, PO Box ABC, Bradley, WV 25818. *Phone:* 304-877-6428 Ext. 3213 or toll-free 800-678-9ABC Ext. 3213. *Fax:* 304-877-5082. *E-mail:* admissions2@abc.edu. *Web site:* http://www.abc.edu/.

Bethany College

Bethany, West Virginia

General Independent, 4-year, coed, affiliated with Christian Church (Disciples of Christ) **Entrance** Moderately difficult **Setting** 1,300-acre rural campus **Total enrollment** 830 **Student-faculty ratio** 14:1 **Application deadline** Rolling (freshmen), rolling (transfer) **Freshman admission** 78% were admitted. Average high school GPA 3.2 **Freshman test scores** SAT critical reading scores over 500: 34.26%; SAT math scores over 500: 35.21%; ACT scores over 18: 77.36%; SAT critical reading scores over 600: 9.38%; SAT math scores over 600: 7.98%; ACT scores over 24: 26.31% **Housing** Yes **Expenses** Tuition & Fees $21,465; Room & Board $8700 **Undergraduates** 47% women, 1% part-time, 2% 25 or older, 0.4% Native American, 2% Hispanic American, 10% African American, 1% Asian American/Pacific Islander **The most frequently chosen baccalaureate fields are** education, communications/journalism, psychology **Academic program** Advanced placement, self-designed majors, internships **Contact** Ms. Karina Dayich, Director of Admission, Bethany College, Office of Admission, Bethany, WV 26032. *Phone:* 304-829-7611 or toll-free 800-922-7611. *Fax:* 304-829-7142. *E-mail:* admission@bethanywv.edu. *Web site:* http://www.bethanywv.edu/.

Bluefield State College

Bluefield, West Virginia

General State-supported, 4-year, coed **Entrance** Noncompetitive **Setting** 45-acre small-town campus **Total enrollment** 1,989 **Student-faculty ratio** 17:1 **Application deadline** Rolling (freshmen), rolling (transfer) **Freshman admission** 79% were admitted. Average high school GPA 3.37 **Freshman test scores** SAT critical reading scores over 500: 36%; SAT math scores over 500: 32%; ACT scores over 18: 58%; SAT critical reading scores over 600: 8%; SAT math scores over 600: 12%; ACT scores over 24: 8% **Housing** No **Expenses** Tuition & Fees: state resident $4596, nonresident $9000 **Undergraduates** 61% women, 20% part-time, 41% 25 or older, 0.4% Native American, 1% Hispanic American, 13% African American, 0.4% Asian American/Pacific Islander **The most frequently chosen baccalaureate fields are** engineering technologies, business/marketing, liberal arts/general studies **Academic program** Advanced placement, honors program, summer session, adult/continuing education programs, internships **Contact** Mr. Kenneth Mandeville, Director of Student Recruitment, Bluefield State College, 219 Rock

Bluefield State College (continued)
Street, Bluefield, WV 24701-2198. *Phone:* 304-327-4067 or toll-free 800-344-8892 Ext. 4065 (in-state); 800-654-7798 Ext. 4065 (out-of-state). *Fax:* 304-325-7747. *E-mail:* bscadmit@bluefieldstate.edu. *Web site:* http://www.bluefieldstate.edu/.

Concord University
Athens, West Virginia

General State-supported, comprehensive, coed **Entrance** Minimally difficult **Setting** 100-acre rural campus **Total enrollment** 2,947 **Student-faculty ratio** 18:1 **Application deadline** Rolling (freshmen), rolling (transfer) **Freshman admission** 60% were admitted. Average high school GPA 3.25 **Freshman test scores** SAT critical reading scores over 500: 42%; SAT math scores over 500: 38%; ACT scores over 18: 83%; SAT critical reading scores over 600: 6%; SAT math scores over 600: 9%; ACT scores over 24: 23% **Housing** Yes **Expenses** Tuition & Fees: state resident $4974, nonresident $11,050; Room & Board $6766 **Undergraduates** 58% women, 17% part-time, 14% 25 or older, 0.2% Native American, 1% Hispanic American, 5% African American, 2% Asian American/Pacific Islander **The most frequently chosen baccalaureate fields are** business/marketing, biological/life sciences, education **Academic program** English as a second language, advanced placement, accelerated degree program, self-designed majors, honors program, summer session, internships **Contact** Mr. Kent Gamble, Director of Enrollment, Concord University, 1000 Vermillion Street, Athens, WV 24712. *Phone:* 304-384-5316 or toll-free 888-384-5249. *Fax:* 304-384-9044. *E-mail:* admissions@concord.edu. *Web site:* http://www.concord.edu/.

Davis & Elkins College
Elkins, West Virginia

General Independent Presbyterian, 4-year, coed **Entrance** Moderately difficult **Setting** 170-acre small-town campus **Total enrollment** 640 **Student-faculty ratio** 10:1 **Application deadline** Rolling (freshmen), rolling (transfer) **Freshman admission** 75% were admitted. Average high school GPA 2.9 **Freshman test scores** SAT critical reading scores over 500: 37.3%; SAT math scores over 500: 30%; ACT scores over 18: 67.2%; SAT critical reading scores over 600: 8%; SAT math scores over 600: 8%; ACT scores over 24: 19% **Housing** Yes **Expenses** Tuition & Fees $19,840; Room & Board $6700 **Undergraduates** 65% women, 11% part-time, 24% 25 or older, 1% Native American, 2% Hispanic American, 4% African American, 1% Asian American/Pacific Islander **The most frequently chosen baccalaureate fields are** business/marketing, education, parks and recreation **Academic program** English as a second language, advanced placement, accelerated degree program, self-designed majors, honors program, summer session, adult/continuing education programs, internships **Contact** Ms. Reneé Heckel, Director of Enrollment Management, Davis & Elkins College, 100 Campus Drive, Elkins, WV 26241. *Phone:* 304-637-1974 or toll-free 800-624-3157 Ext. 1230. *Fax:* 304-637-1800. *E-mail:* admiss@davisandelkins.edu. *Web site:* http://www.davisandelkins.edu/.

Fairmont State University
Fairmont, West Virginia

General State-supported, comprehensive, coed **Entrance** Minimally difficult **Setting** 120-acre small-town campus **Total enrollment** 4,572 **Student-faculty ratio** 17:1 **Application deadline** Rolling (freshmen), rolling (transfer) **Freshman admission** 61% were admitted. Average high school GPA 3.12 **Freshman test scores** SAT critical reading scores over 500: 20%; SAT math scores over 500: 43.6%; ACT scores over 18: 81.1%; SAT critical reading scores over 600: 5.5%; SAT math scores over 600: 12.7%; ACT scores over 24: 18.9% **Housing** Yes **Expenses** Tuition & Fees: state resident $5372, nonresident $11,104; Room & Board $6900 **Undergraduates** 56% women, 14% part-time, 28% 25 or older, 0.4% Native American, 1% Hispanic American, 4% African American, 1% Asian American/Pacific Islander **The most frequently chosen baccalaureate fields are** business/marketing, education, family and consumer sciences **Academic program** English as a second language, advanced placement, accelerated degree program, honors program, summer session, adult/continuing education programs, internships **Contact** Mr. Steve Leadman, Director of Admissions and Recruiting, Fairmont State University, 1201 Locust Avenue, Fairmont, WV 26554. *Phone:* 304-367-4892 or toll-free 800-641-5678. *Fax:* 304-367-4789. *E-mail:* admit@fairmontstate.edu. *Web site:* http://www.fairmontstate.edu/. **Visit Petersons.com and enter keyword Fairmont**

See page 790 for the College Close-Up.

Glenville State College
Glenville, West Virginia

General State-supported, 4-year, coed **Entrance** Noncompetitive **Setting** 331-acre rural campus **Total enrollment** 1,721 **Student-faculty ratio** 18:1 **Application deadline** Rolling (freshmen), 8/24 (transfer) **Freshman admission** 100% were admitted. Average high school GPA 2.9 **Freshman test scores** SAT critical reading scores over 500: 23%; SAT math scores over 500: 22%; ACT scores over 18: 67%; SAT critical reading scores over 600: 4%; SAT math scores over 600: 3%; ACT scores over 24: 13% **Housing** Yes **Expenses** Tuition & Fees: state resident $4888, nonresident $11,702; Room & Board $6460 **Undergraduates** 43% women, 33% part-time **The most frequently chosen baccalaureate fields are** education, business/marketing, social sciences **Academic program** Advanced placement, accelerated degree program, self-designed majors, honors program, summer session, adult/continuing education programs, internships **Contact** Mr. Tommy Oldaker, Admission Counselor, Glenville State College, 200 High Street, Glenville, WV 26351-1200. *Phone:* 304-462-4128 Ext. 6133 or toll-free 800-924-2010. *Fax:* 304-462-8619. *E-mail:* tommy.oldaker@glenville.edu. *Web site:* http://www.glenville.edu/.

Marshall University
Huntington, West Virginia

General State-supported, university, coed **Entrance** Moderately difficult **Setting** 70-acre urban campus **Total enrollment** 13,776 **Student-faculty ratio** 19:1 **Application deadline** Rolling (freshmen), rolling (transfer) **Freshman admission** 86% were admitted. Average high school GPA 3.33 **Freshman test scores** SAT math scores over 500: 40.41%; ACT scores over 18: 91%; SAT math scores over 600: 11.64%; ACT scores over 24: 35% **Housing** Yes **Expenses** Tuition & Fees: state resident $5236, nonresident $12,482; Room & Board $7556 **Undergraduates** 56% women, 17% part-time, 21% 25 or older, 0.4% Native American, 1% Hispanic American, 6% African American, 1% Asian American/Pacific Islander **The most frequently chosen baccalaureate fields are** business/marketing, education, liberal arts/general studies **Academic program** English as a second language, advanced placement, accelerated degree program, honors program, summer session, adult/continuing education programs, internships **Contact** Dr. Tammy Johnson, Director of Admissions, Marshall University, 1 John Marshall Drive, Huntington, WV 25755. *Phone:* 800-642-3499 or toll-free 800-642-3499. *Fax:* 304-696-3135. *E-mail:* admissions@marshall.edu. *Web site:* http://www.marshall.edu/.

Mountain State University
Beckley, West Virginia

General Independent, comprehensive, coed **Entrance** Noncompetitive **Setting** 35-acre small-town campus **Total enrollment** 5,951 **Student-faculty ratio** 14:1 **Application deadline** Rolling (freshmen), rolling (transfer) **Freshman admission** 100% were admitted. Average high school GPA 3.02 **Freshman test scores** ACT scores over 18: 52%; ACT scores over 24: 10% **Housing** Yes **Expenses** Tuition & Fees $8700; Room & Board $6116 **Undergraduates** 67% women, 28% part-time, 58% 25 or older, 1% Native American, 2% Hispanic American, 15%

African American, 2% Asian American/Pacific Islander **The most frequently chosen baccalaureate fields are** health professions and related sciences, liberal arts/general studies, security and protective services **Academic program** English as a second language, advanced placement, accelerated degree program, self-designed majors, summer session, adult/continuing education programs, internships **Contact** Ms. Darlene Brown, Enrollment Coordinator, Mountain State University, PO Box 9003, Beckley, WV 25802-9003. *Phone:* 304-929-1433 or toll-free 800-766-6067 Ext. 1433. *Fax:* 304-253-5072. *E-mail:* gomsu@mountainstate.edu. *Web site:* http://www.mountainstate.edu/.

Visit Petersons.com and enter keyword Mountain

See page 988 for the College Close-Up.

Ohio Valley University

Vienna, West Virginia

General Independent, comprehensive, coed, affiliated with Church of Christ **Entrance** Minimally difficult **Setting** 299-acre small-town campus **Total enrollment** 501 **Student-faculty ratio** 11:1 **Application deadline** 8/15 (freshmen), rolling (transfer) **Freshman admission** 57% were admitted **Freshman test scores** SAT critical reading scores over 500: 28%; SAT math scores over 500: 28%; ACT scores over 18: 85%; SAT critical reading scores over 600: 14%; SAT math scores over 600: 9%; ACT scores over 24: 27% **Housing** Yes **Expenses** Tuition & Fees $17,200; Room & Board $6676 **Undergraduates** 53% women, 13% part-time, 25% 25 or older, 4% Hispanic American, 5% African American **Academic program** English as a second language, advanced placement, honors program, summer session, adult/continuing education programs, internships **Contact** Mrs. Valerie Wright, Admissions Office Manager, Ohio Valley University, 1 Campus View Drive, Vienna, WV 26105. *Phone:* 304-865-6200 or toll-free 877-446-8668 Ext. 6200. *Fax:* 304-865-6001. *E-mail:* admissions@ovu.edu. *Web site:* http://www.ovu.edu/.

Potomac State College of West Virginia University

Keyser, West Virginia

General State-supported, primarily 2-year, coed **Entrance** Noncompetitive **Setting** 18-acre small-town campus **Total enrollment** 1,810 **Student-faculty ratio** 27:1 **Application deadline** Rolling (freshmen), rolling (transfer) **Freshman admission** Average high school GPA 2.78 **Freshman test scores** SAT critical reading scores over 500: 16%; SAT math scores over 500: 17%; ACT scores over 18: 60%; SAT critical reading scores over 600: 3%; SAT math scores over 600: 5%; ACT scores over 24: 10% **Housing** Yes **Undergraduates** 53% women, 26% part-time, 12% 25 or older, 0.2% Native American, 3% Hispanic American, 13% African American, 1% Asian American/Pacific Islander **The most frequently chosen baccalaureate fields are** business/marketing, security and protective services **Academic program** Advanced placement, honors program, summer session, adult/continuing education programs, internships **Contact** Ms. Beth Little, Director of Enrollment Services, Potomac State College of West Virginia University, 75 Arnold Street, Keyser, WV 26726. *Phone:* 304-788-6820 or toll-free 800-262-7332 Ext. 6820. *Fax:* 304-788-6939. *E-mail:* go2psc@mail.wvu.edu. *Web site:* http://www.potomacstatecollege.edu/.

Salem International University

Salem, West Virginia

Contact Ms. Gina Cossey, Vice President, Recruiting and Admissions, Salem International University, PO Box 500, Salem, WV 26426-0500. *Phone:* 304-326-1359 or toll-free 800-283-4562. *Fax:* 304-326-1592. *E-mail:* admissions@salemiu.edu. *Web site:* http://www.salemu.edu/.

Shepherd University

Shepherdstown, West Virginia

General State-supported, comprehensive, coed **Entrance** Moderately difficult **Setting** 320-acre small-town campus **Total enrollment** 4,256 **Student-faculty ratio** 19:1 **Application deadline** Rolling (freshmen), rolling (transfer) **Freshman admission** 94% were admitted. Average high school GPA 3.21 **Freshman test scores** SAT critical reading scores over 500: 51.24%; SAT math scores over 500: 51.55%; ACT scores over 18: 95.51%; SAT critical reading scores over 600: 12.97%; SAT math scores over 600: 13.35%; ACT scores over 24: 30.78% **Housing** Yes **Expenses** Tuition & Fees: state resident $5234, nonresident $13,574; Room & Board $7228 **Undergraduates** 57% women, 20% part-time, 14% 25 or older, 0.4% Native American, 2% Hispanic American, 5% African American, 2% Asian American/Pacific Islander **The most frequently chosen baccalaureate fields are** business/marketing, education, liberal arts/general studies **Academic program** Advanced placement, accelerated degree program, honors program, summer session, adult/continuing education programs, internships **Contact** Mr. Randall Friend, Director of Admissions, Shepherd University, PO Box 5000, Shepherdstown, WV 25443-5000. *Phone:* 304-876-5212 or toll-free 800-344-5231. *Fax:* 304-876-5165. *E-mail:* admissions@shepherd.edu. *Web site:* http://www.shepherd.edu/.

Visit Petersons.com and enter keyword Shepherd

Strayer University–Teays Valley Campus

Scott Depot, West Virginia

General Proprietary, comprehensive, coed **Contact** Admissions Office, Strayer University–Teays Valley Campus, 100 Corporate Center Drive, Scott Depot, WV 25560. *Phone:* 304-760-1700. *Web site:* http://www.strayer.edu/teays_valley.

University of Charleston

Charleston, West Virginia

General Independent, comprehensive, coed **Entrance** Moderately difficult **Setting** 40-acre urban campus **Total enrollment** 1,396 **Student-faculty ratio** 14:1 **Application deadline** Rolling (freshmen), rolling (transfer) **Freshman admission** 79% were admitted. Average high school GPA 3.33 **Freshman test scores** SAT critical reading scores over 500: 45%; SAT math scores over 500: 38%; ACT scores over 18: 88%; SAT critical reading scores over 600: 10%; SAT math scores over 600: 11%; ACT scores over 24: 36% **Housing** Yes **Expenses** Tuition & Fees $24,000; Room & Board $8700 **Undergraduates** 59% women, 3% part-time, 10% 25 or older, 0.3% Native American, 1% Hispanic American, 8% African American, 1% Asian American/Pacific Islander **Academic program** English as a second language, advanced placement, accelerated degree program, self-designed majors, summer session, adult/continuing education programs, internships **Contact** Mr. Alan Liebrecht, Vice President for Enrollment, University of Charleston, 2300 MacCorkle Avenue, SE, Charleston, WV 25304. *Phone:* 304-357-4750 or toll-free 800-995-GOUC. *Fax:* 304-357-4781. *E-mail:* admissions@ucwv.edu. *Web site:* http://www.ucwv.edu/.

Visit Petersons.com and enter keywords University of Charleston

See page 1258 for the College Close-Up.

West Liberty University

West Liberty, West Virginia

General State-supported, comprehensive, coed **Entrance** Minimally difficult **Setting** rural campus **Total enrollment** 2,645 **Student-faculty ratio** 17:1 **Application deadline** Rolling (freshmen), rolling (transfer) **Freshman admission** 79% were admitted. Average high school GPA 3.21 **Freshman test scores** SAT critical reading scores over 500: 22.5%; SAT math scores over 500: 24%; ACT scores over 18: 75.9%; SAT critical reading scores over 600: 1.5%; SAT math scores over 600: 3%; ACT scores over 24: 20% **Housing** Yes **Expenses** Tuition & Fees: state resident $4880, nonresident $11,950; Room & Board $6870 **Undergraduates** 56% women, 13% part-time, 15% 25 or older, 0.2% Native American, 1% Hispanic American, 3% African American, 1% Asian

West Liberty University (continued)

American/Pacific Islander **The most frequently chosen baccalaureate fields are** business/marketing, education, health professions and related sciences **Academic program** Advanced placement, accelerated degree program, self-designed majors, honors program, summer session, adult/continuing education programs, internships **Contact** Ms. Stephanie North, Admissions Counselor, West Liberty University, PO Box 295, West Liberty, WV 26074. *Phone:* 304-336-8078 or toll-free 800-732-6204 Ext. 8076. *Fax:* 304-336-8403. *E-mail:* wladmsn1@westliberty.edu. *Web site:* http://www.westliberty.edu/.

West Virginia State University
Institute, West Virginia

General State-supported, comprehensive, coed **Entrance** Minimally difficult **Setting** 98-acre suburban campus **Total enrollment** 4,003 **Student-faculty ratio** 19:1 **Application deadline** 8/11 (freshmen), 8/11 (transfer) **Freshman admission** Average high school GPA 2.77 **Housing** Yes **Expenses** Tuition & Fees: state resident $4346, nonresident $10,346; Room & Board $6020 **Undergraduates** 60% women, 49% part-time, 37% 25 or older, 0.5% Native American, 1% Hispanic American, 17% African American, 1% Asian American/Pacific Islander **The most frequently chosen baccalaureate fields are** business/marketing, communications/journalism, liberal arts/general studies **Academic program** Advanced placement, accelerated degree program, summer session, adult/continuing education programs, internships **Contact** Mr. Christopher D. Jackson, Interim Director of Recruiting, West Virginia State University, Campus Box 197, PO Box 1000, Ferrell Hall, Room 106, Institute, WV 25112-1000. *Phone:* 304-766-3033 or toll-free 800-987-2112. *Fax:* 304-766-5182. *E-mail:* jacksoc@wvstateu.edu. *Web site:* http://www.wvstateu.edu/.

West Virginia University
Morgantown, West Virginia

General State-supported, university, coed **Entrance** Moderately difficult **Setting** 913-acre small-town campus **Total enrollment** 28,898 **Student-faculty ratio** 23:1 **Application deadline** 8/1 (freshmen), 8/1 (transfer) **Freshman admission** 88% were admitted. Average high school GPA 3.3 **Freshman test scores** SAT critical reading scores over 500: 53.24%; SAT math scores over 500: 60.89%; ACT scores over 18: 91.4%; SAT critical reading scores over 600: 12.15%; SAT math scores over 600: 16.65%; ACT scores over 24: 39.57% **Housing** Yes **Expenses** Tuition & Fees: state resident $5304, nonresident $16,402; Room & Board $7770 **Undergraduates** 45% women, 7% part-time, 7% 25 or older **The most frequently chosen baccalaureate fields are** business/marketing, communications/journalism, engineering **Academic program** English as a second language, advanced placement, accelerated degree program, self-designed majors, honors program, summer session, adult/continuing education programs, internships **Contact** Ms. Kim Guynn, Interim Assistant Director of Admissions, West Virginia University, PO Box 6009, Morgantown, WV 26506-6009. *Phone:* 304-293-2124 or toll-free 800-344-9881. *Fax:* 304-293-3080. *E-mail:* go2wvu@mail.wvu.edu. *Web site:* http://www.wvu.edu/.

West Virginia University at Parkersburg
Parkersburg, West Virginia

Contact Ms. Violet Mosser, Senior Admissions Counselor, West Virginia University at Parkersburg, 300 Campus Drive, Parkersburg, WV 26104. *Phone:* 304-424-8223 Ext. 223 or toll-free 800-WVA-WVUP. *Fax:* 304-424-8332. *E-mail:* violet.mosser@mail.wvu.edu. *Web site:* http://www.wvup.edu/.

West Virginia University Institute of Technology
Montgomery, West Virginia

General State-supported, comprehensive, coed **Entrance** Noncompetitive **Setting** 200-acre small-town campus **Total enrollment** 1,453 **Application deadline** Rolling (freshmen), rolling (transfer) **Housing** Yes **Undergraduates** 26% 25 or older **Academic program** English as a second language, advanced placement, accelerated degree program, self-designed majors, summer session, adult/continuing education programs, internships **Contact** William Willis, Admissions Coordinator, West Virginia University Institute of Technology, 405 Fayette Pike, Montgomery, WV 25136. *Phone:* 304-442-3071 Ext. 3331 or toll-free 888-554-8324. *Fax:* 304-442-3052. *E-mail:* william.willis@mail.wvu.edu. *Web site:* http://www.wvutech.edu/.

Visit Petersons.com and enter keywords West Virginia University

See page 1372 for the College Close-Up.

West Virginia Wesleyan College
Buckhannon, West Virginia

General Independent, comprehensive, coed, affiliated with United Methodist Church **Entrance** Moderately difficult **Setting** 80-acre small-town campus **Total enrollment** 1,416 **Student-faculty ratio** 13:1 **Freshman admission** 81% were admitted. Average high school GPA 3.32 **Freshman test scores** SAT critical reading scores over 500: 41.42%; SAT math scores over 500: 50%; ACT scores over 18: 87%; SAT critical reading scores over 600: 10.11%; SAT math scores over 600: 16.16%; ACT scores over 24: 41% **Housing** Yes **Expenses** Tuition & Fees $23,980; Room & Board $7140 **Undergraduates** 54% women, 3% part-time, 5% 25 or older, 1% Native American, 3% Hispanic American, 8% African American, 1% Asian American/Pacific Islander **The most frequently chosen baccalaureate fields are** business/marketing, education, parks and recreation **Academic program** English as a second language, advanced placement, self-designed majors, honors program, summer session, internships **Contact** John Waltz, Director of Admission, West Virginia Wesleyan College, 59 College Avenue, Buckhannon, WV 26201. *Phone:* 304-473-8510 or toll-free 800-722-9933. *Fax:* 304-473-8108. *E-mail:* admission@wvwc.edu. *Web site:* http://www.wvwc.edu/.

Wheeling Jesuit University
Wheeling, West Virginia

General Independent Roman Catholic (Jesuit), comprehensive, coed **Entrance** Moderately difficult **Setting** 65-acre suburban campus **Total enrollment** 1,361 **Student-faculty ratio** 11:1 **Application deadline** Rolling (freshmen), rolling (transfer) **Freshman admission** 74% were admitted. Average high school GPA 3.5 **Freshman test scores** SAT critical reading scores over 500: 61%; SAT math scores over 500: 59%; ACT scores over 18: 95%; SAT critical reading scores over 600: 15%; SAT math scores over 600: 12%; ACT scores over 24: 43% **Housing** Yes **Expenses** Tuition & Fees $24,390 **Undergraduates** 59% women, 17% part-time, 17% 25 or older, 0.2% Native American, 2% Hispanic American, 2% African American, 1% Asian American/Pacific Islander **The most frequently chosen baccalaureate fields are** business/marketing, health professions and related sciences, psychology **Academic program** English as a second language, advanced placement, accelerated degree program, self-designed majors, honors program, summer session, adult/continuing education programs, internships **Contact** Ms. Beth Loy, Director of Admissions, Wheeling Jesuit University, 316 Washington Avenue, Wheeling, WV 26003. *Phone:* 304-243-2425 or toll-free 800-624-6992 Ext. 2359. *Fax:* 304-243-2397. *E-mail:* bloy@wju.edu. *Web site:* http://www.wju.edu/.

Visit Petersons.com and enter keyword Wheeling

WISCONSIN

Alverno College
Milwaukee, Wisconsin

General Independent Roman Catholic, comprehensive, undergraduate: women only; graduate: coed **Entrance** Moderately difficult **Setting** 46-acre urban campus **Total enrollment** 2,815 **Student-faculty ratio** 13:1 **Application deadline** Rolling (freshmen), rolling (transfer) **Freshman admission** 85% were admitted. Average high school GPA 2.9 **Freshman test scores** ACT scores over 18: 73%; ACT scores over 24: 13% **Housing** Yes **Expenses** Tuition & Fees $18,162; Room & Board $6336 **Undergraduates** 28% part-time, 36% 25 or older, 1% Native American, 13% Hispanic American, 18% African American, 5% Asian American/Pacific Islander **The most frequently chosen baccalaureate fields are** business/marketing, education, health professions and related sciences **Academic program** Advanced placement, self-designed majors, summer session, adult/continuing education programs, internships **Contact** Ms. Holly Schwoerer, Assistant Director for High School Admissions, Alverno College, 3400 South 43 Street, PO Box 343922, Milwaukee, WI 53234-3922. *Phone:* 414-382-6103 or toll-free 800-933-3401. *Fax:* 414-382-6055. *E-mail:* admissions@alverno.edu. *Web site:* http://www.alverno.edu/.

Bellin College
Green Bay, Wisconsin

General Independent, comprehensive, coed, primarily women **Entrance** Moderately difficult **Setting** urban campus **Total enrollment** 304 **Application deadline** Rolling (freshmen), rolling (transfer) **Housing** No **Undergraduates** 22% 25 or older **Academic program** Advanced placement, accelerated degree program, summer session **Contact** Dr. Penny Croghan, Admissions Director, Bellin College, 3201 Eaton Road, Green Bay, WI 54305. *Phone:* 920-433-5803 or toll-free 800-236-8707. *Fax:* 920-433-7416. *E-mail:* admissio@bcon.edu. *Web site:* http://www.bellincollege.edu/.

Beloit College
Beloit, Wisconsin

General Independent, 4-year, coed **Entrance** Very difficult **Setting** 65-acre small-town campus **Total enrollment** 1,407 **Student-faculty ratio** 11:1 **Application deadline** 1/15 (freshmen), rolling (transfer) **Freshman admission** 73% were admitted. Average high school GPA 3.39 **Freshman test scores** SAT critical reading scores over 500: 87.42%; SAT math scores over 500: 88.08%; ACT scores over 18: 99.55%; SAT critical reading scores over 600: 65.57%; SAT math scores over 600: 57.62%; ACT scores over 24: 80.91% **Housing** Yes **Expenses** Tuition & Fees $33,368; Room & Board $6830 **Undergraduates** 57% women, 4% part-time, 2% 25 or older, 1% Native American, 4% Hispanic American, 4% African American, 3% Asian American/Pacific Islander **The most frequently chosen baccalaureate fields are** social sciences, English, visual and performing arts **Academic program** English as a second language, advanced placement, self-designed majors, summer session, adult/continuing education programs, internships **Contact** Mr. James S. Zielinski, Director of Admissions, Beloit College, 700 College Street, Beloit, WI 53511-5596. *Phone:* 608-363-2500 or toll-free 800-9-BELOIT. *Fax:* 608-363-2075. *E-mail:* admiss@beloit.edu. *Web site:* http://www.beloit.edu/.

Visit Petersons.com and enter keyword Beloit

See page 592 for the College Close-Up.

Bryant & Stratton College
Milwaukee, Wisconsin

General Proprietary, primarily 2-year, coed **Entrance** Minimally difficult **Setting** urban campus **Total enrollment** 828 **Student-faculty ratio** 13:1 **Application deadline** Rolling (freshmen), rolling (transfer) **Freshman admission** 89% were admitted **Housing** No **Expenses** Tuition & Fees $14,430 **Undergraduates** 84% women, 44% part-time, 4% Hispanic American, 91% African American, 1% Asian American/Pacific Islander **Academic program** Advanced placement, summer session, adult/continuing education programs, internships **Contact** Ms. Kristin Weiss, Director of Admissions, Bryant & Stratton College, 310 West Wisconsin Avenue, Milwaukee, WI 53203-2214. *Phone:* 414-276-5200. *Web site:* http://www.bryantstratton.edu/.

Bryant & Stratton College—Wauwatosa Campus
Wauwatosa, Wisconsin

General Proprietary, 4-year, coed **Setting** suburban campus **Total enrollment** 1,264 **Student-faculty ratio** 10:1 **Application deadline** Rolling (freshmen), rolling (transfer) **Housing** No **Undergraduates** 86% women, 26% part-time, 48% 25 or older, 0.5% Native American, 5% Hispanic American, 65% African American, 2% Asian American/Pacific Islander **Academic program** Advanced placement, adult/continuing education programs, internships **Contact** Tony Krocak, Director of Admissions, Bryant & Stratton College—Wauwatosa Campus, 10950 W. Potter Road, Wauwatosa, WI 53226. *Phone:* 414-302-7000 Ext. 502. *Web site:* http://www.bryantstratton.edu/.

Cardinal Stritch University
Milwaukee, Wisconsin

Contact Ms. Kristine Bueno, Associate Director of Admissions, Cardinal Stritch University, 6801 North Yates Road, Milwaukee, WI 53217-3985. *Phone:* 414-410-4040 or toll-free 800-347-8822 Ext. 4040. *Fax:* 414-410-4058. *E-mail:* admityou@stritch.edu. *Web site:* http://www.stritch.edu/.

Carroll University
Waukesha, Wisconsin

General Independent Presbyterian, comprehensive, coed **Entrance** Moderately difficult **Setting** 52-acre suburban campus **Total enrollment** 3,403 **Student-faculty ratio** 17:1 **Application deadline** Rolling (freshmen), rolling (transfer) **Freshman admission** 73% were admitted. Average high school GPA 3.3 **Freshman test scores** ACT scores over 18: 96.5%; ACT scores over 24: 43.6% **Housing** Yes **Expenses** Tuition & Fees $22,937; Room & Board $7668 **Undergraduates** 66% women, 16% part-time, 14% 25 or older, 0.3% Native American, 3% Hispanic American, 3% African American, 2% Asian American/Pacific Islander **The most frequently chosen baccalaureate fields are** business/marketing, education, health professions and related sciences **Academic program** English as a second language, advanced placement, self-designed majors, honors program, summer session, adult/continuing education programs, internships **Contact** Mr. James Wiseman, Vice President of Enrollment, Carroll University, 100 North East Avenue, Waukesha, WI 53186-5593. *Phone:* 262-524-7221 or toll-free 800-CARROLL. *Fax:* 262-524-7139. *E-mail:* info@carrollu.edu. *Web site:* http://www.carrollu.edu/.

Visit Petersons.com and enter keywords Carroll University

See page 686 for the College Close-Up.

Carthage College
Kenosha, Wisconsin

Contact Mr. Bradley J. Andrews, Vice President for Enrollment and Student Life, Carthage College, 2001 Alford Park Drive, Kenosha, WI 53140. *Phone:* 262-551-6000 or toll-free 800-351-4058. *Fax:* 262-551-5762. *E-mail:* admissions@carthage.edu. *Web site:* http://www.carthage.edu/.

Columbia College of Nursing
Milwaukee, Wisconsin

General Independent, 4-year, coed **Entrance** Moderately difficult **Setting** urban campus **Total enrollment** 260 **Student-faculty ratio** 13:1 **Application deadline** 8/1 (freshmen), rolling (transfer) **Freshman admission** 46% were admitted. Average high school GPA 2.5 **Freshman test scores** ACT scores over 18: 96%; ACT scores over 24: 34% **Housing** Yes **Expenses** Tuition & Fees $20,950; Room & Board $4600 **Undergraduates** 97% women, 7% part-time, 2% Hispanic American, 13% African American, 3% Asian American/Pacific Islander **Academic program** Advanced placement, honors program, summer session **Contact** Ms. Amy Dobson, Dean of Admissions, Columbia College of Nursing, 2121 East Newport Avenue, Milwaukee, WI 53211-2952. *Phone:* 414-256-1219 or toll-free 800-321-6265. *Fax:* 414-256-0180. *E-mail:* admiss@mtmary.edu. *Web site:* http://www.ccon.edu/.

Concordia University Wisconsin
Mequon, Wisconsin

General Independent, comprehensive, coed, affiliated with Lutheran Church–Missouri Synod **Entrance** Moderately difficult **Setting** 192-acre suburban campus **Total enrollment** 7,178 **Student-faculty ratio** 12:1 **Application deadline** 8/15 (freshmen), rolling (transfer) **Freshman admission** 64% were admitted. Average high school GPA 3.36 **Freshman test scores** ACT scores over 18: 94%; ACT scores over 24: 35.1% **Housing** Yes **Expenses** Tuition & Fees $20,996; Room & Board $7990 **Undergraduates** 64% women, 43% part-time, 6% 25 or older, 1% Native American, 2% Hispanic American, 14% African American, 1% Asian American/Pacific Islander **The most frequently chosen baccalaureate fields are** business/marketing, education, health professions and related sciences **Academic program** English as a second language, advanced placement, accelerated degree program, self-designed majors, summer session, adult/continuing education programs, internships **Contact** Ms. Julie Schroeder, Concordia University Wisconsin, Admissions Office, 12800 N. Lake Drive, Mequon, WI 53097. *Phone:* 262-243-4305 Ext. 4305 or toll-free 888-628-9472. *E-mail:* admission@cuw.edu. *Web site:* http://www.cuw.edu/.

DeVry University
Milwaukee, Wisconsin

General Proprietary, comprehensive, coed **Entrance** Minimally difficult **Total enrollment** 213 **Student-faculty ratio** 9:1 **Application deadline** Rolling (freshmen), rolling (transfer) **Housing** No **Expenses** Tuition & Fees $14,080 **Undergraduates** 51% women, 73% part-time, 72% 25 or older, 1% Native American, 8% Hispanic American, 48% African American, 6% Asian American/Pacific Islander **Academic program** Advanced placement, accelerated degree program, summer session, adult/continuing education programs **Contact** Admissions Office, DeVry University, 411 East Wisconsin Avenue, Suite 300, Milwaukee, WI 53202. *Web site:* http://www.devry.edu/.

DeVry University
Waukesha, Wisconsin

Contact DeVry University, N14 W23833 Stone Ridge Drive, Suite 450, Waukesha, WI 53188-1157. *Web site:* http://www.devry.edu/.

Edgewood College
Madison, Wisconsin

General Independent Roman Catholic, comprehensive, coed, primarily women **Entrance** Moderately difficult **Setting** 55-acre urban campus **Total enrollment** 2,549 **Student-faculty ratio** 11:1 **Application deadline** 8/14 (freshmen), 8/14 (transfer) **Freshman admission** 72% were admitted. Average high school GPA 3.3 **Freshman test scores** ACT scores over 18: 94.2%; ACT scores over 24: 34.7% **Housing** Yes **Expenses** Tuition & Fees $21,042; Room & Board $7234 **Undergraduates** 71% women, 20% part-time, 21% 25 or older, 1% Native American, 4% Hispanic American, 4% African American, 2% Asian American/Pacific Islander **The most frequently chosen baccalaureate fields are** business/marketing, education, health professions and related sciences **Academic program** Advanced placement, accelerated degree program, self-designed majors, honors program, summer session, adult/continuing education programs, internships **Contact** Ms. Christine Benedict, Director of Undergraduate Admissions, Edgewood College, 1000 Edgewood College Drive, Madison, WI 53711-1997. *Phone:* 608-663-2294 or toll-free 800-444-4861 Ext. 2294. *Fax:* 608-663-2214. *E-mail:* admissions@edgewood.edu. *Web site:* http://www.edgewood.edu/.

Herzing University
Madison, Wisconsin

General Proprietary, 4-year, coed, primarily men **Entrance** Moderately difficult **Setting** suburban campus **Total enrollment** 880 **Application deadline** Rolling (freshmen) **Housing** No **Academic program** Advanced placement, accelerated degree program, honors program, adult/continuing education programs, internships **Contact** Mr. Matthew Schneider, Admissions Director, Herzing University, 5218 East Terrace Drive, Madison, WI 53718. *Phone:* 608-663-0806 or toll-free 800-582-1227. *Fax:* 608-249-8593. *E-mail:* info@msn.herzing.edu. *Web site:* http://www.herzing.edu/madison.

ITT Technical Institute
Green Bay, Wisconsin

General Proprietary, primarily 2-year, coed **Entrance** Minimally difficult **Housing** No **Contact** Director of Recruitment, ITT Technical Institute, 470 Security Boulevard, Green Bay, WI 54313. *Phone:* 920-662-9000 or toll-free 888-884-3626. *Fax:* 920-662-9384. *Web site:* http://www.itt-tech.edu/.

ITT Technical Institute
Greenfield, Wisconsin

General Proprietary, primarily 2-year, coed **Entrance** Minimally difficult **Setting** suburban campus **Housing** No **Contact** Director of Recruitment, ITT Technical Institute, 6300 West Layton Avenue, Greenfield, WI 53220-4612. *Phone:* 414-282-9494. *Web site:* http://www.itt-tech.edu/.

ITT Technical Institute
Madison, Wisconsin

General Proprietary, primarily 2-year, coed **Contact** Director of Recruitment, ITT Technical Institute, 2450 Rimrock Road, Suite 100, Madison, WI 53713. *Phone:* 608-288-6301 or toll-free 877-628-5960. *Web site:* http://www.itt-tech.edu/.

Lakeland College
Sheboygan, Wisconsin

General Independent, comprehensive, coed, affiliated with United Church of Christ **Entrance** Minimally difficult **Setting** 240-acre rural campus **Total enrollment** 3,932 **Student-faculty ratio** 17:1 **Application deadline** Rolling (freshmen), rolling (transfer) **Freshman admission** 77% were admitted. Average high school GPA 3 **Freshman test scores** ACT scores over 18: 86%; ACT scores over 24: 23% **Housing** Yes **Expenses** Tuition & Fees $19,640; Room & Board $7016 **Undergraduates** 62% women, 65% part-time, 18% 25 or older, 1% Native American, 2% Hispanic American, 5% African American, 2% Asian American/Pacific Islander **The most frequently chosen baccalaureate fields are** business/marketing, computer and information sciences, education **Academic program** English as a second language, advanced placement, honors program, summer session, adult/continuing education programs, internships **Contact** Mr. Nick Spaeth, Director of Admissions, Lakeland

Lawrence ranks as the best undergraduate institution in Wisconsin, and 41st overall among the nation's 600 best colleges.—Forbes

Lawrence is among the nation's top colleges for professor accessibility (6th) and best college theater (10th).
—The Princeton Review's "The Best 371 Colleges," 2010 edition

We like what others say about us.

(But the only ranking that should matter is your own.)

For the 11th consecutive year, Lawrence University is ranked among the top quarter of the nation's best liberal arts colleges.
—U.S. News and World Report's 2010 "America's Best Colleges"

"...there is no greater educational bargain in the country." —Loren Pope, author of "Colleges That Change Lives"

Lawrence University—home to a world-class liberal arts college and conservatory of music, both devoted exclusively to undergraduate education—believes that college should not be a one-size-fits-all experience. More important, it delivers. Of the 2,000 courses Lawrence teaches each year, two-thirds of them (independent study, research projects, tutorials, studio lessons, and internships) have total enrollments of one—one student working directly with one professor.

Our 1,400 undergraduates come from nearly every state and more than 50 countries to create one of the most internationally diverse and dynamically engaged learning communities in the United States. We hope you will consider joining them.

LAWRENCE UNIVERSITY

APPLETON, WISCONSIN · 1-920-832-6500 · LAWRENCE.EDU/ADMISSIONS

College, PO Box 359, Nash Visitors Center, Sheboygan, WI 53082-0359. *Phone:* 920-565-1007 or toll-free 800-242-3347. *Fax:* 920-565-1215. *E-mail:* admissions@lakeland.edu. *Web site:* http://www.lakeland.edu/.

Lawrence University
Appleton, Wisconsin

General Independent, 4-year, coed **Entrance** Very difficult **Setting** 84-acre small-town campus **Total enrollment** 1,495 **Student-faculty ratio** 9:1 **Application deadline** 1/15 (freshmen), 5/1 (transfer) **Freshman admission** 69% were admitted. Average high school GPA 3.63 **Freshman test scores** SAT critical reading scores over 500: 94%; SAT math scores over 500: 93%; ACT scores over 18: 100%; SAT critical reading scores over 600: 75%; SAT math scores over 600: 73%; ACT scores over 24: 95% **Housing** Yes **Expenses** Tuition & Fees $34,596; Room & Board $7053 **Undergraduates** 54% women, 4% part-time, 1% 25 or older, 0.3% Native American, 2% Hispanic American, 3% African American, 3% Asian American/Pacific Islander **The most frequently chosen baccalaureate fields are** social sciences, psychology, visual and performing arts **Academic program** Advanced placement, self-designed majors, internships **Contact** Mr. Steven T. Syverson, Vice President for Enrollment Management, Lawrence University, PO Box 599, Appleton, WI 54912-0599. *Phone:* 920-832-6500 or toll-free 800-227-0982. *Fax:* 920-832-6782. *E-mail:* excel@lawrence.edu. *Web site:* http://www.lawrence.edu/.

Maranatha Baptist Bible College
Watertown, Wisconsin

General Independent Baptist, comprehensive, coed **Entrance** Noncompetitive **Setting** 60-acre small-town campus **Total enrollment** 859 **Student-faculty ratio** 15:1 **Application deadline** Rolling (freshmen), rolling (transfer) **Freshman admission** 50% were admitted **Freshman test scores** SAT critical reading scores over 500: 75%; ACT scores over 18: 91%; SAT critical reading scores over 600: 30%; ACT scores over 24: 46% **Housing** Yes **Expenses** Tuition & Fees $11,550; Room & Board $6290 **Undergraduates** 57% women, 7% part-time, 4% 25 or older, 2% Hispanic American, 1% African American, 1% Asian American/Pacific Islander **The most frequently chosen baccalaureate fields are** business/marketing, education, liberal arts/general studies **Academic program** Accelerated degree program, summer session, internships **Contact** Dr. James Harrison, Director of Admissions, Maranatha Baptist Bible College, 745 West Main Street, Watertown, WI 53094. *Phone:* 920-206-2327 or toll-free 800-622-2947. *Fax:* 920-261-9109. *E-mail:* admissions@mbbc.edu. *Web site:* http://www.mbbc.edu/.

Marian University
Fond du Lac, Wisconsin

General Independent Roman Catholic, comprehensive, coed **Entrance** Moderately difficult **Setting** 104-acre small-town campus **Total enrollment** 2,841 **Student-faculty ratio** 13:1 **Application deadline** Rolling (freshmen), rolling (transfer) **Freshman admission** 83% were admitted. Average high school GPA 2.94 **Housing** Yes **Expenses** Tuition & Fees $20,900; Room & Board $5640 **Undergraduates** 73% women, 25% part-time, 35% 25 or older, 1% Native American, 3% Hispanic American, 7% African American, 2% Asian American/Pacific Islander **The most frequently chosen baccalaureate fields are** business/marketing, health professions and related sciences, security and protective services **Academic program** English as a second language, advanced placement, accelerated degree program, self-designed majors, honors program, summer session, internships **Contact** Shannon LaLuzerne, Senior Director of Admissions, Marian University, 45 South National Avenue, Fond du Lac, WI 54935-4699. *Phone:* 800-262-7426

Marian University (continued)
or toll-free 800-2-MARIAN Ext. 7652. *Fax:* 920-923-8755. *E-mail:* admit@marianuniversity.edu. *Web site:* http://www.marianuniversity.edu/.

Marquette University
Milwaukee, Wisconsin

General Independent Roman Catholic (Jesuit), university, coed **Entrance** Moderately difficult **Setting** 93-acre urban campus **Total enrollment** 11,689 **Student-faculty ratio** 14:1 **Application deadline** 12/1 (freshmen) **Freshman admission** 66% were admitted **Freshman test scores** SAT critical reading scores over 500: 87.88%; SAT math scores over 500: 88.75%; ACT scores over 18: 100%; SAT critical reading scores over 600: 44.59%; SAT math scores over 600: 52.82%; ACT scores over 24: 84.78% **Housing** Yes **Expenses** Tuition & Fees $30,462 **Undergraduates** 52% women, 5% part-time, 3% 25 or older, 0.4% Native American, 6% Hispanic American, 5% African American, 4% Asian American/Pacific Islander **The most frequently chosen baccalaureate fields are** business/marketing, communications/journalism, social sciences **Academic program** English as a second language, advanced placement, accelerated degree program, honors program, summer session, adult/continuing education programs, internships **Contact** Mr. Robert Blust, Dean of Undergraduate Admissions, Marquette University, PO Box 1881, Milwaukee, WI 53201-1881. *Phone:* 414-288-7004 or toll-free 800-222-6544. *Fax:* 414-288-3764. *E-mail:* admissions@marquette.edu. *Web site:* http://www.marquette.edu/.

Milwaukee Institute of Art and Design
Milwaukee, Wisconsin

Contact Stacey Steinberg, Director of Admissions, Milwaukee Institute of Art and Design, 273 East Erie Street, Milwaukee, WI 53202. *Phone:* 414-847-3259 or toll-free 888-749-MIAD. *Fax:* 414-291-8077. *E-mail:* admissions@miad.edu. *Web site:* http://www.miad.edu/.

Milwaukee School of Engineering
Milwaukee, Wisconsin

General Independent, comprehensive, coed, primarily men **Entrance** Moderately difficult **Setting** 15-acre urban campus **Total enrollment** 2,648 **Student-faculty ratio** 14:1 **Application deadline** Rolling (freshmen), rolling (transfer) **Freshman admission** 67% were admitted. Average high school GPA 3.52 **Freshman test scores** SAT critical reading scores over 500: 87%; ACT scores over 18: 100%; SAT critical reading scores over 600: 48%; ACT scores over 24: 79% **Housing** Yes **Expenses** Tuition & Fees $29,520; Room & Board $7431 **Undergraduates** 19% women, 8% part-time, 14% 25 or older, 1% Native American, 3% Hispanic American, 3% African American, 3% Asian American/Pacific Islander **The most frequently chosen baccalaureate fields are** business/marketing, engineering, engineering technologies **Academic program** English as a second language, advanced placement, summer session, adult/continuing education programs, internships **Contact** Dana-Marie Grennier, Director of Admissions, Milwaukee School of Engineering, 1025 North Broadway, Milwaukee, WI 53202-3109. *Phone:* 414-277-6761 or toll-free 800-332-6763. *Fax:* 414-277-7475. *E-mail:* grennier@msoe.edu. *Web site:* http://www.msoe.edu/.
Visit Petersons.com and enter keyword Engineering

See page 972 for the College Close-Up.

Mount Mary College
Milwaukee, Wisconsin

General Independent Roman Catholic, comprehensive, undergraduate: women only; graduate: coed **Entrance** Moderately difficult **Setting** 80-acre urban campus **Total enrollment** 1,925 **Student-faculty ratio** 13:1 **Application deadline** Rolling (freshmen), rolling (transfer) **Freshman admission** 50% were admitted. Average high school GPA 2.92 **Freshman test scores** ACT scores over 18: 58%; ACT scores over 24: 10% **Housing** Yes **Expenses** Tuition & Fees $22,118; Room & Board $7498 **Undergraduates** 36% part-time, 39% 25 or older **The most frequently chosen baccalaureate fields are** business/marketing, health professions and related sciences, visual and performing arts **Academic program** Advanced placement, accelerated degree program, self-designed majors, honors program, summer session, adult/continuing education programs, internships **Contact** Mary Ellen Strieter, Admission Counselor Assistant/Receptionist, Mount Mary College, 2900 North Menomonee River Parkway, Milwaukee, WI 53222. *Phone:* 414-258-4810 Ext. 219. *Fax:* 414-256-0180. *E-mail:* admiss@mtmary.edu. *Web site:* http://www.mtmary.edu/.
Visit Petersons.com and enter keywords Mount Mary

See page 994 for the College Close-Up.

Northland College
Ashland, Wisconsin

General Independent, 4-year, coed, affiliated with United Church of Christ **Entrance** Moderately difficult **Setting** 130-acre small-town campus **Total enrollment** 602 **Student-faculty ratio** 12:1 **Application deadline** Rolling (freshmen), rolling (transfer) **Freshman admission** 79% were admitted. Average high school GPA 3.33 **Freshman test scores** SAT critical reading scores over 500: 87%; SAT math scores over 500: 77%; ACT scores over 18: 95%; SAT critical reading scores over 600: 46%; SAT math scores over 600: 36%; ACT scores over 24: 54% **Housing** Yes **Expenses** Tuition & Fees $25,241; Room & Board $6930 **Undergraduates** 55% women, 6% part-time, 9% 25 or older, 3% Native American, 2% Hispanic American, 0.3% African American, 1% Asian American/Pacific Islander **The most frequently chosen baccalaureate fields are** biological/life sciences, education, English **Academic program** Advanced placement, self-designed majors, honors program, summer session, internships **Contact** Ralph Stewart, Director of Admissions, Northland College, 1411 Ellis Avenue, Ashland, WI 54806-3925. *Phone:* 715-682-1257 or toll-free 800-753-1840 (in-state); 800-753-1040 (out-of-state). *Fax:* 715-682-1258. *E-mail:* admit@northland.edu. *Web site:* http://www.northland.edu/.

Ripon College
Ripon, Wisconsin

General Independent, 4-year, coed **Entrance** Moderately difficult **Setting** 250-acre small-town campus **Total enrollment** 1,065 **Student-faculty ratio** 15:1 **Application deadline** Rolling (freshmen), rolling (transfer) **Freshman admission** 79% were admitted. Average high school GPA 3.42 **Freshman test scores** SAT critical reading scores over 500: 70%; SAT math scores over 500: 77%; ACT scores over 18: 96%; SAT critical reading scores over 600: 33%; SAT math scores over 600: 40%; ACT scores over 24: 57% **Housing** Yes **Expenses** Tuition & Fees $25,445; Room & Board $7270 **Undergraduates** 51% women, 2% part-time, 2% 25 or older, 1% Native American, 3% Hispanic American, 1% African American, 1% Asian American/Pacific Islander **The most frequently chosen baccalaureate fields are** business/marketing, psychology, social sciences **Academic program** Advanced placement, accelerated degree program, self-designed majors, internships **Contact** Office of Admission, Ripon College, 300 Seward Street, PO Box 248, Ripon, WI 54971. *Phone:* 920-748-8114 or toll-free 800-947-4766. *Fax:* 920-748-8335. *E-mail:* adminfo@ripon.edu. *Web site:* http://www.ripon.edu/.
Visit Petersons.com and enter keyword Ripon

See page 1080 for the College Close-Up.

St. Norbert College
De Pere, Wisconsin

General Independent Roman Catholic, comprehensive, coed **Entrance** Moderately difficult **Setting** 93-acre suburban campus **Total enrollment** 2,175 **Student-faculty ratio** 14:1 **Application deadline** Rolling

(freshmen), rolling (transfer) **Freshman admission** 83% were admitted. Average high school GPA 3.42 **Freshman test scores** ACT scores over 18: 98%; ACT scores over 24: 52% **Housing** Yes **Expenses** Tuition & Fees $26,972; Room & Board $7052 **Undergraduates** 58% women, 3% part-time, 1% 25 or older, 0.4% Native American, 2% Hispanic American, 1% African American, 1% Asian American/Pacific Islander **The most frequently chosen baccalaureate fields are** business/marketing, communications/journalism, education **Academic program** English as a second language, advanced placement, self-designed majors, honors program, summer session, internships **Contact** Ms. Bridget O'Connor, Vice President for Enrollment Management and Communications, St. Norbert College, 100 Grant Street, De Pere, WI 54115-2099. *Phone:* 920-403-3005 or toll-free 800-236-4878. *Fax:* 920-403-4072. *E-mail:* admit@snc.edu. *Web site:* http://www.snc.edu/.
Visit Petersons.com and enter keyword Norbert

See page 1130 for the College Close-Up.

Silver Lake College
Manitowoc, Wisconsin

General Independent Roman Catholic, comprehensive, coed **Entrance** Minimally difficult **Setting** 30-acre rural campus **Total enrollment** 704 **Student-faculty ratio** 6:1 **Application deadline** 8/1 (freshmen), 8/1 (transfer) **Freshman admission** 74% were admitted. Average high school GPA 2.96 **Freshman test scores** ACT scores over 18: 69%; ACT scores over 24: 23% **Housing** Yes **Expenses** Tuition & Fees $21,180; Room & Board $6700 **Undergraduates** 68% women, 63% part-time, 26% 25 or older, 4% Native American, 1% Hispanic American, 4% African American, 1% Asian American/Pacific Islander **The most frequently chosen baccalaureate fields are** business/marketing, education, psychology **Academic program** Advanced placement, accelerated degree program, self-designed majors, summer session, adult/continuing education programs, internships **Contact** Matthew Thielen, Vice President of Student Life and Dean of Students, Silver Lake College, 2406 South Alverno Road, Manitowoc, WI 54220. *Phone:* 920-686-6199 or toll-free 800-236-4752 Ext. 175. *Fax:* 920-684-7082. *E-mail:* admslc@silver.sl.edu. *Web site:* http://www.sl.edu/.

University of Phoenix–Wisconsin Campus
Madison, Wisconsin

General Proprietary, comprehensive, coed **Entrance** Noncompetitive **Setting** urban campus **Total enrollment** 80 **Application deadline** Rolling (freshmen), rolling (transfer) **Housing** No **Expenses** Tuition & Fees $12,525 **Undergraduates** 62% women, 71% 25 or older, 2% Native American, 2% Hispanic American, 3% African American, 2% Asian American/Pacific Islander **The most frequently chosen baccalaureate field is** business/marketing **Academic program** Advanced placement, accelerated degree program **Contact** Ms. Audra McQuarie, Registrar/Executive Director, University of Phoenix–Wisconsin Campus, 4035 South Riverpoint Parkway, Mail Stop CF-L101, Phoenix, AZ 85040. *Phone:* 480-557-6151 or toll-free 800-776-4867 (in-state); 800-228-7240 (out-of-state). *Fax:* 480-643-3068. *E-mail:* audra.mcquarie@phoenix.edu. *Web site:* http://www.phoenix.edu/.

University of Wisconsin–Eau Claire
Eau Claire, Wisconsin

General State-supported, comprehensive, coed **Entrance** Moderately difficult **Setting** 333-acre small-town campus **Total enrollment** 11,046 **Student-faculty ratio** 21:1 **Application deadline** Rolling (freshmen), 7/1 (transfer) **Freshman admission** 67% were admitted **Freshman test scores** SAT critical reading scores over 500: 87.18%; SAT math scores over 500: 89.75%; ACT scores over 18: 99.25%; SAT critical reading scores over 600: 43.59%; SAT math scores over 600: 53.85%; ACT scores over 24: 61.14% **Housing** Yes **Expenses** Tuition & Fees: state resident $6633, nonresident $14,206; Room & Board $5730 **Undergraduates** 58% women, 7% part-time, 7% 25 or older, 1% Native American, 1% Hispanic American, 1% African American, 3% Asian American/Pacific Islander **The most frequently chosen baccalaureate fields are** business/marketing, education, health professions and related sciences **Academic program** English as a second language, advanced placement, accelerated degree program, self-designed majors, honors program, summer session, adult/continuing education programs, internships **Contact** Ms. Kristina Anderson, Executive Director of Enrollment Management and Director of Admissions, University of Wisconsin–Eau Claire, PO Box 4004, Eau Claire, WI 54702-4004. *Phone:* 715-836-5415. *Fax:* 715-836-2409. *E-mail:* admissions@uwec.edu. *Web site:* http://www.uwec.edu/.

University of Wisconsin–Green Bay
Green Bay, Wisconsin

General State-supported, comprehensive, coed **Entrance** Moderately difficult **Setting** 700-acre suburban campus **Total enrollment** 6,664 **Student-faculty ratio** 25:1 **Application deadline** Rolling (freshmen), rolling (transfer) **Freshman admission** 70% were admitted. Average high school GPA 3.25 **Freshman test scores** ACT scores over 18: 97%; ACT scores over 24: 33% **Housing** Yes **Expenses** Tuition & Fees: state resident $6909, nonresident $14,899; Room & Board $6500 **Undergraduates** 64% women, 22% part-time, 22% 25 or older, 2% Native American, 1% Hispanic American, 1% African American, 3% Asian American/Pacific Islander **The most frequently chosen baccalaureate fields are** business/marketing, biological/life sciences, psychology **Academic program** Advanced placement, self-designed majors, summer session, adult/continuing education programs, internships **Contact** Ms. Pam Harvey-Jacobs, Director of Admissions, University of Wisconsin–Green Bay, 2420 Nicolet Drive, Green Bay, WI 54311-7001. *Phone:* 920-465-2111 or toll-free 888-367-8942. *Fax:* 920-465-5754. *E-mail:* uwgb@uwgb.edu. *Web site:* http://www.uwgb.edu/.

University of Wisconsin–La Crosse
La Crosse, Wisconsin

General State-supported, comprehensive, coed **Entrance** Moderately difficult **Setting** 121-acre suburban campus **Total enrollment** 9,890 **Student-faculty ratio** 21:1 **Application deadline** Rolling (freshmen), rolling (transfer) **Freshman admission** 69% were admitted **Freshman test scores** ACT scores over 18: 100%; ACT scores over 24: 69.5% **Housing** Yes **Expenses** Tuition & Fees: state resident $7509, nonresident $15,082; Room & Board $5630 **Undergraduates** 57% women, 5% part-time, 6% 25 or older, 0.4% Native American, 2% Hispanic American, 1% African American, 3% Asian American/Pacific Islander **The most frequently chosen baccalaureate fields are** business/marketing, biological/life sciences, education **Academic program** English as a second language, advanced placement, honors program, summer session, adult/continuing education programs, internships **Contact** Ms. Kathryn Kiefer, Director of Admissions, University of Wisconsin–La Crosse, 1725 State Street, La Crosse, WI 54601. *Phone:* 608-785-8939. *Fax:* 608-785-8940. *E-mail:* admissions@uwlax.edu. *Web site:* http://www.uwlax.edu/.

University of Wisconsin–Madison
Madison, Wisconsin

General State-supported, university, coed **Entrance** Very difficult **Setting** 1,050-acre urban campus **Total enrollment** 42,099 **Student-faculty ratio** 17:1 **Application deadline** 2/1 (freshmen), 2/1 (transfer) **Freshman admission** 57% were admitted. Average high school GPA 3.69 **Freshman test scores** SAT critical reading scores over 500: 90%; SAT math scores over 500: 96.8%; ACT scores over 18: 99.6%; SAT critical reading scores over 600: 59.1%; SAT math scores over 600: 81.5%; ACT scores over 24: 92.5% **Housing** Yes **Expenses** Tuition & Fees: state resident $8314, nonresident $23,063; Room & Board $7157 **Undergraduates** 52% women, 8% part-time, 5% 25 or older, 1% Native American, 4%

University of Wisconsin–Madison (continued)
Hispanic American, 3% African American, 6% Asian American/Pacific Islander **The most frequently chosen baccalaureate fields are** biological/life sciences, business/marketing, social sciences **Academic program** English as a second language, advanced placement, accelerated degree program, self-designed majors, honors program, summer session, adult/continuing education programs, internships **Contact** Office of Undergraduate Admissions, University of Wisconsin–Madison, 716 Langdon Street, Madison, WI 53706-1481. *Phone:* 608-262-3961. *Fax:* 608-262-7706. *E-mail:* onwisconsin@admissions.wisc.edu. *Web site:* http://www.wisc.edu/.

University of Wisconsin–Milwaukee
Milwaukee, Wisconsin

General State-supported, university, coed **Entrance** Moderately difficult **Setting** 90-acre urban campus **Total enrollment** 30,418 **Student-faculty ratio** 21:1 **Application deadline** 7/1 (freshmen), 8/1 (transfer) **Freshman admission** 77% were admitted. Average high school GPA 3.05 **Freshman test scores** SAT critical reading scores over 500: 67.5%; SAT math scores over 500: 70.83%; ACT scores over 18: 88.74%; SAT critical reading scores over 600: 32.5%; SAT math scores over 600: 37.5%; ACT scores over 24: 32.71% **Housing** Yes **Expenses** Tuition & Fees: state resident $8522, nonresident $18,251; Room only $4290 **Undergraduates** 51% women, 17% part-time, 17% 25 or older, 1% Native American, 5% Hispanic American, 7% African American, 5% Asian American/Pacific Islander **The most frequently chosen baccalaureate fields are** business/marketing, education, health professions and related sciences **Academic program** English as a second language, advanced placement, accelerated degree program, self-designed majors, honors program, summer session, adult/continuing education programs, internships **Contact** Ms. Jan Ford, Director, Recruitment and Outreach, University of Wisconsin–Milwaukee, PO Box 413, Milwaukee, WI 53201-0413. *Phone:* 414-229-4397. *Fax:* 414-229-6940. *E-mail:* uwmlook@uwm.edu. *Web site:* http://www.uwm.edu/.

University of Wisconsin–Oshkosh
Oshkosh, Wisconsin

General State-supported, comprehensive, coed **Entrance** Moderately difficult **Setting** 192-acre suburban campus **Total enrollment** 13,002 **Student-faculty ratio** 21:1 **Application deadline** Rolling (freshmen), rolling (transfer) **Freshman admission** 85% were admitted. Average high school GPA 3.24 **Freshman test scores** ACT scores over 18: 95%; ACT scores over 24: 33% **Housing** Yes **Expenses** Tuition & Fees: state resident $6038, nonresident $13,610; Room & Board $5898 **Undergraduates** 59% women, 20% part-time, 16% 25 or older, 1% Native American, 2% Hispanic American, 2% African American, 3% Asian American/Pacific Islander **The most frequently chosen baccalaureate fields are** business/marketing, education, health professions and related sciences **Academic program** English as a second language, advanced placement, accelerated degree program, self-designed majors, honors program, summer session, adult/continuing education programs, internships **Contact** Mr. Richard Hillman, Associate Director of Admissions, University of Wisconsin–Oshkosh, 800 Algoma Boulevard, Oshkosh, WI 54901. *Phone:* 920-424-0202. *E-mail:* oshadmuw@uwosh.edu. *Web site:* http://www.uwosh.edu/.

University of Wisconsin–Parkside
Kenosha, Wisconsin

General State-supported, comprehensive, coed **Entrance** Moderately difficult **Setting** 700-acre suburban campus **Total enrollment** 5,303 **Student-faculty ratio** 20:1 **Application deadline** 8/1 (freshmen), 8/1 (transfer) **Freshman admission** 63% were admitted **Freshman test scores** ACT scores over 18: 77%; ACT scores over 24: 19% **Housing** Yes **Expenses** Tuition & Fees: state resident $7196, nonresident $14,769; Room & Board $6252 **Undergraduates** 55% women, 28% part-time, 25% 25 or older, 0.4% Native American, 9% Hispanic American, 10% African American, 3% Asian American/Pacific Islander **The most frequently chosen baccalaureate fields are** business/marketing, security and protective services, social sciences **Academic program** Advanced placement, accelerated degree program, honors program, summer session, internships **Contact** Mrs. DeAnn Possehl, Director of Student Life, University of Wisconsin–Parkside, PO Box 2000, 900 Wood Road, Kenosha, WI 53141-2000. *Phone:* 262-595-2454. *E-mail:* possehl@uwp.edu. *Web site:* http://www.uwp.edu/.

University of Wisconsin–Platteville
Platteville, Wisconsin

General State-supported, comprehensive, coed **Entrance** Moderately difficult **Setting** 380-acre small-town campus **Total enrollment** 7,648 **Student-faculty ratio** 20:1 **Application deadline** Rolling (freshmen), rolling (transfer) **Freshman admission** 80% were admitted **Freshman test scores** ACT scores over 18: 92.53%; ACT scores over 24: 38.45% **Housing** Yes **Expenses** Tuition & Fees: state resident $6820, nonresident $14,130; Room & Board $5800 **Undergraduates** 36% women, 9% part-time, 9% 25 or older, 1% Native American, 1% Hispanic American, 2% African American, 1% Asian American/Pacific Islander **The most frequently chosen baccalaureate fields are** business/marketing, engineering, engineering technologies **Academic program** English as a second language, advanced placement, self-designed majors, honors program, summer session, adult/continuing education programs, internships **Contact** Ms. Angela Udelhofen, Director of Admissions and Enrollment Management, University of Wisconsin–Platteville, 1 University Plaza, 120 Brigham Hall, Platteville, WI 53818-3099. *Phone:* 608-342-1125 or toll-free 800-362-5515. *Fax:* 608-342-1122. *E-mail:* admit@uwplatt.edu. *Web site:* http://www.uwplatt.edu/.

University of Wisconsin–River Falls
River Falls, Wisconsin

General State-supported, comprehensive, coed **Entrance** Moderately difficult **Setting** 225-acre suburban campus **Total enrollment** 6,728 **Student-faculty ratio** 23:1 **Application deadline** Rolling (freshmen), rolling (transfer) **Freshman admission** 76% were admitted **Freshman test scores** SAT critical reading scores over 500: 47.83%; SAT math scores over 500: 52.17%; ACT scores over 18: 93.3%; SAT critical reading scores over 600: 8.7%; SAT math scores over 600: 21.74%; ACT scores over 24: 32.66% **Housing** Yes **Expenses** Tuition & Fees: state resident $6460, nonresident $14,105; Room & Board $5372 **Undergraduates** 59% women, 7% part-time, 9% 25 or older, 0.3% Native American, 1% Hispanic American, 1% African American, 2% Asian American/Pacific Islander **The most frequently chosen baccalaureate fields are** business/marketing, agriculture, education **Academic program** English as a second language, advanced placement, honors program, summer session, adult/continuing education programs, internships **Contact** Mark Meydam, Director of Admissions, University of Wisconsin–River Falls, 410 South Third Street, River Falls, WI 54022. *Phone:* 715-425-3500. *Fax:* 715-425-0676. *E-mail:* admit@uwrf.edu. *Web site:* http://www.uwrf.edu/.

University of Wisconsin–Stevens Point
Stevens Point, Wisconsin

General State-supported, comprehensive, coed **Entrance** Moderately difficult **Setting** 335-acre small-town campus **Total enrollment** 8,940 **Student-faculty ratio** 20:1 **Application deadline** Rolling (freshmen), rolling (transfer) **Freshman admission** 73% were admitted. Average high school GPA 3.42 **Freshman test scores** SAT critical reading scores over 500: 86.4%; ACT scores over 18: 98.2%; SAT critical reading scores over 600: 50%; ACT scores over 24: 42.8% **Housing** Yes **Expenses** Tuition & Fees: state resident $6530, nonresident $14,104; Room & Board $5612 **Undergraduates** 52% women, 6% part-time,

11% 25 or older, 1% Native American, 1% Hispanic American, 1% African American, 3% Asian American/Pacific Islander **The most frequently chosen baccalaureate fields are** natural resources/environmental science, education, social sciences **Academic program** English as a second language, advanced placement, accelerated degree program, self-designed majors, summer session, adult/continuing education programs, internships **Contact** Ms. Catherine Glennon, Director of Admissions, University of Wisconsin–Stevens Point, 2100 Main Street, Stevens Point, WI 54481-3897. *Phone:* 715-346-2441. *Fax:* 715-346-3296. *E-mail:* admiss@uwsp.edu. *Web site:* http://www.uwsp.edu/.

University of Wisconsin–Stout
Menomonie, Wisconsin

General State-supported, comprehensive, coed **Entrance** Moderately difficult **Setting** 120-acre small-town campus **Total enrollment** 9,015 **Student-faculty ratio** 20:1 **Application deadline** Rolling (freshmen), rolling (transfer) **Freshman admission** 77% were admitted. Average high school GPA 3.2 **Freshman test scores** ACT scores over 18: 91.5%; ACT scores over 24: 26.3% **Housing** Yes **Expenses** Tuition & Fees: state resident $7821, nonresident $15,566; Room & Board $5336 **Undergraduates** 48% women, 15% part-time, 15% 25 or older, 1% Native American, 1% Hispanic American, 1% African American, 3% Asian American/Pacific Islander **The most frequently chosen baccalaureate fields are** business/marketing, education, visual and performing arts **Academic program** Accelerated degree program, honors program, summer session, adult/continuing education programs, internships **Contact** Dr. Pamela Holsinger-Fuchs, Executive Director of Enrollment Services, University of Wisconsin–Stout, Admissions, Bowman Hall, Menomonie, WI 54751. *Phone:* 715-232-2639 or toll-free 800-HI-STOUT. *Fax:* 715-232-2639. *E-mail:* admissions@uwstout.edu. *Web site:* http://www.uwstout.edu/.

University of Wisconsin–Superior
Superior, Wisconsin

General State-supported, comprehensive, coed **Entrance** Moderately difficult **Setting** 230-acre suburban campus **Total enrollment** 2,793 **Student-faculty ratio** 18:1 **Application deadline** Rolling (freshmen), rolling (transfer) **Freshman admission** 68% were admitted **Freshman test scores** ACT scores over 18: 91%; ACT scores over 24: 32% **Housing** Yes **Expenses** Tuition & Fees: state resident $6736, nonresident $14,309; Room & Board $5485 **Undergraduates** 57% women, 19% part-time, 29% 25 or older, 3% Native American, 1% Hispanic American, 2% African American, 1% Asian American/Pacific Islander **The most frequently chosen baccalaureate fields are** business/marketing, communications/journalism, education **Academic program** English as a second language, advanced placement, self-designed majors, honors program, summer session, adult/continuing education programs, internships **Contact** Ms. Tonya Roth, Director of Admission, University of Wisconsin–Superior, Belknap and Catlin, PO Box 2000, Superior, WI 54880-4500. *Phone:* 715-394-8217. *Fax:* 715-394-8407. *E-mail:* admissions@uwsuper.edu. *Web site:* http://www.uwsuper.edu/.

University of Wisconsin–Whitewater
Whitewater, Wisconsin

General State-supported, comprehensive, coed **Entrance** Moderately difficult **Setting** 385-acre small-town campus **Total enrollment** 11,139 **Application deadline** Rolling (freshmen), rolling (transfer) **Freshman admission** 69% were admitted. Average high school GPA 3.2 **Housing** Yes **Expenses** Tuition & Fees: state resident $7439, nonresident $15,012; Room & Board $5028 **Undergraduates** 50% women, 6% part-time, 0.4% Native American, 3% Hispanic American, 5% African American, 2% Asian American/Pacific Islander **The most frequently chosen baccalaureate fields are** business/marketing, communications/journalism, education **Academic program** English as a second language, advanced placement, accelerated degree program, self-designed majors, honors program, summer session, adult/continuing education programs, internships **Contact** Mr. Stephen J. McKellips, Director of Admissions, University of Wisconsin–Whitewater, 800 West Main Street, Whitewater, WI 53190-1790. *Phone:* 262-472-1440 Ext. 1512. *Fax:* 262-472-1515. *E-mail:* uwwadmit@uww.edu. *Web site:* http://www.uww.edu/.

Viterbo University
La Crosse, Wisconsin

General Independent Roman Catholic, comprehensive, coed, primarily women **Entrance** Moderately difficult **Setting** 72-acre suburban campus **Total enrollment** 3,282 **Student-faculty ratio** 12:1 **Application deadline** Rolling (freshmen), rolling (transfer) **Freshman admission** 87% were admitted. Average high school GPA 3.35 **Freshman test scores** ACT scores over 18: 95%; ACT scores over 24: 37% **Housing** Yes **Expenses** Tuition & Fees $20,850; Room & Board $6970 **Undergraduates** 70% women, 26% part-time, 29% 25 or older, 1% Native American, 2% Hispanic American, 2% African American, 2% Asian American/Pacific Islander **The most frequently chosen baccalaureate fields are** business/marketing, education, health professions and related sciences **Academic program** Advanced placement, accelerated degree program, self-designed majors, honors program, summer session, adult/continuing education programs, internships **Contact** Mr. Wayne Wojciechowski, Assistant Academic Vice President, Viterbo University, 900 Viterbo Drive, LaCrosse, WI 54601. *Phone:* 608-796-3085 or toll-free 800-VITERBO Ext. 3010. *Fax:* 608-796-3020. *E-mail:* admission@viterbo.edu. *Web site:* http://www.viterbo.edu/.

Wisconsin Lutheran College
Milwaukee, Wisconsin

General Independent, 4-year, coed, affiliated with Wisconsin Evangelical Lutheran Synod **Entrance** Moderately difficult **Setting** 48-acre suburban campus **Total enrollment** 753 **Student-faculty ratio** 10:1 **Freshman admission** 76% were admitted. Average high school GPA 3.34 **Freshman test scores** ACT scores over 18: 91%; ACT scores over 24: 50% **Housing** Yes **Expenses** Tuition & Fees $21,180; Room & Board $7450 **Undergraduates** 56% women, 7% part-time, 2% 25 or older, 0.4% Native American, 2% Hispanic American, 4% African American, 2% Asian American/Pacific Islander **The most frequently chosen baccalaureate fields are** communications/journalism, psychology, visual and performing arts **Academic program** English as a second language, advanced placement, self-designed majors, summer session, internships **Contact** Ms. Meghan Wieselmann, Admissions Office Manager, Wisconsin Lutheran College, 8800 West Bluemound Road, Milwaukee, WI 53226-9942. *Phone:* 414-443-8718 or toll-free 888-WIS LUTH. *Fax:* 414-443-8547. *E-mail:* meg.wieselmann@wlc.edu. *Web site:* http://www.wlc.edu/.

WYOMING

University of Wyoming
Laramie, Wyoming

General State-supported, university, coed **Entrance** Moderately difficult **Setting** 785-acre small-town campus **Total enrollment** 12,427 **Student-faculty ratio** 14:1 **Application deadline** 8/10 (freshmen), 8/10 (transfer) **Freshman admission** 96% were admitted. Average high school GPA 3.43 **Freshman test scores** SAT critical reading scores over 500: 69.9%; SAT math scores over 500: 74.8%; ACT scores over 18: 95.8%; SAT critical reading scores over 600: 27.1%; SAT math scores over 600: 33.8%; ACT scores over 24: 53.6% **Housing** Yes **Expenses** Tuition & Fees: state resident $3927, nonresident $12,237; Room & Board $8360 **Undergraduates** 53% women, 17% part-time, 21% 25 or older, 1% Native American, 4% Hispanic American, 1% African

University of Wyoming (continued)
American, 1% Asian American/Pacific Islander **The most frequently chosen baccalaureate fields are** business/marketing, education, engineering **Academic program** English as a second language, advanced placement, accelerated degree program, self-designed majors, honors program, summer session, internships **Contact** Aaron Appelhans, Assistant Director of Admissions, University of Wyoming, 1000 East University Avenue, Department 3435, Laramie, WY 82071. *Phone:* 307-766-5160 or toll-free 800-342-5996. *Fax:* 307-766-4042. *E-mail:* why-wyo@uwyo.edu. *Web site:* http://www.uwyo.edu/.

Visit Petersons.com and enter keyword Wyoming

See page 1324 for the College Close-Up.

CANADA

Acadia University
Wolfville, Nova Scotia, Canada

General Province-supported, comprehensive, coed **Entrance** Moderately difficult **Setting** 250-acre small-town campus **Total enrollment** 3,462 **Student-faculty ratio** 10:1 **Application deadline** 7/1 (freshmen), 7/1 (transfer) **Freshman admission** 36% were admitted **Housing** Yes **Expenses** Tuition & Fees: state resident 6648 Canadian dollars, nonresident 7670 Canadian dollars; Room & Board 7985 Canadian dollars **Undergraduates** 56% women, 5% part-time, 8% 25 or older **The most frequently chosen baccalaureate fields are** business/marketing, education, social sciences **Academic program** English as a second language, advanced placement, honors program, summer session, internships **Contact** Ms. Anne Scott, Manager of Admissions, Acadia University, Wolfville, NS B4P 2R6, Canada. *Phone:* 902-585-1016. *Fax:* 902-585-1092. *E-mail:* admissions@acadiau.ca. *Web site:* http://www.acadiau.ca/.

Alberta Bible College
Calgary, Alberta, Canada

Contact Alberta Bible College, 635 Northmount Drive, NW, Calgary, AB T2K 3J6, Canada. *Phone:* toll-free 877-542-9492. *Web site:* http://www.abc-ca.org/.

Alberta College of Art & Design
Calgary, Alberta, Canada

General Province-supported, 4-year, coed **Entrance** Moderately difficult **Setting** 1-acre urban campus **Total enrollment** 1,166 **Student-faculty ratio** 17:1 **Application deadline** 4/1 (freshmen), 3/1 (transfer) **Freshman admission** 46% were admitted **Housing** Yes **Expenses** Tuition & Fees: state resident $5161; Room & Board $9368 **Undergraduates** 69% women, 7% part-time, 21% 25 or older **The most frequently chosen baccalaureate field is** visual and performing arts **Academic program** Advanced placement, summer session, adult/continuing education programs, internships **Contact** Ms. Joy Borman, Director of Admissions, Alberta College of Art & Design, 1407-14 Avenue NW, Calgary, AB T2N 4R3, Canada. *Phone:* 403-284-7689 or toll-free 800-251-8290. *Fax:* 403-284-7644. *E-mail:* admissions@acad.ca. *Web site:* http://www.acad.ca/.

Ambrose University College
Calgary, Alberta, Canada

General Independent, comprehensive, coed, affiliated with The Christian and Missionary Alliance **Entrance** Noncompetitive **Setting** 16-acre urban campus **Student-faculty ratio** 15:1 **Application deadline** Rolling (freshmen), rolling (transfer) **Housing** Yes **Expenses** Tuition & Fees 8640 Canadian dollars; Room & Board 5490 Canadian dollars **Academic program** English as a second language, advanced placement, accelerated degree program, honors program, summer session, adult/continuing education programs, internships **Contact** Admissions Officer, Ambrose University College, 630, 833-4th Avenue SW, Calgary, AB T2P 3T5, Canada. *Phone:* toll-free 800-461-1222. *E-mail:* enrolment@ambrose.edu. *Web site:* http://www.ambrose.edu/.

Athabasca University
Athabasca, Alberta, Canada

General Province-supported, comprehensive, coed **Entrance** Noncompetitive **Setting** 480-acre small-town campus **Total enrollment** 34,171 **Application deadline** Rolling (freshmen), rolling (transfer) **Housing** No **Expenses** Tuition & Fees: state resident 6100 Canadian dollars, nonresident 7150 Canadian dollars **Undergraduates** 55% 25 or older **Academic program** English as a second language, advanced placement, accelerated degree program, self-designed majors, summer session, adult/continuing education programs **Contact** Information Centre, Athabasca University, 1 University Drive, Athabasca, AB T9S 3A3. *Phone:* 800-788-9041 or toll-free 800-788-9041. *Fax:* 780-675-6437. *E-mail:* reginfo@cs.athabascau.ca. *Web site:* http://www.athabascau.ca/.

Bethany Bible College
Sussex, New Brunswick, Canada

General Independent, 4-year, coed, affiliated with Wesleyan Church **Entrance** Moderately difficult **Setting** 57-acre small-town campus **Total enrollment** 203 **Student-faculty ratio** 13:1 **Application deadline** Rolling (freshmen), rolling (transfer) **Freshman admission** 57% were admitted. Average high school GPA 3.41 **Freshman test scores** SAT critical reading scores over 500: 69%; SAT math scores over 500: 38.5%; ACT scores over 18: 100%; ACT scores over 24: 33.5% **Housing** Yes **Expenses** Tuition & Fees $8550; Room & Board $5100 **Undergraduates** 51% women, 3% part-time, 14% 25 or older **The most frequently chosen baccalaureate field is** theology and religious vocations **Academic program** Advanced placement, summer session, internships **Contact** Mrs. Dana Butler, Admissions Coordinator, Bethany Bible College, 26 Western Street, Sussex, NB E4E 5L2, Canada. *Phone:* 506-432-4422 or toll-free 888-432-4422. *Fax:* 506-432-4442. *E-mail:* butlerd@bbc.ca. *Web site:* http://www.bethany-ca.edu/.

Bishop's University
Sherbrooke, Quebec, Canada

General Province-supported, comprehensive, coed **Entrance** Moderately difficult **Setting** 500-acre small-town campus **Total enrollment** 2,291 **Student-faculty ratio** 16:1 **Application deadline** 3/1 (freshmen), 3/1 (transfer) **Freshman test scores** ACT scores over 18: 100%; ACT scores over 24: 30% **Housing** Yes **Expenses** Tuition & Fees: state resident 2883 Canadian dollars, nonresident 6393 Canadian dollars; Room & Board 6900 Canadian dollars **Undergraduates** 56% women, 19% part-time, 21% 25 or older **Academic program** English as a second language, advanced placement, accelerated degree program, self-designed majors, honors program, summer session, adult/continuing education programs, internships **Contact** Mrs. Jacqueline Belleau, Coordinator of Student Recruitment, Bishop's University, 2600 College Street, Sherbrooke, QC J1M 0C8, Canada. *Phone:* 819-822-9600 Ext. 2691 or toll-free 877-822-8200. *Fax:* 819-822-9661. *E-mail:* recruitment@ubishops.ca. *Web site:* http://www.ubishops.ca/.

Visit Petersons.com and enter keyword Bishop's

See page 604 for the College Close-Up.

Brandon University
Brandon, Manitoba, Canada

Contact Murray Kerr, Director of Admissions, Brandon University, 270 18th Street, Brandon, MB R7A 6A9, Canada. *Phone:* 204-727-7352 or toll-free 800-644-7644. *Fax:* 204-728-3221. *E-mail:* kerr@brandonu.ca. *Web site:* http://www.brandonu.ca/.

Briercrest College
Caronport, Saskatchewan, Canada

Contact Mr. Mike Benallick, Director of Admissions, Briercrest College, 510 College Drive, Caronport, SK S0H 0S0, Canada. *Phone:* 306-756-3200 or toll-free 800-667-5199. *Fax:* 403-669-2024. *E-mail:* enrollment@briercrest.ca. *Web site:* http://www.briercrest.ca/.

British Columbia Institute of Technology
Burnaby, British Columbia, Canada

General Province-supported, 4-year, coed **Entrance** Moderately difficult **Setting** 103-acre urban campus **Total enrollment** 22,507 **Freshman admission** 44% were admitted **Housing** Yes **Expenses** Tuition & Fees: state resident 5050 Canadian dollars **Undergraduates** 43% women, 68% part-time **Contact** Ms. Anna Dosen, Supervisor of Admissions, British Columbia Institute of Technology, 3700 Willingdon Avenue, Burnaby, BC V5G 3H2, Canada. *Phone:* 604-432-8496. *Fax:* 604-431-6917. *Web site:* http://www.bcit.ca/.

Brock University
St. Catharines, Ontario, Canada

General Province-supported, university, coed **Entrance** Moderately difficult **Setting** 540-acre urban campus **Total enrollment** 17,493 **Student-faculty ratio** 30:1 **Application deadline** 4/1 (freshmen), 4/1 (transfer) **Freshman admission** Average high school GPA 3 **Housing** Yes **Expenses** Tuition & Fees: state resident 5758 Canadian dollars; Room & Board 7975 Canadian dollars **Undergraduates** 58% women **Academic program** English as a second language, advanced placement, accelerated degree program, self-designed majors, honors program, summer session, adult/continuing education programs, internships **Contact** Mrs. Lynn Thompson-Dovi, International Admissions Officer, Brock University, 500 Glenridge Avenue, L2S 3A1, Canada. *Phone:* 905-688-5550 Ext. 3431. *Fax:* 905-688-5488. *E-mail:* admissns@brocku.ca. *Web site:* http://www.brocku.ca/.

Canadian Mennonite University
Winnipeg, Manitoba, Canada

Contact Mr. Abe Bergen, Director of Enrollment Services, Canadian Mennonite University, 500 Shaftesbury Boulevard, Winnipeg, MB R3P 2N2, Canada. *Phone:* 204-487-3300 Ext. 652 or toll-free 877-231-4570. *Fax:* 204-487-3858. *E-mail:* cu@cmu.ca. *Web site:* http://www.cmu.ca/.

Cape Breton University
Sydney, Nova Scotia, Canada

General Province-supported, comprehensive, coed **Entrance** Moderately difficult **Setting** urban campus **Total enrollment** 3,253 **Student-faculty ratio** 15:1 **Application deadline** 8/1 (freshmen), rolling (transfer) **Housing** Yes **Expenses** Tuition & Fees: state resident $4638, nonresident $5660; Room & Board $6560 **Academic program** English as a second language, honors program, internships **Contact** Brendan MacDonald, Manager, Admissions, Cape Breton University, Box 5300, 1250 Grand Lake Road, Sydney, NS B1P 6L2, Canada. *Phone:* 902-563-1117 or toll-free 888-959-9995. *E-mail:* brendan_macdonald@cbu.ca. *Web site:* http://www.cbu.ca/.

Carleton University
Ottawa, Ontario, Canada

Contact Ms. Jean Mullan, Director, Undergraduate Recruitment Office, Carleton University, 1125 Colonel By Drive, Ottawa, ON K1S 5B6, Canada. *Phone:* 613-520-3663 or toll-free 888-354-4414. *E-mail:* liaison@admissions.carleton.ca. *Web site:* http://www.carleton.ca/.

Centennial College
Scarborough, Ontario, Canada

Contact Enrolment Services, Centennial College, PO Box 631, Station 'A', Scarborough, ON M1K 5E9, Canada. *Phone:* 416-289-5325 or toll-free 800-268-4419. *E-mail:* success@centennialcollege.ca. *Web site:* http://www.centennialcollege.ca/.

Collège Dominicain de Philosophie et de Théologie
Ottawa, Ontario, Canada

General Independent Roman Catholic, comprehensive, coed **Entrance** Noncompetitive **Setting** urban campus **Total enrollment** 216 **Application deadline** 6/1 (freshmen), rolling (transfer) **Freshman admission** 100% were admitted **Housing** Yes **Expenses** Tuition & Fees 3540 Canadian dollars; Room & Board 6600 Canadian dollars **Undergraduates** 60% women, 62% part-time, 79% 25 or older, 1% Hispanic American, 3% Asian American/Pacific Islander **The most frequently chosen baccalaureate fields are** philosophy and religious studies, theology and religious vocations **Academic program** Accelerated degree program, summer session **Contact** Fr. Herve Tremblay OP, Registrar, Collège Dominicain de Philosophie et de Théologie, 96 Empress Avenue, Ottawa, ON K1R 7G3, Canada. *Phone:* 613-233-5696 Ext. 308. *Fax:* 613-233-6064. *E-mail:* registraire@collegedominicain.ca. *Web site:* http://www.collegedominicain.ca/.

Collège universitaire de Saint-Boniface
Saint-Boniface, Manitoba, Canada

Contact Collège universitaire de Saint-Boniface, 200 avenue de la Cathèdrale, Saint-Boniface, MB R2H 0H7, Canada. *Web site:* http://www.ustboniface.mb.ca/.

Columbia Bible College
Abbotsford, British Columbia, Canada

General Independent Mennonite Brethren, 4-year, coed **Entrance** Noncompetitive **Setting** 9-acre urban campus **Total enrollment** 464 **Student-faculty ratio** 17:1 **Application deadline** 8/15 (freshmen), 8/15 (transfer) **Housing** Yes **Expenses** Tuition & Fees $8550 **Undergraduates** 15% 25 or older **The most frequently chosen baccalaureate field is** theology and religious vocations **Academic program** Advanced placement, internships **Contact** Aaron Roorda, Director of Admissions, Columbia Bible College, 2940 Clearbrook Road, Abbotsford, BC V2T 2Z8. *Phone:* 604-853-3358 Ext. 301 or toll-free 800-283-0881. *Fax:* 604-853-3063. *E-mail:* aaron.roorda@columbiabc.edu. *Web site:* http://www.columbiabc.edu/.

Concordia University

Montréal, Quebec, Canada

General Province-supported, university, coed **Entrance** Moderately difficult **Setting** 52-acre urban campus **Total enrollment** 33,595 **Student-faculty ratio** 20:1 **Application deadline** 3/1 (freshmen), 3/1 (transfer) **Freshman admission** 69% were admitted **Housing** Yes **Expenses** Tuition & Fees: state resident 3243 Canadian dollars, nonresident 6843 Canadian dollars; Room & Board 8084 Canadian dollars **Undergraduates** 51% women, 35% part-time, 22% 25 or older **The most frequently chosen baccalaureate fields are** business/marketing, social sciences, visual and performing arts **Academic program** English as a second language, advanced placement, accelerated degree program, self-designed majors, honors program, summer session, adult/continuing education programs, internships **Contact** Ms. Assunta Fargnoli, Assistant Registrar, Concordia University, 1455 de Maisonneuve Boulevard West, Building LB-719-2, Montreal, QC H3G 1M8, Canada. *Phone:* 514-848-2424 Ext. 2628. *Fax:* 514-848-2621. *E-mail:* fargnoli@alcor.concordia.ca. *Web site:* http://www.concordia.ca/.

Concordia University College of Alberta

Edmonton, Alberta, Canada

General Independent Lutheran, comprehensive, coed **Entrance** Moderately difficult **Setting** 15-acre urban campus **Total enrollment** 1,579 **Student-faculty ratio** 18:1 **Application deadline** 6/30 (freshmen) **Freshman admission** 65% were admitted **Housing** Yes **Expenses** Tuition & Fees 6889 Canadian dollars; Room & Board 5250 Canadian dollars **The most frequently chosen baccalaureate fields are** education, business/marketing, psychology **Academic program** Advanced placement, honors program, summer session, internships **Contact** Student and Enrolment Services, Concordia University College of Alberta, 7128 Ada Boulevard, Edmonton, AB T5B 4E4. *Phone:* 780-479-9220 or toll-free 866-479-5200. *Fax:* 780-378-8460. *E-mail:* admits@concordia.ab.ca. *Web site:* http://www.concordia.ab.ca/.

Crandall University

Moncton, New Brunswick, Canada

General Independent Baptist, 4-year, coed **Entrance** Minimally difficult **Setting** 220-acre urban campus **Total enrollment** 765 **Student-faculty ratio** 17:1 **Application deadline** Rolling (freshmen), rolling (transfer) **Freshman admission** 89% were admitted. Average high school GPA 2.67 **Housing** Yes **Expenses** Tuition & Fees 7635 Canadian dollars; Room & Board 5330 Canadian dollars **Undergraduates** 66% women, 10% part-time, 41% 25 or older **The most frequently chosen baccalaureate fields are** education, business/marketing, psychology **Academic program** English as a second language, advanced placement, accelerated degree program, honors program, summer session, adult/continuing education programs, internships **Contact** Mrs. Laura Lutes, Administrative Officer- Admissions and Recruitment, Crandall University, Box 6004, Moncton, NB E1C 9L7, Canada. *Phone:* 506-858-8970 Ext. 6433 or toll-free 888-YOU-N-ABU. *Fax:* 506-858-9694. *E-mail:* Laura.lutes@crandallu.ca. *Web site:* http://www.crandallu.ca/.

Dalhousie University

Halifax, Nova Scotia, Canada

General Province-supported, university, coed **Entrance** Moderately difficult **Setting** 80-acre urban campus **Total enrollment** 15,367 **Student-faculty ratio** 14:1 **Application deadline** 6/1 (freshmen), 6/1 (transfer) **Housing** Yes **Expenses** Tuition & Fees: state resident 6800 Canadian dollars; Room & Board 7940 Canadian dollars **Undergraduates** 56% women, 13% part-time, 18% 25 or older **Academic program** English as a second language, advanced placement, accelerated degree program, honors program, summer session, internships **Contact** Mairead Barry, Associate Registrar and Director of Admissions, Dalhousie University, Office of the Registrar, Halifax, NS B3H 4H6, Canada. *Phone:* 902-494-2148. *Fax:* 902-494-1630. *E-mail:* admissions@dal.ca. *Web site:* http://www.dal.ca/.

Emily Carr Institute of Art + Design

Vancouver, British Columbia, Canada

Contact Admissions, Emily Carr Institute of Art + Design, 1399 Johnston Street, Vancouver, BC V6H 3R9, Canada. *Phone:* 604-844-3800 or toll-free 800-832-7788. *Fax:* 604-844-3801. *Web site:* http://www.eciad.ca/.

Emmanuel Bible College

Kitchener, Ontario, Canada

General Independent, 4-year, coed, affiliated with Missionary Church **Entrance** Moderately difficult **Setting** 12-acre urban campus **Total enrollment** 209 **Application deadline** Rolling (freshmen) **Housing** Yes **Expenses** Tuition & Fees $8771; Room & Board $4934 **Academic program** Accelerated degree program, summer session, internships **Contact** Sherry Mahon, Director of Admissions and Seminars, Emmanuel Bible College, 100 Fergus Avenue, Kitchener, ON N2A 2H2, Canada. *Phone:* 519-894-8900 Ext. 224. *E-mail:* smahon@ebcollege.on.ca. *Web site:* http://www.ebcollege.on.ca/.

Eston College

Eston, Saskatchewan, Canada

Contact Eston College, 730 1st Street E., Box 579, Eston, SK S0L 1A0, Canada. *Phone:* toll-free 888-440-3424. *Web site:* http://www.estoncollege.ca/.

HEC Montreal

Montréal, Quebec, Canada

General Province-supported, comprehensive, coed **Entrance** Moderately difficult **Setting** 9-acre urban campus **Total enrollment** 12,667 **Student-faculty ratio** 23:1 **Application deadline** 3/1 (freshmen) **Freshman admission** 63% were admitted **Housing** Yes **Expenses** Tuition & Fees: state resident 2930 Canadian dollars, nonresident 6463 Canadian dollars; Room only 3197 Canadian dollars **Undergraduates** 51% women, 51% part-time, 51% 25 or older **The most frequently chosen baccalaureate field is** business/marketing **Academic program** English as a second language, self-designed majors, honors program, summer session, adult/continuing education programs **Contact** Mrs. Yolaine Martineau, Office of the Registrar, HEC Montreal, 3000 Chemin de la Cote-Sainte-Catherine, Montreal, QC H3T 2A7. *Phone:* 514-340-6151. *Fax:* 514-340-5640. *E-mail:* admission.info@hec.ca. *Web site:* http://www.hec.ca/.

Heritage Baptist College and Heritage Theological Seminary

Cambridge, Ontario, Canada

General Independent Baptist, comprehensive, coed **Entrance** Noncompetitive **Setting** 7-acre urban campus **Total enrollment** 274 **Student-faculty ratio** 11:1 **Application deadline** 9/1 (freshmen), 9/1 (transfer) **Freshman admission** 100% were admitted **Housing** Yes **Expenses** Tuition & Fees $8420; Room & Board $4320 **Undergraduates** 39% women, 19% part-time, 26% 25 or older **The most frequently chosen baccalaureate fields are** education, theology and religious vocations **Academic program** Advanced placement, summer session, internships **Contact** Mr. Mark Walther, Assistant Dean of Students, Heritage Baptist College and Heritage Theological Seminary, 175 Holiday Inn Drive, New York, NY 10023-6588. *Phone:* 519-651-2869 Ext. 251. *Fax:* 519-651-2870. *E-mail:* mwalther@heritagecollege.net. *Web site:* http://www.heritage-theo.edu/.

Horizon College & Seminary
Saskatoon, Saskatchewan, Canada

General Independent, 4-year, coed, affiliated with Pentecostal Assemblies of Canada **Entrance** Minimally difficult **Setting** 5-acre urban campus **Total enrollment** 58 **Student-faculty ratio** 10:1 **Application deadline** 9/15 (freshmen) **Freshman admission** 69% were admitted **Housing** Yes **Expenses** Tuition & Fees $6196; Room & Board $4592 **Undergraduates** 43% women, 43% part-time, 5% 25 or older **The most frequently chosen baccalaureate field is** philosophy and religious studies **Academic program** Self-designed majors, internships **Contact** Ms. Judy Heyer, Registrar, Horizon College & Seminary, 1303 Jackson Avenue, Saskatoon, SK S7H 2M9, Canada. *Phone:* 306-374-6655 or toll-free 877-374.6655. *Fax:* 306-373-6968. *E-mail:* admissions@horizon.edu. *Web site:* http://www.horizon.edu/.

The King's University College
Edmonton, Alberta, Canada

General Independent interdenominational, 4-year, coed **Entrance** Moderately difficult **Setting** 20-acre suburban campus **Total enrollment** 662 **Student-faculty ratio** 12:1 **Application deadline** Rolling (freshmen), rolling (transfer) **Freshman admission** 81% were admitted. Average high school GPA 3.3 **Housing** Yes **Expenses** Tuition & Fees 9228 Canadian dollars; Room & Board 5390 Canadian dollars **Undergraduates** 57% women, 7% part-time, 17% 25 or older **The most frequently chosen baccalaureate fields are** education, English, psychology **Academic program** English as a second language, advanced placement, summer session, adult/continuing education programs, internships **Contact** Mr. Glenn Keeler, Registrar/Director of Admissions, The King's University College, 9125-50 Street, Edmonton, AB T6B 2H3. *Phone:* 780-465-3500 Ext. 8035 or toll-free 800-661-8582. *Fax:* 780-465-3534. *E-mail:* admissions@kingsu.ca. *Web site:* http://www.kingsu.ca/.

Kwantlen Polytechnic University
Surrey, British Columbia, Canada

General Province-supported, 4-year, coed **Setting** suburban campus **Total enrollment** 12,608 **Student-faculty ratio** 35:1 **Application deadline** Rolling (freshmen), rolling (transfer) **Freshman admission** 41% were admitted **Housing** No **Expenses** Tuition & Fees: state resident 4129 Canadian dollars **Undergraduates** 57% women, 38% part-time, 31% 25 or older **The most frequently chosen baccalaureate fields are** business/marketing, health professions and related sciences, liberal arts/general studies **Academic program** English as a second language, advanced placement, accelerated degree program, self-designed majors, honors program, summer session, adult/continuing education programs, internships **Contact** Admissions, Kwantlen Polytechnic University, 12666—72nd Avenue, Surrey, BC V3W 2M8. *Phone:* 604-599-2000. *Fax:* 604-599-2086. *E-mail:* admission@kwantlen.ca. *Web site:* http://www.kwantlen.ca/.

Lakehead University
Thunder Bay, Ontario, Canada

General Province-supported, comprehensive, coed **Entrance** Moderately difficult **Setting** 345-acre suburban campus **Total enrollment** 7,768 **Application deadline** 9/21 (freshmen), 9/21 (transfer) **Freshman admission** 76% were admitted **Housing** Yes **Expenses** Tuition & Fees: state resident 5495 Canadian dollars, nonresident 5495 Canadian dollars; Room & Board 7170 Canadian dollars **Undergraduates** 58% women, 18% part-time **The most frequently chosen baccalaureate fields are** education, engineering, social sciences **Academic program** Advanced placement, accelerated degree program, honors program, summer session, internships **Contact** Jordana Hughes, Admissions Officer, Lakehead University, 955 Oliver Road, Thunder Bay, ON P7B 5E1, Canada. *Phone:* 807-343-8868 or toll-free 800-465-3959. *Fax:* 807-766-7209. *E-mail:* admissions@lakeheadu.ca. *Web site:* http://www.lakeheadu.ca/.

Laurentian University
Sudbury, Ontario, Canada

General Province-supported, comprehensive, coed **Setting** 700-acre suburban campus **Total enrollment** 8,918 **Application deadline** 4/1 (freshmen), rolling (transfer) **Housing** Yes **Expenses** Tuition & Fees: state resident 5435 Canadian dollars; Room only 3550 Canadian dollars **Academic program** English as a second language, accelerated degree program, honors program, summer session, adult/continuing education programs, internships **Contact** Mr. Ron Smith, Registrar, Laurentian University, Ramsey Lake Road, P3E 2C6, Canada. *Phone:* 705-675-1151. *Fax:* 705-675-4891. *E-mail:* admissions@laurentian.ca. *Web site:* http://www.laurentian.ca/.

Master's College and Seminary
Toronto, Ontario, Canada

General Independent Pentecostal, 4-year, coed **Entrance** Noncompetitive **Setting** urban campus **Total enrollment** 278 **Student-faculty ratio** 11:1 **Application deadline** 8/31 (freshmen), 8/31 (transfer) **Freshman admission** 95% were admitted **Housing** No **Expenses** Tuition & Fees $6176 **The most frequently chosen baccalaureate field is** theology and religious vocations **Academic program** Accelerated degree program, summer session, internships **Contact** Ms. Flora Anthony, Admissions, Master's College and Seminary, 282 Cummer Avenue, Toronto, ON M2M 2E7, Canada. *Phone:* 800-295-6368 or toll-free 800-295-6368 Ext. 243. *Fax:* 416-482-7004. *E-mail:* flora.anthony@mcs.edu. *Web site:* http://www.mcs.edu/.

McGill University
Montréal, Quebec, Canada

General Province-supported, university, coed **Entrance** Very difficult **Setting** 80-acre urban campus **Total enrollment** 31,664 **Student-faculty ratio** 16:1 **Application deadline** 1/15 (freshmen), 1/15 (transfer) **Freshman admission** 54% were admitted. Average high school GPA 3.52 **Freshman test scores** SAT critical reading scores over 500: 99.54%; SAT math scores over 500: 99.55%; ACT scores over 18: 100%; SAT critical reading scores over 600: 91.38%; SAT math scores over 600: 92.97%; ACT scores over 24: 98.74% **Housing** Yes **Expenses** Tuition & Fees: state resident 3468 Canadian dollars, nonresident 7000 Canadian dollars; Room & Board 11,000 Canadian dollars **Undergraduates** 59% women, 17% part-time, 11% 25 or older **The most frequently chosen baccalaureate fields are** business/marketing, biological/life sciences, social sciences **Academic program** English as a second language, advanced placement, accelerated degree program, honors program, summer session, adult/continuing education programs, internships **Contact** Enrollment Services, McGill University, 845 Sherbrooke Street West, James Administration Building, Room 205, Montreal, QC H3A 2T5, Canada. *Phone:* 514-398-3910. *Fax:* 514-398-4193. *E-mail:* admissions@mcgill.ca. *Web site:* http://www.mcgill.ca/.

McMaster University
Hamilton, Ontario, Canada

General Province-supported, university, coed **Entrance** Very difficult **Setting** 300-acre suburban campus **Total enrollment** 25,809 **Student-faculty ratio** 25:1 **Application deadline** 6/1 (freshmen), 6/1 (transfer) **Freshman admission** 68% were admitted **Housing** Yes **Expenses** Room & Board 7225 Canadian dollars **The most frequently chosen baccalaureate fields are** health professions and related sciences, liberal arts/general studies, social sciences **Academic program** English as a second language, advanced placement, accelerated degree program, honors program, summer session, adult/continuing education programs, internships **Contact** Olivia Demerling, Admissions Officer, McMaster University, 1280 Main Street West, Hamilton, ON L8S 4M2, Canada. *Phone:* 905-525-4600. *Fax:* 905-527-1105. *E-mail:* admitmac@mcmaster.ca. *Web site:* http://www.mcmaster.ca/.

Memorial University of Newfoundland

St. John's, Newfoundland and Labrador, Canada

General Province-supported, university, coed **Entrance** Moderately difficult **Setting** 250-acre urban campus **Total enrollment** 17,378 **Student-faculty ratio** 12:1 **Application deadline** Rolling (freshmen), 3/1 (transfer) **Housing** Yes **Expenses** Tuition & Fees: state resident $3044; Room & Board $5968 **Undergraduates** 61% women, 16% part-time, 16% 25 or older **Academic program** English as a second language, advanced placement, accelerated degree program, honors program, summer session, adult/continuing education programs, internships **Contact** Ms. Marian Abbott, Admissions Office, Memorial University of Newfoundland, Elizabeth Avenue, St. John's, NL A1C 5S7, Canada. *Phone:* 709-737-3705. *E-mail:* sturecru@morgan.ucs.mun.ca. *Web site:* http://www.mun.ca/.

Meritus University

Fredericton, New Brunswick, Canada

General Proprietary, comprehensive, coed **Setting** 1-acre urban campus **Application deadline** Rolling (freshmen), rolling (transfer) **Expenses** Tuition & Fees 8250 Canadian dollars **Academic program** Advanced placement **Contact** Mr. Jaime Gardea, Admissions Office, Meritus University, 30 Knowledge Park Drive, Suite 301, Fredericton, NB E3C 2R2, Canada. *Phone:* 800-856-3940 or toll-free 800-856-3940. *Fax:* 506-443-8470. *E-mail:* enrolmentinfo@staff.MeritusU.ca. *Web site:* http://www.meritusu.ca/.

Mount Allison University

Sackville, New Brunswick, Canada

General Province-supported, comprehensive, coed **Entrance** Moderately difficult **Setting** 50-acre small-town campus **Total enrollment** 2,527 **Student-faculty ratio** 16:1 **Application deadline** Rolling (freshmen), rolling (transfer) **Freshman admission** 74% were admitted. Average high school GPA 3.32 **Housing** Yes **Expenses** Tuition & Fees: state resident 7009 Canadian dollars; Room & Board 7389 Canadian dollars **Undergraduates** 58% women, 5% part-time, 6% 25 or older **The most frequently chosen baccalaureate fields are** business/marketing, psychology, social sciences **Academic program** Advanced placement, self-designed majors, honors program, summer session, adult/continuing education programs, internships **Contact** Mr. Matt Sheridan-Jonah, Manager of Admissions, Mount Allison University, 65 York Street, Sackville, NB E4L 1E4, Canada. *Phone:* 506-364-3294. *Fax:* 506-364-2272. *E-mail:* admissions@mta.ca. *Web site:* http://www.mta.ca/.

Mount Royal University

Calgary, Alberta, Canada

Contact Admissions Office, Mount Royal University, 4825 Mount Royal Gate SW, Calgary, AB T3E 6K6, Canada. *Phone:* 403-440-5000 or toll-free 877-440-5001. *Web site:* http://www.mtroyal.ca/.

Mount Saint Vincent University

Halifax, Nova Scotia, Canada

General Province-supported, comprehensive, coed, primarily women **Entrance** Moderately difficult **Setting** 40-acre suburban campus **Total enrollment** 2,946 **Student-faculty ratio** 13:1 **Application deadline** 3/15 (freshmen), 8/15 (transfer) **Freshman admission** 60% were admitted **Housing** Yes **Expenses** Tuition & Fees: state resident 6340 Canadian dollars; Room & Board 7190 Canadian dollars **Undergraduates** 33% 25 or older **The most frequently chosen baccalaureate fields are** business/marketing, communications/journalism, education **Academic program** Honors program, summer session, adult/continuing education programs, internships **Contact** Ms. Heidi Tattrie, Assistant Registrar/Admissions, Mount Saint Vincent University, 166 Bedford Highway, Halifax, NS B3M2J6, Canada. *Phone:* 902-457-6117. *Fax:* 902-457-6498. *E-mail:* admissions@msvu.ca. *Web site:* http://www.msvu.ca/.

Ner Israel Yeshiva College of Toronto

Thornhill, Ontario, Canada

Contact Rabbi Y. Kravetz, Director of Admissions, Ner Israel Yeshiva College of Toronto, 8950 Bathurst Street, Thornhill, ON L4J 8A7, Canada. *Phone:* 905-731-1224.

Nipissing University

North Bay, Ontario, Canada

General Province-supported, comprehensive, coed **Entrance** Moderately difficult **Setting** 290-hectare urban campus **Total enrollment** 3,700 **Freshman admission** Average high school GPA 3 **Housing** Yes **Expenses** Tuition & Fees: state resident 5475 Canadian dollars, nonresident 5475 Canadian dollars; Room only 4500 Canadian dollars **Academic program** Advanced placement, accelerated degree program, honors program, summer session **Contact** Ms. Lori-Ann Beckford, Assistant Registrar-Liaison, Nipissing University, 100 College Drive, Box 5002, North Bay, ON P1B 8L7, Canada. *Phone:* 705-474-3461 Ext. 4518. *Fax:* 705-474-1947. *E-mail:* liaison@nipissingu.ca. *Web site:* http://www.nipissingu.ca/.

Nova Scotia Agricultural College

Truro, Nova Scotia, Canada

General Province-supported, comprehensive, coed **Entrance** Minimally difficult **Setting** 408-acre small-town campus **Total enrollment** 902 **Student-faculty ratio** 12:1 **Application deadline** 8/1 (freshmen) **Freshman admission** 78% were admitted **Housing** Yes **Expenses** Tuition & Fees: state resident $5928; Room & Board $7376 **Undergraduates** 29% 25 or older **The most frequently chosen baccalaureate fields are** agriculture, business/marketing, natural resources/environmental science **Academic program** Advanced placement, summer session, adult/continuing education programs, internships **Contact** Ms. Elizabeth Johnson, Admissions Officer, Nova Scotia Agricultural College, PO Box 550, Truro, NS B2N 5E3, Canada. *Phone:* 902-893-8212 or toll-free 888-700-6722. *Fax:* 902-895-5529. *E-mail:* recruit@nsac.ca. *Web site:* http://nsac.ca/.

NSCAD University

Halifax, Nova Scotia, Canada

General Province-supported, comprehensive, coed **Entrance** Moderately difficult **Setting** 1-acre urban campus **Total enrollment** 1,021 **Student-faculty ratio** 9:1 **Application deadline** 5/15 (freshmen), 2/15 (transfer) **Freshman admission** 75% were admitted **Housing** Yes **Expenses** Tuition & Fees: state resident 5932 Canadian dollars **Undergraduates** 35% 25 or older **The most frequently chosen baccalaureate field is** visual and performing arts **Academic program** Self-designed majors, honors program, summer session, internships **Contact** Mr. Terry Bailey, Director of Admissions and Enrollment Services, NSCAD University, 5163 Duke Street, Halifax, NS B3J 3J6. *Phone:* 902-494-8129. *Fax:* 902-425-2987. *E-mail:* admissions@nscad.ca. *Web site:* http://www.nscad.ca/.

Okanagan College

Kelowna, British Columbia, Canada

Contact Mr. Paul Campo, Okanagan College, 1000 KLO Road, Kelowna, BC V1Y 4X8, Canada. *Phone:* 250-762-5445 Ext. 4332. *E-mail:* pgcampo@okanagan.bc.ca. *Web site:* http://www.okanagan.bc.ca/.

Prairie Bible Institute

Three Hills, Alberta, Canada

General Independent interdenominational, 4-year, coed **Entrance** Minimally difficult **Setting** 130-acre small-town campus **Application deadline** 8/15 (freshmen), 8/15 (transfer) **Housing** Yes **Expenses** Tuition & Fees 9058 Canadian dollars; Room & Board 5100 Canadian dollars **Aca-**

demic program English as a second language, advanced placement, accelerated degree program, adult/continuing education programs, internships **Contact** Mr. Kevin Kirk, Vice President Marketing and Enrollment Management, Prairie Bible Institute, 330 Sixth Avenue North, PO Box 4000, Three Hills, AB T0M 2N0, Canada. *Phone:* 403-443-5511 Ext. 3007 or toll-free 800-661-2425. *E-mail:* admissions@prairie.edu. *Web site:* http://www.pbi.ab.ca/.

Providence College and Theological Seminary

Otterburne, Manitoba, Canada

General Independent interdenominational, comprehensive, coed **Entrance** Noncompetitive **Setting** 100-acre rural campus **Total enrollment** 506 **Student-faculty ratio** 19:1 **Application deadline** Rolling (freshmen), rolling (transfer) **Freshman admission** 87% were admitted **Housing** Yes **Expenses** Tuition & Fees 7260 Canadian dollars; Room & Board 4570 Canadian dollars **Undergraduates** 47% women, 16% part-time **Academic program** English as a second language, accelerated degree program, internships **Contact** Mr. Adrian Enns, Director of College Enrollment, Providence College and Theological Seminary, 10 College Crescent, Otterburne, MB R0A 1G0, Canada. *Phone:* 204-433-7488 or toll-free 800-668-7768. *Fax:* 204-433-7158. *E-mail:* info@prov.ca. *Web site:* http://www.prov.ca/.

Queen's University at Kingston

Kingston, Ontario, Canada

General Province-supported, university, coed **Entrance** Most difficult **Setting** 160-acre urban campus **Total enrollment** 22,601 **Student-faculty ratio** 15:1 **Application deadline** 2/1 (freshmen), 5/15 (transfer) **Freshman test scores** SAT critical reading scores over 500: 84%; SAT math scores over 500: 92%; SAT critical reading scores over 600: 55%; SAT math scores over 600: 70% **Housing** Yes **Expenses** Tuition & Fees: state resident 5908 Canadian dollars; Room & Board 10,259 Canadian dollars **Undergraduates** 61% women, 20% part-time, 4% 25 or older **The most frequently chosen baccalaureate fields are** biological/life sciences, education, engineering **Academic program** English as a second language, advanced placement, accelerated degree program, self-designed majors, honors program, summer session, adult/continuing education programs, internships **Contact** Ms. Wendy Smith, Admission Coordinator, Queen's University at Kingston, Undergraduate Admissions, Gordon Hall, 74 Union St, Kingston, ON K7L 3N6, Canada. *Phone:* 613-533-2218. *Fax:* 613-533-6810. *E-mail:* admission@queensu.ca. *Web site:* http://www.queensu.ca/.

Redeemer University College

Ancaster, Ontario, Canada

General Independent interdenominational, 4-year, coed **Entrance** Moderately difficult **Setting** 86-acre small-town campus **Total enrollment** 918 **Student-faculty ratio** 13:1 **Application deadline** 5/31 (freshmen), 5/31 (transfer) **Freshman admission** 81% were admitted **Freshman test scores** ACT scores over 18: 100%; ACT scores over 24: 64% **Housing** Yes **Expenses** Tuition & Fees 13,690 Canadian dollars; Room & Board 6126 Canadian dollars **Undergraduates** 60% women, 12% part-time **The most frequently chosen baccalaureate fields are** English, business/marketing, history **Academic program** Honors program, summer session, internships **Contact** Recruitment, Redeemer University College, 777 Garner Road East, Ancaster, ON L9K 1J4, Canada. *Phone:* 905-648-2139 Ext. 4280 or toll-free 800-263-6467 Ext. 4280. *Fax:* 905-648-9545. *E-mail:* recruitment@redeemer.ca. *Web site:* http://www.redeemer.ca/.

Rocky Mountain College

Calgary, Alberta, Canada

General Independent, 4-year, coed, affiliated with Missionary Church **Entrance** Noncompetitive **Setting** 1-acre suburban campus **Application deadline** Rolling (freshmen), rolling (transfer) **Housing** Yes **Expenses** Tuition & Fees $9380; Room & Board $3000 **Academic program** Advanced placement, summer session, adult/continuing education programs, internships **Contact** Robert Harris, Director of Enrolment and Marketing, Rocky Mountain College, 4039 Brentwood Road, NW, Calgary, AB T2L 1L1, Canada. *Phone:* 403-284-5100 or toll-free 877-YOUnRMC. *E-mail:* enrolment@rockymountaincollege.ca. *Web site:* http://www.rockymountaincollege.ca/.

Royal Military College of Canada

Kingston, Ontario, Canada

General Federally supported, comprehensive, coed **Entrance** Most difficult **Setting** 90-acre urban campus **Total enrollment** 6,500 **Application deadline** 1/15 (freshmen) **Freshman admission** 40% were admitted **Housing** Yes **Undergraduates** 15% 25 or older **Academic program** English as a second language, honors program **Contact** Lt. Col. Rod McDonald, Registrar, Royal Military College of Canada, PO Box 17000, Station Forces, Kingston, ON K7K 7B4, Canada. *Phone:* 613-541-6000 Ext. 6579. *Fax:* 613-542-3565. *E-mail:* liaison@rmc.ca. *Web site:* http://www.rmc.ca/.

Royal Roads University

Victoria, British Columbia, Canada

General Province-supported, upper-level, coed **Entrance** Moderately difficult **Setting** 565-acre suburban campus **Total enrollment** 3,120 **Housing** No **Expenses** Tuition & Fees: state resident 14,100 Canadian dollars **Academic program** Accelerated degree program, summer session, adult/continuing education programs **Contact** Admissions, Royal Roads University, 2005 Sooke Road, Victoria, BC V9B 5Y2, Canada. *Phone:* 250-391-2511 or toll-free 800-788-8028. *E-mail:* learn.more@royalroads.ca. *Web site:* http://www.royalroads.ca/.

Ryerson University

Toronto, Ontario, Canada

General Province-supported, comprehensive, coed **Entrance** Moderately difficult **Setting** 20-acre urban campus **Total enrollment** 25,181 **Application deadline** 2/1 (freshmen) **Freshman admission** Average high school GPA 3.0 **Housing** Yes **Expenses** Tuition & Fees: state resident 4983 Canadian dollars **The most frequently chosen baccalaureate fields are** business/marketing, engineering, health professions and related sciences **Academic program** English as a second language, advanced placement, honors program, summer session, adult/continuing education programs, internships **Contact** Michelle Beaton, Manager of International Student Recruitment, Ryerson University, 350 Victoria Street, Toronto, ON M5B 2K3. *Phone:* 416-979-5080. *Fax:* 416-979-5067. *E-mail:* inquire@ryerson.ca. *Web site:* http://www.ryerson.ca/.
Visit Petersons.com and enter keyword Ryerson

See page 1094 for the College Close-Up.

St. Francis Xavier University

Antigonish, Nova Scotia, Canada

General Independent Roman Catholic, comprehensive, coed **Entrance** Moderately difficult **Setting** 100-acre small-town campus **Total enrollment** 4,853 **Student-faculty ratio** 17:1 **Application deadline** Rolling (freshmen), rolling (transfer) **Freshman admission** 82% were admitted **Housing** Yes **Expenses** Tuition & Fees 7503 Canadian dollars; Room & Board 7625 Canadian dollars **Undergraduates** 62% women, 50% part-time, 10% 25 or older **Academic program** English as a second language, advanced placement, accelerated degree program, self-designed majors, honors program, summer session, adult/continuing education programs, internships **Contact** Ms. Sarah Murray, Admissions Officer, St. Francis Xavier University, PO Box 5000, Antigonish, NS B2G 2W5, Canada. *Phone:* 902-867-2219 or toll-free 877-867-7839

St. Francis Xavier University (continued)
(in-state); 877-867-STFX (out-of-state). *Fax:* 902-867-2329. *E-mail:* mbarry@stfx.ca. *Web site:* http://www.stfx.ca/.

Saint Mary's University
Halifax, Nova Scotia, Canada

General Province-supported, comprehensive, coed **Entrance** Moderately difficult **Setting** 30-acre urban campus **Application deadline** 7/1 (freshmen), 6/1 (transfer) **Housing** Yes **Expenses** Tuition & Fees: state resident $13,637; Room & Board $7450 **Academic program** English as a second language, accelerated degree program, self-designed majors, honors program, summer session, adult/continuing education programs, internships **Contact** Mr. Greg Ferguson, Director of Admissions, Saint Mary's University, Halifax, NS B3H 3C3, Canada. *Phone:* 902-420-5415. *Fax:* 902-496-8100. *E-mail:* greg.ferguson@smu.ca. *Web site:* http://www.smu.ca/.

Saint Paul University
Ottawa, Ontario, Canada

Contact Admission and Recruitment Office, Saint Paul University, 223 Main Street, Ottawa, ON K1S 1C4, Canada. *Phone:* 613-236-1393 Ext. 8990 or toll-free 800-637-6859. *Fax:* 613-782-3014. *E-mail:* admission@ustpaul.ca. *Web site:* http://www.ustpaul.ca/.

St. Thomas University
Fredericton, New Brunswick, Canada

General Independent Roman Catholic, 4-year, coed **Entrance** Moderately difficult **Setting** 16-acre small-town campus **Total enrollment** 2,426 **Student-faculty ratio** 19:1 **Application deadline** 8/31 (freshmen), 8/31 (transfer) **Freshman admission** 84% were admitted. Average high school GPA 3.3 **Housing** Yes **Expenses** Tuition & Fees 4876 Canadian dollars; Room & Board 6800 Canadian dollars **Undergraduates** 67% women, 10% part-time, 9% 25 or older **The most frequently chosen baccalaureate fields are** English, psychology, social sciences **Academic program** English as a second language, advanced placement, accelerated degree program, self-designed majors, honors program, summer session, internships **Contact** Ms. Kathryn Monti, Director of Admissions, St. Thomas University, Admissions and Welcome Building, Fredericton, NB E3B 5G3, Canada. *Phone:* 506-452-0532. *Fax:* 506-452-0617. *E-mail:* admissions@stu.ca. *Web site:* http://www.stu.ca/.

Simon Fraser University
Burnaby, British Columbia, Canada

General Province-supported, university, coed **Entrance** Moderately difficult **Setting** suburban campus **Total enrollment** 27,081 **Student-faculty ratio** 10:1 **Application deadline** 4/30 (freshmen), 4/30 (transfer) **Freshman admission** 77% were admitted. Average high school GPA 3.2 **Housing** Yes **Expenses** Tuition & Fees: state resident 5258 Canadian dollars; Room & Board 7464 Canadian dollars **Undergraduates** 55% women, 48% part-time, 13% 25 or older **Academic program** English as a second language, advanced placement, honors program, summer session, adult/continuing education programs, internships **Contact** Ms. Louise Legris, Director of Admissions, Simon Fraser University, 8888 University Drive, Burnaby, BC V5A 1S6, Canada. *Phone:* 778-782-3498. *Fax:* 778-782-4969. *E-mail:* undergraduate-admissions@sfu.ca. *Web site:* http://www.sfu.ca/.
Visit Petersons.com and enter keyword Fraser

Southern Alberta Institute of Technology
Calgary, Alberta, Canada

General Province-supported, primarily 2-year, coed **Setting** 96-acre urban campus **Total enrollment** 7,672 **Application deadline** Rolling (freshmen), rolling (transfer) **Housing** Yes **Undergraduates** 42% women, 9% part-time **Academic program** Internships **Contact** Ms. Jennifer Bennett, Registrar/Director, Southern Alberta Institute of Technology, 1301 16th Avenue NW, Calgary, AB T2M 0L4, Canada. *Phone:* 403-284-8857 or toll-free 877-284-SAIT. *Fax:* 403-284-7112. *Web site:* http://www.sait.ca/.

Steinbach Bible College
Steinbach, Manitoba, Canada

General Independent Mennonite, 4-year, coed **Entrance** Minimally difficult **Setting** 16-acre urban campus **Total enrollment** 148 **Student-faculty ratio** 18:1 **Freshman admission** 81% were admitted **Housing** Yes **Expenses** Tuition & Fees 6377 Canadian dollars; Room & Board 4320 Canadian dollars **Undergraduates** 41% women, 36% part-time **Contact** Mrs. Kaylene Buhler, Admissions Counselor, Steinbach Bible College, 50 PTH 12 North, Steinbach, MB R5G 1T4, Canada. *Phone:* 204-326-6451 Ext. 232 or toll-free 800-230-8478. *Fax:* 204-326-6908. *E-mail:* info@sbcollege.ca. *Web site:* http://www.sbcollege.ca/.

Summit Pacific College
Abbotsford, British Columbia, Canada

General Independent, 4-year, coed, affiliated with Pentecostal Assemblies of Canada **Entrance** Moderately difficult **Setting** 101-acre suburban campus **Application deadline** Rolling (freshmen), rolling (transfer) **Housing** Yes **Expenses** Tuition & Fees 6790 Canadian dollars; Room & Board 4988 Canadian dollars **Academic program** Summer session, internships **Contact** Ms. Melody Deeley, Admissions and Registration, Summit Pacific College, Box 1700, Abbotsford, BC V2S 7E7, Canada. *Phone:* 604-851-7225 or toll-free 800-976-8388. *E-mail:* registrar@summitpacific.ca. *Web site:* http://www.summitpacific.ca/.

Télé-université
Québec, Quebec, Canada

Contact Ms. Louise Bertrand, Registraire, Télé-université, 455, rue de l'Église, C.P. 4800, succ. Terminus, Québec, QC G1K 9H5, Canada. *Phone:* 418-657-2262 Ext. 5307 or toll-free 888-843-4333. *E-mail:* info@teluq.uquebec.ca. *Web site:* http://www.teluq.uquebec.ca/.

Thompson Rivers University
Kamloops, British Columbia, Canada

General Province-supported, comprehensive, coed **Setting** 100-acre small-town campus **Total enrollment** 23,419 **Student-faculty ratio** 12:1 **Application deadline** 3/1 (freshmen), 3/1 (transfer) **Freshman admission** 50% were admitted **Housing** Yes **Expenses** Tuition & Fees: state resident 4380 Canadian dollars, nonresident 4380 Canadian dollars; Room only 3900 Canadian dollars **Undergraduates** 27% 25 or older **Academic program** English as a second language, advanced placement, accelerated degree program, honors program, summer session, adult/continuing education programs, internships **Contact** Mr. Josh Keller, Director, Student Recruitment & Liaison, Thompson Rivers University, PO Box 3010, 900 McGill Road, Kamloops, BC V2C 5N3, Canada. *Phone:* 250-828-5008. *Fax:* 250-828-5159. *E-mail:* jkeller@tru.ca. *Web site:* http://www.tru.ca.

Trent University
Peterborough, Ontario, Canada

General Province-supported, university, coed **Entrance** Moderately difficult **Setting** 1,400-acre suburban campus **Total enrollment** 7,817 **Student-faculty ratio** 20:1 **Application deadline** 6/1 (freshmen), 6/1 (transfer) **Freshman admission** 20% were admitted **Housing** Yes **Expenses** Tuition & Fees: state resident 7337 Canadian dollars; Room & Board 9854 Canadian dollars **Undergraduates** 65% women, 18% part-time, 18% 25 or older **Academic program** English as a second language, advanced placement, accelerated degree program, self-designed majors, honors program, summer session **Contact** Lois Fleming, Admissions Officer, Trent University, 1600 West Bank Drive, Peterborough, ON K9J 7B8, Canada. *Phone:* 705-748-1215. *Fax:* 705-748-1629. *E-mail:* leaders@trentu.ca. *Web site:* http://www.trentu.ca/.

Trinity Western University

Langley, British Columbia, Canada

General Independent, comprehensive, coed, affiliated with Evangelical Free Church of America **Entrance** Moderately difficult **Setting** 150-acre suburban campus **Student-faculty ratio** 18:1 **Application deadline** 6/15 (freshmen), 6/15 (transfer) **Housing** Yes **Expenses** Tuition & Fees $17,460; Room & Board $7380 **Academic program** English as a second language, advanced placement, honors program, summer session, internships **Contact** Director of Admissions, Trinity Western University, 7600 Glover Road, Langley, BC V2Y 1Y1, Canada. *Phone:* 604-888-7511 Ext. 3005 or toll-free 888-468-6898. *E-mail:* admissions@twu.ca. *Web site:* http://www.twu.ca/.

Tyndale University College & Seminary

Toronto, Ontario, Canada

Contact Tricia McKenley, Admissions Office Coordinator, Tyndale University College & Seminary, 25 Ballyconnor Court, Toronto, ON M2M 4B3, Canada. *Phone:* 416-218-6757 Ext. 6738 or toll-free 800-663-6052. *E-mail:* admissions@tydale.ca. *Web site:* http://www.tyndale.ca/.

Université de Moncton

Moncton, New Brunswick, Canada

Contact Miss Nicole Savois, Chief Admission Officer, Université de Moncton, Moncton, NB E1A 3E9, Canada. *Phone:* 506-858-4115 or toll-free 800-363-8336. *E-mail:* gallanrm@umoncton.ca. *Web site:* http://www.umoncton.ca/.

Université de Montréal

Montréal, Quebec, Canada

Contact Mr. Pierre Chenard, Registrar, Université de Montréal, CP 6128, Succursale Centre-ville, Montréal, QC H3C 3J7, Canada. *Phone:* 514-343-2214. *Fax:* 514-343-2097. *E-mail:* pierre.chenard@umontreal.ca. *Web site:* http://www.umontreal.ca/.

Université de Sherbrooke

Sherbrooke, Quebec, Canada

Contact Ms. Lisa Bedard or Valerie Bergeron, Admissions Officers, Université de Sherbrooke, 2500, Boulevard de l'Université, Sherbrooke, QC J1K 2R1, Canada. *Phone:* 819-821-7687 or toll-free 800-267-UDES. *Web site:* http://www.usherbrooke.ca/.

Université du Québec à Chicoutimi

Chicoutimi, Quebec, Canada

Contact Mr. Claudio Zoccastello, Admissions Officer, Université du Québec à Chicoutimi, 555, boulevard de L'Université, Chicoutimi, QC G7H 2B1, Canada. *Phone:* 418-545-5005. *E-mail:* czoccast@uqac.uquebec.ca. *Web site:* http://www.uqac.ca/.

Université du Québec à Montréal

Montréal, Quebec, Canada

Contact Ms. Lucille Boisselle-Roy, Admissions Officer, Université du Québec à Montréal, CP 8888, Succursale Centreville, Montréal, QC H2L 4S8, Canada. *Phone:* 514-987-3132. *E-mail:* admission@uqam.ca. *Web site:* http://www.uqam.ca/.

Université du Québec à Rimouski

Rimouski, Quebec, Canada

Contact Ms. Marie Saint Laurent, Admissions Officer, Université du Québec à Rimouski, 300 Allee des Ursulines, CP3300, Rimouski, QC QC G5L 3A1, Canada. *Phone:* 418-724-1433. *E-mail:* philippe_horth@uqar.uquebec.ca. *Web site:* http://www.uqar.ca/.

Université du Québec à Trois-Rivières

Trois-Rivières, Quebec, Canada

Contact Ms. Jean Bois, Admissions Officer, Université du Québec à Trois-Rivières, 3351 blvd des Forges, Case post 500, Trois-Rivières, QC G9A 5H7, Canada. *Phone:* 819-376-5011 or toll-free 800-365-0922. *Fax:* 819-376-5232. *E-mail:* registraire@uqtr.ca. *Web site:* http://www.uqtr.ca/.

Université du Québec, École de technologie supérieure

Montréal, Quebec, Canada

Contact Mme. Francine Gamache, Registraire, Université du Québec, École de technologie supérieure, 1100, rue Notre Dame Ouest, Montréal, QC H3C 1K3, Canada. *Phone:* 514-396-8885. *E-mail:* admission@ets.mtl.ca. *Web site:* http://www.etsmtl.ca/.

Université du Québec en Abitibi-Témiscamingue

Rouyn-Noranda, Quebec, Canada

Contact Mrs. Monique Fay, Admissions Officer, Université du Québec en Abitibi-Témiscamingue, 445 boulevard de l'Université, Rouyn-Noranda, QC J9X 5E4, Canada. *Phone:* 819-762-0971. *E-mail:* micheline.chevalier@uqat.uquebec.ca. *Web site:* http://www.uqat.ca/.

Université du Québec en Outaouais

Gatineau, Quebec, Canada

General Province-supported, university, coed **Entrance** Noncompetitive **Setting** small-town campus **Total enrollment** 5,391 **Housing** Yes **Expenses** Tuition & Fees: state resident $2660, nonresident $6259; Room only $5112 **Academic program** Accelerated degree program, summer session, adult/continuing education programs, internships **Contact** Registrar Office, Université du Québec en Outaouais, CP 1250, Succursale Hull, 101 St-Jean-Bosco, 101 rue Saint-Jean-Bosco, Gatineau, QC J8X 3X7, Canada. *Phone:* 819-595-3900 or toll-free 800-567-1283 Ext. 1840. *Fax:* 819-773-1835. *E-mail:* registraire@uqo.ca. *Web site:* http://www.uqo.ca/.

Université Laval

Québec, Quebec, Canada

Contact Promotion and Recruitment Division, Université Laval, C.P. 2208, succursale Terminus, Quebec, QC G1K 7P4, Canada. *Phone:* 418-656-2764 or toll-free 877-785-2825. *Fax:* 418-656-5216. *E-mail:* info@dap.ulaval.ca. *Web site:* http://www.ulaval.ca/.

Université Sainte-Anne

Church Point, Nova Scotia, Canada

Contact Mrs. Blanche Thériault, Admissions Officer, Université Sainte-Anne, Church Point, NS B0W 1M0, Canada. *Phone:* 902-769-2114 Ext. 116. *E-mail:* admission@ustanne.ednet.ns.ca. *Web site:* http://www.usainteanne.ca/.

University of Alberta
Edmonton, Alberta, Canada

General Province-supported, university, coed **Entrance** Moderately difficult **Setting** 154-acre urban campus **Total enrollment** 37,588 **Student-faculty ratio** 21:1 **Application deadline** 5/1 (freshmen), 5/1 (transfer) **Freshman admission** Average high school GPA 3.6 **Housing** Yes **Undergraduates** 56% women, 6% part-time **Academic program** English as a second language, advanced placement, self-designed majors, honors program, summer session, adult/continuing education programs, internships **Contact** Ms. Patricia Dalton, Associate Registrar/Director of Enrollment Management, University of Alberta, 105 Administration Building, Edmonton, AB T6G 2M7, Canada. *Phone:* 780-492-3113. *Fax:* 780-492-4380. *E-mail:* registrar@ualberta.ca. *Web site:* http://www.ualberta.ca/.

The University of British Columbia
Vancouver, British Columbia, Canada

General Province-supported, university, coed **Entrance** Very difficult **Setting** 1,000-acre urban campus **Total enrollment** 46,671 **Student-faculty ratio** 15:1 **Application deadline** 2/28 (freshmen), 2/28 (transfer) **Freshman admission** 53% were admitted **Housing** Yes **Expenses** Tuition & Fees: state resident 5154 Canadian dollars; Room & Board 6650 Canadian dollars **Undergraduates** 54% women, 31% part-time **Academic program** English as a second language, advanced placement, honors program, summer session, adult/continuing education programs, internships **Contact** Acting Associate Director, Undergraduate Admissions, The University of British Columbia, 1874 East Mall, V6T 1Z1, Canada. *Phone:* 604-822-8999 or toll-free 877-292-1422. *Fax:* 604-822-9888. *E-mail:* registrar.admissions@ubc.ca. *Web site:* http://www.ubc.ca/.

The University of British Columbia–Okanagan
Kelowna, British Columbia, Canada

General Province-supported, university, coed **Entrance** Moderately difficult **Setting** 260-acre urban campus **Total enrollment** 6,104 **Student-faculty ratio** 14:1 **Application deadline** 2/28 (freshmen), 2/28 (transfer) **Freshman admission** 53% were admitted **Housing** Yes **Expenses** Tuition & Fees: state resident 5032 Canadian dollars; Room & Board 5700 Canadian dollars **Undergraduates** 58% women, 22% part-time **Academic program** English as a second language, advanced placement, self-designed majors, honors program, summer session, internships **Contact** International Student Recruitment, The University of British Columbia–Okanagan, 3333 University Way, Kelowna, BC V1V 1V7. *Phone:* 250-807-9447. *Fax:* 250-807-8552. *E-mail:* registrar.admissions@ubc.ca. *Web site:* http://www.ubc.ca/okanagan/welcome.html.

University of Calgary
Calgary, Alberta, Canada

General Province-supported, university, coed **Entrance** Moderately difficult **Setting** 213-hectare urban campus **Total enrollment** 28,069 **Student-faculty ratio** 13:1 **Application deadline** 4/1 (freshmen), 4/1 (transfer) **Freshman admission** 58% were admitted **Housing** Yes **Expenses** Tuition & Fees: state resident 5803 Canadian dollars; Room & Board 7035 Canadian dollars **Undergraduates** 18% 25 or older **The most frequently chosen baccalaureate fields are** health professions and related sciences, business/marketing, social sciences **Academic program** English as a second language, advanced placement, honors program, summer session, adult/continuing education programs, internships **Contact** Kim Vandam, Associate Director of Admissions, University of Calgary, 2500 University Drive NW, Calgary, AB T2N 1N4, Canada. *Phone:* 403-220-3825. *E-mail:* vandam@ucalgary.ca. *Web site:* http://www.ucalgary.ca/.

University of Guelph
Guelph, Ontario, Canada

General Province-supported, university, coed **Entrance** Moderately difficult **Setting** 817-acre urban campus **Total enrollment** 19,530 **Student-faculty ratio** 22:1 **Application deadline** 3/1 (freshmen), 5/1 (transfer) **Freshman admission** 73% were admitted. Average high school GPA 3.5 **Housing** Yes **Expenses** Room & Board $9310 **Academic program** English as a second language, advanced placement, accelerated degree program, self-designed majors, honors program, summer session, internships **Contact** Ms. Mary Haggarty, Admissions Coordinator, University of Guelph, L-3 University Centre, Guelph, ON N1G 2W1, Canada. *Phone:* 519-824-4120 Ext. 58711. *Fax:* 519-766-9481. *E-mail:* usainfo@registrar.uoguelph.ca. *Web site:* http://www.uoguelph.ca/.

See page 1272 for the College Close-Up.

University of King's College
Halifax, Nova Scotia, Canada

General Province-supported, 4-year, coed **Entrance** Moderately difficult **Setting** 4-acre urban campus **Total enrollment** 1,164 **Student-faculty ratio** 21:1 **Application deadline** 3/1 (freshmen), 6/1 (transfer) **Freshman admission** 78% were admitted **Housing** Yes **Expenses** Tuition & Fees: state resident 7207 Canadian dollars, nonresident 7207 Canadian dollars; Room & Board 8410 Canadian dollars **Undergraduates** 58% women, 3% part-time, 3% 25 or older **The most frequently chosen baccalaureate fields are** communications/journalism, liberal arts/general studies **Academic program** Advanced placement, accelerated degree program, self-designed majors, honors program, summer session, internships **Contact** Ms. Jill MacBeath, Admissions and Recruitment Coordinator, University of King's College, Registrar's Office, Halifax, NS B3H 3A1, Canada. *Phone:* 902-422-1271. *Fax:* 902-425-8183. *E-mail:* admissions@ukings.ns.ca. *Web site:* http://www.ukings.ca/.

University of Lethbridge
Lethbridge, Alberta, Canada

General Province-supported, university, coed **Entrance** Moderately difficult **Setting** 576-acre urban campus **Total enrollment** 8,209 **Application deadline** 6/1 (freshmen), 6/1 (transfer) **Freshman admission** 56% were admitted **Housing** Yes **Expenses** Tuition & Fees: state resident 5559 Canadian dollars; Room & Board 6652 Canadian dollars **Undergraduates** 57% women, 10% part-time, 18% 25 or older **The most frequently chosen baccalaureate fields are** business/marketing, health professions and related sciences, psychology **Academic program** English as a second language, accelerated degree program, self-designed majors, summer session, internships **Contact** Ms. Alice Miller, Assistant Registrar, University of Lethbridge, 4401 University Drive, Lethbridge, AB T1K 3M4. *Phone:* 403-320-5700. *Fax:* 403-329-5159. *E-mail:* inquiries@uleth.ca. *Web site:* http://www.uleth.ca/.

University of Manitoba
Winnipeg, Manitoba, Canada

General Province-supported, university, coed **Entrance** Moderately difficult **Setting** 685-acre suburban campus **Total enrollment** 27,476 **Housing** Yes **Expenses** Tuition & Fees: state resident 3419 Canadian dollars; Room & Board 7759 Canadian dollars **Undergraduates** 56% women, 19% part-time **The most frequently chosen baccalaureate fields are** health professions and related sciences, education, liberal arts/general studies **Academic program** English as a second language, advanced placement, accelerated degree program, self-designed majors, honors program, summer session, adult/continuing education programs, internships **Contact** Mr. Peter Dueck, Director of Enrollment Services, University of Manitoba, Winnipeg, MB R3T 2N2, Canada. *Phone:* 204-474-6382. *Web site:* http://www.umanitoba.ca/.

University of New Brunswick Fredericton

Fredericton, New Brunswick, Canada

General Province-supported, university, coed **Entrance** Moderately difficult **Setting** 7,100-acre urban campus **Total enrollment** 10,927 **Student-faculty ratio** 18:1 **Application deadline** 3/31 (freshmen), 3/31 (transfer) **Freshman admission** 83% were admitted **Housing** Yes **Expenses** Tuition & Fees: state resident 5482 Canadian dollars **Undergraduates** 55% women, 14% part-time **Academic program** English as a second language, advanced placement, accelerated degree program, self-designed majors, honors program, summer session, adult/continuing education programs, internships **Contact** Associate Registrar/Admissions, University of New Brunswick Fredericton, PO Box 4400, Fredericton, NB E3B 5A3, Canada. *Phone:* 506-453-4865. *Fax:* 506-453-5016. *E-mail:* unbfacts@unb.ca. *Web site:* http://www.unb.ca/.

University of New Brunswick Saint John

Saint John, New Brunswick, Canada

General Province-supported, comprehensive, coed **Entrance** Moderately difficult **Setting** 250-acre urban campus **Application deadline** Rolling (freshmen), rolling (transfer) **Housing** Yes **Expenses** Tuition & Fees: state resident $6131; Room & Board $5899 **Academic program** English as a second language, advanced placement, accelerated degree program, self-designed majors, honors program, summer session, adult/continuing education programs, internships **Contact** Ms. Sue Ellis Loparco, Admissions Officer, University of New Brunswick Saint John, PO Box 5050, Saint John, NB E2L 4L5, Canada. *Phone:* 506-648-5674 or toll-free 800-743-4333 (in-state); 800-743-5691 (out-of-state). *E-mail:* apply@unbsj.ca. *Web site:* http://www.unb.ca/.

University of Northern British Columbia

Prince George, British Columbia, Canada

General Province-supported, university, coed **Entrance** Noncompetitive **Setting** 1,344-acre suburban campus **Total enrollment** 4,177 **Student-faculty ratio** 10:1 **Application deadline** 3/1 (freshmen), 3/1 (transfer) **Freshman admission** 76% were admitted **Housing** Yes **Expenses** Tuition & Fees: state resident 5394 Canadian dollars; Room only 4524 Canadian dollars **Undergraduates** 42% 25 or older **The most frequently chosen baccalaureate fields are** business/marketing, health professions and related sciences, natural resources/environmental science **Academic program** Advanced placement, self-designed majors, honors program, summer session, internships **Contact** Mr. Grant Kerr, Assistant Registrar-Admissions, University of Northern British Columbia, Office of the Registrar, 3333 University Way, Prince George, BC V2N 4Z9. *Phone:* 250-960-6347. *Fax:* 250-960-6330. *E-mail:* registrar-info@unbc.ca. *Web site:* http://www.unbc.ca/.

University of Ottawa

Ottawa, Ontario, Canada

General Province-supported, university, coed **Entrance** Moderately difficult **Setting** 43-hectare urban campus **Total enrollment** 37,922 **Student-faculty ratio** 23:1 **Application deadline** 6/1 (freshmen) **Freshman admission** 61% were admitted. Average high school GPA 3.26 **Housing** Yes **Expenses** Tuition & Fees: state resident 5583 Canadian dollars; Room & Board 6212 Canadian dollars **Undergraduates** 61% women, 18% part-time, 15% 25 or older **The most frequently chosen baccalaureate fields are** education, health professions and related sciences, social sciences **Academic program** English as a second language, advanced placement, honors program, summer session, internships **Contact** Ms. Caroline Pharand, University of Ottawa, 550 Cumberland Street, PO Box 450, Station A, Ottawa, ON K1N 6N5, Canada. *Phone:* 613-562-5800 Ext. 1593. *Fax:* 613-562-5790. *E-mail:* cpharand@uottawa.ca. *Web site:* http://www.uottawa.ca/.

University of Phoenix–Vancouver Campus

Burnaby, British Columbia, Canada

General Proprietary, comprehensive, coed **Entrance** Noncompetitive **Setting** urban campus **Total enrollment** 292 **Application deadline** Rolling (freshmen), rolling (transfer) **Housing** No **Expenses** Tuition & Fees $12,180 **Undergraduates** 98% 25 or older, 1% Asian American/Pacific Islander **The most frequently chosen baccalaureate field is** business/marketing **Academic program** Advanced placement, accelerated degree program, adult/continuing education programs **Contact** Ms. Audra McQuarie, Registrar/Executive Director, University of Phoenix–Vancouver Campus, 4035 South Riverpoint Parkway, Mail Stop CF-L101, Phoenix, AZ 85040. *Phone:* 480-557-6151 or toll-free 800-776-4867 (in-state); 800-228-7240 (out-of-state). *Fax:* 480-643-3068. *E-mail:* audra.mcquarie@phoenix.edu. *Web site:* http://www.phoenix.edu/.

University of Prince Edward Island

Charlottetown, Prince Edward Island, Canada

General Province-supported, comprehensive, coed **Entrance** Moderately difficult **Setting** 130-acre small-town campus **Total enrollment** 4,200 **Student-faculty ratio** 12:1 **Application deadline** 8/1 (freshmen), 8/1 (transfer) **Freshman admission** 61% were admitted **Housing** Yes **Expenses** Tuition & Fees: state resident 5355 Canadian dollars; Room & Board 7144 Canadian dollars **Undergraduates** 61% women, 16% part-time, 19% 25 or older **Academic program** English as a second language, advanced placement, accelerated degree program, honors program, summer session, internships **Contact** Darcy McCardle, Assistant Registrar, University of Prince Edward Island, 550 University Avenue, Charlottetown, PE C1A 4P3, Canada. *Phone:* 902-566-0634. *Fax:* 902-566-0795. *E-mail:* dmccardle@upei.ca. *Web site:* http://www.upei.ca/.

University of Regina

Regina, Saskatchewan, Canada

General Province-supported, university, coed **Entrance** Minimally difficult **Setting** 445-acre urban campus **Total enrollment** 11,590 **Student-faculty ratio** 17:1 **Application deadline** 7/1 (freshmen), 7/1 (transfer) **Freshman admission** 88% were admitted. Average high school GPA 3.5 **Housing** Yes **Expenses** Tuition & Fees: state resident 5059 Canadian dollars; Room & Board 7772 Canadian dollars **Undergraduates** 61% women, 24% part-time, 25% 25 or older **The most frequently chosen baccalaureate fields are** business/marketing, education, security and protective services **Academic program** English as a second language, advanced placement, self-designed majors, honors program, summer session, adult/continuing education programs, internships **Contact** Ms. Susan Husum, Manager (Admissions), University of Regina, 3737 Wascana Parkway, Regina, SK S4S 0A2, Canada. *Phone:* 306-585-4942 or toll-free 800-664-4756. *Fax:* 306-585-5521. *E-mail:* admissions@uregina.ca. *Web site:* http://www.uregina.ca/.

University of Saskatchewan

Saskatoon, Saskatchewan, Canada

General Province-supported, university, coed **Entrance** Moderately difficult **Setting** 2,425-acre urban campus **Total enrollment** 19,201 **Student-faculty ratio** 16:1 **Application deadline** 5/1 (freshmen), 5/1 (transfer) **Freshman admission** 80% were admitted **Housing** Yes **Expenses** Tuition & Fees: state resident 6935 Canadian dollars; Room & Board 7221 Canadian dollars **The most frequently chosen baccalaureate fields are** health professions and related sciences, business/marketing, visual and performing arts **Academic program** English as a second language, advanced placement, accelerated degree program, honors program, summer session, adult/continuing education programs, internships **Contact** Recruitment and Admissions, University of Saskatchewan, 105 Administration Place, Saskatoon, SK S7N 5A2, Canada. *Phone:*

University of Saskatchewan (continued)
306-966-5788. *Fax:* 306-966-2115. *E-mail:* admissions@usask.ca. *Web site:* http://www.usask.ca/.

University of the Fraser Valley
Abbotsford, British Columbia, Canada

General Province-supported, comprehensive, coed **Setting** urban campus **Application deadline** 1/31 (freshmen), 2/28 (transfer) **Housing** Yes **Academic program** English as a second language, advanced placement, summer session, adult/continuing education programs, internships **Contact** Ms. Robin Smith, Admissions Coordinator, University of the Fraser Valley, 33844 King Road, Abbotsford, BC V2S 7M8, Canada. *Phone:* 604-504-7441 Ext. 4540 or toll-free 808-504-7441. *Fax:* 604-853-0138. *E-mail:* reginfo@ucfv.ca. *Web site:* http://www.ufv.ca/.

University of Toronto
Toronto, Ontario, Canada

General Province-supported, university, coed **Entrance** Very difficult **Setting** 714-hectare urban campus **Total enrollment** 77,899 **Student-faculty ratio** 24:1 **Application deadline** 3/1 (freshmen), 7/1 (transfer) **Freshman admission** 21% were admitted **Housing** Yes **Expenses** Tuition & Fees: state resident 5991 Canadian dollars, nonresident 5991 Canadian dollars; Room & Board 11,500 Canadian dollars **Undergraduates** 55% women, 11% part-time, 27% 25 or older **Academic program** English as a second language, summer session, adult/continuing education programs **Contact** Ms. Merike Remmel, Director of Admissions, University of Toronto, Toronto, ON M5S 1A1, Canada. *Phone:* 416-978-2190. *Fax:* 416-978-7022. *E-mail:* admissions.help@utoronto.ca. *Web site:* http://www.utoronto.ca/uoft.html.

University of Victoria
Victoria, British Columbia, Canada

General Province-supported, university, coed **Entrance** Moderately difficult **Setting** 380-acre suburban campus **Total enrollment** 19,479 **Student-faculty ratio** 27:1 **Application deadline** 4/30 (freshmen), 4/30 (transfer) **Freshman admission** 75% were admitted. Average high school GPA 3.6 **Housing** Yes **Expenses** Tuition & Fees: state resident 5099 Canadian dollars; Room & Board 7988 Canadian dollars **Undergraduates** 56% women, 35% part-time, 22% 25 or older **Academic program** English as a second language, advanced placement, self-designed majors, honors program, summer session, adult/continuing education programs, internships **Contact** Mr. Bruno Rocca, Student Recruitment Director, University of Victoria, PO Box 1700 STN CSC, Victoria, BC V8W 2Y2. *Phone:* 250-721-8121 Ext. 8109. *Fax:* 250-721-6225. *E-mail:* admit@uvic.ca. *Web site:* http://www.uvic.ca/.

University of Waterloo
Waterloo, Ontario, Canada

General Province-supported, university, coed **Entrance** Moderately difficult **Setting** 900-acre suburban campus **Total enrollment** 27,206 **Application deadline** 3/31 (freshmen) **Freshman admission** 58% were admitted **Housing** Yes **Undergraduates** 43% women, 4% part-time **The most frequently chosen baccalaureate fields are** engineering, liberal arts/general studies, mathematics **Academic program** English as a second language, advanced placement, accelerated degree program, self-designed majors, honors program, summer session, internships **Contact** Ms. Nancy Weiner, Associate Registrar, Admissions, University of Waterloo, 200 University Avenue West, Waterloo, ON N2L 3G1, Canada. *Phone:* 519-888-4567 Ext. 32265. *Fax:* 519-746-2882. *E-mail:* registrar@uwaterloo.ca. *Web site:* http://www.uwaterloo.ca/.

The University of Western Ontario
London, Ontario, Canada

General Province-supported, university, coed **Entrance** Very difficult **Setting** 477-hectare suburban campus **Total enrollment** 28,985 **Student-faculty ratio** 20:1 **Application deadline** 6/1 (freshmen), 6/1 (transfer) **Freshman admission** 54% were admitted **Housing** Yes **Expenses** Tuition & Fees: state resident 5874 Canadian dollars; Room & Board 8440 Canadian dollars **Undergraduates** 56% women, 11% part-time, 3% 25 or older **The most frequently chosen baccalaureate fields are** health professions and related sciences, education, social sciences **Academic program** English as a second language, accelerated degree program, self-designed majors, honors program, summer session, adult/continuing education programs, internships **Contact** Undergraduate Recruitment and Admissions, The University of Western Ontario, 1151 Richmond Street, Suite 2, Room 165 Stevenson Lawson Building, London, ON N5A5B8, Canada. *Phone:* 519-661-2100. *Fax:* 519-661-3710. *E-mail:* reg-admissions@uwo.ca. *Web site:* http://www.uwo.ca/.

University of Windsor
Windsor, Ontario, Canada

General Province-supported, university, coed **Entrance** Moderately difficult **Setting** 125-acre urban campus **Total enrollment** 15,999 **Student-faculty ratio** 21:1 **Application deadline** Rolling (freshmen), rolling (transfer) **Freshman admission** 78% were admitted **Housing** Yes **Expenses** Tuition & Fees: state resident 5662 Canadian dollars; Room & Board 8185 Canadian dollars **Undergraduates** 55% women, 22% part-time, 26% 25 or older **Academic program** Advanced placement, accelerated degree program, self-designed majors, honors program, summer session, adult/continuing education programs, internships **Contact** Ms. Charlene Yates, Manager of Undergraduate Admissions, University of Windsor, Office of the Registrar, 401 Sunset Avenue, Windsor, ON N9B 3P4, Canada. *Phone:* 519-253-3000 Ext. 3315 or toll-free 800-864-2860. *Fax:* 519-971-3653. *E-mail:* registr@uwindsor.ca. *Web site:* http://www.uwindsor.ca/.

Visit Petersons.com and enter keyword Windsor

See page 1322 for the College Close-Up.

The University of Winnipeg
Winnipeg, Manitoba, Canada

Contact Mr. Colin Russell, Registrar, The University of Winnipeg, 515 Portage Avenue, Winnipeg, MB R3B 2E9, Canada. *Phone:* 204-786-9776. *Fax:* 204-786-8656. *E-mail:* admissions@uwinnipeg.ca. *Web site:* http://www.uwinnipeg.ca/.

Vancouver Island University
Nanaimo, British Columbia, Canada

General Province-supported, comprehensive, coed **Setting** 110-acre campus **Contact** Ms. Leslie Peterson, Admissions Manager, Vancouver Island University, 900 Fifth Street, Nanaimo, BC V9R 5S5, Canada. *Phone:* 250-740-6355. *Fax:* 250-740-6479. *Web site:* http://www.viu.ca/.

Vanguard College
Edmonton, Alberta, Canada

General Independent, 4-year, coed, affiliated with Pentecostal Assemblies of Canada **Setting** 1-hectare urban campus **Application deadline** 8/19 (freshmen) **Housing** No **Expenses** Tuition & Fees $6040 **Academic program** Advanced placement, accelerated degree program, summer session, internships **Contact** Tim Bratton, Recruitment Director, Vanguard College, 11617 106 Avenue, NW, Edmonton, AB T5H 0S1, Canada. *Phone:* 780-452-0808 Ext. 231 or toll-free 866-222-0808. *Fax:* 780-452-5803. *E-mail:* tbratton@vanguardcollege.com. *Web site:* http://www.vanguardcollege.com/.

Western Christian College
Regina, Saskatchewan, Canada

General Independent, 4-year, coed, affiliated with Church of Christ **Setting** urban campus **Housing** Yes **Expenses** Tuition & Fees 7175

INFLUENCE
STARTS HERE

"I believe there is nothing more powerful than an idea and more noble than to pursue a dream. I want to show young people that if you are motivated and committed, you can achieve great things at any age."

Prerna Chandak BComm '08
One of Chatelaine Magazine's 80 Amazing Women to Watch in 2008
2007 Top 20 Under 20 Award Recipient
CEO, Lemonade Capital

At UWindsor, we're taking responsibility for the future.

To learn more, just ask our faculty, staff and alumni.

University of Windsor
thinking forward

www.uwindsor.ca/beinfluential

Canadian dollars; Room & Board 4800 Canadian dollars **Contact** Ms. Pamela Stonehouse, Registrar, Western Christian College, 100-400 Fourth Avenue, Regina, SK S4T 0H8, Canada. *Phone:* 306-545-1515 Ext. 500. *Fax:* 306-352-2198. *E-mail:* registrar@westernchristian.ca. *Web site:* http://www.westernchristian.ca/.

Wilfrid Laurier University
Waterloo, Ontario, Canada

General Province-supported, comprehensive, coed **Entrance** Minimally difficult **Setting** 40-acre urban campus **Total enrollment** 17,572 **Student-faculty ratio** 25:1 **Application deadline** 5/1 (freshmen), 5/1 (transfer) **Freshman admission** 68% were admitted **Housing** Yes **Expenses** Tuition & Fees: state resident 5953 Canadian dollars; Room & Board 7929 Canadian dollars **Undergraduates** 59% women, 13% part-time, 5% 25 or older **Academic program** English as a second language, advanced placement, accelerated degree program, honors program, summer session, adult/continuing education programs, internships **Contact** Ms. Lois Wood, Associate Registrar, Undergraduate Admissions, Wilfrid Laurier University, 75 University Avenue West, Waterloo, ON N2L 3C5, Canada. *Phone:* 519-884-0710 Ext. 6099. *Fax:* 519-884-8826. *E-mail:* admissions@wlu.ca. *Web site:* http://www.wlu.ca/.

William and Catherine Booth College
Winnipeg, Manitoba, Canada

General Independent religious, 4-year, coed, primarily women **Setting** urban campus **Total enrollment** 322 **Student-faculty ratio** 9:1 **Application deadline** 7/31 (freshmen) **Freshman admission** 71% were admitted **Housing** Yes **Expenses** Tuition & Fees 7380 Canadian dollars; Room & Board 4000 Canadian dollars **Undergraduates** 50% 25 or older **Academic program** Accelerated degree program, honors program, summer session, adult/continuing education programs, internships **Contact** Chantel Burt, Director of Admission, William and Catherine Booth College, 447 Webb Place, Winnipeg, MB R3B 2P2, Canada. *Phone:* 204-924-4867 or toll-free 800-781-6044. *E-mail:* cburt@boothcollege.ca. *Web site:* http://www.boothcollege.ca/.

York University
Toronto, Ontario, Canada

General Province-supported, university, coed **Entrance** Moderately difficult **Setting** 457-acre urban campus **Total enrollment** 53,205 **Student-faculty ratio** 19:1 **Application deadline** 2/1 (freshmen), 2/1 (transfer) **Freshman admission** Average high school GPA 3.4 **Housing** Yes **Expenses** Tuition & Fees: state resident 5761 Canadian dollars; Room & Board 7250 Canadian dollars **Undergraduates** 60% women, 16% part-time, 20% 25 or older **Academic program** English as a second language, advanced placement, accelerated degree program, self-designed majors, honors program, summer session, adult/continuing education programs, internships **Contact** Ms. Amber Holliday, International Recruitment Officer, York University, N301 Bennett Centre for Student Services, 4700 Keele Street, Toronto, ON M3J 1P3, Canada. *Phone:* 416-736-2100 Ext. 60595. *Fax:* 416-736-5741. *E-mail:* aburkett@yorku.ca. *Web site:* http://www.yorku.ca/.

Visit Petersons.com and enter keywords York University

See page 1388 for the College Close-Up.

INTERNATIONAL

BULGARIA

American University in Bulgaria
Blagoevgrad, Bulgaria

Contact Yordanka Melnikliyska, Director of Admissions, American University in Bulgaria, Blagoevgrad 2700, Bulgaria. *Phone:* 359 73 888 218. *Fax:* 359 73 800 174. *E-mail:* admission@aubg.bg. *Web site:* http://www.aubg.bg/.

CAYMAN ISLANDS

International College of the Cayman Islands
Newlands, Cayman Islands

General Independent, comprehensive, coed **Entrance** Moderately difficult **Setting** 3-acre rural campus **Housing** No **Academic program** English as a second language, advanced placement, accelerated degree program, self-designed majors, summer session, adult/continuing education programs, internships **Contact** Ms. Irene Derksen, Director of Admissions, International College of the Cayman Islands, PO Box 136, Savannah Post Office, Newlands, Grand Cayman, Cayman Islands. *Phone:* 345-325-6454. *E-mail:* admissions@icci.edu.ky. *Web site:* http://www.icci.edu.ky/.

EGYPT

The American University in Cairo
Cairo, Egypt

Contact Ms. Randa Kamel, Director of Enrollment Services, The American University in Cairo, The Office of Student Affairs, 420 Fifth Avenue, 3rd Floor, New York, NY 10018-2728. *Phone:* 212-797-5551. *Fax:* 212-797-1974. *E-mail:* randa_k@aucnyo.edu. *Web site:* http://www.aucegypt.edu/.

FRANCE

The American University of Paris
Paris, France

General Independent, comprehensive, coed **Entrance** Moderately difficult **Setting** urban campus **Total enrollment** 614 **Student-faculty ratio** 18:1 **Application deadline** 3/15 (freshmen), 3/15 (transfer) **Freshman admission** 68% were admitted **Housing** Yes **Expenses** Tuition & Fees 25,175 euros; Room & Board 9500 euros **Undergraduates** 72% women, 6% part-time, 3% 25 or older **Academic program** Advanced placement, honors program, summer session, internships **Contact** International Admissions Office, The American University of Paris, 6 rue du Colonel Combes, F-75007 Paris, France. *Phone:* +33 1 40 62 07 20. *Fax:* +33 1 47 05 34 32. *E-mail:* admissions@aup.edu. *Web site:* http://www.aup.edu/.

Visit Petersons.com and enter keywords American University of Paris

See page 472 for the College Close-Up.

Parsons Paris School of Art + Design
Paris, France

Contact Sara Krauskopf, Parsons Paris School of Art + Design, 14 rue Letellier, F-75015 Paris, France. *Phone:* 331 4577 40 17. *Fax:* 331 4577 44 12. *E-mail:* sara.krauskopf@parsons-paris.com. *Web site:* http://www.parsons-paris.com/.

Schiller International University
Paris, France

General Independent, comprehensive, coed **Entrance** Minimally difficult **Setting** urban campus **Total enrollment** 87 **Student-faculty ratio** 4:1 **Application deadline** Rolling (freshmen), rolling (transfer) **Housing** No **Expenses** Tuition & Fees 16,600 euros **Undergraduates** 41% women, 5% part-time **Academic program** English as a second language, advanced placement, accelerated degree program, self-designed majors, honors program, summer session, adult/continuing education programs, internships **Contact** Ms. Kamala Dontamsetti, Associate Director of Admissions, Schiller International University, 300 East Bay Drive, Largo, FL 33770. *Phone:* 727-736-5082 Ext. 234. *Fax:* 727-734-0347. *E-mail:* admissions@schiller.edu. *Web site:* http://www.schiller.edu/.

GERMANY

Schiller International University
Heidelberg, Germany

General Independent, comprehensive, coed **Entrance** Minimally difficult **Setting** urban campus **Total enrollment** 175 **Student-faculty ratio** 9:1 **Application deadline** Rolling (freshmen), rolling (transfer) **Housing** Yes **Expenses** Tuition & Fees 16,600 euros **Undergraduates** 41% women, 2% part-time, 27% 25 or older **Academic program** English as a second language, advanced placement, accelerated degree program, honors program, summer session, adult/continuing education programs, internships **Contact** Ms. Kamala Dontamsetti, Associate Director of Admissions, Schiller International University, 300 East Bay Drive, Largo, FL 33770. *Phone:* 727-736-5082 Ext. 234. *Fax:* 727-734-0359. *E-mail:* kamala_dontamsetti@schiller.edu. *Web site:* http://www.schiller.edu/.

GREECE

American College of Thessaloniki
Pylea, Greece

General Independent, comprehensive, coed **Entrance** Minimally difficult **Setting** 40-acre suburban campus **Total enrollment** 467 **Student-faculty ratio** 14:1 **Application deadline** Rolling (freshmen), rolling (transfer) **Freshman admission** 96% were admitted. Average high school GPA 2.7 **Housing** Yes **Expenses** Tuition & Fees 8200 euros; Room only 4200 euros **Undergraduates** 51% women, 24% part-time, 13% 25 or older **The most frequently chosen baccalaureate fields are** business/marketing, computer and information sciences, history **Academic program** English as a second language, advanced placement, accelerated degree program, summer session, internships **Contact** Mrs. Roula Lebetli, Director of Admissions, American College of Thessaloniki, PO Box 21021, Pylea, GR-555-10 Pylea, Thessaloniki, Greece. *Phone:*

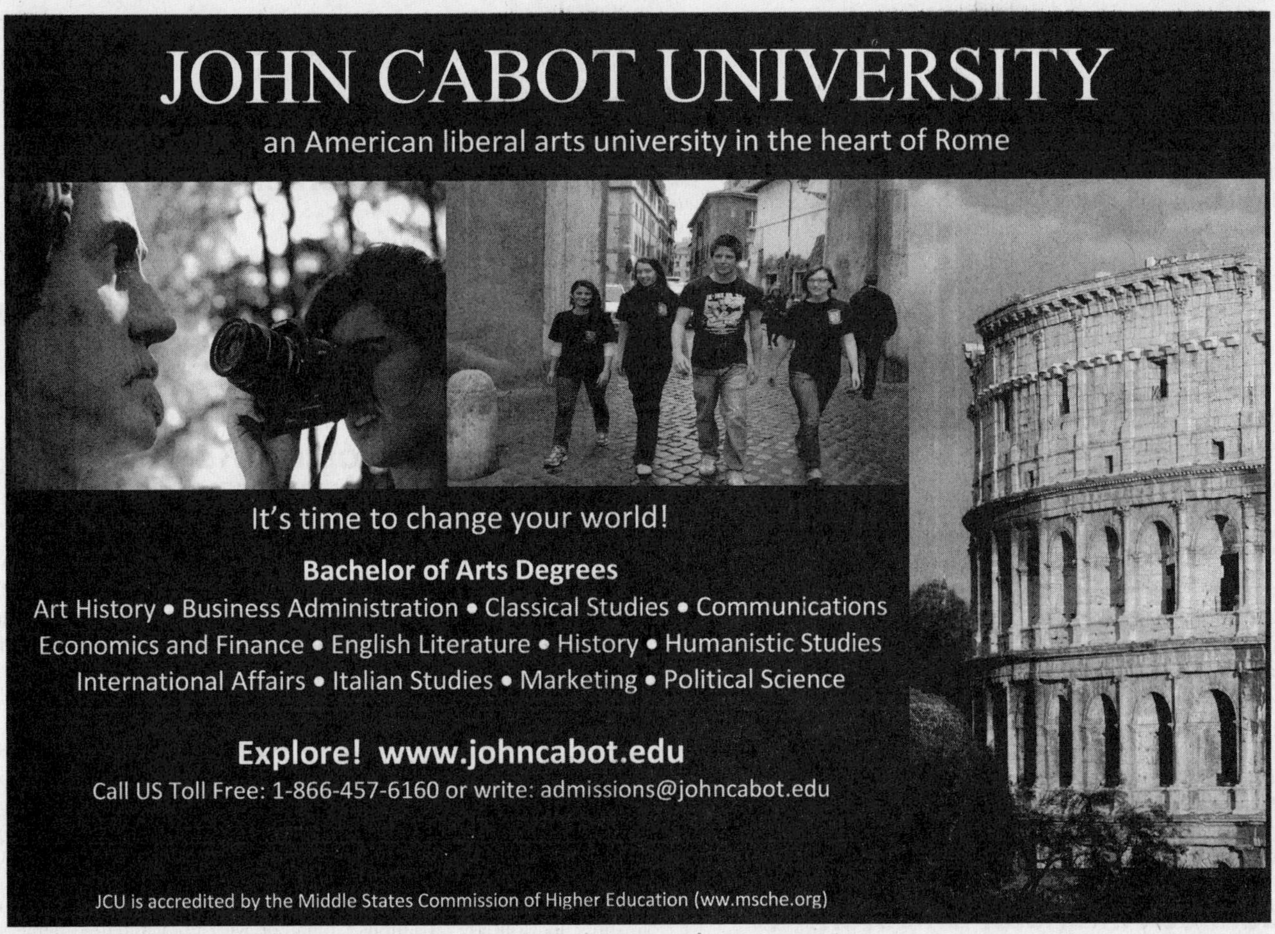

JOHN CABOT UNIVERSITY

an American liberal arts university in the heart of Rome

It's time to change your world!

Bachelor of Arts Degrees

Art History • Business Administration • Classical Studies • Communications
Economics and Finance • English Literature • History • Humanistic Studies
International Affairs • Italian Studies • Marketing • Political Science

Explore! www.johncabot.edu

Call US Toll Free: 1-866-457-6160 or write: admissions@johncabot.edu

JCU is accredited by the Middle States Commission of Higher Education (ww.msche.org)

30 2310-398239. *Fax:* 30 2310-398389. *E-mail:* admissions@act.edu. *Web site:* http://www.act.edu/.

The American University of Athens
Athens, Greece

Contact Ms. Thalia Poulos, Director of Admissions, The American University of Athens, 4 Sohou Street and Kifissias Avenue, Neo Psychiko, GR-115 25 Athens, Greece. *Phone:* 30 210-725-9301. *E-mail:* admissions@aua.edu. *Web site:* http://www.aua.edu/.

Deree College, The American College of Greece
Athens, Greece

Contact Ms. Lucy Kanatsouli, Deree College, The American College of Greece, 6 Gravias Street, GR-153-42 Aghia Paraskevi, Athens, Greece. *Phone:* 30 210-600-9800 Ext. 1322. *E-mail:* dereeadm@hol.gr. *Web site:* http://www.acg.edu/.

IRELAND

Institute of Public Administration
Dublin, Ireland

Contact Dr. Denis O'Brien, Registrar, Institute of Public Administration, 57-61 Lansdowne Road, Dublin 4, Ireland. *Phone:* 353-1-240-3600. *Fax:* 353-1-668-9135. *E-mail:* undergrad@ipa.ie. *Web site:* http://www.ipa.ie/.

ITALY

The American University of Rome
Rome, Italy

Contact Ms. Mara Nisdeo, Director of Admissions, The American University of Rome, Via Pietro Roselli 4, I-00153 Roma, Italy. *Phone:* 39 06-58330919 Ext. 206 or toll-free 888-791-8327. *E-mail:* admissions@aur.edu. *Web site:* http://www.aur.edu/.

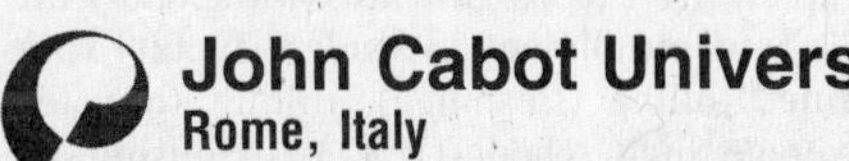

John Cabot University
Rome, Italy

General Independent, 4-year, coed **Entrance** Moderately difficult **Setting** urban campus **Total enrollment** 750 **Student-faculty ratio** 18:1 **Application deadline** 7/15 (freshmen), 7/15 (transfer) **Freshman admission** 51% were admitted. Average high school GPA 3 **Housing** Yes **Expenses** Tuition & Fees $18,600; Room & Board $13,200 **Academic program** English as a second language, advanced placement, honors program, summer session, internships **Contact** Ms. Jill Peacock, Director of Admissions, John Cabot University, Via della Lungara 233, I-00165 Roma, Italy. *Phone:* 39 06 681 9121 or toll-free 866-227-0112. *Fax:* 39 06 589 7429. *E-mail:* admissions@johncabot.edu. *Web site:* http://www.johncabot.edu/.

Visit Petersons.com and enter keyword John

See page 874 for the College Close-Up.

KENYA

United States International University

Nairobi, Kenya

Contact Admissions Director, United States International University, PO Box 14634, Thika Road Kasarani, Nairobi 00800, Kenya. *Phone:* 254-02-3606563. *E-mail:* admit@usiu.ac.ke. *Web site:* http://www.usiu.ac.ke/.

LEBANON

American University of Beirut

Beirut, Lebanon

General Independent, university, coed **Setting** 60-acre urban campus **Total enrollment** 7,507 **Student-faculty ratio** 13:1 **Application deadline** 1/15 (freshmen), 4/30 (transfer) **Freshman admission** 60% were admitted. Average high school GPA 2.96 **Freshman test scores** SAT critical reading scores over 500: 44.6%; SAT math scores over 500: 95.1%; SAT critical reading scores over 600: 8.8%; SAT math scores over 600: 68.3% **Housing** Yes **Expenses** Tuition & Fees $12,495; Room only $2924 **Undergraduates** 48% women, 3% part-time, 1% 25 or older **The most frequently chosen baccalaureate fields are** business/marketing, biological/life sciences, engineering **Academic program** English as a second language, advanced placement, honors program, summer session, internships **Contact** Dr. Salim Kanaan, Director of Admissions Office, American University of Beirut, PO Box 11-0236, Riad El-Solh, 1107 2020, Lebanon. *Phone:* 961 1-374 374 Ext. 2592. *Fax:* 961 1-750 775. *E-mail:* admissions@aub.edu.lb. *Web site:* http://www.aub.edu.lb/.

Lebanese American University

Beirut, Lebanon

Contact Mrs. Nada Badran, Director of Admissions, Lebanese American University, PO Box 13-5053, Beirut, Lebanon. *Phone:* 961 1 786456 Ext. 1162. *Fax:* 961 1 786454. *E-mail:* admissions.beirut@lau.edu.lb. *Web site:* http://www.lau.edu.lb/.

MEXICO

Alliant International University–México City

Mexico City, Mexico

General Independent, comprehensive, coed **Entrance** Moderately difficult **Setting** urban campus **Total enrollment** 53 **Student-faculty ratio** 12:1 **Application deadline** Rolling (freshmen), rolling (transfer) **Freshman admission** Average high school GPA 3.2 **Housing** No **Expenses** Tuition & Fees $8580 **Undergraduates** 38% women, 33% part-time, 40% 25 or older, 14% Hispanic American **Academic program** English as a second language, advanced placement, accelerated degree program, summer session, internships **Contact** Vania Quiroz, Chief Operations Manager, Alliant International University–México City, Hamburgo #115, Col. Juarez, CP06700 Mexico City, Mexico. *Phone:* 52 5555257651. *Fax:* 52 5552642188. *E-mail:* mexicoadmissions@alliant.edu. *Web site:* http://www.alliantmexico.edu/.

Instituto Tecnológico y de Estudios Superiores de Monterrey, Campus Central de Veracruz

Córdoba, Mexico

Contact Ing. Luis Pablo Villareal, Registrar, Instituto Tecnológico y de Estudios Superiores de Monterrey, Campus Central de Veracruz, Avenida Eugenio Garza Sada 1, Apartado Postal 314, 94500 Córdoba, Veracruz, Mexico. *Phone:* 27-13-23-40 Ext. 123. *Web site:* http://www.ver.itesm.mx/.

Instituto Tecnológico y de Estudios Superiores de Monterrey, Campus Chiapas

Tuxtla Gutiérrez, Mexico

Contact Lic. Luis Enrique Cancino, Registrar, Instituto Tecnológico y de Estudios Superiores de Monterrey, Campus Chiapas, Carretera a Tapanatepec Km 149&746, Apartado Postal 312, 29000 Tuxtla Gutiérrez, Chiapas, Mexico. *Phone:* 96-15-1723. *Web site:* http://www.chs.itesm.mx/.

Instituto Tecnológico y de Estudios Superiores de Monterrey, Campus Chihuahua

Chihuahua, Mexico

Contact Ing. Juan Manuel Fernandez, Registrar, Instituto Tecnológico y de Estudios Superiores de Monterrey, Campus Chihuahua, Colegio Militar 4700, Colonia Nombre de Dios, Apartado Postal 728, 31300 Chihuahua, Chihuahua, Mexico. *Phone:* 14-17-48-58 Ext. 117. *Web site:* http://www.chi.itesm.mx/.

Instituto Tecnológico y de Estudios Superiores de Monterrey, Campus Ciudad de México

Ciudad de Mexico, Mexico

Contact Admissions Office, Instituto Tecnológico y de Estudios Superiores de Monterrey, Campus Ciudad de México, Calle del Puente #222 esquina con Periférico, 14380 Colonia Huipulco, Tlalpan, MDF, Mexico. *Phone:* 5-673-6488. *Web site:* http://www.ccm.itesm.mx/.

Instituto Tecnológico y de Estudios Superiores de Monterrey, Campus Ciudad Juárez

Ciudad Juárez, Mexico

Contact Lic. Alberto Trejo, Registrar, Instituto Tecnológico y de Estudios Superiores de Monterrey, Campus Ciudad Juárez, Boulevard Tomas Fernandez y Avenida A J Bermudez, Apartado Postal 3105-J, 32320 Ciudad Juárez, Chihuahua, Mexico. *Phone:* 16-17-88-07 Ext. 113. *Web site:* http://www.cdj.itesm.mx/.

Instituto Tecnológico y de Estudios Superiores de Monterrey, Campus Ciudad Obregón

Ciudad Obregón, Mexico

Contact Lic. Judith Almeida, Registrar, Instituto Tecnológico y de Estudios Superiores de Monterrey, Campus Ciudad Obregón, Dr Norman E Borlaug Km 14, Apartado Postal 662, 85000 Ciudad Obregón, Sonora, Mexico. *Phone:* 64-15-03-12. *Web site:* http://www.cob.itesm.mx/.

Instituto Tecnológico y de Estudios Superiores de Monterrey, Campus Colima

Colima, Mexico

Contact Lic. Manuel Perez Rivera, Registrar, Instituto Tecnológico y de Estudios Superiores de Monterrey, Campus Colima, Prolongacion Ignacio Sandoval s/n, Fraccionamiento Jardines de Vista Hermosa, Apartado

Postal 190, 28010 Colima, Colima, Mexico. *Phone:* 33-12-53-39. *Web site:* http://www.col.itesm.mx/.

Instituto Tecnológico y de Estudios Superiores de Monterrey, Campus Cuernavaca

Temixco, Mexico

Contact Lic. Miguel Angel Machua S., Registrar, Instituto Tecnológico y de Estudios Superiores de Monterrey, Campus Cuernavaca, Paseo de la Reforma 182-A, Colonia Lomas de Cuernavaca, 62000 Temixco, Morelos, Mexico. *Phone:* 73 18-49-57. *Web site:* http://www.mor.itesm.mx/.

Instituto Tecnológico y de Estudios Superiores de Monterrey, Campus Estado de México

Estado de Mexico, Mexico

Contact Prof. Jose de Jesus Molina, Registrar, Instituto Tecnológico y de Estudios Superiores de Monterrey, Campus Estado de México, Carretera Lago de Guadalupe Km. 3.5, Atizapan de Zaragoza, Estado de Mexico 52926, Mexico. *Phone:* 5-873-3600. *Web site:* http://www.cem.itesm.mx/.

Instituto Tecnológico y de Estudios Superiores de Monterrey, Campus Guadalajara

Zapopan, Mexico

Contact Ms. Janet Martell Sotomayor, Registration Director, Instituto Tecnológico y de Estudios Superiores de Monterrey, Campus Guadalajara, Avenida General Ramón Corona 2514, Colonia Nuevo Mexico, 45140 Zapopan, Jalisco, Mexico. *Phone:* 3-669-3006. *Web site:* http://www.gda.itesm.mx/.

Instituto Tecnológico y de Estudios Superiores de Monterrey, Campus Hidalgo

Pachuca, Mexico

Contact Lic. Lizbet Melo, Registrar, Instituto Tecnológico y de Estudios Superiores de Monterrey, Campus Hidalgo, Boulevard Felipe Angeles s/n al lado de la Unidad Deportiva, Apartado Postal 337, 42090 Pachuca, Hidalgo, Mexico. *Phone:* 714-25-00 Ext. 128. *Web site:* http://www.hgo.itesm.mx/.

Instituto Tecnológico y de Estudios Superiores de Monterrey, Campus Irapuato

Irapuato, Mexico

Contact Ing. Marcela Beltrán, Registrar, Instituto Tecnológico y de Estudios Superiores de Monterrey, Campus Irapuato, Paseo Mirador del Valle No. 445, Col. Villas de Irapuato, Apartado Postal 568, 36660 Irapuato, Guanajuato, Mexico. *Phone:* 46-230342. *Web site:* http://www.ira.itesm.mx/.

Instituto Tecnológico y de Estudios Superiores de Monterrey, Campus Laguna

Torreón, Mexico

Contact Ing. Aroldo Camargo Soto, Registrar, Instituto Tecnológico y de Estudios Superiores de Monterrey, Campus Laguna, Paseo del Tecnologico s/n Ampliacion La Rosita, Apartado Postal 506, 27250 Torreón, Coahuila, Mexico. *Phone:* 17-20-66-61 Ext. 23. *Web site:* http://www.lag.itesm.mx/.

Instituto Tecnológico y de Estudios Superiores de Monterrey, Campus León

León, Mexico

Contact Lic. Eddie Villegas, Registrar, Instituto Tecnológico y de Estudios Superiores de Monterrey, Campus León, Avenida Eugenio Garza Sada s/n Colonia Cerro Gordo, Apartado Postal 872, 37120 León, Guanajuato, Mexico. *Phone:* 47-17-10-00 Ext. 131. *Web site:* http://www.leo.itesm.mx/.

Instituto Tecnológico y de Estudios Superiores de Monterrey, Campus Mazatlán

Mazatlán, Mexico

Contact Ing. Martin Ley Urias, Registrar, Instituto Tecnológico y de Estudios Superiores de Monterrey, Campus Mazatlán, Carretera Mazatlan-Higueras, Km 3, Camino al Conchi, Apartado Postal 799, 82000 Mazatlán, Sinaloa, Mexico. *Phone:* 69-80-1143. *Web site:* http://www.maz.itesm.mx/.

Instituto Tecnológico y de Estudios Superiores de Monterrey, Campus Monterrey

Monterrey, Mexico

Contact Lic. Carlos Ordoñez, International Student Advisor, Instituto Tecnológico y de Estudios Superiores de Monterrey, Campus Monterrey, Avenida Eugenio Garza Sada 2501 Sur Colonia Tecnnologico, Sucursal de Correos J, 64849 Monterrey, Nuevo León, Mexico. *Phone:* 52 81 8328 4065 Ext. 3942 or toll-free 52-81-83284065 (in-state); 52-81-83593293 (out-of-state). *Web site:* http://www.mty.itesm.mx/.

Instituto Tecnológico y de Estudios Superiores de Monterrey, Campus Querétaro

Santiago de Querétaro, Mexico

Contact Lic. Marco Vinicio Lopez, Registrar, Instituto Tecnológico y de Estudios Superiores de Monterrey, Campus Querétaro, Avenida Epigmenio González #500, Apartado Postal 37, 76130 Querétaro, Querétaro, Mexico. *Phone:* 42-17-38-25 Ext. 156. *Web site:* http://www.qro.itesm.mx/.

Instituto Tecnológico y de Estudios Superiores de Monterrey, Campus Saltillo

Saltillo, Mexico

Contact Lic. Esteban Ramos, Registrar, Instituto Tecnológico y de Estudios Superiores de Monterrey, Campus Saltillo, Prolongacion Juan de la Barrera 1241 Ote, Apartado Postal 539, 25270 Saltillo, Coahuila, Mexico. *Phone:* 84-15-06-90 Ext. 12. *Web site:* http://www.sal.itesm.mx/.

Instituto Tecnológico y de Estudios Superiores de Monterrey, Campus San Luis Potosí

San Luis Potosí, Mexico

Contact Ing. Consuelo Gonzalez, Registrar, Instituto Tecnológico y de Estudios Superiores de Monterrey, Campus San Luis Potosí, Avenida

Instituto Tecnológico y de Estudios Superiores de Monterrey, Campus San Luis Potosí (continued)

Robles 600, Colonia Jacarandas, Apartado Postal 1473 Suc E, 78140 San Luis Potosí, SLP, Mexico. *Phone:* 48 13-3441 Ext. 14. *Web site:* http://www.slp.itesm.mx/.

Instituto Tecnológico y de Estudios Superiores de Monterrey, Campus Sinaloa

Culiacán, Mexico

Contact Lic. Hugo Guerrero, Registrar, Instituto Tecnológico y de Estudios Superiores de Monterrey, Campus Sinaloa, Boulevard Culiacán 3773, Apartado Postal 69-F, 80800 Culiacán, Sinaloa, Mexico. *Phone:* 67-14-03-69. *Web site:* http://www.sin.itesm.mx/.

Instituto Tecnológico y de Estudios Superiores de Monterrey, Campus Sonora Norte

Hermosillo, Mexico

Contact Ing. Victor Eduardo Perez Orozco, Library and Admissions/Registration Director, Instituto Tecnológico y de Estudios Superiores de Monterrey, Campus Sonora Norte, Carretera Hermosillo-Nogales Km 9, Apartado Postal 216, 83000 Hermosillo, Sonora, Mexico. *Phone:* 62-15-52-05 Ext. 131. *Web site:* http://www.her.itesm.mx/.

Instituto Tecnológico y de Estudios Superiores de Monterrey, Campus Tampico

Altimira, Mexico

Contact Ing. Javier Ponce, Registrar, Instituto Tecnológico y de Estudios Superiores de Monterrey, Campus Tampico, Boulevard Petrocel Km 1.3, Corredor Industrial, Carretera Tampico-Mante, 89120 Altimira, Tamaulipas, Mexico. *Phone:* 126-4-19-79. *Web site:* http://www.tam.itesm.mx/.

Instituto Tecnológico y de Estudios Superiores de Monterrey, Campus Toluca

Toluca, Mexico

Contact Ing. Victor M. Martinez Orta, Registrar, Instituto Tecnológico y de Estudios Superiores de Monterrey, Campus Toluca, Ex-hacienda La Pila, 100 metros al norte de San Antonio Buenavista, 50252 Toluca, Estado de Mexico, Mexico. *Phone:* 72-74-11-92. *Web site:* http://www.tol.itesm.mx/.

Instituto Tecnológico y de Estudios Superiores de Monterrey, Campus Zacatecas

Zacatecas, Mexico

Contact Lic. de Lourdes Zorrilla, Business Affairs Director and Registrar, Instituto Tecnológico y de Estudios Superiores de Monterrey, Campus Zacatecas, Calzada Pedro Coronel #16, Frente al Club Bernades, Municipio de Guadalupe, 98000 Zacatecas, Zacatecas, Mexico. *Phone:* 49 23-00-40. *Web site:* http://www.zac.itesm.mx/.

Universidad de las Americas, A.C.

Mexico City, Mexico

Contact Universidad de las Americas, A.C., Calle de Puebla 223, Col. Roma, 06700 Mexico City, Mexico. *Web site:* http://www.udla.mx/.

Universidad de las Américas–Puebla

Puebla, Mexico

General Independent, university, coed **Entrance** Moderately difficult **Setting** 84-hectare suburban campus **Total enrollment** 6,450 **Student-faculty ratio** 11:1 **Application deadline** 8/2 (freshmen), rolling (transfer) **Freshman admission** 29% were admitted **Housing** Yes **Expenses** Tuition & Fees $11,200; Room & Board $5000 **Undergraduates** 53% women, 29% part-time, 8% 25 or older **The most frequently chosen baccalaureate fields are** business/marketing, computer and information sciences, engineering **Academic program** Advanced placement, accelerated degree program, summer session, internships **Contact** Miss Madet Ruisenor-Quintero, Director of Student Enrollment Office, Universidad de las Américas–Puebla, Ex-Hacienda Santa Catarina Martir S/N, 72820 Puebla, Mexico. *Phone:* 52 229-2024. *E-mail:* sergio.linares@udlap.mx. *Web site:* http://www.udlap.mx/.

Universidad de Monterrey

San Pedro Garza Garcia, Mexico

Contact Universidad de Monterrey, Av. Ignacio Morones Prieto 4500 Pte, 66238 San Pedro Garza García, NL, Mexico. *Phone:* toll-free 800-849-4757. *Web site:* http://www.udem.edu.mx/.

MONACO

The International University of Monaco

Monte Carlo, Monaco

Contact Dr. Gisele Dudognon, Director of Admissions, The International University of Monaco, 2, Avenue Albert II, MC-98000 Principality of Monaco, Monaco. *Phone:* 377 97986 994. *Fax:* 377 92052 830. *E-mail:* gdudognon@monaco.edu. *Web site:* http://www.monaco.edu/.

NICARAGUA

Ave Maria University–Latin American Campus

San Marcos, Nicaragua

General Independent Roman Catholic, 4-year, coed **Entrance** Moderately difficult **Setting** 2-acre small-town campus **Housing** Yes **Expenses** Tuition & Fees $15,244; Room & Board $3200 **Academic program** English as a second language, advanced placement, summer session **Contact** Mr. Patrick Clark, Director of Admissions, Ave Maria University–Latin American Campus, San Marcos, Carazo, Nicaragua. *Phone:* 43 22314-138. *E-mail:* patrick.clark@avemaria.edu.ni. *Web site:* http://www.avemaria.edu.ni/.

NIGERIA

The Nigerian Baptist Theological Seminary

Ogbomoso, Nigeria

Contact Mr. Daniel F. Oroniran, Registrar, The Nigerian Baptist Theological Seminary, PO Box 30, Ogbomoso, Oyo, Nigeria. *Phone:* 038-710011.

SOUTH AFRICA

University of South Africa
Pretoria, South Africa

Contact Contact Centre, University of South Africa, PO Box 392, Pretoria 0003, South Africa. *Phone:* 27-11 670-9000. *Fax:* 012 429 4150. *E-mail:* study-info@unisa.ac.za. *Web site:* http://www.unisa.ac.za/.

SPAIN

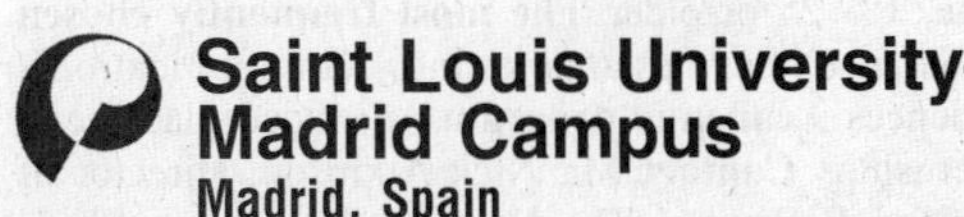

Saint Louis University–Madrid Campus
Madrid, Spain

General Independent Roman Catholic (Jesuit), comprehensive, coed **Entrance** Moderately difficult **Setting** 1-acre urban campus **Student-faculty ratio** 7:1 **Application deadline** 5/31 (freshmen), 5/31 (transfer) **Housing** Yes **Expenses** Tuition & Fees $15,660; Room only $5880 **Academic program** English as a second language, advanced placement, honors program, summer session, internships **Contact** Ms. Maria-Jose Morell, Director of Enrollment Management, Saint Louis University–Madrid Campus, Avenida del Valle, 34, 28003 Madrid, Spain. *Phone:* 34 91-554-5858. *Fax:* 34 91-554-6202. *E-mail:* mmorell@slu.edu. *Web site:* http://spain.slu.edu/.
Visit Petersons.com and enter keyword Madrid

See page 1122 for the College Close-Up.

Schiller International University
Madrid, Spain

General Independent, comprehensive, coed **Entrance** Minimally difficult **Setting** urban campus **Total enrollment** 90 **Student-faculty ratio** 6:1 **Application deadline** Rolling (freshmen), rolling (transfer) **Expenses** Tuition & Fees 16,600 euros **Academic program** English as a second language, advanced placement, accelerated degree program, self-designed majors, summer session, adult/continuing education programs, internships **Contact** Ms. Kamala Dontamsetti, Associate Director of Admissions, Schiller International University, 300 East Bay Drive, Largo, FL 33700. *Phone:* 727-736-5082 Ext. 234. *Fax:* 727-734-0359. *E-mail:* admissions@schiller.edu. *Web site:* http://www.schillermadrid.edu/.

SWITZERLAND

Ecole Hôtelière de Lausanne
Lausanne, Switzerland

Contact Ms. Carvi Stucki Wick, Admissions Director, Ecole Hôtelière de Lausanne, Le Chalet-a-Gobet, CH-1000 Lausanne 25, Switzerland. *Phone:* 41 21 785 1111. *Fax:* 41 21 785 1376. *E-mail:* carvi.stucki@ehl.ch. *Web site:* http://www.ehl.ch/.

Franklin College Switzerland
Sorengo, Switzerland

General Independent, 4-year, coed **Entrance** Moderately difficult **Setting** 10-acre suburban campus **Total enrollment** 434 **Student-faculty ratio** 11:1 **Application deadline** 3/15 (freshmen), 6/15 (transfer) **Freshman admission** 70% were admitted. Average high school GPA 3.26 **Freshman test scores** SAT critical reading scores over 500: 96%; SAT math scores over 500: 79%; ACT scores over 18: 100%; SAT critical reading scores over 600: 61%; SAT math scores over 600: 41%; ACT scores over 24: 68% **Housing** Yes **Expenses** Tuition & Fees $34,400; Room & Board $10,700 **Undergraduates** 65% women, 2% part-time, 1% 25 or older **The most frequently chosen baccalaureate fields are** business/marketing, communications/journalism, social sciences **Academic program** English as a second language, advanced placement, accelerated degree program, honors program, summer session, internships **Contact** U.S. Director of Admissions, Franklin College Switzerland, Via Ponte Tresa 29, CH-6924 Sorengo, Switzerland. *Phone:* 212-922-9650. *Fax:* 212-922-9870. *E-mail:* info@fc.edu. *Web site:* http://www.fc.edu/.
Visit Petersons.com and enter keyword Switzerland

See page 812 for the College Close-Up.

Glion Institute of Higher Education
Glion-sur-Montreux, Switzerland

Contact Admissions, Glion Institute of Higher Education, Route de Glion 111, CH-1823 Glion-sur-Montreux, Switzerland. *Phone:* 41-0 21 989 26 77. *Fax:* 41-0 21 989 26 78. *E-mail:* info@glion.edu. *Web site:* http://www.glion.ch/.

Les Roches International School of Hotel Management
Bluche, Switzerland

Contact Enrollment Management Department, Les Roches International School of Hotel Management, CH-3975 Bluche, Switzerland. *Phone:* 41-021 989 26 44. *Fax:* 41-021 989 26 45. *E-mail:* info@les-roches.ch. *Web site:* http://www.lesroches.cc/.

TAIWAN

Christ's College
Taipei, Taiwan

General Independent religious, 4-year, coed **Contact** Christ's College, 51 Tzu Chiang Road, Tanshui 251 Tapei, Taiwan, Taiwan. *Web site:* http://www.christc.org.tw/.

UNITED ARAB EMIRATES

The American University in Dubai
Dubai, United Arab Emirates

General Proprietary, comprehensive, coed **Setting** urban campus **Total enrollment** 2,611 **Freshman admission** 96% were admitted **Housing** Yes **Undergraduates** 46% women, 19% part-time **Academic program** English as a second language, advanced placement, accelerated degree program, honors program, summer session, internships **Contact** Mrs. Carol Maalouf, Director of Admissions, The American University in Dubai, PO Box 28282, Dubai, United Arab Emirates. *Phone:* 971 4 399 9000 Ext. 170. *Fax:* 971 4 399 8899. *E-mail:* admissions@aud.edu. *Web site:* http://www.aud.edu.

American University of Sharjah
Sharjah, United Arab Emirates

Contact Ali Shuhaimy, Dean of Admissions, American University of Sharjah, PO Box 26666, Sharjah, United Arab Emirates. *Phone:* 971 6 515-5555. *E-mail:* ashuhaimy@aus.edu. *Web site:* http://www.aus.edu/.

UNITED KINGDOM

American InterContinental University–London
London, United Kingdom

General Proprietary, comprehensive, coed **Setting** urban campus **Total enrollment** 700 **Application deadline** Rolling (freshmen), rolling (transfer) **Undergraduates** 18% 25 or older **The most frequently chosen baccalaureate fields are** business/marketing, computer and information sciences, visual and performing arts **Academic program** Accelerated degree program, summer session, adult/continuing education programs **Contact** Mr. Amer Mourad, Vice President of Admissions, American InterContinental University–London, 110 Marylebone High Street, London W1U 4RY, United Kingdom. *Phone:* 877-564-6248 or toll-free 888-567-5888. *Fax:* 877-564-6248. *Web site:* http://www.aiuniv.edu/.

Hult International Business School
London, United Kingdom

General Independent, comprehensive, coed **Entrance** Moderately difficult **Setting** urban campus **Total enrollment** 194 **Application deadline** 6/27 (freshmen) **Expenses** Tuition & Fees 14,200 British pounds **Academic program** Advanced placement, accelerated degree program, self-designed majors, honors program, summer session, internships **Contact** Mrs. Anna Frolander, Executive Director of Undergraduate Admissions, Hult International Business School, 46-47 Russell Square, London WC1B 4JP, United Kingdom. *Phone:* 44 207 341 8555. *E-mail:* anna.frolander@hult.edu. *Web site:* http://www.hult.edu/.

Regent's American College London
London, United Kingdom

Contact Admissions Director, Regent's American College London, Regent's College, Inner Circle, Regent's Park, London NW1 4NS, United Kingdom. *Phone:* 44-0 207 487 7507. *Fax:* 44-0 207 487 7425. *E-mail:* bacl@regents.ac.uk. *Web site:* http://www.bacl.ac.uk/.

Richmond, The American International University in London
Richmond, United Kingdom

General Independent, comprehensive, coed **Entrance** Moderately difficult **Setting** 5-acre urban campus **Total enrollment** 1,043 **Student-faculty ratio** 12:1 **Application deadline** Rolling (freshmen), rolling (transfer) **Freshman admission** 74% were admitted. Average high school GPA 3.15 **Freshman test scores** SAT critical reading scores over 500: 78.94%; SAT math scores over 500: 82.56%; ACT scores over 18: 100%; SAT critical reading scores over 600: 21.05%; SAT math scores over 600: 5.5%; ACT scores over 24: 60% **Housing** Yes **Expenses** Tuition & Fees $27,000; Room & Board $12,900 **Undergraduates** 64% women, 1% part-time, 1% 25 or older **The most frequently chosen baccalaureate fields are** business/marketing, communications/journalism, social sciences **Academic program** Advanced placement, summer session, internships **Contact** Mr. Nick Atkinson, Director of United States Admissions, Richmond, The American International University in London, 343 Congress Street, Suite 3100, Boston, MA 02210-1214. *Phone:* 617-450-5617. *Fax:* 617-450-5601. *E-mail:* us_admissions@richmond.ac.uk. *Web site:* http://www.richmond.ac.uk/. **Visit Petersons.com and enter keyword Richmond**

See page 1076 for the College Close-Up.

Schiller International University
London, United Kingdom

General Independent, comprehensive, coed **Entrance** Minimally difficult **Setting** urban campus **Total enrollment** 383 **Student-faculty ratio** 7:1 **Application deadline** Rolling (freshmen), rolling (transfer) **Housing** Yes **Expenses** Tuition & Fees 10,200 British pounds; Room & Board 6000 British pounds **Academic program** English as a second language, advanced placement, accelerated degree program, self-designed majors, honors program, summer session, adult/continuing education programs, internships **Contact** Ms. Kamala Dontamsetti, Associate Director of Admissions, Schiller International University, 300 East Bay Drive, Largo, FL 33770. *Phone:* 727-736-5082 Ext. 239 or toll-free 800-336-4133. *Fax:* 727-734-0359. *E-mail:* admissions@schiller.edu. *Web site:* http://www.schiller.edu/.

College Close-Ups

ACADEMY OF ART UNIVERSITY

SAN FRANCISCO, CALIFORNIA

The University

In 1929, Academy of Art University founder Richard S. Stephens, who was the advertising creative director of *Sunset* magazine, acted on his belief that "aspiring artists and designers, given proper instruction, hard work, and dedication, can learn the skills needed to become successful professionals." His new school of advertising art consisted of 46 students meeting in one room on San Francisco's Kearny Street.

The instructors, who are professional artists, bring real-world problems, situations, solutions, and practical experience to the students. Thus was born the school's philosophy by the founder: Hire today's best practicing professionals to teach the art and design professionals of tomorrow. At that time, advertising consisted primarily of illustrations, photos, and copy. Consequently, it became necessary to teach beginning students the fundamentals of drawing, painting, color, light, and photography as well as layout and typography.

When Richard A. Stephens succeeded his father as president in 1951, the Foundations Department was added, ensuring all students comprehended the basic principles of traditional art and design. Illustration soon expanded to include fine arts (drawing, painting, sculpture, and printmaking), and advertising design spawned the School of Graphic Design. Fashion (design, textiles, and merchandising) and Interior Design Schools were also added. In 1966, the Academy officially became a college, and in a decade, the Master of Fine Arts degree was offered. Five more buildings were purchased, and by 1992, there were more than 2,500 students.

The leadership of the Academy was then turned over to the third generation, Elisa Stephens, granddaughter of the school's founder. She quickly determined that the school's small School of Computer Arts: New Media had enormous potential to prepare students for multimedia careers when allied with such companies as Silicon Graphics, Pixar, Adobe, and Walt Disney Productions. It is now one of the largest departments at the Academy.

Today, Academy of Art University is the largest private accredited art and design school in the nation with an enrollment of more than 13,000. More than one fifth of the student body is made up of international students. The Academy has thirty facilities that house classrooms, studios, galleries, and residence halls. The students, who are admitted through an open-enrollment policy, aspire to earn A.A., B.A., B.F.A., M.A., M.F.A., or M. Arch. degrees in fourteen majors. Students can study in San Francisco or through the Academy's flexible online programs.

The school maintains a fleet of buses to connect the different points of the campus, all of which are located within the city limits of San Francisco, one of the world's most vibrant and beautiful cities. The instructors, who are 80 percent part-time and made up of working art and design professionals, are recruited from all across the nation, and are drawn to the creative and intellectual center that is the Bay Area. Extensive senior-year internship programs allow students to gain valuable experience and develop strong portfolios in their chosen field before graduation.

The Academy is one of the few art and design schools that believe in nurturing the whole artist; this includes developing athletic talents along with artistic ones. Students can participate in intercollegiate, intramural and club sports.

Academy of Art University is an accredited member of the Western Association of Schools and Colleges (WASC), National Association of Schools of Art and Design (NASAD), Council for Interior Design (BFA), and National Architectural Accrediting Board (NAAB) for M.Arch.

Location

The city of San Francisco is one of the great cultural centers of the world; a melting pot of diversity, ethnicity, and creativity that has spawned major museums and galleries, world-class opera and theaters, dance companies, film production and recording studios, technological innovation, performing artists ranging from classical to popular music, and numerous other cultural opportunities. The city's status as a tourist mecca located on the Pacific Rim ensures that one encounters people from all corners of the world.

The climate is moderate and offers kaleidoscopic blends of sunshine and fog nine months of the year. The Northpoint campus is located at world-famous Pier 39; one can view Alcatraz Island from classroom windows. Four other buildings are two blocks from historic Union Square in the commercial heart of the city. Three other buildings are located near the Financial District. The city offers myriad locations for field trips and studio visits. World-renowned artists display their creations in the Academy's three nonprofit art galleries, which are open to the public. The University is an urban institution that both draws upon and contributes to the cultural wealth of the community in which it resides.

Majors and Degrees

Academy of Art University offers A.A., B.A., B.F.A., M.A., M.F.A., and M.Arch. degrees and certificates in the following majors: advertising (account planning, art direction, copywriting, and television commercials), animation/visual effects (background painting/layout design, character development, game design, storyboard art, VFX/compositing, visual development, and 3-D modeling), architecture (residential, commercial and green architecture), computer arts/new media (computer graphics, digital imaging, new media, and Web design), digital arts and communications (client and service-side Internet design creative programming, information architecture, interactive information graphics, interactive modeling, prototyping/testing, and usability), fashion (fashion design, fashion illustration, knitwear, merchandising, and textiles), fine art (ceramics, metal arts, painting/drawing, printmaking, and sculpture), graphic design (corporate and brand identity, motion graphics, multimedia, package design, print and collateral, and Web site design), illustration (cartooning, children's books, editorial, feature film animation, and 2-D animation), industrial design (furniture, product, toy, and transportation), interior architecture and design (commercial, furniture, and residential), motion pictures and television (acting, advertising/director–camera, cinematography, directing, editing, producing, production design, screenwriting, and special effects), and photography (advertising, digital photography, documentary, fine art, photo illustration, and photojournalism). The Academy's newest program, multimedia communications, teaches students the latest media trends through courses in broadcasting, journalism and production in studios and on location.

Academic Programs

A total of 132 credit units are required to earn a Bachelor of Fine Arts degree, consisting of 18 units of foundations courses, 60 units in the major, 9 units of art electives, and 45 units of liberal arts courses. First-year students must complete six foundations courses before the end of the year. Fundamental courses are related specifically to students' majors to prepare them to begin intense focus courses in their field by the sophomore year. All major courses of study are structured so the student builds upon skills learned the previous semester and advances to the next level of technical or creative proficiency. Some related major courses may be taken concurrently. Each course is worth 3 credits.

Liberal arts courses teach practical applications for forging a professional career in art and design. International students who come from countries where English is not the primary language may take additional ESL classes, as determined by English language proficiency testing. Students are advised to meet with departmental directors at least once during the academic year to have their progress assessed. Portfolios are reviewed before the junior year to determine whether or not a student has progressed sufficiently to continue study at the Academy.

Academic Facilities

The Academy's facilities reflect its commitment to training students for careers in art and design; not only do students have access to some of the most advanced facilities in the nation, but the Academy continually invests in new equipment to ensure that it remains on the cutting edge of technology. By learning on industry-standard equipment, students gain valuable professional skills that make them highly employable.

The Academy's eight-story Digital Arts Center offers students from the Animation and Visual Effects, Computer Arts: New Media, Digital Arts and Communications, Fashion, and Motion Pictures and Television Schools access to an incredible array of technology. The center has a multitude of computer workstations, including Silicon Graphics, Adobe Premier, and autoCAD workstations. Students also have the use of Avid digital-editing suites, multitrack sound-editing studios, a dedicated green-screen studio, and other pieces of video equipment, including Bosch Telecine equipment.

The School of Photography occupies its own building, which houses individual studios and a wide range of equipment, including full-length shooting studios; Hasselblad, Mamyia, Canon, and Sinar cameras; Broncolor, Norman, and Speedotron strobe systems; black-and-white darkrooms; a color lab facility with single-print stations; and the latest technology, such as Macintosh G5 computers for digital imaging and output. In addition, the Academy's modern, professional studio is one of the largest of any photography school in the nation and is ideal for shooting automobiles, motorcycles, and large sets.

Fine Art and Advertising are located in one of the Academy's newest buildings. There are five floors occupied by studio space and labs fully equipped for silkscreen, lithography, book arts, etching/intaglio, and relief painting, as well as a fully functioning advertising agency.

The Academy's Fine Art Sculpture Center is a 58,000-square-foot facility that houses state-of-the-art studios for figure, ceramic, neon/illumination, bronze, metal fabrication, and mold-making sculpture. Students also have use of an off-site bronze-casting facility and foundry. When students graduate from the Academy, they have the opportunity to exhibit in one of the three non-profit galleries located in the heart of downtown San Francisco's premier gallery district. These street-level facilities are an excellent way for students to promote and sell their work and to gain networking experience.

Multimedia Communications and Graphic Design are housed in the Academy's main building in the heart of San Francisco. Multimedia Communications students have access to a professional studio on the building's first floor. And the School of Industrial Design building houses an impressive car collection for inspiration.

The Library houses more than 30,000 books and magazines, as well as 375 CD titles, 150,000 slides, and 2,000 videos. Computers with Internet access are available to students, as well as an online catalog, color scanners, and color and black-and-white copiers. Workshops and electronic study guides are also available. The Academy Resource Center offers all students free learning support services that include study hall, tutoring, mentoring, mid-point review and study-skills workshops, a writing lab, a state-of-the-art multimedia language lab, an English for Art Program, and a Conversation Partner Program.

Costs

Tuition is $670 per credit unit for undergraduates. Full-time students carry either 12 or 15 units per semester. There is a nonrefundable $120 registration fee—$100 is applicable toward tuition. Lab fees run from $25 to $400 per semester, depending on the class. Tuition and fees are subject to change at any time. Art supplies can run from $250 to $500 per semester, depending on the major. The Academy has most of the expensive technical equipment available for students to borrow or use in a lab.

Academy of Art University operates fourteen residence halls within the city. Several housing options are offered, and costs vary from $6600 to $10,000 per academic year (fall and spring semesters). For further information, students may contact the Academy Housing Office directly at housing@academyart.edu or 800-544-2787 (toll-free).

Financial Aid

The Academy offers financial aid packages consisting of grants, loans, and work-study to eligible students with a demonstrated need. Low-interest loans are available to all eligible students, regardless of need. As financial aid programs, procedures, and eligibility requirements change frequently, applicants should contact the Financial Aid Office at financialaid@academyart.edu or 800-544-2787 (toll-free).

Faculty

The Academy averages 950 instructors in fall/spring semester, most of whom are full-time art and design professionals and part-time teachers. The student-teacher ratio for undergraduate classes averages 18:1.

Student Government

Although there is no formal student government, each department has between 2 and 3 student representatives who meet with the president as needed throughout the semester to discuss any student issues.

Admission Requirements

Applicants for the A.A., B.A., and B.F.A. programs must have a high school diploma or GED equivalent. There is no portfolio requirement. M.A. and M.F.A. applicants must have a bachelor's degree and submit a portfolio and statement of intent. International students take written and speech tests to determine which ESL classes may have to be completed. Most ESL classes can be taken in conjunction with art and design classes. All foundations classes offer specialized ESL sections with instructors trained for language assistance. The application fee is $100 for undergraduates. A $500 tuition deposit applies to international applicants.

Application and Information

Students may apply to enter the Academy at the beginning of the spring, fall, or summer semesters. Information in this profile is subject to change. Students should contact Academy of Art University for current information or visit www.academyart.edu.

Prospective Student Services
Academy of Art University
79 New Montgomery Street
San Francisco, California 94105
Phone: 415-274-2222
800-544-2787 (toll-free)
Fax: 415-618-6287
E-mail: info@academyart.edu
Web site: http://academyart.edu

Student working at Academy of Art University.

ADELPHI UNIVERSITY

GARDEN CITY, NEW YORK

The University

Adelphi University, founded in 1896, is Long Island's first private coeducational institution of higher learning. A nonsectarian, independent university, Adelphi welcomes men and women of all backgrounds who display intellectual inquisitiveness, academic commitment, and a desire for achievement and purpose in life. The University enrolls 5,139 undergraduates and 3,348 graduate students. Forty-one states and fifty-seven countries are represented in its diverse student body. The campus is located on 75 landscaped acres in Garden City, New York, 20 miles east of New York City and easily accessible by public transportation. The University also has three off-campus centers: the Manhattan Center in New York City, the Hauppauge Center on Long Island, and the Hudson Valley Center in Poughkeepsie, New York.

Adelphi University's schools and programs include the College of Arts and Sciences; the Honors College; the Schools of Business, Nursing, and Social Work; the Ruth S. Ammon School of Education; the Gordon F. Derner Institute of Advanced Psychological Studies; and adult academic programs in University College.

The University's six residence halls accommodate more than 1,100 students, and construction is underway on a new residence hall to be completed by summer 2011. The Residential Life staff at Adelphi is committed to bringing education to the residence halls. A lecture and discussion series brings faculty members together with students to examine events of the day and issues related to the classroom. In addition, about 200 seminars, workshops, and events are offered each year. Faculty and guest lecturers lead discussions on such topics as American and global politics, ethnic diversity, legal affairs, job interviewing, sexual conduct, and AIDS.

Opportunities for enhancing life beyond the classroom abound at Adelphi. Students participate in intramural and intercollegiate athletics (including nationally ranked men's and women's soccer, women's softball, and men's baseball, basketball, and lacrosse), drama productions, and more than eighty student clubs, community-service groups, and organizations. Students take advantage of the thriving cultural arts programs, including plays, art exhibits, concerts, and lectures; the comprehensive sports and fitness services; and the breathtaking 75-acre campus. Physical education facilities include a swimming pool; basketball court; weight-training and exercise rooms; a large indoor running track; and fields for baseball, lacrosse, soccer, and softball. In addition, a vast array of activities such as movies, exhibits, cabarets, symposia, and field trips are scheduled every semester.

The Adelphi student newspaper (*Delphian*), the yearbook (*Oracle*), and the student literary and arts magazine, *Magnum Opus*, welcome writers and photographers.

In the Ruth S. Harley University Center (UC)—a central meeting place on campus—Adelphi students browse in the full-service bookstore, refresh themselves and relax in one of the center's lounges (commuter students have a special lounge equipped with lockers), eat in the UC Cafeteria, and enjoy a vast array of activities including movies, comedy shows, lectures, dance parties, and musical events. Cultural trips are also offered. The University Center also houses Adelphi's numerous student organizations.

Location

Adelphi's main campus is located in the picturesque and architecturally distinctive suburban community of Garden City, New York, a village of stately homes, historic buildings, and parks. The cultural and commercial resources of New York City and the recreation and entertainment of Long Island are only a short distance away by public or private transit.

Majors and Degrees

Undergraduate studies leading to the degrees of Bachelor of Arts (B.A.), Bachelor of Business Administration (B.B.A.), Bachelor of Fine Arts (B.F.A.), Bachelor of Science (B.S.), and Bachelor of Social Work (B.S.W.) are offered at Adelphi University. Programs of study at Adelphi include: accounting; African American and ethnic studies; anthropology/forensic anthropology; art, with specializations in art history, fine arts and studio art* (ceramics, painting, photography, printmaking, and sculpture), and graphic design*; art education*, Asian studies; biochemistry; biology; business; chemistry; communication sciences and disorders; communications (journalism, media studies, moving image production); computer and management information systems; computer science; criminal justice; dance; economics; education studies, with programs of study in childhood education (STEP) and adolescence education (STEP); English (literature, creative writing); environmental studies; exercise science and sport management; finance; French; gender studies; history; human resource management; interdisciplinary studies; international studies; languages and international studies (political science, business); Latin American studies; management; marketing; mathematics; music; nursing; performing arts** (acting and design technology); philosophy; physical education; physical education/health education; physics; political science; psychology; public service; social work; sociology; Spanish; undecided arts and sciences; and undecided business. (A * indicates that an art portfolio is required; ** indicates that an audition is required.)

Five-year bachelor's/master's programs are offered in Scholars Teacher Education Program (STEP), childhood education, adolescence education, and social work.

Opportunities for preprofessional studies are available in predental, pre-engineering, prelaw, premedicine, preoptometry, and pre-physical therapy/allied health.

Academic Programs

The goal of the academic programs at Adelphi is to provide higher education that cultivates the intellect and prepares students for the future. Consistent with the University's approach to liberal learning, students take part in the University's general education distribution requirements.

A minimum of 120 credits is required for a baccalaureate degree, with a specified number in the chosen major. Double majors and various minors may be elected. Seniors of superior academic ability may be admitted to graduate courses in their major field.

Off-Campus Programs

Adelphi University offers study-abroad programs that can last several weeks or span up to an academic year. Students can participate in Adelphi-run programs in Florence, London, Mexico, Greece, Poland, and the Bahamas, or join programs run by other educational institutions.

Academic Facilities

The University Libraries are composed of the Swirbul Library, the Archives and Special Collections, and the libraries at the Manhattan, Hauppauge, and Hudson Valley centers. These libraries contain 593,920 volumes and 806,642 items in microformat, plus 33,256 audiovisual items, 1,203 periodical subscriptions, and access to over 30,000 electronic titles. The University Libraries are fully automated with holdings accessible through ALICAT (the Adelphi Libraries Catalog Online). As an enhancement of the traditional reference services, online access is provided to 195 research databases.

The Swirbul Library is also the center of information technology on campus. Its amenities include a battery of personal computers that are fully networked for student use, a faculty development lab, and a technology infrastructure that reaches into every classroom and every part of the curriculum to provide Web-based learning and other applications of communication and information media.

The new 18,000-square-foot Adele and Herbert J. Klapper Center for Fine Arts has greatly expanded Adelphi's art studio and classroom space and offers greater opportunity for nonmajors to take art courses. This is in addition to the current state-of-the-art digital graphics design studio and faculty offices and the expansion of drawing studios in Blodgett Hall.

In 2006, Adelphi broke ground on an ambitious construction project to expand and enhance academic, cultural, and athletic facilities. Opened in fall 2008, the new Performing Arts Center showcases prestigious programs in acting, design/technical theater, music, and dance together under one roof. The new center features a 500-seat music performance hall, dance and recital rooms, music practice rooms, temperature-controlled instrument storage rooms, and a black box theater.

The Center for Recreation and Sports, which also opened in fall 2008, is the new home of Adelphi's successful athletics programs. The center's three-story, three-court gym, which converts into a 2,200-seat arena for basketball games and other events, accommodates recreational and intercollegiate athletes and health and physical education students, and can host NCAA tournaments and championships.

Costs

The 2009–10 tuition and fees for full-time undergraduates are $26,230. For students living on campus, additional costs include room ($7590 for a typical double room without air conditioning) and board ($2400 for a basic meal plan).

Financial Aid

The Office of Student Financial Services administers federal and New York State programs that provide funds to assist students in pursuing their academic goals. In addition to grants based on need, Adelphi annually offers almost 1,000 of its own scholarships based on merit, talent, and extracurricular excellence. Ninety-four percent of Adelphi freshmen receive some form of financial aid each year. The average financial aid package award for a full-time freshman is approximately $16,400.

Faculty

At Adelphi, the quality of education is entrusted to its distinguished faculty members, who are noted for their serious commitment to students, as well as for their research and professional contributions. Here, professors, not graduate assistants, teach undergraduate courses, and students learn in small, intimate environments.

Student Government

The Student Government Association is the elected student group that represents the opinions of the full-time undergraduate body to the administration and other groups. The Student Government Association hosts speakers, sponsors awareness days, and serves as a voice for student concerns and interests.

Admission Requirements

Recommended admission qualifications include graduation from a four-year public or private high school or equivalent credentials, four years of English, three years of science, three years of mathematics, two to three years of a foreign language or languages, and 4 additional units chosen from the fields mentioned or from history and social studies. Official test results from the SAT or ACT with writing are required.

Personal interviews and campus tours are strongly recommended for all applicants. Arrangements can be made by contacting the Office of Admissions.

Application and Information

The following admission credentials should be submitted by applicants: a completed application for admission, the $35 nonrefundable application fee, an official secondary school transcript or GED certificate, official results of the SAT or ACT, and letters of recommendation. Transfer students must submit official transcripts from all colleges previously attended.

Adelphi accepts applications on a rolling basis, with admission twice each year for the semesters beginning in September and January. Freshman filing dates are December 1 for early action, February 1 for priority consideration for joint-degree programs, March 1 for regular admission to the fall semester (applications received later are reviewed on a rolling basis), and November 1 for regular admission for the spring semester (applications received later are reviewed on a rolling basis). The nonbinding early-action plan is available only for the September term. An early-action decision means that applicants who submit their completed applications by December 1 receive an admissions decision by December 31 and that they are considered for scholarships and financial aid.

For more information, students should contact:

University Admissions
Adelphi University
Garden City, New York 11530
Phone: 800-ADELPHI (toll-free)
E-mail: admissions@adelphi.edu
Web site: http://www.adelphi.edu

ALBERTUS MAGNUS COLLEGE

NEW HAVEN, CONNECTICUT

The College

Founded in 1925 by the Dominican Sisters of St. Mary of the Springs, Albertus Magnus College educates men and women to become leaders in all walks of life. The College is committed to providing a liberal arts education rooted in the Dominican tradition of scholarship. Professors at Albertus strive to help their students develop in all areas; as much attention is paid to the nurturing of a student's aesthetic, physical, and moral capacities as to his or her intellectual capabilities. In 1992, the College began offering its first graduate-level course of study through the Master of Arts in Liberal Studies program. More recently, the College has expanded its graduate-level offerings to include the Master of Science in Management, the Master of Arts in Art Therapy, the Master of Arts in Leadership, and the Master of Business Administration.

The traditional undergraduate program has a student body of approximately 500 students, who live and learn on the beautiful 50-acre campus in the Prospect Hill neighborhood of New Haven. Another 1,500 students attend graduate programs or accelerated programs for adults. These students come from various parts of the United States (largely the New England area). About 60 percent of the students live on campus in student dormitories that are renovated mansions from the early 1900s. The housing program fosters a strong sense of community spirit, and students often plan workshops, parties, and other social and learning events in their residence halls.

The Campus Center is a hub of student activities, such as comedy shows, live music, contests, and other unique functions. The variety of on-campus organizations includes the Student Government Association, the Campus Activities Board, the multicultural student union, a dance team, the Psychology Club, the Art Club, the Environmental Club, the Business Club, and numerous creative writing options, such as *Breakwater* literary magazine and the English Club. Albertus has recently added a new cyber lounge, the Common Ground, where students can check e-mail, work on homework, and enjoy a cup of coffee.

Students may also share in the excitement of live drama through the College's professionally managed ACT 2 Theatre, providing a number of artistic, academic, and recreational possibilities. In addition, students are encouraged to become part of the New Haven community through extracurricular and volunteer activities. The active Campus Ministry provides opportunities to volunteer, organize campus events, and participate in community service projects.

The Cosgrove, Marcus, Messer Athletic Center houses a 25-yard pool, a Jacuzzi, three racquetball courts, a weight and cardio room, a dance studio, and a gymnasium. In addition to this facility, there are soccer and softball fields, an outdoor track, and several tennis courts. Albertus fields intercollegiate athletic teams in baseball, basketball, cross-country, soccer, tennis, and volleyball for men and basketball, cross-country, soccer, softball, tennis, and volleyball for women. Albertus's teams compete in the NCAA Division III/Great Northeast Athletic Conference (GNAC) and the Eastern College Athletic Conference (ECAC). The Athletic Department also offers an intramural program in some sports.

Location

New Haven is a multicultural city with a population of more than 130,000 people. The city hosts approximately 16,000 students attending the seven colleges and universities in the greater New Haven area. This concentration of students creates exciting choices for social, recreational, and cultural activities for Albertus students. The city has some of the finest theaters in the country, including the Long Wharf and Shubert theaters. There are many fantastic art collections, museums, and movie theaters. Large shopping facilities, excellent restaurants, and several recreational areas are only a short distance from the Albertus Magnus College campus.

Majors and Degrees

The Albertus Magnus College traditional undergraduate program confers the Bachelor of Arts (B.A.), Bachelor of Science (B.S.), and Bachelor of Fine Arts (B.F.A.) degrees. The areas of study include accounting, art (history and studio), art therapy, biology, business administration, chemistry, child development and mental health, communications, computer information systems, creative writing, criminal justice, drama, education (grades 4–12), English, finance, general studies, graphic design, history, humanities, human services, industrial and organizational psychology, international business, marketing, mathematics, performing communications, philosophy/religion, photography, physical sciences, political science, prelaw, premedicine, psychology, Spanish, sports communications, social science, social work, sociology, urban studies, and visual arts.

Academic Programs

Albertus Magnus College is committed to providing a liberal arts education that promotes the pursuit of truth in all its dimensions. The College recognizes the importance of cultivating core competencies and knowledge if students are to meet the challenges and opportunities they encounter in their communities and workplaces. Albertus has recently developed the Insight Program, which serves as the College's core curriculum. Through this program, students build a thinking framework that supports them throughout their lives as they realize their goals. In addition, the Insight Program helps students improve their capabilities in critical and creative thinking; grasp the methods of scientific, quantitative, mathematical, and philosophical reasoning; and appreciate and assess perspectives different from their own. The B.A. and B.S. degrees require 120 credits for graduation and the B.F.A. requires 127 credits. The College's Office of Career Services helps graduating students prepare for career direction and job placement. The Academic Development Center and Writing Center provide personal instruction to students who may benefit from additional help with their schoolwork. The centers also provide services to those students with learning disabilities. Students who show strong academic potential may pursue a course of study through the College's honors program. Students may relate academic study to work experience through a system of academically credited internships. Through the College's system of internships for juniors and seniors, Albertus students have become increasingly involved in the New Haven community and gain valuable, practical, professional training. Often, internships lead to permanent positions with local companies and corporations.

Academic Facilities

Rosary Hall, the College's first building, now houses a library collection of 110,000 volumes, 600 periodicals, 4,400 pieces of microfilm, and full access to the Internet, including LexisNexis, EBSCOhost, and PsycINFO. The interlibrary loan program has access to materials at academic and public libraries across the country. The Media Center has equipment that students may use to produce new materials as well as review older materials. Interlibrary services with other local universities are also available. The New Center for Science, Art and Technology provides the most modern scientific equipment available for students majoring in biological and physical sciences, along with state-of-the-art broadcasting technology for communication students. Aquinas Hall houses the academic computer labs, which are equipped with personal computers, digital scanners, laser printers, and full Internet access. Every classroom in Aquinas Hall is laptop compatible, and the entire campus is engineered for wireless use.

Costs

The costs for the 2009–10 school year are $23,959 for tuition and $9914 for room and board (nineteen meals per week). Expenses for books, travel, and personal supplies vary.

Financial Aid

Albertus Magnus College offers a variety of merit-based scholarships to students who have achieved high academic standing in high school or in their two-year college programs. In addition to scholarships based solely on academics, the College offers scholarships for students who attend Catholic high schools, students who are valedictorians or salutatorians of their high schools, students who live in the New Haven area, and students who have shown a commitment to community service. Interested students should contact the Office of Admission for specific information regarding these and other scholarship opportunities. Scholarships are awarded to eligible students who apply and are accepted to the College prior to March 15.

Approximately 85 percent of the College's students receive financial aid in some form. The College requires that students file the Albertus Magnus College financial aid application form and the Free Application for Federal Student Aid (FAFSA) to be considered for Albertus scholarships and grants, Federal Perkins Loans, Federal Supplemental Educational Opportunity Grants, and Federal Work-Study Program awards. The College awards financial aid on a rolling basis; however, students who are accepted and submit their FAFSA forms by February 28 are given priority.

Faculty

Faculty members at Albertus come from leading universities in the United States and abroad and are one of the College's greatest assets. Ninety percent of the full- and part-time faculty members hold a Ph.D. or the equivalent. Their primary concern is teaching, although the work of many faculty members has been published. Students find faculty members accessible for academic or personal counseling and for campus sports and activities.

Student Government

Through the Student Government Association (SGA), Albertus students have the primary responsibility for governing their own residential and social life. All full-time matriculated students are members of the SGA and, through its committees and officers, manage student government and social affairs and participate in the campus judicial system. Students serve on faculty committees, the Academic Policy Committee, and the Library Committee.

Admission Requirements

Albertus Magnus College welcomes applications from students of all ages, nationalities, and ethnic, cultural, racial, and religious groups. Applicants may be admitted as freshmen or as transfer, provisional, or special students.

In evaluating freshman candidates, the Office of Admission considers a student's application, counselor recommendation, high school transcript, essay, extracurricular activities, and scores on the SAT or ACT. Emphasis is placed on the student's record of performance rather than on the results of standardized tests.

Transfer students are welcome at the College. They must submit high school records, SAT or ACT scores, and college records for evaluation, in addition to the application and the recommendation. Interviews are recommended for freshman and transfer applicants.

More information is available on the College's Web site, http://www.albertus.edu.

Application and Information

The College accepts students for entrance on a rolling admission basis. Students may also apply online at http://www.albertus.edu. As soon as all of a candidate's admission materials have been received, his or her application is considered and notification is made as soon as a decision has been reached.

Application forms, recommendation forms, and information may be obtained by contacting:

Office of Admission
Albertus Magnus College
700 Prospect Street
New Haven, Connecticut 06511-1189
Phone: 203-773-8501
800-578-9160 (toll-free)
Fax: 203-773-5248
E-mail: admissions@albertus.edu
Web site: http://www.albertus.edu

Beautiful Rosary Hall.

ALVERNIA UNIVERSITY

READING, PENNSYLVANIA

The University

Alvernia University, with a total enrollment of more than 2,800 men and women, is a rigorous, caring, and inclusive learning community committed to academic excellence rooted in the Catholic, Franciscan, and liberal arts traditions. With a student-faculty ratio of 13:1, Alvernia offers a personalized environment where the faculty members know and care about each student. Located on a beautiful 121-acre campus on the outskirts of Reading, Alvernia offers a setting conducive to learning and is conveniently accessible. It is chartered by the commonwealth of Pennsylvania, fully accredited by the Middle States Association of Colleges and Schools, and sponsored by the Bernardine Franciscan Sisters.

Alvernia participates in a full range of intercollegiate sports, including baseball, basketball, cross-country, field hockey, golf, ice hockey, lacrosse, soccer, softball, tennis, track and field, and volleyball. The University is a member of the NCAA Division III, the ECAC, and the Commonwealth Conference of the Middle Atlantic States Collegiate Athletic Corporation (MAC), a highly competitive Division III intercollegiate conference. A state-of-the-art turf field and track, opened in 2009, is the latest addition to campus facilities.

Alvernia's growing roster of student events, activities, and organizations offers something for everyone. From ballroom dancing to a new sport, from philosophical debates to three-on-three basketball, from improvisational theatre to community service, there's a club for every interest—and if there isn't, students can start one. The Student Government Association and the Campus Activities Board plan plenty of on-campus entertainment and social events, including comedians, bands, film series, and other events, as well as discounted trips (transportation included) in and around the region.

Students log 40 hours of volunteer service as a graduation requirement, and Alvernia helps them find opportunities to fit their interests, schedule, and talents. Students can tutor schoolchildren, shovel sidewalks for the elderly, stock groceries at a food bank, or practice Spanish language skills on alternative spring break mission trips to Ecuador or Santo Domingo. Giving back, pitching in, helping out, getting involved, making a difference—no matter what it's called, at Alvernia, all that matters is that everyone does it. Service to others is part of the Alvernia experience and reflects the University's core beliefs.

Resident students have several attractive housing options, including traditional and suite-style residence halls and town houses. New residence halls opened in 2003, 2005, and 2009. A student center is the hub of campus life, with the dining hall, the new student-run Crusader Café, wireless Internet access, 24/7 availability for late-night study breaks or between classes, and a lounge with a big-screen television and game room.

Location

Many first-time visitors are surprised to find Alvernia's peaceful, tree-lined grounds and modern campus buildings in Reading, Pennsylvania, a city of 81,000 once known for its national importance to the mining and railroad industries. Downtown Reading, about 3 miles from the campus, offers a mix of cultural and entertainment destinations. Located in the scenic Blue Mountain area of eastern Pennsylvania, Alvernia's campus overlooks Angelica Park, noted for its rustic beauty. Beyond Reading lies Pennsylvania's famous Amish country. The University also has easy access to the metropolitan areas of New York, Philadelphia, Baltimore, and Washington, D.C., where students can take advantage of the cultural, historical, and educational attractions these cities have to offer.

Majors and Degrees

Alvernia University offers the Bachelor of Arts, Bachelor of Science, Bachelor of Science in Nursing, and Associate in Science degrees. Bachelor of Arts or Bachelor of Science candidates can major in the following areas: accounting, addiction studies, athletic training, biochemistry, biology, biology/medical technology, chemistry, chemistry/medical technology, communication, computer information systems, criminal justice administration, education (early childhood, middle school, special, and secondary, with major areas in biology, business computers and information technology, chemistry, English, mathematics, and social studies), English, forensic science, general science, history, human resource management, liberal studies, management, marketing, mathematics, nursing, occupational therapy, philosophy, political science, psychology, social work, sport management, theater, and theology. Students can take double majors in areas that are closely related.

Alvernia University also offers graduate programs leading to the Master of Education, the Master of Business Administration, the Master of Arts in Community Counseling, the Master of Arts in Liberal Studies, the Master of Science in Nursing, and the Master of Occupational Therapy. A Doctor of Philosophy in leadership is also available.

Academic Programs

The academic program is designed to help students to think logically and critically, to comprehend accurately, and to communicate effectively. The University concentrates on the personal development of its students by fostering academic integrity, social responsibility, and moral values. The educational program is based on a commitment to develop the whole person into a responsible individual. Therefore, students not only are required to demonstrate proficiency in those skills demanded by their chosen professional concentration but also are expected to take advantage of the opportunity to grow intellectually and spiritually and to be responsible to themselves and to society.

The Honors Program invites qualified students into an enhanced academic experience. Opportunities include a First Year Honors seminar; service opportunities; intellectual and social support; summer internships in Washington, D.C.; and a variety of imaginative courses. Honors students complete at least three Honors courses plus a senior thesis.

To earn a bachelor's degree, students must complete a minimum of 123 credits, with 54 credits in the liberal arts. Additional requirements vary according to the major program.

Academic Facilities

Alvernia's library facility holds more than 100,000 volumes, including reference works, books for general circulation, and bound periodicals. The library currently subscribes to 400 periodicals covering all areas of study taught at the University, and more than 1,440 volumes of back issues are in the microfilm collection. The library also houses the Audio-Visual Center, which has 23,000 pieces of audiovisual material, including more than 4,750 music records and scores.

A new science wing opened in fall 2006 and houses several modern laboratories for science majors and research facilities for psychology majors. Nursing students have practice clinics featuring current medical equipment and life-sized computer-driven patient simulators.

Costs

For 2009–10, the basic tuition fee was $23,900; room and board were $9126.

Financial Aid

More than 99 percent of the students attending Alvernia receive some type of financial aid. The types of aid most commonly received are Pennsylvania Higher Education Assistance Agency grants for

Pennsylvania residents, Federal Pell Grants, and numerous scholarships from private sources, as well as grants and scholarships from the University itself. This aid is awarded on the basis of academic performance and financial need. The deadline for application for Alvernia University aid is April 1. In addition, Alvernia participates in the federally funded Federal Work-Study Program. Student loans are also available.

Faculty

The faculty consists of 89 full-time and 190 part-time members, each dedicated to teaching and serving the needs of every student. The faculty is as diversified as the many fields of interest that its members represent. Alvernia faculty members publish widely in professional journals and other media; they present papers and moderate conferences in the region and as far away as India, Italy, Mexico, and South Africa; and they serve on boards and committees of professional associations and corporate and community boards. The use of such faculty members is intended to enhance the theoretical portions of professional training with practical professional knowledge.

Student Government

The Student Government Association (SGA) provides an opportunity for individual leadership and development while also determining, in cooperation with the administration and faculty, suitable standards for University and community life. SGA leaders, elected annually by the student body, are responsible for maintaining the student voice when issues on campus arise. Other duties include activities such as social events, a speakers series, and club activities. The SGA also acts as an intermediary between the administration, the faculty, and the student body and maintains order on campus by proposing rules and regulations for the welfare of the University community. It is composed of a president, vice president, secretary, treasurer, and chief justice elected by the student body and is augmented by 2 representatives from each class.

Admission Requirements

Admission requirements normally include a high school diploma with 16 Carnegie units in the following subjects: English, 4 units; mathematics, 2 units; science, 2 units; social studies, 2 units; and modern languages, 2 units. The remaining units may be made up of academic electives. The University is willing to consider good students whose preparation does not include all of these subjects. Nursing students must fulfill the admission requirements established by the Pennsylvania State Board of Nurse Examiners. The State High School Equivalency Diploma is generally recognized as fulfilling the minimum entrance requirements. Applicants to the freshman class are required to take the SAT; the ACT is also acceptable. Outstanding candidates are considered for entrance to Alvernia at the end of their junior year of high school on the basis of requests made by the candidate and the high school. With the approval of their school officials, students may also be admitted to certain courses during their senior year in high school, simultaneously earning credit toward the high school diploma and a college degree.

Application and Information

Applicants should submit an application for admission and enclose the nonrefundable $25 processing fee. The application form may be obtained from the Office of Admissions or from the University's Web site. Applicants should have an official copy of their high school record sent to the Office of Admissions, along with the official results of the SAT or ACT.

A personal interview, while not required, is often desirable for the prospective student. All interested students and their families are invited to visit Alvernia for a tour of the campus and a personal interview with a member of the Admissions Office staff. It is advisable to make an appointment by mail or phone at least one week in advance. The University reserves the right to request an interview if certain aspects of an application need clarification.

Because Alvernia has a rolling admission policy, an applicant is notified of acceptance by the Director of Admissions shortly after the necessary credentials are on file and have been reviewed, generally within one month of the time an application has been completed. To reserve a place in the freshman class, all students must make a $300 deposit by May 1. This deposit is credited to the student's account for the first semester but is not refunded if the student fails to attend. Transfer students should have a grade point average of 2.0 or higher on a 4.0 scale and should be aware that only grades of C or better are eligible for credit transfer. Alvernia accepts a maximum of 75 transfer credits; at least 45 credits that are required for graduation must be earned at Alvernia and must satisfy all graduation requirements. A detailed analysis of credits to be transferred is done only after students have been accepted by the University. For more information or to schedule a visit, students should contact:

Director of Admissions
Alvernia University
Reading, Pennsylvania 19607
Phone: 888-ALVERNIA (258-3764, toll-free)
Fax: 610-790-2873
E-mail: admissions@alvernia.edu
Web site: http://www.alvernia.edu

Friends outside historic Francis Hall on Alvernia's peaceful, tree-lined campus.

COLLEGE CLOSE-UPS

AMERICAN UNIVERSITY

WASHINGTON, D.C.

The University

At American University (AU) in Washington, D.C., students learn from award-winning authors, policymakers, artists, scholars and researchers, filmmakers, lawyers, scientists, and journalists. AU faculty members are both leaders in their fields and committed teachers, and 94 percent have the highest degree in their fields. AU's faculty provides students with the necessary balance between theory and practice with the nation's capital serving as their laboratory for learning. An AU education is more than just what students learn—it's what they do with that knowledge. The 6,000-plus undergraduates at AU are active citizens and strive to serve the world around them via hands-on research, internships, community and volunteer service, and study abroad.

AU's students are a microcosm of the world's diversity. From across the United States and more than 140 countries, they share a desire to shape tomorrow's world. AU actively promotes international understanding, and this is reflected in the University's curriculum offerings, its faculty research, and the regular presence of world leaders on campus.

AU students enjoy the convenience of EagleBuck$, a cashless way to pay on and off campus at the area's most popular businesses. A prepaid, stored-value account that is part of the AU identification card, EagleBuck$ are an easy way for students to obtain food, goods, and services 24 hours a day.

Almost all first-year students and a majority of all students live in on-campus housing. The University's seven smoke-free residence halls have been recently renovated and offer a choice of single-sex or coed floors and special interest options, such as an honors floor. Most rooms house 2 students and have two complete sets of furniture and computer network and telephone access points. Laundry and cooking facilities are available on each floor. In conjunction with the installation of new laundry machines throughout the residence halls, AU has implemented a fully computerized laundry service called eSUDS. Students can use a Web application to check if washers and dryers are available in the nearest laundry room. Using the existing EagleBuck$ system, students activate and pay for laundry service by swiping their student ID card through a special laundry room ID reader. When the wash or dry cycle is complete, the student receives notification via e-mail or text message. Because AU is in a residential neighborhood, students have the option of finding an off-campus apartment within walking distance of the campus. Students have a variety of meal plans from which to choose. AU has a main dining room close to the residence halls and many small cafés. On-campus restaurants include Subway, McDonald's, and Einstein Bros. Bagels.

Nonresidential fraternities and sororities, more than 200 student-run organizations, NCAA Division I championship athletics, and intramural and club sports offer students a myriad of ways to get involved.

Location

American University is located in the residential "Embassy Row" neighborhood of Washington, D.C. Nestled among embassies and ambassadorial residences, AU's campus offers a safe, suburban environment with easy access to Washington's countless cultural destinations via the Metrorail subway system. AU is convenient to Ronald Reagan Washington National Airport, Dulles International Airport, and Baltimore/Washington International Airport as well as to Union Station and interstate highways.

Majors and Degrees

The College of Arts and Sciences awards B.A., B.F.A., and B.S. degrees in the arts, education, humanities, sciences, and social sciences through its twenty academic units. Prelaw and premedical programs are also available.

The School of International Service offers a B.A. in international studies or in language and area studies.

The School of Public Affairs offers a B.A. degree in justice, law and society, and political science. The school also offers CLEG, a unique interdisciplinary program that combines courses in communication, law, economics, and government.

The School of Communication is a professional school that offers training in broadcast journalism, communication studies, foreign language and communication media, print journalism, public communication, and film and media arts.

The Kogod School of Business offers the Bachelor of Science in Business Administration (B.S.B.A.), with specializations in accounting, economics, enterprise management, finance, human resource management, international business, international finance, international management, international marketing, management of information technology, and marketing. The school also offers a B.S. in business administration and language and culture studies (BLC) as well as a B.S. in business and music (BAM).

Academic Programs

Students can choose from numerous programs in the arts and humanities, business, education, international studies, public affairs, sciences, social sciences, or preprofessional programs in law and medicine. Students may decide to double major and have the option of constructing their own interdisciplinary major. Students may major in one AU school and minor in another school or college. Most majors offer the option of pursuing a combined bachelor's/master's program. Students do not need to formally declare a major until the end of their sophomore year.

During the first two years, students choose ten classes from more than 150 specially designed courses in the General Education Program, which is designed for all undergraduate students regardless of major or degree program. Aimed at building a strong intellectual foundation, the courses are drawn from five curricular areas: the creative arts, global and multicultural perspectives, international and intercultural experience, social institutions and behavior, and the natural sciences. Students are required to take two courses in each area, the first of which serves as the foundation course while the second is a more specialized course in an approved sequence. These innovative courses are a vital part of students' intellectual and professional preparation. They improve writing and critical-thinking skills; offer new and balanced scholarship on ethical principles, gender, race, class, and culture; and incorporate quantitative and computing skills as appropriate for their field. In addition, all students are required to complete two courses in English composition and one in college-level mathematics.

The educational goals of the College of Arts and Sciences include teaching students to examine Western and non-Western cultures, appreciate scientific inquiry, master written and oral expression, develop the ability to analyze and synthesize information, and build an understanding of the moral and ethical dimensions that underlie decision making. Working with faculty members and professional academic counselors, students select internships and develop courses of study in more than forty majors in the arts, education, humanities, mathematics, performing arts, sciences, and social sciences. The college's strong liberal arts curriculum is enhanced by the educational, social, cultural, artistic, and scientific resources of Washington, D.C. The individual strengths of each department are heightened by students' ability to cross the lines between disciplines—expanding their educational horizons while acquiring the skills and knowledge required for success in graduate-level study or in their chosen careers.

American's School of International Service (SIS) is the largest of its kind in the United States and offers serious students a breadth of study in international relations. Among the Association of Professional Schools of International Affairs (APSIA), AU's SIS has the largest number of students who are women and members of minority groups. It ranks sixth among APSIA schools in number of international students. The international studies program begins with foundation courses and core field courses to provide students with the tools to explore specific areas of study in greater depth. Students select an area of specialization from among Africa, the Americas, Asia, Europe, the Middle East, or Russia and Central Eurasia. Students also select a functional field of concentration in business, comparative and international race relations, international politics, U.S. foreign policy, Islamic studies, global environmental politics, international communication, international development, international economic policy, or peace and conflict resolution. The language and area studies major provides a strong foundation in language and culture courses. Students choose one of four areas: French/Western Europe, German/Western Europe, Spanish/Latin America, or Russian area studies.

Students in the School of Public Affairs are engaged in learning about local, national, and international politics with a focus on public institutions; public policy; crime; justice; and law. These areas frame a comprehensive program that incorporates classroom learning, individualized research projects, relevant field studies, and professional training. Washington's facilities for scholarly research and work opportunities in public affairs are limitless. Students may participate in the school's leadership and summer programs, and they can get involved in the school's Women and Politics, Public Affairs and Advocacy, or Campaign Management institutes.

The goal of the School of Communication (SOC) is to develop professionally trained communicators who are equipped intellectually and ethically to convey the issues of contemporary society. SOC graduates the third-largest number of communication professionals among U.S. institutions. The curriculum benefits from the environment of Washington, D.C., one of the world's major communications centers. The school emphasizes involving students with Washington's communicators and communication facilities. A strong liberal arts curriculum is required to ensure students' abilities to interpret the world around them.

The Kogod School of Business provides students with a solid foundation in business, including the preparation to be responsible citizens and assume leadership roles in a global business economy. Recognized for academic excellence by the *Wall Street Journal*, Kogod is entrepreneurial, relevant to today's markets, and flexible in its strategies. The school offers a business curriculum derived from a multifunctional view of business that emphasizes critical skills and topics such as communication, e-commerce, teamwork, technology, ethics, and global business. Nearly every major U.S. corporation and many multinational firms have a presence in the Washington, D.C., area, providing Kogod students with limitless opportunities to enhance classroom learning through internship experiences.

Off-Campus Programs

Each year, the University's Career Center provides more than 500 students with internship experience in jobs related to their educational and career goals. Such professional training may be with arts organizations, museums, private business, industry, community and social service organizations, or local, state, and federal governments. Full-time faculty members from nearly all University departments serve as program coordinators.

American University administers its own exciting study-abroad program called AU Abroad. Students can study at more than 145 locations in over forty countries around the world. Built into most of these study programs are opportunities for language immersion and to tour the country, meet and talk with national leaders and academicians, and participate in internships and homestays.

Academic Facilities

The University's facilities include a state-of-the-art language resource center, multimedia design and development labs, and science laboratories. The new Katzen Arts Center features more than 130,000 square feet of space for the fine and performing arts. Athletic facilities include a sports center with indoor and outdoor tracks, soccer and intramural fields, an Olympic-size pool, and a state-of-the-art fitness center. There are fourteen classroom buildings, a 50,000-watt broadcast center, and an interdenominational religious center. The library is a member of the OCLC network, which gives students online access to 2,000 other member libraries. Computing resources are delivered by a fiber-optic network with connections throughout campus, including all residence hall rooms, as well as through wireless access for laptops, PDAs, and smartphones.

Costs

Undergraduate tuition and fees for the 2009–10 academic year are $34,456. Room and board costs average $12,930 for the year. There are several installment payment plans.

Financial Aid

AU recognizes academic achievement and potential and offers merit scholarships to approximately 25 percent of each freshman class. These scholarships are not based on financial need, and no separate application forms are required. The scholarships include awards of up to full tuition. Scholarships are also available for transfer students. The University also supports a multimillion-dollar financial assistance program. Families must apply by February 15 for priority consideration. Some 83 percent of all freshmen receive some sort of financial aid.

Faculty

The faculty represents a rich mix of academic and professional training. Its 578 full-time members are nationally and internationally recognized in their fields, and 94 percent have the highest degree in their field. An important part of American's academic program is the integration of practicing professionals into the faculty. The talent pool available in Washington, D.C., is enormous. Students have the opportunity to learn from professionals from such organizations as the World Bank, Discovery Communications, the Associated Press, the National Endowment for the Arts, the John F. Kennedy Center for the Performing Arts, the National Aeronautics and Space Administration, and other private corporations. These faculty members bring a real-world perspective to the classroom experience. The student-faculty ratio is 14:1. The average undergraduate class size is 23 students.

Student Government

The AU Student Government represents all full-time undergraduates. There are also school and college councils.

Admission Requirements

Admission to AU is selective and competitive. Each freshman applicant is reviewed individually, with careful consideration given to the high school record, SAT or ACT scores (with writing), the essay, extracurricular activities, and letters of recommendation. Special emphasis is given to leadership qualities, creative endeavors, volunteerism, and entrepreneurship. The middle 50 percent of admitted students have grade point averages between 3.55 and 4.03 (school reported) and combined SAT scores between 1210 and 1370 or ACT scores between 27 and 31. The University welcomed 372 transfer students in 2008–09. A minimum GPA of 2.5 (on a 4.0 scale) on all university-level work completed is necessary to be considered competitive for admission. Transfer students should visit the University's Web site for more information.

Application and Information

The deadline for early decision freshmen is November 15, with notification made by December 31. The regular decision deadline is January 15. While most freshmen are admitted for the fall semester, students may also apply for summer- or spring-semester entry. Transfer applicants may apply for all three terms. Students should call or visit the University's Web site for application requirements. The University participates in the Common Application program and accepts both the online and paper application forms. The University also hosts its own online application.

Undergraduate Admissions
American University
4400 Massachusetts Avenue, NW
Washington, D.C. 20016-8001
Phone: 202-885-6000
Fax: 202-885-1025
E-mail: admissions@american.edu
Web site: http://www.american.edu/admissions

THE AMERICAN UNIVERSITY OF PARIS

THE AMERICAN UNIVERSITY OF PARIS
knowledge, perspective, understanding

PARIS, FRANCE

The University

Chartered as a liberal arts college in 1962, The American University of Paris (AUP) is today an urban, independent, international university located at the confluence of France, Europe, and the world. The University aims to provide the finest American undergraduate and graduate programs to students from all national, linguistic, and educational backgrounds, and to take its place as a renowned global center for innovative interdisciplinary research.

To that end, the curriculum is discipline-based, comparative, and cross-cultural. Both student learning and faculty research are driven by a desire for excellence, are shaped by AUP's singular geography and demographic diversity, and directed towards critical twenty-first-century issues. AUP offers an innovative pedagogical model integrating classroom learning and hands-on experience that prepares students to master and to make, to reflect and to apply, to analyze and to act.

The University aims to educate its graduates to communicate well in a world of many languages, to think critically about history, culture, the arts, science, politics, business, communication, and society, to develop creative interdisciplinary approaches to important contemporary challenges, to be both technologically and culturally literate in a world of swift-paced change, to understand the ethical imperatives of living in such a world, and to take their places as responsible actors in communities, civil societies, and countries around the globe.

Americans represent about one third of the student body, Europeans from Moscow to London (more than twenty-five countries) another third, and the final third come about evenly from the Middle East, Africa, Asia, and Latin America.

Students have the opportunity to learn and meet other students through a large number of clubs and organizations. Some of the most popular include WhiteMask Theatre club, AUP's award-winning debate club, Model United Nations, Photo Club, and the A'Cappella Choir.

AUP students also manage several student-run publications, including the biweekly student newspaper, *The Planet; Core,* AUP's humanities journal; *Scripta Politica et Economica;* and *Paris/Atlantic,* a journal of creative work.

AUP offers a liberal arts undergraduate curriculum of fourteen majors and thirty-two minors for the Bachelor of Arts and the Bachelor of Science degrees. In addition, five graduate degrees are offered: the Master of Arts in global communication; Master of Arts in international affairs, conflict resolution, and civil society development; Master of Arts in Middle East and Islamic studies; Master of Public Administration in strategic public policy; and Master of Arts in cultural translation. The University's academic excellence, dynamic classroom experience, and genuinely international/multicultural environment have proven important advantages. Many AUP students go on to the finest graduate schools and careers in the United States, Europe, and elsewhere around the world.

AUP students live off campus, many in the beautiful Parisian neighborhoods near the University. The Housing Office helps AUP students find lodging in chambres de bonne (small private rooms generally found on the top floor of older French apartment buildings), with French hosts, or in apartments.

Location

AUP is an urban institution composed of six buildings centrally located in the seventh arrondissement of Paris, on the Left Bank, near the Eiffel Tower and the Seine. All of the landmarks of this historic city are easily reached by foot or public transportation. AUP students and professors take advantage of the urban campus's proximity to some of the world's best cultural and academic offerings.

Majors and Degrees

Undergraduate students at AUP can earn a Bachelor of Arts or a Bachelor of Science degree. Bachelor of Arts degrees are conferred in applied international finance, art history, comparative literature, European and Mediterranean cultures, film studies, French studies, global communications, history and social sciences, information and communication technologies, international business, international economics, international and comparative politics, and psychology.

Students may also elect to double major or minor in another field. Minors include the following: American studies, applied mathematics, applied statistics, art history, cities: architecture and urban culture, classical civilization, comparative literature, comparative European politics, comparative political communications, computer science, critical theory, development studies, European and Mediterranean cultures, film history and theory, film studies, fine arts, French studies, gender studies, global communications, global studies, history, information technology, international business administration, international economics, international journalism, international law, medieval studies, philosophy, psychology, Renaissance studies, social sciences, and theater and performance.

Academic Programs

Students plan their academic career following guidelines established in the AUP catalog and with the help of a faculty adviser. The bachelor's degree requires a minimum of 120 credit hours. Each completed course counts as 1 to 4 credits toward a degree. Every student at AUP follows a general education program that complements the student's work in the major and runs parallel to it over the course of a student's academic trajectory. The general education program, entitled Envisioning a World of Interdependence, requires students to fulfill the following requirements: FirstBridge, a freshman program of two creatively joined courses linked by a reflective seminar (7 credits); 6 credits of English writing and humanities; proficiency and the ability to engage in intellectual discourse in French; one course in natural or physical science and one course in mathematics; two courses (6 credits) in Comparing Worlds Past and Present: Historical and Cross-Cultural

Understandings; and two courses (6 credits) in Mapping the World: Social Experience and Organization.

The English Foundation program was created for students whose mother tongue is not English and who need to improve their English skills, specifically in writing for academic purposes. This is a one- or two-semester curriculum designed to help students integrate into university education in English.

AUP has a fall and spring semester and one summer term.

The Dean's List, which is published at the end of each semester, includes the names of students who have achieved a distinguished level of academic performance. Chapters of the following honor societies exist at the University: Pi Delta Phi (National French Honor Society), Phi Sigma Iota (International Foreign Language Honor Society), Sigma Tau Delta (National English Honor Society), and Omicron Delta Epsilon (International Economics Honor Society).

Off-Campus Programs

AUP students are welcome to spend one or two semesters in an approved AUP study-abroad program such as the College for International Studies (Spain), Emory (Goizueta Business School), Salve Regina, or the Universities of Miami (Florida) and Cape Town (South Africa), and the global campuses of New York University. Individual arrangements are also possible with other universities.

Academic Facilities

The AUP Library houses more than 72,000 books and more than 6,000 print and electronic periodicals. Other databases, as well as a document delivery service, facilitate materials that are not owned by the library.

ARC@AUP (the Academic Resource Center) is a project designed to link technology to the curriculum and to supplement academic support services at AUP. On the ground floor of the Grenelle Building, ARC provides multiple services to students, including library research stations and video production equipment. Peer tutoring services, including the Writing Lab, are also available in the ARC space.

There are five student computer labs containing 100 IBM and Macintosh computers. Students have free e-mail accounts and Internet access as well as use of a variety of software, printers, projectors, and scanners.

Costs

Information on full-time tuition can be found on the Web site (http://www.aup.edu). Part-time students' tuition is determined on a per-credit basis. Students can estimate paying an additional €10,000 per academic year for housing, meals, and books, not including other discretionary spending.

Financial Aid

AUP offers a program of University-funded scholarships and grants that are awarded both on a student's academic strength and the family's financial circumstances. The maximum award in most cases is 50 percent of the tuition; however, there is a limited number of 75-percent tuition AUP Scholar awards. Students with a good record of academic achievement are eligible for academic merit scholarships. Approximately 40 percent of students receive some form of financial aid from the University.

Faculty

The ratio of students to full-time faculty members is 20:1. The faculty is dedicated to both research and teaching. Eighty percent of the full-time faculty members hold doctoral degrees from the world's most distinguished graduate schools. AUP faculty members represent more than fifteen nationalities; all are at least bilingual. All courses are taught by faculty members. AUP does not use teaching assistants for its courses.

Student Government

At the heart of AUP's student activities is the SGA, an elected body of executive officers, class officers, and departmental student representatives. Organized to deal with issues affecting the student body, AUP's strongly vocal SGA holds weekly Senate meetings, represents student needs to the administration, manages the student activities budget, and plans and promotes social events for the AUP community.

Admission Requirements

AUP evaluates applicants based on the breadth of their program of study, their academic record, the results of national examinations, and the evaluation of teachers and counselors. The applicant's written statement of purpose, as well as evidence of his or her maturity, also weighs heavily. Admission interviews, either in person or by telephone, are strongly encouraged.

Application and Information

Undergraduate candidates living in the United States, Canada, Mexico, Central and South America can submit their application to the following U.S. address which will be forwarded to the Paris office:

The American University of Paris
700 North Colorado Boulevard #502
Denver, Colorado 80206
Phone: 303-993-4326
E-mail: admissions@aup.edu
Web site: http://www.aup.edu

All other undergraduate and graduate school candidates should submit their applications to:

International Admissions Office
The American University of Paris
6, rue du Colonel Combes
75007 Paris
France
Phone: 33-1-40-62-07-20
E-mail: admissions@aup.edu
Web site: http://www.aup.edu

COLLEGE CLOSE-UPS

AMRIDGE UNIVERSITY

MONTGOMERY, ALABAMA

The University

Founded in 1967, Amridge University is an independent, coeducational institution dedicated to the spirit of its ideals and Christian heritage. All Amridge University programs are taught from a Christian perspective. Amridge University is one of the nation's leading universities offering distance learning programs and services to adults nationally. Adding to the prestige of the University is its selection by the U.S. Department of Education as one of fifteen initial participants in the Distance Education Demonstration Program. Amridge University worked with the U.S. Department of Education to develop a national model to help chart the future of distance learning.

Accredited by the Southern Association of Colleges and Schools, Amridge University grants associate, bachelor's, master's, and doctoral degrees, all available via a distance learning format. Graduate degrees are awarded in counseling/family therapy, organizational leadership, and religious studies. These degrees foster leadership, counseling and family therapy skills, knowledge, and biblical and Christian ministry skills. The counseling degrees are designed to help prepare students for licensure. Doctoral degrees include Doctor of Ministry and Doctor of Philosophy degrees. These are advanced professional degrees for community organization and church-related vocations, with a concentration designed to prepare participants to counsel families and individuals.

The policy of Amridge University is to provide reasonable accommodation for persons who are handicapped or disabled as designated in Section 504 of the Rehabilitation Act of 1973 and the Americans with Disabilities Act of 1990. Although the Morgan W. Brown building is not equipped with an elevator, the needs of the physically challenged can be met from the first floor. These include registration, counseling, library facilities, classroom facilities, rest rooms, break room facilities, and others. Ample parking is provided.

Location

Amridge University is located in Montgomery, Alabama, the capital city of the state. Strategically located in the central part of the state between Huntsville and Mobile and Atlanta, Georgia, Montgomery is one of the fastest-growing cities in the state and the region. The city is clean and modern, with beautiful residential areas, parks and playgrounds, and fine schools and universities. Students and families can also enjoy its museums, zoo, and facilities of the capitol building.

Montgomery has two major U.S. Air Force installations: Maxwell Air Force Base and Gunter Annex. Maxwell is where the Air War College is located and is a strategic center for education.

The metropolitan area has a population of more than 350,000 citizens. There are many churches and educational institutions. The city has an abundance of good housing in addition to other advantages.

Majors and Degrees

Undergraduate degrees are awarded in Biblical studies, business, homeland security, human development, human resource management, liberal studies, management communication, and public safety and criminal justice. These degrees promote biblical and Christian ministry skills, human development skills, knowledge in the arts, and management communication skills. Amridge University students are fully matriculated students of Amridge University with full student privileges, rights, and responsibilities.

Academic Programs

Amridge University is primarily a distance learning institution, although there are many classes offered on campus. The academic year consists of three semesters: fall, spring, and summer.

A student must fulfill the required semester hours in a major as well as the basic requirements of the core curriculum. All core and major requirements can be received from the University. Amridge University programs have a traditional structure.

Distance education is approved by the Southern Association of Colleges and Schools and the U.S. Department of Education, ensuring that distance education students receive the same high-quality education as on-campus students. Faculty and student services for students on campus are available to distance learners. Amridge University ensures that students have regular contact with faculty and staff members via e-mail and telephone. No residency is required for undergraduates.

In addition to offering distance learning to a diverse array of individuals, Amridge University is a participating member of the GoArmyEd project. This is an online, streamlined process giving soldiers easy access to obtaining funding for their educations.

Academic Facilities

Amridge University sits stately on a 9-acre campus adjoining Interstate 85. A beautiful building houses the administration offices, classrooms, and Library Resource Center.

Costs

Undergraduate tuition per semester hour is $300.

Financial Aid

Aid from institutionally generated funds is provided on the basis of academic merit, financial need, and other criteria. A limited number of scholarships are available. Priority is given to early applicants.

Federal funding available for undergraduates includes Federal Pell Grants, Federal Supplemental Educational Opportunity Grants (FSEOG), Academic Competitiveness Grant (ACG), the

SMART Grant, the Federal Work-Study Program, and FFEL subsidized and unsubsidized loans. Eighty percent of students receive financial aid.

Faculty

The instructional faculty members total approximately 100. Approximately 65 percent of the full-time faculty members hold doctoral degrees, 100 percent hold master's degrees, and 100 percent hold terminal degrees. Faculty members specialize in their areas and have exceptional training in distance learning delivery.

Student Government

Student volunteers serve as members of the Student Advisory Committee. Volunteers are appointed by the Student Services Team, with recommendations from the deans. The committee meets on a regular term basis and is reorganized on a yearly basis. Concerns, recommendations, and requests are presented directly from the committee to the appropriate University area.

Admission Requirements

Amridge University is open to all persons who are of good character and who are academically qualified. The University has developed a streamlined admissions process to help potential students complete the process in a timely manner so they can begin their studies. As new technologies and processes become available, Amridge University makes every effort to adopt and use the latest technologies to help the admissions process. Transfer students in good academic standing are invited to apply to Amridge University. Prospective students must submit a $75 nonrefundable fee along with the completed application for admission.

Application and Information

For further information, students may contact:

Carl Byrd
Amridge University
1200 Taylor Road
Montgomery, Alabama 36117
Phone: 334-387-7569
800-351-4040 Ext. 7569 (toll-free)
Fax: 334-387-3878
E-mail: carlbyrd@amridgeuniversity.edu
Web site: http://www.amridgeuniversity.edu

COLLEGE CLOSE-UPS

ARCADIA UNIVERSITY

GLENSIDE, PENNSYLVANIA

The University

Arcadia is a top-ranked private university offering bachelor's, master's, and doctoral degrees. Over 3,900 students choose from among seventy-five fields of study. *U.S. News & World Report* ranks Arcadia University among the top 25 master's universities in the North. Arcadia's diverse student population represents a cross section of cultural and socioeconomic backgrounds. Enrollment includes 2,200 undergraduate and 1,700 graduate students. At present, Arcadia students come from forty-six states and nineteen other countries, and 80 percent of the full-time undergraduate population resides on campus.

Arcadia was ranked first in the nation for the percentage of undergraduate students studying abroad in the 2008 *Open Doors* report and has an extensive study-abroad program. Students can choose from over 100 programs in more than fourteen countries.

Campus life, including more than forty-five clubs and organizations, athletics, and cultural and social events, is rich and varied. Community service is an integral part of the Arcadia University experience. Students volunteer on neighborhood improvement projects, work at literacy or gerontology centers, and assist disadvantaged or disabled children. NCAA Division III intercollegiate competition is offered in basketball, field hockey, lacrosse, soccer, softball, swimming, tennis, and volleyball for women and baseball, basketball, golf, soccer, swimming, and tennis for men. Cheerleading, men's lacrosse, and equestrian are offered as club sports, while intramural sports offer other athletic opportunities.

Arcadia offers master's programs in the fields of business administration, counseling psychology, education, English, forensic science, genetic counseling, health education, humanities, international peace and conflict resolution, international relations and diplomacy, physician assistant, and public health. Doctor of Physical Therapy (D.P.T.) and Doctor of Education (Ed.D.) in special education degrees are also offered.

Location

Arcadia, located in metropolitan Philadelphia, features a beautiful rolling campus built around the historic landmark Grey Towers Castle. The University is 12 miles from Center City Philadelphia and only 90 minutes from the Jersey shore and Pennsylvania's Pocono Mountains. Students have access to dozens of museums, galleries, performing arts centers, and nightspots; and historic, government, and commercial sites in the metropolitan area.

Majors and Degrees

Arcadia offers Bachelor of Arts degrees in accounting, acting, art (art history, pre–art therapy, studio art), biology (allied health, biological basis of behavior, biomedical, conservation, forensics, molecular), business administration (economics, international economics, international human resources, international marketing, management, marketing), chemistry (biochemistry, chemical professions, forensics, health professions), communications (cinema studies, corporate, international cinema, print, video), computer science, computing technology (design, technical), criminal justice, digital media/global media, education (elementary and early childhood, elementary, secondary), English (creative writing, professional writing), fashion studies, fine arts (art education, ceramics, graphic design, interior design, metals and jewelry, painting, photography, pre–art therapy, printmaking), global legal studies, health administration, history, interdisciplinary science, international business and culture, international studies (globalization, development and human rights, modern Mediterranean world, global public health), Italian studies, liberal studies (applied social science for the global citizen, individualized), management information systems, mathematics (actuarial science), media industries, modern languages, philosophy, political science (international politics, prelaw and political theory, U.S. politics and policy), psychology (pre–art therapy, human resources), scientific illustration, sociology, sound and music, Spanish, Spanish cultural studies, sport psychology, and theater arts and English. Bachelor of Science degrees are offered in accounting, business administration, chemistry, chemistry and business, computer science, international finance, management information systems, marketing, and mathematics. Bachelor of Fine Arts degrees are awarded to students majoring in acting or studio arts with concentrations in ceramics, graphic design, interior design, metals and jewelry, painting, photography, and printmaking. Preparation for certification in art education is offered in conjunction with the B.F.A. program, as is preparation for graduate study in art therapy. A five-year program combines the Bachelor of Arts in education with a Master of Education in special education.

Arcadia's physician assistant studies 4+2 program provides a four-year undergraduate degree in a related field, followed by two years of study in the Master of Medical Science: Physician Assistant Program at Arcadia. Arcadia undergraduates who satisfy the prerequisites are assured admission to the program. The University also offers a combined undergraduate and graduate (4+2.5) program leading to the Doctor of Physical Therapy, with assured admission for undergraduates who meet established criteria. The International Peace and Conflict Resolution Program provides a four-year undergraduate degree followed by two years of study in the Master of Arts in international peace and conflict resolution. The forensic science program provides a four-year undergraduate program in a related field followed by two years in the Master of Science in Forensic Science (M.S.F.S.) program.

Arcadia offers several five-year programs in education. These include degrees in special education, environmental education, literacy education/reading, literacy education/ESL, technology education, and library science. There also are secondary education certificates available in biology, chemistry, English, mathematics, general science, social studies, and art education.

A dual-degree (3+2) program in engineering is offered in conjunction with Columbia University. An accelerated (3+4) program with Salus University leads to Bachelor of Arts and Doctor of Optometry degrees. A 3+2 program in environmental education leads to a B.A. in biology and a Master of Arts in Education in environmental education. Preprofessional preparation is offered for dentistry, law, medicine, nursing, optometry, veterinary medicine, and other areas.

Academic Programs

Arcadia's new undergraduate curriculum provides a distinctively global, integrative, and personal learning experience that prepares students to contribute and prosper in a diverse and dynamic world. Students are encouraged to design their own path, explore the globe, make intellectual connections, and develop an area of expertise. There are opportunities to study around the world and make connections across disciplines and cultures. Every student pursues a major, participates in cultural experiences, explores areas of inquiry, and develops intellectual practices.

Highly qualified students may enhance their education through the Honors Program, which merges the best of the University's academic traditions with innovative honors courses. The program also features a special experience in Greece. Admission to the Honors Program may occur at the time of acceptance to the University, or after the student has been enrolled at the University for one or more semesters.

Credit toward graduation is granted for scores of 3 or better on Advanced Placement examinations. Exemption from or credit for courses may also be earned through the College-Level Examination Program (CLEP) and locally administered examinations at the discretion of the department concerned.

Arcadia's academic year is divided into two semesters. Three summer sessions are offered, beginning in May and continuing through early August. Most full-time students carry four academic courses in each regular semester; 128 semester hours are required for graduation.

Off-Campus Programs

Arcadia's College of Global Studies, top-ranked in the nation by *U.S. News & World Report,* has one of the largest campus-based international study programs in the U.S. With more than 100 programs around the world, the College of Global Studies supports and implements the University's commitment to international education. Students can spend a summer, semester, or full year abroad for approximately the same cost as remaining on the Glenside campus.

Arcadia offers two distinct opportunities for students to study abroad during their first year of college. The University's London/Scotland/Spain Preview program enables first-year students in good academic standing to spend their spring break in London, Scotland, or Spain for just $495, which includes round-trip airfare, accommodations, and programming. The unique First Year Study Abroad Experience (FY-SAE) gives select incoming students the chance to spend their first or second semester in London or Scotland. Arcadia's First Year Study Abroad Experience and Preview programs have been recognized as among the most innovative international programs in the country by the American Council on Education, *U.S. News & World Report,* and *The Princeton Review.*

In 2007, Arcadia introduced Majors Abroad Programs (MAPs). Students in these majors spend a year (two semesters) abroad, taking general courses as well as major-related courses at an overseas institution.

Off-campus study in the Philadelphia area includes internships and fieldwork in most majors. The University requires students to partake in a global connections experience, which may occur overseas, through a domestic study-away program or locally.

Academic Facilities

The campus includes historical buildings as well as extensive modern facilities. A prime academic resource on Arcadia's campus is Landman Library, which offers students increased technology and access to resources both on campus and around the globe. The newly opened Easton Hall features classrooms with the latest technology, a café, and an outdoor patio and waterfall, which make great places for students, faculty, and staff to interact.

Wireless Internet access is available everywhere on campus and extends to each room in the residence halls. Computer labs—including a Mac lab—are available for student use.

Costs

Tuition for 2009–10 is $30,780. Student fees are $480 per year. Room and board charges are $10,680 per year. Books and supplies for most students cost between $300 to $500 per semester.

Financial Aid

On average, 96 percent of full-time undergraduates receive financial aid, and 95 percent receive grants and scholarships. Every effort is made to see that students requiring financial assistance are able to attend Arcadia. Aid is awarded on the basis of need, as determined by the Free Application for Federal Student Aid (FAFSA) and the Arcadia University Financial Aid Application, and is available in the form of grants, loans, and part-time campus employment or some combination of the three. Scholarships are presented annually to entering first-year and transfer students who have achieved academic distinction or have been recognized for outstanding extracurricular accomplishments. Distinguished Scholarships, ranging from $54,000 to $72,000 over four years, and Achievement Awards, ranging from $4000 to $52,000 over four years, recognize academic excellence, leadership, and extracurricular accomplishments. A limited number of full-tuition scholarships are available to the top entering first-year undergraduates in the applicant pool. To receive full consideration for financial aid, students should complete their applications and submit the FAFSA and the Arcadia University Financial Aid Application by March 1.

A financial aid calculator for students considering full-time undergraduate enrollment is available at http://www.arcadia.edu/calculator. This calculator gives students the chance to estimate their eligibility for federal, state, and Arcadia University financial aid (including merit scholarships).

Faculty

Arcadia University has a faculty with a primary commitment to teaching. The average class size is 16 students, and the ratio of students to faculty members is 13:1. This fosters an environment in which students and faculty members collaborate on research and writing and engage in informal discussions, field trips, and other activities outside the classroom. Ninety-five percent of Arcadia faculty members hold doctorates or terminal degrees, and all courses are taught by faculty members, not graduate assistants.

Student Government

Student life is largely self-regulated by the Student Government Organization (SGO) through the Student Senate. Students serve on most major faculty committees, and student leaders attend Board of Trustees meetings.

Admission Requirements

Students are selected on the basis of educational preparation, intellectual promise, and potential. Enrollment Management staff members review each candidate's credentials. Emphasis is placed on the candidate's academic record, including the type of program followed and the grades and class rank earned. Standardized test scores, counselor and teacher recommendations, participation in school and community activities, and other supporting credentials also are considered.

Freshman applicants must submit an official high school transcript, standardized test scores (SAT or ACT), and counselor and teacher recommendations. Applicants should pursue a college-preparatory program, usually consisting of 16 academic units. Early admission, deferred admission, and advanced placement are available. Students are encouraged to visit the campus for an admissions interview and a student-guided tour.

Transfer applicants may apply for the fall term or at midyear and must submit official college transcripts. In some cases, transfer applicants are required to submit high school transcripts and SAT or ACT scores.

Application and Information

Students are encouraged to submit their applications as early as possible in the senior year. Admission decisions are made on a rolling basis, and applicants are usually notified within four to six weeks of the date of submission of the completed application. For freshman applicants, the priority admissions application deadline for Distinguished Scholarship consideration is January 15. The priority admissions application deadline for Achievement Award consideration is March 1. The admissions application deadline is also March 1. The transfer student deadline for portfolio review, Honors Program, Distinguished Scholarship consideration, and priority admissions is June 15 for fall-term admission.

Requests for further information should be directed to:

Office of Enrollment Management
Arcadia University
450 South Easton Road
Glenside, Pennsylvania 19038-3295
Phone: 215-572-2910
877-ARCADIA (877-272-2342, toll-free)
E-mail: admiss@arcadia.edu
Web site: http://www.arcadia.edu/pet.asp

Grey Towers Castle, Arcadia University.

COLLEGE CLOSE-UPS

ARGOSY UNIVERSITY

ARGOSY UNIVERSITY

The University

Argosy University is a postsecondary institution of higher education offering a variety of degree programs that focus on the human side of success alongside professional competence. For students looking for a more personal approach to education, Argosy University may just be the answer. Drawing upon over thirty years of history, Argosy University has developed a curriculum that focuses on interpersonal skills and practical experience alongside academic learning. Argosy's programs are taught by practicing professionals who bring real-world experience into the classroom. Students graduate with both a solid foundation of knowledge and the power to put it to work. To accommodate busy working adults, many programs at Argosy University have a flexible structure, with both campus and online learning, and evening, weekend, and daytime classes. There are also financial aid options available for students who qualify.

Argosy University is a private institution of higher education dedicated to providing quality professional education programs at the doctoral, master's, bachelor's, and associate degree levels as well as continuing education to individuals who seek to enhance their professional and personal lives. The University emphasizes programs in the behavioral sciences (psychology and counseling), business, education, and the health-care professions. A limited number of preprofessional programs and general education offerings are provided to permit students to prepare for entry into these professional fields. The programs of Argosy University are designed to instill the knowledge, skills, and ethical values of professional practice and to foster values of social responsibility in a supportive, learning-centered environment of mutual respect and professional excellence.

With nineteen campuses nationwide, Argosy University provides students with a network of resources found at larger universities, including a career resources office, an academic resources center, and extensive information access for research. The University's innovative programs feature dynamic, relevant, and practical curricula delivered in flexible class formats. Students enjoy scheduling options that make it easier to fit school into their busy lives. They can choose from day and evening courses, on campus or online. Many students find a combination of both to be an ideal way of continuing their education while meeting family and professional demands.

Most students are full-time working professionals who live within driving distance of the campus. The University does not offer or operate student housing.

Argosy University is accredited by the Higher Learning Commission of the North Central Association and is a member of the North Central Association (30 North LaSalle Street, Suite 2400, Chicago, Illinois 60602; phone: 800-621-7440; Web site: http://ncahlc.org).

Location

Argosy University operates nineteen locations across the U.S. and offers a variety of degree programs online (http://www.argosy.edu). Campus locations include the following:

Atlanta, 980 Hammond Drive, Suite 100, Atlanta, Georgia 30328; phone: 770-671-1200 or 888-671-4777 (toll-free)

Chicago, 225 North Michigan Avenue, Suite 1300, Chicago, Illinois 60601; phone: 312-777-7600 or 800-626-4123 (toll-free)

Dallas, 5001 Lyndon B. Johnson Freeway, Heritage Square, Farmers Branch, Texas 75244; phone: 214-890-9900 or 866-954-9900 (toll-free)

Denver, 7600 E. Eastman Avenue, Denver, Colorado 80231; phone: 303-248-2700 or 866-431-5981 (toll-free)

Hawai'i, 400 ASB Tower, 1001 Bishop Street, Honolulu, Hawaii 96813; phone: 808-536-5555 or 888-323-2777 (toll-free)

Inland Empire, 636 East Brier Drive, Suite 120, San Bernardino, California 92408; phone: 909-915-3800 or 866-217-9075 (toll-free)

Los Angeles, 5230 Pacific Concourse, Suite 200, Los Angeles, California 90045; phone: 310-866-4000 or 866-505-0332 (toll-free)

Nashville, 100 Centerview Drive, Suite 225, Nashville, Tennessee 37214; phone: 615-525-2800 or 866-833-6598 (toll-free)

Orange County, 601 South Lewis Street, Orange County, California 92868; phone: 714-620-3700 or 800-716-9598 (toll-free)

Phoenix, 2233 West Dunlap Avenue, Phoenix, Arizona 85021; phone: 602-216-2600 or 866-216-2777 (toll-free)

Salt Lake City, 121 Election Road, Suite 300, Draper, Utah 84020; phone: 801-601-5000 or 888-639-4756 (toll-free)

San Diego, 1615 Murray Canyon Road, Suite 100, San Diego, California 92108; phone: 619-321-3000 or 866-505-0333 (toll-free)

San Francisco Bay Area, 1005 Atlantic Avenue, Alameda, California 94501; phone: 510-217-4700 or 866-215-2777 (toll-free)

Sarasota, 5250 17th Street, Sarasota, Florida 34235; phone: 941-379-0404 or 800-331-5995 (toll-free)

Schaumburg, 999 North Plaza Drive, Suite 111, Schaumburg, Illinois 60173-5403; phone: 847-969-4900 or 866-290-2777 (toll-free)

Seattle, 2601-A Elliott Avenue, Seattle, Washington 98121; phone: 206-283-4500 or 888-283-2777 (toll-free)

Tampa, 1403 North Howard Avenue, Tampa, Florida 33607; phone: 813-393-5290 or 800-850-6488 (toll-free).

Twin Cities, 1515 Central Parkway, Eagan, Minnesota 55121; phone: 651-846-2882 or 888-844-2004 (toll-free)

Washington, D.C., 1550 Wilson Boulevard, Suite 600, Arlington, Virginia 22209; phone: 703-526-5800 or 866-703-2777 (toll-free)

Argosy University is certified by SCHEV to operate in Virginia.

Argosy University, Nashville is authorized for operation as a postsecondary educational institution by the Tennessee Higher Education Commission.

Majors and Degrees

Argosy University's College of Undergraduate Studies offers Bachelor of Arts (B.A.) programs in liberal arts and psychology as well as Bachelor of Science (B.S.) programs in business administration and criminal justice. Please note that not all degree programs are offered at all locations.

Academic Programs

The Bachelor of Arts (B.A.) in liberal arts program offers an integrative approach to learning which aims to develop competencies in the basic academic areas and disciplines in higher education. It extends the capacity for intellectual inquiry through the incorporation of courses that develop the individual, prepare them for the workplace, and for constructive participation in a global society. The B.A. in liberal arts gives students the opportunity to integrate real world experience with the critical acquisition of a variety of human knowledge and skills that not only encourages sensitivity to the diversity of human cultures, but also creates a desire to achieve personal and professional excellence.

The Bachelor of Arts (B.A.) in psychology program is designed to prepare students to begin a human services career as an entry-level counselor, case manager, or human resources administrator or in management and business services, as well as for graduate study in fields such as counseling, social work, and marriage and family therapy. The program is flexible enough to allow students to pursue opportunities offered by a number of states for credentialing or certification at the bachelor's level.

The Bachelor of Science (B.S.) in business administration degree program is designed to help students focus their academic and professional development consistent with their career objectives and experiences. In addition to the business core, students complete one of the following concentrations: accounting, finance, health-care management, human resources, international business, marketing, and organizational management. Students may choose one of five optional concentrations: customized professional concentration, finance, health-care management, international business, or marketing.

The Bachelor of Science (B.S.) in criminal justice is a practitioner-oriented program that prepares students to become successful professionals in the fields of law enforcement, corrections, probation and parole, and security. The curriculum provides students with critical thinking, communication, research, and professional skills that contribute to career development. In addition to core course work, students will complete two of seven optional concentrations: corrections, forensic psychology, homeland security, management, police, security management, and substance abuse.

Argosy University's bachelor's degree programs are open to students and working professionals with no college experience and those who have attended a community college, junior college, or other university.

Program offerings vary by school.

Academic Facilities

Argosy University libraries provide curriculum support and educational resources including current text materials, diagnostic training documents, reference materials and databases, journals and dissertations, and major and current titles in program areas. There is an online public-access catalog of library resources available throughout the Argosy University system. Students enjoy full remote access to their campus library database, enabling them to study and conduct research at home. Academic databases offer dissertation abstracts, academic journals, and professional periodicals. All library computers are Internet accessible. Software applications include Word, Excel, PowerPoint, SPSS, and various test-scoring programs.

Costs

Tuition varies by program. Students should contact the Argosy University campus of their choice for tuition information.

Financial Aid

Financial aid options are available to students who qualify. Argosy University offers access to federal and state aid programs, merit-based awards, grants, loans, and a work-study program. As a first step, students should complete the Free Application for Federal Student Aid (FAFSA). Prospective students can apply electronically at http://www.fafsa.ed.gov or at the campus. To receive consideration for financial aid and ensure timely receipt of funds, it is best to submit an application promptly.

Faculty

The Argosy University faculty is composed of working professionals who have a passion to help students succeed. Members bring real-world experience and the latest practice innovations to the academic setting. The diverse faculty is widely recognized for contributions to the field. Most hold doctoral degrees. They provide a substantive education that combines comprehensive knowledge with critical skills and practical workplace relevance. Above all, faculty members are committed to their students' personal and professional development.

Student Government

Argosy University campuses offer unique opportunities for student involvement beyond individual programs of study. Most faculty committees include a student representative. In addition, a student group meets with faculty members and administrators regularly to discuss pertinent campus-related issues.

Admission Requirements

Admission requirements differ depending on the number of college credits completed prior to application.

Students who have earned 12 or fewer semester college credits must provide proof of high school graduation or GED and meet one of the following conditions for admission: ACT composite score of 18 or above, or a combined math and verbal SAT score of 870, or minimum ACCUPLACER scores of 86 in sentence skills and 53 in algebra. Applicants who do not meet any of the above conditions for admission will be admitted with academic support if they provide proof of high school graduation or GED and meet one of the following: ACT composite score of 14 to 17, or a combined math and verbal SAT score of 660 to 869, or minimum ACCUPLACER scores of 54 in sentence skills and 36 in arithmetic.

Applicants who have earned 13 or more semester college credits must provide proof of high school graduation or GED and meet one of the following conditions for admission: cumulative college GPA of 2.0 or above or minimum ACCUPLACER scores of 86 for sentence skills and 53 in algebra. Students who do not meet either of the above criteria will be admitted with academic support if they provide proof of high school graduation or GED and meet the following condition: minimum ACCUPLACER scores of 54 in reading and 36 in arithmetic.

Students admitted with academic support are limited to 12 credit hours of study during their first semester (6 credit hours per session). Students admitted with academic support will be required to complete developmental English and/or math courses unless they meet the following conditions: Writing Review (ENG099)—must meet one of the following: a minimum ACCUPLACER score of 86 in sentence skills, or a minimum ACT verbal score of 18, or a minimum SAT verbal score of 425, or completion of a college-level English composition course with a grade of C or above; Mathematics Review I (MAT096)—must meet one of the following: a minimum ACCUPLACER score of 53 in algebra, or a minimum ACT math score of 18, or a minimum SAT math score of 440, or completion of a college-level English composition course with a grade of C or above.

Other admission requirements may include credit hours of qualified transfer credit with a grade of C- or better from a regionally accredited institution or a nationally accredited institution approved and documented by the faculty and dean of the College of Business, or the College of Professional Psychology, at Argosy University or completion of an Associate of Arts or Associate of Science degree from a regionally accredited institution. A maximum of 78 lower-division or 90 total credit hours may be transferred. A minimum written TOEFL score of 500 (paper-based test), 173 (computer-based test), or 61 (Internet-based test) is required for all applicants whose native language is not English or who have not graduated from an institution in which English is the language of instruction.

Official transcripts from approved postsecondary institutions must include a minimum grade point average of 2.0 (on a scale of 4.0) for all academic work completed. Exceptions may be made for extenuating circumstances. All applications must include a completed application form, proof of high school graduation or successful completion of the GED test, official postsecondary transcripts, and a nonrefundable (except in California) application fee. Additional materials are required prior to matriculation. Some programs have additional application requirements or include exceptions to admission requirements. An admissions representative can provide further information.

Please refer to the University's catalog for additional information.

Application and Information

Argosy University accepts students on a rolling admissions basis year-round, depending on availability of required courses. Applications for admission are available online at http://www.argosy.edu or by contacting one of the campus locations.

Argosy University Administrative Office
Phone: 800-377-0617 (toll-free)
Web site: http://www.argosy.edu

THE ART INSTITUTE OF ATLANTA

ATLANTA, GEORGIA

At The Art Institute of Atlanta, students are given the opportunity to learn new ways to apply talent, energy, and skill in the creative arts. The school seeks to provide a curriculum that integrates conceptual and analytical skills with education to prepare students to pursue entry-level employment in the creative arts.

The Art Institute of Atlanta offers fifteen bachelor's degree programs and seven associate degree options to students. Assistance is available to help students with resume writing, networking, and keeping abreast of what employers are looking for in job candidates.

Students come to The Art Institute of Atlanta from across the United States and abroad. The student population includes recent high school graduates, transfer students, and those who have left a previous employment situation to study and train for a new career. Students are creative, competitive, and open to new ideas. They place great value on an education that prepares them to pursue an exciting entry-level position in the arts.

The Art Institute of Atlanta, including its satellite campus and its branch campuses—The Art Institute of Atlanta–Decatur, The Art Institute of Charleston, The Art Institute of Tennessee–Nashville, The Art Institute of Virginia Beach, The Art Institute of Washington, and The Art Institute of Washington–Northern Virginia—is accredited by the Commission on Colleges of the Southern Association of Colleges and Schools to award associate and baccalaureate degrees. Contact the Commission on Colleges at 1866 Southern Lane, Decatur, Georgia 30033-4097 or call 404-679-4500 for questions about the accreditation of The Art Institute of Atlanta.

The Associate in Arts degree in culinary arts and the Bachelor of Science degree in culinary arts management programs at The Art Institute of Atlanta are accredited by the Accrediting Commission of the American Culinary Federation Education Foundation.

The interior design program leading to the Bachelor of Fine Arts degree is accredited by the Council for Interior Design Accreditation, 206 Grandville Avenue, Suite 350, Grand Rapids, Michigan 49503; http://www.accredit-id.org.

The Art Institute of Atlanta is an accredited institutional member of the National Association of Schools of Art and Design (NASAD).

The Art Institute of Atlanta is licensed by the Georgia Nonpublic Postsecondary Education Commission, 2082 East Exchange Place, Suite 220, Tucker, Georgia 30084.

Location

Located in bustling suburban Atlanta, the school is close to public transportation and within walking distance of a shopping center with movie theaters, several restaurants, and stores. One of the city's largest malls is less than a 10-minute drive—or one subway stop from The Art Institute of Atlanta. There are at least thirty restaurants within a 15-minute drive. Students enjoy clubs and concerts, galleries and museums, baseball games, and rollerblading in Piedmont Park. The High Museum of Art, Michael C. Carlos Museum, Atlanta Contemporary Art Center, and dozens of art galleries throughout the city are wonderful resources for creative-minded students.

Programs of Study and Degrees

The Art Institute of Atlanta offers bachelor's degree programs in advertising, audio production, culinary arts management, digital filmmaking and video production, fashion and retail management, food and beverage management, game art and design, graphic design, illustration, interior design, media arts and animation, photographic imaging, visual and game programming, visual effects and motion graphics, and Web design and interactive media.

Associate in Arts degree programs are offered in culinary arts; culinary arts with a concentration in baking and pastry; graphic design; photographic imaging; video production; Web design and interactive media; and wine, spirits, and beverage management.

Diploma programs are offered in advertising design, commercial photography, culinary arts–baking and pastry, culinary arts–skills, digital design, residential interiors, video skills, and Web design.

The culinary arts, culinary arts management, food and beverage management, graphic design, interior design, and Web design and interactive media programs are available in an evening and weekend option format.

Academic Programs

The academic year of The Art Institute of Atlanta is divided into four quarters that begin in January, April, July, and October. Full-time students typically take 16 academic credits per quarter. An associate degree can be earned in as little as six to seven quarters (approximately two years), and a bachelor's degree can be earned in as little as twelve quarters (three to four years). Students may take online classes in order to earn a degree on a flexible schedule, or they may take online classes as a supplement to traditional classroom learning.

Academic Facilities

Facilities at The Art Institute of Atlanta are concentrated in two buildings for easy access. There are Mac and PC computer labs for student use. Specialty labs and studios include a digital editing lab, digital imaging lab, wet photo lab, audio lab, photography studio, video studio, and control room. The school offers art labs, figure and still-life drawing studios, drafting labs, classrooms wired for Internet access, a conference room, and meeting rooms. The Art Institute of Atlanta library holds more than 40,000 items, including books, videotapes, DVDs, CDs, more than 40 online full-text databases, and access to libraries at other local colleges and universities. The Interior Design Department has a special resource library.

Culinary arts students learn in professional teaching kitchens. Creations Dining Lab, the teaching dining room of the culinary arts program, allows students to gain hands-on experience similar to what they'll experience in the real world. Students work under the skilled direction of chef instructors to create lunch and dinner for restaurant patrons.

The Gallery, located on the first floor, is a noncommercial exhibition space that reflects and exemplifies the artwork of professionals, faculty members, students, and graduates in their professional fields. The gallery's goals are to inspire and challenge students through examples of accomplished artists, to provide opportunities to increase public awareness of The Art Institute of Atlanta and its importance in the art community, and to enrich the learning community at the school through exhibitions that demonstrate high levels of excellence.

Costs

Tuition cost varies by program. Prospective students should contact the school for current tuition costs. Other charges include a starting kit for all first-quarter students. Kits vary in price depending on the program of study.

Financial Aid

Financial aid is available for those who qualify. Students who require financial assistance should first complete and submit a Free Application for Federal Student Aid (FAFSA) and meet with a financial aid officer.

Faculty

The Art Institute of Atlanta faculty includes full-time and part-time instructors with professional experience in their respective fields. Faculty members pride themselves on building close personal relationships with students. Most maintain an informal open-door policy and are available to meet with students and student organizations.

Student Government

The Student Advisory Assembly, the representative body of students, meets regularly to discuss policy matters and to plan programs to enhance student life. The assembly offers a valuable opportunity for students to learn the principles of leadership as well as communication and human relations skills. Other organizations dedicated to student life include the Housing Council, International Student Association, Student Activities Board, and Student Ambassadors. Students may take part in several student organizations, such as professional organizations for creative artists, which provide networking and other career opportunities.

Admission Requirements

To apply to The Art Institute of Atlanta, students must submit an application for admission, a 150-word essay, a signed notice regarding transferability for credit earned, and high school transcripts or General Educational Development (GED) test scores. Official reports of SAT, ACT, ASSET, or COMPASS scores must also be given to the school. Finally, students are required to complete an interview with an assistant director of admissions and to present a portfolio of their work. There is a $50 application fee.

Admissions decisions are made by the Admissions Committee, which consists of school faculty and staff members. The committee determines whether an applicant has a reasonable chance to be successful at The Art Institute of Atlanta, based upon the applicant's academic record, essay, and the appropriateness of stated career goals as they relate to the chosen program of study.

For the most recent information regarding admission requirements, please refer to the current academic catalog.

Application and Information

To obtain an application, make arrangements for an interview, or tour the school, prospective students should contact:

The Art Institute of Atlanta
6600 Peachtree Dunwoody Road, N.E.
100 Embassy Row
Atlanta, Georgia 30328-1635
Phone: 770-394-8300
800-275-4242 (toll-free)
Fax: 770-394-0008
Web site: http://www.artinstitutes.edu/atlanta

COLLEGE CLOSE-UPS

The Art Institute of Atlanta; The Art Institute of Atlanta–Decatur[1]; The Art Institute of Austin[2]; The Art Institute of California–Hollywood; The Art Institute of California–Inland Empire; The Art Institute of California–Los Angeles; The Art Institute of California–Orange County; The Art Institute of California–Sacramento; The Art Institute of California–San Diego; The Art Institute of California–San Francisco; The Art Institute of California–Sunnyvale; The Art Institute of Charleston[1]; The Art Institute of Charlotte; The Art Institute of Colorado; The Art Institute of Dallas; The Art Institute of Fort Lauderdale; The Art Institute of Fort Worth[3]; The Art Institute of Houston; The Art Institute of Houston–North[2]; The Art Institute of Indianapolis[4]; The Art Institute of Jacksonville[5]; The Art Institute of Las Vegas; The Art Institute of Michigan; The Art Institute of New York City; The Art Institute of Ohio–Cincinnati[6]; The Art Institute of Philadelphia; The Art Institute of Phoenix; The Art Institute of Pittsburgh; The Art Institute of Portland; The Art Institute of Raleigh–Durham; The Art Institute of Salt Lake City; The Art Institute of San Antonio[2];The Art Institute of Seattle; The Art Institute of Tampa[5]; The Art Institute of Tennessee–Nashville[1,7]; The Art Institute of Tucson; The Art Institute of Vancouver; The Art Institute of Virginia Beach[1,8]; The Art Institute of Washington[1,8]; The Art Institute of Washington–Northern Virginia[1,8]; The Art Institute of York–Pennsylvania; The Art Institutes International–Kansas City; The Art Institutes International Minnesota; The Illinois Institute of Art–Chicago; The Illinois Institute of Art–Schaumburg; Miami International University of Art & Design; The New England Institute of Art.

[1]A branch of The Art Institute of Atlanta
[2]A branch of The Art Institute of Houston
[3]A branch of The Art Institute of Dallas
[4]The Art Institute of Indianapolis is regulated by the Indiana Commission on Proprietary Education, 302 West Washington Street, Room E201, Indianapolis, Indiana 46204, AC-0080
[5]A branch of Miami International University of Art & Design
[6]The Art Institute of Ohio–Cincinnati, 8845 Governors Hill Drive, Suite 100, Cincinnati, Ohio 45249-3317, OH Reg. #04-01-1698B
[7]The Art Institute of Tennessee–Nashville is authorized for operation as a postsecondary educational institution by the Tennessee Higher Education Commission.
[8]Certified by the State Council of Higher Education to operate in Virginia

THE ART INSTITUTE OF ATLANTA–DECATUR

DECATUR, GEORGIA

The Art Institute of Atlanta–Decatur
A branch of The Art Institute of Atlanta

The Art Institute of Atlanta–Decatur provides students with an educational environment and dedicated faculty members committed to preparing students to pursue entry-level positions in the creative arts. Under the guidance of industry professionals, students learn by doing the types of tasks they are likely to encounter in the workplace. In addition, assistance is available to help students with resume writing, networking, and keeping aware of what employers are looking for in job candidates. The school offers seven bachelor's degree programs and two associate degree programs.

The student population includes recent high school graduates, transfer students, and those who have left a previous employment situation to study and train for a new career. Students are creative, competitive, and open to new ideas. They place great value on an education that prepares them to pursue an exciting entry-level position in the arts.

The Art Institute of Atlanta–Decatur places a high value on the quality of student life—both in and out of the classroom. Students participate in a wide variety of activities, including clubs and organizations, community service, and various committees designed to enhance the quality of student life.

The school offers assistance in helping students to secure housing.

The Art Institute of Atlanta–Decatur is a branch campus of The Art Institute of Atlanta. The Art Institute of Atlanta is accredited by the Commission on Colleges of the Southern Association of Colleges and Schools to award associate and baccalaureate degrees. Contact the Commission on Colleges at 1866 Southern Lane, Decatur, Georgia 30033-4097 or call 404-679-4500 for questions about the accreditation of The Art Institute of Atlanta.

The Art Institute of Atlanta–Decatur is licensed by the Georgia Nonpublic Postsecondary Education Commission, 2082 East Exchange Place, Suite 220, Tucker, Georgia 30084.

The Art Institute of Atlanta–Decatur is approved for veterans education benefits. This school is authorized under federal law to enroll nonimmigrant alien students.

Location

Decatur is a diverse, progressive community that retains a small-town feel, with quiet residential areas and historic districts. Decatur has easy access to the bustling city of Atlanta with its varied and plentiful arts, culture, entertainment, and sports venues.

Programs of Study and Degrees

The Art Institute of Atlanta–Decatur offers bachelor's degree programs in advertising, fashion and retail management, game art and design, graphic design, interior design, media arts and animation, and Web design and interactive media.

Associate degrees are offered in graphic design and Web design and interactive media.

Diploma programs are available in advertising design, digital design, residential interiors, and Web design.

Academic Programs

The Art Institute of Atlanta–Decatur operates on a year-round, four-quarter system.

Academic Facilities

The Art Institute of Atlanta–Decatur contains classrooms, Mac and PC computer labs, and a library for student use. There is also a bookstore.

Costs

Tuition cost varies by program. Prospective students should contact the school for current tuition costs. Other charges include a starting kit for all first quarter students. Kits vary in price depending on the program of study.

Financial Aid

Financial aid is available for those who qualify. Students who require financial assistance should first complete and submit a Free Application for Federal Student Aid (FAFSA) and meet with a financial aid officer.

Faculty

Faculty members at The Art Institute of Atlanta–Decatur have professional knowledge that they bring into the classroom. The school's faculty members provide their students with a real-world, relevant educational experience.

Admission Requirements

Applicants must provide proof of high school graduation or achievement of a General Educational Development (GED) certificate as a prerequisite for admission. In lieu of documenting high school graduation or a GED certificate, applicants may provide proof of attaining an associate degree or higher from an accredited institution. An official transcript indicating date of high school graduation, GED certificate (including test scores), or date of college graduation (including degree granted) is required as proof.

All individuals seeking admission to The Art Institute of Atlanta–Decatur are interviewed in person or by phone by an assistant director of admissions, and each applicant must submit an original essay of at least 150 words stating how an education at The Art Institute of Atlanta–Decatur would help the student to achieve career goals. There is a $50 application fee.

For the most recent information regarding admission requirements, please refer to the current academic catalog.

Application and Information

To obtain an application, make arrangements for an interview, or tour the school, prospective students should contact:

The Art Institute of Atlanta–Decatur
One West Court Square, Suite 110
Decatur, Georgia 30030
Phone: 404-942-1800
866-856-6203 (toll-free)
Fax: 404-942-1818
Web site: http://www.artinstitutes.edu/decatur

COLLEGE CLOSE-UPS

The Art Institute of Atlanta; The Art Institute of Atlanta–Decatur[1]; The Art Institute of Austin[2]; The Art Institute of California–Hollywood; The Art Institute of California–Inland Empire; The Art Institute of California–Los Angeles; The Art Institute of California–Orange County; The Art Institute of California–Sacramento; The Art Institute of California–San Diego; The Art Institute of California–San Francisco; The Art Institute of California–Sunnyvale; The Art Institute of Charleston[1]; The Art Institute of Charlotte; The Art Institute of Colorado; The Art Institute of Dallas; The Art Institute of Fort Lauderdale; The Art Institute of Fort Worth[3]; The Art Institute of Houston; The Art Institute of Houston–North[2]; The Art Institute of Indianapolis[4]; The Art Institute of Jacksonville[5]; The Art Institute of Las Vegas; The Art Institute of Michigan; The Art Institute of New York City; The Art Institute of Ohio–Cincinnati[6]; The Art Institute of Philadelphia; The Art Institute of Phoenix; The Art Institute of Pittsburgh; The Art Institute of Portland; The Art Institute of Raleigh–Durham; The Art Institute of Salt Lake City; The Art Institute of San Antonio[2];The Art Institute of Seattle; The Art Institute of Tampa[5]; The Art Institute of Tennessee–Nashville[1,7]; The Art Institute of Tucson; The Art Institute of Vancouver; The Art Institute of Virginia Beach[1,8]; The Art Institute of Washington[1,8]; The Art Institute of Washington–Northern Virginia[1,8]; The Art Institute of York–Pennsylvania; The Art Institutes International–Kansas City; The Art Institutes International Minnesota; The Illinois Institute of Art–Chicago; The Illinois Institute of Art–Schaumburg; Miami International University of Art & Design; The New England Institute of Art.

[1]A branch of The Art Institute of Atlanta
[2]A branch of The Art Institute of Houston
[3]A branch of The Art Institute of Dallas
[4]The Art Institute of Indianapolis is regulated by the Indiana Commission on Proprietary Education, 302 West Washington Street, Room E201, Indianapolis, Indiana 46204, AC-0080
[5]A branch of Miami International University of Art & Design
[6]The Art Institute of Ohio–Cincinnati, 8845 Governors Hill Drive, Suite 100, Cincinnati, Ohio 45249-3317, OH Reg. #04-01-1698B
[7]The Art Institute of Tennessee–Nashville is authorized for operation as a postsecondary educational institution by the Tennessee Higher Education Commission.
[8]Certified by the State Council of Higher Education to operate in Virginia

THE ART INSTITUTE OF AUSTIN

AUSTIN, TEXAS

The Art Institute of Austin provides students with an educational environment and dedicated faculty members committed to preparing students to pursue entry-level positions in the creative arts. Under the guidance of industry professionals, students learn by doing the types of tasks they are likely to encounter in the workplace. In addition, assistance is available to help students with resume writing, networking, and keeping aware of what employers are looking for in job candidates. The school offers ten bachelor's degree programs and three associate degree programs.

The student population includes recent high school graduates, transfer students, and those who have left a previous employment situation to study and train for a new career. Students are creative, competitive, and open to new ideas. They place great value on an education that prepares them to pursue an exciting entry-level position in the arts.

The Art Institute of Austin places a high value on the quality of student life—both in and out of the classroom. Students can participate in a wide variety of activities, including clubs and organizations, community service, and various committees designed to enhance the quality of student life.

The school offers assistance in helping students to secure housing.

The Art Institute of Austin is a branch campus of The Art Institute of Houston. The Art Institute of Houston is accredited by the Commission on Colleges of the Southern Association of Colleges and Schools to award associate and baccalaureate degrees. Contact the Commission on Colleges at 1866 Southern Lane, Decatur, Georgia 30033-4097 or call 404-679-4500 for questions about the accreditation of The Art Institute of Houston.

The Art Institute of Austin holds a certificate of authorization acknowledging exemption from Texas Higher Education Coordinating Board regulations.

Location

Austin is the capital and fourth-largest city in Texas, with a population of nearly 710,000. Austin was number 2 on the list of best big cities in "Best Places to Live" by *Money* magazine in 2006. It's also been called the greenest city in America by MSN. The area is home to numerous cultural organizations, museums, and performing arts venues.

Programs of Study and Degrees

The Art Institute of Austin offers bachelor's degree programs in audio production, culinary management, design and technical graphics, digital filmmaking and video production, fashion and retail management, graphic design, interior design, media arts and animation, photography, and Web design and interactive media.

Associate degrees are offered in culinary arts, graphic design, and Web design and interactive media.

Academic Programs

The Art Institute of Austin operates on a year-round, four-quarter system.

Academic Facilities

The Art Institute of Austin contains classrooms, Mac and PC computer labs, and a library for student use. There is also a bookstore.

Costs

Tuition cost varies by program. Prospective students should contact the school for current tuition costs. Other charges include a starting kit for all first quarter students. Kits vary in price depending on the program of study.

Financial Aid

Financial aid is available for those who qualify. Students who require financial assistance should first complete and submit a Free Application for Federal Student Aid (FAFSA) and meet with a financial aid officer.

Faculty

Faculty members at The Art Institute of Austin have professional knowledge that they bring into the classroom. The school's faculty members provide their students with a real-world, relevant educational experience.

Admission Requirements

Applicants must provide proof of high school graduation or achievement of a General Educational Development (GED) certificate as a prerequisite for admission. In lieu of documenting high school graduation or a GED certificate, applicants may provide proof of attaining an associate degree or higher from an accredited institution. An official transcript indicating date of high school graduation, GED certificate (including test scores), or date of college graduation (including degree granted) is required as proof.

All individuals seeking admission to The Art Institute of Austin are interviewed in person or by phone by an assistant director of admissions, and each applicant must submit an original essay of at least 150 words stating how an education at The

Art Institute of Austin would help the student to achieve career goals. There is a $50 application fee.

For the most recent information regarding admission requirements, please refer to the current academic catalog.

Application and Information

To obtain an application, make arrangements for an interview, or tour the school, prospective students should contact:

The Art Institute of Austin
101 West Louis Henna Boulevard, Suite 100
Austin, Texas 78728
Phone: 512-691-1707
866-583-7952 (toll-free)
Fax: 512-691-1790
Web site: http://www.artinstitutes.edu/austin

COLLEGE CLOSE-UPS

The Art Institute of Atlanta; The Art Institute of Atlanta–Decatur[1]; The Art Institute of Austin[2]; The Art Institute of California–Hollywood; The Art Institute of California–Inland Empire; The Art Institute of California–Los Angeles; The Art Institute of California–Orange County; The Art Institute of California–Sacramento; The Art Institute of California–San Diego; The Art Institute of California–San Francisco; The Art Institute of California–Sunnyvale; The Art Institute of Charleston[1]; The Art Institute of Charlotte; The Art Institute of Colorado; The Art Institute of Dallas; The Art Institute of Fort Lauderdale; The Art Institute of Fort Worth[3]; The Art Institute of Houston; The Art Institute of Houston–North[2]; The Art Institute of Indianapolis[4]; The Art Institute of Jacksonville[5]; The Art Institute of Las Vegas; The Art Institute of Michigan; The Art Institute of New York City; The Art Institute of Ohio–Cincinnati[6]; The Art Institute of Philadelphia; The Art Institute of Phoenix; The Art Institute of Pittsburgh; The Art Institute of Portland; The Art Institute of Raleigh–Durham; The Art Institute of Salt Lake City; The Art Institute of San Antonio[2];The Art Institute of Seattle; The Art Institute of Tampa[5]; The Art Institute of Tennessee–Nashville[1,7]; The Art Institute of Tucson; The Art Institute of Vancouver; The Art Institute of Virginia Beach[1,8]; The Art Institute of Washington[1,8]; The Art Institute of Washington–Northern Virginia[1,8]; The Art Institute of York–Pennsylvania; The Art Institutes International–Kansas City; The Art Institutes International Minnesota; The Illinois Institute of Art–Chicago; The Illinois Institute of Art–Schaumburg; Miami International University of Art & Design; The New England Institute of Art.

[1]A branch of The Art Institute of Atlanta
[2]A branch of The Art Institute of Houston
[3]A branch of The Art Institute of Dallas
[4]The Art Institute of Indianapolis is regulated by the Indiana Commission on Proprietary Education, 302 West Washington Street, Room E201, Indianapolis, Indiana 46204, AC-0080
[5]A branch of Miami International University of Art & Design
[6]The Art Institute of Ohio–Cincinnati, 8845 Governors Hill Drive, Suite 100, Cincinnati, Ohio 45249-3317, OH Reg. #04-01-1698B
[7]The Art Institute of Tennessee–Nashville is authorized for operation as a postsecondary educational institution by the Tennessee Higher Education Commission.
[8]Certified by the State Council of Higher Education to operate in Virginia

THE ART INSTITUTE OF BOSTON AT LESLEY UNIVERSITY

BOSTON, MASSACHUSETTS

The Institute

Founded in 1912, The Art Institute of Boston (AIB) is a professional college of visual arts that offers program and course work designed to prepare students to be professional illustrators, animators, graphic designers, Web designers, photographers, exhibiting fine artists, art teachers, and art therapists. AIB provides students with an intimate, challenging, and supportive environment that balances personal artistic expression with practical professional preparation.

AIB's more than 500 students come from thirty states and fifteen other countries, creating a global community of young artists with a stimulating variety of backgrounds and viewpoints. The nature of the college allows students to form close ties with other students and with faculty and staff members, most of whom are practicing professional artists. Studio classes are small and intimate, with an average of 13 students per instructor, which allows for personal attention and an emphasis on self-exploration and the development of an individual style. Students are prepared for professions in the arts by exposure to the most current trends and technology in their fields and internships and freelance opportunities that provide them with professional connections for career opportunities after graduation.

The University also offers activities such as major exhibitions, student exhibits, lectures, art auctions, special event–related parties, as well as a visiting artist program that brings prominent artists to the campus for lectures and workshops.

AIB's strengths as a professional college of the visual arts are combined with the resources of Lesley University, providing students with expanded educational opportunities that are not usually found at most independent colleges of art, yet preserving the character of a small, private art college.

The University provides a variety of dormitory housing options for students, including residences on the Cambridge campus of Lesley University, near Harvard Square (shuttle service provided).

The Career Resource Center at Lesley University provides career development and job search services to AIB degree candidates and alumni. Students are provided individual assistance and training in job search, career assessment, and decision-making skills that are used throughout a lifetime of employment. Workshops and special events are planned throughout the academic year on a variety of topics. The Artists Resource Center at AIB maintains current job listings and provides information on competitions, fellowships and grants, exhibition opportunities, and other resources for artists. Career counseling also takes place informally with faculty members and advisers within each department.

Master's programs in expressive therapies and art education are offered in conjunction with Lesley University.

Location

Boston is an extraordinary college town. Nearly 230,000 students live and study here every year at seventy institutions of higher learning. The city offers all the human and institutional resources expected in a major cultural, educational, and commercial center. World-class art exhibitions, concerts, lectures, theater, sports, and popular entertainment are among its riches. The spirit is cosmopolitan, but the setting is distinctive to Boston, with its historic neighborhoods, parks, and nearby New England rural and coastal areas.

The Art Institute of Boston students use the city's extensive resources as a part of their learning environment in many ways—for artistic and academic research, for internships and job opportunities, and for personal recreation. Full-time students receive free admission to the Museum of Fine Arts, Boston.

Majors and Degrees

The Art Institute of Boston awards the Bachelor of Fine Arts degree in animation, art history, fine arts, design, illustration, and photography. Students may elect to earn a five-year double-major B.F.A./Diploma in design/fine arts, design/illustration, or illustration/fine arts. AIB students also have the option to study for a dual B.F.A./M.Ed. in art education. An advanced professional certificate two-year studio-intensive program is offered in animation, design, or illustration. AIB also offers a low-residency Master of Fine Arts degree in visual arts.

Candidates for the design program can study advertising and corporate communications, package design, publishing and book design, and Web and multimedia design. The illustration program offers specializations in advertising, animation, book, and editorial. Fine arts students choose from drawing, painting, printmaking, and sculpture as concentrations, with courses available in ceramics, installation, and new media. Photography students specialize in commercial, documentary, fine arts, or media. An intensive precollege program is available for high school students throughout the academic year and the summer.

Academic Programs

AIB's challenging curriculum is structured to provide students with an understanding of the process of visual communication and expression, along with the social, historical, and cultural influences that shape the world and inform their imaginations.

AIB's rigorous first-year foundation includes intensive study in drawing and visual perception. Photography students take a unique foundation, with a direct immersion in the conceptual, technical, and historic aspects of photography. The foundation supplies students with the skills, insights, and fluency of expression that are necessary to meet the challenges of further study in art.

After the foundation year, students choose a major that can include unique specializations, combined majors, and a wide variety of interdisciplinary courses and workshops. Students take core courses in their major and continue with more individualized instruction, working closely with the faculty of working professional artists, toward their personal and professional goals. Students prepare for careers in the visual arts with real world studio assignments and professional internships, giving them valuable firsthand experience in their intended fields.

As an integral part of their study, all degree and diploma students take a blend of required and elective liberal arts courses. These courses are designed to develop effective communication skills, give a firm academic grounding in the history of their major area of study, and allow students to pursue individual interests that stimulate their imaginations and interests.

AIB offers both day and evening degree credit courses during the fall, spring, and summer semesters. In addition, the continuing and professional education program offers evening and weekend courses, workshops, and intensive seminars in the areas of visual arts, liberal arts, and career development to be taken by artists, educators, and professionals.

Off-Campus Programs

AIB students may opt in their junior year to spend a semester abroad. They can choose to study the visual art, history, humanities, language, and culture of Italy at The Art Institute of Florence, of France at Pont-Avon School of Art, or of Ireland at The Burren College of Art. The Illustration and Design Departments offer an exchange with the Willem de Kooning Academy in the Netherlands, Ecole de Communication Visuelle in Paris, and Hochschule für Kunste, Bremen, Germany. Students may take a semester or an intensive year-long course of study and studio work in New York City or spend

COLLEGE CLOSE-UPS

their junior year at one of thirty-five schools in the Association of Independent Colleges of Art and Design (AICAD) located across the country. AIB also offers students the opportunity to take classes at the Boston Architectural College and the Maine Photographic Workshop.

Academic Facilities

The Art Institute of Boston's facilities include five state-of-the-art Macintosh computer laboratories, an animation lab, an updated photography lab with color and black-and-white printers, a digital photography lab, a printmaking lab with etching and lithography presses, a wood shop, and a clay lab with kilns. Senior fine arts students have their own individual studios in which to create.

The Art Institute of Boston was selected to join the New Media Centers Program, a consortium of higher education institutions and digital technology companies dedicated to advancing learning through new media. AIB has newly expanded multimedia programs that use state-of-the-art technology and equipment.

The Art Institute of Boston Library maintains a focused collection, specializing in the fields of fine arts, art history, illustration, design, and photography. The library's collection of more than 11,000 books is focused on modern and contemporary art and design themes. The library has subscriptions to more than 80 current art journals and provides online access to scholarly articles through full-text art databases. Videos and a special collection of rare artists' books are available for use in the library.

The library's visual resources collection contains slides and high quality digital images, which support the art curricula. AIB participates in the ARTstor project, a digital library of nearly a million images in the areas of art, architecture, the humanities, and social sciences.

Access to the library's digital collections of images, scholarly articles, and e-books is available online. Students can also search, request, and renew print materials online.

For research in nonart disciplines, students and faculty have access to the Lesley University Sherrill Library near Harvard Square in Cambridge. The collections of the library are strong in all curricular areas, with an emphasis on education, psychology, human services, management, and expressive arts therapies.

Lesley is affiliated with the Fenway Libraries Online, which allows direct online borrowing privileges and book delivery from additional Boston art libraries. Lesley is also a member of the Fenway Library Consortium, which provides walk-in borrowing privileges at sixteen nearby libraries.

The Art Institute of Boston sponsors a full program of exhibitions and lectures by visiting artists. The gallery presents major exhibitions of contemporary and historical work by established and emerging artists, including the alumni of The Art Institute of Boston. Students have the opportunity to assist in mounting exhibitions and to personally meet visiting artists. A student gallery and reserved areas show student work year-round. Gallery South exhibits the work of student photographers throughout the year, including group and senior exhibitions.

Costs

Tuition for the 2010–11 academic year is $26,850. Room and board costs are $12,800 per year. Material and supply costs vary according to individual and departmental requirements. In general, foundation, fine arts, illustration, and design students spend approximately $1700 per year for supplies, while photography students can expect to spend about $3000 per year, with further expenses dependent upon the equipment chosen by the individual student.

Financial Aid

Approximately 80 percent of students receive aid each year through AIB's active financial aid program. Awards are made on the basis of need as determined by the United States Department of Education, which analyzes all the financial resources of the student. The Financial Aid Office's goal is to help students meet established needs through a combination of Federal Pell Grants, Federal Stafford Student Loans, Federal Work-Study Program awards, other federal grants, scholarships, and state programs.

Various merit-based and need-based scholarships are available. The Art Institute of Boston administers more than $4 million in scholarships, financial aid, and loans for students each year. The application deadline is March 15 for need-based awards.

Faculty

The Art Institute of Boston at Lesley University has 105 full- and part-time faculty members, 81 percent of whom have doctoral or terminal degrees; 90 percent are practicing artists, designers, illustrators, and photographers. The student-faculty ratio is 9:1.

Student Government

Students at the Art Institute of Boston are represented in the Student Government Association of Lesley University. The SGA works to ensure that the needs of the entire student body are being met on campus, and serves as a liaison for all students with faculty, administration, and trustees.

Admission Requirements

In considering applications for admission, The Art Institute of Boston looks for artistic potential and personal commitment. A portfolio of original work is an important part of the application; academic grades, test scores, and extracurricular activities are also strongly considered. A school visit is strongly encouraged, giving applicants the opportunity to present their portfolios, discuss their goals and interests with an admission counselor, and determine how they may benefit from AIB's programs. SAT or ACT scores are required of applicants who have graduated from high school within the past three years.

Application and Information

To ensure a place in the desired program of study and in order to meet application deadlines for financial aid, students are encouraged to apply by the priority application dates of February 15 for fall and November 15 for spring admittance. After these dates, applications are considered and accepted on a rolling basis as long as space allows. A complete application consists of an application form, essay, resume of accomplishments and cocurricular activities, transcript(s) of all courses completed, SAT or ACT test scores (B.F.A. candidates, U.S. only), and a portfolio. Transfer and international applications are accepted and encouraged.

For further information, students should visit the school's Web site or contact an admissions representative at:

Office of Admission
The Art Institute of Boston at Lesley University
700 Beacon Street
Boston, Massachusetts 02215
Phone: 617-585-6710
800-773-0494 Ext. 6710 (toll-free, U.S. and Canada)
E-mail: admissions@aiboston.edu
Web site: http://www.aiboston.edu/info/discover

Studio classes are small and intimate, with an average of 13 students per instructor.

THE ART INSTITUTE OF CALIFORNIA–HOLLYWOOD

The Art Institute of California–Hollywood

NORTH HOLLYWOOD, CALIFORNIA

The Art Institute of California–Hollywood provides students with a creative educational environment. Offering fourteen bachelor's degree programs and six associate degree programs, the school and its dedicated faculty members are committed to preparing students to pursue entry-level positions in the creative arts.

Under the guidance of industry professionals, students learn by doing the types of tasks they are likely to encounter in the workplace. In addition, assistance is available to help students with resume writing, networking, and keeping aware of what employers are looking for in job candidates.

The student population includes recent high school graduates, transfer students, and those who have left a previous employment situation to study and train for a new career. Students are creative, competitive, and open to new ideas. They place great value on an education that prepares them to pursue an exciting entry-level position in the arts.

The Art Institute of California–Hollywood places a high value on the quality of student life inside and outside the classroom. Students can take part in a wide variety of activities, clubs and organizations, community service opportunities, and various student life enhancing committees.

Instructors are encouraged to look for upcoming books and to advise the administration of any books that may prove useful to their students. Students also have access to the public libraries.

The Student Affairs Office helps students who need assistance in locating housing.

The Art Institute of California–Hollywood is accredited by the Accrediting Council for Independent Colleges and Schools (ACICS) to award associate degrees and bachelor's degrees. ACICS is listed as a nationally recognized accrediting agency by the United States Department of Education and is recognized by the Council for Higher Education Accreditation. ACICS can be contacted at 750 First Street NE, Suite 980, Washington, D.C. 20002; phone: 202-336-6780.

The Art Institute of California-Hollywood has been granted approval to operate by the California Bureau for Private Postsecondary and Vocational Education, California Department of Consumer Affairs, 1625 North Market Boulevard, Suite S-308, Sacramento, California 95834; phone: 916-574-8200; www.bppve.ca.gov.

Location

The school is located at the crossroads of California's design, fashion, and entertainment industries, The Art Institute of California–Hollywood is designed with the creative student in mind.

Programs of Study and Degrees

Bachelor's degree programs are offered in culinary management, digital filmmaking and video production, digital photography, fashion design, fashion marketing and management, game art and design, graphic design, industrial design, interior design, media arts and animation, set and exhibit design, visual and game programming, visual effects and motion graphics, and Web design and interactive media.

Associate degree programs are offered in culinary arts, digital photography, fashion design, fashion marketing, graphic design, and Web design and interactive media.

The graphic design and interior design programs are also available in an evening and weekend option format.

Academic Programs

The Art Institute of California–Hollywood operates on a year-round, four-quarter system.

Academic Facilities

The Art Institute of California–Hollywood is home to classrooms, studios, offices, a student lounge, a supply store, and a learning resource center. Equipment provided at The Art Institute of California–Hollywood is specific to the program of study and may include projectors, editing decks, camcorders, PC and Macintosh computers, printers, drafting tables, and kitchen appliances.

Costs

Tuition cost varies by program. Prospective students should contact the school for current tuition costs. Other charges include a starting kit for all first-quarter students. Kits vary in price depending on the program of study.

Financial Aid

Financial aid is available for those who qualify. Students who require financial assistance should first complete and submit a Free Application for Federal Student Aid (FAFSA) and meet with a financial aid officer.

Faculty

Faculty members at The Art Institute of California–Hollywood have professional knowledge that they bring into the classroom. The school's faculty members provide their students with a unique, relevant educational experience.

Admission Requirements

Applicants must provide proof of high school graduation or achievement of General Educational Development (GED) certificate as a prerequisite for admission. In lieu of documenting high school graduation or a GED certificate, applicants may provide proof of attaining an associate degree or higher from an accredited institution. An official transcript indicating date of high school graduation, GED certificate (including test scores), or date of college graduation (including degree granted) is required as proof.

All individuals seeking admission to The Art Institute of California–Hollywood are interviewed in person or by phone by an assistant director of admissions, and each applicant must create an original essay of at least 150 words stating how an education at The Art Institute of California–Hollywood would help the student to achieve career goals. There is a $50 application fee.

For the most recent information regarding admission requirements, please refer to the current academic catalog.

Application and Information

To obtain an application, make arrangements for an interview, or tour the school, prospective students should contact:

The Art Institute of California–Hollywood
5250 Lankershim Boulevard
North Hollywood, California 91601
Phone: 818-299-5100
877-468-6232 (toll-free)
Fax: 818-299-5150
Web site: http://www.artinstitutes.edu/hollywood

COLLEGE CLOSE-UPS

The Art Institute of Atlanta; The Art Institute of Atlanta–Decatur[1]; The Art Institute of Austin[2]; The Art Institute of California–Hollywood; The Art Institute of California–Inland Empire; The Art Institute of California–Los Angeles; The Art Institute of California–Orange County; The Art Institute of California–Sacramento; The Art Institute of California–San Diego; The Art Institute of California–San Francisco; The Art Institute of California–Sunnyvale; The Art Institute of Charleston[1]; The Art Institute of Charlotte; The Art Institute of Colorado; The Art Institute of Dallas; The Art Institute of Fort Lauderdale; The Art Institute of Fort Worth[3]; The Art Institute of Houston; The Art Institute of Houston–North[2]; The Art Institute of Indianapolis[4]; The Art Institute of Jacksonville[5]; The Art Institute of Las Vegas; The Art Institute of Michigan; The Art Institute of New York City; The Art Institute of Ohio–Cincinnati[6]; The Art Institute of Philadelphia; The Art Institute of Phoenix; The Art Institute of Pittsburgh; The Art Institute of Portland; The Art Institute of Raleigh–Durham; The Art Institute of Salt Lake City; The Art Institute of San Antonio[2];The Art Institute of Seattle; The Art Institute of Tampa[5]; The Art Institute of Tennessee–Nashville[1,7]; The Art Institute of Tucson; The Art Institute of Vancouver; The Art Institute of Virginia Beach[1,8]; The Art Institute of Washington[1,8]; The Art Institute of Washington–Northern Virginia[1,8]; The Art Institute of York–Pennsylvania; The Art Institutes International–Kansas City; The Art Institutes International Minnesota; The Illinois Institute of Art–Chicago; The Illinois Institute of Art–Schaumburg; Miami International University of Art & Design; The New England Institute of Art.

[1]A branch of The Art Institute of Atlanta
[2]A branch of The Art Institute of Houston
[3]A branch of The Art Institute of Dallas
[4]The Art Institute of Indianapolis is regulated by the Indiana Commission on Proprietary Education, 302 West Washington Street, Room E201, Indianapolis, Indiana 46204, AC-0080
[5]A branch of Miami International University of Art & Design
[6]The Art Institute of Ohio–Cincinnati, 8845 Governors Hill Drive, Suite 100, Cincinnati, Ohio 45249-3317, OH Reg. #04-01-1698B
[7]The Art Institute of Tennessee–Nashville is authorized for operation as a postsecondary educational institution by the Tennessee Higher Education Commission.
[8]Certified by the State Council of Higher Education to operate in Virginia

THE ART INSTITUTE OF CALIFORNIA–INLAND EMPIRE

SAN BERNARDINO, CALIFORNIA

The Art Institute of California–Inland Empire helps students to cultivate and refine the talents and skills that are needed to pursue entry-level positions in the creative arts. Classes are taught in an environment that encourages learning, leadership, and creativity. The school offers nine bachelor's degree programs and three associate degree programs.

Faculty and staff members strive to foster development and cultivate artistic growth. Students are given opportunities to develop leadership skills and build relationships. In addition, assistance is available to help students with resume writing, networking, and keeping abreast of what employers are looking for in job candidates.

The Art Institute of California–Inland Empire places a high value on the quality of student life both in and out of the classroom. Students can participate in a wide variety of activities, including clubs and organizations, community service opportunities, and various committees designed to enhance the quality of student life.

The Residential Life and Housing Department provides information on independent housing options to all enrolled students requesting such assistance. The Residential Life and Housing staff members coordinate a variety of activities and are available to assist students in arranging suitable living accommodations.

Students come to The Art Institute of California–Inland Empire from throughout the United States. The student population includes recent high school graduates, transfer students, and those who have left a previous employment situation to study and train for a new career. Students are creative, competitive, and open to new ideas.

The Art Institute of California–Inland Empire is accredited by the Accrediting Commission of Career Schools and Colleges (ACCSC) as a branch of The Art Institute of California–San Diego. ACCSC may be contacted at 2101 Wilson Boulevard, Suite 302, Arlington, Virginia 22201; phone: 703-247-4212.

The Art Institute of California–Inland Empire has been granted approval to operate by the California Bureau for Private Postsecondary and Vocational Education, California Department of Consumer Affairs, 1625 North Market Boulevard, Suite S-308, Sacramento, California 95834; phone: 916-574-8200; http://www.bppve.ca.gov.

Location

The Art Institute of California–Inland Empire is located in San Bernardino. Within a short drive from the school, students can enjoy mountains, deserts, Los Angeles, or Mexico. Surfing, water sports, tennis, golf, jogging, mountain biking, and many other outdoor activities are supported by the region's mild climate.

Programs of Study and Degrees

The Art Institute of California–Inland Empire offers bachelor's degrees in audio production, culinary management, fashion and retail management, fashion design, game art and design, graphic design, interior design, media arts and animation, and Web design and interactive media.

Students may also pursue associate degrees in baking and pastry, culinary arts and graphic design.

The culinary arts, graphic design, and interior design programs are available in an evening and weekend option format.

Academic Programs

The academic year is divided into four quarters, beginning in January, April, July, and October. Each program is offered on a year-round basis, allowing students to continue to work uninterrupted toward their degrees.

Academic Facilities

The Art Institute of California–Inland Empire occupies approximately 25,000 square feet. In addition to classrooms, studios, laboratories, offices, a student lounge, a library, and an exhibition gallery, The Art Institute of California–Inland Empire maintains an art supply store for the convenience of students. Equipment provided at The Art Institute of California–Inland Empire is specific to the program of study. This includes, but is not limited to, projectors, editing decks, PC and Macintosh computers, and printers.

Costs

Tuition cost varies by program. Prospective students should contact the school for current tuition costs. Other charges include a starting kit for all first-quarter students. Kits vary in price, depending on the program of study.

Financial Aid

Financial aid is available for those who qualify. Students who require financial assistance should first complete and submit a Free Application for Federal Student Aid (FAFSA) and meet with a financial aid officer.

Faculty

The Art Institute of California–Inland Empire faculty consists of full-time and part-time instructors, many of whom have advanced degrees and professional experience in their respective fields.

Student Government

The Student Federation is responsible for student government and acts as a liaison between the student body and faculty and staff members.

Admission Requirements

Applicants must provide proof of high school graduation or achievement of a General Educational Development (GED) certificate as a prerequisite for admission. In lieu of documenting high school graduation or a GED certificate, applicants may provide proof of attaining an associate degree or higher from an accredited institution. An official transcript indicating date of high school graduation, GED certificate (including test scores), or date of college graduation (including degree granted), is required as proof.

All individuals seeking admission to The Art Institute of California–Inland Empire are interviewed in person or by phone by an assistant director of admissions, and each applicant must create an original essay of at least 150 words stating how an education at the school would help the student to achieve career goals. There is a $50 application fee.

For the most recent information regarding admission requirements, please refer to the current academic catalog.

Application and Information

To obtain an application, make arrangements for an interview, or tour the school, prospective students should contact:

The Art Institute of California–Inland Empire
674 East Brier Drive
San Bernardino, California 92408
Phone: 909-915-2100
800-353-0812 (toll-free)
Fax: 909-915-2130
Web site: http://www.artinstitutes.edu/inlandempire

COLLEGE CLOSE-UPS

The Art Institute of Atlanta; The Art Institute of Atlanta–Decatur[1]; The Art Institute of Austin[2]; The Art Institute of California–Hollywood; The Art Institute of California–Inland Empire; The Art Institute of California–Los Angeles; The Art Institute of California–Orange County; The Art Institute of California–Sacramento; The Art Institute of California–San Diego; The Art Institute of California–San Francisco; The Art Institute of California–Sunnyvale; The Art Institute of Charleston[1]; The Art Institute of Charlotte; The Art Institute of Colorado; The Art Institute of Dallas; The Art Institute of Fort Lauderdale; The Art Institute of Fort Worth[3]; The Art Institute of Houston; The Art Institute of Houston–North[2]; The Art Institute of Indianapolis[4]; The Art Institute of Jacksonville[5]; The Art Institute of Las Vegas; The Art Institute of Michigan; The Art Institute of New York City; The Art Institute of Ohio–Cincinnati[6]; The Art Institute of Philadelphia; The Art Institute of Phoenix; The Art Institute of Pittsburgh; The Art Institute of Portland; The Art Institute of Raleigh–Durham; The Art Institute of Salt Lake City; The Art Institute of San Antonio[2];The Art Institute of Seattle; The Art Institute of Tampa[5]; The Art Institute of Tennessee–Nashville[1,7]; The Art Institute of Tucson; The Art Institute of Vancouver; The Art Institute of Virginia Beach[1,8]; The Art Institute of Washington[1,8]; The Art Institute of Washington–Northern Virginia[1,8]; The Art Institute of York–Pennsylvania; The Art Institutes International–Kansas City; The Art Institutes International Minnesota; The Illinois Institute of Art–Chicago; The Illinois Institute of Art–Schaumburg; Miami International University of Art & Design; The New England Institute of Art.

[1]A branch of The Art Institute of Atlanta
[2]A branch of The Art Institute of Houston
[3]A branch of The Art Institute of Dallas
[4]The Art Institute of Indianapolis is regulated by the Indiana Commission on Proprietary Education, 302 West Washington Street, Room E201, Indianapolis, Indiana 46204, AC-0080
[5]A branch of Miami International University of Art & Design
[6]The Art Institute of Ohio–Cincinnati, 8845 Governors Hill Drive, Suite 100, Cincinnati, Ohio 45249-3317, OH Reg. #04-01-1698B
[7]The Art Institute of Tennessee–Nashville is authorized for operation as a postsecondary educational institution by the Tennessee Higher Education Commission.
[8]Certified by the State Council of Higher Education to operate in Virginia

THE ART INSTITUTE OF CALIFORNIA–LOS ANGELES

The Art Institute of California–Los Angeles

SANTA MONICA, CALIFORNIA

The Art Institute of California–Los Angeles prepares students to pursue entry-level positions in creative careers in the arts. The school strives to provide quality programs and services that foster the development of student potential. The Art Institute of California–Los Angeles is housed in a 107,000-square-foot building that was designed with the creative student in mind. Bright, spacious classrooms, studios, and labs offer a productive working atmosphere.

The school currently offers twelve bachelor's degree programs and five associate degree programs. Each program is offered on a year-round basis, allowing students to continue to work uninterrupted toward their degrees. An impressive faculty of working professionals strives to strengthen students' skills and cultivate their talents. Each student has an academic adviser, who helps to devise career strategies and choose courses consistent with the student's career goals. Programs are carefully defined with support and contributions from the professional community. Curricula are reviewed regularly to keep up with the needs of a changing marketplace.

The student population includes recent high school graduates, transfer students, and those who have left a previous employment situation to study and train for a new career. Students are creative, competitive, and open to new ideas. They place great value on an education that prepares them for an exciting entry-level position in the arts.

Assistance is available to help students with resume writing, networking, and keeping aware of what employers are looking for in job candidates.

The Office of Residential Life and Housing is committed to providing students with comfortable and convenient housing options. The Art Institute of California–Los Angeles contracts with several local luxury apartment complexes to provide housing to students. Professional residential life staff members live on-site and are available to address student needs. The fully furnished apartment units are located in gated and courtesy-patrolled communities that include on-site parking, fitness centers, swimming pools, and computer rooms. Direct shuttle service is available from school-sponsored housing sites to The Art Institute of California–Los Angeles. The school also provides accommodations to qualified students with disabilities. The Disability Services Office assists qualified students in acquiring reasonable and appropriate accommodations and in supporting their success at the school.

A wide variety of clubs and organizations are available to students, including the Culinary Club, International Student Club, BAMF (comics: writing, drawing, analysis), and Black Ops (PC gaming). The Non-Traditional Student Resource (NTSR) serves as a communication network, fostering a comfortable academic and social atmosphere while providing a support system for nontraditional students.

The Art Institute of California–Los Angeles is accredited by the Accrediting Council for Independent Colleges and Schools (ACICS) to award diplomas, associate degrees, and bachelor's degrees. ACICS is listed as a nationally recognized accrediting agency by the United States Department of Education and is recognized by the Council for Higher Education Accreditation. ACICS can be contacted at 750 First Street NE, Suite 980, Washington, D.C. 20002; phone: 202-336-6780.

The Art Institute of California–Los Angeles has been granted approval to operate by the California Bureau for Private Postsecondary and Vocational Education, California Department of Consumer Affairs, 1625 North Market Boulevard, Suite S-308, Sacramento, California 95834; phone: 916-574-8200; http://www.bppve.ca.gov.

Location

Located in Los Angeles, the arts and entertainment capital of the world, The Art Institute of California–Los Angeles is within easy driving distance of the Pacific Coast Highway, Century City, and downtown. The city offers a rich diversity of food, fashion, architecture, entertainment, languages, world views, and religions that are showcased in numerous community and ethnic festivals throughout the year. Leisure activities include hiking on Santa Monica Mountain trails or visits to the Getty Museum, Los Angeles County Museum of Art, or Los Angeles Zoo. Students may also enjoy dining and shopping on Santa Monica's Third Street Promenade or in nearby Westwood Village. Music and theater venues include the Hollywood Bowl, the Greek Theatre, the Music Center, and the Dorothy Chandler Pavilion. Other popular destinations are Watts Towers, the La Brea Tar Pits, Hollywood Boulevard's Walk of Fame, and Mann's Chinese Theater.

Programs of Study and Degrees

The Art Institute of California–Los Angeles offers Bachelor of Science degree programs in audio production, culinary management, digital filmmaking and video production, fashion design, fashion marketing and management, game art and design, game programming, graphic design, interior design, media arts and animation, visual effects and motion graphics, and Web design and interactive media.

Associate of Science degree programs are available in baking and pastry, culinary arts, graphic design, video production, and Web design and interactive media.

Diplomas are offered in baking and pastry and the art of cooking.

The culinary arts, culinary management, graphic design, and interior design programs are available in an evening and weekend option format.

Academic Programs

The academic year is divided into four quarters that begin in January, April, July, and October. Associate degree candidates must complete 112 academic credits to graduate, including 28 general education credits. These are generally earned over seven quarters. Bachelor's degree candidates must complete 192 credits, including 56 general education credits. These are generally earned over eleven quarters. All students must complete their programs of study with a minimum 2.0 cumulative GPA to meet graduation requirements.

Academic Facilities

Located at 31st Street in the city of Santa Monica, The Art Institute of California–Los Angeles provides equipment that

COLLEGE CLOSE-UPS

includes projectors, editing decks, PC and Macintosh computers, printers, and well-equipped kitchens. The library collection includes approximately 15,000 books, 260 periodical subscriptions, and 1,650 items of digital and audiovisual materials. The library is equipped with eight computer stations, has Internet access, and subscribes to online databases. In addition to classrooms, studios, laboratories, offices, a student lounge, a learning resource center, and an exhibition gallery, the school also maintains an art supply store for the convenience of its students.

Costs

Tuition cost varies by program. Prospective students should contact the school for current tuition costs. Other charges include a starting kit for all first-quarter students. Kits vary in price depending on the program of study.

Financial Aid

Financial aid is available for those who qualify. Students who require financial assistance should first complete and submit a Free Application for Federal Student Aid (FAFSA) and meet with a financial aid officer.

Faculty

The Art Institute of California–Los Angeles faculty comprises full-time and part-time instructors, many with advanced degrees and professional experience in their respective fields.

Student Government

The Associated Student Council provides a forum to discuss student issues, facilitates the exchange of ideas and information among students, and acts as a liaison between students and members of the faculty and administration; it also organizes student activities at the school and provides student leadership opportunities. In addition, the Activities and Events Council consists of an elected board, representatives from each student organization, and other interested students.

Admission Requirements

The admission process at The Art Institute of California–Los Angeles includes a student interview with the admissions office (either in person or by phone) and submission of a completed application form, a 150-word essay, high school transcripts or General Educational Development (GED) test scores, and official SAT or ACT scores. There is a $50 application fee.

For the most recent information regarding admission requirements, please refer to the current academic catalog.

Application and Information

To obtain an application, make arrangements for an interview, or tour the school, prospective students should contact:

The Art Institute of California–Los Angeles
2900 31st Street
Santa Monica, California 90405-3035
Phone: 310-752-4700
888-646-4610 (toll-free)
Fax: 310-752-4708
Web site: http://www.artinstitutes.edu/losangeles

The Art Institute of Atlanta; The Art Institute of Atlanta–Decatur[1]; The Art Institute of Austin[2]; The Art Institute of California–Hollywood; The Art Institute of California–Inland Empire; The Art Institute of California–Los Angeles; The Art Institute of California–Orange County; The Art Institute of California–Sacramento; The Art Institute of California–San Diego; The Art Institute of California–San Francisco; The Art Institute of California–Sunnyvale; The Art Institute of Charleston[1]; The Art Institute of Charlotte; The Art Institute of Colorado; The Art Institute of Dallas; The Art Institute of Fort Lauderdale; The Art Institute of Fort Worth[3]; The Art Institute of Houston; The Art Institute of Houston–North[2]; The Art Institute of Indianapolis[4]; The Art Institute of Jacksonville[5]; The Art Institute of Las Vegas; The Art Institute of Michigan; The Art Institute of New York City; The Art Institute of Ohio–Cincinnati[6]; The Art Institute of Philadelphia; The Art Institute of Phoenix; The Art Institute of Pittsburgh; The Art Institute of Portland; The Art Institute of Raleigh–Durham; The Art Institute of Salt Lake City; The Art Institute of San Antonio[2];The Art Institute of Seattle; The Art Institute of Tampa[5]; The Art Institute of Tennessee–Nashville[1,7]; The Art Institute of Tucson; The Art Institute of Vancouver; The Art Institute of Virginia Beach[1,8]; The Art Institute of Washington[1,8]; The Art Institute of Washington–Northern Virginia[1,8]; The Art Institute of York–Pennsylvania; The Art Institutes International–Kansas City; The Art Institutes International Minnesota; The Illinois Institute of Art–Chicago; The Illinois Institute of Art–Schaumburg; Miami International University of Art & Design; The New England Institute of Art.

[1]A branch of The Art Institute of Atlanta
[2]A branch of The Art Institute of Houston
[3]A branch of The Art Institute of Dallas
[4]The Art Institute of Indianapolis is regulated by the Indiana Commission on Proprietary Education, 302 West Washington Street, Room E201, Indianapolis, Indiana 46204, AC-0080
[5]A branch of Miami International University of Art & Design
[6]The Art Institute of Ohio–Cincinnati, 8845 Governors Hill Drive, Suite 100, Cincinnati, Ohio 45249-3317, OH Reg. #04-01-1698B
[7]The Art Institute of Tennessee–Nashville is authorized for operation as a postsecondary educational institution by the Tennessee Higher Education Commission.
[8]Certified by the State Council of Higher Education to operate in Virginia

THE ART INSTITUTE OF CALIFORNIA–ORANGE COUNTY

SANTA ANA, CALIFORNIA

The Art Institute of California–Orange County

The Art Institute of California–Orange County helps prepare students to pursue entry-level positions in the creative arts through an environment that encourages academic freedom, responsible decision making, and critical thinking. A collaborative environment encourages personal and professional growth while promoting teamwork and communication. The Art Institute of California–Orange County offers thirteen bachelor's degree programs and five associate degree programs.

Students are taught professional skills; instructors and staff members assist students in portfolio development and professional resume creation. Many gain on-the-job skills through participation in internships or externships at local companies and nationally recognized corporations. Assistance is available to help students with resume writing, networking, and keeping abreast of what employers are looking for in job candidates.

Students come from across the country and abroad. The student population includes recent high school graduates, transfer students, and those who have left a previous employment situation to study and train for a new career.

The Art Institute of California–Orange County offers school-sponsored housing, featuring furnished apartment units that include laundry facilities, a fitness center, a pool, a spa, and tennis courts. Each unit is within walking distance of a variety of restaurants, grocery stores, and retail establishments. Apartment information and roommate referrals are available to enrolled students who choose to live outside of school-sponsored housing.

The school provides an environment that encourages involvement in a wide variety of academic and nonacademic activities. Student organizations include chapters of AIGA, International Game Developers Association (IGDA), and American Society of Interior Designers. Clubs include the Multimedia and Web Design Club, the OC Ad Club, Women in Animation, and the Classic Game Club. Music Madness, Pizza with the Prez, All-School Picnic, Drive-in Movie Night, Stress Relief Events, and Meet the Pros—a professional speaker series—are just a few of the many school-sponsored offerings.

The Art Institute of California–Orange County is accredited by the Accrediting Council for Independent Colleges and Schools to award diplomas, associate degrees, and bachelor's degrees. The Accrediting Council for Independent Colleges and Schools (ACICS) is listed as a nationally recognized accrediting agency by the United States Department of Education and is recognized by the Council for Higher Education Accreditation. ACICS can be contacted at 750 First Street NE, Suite 980, Washington, D.C. 20002; phone: 202-336-6780.

The Art Institute of California–Orange County has been granted approval to operate by the California Bureau for Private Postsecondary and Vocational Education, California Department of Consumer Affairs, 1625 North Market Boulevard, Suite S-308, Sacramento, California 95834; phone: 916-574-8200; http:// www.bppve.ca.gov.

The interior design program leading to the Bachelor of Science degree is accredited by the Council for Interior Design Accreditation, 206 Grandville Avenue, Suite 350, Grand Rapids, Michigan 49503; http://www.accredit-id.org.

Location

The Art Institute of California–Orange County is strategically located in the heart of the booming southern California region that includes the counties of Orange, Los Angeles, San Diego, and Ventura. Southern California is a central hub of the entertainment, advertising, design, aerospace, and culinary industries. Orange County offers 42 miles of beautiful, sandy Pacific Ocean coastline, and wilderness parks are minutes away for camping, hiking, and biking. The area has more than 250 sunny days a year and is home to Disneyland, Knott's Berry Farm, and world-renowned cultural events, including the annual Laguna Beach Festival of the Arts.

Programs of Study and Degrees

Bachelor of Science degrees are available in advertising, culinary management, digital filmmaking and video production, fashion design, fashion marketing and management, game art and design, graphic design, industrial design, interior design, media arts and animation, visual and game programming, visual effects and motion graphics, and Web design and interactive media.

Associate of Science degrees are offered in baking and pastry, culinary arts, digital photography, graphic design, and Web design and interactive media.

Diploma programs are offered in baking and pastry and the art of cooking.

The culinary arts, culinary management, graphic design, and interior design programs are available in an evening and weekend option format.

Academic Programs

A bachelor's degree requires the completion of 192 credits, while an associate degree requires the completion of 112 academic credits. The academic year is divided into four quarters that begin in January, April, July, and October. Each program is offered on a year-round basis, allowing students to continue to work uninterrupted toward their degrees.

The school arranges study trips to local cultural and commercial sites. These visits offer an opportunity for valuable exposure to places and events relating to the student's field of study. In addition, out-of-town seminars and visits may be planned in individual programs.

The Student Tutoring Program is a peer-to-peer tutoring assistance program that is available to all current students. Each tutor has unique qualifications in his or her area of expertise.

Academic Facilities

The Art Institute of California–Orange County was designed with the creative student in mind. Light, spacious classrooms and well-equipped studios, professional-skill kitchens, and computer labs offer a productive working atmosphere to explore and render creativity. On-site equipment includes projectors, editing decks, camcorders, Windows NT and Macintosh computers, printers, and well-equipped kitchens. The Library/Learning Resources Center develops and maintains a readily available collection of books, periodicals, audiovisual materials, and CDs. Remote access to information sources is available through the Internet. Resources focus on creative art, design, and multimedia production as well as support for general education enhancement in the fine arts, humanities, social sciences, and communication. The school also maintains an art supply store for the convenience of its students. 50 Forks, a dining lab that operates as a full-service restaurant, is overseen by professional chef faculty members and operated by upper-level culinary students as a final passage prior to graduation.

Costs

Tuition cost varies by program. Prospective students should contact the school for current tuition costs. Other charges include a starting kit for all first-quarter students. Kits vary in price depending on the program of study.

Financial Aid

Financial aid is available for those who qualify. Students who require financial assistance should first complete and submit a Free Application for Federal Student Aid (FAFSA) and meet with a financial aid officer.

Faculty

The faculty members at The Art Institute of California–Orange County bring a professional perspective and industry standards into the classroom to better prepare students for entry-level positions upon graduation.

Student Government

The President's Club is a group of students who promote the philosophy of "students helping students." Members act as emissaries for the school and as a liaison between students and faculty and staff members. The club assists new students as well as helping in the organization and promotion of campus activities. Student members must be nominated for the organization by a member of the faculty or staff.

Admission Requirements

Prospective students must hold a high school diploma or General Educational Development (GED) certificate or have earned a bachelor's degree or higher from an accredited institution. High school seniors who have not yet graduated should submit a partial transcript that indicates their expected graduation date. All prospective students are required to submit two essays of approximately one page in length describing what they expect from the school and how an education at The Art Institute of California–Orange County may help them to reach their career goals. Applicants are interviewed either in person or by telephone by an assistant director of admissions. In addition, other standardized exams, such as the SAT or ACT, may be considered. Prospective students may apply at any time prior to the start of the upcoming quarter, and applications may be submitted online or mailed directly to the school. There is a $50 application fee.

For the most recent information regarding admission requirements, please refer to the current academic catalog.

Application and Information

To obtain an application, make arrangements for an interview, or tour the school, prospective students should contact:

The Art Institute of California–Orange County
3601 West Sunflower Avenue
Santa Ana, California 92704-7931
Phone: 714-830-0200
888-549-3055 (toll-free)
Fax: 714-556-1923
Web site: http://www.artinstitutes.edu/orangecounty

COLLEGE CLOSE-UPS

The Art Institute of Atlanta; The Art Institute of Atlanta–Decatur[1]; The Art Institute of Austin[2]; The Art Institute of California–Hollywood; The Art Institute of California–Inland Empire; The Art Institute of California–Los Angeles; The Art Institute of California–Orange County; The Art Institute of California–Sacramento; The Art Institute of California–San Diego; The Art Institute of California–San Francisco; The Art Institute of California–Sunnyvale; The Art Institute of Charleston[1]; The Art Institute of Charlotte; The Art Institute of Colorado; The Art Institute of Dallas; The Art Institute of Fort Lauderdale; The Art Institute of Fort Worth[3]; The Art Institute of Houston; The Art Institute of Houston–North[2]; The Art Institute of Indianapolis[4]; The Art Institute of Jacksonville[5]; The Art Institute of Las Vegas; The Art Institute of Michigan; The Art Institute of New York City; The Art Institute of Ohio–Cincinnati[6]; The Art Institute of Philadelphia; The Art Institute of Phoenix; The Art Institute of Pittsburgh; The Art Institute of Portland; The Art Institute of Raleigh–Durham; The Art Institute of Salt Lake City; The Art Institute of San Antonio[2];The Art Institute of Seattle; The Art Institute of Tampa[5]; The Art Institute of Tennessee–Nashville[1,7]; The Art Institute of Tucson; The Art Institute of Vancouver; The Art Institute of Virginia Beach[1,8]; The Art Institute of Washington[1,8]; The Art Institute of Washington–Northern Virginia[1,8]; The Art Institute of York–Pennsylvania; The Art Institutes International–Kansas City; The Art Institutes International Minnesota; The Illinois Institute of Art–Chicago; The Illinois Institute of Art–Schaumburg; Miami International University of Art & Design; The New England Institute of Art.

[1]A branch of The Art Institute of Atlanta
[2]A branch of The Art Institute of Houston
[3]A branch of The Art Institute of Dallas
[4]The Art Institute of Indianapolis is regulated by the Indiana Commission on Proprietary Education, 302 West Washington Street, Room E201, Indianapolis, Indiana 46204, AC-0080
[5]A branch of Miami International University of Art & Design
[6]The Art Institute of Ohio–Cincinnati, 8845 Governors Hill Drive, Suite 100, Cincinnati, Ohio 45249-3317, OH Reg. #04-01-1698B
[7]The Art Institute of Tennessee–Nashville is authorized for operation as a postsecondary educational institution by the Tennessee Higher Education Commission.
[8]Certified by the State Council of Higher Education to operate in Virginia

THE ART INSTITUTE OF CALIFORNIA–SACRAMENTO

SACRAMENTO, CALIFORNIA

The Art Institute of California–Sacramento

The Art Institute of California–Sacramento provides students with an educational environment and dedicated faculty members committed to preparing students to pursue entry-level positions in the creative arts. Under the guidance of industry professionals, students learn by doing the types of tasks they are likely to encounter in the workplace. In addition, assistance is available to help students with resume writing, networking, and keeping aware of what employers are looking for in job candidates. The school offers seven bachelor's degree programs and four associate degree programs.

The student population includes recent high school graduates, transfer students, and those who have left a previous employment situation to study and train for a new career. Students are creative, competitive, and open to new ideas. They place great value on an education that prepares them to pursue an exciting entry-level position in the arts.

The Art Institute of California–Sacramento places a high value on the quality of student life—both in and out of the classroom. Students participate in a wide variety of activities, including clubs and organizations, community service, and various committees designed to enhance the quality of student life.

The school offers assistance in helping students secure housing.

The Art Institute of California–Sacramento is accredited by the Accrediting Council for Independent Colleges and Schools (ACICS) to award diplomas, associate degrees, and bachelor's degrees. ACICS is listed as a nationally recognized accrediting agency by the United States Department of Education and is recognized by the Council for Higher Education Accreditation. ACICS can be contacted at 750 First Street NE, Suite 980, Washington, D.C. 20002; phone: 202-336-6780.

The Art Institute of California–Sacramento has been granted approval to operate by the California Bureau for Private Postsecondary and Vocational Education, California Department of Consumer Affairs, 1625 North Market Boulevard, Suite S-308, Sacramento, California 95834; phone: 916-574-8200; http://www.bppve.ca.gov.

Location

Sacramento's metropolitan population of more than 2 million means that students have access to recreation and the arts. In addition to state government, the city is a major transportation and commerce hub linking the east with California's coastal cities.

Programs of Study and Degrees

Bachelor's degree programs are offered in culinary management, digital filmmaking and video production, game art and design, graphic design, interior design, media arts and animation, and Web design and interactive media.

Associate degrees are offered in baking and pastry, culinary arts, graphic design, and Web design and interactive media.

Diploma programs are available in baking and pastry and the art of cooking.

Academic Programs

The Art Institute of California–Sacramento operates on a year-round, four-quarter system.

Academic Facilities

The Art Institute of California–Sacramento contains classrooms, Mac and PC computer labs, and a library for student use. There is also a bookstore.

Costs

Tuition cost varies by program. Prospective students should contact the school for current tuition costs. Other charges include a starting kit for all first quarter students. Kits vary in price depending on the program of study.

Financial Aid

Financial aid is available for those who qualify. Students who require financial assistance should first complete and submit a Free Application for Federal Student Aid (FAFSA) and meet with a financial aid officer.

Faculty

Faculty members at The Art Institute of California–Sacramento have professional knowledge that they bring into the classroom. The school's faculty members provide their students with a real-world, relevant educational experience.

Admission Requirements

Applicants must provide proof of high school graduation or achievement of a General Educational Development (GED) certificate as a prerequisite for admission. In lieu of documenting high school graduation or a GED certificate, applicants may provide proof of attaining an associate degree or higher from an accredited institution. An official transcript indicating date of high school graduation, GED certificate (including test scores), or date of college graduation (including degree granted) is required as proof.

All individuals seeking admission to The Art Institute of California–Sacramento are interviewed in person or by phone by an assistant director of admissions, and each applicant must create an original essay of at least 150 words stating how an education at The Art Institute of California–Sacramento would help the student achieve career goals. There is a $50 application fee.

For the most recent information regarding admission requirements, please refer to the current academic catalog.

Application and Information

To obtain an application, make arrangements for an interview, or tour the school, prospective students should contact:

The Art Institute of California–Sacramento
2850 Gateway Oaks Drive, Suite #100
Sacramento, California 95833
Phone: 916-830-6320
800-477-1957 (toll-free)
Fax: 916-830-6344
Web site: http://www.artinstitutes.edu/sacramento

COLLEGE CLOSE-UPS

The Art Institute of Atlanta; The Art Institute of Atlanta–Decatur[1]; The Art Institute of Austin[2]; The Art Institute of California–Hollywood; The Art Institute of California–Inland Empire; The Art Institute of California–Los Angeles; The Art Institute of California–Orange County; The Art Institute of California–Sacramento; The Art Institute of California–San Diego; The Art Institute of California–San Francisco; The Art Institute of California–Sunnyvale; The Art Institute of Charleston[1]; The Art Institute of Charlotte; The Art Institute of Colorado; The Art Institute of Dallas; The Art Institute of Fort Lauderdale; The Art Institute of Fort Worth[3]; The Art Institute of Houston; The Art Institute of Houston–North[2]; The Art Institute of Indianapolis[4]; The Art Institute of Jacksonville[5]; The Art Institute of Las Vegas; The Art Institute of Michigan; The Art Institute of New York City; The Art Institute of Ohio–Cincinnati[6]; The Art Institute of Philadelphia; The Art Institute of Phoenix; The Art Institute of Pittsburgh; The Art Institute of Portland; The Art Institute of Raleigh–Durham; The Art Institute of Salt Lake City; The Art Institute of San Antonio[2];The Art Institute of Seattle; The Art Institute of Tampa[5]; The Art Institute of Tennessee–Nashville[1,7]; The Art Institute of Tucson; The Art Institute of Vancouver; The Art Institute of Virginia Beach[1,8]; The Art Institute of Washington[1,8]; The Art Institute of Washington–Northern Virginia[1,8]; The Art Institute of York–Pennsylvania; The Art Institutes International–Kansas City; The Art Institutes International Minnesota; The Illinois Institute of Art–Chicago; The Illinois Institute of Art–Schaumburg; Miami International University of Art & Design; The New England Institute of Art.

[1]A branch of The Art Institute of Atlanta
[2]A branch of The Art Institute of Houston
[3]A branch of The Art Institute of Dallas
[4]The Art Institute of Indianapolis is regulated by the Indiana Commission on Proprietary Education, 302 West Washington Street, Room E201, Indianapolis, Indiana 46204, AC-0080
[5]A branch of Miami International University of Art & Design
[6]The Art Institute of Ohio–Cincinnati, 8845 Governors Hill Drive, Suite 100, Cincinnati, Ohio 45249-3317, OH Reg. #04-01-1698B
[7]The Art Institute of Tennessee–Nashville is authorized for operation as a postsecondary educational institution by the Tennessee Higher Education Commission.
[8]Certified by the State Council of Higher Education to operate in Virginia

THE ART INSTITUTE OF CALIFORNIA–SAN DIEGO

SAN DIEGO, CALIFORNIA

The Art Institute of California–San Diego

The Art Institute of California–San Diego helps prepare students to pursue entry-level positions in the creative marketplace by teaching professional skills. Instructors and staff members direct students' portfolio development and resume creation, while partnerships with local and national employers help to deliver relevant education that can benefit both students and employers. The school offers eleven bachelor's degrees options as well as four associate degree programs.

Academic programs are carefully created with the support and contributions of members of the professional community through Program Advisory Committees. Curricula are further reviewed by faculty members and industry professionals to ensure that they assist students in preparing for the needs of a changing marketplace.

Career Services keeps track of employer satisfaction and industry trends to provide employers with candidates who fulfill their needs while working to assist in graduates' career goals. In addition, assistance is available to help students with resume writing, networking, and keeping aware of what employers are looking for in job candidates.

Students come to The Art Institute of California–San Diego from across the United States and abroad. The student population includes recent high school graduates, transfer students, and those who have left a previous employment situation to study and train for a new career. Students are creative, competitive, and open to new ideas. They place great value on an education that prepares them to pursue an exciting entry-level position in the arts.

Students may join the Advertising Club, AIGA, the Comic Club, the Level Design Club, the Theatre Club, and the interactive or 3-D clubs. Art Institute of California–San Diego students help the national Ad Club by designing and producing collateral as well as participating in such events as holiday parties, media auctions, and creative shows. Students may also serve on the Student Council, which plans school social and cultural events.

Students may live in school-sponsored housing at The Club at River Run, located 1.5 miles from the school and adjacent to the trolley line. Four students share a two-bedroom, fully furnished apartment. The complex offers many amenities, including a swimming pool, Jacuzzi, tennis courts, fitness center, and a clubhouse. Two resident assistants live in the complex and have organized events such as potlucks, bowling nights, video game tournaments, cookouts, pizza parties, and faculty-student dinners. Security is provided by on-site management during the day and courtesy patrols in the evening hours. Supermarkets, banks, coffee shops, and fast food are conveniently located nearby. The Student Affairs Department provides information on roommate referrals and apartment rentals.

The Art Institute of California–San Diego is accredited by the Accrediting Commission of Career Schools and Colleges (ACCSC) which may be contacted at 2101 Wilson Boulevard, Suite 302, Arlington, Virginia 22201; phone: 703-247-4212.

The Associate of Science degree in culinary arts is accredited by the Accrediting Commission of the American Culinary Federation Education Foundation.

The Art Institute of California–San Diego has been granted approval to operate by the California Bureau for Private Postsecondary and Vocational Education, California Department of Consumer Affairs, 1625 North Market Boulevard, Suite S-308, Sacramento, California 95834; phone: 916-574-8200; http://www.bppve.ca.gov.

Location

Within a 2-hour drive are mountains, deserts, Los Angeles, Mexico, surfing, water sports, tennis, golf, jogging, mountain biking, and beaches. San Diego offers many regional shopping centers as well as picturesque spots, including the San Diego Zoo, Wild Animal Park, Sea World, Seaport Village, Old Town, Horton Plaza, the Gaslamp District, and La Jolla. The opera, symphony, live theater district, professional and collegiate athletic events, and concerts are also nearby. San Diego's average daytime temperature is 70 degrees, and the city averages 267 sunny days each year.

Programs of Study and Degrees

The Art Institute of California–San Diego offers bachelor's degree programs in advertising, audio production, culinary management, fashion design, fashion marketing and management, game art and design, graphic design, interior design, media arts and animation, visual and game programming, and Web design and interactive media.

Associate degree programs are available in advertising, baking and pastry, culinary arts, and graphic design.

The graphic design and interior design programs are also available in an evening and weekend option format.

Academic Programs

The Art Institute of California–San Diego operates on a year-round, four-quarter system.

Academic Facilities

The Art Institute of California–San Diego is home to a student book and supply store, student lounge, computer labs with both PC and Macintosh computers, art production studios, life drawing rooms, culinary kitchens and storage, an Interior Design Resource Center, a Learning Resource Center (LRC), administrative offices, and classrooms.

Light, spacious classrooms and well-equipped studios are designed to breed creativity. The library and Learning Resource Center provide a readily available collection of books, periodicals, audiovisual materials, and CDs as well as access to remote sources through the Internet. Resources focus on creative art, design, and multimedia production as well as support for general education enhancement in the fine arts, humanities, social sciences, and communication. The Palette is a restaurant open to the public that is operated by senior-level culinary students and overseen by faculty members who are professional chefs.

Costs

Tuition cost varies by program. Prospective students should contact the school for current tuition costs. Other charges include a starting kit for all first-quarter students. Kits vary in price depending on the program of study.

Financial Aid

Financial aid is available for those who qualify. Students who require financial assistance should first complete and submit a Free Application for Federal Student Aid (FAFSA) and meet with a financial aid officer.

Faculty

The Art Institute of California–San Diego has part-time and full-time faculty members, many of whom are experienced in their respective fields. By tapping the experience of industry professionals, the school is able to bring a professional perspective into the classroom.

Admission Requirements

Prospective students must be high school graduates or hold a General Educational Development (GED) certificate. High school seniors who have not yet graduated should submit a partial transcript that indicates their expected graduation date. All prospective students are required to write an essay of approximately 150 words describing how an education at The Art Institute of California–San Diego will help them to attain their creative goals. An interview, either in person or by telephone, is required. SAT or ACT scores may also be considered. Applications may be submitted online or mailed to the school. There is a $50 application fee.

For the most recent information regarding admission requirements, please refer to the current academic catalog.

Application and Information

To obtain an application or make arrangements for an interview or tour of the school, prospective students should contact:

The Art Institute of California–San Diego
7650 Mission Valley Road
San Diego, California 92108-4423
Phone: 858-598-1200
866-275-2422 (toll-free)
Fax: 619-291-3206
Web site: http://www.artinstitutes.edu/sandiego

The Art Institute of Atlanta; The Art Institute of Atlanta–Decatur[1]; The Art Institute of Austin[2]; The Art Institute of California–Hollywood; The Art Institute of California–Inland Empire; The Art Institute of California–Los Angeles; The Art Institute of California–Orange County; The Art Institute of California–Sacramento; The Art Institute of California–San Diego; The Art Institute of California–San Francisco; The Art Institute of California–Sunnyvale; The Art Institute of Charleston[1]; The Art Institute of Charlotte; The Art Institute of Colorado; The Art Institute of Dallas; The Art Institute of Fort Lauderdale; The Art Institute of Fort Worth[3]; The Art Institute of Houston; The Art Institute of Houston–North[2]; The Art Institute of Indianapolis[4]; The Art Institute of Jacksonville[5]; The Art Institute of Las Vegas; The Art Institute of Michigan; The Art Institute of New York City; The Art Institute of Ohio–Cincinnati[6]; The Art Institute of Philadelphia; The Art Institute of Phoenix; The Art Institute of Pittsburgh; The Art Institute of Portland; The Art Institute of Raleigh–Durham; The Art Institute of Salt Lake City; The Art Institute of San Antonio[2];The Art Institute of Seattle; The Art Institute of Tampa[5]; The Art Institute of Tennessee–Nashville[1,7]; The Art Institute of Tucson; The Art Institute of Vancouver; The Art Institute of Virginia Beach[1,8]; The Art Institute of Washington[1,8]; The Art Institute of Washington–Northern Virginia[1,8]; The Art Institute of York–Pennsylvania; The Art Institutes International–Kansas City; The Art Institutes International Minnesota; The Illinois Institute of Art–Chicago; The Illinois Institute of Art–Schaumburg; Miami International University of Art & Design; The New England Institute of Art.

[1]A branch of The Art Institute of Atlanta
[2]A branch of The Art Institute of Houston
[3]A branch of The Art Institute of Dallas
[4]The Art Institute of Indianapolis is regulated by the Indiana Commission on Proprietary Education, 302 West Washington Street, Room E201, Indianapolis, Indiana 46204, AC-0080
[5]A branch of Miami International University of Art & Design
[6]The Art Institute of Ohio–Cincinnati, 8845 Governors Hill Drive, Suite 100, Cincinnati, Ohio 45249-3317, OH Reg. #04-01-1698B
[7]The Art Institute of Tennessee–Nashville is authorized for operation as a postsecondary educational institution by the Tennessee Higher Education Commission.
[8]Certified by the State Council of Higher Education to operate in Virginia

THE ART INSTITUTE OF CALIFORNIA–SAN FRANCISCO

The Art Institute of California–San Francisco

SAN FRANCISCO, CALIFORNIA

The Art Institute of California–San Francisco helps students cultivate and refine the talents and skills that are needed to pursue entry-level positions in the creative arts. Curricula are taught in an environment that encourages free expression, leadership, and responsible decision making. The school offers twelve bachelor's degree programs to students, as well as six associate degree programs, a diploma program, and a master's degree in computer animation.

Faculty and staff members strive to foster development and cultivate artistic growth. Students are given opportunities to develop leadership skills and build relationships. In addition, assistance is available to help students with resume writing, networking, and keeping abreast of what employers are looking for in job candidates.

The Art Institute of California–San Francisco places a high value on the quality of student life both in and out of the classroom. Students can participate in a wide variety of activities, including clubs and organizations, community service opportunities, and various committees designed to enhance the quality of student life. Numerous all-school programs and events are planned throughout the year to meet the educational, developmental, and social needs of students. The Art Institute of California–San Francisco also includes a student gallery, a student lounge, staff offices, and an art supply store.

The Art Institute of California–San Francisco helps students to obtain comfortable, affordable housing. The school has two housing locations. Westlake Village Apartments in Daly City offers studio apartments for 2 occupants. Two-bedroom units for 4 occupants are also available. The Fillmore Center in San Francisco offers two- and three-bedroom units for 6 occupants. All apartments are furnished with a full kitchen and one or two bathrooms. Both housing sites are conveniently located within a 20-minute commute of the school, using public transportation. Students may also choose to live in independent housing; those who decide to live off campus are encouraged to begin their housing search early. Roommate referral services are available.

Students come to The Art Institute of California–San Francisco from throughout the United States and abroad. The student population includes recent high school graduates, transfer students, and those who have left a previous employment situation to study and train for a new career. Students are creative, competitive, and open to new ideas. They place great value on an education that prepares them for an exciting entry-level position in the arts. Many clubs and organizations are specific to programs of study, while others are geared toward student interest in photography, the environment, and campus activities. Students also take advantage of San Francisco's clubs, concerts, museums, ethnic restaurants, and Golden Gate Park. Local activities and clubs include the San Francisco Siggraph Chapter, Graphic Design Guild, San Francisco Fashion Group, and Game Developers Local Chapter. In addition, students have attended events such as the International Game Developers Conference, MacWorld, and the HOW Conference.

The Art Institute of California–San Francisco, is accredited by the Accrediting Council for Independent Colleges and Schools (ACICS) to award associate and bachelor's degrees. The ACICS is listed as a nationally recognized accrediting agency by the United States Department of Education and is recognized by the Council for Higher Education Accreditation. ACICS can be contacted at 750 First Street NE, Suite 980, Washington, D.C. 20002; phone: 202-336-6780.

The Art Institute of California–San Francisco has been granted approval to operate by the California Bureau for Private Postsecondary and Vocational Education, California Department of Consumer Affairs, 1625 North Market Boulevard, Suite S-308, Sacramento, California 95834; phone: 916-574-8200; http://www.bppve.ca.gov.

Location

The Art Institute of California–San Francisco is located on Market Street, in the center of downtown San Francisco. San Francisco is home to the Golden Gate Bridge, Alcatraz Island, and the Haight-Ashbury district. With a population of more than 700,000, San Francisco has the highest concentration of arts organizations in the world. Students have access to public libraries, including the Center of Performing Arts Library, with its specialized sections on fashion and costuming. Natural attractions include the rolling hills and mountains in nearby wine country and dramatic vistas overlooking the Pacific, which provide options for hiking, biking, and other outdoor activities. Asian, Hispanic, and Italian neighborhoods are within walking distance. Public transportation, including cable cars, is available. The Bay Area and nearby Silicon Valley are home to leading new-media companies.

Programs of Study and Degrees

Bachelor's degrees are offered in advertising, audio production, culinary management, digital filmmaking and video production, fashion design, fashion marketing and management, game art and design, graphic design, interior design, media arts and animation, visual and game programming, and Web design and interactive media.

Associate degrees are available in baking and pastry, culinary arts, fashion design, fashion marketing, graphic design, and Web design and interactive media.

A Master of Fine Arts degree is offered in computer animation.

A diploma program is offered in baking and pastry.

Academic Programs

The academic year is divided into four quarters, beginning in January, April, July, and October. A bachelor's degree requires completion of 192 credits. An associate degree requires completion of 112 academic credits.

Academic Facilities

The school's 37,000 square feet houses classrooms, studios, offices, an exhibition gallery, a Learning Resource Center with library and research facilities, a student art supply store, and computer labs with Internet connections. The library is constantly updated and supplemented with new acquisitions. At The Art Institute of California–San Francisco, the library offers a collection of books, magazines, newspapers, videos, CDs, and slides that supports program-specific technology. Light, spacious classrooms and equipped studios and computer labs offer a productive working atmosphere in which students can explore and render their creativity.

Costs

Tuition cost varies by program. Prospective students should contact the school for current tuition costs. Other charges include a starting kit for all first-quarter students. Kits vary in price, depending on the program of study.

Financial Aid

Financial aid is available for those who qualify. Students who require financial assistance should first complete and submit a Free Application for Federal Student Aid (FAFSA) and meet with a financial aid officer.

Faculty

The Art Institute of California–San Francisco faculty consists of full-time instructors and part-time instructors, many of whom have advanced degrees and professional experience in their respective fields.

Student Government

The Student Federation is responsible for student government and acts as a liaison between the student body and faculty and staff members.

Admission Requirements

Prospective students must submit an application for admission, record of proof of high school graduation or a General Educational Development (GED) certificate, high school transcripts, and SAT or ACT scores, if available. High school seniors who have not yet graduated should submit a partial transcript that indicates their expected graduation date. Portfolios are welcomed but are not required. Applicants are evaluated on the basis of their previous education, background, and stated or demonstrated interest in the school's programs. Students must be interviewed either in person or via telephone by an Assistant Director of Admissions. Prospective students may apply at any time prior to the start of the upcoming quarter. There is a $50 application fee.

For the most recent information regarding admission requirements, please refer to the current academic catalog.

Application and Information

To obtain an application, make arrangements for an interview, or tour the school, prospective students should contact:

The Art Institute of California–San Francisco
1170 Market Street
San Francisco, California 94102-4928
Phone: 415-865-0198
888-493-3261 (toll-free)
Fax: 415-863-6344
Web site: http://www.artinstitutes.edu/sanfrancisco

COLLEGE CLOSE-UPS

The Art Institute of Atlanta; The Art Institute of Atlanta–Decatur[1]; The Art Institute of Austin[2]; The Art Institute of California–Hollywood; The Art Institute of California–Inland Empire; The Art Institute of California–Los Angeles; The Art Institute of California–Orange County; The Art Institute of California–Sacramento; The Art Institute of California–San Diego; The Art Institute of California–San Francisco; The Art Institute of California–Sunnyvale; The Art Institute of Charleston[1]; The Art Institute of Charlotte; The Art Institute of Colorado; The Art Institute of Dallas; The Art Institute of Fort Lauderdale; The Art Institute of Fort Worth[3]; The Art Institute of Houston; The Art Institute of Houston–North[2]; The Art Institute of Indianapolis[4]; The Art Institute of Jacksonville[5]; The Art Institute of Las Vegas; The Art Institute of Michigan; The Art Institute of New York City; The Art Institute of Ohio–Cincinnati[6]; The Art Institute of Philadelphia; The Art Institute of Phoenix; The Art Institute of Pittsburgh; The Art Institute of Portland; The Art Institute of Raleigh–Durham; The Art Institute of Salt Lake City; The Art Institute of San Antonio[2];The Art Institute of Seattle; The Art Institute of Tampa[5]; The Art Institute of Tennessee–Nashville[1,7]; The Art Institute of Tucson; The Art Institute of Vancouver; The Art Institute of Virginia Beach[1,8]; The Art Institute of Washington[1,8]; The Art Institute of Washington–Northern Virginia[1,8]; The Art Institute of York–Pennsylvania; The Art Institutes International–Kansas City; The Art Institutes International Minnesota; The Illinois Institute of Art–Chicago; The Illinois Institute of Art–Schaumburg; Miami International University of Art & Design; The New England Institute of Art.

[1]A branch of The Art Institute of Atlanta
[2]A branch of The Art Institute of Houston
[3]A branch of The Art Institute of Dallas
[4]The Art Institute of Indianapolis is regulated by the Indiana Commission on Proprietary Education, 302 West Washington Street, Room E201, Indianapolis, Indiana 46204, AC-0080
[5]A branch of Miami International University of Art & Design
[6]The Art Institute of Ohio–Cincinnati, 8845 Governors Hill Drive, Suite 100, Cincinnati, Ohio 45249-3317, OH Reg. #04-01-1698B
[7]The Art Institute of Tennessee–Nashville is authorized for operation as a postsecondary educational institution by the Tennessee Higher Education Commission.
[8]Certified by the State Council of Higher Education to operate in Virginia

THE ART INSTITUTE OF CALIFORNIA–SUNNYVALE

SUNNYVALE, CALIFORNIA

The Art Institute of California–Sunnyvale provides students with an educational environment and dedicated faculty members who are committed to preparing students to pursue entry-level positions in the creative arts. Under the guidance of industry professionals, students learn by doing the types of tasks they are likely to encounter in the workplace. In addition, assistance is available to help students with resume writing, networking, and keeping aware of what employers are looking for in job candidates. The school offers eight bachelor's degree programs and three associate degree programs.

The student population includes recent high school graduates, transfer students, and those who have left a previous employment situation to study and train for a new career. Students are creative, competitive, and open to new ideas. They place great value on an education that prepares them to pursue an exciting entry-level position in the arts.

The Art Institute of California–Sunnyvale places a high value on the quality of student life—both in and out of the classroom. Students can participate in a wide variety of activities, including clubs and organizations, community service, and various committees designed to enhance the quality of student life.

The school offers assistance in helping students to secure housing.

The Art Institute of California–Sunnyvale, a branch of The Art Institute of California–Hollywood, is accredited by the Accrediting Council for Independent Colleges and Schools (ACICS) to award associate degrees and bachelor's degrees. ACICS is listed as a nationally recognized accrediting agency by the United States Department of Education and is recognized by the Council for Higher Education Accreditation. ACICS can be contacted at 750 First Street NE, Suite 980, Washington, D.C. 20002; phone: 202-336-6780.

The Art Institute of California–Sunnyvale has been granted temporary approval to operate by the California Bureau for Private Postsecondary and Vocational Education (California Department of Consumer Affairs, 1625 North Market Boulevard, Suite S-308, Sacramento, California 95834; phone: 916-574-8200; http://www.bppve.ca.gov) in order to enable the bureau to conduct a quality inspection of the institution.

Location

Sunnyvale, a town of over 131,000 people, is one of the major cities that make up California's Silicon Valley. It's located between the San Francisco Bay and San Jose, providing easy access to cultural exhibitions, art museums, professional sports, and other entertainment options.

Programs of Study and Degrees

Bachelor's degree programs are offered in culinary management, digital filmmaking and video production, fashion marketing and management, game art and design, graphic design, interior design, media arts and animation, and Web design and interactive media.

Associate degrees are offered in culinary arts, graphic design, and Web design and interactive media.

Academic Programs

The Art Institute of California–Sunnyvale operates on a year-round, four-quarter system.

Academic Facilities

The Art Institute of California–Sunnyvale is a 53,000 square-foot facility that contains classrooms, Mac and PC computer labs, and a library for student use. There is also a bookstore.

Costs

Tuition cost varies by program. Prospective students should contact the school for current tuition costs. Other charges include a starting kit for all first quarter students. Kits vary in price depending on the program of study.

Financial Aid

Financial aid is available for those who qualify. Students who require financial assistance should first complete and submit a Free Application for Federal Student Aid (FAFSA) and meet with a financial aid officer.

Faculty

Faculty members at The Art Institute of California–Sunnyvale have professional knowledge that they bring into the classroom. The school's faculty members provide their students with a real-world, relevant educational experience.

Admission Requirements

Applicants must provide proof of high school graduation or achievement of a General Educational Development (GED) certificate as a prerequisite for admission. In lieu of documenting high school graduation or a GED certificate, applicants may provide proof of attaining an associate degree or higher from an accredited institution. An official transcript indicating date of high school graduation, GED certificate (including test scores), or date of college graduation (including degree granted) is required as proof.

All individuals seeking admission to The Art Institute of California–Sunnyvale are interviewed in person or by phone by an assistant director of admissions, and each applicant must create an original essay of at least 150 words stating how an education at The Art Institute of California–Sunnyvale would help the student to achieve career goals. There is a $50 application fee.

For the most recent information regarding admission requirements, please refer to the current academic catalog.

Application and Information

To obtain an application, make arrangements for an interview, or tour the school, prospective students should contact:

The Art Institute of California–Sunnyvale
1120 Kifer Road
Sunnyvale, California 94086
Phone: 408-962-6400
866-583-7961 (toll-free)
Fax: 408-962-6498
Web site: http://www.artinstitutes.edu/sunnyvale

COLLEGE CLOSE-UPS

The Art Institute of Atlanta; The Art Institute of Atlanta–Decatur[1]; The Art Institute of Austin[2]; The Art Institute of California–Hollywood; The Art Institute of California–Inland Empire; The Art Institute of California–Los Angeles; The Art Institute of California–Orange County; The Art Institute of California–Sacramento; The Art Institute of California–San Diego; The Art Institute of California–San Francisco; The Art Institute of California–Sunnyvale; The Art Institute of Charleston[1]; The Art Institute of Charlotte; The Art Institute of Colorado; The Art Institute of Dallas; The Art Institute of Fort Lauderdale; The Art Institute of Fort Worth[3]; The Art Institute of Houston; The Art Institute of Houston–North[2]; The Art Institute of Indianapolis[4]; The Art Institute of Jacksonville[5]; The Art Institute of Las Vegas; The Art Institute of Michigan; The Art Institute of New York City; The Art Institute of Ohio–Cincinnati[6]; The Art Institute of Philadelphia; The Art Institute of Phoenix; The Art Institute of Pittsburgh; The Art Institute of Portland; The Art Institute of Raleigh–Durham; The Art Institute of Salt Lake City; The Art Institute of San Antonio[2]; The Art Institute of Seattle; The Art Institute of Tampa[5]; The Art Institute of Tennessee–Nashville[1,7]; The Art Institute of Tucson; The Art Institute of Vancouver; The Art Institute of Virginia Beach[1,8]; The Art Institute of Washington[1,8]; The Art Institute of Washington–Northern Virginia[1,8]; The Art Institute of York–Pennsylvania; The Art Institutes International–Kansas City; The Art Institutes International Minnesota; The Illinois Institute of Art–Chicago; The Illinois Institute of Art–Schaumburg; Miami International University of Art & Design; The New England Institute of Art.

[1]A branch of The Art Institute of Atlanta
[2]A branch of The Art Institute of Houston
[3]A branch of The Art Institute of Dallas
[4]The Art Institute of Indianapolis is regulated by the Indiana Commission on Proprietary Education, 302 West Washington Street, Room E201, Indianapolis, Indiana 46204, AC-0080
[5]A branch of Miami International University of Art & Design
[6]The Art Institute of Ohio–Cincinnati, 8845 Governors Hill Drive, Suite 100, Cincinnati, Ohio 45249-3317, OH Reg. #04-01-1698B
[7]The Art Institute of Tennessee–Nashville is authorized for operation as a postsecondary educational institution by the Tennessee Higher Education Commission.
[8]Certified by the State Council of Higher Education to operate in Virginia

THE ART INSTITUTE OF CHARLESTON

CHARLESTON, SOUTH CAROLINA

The Art Institute of Charleston provides students with an educational environment and dedicated faculty members who are committed to preparing students to pursue entry-level positions in the creative arts. Under the guidance of industry professionals, students learn by doing the types of tasks they are likely to encounter in the workplace. In addition, assistance is available to help students with resume writing, networking, and keeping aware of what employers are looking for in job candidates. The school offers seven bachelor's degree programs and five associate degree programs.

The student population includes recent high school graduates, transfer students, and those who have left a previous employment situation to study and train for a new career. Students are creative, competitive, and open to new ideas. They place great value on an education that prepares them to pursue an exciting entry-level position in the arts.

The Art Institute of Charleston places a high value on the quality of student life—both in and out of the classroom. Students can participate in a wide variety of activities, including clubs and organizations, community service, and various committees designed to enhance the quality of student life.

The school offers assistance in helping students to secure housing.

The Art Institute of Charleston is a branch campus of The Art Institute of Atlanta. The Art Institute of Atlanta is accredited by the Commission on Colleges of the Southern Association of Colleges and Schools to award associate and baccalaureate degrees. Contact the Commission on Colleges at 1866 Southern Lane, Decatur, Georgia 30033-4097 or call 404-679-4500 for questions about the accreditation of The Art Institute of Atlanta.

The Art Institute of Charleston is licensed by the South Carolina Commission on Higher Education, 1333 Main Street, Suite 200, Columbia, South Carolina 29201; phone: 803-737-8860. Licensure indicates only that minimum standards have been met; it is not equal to or synonymous with accreditation by an accrediting agency recognized by the U.S. Department of Education.

Location

The school's Market Street location is close to arts, historical, and cultural organizations, allowing students to experience all that Charleston has to offer.

Programs of Study and Degrees

Bachelor's degree programs are offered in culinary arts management, digital filmmaking and video production, fashion and retail management, graphic design, interior design, photographic imaging, and Web design and interactive media.

Associate degrees are offered in culinary arts; culinary arts with a concentration in baking and pastry; graphic design; Web and interactive media; and wine, spirits, and beverage management.

Certificate programs are available in commercial photography and culinary arts–skills.

Academic Programs

The Art Institute of Charleston operates on a year-round, four-quarter system.

Academic Facilities

The Art Institute of Charleston contains classrooms, Mac and PC computer labs, and a library for student use. There is also a bookstore.

Costs

Tuition cost varies by program. Prospective students should contact the school for current tuition costs. Other charges include a starting kit for all first quarter students. Kits vary in price depending on the program of study.

Financial Aid

Financial aid is available for those who qualify. Students who require financial assistance should first complete and submit a Free Application for Federal Student Aid (FAFSA) and meet with a financial aid officer.

Faculty

Faculty members at The Art Institute of Charleston have professional knowledge that they bring into the classroom. The school's faculty members provide their students with a real-world, relevant educational experience.

Admission Requirements

Applicants must provide proof of high school graduation or achievement of a General Educational Development (GED) certificate as a prerequisite for admission. In lieu of documenting high school graduation or a GED certificate, applicants may provide proof of attaining an associate degree or higher from an accredited institution. An official transcript indicating date of high school graduation, GED certificate (including test scores), or date of college graduation (including degree granted) is required as proof.

All individuals seeking admission to The Art Institute of Charleston are interviewed in person or by phone by an assistant director of admissions, and each applicant must create an original essay of at least 150 words stating how an education at The Art Institute of Charleston would help the student to achieve career goals. There is a $50 application fee.

For the most recent information regarding admission requirements, please refer to the current academic catalog.

Application and Information

To obtain an application, make arrangements for an interview, or tour the school, prospective students should contact:

The Art Institute of Charleston
24 North Market Street
Charleston, South Carolina 29401-2623
Phone: 843-727-3500
866-211-0107 (toll-free)
Fax: 843-727-3440
Web site: http://www.artinstitutes.edu/charleston

COLLEGE CLOSE-UPS

The Art Institute of Atlanta; The Art Institute of Atlanta–Decatur[1]; The Art Institute of Austin[2]; The Art Institute of California–Hollywood; The Art Institute of California–Inland Empire; The Art Institute of California–Los Angeles; The Art Institute of California–Orange County; The Art Institute of California–Sacramento; The Art Institute of California–San Diego; The Art Institute of California–San Francisco; The Art Institute of California–Sunnyvale; The Art Institute of Charleston[1]; The Art Institute of Charlotte; The Art Institute of Colorado; The Art Institute of Dallas; The Art Institute of Fort Lauderdale; The Art Institute of Fort Worth[3]; The Art Institute of Houston; The Art Institute of Houston–North[2]; The Art Institute of Indianapolis[4]; The Art Institute of Jacksonville[5]; The Art Institute of Las Vegas; The Art Institute of Michigan; The Art Institute of New York City; The Art Institute of Ohio–Cincinnati[6]; The Art Institute of Philadelphia; The Art Institute of Phoenix; The Art Institute of Pittsburgh; The Art Institute of Portland; The Art Institute of Raleigh–Durham; The Art Institute of Salt Lake City; The Art Institute of San Antonio[2]; The Art Institute of Seattle; The Art Institute of Tampa[5]; The Art Institute of Tennessee–Nashville[1,7]; The Art Institute of Tucson; The Art Institute of Vancouver; The Art Institute of Virginia Beach[1,8]; The Art Institute of Washington[1,8]; The Art Institute of Washington–Northern Virginia[1,8]; The Art Institute of York–Pennsylvania; The Art Institutes International–Kansas City; The Art Institutes International Minnesota; The Illinois Institute of Art–Chicago; The Illinois Institute of Art–Schaumburg; Miami International University of Art & Design; The New England Institute of Art.

[1]A branch of The Art Institute of Atlanta
[2]A branch of The Art Institute of Houston
[3]A branch of The Art Institute of Dallas
[4]The Art Institute of Indianapolis is regulated by the Indiana Commission on Proprietary Education, 302 West Washington Street, Room E201, Indianapolis, Indiana 46204, AC-0080
[5]A branch of Miami International University of Art & Design
[6]The Art Institute of Ohio–Cincinnati, 8845 Governors Hill Drive, Suite 100, Cincinnati, Ohio 45249-3317, OH Reg. #04-01-1698B
[7]The Art Institute of Tennessee–Nashville is authorized for operation as a postsecondary educational institution by the Tennessee Higher Education Commission.
[8]Certified by the State Council of Higher Education to operate in Virginia

THE ART INSTITUTE OF CHARLOTTE

CHARLOTTE, NORTH CAROLINA

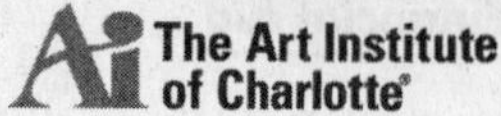

The Art Institute of Charlotte prepares students to pursue entry-level employment in the creative arts. Students learn through programs of study that reflect the needs of a changing job market. Courses are taught by faculty members who have professional experience in their fields of expertise. The school offers seven bachelor's degree programs and five associate degree programs.

Students come to The Art Institute of Charlotte from throughout the southeastern United States and abroad. The student population includes recent high school graduates, transfer students, and those who have left a previous employment situation to study and train for a new career. Students are creative, competitive, and open to new ideas. They place great value on an education that prepares them to pursue an exciting entry-level position in the arts.

Student housing options include apartments that comfortably accommodate 4 students in two-bedroom, two-bath units complete with living room, dining area, and full kitchen. Students submit a roommate preference form and are assigned to apartments by the housing staff. The apartments are located close to The Art Institute of Charlotte and shopping, dining, and entertainment venues.

Students enrolled in The Art Institute of Charlotte can get involved in student-led activities through the Student Affairs Department. Activities stimulate cultural awareness, creativity, and social and professional development. Students enrolled in the Interior Design Program may join the Interior Design Student Association. In addition, academic departments regularly organize trips to the International Home Furnishing Market in High Point, North Carolina, as well as to local museums and galleries.

Services are available to assist students with resume writing, networking, and keeping aware of what employers are looking for in job applicants.

The Art Institute of Charlotte is accredited by the Accrediting Council for Independent Colleges and Schools (ACICS) to award certificates, associate degrees, and bachelor's degrees. ACICS is listed as a nationally recognized accrediting agency by the United States Department of Education and is recognized by the Council for Higher Education Accreditation. ACICS can be contacted at 750 First Street NE, Suite 980, Washington, D.C. 20002; phone: 202-336-6780.

The Art Institute of Charlotte is licensed to award certificates by the North Carolina State Board of Community Colleges and is licensed to award associate and bachelor's degrees by the Board of Governors of the University of North Carolina.

Location

Charlotte mixes the characteristics of a large urban center with the charm of suburban life. With a mild climate and central location, Charlotte residents are only 2 hours from the Blue Ridge Mountains and 3 hours from the Atlantic coast. Charlotte is known for its arts community, sports, shopping, and restaurants. More than 300 Fortune 500 companies have offices in Charlotte, the nation's second-largest banking center. The city is the nation's fifth-largest urban region, with 6.3 million people living within a 100-mile radius.

Programs of Study and Degrees

Bachelor's degree programs are available in culinary arts management, digital filmmaking and video production, fashion marketing and management, graphic design, interior design, photography, and Web design and interactive media.

Associate degree programs are offered in culinary arts, fashion marketing, graphic design, interior design, and Web design and interactive media.

A certificate program is available in Web design.

Academic Programs

The Art Institute of Charlotte operates on a year-round, four-quarter system.

Academic Facilities

The Art Institute of Charlotte facility has computer labs for student use. Additional computers are available in the library. Studios, classrooms, and meeting rooms are available for students and faculty members.

Costs

Tuition cost varies by program. Prospective students should contact the school for current tuition costs. Other charges include a starting kit for all first quarter students. Kits vary in price depending on the program of study.

Financial Aid

Financial aid is available for those who qualify. Students who require financial assistance should first complete and submit a Free Application for Federal Student Aid (FAFSA) and meet with a financial aid officer.

Faculty

Faculty members at The Art Institute of Charlotte are experienced instructors, many of whom have professional experience outside of the classroom. There are full- and part-time faculty members at the school.

Admission Requirements

Applicants must be high school graduates or have a General Educational Development (GED) certificate. A 150-word written essay is required, as are high school transcripts and any records from other academic institutions attended. All interested students are interviewed in person or over the phone. Following this interview, prospective students complete an application for admission and submit the enrollment fee. Applicants who have taken the SAT or ACT are encouraged to submit their scores to the Admissions Office for evaluation. There is a $50 application fee.

For the most recent information regarding admission requirements, please refer to the current academic catalog.

Application and Information

To obtain an application or make arrangements for an interview or tour of the school, prospective students should contact:

The Art Institute of Charlotte
Three LakePointe Plaza
2110 Water Ridge Parkway
Charlotte, North Carolina 28217-4536
Phone: 704-357-8020
800-872-4417 (toll-free)
Fax: 704-357-1133
Web site: http://www.artinstitutes.edu/charlotte

COLLEGE CLOSE-UPS

The Art Institute of Atlanta; The Art Institute of Atlanta–Decatur[1]; The Art Institute of Austin[2]; The Art Institute of California–Hollywood; The Art Institute of California–Inland Empire; The Art Institute of California–Los Angeles; The Art Institute of California–Orange County; The Art Institute of California–Sacramento; The Art Institute of California–San Diego; The Art Institute of California–San Francisco; The Art Institute of California–Sunnyvale; The Art Institute of Charleston[1]; The Art Institute of Charlotte; The Art Institute of Colorado; The Art Institute of Dallas; The Art Institute of Fort Lauderdale; The Art Institute of Fort Worth[3]; The Art Institute of Houston; The Art Institute of Houston–North[2]; The Art Institute of Indianapolis[4]; The Art Institute of Jacksonville[5]; The Art Institute of Las Vegas; The Art Institute of Michigan; The Art Institute of New York City; The Art Institute of Ohio–Cincinnati[6]; The Art Institute of Philadelphia; The Art Institute of Phoenix; The Art Institute of Pittsburgh; The Art Institute of Portland; The Art Institute of Raleigh–Durham; The Art Institute of Salt Lake City; The Art Institute of San Antonio[2];The Art Institute of Seattle; The Art Institute of Tampa[5]; The Art Institute of Tennessee–Nashville[1,7]; The Art Institute of Tucson; The Art Institute of Vancouver; The Art Institute of Virginia Beach[1,8]; The Art Institute of Washington[1,8]; The Art Institute of Washington–Northern Virginia[1,8]; The Art Institute of York–Pennsylvania; The Art Institutes International–Kansas City; The Art Institutes International Minnesota; The Illinois Institute of Art–Chicago; The Illinois Institute of Art–Schaumburg; Miami International University of Art & Design; The New England Institute of Art.

[1]A branch of The Art Institute of Atlanta
[2]A branch of The Art Institute of Houston
[3]A branch of The Art Institute of Dallas
[4]The Art Institute of Indianapolis is regulated by the Indiana Commission on Proprietary Education, 302 West Washington Street, Room E201, Indianapolis, Indiana 46204, AC-0080
[5]A branch of Miami International University of Art & Design
[6]The Art Institute of Ohio–Cincinnati, 8845 Governors Hill Drive, Suite 100, Cincinnati, Ohio 45249-3317, OH Reg. #04-01-1698B
[7]The Art Institute of Tennessee–Nashville is authorized for operation as a postsecondary educational institution by the Tennessee Higher Education Commission.
[8]Certified by the State Council of Higher Education to operate in Virginia

THE ART INSTITUTE OF COLORADO

DENVER, COLORADO

The Art Institute of Colorado has a mission to provide programs that prepare graduates to pursue entry-level jobs in the creative arts. Programs are developed with and taught by experienced educators, either in traditional classroom settings or through online courses. The school offers fourteen bachelor's degree programs, seven associate degree programs, and two diploma programs. Continuing education is available through the Department of Continuing Education at The Art Institute of Colorado.

The student population includes recent high school graduates, transfer students, and those who have left a previous employment situation to study and train for a new career. Students are creative, competitive, and open to new ideas. They place great value on an education that prepares them for an exciting entry-level position in the arts.

The Art Institute of Colorado students come from across the country and around the world. They are dedicated men and women who strive for excellence. International students are provided assistance through the International Student Advisement Office. This office provides a variety of support services and enrichment activities designed to meet the needs of international students.

The school is committed to helping students throughout their education experience, both in and out of the classroom, with such issues as the transition to academic life and involvement in student activities. In addition, assistance is available to help students with resume writing, networking, and keeping aware of what employers are looking for in job candidates. A variety of support services are available to help qualified students with counseling needs and disability services.

Student Affairs offers a wide variety of student activities to encourage social networking and stress management, including social and athletic events, a quarterly student art show, and creativity-enhancing activities and field trips. In addition, most academic departments sponsor student chapters of professional associations, including the American Culinary Federation, AIGA, American Society of Interior Designers, Industrial Designers of America, and Colorado Game Developers Association.

The Art Institute of Colorado's housing facility, the Towers, offers a variety of living accommodations in a fully equipped, partially furnished, apartment-style complex. An on-site professional staff member is available to coordinate activities and to help residents become acquainted with each other and with The Art Institute of Colorado.

The Art Institute of Colorado is accredited by the Higher Learning Commission and is a member of the North Central Association, 30 North LaSalle Street, Suite 2400, Chicago, Illinois, 60602-2504; http://www.ncahlc.org.

The Art Institute of Colorado is authorized to award diplomas, associate of applied science degrees, and bachelor of arts degrees by the Colorado Department of Higher Education, Commission on Higher Education, 1380 Lawrence Street, Suite 1200, Denver, Colorado 80202.

The Associate of Applied Science in culinary arts degree program is accredited by the Accrediting Commission of the American Culinary Federation Education Foundation.

The interior design program leading to the Bachelor of Arts degree is accredited by the Council for Interior Design Accreditation, 206 Grandville Avenue, Suite 350, Grand Rapids, Michigan 49503; http://www.accredit-id.org.

The Associate of Applied Science in kitchen and bath design degree program is accredited by the National Kitchen & Bath Association (NKBA). NKBA can be contacted at 687 Willow Grove Street, Hackettstown, New Jersey 07840; phone: 800-THE-NKBA; http://www.nkba.org.

Location

The Art Institute of Colorado is located in Denver, home to many major corporations and high-technology companies. Located near galleries, museums, and theaters, The Art Institute of Colorado provides easy access to music and dance performances at both the Performing Arts Complex and Red Rocks Amphitheater. Denver is a 1-hour drive from world-class skiing and water sports, amid the Rocky Mountains' breathtaking scenery. The city itself offers ample opportunities for biking, hiking, in-line skating, and viewing professional sports.

Programs of Study and Degrees

Bachelor's degrees are offered in culinary management, design and technical graphics, design management, digital filmmaking and video production, fashion design, fashion retail management, food and beverage management, graphic design, industrial design, interior design, media arts and animation, photography, visual effects and motion graphics, and Web design and interactive media.

Associate degree programs are available in baking and pastry, culinary arts, graphic design, kitchen and bath design, photography, video production, and Web design and interactive media.

Diploma programs are offered in baking and pastry, and the art of cooking.

The culinary arts, fashion retail management, graphic design, interior design, and photography programs are available in an evening and weekend option format.

Academic Programs

The Art Institute of Colorado offers Bachelor of Arts degree programs that are designed to be thirty-six months in length. Associate degree programs are designed to take twenty-one months to complete.

Academic Facilities

The Art Institute of Colorado computer labs contain more than 250 PC and Macintosh computers. Photography, audiovisual, and technology equipment is available for students to check out through the Media Services Department. Equipment includes analog and digital still cameras as well as audio and lighting equipment.

The library at The Art Institute of Colorado has a collection of 20,000 titles, including books, videotapes, DVDs, and magazines. The library subscribes to more than 200 periodicals and holds up to ten years of back-issue archives supporting major subject areas taught at the school. Tables for group work and Internet terminals for research are available in the library. The Service Bureau is an on-campus facility dedicated to meeting the printing and scanning needs of students.

Costs

Tuition cost varies by program. Prospective students should contact the school for current tuition costs. Other charges include a starting kit for all first-quarter students. Kits vary in price, depending on the program of study.

Financial Aid

Financial aid is available for those who qualify. Students who require financial assistance should first complete and submit a Free Application for Federal Student Aid (FAFSA) and meet with a financial aid officer.

Faculty

The Art Institute of Colorado faculty members are professionals, many of whom have real-world experience in creative arts careers. The school's faculty members encourage students to cultivate conceptual, creative, and problem-solving skills. There are full-time and part-time faculty members.

Admission Requirements

All applicants are evaluated on the basis of previous education, background, and stated or demonstrated interest in a career program. Applicants must provide high school or college transcripts and an essay of approximately 150 words stating how an education at The Art Institute of Colorado will help them attain their creative goals. Portfolios are welcome but not required. Applicants who have taken the SAT or ACT are encouraged to submit scores for evaluation. There is a $50 application fee.

For the most recent information regarding admission requirements, please refer to the current academic catalog.

Application and Information

To obtain an application, make arrangements for an interview, or tour the school, prospective students should contact:

The Art Institute of Colorado
1200 Lincoln Street
Denver, Colorado 80203-2172
Phone: 303-837-0825
800-275-2420 (toll-free)
Fax: 303-860-8520
Web site: http://www.artinstitutes.edu/denver

The Art Institute of Atlanta; The Art Institute of Atlanta–Decatur[1]; The Art Institute of Austin[2]; The Art Institute of California–Hollywood; The Art Institute of California–Inland Empire; The Art Institute of California–Los Angeles; The Art Institute of California–Orange County; The Art Institute of California–Sacramento; The Art Institute of California–San Diego; The Art Institute of California–San Francisco; The Art Institute of California–Sunnyvale; The Art Institute of Charleston[1]; The Art Institute of Charlotte; The Art Institute of Colorado; The Art Institute of Dallas; The Art Institute of Fort Lauderdale; The Art Institute of Fort Worth[3]; The Art Institute of Houston; The Art Institute of Houston–North[2]; The Art Institute of Indianapolis[4]; The Art Institute of Jacksonville[5]; The Art Institute of Las Vegas; The Art Institute of Michigan; The Art Institute of New York City; The Art Institute of Ohio–Cincinnati[6]; The Art Institute of Philadelphia; The Art Institute of Phoenix; The Art Institute of Pittsburgh; The Art Institute of Portland; The Art Institute of Raleigh–Durham; The Art Institute of Salt Lake City; The Art Institute of San Antonio[2];The Art Institute of Seattle; The Art Institute of Tampa[5]; The Art Institute of Tennessee–Nashville[1,7]; The Art Institute of Tucson; The Art Institute of Vancouver; The Art Institute of Virginia Beach[1,8]; The Art Institute of Washington[1,8]; The Art Institute of Washington–Northern Virginia[1,8]; The Art Institute of York–Pennsylvania; The Art Institutes International–Kansas City; The Art Institutes International Minnesota; The Illinois Institute of Art–Chicago; The Illinois Institute of Art–Schaumburg; Miami International University of Art & Design; The New England Institute of Art.

[1]A branch of The Art Institute of Atlanta
[2]A branch of The Art Institute of Houston
[3]A branch of The Art Institute of Dallas
[4]The Art Institute of Indianapolis is regulated by the Indiana Commission on Proprietary Education, 302 West Washington Street, Room E201, Indianapolis, Indiana 46204, AC-0080
[5]A branch of Miami International University of Art & Design
[6]The Art Institute of Ohio–Cincinnati, 8845 Governors Hill Drive, Suite 100, Cincinnati, Ohio 45249-3317, OH Reg. #04-01-1698B
[7]The Art Institute of Tennessee–Nashville is authorized for operation as a postsecondary educational institution by the Tennessee Higher Education Commission.
[8]Certified by the State Council of Higher Education to operate in Virginia

THE ART INSTITUTE OF DALLAS

DALLAS, TEXAS

The Art Institute of Dallas provides programs that help prepare students to pursue entry-level positions in the creative arts. Courses are taught by experienced faculty members in an environment that seeks to encourage expression, leadership, and responsible decision making. The Art Institute of Dallas offers ten bachelor's degree programs and eight associate degree programs.

The student population includes recent high school graduates, transfer students, and those who have left a previous employment situation to study and train for a new career. Students are creative, competitive, and open to new ideas. They place great value on an education that prepares them to pursue an exciting entry-level position in the arts.

The Art Institute of Dallas is an international experience—one that is culturally diverse and creatively stimulating. Students attend the school from nearly forty countries. An international student adviser is available to assist students with their cultural adjustments and immigration matters.

The school provides students with employment assistance classes, individual employment assistance, and printed job-search information. Training includes job-search skills and interviewing techniques. Students can also receive portfolio counseling from The Art Institute of Dallas staff members.

Movie nights, sports activities, and field trips are part of The Art Institute of Dallas experience. Students can also get involved in the local area via community service opportunities. Through class projects and honors endeavors, students have assisted local charities in the development of their media campaigns. Numerous organizations are available for students to volunteer based on special interest areas.

Many students live at The Falls at Highpoint, a controlled-access apartment complex approximately 3 miles from The Art Institute of Dallas. Students may take advantage of value-priced food at the school's Sunrise Deli.

The Art Institute of Dallas is accredited by the Commission on Colleges of the Southern Association of Colleges and Schools to award associate degrees and baccalaureate degrees. Contact the Commission on Colleges at 1866 Southern Lane, Decatur, Georgia 30033-4097 or call 404-679-4500 for questions about the accreditation of The Art Institute of Dallas.

The Art Institute of Dallas holds a certificate of authorization acknowledging exemption from Texas Higher Education Coordinating Board regulations. The Art Institute of Dallas is licensed by the Arkansas State Board of Private Career Education. The Art Institute of Dallas is licensed by the Oklahoma Board of Private Vocational Schools, 3700 North Classen Boulevard, Suite 250, Oklahoma City, Oklahoma 73118; phone: 405-528-3370.

The certificate in art of cooking and the Associate of Applied Science degree in culinary arts programs are accredited by the Accrediting Commission of the American Culinary Federation Education Foundation.

The interior design program leading to the Bachelor of Fine Arts degree is accredited by the Council for Interior Design Accreditation, 206 Grandville Avenue, Suite 350, Grand Rapids, Michigan 49503; http://www.accredit-id.org.

Location

The school is located in the Dallas/Fort Worth area, which has one of the lowest cost-of-living indexes of any major metropolitan area. The Dallas/Fort Worth area offers a diverse range of cultural and recreational activities, including the Dallas Symphony, Mesquite Rodeo, Six Flags, Lone Star Park, concerts in the West End, and national sports teams. Many major employers have relocated to the Dallas/Fort Worth area due to its positive economic environment.

Programs of Study and Degrees

The Art Institute of Dallas offers bachelor's degree programs in advertising design, culinary management, digital filmmaking and video production, fashion and retail management, fashion design, graphic design, interior design, media arts and animation, photography, and Web design and interactive media.

Associate degree programs include baking and pastry, culinary arts, fashion design, graphic design, kitchen and bath design, photography, restaurant and catering management, and video production.

A certificate program is available in the art of cooking.

The culinary arts, graphic design, and interior design programs, as well as the Bachelor of Fine Arts in fashion design program, are available in an evening and weekend option format.

Academic Programs

Associate degree programs can be completed as little as twenty-one months. Bachelor's degree programs can be completed in as little as thirty-six months.

Academic Facilities

Computer labs offering PC and Macintosh computers are available for student use. The Art Institute of Dallas library supports the student community's information and imaging needs. In 1996, the library was officially named for its founder and first librarian, Mildred M. Kelley. The library maintains a collection of books, periodical titles in both print and full-text electronic versions, videotapes, photographic slides, and visual reference cards. In addition, it provides reference services and instruction in the use of library services and facilities, electronic database searching, and research techniques.

The Academic Improvement Center provides tutoring services in the areas of general study skills, mathematics, writing, reading, and basic computer application skills. The center is open Monday through Friday and provides academic testing (ASSET, Learning Styles Assessment) on a weekly basis.

Costs

Tuition cost varies by program. Prospective students should contact the school for current tuition costs. Other charges include a starting kit for all first quarter students. Kits vary in price depending on the program of study.

Financial Aid

Financial aid is available for those who qualify. Students who require financial assistance should first complete and submit a Free Application for Federal Student Aid (FAFSA) and meet with a financial aid officer.

Faculty

Led by an executive committee and a group of academic department directors, faculty members seek to deliver student-centered education, and curriculum content is regularly reviewed. There are full-time and part-time faculty members.

Student Government

The Student Ambassador Organization promotes high-quality representation of the student body. The group provides a channel of communication among students, the administration, and faculty members.

Admission Requirements

Applicants are required to write a paragraph of approximately 300 words stating how The Art Institute of Dallas may help them reach their creative goals. Applicants must present proof of high school graduation or a General Educational Development (GED) certificate as well as their accomplishments and core academic courses. Successful admission depends on QPA, accomplishments, SAT or ACT scores, and a personal interview with admission representatives. Applicants who do not submit a transcript of GED scores are required to take additional testing.

To enroll, students must submit an admission application and an enrollment agreement along with a $50 application fee.

For the most recent information regarding admission requirements, please refer to the current academic catalog.

Application and Information

To obtain an application, make arrangements for an interview, or tour the school, prospective students should contact:

The Art Institute of Dallas
8080 Park Lane, Suite 100
Dallas, Texas 75231-5993
Phone: 214-692-8080
800-275-4243 (toll-free)
Fax: 214-750-9460
Web site: http://www.artinstitutes.edu/dallas

The Art Institute of Atlanta; The Art Institute of Atlanta–Decatur[1]; The Art Institute of Austin[2]; The Art Institute of California–Hollywood; The Art Institute of California–Inland Empire; The Art Institute of California–Los Angeles; The Art Institute of California–Orange County; The Art Institute of California–Sacramento; The Art Institute of California–San Diego; The Art Institute of California–San Francisco; The Art Institute of California–Sunnyvale; The Art Institute of Charleston[1]; The Art Institute of Charlotte; The Art Institute of Colorado; The Art Institute of Dallas; The Art Institute of Fort Lauderdale; The Art Institute of Fort Worth[3]; The Art Institute of Houston; The Art Institute of Houston–North[2]; The Art Institute of Indianapolis[4]; The Art Institute of Jacksonville[5]; The Art Institute of Las Vegas; The Art Institute of Michigan; The Art Institute of New York City; The Art Institute of Ohio–Cincinnati[6]; The Art Institute of Philadelphia; The Art Institute of Phoenix; The Art Institute of Pittsburgh; The Art Institute of Portland; The Art Institute of Raleigh–Durham; The Art Institute of Salt Lake City; The Art Institute of San Antonio[2];The Art Institute of Seattle; The Art Institute of Tampa[5]; The Art Institute of Tennessee–Nashville[1,7]; The Art Institute of Tucson; The Art Institute of Vancouver; The Art Institute of Virginia Beach[1,8]; The Art Institute of Washington[1,8]; The Art Institute of Washington–Northern Virginia[1,8]; The Art Institute of York–Pennsylvania; The Art Institutes International–Kansas City; The Art Institutes International Minnesota; The Illinois Institute of Art–Chicago; The Illinois Institute of Art–Schaumburg; Miami International University of Art & Design; The New England Institute of Art.

[1]A branch of The Art Institute of Atlanta
[2]A branch of The Art Institute of Houston
[3]A branch of The Art Institute of Dallas
[4]The Art Institute of Indianapolis is regulated by the Indiana Commission on Proprietary Education, 302 West Washington Street, Room E201, Indianapolis, Indiana 46204, AC-0080
[5]A branch of Miami International University of Art & Design
[6]The Art Institute of Ohio–Cincinnati, 8845 Governors Hill Drive, Suite 100, Cincinnati, Ohio 45249-3317, OH Reg. #04-01-1698B
[7]The Art Institute of Tennessee–Nashville is authorized for operation as a postsecondary educational institution by the Tennessee Higher Education Commission.
[8]Certified by the State Council of Higher Education to operate in Virginia

THE ART INSTITUTE OF FORT LAUDERDALE

FORT LAUDERDALE, FLORIDA

The Art Institute of Fort Lauderdale trains and prepares individuals to pursue entry-level positions in the creative arts. Professional development is encouraged through curricula that emphasize the communication, reasoning, and technical skills potential employers seek. The Art Institute of Fort Lauderdale offers fourteen bachelor's degree and eight associate degree programs.

The Career Services Office offers job search assistance to help students find part-time employment while attending The Art Institute of Fort Lauderdale and entry-level positions in the arts following graduation. Students may also join professional organizations, which may put them in contact with professionals from their chosen field.

The student population includes recent high school graduates, transfer students, and those who have left a previous employment situation to study and train for a new career. Students are creative, competitive, and open to new ideas.

Student clubs and organizations have been formed in multimedia, illustration, graphic design, philosophy, fashion design, animation, industrial design, and photography.

School-sponsored housing facilities are close by and are available to those students who prefer a traditional, residential-life environment. Housing facilities allow for easy access to beaches, boating, parks, and shopping. Independent housing information and roommate referrals are also available.

The Art Institute of Fort Lauderdale is accredited by the Accrediting Council for Independent Colleges and Schools (ACICS) to award diplomas, associate degrees, and bachelor's degrees. ACICS is listed as a nationally recognized accrediting agency by the United States Department of Education and is recognized by the Council for Higher Education Accreditation. ACICS can be contacted at 750 First Street NE, Suite 980, Washington, D.C. 20002; phone: 202-336-6780.

The Art Institute of Fort Lauderdale is licensed by the Commission for Independent Education, Florida Department of Education. Additional information regarding this institution may be obtained by contacting the commission at 325 West Gaines Street, Suite 1414, Tallahassee, Florida 32399-0400; phone: 888-224-6684 (toll-free).

The Associate of Science degree in culinary arts and the Bachelor of Science degree in culinary management are accredited by the Accrediting Commission of the American Culinary Federation Education Foundation.

The interior design program leading to the Bachelor of Science degree is accredited by the Council for Interior Design Accreditation, 206 Grandville Avenue, Suite 350, Grand Rapids, Michigan 49503; http://www.accredit-id.org.

Location

Surrounded by waterways, Fort Lauderdale is known as "The Venice of America." The area has an average temperature of 70 degrees in the winter and offers many opportunities for fun in the sun. The Art Institute of Fort Lauderdale is close to 23 miles of beaches, shopping districts, museums, historical sites, restaurants, and nightclubs. Located between Miami and Palm Beach, Fort Lauderdale's many attractions include its world-famous beach, the picturesque Riverwalk, and Las Olas Boulevard—a centerpiece of fashion, fine dining, and entertainment. Tourists and residents alike enjoy the Broward Center for the Performing Arts, Museum of Discovery and Science, Museum of Art, and Old Fort Lauderdale Village and Museum. Fort Lauderdale also supports a diverse range of industries, including marine, manufacturing, finance, insurance, real estate, high technology, avionics/aerospace, and film and television production.

Programs of Study and Degrees

The Art Institute of Fort Lauderdale offers Bachelor of Science degree programs in advertising, culinary management, digital filmmaking and video production, fashion design, fashion merchandising, game art and design, graphic design, illustration, industrial design, interior design, media arts and animation, photography, visual effects and motion graphics, and Web design and interactive media.

Associate of Science degree programs are available in baking and pastry, culinary arts, fashion design, graphic design, interior design, photography, video production, and Web design and interactive media.

Diploma programs are offered in art of cooking and residential design.

Academic Programs

The Art Institute of Fort Lauderdale offers Bachelor of Science degree programs, Associate of Science degree programs, and diploma programs.

Academic Facilities

The Art Institute of Fort Lauderdale occupies approximately 140,000 square feet in four separate buildings. The school has computer and program-specific labs, including those for animation, digital sound, CAD, and fashion design and the Digital Imaging Center. PC and Macintosh computers in a number of labs are available to students. Software programs include industry-relevant programs such as Premiere, Dreamweaver, Final Cut Pro, Quark, Illustrator, Photoshop, AutoCAD, Gerber, 3-D Max, Painter, Director, Flash, and Maya. The Nevin C. Meinhardt Memorial Library features a collection of books, periodicals, audiovisual materials, and online databases. The library provides access to remote resources through the Internet and cooperative agreements with other area libraries.

In addition, culinary students receive hands-on training in the bakery and presentation kitchens. The Chef's Palette is an on-site restaurant where students learn firsthand what it takes to operate and manage a restaurant. The Mark K. Wheeler Gallery is located on the first floor of the main building.

Costs

Tuition cost varies by program. Prospective students should contact the school for current tuition costs. Other charges include a starting kit for all first-quarter students. Kits vary in price depending on the program of study.

Financial Aid

Financial aid is available for those who qualify. Students who require financial assistance should first complete and submit a Free Application for Federal Student Aid (FAFSA) and meet with a financial aid officer.

Faculty

The Art Institute of Fort Lauderdale consists of both full-time and part-time professional faculty members, many of whom have advanced degrees and experience in their chosen fields.

Student Government

All students have the right to participate and vote in Student Government elections and referenda. The Student Government works with faculty and staff members to provide numerous events, including student socials, community outreach programs, volunteer work, and student service events.

Admission Requirements

Admission to The Art Institute of Fort Lauderdale requires a completed application form, evidence of high school graduation or successful completion of the General Educational Development (GED) test, and an essay on how the school may assist in achieving the applicant's creative goals. Applicants are also required to schedule an interview with an admissions representative and, if financial aid is needed, to complete the FAFSA and PLUS loan forms found in the application packet. There is a $50 application fee.

For the most recent information regarding admission requirements, please refer to the current academic catalog.

Application and Information

To obtain an application, make arrangements for an interview, or tour the school, prospective students should contact:

The Art Institute of Fort Lauderdale
1799 S.E. 17th Street
Fort Lauderdale, Florida 33316-3013
Phone: 954-463-3000
800-275-7603 (toll-free)
Fax: 954-728-8637
Web site: http://www.artinstitutes.edu/fortlauderdale

COLLEGE CLOSE-UPS

The Art Institute of Atlanta; The Art Institute of Atlanta–Decatur[1]; The Art Institute of Austin[2]; The Art Institute of California–Hollywood; The Art Institute of California–Inland Empire; The Art Institute of California–Los Angeles; The Art Institute of California–Orange County; The Art Institute of California–Sacramento; The Art Institute of California–San Diego; The Art Institute of California–San Francisco; The Art Institute of California–Sunnyvale; The Art Institute of Charleston[1]; The Art Institute of Charlotte; The Art Institute of Colorado; The Art Institute of Dallas; The Art Institute of Fort Lauderdale; The Art Institute of Fort Worth[3]; The Art Institute of Houston; The Art Institute of Houston–North[2]; The Art Institute of Indianapolis[4]; The Art Institute of Jacksonville[5]; The Art Institute of Las Vegas; The Art Institute of Michigan; The Art Institute of New York City; The Art Institute of Ohio–Cincinnati[6]; The Art Institute of Philadelphia; The Art Institute of Phoenix; The Art Institute of Pittsburgh; The Art Institute of Portland; The Art Institute of Raleigh–Durham; The Art Institute of Salt Lake City; The Art Institute of San Antonio[2];The Art Institute of Seattle; The Art Institute of Tampa[5]; The Art Institute of Tennessee–Nashville[1,7]; The Art Institute of Tucson; The Art Institute of Vancouver; The Art Institute of Virginia Beach[1,8]; The Art Institute of Washington[1,8]; The Art Institute of Washington–Northern Virginia[1,8]; The Art Institute of York–Pennsylvania; The Art Institutes International–Kansas City; The Art Institutes International Minnesota; The Illinois Institute of Art–Chicago; The Illinois Institute of Art–Schaumburg; Miami International University of Art & Design; The New England Institute of Art.

[1]A branch of The Art Institute of Atlanta
[2]A branch of The Art Institute of Houston
[3]A branch of The Art Institute of Dallas
[4]The Art Institute of Indianapolis is regulated by the Indiana Commission on Proprietary Education, 302 West Washington Street, Room E201, Indianapolis, Indiana 46204, AC-0080
[5]A branch of Miami International University of Art & Design
[6]The Art Institute of Ohio–Cincinnati, 8845 Governors Hill Drive, Suite 100, Cincinnati, Ohio 45249-3317, OH Reg. #04-01-1698B
[7]The Art Institute of Tennessee–Nashville is authorized for operation as a postsecondary educational institution by the Tennessee Higher Education Commission.
[8]Certified by the State Council of Higher Education to operate in Virginia

THE ART INSTITUTE OF FORT WORTH

FORT WORTH, TEXAS

The Art Institute of Fort Worth provides students with an educational environment and dedicated faculty members committed to preparing students to pursue entry-level positions in the creative arts. The school offers six bachelor's degree programs and two associate degree programs.

Under the guidance of industry professionals, students learn by doing the types of tasks they are likely to encounter in the workplace. In addition, assistance is available to help students with resume writing, networking, and keeping aware of what employers are looking for in job candidates.

The student population includes recent high school graduates, transfer students, and those who have left a previous employment situation to study and train for a new career. Students are creative, competitive, and open to new ideas. They place great value on an education that prepares them to pursue an exciting entry-level position in the arts.

The Art Institute of Fort Worth places a high value on the quality of student life—both in and out of the classroom. Students can participate in a wide variety of activities, including clubs and organizations, community service opportunities, and various committees designed to enhance the quality of student life.

The school's Learning Resource Center helps to meet students' needs for the programs taught at The Art Institute of Fort Worth. It is updated and supplemented with new acquisitions. Instructors are encouraged to look for upcoming books and to advise the administration of any books that may prove useful to their students. Students also have access to the public libraries.

The Student Affairs Office helps students who need assistance in locating housing.

The Art Institute of Fort Worth is a branch of The Art Institute of Dallas. The Art Institute of Dallas is accredited by the Commission on Colleges of the Southern Association of Colleges and Schools to award associate and baccalaureate degrees. Contact the Commission on Colleges at 1866 Southern Lane, Decatur, Georgia 30033-4097 or call 404-679-4500 for questions about the accreditation of The Art Institute of Dallas.

The Art Institute of Fort Worth holds a certificate of authorization acknowledging exemption from Texas Higher Education Coordinating Board regulations.

Location

Downtown Fort Worth is known for its art deco style buildings and culture, including theater, museums, and music. The city is also known for the popular Fort Worth Stockyards historic district.

Programs of Study and Degrees

Bachelor's degree programs are offered in advertising design, fashion and retail management, graphic design, interior design, photography, and Web design and interactive media.

Associate degree programs are offered in graphic design and Web design and interactive media.

Academic Programs

The Art Institute of Fort Worth operates on a year-round, four-quarter system.

Academic Facilities

The Art Institute of Fort Worth contains classrooms, studios, offices, a student lounge, a supply store, and a learning resource center. Equipment provided is specific to the program of study and may include projectors, editing decks, camcorders, PC and Macintosh computers, and printers.

Costs

Tuition cost varies by program. Prospective students should contact the school for current tuition costs. Other charges include a starting kit for all first quarter students. Kits vary in price depending on the program of study.

Financial Aid

Financial aid is available for those who qualify. Students who require financial assistance should first complete and submit a Free Application for Federal Student Aid (FAFSA) and meet with a financial aid officer.

Faculty

Faculty members at The Art Institute of Fort Worth have professional knowledge that they bring into the classroom. The school's faculty members provide their students with a unique, relevant educational experience. Faculty members are employed on both a full- and part-time basis.

Admission Requirements

Applicants must provide proof of high school graduation or achievement of a General Educational Development (GED) certificate as a prerequisite for admission. In lieu of documenting high school graduation or a GED certificate, applicants may provide proof of attaining an associate degree or higher from an accredited institution. An official transcript indicating date of high school graduation, GED certificate (including test scores), or date of college graduation (including degree granted) is required as proof.

All individuals seeking admission to The Art Institute of Fort Worth are interviewed in person or by phone by an assistant director of admissions, and each applicant must create an original essay of at least 150 words stating how an education at The Art Institute of Fort Worth would help the student to achieve career goals. There is a $50 application fee.

For the most recent information regarding admission requirements, please refer to the current academic catalog.

Application and Information

To obtain an application, make arrangements for an interview, or tour the school, prospective students should contact:

The Art Institute of Forth Worth
7000 Calmont Avenue, Suite 150
Fort Worth, Texas 76116
Phone: 817-210-0808
888-422-9686 (toll-free)
Fax: 817-210-0901
Web site: http://www.artinstitutes.edu/fortworth

COLLEGE CLOSE-UPS

The Art Institute of Atlanta; The Art Institute of Atlanta–Decatur[1]; The Art Institute of Austin[2]; The Art Institute of California–Hollywood; The Art Institute of California–Inland Empire; The Art Institute of California–Los Angeles; The Art Institute of California–Orange County; The Art Institute of California–Sacramento; The Art Institute of California–San Diego; The Art Institute of California–San Francisco; The Art Institute of California–Sunnyvale; The Art Institute of Charleston[1]; The Art Institute of Charlotte; The Art Institute of Colorado; The Art Institute of Dallas; The Art Institute of Fort Lauderdale; The Art Institute of Fort Worth[3]; The Art Institute of Houston; The Art Institute of Houston–North[2]; The Art Institute of Indianapolis[4]; The Art Institute of Jacksonville[5]; The Art Institute of Las Vegas; The Art Institute of Michigan; The Art Institute of New York City; The Art Institute of Ohio–Cincinnati[6]; The Art Institute of Philadelphia; The Art Institute of Phoenix; The Art Institute of Pittsburgh; The Art Institute of Portland; The Art Institute of Raleigh–Durham; The Art Institute of Salt Lake City; The Art Institute of San Antonio[2];The Art Institute of Seattle; The Art Institute of Tampa[5]; The Art Institute of Tennessee–Nashville[1,7]; The Art Institute of Tucson; The Art Institute of Vancouver; The Art Institute of Virginia Beach[1,8]; The Art Institute of Washington[1,8]; The Art Institute of Washington–Northern Virginia[1,8]; The Art Institute of York–Pennsylvania; The Art Institutes International–Kansas City; The Art Institutes International Minnesota; The Illinois Institute of Art–Chicago; The Illinois Institute of Art–Schaumburg; Miami International University of Art & Design; The New England Institute of Art.

[1]A branch of The Art Institute of Atlanta
[2]A branch of The Art Institute of Houston
[3]A branch of The Art Institute of Dallas
[4]The Art Institute of Indianapolis is regulated by the Indiana Commission on Proprietary Education, 302 West Washington Street, Room E201, Indianapolis, Indiana 46204, AC-0080
[5]A branch of Miami International University of Art & Design
[6]The Art Institute of Ohio–Cincinnati, 8845 Governors Hill Drive, Suite 100, Cincinnati, Ohio 45249-3317, OH Reg. #04-01-1698B
[7]The Art Institute of Tennessee–Nashville is authorized for operation as a postsecondary educational institution by the Tennessee Higher Education Commission.
[8]Certified by the State Council of Higher Education to operate in Virginia

THE ART INSTITUTE OF HOUSTON

HOUSTON, TEXAS

At The Art Institute of Houston, students develop practical skills that prepare them to pursue entry-level positions in the creative arts. Programs incorporate traditional liberal arts and hands-on instruction. Twelve bachelor's degrees and five associate degree programs are offered at the school.

Students come to The Art Institute of Houston from throughout the United States and abroad. The student population includes recent high school graduates, transfer students, and those who have left a previous employment situation to study and train for a new career. Students are creative, competitive, and open to new ideas. They place great value on an education that prepares them to pursue an exciting entry-level position in the arts.

Students may take part in a number of clubs, social activities, and volunteer service projects in the community. Student activities include professional organizations such as the National Technical Honors Society, American Society of Interior Designers (ASID), and AIGA. Clubs include Baking and Pastry, Great Chefs, and Poetry.

The Art Institute of Houston will help students pursue entry-level employment after graduation. Job search training in the classrooms, one-on-one efforts, and an on-campus job fair for potential employers assist students in achieving this goal.

Many students live in The Park at Voss, a controlled-access apartment complex located 2.8 miles from the school and one block from the Metro bus line. The most common living arrangement at this complex is a two-bedroom, two-bath apartment shared by 4 students. Double and single student-apartment options are limited and based on seniority and availability.

One-on-one peer tutoring is available, and many faculty members provide tutoring and workshops that are specific to the courses they instruct. Art Institute of Houston mentors devote approximately 2 hours per week to assisting new students in their adjustment to both academic life and their new surroundings. In addition, assistance is available to help students with resume writing, networking, and keeping aware of what employers are looking for in job candidates.

The Art Institute of Houston is accredited by the Commission on Colleges of the Southern Association of Colleges and Schools to award associate degrees and baccalaureate degrees. Contact the Commission on Colleges at 1866 Southern Lane, Decatur, Georgia 30033-4097 or call 404-679-4500 for questions about the accreditation of The Art Institute of Houston.

The Bachelor of Science degree in culinary management, the Associate of Applied Science degree in baking and pastry, the Associate of Applied Science degree in culinary arts, and the diploma program in culinary arts are accredited by the Accrediting Commission of the American Culinary Federation Education Foundation.

The interior design program leading to the Bachelor of Arts degree is accredited by the Council for Interior Design Accreditation, 206 Grandville Avenue, Suite 350, Grand Rapids, Michigan 49503; http://www.accredit-id.org.

The Art Institute of Houston holds a certificate of authorization acknowledging exemption from Texas Higher Education Coordinating Board Regulations.

Location

The Art Institute of Houston is close to several major art museums, a premier opera, a ballet, a symphony, and live theater companies. Culturally diverse, Houston has several international ethnic communities, great restaurants, and an eclectic nightlife as well as national sports teams. The city features a mild, semitropical climate and sunny beaches in nearby Galveston and Mexico.

Programs of Study and Degrees

The Art Institute of Houston offers bachelor's degree programs in audio production, culinary management, design and technical graphics, digital filmmaking and video production, fashion and retail management, food and beverage management, graphic design, interior design, media arts and animation, photography, visual effects and motion graphics, and Web design and interactive media.

Associate degree programs are available in baking and pastry, culinary arts, graphic design, restaurant and catering management, and Web design and interactive media.

A diploma program is offered in culinary arts.

The bachelor's degree programs in culinary management, interior design, and Web design and interactive media, as well as the Associate of Applied Science degree program in culinary arts are available in an evening and weekend option format.

Academic Programs

The academic year is divided into four quarters of approximately eleven weeks each. Students may start their program of study in any quarter. Bachelor's degrees can be earned upon completion of 180 academic credits over approximately twelve quarters. Associate degrees are earned upon completion of 90 to 108 academic credits, depending on the program, and can take seven to eight quarters. Diploma programs require the completion of 61 academic credits. Online programs are offered in two sessions per academic quarter.

Academic Facilities

The Art Institute of Houston Resource Center collection consists of approximately 28,000 books, 1,700 videos, 200 journals, 4 databases, and 850 discs containing imagery files, sound files, and software tutorials. The center includes twenty-eight computer stations for patron use. PCs provide access to the online catalog, the Internet, and some Microsoft Office products. Macintosh computers provide access to the online catalog and Internet and to the software that is utilized in design classes. Complimentary scanning and printing are available.

Costs

Tuition cost varies by program. Prospective students should contact the school for current tuition costs. Other charges include a starting kit for all first-quarter students. Kits vary in price depending on the program of study.

Financial Aid

Financial aid is available for those who qualify. Students who require financial assistance should first complete and submit a Free Application for Federal Student Aid (FAFSA) and meet with a financial aid officer.

Faculty

The Art Institute of Houston faculty members have professional experience in their chosen fields, and many hold advanced degrees. There are full-time and part-time faculty members.

Student Government

The Student Government is the primary vehicle for student participation in institutional decision making. The Student Government acts as a voice on behalf of the student body and sponsors speakers, workshops, seminars, and other activities. When students seek change or have a request that affects the student body as a whole, Student Government serves as a forum for discussion and decision making. All students are eligible to belong to Student Government.

Admission Requirements

Admission to The Art Institute of Houston begins with an interview with an assistant director of admissions, either in person or by phone. Upon approval, students submit an application for admission and an enrollment agreement. Prospective students must be high school graduates, hold a General Educational Development (GED) certificate, or have earned an associate degree or higher from an accredited institution. The Art Institute of Houston considers alternative documentation from students who have completed high school or its equivalent but cannot provide the usual documentation. (The president of The Art Institute of Houston must approve all exceptions.) Evaluations are based on an applicant's previous education, background, and stated or demonstrated interest in a particular program. Portfolios are required for admission to the media arts and animation program; they are welcomed for other programs but not required. Applicants who have taken the SAT or ACT are encouraged to submit their scores for evaluation. There is a $50 application fee.

For the most recent information regarding admission requirements, please refer to the current academic catalog.

Application and Information

To obtain an application, make arrangements for an interview, or tour the school, prospective students should contact:

The Art Institute of Houston
1900 Yorktown Street
Houston, Texas 77056-4197
Phone: 713-623-2040
800-275-4244 (toll-free)
Fax: 713-966-2797
Web site: http://www.artinstitutes.edu/houston

The Art Institute of Atlanta; The Art Institute of Atlanta–Decatur[1]; The Art Institute of Austin[2]; The Art Institute of California–Hollywood; The Art Institute of California–Inland Empire; The Art Institute of California–Los Angeles; The Art Institute of California–Orange County; The Art Institute of California–Sacramento; The Art Institute of California–San Diego; The Art Institute of California–San Francisco; The Art Institute of California–Sunnyvale; The Art Institute of Charleston[1]; The Art Institute of Charlotte; The Art Institute of Colorado; The Art Institute of Dallas; The Art Institute of Fort Lauderdale; The Art Institute of Fort Worth[3]; The Art Institute of Houston; The Art Institute of Houston–North[2]; The Art Institute of Indianapolis[4]; The Art Institute of Jacksonville[5]; The Art Institute of Las Vegas; The Art Institute of Michigan; The Art Institute of New York City; The Art Institute of Ohio–Cincinnati[6]; The Art Institute of Philadelphia; The Art Institute of Phoenix; The Art Institute of Pittsburgh; The Art Institute of Portland; The Art Institute of Raleigh–Durham; The Art Institute of Salt Lake City; The Art Institute of San Antonio[2];The Art Institute of Seattle; The Art Institute of Tampa[5]; The Art Institute of Tennessee–Nashville[1,7]; The Art Institute of Tucson; The Art Institute of Vancouver; The Art Institute of Virginia Beach[1,8]; The Art Institute of Washington[1,8]; The Art Institute of Washington–Northern Virginia[1,8]; The Art Institute of York–Pennsylvania; The Art Institutes International–Kansas City; The Art Institutes International Minnesota; The Illinois Institute of Art–Chicago; The Illinois Institute of Art–Schaumburg; Miami International University of Art & Design; The New England Institute of Art.

[1]A branch of The Art Institute of Atlanta
[2]A branch of The Art Institute of Houston
[3]A branch of The Art Institute of Dallas
[4]The Art Institute of Indianapolis is regulated by the Indiana Commission on Proprietary Education, 302 West Washington Street, Room E201, Indianapolis, Indiana 46204, AC-0080
[5]A branch of Miami International University of Art & Design
[6]The Art Institute of Ohio–Cincinnati, 8845 Governors Hill Drive, Suite 100, Cincinnati, Ohio 45249-3317, OH Reg. #04-01-1698B
[7]The Art Institute of Tennessee–Nashville is authorized for operation as a postsecondary educational institution by the Tennessee Higher Education Commission.
[8]Certified by the State Council of Higher Education to operate in Virginia

THE ART INSTITUTE OF HOUSTON–NORTH

HOUSTON, TEXAS

Offering five bachelor's degree programs and one associate degree program, the Art Institute of Houston–North provides students with a creative educational environment. The school's dedicated faculty members are committed to preparing students to pursue entry-level positions in the creative arts.

Under the guidance of industry professionals, students learn by doing the types of tasks they are likely to encounter in the workplace. In addition, assistance is available to help students with resume writing, networking, and keeping aware of what employers are looking for in job candidates.

The student population includes recent high school graduates, transfer students, and those who have left a previous employment situation to study and train for a new career. Students are creative, competitive, and open to new ideas. They place great value on an education that prepares them for an exciting entry-level position in the arts.

The Art Institute of Houston–North places a high value on the quality of student life inside and outside the classroom. Students take part in a wide variety of activities, clubs and organizations, community service opportunities, and various student life enhancing committees.

Instructors are encouraged to look for upcoming books and to advise the administration of any books that may prove useful to their students. Students also have access to the public libraries.

The Student Affairs Office helps students who need assistance in locating housing.

The Art Institute of Houston–North is a branch campus of The Art Institute of Houston. The Art Institute of Houston is accredited by the Commission on Colleges of the Southern Association of Colleges and Schools to award associate and baccalaureate degrees. Contact the Commission on Colleges at 1866 Southern Lane, Decatur, Georgia 20033-4097 or call 404-679-4500 for questions about the accreditation of The Art Institute of Houston.

The Art Institute of Houston–North holds a certificate of authorization acknowledging exemption from Texas Higher Education Coordinating Board Regulations.

Location

A growing and exciting "edge city," northwest Houston is coming into its own as a center for the visual and performing arts, education, shopping, and recreation catering to the young—and the young at heart. Lakes and streams, forested parks, and safe neighborhoods can all be found just minutes from Houston's central business district.

Programs of Study and Degrees

Bachelor's degree programs are offered in fashion and retail management, graphic design, interior design, media arts and animation, and photography.

An associate degree program is offered in graphic design.

Academic Programs

The Art Institute of Houston–North operates on a year-round, four-quarter system.

Academic Facilities

The Art Institute of Houston–North is home to classrooms, studios, offices, a student lounge, a supply store, and a learning resource center. Equipment provided at The Art Institute of Houston–North is specific to the program of study and may include projectors, editing decks, camcorders, and PC and Macintosh computers.

Costs

Tuition cost varies by program. Prospective students should contact the school for current tuition costs. Other charges include a starting kit for all first quarter students. Kits vary in price depending on the program of study.

Financial Aid

Financial aid is available for those who qualify. Students who require financial assistance should first complete and submit a Free Application for Federal Student Aid (FAFSA) and meet with a financial aid officer.

For the most recent information regarding admission requirements, please refer to the current academic catalog.

Faculty

Faculty members at The Art Institute of Houston–North have professional knowledge that they bring into the classroom. The school's faculty members provide their students with a hands-on, industry-relevant educational experience.

Admission Requirements

Applicants must provide proof of high school graduation or achievement of a General Educational Development (GED) certificate as a prerequisite for admission. In lieu of documenting high school graduation or a GED certificate, applicants may provide proof of attaining an associate degree or higher from an accredited institution. An official transcript indicating date of high school graduation, GED certificate (including test scores), or date of college graduation (including degree granted) is required as proof.

All individuals seeking admission to The Art Institute of Houston–North are interviewed in person or by phone by an assistant director of admissions, and each applicant must create an original essay of at least 150 words stating how an education at The Art Institute of Houston–North would help the student to achieve career goals. There is a $50 application fee.

Application and Information

To obtain an application, make arrangements for an interview, or tour the school, prospective students should contact:

The Art Institute of Houston–North
10740 North Gessner Drive, Suite 190
Houston, Texas 77064
Phone: 281-671-3381
866-830-4450 (toll-free)
Fax: 281-671-3550
Web site: http://www.artinstitutes.edu/houston-north

COLLEGE CLOSE-UPS

The Art Institute of Atlanta; The Art Institute of Atlanta–Decatur[1]; The Art Institute of Austin[2]; The Art Institute of California–Hollywood; The Art Institute of California–Inland Empire; The Art Institute of California–Los Angeles; The Art Institute of California–Orange County; The Art Institute of California–Sacramento; The Art Institute of California–San Diego; The Art Institute of California–San Francisco; The Art Institute of California–Sunnyvale; The Art Institute of Charleston[1]; The Art Institute of Charlotte; The Art Institute of Colorado; The Art Institute of Dallas; The Art Institute of Fort Lauderdale; The Art Institute of Fort Worth[3]; The Art Institute of Houston; The Art Institute of Houston–North[2]; The Art Institute of Indianapolis[4]; The Art Institute of Jacksonville[5]; The Art Institute of Las Vegas; The Art Institute of Michigan; The Art Institute of New York City; The Art Institute of Ohio–Cincinnati[6]; The Art Institute of Philadelphia; The Art Institute of Phoenix; The Art Institute of Pittsburgh; The Art Institute of Portland; The Art Institute of Raleigh–Durham; The Art Institute of Salt Lake City; The Art Institute of San Antonio[2];The Art Institute of Seattle; The Art Institute of Tampa[5]; The Art Institute of Tennessee–Nashville[1,7]; The Art Institute of Tucson; The Art Institute of Vancouver; The Art Institute of Virginia Beach[1,8]; The Art Institute of Washington[1,8]; The Art Institute of Washington–Northern Virginia[1,8]; The Art Institute of York–Pennsylvania; The Art Institutes International–Kansas City; The Art Institutes International Minnesota; The Illinois Institute of Art–Chicago; The Illinois Institute of Art–Schaumburg; Miami International University of Art & Design; The New England Institute of Art.

[1]A branch of The Art Institute of Atlanta
[2]A branch of The Art Institute of Houston
[3]A branch of The Art Institute of Dallas
[4]The Art Institute of Indianapolis is regulated by the Indiana Commission on Proprietary Education, 302 West Washington Street, Room E201, Indianapolis, Indiana 46204, AC-0080
[5]A branch of Miami International University of Art & Design
[6]The Art Institute of Ohio–Cincinnati, 8845 Governors Hill Drive, Suite 100, Cincinnati, Ohio 45249-3317, OH Reg. #04-01-1698B
[7]The Art Institute of Tennessee–Nashville is authorized for operation as a postsecondary educational institution by the Tennessee Higher Education Commission.
[8]Certified by the State Council of Higher Education to operate in Virginia

THE ART INSTITUTE OF INDIANAPOLIS

INDIANAPOLIS, INDIANA

The Art Institute of Indianapolis provides students with an educational environment and dedicated faculty members committed to preparing students to pursue entry-level positions in the creative arts. The school offers eight bachelor's degree programs and four associate degree programs.

Under the guidance of industry professionals, students learn by doing the types of tasks they are likely to encounter in the workplace. In addition, assistance is available to help students with resume writing, networking, and keeping aware of what employers are looking for in job candidates.

The student population includes recent high school graduates, transfer students, and those who have left a previous employment situation to study and train for a new career. Students are creative, competitive, and open to new ideas. They place great value on an education that prepares them to pursue an exciting entry-level position in the arts.

The Art Institute of Indianapolis places a high value on the quality of student life—both in and out of the classroom. Students can participate in a wide variety of activities, including clubs and organizations, community service opportunities, and various committees designed to enhance the quality of student life.

The school's Learning Resource Center helps to meet students' needs for the programs taught at The Art Institute of Indianapolis. It is constantly updated and supplemented with new acquisitions. Instructors are encouraged to look for upcoming books and to advise the administration of any books that may prove useful to their students. Students also have access to the public libraries.

The Student Affairs Office helps students who need assistance in locating housing.

The Art Institute of Indianapolis is accredited by the Accrediting Commission of Career Schools and Colleges (ACCSC) as a branch of The Art Institute of Las Vegas. ACCSC may be contacted at 2101 Wilson Boulevard, Suite 302, Arlington, Virginia 22201; phone: 703-247-4212.

This institution is regulated by the Indiana Commission on Proprietary Education, 302 West Washington Street, Room E201, Indianapolis, Indiana 46204; phone: 800-227-5695 (toll-free) or 317-232-1320. AC-0080

Location

Located in the northwest part of Indianapolis, at the Pyramids, the school is within minutes of a thriving metropolis. The Pyramids are situated on 45 acres, with a 25-acre lake. The Pyramids are adjacent to I-465 for convenient travel to all major thoroughfares.

Programs of Study and Degrees

Bachelor's degree programs are offered in culinary management, digital photography, fashion and retail management, fashion design, graphic design, interior design, media arts and animation, and Web design and interactive media.

Associate degree programs are offered in baking and pastry, culinary arts, digital photography, and graphic design. Certificates are available in baking and pastry, culinary arts, digital design, and residential design.

Academic Programs

The Art Institute of Indianapolis operates on a year-round, four-quarter system.

Academic Facilities

The Art Institute of Indianapolis occupies approximately 15,000 square feet, including classrooms, studios, offices, a student lounge, a supply store, and a learning resource center. Equipment provided at The Art Institute of Indianapolis is specific to the program of study and may include projectors, editing decks, camcorders, PC and Macintosh computers, printers, drafting tables, and kitchen appliances.

Costs

Tuition cost varies by program. Prospective students should contact the school for current tuition costs. Other charges include a starting kit for all first quarter students. Kits vary in price depending on the program of study.

Financial Aid

Financial aid is available for those who qualify. Students who require financial assistance should first complete and submit a Free Application for Federal Student Aid (FAFSA) and meet with a financial aid officer.

Faculty

Faculty members at The Art Institute of Indianapolis have professional knowledge that they bring into the classroom. The school's faculty members provide their students with a unique, relevant educational experience. Faculty members are employed on both a full- and part-time basis.

Admission Requirements

Applicants must provide proof of high school graduation or achievement of a General Educational Development (GED) certificate as a prerequisite for admission. In lieu of documenting high school graduation or a GED certificate, applicants may provide proof of attaining an associate degree or higher from an accredited institution. An official transcript indicating date of high school graduation, GED certificate (including test scores), or date of college graduation (including degree granted) is required as proof.

All individuals seeking admission to The Art Institute of Indianapolis are interviewed in person or by phone by an assistant director of admissions, and each applicant must create an original essay of at least 150 words stating how an education at The Art Institute of Indianapolis would help the student to achieve career goals. There is a $50 application fee.

For the most recent information regarding admission requirements, please refer to the current academic catalog.

Application and Information

To obtain an application, make arrangements for an interview, or tour the school, prospective students should contact:

The Art Institute of Indianapolis
3500 Depauw Boulevard, Suite 1010
Indianapolis, Indiana 46268-6124
Phone: 317-613-4800
866-441-9031 (toll-free)
Fax: 317-613-4808
Web site: http://www.artinstitutes.edu/indianapolis

The Art Institute of Atlanta; The Art Institute of Atlanta–Decatur[1]; The Art Institute of Austin[2]; The Art Institute of California–Hollywood; The Art Institute of California–Inland Empire; The Art Institute of California–Los Angeles; The Art Institute of California–Orange County; The Art Institute of California–Sacramento; The Art Institute of California–San Diego; The Art Institute of California–San Francisco; The Art Institute of California–Sunnyvale; The Art Institute of Charleston[1]; The Art Institute of Charlotte; The Art Institute of Colorado; The Art Institute of Dallas; The Art Institute of Fort Lauderdale; The Art Institute of Fort Worth[3]; The Art Institute of Houston; The Art Institute of Houston–North[2]; The Art Institute of Indianapolis[4]; The Art Institute of Jacksonville[5]; The Art Institute of Las Vegas; The Art Institute of Michigan; The Art Institute of New York City; The Art Institute of Ohio–Cincinnati[6]; The Art Institute of Philadelphia; The Art Institute of Phoenix; The Art Institute of Pittsburgh; The Art Institute of Portland; The Art Institute of Raleigh–Durham; The Art Institute of Salt Lake City; The Art Institute of San Antonio[2];The Art Institute of Seattle; The Art Institute of Tampa[5]; The Art Institute of Tennessee–Nashville[1,7]; The Art Institute of Tucson; The Art Institute of Vancouver; The Art Institute of Virginia Beach[1,8]; The Art Institute of Washington[1,8]; The Art Institute of Washington–Northern Virginia[1,8]; The Art Institute of York–Pennsylvania; The Art Institutes International–Kansas City; The Art Institutes International Minnesota; The Illinois Institute of Art–Chicago; The Illinois Institute of Art–Schaumburg; Miami International University of Art & Design; The New England Institute of Art.

[1]A branch of The Art Institute of Atlanta
[2]A branch of The Art Institute of Houston
[3]A branch of The Art Institute of Dallas
[4]The Art Institute of Indianapolis is regulated by the Indiana Commission on Proprietary Education, 302 West Washington Street, Room E201, Indianapolis, Indiana 46204, AC-0080
[5]A branch of Miami International University of Art & Design
[6]The Art Institute of Ohio–Cincinnati, 8845 Governors Hill Drive, Suite 100, Cincinnati, Ohio 45249-3317, OH Reg. #04-01-1698B
[7]The Art Institute of Tennessee–Nashville is authorized for operation as a postsecondary educational institution by the Tennessee Higher Education Commission.
[8]Certified by the State Council of Higher Education to operate in Virginia

THE ART INSTITUTE OF JACKSONVILLE

JACKSONVILLE, FLORIDA

The Art Institute of Jacksonville helps students cultivate and refine the talents and skills that can lead to entry-level positions in the creative arts. Classes are taught in an environment that encourages learning, leadership, and creativity. The school offers eight bachelor's degree programs and three associate degree programs.

Faculty and staff members strive to foster development and cultivate artistic growth. Students are given opportunities to develop leadership skills and build relationships. In addition, assistance is available to help students with resume writing, networking, and keeping abreast of what employers are looking for in job candidates.

The Art Institute of Jacksonville places a high value on the quality of student life both in and out of the classroom. Students can participate in a wide variety of activities, including clubs and organizations, community service, and various committees designed to enhance the quality of student life.

Students come to The Art Institute of Jacksonville from throughout the United States. The student population includes recent high school graduates, transfer students, and those who have left a previous employment situation to study and train for a new career. Students are creative, competitive, and open to new ideas.

The school provides information on independent housing options to all enrolled students requesting such assistance.

Miami International University of Art & Design and its branch campuses The Art Institute of Jacksonville and The Art Institute of Tampa are accredited by the Commission on Colleges of the Southern Association of Colleges and Schools to award diplomas, associate, baccalaureate, and master's degrees. Contact the Commission on Colleges at 1866 Southern Lane, Decatur, Georgia 30033-4097; or call 404-679-4500 for questions about the accreditation of Miami International University of Art & Design.

The Art Institute of Jacksonville is licensed by the Commission for Independent Education, Florida Department of Education. Additional information regarding this institution may be obtained by contacting the Commission at 325 West Gaines St., Suite 1414, Tallahassee, Florida 32399-0400; phone: 888-224-6684 (toll-free).

Location

The Art Institute of Jacksonville is located in Jacksonville, Florida's largest city. With mild winters and warm summers, Jacksonville is a popular tourist destination. The Jacksonville beaches, Florida Theater, and professional sports teams are exciting entertainment options within the region.

Programs of Study and Degrees

Bachelor's degrees are offered in culinary management, digital filmmaking and video production, digital photography, fashion and retail management, graphic design, interior design, media arts and animation, and Web design and interactive media.

Students may also pursue associate degrees in culinary arts, graphic design, or Web design and interactive media design.

A diploma program is offered in culinary arts–skills.

Academic Programs

The academic year is divided into four quarters, beginning in January, April, July, and October. Each program is offered on a year-round basis, allowing students to continue to work uninterrupted toward their degrees.

Academic Facilities

The Art Institute of Jacksonville is located on Baypine Road in Jacksonville, Florida. The school has a bookstore, Mac and PC computer labs, and classrooms.

Costs

Tuition cost varies by program. Prospective students should contact the school for current tuition costs. Other charges include a starting kit for all first-quarter students. Kits vary in price depending on the program of study.

Financial Aid

Financial aid is available for those who qualify. Students who require financial assistance should first complete and submit a Free Application for Federal Student Aid (FAFSA) and meet with a financial aid officer.

Faculty

The Art Institute of Jacksonville faculty consists of full-time and part-time instructors, many of whom have advanced degrees and professional experience in their respective fields.

Student Government

The Student Federation is responsible for student government and acts as a liaison between the student body and faculty and staff members.

Admission Requirements

Applicants must provide proof of high school graduation or achievement of a General Educational Development (GED) certificate as a prerequisite for admission. In lieu of documenting high school graduation or a GED certificate, applicants may provide proof of attaining an associate degree or higher from an accredited institution. An official transcript indicating date of high school graduation, GED certificate (including test scores), or date of college graduation (including degree granted) is required as proof.

All individuals seeking admission to The Art Institute of Jacksonville are interviewed in person or by phone by an assistant director of admissions, and each applicant must submit an original essay of at least 150 words stating how an education at the school would help the student to achieve career goals. There is a $50 application fee.

For the most recent information regarding admission requirements, please refer to the current academic catalog.

Application and Information

To obtain an application, make arrangements for an interview, or tour the school, prospective students should contact:

The Art Institute of Jacksonville
8775 Baypine Road
Jacksonville, Florida 32256-8528
Phone: 904-486-3000
800-924-1589 (toll-free)
Fax: 904-732-9423
Web site: http://www.artinstitutes.edu/jacksonville

The Art Institute of Atlanta; The Art Institute of Atlanta–Decatur[1]; The Art Institute of Austin[2]; The Art Institute of California–Hollywood; The Art Institute of California–Inland Empire; The Art Institute of California–Los Angeles; The Art Institute of California–Orange County; The Art Institute of California–Sacramento; The Art Institute of California–San Diego; The Art Institute of California–San Francisco; The Art Institute of California–Sunnyvale; The Art Institute of Charleston[1]; The Art Institute of Charlotte; The Art Institute of Colorado; The Art Institute of Dallas; The Art Institute of Fort Lauderdale; The Art Institute of Fort Worth[3]; The Art Institute of Houston; The Art Institute of Houston–North[2]; The Art Institute of Indianapolis[4]; The Art Institute of Jacksonville[5]; The Art Institute of Las Vegas; The Art Institute of Michigan; The Art Institute of New York City; The Art Institute of Ohio–Cincinnati[6]; The Art Institute of Philadelphia; The Art Institute of Phoenix; The Art Institute of Pittsburgh; The Art Institute of Portland; The Art Institute of Raleigh–Durham; The Art Institute of Salt Lake City; The Art Institute of San Antonio[2];The Art Institute of Seattle; The Art Institute of Tampa[5]; The Art Institute of Tennessee–Nashville[1,7]; The Art Institute of Tucson; The Art Institute of Vancouver; The Art Institute of Virginia Beach[1,8]; The Art Institute of Washington[1,8]; The Art Institute of Washington–Northern Virginia[1,8]; The Art Institute of York–Pennsylvania; The Art Institutes International–Kansas City; The Art Institutes International Minnesota; The Illinois Institute of Art–Chicago; The Illinois Institute of Art–Schaumburg; Miami International University of Art & Design; The New England Institute of Art.

[1]A branch of The Art Institute of Atlanta
[2]A branch of The Art Institute of Houston
[3]A branch of The Art Institute of Dallas
[4]The Art Institute of Indianapolis is regulated by the Indiana Commission on Proprietary Education, 302 West Washington Street, Room E201, Indianapolis, Indiana 46204, AC-0080
[5]A branch of Miami International University of Art & Design
[6]The Art Institute of Ohio–Cincinnati, 8845 Governors Hill Drive, Suite 100, Cincinnati, Ohio 45249-3317, OH Reg. #04-01-1698B
[7]The Art Institute of Tennessee–Nashville is authorized for operation as a postsecondary educational institution by the Tennessee Higher Education Commission.
[8]Certified by the State Council of Higher Education to operate in Virginia

THE ART INSTITUTE OF LAS VEGAS

HENDERSON, NEVADA

The Art Institute of Las Vegas provides education programs that prepare students to pursue entry-level positions in the creative arts. Located in the prestigious Green Valley area of Henderson in the Las Vegas Valley, the school occupies approximately 48,000 square feet and currently offers twelve bachelor's degree programs and three associate degree programs.

Each program is offered on a year-round basis, allowing students to work uninterrupted toward their degrees. The faculty members strive to strengthen the students' skills and cultivate their talents through programs carefully designed with the support and contributions of leading members of the professional community. Instructional methods include lectures, demonstrations, labs, one-on-one tutorials, and periodic examinations. Courses may include internships, field trips, online courses, and independent studies. The curricula are reviewed periodically to ensure that they meet the needs of a changing marketplace.

Students come to The Art Institute of Las Vegas from across the United States and abroad. The student population includes recent high school graduates, transfer students, and those who have left a previous employment situation to study and train for a new career. Students are creative, competitive, and open to new ideas. They place great value on an education that prepares them for an exciting entry-level position in the arts.

Students are expected to gain an understanding of theoretical and practical knowledge appropriate to their degree objectives, complete specific courses, and develop critical and analytical learning abilities along with values that contribute to lifelong learning.

The Career Services Department helps students to launch a job search and can assist in locating part-time employment while students are still in school. The department assists students with resume writing, networking, and keeping abreast of what employers are looking for in job applicants.

The Art Institute of Las Vegas school-sponsored housing facility offers a variety of living accommodations in a fully-equipped, partially furnished, apartment-style complex. A resident adviser lives in the housing facility and assists students in coordinating activities, meeting each other, and learning about the school.

The Student Affairs Office is the key contact for all international students. This office provides a variety of support services and enrichment activities to meet the needs of international students.

The Art Institute of Las Vegas holds film festivals, portfolio shows, and other activities for students. Counseling services are available to all students while attending the school. The school provides confidential short-term counseling for individuals and groups in accordance with professional, legal, and ethical codes of the counseling profession.

The Art Institute of Las Vegas is accredited by the Accrediting Commission of Career Schools and Colleges (ACCSC). ACCSC may be contacted at 2101 Wilson Boulevard, Suite 302, Arlington, Virginia 22201; phone: 703-247-4212.

The Art Institute of Las Vegas is licensed to operate by the Commission on Postsecondary Education, 1820 East Sahara Avenue, Suite 111, Las Vegas, Nevada 89104; phone: 702-486-7330.

Location

Las Vegas provides sunny days, museums, libraries, parks, gift shops, and historical sites. Just outside the city are some of the world's most beautiful natural wonders, including the Grand Canyon, Red Rock Canyon, Death Valley, Hoover Dam, and Valley of Fire State Park. Nearly 1.5 million residents live in the Las Vegas metro area.

Programs of Study and Degrees

The school offers bachelor's degree programs in audio production, culinary management, digital filmmaking and video production, digital photography, fashion and retail management, food and beverage management, game art and design, graphic design, interior design, media arts and animation, visual effects and motion graphics, and Web design and interactive media.

Associate degree programs are available in baking and pastry, culinary arts, and drafting technology and design.

Academic Programs

To receive an associate degree, a student must complete a minimum of 112 quarter credits, with 28 quarter credits in general education courses and 84 quarter credits in a specialty area. To receive a bachelor's degree, a student must complete a minimum of 192 quarter credits, with 48 quarter credits in general education courses and 114 quarter credits in a specialty area. For both degrees, the student must achieve a cumulative GPA of 2.0 or higher, meet portfolio or other requirements, and satisfy all financial obligations to the school. A limited number of courses are available online for an additional fee per course.

Academic Facilities

The Art Institute of Las Vegas houses classrooms, studios, offices, a student lounge, a supply store, Mac and PC labs, faculty and staff offices, and the Learning Resource Center, with library and reference materials. In addition, program-specific equipment, including projectors, editing decks, camcorders, printers, drafting tables, and kitchen appliances are provided to help students complete their projects. Students also have access to the public libraries and the University of Nevada–Las Vegas campus library.

Costs

Tuition cost varies by program. Prospective students should contact the school for current tuition costs. Other charges

COLLEGE CLOSE-UPS

include a starting kit for all first quarter students. Kits vary in price depending on the program of study.

Financial Aid

Financial aid is available for those who qualify. Students who require financial assistance should first complete and submit a Free Application for Federal Student Aid (FAFSA) and meet with a financial aid officer.

Faculty

The Art Institute of Las Vegas faculty includes full-time and part-time instructors, many of whom have advanced degrees and professional experience in their respective fields of study.

Admission Requirements

As a prerequisite for admission, a prospective student must be a high school graduate, hold a General Educational Development (GED) certificate, or have earned a bachelor's degree or higher from an accredited institution of postsecondary education. Each prospective student is interviewed, either in person or by telephone, by an assistant director of admissions to determine whether the student and school are a good fit. Portfolios may qualify the student for advanced placement, and applications may be submitted any time prior to the start of the next quarter. There is a $50 application fee.

For the most recent information regarding admission requirements, please refer to the current academic catalog.

Application and Information

To obtain an application, make arrangements for an interview, or tour the school, prospective students should contact:

The Art Institute of Las Vegas
2350 Corporate Circle
Henderson, Nevada 89074-7737
Phone: 702-369-9944
800-833-2678 (toll-free)
Fax: 702-992-8458
Web site: http://www.artinstitutes.edu/lasvegas

COLLEGE CLOSE-UPS

The Art Institute of Atlanta; The Art Institute of Atlanta–Decatur[1]; The Art Institute of Austin[2]; The Art Institute of California–Hollywood; The Art Institute of California–Inland Empire; The Art Institute of California–Los Angeles; The Art Institute of California–Orange County; The Art Institute of California–Sacramento; The Art Institute of California–San Diego; The Art Institute of California–San Francisco; The Art Institute of California–Sunnyvale; The Art Institute of Charleston[1]; The Art Institute of Charlotte; The Art Institute of Colorado; The Art Institute of Dallas; The Art Institute of Fort Lauderdale; The Art Institute of Fort Worth[3]; The Art Institute of Houston; The Art Institute of Houston–North[2]; The Art Institute of Indianapolis[4]; The Art Institute of Jacksonville[5]; The Art Institute of Las Vegas; The Art Institute of Michigan; The Art Institute of New York City; The Art Institute of Ohio–Cincinnati[6]; The Art Institute of Philadelphia; The Art Institute of Phoenix; The Art Institute of Pittsburgh; The Art Institute of Portland; The Art Institute of Raleigh–Durham; The Art Institute of Salt Lake City; The Art Institute of San Antonio[2];The Art Institute of Seattle; The Art Institute of Tampa[5]; The Art Institute of Tennessee–Nashville[1,7]; The Art Institute of Tucson; The Art Institute of Vancouver; The Art Institute of Virginia Beach[1,8]; The Art Institute of Washington[1,8]; The Art Institute of Washington–Northern Virginia[1,8]; The Art Institute of York–Pennsylvania; The Art Institutes International–Kansas City; The Art Institutes International Minnesota; The Illinois Institute of Art–Chicago; The Illinois Institute of Art–Schaumburg; Miami International University of Art & Design; The New England Institute of Art.

[1]A branch of The Art Institute of Atlanta
[2]A branch of The Art Institute of Houston
[3]A branch of The Art Institute of Dallas
[4]The Art Institute of Indianapolis is regulated by the Indiana Commission on Proprietary Education, 302 West Washington Street, Room E201, Indianapolis, Indiana 46204, AC-0080
[5]A branch of Miami International University of Art & Design
[6]The Art Institute of Ohio–Cincinnati, 8845 Governors Hill Drive, Suite 100, Cincinnati, Ohio 45249-3317, OH Reg. #04-01-1698B
[7]The Art Institute of Tennessee–Nashville is authorized for operation as a postsecondary educational institution by the Tennessee Higher Education Commission.
[8]Certified by the State Council of Higher Education to operate in Virginia

THE ART INSTITUTE OF MICHIGAN

NOVI, MICHIGAN

The Art Institute of Michigan provides students with an educational environment and dedicated faculty members committed to preparing students to pursue entry-level positions in the creative arts. Under the guidance of industry professionals, students learn by doing the types of tasks they are likely to encounter in the workplace. In addition, assistance is available to help students with resume writing, networking, and keeping aware of what employers are looking for in job candidates. The school offers seven bachelor's degree programs and four associate degree programs.

The school offers assistance in helping students to secure housing.

The student population includes recent high school graduates, transfer students, and those who have left a previous employment situation to study and train for a new career. Students are creative, competitive, and open to new ideas. They place great value on an education that prepares them for an exciting entry-level position in the arts.

The Art Institute of Michigan places a high value on the quality of student life—both in and out of the classroom. Students can participate in a wide variety of activities, including clubs and organizations, community service, and various committees designed to enhance the quality of student life.

The Art Institute of Michigan, as a branch of the Illinois Institute of Art, is accredited by the Higher Learning Commission and is a member of the North Central Association, 30 North LaSalle Street, Suite 2400, Chicago, Illinois 60602; http://www.ncahlc.org.

The Art Institute of Michigan is licensed under the laws of the Michigan Department of Labor and Economic Growth.

Location

Novi, a town of over 52,000, is a suburb of Detroit. One of the fastest-growing cities in Michigan, Novi is home to the Motorsports Hall of Fame of America and Twelve Oaks Mall and is just a short drive from the cultural, entertainment, and sports facilities of Detroit.

Programs of Study and Degrees

The Art Institute of Michigan offers bachelor's degree programs in advertising, culinary management, digital photography, fashion marketing and management, interior design, visual communications, and Web design and interactive media.

Associate degrees are offered in culinary arts, fashion merchandising, graphic design, and Web design and interactive media.

A certificate program is offered in professional baking and pastry.

Academic Programs

The Art Institute of Michigan operates on a year-round, four-quarter system.

Academic Facilities

The Art Institute of Michigan contains classrooms, Mac and PC computer labs, and a library for student use. There is also a bookstore.

Costs

Tuition cost varies by program. Prospective students should contact the school for current tuition costs. Other charges include a starting kit for all first quarter students. Kits vary in price depending on the program of study.

Financial Aid

Financial aid is available for those who qualify. Students who require financial assistance should first complete and submit a Free Application for Federal Student Aid (FAFSA) and meet with a financial aid officer.

Faculty

Faculty members at The Art Institute of Michigan have professional knowledge that they bring into the classroom. The school's faculty members provide their students with a real-world, relevant educational experience. The faculty consists of both full-time and part-time employees.

Admission Requirements

Applicants must provide proof of high school graduation or achievement of a General Educational Development (GED) certificate as a prerequisite for admission. In lieu of documenting high school graduation or a GED certificate, applicants may provide proof of attaining an associate degree or higher from an accredited institution. An official transcript indicating date of high school graduation, GED certificate (including test scores), or date of college graduation (including degree granted) is required as proof.

All individuals seeking admission to The Art Institute of Michigan are interviewed in person or by phone by an assistant director of admissions, and each applicant must submit an original essay of at least 150 words stating how an education at The Art Institute of Michigan would help the student to achieve career goals.

There is a $50 application fee.

For the most recent information regarding admission requirements, please refer to the current academic catalog.

Application and Information

To obtain an application, make arrangements for an interview, or tour the school, students should contact:

The Art Institute of Michigan
28125 Cabot Drive, Suite 120
Novi, Michigan 48377
Phone: 248-675-3800
800-479-0087 (toll-free)
Fax: 248-675-3830
Web site: http://www.artinstitutes.edu/detroit

COLLEGE CLOSE-UPS

The Art Institute of Atlanta; The Art Institute of Atlanta–Decatur[1]; The Art Institute of Austin[2]; The Art Institute of California–Hollywood; The Art Institute of California–Inland Empire; The Art Institute of California–Los Angeles; The Art Institute of California–Orange County; The Art Institute of California–Sacramento; The Art Institute of California–San Diego; The Art Institute of California–San Francisco; The Art Institute of California–Sunnyvale; The Art Institute of Charleston[1]; The Art Institute of Charlotte; The Art Institute of Colorado; The Art Institute of Dallas; The Art Institute of Fort Lauderdale; The Art Institute of Fort Worth[3]; The Art Institute of Houston; The Art Institute of Houston–North[2]; The Art Institute of Indianapolis[4]; The Art Institute of Jacksonville[5]; The Art Institute of Las Vegas; The Art Institute of Michigan; The Art Institute of New York City; The Art Institute of Ohio–Cincinnati[6]; The Art Institute of Philadelphia; The Art Institute of Phoenix; The Art Institute of Pittsburgh; The Art Institute of Portland; The Art Institute of Raleigh–Durham; The Art Institute of Salt Lake City; The Art Institute of San Antonio[2];The Art Institute of Seattle; The Art Institute of Tampa[5]; The Art Institute of Tennessee–Nashville[1,7]; The Art Institute of Tucson; The Art Institute of Vancouver; The Art Institute of Virginia Beach[1,8]; The Art Institute of Washington[1,8]; The Art Institute of Washington–Northern Virginia[1,8]; The Art Institute of York–Pennsylvania; The Art Institutes International–Kansas City; The Art Institutes International Minnesota; The Illinois Institute of Art–Chicago; The Illinois Institute of Art–Schaumburg; Miami International University of Art & Design; The New England Institute of Art.

[1]A branch of The Art Institute of Atlanta
[2]A branch of The Art Institute of Houston
[3]A branch of The Art Institute of Dallas
[4]The Art Institute of Indianapolis is regulated by the Indiana Commission on Proprietary Education, 302 West Washington Street, Room E201, Indianapolis, Indiana 46204, AC-0080
[5]A branch of Miami International University of Art & Design
[6]The Art Institute of Ohio–Cincinnati, 8845 Governors Hill Drive, Suite 100, Cincinnati, Ohio 45249-3317, OH Reg. #04-01-1698B
[7]The Art Institute of Tennessee–Nashville is authorized for operation as a postsecondary educational institution by the Tennessee Higher Education Commission.
[8]Certified by the State Council of Higher Education to operate in Virginia

THE ART INSTITUTE OF OHIO–CINCINNATI

CINCINNATI, OHIO

The Art Institute of Ohio–Cincinnati

COLLEGE CLOSE-UPS

The Art Institute of Ohio–Cincinnati offers education programs that prepare students to pursue entry-level employment in the creative arts. The school offers eight bachelor's degree programs and six associate degree programs.

The Art Institute of Ohio–Cincinnati includes more than 35,000 square feet of classroom, laboratory, and office space designed according to the school's specifications for its design programs.

Students come to The Art Institute of Ohio–Cincinnati from throughout the United States. The student population includes recent high school graduates, transfer students, and those who have left a previous employment situation to study and train for a new career. Students are creative, competitive, and open to new ideas. They place great value on an education that prepares them to pursue an exciting entry-level position in the arts.

Student life is an integral part of The Art Institute of Ohio–Cincinnati experience. The Office of Student Affairs sponsors a variety of events, including intramural sports, dances, parties, lunch-and-learn sessions, and off-campus trips.

The Art Institute of Ohio–Cincinnati, as a branch of the Illinois Institute of Art, is accredited by the Higher Learning Commission and a member of the North Central Association, 30 North LaSalle Street, Suite 2400, Chicago, Illinois 60602; http://.www.ncahlc.org.

The Art Institute of Ohio–Cincinnati holds a provisional certificate of authorization for its academic programs by the Ohio Board of Regents, 30 East Broad Street, Columbus, Ohio 43215; phone: 614-466-6000. The provisional authorization expires on December 31, 2012.

The Art Institute of Ohio–Cincinnati is licensed by the Ohio State Board of Career Colleges and Schools, 35 East Gay Street, Columbus, Ohio 43266-0591; phone: 614-466-2752. OH Reg. # 04-01-1698B.

The Art Institute of Ohio–Cincinnati is regulated by the Indiana Commission on Proprietary Education, 302 West Washington Street, Room E201, Indianapolis, Indiana 46204-2767; phone: 317-232-1320 (in-state) or 800-227-5695 (toll-free). AC0165.

Location

Cincinnati is home to major-league sporting events, concerts, a professional symphony, theater, Kings Island, award-winning restaurants, and downtown entertainment districts that offer exciting nightlife. The city is known for its great beauty, with steep hills, wooded suburbs, a picturesque downtown riverfront, and four distinct seasons.

Programs of Study and Degrees

Bachelor's degree programs are available in advertising, culinary management, digital filmmaking and video production, fashion marketing and management, interior design, media arts and animation, visual communications, and Web design and interactive media.

Associate degree programs include culinary arts, fashion merchandising, graphic design, interior design, video production, or Web design and interactive media.

A diploma programs is offered in baking and pastry.

Academic Programs

The Art Institute of Ohio–Cincinnati operates on a year-round, four-quarter system.

Academic Facilities

The Art Institute of Ohio–Cincinnati provides easy access to the technology, tools, and facilities needed to complete projects in all disciplines. Students may produce work in an environment that is appropriate for their chosen creative endeavors. The facilities include media presentation rooms for special instructional needs, libraries that provide instructional resources, and academic support for both faculty members and students.

Costs

Tuition costs vary by program. Prospective students should contact the school for current tuition costs. Other charges include a starting kit for all first-quarter students. Kits vary in price, depending on the program of study.

For the most recent information regarding admission requirements, please refer to the current academic catalog.

Financial Aid

Financial aid is available for those who qualify.

Faculty

The Art Institute of Ohio–Cincinnati's faculty members have experience in their fields and are committed to the academic and technical preparation of their students. Faculty members are employed on both a part-time and full-time basis.

Admission Requirements

Applicants to The Art Institute of Ohio–Cincinnati must demonstrate proof of high school graduation or its equivalent. An official copy of the high school transcript or General Educational Development (GED) certificate is required. Candidates are interviewed and must write an essay on how an education at The Art Institute of Ohio–Cincinnati can help them reach their career goals.

Each applicant's academic transcript and completed essay are evaluated by the Admissions Acceptance Committee. A separate application and enrollment form must be completed and signed by the applicant and then submitted to The Art Institute of Ohio–Cincinnati. There is an application fee of $50.

Application and Information

To obtain an application or make arrangements for an interview or tour of the school, prospective students should contact:

The Art Institute of Ohio–Cincinnati
8845 Governors Hill Drive
Cincinnati, Ohio 45249-3317
Phone: 513-833-2400
866-613-5184 (toll-free)
Fax: 877-477-8486 (toll-free)
Web site: http://www.artinstitutes.edu/cincinnati

COLLEGE CLOSE-UPS

The Art Institute of Atlanta; The Art Institute of Atlanta–Decatur[1]; The Art Institute of Austin[2]; The Art Institute of California–Hollywood; The Art Institute of California–Inland Empire; The Art Institute of California–Los Angeles; The Art Institute of California–Orange County; The Art Institute of California–Sacramento; The Art Institute of California–San Diego; The Art Institute of California–San Francisco; The Art Institute of California–Sunnyvale; The Art Institute of Charleston[1]; The Art Institute of Charlotte; The Art Institute of Colorado; The Art Institute of Dallas; The Art Institute of Fort Lauderdale; The Art Institute of Fort Worth[3]; The Art Institute of Houston; The Art Institute of Houston–North[2]; The Art Institute of Indianapolis[4]; The Art Institute of Jacksonville[5]; The Art Institute of Las Vegas; The Art Institute of Michigan; The Art Institute of New York City; The Art Institute of Ohio–Cincinnati[6]; The Art Institute of Philadelphia; The Art Institute of Phoenix; The Art Institute of Pittsburgh; The Art Institute of Portland; The Art Institute of Raleigh–Durham; The Art Institute of Salt Lake City; The Art Institute of San Antonio[2];The Art Institute of Seattle; The Art Institute of Tampa[5]; The Art Institute of Tennessee–Nashville[1,7]; The Art Institute of Tucson; The Art Institute of Vancouver; The Art Institute of Virginia Beach[1,8]; The Art Institute of Washington[1,8]; The Art Institute of Washington–Northern Virginia[1,8]; The Art Institute of York–Pennsylvania; The Art Institutes International–Kansas City; The Art Institutes International Minnesota; The Illinois Institute of Art–Chicago; The Illinois Institute of Art–Schaumburg; Miami International University of Art & Design; The New England Institute of Art.

[1]A branch of The Art Institute of Atlanta
[2]A branch of The Art Institute of Houston
[3]A branch of The Art Institute of Dallas
[4]The Art Institute of Indianapolis is regulated by the Indiana Commission on Proprietary Education, 302 West Washington Street, Room E201, Indianapolis, Indiana 46204, AC-0080
[5]A branch of Miami International University of Art & Design
[6]The Art Institute of Ohio–Cincinnati, 8845 Governors Hill Drive, Suite 100, Cincinnati, Ohio 45249-3317, OH Reg. #04-01-1698B
[7]The Art Institute of Tennessee–Nashville is authorized for operation as a postsecondary educational institution by the Tennessee Higher Education Commission.
[8]Certified by the State Council of Higher Education to operate in Virginia

THE ART INSTITUTE OF PHILADELPHIA

PHILADELPHIA, PENNSYLVANIA

The Art Institute of Philadelphia provides education programs that prepare students to pursue an entry-level job in the creative arts. The school offers thirteen bachelor's degree programs and nine associate degree programs.

Students come to The Art Institute of Philadelphia from across the country and abroad. The student body includes a diverse population—from men and women who enrolled directly after completing high school to those who transferred in from colleges and universities to those who have left employment to prepare for new careers.

Students at The Art Institute of Philadelphia have the opportunity to join such professional organizations as AIGA, the American Society of Interior Designers (ASID), and the Future Faces of Fashion Association.

Whether in the student lounge, the gallery, The Art Institute of Philadelphia Supply Store, or the extensive resource center, the daily gathering of students and faculty and staff members can make it easy to feel the energy, caring, and commitment that underlie an education at The Art Institute of Philadelphia. Classes are structured to be as close to a professional work environment as possible. Students practice their skills in labs and studios featuring industry-relevant technologies.

Assistance is available to help students with resume writing, networking, and keeping abreast of what employers are looking for in job candidates. The school offers a skills-enhancement program designed to help students prepare for college-level English and math courses, and confidential counseling is available when academic or personal problems create roadblocks to success.

The Student Services Department helps enrolled students to locate appropriate housing. Options include school-sponsored, apartment-style housing and independent apartment living.

The Art Institute of Philadelphia is accredited by the Accrediting Council for Independent Colleges and Schools (ACICS) to award diplomas, associate degrees, and bachelor's degrees. ACICS is listed as a nationally recognized accrediting agency by the United States Department of Education and is recognized by the Council for Higher Education Accreditation. ACICS can be contacted at 750 First Street NE, Suite 980, Washington, D.C. 20002; phone: 202-336-6780.

The Art Institute of Philadelphia is authorized by the Pennsylvania Department of Education to confer Bachelor of Science degrees, Associate of Science degrees, and diplomas. The Department of Education can be contacted at Commonwealth of Pennsylvania, Department of Education Office of Postsecondary and Higher Education, 333 Market Street, Harrisburg, Pennsylvania 17126; phone: 717-783-6788.

The Associate of Science in culinary arts degree program is accredited by the Accrediting Commission of the American Culinary Federation Education Foundation.

Location

Philadelphia is the birthplace of American democracy. The City of Brotherly Love surrounds the largest municipal landscaped park in the world, with tree-lined streets and an elegant blend of contemporary and historic architecture. Philadelphia has a renowned symphony orchestra, theater, film, jazz, and opera. With thirty-two major museums—including the expansive collections at the Museum of Art—the city is also home to fine shopping at locations such as the European-style Bourse, with its fifty international boutiques and restaurants, and to sports teams, such as baseball's Phillies, the NFL's Eagles, the NBA's 76ers, and the NHL's Flyers.

Programs of Study and Degrees

The Art Institute of Philadelphia offers bachelor's degree programs in advertising, audio production, culinary management, digital filmmaking and video production, fashion design, fashion marketing, graphic design, industrial design technology, interior design, media arts and animation, photography, visual effects and motion graphics, and Web design and interactive media.

Associate degree programs are offered in culinary arts, digital filmmaking and video production, fashion design, fashion marketing, graphic design, interior design, photography, visual merchandising, and Web design and interactive media.

Diploma programs in baking and pastry and in culinary arts are also available.

The baking and pastry program and the Associate of Science in culinary arts program are available in an evening and weekend option format.

Academic Programs

School quarters are eleven weeks long, and academic programs are between six and twelve quarters in length. Programs are offered on a year-round basis, allowing for strong continuity and the ability to work uninterrupted toward a degree.

The Art Institute of Philadelphia arranges student trips to local cultural and commercial sites. These visits can be an integral part of each student's learning experience. In addition to local student trips to support the curriculum, out-of-town seminars and visits are planned within individual programs.

Academic Facilities

The Art Institute of Philadelphia occupies nearly 86,000 square feet of space on Chestnut Street. Designated a historical site by the Philadelphia Historical Commission, the Art Deco building became home to The Art Institute of Philadelphia in 1982. In addition to classrooms, studios, laboratories, offices, a learning resource center, and the exhibition gallery, the school maintains an impressive gallery and an art supply store for the convenience of students. Additional space at 1610 Chestnut Street adds approximately 40,000 square feet of offices, classrooms, and computer labs.

The culinary arts programs are housed at 2300 Market Street. Three large kitchens are contained within the building, along with a bake shop, a skills kitchen, and an à la carte kitchen.

Computer lab facilities at the school include the PAD System (computerized patternmaking) as well as Intergraph Visual Workstations, PCs and Macs, Avid video labs, and a television station.

Costs

Tuition cost varies by program. Prospective students should contact the school for current tuition costs. Other charges include a starting kit for all first-quarter students. Kits vary in price depending on the program of study.

Financial Aid

Financial aid is available for those who qualify. Students who require financial assistance should first complete and submit a Free Application for Federal Student Aid (FAFSA) and meet with a financial aid officer.

Faculty

The school employs full-time and part-time faculty members. The Art Institute of Philadelphia faculty members, many of whom have professional experience in their industry, have credentials and reputations within their respective fields. Faculty members, the academic department director, and the dean of education provide academic counseling, evaluating student projects for the purpose of helping students to prepare a professional portfolio.

Admission Requirements

High school graduation or a General Educational Development (GED) certificate is a prerequisite for admission. All applicants are evaluated on the basis of previous education and their background/interest in the program of interest. Portfolios are welcomed but not required.

The Art Institute of Philadelphia operates on a rolling admissions basis. High school and/or college transcripts must be submitted to The Art Institute of Philadelphia at least one month prior to starting classes. There is a $50 application fee.

For the most recent information regarding admission requirements, please refer to the current academic catalog.

Application and Information

To obtain an application, make arrangements for an interview, or tour the school, prospective students should contact:

The Art Institute of Philadelphia
1622 Chestnut Street
Philadelphia, Pennsylvania 19103-5119
Phone: 215-567-7080
800-275-2474 (toll-free)
Fax: 215-405-6399
Web site: http://www.artinstitutes.edu/philadelphia

COLLEGE CLOSE-UPS

The Art Institute of Atlanta; The Art Institute of Atlanta–Decatur[1]; The Art Institute of Austin[2]; The Art Institute of California–Hollywood; The Art Institute of California–Inland Empire; The Art Institute of California–Los Angeles; The Art Institute of California–Orange County; The Art Institute of California–Sacramento; The Art Institute of California–San Diego; The Art Institute of California–San Francisco; The Art Institute of California–Sunnyvale; The Art Institute of Charleston[1]; The Art Institute of Charlotte; The Art Institute of Colorado; The Art Institute of Dallas; The Art Institute of Fort Lauderdale; The Art Institute of Fort Worth[3]; The Art Institute of Houston; The Art Institute of Houston–North[2]; The Art Institute of Indianapolis[4]; The Art Institute of Jacksonville[5]; The Art Institute of Las Vegas; The Art Institute of Michigan; The Art Institute of New York City; The Art Institute of Ohio–Cincinnati[6]; The Art Institute of Philadelphia; The Art Institute of Phoenix; The Art Institute of Pittsburgh; The Art Institute of Portland; The Art Institute of Raleigh–Durham; The Art Institute of Salt Lake City; The Art Institute of San Antonio[2];The Art Institute of Seattle; The Art Institute of Tampa[5]; The Art Institute of Tennessee–Nashville[1,7]; The Art Institute of Tucson; The Art Institute of Vancouver; The Art Institute of Virginia Beach[1,8]; The Art Institute of Washington[1,8]; The Art Institute of Washington–Northern Virginia[1,8]; The Art Institute of York–Pennsylvania; The Art Institutes International–Kansas City; The Art Institutes International Minnesota; The Illinois Institute of Art–Chicago; The Illinois Institute of Art–Schaumburg; Miami International University of Art & Design; The New England Institute of Art.

[1]A branch of The Art Institute of Atlanta
[2]A branch of The Art Institute of Houston
[3]A branch of The Art Institute of Dallas
[4]The Art Institute of Indianapolis is regulated by the Indiana Commission on Proprietary Education, 302 West Washington Street, Room E201, Indianapolis, Indiana 46204, AC-0080
[5]A branch of Miami International University of Art & Design
[6]The Art Institute of Ohio–Cincinnati, 8845 Governors Hill Drive, Suite 100, Cincinnati, Ohio 45249-3317, OH Reg. #04-01-1698B
[7]The Art Institute of Tennessee–Nashville is authorized for operation as a postsecondary educational institution by the Tennessee Higher Education Commission.
[8]Certified by the State Council of Higher Education to operate in Virginia

THE ART INSTITUTE OF PHOENIX

PHOENIX, ARIZONA

The Art Institute of Phoenix offers creative education programs, utilizing program-specific technology, to help students bring their creative goals to life. Graduates are prepared to pursue entry-level positions using the specialized skills and competencies employers seek. The school offers thirteen bachelor's degree programs and three associate degree programs.

Students come to The Art Institute of Phoenix from across United States and abroad. The student population includes recent high school graduates, transfer students, and those who have left a previous employment situation to study and train for a new career. Students are creative, competitive, and open to new ideas. They place great value on an education that prepares them to pursue an exciting entry-level position in the arts. Assistance is available to help students with resume writing, networking, and keeping abreast of what employers are looking for in job candidates.

The Art Institute of Phoenix provides Internet access for students throughout the school. Students may also utilize multiple computer labs, a Learning Resource Center, a student supply store, a Career Services Center, and a student lounge. Many student organizations and clubs exist to build friendships with like-minded classmates who are also refining their creative talents.

Through a special arrangement with select apartment complexes close to the school, The Art Institute of Phoenix offers students the opportunity to live in nearby furnished apartments.

The Art Institute of Phoenix is accredited by the Accrediting Council for Independent Colleges and Schools (ACICS) to award diplomas, associate degrees, and bachelor's degrees. ACICS is listed as a nationally recognized accrediting agency by the United States Department of Education and is recognized by the Council for Higher Education Accreditation. ACICS can be contacted at 750 First Street NE, Suite 980, Washington, D.C. 20002; phone: 202-336-6780.

The Associate of Applied Science in culinary arts degree program is accredited by the American Culinary Federation Foundation, Inc. Accrediting Commission.

The interior design program leading to the Bachelor of Arts degree is accredited by the Council for Interior Design Accreditation, 206 Grandville Avenue, Suite 350, Grand Rapids, Michigan 49503; http://www.accredit-id.org.

The Art Institute of Phoenix is authorized by the Arizona State Board for Private Postsecondary Education, 1400 West Washington Street, Room 2560, Phoenix, Arizona 85007; phone: 602-542-5709; http://azppse.state.az.us.

Location

Phoenix is one of the fastest-growing metropolitan areas in the country. Located in the heart of the beautiful Sonoran Desert, Phoenix is the gateway to cool pine forests, the red rock towers of Sedona, and the Grand Canyon. The city offers sun-filled days and a nightlife that ranges from top comedy and music clubs to the Phoenix Art Museum and Phoenix Symphony Orchestra. Professional sports teams include the Diamondbacks, Suns, Cardinals, and Coyotes.

Programs of Study and Degrees

The Art Institute of Phoenix offers bachelor's degree programs in advertising, audio production, culinary management, digital filmmaking and video production, digital photography, fashion marketing, game art and design, graphic design, interior design, media arts and animation, visual and game programming, visual effects and motion graphics, and Web design and interactive media.

Associate of Applied Science degree programs are offered in baking and pastry arts, culinary arts, and graphic design.

The culinary arts, culinary management, graphic design, and Web design and interactive media programs are also available in an evening and weekend option format.

Academic Programs

The Art Institute of Phoenix is in session year-round. Depending on the program, students can graduate in nine to thirty-six months with a diploma, an Associate of Applied Science degree, or a Bachelor of Arts degree in their chosen field.

Academic Facilities

The Art Institute of Phoenix is located in a four-story building in the northwest corner of Phoenix. Students enjoy scenic mountain views from many of the building's large picture windows. With sun streaming into classrooms and computer laboratories, student creativity flows easily. Classroom and computer laboratory facilities are well maintained, with a full-time technology manager on-site. The culinary arts kitchens are spacious and filled with commercial equipment similar to that which students will work with in entry-level positions. Digital media production students have access to a full television studio and control room, along with editing suites to complete their work.

Costs

Tuition cost varies by program. Prospective students should contact the school for current tuition costs. Other charges include a starting kit for all first-quarter students. Kits vary in price depending on the program of study.

Financial Aid

Financial aid is available for those who qualify. Students who require financial assistance should first complete and submit a Free Application for Federal Student Aid (FAFSA) and meet with a financial aid officer.

Faculty

The Art Institute of Phoenix offers personal attention from knowledgeable, professional instructors. Many of the faculty members are working professionals who bring practical knowledge and professional experience to the classroom. The faculty members at The Art Institute of Phoenix are available for student appointments to discuss academic issues. Faculty members also offer tutoring to students in need of extra help. Faculty members are employed on both a part-time and full-time basis.

Student Government

The President's Club is a school organization that promotes the philosophy of "students helping students." Those students selected to join the club assist new students with adjusting to life in Phoenix, studies at The Art Institute of Phoenix, and school activities. Criteria for selection into this club are a minimum GPA of 3.0 at The Art Institute of Phoenix, good attendance, completion of at least one full quarter of study, a desire to assist other students, and responsible behavior.

Admission Requirements

Many prospective students meet with an assistant director of admissions to discuss future goals and plan the admissions process. For admission to The Art Institute of Phoenix, students are evaluated on the basis of previous education, background, and a demonstrated interest in the selected program. Portfolio submission is encouraged but not required.

As part of the application process, students must write an essay stating how an education at The Art Institute of Phoenix will help them to attain their creative goals. Successful admission into The Art Institute of Phoenix and a satisfactory program start is dependent upon the essay; grade point average, as evidenced in transcript evaluation; an evaluation of General Educational Development (GED) test scores; a review of nationally based exams (preferred but not required), such as the SAT or ACT; and a personal interview with an assistant director of admissions. There is a $50 application fee.

For the most recent information regarding admission requirements, please refer to the current academic catalog.

Application and Information

To obtain an application, make arrangements for an interview, or tour the school, prospective students should contact:

The Art Institute of Phoenix
2233 West Dunlap Avenue
Phoenix, Arizona 85021-2859
Phone: 602-331-7500
800-474-2479 (toll-free)
Fax: 602-331-5301
Web site: http://www.artinstitutes.edu/phoenix

COLLEGE CLOSE-UPS

The Art Institute of Atlanta; The Art Institute of Atlanta–Decatur[1]; The Art Institute of Austin[2]; The Art Institute of California–Hollywood; The Art Institute of California–Inland Empire; The Art Institute of California–Los Angeles; The Art Institute of California–Orange County; The Art Institute of California–Sacramento; The Art Institute of California–San Diego; The Art Institute of California–San Francisco; The Art Institute of California–Sunnyvale; The Art Institute of Charleston[1]; The Art Institute of Charlotte; The Art Institute of Colorado; The Art Institute of Dallas; The Art Institute of Fort Lauderdale; The Art Institute of Fort Worth[3]; The Art Institute of Houston; The Art Institute of Houston–North[2]; The Art Institute of Indianapolis[4]; The Art Institute of Jacksonville[5]; The Art Institute of Las Vegas; The Art Institute of Michigan; The Art Institute of New York City; The Art Institute of Ohio–Cincinnati[6]; The Art Institute of Philadelphia; The Art Institute of Phoenix; The Art Institute of Pittsburgh; The Art Institute of Portland; The Art Institute of Raleigh–Durham; The Art Institute of Salt Lake City; The Art Institute of San Antonio[2];The Art Institute of Seattle; The Art Institute of Tampa[5]; The Art Institute of Tennessee–Nashville[1,7]; The Art Institute of Tucson; The Art Institute of Vancouver; The Art Institute of Virginia Beach[1,8]; The Art Institute of Washington[1,8]; The Art Institute of Washington–Northern Virginia[1,8]; The Art Institute of York–Pennsylvania; The Art Institutes International–Kansas City; The Art Institutes International Minnesota; The Illinois Institute of Art–Chicago; The Illinois Institute of Art–Schaumburg; Miami International University of Art & Design; The New England Institute of Art.

[1]A branch of The Art Institute of Atlanta
[2]A branch of The Art Institute of Houston
[3]A branch of The Art Institute of Dallas
[4]The Art Institute of Indianapolis is regulated by the Indiana Commission on Proprietary Education, 302 West Washington Street, Room E201, Indianapolis, Indiana 46204, AC-0080
[5]A branch of Miami International University of Art & Design
[6]The Art Institute of Ohio–Cincinnati, 8845 Governors Hill Drive, Suite 100, Cincinnati, Ohio 45249-3317, OH Reg. #04-01-1698B
[7]The Art Institute of Tennessee–Nashville is authorized for operation as a postsecondary educational institution by the Tennessee Higher Education Commission.
[8]Certified by the State Council of Higher Education to operate in Virginia

THE ART INSTITUTE OF PITTSBURGH

PITTSBURGH, PENNSYLVANIA

At The Art Institute of Pittsburgh, students are given the opportunity to learn new ways to apply creative talent, energy, and skills to a world of commercial and culinary arts, design, and technology. With fifteen bachelor's and eight associate degree programs, the school prepares students to pursue entry-level positions in the creative arts.

The school is located within a renovated historic landmark building with ten floors of fully networked, industry-standard computer labs and specialty facilities. Four kitchens, editing suites, digital photography labs, a television production studio, and an industrial design machine shop allow students to gain expertise in their fields of study.

The student population includes recent high school graduates, transfer students, and those who have left a previous employment situation to study and train for a new career. Students are creative, competitive, and open to new ideas. They place great value on an education that prepares them for an exciting entry-level position in the arts. The Art Institute of Pittsburgh Student Affairs Department arranges school activities and events. The department also employs a student activities coordinator who plans various events, theme parties, and clubs. Events are communicated via weekly and quarterly newsletters as well as through a television network. A cross-program Student Council represents the needs and issues of the entire student body. The school also supports approximately twenty clubs and intramural sports teams and oversees the activities and concerns of school-sponsored housing residents. The Student Life Department offers counseling services.

Students at The Art Institute of Pittsburgh may find reasonably priced housing within a 5- to 10-minute walk of the school through the school's Housing Department. Amenities include cable/Internet service, laundry facilities, and easy access to public transportation.

The Art Institute of Pittsburgh is accredited by the Middle States Commission on Higher Education, 3624 Market Street, Philadelphia, Pennsylvania 19104; phone: 267-284-5000; http://www.msche.org. The Middle States Commission on Higher Education is an institutional accrediting agency recognized by the U.S. Secretary of Education and the Council for Higher Education Accreditation.

The Art Institute of Pittsburgh is authorized by the Pennsylvania Department of Education to confer Bachelor of Science degrees, Associate of Science degrees, and diplomas. The Department of Education can be contacted at Commonwealth of Pennsylvania, Department of Education Office of Postsecondary and Higher Education, 333 Market Street, Harrisburg, Pennsylvania 17126; phone: 717-783-6788.

The Associate of Science degree in culinary arts and the Bachelor of Science degree in culinary management are accredited by the Accrediting Commission of the American Culinary Federation Education Foundation.

The interior design program leading to the Bachelor of Science degree is accredited by the Council for Interior Design Accreditation, 206 Grandville Avenue, Suite 350, Grand Rapids, Michigan 49503; http://www.accredit-id.org.

Location

The Art Institute of Pittsburgh is nestled in the heart of downtown Pittsburgh's Golden Triangle. Pittsburgh is a thriving metropolis, sprawling over 55 square miles. It is situated halfway between New York City and Chicago and is within a 2-hour flight or a one-day drive of more than 70 percent of the U.S. population.

Pittsburgh is the international headquarters of many technology-driven businesses. Culture abounds, with summer concerts in the downtown's Market Square at no charge, new theaters, thriving nightlife districts, quaint coffee shops, and retail merchants on every corner. The Pittsburgh Steelers' stadium and the Pirates' waterfront PNC Park adorn the city's North Shore. Pittsburgh is serviced by Greater Pittsburgh International Airport, one of the largest and most retail-developed airports in the country.

Programs of Study and Degrees

The Art Institute of Pittsburgh offers bachelor's degree programs in advertising, culinary management, digital filmmaking and video production, entertainment design, fashion and retail management, fashion design, game art and design, graphic design, hotel and restaurant management, industrial design, interior design, media arts and animation, photography, visual effects and motion graphics, and Web design and interactive media.

Associate of Science degree programs are offered in baking and pastry, culinary arts, digital filmmaking and video production, graphic design, industrial design technology, kitchen and bath design, photography, and Web design and interactive media.

Diploma programs are offered in the art of cooking, digital design, and Web design.

Academic Facilities

The Art Institute of Pittsburgh is located in a fully networked, 170,000-square-foot historic landmark building. The facility has interchangeable classroom, computer, and cell animation labs with extended access to Macintosh and PC computers and design and animation software. Photography students use a digital darkroom as well as traditional wet labs and printing stations. Interior design students have access to a fabric and textile research facility and computer-aided drawing software. The building is equipped with a television studio, digital editing suites, and Foley audio studio to support the video production curriculum. An industrial design shop is available. The Art Institute of Pittsburgh also contains a program-oriented library.

Culinary students learn in an environment similar to what they'll see in the industry, with professional kitchens and A Taste of Art, a working restaurant where culinary students serve the public.

Costs

Tuition cost varies by program. Prospective students should contact the school for current tuition costs. Other charges include a starting kit for all first-quarter students. Kits vary in price depending on the program of study.

Financial Aid

Financial aid is available for those who qualify. Students who require financial assistance should first complete and submit a Free Application for Federal Student Aid (FAFSA) and meet with a financial aid officer.

Faculty

The Art Institute of Pittsburgh faculty and staff members are professionals, many of whom are drawn from the ranks of industry. The school's faculty consists of full-time and part-time instructors who teach students how to cultivate conceptual, creative, and problem-solving skills.

In addition, assistance is available to help students with resume writing, networking, and keeping abreast of what employers are looking for in job candidates.

Admission Requirements

A prospective student must be a high school graduate with a high school QPA of 2.0 or higher (2.5 or higher QPA required for admission into game art and design), hold a General Educational Development (GED) certificate, or have a bachelor's degree or higher as a prerequisite for admission. Students who have completed high school or its equivalent but cannot provide the necessary documentation may provide alternate documentation to satisfy this requirement. The president of The Art Institute of Pittsburgh must approve all exceptions. A student who holds a bachelor's degree or higher may submit proof of the degree to satisfy the high school graduation or General Educational Development (GED) requirement. There is a portfolio requirement for media arts and animation and game art and design program candidates.

All applicants are evaluated on the basis of their previous education, background, and stated or demonstrated interest in their program of choice. Applicants who have taken the SAT or ACT are encouraged to submit scores to the Admissions Office for evaluation.

Applications are accepted on a rolling basis. An application for admission must be completed and signed by the applicant and be submitted along with an essay stating how The Art Institute of Pittsburgh can help the student to attain his or her creative goals. There is a $50 application fee.

For the most recent information regarding admission requirements, please refer to the current academic catalog.

Application and Information

To obtain an application, make arrangements for an interview, or tour the school, prospective students should contact:

The Art Institute of Pittsburgh
420 Boulevard of the Allies
Pittsburgh, Pennsylvania 15219-1301
Phone: 412-263-6600
800-275-2470 (toll-free)
Fax: 412-263-6667
Web site: http://www.artinstitutes.edu/pittsburgh

The Art Institute of Atlanta; The Art Institute of Atlanta–Decatur[1]; The Art Institute of Austin[2]; The Art Institute of California–Hollywood; The Art Institute of California–Inland Empire; The Art Institute of California–Los Angeles; The Art Institute of California–Orange County; The Art Institute of California–Sacramento; The Art Institute of California–San Diego; The Art Institute of California–San Francisco; The Art Institute of California–Sunnyvale; The Art Institute of Charleston[1]; The Art Institute of Charlotte; The Art Institute of Colorado; The Art Institute of Dallas; The Art Institute of Fort Lauderdale; The Art Institute of Fort Worth[3]; The Art Institute of Houston; The Art Institute of Houston–North[2]; The Art Institute of Indianapolis[4]; The Art Institute of Jacksonville[5]; The Art Institute of Las Vegas; The Art Institute of Michigan; The Art Institute of New York City; The Art Institute of Ohio–Cincinnati[6]; The Art Institute of Philadelphia; The Art Institute of Phoenix; The Art Institute of Pittsburgh; The Art Institute of Portland; The Art Institute of Raleigh–Durham; The Art Institute of Salt Lake City; The Art Institute of San Antonio[2];The Art Institute of Seattle; The Art Institute of Tampa[5]; The Art Institute of Tennessee–Nashville[1,7]; The Art Institute of Tucson; The Art Institute of Vancouver; The Art Institute of Virginia Beach[1,8]; The Art Institute of Washington[1,8]; The Art Institute of Washington–Northern Virginia[1,8]; The Art Institute of York–Pennsylvania; The Art Institutes International–Kansas City; The Art Institutes International Minnesota; The Illinois Institute of Art–Chicago; The Illinois Institute of Art–Schaumburg; Miami International University of Art & Design; The New England Institute of Art.

[1]A branch of The Art Institute of Atlanta
[2]A branch of The Art Institute of Houston
[3]A branch of The Art Institute of Dallas
[4]The Art Institute of Indianapolis is regulated by the Indiana Commission on Proprietary Education, 302 West Washington Street, Room E201, Indianapolis, Indiana 46204, AC-0080
[5]A branch of Miami International University of Art & Design
[6]The Art Institute of Ohio–Cincinnati, 8845 Governors Hill Drive, Suite 100, Cincinnati, Ohio 45249-3317, OH Reg. #04-01-1698B
[7]The Art Institute of Tennessee–Nashville is authorized for operation as a postsecondary educational institution by the Tennessee Higher Education Commission.
[8]Certified by the State Council of Higher Education to operate in Virginia

THE ART INSTITUTE OF PORTLAND

PORTLAND, OREGON

At The Art Institute of Portland, students and faculty members share ideas and work together to provide an opportunity to develop skills in the creative arts. Friendships and potential career contacts can be made as new designs emerge and become a part of the vibrant creative culture. The Art Institute of Portland is committed to preparing students to pursue entry-level positions in the arts. The school offers eighteen bachelor's degree programs and four associate degree programs.

The Art Institute of Portland provides educational programs created to instruct students in skills useful for everyday performance in the workplace. Education is offered along two main tracks in the fields of design and management. Programs include course work in communications, the humanities, social sciences, natural science, and mathematics. In addition, students have access to a wide variety of educational experiences, including workshops, seminars, and internships.

The Art Institute of Portland seeks to provide a diverse, challenging, rewarding educational experience to its students. The Student Affairs Department helps students to enrich their academic experience through student clubs and organizations, school activities, counseling and disability services, and housing services. Student clubs include the American Society of Interior Designers (ASID), Fight Club, Rorschach Writers Guild, and the S.T.A.C. (Student Action Committee).

Students come to The Art Institute of Portland from throughout the United States and abroad. The student population includes recent high school graduates, transfer students, and those who have left a previous employment situation to study and train for a new career. Students are creative, competitive, and open to new ideas. They place great value on an education that prepares them to pursue an exciting entry-level position in the arts.

Assistance is available to help students with resume writing, networking, and keeping abreast of what employers are looking for in job candidates.

The Art Institute of Portland offers housing assistance to all students. School-sponsored housing is available. Resident assistants are trained by the housing staff to help students become acquainted with each other through social and academic activities. Apartment information and roommate referrals are also available for students who choose to live off-campus.

The Art Institute of Portland is accredited by the Northwest Commission on Colleges and Universities (NWCCU), an institutional accrediting body recognized by the United States Department of Education. NWCCU can be contacted at 8060 165th Avenue NE, Suite 100, Redmond, Washington 98052-3981.

The interior design program leading to the Bachelor of Fine Arts degree is accredited by the Council for Interior Design Accreditation, 206 Grandville Avenue, Suite 350, Grand Rapids, Michigan 49503; http://www.accredit-id.org.

Location

Portland is the largest city in Oregon, located on the Willamette River near its junction with the Columbia River. Since 1888, Portland has been known as the Rose City because of the thousands of flowers that bloom in Washington Park. Natural attractions include the Columbia River Gorge's 3,000-foot-high basaltic cliffs, Multnomah Falls, and Mount Hood—the site of America's longest ski season. Portland also has a wide array of coffee shops, Native American art galleries, bookstores, and brew pubs as well as the Oregon Symphony, Tygres Heart Shakespeare Company, Musical Theater Company, Portland Opera, Baroque Orchestra, Northwest Afrikan American Ballet, Oregon Ballet Theatre, and Mount Hood Festival of Jazz.

Portland is home to many large apparel companies—students in the apparel accessory design and the apparel design programs have the advantage of learning from talented professionals in the industry. In addition, The Art Institute of Portland has built valuable relationships with the Oregon Film and Video Office and the Oregon Media Production Association.

Programs of Study and Degrees

Bachelor's degrees are available in advertising, apparel accessory design, apparel design, culinary management, design management, design research, design visualization, digital film and video, fashion marketing, game art and design, graphic design, industrial design, interior design, media arts and animation, photography and design, visual and game programming, visual effects and motion graphics, and Web design and interactive media.

Associate degrees are offered in apparel accessory design, apparel design, culinary arts, and graphic design.

Diploma programs are offered in baking and pastry and the art of cooking.

A minor in sustainability is offered with the bachelor's degree programs in apparel accessory design, apparel design, culinary management, design management, design research, fashion marketing, industrial design, and interior design.

Academic Programs

The academic year is divided into four quarters, beginning in January, April, July, and October. To earn a bachelor's degree, students must complete, at minimum, 180 academic credits. To earn an associate degree, students must earn, at minimum, 105 academic credits.

Academic Facilities

With more than 80,000 square feet of space, The Art Institute of Portland houses computer labs where students work on Macs and PCs using various software applications related to their programs of study. The Art Institute of Portland Gallery serves as a noncommercial exhibition space that reflects and exemplifies the artwork of professionals, faculty members, students, and graduates. Students learn more about industry-related media gear at the Equipment Cage and create high-resolution prints of their projects in the school's Print Service Center. The library's specialized collection is organized around the college curriculum, featuring books, journals and magazines, videos, DVDs, and CD-ROMs.

Culinary students learn in an environment similar to what they'll see in the industry, with professional kitchens that enable them to gain hands-on, real-world experience.

Costs

Tuition varies by program. Prospective students should contact the school for current tuition costs. Other charges include a starting kit for all first-quarter students. Kits vary in price depending on the program of study.

Financial Aid

Financial aid is available for those who qualify. Students who require financial assistance should first complete and submit a Free Application for Federal Student Aid (FAFSA) and meet with a financial aid officer.

Faculty

The Art Institute of Portland faculty consists of full-time and part-time instructors, many of whom have degrees and professional experience in their respective fields. The faculty members bring this knowledge and experience to their instruction.

Admission Requirements

Prospective students must submit an essay of approximately 150 words in which they describe the ways an education at The Art Institute of Portland may help to meet their creative objectives. Portfolios are encouraged but not required. An application for admission and enrollment agreement must be submitted to the school. Applicants who have taken the SAT or ACT should also submit these test scores. Each individual seeking admission is interviewed by an assistant director of admissions in order to explore the applicant's background, interests, and goals. There is a $50 application fee.

For the most recent information regarding admission requirements, please refer to the current academic catalog.

Application and Information

To obtain an application or make arrangements for an interview or tour of the school, prospective students should contact:

The Art Institute of Portland
1122 N.W. Davis Street
Portland, Oregon 97209-2911
Phone: 503-228-6528
888-228-6528 (toll-free)
Fax: 503-227-1945
Web site: http://www.artinstitutes.edu/portland

The Art Institute of Atlanta; The Art Institute of Atlanta–Decatur[1]; The Art Institute of Austin[2]; The Art Institute of California–Hollywood; The Art Institute of California–Inland Empire; The Art Institute of California–Los Angeles; The Art Institute of California–Orange County; The Art Institute of California–Sacramento; The Art Institute of California–San Diego; The Art Institute of California–San Francisco; The Art Institute of California–Sunnyvale; The Art Institute of Charleston[1]; The Art Institute of Charlotte; The Art Institute of Colorado; The Art Institute of Dallas; The Art Institute of Fort Lauderdale; The Art Institute of Fort Worth[3]; The Art Institute of Houston; The Art Institute of Houston–North[2]; The Art Institute of Indianapolis[4]; The Art Institute of Jacksonville[5]; The Art Institute of Las Vegas; The Art Institute of Michigan; The Art Institute of New York City; The Art Institute of Ohio–Cincinnati[6]; The Art Institute of Philadelphia; The Art Institute of Phoenix; The Art Institute of Pittsburgh; The Art Institute of Portland; The Art Institute of Raleigh–Durham; The Art Institute of Salt Lake City; The Art Institute of San Antonio[2];The Art Institute of Seattle; The Art Institute of Tampa[5]; The Art Institute of Tennessee–Nashville[1,7]; The Art Institute of Tucson; The Art Institute of Vancouver; The Art Institute of Virginia Beach[1,8]; The Art Institute of Washington[1,8]; The Art Institute of Washington–Northern Virginia[1,8]; The Art Institute of York–Pennsylvania; The Art Institutes International–Kansas City; The Art Institutes International Minnesota; The Illinois Institute of Art–Chicago; The Illinois Institute of Art–Schaumburg; Miami International University of Art & Design; The New England Institute of Art.

[1]A branch of The Art Institute of Atlanta
[2]A branch of The Art Institute of Houston
[3]A branch of The Art Institute of Dallas
[4]The Art Institute of Indianapolis is regulated by the Indiana Commission on Proprietary Education, 302 West Washington Street, Room E201, Indianapolis, Indiana 46204, AC-0080
[5]A branch of Miami International University of Art & Design
[6]The Art Institute of Ohio–Cincinnati, 8845 Governors Hill Drive, Suite 100, Cincinnati, Ohio 45249-3317, OH Reg. #04-01-1698B
[7]The Art Institute of Tennessee–Nashville is authorized for operation as a postsecondary educational institution by the Tennessee Higher Education Commission.
[8]Certified by the State Council of Higher Education to operate in Virginia

THE ART INSTITUTE OF RALEIGH-DURHAM

DURHAM, NORTH CAROLINA

The Art Institute of Raleigh-Durham

The Art Institute of Raleigh-Durham provides students with a creative educational environment and dedicated faculty members committed to preparing students to pursue entry-level positions in the creative arts. The Art Institute of Raleigh-Durham offers five bachelor's degree programs and four associate degree programs.

Under the guidance of industry professionals, students learn by doing the types of tasks they are likely to encounter in the workplace. In addition, assistance is available to help students with resume writing, networking, and keeping aware of what employers are looking for in job candidates.

The student population includes recent high school graduates, transfer students, and those who have left a previous employment situation to study and train for a new career. Students are creative, competitive, and open to new ideas. They place great value on an education that prepares them to pursue an exciting entry-level position in the arts.

The Art Institute of Raleigh-Durham places a high value on the quality of student life inside and outside the classroom. Students take part in a wide variety of activities, clubs and organizations, community service opportunities, and various student life enhancing committees.

Instructors are encouraged to look for upcoming books and to advise the administration of any books that may prove useful to their students. Students also have access to the public libraries.

The Student Affairs Office helps students who need assistance in locating housing.

The Art Institute of Raleigh-Durham, a branch of The Art Institute of Charlotte, is accredited by the Accrediting Council for Independent Colleges and Schools (ACICS) to award associate degrees and bachelor's degrees. ACICS is listed as a nationally recognized accrediting agency by the United States Department of Education and is recognized by the Council for Higher Education Accreditation. ACICS can be contacted at 750 First Street NE, Suite 980, Washington, D.C. 20002; phone: 202-336-6780.

The Art Institute of Raleigh–Durham is licensed by the Board of Governors of the University of North Carolina to confer Associate of Applied Science and Bachelor of Art degrees.

Location

The Art Institute of Raleigh-Durham is located in the heart of the downtown Durham historical and entertainment district. This area of North Carolina is known as the Research Triangle, with a population of over 1.6 million people.

Programs of Study and Degrees

Bachelor's degree programs are offered in culinary management, fashion marketing and management, graphic design, interior design, and Web design and interactive media.

Associate degree programs are offered in culinary arts, fashion marketing, graphic design, and Web design and interactive media.

Academic Programs

The Art Institute of Raleigh-Durham operates on a year-round, four-quarter system.

Academic Facilities

The Art Institute of Raleigh-Durham is home to classrooms, studios, offices, a student lounge, a supply store, and a learning resource center. Equipment provided at The Art Institute of Raleigh-Durham is specific to the program of study and may include projectors, editing decks, camcorders, PC and Macintosh computers, printers, drafting tables, and kitchen appliances.

Costs

Tuition cost varies by program. Prospective students should contact the school for current tuition costs. Other charges include a starting kit for all first quarter students. Kits vary in price depending on the program of study.

Financial Aid

Financial aid is available for those who qualify. Students who require financial assistance should first complete and submit a Free Application for Federal Student Aid (FAFSA) and meet with a financial aid officer.

Faculty

Faculty members at The Art Institute of Raleigh-Durham have professional knowledge that they bring into the classroom. The school's faculty members provide their students with a unique, relevant educational experience. Faculty members are employed on both a part-time and full-time basis.

Admission Requirements

Applicants must provide proof of high school graduation or achievement of a General Educational Development (GED) certificate as a prerequisite for admission. In lieu of documenting high school graduation or a GED certificate, applicants may provide proof of attaining an associate degree or higher from an accredited institution. An official transcript indicating date of high school graduation, GED certificate (including test scores), or date of college graduation (including degree granted) is required as proof.

All individuals seeking admission to The Art Institute of Raleigh-Durham are interviewed in person or by phone by an assistant director of admissions, and each applicant must create an original essay of at least 150 words stating how an education at The Art Institute of Raleigh-Durham would help the student to achieve career goals. There is a $50 application fee.

For the most recent information regarding admission requirements, please refer to the current academic catalog.

Application and Information

To obtain an application, make arrangements for an interview, or tour the school, prospective students should contact:

The Art Institute of Raleigh-Durham
410 Blackwell Street, Suite 200
Durham, North Carolina 27701
Phone: 919-317-3050
888-245-9593 (toll-free)
Fax: 919-317-3231
Web site: http://www.artinstitutes.edu/raleigh-durham

The Art Institute of Atlanta; The Art Institute of Atlanta–Decatur[1]; The Art Institute of Austin[2]; The Art Institute of California–Hollywood; The Art Institute of California–Inland Empire; The Art Institute of California–Los Angeles; The Art Institute of California–Orange County; The Art Institute of California–Sacramento; The Art Institute of California–San Diego; The Art Institute of California–San Francisco; The Art Institute of California–Sunnyvale; The Art Institute of Charleston[1]; The Art Institute of Charlotte; The Art Institute of Colorado; The Art Institute of Dallas; The Art Institute of Fort Lauderdale; The Art Institute of Fort Worth[3]; The Art Institute of Houston; The Art Institute of Houston–North[2]; The Art Institute of Indianapolis[4]; The Art Institute of Jacksonville[5]; The Art Institute of Las Vegas; The Art Institute of Michigan; The Art Institute of New York City; The Art Institute of Ohio–Cincinnati[6]; The Art Institute of Philadelphia; The Art Institute of Phoenix; The Art Institute of Pittsburgh; The Art Institute of Portland; The Art Institute of Raleigh–Durham; The Art Institute of Salt Lake City; The Art Institute of San Antonio[2];The Art Institute of Seattle; The Art Institute of Tampa[5]; The Art Institute of Tennessee–Nashville[1,7]; The Art Institute of Tucson; The Art Institute of Vancouver; The Art Institute of Virginia Beach[1,8]; The Art Institute of Washington[1,8]; The Art Institute of Washington–Northern Virginia[1,8]; The Art Institute of York–Pennsylvania; The Art Institutes International–Kansas City; The Art Institutes International Minnesota; The Illinois Institute of Art–Chicago; The Illinois Institute of Art–Schaumburg; Miami International University of Art & Design; The New England Institute of Art.

[1]A branch of The Art Institute of Atlanta
[2]A branch of The Art Institute of Houston
[3]A branch of The Art Institute of Dallas
[4]The Art Institute of Indianapolis is regulated by the Indiana Commission on Proprietary Education, 302 West Washington Street, Room E201, Indianapolis, Indiana 46204, AC-0080
[5]A branch of Miami International University of Art & Design
[6]The Art Institute of Ohio–Cincinnati, 8845 Governors Hill Drive, Suite 100, Cincinnati, Ohio 45249-3317, OH Reg. #04-01-1698B
[7]The Art Institute of Tennessee–Nashville is authorized for operation as a postsecondary educational institution by the Tennessee Higher Education Commission.
[8]Certified by the State Council of Higher Education to operate in Virginia

THE ART INSTITUTE OF SALT LAKE CITY

DRAPER, UTAH

The Art Institute of Salt Lake City provides students with an educational environment and dedicated faculty members who are committed to preparing students to pursue entry-level positions in the creative arts. Under the guidance of industry professionals, students learn by doing the types of tasks they are likely to encounter in the workplace. In addition, assistance is available to help students with resume writing, networking, and keeping aware of what employers are looking for in job candidates. The school offers eight bachelor's degree programs, and three associate degree programs.

The student population includes recent high school graduates, transfer students, and those who have left a previous employment situation to study and train for a new career. Students are creative, competitive, and open to new ideas. They place great value on an education that prepares them to pursue an exciting entry-level position in the arts.

The school offers assistance in helping students to secure housing.

The Art Institute of Salt Lake City is accredited by the Accrediting Commission of Career Schools and Colleges (ACCSC) as a branch of The Art Institute of Las Vegas. ACCSC may be contacted at 2101 Wilson Boulevard, Suite 302, Arlington, Virginia 22201; phone: 703-247-4212.

The Art Institute of Salt Lake City is exempt from registration pursuant to the Utah Postsecondary Proprietary School Act. Any questions should be directed to the Utah Division of Consumer Protection (UDCP), 160 East 300 South, Second Floor, Salt Lake City, Utah 84114; phone: 801-530-6601.

Location

Draper is located in the Wasatch Mountains at the south end of the Salt Lake Valley. The city has long been known as a premier hang-gliding destination with breathtaking views. Draper is fast becoming a hub for new development in the Salt Lake and Utah Valleys.

Programs of Study and Degrees

Bachelor's degree programs are offered in culinary management, digital filmmaking and video production, digital photography, game art and design, graphic design, interior design, media arts and animation, and Web design and interactive media.

Associate degrees are offered in baking and pastry, culinary arts, and graphic design.

Academic Programs

The Art Institute of Salt Lake City operates on a year-round, four-quarter system.

Academic Facilities

The Art Institute of Salt Lake City contains classrooms, Macintosh and PC computer labs, and a library for student use. There is also a bookstore.

Costs

Tuition cost varies by program. Prospective students should contact the school for current tuition costs. Other charges include a starting kit for all first-quarter students. Kits vary in price depending on the program of study.

Financial Aid

Financial aid is available for those who qualify. Students who require financial assistance should first complete and submit a Free Application for Federal Student Aid (FAFSA) and meet with a financial aid officer.

Faculty

Faculty members at The Art Institute of Salt Lake City have professional knowledge that they bring into the classroom. The school's faculty members provide their students with a real-world, relevant educational experience. Faculty members are employed on both a part-time and full-time basis.

Admission Requirements

Applicants must provide proof of high school graduation or achievement of a General Educational Development (GED) certificate as a prerequisite for admission. In lieu of documenting high school graduation or a GED certificate, applicants may provide proof of attaining an associate degree or higher from an accredited institution. An official transcript indicating date of high school graduation, receipt of a GED certificate (including test scores), or date of college graduation (including degree granted) is required as proof.

All individuals seeking admission to The Art Institute of Salt Lake City are interviewed in person or by phone by an assistant director of admissions, and each applicant must create an original essay of at least 150 words stating how an education at The Art Institute of Salt Lake City would help the student to achieve career goals. There is a $50 application fee.

For the most recent information regarding admission requirements, please refer to the current academic catalog.

Application and Information

To obtain an application, make arrangements for an interview, or tour the school, prospective students should contact:

The Art Institute of Salt Lake City
121 West Election Road, Suite 100
Draper, Utah 84020-9492
Phone: 801-601-4700
800-978-0096 (toll-free)
Fax: 801-601-4724
Web site: http://www.artinstitutes.edu/saltlakecity

COLLEGE CLOSE-UPS

THE ART INSTITUTE OF SAN ANTONIO

SAN ANTONIO, TEXAS

The Art Institute of San Antonio provides students with a creative educational environment and dedicated faculty members committed to preparing students to pursue entry-level positions in the creative arts. The Art Institute of San Antonio offers seven bachelor's degree programs and three associate degree programs.

Under the guidance of industry professionals, students learn by doing the types of tasks they are likely to encounter in the workplace. In addition, assistance is available to help students with resume writing, networking, and keeping aware of what employers are looking for in job candidates.

The student population includes recent high school graduates, transfer students, and those who have left a previous employment situation to study and train for a new career. Students are creative, competitive, and open to new ideas. They place great value on an education that prepares them to pursue an exciting entry-level position in the arts.

The Art Institute of San Antonio places a high value on the quality of student life inside and outside the classroom. Students take part in a wide variety of activities, clubs and organizations, community service opportunities, and various student life enhancing committees.

Instructors are encouraged to look for upcoming books and to advise the administration of any books that may prove useful to their students. Students also have access to the public libraries.

The Student Affairs Office helps students who need assistance in locating housing.

The Art Institute of San Antonio is a branch of The Art Institute of Houston. The Art Institute of Houston is accredited by the Commission on Colleges of the Southern Association of Colleges and Schools to award associate and baccalaureate degrees. Contact the Commission on Colleges at 1866 Southern Lane, Decatur, Georgia 30033-4097 or call 404-679-4500 for questions about the accreditation of The Art Institute of Houston.

The Art Institute of San Antonio holds a certificate of authorization acknowledging exemption from Texas Higher Education Coordinating Board regulations.

Location

San Antonio, the second-largest city in Texas, is one of the fastest growing areas in the United States. There are five Fortune 500 companies in the area, and visitors and locals alike enjoy the River Walk, Majestic Theatre, Alamo complex, and Spanish Governor's Palace.

Programs of Study and Degrees

Bachelor's degree programs are offered in culinary management, fashion and retail management, graphic design, interior design, media arts and animation, photography, and Web design and interactive media.

Associate degree programs are offered in culinary arts, graphic design, and Web design and interactive media.

Academic Programs

The Art Institute of San Antonio operates on a year-round, four-quarter system.

Academic Facilities

The Art Institute of San Antonio is home to classrooms, studios, offices, a student lounge, a supply store, and a learning resource center. Equipment provided at The Art Institute of San Antonio is specific to the program of study and may include projectors, editing decks, camcorders, PC and Macintosh computers, printers, drafting tables, and kitchen appliances.

Costs

Tuition cost varies by program. Prospective students should contact the school for current tuition costs. Other charges include a starting kit for all first-quarter students. Kits vary in price depending on the program of study.

Financial Aid

Financial aid is available for those who qualify. Students who require financial assistance should first complete and submit a Free Application for Federal Student Aid (FAFSA) and meet with a financial aid officer.

Faculty

Faculty members at The Art Institute of San Antonio have professional knowledge that they bring into the classroom. The school's faculty members provide their students with a unique, relevant educational experience. Faculty consists of both part-time and full-time employees.

Admission Requirements

Applicants must provide proof of high school graduation or achievement of a General Educational Development (GED) certificate as a prerequisite for admission.

In lieu of documenting high school graduation or a GED certificate, applicants may provide proof of attaining an associate degree or higher from an accredited institution. An official transcript indicating date of high school graduation, GED certificate (including test scores), or date of college graduation (including degree granted) is required as proof.

All individuals seeking admission to The Art Institute of San Antonio are interviewed in person or by phone by an assistant director of admissions, and each applicant must create an original essay of at least 150 words stating how an education at The Art Institute of San Antonio would help the student to achieve career goals. There is a $50 application fee.

For the most recent information regarding admission requirements, please refer to the current academic catalog.

Application and Information

To obtain an application, make arrangements for an interview, or tour the school, prospective students should contact:

The Art Institute of San Antonio
10000 IH-10 West
Suite 200
San Antonio, Texas 78230
Phone: 888-222-0040 (toll-free)
Web site: http://www.artinstitutes.edu/sanantonio

The Art Institute of Atlanta; The Art Institute of Atlanta–Decatur[1]; The Art Institute of Austin[2]; The Art Institute of California–Hollywood; The Art Institute of California–Inland Empire; The Art Institute of California–Los Angeles; The Art Institute of California–Orange County; The Art Institute of California–Sacramento; The Art Institute of California–San Diego; The Art Institute of California–San Francisco; The Art Institute of California–Sunnyvale; The Art Institute of Charleston[1]; The Art Institute of Charlotte; The Art Institute of Colorado; The Art Institute of Dallas; The Art Institute of Fort Lauderdale; The Art Institute of Fort Worth[3]; The Art Institute of Houston; The Art Institute of Houston–North[2]; The Art Institute of Indianapolis[4]; The Art Institute of Jacksonville[5]; The Art Institute of Las Vegas; The Art Institute of Michigan; The Art Institute of New York City; The Art Institute of Ohio–Cincinnati[6]; The Art Institute of Philadelphia; The Art Institute of Phoenix; The Art Institute of Pittsburgh; The Art Institute of Portland; The Art Institute of Raleigh–Durham; The Art Institute of Salt Lake City; The Art Institute of San Antonio[2];The Art Institute of Seattle; The Art Institute of Tampa[5]; The Art Institute of Tennessee–Nashville[1,7]; The Art Institute of Tucson; The Art Institute of Vancouver; The Art Institute of Virginia Beach[1,8]; The Art Institute of Washington[1,8]; The Art Institute of Washington–Northern Virginia[1,8]; The Art Institute of York–Pennsylvania; The Art Institutes International–Kansas City; The Art Institutes International Minnesota; The Illinois Institute of Art–Chicago; The Illinois Institute of Art–Schaumburg; Miami International University of Art & Design; The New England Institute of Art.

[1]A branch of The Art Institute of Atlanta
[2]A branch of The Art Institute of Houston
[3]A branch of The Art Institute of Dallas
[4]The Art Institute of Indianapolis is regulated by the Indiana Commission on Proprietary Education, 302 West Washington Street, Room E201, Indianapolis, Indiana 46204, AC-0080
[5]A branch of Miami International University of Art & Design
[6]The Art Institute of Ohio–Cincinnati, 8845 Governors Hill Drive, Suite 100, Cincinnati, Ohio 45249-3317, OH Reg. #04-01-1698B
[7]The Art Institute of Tennessee–Nashville is authorized for operation as a postsecondary educational institution by the Tennessee Higher Education Commission.
[8]Certified by the State Council of Higher Education to operate in Virginia

THE ART INSTITUTE OF SEATTLE

SEATTLE, WASHINGTON

The Art Institute of Seattle provides programs that prepare graduates to pursue entry-level employment in the creative arts. Programs are developed with and taught by experienced educators. The Art Institute of Seattle has a proud history both as a part of the Seattle community and as a contributor to the Northwest's creative industries. The Art Institute of Seattle offers twelve bachelor's degree programs and twelve associate degree programs.

The Career Services Department works with students to refine their presentations to potential employers. The department also helps provide student advisers with insight into each student's specialized skills and interests. Specific career advising occurs during the last two quarters of a student's education. Interviewing techniques and resume-writing skills are developed, and students receive portfolio advising from faculty members.

Students come to The Art Institute of Seattle from throughout the United States and abroad. The student population includes recent high school graduates, transfer students, and those who have left a previous employment situation to study and train for a new career. Students are creative, competitive, and open to new ideas. They place great value on an education that prepares them to pursue an exciting entry-level position in the arts.

The Art Institute of Seattle places high importance on student life, both inside and outside the classroom. The school provides an environment that encourages involvement in a wide variety of activities, including clubs and organizations, community service opportunities, and various committees designed to enhance the quality of student life. Numerous all-school programs and events are planned throughout the year to meet students' needs.

The Student Affairs Department offers a variety of services to students to help them make the most of their educational experience. These services include both school-sponsored and independent housing options.

The Art Institute of Seattle is accredited by the Northwest Commission on Colleges and Universities (NWCCU), an institutional accrediting body recognized by the United States Department of Education.

The Art Institute of Seattle is licensed under Chapter 28c.10RCW; inquiries or complaints regarding this or any other private vocational school may be made to the Workforce Training and Education Coordinating Board, 128 10th Avenue SW, P.O. Box 43105, Olympia, Washington 98504-3105; phone: 360-753-5662.

The Associate of Applied Arts in culinary arts degree program is accredited by the Accrediting Commission of the American Culinary Federation Education Foundation.

Location

The Art Institute of Seattle is located in the city's Belltown district. Founded by Native Americans and traders, the city has retained respect for its different cultures and customs. People from all over the world come to study, work, and live in this city that is known for its friendly people and beautiful natural surroundings.

World-class companies, such as Microsoft, Boeing, Starbucks, Amazon.com, and Nordstrom, make their global headquarters in Seattle. As a gateway to the Pacific Rim, Seattle is a crossroads where creativity, technology, and business meet.

Programs of Study and Degrees

Bachelor's degree programs are available in audio design technology, culinary arts management, digital filmmaking and video production, fashion design, fashion marketing, game art and design, graphic design, industrial design, interior design, media arts and animation, photography, and Web design and interactive media.

Associate degrees are available in animation art and design, audio production, baking and pastry, culinary arts, fashion design, fashion marketing, graphic design, industrial design technology, interior design, photography, video production, and Web design and interactive media.

Diploma programs are offered in baking and pastry, digital design, residential design, and the art of cooking.

Academic Programs

The Art Institute of Seattle operates on a year-round, quarterly basis. Each quarter totals eleven weeks. Bachelor's degree programs are twelve quarters in length.

Academic Facilities

The Art Institute of Seattle is an urban campus that comprises three facilities. The school houses classrooms, audio and video studios, a student store, student lounges, copy centers, a gallery, a woodshop, a sculpture room, fashion display windows, a resource center, a technology center, and culinary facilities. The Art Institute of Seattle is also home to a student-run, public restaurant.

Costs

Tuition cost varies by program. Prospective students should contact the school for current tuition costs. Other charges include a starting kit for all first quarter students. Kits vary in price depending on the program of study.

Financial Aid

Financial aid is available for those who qualify. Students who require financial assistance should first complete and submit a Free Application for Federal Student Aid (FAFSA) and meet with a financial aid officer.

Faculty

Faculty members at The Art Institute of Seattle are experienced professionals, many of whom bring real-world knowledge into the classroom. There are full-time and part-time faculty members.

Admission Requirements

A student seeking admission to The Art Institute of Seattle is required to interview with an admissions representative (in person or over the phone). Applicants are required to have a high school diploma or a General Educational Development (GED) certificate and to submit an admissions application and an essay describing how an education at The Art Institute of Seattle may help the student to achieve career goals. For advanced placement, additional information, including college transcripts, letters of recommendation, or portfolio work, may be required. Students may apply for admission online.

The Art Institute of Seattle follows a rolling admissions schedule. Students are encouraged to apply for their chosen quarter early so that they may take advantage of orientation activities. Students may also apply until the actual start date for any given quarter, depending on space availability. There is a $50 application fee.

For the most recent information regarding admission requirements, please refer to the current academic catalog.

Application and Information

To obtain an application, make arrangements for an interview, or tour the school, prospective students should contact:

The Art Institute of Seattle
2323 Elliott Avenue
Seattle, Washington 98121-1642
Phone: 206-448-6600
800-275-2471 (toll-free)
Fax: 206-269-0275
Web site: http://www.artinstitutes.edu/seattle

The Art Institute of Atlanta; The Art Institute of Atlanta–Decatur[1]; The Art Institute of Austin[2]; The Art Institute of California–Hollywood; The Art Institute of California–Inland Empire; The Art Institute of California–Los Angeles; The Art Institute of California–Orange County; The Art Institute of California–Sacramento; The Art Institute of California–San Diego; The Art Institute of California–San Francisco; The Art Institute of California–Sunnyvale; The Art Institute of Charleston[1]; The Art Institute of Charlotte; The Art Institute of Colorado; The Art Institute of Dallas; The Art Institute of Fort Lauderdale; The Art Institute of Fort Worth[3]; The Art Institute of Houston; The Art Institute of Houston–North[2]; The Art Institute of Indianapolis[4]; The Art Institute of Jacksonville[5]; The Art Institute of Las Vegas; The Art Institute of Michigan; The Art Institute of New York City; The Art Institute of Ohio–Cincinnati[6]; The Art Institute of Philadelphia; The Art Institute of Phoenix; The Art Institute of Pittsburgh; The Art Institute of Portland; The Art Institute of Raleigh–Durham; The Art Institute of Salt Lake City; The Art Institute of San Antonio[2];The Art Institute of Seattle; The Art Institute of Tampa[5]; The Art Institute of Tennessee–Nashville[1,7]; The Art Institute of Tucson; The Art Institute of Vancouver; The Art Institute of Virginia Beach[1,8]; The Art Institute of Washington[1,8]; The Art Institute of Washington–Northern Virginia[1,8]; The Art Institute of York–Pennsylvania; The Art Institutes International–Kansas City; The Art Institutes International Minnesota; The Illinois Institute of Art–Chicago; The Illinois Institute of Art–Schaumburg; Miami International University of Art & Design; The New England Institute of Art.

[1]A branch of The Art Institute of Atlanta
[2]A branch of The Art Institute of Houston
[3]A branch of The Art Institute of Dallas
[4]The Art Institute of Indianapolis is regulated by the Indiana Commission on Proprietary Education, 302 West Washington Street, Room E201, Indianapolis, Indiana 46204, AC-0080
[5]A branch of Miami International University of Art & Design
[6]The Art Institute of Ohio–Cincinnati, 8845 Governors Hill Drive, Suite 100, Cincinnati, Ohio 45249-3317, OH Reg. #04-01-1698B
[7]The Art Institute of Tennessee–Nashville is authorized for operation as a postsecondary educational institution by the Tennessee Higher Education Commission.
[8]Certified by the State Council of Higher Education to operate in Virginia

THE ART INSTITUTE OF TAMPA

TAMPA, FLORIDA

The Art Institute of Tampa provides education programs created to help students pursue entry-level employment in the creative arts. Students are encouraged to gain an understanding of theoretical and practical knowledge appropriate to their degree objectives, demonstrated through measurable student-learning outcomes specified for each degree program. The Art Institute of Tampa offers twelve bachelor's degree programs and five associate degree programs.

The student population includes recent high school graduates, transfer students, and those who have left a previous employment situation to study and train for a new career. Students are creative, competitive, and open to new ideas. They place great value on an education that prepares them to pursue an exciting entry-level position in the arts.

Classes are sized to allow for individual attention, and course work is developed by industry leaders who are familiar with the professional workplace. Many faculty members work outside of the classroom and bring back practical knowledge that provides students with a relevant, hands-on education. In addition, assistance is available to help students with resume writing, networking, and keeping abreast of what employers are looking for in job candidates.

The active contribution of students to college life supports the creative and intellectual evolution of everyone at The Art Institute of Tampa. Although some students arrive with previous experience in their program fields, others arrive with only their desire to learn. Students come to The Art Institute of Tampa from private schools, public schools, and homeschool environments.

Housing placement assistance is available through referrals and other local resources.

Miami International University of Art & Design and its branch campuses The Art Institute of Jacksonville and The Art Institute of Tampa are accredited by the Commission on Colleges of the Southern Association of Colleges and Schools to award diplomas, associate, baccalaureate, and master's degrees. Contact the Commission on Colleges at 1866 Southern Lane, Decatur, Georgia 30033-4097; or call 404-679-4500 for questions about the accreditation of Miami International University of Art & Design.

The Art Institute of Tampa is licensed by the Commission for Independent Education, Florida Department of Education. Additional information regarding this institution may be obtained by contacting the commission at 325 West Gaines Street, Suite 1414, Tallahassee, Florida 32399-0400; phone: 888-224-6684 (toll-free).

The Associate of Arts degree program in culinary arts is accredited by the Accrediting Commission of the American Culinary Federation Education Foundation.

Location

Located in Tampa's bustling business district, The Art Institute of Tampa is situated across from Raymond James Stadium and Al Lopez Park, comprising 126 acres of Florida's fauna and flora. Tampa's balmy climate makes the outdoors enjoyable year-round. Residents enjoy bicycling, jogging, sunbathing, walking, in-line skating, swimming, sport fishing, scuba diving, and snorkeling. Gyms and dance studios offer opportunities for aerobics, weight lifting, ballet, kickboxing, and the martial arts. Local attractions include Busch Gardens, the Florida Aquarium, Lowry Park Zoo, the Tampa Museum of Art, Shakespeare in the Park, the Clearwater Jazz Festival, and the world-renowned Salvador Dalí Museum. Sports fans follow the Tampa Bay Buccaneers, Devil Rays, or Lightning, and popular nightlife spots include Channelside, Bay Street, and Ybor City, the center of the city's bustling music scene. Theater, symphony, and dance performances; museums; and a diverse range of art galleries showcase some of the world's greatest talent. Situated on the west coast of Florida, the Tampa Bay area has grown to become one of the most populous and affluent regions in Florida. With its unique blend of urban excitement and natural beauty, there really is something for everyone who lives in the beautiful, diverse communities connected by green spaces and waterways.

Programs of Study and Degrees

The Art Institute of Tampa offers bachelor's degrees in advertising, culinary management, digital filmmaking and video production, digital photography, fashion and retail management, food and beverage management, game art and design, graphic design, interior design, media arts and animation, visual effects and motion graphics, and Web design and interactive media.

Associate degrees are available in baking and pastry; culinary arts; graphic design; Web design and interactive media; and wine, spirits, and beverage management (participation in the program for those under 21 years of age will be conducted in accord with state law regarding the possession and consumption of alcoholic beverages).

A diploma is available in baking and pastry.

Academic Programs

The academic year is divided into four quarters, beginning in January, April, July, and October. Bachelor's degrees require the completion of 192 credits, and associate degrees require completion of 112 academic credits.

Academic Facilities

The school's facility features cross-platform computer labs, a resource library, a gallery, and a student lounge. The Art Institute of Tampa offers each student easy access to the technology, tools, and facilities needed to complete projects in all disciplines.

Costs

Tuition cost varies by program. Prospective students should contact the school for current tuition costs. Other charges include a starting kit for all first-quarter students. Kits vary in price, depending on the program of study.

Financial Aid

Financial aid is available for those who qualify. Students who require financial assistance should first complete and submit a Free Application for Federal Student Aid (FAFSA) and meet with a financial aid officer.

Faculty

The Art Institute of Tampa faculty consists of full-time and part-time instructors. Instructors bring professional knowledge to their teaching, and many work in their fields of expertise outside of the classroom.

Student Government

Student leadership is fundamental to academic success and is a way to network with and meet other students. Student leaders serve as role models for peers and act as student advocates for the school. Student leadership programs at The Art Institute of Tampa are designed to support the mission of the school, help students refine interpersonal skills, implement positive change for the student body, and promote school and community spirit. Students may become active members of The Art Institute of Tampa Student Government, start or join a university club, or attend school-sponsored seminars designed to improve leadership skills.

Admission Requirements

Applicants must demonstrate proof of high school graduation or its equivalent in order to receive final acceptance. An official copy of a high school transcript or General Educational Development (GED) transcript is required. Applicants are also required to interview with the school (either in person or by telephone) and write an essay of approximately 150 words in length describing how an education at The Art Institute of Tampa will help them attain creative goals. The Admissions Acceptance Committee determines the compatibility of the applicant with the school and reserves the right to request the results of the SAT or ACT exam and other additional information. A separate application and enrollment form must be completed and signed by the applicant. Prospective students may apply at any time of the year. Applications may be submitted online or mailed to the school. There is a $50 application fee.

For the most recent information regarding admission requirements, please refer to the current academic catalog.

Application and Information

To obtain an application, make arrangements for an interview, or tour the school, prospective students should contact:

The Art Institute of Tampa
Parkside at Tampa Bay Park
4401 North Himes Avenue, Suite 150
Tampa, Florida 33614-7086
Phone: 813-873-2112
866-703-3277 (toll-free)
Fax: 813-873-2171
Web site: http://www.artinstitutes.edu/tampa

COLLEGE CLOSE-UPS

The Art Institute of Atlanta; The Art Institute of Atlanta–Decatur[1]; The Art Institute of Austin[2]; The Art Institute of California–Hollywood; The Art Institute of California–Inland Empire; The Art Institute of California–Los Angeles; The Art Institute of California–Orange County; The Art Institute of California–Sacramento; The Art Institute of California–San Diego; The Art Institute of California–San Francisco; The Art Institute of California–Sunnyvale; The Art Institute of Charleston[1]; The Art Institute of Charlotte; The Art Institute of Colorado; The Art Institute of Dallas; The Art Institute of Fort Lauderdale; The Art Institute of Fort Worth[3]; The Art Institute of Houston; The Art Institute of Houston–North[2]; The Art Institute of Indianapolis[4]; The Art Institute of Jacksonville[5]; The Art Institute of Las Vegas; The Art Institute of Michigan; The Art Institute of New York City; The Art Institute of Ohio–Cincinnati[6]; The Art Institute of Philadelphia; The Art Institute of Phoenix; The Art Institute of Pittsburgh; The Art Institute of Portland; The Art Institute of Raleigh–Durham; The Art Institute of Salt Lake City; The Art Institute of San Antonio[2];The Art Institute of Seattle; The Art Institute of Tampa[5]; The Art Institute of Tennessee–Nashville[1,7]; The Art Institute of Tucson; The Art Institute of Vancouver; The Art Institute of Virginia Beach[1,8]; The Art Institute of Washington[1,8]; The Art Institute of Washington–Northern Virginia[1,8]; The Art Institute of York–Pennsylvania; The Art Institutes International–Kansas City; The Art Institutes International Minnesota; The Illinois Institute of Art–Chicago; The Illinois Institute of Art–Schaumburg; Miami International University of Art & Design; The New England Institute of Art.

[1]A branch of The Art Institute of Atlanta
[2]A branch of The Art Institute of Houston
[3]A branch of The Art Institute of Dallas
[4]The Art Institute of Indianapolis is regulated by the Indiana Commission on Proprietary Education, 302 West Washington Street, Room E201, Indianapolis, Indiana 46204, AC-0080
[5]A branch of Miami International University of Art & Design
[6]The Art Institute of Ohio–Cincinnati, 8845 Governors Hill Drive, Suite 100, Cincinnati, Ohio 45249-3317, OH Reg. #04-01-1698B
[7]The Art Institute of Tennessee–Nashville is authorized for operation as a postsecondary educational institution by the Tennessee Higher Education Commission.
[8]Certified by the State Council of Higher Education to operate in Virginia

THE ART INSTITUTE OF TENNESSEE–NASHVILLE

NASHVILLE, TENNESSEE

The Art Institute of Tennessee–Nashville
A branch of The Art Institute of Atlanta

The Art Institute of Tennessee–Nashville helps students to cultivate and refine the talents and skills that are needed to pursue entry-level positions in the creative arts. Classes are taught in an environment that encourages learning, leadership, and creativity. The school offers nine bachelor's degree programs and four associate degree programs.

Faculty and staff members strive to foster development and cultivate artistic growth. Students are given opportunities to develop leadership skills and build relationships. In addition, assistance is available to help students with resume writing, networking, and keeping abreast of what employers are looking for in job candidates.

The Art Institute of Tennessee–Nashville places a high value on the quality of student life both in and out of the classroom. Students participate in a wide variety of activities, including clubs and organizations, community service opportunities, and various committees designed to enhance the quality of student life.

The school provides information on independent housing options to all enrolled students requesting such assistance.

Students come to The Art Institute of Tennessee–Nashville from throughout the United States. The student population includes recent high school graduates, transfer students, and those who have left a previous employment situation to study and train for a new career. Students are creative, competitive, and open to new ideas.

The Art Institute of Tennessee–Nashville is a branch campus of The Art Institute of Atlanta. The Art Institute of Atlanta is accredited by the Commission on Colleges of the Southern Association of Colleges and Schools to award associate and baccalaureate degrees. Contact the Commission on Colleges at 1866 Southern Lane, Decatur, Georgia 30033-4097 or call 404-679-4500 for questions about the accreditation of The Art Institute of Atlanta.

The Art Institute of Tennessee–Nashville is authorized for operation as a postsecondary educational institution by the Tennessee Higher Education Commission.

Location

The Art Institute of Tennessee–Nashville is located close to downtown, providing students with ease of access, opportunities to volunteer for civic organizations, and the ability to enjoy all the culture and excitement that the city of Nashville has to offer.

Programs of Study and Degrees

The Art Institute of Tennessee–Nashville offers bachelor's and associate degrees. Bachelor's degrees are offered in audio production, culinary arts management, digital filmmaking and video production, fashion and retail management, graphic design, interior design, media arts and animation, photographic imaging, and Web design and interactive media.

Associate degrees are available in culinary arts, graphic design, video production, and Web design and interactive media.

Diploma programs are offered in culinary arts–baking and pastry and culinary arts–skills.

Academic Programs

The academic year is divided into four quarters, beginning in January, April, July, and October. Each program is offered on a year-round basis, allowing students to continue to work uninterrupted toward their degrees.

Academic Facilities

The Art Institute of Tennessee–Nashville has a bookstore, Mac and PC computer labs, and classrooms.

Costs

Tuition cost varies by program. Prospective students should contact the school for current tuition costs. Other charges include a starting kit for all first-quarter students. Kits vary in price, depending on the program of study.

Financial Aid

Financial aid is available for those who qualify. Students who require financial assistance should first complete and submit a Free Application for Federal Student Aid (FAFSA) and meet with a financial aid officer.

Student Government

The Student Federation is responsible for student government and acts as a liaison between the student body and faculty and staff members.

Admission Requirements

Applicants must provide proof of high school graduation or achievement of a General Educational Development (GED) certificate as a prerequisite for admission. In lieu of documenting high school graduation or a GED certificate, applicants may provide proof of receiving an associate degree or higher from an accredited institution. An official transcript indicating date of high school graduation, receipt of a GED certificate (including test scores), or date of college graduation (including degree granted) is required as proof.

All individuals seeking admission to The Art Institute of Tennessee–Nashville are interviewed in person or by phone by an assistant director of admissions, and each applicant must write an original essay of at least 150 words stating how an education at the school would help the student achieve career goals. There is a $50 application fee.

For the most recent information regarding admission requirements, please refer to the current academic catalog.

Application and Information

To obtain an application, make arrangements for an interview, or tour the school, prospective students should contact:

The Art Institute of Tennessee–Nashville
100 Centerview Drive, Suite 250
Nashville, Tennessee 37214-3439
Phone: 615-874-1067
866-747-5770 (toll-free)
Fax: 615-874-3530
Web site: http://www.artinstitutes.edu/nashville

COLLEGE CLOSE-UPS

The Art Institute of Atlanta; The Art Institute of Atlanta–Decatur[1]; The Art Institute of Austin[2]; The Art Institute of California–Hollywood; The Art Institute of California–Inland Empire; The Art Institute of California–Los Angeles; The Art Institute of California–Orange County; The Art Institute of California–Sacramento; The Art Institute of California–San Diego; The Art Institute of California–San Francisco; The Art Institute of California–Sunnyvale; The Art Institute of Charleston[1]; The Art Institute of Charlotte; The Art Institute of Colorado; The Art Institute of Dallas; The Art Institute of Fort Lauderdale; The Art Institute of Fort Worth[3]; The Art Institute of Houston; The Art Institute of Houston–North[2]; The Art Institute of Indianapolis[4]; The Art Institute of Jacksonville[5]; The Art Institute of Las Vegas; The Art Institute of Michigan; The Art Institute of New York City; The Art Institute of Ohio–Cincinnati[6]; The Art Institute of Philadelphia; The Art Institute of Phoenix; The Art Institute of Pittsburgh; The Art Institute of Portland; The Art Institute of Raleigh–Durham; The Art Institute of Salt Lake City; The Art Institute of San Antonio[2];The Art Institute of Seattle; The Art Institute of Tampa[5]; The Art Institute of Tennessee–Nashville[1,7]; The Art Institute of Tucson; The Art Institute of Vancouver; The Art Institute of Virginia Beach[1,8]; The Art Institute of Washington[1,8]; The Art Institute of Washington–Northern Virginia[1,8]; The Art Institute of York–Pennsylvania; The Art Institutes International–Kansas City; The Art Institutes International Minnesota; The Illinois Institute of Art–Chicago; The Illinois Institute of Art–Schaumburg; Miami International University of Art & Design; The New England Institute of Art.

[1]A branch of The Art Institute of Atlanta
[2]A branch of The Art Institute of Houston
[3]A branch of The Art Institute of Dallas
[4]The Art Institute of Indianapolis is regulated by the Indiana Commission on Proprietary Education, 302 West Washington Street, Room E201, Indianapolis, Indiana 46204, AC-0080
[5]A branch of Miami International University of Art & Design
[6]The Art Institute of Ohio–Cincinnati, 8845 Governors Hill Drive, Suite 100, Cincinnati, Ohio 45249-3317, OH Reg. #04-01-1698B
[7]The Art Institute of Tennessee–Nashville is authorized for operation as a postsecondary educational institution by the Tennessee Higher Education Commission.
[8]Certified by the State Council of Higher Education to operate in Virginia

THE ART INSTITUTE OF TUCSON

TUCSON, ARIZONA

COLLEGE CLOSE-UPS

The Art Institute of Tucson provides students with a creative educational environment and dedicated faculty members committed to preparing students to pursue entry-level positions in the creative arts. The school offers ten bachelor's degree programs and three associate degree programs.

Under the guidance of industry professionals, students learn by doing the types of tasks they are likely to encounter in the workplace. In addition, assistance is available to help students with resume writing, networking, and keeping aware of what employers are looking for in job candidates.

The student population includes recent high school graduates, transfer students, and those who have left a previous employment situation to study and train for a new career. Students are creative, competitive, and open to new ideas. They place great value on an education that prepares them to pursue an exciting entry-level position in the arts.

The Art Institute of Tucson places a high value on the quality of student life inside and outside the classroom. Students take part in a wide variety of activities, clubs and organizations, community service opportunities, and various student life-enhancing committees.

Instructors are encouraged to look for upcoming books and to advise the administration of any books that may prove useful to their students. Students also have access to the public libraries.

The Student Affairs Office helps students who need assistance in locating housing.

The Art Institute of Tucson is accredited by the Accrediting Council for Independent Colleges and Schools (ACICS) to award associate degrees and bachelor's degrees. ACICS is listed as a nationally recognized accrediting agency by the United States Department of Education and is recognized by the Council for Higher Education Accreditation. ACICS can be contacted at 750 First Street NE, Suite 980, Washington, D.C. 20002; phone: 202-336-6780.

The Art Institute of Tucson is licensed, approved, and regulated by the Arizona State Board for Private Postsecondary Education.

Location

Tucson is a fast-growing, progressive metropolitan area with an incredibly rich cultural heritage. Arizona, also known as the Grand Canyon state, today combines the cultures of the United States and Mexico with continued influence from past settlement by Native Americans, Spanish explorers, and Anglo frontiersmen. The result is a diverse mix of people, architecture, food, and communities that can serve as a catalyst for inspiring our students' creativity.

Programs of Study and Degrees

Bachelor's degree programs are offered in advertising, culinary arts, digital filmmaking and video production, digital photography, fashion design, fashion marketing, graphic design, interior design, media arts and animation, and Web design and interactive media.

Associate degree programs are offered in baking and pastry, culinary arts, and graphic design.

Academic Programs

The Art Institute of Tucson operates on a year-round, four-quarter system.

Academic Facilities

The Art Institute of Tucson is home to classrooms, studios, offices, a student lounge, a supply store, and a learning resource center. Equipment provided at The Art Institute of Tucson is specific to the program of study and may include projectors, editing decks, camcorders, PC and Macintosh computers, printers, drafting tables, and kitchen appliances.

Costs

Tuition cost varies by program. Prospective students should contact the School for current tuition costs. Other charges include a starting kit for all first-quarter students. Kits vary in price depending on the program of study.

Financial Aid

Financial aid is available for those who qualify. Students who require financial assistance should first complete and submit a Free Application for Federal Student Aid (FAFSA) and meet with a financial aid officer.

Faculty

Faculty members at The Art Institute of Tucson have professional knowledge that they bring into the classroom. The School's faculty members provide their students with a unique, relevant educational experience. Faculty consists of both part-time and full-time employees.

Admission Requirements

Applicants must provide proof of high school graduation or achievement of a General Educational Development (GED) certificate as a prerequisite for admission.

In lieu of documenting high school graduation or a GED certificate, applicants may provide proof of attaining an associate degree or higher from an accredited institution. An official transcript indicating date of high school graduation, GED certificate (including test scores), or date of college graduation (including degree granted) is required as proof.

All individuals seeking admission to The Art Institute of Tucson are interviewed in person or by phone by an assistant director of admissions, and each applicant must create an original essay of at least 150 words stating how an education at The Art Institute of Tucson would help the student to achieve career goals. There is a $50 application fee.

For the most recent information regarding admission requirements, please refer to the current academic catalog.

Application and Information

To obtain an application, arrange for an interview, or tour the school, prospective students should contact:

The Art Institute of Tucson
5099 East Grant Road
Suite 100
Tucson, Arizona 85712
Phone: 520-318-2700
866-690-8850 (toll-free)
Fax: 520-881-4794
Web site: http://www.artinstitutes.edu/tucson

COLLEGE CLOSE-UPS

The Art Institute of Atlanta; The Art Institute of Atlanta–Decatur[1]; The Art Institute of Austin[2]; The Art Institute of California–Hollywood; The Art Institute of California–Inland Empire; The Art Institute of California–Los Angeles; The Art Institute of California–Orange County; The Art Institute of California–Sacramento; The Art Institute of California–San Diego; The Art Institute of California–San Francisco; The Art Institute of California–Sunnyvale; The Art Institute of Charleston[1]; The Art Institute of Charlotte; The Art Institute of Colorado; The Art Institute of Dallas; The Art Institute of Fort Lauderdale; The Art Institute of Fort Worth[3]; The Art Institute of Houston; The Art Institute of Houston–North[2]; The Art Institute of Indianapolis[4]; The Art Institute of Jacksonville[5]; The Art Institute of Las Vegas; The Art Institute of Michigan; The Art Institute of New York City; The Art Institute of Ohio–Cincinnati[6]; The Art Institute of Philadelphia; The Art Institute of Phoenix; The Art Institute of Pittsburgh; The Art Institute of Portland; The Art Institute of Raleigh–Durham; The Art Institute of Salt Lake City; The Art Institute of San Antonio[2];The Art Institute of Seattle; The Art Institute of Tampa[5]; The Art Institute of Tennessee–Nashville[1,7]; The Art Institute of Tucson; The Art Institute of Vancouver; The Art Institute of Virginia Beach[1,8]; The Art Institute of Washington[1,8]; The Art Institute of Washington–Northern Virginia[1,8]; The Art Institute of York–Pennsylvania; The Art Institutes International–Kansas City; The Art Institutes International Minnesota; The Illinois Institute of Art–Chicago; The Illinois Institute of Art–Schaumburg; Miami International University of Art & Design; The New England Institute of Art.

[1]A branch of The Art Institute of Atlanta
[2]A branch of The Art Institute of Houston
[3]A branch of The Art Institute of Dallas
[4]The Art Institute of Indianapolis is regulated by the Indiana Commission on Proprietary Education, 302 West Washington Street, Room E201, Indianapolis, Indiana 46204, AC-0080
[5]A branch of Miami International University of Art & Design
[6]The Art Institute of Ohio–Cincinnati, 8845 Governors Hill Drive, Suite 100, Cincinnati, Ohio 45249-3317, OH Reg. #04-01-1698B
[7]The Art Institute of Tennessee–Nashville is authorized for operation as a postsecondary educational institution by the Tennessee Higher Education Commission.
[8]Certified by the State Council of Higher Education to operate in Virginia

THE ART INSTITUTE OF VIRGINIA BEACH

VIRGINIA BEACH, VIRGINIA

The Art Institute of Virginia Beach provides students with a creative educational environment and dedicated faculty members committed to preparing students to pursue entry-level positions in the creative arts. The school offers eight bachelor's degree programs and three associate degree programs.

Under the guidance of industry professionals, students learn by doing the types of tasks they are likely to encounter in the workplace. In addition, assistance is available to help students with resume writing, networking, and keeping aware of what employers are looking for in job candidates.

The student population includes recent high school graduates, transfer students, and those who have left a previous employment situation to study and train for a new career. Students are creative, competitive, and open to new ideas. They place great value on an education that prepares them to pursue an exciting entry-level position in the arts.

The Art Institute of Virginia Beach places a high value on the quality of student life inside and outside the classroom. Students take part in a wide variety of activities, clubs and organizations, community service opportunities, and various student life-enhancing committees.

Instructors are encouraged to look for upcoming books and to advise the administration of any books that may prove useful to their students. Students also have access to the public libraries.

The Student Affairs Office helps students who need assistance in locating housing.

The Art Institute of Virginia Beach is a branch campus of The Art Institute of Atlanta. The Art Institute of Atlanta is accredited by the Commission on Colleges of the Southern Association of Colleges and Schools to award associate and baccalaureate degrees. Contact the Commission on Colleges at 1866 Southern Lane, Decatur, Georgia 30033-4097 or call 404-679-4500 for questions about the accreditation of The Art Institute of Atlanta.

The Art Institute of Virginia Beach, a branch of The Art Institute of Atlanta, is certified to operate in Virginia by the State Council of Higher Education for Virginia, James Monroe Building, 101 North Fourteenth Street, Richmond, Virginia 23219; phone: 804-225-2600.

Location

Virginia Beach gives students easy access to cultural and recreational opportunities. Located at the mouth of the Chesapeake Bay, Virginia Beach is home to nearly 450,000 people, miles of beach, and many historic sites.

Programs of Study and Degrees

Bachelor's degree programs are offered in advertising, culinary arts management, fashion and retail management, graphic design, interior design, media arts and animation, photographic imaging, and Web design and interactive media.

Associate degree programs are offered in culinary arts, graphic design, and Web design and interactive media.

Academic Programs

The Art Institute of Virginia Beach operates on a year-round, four-quarter system.

Academic Facilities

The Art Institute of Virginia Beach is home to classrooms, studios, offices, a student lounge, a supply store, and a learning resource center. Equipment provided at The Art Institute of Virginia Beach is specific to the program of study and may include projectors, editing decks, camcorders, PC and Macintosh computers, printers, drafting tables, and kitchen appliances.

Costs

Tuition cost varies by program. Prospective students should contact the school for current tuition costs. Other charges include a starting kit for all first-quarter students. Kits vary in price depending on the program of study.

Financial Aid

Financial aid is available for those who qualify. Students who require financial assistance should first complete and submit a Free Application for Federal Student Aid (FAFSA) and meet with a financial aid officer.

Faculty

Faculty members at The Art Institute of Virginia Beach have professional knowledge that they bring into the classroom. The school's faculty members provide their students with a unique, relevant educational experience. Faculty consists of both part-time and full-time employees.

Admission Requirements

Applicants must provide proof of high school graduation or achievement of a General Educational Development (GED) certificate as a prerequisite for admission.

In lieu of documenting high school graduation or a GED certificate, applicants may provide proof of attaining an associate degree or higher from an accredited institution. An official transcript indicating date of high school graduation, GED certificate (including test scores), or date of college graduation (including degree granted) is required as proof.

All individuals seeking admission to The Art Institute of Virginia Beach are interviewed in person or by phone by an assistant director of admissions, and each applicant must create an original essay of at least 150 words stating how an education at The Art Institute of Virginia Beach would help the student to achieve career goals. There is a $50 application fee.

For the most recent information regarding admission requirements, please refer to the current academic catalog.

Application and Information

To obtain an application, make arrangements for an interview, or tour the school, prospective students should contact:

The Art Institute of Virginia Beach
Two Columbus Center
4500 Main Street, Suite 100
Virginia Beach, Virginia 23462
Phone: 757-493-6700
877-437-4428 (toll-free)
Fax: 757-493-6800
Web site: http://www.artinstitutes.edu/virginia-beach

The Art Institute of Atlanta; The Art Institute of Atlanta–Decatur[1]; The Art Institute of Austin[2]; The Art Institute of California–Hollywood; The Art Institute of California–Inland Empire; The Art Institute of California–Los Angeles; The Art Institute of California–Orange County; The Art Institute of California–Sacramento; The Art Institute of California–San Diego; The Art Institute of California–San Francisco; The Art Institute of California–Sunnyvale; The Art Institute of Charleston[1]; The Art Institute of Charlotte; The Art Institute of Colorado; The Art Institute of Dallas; The Art Institute of Fort Lauderdale; The Art Institute of Fort Worth[3]; The Art Institute of Houston; The Art Institute of Houston–North[2]; The Art Institute of Indianapolis[4]; The Art Institute of Jacksonville[5]; The Art Institute of Las Vegas; The Art Institute of Michigan; The Art Institute of New York City; The Art Institute of Ohio–Cincinnati[6]; The Art Institute of Philadelphia; The Art Institute of Phoenix; The Art Institute of Pittsburgh; The Art Institute of Portland; The Art Institute of Raleigh–Durham; The Art Institute of Salt Lake City; The Art Institute of San Antonio[2];The Art Institute of Seattle; The Art Institute of Tampa[5]; The Art Institute of Tennessee–Nashville[1,7]; The Art Institute of Tucson; The Art Institute of Vancouver; The Art Institute of Virginia Beach[1,8]; The Art Institute of Washington[1,8]; The Art Institute of Washington–Northern Virginia[1,8]; The Art Institute of York–Pennsylvania; The Art Institutes International–Kansas City; The Art Institutes International Minnesota; The Illinois Institute of Art–Chicago; The Illinois Institute of Art–Schaumburg; Miami International University of Art & Design; The New England Institute of Art.

[1]A branch of The Art Institute of Atlanta
[2]A branch of The Art Institute of Houston
[3]A branch of The Art Institute of Dallas
[4]The Art Institute of Indianapolis is regulated by the Indiana Commission on Proprietary Education, 302 West Washington Street, Room E201, Indianapolis, Indiana 46204, AC-0080
[5]A branch of Miami International University of Art & Design
[6]The Art Institute of Ohio–Cincinnati, 8845 Governors Hill Drive, Suite 100, Cincinnati, Ohio 45249-3317, OH Reg. #04-01-1698B
[7]The Art Institute of Tennessee–Nashville is authorized for operation as a postsecondary educational institution by the Tennessee Higher Education Commission.
[8]Certified by the State Council of Higher Education to operate in Virginia

THE ART INSTITUTE OF WASHINGTON

ARLINGTON, VIRGINIA

The Art Institute of Washington provides education programs that prepare students to pursue entry-level careers in the creative arts. Programs of study are designed with the support and contributions of the professional community. The curricula are reviewed regularly to help ensure that students are trained to meet the needs of a changing marketplace. The Art Institute of Washington offers fourteen bachelor's degree programs and eight associate degree programs.

The student population includes recent high school graduates, transfer students, and those who have left a previous employment situation to study and train for a new career. Students are creative, competitive, and open to new ideas. They place great value on an education that prepares them to pursue an exciting entry-level position in the arts.

The School's blend of theoretical study and practical skill building gives graduates a foundation on which to build creative goals. Students who attend The Art Institute of Washington are given opportunities to develop leadership skills and build relationships within their fields.

Services are available to assist students with resume writing, networking, and keeping abreast of what employers are looking for in job applicants.

Getting involved and becoming an active participant in the School is an important part of a student's educational experience. Many activities take place each quarter that provide opportunities for students to connect with peers, members of the staff and faculty, and members of the local community. Student ambassadors assist new students in their adjustment to the college and serve as hosts to important visitors. Students may also join student clubs, get involved in student leadership functions, and participate in social events, including student art shows. Art Institute of Washington students also volunteer for local charities.

Residential communities provide a living-learning environment that is conducive to study, relaxation, and entertainment. The Art Institute of Washington provides housing in the Rosslyn neighborhood of Arlington. Apartments are carpeted and fully furnished and include a washer and dryer. Residence life advisers live on-site to assist students with academic and personal matters and to organize a wide variety of social and educational programs.

The Art Institute of Washington is a branch campus of The Art Institute of Atlanta. The Art Institute of Atlanta is accredited by the Commission on Colleges of the Southern Association of Colleges and Schools to award associate and baccalaureate degrees. Contact the Commission on Colleges at 1866 Southern Lane, Decatur, Georgia 30033-4097 or call 404-679-4500 for questions about the accreditation of The Art Institute of Atlanta.

The Associate in Arts in culinary arts and culinary arts with a concentration in baking and pastry degree programs are accredited by the American Culinary Federation (ACF).

The interior design program leading to the Bachelor of Fine Arts is accredited by the Council for Interior Design Accreditation, 206 Grandville Avenue, Suite 350, Grand Rapids, Michigan 49503; http://www.accredit-id.org.

Certified by the State Council of Higher Education for Virginia (SCHEV) to operate in Virginia.

Location

Located in Arlington, Virginia, directly across the Potomac River from Washington, D.C., The Art Institute of Washington occupies the ground floor and the ninth through twelfth floors of the Ames Center. The area is home to a variety of activities, including professional sports, first-rate theatrical and musical entertainment, beautiful parks, and cultural events. Some of the most popular places to visit are the Washington Monument, Lincoln Memorial, Vietnam and Korean War Memorials, Arlington National Cemetery, Smithsonian Institution and Museums, and Capitol Building. The Arlington community is home to the Fashion Center at Pentagon City, with its more than 150 stores, and the Crystal City Underground and Plaza Shops, which hosts more than 120 retail shops. In addition, Arlington has more than 170 county parks and playgrounds, including over 80 miles of bicycle routes and jogging trails.

Programs of Study and Degrees

Bachelor's degrees are available in advertising, audio production, culinary arts management, digital filmmaking and video production, fashion and retail management, food and beverage management, game art and design, graphic design, interior design, media arts and animation, photographic imaging, visual and game programming, visual effects and motion graphics, and Web design and interactive media.

Associate degrees are offered in audio production; culinary arts; culinary arts with a concentration in baking and pastry; graphic design; photographic imaging; video production; Web design and interactive media; and wine, spirits, and beverage management.

Diploma programs are available in advertising design, commercial photography, culinary arts–baking and pastry, culinary arts–skills, digital design, video skills, and Web design.

The culinary arts and associate in graphic design programs are available in an evening and weekend option format.

Academic Programs

The academic year is divided into four quarters, beginning in January, April, July, and October. Students may begin their program of study during any quarter. Bachelor's degrees require the completion of 192 credit hours, and associate degree programs require completion of 96 to 112 credit hours.

Academic Facilities

The School's setting in the Ames Center consists of classrooms, studios, computer labs, a student lounge, administrative offices for staff and faculty members, and a Learning Resource Center with a library and reference materials. The building also houses the student counseling center, the tutoring center, teaching kitchens and dining lab, an art supply store, and an exhibition gallery, as well as a television studio and sound stage.

Costs

Tuition cost varies by program. Prospective students should contact the School for current tuition costs. Other charges include a starting kit for all first-quarter students. Kits vary in price, depending on the program of study.

Financial Aid

Financial aid is available for those who qualify. Students who require financial assistance should first complete and submit a Free Application for Federal Student Aid (FAFSA) and meet with a financial aid officer.

Faculty

The Art Institute of Washington faculty consists of full-time and part-time members, many of whom have professional experience in their industries. The faculty prides itself on building close personal relationships with the students. Most faculty and staff members maintain an informal, open-door policy and are available for student questions and suggestions.

Admission Requirements

Prospective students must interview, either by telephone or in person, with a member of the admissions staff in order to explore the student's background and interests and how they relate to The Art Institute of Washington's programs. To apply, students must submit a completed application for admission, including an essay, high school transcripts or General Educational Development (GED) test scores, SAT or ACT scores, and a $50 nonrefundable application fee. Prospective students may apply at any time of the year. Applications may be submitted online or mailed to the School.

For the most recent information regarding admission requirements, please refer to the current academic catalog.

Application and Information

To obtain an application, make arrangements for an interview, or tour the school, prospective students should contact:

The Art Institute of Washington
1820 North Fort Myer Drive
Arlington, Virginia 22209-1802
Phone: 703-358-9550
877-303-3771 (toll-free)
Fax: 703-358-9759
Web site: http://www.artinstitutes.edu/arlington

COLLEGE CLOSE-UPS

The Art Institute of Atlanta; The Art Institute of Atlanta–Decatur[1]; The Art Institute of Austin[2]; The Art Institute of California–Hollywood; The Art Institute of California–Inland Empire; The Art Institute of California–Los Angeles; The Art Institute of California–Orange County; The Art Institute of California–Sacramento; The Art Institute of California–San Diego; The Art Institute of California–San Francisco; The Art Institute of California–Sunnyvale; The Art Institute of Charleston[1]; The Art Institute of Charlotte; The Art Institute of Colorado; The Art Institute of Dallas; The Art Institute of Fort Lauderdale; The Art Institute of Fort Worth[3]; The Art Institute of Houston; The Art Institute of Houston–North[2]; The Art Institute of Indianapolis[4]; The Art Institute of Jacksonville[5]; The Art Institute of Las Vegas; The Art Institute of Michigan; The Art Institute of New York City; The Art Institute of Ohio–Cincinnati[6]; The Art Institute of Philadelphia; The Art Institute of Phoenix; The Art Institute of Pittsburgh; The Art Institute of Portland; The Art Institute of Raleigh–Durham; The Art Institute of Salt Lake City; The Art Institute of San Antonio[2];The Art Institute of Seattle; The Art Institute of Tampa[5]; The Art Institute of Tennessee–Nashville[1,7]; The Art Institute of Tucson; The Art Institute of Vancouver; The Art Institute of Virginia Beach[1,8]; The Art Institute of Washington[1,8]; The Art Institute of Washington–Northern Virginia[1,8]; The Art Institute of York–Pennsylvania; The Art Institutes International–Kansas City; The Art Institutes International Minnesota; The Illinois Institute of Art–Chicago; The Illinois Institute of Art–Schaumburg; Miami International University of Art & Design; The New England Institute of Art.

[1]A branch of The Art Institute of Atlanta
[2]A branch of The Art Institute of Houston
[3]A branch of The Art Institute of Dallas
[4]The Art Institute of Indianapolis is regulated by the Indiana Commission on Proprietary Education, 302 West Washington Street, Room E201, Indianapolis, Indiana 46204, AC-0080
[5]A branch of Miami International University of Art & Design
[6]The Art Institute of Ohio–Cincinnati, 8845 Governors Hill Drive, Suite 100, Cincinnati, Ohio 45249-3317, OH Reg. #04-01-1698B
[7]The Art Institute of Tennessee–Nashville is authorized for operation as a postsecondary educational institution by the Tennessee Higher Education Commission.
[8]Certified by the State Council of Higher Education to operate in Virginia

THE ART INSTITUTE OF WASHINGTON–NORTHERN VIRGINIA

DULLES, VIRGINIA

The Art Institute of Washington—Northern Virginia
A branch of The Art Institute of Atlanta

The Art Institute of Washington—Northern Virginia provides students with a creative educational environment and dedicated faculty members committed to preparing students to pursue entry-level positions in the creative arts. The school offers seven bachelor's degree programs and two associate degree programs.

Under the guidance of industry professionals, students learn by doing the types of tasks they are likely to encounter in the workplace. In addition, assistance is available to help students with resume writing, networking, and keeping aware of what employers are looking for in job candidates.

The student population includes recent high school graduates, transfer students, and those who have left a previous employment situation to study and train for a new career. Students are creative, competitive, and open to new ideas. They place great value on an education that prepares them to pursue an exciting entry-level position in the arts.

The Art Institute of Washington–Northern Virginia places a high value on the quality of student life inside and outside the classroom. Students take part in a wide variety of activities, clubs and organizations, community service opportunities, and various student life-enhancing committees.

Instructors are encouraged to look for upcoming books and to advise the administration of any books that may prove useful to their students. Students also have access to the public libraries.

The Student Affairs Office helps students who need assistance in locating housing.

The Art Institute of Washington–Northern Virginia is a branch campus of The Art Institute of Atlanta. The Art Institute of Atlanta is accredited by the Commission on Colleges of the Southern Association of Colleges and Schools to award associate and baccalaureate degrees. Contact the Commission on Colleges at 1866 Southern Lane, Decatur, Georgia 30033-4097 or call 404-679-4500 for questions about the accreditation of The Art Institute of Atlanta.

The Art Institute of Washington–Northern Virginia, a branch of The Art Institute of Atlanta, is certified by the State Council for Higher Education in Virginia, James Monroe Building, 101 North Fourteenth Street, Richmond, Virginia 23219; phone: 804-225-2600.

Location

Dulles is part of the Washington D.C. metropolitan area, with a regional population of 5.3 million people. Several large corporations, including MCI and AOL, are based here. The close proximity of Dulles to the nation's capital provides students the opportunity to experience the arts, museums, and national monuments. Students can enjoy performances by the National Symphony Orchestra, Washington National Opera, or the Washington Ballet at the John F. Kennedy Center for the Performing Arts. The area also offers five professional sports teams: the Wizards, Capitals, Nationals, D.C. United, and Redskins.

Programs of Study and Degrees

Bachelor's degree programs are offered in advertising, fashion and retail management, graphic design, interior design, media arts and animation, photographic imaging, and Web design and interactive media.

Associate degree programs are offered in graphic design and Web design and interactive media.

Academic Programs

The Art Institute of Washington–Northern Virginia operates on a year-round, four-quarter system.

Academic Facilities

The Art Institute of Washington–Northern Virginia is home to classrooms, studios, offices, a student lounge, a supply store, and a learning resource center. Equipment provided at The Art Institute of Washington–Northern Virginia is specific to the program of study and may include projectors, editing decks, camcorders, PC and Macintosh computers, printers, and drafting tables.

Costs

Tuition cost varies by program. Prospective students should contact the school for current tuition costs. Other charges include a starting kit for all first-quarter students. Kits vary in price depending on the program of study.

Financial Aid

Financial aid is available for those who qualify. Students who require financial assistance should first complete and submit a Free Application for Federal Student Aid (FAFSA) and meet with a financial aid officer.

Faculty

Faculty members at The Art Institute of Washington–Northern Virginia have professional knowledge that they bring into the classroom. The school's faculty members provide their students with a unique, relevant educational experience. Faculty consists of both part-time and full-time employees.

Admission Requirements

Applicants must provide proof of high school graduation or achievement of a General Educational Development (GED) certificate as a prerequisite for admission.

In lieu of documenting high school graduation or a GED certificate, applicants may provide proof of attaining an associate degree or higher from an accredited institution. An official transcript indicating date of high school graduation, GED certificate (including test scores), or date of college graduation (including degree granted) is required as proof.

All individuals seeking admission to The Art Institute of Washington–Northern Virginia are interviewed in person or by phone by an assistant director of admissions, and each applicant must create an original essay of at least 150 words stating how an education at The Art Institute of Washington–Northern Virginia would help the student to achieve career goals. There is a $50 application fee.

For the most recent information regarding admission requirements, please refer to the current academic catalog.

Application and Information

To obtain an application, make arrangements for an interview, or tour the school, prospective students should contact:

The Art Institute of Washington–Northern Virginia
The Corporate Office Park at Dulles Town Center
21000 Atlantic Blvd., Suite 100
Dulles, Virginia 20166
Phone: 571-449-4400
888-627-5008 (toll-free)
Fax: 571-449-4500
Web site: http://www.artinstitutes.edu/northern-virginia

COLLEGE CLOSE-UPS

The Art Institute of Atlanta; The Art Institute of Atlanta–Decatur[1]; The Art Institute of Austin[2]; The Art Institute of California–Hollywood; The Art Institute of California–Inland Empire; The Art Institute of California–Los Angeles; The Art Institute of California–Orange County; The Art Institute of California–Sacramento; The Art Institute of California–San Diego; The Art Institute of California–San Francisco; The Art Institute of California–Sunnyvale; The Art Institute of Charleston[1]; The Art Institute of Charlotte; The Art Institute of Colorado; The Art Institute of Dallas; The Art Institute of Fort Lauderdale; The Art Institute of Fort Worth[3]; The Art Institute of Houston; The Art Institute of Houston–North[2]; The Art Institute of Indianapolis[4]; The Art Institute of Jacksonville[5]; The Art Institute of Las Vegas; The Art Institute of Michigan; The Art Institute of New York City; The Art Institute of Ohio–Cincinnati[6]; The Art Institute of Philadelphia; The Art Institute of Phoenix; The Art Institute of Pittsburgh; The Art Institute of Portland; The Art Institute of Raleigh–Durham; The Art Institute of Salt Lake City; The Art Institute of San Antonio[2];The Art Institute of Seattle; The Art Institute of Tampa[5]; The Art Institute of Tennessee–Nashville[1,7]; The Art Institute of Tucson; The Art Institute of Vancouver; The Art Institute of Virginia Beach[1,8]; The Art Institute of Washington[1,8]; The Art Institute of Washington–Northern Virginia[1,8]; The Art Institute of York–Pennsylvania; The Art Institutes International–Kansas City; The Art Institutes International Minnesota; The Illinois Institute of Art–Chicago; The Illinois Institute of Art–Schaumburg; Miami International University of Art & Design; The New England Institute of Art.

[1]A branch of The Art Institute of Atlanta
[2]A branch of The Art Institute of Houston
[3]A branch of The Art Institute of Dallas
[4]The Art Institute of Indianapolis is regulated by the Indiana Commission on Proprietary Education, 302 West Washington Street, Room E201, Indianapolis, Indiana 46204, AC-0080
[5]A branch of Miami International University of Art & Design
[6]The Art Institute of Ohio–Cincinnati, 8845 Governors Hill Drive, Suite 100, Cincinnati, Ohio 45249-3317, OH Reg. #04-01-1698B
[7]The Art Institute of Tennessee–Nashville is authorized for operation as a postsecondary educational institution by the Tennessee Higher Education Commission.
[8]Certified by the State Council of Higher Education to operate in Virginia

THE ART INSTITUTE OF YORK–PENNSYLVANIA

YORK, PENNSYLVANIA

The Art Institute of York–Pennsylvania

The Art Institute of York–Pennsylvania provides students with an educational environment and dedicated faculty members who are committed to preparing students to pursue entry-level positions in the creative arts. Professional academic courses encourage the achievement of self-knowledge and the development of critical thinking. Under the guidance of industry professionals, students learn by doing the types of tasks they are likely to encounter in the workplace. In addition, assistance is available to help students with resume writing, networking, and keeping aware of what employers are looking for in job candidates.

Courses are taught in a studio or lab setting. While at the school, students can access the wireless network to check mail, hand in assignments, and work on a project, anywhere on campus. The school offers five bachelor's degree programs and two associate degree programs.

The Art Institute of York–Pennsylvania is accredited by the Accrediting Commission of Career Schools and Colleges (ACCSC). ACCSC may be contacted at 2101 Wilson Boulevard, Suite 302, Arlington, Virginia 22201; phone: 703-247-4212.

The Art Institute of York–Pennsylvania is authorized by the Pennsylvania Department of Education to confer the Bachelor of Science degrees and Associate of Science degrees. The Department of Education can be contacted at the Commonwealth of Pennsylvania, Department of Education Office of Postsecondary and Higher Education, 333 Market Street, Harrisburg, Pennsylvania 17126; phone: 717-783-6788.

Location

The Art Institute of York–Pennsylvania is located in York, a suburban area in south-central Pennsylvania. Surrounded by sprawling hills and Amish farmlands, York offers visitors an abundance of shopping areas and museums and three centuries of American history, including battlefields from the Revolutionary and Civil wars. York is a 30-minute drive from Hershey and Harrisburg, Pennsylvania; approximately a 90-minute drive from Philadelphia; and a 1-hour drive from Baltimore, Maryland.

Programs of Study and Degrees

Bachelor's degree programs are offered in fashion and retail management, graphic design, interior design, media arts and animation, and Web design and interactive media.

Associate degrees are offered in graphic design and kitchen and bath design.

Academic Programs

The Art Institute of York–Pennsylvania operates on a year-round, four-quarter system.

Academic Facilities

The Art Institute of York–Pennsylvania is housed within a 38,000-square-foot building in suburban York, Pennsylvania. The facility contains classrooms and studios, a student computer commons, a gallery, an art store, and a library.

In association with the York Martin Memorial Library, The Art Institute of York–Pennsylvania houses a 1,000-square-foot library on the first floor of the school. In addition to general reference books, the library houses titles specifically related to programs offered at the school. The library features interlibrary loan, CD-ROM-based reference materials, and PC business software for use by students and the public.

Costs

Tuition cost varies by program. Prospective students should contact the school for current tuition costs. Other charges include a starting kit for all first quarter students. Kits vary in price depending on the program of study.

Financial Aid

Financial aid is available for those who qualify. Students who require financial assistance should first complete and submit a Free Application for Federal Student Aid (FAFSA) and meet with a financial aid officer.

Faculty

Faculty members at The Art Institute of York–Pennsylvania are professionals, many of whom have experience in their fields of expertise. The school has full-time and part-time faculty members, who provide their students with a unique, relevant educational experience.

Admission Requirements

The Art Institute of York–Pennsylvania encourages interested students to apply early. To apply, students must possess a high school diploma or General Educational Development (GED) certificate and a minimum SAT score of 800 (at least 400 math and 400 verbal) or a minimum ACT score of 16. A portfolio review may be required. There is a $50 application fee.

For the most recent information regarding admission requirements, please refer to the current academic catalog.

Application and Information

To obtain an application or make arrangements for an interview or tour of the school, prospective students should contact:

The Art Institute of York–Pennsylvania
1409 Williams Road
York, Pennsylvania 17402-9012
Phone: 717-755-2300
800-864-7725 (toll-free)
Fax: 717-840-1951
Web site: http://www.artinstitutes.edu/york

The Art Institute of Atlanta; The Art Institute of Atlanta–Decatur[1]; The Art Institute of Austin[2]; The Art Institute of California–Hollywood; The Art Institute of California–Inland Empire; The Art Institute of California–Los Angeles; The Art Institute of California–Orange County; The Art Institute of California–Sacramento; The Art Institute of California–San Diego; The Art Institute of California–San Francisco; The Art Institute of California–Sunnyvale; The Art Institute of Charleston[1]; The Art Institute of Charlotte; The Art Institute of Colorado; The Art Institute of Dallas; The Art Institute of Fort Lauderdale; The Art Institute of Fort Worth[3]; The Art Institute of Houston; The Art Institute of Houston–North[2]; The Art Institute of Indianapolis[4]; The Art Institute of Jacksonville[5]; The Art Institute of Las Vegas; The Art Institute of Michigan; The Art Institute of New York City; The Art Institute of Ohio–Cincinnati[6]; The Art Institute of Philadelphia; The Art Institute of Phoenix; The Art Institute of Pittsburgh; The Art Institute of Portland; The Art Institute of Raleigh–Durham; The Art Institute of Salt Lake City; The Art Institute of San Antonio[2];The Art Institute of Seattle; The Art Institute of Tampa[5]; The Art Institute of Tennessee–Nashville[1,7]; The Art Institute of Tucson; The Art Institute of Vancouver; The Art Institute of Virginia Beach[1,8]; The Art Institute of Washington[1,8]; The Art Institute of Washington–Northern Virginia[1,8]; The Art Institute of York–Pennsylvania; The Art Institutes International–Kansas City; The Art Institutes International Minnesota; The Illinois Institute of Art–Chicago; The Illinois Institute of Art–Schaumburg; Miami International University of Art & Design; The New England Institute of Art.

[1]A branch of The Art Institute of Atlanta
[2]A branch of The Art Institute of Houston
[3]A branch of The Art Institute of Dallas
[4]The Art Institute of Indianapolis is regulated by the Indiana Commission on Proprietary Education, 302 West Washington Street, Room E201, Indianapolis, Indiana 46204, AC-0080
[5]A branch of Miami International University of Art & Design
[6]The Art Institute of Ohio–Cincinnati, 8845 Governors Hill Drive, Suite 100, Cincinnati, Ohio 45249-3317, OH Reg. #04-01-1698B
[7]The Art Institute of Tennessee–Nashville is authorized for operation as a postsecondary educational institution by the Tennessee Higher Education Commission.
[8]Certified by the State Council of Higher Education to operate in Virginia

THE ART INSTITUTES INTERNATIONAL–KANSAS CITY

The Art Institutes International–Kansas City™

LENEXA, KANSAS

The Art Institutes International–Kansas City provides students with an educational environment and dedicated faculty members committed to preparing students to pursue entry-level positions in the creative arts. The School offers eight bachelor's degree programs and three associate degree programs.

Under the guidance of industry professionals, students learn by doing the types of tasks they are likely to encounter in the workplace. In addition, assistance is available to help students with resume writing, networking, and keeping aware of what employers are looking for in job candidates.

The student population includes recent high school graduates, transfer students, and those who have left a previous employment situation to study and train for a new career. Students are creative, competitive, and open to new ideas. They place great value on an education that prepares them to pursue an exciting entry-level position in the arts.

The Art Institutes International–Kansas City places a high value on the quality of student life inside and outside the classroom. Students can take part in a wide variety of activities, clubs and organizations, community service opportunities, and various student life-enhancing committees.

Instructors are encouraged to look for upcoming books and to advise the administration of any books that may prove useful to their students. Students also have access to the public libraries.

The Student Affairs Office helps students who need assistance in locating housing.

The Art Institutes International–Kansas City is accredited by the Accrediting Council for Independent Colleges and Schools (ACICS) to award associate and bachelor's degrees. ACICS is listed as a nationally recognized accrediting agency by the United States Department of Education and is recognized by the Council for Higher Education Accreditation. ACICS can be contacted at 750 First Street NE, Suite 980, Washington, D.C. 20002; phone: 202-336-6780.

The Kansas Board of Regents has approved The Art Institutes International–Kansas City to operate in the state of Kansas. The Kansas Board of Regents may be contacted at the following address: Kansas Board of Regents, Private Postsecondary Education Division, 1000 Southwest Jackson Street, Suite 520, Topeka, Kansas 66612-1368; phone: 785-296-0911; fax: 785-296-4526.

Location

Lenexa is part of the Kansas City metropolitan area of nearly two million people. Kansas City's contributions to jazz and the blues are well known. The city is also home to over 200 fountains and more boulevards than any city besides Paris.

Programs of Study and Degrees

Bachelor's degree programs are offered in advertising, culinary arts, digital filmmaking and video production, fashion marketing, graphic design, interior design, photography, and Web design and interactive media.

Associate degree programs are offered in baking and pastry arts, culinary arts, and graphic design.

Academic Programs

The Art Institutes International–Kansas City operates on a year-round, four-quarter system.

Academic Facilities

The Art Institutes International–Kansas City is home to classrooms, studios, offices, a student lounge, a supply store, and a learning resource center. Equipment provided at The Art Institutes International–Kansas City is specific to the program of study and may include projectors, editing decks, camcorders, PC and Macintosh computers, printers, drafting tables, and kitchen appliances.

Costs

Tuition cost varies by program. Prospective students should contact the School for current tuition costs. Other charges include a starting kit for all first quarter students. Kits vary in price depending on the program of study.

Financial Aid

Financial aid is available for those who qualify. Students who require financial assistance should first complete and submit a Free Application for Federal Student Aid (FAFSA) and meet with a financial aid officer.

Faculty

Faculty members at The Art Institutes International–Kansas City are hired on both a part-time and full-time basis. Faculty members have professional knowledge that they bring into the classroom. The School's faculty members provide their students with a unique, relevant educational experience.

Admission Requirements

Applicants must provide proof of high school graduation or achievement of a General Educational Development (GED) certificate as a prerequisite for admission. In lieu of documenting high school graduation or a GED certificate, applicants may provide proof of attaining an associate degree or higher from an accredited institution. An official transcript indicating date of high school graduation, GED certificate (including test scores), or date of college graduation (including degree granted) is required as proof.

All individuals seeking admission to The Art Institutes International–Kansas City are interviewed in person or by phone by an assistant director of admissions, and each applicant must create an original essay of at least 150 words stating how an education at The Art Institutes International–Kansas City would help the student to achieve career goals. There is a $50 application fee.

For the most recent information regarding admission requirements, please refer to the current academic catalog.

Application and Information

To obtain an application, arrange for an interview, or tour the school, prospective students should contact:

The Art Institutes International–Kansas City
8208 Melrose Drive
Lenexa, Kansas 66214
Phone: 913-217-4600
866-530-8508 (toll-free)
Fax: 913-217-4690
Web site: http://www.artinstitutes.edu/kansascity

COLLEGE CLOSE-UPS

The Art Institute of Atlanta; The Art Institute of Atlanta–Decatur[1]; The Art Institute of Austin[2]; The Art Institute of California–Hollywood; The Art Institute of California–Inland Empire; The Art Institute of California–Los Angeles; The Art Institute of California–Orange County; The Art Institute of California–Sacramento; The Art Institute of California–San Diego; The Art Institute of California–San Francisco; The Art Institute of California–Sunnyvale; The Art Institute of Charleston[1]; The Art Institute of Charlotte; The Art Institute of Colorado; The Art Institute of Dallas; The Art Institute of Fort Lauderdale; The Art Institute of Fort Worth[3]; The Art Institute of Houston; The Art Institute of Houston–North[2]; The Art Institute of Indianapolis[4]; The Art Institute of Jacksonville[5]; The Art Institute of Las Vegas; The Art Institute of Michigan; The Art Institute of New York City; The Art Institute of Ohio–Cincinnati[6]; The Art Institute of Philadelphia; The Art Institute of Phoenix; The Art Institute of Pittsburgh; The Art Institute of Portland; The Art Institute of Raleigh–Durham; The Art Institute of Salt Lake City; The Art Institute of San Antonio[2];The Art Institute of Seattle; The Art Institute of Tampa[5]; The Art Institute of Tennessee–Nashville[1,7]; The Art Institute of Tucson; The Art Institute of Vancouver; The Art Institute of Virginia Beach[1,8]; The Art Institute of Washington[1,8]; The Art Institute of Washington–Northern Virginia[1,8]; The Art Institute of York–Pennsylvania; The Art Institutes International–Kansas City; The Art Institutes International Minnesota; The Illinois Institute of Art–Chicago; The Illinois Institute of Art–Schaumburg; Miami International University of Art & Design; The New England Institute of Art.

[1]A branch of The Art Institute of Atlanta
[2]A branch of The Art Institute of Houston
[3]A branch of The Art Institute of Dallas
[4]The Art Institute of Indianapolis is regulated by the Indiana Commission on Proprietary Education, 302 West Washington Street, Room E201, Indianapolis, Indiana 46204, AC-0080
[5]A branch of Miami International University of Art & Design
[6]The Art Institute of Ohio–Cincinnati, 8845 Governors Hill Drive, Suite 100, Cincinnati, Ohio 45249-3317, OH Reg. #04-01-1698B
[7]The Art Institute of Tennessee–Nashville is authorized for operation as a postsecondary educational institution by the Tennessee Higher Education Commission.
[8]Certified by the State Council of Higher Education to operate in Virginia

THE ART INSTITUTES INTERNATIONAL MINNESOTA

MINNEAPOLIS, MINNESOTA

The Art Institutes International Minnesota provides students with an educational environment and dedicated faculty members committed to preparing students to pursue entry-level positions in the creative arts. The School offers twelve bachelor's degree programs and six associate degree programs.

Under the guidance of industry professionals, students learn by doing the types of tasks they are likely to encounter in the workplace. In addition, assistance is available to help students with resume writing, networking, and keeping aware of what employers are looking for in job candidates.

The student population includes recent high school graduates, transfer students, and those who have left a previous employment situation to study and train for a new career. Students are creative, competitive, and open to new ideas. They place great value on an education that prepares them to pursue an exciting entry-level position in the arts.

The Art Institutes International Minnesota places a high value on the quality of student life inside and outside the classroom. Students can take part in a wide variety of activities, clubs and organizations, community service opportunities, and various student life-enhancing committees.

Instructors are encouraged to look for upcoming books and to advise the administration of any books that may prove useful to their students. Students also have access to the public libraries.

The Student Affairs Office helps students who need assistance in locating housing.

The Art Institutes International Minnesota is accredited by the Accrediting Council for Independent Colleges and Schools (ACICS) to award certificates, associate degrees, and bachelor's degrees. ACICS is listed as a nationally recognized accrediting agency by the United States Department of Education and is recognized by the Council for Higher Education Accreditation. ACICS can be contacted at 750 First Street NE, Suite 980, Washington, D.C. 20002; phone: 202-336-6780.

The Art Institute International Minnesota is registered as a private institution with the Minnesota Office of Higher Education (1450 Energy Park Drive, Suite 350, St. Paul, Minnesota 55108; phone: 651-642-0567; http://www.ohe.state.mn.us) pursuant to sections 136A.61 to 136A.71.

The Associate in Applied Science degree in culinary arts program is accredited by the American Culinary Federation (ACF).

Location

Minneapolis is a thriving environment for creative minds; home to culture, arts, and entertainment. The Twin Cities region has many Fortune 500 companies, including Target, Best Buy, 3M, and General Mills. The area is also home to a top design and advertising market and is a major U.S. business hub.

Programs of Study and Degrees

Bachelor's degree programs are offered in advertising, culinary management, design management, digital film and video production, fashion and retail management, graphic design, hospitality management, interior design, media arts and animation, photography, visual effects and motion graphics, and Web design and interactive media.

Associate in Applied Science degree programs are offered in baking and pastry, culinary arts, graphic design, interior design, interior planning with AutoCAD, and Web design and interactive media.

Certificate programs are offered in baking and pastry and the art of cooking.

The certificate in baking and pastry and the programs in culinary arts, culinary management, graphic design, the art of cooking, and Web design and interactive media are available in an evening and weekend option format.

Academic Programs

The Art Institutes International Minnesota operates on a year-round, four-quarter system.

Academic Facilities

The Art Institutes International Minnesota is home to classrooms, studios, offices, a student lounge, a supply store, and a learning resource center. Equipment provided at The Art Institutes International Minnesota is specific to the program of study and may include projectors, editing decks, camcorders, PC, and Macintosh computers, printers, drafting tables, and kitchen appliances.

Costs

Tuition cost varies by program. Prospective students should contact the School for current tuition costs. Other charges include a starting kit for all first-quarter students. Kits vary in price depending on the program of study.

Financial Aid

Financial aid is available for those who qualify. Students who require financial assistance should first complete and submit a Free Application for Federal Student Aid (FAFSA) and meet with a financial aid officer.

Faculty

Faculty members at The Art Institutes International Minnesota have professional knowledge that they bring into the classroom. The School's faculty members provide their students with a unique, relevant educational experience.

Admission Requirements

Applicants must provide proof of high school graduation or achievement of a General Educational Development (GED) certificate as a prerequisite for admission. In lieu of documenting high school graduation or a GED certificate, applicants may provide proof of attaining an associate degree or higher from an accredited institution. An official transcript indicating date of high school graduation, GED certificate (including test scores), or date of college graduation (including degree granted) is required as proof.

All individuals seeking admission to The Art Institutes International Minnesota are interviewed in person or by phone by an assistant director of admissions, and each applicant must create an original essay of at least 150 words stating how an education at The Art Institutes International Minnesota would help the student to achieve career goals. There is a $50 application fee.

For the most recent information regarding admission requirements, please refer to the current academic catalog.

Application and Information

To obtain an application, arrange for an interview, or tour the school, prospective students should contact:

The Art Institutes International Minnesota
15 South 9th Street
Minneapolis, Minnesota 55402-3105
Phone: 612-332-3361
800-777-3643 (toll-free)
Fax: 612-332-3934
Web site: http://www.artinstitutes.edu/minneapolis

The Art Institute of Atlanta; The Art Institute of Atlanta–Decatur[1]; The Art Institute of Austin[2]; The Art Institute of California–Hollywood; The Art Institute of California–Inland Empire; The Art Institute of California–Los Angeles; The Art Institute of California–Orange County; The Art Institute of California–Sacramento; The Art Institute of California–San Diego; The Art Institute of California–San Francisco; The Art Institute of California–Sunnyvale; The Art Institute of Charleston[1]; The Art Institute of Charlotte; The Art Institute of Colorado; The Art Institute of Dallas; The Art Institute of Fort Lauderdale; The Art Institute of Fort Worth[3]; The Art Institute of Houston; The Art Institute of Houston–North[2]; The Art Institute of Indianapolis[4]; The Art Institute of Jacksonville[5]; The Art Institute of Las Vegas; The Art Institute of Michigan; The Art Institute of New York City; The Art Institute of Ohio–Cincinnati[6]; The Art Institute of Philadelphia; The Art Institute of Phoenix; The Art Institute of Pittsburgh; The Art Institute of Portland; The Art Institute of Raleigh–Durham; The Art Institute of Salt Lake City; The Art Institute of San Antonio[2];The Art Institute of Seattle; The Art Institute of Tampa[5]; The Art Institute of Tennessee–Nashville[1,7]; The Art Institute of Tucson; The Art Institute of Vancouver; The Art Institute of Virginia Beach[1,8]; The Art Institute of Washington[1,8]; The Art Institute of Washington–Northern Virginia[1,8]; The Art Institute of York–Pennsylvania; The Art Institutes International–Kansas City; The Art Institutes International Minnesota; The Illinois Institute of Art–Chicago; The Illinois Institute of Art–Schaumburg; Miami International University of Art & Design; The New England Institute of Art.

[1]A branch of The Art Institute of Atlanta
[2]A branch of The Art Institute of Houston
[3]A branch of The Art Institute of Dallas
[4]The Art Institute of Indianapolis is regulated by the Indiana Commission on Proprietary Education, 302 West Washington Street, Room E201, Indianapolis, Indiana 46204, AC-0080
[5]A branch of Miami International University of Art & Design
[6]The Art Institute of Ohio–Cincinnati, 8845 Governors Hill Drive, Suite 100, Cincinnati, Ohio 45249-3317, OH Reg. #04-01-1698B
[7]The Art Institute of Tennessee–Nashville is authorized for operation as a postsecondary educational institution by the Tennessee Higher Education Commission.
[8]Certified by the State Council of Higher Education to operate in Virginia

ASBURY COLLEGE

WILMORE, KENTUCKY

The College

Located 20 minutes south of Lexington, Kentucky, Asbury College is a private, residential, liberal arts institution committed to academic excellence and spiritual vitality. Founded in 1890, the College offers fifty undergraduate majors, a degree-completion program, and several graduate programs in education and social work.

The mission of Asbury College, as a Christian liberal arts college in the Wesleyan-Holiness tradition, is to equip men and women, through a commitment to academic excellence and spiritual vitality, for a lifetime of learning, leadership, and service to the professions, society, the family, and the Church, thereby preparing them to engage their cultures and advance the cause of Christ around the world.

A distinguishing mark of Asbury's Christian community is that the members are committed to a set of basic principles that are considered essential to maintain the spirit and health of the community. At Asbury College, the basic tenet of the community is found in Jesus's two great commandments in Matthew 22:37–40: "You shall love the Lord your God with all your heart, and with all your soul, and with all your mind . . . And . . . you shall love your neighbor as yourself." Thus, members of the Asbury community seek to love God and practice self-sacrificial love in relationship to others. Such disciplined community living is inherent preparation for servant-leaders who give their lives to fulfill a cause greater than themselves.

Citing the Christian and academic reputation of the College as their primary reason for selecting Asbury, 314 new freshmen were enrolled in fall 2009. The current undergraduate enrollment is 1,313 students from forty-four states and eleven countries. Kentucky, Ohio, Indiana, Pennsylvania, and Georgia are the five states that are represented the most. Asbury offers majors and programs of study within the liberal arts curriculum and confers the degrees of Bachelor of Arts and Bachelor of Science in education. The most popular majors are in the departments of communication arts, education, psychology, equine management, bible-theology, and history.

Organizations and clubs are an important part of student life at Asbury College. Positions on the *Collegian* (student newspaper) and the *Asburian* (yearbook) are open to all students. Students can become involved in the IMPACT and Reach Out programs (community involvement), Acting on AIDS, Art, Speech, English, Foreign Student, French, and Spanish Clubs. Students may also participate in the Women's Vocal Ensemble, Men's Glee Club, Jazz Ensemble, Chorale, and Concert Band. Student honor societies include Alpha Psi Omega (drama), Phi Alpha Theta (history), Phi Sigma Tau (philosophy), Sigma Zeta (science and mathematics), Sigma Tau Delta (English), and Sigma Delta Pi (Spanish). Among the professional organizations that students may join are the American Guild of Organists, the Music Educators National Conference, the Kentucky Intercollegiate Press Association, the Student National Education Association, and the Student Association for Health, Physical Education and Recreation.

Asbury recognizes the value of athletics and maintains a program of intramural and intercollegiate sports. Asbury is a member of the NAIA and offers athletic scholarships to athletes in every sport. Intercollegiate sports for men are baseball, basketball, cross-country, golf, soccer, swimming and diving, and tennis. For women, basketball, cheerleading, cross-country, golf, soccer, softball, swimming and diving, tennis, and volleyball are offered. Intramural activities include basketball, flag football, golf, soccer, softball, tennis, Ultimate Frisbee, volleyball, and walleyball. The College also sponsors a Christian witness gymnastics team that tours each spring semester, called the Tumbling Team.

Eighty-five percent of Asbury students reside in College residence halls. Duplexes for married students are available. Counseling and health services are available to all students. Asbury maintains a well-equipped clinic with a competent, experienced staff consisting of registered nurses and a physician.

Location

Wilmore, a safe community of approximately 6,000, is located in the heart of the famous Bluegrass region, 15 miles southwest of Lexington, Kentucky, the second-largest city in the commonwealth. The campus consists of more than 360 acres, including a horse farm and ropes challenge course on the Kentucky Palisades. The main campus area is considered a "walking campus."

Surrounding Wilmore are reminders of the state's pioneer history, including Fort Harrod, Boonesborough, and Shakertown, a restored religious community dating from the 1800s. Near Lexington is the Kentucky Horse Park, and the airport is only 20 minutes away from campus. Camping, rock-climbing, boating, and fishing are available at nearby Red River Gorge and Natural Bridge, and Mammoth Cave National Park is 2½ hours from Wilmore.

Lexington has theaters, an opera house, a symphony orchestra, and Rupp Arena, where programs ranging from performances by well-known musicians to basketball games are presented.

Majors and Degrees

Asbury College confers the degrees of Bachelor of Arts and the Bachelor of Science in education. Undergraduate majors are available in accounting, ancient languages, art, bible and theology (preministry or preseminary), biblical languages, biochemistry, biology, business management, chemistry, Christian ministries, communications, computational mathematics, creative writing, elementary education, engineering (with the University of Kentucky), English, equine management, exercise science, financial mathematics, French, health science, history, journalism, mathematics, media communication, middle school education, missions, music, music business, P–12 education (art, French, health and physical education, Latin, music, and Spanish), pre-therapy and occupational therapy, philosophy, physical science, political science, psychology, recreation, secondary education (biological science, chemistry, English, English as a second language, mathematics, and social studies), social work, sociology, Spanish, sport management, theater and cinema, worship arts, and youth ministries.

Academic Programs

Asbury College operates on a sixteen-week semester system with one 4-week summer session. To qualify for graduation, students must complete a minimum of 124 semester hours with an overall grade point average of at least 2.0 and 2.5 in teacher education programs.

The liberal arts core requirements are as follows: Foundations for Spiritual Life and Growth, 9 credits; communication, 3 credits; mathematics, 0–3 credits; English, 6 credits; world language, 0–9 credits; sciences with a lab, 4 credits; fine arts, 3 credits;

social sciences, 3 credits; physical education, 2 credits; cross-cultural experience, 0–3 credits; leadership, 3 credits; and history and philosophy, 6 credits.

Students may be granted college credit for satisfactory performance on AP tests in certain subjects. Advanced standing in foreign language is also available to qualifying students. Further detailed information is available from the College.

Off-Campus Programs

Qualified students may participate in the American Studies Program in Washington, D.C.; the Holy Land Studies Program in Israel; the Wesleyan Urban Coalition Program in Chicago; Martha's Vineyard; Los Angeles Film School; and other bestsemester.com programs, as well as in the Latin American Studies Program.

Academic Facilities

College facilities that are available to students include a computer center and several well-equipped chemistry, biology, physics, and computer laboratories. The College also has a radio station and an outstanding TV studio with a 24-hour cable station. The Kinlaw Library, completed in 2001, is a 72,000-square-foot facility that houses the College's 168,000-volume collection, as well as the Kirkland Learning Resources Center. With wireless service available, computer, media, and curriculum labs are included in the building.

Costs

For 2009–10 annual expenses are $23,577 for tuition and $5620 for room and board.

Financial Aid

More than 90 percent of the College's students receive some type of financial assistance. The various aid programs include academic scholarships, Federal Pell Grants, Federal Supplemental Educational Opportunity Grants, Kentucky Higher Education Assistance Authority Grants, Federal Perkins Loans, Federal Stafford Student Loans, state loans, institutional grants and loans, institutional employment, and Federal Work-Study Program awards. Asbury offers honor scholarships, including a few full tuition grants. National Merit Finalists receive 70 percent tuition scholarships. There are merit scholarships available for athletes, musicians, and theater participants as well.

To apply for aid, students should complete the Free Application for Federal Student Aid (FAFSA). Priority consideration is given to those who file before March 1. Financial need is defined as the difference between the amount a family can pay and the total expenses for the academic year. If there is a deficit, the student is considered to have financial need. The awards are made on the basis of financial need. Notification of awards begins early in April. For more information, students may contact the financial aid office at 859-858-3511 Ext. 2195 or 800-888-1818 Ext. 2195 (toll-free).

Faculty

Asbury has a full-time faculty of about 80 members. The part-time faculty usually numbers 70 members. Each student has a faculty adviser, who is personally interested in each student and willing to assist advisees in any way possible. Faculty members are approachable and many open their homes to students, leading Bible studies or homework sessions. Asbury's faculty-student ratio is 1:15. Approximately 75 percent of the full-time faculty members hold earned terminal degrees in their fields.

Student Government

The objectives of the student government organization are to act as a unifying force, bringing the institution as a whole into vital contact with current issues in college life; to help students find opportunities in college life in a mature Christian spirit, through recommendation and administration; and to promote an atmosphere for intellectual, spiritual, and cultural development. Regulations for student life are explained in the student handbook. The use of tobacco, alcoholic beverages, and illegal drugs is strictly prohibited.

Admission Requirements

The Asbury College faculty strongly recommends that applicants should have completed the following requirements in grades 9 through 12: 4 years of English, including 1 year of composition; 3 or 4 years of mathematics (algebra, geometry, advanced algebra, and other advanced math); 2 years of social studies, of which 1 year should be history; 2 or 3 years of laboratory science; and 2 years of the same foreign language. Applicants should have a grade point average of at least 2.5. Students should take the ACT examination (and have a minimum ACT composite score of 22) or the SAT (minimum score of 1020 with the combined reading and math scores). Freshmen entering Asbury have had an average ACT composite score of 24.6, an SAT combined score of 1163, and a high school grade point average of 3.58. Transfer students must have maintained an average of 2.5 or better at the college or university last attended.

Application and Information

Students may apply for freshman admission during the spring of their junior year or during their senior year in high school. An official transcript and Christian Character Reference Form are required for each student. Enrollment is cut off at resident capacity. Admission decisions are made and financial assistance is awarded by Asbury College without regard to race, color, sex, national origin, or handicap.

Further information may be obtained by contacting:

Office of Admissions
Asbury College
Wilmore, Kentucky 40390
Phone: 859-858-3511 Ext. 2142
800-888-1818 Ext. 2142 (toll-free)
Fax: 859-858-3921
Web site: http://www.asbury.edu

Asbury helped broadcast the 2008 Olympics in Beijing.

ASSUMPTION COLLEGE

WORCESTER, MASSACHUSETTS

The College

Assumption College, established in 1904 by the Augustinians of the Assumption, is a coeducational institution known for its classic liberal arts curriculum and strong academic programs in business and professional studies. The College's 2,113 undergraduates choose among thirty-nine majors and forty-four minors, gaining a depth and breadth of knowledge that is the foundation of lifelong success. Their educational experience is grounded in the rich Catholic intellectual tradition, which cultivates both the intellect and personal values students need to meet the demands of a constantly changing world. Undergraduates and graduate students interact closely with faculty members and staff in a thriving community that develops graduates known for critical intelligence, thoughtful citizenship, and compassionate service.

The academic atmosphere is marked by individual attention and the quest for personal excellence. With a student-faculty ratio of just 12:1, Assumption's professors serve as mentors, who challenge students to ask questions, find their own answers, and grow—intellectually, socially, and spiritually. Students are encouraged to gain hands-on experience at internships and to participate in individual research projects. Within six months of graduation, 97 percent of the graduates are either employed or in graduate school.

At Assumption, 90 percent of the undergraduates live on campus and housing is guaranteed for all four years. The campus is lively seven days a week with academic programming, activities sponsored by student clubs and organizations, community service opportunities, campus ministry programs, and intercollegiate, intramural, and club sports. The College's state-of-the-art recreation center supports the well-being of all students.

Location

Spreading across 185 acres, the College's beautiful campus is situated in a residential neighborhood just minutes from downtown Worcester, Massachusetts. Worcester, the second largest city in New England, is a vibrant college town, home to 30,000 students. The city offers extensive opportunities for entertainment, internships, and community service. Great restaurants, cultural venues and programs, retail and entertainment options, and professional sports teams provide students with many off-campus activities. Worcester is also centrally located, with Boston, Providence, Rhode Island, and Hartford, Connecticut, each an hour's drive away. There is regular commuter rail service to Boston.

Majors and Degrees

The College offers thirty-nine Bachelor of Arts degrees. The most popular programs include English (concentrations in literature or writing and mass communications), history, political science, psychology, the natural sciences (biology, biotechnology and molecular biology, chemistry, and environmental science), education, human services and rehabilitation studies, and business disciplines such as accounting, international business, management, marketing, and organizational communication. Minors are offered in forty-four areas.

The College offers graduate degrees in business, special education, school counseling, counseling psychology, and rehabilitation counseling. The College also has agreements with a number of highly regarded institutions so that students can continue their education in medical technology, engineering (a 3–2 program with University of Notre Dame), and law (3–3 programs with Duquesne and Western New England Law Schools). Joint seven-year programs are also available for those interested in physical therapy, podiatry, or optometry.

Preprofessional preparation is available for dentistry, medicine, and law.

Academic Programs

The College's classic liberal arts curriculum promotes the lively discussion of the books, ideas, people, and events that have shaped civilization. Faculty members and students explore the rich Catholic intellectual tradition as they seek truth and the nature of the world.

Assumption also offers academic programs and courses that help students achieve their full potential. The College's first-year program engages new students with linked courses from two disciplines and coordinated activities that complement classroom experiences. The same 20 students take courses in the fall and spring semesters, enabling them to make important intellectual connections, while getting to know other students. The honors program and the Fortin and Gonthier Foundations of Western Civilization Program encourage students to challenge themselves intellectually. Air Force and Army ROTC are also available.

Assumption College follows a traditional two-semester calendar, from late August to mid-May, as well as an optional January intersession. The Graduate School and the Center for Continuing and Career Education also offer two summer sessions for students.

Undergraduates complete a core curriculum that provides a strong foundation in the liberal arts. Students must complete 120 credit hours in all the academic programs to earn a degree.

Off-Campus Programs

The College and twelve other institutions of higher learning created the Colleges of Worcester Consortium to offer the 30,000 college students in the area even greater academic and social opportunities. Assumption students may cross-register for academic credit at any of the participating colleges and enjoy their social and cultural events. Free transportation to many other participating institutions is available.

Eligible students may choose to spend a semester or a year abroad. The College's students have studied abroad in Australia, Austria, Chile, China, Costa Rica, the Czech Republic, England, France, Germany, Greece, Ireland, Italy, Japan, the Netherlands, Spain, and other locations.

Students explore their professional choices and broaden their workplace skills at local, regional, national, and international internships. In recent years, they have interned at PBS, the U.S. House of Representatives, Ralph Lauren, the Hungarian Embassy, Smith Barney, Fidelity, *The Daily Show with Jon Stewart*, ABC News, Dean Witter Reynolds, AT&T, and Sony Japan.

Academic Facilities

The College has invested more than $60 million to enhance the campus facilities. Nearly the entire campus is wireless.

The Testa Science Center houses the Department of Natural Sciences and features multiuse classrooms with state-of-the-art technology, ten teaching laboratories, seven laboratories dedicated for faculty and student research, a working greenhouse, conference rooms, and student lounge areas.

The Information Technology Center houses computer labs, technology-rich classrooms, and experienced support staff. Students can learn Web authoring, graphics and animation, digital video, and multimedia production. The digital audio studio is available for all students and faculty members.

Assumption offers a variety of housing options to accommodate the 90 percent of students who live on campus. There are traditional residence halls, suites, a living and learning residence, and apartments. All resident students have individual hard-wired and wireless Internet access in their rooms. The outstanding stadium and athletic facilities support the College's 23 NCAA Division II intercollegiate teams, many recreational programs, and the physical well-being of the entire campus community.

Costs

For 2009–10, tuition was $29,806; room and board were $10,070. The board plan is required for all first-year students. Student fees totalled $880. The total for tuition, room and board, and fees was $40,756.

Financial Aid

The College offers financial aid based on demonstrated need and scholastic achievement. The College requires that students submit the Free Application for Federal Student Aid (FAFSA) which is available on January 1. This form should be filed by February 1, so that the College can consider the information as it makes financial aid awards.

All applicants for admission are considered for merit awards up to $20,000 per year. Funds awarded through this program reflect the College's commitment to academic excellence and student leadership.

Faculty

Approximately 90 percent of the Assumption College faculty members hold doctoral or terminal degrees. They are active scholars in their fields, presenting their ideas and research at professional conferences, writing books and articles, and publishing in journals. With a student-to-faculty ratio of 12:1, professors get to know the students—to mentor, encourage, and help students succeed. Professors work closely with students and challenge them to explore new paths of knowledge and make their own discoveries. All of Assumption's academic advisors are full-time faculty members.

Student Government

There are more than sixty clubs and organizations on campus, offering students opportunities in community service, sports, academics, leadership, and special interests. The Student Government Association (SGA), the elected representatives of the student body, coordinates official communication between the student community and the College administration and officially recognizes student clubs and activities.

Admission Requirements

All applicants must graduate from an accredited secondary school with a minimum of 18 academic units. These units should include 4 years of English, 3 years of mathematics, 2 years of a foreign language, 2 years of history, 2 years of science, and 5 additional academic units.

Admission to Assumption is test-score optional. When submitting an application an essay and recommendations are required. Interviews are recommended, but not required.

The number of solid academic courses, including the number of honors or Advanced Placement-level courses, is considered during the application review process.

The Admissions Committee understands that grading standards vary from school to school, or from one course to another. Class rank provides some context within which to place the grades of students applying from a given school. Some schools also provide grade distribution charts. The Committee also considers whether the applicant's grade point average or rank in class is weighted or unweighted.

Application and Information

Campus visits are strongly recommended. Appointments can be scheduled Monday through Friday. Group Information Sessions are held most Saturdays in the fall.

Applicants must submit a completed application, a $50 application fee, official transcripts, a recommendation, and an essay. Applications for early action must be received by November 15. The deadline for regular admission is February 15. Students may apply by completing the College's application, the Common Application and Supplement, or the Universal Application. Apply online at the College's Web site, http://www.assumption.edu, http://www.commonapp.org, or http://www.universalcollegeapp.com.

For more information, students should contact:

Office of Admissions
Assumption College
500 Salisbury Street
P.O. Box 15005
Worcester, Massachusetts 01609-1296
Phone: 508-767-7285
866-477-7776 (toll-free)
E-mail: admiss@assumption.edu
Web site: http://www.assumption.edu

The flagship of Assumption's six-year, $60-million physical plant expansion program is the Testa Science Center.

AURORA UNIVERSITY

AURORA, ILLINOIS

The University

Aurora University was founded in 1893. The school has grown substantially over the years and has taken on many new challenges. In 1938, it was one of the first small colleges to achieve regional accreditation. In 1947, the college's evening program was instituted—one of the nation's first adult education programs at a liberal arts college. In 1985, Aurora College was reorganized as Aurora University, reflecting both the increased size of the institution and the needs associated with its many new programs. In addition to the College of Arts and Sciences, the University comprises the College of Education (including health and physical education) and the College of Professional Studies (social work, nursing, and business). Today, the University enrolls 4,300 students in more than forty undergraduate programs and eleven graduate degree programs in business, social work, and education. An Ed.D. degree is offered in educational leadership. Degree programs are also offered on the shores of Geneva Lake in Williams Bay, Wisconsin. Degree programs include the B.S. in communication, business leadership, and recreation administration; the RN to B.S.N.; the Master of Arts in Teaching; the M.A. in reading instruction; the M.A. in special education; the M.S. in recreation administration; the M.B.A.; a weekend M.S.W. program; and the Ed.D. degree.

The University's student body includes 600 on-campus, traditional-age students; 1,400 undergraduate commuters; 1,900 graduate students; and more than 400 students at the George Williams College campus. The majority of Aurora's students come from the upper-Midwest region, but twenty states are also represented.

Social life is based on campus, and most activities are campuswide. Aurora has more than fifty musical, literary, religious, social, and service clubs and organizations. There are also opportunities to be involved in theater and the highly regarded University Chorale. Aurora University has a long history of excellence in both intercollegiate and intramural athletics. A member of the NCAA Division III, Aurora fields intercollegiate teams in baseball, basketball, cross-country, football, golf, indoor track, lacrosse, soccer, softball, tennis, track, and volleyball, often with championship results.

Aurora University is accredited at the bachelor's, master's, and doctoral degree levels by the Higher Learning Commission of the North Central Association of Colleges and Schools, and its programs are accredited by the Commission on Collegiate Nursing Education, Illinois Department of Professional Regulation, Council on Social Work Education, National Recreation and Park Association/American Association of Leisure and Recreation, and Association of Collegiate Business Schools and Programs. The College of Education is also accredited by the National Council for Accreditation of Teacher Education.

Location

Aurora University is located in an attractive residential neighborhood on the southwest side of Aurora, Illinois, which has a population of more than 170,000 and is the state's second-largest city. The 32-acre main campus is located only minutes from the Illinois Research and Development Corridor, the site of dozens of nationally and internationally based businesses and industries. Located within an hour's drive or train ride is Chicago, one of the most vibrant cities in the world.

Majors and Degrees

The Bachelor of Arts degree is awarded in accounting, art, biology, business administration, business and commerce, coaching and youth sport development, communication, computer science, criminal justice, elementary education, English, finance, history, management information technology, marketing, organizational management, physical education (K–12 teacher certification), political science, psychology, religion, sociology, Spanish, special education, and theater. The Bachelor of Science degree is awarded in accounting, actuarial science, athletic training, biology, business administration, business and commerce, computer science, finance, health science (allied health, predentistry, premedicine, and pre–veterinary studies), management information technology, marketing, mathematics, organizational management, physical education (fitness and health promotion), and recreation administration. The Bachelor of Science in Nursing and the Bachelor of Science in social work are also offered. The University offers supplemental majors in prelaw and secondary education as well as the YMCA Senior Director Certificate Program.

Academic Programs

Aurora University prides itself on its first-year program, which ensures that entering students make a successful transition to college. The only private college in Illinois selected to be part of a national project to create a model of excellence for the first college year, Aurora University recognizes the unique needs of freshmen.

Aurora University offers academic programs combining a liberal arts foundation with majors emphasizing career preparation and selected concentrations. Graduates are educated to be purposeful, ethical, and proficient—equipped for worthwhile careers and productive lives and for venturing forth into a changing world.

To earn a bachelor's degree, students are required to fulfill the general education core curriculum of the University and the major requirements for an approved major; complete at least 120 semester hours with a GPA of at least 2.0 on a 4.0 scale, including at least 52 semester hours at a senior college; and complete at least 30 semester hours, including the last 24 for the degree and at least 18 in the major, at Aurora University.

Entering freshmen who qualify and are highly motivated are invited to join the Honors Program. Students with an ACT score of 25 or above and a high school GPA of at least 3.0 on a 4.0 scale are invited to join. Those in the program participate in innovative seminars, service learning, advanced course work, and other special and cultural events.

Aurora University accepts credits earned through APP, CLEP, and DANTES. In addition, credit based on portfolio assessment is available to students who have significant prior learning from career experience or individual study.

The University observes a semester calendar (two 16-week semesters), with classes beginning in late August and concluding in early May. A three-week May Term offers exciting course work, including international study/travel and unique intensive courses.

Off-Campus Programs

Aurora University offers travel-study programs abroad and within the United States. Recent travel/study destinations included China, Costa Rica, France, England, Italy, South Africa, Mexico, and

Greece. The University also has off-campus classes in various locations in Illinois and Wisconsin and fifteen degree programs at the University's George Williams campus near Lake Geneva, Wisconsin.

Academic Facilities

The major buildings at Aurora are marked by the distinctive, red-tiled roofs specified by Charles Eckhart in his donation for the original campus. Dunham Hall houses state-of-the-art computer facilities as well as the Schingoethe Center for Native American Cultures. The newest classroom building houses the Institute for Collaboration, which brings together education, health and human services, business, and government to facilitate the development of collaborative leadership. Other facilities include the fully equipped Perry Theatre, the Parolini Fine Arts Center, science labs, a flora-fauna complex, and the College Commons. Music practice rooms, piano labs, and a spacious art studio are housed in the Parolini Music Center. The Charles B. Phillips Library has more than 99,000 volumes, 7,000 multimedia materials, and approximately 518 current periodical subscriptions. In addition, the library provides access to approximately 3,700 journals in electronic full text and interfaces with sixty-four other universities.

Costs

Tuition for the 2009–10 school year is $18,000 for full-time students (24–34 semester hours per year), and yearly room and board costs average $7850.

Financial Aid

Aurora University's financial aid program has been designed to make it possible for any academically qualified student to afford the benefits of a private education. The University works with students to determine the amount of their costs and to identify all available resources so students can meet these expenses. Financial aid is awarded based on financial need as reported on the FAFSA. In addition to need-based financial aid, Aurora University offers academic scholarships, including the Board of Trustees Scholarship, Crimi Scholarship, Deans' Scholarship, Solon B. Cousins Scholarship, Aurora University Opportunity Grant, and transfer scholarships.

Faculty

The favorable student-faculty ratio of 15:1 ensures that students receive plenty of individual attention in class. Instructors also make time for students outside of class, acting as mentors and advisers, and they are eager to answer questions and join students in campus activities.

Student Government

The student body is represented by the Aurora University Student Association (AUSA), which provides funding for over fifty student groups on campus. Students are also active members of committees ranging from faculty searches to ad hoc task forces and are provided with certain voting privileges.

Admission Requirements

The Aurora University Committee on Admission considers the complete record of a candidate for admission. The University seeks qualified students from varied geographical, cultural, economic, racial, and religious backgrounds. Admission requirements include an ACT score of 19 or above, a high school GPA of 2.5 or above, and a college-preparatory curriculum. Two general qualities are considered in each candidate: academic ability, enabling the student to benefit from a high-quality academic program, and a diversity of talents and interests that can contribute to making the campus community a better and more interesting place for learning. An application for admission to Aurora University is considered on the basis of the academic ability, achievements, activities, and motivation of the student. Candidates for the Honors Program must have an ACT score of 25 or higher and a high school GPA of at least 3.0 on a 4.0 scale. Transfer students with fewer than 30 semester hours of credit should apply in the same manner as freshman applicants. Transfer students with more than 15 semester hours may be admitted to Aurora University if they have a transferable overall GPA of 2.5 or higher. Aurora accepts a maximum of 90 semester hours of transfer credits from a combination of two- and four-year schools. A maximum of 68 semester hours may be transferred from two-year schools. For further information, students should contact a transfer counselor in the Office of Admission and Financial Aid.

Application and Information

To apply for admission to Aurora University, the following items should be sent to the Office of Admission and Financial Aid: a completed application form, an official transcript from the guidance counselor, and official ACT or SAT scores. Transfer students should submit official transcripts from each college or university attended, along with the completed application.

For applications and further information, students may contact:

Office of Admission and Financial Aid
Aurora University
347 South Gladstone Avenue
Aurora, Illinois 60506
Phone: 630-844-5533
800-742-5281 (toll-free)
E-mail: admission@aurora.edu
Web site: http://www.aurora.edu

A view of Eckhart Hall at Aurora University in Aurora, Illinois.

AUSTIN COLLEGE

SHERMAN, TEXAS

The College

One of the finest selective liberal arts and sciences colleges in the nation, Austin College seeks students with evidence of academic ability and achievement, an eagerness for intellectual challenge and self-exploration, and a value-centered approach to their involvement. The learning environment is well suited to students who want to be known and challenged by faculty members and peers alike. The majority of students live on campus, creating a dynamic living and learning environment. Founded in 1849, Austin College is affiliated through a covenant relationship with the Presbyterian Church (U.S.A.). The liberal arts and sciences foundation develops lifelong learning abilities, such as thinking critically, solving problems, and communicating with others, and nurtures the whole person through academic, co-curricular, and social involvement.

International education and global awareness are priorities of the College, and more than 70 percent of Austin College graduates spend at least one month in international study during their college experience.

Austin College has an enrollment of approximately 1,350 students. The students are predominantly 18–21 years old, come from thirty-four states and twenty-eight countries, and represent a diversity of ethnicity, religion, and experience.

Opportunities for involvement include more than sixty student organizations, ranging from academic to special interest to local fraternities and sororities. Involvement in music, theater, and art programs is available to all students regardless of major. Intercollegiate athletics through membership in the Southern Collegiate Athletic Conference include six sports for men and six for women, and many students take part in intramural activities. The College maintains a 29-acre recreational area on Lake Texoma, about 20 minutes from the campus. All students are encouraged to participate in volunteer service and be involved in the community.

Austin College offers guidance to students through Career Services, the Academic Skills Center, and Health Services. The campus dining service offers many food options for students each day. The campus offers coed and single-sex residence halls as well as apartments and suites that are available to juniors and seniors. Students of German, French, Japanese, Chinese, and Spanish may choose to live in the language residence, where the target languages are spoken in common areas.

Many students continue on to graduate and professional study and enjoy successful acceptance rates at these institutions. Austin College graduates can be found around the world in exciting and successful careers, and graduates regularly earn prestigious national honors.

Location

Austin College is located in Sherman, Texas, approximately 30 minutes north of the greater Dallas metroplex. Sherman is a small city of approximately 35,000 that *Money* magazine includes among the top 15 percent of the 300 "most livable small cities" in the U.S. Sherman offers students plenty of cultural, religious, and social opportunities, and nearby Lake Texoma offers many additional recreational opportunities. For those seeking "big-city" excitement, the Dallas–Fort Worth metroplex is a short drive south on U.S. Highway 75.

Majors and Degrees

The Bachelor of Arts degree is offered in American studies, art, Asian studies, biochemistry, biology, business administration, chemistry, classical civilization, classics, communication studies (media studies, speech and social interaction, or theater emphasis), computer science, economics, education (through the master's program), English, environmental studies, French, German, history, international economics and finance, international relations, Japanese, Latin, Latin American and Iberian studies, mathematics, music, philosophy, physics, political science, psychology, religious studies, sociology, and Spanish. Minors and interdisciplinary majors are also available in anthropology, art history, cognitive science, community service and policy, educational psychology, ethics, exercise and sport science, film studies, gender studies, Southwestern and Mexican studies, and Western intellectual tradition. In addition, the Special Degree Program allows students to design an individualized major incorporating various interests.

Through the Austin Teacher Program, a special five-year teacher education program, a student earns both the Bachelor of Arts degree in a major of choice and the Master of Arts in Teaching degree.

Austin College also has excellent preprofessional programs in engineering, health sciences, law, and theology.

Academic Programs

Making connections across disciplines and discovering the "bigger picture" bring learning to life. The Austin College curriculum emphasizes both depth and breadth of study. In the fall of the freshman year, all students take a seminar course that introduces them to the inquisitive learning style that defines Austin College. Instead of requiring every student to take a prescribed list of general education courses, Austin College uses a more flexible system that gives students control over their learning experience. Students fulfill the depth dimension by completing a major in a field of specialization plus a minor (or second major) in another field. The breadth dimension offers students the opportunity to explore across the disciplines in areas of personal interest. By careful selection of a minor, students may meet the goals of the breadth dimension while achieving some depth of study in a second field.

Students seeking a nontraditional major or minor may pursue the Special Program Option, in which study is individually designed. The program is particularly adaptable to the needs of students interested in studying interdisciplinary subject areas or in preparing for unique career fields.

Austin College has a 4-1-4 calendar year. Four courses are taken in the fall and spring terms, and one course is completed during the January term. Summer courses are also available. The January term offers an opportunity for in-depth study of one academic or special interest, travel courses, internships, and individualized study.

The College also offers the four-year Posey Leadership Institute, which combines course work, international study, volunteer service, an internship, involvement with a community mentor, and interaction with national and international leaders to develop awareness of leadership skills and styles. Membership in the Posey Leadership Institute is competitive and limited in number and includes a scholarship.

Off-Campus Programs

Students have opportunities for study in England, France, Germany, Spain, Japan, and other countries through the Institute of European and Asian Studies. They participate in the Washington Semester and Washington Summer Symposium as well. Students also can become involved in field study through the social sciences laboratory or individually arranged programs.

Academic Facilities

The College's excellent facilities include the Robert J. and Mary Wright Campus Center, science classrooms and laboratories, a computer center, the new Forster Art Studio Complex, two theaters, the Robert T. Mason Athletic-Recreation Complex, and the Jordan Family Language House, which offers a residential language immersion program in Chinese, French, German, Japanese, and Spanish. Abell Library Center includes more than 300,000 volumes and 900 periodicals to maximize research and learning opportunities. A campuswide fiber-optic computer network and wireless access in many campus locations provide access to on-campus resources and the Internet. Five environmental research areas are all within a short drive of the campus.

Costs

The basic tuition and fees charge for students entering in 2008–09 was $26,555 and room and board charges were $8657, for a total of $35,212.

Financial Aid

Assistance is given in three forms: grants and/or scholarships, loans, and on-campus jobs. Students applying for need-based financial aid should request a financial aid application from Austin College and should also submit the Free Application for Federal Student Aid (FAFSA). Competitive awards, based on merit rather than on financial need, are also available. Students who wish to be considered for general scholarship awards must indicate such on the Common Application Supplement for Austin College. Separate applications are necessary for the competitive scholarships: full-tuition Presidential Scholarships, Posey Leadership Institute Scholarships, Hallam Citizen Scholarships, Center for Southwestern and Mexican Studies Scholarships, John D. Moseley Alumni Fellowships and Scholarships, Sara Bernice Moseley Scholarships for Presbyterian Students, and fine arts scholarships in art, music, and theater. More than 90 percent of students receive some form of financial assistance.

Faculty

Of the 106 full-time faculty members, 98 percent hold terminal degrees. Faculty members holding earned doctorates teach at all levels. In addition to carrying out their academic and professional responsibilities, faculty members participate in the governance of the College and serve as students' mentors. With a student-faculty ratio of 12:1 and an average class size of 22, the emphasis at Austin College is on classroom excellence.

Student Government

Under a community-government partnership plan, in which students and members of the faculty and administration are all participants, student involvement and leadership are important aspects of College governance. The College is committed to high principles in scholarship and general behavior.

Admission Requirements

Admission is competitive, with four times the number of applicants as places in the freshman class. Transfer students are subject to the same rigorous standards required of freshman applicants. Students who cannot fulfill these requirements are considered on an individual basis. All admission credentials for fall freshman applicants must be received by the Office of Admission by one of the following deadlines: December 1 for Early Action I applicants, January 15 for Early Action II applicants (and for scholarship applicants), and March 1 for Regular Decision applicants. Students who apply for admission after March 1 are considered on a space-available basis. To reserve a place in the entering class, a $350 deposit is required by May 1. The College's early admission program allows qualified students to enroll after their junior year of high school. Admission to Austin College is on an equal basis, regardless of age, color, disability, race, sex, sexual orientation, religion, national origin, or status as a veteran.

Application and Information

Austin College exclusively accepts the Common Application. Prospective students may apply online or download a copy at http://www.commonapp.org. Students also may obtain a copy from their high school guidance counselor or by calling Austin College. The Common Application Supplement for Austin College also is required. A completed application form, SAT Reasoning Test or ACT with writing scores, two letters of reference, and a transcript from each high school and college attended must be submitted to Austin College.

For more information, students should contact:

Office of Admission
Austin College
900 North Grand Avenue, Suite 6N
Sherman, Texas 75090
Phone: 903-813-3000
800-KANGAROO (526-4276, toll-free)
Fax: 903-813-3198
E-mail: admission@austincollege.edu
Web site: http://www.austincollege.edu

Austin College's tree-lined walkways, landscaped plazas, and green expanses provide a backdrop for the mixture of historical and modern buildings on the campus of the 160-year-old college.

BABSON COLLEGE

WELLESLEY, MASSACHUSETTS

The College

Since its founding in 1919, Babson College has focused on educating business leaders capable of initiating and managing change, navigating ethical choices, and solving the problems of today and tomorrow. Students are immersed in an enriching environment that fosters leadership, teamwork, creativity, communication, diversity, and ethics. The 2009–10 undergraduate enrollment was 812 women and 1,086 men. An independent, coeducational institution, Babson is accredited by AACSB International–The Association to Advance Collegiate Schools of Business, the New England Association of Schools and Colleges, and the European Quality Improvement System (EQUIS).

Babson is a residential college and is a 24-hours-a-day, seven days-a-week community alive with intellectual, cultural, athletic, and social activities. Approximately 85 percent of the undergraduate student body lives on campus in fourteen residence halls. Housing options include coed residence halls, fraternity and sorority housing, and substance-free, multicultural, entrepreneurial, and other specialty-themed housing.

Babson College is an NCAA Division III school, and most of the College's intercollegiate teams compete in the New England Women's and Men's Athletic Conference (NEWMAC). There are twenty-two men's and women's varsity sports teams, with additional club and intramural sports available to all students.

The Webster Center features an indoor, 200-meter, six-lane track; a field house; a gymnasium with three basketball courts; a racquetball court; a 25-yard, six-lane pool with 1- and 3-meter diving boards; a fitness center; squash courts; and a dance/aerobics studio. The Babson Skating Center features a 600-seat skating arena. Outdoor facilities include eight tennis courts, a new AstroTurf field, a game field, a renovated softball diamond, a baseball field, two sand-based varsity fields, and a club rugby field.

Location

Babson's beautiful 370-acre campus is in Wellesley, Massachusetts, 14 miles west of Boston, a city renowned for its cultural and recreational opportunities. More than sixty colleges and universities bring more than 250,000 college students to the Boston area, making it one of the world's best college towns for cultural exchange and research.

Majors and Degrees

Babson offers a Bachelor of Science degree, a Master of Business Administration degree, three Master of Science degree programs, and executive education programs for business professionals.

Academic Programs

The curriculum breaks down the artificial barriers between disciplines by emphasizing an integrated, holistic approach to learning. The curriculum integrates core competencies, key business disciplines, and the liberal arts into foundation, intermediate, and advanced programs. Babson's core competencies include rhetoric, quantitative analysis, entrepreneurial and creative thinking, global and multicultural perspectives, ethics and social responsibility, leadership and teamwork, and critical and integrative thinking.

These learning outcomes are introduced and reinforced as students' progress through the undergraduate curriculum. The Foundation Program lays the groundwork, raising students' abilities to formulate, explore, and reflect critically. In the second year, students proceed to the Intermediate Program, which adds breadth, elaborates issues, and exposes them to more disciplinary and interdisciplinary analyses. The Advanced Program challenges students to think about issues with increased confidence, independence, and creativity.

Foundation Program courses may include quantitative methods with calculus, probability and statistics, financial accounting, rhetoric, arts and humanities, history and society, business law, science, and Foundations of Management and Entrepreneurship (FME), a yearlong immersion into the world of start-ups, where student teams actually create their own businesses, receiving grants of up to $3000 to cover costs. Babson is the only U.S. school to teach the management core curriculum as an integrated three-semester course where all aspects of business are covered, including accounting, marketing, finance, management operations, strategy, organizational behavior, IT sales, and economics.

In the Advanced Program, students are free to expand and fine-tune core competencies as they reflect on their own career and life goals. During this time, students take courses in advanced management and liberal arts electives. Babson offers twenty-four optional concentrations in both business and liberal arts disciplines. This way, students may further plan their own course of study by focusing on certain areas of interest while continuing to benefit from Babson's interdisciplinary approach to learning. Students also have the opportunity to participate in field-based experiences such as an internship or consulting experience. Special programs, such as the Weissman program, the Honors Program, the Women's Leadership Program, the Management Consulting Field Experience, the Babson College Fund (student-managed endowment), Master of Science in Accounting (M.S.A.), and Independent Research allow students to take advantage of customized learning opportunities at Babson.

Babson's flexible curriculum allows students to pursue courses that appeal to them and align with their goals. To aid in the decision-making process, students receive guidance from faculty mentors and professional staff throughout their four years.

To earn the Bachelor of Science degree, students are required to complete a minimum of 128 semester hours with a C average or better, with a minimum of 63 credits in the liberal arts (including 20 credits in advanced liberal arts). Transfer students must complete a minimum of 64 semester hours at Babson. Once a student has earned 96 credits, all remaining credits must be earned at Babson, at a Babson-approved cross-registration program, or at a Babson-affiliated Study Abroad Program.

Entering students may be granted credit or advanced course placement for successful scores on Advanced Placement (AP) examinations administered by the College Board as well as some courses in the International Baccalaureate (IB) curriculum.

The College operates on a two-semester academic calendar; semesters run from September to December and from late January through May. An optional credit-bearing three-week winter session is offered in January, and two summer sessions are offered—one from late May to early July and one from mid-July to mid-August.

Off-Campus Programs

In addition, Babson has a partnership with Wellesley College and the Franklin W. Olin College of Engineering, an independent institution that opened in 2001 and is located on a 70-acre site adjacent to Babson. Babson, Olin, and Wellesley are collaborating academically and cocurruculary in order to provide extraordinary opportunities in all aspects of the student experience, including joint academic and research programming, student life programming, and lecture series.

Babson students can also take a course each semester at one of the other area colleges, including Brandeis University and Regis College, for full academic credit. These off-campus programs offer greater access to liberal arts courses, including a wide range of foreign languages.

Babson's vibrant study-abroad program enables students to spend either a summer or one or both semesters of their junior year overseas at a college or university. Currently, forty-seven programs are offered in twenty-six countries, and full academic credit is given for approved management and liberal arts courses.

Academic Facilities

Horn Library houses an extensive business collection of print, media, and computerized information resources. Students have campus-wide access to newspapers, journals, investment analyst reports, corporate records, directories, and international information. They also benefit from numerous electronic research and news services that supplement a selection of the best business and liberal arts books, newspapers, journals, CD-ROMs, audiocassettes, videocassettes, and videodiscs.

Horn Computer Center is equipped with a lab that remains open 24 hours a day. Wireless access is available throughout the campus. Every incoming Babson undergraduate student receives a leased laptop computer with integrated Wi-Fi wireless technology.

Other facilities are the Donald W. Reynolds Campus Center, the Richard W. Sorenson Family Visual Arts Center, the Richard W. Sorenson Center for the Arts, the Stephen D. Culter Center for Investments and Finance, the Glavin Family Chapel, and the Arthur M. Blank Center for Entrepreneurship.

Costs

For 2010–11, tuition and fees are $39,040. The total estimated cost for a residential student is $51,916.

Financial Aid

Babson is committed to educating students from diverse backgrounds; applying for financial aid does not affect a student's chances of being admitted to Babson College. Financial assistance is awarded on merit and demonstrated financial need. Assistance for students begins with consideration for student loans and work-study. Those with need beyond the loan and work-study amounts are also considered for Babson grants.

In 2008–09, nearly 40 percent of all first-year students received need-based Babson grants. More than half of Babson students receive some form of financial assistance. Students should note that need-based financial assistance is available to U.S. citizens and permanent residents of the United States. Babson's merit scholarships include Weissman Scholarships, Presidential Scholarships, the Women's Leadership Awards, and the Diversity Leadership Awards. Application for aid is made by submitting the Free Application for Federal Student Aid (FAFSA) and the Financial Aid PROFILE of the College Scholarship Service. The application deadline for first-year undergraduate students is January 15. For transfer students and September enrollment, the deadline is April 1, and November 1 for January enrollment.

Faculty

Because of Babson's close-knit community, students are able to form close relationships with the faculty. Of the 239 faculty members, 159 are full-time, and 92 percent of the full-time faculty members hold a doctoral degree or its equivalent. Faculty members are accomplished entrepreneurs, executives, scholars, authors, researchers, poets, and artists who bring an intellectual diversity that adds depth to Babson's educational programs and offers students a rich, challenging experience. Babson's student-faculty ratio is 14:1, with an average class size of 29. Most importantly, faculty members teach 100 percent of the courses.

Student Government

Students are encouraged to take an active role in campus activities and student government. The Student Government Association promotes students' interests; allocates funds to campus organizations for academic, social, and recreational activities; licenses student-run businesses; and helps formulate and maintain student regulations. There are over seventy student clubs and organizations currently on campus.

Admission Requirements

In selecting new students, the admission office considers each candidate's biographical data, transcripts, test scores, personal statements, and references. Evaluation is based upon comparisons of the qualifications of those who apply. To a large extent, the degree of competition is set by the caliber of the applicants themselves. Consideration is given to the depth and rigor of each candidate's academic program, academic motivation and achievement, and progress from one year to the next. Prospective students are strongly encouraged to have completed or be currently enrolled in a precalculus math class.

The Admission Committee carefully reviews courses taken, math aptitude, and standardized test scores. Reading and writing skills as well as verbal expression are measured using English grades, essays, and standardized test scores. Intangible personal qualities are also important—leadership, creativity, enthusiasm, and an overall good fit with Babson that includes a willingness to contribute to the community in meaningful and positive ways. There is no standard format for submitting this information, so Babson relies on letters of recommendation, references, and personal statements. In addition, the College evaluates extracurricular activities and work experience, seeking candidates who have exceptional leadership qualities and have participated in activities that have potential carryover to college. Efforts are made to enroll students with diverse backgrounds and experiences.

The College offers three application plans: regular decision, early decision, and early action. For more information about these plans and their deadlines, prospective students should visit the College's Web site (http://www.babson.edu/ugrad). Campus visits and group information sessions with an admission counselor are strongly recommended.

Application and Information

For further information or application forms, students should contact:

Lunder Undergraduate Admission Center
Babson College
Babson Park, Massachusetts 02457-0310
Phone: 781-239-5522
800-488-3696 (toll-free)
Fax: 781-239-4006
E-mail: ugradadmission@babson.edu
Web site: http://www.babson.edu/ugrad

BALDWIN-WALLACE COLLEGE

BEREA, OHIO

The College

Founded in 1845, Baldwin-Wallace College (B-W) in Berea, Ohio, is an accredited institution affiliated with the United Methodist Church that blends the hallmarks of a traditional liberal arts education with an emphasis on professional preparation. Baldwin-Wallace celebrates a long history of diversity and prides itself as being one of the first colleges in Ohio to admit students without regard to race or gender. That spirit of inclusiveness has flourished and evolved into a personalized approach to education—one that stresses individual growth as students learn to learn, respond to new ideas, adapt to new situations, and prepare for the certainty of change.

B-W's reputation as one of the most respected independent colleges in Ohio has led to consistent growth over the past decade and enrollment of approximately 3,100 full-time undergraduate students. The student profile shows that 25 percent of incoming freshmen come from the top 10 percent of their high school classes, with more than 50 percent in the top quarter. In addition to the traditional-aged college student, Baldwin-Wallace has helped adult learners for more than fifty years to develop skills, redirect careers, and enhance lives. Today, 500 adult learners of all ages participate in evening and weekend classes in a variety of programs that are designed to accommodate the varying learning styles and schedules of busy adult learners. Another 700 students are enrolled in part-time graduate programs in education and business administration.

Baldwin-Wallace College is an academic community committed to the liberal arts and sciences as the foundation for lifelong learning. The College fulfills this mission through a rigorous academic program that is characterized by excellence in teaching and learning within a challenging, supportive environment that enhances students' intellectual and personal growth. Baldwin-Wallace College is committed to the success of its students. In addition to receiving a top-notch liberal arts education, students also enjoy numerous opportunities for internships, faculty-directed research, and service-learning programs. Moreover, students work with their faculty adviser to develop personal action plans that are designed to help each individual student prepare fully for life after college. These programs and approaches are enhanced by B-W's student-focused faculty, close-knit community, and rich College traditions. In all, Baldwin-Wallace College provides a truly unique place to study and prepare for future success.

More than 90 percent of Baldwin-Wallace graduates find employment or enter graduate or professional school within nine months of graduation. Recent Baldwin-Wallace graduates have been accepted at some of the finest graduate schools in the world, including Carnegie Mellon, Case Western Reserve, Cornell, Eastman School of Music, Harvard, Johns Hopkins, Rice, William and Mary, and the Universities of Michigan and Virginia.

Location

B-W students enjoy the best of both worlds. Berea, Ohio, with its tree-lined streets, picturesque homes, and population of 19,000, is an ideal college town. At the same time, students are only 20 minutes from the heart of Cleveland, which is home to Fortune 500 companies as well as unique recreational and cultural opportunities. Cleveland is home to outstanding museums and galleries, professional sporting events, a world-class orchestra, exciting nightlife, and an extensive park system.

Majors and Degrees

Baldwin-Wallace offers the Bachelor of Arts (B.A.), Bachelor of Science (B.S.), Bachelor of Science in Education (B.S.E.), Bachelor of Music (B.M.), and Bachelor of Music in Education (B.M.E.) degrees. Majors include accounting, art history, art studio, athletic training, biology, broadcasting and mass communications, business, chemistry, communication disorders, communication studies, computer information systems, computer science, criminal justice, economics, education, English, English creative writing, exercise science, film studies, finance, French, German, health-care management, health promotion and education, history, human resource management, international business, international studies, management, marketing, mathematical economics, mathematics, medical technology, neuroscience, philosophy, physical education, physics, political science, pre-engineering, pre–physical therapy, psychology, public relations, religion, sociology, Spanish, sport management, sustainability, and theater. The Conservatory of Music offers majors in music composition, music education, music history and literature, music in the liberal arts, music management, music performance, music theater, music theory, and music therapy.

Academic Programs

More than fifty majors and several 3-2 cooperative and pre-professional programs are available to traditional B-W undergraduates. Evening and weekend programs include thirteen majors and six certificate programs.

Off-Campus Programs

Baldwin-Wallace College has institutional partnerships with several other universities around the globe, some of which include Edge Hill College (England), University of the Sunshine Coast (Australia), Ewha University (Korea), Bohme Jesus (Brazil), University of Osnabrück (Germany), Kansai Gaidai University (Japan), Hong Kong Baptist University (China), University of Hull (England), Athlone Institute of Technology (Ireland), Galway Mayo Institute of Technology (Ireland), American Business School in Paris, York St John University (England), Washington Center, New York Media Institute at Marist College, Christ College (India), and American University (Washington, D.C.).

In addition to traditional study-abroad programs, with students studying and living on a particular campus for the semester, B-W features a series of focused-study tours that are led by B-W faculty and staff members and examine specific topics or geographic regions. Some programs involve homestays, while others use hostels and hotels. Quite literally, students learn while on the road. Study tours are offered in alternating academic years.

B-W often sponsors faculty-led two- to three-week seminars for credit in May, which are perfect for students who seek an international experience but do not want to be away for extended periods. Destinations have included Vienna, Prague, and Budapest. Spring trips in 2008 included India and China, and there was a Seminar in Europe as well as an environmental excursion to Ecuador. Most locations for study-abroad programs offered during the academic year—such as Australia, China, England, Korea, and Spain—are also offered during the summer term. The Semester at Sea program sends students to ten different countries—such as Brazil, Egypt, India, Japan, and Vietnam—aboard a 23,000-ton ship with 600 other college undergraduates.

Academic Facilities

The Ritter Library offers special programs, including instruction on how to use the library and a reference service to help students find specific information quickly. The library's 250 convenient online databases, 45 million OhioLINK books, and 20,000 electronic and print periodicals offer a wealth of information. The Jones Music Library is located on the lower level of Merner-Pfeiffer Hall. Jones is the only lending music library on campus, and its collection of nearly 40,000 items composes a significant portion of Baldwin-Wallace College's music holdings. The Riemenschneider Bach Institute, located on the floor above the Jones Music Library, is the other music library at B-W and functions primarily as a research library. The institute is a world-renowned Bach center—the guardian of priceless Bach-related manuscripts and first editions and the publisher of *BACH: Journal of the Riemenschneider Bach Institute,* an international journal. The institute's facilities include a research library and a vault for manuscripts and rare books. Other resources include twenty campus computer labs; a 4,000-watt campus radio station; a multimedia lab for video digitizing and editing, Web site development, computer animation, and more; an on-campus gallery showcasing the work of student, faculty, and area artists; and the Burrell Memorial Observatory. The neuroscience lab includes a two-room vivarium, a small-animal surgery room, a neurophysical laboratory, and several rooms dedicated to behavioral observation and computer analysis.

Costs

In 2009–10, full-time (12–18 credit hours) liberal arts students pay $32,190 per academic year in tuition, room, board, and fees. Conservatory students pay $34,238 per academic year.

Financial Aid

Baldwin-Wallace's tuition ranks among the lowest and most affordable of private colleges in Ohio. To help students and their families meet the cost of a high-quality education, B-W awards more than $50 million annually to students in the form of scholarships, grants, loans, and work-study opportunities. B-W is committed to working with students and their families to offer financial support in terms of scholarships, grants, loans from government and private sources, and an array of campus employment opportunities. Nearly 100 percent of Baldwin-Wallace students receive some sort of financial assistance.

Merit scholarships range from $1000 to $13,000 and are awarded to academically exceptional incoming freshmen. The College also offers competitive awards, ranging from $1000 to $4000. Baldwin-Wallace provides scholarships for transfer students. More information is available from the Office of Financial Aid.

Faculty

Close relationships are at the heart of the B-W experience. Most classes average only 19 students, and the student-faculty ratio is 15:1. Professors share their wisdom and experience on a one-to-one basis, helping students choose classes or assisting students in their search for the perfect internship. Faculty members regularly give out their home phone numbers. From corporate executives and lifelong educators to environmentalists and practicing psychologists, B-W's more than 300 full-time and part-time faculty members bring impressive credentials from their fields. Nearly 80 percent have earned the highest degree in their field. They are dedicated and talented teachers who want to provide an educational experience that goes well beyond the textbook.

Student Government

Student Government consists of three branches—the legislative, the executive, and the judicial. The Student Senate is the official representative body of the students of Baldwin-Wallace College. All meetings are open, and all students are welcome to participate. Senators meet with College administrators and faculty members to express the opinions of the student body in matters affecting student life and to establish and fund official student organizations. The president and vice president of the student body lead the executive branch of Student Government and work closely with the Senate to express student body views to the College faculty and administration. The judicial branch of Student Government consists of the supreme court of the student body, which hears cases pertaining to Student Government and the clubs it funds. Elections for student body government occur each February. All class officers are elected by the student body and help in planning various events on campus, including Homecoming, April Reign, and senior class events.

Admission Requirements

Applicants must submit the completed application (electronic or paper), a high school transcript, a teacher recommendation, the Secondary School Record Request Form, and the $25 application fee (waived if applying online). SAT and ACT results are optional. (In lieu of standardized test results, students must submit a graded writing sample.) Transfer applicants also must submit college or university transcripts. Candidates applying to the Conservatory of Music also must complete the Conservatory Audition Portfolio.

Application and Information

The deadline for undergraduate admission is May 1. The priority admission deadline is March 1. Applicants are notified, beginning November 1, on a rolling basis within four to six weeks of receipt of a completed application.

Office of Admission
Baldwin-Wallace College
275 Eastland Road
Berea, Ohio 44017-2088
Phone: 440-826-2222
877-BW-APPLY (toll-free)
Fax: 440-826-3830
E-mail: info@bw.edu
Web site: http://www.bw.edu/admission

BARD COLLEGE AT SIMON'S ROCK

GREAT BARRINGTON, MASSACHUSETTS

The College

Simon's Rock is the only four-year residential college of the liberal arts and sciences specifically designed to provide bright, highly motivated students with the opportunity to begin college after the tenth or eleventh grade. Students who successfully complete the requirements receive the Associate of Arts (A.A.) degree after two years of study and the Bachelor of Arts (B.A.) degree after four. Full- and partial-tuition scholarships are available. The average age of entering students is 16.

Simon's Rock challenges the traditional assumption that students must be 18 before they can be asked to develop seriously their intelligence, imagination, and self-discipline. Students at Simon's Rock pursue an academic program that enables them to fulfill their potential at an age when their interest, energy, and curiosity are at a peak.

The College was founded in 1964 by Elizabeth Blodgett Hall and first admitted students in 1966. In 1979, Simon's Rock became a part of Bard College, located 50 miles away at Annandale-on-Hudson, New York.

Simon's Rock has been a model for a rapidly growing early college movement across the U.S. For more than forty years, Simon's Rock has proven that highly motivated students of high school age are fully capable of engaging in college work; that they are best able to develop in a small-college environment; that serving these students well requires a faculty committed to distinction in teaching and scholarship, as well as active participation in the students' social and personal development; and that a coherent general education in the liberal arts and sciences should be the foundation for early college students.

Location

The College is built on over 200 rolling and wooded acres 2 miles west of Great Barrington, a town of 8,500, in the Berkshire Hills of western Massachusetts. Boston and New York City are 140 miles away; Albany and Springfield are 40 miles away. The Berkshires' natural beauty and wide variety of cultural attractions make the area an unusually attractive place in which to live. The countryside provides excellent terrain for hiking, bicycling, cross-country and Alpine skiing, canoeing, and climbing. The Tanglewood Music Festival, Jacob's Pillow Dance Festival, and numerous summer theaters are located in nearby towns. Great Barrington itself is a thriving business community with a variety of schools and service agencies in which Simon's Rock students work and volunteer.

Majors and Degrees

Simon's Rock offers programs leading to the A.A. and B.A. degrees in the liberal arts and sciences. Students may complete their B.A. studies with a concentration in most traditional disciplines or choose one of several interdisciplinary concentrations.

Academic Programs

The academic program at Simon's Rock combines a core curriculum in the liberal arts and sciences with extensive opportunities for students to pursue their own interests through electives, tutorials, and independent study.

Because Simon's Rock students begin college without completing high school, the College is particularly conscious of its responsibility to ensure that all students develop the skills and knowledge expected of an educated person. The core curriculum comprises approximately half of students' total academic load during their first two years. Requirements include a writing and thinking workshop, which new students attend during the week before the regular semester begins; first-year, sophomore, and cultural perspectives seminars; and courses in the arts, mathematics, natural science, and foreign language. The College also requires that students participate in a recreational athletics program and attend a series of health and wellness programs.

All new students are assigned a faculty adviser, who meets with them weekly during their first semester and regularly throughout the rest of their career at Simon's Rock. Classes are small, faculty members are accessible, and the opportunities for students to pursue diverse interests are extensive.

The curriculum of the first two years at Simon's Rock leads to the A.A. in liberal arts. Students who successfully complete the A.A. requirements may continue at Simon's Rock for a B.A. or transfer to another college or university to complete their baccalaureate degree. Close to half of each class remains to complete a B.A. at Simon's Rock in one of approximately forty concentrations; the remainder of the students transfer. Through the sophomore planning process, students receive individualized guidance from staff in the Win Student Resource Commons as they explore options for their last two years of undergraduate study.

Students wishing to stay at Simon's Rock for a B.A. must apply for admission to a concentration through a process called Moderation. Each student meets with a group of faculty in their area(s) of interest to review the student's accomplishments and together plan the remainder of the student's education program. Students suggest and are advised of junior- and senior-year opportunities. These traditionally include advanced seminars, independent study involvement in faculty research projects, specialized tutorials, internships, courses at Bard, and a possible semester or full year of study abroad.

The senior thesis is the focus of each B.A. student's final year. Drawing on the skills in analysis and synthesis acquired during the previous three years, students devote themselves wholeheartedly to the project and to learning, which has been personally defined and developed. Recent theses have taken many forms: critical studies in literature, sociological research, musical compositions, creative fiction, translations, scientific experiments, mathematical problem solving, artistic exhibitions and performances, and various combinations of these forms.

The regular academic program is supplemented by a number of signature programs. The Simon's Rock/Columbia University Engineering Program offers three years at Simon's Rock and two years in the engineering school at Columbia University in New York, at the end of which students receive both a B.A. from Simon's Rock and a B.S. from Columbia's School of Engineering and Applied Science. Simon's Rock also offers similar arrangements with the engineering schools at Dartmouth University and Washington University in St. Louis.

Through Simon's Rock Scholars at Oxford, a select group of Simon's Rock students are admitted to spend their junior year at Lincoln College of the University of Oxford in England each year. Founded in 1427, Lincoln College is one of the oldest and most esteemed of the Oxford Colleges. Simon's Rock Scholars at Oxford are full members of Lincoln College, live on the grounds at Lincoln, are taught by the regular faculty members at Oxford, and have access to the rich resources and facilities of the University.

Simon's Rock has recently formalized a program in creative writing through which students will be able to spend up to a full year at the Centre for New Writing at the University of Manchester in the UK. Launched in September 2007, the Centre was designed to develop and refine the creative and critical work of its students, explore and research collaboration between creative and critical writing, and broaden access to literature and writers in the region. Founded on the principle that good reading and good writing naturally go together, the Centre's goal is to be a place where the best, most interesting contemporary literature is both written and written about.

The proseminar in Social Scientific Inquiry, an in-house program commencing in the 2008–09 academic year, provides students with an opportunity for immersion in social theory, social research, and social action through intensive interaction with scholars active across the broad spectrum of the disciplines.

Simon's Rock students also have the opportunity to study at Bard College at Annandale. Upper-college (B.A.) students can take classes at Bard's campus in Annandale-on-Hudson, New York, or work on their senior theses while spending a semester in residence at the Annandale campus. Students can also take advantage of Bard's study-abroad programs; its groundbreaking Manhattan-based Globalization and International Affairs Program; and the Bard Rockefeller Program, a collaborative venture with Rockefeller University offering advanced research opportunities in medicine and the sciences.

Off-Campus Programs

Students pursue a variety of study-abroad programs and options. The Simon's Rock Win Resource Commons works with students to find study-abroad opportunities suited to their goals and interests. They use established independent programs (the School for Field Studies, Semester at Sea, Global Routes), programs through other schools (Oxford University, the Sorbonne, Bogazici University in Istanbul, Turkey), and special Simon's Rock programs (fieldwork in geography in China and in politics and culture in Ghana). The result is something very different from the standard tour of famous sites. Students have recently taken intensive math instruction at Central European University in Budapest, Hungary; helped build a school in a remote village in northern Thailand; and served as apprentices to dancers, drummers, mask carvers, and batik artists in Bali. Students can also take advantage of Bard's study-abroad and international programs, including special arrangements with universities in Germany, Russia, and South Africa and intensive language immersion programs in China, France, Germany, Italy, Japan, Morocco, Mexico, and Russia. Programs can last for a semester, a full academic year, or shorter periods during the breaks.

Academic Facilities

The Fisher Science and Academic Center houses the College's biology, chemistry, ecology, and physics laboratories; research labs for faculty members and students; classrooms and tutorial rooms; a sixty-seat lecture center; and faculty offices. The Daniel Arts Center, which opened in the fall of 2004, incorporates a 350-seat theater and concert hall, a black box theater, a dance studio, and rehearsal facilities; painting, drawing, photography, ceramics, metalworking, printmaking, 3-D, video production, and digital arts studios; exhibition areas; and spaces for large-scale art and set construction. A music hall, a recording studio, and music practice rooms are also available to students in the arts. The campus library houses 68,000 volumes and collections of recordings and periodicals, a listening room, and a language laboratory. Simon's Rock students also have access to the Bard College library. An interlibrary loan system provides access to other college and university collections. The Kilpatrick Athletic Center includes squash courts, a basketball court, an elevated track, a swimming pool, and a full-service fitness center.

Costs

For 2009–10, tuition and fees were $40,170, and room and board were $10,960. For first-year students, there is also an orientation fee.

Financial Aid

Simon's Rock is committed to making an early college education available to a diverse group of highly motivated, academically qualified students. U.S. citizens and permanent residents are eligible to apply for federal and state financial assistance programs as well as institutional scholarships and grants. International students are eligible to receive Simon's Rock scholarships and grants. Approximately 80 percent of students receive some form of financial aid.

Applicants wishing to be considered for an Acceleration to Excellence Program merit scholarship must submit their applications by February 1.

Faculty

The College has approximately 40 full-time faculty members, most of whom hold either an earned doctorate or an equivalent terminal degree in their field. Simon's Rock supplements this full-time faculty with visiting scholars, regular adjunct faculty members in music and studio arts, and part-time faculty members in other areas as needed. Faculty members are distinguished not only by their excellence in teaching and advising but also by their sensitivity to the particular developmental needs of the College's younger students.

Student Government

Students at Simon's Rock participate in the decision making and governance of the community through elected and appointed positions on College committees that oversee academic and social life. The campus is characterized by respect for individual rights and a strong sense of community.

Admission Requirements

Simon's Rock seeks students who are smart, independent-minded, self-directed, creative, and passionate about learning. The admission staff recognizes its special responsibility to work closely with prospective students and their parents to ensure that the decision to enter Simon's Rock is the right one. For this reason, a personal interview is required of each applicant. The application also requires an official high school transcript, two letters of recommendation, writing samples, and a parent's statement. Standardized test scores are optional for most applicants; however, international students for whom English is not a first language must submit TOEFL scores.

Application and Information

Candidates should submit their materials by May 31 for fall admission. Applications are reviewed on a rolling basis year-round, and early application is strongly encouraged. Applicants are generally notified as to the Admission Committee's decision within several weeks of the time they complete their applications. The application fee is $50.

To schedule an interview or request further information, students should contact:

Office of Admission
Bard College at Simon's Rock
84 Alford Road
Great Barrington, Massachusetts 01230-2499
Phone: 800-235-7186 (toll-free)
Fax: 413-541-0081
E-mail: admit@simons-rock.edu
Web site: http://www.simons-rock.edu

COLLEGE CLOSE-UPS

BARNARD COLLEGE

NEW YORK, NEW YORK

The College

Barnard College was among the pioneers in the late nineteenth-century crusade to make higher education available to young women. Founded in 1889, it became affiliated with the Columbia University system in 1900 and today serves 2,360 students who come from nearly every state and almost forty countries. It remains a partner of the university, and students at the two schools may cross-register for courses at either institution. Barnard students have access to Columbia University libraries, and graduates receive their degree from the university. Despite this close connection, Barnard College remains a small, independent liberal arts college, devoted solely to the undergraduate education of women. The College maintains its own Board of Trustees, faculty, and administrative staff; its own endowment; an independent admissions process; and sole ownership of its property and physical plant. It offers the intimacy of a small college with all the added advantages of a major university.

The self-contained Barnard campus occupies 4 acres of urban property along Broadway between 116th and 120th streets. Barnard Hall, with its newly renovated Ethel S. LeFrak '41 and Samuel J. LeFrak Gymnasium and Julius S. Held Lecture Hall, stands opposite the main gates of the College, while the south end of the campus contains the Brooks, Reid, Hewitt, and Sulzberger residence halls complex. Additional housing is located nearby, and some options for coed housing with Columbia are available. Students are guaranteed housing for all four years at Barnard. The College is currently building a new state-of-the-art student center called the Nexus, which is scheduled to open winter 2009. The Nexus will house student leadership offices, a cafe, a theater, and lounges.

Location

Barnard is located on the upper west side of Manhattan, in the safe and quiet Morningside Heights neighborhood, directly across from Columbia University. Abounding with cultural, educational, internship, and professional opportunities, New York is Barnard's laboratory.

Majors and Degrees

Students can earn a Bachelor of Arts in the following subjects: Africana studies, American studies, ancient studies, anthropology, architecture, art history, Asian and Middle Eastern cultures, astronomy, biochemistry, biological sciences, chemistry, classics (Greek and Latin), comparative literature, computer science, dance, economics, education, English, environmental biology, environmental science, film studies, foreign area studies, French, German, history, human rights studies, Italian, Jewish studies, mathematics and applied mathematics, medieval and Renaissance studies, music, neuroscience, philosophy, physics, political science, psychology, religion, Russian and Slavic studies, sociology, Spanish and Latin American cultures, statistics, theater, urban studies, and women's studies.

Barnard College also offers double- and joint-degree programs in cooperation with other schools within the Columbia University community. These include a five-year (3-2) program offered in conjunction with the School of International Affairs, in which a student earns both an A.B. degree and a Master in International Affairs (M.I.A.) or a Master of Public Administration (M.P.A). In cooperation with the School of Law, Barnard offers an accelerated program in interdisciplinary legal education, whereby selected students can begin their legal studies after three years of undergraduate course work. Through the School of Engineering and Applied Science, Barnard students can pursue a five-year (3-2) program in all branches of engineering, including aerospace, civil, and electrical engineering, leading to both an A.B. and a B.S. degree. In cooperation with the School of Dentistry, a limited number of students may enter the Columbia University School of Dental and Oral Surgery after three years of undergraduate work at Barnard. Outside the university, a student can earn both an A.B. degree and a Master of Music (M.M.) in a five-year (3-2) program with the Juilliard School. Through an agreement with List College of the Jewish Theological Seminary, students can earn an A.B. degree from Barnard and a bachelor's degree in Hebrew literature.

Academic Programs

Two required courses, First-Year Seminar and First-Year English, set the foundation for a Barnard education with small classes limited to 16 students. General education requirements are organized around nine Ways of Knowing that reflect the breadth and depth of a true liberal arts education while building the skills of analysis, independent thought, and self-expression. The Ways of Knowing offer a flexible structure and a wide array of courses under the following categories: reason and values, social analysis, cultures in comparison, language, laboratory science, quantitative and deductive reasoning, historical studies, literature, and visual and performing arts.

Advanced placement and I.B. credit are available. Barnard operates on a two-semester calendar, with classes beginning in early September. The fall semester ends in mid-December; classes resume for the spring semester in mid-January and end in mid-May.

Off-Campus Programs

As independent affiliates of Columbia University, Barnard students have open access to the courses, libraries, and other facilities of Columbia. With special permission, students may also register for selected classes in Columbia's graduate and professional schools. A program offered in cooperation with the Jewish Theological Seminary, located two blocks north of Barnard, allows qualified students to take courses for credit. In a similar exchange with both the Juilliard School and the nearby Manhattan School of Music, qualified Barnard students may take music lessons in a conservatory setting.

Under the auspices of Reid Hall in Paris, a Barnard-Columbia facility, several semester-long and full-year programs are offered. Students of classics are eligible to study at the Intercollegiate Center for Classical Studies in Rome. Qualified students may also study at Oxford (Somerville College), Cambridge (Newnham College), the University of London (University College, London School of Economics, King's College, or Queen Mary College), or the University of Warwick. Qualified students are also eligible to study in Germany, Italy, Japan, and more than 300 programs in sixty countries worldwide. Students may also participate in exchange programs with Spelman College in Atlanta and Howard University in Washington, D.C.

Barnard's metropolitan location offers its students a variety of work experiences through its extensive program of more than 2,500 internships. More than two thirds of Barnard students participate in internships throughout the academic year and summer; approximately one third of these internship opportunities receive stipends.

Academic Facilities

Milbank Hall, the oldest building on the campus, houses administrative and faculty offices, classrooms, the Arthur Ross Greenhouse, and the Minor Latham Playhouse. Fourteen-story Altschul

Hall, devoted mainly to the sciences, has classrooms, department offices, and modern laboratory equipment.

Wollman Library offers three floors of reading areas and more than 170,000 volumes in open stacks. Students also have access to the 8 million volumes within the Columbia University library system.

Currently under construction, the Nexus, a 70,000-square-foot state-of-the-art facility, will expand and increase the space available for teaching, for learning, for student activities, for dining, and for large lectures and theatrical productions.

Costs

Tuition and fees for 2010–11 are yet to be announced. Room and board costs have not yet been determined.

Financial Aid

Financial aid supplied or administered by Barnard is awarded on demonstrated need as determined by federal regulations and the College's Office of Financial Aid. Barnard gives no merit or athletic scholarships. College aid is supplementary to family resources. Once need has been established, Barnard is committed to covering 100 percent of demonstrated need for U.S. citizens and permanent residents through a combination of grants, loans, and work-study. Approximately 55 percent of the students at Barnard receive some form of financial aid. A limited number of scholarships are available to international citizens.

Barnard College has a need-blind admission policy in which all applications are judged on merit without reference to the applicant's financial circumstances.

Faculty

Barnard College employs 319 teaching faculty members. The student-faculty ratio is 10:1. The faculty includes editors of leading scholarly journals, prize-winning novelists and translators, and frequent winners of awards from respected foundations, corporations, and government agencies. They are actively engaged in research and publication in their respective fields, but they regard teaching as their primary commitment. All students have faculty advisers who assist them in selecting courses and designing individual academic programs.

Student Government

Every Barnard student is a member of the Student Government Association, which sponsors numerous extracurricular activities. These include the College newspaper, the literary magazine, dramatic groups, political and religious organizations, and preprofessional and departmental clubs. Cooperation between Barnard and Columbia groups is common and seamless. Students, faculty members, and administrators serve on tripartite committees and share responsibility for policy recommendations on curriculum, housing, financial aid, orientation, and the library.

Admission Requirements

The Committee on Admissions selects young women of proven academic strength who exhibit the potential for further intellectual growth. Careful consideration is given to candidates' high school records, recommendations, writing skills, standardized test scores, and special abilities and interests. While admission is highly selective, no one criterion determines acceptance. Each applicant is considered in terms of her individual qualities of mind and spirit and her potential for successfully completing her program of study at Barnard.

Candidates for admission to the first-year class must have taken a college-preparatory program at an approved secondary school or have an equivalent level of education. A recommended program comprises 4years of work in English, 3 or more years in mathematics, 3 or more years in a foreign language, 3 or more years in science (with laboratory), and 3 or more years in history. Barnard also requires candidates to submit scores from the SAT Reasoning Test, along with two SAT Subject Tests. Alternatively, students may submit scores from the ACT with writing in place of the SAT and subject tests. Students educated in a non-English-speaking setting or who have studied in English for less than five years should take the TOEFL exam as well. An interview is recommended but not required.

Application and Information

Applicants for first-year admission should apply to Barnard in the fall of their senior year of high school. Applications must be received by January 1 and should be accompanied by a nonrefundable fee of $55. Students are notified of the admission decision in early April. Well-qualified high school seniors who have selected Barnard as their first-choice college may apply under the binding early decision Plan. Early decision applications must be submitted by November 15. Barnard accepts transfer students to the sophomore and junior classes. Transfer applications must be submitted by April 1 for consideration for September enrollment and by November 1 for consideration for January enrollment.

For more information about Barnard College, students should contact:

Jennifer Gill Fondiller
Dean of Admissions
Barnard College
3009 Broadway
New York, New York 10027
Phone: 212-854-2014
Fax: 212-854-6220
E-mail: admissions@barnard.edu
Web site: http://www.barnard.edu

A view of Milbank Hall from McIntosh Plaza at Barnard College.

BARRY UNIVERSITY

MIAMI SHORES, FLORIDA

The University

Barry University is an independent Catholic university. Founded in 1940 by the Dominican Sisters of Adrian, Michigan, the University provides a multicultural student body with a high-quality education; a caring environment; and a religious dimension, which encourages a commitment to community service. Classes are small, so students receive personal attention from distinguished faculty members and advisers. The student-faculty ratio is 14:1.

The palm-tree lined main campus featuring Spanish-style architecture is in Miami Shores. The University also offers adult and continuing education programs at more than twenty-five additional sites from South Miami to Tallahassee. Students come from all compass points, age groups, ethnicities, and faith perspectives, representing nearly all fifty states and close to 120 countries. Of the nearly 9,000 students enrolled, more than 3,000 are traditional undergraduate students and nearly 5,500 are graduate and continuing education students.

Barry offers more than sixty undergraduate majors and more than fifty graduate degree programs in the arts and sciences, business, education, health sciences, human performance and leisure sciences, law, podiatric medicine, and social work. Some are five-year bachelor's-to-master's programs. Students can also gain hands-on professional experience before graduation through internships.

Resident students live in eight air-conditioned residence halls and three apartment buildings. Each room includes cable and high-speed Internet access. All students may keep cars on campus. The University's Department of Commuter Affairs serves as a resource center for commuter students.

Barry holds membership in twenty honor societies and hosts more than sixty student organizations, including the dance club, gospel choir, the Campus Activities Board, and the *Buccaneer* student newspaper, as well as fraternities and sororities. Barry also promotes community service through organizations including Best Buddies, Habitat for Humanity, Alternative Spring Break, and Pals-4-Paws animal rescue.

The 78,000-square-foot R. Kirk Landon Student Union houses the offices of student services and student organizations as well as a bookstore, dining room, snack bar, game room, and more. A fully equipped fitness center features weight and cardio equipment.

The University fields twelve intercollegiate athletic teams that participate in the NCAA Division II and the Sunshine State Conference. The Buccaneers have won seven national championships. Nearly 60 percent of Barry's student-athletes achieve grade point averages above 3.0. Intramural sports include basketball, flag football, soccer, softball, and table tennis.

The University is accredited by the Southern Association of Colleges and Schools to award bachelor's, master's, specialist, and doctoral degrees. Barry also holds a number of accreditations from professional organizations for specific programs.

Location

Barry University is located in sunny Miami Shores, Florida, just 5 miles from the ocean and minutes from the dynamic city of Miami. South Florida is an international business, tourism, and entertainment hub offering a wide range of internship options and a vibrant cultural scene. Highlights include Urban Beach Week, the Calle Ocho street festival, the Miami International Book Fair, and the Art Basel Miami Beach contemporary art festival. The New World Symphony, the Miami International Film Festival, and the Miami City Ballet provide a full season of performances. South Florida also hosts the Miami Dolphins football team, the Miami Heat basketball team, the Florida Marlins baseball team, and the Florida Panthers hockey team. The hospitable climate allows for swimming, sailing, scuba diving, golf, tennis, soccer, and other outdoor activities year-round, and the natural beauty of the Florida Keys, Everglades, and coral reefs are just a day trip away.

Majors and Degrees

Barry University offers the Bachelor of Arts degree in advertising, art (art history, ceramics, graphic design, and painting and/or drawing), broadcast communication, communication studies, English (literature and professional writing), history, international studies, music, philosophy, photography (biomedical/forensic), prelaw, public relations, Spanish (language and literature and translation and interpretation), theater (acting, dance theater, technical theater), and theology.

The Bachelor of Science degree is offered in accounting, athletic training (premedicine and pre–physical therapy specializations and a five-year seamless B.S. to M.S.), biology (clinical, marine, and preprofessional), cardiovascular perfusion, chemistry (biochemistry, environmental chemistry, predental, premedical, prep-harmacy, and pre-veterinary), computer information sciences, computer science, criminology, elementary education (ESOL, autism, gifted, and reading endorsements), exercise science (premedical and pre–physical therapy specializations and a five-year seamless B.S. to M.S.), exceptional student education (ESOL endorsement), finance, international business, management, marketing, mathematical sciences (computational, general, and statistics/actuarial science), physical education (grades K–12), political science, psychology (industrial/organizational), sociology, and sport management (diving industry, golf industry, and five-year seamless B.S. to M.S.). There is also a five-year seamless B.S. to M.S. degree in education, with three specializations: infancy through early childhood (birth–grade 3), early and middle childhood (K–6), and special education (K–12).

The University also offers the Bachelor of Science in Nursing, the Bachelor of Fine Arts (art and photography), the Bachelor of Music (instrumental performance; sacred music; and voice, opera, and musical theater), and the Bachelor of Social Work.

Minor concentrations are available in specific subject areas as well as in the interdisciplinary areas of Africana studies, film studies, journalism, peace studies, social sciences, and women's studies.

Accelerated undergraduate degree programs are offered for working adults through Barry's evening and weekend programs.

Academic Programs

The University operates on a semester plan. The first semester extends from the end of August to mid-December, and the second semester extends from mid-January to early May. Two 6-week sessions are offered during the summer. Students must maintain a minimum cumulative grade point average of 2.0 (or C) and earn a minimum of 120 credits for a degree. Of these 120 credits, 9 must be in philosophy and theology, 9 in communication—oral and written, 9 in humanities and arts, 9 in physical or natural sciences and mathematics, and 9 in social and behavioral sciences. The traditional full-time academic load is 12 to 18 credits each semester and 6 credits each summer term. Candidates for degree programs may elect a major and area of specialization and must satisfy all requirements of the program that they choose to follow, including all professional preparation requirements. Internships are required for many majors.

An ELS Language Centers program is available to international students needing to increase language proficiency. The Center for Advanced Learning offers a program designed to assist students with learning disabilities who have the intellectual potential and motivation to complete a four-year degree.

The Honors Program offers an active, interdisciplinary honors curriculum designed to add breadth and depth to the educational experience.

Off-Campus Programs

Barry University offers summer programs abroad in places such as Europe and China. Barry is also a member of the College Consortium for International Studies, enabling students to participate in programs offered by member colleges and universities in more than thirty countries. Barry University students may enroll in Air Force ROTC courses through cross-registration at a nearby university.

Academic Facilities

At Barry, students find the high-quality resources they need to support their education. Campus facilities include the Monsignor William Barry Library, an extensive library network, photography and digital imaging labs, a human performance lab, an athletic training room, a biomechanics lab, a full-service digital television production studio, an academic computing center, multimedia business classrooms, art studios, a performing arts center, a nursing lab and resource center, and several other labs dedicated to Barry's health, science, and education programs.

Costs

For 2009–10, tuition for full-time undergraduate students for the academic year was $26,400. Student services fees are included in tuition. Room and board costs averaged $9000, based on a double-occupancy room. Expenses such as books, supplies, laboratory or other special fees, and transportation are not included in these costs.

Financial Aid

Close to 90 percent of all undergraduate students at Barry University receive some form of financial aid. Barry offers an excellent scholarship program, awarding aid each year to students who have demonstrated academic success and promise. These scholarships may be renewed for up to four years as long as the student meets the renewal criteria. Barry need-based grants and athletic scholarships are also available. Barry also participates in the full array of federal and state of Florida financial aid programs.

To be considered for financial assistance, applicants must submit the Free Application for Federal Student Aid (FAFSA). Additional information may be obtained by calling the Office of Financial Aid at 305-899-3673 or 800-695-2279 (toll-free) or by e-mail at finaid@mail.barry.edu.

Faculty

Faculty members are easily accessible to students and are committed to providing individualized attention. More than 80 percent of faculty members hold a Ph.D. or terminal degree in their field of study. The student-faculty ratio is 14:1.

Student Government

The Student Government Association serves as a liaison between the student body and the administration and faculty. All undergraduate students are members of the association, which is governed by an Executive Board comprising 4 members, and the Senate, which consists of 7 elected representatives. Unless otherwise specified, Senate meetings are open, and students are invited and encouraged to attend the weekly sessions.

Admission Requirements

In reviewing the credentials of students seeking admission, Barry University considers an applicant's composite efforts. Candidates must present the following materials: the completed application form, official high school or college transcripts, and the results of the SAT or ACT.

Application and Information

The University reviews applications as they are completed. Students are advised of their acceptance once the admissions staff has reviewed all required documents. Students may apply any time after completion of their junior year in high school. It is advisable to apply early. The student's completed application form and supporting credentials should be sent to the Office of Admissions. Students may also apply online at http://www.barry.edu/mybarry.

Ms. Magda Castineyra
Director of Undergraduate Admissions
Barry University
Division of Enrollment Services
11300 Northeast Second Avenue
Miami Shores, Florida 33161-6695
Phone: 305-899-3100
800-695-2279 (toll-free)
Fax: 305-899-2971
E-mail: admissions@mail.barry.edu
Web site: http://www.barry.edu

Barry's palm-tree lined main campus offers an outstanding environment for quiet reflection and study.

BARTON COLLEGE

WILSON, NORTH CAROLINA

The College

Founded in 1902 as the first degree-granting institution in eastern North Carolina, Barton College opened its doors to 107 students with one building on 5 acres of campus. Today, Barton welcomes approximately 1,200 students from twenty-four states and nine countries to a campus of twenty-six buildings on 65 acres.

The College offers several avenues of assistance for students, especially during the freshman year, including an innovative freshman advising program designed to assist students in making the transition from home and high school to college and residence hall life. All freshmen meet with their adviser three times a week in a classroom seminar setting. Outside the classroom experience, the First-Year Seminar program also offers exposure to a variety of cultural and social events, including concerts, lectures, art exhibits, theater productions, and sports events. Inside the classroom, Barton's student-centered core curriculum enhances academic success and provides students with an outstanding foundation from which the total liberal arts experience is achieved.

Barton's Student Affairs Program includes residence life programs, special activities, fellowship programs, and counseling services that provide for the students' cultural, social, spiritual, and emotional development. In addition, Barton has fifty clubs and organizations in which students can be involved, including academic organizations, specialty clubs, fraternities, and sororities. Another vital component of student life is the Career Services Center. The center provides a vigorous on-campus recruiting program that brings approximately 100 recruiters to Barton's campus annually, representing corporations, government, and educational areas. In addition, several hundred other employers seek to hire Barton students each year. Barton's graduates rank exceptionally well in obtaining employment in their chosen field of study, and their salaries are competitive with those of students from other North Carolina colleges and universities.

On-campus housing is provided in five residence halls: East Campus Suites, Hilley, Hackney, Waters, and Wenger. All five facilities feature cable television and Internet access in each room. East Campus Suites is Barton's newest residence hall for juniors and seniors and offers additional amenities and more independence.

Offering a strong, competitive sports program, Barton College's Bulldogs compete in the NCAA Division II and the Conference Carolinas. The intercollegiate sports program includes women's basketball, cross-country, fast-pitch softball, soccer, tennis, and volleyball; and men's baseball, basketball, cross-country, golf, soccer, and tennis. In 2007, the Barton College men's basketball team won the NCAA Division II National Championship. Also, in recent years, Barton has won the Joby Hawn Award multiple times, recognizing the College as having the best overall athletics program within the Conference Carolinas. A wide variety of intramural sports are also offered to the entire campus community. All students and especially those involved in Barton's intramural, physical education, and athletic programs benefit from the Kennedy Recreation and Intramural Center that features an indoor swimming pool, walking/jogging areas, an auxiliary gym, and a weight/fitness room. Barton also has a twelve-court tennis complex to add to its outstanding facilities package.

The 30-acre Barton College Athletic Complex includes the award-winning Nixon Baseball Field, the Jeffries Softball Field, and a newly lighted soccer field, in addition to several practice fields and the Scott Davis Field House.

Location

Wilson is in the coastal plain region of eastern North Carolina. The city provides an excellent home for the College and is within easy driving distance of several metropolitan areas and scenic attractions. The state capital of Raleigh is a 35-minute drive to the west; to the north, Richmond, Virginia, is 2 hours away and Washington, D.C., is 4 hours away. The beautiful Atlantic coast of North Carolina is 100 miles from the campus, and the scenic Blue Ridge Mountains are easily accessible. Located on Interstate 95, Wilson is also accessible by U.S. Routes 264, 117, and 301 and North Carolina Routes 42 and 58. Wilson is 45 minutes from Raleigh/Durham International Airport. Amtrak has daily service with one northbound and one southbound departure.

The College's historic neighborhood is just a few minutes from busy downtown Wilson. Banks, theaters, shopping centers, and restaurants are close by. Many of Wilson's arts and cultural events take place on the College campus. The Wilson community (approx. population 50,000) enjoys a mild climate that has an average annual temperature of 65 degrees.

Majors and Degrees

Barton College offers six baccalaureate degrees: Bachelor of Arts, Bachelor of Science, Bachelor of Fine Arts, Bachelor of Nursing, Bachelor of Social Work, and Bachelor of Liberal Studies. These degrees are administered by five schools.

The School of Arts and Sciences offers programs in art education (K–12), art and design (with concentrations in ceramics, graphic design, painting, and photography), athletic training, biology, (preprofessional programs in dentistry, medical technology, medicine, physical therapy, and veterinary medicine), chemistry (preprofessional program in pharmacy), English*, environmental science, fitness management, history, mass communications (concentrations include audio recording technology, broadcast/video production, print and electronic journalism), mathematics (preprofessional program in engineering), physical education (with teacher licensure), political science (concentrations include business and prelaw), psychology, religion and philosophy, social studies (with teacher licensure), Spanish*, sport management, and theater (concentrations include design, management, and performance).

The School of Behavioral Sciences offers programs in criminology and criminal justice, gerontology, and social work.

The School of Business offers programs in accounting, business management, and management of human resources.

The School of Education offers programs in education of the deaf and hard of hearing (K–12), elementary education (K–6), middle school education (6–9), and special education: general curriculum (K–6).

The School of Nursing offers a program in nursing.

*Programs indicated with an asterisk (*) are available with or without a teacher licensure program.

Minors can be earned in accounting, American studies, art and design, biology, business administration, chemistry, communications, computer information systems, criminal justice and criminology, economics, English, finance, geography, gerontology, history, international business, management, mathematics, physical education, political science, psychology, religion and philosophy, Spanish, strength and conditioning, theater, and writing.

Academic Programs

Barton College offers a strong liberal arts tradition, and students follow a core curriculum during their freshman and sophomore years. Through a carefully guided advising program they declare a major area of study at the end of their freshman year or at the beginning of their sophomore year. At that point, they begin an intense and challenging program of study in their chosen field while completing general college requirements.

Expanded travel opportunities and concentrated study are enhanced by Barton's 4-1-4 semester system featuring the January Term.

Barton College's athletic training education, nursing, education, and social work programs are nationally accredited programs. The School of Business majors continue to be popular areas of study. Barton is one of the few colleges on the East Coast to offer a program for the education of the deaf and the hard of hearing. Also unique is the audio recording technology program, which features a 32-track digital recording studio. The School of Behavioral Sciences offers a social work degree program, a gerontology major, and a criminology and criminal justice major with law enforcement certification available to students choosing that track.

Off-Campus Programs

Each year students participate in faculty-led trips to different areas of the world. Students recognize this travel as an excellent opportunity to enrich their college experience. Depending on the nature and destination of the travel, students may obtain college credit for their participation. Barton also has exchange agreements with colleges in Europe and Asia for extended overseas study offered in conjunction with a global focus emphasis.

Academic Facilities

Barton College has a fiber-optic underground network that includes an infrastructure of data, voice, and video wiring across campus. The Willis N. Hackney Library is open 87.5 hours per week to serve the College community. The library's offerings include over 169,000 volumes, more than 22,000 electronic books, and a substantial collection of non-print materials. It subscribes to approximately 390 periodicals and newspapers in print and microform format and provides full-text access to over 13,000 periodicals in online databases, which are accessible to Barton users both on and off campus. The curriculum lab, located on the second floor of Hackney Library, includes copies of textbooks and other resource materials used in the North Carolina public schools. Hackney Library is also a depository for selected U.S. government documents and offers Internet access to a wide variety of resources. The library has an automated cataloging system that is accessible via the Internet. Computers for research and other uses are available at the library to both the Barton community and the public. A wireless computer network and loaner wireless laptops are also available to Barton students.

The newest teaching facility is the Lauren Kennedy and Alan Campbell Theatre, which opened in 2009. This innovative black box theater provides a flexible and adaptable space for teaching and performance.

Located on the first floor of J. W. Hines Hall are two computer labs for classes and individual student use. Computer labs are also available for student use in the Nixon Nursing Building, the Belk Education Building, Hamlin Student Center, and Moye Science Hall. Belk Education Building houses the Merck Science and Mathematics Instructional Lab. The Sam and Marjorie Ragan Writing Center supplements Barton's commitment to language and writing as vital components of the liberal arts curriculum.

WEDT-TV, a local cable television station operated by Barton College and staffed by Barton students, is located in the Roma Hackney Music Building. The TV studio provides equipment and facilities for study and use in video and audio production. The Hackney Music Building also houses classrooms, the College's library for recordings and musical scores, and the Sara Lynn Kennedy Recording Studio. Moye Science Hall provides classrooms, laboratories, a greenhouse, and research-related study areas for students. The Nixon Nursing Building houses classrooms and a laboratory for the nursing program, as well as a multimedia center with a projection system used for a broad range of lecture and teaching purposes. Case Art Building provides classrooms, class studios, and two art galleries for Barton's permanent art collection and visiting exhibits. The art building also houses computer graphics, digital imaging, and darkroom labs.

Costs

Expenses for the 2009–10 year included tuition, $19,100; room, $3230; board plan, $3782; and combined fees, $1548. These totaled $27,660 for the year. The estimated cost of books per semester is $600. Rates for East Campus Suites are not listed because of limited availability; this facility is reserved for juniors and seniors.

Financial Aid

The objective of the financial aid program at Barton College is to provide financial assistance to qualified students who would not otherwise be able to begin or continue their college education. Financial aid is awarded on the basis of need. (Financial need exists when the total cost of education exceeds the amount of money a student and family can reasonably make available from income and assets.) Barton College requires that all applicants for financial aid complete the Free Application for Federal Student Aid (FAFSA) as a means of determining financial need. Approximately 90 percent of Barton students receive financial aid. Aid comes from federal, state, and institutional resources and may be awarded as scholarships, grants, loans, or work-study. In addition, many students apply for part-time jobs on campus or in the community.

Students are encouraged to apply early for financial aid and should have their completed application in the Financial Aid Office by June 1 in order to ensure receipt of awards by the beginning of the fall semester. Every effort is made to process completed applications received after this date; however, earlier applications receive top priority in the awards process.

Faculty

Faculty members at Barton College recognize the importance of personalized attention for the students' learning experience. Because of the 11:1 student-faculty ratio, professors at Barton are able to teach small classes and have the opportunity to meet and to get to know their students as individuals. Faculty members make every effort to be accessible to students between classes and during regularly scheduled office hours. Professors at Barton are committed to the success of their students.

Student Government

The Student Government Association (SGA) of Barton College provides students with opportunities to express themselves on issues of concern. Student government also provides a setting for studying the democratic process. The officers of the SGA are elected by the members of the student body, and the president of the SGA serves as an ex officio member of the College Board of Trustees.

Admission Requirements

To be considered for admission to Barton College, a student must have a high school diploma or its equivalent with a minimum total of 13 college-preparatory units. The following courses are recommended: English, 4 units; mathematics, 3 or more units (algebra I, geometry, and algebra II are required); natural sciences, 2 or more units (one lab science is required); social sciences, 3 or more units; and foreign language, 2 or more units (encouraged, but not required). A student applying for admission must also take the SAT or ACT and achieve a score that, when considered along with the high school record, predicts probable success in college. Students interested in transferring to Barton College should contact the Office of Admissions for requirements.

Application and Information

To apply for admission to the College, a student must submit a completed application, a nonrefundable $25 application fee ($50 for international students), and an official transcript of high school credits. A copy of SAT or ACT scores should be sent to the Office of Admissions by the testing agency. International applicants whose native language is not English must also submit the results of the Test of English as a Foreign Language (TOEFL). Students are encouraged to apply early and are usually notified of a decision within two weeks of the admission office's receipt of the completed application and information.

For further information, students may contact:

Office of Admissions
Barton College
Box 5000
Wilson, North Carolina 27893-7000
Phone: 252-399-6317
800-345-4973 (toll-free)
Fax: 252-399-6572
E-mail: enroll@barton.edu
Web site: http://www.barton.edu

BASTYR UNIVERSITY

KENMORE, WASHINGTON

The University

An undergraduate education at Bastyr University is the first step on a path leading to a richly rewarding future in the dynamic field of science-based natural health. Bastyr's unparalleled programs are based on a mind-body-spirit approach to wellness, with a challenging curriculum that prepares students to further their goals in scientific, medical, and wellness-related fields. Expertise in natural and holistic healing is increasingly in demand, so graduates with degrees in the natural health sciences fulfill an important role in the marketplace.

Bastyr University is a world-renowned institution of natural health arts and sciences, with a reputation as a leader and innovator in the field. Founded as a naturopathic medical college in 1978, Bastyr has since expanded its offerings to become a multidisciplinary university with a wide range of graduate and undergraduate educational opportunities. The foundation of Bastyr University's entire curriculum rests on the integration of modern science with traditional healing methods.

As a small independent university, Bastyr offers students a strong sense of community with abundant academic and personal support. Undergraduate students enjoy a collegial relationship with graduate students as well as with faculty and staff members.

Bastyr undergraduate students are goal-oriented individuals who bring a passionate interest and intense focus to their areas of study. They thrive on diversity and individual expression, and they continually seek out opportunities to grow both intellectually and personally.

As part of its mission to improve the well-being of the human community, Bastyr University conducts research studies at its research institute and delivers premier care at its natural health care clinic. The Bastyr University Research Institute is devoted to the evaluation of natural medicine practices and the exploration of natural therapies for serious chronic diseases. Participation in research projects is available to a select number of students. The University's teaching clinic in Seattle, Bastyr Center for Natural Health, is the largest natural health clinic in the Northwest and provides the main venue for graduate students' clinical training.

In 1989, Bastyr University became the first naturopathic school to achieve accreditation and is accredited by the Northwest Commission on Colleges and Universities.

Location

The Bastyr University campus is located in Kenmore, Washington, just north of Seattle, in the heart of the picturesque Pacific Northwest. Bastyr's inviting campus environment is a strong attraction for students, who find it uniquely suited to the study of healing practices. Adjacent to the University's 51 acres of fields and gardens are miles of wooded trails winding through the 316-acre St. Edward State Park on the northeast shore of Lake Washington. The park also features a public swimming pool, outdoor volleyball courts, tennis courts, and playfields, which are available to Bastyr students.

Seattle is one of the most attractive cities in the Pacific Northwest and has easy access to mountains, ocean beaches, lakes, and numerous national, state, and city parks. Several ski areas are within an hour's drive, and there are plentiful opportunities for hiking, camping, and other outdoor recreation. The city offers a full range of museums, theaters, fine restaurants, a major opera company, a symphony orchestra, major-league sports, and outdoor activities.

Majors and Degrees

Bastyr University offers several two-year, upper-division programs that lead to Bachelor of Science degrees. Undergraduates may choose majors in exercise science and wellness, health psychology, herbal sciences, nutrition, nutrition and culinary arts, nutrition and exercise science, or a combined B.S./M.S. program in acupuncture and Oriental medicine (AOM) that is designed to meet the requirements for national licensure in acupuncture. Students can also choose a double major.

Academic Programs

In each degree program at Bastyr, students learn to integrate the pursuit of physical health with the mental, spiritual, and environmental factors involved in wellness.

The Bachelor of Science with a major in nutrition provides students with a comprehensive education that merges the science of nutrition with a broader view of wellness, community and the environment. Bastyr's experienced faculty guides students through the physiological, biochemical, socioeconomic, political, and psychological aspects of human nutrition. This B.S. degree program can be combined with the Didactic Program in Dietetics for those interested in becoming registered dietitians (RD). Bastyr University's Didactic Program in Dietetics has been approved by the American Dietetic Association Council on Education.

The new Bachelor of Science with a major in nutrition and culinary arts is one of the nation's first degree programs of its kind, combining the rigorous sciences of human metabolism, nutrition, and food with a full spectrum of culinary skill development. With a whole food philosophy at its core, this innovative degree will prepare graduates for enhanced career opportunities in areas that require knowledge of both nutrition and the culinary arts.

The new Bachelor of Science with a major in nutrition and exercise science integrates the University's unique whole-food approach with exercise physiology and holistic health and wellness. Students learn about the impact that nutrition and physical activity have on health and wellness. Graduates may develop careers in the areas of community health and fitness or disease prevention and health promotion, including strength and conditioning coaches and personal trainers. This degree also prepares students for graduate work in related health science fields.

The Bachelor of Science with a major in exercise science and wellness combines a rigorous, in-depth study of the body's physiology and mechanics with a focus on nutrition, stress management, and holistic wellness. Graduates are prepared to work in the fitness and wellness industry and possess the educational requirements needed to achieve exercise certification from the American College of Sports Medicine and other professional exercise affiliates.

The Bachelor of Science with a major in health psychology offers a solid foundation in core psychology with a progressive focus on the relationship between health and the body, mind, and spirit. Students learn the tools to improve people's quality of life and to address systemic problems in society and social institutions. Students may enroll in one of two tracks: health psychology, or psychology and human biology (psychology premed).

The Bachelor of Science with a major in herbal sciences provides a thorough and scientifically rigorous introduction to herbal medicine, including plant identification and pharmacology. The program also imparts real-world skills and expertise in the herbal products industry and introduces the student to concepts of disease prevention and health maintenance using medicinal herbs.

Bastyr's acupuncture and Oriental medicine program combines the ancient wisdom and time-honored traditions of Oriental medicine with the rigors of contemporary medical science. The combined B.S./M.S. option in acupuncture and Oriental medicine is generally a 3.5 year program. A certificate program for additional study in Chinese herbal medicine is also offered. The University's acupuncture and Oriental medicine programs are accredited by the Accreditation Commission for Acupuncture and Oriental Medicine (ACAOM) and meet the requirements of the national certification exam.

In addition to its undergraduate programs, the University offers master's programs in nutrition and in acupuncture as well as doctoral programs in naturopathic medicine and in acupuncture and Oriental medicine.

Academic Facilities

The University's 186,000-square-foot facility houses a wealth of resources dedicated to students, including a comprehensive bookstore, numerous scientific laboratories, a whole-food nutrition kitchen, research facilities, a gourmet vegetarian cafeteria, dormitory space, and wireless Internet access and computer labs.

The University also maintains a medical library with extensive resources for conventional and natural medicine. These include more than 19,000 volumes; 250 journal subscriptions; special collections in the areas of nutrition, herbal sciences, psychology, and exercise science; and access to many health and natural medicine databases. Students at Bastyr University are also eligible to use the Health Sciences Library at the University of Washington.

Costs

Tuition for the 2009–10 academic year was $505 per credit for 1 to 11.5 credits and $6050 per quarter for 12–16 credits; the cost for each additional credit over 16 is $320. The total cost of tuition and fees for a full-time student for the academic year was $19,050 ($23,207 for the combined B.S./M.S. AOM program), depending on the number of credits needed to complete a program. Students can expect to spend approximately $1125 per year on books and supplies ($1625 for the combined B.S./M.S. program).

Bastyr University is constructing a new eco-friendly, LEED-certified student housing village that will be ready for occupancy in summer 2010. The complex has the capacity to house 132 students in twelve individual rooms in each of eleven cottage-style buildings. The three-story cottages will connect to a series of garden paths, courtyards, and outdoor living spaces designed to be energy efficient.

Many students also live in shared housing facilities off campus; the average rent per person ranges from $400 to $900 per month. The Office of Student Affairs maintains listings of available housing, which are also listed on Bastyr's Web site at www.bastyr.edu/housing. The Washington Financial Aid Association estimates that living expenses for nine months, including transportation and personal expenses, average $1405 per month.

Financial Aid

Students are eligible to participate in state and federal financial aid programs, including the Washington State Need Grant, Washington State Education Opportunity Grant, Federal Pell Grant, Federal Supplemental Educational Opportunity Grant (FSEOG), Federal Stafford Student Loan, Federal Perkins Loan, and the Federal Work-Study Program. Applicants seeking financial aid should complete the application process by May 15. Financial aid information is provided by the University on request.

Faculty

Bastyr University students enjoy a 9:1 student-faculty ratio with professors who are approachable and accessible. There are 49 core and 95 adjunct faculty members, many of whom teach in both the undergraduate and graduate programs. More than 80 percent hold advanced or doctoral degrees. All faculty members are involved in teaching and are dedicated to providing students with programs of the highest quality.

Student Government

Students have a variety of opportunities for contributing to the operation of the Bastyr community. The Student Council makes decisions about social activities, school policies, and budget items affecting students. Each class and program is represented on the council. Students also serve on the Curriculum Review, Library, and Resident Selection committees; the Appeals Board; and ad hoc committees.

Admission Requirements

Admission is based on academic achievement, personal and social development, and demonstrated humanistic qualities. Credentials to be submitted include all official transcripts, a completed application form, and a $60 application fee. The minimum prerequisite for the bachelor's programs is two years of college-level general education (90 quarter or 60 semester credits), including those distribution and course requirements described below. Students must take the following distribution of general education courses, which are not counted toward any other requirements: arts and humanities, 15 quarter credits; social sciences, 15 quarter credits; and natural sciences and mathematics, 12 quarter credits. In addition, specific required courses include 9 quarter credits of English composition and/or literature, 4 quarter credits of intermediate algebra, 8 quarter credits of general chemistry (science-major level, with lab), 4 quarter credits of general biology (with lab), 3 quarter credits of general psychology, and 3 quarter credits of public speaking. Nutrition majors are required to have taken 5 quarter credits of introductory nutrition. Herbal sciences majors are required to have 3 quarter credits of botany. A minimum 2.25 overall GPA and a C or better in all basic proficiency and science requirement courses are needed.

Application and Information

Applications should be submitted to the University by March 15 for priority consideration for fall admission. Late applications are considered if space is available. Application may be made by submitting the Bastyr University undergraduate application with a $60 nonrefundable fee and all official transcripts. Online applications are also available and can be accessed at http://www.bastyr.edu/admissions.

Prospective students are encouraged to visit the campus or attend recruiting events in their region. For further information, students should contact:

Admissions Office
Bastyr University
14500 Juanita Drive NE
Kenmore, Washington 98028
Phone: 425-602-3330
E-mail: admissions@bastyr.edu
Web site: http://www.bastyr.edu/sub/adtrack.asp?adid=pe01

Students on the Bastyr Kenmore campus.

BAY STATE COLLEGE

BOSTON, MASSACHUSETTS

The College

Founded in 1946, Bay State College is a private, independent coeducational institution located in Boston's historic Back Bay. Since its founding, Bay State College has been preparing graduates for outstanding careers and continued education.

The College primarily offers associate degrees and has expanded into bachelor's degree offerings. The educational experience offered through the variety of associate and bachelor's degree programs prepares students to excel in the career of their choice. Personalized attention is the cornerstone of a Bay State College education. Through the transformative power of its core values of quality, respect, and support, Bay State College has been able to assist students with setting and achieving goals that prepare them for careers and continued education. In fact, with its First-Year Experience, a 1-credit course all students must complete, Bay State College students are exposed to the concept of "action planning." The Bay State College action plan is designed to help students identify their goals and set about a course of action to achieve those goals. Students review their action plan each semester with their academic adviser and evaluate how they are progressing on their plan. This is just one method Bay State College graduates apply to their lives beyond college. The ability to identify, set, and achieve goals is a trait all people aspire to master.

Recognizing that one of the most important aspects of college is life outside the classroom, the Office of Student Affairs seeks to provide services to Bay State College students from orientation through graduation and beyond. There are many clubs and organizations on campus, such as the Criminal Justice Society, the Early Childhood Education Club, the Student Government Association, and the Entertainment Management Association. Bay State College students enjoy the opportunity to create clubs and organizations that meet their interests. Special events throughout the year include a fashion show and a host of events produced by the Entertainment Management Association. Students also enjoy professional sports teams such as the Boston Celtics and the Boston Red Sox.

To support the overall wellness of the student body, Bay State has partnered with the Body Evolver Fitness Club, where students can take advantage of a wide variety of fitness equipment and classes at a discounted rate.

One of the unique aspects of living at Bay State College is the residence halls. With their location in the historic Back Bay, the buildings are original Victorian town houses and brownstones. Each building has its own character and charm, making living on campus a distinctive experience. Each building has a computer lab with free Internet access, coin-operated laundry, vending machines, a house phone with free local calling, and a social lounge that includes cable television and a microwave oven. Each student room has basic cable service and access to a wireless Internet network.

The Career Services office offers lifetime career assistance to both current students and alumni, continuing to provide assistance and support to them throughout their careers, with career-management counseling, workshops, career panels, guest speakers, resume and cover letter reviews, interview preparation, and job listings.

Bay State College is accredited by the New England Association of Schools and Colleges; is authorized to award the Associate in Science, Associate in Applied Science, and three Bachelor of Science degrees by the commonwealth of Massachusetts; and is a member of several professional educational associations. The College's medical assisting program is accredited by the Accrediting Bureau of Health Education Schools (ABHES). The physical therapist assistant studies program is accredited by the Commission on Accreditation in Physical Therapy Education (CAPTE) of the American Physical Therapy Association (APTA).

Location

Located in the historic city of Boston, Massachusetts, and surrounded by dozens of colleges and universities, Bay State College is an ideal setting in which to pursue a college degree. Tree-lined streets around the school are mirrored in the skyscrapers of the Back Bay. The College is located within walking distance of several major-league sports franchises, concert halls, museums, the Freedom Trail, Boston Symphony Hall, the Boston Public Library, and the Boston Public Garden. World-class shopping and major cultural and sporting events help make college life an experience that students will always remember. The College is accessible by the MBTA, commuter rail, and bus and is near Boston Logan International Airport.

Majors and Degrees

Bay State College is continually reviewing, enhancing, and adding new programs to help graduates remain industry-current in their respective fields.

Bachelor's degrees are offered in entertainment management, fashion merchandising, and management.

Associate degrees are offered in business administration, criminal justice, early childhood education, entertainment management (with a concentration in recording arts production), fashion design, fashion merchandising, health studies, medical assisting, physical therapist assistant studies, retail business management, and travel and hospitality management.

Academic Programs

Bay State College operates on a semester calendar. The fall semester runs from early September to late December. The spring semester runs from late January to mid-May. A satellite campus is located in Middleborough, Massachusetts.

Bay State College also offers courses to working adults in its Continuing and Professional Education Division. The courses, offered in eight-week sessions, allow more flexibility for students who must balance work and family commitments while pursuing their education.

Off-Campus Programs

The internship program, available in all major areas of study, provides students with practical field experience, enabling them to hone their skills and gain insight into the various technologies employed in their respective fields. Fieldwork is a requirement for many majors and is a great opportunity for students to build resumes, apply what they have learned in the classroom, and gain a competitive advantage in the job market.

Students from Bay State College are among the 250 students participating in the Walt Disney World College Program. During their stay at Walt Disney World, students receive on-the-job training and classroom experience. This is just one of the many internship possibilities for students each year at Bay State College.

Academic Facilities

The library has a combined book collection of approximately 5,300 books. In addition, Bay State College has 100 periodicals and 200 audiovisual titles. The College's sixty computers have access to the Internet and several databases for magazine and journal articles, including ProQuest Academic, LexisNexis Academic, JSTOR, Infotrac, Newsbank, EBSCO, the Internet Public Library, and the Library of Congress Research Tools. The library also participates in an interlibrary-loan program with the Boston Regional Library System.

Costs

Tuition for 2009–10 for full-time students was $19,875 per year; for the physical therapist assistant studies program full-time tuition in 2008–09 was $20,500 per year, plus a $475 lab fee. Room and board for 2009–10 were $11,800 per year; application fee, $40; student services fee, $375; and student activity fee, $50. The cost of books and additional fees varies by major. A residence hall security deposit of $200 and a technology fee of $250 are required of all resident students.

Financial Aid

Bay State College offers the following financial aid programs to qualified students: Bay State College grant, which ranges from $500 to $4000; Federal Pell Grant; MASSGrant/State Scholarship; Federal Supplemental Educational Opportunity Grant; Massachusetts No Interest Loan; Federal Perkins Loan; and Federal Direct Stafford/Ford Loan. The College also offers numerous part-time employment and work-study opportunities during the academic year.

Faculty

There are 41 faculty members, with the majority holding advanced degrees and several holding doctoral degrees. The student-faculty ratio is 15:1.

Student Government

The Student Association serves as the voice of the Bay State College student body. It consists of a group of elected student representatives from the various academic programs. Roles and responsibilities of Student Association members include providing input on College policies and procedures, assuming leadership roles on campus, acting as a voice of the student body, and planning activities and events. Elections are held every fall, and all students are encouraged to vote. The group comprises representatives from each College department, club, and organization, and membership spans all four class years.

Admission Requirements

An applicant to Bay State College must be a high school graduate, a current high school student working toward graduation, or a recipient of a GED certificate. The Office of Admissions recommends that applicants to the associate degree programs have a minimum 2.0 GPA on a 4.0 scale; if available, applicants may submit SAT or ACT scores. Applicants must receive the recommendation of a Bay State College admissions officer. Applicants to the bachelor's degree programs must have a minimum 2.3 GPA on a 4.0 scale and must also submit SAT or ACT scores. A personal interview is highly recommended for all students, and parents are encouraged to attend. Students are responsible for arranging for their official high school transcripts, test scores, and letters of recommendation to be submitted to Bay State College. International applicants must also submit high school transcripts translated into English with an explanation of the grading system, a TOEFL score of at least 500 on the paper-based exam or 173 on the computer-based exam if English is not the native language, and financial documentation. The physical therapist assistant studies program and Evening Division have different or additional admission requirements. For more information about these programs, students should visit the Web site at http://www.baystate.edu.

The Bay State College Admissions Office notifies applicants of a decision within three weeks of receipt of the transcript and other required documents. When a student is accepted to Bay State College, there is a $100 nonrefundable tuition deposit required to ensure a place in the class, which is credited toward the tuition fee. Deposits are due within thirty days of acceptance. Once a student is accepted, a Bay State College representative creates a personalized financial plan that provides payment options for a Bay State College education.

Application and Information

Applications are accepted on a rolling basis. A $40 application fee is due with the application. The fall tuition payment due date is July 1; the spring tuition payment due date is December 1.

Applications should be submitted to:

Admissions Office
Bay State College
122 Commonwealth Avenue
Boston, Massachusetts 02116
Phone: 800-81-LEARN (toll-free)
Fax: 617-536-1735
E-mail: admissions@baystate.edu
Web site: http://www.baystate.edu

BEACON COLLEGE

LEESBURG, FLORIDA

The College

The mission of Beacon College is to offer academic degree programs exclusively for students with learning disabilities (LD), attention-deficit hyperactivity disorder (ADHD), or gifted LD. Students are not defined by their learning disabilities—they are people with interests, concerns, and wishes about what they want to do during their college years and beyond. Beacon offers a fun, supportive, collegiate atmosphere that facilitates academic success, recognizes personal accomplishments, and fosters lifelong friendships.

Beacon College takes seriously its responsibility to assist students in determining realistic goals, discovering personal abilities and interests, and realizing their potential. Beacon combines educational support services with a student life program that contributes to the cultural, social, and intellectual development of all students. New technologies enable students to learn to manage many problems inherent with learning disabilities. Students receive intensive and proactive academic mentoring, appropriate test accommodations, and classroom instruction in a variety of learning modalities. The College also provides support services outside the classroom through the Writing Center and academic mentoring, field placement opportunities in all majors, an emphasis on small classes and supplemental instruction, an outstanding faculty, and academic advisers who have the education and/or training needed to facilitate the growth of students with learning differences.

Out-of-the-classroom experiences are invaluable in the personal development of well-rounded students. Activities include involvement in global/cultural awareness events, social outings, health and wellness programs, leadership education, and community service. The College hosts a variety of on- and off-campus activities that include outdoor/nature experiences, sporting events, cultural/ethnic festivals, musical and arts entertainment, relationship and leadership building, and health education and fitness programs.

The Beacon Activities Council, along with the support and advisement of the Coordinator of Student Activities, plan, schedule, and carry out college-sponsored cocurricular activities. The activities calendar is available online and updated regularly with descriptions of each event. In addition, the Student Services Office maintains an up-to-date list of all student-run organizations and encourages the initiation of new clubs and organizations.

Residential life plays a key part in student development, offering a supportive living environment that fosters interpersonal skills and positive life experiences. The Director of Student Life and the residential assistants (RAs) are trained professionals who provide guidance, support, and assistance. This unique and rewarding housing system allows students to live in apartment-style facilities and develop independent living skills while attending college. The Beacon Village Apartments are equipped with a full-size kitchen (including a dishwasher, a self-cleaning oven, and a refrigerator), a washer/dryer, basic cable television, Internet access, and ceiling fans throughout. The complex is within walking distance of the education building and all campus buildings. Recreational highlights include a swimming pool, a basketball court, a tennis/volleyball court, and a gazebo area.

Location

Situated in the city of Leesburg, Beacon College is approximately 50 miles northwest of Orlando in central Florida, and the Orlando International Airport is about an hour's drive from campus. Central Florida is one of the most beautiful, versatile, and popular vacation destinations in the state—an area of unmatched natural beauty and old Florida charm, all within minutes of the theme park thrills of nearby Orlando and Tampa and the glorious sands of both coasts. Central Florida is also known for its outdoor activities and wildlife, with more than 550 freshwater lakes, making it an ideal spot for anglers, boaters, water-skiers, bicyclists, hikers, bird watchers, and nature enthusiasts. Leesburg has devoted 15 percent of its land area to parks and recreational activities. Local organizations in Mount Dora, Eustis, and Leesburg sponsor outstanding art and theater productions, festivals, and community events. There are quaint downtown streets with period architecture and recreational opportunities, as well as shopping in numerous discount and factory outlets and several upscale malls.

Majors and Degrees

Beacon College offers the Associate of Arts (A.A.) and Bachelor of Arts (B.A.) degrees in three majors—computer information systems (CIS), human services (HS), and liberal studies (LS).

Academic Programs

The computer information systems program offers students the opportunity to learn about the latest technology used in the marketplace and explore a vast number of career choices. Students can choose one of the two tracks to meet their specific career goals: information systems or Web and digital media. The former provides students with a thorough background of incorporating technology into the corporate world, while the latter gives students a basic understanding of creating professional digital media and Web pages.

A career in human services involves helping people to adapt, change, and cope with physical and social conditions in their environment. The HS program provides a comprehensive knowledge of the theoretical foundations of the social sciences and offers practical experience in the professional fields associated with public and community services. This major field of study focuses on psychological and sociological approaches to understanding the holistic development of individuals, families, and communities. Through field placements, students gain work experience designed to facilitate employment in the human services field or further study in a graduate degree program.

The liberal studies program provides a broad-based liberal arts education for students seeking intellectual and personal change. Through LS, students are exposed to a variety of subjects designed to establish a basis for effective lifelong learning and attainment of personal goals. Students learn communication and critical-thinking skills and how to interpret human experience through studies of aesthetic, historical, ethical, and cultural foundations. Students help design their degree by choosing courses in areas of emphasis and minors and by completing internship hours directed toward employment or continuing education.

Students must complete at least 60 credit hours to earn an A.A. degree and 120 credit hours to earn a B.A. degree with a minimum cumulative GPA of 2.0. The general education requirement for all students is 36 credit hours: 9 credit hours in English and communication, 6 in computer information systems, 6 in the humanities and fine arts, 6 in mathematics and natural science, 6 in the social/behavioral sciences, and 3 in critical thinking.

The HS and LS programs require a minimum number of credit hours in the major: 18 credit hours for the associate degree and 36 credit hours for the bachelor's degree. The CIS major requires 21 credit hours in a CIS sequence for the A.A. degree or 36 credit hours for the B.A degree. Students may also choose a minor concentration, which requires at least 18 credit hours, in areas of business management, computer information systems, education, English/literature, history, psychology, and Web and digital media.

Off-Campus Programs

During the summer, Beacon College offers an international cultural studies program, building upon the current requisite global-learning perspective and affording each student a life-changing experience. Programs have included such countries as Australia,

England, France, Germany, Greece, Ireland, Italy, New Zealand, Russia, Spain, Sweden, and Switzerland.

Students gain valuable work experience that focuses on defining career goals through internships in the community. In the Field Placement Program, students develop a transitional plan while taking courses in the psychology and the culture of the workplace.

Academic Facilities

The Beacon College Learning Resource Center (LRC) provides access to the library, the Writing Center, and academic mentoring offices. Dedicated to providing flexible, diverse, and user-centered information services and technology, the Beacon College Library is the focal point of academic life on campus. The library staff has created an inviting environment open to innovation and focused on continuous improvement in resources and accommodations. The library's collection includes more than 23,000 volumes, 38,000 electronic book titles, 100 periodicals in print, 65 full-text databases, 1,000 audiovisual materials, and more than 600 items in its specialized learning disabilities collection. The collection is curriculum based and supports students and faculty in their research efforts. Supplemental materials can be requested through interlibrary loan or acquired through the College's cooperative agreements with local libraries.

The Writing Center offers assistance and support for every phase of the writing process, helping all students develop their critical-thinking skills through a focus on the reading and writing processes necessary for the successful completion of college-level writing for both the advanced and struggling writer.

The College's computer center is equipped with multimedia technology and networked computer workstations. In addition to word processing, e-mail, and Web access, the computer center provides page scanners, voice-activated dictation software, and computerized reading programs to enhance and support the learning process of all students. Individual workstations ensure ready access to systems technology, including technology that assists students with specific learning disabilities.

Costs

In 2010–11, full-time tuition is $27,810 for the academic year. Room and board total $8150 per academic year (two semesters).

Financial Aid

The Office of Financial Aid makes a variety of scholarships, grants, work opportunities, and loans available to eligible students. Many students qualify for some form of financial aid and are encouraged to apply for aid by completing the Beacon College financial aid application and the Free Application for Federal Student Aid (FAFSA) at http://www.fafsa.ed.gov.

Faculty

The Beacon College faculty is committed to helping students achieve individual success. Faculty members facilitate instruction by designing appropriate learning opportunities that reflect an understanding of different learning styles and a variety of learning differences. Team meetings allow faculty to discuss teaching methods and effective intervention techniques, while assessing student progress. An emphasis on self-awareness and critical thinking focused on strategies for lifelong learning are facilitated by faculty and students working together. A low student-faculty ratio provides the opportunity for individual attention, while fostering the competencies necessary for success. The average class size is 12 students. About 80 percent of full-time faculty members hold terminal master's or doctoral degrees.

Student Government

The Student Government Association is dedicated to improving student life and campus involvement through student-led initiatives.

Admission Requirements

To give each candidate full consideration, the Beacon College admissions committee evaluates applicant files only when they are deemed complete. Applicants must submit the completed application, the nonrefundable $50 application fee, a college essay, a recent educational evaluation, official high school transcripts, and three letters of recommendation. Transfer credits are considered based upon official transcripts from an accredited college/university. Official ACT or SAT scores are not mandatory.

The educational evaluation must include a clear diagnosis of learning disability or ADD/HD, or LD Gifted; Wechsler scales (preferably WAIS-IV), with full-scale, cluster, and subtest scores; and achievement assessments (such as Woodcock Johnson or WIAT), with grade-equivalence reporting in reading, writing, or mathematics. An interview may be required. Though not mandatory, it is highly recommend that all candidates visit the campus to fully evaluate the College's academic and student life.

Beacon College accepts applications from English-speaking nonimmigrant students. All accepted international students are required to purchase an insurance policy before the I-20 is issued. All guidelines and application requirements are outlined in the application packet (available online).

Application and Information

Beacon College accepts students on a rolling basis, but the preferred application deadlines are May 1 and November 1 for the fall and spring semesters, respectively. Candidates who apply after the priority deadline are processed on a space-available basis. Candidates are encouraged to apply after the deadline dates until spaces are filled. A $750 nonrefundable deposit is due upon receipt of enrollment contract and is applied to first semester fees.

Office of Admissions
Beacon College
105 East Main Street
Leesburg, Florida 34748
Phone: 352-638-9731
Fax: 352-787-0796
E-mail: admissions@beaconcollege.edu
Web site: http://www.beaconcollege.edu/

Beacon College students head back to Beacon Village Apartments after class.

BELMONT UNIVERSITY

NASHVILLE, TENNESSEE

The University

Nationally recognized programs thrive on the Belmont University campus, which is located in the heart of the state capital, known both as Music City, U.S.A., and the Athens of the South (for its many educational institutions). Nashville offers big-city advantages with small-town charm.

Belmont's vision is to be a leader among teaching universities, bringing together the best of liberal arts and professional education in a Christian community of learning and service. Central to the fulfillment of that vision are faculty members who have a passion for teaching and the belief that premier teaching is interactive, technology-supported, motivational, creative, and exciting.

With an enrollment of approximately 5,000 students, Belmont is the second-largest of Tennessee's private colleges and universities.

In addition to the twenty-five international countries represented in the student body, Belmont University attracts students from every state in the United States. The culturally diverse institution is committed to listening and learning from everyone. Students of today are helping shape the way students of tomorrow will be educated.

Belmont's beautiful, antebellum campus reflects a long, rich history that dates back to the nineteenth century, when the grounds were Adelicia Acklen's Belle Monte estate. University buildings that were erected over the past 110 years flank the Italianate mansion, which is still used by the campus. On the way to classes that prepare them for the twenty-first century, students enjoy Victorian gardens, statuary, and gazebos that recall a treasured past.

Two prestigious women's schools preceded the comprehensive liberal arts institution: the original Belmont College (1890–1913) and Ward-Belmont (1913–1951). In 1951, the Tennessee Baptist Convention founded the second Belmont College (1951–1991), with an initial coeducational enrollment of 136 students. Soon after celebrating 100 years of education on the same campus, the institution became a university in 1991, culminating a decade of dramatic growth and progress.

In addition to seven baccalaureate degrees, Belmont University offers twelve graduate degrees: the Master of Accountancy, the Master of Arts in Teaching, the Master of Business Administration, the Master of Sport Administration, the Master of English, the Master of Music, the Master of Education, the Master of Science in Nursing, the Master of Science in Occupational Therapy, the Doctor of Occupational Therapy, the Doctor of Pharmacy, and the Doctor of Physical Therapy.

Location

Belmont University occupies a 75-acre campus in southeast Nashville. With a metropolitan area of roughly a million residents, Nashville is a cultural, educational, health-care, commercial, and financial center in the mid-South. Practical educational opportunities, offered through diverse curriculums, provide students with the hands-on experience they need in preparation for a meaningful career. The city's location halfway between the northern and southern boundaries of the United States, with three intersecting interstate highways and an international airport, makes it accessible to students from across the country.

Majors and Degrees

Belmont University is accredited by the Commission on Colleges of the Southern Association of Colleges and Schools to award baccalaureate, master's, and doctoral degrees. Belmont grants seven undergraduate degrees: the Bachelor of Arts, the Bachelor of Business Administration, the Bachelor of Fine Arts, the Bachelor of Music, the Bachelor of Science, the Bachelor of Science in Nursing, and the Bachelor of Social Work. Majors or concentrations are offered in accounting, applied discrete mathematics, art (art education, art history, design communications, and studio art), Asian studies, audio and video production, audio engineering technology, biblical languages, biblical studies, biochemistry and molecular biology, biology, business administration, chemistry, Christian ethics, Christian leadership, classics, communication studies, computer science, early childhood education, economics, engineering physics, English, entertainment industry studies, entrepreneurship, environmental science, European studies, exercise science, finance, French, German, health, history, information systems management, international business, international economics, international politics, journalism, management, marketing, mass communication, mathematics, medical imaging technology, medical physics, medical technology, middle school education, music (church music, commercial music, music composition, music education, music with an outside minor, musical theater, music performance, piano pedagogy, music theory), music business, neuroscience, nursing, organizational and corporate communications, pharmaceutical studies, philosophy, physical education and health, physics, politics and public law, political science, psychology, public relations, religion and the arts, religious studies, science and engineering management, social entrepreneurship, social work, sociology, songwriting, Spanish, theater and drama, video production, and Web programming and development.

Academic Programs

Uniquely positioned to provide the best of liberal arts and professional education, Belmont University offers celebrated professional programs structured to provide an academically well-rounded education. Belmont University operates on a two-semester schedule with classes beginning in late August and ending in early May. Two summer sessions are also offered. The academic program is arranged by school: the College of Arts and Sciences, the College of Business Administration, the Gordon E. Inman College of Health Sciences and Nursing, the College of Visual and Performing Arts, the Mike Curb College of Entertainment and Music Business, and the School of Religion.

In addition to the degrees offered through the schools, Belmont University offers an honors program, which was created to provide an enrichment opportunity for students who have potential for superior academic performance and who seek added challenge and breadth to their studies. Students enrolled in the honors program are led in designing and working through a flexible, individual curriculum and interdisciplinary general education curriculum by a private tutor who is an honors faculty member.

The University's advancements in undergraduate research are credited to a faculty committed to helping students practice their disciplines. The annual Belmont Undergraduate Research Symposium puts Belmont at the forefront of this national movement by providing a public forum for in-depth research at the undergraduate level.

Off-Campus Programs

Belmont University has contracts for dual-degree programs with Auburn University and University of Tennessee, Knoxville. These programs require three years of study at Belmont University followed by approximately two years of study at one of the above institutions. The course of study at Belmont must be mathematics, physics, or chemistry. Following completion of the academic requirements at both institutions, a student is awarded a Bachelor of Science degree from Belmont University and the appropriate degree from the second institution.

Several programs at Belmont have agreements with area organizations to provide students practical training. Nursing students gain clinical experience at all fourteen local area hospitals and other clinical agencies. Education students gain classroom experience in Metro-Davidson County Schools. Music business students gain real-world experience through internships in the Nashville music industry and in Los Angeles and New York City through the Belmont West and East (respectively) programs of study and internships.

Through a wide variety of international study programs on the six populated continents, Belmont offers students the opportunity to broaden and deepen their education while earning credit hours toward their degrees. These programs, which range in duration from two weeks to a year, are available in Australia, the Bahamas, China, Costa Rica, England, France, Germany, Hong Kong, Ireland, Italy, Mexico, New Zealand, Russia, Scotland, South Africa, and Spain.

Academic Facilities

Belmont offers a quiet, secluded environment, and classes are held in nine buildings with the library and other facilities located in proximity to those classrooms.

The Lila D. Bunch Library includes a microcomputer center, multimedia room, and group study rooms. Adjacent to it is the 3,000-square-foot Leu Art Gallery. Located next to the library is the Leu Center for the Visual Arts, featuring state-of-the-art studios with natural lighting and spacious work areas.

The Sam A. Wilson School of Music Building houses classrooms, a resource room, seminar rooms, studio/offices, music practice rooms, a piano lab, and a music technology lab.

The Jack C. Massey Business Center provides classrooms, office space, study lounges, seminar and conference rooms, a copy center, a post office, and a convenience store. A state-of-the-art learning center includes five computer labs. In addition, Massey Business Center houses the 9,000-square-foot Center for Music Business, which provides classrooms, an academic resource center, two state-of-the-art recording studios and control rooms, four isolation booths, a MIDI pre–postproduction room, and an engineering repair shop.

The recently opened Gordon Inman Center for Health Sciences and Nursing houses Belmont's nursing, social work, and occupational therapy programs. Students train in state-of-the-art labs and classrooms that include lift equipment to teach student safety, simulated mannequins that respond to basic stimuli, and apartments to teach social work students how to work with clients with special needs.

Costs

Belmont's tuition and fees are $22,360 per academic year in 2009–10. Room and board in campus residence halls are $8070.

Financial Aid

More than 75 percent of Belmont's students receive some type of financial assistance. The financial aid program at Belmont combines merit-based assistance with need-based assistance to make the University program affordable. Institutional merit awards range from full tuition Presidential Scholarships to performance scholarships. Also included are many levels of academic merit awards. Belmont University also administers traditional state and federal need-based programs, including the Federal Pell Grant, Federal Stafford Student Loan, Federal Perkins Loan, Federal PLUS loan, and Tennessee Student Assistance Grants and Scholarships. Campus employment is available. Parents may arrange monthly tuition payments through an outside vendor. To apply for assistance, the student must complete the Free Application for Federal Student Aid (FAFSA).

Faculty

A highly competent faculty is the paramount attribute of a strong institution of higher education. Belmont University has faculty members who are dedicated to their profession and to the University. Of the more than 200 full-time faculty members, 65 percent hold terminal degrees. Another 30 percent of faculty members have completed formal studies beyond the master's degree.

The influence of the Belmont University faculty is felt beyond the campus. Faculty members are active in church, civic, professional, and academic associations; frequently speak to various groups; and often write for denominational and secular publications. Most faculty members have traveled extensively and many have experienced life in other regions of the United States and abroad.

Student Government

A liaison between the University and student body, the Student Government Association seeks to address educational, social, and spiritual needs of students. As a service organization for the student body, it offers opportunity for campus involvement, acts as the coordinating body for all student organizations, serves as a resource for the campus community, and represents student interests to the faculty and administration.

Admission Requirements

Applicants are considered based on the total picture a student's credentials present. High school students are considered competitive for admission if they present a rigorous course of college-preparatory academic studies. Students should have an above-average academic and cumulative grade point average and rank in the top half of their graduating class. Any college-level work is also expected to be at the above-average level. A strong correlation between high school grades and entrance examination scores is expected. The personal supplement information, a resume of activities, and recommendations are also strongly considered as positive indicators of success at Belmont. Additional requirements, such as portfolios or auditions, are considered in conjunction with the academic credentials for those programs that require them. Each application is considered on an individual basis. No two applicants present the same credentials or the same degree of "fit" with the University. The University desires to work with each student to determine the likelihood for that student to enroll, graduate, and benefit from the Belmont educational experience.

Application and Information

Further information and application materials may be obtained by contacting:

Office of Admissions
Belmont University
1900 Belmont Boulevard
Nashville, Tennessee 37212
Phone: 615-460-6785
800-56ENROLL (toll-free)
Fax: 615-460-5434
E-mail: admissions@belmont.edu
Web site: http://www.belmont.edu

Belmont University students enjoy a beautiful antebellum campus located in thriving metropolitan Nashville.

COLLEGE CLOSE-UPS

BELOIT COLLEGE

BELOIT, WISCONSIN

The College

Beloit College is an independent, national college of liberal arts and sciences that engages the intelligence, imagination, and curiosity of its students. Beloit's focus is on teaching and on the close collaboration that takes place among students and faculty members in small classroom and lab settings. Undergraduates learn to approach the complex problems of the world ethically and thoughtfully in an academic community that values and emphasizes international and interdisciplinary perspectives and the integration of knowledge with experience.

Beloit is Wisconsin's first college, founded in 1846 to serve a frontier society. Today, a geographically diverse population of 1,250 students is drawn to Beloit's residential campus from nearly all North American states and more than forty other countries. Eight percent come from countries outside the United States, 15 percent of U.S. students are non-Caucasian, and a variety of religious orientations and socioeconomic backgrounds are represented on campus. Beloit students are equally diverse in their academic choices. No more than 10 percent of the seniors are represented in any one of more than fifty majors available.

Beloit students are informed and experienced in political and social issues, and they place a premium on individual expression. The range of student activities reflects the spectrum of their interests and involvement. Beloit students serve on College governance committees, establish organizations, manage an annual music festival, and host their own radio and cable TV shows. In a given week, students may have the choice of attending (or organizing) a lecture series, a movie, music performances, a poetry reading, or an environmental debate. Seventy percent of Beloit's students participate in club, intramural, or varsity athletics and use the College's athletic complex adjacent to the residential side of campus. Those who live on campus (and nearly all do) may choose to live in residence halls, on quiet floors or substance-free floors, in one of three fraternity houses or three sorority houses, or in one of the special-interest houses, which include houses that form around students' interests, such as particular languages, gay and lesbian issues, anthropology, the arts, black student issues, faith and spirituality, music, the environment, peace and justice issues, science fiction and fantasy, Latino student issues, and women's issues. Two new town-house complexes have been constructed in the past five years and offer roomy, apartment-style living for juniors and seniors. Meals, served in two dining halls on campus, are offered on a twenty-meal weekly plan and include organic, vegetarian, and vegan meal options.

New students quickly become part of this active and diverse environment through First-Year Initiatives (FYI), an innovative program that places new students in interdisciplinary seminars taught by experienced professors and staff members. These seminars begin the first day students arrive on campus and provide an academic grounding and a social base. They also begin two years of advising by faculty members, which is designed to assist students in their adjustment to Beloit and to bolster campus involvement. FYI leads students into a curriculum that is open and collaborative.

Location

Beloit's 40-acre campus is located on the border between Wisconsin and Illinois, 90 miles northwest of Chicago, 50 miles south of Madison, and 70 miles southwest of Milwaukee, in a small city that Margaret Mead once called "American society in a microcosm." Students may take advantage of the resources of the three major metropolitan areas, and Beloit's hospital, clinics, manufacturers, and various civic and service organizations provide numerous internship, job shadowing, enrichment, and community outreach opportunities. The academic buildings of Beloit College cluster around lawns dotted with ancient North American Indian mounds, while across the campus, newly renovated residence halls encourage interaction among resident students. A 25-acre athletic field and Strong Memorial Stadium are located a few blocks east of the main campus.

Majors and Degrees

Beloit awards Bachelor of Arts and Bachelor of Science degrees in nineteen departments and more than fifty fields of study. In the natural sciences and mathematics division, students may choose majors from the departments of biology, biochemistry, chemistry, environmental studies, geology, mathematics and computer science, and physics. In the social sciences division, students may choose majors from the departments of anthropology, economics and management, education and youth studies, political science and international relations, psychology, and sociology. In the arts and humanities division, majors are offered in the departments of art and art history, classics, English, history, modern languages and literatures, music, philosophy and religious studies, theater arts, and women's and gender studies. Students are also encouraged to create a unique interdisciplinary major. The College offers departmental minors in anthropology, studio art and art history, biology and society, chemistry, computer science, English, geology, history, integrative biology, international economics, management, mathematics, music, philosophy, physics, political economy, political science, and religious studies. Permanent interdisciplinary minors include African studies, American studies, ancient Mediterranean studies, Asian studies, computational visualization and modeling, environmental studies, European studies, health and society, interdisciplinary studies, journalism, Latin American studies, legal studies, medieval studies, museum studies, peace and justice studies, performing arts, Russian studies, and women's and gender studies.

Beloit offers 3-2 cooperative programs for students interested in engineering and environmental management and forestry; preprofessional programs in dentistry, law, and medicine; and a cooperative program that guarantees qualified graduates entry into a master's degree program in nursing. These programs, which have strong advisory and internship components, complement a major in an appropriate discipline. Beloit students may also earn teaching certification.

Academic Programs

Beloit's academic calendar consists of two 14-week semesters with one-week midterm breaks. At the end of the sophomore year, students are required to declare a major and may choose to add a second major, a minor, or teaching certification. Sophomore students work with faculty advisers to define academic and personal goals, including completion of graduation requirements and the declaration of majors, and develop a plan—which may include internships, independent research, or study abroad—for accomplishing them. A structured program called My Academic Plan (MAP) allows students to shape their time at Beloit to ensure they will reach their goals. In addition, Beloit's open curriculum requires two classes from each of the three academic divisions plus an interdisciplinary course, three writing-intensive courses, and significant contact with a culture not one's own. Thirty-one units are required for graduation, each unit representing the equivalent of a course of study involving 4 hours of class time a week per semester.

Off-Campus Programs

Beloit has a century-old tradition of domestic and international off-campus study opportunities, and more than half of new Beloit graduates will have studied and/or conducted research in such a program. Domestic programs include an opportunity to study at the Marine Biological Laboratory at Woods Hole in Massachusetts; a science semester at the Oak Ridge National Laboratory in Knoxville, Tennessee; a semester in the arts, an urban studies program, and a Newberry Library semester in the humanities, all in Chicago; and a Washington Semester at American University in Washington, D.C. Internships, field terms, and summer employment opportunities are arranged through the Office of Field and Career Services. Anthropology field training programs and geology field expeditions take students to domestic and international locations, and additional experiential opportunities exist through Beloit's membership in the Keck Consortium in Geology and the Pew Midstates Science and Mathematics Consortium.

At Beloit College, study abroad is more of an expectation than a luxury. Whether through Beloit's own extensive programs or the Associated Colleges of the Midwest (ACM) and independent programs, Beloit students have studied in more than forty countries worldwide, from Australia to Zimbabwe.

Academic Facilities

Beloit's historic brick and stone buildings coexist with innovative contemporary structures such as the Center for the Sciences, the College's newest academic building, which opened for classes in 2008. The environmentally conceived, 117,000 square-foot center capitalizes on natural light and includes a vegetated roof, high recycled/reused content, water management systems, and other sustainable features. The U.S. Green Building Council (USGBC) has awarded Platinum-level LEED certification to this new facility. Platinum is the highest rating offered by the USGBC and the science center is one of only three buildings in Wisconsin that has received this distinction. While providing a physical space that parallels the quality of Beloit's highly ranked science programs, the Center for the Sciences is also a teaching building; its advanced technology allows students to conduct research on how the building consumes energy. The Center houses student and faculty offices, classrooms and labs, conference rooms, and an atrium. The Logan Museum of Anthropology and the Wright Museum of Art are world-class teaching museums that offer students excellent resources for research and work experience. The Neese Performing Arts Theatre complex features a large thrust stage theater, a black-box theater, a scenic design studio, and a complete costume shop. The World Affairs Center is the hub of language and literature study and includes the College's language lab. Nearly 250 student-accessible computer workstations are located throughout campus, with a combination of wireless and wired network Internet access in academic buildings. Residence halls have a wired Internet connection for every student. Beloit's library collection is in excess of half a million holdings and provides individual and group study areas, computer labs, and extensive listening and viewing areas for the use of audiovisual materials. A 6,000-square-foot center for entrepreneurship in downtown Beloit provides physical space, office resources, and a recording studio where students can put venture plans of their own design into action.

Costs

Tuition for the 2010–11 academic year is $34,808, fees are $230, a double room is $3512, and board (twenty-meal plan) is $3652, for a total comprehensive fee of $42,202. While the cost of books and incidental expenses varies, it totals about $1500.

Financial Aid

Beloit College is committed to making the Beloit experience affordable to all qualified students. The financial aid program recognizes two criteria—scholastic ability and financial need—that may qualify students for awards. During the 2009–10 academic year, about 91 percent of first-year students received financial assistance through grants, loans, or work-study. The College also awards merit scholarships.

In 2009, new students from families with incomes below $50,000 received an average grant of $28,300; qualifying students from families with incomes above $100,000 received an average grant of $14,500. Beloit's attention to providing students high value has won the College recognition in the Princeton Review's guides, the *Fiske Guide to Colleges,* and *U.S. News & World Report* as among the nation's "best buys" in top colleges.

Faculty

The focus of Beloit's faculty is great teaching. Beloit professors are drawn to work in a setting that emphasizes discussion and collaborative learning in small classes. Of the 123 full-time faculty members, 96 percent hold the highest academic degree in their field. All classes are taught by professors. In classrooms, it is easy for students and faculty members to become immersed in their work, since the student-faculty ratio is 11:1 and the average class size is 15 students. All Beloit professors are also academic advisers who are involved in students' academic concerns as well as their adjustment to life at the College. Discussions begun in the classroom are often continued in an informal setting, such as at a basketball game or over dinner at a professor's house.

Student Government

Students at Beloit are actively involved in the governance of the College. The Beloit Student Congress is the College's student government. Its committees (Governance Committee, Publicity Committee, Food Committee, Organization Task Force, and Programming Board) allow the Congress to focus on representing the student body and meeting its goals. In addition to this entirely student-run governing body, students are elected to the College's Academic Senate and serve as voting members of major College committees. Students also sit on all academic search committees.

Admission Requirements

Admission to Beloit is selective. Beloit seeks applicants with special qualities and talents, as well as those from diverse ethnic, geographic, and economic backgrounds. When reviewing applications, the transcript is the most important element. Beloit has no absolute secondary school requirements but recommends a rigorous college-preparatory program. This includes 4 years of English, 4 years of college-preparatory mathematics, 4 years of laboratory science, 4 years of history or social science, and 4 years of a foreign language. Seventh-semester grades may be required. A counselor recommendation is a required part of the application. One teacher recommendation is also required. The essay component of Beloit's application is critical. There is no required topic, so students should write about a topic they believe will represent them well. Either SAT or ACT test scores are required, but they are the least important part of the application. Beloit does not consider the SAT or ACT writing exam for purposes of admission. Interviews are not required for admission but are encouraged. Off-campus alumni interviews can be arranged if a student would like to interview but cannot travel to the campus. Transfer applications are considered for August or January entrance. Applicants must hold at least a B- average at an accredited college or university.

Application and Information

Beloit has modified rolling admissions, so students may apply at any time. For priority consideration, both in admissions and in financial aid, however, students should file their applications by January 15. Students who apply by this date are mailed notification by early March. Early Action 1 applications are due November 1, with notification December 15; Early Action 2 applications are due December 1, with notification January 15. Students who wish to be considered for merit scholarships are strongly encouraged to apply under the Early Action plan. Transfer applications for the fall term are due by March 15 and for the spring term, by November 1. Notification for transfer applications is rolling. For more information, students should contact:

Admissions Office
Beloit College
700 College Street
Beloit, Wisconsin 53511
Phone: 608-363-2500
800-9-BELOIT (toll-free)
Fax: 608-363-2075
E-mail: admiss@beloit.edu
Web site: http://www.beloit.edu

Middle College, which houses the Admissions Office, is at the center of Beloit's New England–style campus.

BENEDICTINE UNIVERSITY

LISLE, ILLINOIS

The University

Benedictine University was founded in 1887 as St. Procopius College. One hundred twenty-three years later, the University remains committed to providing a high-quality, Catholic, liberal education for men and women. The undergraduate enrollment is more than 3,300 students. The student body comprises students of diverse ages, religions, races, and national origins. Twenty-five percent of the full-time students reside on campus.

Benedictine University is situated on a rolling, tree-covered 108-acre campus of twenty major buildings with air-conditioned classrooms and modern, well-equipped laboratories. A student athletic center features three full-size basketball courts, three tennis courts, and training facilities. All of the residence halls are comfortable and spacious and have access to the Internet. On-campus apartments offer one-, two-, and four-bedroom residences. Other features include a scenic lake; a student center with dining halls, lounges, a chapel, a bookstore, and meeting rooms; and the Village of Lisle–Benedictine University Sports Complex, featuring a lighted multipurpose football/soccer stadium with a nine-lane track and lighted baseball and softball fields.

Benedictine University is highly competitive in varsity sports, with a total of nineteen sports. Men's varsity sports are baseball, basketball, cross-country, football, golf, soccer, and track and field (indoor and outdoor). Women's varsity sports are basketball, cheerleading, cross-country, dance, golf, soccer, softball, tennis, track and field (indoor and outdoor), and volleyball. Aside from varsity and intramural athletic programs, forty organizations and clubs exist on campus, including student government, a student newspaper, an orchestra, a jazz group, an African-American Student Union, a Muslim Student Association, the Association of Latin American Students, campus ministry, and various other extracurricular and academic organizations.

Partnerships support the University's growth in the twenty-first century. In 2003, Benedictine and Springfield College in Illinois partnered to bring Benedictine programs and services to the Springfield area, Illinois' state capital. Benedictine partnered in 2004 with Shenyang University of Technology and Shenyang Jianzhu University in China to bring Master of Business Administration and Master of Science in management information systems programs overseas, as demands are high for American business programs. Benedictine opened the Moser Center in Naperville in 2006 to meet the needs of adult students and area businesses.

At Benedictine University, the environment is strengthened by success, not size. Renowned faculty members know students by name and care as much about each student's progress as they do about their own research. Those personal relationships have produced superb results. Benedictine graduates are accepted into some of the most prestigious graduate programs in the country. Approximately two thirds of Benedictine graduates who apply to medical school are accepted, in addition to similar ratios for other health-related professional schools (optometry, pharmacy, physical therapy, and podiatry). The liberal arts curriculum has helped place the University among some of the finest small private schools in the nation.

U.S. News & World Report's 2010 rankings listed Benedictine University as a Top School in the Midwest and sixth in Illinois for campus diversity.

The graduate division offers the following graduate degrees in the business, education, and health areas: the Doctor of Philosophy (Ph.D.) in organization development; the Doctor of Education (Ed.D.) in higher education and organizational change; the Master of Business Administration (M.B.A.); the Master of Arts in Education (M.A.Ed.); the Master of Education (M.Ed.); the Master of Science (M.S.) in accountancy, clinical psychology, clinical exercise physiology, leadership, management and organizational behavior, management information systems, nutrition and wellness, and science content and process; and the Master of Public Health (M.P.H.).

Adult undergraduate accelerated programs, taught by distinguished faculty members, are available in the following areas: accounting (B.B.A.), management (B.A.M.), management and organizational behavior (B.B.A.), nursing (B.S.), and organizational leadership (B.A.). The University also offers an Associate of Arts in business administration in an accelerated format.

Location

Benedictine University is 25 miles west of Chicago, in suburban Lisle near Naperville, and is easily accessible from the city and suburbs via the interstate highway system. Metra trains stop in Lisle, and O'Hare International Airport is only a 30-minute drive. In addition to the many social and cultural offerings of the Chicago metropolitan area, the University enjoys the proximity and use of Argonne National Laboratory, Fermi National Accelerator Laboratory, the Morton Arboretum, a ski hill, a riding stable, and several golf courses. The University's location in the high-tech East-West Tollway corridor gives students opportunities for internships and employment.

Majors and Degrees

Benedictine University offers programs leading to the Bachelor of Arts, Bachelor of Business Administration, Bachelor of Science, and Bachelor of Fine Arts. Programs are offered in accounting, bilingual journalism, biochemistry/molecular biology, biology (B.A. and B.S.), business and economics (concentration in sports management), business with science applications, chemistry, clinical laboratory science, communication arts (concentration in sports communication), computer information systems, computer science, diagnostic medical sonography, economics, elementary education, engineering science, English language and literature, environmental science, finance, fine arts, global studies, health science, history, international business and economics, international studies (concentration in business and political science), management and organizational behavior, marketing, mathematics (concentration in actuarial science), medical humanities, music (concentration in chamber music), music education, nuclear medicine technology, nutrition (concentration in dietetics), philosophy, physical education, physics (concentration in biological physics, engineering physics and physics), political science (concentration in prelaw), prepharmacy, preprofessional health programs (concentration in chiropractic, dentistry, medicine, occupational therapy, optometry, physical therapy, podiatry, and veterinary medicine), psychology, radiation therapy, secondary education, social science, sociology (concentration in criminal justice), Spanish, special education, studio art, theology, and writing and publishing.

In many areas of study, students may opt for a double major. Preprofessional health programs include chiropractic, dentistry, medicine, occupational therapy, optometry, physical therapy, podiatry, and veterinary medicine. Combined professional programs are available with cooperating institutions in clinical laboratory science, nuclear medicine technology, and engineering. A joint engineering program is offered with the Illinois Institute of Technology. A registered nurse may earn a Bachelor of Science degree in nursing. Teacher certification is available in the following majors: biology, business and economics, chemistry, English language and literature, mathematics, physical education, physics, social science, and Spanish.

Academic Programs

For graduation, a student must earn at least 120 semester hours, 55 of which must be completed at a four-year regionally accredited college. At least the final 45 semester hours must be completed at Benedictine University. The University makes selective exceptions to the normal academic residency requirement of 45 semester hours for adults who are eligible for the Degree Completion Program. Eligibility is limited to those who have nearly completed their undergraduate studies but, for reasons of employment, career change, or family situation, found it necessary to interrupt their studies.

The Second Major Program is designed for people who already have a degree in one area and would like to gain expertise in another. This program allows the student to concentrate on courses that fulfill the requirements of a second major. The student receives a certificate upon completion.

Each year, a select number of talented and motivated prospective students are invited to participate in the Scholars Program. The program is designed to enhance the college experience by developing students' international awareness and strengthening their leadership ability.

Off-Campus Programs

Benedictine University is a member of a three-school consortium in the west suburban Chicago area through which students are able to take classes at the other member colleges. Study abroad and internships abroad are encouraged to complement a liberal education.

Academic Facilities

The Kindlon Hall of Learning and the Birck Hall of Science bring science and technology to new levels. The Birck Hall of Science houses state-of-the art computer labs, specialized science labs, a research center, and the Jurica-Suchy Nature Museum.

The Kindlon Hall of Learning houses computer labs, classrooms, multimedia labs, offices, and student lounges. It is also home to the Benedictine Library, which houses more than 120,000 volumes and can be found in the building's impressive five-story tower. The library is also equipped with eleven group study rooms, a computer lab, and an instruction room.

Benedictine University has distance education classrooms that provide students with the capability to interact globally with other colleges and universities in a classroom setting. Scholl Hall houses classrooms and faculty and administrative offices.

Costs

The cost of tuition for the 2009–10 academic year was $21,600. The average cost of room and board is $6943. Mandatory fees total $710 and include health, technology, and student activity fees.

Financial Aid

In 2008–09, Benedictine University freshmen received approximately $6.1 million from financial aid sources that included loans, scholarship and grants, tuition remission, and employment opportunities. Ninety-six percent of the freshman class received financial aid. The average package was $15,842. Benedictine University has dedicated more than $12 million of the annual budget to providing grants and scholarships to its students. Students who wish to apply for aid must complete the Free Application for Federal Student Aid (FAFSA) and the Benedictine University application for admission.

Faculty

The 13:1 student-faculty ratio allows for close interaction between students and faculty members. Of the 115 full-time faculty members, 86 percent hold a Ph.D. or the terminal professional degree in their respective fields. All students are assigned a faculty member as an adviser to help plan programs of study.

Student Government

All full-time enrolled students are automatically members of the student government. The Student Government Association (SGA) is a representative body elected annually by the students to represent their interests. The SGA is responsible for the annual allocation of the student activity fee.

Admission Requirements

The Benedictine University admission philosophy is to select students who are expected to perform successfully in the University's academic programs and become active members of the University community. Typically, Benedictine University's freshman students are in the top third of their high school graduating class, with about 50 percent in the top quarter, and report better-than-average ACT or SAT scores. A minimum of 16 units in academic subjects is required, including 4 units of English, 1 unit of algebra, 1 unit of geometry, 1 unit of history, 1 unit of laboratory science, and 2 units of foreign language. Benedictine University does admit some students who fall below these standards. These applicants receive individual consideration by the Academic Admissions Committee. When appropriate, the committee will place conditions and/or restrictions upon students to help them reach their academic potential.

Students interested in transferring to Benedictine University must have a minimum cumulative average of C (2.0 on a 4.0 scale) or better from all colleges previously attended. Official transcripts from all colleges attended must be submitted directly to the Enrollment Center for evaluation. If fewer than 20 semester hours of transfer credit are submitted, an official high school transcript and SAT or ACT scores are required, and the general admission high school curriculum requirements must also be satisfied. Credits transferred from other institutions are evaluated on the basis of their equivalent at Benedictine University. Grades of D are accepted as transfer credit but do not satisfy Benedictine University requirements, which demand a minimum grade of C.

Requests for admission are considered without regard to the applicant's race, religion, gender, age, or disability.

Application and Information

Applications are reviewed on a rolling basis. Students are encouraged to apply for admission at any time after completing their junior year of high school. Transfer students may apply for admission during their last semester or quarter before anticipated transfer to Benedictine University. Earlier applications are encouraged for scholarship and financial aid opportunities.

For further information, students should contact:

Enrollment Center
Benedictine University
5700 College Road
Lisle, Illinois 60532
Phone: 630-829-6300
888-829-6363 (toll-free outside Illinois)
Fax: 630-829-6301
E-mail: admissions@ben.edu
Web site: http://www.ben.edu

The Birck Hall of Science houses science labs, classrooms, offices, a lecture hall, and the Jurica-Suchy Nature Museum.

BENTLEY UNIVERSITY

WALTHAM, MASSACHUSETTS

The University

Bentley University is a national leader in business education. Centered on education and research in business and related professions, Bentley blends the breadth and technological strength of a university with the values and student focus of a small college. A Bentley education integrates an unparalleled array of business courses with hands-on technology experience and the liberal arts. In addition, Bentley has a master's candidate program that allows students to earn a bachelor's degree and a master's degree in only five years rather than the usual six. Bentley also offers two doctoral programs: accountancy and business.

About 97 percent of Bentley freshmen live on campus, creating a spirited sense of community. Housing includes twenty-three residence halls and apartment-style buildings, featuring a choice of single-, double-, or triple-occupancy dorm rooms; apartments; or suites. Housing is guaranteed to students for all four years. All residence halls are air-conditioned and carpeted and have common areas, which typically include study lounges, exercise facilities, TV lounges, and game rooms. Halls are renovated regularly to keep pace with student needs.

Bentley students live and learn in a multicultural environment that reflects and prepares them to thrive in today's diverse work world. International students representing more than seventy countries are part of the Bentley community.

All students explore the topic of diversity in courses that promote respect for different perspectives, break down stereotypes, and embrace the vitality that a varied student body adds to the university experience. Supporting this commitment are offices such as the Multicultural Center, Spiritual Life Center, Center for International Students and Scholars, and the Women's Center.

The Student Center is the hub of campus activity and is home to Seasons Dining Room and Mongolian Grill; the Blue Line pub, which offers entertainment nearly every night; and more than 100 student clubs and organizations. Opportunities to get involved run the gamut of academic groups, the performing arts, campus media, fraternity and sorority life, and cultural organizations. Sponsored events and informal get-togethers are a regular part of campus life.

The Miller Center for Career Services (CSS) offers resources including an on-campus recruiting program involving 500 national and international companies; an online job-listing service available to Bentley students and alumni; an electronic database of student and alumni resumes; career fairs; and workshops on topics such as effective resume writing, interviewing, and job-search strategies. Thanks to these and other programs, 98 percent of Bentley students find employment or enroll in graduate school within six months of graduation. The median annual salary for 2009 graduates was over $50,000.

Extensive athletic programs are a Bentley hallmark. Students choose among intramural and recreational sports and twenty-three varsity teams in NCAA Divisions I and II. The Dana Athletic Center houses a weight and fitness complex, an aerobics room, a full-service food court, a suspended track, refurbished locker rooms, and function spaces. It also holds a gym and basketball court, volleyball and racquetball courts, a competition-size pool with a diving tank, and saunas. Outdoor facilities include soccer and baseball fields, a track, lighted tennis courts, and other grass and Astroturf fields.

Location

Bentley's location, just minutes west of Boston, puts the city's many resources within easy reach. As the country's ultimate university town, Boston's options range from theater to art exhibits, dance clubs to alternative rock concerts, and championship sports to world-class shopping. Students do not need a car to get around. The free Bentley shuttle makes regular trips to Harvard Square in Cambridge, which is a great area to explore and just a quick subway ride from the heart of Boston. The city also offers students many opportunities for internships and jobs after graduation.

Majors and Degrees

Bentley offers a strong curriculum, focusing on business, technology, and the liberal arts, which provides students with many options for shaping an academic program that fits their skills, interests, and career goals. Bachelor of Science (B.S.) degree programs enable students to gain in-depth knowledge and skills in specific business disciplines: accountancy, computer information systems, corporate finance and accounting, economics–finance, finance, information design and corporate communication, information systems audit and control, management, managerial economics, marketing, and mathematical sciences.

Bentley also offers Bachelor of Arts (B.A.) degree programs, with majors in global studies, history, liberal arts, media and culture, and philosophy. In addition, students can choose from a number of minors and concentration programs that offer them the opportunity to develop expertise in an area outside their chosen major.

The Liberal Studies Major (LSM), an optional double major for business students, can be combined with any business program. It provides students with a competitive edge in today's economy and the broad-based skills essential in all areas of life. The LSM allows students to combine courses that fulfill general education requirements with related electives to pursue one of many concentrations, such as ethics and social responsibility, global perspectives, or health and industry. Students take the same number of courses but add another credential to their degree, helping them stand out to future employers.

Academic Programs

The 4,200 undergraduates who study at Bentley benefit from a unique integration of business and the liberal arts. As the largest business school in New England, Bentley offers remarkable depth in subjects such as accountancy, computer information systems, finance, information design and corporate communication, marketing, and management. In addition, there is a strong commitment to the liberal arts, which allows students to build skills in critical thinking, decision making, communication, and other areas essential to becoming a well-rounded, contributing member of the community. Ethics and social responsibility, which are key themes woven into both business and liberal arts offerings, are supported by Bentley's internationally renowned Center for Business Ethics and prestigious Service-Learning Center.

Over the course of four years, Bentley students develop a solid understanding of the latest technologies and the ways that businesses use them to stay competitive. They learn how to analyze and manage the mountains of information that drive today's business world.

The focus on information technology begins early, as all Bentley freshmen receive a laptop that is fully loaded and network ready. With computer ports and wireless coverage all over the campus—in classrooms, residence hall rooms, dining halls, and the library—students have incredibly fast and convenient access to the Internet, the Bentley network, and many other information sources. This commitment to high-tech learning is supported by an array of academic resources, including classrooms equipped with multimedia technology, student computer laboratories, and a Virtual Lab that offers online access to specialized software from anywhere on campus. Bentley is also home to six high-tech learning labs that give students hands-on experience with the technology they need for their careers.

Off-Campus Programs

Hands-on experience is emphasized across the Bentley curriculum. Internships, group consulting projects, study abroad, service-learning assignments, and other opportunities allow students to apply classroom theory in the workplace and community.

Each year, through Bentley's Service-Learning Center, hundreds of students build valuable skills in business, communication, and teamwork while assisting nonprofit and community-based organizations both locally and internationally.

Bentley students can gain valuable insight into different countries and cultures by studying abroad. Programs that run for one week, one semester, or a full academic year take students to places such as Australia, Brazil, China, Egypt, England, France, Ghana, Hungary, India, Italy, South Africa, and Spain.

Internships in the U.S. and abroad enable students to fine-tune skills, explore interests, and make valuable connections. Recently, students held internships at L'Oreal in both the Caribbean and London, Reebok in Massachusetts, and at the Cannes Film Festival in France, to name a few. The Center for Career Services works with academic departments to coordinate internships, which typically offer course credit toward a Bentley degree. In 2009, 35 percent of Bentley graduates found full-time employment as a direct result of their internships.

Academic Facilities

Concepts and theories taught in the classroom are put to use in several hands-on, high-tech learning laboratories—each among the first of its kind in higher education—that include the financial Trading Room, Center for Marketing Technology, Accounting Center for Electronic Learning and Business Measurement, Center for Languages and International Collaboration, Media Arts Lab, and Design and Usability Center.

Bentley's financial Trading Room, the largest in higher education, combines state-of-the-art technology and real-time data to offer first-hand exposure to financial concepts. In simulated trading sessions, students build investment portfolios and analyze financial risk. Trading Room resources include Bloomberg, FactSet, DataStream, Wonda, and Thomson One Analytics.

The Center for Marketing Technology (CMT) houses the high-end hardware and software applications that are revolutionizing the marketing of products and services. Students learn the latest strategies for testing consumer preferences, creating ad campaigns, using databases to make marketing decisions, and more. CMT resources include Perseus Survey, SPSS, Qualitap, QuarkExpress, and other tools for exploring the complex forces that drive buying and selling in a global economy.

The Accounting Center for Electronic Learning and Business Management (ACELAB) introduces students to the cutting-edge tools and technologies that are reshaping the accounting profession. Students gain experience with auditing, tax preparation software, and other professional applications—skills they apply to tasks such as developing an accounting system and analyzing operational data for management decision making. Resources include software from industry leaders such as SAP and Oracle.

The Center for Languages and International Collaboration (CLIC) is a key resource for language courses, international studies majors, and all students who have an interest in global issues. The center features two satellite dishes and videoconference technology to promote collaboration among Bentley students and their counterparts overseas.

The Media Arts Lab features state-of-the-art resources for video production and editing as well as digital photography. The lab also provides students with industry-standard software programs for screenwriting, sound mixing, graphic design, and DVD authoring.

The Design and Usability Center (DUC) offers one of the most sophisticated testing facilities in the world. The DUC features two state-of-the-art testing labs ideal for usability testing, focus groups, and design workshops. Students use the same applications employed by technical communicators, Web developers, user-interface designers, and usability specialists. The goal is to create information technology products that users can intuitively understand and easily employ.

The Bentley Library supports the University's academic programs with more than 140,000 book titles and 700 periodical subscriptions. The library is also well connected to sophisticated electronic databases such as Dow Jones/Bridge News Retrieval, LexisNexis, Westlaw, and InfoTrac 2000. The library houses group study rooms, research computers, an art gallery, and a café.

Costs

Tuition for resident and nonresident students during the 2009–10 academic year was $34,360. Room and board (double room, meal plan) costs were $11,740. Additional expenses include books, supplies, laptop computer, and personal and travel expenses.

Financial Aid

Bentley administers about $79 million in undergraduate financial aid every year to ensure that all academically qualified students have access to educational choices regardless of financial resources. Assistance comprises scholarships, grants, loans, employment, and payment plans. Currently, more than 70 percent of Bentley's undergraduates receive some form of financial assistance in the form of grants, scholarships, loans, and/or work eligibility.

Faculty

Bentley faculty members are respected teacher-scholars known equally well for their classroom skills and cutting-edge research. They bring practical, real-world experience to the classroom, based on years of professional involvement in their chosen fields. Faculty research focuses on issues of prime importance to current business practice, particularly topics where business intersects with technology and/or with the liberal arts. Much of the research is conducted in partnership with leading corporations and organizations. A student-faculty ratio of 12:1 and average class size of 24 ensure a personal experience for Bentley students. All courses are taught by professors; there are no teaching assistants.

Student Government

Bentley has a number of student governing associations, including the Student Government Association, Senior Class Cabinet, Greek Council, Hall Council Advisory Board, Media Board, Panhellenic Council, and the Graduate Student Association.

Admission Requirements

Students applying for admission to Bentley are encouraged to complete a competitive university preparatory program. Recommendations include 4 years of English, 4 years of mathematics (preferably algebra I and II, geometry, and precalculus or its equivalent), and 3 to 4 years each of history, laboratory science, and a foreign language.

Along with the application, students must submit a secondary school transcript, letters of recommendation from a teacher and a counselor, and official scores of either the SAT or ACT, including the ACT writing test. The University has special applications for international students and transfer students. Applicants who are nonnative speakers of English must also have official scores of the Test of English as a Foreign Language (TOEFL) forwarded to the Office of Undergraduate Admission.

Application and Information

Bentley University accepts the Common Application. The application deadline for students planning to enter in September is January 15. For students planning to begin study in January, the deadline is November 15. Candidates for the fall semester are notified by April 1; spring semester candidates are notified on a rolling basis.

The early decision program is designed for academic achievers for whom Bentley is their first choice. Students who are admitted through this binding program agree to withdraw any applications submitted to other universities. The early decision application deadline is November 1.

The early action program is designed for students who are seriously considering Bentley but are not prepared to commit through the early decision program. This program provides students with an earlier admission decision but gives them the ability to consider other options. The application deadline is November 15.

For more information, students should contact:

Office of Undergraduate Admission
Bentley University
175 Forest Street
Waltham, Massachusetts 02452-4705
Phone: 781-891-2244
800-523-2354 (toll-free)
Fax: 781-891-3414
E-mail: ugadmission@bentley.edu
Web site: http://www.bentley.edu

BERKLEE COLLEGE OF MUSIC

BOSTON, MASSACHUSETTS

Berklee college *of* music

The College

Berklee College of Music was founded on the revolutionary principle that the best way to prepare students for careers in music is through the study and practice of contemporary music. For more than half a century, the college has evolved to reflect the state-of-the-art of music and the music business. With more than a dozen performance and non-performance majors, a diverse and talented student body of 4,000 students representing more than seventy countries, and a music industry "who's who" of alumni, Berklee is the world's premier learning lab for the music of today—and tomorrow.

Berklee has proven its commitment to this approach by wholeheartedly embracing change. The musical landscape looks nothing like it did when Berklee was founded in 1945, but the college has remained current by supplementing its core curriculum with studies in emerging musical genres and indispensable new technology. Berklee also has responded to important developments in music education and music therapy, making good on its promise to improve society through music.

At Berklee, students acquire a strong foundation of contemporary music theory and technique, then build upon that foundation by learning the practical, professional skills needed to sustain a career in music. Majors such as music production and engineering, film scoring, music business/management, music synthesis, songwriting, and music therapy, as well as traditional mainstays of performance and composition, lead toward either a fully accredited four-year baccalaureate degree or a professional diploma. Perhaps more importantly, they prepare students for employment in the music industry.

Berklee attracts a diverse range of students who reflect the multiplicity of influences in today's music, be it jazz, rock, hip-hop, country, gospel, electronica, Latin, or funk. The college is a magnet for aspiring musicians from every corner of the earth, which gives the school a uniquely international flavor. Of all U.S. colleges and universities, Berklee has one of the largest percentages of undergraduates from outside the United States—25 percent. Reflecting the interplay between music and culture, Berklee creates an environment where aspiring music professionals learn how to integrate new ideas and showcase their distinctive skills in an evolving community.

The College's alumni form an ever-widening network of industry professionals who use their openness, virtuosity, and versatility to take music in surprising new directions. Notable alumni include BT, Gary Burton, Terri Lyne Carrington, Bruce Cockburn, Juan Luis Guerra, Roy Hargrove, Quincy Jones, Diana Krall, Aimee Mann, Arif Mardin, Branford Marsalis, Danilo Perez, John Scofield, Howard Shore, Alan Silvestri, Luciana Souza, Susan Tedeschi, and Gillian Welch.

Location

Berklee College of Music is located in Boston's Fenway Cultural District. An international hub of intellectual and creative exploration, the neighborhood includes treasure-filled museums and galleries and world-class performing arts centers such as Symphony Hall, the Wang Center, and the Berklee Performance Center. Boston is also home to many of the world's other great colleges and universities. In addition to the music made at Berklee, there is a lively club and concert scene in the area with coffee houses featuring folk and bluegrass music; neighborhood clubs offering jazz, reggae, and world music; and clubs specializing in rock, blues, dance, urban, and country-western music.

Berklee students participate in intramural sports and fitness programs at nearby institutions; watch Boston's professional sports teams play in the new TD Banknorth Garden or at Fenway Park or other area sports venues; attend theater, club, and concert hall events year-round throughout the city; and walk, skate, or bike through the city's many scenic parks and public gardens. The College is located within walking distance of Boston's public transportation system, allowing students to take advantage of all that Boston has to offer.

Majors and Degrees

Berklee offers a Bachelor of Music (B.M.) degree program and a four-year program leading to a professional diploma. Students may choose to major in composition, contemporary writing and production, film scoring, jazz composition, music business/management, music education, music production and engineering, music synthesis, music therapy, performance, professional music, and songwriting. The College also offers a five-year, dual-major option in which students graduate with an even more marketable education that expands their career options in the music industry.

Academic Programs

The Bachelor of Music program offers a complete music curriculum combined with liberal arts courses such as English, history, languages, mathematics, philosophy, and physical or social science. Intensive concentration in music subjects provides students with the necessary tools for developing their musical talents to the fullest and preparing for the multifaceted and ever-changing demands of today's professional music. The degree program is especially appropriate for students who wish to earn a formal degree; are interested in pursuing a career in music education, music therapy, or business/management; or want to continue their studies at the graduate level.

The diploma is designed for students who want to focus exclusively on contemporary music studies and still get the benefits of a Berklee experience.

All students must complete the core music curriculum, which consists of harmony, arranging, ear training, and introduction to music technology; instrumental studies; ensembles and instrumental labs; and the concentrate courses designated for each major. All degree candidates must complete the general education curriculum and traditional music studies courses.

Off-Campus Programs

Through the Professional Arts Consortium (ProArts), an association of six area institutions of higher education dedicated to the performing and visual arts, Berklee students can take courses at leading Boston area arts institutions in such areas as communications, modern dance, visual arts, ballet, architectural and graphic design, theater arts, and liberal arts. The other members of the consortium are Boston Architectural Center, the Boston Conservatory, Emerson College, Massachusetts College of Art, and the School of the Museum of Fine Arts.

Students who major in music business/management may be eligible to receive credit for their Berklee course work toward an M.B.A. from Suffolk University.

The Berklee International Network is a shared endeavor designed to promote the effectiveness of contemporary music education among members and to advance the value of contemporary music education internationally. Berklee faculty and staff members visit network member schools annually to conduct workshops and clinics and to audition students for scholarships for full-time study at Berklee. There are currently fifteen members of the network: Fundacio L'Aula de Musica Moderna i Jazz in Barcelona, Spain; Rimon School of Jazz and Contemporary Music in Ramat Hasharon (Tel Aviv), Israel; Phillipos Nakas Conservatory in Athens, Greece; Music Academy International in Nancy, France; American School of Modern Music in Paris, France; Instituto de Musica Contemporanea Universidad San Francisco de Quito in Quito, Ecuador; Pop and Jazz Conservatory in Helsinki, Finland; Koyo Conservatoire in Kobe, Japan; PAN School of Music in Tokyo, Japan; Jazz and Rock Schule in Freiburg, Germany; International College of Music in Kuala Lumpur, Malaysia; Academia de Musica Fermatta, Mexico City, Mexico; Conservatorio Souza Lima in São Paulo, Brazil; Seoul Jazz Academy in Seoul, Korea; and the Newpark Music Centre in Dublin, Ireland.

Academic Facilities

Berklee students have the chance to work in the College's state-of-the-art music technology facilities, using some of the most sophisticated recording and synthesis equipment currently available, in addition to facilities specifically designed for the areas of composition, arranging, and film scoring. The facilities at Berklee are furnished with the instruments and equipment that are being used in the world beyond the classroom. Berklee's performance facilities include the Berklee Performance Center, a 1,200-seat concert hall hosting more than 300 student, faculty, and other concerts each year; Cafe 939, a state-of-the-art, all-ages, student-run music venue and coffee house; four recital halls equipped with a variety of sound reinforcement systems; more than forty ensemble rooms; seventy-five private instruction studios; 300 private practice rooms; and an outdoor concert pavilion.

Technological facilities include the Recording Studio Complex, consisting of thirteen studio facilities that include 8-, 16-, and 24-track digital and analog recording capability; synthesis labs, featuring more than 250 MIDI-equipped synthesizers, drum machines, sequencers, and computers, including hard-disk recording; the Learning Center, equipped with forty computer-based MIDI workstations; the Professional Writing Division MIDI Lab; and film scoring labs, providing professional training in the areas of film music composition, editing, sequencing, and computer applications.

Costs

Tuition and fees for the 2008–09 year were $31,776. Room and board fees were $14,360. Although the cost of books tends to vary among students, it is estimated at about $800 per year.

Financial Aid

A very large percentage of the student body receives some form of financial aid, so no student should allow financial barriers to stop him or her from applying to the College. Funds are available from many different sources, including Berklee and federal and state programs. Students are eligible for merit-based scholarships and, in cases of demonstrated need, federal assistance is provided. Subsidized loans, a tuition-installment plan, and campus employment are also available. Financial aid counselors are available to students and their families to discuss the various options available to them. Students should be aware that there are specific deadlines for federal and state fund applications and for scholarships. Berklee awards $20 million in scholarships each year to students from all over the world who demonstrate the potential to succeed in today's music industry.

Berklee's Office of Scholarships and Student Employment provides extensive opportunities for both domestic and international students to apply for merit-based scholarships via audition (entering students) or submission of an achievement portfolio (continuing and returning students who have successfully completed a minimum of two semesters).

Faculty

The personal attention students receive from teachers at Berklee guides them beyond the theoretical so that they can apply what they've learned in their next ensemble rehearsal, evening jam session, or gig. All instruction is administered by Berklee's more than 500 faculty members. Teachers are talented artists who demonstrate their commitment to music education in the classroom and beyond. Most faculty members also write and arrange music, perform in concert halls and clubs, make recordings, or perform on television and radio, and some do it all. All faculty members bring to the classroom knowledge of music and the wisdom that comes from professional music experience.

Student Government

Berklee's broad-based system of governance relies on participation from all areas of the college community. The Council of Students represents the voice and perspectives of students regarding all of the issues reviewed by the college. Students are also asked to serve on a wide variety of college committees that advise administrators on such topics as the college's master plan, honorary degree recipients, website, and academic and student policies. And many of our student leaders have opportunity to meet with the president, vice presidents, and trustees during the academic year to discuss current issues, concerns, and institutional activities.

Admission Requirements

Berklee's board of admissions seeks students who show high potential; who are creative, collaborative, and who have something extra that sets them apart. The College considers every aspect of an applicant's strengths and looks for candidates who reflect the rich diversity of Berklee's curriculum, with high musical aptitude as players or writers; or in business, production, music therapy, or music education.

The College takes into consideration both academics as well as musical aptitude. Berklee does not have specific GPA or test score requirements, nor does it have any specific class ranking requirements. The audition and interview process, along with a comprehensive and holistic evaluation of each applicant, provides the College with a wealth of information to assess students' ability to succeed at Berklee.

Application and Information

Berklee uses fixed application deadlines for each semester of entry. Applying to the College is a three-step process. All applicants must submit an online application, participate in a live audition and interview, and mail in the appropriate transcripts to be considered for full-time enrollment at the College.

The online application has two parts. Section one of the application asks that students provide us with their personal contact information, including whether they are a vocalist or instrumentalist, their preferred audition location, and responses to fourteen questions that will be used in their interview. A live audition and interview is required as part of the application. A complete listing of audition dates, deadlines, and locations throughout the world is available on Berklee's website.

Section two of the application asks that students provide information about their musical and academic background. All supporting materials must be postmarked by the posted deadline date. To learn more about how to apply to the college, and information about the audition and interview experience, students should visit our online tour.

For further information, students should contact:

Office of Admissions
Berklee College of Music
1140 Boylston Street
Boston, Massachusetts 02215
Phone: 617-266-2222 (worldwide)
800-BERKLEE (toll-free in the U.S. and Canada)
Fax: 617-747-2047
E-mail: admissions@berklee.edu
Web site: http://www.berklee.edu

Berklee College of Music student using state-of-the-art music technology.

BETHEL UNIVERSITY

ST. PAUL, MINNESOTA

The University

Bethel University began its Christian liberal arts program in 1945 but traces its roots to Bethel Seminary, founded in 1871. The University encourages growth and learning in a distinctly Christian environment, continually striving to help students discover and develop the skills God has given them. Campus lifestyle expectations have been designed to build unity within diversity. All Bethel students, faculty members, and staff members are expected to follow those expectations during their time as members of the Bethel community. Bethel's approximately 6,200 students represent a range of national and international cultures. Most of Bethel's undergraduate students are between 18 and 22 years of age, but older and younger students bring a welcome variety to campus life. Bethel students are involved in a wealth of cocurricular activities, from music to ministry, Bible study to broadcasting, theater to tennis, and art to athletics. Bethel sports teams compete in NCAA Division III and the Minnesota Intercollegiate Athletic Conference, and several teams are conference champions or annual championship contenders. The Sports and Recreation Center is used almost continuously for intercollegiate and intramural sports events as well as personal recreation, and the Community Life Center provides a 1,700-seat performance hall and chapel.

The campus, built in the 1970s, is the newest among Minnesota colleges and universities. Versatile buildings are centers for the sciences, humanities, physical education, learning resources, and fine arts. A series of skyways and breezeways connect the facilities and make getting to and from class a pleasure—even in the heart of winter. A spacious new lakeside student center opened in spring 2009. Residence life at Bethel takes many forms. Traditional college dorm rooms, spacious suites, town houses—whatever their preference, Bethel students find a warm, family atmosphere in the living areas. All freshman and sophomore students, except those who are married or living with their parents while in attendance, are required to live in University housing.

In addition to the undergraduate programs listed below, Bethel's Graduate School offers accelerated Master of Arts degrees in communication, counseling psychology, education K–12, literacy education, nursing, organizational leadership, and teaching; a Master of Education degree in special education; a doctoral degree in educational administration; and a Master of Business Administration degree.

Location

The Bethel campus borders Lake Valentine in Arden Hills and comprises 231 acres of beauty and tranquility, conducive to study and leisure. Just 15 minutes from downtown St. Paul and Minneapolis, Bethel enjoys the benefits of both cities, which are noted nationally for their high quality of life. The Twin Cities are home to the headquarters of most of Minnesota's large corporations as well as more than thirty major shopping centers and one of the world's largest shopping malls, the Mall of America. Culture thrives in the cities with an international array of music, theater, and art. At the all-weather Metrodome, the Target Center, and the Xcel Energy Center, sports fans cheer their favorite pro teams—the Minnesota Vikings, Twins, Timberwolves, and Wild. Abundant recreation exists year-round in this busy metropolis, which offers more than 900 lakes and 500 parks.

Majors and Degrees

The Bachelor of Arts (B.A.) degree is offered, with majors in accounting and finance, art, athletic training, biblical and theological studies, biology, business, business and political science, chemistry, communication studies, community health, computer science, economics, economics and finance, education, engineering science, English literature, English literature and writing, environmental studies, French, history, international relations, journalism, mathematics, media communication, music, philosophy, physics, political science, psychology, reconciliation studies, sacred music, social work, sociocultural studies, Spanish, teaching English as a foreign language, teaching English as a second language, theater arts, Third World studies, and youth ministry.

The Bachelor of Science (B.S.) degree is offered, with majors in applied physics, biochemistry/molecular biology, biology, chemistry, computer science, environmental science, exercise science, nursing, and physics. The Bachelor of Music (B.Mus.) degree is offered in applied performance. The Bachelor of Music Education (B.Mus.Ed.) degree is offered with an emphasis in instrumental K–12 or vocal K–12. Numerous preprofessional programs are offered as well.

Academic minors are available in most of the major disciplines listed above and in the following areas: Asian studies, athletic coaching, biblical languages (Hebrew and Greek), classics, creative writing, cross-cultural mission, entrepreneurship, family studies, film studies, German, leadership studies, management information systems, modern world languages, religious studies, and social welfare studies.

In addition to its seminary programs and traditional undergraduate degree programs, Bethel offers several career-relevant undergraduate degree programs for adults.

Academic Programs

Bethel offers sixty-seven majors within seventy-eight fields of study. The University was named among the top Midwestern universities by *U.S. News & World Report* for 2008. Students are required to take classes that will give them a broad view of the world and their role in it as Christians. General education classes are grouped around the following themes: personal development; biblical foundations; math, science, and technology; and global perspectives. In addition, in order to graduate, all Bethel students must meet a language proficiency requirement, partake in an off-campus cross-cultural experience, and complete a capstone course in contemporary Christian issues.

Bethel University follows a semester calendar consisting of two 15-week semesters and a three-week interim in January. A full-time academic load for each semester is 12 to 18 credits. To graduate, students must complete a minimum of 122 credits with a cumulative grade point average of at least 2.0 and a minimum 2.25 grade point average in their majors. Also required are 51–52 credits of general education. Bethel awards advanced-placement credit in recognition of learning that has been achieved apart from a college or university classroom situation. A maximum of 30 advanced-placement credits can be applied toward a degree program. Students may also individualize their academic programs through directed studies with faculty members and through academic internships with off-campus institutions.

Off-Campus Programs

Bethel students may study in almost any country and across the United States as part of their education. Off-campus extension programs include the American Studies Program of the Council for Christian Colleges and Universities, which provides internship opportunities in Washington, D.C. The council also sponsors a Latin American Studies Program, which offers students an opportunity to study in Costa Rica. The Los Angeles Film Studies Center gives students of any major a semester of learning and working experience in Los Angeles, the world's film capital. The Christian College Consortium Visitor Program is designed to allow students to take advantage of course offerings and varied experiences on other Christian college and university campuses throughout the United States. The Au Sable Institute in Michigan offers intensive courses in environmental studies. Through the Upper Midwest Association for Intercultural Education, Bethel students study abroad during interim. In the fall semester of alternate years, Bethel students can study and travel in France, Great Britain, Ireland, and Northern Ireland under the direction of a faculty member from the Bethel University Department of English. Other Bethel-sponsored programs include Europe Term, Guatemala Term, Spain Term, Thailand Term, South Africa Term, and the New York Center for Art & Media Studies. Additional opportunities available to Bethel students include the Australia Studies Centre, Australia Term, China Studies Program, Creation Care Study Program, Hong Kong Baptist University, Lithuania Christian College, Middle East Studies Program, Russian Studies Program, Scholars' Semester in Oxford, Tokyo Christian University, Uganda Studies Program, Oxford Summer Programme, Contemporary Music Center, The Oregon Extension, and Washington Journalism Center.

Academic Facilities

Bethel's Community Life Center offers a beautiful hall with outstanding acoustical design that makes it one of the best performance facilities in the upper Midwest. The Bethel science labs and music practice rooms are modern and well equipped. Approximately four plays are performed each year in the Bethel Theatre.

The Bethel University Library Web site serves as a portal to more than 184,000 volumes located in the library, including books, music CDs, and more than 14,000 videos/DVDs; more than 30,000 full-text periodicals online and 1,593 hard-copy journal titles; over 18,000 e-books; more than 100 online databases; a bibliographic manager; an e-mail and chat reference service; a "Research Wizard"; interactive tutorials; and interlibrary-loan access to more than 2 million volumes within the consortium. Services in the library include an "Information Commons," which provides research, technical, and multimedia assistance; wireless access to the Internet; laptops, digital cameras, portable DVD players, and much more equipment for checkout; seventy general-use computers; a full-service AV department; individual and small-group study areas; listening/viewing rooms; multimedia production space; reference; faculty technology consulting; and instruction. Bethel students are assigned computer accounts, allowing them access to a wealth of academic and specialized computing services.

Costs

For 2010–11, tuition is $27,950 and room and board costs are $8220. Bethel University tuition costs are lower than average for Minnesota private colleges and universities. Housing costs are set each spring for incoming freshmen and transfer students. For students who live in Bethel housing all four years, the room rate for their incoming freshman year is frozen for the remainder of their college career. Freshmen living on campus must purchase the three-meal-per-day basic meal plan; upperclass students may choose from a variety of meal plans. The actual cost of attending Bethel depends on the amount of financial aid a student receives.

Financial Aid

Bethel University strives to make it financially possible for every qualified student to attend. Each year, more than 90 percent of the students receive some kind of financial aid, including scholarships, grants, loans, and assistance in the form of on-campus employment. Students who wish to be considered for financial aid must first be admitted to the University and then submit both the Free Application for Federal Student Aid (FAFSA) and a Bethel University Financial Aid Application. Bethel's priority deadline is April 15 of each year. Students who have completed and mailed all necessary forms by this date receive first consideration.

Faculty

Nothing determines the quality of a university more than the people who teach there. Bethel professors combine strong academic credentials with a commitment to Jesus Christ. Bethel faculty members are known for being warm and caring. It is not hard to receive personal attention, since there are only 15 students to every faculty member. Professors are very accessible to students during regular office hours as well as at other times. Of Bethel's 202 full-time faculty members, more than 80 percent—and virtually all tenured faculty members—have earned doctorates. The Bethel faculty is complemented by 121 part-time instructors.

Student Government

The Bethel Student Association empowers students by providing them with opportunities, resources, and responsibility. The student leaders involved represent the student body to the staff and faculty as well as implement programs and activities that are student focused and driven. The Executive Team is composed of the student body president, student body vice president, and 8 executive directors. Each executive director manages a distinct branch of the student government, which fulfills a specific function within the organization.

Admission Requirements

Bethel University seeks students who desire an education based on strong academics in a Christian environment. To be considered for admission, the student must graduate from an accredited high school or equivalent, rank in the top 50 percent of his or her high school class, and meet minimum test score requirements (92 on the PSAT, 920 on the SAT, or 21 on the ACT). Transcripts, two references, and commitment to Bethel's covenant (lifestyle statement) are also required. Bethel recommends that students take 4 years of English, 3 years of mathematics, 3 years of science, and 2 years of social studies while in high school. Transfer students with a 2.5 or higher cumulative college GPA are also welcome. On-campus interviews are not required but are strongly recommended.

Application and Information

Students wishing to apply for admission to Bethel must send the following: a completed Bethel application form with a $25 nonrefundable application fee (waived before November 1); test scores from the PSAT, SAT, or ACT; an essay; a list of courses currently in progress; transcripts of all course work completed at the high school and college levels; and the names of two references: an academic reference and a spiritual reference. Students considering Bethel should apply in the fall of their senior year. The Office of Admissions reviews applications throughout the year. Early action decisions are made for students who submit applications by November 1.

For further information about specific Bethel programs and campus visit opportunities, students should contact:

Office of Admissions
Bethel University
3900 Bethel Drive
St. Paul, Minnesota 55112
Phone: 651-638-6242
800-255-8706 Ext. 6242 (toll-free)
Fax: 651-635-1490
E-mail: BUadmissions-cas@bethel.edu
Web site: http://www.bethel.edu

Bethel's Community Life Center.

BIRMINGHAM–SOUTHERN COLLEGE

BIRMINGHAM, ALABAMA

The College

Birmingham-Southern College (BSC) was created through a merger of Southern University (established in 1856) and Birmingham College (established in 1898). Since 1959, when *Harper's Magazine* called it "one of the leading small colleges in the South," Birmingham-Southern continues to be recognized nationally for its quality academics, its value, and its safety preparedness. The 2009 issue of the *Fiske Guide to Colleges* includes Birmingham-Southern as one of twenty-six private institutions in the nation named as a best buy for the "quality of the academic offerings in relation to the cost of attendance." Loren Pope's *Colleges That Change Lives* includes BSC as one of forty colleges and universities that are "outdoing the Ivy League schools and the major universities in producing winners." The *Princeton Review* includes the college as one of "America's Best Value Colleges" and one of the "Best 371 Colleges." Birmingham-Southern was the only institution of higher learning in Alabama to receive an "A" for safety preparedness in a 2008 *Reader's Digest* survey, and BSC was ranked ninth in the nation overall, making it the top-ranked liberal arts college in America. The Center for College Affordability and Productivity and Forbes.com rank BSC first among colleges and universities in Alabama based on student satisfaction while in college and success after college, and the College was also named to the 2008 President's Higher Education Community Service Honor Roll for helping to build a culture of service and civic engagement in the nation.

Birmingham-Southern is accredited by AACSB International—The Association to Advance Collegiate Schools of Business and is a Phi Beta Kappa institution.

Each year, Birmingham-Southern ranks first in Alabama and among the nation's best in percentage of all graduates accepted to medical, dental, or health career programs; the College also ranks high nationally in graduates accepted to law school.

Birmingham-Southern competes in NCAA Division III athletics and supports twenty-one varsity sports. New sports include football, men's and women's indoor and outdoor track and field, and men's and women's lacrosse. The College has more than eighty clubs and organizations and intramural sports. Its enrollment has grown to more than 1,500 students per year.

Location

Located on a 197-acre hilltop campus in western Birmingham, the College is just 3 miles via I-59/20 from the downtown business district. Birmingham, which is Alabama's largest city, has been honored by the U.S. Conference of Mayors as the "Most Livable City in America" and offers fine restaurants, museums, city and state parks, and theater. Its offerings are supplemented by the activities of four other Birmingham colleges. Birmingham's 17,000-seat Civic Center is the setting for many outstanding cultural and athletic events.

Majors and Degrees

Birmingham-Southern offers the undergraduate degrees of Bachelor of Arts, Bachelor of Science, Bachelor of Music, Bachelor of Music Education, and Bachelor of Fine Arts. Departmental majors include accounting, art, art history, biology, business administration, chemistry, computer science, dance, economics, education, engineering (3-2 program), English, environmental studies (3-2 program), French, German, history, mathematics, music, nursing (3-2 program), philosophy, physics, political science, psychology, religion, sociology, Spanish, theater arts, and urban environmental studies. Individualized and interdisciplinary majors are also available.

Academic Programs

The College operates on a 4-1-4 calendar. Thirty-six units are required for the bachelor's degree; these comprise 32 regular term units and 4 Interim Term units. The minimum residence requirement is two years. In addition to its traditional liberal arts programs, Birmingham-Southern offers a number of individualized learning opportunities to meet students' special needs and career goals. These are the Honors Program, the Mentor Program, leadership studies, independent study, the student internship program, individualized majors, and the Interim Term. The College emphasizes international opportunities for students through course offerings, visitors to the campus, and international travel/study programs. Through the Associated Colleges of the South, the College offers international programs in England, Brazil, and Central Europe.

Credit is available through Advanced Placement tests and also may be earned through a College-approved internship program.

Birmingham-Southern offers several special programs, including a one-week Student Leaders in Service program and a dual-enrollment program that enables high school seniors to take college-credit courses.

Off-Campus Programs

The College sponsors an internship program, through which students may earn credit for actual work experience. Depending on their major, students may be assigned positions in business, government, industry, human services, or other preprofessional areas of interest. In addition, students may take part in a cooperative exchange program that enables them to take courses at the University of Alabama at Birmingham, Miles College, or Samford University. They also may participate in Army ROTC at the University of Alabama at Birmingham or Air Force ROTC at Samford University.

Academic Facilities

Birmingham-Southern College features several new facilities, including the Norton Campus Center, the Striplin Physical Fitness Center, the Stephens Science Center, the Admission Welcome Center, the Athletics Complex, and the Urban Environmental Park. BSC is home to the Meyer Planetarium, the first public planetarium in Alabama. The only split-revolve-lift stage in the country is housed in the College Theatre. Six fraternity houses on fraternity row recently opened, and a major renovation to Daniel Men's Residence Hall resulted in suite-style living. A newly renovated Humanities Center also recently opened, and two new residence halls are under construction to provide suite-style living for 167 men and women.

Costs

Tuition at BSC for 2009–10 was $25,800, and room and board fees average $8000. There is a $390 student activity fee and $556 IT fee. Estimated expenses for books and supplies are $1160. Transportation and personal expenses are additional costs.

Financial Aid

Birmingham-Southern feels strongly that well-qualified students should have an opportunity for a college education regardless of economic circumstances. More than 98 percent of the

College's students receive financial aid of some kind. Birmingham-Southern students received more than $27 million in aid last year. Scholarships and grants range from $1000 to full tuition and may be renewed annually. Each student requesting financial assistance must submit the Free Application for Federal Student Aid (FAFSA). With the exception of the College's competitive scholarship programs and the Alabama Student Grant, all financial assistance awarded through the Office of Financial Aid is based on a demonstrated need determined from the required forms. Preference is given to those students who file by the March 1 priority deadline. In addition to the need-based programs, Birmingham-Southern awards more than $1.5 million in merit-based scholarships through a scholarship competition that is held in the spring.

Faculty

The faculty is composed of 115 full-time and 55 part-time teaching members; approximately 96 percent hold a Ph.D. degree or the terminal degree in their field. In addition to teaching, the faculty's major responsibility is advising students. Faculty members are actively involved in cocurricular activities that are planned primarily for students, and all are assigned a limited number of student advisees. They work closely with these students in planning and developing individual programs to fulfill the students' career interests. The student-faculty ratio is 12:1, and no freshman English class has more than 16 students.

Student Government

The Student Government Association of the College is chartered to operate under a constitution developed by the students, faculty members, and administration. Through a large measure of self-government, this organization helps provide a well-balanced intellectual, educational, and social cocurricular program for all students. The Honor Code makes each student responsible for upholding the social and academic standards of the College. Students serve on numerous College committees.

Admission Requirements

Approximately 425 freshmen enroll each year and are selected on the basis of high school record, ACT or SAT scores, academic courses attempted, an admission essay, an interview, and recommendations of school officials. Applicants are expected to have completed at least 16 units of course work, 12 of which must be in academic subjects. Four units of English and at least 2 units each of mathematics, history, science, and social sciences are required, and 2 units of a foreign language are recommended. Students are encouraged to take more than the minimum units required in academic subjects.

Although an interview is not required except in the case of early admission, each applicant is encouraged to visit the campus and talk with an admission counselor or the Dean of Enrollment Management.

Transfer applicants must have at least a C average (2.0 on a 4.0 scale) on a full schedule of courses that are acceptable to Birmingham-Southern and a status of good standing with a clear academic and social record from the last college attended. If the applicant has attended more than one college, his or her overall average at these schools must meet the minimum academic year grade point average required at Birmingham-Southern. Transfer students may enroll at the beginning of any term.

Application and Information

The College considers applications on a rolling admission basis. The priority deadline for scholarship applications is a January 1 postmark.

Preview Days are held in September, October, November, and April, and the College offers two Preview Days during the summer.

Inquiries concerning admission should be addressed to:

Sheri S. Salmon
Dean of Enrollment Management
Birmingham-Southern College
900 Arkadelphia Road
Box 549008
Birmingham, Alabama 35254
Phone: 205-226-4696
800-523-5793 (toll-free)
E-mail: admission@bsc.edu
Web site: http://www.bsc.edu

A view of the campus at Birmingham-Southern College.

BISHOP'S UNIVERSITY

SHERBROOKE, QUEBEC, CANADA

The University

Since 1843 Bishop's University has provided students from across Canada and around the world with a sound and liberal education. Today, Bishop's offers undergraduate degrees in business, education, humanities, natural sciences, and social sciences to 1,900 students from every Canadian province, twenty U.S. states, and sixty-five countries around the world. Although it is located in Quebec, Bishop's is an English-language university in a bilingual setting. The mission of Bishop's University is to provide a sound and liberal education at the undergraduate level. The goal is the education of individuals to realize their full potential in their intellectual, spiritual, social, and physical dimensions. To this end, Bishop's emphasizes excellence in teaching enriched by scholarship and research. Furthermore, the University encourages frequent interactions among students and faculty members, participation in nonacademic activities, a keen sense of responsibility to others, and an openness within as well as a commitment to the Quebec, Canadian, and international communities.

In September 2009, 1,854 full-time undergraduate students were enrolled at Bishop's, making it one of the smallest universities in Canada. The University expects to have nearly 2,000 full-time students enrolled by September 2010. Sixty percent of students come from outside the province of Quebec and 25 percent list French as their first language. The average class size in first-year courses is 40 students; in upper-level courses, the average drops to 17 students. First-year students are guaranteed housing in one of seven residence halls on campus. All rooms are single or double and are wired for Internet access.

Athletics plays a major role at Bishop's. Varsity sports include football and golf for men, soccer for women, and alpine skiing, basketball, and rugby for both men and women. Club sports include men's lacrosse and women's ice hockey. Bishop's is blessed with excellent facilities and numerous extracurricular activities. The Athletic Complex includes two gyms, two weight rooms, an indoor pool, an indoor running track, six squash courts, an aerobics studio, and ten outdoor tennis courts (including six lighted courts). Construction is scheduled to begin in 2010 on a $30-million expansion and renovation to the sports and wellness complex. Its multi-sport stadium has a state-of-the-art turf field. Bishop's has a nine-hole golf course on campus and 124 kilometers (77 miles) of bike trails and cross-country ski paths that begin on the campus. The region is also surrounded by excellent skiing and snowboarding mountains. More than fifty clubs and organizations offer a variety of student activities, including the Student Representative Council, a student-run newspaper, the yearbook, the debating team, and the Big Buddies Association.

Location

Bishop's is a peaceful, residential campus in the borough of Lennoxville, just minutes away from downtown Sherbrooke, one of the largest cities in Quebec. The Eastern Townships of Quebec—a region blessed with some of the finest outdoor recreational opportunities in Canada—is also less than a day's drive from Ottawa, Toronto, Boston, and New York City. Nearby are the dynamism of Montreal, Quebec City, and the American-border states of Vermont, New Hampshire, and Maine. Sherbrooke topped the *Canadian Business'* sixth annual ranking of the best places to set up a business. The survey also cited Sherbrooke's eight post-secondary educational institutions, including two universities. "This gives Sherbrooke one of the highest concentrations of brains, students and R&D on the continent, and contributes a billion dollars to the local economy."

Majors and Degrees

Bishop's offers Bachelor of Arts (B.A.), Bachelor of Business Administration (B.B.A.), Bachelor of Commerce and Science (B.C.S.), Bachelor of Education (B.Ed.), and Bachelor of Science (B.Sc.) degree programs. Programs are available in biology, biochemistry, business administration, chemistry, classical studies, computer science, drama, economics, education (elementary or secondary), English, French and Québécois studies, fine arts, health science, history, liberal arts, mathematics, modern languages, music, philosophy, physics, political studies, psychology, religion, sociology, and women's studies. Students can also enroll in interdisciplinary programs.

Academic Programs

Students are encouraged to study outside of their division and to choose minors or double majors. Many students combine very diverse studies—such as double majors in business and drama, a major in biology and a minor in the fine arts, or a major in political studies and a minor in sociology.

Prospective students are encouraged to choose a specific major when applying to Bishop's. The major normally requires that a student take sixteen courses, or 48 credits, within one discipline. A wide range of complementary courses or a major or minor in another subject area may be added during the course of a student's degree and completed in conjunction with the original major. A minor requires eight courses, or 24 credits, within a single concentration and is added to a student's program during the course of a student's degree program.

The honors course of study is the most highly specialized concentration of courses within a degree. Students must normally take the majority of their courses (twenty courses or 60 credits) in one discipline, as designated by the department concerned, while maintaining a high academic standing. An honors degree is normally declared during a student's second or third year of study and is based on academic performance. Students who intend to pursue graduate studies are strongly urged to consider an honors degree.

Off-Campus Programs

Full-time students with a 70 percent or better cumulative GPA and who are enrolled in their first degree can apply to participate in an exchange program. Bishop's University has exchange agreements with universities in several different countries, and new possibilities are added every year. Students may consider Australia, Belgium, England, Finland, France, Germany, Korea, Mexico, Netherlands, Norway, South Africa, Spain, Sweden, Switzerland, and the United States. Most students who participate go in either the second year of a three-year Bishop's degree program or the third year of a four-year degree program. Other arrangements are possible.

Academic Facilities

Most of Bishop's classroom and laboratory facilities have recently been renovated or are scheduled to be renovated in the near future. The Cole Computer Centre houses the main computer systems and wireless connectivity. More than 650 desktop computers and five general-purpose and departmental labs provide a 10:1 student-computer ratio. Stand-up e-mail workstations for all students and staff and faculty members are located throughout the campus.

The Dobson-Lagassé Centre for Entrepreneurship, established to assist start-up businesses with rapid access to strategic information, provides assistance in writing business plans and flexible mentoring for better business performance. The Eastern Townships Research Centre was established in 1982 to foster and stimulate research on historical, cultural, and social aspects of the Eastern Townships. The Curry Wildlife Refuge, a 3-hectare wetland conservation area, acts as an on-campus laboratory.

The Foreman Art Gallery serves as a forum for the presentation and examination of the visual arts through a program of contemporary and historical exhibitions as well as a lecture series and films. The Centennial Theatre seats 575 and accommodates a variety of theatrical productions, concerts, and guest speakers as well as weekly films. There is also a multipurpose studio theater (in-the-round) with seating for 175. First constructed in 1897 and completely renovated in 1991, Bandeen Hall is a 156-seat recital hall that combines outstanding acoustics and modern equipment with the grace and charm of a nineteenth-century structure.

The John Bassett Memorial Library, with a seating capacity of 500, houses a collection of 590,577 items. The library has a computer lab with twenty-seven workstations, six laptop ports, and wireless access to the Internet. In addition to books and audiovisual materials, the collection includes subscriptions to 18,408 print and online periodical titles and twenty-six electronic products, such as abstracts, company reports, and full-text online journals.

The Johnson Science Labs is scheduled to undergo a $5-million upgrade and renovation in the spring of 2010, providing state-of-the-art science facilities for student and faculty research.

Costs

In 2009, Quebec residents paid Can$65.60 per credit, while out-of-province Canadian residents paid Can$183.36 per credit. International students enrolled in a science, mathematics, computer science, drama, music, or fine art program paid Can$500.53 per credit, while all other disciplines cost Can$448.13 per credit. All students paid Can$457.50 in fees. The room-only portion of the residence fees during the academic year was from Can$406 per month for a double room and Can$510 per month for a single room with a semiprivate bathroom. All residents selected a meal plan, which varied in cost from Can$424 to Can$454 per month.

Estimated costs for full-time international students are between Can$13,500 and Can$15,000 for tuition and student fees (including health coverage) for two semesters. Room and board in campus residence with a full meal plan cost approximately Can$6900 for two semesters.

Financial Aid

Renewable entrance scholarships, ranging from Can$1000 to Can$4000, are guaranteed for all Canadian and CEGEP students who meet the scholarship criteria. To be eligible for an academic scholarship, students must apply to Bishop's no later than March 1, and recipients are notified no later than May 1. In addition, there are ten Can$2000 admission scholarships awarded to students from the American high school system. The University also grants a number of awards and bursaries to students in financial need who meet specific criteria. For example, students who have demonstrated outstanding records of leadership may be eligible for an APEX (Awards for Peer Excellence) of Can$1000 for one year.

Faculty

Faculty members are loyal, committed teachers who deem personal interaction with undergraduate students to be a priority. They have chosen to teach at Bishop's because it is possible to know and appreciate each of their students on an individual basis. In all divisions and schools, professors are involved in interesting and exciting research activities, ranging from complex chemical experiments to political and literature studies to the creation of new works of art and music. The student-faculty ratio is 17:1.

Student Government

The Bishop's University Students' Representative Council (SRC) is a nonprofit student-run organization to which all students automatically belong. The SRC provides students with a voice in student-related issues, not only at the University level but also at the provincial and national level. The SRC comprises a 5-member executive branch (the president, the academic vice president, the internal vice president, the external vice president, and the director of finance), which, with 5 student senators, 6 students-at-large, and 1 corporate representative, forms the 17-member Executive Council.

Admission Requirements

Bishop's invites applications from students interested in participating academically and socially in the University. Acceptance to the University is based upon a review of a student's past academic record in CEGEP, secondary, or postsecondary studies. School performance and the quality of academic work are the most important criteria used in judging the probability of an applicant's success at the university level and in determining their eligibility for admission.

CEGEP applicants must complete a DEC and enter a 93-credit (three-year) program. Canadian high school applicants must have a high school diploma and a minimum 75 percent overall average on academic courses. U.S. high school applicants must have their high school diploma and submit SAT or ACT scores. Transfer applicants are assessed on an individual basis. Adjustments in degree length may be made for International Baccalaureate or Advanced Placement courses. Students are encouraged to visit the Web site for application and program requirements (http://www.ubishops.ca).

Applicants should submit a completed application form (online at https://www.gobishops.ca), an academic transcript of work completed to the end of the previous semester (student copies are accepted from CEGEP and Ontario applicants, but all others must submit an official transcript), the Can$60 application fee, and a copy of their birth certificate (and Canadian permanent resident documentation, if applicable).

Application and Information

Those planning to begin their studies at Bishop's in September must apply by March 1, though earlier applications are encouraged. The application deadline for January admission is October 15. Admission may be limited by space availability after these dates. Those who apply by the deadlines should have a response within three weeks.

Jock Phippen
Director of Enrolment Management
Bishop's University
Sherbrooke, Quebec J1M 1Z7
Canada
Phone: 819-822-9600, Ext. 2631
877-822-8200 (toll-free)
Fax: 819-822-9661
E-mail: jphippen@ubishops.ca
Web site: http://www.gobishops.ca

BLOOMFIELD COLLEGE

BLOOMFIELD, NEW JERSEY

The College

Founded in 1868, Bloomfield College (BC) is an independent, four-year, liberal arts college enrolling more than 2,300 students from around the world. The College's mission is to prepare students to attain academic, personal, and professional excellence in a multicultural and global society. Bloomfield College offers more than sixty degree programs in the liberal arts and sciences, creative arts and technology, and professional studies, which include accounting, business administration, computer information systems, criminal justice, education, game development, network engineering, nursing, pre-chiropractic studies, the sciences, and more.

Bloomfield is accredited by the Middle States Association of Colleges and Schools, and the nursing program is accredited by the Commission on Collegiate Nursing Education and the New Jersey Board of Nursing. The College is chartered by the state of New Jersey, and its academic programs are approved by the New Jersey Commission on Higher Education. The accounting program is a Registered Accounting Curriculum for Public Accountancy in the state of New Jersey and meets the state's educational requirements for candidates applying to sit for the CPA examination.

Students have many opportunities to engage in cocurricular programs that enrich their educational experience. In addition to student government, Nursing Student Association, Association of Latin American Students, International Student Association, Haitian Student Association, and other clubs and organizations, students can actively participate in various service-learning, global awareness, professional, and leadership development programs and activities. Campus publications include *In Print,* the College yearbook, and *On the Green,* a magazine for alumni and friends.

The Student Center is the social and recreational focus of the College community and houses meeting rooms, a snack bar, lounges, and the Center for Student Leadership and Engagement, which provides opportunities for student socialization, leadership, and cocurricular learning.

Bloomfield College has a full program of championship NCAA Division II intercollegiate sports, intramural sports, and recreational activities. Men's intercollegiate sports include baseball, basketball, cross-country, soccer, and tennis. Women's intercollegiate sports are basketball, cross-country, soccer, softball, and volleyball. Bloomfield College is also a member of the Central Atlantic Collegiate Conference (CACC), the Eastern College Athletic Conference (ECAC), and the New Jersey Association of Intercollegiate Athletics for Women (NJAIAW).

In addition to general on-campus housing, the College provides special residence halls for first-year students, theme houses, and a new suite-style residence hall. A complete residence-life program provides academic, social, and recreational programs for resident students.

The Center for Academic Development offers individual tutoring and group workshops to all students. Academic advising is ongoing, and students meet with their adviser before registering each semester.

Other support services include the Honors Program, Support for Achievement in Graduate Education, Educational Opportunity Fund Program, career counseling and placement, women's services, and the Wellness Center, which includes health services, the chaplain, and personal counseling. An extensive English for Academic Purposes program for students for whom English is a second language is also offered.

Location

Located in Bloomfield, New Jersey, a suburban, residential community 12 miles from New York City, the College attracts resident students from areas around the world as well as commuter students from the New Jersey/New York metropolitan area. Bloomfield is easily accessible by bus, train, or car from northern New Jersey, New York City, and Rockland and Westchester counties in New York.

Majors and Degrees

Bloomfield College offers more than sixty academic programs in the Bachelor of Arts and Bachelor of Science degrees. Majors and their concentrations include accounting, allied health technologies (diagnostic medical sonography, nuclear medicine technology, respiratory care, and vascular medicine technology), biology (general biology, prechiropractic studies, premedical studies, and pre-podiatric studies), business administration (with specializations in economics, finance, human resource management, international business management, management, management information systems, marketing, and supply chain management), chemistry (biochemistry, general chemistry, and premedical), clinical laboratory science (cytotechnology and medical laboratory science), computer information systems (database, network/ security, and programming), creative arts and technology (animation, digital video, fine arts, game development, graphics for print and digital media, interactive multimedia, and music technology), e-commerce (applications design, applications programming, and support/implementation), education (elementary/ early childhood, elementary with subject matter specialization, secondary, and special education), English (communications, literature, and writing), history, mathematics (applied mathematics), network engineering (Internet technology and LAN specialist), nursing (generic nursing and RN to B.S.N.), philosophy, political science (general, human services, public administration, and public policy), psychology (general psychology and human services), religion, and sociology (criminal justice, general sociology, and human services).

Bloomfield College maintains a joint Bachelor of Science/Doctor of Chiropractic degree program with thirteen accredited chiropractic colleges. Three versions of the prechiropractic program are offered, each preparing students for admission to colleges offering the Doctor of Chiropractic (D.C.) degree.

Bloomfield offers certificate programs in digital media, diversity training, game design, game programming, gerontology, network engineering, and supply chain management. In addition to the traditional format, there is also an accelerated version of the RN to B.S.N. program which allows the degree to be completed more quickly.

The College recently launched its first postgraduate degree, the Master of Accounting (M.Acc.). The M.Acc. program provides a strong technical foundation as well as a practical understanding of the context in which business decisions must be evaluated. This ten-course program is designed to be completed in two academic years with courses being offered year-round. The curriculum allows students to meet the 150-hour rule currently required by most states to sit for the CPA exam.

Academic Programs

Degree candidacy requires the successful completion of at least 33 course units; a full course unit is equivalent to 4 semester hours. A minimum of 16 course units must be completed at an advanced level. Four categories of courses are offered at the College: general education courses, distribution courses, specific major and major required courses, and elective courses. Course requirements for the degree vary among majors.

Other special programs available at Bloomfield include an RN to B.S.N. transfer program for registered nurses who already have a two-year degree; the Educational Opportunity Fund Program, a state-funded program of educational and special services for disadvantaged students; English as a second language; an honors program; and various internship programs.

The Bloomfield College academic calendar consists of fifteen-week fall and spring semesters and an optional summer session consisting of two 7-week terms.

Off-Campus Programs

Bloomfield College is a member of the College Consortium for International Studies (CCIS). Students have the choice of more than seventy-five study-abroad programs in thirty countries around the world, for a semester, a summer, or a full academic year.

Academic Facilities

Renovated Talbott Hall is the technology hub and media center of the College. The lower level houses classrooms featuring laptop and desktop computers, conference rooms, a general computer lab, and a comfortable lounge area. A Web-based radio station, which is part of the College's communications program, occupies the lower mezzanine area level.

The Bloomfield College library houses a collection of more than 68,000 titles, including subscriptions to more than 520 periodicals, an up-to-date reference collection, and thousands of reels of microfilm and microfiche as well as musical recordings and scores, films, and DVDs. The library has an online card catalog, thousands of electronic journals available through 15 databases, and holds a variety of CD-ROMs in the humanities, nursing, and social sciences. Bloomfield College's library holds a unique selection of books about Broadway and theater arts known as the Larry Qualls Collection. Library instruction and research assistance make the library a complete learning center. The library also contains the Media Center, which consists of three electronic classrooms, a distance learning room, and a screening room.

In addition to numerous computer labs, the College has wireless connectivity in most buildings on campus, including the library, the Student Center, and student residences, with plans for many more locations.

Costs

Tuition in 2010–11 for full-time students is $20,800 per year. Room and board for resident students are $10,600 per year. Fees total approximately $1200.

Financial Aid

Bloomfield College students receive approximately $38 million in scholarships and financial aid, with more than 90 percent of the full-time day student population receiving some form of financial assistance. Academic scholarships are administered by the Office of Admission; athletic scholarships are administered by the athletics department. College, state, and federal programs, such as grants, loans, and work-study, are administered by the Office of Financial Aid. The priority deadline for filing the FAFSA for Bloomfield College financial aid is March 15. Applicants who meet the March 15 deadline are considered for Bloomfield College scholarships and campus-based financial aid, including PACE, an interest-free loan for parents.

Faculty

A highly qualified and diverse faculty instructs more than 2,100 students of all ages in day, evening, and accelerated sessions, with a student-faculty ratio of 14:1. Approximately 75 percent of the full-time faculty members have earned doctorates or terminal degrees.

Student Government

The Bloomfield College Student Government serves as a vehicle of communication for student concerns, interests, and educational needs. The administrative staff and the College faculty serve as advisers to all student government activities and enterprises.

Admission Requirements

Bloomfield College admits qualified applicants who demonstrate the motivation, desire, and potential to benefit from and contribute to programs of study in the liberal arts and sciences, creative arts and technology, and professional studies. The College evaluates applicants in a comprehensive manner, with emphasis placed on the applicant's academic history, quality of curriculum, performance on standardized tests such as SAT and/or ACT, extracurricular involvement, results of one-on-one interviews, and recommendations from teachers and counselors. Once admitted, students are placed according to their academic preparation and achievement.

Application and Information

All applicants are encouraged to visit the College to discuss their academic and career plans with an admission counselor. Accepted students may participate in the Bloomfield overnight program where they can experience the campus firsthand and talk with students, faculty members, and administrators about academic programs and student activities, as well as the issues of admission and financial assistance. Applications are accepted throughout the year, with a priority application deadline of March 14 for the fall semester and November 15 for the spring semester. Applicants are notified within two weeks of the College's receipt of required materials. Applications received after these dates are considered on a space-available basis. Admission is open to all qualified students without regard to race, color, creed, religion, national or ethnic origin, sex, age, or physical disability. The College welcomes applications from high school seniors, transfer students, and adult students returning to school. Students may apply online at http://www.bloomfield.edu/apply. For further information, students should contact:

Bloomfield College Office of Admission
One Park Place
Bloomfield, New Jersey 07003
Phone: 973-748-9000 Ext. 230
800-848-4555 (toll-free)
E-mail: admission@bloomfield.edu
Web site: http://www.bloomfield.edu/admissions

BOSTON COLLEGE

CHESTNUT HILL, MASSACHUSETTS

The University

Boston College (BC) was founded in 1863 by the Jesuits to serve the sons of Boston's Irish immigrants. Today a coeducational university on more than 205 acres in Chestnut Hill, BC may seem a world apart from the small school in the crowded heart of Boston that was its first home. Through more than fourteen decades of growth and change, however, BC has held fast to the Jesuit ideals that inspired its founders. A Jesuit education today, as a century ago, is grounded in the liberal arts and in a commitment to the service of others.

Undergraduates may enroll in the College of Arts and Sciences, the Wallace E. Carroll School of Management, the Connell School of Nursing, or the Lynch School of Education.

BC's 9,000 undergraduates come from many backgrounds. The university draws from nearly all fifty states and more than fifty countries. Students' religious and cultural backgrounds are similarly diverse. Today, the university's AHANA (African American, Hispanic, Asian, and Native American) and international students make up nearly 25 percent of the undergraduate student body.

In today's complex and increasingly diverse world, the university believes that the best education is one that broadens a student's capacity to reason, think, and make critical judgments in a wide range of areas. Thus, each BC student fulfills a core of liberal arts courses from which he or she can pursue degrees in more than fifty areas of study and choose from more than 1,400 course offerings throughout the university.

According to several recent national publications, BC is in the top tier of the nation's colleges and universities. The foundation for that achievement is the university's scholars and researchers—679 full-time professionals who make up the faculty. The kinship between teachers and students is one of the hallmarks of a BC education; that relationship is nurtured by a student-teacher ratio of 13:1. The median class size at the university is 20 students.

At BC, learning continues beyond the classroom in more than 200 student-run organizations. These include student government, honor societies, language and cultural organizations, performance ensembles, political groups, preprofessional clubs, publications, and service organizations. BC also sponsors thirteen varsity teams for men and sixteen for women, all of which compete at the NCAA Division I level. The College also supports sixty club and intramural sports.

Location

Located in the Chestnut Hill section of Newton, BC sits on the doorstep of one of America's great cities, a center of culture and education for more than three centuries. It is an energetic, cosmopolitan city that draws life and enthusiasm from the more than 200,000 college students in residence during the academic year. Located just 6 miles from downtown Boston and with easy access to the city via the trolley system that stops at the foot of the campus, BC offers the best of both worlds: a scenic suburban setting neighboring an exciting metropolitan center.

Majors and Degrees

The College of Arts and Sciences (A&S) is the oldest and largest of the four undergraduate schools at BC. A&S students must complete thirty-eight 1-semester courses, thirty-two of which are in A&S departments. The normal course load is five courses per semester for the first three years and four courses per semester during the senior year. The undergraduate curriculum includes the university Core Curriculum and ten to twelve courses in the major field, with the remainder of courses chosen as electives. A&S offers degrees in the following areas: art history, biochemistry, biology, chemistry, classical studies, communication, computer science, economics, English, environmental geosciences, film studies, French, geology, geology and geophysics, geophysics, German studies, Hispanic studies, history, independent major, international studies, Italian, linguistics, mathematics, music, philosophy, physics, political science, psychology, Russian, Slavic studies, sociology, studio art, theater, and theology. Preprofessional advisement is also available in medical, dental, veterinary, and legal programs. Students can also select from twenty-one departmental minors, or nineteen interdisciplinary minors.

The Carroll School of Management educates students to be leaders in business and industry and in public agencies, educational institutions, and service organizations. The Carroll School offers concentrations in accounting, computer science, corporate reporting and analysis, economics, finance, general management, human resource management, information systems, marketing, and operations and strategic management.

The Lynch School of Education prepares students for education and human services professions. Programs provide a general education, professional preparation, and specialized education in the major field. Fieldwork in area schools is closely linked to course work in each specialization. The Lynch School awards degrees upon completion of thirty-eight courses, including the University Core, a major field of study in education, and a second major in a subject field or an interdisciplinary area in A&S that complements the student's program. Areas of specialization include early childhood education, elementary education, human development, and secondary education. The Lynch School also offers interdisciplinary majors in American heritages, general science, mathematics/computer science, and perspectives on Spanish America.

The Connell School of Nursing offers a four-year program of study leading to a Bachelor of Science degree. The three major components to the curriculum are nursing major courses, electives, and the required University Core. In all courses, principles of wellness, illness, rehabilitation, and health maintenance serve as a theoretical basis in preparing students for professional nursing practice. Nursing courses include traditional classes, simulated and audiovisual laboratory activities on campus, and clinical learning activities in health-care settings.

Academic Programs

Every BC education is centered on a core curriculum—a set of required courses. BC offers a core curriculum because it believes in the unity of knowledge. While the core, which is continually reviewed by a committee of faculty members, varies somewhat by school, its common elements include literature, natural science, writing, philosophy, theology, social science, modern European history, mathematics, fine arts, and the study of a non-European culture.

There is a wide variety of extraordinary academic programs available to BC students to enhance their educational experience. They include, among others, honors programs within each of the university's four undergraduate schools, Undergraduate Faculty Research Fellows, the Scholar of the College, PULSE, and Perspectives on Western Culture.

Off-Campus Programs

BC encourages all students to take part in internship programs. More than half of BC undergraduates participate in at least one internship or prepracticum placement during their college years. Internships can be paid or unpaid and may take place during the academic year or the summer; some carry academic credit.

BC students may take on the challenge of international study in more than seventy programs administered by BC at universities in more than thirty countries. BC students who study abroad typically do so in their junior year, but there is also a range of full-year and summer-abroad opportunities. The Office of International Programs helps students with program selection and applications and maintains a library of reference books and professional evaluations of international study programs.

Academic Facilities

BC's eight libraries contain more than 2.4 million printed volumes, over 4.2 million items in microform, approximately 213,086 government documents, more than 9,000 serial subscriptions, and a wide collection of films and archival items. The resources of the library system range from some of Europe's earliest printed books to hundreds of computerized databases. Students with personal computers have dorm-room access to these databases as well as to Quest and other library information sources through Agora, the campus information network. Additionally, all of BC's libraries and classrooms offer a wireless network that provides access to these resources and the Internet.

Research laboratories in the state-of-the-art science facilities have been specially designed to accommodate the advanced instrumentation required for modern science and to provide flexibility for accommodating new equipment. The $85-million expansion to the Higgins Biology and Physics Center was carefully designed to place classrooms, laboratories, computer facilities, and office space in proximity and to facilitate interaction among faculty members, researchers, and students. In addition to the Center's seventeen new teaching laboratories, special working labs are designed and outfitted for research and teaching in the fields of biology and physics.

Costs

Tuition for the 2009–10 academic year was $39,130, which included a student activity fee and campus health fee. The total for room and board was $11,840, which includes the board plan. Freshman mandatory fees include a one-time required charge of $430 for first year orientation and student identification.

Financial Aid

BC maintains a financial aid program to assist deserving and qualified students who might otherwise not be able to attend the university. Boston College is committed to providing funds to meet the full demonstrated need of every admitted student who applies for financial aid. Overall, 65.7 percent of students receive some form of financial aid. Assistance for freshmen alone included more than $19 million in need-based grants. The university offers financial aid to students based on need as demonstrated by completion of the College Scholarship Service's Financial Aid PROFILE and the Free Application for Federal Student Aid (FAFSA). All requirements and deadlines and complete instructions are available in BC admission literature. An application for financial aid in no way affects a decision on admission.

Each year, BC chooses 15 incoming freshmen as Presidential Scholars to receive merit-based, full-tuition scholarships. Students are selected from all candidates who apply through the Early Action program.

Faculty

BC has 679 full-time faculty members. Of these faculty members, 98 percent hold doctoral degrees. The nearly 100 Jesuits living on the BC campus make up one of the largest Apostolic Jesuit communities in the world. Nearly half of these members are active in the College's administration and teaching.

Student Government

The Undergraduate Government of Boston College (UGBC), formed in 1968, is led by the president and vice president, who are elected in the spring of each year by the entire student body. UGBC's goal is to serve the students by providing services and opportunities and by representing them in the best manner possible to the university community. To accomplish this goal, UGBC provides many educational, social, and cultural programs, such as concerts, lectures, roundtables, and more.

Admission Requirements

The undergraduate admission staff pays particular attention to students who have done well in a demanding college-preparatory curriculum, including Advanced Placement (AP) and honors courses when available. For the class of 2012, there were 30,845 applications for 2,167 places. The majority of incoming freshmen ranked comfortably in the top 10 percent of their high school class. The SAT scores of the middle half of admitted freshmen were 1870–2140. On the ACT, scores of the middle half were between 28 and 32.

Application and Information

Students applying to Boston College for a place in the freshman class must complete both the Common Application and the Boston College Supplemental Application. All applicants should submit the BC Supplemental Application as soon as they have decided to apply to Boston College. Students are encouraged to apply via BC's Web site at http://www.bc.edu/applications but may also apply at http://www.commonapp.org.

Students applying through the regular admission program must submit the Common Application and all other required forms, along with the $70 application fee, by January 1. Candidates are notified of action taken on their application in early April. Admitted students intending to matriculate are required to forward a confirmation fee to the Admission Office postmarked by May 1.

Students with superior academic credentials who view Boston College as a top choice may apply through the nonbinding early action program. These applicants must submit both application forms, along with the $70 application fee, by November 1. Candidates learn of their admission decision before December 25 but have the standard deadline (May 1) to reserve their places as freshmen. Boston College does permit students to apply under early action if they have applied to an early decision college.

BC accepts transfer applicants each semester. Transfer candidates should request applications for transfer admission from the Office of Undergraduate Admission or via the Web site at http://www.bc.edu/transfer. In addition to high school records and standardized test results, transfer applicants must furnish transcripts from all postsecondary institutions they have attended.

For more information, students should contact:

Office of Undergraduate Admission
Devlin Hall 208
Boston College
Chestnut Hill, Massachusetts 02467
Phone: 617-552-3100
800-360-2522 (toll-free)
Fax: 617-552-0798
Web site: http://www.bc.edu

Located just 6 miles from downtown Boston, Boston College offers the best of both worlds: a scenic suburban setting neighboring an exciting metropolitan center.

COLLEGE CLOSE-UPS

BOSTON UNIVERSITY

BOSTON, MASSACHUSETTS

The University

Boston University is a private teaching and research university located on the banks of the Charles River in Boston. Boston University is a dynamic community, which encourages creativity and innovation in both its students and faculty. The faculty comprises some of the world's foremost experts who are dedicated to the art of teaching. The average class size is 27 students. Together, the ten undergraduate schools and colleges offer more than 250 major and minor areas of concentration. Students may choose from programs of study in areas as diverse as biochemistry, broadcast journalism, business, mechanical engineering, elementary education, international relations, physical therapy, psychology, and theater arts. With a student body representing all fifty states and more than 100 countries, Boston University has one of the most culturally diverse student bodies in the United States. The campus community supports more than 500 different student organizations, ranging from ice broomball teams to performing arts groups, community service activities to student government, and clubs with cultural and professional as well as academic affiliations.

Location

Boston is an international center of cultural and intellectual activity, with a concentration of facilities for higher education unrivaled throughout the world. Home to many fine museums, baseball's Fenway Park, an active theater district, and the Boston Symphony Orchestra, the city has a vibrant energy all its own. During the academic year 1 in 5 residents is a college student, making Boston the ultimate college town.

Majors and Degrees

Boston University grants the B.A., B.S., B.S.B.A., B.S.Ed., B.A.S., B.L.S., B.A.A., Mus.B., and B.F.A. undergraduate degrees. Of the University's seventeen schools and colleges, ten offer opportunities for undergraduate study. The following list indicates the range of undergraduate programs available.

Students in the College of Arts and Sciences(CAS) may concentrate in American studies; ancient Greek; ancient Greek and Latin; anthropology; anthropology and religion; archaeology; art history; astronomy; astronomy and physics; biochemistry and molecular biology; biology; biology with a specialization in behavioral biology; biology with a specialization in cell biology, molecular biology, and genetics; biology with a specialization in ecology and conservation biology; biology with a specialization in neurobiology; biology with a specialization in quantitative biology; chemistry; chemistry with specialization in biochemistry; chemistry with specialization in teaching; Chinese language and literature; classical civilization; classics and philosophy; classics and religion; comparative literature; computer science; earth sciences; East Asian studies; economics; economics and mathematics; English; environmental analysis and policy; environmental science; French language and literature; geography with a specialization in human geography; geography with a specialization in physical geography; geophysics and planetary sciences; German language and literature; Hispanic language and literatures; history; international relations; Italian studies; Japanese language and literature; Latin; Latin American studies; linguistics; linguistics and philosophy; marine science; mathematics; mathematics and computer science; mathematics and philosophy; music (nonperformance); neuroscience; philosophy; philosophy and physics; philosophy and political science; philosophy and psychology; philosophy and religion; physics; political science; predentistry; prelaw; premedicine; pre-veterinary medicine; psychology; religion; Russian language and literature; Russian/East European studies; and sociology. Special curricula include seven-year accelerated programs in liberal arts and dentistry and liberal arts and medicine; the Modular Medical Integrated Curriculum; a dual-degree program; and various combined B.A./M.A. degree programs.

The College of Fine Arts (CFA) offers programs in the School of Music (composition and theory, music education, musicology, and performance), the School of Theater (acting, design, management, production, and theater arts), and the School of Visual Arts (art education, graphic design, painting, and sculpture).

The College of General Studies (CGS) offers a two-year liberal-arts-based program that features a core curriculum and intensive team teaching. It is designed so that students continue as juniors in the degree-granting schools and colleges of the University.

The College of Communication (COM) offers major programs of undergraduate study in film, television, journalism (with specialization available in broadcast journalism, magazine journalism, news-editorial journalism, and photojournalism), mass communication, advertising, and public relations.

Majors in the College of Engineering (ENG) include biomedical engineering, computer engineering, electrical engineering, mechanical engineering, mechanical engineering with specialization in aerospace, and mechanical engineering with specialization in manufacturing.

The College of Health and Rehabilitation Sciences: Sargent College (SAR) offers programs in athletic training; health science; human physiology; nutrition; and speech, language, and hearing sciences as well as a five-year combined B.S./M.S. degree program in occupational therapy, a six-year B.S./D.P.T. program in physical therapy, and a six-year B.S. in athletic training/D.P.T. in physical therapy program.

Areas of concentration in the School of Education (SED) include bilingual education, deaf studies, early childhood education, elementary education, English education, history and social science education, Latin and classical studies education, mathematics education, modern foreign language education, science education, and special education.

The Science and Engineering Program (SEP) offers a four-semester program for those students interested in studying the natural sciences or engineering. It is designed so that students continue as juniors in either the College of Engineering or a science program in the College of Arts and Sciences.

The School of Hospitality Administration (SHA) offers a rigorous program in the management of hotels, restaurants, food and beverage service, travel and tourism, and entertainment.

Concentrations in the School of Management (SMG) include accounting, business law, entrepreneurship, finance, general management, international management, management information systems, marketing, operations and technology management, and organizational behavior.

Academic Programs

A Boston University education combines the elements of a traditional liberal arts education with training for the professions. Highly qualified freshmen may be invited to participate in the University Honors College.

Boston University has more than seventy programs that take students around the world. Internships, fieldwork, and study-abroad opportunities are offered on six continents within twenty-six countries, including the U.S. BU has a series of programs and internships in a variety of locations, including Auckland, Beijing, Dresden, Dublin, Geneva, Haifa, London, Los Angeles, Madrid, Paris, Sydney, and Washington, D.C. Programs offered include studies in art/architecture, business/economics, engineering, human health services, journalism/communications, visual/performing arts, and many more. Fieldwork programs may be found in locations that include Belize,

Ecuador, and Spain, with study-abroad options that include programs in Auckland, Burgos, Dresden, Grenoble, Haifa, Madrid, Niamey, Oxford, Padova, Quito, and Venice. Summer study programs exist in Argentina, Australia, China, England, France, Ireland, Italy, Peru, Senegal, Spain, and the United States.

Boston University operates on a calendar of two semesters and two summer terms. Students generally take four courses each semester; thirty-two courses are required for graduation. Most degree programs are built around a core of humanities and social and natural sciences. Concentrations require eight to thirteen courses. Electives generally total 30–40 percent of the courses taken, allowing for interdisciplinary study.

Academic Facilities

Three of the newest facilities on campus are the School of Hospitality Administration Building, a fully wireless facility with dedicated space for student activities and career recruitment and a hospitality library; the Agganis Arena; and the Fitness and Recreation Center. A life science and engineering facility, with 187,000 square feet of laboratory and research space for the biology, bioinformatics, chemistry, and bioengineering departments, also opened recently. Boston University's state-of-the-art Photonics Center features classroom and laboratory space for the College of Engineering as well as labs designed to support industry partners who seek to develop new photonics-based products. The School of Management building represents one of the most technologically advanced educational facilities in the country, with more than 4,000 data and communications ports and a dedicated career center and management library.

Through Boston University Information Services and Technology, students have access to public computing facilities equipped with workstations, terminals, and laser printers as well as a high-speed campus network interconnecting all computer resources and linking them to the Internet. An 890-seat proscenium theater, studio space for visual arts students, practice rooms for music, and a 575-seat music performance center are indicative of Boston University's support for the arts. More than 2.8 million library volumes and more than 4.7 million microform units are contained in Mugar Memorial Library, where the Twentieth-Century Archives are held, including the papers of Martin Luther King Jr., Theodore Roosevelt, Robert Frost, and Bette Davis.

Costs

Tuition for 2009–10 was $37,910; estimated room and board costs were $11,848. University and college fees were $530. These costs are exclusive of books, supplies, travel, and personal expenses.

Financial Aid

The Boston University Financial Assistance office has a variety of grants, scholarships, student loans, and student employment opportunities available to those who request help in meeting the expenses of attending Boston University. Information about credit-based financing options is also provided to students and parents. Need-based aid is offered to eligible students. Merit awards are offered to selected students.

Financial aid offered on the basis of calculated financial eligibility may include Boston University grants, state and federal grants, loans, Federal Work-Study, and other part-time employment. Boston University makes every effort to assist students with calculated financial eligibility, however, funds are limited and it is not possible to meet the eligibility of all applicants for financial aid. Priority for a Boston University grant is given to those students with the strongest academic records. Nevertheless, all applicants who anticipate the need for financial aid are encouraged to apply. In addition, Boston University believes in recognizing and rewarding outstanding high school seniors for their academic and other accomplishments. The University is therefore committed to offering a variety of merit awards.

Faculty

Students are taught by faculty members who distinguish themselves through their ability, experience, research, and publications. In addition to fulfilling their classroom responsibilities, faculty members are accessible as academic and career advisers who assist students in obtaining internships as well research opportunities.

Student Government

Each school and college has its own student government, which regulates student affairs within the school or college. The University-wide student governing body, the Student Union, has representation from all University schools and colleges. Each residence also has its own student government, composed of elected representatives from each floor.

Admission Requirements

The Board of Admissions considers each candidate individually. Primary emphasis is placed on the strength of the secondary school record, but required test scores (SAT or ACT), character, breadth of interest, school recommendations, and other personal qualifications are also carefully evaluated. Students are required to submit the SAT or the ACT (with Writing Test). Results of the ACT that do not include the Writing Test will not meet the requirement for admission. Students taking the SAT will also be required to submit the results of two SAT Subject Tests in different subject areas. Students taking the ACT (with Writing Test) do not need to submit Subject Tests. Prospective students should see the Requirements and Standards chart at http://www.bu.edu/admissions/apply/ freshmen/ program-requirements/ for a full listing of the standardized testing requirements. Secondary school graduation or an equivalency diploma is required of all candidates; for the College of Fine Arts, an audition or a portfolio is required. For certain programs, interviews and additional SAT Subject Test scores are required.

Students with earned credit from other colleges may be admitted. Applicants are considered for September or January entrance. Transfer students are not eligible for admission to the Accelerated Liberal Arts Medical or Dental Programs, the College of General Studies, or the Science and Engineering Program. January admission to the College of Fine Arts School of Theatre is also not available to transfer students. Boston University offers programs of early decision (binding agreement), early admission, and deferred admission.

Boston University admits qualified students regardless of their race, color, national origin, religion, sex, age, or disability to all its programs and activities.

Application and Information

Boston University requires the Common Application and the Boston University Supplement. Information on applying is available online at http://www.bu.edu/admissions/apply. The deadline for applications is January 1. Applicants for Early Decision must apply by November 1. Accelerated program applicants, Trustee Scholar nominees, Dr. Martin Luther King Jr. Scholarship nominees, and Alexander Graham Bell Scholarship nominees must file by December 1. Candidates for financial aid should complete the College Scholarship Service (CSS) Financial Aid PROFILE and the Free Application for Federal Student Aid (FAFSA) by February 15. Transfer students applying for September admission should submit their applications, CSS/Financial Aid PROFILE forms, and Free Application for Federal Student Aid (FAFSA) forms by April 1 or by November 1 for January admission.

Boston University Admissions
121 Bay State Road
Boston, Massachusetts 02215

Phone: 617-353-2300
E-mail: admissions@bu.edu
Web site: http://www.bu.edu/admissions

BOWIE STATE UNIVERSITY

BOWIE, MARYLAND

The University

Bowie State University began as a normal school in the city of Baltimore in 1865, and it has evolved over the years into a four-year, coeducational, liberal arts institution. It is currently situated on a beautiful 500-acre campus in Prince Georges County, Maryland, and offers both graduate and undergraduate programs of study. Teacher education programs were established in 1925; in 1935, with state authorization, a four-year program for the training of elementary school teachers was begun and the school became the Maryland State Teachers College at Bowie. In 1951, with the approval of the State Board of Education, its governing body at the time, the college established a teacher-preparation curriculum for the training of teachers for the core program in the junior high schools. Ten years later, permission was granted to institute a teacher-training program for secondary education. A liberal arts program was established in 1963, and the institution's name was changed to Bowie State College. In 1988, Bowie State achieved university status and joined the University System of Maryland (USM).

Bowie State University's physical plant is valued at more than $225 million, and its current enrollment is 5,617 students, 1,217 of whom are in the Graduate School. The University has twenty-two buildings on campus with the addition of the $21-million state-of-the-art Center for Learning and Technology that opened in 2000, the $11.8-million Computer Science Center that opened in 2002, and the new $19-million Center for Business and Graduate Studies opened in 2007. Two of the buildings, the Communication Arts Center and the physical education complex, were completed in 1973, and an administration building opened in 1977. Seven residence halls, including Goodloe Hall and Alex Haley Hall, a state-of-the-art residence hall that houses honors students, house approximately 850 students. In addition, a 460-bed apartment-style residence hall, Christa McAuliffe, was completed in 2004. The $2.6-million physical education complex houses a 3,000-seat basketball arena, an Olympic-size swimming pool with underwater viewing windows and facilities for 200 spectators, an apparatus gymnasium, a dance studio, a wrestling room, a weight-training room, eight handball/squash courts, a therapy room, and offices for instructors and coaches. The $5.5-million University Activities Center includes a cafeteria. Bowie State has broken ground for its new $79 million Fine and Performing Arts Center. The 123,000-square-foot building will include a 400-seat main theater, a 200-seat black box theater, a 200-seat recital hall, an art gallery, classrooms, labs, and offices.

Bowie State University considers the student activities program a vital part of the total educational program. Students have access to more than forty different activities. These include student government, the student union, intercollegiate athletics, eight fraternities and sororities, numerous departmental clubs and preprofessional organizations, and music and drama organizations.

The Graduate School grants the Master of Arts in counseling psychology, English, human resource development, mental health counseling, organizational communications, school psychology, and teaching (M.A.T.); the Master of Business Administration; the Master of Education in elementary education, reading education, school administration and supervision, school counseling, secondary education, and special education; the Master of Public Administration; and the Master of Science in applied computational mathematics, computer science, management information systems, and nursing. The Doctor of Education is granted in educational leadership and the Applied Doctor of Science is granted in computer science. The Adler-Dreikurs Institute of Human Relations at Bowie State University is the first fully accredited master's-degree-granting Adlerian institute in the United States.

Bowie State University admits students without regard to sex, religion, or nationality, and the University does not discriminate on the basis of race, creed, color, national or ethnic origin, age, sex, or handicap. The University is accredited by the Middle States Association of Colleges and Schools and approved by the Maryland State Department of Education. Its programs in teacher education, social work education, nursing, business, and computer science are accredited by the National Council for Accreditation of Teacher Education, the National Council on Social Work Education, the National League for Nursing Accrediting Commission, the Maryland Board of Nursing, the Association of Collegiate Business Schools and Programs, and the Computer Science Accreditation Commission of the Computing Sciences Accreditation Board, respectively.

Location

Bowie, Maryland, is in a triangle formed by Annapolis (20 miles east), Baltimore (25 miles north), and Washington, D.C. (17 miles southwest). The suburban setting provides an ideal, safe environment for students and scholars, with access to all of the important cultural, governmental, and business activities in any of the three metropolitan areas.

Majors and Degrees

Bowie State University offers the Bachelor of Arts or Bachelor of Science degree with majors in biology, business administration, communications media, computer science, computer technology, early childhood education, elementary education, English, English education, fine art, government, history, mathematics, nursing, child and adolescent studies, psychology, science education, social work, sport management, sociology/criminal justice, and technology. A dual-degree program is offered in engineering.

Academic Programs

The University operates on a semester calendar. Academic offerings are housed under four schools (School of Arts and Sciences, School of Education, School of Professional Studies, and the new School of Business) and can be divided into four main areas: humanities, science and mathematics, social sciences, and education. To receive a bachelor's degree, a student must earn a minimum of 120 semester hours with a cumulative grade point average of 2.0 or better. Students are provided the opportunity to complete the General Education Program, acquire lifelong learning skills for a competitive world, and make a successful transition into their junior year. General studies requirements include communication skills, 9 hours; humanities, 9 hours; social sciences, 18 hours; science and mathematics, 9 hours; and physical education, 2 hours. The remaining credit hours can be electives or from major and minor areas of interest. Students must also pass the test of Proficiency in the English Language and must take the national standardized test in their major area.

The Honors Program is designed for students with outstanding academic records and potential and provides a special educational opportunity for young adults with exceptional talent. The program is comprehensive and multidisciplinary in structure and interdisciplinary in application. It has been designed to provide a creative approach to the teaching/learning process and to present activities that encourage the shaping of students' own experiences.

The Special Services Project is a federally funded program designed to retain and graduate first-generation, low-income, and disabled students who have been admitted to Bowie State University. The purpose of the project is to help students overcome academic and nonacademic barriers to academic success, through participation in specially designed activities, including counseling, tutoring, and workshops on test taking and study skills.

Through the Cooperative Education Program, a student may choose either the alternate or parallel programs of study and work in business, industry, government, or a social-service agency. This program is open to Bowie State students who have completed at least one academic year with a minimum cumulative grade point average of 2.0.

The University participates in the College-Level Examination Program (CLEP), administered by the Educational Testing Service for the College Board, and in the Defense Activity for Non-Traditional Education Support (DANTES) program. The University also has a program for awarding students credit for learning acquired through life and work experience. Under this program, students document their backgrounds in a portfolio, which is reviewed by the faculty. Through all of these programs, qualified students may receive up to 30 credit hours toward their degree. In addition, the University offers an Army ROTC program. Two-year and three-year scholarships are available.

Academic Facilities

The Communication Arts Center, a $6.5-million building that houses the humanities division, contains classrooms, offices, conference rooms, and studio-laboratories and seats approximately 1,000 patrons. The $8.8-million, 345,514-volume Thurgood Marshall Library is centrally located on campus and provides excellent equipment and reference departments for the student body. The microfilm file contains 474,196 items; periodicals number 767. Campus research facilities include science laboratories, television and radio studios, language laboratories, and the Adler-Dreikurs Institute. Access to the library collection is provided through Victor Web, the electronic catalog that also links users to millions of USM volumes. The new Center for Learning and Technology, the main classroom building, features a new supercomputer (one of the fastest computers in the world), fourteen electronic classrooms, two interactive lecture halls, three computer labs, one speech lab, and a 300-seat auditorium and conference center. In addition, the new Computer Science Center has five classrooms and thirteen labs. Finally, the Center for Business and Graduate Studies, which opened in 2007, provides modern classrooms, labs, study space, offices, and administrative support space for the School of Business and the Division of Graduate Studies.

Costs

In 2009–10, the annual cost of tuition, fees, board, and room for a freshman who is a Maryland resident averaged $13,000; for a non-Maryland resident, the cost averaged $25,000. The annual cost for a commuting student who is a Maryland resident was about $7000; the cost for a commuting student who is not a Maryland resident was about $17,000.

Financial Aid

Federal Pell Grants, Supplemental Grants, Work-Study, Perkins Loans, and Direct Loans are available. University scholarships, tuition waivers, and diversity grants are awarded. Most awards are based on need. Academic scholarships could be offered to students with cumulative weighted grade point averages of at least 3.3 and minimum SAT (reading and math) scores of 1100. In addition, merit awards are given for athletics, music and fine arts, and ROTC. More than 77 percent of all undergraduate students receive some form of financial aid. Deadlines are March 1 for the fall semester and November 15 for the spring semester.

Faculty

More than 85 percent of the 160 full-time faculty members have earned doctoral degrees. The faculty-student ratio is 1:18.

Student Government

All students are members of the Student Government Association, which, in cooperation with the administration, sets the standards for student life. Students are encouraged to assume leadership roles and to participate in the various programs and activities of the University. The Residence Hall Council provides opportunities for students to participate in the administration of residence life and in the cultural growth of the campus community.

Admission Requirements

Maryland residents applying for admission should have a minimum cumulative grade point average in their core high school courses of 2.0 (on a 4.0 scale) and a minimum SAT (reading and math only) score of 900 (or a minimum ACT score of 19). A sliding scale is used for students who have higher grade point averages or SAT scores. Conditional admission may be offered to students with a minimum cumulative grade point average of 2.0 and minimum SAT (reading and math only) scores of 830 to 899 (or a minimum ACT score of 17). Applicants must have earned a high school diploma or a GED certificate. The following courses are required: English, 4 credits; social science/history, 3 credits; mathematics (algebra I, algebra II, and geometry), 3 credits; laboratory sciences, 2 credits; foreign language, 2 credits; and electives, 6 credits. A $40 application fee is charged, and a health certificate must be submitted before entering the University.

Transfer students must have a minimum 2.0 cumulative grade point average for a minimum of 24 transferable credits, or SAT scores are required. International students and mature adults are encouraged to apply.

Application and Information

The application deadline is April 1 for the fall semester and November 1 for spring. Students should apply online at http://www.bowiestate.edu/apply.

Admissions Office
Bowie State University
Bowie, Maryland 20715-9465
Phone: 301-860-3415
410-880-4100 Ext. 3415 (from the Baltimore-Columbia area)
877-77-BOWIE (toll-free)
Fax: 301-860-3518
E-mail: undergradadmissions@bowiestate.edu
Web site: http://www.bowiestate.edu

Flags representing the international student population of Bowie State University frame the entrance to the 500-acre campus.

COLLEGE CLOSE-UPS

BRIDGEWATER STATE COLLEGE

BRIDGEWATER, MASSACHUSETTS

The College

Bridgewater State College was founded in 1840 and has grown from a teacher-preparation school of 28 students to a comprehensive liberal arts institution that enrolls more than 10,000 students each year (7,200 undergraduates) in day, evening, and summer programs.

The College offers students a lively cultural, social, and recreational life to enhance their learning experience. The Adrian Tinsley Center, Rondileau Campus Center, and East Campus Commons are the settings for many of the student-life activities. Cultural, educational, and entertainment programs, including lectures by guest speakers, concerts, exhibits, and movies, are regularly featured at the Campus Center, while a wide selection of fitness activities are available in the Tinsley Center. The College offers more than 100 student clubs and organizations in a variety of interest areas. Intercollegiate varsity athletic teams compete under NCAA Division III. Men's teams include baseball, basketball, cross-country, football, soccer, swimming, tennis, track and field, and wrestling. Teams for women include basketball, cross-country, field hockey, lacrosse, soccer, softball, swimming, tennis, track and field, and volleyball. A number of club sports are open to students, including cheerleading, equestrian, karate, Ultimate Frisbee, men's ice hockey and lacrosse, and women's rugby.

The Bridgewater State College campus has ten residence halls and thirty-four academic/administrative buildings spread over its 235-acre campus. The atmosphere at Bridgewater is friendly and informal, based on the concept that the College is a diverse community of people with shared interests and goals. A number of important student services (including career, academic, and personal counseling; disability and health services; and housing assistance) are available.

The College offers programs leading to the bachelor's degree in more than thirty different areas of study through the Schools of Arts and Sciences, Business, and Education and Allied Studies.

Bridgewater's School of Graduate Studies offers degrees, including the Master of Arts, Master of Arts in Teaching, Master of Public Administration, and Master of Science, in fields such as management, criminal justice, computer science, English, teacher education, physical education, and psychology. Advanced certificates in teaching are also awarded.

Location

Bridgewater State College is located in Bridgewater, Massachusetts, a community of more than 25,000 people approximately 30 miles south of Boston and 25 miles north of Cape Cod. The area is near many cultural, recreational, and historic sites. Commuter train service to and from Boston operates from early morning to late evening, seven days a week. The Bridgewater train station is located in the center of the College's campus.

Majors and Degrees

Bridgewater State College confers the Bachelor of Arts, Bachelor of Science, and Bachelor of Science in Education degrees.

Undergraduate majors are offered in accounting and finance, anthropology, art, aviation science (airport management, aviation management, flight training), biology, business (see "management"), chemistry, chemistry-geology, communication arts and sciences (communication studies, dance education, speech communication, theater arts, theater education), computer science, criminal justice, early childhood education, earth sciences, economics, elementary education, English, geography, health education, history, management (energy and environmental resources management, general management, global management, information systems management, marketing transportation), mathematics, music, philosophy, physical education, physics, political science, psychology, secondary education, social work, sociology, Spanish, and special education (including communication disorders).

Academic Programs

Bridgewater State College offers a full range of study in more than thirty degree areas. The goal of the academic program is to prepare broadly educated individuals in the liberal arts and the professions. The Academic Achievement Center provides academic counseling and assistance to all freshmen and transfer students. All students must complete the Core Curriculum of general education courses to earn a bachelor's degree. Students must complete 120 semester hours of credit, of which at least 30–36 hours must be taken in a major field of study. Selected students may enroll in departmental or College-wide honors programs.

The College operates on a traditional two-semester calendar and offers two 5-week summer sessions and a number of intensive courses over the summer months.

Off-Campus Programs

Bridgewater State College participates in three programs that allow students to take courses for credit at other institutions of higher education. First, College Academic Program Sharing (CAPS) provides full-time students with the opportunity to take courses offered at any of the other state colleges in Massachusetts. The College is also a member of the Southeastern Association for Cooperation of Higher Education in Massachusetts (SACHEM), a consortium of public and private colleges that includes Bristol Community, Cape Cod Community, Dean, Massasoit Community, Stonehill, and Wheaton Colleges; Massachusetts Maritime Academy; and the University of Massachusetts Dartmouth. Finally, Bridgewater participates in the National Student Exchange Program, which allows students to spend a term at other public colleges and universities in the United States.

Students are encouraged to pursue internships within their major field that provide opportunities to earn college credit while gaining practical experience. Faculty advisers assist students in securing internships in which they work with professionals in business, industry, education, and government.

Academic Facilities

The John Joseph Moakley Center for Technological Applications, named in honor of the late congressman from Massachusetts, is the hub of the College's campuswide voice, data, and video network. Technological resources in the building include a series of technology-integrated classrooms, an open-access computer lab, a television studio and control room, a teleconference facility, and a large lecture hall with integrated, computer-based display technology.

The Clement C. Maxwell Library is a four-story facility that seats 2,500 and has more than 300,000 books, 1,102 periodicals, and 19,500 journals on its information network. Other major resources on campus include an astronomy observatory, radio and television production facilities, a Teacher Technology Center, and the new Tinsley Athletic Center, which houses classrooms, laboratories, a fitness center, an NCAA-regulation gymnasium and basketball court, and meeting areas.

Costs

For 2009–10, tuition for full-time study was $910 per year for Massachusetts residents and $7050 per year for out-of-state students. Fees were $5563 per year, books averaged $800, and room and board averaged $8116. These expenses are all subject to change.

Financial Aid

Many sources of financial aid are available to Bridgewater students, including Federal Pell Grants, Federal Supplemental Educational Opportunity Grants, Federal Perkins Loans, Federal Stafford Student Loans, HELP loans, alumni scholarships, and Federal Work-Study Program awards. The Financial Aid Office has an informative brochure detailing methods of application and guidelines for qualification. For a copy, prospective applicants should write to the Financial Aid Office or telephone 508-531-1341. Students are required to submit the Free Application for Federal Student Aid (FAFSA). Applications for financial aid for the fall semester must be received by March 1.

Faculty

The College faculty has 306 full-time members; 90 percent hold terminal degrees in their area. Since the student-faculty ratio is 19:1 and the emphasis of the faculty is on classroom instruction, there are many opportunities for personal contact and interaction between faculty members and students at Bridgewater. Students discover that faculty members are interested in them as individuals and are eager to help them succeed. Graduate students do not teach any courses.

Student Government

Every Bridgewater student is automatically a member of the Student Government Association. Bridgewater's special philosophy of maintaining a College community means that all the people who are part of it—students, faculty and staff members, administrators, and alumni—are partners in an educational program whose goal is academic excellence. The Student Government Association is the official representative of the students' point of view, and its officers, elected by the students themselves, organize activities and projects that benefit the student body and the College as a whole.

Admission Requirements

The basic aim of the admission requirements is to ensure the selection of students who have demonstrated intellectual capacity, motivation, and character and who have a record of scholastic achievement. Consideration is given to applicants regardless of their race, religion, national origin, sex, age, color, ethnic origin, or handicap. Three important factors are considered in the freshman admission process: secondary school preparation, SAT or ACT test scores, and personal qualifications. Prior to acceptance, secondary school students are required to pass 16 college-preparatory units: 4 years of English; 3 years of mathematics, including algebra I and II and geometry; 3 years of science, including 2 years of laboratory science; 2 years of history/social science, including 1 year of U.S. history; 2 years of the same foreign language; and two college-preparatory-level electives. High school students are encouraged to elect additional courses in music, art, and computer science. An essay/personal statement is required. Recommendations are not required but may be submitted with other application materials. Transfer students must submit an official transcript from each college previously attended.

The College also encourages qualified international students to apply for admission. The application procedures should be completed at least six months before the desired date of enrollment. Scores on the Test of English as a Foreign Language (TOEFL) are required from students whose first language is not English. An external evaluation of any transcripts from non-U.S. institutions and an Affidavit of Financial Support are also required.

Application and Information

Applications for freshman admission should be filed with the $25 application fee on or before February 15 for priority consideration. Freshmen seeking on-campus housing must apply before February 15. Students who wish to transfer to Bridgewater from another college should apply by November 1 for January entrance or by April 1 for September entrance for priority consideration.

Students choosing the early action option must submit an application and all supporting materials no later than November 15. Early action candidates are sent a decision letter by December 15.

Students are invited to attend on-campus Friday Admission Information Sessions, which are followed by a student-led tour of the campus. General campus tours are also offered Monday through Thursday at 11 a.m. and 3 p.m. while classes are in session. Appointments can be scheduled by calling the Office of Admission.

An application form and further information may be obtained by contacting:

Office of Admission
Bridgewater State College
Bridgewater, Massachusetts 02325
Phone: 508-531-1237
Fax: 508-531-1746
E-mail: admission@bridgew.edu
Web site: http://www.bridgew.edu

BROOKLYN COLLEGE OF THE CITY UNIVERSITY OF NEW YORK

BROOKLYN, NEW YORK

The College

Since its founding in 1930, Brooklyn College has distinguished itself as one of the nation's leading public institutions of higher learning. The College is situated on a 26-acre campus in the most dynamic New York City borough. It has been repeatedly cited for its physical beauty and for its state-of-the-art facilities.

Brooklyn College enrolls over 17,000 undergraduate and graduate students, in more than 130 programs in the humanities, education, the arts, business, sciences, and social sciences leading to bachelor's and master's degrees and advanced certificates. As one of the eleven senior colleges of the City University of New York, it shares the mission of the University, whose primary goals are access and excellence.

The tradition of academics is reflected in the accomplishments of the College's graduates and faculty members. Brooklyn College ranks nineteenth nationally in the number of undergraduates who have gone on to receive Ph.D. degrees, and it has a faculty distinguished by master teaching and scholarly achievement. Ninety percent of the full-time faculty members hold the highest degree in their field. Among them are Fulbright, Guggenheim, and MacArthur Foundation fellows; an Obie Award–winning playwright; Pulitzer Prize and National Book Award–winning authors; and award-winning scientists and musicians. The College's School of Education is rated among the top twenty such programs in the country, and its M.F.A. program was recently rated fifteenth in the country, above Sarah Lawrence College.

The College has an ambitious program of expansion and renewal. The newly renovated and expanded College library is the most technologically advanced facility in the CUNY system. The College's recently opened West Quad Center has state-of-the-art physical education and athletic facilities, including a swimming pool, competition and practice gymnasiums, racquetball courts, a fitness center, and teaching and research labs. It also consolidates student services offices, along with a one-stop services center to maximize convenient access to transactions and information.

Brooklyn College's students participate in more than 140 chartered campus groups, including academic clubs, service and honor societies, athletics groups, special interest groups, and performing arts organizations. Special lectures, concerts, and events are scheduled throughout the year. On the campus quad and in the Student Center, fraternities and sororities provide social and community service activities. The Hillel Foundation, Intervarsity Christian Fellowship, and Newman Center are among the many special interest clubs on campus. Students publish newspapers, magazines, and journals, and also operate WBCR, the Brooklyn College radio station.

The staff of experienced career professionals at the Magner Center for Career Development and Internships assists students who are exploring career options or building their resume while they study. The College typically places more than 1,600 students in internships each academic year, giving them a head start toward achieving their career goals. Many of the internships are paid, within Fortune 500 companies, nonprofit organizations, government, and the arts. The Center is also available to alumni seeking to develop the skills necessary to attain their career goals.

The newly redesigned Center for Student Disability Services provides counseling and assistance to students with disabilities to ensure that they have complete access to College programs and facilities. College and departmental counseling programs provide students with academic and personal counseling. Career, preprofessional, veterans', and psychological counseling services, as well as a health clinic and child care for students are also available.

Location

Brooklyn College is located in the residential Midwood section of Brooklyn, a short subway ride from Manhattan. The many different cultures of Brooklyn contribute to the wide ethnic diversity of the College's student and teacher population. The availability of a variety of New York City cultural events and institutions enriches students' educational experience. Subway and bus transportation to all points inside and outside the borough is easily accessible from the College.

Majors and Degrees

Brooklyn College awards the Bachelor of Arts (B.A.), Bachelor of Science (B.S.), Bachelor of Music (B.Mus.), Bachelor of Fine Arts (B.F.A.), Bachelor of Science/Master of Professional Studies (B.S./M.P.S.), and Bachelor of Business Administration (B.B.A.) degrees.

Majors are available in the following areas: accounting; Africana studies; American studies; anthropology; art; art history; art studio; biology; broadcast journalism; business administration; business, finance, and management; business information systems; Caribbean studies; chemistry; children's studies; classics; communication; comparative literature; computer science; creative writing; economics; education (childhood education, early childhood education, secondary education with certification in eleven subject areas); English; environmental studies; film; French; geology; health and nutrition sciences; history; information systems; Italian; journalism; Judaic studies; linguistics; mathematics; mathematics-computational; media studies; multimedia computing; music; music composition; music performance; philosophy; physical education; physics; political science; psychology; Puerto Rican and Latino studies; religion; Russian; sociology; Spanish; speech; speech-language pathology, audiology, speech and hearing science; television and radio; theater; and women's studies.

Certificate programs are offered in accounting, computers and programming, and film; credits earned in these programs are also applicable toward a baccalaureate degree.

A 4½-year Business Information Systems program leads to Bachelor of Science and Master of Professional Studies (B.S./M.P.S.) degrees.

An eight-year coordinated honors program with SUNY's Brooklyn Health Science Center leads to B.A. and M.D. degrees and is limited to 15 students per year who are admitted in the fall following their high school graduation.

A two-year coordinated engineering program includes attending Brooklyn College for two years of pre-engineering studies and then transferring to Polytechnic University, City College, or the College of Staten Island for an additional two years of study to fulfill the B.S. degree requirements in a specific engineering field.

Qualified students can earn a Brooklyn College B.A. or B.S. degree by satisfactorily completing all requirements for graduation except 30 elective credits, and also satisfactorily completing at least one year's work in an accredited dental, engineering, law, medical, optometry, podiatry, or veterinary school.

Academic Programs

A Brooklyn College liberal arts education consists of the College-wide core curriculum, which provides a diverse educational experience in the liberal arts and sciences for all students; major studies, which comprise specialized, intensive study in one discipline or an interdisciplinary program; and elective courses, selected from more than seventy-five areas. This three-pronged curriculum prepares students to make appropriate career and personal choices by developing their critical and independent thinking skills, their ability to acquire and organize knowledge, and their proficiency with both verbal and written communication. Students pursuing a bachelor's degree must successfully complete a minimum of 120 credits.

The academic calendar consists of a fall and a spring semester. Two summer sessions and a January intersession are available. Classes are offered in day, evening, and weekend sessions.

The Honors Academy includes: the Scholars Program, offering students who combine academic excellence with initiative and inquisitiveness the opportunity to take classes and courses that are only for members of the program; the Coordinated B.A./M.D. Program (described above); the William E. Macaulay Honors College Program, which consists of a challenging honors curriculum and cultural experiences, as well as a full-tuition scholarship, internship opportunities, and an academic expense account; the Mellon Mays Undergraduate Fellowship, a two-year program for members of minority groups who are considering scholarly study in the humanities; the Minority Access Research Careers Program; and the Coordinated Engineering Honors Program.

Students who have completed college-level courses in high school may be considered for exemption, with or without credit, from equivalent college courses on the basis of Advanced Placement tests given by the College Board. Brooklyn College gives exemption examinations in subjects not offered by the College Board. Students completing three years of foreign language in high school are exempt from the College's language requirement.

Academic Facilities

The College's magnificent library is much more than a traditional academic library; it is a comprehensive information center with extensive physical and digital collections, the College archives, a new media center, and both academic and administrative computing. The library's growing collections include approximately 15,000 electronic subscriptions and works of reference, 50,000 electronic books, 1.3 million volumes, 1.6 million microfilms, 50,000 serials, and 25,000 rich media items (sound recordings, videotapes, and DVDs). The library's twenty-two group-study rooms, five computer classrooms, and 600-plus computers make it the campus's premier study and research space.

Students have access to over 1,000 state-of-the-art computers in various public computer labs, each with extensive operating hours, including the Library Café that combines casual computing, a Starbucks, and 24/7 computer availability. Scores of specialized computer labs and high-tech learning spaces support the College's many programs.

The West Quad Center includes extensive state-of-the-art physical education and recreation facilities and a huge consolidated student services center offering one-stop service for most student administrative transactions.

Other special facilities include a walk-in learning and tutoring center, a language laboratory, art studios, an advanced color television production studio, a fully operational advanced radio station, a working journalism newsroom, film production and editing facilities, a speech and hearing clinic, psychological laboratories, laser laboratories, an aquatic research center whose projects were aboard the space shuttle, a nuclear physics laboratory, and much more.

The Brooklyn Center for the Performing Arts at Brooklyn College presents music, dance, and theater productions. It includes a 2,500-seat auditorium, a theater, a recital hall, and a workshop theater. Construction is beginning on a new $50-million center for the performing arts, which will serve the Conservatory of Music, the Department of Theater, and related disciplines.

Costs

In 2009–10, New York State residents paid tuition of $2300 per semester for full-time students, $195 per credit for part-time students, and $285 per credit for non-degree resident students. Non–New York State residents and international students paid tuition of $415 per credit whether they were full- or part-time students and $610 per credit for non-degree students. (All students pay per credit for summer session and intersession courses.) The College is an easily accessible commuter institution with many housing options nearby, including a new residence hall scheduled to open during the fall 2010 semester.

Financial Aid

Admission, financial aid, and scholarship decisions are made independently of each other, and an application for aid does not hinder a student's opportunity for admission. Financial assistance is available for eligible students through state and federal grant, loan, and work-study programs.

New students, especially those with strong high school or college academic records and SAT scores, are encouraged to apply for annual scholarships. Continuing students may qualify for one of the more than 400 scholarships, prizes, and awards that are given each year to Brooklyn College students. The requirements vary for each award, but recipients are chosen based on academic performance, financial need, and other criteria that may be stipulated by the donors. Scholarships range from $100 to $4000 per year.

Faculty

The College has an outstanding faculty (537 full-time and 837 part-time) whose members have demonstrated excellence in teaching and scholarly research. Faculty members assist in the academic advisement of entering students and provide counseling to students majoring in their department. They also hold regular office hours and are generally available to support student activities.

Student Government

Brooklyn College has three student government organizations on campus: one for undergraduate day students, one for undergraduate evening students, and one that represents graduate students. Student government is expected to advocate for the interests of the student body, provide a venue for making decisions that can shape students' academic futures, and help improve campus life by creating and maintaining student services. Students also serve on the Policy Council, the major college-wide governing body.

Admission Requirements

Brooklyn College admits freshmen and transfers for both the fall and spring semesters. Regular freshman admission is based on the student having a minimum of an 81 average in their academic subjects and a minimum SAT of 1000 or the equivalent ACT scores. Freshman students should demonstrate successful completion of at least 12 or more high school academic units (of which at least 5 units must include 2 or more years of English and 2 or more years of math). The recommended high school preparation for the College's curriculum is 4 years of English, 4 years of social studies, 3 years of mathematics, 3 years of science, and 3 years of a foreign language. Highly qualified high school juniors may apply for early admission directly at the Admissions Office of the College.

The Search for Education, Elevation, and Knowledge (SEEK) Program at Brooklyn College is committed to helping students from educationally and financially disadvantaged backgrounds meet their educational goals through tutoring and mentoring. Students must fill out a separate section on the CUNY application for the SEEK Program.

Freshmen seeking admission to the Brooklyn College Honors Academy which includes the Scholars Program, Macaulay Honors College Program, and the B.A./M.D. Program must present a high school average of 90 or better, exceptional SAT or ACT scores, letters of recommendation, an essay, and a personal interview.

Transfer students are admitted to the college with a minimum of a 2.3 cumulative average on prior coursework. In addition, students with fewer than 25 credits completed must also meet the regular freshman requirements.

Application and Information

Application for admission to the undergraduate programs for the fall or spring semester should be made online via the College's Web site at http://www.brooklyn.edu/pug. Some honors programs, fellowships, and coordinated programs have special applications or application requirements, which can be obtained at the College's Web site. Undergraduate applications are processed by the City University of New York's central processing center (University Applications Processing Center–UAPC) and while applications for admission are processed on a rolling basis, applicants who apply before February 1 for fall admission and before October 1 for spring have the best opportunity for admission consideration, comprehensive advisement, and course registration. The CUNY Honors College Program applicants are required to apply by November 1 (early decision) and December 15 (regular decision) for fall admission.

For additional information or to arrange to meet with an admissions counselor, please visit the College's Web site.

Office of Admissions
Brooklyn College
West Quad Center, Room 222
2900 Bedford Avenue,
Brooklyn, New York 11210
Phone: 718-951-5001
E-mail: adminqry@brooklyn.cuny.edu
Web site: http://www.brooklyn.edu/pug

BROWN MACKIE COLLEGE–ALBUQUERQUE

ALBUQUERQUE, NEW MEXICO

The College

Brown Mackie College–Albuquerque is one of over twenty locations in the Brown Mackie College system of schools (www.brownmackie.edu), which is dedicated to providing educational programs that prepare students to pursue entry-level positions in a competitive, rapidly changing workplace. Brown Mackie College schools offer bachelor's degree, associate degree, certificate, and diploma programs in health sciences, business, information technology, legal studies, and design to over 19,000 students in the Midwest, Southeast, Southwest, and Western United States.

Brown Mackie College was originally founded and approved by the Board of Trustees of Kansas Wesleyan College in Salina, Kansas on July 30, 1892. In 1938, the College was incorporated as the Brown Mackie School of Business under the ownership of Perry E. Brown and A.B. Mackie, former instructors at Kansas Wesleyan University in Salina, Kansas. Their last names formed the name of Brown Mackie. By January 1975, with improvements in curricula and higher degree-granting status, the Brown Mackie School of Business became Brown Mackie College.

Brown Mackie College–Albuquerque is accredited by the Accrediting Council for Independent Colleges and Schools (ACICS) to award bachelor's degrees, associate degrees, and certificates. ACICS is listed as a nationally recognized accrediting agency by the United States Department of Education and is recognized by the Council for Higher Education Accreditation. ACICS can be contacted at 750 First Street NE, Suite 980, Washington, D.C. 20002; phone: 202-336-6780.

Location

Brown Mackie College–Albuquerque is conveniently located at 10500 Copper Avenue NE, in Albuquerque, New Mexico. The College has a generous parking area and is easily accessible by public transportation.

Programs of Study and Degrees

Brown Mackie College–Albuquerque provides higher education to traditional and nontraditional students through bachelor's degree, associate degree, and diploma programs that assist in enhancing their career opportunities, broadening their perspectives through appropriate general education courses, thinking independently and critically, and improving problem-solving abilities. The College strives to develop within its students the desire for lifelong and continued education.

The Bachelor of Science degree (180 credits) is awarded in business administration, criminal justice, health-care management, and legal studies.

The Associate of Applied Science degree (96 credits) is awarded in accounting technology, architectural design and drafting technology, business management, criminal justice, health-care administration, information technology, medical assisting, paralegal studies, pharmacy technology, surgical technology, and veterinary technology.

The College offers diploma programs (48 credits) in accounting, business, criminal justice, medical assistant, and paralegal assistant studies.

Academic Programs

Each College quarter comprises twelve weeks. Bachelor's degree programs require a minimum of sixteen quarters to complete. Associate degree programs require a minimum of eight quarters to complete. Programs are offered on a year-round basis, providing students with the ability to work uninterrupted toward completion of their programs. The College offers all programs in a unique One Course a Month format. This allows students to focus studies on only one course for four weeks. This schedule has proven convenient for students with multiple obligations such as jobs and family.

Academic Facilities

A modern facility, Brown Mackie College–Albuquerque offers more than 35,000 square feet. The College is equipped with multiple computer labs, housing over 100 computers. High-speed access to the Internet and other online resources are available to students and faculty. Multimedia classrooms are outfitted with overhead projectors, VCR/DVD players, and computers.

The campus is nonresidential; public transportation and ample parking at no cost are available. The campus is a smoke-free facility.

Costs

Tuition in the 2010–11 academic year for all bachelor's and associate degrees and certificates is $266 per credit hour; fees are $15 per credit hour. Tuition for the surgical technology program is $310 per credit hour; fees are $15 per credit hour. The cost of textbooks and other instructional materials varies by program.

Financial Aid

Financial aid is available for those who qualify. The College maintains a full-time staff of financial aid professionals to assist qualified students in obtaining the financial assistance they require to meet their educational expenses. Available resources include federal and state aid, student loans from private lenders, and Federal Work-Study opportunities, both on and off college premises.

Each year, the College makes available scholarships of $1000 each to qualifying seniors from area high schools. No more than one scholarship is awarded per high school. In order to qualify, a senior must have graduated from a participating high school, must be maintained a cumulative grade point average of at least 2.0, and submitted a brief essay. The student's extracurricular activities and community service are also considered. These scholarships are available only to students enrolling in one of the College's degree programs. Students awarded the scholarship must enroll at Brown Mackie College–Albuquerque between June and September immediately following their high school graduation. Applications for these scholarships can be obtained from the guidance departments of participating high schools. These applications must be completed and returned to the College by March 31.

Faculty

Experienced faculty members provide academic support and are committed to the academic and technical preparation of their students. The College has both full-time and part-time instructors, with a student-faculty ratio of 15:1.

Admission Requirements

Each applicant for admission is assigned an Assistant Director of Admissions who directs the applicant through the steps of the admissions process. They provide information on curriculum, policies, procedures, and services and assist the applicant in setting necessary appointments and interviews. To qualify for admission, each applicant must provide documentation of graduation from an accredited high school or from a state-approved secondary education curriculum or provide official documentation of high school graduation equivalency. All transcripts become the property of the College. Admission to the College is based on the applicant meeting the stated requirements, a review of the applicant's previous educational records, and a review of the applicant's career interests. If previous academic records indicate the College's education and training programs would not benefit the applicant, the College reserves the right to advise the applicant not to enroll. Special requirements for enrollment into certain programs are discussed in the descriptions of those programs.

For the most recent information regarding admission requirements, prospective students should refer to the current academic catalog.

Application and Information

Applicants must complete and submit an application form, along with documentation of graduation from an accredited high school or state-approved secondary education curriculum or official documentation of high school graduation equivalency.

For additional information, prospective students should contact:

Director of Admissions
Brown Mackie College–Albuquerque
10500 Copper Avenue
Albuquerque, New Mexico 87123
Phone: 505-559-5200
Fax: 505-559-5222
E-mail: bmcalbadm@brownmackie.edu
Web site: http://www.brownmackie.edu/Albuquerque

BROWN MACKIE COLLEGE–BOISE

BOISE, IDAHO

The College

Brown Mackie College–Boise is one of over twenty locations in the Brown Mackie College system of schools (www.brownmackie.edu), which is dedicated to providing educational programs that prepare students to pursue entry-level positions in a competitive, rapidly changing workplace. Brown Mackie College schools offer bachelor's degree, associate degree, certificate, and diploma programs in health sciences, business, information technology, legal studies, and design to over 19,000 students in the Midwest, Southeast, Southwest, and Western United States.

Brown Mackie College–Boise is accredited by the Accrediting Council for Independent Colleges and Schools to award bachelor's degrees, associate degrees, and diplomas. The Accrediting Council for Independent Colleges and Schools is listed as a nationally recognized accrediting agency by the United States Department of Education and is recognized by the Council for Higher Education Accreditation. ACICS can be contacted at 750 First Street NE, Suite 980, Washington, D.C. 20002-4241; phone: 202-336-6780.

The occupational therapy assistant program is pending accreditation by the Accreditation Council for Occupational Therapy Education (ACOTE) of the American Occupational Therapy Association (AOTA), 4720 Montgomery Lane, P.O. Box 31220, Bethesda, Maryland 20824-1220; phone: 301-652-2682.

Location

Brown Mackie College–Boise is conveniently located at 9050 West Overland Road in Boise, Idaho. The College has a generous parking area and is easily accessible by public transportation.

Programs of Study and Degrees

Brown Mackie College–Boise provides higher education to traditional and nontraditional students through bachelor's degree, associate degree, and diploma programs that assist in enhancing their career opportunities, broadening their perspectives through appropriate general education courses, thinking independently and critically, and improving problem-solving abilities.

The Bachelor of Science degree (180 credits) is awarded in business administration, criminal justice, health-care management, and legal studies.

The Associate of Science degree (96 credits) is awarded in accounting technology, bioscience laboratory technology, business management, criminal justice, health-care administration, information technology, medical assisting, paralegal studies, and surgical technology.

The Associate of Applied Science degree is awarded in architectural design and drafting technology, occupational therapy assistant (100 credits), and veterinary technology (96 credits).

The College offers a diploma program (48 credits) in accounting, business, criminal justice, dental assistant studies, medical assistant studies, and paralegal assistant studies.

Academic Programs

Each College quarter comprises twelve weeks. Bachelor's degree programs require a minimum of sixteen quarters to complete. Associate degree programs require a minimum of eight quarters to complete. Programs are offered on a year-round basis, providing students with the opportunity to work uninterrupted toward completion of their programs. The College offers all programs in a unique One Course a Month format. This allows students to focus studies on only one course for four weeks. This schedule has proven convenient for students with multiple obligations such as jobs and family.

Academic Facilities

Opened in 2008, this modern facility offers more than 40,000 square feet of tastefully decorated classrooms, laboratories, and office space designed to specifications of the College for its business, medical, and technical programs. Instructional equipment is comparable to current technology used in business and industry today. Modern classrooms for special instructional needs offer multimedia capabilities with surround sound and overhead projectors accessible through computer, DVD, or VHS. Internet access and instructional resources are available at the College's library. Experienced faculty members provide academic support and are committed to the academic and technical preparation of their students.

The campus is nonresidential; public transportation and ample parking at no cost are available.

Costs

Tuition for programs in the 2010–11 academic year is $275 per credit hour, with a $15 per credit hour general fee applied to instructional costs for activities and services. Textbooks and other instructional materials varied by program. Tuition for certain occupational therapy assistant courses is $365 per credit hour with a $15 per credit fee applied to instructional costs for activities and services. Tuition for certain surgical technology courses is $310 per credit hour with a $15 per credit fee applied to instructional costs for activities.

Financial Aid

Financial aid is available for those who qualify. The College maintains a full-time staff of financial aid professionals to assist qualified students in obtaining financial assistance. The College participates in several student aid programs. Forms of financial aid available through federal resources include the Federal Pell Grant Program, Federal Supplemental Educational Opportunity Grant (FSEOG) Program, Federal Work-Study Program, Federal Perkins Loan Program, Federal Stafford Student Loan Program (subsidized and unsubsidized), and the Federal PLUS Loan Program.

Each year, the College makes available President's Scholarships of $1000 each to qualifying seniors from area high schools. No more than one scholarship is awarded per high school. In order to qualify, a senior must be graduating from a participating high school, must be maintaining a cumulative grade point average of at least 2.0, and must submit a brief essay. The student's extracurricular activities and community service are also considered. The President's Scholarship is available only to students enrolling in one of the College's degree programs.

Students awarded the scholarship must enroll at Brown Mackie College–Boise between June and September immediately following their high school graduation. Applications for these scholarships can be obtained from the guidance departments of participating high schools. These applications must be completed and returned to the College by March 31.

Faculty

There are 17 full-time and 34 part-time faculty members at the College. The average student-faculty ratio is 15:1. Each student is assigned a program director as an adviser.

Admission Requirements

Each applicant for admission is assigned an Assistant Director of Admissions who directs the applicant through the steps of the admissions process. They provide information on curriculum, policies, procedures, and services, and assist the applicant in setting necessary appointments and interviews. To qualify for admission, each applicant must provide documentation of graduation from an accredited high school or from a state-approved secondary education curriculum or provide official documentation of high school graduation equivalency. All transcripts become the property of the College.

As part of the admission process, students are given an assessment of academic skills. Although the results of this assessment do not determine eligibility for admission, they provide the College with a means of determining the need for academic support as well as a means by which the College can evaluate the effectiveness of its educational programs. All new students are required to complete this assessment, which is readministered at the end of the student's program so results may be compared with those of the initial administration.

In addition to the College's general admission requirements, applicants enrolling in the occupational therapy assistant program must document one of the following: a high school cumulative grade point average of at least 2.5, a score on the GED examination of at least 57 (557 if taken on or after January 15, 2002), or completion of 12 quarter-credit hours or 8 semester-credit hours of collegiate course work with a grade point average of at least 2.5. Credit hours may not include Professional Development (CF 1100), the Brown Mackie College–Boise course. Students entering the program must also have completed a biology course with a grade of at least a C (or an average of at least 2.0 on a 4.0 scale).

For the most recent information regarding admission requirements, prospective students should refer to the current academic catalog.

Application and Information

Applicants must complete and submit an application form, along with documentation of graduation from an accredited high school or state-approved secondary education curriculum or official documentation of high school graduation equivalency.

For additional information, prospective students should contact:

Director of Admissions
Brown Mackie College–Boise
9050 W. Overland Road, Suite 100
Boise, Idaho 83709
Phone: 208-321-8800
888-810-9286 (toll-free)
Fax: 208-375-3249
E-mail: bmcboiadm@brownmackie.edu
Web site: http://www.brownmackie.edu/Boise

COLLEGE CLOSE-UPS

BROWN MACKIE COLLEGE–FORT WAYNE

FORT WAYNE, INDIANA

The College

Brown Mackie College–Fort Wayne is one of over twenty locations in the Brown Mackie College system of schools (www.brownmackie.edu), which is dedicated to providing educational programs that prepare students to pursue entry-level positions in a competitive, rapidly changing workplace. Brown Mackie College schools offer bachelor's degree, associate degree, certificate, and diploma programs in health sciences, business, information technology, legal studies, and design to over 19,000 students in the Midwest, Southeast, Southwest, and Western United States.

Brown Mackie College–Fort Wayne is one of the oldest institutions of its kind in the country and the oldest in the state of Indiana. Established in 1882 as the South Bend Commercial College, the school later changed its name to Michiana College. In 1930, the College was incorporated under the laws of the state of Indiana and was authorized to confer associate degrees and certificates in business. In 1992, the College in South Bend added a branch location in Fort Wayne, Indiana. In 2004, Michiana College changed its name to Brown Mackie College–Fort Wayne. Brown Mackie College–Fort Wayne is owned and operated by Education Management Corporation (EDMC), 210 Sixth Avenue, 33rd Floor, Pittsburgh, Pennsylvania 15222-2603. EDMC has been in business for over forty years and is one of the largest providers of private post-secondary education in North America with eighty-nine campus locations in twenty-eight states and Canada.

Brown Mackie College–Fort Wayne is accredited by the Accrediting Council for Independent Colleges and Schools (ACICS) to award bachelor's degrees, associate degrees, diplomas, and certificates. ACICS is listed as a nationally recognized accrediting agency by the Department of Education. Its accreditation of degree-granting institutions also is recognized by the Council for Higher Education Accreditation. ACICS can be contacted at 750 First Street NE, Suite 980, Washington, D.C. 20002-4241; phone: 202-336-6780.

The College's Associate of Science in medical assisting program is accredited by the Commission on Accreditation of Allied Health Education Programs (1361 Park Street, Clearwater, Florida 33756; phone: 727-210-2350; Web site: www.caahep.org), upon the recommendation of the Medical Assisting Education Review Board (MAERB).

The medical assisting degree program (optional certification) is accredited by the American Association of Medical Assistants (AAMA). Graduates are eligible at their option to sit for the AAMA Certification/Recertification Examination of Medical Assistants. Graduates who pass this examination are awarded the Certified Medical Assistant (CMA) credential. A CMA must be recertified every five years through continuing education or reexamination. Examinations are generally administered in June and January. Further information can be obtained by contacting the Medical Assisting Program Director or by contacting AAMA Certification Department, 20 North Wacker Drive, Suite 1575, Chicago, Illinois 60606-2903; phone: 312-424-3100.

The occupational therapy assistant program is accredited by the Accreditation Council for Occupational Therapy Education (ACOTE) of the American Occupational Therapy Association (AOTA), 4720 Montgomery Lane, P.O. Box 31220, Bethesda, Maryland 20824-1220; phone: 301-652-2682. In order to practice as occupational therapy assistants, graduates must pass the certification examination for the certified occupational therapy assistant. Application for such examination is arranged through the National Board for Certification in Occupational Therapy, Inc. (NBCOT). Graduates may request application materials and the candidate handbook from NBCOT or apply online. For further information, graduates should contact NBCOT, 800 South Frederick Avenue, Suite 200, Gaithersburg, Maryland 20877-4150; phone: 301-990-7979; Web site: www.nbcot.org.

To practice as an occupational therapy assistant in Indiana, a graduate must be certified by the state. Graduates may apply for a temporary permit to work between graduation and successful completion of certification examination. For information on application procedures for either a temporary permit or permanent state endorsement, graduates should contact the Occupational Therapy Committee, Health Professions Bureau, Indiana Government Center South, 402 West Washington Street, Room 041, Indianapolis, Indiana 46204; phone: 317-232-2960; Web site: www.in.gov/hpb/boards/otc/; hbp6@hpb.state.in.us.

The College's diploma program in practical nursing is accredited by the Indiana State Board of Nursing, 402 West Washington Street, Room W066, Indianapolis, Indiana 46204; phone: 317-234-2043. Graduates are eligible to complete two applications: the National Council Licensure Examination (NCLEX) and the Indiana licensure application. Indiana applications for licensure by examination must be completed by each candidate and be submitted to the Health Professions Bureau. Registration with NCLEX must be completed according to the instructions in the NCLEX Candidate Bulletin. Both the Indiana licensure application and the NCLEX registration process must be completed before eligibility to take the examination can be granted by the Indiana Board of Nursing. Graduates may obtain further information by contacting the Indiana State Board of Nursing, 402 West Washington Street, Room W066, Indianapolis, Indiana 46204; phone: 317-234-2043; Web site: www.ai.org/hpb.

The surgical technology program is accredited by the Accrediting Bureau of Health Education Schools (ABHES). Graduates of this program are eligible at their option to sit for the CST Certification Examination of Surgical Technologists. Graduates who pass this examination are awarded the Certified Surgical Technologist (CST) credential. A CST must be recertified every four years through continuing education or reexamination. Further information can be obtained by contacting the Surgical Technology Program Director or by contacting the ABHES, 7777 Leesburg Pike, Suite 314 North, Falls Church, Virginia 22043; phone: 703-917-9503; Web site: www.abhes.org.

The College is licensed and regulated by the Indiana Commission on Proprietary Education, 302 West Washington Street, Room E201, Indianapolis, Indiana 46204; phone: 800-227-5695 (toll-free) or 317-232-1320. (Indiana advertising code: AC-0109.)

Location

Brown Mackie College–Fort Wayne is located at 3000 East Coliseum Boulevard in Fort Wayne, Indiana. The College facility is accessible by public transportation. Ample parking is provided at no additional charge. For added convenience, the College also operates a learning site at 2135 South Hannah Drive in Fort Wayne.

Programs of Study and Degrees

Brown Mackie College–Fort Wayne provides higher education to traditional and nontraditional students through bachelor's degree, associate degree, diploma, and certificate programs that assist them in enhancing their career opportunities, broadening their perspectives through appropriate general education courses, thinking independently and critically, and improving problem-solving abilities. The College strives to develop within its students the desire for lifelong and continued education.

The Bachelor of Science degree (184 credits) is awarded in business administration, criminal justice, legal studies, and health-care management (180 credits).

The Associate of Science degree (96 credits) is awarded in accounting technology, business management, computer software technology, criminal justice, health-care administration, medical assisting, office management, paralegal studies, and surgical technology.

The Associate of Applied Science degree (96 credits) is awarded in biomedical equipment technology, dietetics technology, health and fitness training, occupational therapy assistant studies, and physical therapist assistant studies.

A diploma (76 credits) is awarded in practical nursing.

The College offers certificate programs (48 credits) in accounting, business, computer software applications, criminal justice, medical assistant studies, and paralegal assistant studies.

Academic Programs

Each College quarter comprises twelve weeks. Bachelor's degree programs require a minimum of sixteen quarters to complete. Associate degree programs require a minimum of eight quarters to complete. Programs are offered on a year-round basis, providing students with the ability to work uninterrupted toward their degrees. The College offers all programs in a unique One Course a Month format. This allows students to focus studies on only one course for four weeks. This schedule has proven convenient for students with multiple obligations such as jobs and family.

Academic Facilities

In 2005, the campus located in a 75,000-square-foot facility at 3000 East Coliseum Boulevard. Record enrollment allowed the institution to triple in size in less than one year. The three-story building offers a modern, professional environment for study. Ten classrooms are outfitted as "classrooms of the future," with an instructor workstation, full multimedia capabilities, a surround sound system, and projection screen that can be accessed by computer, DVD, or VHS equipment. The Brown Mackie College–Fort Wayne facility includes a criminal justice lab, surgical technology labs, medical labs, computer labs, and occupational and physical therapy labs, as well as a library and bookstore. The labs provide students with hands-on opportunities to apply knowledge and skills learned in the classroom. Students are welcome to use the labs when those facilities are not in use for scheduled classes.

The College is nonresidential; public transportation and ample parking at no cost are available. The campus is a smoke-free facility.

Costs

Tuition in the 2010–11 academic year is $266 per credit hour with fees of $15 per credit hour for all programs except practical nursing, surgical technology, personal fitness training, occupational therapy assistant studies, and physical therapist assistant studies. Textbooks and other instructional materials vary by program. For the practical nursing program, tuition is $325 per credit hour; fees are $25 per credit hour. For the surgical technology program, tuition is $310 per credit hour; fees are $15. Tuition for the personal fitness training program is $275 per credit hour; fees are $25 per credit hour. Textbook expenses are estimated at $400 for the first term, $600 for the second term, and $100 for the third, fourth, and fifth terms. For certain courses in the occupational therapy assistant studies and physical therapist assistant studies programs, tuition is $365 per credit hour; fees are $15 per credit hour. Textbook expenses are estimated at $370 per quarter for the first six terms and $460 for the seventh term.

Financial Aid

The College maintains a full-time staff of financial aid professionals to assist qualified students in obtaining financial assistance. The College participates in several student aid programs. Forms of financial aid available through federal resources include the Federal Pell Grant Program, Federal Supplemental Educational Opportunity Grant (FSEOG) Program, Federal Work-Study Program, Federal Perkins Loan Program, Federal Stafford Student Loan Program (subsidized and unsubsidized), and the Federal PLUS Loan Program. Eligible students may apply for Indiana state awards, such as the Frank O'Bannon Grant Program (formerly the Indiana State Grant Program), the Higher Education Award, and Twenty-First Century Scholarships for high school students; for the Core 40 awards; and for veterans' educational benefits. For further information, students should contact the College Student Financial Services Office.

Each year, the College makes available President's Scholarships of $1000 each to qualifying seniors from area high schools. No more than one scholarship is awarded per high school. In order to qualify, a senior must have graduated from a participating high school, maintained a cumulative grade point average of at least 2.0, and submitted a brief essay. The student's extracurricular activities and community service are also considered. The President's Scholarship is available only to students enrolling in one of the College's degree programs. Students awarded the scholarship must enroll at Brown Mackie College–Fort Wayne between June and September immediately following their high school graduation. Applications for these scholarships can be obtained from the guidance departments of participating high schools. These applications must be completed and returned to the College by March 31.

Faculty

The College has 45 full-time and 80 part-time instructors, with a student-faculty ratio of 15:1. Each student is assigned a faculty adviser.

Admission Requirements

Each applicant for admission is assigned an Assistant Director of Admissions, who directs the applicant through the steps of the admissions process, providing information on curriculum, policies, procedures, and services and assisting the applicant in setting necessary appointments and interviews. To qualify for admission, each applicant must provide documentation of graduation from an accredited high school or from a state-approved secondary education curriculum or provide official documentation of high school graduation equivalency. All transcripts become the property of the College. Admission to the College is based on the applicant meeting the stated requirements, a review of the applicant's previous educational records, and a review of the applicant's career interests. If previous academic records indicate the College's education and training programs would not benefit the applicant, the College reserves the right to advise the applicant not to enroll. Special requirements for enrollment into certain programs are discussed in the descriptions of those programs.

In addition to the College's general admission requirements, applicants enrolling in the practical nursing program must document the following, which must be completed and a record of proof must appear in the student's file prior to the start of the nursing fundamentals course. No student will be admitted to a clinical agency unless all paperwork is completed. This paperwork is a requirement of all contracted agencies. This paperwork includes records of (1) a complete physical, current to within six months of admission; (2) a two-step Mantoux test that is kept current throughout schooling; (3) a hepatitis B vaccination or signed refusal; (4) up-to-date immunizations, including tetanus and rubella; (5) a record of current CPR certification that is maintained throughout the student's clinical experience; and (6) hospitalization insurance or a signed waiver.

Application and Information

Applicants must complete and submit an application form, along with documentation of graduation from an accredited high school or state-approved secondary education curriculum or official documentation of high school graduation equivalency.

For additional information, prospective students should contact:

Director of Admissions
Brown Mackie College–Fort Wayne
3000 East Coliseum Boulevard
Fort Wayne, Indiana 46805
Phone: 260-484-4400
866-433-2289 (toll-free)
Fax: 260-484-2678
E-mail: bmcfwaadm@brownmackie.edu
Web site: http://www.brownmackie.edu/FortWayne

COLLEGE CLOSE-UPS

BROWN MACKIE COLLEGE–GREENVILLE

GREENVILLE, SOUTH CAROLINA

The College

Brown Mackie College–Greenville is one of over twenty locations in the Brown Mackie College system of schools (www.brownmackie.edu), which is dedicated to providing educational programs that prepare students to pursue entry-level positions in a competitive, rapidly changing workplace. Brown Mackie College schools offer bachelor's degree, associate degree, and certificate programs in health sciences, business, information technology, and legal studies to over 19,000 students in the Midwest, Southeast, Southwest, and Western United States.

Brown Mackie College was originally founded and approved by the Board of Trustees of Kansas Wesleyan College in Salina, Kansas on July 30, 1892. In 1938, the College was incorporated as The Brown Mackie School of Business under the ownership of Perry E. Brown and A.B. Mackie, former instructors at Kansas Wesleyan University in Salina, Kansas. Their last names formed the name of Brown Mackie. By January 1975, with improvements in curricula and higher degree-granting status, The Brown Mackie School of Business became Brown Mackie College.

Brown Mackie College–Greenville is accredited by the Accrediting Council for Independent Colleges and Schools (ACICS) to award bachelor's degrees, associate degrees, and certificates. ACICS is listed as a nationally recognized accrediting agency by the United States Department of Education and is recognized by the Council for Higher Education Accreditation. ACICS can be contacted at 750 First Street NE, Suite 980, Washington, D.C. 20002-4241; phone: 202-336-6780.

Location

Brown Mackie College–Greenville is conveniently located at Two Liberty Square, 75 Beattie Place, Suite 100, in Greenville, South Carolina. The College has a generous parking area and is easily accessible by public transportation.

Programs of Study and Degrees

Brown Mackie College–Greenville provides higher education to traditional and nontraditional students through bachelor's degree, associate degree, and certificate programs that assist in enhancing their career opportunities, broadening their perspectives through appropriate general education courses, thinking independently and critically, and improving problem-solving abilities. The College strives to develop within its students the desire for lifelong and continued education.

The Bachelor of Science degree (180 credits) is awarded in business administration, criminal justice, health-care management, and legal studies.

The Associate of Applied Science degree is awarded in accounting technology, business management, criminal justice, health-care administration, information technology, medical assisting, office management, paralegal studies, and surgical technology.

The certificate is awarded in accounting, business, criminal justice, medical assistant studies, and paralegal assistant studies.

Academic Programs

Each College quarter comprises twelve weeks. Bachelor's degree programs require a minimum of sixteen quarters to complete. Associate degree programs require a minimum of eight quarters to complete. Programs are offered on a year-round basis, providing students with the ability to work uninterrupted toward completion of their degrees. The College offers all programs in a unique One Course a Month format. This allows students to focus studies on only one course for four weeks. This schedule has proven convenient for students with multiple obligations such as jobs and family.

Academic Facilities

A modern facility, Brown Mackie College–Greenville offers more than 25,000 square feet. The College is equipped with multiple computer labs housing over sixty computers. High-speed access to the Internet and other online resources are available for students and faculty. Multimedia classrooms are outfitted with overhead projectors, VCR/DVD players, and computers.

The campus is nonresidential; public transportation and ample parking at no cost are available. The campus is a smoke-free facility.

Costs

Tuition in the 2010–11 academic year for most bachelor's and associate degrees and certificates is $260 per credit hour; fees are $15 per credit hour. Tuition for the surgical technology program is $310 per credit hour; fees are $15 per credit hour. The cost of textbooks and other instructional expenses varies by program.

Financial Aid

Financial aid is available for those who qualify. The College maintains a full-time staff of financial aid professionals to assist qualified students in obtaining the financial assistance they require to meet their educational expenses. Available resources include federal and state aid, student loans from private lenders, and Federal Work-Study opportunities, both on and off college premises.

Each year, the College makes available President's Scholarships of $1000 each to qualifying seniors from area high schools. No more than one scholarship is awarded per high school. In order to qualify, a senior must have graduated from a participating high school, maintained a cumulative grade point average of at least 2.0, and submitted a brief essay. The student's extracurricular activities and community service are also considered. The President's Scholarship is available only to students enrolling in one of the College's degree programs. Students awarded the scholarship must enroll at Brown Mackie College–Greenville between June and September immediately following their high school graduation. Applications for these scholarships can be obtained from the guidance departments of participating high schools. These applications must be completed and returned to the College by March 31.

Faculty

Experienced faculty members provide academic support and are committed to the academic and technical preparation of their students. The College has 5 full-time and 10 part-time instructors, with a student-faculty ratio of 24:1. Each student is assigned a faculty adviser.

Admission Requirements

Each applicant for admission is assigned an Assistant Director of Admissions who directs the applicant through the steps of the admissions process. They provide information on curriculum, policies, procedures, and services and assist the applicant in setting necessary appointments and interviews. To qualify for admission, each applicant must provide documentation of graduation from an accredited high school or from a state-approved secondary education curriculum or provide official documentation of high school graduation equivalency. All transcripts become the property of the College. Admission to the College is based on the applicant meeting the stated requirements, a review of the applicant's previous educational records, and a review of the applicant's career interests. If previous academic records indicate the College's education and training programs would not benefit the applicant, the College reserves the right to advise the applicant not to enroll. Special requirements for enrollment into certain programs are discussed in the descriptions of those programs.

For the most recent information regarding admission requirements, prospective students should refer to the current academic catalog.

Application and Information

Applicants must complete and submit an application form along with documentation of graduation from an accredited high school or state-approved secondary education curriculum or official documentation of high school graduation equivalency.

For additional information, prospective students should contact:

Director of Admissions
Brown Mackie College–Greenville
Two Liberty Square
75 Beattie Place, Suite 100
Greenville, South Carolina 29601
Phone: 864-239-5300
Fax: 864-232-4094
E-mail: bmcgrweb@brownmackie.edu
Web site: http://www.brownmackie.edu/greenville

BROWN MACKIE COLLEGE–INDIANAPOLIS

INDIANAPOLIS, INDIANA

The College

Brown Mackie College–Indianapolis is one of over twenty locations in the Brown Mackie College system of schools (http://www.brownmackie.edu), which is dedicated to providing educational programs that prepare students to pursue entry-level positions in a competitive, rapidly changing workplace. Brown Mackie College's system of schools offer bachelor's degree, associate degree, certificate, and diploma programs in health sciences, business, information technology, legal studies, and design to more than 19,000 students in the Midwest, Southeast, Southwest, and Western United States.

Brown Mackie College–Indianapolis was founded in 2007 as a branch of Brown Mackie College–Findlay, Ohio.

Brown Mackie College–Indianapolis is accredited by the Accrediting Council for Independent Colleges and Schools to award bachelor's degrees, associate degrees, and certificates. The Accrediting Council for Independent Colleges and Schools is listed as a nationally recognized accrediting agency by the United States Department of Education and is recognized by the Council for Higher Education Accreditation. ACICS can be contacted at 750 First Street NE, Suite 980, Washington, D.C. 20002; phone: 202-336-6780.

The College is licensed and regulated by the Indiana Commission on Proprietary Education, 302 West Washington Street, Indianapolis, Indiana 46204; phone: 317-232-1320 or 800-227-5695 (toll-free). (Indiana advertising code: AC-0078.)

The occupational therapy assistant program is accredited by the Accreditation Council for Occupational Therapy Education (ACOTE) of the American Occupational Therapy Association (AOTA), 4720 Montgomery Lane, P.O. Box 31220, Bethesda, Maryland 20824-1220; phone: 301-652-2682.

Location

Brown Mackie College–Indianapolis is conveniently located at 1200 North Meridian Street in Indianapolis, Indiana. The College has a generous parking area and is easily accessible by public transportation.

Programs of Study and Degrees

Brown Mackie College–Indianapolis provides higher education to traditional and nontraditional students through bachelor's degree, associate degree, diploma, and certificate programs that assist them in enhancing their career opportunities, broadening their perspectives through appropriate general education courses, thinking independently and critically, and improving problem-solving abilities. The College strives to develop within its students the desire for lifelong and continued education.

The Bachelor of Science degree (180 credits) is awarded in business administration, criminal justice, and legal studies.

The Associate of Science degree (96 credits) is awarded in business management, criminal justice, health-care administration, medical assisting, and paralegal studies. The Associate of Applied Science degree (100 credits) is awarded in occupational therapy assistant studies.

A diploma program (76 credits) in practical nursing is offered.

The College offers certificate programs (48 credits) in business and medical assistant studies.

Academic Programs

Each College quarter comprises twelve weeks. Bachelor's degree programs require a minimum of sixteen quarters to complete. Associate degree programs require a minimum of eight quarters to complete. Programs are offered on a year-round basis, providing students with the ability to work uninterrupted toward their degrees. The College offers all programs in a unique One Course a Month format. This allows students to focus studies on only one course for four weeks. This schedule has proven convenient for students with multiple obligations such as jobs and family.

Academic Facilities

Opened in January 2008, this modern facility offers more than 22,000 square feet of tastefully decorated classrooms, laboratories, and office space designed to the specifications of the College for its business, health-care, and technical programs. Instructional equipment is comparable to current technology used in business and industry today. Modern classrooms for special instructional needs offer multimedia capabilities with surround sound and overhead projectors accessible through computer, DVD, or VHS. Internet access and instructional resources are available at the College's library. Experienced faculty members provide academic support and are committed to the academic and technical preparation of their students.

The campus is nonresidential; public transportation and ample parking at no cost are available.

Costs

Tuition for most programs in the 2010–11 academic year is $283 per credit hour and fees are $15 per credit hour, with some exceptions. Tuition for the practical nursing diploma program is $325 per credit hour with a $25 per credit hour general fee applied to instructional costs for activities and services. For certain occupational therapy assistant studies courses the tuition is $283 per credit hour for general courses and $365 per credit hour for program-specific courses. General fees are $15 per credit hour.

Financial Aid

Financial aid is available to those who qualify. The College maintains a full-time staff of financial aid professionals to assist qualified students in obtaining the financial assistance they require to meet their educational expenses. Available resources include federal and state aid, student loans from private lenders, and federal work-study opportunities, both on and off college premises.

Each year, the College makes available scholarships of $1000 each to qualifying seniors from area high schools. No more than one scholarship is awarded per high school. In order to qualify, a senior must be graduating from a participating high school, must be maintaining a cumulative grade point average of at least 2.0, and must submit a brief essay. The student's extracurricular activities and community service are also considered. These scholarships are available only to students enrolling in one of the College's degree programs. Students awarded the scholarship must enroll at Brown Mackie College–Indianapolis between June and September immediately following their high school graduation. Applications for these scholarships can be obtained from the guidance departments of participating high schools. These applications must be completed and returned to the College by March 31.

Faculty

The College has 2 full-time and 6 part-time instructors, with a student-faculty ratio of 21:1. Faculty members provide tutoring and additional academic services to students as needed.

Admission Requirements

Each applicant for admission is assigned an Assistant Director of Admissions, who directs the applicant through the steps of the admissions process, providing information on curriculum, policies, procedures, and services and assisting the applicant in setting necessary appointments and interviews. To qualify for admission, each applicant must provide documentation of graduation from an accredited high school or from a state-approved secondary education curriculum or provide official documentation of high school graduation equivalency. All transcripts become the property of the College. Admission to the College is based on the applicant meeting the stated requirements, a review of the applicant's previous educational records, and a review of the applicant's career interests. If previous academic records indicate the College's education and training programs would not benefit the applicant, the College reserves the right to advise the applicant not to enroll. Special requirements for enrollment into certain programs are discussed in the descriptions of those programs.

In addition to the College's general admission requirements, applicants enrolling in the practical nursing program must document the following: fulfillment of Brown Mackie College–Indianapolis general requirements; complete physical (must be current to within six months of admission); two-step Mantoux TB skin test (must be current throughout schooling); hepatitis B vaccination or signed refusal; up-to-date immunizations, including tetanus and rubella; record of current CPR certification (certification must be current throughout the clinical experience through health-care provider certification or the American Heart Association); and hospitalization insurance or a signed waiver.

For the most recent information regarding admission requirements, please refer to the current academic catalog.

Application and Information

Applicants must complete and submit an application form, along with documentation of graduation from an accredited high school or state-approved secondary education curriculum or official documentation of high school graduation equivalency.

For additional information, prospective students should contact:

Senior Director of Admissions
Brown Mackie College–Indianapolis
1200 North Meridian Street, Suite 100
Indianapolis, Indiana 46204
Phone: 866-255-0279 (toll-free)
Fax: 317-632-4557
E-mail: bmcindadm@brownmackie.edu
Web site: http://www.brownmackie.edu/Indianapolis

BROWN MACKIE COLLEGE–LOUISVILLE

LOUISVILLE, KENTUCKY

The College

Brown Mackie College–Louisville is one of over twenty locations in the Brown Mackie College system of schools (www.brownmackie.edu), which is dedicated to providing educational programs that prepare students to pursue entry-level positions in a competitive, rapidly changing workplace. Brown Mackie College schools offer bachelor's degree, associate degree, certificate, and diploma programs in health sciences, business, information technology, legal studies, and design to over 19,000 students in the Midwest, Southeast, Southwest, and Western United States.

Brown Mackie College–Louisville opened in 1972 as RETS Institute of Technology. The first RETS school was founded in 1935 in Detroit in response to the rapid growth of radio broadcasting and the need for qualified radio technicians. The RETS Institute changed its name to Brown Mackie College–Louisville in 2004.

Brown Mackie College–Louisville is accredited by the Accrediting Council for Independent Colleges and Schools (ACICS) to award bachelor's degrees, associate degrees, diplomas, and certificates. ACICS is listed as a nationally recognized accrediting agency by the United States Department of Education and is recognized by the Council for Higher Education Accreditation. ACICS can be contacted at 750 First Street NE, Suite 980, Washington, D.C. 20002-4241; phone: 202-336-6780.

Brown Mackie College–Louisville is licensed by the Kentucky Council on Postsecondary Education for all programs offered by the College. The council is located at 1024 Capital Center Drive, Suite 320 Frankfort, Kentucky 40601.

The Brown Mackie College–Louisville's Associate of Applied Science degree in surgical technology is accredited by both the Accrediting Bureau of Health Education Schools, 7777 Leesburg Pike, Suite 314N, Falls Church, Virginia 22043; phone: 703-917-9503 and the Commission on Accreditation of Allied Health Education Programs, 1361 Park Street, Clearwater, Florida 33756.

The occupational therapy assistant studies program has applied for accreditation by the Accreditation Council for Occupational Therapy Education (ACOTE) of the American Occupational Therapy Association (AOTA), located at 4720 Montgomery Lane, P.O. Box 31220, Bethesda, Maryland 20824; phone: 301-652-AOTA.

The veterinary technology program is accredited as a program for educating veterinary technicians by the American Veterinary Medical Association (AVMA), 1931 North Meacham Road, Suite 100, Schaumburg, Illinois 60173.

The Brown Mackie College–Louisville diploma program in practical nursing is approved by the Kentucky Board of Nursing, 312 Whittington Parkway, Suite 300, Louisville, Kentucky 40222.

Location

Brown Mackie College–Louisville is conveniently located at 3605 Fern Valley Road in Louisville, Kentucky. The College has a generous parking area and is easily accessible by public transportation.

Programs of Study and Degrees

Brown Mackie College–Louisville provides higher education to traditional and nontraditional students through bachelor's degree, associate degree, and diploma programs that assist in enhancing their career opportunities, broadening their perspectives through appropriate general education courses, thinking independently and critically, and improving problem-solving abilities.

The Bachelor of Science degree (180 credits) is awarded in business administration, criminal justice, health-care management, and legal studies.

The Associate of Applied Business degree (96 credits) is awarded in accounting technology, business management, computer networking and applications, criminal justice, and paralegal studies.

The Associate of Applied Science degree (96 credits) is awarded in biomedical equipment technology, early childhood education, electronics, graphic design, health-care administration, medical assisting, occupational therapy assistant studies (100 credits), pharmacy technology, surgical technology, and veterinary technician studies.

The College offers a diploma program (48 credits) in practical nursing.

The College offers a certificate program (24 credits) in computer networking.

Academic Programs

Each College quarter comprises twelve weeks. Bachelor's degree programs require a minimum of sixteen quarters to complete. Associate degree programs require a minimum of eight quarters to complete. Programs are offered on a year-round basis, providing students with the ability to work uninterrupted toward completion of their programs. The College offers all programs in a unique One Course a Month format. This allows students to focus studies on only one course for four weeks. This schedule has proven convenient for students with multiple obligations such as jobs and family.

Academic Facilities

Brown Mackie College–Louisville has more than 42,000 square feet of multipurpose classrooms, including networked computer laboratories, electronics laboratories, veterinary technology labs, medical labs, nursing labs, a resource center, and offices for administrative personnel as well as for student services such as admissions, student financial services, and career-services assistance. In 2009, an additional 6,000 square feet was opened at the Louisville location. Included in this build-out are an occupational therapy lab, a criminal justice lab, additional classrooms, and faculty space. In 2010, an additional 25,000 square feet is scheduled to open at this location. Plans for this build-out include a biomedical equipment lab, additional classrooms, a career services center, and additional faculty/administration space.

The College is nonresidential; ample parking at no cost is available. The campus is a smoke-free facility.

Costs

Tuition for most programs in the 2010–11 academic year is $266 per credit hour. The practical nursing diploma program is $325 per credit hour, the surgical technology program is $310 per credit hour, the occupational therapy program is $365 per credit hour, and computer networking courses are $300 per credit hour. The length of the program determines total cost. The cost of textbooks and other instructional materials varies by program.

Financial Aid

Financial aid is available for those who qualify. The College maintains a full-time staff of financial aid professionals to assist qualified students in obtaining financial assistance. The College participates in several student aid programs. Forms of financial aid available through federal resources include the Federal Pell Grant Program, Federal Supplemental Educational Opportunity Grant (FSEOG) Program, Federal Work-Study Program, Federal Perkins Loan Program, Federal Stafford Student Loan Program (subsidized and unsubsidized), and the Federal PLUS Loan Program.

Each year, the College makes available President's Scholarships of $1000 each to qualifying seniors from area high schools. No more than one scholarship is awarded per high school. In order to qualify, a senior must have graduated from a participating high school, maintained a cumulative grade point average of at least 2.0, and submitted a brief essay. The student's extracurricular activities and community service are also considered. The President's Scholarship is available only to students enrolling in one of the College's degree programs. Students awarded the scholarship must enroll at Brown Mackie College–Louisville between June and September immediately following their high school graduation. Applications for these scholarships can be obtained from the guidance departments of participating high schools. These applications must be completed and returned to the College by March 31.

Faculty

There are 45 full-time and over 100 part-time faculty members at the College. The average student-faculty ratio is 20:1.

Admission Requirements

Each applicant for admission is assigned an Assistant Director of Admissions, who directs the applicant through the steps of the admissions process, providing information on curriculum, policies, procedures, and services and assisting the applicant in setting necessary appointments and interviews.

To qualify for admission, each applicant must provide documentation of graduation from an accredited high school or from a state-approved secondary education curriculum or provide official documentation of high school graduation equivalency. All transcripts become the property of the College. Admission to the College is based on the applicant meeting the stated requirements, a review of the applicant's previous educational records, and a review of the applicant's career interests. If previous academic records indicate the College's education and training programs would not benefit the applicant, the College reserves the right to advise the applicant not to enroll. Special requirements for enrollment into certain programs are discussed in the descriptions of those programs.

In addition to the College's general admission requirements, applicants enrolling in either the occupational therapy assistant program or the surgical technology program must document one of the following: a high school cumulative grade point average of at least 2.5, a score on the GED examination of at least 57 (557 if taken on or after January 15, 2002), or completion of 12 quarter-credit hours or 8 semester-credit hours of collegiate course work with a grade point average of at least 2.5. Credit hours may not include Professional Development (CF 1100), the Brown Mackie College–Louisville course. Students entering the program must also have completed a biology course with a grade of at least a C (or an average of at least 2.0 on a 4.0 scale).

In addition to the College's general admission requirements, applicants enrolling in the practical nursing program must document the following, which must be completed and a record of proof must appear in the student's file prior to the start of the nursing fundamentals course. No student will be admitted to a clinical agency unless all paperwork is completed. The paperwork is a requirement of all contracted agencies. This paperwork includes records of (1) a complete physical, current to within six months of admission; (2) a two-step Mantoux test that is kept current throughout schooling; (3) a hepatitis B vaccination or signed refusal; (4) up-to-date immunizations, including tetanus and rubella; (5) a record of current CPR certification that is maintained throughout the student's clinical experience; and (6) hospitalization insurance or a signed waiver.

For the most recent information regarding admission requirements, prospective students should refer to the current academic catalog.

Application and Information

Applicants must complete and submit an application form along with documentation of graduation from an accredited high school or completion of state-approved secondary education curriculum or provide official documentation of high school graduation equivalency.

For additional information, prospective students should contact:

Director of Admissions
Brown Mackie College–Louisville
3605 Fern Valley Road
Louisville, Kentucky 40219
Phone: 502-968-7191
800-999-7387 (toll-free)
Fax: 502-357-9956
E-mail: bmcloadm@brownmackie.edu
Web site: http://www.brownmackie.edu/Louisville

BROWN MACKIE COLLEGE–MERRILLVILLE

MERRILLVILLE, INDIANA

COLLEGE CLOSE-UPS

The College

Brown Mackie College–Merrillville is one of over twenty locations in the Brown Mackie College system of schools (www.brownmackie.edu), which is dedicated to providing educational programs that prepare students to pursue entry-level positions in a competitive, rapidly changing workplace. Brown Mackie College schools offer bachelor's degree, associate degree, certificate, and diploma programs in health sciences, business, information technology, legal studies, and design to over 19,000 students in the Midwest, Southeast, Southwest, and Western United States.

Founded in 1890 by A. N. Hirons as LaPorte Business College in LaPorte, Indiana, the institution later became known as Commonwealth Business College. In 1919, ownership was transferred to Grace and J. J. Moore, who successfully operated the College under the name of Reese School of Business for several decades. In 1975, the College came under the ownership of Steven C. Smith as Commonwealth Business College. A second location, now known as Brown Mackie College–Merrillville, was opened in 1984 in Merrillville, Indiana.

Brown Mackie College–Merrillville is accredited by the Accrediting Council for Independent Colleges and Schools (ACICS) to award bachelor's degrees, associate degrees, certificates, and diplomas. ACICS is listed as a nationally recognized accrediting agency by the United States Department of Education and is recognized by the Council for Higher Education Accreditation. ACICS can be contacted at 750 First Street NE, Suite 980, Washington, D.C. 20002; phone: 202-336-6780. The College is licensed and regulated by the Indiana Commission on Proprietary Education, 302 West Washington Street, Indianapolis, Indiana 46204; phone: 800-227-5695 (toll-free) or 317-232-1320. (Indiana advertising code: AC-0138.)

Brown Mackie College–Merrillville's medical assisting Associate of Science degree program is accredited by the Accrediting Bureau of Health Education Schools. The College's surgical technology Associate of Science degree program is accredited by the Accrediting Bureau of Health Education Schools.

The surgical technology Associate of Science degree is accredited by the Commission on Accreditation of Allied Health Education Programs (www.caahep.org) upon the recommendation of the Accreditation Review Committee on Education in Surgical Technology of the Commission on Accreditation of Allied Health Education Programs, 1361 Park Street, Clearwater, Florida 33756; phone: 727-210-2350.

The occupational therapy assistant studies Associate of Applied Science degree is accredited by the Accreditation Council for Occupational Therapy Education (ACOTE) of the American Occupational Therapy Association (AOTA), 4720 Montgomery Lane, P.O. Box 31220, Bethesda, Maryland 20824-1220: phone: 301-652-2682.

The College is a nonresidential, smoke-free institution.

Location

Brown Mackie College–Merrillville is conveniently located in northwest Indiana at 1000 East 80th Place, Merrillville, in the Twin Towers business complex just west of the intersection of U.S. Route 30 and Interstate 65. A spacious parking lot provides ample parking at no additional charge.

Programs of Study and Degrees

Brown Mackie College–Merrillville provides higher education to traditional and nontraditional students through bachelor's degree, associate degree, diploma, and certificate programs that assist in enhancing their career opportunities, broadening their perspectives through appropriate general education courses, thinking independently and critically, and improving problem-solving abilities. The College strives to develop within its students the desire for lifelong and continued education.

The Bachelor of Science degree is awarded in business administration (184 credits), criminal justice (184 credits), health-care management (180 credits), and legal studies (184 credits).

The Associate of Science degree (96 credits) is awarded in accounting technology, administration in gerontology, business management, computer software technology, criminal justice, medical assisting studies, medical office management, paralegal studies, and surgical technology.

The Associate of Applied Science degree (100 credits) is awarded in health and fitness training, occupational therapy assistant studies, and dietetics technology.

A diploma program (76 credits) in practical nursing is offered.

The College offers certificate programs (48 credits) in accounting, business, computer software applications, criminal justice, fitness trainer studies, medical assistant studies, and paralegal assistant studies.

Academic Programs

Each College quarter comprises ten to twelve weeks. Bachelor's degree programs require a minimum of sixteen quarters to complete. Associate degree programs require a minimum of eight quarters to complete. Programs are offered on a year-round basis, providing students with the ability to work uninterrupted toward completion of their programs. The College offers all programs in a unique One Course a Month format. This allows students to focus on only one course for four weeks. This schedule has proven convenient for students with multiple obligations such as jobs and family.

Academic Facilities

Occupying 26,000 square feet, Brown Mackie College–Merrillville was opened to students in October 1998 in the Twin Towers complex of Merrillville and comprises several instructional rooms, including five computer labs with networked computers and four medical laboratories. The administrative offices, college library, and student lounge are all easily accessible to students. The College bookstore stocks texts, courseware, and other educational supplies required for courses at the College. Students also find a variety of personal, recreational, and gift items, including apparel, supplies, and general merchandise incorporating the College logo. Hours are posted at the bookstore entrance.

Costs

Tuition for most programs in the 2010–11 academic year is $266 per credit hour, with some exceptions. The practical nursing diploma program is $325 per credit hour. For the surgical technology program, the tuition is $310 per credit hour, and fees are $15 per credit hour. For certain courses in the occupational therapy assistant program, the tuition is $365 per credit hour. The length of the program determines total cost. Textbook fees vary according to program.

Financial Aid

Financial aid is available to those who qualify. The College maintains a full-time staff of financial aid professionals to assist qualified students in obtaining financial assistance. The College participates in several student aid programs. Forms of financial aid available through federal resources include the Federal Pell Grant Program, Federal Supplemental Educational Opportunity Grant (FSEOG) Program, Federal Work-Study Program, Federal Perkins Loan Program, Federal Stafford Student Loan Program (subsidized and unsubsidized), and the Federal PLUS Loan Program. Eligible students may apply for Indiana state awards, such as the Higher Education Award and Twenty-First Century Scholarships for high school students, the Core 40 awards, and veterans' educational benefits. Students with physical or mental disabilities that are a handicap to employment may be eligible for training services through the state's Bureau of Vocational Rehabilitation. For further information, students should contact the College's Student Financial Services Office.

Each year, the College makes available scholarships of $1000 each to qualifying seniors from area high schools. No more than one scholarship is awarded per high school. In order to qualify, a senior must be graduating from a participating high school, must be maintaining a cumulative grade point average of at least 2.0, and must submit a brief essay. The student's extracurricular activities and community service are also considered. These scholarships are available only to students enrolling in one of the College's degree programs. Students awarded the scholarship must enroll at Brown Mackie College–Merrillville between June and September immediately following their high school graduation. Applications for these scholarships can be obtained from the guidance departments of participating high schools. These applications must be completed and returned to the College by March 31.

Faculty

There are approximately 60 full-time and 25 part-time faculty members at the College, practitioners in their fields of expertise. The average student-faculty ratio is 17:1.

Admission Requirements

Each applicant for admission is assigned an Assistant Director of Admissions who directs the applicant through the steps of the admissions process, providing information on curriculum, policies, procedures, and services and assisting the applicant in setting necessary appointments and interviews. To qualify for admission, each applicant must provide documentation of graduation from an accredited high school or completion of a state-approved secondary education curriculum or provide official documentation of high school graduation equivalency. All transcripts become the property of the College.

As part of the admission process, students are given an assessment of academic skills. Although the results of this assessment do not determine eligibility for admission, they provide the College with a means of determining the need for academic support as well as a means by which the College can evaluate the effectiveness of its educational programs. All new students are required to complete this assessment, which is readministered at the end of the student's program so results may be compared with those of the initial administration.

In addition to the College's general admission requirements, applicants enrolling in the practical nursing program must document the following, which must be completed, and a record of proof must appear in the student's file prior to the start of the nursing fundamentals course. No student will be admitted to a clinical agency unless all paperwork is completed. The paperwork is a requirement of all contracted agencies. This paperwork includes records of (1) a complete physical, current to within six months of admission, (2) a two-step Mantoux test that is kept current throughout schooling, (3) a hepatitis B vaccination or signed refusal, (4) up-to-date immunizations, including tetanus and rubella, (5) a record of current CPR certification that is maintained throughout the student's clinical experience, and (6) hospitalization insurance or a signed waiver.

For the most recent information regarding admission requirements, please refer to the current academic catalog.

Application and Information

Applicants must complete and submit an application form along with documentation of graduation from an accredited high school or completion of state-approved secondary education curriculum or provide official documentation of high school graduation equivalency. For additional information, prospective students should contact:

Brown Mackie College–Merrillville
1000 East 80th Place, Suite 101N
Merrillville, Indiana 46410
Phone: 219-769-3321
800-258-3321 (toll-free)
Fax: 219-738-1076
E-mail: bmcmeadm@brownmackie.edu
Web site: http://www.brownmackie.edu/Merrillville

BROWN MACKIE COLLEGE–MIAMI

MIAMI, FLORIDA

The College

Brown Mackie College–Miami is one of over twenty locations in the Brown Mackie College system of schools (www.brownmackie.edu), which is dedicated to providing educational programs that prepare students to pursue entry-level positions in a competitive, rapidly changing workplace. Brown Mackie College schools offer bachelor's degree, associate degree, certificate, and diploma programs in health sciences, business, information technology, legal studies, criminal justice, early childhood education, and design to over 19,000 students in the Midwest, Southeast, Southwest, and Western United States.

Brown Mackie College–Miami is accredited by the Accrediting Council for Independent Colleges and Schools (ACICS) to award bachelor's degrees and associate degrees. ACICS is listed as a nationally recognized accrediting agency by the United States Department of Education and is recognized by the Council for Higher Education Accreditation. ACICS can be contacted at 750 First Street, NE, Suite 980, Washington, D.C. 20002-4241; phone: 202-336-6780.

The College is a nonresidential, smoke-free institution.

Location

Brown Mackie College–Miami occupies space within the newly renovated One Herald Plaza in Miami, Florida. It is conveniently located adjacent to the OMNI Metro Mover and bus stop, with access to Metro Rail and Florida's regional Tri-Rail system. Ample parking is also available.

Programs of Study and Degrees

Brown Mackie College–Miami provides higher education to traditional and nontraditional students through bachelor's degree and associate degree programs that assist them in enhancing their career opportunities, broadening their perspectives through appropriate general education courses, thinking independently and critically, and improving problem-solving abilities. The College strives to develop within its students the desire for lifelong and continued education.

The Bachelor of Science degree (180 credits) is awarded in business administration, criminal justice, and health-care management.

The Associate of Science degree (96 credits) is awarded in accounting technology, business management, criminal justice, early childhood education, health-care administration, information technology, medical assisting, and paralegal studies.

Academic Programs

Each College quarter comprises twelve weeks. Bachelor's degree programs require a minimum of sixteen quarters to complete. Associate degree programs require a minimum of eight quarters to complete. Programs are offered on a year-round basis, providing students with the ability to work uninterrupted toward their degrees. The College offers all programs in a unique One Course a Month format. This allows students to focus studies on only one course for four weeks. This schedule has proven convenient for students with multiple obligations such as jobs and family.

Academic Facilities

Brown Mackie College–Miami is conveniently located at One Herald Plaza. The College recently moved its main campus from Biscayne Boulevard to occupy 50,000 square feet on the top floor of the Miami Herald building, which sits on beautiful Biscayne Bay and offers a clear view of Miami's famous South Beach.

The College offers hands-on experiences in its many labs, including a criminal justice lab featuring facial recognition software along with a multitude of forensic equipment. The computer-networking lab has eight computer classrooms and offers students a modern and professional environment for study. Each student has access to the technology, tools, and facilities needed to complete projects in each subject area. Students are welcome to use the labs when they are not being used for scheduled classes. The new location features a comfortable student lounge as well as an on-site eatery available during all class shifts. The College bookstore offers retail items including college ware, as well as textbooks and kits specific to programs of study.

The College still maintains a learning center in the OMNI building across the street from the main campus until the second phase of construction is completed at the Herald building. This learning center offers two medical assisting labs and an additional computer classroom. The learning center also offers a library that is available to Brown Mackie College–Miami students as part of a shared-service agreement with Miami International University of Art & Design. The collection includes more than 20,000 volumes, including books and visual aids. In addition, the library subscribes to more than 200 periodicals specific to the academic programs offered.

Costs

Tuition in the 2010–11 academic year for all programs is $336 per credit hour; fees are $15 per credit hour. Textbooks and other instructional materials vary by program.

Financial Aid

Financial aid is available for those who qualify. The College maintains a full-time staff of financial aid professionals to assist qualified students in obtaining financial assistance. The College participates in several student aid programs. Forms of financial aid available to qualified students through federal resources include the Federal Pell Grant Program, Federal Supplemental Educational Opportunity Grant (FSEOG) Program, Federal Work-Study Program, Federal Perkins Loan Program, Federal Stafford Student Loan Program (subsidized and unsubsidized), Federal PLUS loan program, and Florida State grant program. Eligible students may apply for veterans' educational benefits. Students with physical or mental disabilities that are a handicap to employment may be eligible for training services through the state Agency for Vocational Rehabilitation. For further information, students should contact the College Student Financial Services Office.

Each year, the College makes available President's Scholarships of $1000 each to qualifying seniors from area high schools. No more than one scholarship is awarded per high school. In order to qualify, a senior must be graduating from a participating high school, must be maintaining a cumulative grade point average of at least 2.0, and must submit a brief essay. The student's extracurricular activities and community service are also considered. The President's Scholarship is available only to students enrolling in one of the College's degree programs. Students awarded the scholarship must enroll at Brown Mackie College–Miami between June and September immediately following their high school graduation. Applications for these scholarships can be obtained from the guidance departments of participating high schools. These applications must be completed and returned to the College by March 31.

Faculty

There are 15 full-time and 27 adjunct faculty members at the College. The average student-faculty ratio is 20:1.

Admission Requirements

Each applicant for admission is assigned an Assistant Director of Admissions, who directs the applicant through the steps of the admissions process, providing information on curriculum, policies, procedures, and services and assisting the applicant in setting necessary appointments and interviews. To qualify for admission, applicants must be a graduate of a public or private high school or a correspondence school or education center that is accredited by an agency that is recognized by the U.S. or State of Florida Department of Education or any of its approved agents. As part of the admissions process, applicants must sign a document attesting to graduation or completion and containing the information to obtain verification of such. Verification must be obtained within the first term. All transcripts become the property of the College. Admission to the College is based on the applicant meeting the stated requirements, a review of the applicant's previous educational records, and a review of the applicant's career interests. If previous academic records indicate the College's education and training programs would not benefit the applicant, the College reserves the right to advise the applicant not to enroll. Special requirements for enrollment into certain programs are discussed in the descriptions of those programs.

Students are given an assessment of academic skills during the first two weeks of class. Although the results of this assessment do not determine eligibility for admission, they provide the College with a means of determining the need for academic support as well as a means by which the College can evaluate the effectiveness of its educational programs. All new students are required to complete this assessment.

For the most recent information regarding admission requirements, please refer to the current academic catalog.

Application and Information

Applicants must complete and submit an application form.

Director of Admissions
Brown Mackie College–Miami
One Herald Plaza
Miami, Florida 33132-1418
Phone: 305-341-6600
866-505-0335 (toll-free)
Fax: 305-373-8814
E-mail: bmmiaadm@brownmackie.edu
Web site: http://www.brownmackie.edu/Miami

BROWN MACKIE COLLEGE–MICHIGAN CITY

MICHIGAN CITY, INDIANA

The College

Brown Mackie College–Michigan City is one of over twenty locations in the Brown Mackie College system of schools (www.brownmackie.edu), which is dedicated to providing educational programs that prepare students to pursue entry-level positions in a competitive, rapidly changing workplace. Brown Mackie College schools offer bachelor's degree, associate degree, certificate, and diploma programs in health sciences, business, information technology, legal studies, and design to over 19,000 students in the Midwest, Southeast, Southwest, and Western United States.

Founded in 1890 by A. N. Hirons as LaPorte Business College in LaPorte, Indiana, the institution later became known as Commonwealth Business College. In 1919, ownership was transferred to Grace and J. J. Moore, who successfully operated the College under the name of Reese School of Business for several decades. In 1975, the College came under the ownership of Steven C. Smith as Commonwealth Business College. In 1997, the College relocated to its present site in Michigan City, Indiana. The College was acquired by Education Management Corporation (EDMC) on September 2, 2003, and changed its name to Brown Mackie College–Michigan City in November 2004.

Brown Mackie College–Michigan City is accredited by the Accrediting Council for Independent Colleges and Schools (ACICS) to award bachelor's degrees, associate degrees, and certificates. ACICS is listed as a nationally recognized accrediting agency by the United States Department of Education and is recognized by the Council for Higher Education Accreditation. ACICS can be contacted at 750 First Street NE, Suite 980, Washington, D.C. 20002; phone: 202-336-6780.

The College's medical assisting degree program is accredited by the Commission on Accreditation of Allied Health Education Programs (CAAHEP), 1361 Park Street, Clearwater, Florida 33756; phone: 727-210-2350, upon the recommendation of the Curriculum Review Board of the American Association of Medical Assistants Endowment (AAMAE).

The College's surgical technology program is accredited by the Commission on Accreditation of Allied Health Education Programs (CAAHEP), 1361 Park Street, Clearwater, Florida 33756; phone: 727-210-2350, on recommendation of the Curriculum Review Board of the American Association of Medical Assistants Endowment (AAMAE).

The College's veterinary technology degree program is accredited by the AVMA as a program for educating veterinary technicians.

The Indiana advertising code for Brown Mackie College–Michigan City is AC-0138.

The College is a nonresidential, smoke-free institution.

Location

Brown Mackie College–Michigan City is conveniently located in northwest Indiana, at 325 East U.S. Highway 20, Michigan City, 1 mile north of Interstate 94, near the intersection of routes 20 and 421. Additional parking spaces were added in 2002, providing students and employees with ample parking at no additional charge.

Programs of Study and Degrees

Brown Mackie College–Michigan City provides higher education to traditional and nontraditional students through bachelor's degree, associate degree, and certificate programs that assist in enhancing their career opportunities, broadening their perspectives through appropriate general education courses, thinking independently and critically, and improving problem-solving abilities. The College strives to develop within its students the desire for lifelong and continued education.

The Bachelor of Science degree (184 credits) is awarded in business administration, criminal justice, health-care management (180 credits) and legal studies.

The Associate of Science degree (96 credits) is awarded in accounting technology, business management, computer software technology, criminal justice, early childhood education, health and therapeutic massage, health-care administration, medical assisting, medical office management, paralegal studies, surgical technology, and veterinary technology.

The College offers certificate programs (48 credits) in accounting, business, computer software applications, criminal justice, medical assistant studies, medical coding and billing, and paralegal assistant studies.

Academic Programs

Each College quarter comprises twelve weeks. Bachelor's degree programs require a minimum of sixteen quarters to complete. Associate degree programs require a minimum of eight quarters to complete. Programs are offered on a year-round basis, providing students with the ability to work uninterrupted toward their degrees. The College offers all programs in a unique One Course a Month format. This allows students to focus studies on only one course for four weeks. This schedule has proven convenient for students with multiple obligations such as jobs and family.

Academic Facilities

In 2002, the College underwent a major renovation and added 3,360 square feet, for a total of 10,338 square feet of occupancy. An additional medical laboratory, a larger library, new classrooms, and a bookstore were added. All classrooms and the library are equipped with new technology, including multimedia projectors, surround-sound audio systems, VCRs, and DVD players. Five of the ten new classrooms are equipped with networked computer systems. The two medical laboratories contain newly acquired medical equipment and instructional tools and supplies. Administrative offices are easily accessible to students.

Costs

Tuition in the 2010–11 academic year is $266 per credit hour and fees are $15 per credit hour. For the surgical technology program, the tuition is $310 per credit hour and fees are $15 per credit hour. Textbook fees vary according to the program.

Financial Aid

The College maintains a full-time staff of financial aid professionals to assist qualified students in obtaining financial assistance. The College participates in several student aid programs. Forms of financial aid available to qualified students through federal resources include the Federal Pell Grant Program, Federal Supplemental Educational Opportunity Grant (FSEOG) Program, Federal Work-Study Program, Federal Stafford Student Loan Program (subsidized and unsubsidized), and Federal PLUS loan program.

Eligible students may apply for Indiana state awards, such as the Higher Education Award and Twenty-First Century Scholarships for high school students, the Core 40 awards, and veterans' educational benefits. Students with physical or mental disabilities that are a handicap to employment may be eligible for training services through the state's Bureau of Vocational Rehabilitation. For further information, students should contact the College Student Financial Services Office.

Each year, the College makes available scholarships of $1000 each to qualifying seniors from area high schools. No more than one scholarship is awarded per high school. In order to qualify, a senior must be graduating from a participating high school, must be maintaining a cumulative grade point average of at least 2.0, and must submit a brief essay. The student's extracurricular activities and community service are also considered. These scholarships are available only to students enrolling in one of the College's degree programs. Students awarded the scholarship must enroll at Brown Mackie College–Michigan City between June and September immediately following their high school graduation. Applications for these scholarships can be obtained from the guidance departments of participating high schools. These applications must be completed and returned to the College by March 31.

Faculty

There are 9 full-time and 31 part-time faculty members at the College. The average student-faculty ratio is 13:1. Each student is assigned a faculty adviser.

Admission Requirements

Each applicant for admission is assigned an Assistant Director of Admissions, who directs the applicant through the steps of the admissions process, providing information on curriculum, policies, procedures, and services and assisting the applicant in setting necessary appointments and interviews. To qualify for admission, each applicant must provide documentation of graduation from an accredited high school or completion of a state-approved secondary education curriculum or provide official documentation of high school graduation equivalency. All transcripts become the property of the College.

As part of the admission process, students are given an assessment of academic skills. Although the results of this assessment do not determine eligibility for admission, they provide the College with a means of determining the need for academic support, as well as a means by which the College can evaluate the effectiveness of its educational programs. All new students are required to complete this assessment, which is readministered at the end of the student's program so results may be compared with those of the initial administration.

For the most recent information regarding admission requirements, please refer to the current academic catalog.

Application and Information

Applicants must complete and submit an application form along with documentation of graduation from an accredited high school or completion of a state-approved secondary education curriculum or provide official documentation of high school graduation equivalency. For additional information, prospective students should contact:

Director of Admissions
Brown Mackie College–Michigan City
325 East U.S. Highway 20
Michigan City, Indiana 46360
Phone: 219-877-3100
800-519-2416 (toll-free)
Fax: 219-877-3110
E-mail: bmcmcadm@brownmackie.edu
Web site: http://www.brownmackie.edu/MichiganCity

BROWN MACKIE COLLEGE–NORTHERN KENTUCKY

FORT MITCHELL, KENTUCKY

BROWN MACKIE COLLEGE
NORTHERN KENTUCKY™

The College

Brown Mackie College–Northern Kentucky is one of over twenty locations in the Brown Mackie College system of schools (www.brownmackie.edu), which is dedicated to providing educational programs that prepare students to pursue entry-level positions in a competitive, rapidly changing workplace. Brown Mackie College's system of schools offer bachelor's degree, associate degree, certificate, and diploma programs in health sciences, business, information technology, legal studies, and design to more than 19,000 students in the Midwest, Southeast, Southwest, and Western United States.

The College was founded in Cincinnati, Ohio, in February 1927 as a traditional business college. In May 1981, the College opened a branch location in northern Kentucky, which moved in 1986 to its current location in Fort Mitchell.

Brown Mackie College–Northern Kentucky is accredited by the Accrediting Council for Independent Colleges and Schools (ACICS) to award bachelor's degrees, associate degrees, and certificates. ACICS is listed as a nationally recognized accrediting agency by the United States Department of Education and is recognized by the Council for Higher Education Accreditation. ACICS can be contacted at 750 First Street NE, Suite 980, Washington, D.C. 20002; phone: 202-336-6780.

The occupational therapy assistant studies program has applied for accreditation by the Accreditation Council for Occupational Therapy Education (ACOTE) of the American Occupational Therapy Association (AOTA), located at 4720 Montgomery Lane, P.O. Box 31220, Bethesda, Maryland 20824; phone: 301-652-AOTA.

The Ohio registration number is 03-09-1686T.

Location

Brown Mackie College–Northern Kentucky is conveniently located at 309 Buttermilk Pike in Fort Mitchell, Kentucky. A spacious parking lot provides ample parking at no additional charge.

Programs of Study and Degrees

Brown Mackie College–Northern Kentucky provides higher education to traditional and nontraditional students through bachelor's degree, associate degree, and diploma programs that assist them in enhancing their career opportunities, broadening their perspectives through appropriate general education courses, thinking independently and critically, and improving problem-solving abilities. The College strives to develop within its students the desire for lifelong and continued education.

The Bachelor of Science degree is awarded in business administration (184 credits), criminal justice (184 credits), health-care management (180 credits), and legal studies (184 credits).

The Associate of Applied Business degree (96 credits) is awarded in accounting technology, business management, computer software technology, criminal justice, health-care administration, information technology, and paralegal studies.

The Associate of Applied Science degree (96 credits) is awarded in computer-aided design and drafting technology, medical assisting, occupational therapy assistant studies (100 credits), pharmacy technology, and surgical technology.

The College offers a diploma program (76 credits) in accounting, business, computer applications, computer software applications, medical assistant studies, and practical nursing.

Academic Programs

Each College quarter comprises ten to twelve weeks. Bachelor's degree programs require a minimum of sixteen quarters to complete. Associate degree programs require a minimum of eight quarters to complete. Programs are offered on a year-round basis, providing students with the ability to work uninterrupted toward their degrees. The College offers all programs in a unique One Course a Month format. This allows students to focus studies on only one course for four weeks. This schedule has proven convenient for students with multiple obligations such as jobs and family.

Academic Facilities

Brown Mackie College–Northern Kentucky offers media presentation rooms for special instructional needs and a library that provides instructional resources and academic support for both faculty members and students.

The campus is nonresidential; public transportation and ample parking at no cost are available. The campus is a smoke-free facility.

Costs

Tuition for the 2010–11 academic year is $266 per credit hour and general fees are $15 per credit hour, with some exceptions. The practical nursing program tuition is $325 per credit hour and general fees are $25 per credit hour. The surgical technology tuition is $310 per credit hour. Tuition for the occupational therapy assistant program is $266 per credit hour for general courses and $365 per credit hour for program-specific courses. The cost of textbooks and other instructional materials varies by program.

Financial Aid

Financial aid is available to those who qualify. The College maintains a full-time staff of financial aid professionals to assist qualified students in obtaining financial assistance. The College participates in several student aid programs. Forms of financial aid available through federal resources include Federal Pell Grants, Federal Supplemental Educational Opportunity Grants (FSEOG), Federal Work-Study Program awards, Federal Perkins Loans, Federal Stafford Student Loans (subsidized and unsubsidized), and Federal PLUS loans. Eligible students may apply for veterans' educational benefits. Students with physical or mental disabilities that are a handicap to employment may be eligible for training services through the state Vocational Rehabilitation Agency. For further information, students should contact the College Student Financial Services Office.

Each year, the College makes available President's Scholarships of $1000 each to qualifying seniors from area high schools. No more than one scholarship is awarded per high school. In order to qualify, a senior have graduated from a participating high school, maintained a cumulative grade point average of at least 2.0, and submitted a brief essay. The student's extracurricular activities and community service are also considered. The President's Scholarship is available only to students enrolling in one of the College's degree programs. Students who receive the scholarship must enroll at Brown Mackie College–Northern Kentucky between June and September immediately following their high school graduation. Applications for these scholarships can be obtained from the guidance departments of participating high schools. These applications must be completed and returned to the College by March 31.

Faculty

There are 11 full-time and 20 part-time faculty members. The student-faculty ratio is 15:1.

Admission Requirements

Each applicant for admission is assigned an Assistant Director of Admissions, who directs the applicant through the steps of the admissions process, providing information on curriculum, policies, procedures, and services and assisting the applicant in setting necessary appointments and interviews. To qualify for admission, each applicant must provide documentation of graduation from an accredited high school or from a state-approved secondary education curriculum or provide official documentation of high school graduation equivalency. All transcripts become the property of the College. Admission to the College is based upon the applicant meeting the stated requirements, a review of the applicant's previous education records, and a review of the applicant's career interests. If previous academic records indicate the College's education and training programs would not benefit the applicant, the College reserves the right to advise the applicant not to enroll. Special requirements for enrollment into certain programs are discussed in the descriptions of those programs.

In addition to the College's general admission requirements, applicants enrolling in the practical nursing program must document the following, which must be completed, and a record of proof must appear in the student's file prior to the start of the nursing fundamentals course. No student will be admitted to a clinical agency unless all paperwork is completed. The paperwork is a requirement of all contracted agencies. This paperwork includes records of (1) a complete physical, current to within six months of admission; (2) a two-step Mantoux test that is kept current throughout schooling; (3) a hepatitis B vaccination or signed refusal; (4) up-to-date immunizations, including tetanus and rubella; (5) a record of current CPR certification that is maintained throughout the student's clinical experience; and (6) hospitalization insurance or a signed waiver.

For the most recent information regarding admission requirements, prospective students should refer to the current academic catalog.

Application and Information

Applicants must complete and submit an application form, along with documentation of graduation from an accredited high school or state-approved secondary education curriculum or official documentation of high school graduation equivalency.

For additional information, prospective students should contact:

Director of Admissions
Brown Mackie College–Northern Kentucky
309 Buttermilk Pike
Fort Mitchell, Kentucky 41017
Phone: 859-341-5627
800-888-1445 (toll-free)
Fax: 859-341-6483
E-mail: bmcnkadm@brownmackie.edu
Web site: http://www.brownmackie.edu/NorthernKentucky

BROWN MACKIE COLLEGE–PHOENIX

PHOENIX, ARIZONA

The College

Brown Mackie College–Phoenix is one of over twenty locations in the Brown Mackie College system of schools (www.brownmackie.edu), which is dedicated to providing educational programs that prepare students to pursue entry-level positions in a competitive, rapidly changing workplace. Brown Mackie College schools offer bachelor's degree, associate degree, certificate, and diploma programs in health sciences, business, information technology, legal studies, and design to over 19,000 students in the Midwest, Southeast, Southwest, and Western United States.

Brown Mackie College–Phoenix was founded in 2009 as a branch of Brown Mackie College–Tucson, Arizona.

Brown Mackie College–Phoenix is accredited by the Accrediting Council for Independent Colleges and Schools (ACICS) to award bachelor's degrees, associate degrees, and diplomas. ACICS is listed as a nationally recognized accrediting agency by the United States Department of Education and is recognized by the Council for Higher Education Accreditation. ACICS can be contacted at 750 First Street NE, Suite 980, Washington, D.C. 20002; phone: 202-336-6780.

The occupational therapy assistant studies program has applied for accreditation by the Accreditation Council for Occupational Therapy Education (ACOTE) of the American Occupational Therapy Association (AOTA), located at 4720 Montgomery Lane, P.O. Box 31220, Bethesda, Maryland 20824-1220; phone: 301-652-2682.

This institution is licensed by the Arizona State Board for Private Postsecondary Education, 1400 West Washington Street, Room 260, Phoenix, Arizona 85007; phone: 602-542-5709.

The College is a nonresidential, smoke-free institution.

Location

Brown Mackie College–Phoenix is conveniently located at 13430 North Black Canyon Highway in Phoenix, Arizona. The College has a generous parking area and is easily accessible by public transportation.

Programs of Study and Degrees

Brown Mackie College–Phoenix provides higher education to traditional and nontraditional students through bachelor's and associate degree programs that assist in enhancing their career opportunities, broadening their perspectives through appropriate general education courses, thinking independently and critically, and improving problem-solving abilities. The College strives to develop within its students the desire for lifelong and continued education.

The Bachelor of Science degree (180 credits) is awarded in business administration, criminal justice, health-care management, and legal studies.

The Associate of Science degree (96 credits) is awarded in accounting technology, business management, criminal justice, health-care administration, information technology, medical assisting, paralegal studies, and surgical technology.

The Associate of Applied Science degree (96 credits) is awarded in occupational therapy assistant studies.

Academic Programs

Each College quarter comprises twelve weeks. Bachelor's degree programs require a minimum of sixteen quarters to complete. Associate degree programs require a minimum of eight quarters to complete. Programs are offered on a year-round basis, providing students with the ability to work uninterrupted toward completion of their programs. The College offers all programs in a unique One Course a Month format. This allows students to focus studies on only one course for four weeks. This schedule has proven convenient for students with multiple obligations such as jobs and family.

Academic Facilities

Brown Mackie College–Phoenix has a variety of classrooms including computer labs housing the latest technology in the industry. High-speed access to the Internet and other online resources are available for students and faculty. Multimedia classrooms provide a learning environment equipped with overhead projectors, TVs, DVD/VCR players, computers, and sound systems.

Costs

Tuition for programs in the 2010–11 academic year is $250 per credit hour, with a $15 per credit hour general fee applied to instructional costs for activities and services. For the surgical technology program, the tuition is $275 per credit hour with a $15 per credit hour general fee applied to instructional costs for activities. Textbooks and other instructional materials vary by program.

Financial Aid

Financial aid is available for those who qualify. The College maintains a full-time staff of financial aid professionals to assist qualified students in obtaining financial assistance. The College participates in several student aid programs. Forms of financial aid available to those who qualify through federal resources include the Federal Pell Grant Program, Federal Supplemental Educational Opportunity Grant (FSEOG) Program, Federal Work-Study Program, Federal Perkins Loan Program, Federal Stafford Student Loan Program (subsidized and unsubsidized), and the Federal PLUS Loan Program.

Each year, the College makes available President's Scholarships of $1000 each to qualifying seniors from area high schools. No more than one scholarship is awarded per high school. In order to qualify, a senior must be graduating from a participating high school, must be maintaining a cumulative grade point average of at least 2.0, and must submit a brief essay. The student's extracurricular activities and community service are also considered. The President's Scholarship is available only to students enrolling in one of the College's degree programs. Students awarded the scholarship must enroll at Brown Mackie College–Phoenix between June and September immediately following their high school graduation. Applications for these scholarships can be obtained from the guidance departments of participating high schools. These applications must be completed and returned to the College by March 31.

Faculty

Experienced faculty members provide academic support and are committed to the academic and technical preparation of their students. The College has both full- and part-time faculty members. The average student-faculty ratio is 12:1. Each student is assigned a program director as an adviser.

Admission Requirements

Each applicant for admission is assigned an Assistant Director of Admissions, who directs the applicant through the steps of the admissions process, providing information on curriculum, policies, procedures, and services and assisting the applicant in setting necessary appointments and interviews. To qualify for admission, each applicant must provide documentation of graduation from an accredited high school or from a state-approved secondary education curriculum or provide official documentation of high school graduation equivalency. All transcripts become the property of the College.

For the most recent information regarding admission requirements, please refer to the current academic catalog.

Application and Information

Applicants must complete and submit an application form, along with documentation of graduation from an accredited high school or state-approved secondary education curriculum or official documentation of high school graduation equivalency.

For additional information, prospective students should contact:

Director of Admissions
Brown Mackie College–Phoenix
13430 N. Black Canyon Highway, Suite 190
Phoenix, Arizona 85029
Phone: 602-337-3044
866-824-4793 (toll-free)
Fax: 480-375-2450
E-mail: bmcpxadmn@brownmackie.edu
Web site: http://www.brownmackie.edu/Phoenix

COLLEGE CLOSE-UPS

BROWN MACKIE COLLEGE–ST. LOUIS

FENTON, MISSOURI

The College

Brown Mackie College–St. Louis is one of over twenty locations in the Brown Mackie College system of schools (www.brownmackie.edu), which is dedicated to providing educational programs that prepare students to pursue entry-level positions in a competitive, rapidly changing workplace. Brown Mackie College schools offer bachelor's degree, associate degree, certificate, and diploma programs in health sciences, business, information technology, legal studies, and design to over 19,000 students in the Midwest, Southeast, Southwest, and Western United States.

Brown Mackie College was originally founded and approved by the Board of Trustees of Kansas Wesleyan College in Salina, Kansas on July 30, 1892. In 1938, the College was incorporated as The Brown Mackie School of Business under the ownership of Perry E. Brown and A.B. Mackie, former instructors at Kansas Wesleyan University in Salina, Kansas. Their last names formed the name of Brown Mackie. By January 1975, with improvements in curricula and higher degree-granting status, The Brown Mackie School of Business became Brown Mackie College.

Brown Mackie College–St. Louis is accredited by the Accrediting Council for Independent Colleges and Schools (ACICS) to award bachelor's degrees, associate degrees, and diplomas. ACICS is listed as a nationally recognized accrediting agency by the United States Department of Education and is recognized by the Council for Higher Education Accreditation. ACICS can be contacted at 750 First Street NE, Suite 980, Washington, D.C. 20002; phone: 202-336-6780.

Location

Brown Mackie College–St. Louis is conveniently located at 2 Soccer Park Road in Fenton, Missouri. The College has a generous parking area and is easily accessible by public transportation.

Programs of Study and Degrees

Brown Mackie College–St. Louis provides higher education to traditional and nontraditional students through bachelor's and associate degree programs that assist in enhancing their career opportunities, broadening their perspectives through appropriate general education courses, thinking independently and critically, and improving problem-solving abilities. The College strives to develop within its students the desire for lifelong and continued education.

The Bachelor of Science degree (184 credits) is awarded in business administration, criminal justice, health-care management (180 credits), and legal studies.

The Associate of Applied Science degree (96 credits) is awarded in accounting technology, architectural design and drafting technology, business management, criminal justice, health-care administration, information technology, medical assisting, office management, paralegal studies, pharmacy technology, and surgical technology.

The College offers diploma programs (48 credits) in accounting, business, criminal justice, medical assistant studies, and paralegal assistant studies.

Academic Programs

Each College quarter comprises twelve weeks. Bachelor's degree programs require a minimum of sixteen quarters to complete. Associate degree programs require a minimum of eight quarters to complete. Programs are offered on a year-round basis, providing students with the ability to work uninterrupted toward completion of their programs. The College offers all programs in a unique One Course a Month format. This allows students to focus studies on only one course for four weeks. This schedule has proven convenient for students with multiple obligations such as jobs and family.

Academic Facilities

A modern facility, Brown Mackie College–St Louis offers more than 30,000 square feet. The College is equipped with multiple computer labs, housing over 200 computers. High-speed access to the Internet and other online resources are available for students and faculty. Multimedia classrooms are outfitted with overhead projectors, VCR/DVD players, and computers.

The campus is nonresidential; public transportation and parking at no cost are available. The campus is a smoke-free facility.

Costs

Tuition in the 2010–11 academic year for all bachelor's and associate degrees and diploma programs is $260 per credit hour; fees are $15 per credit hour. Tuition for the surgical technology program is $310 per credit hour; fees are $15 per credit hour. The cost of textbooks and other instructional materials varies by program.

Financial Aid

Financial aid is available for those who qualify. The College maintains a full-time staff of financial aid professionals to assist qualified students in obtaining the financial assistance they require to meet their educational expenses. Available resources include federal and state aid, student loans from private lenders, and Federal Work-Study opportunities, both on and off college premises.

Each year, the College makes available scholarships of $1000 each to qualifying seniors from area high schools. No more than one scholarship is awarded per high school. In order to qualify, a senior must have graduated from a participating high school, maintained a cumulative grade point average of at least 2.0, and submitted a brief essay. The student's extracurricular activities and community service are also considered. These scholarships are available only to students enrolling in one of the College's degree programs. Students awarded the scholarship must enroll at Brown Mackie College–St. Louis between June and September immediately following their high school graduation. Applications for these scholarships can be obtained from the guidance departments of participating high schools. These applications must be completed and returned to the College by March 31.

Faculty

Experienced faculty members provide academic support and are committed to the academic and technical preparation of their students. The College has 3 full-time and 3 part-time instructors, with a student-faculty ratio of 20:1.

Admission Requirements

Each applicant for admission is assigned an Assistant Director of Admissions who directs the applicant through the steps of the admissions process. They provide information on curriculum, policies, procedures, and services and assist the applicant in setting necessary appointments and interviews. To qualify for admission, each applicant must provide documentation of graduation from an accredited high school or from a state-approved secondary education curriculum or provide official documentation of high school graduation equivalency. All transcripts become the property of the College. Admission to the College is based on the applicant meeting the stated requirements, a review of the applicant's previous educational records, and a review of the applicant's career interests. If previous academic records indicate the College's education and training programs would not benefit the applicant, the College reserves the right to advise the applicant not to enroll. Special requirements for enrollment into certain programs are discussed in the descriptions of those programs.

For the most recent information regarding admission requirements, prospective students should refer to the current academic catalog.

Application and Information

Applicants must complete and submit an application form, along with documentation of graduation from an accredited high school or state-approved secondary education curriculum or official documentation of high school graduation equivalency.

For additional information, prospective students should contact:

Director of Admissions
Brown Mackie College–St. Louis
2 Soccer Park Road
Fenton, Missouri 63026
Phone: 636-651-3290
Fax: 636-651-3349
E-mail: bmcstladm@brownmackie.edu
Web site: http://www.brownmackie.edu/StLouis

COLLEGE CLOSE-UPS

BROWN MACKIE COLLEGE–SOUTH BEND

SOUTH BEND, INDIANA

COLLEGE CLOSE-UPS

The College

Brown Mackie College–South Bend is one of over twenty locations in the Brown Mackie College system of schools (www.brownmackie.edu), which is dedicated to providing educational programs that prepare students to pursue entry-level positions in a competitive, rapidly changing workplace. Brown Mackie College schools offer bachelor's degree, associate degree, certificate, and diploma programs in health sciences, business, information technology, legal studies, and design to over 19,000 students in the Midwest, Southeast, Southwest, and Western United States.

The College is one of the oldest institutions of its kind in the country and the oldest in the state of Indiana. Established in 1882 as the South Bend Commercial College, the school later changed its name to Michiana College. In 1930, the school was incorporated under the laws of the state of Indiana and was authorized to confer associate degrees and certificates in business. The College relocated to East Jefferson Boulevard in 1987. In September 2009, Brown Mackie College–South Bend officially opened a new 46,000-square-foot facility at 3454 Douglas Road in South Bend, Indiana.

Brown Mackie College–South Bend is accredited by the Accrediting Council for Independent Colleges and Schools (ACICS) to award bachelor's degrees, associate degrees, diplomas, and certificates. ACICS is listed as a nationally recognized accrediting agency by the United States Department of Education and is recognized by the Council for Higher Education Accreditation. ACICS can be contacted at 750 First Street NE, Suite 980, Washington, D.C. 20002; phone: 202-336-6780.

The Brown Mackie College–South Bend medical assisting Associate of Science degree program is accredited by the Commission on Accreditation of Allied Health Education Programs (www.caahep.org) upon the recommendation of the Curriculum Review Board of the American Association of Medical Assistants Endowment (AAMAE).

The occupational therapy assistant studies program is accredited by the Accreditation Council for Occupational Therapy Education (ACOTE) of the American Occupational Therapy Association (AOTA), located at 4720 Montgomery Lane, P.O. Box 31220, Bethesda, Maryland 20824-1220; phone: 301-652-2682.

The physical therapist assistant studies program at the South Bend location is accredited by the Commission on Accreditation in Physical Therapy Education (CAPTE) of the American Physical Therapy Association (APTA), 1111 North Fairfax Street, Alexandria, Virginia 22314; phone: 703-706-3241.

The practical nursing program is accredited by the Indiana State Board of Nursing, 402 West Washington Street, Room W066, Indianapolis, Indiana 46204; phone: 317-234-2043.

The Indiana advertising code for Brown Mackie College–South Bend is AC-0110.

The College is a nonresidential, smoke-free institution.

Location

Brown Mackie College–South Bend is conveniently located at 3454 Douglas Road in South Bend, Indiana. The College has a generous parking area and is also easily accessible by public transportation.

Programs of Study and Degrees

Brown Mackie College–South Bend provides higher education to traditional and nontraditional students through bachelor's degree, associate degree, diploma, and certificate programs that assist in enhancing their career opportunities, broadening their perspectives through appropriate general education courses, thinking independently and critically, and improving problem-solving abilities.

The Bachelor of Science degree (184 credits) is awarded in business administration, criminal justice, health-care management (180 credits), and legal studies.

The Associate of Science degree (96 credits) is awarded in accounting technology, business management, computer software technology, criminal justice, early childhood education, health-care administration, health and therapeutic massage, information technology, medical assisting, paralegal, and veterinary technology.

The Associate of Applied Science degree (100 credits) is awarded in occupational therapy assistant studies and physical therapist assistant studies.

The College offers a diploma program (76 credits) in practical nursing.

The College offers the following certificate programs (48 credits): accounting, business, computer software applications, criminal justice, medical assistant studies, and paralegal assistant studies.

Academic Programs

Each College quarter comprises twelve weeks. Bachelor's degree programs require a minimum of sixteen quarters to complete. Associate degree programs require a minimum of eight quarters to complete. Programs are offered on a year-round basis, providing students with the ability to work uninterrupted toward completion of their programs. The College offers all programs in a unique One Course a Month format. This allows students to focus studies on only one course for four weeks. This schedule has proven convenient for students with multiple obligations such as jobs and family.

Academic Facilities

Brown Mackie College–South Bend's new location has a generous parking area and is easily accessible by public transportation. The College's smoke-free, three-story 46,000 square foot building offers a modern, professional environment for study. The facility offers "classrooms of the future," with instructor workstations and full multimedia capabilities that include surround sound and projection screens that can be accessed by computer, DVD, and VHS machines. The new facility includes medical, computer, and occupational and physical therapy labs, as well as a library and bookstore. The labs provide students with hands-on opportunities to apply knowledge and skills learned in the classroom. The veterinary technology lab is 2,600 square feet and includes surgery areas, treatment areas, and kennels.

Costs

Tuition for programs in the 2010–11 academic year is $266 per credit hour, with a $15 per credit hour general fee applied to instructional costs for activities and services. Textbooks and other instructional materials vary by program. Tuition for all courses in the practical nursing program is $325 per credit hour, with a $25 per credit hour general fee applied to instructional costs for activities and services. Tuition for certain courses in the physical therapist assistant program is $365 per credit hour. Tuition for certain courses in the occupational therapy assistant program is $365 per credit hour.

Financial Aid

Financial aid is available for those who qualify. The College maintains a full-time staff of financial aid professionals to assist qualified students in obtaining financial assistance. The College participates in several student aid programs. Forms of financial aid available through federal resources include the Federal Pell Grant Program, Federal Supplemental Educational Opportunity Grant (FSEOG) Program, Federal Work-Study Program, Federal Perkins Loan Program, Federal Stafford Student Loan Program (subsidized and unsubsidized), and the Federal PLUS Loan Program.

Eligible students may apply for Indiana state awards, such as the Frank O'Bannon Grant Program (formerly the Indiana Higher Education Grant) and Twenty-First Century Scholars Program for high school students, the Core 40 awards, and veterans' educational benefits. Students with physical or mental disabilities that are a handicap may be eligible for training services through the state's Bureau of Vocational Rehabilitation. For further information, students should contact the College Student Financial Services Office.

Each year, the College makes available President's Scholarships of $1000 each to qualifying seniors from area high schools. No more than one scholarship is awarded per high school. In order to qualify, a senior must be graduating from a participating high school, must be maintaining a cumulative grade point average of at least 2.0, and must submit a brief essay. The student's extracurricular activities and community service are also considered. The President's Scholarship is available only to students enrolling in one of the College's degree programs. Students awarded the scholarship must enroll at Brown Mackie College–South Bend between June and September immediately following their high school graduation. Applications for these scholarships can be obtained from the guidance departments of participating high schools. These applications must be completed and returned to the College by March 31.

Faculty

There are 29 full-time and 46 part-time faculty members at the College. The average student-faculty ratio is 12:1. Each student is assigned a program director as an adviser.

Admission Requirements

Each applicant for admission is assigned an Assistant Director of Admissions, who directs the applicant through the steps of the admissions process, providing information on curriculum, policies, procedures, and services; and assisting the applicant in setting necessary appointments and interviews. To qualify for admission, each applicant must provide documentation of graduation from an accredited high school or from a state-approved secondary education curriculum or provide official documentation of high school graduation equivalency. All transcripts become the property of the College.

Admission to the College is based on the applicant meeting the stated requirements, a review of the applicant's previous educational records, and a review of the applicant's career interests. If previous academic records indicate the College's education and training programs would not benefit the applicant, the College reserves the right to advise the applicant not to enroll. Special requirements for enrollment into certain programs are discussed in the descriptions of those programs.

In addition to the College's general admission requirements, applicants enrolling in the occupational therapy assistant or physical therapist assistant programs must document one of the following: a high school cumulative grade point average of at least 2.5, a score on the GED examination of at least 57 (557 if taken on or after January 15, 2002), or completion of 12 quarter-credit hours or 8 semester-credit hours of collegiate course work with a grade point average of at least 2.5. Credit hours may not include Professional Development (CF 1100), the Brown Mackie College–South Bend course. Students entering either program must also have completed a biology course with a grade of at least a C (or an average of at least 2.0 on a 4.0 scale).

In addition to the College's general admission requirements, applicants enrolling in the practical nursing program must document the following: fulfillment of Brown Mackie College–South Bend general requirements; complete physical (must be current to within six months of admission); two-step Mantoux TB skin test (must be current throughout schooling); hepatitis B vaccination or signed refusal; up-to-date immunizations, including tetanus and rubella; record of current CPR certification (certification must be current throughout the clinical experience through health-care provider certification or the American Heart Association); and hospitalization insurance or a signed waiver.

For the most recent administration regarding admission requirements, please refer to the current academic catalog.

Application and Information

Applicants must complete and submit an application form, along with documentation of graduation from an accredited high school or state-approved secondary education curriculum or official documentation of high school graduation equivalency.

For additional information, prospective students should contact:

Director of Admissions
Brown Mackie College–South Bend
3454 Douglas Road
South Bend, Indiana 46635
Phone: 574-237-0774
800-743-2447 (toll-free)
Fax: 574-237-3585
E-mail: bmcsbadm@brownmackie.edu
Web site: http://www.brownmackie.edu/SouthBend

BROWN MACKIE COLLEGE–TUCSON

TUCSON, ARIZONA

The College

Brown Mackie College–Tucson is one of over twenty locations in the Brown Mackie College system of schools (www.brownmackie.edu), which is dedicated to providing educational programs that prepare students to pursue entry-level positions in a competitive, rapidly changing workplace. Brown Mackie College schools offer bachelor's degree, associate degree, and diploma programs in health sciences, business, information technology, legal studies, and design to over 19,000 students in the Midwest, Southeast, Southwest, and Western United States.

Brown Mackie College was originally founded and approved by the Board of Trustees of Kansas Wesleyan College in Salina, Kansas on July 30, 1892. In 1938, the College was incorporated as The Brown Mackie School of Business under the ownership of Perry E. Brown and A.B. Mackie, former instructors at Kansas Wesleyan University in Salina, Kansas. Their last names formed the name of Brown Mackie. By January 1975, with improvements in curricula and higher degree-granting status, The Brown Mackie School of Business became Brown Mackie College.

Brown Mackie College entered the Arizona market in 2007 when it purchased a school that had been previously established in the Tucson area. That school had an established history in the community and was converted into what is now known as Brown Mackie College–Tucson. The historical timeline of Brown Mackie College–Tucson started in 1972 when Rockland West Corporation first formed a partnership with Lamson Business College. At that time the school was a career college which offered only short term programs focusing on computer training and secretarial skills. In 1994 the College became accredited as a junior college and began offering associate degrees in academic subjects. The mission was then modified to include the goal of instilling in graduates an appreciation for lifelong learning through the general education courses which became a part of every program.

In 1996 the College applied for and received status as a senior college by the Accrediting Commission of Independent Colleges and Schools. This gave the school the ability to offer course work leading to a Bachelor of Science degree in business administration. Since then the program offerings for bachelor's and associate degrees have expanded.

In 1986, the campus moved from 5001 East Speedway to the 4585 East Speedway location where it remains today. In 2008, two of the College's three buildings were remodeled which resulted in updated classrooms; networked computer laboratories; new medical, surgical technology ,and forensics laboratories; a larger library and offices for student services such as academics, admissions, and student financial services; and a full-service college store. In 2009 the third building was remodeled and provides newer classrooms and a new career services department.

Brown Mackie College–Tucson is accredited by the Accrediting Council for Independent Colleges and Schools (ACICS) to award bachelor's degrees, associate degrees, and certificates. ACICS is listed as a nationally recognized accrediting agency by the United States Department of Education and is recognized by the Council for Higher Education Accreditation. ACICS can be contacted at 750 First Street NE, Suite 980, Washington, D.C. 20002; phone: 202-336-6780.

This institution is licensed by the Arizona State Board for Private Postsecondary Education, 1400 West Washington Street, Room 260, Phoenix, Arizona 85007; phone: 620-543-5709.

Location

Brown Mackie College–Tucson is conveniently located at 4585 East Speedway Boulevard in Tucson, Arizona. The College has a generous parking area and is also easily accessible by public transportation.

Programs of Study and Degrees

Brown Mackie College–Tucson provides higher education to traditional and nontraditional students through bachelor's degree, associate degree, and diploma programs that assist in enhancing their career opportunities, broadening their perspectives through appropriate general education courses, thinking independently and critically, and improving problem-solving abilities. The College strives to develop within its students the desire for lifelong and continued education.

The Bachelor of Science degree (184 credits) is awarded in accounting, business administration, criminal justice, health-care management (180 credits), information technology, and legal studies.

The Associate of Science degree (96 credits) is awarded in accounting technology, business management, computer networking and security, criminal justice, early childhood education, health-care administration, information technology, medical assisting, paralegal studies, and surgical technology.

The Associate of Applied Science degree is awarded in biomedical equipment technology (96 credits), health and fitness training, and occupational therapy assistant studies (100 credits).

A diploma (76 credits) is awarded in fitness trainer studies.

Academic Programs

Each College quarter comprises twelve weeks. Bachelor's degree programs require a minimum of sixteen quarters to complete. Associate degree programs require a minimum of eight quarters to complete. Programs are offered on a year-round basis, providing students with the ability to work uninterrupted toward their degrees. The College offers all programs in a unique One Course a Month format. This allows students to focus studies on only one course for four weeks.

This schedule has proven convenient for students with multiple obligations such as jobs and family.

Academic Facilities

A modern facility, Brown Mackie College–Tucson offers more than 31,000 square feet. The College is equipped with multiple computer labs housing over 200 computers. High-speed access to the Internet and other online resources are available for students and faculty. Multimedia classrooms are outfitted with overhead projectors, VCR/DVD players, and computers. The campus is nonresidential; public transportation and parking at no cost are available.

Costs

Tuition in the 2010–11 academic year for most bachelor's, associate, and diploma programs is $294 per credit hour; fees are $15 per credit hour. Tuition for the surgical technology program is $310 per credit hour; fees are $15 per credit hour. Tuition for certain courses in the occupational therapy assistant program is $365 per credit hour; fees are $15 per credit hour. Textbook and other instructional expenses vary by program.

Financial Aid

Financial aid is available for those who qualify. The College maintains a full-time staff of financial aid professionals to assist qualified students in obtaining the financial assistance they require to meet their educational expenses. Available resources include federal and state aid, student loans from private lenders, and Federal Work-Study opportunities, both on and off college premises.

Each year, the College makes available scholarships of $1000 each to qualifying seniors from area high schools. No more than one scholarship is awarded per high school. In order to qualify, a senior must be graduating from a participating high school, must be maintaining a cumulative grade point average of at least 2.0, and must submit a brief essay. The student's extracurricular activities and community service are also considered. These scholarships are available only to students enrolling in one of the College's degree programs. Students awarded the scholarship must enroll at Brown Mackie College—Tucson between June and September immediately following their high school graduation. Applications for these scholarships can be obtained from the guidance departments of participating high schools. These applications must be completed and returned to the College by March 31.

Faculty

Experienced faculty members provide academic support and are committed to the academic and technical preparation of their students. The College has 15 full-time and 35 part-time instructors, with a student-faculty ratio of 12:1. Each student is assigned a faculty adviser.

Admission Requirements

Each applicant for admission is assigned an Assistant Director of Admissions who directs the applicant through the steps of the admissions process. They provide information on curriculum, policies, procedures, and services and assist the applicant in setting necessary appointments and interviews. To qualify for admission, each applicant must provide documentation of graduation from an accredited high school or from a state-approved secondary education curriculum or provide official documentation of high school graduation equivalency. All transcripts become the property of the College. Admission to the College is based on the applicant meeting the stated requirements, a review of the applicant's previous educational records, and a review of the applicant's career interests. If previous academic records indicate the College's education and training programs would not benefit the applicant, the College reserves the right to advise the applicant not to enroll. Special requirements for enrollment into certain programs are discussed in the descriptions of those programs.

For the most recent information regarding admission requirements, please refer to the current academic catalog.

Application and Information

Applicants must complete and submit an application form, along with documentation of graduation from an accredited high school or state-approved secondary education curriculum or official documentation of high school graduation equivalency.

For additional information, prospective students should contact:

Director of Admissions
Brown Mackie College–Tucson
4585 East Speedway Boulevard, Suite 204
Tucson, Arizona 85712
Phone: 520-319-3300
Fax: 520-325-0108
E-mail: bmctuadm@brownmackie.edu
Web site: http://www.brownmackie.edu/Tucson

BROWN MACKIE COLLEGE–TULSA

TULSA, OKLAHOMA

The College

Brown Mackie College–Tulsa is one of over twenty locations in the Brown Mackie College system of schools (www.brownmackie.edu), which is dedicated to providing educational programs that prepare students to pursue entry-level positions in a competitive, rapidly changing workplace. Brown Mackie College schools offer bachelor's degree, associate degree, certificate, and diploma programs in health sciences, business, information technology, legal studies, and design to over 19,000 students in the Midwest, Southeast, Southwest, and Western United States.

Brown Mackie College–Tulsa was founded in 2008 as a branch of Brown Mackie College–South Bend, Indiana.

Brown Mackie College–Tulsa is accredited by the Accrediting Council for Independent Colleges and Schools (ACICS) to award bachelor's degrees, associate degrees, and diplomas. ACICS is listed as a nationally recognized accrediting agency by the United States Department of Education and is recognized by the Council for Higher Education Accreditation. ACICS can be contacted at 750 First Street NE, Suite 980, Washington, D.C. 20002; phone: 202-336-6780.The College is licensed by the Oklahoma Board of Private Vocational Schools (OBPVS), 3700 North Classen Boulevard, Suite 250, Oklahoma City, Oklahoma 73118; phone: 405-528-3370.

Location

Brown Mackie College–Tulsa is conveniently located at 4608 South Garnett Road, Suite 110 in Tulsa, Oklahoma. The College has a generous parking area and is easily accessible by public transportation.

Programs of Study and Degrees

Brown Mackie College–Tulsa provides higher education to traditional and nontraditional students through bachelor's degree, associate degree, and diploma programs that assist in enhancing their career opportunities, broadening their perspectives through appropriate general education courses, thinking independently and critically, and improving problem-solving abilities. The College strives to develop within its students the desire for lifelong and continued education.

The Bachelor of Science degree (180 credits) is awarded in business administration, criminal justice, health-care management, and legal studies.

The Associate of Applied Science degree (96 credits) is awarded in accounting technology, business management, criminal justice, health-care administration, information technology, medical assisting, occupational therapy assistant studies, office management, paralegal studies, and surgical technology.

The College offers diploma programs (48 credits) in accounting, business, criminal justice, medical assistant studies, and paralegal assistant studies.

Academic Programs

Each College quarter comprises twelve weeks. Bachelor's degree programs require a minimum of sixteen quarters to complete. Associate degree programs require a minimum of eight quarters to complete. Programs are offered on a year-round basis, providing students with the ability to work uninterrupted toward completion of their programs. The College offers all programs in a unique One Course a Month format. This allows students to focus studies on only one course for four weeks. This schedule has proven convenient for students with multiple obligations such as jobs and family.

Academic Facilities

Opened in 2008, this modern facility offers more than 25,000 square feet of tastefully decorated classrooms, laboratories, and office space designed to specifications of the College for its business, medical, and technical programs. Instructional equipment is comparable to current technology used in business and industry today. Modern classrooms for special instructional needs offer multimedia capabilities with surround sound and overhead projectors accessible through computer, DVD, or VHS. Internet access and instructional resources are available at the College's library. Experienced faculty members provide academic support and are committed to the academic and technical preparation of their students.

The campus is nonresidential; public transportation and ample parking at no cost are available.

Costs

Tuition for programs in the 2010–11 academic year is $250 per credit hour, with a $15 per credit hour general fee applied to instructional costs for activities and services. Tuition for the occupational therapy program courses is $365 per credit hour with a $15 per credit hour general fee applied to instructional costs for activities. Textbooks and other instructional materials vary by program.

Financial Aid

Financial aid is available for those who qualify. The College maintains a full-time staff of financial aid professionals to assist qualified students in obtaining financial assistance. The College participates in several student aid programs. Forms of financial aid available through federal resources include the Federal Pell Grant Program, Federal Supplemental Educational Opportunity Grant (FSEOG) Program, Federal Work-Study Program, Federal Perkins Loan Program, Federal

Stafford Student Loan Program (subsidized and unsubsidized), and the Federal PLUS Loan Program.

Admission Requirements

Each applicant for admission is assigned an Assistant Director of Admissions, who directs the applicant through the steps of the admissions process, providing information on curriculum, policies, procedures, and services and assisting the applicant in setting necessary appointments and interviews. To qualify for admission, applicants must be a graduate of a public or private high school or a correspondence school or education center that is accredited by an agency that is recognized by the U.S. or State of Oklahoma Department of Education or any of its approved agents. As part of the admissions process applicants must sign a document attesting to graduation or completion and containing the information to obtain verification of such. Verification must be obtained within the first term (90 days) or the student will be withdrawn from the institution following established guidelines for withdrawn students noted in the catalog. Title IV aid will not be dispersed until verification of graduation or completion has been received by the College. All transcripts become the property of the College.

Students are given an assessment of academic skills. Although the results of this assessment do not determine eligibility for admission, they provide the College with a means of determining the need for academic support.

For the most recent information regarding admission requirements, please refer to the current academic catalog.

Application and Information

Applicants must complete and submit an application form, along with documentation of graduation from an accredited high school or state-approved secondary education curriculum or official documentation of high school graduation equivalency.

For additional information, prospective students should contact:

Director of Admissions
Brown Mackie College–Tulsa
4608 South Garnett Road, Suite 110
Tulsa, Oklahoma 74146
Phone: 918-628-3700
888-794-8411 (toll-free)
Fax: 918-828-9083
E-mail: bmctuladm@brownmackie.edu
Web site: http://www.brownmackie.edu/Tulsa

BRYANT UNIVERSITY

SMITHFIELD, RHODE ISLAND

The University

Founded in 1863, Bryant University is seeking to shift paradigms in undergraduate education by shattering the belief that liberal arts and business are separate paths.

Throughout its 147-year history, Bryant has empowered students to achieve their personal best in life and their chosen professions. The University is the choice for individuals seeking the best integration of business and liberal arts, using state-of-the-art technology. Bryant's innovative real-world curriculum is made even more profound by an unwavering focus on character and ethics. The result is a transformative, life-defining experience that can help students take full advantage of the opportunities and challenges that are ahead.

Bryant's 3,347 full-time undergraduate students represent twenty-seven states and fifty countries, with 87 percent of students living on campus. Students enjoy the advantages of small classes and close relationships among fellow students, faculty members, and administrators. In this environment, students come to understand the interaction between various academic disciplines and their practical applications in the global community.

All of Bryant's rigorous academic programs are accredited by the New England Association of Schools and Colleges (NEASC). The University's College of Business is accredited by AACSB International—The Association to Advance Collegiate Schools of Business—a distinction earned by only 5 percent of universities worldwide.

Sports and recreation play an integral role in the health and well-being of students. The Elizabeth and Malcolm Chace Wellness and Athletic Center features a fully equipped fitness center, a six-lane swimming pool, circuit-training equipment and free weights, and a group exercise room, with forty-four different fitness classes offered every week. Students participate in and root for Bryant's twenty-two intercollegiate varsity sports teams, which compete at the Division I level. In addition, students can take part in club and intramural sports throughout the academic year. Teams compete on a variety of well-maintained athletic fields, and spectators can watch from the 4,000-seat Bulldog Stadium.

Bryant has more than eighty student clubs and organizations that benefit many social causes, provide recreational enjoyment, promote intellectual exploration, and offer opportunities to develop new talents and passions. The Student Programming Board, the Intercultural Center, the Arts and Culture Club, the Marketing Association, and the Student Senate are just a few of the organizations that involve students in campus life. There are many places on and off campus for students to gather and enjoy music, comedy, and other kinds of entertainment.

The John H. Chafee Center for International Business, located on campus, links Bryant students directly to regional businesses that operate globally. Additionally, the University's U.S.-China and Confucius Institutes forge academic, business, and cultural partnerships between Bryant University and higher learning institutions, business enterprises, and governmental offices in China.

Location

Bryant University is situated on a beautiful 428-acre campus in Smithfield, Rhode Island, only 15 minutes from the state capital, Providence; 45 minutes from Boston; and 3 hours from New York City. Students can enjoy an array of activities on and off campus as well as excellent restaurants, cultural activities, and sports events in the area.

Students are able to take advantage of internship and employment opportunities at many small and large businesses, Fortune 500 companies, and not-for-profit organizations within driving distance of the Bryant campus. Transportation includes buses (free for students) that travel to and from campus, a train station in Providence, and airports near Providence and in Boston.

Majors and Degrees

Bryant's College of Arts and Sciences offers degrees in actuarial mathematics, applied economics, applied mathematics and statistics, applied psychology, communication, environmental science, global studies, history, literary and cultural studies, politics and law, and sociology. The College of Business offers degrees in business administration with concentrations in accounting, computer information systems, entrepreneurship, finance, financial services, management, and marketing; information technology; and international business with concentrations in computer information systems, finance, management, and marketing.

Bryant offers twenty-eight minors in business and liberal arts. To view all of the University's areas of study, visit http://www.bryant.edu/areasofstudy.

Bryant's Graduate School of Business offers a full-time or part-time Master of Business Administration (M.B.A.), a Master of Science in Taxation (M.S.T.), and a Master of Professional Accountancy (M.P.Ac.).

Academic Programs

A Bryant education focuses on engagement and balances academic theory with practical reality. Its programs deliver the highest standards of academic excellence, character, and ethics in a global, real-world context.

Students must complete a core curriculum that integrates business, liberal arts, and technology. Graduation requirements include a minimum of 123 semester hours. Bryant University operates on a semester plan.

Entering students may receive credit through the Advanced Placement (AP) Program or the College-Level Examination Program (CLEP) administered by the College Board. Credit is also awarded for International Baccalaureate (IB) higher-level exams. The Honors Program is an excellent vehicle for highly motivated students to stretch their intellectual limits.

Bryant also participates in the Army ROTC Program.

Off-Campus Programs

The Amica Center for Career Education, named one of the top 10 university career and job placement services in the country by the Princeton Review, offers students opportunities to expand their learning beyond the classroom. Through relationships with more than 300 companies, the center helps students secure practical internships at organizations such as Fidelity Investments, PricewaterhouseCoopers, Walt Disney World, the New England Patriots, Textron, local and national media outlets, and a variety of nonprofit organizations. The Amica Center also helps graduating seniors identify and pursue job opportunities.

Qualified students may participate in Bryant's Study Abroad Program and choose to study with partners in forty-six different countries. The University also offers a Sophomore International

Experience, a two-week overseas course where students learn about other cultures and how businesses operate globally.

Academic Facilities

Bryant's modern campus is anchored by the Unistructure, the center of academic and social activity. The Bryant Center houses the bookstore, student organization offices, and a food court. The Koffler Center and the Communications Complex feature several computer labs, a state-of-the-art digital television studio and editing suites, and Bryant's student-run radio station.

The George E. Bello Center for Information and Technology has an abundance of wired and wireless connectivity and banks of high-speed computers. The C.V. Starr Financial Markets Center receives real-time data via live feeds through Reuters 3000, the same system used by top international financial institutions. The Bello Center also houses the Douglas and Judith Krupp Library. It holds more than 150,000 volumes and thousands of reference databases and online resources, making it one of the most comprehensive business library collections in the region.

As part of their tuition, all first-year students receive a laptop computer that is network ready and fully loaded with software. Students can work on their laptops virtually anywhere on Bryant's wireless campus. Every three years, instructional computers in the classrooms are upgraded or replaced.

Costs

For 2010–11, tuition is $33,033, which includes personal use of a laptop computer for entering students. Residence hall room and board fees are $12,215 and there is a $312 student activity fee. Tuition and fees are subject to change. Most students (87 percent) live on campus. There are a variety of housing arrangements, including the first-year complex, suite-style residence halls, and townhouses for seniors. There are special fees for summer and winter sessions.

Financial Aid

Bryant has a comprehensive program of merit- and need-based financial aid. Eighty-nine percent of Bryant students received some form of financial aid in 2009. Merit scholarships, need-based grants, loans, and work-study awards are available. Students interested in applying for financial assistance in the form of need-based grants, work-study, and education loans must file a Free Application for Federal Student Aid (FAFSA). The FAFSA can be found online at http://www.fafsa.ed.gov. The FAFSA filing deadline at Bryant University is February 15. The FAFSA can be submitted as early as January 1. For more information, students should contact the Director of Financial Aid.

Faculty

Bryant faculty members are dedicated to helping students develop their intellectual potential. They continuously engage in research, publishing, consulting, community service, and practical experience. With a 17:1 student-faculty ratio, each student can develop relationships with faculty members for guidance and support. Among the faculty members at Bryant are a practicing clinical psychologist, a nationally respected expert in advertising effectiveness and public policy, and the Poet Laureate Emeritus of Rhode Island.

Student Government

The Student Senate, the student governing body, serves as a channel of communication between students, faculty members, and administrators.

Admission Requirements

Bryant University seeks students who are motivated learners and have a history of academic achievement. Minimum entrance requirements include 4 years each of English and preparatory mathematics, including a year beyond algebra II (with a preference for precalculus or calculus in the senior year), and 2 years each of history or social science, a laboratory science, and a foreign language. Remaining secondary course work should be in a foreign language, mathematics, science, and social studies. Entering students may receive credit through the Advanced Placement (AP) Program or the College-Level Examination Program (CLEP) administered by the College Board. Credit is also awarded for International Baccalaureate (IB) higher-level exams.

SAT or ACT scores must be submitted. The Admission Committee considers recommendations from the secondary school guidance office and faculty members concerning character and personal qualifications that are not in the academic record. Interviews, though not required, may be scheduled in advance of a campus visit.

Application and Information

Applications must be submitted to the Office of Admission with a nonrefundable fee of $50 by November 15 (early decision I), December 1 (early action), January 14 (early decision II), or February 1 (regular decision). It is the responsibility of the applicant to request that the secondary school guidance office send a copy of their school record, and SAT or ACT scores, directly to Bryant University. International applicants must also submit TOEFL scores and a completed Certification of Finances form.

For admission information:
Director of Admission
Bryant University
1150 Douglas Pike
Smithfield, Rhode Island 02917-1285
Phone: 401-232-6100
800-622-7001 (toll-free)
Fax: 401-232-6741
E-mail: admission@bryant.edu
Web site: http://admission.bryant.edu

For financial aid information:
Director of Financial Aid
Phone: 401-232-6020
800-248-4036 (toll-free)
Fax: 401-232-6319
E-mail: finaid@bryant.edu
Web site: http://admission.bryant.edu

Founded in 1863, Bryant University strives to blend a liberal arts and business education.

BRYN MAWR COLLEGE

BRYN MAWR, PENNSYLVANIA

The College

Bryn Mawr women are leaders in the classroom, in the studio, in the laboratory, and on the field. They are women who share an intense intellectual commitment, a purposeful vision of their lives, and a common desire to make a meaningful contribution to the world.

Bryn Mawr women empower each other to engage with the world beyond the campus, too, by testing the boundaries of knowledge in a number of ways. Through advanced research projects, summer internships, and collaborative research with faculty members, students are involved in the local, national, and global communities. Bryn Mawr's Katherine Houghton Hepburn Center for Women in Public Life, Office of Civic Engagement, and the Praxis Program, which integrates fieldwork with theoretical study, provide students with extensive opportunities for internships in Philadelphia, where they may apply knowledge far beyond the classroom. Many students pursue independent and interdepartmental majors with faculty permission. Joint academic programs also exist with Haverford, Swarthmore, and the University of Pennsylvania.

Bryn Mawr alumnae are physicians, economists, entrepreneurs, scholars, filmmakers, journalists, jurists, writers, and scientists whose achievements are marked by originality of thought and direction. Bryn Mawr's prestigious alumnae include the first woman to be president of Harvard University, one of the first women to receive the Nobel Peace Prize, the first woman neurosurgeon, and the first and only woman to receive four Academy Awards.

Diversity is central to Bryn Mawr's mission as an extraordinary liberal arts college, improving the academic experience and enriching the campus community. Students of color and international students make up nearly 40 percent of the undergraduate enrollment. Bryn Mawr's student body is composed of women from forty-seven states and fifty-eight other countries. Above all else, Bryn Mawr women share a tremendous respect for individual differences, not merely a passive tolerance of other lifestyles and points of view. The result is a community that resounds with the energy, healthy friction, and range of perspectives that can only come from true cultural and ideological diversity. The diversity that Bryn Mawr students experience, in and out of the classroom, helps prepare them for confident global citizenship and leadership, skills needed by the next generation of world leaders. These women share a commitment to a community that is based on inclusion and support, reinforced by Bryn Mawr's Honor Code, a set of principles stressing personal integrity and mutual respect. In the words of one graduating senior, "This is a place where being yourself makes you feel part of something larger than yourself. A strong sense of self is what we all have in common."

Bryn Mawr is a charter member of the Centennial Conference and is home to twelve NCAA varsity athletic teams. Students may compete in badminton, basketball, crew, cross-country, field hockey, lacrosse, soccer, swimming, tennis, indoor track and field, outdoor track and field, and volleyball. A $7-million upgrade and renovation of the Bern-Schwarz Gymnasium, due to be completed in fall 2010, will offer both students and athletes enhanced spaces for training, fitness, and aquatics. Renovation and improvement of the Goodhart Theatre was completed in the fall of 2009, with major upgrades to accommodate student interest in performing arts.

Bryn Mawr students participate in more than 100 active student organizations. The tricollege community of Haverford, Swarthmore, and Bryn Mawr Colleges also sponsors many student groups and activities.

Location

Bryn Mawr College is located on a 135-acre suburban campus, 11 miles west of Philadelphia. Bryn Mawr's campus is graceful and serene and has a deep engagement with the wider world. Bryn Mawr women enjoy a rich academic and social life on their own campus and at neighboring tricollege partners Haverford and Swarthmore Colleges as well as the University of Pennsylvania.

Bryn Mawr's relationship with Haverford College is particularly close and students participate in many bicollege extracurricular activities, including the orchestra, the chorus, the drama program, and a bicollege newspaper. A 20-minute walk or a 5-minute ride on the bicollege "Blue Bus" brings students from one campus to the other.

Almost all students live on campus in one of thirteen main residence halls. These buildings, which include a multicultural residence for students interested in foreign languages and culture, range from university Gothic to postmodern in style. Two of the buildings are listed on the National Register of Historic Places, and one is also a National Historic Landmark.

Majors and Degrees

Bryn Mawr College grants the Bachelor of Arts (A.B.) degree with majors, minors, and concentrations in more than forty areas: Africana studies, anthropology, astronomy, biology, chemistry, classical and Near Eastern archaeology, classical languages, classical studies, comparative literature, computational methods, computer science, creative writing, dance, East Asian studies, economics, education, English, environmental studies, film studies, fine arts, French and French studies, gender and sexuality, geology, German and German studies, Greek, growth and structure of cities, Hebrew and Judaic studies, Hispanic and Hispanic-American studies, history, history of art, international studies, Italian, Latin, linguistics, mathematics, music, neural and behavioral sciences, peace and conflict studies, philosophy, physics, political science, psychology, religion, Romance languages, Russian, sociology, Spanish, and theater and theater studies.

There are nearly 3,000 course exchanges between Bryn Mawr and Haverford each year, selected from a jointly published course list. Bryn Mawr students may major in any of Haverford's coordinate departments or in astronomy, classics, music, or religion while earning a Bachelor of Arts degree from Bryn Mawr. A new major in linguistics offered through Swarthmore College is also available. Finally, Haverford, Swarthmore, and Bryn Mawr have joined together to form the Middle East Studies Initiative.

Academic Programs

The Bryn Mawr curriculum is designed to encourage breadth of learning and training in the fundamentals of scholarship in the first two years, and mature, sophisticated, in-depth study in a major program during the last two years. Its overall purpose is to challenge the student and prepare her for the lifelong pleasure and responsibility of educating herself and playing a responsible role in contemporary society. The curriculum encourages independence within a rigorous but flexible framework. Each student chooses and plans her major in consultation with her dean and faculty adviser. Some students take advantage of this freedom to design an independent major, while others fashion their own intellectual perspectives by enrolling in courses that span academic fields or assisting with a faculty member's research project.

With certain restrictions, full-time Bryn Mawr students may also take courses at Swarthmore College, the University of Pennsylvania, and Villanova University during the academic year without paying additional fees.

Off-Campus Programs

Bryn Mawr is only 20 minutes by car or seven short stops by train from the vast cultural and professional resources of Philadelphia, the nation's sixth-largest city. Philadelphia is an incredible resource for Bryn Mawr—a truly accessible city rich with cultural and professional resources, including the Philadelphia Museum of Art, the Philadelphia Orchestra, the Pennsylvania Ballet, numerous theaters, professional sports teams, and some of the nation's most important historic sites, as well as internship opportunities in Center City law firms, art galleries, government agencies, hospitals, TV studios, banks, and schools. When Philadelphia seems too small, 1 in 3 Bryn Mawr students participate in one of more than seventy study-abroad programs from Stockholm to South Africa.

Academic Facilities

Bryn Mawr ranks among the top ten of all U.S. colleges and universities in the percentage of graduates going on to earn a Ph.D. Bryn Mawr students have unlimited access to libraries and laboratories equal to those of many graduate programs, allowing students to pursue independent research at a level unavailable at most undergraduate institutions. These resources include an extensive array of laboratory equipment for the study of science, such as a robotics lab, laser with rangefinder, DNA analyzers, and a geological subsurface profiling system. More than 1 million volumes in a network of open-stack libraries are available to Bryn Mawr students, as well as access to the libraries of both Haverford and Swarthmore Colleges via the Tripod Library System. In addition, the College has recently enhanced several of its buildings to support student inquiry in all of the liberal arts, including a $19-million renovation of the Marjorie Goodhart Theater which consists of a new state-of-the-art theater, practice rooms, a teaching theater, and scene shop; the upgrade of Dalton Hall, home to Bryn Mawr's social science labs and classrooms; and Bettws-y-Coed, a center for the study of psychology complete with new labs, faculty offices, and meeting rooms. Four former faculty residences have also been renovated to house the student activities village, Cambrian Row.

Costs

In 2009–10, Bryn Mawr tuition, room and board, and fees totaled $50,034.

Financial Aid

To apply for financial aid, students must submit the Free Application for Federal Student Aid (FAFSA), the College Scholarship Service (CSS) PROFILE form, and if applicable, the CSS Noncustodial Parent PROFILE. The College also requires a signed copy of the custodial and noncustodial parents' and student's most recent federal income tax returns, including W-2 forms, and all schedules and attachments. Tax returns must be submitted to The College Board's Institutional Documentation Service (IDOC). Applicants who are not citizens of the U.S. may file the (CSS) PROFILE or may instead submit the International Student Financial Aid Application directly to the Financial Aid Office. Non–U.S. citizens must also submit letters (in English) from their parents' employers stating gross income and the value of any perquisites, subsidies, and benefits directly to the Financial Aid Office. Prospective freshmen are notified of the admission and financial aid decisions at the same time.

Faculty

The Bryn Mawr faculty has 158 full-time members, of whom 49 percent are women and 15 percent are professors of color. The College's student-faculty ratio is 8:1. Few colleges or universities can genuinely claim the intellectual curiosity, intensity, and passion found at Bryn Mawr. Classes are small (many have fewer than 15 students), and faculty members come to know their students as individuals. That means more than just being on a first-name basis. In fact, Bryn Mawr faculty members, world-renowned leaders in their fields, regard their students as junior colleagues, fully capable of working at a high level, developing their own ideas, and making important contributions. It is in this way that, perhaps more than at any other school, Bryn Mawr feels like a graduate school on an undergraduate level.

Student Government

Bryn Mawr's culture of innovative leadership dates back to 1892 and the founding of the Student Self-Government Association (SGA), the oldest undergraduate governing body in the country. SGA gives Bryn Mawr students the responsibility of running many campus organizations and activities and participating in discussion and resolution of important issues, such as curriculum and faculty appointments.

Admission Requirements

Bryn Mawr's freshman class of about 350 is selected from applicants from all parts of the United States and the world. The Admissions Committee, composed of admissions officers, professors, and current students, looks for an excellent school and test record and asks the applicant's counselor and teachers for an estimate of her character and readiness for college. Such qualities as integrity, vitality, a sense of humor, independence, and sensitivity to others are important, as are any special talents or interests. Early decision, early admission, deferred entrance, and advanced placement options are available to qualified students.

Basic high school academic requirements include 4 years of English, 3 years of mathematics, at least 1 year each of a laboratory science and history, and a solid foundation in at least one foreign language. However, most applicants are well prepared for the academic rigor of Bryn Mawr and have taken at least three lab science courses as well as mathematics courses that include trigonometry. Bryn Mawr's has adopted a "test flexible" admissions policy which allows students to submit a combination of the SAT, SAT Subject Tests, the ACT, and AP exam scores. Complete details on the "test flexible" policy may be found on the Bryn Mawr Web site. For tests scores to be considered in the application process, tests must be taken by November of the senior year for early decision applicants and January for regular decision applicants. An interview, either at the College or with a local alumnae representative, is also strongly recommended. Application forms should be submitted by November 15 for fall early decision applicants, by January 1 for winter early decision applicants, and by January 15 for regular decision applicants.

Transfer students must complete a minimum of two years of work at Bryn Mawr to qualify for the A.B. degree.

Bryn Mawr exclusively accepts the Common Application for all admission plans.

Application and Information

The Admissions Office is open from 9 a.m. to 5 p.m. on weekdays and, during the fall, from 9 a.m. to 1 p.m. on Saturdays. Bryn Mawr accepts the Common Application, which can be found online (http://www.commonapplication.org). For further information, an application form, or the name of a local alumnae representative, prospective students should contact:

Bryn Mawr College Office of Admissions
101 North Merion Avenue
Bryn Mawr, Pennsylvania 19010-2899
Phone: 610-526-5152
Fax: 610-526-7471
E-mail: admissions@brynmawr.edu
Web site: http://www.brynmawr.edu
http://www.brynmawr.edu/admissions/applicationoptions.shtml (to apply online)

BUCKNELL UNIVERSITY

LEWISBURG, PENNSYLVANIA

The University

Founded in 1846 as a "literary institution" in the "wilds of Pennsylvania," Bucknell University has long embraced academic vigor. Today, Bucknell is a top-ranked university offering a personalized and comprehensive liberal arts education to exceptionally talented students from across the U.S. and around the world. With academic programs in the arts, engineering, humanities, management, and social and natural sciences, and broad opportunities outside of class, Bucknell is now much more than a literary institution: It is a place that prepares students for success in an increasingly complex and interconnected global society.

Bucknell's 3,450 undergraduates can choose from more than fifty majors and sixty minors. Students can build robots, write and perform in their own plays, or debate solutions to the crisis in Sudan. Engineers can make art, artists can analyze DNA, and philosophers can make music. Each student chooses his or her own pathway, but what unites everyone is a shared passion for learning and a desire to achieve deeper levels of understanding about life and the world.

Bucknell's faculty creates an environment of free-flowing ideas and stimulating discussions. Professors teach every class, getting to know students personally and challenging them to do their best. The professors are also dedicated scholars who frequently receive awards and grants for their work. Often, they engage students in research and creative projects outside of class. By doing so, they provide students with mentorship and guidance for the future.

Outside of class, students participate in myriad activities. Bucknell offers Division I athletics along with intramural and club sports, active Greek life programs, and more than 150 student-run clubs and organizations. These organizations focus on anything from social and environmental causes to cultural awareness, poetry slams, dance, pottery, or politics. Students can enrich their religious and spiritual lives through multiple University and student-led faith organizations.

The University is a residential campus, requiring nearly all of its undergraduates to live on campus. Living on campus does not, however, mean students are isolated from the "real" world—quite the opposite is true. Visiting scholars and speakers come to Bucknell nearly every week, and much of the curriculum focuses on cultures, societies, and economies around the globe. Learning happens off campus, too. Students frequently perform service work in places as close as the local nursing home and as far away as Nicaragua. They secure summer internships with nonprofit organizations and corporations. They study abroad through one of University's own "in" programs or 130 other approved programs in Africa, Asia, Europe, and South America. And after they graduate, they live and work all over the world.

Alumni of Bucknell succeed in their careers because they offer a combination of skills, knowledge, and flexibility of mind that employers seek. To prepare students, the University offers career services including advising, networking, mock interviews, internship and externship support, and employer fairs to students throughout their four years at Bucknell. The placement rate is consistently high: 93 percent of the class of 2008 was employed or in graduate school within six months of graduation.

Location

With its green spaces, red brick buildings, and striking vistas, Bucknell's campus is a quintessential college environment in the heart of scenic central Pennsylvania. The shops of downtown Lewisburg lie within walking distance of campus. The University is located within a 3 to 4 hours' drive of most of the major Eastern cities, including New York City; Washington, D.C.; Philadelphia; and Pittsburgh.

Majors and Degrees

Bucknell provides students with a choice of more than fifty majors in a variety of liberal arts and professional fields. Bachelor of Arts degrees are available in animal behavior, anthropology, art, art history, combined art and art history, biology, chemistry, classics (Greek or Latin concentrations), comparative humanities, computer science, East Asian studies (China or Japan concentrations), economics, education, English (creative writing or film/media studies concentrations), environmental geology, environmental studies, French, geography, geology, German, history, international relations (Africa, Europe, East Asia, Latin America, Middle East, North America, or Russia concentrations), Latin American studies, mathematics (general, pure mathematics, or statistics concentrations), music, philosophy, physics, political science, psychology, religion, Russian, sociology (general, human services, or legal studies concentrations), Spanish, theater, and women's and gender studies.

The music program offers a Bachelor of Music degree with majors in music composition, music education, music history, and performance.

Bachelor of Science degrees are available in animal behavior, biology, cell biology and biochemistry, chemistry, computer science, economics and mathematics, engineering (in the disciplines of biomedical, chemical, civil, computer, electrical, and mechanical engineering as well as a degree in computer science and engineering), environmental geology, environmental studies, geology, mathematics (general, pure mathematics, or statistics concentrations), neuroscience, and physics.

Bachelor of Science in Business Administration degrees are available in accounting and management.

Bachelor of Science in Education degrees are available in early childhood development and elementary education.

In consultation with an academic adviser, students also may design their own major based around their individualized educational goals. Select engineering students also have the option of completing one of two five-year interdisciplinary programs; these programs lead to a B.S. in an engineering field and either a B.A. in another discipline or a specially designed Bachelor of Management for Engineers degree.

Academic Programs

Requirements for each degree program vary, but all students are required to complete three writing courses. Special programs are offered to encourage each student's personal and intellectual development. Examples include the first-year foundation seminars, an introductory engineering course open to students in the College of Arts and Sciences, and Bucknell's Residential College program. The Residential Colleges are seven themed-based options for first-year students that combine classroom and out-of-class activities into a living and learning experience. The themes are the arts, environmental issues, global affairs, humanities, languages and cultures, social justice, and society and technology.

Off-Campus Programs

Bucknell University's Office of International Education offers one of the largest study-abroad programs available at an undergraduate liberal arts institution. The current graduating class has sent more than 45 percent of its students to study abroad for a year, a semester, and/or a summer. Bucknell sponsors four of its own semester-long "Bucknell In" programs: Bucknell in Barbados, Bucknell in London, Bucknell en France, and Bucknell en España. During the summer, the University offers "Bucknell In" programs in Barbados, Northern Ireland, Nicaragua, and the Virgin Islands.

In addition to Bucknell-run programs, the University is affiliated with 130 other programs worldwide. Shorter-term service- and learning-abroad programs are also available, along with internship programs in Philadelphia or Washington, D.C. Financial aid, grants, and scholarships apply toward study abroad.

Academic Facilities

Bucknell's 450-acre campus includes facilities for art, engineering, music, the sciences, theater, and dance and a 1,200-seat performance hall. Bertrand Library holds 833,000 volumes, provides access to more than 26,000 periodicals, and offers thousands of audiovisual materials. Computer labs are available across campus, and most of campus is wireless-accessible. Classrooms are equipped with projectors and computers, some with computers for each student. All student residences are connected to the residential network, featuring a high-speed data connection for each student. Science and engineering programs have sophisticated instrumentation available for student use.

Costs

The cost of tuition and fees for 2009–10 was $50,320, including $40,594 for tuition, $9504 for room and board, and $222 for student fees.

Financial Aid

More than $62 million in total financial aid was awarded to students in 2009, with an average award of $25,000. More than 63 percent of all students received some form of aid, including government grants and loans. Financial aid applicants must file the Financial Aid PROFILE with the College Scholarship Service before January 15.

Faculty

Bucknell has more than 330 full-time and 23 part-time members on the teaching faculty; 97 percent of full-time faculty members hold doctorates or appropriate terminal degrees. The student-faculty ratio is 10:1. Professors teach first-year students as well as advanced students; no classes are taught by graduate students.

Bucknell's professors uphold the teacher-scholar ideal, through which they are committed to providing an excellent undergraduate education and also actively pursuing their scholarly work. Many students collaborate with faculty members in research, and projects regularly lead to joint publications or presentations at professional meetings.

Student Government

The Bucknell Student Government serves as the official voice of Bucknell's students. It dispenses funds for most student clubs and organizations, and its representatives serve on standing committees of the Board of Trustees and other University governance groups.

Admission Requirements

Admission decisions focus on the quality of preparation as demonstrated by achievement in rigorous high school courses, SAT or ACT scores, special talent, significant contribution to school or community, and evidence of strong character and integrity. A demonstrated interest in the University and strong essays weigh heavily in the admissions process. The University seeks qualified students from all backgrounds throughout the United States and abroad.

Application and Information

Regular Decision applications should be filed before January 15 of the senior year in high school for notification by April 1. SAT and/or ACT results must be submitted before March 1. Early Decision candidates may apply for Early Decision–Round One consideration by November 15 or Early Decision–Round Two consideration by January 15. Applications for transfer students should be submitted by March 15 for studies beginning the following fall and by November 1 for the spring semester.

Robert G. Springall
Dean of Admissions
Bucknell University
Lewisburg, Pennsylvania 17837
Phone: 570-577-1101
Fax: 570-577-3538
E-mail: admissions@bucknell.edu
Web site: http://www.bucknell.edu

The Academic Quad is the hub of campus, where students and faculty members greet each other between classes and soak up the sun on warm days. The tower of Bertrand Library is both a landmark and a symbol of University life.

BUFFALO STATE COLLEGE, STATE UNIVERSITY OF NEW YORK

Buffalo State
State University of New York

BUFFALO, NEW YORK

The College

Buffalo State is the college of choice for high-achieving students who want to develop close relationships with professors—a major contributor to college success. Most classes have fewer than 40 students and the student-faculty ratio is 17:1. And professors, not graduate students, teach even introductory courses. Buffalo State offers more than 160 programs for undergraduate students and sixty graduate programs on a safe, convenient campus located in the heart of Buffalo's historic cultural corridor.

Buffalo State graduates are highly sought after by employers. Internships and service-learning opportunities provide students with the real-world experience necessary for success in the marketplace. Buffalo State students gain experience in such places as museums, hospitals, political offices, schools, police laboratories, banks and investment firms, advertising agencies, and engineering firms.

Of a total enrollment of more than 11,000 students, approximately 9,000 are undergraduates. Most students come from New York State, but the College has a growing number of out-of-state and international students, including those from nearby southern Ontario.

Buffalo State is known for its excellent teacher training programs. Its professional education programs have been continuously accredited by the National Council for Accreditation of Teacher Education (NCATE) since 1954. NCATE is a national, professional organization that evaluates teacher preparation programs to ensure that they meet rigid standards of excellence. Graduates from Buffalo State are recruited by school districts throughout the United States.

Buffalo State also offers a healthy mix of traditional and unusual majors. The College has one of the largest and most diverse arts programs in the state, from design (jewelry, furniture, interior, and more) to performing arts to fashion and textile technology. Buffalo State's science, technology, engineering, and mathematics (STEM) programs have received millions of dollars in support in recent years; demand for Buffalo State graduates is 100 percent in some majors. Two new undergraduate degree programs—the B.A. in television and film arts and the B.A. in writing—are designed to provide graduates with a unique blend of a liberal arts worldview and hands-on skills.

The Sports Arena, housing Buffalo's only college ice hockey rink, is home to the NCAA Division III Bengals varsity teams, which include nineteen men's and women's teams. In addition, club and intramural teams involve students in friendly competition in sports such as basketball, dodge ball, racquetball, softball, and more. The sports complex also includes outdoor fields, an indoor arena, a pool, dance studios, weight rooms, and a student fitness center.

A variety of living and learning options are available on campus, including suite- and apartment-style housing and special floors for honors and international students. Attractive off-campus housing is readily available in surrounding residential neighborhoods.

More than 100 student organizations—from the radio station and volunteer groups to sororities and fraternities—allow students to meet new people, take breaks from classes, and develop leadership skills.

Location

Buffalo State is definitely not the place for students wishing to attend a school surrounded by cow pastures. Buffalo State is the only SUNY comprehensive college located in a major city. The College is situated in the Elmwood Museum District adjacent to Delaware Park, the world-famous Albright-Knox Art Gallery, the Buffalo and Erie County Historical Society, Hoyt Lake, and the Buffalo Zoo. Students find trendy restaurants, shops, and coffee bars within walking distance of campus. Outdoor sports, from kayaking to downhill skiing, are minutes away. Buffalo, which is home to the NFL's Bills and the NHL's Sabres, is minutes from Niagara Falls, less than 2 hours from Toronto, and a day's drive—or an hour's flight—from New York City and Boston. The Buffalo Niagara International Airport is 15 minutes from campus, with daily service to major metropolitan areas.

Majors and Degrees

The College's academic departments are organized within four schools: Arts and Humanities, Education, Natural and Social Sciences, and Professions. More than 90 majors are available.

From the stage to the classroom, School of Arts and Humanities programs instill students with a passion for learning, and foundation for critical thinking, artistic inventiveness, and cultural awareness that lasts a lifetime. These invaluable skills serve our graduates well in career fields that are as vast and varied as our course selection. Majors include art, art education, art history, arts and letters, communication studies, communication design, English, English education, French education, French language and literature, humanities, individualized studies, interior design, journalism, media production, music, music education, painting, philosophy, photography, printmaking, public communication, sculpture, Spanish education, Spanish language and literature, television and film arts, theater, and writing.

The School of Education has a distinguished history of preparing leaders and educators to excel in a wide range of classroom settings. Students learn through a strong and diverse on-campus curriculum as well as through direct student teacher experiences. Majors include business and marketing education, career and technical education, childhood education, early childhood and childhood education, early childhood education, exceptional education, and individualized studies.

Programs in the School of Natural and Social Sciences help students develop skills in analytical thinking, quantitative methods, problem solving, critical thinking, and effective communication. Students are taught to use the facts, concepts, and principles learned in the field and in the classroom for practical application. Majors include anthropology, applied mathematics, applied sociology, biology, biology education, chemistry, chemistry education, earth science education, earth sciences, economics, forensic chemistry, geography, geology, history, individualized studies, mathematics, mathematics education, physics, physical education, physics engineering (3-2 cooperative program), political science, psychology, social studies education, sociology, urban and regional analysis and planning.

The School of the Professions educates future professionals to lead within diverse settings and participate in community and professional life through partnerships. The school prepares graduates for productive and successful careers in a global society. Majors include business administration, computer information systems, criminal justice, dietetics, electrical engineering technology: electronics, electrical engineering technology: power and machines, fashion and textile, technology, health and wellness, hospitality administration, individualized studies, industrial technology, mechanical engineering technology, social work, speech-language pathology, and technology education.

Fifty-six departmental minors are available.

The College offers advisement programs for an increasing number of prelaw, premedical, and prehealth students who are preparing for graduate study in dentistry, law, medicine, or veterinary science.

Academic Programs

All Buffalo State undergraduate students must complete a minimum of 120 credit hours to qualify for a bachelor's degree. The College recently implemented a "required courses" program called Intellectual Foundations. Intellectual Foundations builds the intellectual and creative foundations for a student's future at the college and beyond.

It begins with the Foundations of Inquiry (BSC 101), a course required in the student's first year at Buffalo State, and continues with fifteen to twenty more courses, most of which would be completed in the first two years at the college. BSC 101 introduces the college's liberal arts curriculum and lays a foundation of critical thinking and basic research skills. Each section of BSC 101 focuses on one or more interdisciplinary topics while exploring interconnections among the arts, humanities, natural sciences and social sciences.

Buffalo State offers an All-College Honors Program as well as honors sequences in eleven majors. Learning communities—open to all freshmen—involve small groups of students who take the same block of thematically related classes, taught by teams of faculty members. These students have access to special gathering places on campus, equipped with computers and kitchens, where they can meet and study with other students in the program and their professors.

The College operates on a semester basis, with a three-week intersemester term in January. A summer program of three 4-week sessions is also offered.

Off-Campus Programs

Several off-campus educational opportunities provide flexibility to broaden intellectual horizons and tailor learning to individual interests and career goals. These opportunities include internships, independent study projects, clinical practice, workshops, exchange opportunities at more than 175 other U.S. colleges and universities, study-abroad programs at more than 300 institutions around the world, credit for experiential learning, and the ability to cross-register or complete degrees at other schools through special arrangement. All options carry college credit.

Academic Facilities

The 125-acre campus is built for academic excellence, beginning with E. H. Butler Library. Its holdings include more than 530,000 books, 12,000 audiovisual items, subscriptions to hundreds of print periodicals, over 100 databases that provide full-text articles from more than 27,000 serials and journals, and multimedia databases that offer sound files and images. Library databases are accessible both on and off campus, allowing students to conduct research any time of the day or night, right from their desktop.

Students have access to 1,500 computer workstations in 150 labs and classrooms throughout campus. Every student has a personal computer account with continuous e-mail and Internet access, as well as individual network accounts for file storage and Web pages. Residence halls are wired with high-speed Internet ports.

The College's new $33-million Burchfield Penney Art Center opened in fall 2008. This spectacular museum designed by world-class architectural firm Gwathmey Siegel & Associates\ houses the world's largest collection of works by watercolorist Charles E. Burchfield, and is the latest addition to Buffalo's museum district. The museum boasts extensive exhibition space, classrooms, a conservation lab, an auditorium, and a café.

A $6.5-million renovation of the Campbell Student Union's residential and retail dining centers was completed prior to the 2008–09 academic year. Other planned construction includes a $93-million renovation of the Science and Mathematics Complex and a new $43-million technology building. A new football stadium is under consideration. An 856-seat auditorium in stately Rockwell Hall houses the Performing Arts Center. Broadcast majors gain hands-on experience through the College's television studio and radio station (WBNY-FM 91.3). The Warren Enters Theater is a $2.6-million state-of-the-art learning laboratory. The campus also offers several other "learning lab" opportunities for students: the Buckham Campus School (a K–8 Buffalo public school), Campus House (a private faculty-staff club operated by hospitality administration students), the Speech-Language-Hearing Clinic, and the Whitworth Ferguson Planetarium. Buffalo State's Great Lakes Center for Environmental Research and Education, located 1 mile from campus on Buffalo's waterfront, features a fleet of research vessels and an on-shore field station.

Costs

For academic year 2009–10, full-time tuition for in-state students was $4970; fees were $1037. Out-of-state students paid $12,870 per year in tuition and $1037 in fees. On-campus room and board costs were $9726. Books, supplies, and personal expenses, including transportation, were estimated at $3100 per year. Costs are subject to change.

Financial Aid

About 77 percent of Buffalo State undergraduates receive financial assistance through grants, scholarships, loans, and employment averaging $9473 per year. The Financial Aid Office helps students find ways to pay for their college education. The office oversees distribution of more than $28 million in federal and state grants, loans, and student employment annually. In addition, more than 125 scholarship funds are managed by the Financial Aid Office.

For information on financial aid or scholarships, students may visit http://www.fafsa.ed.gov or Buffalo State's Web site, listed in the Application and Information section. The recommended filing date for submission of aid applications for fall semester is March 15. Applications received after published deadlines are processed on a first-come, first-served basis, with awards subject to availability of funds.

Faculty

Buffalo State's faculty consists of 429 full-time and 358 part-time members. Eighty percent of the full-time faculty members have earned doctorates or terminal degrees in their fields. Faculty members are scholars, actively involved in research, publishing, and the arts. Buffalo State does not rely on teaching assistants or graduate students for classroom instruction. The College is especially proud of its 55 recipients of the SUNY Chancellor's Award for Excellence in Teaching. Faculty members provide academic advisement for majors. Professional staff members provide academic advisement for undeclared students, tutoring, personal and career counseling, and health care.

Student Government

United Students Government (USG) represents the interests of all students and encourages their participation in educational, recreational, cultural, and social activities. USG offers a variety of services and programs, including concerts, a campus newspaper, the Whispering Pines college camp, and a dental clinic funded through the mandatory student activity fee.

Admission Requirements

Buffalo State accepts both proven and promising students who demonstrate the ability to complete college-level work. Admission counselors look for a broad, balanced high school education that includes study in English, foreign language(s), mathematics, science, and social studies.

Admission decisions are based on a variety of factors, including performance in rigorous college-preparatory course work, standardized test scores (SAT or ACT), rank in class, and recommendations from teachers and school counselors. Satisfactory results on the General Educational Development (GED) test are also acceptable. For transfer students, a minimum grade point average of 2.0 out of 4.0 is required for consideration, although some programs require a higher grade point average.

Buffalo State welcomes applications from international students (contact: International Student Affairs Office, telephone: 716-878-5331, http://www.buffalostate.edu/offices/isa).

Application and Information

Candidates must complete the State University of New York application, available from the Buffalo State Admissions Office, high school guidance offices, college transfer offices, or online at http://www.suny.edu/student. Decisions are made on a rolling basis beginning in mid-September for spring applicants, and in mid-December for fall applicants. Processing of applications continues until new-student enrollment goals have been met. Campus visits are recommended.

Admissions Office
Moot Hall 110
Buffalo State College
1300 Elmwood Avenue
Buffalo, New York 14222-1095

Phone: 716-878-4017
Fax: 716-878-6100
E-mail: admissions@buffalostate.edu
Web site: http://www.buffalostate.edu

BUTLER UNIVERSITY

INDIANAPOLIS, INDIANA

The University

Butler University has a proud tradition of excellence and innovation. Challenging and enabling students to meet their personal and professional goals has guided the University since 1855. Today, Butler is a nationally recognized comprehensive university with a total undergraduate enrollment of more than 3,800 students. Butler is accredited by the Higher Learning Commission of the North Central Association of Colleges and Schools.

Butler students represent almost every state in the nation and fifty-two countries, reflecting a diversity of cultures, interests, aspirations, personalities, and experiences. Students can choose from a number of housing options, including a newly built upperclass residential apartment village, an apartment-style residence hall, one all-women residence hall with an optional living-learning center, two coeducational residence halls with optional living-learning centers, fraternities, and sororities. A health and recreation complex is equipped with recreation courts, an indoor jogging track, an aquatics area, a weight and fitness space, a lounge, and a juice bar. Since opening in 2006, the complex has also won two national awards, including one for innovative architecture and design and one for its outstanding indoor sports facilities.

There are more than 140 official student organizations, fourteen Greek organizations, and nineteen Division I varsity athletic teams. Students take advantage of Broadway shows at Butler's Clowes Memorial Hall, the city's premier performing arts center. Basketball fans cheer on the Bulldogs at the 10,000-seat historic Hinkle Fieldhouse, where the final game in the movie *Hoosiers* was filmed.

Located near the center of campus, Atherton Union serves as a natural gathering space for students. Atherton Union has numerous amenities, including e-mail stations, wireless capabilities, a 24-hour computer lab, Starbucks coffee shop, bookstore, food court, dining hall, and convenience store. Atherton is also home to the Efroymson Diversity Center. The center houses the Office of Diversity Programs, Office of International Student Services and a number of student organizations.

Graduate degrees include business administration, creative writing, education administration (EPPSP), effective teaching and leadership, English, history, music conducting, music composition, music education, music history, music theory, music performance, piano pedagogy, pharmaceutical science, physician assistant, public accounting, and school counseling. In addition, Butler offers a doctor of pharmacy (Pharm.D.) program. A dual Pharm.D./M.B.A. program allows pharmacy students to develop management skills and entrepreneurial capabilities in conjunction with pharmacy experience while earning both a Pharm.D. and an M.B.A. in six years.

Location

Butler University is located on 290 acres of Indianapolis' historic Butler-Tarkington neighborhood, which is also home to Indiana's governor. The campus maintains its heritage with centuries-old trees; open, landscaped malls; curving sidewalks; and fountains. Most of the University's full-time students live on campus and enjoy a nature preserve, prairie, historical canal, formal botanical garden, an observatory, and jogging paths.

Just 6 miles from downtown Indianapolis, Butler's urban location offers internship opportunities that provide excellent graduate school and career preparation. Indianapolis, Indiana's state capital and the thirteenth-largest city in the nation, boasts a variety of cultural activities, including the Indianapolis Symphony Orchestra, the Indiana Repertory Theatre, the Indianapolis Museum of Art (just two blocks from campus), the Eiteljorg Museum, the Indiana State Museum, and the world's largest children's museum.

The Indianapolis Motor Speedway is the anchor of Indianapolis' professional sports, while basketball, football, hockey, and baseball have homes in three major sports arenas. Indianapolis is home to the NCAA headquarters, its Hall of Champions, and the men's and women's Big Ten basketball championships. In 2012, Indianapolis will host the Super Bowl. Butler has been the proud co-host of the NCAA Final Four championship in 1991, 1997, 2000, 2006, and 2010.

Majors and Degrees

As a comprehensive university with a strong liberal arts foundation, Butler is committed to graduating students who have a well-rounded yet focused education. A core curriculum affords students the opportunity to gain knowledge in the humanities, the arts, social sciences, natural sciences, and mathematics.

Baccalaureate degrees are offered through Butler's five colleges: Business Administration, Education, Liberal Arts and Sciences, Pharmacy and Health Sciences, and Fine Arts. Unique programs include the engineering dual-degree program, offered jointly by Butler University and the Purdue School of Engineering and Technology at Indianapolis. Students receive both a Butler Bachelor of Science degree in a selected liberal arts and sciences major (biology, chemistry, computer science, economics, mathematics, physics or science, technology and society) and a Purdue Bachelor of Science degree in biomedical, computer, electrical, or mechanical engineering.

For students who are undecided about their major field of study, there is an Exploratory Studies Program, where students develop a personalized academic plan to help choose the major that best suits their interests and abilities.

The College of Education is dedicated to preparing outstanding teachers. The administration and the faculty and staff members of the College of Education are committed to providing the best possible learning experience for students. For the past eight years, the College has experienced a 99 percent (or above) placement rate for its students, an indicator that Butler students place first in education. Undergraduate majors offered through the College are early and middle childhood education and middle and secondary education.

The College of Liberal Arts and Sciences creates lifelong learners. The College affirms the central role of liberal arts education while offering opportunities for specialization. Majors include actuarial science, anthropology, biological sciences, chemistry, classical studies, communication disorders (speech language pathology), communication studies, computer science, economics, English, French, French and business studies, German, German and business studies, history, individualized major, international studies, journalism, literature and writing, mathematics, philosophy, philosophy and religion, physics, political science, psychology, public and corporate communications, religion, science technology and society, sociology, sociology and criminal justice, software engineering, Spanish, Spanish and business studies, and urban affairs.

The College of Business Administration prepares students to be tomorrow's business leaders through hands-on experiential learning and two required internships. A unique program in the College—the Butler Business Accelerator—allows students to serve as consultants for central Indiana businesses. Majors in the College include accounting, economics, international management, management information systems, and marketing.

The Jordan College of Fine Arts integrates intensive conservatory training with broad objectives and a strong academic curriculum. The College is well respected for its tradition of educating students as emerging professionals in the arts. Majors offered are applied composition, arts administration, dance, electronic media studies–journalism, electronic media studies–video, multimedia studies, music, music history, music theory, music education, piano pedagogy, recording industry studies, and theater.

College of Pharmacy and Health Sciences graduates serve society as caring, ethical health professionals and community leaders. The College's professional programs combine intensive classroom education with clinical experiences in the professional phases of the degrees. Majors offered are pharmacy and physician assistant.

Butler offers preprofessional programs in dentistry, law, medicine, optometry, physical therapy, seminary, and veterinary medicine.

Preprofessional programs supplement a major, and are designed to prepare students for professional school and graduate school placement.

Academic Programs

All candidates for the baccalaureate degree must complete the University core requirements and at least 45 semester hours of work. Thirty of the 45 hours must be in the college granting the degree. Eligible students may participate in the honors program. By the end of the sophomore year, honors course work is generally completed. Students then begin the next phase, an independent study to help them research, write, and eventually present their honors thesis. Butler is a sponsoring institution for the National Merit Scholarship Program. Butler also offers advanced placement with appropriate academic credit in most subjects covered by either the AP examinations or the CLEP tests. Students may choose to enroll in Air Force and Army ROTC programs.

Butler students have the chance to originate research projects and participate in them with faculty members and then develop these projects into professional presentations and publications. Hundreds of Butler students present their projects at the Undergraduate Research Conference, hosted by Butler every April. In addition, the Butler Summer Institute awards accepted students a $2000 grant plus housing while they work on summer research projects with faculty members.

Off-Campus Programs

Butler offers more than 110 study abroad programs in over forty countries to meet the diverse needs of the student population. Butler students have studied in Argentina, Australia, Chile, Costa Rica, England, Ireland, Mexico, New Zealand, Northern Ireland, and Scotland. Students can choose to study for a semester, academic year, or summer term.

Academic Facilities

Butler's academic facilities include the latest technology. These include Mac and PC computers, wireless and Ethernet connections in every residence hall room and all classrooms, multimedia classrooms, language labs, international studies center, electronic card access into most buildings, access to Internet2, e-portfolios, and four 24-hour campus computer labs plus one in each residence hall. Additionally, some classrooms have lecture-capture capabilities for student playback via the Web, and SmartBoards, which allow instructors to e-mail class notes directly from the white board.

The Richard M. Fairbanks Center for Communication and Technology includes state-of-the-art classrooms, laboratories, conference rooms, television studios, graphics production and editing facilities, recording studios, student newspaper offices, online magazine production space, and speaker labs.

Many student performances, including theater, dance, and music, can be seen in Butler's 2,200-seat Clowes Memorial Hall and the 140-seat Eidson-Duckwall Recital Hall. The Holcomb Observatory and Planetarium houses the largest telescope in the state of Indiana, a 38-inch Cassegrain reflector. Butler's libraries house approximately 250,000 monograph volumes, 110,000 government documents, 1,500 current journal subscriptions, 14,000 audiovisual materials, and more than 17,000 musical scores. The library system also features a searchable computer database, rare books collection, archives, online catalog access, and research tools.

Costs

For the 2009–10 academic year, tuition was $28,460 for full-time undergraduate students. Average room and board were $9500 per year. Books are estimated at $800 per semester, and other fees are estimated at $800. Tuition for the professional pharmacy program was $30,780 and $34,130 for the sixth year. Tuition for the professional health sciences program was $30,780 and $440 per hour for the fifth year master of physician assistant program.

Financial Aid

Butler University offers a variety of financial assistance programs based on the demonstration of academic excellence, performance talent, or financial need. Butler awards merit-based academic scholarships to students who have displayed outstanding high school achievement and have excelled in leadership and community service. Performance awards are available in the areas of music, dance, theater, and athletics. Scholarships are also offered in selected majors. On-campus employment and work-study programs are also available. All students who seek need-based financial assistance are required to file the Free Application for Federal Student Aid (FAFSA).

The University offers National Merit, National Achievement, and National Hispanic Recognition Program scholarships. Semifinalists in these programs are guaranteed a minimum Freshman Academic Scholarship. However, based on academic screening, these students may qualify for a higher award. Finalists in these programs who designate Butler as their sponsor and file their FAFSA by March 1 are eligible for an additional award that ranges from $750 to $2000.

The University also offers Dr. John Morton-Finney Leadership Program Awards to students who exhibit leadership and a commitment to diversity in their high schools and communities. Awards are based on class rank, SAT/ACT scores, leadership roles in school and the community, and an on-campus interview. These awards include an expectation of continued campus and community leadership while at Butler.

Faculty

Teaching is the top priority for Butler's 328 full-time faculty members; 81 percent hold the highest (terminal) degree in their fields. Many are active in national research programs, write for publications, counsel in government and business, and participate in the arts. With a comfortable teaching load, Butler's faculty members have time to work with students individually. The student-faculty ratio is 11:1. All classes are taught by professors; there are no teaching assistants.

Student Government

As the official student governing body, Student Government Association (SGA) is the liaison between faculty and administration members. The organization is also responsible for budgeting funds from the student activity fee. These funds promote SGA's Program Board activities, including the film series, concerts, and all campus special events as well as the purchase of the Butler yearbook, *The Drift*.

Admission Requirements

Applicants are expected to complete a minimum of 14 academic units in high school, including 4 years of English, 3 years each of laboratory sciences (must include biology and chemistry), 3 years of mathematics (must include algebra 1, geometry, and algebra 2), 2 years each of history or social studies, and 2 years of the same foreign language. A candidate for admission typically ranks in the upper third of his or her high school class and should submit satisfactory results of the SAT or the ACT, including the optional Writing Test. The Jordan College of Fine Arts requires an audition. In addition to these factors, the Admission Committee considers the applicant's leadership skills, course selection, academic performance, and a writing sample. Students who wish to transfer from another regionally accredited college or university are considered if they are in good standing and have a grade point average of 2.0 or better in their previous academic work. Transfer students must submit official transcripts of all college work.

Application and Information

Butler offers three nonbinding admission programs: early action, November 15; early action II, January 15; and regular decision, February 15.

Campus visits are strongly recommended, though not required, and are arranged on a daily basis. Several open-house programs are also scheduled throughout the year. Interested students and their families are encouraged to visit http://go.butler.edu to make arrangements for campus visits.

Office of Admission
Butler University
4600 Sunset Avenue
Indianapolis, Indiana 46208-3485
Phone: 317-940-8100
888-940-8100 (toll-free)
Fax: 317-940-8150
E-mail: admission@butler.edu
Web site: http://go.butler.edu

CABRINI COLLEGE

RADNOR, PENNSYLVANIA

The College

Cabrini College is a residential Catholic college that welcomes students of all faiths and cultures. Founded in 1957 by the Missionary Sisters of the Sacred Heart of Jesus, Cabrini is located on 112 acres in the Main Line suburb of Radnor, Pennsylvania. Cabrini serves 3,500 men and women in undergraduate and graduate programs in the liberal arts and sciences and professional studies.

At Cabrini, students find new experiences, challenges, fascinating ideas, and peers who share similar beliefs and values. The campus—where the student is encouraged to develop as a whole person—is centered on four core values: community, respect, vision, and dedication to excellence.

The National Survey of Student Engagement consistently shows that Cabrini first-year students and seniors score higher than those at more than 700 colleges and universities in several benchmarks of effective educational practice, such as level of academic challenge, student-faculty interaction, enriching educational experiences, and supportive campus environment.

Cabrini's commitment to social justice spans more than two decades. It was among the first in higher education to implement community service into the curriculum and the first in Pennsylvania to require community service of all undergraduates. In 2005, Cabrini signed a formal agreement with Catholic Relief Services (CRS) to support global service initiatives.

More than 66 percent of Cabrini's full-time undergraduate students live on campus in a variety of housing accommodations, including traditional residence halls for men and women, residential houses, and a 120-bed, apartment-style complex. The College provides a full range of services to students, including placement, career, and personal counseling; a tutoring program; and health services. Students can participate in eighteen intercollegiate sports for men and women as well as an intramural sports program. Other popular extracurricular activities are the theater program, the College chorus, departmental clubs, professional organizations like the Accounting Association and the American Institute for Graphic Arts, and campus ministry. Students are encouraged to join the College's award-winning newspaper, the literary journal, and the yearbook. The campus radio station, WYBF-FM, and television studio are available to all students.

At the graduate level, Cabrini offers a Master of Education degree, numerous teacher certifications, and a Master of Science degree in organization leadership.

Location

Cabrini is located on a wooded, spacious 112-acre suburban campus, just minutes from the King of Prussia shopping mall and 30 minutes from Philadelphia. Students can take advantage of the city's many cultural, social, and educational opportunities, including trips to museums, historic sites, musical performances, and sporting events. Cabrini is also close to many other Philadelphia-area colleges, which sponsor activities of interest to students.

Majors and Degrees

Cabrini offers the Bachelor of Arts degree, with major programs in American studies, communication, English, French (through an affiliate agreement with Eastern University), graphic design, history, liberal studies, philosophy, political science, psychology, religious studies, sociology, and Spanish. The Bachelor of Science degree is offered, with major programs in accounting, biology, business administration, chemistry, computer information science, exercise science and health promotion, finance, human resource management, marketing, and mathematics. An individualized major, which is designed by the student using existing courses, can lead to a B.A. degree. The Bachelor of Social Work degree, which is accredited by the Council on Social Work Education, is awarded to graduates completing the social work major. The Bachelor of Science in Education degree is available, with majors in early childhood, educational studies, elementary, and special education; these programs also lead to teacher certification in each of the three fields (except for the educational studies major). Education majors are certified to teach in Pennsylvania and reciprocating states. Teacher certification for secondary education is offered in biology, chemistry, communications, English, mathematics, and social studies (concentration in history or sociology). Preprofessional programs in dentistry, nursing, occupational therapy, pharmacy, podiatry, and physical therapy are designed by faculty advisers to meet the needs of individual students. Academic concentrations include advertising, economics, international business, journalism and writing, nonprofit management, professional communication, public administration, social justice, theater, and video/audio/recording arts/photography/new communication technology. Students can enter Cabrini College as undeclared.

Academic Programs

"Justice Matters"—the College's new liberal arts core curriculum—includes a sequence of developmentally linked, writing-intensive courses taken in the first, second, and third years, and a capstone project in the fourth year. It defines the Contemporary Cabrinian Education through Academic Excellence, Social Justice, and Transformational Learning.

Within each major, Cabrini's curriculum is designed to help students develop professional skills in their chosen career field. Classroom instruction in all majors is supplemented by various forms of experiential learning. Many programs have required internships, through which upperclass students can earn academic credit for working in a job related to their major program.

Cooperative Education is another form of experiential learning for all students to gain on-the-job experience in a field they may wish to pursue, and most co-ops are paid positions.

All education majors participate in fieldwork beginning in the sophomore year. Social work majors spend 600 hours in direct practice before graduation. Cabrini students can choose a double major, and a free elective system encourages students to broaden their academic backgrounds.

Students may pursue their studies on a full-time or part-time basis during the school year. The College enables students to take courses in the evening, on Saturday, or during the summer. The College also is beginning to offer more courses online.

Off-Campus Programs

Cabrini participates with area colleges in a number of cooperative programs that enrich educational opportunities. Through an exchange program with nearby Eastern University, Rosemont College, Valley Forge Military College, and all institutions in the Southeastern Pennsylvania Consortium of Higher Education (SEPCHE), full-time students may elect courses offered on the other campuses; no additional tuition fees are charged, and credit is automatically transferred. Cabrini also maintains affiliations with the Pennsylvania College of Podiatric Medicine for an accelerated medical program and KAJEM Recording Arts Studio for communication.

Academic Facilities

Cabrini's 186,000-volume library, which includes subscription to 240 periodicals, serves as a comprehensive resource for students. The library continues to expand its collection of electronic resources and now provides access to more than 50,000 electronic periodicals in a wide range of disciplines. Cabrini is a member of the TCLC (Tri-State College Library Cooperative), SEPCHE (Southeast Pennsylvania Consortium for Higher Education), and PALCI (Pennsylvania Academic Library Consortium, Inc.) so additional resources at other libraries in the area are just a keystroke away. Research assistance is available via phone, chat, text messaging, and in person. The College's computer laboratory, which is open to all students, and five state-of-the-art-computer classroom facilities are equipped with IBM or Macintosh computers. Research facilities include the biology, chemistry, and psychology laboratories. A modern, fully equipped communication center houses the College's television studio, FM radio station, newsroom (with facilities for desktop publishing), and graphic design laboratory.

A great resource for education majors is the Children's School. Education majors have the opportunity to observe, do fieldwork, and student teach at the school. The College's educational resource center provides students with access to teaching materials, ranging from videos and transparencies to children's literature.

The Antoinette Iadarola Center for Science, Education, and Technology provides the ideal setting for learning and discovery. The three-story facility underscores Cabrini's commitment to the sciences by providing state-of-the-art equipment, study space and training, and research and experimentation opportunities. The facility is designed to provide labs and classrooms for science majors and nonmajors, with smart technology in every lab, enhancing the learning experience. The building also includes a high-tech sixty-seat lecture hall, which features stadium seating for classes, seminars, workshops, and outreach programs.

The science education classroom is designed specifically for education majors and secondary education certification; this classroom helps students learn innovative ways to teach science to children in grades K–12. Labs for anatomy and physiology, microbiology, life sciences, and biotechnology complement research labs and a resource center for faculty members and students. Equipment includes fluorescent, phase, and inverted microscopes; a flow cytometer; and recombinant DNA and cell facilities. The Center's top floor houses the general chemistry, organic chemistry, and analytical chemistry labs; specialized instrumentation rooms; and a chemistry resource center as well as research labs for faculty members and students.

Majors include biology/biological sciences, biology/premedicine, biology/biotechnology, and chemistry. Non-degree-granting pre–allied health programs include those in nursing, occupational therapy, pharmacy, and physical therapy. Various science and technology-focused minors and concentrations are also available for students to explore science within the context of their chosen area of study.

The Center also houses the Center for Teaching and Learning, a learning commons that provides individualized support for students in math, writing, and specific subjects.

Costs

Tuition for full-time students in 2009–10 is $30,120; average room and board cost $11,400 for the year. General fees of $910 cover student registration, health services, activities, library use, testing, and publications. Fees for laboratory and other courses vary. Textbooks and supplies are approximately $1050 per year. Students with cars secure a $95 parking permit annually.

Financial Aid

Last year, 96 percent of Cabrini's undergraduates shared more than $23 million in financial aid in the form of scholarship, grant, loan, and work-study funds. The College itself offered more than $10 million through a variety of institutional scholarship programs. In addition, eligible students can receive funds through federal programs such as Pell Grants, Supplemental Educational Opportunity Grants, and the Federal Work-Study Program, which is a student employment program. Pennsylvania students may also be eligible for a Pennsylvania State Grant. Sometimes out-of-state students may be able to receive grants from their own states. In addition to the Federal Work-Study Program, the College offers its own Work-Grant Program to help students with tuition costs. Applicants for all federal financial aid, plus any aid that is based on financial need, must submit the Free Application for Federal Student Aid (FAFSA) as soon as the form becomes available on January 1. The FAFSA is available by going online to http://www.fafsa.ed.gov. All financial aid is offered for a one-year period but is renewable.

Faculty

Cabrini's average class size is 19 students, and the College's faculty members are committed to developing and challenging the individual skills of each student. Faculty members are known for their dedication to teaching and getting to know their students personally. Each full-time student has a faculty adviser who assists in arranging a program that is designed to meet the student's objectives.

Student Government

The Student Government Association (SGA) of Cabrini College facilitates all communication pertaining to students within the College community. The association exists to make known the views of the student body and to look after its interests with respect to the faculty members, administration, and educational policies of the College.

Admission Requirements

Admissions considers applicants on the basis of their high school record, SAT or ACT scores, class rank, and other indicators of potential to succeed in college-level studies, such as recommendations. Applications for admission are reviewed without regard to sex, race, creed, color, national origin, age, or handicap. Applicants should be graduates of an accredited high school (or present equivalent credentials) and have a minimum of 15 units of credit: 4 in English, 2 in a foreign language, 3 in college-preparatory mathematics, 3 in science, and 3 in social studies. Cabrini also conducts an early admission program through which students with superior ability and a sound academic background may begin college studies at the end of the junior year in high school. Applicants may apply for advanced standing at Cabrini through the Advanced Placement (AP) Program and the College-Level Examination Program (CLEP) of the College Board. The College's Office of Graduate and Professional Studies administers CLEP and DANTES tests.

Cabrini welcomes transfer students from other accredited institutions. Applicants should have a minimum GPA of 2.0 to be considered for transfer. Students transferring from Bucks County Community College, Community College of Philadelphia, Manor College, Delaware County Community College, Montgomery County Community College, Harcum College, Harrisburg Area Community College, Peirce College, Reading Community College, or Valley Forge Military College with an A.A. or A.S. degree and a minimum 2.5 GPA receive credit for all previous course work. Two-year-college students are encouraged to follow a course of liberal and general studies during their first two years at another institution if they expect to continue their studies at a four-year college such as Cabrini.

A campus visit, while not required, is recommended for prospective students. The Admissions Office offers individual interviews and group information sessions on weekdays and select Saturdays. Students conduct campus tours, which may include class visits and informal meetings with faculty members and administrators. Those planning to visit the campus should contact Admissions for information. In addition, representatives of the College visit high schools in various cities.

Application and Information

Applicants for freshman admission are requested to have SAT or ACT scores and official high school transcripts sent to the Admissions Office along with the application for admission. Transfer students must submit an application and high school and college transcripts. A nonrefundable application fee of $35 must accompany the application. The Admissions Office maintains a rolling admission policy until the class is filled and takes action on an application when all the necessary credentials are on file. Students can apply online at https://duapp2.cabrini.edu/apply/app.

For more information, students may contact:

Admissions Office
Cabrini College
610 King of Prussia Road
Radnor, Pennsylvania 19087-3698
Phone: 610-902-8552
800-848-1003 (toll-free)
E-mail: admit@cabrini.edu
Web site: http://www.cabrini.edu

COLLEGE CLOSE-UPS

CALDWELL COLLEGE

CALDWELL, NEW JERSEY

The College

Caldwell College is a Catholic, coeducational four-year liberal arts institution rooted in a proud 800-year Dominican tradition of rigorous scholarship, committed teaching, and ethical values. Founded in 1939 by the Sisters of St. Dominic, Caldwell College helps students achieve their full intellectual and personal potential in a supportive community.

The College's most popular offerings include undergraduate degrees in business, psychology, and education. Caldwell has twenty-nine undergraduate degrees, seventeen graduate programs, and a Caldwell Scholars Program. The adult undergraduate program encourages adults to return to college to complete their degree, earn a new degree, or simply learn for pleasure. Day, evening, Saturday, and distance learning courses highlight the importance of lifelong learning. Accelerated options combine the curricular opportunities of the distance education program with traditional on-campus offerings. Post-baccalaureate programs in applied behavior analysis (ABA), pastoral ministry, special education, and teacher certification are available.

The Center for Graduate and Continuing Studies meets the academic needs of the College's adult students. The center provides adult learners, in undergraduate or graduate programs, with excellence in teaching, caring academic support, and learning options that work with their busy lives.

Master's degrees are offered in applied behavior analysis (ABA), which is a highly effective treatment for autism; business administration (accounting, nonprofit management); counseling psychology (art therapy, mental health counseling, school counseling); curriculum and instruction (special education, supervisor certification); educational administration; pastoral ministry (church administration); and special education (general teacher and certification, learning disabilities). Educational administration is also offered in a fast-track Off-Campus Leadership Development Program. Post-master's programs in educational principal's and supervisor's certification, a professional counselor licensing credential, and post-master's specializations in art therapy and school counseling are offered. A Director of School Counseling program is available. Combined bachelor's-master's programs are available to qualified students in art therapy, business, psychology, school counseling, and theology.

The Career Planning and Development Office assists students with all aspects of career exploration and the job search process. The office provides ongoing career counseling, an extensive career library, self-assessment tools, graduate-study information, and online resources to help students clarify personal and professional goals and explore academic and career opportunities. Career planning and development counselors assist students with resume writing, interview preparation, and career research.

Caldwell College sponsors work-based internship and cooperative education opportunities that encourage students to integrate work experience with classroom learning. Program participants explore possible careers and develop valuable contacts in their field of interest, which often lead to employment offers. The Career Planning and Development Office assists students and alumni who are seeking full- and part-time employment. Caldwell College alumni also participate in career-related panels and workshops. The College's Business Advisory Council, which includes about 40 members from major corporations throughout New Jersey, helps business leaders and educators share their resources so both students and the business community can prepare for the challenges of the global marketplace. Through guest lecturers, classroom interaction with corporate leaders, mentoring programs, and the availability of significant career counseling, students learn how to be successful in today's workplace.

Caldwell College enrolls approximately 2,300 full-time, part-time, and graduate students. Approximately 84 percent of the full-time students are from New Jersey. In addition, the College's rich cultural diversity attracts individuals from northeastern and mid-Atlantic states and from more than twenty-six other countries. The cultural mix of students includes African American (13 percent), Hispanic (10 percent), Asian American (2 percent), and international (4 percent) students. Fully qualified faculty members and a 13:1 student-faculty ratio provide close, personal attention.

About 45 percent of full-time students live on campus. Single, double, triple, and a few quad rooms are available. A new 200-bed, apartment-style residence hall opened in August 2007. The food service features extended hours and an expanded menu, with both American and international food selections. All students may have a car on campus. A variety of clubs and organizations are available. Guest artists, musicians, authors, and speakers appear on campus regularly, and there are dances and other activities. An on-campus fitness center, equipped with cardiovascular equipment, provides students with health and exercise opportunities. Caldwell fields NCAA Division II teams in men's baseball, basketball, golf, soccer, and tennis and in women's basketball, cross-country, soccer, softball, tennis, and volleyball and sponsors a variety of recreational sports. The 60,000-square-foot George R. Newman Student Activities and Recreation Center opened in 2002.

Location

Located on a beautiful, secure 70-acre campus 20 miles west of New York City, students participate in numerous educational, cultural, and social experiences while enjoying the relaxed atmosphere of campus life. A variety of shops and restaurants are within walking distance. Area attractions include theaters, museums, parks, ski resorts, malls, professional sports arenas, the New Jersey Performing Arts Center, and the New Jersey shore. Many corporate headquarters are easily accessible and provide a variety of internship opportunities. The College can be reached by public transportation and is near major highways, including the Garden State Parkway, the New Jersey Turnpike, and Interstates 80, 280, and 287.

Majors and Degrees

Caldwell College offers twenty-nine undergraduate Bachelor of Arts (B.A.), Bachelor of Science (B.S.), and Bachelor of Fine Arts (B.F.A.) degrees. A multidisciplinary major is offered. The College also offers an individualized major for students seeking to design their own course work with administrative approval. The B.A. is offered in art, biology, chemistry, communication arts, criminal justice, elementary education, English, French, history, an individualized major, mathematics, music, political science, psychology, social studies, sociology, Spanish, and theology. The B.S. is offered in accounting, business administration, computer information systems, computer science, financial economics, international business, management, marketing, and medical technology. The B.F.A. is offered in art. The Division of Education offers teacher certification programs in elementary education (nursery–grade 8) and for teaching grades K–12 in art, biology, English, French, mathematics, music, social studies, Spanish, and special education as well as a P–3 certification. A dual certification program is available to registered nurses who wish to obtain school nurse certification and teacher of health endorsement.

Academic Programs

Eligibility for a degree requires completion of a minimum of 120 credits and a GPA of at least 2.0 (C). Students must also complete major courses with a minimum grade of C and satisfy all other departmental requirements. All programs require that students successfully pass a form of outcomes assessment in the senior year. Liberal arts requirements include courses in computer literacy, English, fine arts, foreign language, history, mathematics, natural sciences, philosophy, physical education, public speaking, religious studies, and social sciences. A Writing Across the Curriculum program systematically develops a student's ability to write well, regardless of his or her major. Opportunities for independent study, internships, co-ops, double majors, minors, and certificate programs are available. The Caldwell Scholars Program challenges exceptional students with both interdisciplinary studies and a directed honors project and is supplemented by guest lecturers.

Scores of 3, 4, or 5 on the College Board's Advanced Placement tests earn advanced placement or credit for completed work. Students may receive credit for knowledge gained through independent study or experience through the College-Level Examination Program (CLEP). Adult students can earn credit through Caldwell's Prior Learning Assessment Policy, provided they can demonstrate acquired knowledge that corresponds to course requirements. Course selection is determined by placement test results, and international students may be required to enroll in credit-bearing, advanced-level English for nonnative speakers (ENNS) courses.

Caldwell College currently has fourteen joint-degree affiliation programs, which give students the opportunity to attain professional degrees in an accelerated period of time and to save a year of Caldwell College tuition. Some of the affiliated schools for medical degrees include St. George's University's School of Medicine and Veterinary Medicine in Grenada, UMDNJ's New Jersey Medical School, and Columbia University, College of Physicians and Surgeons. An affiliation with Rutgers University enables qualified students to earn a B.A. degree in sociology from Caldwell and an M.S.W. from Rutgers School of Social Work in five years. Caldwell recently added an agreement with Seton Hall University for a combined B.A. in biology and M.S. in athletic training. This five-year program enables qualified candidates to take three years of course work at Caldwell, then two years at Seton Hall, earning both B.A. and M.S. degrees. Affiliation programs also include seven-year accelerated programs and eight-year traditional routes. The seven-year programs are highly competitive, and students must be accepted by both the affiliated institution and Caldwell and maintain the mandatory GPAs and test scores.

Off-Campus Programs

The College has exchange-program agreements with Duksung Women's University and Catholic University of Korea that provide students with broad opportunities to better prepare themselves for the global marketplace. Caldwell also offers short-term travel experiences, usually up to three weeks in length and during the winter or summer session, to numerous locations. Students are accompanied by faculty members, who design and present courses in a variety of academic disciplines. Caldwell is also affiliated with the Washington Semester Program of American University, Washington, D.C.

Academic Facilities

To better focus on its desire to excel in the teaching of math and science, Caldwell College used nearly $2 million in federal grants to help establish the Center for Excellence for Teaching on the campus. The College renovated the biology, physics, and chemistry labs and plans to serve as a regional hub to implement innovative teacher preparation programs that will emphasize the effective use of classroom technology, refinement of math and science training, special education teacher training, and developing programs for disadvantaged students.

Campus facilities include a library, four classroom and administrative buildings, and a theater. An academic building, which opened in 1997, features a 120-seat lecture hall and faculty and administrative offices. A psychology lab is equipped with computers and specialized state-of-the-art hardware and software for conducting psychological studies related to class work and for independent student and faculty psychological research. The lab provides equipment for observing and collecting behavioral data, student role-playing, and developing counseling skills. Wide-screen video and computer graphics capability and satellite reception are available. Jennings Library contains 146,350 volumes, subscribes to 443 periodicals, and provides access to more than 21,500 journal titles in 53 full-text databases. Off-campus access to the online public-access catalog and online databases is available. Full-text databases support the major curricular areas. A curriculum lab has texts for grades K–12, visual aids, and other resources. The Media Center is equipped with VHS, DVD, and CD listening equipment for use in classroom assignments.

The Department of Art contains a gallery studio featuring professional and student work. The Communication Arts Department's facilities include a television studio, a digital editing suite, a public speaking lab, and a radio studio. Students may produce and perform TV and radio shows, which are broadcast to the entire campus community.

Computer labs, with up-to-date personal computers, software, and multimedia equipment, offer free scanning and laser printing. Other computer labs are dedicated to specific areas of study, including art, education, ENNS, math, music, the sciences, video editing, and writing. There are two technology-rich classrooms, the Academic Computer Classroom and the Business Computer Classroom, and twelve technology-enhanced classrooms that are equipped with digital audio and video and computer equipment. All offices, classrooms, labs, and dorm rooms are connected to the campus network and the Internet.

Costs

For the 2008–09 academic year, full-time tuition and fees were $23,600 and campus room and board were approximately $8300. Adult undergraduate tuition was $565 per credit hour, and graduate tuition was $708 per credit hour.

Financial Aid

Approximately 80 percent of the current full-time undergraduate students receive financial aid from federal sources that include the Pell Grant, Stafford Student Loan, Work-Study, and Supplemental Educational Opportunity Grant programs. Caldwell College offers scholarships for academic and athletic excellence, special interest and privately sponsored scholarships, tuition grants, and campus employment. New Jersey offers tuition aid grants for state residents. The New Jersey Educational Opportunity Fund (EOF) makes it possible for all students, especially the educationally and economically disadvantaged for whom college might otherwise be an unrealistic goal, to pursue higher education. All financial aid applicants must file the Free Application for Federal Student Aid (FAFSA). The priority filing deadline is April 1.

Faculty

There are 83 full-time faculty members, with 84 percent having earned their doctoral/terminal degree, and 10 part-time faculty members. There are 4 full-time ENNS and Academic Support Center instructors and 123 adjunct faculty members.

Student Government

Caldwell College's students, through the Student Government Association and the Resident Council, shape many nonacademic policies and regulations. Students help determine total College policy through representation on several College standing committees.

Admission Requirements

The Office of Undergraduate Admissions individually reviews each applicant's high school record, SAT or ACT scores (with essay score), essay, letters of recommendation, and class rank (when available) to determine the student's ability to succeed at Caldwell College. International students must submit proof of their TOEFL score with their applications. Students must complete at least 16 high school academic units, including 4 years of English, 2 of foreign language, 2 of mathematics, 2 of science, and 1 of history. Transfer applicants must submit an official transcript from each college and university attended. If they have earned fewer than 30 credits, they must also submit a high school transcript and SAT/ACT scores with the essay score. Caldwell College does not discriminate against applicants on the basis of race, color, creed, age, national or ethnic origin, or handicap.

Application and Information

Caldwell College has a rolling admissions policy, accepting applicants throughout the year, based on availability. An early action admissions program allows students who apply by December 1 to have a decision by January 1. The priority application deadline for freshmen is April 1 (July 15 for transfer students). There is a nonrefundable $40 application fee. Applicants are notified of their admission eligibility after their credentials have been evaluated.

Office of Admissions
Caldwell College
120 Bloomfield Avenue
Caldwell, New Jersey 07006-6195
Phone: 973-618-3500
888-864-9516 (toll-free outside New Jersey)
Fax: 973-618-3600
E-mail: admissions@caldwell.edu
Web site: http://www.caldwell.edu

COLLEGE CLOSE-UPS

CALIFORNIA COLLEGE OF THE ARTS

SAN FRANCISCO AND OAKLAND, CALIFORNIA

The College

California College of the Arts (CCA), founded in 1907, offers studies in twenty undergraduate and seven graduate majors in the areas of fine arts, architecture, design, and writing. The College has world-class facilities at its two campuses in San Francisco and Oakland. Students and faculty members create a supportive community of friends, colleagues, and mentors in an intimate, private-college environment.

CCA alumni have been at the forefront of nearly every major art movement of the past century and its students begin making their mark well before graduation. Students from nearly every CCA program participated in the high-profile 2009 Solar Decathlon, winning several awards. A CCA animation student was one of only 12 selected (out of 2,500 applicants) for a Pixar internship in 2008. And one of the College's industrial design students recently signed a contract with Universal Toys to manufacture a toy he first conceived as a class project.

BusinessWeek magazine named CCA one of the world's best design schools in 2009. CCA is accredited by the Western Association of Schools and Colleges, the National Association of Schools of Art and Design, the National Architectural Accrediting Board, and the Council for Interior Design Accreditation.

CCA has approximately 1,400 undergraduate and 400 graduate students. In the undergraduate population, 62 percent are women, 38 percent are men, 33 percent are from underrepresented populations, and 9 percent are international students. Of the entering class, 54 percent are first-time freshmen and 46 percent are transfer and second-degree students. About 32 percent come from out of state.

About 80 percent of first-year students live on campus. Throughout the year, the residential-life staff hosts social and educational programs ranging from movie nights to museum trips and professional lectures.

Students are encouraged to join existing clubs and organizations or to form new ones. They are active in preprofessional groups, including the American Institute of Architecture Students (AIAS), American Institute of Graphic Arts (AIGA), Industrial Designers Society of America (IDSA), and International Interior Design Association (IIDA).

Location

The San Francisco Bay Area is known for creative and technological innovation, environmental leadership, and thriving art and design communities. It is home to world-class museums and alternative galleries as well as active endeavors in theater, music, dance, film, and literature. Beaches, the Napa Valley, Mendocino, Monterey, Lake Tahoe, and Yosemite are all close by.

CCA's San Francisco campus spans a city block in the Potrero Hill neighborhood, near the design district. The Oakland campus occupies 4 acres in the Rockridge neighborhood, 3 miles from the University of California, Berkeley. A free shuttle connects the campuses and residence halls. Both campuses are easily accessible via public transportation.

Majors and Degrees

CCA offers the Bachelor of Fine Arts (B.F.A.) degree in animation, ceramics, community arts, fashion design, film, furniture, glass, graphic design, illustration, industrial design, interior design, jewelry/metal arts, painting/drawing, photography, printmaking, sculpture, and textiles. The College offers the Bachelor of Arts (B.A.) degree in visual studies and writing and literature. CCA also offers a bachelor of architecture (B.Arch.) degree, a five-year program.

CCA offers seven graduate programs: the M.F.A. in design, fine arts, and writing; the M.A. in curatorial practice and visual and critical studies; the M.Arch. in architecture; and the M.B.A. in design strategy. Graduate fine arts media areas include ceramics, film, furniture, glass, jewelry/metal arts, painting/drawing, photography, printmaking, sculpture, social practice, and textiles.

Academic Programs

The B.F.A. requires the completion of 126 semester units (75 in studio work and 51 in humanities and sciences). The B.A. requires 126 semester units (51 in humanities and sciences, 36 in the major, and 39 in studio work). The B.Arch. requires 165 semester units, including the core program and a 9-semester major program.

Undergraduates begin with a core curriculum, which covers a variety of artistic media, principles, and processes as well as writing, literature, art history, and critical theory.

CCA operates on a two-semester academic calendar with a six-week summer session. Summer programs include the Pre-College Program for high school students (participants earn college credit). Continuing education programs are offered throughout the year.

Off-Campus Programs

Qualified upper-division students may spend a semester at one of thirty-two other U.S. art schools through the Association of Independent Colleges of Art and Design (AICAD). Students may cross-register at Mills College or Holy Names University, both in Oakland.

Through the International Exchange Program, students may spend a semester at one of more than thirty colleges of art and design around the world. CCA also offers summer study-abroad courses.

Academic Facilities

The Oakland campus is home to the first-year program and the programs in animation, ceramics, community arts, glass,

COLLEGE CLOSE-UPS

jewelry/metal arts, photography, printmaking, sculpture, textiles, visual studies, and writing and literature. Animation students have state-of-the-art studios and equipment for digital video, film, and sound production. The ceramics facilities include numerous gas and electric kilns. Sculpture facilities include a bronze foundry, a waxworking area, a plaster and mold-making room, a metal fabrication studio, and a woodshop. Textiles facilities include a computerized weaving lab, a digital Jacquard TC-1 loom, and a fiber sculpture studio. For printmaking there are lithography presses, a 40x60 American French Tool etching press, a silkscreening and papermaking complex, and a letterpress lab. The two-floor photography center has darkrooms for black-and-white and color printing, a 42-inch RA4 color processor, and a mural darkroom.

The San Francisco campus houses the programs in architecture, fashion design, film, furniture, graphic design, illustration, industrial design, interior design, and painting/drawing as well as all of the graduate programs. There is a state-of-the-art digital production facility and stage. The wood and furniture facilities include a bench room, a machine room, and a spray booth. Seniors in the painting/drawing program have individual studios, as do all fine arts graduate students.

Media centers offer equipment for checkout. The fourteen dedicated computer labs are available to all students 16 to 24 hours daily, whenever they are not being used for classes. The labs have Intel-based Macintosh computers and a complete range of software. Available hardware includes slide and flatbed scanning devices, Cintiq displays, audio/video decks, graphics tablets, CD/DVD burners, and large-format color printers. There is a rapid prototyping studio for 3-D printing.

CCA's libraries hold more than 60,000 titles. They subscribe to approximately 300 hard-copy periodicals and more than 2,500 full-text online periodicals. On the San Francisco campus there is also an extensive materials library.

The campuses have several spaces for student exhibitions. The CCA Wattis Institute for Contemporary Arts, on the San Francisco campus, presents exhibitions of internationally prominent contemporary artists.

Costs

Tuition for the 2009–10 year was $32,904 for full-time undergraduates and $1371 per unit for part-time students. Tuition is the same for California and out-of-state residents. Campus housing costs an additional $6870. Total costs for 2009–10 were $47,854, which includes $33,254 in tuition and fees, $9650 for room and board, $1500 for books and supplies, and $3450 for miscellaneous expenses.

Financial Aid

In 2009–10, 81 percent of CCA students received financial aid from some source. Approximately 78 percent received CCA scholarships. The college offers financial aid in the form of scholarships, grants, loans, and work-study programs. There are both need- and merit-based awards.

Students seeking merit scholarships must submit their admissions application by February 1. Students applying for financial assistance in 2010–11 should submit the FAFSA by March 1. CCA continues to award aid after March 1 as funding permits. Students can apply for grants and loans throughout the year. CCA is approved for veterans who wish to attend under the Veterans Administration Educational Benefits Program. CCA offers an interest-free payment plan.

Faculty

CCA's faculty includes 500 artists, architects, designers, writers, and scholars, most of whom combine teaching with professional work in their respective fields. The average class size is 18. Faculty members serve as advisers to first-year students.

Student Government

The Student Council includes students from all areas of CCA and sponsors extracurricular activities, including films, receptions, and gallery excursions.

Admission Requirements

Admitted undergraduates must have a high school diploma or equivalent. Applications are reviewed on an individualized basis, taking into account academic achievements, creative abilities, individual achievements and activities, a personal essay, recommendations, and a portfolio.

Application and Information

For undergraduates, there are two priority deadlines for fall admission: February 1 and March 1. Those interested in applying for merit scholarships should submit their applications by February 1. The priority deadline for spring undergraduate applicants is October 1. Students who meet the admissions priority deadlines receive first consideration for housing, financial aid, and course selection. Applications are reviewed in the order they are received. There is a nonrefundable application fee of $60. It is possible to register for courses as a nondegree student (on a space-available basis).

Students may apply online at http://www.cca.edu/admissions. To request forms and brochures, the college viewbook, or any additional information, please contact:

Office of Enrollment Services
California College of the Arts
1111 Eighth Street
San Francisco, California 94107-2247
Phone: 800-447-1ART (toll-free)
Fax: 415-703-9539
Web site: http://www.cca.edu

COLLEGE CLOSE-UPS

CALIFORNIA LUTHERAN UNIVERSITY

THOUSAND OAKS, CALIFORNIA

The University

California Lutheran University (CLU) was founded in 1959, but its history goes back much farther than that. CLU is part of a 500-year-old tradition of Lutheran higher education—a tradition begun on a university campus as a teaching and reforming movement, a tradition of thoughtful investigation and bold discovery.

Following in this tradition, CLU insists on wide-ranging, critical inquiry into matters of both faith and reason. Students are encouraged to investigate personal beliefs that impact their educational and career choices and are asked to reflect on how their intellectual and spiritual convictions come together to define them as a whole person. Ultimately, the goal of CLU is to educate leaders for a global society who are strong in character and judgment, confident in their identity and vocation, and committed to service and justice. The individual exploration of truth is only a starting point for the whole educational experience by which students and professors work together to seek answers to the intellectual and professional questions that face world citizens.

CLU's 225-acre campus is home to 2,129 undergraduate and 1,282 graduate students from across the nation and around the world who represent a diversity of faiths and cultures. CLU provides access to a wide variety of organizations, sports, and other activities, providing ample opportunities for students to develop their leadership skills. KCLU-FM, a National Public Radio affiliate on the CLU campus, provides a valuable service to the community and a learning opportunity for students.

Master's degrees are awarded in business administration, computer science, education, marriage and family counseling, psychology, and public policy and administration. The NCATE-accredited School of Education offers an Ed.D. in educational leadership as well as a number of credential and certificate programs. International M.B.A. and post-M.B.A. programs are offered through the School of Business.

CLU is accredited by the Western Association of Schools and Colleges and is ranked in the top twenty by *U.S. News & World Report.*

Location

Poised at the intersection of the Americas on the Pacific Rim, CLU's location helps prepare students for careers in a global society. Thousand Oaks, which is located in one of America's significant technology corridors, the "101 Corridor," offers the conveniences of an urban area but is situated in an area of scenic natural beauty with open spaces and rolling hills. Because of its location midway between downtown Los Angeles and Santa Barbara and 15 miles inland from the Pacific Ocean, CLU offers students numerous recreational and cultural opportunities as well as internship and career opportunities in government, entertainment, and social services.

Majors and Degrees

CLU offers thirty-six majors within the College of Arts and Science, the School of Business, and the School of Education. In addition, undergraduate preprofessional preparation is available in law, medicine, and health-related fields. Undergraduate degrees are offered in accounting, art, biochemistry and molecular biology, bioengineering, biology, business administration, chemistry, communication, computer information systems, computer science, criminal justice, economics, English, environmental science, exercise science and sports medicine, French, geology, German, history, interdisciplinary studies, international studies, liberal studies (education), marketing communication, mathematics, multimedia, music, philosophy, physics, political science, psychology, religion, social science, sociology, Spanish, and theater arts. Minors are offered in art, bioengineering, biology, business administration, chemistry, church music, communication, computer science, economics, English, environmental studies, ethnic studies, French, gender and women's studies, geography, geology, German, Greek, history, international business, international studies, legal studies, mathematics, multimedia, music, philosophy, physics, political science, psychology, religion, religion minor with church vocations, religion minor with youth ministry, sociology, Spanish, and theater arts.

Academic Programs

CLU's integrated curriculum helps students comprehend issues from a variety of perspectives. Students learn to ask the right questions and to think critically in order to analyze, process, transform, and communicate information. With thirty-six majors and thirty-one minors, students are encouraged to sample classes widely to build a broad base of knowledge. CLU feels that while planning for a career is important, the type of education that prepares students for a changing world is one of the greatest gifts a college education can provide.

At the heart of CLU's academic program is a general education curriculum called Core 21. Students' views of the world expand as they learn how disciplines connect in this interdisciplinary approach. Core 21 extends through all four years, beginning with Freshman Seminar. CLU realizes that students' interests may not fit neatly into an academic box. Whether a student enters college with a definite major in mind or an awareness of the areas he or she wants to explore, CLU's curriculum offers distinctive ways to combine academic interests and goals with practical career preparation.

Students who wish to delve deeper into the life of the mind in smaller, seminar-style classes may also have access to the Honors Program. Honors courses bring students and faculty members together to contemplate issues of enduring human concern as well as contemporary problems facing society. Students who successfully complete the requisite honors courses over four years are awarded University Honors at graduation. A second honors program, Departmental Honors, is open to junior and senior students who wish to participate in prolonged, mentored scholarship with a faculty member in their chosen major field.

Off-Campus Programs

Students may take courses abroad while maintaining their student status at CLU by enrolling in one of the more than forty study-abroad programs offered. The University offers ongoing study, internship, and exchange programs in Austria, Belgium, Germany, Hong Kong, India, Mexico, Sweden, Tanzania, and Thailand. CLU also offers a Washington, D.C., semester for students in every field of study. This program allows students to live, study, and work in the nation's capital while earning a full semester of academic credit. While completing their professional internship and taking two academic courses, they also participate in orientation sessions, field trips, meetings with experts, and seminars on current events. Students are housed in furnished condominiums across the Potomac River in Arlington, Virginia.

Academic Facilities

The most recent addition to the CLU campus is Trinity Hall, a 220-bed residence hall. Several new athletic arenas have just been completed, including the 96,000-square-foot Gilbert Sports and Fitness Center, featuring two gymnasiums, an events center, fitness and strength conditioning centers, dance studios, and a Hall of Fame; the Samuelson Aquatics Center, consisting of a 50-meter by 25-yard pool and diving well, providing the swimming, diving, and water polo teams with an Olympic-quality facility in which to train and compete; the George "Sparky" Anderson baseball field and Ullman Stadium; and the new Hutton softball field.

The campus is distinctive in its combination of mid-century modern and classic-contemporary architecture. The 600-seat Samuelson Chapel, with its towering wall of stained glass, mahogany carvings, and handcrafted Steiner-Reck organ, anchors the campus, which also includes the state-of-the-art Ahmanson Science Center, Pearson Library, and Soiland Humanities Center. The Preus-Brandt Forum is a 250-seat lecture/performance center equipped with modern sound and lighting equipment.

Costs

Tuition for the 2009–10 academic year is $28,980 (12–17 credits per semester). Room and board for the year is $10,090. Student fees are $250 per year.

Financial Aid

Available assistance includes need-based and non-need-based University scholarships; low-interest, long-term loans from external sources; Federal Supplemental Educational Opportunity Grants; Federal Pell Grants; and Federal Work-Study Program positions. Part-time jobs are available both on and off campus. Applicants for aid should submit the Free Application for Federal Student Aid (FAFSA). The parents' and/or student's most recent IRS 1040 form must also be submitted. The priority application deadline is March 1. CLU scholarships are awarded based on the submission of a completed application.

Faculty

At CLU, professors care passionately about teaching and students. CLU's average class size of 22 students enables faculty members to know their students and enables students to develop relationships with mentors. Students have lively, in-depth discussions with the highly trained faculty members who teach their classes. Eighty-one percent of the full-time faculty members have earned their doctoral or terminal degree. They bring a depth of intellectual expertise and academic curiosity to the classroom. Among the faculty members are a former senior economist of the United Nations Development Programme, as well as master scholars in everything from media law and Mexican narrative to artificial intelligence and classical and quantum chaos. The list of their areas of research and interests—the social psychology of moral development, molecular evolution, economic and business forecasting models, and politics in movies, to name a few—brings a broad and beneficial foundation to students' liberal arts experience.

Student Government

All undergraduate students carrying 9 or more units are automatically members of the Associated Students of California Lutheran University by virtue of their enrollment in the University. Student governance, including allocation of the student activity fee, is conducted by student body–elected officials.

Admission Requirements

Applicants for admission must complete the application form (the CLU application or the Common Application may be used) and submit a high school transcript, SAT or ACT scores, one recommendation, an essay/personal statement, and a $45 nonrefundable application fee ($25 for online applications). An interview is not required but is strongly recommended. International students whose native language is not English must also submit TOEFL or IELTS scores. All students are expected to have followed the most competitive college-prep curriculum available to them at their high school. Transfer students must also send a transcript of all completed college work (if more than 28 semester units of college work have been completed, SAT/ACT scores are not required).

Application and Information

The Early Action (EA) deadline is November 15. The Regular Decision Round 1 deadline is January 15, and the Regular Decision Round 2 deadline is March 15. For additional information, interested students should contact:

Office of Admission
California Lutheran University
60 West Olsen Road #1350
Thousand Oaks, California 91360-2700
Phone: 805-493-3135
877-CLU-FOR-U (toll-free)
Fax: 805-493-3114
E-mail: admissions@CalLutheran.edu
Web site: http://www.CalLutheran.edu

At CLU, professors care passionately about teaching and students.

CALIFORNIA UNIVERSITY OF PENNSYLVANIA

CALIFORNIA, PENNSYLVANIA

The University

California University of Pennsylvania, a member of Pennsylvania's State System of Higher Education, traces its origin to the establishment of an academy in the town of California, Pennsylvania, in 1852. It has as its mission "Building character and building careers." California University began as a teacher-preparation school and has evolved into a multipurpose university that grants both undergraduate and graduate degrees.

Since 2006, California has been included annually in the *Princeton Review's* "Best Northeastern Colleges." California University was also included in the *Templeton Guide to Character Building Colleges* and the *Making a Difference College and Graduate Guide*, the distinctive guide for students who want to use their education to make a better world. The University adopted integrity, civility, and responsibility as its core values in 1998 and encourages all members of the community to aspire to these high ideals in order to make the University community, and the world, a better place.

The campus and recreational facilities, consisting of 190 acres with forty-six primary buildings, are nestled on a bend of the Monongahela River. The Natali Student Center, which is located in the center of the campus, houses the student information center, dining facilities, movie theater, convenience store, food court, bookstore, ATM machine, and a variety of student organizations, including the Commuter Center and the University radio (WCAL) and television (CUT) stations. The recreational complex, Roadman Park, is located less than 1½ miles from the campus. Tennis courts; running tracks; picnic areas; baseball, softball, rugby, and soccer fields; and the football stadium are located there.

The current enrollment is about 7,200 undergraduate and 1,800 graduate students. About 4,000 undergraduate students commute, 1,500 live on campus in six recently completed air-conditioned residence halls, 750 live off campus in a new garden-style apartment complex that is affiliated with the University, and the rest live in off-campus fraternity or sorority houses, rental units, or private homes.

At the University, students have the opportunity to select the living arrangement that best fits their personal needs and preferences. Lower-campus residence halls provide the perfect environment for being in the center of all academic and recreational activities. On-campus living also provides an environment that offers structure, with tremendous convenience to classrooms, dining, Natali Student Center, and Manderino Library. A variety of room configurations allow students to choose from 1, 2, or 3 roommates or suitemates.

Great for more independent living, the apartments at Vulcan Village are located less than 1½ miles from campus, adjacent to Roadman Park. There are a variety of configurations, most of which have private baths. Vulcan Village also provides a clubhouse with a fully equipped fitness center, a recreation room with various games, a computer lab, and a media room. Other amenities include an outdoor swimming pool and sand volleyball and basketball courts. A shuttle service connects Vulcan Village to the main campus.

The University offers students the convenience of an on-campus Health Center, which is staffed by registered nurses and a nurse practitioner. A medical director/physician has regularly scheduled office hours.

The Counseling Center, which is staffed by professionals, is available to all students and provides psychological services. The University also offers drug and alcohol education programs that include consultation, intervention, counseling, education, awareness programs, and substance-free activities.

Location

The campus is located in the borough of California, Pennsylvania, a community of 6,000 people. It is approximately 35 miles south of Pittsburgh in the foothills of the Allegheny Mountains, near Pennsylvania's Laurel Highlands recreational area. Professional baseball, football, and hockey, as well as a variety of cultural activities, are available in Pittsburgh. The area in which the University is located has a number of significant historical sites related to the pre–Revolutionary War era. The University also offers students the option of off-campus classes in Canonsburg at the Southpointe Technology Park.

Majors and Degrees

California University of Pennsylvania offers the following baccalaureate degree programs: Bachelor of Arts, Bachelor of Fine Arts, Bachelor of Science, Bachelor of Science in Athletic Training, Bachelor of Science in Education, Bachelor of Science in Nursing, and Bachelor of Science in Sports Management. Associate of Arts, Associate of Science, and Associate of Applied Science degrees are also offered.

The liberal arts majors include art, communication studies (language and literacy, public relations, radio/television, and speech concentrations available), criminal justice, English (creative writing, journalism, and literature concentrations available), French, graphic design, history, international studies (business and economics, geography, modern languages, and political science concentrations available), philosophy, political science (campaign management, prelaw, and public policy concentrations available), psychology (industrial-organizational psychology concentration available), sociology (applied sociology concentration available), Spanish, and theater.

The Bachelor of Science in Education includes majors in athletic training, communication disorders, early childhood education, elementary education, secondary education (art, biology, chemistry, communication, comprehensive social sciences, earth and space science, English, French, mathematics, physics, and Spanish), special education, and technology education. Dual majors are available in many education programs. The College of Education and Human Services also offers bachelor's degrees in gerontology, social work, and sport management, with concentrations in professional golf management and wellness and fitness.

The Eberly College of Science and Technology offers majors in the areas of administration and management, biology, business administration (accounting, business administration, business economics, computer-based systems management, finance, human resources management, management, and marketing), computer information systems, computer science, earth science, electrical engineering technology, environmental earth science, environmental studies (ecology, environmental science, and fisheries and wildlife concentrations) geography (geographic information systems and travel and tourism concentrations), geology, graphic communication technology, natural sciences (biology, chemistry, earth science, geology, mathematics, natural sciences interdisciplinary, and physics), parks and recreation management, and pre–health professions (pre–chiropractic medicine, predentistry, premedicine, pre–mortuary science, preoptometry, pre–osteopathic medicine, prepharmacy, pre–podiatric medicine, and pre–veterinary medicine). A cooperative nursing program is offered with the Community College of Allegheny County. The

University offers an upper-division Bachelor of Science in Nursing degree program for students who have completed an RN program.

Academic Programs

Each bachelor's degree requires a minimum of 120 semester hours of credit. A general education requirement of 51 credits is distributed among the following areas: building a sense of community (1 credit), communication skills (9 credits), critical-thinking skills (3 credits), fine arts (3 credits), health and wellness (3 credits), humanities (3 credits), mathematics (3 credits), multicultural awareness (3 credits), natural sciences (8 credits), social sciences (6 credits), technological literacy (6 credits), and values (3 credits). An honors program provides an opportunity for an enhanced educational experience to students who meet the criteria. Honors students have the option of living in the new Honors Residence Hall, which offers numerous outstanding amenities, including a private library. Wireless Internet connections are available throughout campus. Applications of all incoming first-year and transfer students are reviewed, and those with the highest indicators of past and future academic success are invited to participate in the honors program.

Academic Facilities

The University has traditional library holdings of more than 360,000 volumes, more than 1 million microform units, nearly 1,500 periodical titles, and U.S. government documents. It is a member of the Keystone Library Network, which provides access to library holdings, databases, and electronic resources among fourteen State System of Higher Education libraries. This virtual library electronically links users to a variety of information sources and delivers both text and multimedia sources immediately and seamlessly from any location. The 80,400-square-foot Eberly Science and Technology Center features state-of-the-art science and computer laboratories and is one of the premier teaching facilities on campus. Every residence hall room is wired with fiber optics so that students can bring computers, plug them in, and have immediate access to the Internet and all its resources. For students who do not have computers of their own, there is a computer lab on every floor of the residence halls. Numerous specialized computer facilities are available across the campus, including ones devoted to meteorology, math and computer science, word processing, accounting, CAD-CAM, robotics, teacher education, art, and chemistry.

Costs

The 2009–10 tuition for a resident of Pennsylvania attending full-time (12 to 18 credits) was $2777 per semester. For a full-time nonresident, tuition was $4444 per semester. Room costs for 2009–10 ranged from $2853 to $4162. Board prices ranged from $1284 to $1576. Based on a full-time schedule, fees for 2009–10 included a $103 technology fee, an $85 service fee, a $260 Student Association fee, an $81 student union building fee, an $84 student center operations and maintenance fee, and a $277 academic support fee. The cost of books, materials, and supplies varies with each program.

Financial Aid

California University of Pennsylvania has available a number of types of financial aid, including student employment, grant and scholarship aid through the Pennsylvania Higher Education Assistance Agency, federal grants, and student loans. A number of non-need-based academic scholarships are available for talented students. All students must complete the Pennsylvania State Grant and federal financial aid application for need-based aid. The Director of Financial Aid at the University administers all student aid. Overall, 98 percent of student need is met for students who are awarded need-based aid.

Faculty

Classes are taught by nearly 300 full-time faculty members; no classes are taught by graduate assistants. Terminal degrees are held by more than 78 percent of the full-time faculty members. Faculty advisers are assigned based on the student's major, department, or school.

Student Government

Student government at California University of Pennsylvania regulates cocurricular activities. It furthers the quality of student life by encouraging and funding diverse student activities, providing experiences in the principles and practices of democratic government, supplying a forum for general student interest, and improving and promoting the cultural standards of the University. Students sit on many important University committees, including the University Forum, and have a voice in most policy decisions.

Admission Requirements

California University of Pennsylvania welcomes applications from all qualified persons. Admission standards have been established by California University of Pennsylvania for the purpose of ascertaining which prospective students are most likely to succeed at the University. An applicant for admission should have graduated from an accredited four-year high school or should possess an equivalency diploma issued by a state department of education. All applicants should submit to the University evidence of their ability to do college-level work, as indicated by such tests as the College Board's SAT. All applicants are required to have a Social Security number.

Application and Information

Prospective students should obtain, complete, and return an application form, along with the Secondary School Record (which is completed by the high school guidance counselor). A nonrefundable application fee of $25 must accompany the application. Students can apply and pay online at the University's Web site. A student who would like to transfer to California University of Pennsylvania should complete the application form (hard copy or online) and forward it to the Admissions Office with a nonrefundable check or money order for $25 or pay online. Official transcripts from all colleges and universities attended must be sent to the Admissions Office.

For additional information regarding admission, students should contact:

Dr. William Edmonds
Director of Admissions
California University of Pennsylvania
250 University Avenue
California, Pennsylvania 15419
Phone: 724-938-4404
888-412-0479 (toll-free)
E-mail: inquiry@calu.edu
Web site: http://www.calu.edu

Students on the campus of California University of Pennsylvania.

CALVIN COLLEGE
GRAND RAPIDS, MICHIGAN

The College

Calvin College is an institution that values both intellect and faith; this view affects every area of campus life, from the content of each course to service-learning opportunities and life in the residence halls. Calvin is one of the nation's largest and most respected Christian colleges. The 2009 fall enrollment was 4,092. Calvin maintains a strong affiliation with the Christian Reformed Church, and students from more than fifty other church denominations across North America and around the world choose Calvin for its unique curriculum and faith-based mission.

Calvin is deeply committed to being a diverse community and is taking deliberate steps to increase opportunities for women, members of underrepresented minority groups, and students with disabilities. At Calvin, students are challenged not only to obtain an outstanding education and to prepare for a career but also to live lives of commitment and service.

Students come from nearly every state and forty-eight countries. Most students are between 18 and 22 years old; however, those pursuing the Master of Education (M.Ed.) add to the age diversity on campus. The Broene Counseling Center offers career counseling and career resource services as well as personal counseling. Career Development assists students from their first year through their last, equipping them for interviews, internships, and searching for full-time employment upon graduation.

A wide variety of co-curricular opportunities are available, including music, theater, athletics, art, culture, service, and campus ministries. Calvin's Service-Learning Center provides opportunities for academically based service learning in addition to such programs as big brothers/big sisters, services for the elderly, and school tutoring. Calvin is an NCAA Division III school and participates in the Michigan Intercollegiate Athletic Association; Calvin's athletic teams regularly are ranked nationally in Division III. The men's basketball team won the national championship in 1992 and 2000; the women's cross-country team captured the national championship in 1998 and 1999 and took second place honors in 2008. In 2000, 2003, 2004, and 2007, the men's cross-country team won the national championship. The men's ice-hockey club won the 2004 ACHA DIII national championship.

The 400-acre campus is a modern, well-planned community; its oldest academic building was erected in 1960. Fifteen residence halls, eleven apartment buildings, and two spacious dining halls accommodate 2,600 resident students. High-speed computing is available throughout the campus, and wireless service is offered in the residence halls and many campus locations. Calvin's new $55-million athletic complex features a 5,000-seat arena, an indoor track and tennis center, a health center, and an aquatics center with a 50-meter by 25-yard pool. Calvin's outdoor athletic sites include baseball and softball diamonds, a premier soccer field with seating for 1,500 and two practice fields, an eight-lane track, a six-court tennis facility, a paved jogging path, and two sand volleyball courts.

Location

Calvin's beautifully wooded campus, which includes a 100-acre ecosystem preserve, is located in the suburbs of Grand Rapids, a metropolitan area of more than 600,000 people. Hundreds of restaurants, dozens of theaters, seven shopping malls, and a fine selection of museums and parks are within a short drive. Lake Michigan beaches, ski areas, parks, and trails are within a 40-minute drive. Cultural and community activities take place weekly on the Calvin campus, on the campuses of six other local colleges, and at DeVos Hall and VanAndel Arena in downtown Grand Rapids. City bus routes include a stop at Calvin's campus.

Majors and Degrees

The Bachelor of Arts and Bachelor of Science degrees are offered, with major concentrations in accounting, art, art history, Asian studies, biochemistry, biology, biotechnology, business, chemistry, Chinese, classical civilization, classical languages, communication arts and sciences, computer science, digital communications, Dutch, early childhood education, economics, elementary and secondary education, engineering, English, environmental science, environmental studies, exercise science, film studies, French, geography, geology, German, Greek, health education, history, information systems, international development studies, international relations, Japanese, Latin, mathematics and statistics, media production, media studies, music, nursing, philosophy, physical education, physics/astronomy, political science, psychology, public administration, recreation, religion, social work, sociology, Spanish, special education, speech pathology and audiology, sport management, and theater. The Bachelor of Fine Arts (B.F.A.) degree in art is offered in addition to the B.A. degree in art.

Professional programs include engineering (chemical, civil/environmental, electrical/computer, mechanical), natural resources, prearchitecture, prelaw, premedicine/predentistry, prepharmacy, pre–physical therapy, pre–seminary studies, social work, and elementary, secondary, and special education. Minor concentrations are available in African and African diaspora studies, archaeology, congregational studies, dance, English as a second language, gender studies, journalism, medieval studies, ministry studies, missions, urban studies, writing, and youth ministry leadership. Calvin offers a Master of Education degree (M. Ed); a master's program in speech pathology is pending accreditation.

Academic Programs

Calvin College maintains a strong commitment to a liberal arts curriculum as an integral way to help students understand God's world and their place in it. The College follows a 4-1-4 academic calendar, consisting of two four-month semesters with a three-week January Interim term. Graduation requires the successful completion of 124 semester hours.

Calvin's core curriculum begins with a first-year gateway course, Developing a Christian Mind, and ends with a capstone course in the senior year. Core curriculum requirements include foreign language, history, literature and arts, mathematics, natural sciences, philosophy, physical education, religion, social sciences, and written and spoken rhetoric. Some requirements can be satisfied by advanced high school work in foreign language, literature, and natural sciences. Qualified students can earn course exemption and/or credit by completing college-level work in high school or by examination. Satisfactory scores on Advanced Placement (AP), International Baccalaureate (I.B.), and/or CLEP exams are also accepted.

Incoming students with an ACT composite of at least 29 who are interested in nursing and meet other admissions requirements will receive automatic admission to Calvin's nursing program. Incoming students with an ACT composite of at least 29 or current Calvin students with a grade point average of 3.3 or higher are invited to participate in the Honors Program for advanced-level courses, interdisciplinary courses, and co-curricular opportunities. Students can also benefit from services offered by the Office of Student Academic Services, which provides academic counseling, tutoring, training in study skills, and review courses in key subjects.

Off-Campus Programs

Study-abroad programs for a semester or a year are offered in Austria, Belize, China, Costa Rica, France, Germany, Ghana, Great Britain, Honduras, Hungary, Japan, the Netherlands, and Spain. Students register for courses in various subjects, and the credits earned are applied toward graduation requirements. The Chicago Semes-

ter program, the Oregon Extension Program, and the Au Sable Institute of Environmental Studies are offered in cooperation with Calvin and other colleges. Students can also participate in programs of the Council for Christian Colleges and Universities: the American Studies Program in Washington, D.C.; the Latin American Studies Program in Central America; a Film Studies Program in Hollywood; a Middle East Studies Program in Cairo, Egypt; and a Russian Studies Program in Moscow. Calvin's Study in Spain Program is one option students may choose to fulfill their foreign language requirement. Many courses offered during the Interim are also taught abroad.

Academic Facilities

The four-floor Science Complex features a center core of laboratories, an atom trapper, and an observatory. The Engineering Building provides space for engineering students and faculty members to do research, design work and project construction. The DeVries Hall of Science includes medical research laboratories and classrooms. The Spoelhof College Center houses administrative offices, a social research center, an art gallery, six art studios, and a 340-seat auditorium. The Covenant Fine Arts Center is scheduled to reopen in the fall of 2010, with additional spaces for classes, music rehearsals and performances, and art exhibitions.

The Hekman Library–Hiemenga Hall complex includes a five-level, computerized library containing more than 800,000 bound volumes, 2,750 periodicals, an extensive collection of microfiche, records and tapes, and government publications; more than 1,500 students can be comfortably seated at study carrels and tables. The complex also houses the Information Technology Center, the Calvin Center for Christian Scholarship, the Meeter Center for Calvinism Studies, a distance learning classroom, a TV studio, a graphics production lab, and a curriculum center for teacher education students. The 55,000-square-foot DeVos Communications Center is home to a 150-seat video theater, a television studio, an audio studio, digital audio and video editing labs, and a speech pathology and audiology clinic. The Prince Conference Center houses seminars, meetings, and retreats.

Costs

Tuition and fees for 2009–10 were $23,810; tuition for the Interim was free for full-time students enrolled for at least one semester. Room and board charges were $8275 for resident students with a twenty-one-meal-per-week plan (ten- and fifteen-meal-per-week plans are also available). About $800 is needed for textbooks.

Financial Aid

Over 70 percent of first year students are awarded an academic scholarship in amounts ranging from $10,000 to $1,000. Sixty percent of Calvin students receive need-based financial aid; demonstrated need is the most important criterion in determining eligibility. Students wishing to be considered for financial aid must be admitted to the College and must submit the Free Application for Federal Student Aid (FAFSA) and Calvin's Supplemental Application for Financial Aid. February 15 is the filing deadline for maximum consideration. Financial awards to eligible applicants consist of state and federal grants, loans, Federal Work-Study Program funds, and institutional grants and scholarships. Part-time employment is available on campus, and placement preference is given to students with financial need. Calvin's Student Employment Office also helps students find off-campus employment.

Faculty

Calvin's outstanding faculty members have distinguished themselves through publication and research, yet each is available 10–15 hours per week outside of class for academic and personal counseling. More than 81 percent have earned the highest academic degree in their field. Each faculty member is a professing Christian, committed to the integration of his or her personal faith and discipline. There are over 320 full-time and 98 part-time faculty members; the faculty-student ratio is 1:12.

Student Government

The 27-member Student Senate supervises most student activities and oversees the budgets for student publications, homecoming, the film arts, and the Service-Learning Center. Student members serve on most faculty committees governing the College. Each residence hall has its own governing council and judiciary committee. Campus rules are designed to build a Christian academic community. Calvin attempts to aid student development and responsible action by clearly expressing its expectations and de-emphasizing regulations.

Admission Requirements

Applicants should be graduates of an accredited high school program and should have completed satisfactorily at least 15 units of college-preparatory work, including 3 in English and 3 in algebra and geometry. Applicants with high school averages of C+ (2.5) or higher who score above 20 on the ACT composite or above 470 on both the math and critical reading sections of the SAT are normally given regular admission. Applicants with lower grades and scores, or those with deficiencies in their high school preparation, may be admitted under special conditions. International students should refer to http://www.calvin.edu/international for application procedures. Students who come from a non-English-speaking culture must submit results of the TOEFL or IELTS or provide other documentation of English-language proficiency.

Application and Information

Applicants must submit a completed application form, a high school or college transcript, results of either the ACT or SAT, and an educational recommendation completed by a teacher or counselor. Admission decisions are made on a rolling basis beginning in mid-October. Applicants for fall admission are urged to complete their file before February 1; the deadline for admission is August 15 for U.S. and Canadian applicants and April 1 for international applicants, as long as space is available. Students and parents are strongly encouraged to visit the campus. The "Fridays at Calvin" campus visit program provides an excellent opportunity to experience life at Calvin firsthand. For more information about Calvin or to register for a visit, students should contact:

Office of Admissions and Financial Aid
Calvin College
3201 Burton Street, SE
Grand Rapids, Michigan 49546
Phone: 616-526-6106 (admissions)
616-526-6134 (financial aid)
616-526-8480 (TTY)
800-688-0122 (toll-free in North America)
Fax: 616-526-6777
E-mail: admissions@calvin.edu
finaid@calvin.edu
Web site: http://www.calvin.edu

Recognized as one of the finest research libraries in western Michigan, the Hekman Library is a hub of student and faculty activity on the Calvin College campus.

COLLEGE CLOSE-UPS

CAMPBELL UNIVERSITY

BUIES CREEK, NORTH CAROLINA

The University

Founded in 1887, Campbell University has the distinction of being North Carolina's second-largest private undergraduate institution. In 1979, the name of the institution was changed from Campbell College to Campbell University. Its current enrollment for all campuses is about 9,600 students. There are more than 4,300 students at the main campus in Buies Creek. In an average year, Campbell attracts students from all 100 North Carolina counties, all fifty states, and fifty other countries. Seventy-five percent of the students come from North Carolina. Members of minority groups make up 25 percent of the student body.

Campbell University is Baptist affiliated. Approximately 48 percent of its students are Baptist, but young people of twenty-three other faiths complete the student body. It is concerned with maintaining, for living and learning, an environment consistent with Christian ideals. Among the extracurricular activities available at Campbell are band, choir, and drama groups; religious, political, professional, social, and academic groups; and intercollegiate sports, campus recreation, intramural sports, and club sports.

In athletics, the University is a member of NCAA Division I (Athletic Sun Conference) for men and women (with the exception of football, swimming, and wrestling). Men's sports include baseball, basketball, cheerleading, cross-country, football, golf, soccer, tennis, track and field, and wrestling. Women's sports include basketball, cheerleading, cross-country, golf, soccer, softball, swimming, tennis, track and field, and volleyball.

The $30-million John W. Pope Jr. Convocation Center was completed in 2008. The facility can house 3,000 spectators for athletic events and up to 5,000 for special concerts and graduation ceremonies. Phase I of the Barker-Lane Stadium was completed in 2008. Seating will be available for an estimated 10,000 students and visitors when the stadium is completed.

A number of activities are available on campus during the summer for school-age students. Campbell University hosts an array of camps, including band, basketball, golf, volleyball, and others. During the ten-week period, Campbell accommodates more than 5,000 students.

The University also has campuses offering a variety of undergraduate and graduate courses at Fort Bragg, Morrisville (RTP), Pope AFB, and Camp Lejuene, North Carolina.

Location

Buies Creek is a small, well-kept residential community in Harnett County, where North Carolina's coastal plain and Piedmont meet just east of the center of the state. The region is one of the most progressive for education and research in the Southeast. Campbell's main campus is just a 45-minute drive south of Raleigh, the state's capital; and 30 minutes north of Fayetteville. Students are also within an hour's drive of Research Triangle Park and the city of Durham.

Majors and Degrees

Campbell University confers seven undergraduate degrees: Bachelor of Arts, Bachelor of Science, Bachelor of Applied Science, Bachelor of Business Administration, Bachelor of Health Science, and Bachelor of Social Work and an Associate in Arts degree. The major, minor, track, and/or concentration may be in any one of the following fields: accounting, advertising, art, athletic training, biblical studies, biochemistry, biological sciences, biology, birth–kindergarten, broadcasting and electronic media, business administration, chemistry, Christian history, Christian ministry, church music, clinical research, communication studies, comprehensive music, criminal justice administration, drama and Christian ministry, economics, education, educational studies (no licensure), elementary education, English, environmental science, exercise science, exercise and sport science, financial planning, fitness/wellness management, French, general science, government, graphic design, health and physical education, health communications, history, homeland security, honors interdisciplinary minor, information security, information technology management, information technology and security, international business, international studies, K–12 education, journalism, kinesiology, mathematics, middle grades education, military science, music, music composition, music education, PGA golf management, pharmaceutical sciences, piano pedagogy, political science, predentistry, pre-engineering, prelaw, premedicine, preoptometry, prepharmacy, pre–physical therapy, pre–physician's assistant studies, preprofessional, pre–veterinary science, psychology, public administration, public policy, public relations, religion, secondary education, social science, social work, Spanish, special education, sport business program, sport management, studio art, study abroad, teaching fellows, theater arts, trust and wealth management, and U.S. Army ROTC.

Academic Programs

The curriculum of Campbell University is designed to meet students' individual needs and interests. During their first two years, students follow a general course of study, the General College Curriculum, to broaden their backgrounds in the basic fields of knowledge. By the end of their sophomore year, they should have selected a major subject for specialized study during their final two years. Basic curriculum requirements for the first two years in semester hours are math, 6; English, 12; social studies, 6; natural science, 8; religion, 6; music, art appreciation, or drama, 3; foreign language, up to 9, depending on high school credits and the program of study; and health and physical education, 3. Candidates for a degree must earn a minimum of 128 semester hours, including the 3 in health and physical education, while maintaining at least a C average in academic course work; must complete a minimum of 32 semester hours in the departmental major at Campbell; and must average C or better in all courses required for the major. Candidates for the Associate in Arts degree must complete 64 semester hours of work and have at least a 2.0 GPA on all work required for graduation and at least a 2.0 GPA on 80 percent of all work attempted. The University calendar enables students to complete first-semester course work and examinations before Christmas vacation and end the spring session by the middle of May.

Campbell offers a complete curriculum of evening courses at its nearby RTP and Fort Bragg campuses. The Fort Bragg campus is primarily a service for military personnel on active duty, but classes are open to civilian students.

Campbell offers the nation's first undergraduate program in trust and wealth management and since 1968 has been training prospective trust officers for the banks and trust companies of the region. Campbell also sponsors the Southeastern Trust School, a summer institute for trust officers.

Campbell's College of Pharmacy and Health Sciences has served the health-care needs of North Carolina and beyond for more than twenty years, paving the path for minority student recruitment and education enhancement through the Advancement for Underrepresented Minority Pharmacists Program. The school's curriculum is designed to focus on Pharmacy College Admission Test preparation, educational seminars, and a mentoring program in order to better prepare students for a career in pharmacy. Campbell's pharmacy students have maintained a 99 percent passage rate on the national board exams and 99 percent on state board exams.

Campbell's School of Education was established in 1985 in response to the need for fully qualified educators for the educational system of North Carolina and the country. School of Education students continue their history of academic excellence, posting a passage rate for the Praxis II exam of 98 percent in 2009. The School of

Education was selected as a North Carolina Teaching Fellow School, joining thirteen public and four private institutions across the state.

The Military Science Department offers Army Reserve Officer Training Corps (ROTC) classes, leading to a commission as an officer in the Active, Reserve, or National Guard component of the United States Army. Campbell's ROTC program is one of the best in the nation, earning the MacArthur Award three times since 1989 as the premier leadership-training program in the nation. It has also been recognized an additional five times as a part of the winning regional brigade. This annual award is given jointly by the MacArthur Foundation and the U.S. Army Cadet Command. The Campbell training program is one of the best preparations possible for the nation's future leaders.

Off-Campus Programs

Credit may be earned in off-campus settings through apprenticeships or internships in communications, government, public education, religious education, psychology, social work, trust management, and other fields. Campbell's philosophy on internships is department based. Departmental inquiries are welcomed. The American Studies Program in Washington, D.C.; the Los Angeles Film Studies Center in Hollywood, California; and the Summer Institute of Journalism, also in Washington, D.C., each offer a semester-long internship program. New study-abroad opportunities also allow students to study in Costa Rica, England (Oxford), Hawaii, and Tanzania.

Academic Facilities

The $11-million Lundy-Fetterman School of Business building provides 76,000 square feet of space for state-of-the-art classrooms, a computer lab, several breakout rooms, and a library. The Leslie H. Campbell Hall of Science provides the individual student with newly renovated lab facilities for research projects, which the University encourages in four sciences. Campbell's own computer center is supplemented by more than twenty departmental labs offering both PC and Macintosh computers. It is linked with the Triangle Universities Computation Center of the North Carolina Educational Computer Service. Campbell's Carrie Rich Library houses a collection of more than 218,000 volumes, in addition to interlibrary loans and microforms; breakout rooms for group study; and laptop computers that may be checked out by students. The D. Rich Memorial Building, housing Turner Auditorium, and the four-story Fred L. Taylor Hall of Religion contain classrooms and faculty offices. The Taylor Bott Rogers Fine Arts Complex, containing 48,820 square feet of space, is well equipped for the wide range of events staged by active music, drama, and art groups. A 7,000-square-foot, $4-million research facility supports the Master of Science programs in pharmaceutical sciences and clinical research. Maddox Hall, a new $7.7-million College of Pharmacy and Health Sciences teaching facility, offers 42,000 square feet dedicated to pharmacy students. Keith Hills housing development and golf course provides a 27-hole course for students and the community.

Costs

The 2010–11 comprehensive fee for tuition and general fees is $22,520. On-campus room and board starts at $7800.

Financial Aid

Campbell University has private and institutional scholarships, federal grants, loans, and Federal Work-Study Program awards. Loans are available through the Federal Stafford Student Loan Program and the Federal Perkins Loan Program. Needs analysis forms (Free Application for Federal Student Aid) are available on January 1 and are due in the Financial Aid Office by March 15 if the applicant wishes to be considered for a maximum award. Eighty-eight percent of the student body received financial assistance in 2009–10. All assistance is offered without regard to race, creed, or national origin.

Faculty

The faculty consists of 193 professors, of whom approximately 89 percent have earned the doctorate or the highest degree in their field. Eighty-one percent of classes have fewer than 50 students. Campbell's student-faculty ratio is 18:1.

Student Government

Through the Student Government Association (SGA), the student body has an opportunity for self-government and a means to channel ideas and wishes to the proper administrative personnel. The SGA is composed of executive, judicial, and legislative branches. The executive officers are the president, vice president, secretary, treasurer, parliamentarian, chaplain, representatives of men's and women's communities, and a representative for commuting students. The legislative branch includes the Student Congress, made up of representatives from each of the four classes elected by popular vote.

Admission Requirements

The minimum requirements for admission to Campbell include graduation from high school or equivalent credentials, with at least 13 nonvocational units, which must include 4 in English, 3 in college-preparatory mathematics (including 2 of algebra and 1 of geometry), 2 in social sciences (1 must be in United States history), and 2 in natural sciences (1 must be a laboratory science). Two units of a foreign language are highly desirable. Acceptable scores must be earned on the SAT or the ACT.

Application and Information

An application for admission, accompanied by a $35 nonrefundable application fee, must be filed. Students may also apply online. When all records are on file, the Admissions Committee notifies the student of its decision. Application forms and further information may be requested from:

Office of Admissions
Campbell University
P.O. Box 546
Buies Creek, North Carolina 27506
Phone: 910-893-1290
910-893-1417 (international)
800-334-4111 (toll-free)
E-mail: adm@campbell.edu
Web site: http://www.campbell.edu/

Students on the lawn in front of the Fine Arts Complex and Lundy-Fetterman School of Business/Folwell Fountain.

COLLEGE CLOSE-UPS

CANISIUS COLLEGE

BUFFALO, NEW YORK

The College

Canisius College offers the best in high-quality academic programs and facilities as well as outstanding faculty members who are leaders in their fields. With more than seventy distinct majors, minors, and special programs and an exciting urban location to support internships and out-of-class experiences, Canisius College prepares students for success. Canisius is a place where leaders are made.

Canisius College offers a state-of-the-art campus with enhanced technology in academic and living facilities. Canisius housing is like a home away from home, not just a temporary living accommodation. Bosch and Frisch Residence Halls, which were recently renovated, and Dugan Hall, which opened in 2005, are the primary residences for first-year students at Canisius. Apartment-style living is available to sophomores, juniors, and seniors in one of the many town-house complexes and apartment buildings on campus. Specialty housing options include George Martin Honors Hall, available to students in the All-College Honors Program, and the Intercultural Living Center, a learning community residence for international and U.S. students. All campus housing is equipped with high-speed, wireless Internet access and cable television.

Students have opportunities to develop leadership skills through involvement in student clubs and organizations, research, and service learning. There is something for everyone at Canisius. There are more than 100 college-sponsored student clubs and organizations and a wide range of athletic teams from which to choose. The students are not only leaders in the classroom but also on the NCAA Division I athletic field. Most of the sixteen Golden Griffin teams compete in the Metro Atlantic Athletic Conference (MAAC), in which a majority of the champions receive an entry into their respective NCAA tournaments. Since joining the MAAC in 1989, men's basketball, baseball, women's cross-country, men's lacrosse, men's soccer, and softball have claimed conference titles.

Location

Canisius College's urban setting is a significant advantage for students who are seeking internship, research, and service learning opportunities because of the proximity to a wide range of businesses and organizations.

Canisius is located on 62 acres in a residential neighborhood in north-central Buffalo. Buffalo is a great college town that has it all: professional sports teams, a world-renowned art gallery, historic architecture, and scenic parks and waterways all within minutes from campus.

The internationally known Albright-Knox Art Gallery holds one of the world's finest collections of nineteenth- and twentieth-century American and European works of art. Buffalo is also home to the Buffalo Philharmonic Orchestra and the Studio Arena Theatre, which provides a wide variety of theater experiences.

The Metro Rail rapid transit system connects the College with some of Buffalo's most exciting venues, including HSBC Arena, home of the National Hockey League's Buffalo Sabres. The arena also hosts college basketball with Canisius' Golden Griffins as well as major popular and rock music concerts. During the summer, students can catch Buffalo Bisons Triple-A baseball games at Dunn Tire Park. At Ralph Wilson Stadium, in Orchard Park, the Buffalo Bills are a focal point throughout the football season.

The Buffalo Zoo and Delaware Park, a 350-acre park with a lake and a golf course, are located less than a mile from the campus.

Majors and Degrees

The College of Arts and Sciences is the largest and most diverse of Canisius' three academic divisions, with majors in the natural and social sciences, humanities, and preprofessional studies. It also houses the core curriculum, which strengthens fundamental critical thinking, oral, and written communication skills and helps enhance students' understanding of other cultures. The College of Arts and Sciences offers programs leading to bachelor's degrees in anthropology, art history, biochemistry, bioinformatics, biology, chemistry, clinical laboratory science, communication studies, computer science, criminal justice, digital media arts, economics, English, environmental science, European studies, history, international relations, mathematics and statistics, modern languages (French, German, and Spanish), music, philosophy, physics, political science, psychology, religious studies and theology, sociology, and urban studies.

The Richard J. Wehle School of Business offers a well-rounded business curriculum to complement the liberal arts courses in the major, which gives the student an understanding of the broad and interrelated nature of business issues. There are programs leading to the B.S. degree in accounting, accounting information systems, economics, entrepreneurship, finance, information systems, international business, management, and marketing. All the business programs are accredited by the AACSB International–The Association to Advance Collegiate Schools of Business.

The School of Education and Human Services offers degrees that lead to teacher certification at the early childhood, childhood, middle childhood, or adolescent level, such as adolescence education, athletic training/sports medicine, childhood education, early childhood education, physical education, and special education. All programs are accredited by the National Council for Accreditation of Teacher Education (NCATE).

Canisius also offers diverse and flexible academic programs, such as fashion merchandising (in conjunction with the Fashion Institute of Technology), fine arts, and military science, and certification programs in gerontology and women's studies. Preprofessional programs are available in dentistry, engineering, law, medicine, pharmacy, and veterinary medicine. Canisius also has an early assurance of admission agreement for New York State residents, with the Schools of Medicine and Dental Medicine of SUNY at Buffalo and SUNY Medical School at Syracuse. Seven-year joint-degree programs exist between Canisius and the SUNY Buffalo School of Dental Medicine, the Ohio College of Podiatric Medicine, the New York College of Podiatric Medicine, the SUNY College of Optometry, and the Lake Erie College of Osteopathic Medicine. A new five-year engineering degree program with SUNY at Buffalo and Penn State Behrend allows students to get a bachelor's degree from Canisius and the other institution, and a five-year combined-degree program leads to the B.A. in a major in one of the liberal arts disciplines and a Master of Business Administration degree.

Academic Programs

To earn a bachelor's degree from Canisius College, students must complete forty courses and a minimum of 120 credit hours. Within each curriculum, the courses are distributed into three areas: core curriculum, major field requirements, and free electives. The College requires that students complete a rounded program of humanistic studies embracing literature, the physical and social sciences, oral and written communication, philosophy, history, and religious studies.

The All-College Honors Program is available for qualified students. This program includes rigorous exploration of the arts and sciences in an enriched curriculum with close faculty supervision and small classes. Students may also obtain college credit through the Advanced Placement Program of the College Board, the International Baccalaureate Program or through college courses offered in their high schools. Students with scores of 3 or better on Advanced

Placement tests, 4 or better on International Baccalaureate tests or grades of C or better in college-level courses are considered for credit and advanced standing.

Off-Campus Programs

Many Canisius students choose to spend a semester or a year studying abroad, improving their fluency in another language, and opening the doors to exciting personal and professional opportunities. Canisius administers semester-abroad programs in Australia, Belgium, China, El Salvador, England, France, Germany, Ireland, Italy, Japan, Puerto Rico, Spain, and Sweden. Service immersion experiences also allow students to gain community service experience in the Appalachia region, Jamaica, El Salvador, India , Mexico, New York City, and Poland. The Office of International Student Programs assists students in selecting a study-abroad program, organizes a predeparture orientation, and assists students upon their return to the United States.

Students majoring in international relations and political science may participate in programs in Washington, D.C., or Albany, New York, which have been designed to give students practical experience in their fields.

Academic Facilities

Canisius has invested nearly $120 million over the last thirteen years to create state-of-the-art technology classrooms, residence halls, and cultural and recreational spaces. In addition, the campus provides wireless access in every building and residence hall. Instructional computing facilities include duel-platform computers located in general-purpose labs and teaching labs. The College offers fifty laptops students can check out for use within the library as well as e-mail and Internet stations at various convenient locations on campus.

Costs

For the academic year 2009–10, tuition and fees were $29,512, and room and board were $10,556. Books and supplies were estimated to cost $700. An additional $1130 per year was recommended for travel and personal expenses.

Financial Aid

Of the class of 2012, 98 percent receive some form of financial aid, and the average award is $23,219. This aid includes Canisius College scholarships and grants, state grants, state and federal loans, federal grants, and Federal Work-Study Program awards. Applications for financial aid should be completed by February 15. The Free Application for Federal Student Aid (FAFSA) and the TAP application (New York State residents only) must be filed before consideration can be given to applicants.

Faculty

The Canisius College faculty consists of 226 full-time teachers, including Jesuits and laymen and women. More than 94 percent hold doctorates or other terminal degrees. The primary emphasis of the faculty members is teaching, and many serve as academic advisers. The student-faculty ratio is 12:1.

Student Government

The Undergraduate Student Association comprises the entire undergraduate student body and is represented by elected officers who serve on the Student Senate. The senate assists and supervises student activities and advocates on behalf of the students, presenting their views to the College administration. In addition, students serve on many College committees.

Admission Requirements

Students' applications for admission are evaluated on a combination of factors, including a student's academic ability, strength of character, high school record, rank in class, an essay, aptitude tests (SAT or ACT), extracurricular activities, and recommendations. An applicant to the College is encouraged to pursue a challenging college-preparatory program in high school. This program of studies should include a minimum of 16 units of credit in the academic subjects of English, foreign language, mathematics, science, and social studies. Recommendations from teachers or school counselors are strongly encouraged, and they are considered in reviewing applications for admission. Campus interviews are strongly recommended and in some cases may be required.

Transfer students are welcome and are admitted to Canisius in the fall and spring semesters. In addition to meeting the academic standards required of all entering students, transfer students are considered for admission if they have a minimum 2.0 cumulative quality point average when transferring from either a two-year or a four-year accredited institution.

Canisius College does not discriminate on the basis of age, race, religion or creed, color, sex, national or ethnic origin, sexual orientation, marital status, veteran's status, genetic predisposition or carrier status, or disability in administration of its educational policies, employment practices, admissions policies, scholarship and loan programs, and athletic and other school-administered programs.

Application and Information

Students are encouraged to submit their applications for admission in the fall of their senior year in high school. Application forms are available from the Office of Admissions, or fee-waived applications can be found on the Web at http://www.canisius.edu/admissions. Students may also apply using the Common Application. The completed application form should be presented to the high school counselor, to be forwarded to the Office of Admissions with an official high school transcript, SAT or ACT scores, and any letters of recommendation. Arrangements for interviews may be made by contacting the Office of Admissions at least one week in advance of the desired date for a visit.

Canisius considers applications under a rolling admission policy. Students applying by November 15 are notified of admission decision by December 15, along with scholarship notification. Students are encouraged to apply no later than March 1 for full and equal consideration.

For application forms and additional information, students should contact:

Admissions Office
Canisius College
2001 Main Street
Buffalo, New York 14208
Phone: 716-888-2200
800-843-1517 (toll-free)
Fax: 716-888-3230
E-mail: admissions@canisius.edu
Web site: http://www.canisius.edu/admissions

Canisius College is the ideal size for each individual to be an important part of campus life.

CAPITAL UNIVERSITY

COLUMBUS, OHIO

The University

Since its founding in 1830 by the Lutheran Church, Capital University has earned a reputation for academic excellence and affordability, an accomplishment that earned Capital recognition as one of the top regional universities by *U.S. News & World Report.* The University's undergraduate and graduate programs combine personal attention with a balanced liberal arts and professional studies education to prepare students for lifelong learning, leadership, and service. Students also benefit from the attention faculty and staff members pay to their moral, social, and ethical development. Students at Capital are part of the "CAP Family," a family that cares about the total growth and well-being of each of its members.

Five schools comprise The College at Capital University: the Conservatory of Music and School of Communication; the School of Humanities; the School of Management and Leadership; the School of Natural Sciences, Nursing, and Health; and the School of Social Sciences and Education. In addition to the 60 majors and 40 minors available to undergraduates, graduate students can earn master's degrees in business, music education and nursing, as well as the juris doctor and four other advanced degrees from Capital University Law School. The university also offers adult learners an opportunity to balance their lives and their goals as they complete their undergraduate degree through the Center for Lifelong Learning. Of the approximately 3,600 students enrolled at Capital, more than 1,800 are traditional undergraduates. Approximately 65 percent of these students reside on campus in the University's six residence halls, including suite-style housing and apartments for upperclass students.

There are more than seventy student organizations, including a number of musical groups that are open to music and nonmusic majors alike. Other opportunities for involvement include preprofessional groups, theater, the student newspaper, departmental organizations, and the debate team. Numerous opportunities for volunteerism and service projects also exist. Approximately 20 percent of Capital's undergraduates are members of the nine social fraternities and sororities on campus.

There is an active and influential student government on the Capital campus. Students are elected in campuswide elections each spring. Through this organization, students have the opportunity to gain leadership experiences.

As a university affiliated with the Evangelical Lutheran Church in America, Capital believes that the religious, social, racial, and ethnic diversity found on campus enhances each student's development. In this spirit, worship, study, and extracurricular opportunities are offered in a cooperative, ecumenical way.

Varsity and intramural athletics are offered for men and women. The eight varsity sports for men are baseball, basketball, cross-country, football, golf, soccer, tennis, and track. Women's varsity sports are basketball, cross-country, golf, soccer, softball, tennis, track, and volleyball. Capital's sports teams are sanctioned by the National Collegiate Athletic Association Division III, and the University is a member of the Ohio Athletic Conference. Intramural sports are also a big part of campus life. In addition, Capital's fitness rooms and activities such as aerobics provide options for students who want to develop their own individual fitness programs.

Location

Capital is located in the Columbus suburb of Bexley, which is primarily a residential community with a number of small shops and restaurants. Downtown Columbus is just 3 miles from campus and easily reached by city buses. As the fifteenth-largest city in the country and part of a major metropolitan area, Columbus offers a wide variety of social and cultural opportunities. Students can enjoy performances by BalletMet, Opera Columbus, or the Columbus Jazz Orchestra, or they may visit the more than fifty art galleries in the area. Students may follow professional sports by attending the games of the Columbus Crew (Major League Soccer), the Columbus Blue Jackets (National Hockey League), or the Columbus Clippers (AAA franchise of the Cleveland Indians). There is also an expansive network of parks and recreation facilities, bike trails, and the Columbus Zoo. Many of the city's attractions are free or offer substantial student discounts. In addition, as Ohio's capital and largest city, Columbus is the home of many national and international corporations. These companies offer Capital students unlimited opportunities for internships and employment after graduation.

Majors and Degrees

Capital University offers the Bachelor of Arts degree in art, art therapy, athletic training, biochemistry, biology, business (accounting, financial economics, leadership and management, and marketing), chemistry (major approved by the American Chemical Society), communication, computer science, criminology, economics, education, English (literature and professional writing), environmental science, exercise science, health and fitness management, history, international studies, mathematics, modern languages (French and Spanish), organizational communication, philosophy, political science, professional studies, psychology, public administration, public relations, radio-television, religion, sociology, and theater studies. Preparation for professional programs is available in dentistry, medicine, optometry, pharmacy, physical therapy, physician assistant studies, and veterinary medicine. Prelaw and pre-seminary studies help prepare students for graduate studies in religion and the legal profession.

Capital also offers the Bachelor of Science in Nursing (approved by the National League for Nursing Accrediting Commission) and Bachelor of Social Work (approved by the Council on Social Work Education). For music students, Capital offers a Bachelor of Music in composition, jazz studies, keyboard pedagogy (church music, organ, and piano), music education (vocal and instrumental), music industry, music media, music merchandising, music technology, and performance (instrumental, organ, piano, and vocal). The Bachelor of Arts in music is also offered.

A program in engineering, which leads to dual degrees, is offered in cooperation with Washington University in St. Louis and Case Western Reserve University in Cleveland. A similar dual-degree program in pre–occupational therapy is also offered in conjunction with Washington University and the University of Indianapolis.

Academic Programs

The academic year consists of two semesters, the first of which begins in late August and ends in December. The second semester begins in early January and ends in early May. Summer classes are available.

In addition to taking courses related to their field of study, all undergraduate students take courses that fulfill a set of general education goals and bring together the University's academic, scientific, religious, and artistic disciplines.

Learning is not confined to the classroom at Capital. All undergraduate students, regardless of their major, may participate in an internship that allows them to apply newly learned skills to on-the-job situations.

Faculty advisers help students select a major, choose appropriate classes, and suggest career options. In addition, staff members in Capital's Career Services Office help students plan careers, provide instruction in resume writing and interviewing, and share information about graduate schools. On-campus recruiting sessions and a job-referral service also enhance employment opportunities.

Off-Campus Programs

At Capital, one way students learn more about other cultures and countries is through international study.

Capital is the only school in the country that offers a semester of undergraduate study at the Zoltán Kodály Pedagogical Institute of Music in Hungary for students in the Conservatory of Music.

In addition, Capital's Office of International Education offers overseas study opportunities in countries around the world, including China, Ecuador, France, Germany, Israel, the Netherlands, Spain, and Tanzania.

Closer to home, students may participate in a semester internship in one of thousands of organizations in the nation's capital through an arrangement with the Washington Center. In addition, cross-registration for enrolled students is available with Columbus College of Art and Design, Columbus State Community College, Ohio Dominican University, The Ohio State University, Otterbein College, and other area colleges and universities.

Academic Facilities

Capital's campus consists of twenty-four buildings. Through CAP-Net, Capital's campuswide voice, data, and video network, every residence hall room, classroom, and office is connected to the Internet and the Web. Through the library's connection to OhioLINK, students have access to more than 10 million items held by fifty libraries throughout the state. Information Technology provides a television studio and computer labs for student use. The Advanced Computational Studies Laboratory includes an array of computer hardware that allows students to access an extensive collection of scientific software and to simulate a parallel computing environment. A state-of-the-art technology classroom and language lab enhance teaching and learning. Nursing students may also use the microcomputers and instructional software contained in the School of Nursing's Helene Fuld Health Trust Learning Resources Laboratory. For the art lover, Chagall, Picasso, and Warhol are as close as Capital's Blackmore Library, which houses the University's Schumacher Gallery and its 2,500-piece collection.

Costs

In 2009–10, tuition and fees were $28,480. Room and board fees were $7510.

Financial Aid

Approximately 99 percent of Capital's undergraduate students receive some form of financial assistance. To apply, a student must file the Free Application for Federal Student Aid (FAFSA).

University scholarships are awarded to incoming freshmen and transfer students on the basis of academic achievement (and standardized test scores for freshmen). Full-tuition scholarships (Collegiate Fellowships) are awarded to incoming freshmen based on academic achievement and an on-campus competition. Music scholarships and participation awards are granted based on music ability as demonstrated during an audition. Additional grants are available for leadership, underrepresented or disadvantaged students, and out-of-state residents.

Faculty

The University has 230 full- and part-time faculty members for its undergraduate programs. The student-faculty ratio is 10:1.

Admission Requirements

Capital University admits qualified students regardless of race, color, religion, gender, age, disability, or national or ethnic origin to all the rights, privileges, programs, and activities generally accorded or made available to the students at the University.

To be considered for admission to any of the undergraduate programs, students must submit copies of their high school transcript, ACT or SAT scores, and a counselor recommendation. Applicants to the Conservatory of Music must also arrange for an audition, either in person or by videotape. There are special admission requirements for the Department of Nursing, and students should contact the Admission Office for details. Scores on Advanced Placement tests and College-Level Examination Program subject examinations are accepted as additional indicators of an applicant's ability, and course credit may be awarded for satisfactory scores on these examinations. Campus visits are encouraged. Arrangements for a tour of the campus and an interview, class visits, and appointments with professors may be made through the Admission Office. When an admission representative visits high schools, interested students in the area are notified and encouraged to meet with the representative. Transfer applicants must be in good social and academic standing and have a minimum grade point average of 2.25 at the institutions they attended previously. International applicants must submit official secondary school transcripts and photocopies of school-leaving certificates, TOEFL scores, SAT scores if available, and recommendation letters from a guidance counselor or headmaster and from a teacher.

Application and Information

Applications for admission may be submitted starting September 1 for the following year. Applicants are notified of their status as soon as their application is complete. The priority application deadline for the fall semester is April 15. Applications received after April 15 are reviewed on a space-available basis.

Director of Admission
Capital University
1 College and Main
Columbus, Ohio 43209-2394
Phone: 614-236-6101
866-544-6175 (toll-free)
Fax: 614-236-6926
E-mail: admissions@capital.edu
Web site: http://www.capital.edu

Undergraduate students at Capital University are encouraged to explore original research projects, independently or with other students and faculty members, then present their findings at local, national, and international conferences.

CARLETON COLLEGE

NORTHFIELD, MINNESOTA

The College

Since its inception in 1866, Carleton College has been a coeducational, residential, liberal arts college. Sponsored initially by the Congregationalists, Carleton opened its doors in 1867 as Northfield College. Four years later, William Carleton of Charlestown, Massachusetts, donated $50,000 to the fledgling college, the result of which was the change of name from Northfield to Carleton. Binding church ties were dropped long ago, and the College continues to welcome students from a kaleidoscope of races, religions, and cultures.

Today, first-year classes number about 490 to 510, and the student body is approximately 50 percent men. The on-campus enrollment of about 1,800 includes students from virtually every state and about twenty-five other countries. About a quarter are from Minnesota, and the next most represented states are Illinois, California, Wisconsin, New York, Massachusetts, Oregon, and Washington. About 20 percent are students who are members of minority groups, and 10 percent are the first generation of their families to attend college.

Most first-year students choose to take a first-year seminar, some of which deal with contemporary problems or concerns, others with more esoteric material. Many upperclass students do at least some independent study in their major, and a significant number of students take advantage of internship and work experience.

Though academic work takes top priority, Carleton students are actively involved in over 100 organizations, clubs, and other activities, ranging from the Quiz Bowl team (which won the nationals in 2007), and the improvisational comedy troupe Cujokra to Ultimate Frisbee (Carleton's women's team won the national intercollegiate championship in 2000, and the men's team won in 2001) and one of the top Model United Nations teams in the country. Musicians can play in the orchestra or smaller ensembles or sing in the choir, the Carleton Singers, or one of six a cappella groups. Athletes can participate in one of ten varsity sports for men or eleven for women, one of eighteen competitive club teams, or any of fifteen intramural sports.

Normally, 96 percent of Carleton first-year students return for their sophomore year. The most recent figures available show that 89 percent of first-year students graduated in four years or less, and 93 percent graduated within five years.

Location

Northfield is about 35 miles from the Minneapolis–St. Paul International Airport and 40 miles from the downtown Twin Cities. Once a traditional small agrarian community, Northfield is also the home of St. Olaf College and several multinational businesses, and a number of its residents now commute to the Twin Cities. Most of the buildings in downtown Northfield look much as they did at the turn of the century. A revitalized riverbank and a core of downtown businesses and shops make for pleasant afternoon and evening strolls.

Majors and Degrees

Carleton grants only one undergraduate degree, the Bachelor of Arts. Majors offered are African/African American studies, American studies, art history, biology, chemistry, cinema and media studies, classical languages, classical studies, computer science, economics, English, French, French and Francophone studies, geology, German, Greek, history, international relations, Latin, Latin American studies, mathematics, music, philosophy, physics, political science, psychology, religion, Romance languages, Russian, sociology and anthropology, Spanish, studio art, theater arts, and women's studies. Students may also self-design their own majors.

In addition to a major, students may elect to study one of sixteen concentrations, integrated interdisciplinary programs that cut across traditional boundaries of academic disciplines and serve to both strengthen and complement the major: African/African American studies, archaeology, biochemistry, cognitive studies, cross-cultural studies, East Asian studies, educational studies, environmental and technology studies, French and Francophone studies, Latin American studies, media studies, medieval and Renaissance studies, political economy, Russian studies, South Asian studies, and women's studies.

Special programs are available in dance, Hebrew/Judaic studies, linguistics, and literary and cultural studies. Carleton offers a teacher education program leading to a secondary teaching license in art, English, French, German, mathematics, Russian, science, the social studies, or Spanish. Elementary licensure is available only in art and world languages, French, German, and Spanish. The joint liberal arts–engineering program, commonly known as the 3-2 program, is offered in conjunction with either Columbia University or Washington University (St. Louis).

Academic Programs

Carleton's avowed purpose is to provide a liberal arts education of the highest quality. The College teaches the basic skills upon which all higher achievements rest: to read perceptively, to write and speak clearly, and to think analytically. The Carleton education aims to nurture a sense of curiosity and intellectual adventure, an awareness of method and purpose in a variety of fields, and an affinity for quality and integrity wherever they may be found. These values prepare Carleton graduates to lead fully realized lives in a diverse and changing world.

To this end, the Carleton curriculum balances a traditional emphasis upon classic fields of study, or disciplines, with a complementary offering of distribution courses, electives, and interdisciplinary programs. To be awarded the Bachelor of Arts degree, a student must take at least thirty-five courses, two of which must come from arts and literature, two from the humanities, three from the social sciences, and three from mathematics and the natural sciences. In addition, everyone must take at least one course that is centrally concerned with a culture different from his or her own. All students must also satisfy two proficiency requirements: the writing of English and the learning of a second language.

Carleton students normally choose a major during the spring term of their sophomore year. In any given year, 12–18 students graduate with double majors, and about 15 graduate with special majors. All students must complete an integrative exercise, which could include a comprehensive examination, an extensive research project, a major paper, or a public lecture, in their major field, usually in the senior year. Carleton's academic year is composed of three 10-week-long terms: fall, winter, and spring.

Off-Campus Programs

Two thirds of Carleton students spend at least one term completing an off-campus program. During any one academic year, more than 350 students are involved in off-campus study in locations such as Australia, Japan, China, England, India, Mexico, Costa Rica, Western Africa, and Washington, D.C. Each year the College sponsors as many as ten faculty-led off-campus seminars for Carleton students. Through membership in a number of consortia, Carleton students may participate in more than twenty additional international programs lasting from a semester to a full year. Students may also select from a list of programs sponsored by other institutions, consortia, and agencies that Carleton has evaluated and approved for academic credit, or they can request approval of a program that they and their academic advisers believe will further their educational goals.

Academic Facilities

The Carleton campus consists of more than 900 acres of land, about 800 of which are the Arboretum, a game and nature preserve used regularly as an outdoor laboratory for biology, chemistry, and geology as well as a recreational area. Twenty miles of running and skiing trails crisscross the "arb," which *Runner's World* has named the best place to run in the state of Minnesota.

Approximately forty buildings are found on the College's main campus of nearly 100 acres. Ten are student residence halls ranging in capacity from 110 to 205. Built in 2000, an 80,000-square-foot field house/recreation center offers an indoor track, a climbing wall, and eighty weight-training and fitness machines. The Music and Drama Center offers a concert hall seating 500 and a theater seating 460, joined by a gallery, ensemble rooms, practice rooms, dressing rooms, and scenery and costume storage rooms. Three buildings are devoted to the sciences: Olin (physics and psychology), Mudd (chemistry and geology), and Hulings (biology). Goodsell Observatory houses a 16-inch visual refractor telescope and an 8-inch photographic refractor telescope. The four-story Center for Mathematics and Computing (CMC) offers computer labs open around-the-clock. Along with six other labs distributed around campus, they provide easy access to a wide range of applications, free printing, and specialized multimedia equipment. The campus has more than 600 advanced workstations and personal computers, all of which are linked to the high-speed campus network and Internet2. In the residence halls, every room provides Internet connections, allowing students to plug in their own computers for access to the campus network. Wireless networks are also available in many locales.

Costs

For 2009–10, tuition was $39,546; fees, $231; and room and board, $10,428. Travel costs vary. Books, supplies, and personal expenses are estimated to be about $1200.

Financial Aid

Carleton meets the full demonstrated financial need of every student admitted to the College and continues meeting each student's need for four years or until graduation. An on-campus job of 8 to 10 hours per week and a loan opportunity are included in nearly every financial aid package. In 2008–09, about 80 percent of Carleton students received a total of more than $26 million in financial aid or scholarships from all sources. Fifty-five percent received grant assistance; the average need-based grant was $25,608. The only non-need scholarships the College offers are sixty-five to seventy-five Carleton-sponsored National Merit, National Achievement, and National Hispanic Scholarships.

Faculty

All Carleton classes are taught by faculty members rather than graduate students or teaching assistants. Of the 207 faculty members, 184 are full-time, resulting in a student-faculty ratio of 9:1. Of those full-time faculty members, 95 percent hold the highest degree in their academic field. The average class size is about 18, and the average lab size is 15. Most faculty members also serve as academic advisers.

Student Government

Students are actively involved in the governance of the College. Directly below the Board of Trustees is the College Council, chaired by the President, which is composed of 5 faculty members, 5 students, 5 staff members, 1 trustee, and 1 alumnus. The three major policy committees, Education and Curriculum, Student Life, and the Budget Committee, are also made up of faculty members, students, and staff members. Every student is a member of the Carleton Student Association (CSA). Three officers and 16 senators are elected annually to serve as the CSA Senate, which, among other duties, manages the student activities budget.

Admission Requirements

Carleton normally receives about 4,900 applications for the approximately 500 places available in the first-year class. Admission is based on several considerations: superior academic achievement, personal qualities and interests, participation in extracurricular activities, and potential for development as a student and a graduate of the College. The Admissions Committee weighs all factors to ensure that those students offered admission are not only adequately prepared for the academic work but also will benefit from their total experience at Carleton and are likely to add significantly to the College through their individual talents and personal qualities.

Application and Information

Students interested in applying for admission should contact the Office of Admissions. Interviews, with either a staff member or an alumni admissions representative, are recommended but not required. A visit to the campus is strongly encouraged. During the academic year, overnight stays, interviews, and class visits are usually available but must be scheduled in advance.

Students who decide that Carleton is their first-choice college are encouraged to apply for early decision by November 15, first round, or by January 15, second round. The application deadline for regular decision is January 15. Regular decision candidates are notified before April 15, and the candidate's reply date is May 1. For more information, prospective students should contact:

Office of Admissions
Carleton College
100 South College Street
Northfield, Minnesota 55057
Phone: 507-222-4190
800-995-2275 (toll-free)
Fax: 507-222-4526
E-mail: admissions@acs.carleton.edu
Web site: http://www.carleton.edu

An aerial view of the Carleton College campus.

COLLEGE CLOSE-UPS

CARLOS ALBIZU UNIVERSITY

MIAMI, FLORIDA

The University

Carlos Albizu University (CAU) is dedicated to the study and understanding of human endeavors from a holistic, dynamic, and integrated perspective. The University's programs have produced culturally sensitive professionals who are capable of serving the diverse population of the global community. The University is regionally accredited by the Middle States Commission on Higher Education and is licensed by the Florida Department of Education Commission for Independent Education.

The University's mission is achieved through advanced training, research, the dissemination of scientific and cultural information, and the provision of professional services with sensitivity toward culturally diverse constituencies. Through its expert faculty, CAU offers exciting and challenging programs to more than 2,000 students, who represent more than forty countries. Classes are small, with flexible schedules to meet the students' needs.

In addition to its undergraduate programs, the University also offers the following master's degree programs: an accelerated Master of Business Administration (M.B.A.); a Master of Science in psychology, with majors in marriage and family therapy, mental health counseling, and school counseling; and a Master of Science in industrial and organizational psychology that has been ranked by independent researchers among the top third of programs of its kind in the nation. CAU also offers Master of Science degree programs in exceptional student education (ESSE) and in teaching English to speakers of other languages (TESOL). CAU's APA-accredited Doctor of Psychology (Psy.D.) program offers concentrations in child psychology, clinical neuropsychology, forensic psychology, and general psychology.

CAU was founded in 1966 in Puerto Rico with the specific objective of offering a Master of Science degree in clinical psychology. At that time, very few mental health professionals worked on the island, and most of them received their professional education outside of Puerto Rico. CAU enabled these professionals to receive training that was specifically adapted to Puerto Rican sociocultural realities. A thriving and modern 18-acre campus was established in Miami in 1980, offering graduate psychology programs that are sensitive to cultural and ethnic issues.

In 2000, the two-campus institution was renamed Carlos Albizu University as a posthumous honor to its founder, becoming the only fully accredited secular university in the United States named in honor of a Hispanic. CAU proudly recognizes Dr. Albizu's distinguished career as a professor of psychology and his service as the first president of the National Hispanic Psychological Association.

Location

The University is located in the new city of Doral in Miami-Dade County, Florida. Multiple dining, shopping, and entertainment venues are located just around the corner from the Miami campus, and the world-famous art deco district of Miami Beach is only 25 minutes away. In addition, many national and international companies have their headquarters in the area neighboring the campus. Rich in multicultural diversity and laden with the complex socioeconomic and psychosocial realities that accompany such diversity, Miami has become a multicultural and international center as well as the home of many who have moved to the U.S. from Latin America and the Caribbean.

Majors and Degrees

At the Miami campus, the University offers the following undergraduate programs: a Bachelor of Science (B.S.) degree in psychology, a Bachelor of Business Administration (B.B.A.) degree, a Bachelor of Arts (B.A.) in elementary education, and certificate programs in early childhood education (ECE) and in English for speakers of other languages (ESOL).

Academic Programs

A bachelor's degree requires completion of 120 to 124 credits, including 48 to 60 credits in foundation courses, 43 to 48 credits in core major courses, and the rest in concentrations or electives. The B.S. in psychology and the B.A. in elementary education may receive a maximum of 90 transfer credits from an accredited institution of higher learning. The Bachelor of Business Administration may receive a maximum of 72 transfer credits. Students must have an overall grade point average (GPA) of at least 2.0 in order to be admitted; the GPA within the program of study must be maintained at 2.25 to 2.5, depending on the program.

Independent study allows students to take a regular course from an instructor on an individual or small-group basis rather than in a classroom setting. With the approval of a professor and the program director, a student may take a maximum of 9 hours of independent study after competing at least 24 hours of traditional study. Special project courses allow students to design courses to fit their particular interests.

The academic year is divided into three 15-week academic terms: spring (January to April), summer (May to August), and fall (September to December).

Academic Facilities

The Albizu Library's collection includes printed and nonprinted materials in the behavioral sciences, psychology, psychiatry, and mental health. The collection also includes a number of volumes and resources on business, management, marketing, economics, accounting, and finance, as well as subscriptions to the leading management journals and publications. Additional resources are offered in the areas of curriculum development, elementary education, special education, and classroom management. CAU students have access to the leading online databases, such as EBSCO and ProQuest. A special collection of materials on cross-cultural topics is also housed in the library, and there is a collection of testing materials for different disciplines.

The CAU campus offers it students many facilities and features similar to those offered at a larger university while also providing the personal attention afforded by a small university. The University features five computer labs, a student lounge, cafeteria, indoor and outdoor study areas, and the Albizu Library. The University has wireless Internet connections available throughout the campus and has technologically equipped classrooms.

CAU is home to the Goodman Psychological Services Center. This is a unique resource to both the students training to become practitioners in the field of psychology and to the community. The students are given the opportunity to hone clinically acquired skills while providing supervised mental health services to CAU's local community. Since 1980, the Goodman Center has provided services to more than ten thousand members of the community and continues to contribute to the availability of affordable mental health care to underserved populations.

Costs

Undergraduate tuition for 2008–09 was $305 per credit ($385 per credit for upper division business programs). Other expenses include a global fee of $248 per session.

Financial Aid

More than 75 percent of CAU's students receive financial aid. Recipients must be U.S. citizens or eligible noncitizens who are enrolled for at least 6 credits. In addition, students must not be in default or owe repayment on a grant. Financial aid applications must be received by June 1 for fall enrollment, October 1 for spring enrollment, and March 1 for summer enrollment. In accordance with Title IV regulations, an undergraduate student is considered to be full-time when enrolled in 12 or more credits and part-time when enrolled in 6 to 11 credits of study. Available grants include the Federal Pell Grant, the Federal Supplemental Opportunity Educational Grant, the Florida State Assistance Grant, and the Florida Bright Futures Scholarship. Fifteen $1000 Albizu Scholarships are offered each term. Tuition assistance of 20 percent is available to government employees for qualifying programs. Federal Stafford Student Loans and Federal PLUS loans are available with interest rates that do not exceed 9 percent.

Faculty

The faculty consists of approximately 100 full-time and part-time instructors, all of whom have advanced degrees (master's or higher) in their respective programs of study and are members of professional organizations related to their fields of interest and research.

Student Government

The Student Council seeks to promote communication, cooperation, and understanding among students and members of the faculty and administration and suggests ways to promote the best interests and objectives of the academic community. The Student Council's functions are regulated by the applicable dispositions of the General Regulations for Students of the CAU.

Admission Requirements

Undergraduate applicants must submit the following items to be considered for admission: a completed and signed application form; official transcripts from all high schools, colleges, or universities previously attended; letters of recommendation; a resume; and a $25 application fee. Undergraduate applicants must present a GPA of 2.0 or higher to be considered for admission. Graduate degree programs follow different admission standards and procedures.

International students applying for admission must comply with current immigration regulations and submit their academic records to authorized agencies for verification of their equivalency to course work offered in the United States. In addition, they should have all admission credentials on file at least ninety days prior to the beginning of the term of expected enrollment.

Transfer students may transfer credits earned from an accredited college or university. Education and training must have been received in an accredited institution of higher education that at the time of training was accredited by an accrediting organization recognized by the U.S. Department of Education. Students may apply for prior learning credits for college-level course work, work experience, military service, or analogous learning outside of the traditional classroom.

After all materials have been received, the applicant's completed file is forwarded to the appropriate undergraduate program and reviewed by a faculty member. At the discretion of the director of the undergraduate program, the applicant is scheduled for an interview. Upon admission to the program, a faculty adviser is assigned to the prospective student.

CAU does not discriminate against any student with special needs and/or conditions who is otherwise eligible and who meets program and professional performance standards and expectations.

Application and Information

Applications must be received prior to the beginning of the term of enrollment for which the applicant is requesting admission. Out-of-state and international applicants should submit all admission documents at least ninety days prior to the beginning of the term of expected enrollment. Applications may be submitted online or mailed to:

Miami Campus
Carlos Albizu University
2173 Northwest 99th Avenue
Miami, Florida 33172
Phone: 305-593-1223 Ext. 137
888-GO-TO-CAU (toll-free)
Fax: 305-592-7930
Web site: http://www.mia.albizu.edu

CARLOW UNIVERSITY

PITTSBURGH, PENNSYLVANIA

The University

Carlow University was founded in 1929 in response to a local need for a Catholic women's college. The mission of the University is to involve people, primarily women, in a process of self-directed lifelong learning that frees them to think clearly and creatively, to discover and to challenge or affirm cultural and aesthetic values, to respond reverently to God and others, and to render competent and compassionate service in personal and professional life. Although Carlow makes explicit its strong continuing commitment to the education of women, it welcomes men. The University's mission has been confirmed over the years by the growing number of students who come seeking a solid liberal arts education as well as strong career preparation. In addition to its undergraduate programs, the University offers an M.B.A., an M.F.A., and other graduate degrees.

Current enrollment exceeds 2,300 students. Carlow's students have various backgrounds and come mainly from the Middle Atlantic states; the majority are from western Pennsylvania.

Placement and career counseling, free professional and peer tutorial services, the Center for Academic Achievement, the Disabilities Service Office, student health, personal counseling programs, and campus ministry are support services available to students.

Cocurricular organizations include the Student Government Association, the Commuter Student Association, the International Student Association, the *Purple Menace* newspaper, and United Black Students, among many others.

The University has a large group of students involved in community service and volunteerism. Spring break service projects have taken students to Jamaica, the Virgin Islands, Arizona, Arkansas, Texas, Ireland, and many other locations. Academic- or career-oriented organizations include Alpha Phi Omega (national service/honor society), American Chemical Society, Beta Beta Beta (biology club), Business Leaders of Carlow, the Council for Exceptional Children, Kappa Delta Epsilon (for education majors), Social Work Organization, Student Nurses Association of Pennsylvania, Phi Chi Theta (business fraternity), and the Psychology Club. Special-interest groups include Blessed, the Gospel choir; the Environmental Clean-up Organization; Pep Band; Spirit; Student Athlete Association; Theater Group; and Women in Communication (WIC).

The athletic program includes women's intercollegiate basketball, soccer, softball, tennis, and volleyball as well as a selection of physical education courses, including aerobics, fitness and weight control, martial arts/self-defense, modern dance, water aerobics, weight training, and yoga. Wellness and fitness services include individual health assessment, fitness programming, and nutrition counseling.

Popular campus events include entertainment, film series, carnivals, Homecoming, Mercy Founders Week, a St. Patrick's Day celebration and parade, the International Festival, Black History Month events, Women's History Month events, and theater productions.

The University's central location gives students opportunities for internships in various businesses and agencies. Students in health-related fields complete their clinical experiences in the many fine teaching hospitals and private health-care facilities in the city of Pittsburgh. City buses stop in front of the campus, and campus parking is available for commuting students.

Location

Carlow University is located on a 15-acre campus in the heart of Oakland, one of the nation's biggest college towns and the educational, cultural, and medical center of Pittsburgh. Nine other colleges and universities at which students can cross-register are within walking distance or just minutes away by bus. Schenley Park, Carnegie Library and Museums, Phipps Conservatory, Carnegie Music and Lecture Halls, and the Oakland shopping district are all a short walk from the campus. Downtown Pittsburgh is only a 10-minute bus ride away. Greater Pittsburgh International Airport is a 30-minute drive from the Carlow campus.

Majors and Degrees

Carlow University grants the undergraduate degrees of Bachelor of Arts, Bachelor of Science, Bachelor of Science in Nursing, and Bachelor of Social Work. Programs include accounting, art, art/art education, art/art history, art/ceramics, art/graphic design, art/interactive media design, art/painting and drawing, art/photography, art with a certificate in art therapy preparation, biology (with concentrations in forensic medical and legal investigations/autopsy specialization, human biology, molecular cell and biotechnology, and organismal/ecological biology), business management, business management/communication, chemistry, communication studies, creative writing, early childhood education, elementary education, English, forensic accounting, health science (available to students who have previously earned an associate degree), history, human resource management and technology, information systems management, liberal studies, marketing, mathematics, nursing, philosophy, political science, professional writing, professional writing/business, psychology, public policy and leadership, scientific/medical marketing, social work, sociology, sociology/criminal justice, Spanish, special education, and theology. An independent major, designed by the student, may also be arranged.

Certification programs are offered in forensic accounting, perfusion technology (biology majors only) and secondary education (biology, chemistry, English, general science, mathematics, and social studies).

Preprofessional programs include athletic training, dentistry, law, medicine, occupational therapy, optometry, osteopathy, pharmacy, physical therapy, physician assistant studies, podiatry, and veterinary medicine.

The University offers 3-2 programs in engineering in three areas: biology/environmental engineering, chemistry/chemical engineering, and mathematics/engineering. In addition, there are a 3-2 program in environmental science and a 3-3 B.A./J.D. law program.

Academic Programs

Carlow's primary concern is the development of the student as a lifelong learner. To this end, members of the Carlow community—students, faculty, and staff—recognize the integrity and value of each person in the daily life and work of the University. The academic programs are broad and flexible, including opportunities for double majors, single majors with certification in education, minors, certificate programs, and changes of major. Transfer students are warmly welcomed.

The University operates on the two-semester system, August to December and January to May. Summer sessions, a variable number of weeks in length, are offered every year. Most courses carry 3 credits (laboratory courses, among others, carry 4 credits). Students normally take five courses each semester. Each student must demonstrate basic competence in English composition, speech and interpersonal communication, reading comprehension, and mathematics. Required of all students is one course each in a lab science, history, literature, mathematics, social/

behavioral science (such as psychology or sociology), theology, fine arts, philosophy, women's studies, and political science or economics, as well as one global perspective course. Students are also required to take an interdisciplinary course, which is selected from a variety of subject areas. Students in nursing, education, social work, psychology, management, and perfusion technology are required to do fieldwork as part of their program. Field placements and internships are guaranteed and encouraged in all areas of study. An honors program is open to eligible students. After the first semester of the first year, one course per semester (outside of the major) may be taken on a pass-fail basis. Some courses may be challenged, for credit or exemption, by passing an examination. CLEP general exam credits may be used for this purpose as well.

The University gives women and men the opportunity to return to the classroom at various stages of their lives. Adult learners may enroll in full-time and part-time degree programs, noncredit enrichment courses, seminars, and workshops. Scheduling options include day, evening, accelerated, weekend, and online courses.

Academic Facilities

Grace Library, a five-level multipurpose learning center in the heart of the campus, currently contains more than 100,000 books, subscribes to over 350 print journals, and offers access to more than 4,500 online journals. The library houses the offices of the President and Provost. The Center for Academic Achievement, the mail room, the bookstore, Academic Affairs, the Center for Career Enrichment, Printing Services, the International Poetry Forum, University Archives, and computer laboratories are also located here. Kresge Theatre, a 300-seat auditorium, is located on the fifth level as well.

Curran Hall houses the School of Nursing and includes a state-of-the-art nursing skills lab and conference and seminar rooms. Frances Warde Hall is a residence hall that also houses the School of Education, art labs, student affairs offices, and the campus café. Antonian Hall houses the 1,000-seat Sister Rosemary Heyl Theatre, the School for Social Change, the fine arts department, and classrooms as well as administrative offices for admissions, financial aid, advising, the registrar, and student accounts.

The cafeteria and the Campus School of Carlow University (kindergarten through grade 8) are located in Tiernan Hall. St. Joseph Hall contains the gymnasium, fitness center, and swimming pool, and Aquinas Hall houses classrooms, the humanities division, the International Student Center, and faculty and staff offices.

Carlow's A. J. Palumbo Hall of Science and Technology houses state-of-the-art teaching/research laboratories in physics, organic and advanced chemistry, genetics, cell biology, and gross anatomy; a herbarium to store dry plant specimens; a greenhouse; an amphitheater for scientific presentations; and the Bayer Children's Science Learning Laboratory.

Carlow University's campus computer network features Internet accounts and e-mail, network and Internet access from any location on campus. There is one network port per pillow in the residence halls.

Costs

Tuition and fees for 2010–11 are $22,600 for full-time students. Room and board charges for the year are $8900 for double occupancy.

Financial Aid

Financial aid in the form of grants, scholarships, loans, and student employment is available to eligible applicants. More than 90 percent of all full-time students receive some type of financial assistance. The University expects that most aid recipients assume a portion of their expenses through loans and/or part-time employment. Job opportunities are available on campus in a wide variety of positions, and students are placed, whenever possible, in positions that coincide with their skills and interests. Basketball, soccer, softball, tennis, and volleyball scholarships are also available.

Faculty

Carlow's student-faculty ratio is 12:1, and faculty members are readily available to help plan individualized programs of study, to provide assistance relating to field placements and internships, and to assist in career preparation. The student's major adviser is normally a faculty member in the department.

Student Government

All registered students are members of the Student Government Association (SGA). Through the SGA, students act as equal participants with the administration, faculty, and staff in general governance. The SGA promotes the general welfare of the students and is the advocate to ensure that the academic, social, and spiritual needs of students are met. SGA is empowered to charter all student organizations.

Admission Requirements

Applicants are evaluated on the basis of their secondary school record, class rank, and scores on the SAT or ACT. The Committee on Admissions recognizes that school curricula vary greatly and always gives careful consideration to the application of an able student whose course work or grading scale is more challenging or whose preparation differs from the traditional program. A personal interview is strongly recommended but not required. Overnight visits, a day of classes, campus tours, and meals are available and are strongly encouraged. Throughout the year, the University sponsors programs that give candidates the opportunity to tour the campus and meet faculty and staff members and Carlow students.

Application and Information

Although Carlow subscribes to the rolling admission plan, high school students are encouraged to submit an application early in the first semester of the senior year. Students interested in early notification should apply by September 30. The University's priority admission and scholarship deadline is February 15.

Students may apply online or request an application form by contacting:

Office of Admissions
Carlow University
3333 Fifth Avenue
Pittsburgh, Pennsylvania 15213
Phone: 412-578-6059
800-333-2275
E-mail: admissions@carlow.edu
Web site: http://www.carlow.edu

CARNEGIE MELLON UNIVERSITY

Carnegie Mellon

PITTSBURGH, PENNSYLVANIA

The University

Since its beginning more than 100 years ago, Carnegie Mellon has evolved into an institution consistently ranked in the top 25 for its unique approach to education and research. Students become experts in fields ranging from business, the fine arts, and computer science to humanities, the sciences, and engineering—far more than steel magnate and philanthropist Andrew Carnegie first envisioned when he founded Carnegie Mellon as a technical school in 1900.

Carnegie Mellon is world renowned for its left-brain and right-brain thinking that unite within the University's collaborative culture and are the foundation of learning at Carnegie Mellon. Students acquire a depth and breadth of knowledge while sharpening problem-solving, critical-thinking, creative, and quantitative skills. The University's unique approach to education develops sound critical judgment, resourcefulness, and professional ethics through interdisciplinary and hands-on experiences. Graduates go on to become the innovative leaders and problem solvers of tomorrow.

Students in this private coeducational university come from all fifty states and more than forty countries. Each year, Carnegie Mellon enrolls a diverse freshman class of approximately 1,400 students from a variety of social and cultural backgrounds with a wide range of academic and artistic interests. The total undergraduate population is 5,800. Approximately 13 percent of the student body identifies with an ethnic minority population such as African American, Hispanic/Latino American, or Native American. The international student population makes up 13 percent of the student body.

Carnegie Mellon spans the best of both worlds; its traditional 150-acre campus is located minutes from downtown Pittsburgh, yet it is surrounded by residential neighborhoods. Student activities include more than 150 clubs and organizations, varsity and intramural sports, fraternities and sororities, and student government. Off campus, students can take advantage of three culturally active neighborhoods (all within walking distance), the largest public park in Pittsburgh, urban and suburban shopping, excellent sightseeing, professional sports, museums, art galleries, and amusement parks.

Approximately 80 percent of students live in University housing, which is guaranteed for all four years, provided students remain in the housing system, and ranges from traditional residence halls, special-interest housing, and apartment buildings to fraternity and sorority housing. Freshmen are required to live in University housing.

Carnegie Mellon students come away from their undergraduate experience poised to be trendsetters, whether in the business world, the art community, or graduate school. Students not only gain the knowledge necessary to succeed professionally, they also learn how to maximize their creativity, intellectual playfulness, and analytical skills in order to survive in an ever-changing global environment. The University strives to produce graduates who are adaptable, resourceful, and independent—graduates who communicate effectively, strive to be leaders, and understand their professional and social responsibilities.

High school juniors can participate in Carnegie Mellon's six-week summer Pre-College programs, in which students have the opportunity to take college course work, meet people from all over the country, live like true college students, and explore the city of Pittsburgh. Students can take two regular Carnegie Mellon courses for full credit in disciplines such as engineering, humanities, computer science, or the sciences; immerse themselves in the fine arts studio or conservatory-based courses to determine their level of interest for study at the college level in architecture, art, design, drama, or music; or attend the National High School Game Academy, in which students learn interactive digital game development through hands-on experience.

In addition to bachelor's degrees, Carnegie Mellon offers master's and doctoral degrees.

Location

Carnegie Mellon is located 5 miles from the downtown area in the Oakland neighborhood of Pittsburgh. Home to several of the city's colleges, universities, museums, and hospitals, Oakland offers many activities and resources to area students. Although Carnegie Mellon has the collegiate feel of a suburban campus, the surrounding Pittsburgh community provides all of the cultural and social advantages of a big city. The University is approximately 1 hour from some of the best skiing in the East and is only a short plane ride from many major metropolitan areas, including Boston, New York City, Chicago, Philadelphia, and Washington, D.C.

Majors and Degrees

Undergraduate majors at Carnegie Mellon include business administration, computer science, engineering (biomedical engineering*, chemical engineering, civil and environmental engineering, electrical and computer engineering, engineering and public policy*, materials science engineering, and mechanical engineering), fine and performing arts (architecture, art, design, drama, and music), information systems, liberal arts and professional studies (economics, English, history, information systems, modern languages, philosophy, political science, psychology, social and decision sciences, and statistics), and the sciences (biological sciences, chemistry, mathematical sciences, and physics). The Bachelor of Computer Science and Arts (B.C.S.A.), Bachelor of Humanities and Arts (B.H.A.), and Bachelor of Science and Arts (B.S.A.) degree programs are also available, as are many interdepartmental majors. (* indicates double majors only.)

Academic Programs

There is no core curriculum at Carnegie Mellon. The only required classes are Computing@CarnegieMellon (C@CM) and a first-year writing course. Each college has its own requirements for graduation.

Students at Carnegie Mellon have the freedom to design courses of study that cross over majors and disciplines. In fact, some students have double majors, minors, or concentrations in areas other than their principal major. It is not unusual to find an engineering student with a double major in music or an English major with a minor in business administration.

The Bachelor of Computer Science and Arts, Bachelor of Humanities and Arts, and Bachelor of Science and Arts degree programs are unique, nonperformance-based programs that allow students to pursue interdisciplinary programs in the fine arts and either computer science, humanities and social sciences, or the pure sciences. Other special programs include Army, Navy, and Air Force ROTC; self-defined majors and interdepartmental major options in the College of Humanities and Social Sciences; prelaw and premedicine advising programs; and five-year combined bachelor's/master's degree programs.

Carnegie Mellon has nearly unlimited opportunities for students to participate in undergraduate research, sometimes as early as the second semester of the freshman year. Many departments offer research training courses and research programs during the academic year and summer. Students can work on research in groups, individually with a professor, or independently through Carnegie Mellon's Small Undergraduate Research Grant (SURG) program.

Off-Campus Programs

Carnegie Mellon students can take one course per semester at any of the following colleges and universities in Pittsburgh for full credit: the University of Pittsburgh, Carlow College, Chatham University, Duquesne University, La Roche College, Point Park University, Robert Morris University, Pittsburgh Theological Seminary, and the Community College of Allegheny County.

Carnegie Mellon has numerous study-abroad programs, including university exchange programs in Chile, Singapore, Mexico, Japan, and Switzerland. More than 350 students take advantage of study abroad each year. Students may also take advantage of study-abroad opportunities through their department or another university.

Academic Facilities

Carnegie Mellon has a 150-acre main campus with a few outlying research buildings. The campus contains more than fifty academic and administrative buildings and three libraries. The Hunt, Engineering and Science, and Mellon Institute Libraries contain more than 1 million volumes and thousands of periodicals. An international online resource sharing system and reciprocal borrowing between Carnegie Mellon and other local universities provide students with almost unlimited library resources.

A wireless network spans all academic, administrative, and residence hall buildings as well as key outdoor areas across campus. Public computing labs, known as clusters, offer more than 400 Macintosh, Windows, and Linux workstations. To help tackle computer-intensive calculations or produce dazzling multimedia presentations, color scanners, audio mixers, microphones, and cutting-edge high-definition video (HDV) camera and editing equipment are also available.

For students with their own computers, all of the residence hall rooms are wired to the Andrew network—Carnegie Mellon's high-speed computer network that links the campus and provides access to the outside world. Carnegie Mellon was the first university campus to offer wireless networking.

In addition to academic facilities, Carnegie Mellon features the University Center—a centralized building with eateries and recreational facilities, the historic Kresge Theater for Performing Arts, studio and black-box theaters, art galleries, abundant studio and rehearsal space, a gymnasium, and numerous research laboratories.

Costs

Carnegie Mellon's costs for the 2009–10 academic year included tuition and fees of $42,100 and room and board of $10,750. Books, supplies, and personal expenses were estimated at $2400. The total cost was approximately $55,250. International students also paid an additional $2200 for required health insurance.

Financial Aid

Carnegie Mellon is a need-blind institution, meaning that students' personal financial information is not considered in the admission process. Approximately 59 percent of the freshman class receives financial aid (U.S. citizens and eligible noncitizens).

Carnegie Mellon uses Federal Methodology to determine financial aid eligibility. The forms required to apply for financial assistance are the Free Application for Federal Student Aid (FAFSA), the Carnegie Mellon Financial Aid Form, parental W-2s, and both parental and student tax returns. Financial aid packages usually include a combination of loans, grants, and work-study allowances.

Carnegie Mellon also offers the Carnegie Scholarship, a need- and merit-based scholarship, awarded to academically and artistically talented middle-income students who qualify for little to no need-based financial aid. Carnegie Scholarships are open to all qualified U.S. citizens and permanent residents, regardless of race or national origin. In order to be considered for the Carnegie Scholarship, students must file the FAFSA. Students are also encouraged to apply for outside scholarships as a source of aid.

Faculty

Carnegie Mellon has more than 1,200 teaching and research faculty members and a student-faculty ratio of 10:1. The average class size is 25 to 35 students. Faculty members are practicing professionals at the forefront of their respective fields who often teach both undergraduate and graduate courses. Carnegie Mellon's classes are taught by faculty members, not teaching assistants. Professors, instructors, and lecturers are in the classroom, lab, studio, or workplace creating new knowledge on a daily basis and passing that knowledge on to their students. Undergraduates have the opportunity to work on groundbreaking research projects with award-winning faculty members, many times one-on-one, through assistantships, internships, work-study positions, and extracurricular organizations.

Student Government

Carnegie Mellon's Student Senate is composed of representatives from each college at Carnegie Mellon and exists to promote the welfare of the campus community, distribute budget funds to student groups, provide a liaison between students and the administration, and inform the student body of proposals and changes.

Admission Requirements

Carnegie Mellon looks for strong students, both academically and socially, who have a wide range of interests and activities. There are no minimum grade requirements or standardized test scores, although most of Carnegie Mellon's students tend to have strong test scores and are at the top of their classes. The University uses standardized test scores, including the SAT Reasoning Test (or ACT with Writing Test) and SAT Subject Tests; high school performance; evidence of leadership; honors and awards earned; and extracurricular activities to make admission decisions. Recommendations from a guidance counselor and a teacher are required along with a personal statement and essay. Interviews with admission counselors are recommended but not required.

Carnegie Mellon also requires the TOEFL or IELTS if the student's native language is not English. Carnegie Mellon requires TOEFL scores of 250 or better on the CBT TOEFL, 600 or better on the pencil and paper TOEFL, 100 or better on the Internet-based TOEFL, or an IELTS score of 7 or above.

Carnegie Mellon strives to build a class of students that is racially, socially, economically, and geographically diverse. The University is committed to recruiting students from traditionally underrepresented backgrounds, including African Americans, Hispanic/Latino Americans, and Native Americans. Transfer students are also welcome.

Application and Information

Carnegie Mellon has three types of decision plans: early admission, early decision, and regular decision.

Early admission is for high school juniors who wish to skip their senior year to go directly to college. In addition to academic strength, early admission candidates must display maturity and have strong teacher and guidance counselor recommendations. The application deadline for early admission is January 1 (December 1 for fine arts), and candidates are notified between March 15 and April 15.

Early decision is offered for students who declare Carnegie Mellon as their first choice. Early decision is a binding agreement; if admitted, students are expected to enroll. The University offers two early decision plans. The deadline for Early Decision I is November 1 (there is no Early Decision I for acting, music, theater, directing, composition, voice, flute, or B.C.S.A./B.H.A./B.S.A.), and candidates are notified of a decision by December 15. The deadline for Early Decision II is December 1 (there is no Early Decision II for architecture, art, design, drama, music, or B.C.S.A./B.H.A./B.S.A.), and candidates are notified by January 15.

Regular decision is the most popular plan. Applications are due by January 1 (December 1 for fine arts), and notification occurs between March 15 and April 15.

Students interested in learning more about Carnegie Mellon can arrange to visit the campus. Throughout most of the year, the University offers group information sessions, campus tours, and personal interviews, which are recommended, but not required, for admission.

Group information sessions and hometown or alumni interviews are available for students who cannot come to Pittsburgh. University representatives travel across the United States during the fall of every year. Students should visit http://www.cmu.edu/admission to see the current travel schedule.

For more information, students should contact:

Carnegie Mellon Office of Admission
5000 Forbes Avenue
Pittsburgh, Pennsylvania 15213-3890
Phone: 412-268-2082
Fax: 412-268-7838
E-mail: undergraduate-admissions@andrew.cmu.edu
Web site: http://www.cmu.edu/admission/

Carnegie Mellon University, located in Pittsburgh, Pennsylvania, is one of America's leading universities.

CARROLL COLLEGE

HELENA, MONTANA

The College

Student centered and affordable, Carroll College is a private, Catholic college located in Montana's state capital. Carroll is nationally recognized for excellence in academics, athletics, and extracurricular competition. With a student body of 1,500 and most classes averaging 20 or fewer students, Carroll offers each student personalized attention and mentoring from outstanding expert faculty members. Carroll's faculty is results-oriented, assisting students in classwork, research, job searches, and graduate school admissions. This personal touch is also reflected by Carroll's award-winning financial aid staff, committed to offering generous grants and scholarships which are available to 95 percent of all students, with financial aid awards continuing through all four years of a student's education. Finally, Carroll is committed to making sure students can enroll in the courses needed to complete their majors in four years. This can save Carroll students time and money.

In national competition, Carroll wins high honors. Carroll's Fighting Saints football team has won five NAIA national championships, all while maintaining a record number of nationally recognized academic scholar-athletes. In the 2009–10 season, all nine of Carroll's athletic teams were honored as NAIA Scholar Teams, earning at least a 3.0 team GPA, and Carroll's soccer team led the nation in 2007–08 for the highest GPA in the NAIA. The Carroll Talking Saints forensics team, a training ground for future attorneys, politicians, and business professionals, is ranked in the top five of all colleges and universities of all sizes nationwide and has reigned as the Northwest regional champion for the past twenty years.

Eighty-four percent of Carroll pre-med students applying to medical school are accepted, while the national average for medical school acceptance hovers near 50 percent. Carroll students taking all sections of the nationwide Uniform Certified Public Accountant Examination enjoy a first-time pass rate three times the national average.

Distinctive to Carroll is its dedication to service learning and social justice. Starting from the first semester of freshman year, students embark on professor-led projects to help underserved people while examining the deeper issues involved. These projects take students into the community, where they offer volunteer hours and research expertise to organizations such as the local food bank, homeless shelter, and schools. Service abroad is available several times a year to Carroll students. Recent trips include student journeys to Haiti to provide medical care and Carroll's student chapter of Engineers Without Borders constructed an integrated sewer, farm irrigation, and fish hatchery system at a Mexican orphanage. Students have also volunteered their medical and engineering skills at a Guatemalan school and clinic. Students can also create their own social justice project. As an example, for four years, students have led an award-winning fundraiser to benefit St. Jude Children's Research Hospital and raised over $100,000.

The College's commitment to service is also embodied in many of Carroll's programs, including the Human-Animal Bond minor, the first of its kind in the nation, which educates students to train dogs and horses as service and therapy animals with a foundation in psychology. Carroll's Hunthausen Peace and Justice Center fosters service work and hosts guest speakers and special events to raise awareness about social justice issues. The Center also provides financial and moral support to students who answer the call to serve others.

Founded in 1909, Carroll College is accredited by the Northwest Association of Schools and Colleges. The College is a member of the National Association of Independent Colleges and Universities, the American Council on Education, the Council of Independent Colleges, the Association of Catholic Colleges and Universities, and the Western Independent College Fund.

Location

Helena, the state capital, nestles in the heart of southwestern Montana's Rocky Mountains. It is a wonderland for hikers, mountain bikers, climbers, skiers and boarders, kayakers, and enthusiasts of almost every outdoor sport. Carroll's Adventures and Mountaineering Program guides hundreds of students on backpacking, camping, rock-climbing, and snow exploits in addition to sponsoring outdoor survival clinics and extreme sport film screenings.

The Great Divide Ski Area is a 45-minute trek from Carroll. Two internationally top-rated world-class ski resorts are easy day trips and four other outstanding ski hills are about 2½ hours from campus.

Majors and Degrees

Carroll College offers a four-year Bachelor of Arts degree program. Its majors and areas of concentration include accounting; biology; biochemistry-molecular biology; business administration (with concentrations in economics, finance, international business, management, and marketing); chemistry; civil engineering; civil engineering with a concentration in environmental engineering; classical studies; communication studies; community health; computer information systems (CIS); computer science; elementary education; engineering (3-2 and 4-2 programs); engineering mechanics; English literature; English writing; environmental studies (with concentrations in biology, chemistry, community formation, culture integration, and public policy and management); ethics and values studies; French; health and physical education (with concentrations in K–12 and sport management); health science; history; international relations; mathematics (with a cognate concentration); nursing; philosophy; political science; psychology; public administration; public relations (with concentrations in marketing, print journalism, and TV production); secondary education (with concentrations in biology, chemistry, communication studies, English, history, mathematics, political science, and social studies); sociology; Spanish; Spanish education (K–12); theater (with concentrations in acting/directing and design/stagecraft); and theology (with concentrations in contextual and systematic).

Under the 3-2 engineering program, students attend Carroll for three years and then transfer to an affiliate school to complete specialized studies. Upon completion, students receive two degrees, one from Carroll and one from the affiliate school. Affiliate schools are Columbia, Gonzaga, Montana State–Bozeman, Montana Tech, and the Universities of Minnesota, Notre Dame, and Southern California.

Carroll offers preprofessional programs in dentistry, law, medicine, optometry, pharmacy, physical therapy, physician's assistant studies, seminary, and veterinary medicine. Carroll also offers various two-year Associate of Arts degrees.

Academic Programs

The academic year consists of fall and spring semesters and a limited summer term. Carroll's Bachelor of Arts degree program requires that all students study the arts, sciences, humanities, and social sciences for at least four of their eight semesters at Carroll.

Minors and special course offerings include anthropology, arts management and administration, dance, economics, gender studies, geographic information system (GIS) certification, the Honors Scholars Program, languages (including French, German, Greek, Latin, linguistics, and Spanish), Latin American studies, military science (ROTC), music, physics, special education, study abroad, television production, and visual arts.

Off-Campus Programs

Study-abroad opportunities round out Carroll's academic offerings. Carroll has provided students professor-led study-abroad opportunities to every continent except Antarctica. Carroll's Study Abroad Office also arranges for students to enter exchange programs and to perform independent study abroad at colleges and universities worldwide.

Academic Facilities

Carroll College offers learning facilities with the latest technology, including multiple touch-activated projected computer screens (known as SmartBoards) and real-time electronic classroom voting. The Fortin Science Center provides outstanding chemistry and biology laboratories. In 2008 and 2009, biology labs were remodeled to create an updated undergraduate research center, allowing Carroll students access to professional-caliber facilities and equipment for their scientific research. The Nursing Department's training facility is the regional leader, with a realistic ER triage unit and an extensive array of the most advanced patient-simulation equipment available, including SimMan and SimBaby. The Civil Engineering Laboratory houses professional-grade machinery and materials, including hydraulics-, machinery-, and structures-testing capabilities and a model water-treatment plant. Carroll's four coed residence halls provide classrooms, computer labs, chapels, and art galleries.

Costs

For the 2009–10 academic year, Carroll's tuition and fees totaled $22,044; room and board fees were $7188, and the technology and activities fee was $380. Other general personal expenses included books, supplies, and transportation. Generous financial aid provides substantial discounts to almost all students (see Financial Aid below).

Financial Aid

Because of the College's generous financial aid packages and an established likelihood of graduating in four years, Carroll students matriculate with around the same debt as state-school alumni. In the 2008–09 academic year, Carroll awarded an average of over $18,000 in financial aid packages to freshmen. Ninety-five percent of Carroll's full-time, degree-seeking students receive College-sponsored, state, and federal financial aid. Carroll's merit scholarships range from $4000 to $11,500 annually.

The average four-year graduation rate of Carroll College students is 86 percent, compared the national private college average of 79 percent and the national state university average of 49 percent. An earlier graduation can lower graduates' debts and improve their lifetime earning potential. As a result, Carroll's student loan repayment default rate remains one of the lowest in the nation. Carroll was recently recognized with an award from the Montana Guaranteed Student Loan Program for achieving the lowest loan default rate in Montana, which points to the value of a Carroll education and the proven success of Carroll alumni in obtaining well-paying jobs in their chosen professions upon graduation.

More information on Carroll scholarships is available at the College Web site at http://www.carroll.edu/finaid/. To receive priority consideration for scholarships, students must have a complete admission file by February 15. Carroll requires students interested in need-based financial assistance to submit the Free Application for Federal Student Aid (FAFSA), available from high school counselors or at http://www.fafsa.ed.gov, as early as possible after January 1.

Faculty

Carroll's 78 full-time and 71 adjunct faculty members are expert teachers and experts in their fields, with almost all holding doctorate or terminal degrees. Professors, not graduate students, instruct all Carroll courses.

Carroll's faculty members are consistently recognized for their excellence, earning Fulbright Scholarships and winning National Endowment for the Arts and National Endowment for the Humanities grants and awards for leadership and scholarship in their fields. In the sciences, Carroll professors perform groundbreaking research across the globe and lead student research in biology, chemistry, history, psychology, and many other disciplines. Widely published in the humanities and sciences, Carroll professors are also student-centered, placing a particular emphasis on mentoring students and maintaining extensive office hours and other opportunities for students seeking academic help and personal guidance. Students take advantage of opportunities to dine with professors in their homes and participate in activities such as game nights and music sessions at professors' residences. Professors actively assist students in applying for employment and graduate school and often play pivotal roles in their students' obtaining initial job offers, internships, graduate school placement, and research/graduate teaching fellowships.

Student Government

The Associated Students of Carroll College helps students communicate with the administration and make important decisions about campus activities and student life. All students vote to elect the campus president, vice president, executive secretary and treasurer, and each class (freshman, sophomore, junior, and senior) elects four student senators to represent them in campus decision making. Carroll's House of Representatives includes leaders of each campus club. The Carroll Activities Board assists students in starting their own clubs and leading their own projects, including a variety of campus events such as concerts, film festivals, comedy nights, and charity fund-raisers. Students are always welcome to write for Carroll's student newspaper, literary magazine, and yearbook; be a DJ on Carroll KROL-FM radio; film and report news as an intern reporter/anchor at Saints TV (aired on our NBC affiliate station on campus); and make indie movies for the annual Carroll film festival. Campus clubs include those devoted to service work; faith; social justice activism; professions like engineering, psychology, health care, and education; the environment and recycling; outdoor adventure; politics; international students; dance; rodeo; and astronomy.

Admission Requirements

Degree candidates are those who have applied through the Office of Admission for a course of study leading to the Bachelor of Arts degree. Degree candidates may be enrolled on a full- or part-time basis. Admission decisions are based upon a student's high school performance high school, personal essay, a secondary school report, letters of recommendation, demonstrated commitment to intellectual achievement, and performance on standardized college entrance exams.

When applying for admission, candidates must submit the application form, official transcripts from the high school and all colleges previously attended, a secondary school report and/or a letter of recommendation, ACT or SAT scores, and a $35 nonrefundable application fee. There is no fee for online applications at http://www.carroll.edu/admission/applying or through the Common Application at https://www.commonapp.org/. Transfer students who have successfully completed more than 24 college semester credits with at least a C (2.5) grade average are not required to submit high school transcripts or ACT or SAT scores.

Application and Information

Carroll College has a rolling admission policy with a regular admission deadline of February 15 for incoming freshmen and international applicants or March 15 for transfer applicants. Students should note that late submission of material may jeopardize financial aid awards and course registration. Students can apply online at the Carroll Web site or through the Common Application Web site.

For application forms or more information, students should contact:

Director of Admission
Carroll College
1601 North Benton Avenue
Helena, Montana 59625-0002
Phone: 406-447-4384
800-992-3648 (toll-free)
E-mail: admission@carroll.edu
Web site: http://www.carroll.edu

Carroll College's St. Charles Hall.

CARROLL UNIVERSITY

WAUKESHA, WISCONSIN

The University

Carroll University was chartered by the territorial legislature of Wisconsin in 1846. Carroll University is affiliated with the Presbyterian Church (U.S.A.) but is nonsectarian and ecumenical.

The University realizes that personalized education is the special province of a small college and recognizes the variety of students' individual needs and preferences. Carroll's student body is diverse, with representation from twenty-five states and thirty-three countries. The campus has more than 2,500 full-time men and women, as well as more than 650 part-time students. In addition, there are more than 200 graduate students on the Carroll campus.

Many opportunities exist for cocurricular involvement. Three fraternities and four sororities draw participation from about 13 percent of the students. A broad variety of special interest organizations provide a full program of campus activities in addition to the all-campus social, intellectual, and athletic events that are scheduled throughout the year. The University's facilities for recreation and athletics include the Van Male Fieldhouse, which has a basketball court; an indoor track; indoor facilities for badminton, tennis, and volleyball; and a pool. The adjacent Ganfield Gymnasium provides additional space for athletics and recreation. A football field, soccer field, new outdoor track, and softball diamond are also available.

In addition to the bachelor's degrees Carroll offers, the University also grants the master's degree in education and software engineering as well as a clinical doctorate in physical therapy.

Location

The University is located in the city of Waukesha, a residential community of 68,000 people, which is 18 miles west of Milwaukee and 100 miles north of Chicago. The University's proximity to these two major urban centers and to the settings associated with Wisconsin's famous outdoor sports and leisure activities provides Carroll students with numerous opportunities for recreation, entertainment, and enrichment.

Majors and Degrees

Carroll University grants the B.A., B.S., B.M.E. (Bachelor of Music Education), and B.S.N. (Bachelor of Science in Nursing) degrees. Areas of study include accounting, actuarial science, applied physics, art, athletic training, biochemistry, biology, business administration (finance, human resources, management, management information systems, marketing, small-business management), chemistry, communication, computer science (information systems, software engineering), criminal justice, diagnostic medical sonography, education (adaptive, early childhood, elementary, secondary), English, environmental science, European studies, exercise science, forensic science, global studies, graphic communication, history, information technology (Web application development, business and social applications), journalism, marine biology, mathematics, music, music education, nursing, oceanography, organizational leadership, philosophy, politics and economics, photography, physical education, physical therapy, politics, print management, psychology, public relations, radiologic technology, recreation management, religious studies, self-designed major, sociology, Spanish, theater arts, and writing.

Academic Programs

The University currently operates on a semester calendar. All students must complete 128 credits with a C average or better. A major, generally consisting of 40 credits, must be completed. General education requirements include the First Year Seminar, English, liberal studies distribution courses, and a capstone experience. B.A. students must take two years of a modern language or the equivalent. B.S. students must take mathematics and either a computer science or logic course. Students may also select a second major or they may select a minor, which generally requires 16 to 28 credits. The honors program offers intensive sections of courses in the arts and sciences for academically talented students.

Advanced placement or credit may be granted to students who have completed the appropriate College Board Advanced Placement examinations. Credit may be granted for a score at or above the 75th percentile on the humanities, natural science, or social science general examination of the College-Level Examination Program (CLEP). Scores on CLEP subject examinations may also qualify to be approved for credit. A total of not more than 48 credit hours may be awarded through CLEP general and subject examinations.

Off-Campus Programs

The New Cultural Experiences Program gives all Carroll students the opportunity to study in a different cultural setting. Students may plan an individual program or participate in a planned group experience involving other students and Carroll faculty members. Group experiences are offered in locations such as Australia, Belize, England, and Japan and countries in Europe and Africa. Other off-campus programs include the Washington Semester, the United Nations Semester, and the Junior Year Abroad. In addition, career internships are provided in the Milwaukee-Waukesha area for students interested in gaining practical work experience in their proposed career field. All of these programs carry degree credit; the amount depends upon the nature and duration of the experience.

Academic Facilities

The University library houses more than 150,000 volumes, 18,000 microforms, and 400 periodicals. The Department of Education is in the Barstow Building with the Modern Language and Communication Departments. Rankin Hall houses the Departments of Biology, Psychology, and Religious Studies, as well as the psychology laboratories. Maxon Hall houses the Departments of Geography and Mathematics. It also contains the laboratories for advanced chemistry; the geography laboratory, with independent-study booths and audiovisual instruments; a darkroom; a cartography laboratory; a map library; and a National Weather Service observation station. The chemistry and physics laboratories are in Lowry Hall. All science laboratories are provided with up-to-date equipment. Main Hall houses classrooms for all academic areas. MacAllister Hall is home to the Departments of English, History, Politics, and Philosophy.

The Shattuck Music Center houses a recital hall that seats 150, an auditorium that seats 1,350, and a Schantz seventy-two-stop pipe organ. The Department of Music has a large band-practice room, teaching studios, a multisensing room, a computerized music laboratory, and classrooms. The Humphrey Building houses the Art Department and Humphrey Memorial Chapel. The University's physical therapy program is located adjacent to the University's athletic complex. A state-of-the-art nursing lab is found in the lower level of the Theatre Arts Building.

Costs

For 2009–10, the tuition was approximately $22,470 and room and board were $7023.

Financial Aid

Approximately 98 percent of Carroll's students receive some form of financial aid. Aid is based on need, as determined by the U.S. Department of Education's Free Application for Federal Student Aid (FAFSA), as well as on scholastic ability and achievement. Generally, students receive a package consisting of a scholarship, a grant, a loan, and/or campus employment.

Various merit scholarships are available to students. Merit scholarships range from $24,000 to $44,000 over four years and are determined by a student's ACT or SAT scores and class rank. Students who attend high schools that do not rank are not excluded from consideration for any academic scholarships. Additional scholarships are awarded to qualified students who are interested in music, theater, history, art, math, or the sciences. Students should contact the Office of Admission for details.

Faculty

The student-faculty ratio at Carroll is approximately 16:1. More than 85 percent of faculty members hold a doctorate in their specialized area of study. There are more than 100 full-time faculty members at Carroll.

Student Government

Through election to the Student Senate and College Activities Board, students have responsibility for nonacademic matters affecting their lives at the University. In addition, there is voting student representation on all University committees, and there are student observers on the Board of Trustees.

Admission Requirements

Carroll's admission procedure is intended to ensure academic and personal success for accepted students. Each candidate is evaluated individually; evidence of the interest in and ability to do college-level work is important. The University exercises careful selection, but no candidate is disqualified because of race, color, religion, sex, national origin, age, disability, sexual orientation, or veteran status.

Application and Information

To be considered, each candidate for freshman admission must submit the following materials: a completed application for admission, a transcript from an accredited high school showing progress toward or completion of 15 units of work and graduation, a satisfactory personal evaluation from the high school, and scores on the SAT or ACT. Transfer students must submit a transcript from every college attended previously and a statement of good standing. Admission decisions are made on a rolling basis until the class is filled. There are no deadlines, but early application is recommended.

Admission to the University may be granted following the completion of three years of high school work, provided that the high school indicates that this is in the applicant's best interest. The candidate may or may not have completed the course work required for high school graduation at the time of admission, but he or she must show unusual promise and achievement.

For more information about Carroll University, prospective students should contact:

Admission Office
Carroll University
100 North East Avenue
Waukesha, Wisconsin 53186
Phone: 262-524-7220
800-CARROLL (toll-free)
E-mail: info@carrollu.edu
Web site: http://www.carrollu.edu

CARSON-NEWMAN COLLEGE

JEFFERSON CITY, TENNESSEE

The College

Founded in 1851 by Tennessee Baptists, Carson-Newman (C-N) is a private, coeducational, Christian liberal arts college. The College has an enrollment of approximately 2,000 undergraduate and over 150 graduate students. The average class size is 16 students, and the ratio of men to women is 1:1. Each fall, Carson-Newman enrolls approximately 550 new undergraduate students. While Carson-Newman students come primarily from the Southeastern states, thirty-two states are represented.

In addition to its outstanding academics, C-N also provides many opportunities for student involvement in various clubs and organizations, nationally recognized varsity athletics, intramural athletics, music and drama groups, an award-winning forensics team, and many other extracurricular activities. The majority of C-N students live on campus in one of the four residence halls or two apartment complexes.

Carson-Newman also offers graduate programs. Programs in education are available, leading to Master of Arts in Teaching (M.A.T.) degrees in curriculum and instruction and in English as a second language and Master of Education M.Ed.) degrees in curriculum and instruction, educational leadership, and school counseling. A Master of Science in Nursing (M.S.N.) degree is also offered. Beginning in the spring of 2010, C-N will also offer an M.B.A. program.

Location

C-N is conveniently located in eastern Tennessee, just 30 miles from Knoxville, which has a population of 450,000, and 45 miles from Gatlinburg, the gateway to the Great Smoky Mountains. Students appreciate the diverse opportunities available in the city and in the outdoor areas. Shopping, dining, and entertainment opportunities are available near the College.

Majors and Degrees

The nine academic divisions of the College are Business, Education, Family and Consumer Sciences, Fine Arts, Humanities, Natural Sciences and Mathematics, Nursing, Religion, and Social Sciences. C-N awards Bachelor of Arts, Bachelor of Music, Bachelor of Science, and Bachelor of Science in Nursing degrees. In addition, an Associate of Arts in Christian ministries degree is also offered.

Majors are available in art (art, photography), athletic training, business (accounting, business administration, international economics, general business, management), church recreation, communication studies and theater (advertising/public relations, journalism, media ministry, radio/television/film, speech), computer information systems (computer studies, data processing), education (athletic coaching, elementary education, physical education/health, secondary certification, special education), English (creative writing, literature), family and consumer sciences (child and family studies, consumer services, foods and nutrition, interior design and retail), early childhood education, foreign language (biblical languages, French, Spanish), general studies, history, human services, individual directions, mathematics, military science/U.S. Army ROTC or U.S. Air Force ROTC, music (church music, music composition, music education, music theory, music with an outside field, piano and organ performance, vocal performance), natural and physical science (biochemistry, biology, chemistry, physics), nursing, philosophy (philosophy, philosophy/religion), political science, psychology (applied psychology, social entrepreneurship), religion, sociology, and sport science (exercise science).

The College offers extremely strong curricula in preprofessional programs and health professions. Preprofessional programs are offered in dentistry, health information management, law, medicine, occupational therapy, optometry, physical therapy, and veterinary medicine. In cooperation with several other institutions, C-N offers binary degrees (2-3 and 3-2 programs) in medical technology, pharmacy, and physician assistant studies.

Academic Programs

The College operates on a traditional semester system. May term is a three-week intensive period of study giving students the opportunity to earn 3 credit hours. Summer terms are also offered.

All baccalaureate degrees require completion of 128 semester hours. Students must complete the C-N liberal arts core requirements and a total of 36 semester hours at the junior/senior level. Specific course requirements vary depending on major and degree program. Honors courses, independent study, and internships are available to students who qualify. Advanced credit is available for students who achieve required scores on AP exams, CLEP tests, and C-N departmental examinations.

New students are assigned a faculty adviser, who assists with course selection and student concerns. Career planning and tutoring services are also available through the Life Directions Center. The College's exceptionally high placement rate in professional programs in medicine, law, business, and theological study is testimony to the excellence of its rigorous academic program.

Off-Campus Programs

Students have the opportunity to spend an entire semester abroad by participating in the London Semester and other study-abroad opportunities. C-N, along with International Enrichment, Inc., provides all academic and nonacademic support services.

The Washington Semester is available as an internship program primarily for political science and prelaw majors. Through the program, students earn credit for work in the nation's capital. Art and foreign language majors may earn credit while studying and traveling throughout Europe during the three-week May term.

Academic Facilities

C-N offers the facilities and resources necessary for the enrichment of each student's education. Facilities include numerous computer labs; a campuswide computer network; a media service center; two theaters for drama production; Thomas Recital Hall, which is in one of the finest music facilities in the Southeast; two art galleries and twenty-three individual art studios; the Stephens-Burnette Library, with more than 500,000 volumes; and an award-winning 96,000-square-foot Student Activities Center. The new family and consumer science building, Blye-Poteat Hall, opened in fall 2007, and the new business building, Ted Russell Hall, opened in spring 2009.

Costs

The annual cost at Carson-Newman, including room, board, and tuition, is well below the national average for four-year private colleges. Tuition for 2009–10 is $17,850, room averages $2400, board averages $3050, the student activity fee is approximately $425, and the technology fee is approximately $425. Total direct charges are approximately $24,150. Students should allow approximately $800 for books per year.

Financial Aid

Carson-Newman allocates thousands of dollars each year to help supplement the resources of families. Financial aid awards are tailored to meet students' economic needs. Carson-Newman participates in all state and federal aid programs and awards aid based on demonstrated need as documented by a need analysis form, such as the Free Application for Federal Student Aid (FAFSA). Carson-Newman also awards academic scholarships based on achievement. The priority deadline for filing financial assistance forms is March 1.

Faculty

C-N faculty members are known for their interaction with students both inside and outside of classes. The student-faculty ratio at C-N is 13:1, so students are sure to receive individual attention. Faculty members are involved in scholarly pursuits such as authoring books, leading national scholastic organizations, and research, but their primary focus is teaching.

Student Government

The Student Government Association (SGA) represents the entire student body by voicing student concerns in campus affairs. The purpose of SGA is to promote the welfare of every student through justice, to protect individual rights and freedoms, to encourage high standards of conduct, and to train students in the general principles of self-government.

Admission Requirements

Carson-Newman College seeks applicants who demonstrate academic preparation and who possess an appreciation of and sensitivity to a Christian education and a liberal arts curriculum. Carson-Newman accepts applications for freshman and transfer admission for each term of enrollment (fall, spring, and summer). Freshman candidates must have a GPA of 2.25 or higher and a minimum score of 900 on the SAT (450 critical reading and 450 math) or 19 on the ACT; they must also rank in the top half of their high school graduating class. Transfer applicants must have a minimum cumulative GPA of 2.0 in courses that transfer to Carson-Newman. Additional information on admission requirements can be obtained on the Carson-Newman College Office of Admissions Web site.

Application and Information

Applicants must submit a free online application for admission, official transcripts, and test scores. Admission decisions are made on a rolling basis, and students are notified within two weeks of receipt of all required documents. The application deadline is May 1 for the fall semester or December 1 for the spring semester. Applicants who wish to be considered for merit scholarships should apply by December 31.

For additional information, students should contact the Office of Undergraduate Admissions at 865-471-3223 or visit http://www.cn.edu.

Office of Undergraduate Admissions
Carson-Newman College
Jefferson City, Tennessee 37760
Phone: 865-471-3223
800-678-9061 (toll-free)
E-mail: admitme@cn.edu
Web site: http://www.cn.edu

Students on the Carson-Newman campus.

CASE WESTERN RESERVE UNIVERSITY

CLEVELAND, OHIO

The University

Ranking consistently among the top private universities in the United States, Case Western Reserve University offers unlimited opportunities for motivated students. Its faculty members challenge and support students to help them flourish, and its partnerships with world-class cultural, educational, and scientific institutions ensure that undergraduate education extends beyond the classroom.

Challenging and innovative academic programs and experiential learning opportunities are at the core of the Case experience. Case's 10:1 student-faculty ratio allows students to have close interaction with professors. Co-ops, internships, study abroad, and other experiential opportunities bring theory to life in amazing settings, and nearly every student participates in research or independent study.

Although Case Western Reserve was formed in 1967 by the merger of Western Reserve University and Case Institute of Technology, it traces its roots back to the 1826 founding of Western Reserve College, making Case both a young university and one of the oldest private colleges in the nation. Currently, more than 4,300 undergraduates are enrolled in programs in engineering, science, management, nursing, the arts, the humanities, and the social and behavioral sciences. Students access Case's graduate and professional schools in applied social sciences, dental medicine, graduate studies, law, management, medicine, and nursing. Several undergraduate programs and majors combine undergraduate and graduate and professional degrees and resources. Examples are five-year B.A./M.A. or B.S./M.S. degrees, including a five-year B.S./M.S. degree in engineering and management, and dual admission to undergraduate and professional school. In addition, collaborative arrangements with neighboring cultural and health-care institutions enable the University to provide special opportunities in other fields, such as art history, offered in conjunction with the renowned Cleveland Museum of Art.

Nearly every type of student interest group, from political organizations to multiethnic student unions, is represented on campus. Campus Greek life consists of sixteen national fraternities and seven sororities, with approximately 30 percent of undergraduate students participating. Residence halls are coeducational, and 81 percent of the students reside on campus.

A charter member of the University Athletic Association, an NCAA Division III conference, Case has won championships in cross-country, football, softball, track and field, and wrestling. Twenty percent of undergraduates wear the blue-and-white varsity uniform, and 70 percent join an intramural team. Club sports include fencing, golf, ice hockey, skiing, and Ultimate (Frisbee).

Location

Case is located in University Circle, a unique cultural district comprising 550 acres of parks, gardens, museums, schools, hospitals, churches, and human service institutions. The Cleveland Museum of Art, the Cleveland Museum of Natural History, and Severance Hall, home of the Cleveland Orchestra, are within walking distance; downtown Cleveland is 10 minutes away by car or public transportation. Partnerships in education and research among University Circle institutions enable students to make full use of resources beyond those of the University itself, and students receive free access to these and other local institutions, including the downtown Rock and Roll Hall of Fame and Museum.

Majors and Degrees

Case has a single-door admission policy—once students are admitted, they can pursue any major(s) they wish. Programs of study leading to the Bachelor of Arts degree include anthropology, art history (joint program with the Cleveland Museum of Art), Asian studies, astronomy, biochemistry, biology, chemistry, classics, cognitive science, communication sciences (collaborative program with the Cleveland Hearing and Speech Center), computer science, dance, economics, English, environmental geology, environmental studies, French, French and Francophone studies, geological sciences, German, German studies, history, history and philosophy of science, international studies, Japanese studies, mathematics, music (joint program with the Cleveland Institute of Music), nutrition, nutritional biochemistry and metabolism, philosophy, physics, political science, psychology, religious studies, sociology, Spanish, statistics, theater, and world literature. The following B.A. programs are available as a second major only: American studies, evolutionary biology, gerontological studies, natural sciences, prearchitecture, teacher education, and women's studies.

Bachelor of Science degrees are offered in the following fields: accounting, aerospace engineering, applied mathematics, art education (joint program with the Cleveland Institute of Art), astronomy, biochemistry, biology, biomedical engineering, chemical engineering, chemistry, civil engineering, computer engineering, computer science, electrical engineering, engineering physics, geological sciences, management (business), materials science and engineering, mathematics, mathematics and physics (combined major), mechanical engineering, music education, nursing, nutrition, nutritional biochemistry and metabolism, physics, polymer science and engineering, statistics, systems and control engineering, systems biology, and an undesignated engineering major.

Minor areas of concentration include artificial intelligence, art studio, childhood studies, Chinese, electronics, entrepreneurship, ethnic studies, finance, history of science and technology, Italian, Japanese, Judaic studies, management information and decision systems, marketing, photography, public policy, Russian, sports medicine, and teacher licensure. In addition, most major subjects are available as minors. A minor in electrical engineering is available to students pursuing any other engineering major.

Students may work toward a combined B.A./B.S. degree or integrate undergraduate and graduate studies to complete both the bachelor's and master's degrees in five years or less. Students who are interested in both the liberal arts and engineering can benefit from the Binary Program. Students spend three years at one of forty participating liberal arts colleges and then spend two years at Case studying engineering or a related field. Graduates of this program receive both a B.A. and a B.S. degree.

Academic Programs

Students in all majors participate in SAGES, the Seminar Approach to General Education and Scholarship program. SAGES consists of four innovative and engaging seminars that emphasize written and verbal communication skills and concludes with a Senior Capstone project. As a result, all Case students benefit from building on these important skills throughout their undergraduate education. Through a combination of core curricula, major requirements, and minors or approved course sequences, all undergraduates receive a broad educational base as well as specialized knowledge in their chosen fields.

The University offers students opportunities for independent research and internships in business, health care, government, and the arts. A co-op option providing two 7-month work periods in industry or government is available for majors in engineering, science, management, accounting, and computer science.

The Senior Year in Professional Studies option allows B.A. candidates who are admitted during their junior year to Case's Schools of Applied Social Sciences, Dental Medicine, Management, Medicine, or Nursing to substitute the first year of professional school for their senior year.

High school seniors who are exceptionally well qualified in specific fields are eligible for the Pre-professional Scholars Program (PPSP), which is offered in association with the Schools of Applied Social Sciences, Dental Medicine, Law, and Medicine. Each PPSP student is awarded admission to Case as an undergraduate and conditional admission to the appropriate professional school upon completion of the entrance requirements set by each school.

The University has two 4-month semesters and one 4- to 8-week summer session.

Off-Campus Programs

Selected students may enroll as juniors and seniors in the Washington Semester program, which is conducted each spring at American

University. Students with a B average or higher may participate in the Junior Year Abroad program. Up to 36 hours of credit may be granted for study at an international university. Engineering students can participate in a Global Exchange with universities such as Waseda in Tokyo, Japan. Students may also cross-register at other Cleveland-area colleges and universities for one course per semester.

Academic Facilities

The $30-million Kelvin Smith Library is located in the heart of the campus. Through reciprocal borrowing arrangements, Case students have access to the holdings of the Cleveland Public Library as well as the libraries of five University Circle institutions; the members of OhioLINK, a network that includes state colleges and universities; the State Library of Ohio; and several private institutions. Case is classified by the Carnegie Foundation as a university with very high research activity (RU/VH), and its lab facilities are state of the art. The University operates two astronomical observatories, a biological field station, a $6-million undergraduate engineering lab, and nearly 100 other designated research centers and laboratories. The University's high-speed communications network links every residence hall room with computing centers, libraries, and databases on and off campus. Case's wireless network is one of the largest in the U.S. Other computer facilities on campus offer various models of computers and a wide variety of software programs, available free of charge to Case students.

The University Farm, located in nearby Hunting Valley, Ohio, offers educational opportunities in natural settings. Its 389 acres encompass a variety of deciduous forests, ravines, waterfalls, meadows, ponds, and a self-contained natural watershed.

Costs

For 2009–10, tuition and compulsory health and laboratory fees totaled $35,900. Room and board cost an average of $10,890. Required fees totaled $1843.

Financial Aid

Financial aid consisting of grants, loans, and work assistance is awarded on the basis of a student's need. Applicants must file the Free Application for Federal Student Aid (FAFSA) as well as Case's own financial aid application. A signed copy of the most recent federal tax return (Form 1040) is also required. Students are automatically considered for merit-based scholarships when they apply to the University; these awards range from $500 to 80 percent of tuition.

Faculty

The undergraduate student-faculty ratio at Case is 10:1. Ninety-six percent of credit hours are taught by faculty members, not graduate students. Each college provides counselors who are available for both academic and personal advice. Once a major has been chosen, a member of the department in which the student is majoring acts as his or her academic adviser.

Case counts 14 Nobel laureates among its alumni and current and former faculty members, including the first American scientist ever to receive the prize. Undergraduate students have several opportunities to partner with faculty members on research or special projects, allowing for valuable learning opportunities, mentoring, networking, and personal development.

Student Government

Case's Undergraduate Student Government represents all undergraduate students. The assembly acts as a liaison between undergraduate students and the faculty, administration, and other groups; grants recognition to undergraduate organizations; and has the responsibility and authority to allocate funds from student activity fees to student organizations. The Residence Hall Association is a governing body for on-campus living, the University Program Board plans special events, and the Interfraternity Congress and Panhellenic Council govern the Greek community.

Admission Requirements

It is recommended that students pursue 4 units of English, 3 units of math, 3 units of science (2 of which must be laboratory science), 3 units of social studies, and 2 units of foreign language. The University recommends that applicants interested in engineering and the sciences have an additional unit of math and laboratory science. For students interested in the liberal arts, it is recommended that students take an additional unit of social studies and foreign language. An informational interview is not a required part of the admission process, but it is strongly recommended as the best way to learn about the University. To receive full consideration for admission and scholarships, students must take the SAT or ACT prior to their selected application deadline.

Application and Information

Students who wish to receive early notification of their admission status may apply for early action by November 15; they are notified by January 1. The final application deadline is January 15 for notification by April 1. Application deadlines for transfer students are May 15 for fall admission and October 15 for spring admission. The application deadline for the Pre-professional Scholars Program (medicine, dentistry, law, or social work) is December 1. Students can apply to Case via the free online Common Application. The fall semester begins in late August.

Interviews with admission professionals, campus visits, group information sessions, and other resources are available to all prospective students. For more information, students should contact:

Office of Undergraduate Admission
Case Western Reserve University
10900 Euclid Avenue
Cleveland, Ohio 44106-7055
Phone: 216-368-4450
E-mail: admission@case.edu
Web site: http://admission.case.edu

Case Western Reserve University students on campus.

COLLEGE CLOSE-UPS

CASTLETON STATE COLLEGE

CASTLETON, VERMONT

The College

Castleton State College was founded in 1787; it was the first institution of higher learning in Vermont and the eighteenth in the United States. The 165-acre campus is located in Castleton, a historic Vermont village. Sixty-five percent of the 1,800 full-time undergraduate students at the College are Vermonters; the balance of the student population comes from New England and the Middle Atlantic states.

Castleton is committed to providing an undergraduate education in which the liberal arts and career preparation complement each other. Through an innovative program called Soundings, freshmen earn academic credit by attending a series of special events that include theater, music, dance, film, debate, and opinion from influential people. New students also participate in the First-Year Seminar, giving them the opportunity to develop the skills of a successful college student. First-year students may apply for the College's Honors Program. Community service and internships play an important role in a Castleton education.

There are ten major residence halls. Together, the residences accommodate nearly 900 students. Each residence hall room is equipped with at least two Internet hookups and wireless access, which give each student the opportunity to access the Web and e-mail using their own personal computer. There is no additional charge for this service. Each room is also equipped with cable TV connections. Off-campus housing is available in the Castleton, Fair Haven, and Rutland areas. Students who live on campus eat in Huden Dining Hall. All students are allowed to have automobiles on campus.

More than forty clubs and organizations provide a wide variety of student activities that include club sports, an FM radio station, the student newspaper, and an active outing club. Other clubs relate to college majors and future careers; still others serve the College or local community. Castleton is a member of the North Atlantic Conference of NCAA Division III. Castleton offers twenty intercollegiate sports. Men compete in baseball, basketball, cross-country running, football, golf, ice hockey, lacrosse, skiing, soccer, and tennis. Women compete in basketball, cross-country running, field hockey, ice hockey, lacrosse, skiing, soccer, softball, tennis, and volleyball. A majority of Castleton's students are involved in the intramural and recreational sports program.

In the fall of 2009, Castleton completed a $25.7-million project which included renovation and expansion of the Campus Center and the gymnasium, construction of a stadium, and improvements to the athletic fields.

Location

The campus is 12 miles west of Rutland, one of Vermont's largest cities. Montreal, Boston, Hartford, Albany, and New York City are all within easy driving distance. Amtrak passenger trains to and from New York City stop in the village of Castleton. Killington and Pico ski areas, Lake Bomoseen, and the Green Mountains provide excellent recreational opportunities and an exceptional living and learning environment.

Majors and Degrees

Castleton State College offers B.A. or B.S. degrees in more than thirty areas of study: accounting, American literature, art, athletic training, biology, children's literature, computer information systems, communication, criminal justice, digital media, elementary education, environmental science, exercise science, forensic psychology, geology, health science, history, journalism, management, marketing, mass media, mathematics, music, music education, natural science, nursing, physical education, psychology, public relations, secondary education, social work, sociology, Spanish, special education, sports administration, theater arts, and world literature. Associate degrees can be earned in business, communication, computer programming, criminal justice, general studies, or nursing.

Academic Programs

The Castleton curriculum is designed to provide the student with a strong liberal arts background plus the opportunity for career preparation in a specific area. All four-year students are required to complete a core of general education requirements during the four-year degree program. The first year of study can be used by the undecided student to explore various areas of interest. The student with a specific career interest may begin study in the major field as a freshman, although four-year students are not required to formally declare their major until the end of the sophomore year.

Castleton students typically enroll in five courses each semester. The academic calendar consists of two 15-week semesters and three 4-week summer sessions. Grading is traditional, and a pass/no-pass option is available. Internships and field experiences complement many of the academic programs at Castleton and are required in the communication, criminal justice, social work, and education programs.

Students may transfer internally from two-year to four-year programs in business, communication, computer information systems, criminal justice, and general studies. Students who transfer to Castleton after graduating from an accredited two-year college are granted full transfer credit for all academic work up to 64 credits or the number required for the associate degree.

Freshman students achieving at least a 3.5 grade point average in their first year at Castleton are recognized by the Castleton Chapter of Phi Eta Sigma, a national honor society that recognizes freshman scholastic achievement in colleges throughout the country. Outstanding junior and senior scholars are recognized by the Castleton Chapter of Alpha Chi. Pinnacle, the honor society for nontraditional students, honors qualified candidates. There are honor societies in theater arts, education, psychology, and Spanish. Students who have achieved a 4.0 grade point average are named to the President's List of Outstanding Students and those with a 3.5 grade point average or better to the Dean's List.

Academic Facilities

The Calvin Coolidge Library houses a collection of more than 500,000 books, periodicals, microforms, and nonprint media. Access to Castleton's library resources and outside scholarly sources is made possible through numerous online and CD databases; a sophisticated, networked electronic library system; the Internet; and strong consortial relationships within the state of Vermont. An audiovisual media facility provides a wide range of audiovisual equipment, including digital video editing, digital cameras, and presentation equipment.

Castleton's Stafford Academic Center houses the Computing Center, a high-tech multimedia lecture hall, distance learning classrooms, and the Departments of Education, Mathematics, and Nursing.

The Spartan Athletic Complex houses Glenbrook Gymnasium, the athletic training room, a swimming pool, two racquetball courts, a new fitness center, and a large indoor activity area.

The Fine Arts Center contains a 500-seat auditorium; facilities for art, drama, dance, and music. A new television studio is due to open in 2010 in an addition to Leavenworth Hall.

The Jeffords Center, which was renovated and expanded in the spring and summer of 2007, houses science classrooms and laboratories, a state-of-the-art auditorium, laboratories for faculty and student research projects, and a greenhouse. An astronomical observatory is a short walk away.

There are more than 225 personal computers designated for student use located in labs across the campus.

Costs

Costs for 2009–10 were as follows: tuition for Vermont residents, $7992, and for nonresidents, $17,232. Room and board expenses totaled $7808. Annual fees were $828. The orientation and registration for new students was $200.

Financial Aid

Eighty percent of Castleton's full-time undergraduate students receive financial assistance from federal, state, College, or other sources. Grants, loans, and work-study jobs are available for qualified students. Applicants for financial aid should file the Free Application for Federal Student Aid (FAFSA) form by February 15 of the senior year in high school. All financial aid awards are based on need.

Most Castleton scholarships are awarded as part of the College's Honors Scholarship Program. Amounts range from $1000 to $6000 per year. First-year students who have a combined critical reading and math SAT score of at least 1100 and have a GPA of at least 3.3 on a 4.0 scale are eligible for one of these scholarships. Additional scholarships are available to new students based on certain academic credentials, service to their community, and financial need. There are also special scholarships for students wishing to study music or Spanish.

Faculty

The full-time faculty at Castleton consists of 90 men and women, 96 percent of whom hold terminal degrees in their field. Adjunct faculty members, many of them local businesspeople and members of the professions, complement the efforts of the full-time faculty. The student-faculty ratio is 14:1. Each student has a faculty member as an adviser.

Student Government

The Student Association is the chief vehicle of student government. All students who are registered for 8 or more credit hours are members. Elected representatives hold membership on most College committees, including the Curriculum and Cultural Affairs Committees. Students are also able to develop leadership qualities by participating in the various clubs and other organizations on campus.

Admission Requirements

Applicants are evaluated on the basis of their secondary school records, standardized test scores, and recommendations. Admission is granted to those applicants who have demonstrated their ability and potential to meet the challenges of a postsecondary learning experience.

Application and Information

Students may apply for admission through the Castleton Web site. Under Castleton's rolling admission policy, applications are processed throughout the year, and candidates are notified of the admission decision as soon as their folders are complete. Students are admitted in the fall and spring semesters.

For more information about Castleton State College or to arrange a campus visit, students should contact:

Director of Admissions
Castleton State College
Castleton, Vermont 05735
Phone: 802-468-1213
800-639-8521 (toll-free)
Fax: 802-468-1476
E-mail: info@castleton.edu
Web site: http://www.castleton.edu

On the grounds of Castleton State College.

CEDAR CREST COLLEGE

ALLENTOWN, PENNSYLVANIA

The College

Cedar Crest College was founded in 1867 and for more than 142 years has taken a bold approach to education by providing women with the competitive edge needed to succeed. A liberal arts college by design, Cedar Crest prepares women to lead in a global society. Approximately 1,900 students attend the College annually, representing thirty-two states and twenty countries.

Cedar Crest College has more than thirty academic programs and faculty members who put a unique spin on traditional majors such as business and marketing, communication, English, and performing arts. In addition, Cedar Crest College has renowned programs in forensic science (one of fourteen accredited programs in the country and the only one affiliated with a women's college), social work (the only accredited program in the Lehigh Valley), and genetic engineering (one of the oldest programs in the country).

The College's health and wellness program has received a gold award for student health, wellness, and counseling from the National Association of Student Personnel Administrators. The health and wellness initiative includes personal sports training; nutrition counseling; and a full schedule of dance, yoga, and aerobics classes. The Rodale Aquatic Center for Civic Health, a state-of-the-art, two-pool complex, offers health and fitness opportunities for the entire campus community. The campus also has tennis courts; regulation fields for field hockey, lacrosse, soccer, and softball; and a fitness center.

Cedar Crest students participate in eight NCAA Division III intercollegiate sports: basketball, cross-country, field hockey, lacrosse, soccer, softball, tennis, and volleyball. The College offers two club sports, equestrian and swimming. The Falcons belong to the Colonial States Athletic Conference (CSAC) and compete against institutions in Pennsylvania, New Jersey, and Delaware. Cedar Crest student-athletes successfully integrate their studies with athletics. The CSAC recently awarded Cedar Crest student-athletes the first institutional achievement award for earning the highest grade point average in the Conference.

Cedar Crest students hold leadership positions in more than forty clubs and organizations on campus. Student clubs range from the Student Government Association and Student Activities Board to the Literary Club and Biology Club. The College prepares women to lead, not just in college, but for life. Leadership retreats and community service opportunities are held throughout the year. The campus completes more than 20,000 hours in community service annually. Service opportunities are available throughout the Lehigh Valley at schools, hospitals, animal shelters, and Habitat for Humanity. At Cedar Crest, students serve early and often.

Cedar Crest upperclass students have the opportunity to live and learn together in the College's living-learning communities. These communities focus on a variety of relevant and timely topics such as global social justice and the environment. They bring together students who share a common interest, regardless of major or career focus. Sharing perspectives and lifestyles in this group setting enhances the students' educational journey as they gain intellectual appreciation and global awareness, apply and hone leadership skills, and make a difference locally and globally. It is the epitome of the seamless college experience as students live together, take a house class together, travel together, and develop close relationships with a faculty member affiliated with the community.

Through the Career Planning Office, students are placed in competitive internships near the campus and in major cities.

Cedar Crest's academic programs are fully accredited by the Middle States Association of Colleges and Schools and, where appropriate, by the American Academy of Forensic Science, American Medical Association, American Dietetic Association, American Bar Association, National League for Nursing Accrediting Commission, National Council on Social Work Education, and the Departments of Education of New York, New Jersey, and Pennsylvania. The College offers master's degrees three fields: education, forensic science, and nursing.

Location

Students enjoy Cedar Crest's parklike campus, nestled in the heart of the Lehigh Valley in the West End of Allentown, Pennsylvania. The campus is a beautiful 84-acre nationally registered arboretum with more than 130 species of trees. The College is within easy distance of the extensive Allentown park system, high-end retail shopping, well-known restaurants, cultural activities, and the Pocono ski and outdoor resorts.

Cedar Crest is located in "College Valley," home to more than 32,000 students at eight colleges within 20 minutes of campus. Students can participate in student- and faculty-led trips to nearby Philadelphia (less than one hour) and New York City (less than two hours). Students can explore the metropolitan areas of the East Coast, like Washington D.C., Baltimore, and Boston, while enjoying the benefits of a small, suburban campus.

Majors and Degrees

Cedar Crest offers more than thirty fields of study in the arts, humanities, social sciences, business, and sciences. The combination of majors and course offerings provides students with a strong liberal arts background. The College also offers preprofessional programs in dentistry, law, medicine, and veterinary medicine. The well-respected academic program provides support for students as they create an academic experience that is both personal and practical. Students are expected to be involved in planning their academic pathway from the very beginning.

Academic Programs

Self-designed majors, double majors, minors, and individual and group research projects are available and reflect the academic emphasis at the undergraduate level. Students may begin research as early as their first year on campus. Students can begin writing for the campus newspaper or hosting their own radio shows early in their college career.

The Honors Program at Cedar Crest is cross-disciplinary and designed for women who have demonstrated exceptional academic and intellectual curiosity and achievement. It embraces the traditional liberal arts philosophy and provides students with a unique opportunity for growth and enrichment in an environment whose hallmark is an engaged faculty, diverse coursework, and graduate-level research experience.

Through a consortium with the Lehigh Valley Colleges, Cedar Crest upperclass students may cross-register and take courses at Lehigh and DeSales Universities and Lafayette, Moravian, and Muhlenberg Colleges at no additional cost.

Off-Campus Programs

Cedar Crest women are encouraged to pursue internships in their area of study. Internships enable students to gain practical experience at major corporations, national nonprofit organizations, and health-care facilities. Some Cedar Crest students have served internships with CNN, as a foreign correspondent with the United Nations, and with the FBI, working on a database for DNA fingerprinting.

The College stresses the importance of global awareness and encourages students to take advantage of study-abroad opportunities.

Academic Facilities

Learning spaces include hospital simulation labs, a ceramic studio, a state-of-the art nutrition laboratory, music practice rooms, *The Crestiad* newsroom, dance and art studios and workshops, theaters, up-to-date genetic engineering laboratories, forensic science laboratories, a papermaking studio, and a greenhouse.

Cedar Crest students socialize and dine in the Tompkins College Center, the hub of student activity. The center is home to Samuels Theatre, club meeting rooms, the dining hall, and the Falcon's Nest café.

Costs

For 2010–11, tuition is $28,967; room and board are $9890.

Financial Aid

Student applications are reviewed for scholarship eligibility at the time of acceptance. The College's scholarships are awarded based on high school merit, leadership, and service. The College holds an annual scholarship competition that awards one high-achieving student a full tuition scholarship for four years.

The financial aid program at Cedar Crest is based on financial need and includes grants, loans, and employment. Students applying for need-based financial aid should file the Free Application for Federal Student Aid (FAFSA).

Faculty

The Cedar Crest faculty is an exceptional group that wants students to succeed. Not only do they offer unique courses, which take a nontraditional approach to many traditional academic programs, but faculty members may also be working artists, published writers, accomplished actors, business professionals for world renowned corporations, or scientists making discoveries that will impact us all. They strive to ensure that student learning extends beyond the classroom.

Cedar Crest students meet one-on-one with a faculty mentor to build course schedules and discuss future plans. Students also work closely with faculty on groundbreaking research in all disciplines. This research can lead to national presentations and professional publications.

Admission Requirements

Cedar Crest welcomes applications from first-year students entering after high school and those seeking to transfer from another college or university. The admissions process is individualized and holistic. Criteria considered include academic course work and strength of program, completion of a college preparatory program, standardized test scores, personal statements, recommendation letters, leadership experience and potential, community service, employment, and special talents.

Application and Information

Applications are reviewed on a rolling basis, so they are processed and evaluated as soon as all materials have been received. Acceptances begin September 15. The priority deadline for scholarship review is February 15.

Students can apply online at http://www.cedarcrest.edu/apply or through the Common Application at https://www.commonapp.org.

Senior Executive Vice President for Enrollment Management
Cedar Crest College
100 College Drive
Allentown, Pennsylvania 18104-6196
Phone: 800-360-1222 (toll-free)
Fax: 610-606-4647
E-mail: admissions@cedarcrest.edu
Web site: http://www.cedarcrest.edu

CHADRON STATE COLLEGE

CHADRON, NEBRASKA

The College

Chadron State College (CSC) challenges and prepares students to realize academic, personal, and professional success. These successes are developed through experiences in activities on and off campus. Founded in 1911 as Nebraska State Normal School, Chadron State has a proven record of graduates who excel. The professors are approachable and work closely with the students. The total fall 2008 enrollment was slightly over 2,600 students. The majority of the student population comes from Nebraska, Wyoming, South Dakota, and Colorado; sixteen other countries are also represented on the campus. Approximately 41 percent of the undergraduate students are men and 59 percent are women.

A combination of academic offerings and faculty expertise enhances the rewards from students' efforts at Chadron State College. Chadron State offers Bachelor of Arts, Bachelor of Science, Bachelor of Applied Sciences, and Bachelor of Science in education programs (four-year degrees) as well as the Master of Arts in Education, Master of Business Administration, Master of Science in Education, Specialist in Education, and Master of Science in Organizational Management. The College is accredited by the Higher Learning Commission of the North Central Association of Colleges and Schools, the National Council for Accreditation of Teacher Education, the Council on Social Work Education, and the Nebraska State Department of Education.

A college campus environment in beautiful northwest Nebraska makes the location a great place to live and study. Tall, pine-covered buttes extend across the south end of the campus. A national forest is nearby and two state parks are within driving distance of the College. Chadron State College has six spacious residence halls, a physical activity center with an indoor track, three versatile basketball/tennis/volleyball courts, a weight-training room, three racquetball courts, and specialized classrooms for dance, cardiovascular exercise, and gymnastics. Chadron State also has a student center, a fine arts building with two theaters, an educational technology and distance learning center, and a Coffee Café in the basement of the library. More than sixty campus clubs and organizations, numerous intramural leagues, and eleven intercollegiate NCAA Division II athletic teams offer opportunities for involvement and entertainment. The newest addition is women's softball.

Location

Chadron is a community of approximately 6,000 people. Located at the junction of U.S. Highways 385 and 20, Chadron has a low crime rate. The national forest and state parks surrounding the city of Chadron provide a beautiful recreational aspect to the College. Students enjoy hiking, mountain biking, hunting, fishing, and camping as favorite pastimes. Fort Robinson, 28 miles west, was once a colorful frontier military post. The Hudson-Meng Bison Kill Site, the Agate Fossil Beds, and the Mammoth Site are close by. The Black Hills of South Dakota are only an hour's drive to the north.

A commuter airline connects Denver, Colorado, and Chadron. The Denver Coach is also available in and out of Chadron. Several fast food businesses and fine dining restaurants provide dining opportunities. The College brings nationally and internationally known entertainers and fine arts attractions to the city of Chadron regularly.

Majors and Degrees

Bachelor of Arts degrees are awarded in art (with options in graphic design and art studio), business administration (with options in accounting, agribusiness, economics, finance, management, management information systems, and marketing), communication arts (with options in public relations, journalism, and communication), English and literature, family and consumer sciences (with options in child development, design and merchandising, hospitality management, and human services), history, industrial management, justice studies (with options in criminal justice and legal studies), library media, music (with options in music performance and commercial music business), psychology (with options in general psychology and substance abuse), recreation, social work, and theater.

Bachelor of Science degrees are awarded in biology (with options in environmental studies, general biology, and human biology), chemistry, clinical laboratory science (medical technology), health sciences, mathematics, physical science (with options in chemistry, geoscience, and physics), and range management (with options in rangeland livestock production, and range management). A minor in wildlife management is available.

A Bachelor of Applied Sciences (B.A.S.) degree is available. This program is designed for individuals who have completed an Associate of Science or Associate of Applied Science degree from an accredited technical or community college. The B.A.S. degree is intended to enhance technical learning with general education courses and advanced technical support courses to meet the student's individual career and education goals. Options may be selected in agricultural operations, health care, industrial trades, or management services.

The Bachelor of Science in Education is offered in art (K–12), basic business education, biology, chemistry, earth science, economics, English, English (4–9), extended health education, family and consumer sciences (4–9 and 7–12), health and physical education (7–12), health education (7–12), history, industrial technology (7–12), language arts (7–12), mathematics (4–9 and 7–12), middle grades (4–9), music (K–12) and vocal music (K–8), natural science, physical education (K–8 and 7–12), physical science, physics, social science, Spanish, theater, trade and industrial education (10–12), and vocational business education.

Academic Programs

Chadron State College has an academic year that is divided into fall, spring, and summer semesters. Students seeking a baccalaureate degree from Chadron State College must complete the requirements for the program in addition to the general studies requirements. Bachelor of Arts and Bachelor of Science in education degrees are granted upon completion of a minimum total of 125 credit hours—45 of which must be at the 300 or 400 (junior or senior) level. A grade point average of at least 2.0 (on a 4.0 scale) must be maintained for the Bachelor of Arts programs, and a GPA of at least 2.5 must be maintained for the Bachelor of Science in education programs. No more than 66 credit hours may be transferred or applied toward a baccalaureate degree from a two-year institution.

Students who possess either an A.S. or A.A.S. degree may pursue the Bachelor of Applied Science degree. Degree requirements for the B.A.S. degree include a minimum of 125 credit hours, 45 credit hours of upper-division course work (24 of the last 30 credit hours must be from CSC), 40 credit hours of CSC general studies, 36 credit hours of upper-division courses to support the student's chosen option, and a cumulative GPA of at least 2.0 (on a 4.0 scale). Prospective students should contact the Extended Campus Programs Office for an application.

Chadron State College offers alternative options for earning credit. Course work may be supplemented by internships and a cooperative learning program. Travel opportunities for credit during the school year and the summers are available. Independent studies and the College-Level Examination Program (CLEP) are available as well.

Off-Campus Programs

Several low-cost tours and field trips are arranged by the College, usually in the spring and summer months. Internships are encouraged for junior and senior students. Summer travel opportunities are developed, for which students may receive credit. In the past, student groups have gone to Europe, Japan, Canada, Nassau, and Mexico as well as various parts of the United States, including Alaska and Hawaii.

Academic Facilities

The Reta King Library currently contains over 161,000 books, 384,867 microform titles, more than 43,760 bound periodicals, and 480 current periodicals. The library provides two computer laboratories, photocopiers, and microfilm/microfiche readers for student and faculty use. Students also have access to the online catalogs of the two other state colleges in Nebraska and an electronic database with access to 19,840 full-text and 61,628 eBooks. The Internet is readily accessible in the residence halls and classroom buildings. Wireless access is provided in various locations across campus including the Student Center and Library. The College has more than 400 computers, including PCs and Macintosh computers for student use in the computer labs, classrooms, library, and residence halls. Laptop computers may also be checked out in the library.

Costs

For the 2009–10 academic year, the cost of tuition for 15 credit hours, fees, room, and board for Nebraska residents was $9475. For nonresident students, the cost was $13,150. Other expenses such as books, travel, and supplies cost approximately $3000. Nonresidents may become eligible to pay resident tuition by either qualifying for the Non-Resident Scholars Program, the Student Opportunity Award, or completing requirements for obtaining legal Nebraska residency.

Financial Aid

Undergraduate students should file the Free Application for Federal Student Aid (FAFSA) online. After receiving the results from the processor, students should forward them to the College Director of Financial Aid. Undergraduate applications for financial assistance provide consideration for the Federal Pell Grant, Federal Work-Study, Federal Perkins Loan, Federal Supplemental Educational Opportunity Grant, Federal PLUS, and Federal Family Education Loan Programs as well as the State Scholarship Award Program and Student Assistance Program. A monthly payment plan is available through the Business Office. CSC provides electronic FAFSA processing.

Faculty

The College currently has a teaching faculty of 139 members (95 full-time, 74 percent of whom have terminal degrees). Faculty members are involved in student activities, and the vast majority of the undergraduate classes are taught by faculty members. The student–undergraduate faculty ratio of 17:1 allows close relationships between faculty members and students.

Student Government

A large number of students are actively involved in the student government. Numerous committees and organizations, including Student Senate, make an impact on the College. Students take part in decisions concerning scholastic, collegiate, intellectual, recreational, social, and cultural activities on and off campus.

Admission Requirements

The College has an open-admission policy for all students. Chadron State College welcomes inquiries regarding the College's programs and admission requirements. To ensure a more successful college career, Chadron State recommends that a student pursue the following courses in high school: 4 units of English; 3 units of mathematics; 3 units of social studies, including 1 unit of American history and 1 unit of global studies; 2 units of laboratory science; and other academic courses selected from areas such as foreign language, visual or performing arts, and computer literacy. Applications for admission should be submitted by currently enrolled high school students between the beginning of their last year and one month prior to the beginning of the term for which they seek admission. Individuals who have completed high school should submit their application materials at least one month prior to the beginning of the term for which they wish to be admitted.

Application and Information

Freshman applicants should submit a completed application for admission; an official high school transcript reflecting a graduation date, class rank, and overall grade point average; and ACT or SAT scores. Scores from the ACT/SAT are not required for students who graduated from high school five or more years prior to enrollment at Chadron State. Home-schooled students are accepted with a home school transcript and ACT/SAT scores.

Freshmen who have earned college credit and transfer students should submit a completed application for admission and official transcripts from all colleges or universities previously attended. If the student has attempted fewer than 12 semester hours of credit, he or she must also submit an official high school transcript, including ACT or SAT scores. Campus visits are encouraged. For more information, students should contact:

Ms. Tena Cook
Director of Admissions
Chadron State College
1000 Main Street
Chadron, Nebraska 69337-2690
Phone: 308-432-6263
800-242-3766 (toll-free)
Fax: 308-432-6229
E-mail: inquire@csc.edu
Web site: http://www.csc.edu

CHAPMAN UNIVERSITY

ORANGE, CALIFORNIA

The University

During its more than 148-year history, Chapman has evolved from a small, traditional liberal arts college that was founded in 1861 by members of the First Christian Church (Disciples of Christ) into a midsized comprehensive liberal arts and sciences university that is distinguished for its nationally recognized programs in film and television production, business and economics, theater, dance, music, education, and the natural and applied sciences. The mission of Chapman University is to provide personalized education of distinction that leads to inquiring, ethical, and productive lives as global citizens.

Chapman's parklike ivy-covered, tree-lined campus features a blending of fully refurbished historic structures with the newest in state-of-the-art Internet and satellite-connected learning environments. Five residence halls and six on-campus apartment buildings are conveniently located on the edge of the campus. Prominent in the center of the campus is Liberty Plaza, featuring a raised replica of a Lincoln chair that views a 5-ton section of the Berlin Wall.

Chapman University's academic structure includes the Wilkinson College of Humanities and Social Sciences, the Dodge College of Film and Media Arts, the AACSB International–accredited Argyros School of Business and Economics, the CTC-approved School of Education, the ABA-accredited School of Law, the Schmid College of Science, and the College of Performing Arts, which includes the NASM-accredited Conservatory of Music and NASD-accredited Department of Dance. Other nationally accredited programs include the APTA-accredited Doctor of Physical Therapy program. Chapman has been further recognized by the Templeton Foundation as one of only 100 colleges nationally to be designated as a Templeton Foundation "Character-Building College" for its emphasis on global citizenry and for student involvement in community action and stewardship activities.

In addition to just over 6,000 undergraduate, graduate, and professional school students enrolled on the campus in Orange, Chapman also enrolls another 8,000 undergraduate and graduate students annually through its Chapman University College and associated network of thirty University College corporate campus centers, serving primarily working adults with evening and weekend program formats, located in California and Washington.

The University environment is electric, involving, and outdoor-oriented. Along with the obvious benefits associated with the southern California climate, Chapman students enjoy a dynamic and involving student activities program. Although predominantly from California, Chapman students come from more than forty states; in addition, approximately 10 percent of its students come from thirty-four other countries. Over the past five years, Chapman students have been named Truman Scholars, Coro Fellows, *USA Today* All-USA College Academic Team members, NCAA All-Americans, and NCAA Academic All-Americans. Chapman's long and distinguished heritage in intercollegiate athletics includes five NCAA national championships in baseball, tennis, and softball. Chapman competes as an independent in the NCAA Division III level and fields teams in baseball, basketball (m/w), crew (m/w), cross-country (m/w), football, golf, lacrosse, soccer (m/w), softball, swimming (w), tennis (m/w), track and field (m/w), volleyball (w), and water polo (m/w). Approximately 20 percent of Chapman's student body participates in intercollegiate athletics. In 2007–08, 4 student-athletes were named as NCAA All-Americans and 8 as NCAA Academic All-Americans.

More than seventy clubs and organizations are available, many with commitments to a wide range of community service efforts. Chapman's Greek system includes six nationally chartered fraternities for men and five nationally chartered sororities for women. A comprehensive intramural sports program involves myriad sports activities for all campus community members throughout the school year. On-campus intercollegiate athletic events as well as music, art, and theater productions provide students with extensive extracurricular activity options. Chapman's proximity to area recreational and cultural opportunities allows Chapman students to enjoy the essence of what makes Orange County's south coast area an enviable environment in which to live and learn.

Prominent Chapman alumni include the Honorable Loretta Sanchez '88, member of Congress; the Honorable David Bonior '72, member of Congress; CNBC World anchorwoman, Bettina Chua '88; television and film producers John Copeland '73, Jon Garcia '93, and John David Currey '98; cinematographer Gene Jackson '70; television sports analyst Steve Lavin '88; major-league baseball executive Gordon Blakely '76; major-league baseball Cy Young Award winner Randy Jones '72 ; Tony Award nominee and star of Broadway's *Showboat,* Michel Bell '68; resident tenor at the Staatsoper-Vienna John Nuzzo '91; and former U.S. Ambassador to Spain and philanthropist George L. Argyros '65.

Location

Orange County, California, has been rated by *Places Rated Almanac* as "the #1 place to live in North America," citing superior climate, cultural, recreational, educational, and career-entree opportunities. Los Angeles is 35 miles to the north, and San Diego is 80 miles to the south. Nearby entertainment venues include Disneyland, Knott's Berry Farm, the Orange County Performing Arts Center, major-league baseball, and hockey. Pristine West Coast beaches are less than 10 miles from the campus, and seasonal snow skiing is 90 minutes away. The average year-round temperature on campus is 71°F, and the prevailing sea breeze coming off nearby southwest-facing beaches keeps the air clean and smog free.

Majors and Degrees

Chapman awards the Bachelor of Arts degree in the fields of art, biology, chemistry, communications, dance, economics, English and comparative literature, film and television, French, history, liberal studies (teaching), music, peace studies, philosophy, physical education, political science, psychology, religion, social science, sociology, Spanish, and theater. The Bachelor of Fine Arts degree is offered in creative writing, dance performance, film production, graphic design, studio art, television and broadcast journalism, and theater performance. The Bachelor of Science degree is offered in accounting, applied mathematics, biology, business administration, chemistry, computer information systems, computer science, and natural science. The Bachelor of Music degree is granted in composition, conducting, music education (vocal and instrumental), music performance (vocal and instrumental), and music therapy. Preprofessional or prevocational programs are offered in dentistry, law, medicine, physical therapy, social service, teaching, theology, and veterinary medicine.

Academic Programs

Possibly unique to Chapman is the University's relationship with the professional mentoring program, Inside Track. In addition to traditionally assigned academic advisers from various disciplines and tutoring services provided by the Center for Academic Success, each freshman is also assigned a life coach with whom they meet once weekly to develop critical skills, set goals, and address the many challenges that might interfere with their success. Coaching sessions are focused on personal development, assistance with planning and organization, and, most important, motivation and encouragement. Working in partnership with University administrators and faculty, Inside Track provides an invaluable safety net for students, helping to improve academic preparedness and performance.

The requirements for graduation are commensurate with the liberal arts philosophy of education maintained by Chapman. The program of studies is designed to ensure a breadth of subject matter selection in the liberal arts as well as depth of preparation in the student's major field. The minimum graduation requirements include successful completion (C average) of 124 semester credits, of which 36 must be earned in the upper division. Competence in reading, written communication, oral communication, computation, and library usage is required of all students. Chapman's general education sequence provides a broad introduction to the humanities, social sciences, and natural sciences. Students select general education classes with the guidance of their faculty adviser. A maximum of 32 semester credits may be gained through Advanced Placement (AP), College-Level Examination Program (CLEP), and departmental examinations.

Chapman's academic year operates on a 4-1-4 modified semester system. January is reserved for an optional Interterm. The University College corporate campus locations offer five 10-week terms annually.

Ample opportunities are available for alternative learning experiences. Internships and cooperative education programs are recommended. Students may also undertake in-depth individual study or research in their major field in conjunction with a faculty member.

Academic Facilities

Major facilities additions to the Chapman campus over the past few years include the completion of the 100,000-square-foot Leatherby Libraries complex, housing eight discipline-specific individual libraries, a sculpture garden, a cyber courtyard, and a 24-hour study commons and coffee bar; the Oliphant Hall addition to the School of Music, which includes 24,000 square feet featuring fourteen teaching studios, a sixty-seat lecture hall, music therapy laboratory, and orchestra hall; and the new Interfaith Center, which features the 12,500-square-foot Wallace All-Faiths Chapel. The 90,000-square-foot Argyros Forum includes the primary campus dining area and conference and classroom facilities. The 1,000-seat Memorial Auditorium is listed on the National Register of Historic Places. Athletic facilities include the 4,000-seat Hutton Sports Center arena, four championship tennis courts, and training and fitness facilities for the campus and surrounding community. A new 2,000-seat outdoor stadium and a 500-seat swim stadium/Olympic pool complex were recently completed. Arnold Beckman Hall is the center for business and information technology, including the Argyros School of Business and Economics, the A. Gary Anderson Center for Economic Research, the Ralph Leatherby Center for Entrepreneurship and Business Ethics, the Walter Schmid Center for International Business, and the Hobbs Institute for Real Estate, Law, and Environmental Studies. The College of Performing Arts facilities include the 250-seat repertory-style Waltmar Theatre and the Guggenheim Art Gallery. The Hashinger Science Center features laboratories for nuclear science, radiation, crystallography, genetics, food science, and physical therapy.

Costs

For the 2009–10 academic year, full-time tuition and fees (including accident and sickness fee, health center fee, and associated student membership fee) will be $36,764. Annual room and board costs averaged $12,000. The estimated cost for books was $1000 per year.

Financial Aid

More than 85 percent of Chapman students benefit from some form of financial aid or scholarship assistance. Need-based financial awards include a combination of grants, scholarships, loans, and work-study jobs on campus. Awards are renewable, assuming that students complete the annual application process on time. By using a combination of Chapman's internal resources and federal and state funding, an individual financial aid package can be tailored in an attempt to meet the student's financial need. Merit and talent scholarship awards, regardless of financial need, round out the types of financial assistance that Chapman offers.

Faculty

The University's faculty is composed of 280 full-time and 258 part-time members, more than 80 percent of whom hold doctoral or other terminal degrees. Their primary commitment is to undergraduate teaching, although most are also actively involved in scholarly research and publication. Many faculty members teach both undergraduate and graduate courses. Teaching assistants or graduate assistants are not used for the instruction of undergraduate classes. Chapman's favorable student-faculty ratio of 16:1 allows extensive interaction between the faculty members and students.

Student Government

Chapman has an associated student government that actively participates in the administration of the University.

Admission Requirements

Admission to Chapman is selective. In 2009, admission was granted to 48 percent of the applicant pool. The University is interested in admitting students whose prior records indicate that they will be successful in a competitive collegiate environment. Freshman applicants are considered for admission based primarily on the nature and sequence of their high school course work, the grade point average achieved, and their results on either the SAT or ACT examination. Transfer candidates are considered for admission on the basis of their course work and cumulative grade point average earned at other regionally accredited postsecondary institutions.

Application and Information

Chapman University is an exclusive user of the Common Application (http://www.commonapp.org). Candidates are strongly encouraged to visit and tour the campus and participate in an information session led by an admission officer. Arrangements for a group information session and campus tour can be made through the Office of Admission. Freshman applicants can choose either a nonbinding November 15 early action application deadline or the January 15 regular application deadline. Transfer applicants must apply before the March 15 transfer deadline. Freshman candidates who apply after January 15 and transfer candidates who apply after March 15 are considered on a space-available basis. For further information, students should contact:

Office of Admission
Chapman University
One University Drive
Orange, California 92866
Phone: 714-997-6711
888-CUAPPLY (toll-free)
Fax: 714-997-6713
E-mail: admit@chapman.edu
Web site: http://www.chapman.edu

CHATHAM UNIVERSITY

PITTSBURGH, PENNSYLVANIA

chatham
UNIVERSITY

The University

Founded in 1869, Chatham University is a coed university with a women's college at its historic heart. Chatham University provides students with a solid education built upon strong academics, public leadership, and global understanding. Chatham's Shadyside Campus is located on historic Woodland Road in Pittsburgh's Shadyside neighborhood, while its Eden Hall Campus is located 45 minutes north in Richland Township.

The University houses three distinctive colleges. Chatham College for Women provides academic and cocurricular programs for undergraduate women and embodies the traditions and rituals of one of the nation's oldest colleges for women. The College for Graduate Studies offers women and men both master's and doctoral programs. The College for Continuing and Professional Studies provides online and hybrid undergraduate and graduate degree programs for women and men, certificate programs, and community programming.

The University's total student body of almost 2,300 represents forty-four states and twenty-six other countries. Members of minority groups and international students compose 14 percent of the total student body. Resident and commuting students participate actively in the numerous professional, academic, social, and special-interest organizations at the University. Each year, Chatham students complete thousands of hours of community service with organizations throughout the region.

Chatham College for Women offers NCAA Division III intercollegiate competition in basketball, cross-country, ice hockey, soccer, softball, swimming and diving, tennis, volleyball, and water polo as well as intramural and recreational competition in other sports. Chatham's Athletic and Fitness Center includes an eight-lane competition pool, a gymnasium, squash courts, cardio rooms, a climbing wall, a running track, and exercise and dance studios.

All incoming undergraduate students receive tablet PCs that can access the University's wireless network and are incorporated into the curriculum for in-class note-taking, research, and online learning. Students are assessed a technology fee each year to lease the computers, which they own upon graduation.

All residence halls have computer labs and high-speed network printers as well as network ports in each room. Central computer equipment supports e-mail, computer-mediated courseware, personal Web pages, and file and print servers. Chatham participates in campuswide software license agreements that permit students to install select productivity software on their personal machines at no additional cost.

Location

Chatham's suburban, historic Shadyside Campus is located minutes from downtown Pittsburgh and features towering trees, wandering paths, and century-old mansions that serve as residence halls. The Shadyside Campus includes Chatham Eastside, a new LEED Silver facility that houses the University's interior architecture, landscape architecture, occupational therapy, physical therapy, and physician assistant studies programs. The University's new 388-acre Eden Hall Campus is located north of the city in Richland Township and is the home of Chatham's new School of Sustainability and the Environment.

Pittsburgh is one of the safest and most dynamic green cities in the country and is headquarters to major businesses and industries in finance, health care, and technology. Eclectic neighborhoods reflect Pittsburgh's historic qualities and appeal to a wide audience. Students may ride public transportation free within Allegheny County simply by presenting their Chatham ID. Arts and entertainment options range from the Pittsburgh Symphony to world-renowned opera, ballet, and theater companies and museums. For sports enthusiasts, Pittsburgh offers the Penguins, Pirates, and Steelers professional ice-hockey, baseball, and football teams. Pittsburgh has also been rated America's Most Livable City by *Places Rated Almanac* and Most Livable City in the U.S. and twenty-ninth Most Livable City Worldwide by *The Economist.* Bus, rail, and air connections are available to and from most major cities. For more information, students should visit http://www.pittsburghregion.org.

Majors and Degrees

Chatham University offers the following majors leading to a Bachelor of Arts or Bachelor of Science degree: accounting, art history, arts management, biochemistry, biology, chemistry, cultural studies, economics, education (elementary, early childhood, secondary, environmental science, visual arts), engineering (3-2 program), English, environmental policy, environmental science (B.A. or B.S.), exercise science, film and digital video-making, forensics, French and francophone studies, history, interior architecture, international business, international studies, landscape studies certificate, management, marketing, mathematics, music, physics, political science, policy studies (global or public), professional communication (broadcast journalism, print journalism, professional writing, public relations), psychology, social work, Spanish and Hispanic studies, visual arts (emerging media, photography or studio arts), and women's studies. Students may choose a traditional major, an interdisciplinary major, a double major, or a self-designed major.

Preprofessional programs are offered in education and law, medicine and health professions, physical therapy, teaching certification, and veterinary medicine. A joint-degree engineering program is offered with Carnegie Mellon University and the University of Pittsburgh. Teacher certification is available through the education program in early childhood, elementary, environmental, school counseling, secondary education, and special education.

The Accelerated Graduate Program enables qualified undergraduate students to become candidates for admission to one of the University's graduate programs during their junior year, enabling them to earn both a bachelor's and master's degree in as little as five years. The following degree programs are included: Doctor of Physical Therapy, Master of Accounting, Master of Arts in Food Studies, Master of Arts in Landscape Studies, Master of Arts in Teaching, Master of Business Administration, Master of Fine Arts in Film and Digital Technology, Master of Fine Arts in Creative Writing, Master of Interior Architecture, Master of Landscape Architecture, and Master of Science in Biology. Chatham also offers its Accelerated Graduate Program with the prestigious H. John Heinz III School of Public Policy at Carnegie Mellon University. Students may apply during their junior year to one of the following Heinz School programs: Master of Arts Management, Master of Information Systems Management, Master of Science in Healthcare Policy and Management, and Master of Science in Public Policy and Management. Accepted students take courses at both Chatham and the Heinz School during their senior year and earn a bachelor's degree from Chatham and a master's degree from Carnegie Mellon.

Academic Programs

Chatham's general education curriculum includes six required interdisciplinary courses, plus analytical reasoning, an international or intercultural experience, and wellness courses. Graduation requirements include the general education courses, a major, and the Senior Tutorial—an original research/capstone project. Students are mentored one-on-one by a faculty member throughout the tutorial process. The project provides an excellent bridge to graduate and professional schools and strong preparation for law and medical schools.

The University's 4-4-1 academic calendar consists of fall and spring terms plus a three-week "Maymester" which features study abroad, concentrated study, experimental projects, travel and field experiences, internships, interdisciplinary study, and student exchanges with other institutions.

The First-Year Student Sequence introduces students to the faculty and the University community and its culture and provides opportunities to learn about the resources of the urban environment and study issues of concern to women. Interactive seminar courses provide students with the analytical and communication skills essential for successful academic performance.

Chatham's Programs for Academic Success, Career Development, and Educational Enrichment (PACE) offers students a comprehensive approach to academic and career planning as well as an academic support network designed to maximize each student's academic success. Career services include counseling for undecided students, student internships, placement, workshops, recruitment, and mentor programs.

The Rachel Carson Institute honors Chatham's 1929 alumna and her commitment to the environment. The Pennsylvania Center for Women, Politics, and Public Policy introduces students to the world of politics, public policy, and civic engagement. The Center for Women's Entrepreneurship provides support for women entrepreneurs in the Pittsburgh region.

Off-Campus Programs

Chatham students may at no additional cost register for classes at any of Pittsburgh's eight other colleges and universities, including Carnegie Mellon and the University of Pittsburgh, both of which are within walking distance of the campus and also accessible via free shuttle service. Chatham Abroad involves a three-week travel experience with faculty members during Maymester of the sophomore year; past Chatham Abroad trips featured Belize, Egypt, England, France, the Galapagos Islands, Ireland, Italy, Morocco, Russia, and Spain for an additional fee.

Chatham students may participate in up to six internships related to their major and career goals before they graduate. Recent examples include American Cancer Society, Children's Institute, East End Cooperative Ministry, Girl Scouts, Global Links, Greater Pittsburgh Community Food Bank, Pittsburgh Action Against Rape, Race for the Cure, Sojourner House, Womansplace, Women and Girls Foundation of Southwest Pennsylvania, YWCA, and numerous sites in Pittsburgh's corporate, nonprofit, government, health-care, and communications communities.

Academic Facilities

The Jennie King Mellon (JKM) Library serves the Chatham community as a primary research, study, and resource center. Students may access the Library's approximately 90,000 volumes, almost 250 current print journals, over 26,000 full-text electronic journals, and over 50 online databases through the library's Web page. The Library offers a wide variety of information and instructional services, interlibrary loan, database searching workshops, course-related instruction, and individual research consultations. Librarians are available for research assistance during all open library hours via phone, e-mail, and IM Reference, as well as in person. Individual study rooms, special seminar rooms, and a 24/7 study room are also offered. Through consortium memberships, the library provides access to materials from hundreds of academic libraries nationwide.

The Science Laboratory Complex houses state-of-the-art science laboratories and individual laboratory units. Psychology and language laboratories and audiovisual facilities are also available. The Broadcast Studio contains sophisticated audio- and video-editing technology, including Macintosh G5 computers, as well as a multifunctional studio. Chatham's Art and Design Center features fine and applied art studios, a computer lab, and classroom space as well as gallery and student exhibition space.

Costs

For 2009–10, full-time tuition was $27,270 per year, and room and board were approximately $8700. A one-time deposit of $150 for tuition and $150 for on-campus housing is paid by newly admitted students and is applied to first-semester charges. Regularly enrolled full-time students pay no additional costs for Maymester courses, except for special supplies or travel. Music lessons and art supplies are additional. Students must have health and accident insurance. A technology fee is assessed for the laptop PC program.

Financial Aid

Financial aid is awarded on the basis of an individual's financial need, as determined through the Free Application for Federal Student Aid. The awards combine grants, loans, and employment. The priority financial aid deadline is May 1. Sources of financial aid include Chatham University grants and loans, state grants, Federal Pell Grants, Federal Supplemental Educational Opportunity Grants, federally funded student loans, and jobs provided under the Federal Work-Study Program. Chatham Merit scholarships for entering students are awarded without regard to need on the basis of high academic achievement and an on-campus interview. Scholarships begin at approximately $4000 and continue up to $20,000, and are awarded based on the student's match with Chatham's mission as well as the academic merits on her application for admission. Minna Kaufmann Ruud Scholarships are available for students with exceptional ability in vocal music, based on an on-campus audition. Approximately 98 percent of undergraduate students receive aid administered by the University.

Faculty

The undergraduate student-teacher ratio of 9:1 ensures individual consideration and interaction between students and faculty members. Each student is assigned a faculty member who serves as her adviser through the completion of her degree program, including the Senior Tutorial capstone project. Ninety-eight percent of all undergraduate faculty members hold terminal degrees.

Admission Requirements

Evaluation is made on the basis of the prospective student's academic record, recommendations, essay, involvement in activities, and other submitted material. Chatham seeks to enroll students representing a variety of cultural, geographical, racial, religious, and socioeconomic backgrounds, with diverse talents in academic and creative areas. The admissions requirements now include a Standardized Test-Optional Policy. Applicants may choose to submit a graded writing sample and resume or a list of curricular and cocurricular activities as well as a portfolio or special project/activity in lieu of SAT or ACT scores. These materials are reviewed by Chatham faculty members and may be applied toward the scholarship review process.

It is strongly recommended that candidates arrange to visit the University for a personal appointment, a student-guided campus tour, observation of one or more classes, and conversations with faculty and staff members and students. Early entrance is available for well-qualified and mature students who wish to begin at the end of their junior year in high school; early-entrance candidates must have an on-campus interview. Chatham welcomes the opportunity to discuss future educational plans with transfer candidates in good academic standing, including junior college and community college graduates. Chatham grants college course credit for grades of 4 or 5 on the Advanced Placement (AP) examinations. Certain prerequisites in course offerings may be fulfilled by attaining scores of 3, 4, or 5.

Application and Information

Candidates for admission must file an application with the Admissions Office, together with a $35 nonrefundable processing fee. A free online application is available on the University's Web site. Applications are accepted on a rolling basis.

Vice President of Admissions and Financial Aid
Office of Admissions
Chatham University
Woodland Road
Pittsburgh, Pennsylvania 15232
Phone: 412-365-1290
800-837-1290 (toll-free)
Fax: 412-365-1609
E-mail: admissions@chatham.edu
Web site: http://www.chatham.edu

A view of the Chatham University campus.

CHESTNUT HILL COLLEGE

PHILADELPHIA, PENNSYLVANIA

The College

Chestnut Hill College is a four-year, coeducational, Catholic liberal arts college. Founded in 1924 by the Sisters of St. Joseph, it is situated on a 75-acre campus overlooking the Wissahickon Creek. Enrolling more than 2,000 students, Chestnut Hill College is a diverse community of learners. Working adults are enrolled in the accelerated evening and weekend undergraduate program (School of Continuing and Professional Studies). In addition to its undergraduate degrees, Chestnut Hill awards the M.Ed., M.A., and M.S. (School of Graduate Studies) in seven fields, including administration of human services; clinical and counseling psychology; education; holistic spirituality; holistic spirituality and health care; holistic spirituality and spiritual direction; and international business, language, and culture. The College also awards a doctoral degree in clinical psychology (Psy.D.).

When it comes to student activities, students enthusiastically engage in the many clubs and organizations available and participate in everything from aerobics and horseback riding to golf and archery. The College is a member of NCAA Division II and competes in baseball (men), basketball (men and women), cross-country (men and women), golf (men and women), lacrosse (men and women), soccer (men and women), softball (women), tennis (men and women), and volleyball (women). A swimming pool, a gymnasium, a fitness room, and outdoor basketball and tennis courts provide excellent athletic facilities for Chestnut Hill's students.

Location

Chestnut Hill College is situated in a beautiful historical area at the northwestern edge of Philadelphia. The College is bounded by the wooded hills of Fairmount Park, yet it is only a 30-minute ride by train or car to downtown Philadelphia where students can enjoy a wide variety of dining, cultural, and sporting events. Among the many attractions are the museums that grace Philadelphia, from its landmark Art Museum to the Rodin Museum, the Living History Museum, the Franklin Institute, and numerous others. The city's history is reflected throughout but is most prominent in the areas surrounding Independence Hall, Society Hill, and Penn's Landing. In addition, more than seventy colleges, universities, and medical schools in the area offer opportunities for socialization and an extensive range of activities.

One mile beyond Chestnut Hill College on Germantown Avenue is the well-known area of Philadelphia also called Chestnut Hill. Reminiscent of a colonial village, this section of Philadelphia provides convenient opportunities for shopping, cultural experiences, and transportation to downtown Philadelphia. Chestnut Hill is a school in a suburban setting with all the advantages of a cosmopolitan experience—located where the northwest corner of the city meets the suburbs.

Majors and Degrees

The Bachelor of Arts, Bachelor of Science, and Bachelor of Music degrees are offered with majors in accounting; biochemistry; biology; business administration; chemistry; communications and technology; computer and information science; computer and information technology; criminal justice; early childhood education (with an option of Montessori certification); early childhood and elementary education; elementary education; English literature; English literature and communications; environmental science; forensic sciences; French; history; human services; international business, language, and culture; marketing; mathematics; mathematical and computer science; molecular biology; music; music education; political science; psychology; secondary education certification in various disciplines; sociology; and Spanish.

Dual degrees (B.S./M.S.) are offered in education; human services; psychology; and international business, language, and culture.

Academic Programs

The academic year consists of two 15-week semesters. There are also two 6-week summer sessions.

As a liberal arts college, Chestnut Hill offers courses of study that provide the student with a broad background in the fine arts and humanities, a knowledge of science, and a keen awareness of the social problems of the day, as well as intensive, in-depth study in a major field.

Chestnut Hill College confers a B.S., B.M., or B.A. degree to students who earn 120 semester hours of credit and satisfy specific requirements set by the faculty. Core seminars are interdisciplinary and provide opportunities for experiential learning. In addition, students must take 6 semester hours of religious studies, 6 hours beyond the elementary level in a classical or modern foreign language, and 3 hours in a writing course (unless exempted by the English department). Focused on six perspectives (historical, literary, artistic, scientific, behavior, and problem solving and analysis), the Ways of Knowing component of the core curriculum is designed to introduce students to different learning methodologies and strategies.

A student with the ability and proper motivation may be permitted to major in two departments. The student must consult with the chair of each department to determine the feasibility of the proposal and then submit it to the dean of the college for approval. It is understood that the student will satisfy the requirements of both departments.

Each year, selected first-year students and sophomores are invited into an interdepartmental honors program that challenges intellectual initiative and provides the opportunity for independent study and seminar discussion. The completion of the four honors courses and an honors paper satisfies all distributional requirements. Students may apply for admission at the beginning of their first year or sophomore year.

Sophomores of high scholastic standing are invited by their major departments to engage in a program of independent study during their junior and senior years. This opportunity for independent study and original research culminates in an honors thesis, which is a prerequisite for the conferring of honors at graduation.

Off-Campus Programs

Students have the advantages of two campuses and two curricula through an agreement with La Salle University, which allows students from either school to register for courses at the other institution for full credit without paying extra tuition. Public transportation is available between the two schools.

At Chestnut Hill College, a student may take advantage of the interim between semesters by coordinating travel and study. Students, with the assistance of one or more of their professors, can use their imagination and interests to develop an off-campus program. Should the program be lengthier than the interim allows, students may schedule their travel and study for the summer. Past intersession programs have included studies of French culture in Paris, women in English literature in London, and marine biology in Florida.

Chestnut Hill College participates in a consortium arrangement with seven colleges throughout the nation, founded by the Sisters of St. Joseph. As participants, students can study at any other member institution for a semester or a year, while maintaining status as full-time Chestnut Hill students.

An average of B or above and approval of the academic dean allow an upperclass student to pursue organized study in another country. The major department must approve the course of study. In recent years, Chestnut Hill College students have enrolled in institutions in London, Madrid, Rome, Salzburg, Vienna, and other European centers. Chestnut Hill College maintains agreements with Regent's College London, the Sorbonne and the American Business School in Paris, the Centre d'Etudes Franco-Americain de Management in Lyons, and Seisen University in Japan for study abroad.

The growing interest of students in acquiring on-the-job experience while still in college has prompted the development of many departmental internship programs, which provide students with the opportunity to gain professional experience in their major while earning academic credit. Chestnut Hill has also an office of career development, through which Chestnut Hill College assists students in finding jobs that correspond to their career interests and academic pursuits. Co-op students work and attend classes in alternate periods, earning academic credit for their practical experience.

Academic Facilities

Chestnut Hill College's Logue Library houses a collection of approximately 139,585 volumes and 544 current periodicals, a rare book room that contains first editions and special editions, the Gruber Theater, the fine Curriculum Library for elementary education, and an Irish literature collection. Well-equipped science laboratories, a math center, a multimedia technology center, a writing enrichment center, individual practice rooms for music students, a spacious art studio, a planetarium, and an observatory are among the many other outstanding facilities on campus. Martino Hall, which opened in 2000 and was designed to maintain the architectural history of the College, provides room for a performance center, gymnasium, or convocation center. The second and third floors house "smart" classrooms. Fitzsimmons Hall opened its doors in fall 2006 offering resident students suite-style living accommodations. The College recently acquired the neighboring 35-acre Sugerloaf Mansion estate and renovations are scheduled to complete in spring 2010. This new facility will offer additional resident housing, classrooms, a second student dining facility, office space, and conferencing capability.

Costs

General expenses for 2010–11 are tuition $28,100; and room and board between $8500 and $9500.

Financial Aid

Financial aid is available in the form of academic scholarships, loans, work-study programs, federal grants, and Chestnut Hill College grants. Most of these are based on financial need and are awarded in financial aid packages that combine various forms of aid and are tailored to each student's need. More than 75 percent of Chestnut Hill College students receive financial aid to meet College costs. All applicants for aid should file a copy of the Free Application for Federal Student Aid (FAFSA). Merit-based scholarships and awards are granted for academic achievement.

Faculty

Evidence of Chestnut Hill's vitality can be seen in its faculty. While their primary interest is teaching, faculty members are also engaged in research, publication, travel, and other professional activities. More than 82 percent of the faculty members hold terminal degrees. The men and women who make up this group are deeply interested in both their subject and their students. Their qualifications include international degrees from Bangalore University (India), the University of London, and the University of Paris, and domestic degrees from Boston College, Bryn Mawr College, Catholic University of America, Columbia University, Creighton University, Duke University, Fordham University, Harvard University, Middlebury College, the New School for Social Research, New York University, Purdue University, Saint Louis University, Temple University, and the Universities of Arizona, Delaware, Massachusetts, Minnesota, Montana, New Mexico, North Carolina, Notre Dame, and Pennsylvania. Chestnut Hill College's faculty-student ratio is 1:12.

Student Government

A student at Chestnut Hill College has the opportunity to think independently and approach decisions creatively. Students, in conjunction with members of the faculty and administration, make judgments concerning all collegiate affairs. Several organizations provide structure for the decision-making process. Students join members of the faculty and administration on the Curriculum Committee and the College Council. The Academic, Social-Cultural, and Student Affairs Committees of the Student Organization identify, represent, and meet campus needs.

Admission Requirements

Chestnut Hill College welcomes students whose aptitudes and academic records show a desire to accept a challenge. Applications are judged by the Admissions Committee on the basis of intellectual ability, academic achievement (class rank and performance in high school, including completion of 16 academic units), and SAT or ACT results.

Students should submit a completed application, application fee, SAT or ACT scores, and a high school transcript. Letters of recommendation, a personal statement, and other supporting documentation are strongly encouraged. An interview is recommended and may be required. A student wishing to transfer to Chestnut Hill College is asked to submit a transcript from all colleges previously attended.

Application and Information

Applications are processed on a rolling admission system. To arrange an interview or to obtain more detailed information about the academic program, students should contact:

Office of Admissions
School of Undergraduate Studies
Chestnut Hill College
9601 Germantown Avenue
Philadelphia, Pennsylvania 19118
Phone: 215-248-7001
800-248-0052 (toll-free)
E-mail: chcapply@chc.edu
Web site: http://www.chc.edu

CHRISTIAN BROTHERS UNIVERSITY

MEMPHIS, TENNESSEE

The University

Students from all over the country and the world come to Christian Brothers University (CBU) in midtown Memphis for its distinctive, vibrant, and vigorous educational programs. CBU provides students with choices that impact their opportunities in the future. CBU offers an education based individualized attention, not huge lecture halls. Faculty, staff, and students are available and accessible to help new students find the right major, the right schedule, and the right extracurricular activities. CBU strives to prepare each student for the future.

CBU's students, faculty, administration, and alumni are part of a much larger Catholic educational network. In the 1600s, Saint John Baptist de La Salle began a new system of schools in which teachers assist parents in the educational, ethical, and religious formation of their children. Today, the Lasallian Community, the ongoing home of De La Salle's tradition and spirit, is alive and functioning in 80 countries and in more than 1,000 educational institutions. CBU, founded in 1871, is one of six Lasallian universities in the United States. Excellence in teaching and individualized attention are hallmarks of the University. CBU prepares students for professional careers and advanced study in the arts, business, engineering, and sciences, and for lives of moral responsibility and constructive community involvement.

There are more than 1,700 students from twenty-five states and seventeen countries enrolled at CBU. Twenty-four percent of the students ranked in the top 10 percent of their class. Twenty-seven different faiths are represented in the student body; 20 percent of the students are Catholic. Religious observances are not required, but students are encouraged to practice their faith openly and actively.

More than half of first-year students at CBU live on campus in residence halls or student apartments. All residence halls are networked, providing free e-mail and Internet access. In addition, each room is wired for free local telephone service and cable television. A wireless network is available in most major buildings across the campus, as well as outdoors in the Buckman Quad. Students also have access to hundreds of PCs across the campus in University-maintained labs.

There is always something happening at CBU. The extensive calendar of activities and events includes concerts, dances, picnics, cultural programs, and a busy year-round intramural sports program. CBU has an active and involved Student Government Association and there are numerous clubs and organizations to help students connect with one another. There are over forty student groups including fraternities, sororities, philanthropic clubs, and religious organizations. There are also clubs that assist students in their major field of study. Opportunities are available for student participation in University theater, art, and music programs.

CBU student-athletes strive for excellence, both in the classroom and on the field. CBU competes in the NCAA Division II Gulf South Conference (GSC) in women's basketball, cross-country, golf, soccer, softball, tennis, and volleyball and men's baseball, basketball, cross-country, golf, soccer, and tennis. CBU consistently finishes among the leaders of the GSC and NCAA Division II for student-athlete success in the classroom. Its nearly 200 student-athletes routinely post a combined GPA above 3.0 and dominate the GSC All-Academic teams. Their success extends to the playing field with twenty-eight conference championships, ten regional championships, and a national championship. In addition to these teams, CBU offers bowling and men's lacrosse as club sports and has an active intramural sports program. There are fitness and recreational facilities on campus, including an outdoor basketball court, a sand volleyball court, and a swimming pool.

CBU is accredited by the Commission on Colleges of the Southern Association of Colleges and Schools to award the bachelor's and master's degrees. Programs at the graduate level include master's degree programs in business administration, Catholic studies, education, educational leadership, and engineering management.

Location

The 75-acre wooded CBU campus is in the heart of midtown Memphis, a blend of big city and Southern culture. Memphis offers a world of opportunity and adventure. The banks of the Mississippi River come alive each May during the Beale Street Music Festival, which hosts a long list of great acts. The world-renowned Memphis in May also hosts its annual Barbecue Festival, with teams competing to create the best of the hometown favorite.

Live music is a Memphis tradition on legendary Beale Street and at clubs and venues throughout the city. The Memphis Grizzles play a season of NBA games in the FedExForum and the retro-style AutoZone Park hosts the Memphis Redbirds, the Triple-A farm team for the St. Louis Cardinals.

The nearby Cooper-Young District—an energetic and artsy blend of restaurants, shops, and coffeehouses—is a neighborhood hotspot for CBU students and hosts an annual arts and music festival. Nationally noted restaurants, a resurgence of the downtown entertainment district, and acres of lush, green parks help to round out the entertainment options in Memphis.

Majors and Degrees

The University awards Bachelor of Arts (B.A.), Bachelor of Science (B.S.), and Bachelor of Fine Arts (B.F.A.) degrees. Majors include accounting, applied psychology, biochemistry, biology (with a concentration available in environmental studies), biomedical science, business administration (with concentrations in finance, human resource management, international business, management, management information systems, marketing, and sports management), chemical and biochemical engineering, chemistry (with concentrations available in premed, preforensics, and prepharmacy), civil engineering, computer science, cultural studies (grades 4–8)*, electrical and computer engineering, engineering management (with concentrations available in packaging and information systems), engineering physics, English, English for corporate communications, history, liberal studies (grades K–6)*, mathematics, mechanical engineering, natural science, physics, prelaw, preprofessional health programs, psychology, religion and philosophy, special education (grades K–12)*, and studio art (with concentrations available in art therapy, art education, and graphic design). *Licensure offered at the M.A.T. level.

Academic Programs

With majors in the arts, business, engineering, and sciences, CBU offers excellent educational options while focusing on individualized attention. CBU's top-notch faculty teaches all classes and labs, encouraging CBU students to achieve above and beyond their potential and expectations. CBU's academically rigorous education also focuses on moral responsibility and community involvement and embraces diversity. Internships and the latest state-of-the-art software and research equipment give students the chance to actively participate in their own education.

The School of Arts is the heart of the educational experience at CBU. A liberal arts education is as much about living as it is about working. Through the arts, students are encouraged to acquire intellect, clarify values, celebrate cultural diversity, and encourage compassion for others. These goals are sought and achieved within an atmosphere of free inquiry, dialogue, and interfaith concern. The School of Arts has a reputation for producing quality teachers. Within the first year after completion of the teaching licensure requirements, 95 percent of CBU-prepared candidates are employed in the local and regional public and private schools.

The School of Business leads students through a rigorous academic curriculum with an emphasis on analytical capability, global awareness, real-world experience, and ethical, levelheaded decision making. CBU's market-oriented and technology-focused approach arms students with the skills necessary for immediate employment in business, industry, and government. The business faculty possesses real-world experience, and CBU graduates include a circuit court judge, a Hollywood entertainment executive, a technology company vice-president, and a member of the New York Stock Exchange.

The School of Engineering is a nationally recognized, ABET-accredited program that blends small classes with unrivaled equipment, tremendous internships, and flexible curricula to prepare graduates for direct entry to the engineering profession or graduate school. Students work in state-of-the-art laboratories where hands-on experience teaches them to design, construct, and test ideas. Engineering students complete projects, collaborate in teams, and learn to communicate their ideas effectively, emerging ready and able to meet today's technological challenges. The School recently celebrated fifty years of graduating engineers in Memphis.

The School of Sciences offers a rigorous but supportive program in the sciences and mathematics to prepare students for graduate study and a career in the health professions, research, computers and technology, and teaching licensure. Classes and labs are small and always taught by faculty members in a personalized, hands-on setting with up-to-date instrumentation. Prehealth students historically enjoy professional school acceptance rates far above the national average to medical and pharmacy schools.

A degree from CBU deals with the subject matter of a specific major, but also helps the graduate find a unique place in society and the world. The educational experience at CBU creates graduates who have the ability to think clearly, confidently, and creatively. CBU graduates are people who can turn challenges into opportunities, problems into solutions, and questions into answers.

Off-Campus Programs

At CBU, a student's education does not begin and end in the classroom. Several opportunities exist for CBU students to engage in travel and study abroad. The Study Abroad Program at CBU exposes students and faculty to other countries, cultures, and languages with regularly scheduled study trips to locations around the globe. Students can also spend an entire semester or a summer session abroad. More information is available online at http://www2.cbu.edu/cbu/Academics/studyabroad/.

In addition, CBU offers internships and mentor projects that pair students with either a faculty member or a researcher at a well-known institution such as FedEx, International Paper, AutoZone, Morgan Keegan, St. Jude Children's Research Hospital, and Buckman Laboratories. Volunteer opportunities abound at nonprofit organizations, religious communities, and multicultural centers.

Academic Facilities

Plough Memorial Library is housed in a three-story building centrally located on campus and contains more than 154,000 volumes and 532 current periodical subscriptions. Access to the library's collections is provided through an online catalog and automated circulation system. The library cooperates with Memphis-area academic libraries to provide reciprocal borrowing privileges for students, faculty, and staff members. Materials can be borrowed from other libraries around the country through the interlibrary loan service. Additional collections are available in the Brother I. Leo O'Donnell Archives, which traces the 137-year history of the University and includes the Leslie H. Kuehner Napoleon Collection, the Higgins Collection on the history of Bolivia, and the De La Salle Christian Brothers Midwest Province Archival Record and Museum Collections. The Beverly and Sam Ross Gallery offers students the opportunity for an enjoyable educational experience through regularly scheduled art exhibits.

Costs

Tuition and fees for the 2009–10 academic year were $23,730. Room and board and books averaged $6640.

Financial Aid

The Christian Brothers founded their schools on the principle that an education should be available to anyone, regardless of socioeconomic status. Still true to that mission, CBU provides generous scholarship and financial aid packages, along with individualized advice on finding and obtaining any and all financial resources that might be available. Over 90 percent of the current CBU students receive some sort of financial assistance based on need and/or merit. More information is available from the Student Financial Assistance Office at 901-321-3305 or 877-255-0032 (toll-free) or via e-mail at finaid@cbu.edu.

Faculty

CBU has 99 full-time faculty members, all of whom hold at least a master's degree; 83.8 percent hold doctorates or the highest degrees in their field. No courses are taught by teaching assistants. The student-faculty ratio is 13:1.

Student Government

Programs aimed at the cultural, educational, and entertainment interests of the student body are arranged and conducted with the advice and assistance of the Student Government Programming Council, which serves as a voice for the student body. The Programming Council, with assistance from the Director of Student Activities, plans, coordinates, and implements a variety of student activities that are publicized through the CBU Web site, social media outlets, e-mails, campus bulletin boards, various campus publications, and posters on campus.

Admission Requirements

Students must have graduated from an approved secondary school, have a scholastic average of at least 2.5 and achieve satisfactory scores on the ACT or SAT. Applicants should submit the completed application form, the $25 application fee, an official high school transcript, official ACT or SAT scores, an essay or personal statement, and the completed health form. Transfer students should also submit official transcripts from all colleges attended. International students must also provide proof of English proficiency and a declaration of finances.

Application and Information

Admission is selective, and students are encouraged to apply as early as possible. The preferred application date is May 1 for the fall semester and January 1 for the spring semester. Students who apply after these dates are considered for admission on a space-available basis. Applications are reviewed on a rolling-admissions basis. Applicants are encouraged to submit complete admission credentials for the Early Scholars Program by December 1 for earlier notification of scholarship awards. The early action admissions program is nonbinding.

Office of Admissions
Christian Brothers University
650 East Parkway South
Memphis, Tennessee 38104

Phone: 901-321-3205
800-288-7576 (toll-free)
E-mail: admissions@cbu.edu
Web site: http://www.cbu.edu

CHRISTOPHER NEWPORT UNIVERSITY

NEWPORT NEWS, VIRGINIA

The University

Christopher Newport University (CNU) was founded in 1960 and enrolls 4,800 students in more than seventy areas of study (including three 5-year master's degree programs). The University takes pride in its "student-first, teaching-first" community. Small classes taught by veteran faculty members, a beautiful and safe campus, and one of the nation's finest sports programs make CNU a distinctive choice among Virginia's public universities.

At CNU, students are challenged to thrive academically. Each fall, the President's Leadership Program accepts approximately 300 high-achieving freshmen who have exhibited leadership characteristics in their schools and communities. Through the four-year Honors Program, academically talented students enjoy a rich educational experience, participating in challenging courses and cultural/intellectual activities. CNU students also actively participate in community service and service learning, hallmarks of the University.

Location

CNU ranks as one of the safest midsize campuses in Virginia. Its picturesque 260-acre campus and superb residential facilities receive high praise from students and visitors alike. The University is located on the Virginia Peninsula in suburban Newport News. It is adjacent to Mariners' Museum Park, a pristine 550-acre nature preserve with miles of jogging trails around Lake Maury and along the James River.

CNU is 35 miles from the pounding surf and rolling dunes of Virginia Beach, 25 miles from historic Williamsburg, 75 miles from Richmond, and 150 miles from Washington, D.C. Students enjoy the year-round moderate climate, the short driving distance to the beach, and the region's diverse recreational opportunities.

Majors and Degrees

CNU's academic programs fall within three colleges: the College of Arts and Humanities, the College of Natural and Behavioral Sciences, and the College of Social Sciences (which includes the Joseph W. Luter III School of Business). CNU offers the Bachelor of Arts degree in American studies (concentrations in humanities and social science), communication studies, English (concentrations in film studies, literature, and writing), fine arts (concentrations in art history and studio art), foreign language (majors in French, German, and Spanish), history (interdisciplinary prelaw program available), interdisciplinary studies, philosophy (concentrations in preseminary studies and religious studies), political science, psychology, and sociology (social work major and concentrations in anthropology, criminology, and education and socialization).

Students may choose the Bachelor of Music degree (concentrations in performance, theory/composition, choral music education, and instrumental music education) or the Bachelor of Science degree in interdisciplinary studies. A special curriculum is offered in jazz studies. A Bachelor of Arts in theater is offered (concentrations in acting, arts administration, design/technology, directing and dramatic literature, music theater/dance, and theater studies).

Minors are available in American studies, anthropology, art history/studio art, childhood studies, civic engagement and social entrepreneurship, classical civilization, communication studies, film studies, French, German, gerontology, history, journalism, Latin classical studies, leadership studies, music, philosophy and religious studies, political science, psychology, sociology, Spanish, theater arts, women's and gender studies, U.S. national securities studies, and writing.

Also offered in the sciences are the Bachelor of Arts degree in biology, interdisciplinary studies, and mathematics; and the Bachelor of Science degree in applied physics, biology (preprofessional programs in dental, medical, and veterinary studies), chemistry, computer engineering, computer science, environmental science, information systems, interdisciplinary studies, mathematics, and psychology. Minors are available in applied physics, biology, chemistry, computer science, and mathematics.

The Luter School of Business, accredited by AACSB International—The Association to Advance Collegiate Schools of Business, offers the Bachelor of Science in Business Administration degree, with majors in accounting, economics, finance, management, and marketing and minors in business administration and economics.

Academic Programs

To be eligible for an undergraduate degree, students must successfully complete 120 academic semester hours. The last 45 semester hours of credit must be taken in residence.

The first two years of all students' academic programs require successful completion of the Liberal Learning Core requirements in such areas as English (writing), foreign language, humanities, laboratory science, mathematics, social science, and various areas of inquiry. New, innovative freshman seminars allow students to explore unique interdisciplinary courses.

At CNU, students also enjoy unique opportunities for specialized study. The premed and prehealth program includes academic and career advising, mentoring, clinical internships, and expert guidance throughout the application process. Through an agreement between CNU and Eastern Virginia Medical School (EVMS), selected students may receive early assurance of a position in medical school at EVMS upon satisfactory completion of their undergraduate degree program and their continued high academic achievement.

With the Master of Arts in Teaching (M.A.T.), students major in a specific content area, receiving a bachelor's degree after four years. In the fifth year they complete graduate-level professional courses and a semester of student teaching.

Students interested in attending law school reap the benefits of hands-on advising and mentoring provided by the prelaw program. While not a degreed program, it prepares students in departments across campus for law school admittance and success.

First-year students may participate in Learning Communities. Students in these groups live together, take classes together, and are guided by an upper-class student dedicated to their academic success.

Off-Campus Programs

The University actively supports study abroad for all its students and sponsors a variety of international study programs each year that promote cross-cultural education and growth. Students have recently participated with faculty members in study-abroad programs in Belgium, China, England, France, Germany, Holland, Ireland, Italy, Kenya, Morocco, and Spain. CNU offers top students the opportunity to study at Oxford University each summer. CNU provides up to $5000 for international study to students who participate in the President's Leadership Program. Students may also travel to Europe with the CNU Chamber Singers or worldwide with CNU's award-winning Model U.N. Club.

Students also broaden their education through internships. Each year they receive opportunities with prominent organizations like NASA; the Thomas Jefferson National Laboratory; the Secret Service; and countless media, health-care, education, and social-service firms and agencies, among others.

Academic Facilities

CNU's academic buildings contain a variety of small classrooms and auditoriums, computer laboratories, specialty laboratories, an instructional technology center, and a greenhouse/herbarium.

Students have access to more than 1,200 computer workstations on campus as well as e-mail and Internet access in the residential facilities. Wireless access is available in all public areas. Top-rated, state-of-the-art residence halls and upperclass apartments accommodate 3,000 students on campus.

In 2010 CNU celebrated the opening of a new academic home for all of the liberal arts, the Lewis Archer McMurran Jr. Hall, which provides more than 82,000 square feet of teaching and learning spaces. A new $80-million integrated science center is under construction.

The University has completed $500 million in new facilities over the past decade, creating an impressive and appealing "home" for its students and faculty. An additional $500 million in capital construction is scheduled to take place by 2020.

The dazzling Paul and Rosemary Trible Library opened in 2008 with more than 100,000 square feet for information technology and traditional library collections. As the intellectual center of the campus, the library features a fourteen-story tower, lighted day and night, and a 1,600-square-foot coffee shop with adjacent study rooms. The dazzling rotunda in the Trible Library and its many elegant study spaces have created an outstanding academic home for study.

CNU is home to the $16-million Freeman Sports and Convocation Center, the $64-million Ferguson Center for the Arts (designed by I. M. Pei), and the $35-million David Student Union. At the Ferguson Center, CNU hosts internationally recognized performers like Andrea Bocelli, David Copperfield, Whoopi Goldberg, and B.B. King, among others. Students may attend these performances for between $5 and $15.

Costs

In-state tuition for full-time students for the 2009–10 academic year was $8050; nonresident tuition for full-time students was $15,992. Books and supplies average $750–$1000 per year. The room and board rate for the 2009–10 academic year was $9240.

Financial Aid

The University's financial aid programs serve approximately 50 percent of the student body. CNU offers every form of federally funded financial aid and more than 200 renewable merit scholarships for freshmen. The President's Leadership Program offers a minor in leadership studies and up to $5000 per year for academically superior students, regardless of need. The Honors Program offers scholarships of up to $5000 per year and gives students priority registration and the opportunity to develop their own path of courses instead of being tied to core requirements.

Faculty

Nearly 90 percent of CNU faculty members hold the highest degree in their professional field. Faculty members are chosen at CNU only if teaching is their top priority. They are advisers, mentors, and friends to their students, placing great emphasis on undergraduate research and preparation for graduate school.

Student Government

With more than 100 student clubs and organizations, students find no shortage of opportunities for campus involvement.

The University also encourages students to participate in the formulation of rules, regulations, and policies directly affecting student life. Students may get involved with the University's committees and councils. CNU is a community of honor, and all freshmen take an honor pledge during their Welcome Week orientation activities.

Admission Requirements

CNU welcomes applications from Virginia residents and out-of-state students whose education includes a strong college-preparatory curriculum and a record of success. Of the students accepted into the freshman class, the midrange (middle 50 percent) SAT score was 1100 to 1280 (critical reading and math); the average GPA was 3.6 on a 4.0 scale. CNU applicants may also submit the ACT exam, with or without the writing sample. Superior students with a GPA of 3.5 or better may apply to the University without submitting an SAT or ACT score.

Application and Information

Applications, viewbooks, and additional information may be obtained from the University's Web site or by contacting:

Christopher Newport University
Admissions Office
1 University Place
Newport News, Virginia 23606-2998
Phone: 757-594-7015
757-594-7938 (TDD)
800-333-4CNU (toll-free)
E-mail: admit@cnu.edu
Web site: http://www.cnu.edu

Trible Library is the intellectual center of Christopher Newport University.

THE CITADEL, THE MILITARY COLLEGE OF SOUTH CAROLINA

CHARLESTON, SOUTH CAROLINA

The College

The Citadel, founded in 1842, has a rich and storied history. Though it has been greatly expanded and modernized, it is basically the same distinctive institution it was when founded. The College's mission is to educate and prepare graduates to become principled leaders in all walks of life by instilling core values—academics, duty, honor, morality, discipline, diversity—in a challenging intellectual environment. The Citadel remains a stronghold of duty, self-discipline, and high ideals in a changing American society.

As a classic military college, The Citadel emphasizes the value of a strict indoctrination for first-year students, who are called knobs. The disciplined lifestyle that begins in the knob year binds cadets into a lifelong, close-knit camaraderie that is one of the strongest forces in their lives after graduation.

Citadel graduates have fought in every American conflict since the Mexican War. Cadets from The Citadel fired the first shots of the Civil War. The Corps flag displays nine battle streamers earned in that war. Citadel graduates continue to serve their country with distinction in all branches of the armed services.

The Corps of Cadets numbers approximately 2,100 young men and women and represents nearly every state in the U.S. and many other countries. All cadets are required to reside in barracks. A physical education center provides splendid facilities for physical education and individual and team sports unrelated to varsity events. The student activities building, named for General Mark W. Clark, the late president emeritus, houses the Honor Court room, reception lounge, Office of Cadet Activities, photograph darkroom, student publication offices, canteen, barber shop, auditorium, billiard room, gift shop, and post office. The beautiful Summerall Chapel, which is a shrine of religion, patriotism, and remembrance, is flexibly designed for use by major denominational groups.

The Citadel, a member of NCAA Division I (football division I-AA) and the Southern Conference, fields sixteen men's and women's intercollegiate athletic teams. Cadets take part in the almost fifty club and intramural sports programs, which include bicycling, bowling, boxing, crew, fencing, gymnastics, ice hockey, judo, karate, lacrosse, pistol, rugby, sailing, scuba diving, skydiving, volleyball, and waterskiing. The Citadel has its own boating center with canoes, power boats, and sailboats available for cadets' use.

Location

The Citadel is located in one of America's most historic cities, Charleston, South Carolina. The beautiful 100-acre campus is bordered by the Ashley River and historic Hampton Park. The climate is ideal, with an average temperature of 67 degrees. Many excellent ocean beaches are nearby. The Citadel's very own beach house is located just a few minutes away on the lush Isle of Palms. Charleston is famous for its pre-Revolutionary houses and gardens, outstanding restaurants, golf courses, and cultural centers. Entertainment and nightlife abound.

Charleston is served by Amtrak, an international airport, two bus lines, seven taxi companies, a limousine service, and fifteen rental-car firms. The city's transit system stops at The Citadel's main entrance. The campus is readily accessible via Interstate 26 or U.S. Highway 17.

Majors and Degrees

Organized into five schools, The Citadel offers twenty majors and twenty-six minor areas of academic concentration. This provides cadets with academic opportunities normally expected only at a university, combined with the personalized attention afforded by a small college. Bachelor of Arts degrees are available in chemistry, criminal justice, English, history, mathematics, modern languages (French, German, and Spanish), political science, and psychology. Bachelor of Science degrees are offered in biology, business administration, chemistry, civil engineering, computer science, education, electrical engineering, mathematics, physical education, and physics.

Academic Programs

The Citadel provides a sound education reinforced by the best features of a disciplined environment.

All cadets participate in one of the Reserve Officers' Training Corps programs—Army, Air Force, or Naval/Marine Corps. These programs do not require students to accept a commission or be committed to active duty.

The educational requirements of all majors ensure that The Citadel graduate is conversant with literature, history, and the natural and social sciences. Cadets learn to think critically by confronting issues raised in challenging courses.

The Citadel Honors Program is a specially designed educational experience that meets the needs of students with an outstanding record of academic achievement and a sense of intellectual adventure. While pursuing any one of the twenty degree programs offered by The Citadel, Honors students take a series of general education Honors courses concentrated in their first two years and an Honors seminar in their third and fourth years.

The Citadel—a fully accredited, four-year, coeducational, comprehensive senior college—is a member of the Southern Association of Colleges and Schools, the American Council on Education, the American Association of Colleges for Teacher Education, and the Association of American Colleges. The business administration department is accredited by AACSB International–The Association to Advance Collegiate Schools of Business. The civil and environmental engineering and electrical and computer engineering departments are accredited by the Accreditation Board for Engineering and Technology. The chemistry department is accredited by the American Chemical Society. The education department is accredited by the National Council for Accreditation of Teacher Education and the National Association of State Directors of Teacher Education and Certification.

Off-Campus Programs

The Citadel's Office of International Studies provides a variety of study-abroad and internship opportunities for cadets who are interested in a semester or year abroad.

Academic Facilities

Twenty-four major buildings are efficiently grouped around a huge parade ground to provide maximum convenience for students. Among the College's academic facilities are the Daniel Library, two engineering buildings, multimedia classrooms, and computer facilities located in all academic areas. The entire campus is linked to a fiber-optic network. Through a consortium arrangement, other local college libraries and facilities are available to cadets. Cadet barracks provide computer connections to the campus wide network and the Internet for each cadet in every room. Wireless service allows members of The Citadel community to access the campus network and the Internet from areas around campus.

Costs

The Citadel's extremely competitive fee structure includes uniforms, room, board, books, dry cleaning, laundry, athletic events, student publications, infirmary care, and haircuts. The total annual fees for 2009–10 by residence and by class: for residents of South Carolina, fees for first-year students were $21,729, and for sophomores, juniors, and seniors, $17,663. For out-of-state students, fees for first-year students were $35,539, and for sophomores, juniors, and seniors, $31,473.

Financial Aid

The Citadel offers two types of financial assistance: financial aid, which consists of loans and grants awarded on the basis of need, and scholarships, which are awarded on the basis of merit. In 2008, more than 76 percent of the Cadet Corps received financial aid and 49 percent received scholarships, ranging from several hundred dollars a year to complete expenses for four years. To be considered for financial aid or scholarships, students must submit an application for admission; a separate scholarship application for new students is not required. The deadline for applying for need-based financial aid is February 28 of the senior year in high school.

Faculty

All courses at The Citadel are taught by dedicated faculty members, more than 95 percent of whom hold doctoral degrees. The student-faculty ratio is 17:1. All faculty members are required to set aside time for counseling and assisting cadets with their studies.

Student Government

Cadets form a regiment, composed of a band and bagpipe unit, a ceremonial artillery unit, and four battalions of four to five companies each. Student authority is entrusted to the chain of command and the elected class officials.

A principal aspect of student government is the honor code. Under that code, a cadet does not lie, cheat, steal, or tolerate those who do. An Honor Committee elected by cadets administers the code.

Admission Requirements

Applicants must be unmarried, between 17 and 23 years of age, physically qualified for enrollment in ROTC, and graduates of an accredited secondary school or have satisfactorily completed the General Educational Development examination. The required high school subjects are 4 units of English; 3 units of mathematics (algebra I, algebra II, and geometry); 3 years of laboratory science (biology, chemistry, and a third unit that must have biology or chemistry as a prerequisite); 2 years of the same foreign language; 2 units of social science; 4 units of electives; 1 unit of U.S. history; and 1 unit of physical education or ROTC. Additional course work in mathematics and foreign language is recommended. Other considerations include the applicant's rank in class, academic performance, and scores on either the SAT or ACT. Extracurricular activities are viewed as indications of leadership and desirable character traits. All factors are weighed in the final determination of the applicant's qualifications. The Citadel actively seeks and encourages applications for admission without regard to gender, race, or ability to pay. Applicants are encouraged to apply upon completion of their junior year in high school.

Application and Information

Applications may be made at the end of the junior year in secondary school. Prospective cadets should arrange to have their SAT or ACT scores forwarded to The Citadel. While applicants are welcome to visit the campus at any time, special programs are arranged on a designated schedule, during which the accepted applicants reside in barracks. Inquiries should be addressed to:

Office of Admissions
The Citadel, The Military College of South Carolina
171 Moultrie Street
Charleston, South Carolina 29409
Phone: 800-868-1842 (toll-free)
E-mail: admissions@citadel.edu
Web site: http://www.citadel.edu

Members of the Corps of Cadets stand in formation on the quadrangle within one of The Citadel's five battalions.

CITY COLLEGE OF THE CITY UNIVERSITY OF NEW YORK

NEW YORK, NEW YORK

COLLEGE CLOSE-UPS

The College

Since its founding in 1847, the City College of New York (CCNY) has stressed the dual goals of offering access to higher education combined with academic excellence. That policy has had remarkable results, making CCNY one of America's greatest educational success stories. For example, 9 Nobel Prize winners are City College graduates, as is former Secretary of State Colin Powell and INTEL cofounder Andrew Grove, placing CCNY's graduates among the nation's leaders. The College ranks among the top dozen in the number of alumni who are members of the prestigious National Academy of Engineering and in producing graduates who have become America's leading business executives. Reflecting the College's commitment to equal educational opportunity, CCNY is also one of the nation's leaders in producing minority engineering graduates and in the number of black graduates who gain admission to medical school.

Overall, CCNY graduates exceed the national average in obtaining admission to medical school. The College has more full-time doctoral students in campus-based programs than all of the other City University of New York (CUNY) colleges combined. CCNY houses several major centers and institutes, including the CUNY Institute for Transportation Systems, the Colin Powell Center for Policy Studies, and the New York State Structural Biology Center, and offers the largest undergraduate research program in the metropolitan area.

The College offers students a wide variety of social activities; more than 100 clubs are organized on campus. Students can also participate in numerous intercollegiate and intramural sports. There are thirteen varsity teams for men and women.

In fall 2006, the first residence hall at City College, The Towers, opened on South Campus. The campus is a hub of construction activity, with the new School of Architecture and two new science buildings scheduled to open in the next four years.

Location

The City College campus occupies 36 acres in Manhattan along Convent Avenue from 131st to 141st Streets in the area known as Hamilton Heights. The surrounding neighborhoods are predominantly residential, although there are shopping areas west of the campus along Broadway and south toward 125th Street.

Majors and Degrees

The College of Liberal Arts and Science offers the Bachelor of Arts (B.A.), the Bachelor of Science (B.S.), and the Bachelor of Fine Arts (B.F.A.) degrees in the following majors: advertising, American studies, anthropology, area studies, art, art history, biochemistry, biology, chemistry, communication, comparative literature, creative writing, earth and atmospheric science, economics, electronic design and multimedia, English, film and video production, foreign languages and literature, history, international studies, management and administration, mathematics, music (performance, sonic arts technology, theory), optometry (combined B.S./O.D.), philosophy, physics, political science, prelaw, premedical studies, psychology, public relations, sociology, theater, and women's studies.

The School of Architecture, Urban Design, and Landscape Architecture offers a B.S. in architecture and the five-year Bachelor of Architecture.

The Sophie Davis School of Biomedical Education provides a seven-year B.S./M.D. curriculum for highly qualified high school graduates who reside in New York State. The Physician's Assistant Program, also part of the School of Biomedical Education, offers a B.S. degree and is a joint program between City College and Harlem Hospital. This is an upper-division (junior and senior years) program.

The School of Education offers programs that lead to the Bachelor of Science in Education (B.S.Ed.) in the following majors: bilingual education, early childhood education, and elementary education. In addition, students are prepared to teach a wide variety of subjects in secondary schools.

The Grove School of Engineering offers the Bachelor of Engineering (B.E.) degree in the fields of biomedical, chemical, civil, computer, electrical, environmental, and mechanical engineering and the B.S. in computer science.

The Center for Worker Education is an off-site program that helps adults return to college while continuing their full-time employment. Students can complete a bachelor's degree program in the evening.

Academic Programs

City College includes the College of Liberal Arts and Science and the largest complex of professional schools in the City University. These include the Schools of Architecture and Education, the Sophie Davis School of Biomedical Education, and the Grove School of Engineering. Accelerated five-year combined undergraduate/graduate degree programs are available in economics, English, history, mathematics, and psychology.

A Freshman Honors Program is available for qualified students who are interested in advanced research work and independent study. City College is one of seven campuses that form the consortium in the Macaulay Honors College program. The Macaulay Honors College program is designed to provide an outstanding educational opportunity to academically gifted students by offering a challenging undergraduate experience shaped by the combined resources of CUNY and New York City. Macaulay students are designated University Scholars and each receives a full-tuition scholarship; a $7500 Opportunities Fund to pursue global learning, independent research, and internship opportunities; a laptop; and a Cultural Passports granting free or reduced-price admission to arts and educational institutions throughout New York City.

Cooperative education internships are also provided for interested applicants. Such programs as Minority Access to Research Careers (MARC), Minority Biomedical Research Support (MBRS), and City College Research Scholars (CRS) provide paid and volunteer opportunities to do research at various institutions.

City College has a core curriculum that is founded on a strong liberal arts base and is designed to ensure the continued quality and relevance of its academic programs. The core curriculum reflects a global vision of human achievement in an increasingly interdependent world and is designed to provide City College students with superior academic preparation while enhancing their capacity to think critically and creatively. The College has a long history of encouraging independent thought and initiative and continues to foster an educational atmosphere in which students can explore and develop their interests and talents.

For most bachelor's degree programs, the total number of credits necessary to earn a degree is 120; a bachelor's degree in engineering requires up to 136 credits. The College works on a semester calendar and offers three summer sessions (one7½-week session and two 4-week sessions) and a winter session.

Off-Campus Programs

City College has exchange programs in Austria, China, England, Germany, and Morocco as well as a summer program in the Dominican Republic. Students are able to spend a semester, a full academic year, a summer term, or a winter term at one of the cooperating schools. Through a cooperative arrangement, students are also able to take courses at the various branches of the City University.

Academic Facilities

New facilities add a modern tone to the original neo-Gothic buildings, which have been designated state and national landmarks. In addition, a $200-million renovation of the neo-Gothic buildings has been completed. The thirteen-story Robert E. Marshak Science Building houses more than 200 teaching and research laboratories, a planetarium, a weather station, an electron microscope, laser research facilities, a science and engineering library, and a major physical education complex. The Grove School of Engineering has more than forty research laboratories. Aaron Davis Hall contains a 750-seat proscenium theater, a 200-seat experimental theater, and a seventy-five-seat studio workshop for rehearsals. The North Academic Center occupies three full city blocks and has 2,000 classrooms, laboratories, lecture halls, offices, and dining and student activity areas. It includes the Morris Raphael Cohen Library, which houses more than 1.3 million volumes, one of the largest collections in the City University.

Computer facilities are extensive at City College. The Computation Center provides services to meet instructional, administrative, and research needs. Numerous computer labs are located throughout the College, utilizing microcomputers and minicomputers to provide research and academic services to students and faculty and staff members.

Costs

In 2008–09 for students who were residents of New York State, the tuition for full-time attendance (12 or more credits or the equivalent) was $2000 per semester, or $4000 per year. Part-time students who were residents of New York State paid $170 per credit. Tuition for out-of-state and international students was $360 per credit. Tuition and fees are subject to change. Books, supplies, and commuting and personal expenses average $5905 a year for full-time students who live with their parents and $12,916 for students who live on their own, excluding tuition and moderate activity fees. The cost for housing in the recently constructed Towers residence hall is from $8600 to $14,040 per academic year.

Financial Aid

Financial assistance is available for eligible City College students through state and federal programs. Students who wish to apply for financial aid must file the Free Application for Federal Student Aid (FAFSA) and the TAP/APTS Application and CUNY Supplement. Among the forms of financial aid available are Federal Supplemental Educational Opportunity Grants, Federal Perkins Loans, and Federal Work-Study Program awards. A large percentage of City College students receive some type of aid. For information, students should contact the Financial Aid Office at City College at 212-650-5819.

The City College of New York Scholarship Program offers a variety of scholarships to entering freshman and transfer students. Freshman applicants should have a minimum combined score of 1100 on the critical reading and math section of the SAT or a 24 on the ACT, and a high school average of 85. Transfer students should have a minimum GPA of 3.0. The scholarship application deadline was February 2. For information about the scholarships available, including deadlines, eligibility, and criteria, students should visit the Web site at http://www.ccny.cuny.edu/admissions.

Faculty

City College's outstanding faculty represents a broad range of disciplines, and many members have earned the nation's highest forms of recognition—Guggenheim and Fulbright awards as well as grants that amount to millions of dollars annually in support of their research and scholarship. Eighty-five percent of the faculty members hold Ph.D. degrees. The student-teacher ratio is 14:1.

Student Government

Students have traditionally played an active role in campus government. Each year, two different senates are elected at the undergraduate level: one each for the day and evening divisions. Student government funds pay for the activities of student organizations, which send representatives to a student-faculty administrative committee that advises the College president on matters of an extracurricular nature. Through their representatives, students are given a voice on departmental committees, and they vote on matters of educational policy, budget, and faculty appointments and reappointments.

Admission Requirements

In determining admission to City College, the following factors are considered: a student's overall high school academic average from grades 9 through 12, the total number of academic units completed (New York State Regents courses), and the combined SAT score obtained on the Critical Reading and Mathematics sections of the exam. These factors are weighted together to determine eligibility. The College recommends that students preparing to apply to programs at City College complete 4 years of English, 4 years of social studies, 3 years of sequential math (or its equivalent), 2 years of laboratory science, 2 years of a foreign language, and 1 year of performing or visual arts in high school as the academic preparation needed for success and admission to the College. Qualified high school juniors may apply for early admission. Students who take the General Educational Development test (GED) and receive a score of at least 3250 (325 old scoring) are accepted to the City College. Students with special educational and financial needs may qualify for admission to the Search for Education, Elevation, and Knowledge (SEEK) Program. City College accepts students who wish to transfer from other post-secondary institutions. Requirements for admission vary according to the program and the number of credits completed. Applicants should contact the College for information about admission as a transfer student.

Application and Information

Applications to City College are processed through the City University of New York Processing Center. Although applications are processed on a rolling basis, students who wish a prompt response should adhere to the initial deadline dates of October 1 (spring admission) and March 15 (fall admission). Applications from qualified students that are received after these deadlines are processed on a space-available basis. Students applying to Macaulay Honors College must apply by November 1 for early decision and by December 15 for regular decision. All applications to The City College of New York must be completed online at www.cuny.edu/apply. For more information about admissions to City College contact the Office of Admissions.

Office of Admissions
The City College of the City University of New York
160 Convent Avenue, A-101
New York, New York 10031

Phone: 212-650-6977
E-mail: admissions@ccny.cuny.edu
Web site: http://www.ccny.cuny.edu/admissions

CLARKSON UNIVERSITY

POTSDAM, NEW YORK

The University

Founded in 1896, Clarkson stands out among America's private, nationally ranked research institutions because of its dynamic collaborative learning environment, innovative degree and research programs, and unmatched record of accomplishment for producing leaders and innovators.

The University attracts 3,000 enterprising students from diverse backgrounds (including some 400 graduate students) who thrive in rigorous programs in engineering, arts, sciences, business, and health sciences and in the University's close-knit, residential learning/living community. Clarkson defies convention in the classroom, in its laboratories, and by the impact its graduates have in the world. The University is New York State's highest-ranked small research institution. However, size is Clarkson's advantage—fostering leadership and problem-solving skills and readily affording students and faculty members the flexibility to span the boundaries of traditional academic areas.

Clarkson students also enjoy extraordinary opportunities to pursue faculty-mentored research. They gain professional experience through internships and co-ops with corporations and government organizations and can broaden their perspectives through a wide range of study-abroad opportunities.

Top graduate schools welcome Clarkson graduates to study medicine, law, and other professions. Johns Hopkins, MIT, Princeton, Yale, Caltech, Rice, and Stanford are just some of the schools chosen by Clarkson students.

Clarkson's 98 percent placement rate is among the nation's highest, with the most recent starting salaries averaging more than $52,000. Clarkson is a key recruitment source for many of America's industry leaders, including General Electric, Alcoa, Xerox, Accenture, IBM, and Procter & Gamble. In fact, 1 in 6 Clarkson alumni is already a CEO, president, vice president, or company owner.

Clarkson's active campus also offers a wide variety of extracurricular activities, including more than eighty clubs and interest groups. Students publish a lively campus newspaper and run campus radio and television stations. Active professional and honor societies enrich the campus experience.

There are Division I men's and women's hockey teams, as well as, seventeen Division III intercollegiate athletic teams for women and men. Recreational facilities include a field house and gym with racquetball, basketball, and indoor tennis courts; a state-of-the-art fitness center; and a swimming pool.

Location

Clarkson is located in Potsdam, the quintessential "college town," nestled in the foothills of the northern Adirondack region of New York. The beautiful Northeast corner of the state is the home of the 6-million-acre Adirondack Park. Within 2 hours of the campus are Lake Placid and the cosmopolitan Canadian cities of Montreal and Ottawa.

Majors and Degrees

Undergraduate degree programs offered are aeronautical engineering, American studies, applied mathematics and statistics, Areté (liberal arts/business), biology, biomolecular engineering, biomolecular science, management, chemical engineering, chemistry, civil engineering, communication, computer engineering, computer science, digital arts and sciences, electrical engineering, engineering and management, environmental engineering, environmental health science, environmental science and policy, financial information and analysis, global supply chain management, history, humanities, information systems and business processes, innovation and entrepreneurship, liberal studies, mathematics, mechanical engineering, physical therapy (pre–physical therapy leading to a doctorate), physics, political science, psychology, social sciences, and software engineering.

First-year students who are still deciding on a major may begin in a general program in business studies, engineering studies, science studies, or university studies.

Clarkson offers a University honors program, a three-year bachelor's degree option, a five-year B.S./M.S. in chemistry/biochemistry, a five-year B.S./M.B.A., and preprofessional programs in dentistry, law, medicine, physical therapy, and veterinary science.

Academic Programs

Clarkson's historic strengths in business, engineering, liberal arts, and science remain at the core of the curriculum. These programs have also been combined into cutting-edge, cross-disciplinary majors: biomolecular science, digital arts and sciences, environmental science and policy, information technology, interdisciplinary engineering and management, and software engineering.

A dynamic, hands-on approach to learning is one of the hallmarks of a Clarkson education. Clarkson students learn about business by actually starting a business. They conduct scientific research alongside distinguished faculty mentors in state-of-the-art laboratories. The University's undergraduate research program has produced 19 Goldwater Scholars since the highly competitive national scholarship program was launched in 1986.

National rankings and honors include the following: among the 125 "Best National Universities–Doctoral," *U.S. News & World Report,* 2009; among the "Best Undergraduate Engineering Programs," *U.S. News & World Report,* 2009; among the "Top 20 Wired Campuses," in *PC Magazine* and the *Princeton Review* 2007; the Supply Chain Management Program ranks thirteenth in the nation, *U.S. News & World Report,* 2009; and among the best business schools in the nation, the *Princeton Review's Best 282 Business Schools,* 2007 edition. The undergraduate program in innovation and entrepreneurship is ranked number twenty-two among 700 U.S. higher educational institutions by the *Princeton Review* and *Entrepreneur* magazine, 2006.

Clarkson was also ranked among the top 100 graduate schools in environmental engineering and civil engineering by *U.S. News & World Report's* "Best Graduate Programs," 2009.

In addition, Clarkson's award-winning Student Projects for Engineering Experience and Design (SPEED) program promotes multidisciplinary, project-based extracurricular learning opportunities for more than 400 undergraduates annually. Some fifteen design teams compete in national and regional collegiate competitions that involve design and analysis, teamwork, and communication skills.

Off-Campus Programs

Students benefit from the resources of the Associated Colleges of the St. Lawrence Valley, which comprises Clarkson University, St. Lawrence University, SUNY Canton, and SUNY Potsdam. Benefits for students include opportunities to participate in activities ranging from clubs to concerts, interlibrary exchange, and cross-registration that allows students to pursue two courses per year at member colleges at no extra cost.

Academic Facilities

The University's 640-acre wooded campus is the site of forty-six buildings that comprise more than 1.2-million square feet of assignable space. Dedicated exclusively to instructional programs are more than 375,000 square feet, including some 54,000 square feet of traditional classrooms and more than 168,000 square feet assigned as laboratory areas. In the Center for Advanced Materials Processing (a New York State Center for Advanced Technology), there are seventy state-of-the-art research labs, including many related to nanotechnology and environmental research. Others include a multidisciplinary engineering and project laboratory for team-based projects, such as the mini-Baja and Formulae SAE racers, a robotics laboratory, a high-voltage lab, electron microscopy, a Class 10 clean room, a polymer fabrication lab, crystal growth labs, and a structural testing lab. School of Arts and Sciences facilities include a virtual-reality laboratory, the Clarkson Open Source Institute, a molecular design laboratory, a human brain electrophysiology laboratory, and other specialized facilities. In 2008, a 16,000-square-foot Technology Advancement Center was opened.

Bertrand H. Snell Hall houses the School of Business and the School of Arts and Sciences administrative offices as well as fully networked classrooms and study spaces and collaborative centers that feature wireless network access and videoconferencing capabilities. The facility includes three academic centers, which are available to all students: the Shipley Center for Innovation, the Center for Global Competitiveness, and the Eastman Kodak Center for Excellence in Communication. The Center for Health Sciences at Clarkson is a regional center of excellence for education, treatment, and research in physical rehabilitation and other health sciences.

Costs

Tuition was $32,220 for the 2009–10 year, room (2-person) was $5890, and the meal plan was $5228. Student fees totaled $690. In addition, students usually spend about $2000 annually on books, supplies, travel, and personal expenses.

Financial Aid

The University offers a variety of scholarships and loans, including state and federal student loans, state scholarships and awards, individual scholarships, federal grants, and federal work-study programs.

Faculty

Clarkson's 190 full-time faculty members teach undergraduate and graduate classes, with graduate students assisting only in undergraduate lab sciences. With an excellent student-faculty ratio of 15:1, undergraduates benefit from regular interaction with the school's faculty members and small class sizes (especially at the upper levels). The University attracts teacher/scholars who are also highly regarded scholars in their fields. 96 percent hold a doctorate.

Student Government

The Student Senate and the Interfraternity Council combine to form the student government at Clarkson University. The former supervises all extracurricular activities (except athletics) and has responsibility for the allocation of student activity funds and for other appropriate business. The latter prescribes standards and rules for fraternities. Students are involved in the formation of University policies through membership, with faculty and staff representatives, on all important committees.

Admission Requirements

Clarkson recommends that prospective students follow a challenging secondary school curriculum that includes mathematics, science, and English. Candidates for entrance to the Wallace H. Coulter School of Engineering or students pursuing a degree in the sciences or an interdisciplinary engineering and management degree should have successfully completed secondary school courses in physics and chemistry. All candidates for admission are required to take the SAT or ACT. SAT Subject Tests are optional. The high school record is the most important factor in an admission decision. International students for whom English is a second language must submit a minimum TOEFL score of 550 (paper-based) or 212 (computer-based). All applicants must include a personal statement of 250 to 500 words describing a special interest, experience, or achievement.

Students achieving scores of 4 or better on the College Board's Advanced Placement examinations are considered for advanced placement and credit in virtually all academic areas. Advanced standing is most common in English, mathematics, and science.

An early decision plan is offered on a "first-choice" basis; this plan does not prohibit the student from making other applications, but it does commit the student to withdrawing other applications if accepted at Clarkson.

Although not required, a personal interview with a member of the Office of Admission is highly recommended, especially for early decision candidates. Interviews on campus should be arranged by letter or telephone at least one week prior to the intended visit. The Office of Admission is open Monday through Friday, from 8 a.m. to 4:30 p.m., and Saturday by appointment. The University welcomes visitors to the campus and makes arrangements, as requested, for families to tour and meet with academic and other departments on campus.

Application and Information

Office of Undergraduate Admission
Holcroft House
Clarkson University
P.O. Box 5605
Potsdam, New York 13699-5605
Phone: 315-268-6480
800-527-6577 (toll-free)
Fax: 315-268-7647
E-mail: admission@clarkson.edu
Web site: http://www.clarkson.edu

Clarkson is a leader in project-based learning, providing students with strong communication skills, leadership ability, and technological skill in their fields.

CLARK UNIVERSITY

WORCESTER, MASSACHUSETTS

The University

Founded in 1887, Clark is a private, liberal arts-based research university committed to scholarship that addresses social imperatives in a global context. Clark enrolls approximately 2,200 undergraduate and 1,000 graduate students. Undergraduates are offered a broad and deep liberal arts education that enables them to address the complex scientific, social, and economic challenges facing the world through hands-on research, in-depth exploration, and practical problem solving. Clark's focused areas of research excellence are backed by strong Ph.D. and master's-degree programs that engage graduate students from around the world in relevant, challenging, and innovative research that transforms communities. Research is a central component of Clark's mission, and the University has a tradition of challenging convention in the quest for new knowledge. Today, Clark continues this legacy of innovation with a research program that focuses on such areas as urban education, environmental issues and policies, management, health care, child and family welfare, holocaust and genocide studies, and international development and social change, generating findings and insights that directly benefit the communities the University serves.

Of the undergraduate students, about 60 percent are women, 8 percent are international students, and 70 percent live on campus. Students are guaranteed housing in one of nine residence halls for their first two years at Clark. Students can live with other freshmen in one of Clark's three First-Year Experience residence halls, or with upperclass students in one of the mixed-class residence halls. Housing options for upperclass students include suites (which resemble an apartment with a separate entry door, living room, and bathroom).

Clark's students are passionate about ideas, causes, and events beyond themselves; and are empowered to seek out and become involved in the many cocurricular opportunities available both on campus and off. Students can participate in more than 100 clubs and organizations.

Clark University is a Division III member of the National Collegiate Athletic Association and maintains highly competitive varsity athletic teams in a variety of sports. Men compete in baseball, basketball, cross-country, hockey, lacrosse, rowing, soccer, swimming and diving, and tennis. Women compete in basketball, cross-country, field hockey, rowing, soccer, softball, swimming and diving, tennis, and volleyball. Sixty-five percent of undergraduate students participate in intercollegiate, intramural, club, wellness, or recreational programs.

Clark's intramural program gives students the opportunity to compete and have fun without the demands of varsity athletics. Approximately half of the student body participates in the intramural program, which also encourages participation by Clark's faculty, staff, and alumni.

Location

Located in the heart of New England and about 40 miles west of Boston, Worcester (pronounced "wooster") is within easy reach of many cultural and recreational opportunities. With a population of approximately 175,000, the city is home to a broad mix of immigrants, from Armenian to French-Canadian to Vietnamese, who have lent their distinctive cultures to Worcester neighborhoods, restaurants, and places of worship. Worcester is also recognized as one of the ten most livable cities in the U.S. by *Forbes* magazine. Nearby attractions include Old Sturbridge Village and the Worcester Horticultural Society's Tower Hill Botanical Garden. Wachusett Mountain provides opportunities for skiing and hiking.

Majors and Degrees

Bachelor's degrees are offered in ancient civilization, art history, biochemistry/molecular biology, biology, business management, chemistry, communication and culture, comparative literature, computer science, economics, English, environmental science, foreign languages and literatures, French, geography, global environmental studies, government and international relations, history, international development and social change, mathematics, music, philosophy, physics, psychology, screen studios, sociology, Spanish, studio art, theater arts, and women's and gender studies. Students can also design their own major.

Academic Programs

Clark's challenging liberal arts curriculum encourages students to think critically, comprehend major global challenges, and develop the breadth of capabilities necessary for success in career and citizenship. Clark provides students many of the benefits typically associated with an excellent liberal arts college, including small classes, a strong sense of community, extensive cocurricular opportunities, and faculty members passionate about teaching and mentoring students. In addition, as a research university, Clark offers students the opportunity to participate in cutting-edge scholarship and creative work, working side-by-side with faculty members and graduate students, many of whom are international leaders in their fields. The smaller scale of the institution fosters close, active collaborations among faculty members, graduate students, and undergraduates. The University's dynamic learning environment and social values encourage students to seek out innovative solutions to real-world problems and create positive change in the community and the world.

Clark University's Program of Liberal Studies introduces students to the ways in which different fields and disciplines organize ideas and address questions. Students have the opportunity to engage in original research and creative work and present their results at campuswide celebrations of student accomplishments. Other academic opportunities include a university-wide innovation and entrepreneurship program, a rich array of internship and study-abroad options, and a variety of summer research opportunities. The International Studies Stream provides a broad-based international experience for students through courses, speakers, programs, internships, and study-abroad opportunities.

Clark has received national attention for its accelerated degree program that allows students to complete both a B.A. degree and a master's degree in five years, with fifth-year tuition waived for eligible students.

Off-Campus Programs

Studying abroad can enrich and strengthen students' academic program, help perfect their language skills, and broaden their horizons. Clark offers more than thirty opportunities to study abroad in both foreign-language and English-language programs. Students must declare a major before choosing a program.

An academic internship is a credit-bearing, career-related work experience of limited duration in which an individual takes on responsible roles outside the traditional university environment in a nonprofit organization, government office, or for-profit business. The Clark Recruiter, an online career management system, typically lists more than 300 internships every year. For assistance, students can make a one-on-one appointment with a counselor in the Office of Career Services.

Academic Facilities

In the past decade, Clark has made major investments in facilities to support faculty scholarship, including the Traina Center for the Arts, the Lasry Center for the Biosciences, and the Academic Commons at Goddard Library. The University's main library, Goddard, is a cutting-edge facility for research, teaching, and learning. In addition to the archives and special collections, traditional and electronic resources are available, including Goddard's collection of more than 375,000 volumes, 275,000 monographs, subscriptions to 1,500 periodicals, full Internet access, nearly 50 subject-specific databases, and a public online catalog available twenty-four hours a day. Clark students and faculty also have access to the library collections of thirteen other colleges and universities in the Worcester Consortium.

Clark's research institutes and centers—which include the Mosakowski Institute for Public Enterprise, the George Perkins Marsh Institute, the Clark Labs for Cartographic Analysis, the Jacob Hiatt Center for Urban Education, the Heinz Werner Institute for Development Analysis, and the Strassler Center for Holocaust and Genocide Studies—build on a foundation of interdisciplinary scholarship, with faculty and students working across boundaries to develop innovative solutions to a wide range of contemporary challenges.

Costs

For the 2010–11 academic year, tuition is $36,100, and the student activity fee is $320. Housing varies between $4000 and $7700; meal plans range between $2800 and $3500.

Financial Aid

The Office of Financial Assistance works closely with families to explore a range of financial options. A financial aid package usually comprises grants, loans, and employment. Around 90 percent of students receive some form of financial assistance. In 2009, Clark awarded approximately $36 million in financial assistance. Merit-based scholarships are available, and eligible students can receive scholarships of up to $18,000. Eighty-five percent of the most recent incoming first-year class received University scholarships.

Faculty

Faculty members take pride in serving as scholars, teachers, and mentors. There are 187 full-time faculty members, 96 percent of whom hold a doctorate or terminal degree in their field. The student-to-faculty ratio is 10:1. All undergraduate courses are taught by the faculty members, not graduate students.

Student Government

The Student Council advances the interests of students and ensures that students play a vital role in decisions at the University. Student Council members, elected every semester, work to maximize student influence at Clark.

Admission Requirements

The admissions committee recommends that applicants have a strong senior year course load (at least four, preferably five, solid academic courses). In addition, students should have taken, at minimum, 4 years of English, 3 of mathematics, 3 of science, 2 of social science, and 2 of a foreign language, as well as other electives, including the arts.

Students must submit the completed application, the $55 nonrefundable application fee, transcripts of all high school and college work completed, official ACT or SAT scores, and two letters of recommendation. Transfer students should also include a statement explaining why they wish to attend Clark University. All students whose native language is not English are encouraged to take the TOEFL. Students can apply online using the common or the universal application; paper applications are also accepted.

Application and Information

The application deadlines for the fall and spring semesters are January 15 and November 1 for freshmen, April 1 and November 1 for transfer students, and January 15 for international students.

Office of Admissions
Clark University
950 Main Street
Worcester, Massachusetts 01610
Phone: 508-793-7711
800-462-5275 (toll-free)
Fax: 508-793-8821
E-mail: admissions@clarku.edu
Web site: http://www.clarku.edu/

CLAYTON STATE UNIVERSITY

MORROW, GEORGIA

The University

Clayton State University is an outstanding metropolitan institution located 15 miles southeast of downtown Atlanta. The school was established in 1969 in Morrow, Georgia. Today, Clayton State University offers associate, bachelor's, and master's degrees to approximately 6,500 students, and further serves the needs of the community through a variety of continuing education programs and a dual-enrollment program that serves participating area high school juniors and seniors. Clayton State combines the resources and opportunities of the University System of Georgia and the cosmopolitan city of Atlanta with the advantages of a small university with close faculty-student relations. Clayton State students can cross-register in courses at nineteen public and private universities in the Atlanta region through the Atlanta Regional Consortium of Higher Education (ARCHE).

Situated on a gorgeous lakeside campus, Clayton State's convenient main location in Morrow provides easy access to the metropolitan Atlanta area, enabling students to take advantage of a variety of internship and career opportunities. There are also two oncvenient, alternate sites offering undergraduate course work in Peachtree City and McDonough, Georgia. Metropolitan Atlanta is an international center for business, transportation, communications, information technology, science, health care, and numerous other industries. It offers vast educational, entertainment, and cultural opportunities as well as a sunny, mild climate.

Clayton State is a 100-percent laptop university on a wireless campus with innovative smart classrooms. It was the third public university in the nation to require notebook computers of all students and faculty members. Every Clayton State student must own or have daily access to a notebook computer to use for academic assignments and communications.

Clayton State University is accredited by the Commission on Colleges of the Southern Association of Colleges and Schools (SACS) to award associate, bachelor's, and master's degrees. The nursing program is accredited by the Commission on Collegiate Nursing Education (CCNE). The dental hygiene program is accredited by the Commission on Dental Accreditation of the American Dental Association. The middle-level education program is accredited by the National Council for Accreditation of Teacher Education (NCATE). The music degree programs are accredited by the National Association of Schools of Music (NASM). The business degree is accredited by AACSB International–The Association to Advance Collegiate Schools of Business. The paralegal studies program is accredited by the American Bar Association (ABA). The health-care management program is certified by the Association of University Programs in Health Administration (AUPHA).

Clayton State offers a variety of student services, including career counseling and job placement assistance. The Center for Academic Success helps students strengthen their learning skills through tutoring, multimedia instruction, and academic workshops.

According to the 2009 *U.S. News & World Report* ranking of colleges, Clayton State has the most diverse student population among comprehensive baccalaureate-level colleges and universities in the southern United States. Students at Clayton State represent every region of the U.S. and some twenty-five countries.

Student activities at Clayton State include dances, concerts, films, festivals, lectures, recitals, drama presentations, and visual artists-in-residence. Students participate in more than seventy campus clubs and organizations. *Cygnet,* Clayton State's literary and arts journal, publishes selected works of student poetry, prose, and art. The University's62,000-square-foot, state-of-the-art student activities center houses a two-court gymnasium, fitness areas (including cardiovascular equipment and free weights), and an aerobics studio. In addition, the facility has meeting rooms for student organizations and clubs, a ballroom, and a game room.

Clayton State University is a member of the NCAA Division II Peach Belt Conference. The twelve intercollegiate teams consistently advance to their respective national tournaments. In 2009, Clayton State had four athletes who received all-American honors. Men's athletic teams include basketball, soccer, golf, cross-country, and track and field. Women's athletic teams include basketball, soccer, tennis, cross-country, and track and field. Students may also audition for the cheerleading squad. Prospective students who would like to be considered for athletic recruitment to Clayton State should go online to http://athletics.clayton.edu and click on Recruiting Info.

All first-time, full-time freshmen are required to live on campus. Clayton State opened Laker Hall in August 2008. The residence hall houses approximately 450 students. This state-of-the-art gigaplex building features four-bedroom, two-bath suites with kitchenettes. In addition, residents have on-site access to study lounges, wireless high-speed Internet, cable television, interactive laundry facilities, a game room, and many social activities.

Shops, restaurants, grocery stores, and shopping centers are within a short distance of the main campus.

Location

Nestled on a wooded 163-acre campus with five lakes in suburban Atlanta, Clayton State's setting is peaceful, safe, and conducive to learning. The University is near the crossroads of three major interstate highways and is 15 minutes from Hartsfield-Jackson Atlanta International Airport. Atlanta has a large college-student population, with more than forty postsecondary institutions in the region. With a population of over 5.7 million, the metropolitan Atlanta area offers *Fortune 500* internships, a wide range of affordable housing, and jobs after graduation.

Majors and Degrees

Clayton State offers associate and bachelor's degree programs and certificates. Four-year programs offered are the Bachelor of Arts (B.A.) in communication and media studies, English, history, liberal studies, middle-level education, music, and theater; the Bachelor of Business Administration (B.B.A.) in accounting, business (general), management, marketing, and supply chain management; the Bachelor of Information Technology (B.I.T.); the Bachelor of Music (B.M.) in composition, music education, and performance; the Bachelor of Science (B.S.) in biology, criminal justice, government, health and fitness management, health-care management, integrative studies, mathematics, political science, psychology and human services, and sociology; the Bachelor of Science (B.S.) in computer science (emphasis in computer gaming); the Bachelor of Science in Dental Hygiene (B.S.D.H.); the Bachelor of Science in Information Technology (B.S.I.T.); the Bachelor of Science in Legal Studies (B.S.); the Bachelor of Science in Nursing (B.S.N.) in basic licensure or for existing RNs; and the Bachelor of Applied Science (B.A.S.) degree in administrative management and technology management. The interdisciplinary bachelor's degree in the communication and media studies program provides an integrated multimedia program for students who enjoy writing, drawing, photography, Web design, film, and writing for digital media.

The Regents' Engineering Transfer Program (RETP) is designed for students who intend to transfer into engineering at Georgia Tech or other engineering programs. The dual-degree engineering program with Georgia Tech is a five-year program for students wishing to complete a bachelor's degree at Clayton State as well as a bachelor's degree in engineering from Georgia Tech. A number of programs are designed for students interested in preprofessional tracks, including predentistry, pre-engineering, prelaw, premedicine, prepharmacy, and pre–veterinary medicine.

Academic Programs

The academic year consists of two semesters, a special summer session for study-abroad programs, two short summer terms, and one regular summer term. Clayton State students benefit from a faculty-student ratio of 1:18 in challenging, small classes that offer personal attention from experienced faculty members committed to helping students succeed and reach their goals. Clayton State students engage in opportunities to expand their horizons through faculty research collaborations where they may present or publish their findings together. Students in the liberal studies and integrative studies programs may design their own degree programs. Some programs require students to complete internships in Atlanta and other regions. Clayton State students can also experience global learning through a variety of study-abroad opportunities.

Outstanding freshmen may apply to participate in the Clayton State honors program. Honors students participate in enhanced honors courses, are eligible for special scholarships and early registration, and graduate with an honors diploma seal and recognition at commencement.

Off-Campus Programs

The University currently participates in study-abroad programs sponsored by the European, African, Asian, and Americas Councils of the University System of Georgia. These summer programs, which can be funded by financial aid or HOPE scholarships, offer students up to five weeks of residence in a college environment abroad while earning academic course credit. Clayton State also participates in a student-exchange program with the University of Northumbria in Newcastle, England, in which students can study for a semester or academic year abroad, with the credit earned counting toward their academic program at Clayton State. Similar programs may be available in other countries including France, Italy, Spain, and Russia.

The University System of Georgia also participates in the Academic Common Market, which allows students from fourteen states in the Southeast to major in specialized programs not offered in their home states while paying the tuition rate for Georgia students.

Academic Facilities

Clayton State's striking James Baker University Center is an exciting facility for learning that includes classrooms; meeting rooms; faculty, administrative, and student organization offices; the College of Information and Mathematical Sciences; dining services; the HUB, the campus's computer help desk; and more than 2,000 data drops. Its vaulted ceilings, three-story atrium, and soaring window walls make it a bright and cheerful place for the University community.

Connected to the elegant Baker University Center, the Clayton State library houses a substantial collection of books, microfilm, periodicals, and more than 16,000 pieces of audiovisual software, including slides, videotapes, audiotapes, CDs, and filmstrips. Through the OCLC/SOLINET network, the library has access to the book and periodical holdings of nearly 14,000 academic, public, and special libraries. Clayton State participates in GALILEO, the statewide library initiative, which provides access to numerous periodical and information databases and more than 2,000 full-text periodicals. In addition, the library subscribes to several other electronic and CD-ROM databases. The library seats 450 at tables and study carrels, and specially adapted carrels have been designed for audiovisual playback. Sixty carrels are equipped with Internet connections.

The campus offers the world-famous, acoustically-perfect concert hall, Spivey Hall, the most frequently recorded concert venue on National Public Radio's *Performance Today*. Spivey Hall has developed one of the nation's premier classical, jazz, and world-music series, and its performing artists often teach master classes, giving Clayton State students a rare opportunity for instruction and critiques from established music professionals.

Adjacent to Spivey Hall, the music education building houses two large choral and instrumental rehearsal rooms, several ensemble rooms, and eighteen practice rooms. Students have access to state-of-the-art technology in the recording studio and in the electronic music, keyboard, and vocal pedagogy labs.

Clayton Theatre offers several productions each year. *The productions are student centered but feature professional directors and designers.*

The Georgia Archives and the National Archives for the Southeast border the campus. Both provide exceptional primary-source research materials for Clayton State's history and political science students. Clayton State is the only university in the U.S. with national and state archives adjacent to its campus.

Costs

For the 2009–10 academic year, tuition and fees were $3934 for in-state residents and $13,232 for out-of-state residents. Room and board were $8078. More information about tuition and fees can be found at http://adminservices.clayton.edu/registrar/fees.htm.

Financial Aid

Clayton State offers assistance to students who need financial support to continue their education. Students can participate in federally funded and state-supported grant and loan programs, including HOPE, the lottery-funded scholarship program for Georgia residents. The University also offers outstanding students a variety of academic and talent scholarships. For more information, students should contact the Financial Aid Office at 678-466-4185 or financialaid@clayton.edu.

Faculty

Clayton State has 197 faculty members; 75 percent hold the highest degrees in their fields.

Student Government

The Student Government Association (SGA) works as an advisory body to the University administration and Student and Enrollment Services Committee. SGA maintains the general welfare of the student body by providing students with necessary information that may be of concern and by providing a means for student input and opinion in the organization and operation of student affairs. SGA selects students to serve on campus advisory committees.

Admission Requirements

Clayton State University uses rolling admission, meaning applications are reviewed and admissions decisions are made when all necessary materials and credentials are received. The deadline for submission of all application materials for fall admission is July 15. Clayton State encourages all students to apply and complete their applications for fall admission early to maximize their opportunities for financial aid. The priority and final deadlines for financial aid are listed at http://adminservices.clayton.edu/financialaid/.

Clayton State seeks to attract academically talented students who are likely to succeed.

For freshman admission to Clayton State, applicants must graduate from accredited high schools and have completed college-preparatory curricula. Georgia high school graduates must receive college preparatory diplomas. Prospective freshman students are evaluated for admission using the Freshman Index, which combines a student's high school grade point average (reflecting the successful completion of College Preparatory Curriculum [CPC] units) and either ACT or SAT test scores. For transfer admissions, students must have already completed a minimum of 30 transferable semester credits with a minimum 2.0 GPA.

Application and Information

Prospective freshman applicants must submit a completed application for admission, application fee of $40, official high school transcripts, and either SAT or ACT test scores. Prospective transfer applicants must submit a completed application for admission, application fee of $40, official high school transcript or GED results, and all official college or university transcripts. High school and/or college transcripts must be official copies in sealed, unopened envelopes. Test scores (SAT and SAT Subject Tests, ACT, and AP) must be submitted directly from the testing service or appear on official high school transcripts. In cases requiring the SAT subject tests, the University provides information about which tests are needed and what scores are acceptable. The TOEFL is required for international students who are not native speakers of English and who have not completed their education in an English-speaking country. The admissions application deadlines are July 1 for fall semester, December 1 for spring semester, and April 1 for summer semester.

Office of Recruitment and Admissions
Clayton State University
2000 Clayton State Boulevard
Morrow, Georgia 30260
Phone: 678-466-4115
866-339-2800 (toll-free)
Fax: 678-466-4149
E-mail: csu-info@clayton.edu
Web site: http://www.clayton.edu

CLEMSON UNIVERSITY

CLEMSON, SOUTH CAROLINA

The University

One of the country's most selective public research universities, Clemson was founded in 1889 with a mission to be a "high seminary of learning" dedicated to teaching, research, and service. Today, these three concepts remain at the heart of the University and provide the framework for an exceptional educational experience.

At Clemson University, professors take the time to get to know students and to explore innovative ways of teaching. Exceptional teaching is one reason Clemson's retention and graduation rates rank among the highest in the country among public universities.

Exceptional teaching is also why Clemson continues to attract an increasingly talented student body. In 2009, roughly half of the entering freshmen were ranked in the top 10 percent of their high school classes, and the freshman class averaged 1225 on the critical reading and math sections of the SAT—one of the highest averages among the nation's public research universities.

Clemson is committed to world-class research. With over $140 million in sponsored research support annually, Clemson is one of the National Science Foundation's top-100 research universities. Undergraduates have the opportunity to work closely with faculty members on exciting and challenging research projects.

The University also encourages faculty members to engage their classes through service-learning. One example of this is the Clemson Elementary Outdoors project, in which more than 750 Clemson students from a broad range of disciplines helped research and design outdoor learning areas for the city's elementary school. Clemson has received national recognition for its innovative Communication-Across-the-Curriculum (CAC) program, in which professors focus on providing students with real-life challenges that require them to think and communicate effectively. At Clemson, CAC has become a standard teaching method used in nearly every department.

From cheering the Tigers at a football game to socializing at the Hendrix Student Center, Clemson students can participate in a wide variety of activities outside the classroom. The more than 300 campus clubs and organizations include fraternities and sororities, honoraries, international, military, performing arts, political, professional, religious, service, social interest, special interest, sports and fitness, student media, and union programs and activities.

With 19 intercollegiate sports, Clemson offers exciting spectator sports all year long. Clemson is a charter member of the Atlantic Coast Conference (ACC) and is an NCAA Division I school. Admission to regular-season events played at Clemson is included in University fees for full-time students.

Clemson University is accredited by the Commission on Colleges of the Southern Association of Colleges and Schools (1866 Southern Lane, Decatur, Georgia 30033-4097; phone: 404-679-4501) to award bachelor's, master's, specialist, and doctoral degrees.

Location

Approximately midway between Charlotte, North Carolina, and Atlanta, Georgia, Clemson University is located on 1,400 acres of beautiful rolling hills within the foothills of the Blue Ridge Mountains and along the shores of Lake Hartwell. Great weather and proximity to natural wonders and large cities offer year-round recreational opportunities.

The University's enrollment of just over 18,000 undergraduate and graduate students makes it a defining presence in Clemson, South Carolina, a town of about 12,000. Most students live on campus in one of the twenty-one residence halls and four apartment complexes, which are within a 10-minute walk to class or downtown.

Majors and Degrees

Clemson offers more than seventy undergraduate and approximately 100 graduate degree programs through five academic colleges: Agriculture, Forestry, and Life Sciences; Architecture, Arts, and Humanities; Business and Behavioral Science; Engineering and Science; and Health, Education, and Human Development. Students can earn Bachelor of Arts, Bachelor of Science, or preprofessional degrees in accounting; agricultural and applied economics; agricultural education; agricultural mechanization and business; animal and veterinary sciences; wildlife and fisheries biology; architecture; biochemistry; biological sciences; biosystems engineering; ceramic and materials engineering; chemical engineering; chemistry; civil engineering; communication studies; computer engineering; computer information systems; computer science; construction science and management; early childhood education; economics; electrical engineering; elementary education; English; environmental and natural resources; financial management; fine arts; food science; forest resource management; genetics; geology; graphic communications; health science; history; horticulture; industrial engineering; industrial management; landscape architecture; language and international health; language and international trade; management; marketing; mathematical sciences; mathematics teaching; mechanical engineering; microbiology; modern languages; nursing; packaging science; parks, recreation, and tourism management; philosophy; physics; political science; polymer and textile chemistry; preprofessional health studies; pre–rehabilitation sciences; pre–veterinary medicine; production studies in performing arts; professional golf management; psychology; science teaching; secondary education; sociology; special education; technology and human resource development; textile management; and turfgrass.

Academic Programs

Clemson's academic year is divided into two semesters. The fall semester begins in mid-August, the spring semester in early January. Two summer sessions and one Maymester are also available. Students average 16 credit hours per semester. Clemson requires all students to complete some general education classes specified by the University before graduation. The number of completed credit hours required for graduation varies, depending on the major.

Calhoun Honors College is a University-wide program with roughly 980 students, including approximately 250 freshmen each year. Calhoun Scholars may also choose to pursue departmental honors within their specific academic discipline. In addition, EUREKA! (Experiences in Undergraduate Research, Exploration, and Knowledge Advancement) is a unique and exciting program that enables honors students to pursue research and scholarly activities with faculty members across all disciplines. The advantages of membership include priority registration, extended library loan privileges, honors research grants, and honors housing.

The National Scholars Program is a highly selective program for exceptional students who strive to meet their highest intellectual potential. One of its goals is to develop the interests and talents students need to compete for Rhodes, Marshall, and Truman scholarships; Fulbright Grants; National Science Foundation Graduate Fellowships; and other prestigious international fellowships.

Clemson's nationally recognized Programs for Educational Enrichment and Retention (PEER) is committed to improving academic performance of underrepresented students in engineering and science. Today, thanks in large part to PEER, the six-year graduation rate for African American first-time freshmen is above the national average.

The Women in Science and Engineering (WISE) program focuses on recruiting women into science and engineering and helping them succeed in college and their careers. WISE offers support activities such as mentoring programs, career planning, and study groups.

Tutoring, supplemental instruction, academic skills workshops, and academic counseling are also available free to all Clemson students through the Academic Support Center.

Off-Campus Programs

Clemson's study-abroad and off-campus programs give students the opportunity to study almost anywhere in the world. The International Student Exchange Program and the Clemson Exchange Program allow students to enroll for a summer, semester or full academic year at one of over 100 universities throughout the world. About 28 percent of the student body enriched their education through study abroad last year. Students in a variety of majors have opportunities at the Archbold Center in Dominica; the Daniel Center in Genoa, Italy; the Clemson University Brussels Center in Belgium; and other locations.

Clemson undergraduates have worked at more than 360 companies through Cooperative Education. Participating students alternate periods of academic study with periods of related work in a business, industry, agency, or organization.

Academic Facilities

The Clemson campus is home to a blend of historic buildings and advanced research facilities surrounded by stately trees and lush greenery.

The Libraries and the Division of Computing and Information Technology are committed to providing students and faculty members with the latest ways to access information. Clemson's main library, the Robert M. Cooper Library, is located at the center of campus and provides students with a variety of services and up-to-date collections. The University's wireless networking capability lets students communicate with professors and classmates, read online course materials, check e-mail, and conduct research, all from their own laptops. Students are required to complete an electronic portfolio prior to graduation, allowing them the opportunity to present themselves through a creative venue to prospective employers and graduate schools.

The campus offers an array of facilities and programs designed to enhance a student's entire educational experience. These include the Pearce Center for Professional Communication, Class of 1941 Studio for Student Communication, Rutland Center for Ethics, and Academic Support Center.

Clemson real estate holdings also include more than 32,000 acres of forestry and agricultural lands throughout the state, the majority of which are dedicated to the University's research and service missions.

Costs

For the 2009–10 academic year, undergraduate tuition and fees were $11,478 for South Carolina residents and $25,788 for out-of-state residents. Room and board costs were approximately $6774, and books and supplies were $922. The one-time laptop computer cost was about $1250.

Financial Aid

Financial aid is usually awarded on the basis of need to supplement the amount students and their parents can contribute to college expenses. The University also awards some scholarships based entirely on academic merit. Clemson offers financial aid in the form of grants, scholarships, loans, and part-time employment.

Entering freshmen are evaluated on a competitive basis for scholarships using the admission application. There is no separate scholarship application. For Academic Recruiting Scholarships, students are ranked based on test scores, high school rank-in-class, and other academic factors. In past years, students offered one of these merit scholarships normally had a minimum SAT score of 1350 (combined score from critical reading and mathematics sections), or an ACT of at least 31, and were ranked no lower than the top 10 percent of their senior class. Stipends for in-state residents range from $500 per year to the full cost of attendance. Merit scholarships for out-of-state students range from $2500 per year to the full cost of attendance. Academic Recruiting Scholarships are available only to entering freshmen and are renewable for three additional years provided that the minimum standards are maintained. The application for admission is the first step for prospective freshmen to be considered for merit awards.

General University Scholarships are awarded to both entering freshmen and upperclassmen. To be considered for scholarships, upperclassmen must have a minimum cumulative GPR of at least 2.5. These scholarships may have special criteria set up by the donor, such as a certain residency, major, or career interest. Because of the restrictions on many of these scholarships, it is impossible to predict the recipients. However, the scholarship selection process is very competitive. Stipends range from $250 to $7500.

Faculty

Clemson has over 1,000 full-time faculty members, of whom 86 percent hold a Ph.D. or terminal degree in their fields. In addition, the University has over 150 part-time faculty members. Faculty honors include the Fulbright Scholarship, Guggenheim Fellowship, National Science Foundation CAREER Award, National Institutes of Health Senior Scientist Award, and American Academy of Arts and Sciences membership. The average class size is 29, and the student-to-faculty ratio is 16:1.

Admission Requirements

Each year, the University receives about 17,000 applications for a fall freshman class of 2,950. Transfer applications are received from about 2,000 students, of whom Clemson enrolls 900. Undergraduate applications are available online at http://www.clemson.edu.

For freshman applicants, the following factors are considered: class standing, standardized test scores (SAT or ACT), high school curriculum, grades, and choice of major. All entering freshmen must have completed 4 credits of English, 3 credits of mathematics, 3 credits of laboratory science, 3 credits of a foreign language (in the same language), 3 credits of social sciences, 2 credits in other areas, and 1 credit of physical education.

To be considered for transfer admission, candidates must have completed a full year of college study (a minimum of 30 semester hours or 45 quarter hours of transferable work), earned a cumulative grade point average of at least 2.5 on a 4.0 scale (3.0 preferred), and completed freshman-level courses in English, science, and mathematics for their intended major at Clemson.

Application and Information

Application deadlines for freshman admissions are December 1 (priority date for fall enrollment), May 1 (fall semester deadline), and December 15 (for the spring semester). For transfer admissions, the application deadlines are July 1 (for the fall semester) and December 15 (for the spring semester).

Office of Admissions
Clemson University
105 Sikes Hall, Box 345124
Clemson, South Carolina 29634-5124
Phone: 864-656-2287
Fax: 864-656-2464
E-mail: cuadmissions@clemson.edu
Web site: http://www.clemson.edu
http://twitter.com/BeAClemsonTiger (Twitter)

CLEVELAND INSTITUTE OF MUSIC

CLEVELAND, OHIO

The Institute

The mission of the Cleveland Institute of Music (CIM) is to provide exceptionally talented students from around the world an outstanding, thoroughly professional education in the art of music performance and related musical disciplines. The Institute embraces the legacy of the past and promotes the continuing evolution of music within a supportive and nurturing environment. The Institute also provides rigorous training in programs for gifted precollege musicians and serves as a resource for the community, with training for individuals of all ages and abilities.

A guiding principle at the Institute maintains that a liberal arts education contributes to a broad, humanistic perspective and is a vital component of the undergraduate curriculum. Equally important is the faculty's commitment to incorporating new technologies to complement and enhance the educational program.

The distinguished faculty of the Institute aims to develop the full artistic potential of all of its students. Through performance and teaching, the faculty and administration are dedicated to passing along their knowledge and love for this great art and to providing the bridge to an exciting and fulfilling career.

Founded in 1920, the Cleveland Institute of Music maintains its current size of approximately 450 undergraduate and graduate students and 90 full- and part-time faculty members by controlling the enrollment through carefully balanced admission policies, thus ensuring personal, individual attention for each student. In admitting the optimum number of students to each performance area rather than an unlimited number, CIM maximizes the performance experiences of its students so that they are well prepared to meet the challenges of professional life. The achievements of the Cleveland Institute of Music's alumni throughout the world are indicative of the Institute's commitment to high quality and professionalism. The distinguished-artist faculty includes the principals and other section players of The Cleveland Orchestra, a neighboring institution with which the Institute has a close relationship. All collegiate-level instruction is conducted by members of the CIM faculty and not by teaching assistants.

About 25 percent of CIM's students are in residence at Cutter House, the Institute's residence hall, which is adjacent to the school's main building. In addition to having the usual amenities, each room is connected to the computer network operated by Case Western Reserve University (CWRU), whose campus borders that of CIM. Since all residents are CIM students, practice is permitted in the rooms of Cutter House. Residence hall accommodations are required for freshmen and sophomores.

In addition to the programs of study listed under the Majors and Degrees section, the Cleveland Institute of Music offers programs leading to the following graduate degrees and diplomas: Master of Music, Doctor of Musical Arts, Artist Diploma, and Professional Studies.

Location

CIM is located in University Circle, a cultural, educational, and scientific center situated approximately 4 miles east of downtown Cleveland. University Circle comprises more than thirty institutions that together constitute one of the largest diversified cultural complexes in the world. The complex includes museums, libraries, concert halls, colleges and universities, hospitals, gardens, churches, and temples. Occupying 500 acres in one of the most beautiful areas in the city, the facilities of University Circle offer extensive opportunities for serious study in many fields.

Located within easy walking distance of CIM are Case Western Reserve University, with which CIM cooperates in the Joint Music Program, and Severance Hall, the spectacularly restored home of The Cleveland Orchestra, whose rehearsals are open to CIM students by special arrangement. Students may also visit the Cleveland Museum of Art and enjoy its world-famous collections as well as its annual concert series, featuring world-renowned performers. Easily accessible to Institute students are numerous other University Circle institutions, such as the Cleveland Institute of Art, the Cleveland Play House, the Cleveland Museum of Natural History, the Western Reserve Historical Society, the Crawford Auto-Aviation Museum, and the Cleveland Botanical Garden.

Majors and Degrees

Students may major in audio recording, bassoon, bass trombone, cello, clarinet, collaborative piano, composition, double bass, eurhythmics, flute, guitar, harp, harpsichord, horn, oboe, orchestral conducting, organ, piano, Suzuki cello pedagogy, Suzuki violin pedagogy, timpani and percussion, trombone, trumpet, tuba, viola, violin, and voice.

Through the Joint Music Program with Case Western Reserve University, five-year double-degree programs are available to CIM students. Of the two degrees earned by students in these programs, the Bachelor of Music is one component. Both B.M./B.A. and B.M./B.S. programs may be structured within music or with the CWRU component in a nonmusic field.

Academic Programs

CIM programs offer intensive and comprehensive preparation for professional careers in music. All courses at the school revolve around a core of studies in theory, music history, and literature; the core is designed to provide a thorough musical education. At the undergraduate level, additional educational breadth is provided by required liberal arts courses.

An unusually intense performance environment involves students in a wide repertoire, including solo, chamber, orchestral, and operatic literature.

The development of the disciplines and skills required of a solo performer is an integral part of a student's training at CIM. This training, involving access to faculty members and visiting artists who are practicing professionals, is augmented by the many master classes, repertoire classes, and recitals offered annually. A concerto competition is held each semester, and approximately 6 to 8 students are selected for either public performances or readings with orchestra.

The orchestral training programs are designed to develop and maintain the disciplines and skills essential in making the smoothest possible transition from school to professional life. Sectional rehearsals and orchestral repertoire classes are conducted by principals of The Cleveland Orchestra. CIM's two symphony orchestras present approximately twenty concerts during the academic year, including multiple performances of two fully staged operas. The orchestras also provide a vehicle by which students in the Composition Department may hear and record readings of their works.

The sequence of opera courses is devoted to the principles of theory and practice of the various arts that combine to create an operatic performance. Emphasis is placed on vocal, musical, stylistic, linguistic, and dramatic techniques. Study stresses the application of these elements to role preparation for operas of different historical periods.

Started in 1969, the Joint Music Program between CWRU and CIM represents one of the strongest and most successful academic alliances in the U.S. It is a formal agreement for degree study at both the undergraduate and graduate levels. Each institution focuses on its strengths, which complement those of the partner institution. CIM concentrates on the education and training of professionals skilled in the art of performance, composition, and other related disciplines. CWRU concentrates on the fields of music history, musicology, music education, and early music performance.

Campuses for each institution are adjacent, allowing for easy access to classes and lessons and providing opportunities for regular exchanges of ideas for joint projects.

At its simplest level, the Joint Music Program provides CWRU music majors with instrumental, vocal, and composition lessons, as well as theory classes at CIM. It provides CIM students with music history and general education classes at CWRU. The program also provides a shared Audio Recording Degree Program; a partnership between CIM's library and CWRU's Kulas Music Library, with each collection complementing the other; academic advisement for D.M.A. candidates; and distance learning partnerships, with CIM adding an arts focus to CWRU's advanced Internet2 network.

CIM operates on a two-semester calendar, with fall examinations preceding the Christmas holiday recess.

Academic Facilities

CIM recently completed a $40-million expansion project that adds practice, teaching, and performance space to its facility. The project provides two major additions, including a new state-of-the-art recital hall and new façade at its main entrance. The recital hall seats 250 in a visually and acoustically outstanding space for recitals and chamber music. Another addition at the rear of the main building includes practice rooms, teaching studios, audio recording and distance learning studios, administrative space, a new student lounge, and an outdoor patio.

Cleveland Institute of Music's main building includes a concert hall, classrooms, teaching studios, practice rooms, a library, a eurhythmics studio, an orchestra library, an opera theater workshop and studio, and a music store. Through connection of the entire facility to Case Western Reserve University's computer network, CIM also provides wireless Internet access as well as a Technology Learning Center that enables students to become aware of and accustomed to the ways in which music and technology go hand in hand.

CIM's Robinson Music Library holds excellent print collections in all areas of study at the Institute, with emphasis on performance editions of solo, chamber, and orchestral music and books focusing on Western classical music. It also has a growing collection of electronic resources, including streamed audio subscriptions. The Library Media Center provides distributed sound access to the extensive audiovisual collection, enabling simultaneous listening possibilities in its multimedia carrels and group multimedia rooms. A shared online system with Case Western Reserve University permits the viewing of CWRU library holdings from online public catalogs in the CIM library. There is also wireless computer access in the library.

The residence hall, Cutter House, is adjacent to CIM's main building. In addition to the usual amenities, each room has fiber-optic computer access. Also adjacent to CIM's main building is the Hazel Road Annex, an additional facility for individual practice, chamber music, rehearsal and coaching, master classes, and class recitals.

Costs

A comprehensive catalog, including information on costs as well as other areas of vital interest, is available on CIM's admission Web page (http://www.cim.edu/admission).

Financial Aid

The Cleveland Institute of Music offers outstanding professional training for talented musicians. While such training can be costly, CIM provides many forms of financial assistance, including scholarships, fellowships, work-study awards, and loans. Awards are available to full-time students and are based upon both musical capability and financial need. Entrance auditions as well as financial need serve as the basis for determining the eligibility of new students. More than 95 percent of CIM students receive some form of financial assistance. Further information is available by contacting the Institute's Director of Financial Aid.

Faculty

The distinguished faculty of performers, composers, and teachers, led by CIM's President, Joel Smirnoff, includes more than 40 members of the renowned Cleveland Orchestra and many other outstanding musicians. All liberal arts course offerings are taught by members of the faculty of Case Western Reserve University.

Student Government

The Student Government is the representative organization of the student body. Members are elected annually by the students. The organization carries on an active dialogue with the administration and addresses the daily and long-term needs of currently enrolled students.

Admission Requirements

Acceptance for study at the Cleveland Institute of Music is determined by musical talent, achievement, and academic performance. The Institute expects applicants to have achieved a sufficient musical and academic background demonstrating their potential for successful completion of the intended course of study. Audition appointments are scheduled through the Admission Office upon receipt of application. Candidates are required to submit two letters of recommendation from appropriate musically qualified individuals as well as all appropriate academic transcripts. Freshman applicants who are U.S. citizens or permanent residents must also submit scores on either the SAT or ACT. International applicants for whom English is a second language must submit scores on the Test of English as a Foreign Language (TOEFL); the minimum TOEFL score requirement for degree study is 79 (iBT).

CIM does not discriminate on the basis of race, color, national or ethnic origin, citizenship, religion, age, sex, sexual orientation, or disability in its admission and scholarship policies, in the educational programs or activities it operates, or in employment.

Application and Information

The application deadline is December 1. An appointment for an entrance audition and the required admission examinations is scheduled by the Admission Office upon receipt of application. The application process must be completed online. There is a $100 application fee.

Director of Admission
Cleveland Institute of Music
11021 East Boulevard
Cleveland, Ohio 44106
Phone: 216-795-3107
Web site: http://www.cim.edu

CIM production of Mozart's *The Magic Flute.*

COLBY–SAWYER COLLEGE

NEW LONDON, NEW HAMPSHIRE

The College

Colby-Sawyer College, a coeducational, residential, undergraduate college founded in 1837, evolved from the New England academy tradition and has been engaged in higher education since 1928. The College provides programs of study that innovatively integrate the liberal arts and sciences with professional preparation. Through all of its programs, the College encourages students of varied backgrounds and abilities to realize their full intellectual and personal potential so they may gain understanding about themselves, others, and the major forces shaping our rapidly changing world. At present, students come from all over the United States and eight other countries, with nearly 70 percent of the students coming from outside of New Hampshire. Within the last ten years, two suite-style residence halls have been built to accommodate the College's steady growth in enrollment.

Student athletic involvement occurs at the varsity, club, intramural, and recreational levels. There are ten varsity sports for women (NCAA Division III basketball, cross-country, lacrosse, soccer, swimming and diving, tennis, track and field, and volleyball; ECSC Alpine ski racing; and IHSA riding) and nine for men (NCAA Division III baseball, basketball, cross-country, soccer, swimming and diving, tennis, and track and field; ECSC Alpine ski racing; and IHSA riding). Athletic successes include a men's basketball team that competed in the NCAA tournaments from 2001 to 2003; a track and field team that produced 2 All-Americans in 2004 and 2005 and sent individual qualifiers to the NCAA Championships in 2000, 2002, 2004, 2005, and 2006; and conference championships for men's baseball in 1998 and 1999, men's basketball in 2001–03, women's volleyball in 1999, 2003, and 2005, and women's basketball in 1997–99, 2005–06, and 2008. The women's basketball team also competed in the 2001–04 ECAC tournaments as well as the NCAA tournaments in 1997–99, 2005, and 2008. The women's volleyball team also made appearances at the NCAA tournaments in 1999, 2003, and 2005. Colby-Sawyer's equestrian team was the national champion in 1989 and 1994 as well as the reserve national champion in 1998 and has sent riders to the IHSA national team every year since 1987. For the past ten seasons, the Alpine ski racing team has competed in the USCSA National Championships, where, in 2009, the men's team won the national championship and the women's team finished third. In 2005, they placed both teams within the top three. The women's team finished second in 2008. The Alpine ski racing team has produced 100 All-American citations since 1988. The Colby-Sawyer Chargers compete as a member of the Commonwealth Coast Conference.

The College is accredited by the New England Association of Schools and Colleges, and professional programs also carry the appropriate accreditations. Colby-Sawyer has consistently received recognition as one of the top colleges in its category.

Location

Colby-Sawyer's 200-acre campus is located on the crest of a hill in New London, New Hampshire. Its beautifully maintained grounds and stately Georgian architecture create a picturesque and safe environment that is conducive to learning. The College is located in the heart of the Dartmouth–Lake Sunapee region, a four-season recreational and cultural community known for the natural beauty of its lakes and mountains. Boston is only 1½ hours south and Montreal is 3½ hours north. Students have access to major cities by College van or public bus. The nearby seacoast at Portsmouth, and surrounding lakes, mountains, and state parks provide opportunities for biking, camping, canoeing, golf, hiking, ice skating, Nordic and Alpine skiing, swimming, and tennis. Arts and cultural opportunities can be found in New London as well as in nearby Concord, the state capital, and Hanover, the home of Dartmouth College.

Majors and Degrees

Colby-Sawyer offers bachelor's degrees in many fields. Majors include art history; art-graphic design; art-studio art; biology; business administration; child development; communication studies; creative writing; English; environmental sciences; environmental studies; exercise and sport sciences with specializations in athletic training, exercise science, and sport management; history, society and culture; nursing; and psychology. Other programs include a coaching certificate program, and prelaw, premedicine, pre–physical therapy, and preveterinary tracks.

Academic Programs

Colby-Sawyer College faculty and staff are excellent at working with students who are undecided on a major and they are highly qualified to help students explore their values, talents, and academic and career interests. At Colby-Sawyer College, it is believed that knowledge and experience nurture each other. Therefore, the combination of classroom learning and professional experience is an integral part of each student's education.

All students begin their liberal education at Colby-Sawyer by selecting a Pathway Seminar. Students choose a topic they are interested in learning more about, pose questions that are personally relevant, and search for answers through experiences in several liberal arts areas. They return to these themes in a seminar in their sophomore year, applying all they have learned to answer their own questions and share insights with classmates on such topics as "Sound: From Physics to Fantasia" and "Rituals, Excellence, and Challenge: The Ancient and Modern Games."

Colby-Sawyer's Wesson Honors Program offers an environment conducive to intellectual exploration and creativity beyond that which is available in the general curriculum. This program is carefully designed to advance and polish critical skills of each participating student.

Through a carefully crafted program offered by the Harrington Center for Career Development, all students are encouraged throughout their four years of study to continue to clarify their interests and goals and to gain practical experiences through student employment, internships, and voluntary service to the community.

Internships are a key element in career development and are required for almost all majors. Colby-Sawyer has an impressive roster of internship opportunities available, and through the internship experience, students often receive their first offer of a permanent position. During the internship, students have an opportunity to work directly with professionals in their field of study while developing valuable contacts who can serve as references and career mentors. Organizations that have recently accepted Colby-Sawyer interns include Merrill Lynch, the Minnesota Twins, Continental Cable, Beth Israel Hospital, Blue Cross/Blue Shield, Harvard University Athletic Department, the Buffalo Bisons, the New England Patriots, Nantucket Nectars, the Currier Gallery of Art, the Basketball Hall of Fame, the Olympic Regional Development Authority, Channel 7 (Boston), the Appalachian Mountain Club, and CNN.

Off-Campus Programs

Colby-Sawyer encourages students to study abroad for a semester or a year. The study-abroad adviser works closely with students to select an experience and a school best suited to their individual needs and interests. Students have studied in England, Poland, Australia, Spain, New Zealand, France, Italy, Ireland, Scotland, Switzerland, and many other countries.

Additionally, Colby-Sawyer offers an innovative program for students interested in studying abroad called Global Beginnings. Global Beginnings is a first semester freshmen study abroad program designed for students seeking international travel and cultural exploration. This adventurous program combines the traditional Colby-Sawyer educational experience, as accompanying Colby-Sawyer professors teach classes, with the benefits of cultural immersion. Past locations for Global Beginnings have included Paris/Strasbourg, France and Florence, Italy.

Colby-Sawyer's membership in the fourteen-college New Hampshire College and University Council (NHCUC) allows students to enroll in other NHCUC institutions for a course or for an entire semester.

Academic Facilities

The Susan Colgate Cleveland Library/Learning Center is housed in a unique five-level structure constructed from two pre–Civil War dairy barns masterfully transformed into a warm and inviting facility that has won regional and national architectural awards. Housed in the Library/Learning Center, the Academic Development Center provides academic support services for all students. The staff consists of faculty members, learning specialists, and student academic counselors who work with students to strengthen their writing, math, and research skills, as well as their study skills, such as time management, note-taking, and exam preparation. Colby-Sawyer's English Language and American Culture Program provides support for international students and others whose first language is not English. Among the services available to students with diagnosed learning differences are classroom modifications, personal counseling, and professional as well as peer tutoring. The Library/Learning Center also houses a curriculum lab, an audiovisual room, thirty PC workstations for Internet and library database access, a twelve-station wireless lab, and a networked computer classroom with twenty-five PCs and interactive multimedia teaching equipment. Interlibrary loan service provides access to an extensive array of library holdings throughout New England and the nation.

The magnificent 63,000-square-foot Dan and Kathleen Hogan Sports Center was designed to meet the athletic and recreational needs of Colby-Sawyer College students and members of the local community. This sports center contains a large field house with newly installed maple-wood floors; a suspended walking/jogging track; a six-lane, competition-size swimming pool; and a fitness center furnished with equipment such as StairMasters, Body Master stations, treadmills, rowing ergometers, Nordic cross-country skiing tracks, a Universal gym, stationary bicycles, and a complete selection of free weights. The Hogan Center also houses the Sports Medicine Clinic, which is fully equipped with the latest technology to support the Exercise and Sport Sciences Program.

Opened in 2004, the Curtis L. Ivey Science Center is one of Colby-Sawyer's finest academic facilities and houses the Natural Science and Environmental Studies Programs. Set against nearby Mt. Kearsarge, this beautiful two-story, 33,000-square-foot building consists of a variety of classrooms, laboratories, and offices as well as a 180-seat lecture hall. One of these laboratories focuses on spatial ecology and performs grant-funded research utilizing Geographic Information Systems (GIS) and Global Positioning Systems (GPS) technology.

The nursing program features a Nursing and Health Laboratory containing resources that simulate clinical practice settings. Students also have access to a computer laboratory with software that helps to prepare them for clinical experiences. The nursing program is enriched by its relationship with Dartmouth Hitchcock Medical Center, one of the most well-equipped and technologically advanced teaching hospitals in North America.

The Colby-Sawyer campus computing array includes a campus network with wireless Internet access, five computer laboratory/classrooms, and six mobile multimedia teaching stations, which provide computer graphics, audio, and video capabilities employing the latest digital technology. Computing facilities are equipped with the latest Microsoft Windows applications and laser printers for student use. The College now has a 5:1 student-computer ratio.

The Frances Lockwood Bailey Graphic Design Studios are the center of the graphic design facilities. These studios are equipped with computers loaded with the latest versions of graphic design software programs and desktop publishing capability. Students create graphic images while working with digital scanning and optical character recognition, still-video photography, and VCR, video camera, and other state-of-the-practice images. Advanced student projects are sent to professional imaging centers to create high-resolution hard copy.

Costs

Tuition, room, and board for 2009–10 were $41,950. Approximately $1750 should be allowed for books, supplies, personal expenses, and travel, depending on where students live.

Financial Aid

Through its Financial Aid Program, Colby-Sawyer encourages the attendance of students from a variety of ethnic and cultural backgrounds, economic levels, and geographic regions. Currently, 91 percent of the students receive some form of financial assistance, and Colby-Sawyer provides more than $9 million a year in financial aid and scholarships. Both need-based and merit awards are available, including merit awards for outstanding academic achievement, community service, student leadership, and special talent in art, creative writing, or original research. Each applicant for need-based aid must submit the Free Application for Federal Student Aid (FAFSA). Priority is given to students whose completed forms are received before March 1. A modest amount of financial assistance is available for international students.

Faculty

Colby-Sawyer has a distinguished faculty and staff dedicated to undergraduate teaching, and a personalized education is ensured by an 11:1 student-faculty ratio and average class size of 16. At Colby-Sawyer, senior faculty members teach first-year students as well as students in the upper classes.

Student Government

The Student Government Association (SGA) is structured to provide considerable interaction among students, faculty members, and staff, and the SGA allocates the resources that fund a multitude of involvement and leadership opportunities outside the classroom. Campus activities include the Campus Activities Board, Dance Club, Alpha Chi Honor Society, yearbook, radio station (WSCS 90.9 FM), Drama Club, Admissions Key Association, Art Students Society, Student Nurses Association, *The Courier* (student newspaper), community service, and numerous clubs and intramural teams.

Admission Requirements

The College requires prospective students to present at least 15 units of college-preparatory work. This would usually include 4 years of English, 3 years of mathematics, 3 or more years of social studies, 2 years of a foreign language, and 2 or more years of a laboratory science.

While an admissions interview is not required, every applicant is strongly encouraged to visit Colby-Sawyer for a tour and interview. Interviews often play an important part in the final admissions decision.

Application and Information

Colby-Sawyer College receives and considers applications throughout the year. Beginning in September, applications are reviewed as soon as they become complete, and candidates are notified as soon as the admissions decision is finalized. A completed application includes a transcript of the candidate's high school work (including first-quarter grades for the senior year), one letter of recommendation (from a teacher or a guidance professional), a personal statement, and a $45 nonrefundable application fee. SAT or ACT scores may be submitted, but are not required. Application forms and additional information may be obtained by contacting:

Office of Admissions
Colby-Sawyer College
541 Main Street
New London, New Hampshire 03257
Phone: 603-526-3700
800-272-1015 (toll-free)
Fax: 603-526-3452
E-mail: admissions@colby-sawyer.edu
Internet: http://www.colby-sawyer.edu

THE COLLEGE OF MOUNT ST. JOSEPH

CINCINNATI, OHIO

The College

The College of Mount St. Joseph offers a variety of academic programs, a faculty known for high standards of excellence and innovation, and student activities that include twenty-two NCAA Division III sports teams. Small class sizes and individual attention, as well as opportunities for leadership and service learning, contribute to a positive college experience and student success. Founded in 1920 by the Sisters of Charity, the Mount is a private, Catholic college that emphasizes values, integrity, and social responsibility.

Specialized services are also part of a Mount education and include renewable scholarships, financial aid, cooperative education, multicultural programs, the Wellness Center, child-care services for students with children, and on-campus housing. A new Success Coaching program provides first-year students with guidance from an assigned professional staff member trained to help them address first-year challenges and achieve their goals.

A wireless network enables students to e-mail faculty members, check grades, complete research, and register for classes anytime, from anywhere. Spacious rooms are available in the newly renovated Seton Center Residence Hall, with some offering private bedrooms, a bath, and a shared living area for studying and socializing. Resident students may keep cars on campus. The close-knit campus community is part of a living and learning environment that encourages and nurtures the personal and academic growth of each student.

The undergraduate student body consists of students from eighteen states and four countries. Sixty-three percent of undergraduate students are women, and 11 percent are members of minority groups. The average freshman has an ACT score of 21 and/or a combined SAT score of 995 and a high school GPA of 3.19. Seventy-two percent of all freshman students attended a public high school. Seventy-two percent of freshman applicants are accepted.

There are more than thirty clubs and organizations at the College. These include student government, the student newspaper, academic honor societies, environmental clubs, social clubs, symphonic and community concert bands, jazz and percussion ensembles, chorale groups, theater/drama clubs, political clubs, and intramural athletics. Events and activities include Homecoming, spring break service trips, Exam Jam, and Little Sibs Weekend.

The Mount offers a full intercollegiate athletic program for men and women. Women's programs include basketball, cheerleading, cross-country, dance, golf, lacrosse, soccer, softball, tennis, track and field, and volleyball. Programs for men include baseball, basketball, cross-country, football, golf, lacrosse, soccer, tennis, track and field, volleyball, and wrestling. The Mount Lions compete in the NCAA Division III as a member of the Heartland Collegiate Athletic Conference.

Students at the Mount ranked the College higher than their peers at similar institutions did, according to the 2008 Noel Levitz Student Satisfaction Inventory, which is conducted nationwide. In particular, students noted the Mount's strengths in emphasizing values, ethical responsibility and critical thinking; opportunities to co-op and gain professional experience; and campus experiences that support individual growth.

The Mount is fully accredited by the Higher Learning Commission of the North Central Association of Colleges and Schools. The College is consistently ranked among the top Midwest regional universities for quality and value by *U.S. News & World Report* in its guide to America's Best Colleges.

Location

Located 15 minutes from downtown Cincinnati, the College is situated on a 92-acre suburban campus overlooking the Ohio River and is easily accessible from the airport, bus terminal, railway station, and interstate. Well known for its scenic and rolling hills, greater Cincinnati offers numerous parks, cultural and arts events, museums, theaters, professional athletics, shopping areas, and a wide assortment of fine restaurants. Mount students often join other students attending colleges and universities in and around Cincinnati to participate in social and service activities.

Majors and Degrees

The Mount awards bachelor's degrees in the following areas: accounting, art, art education, art history, athletic training, biochemistry, biology, business administration, business administration/mathematics, chemistry, chemistry/mathematics, communication studies, computer information systems, criminology/sociology, English, fine arts, general studies, graphic design, history, inclusive early childhood education, interactive media design and computing, interdisciplinary liberal studies, interior design, mathematics, mathematics/business administration, mathematics/chemistry, middle childhood education, music, natural science, nursing, paralegal studies, psychology, religious education, religious pastoral ministry, religious studies, social work, sociology, special education, and sport management.

Preprofessional studies are offered in a number of areas, including prehealth, premedicine, pre–art therapy, and prelaw.

Associate degrees are offered in accounting, art, business administration, communication studies, computer information systems, general studies, graphic design, interior design, and paralegal studies.

Certificate programs in gerontology, iDesign (Web and interactive design), nonprofit leadership, and paralegal studies are available, as are teacher licensure programs.

For the state of Ohio licensure in education, the Mount offers programs in adolescent and young adults, inclusive early childhood, middle childhood, multiage, and intervention specialist/special education. Licensure programs for other states are also available.

Academic Programs

To help students explore options in choosing a major, the Academic Exploration Program provides advising, career counseling, and the opportunity to attend linked courses with classmates who are also undecided.

In recognition of its commitment to provide cooperative education experiences in all baccalaureate majors, the Mount's program has received top honors from the Ohio Cooperative Education Association. Students may participate as early as the second semester of their sophomore year and gain paid work experience in their field of study. More than 100 local corporations, businesses, health-care facilities, schools, and nonprofits hire co-ops from the Mount. Other opportunities for practical experience and career development are available through the Career and Experiential Learning Center, on-campus recruiting programs, networking opportunities, and resume services.

In compliance with Section 504 of the Rehabilitation Act of 1973, the Mount provides academic adjustments and auxiliary aids for students with physical or mental impairments that substantially limit or restrict one or more of such major life activities as walking, seeing, hearing, or learning.

The College provides these reasonable academic adjustments and auxiliary aids to eligible students at no charge, according to students' individual needs. Advocacy assistance on disability-related issues is also provided. Eligibility depends on the nature of the impairment and its impact on the particular individual, and is based on documentation from a qualified professional.

Students whose primary disability is a specific learning disability and/or ADHD may apply to Project EXCEL, which addresses the needs of this specific group of students through a comprehensive academic support system. Project EXCEL is a fee-for-service program. Students must be admitted to the College of Mount St. Joseph before applying for Project EXCEL.

All majors are backed by a strong liberal arts curriculum that encourages students to develop skills in analytical thinking, problem solving, decision making, and communication. Students must earn 128 credit hours for a bachelor's degree, with 52 of those credits from the liberal arts and sciences core. For an associate degree, students must earn 64 credit hours, with 27 to 28 of those credits from the liberal arts and sciences core.

The academic year consists of fall and spring semesters and two summer terms. Classes are held in day, evening, or weekend time frames.

Off-Campus Programs

Study-abroad programs are available in London, England. Travel study programs to Africa, Eastern Europe, Egypt, England, Greece, Ireland, Italy, and Japan are also offered. Immersion courses introduce students to the cultures and histories of Pine Ridge Indian Reservation, South Dakota; Tierra Madre Mission, New Mexico; and Appalachia.

Academic Facilities

The Mount's campus features a totally wireless environment as well as up-to-date facilities, including electronic classrooms. The Computer Learning Center offers all students access to IBM and Macintosh systems that support more than 500 different software packages. Students in health sciences learn in laboratories on the campus and benefit from the College's partnerships with nearby hospitals and clinics.

The Mount's Learning Center, which includes a math center and a writing center, offers peer and professional tutoring as well as diagnostic testing.

The library is home to more than 96,000 volumes of books, journals, videotapes, DVDs, and CDs. Patrons have access to more than 140 databases, thousands of electronic books, and hundreds of Web sites specifically chosen for students, faculty, and staff. Through its wide variety of services, the library plays an active role in the College's educational process. Some of these services include interlibrary loan, in-person and online research help, traditional and electronic course reserves, instructional sessions designed for specific courses, a group study room, and full Internet access.

Costs

For the 2009–10 academic year, full-time tuition was $22,000. Part-time tuition (less than 12 hours) was $465 per hour. Room costs ranged from $3526 to $6066 a year, and costs for board ranged from $3426 to $3626 a year. The College offers private and semiprivate housing accommodations and a variety of meal plans. A general fee of $800 a year covers student activities, technology, counseling, student and academic support services, and logistical services. The cost of books varies, depending on course load and major.

Financial Aid

The Mount offers academic scholarship programs in the areas of scholastic achievement and leadership, based on merit or on a combination of merit and need. Many scholarships are renewable each year. Ninety-three percent of full-time undergraduate students receive some form of financial aid, and the average financial aid package is $14,948. The most common are federal, state, or College grants; work-study awards; and loans. Part-time employment may be available on the campus or in the metropolitan area. Interested students should inquire early in their senior year of high school.

Students needing financial support must submit the Free Application for Federal Student Aid (FAFSA) no later than April 15 prior to the fall semester. Most College-sponsored scholarships are awarded on a rolling basis.

Faculty

There are 114 full-time professors at the College. Faculty members have been recognized regionally and nationally for their research and expertise outside the classroom as well as for their contributions as teachers, particularly in the fields of art, science, math, sociology, and education. The student-faculty ratio of 12:1 encourages personal interaction between students and professors.

Student Government

All matriculated students at the Mount are members of the Student Government Association (SGA). Its purpose is to help students understand their rights, privileges, and responsibilities, as well as maintain effective communication with the faculty, staff, and administration.

The SGA encourages students to participate in College governance through active membership on College committees and by assisting in the development of policies that affect student life.

Programs and activities sponsored by SGA include Campus Fair, community service projects, fund-raising events, and social activities such as movies and dances.

Admission Requirements

The Mount reviews every candidate's request for admission. Credentials should include evidence of a college-preparatory high school curriculum, grade point average, standardized test scores, leadership, and extracurricular activities. In addition, personal background and attributes as well as life circumstances are taken into consideration.

Application and Information

Decisions on offers of admission are generally made within two weeks of the date the application process is completed. The application fee is $25, which is not refundable and does not apply toward tuition. Students who want to learn more about the Mount may arrange a visit by contacting the Office of Admission. In addition to individual appointments, the College schedules Get Acquainted Days and Discovery Days throughout the year, giving students and their parents the opportunity to visit the campus, explore academic programs, and take a tour.

Office of Admission
College of Mount St. Joseph
5701 Delhi Road
Cincinnati, Ohio 45233-1672
Phone: 513-244-4531
800-654-9314 (toll-free)
Web site: http://www.msj.edu/admission

The College of Mount St. Joseph provides a liberal arts and professional education that integrates learning and life through academic excellence, respect for others and service.

COLLEGE CLOSE-UPS

THE COLLEGE OF NEW JERSEY

EWING TOWNSHIP, NEW JERSEY

The College

The College of New Jersey (TCNJ) welcomes students who have the talent and motivation to succeed in a highly rigorous academic environment. A public institution founded in 1855, the College enrolls about 5,600 full-time undergraduates, two thirds of whom reside on campus. Today it is heralded by *U.S. News & World Report* as well as *Barron's* as one of the most competitive schools in the nation, public or private. TCNJ serves a diverse student body, preparing graduates to be leaders in their chosen fields.

TCNJ has set the standard for public higher education. Students report they find TCNJ large enough to provide a full range of academic and extracurricular choices, yet small enough to be a genuine residential community of friends and fellow learners. With professors easily available in and out of class and facilities of enviable quality, TCNJ today represents an exceptional value in higher education.

The College of New Jersey's academic approach combines those of both traditional liberal arts schools and professional schools. A liberal learning curriculum ensures that all students are grounded in the beliefs and values of a civic responsibility and intellectual and scholarly growth and that they receive a well-rounded education in the liberal arts. Interdisciplinary studies, internships, research, and faculty mentoring all are part of an educational approach designed to produce successful leaders. While a very high percentage of graduates find immediate employment related to their fields of study, more than 20 percent go directly into graduate schools across the country.

All first- and second-year students are guaranteed on-campus housing, and most juniors and seniors continue to live on campus. Rooming arrangements are quite flexible, from doubles in freshman residence halls to suites and single rooms in campus town houses or apartments for upperclass students. A nationally recognized residence life program and more than 150 student organizations offer numerous opportunities for friendship, personal growth, and leadership. An exceptional 96 percent of first-year students return for their sophomore year.

The arts flourish in two theaters, a recital hall, an art gallery, and numerous other campus venues. Student performances, professional groups on tour, and a large variety of films, lectures, local bands, and solo entertainers fill the academic year with cultural options—many of them free, the rest at low cost.

Student wellness has a high priority, with many facilities for recreation and physical conditioning. In Packer Hall, the campus has access to a larger fitness center, a 25-meter swimming and diving pool, and a basketball court. The Student Recreation Center offers racquetball courts, four tennis courts that are convertible to basketball or volleyball use, a weight room, and an indoor track. Other facilities include a lighted Astroturf field, eight lighted outdoor tennis courts, an outdoor "beach" volleyball court, and numerous athletic fields.

As a Division III member of the National Collegiate Athletic Association, TCNJ offers twenty-one sports: eleven for men and ten for women. Since 1979, TCNJ student-athletes have amassed thirty-six national championships and twenty-nine runner-up awards, more than any other Division III institution in the country. In addition to its NCAA athletics, TCNJ offers a wide variety of recreation programs for intramural competition and self-governing sports clubs. More than 3,500 students play with these less demanding, but spirited and competitive teams, each year, some of which have intercollegiate schedules.

The College's undergraduate programs are accredited by the Middle States Association of Colleges and Schools and by professional associations in engineering, nursing, chemistry, music, education, education of the deaf, computer science, and business.

Location

The College of New Jersey is set on 289 acres in suburban Ewing Township, approximately 15 minutes from downtown Princeton; 10 minutes from Bucks County, Pennsylvania; and 5 miles from the state capital of Trenton. Woodlands and lakes surround the thirty-nine major academic and residential buildings. The campus is 30 miles from the theaters and museums of Philadelphia and 60 miles from those in New York City.

Majors and Degrees

The College of New Jersey offers programs leading to the Bachelor of Arts, Bachelor of Fine Arts, Bachelor of Music, Bachelor of Science, and Bachelor of Science in Nursing degrees.

The B.A. is awarded in art education; art history; communication studies; economics; English, including journalism and professional writing options; history; interactive multimedia; international studies; mathematics and statistics; philosophy; political science; psychology; sociology; Spanish; and women's and gender studies. The B.F.A. is awarded in digital arts, and fine art and graphic design. The B.M. is awarded in music (performance and education). The B.S. is granted in accountancy, biology, biomedical engineering, business administration (finance, general business, information systems management, international business, management, and marketing), chemistry, computer engineering, computer science, early childhood education, economics, education for the hearing-impaired, electrical engineering, elementary education, engineering science, health and physical education, law and justice, mechanical engineering, physics, special education, and technology education. Teacher preparation is available in many arts and science majors.

TCNJ offers a five-year combined Master of Arts in Teaching degree with dual certification in deaf and hard-of-hearing and elementary education. Students may also enroll in a seven-year B.S./M.D. degree program with UMDNJ—New Jersey Medical School (Newark) or a seven-year B.S./O.D. degree program with the State University of New York College of Optometry. Students may apply to TCNJ for a 4½-year combined B.S./M.A. program in law and justice with Rutgers, The State University of New Jersey (Newark). The College also offers a Medical Careers Advisory Committee for premed students and a Pre-Law Advisement Committee for students planning a career in law.

Academic Programs

All academic courses contain a significant out-of-class requirement and provide for even more student-faculty interaction. All baccalaureate degrees require at least thirty-two courses, including a core curriculum in the traditional arts and sciences.

The thirty-week year is divided into fall and spring semesters; the summer session offers courses in two 5-week sessions and one 6-week session. The average class size for freshman-level lectures is 24 students and for upper-division lectures, 22 students.

All first-year students participate in a program linking residential learning in small classes taught by full-time faculty members. Seminars, independent studies, and capstone courses give many students the opportunity for challenging advanced study in close collaboration with faculty members. TCNJ students publish the results of these endeavors or present them at national and regional conferences.

The honors program offers students the particularly challenging academic experiences that allow normal progress toward the degree. Whenever possible, honors courses have an interdisciplinary perspective and curriculum, concentrating on central themes within significant periods in the cultural development of civilization. Honors courses in the major consist of either specially designated sections or independent study. All honors classes are small, personal, and stimulating.

Off-Campus Programs

TCNJ offers students a variety of full-year and one-semester programs of study abroad as well as study at other state colleges and universities within the United States. Exchange programs are available in Australia, Austria, Canada, Denmark, France, Germany, Greece, Israel, Japan, Mexico, the United Kingdom, and twenty-three other countries. National exchanges are available at more than 130 participating institutions in the United States, the U.S. Virgin Islands, Puerto Rico, and Guam. The College of New Jersey hosts the New Jersey State Consortium for International Studies.

Academic Facilities

The College of New Jersey is nearing the end of a ten-year, $250-million campus-planning initiative. Within the past several years, TCNJ has built and opened a Science Complex, Biology Building, Social Science Building, College Spiritual Center, and state-of-the-art library, which serves as the intellectual and social hub of the campus. Campuswide networking provides full Internet accessibility from all residence hall rooms and more than twenty student computing laboratories.

Costs

Costs are relatively low because of state funding. For 2008–09, full-time undergraduate tuition and fees were $12,308 for New Jersey residents and $20,415 for out-of-state students. Room and board charges for the academic year, with a middle meal plan, averaged $9612.

Financial Aid

Approximately half of the full-time undergraduates receive some form of financial aid, such as federal, state, and institutional grants; merit scholarships; student employment; and loan assistance. The Free Application for Federal Student Aid (FAFSA) or Renewal FAFSA is used to apply for all types of aid.

Scholarships and grants include the College of New Jersey Merit Scholars Program, the New Jersey Edward J. Bloustein Distinguished Scholars Program, the New Jersey Tuition Aid Grant, Federal Pell Grants, Federal Supplemental Educational Opportunity Grants (FSEOG), Educational Opportunity Fund (EOF) Promise Award, and Army and Air Force ROTC Scholarships, as well as other institutional scholarships. Loans include the Federal Subsidized and Unsubsidized Stafford Loans, the Federal Perkins Loan, the Federal Parent Loan for Undergraduate Students (PLUS), the New Jersey CLASS Loan, nursing loans, and short-term emergency loan funds. Student employment options include the need-based Federal Work-Study Program (on- and off-campus positions) as well as institutionally supported campus jobs.

Faculty

The approximately 335 full-time members of the College of New Jersey faculty are teachers and scholars. While teaching is their primary commitment, they are also active researchers, authors, artists, performers, and regular contributors in their academic disciplines. No classes are taught by graduate assistants. The student-faculty ratio is 12:1. From their first day, students study with faculty members who may be researching new ways to use solar energy; writing a new text, play, or novel; or investigating the life cycle of desert ferns. Members of the faculty have attracted many significant grants, fellowships, and awards, including the Bancroft Prize in history, Fulbright Scholarships, and grants from the National Science Foundation, the National Institute for Advanced Study, the Guggenheim Foundation, and the National Endowment for the Humanities. Faculty members mentor their students, preparing them for careers, graduate and professional schools, and prestigious fellowships such as the Fulbright, Truman, and Marshall Fellowships recently awarded to TCNJ students.

Student Government

The Student Government Association, comprising all undergraduate students at the College, is governed by elected representatives. The Residence Hall Association provides the mechanism for student input into campus housing policies, and members of the Student Finance Board oversee and administer approximately $500,000 in student funds. The College Union Board sponsors a wide range of special events, including visits by John Leguizamo, Cornel West, and George Carlin.

Admission Requirements

The College of New Jersey seeks students who can succeed in a highly selective academic program and who show intellectual curiosity, academic talent, and the potential to contribute to the life of the College. The College is committed to attracting students from diverse economic, racial, social, and geographic backgrounds. A high school record of at least 16 college-preparatory credits, high school class rank, SAT scores, and special interests, skills, and qualities of all kinds can be influential. Certain departments, such as art and music, use additional criteria to evaluate candidates seeking admission into their programs.

Application and Information

The College of New Jersey is a member of the Common Application. The deadline for applications for January admission is November 15 and for September admission, February 15. There is a $70 application fee. Candidates who apply only to the College of New Jersey under the early decision plan may apply before November 15 and will be notified on or before December 15. Students applying in to the seven-year medical program or as a biology major must apply by January 1. For September admission, the College subscribes to the candidates' reply date of May 1 for payment of $300.

For more information, students should contact:

Dean of Admissions
The College of New Jersey
P.O. Box 7718
Ewing, New Jersey 08628-0718
Phone: 609-771-2131
Web site: http://www.tcnj.edu

Students take a break in front of Green Hall.

COLLEGE OF NOTRE DAME OF MARYLAND

BALTIMORE, MARYLAND

The College

College of Notre Dame of Maryland is a vibrant women's college located in northern Baltimore. Founded and sponsored by the School Sisters of Notre Dame, the College was established in 1895 and was the first Catholic college for women to award the four-year baccalaureate degree.

Today's students are achievement-oriented and preparing for rewarding careers. They are deeply involved in their college and their community. At Notre Dame, students are challenged and supported in achieving more than they ever imagined—personally and professionally. They shape their lives for today and for the future. They learn for life.

Notre Dame's mission is to educate women as leaders. Undergraduate and graduate programs challenge students to strive for intellectual and professional excellence, to build inclusive communities, to engage in service to others, and to promote social responsibility. The Women's College has a close-knit community of approximately 500 students, both residents and commuters. About a third of Notre Dame's students are women who are members of minority groups.

Innovative programs for women and men have enabled the College to expand its educational reach. In 1972, the College initiated the Continuing Education (CE) program, offering women age 25 and older the opportunity to study and earn bachelor's degrees. Today, CE has been fully integrated into the Women's College. In 1975, the Weekend College was established to serve employed students by offering conveniently scheduled classes. In 1984, Graduate Studies began offering master's programs. In 2003, the College launched its Accelerated College for working professionals, further establishing partnerships with business and health-care organizations throughout the area. Most recently, the College instituted its first doctoral program, a Ph.D. in instructional leadership for changing populations. The College opened its School of Pharmacy in fall 2009 with an inaugural class of 70 students. The English Language Institute (ELI), which opened in 1983, offers English as a second language and American culture classes. The Renaissance Institute, a noncredit membership program for students age 50 and older, rounds out the College's educational offerings.

There are approximately 800 women and men in the part-time undergraduate programs in Notre Dame's Weekend College and Accelerated College. Graduate Studies serves more than 1,500 students, both women and men. In fall 2009, the total enrollment (approximately 3,000) in all degree programs and ELI represented approximately twenty states, Guam, and more than twenty other countries. Students participate in a range of campus groups, including student media, performing arts, service, honor societies, academic interest groups, and more.

Notre Dame's Gators participate in eight NCAA Division III sports: basketball, field hockey, lacrosse, soccer, softball, swimming, tennis, and volleyball. The Marion Burk Knott Sports and Activities Complex houses the gymnasium, a fitness center, a dance and exercise studio, and several racquetball courts.

There also are two residence halls: Doyle Hall for first-year students and sophomores and Mary Meletia Hall for juniors and seniors. The recently renovated Marikle Chapel of the Annunciation is the spiritual center of the campus. Daily masses and special events are held in this beautiful chapel in Theresa Hall.

College of Notre Dame of Maryland is accredited by the Middle State Association of Colleges and Schools and the National Council for Accreditation of Teacher Education.

Location

Located on the North Charles Street college corridor in northern Baltimore, Notre Dame's beautiful campus is situated on 58 wooded and landscaped acres in a residential area. The College also holds classes for part-time students pursuing bachelor's and master's degrees at sites in other regions of Maryland.

The College is just 15 minutes from downtown Baltimore, which is renowned for its vibrant Inner Harbor that features shops and restaurants, the National Aquarium in Baltimore, Maryland Science Center, and more. Annapolis, the state capital, and Washington, D.C., are also nearby.

Baltimore truly is a college town, with a number of diverse colleges and universities in the area. Notre Dame is part of the Baltimore Collegetown Network, a group of fifteen colleges that work together to encourage students to participate in social and academic events and programs on each other's campuses. The network sponsors a free shuttle that has a stop at Notre Dame.

Majors and Degrees

Twenty-seven majors are available to students, many with concentration options so that students can further customize their area of study. The majors are art (art history, photography, pre–museum studies, studio art), biology, biology/psychology, business (accounting), chemistry, (pharmacy studies, preprofessional) classical studies, communication arts, computer information systems, computer science, criminology/social deviance (forensic psychology, women and social deviance), digital media arts, economics, education (early childhood, elementary, secondary, special education, TESOL), English (drama, creative writing), history (pre–museum studies, social studies secondary education), international studies (international business, international relations), liberal arts, mathematics, modern foreign languages (French, Spanish, dual language), philosophy, physics, political science (international relations, law and civic engagement, public service), psychology, radiological sciences, and religious studies. Dual-degree programs are also available in engineering and nursing.

Students may choose to minor in most of the major areas or in Asian studies, entrepreneurship, Latin American studies, music, peace and justice studies, women's studies, or writing.

Academic Programs

Students take both general education studies courses and those required for their chosen majors. The general education curriculum provides a coherent yet broad intellectual experience of study in the liberal arts tradition. Through general education studies, students are expected to refine their personal value system, integrate the arts and sciences, develop a global perspective, expand their critical-thinking abilities, and enhance their communication skills.

Courses are required in English composition, fine arts, foreign language, history, literature, mathematics, oral communication, natural science with a lab, philosophy, physical education, social science, and religious studies.

Study and personal behavior are guided by an Honor Code that students pledge to follow beginning early in their first year. Examinations are unsupervised and academic honesty is expected. It is assumed that all work submitted is a student's own. Students and faculty members are deeply committed to the Honor Code, resulting in an academic environment that is grounded in integrity.

Notre Dame is dedicated to experiential learning. Courses integrate service-learning projects that allow students to apply classroom knowledge and skills while meeting community needs. The College's exceptionally strong internship program matches students with credit-bearing experiences in professional settings, helping them to refine career plans and strengthen their resumes.

Exceptionally motivated students of outstanding ability are invited to join the Elizabeth Morrissy Honors Program. Exciting, often interdisciplinary courses bring Notre Dame's excellent liberal arts education to another level and challenge students to stretch themselves intellectually.

Other students may join the Renaissance Professional Scholars (RP) or Transformational Leaders (TL) Programs where students are allowed to design programs of study that will be uniquely their own. The RP Scholars Program allows students to combine advanced courses with career-related experiences to expand their major program of study and connect to experiential learning options that will enhance their career potential. The TL Program will give students the chance to earn the certificate in leadership and social change and allow them to gain the knowledge and experience that will empower them to be leaders who can truly make change happen.

College of Notre Dame also offers "Chart Your Course," a program for students who have not yet declared their majors, and Personal Pathways programs for students pursuing preprofessional tracks including predental, prelaw, premedical, prepharmacy, and preveterinary.

The College's School of Pharmacy welcomed its inaugural class of 70 students in fall 2009. First-year students entering the Women's College who are interested in pharmacy studies should consult the prepharmacy coordinator about the appropriate curriculum to pursue. Students may complete a science degree and then apply to the School of Pharmacy or complete the prerequisites only. An intensive 3+4 program in biology or chemistry plus pharmacy is available to qualified first-year Women's College students.

Off-Campus Programs

The College is dedicated to providing an education that is truly international, and study abroad is greatly encouraged. The College sponsors academic programs in twenty-one countries in Europe, Asia, Latin America, North America, South America, and Australia. Students receive Notre Dame credit for their work; financial aid is applicable to study abroad.

Short-term experiences, generally two- to three-week study tours during January or the summer, offer another option for students.

Locally, College of Notre Dame of Maryland has cooperative arrangements with Johns Hopkins University, Loyola University Maryland, Maryland Institute College of Art, Coppin State University, Morgan State University, Towson University, and Goucher College. This allows full-time Women's College students to register for one class per semester at an area college or university and expands academic options for students.

Academic Facilities

The College has several historic and renovated academic buildings. Knott Science Center features state-of-the-art chemistry and biology laboratories. A planetarium and a rooftop greenhouse are special features of Knott. Historic Gibbons Hall, which is recognizable by its landmark tower, has classrooms with hardwood floors and 10-foot windows. The WCND television and radio studios are housed on the fourth floor in the Communication Arts Department.

The College's main computer center is located in Virginia Rice Kelly Hall and hosts both academic and administrative computing. Networked computer labs include a total of seventy workstations (PCs and Macs). Students can access the Internet and their e-mail accounts at locations throughout the campus and through the College's wireless network. Residence hall rooms are fully wired. There is also a campus video network for both station access and internal cable television production.

The Loyola/Notre Dame Library supports the education programs of both College of Notre Dame and neighboring Loyola University Maryland. The library's Web site is the gateway to a wealth of information, including numerous full-text databases, the library's shared catalog, and the full resources of the Internet. The newly expanded and renovated four-level structure houses more than 400,000 bound volumes and 820 print and 39,000 electronic periodicals, plus 16,000 media items, and microfilm and microfiche units.

The Sister Kathleen Feeley International Center houses ELI and the Office of International Programs. LeClerc Hall is home to the Music Department and a large auditorium for performances and public lectures. Part-time programs for women and men are centralized in Fourier Hall, which features art exhibits in the Gormley Gallery on the second floor.

Costs

The cost for the 2009–10 academic year at College of Notre Dame was $36,450, exclusive of major travel expenses. Tuition was $26,500 and room and board were $9200. Student fees were $750. Additional special academic and nonacademic fees, such as book fees and fees for instrumental lessons, are charged as they apply to a particular student. Fees are subject to change.

Financial Aid

The College works with each student to develop a package that makes Notre Dame an affordable option. Financial assistance consists of scholarships, grants, loans, and paid, part-time employment. Awards are based on need, academic merit, leadership, or achievement. A Free Application for Federal Student Aid (FAFSA) must be completed each year to apply for financial aid.

Faculty

Notre Dame has 102 full-time and 11 half-time faculty members, all of whom hold a master's or doctoral degree. Associate faculty members with exceptional professional and academic experience teach some courses. The undergraduate student-faculty ratio is 12:1.

Student Government

Notre Dame's Student Association provides a vehicle for every Women's College student to participate in the life of the College. Through self-government, participation in college-wide decision making, and planning a vital social life, the Student Association exists to ensure that every student can contribute to a rewarding college experience.

There are five organizations within the Student Association that are coordinated by the Executive Committee: the Student Senate, the Inter-Organization Council, the Apportionment Board, the Honor Board, and the Board of Trustees Representative. The Student Senate includes representatives from each class. The Inter-Organization Council coordinates the programming of more than twenty campus groups. The Honor Board educates the community about the Honor Code and conducts hearings on alleged violations. The Apportionment Board allocates funds for student groups and activities. The student representative to the Board of Trustees is elected by the students to convey their concerns to the board.

Admission Requirements

The Committee on Admissions considers the quality of each student's academic curriculum, grades in academic/college-preparatory or college-level liberal arts and sciences courses, standardized test scores (SAT or ACT for first-year applicants only), essay, resume, and letter of recommendation.

High school students are encouraged to complete courses in English, mathematics, laboratory science, social science, and foreign language in order to be considered favorably. A minimum of 18 units is required for admission for first-year students. Students applying for the Elizabeth Morrissy Honors Program typically have completed numerous Advanced Placement, honors, or International Baccalaureate courses in high school.

Transfer applicants are encouraged to complete at least 12 college credits in liberal arts and science courses prior to submitting an application.

Application and Information

Applications are reviewed and students are accepted on a rolling basis. Students should apply early for best consideration for scholarships and the Morrissy Honors Program. The priority deadline is February 15 for first-year students and March 15 for transfer students for fall admission; December 15 is the deadline for spring admission for first-year and transfer students.

For additional information, students should contact:

Office of Admissions
College of Notre Dame of Maryland
4701 North Charles Street
Baltimore, Maryland 21210
Phone: 410-532-5330
800-435-0200 (toll-free)
E-mail: admiss@ndm.edu
Web site: http://www.ndm.edu

COLLEGE OF SAINT ELIZABETH

MORRISTOWN, NEW JERSEY

The College

The College of Saint Elizabeth (CSE), which celebrated its 110th anniversary in 2009, is the oldest college for women in New Jersey. In addition, CSE is one of the first Catholic colleges in the U.S. to award degrees to women. A Catholic institution in the liberal arts tradition, CSE includes a women's college, coeducational adult undergraduate and graduate degree programs, and one doctoral program. An enrollment of more than 2,100 students fosters considerable student-faculty interaction and a spirit of campuswide encouragement and support. An emphasis is placed on opportunities for individual growth through academic, spiritual, cultural, leadership, and civic experiences.

Located on a 200-acre campus, CSE's buildings command a wide view of the surrounding hills. Sixty-six percent of the women's college students live on campus. Although a majority hails from New Jersey, students represent more than 20 countries and other states. Two attractive residence halls provide ample private and double rooms. Each residence hall has kitchenettes, laundry facilities, a mailroom, lounges, and conference rooms. The student center contains a swimming pool, a gymnasium, a fitness center, a dining room, a newly renovated lounge area, and the College store. The Annunciation Center, a multipurpose arts and education facility, houses state-of the-art music, drama, and art studios and a 560-seat performance center.

Students may belong to extracurricular organizations associated with their academic interests, which include a number of Greek-letter honor and professional societies and student affiliates of the American Chemical Society. In addition, CSE has a variety of organizations such as the Elizabeth Singers, the International/Intercultural Club, the College Activities Board, Campus Ministry, the Students Take Action Committee, Volunteer Services, Student Government, and varsity athletics. The College is affiliated with the North Eastern Athletic Conference (NEAC), the Eastern Colleges Athletic Conference (ECAC), and competes in basketball, cross-country, lacrosse, soccer, softball, swimming, tennis, and volleyball at the NCAA Division III level. A rich calendar of social, cultural, and recreational events is available at the College of Saint Elizabeth. Students frequently socialize with their peers from Drew University and Fairleigh Dickinson University (FDU), two nearby coeducational institutions within walking distance of the campus. Career Services provides assistance with career preparation, internships, and graduate study.

Location

Morristown is located in the rapidly growing corporate center of historical Morris County. Neighboring towns and cities, only minutes from the campus, offer facilities for shopping and recreation. The College is an hour from the cultural and social opportunities of New York City by car, train, or bus and is near the campuses of Fairleigh Dickinson, Seton Hall, Drew, and the County College of Morris. Newark Liberty International Airport is approximately 30 minutes and two New York airports are approximately 1 hour from the campus. Local bus routes are easily accessible, and New Jersey Transit, which has a stop at the campus gate, provides excellent rail commuter service from New York City, Hoboken, Newark, the Oranges, Short Hills, Maplewood, Millburn, Summit, Chatham, Madison, and Dover. Routes 287, 80, 280, 46, 78, 24, and 10 are located close by.

Majors and Degrees

The Bachelor of Arts is offered in American studies, art, biology, chemistry, communications, computer information systems, economics, English, global studies, history, individualized special major, justice studies, mathematics, music, philosophy, psychology, sociology, Spanish, teacher education (multiple levels), and theology. The Bachelor of Science is offered in biochemistry, biology, business administration, chemistry, clinical laboratory sciences (with University of Medicine and Dentistry of NJ), computer science, and foods and nutrition. The Bachelor of Science in Nursing degree is offered as an upper-division nursing program. In addition to CSE's combined B.A. /M.A. degrees in business administration and justice studies, and the B.S./M.S. in Foods and Nutrition, the College offers a combined B.S./M.S. physician assistant degree as a joint program with Seton Hall University.

In addition to the undergraduate majors and degrees listed, the College offers the M.A. degree in counseling psychology, education, educational leadership, forensic psychology and counseling, justice administration and public service, and theology; the M.S. degree in health-care management, management, nursing, and nutrition; and the Ed.D. degree in educational leadership.

Seven-week courses are offered in the evenings. Courses are also given during the summer and winter intersession. Adult undergraduate degree programs are offered in business administration (human resources management, management, or marketing), computer science, foods and nutrition, justice studies, nursing, psychology, and theology.

Academic Programs

The requirements for a B.A., B.S., or B.S.N. degree are 128 semester hours of academic credit, competency in writing, First Year Seminar (not required of adult students), 2 credits in fitness/wellness, and successful completion of the comprehensive examination in the major subject. A minimum of 32 credits is required in the major. The core curriculum requires that students take between 36 and 44 credits distributed among five cluster areas: Literature/Fine Arts/Language; Social and Behavioral Sciences; Natural and Physical Sciences and Mathematics and Computer Science; Philosophy, Theology, and History; and Perspectives on an Interdependent World. The remaining courses are free electives.

Career preparation includes studies in accounting, business management, computer information systems, computer science, criminal justice and legal studies, foods and nutrition, gerontology, human resource management, management, marketing, premedicine, pre–veterinary studies, secondary education, and social work. Education majors may obtain state certification and/or endorsement in early childhood or special education. In addition, the College has a highly successful leadership program, which prepares students for post-graduate success.

Students interested in becoming registered dietitians may enroll in the dietetic internship program if they hold a baccalaureate degree and meet the current American Dietetic Association course work requirements.

Independent study, field experience, internships, study-abroad opportunities, honors, leadership, and accelerated programs, minors, and double majors are available for qualified students. Successful scores on Advanced Placement tests are honored for placement or credit. Credit is given for successful scores on CLEP subject examinations with essays; on the Thomas Edison College Examination Program (TECEP) examinations; on the Regents College Examination in nursing, DANTES, and ACE College Credit Recommendation; and on portfolio assessment of prior learning.

Off-Campus Programs

A cross-registration policy exists with nearby Fairleigh Dickinson and Drew Universities. Qualified students may study abroad during the junior year or in the summer. A January intersession program and summer sessions provide opportunities for short-term courses and off-campus experiences. Students have opportunities in Morris County for volunteer service, field experience, and internships in local agencies, institutions, and the corporate headquarters of numerous multinational corporations.

Academic Facilities

Students majoring in biology and chemistry conduct independent research projects under the guidance of highly qualified professors and in conjunction with local research companies. The College has several well-equipped microcomputer laboratories and extensive software. Mahoney Library is an air-conditioned facility that provides group and individual study areas. The library's collection includes 165 databases, 399 print journals, 561 electronically owned journals, 43,435 electronic journals, 1,571 DVDs and videos, and 117,057 monographs. The Phillips Library of Rare Books and Manuscripts houses a variety of special collections. The library is a selective depository for U.S. government documents. Seventeen Internet workstations provide access to the Internet and a classroom area to provide library and information literacy classes year-round. The library's Web page provides a portal for all services, including a shared online catalog with Fairleigh Dickinson University's library. In addition, there are reciprocal borrowing privileges between FDU and CSE. Media Services provides academic support services to the CSE community in all areas of traditional/non-traditional audio-visual equipment, video conferencing distance education, video/television projects, and stage performance. A TV production studio, an editing suite, and a videoconferencing classroom are housed in the Media Services area.

Costs

Tuition and fees in 2009–10 for incoming full-time freshmen were $25,375 and room and board were $10,904. Other incidental expenses, such as travel, entertainment, clothes, books, and personal expenses, were estimated at $3350. Part-time undergraduate students paid $623 per credit.

Financial Aid

Approximately 95 percent of full-time undergraduate students at the College of Saint Elizabeth receive financial aid. Aid is available from the College itself in the form of scholarships, grants-in-aid, and campus employment and from the federal and state governments in the form of scholarships, grants, loans, and employment. Students who wish to be considered for grants, loans, and campus employment should apply to the College by March 1 for the fall semester and by November 1 for the spring semester. Campus employment is available in the residence halls, laboratories, the library, and College offices, and a limited number of work-study opportunities for qualified students are available both on and off campus. Transfer scholarships are also available.

Faculty

The faculty-student ratio is 1:11. Eighty-six percent of the full-time instructional faculty members for 2009–10 had the highest degree in their field. Several faculty members hold additional professional credentials. The goals of the faculty are to teach effectively, to be readily available to students, and to pursue research.

Student Government

Students participate in the governance of the College through the Student Organization. The Student Organization elects members to the student government, which serves as the student executive branch. Student views on student activities, clubs, and organizations are expressed and acted on through a committee structure. The academic life, student life, and lectures and concerts committees of the College are composed of both faculty members and students and are engaged in determining methods of implementing institutional goals and increasing student satisfaction with campus life. Students are encouraged to participate fully in the academic community and to exercise considerable influence in social and extracurricular activities. There is an open atmosphere on campus, and students have access to the deans and the president.

Admission Requirements

The College looks for students whose aptitude and academic record demonstrate the ability to meet academic challenges. Normally, a student interested in admission to the College should complete 16 academic units by the end of her senior year, including 3 years of English; 2 years of college-preparatory mathematics, including algebra; 2 years of the same foreign language; 1 year of U.S. history; 1 unit of laboratory science and 1 additional unit of science; and six upper-level academic electives. Applicants must submit either SAT or ACT scores. International students must send scores on the Test of English as a Foreign Language (TOEFL). Students applying to the College should submit a secondary school transcript, including courses currently in progress, plus two letters of recommendation from persons who can attest to their academic potential. Students are encouraged to have an on-campus interview and visit the campus. Open houses are held each spring and fall. Well-qualified students who are recommended by their high school principals may be accepted after three years of high school. Transfers from two- and four-year colleges are accepted for the fall and spring semesters. Through articulation agreements, an applicant who has earned an A.A. degree in a transfer program at an accredited two-year college is eligible for admission with junior-class standing. Adult students must submit secondary and previous college transcripts (if any) in addition to the application.

Application and Information

For further information, students may contact:

College of Saint Elizabeth
2 Convent Road
Morristown, New Jersey 07960-6989
Phone: 800-210-7900 (toll-free)
Fax: 973-290-4710
E-mail: apply@cse.edu
Web site: http://www.cse.edu

Students at the College of Saint Elizabeth.

The College of Saint Elizabeth has filed compliance with the Department of Education (formerly Department of Health, Education, and Welfare) under Title VI–Civil Rights Act of 1964, Title IX–Education Amendment of 1972, and the regulations issued by the then Department of Health, Education, and Welfare in implementation thereof, and Section 504 of the Rehabilitation Act of 1973, as amended.

THE COLLEGE OF SAINT ROSE

ALBANY, NEW YORK

COLLEGE CLOSE-UPS

The College

The College of Saint Rose is an independent, residential, coeducational institution where academics and career preparation are top priorities. The College's progressive liberal education core prepares students to dive into one of the College's sixty-six undergraduate fields of study, most of which incorporate a field experience or internship component. The College offers small class sizes, with a student-faculty ratio of 14:1 and an experienced, mentoring faculty. *Money* magazine and *U.S. News & World Report* have ranked Saint Rose as one of the top colleges in the Northeast and the nation, based on such factors as affordability and high academic quality. With the capital of New York as its convenient location and a distinctly personal learning atmosphere on campus, the College of Saint Rose is a place where students realize they will be challenged intellectually and have the ability to change the world.

Saint Rose was founded in 1920 by the Sisters of Saint Joseph of Carondelet and is a distinguished college interwoven within a remarkable city. The campus is part of the fabric of the city and the students and faculty members the threads that make it whole. The College is located in an area that gives it a distinct educational advantage and a college dedicated to cultivating intellectual dynamic leaders appreciative of diversity and active citizenship. The College encompasses eighty buildings, including the new Massry Center for the Arts, the Thelma P. Lally School of Education, a state-of-the-art Science Center, a high-tech music studio, and the Hubbard Interfaith Sanctuary.

Saint Rose students make up a community of leaders. Most of the 3,000 undergraduates at Saint Rose come from twenty-two states and sixteen different countries. The College of Saint Rose actively seeks to enroll students of all backgrounds who can contribute to and benefit from the experience of shared learning and academic success.

Campus housing includes traditional and suite-style residence halls and town houses as well as more than thirty Victorian homes. Each house has its own history and character, with unique wraparound porches and stained-glass windows.

Students participate in organized social activities as well as ten associations related to academic majors. The College of Saint Rose is a member of the National Collegiate Athletic Association (NCAA) Division II and the Northeast-10 Conference. Intercollegiate teams include men's baseball and golf; men's and women's basketball, cross-country, soccer, swimming, tennis, and track and field; and women's softball and volleyball.

Although students ultimately attend Saint Rose to receive a superior education, they also participate in organized social activities that enhance the Saint Rose experience. Saint Rose students belong to more than thirty groups that include academic-related clubs as well as special-interest clubs. They also play in ten to fifteen intramural programs and produce three publications—the award-winning *Chronicle* weekly student newspaper, the *Sphere* literary magazine, and *Reflections,* the College's yearbook.

Location

Saint Rose is located in the historic Pine Hills neighborhood of Albany. With more than 60,000 college students in the area, there are always things to do and people to meet. A wide variety of restaurants, shops, museums, malls, and theaters are within walking distance or are easily accessible by buses that stop at Saint Rose.

Majors and Degrees

The College of Saint Rose offers programs of study in the fields of accounting, American studies, art education (K–12), biochemistry, biology, biology education (7–12), biology/cytotechnology, bioinformatics, business administration, chemistry, chemistry education (7–12), childhood education, childhood education/special education, communication sciences and disorders, communications, computer information systems, computer science, criminal justice, early childhood education, early childhood/special education, earth science (7–12), English, English education (7–12), environmental affairs, exploratory, forensic science, geology, graphic design, history, history/political science, mathematics, mathematics education (7–12), medical technology, music education (K–12), music industry, political science, prelaw, premedicine, pre–veterinary studies, psychology, religious studies, social studies education (7–12), social work, sociology, Spanish, Spanish education (7–12), sport management, studio art, technology education, and women's studies.

Academic Programs

The College offers qualified students the opportunity to pursue accelerated bachelor's/master's degrees in approximately five years of study. The College offers these options in accounting, business, communications sciences and disorders (speech therapy), computer information systems, computer science, English, history, and M.B.A.

Qualified students may also participate in other special programs: a 3+3 option with Albany Law School, a 3+1 medical technology option with Albany College of Pharmacy or Rochester, and a 3+2 engineering option with Union College, Clarkson University, Rensselaer Polytechnic Institute, or Alfred University. Students in these programs complete selected bachelor's degree programs at Saint Rose in three years and transfer to the cooperating institution to finish the professional program.

Students are provided with assistance in planning their programs of study by faculty advisers in their major areas and by the Office of Academic Advisement. They may elect double majors or minors or may design their own programs within the guidelines set by the interdepartmental studies major.

To earn a bachelor's degree, a student must complete a minimum of 122 credits, including, for most majors, the liberal education curriculum requirement of 42 credits, two courses in physical education, and the major requirements as specified. A minimum of 60 credits must be earned on the Saint Rose campus or at one of the colleges in the Hudson-Mohawk Association of Colleges and Universities through cross-registration.

The College operates on a semester calendar, with a fall term extending from August to December and a spring term from January to May. Two summer session programs offer undergraduate and graduate evening courses.

Off-Campus Programs

Saint Rose students can study in one of more than thirty countries, which is made possible by the school's affiliations with the College Consortium for International Studies, Regent's College in London, and the Center for Cross-Cultural Study. All study-abroad opportunities are offered at the same price as Saint Rose tuition (plus airfare and personal expenses), including the Saint Rose financial aid package. All credits count toward the student's degree.

Academic Facilities

The Christian Plumeri Sports Complex is scheduled to open in spring 2010. The College has invested more than $2.5 million to create an outdoor sports complex with a baseball field, softball field, and an artificial turf soccer/lacrosse field as well as a natural grass practice field. These fields will be home for the Saint Rose Golden Knights, who have regularly won bids to Northeast-10 conference and Division II national tournaments, as well as for the College's intramural and club sports.

The College's new $14-million Massry Center for the Arts is a distinctive facility that not only provides a learning environment for music and art but also gives musical and visual artists a prime location to showcase their work to the College community and the public. The 46,000-square-foot facility features a state-of-the-art performance hall, acoustically congruent and separate instrumental and choral rehearsal suites, applied teaching studios, piano keyboard laboratories, smart classrooms, and an art gallery.

Also scheduled to open in spring 2010 is the new Center for Communications and Interactive Media. This 20,000 square foot facility is designed to house new TV and radio studios, a live recording studio, a video and film viewing room, multimedia computer labs, and offices for the College's communications and music industry faculty. It joins the Massry Center for the Arts and the Campus Theatre to form an arts and communications section of the Saint Rose campus.

A recent partnership with IBM and a $7-million technology upgrade greatly enhanced the speed and performance of the College's network, providing the infrastructure for wireless networking, videoconferencing, streaming media, and Blackboard, the Web-based instruction tool. The campuswide network provides wireless access across the campus including the campus center, the library, and all of the residence halls.

The Center for Art and Design houses the student art gallery as well as extensive photography labs, graphic design computers, and one of the largest screen-printing facilities in the state of New York. The College's Music Center features the Saints and Sinners Sound Studio, a music library, a performance hall, and practice rooms. Science and mathematics majors have access to the latest equipment and research facilities in the College's 27,000-square-foot Science Center.

The $15-million, 56,000-square-foot Thelma P. Lally School of Education features a multimedia education forum, classrooms, computer labs, offices, an education and curriculum library, a laboratory nursery school, and a multidisciplinary services clinic. The school provides a learning and teaching environment in which technology plays a critical role and where teachers, parents, and students exchange ideas on how to make the American education system second to none.

With the creation of the $7.5-million Events and Athletics Center, the College of Saint Rose plans to provide an on-campus venue worthy of welcoming best-selling authors, Nobel Prize winners, and world-famous performers. This space is also designed to serve as a unique collegiate basketball venue in the Capital Region, large enough to accommodate the Golden Knights' loyal fan base. In addition, Saint Joseph's Hall, one of Saint Rose's original buildings, received a $5.5-million renovation, turning the building into a student service hub centralized around the College's Student Solution Center.

Costs

Tuition for 2007–08 was $19,960. Room and board costs averaged $8558 per year, depending on the meal plan chosen by the student. Estimated annual costs for books and personal expenses are $1000 and $1400, respectively.

Financial Aid

More than 95 percent of the students receive scholarships and financial assistance. The College of Saint Rose participates in the Federal Pell Grant, FSEOG, TAP, and Federal Work-Study programs and in the Federal Perkins Loan and Federal Stafford Loan Programs. The College provides ample aid in the form of grants, service awards, and scholarships for need or academic achievement. Candidates for financial assistance must file the Free Application for Federal Student Aid. ISIR and SAR forms should be on file in the Financial Aid Office by March 1. Students interested in being considered for academic scholarships must apply to the College by February 1.

Faculty

Saint Rose has a full-time faculty of 194 members, with a student-faculty ratio of 14:1. The average class size is 20–25 students, with more than 55 percent of classes having less than 20 students.

Student Government

The Student Association (SA) consists of elected students who want to make life at the College as enjoyable, interesting, and meaningful as possible. It budgets student funds, appoints representatives to College policymaking committees, and assists individual students and clubs in planning and carrying out projects. It also provides an organ of self-government, promotes an exchange of ideas within the College community, fosters opportunities beyond those offered in the formal curriculum, and advances the welfare of the entire College community. SA also oversees the College's thirty clubs and organizations.

Admission Requirements

The College wishes to admit students who show evidence of strong academic motivation and the ability to benefit from a challenging liberal and professional education. Admission decisions are made after careful study of all the data available for each candidate. Interviews are strongly recommended but not required. Freshman applicants should submit a high school transcript, a letter of recommendation from a teacher or guidance counselor, and scores on the SAT or ACT.

Transfer applicants must submit high school and college transcripts, a letter of recommendation from a college instructor, and a written statement of the reasons for transfer.

Application and Information

The College has an early action (nonbinding) application deadline of December 1. Students are accepted for admission for the fall and spring semesters on a rolling admissions basis. Interested students must apply by February 1 to be considered for academic scholarships ranging from $3000 to full tuition for each undergraduate year. New students who are accepted for admission are asked to submit a $300 enrollment deposit to secure their place in the new class. Information on all aspects of the campus and the academic programs can be obtained by contacting the Office of Admissions; this office also can arrange personal interviews, campus tours, classroom visits, and overnight accommodations.

Office of Undergraduate Admissions
The College of Saint Rose
432 Western Avenue
Albany, New York 12203
Phone: 518-454-5150
800-637-8556 (toll-free)
Fax: 518-454-2013
E-mail: admit@strose.edu (admissions)
finaid@strose.edu (financial aid)
Web site: http://www.strose.edu

Located in the historic Pine Hills neighborhood of Albany, New York, the Saint Rose campus features a mix of classic brick buildings and new stone and glass structures, with the Campus Green at its center. The border of the campus is outlined by more than thirty restored historic Victorian houses featuring wraparound porches and stained-glass windows.

COLLEGE CLOSE-UPS

COLLEGE OF STATEN ISLAND OF THE CITY UNIVERSITY OF NEW YORK

STATEN ISLAND, NEW YORK

CSI CUNY
World class, right here!

The College and The University

Founded in 1976 from the merger of two existing colleges, the College of Staten Island (CSI) is a four-year senior college within the City University of New York (CUNY) and is Staten Island's only public institution of higher learning. CSI is dedicated to both access and excellence and currently serves over 13,000 students.

The College of Staten Island was established through the union of Staten Island Community College (CUNY's first community college, founded in 1955) and Richmond College (CUNY's first upper-division college, founded in 1965).

The College ensures that students receive a thorough liberal arts education through core requirements which include classes in the arts and humanities, mathematics, science, and social sciences. Requirements for the associate degree provide a curriculum based on study in a specific area which is often directed toward a career. Requirements for the bachelor's degree provide disciplined and cumulative programs of study in fifty-three majors.

The Campus Center incorporates cocurricular activities for a complete personal growth experience. The two-story rotunda space at the heart of the structure contains the main dining facilities, the College's health services, a bookstore, offices for student organizations, study and sleep lounges, a small performance/cafe space, game rooms with the latest game consoles, and the state-of-the-art studios of WSIA, the student-operated FM radio station.

Location

CSI is located on a sprawling 204-acre campus located in the heart of Staten Island. The campus is the largest site for a college (public or private) within New York City and with its scenic landscape; the grounds and facilities create a rural oasis in an urban setting. Classrooms and academic offices are located in fourteen neo-Georgian buildings that form two quadrangles connected by the campus walk, which extends between the library and the Campus Center. Five well-built and equipped buildings—the library, the Campus Center, the Biological Sciences/Chemical Sciences building, the Center for the Arts, and the Sports and Recreation Center—provide outstanding facilities for scholastic and community-based activities.

CSI's location offers students the best of two worlds, with Staten Island providing a suburban environment with some of the most interesting landscapes in the metropolitan area, while Manhattan, the center of cultural and social life of the city, is only 25 minutes from the island by ferry. The Verrazano-Narrows Bridge provides direct access to the island from Brooklyn.

Majors and Degrees

CSI offers an Associate in Arts degree in liberal arts and sciences. The Associate in Science degree is offered in engineering science, liberal arts and sciences, and liberal arts and sciences with a prearchitecture concentration. The Associate in Applied Science degree is offered in business, civil engineering technology, computer technology, electrical engineering technology, medical laboratory technology, and nursing.

The Bachelor of Arts degree is conferred in African American studies; American studies; art; art with a photography concentration; cinema studies; economics; English; English with a dramatic literature concentration; history; international studies; music; philosophy; political science; psychology; science, letters, and society; sociology/anthropology; social work; Spanish; and women's studies.

The Bachelor of Science degree is offered in accounting; art; art with a photography concentration; biochemistry; bioinformatics; biology; business; business with a finance concentration, an international business concentration, a management concentration, or a marketing concentration; chemistry; communications; computer science; computer science/mathematics; dramatic arts; economics; economics with a business specialization or a finance specialization; engineering science; information systems; mathematics; medical technology; music; music with an electronics concentration; nursing (upper-division program); physician assistant studies; and physics.

In addition to the exciting array of undergraduate degrees and majors available, CSI also awards the Master of Arts degree in cinema and media studies, English, environmental science, and history and liberal studies; and the Master of Science degree in biology, computer science, neuroscience, mental retardation and developmental disabilities, and nursing education. Special education and post-master's advanced certificates are offered in leadership in education, nursing education, and nursing cultural competence.

The graduate teacher education program prepares students to teach at the early childhood, elementary, and secondary levels. The academic work and field experience meet the requirements for the certification and licensing examinations given by the state and city of New York.

Further, CSI collaborates with the CUNY Graduate School and University Center and Brooklyn College in a doctoral program in polymer chemistry; with the Graduate School and University Center in doctoral programs in computer science, physical therapy, and physics; and in concert with the Center for Developmental Neurosciences and Developmental Disabilities, the College participates in CUNY doctoral subprograms in neuroscience (biology) and learning processes (psychology).

Academic Programs

CSI offers two-year programs in career areas and in liberal arts and sciences and four-year programs with majors in the traditional fields of study. General education requirements have been established for all degrees. The associate degree programs require 60–64 credits, depending on the field; the bachelor's degree programs require 120 credits, with a few exceptions. Credit may be awarded for experiential learning, internships, and independent study and credit may also be earned by examination. Minors may be taken in several fields, and double majors are permitted. Students may graduate with honors in their field of study in most bachelor's degree majors.

The College follows a two-semester calendar, with classes scheduled both day and evening. The Office of Weekend and Evening Services offers a variety of course combinations leading to associate and bachelor's degrees, providing opportunities for nontraditional students with weekday career commitments to pursue a college education at more convenient times. Intensive summer and winter sessions are also offered to students who would like to complete their degrees more quickly.

Off-Campus Programs

The College gives a number of courses for credit at off-campus locations throughout the city through internships at major corporations and other fieldwork. Study-abroad opportunities are available through CSI's Center for International Service which offers students the option of earning academic credit for study in China, Denmark, Ecuador, England, Greece, Italy, Spain, or South Africa.

Academic Facilities

The academic buildings are designed to house approximately 300 modern laboratories and classrooms. Each also houses a study lounge for students, departmental and program offices, and offices for faculty members. Academic and research programs are served by a computer network that allows students and faculty members full access to specialized software, the Internet, online library resources, and e-mail. All major computer languages and software packages are supported. The College is a wireless campus, and its network is available to all students.

The Center for the Arts complex provides facilities for teaching in the instructional wing and areas of public assembly in the public wing. The complex of public facilities includes a 900-seat auditorium, a 450-seat fully equipped theater, a recital hall, an experimental theater, an art gallery, and a conference center. Classrooms, lecture halls, studios, and offices for faculty members are located in the instructional wing.

The CSI Library is staffed with 14 full-time librarians and 7 adjunct librarians who also hold faculty status and rank. In addition, the library also has 40 support staff members. The library's total collection consists of approximately 235,000 books; 900 print journal subscriptions; 77 electronic databases with more than 26,000 full-text journals; 3,000 videos and films; and more than 4,000 sound recordings. The library's online catalog, CUNY+Plus, provides complete access to the collections, including access to holdings of other CUNY libraries. Students also have electronic access to database and research tools 24 hours a day via the Internet. In addition, the library maintains a collection of current textbooks donated by the CSI Student Government. These and other course materials are available at the Reserve Desk. Wireless laptops are loaned to students for use throughout the library. The library building also houses the office of Instructional Support Services and the Cybercafé which offers Starbucks coffee.

The laboratory science building provides facilities for teaching and for two research centers: the Center for Environmental Science and the Center for Developmental Neuroscience and Developmental Disabilities. It consists of a research wing and an instructional wing. State-of-the-art laboratories serve students and faculty members in their teaching and research.

The CSI Astrophysical Observatory is a world-class resource which has been recognized by the International Astronomical Union as an official asteroid tracking station.

The Sports and Recreation Center is a 77,000-square-foot multipurpose facility providing basketball, handball/paddleball, racquetball, and volleyball courts; locker rooms; a gym; instructional areas; an indoor 25-meter swimming pool; and offices for faculty members. Recreational fields occupy the meadows in the northwest quadrant of the campus, providing a green and landscaped open area at the main approach to the campus that includes a running track, indoor and outdoor tennis courts, a soccer field, handball/paddleball courts, softball fields, and a semiprofessional baseball field (original home field to the Staten Island Yankees minor-league baseball team).

Costs

For 2008–09, undergraduate New York State (NYS) tuition was $170 per credit for part-time matriculated students, $2000 per semester for full-time matriculated students, and $250 per credit for nondegree students. Out-of-state full- and part-time students were charged $360 per credit, and nondegree students were charged $530 per credit. Graduate NYS resident tuition was $3200 per semester for students attending the College full-time, $270 per credit for part-time students, and $65 per hour for excess hours. Nonresidents were charged $500 per credit for full- and part-time attendance with $85 per hour for excess hours.

Financial Aid

Financial aid is available through state and federal programs and includes the New York State Tuition Assistance Program (TAP) awards, Federal Pell Grants, Federal Supplemental Educational Opportunity Grants (FSEOG), Search for Elevation and Education through Knowledge (SEEK) awards, scholarships, Federal Work-Study Program awards, and student loan programs. Information about programs, application procedures, and deadlines is available from the Financial Aid Office.

CSI Presidential Scholarships are awarded annually to full-time students on academic proficiency and service. In addition, endowments have been established for scholarships in a number of fields. Further information about scholarships is available from the Career and Scholarship Center.

Faculty

The College has a full-time faculty of 300, of whom approximately 80 percent hold a doctoral degree or the equivalent. The faculty members have made significant contributions in many areas of scholarship, creativity, and public service. Numerous faculty members have received prestigious grants and awards, and more than 30 serve as members of CUNY's doctoral faculty.

Student Government

A single body (Senate) comprised of 20 elected students represents the interests of the College's students, serving as liaison to faculty and administrators. The Senate derives funding from the Student Activity Fee and through its various commissions and committees, the student government sponsors many academic and nonacademic programs.

Admission Requirements

A freshman applicant for admission to a bachelor's degree program must pass the three CUNY Freshman Skills Assessment Tests unless he or she qualifies for exemption based on a satisfactory performance on the SAT or ACT standardized tests or Regents Examinations. Admission to a bachelor's degree program is determined by an applicant's score on the College's admissions index. The index is based on the applicant's high school courses and academic average and the combined verbal and mathematics SAT scores. An applicant whose score reaches or exceeds the College's minimum index number is admitted to a bachelor's degree program. A faculty admissions committee may consider the admission of applicants whose scores approach the College's minimum index number. Transfer students to baccalaureate programs who have fewer than 25 credits must have a GPA of at least 2.0 and must meet freshman entrance criteria. Students must have passed the CUNY Freshman Skills Assessment Tests in mathematics, writing, and reading prior to enrolling in a bachelor's degree program or if they are transferring from another college in CUNY.

Entering first-year students may be admitted to two-year programs if they have graduated from an accredited high school or have earned an equivalency diploma (GED) with a satisfactory score.

As a general rule, the College requires a grade point average equivalent to at least a C for transfer as a matriculated student into a two-year degree program.

Application and Information

Requests for further information and application materials should be directed to:

Office of Recruitment and Admissions
North Administration Building (2A-103)
College of Staten Island
City University of New York
2800 Victory Boulevard
Staten Island, New York 10314

Phone: 718-982-2010
E-mail: admissions@mail.csi.cuny.edu
Web site: http://www.csi.cuny.edu

COLLEGE OF THE ATLANTIC

BAR HARBOR, MAINE

The College

Located between the Atlantic Ocean and Acadia National Park, College of the Atlantic (COA) offers two degrees: a B.A. and a M.Phil., both in human ecology. In pursuit of this degree, students consider their individual passions to create their own academic trajectories, integrating knowledge from all academic disciplines and personal experience to fulfill the mission of human ecology: investigating and improving relationships between humans and our social, natural, built, and virtual communities. COA's small size and individualized curriculum emphasizes mentoring: tutorials and intensive seminar-style classes are encouraged. Faculty-student interchanges are as common in the college's single dining room as during faculty office hours.

Founded in 1969, COA's approach to education is distinctive in several ways. With one major, there are no departments, education is truly interdisciplinary, and all students fashion an individual course of study to satisfy their academic and personal goals. As much as possible, students learn by doing, combining academic rigor with practical application, to the point that recent students have created first-in-the nation legislation for Maine, lobbied on the international stage, completed novels, and presented independent research at international conferences. Readings are frequently from primary sources. The intensity of the intellectual relationship has led some to describe COA as a graduate school for undergraduates.

Beyond this, COA is a democratic institution, with students involved at all levels of governance and a weekly campus meeting to discuss current campus issues and decisions. Major decisions must be brought to an All-College Meeting; most committees include participation by students.

Enrollment for the 2008–09 school year was 323, about ⅜ men. COA has a strong international student presence, with nearly 20 percent of its student body from outside the United States. Given its location, many students enjoy the outdoors. The College also sponsors films, speakers, concerts, and dances, and students hold informal parties, musical get-togethers, and open mics. Students, faculty members, and staff members form a close-knit community.

In addition to its undergraduate degree, the College also offers a Master of Philosophy (M.Phil.) in human ecology.

Location

The College is located in the town of Bar Harbor on Mount Desert Island, Maine, also home to Acadia National Park. Connected to the mainland by a causeway, the large, scenic, mountainous island lies 300 miles north of Boston and 40 miles east of Bangor. In the summer, Bar Harbor teems with tourists. When students return in the fall, the traffic reverses direction and Bar Harbor becomes a quiet coastal Maine village. The Atlantic Ocean and Acadia National Park provide ample opportunities for such outdoor recreational activities as swimming, fishing, canoeing, kayaking, rock climbing, hiking, biking, cross-country skiing, and snowshoeing. Cooperative programs with the Jackson Laboratory, the Mount Desert Island Biological Laboratory, the national park, and the local public school system broaden the scope of COA's educational activities on the island. The College's two island research stations and 73-acre organic farm expand COA's local resources. A new Trans-Atlantic Partnership in Sustainable Food Systems further broadens the College, linking it with an organic research farm in the United Kingdom and a German graduate school.

Majors and Degrees

College of the Atlantic awards the Bachelor of Arts in human ecology. Human ecology emphasizes the understanding of interrelationships between humans and the social, natural, and built environments. Students may develop individualized programs in many areas, including community development, environmental science, green and sustainable business, humanities, international and regional studies, landscape design, literature and writing, marine studies, natural history museum studies, public policy, sustainable agriculture, teacher certification, and visual arts.

Academic Programs

The academic program is designed to develop an ecological perspective through the understanding of social, biological, artistic, and technological interrelationships. Students acquire the skills necessary to enter the fields of science, education, business, law, design, the arts, health, social services, policy and planning, journalism, literature, medicine, agriculture, landscaping, architecture, and many other fields. Sixty percent of COA's alumni have pursued graduate or professional education at some of the country's leading institutions. Small, discussion-based classes are the foundation of the curriculum at COA. Student-initiated workshops, independent studies, intensive tutorials, internships, and senior projects also provide essential learning experiences. Applied learning is the norm, not the exception.

To qualify for graduation, students must complete required interdisciplinary course work, write an essay on human ecology, perform community service, and complete a one-term internship and a one-term capstone project.

College of the Atlantic accepts up to two years of transfer credits from accredited colleges if the grades earned were C or better and were earned in courses of an academic nature.

Off-Campus Programs

The College's academic program is augmented by exchange agreements with the University of Maine at Orono; the Palacky University in Olomouc, Czech Republic; the Olin College of Engineering in Needham, Massachusetts; the Organic Research Centre at Elm Farm in the United Kingdom, the University of Kassel in Germany, the SALT Institute for Documentary Studies, and the National Outdoor Leadership School (NOLS). Students may also spend a term in COA's study-abroad program in the Yucatan Peninsula in Mexico or in Guatemala, or join courses offered in Canada, France, and the Caribbean. The Eco League consortium allows students to study for up to one year at Alaska Pacific University, Green Mountain College, Northland College, or Prescott College.

Academic Facilities

Thorndike Library has more than 48,000 print and multimedia titles and provides access to a variety of subscription-based electronic resources. Access to material in libraries throughout the world is available via the library's interlibrary loan service. COA has zoology, botany, and chemistry laboratories; a herbarium; greenhouses; design and ceramics studios; a gallery; state-of-the-art computer facilities, including a Geographic Information Systems Lab and a green design/graphics computer lab; research boats for marine research and to ferry students and faculty members to College-owned island research stations in the Gulf of Maine; a community garden on campus, and a 73-acre working organic farm. Exhibits at the College's George B. Dorr

Museum of Natural History and the Bar Harbor Whale Museum are made by students, and students run many of the museum programs.

Costs

The total cost for the 2009–10 academic year is about $41,550. This includes $33,060 for tuition, $5400 for rooming, and $3090 for board.

Financial Aid

Nearly three-quarters of the College's students receive some form of financial aid. The Free Application for Federal Student Aid and the College's own form are required by the College to determine a student's eligibility for assistance. COA offers merit scholarships as well as need-based aid. Aid is based on established need and academic merit. Financial aid packages generally consist of a combination of scholarships, work-study awards, and loans.

Faculty

With a faculty of 28 full-time and 12 part-time teachers, the student-faculty ratio is 10:1. Ninety percent of the full-time faculty members have Ph.D.'s or the equivalent. Courses offered by regular visiting faculty members supplement the curriculum. The primary commitment of the COA faculty is teaching and advising undergraduate students.

Student Government

The College governance system is a combination of pure and representative democracy. Students participate in all facets of decision making and serve on all standing committees. Major policy decisions are brought for review to the All-College Meeting, where members of the faculty, staff, and student body each have one vote.

Admission Requirements

The Admission Committee, composed of students, staff members, and faculty members, seeks students who have an enthusiastic, creative, and active approach to learning, a commitment to community service, a strong record of academic achievement, and accompanying intellectual strengths. These qualities should be supplemented with appropriate personal qualities enabling a student to learn in an environment requiring a high degree of self-motivation.

The COA application form contains a series of essay questions that require students to think carefully about College of the Atlantic's educational focus. The application is designed to encourage prospective students to reflect on and express personal reasons for choosing a small college with a focus on human ecology. The answers to these questions, teacher and counselor references, past academic records, and personal interviews are used by the Admission Committee in arriving at its decision. Standardized test scores are optional.

Admission procedures and standards are the same for transfer students as for freshman applicants. Special emphasis is placed on the transfer applicant's college transcript and recommendations. The transfer of credits is determined on an individual basis. All transferring students are required to complete a minimum of two years of study at COA. Applications are also accepted from students at other institutions who wish to spend time at the College as visiting students.

Application and Information

Prospective students are encouraged to visit the College in order to sit in on classes, talk with students and faculty members, and acquire an understanding of the College's individualized educational style. COA employs a deadline of February 15 for fall admission for first-year students, but offers two early decision options: a December 1 deadline, followed by a January 10 deadline. Transfer students must apply by April 1. Decisions for first-year students are mailed on or about April 1 and on or about April 25 for transfer students. Applicants for winter term should apply by November 15 and for spring term by February 15. Application materials may be obtained by writing to the College or by telephoning the Admission Office at the number below. The application fee is $45. COA endorses the policy set by the National Association of College Admission Counselors, whereby regular admission students have the right to defer accepting any offer of admission until May 1.

Director of Admission
College of the Atlantic
105 Eden Street
Bar Harbor, Maine 04609
Phone: 207-288-5015
800-528-0025 (toll-free)
Fax: 207-288-4126
E-mail: inquiry@coa.edu
Web site: http://www.coa.edu

Seabird research at the Alice Eno Biological Station on Great Duck Island.

THE COLLEGE OF WOOSTER

WOOSTER, OHIO

The College

The College of Wooster engages every student in a process of learning that places the student at its center. This ability to democratize excellence—and to infuse students with self-reliance—gives Wooster incomparable value. Some colleges reserve that heightened experience for honors students; Wooster honors every student with personal attention and the tools to develop his or her own vision. The College of Wooster acts on the conviction that everyone can benefit from an honors education. At Wooster, that philosophy enhances the entire college experience. Small classes and an accessible faculty committed to teaching ensure individual attention for every student, from First-Year Seminar to senior year, when students work one-on-one with a faculty adviser on an Independent Study project that pulls together everything they have learned in their first three years at Wooster.

Founded as a Presbyterian college in 1866, Wooster has been an independent, residential college of the liberal arts and sciences since 1969. With small classes (61 percent have fewer than 20 students) and an 11:1 student-faculty ratio, students receive close attention both in and out of the classroom.

Wooster's 1,800 students come from forty-five states and twenty-six countries from all backgrounds and life experiences. They are serious about their academic lives, but they are just as intense about exploring their other interests—and having fun.

Ninety-eight percent of Wooster students live on campus. First-year students can choose to live with their First-Year Seminar classmates or a mix of students from all years. After the first year, the options multiply. Wooster's program houses allow students to live with a group of 7 to 14 others who share their interests. Together, they work on a service project in the community throughout the year, from Habitat for Humanity to the Humane Society.

Close to a third of Wooster students follow their passion for making music through three choirs, a symphony orchestra, symphonic and marching bands, a jazz ensemble, four a cappella groups, and other ensembles. Another third participate in intercollegiate athletics. Wooster has produced 39 All Americans in the past five years and won 67 NCAC championships since 1985.

From the improv group Don't Throw Shoes, to the student-run investment club (managing a $1-million portfolio for the College's endowment), and the cricket team to the radio station, there is something for just about every interest.

Location

The College is located in Wooster, Ohio, a city of approximately 26,000. Wooster is 55 miles southwest of Cleveland and 30 miles southwest of Akron. An unusually close relationship exists between the College and the community. College-community activities include the Wooster Symphony, the Ambassadors Program, and a variety of volunteer and internship experiences.

Majors and Degrees

The College of Wooster offers the degrees of Bachelor of Arts, Bachelor of Music, and Bachelor of Music Education. A student may choose from more than fifty majors and programs of study, including Africana studies; anthropology; archaeology; art history; art–studio; biochemistry and molecular biology; biology; business economics; chemical physics; chemistry; classical studies (Greek, Latin, classical civilization); communication sciences and disorders; communication studies; comparative literature; computer science; cultural area studies (African studies, East Asia Studies, Latin American studies, modern Western Europe, Russia and East Europe studies, and South Asia studies), economics; English; French; geology; German (language, literature, culture); history; international relations; mathematics; music; music education; music history and literature; music performance; music theory–composition; music therapy; neuroscience; philosophy; physics; political science; psychology; religious studies; Russian studies; sociology; Spanish; student-designed major (e.g., journalism, sports medicine); theater and dance; urban studies; and women's, gender, and sexuality studies. In addition, minors are available in most areas as well as Chinese, education (with licensure in elementary or secondary teaching), environmental studies, film studies, international business, and physical education.

Wooster offers dual-degree programs in cooperation with other institutions; such programs lead to either two bachelor's degrees (one from each institution) or a bachelor's degree from Wooster and a master's from the cooperating institution. The dual-degree programs are in the areas of architecture, dentistry, engineering, forestry and environmental studies, nursing, polymer science, and social work.

The College also offers a preprofessional advising program to support those students who want to combine the study of liberal arts with preparation for a specific profession. The preprofessional advising programs provide students with advice on the development of an appropriate academic program, cocurricular and volunteer experiences, guidance on summer research opportunities, lectures by leaders in the various professions, and information about the process of selecting and applying to graduate and professional schools. Wooster's preprofessional programs are in the areas of architecture, business, engineering, forestry and environmental studies, heath professions, law, seminary studies, and social work.

Academic Programs

Students begin their academic journey begins with First-Year Seminar, a writing-intensive course that exercises their intellect and sharpens their critical faculties. In a class of no more than 15, with a professor who is also their academic adviser, students approach a wide range of texts, questioning and analyzing them to tease out meaning and then formulating arguments through extensive writing and discussion.

To ensure that they are conversant with forms of inquiry and discourse in a range of disciplines, students select courses in each of three areas: arts and humanities, history and social sciences, and mathematical and natural sciences. They also gain insight into other cultures through a course in global and cultural perspectives and another in religious perspectives.

Once a major is selected, students engage with the scholarship of that field, master its particular methodologies, and have numerous opportunities to work with faculty members on research projects (as early as the second semester of the first year), participate in internships, or study abroad.

It all culminates in the senior Independent Study (I.S.) project. Working one-on-one with a faculty adviser over the course of a year, students conduct research, create art, or shape a performance that demonstrates their understanding of a discipline and their ability to communicate that knowledge to others. It is called Independent Study, but it is a journey that the student and the faculty adviser take together. Students are guaranteed a 1:1 student-faculty ratio for one class each semester of their senior year. In weekly, hour-long, one-on-one meetings, the adviser helps refine and focus the topic, suggests areas for exploration, asks questions that provoke thought and creativity, and evaluates progress. Students, in turn, review and synthesize literature related to the subject, plan and conduct research in the lab, or work to realize a creative vision in the studio, recital hall, or theater. Students present drafts of their work to their advisers, who offer extensive thoughtful feedback as close collaborators.

If the I.S. project requires travel or special equipment or supplies, the College's Henry J. Copeland Fund for Independent Study can help. In a typical year, the fund disburses more than $90,000 to support a diverse array of student projects, from studying the lives of West African immigrants in Paris or producing a documentary on survivors of Hiroshima to researching ways to purify methane gas to permit its use as a renewable energy source. When the I.S. is complete, students may find themselves presenting the results at a national conference in their discipline or coauthoring papers with their advisers. (Geology professor Mark Wilson has published articles with more than 40 student coauthors.)

Throughout the I.S. project, students learn not just about a specific topic but also about how to break down any complex project into manageable pieces, develop a plan of action, and follow it through. Students learn how to analyze a problem, gather and evaluate information, propose a solution, test its validity, and communicate the results clearly and persuasively. The completed I.S. gives employers tangible proof of resourcefulness, creativity, and communication skills. It also marks the student as an independent scholar who is ready to take on graduate-level research wherever his or her interests lead.

To get a full sense of the range of possibilities, students should check out the I.S. database or listen to Wooster students talk about their projects. Go to http://www.wooster.edu/ and click on Independent Study.

Off-Campus Programs

Students who wish to enrich their undergraduate experience by overseas study may choose from a variety of fully accredited programs. Wooster sponsors a number of its own off-campus programs in the United States and abroad, and through its membership in the Great Lakes Colleges Association and its affiliations, offers off-campus study opportunities in more than fifty countries spanning the globe.

A variety of off-campus opportunities within the United States provide both academic and internship experiences. The Washington Semester and the Semester at the United Nations offer extensive possibilities in national and international government. There is also a fine-arts semester in New York City. Other internship possibilities exist in business, the humanities, the natural sciences, and psychology.

Academic Facilities

The College libraries consist of the Andrews Library, the adjacent Flo K. Gault Library for Independent Study, and the nearby Timken Science Library in Frick Hall. Together, they contain more than 1 million books, periodicals, microforms, electronic journals, videotapes, and audio recordings. As a member of CONSORT and OhioLINK, the libraries can provide almost any book from Ohio's academic libraries within two to three days. The libraries subscribe to a wide variety of electronic databases and to some 5,000 periodicals in electronic form, all available campuswide via the computing network. The libraries house more than 300 study carrels, each of which is equipped with electrical and data connections.

Computing is an important part of Wooster's academic environment. All academic buildings and residence hall rooms are connected to the campus network. The Taylor Hall computer center houses fifty-two terminals for student use while the Wired Scot, a cyber café, features twenty-two PC workstations with Internet access, two large plasma-screen TVs, and wireless Internet access throughout the building.

The College's science facilities contain the most up-to-date laboratory equipment, libraries, computer terminals, and instrumentation, including ultraviolet, visible, fluorescence, and infrared spectrometers; a scanning electron microscope; an atomic force microscope; a nuclear magnetic resonance spectrometer; a mass spectrometer; an X-ray diffractometer; and various chromatographs.

Wooster's Learning Center provides academic support for students, and priority is given to students with identified learning disabilities. Professional staff work with individual students on time management, organization skills, and effective study strategies. Wooster's Writing Center provides writing assistance through one-to-one tutorial sessions and group workshops covering all aspects of the writing process.

The Freedlander Theatre complex contains excellent technical equipment and a separate theater for students' experimental productions. The speech facility houses a radio station and a speech and hearing clinic that also serves the community.

The Scheide Music Center, a 35,000-square-foot complex, contains five classrooms, eleven teaching studios, twenty-three soundproof practice rooms, a music library, and a listening lab. The Timken Rehearsal Hall and the acoustically balanced Gault Recital Hall are "tunable" so that the halls can be rendered "live" to greater or lesser degrees.

The Ebert Art Center has expansive space for studio art and art history. The building includes classrooms, individual studios for senior studio art majors, and the Sussel and Burton D. Morgan Art Galleries.

Costs

The comprehensive fee (room, board, tuition, and fees) for 2009–10 was $43,900.

Financial Aid

Financial assistance is awarded on merit and/or need. Need-based aid is determined by the Free Application for Federal Student Aid (FAFSA). Merit aid is awarded when students are admitted to the College. Applications for need-based aid should be submitted by February 15.

The College of Wooster believes in recognizing individual talent and hard work. Thus, Wooster offers merit-based scholarships that range from $1000 to $23,000 in a number of academic, performance, and leadership areas. All scholarship awards are applicable only toward tuition and are renewable for four years. In all, the College awards more than $32 million in merit and need-based aid to admitted students each year. Students should contact the Office of Admissions to request detailed information about scholarship opportunities.

Faculty

The faculty, 98 percent of whom hold a doctoral degree or terminal degree in their field, are dedicated to meeting the educational needs of individual students; they strive to help them realize their inherent potential. The student-faculty ratio is 11:1.

Student Government

The Campus Council, which consists of representatives from the student body, faculty, and administration, is the main legislative body in the areas of student life and cocurricular affairs. The Student Government Association, the Black Students Association, and the International Student Association also contribute to policymaking at Wooster. Students may attend open meetings of the faculty and are represented on several faculty committees.

Admission Requirements

A candidate for admission to the College should have earned a minimum of 16 academic units in high school, with emphases in English, foreign language, mathematics, natural science, and social studies. The student must present satisfactory scores on either the SAT or the ACT. No College Board Subject Test scores are required.

The deadline for regular admission is February 15. Students are notified of the decision by April 1 and must reply by May 1. Early decision applicants must apply by November 15 and are notified on December 15. Early action candidates must apply by December 15 and are notified by January 15. Students are encouraged to visit the campus and have a personal interview.

The College of Wooster does not discriminate on the basis of age, sex, race, creed, national origin, handicap, sexual orientation, political affiliation, or veteran or military status in the admission of students or in their participation in College educational programs, activities, financial aid, or employment.

Application and Information

Vice President for Enrollment
Office of Admissions
The College of Wooster
Wooster, Ohio 44691

Phone: 330-263-2000 Ext. 2270 or 2322
800-877-9905 (toll-free)
Fax: 330-263-2621
E-mail: admissions@wooster.edu
Web site: http://www.wooster.edu

COLUMBIA UNIVERSITY

Columbia College/The Fu Foundation School of Engineering and Applied Science

NEW YORK, NEW YORK

The University

In 1754, King George II granted a charter to a group of New York citizens to found King's College, dedicated to instruction in "the Learned Languages and the Liberal Arts and Sciences." In its early days, King's College taught such students as Alexander Hamilton, John Jay, Robert Livingston, and Gouverneur Morris. After the Revolution, New York State issued the college a new charter with a more patriotic name—Columbia. In 1897, Columbia moved to a new site in Morningside Heights on the Upper West Side of Manhattan. The architectural firm of McKim, Mead and White, the preeminent architects of their day, designed an open central enclave six blocks long, with a majestic domed and colonnaded library at the center. To this day, it remains one of New York's most impressive settings.

Today, Columbia College and The Fu Foundation School of Engineering and Applied Science (Columbia Engineering) offer their students unique advantages; they are at the same time small, selective colleges and integral components of a major research university.

The College enrolls approximately 4,100 students; the Columbia Engineering student body is roughly 1,400. Students come from all fifty states and over ninety countries. They represent a dazzling array of ethnic, social, economic, cultural, religious, and geographic backgrounds. The diversity of Columbia's student body reflects the diversity of New York City, the world's most international city.

Columbia guarantees four years of on-campus housing to all entering first-year students. Ninety-five percent of undergraduates remain in University residence halls for all four years.

Columbia students take part in extracurricular groups of all kinds: artistic (theater, musical, and dance), athletic (thirty-one Division I varsity sports and dozens of club and intramural sports), communications (the *Columbia Daily Spectator*, the *Columbia Journal of Literary Criticism*, WKCR-FM, a campus television station, and many others), community service (Amnesty International, Big Brother/Big Sister programs, after-hours tutoring programs, a volunteer ambulance squad, and partnerships with dozens of hospitals, soup kitchens, and homeless shelters), and preprofessional (the Charles Drew Pre-Medical Society and the National Society of Black Engineers). Other groups represent students' ethnic, religious, political, and gender identities. There are thirty-three fraternities and sororities. Alfred Lerner Hall houses office and meeting space for student organizations, a theater, a cinema, the Center for Student Advising, and many dining options.

Location

Columbia shares its Morningside Heights neighborhood with a number of other famous institutions: Barnard College, the Cathedral of St. John the Divine, Union Theological Seminary, Jewish Theological Seminary, and the Manhattan School of Music, to name a few. Most of the faculty members from Columbia and the other surrounding schools make their homes in the neighborhood. Morningside Heights is an area known for bookstores, wonderfully varied restaurants, and merchants that cater to student tastes, student budgets, and student hours.

Students are encouraged and assisted in making full use of New York's breathtaking variety of cultural, recreational, and professional resources. Through the Columbia University Arts Initiative, students can receive discounted tickets to Broadway shows, film screenings, art galleries, and a multitude of cultural events in New York City. Passport to NYC offers students free access to thirty museums throughout the city. Columbia students can be found any day of the week exploring the Metropolitan Museum of Art, the Museum of Modern Art, the Guggenheim Museum, the Museum of African Art, the Museo del Barrio, the Asia Society, or any other of the city's hundreds of museums and galleries. Any evening, they might be discovering the theatrical offerings on, off, or "off-off" Broadway (or on campus); attending the opera, ballet, or symphony at Lincoln Center; taking in a movie on campus or in one of New York's 400-plus cinemas; enjoying jazz in Greenwich Village or blues at the Apollo; sampling *pai gwat* in Chinatown; or biking or boating in Central Park. Columbia's internship programs offer students opportunities to explore a career possibility in depth; nowhere else in the world does the concentration of industries allow such a range of possibilities. New York's public transportation system puts the entire city within easy reach of Columbia students; the campus is directly served by a subway line and five bus routes.

Majors and Degrees

Columbia College grants the B.A. degree in approximately ninety programs of study in the humanities, social sciences, and pure sciences, including many interdisciplinary majors. Columbia Engineering grants the B.S. degree in more than fifteen engineering fields. A five-year program that begins in either school allows students to receive both a B.A. from Columbia College and a B.S. from Columbia Engineering.

Joint degree programs offer selected students the opportunity to combine their undergraduate work with study in Columbia University's schools of law and international affairs and with the Juilliard School.

Academic Programs

Columbia has maintained a coherent and relevant curriculum since the time of the First World War, when it introduced the renowned Core Curriculum, a program of general education that has served as a model for hundreds of colleges around the country. One of the two oldest courses in the core is Contemporary Civilization, a year-long historical survey of Western Civilization's religious, political, and moral philosophies; the second is Literature Humanities, a year-long introduction to western culture's most seminal and meaningful literary works. A second year of humanities offers a semester each of music and art appreciation, encouraging students to experience the cultural treasures of New York City. The Global Core requirement enlarges the scope of inquiry beyond the Western focus in order to promote learning and thought about the variety of cultures and the diversity of traditions that interact in the United States and the world today. The Frontiers of Science course outlines the approaches that scientists take to answer interesting problems in the natural world and introduces students to scientific research methods. The Core Curriculum exposes Columbia's multicultural student body to a variety of disciplines, preparing them for the complex questions and issues of modern society.

One hallmark that distinguishes a Columbia Engineering education from that of other prestigious engineering schools is the number of nonengineering courses that every Columbia Engineering undergraduate takes; almost a quarter of a student's program is in the humanities and social sciences and includes components of the Core Curriculum. Alumni often cite this feature of their Columbia Engineering education as the most important reason for success in their careers. All engineering students also take a first-year design class, the country's only hands-on, community-based learning course. Teams of students work with nonprofit organizations and community service agencies to solve real-world engineering design problems. For example, students worked at the Amsterdam Nursing Home to design a non-weight bearing walker for its residents and at Downtown Little League to design a safer dugout.

Off-Campus Programs

Columbia students, with the help of an adviser, may choose from 150 study-abroad programs on every continent, many of which are Columbia-specific programs.

Columbia maintains at Reid Hall, its Paris campus, several undergraduate programs. Courses at Reid Hall are quite varied, permitting students to work not only in the areas of French language, literature, and culture but also in several other fields throughout the range of the humanities and social sciences. In addition, a yearlong program includes course work in the French university system.

Columbia was the first U.S. college to offer an integrated year-abroad program with the Universities of Oxford and Cambridge. Other programs allow students to work at the University of Kyoto in Japan or at the Free University of Berlin in Germany.

Academic Facilities

Columbia has the eighth-largest research library system in North America, consisting of 9.5 million volumes and 26 million manuscripts within 3,000 collections. Included in Columbia's twenty-five libraries are collections of particular significance, including those of the Avery Architectural and Fine Arts Library, the Starr East Asian Library, the Rare Book and Manuscript Library, and the Burke Library of Union Theological Seminary. All divisions are open to Columbia undergraduates. Columbia University Information Technology has five mainframe computers used for academic research and instruction as well as clusters of microcomputers, terminals, and printers; it has remote units and terminals all over campus, including in residence halls, to guarantee accessibility. The chemistry building, Havemeyer Hall, houses modern laboratory facilities for research and undergraduate instruction. Students may also make use of outstanding facilities throughout the University, including an electronic music lab, a cyclotron, an oral history collection, the facilities and programs of the Lamont-Doherty Earth Observatory, and oceanographic research ships. Construction recently began on the new Interdisciplinary Science Building, fourteen stories housing classrooms, research space, a café, and a new science library.

Costs

Tuition for the 2009–10 academic year was $39,296. Room and board for all first-year students were $10,228. With typical fees, books, and supplies, the total cost of a year at Columbia was approximately $54,789.

Financial Aid

All first-year candidates who are U.S., Canadian, or Mexican citizens, or have U.S. permanent resident or political refugee status, are considered for admission without regard to their financial need. International students who do not fit into the above categories should be aware that their admissions process is not need-blind and that their applications are read in a more selective process. Regardless of citizenship, Columbia meets the full demonstrated need of every student admitted as a first-year for all four years of study. Recently, Columbia eliminated loans for all students receiving financial aid and replaced them with University grant money. Parental contributions have also been significantly reduced for a large portion of students receiving financial aid. Financial aid deadlines are November 14 for early decision candidates and March 2 for regular decision candidates. Prospective students should go to http://www.studentaffairs.columbia.edu/finaid/ for information on specific requirements and deadlines. All financial aid at Columbia is based on need; no aid is given in the form of academic, athletic, artistic, or other merit awards. The Office of Financial Aid and Educational Financing believes that cost should not be a barrier to students pursuing their educational dreams.

Faculty

The student-to-faculty ratio is 7:1. Core curriculum classes are capped at 22 students, and over 75 percent of classes have 20 students or less. The Columbia faculty is committed to both teaching and research, and all faculty members teach undergraduates, even the president of the University. All faculty members maintain office hours, and each student receives a faculty adviser from the department that he or she chooses as a major.

Student Government

Each undergraduate division has its own student council and elects representatives to the Columbia University Senate.

Admission Requirements

The Columbia first-year class of 1,341 students is selected from a much larger pool of applicants through a holistic, committee-based review process. Candidates for admission are expected to demonstrate the necessary ability and interest to do successful college work in a variety of disciplines as required for the Columbia degree. The following secondary school preparation is recommended: 4 years of English, including meaningful work in literature and writing; 3 (preferably 4) years of mathematics, including precalculus and calculus where offered; 3 (preferably 4) years of history and social studies; 3 or more years of the same foreign language; and 3 (preferably 4) years of laboratory science (including chemistry and physics where available). The Admissions Committee recognizes that secondary schools vary in offerings and standards; consideration is given to applicants whose preparations differ from the recommended course of study but have taken advantage of what their schools offer.

Standardized tests are required for admission, according to the following guidelines. Students may take the SAT, which consists of three sections, each graded on an 800-point scale. Students who take the test more than once are evaluated on the highest score they receive in any individual section. Applicants may alternately take the ACT, which is graded on a 36-point scale. Students taking the test more than once are evaluated on the highest composite score they receive. The writing component of the ACT is mandatory for candidates for Columbia.

In addition to either the SAT or ACT, students must also take two SAT Subject Tests. For Columbia College, they may take any two tests; for The Fu Foundation School of Engineering and Applied Science, they must take any mathematics test and either the physics or the chemistry test.

Students who attend a school that does not give conventional grades or who are homeschooled must take two additional SAT Subject Tests in addition to all requirements outlined above for Columbia College or The Fu Foundation School of Engineering and Applied Science.

It is absolutely imperative that applicants have the testing service report their standardized test scores directly to either Columbia College (SAT code 2116, ACT code 2717) or The Fu Foundation School of Engineering and Applied Science (SAT code 2111, ACT code 2719), as appropriate.

Transfer students may enter Columbia in September only.

The College has a Visiting Students Program, which allows students to attend for one or both semesters of their sophomore, junior, or senior year.

Application and Information

The postmark deadline for applications is the first business day after January 1. Candidates are notified of the Admissions Committee's decisions on or about April 1. Admitted candidates must respond to Columbia's offer of admission by May 1. Candidates for whom Columbia is their definite first choice may apply under the early decision plan; the deadline is November 1 for all application material, and a decision is rendered by December 15. Candidates admitted to Columbia under early decision are required to withdraw their applications to other colleges. The application fee is $70. The fee may be waived if a school official testifies that the fee would cause the candidate's family financial hardship. The application materials are available online. For further information or for applications, interested students should contact:

Office of Undergraduate Admissions
Columbia University
1130 Amsterdam Avenue, MC2807
New York, New York 10027

Phone: 212-854-2522
Fax: 212-854-1209
E-mail: ugrad-ask@columbia.edu
Web site: http://www.studentaffairs.columbia.edu/admissions

COLUMBIA UNIVERSITY, SCHOOL OF GENERAL STUDIES

NEW YORK, NEW YORK

The University and The School

The School of General Studies (GS) of Columbia University is one of the finest liberal arts colleges in the United States created specifically for returning and nontraditional students seeking a rigorous, traditional, Ivy League undergraduate degree full- or part-time. Most students at GS have, for personal or professional reasons, interrupted their education, never attended college, or are only able to attend part-time. GS is unique among colleges of its type, because its students are fully integrated into the Columbia undergraduate curriculum: they take the same courses with the same faculty members and earn the same degree as all other Columbia undergraduates.

GS students come from varied backgrounds and all walks of life. Many students work full-time while pursuing a degree, and many have family responsibilities; others attend classes full-time and experience Columbia's more traditional college life. In the classroom, the diversity and varied personal experience of the student body promote discussion and debate, fostering an environment of academic rigor and intellectual development. GS has approximately 1,300 undergraduate degree candidates and more than 400 postbaccalaureate premedical students. The average age of a GS student is 29. More than 60 percent of GS students attend classes full-time.

In addition to its bachelor's degree program, GS offers combined undergraduate/graduate degree programs with Columbia's Schools of Social Work, International and Public Affairs, Law, Business, Dental Medicine, Teachers College, and the College of Physicians and Surgeons. More than 70 percent of the students go on to earn advanced degrees after graduation.

GS is home to the oldest and largest postbaccalaureate premedical program in the United States. In the past, the acceptance rate for GS postbaccalaureate premedical program students applying to U.S. medical schools is up to and above 90 percent.

Location

Columbia University is located in Morningside Heights, on the Upper West Side of Manhattan. The University's neighbors include the Union Theological Seminary, the Jewish Theological Seminary, the Manhattan School of Music, St. Luke's Hospital, Riverside Church, and the Cathedral of St. John the Divine. The diversity of intellectual and social activities offered by these institutions is one of Columbia's great assets as a university; another is New York City itself, which offers Columbia students a rich and almost boundless variety of social, cultural, and recreational opportunities that are themselves an education.

Majors and Degrees

The School of General Studies grants the B.A. and B.S. degrees and offers the following majors: African studies; African American studies; American studies; ancient studies; anthropology; applied mathematics; archaeology; architecture; architecture, history and theory; art history; art history–visual arts; Asian American studies; astronomy; astrophysics; biochemistry; biology; biophysics; chemistry; classical studies; classics; comparative ethnic studies; comparative literature and society; computer science; computer science–mathematics; creative writing; dance; drama and theater arts; earth science; East Asian studies; East Central European studies; economics; economics–mathematics; economics–operations research; economics–philosophy; economics–political science; economics–statistics; English and comparative literature; environmental biology; environmental science; evolutionary biology of the human species; film studies; French; French and Francophone studies; German literature and cultural history; Hispanic studies; history; information science, Italian cultural studies; Italian literature; Latin American and Caribbean studies; Latino studies; mathematics; mathematics–statistics; Middle East and Asian languages and cultures; music; neuroscience and behavior; philosophy; physics; political science; political science-statistics; psychology; regional studies; religion; Russian language and culture; Russian literature and culture; Slavic studies; sociology; statistics; urban studies; visual arts; women's and gender studies; and Yiddish studies. Individually designed majors are also available. In addition, the School offers two undergraduate dual-degree programs: one in conjunction with Columbia's School of Engineering and Applied Science and the other in conjunction with the Jewish Theological Seminary.

Academic Programs

The School of General Studies offers a traditional liberal arts education designed to provide students with the broad knowledge and intellectual skills that foster continued education and growth in the years after college as well as providing a sound foundation for positions of responsibility in the professional world.

Requirements for the bachelor's degree comprise three elements: (1) core requirements, intended to develop in students the ability to write and communicate clearly; to understand the modes of thought that characterize the humanities, social sciences, and sciences; to gain familiarity with central cultural ideas through literature, fine arts, and music; and to acquire a working proficiency in a foreign language; (2) major requirements, designed to give students sustained and coherent exposure to a particular discipline in an area of strong intellectual interest; and (3) elective courses, in which students pursue particular interests and skills for their own personal growth or for their relationship to future professional or personal objectives. Students are required to complete a minimum of 124 credits for the bachelor's degree; 60 of these may be in transfer credit, but at least 64 credits (including the last 30 credits) must be completed at Columbia. In addition to the usual graduation honors (cum laude, magna cum laude, and summa cum laude), honors programs for superior students are available in a majority of the University's departments.

Off-Campus Programs

Columbia students may enhance their academic experiences through various study-abroad programs around the world. For example, students may spend a term at the Reid Hall Program in the Montparnasse district of Paris, the Berlin Consortium for German Studies, the Kyoto Consortium for Japanese Studies, or the Language Program in Beijing, China. In addition, students may apply to participate in one of the Columbia-approved study-abroad programs located in countries around the world.

Academic Facilities

The Columbia University libraries constitute the nation's sixth-largest academic library system, with a collection of more than 9.5 million volumes, more than 5 million microform pieces, 26 million manuscript items, and 600,000 rare books. Of the twenty-two libraries in the system, five are designated Distinctive Collections because of their unusual depth and nationally recognized excellence. All library divisions are available to GS students. The University's Computer Center is one of the largest and most powerful university installations in the world and has remote units and terminals in several parts of the campus to enhance its accessibility. The Fairchild Life Sciences Building houses research facilities, laboratories, electron microscopes, and a vast amount of biochemical equipment used for teaching and research. The University's physics building has been the scene of many important developments in the recent history of physics, including the invention of the laser and the first U.S. demonstration of nuclear fission.

Costs

For the 2009–10 academic year, tuition is $1270 per credit, monthly living expenses (including rent) were about $1600, fees were approximately $1800, and books were $1000 to $1300.

Financial Aid

The School of General Studies awards financial aid based upon need and academic ability. Approximately 70 percent of GS degree candidates receive some form of financial aid, including Federal Pell Grants, New York State TAP Grants, Federal Stafford and unsubsidized Stafford Loans, Federal Perkins Loans, General Studies Scholarships, and Federal Work-Study Program awards. Priority application deadlines for new students are June 1 for the fall semester and October 15 for the spring semester. The average scholarship award ranges from $6000 to $8000 for first-year students.

Faculty

The faculty of the School of General Studies, which is shared with Columbia College, the Graduate School of Arts and Sciences, and the School of International and Public Affairs, includes distinguished scholars in virtually every discipline. Of the School's more than 1,000 faculty members, over 99 percent hold a Ph.D. Students, whether full-time or part-time, have many opportunities to work closely with faculty members, both in small classes and in research projects. Faculty members also serve as advisers to students majoring in their area of study and maintain regular office hours to see students.

Student Government

One student of the School represents GS students in the University Senate, a decision-making body comprising students, faculty members, and administrative staff members from each division of the University. In addition, 2 GS students sit as voting members on the Committee on Instruction, which oversees the curriculum of the School. The General Studies Student Council elects officers each year and sponsors activities for students. *The Observer,* the School's student-run magazine, is published several times each year. The Premedical Association (PMA) sponsors events related to the medical school admissions process.

Admission Requirements

The GS admission policy is geared to the maturity and varied backgrounds of its students. Aptitude and motivation are considered along with past academic performance, standardized test scores, and employment history. The School's admission decisions are based on a careful review of each application and reflect the Admissions Committee's considered judgment of the applicant's maturity, academic potential, and present ability to undertake course work at Columbia.

Admission requirements include a completed application form; a 1,500- to 2,000-word autobiographical statement describing the applicant's past educational history and work experience, present situation, and future plans; two letters of recommendation from academic or professional evaluators; an official high school transcript; official transcripts from all colleges and universities attended; official SAT or ACT scores (applicants may take the General Studies Admissions Examination); and a nonrefundable application fee of $65.

Students from outside the United States may apply to the School of General Studies to start or complete a baccalaureate degree. In addition to the materials described above, international applicants must submit official TOEFL scores.

Application and Information

Application deadlines are March 1 for early action (nonbinding), and June 1 for the fall semester, October 1 for early action (nonbinding), and November 1 for the spring semester, and April 1 for the summer semester. Applicants from countries outside the U.S. are urged to apply by August 15 for the spring semester and April 1 for the fall semester. Applications are reviewed as they are completed, and applicants are notified of decisions shortly thereafter.

For more information, students should contact:

Curtis M. Rodgers, Dean of Enrollment Management
Office of Admissions and Financial Aid
School of General Studies
408 Lewisohn Hall
2970 Broadway
Columbia University, Mail Code 4101
New York, New York 10027
Phone: 212-854-2772
E-mail: gsdegree@columbia.edu
Web site: http://www.gs.columbia.edu

The Low Memorial Library/Visitors Center.

THE CULINARY INSTITUTE OF AMERICA

HYDE PARK, NEW YORK

COLLEGE CLOSE-UPS

The Institute

The Culinary Institute of America (CIA) is a private, not-for-profit college dedicated to providing the world's best undergraduate education in culinary arts and baking and pastry arts. Guided by its core values of excellence, leadership, professionalism, ethics, and respect for diversity, the CIA strives to foster an atmosphere where students can develop both professionally and personally. At the CIA, aspiring culinarians gain the general knowledge and specific skills they need to grow into positions of leadership in the foodservice and hospitality industry, the largest private employer in the United States.

Founded in 1946, The Culinary Institute of America today enrolls more than 2,800 students from virtually every state and thirty countries around the world, all united by their shared passion for food. The CIA student body has a balance of recent high school graduates and adults returning to higher education.

As the world's premier culinary college, the CIA is renowned for its degree programs, extraordinary faculty, and outstanding educational facilities. All CIA degree programs emphasize professional, hands-on learning in the college's kitchens, bakeshops, and restaurants. CIA classes span the culinary globe, exploring great cultures, cooking techniques, and cuisines to prepare students for the diversity and creativity of the foodservice industry. Classes are taken in a progressive sequence optimized to build skills, food knowledge, and production experience. These studies culminate in operating courses that give students both kitchen and front-of-the-house experiences in the college's famous restaurants. Bachelor's degree students also focus on foodservice management development, with a broad range of business management and liberal arts courses.

CIA students enjoy an active campus life, with a variety of year-round fitness programs, intramural and club sports, student clubs, and extracurricular activities such as ski and camping trips, on-campus live entertainment events, presentations by leading chefs and industry executives, and cook-offs. The college's Student Recreation Center includes a six-lane pool, a gymnasium, racquetball courts, an aerobics studio, a fitness center and free-weight room, a game room, outdoor tennis courts, and the Courtside Café and Pub. Four coed residence halls and six Adirondack-style lodges house approximately 1,700 students on campus. The college's dining plan provides students with two meals per instructional day.

The Culinary Institute of America is accredited by the Middle States Commission on Higher Education, 3624 Market Street, Philadelphia, Pennsylvania 19104 (telephone: 215-662-5000). The Middle States Commission on Higher Education is an institutional accrediting agency recognized by the U.S. Secretary of Education and the Council for Higher Education Accreditation.

The CIA is also accredited by the Accrediting Commission of Career Schools and Colleges (ACCSC). The certificate of accreditation is available for viewing on the wall of the President's Wing on the second floor of Roth Hall at the college's Hyde Park, New York, campus. Supporting documentation can be reviewed in the office of the Associate Vice President of Planning, Research, and Accreditation, located on the third floor of Roth Hall. Information related to tuition charges, fees, and length of comparable programs at other institutions may be obtained from the ACCSC at 2101 Wilson Boulevard, Suite 302, Arlington, Virginia 22201 (telephone: 703-247-4212).

Location

The CIA's scenic 170-acre campus is set along the east bank of the Hudson River in Hyde Park, New York, conveniently located 1½–2 hours from New York City and Albany.

The Mid-Hudson region's attractions and recreational opportunities offer something for everyone in both rural and urban settings. There are a number of state parks and historic sites throughout the area. Students can taste wines at local vineyards, visit farmer's markets, and pick apples at nearby orchards. To the west lie the Catskill and Shawangunk Mountains, with many opportunities for hiking, skiing, rock climbing, mountain biking, and sightseeing. Concerts, plays, films, and other cultural and special events are offered regularly at the many colleges, theaters, and community facilities throughout the Hudson Valley and Catskill regions. In addition, students can take advantage of the campus's proximity to New York City to experience the culture, arts, and nightlife of this exciting city and food mecca.

Majors and Degrees

The Culinary Institute of America awards the degree of Bachelor of Professional Studies (B.P.S.) in baking and pastry arts management and in culinary arts management, as well as the degree of Associate in Occupational Studies (A.O.S.) in baking and pastry arts and in culinary arts.

Academic Programs

At the core of The Culinary Institute of America's curriculum lies more than 1,300 hours of hands-on instruction in its kitchens and bakeshops as well as classes developing the managerial skills and creative thinking that today's culinary professional requires. Students learn about foods, cooking and baking techniques, cuisines, and business fundamentals while advancing through skills and production kitchens. They also gain invaluable experience in a paid externship program and by cooking and serving in the college's bakery café or in some of the four fine-dining public restaurants on campus. Bachelor's degree students also take courses in marketing, communications, psychology, foreign languages and cultures, accounting and the use of computers in the food business, and financial and human resources management.

Students must earn 132 total credits in culinary arts management or in baking and pastry arts management to graduate with a bachelor's degree. Students must earn 69 total credits in culinary arts or in baking and pastry arts to graduate with an associate degree.

Off-Campus Programs

All students work in externships for a minimum of eighteen weeks (600 hours). These externships provide students with valuable on-the-job experience at one of more than 1,200 top foodservice and hospitality properties—such as hotels, restaurants, and resorts—around the world. B.P.S. students also participate in a travel seminar to one of a number of exciting destination choices—Northern and Southern California, Spain, Italy, and China—where they can learn from local purveyors and visit area restaurants, wineries, and vineyards.

Academic Facilities

CIA students learn the fundamentals of the culinary and baking and pastry arts in the college's forty-one professionally equipped production kitchens and bakeshops and five student-staffed public restaurants on campus—the American Bounty Restaurant,

Escoffier Restaurant, Ristorante Caterina de' Medici, St. Andrew's Café, and Apple Pie Bakery Café. Classes are centered in the college's main building, Roth Hall, as well as in the Shunsuke Takaki School of Baking and Pastry, General Foods Nutrition Center, and Colavita Center for Italian Food and Wine. The CIA regularly hosts world-renowned chefs for lectures, cooking demonstrations, and discussions with students in its Danny Kaye Theatre, Anheuser-Busch Theatre, and Ecolab Theatre. Other valuable academic resources include the 84,000-volume Conrad N. Hilton Library, which contains the largest culinary collection of any culinary school; audiovisual programs to supplement course work; computer labs and workstations; and a wireless network that allows students to access online resources from almost anywhere on campus.

Costs

Freshman tuition for academic year 2010–11 is $24,360. Board is $1260 per semester, which includes two meals per instructional day. Housing costs range from $2000 to $3635 per semester, depending on the room to which the student is assigned.

Additional required fees for the freshman year include a confirmation fee of $100, equipment fees of $1680 for culinary supplies or $1580 for baking and pastry supplies, and a general fee of $550 per semester, which includes student activity and exam fees, as well as secondary student accident insurance. The CIA offers students a tuition installment plan. Details are available from the college's Bursar's Office.

Financial Aid

Approximately 90 percent of the CIA's students receive financial aid in the form of scholarships, grants, loans, and work-study. Federal programs offered at the college include the Federal Pell Grant, Federal Supplemental Educational Opportunity Grant (FSEOG), Academic Competitiveness Grant, Federal Subsidized Stafford Loan, Federal Unsubsidized Stafford Loan, Federal Perkins Loan, Federal Work-Study Program (which provides a variety of on-campus and community service jobs to eligible students), Federal PLUS, and veterans' benefits. Students should also investigate their own state's programs and apply if those grants or scholarships can be used in New York State.

Students who have applied for admission or who are currently enrolled at the CIA may apply for scholarships offered by various organizations in the foodservice industry. A list of these scholarships, which are administered by the college, is available from the Financial Aid Office.

Faculty

The college's faculty is composed of more than 140 chefs and instructors from sixteen countries whose credentials and industry experience are unmatched in culinary education. The 18:1 student-faculty ratio in hands-on classes provides student support and mentoring, while giving students the opportunity to work in an environment closely representative of the foodservice industry.

Student Government

All students in good standing are members of the Student Government Association (SGA). The association's Executive Board acts as a liaison between students and the administration. The SGA helps support student activities and funds all student clubs and committees.

Admission Requirements

The Admissions Committee seeks candidates who have demonstrated a commitment to a culinary career and who have the personal initiative, confidence, and motivation to succeed. The basic requirements are successful completion of a secondary school education or its equivalent and some experience in the foodservice and hospitality industry. The applicant's educational record is evaluated on the basis of overall performance and the type of program taken. Academics and leadership ability are key requirements for the B.P.S. programs. SATs or ACTs are strongly recommended but not required.

Preference is given to candidates who have worked in foodservice, particularly in a kitchen that offers a varied menu. Before entering the program, students should have had about six months of hands-on food preparation in a kitchen in which at least 50 percent of the food is made on the premises.

Applicants must submit a formal application for admission, a nonrefundable $50 application fee, an official secondary school transcript (not a student copy), an essay of between 400 and 500 words, and an official college transcript, if applicable. Students applying directly from high school may include an optional secondary school report. In addition, A.O.S. candidates must provide one recommendation, and B.P.S. applicants must provide two. Bachelor's degree candidates must also participate in an on-campus or telephone interview.

Application and Information

Students may apply for admission to the CIA year-round, as the college offers multiple enrollment seasons from which to choose. Applicants should submit their materials according to the enrollment schedule (available at the Web site listed below) that corresponds to the season they are interested in beginning the degree program. Students are notified of an admission decision according to that schedule. For information, to schedule a tour, or to participate in an Open House program, students should contact:

Admissions Office
The Culinary Institute of America
1946 Campus Drive
Hyde Park, New York 12538-1499
Phone: 800-CULINARY (toll-free)
E-mail: admissions@culinary.edu
Web site: http://www.ciachef.edu

Set along the banks of the Hudson River, The Culinary Institute of America campus lies on 170 scenic acres in historic Hyde Park, New York.

CURRY COLLEGE

MILTON, MASSACHUSETTS

The College

The mission of Curry College, a private institution, is to develop liberally educated persons who are able to gain and to apply knowledge humanely, intelligently, and effectively in a complex, changing world. To achieve its mission, Curry College promotes individual intellectual and social growth by engaging its students in achieving these educational goals: thinking critically, communicating effectively, understanding context, appreciating aesthetic experience, defining a personal identity, examining value systems, and adapting and innovating. The College's curriculum and programs focus on the two hallmarks of the Curry education: a high respect for the individuality of every student and a developmental approach to learning that maximizes opportunities for achievement. One-on-one faculty-student relationships provide many opportunities for personalized instruction and close interaction. Full student counseling and other support services are provided.

The current undergraduate enrollment is 2,000 men and women. Curry students have access to a wide range of cocurricular activities, including the Student Government Association, the student-run newspaper, the yearbook, the *Curry Arts Journal*, several organizations for the performing arts, and the award-winning, student-run radio station. The Office of Student Activities and the Campus Activities Board provide a variety of special events. A full schedule of men's and women's Division III and intramural sports is also provided. Varsity sports for men are baseball, basketball, football, ice hockey, lacrosse, soccer, and tennis; women's varsity sports are basketball, cross-country, lacrosse, soccer, softball, and tennis.

Now well into its second century of providing distinguished educational service, Curry College was founded in Boston in 1879. It was named in honor of its founders, Samuel Silas Curry and Anna Barright Curry. The College moved to its present site in Milton in 1952. In 1974, it absorbed the Perry Normal School, and, in 1977, it entered into a collaborative relationship with Children's Hospital Medical Center, which resulted in the establishment of Curry's Division of Nursing Studies. Curry College is accredited by the New England Association of Schools and Colleges; the nursing program is accredited by the National League for Nursing Accrediting Commission. Curry also offers four masters degree programs, which include a Master of Education (M.Ed.), an M.A. in criminal justice, an M.S. in nursing and a Master of Business Administration (M.B.A.).

Location

Curry is ideally situated in Milton, Massachusetts, a largely residential suburb located near the exceptional resources of Boston. The greater Boston area provides students with a diversity of cultural, educational, recreational, and sports activities. A wide variety of corporations, hospitals, agencies, broadcasting stations, and schools provide excellent internship and job opportunities for Curry students. The College operates a shuttle bus to the MBTA trains, which provide easy access to Boston. Curry students have the benefit of a traditional, wooded New England campus and access to the excitement of a large city.

Majors and Degrees

Curry College awards the following Bachelor of Arts (B.A.) degrees : biology; child, youth, and community education; communication (with concentrations in corporate communication, film studies, journalism, public communication, public relations, radio broadcasting, relational communication, television/digital video, and theater); criminal justice; early childhood education; elementary education; English (with concentrations in American studies, creative writing, literary genre and movements, traditional literary heritage, journalism, professional writing, and women in literature); environmental science; graphic design; information technology; management (with concentrations in accounting, entrepreneurship, finance, human resources, marketing, residential property management, and sports management); philosophy; politics and history; psychology (with a concentrations in counseling, developmental psychology, gerontology, health, and substance-abuse counseling); sociology (with concentrations in ethnic and gender studies and service in the community); special education; and visual arts (with a concentration in studio arts). Curry College awards the following Bachelor of Science (B.S.) degrees: health and nursing. Special minors are available in numerous areas, including applied computing, dance, music, religion, Spanish, Web development, women's studies, and writing to name a few. Provision is also made for students to design majors in areas in which they have a special interest.

Academic Programs

A central liberal arts curriculum, which is required for all students, incorporates a variety of academic disciplines into every student's plan of study. Curry's programs also integrate theoretical classroom learning with a wide variety of field internships in the greater Boston area.

Curry College operates on a two-semester calendar with a summer session. To graduate, students must complete at least 120 credit hours for a B.A. degree or B.S. degree. In both cases, a minimum 2.0 cumulative average must be achieved.

Curry allows students to gain advanced standing in a variety of ways: through successful scores on College-Level Examination Program (CLEP) tests, through credit earned at other accredited colleges and universities, and through end-of-course proficiency examinations. Credit may also be granted for experiential education, such as internships, that have occurred outside the traditional academic environment.

Many academic programs enrich and facilitate the Curry education. The First Year Seminar, the Honors Program, the Women's Studies Program, the Essential Skills Center, and the Field Experience Program are representative of that focus on special interests and diverse learning needs.

The Program for Advancement of Learning (PAL) is a credited program designed to help intelligent, motivated, language-based learning-disabled students to achieve at the college level. PAL provides individual or small-group instruction, textbooks on tape, and untimed examinations, as well as a variety of other applied technologies. Students must apply to the PAL program in order to take advantage of PAL's services. Students receive credit for enrollment in the program for the first year and are able to continue in the program as long as needed.

Off-Campus Programs

Curry students may earn up to 30 credit hours for field internships with outside firms, agencies, radio stations, hospitals, schools, or similar organizations. In consultation with faculty members, students develop learning contracts that articulate their educational and personal goals and establish criteria for the evaluation of their field experience. Students may also arrange to study abroad or at another institution within the United States while enrolled at Curry.

Academic Facilities

The Levin Memorial Library houses more than 110,000 volumes, 650 periodicals, and 10,000 microforms. It is a designated depository for U.S. government documents. The library also houses the Essential Skills Center, where students may secure assistance in reading, writing, mathematics, and the development of study skills. Three computer laboratories contain more than 100 Macintosh and IBM computers, laser printers, color printers, and state-of-the-art optical scanning equipment. The entire campus is networked and linked to the Internet. The library is also home to the Educational Technology Center, which is a host of resources and materials for all of the Education students.

The Science Building includes five laboratories while the Kennedy Academic Center houses a simulated hospital room for use as a nursing laboratory; the Nursing Resource Center, which is equipped with an interactive video lab; and a laboratory for experimental psychology equipped with biofeedback, computer control, and animal and human learning facilities. The Learning Center, with its own computer lab, maintains a complete tape library of all textbooks used at the College. The Hafer Academic Center houses the Experiential Education Office; the Career Planning and Placement Office; the Academic Advising Office; the Hirsh Communication Center, which features a state-of-the-art television studio; and the Parent's Lounge, which hosts student art exhibits. In addition, Curry students operate and maintain WMLN-FM, the College's 172-watt radio station.

The Academic and Performance Center is a three-story, 30,000-square-foot facility that features a 250-seat multipurpose auditorium, state-of-the-art classrooms equipped with wireless laptop connectivity and Smart Board technology, breakout conference rooms, a stock-trading classroom, and a café-style food court in the main atrium.

In the fall of 2009, Curry College opened a new student center. The 84,000-square-foot facility is full of state-of-the-art areas for dining, studying, athletics, student activities, or simply lounging around. The student center has become a place to study between classes, to meet up with friends for dinner, work out, or even take on your roommate in a game of billiards or foosball.

Costs

Tuition for the 2009–10 academic year was $28,000. Room and board were $11,110 (based on a fourteen-meal plan). The cost of the Program for Advancement of Learning (PAL) was $5700. The cost of books, supplies, and personal expenses varies from $900 to $1200.

Financial Aid

Curry provides financial assistance for students who need funding in order to attend college. The financial aid program consists of federal, state, and Curry College scholarships, grants, work-study awards, student assistant jobs, and loans. Approximately 70 percent of the student body receives financial aid. All students applying for financial aid must submit the Free Application for Federal Student Aid (FAFSA) by March 1. Students applying for financial aid should contact the financial aid office.

Faculty

There are 113 full-time faculty members at Curry, about half of whom hold earned doctoral degrees. In addition, each year the College hires highly qualified part-time faculty members and visiting lecturers to augment its teaching staff. Although primarily a teaching faculty, many of Curry's faculty members are engaged in writing, research, and consulting.

Student Government

The general purpose of the Student Government Association (SGA) is the advancement of the College community and the promotion of the general welfare of the students. The SGA seeks to increase student involvement in the formulation of College policies, communicate effectively with all constituencies of the College, and promote student participation within the institution. Members of the SGA serve on the Joint Committee on Communication of the Board of Trustees.

Admission Requirements

Curry College accepts all students who have the necessary preparation and educational background to meet the requirements of the College, regardless of race, religion, national or ethnic origin, age, sex, sexual orientation, or physical handicap. Freshman students are selected on the basis of a combination of the following: secondary school record, scores on the SAT or ACT, recommendation of the secondary school, and the candidate's readiness for college. To be considered for admission, students must generally present at least 16 units of high school work, preferably at the college preparatory level, from an approved secondary school. A recommended program of studies includes: 4 years of English, at least 3 years of mathematics, 2 years of a foreign language, 2 years of science (including at least 1 of a laboratory science), and 2 years of social studies. Applicants should contact the Admission Office to discuss any possible exceptions to these requirements. A GED certificate is acceptable in lieu of a high school diploma. Curry College seeks well-rounded students who can contribute to the Curry community in athletic, artistic, and social endeavors as well as in the academic sphere.

Application and Information

Curry's recommended application deadline is April 1; however, Curry operates on a rolling admission basis. Admission options, such as early decision, deferred entrance, and advanced placement, are also available. Students may apply for September or January entrance. Applicants for the nursing program may only apply for the fall semester. Applicants must submit an application and fee, an official high school transcript, scores from the SAT or ACT, and a counselor's recommendation. In addition, transfer students must submit official college transcripts, along with a College Official's Report form. If English is not the primary language of the applicant, then results of the Test of English as a Foreign Language (TOEFL) must be submitted. An interview is optional but not required. The Admission Committee evaluates each application as soon as all required credentials are received, beginning in January.

Applicants to the Program for Advancement of Learning (PAL) must submit a completed application by March 1. In addition to the criteria listed above, PAL applicants must submit the results of a recently administered Wechsler Adult Intelligence Scale (WAIS-R) test. Achievement testing in reading comprehension, written language, and math must also be submitted. The SAT or ACT requirement is waived for PAL applicants. Final decisions on admission to the program are made once all credentials are complete.

For more information about Curry College, students should contact:

Jane Patricia Fidler
Dean of Admission
Curry College
Milton, Massachusetts 02186
Phone: 617-333-2210
800-669-0686 (toll-free)
Fax: 617-333-2114
E-mail: curryadm@curry.edu
Web site: http://www.curry.edu

The suburban campus of Curry College is only minutes from the city of Boston.

DAEMEN COLLEGE

AMHERST, NEW YORK

The College

Daemen College is a private, career-oriented liberal arts college serving approximately 2,500 students in Amherst, New York.

The mission of Daemen College is to prepare students for life and leadership in an increasingly complex world. Founded on the principle that education should elevate human dignity and foster civic responsibility and compassion, the College seeks to integrate the intellectual qualities acquired through study of the liberal arts with the education necessary for professional accomplishment. This integration, which recognizes equal value in liberal studies and professional programs, aims at preparing graduates who are dedicated to the health and well-being of both their local and global communities.

With a Daemen education, students acquire the skills to solve problems creatively and think critically. They are comfortable with diversity and recognize the importance of a global perspective. They are able to work with others and be invigorated by environments that present challenges and demand innovation. Daemen students are expected to be active participants in their own education and informed citizens who understand that learning is a lifelong journey.

At the heart of Daemen's integrated learning experience is the relationship that can develop between the College's faculty members and its students. Daemen prides itself on maintaining a student-centered atmosphere and a close professional and collaborative association among all members of the College community. Assisted by a supportive faculty, Daemen students are encouraged to pursue goals beyond their initial expectations, to respond to academic challenges, and to develop habits of mind that enrich their lives and their community.

Modern apartment-style residence halls provide separate housing for men and women, in addition to the existing five-story residence hall for freshmen. All residence halls have kitchens, laundry facilities, lounges, and in-room phone/Internet connections. Breakfast, lunch, and dinner are served on weekdays in the Wick Student Center. Brunch and dinner are served on Saturdays and Sundays. Adequate parking is available.

Over fifty student organizations, themed dinners, movie nights, musical theater, internationally famous speakers, and more contribute to a dynamic campus life.

Location

Daemen's suburban 39-acre campus is located in Amherst, New York. Daemen is just minutes away from the city of Buffalo, renowned for the arts, offering exceptional theater, music, art, restaurants, and major league sports. The city is very close to scenic Niagara Falls and Canada. The campus is easily accessible by the major rail, plane, and motor routes that serve Buffalo.

Majors and Degrees

Daemen's Division of Arts and Sciences is designed to provide broad exposure to multiple disciplines that aid students in developing the intellectual and civic competencies that prepare them for life in an increasingly complex society. The career possibilities are nearly endless, as many graduates have gone on to successful leadership in corporations, human service agencies, government, the arts, educational organizations, religious institutions, environmental organizations, medicine, law, veterinary medicine, and research-related fields. Preparation for advanced health-related careers is a strength of the natural science department at Daemen College. The faculty is committed to each student's success, and the College has considerable expertise in teaching the basic sciences that are prerequisites for medical studies.

Daemen's Division of Health and Human Services is designed to provide students with the unique opportunity to work with and learn from both scholars and practitioners—an experience that is critical to understanding the relationship between academic course work and practical application. Experienced and dedicated faculty members provide students with a balanced education through innovative and contemporary courses, exceptional professional internships, field placements, clinical experiences, and pioneering research opportunities. Daemen is dedicated to providing a broad-based education to prepare individuals for the demands of professional and scholarly roles in the health and human services fields. Daemen's liberal arts core and professional curricula ensure that its students integrate liberal studies with their professional education to prepare them for life and leadership.

Majors at Daemen include: accounting; art, with an emphasis in applied design/printmaking, drawing/illustration, graphic design, painting/sculpture, or visual arts education K–12; athletic training (B.S./M.S.); biology, with an emphasis available in biochemistry, adolescence education 7–12, or environmental studies; biochemistry, with several preprofessional programs available; business administration, with an emphasis available in human resource management, international business, management information systems, marketing, or sports management; education, with an emphasis in childhood education 1–6, childhood education/special education 1–6, or early childhood education/special education B–2; English, with an emphasis available in adolescence education 7–12 or communication/public relations; French, with an emphasis available in adolescence education 7–12; health care studies, with an emphasis available in community health, health and fitness training, or complementary and alternative health care practices; history and government, with an emphasis available in adolescence education 7–12; mathematics, with an emphasis available in adolescence education 7–12; natural sciences, with an emphasis available in environmental studies, forensic science, or health science; nursing; political science; physical therapy (B.S./D.P.T.); physician assistant (B.S./M.S.); psychology, with an emphasis available in human services; religious studies; social work; and Spanish, with an emphasis available in adolescence education 7–12. Preprofessional programs are available in pre-dentistry, prelaw, premedicine, and preveterinary.

Academic Programs

Daemen's competency-based core curriculum (sometimes referred to as general education requirements) places the College among the national leaders in innovation and creativity. The core is comprised of 45 hours or fifteen courses that help students master the seven core competencies. The core relies on several innovative features, including linked course work taught within the framework of learning communities, a progressive composition program, interdisciplinary courses that break down barriers among majors, and opportunities for extended research and public presentation.

Daemen offers some of its core curriculum courses in a format known as Learning Communities. This format allows students to move through the core curriculum in smaller groups made up of students from different backgrounds with differing majors and extracurricular interests. In a learning community, a common topic, issue, or subject is studied from the perspective of two or more majors, making for a higher level of critical thinking. Such thinking is necessary for solving problems—be they in a student's professional life or in the nation and the world.

The Student/Faculty Interdisciplinary Think Tank offers students the opportunity to work with a faculty member on a significant research project. Students receive research scholarships and acknowledgement of their work through publications, showings, presentations, or other forms of public recognition.

Daemen has a close professional and collaborative association among all members of the College's community while maintaining a student-centered atmosphere. Assisted by a supportive faculty, Daemen students are encouraged to pursue goals beyond their initial expectations, to respond to academic challenges, and to develop habits of mind that enrich their lives and their community.

The Honors Program at Daemen College provides many opportunities and challenges for outstanding undergraduate students. Students can enhance their learning experience by designing an individual Honors Tutorial or Honors Contract, participating in an interdisciplinary Honors

Colloquium, and sharing their talents with the Daemen community. Honors students have their own organization to direct and oversee student activities on campus.

Off-Campus Programs

Alongside the outstanding and innovative courses that provide the academic foundation at Daemen, there are many other opportunities to enhance a student's education, such as international programs, service learning, and internships.

Daemen's Office of Global Programs operates and coordinates distinctive international programs designed to facilitate students' professional aspirations. In today's global economy, it is vital that students learn about different cultures, political systems, and histories. International study is a staple of the Daemen experience and the College offers semesters abroad, summer programs, and accelerated January term trips.

Daemen believes strongly in learning through service. During their time at Daemen, virtually all undergraduate students engage in various service learning activities. Students from every major and class level participate as individuals or groups in short- and long-term projects or assignments that benefit the local, national, or global communities. Daemen students work with environmental organizations; assist refugee groups; build environmental agencies; help with programs to benefit the needy; serve residents of nursing homes, hospitals, and clinics; tutor children; mentor in city schools; and work on other service projects in various cities throughout the city and the world. These are just a few of the possibilities. More Daemen seniors reported being involved in community-based projects as part of a regular course than did their peers at other institutions as reported in the National Survey of Student Engagement.

Daemen was awarded the Presidential Points of Light National Service Award for students' volunteer work and service learning activities. In addition, Daemen founded and operates the Center for Sustainable Communities and Civic Engagement and is founder and headquarters for the Western New York Service Learning Coalition.

Daemen's Office of Career Development and Cooperative Education Center provides students and graduates with a wide variety of services specially geared to the vocational and self-development needs of the College community before and after graduation. The Center helps students to find an internship or co-op position so they can gain real-world experience in their area of interest. Students benefit by experiencing what careers in their fields are really like. As an added bonus, internship employers frequently offer Daemen interns full-time positions. Internships are available in a wide range of fields, including business, the sports industry, the arts, industry, government, health-related entities, nonprofit organizations, educational institutions, and cultural organizations. The opportunities are local, national, or international—including excellent opportunities with the Washington Internship Institute.

Daemen students are well prepared for professional success. The vast majority of them obtain a position of choice or admission to graduate study in less than a year after graduation. They are leaders in their communities, with a strong dedication to the improvement of the communities in which they live.

Academic Facilities

The Daemen College Research and Information Commons establishes Daemen as a "green" leader among the Western New York region's academic institutions. The building is a technological showcase—a hub of academic research, as well as the academic and social heart of the campus. Art department facilities include ten large studios and one of the largest bronze-casting foundries of any college in the country. Students of French and Spanish find a well-equipped language laboratory in the main classroom building. The beautiful and modern Business Building houses all of the business classrooms, including breakout rooms, which are used for smaller discussion groups. There is also a computer lab, which has fifty Pentium (IBM compatible) computers.

Costs

For the 2009–10 academic year, tuition and fees were $20,720, and room and board were $9450.

Financial Aid

Daemen makes a conscious effort to award financial assistance based upon academic achievement and financial need. In the 2007–08 academic year, 95 percent of full-time Daemen undergraduates received some kind of financial aid. The average award made to full-time undergraduates was approximately $15,000. Daemen College participates in all federal and state financial aid programs and has private sources of scholarship monies to award to eligible students.

Faculty

Class size ranges from about 10 to 20 students, enabling faculty members to get to know the interests and goals of each student.

Student Government

All students are members of the Student Association. The controlling body, or Senate, is comprised of officers and representatives who are elected each year. A Programming Board works with the Student Activities Director and others to plan a well-rounded program of extracurricular activities. Students also serve on advisory committees to the president, the academic dean, and others within the College community.

Admission Requirements

Beginning with the class entering in fall 2009, Daemen College will no longer require applicants to submit standardized test scores (SAT, ACT) as part of the admission application. The decision to make test scores optional reflects Daemen's commitment to enrolling students who reflect intellectual curiosity, persistence in reaching a goal, talent, motivation, and determination to make a difference in their lives and the lives of others. The College relies on high school GPA, transcripts (including grade performance and rigor of courses selected), extracurricular activities, class rank, and counselor or teacher recommendations in making admission decisions. Strong writing skills, a solid secondary school program, and a student's potential for making an important contribution to the campus community are valued. Daemen will also consider applications from students whose preparation is unusual and who can provide strong recommendations as to their ability to succeed in a college program of study.

Students interested in attending Daemen College should contact the Office of Admissions at 800-462-7652 to arrange an appointment for an interview and campus tour.

Application and Information

For application forms, a catalog, or further information, students should contact:

Daemen College
4380 Main Street
Amherst, New York 14226
Phone: 716-839-8225
800-462-7652 (toll-free)
E-mail: admissions@daemen.edu
Web site: http://www.daemen.edu/admissions

While Daemen College is small enough so that all students receive individual attention, it still offers a broad range of programs and facilities.

No person shall, on the basis of sex, race, color, ethnic and national origin, handicap, religion, or age, be denied admission or be subjected to discrimination in admission to Daemen College.

COLLEGE CLOSE-UPS

DELAWARE VALLEY COLLEGE

DOYLESTOWN, PENNSYLVANIA

The College

Founded in 1896, Delaware Valley College (DVC) is a private, coeducational four-year college enrolling approximately 1,650 full-time students. Over the years, the College has concentrated on producing graduates who can fill employers' needs. Today, DVC's curriculum has expanded to include a broad range of programs in agriculture, business, science, education, and liberal arts.

Students attend Delaware Valley College, first and foremost, to prepare themselves for a professional career. The placement record of Delaware Valley College graduates is outstanding, proving that the time-honored educational philosophy of "scholarship with applied experience" works. An extremely high proportion of graduates find employment in their major field of study or enter graduate school within six months of graduation.

In addition to its academic programs, the College offers a wide range of extracurricular activities and events. More than fifty special-interest organizations exist, many of which are linked with a specific major. Student publications include the weekly *RamPages* (newspaper), the *Cornucopia* (yearbook), and the *Gleaner* (literary magazine). The College band and chorale give students the chance to demonstrate their musical talents. There are active minority and international clubs on campus. The DVC Volunteer Corps lines up opportunities for student service to the community in a variety of settings that are relevant to the student's academic major. A-Day, the student-run campuswide fair, annually attracts 50,000 visitors who enjoy the festival, the entertainment, and the academically oriented projects. Such projects as livestock judging, plant sales, chemistry magic shows, computer-aided design demonstrations, a model rainforest habitat, and equestrian events all demonstrate the expertise of DVC students.

Seventy percent of students live on campus in ten residence halls. A full range of intercollegiate and intramural athletics programs (NCAA Division III, ECAC, and MAC) for both women and men is offered. All elements of the College's educational and recreational programs are in place to develop students as open-minded professionals who are capable of expanding their horizons in a future of unlimited possibilities.

On the graduate level, Delaware Valley College offers a Master in Business Administration degree program, a Master of Business Administration in Food and Agribusiness, as well as a Master of Educational Leadership.

Location

The College is located in historic Bucks County, Pennsylvania, approximately 30 miles north of Philadelphia and 70 miles southwest of New York City. Bucks County is one of the fastest-growing areas in the United States, yet it maintains its rich historical and agricultural heritage. The central Bucks County area is also rich in libraries, museums, and additional cultural resources, further enhancing the educational opportunities of Delaware Valley College students. The Pennsylvania and New Jersey Turnpikes provide quick access to the College. A commuter railway system links the College with Philadelphia, providing daily scheduled arrivals and departures. The College enjoys a mutually beneficial relationship with its surrounding community. Many students find convenient employment opportunities with local businesses, and the community benefits from the many events and activities that are held on campus.

Majors and Degrees

Delaware Valley College awards Bachelor of Science degrees in agribusiness, agronomy and environmental science, animal science, biochemistry, biology, business administration, chemistry, criminal justice, dairy science, environmental design, food science and management, horticulture, information technology and management, ornamental horticulture, psychology, and secondary education. A Bachelor of Arts degree is awarded in English. Within the degree programs, students are given the opportunity to focus their attention on a number of options, minors, and specializations, such as accounting, biotechnology, business management, ecological landscape design, ecology, equine science and management, equine studies, floriculture, food service systems management, food technology, landscape contracting and management, marketing, microbiology, plant science, small-animal science, sports management, turfgrass management, media and communication, and zoo science.

DVC also offers preprofessional preparation in dentistry, law, medicine, optometry, and veterinary medicine.

Academic Programs

All courses are taught from a liberal arts perspective, which broadens the students' appreciation of their cultural heritage. The College is committed to producing graduates who are not only technically competent but also skilled in the use of language, mathematics, and computers. The entire academic program is designed to contribute to the total educational growth of the student and provides him or her with the opportunity to participate in special methods and techniques courses that coordinate theory with practice. The College stresses a practical, hands-on approach to learning. The curriculum includes a required 24-week Employment Program, through which students gain practical work experience in their field while still in college. The Employment Program provides valuable entries on student resumes as it builds meaningful skills.

The academic calendar consists of two 15-week semesters, a January term, and two 6-week summer sessions.

Academic Facilities

Many of the courses taught at Delaware Valley College are laboratory or field oriented. Facilities include many lecture rooms, laboratories containing the most up-to-date equipment, and approximately 550 acres of cultivated and forested lands, which offer a variety of field laboratory situations. In addition, the recently acquired 174-acre Roth Farm is being developed and maintained with the help of students and various DVC departments as a "working history farm" to demonstrate agricultural and food production practices from the 1890–1910 era.

Delaware Valley College students benefit from the low student-laboratory ratio. This enables ready access to equipment, which is imperative to learning. Specifically, the College utilizes biology, chemistry, physics, plant science, and animal science laboratories. Facilities include a tissue culture laboratory, a food processing plant, a greenhouse-laboratory complex, a dairy, a small-animal science center, equine breeding barns, and an indoor equestrian center. The campus is itself a recognized arboretum that is managed by students and faculty members. These facilities are all supported by the Krauskopf Memorial Library, which houses some 80,000 publications.

Costs

For 2009–10, tuition and fees are $27,292, room is $4420, and board is $5330 for a twenty-one-meal plan.

Financial Aid

The College is committed to providing financial assistance so that every student is able to meet the costs of obtaining a college education. DVC offers to students of academic promise faculty scholarships and faculty grants. It participates with the federal government in the Federal Pell Grant Program, the Federal Supplemental Educational Opportunity Grant Program, the Federal Perkins Loan Program, and the Federal Work-Study Program. More than 90 percent of the College's total student body receives some type of financial aid; the average award package totaled $21,600 for 2008–09.

Faculty

All courses at Delaware Valley College are taught by faculty members who combine professional expertise with deep theoretical knowledge and are devoted to the teaching profession. Courses are never taught by graduate students. The faculty numbers approximately 200 full- and part-time instructors, who are friendly and accessible and always ready to help individual students make the most of the educational opportunities offered by the College. The teacher-student ratio is 1:18.

Student Government

Students are encouraged to make the most of extracurricular activities to ensure that their education includes as many different experiences as possible. The student government acts to coordinate the activities of all organizations on campus and sponsors a variety of mixers, movies, concerts, and speakers.

Admission Requirements

In reviewing applications for admission, the College takes into consideration the quality of a student's high school work, scores on the SAT or ACT, class rank, the guidance counselor's recommendation, and the level of a student's motivation, as determined by extracurricular activities. A personal interview is recommended.

Application and Information

For more information about Delaware Valley College and its academic, athletic, and financial aid programs, students should contact:

Office of Admissions
Delaware Valley College
700 East Butler Avenue
Doylestown, Pennsylvania 18901-2697

Phone: 215-489-2211
800-2DELVAL (toll-free)
Fax: 215-230-2968
E-mail: admitme@delval.edu
Web site: http://www.delval.edu

Students relaxing in front of Lasker Hall.

COLLEGE CLOSE-UPS

DENISON UNIVERSITY
GRANVILLE, OHIO

The University

Denison University (DU) is a private, four-year, residential liberal arts college that provides a rigorous and challenging education while preparing students for lives of leadership and service. The University was founded in 1831, when the Ohio Baptist Education Society established the Granville Literary and Theological Institution. The University was given its present name and moved to its current location in the 1850s. Denison has more than 30,000 alumni, and, as of June 2009, an endowment of $550 million. The Denison Annual Fund received more than $5 million in gifts from alumni, parents, and friends during fiscal year 2008–09. Historic Cleveland Hall, built in 1904, has been completely renovated and renamed Bryant Arts Center. It houses both the studio art and art history departments and offers state-of-the-art facilities for ceramics, painting, printmaking, photography, and digital media. Both the Samson Talbot Hall of Biological Science and the Burton D. Morgan Center for student, faculty, and alumni-related activities, completed in 2003, further enhance the beautiful campus. Other newer buildings are the F. W. Olin Science Hall, Mitchell Recreation and Athletics Center, McPhail Center for Environmental Studies, and eight suite-style residence halls. The University is proud of the 649 outstanding members of the class of 2013, over 50 percent of whom were in the top 10 percent of their graduating class.

Denison has achieved a national reputation based upon its lengthy cultural heritage, the vitality of its intellectual and ethical concerns, and the performance of its graduates. Extensive personal, career, and professional school counseling is available to students. Approximately 40 percent of Denison students take part in at least one of the University's summer internship programs by the time they graduate. More than half of Denison's graduates enroll in graduate or professional schools within ten years of graduation. Denison students are consistent finalists for a number of postgraduate awards, including the Rhodes and Marshal scholarships. The University has had 11 National Science Foundation Fellows, 11 Goldwater Science scholars, 2 Truman Scholars, 1 Udall Fellow, 1 Charles B. Rangel International Affairs Fellowship, and 49 Fulbright Scholarship winners in the last seventeen years. This year, 23 Denison students have applied for Fulbright Scholarships.

As a residential college, Denison requires its students to live in University housing all four years and offers a variety of housing options in its thirty-six residence halls. A full slate of social and cultural events is scheduled each semester. Twenty-six percent of the approximately 2,100 students join the sixteen fraternities and sororities present on campus. The Denison International Student Association, the Black Student Union, the Asian-American Student Union, and La Fuerza Latina help to enrich the campus community.

Twenty-three intercollegiate sports for men and women and a wide variety of club sports are available. The Mitchell Recreation and Athletics Center and the Physical Education Center serve as the focal point for intercollegiate sports for men and women, all student athletic recreation, physical education classes, and club sports. The Mitchell Center includes a six-lane, 200-meter indoor track, four state-of-the-art indoor tennis courts, a spacious strength room, a modern fitness apparatus room, a large multipurpose and aerobics room, and international squash courts. The Physical Education Center is home to the Alumni Memorial Field House with its recreational track and three hardwood basketball/volleyball courts; Livingston Gym, home of varsity basketball and volleyball with seating for 3,000; Gregory Pool, a six-lane, 25-yard competition and recreation facility; and five racquetball/handball courts. More than 75 percent of Denison students participate in athletics or recreational activities. DU's varsity teams have won a record eleven North Coast Athletic Conference All-Sports titles and have captured 104 conference championships since 1984, the founding year of the Conference.

Location

The 900-acre Denison campus is located on a ridge overlooking the village of Granville, in central Ohio. Founded in 1805 by settlers from Massachusetts, Granville bears a marked resemblance to a New England village. Columbus, the state capital and sixteenth largest U.S. city, 27 miles to the west, is the nearest major city and is served by numerous national airlines. Newark, 7 miles to the east, is an industrial city of 50,000 people. Granville has several fine restaurants and some shopping facilities, but those seeking the larger department stores go to nearby Easton Town Center or downtown Columbus. The University is a cultural and recreational center for the local community, and the Denison Community Association encourages student participation in community service activities, providing more than 18,000 hours of volunteer fieldwork each year. State parks, lakes, bike trails, and ski areas are nearby.

Majors and Degrees

Denison offers the degrees of Bachelor of Arts, Bachelor of Science, and Bachelor of Fine Arts. Departmental, interdepartmental, and individually designed majors, as well as concentrations within departments, are available within the degree programs. The B.A. can be earned through departmental programs in art (history or studio), biology, chemistry, cinema, communication, computer science, dance, economics, English (literature or writing), environmental studies, geosciences, history, international studies (as a double major), Latin, mathematics, modern languages (French, German, and Spanish), music, philosophy, physics, political science, psychology, religion, sociology/anthropology, and theater. The B.A. can also be earned through interdepartmental programs in black studies; East Asian studies; educational studies; philosophy, politics, and economics (PPE); and women's studies. The B.S. is offered in biochemistry, biology, chemistry, computer science, geosciences, mathematics, physics, and psychology. The B.F.A. major is art (studio).

Preprofessional preparation is available in business, dentistry, engineering, environmental management, forestry, law, medical technology, medicine, nursing, occupational therapy, and veterinary science. Denison offers 3-2 programs in engineering with Rensselaer Polytechnic Institute, Washington University in St. Louis, Case Western Reserve University, and Columbia University; in forestry and environmental management with Duke University; and in medical technology with Rochester General Hospital. A 3-4 program in dentistry with Case Western Reserve Dental School is also available along with a cooperative program with Case Western's Weatherhead School of Management for entrance into a year-long M.S. program.

Academic Programs

Denison expects its students to benefit from exposure to a broad liberal arts education and to achieve proficiency in a major field. University degree requirements include successful completion of approximately thirty-five courses (127 semester hours) with a 2.0 or better average, both overall and in the major and minor fields; fulfillment of all general education requirements; passing comprehensive examinations if required in the major; and fulfillment of minimum residence requirements. Approximately one third of a student's course work (thirteen courses) must be chosen from core course offerings in the humanities, sciences, social sciences, and fine arts. Another third is in the major field of study, and the remainder is in electives. There are opportunities for directed and independent study. Students may receive advanced placement or credit through College Board Advanced Placement (AP) tests or International Baccalaureate higher level examinations. Credit is given for an AP score of 4 or 5. Denison's academic calendar consists of two semesters and an optional summer internship program, which includes internships and travel seminars. The academic year begins in late August and ends in early May.

Off-Campus Programs

Denison cooperates in off-campus study programs approved by recognized American colleges and universities and by the Great Lakes Colleges Association. Qualified students may participate for a semester or a year of international study in Africa, Asia, the Caribbean, Europe, Latin America, the Middle East, or Oceania. Domestic programs, offered on a one- or two-semester basis, include the Washington Semester; the Philadelphia Center; the New York Arts Program; the S.E.A. Semester; the Williams-Mystic Semester; the National Theatre Institute; the Headlong Performance Institute; the Oak Ridge, Tennessee Science Semester; the Newberry Library Program in Chicago; the Border Studies Program; and linkages with historically black universities. Nearly 50 percent of the student body participates in an off-campus program by the time of graduation.

Academic Facilities

As a member of the Five Colleges of Ohio consortium, Denison offers access through a combined online catalog to a collection of 2.8 million volumes that can be accessed from computers anywhere on campus via the campus network. As a member of the OhioLINK statewide academic library consortium, library users also have ready access to more than 46 million titles from Ohio's library holdings. The William Howard Doane Library, one of thirteen academic and administrative buildings on the academic and science quadrangles, has on-campus collections of more than 460,349 volumes, 359,441 government documents, and nearly 165,000 (paper, electronic, and microform) periodical subscriptions. More than 650 Macintosh and Dell personal computers are available for student use in forty-three public and departmental labs and student clusters. A network outlet is available to every student living in a residence hall and wireless network zones are campuswide. Network services include central multiuser computers and servers, personal and departmental Web server space, free laser printing, hundreds of software packages, student and staff Web portals and e-mail. Approximately 98 percent of Denison's students own computers. Laptops may be used online from almost anywhere on campus, indoors or outdoors. For more information, students should refer to the library or computing links on the home page of the Denison Web site, listed in this description.

Samson Talbott Hall of Biological Science features flexible teaching labs and interactive lecture and seminar rooms crowned by a spectacular greenhouse. The Chemistry Center contains well-equipped laboratories and a 292-seat circular auditorium. Features of the $7.2-million F. W. Olin Science Hall include a forty-two-seat planetarium with a Zeiss Skymaster projector, a laser spectrometer, and computer-based learning centers for physics and astronomy, geology and geography, and mathematics and computer science. The fine arts quadrangle on the lower campus is made up of six buildings with classrooms and performance facilities for art, music, theater and cinema, and dance. Burke Hall features a recital hall, a theater workshop, and the Denison Museum. Other buildings are the Theatre Arts Building; the Doane Dance Building; Burton Hall, which houses the Department of Music; the newly dedicated Bryant Arts Center, for studio art and art history courses; and the Cinema Building, the center of Denison's nationally recognized cinematography program.

Costs

Annual charges for the 2009–10 academic year are as follows: tuition, $35,650; room and board, $9160; and student fees, $910. An estimated $1800 for books, travel, and personal expenses brings the total annual cost to $47,520.

Financial Aid

In 2008–09, Denison students received more than $57 million in financial assistance. More than 70 percent was awarded from Denison funds. Financial aid packages based on need are composed of grants, loans, and employment on campus. Applicants for both federal and Denison grant aid must complete a Free Application for Federal Student Aid (FAFSA) as early as possible after January 1 and request that the information be sent to Denison. In addition to the institutional need-based grants, Denison offers more than 1,000 merit-based scholarships to first-year students, which range from $8000 to $35,000. Denison awards up to twenty Paschal Carter Scholarships for selected first-year applicants who earn National Merit Finalist status as determined by the National Merit Scholarship Corporation. It approximates full tuition, and the amount of the award stays constant during a student's enrollment at Denison. Alumni Awards in the amounts of $14,000 and $8000, recognizing academic achievement, leadership, and talent, are also offered. The financial aid decision is entirely separate from the admission decision. For more information, students should write to Denison's Office of Financial Aid and ask for the financial aid brochure.

Faculty

Denison's 203 full-time faculty members are deeply committed to teaching and to students. Many have national reputations in their fields; each year faculty members win national awards for teaching excellence. One hundred percent of faculty members have an earned doctorate or terminal degree in their fields. The faculty-student ratio is 1:10. Small classes (average class size is 19) and unique opportunities for one-on-one research with a faculty member encourage active learning. In 2009, about 120 summer scholars did research with their professors on campus. All incoming first-year students are assigned a faculty adviser to assist with course selection and to ease the transition to college life.

Student Government

Through the Denison Campus Governance Association, students budget and direct such campus organizations as the Student Senate, FM radio station, Denison Film Society, and campus newspaper. Students are strongly represented on the governance councils of the University.

Admission Requirements

Entering first-year students must have earned at least 16 academic credits in secondary school, including 4 years of college-preparatory English. Strongly recommended are 3 years each of mathematics, science, foreign language, and social studies. A candidate for admission must file a formal application and an essay. Submission of the results of the SAT or the ACT is optional. SAT Subject Tests are not required, although students may provide these scores as additional information in support of their application for admission. International applicants must submit the results of the Test of English as a Foreign Language (TOEFL) or the results of the SAT. The Admissions Committee is particularly interested in the rigor of the academic program and the grade point average. Other selection criteria are written references from a college adviser and an academic teacher, extracurricular and personal accomplishments, and the student's essay on the application. An interview is strongly encouraged. It is Denison's goal to enroll academically talented students. Denison University admits students of any race, color, religion, age, personal handicap, sex, sexual orientation, veteran status, and national or ethnic origin.

Application and Information

First-Choice Early Decision candidates should apply by November 15 or January 15, with rolling notification through the middle of January. All admitted early decision candidates must send an enrollment deposit within two weeks of notification of acceptance. Students interested in applying for admission under regular application status and for merit-based scholarship consideration must apply by January 15. Those deferred under early decision and all regular applicants are given a final decision by mid-March. Admitted candidates must respond to the admission offer by May 1.

Director of Admissions
Denison University
Box 740
Granville, Ohio 43023-0740
Phone: 740-587-6276
800-336-4766 (toll-free)
E-mail: admissions@denison.edu
Web site: http://www.denison.edu

Denison—preparing students for a lifetime of leadership and learning.

DEPAUL UNIVERSITY

CHICAGO, ILLINOIS

The University

DePaul University is nationally recognized for providing students with a widely respected, immediately applicable education through highly interactive course work and an integrated service-learning approach. More than 150 undergraduate degree programs combine practical expertise with classic, broad-based liberal studies, preparing students for both immediate and long-term success. Located in the heart of Chicago, DePaul University offers students unparalleled access to internships and learning opportunities with many of the nation's top corporations and organizations as well as a rich array of cultural events and institutions. The only one of the nation's ten largest private universities to make teaching its primary focus, DePaul provides an interactive learning environment through expert instruction and small class sizes. More than 98 percent of classes are taught by faculty members.

In fall 2009, DePaul enrolled 25,072 students, retaining its place as the nation's largest Catholic university. Of the 16,199 undergraduates, 2,531 were freshmen. The student body is diverse—about one third of all undergraduates are students of color. The incoming freshmen are also high caliber, with an average high school GPA of 3.5 and more than 20 percent graduating in the top 10 percent of their class.

The mid-50 percent range for the ACT is 22–27; the mid-50 percent range for the SAT is 1040–1250. With a wide range of backgrounds and perspectives, students learn from each other through DePaul's discussion- and project-oriented approach.

In addition to its baccalaureate programs, DePaul offers more than 130 graduate programs, including master's degrees in accountancy, business, computer science, education, liberal arts and sciences, and music; the Master of Fine Arts (M.F.A.) in theater; the Juris Doctor (J.D.); the Master of Law in health law, intellectual property, and taxation; and doctoral programs in computer science, education, philosophy, and psychology.

Recognized by *U.S. News & World Report* for its service-learning program, DePaul takes full advantage of its Chicago location. Professors have long-lasting professional relationships with corporations, government agencies, cultural and civic organizations, and a wide array of nonprofits. Students tap into these connections for internships, mentors, class projects, professional contacts, and more. DePaul has nearly 140,000 alumni, with more than 90,000 residing in the metropolitan area, providing students with a network locally and around the world.

DePaul sponsors more than 200 student organizations that provide opportunities for leadership, service, professional development, socializing, sports, recreation, and special interests.

Students enjoy the excitement and pride of collegiate sports through the DePaul Blue Demons, who participate in NCAA Division I sports as part of the Big East Conference. Women's sports include basketball, cross-country, soccer, softball, tennis, track and field, and volleyball. Men's sports include basketball, cross-country, golf, soccer, tennis, and track and field. Intramural sports programs, as well as club athletics, also are available throughout the year.

Location

DePaul has six campuses in the Chicago metropolitan area and takes full advantage of its culturally and academically rich environment. The Loop Campus is just blocks from Chicago's business district, the Art Institute, Orchestra Hall, Millennium Park, and Lake Michigan. The 40-acre Lincoln Park Campus, just 5 miles north of the Loop Campus, provides a classic residential-college experience surrounded by an urban assortment of stores, theaters, restaurants, and music clubs. From either campus, a short walk or ride on public transit enables students to browse unique shops or visit museums, the zoo, ethnic neighborhoods, and professional sports arenas, such as Wrigley Field and the United Center. DePaul undergraduate students taking 12 or more credit hours are eligible to receive the CTA U-Pass, providing them unlimited rides on CTA-operated bus and rail lines 24 hours per day and seven days per week.

DePaul's four suburban campuses (Naperville, Oak Forest, Rolling Meadows, and O'Hare) provide convenient locations for adult and graduate students to pursue degree programs.

Majors and Degrees

Bachelor of Arts, Bachelor of Fine Arts, Bachelor of Music, Bachelor of Science, Bachelor of Science in Commerce, and Bachelor of Science in Physical Education degrees are offered through DePaul's undergraduate colleges. More than 150 undergraduate majors and nearly 100 minors are available. Double majors and minors may be taken in many areas of study.

The College of Liberal Arts and Sciences offers programs in African and black diaspora studies; allied health technologies; American studies; anthropology; Arabic studies; art, media, and design; Asian American studies; biological sciences; Catholic studies; chemistry; Chinese studies; cities; community service studies; comparative literature; economics; English; environmental science; environmental studies; French; geographic information systems; geography; German; history; history of art and architecture; international studies; Irish studies; Islamic world studies; Italian; Japanese studies; Latin American and Latino studies; LGBTQ studies; mathematical sciences; mathematics and computer science; nursing (for registered nurses/B.S.N. completion only); peace, conflict resolution, and social justice; philosophy; physics; political science; preprofessional studies (dentistry, engineering, health, law, medicine, osteopathy, veterinary medicine); professional writing; psychology; public policy (environmental studies, urban studies); religious studies; scientific data analysis and visualization; sociology; Spanish; and women's and gender studies.

The College of Computing and Digital Media offers programs in animation, computer games development, computer graphics and motion technology, computer science, digital cinema, interactive media, information assurance and security engineering, information systems, information technology, math/computer science, and network technology.

The School of Education offers programs in early childhood education, elementary education, music education (joint program with the School of Music), physical education (sport and fitness management and teaching), secondary education (art, biology, chemistry, English, environmental science, history, mathematics, physics, social science), and world languages education (Chinese, French, German, Italian, Japanese, and Spanish).

The College of Commerce offers programs in accountancy, business administration, e-business, economics, finance, hospitality leadership, management, management information systems, marketing, and real estate.

The College of Communication offers programs in communication and media, communication studies, public relations and advertising, media and cinema studies, and journalism.

The School of Music offers programs in music, composition, jazz studies, music education, music performance, performing arts management, and sound recording technology.

The Theatre School offers programs in acting, costume design, costume technology, dramaturgy/criticism, lighting design, playwriting, scenic design, sound design, stage management, theater arts, theater management, and theater technology.

Students interested in pursuing engineering have the opportunity to complete a five-year joint program with the Illinois Institute of Technology (IIT). This dual-degree program includes three years of study at DePaul and two years at an accredited school of engineering.

Academic Programs

Each college follows the liberal studies program, which has two components. The first, called the common core, emphasizes communication, quantitative skills, and intellectual abilities and introduces the University's small-group, highly interactive educational approach. The second part, learning domains, focuses mainly on the subjects that make up the classic liberal arts and sciences curriculum. Breadth of learning is assured by requiring students to do course work in six learning domains: arts and literature; philosophical inquiry; religious dimensions; scientific inquiry; self, society, and the modern world; and understanding the past.

In autumn quarter, all freshmen take a course that introduces some facet of the intellectual resources of the city, emphasizes DePaul's roles and mission in the city, and provides opportunities to connect classroom learning with persons, communities, and institutions in Chicago. Students select either an Explore Chicago or a Discover Chicago course. Discover Chicago courses combine classroom work and an intensive immersion week. In either type of course, the faculty instructor serves as the academic adviser until students declare a major and are assigned a departmental adviser.

The liberal studies curriculum is integrated into each year of study at DePaul. Students complete a sophomore multiculturalism requirement, junior experiential learning requirement, and senior capstone requirement.

The academic year comprises three quarters. Incoming freshmen may enter with previously earned credit from Advanced Placement, CLEP, or International Baccalaureate. Incoming transfer students may combine earned credit through credit by exam and transferable credit hours from two-year institutions (up to 99 quarter hours/66 semester hours) and from four-year institutions (up to 132 quarter hours/88 semester hours). In some cases, degree requirements can be completed in three years. Advanced undergraduates may take graduate courses. Undergraduates in any college may apply to the Honors Program, which emphasizes cross-cultural and interdisciplinary perspectives with a challenging curriculum that satisfies the required liberal studies core. (Program participation is noted on the students' transcripts.) College-specific honors programs also are offered in accountancy, computer science, finance, and marketing.

Off-Campus Programs

DePaul University has study abroad programs in numerous locations throughout the world. Students study in Australia, Belgium, China, England, France, Germany, Greece, Hungary, Ireland, Italy, Japan, Mexico, Poland, Spain, and Turkey—just to name a few. DePaul sponsors full-year and short-term study tours in order to accommodate students' interests and academic program requirements.

Academic Facilities

The DePaul Center, a $70-million teaching, learning, research, and student services complex, is the cornerstone of the six-building Loop Campus. The CDM Center, home of the College of Computing and Digital Media, offers more than a dozen specialized labs as well as a digital animation studio. The Merle Reskin Theatre provides a 1,400-seat performance space for the theater and music school performances. Wireless networks and other technological upgrades have been implemented at most other academic facilities at all campuses.

All the academic and residential facilities on the 40-acre Lincoln Park Campus are either new or recently rehabbed. Notable buildings include the student center, Ray Meyer Fitness and Recreation Center, Richardson Library, and Sullivan Athletic Center. Two state-of-the-art science buildings have been built recently. The $12-million William McGowan Biological and Environmental Sciences Center includes classrooms, biology, computer, and environmental science laboratories, faculty research suites, and a greenhouse. The Monsignor Andrew J. McGowan Environmental Science and Chemistry Building opened in winter 2009 and was awarded Gold-level LEED certification for its green features.

Costs

For the 2009–10 academic year, full-time tuition for the College of Liberal Arts and Sciences, the College of Commerce, the College of Communication, the College of Computing and Digital Media, and the School of Education was $26,765. Tuition for the School of Music and The Theatre School was $29,630 and guaranteed for four years. Average room and board costs for 2009–10 were $10,500.

Financial Aid

DePaul structures its financial aid program to assist as many students as possible. Scholarships, grants, loans, and work-study opportunities are awarded singly or, more commonly, are combined in a financial aid package to meet the demonstrated financial need of the student. About 70 percent of full-time DePaul undergraduate students receive some form of financial aid. Merit scholarships for freshmen and transfer students are based on academic and extracurricular accomplishments. Institutional merit scholarships for freshmen, with values ranging from $4000 to $15,500 per year for four years, are based on consideration of class rank, grade point average, and SAT or ACT scores, without regard to need. Select freshmen admitted for the fall term are invited to apply upon admission for service and leadership scholarships with values ranging from $8500 to $15,500. Institutional scholarships for transfer students range from $2000 to $7000 and may be awarded to students who have a cumulative GPA of 3.5 or above and a minimum of 30 semester (44 quarter) hours of transferable credit before enrolling at DePaul. All other financial aid programs, except art, athletic, music, and theater talent awards, are based primarily on need.

Students who wish to apply for aid must complete the Free Application for Federal Student Aid (FAFSA) and the DePaul application for admission. Application and notification of aid decisions are on a rolling basis. Students are encouraged to apply and file their FAFSA before February 15 to receive maximum consideration.

Faculty

In the fall of 2009, about 88 percent of the full-time faculty members held a doctoral degree or terminal degree in their field. Faculty members are selected for their teaching ability and conduct 98 percent of all university classes. In addition to teaching, DePaul's faculty members also consult with organizations throughout the metropolitan area and world, engage in research, publish in their fields of expertise, and participate in service.

Admission Requirements

Current high school students may be considered for admission on the basis of six or more semesters of high school work. However, by the time of enrollment the students must have graduated from an accredited secondary school with 4 units in English, 3 in mathematics, 3 in science (2 of which must be lab sciences), and 2 in social sciences. Applicants should have a solid GPA and present strong ACT or SAT scores. Applicants must submit a high school counselor's recommendation. The School of Music and The Theatre School require auditions or interviews for admission. Advanced placement and credit for dual enrollment while still in high school are available.

Transfer students are welcome. To be considered for admission, transfers must be in good standing (eligible to enroll) at the last college/university attended and must have earned a minimum cumulative GPA of 2.0 (C average). College of Commerce, School of Education, and School of Music applicants must have a cumulative GPA of 2.5 or better; registered nurses interested in the B.S.N. completion program must have at least a 2.5 cumulative GPA and licensure from the state of Illinois. Students who have completed fewer than 30 semester hours (44 quarter hours) of transferable credit need to submit an official high school transcript and ACT/SAT scores.

Application and Information

For freshman applicants, the non-binding early action deadline is November 15. To receive strongest consideration for merit scholarships as well as priority registration for orientation and housing, students should apply by November 15. Applicants who are admitted under the early action program receive their decision by January 15. The application deadline for regular notification is February 1 and students receive an admission decision by March 15. After February 1, applications are considered on a space-available basis.

The Theatre School and School of Music applicants are not eligible to participate in the early action program. Application materials to the School of Music and the Theatre School must be received by January 15. Admission decisions are made by April 1.

Application deadlines for transfer students vary by start term: August 1 for fall (September), November 1 for winter (January), March 1 for spring (March), and May 1 for summer (June). Students who apply for admission after the deadlines will have their application considered on a space-available basis.

Campus visits and overnight stays are available for applicants. Interested students and their families are encouraged to call the admission office to arrange a visit.

For further information, prospective students should contact:

Office of Admission
DePaul University
1 East Jackson Boulevard
Chicago, Illinois 60604-2287
Phone: 312-362-8300
800-4DEPAUL (toll-free outside Illinois)
E-mail: admission@depaul.edu
Web site: http://www.depaul.edu

DESALES UNIVERSITY

CENTER VALLEY, PENNSYLVANIA

The University

DeSales University is a private, four-year Catholic university for men and women that is administered by the Oblates of St. Francis de Sales. Its mission is to provide high-quality higher education according to the philosophy of Christian humanism. The University imparts knowledge about, and develops talents for, personal, familial, and societal living, enriching the human community and enhancing the dignity of the individual through its educational endeavors. The University is accredited by the Middle States Association of Colleges and Schools.

In 1961, Joseph McShea was appointed Bishop of the new Allentown Diocese. At the time, the Diocese did not include a Catholic college for men. At the request of Bishop McShea, the Oblates of St. Francis de Sales agreed to assume responsibility for establishing a liberal arts college to serve this need. Allentown College of St. Francis de Sales received a charter to grant bachelor's degrees in 1964, and the first classes began in 1965. The College became coeducational in 1970; throughout the 1980s and 1990s, it began to offer graduate and cooperative education programs. These changes led to the college attaining university status, and it was renamed DeSales University in 2001.

Today, DeSales is home to more than 2,500 undergraduate and graduate students. Life on campus best illustrates DeSales' identity as a Christian humanist institution. Approximately 70 percent of the University's 1,600 undergraduate students live on campus and take full advantage of the rich opportunities provided. Students participate in more than forty clubs and organizations that encompass art, politics, and intramural sports; sixteen athletic teams competing in the NCAA Division III, including basketball, soccer, field hockey, and lacrosse; social outreach; student activities; and a Campus Ministry that enables students to participate in retreats and social justice groups. Billera Hall houses facilities for intercollegiate and intramural sports and fitness activities. The Bishop McShea Student Union contains health services and counseling offices. The Labuda Center for the Performing Arts houses the largest department in the University and is proud of its thirty-five-year history of success. The newly expanded University Center includes the University bookstore and expanded meeting space in addition to the food court, student dining facility, and student lounge. Eight suite-style residence halls offer a range of living options, including living-learning communities, which allows students with common interests to live together.

Location

The Lehigh Valley contains three cities, including Allentown, the third-largest city in Pennsylvania; Bethlehem; and Easton. The region offers a wide range of year-round recreational activities, from skiing and skating in the winter to golf and swimming in the summer, and theater, dance, fine dining, shopping, and music year-round.

The Lehigh Valley has a wide variety of museums, art galleries, and concert venues for every taste and age group, while farmers' markets are a common sight throughout the region. Amusement parks like Dorney Park and Wildwater Kingdom and the Crayola Factory are nearby, as are Kutztown Festival and other annual celebrations. The Promenade Shops at Saucon Valley offer more than sixty-five stores and restaurants and a state-of-the-art movie theater. For those wanting to travel beyond the region, the Lehigh Valley is less than 2 hours from New York City and 1 hour from Philadelphia.

Majors and Degrees

The University offers undergraduate degrees in more than thirty programs, including accounting, biochemistry, biology, chemistry, communications, computer science, criminal justice, dance, digital art, elementary education, English, finance, history, international business, law and society, liberal studies, management, management of information technology, marketing, marriage and family studies, mathematics, nursing, pharmaceutical marketing, philosophy, physician assistant studies, political science, premedicine, psychology, Spanish, sport and exercise science, sport management, television and film, theater, and theology.

Academic Programs

Students must complete forty courses with a minimum GPA of 2.0 to earn a bachelor's degree. Each degree program has three components. The General Education Core requires completion of sixteen courses, including two courses in English; three physical education courses; two courses in a foreign language or world cultures; two courses in history or political science; one course in art or music; one course in literature; five courses in modes of thinking, concentrating on literature, mathematics, natural science, philosophy, and social science; and three courses in theology. The major provides a thorough and systematic study of one subject area. The major requires completion of sixteen courses. As an alternative, a student may choose to enroll in a special degree program, which may extend the number of required courses. Electives comprise the remaining eight course requirements. Electives provide opportunities for learning in areas of special interest outside the student's major. Some students may want to consider a dual major, in which case the student must complete the requirements of both fields of study. Students who wish to complete a minor must take six courses within that field of study.

Off-Campus Programs

DeSales encourages qualified students to study abroad during the summer and/or the academic year. Through an affiliation with the Lehigh Valley Association of Independent Colleges, the University offers qualified students in a number of disciplines the opportunity to spend a summer or semester in Germany, Italy, Mexico, Spain, or other countries. During the fall semester of their junior year, full-time students majoring in theology, philosophy, marriage and family studies, and history are encouraged to study abroad in DeSales University's program at the American University of Rome. Shorter, more intensive trips are offered to all students through a variety of clubs, organizations, and academic programs. Recent trips have taken DeSales students to South Africa, India, Peru, Romania, and other countries.

Academic Facilities

The campus contains twenty-four buildings. A state-of-the-art 37,000-square-foot Science Center houses classrooms and laboratories for the natural sciences. Trexler Library contains more than 550,000 items, including 132,000 volumes and 40,000 electronic books, more than 12,000 electronic journals and newspapers, and 400,000 microfiche items. The periodical collection includes 550 paper and microform subscriptions. Collections of the other five independent colleges of the Lehigh Valley, totaling more than 1 million volumes, are available through an interlibrary loan system.

The University maintains ten computing laboratories or classrooms. The Academic Computing Center contains approximately sixty PCs in its main area, while ACC Computing Classroom houses twenty-three systems. Dooling Hall has three dedicated computing classrooms, each containing approximately twenty-five workstations. Trexler Technology Center contains forty-nine PC systems for both public use and classroom support. Each computing area is supported by at least one high-volume laser printer. All systems have Internet access and contain a suite of both application and network software.

Costs

In 2009–10, full-time tuition was $26,000 per academic year. Other annual fees included a Student Center fee and a technology fee totaling $1235. For students living on campus, room and board cost $9750 per year.

Financial Aid

Nearly 90 percent of incoming students receive some form of financial aid. Students must complete the Free Application for Federal Student Aid and mail it to the processing center indicated on the form with DeSales University's Title IV code number, which is 003986, after January 1 of the student's senior year. The Office of Financial Aid processes requests for assistance on both a date priority and a financial need basis. The types and amounts of assistance a student will receive are specified in an award letter. The package also provides students and parents with a payment options letter, which outlines the three ways a student can finance the remaining cost of education. Parents may apply for a Federal Parent Loan for Undergraduate Students, students may apply for an alternative loan, or they may take advantage of a monthly billing plan.

All applicants are automatically considered for merit scholarships, which are awarded to incoming first-year students based upon academic achievement. Priority consideration is given to students who apply by December 1 of their senior year. Scholarships include Presidential Scholarships, which can award up to full tuition to students who earn a combined SAT score (math and critical reasoning sections) of at least 1300 (29 ACT) and rank in the top 5 percent of their high school class; Trustee Scholarships of $6000 to $10,000 for students who achieve a combined SAT score (math and critical reasoning sections) of at least 1200 (27 ACT) and rank in the top 15 percent of their high school class; and DeSales Scholarships of $4000 for students who achieve a combined SAT score (math and critical reasoning sections) of at least 1100 (24 ACT) and rank in the top 25 percent of their high school class. Department Scholarships are awarded to students who attend scholarship day and demonstrate excellence in their field of study.

Faculty

There are 103 full-time faculty members teaching at the University. Eighty-five percent of the professors have a doctorate or the highest degree in their specialty. The average class size is 18 students, and the student-faculty ratio is 15:1. Students are assigned a faculty member from their chosen field of study to serve as an academic adviser; undeclared students are assigned to a faculty member who assists them in planning courses, deciding upon a major, and moving toward declaring a major.

Student Government

The Student Government Association is the liaison between the students and the administration. The Executive Board and each of the four undergraduate classes elect a president, vice president, secretary, and treasurer, for a total of 20 officers.

Admission Requirements

Admission is based on past academic achievement, particularly within a college-preparatory course of study, as well as the student's potential for future growth. Preferably, this includes four years of English; three to four years of college-preparatory mathematics; two years of modern, foreign, or classical language; and at least two laboratory science courses. Quality of academic performance is the single most important factor in the decision-making process.

Application and Information

DeSales University uses a rolling admissions process; the school notifies applicants of their admission status within four weeks of receiving all application materials. To apply, students must submit a completed application, official high school or home school transcripts, official SAT or ACT scores, two letters of recommendation, and the $30 application fee. An on-campus interview is recommended but not required. For maximum consideration for scholarships, students are encouraged to apply by December 1.

Prospective students may direct their applications or requests for additional information to:

Admissions Office
DeSales University
2755 Station Avenue
Center Valley, Pennsylvania 18034-9568
Phone: 610-282-1100
E-mail: admiss@desales.edu
Web site: http://www.desales.edu

DOMINICAN UNIVERSITY OF CALIFORNIA

SAN RAFAEL, CALIFORNIA

The University

Dominican University of California is an independent, international, learner-centered university of Dominican heritage. It offers a beautiful setting, a close-knit community of over 2,000 students, and an intimate social environment that is an important context for academic goals and personal development.

The University offers many services that support its educational programs. It provides tutoring, career, and personal counseling without charge to Dominican students; offers housing, health, and job placement services; and helps students make the most of their college experience by its readiness to assist them in resolving problems.

The University and the Associated Students of Dominican University sponsor a number of campus activities each year for both resident and nonresident students. Dominican supports twelve intercollegiate teams that compete in the NCAA's Pacific Western Conference: men's and women's basketball, golf, cross-country, and soccer; men's lacrosse; and women's softball, tennis, and volleyball. Students can participate in the chorus, drama group, literary magazine, campus newspaper, campus ministry activities, special interest clubs, dances, and other social events.

Campus Ministry responds to the spiritual needs of Catholic and non-Catholic members of the University community. Catholic liturgies, ecumenical activities for students of all faiths, and community service projects are scheduled throughout the year.

Graduate degrees (M.A., M.S., M.S.N., M.S.O.T., M.F.T., and M.B.A.) are granted in biological sciences, counseling psychology, education, global management, humanities, nursing, occupational therapy, strategic leadership, and sustainable enterprise (Green MBA®).

The University is approved by the California Commission on Teacher Credentialing to prepare and recommend candidates for credentials in elementary, secondary, and special education.

Four residence halls of varied architecture accommodate more than 600 students; there is a dining hall for resident students and others who wish to purchase meals on campus. Forest Meadows, which comprises approximately 25 acres, is the site of the Conlan Recreation Center, a soccer field, tennis courts, and an outdoor amphitheater, where commencement exercises are held. The Recreation Center features regulation basketball and volleyball courts, two cross-courts for volleyball and basketball, and 1,285 spectator seats. It also features a weight-training and fitness room, a multipurpose room, lockers, athletic department offices, and conference rooms. Outside are a six-lane, recreational swimming pool and grassy patio area.

Location

The University is located on 80 wooded acres in scenic Marin County, which is 12 miles north of San Francisco and within a half hour's drive of Pacific Ocean beaches.

Majors and Degrees

A broad range of degrees and certificate and credential programs are offered in letters, the arts and sciences, and professional and preprofessional disciplines.

Undergraduate degrees (B.A., B.S., B.S.N., and B.F.A.) are awarded in the academic areas of art, art history, biological sciences (with concentrations in ecology, environmental science, general biology, molecular cell biology, and premedical studies), business administration (with concentrations in accounting, finance, international business, management, management information systems, and marketing), communications (with concentrations in broadcast media, cinema, journalism, and print), dance (LINES ballet), English, English with a writing emphasis, health science (pre–occupational therapy), history, humanities, interdisciplinary studies, international studies, liberal studies (teacher education), music, music with a performance concentration, nursing, political science, psychology, religion, and women and gender studies.

Minors are offered in chemistry, environmental studies, Latin American studies, leadership studies, mathematics, philosophy, prelaw, and sports management.

Academic Programs

The General Education Program offers more than a brief exposure to the major areas of knowledge in the humanities, arts, and natural and social sciences. It is designed to provide a sequence of courses with a thematic focus that integrates the wisdom and perspectives of several disciplines. The focus assists students in discovering relationships between areas of knowledge, beliefs, cultures, and peoples that differ globally and historically, as well as in acquiring an awareness of tradition, a love of discovery, a respect for the diversity of the human condition, and a realization of human interdependence. Courses within the General Education Program also expose students to a variety of learning experiences, including discussion, lectures, seminars, simulations, practicums, and quiet reflection.

A strong internship program offers students job experience in areas of their choice.

An evening bachelor's degree–completion program (Pathways) for nontraditional learners is also available.

The ELS Language Centers program provides intensive, high-quality English instruction to prepare international students to enter American colleges and universities. Completion of the ELS Language Centers Program level 112 satisfies Dominican's English requirement for admission for international students.

Off-Campus Programs

Dominican offers exchange programs with Aquinas College, Grand Rapids, Michigan; Barry University, Miami, Florida; the College of New Rochelle, New Rochelle, New York; and St. Thomas Aquinas College, Sparkill, New York. These programs enable students matriculated at any one of the five colleges to spend a semester on a campus in a different part of the country, taking advantage of its location and programs. Students pay tuition on their home campus and room and board on the host campus. Further information about the program, which is recommended for students in the sophomore or junior year, is available in the campus Service Center.

Individualized programs for study in other countries may be planned in consultation with the Academic Advising Center, the student's academic adviser, and the transcript evaluator. Dominican grants credit for international study only after a student who obtained prior approval of the program of study has returned to the campus and enrolled for the following year.

Academic Facilities

Archbishop Alemany Library houses more than 100,000 volumes in open stacks; 3,200 reels of microfilm; 775 videocassettes, 225 audiocassettes, and compact discs; and subscriptions to 375 periodicals in print and another 19,000 periodical titles in full text online. Reference services, including access to a variety of computerized databases and indexes, and multimedia facilities are provided to assist students with their studies and assignments. The library also houses the Fletcher Jones Computer Laboratory, an art gallery, a listening room, and a fireplace corner.

Guzman Hall, Albertus Magnus Hall, Bertrand Hall, and the San Marco Art Studios together house faculty offices, science laboratories, lecture halls, a computer center, art galleries and studios, and classrooms. Angelico Hall houses an 850-seat concert auditorium and theater, music studios and practice rooms, and faculty offices.

In 2005, ground was broken on a new $20-million, 35,000-square-foot science and technology facility. The Science Center opened for the fall 2007 classes, featuring more than thirty teaching, research, and computer technology labs.

Costs

Undergraduate full-time tuition (12–17 units per semester) was $33,270 per year for 2009–10. Fees were $300; room and board (a fourteen-meal-per-week plan) cost approximately $12,000 for the year.

Financial Aid

Financial aid is awarded on the basis of need and merit. Merit awards are available for both freshmen and transfer students based on academic achievement. Dominican University of California participates in various federal and state need-based financial aid programs and also has its own financial aid funds, donated by generous alumni and friends, available to help meet University costs.

Need-based financial aid comes in the form of scholarships, grants, part-time employment, and loans. The federal and state financial aid programs are the Federal Supplemental Educational Opportunity Grant, Federal Pell Grant, Federal Work-Study Program, Federal Stafford Student Loan, CLAS/PLUS loan, and Cal Grants A and B. Eligibility for need-based aid is determined after the student, who must be a citizen or permanent resident of the United States, files the Free Application for Federal Student Aid (FAFSA) and the Dominican Financial Aid Application. The need-based financial aid deadline for first-priority consideration is March 2, although late applications are accepted. Student assistantship positions are also available for graduate students.

Faculty

Students find themselves intellectually challenged by the faculty members, who hold degrees from colleges and universities throughout the world and who are committed to individualized teaching and careful supervision of students' development. Seventy-nine percent of Dominican University's full-time faculty members have terminal degrees (the highest obtainable degree in their field). The student-faculty ratio is 11:1.

Student Government

The primary vehicle through which students plan and provide activities, distribute activity funds, and represent themselves to the University's administration and broader community is ASDU—the Associated Students of Dominican University. ASDU is the student association and the student government body. Through elected and appointed representatives to various Dominican committees and governing groups, students may voice their opinions on institutional matters.

Admission Requirements

Dominican University of California welcomes applications from prospective students of all ages, religions, races, and national origins. The University believes that academic potential is measured by more than grades alone. Each candidate for admission is given individual consideration and is evaluated by the Admissions Office on the basis of the student's past scholastic record, present motivation, and potential intellectual development, as indicated by all of the admission materials submitted.

Recommended for undergraduate admission is graduation from an accredited high school with a total of at least 15 units in college-preparatory subjects, to include the following: 4 years of English, 2 years of the same foreign language, 2 years of college-preparatory mathematics (algebra, geometry, algebra 2/trigonometry), 2 years of laboratory sciences to be taken in grades 10–12, and 1 year of U.S. history (1 year of world history or Western civilization is an acceptable alternative for international students). The University encourages students to choose additional courses in at least two of the following areas: English, history, foreign language, social science, advanced mathematics, laboratory science, music, art, and computer science.

Dominican University of California admits highly qualified students after the completion of their junior year in high school if they have fulfilled all admission requirements for freshman standing or passed an equivalency exam and arranged a conference with a member of the admission staff prior to acceptance.

High school seniors wishing to take up to two Dominican courses per semester to meet high school graduation requirements may do so with the written permission of their high school principal or counselor. Arrangements must be made through Academic Advising and Support Services.

Application and Information

The Admissions Office makes its decision on each freshman candidate after receiving his or her completed application form with a $40 nonrefundable fee; an official high school transcript to date; one recommendation from a teacher, administrator, or counselor; scores from either the SAT or the ACT; and a personal essay, as described in the application. For information about the SAT, students should write to Educational Testing Service, 1947 Center Street, Berkeley, California 94704 or P.O. Box 592, Princeton, New Jersey 08541. For information about the ACT, students should write to American College Testing Program, Operations Division, P.O. Box 168, Iowa City, Iowa 52243.

Transfer students must also submit the application form, a $40 fee, and their high school transcript if they have fewer than 24 transfer units. In addition, they must send official college transcripts to date; a personal essay, as described in the application; proof of high school graduation; and one academic letter of recommendation or one professional letter of reference.

International students should fulfill the admission requirements for native students; however, an SAT or ACT score is not required. Passing scores for the Test of English as a Foreign Language (TOEFL) of at least 550 (paper-based) or 80 (Internet-based) or official certification of achieving level 112 in the ELS program may be submitted in lieu of SAT or ACT scores. All transcripts must be translated into English and evaluated by an accredited evaluation agency. In addition, a notarized declaration of finances in U.S. dollars must be submitted.

An interview with a member of the admission staff is strongly recommended to enable the candidate and the University to become acquainted with one another.

Students may apply online at the University's Web site, or they may obtain application forms and information by contacting:

Office of Admissions
Dominican University of California
50 Acacia Avenue
San Rafael, California 94901-2298
Phone: 415-485-3204
888-323-6763 (toll-free)
Fax: 415-485-3214
E-mail: enroll@dominican.edu
Web site: http://www.dominican.edu

COLLEGE CLOSE-UPS

DREXEL UNIVERSITY

PHILADELPHIA, PENNSYLVANIA

The University

Drexel, a private, nonsectarian, coeducational university, has maintained a reputation for academic excellence since its founding in 1891. Its technologically focused academic programs prepare undergraduates for graduate school and a variety of careers. Full-time professional experience through the cooperative education program is a vital part of a Drexel education. Students gain professional experience in jobs related to their career interests by alternating classroom study with periods of full-time employment.

Drexel University grants bachelor's, master's, and doctoral degrees. Last year's undergraduate enrollment numbered 11,003 full-time students representing forty-eight states and ninety-five other countries.

Drexel is committed to expanding their already vast educational opportunities. In 2006, Drexel admitted 181 students to the new Earle Mack School of Law. The School of Law is the first law school to be founded by a major research university in thirty years. In January of 2009, Drexel opened the Sacramento Center for Graduate Studies in Sacramento, California. The Center offers a variety of hybrid graduate degrees by combining online and traditional classroom teaching methods. Drexel University has had great strength in the areas of engineering, science, business, and health care.

Nine residential halls house more than 3,500 students on campus. In conjunction with Drexel's fourteen fraternities and ten sororities, the Campus Activities Board sponsors events such as dances, lectures, excursions, and films. Students take part in a variety of extracurricular activities, including musical groups, a recording studio, Mad Dragon Records, a dance ensemble, theatrical productions, a student-run newspaper, a radio station, and a cable TV station. Drexel offers sixteen NCAA Division I varsity athletic programs, competes in the Colonial Athletic Association Conference, and produces some of the nation's top student athletes in both the academic and athletic arenas. The University sponsors intramural and club sports.

Location

Drexel sits at the heart of the nation's fifth-largest metropolitan area. Philadelphia offers history, culture, nightlife, major-league sports, and great food. The region is also a huge college town, with the highest concentration of universities and colleges in the country. Drexel's immediate neighbor is the University of Pennsylvania, in a neighborhood they share called "University City." With thousands of student residents, University City is a great place for students to spend their college years. The whole region is accessible. Public transportation runs right through the campus. A short walk takes students to Amtrak's 30th Street Station to catch a commuter train to the suburbs; New York City; Washington, D.C.; or beyond.

Majors and Degrees

From computer engineering to media arts and design and from health sciences to business administration, whatever their major, students at Drexel are at the forefront of their field. Offering seventy-three undergraduate programs, Drexel University comprises thirteen colleges and schools, including the Pennoni Honors College. Drexel's academic majors and concentrations include accounting, anthropology, applied engineering technology, architectural engineering, architecture, behavioral health counseling, biological sciences, biomedical engineering, business administration, business and engineering, chemical engineering, chemistry, civil engineering, communication, computer engineering, computer science, construction management, criminal justice, culinary arts, culinary science, dance, design and merchandising, digital media, economics, education, electrical engineering, engineering, engineering for still-deciding students®, English, entertainment and arts management, entrepreneurship, environmental engineering, environmental science, fashion design, film and video, finance, general business for still-deciding students®, general humanities and social sciences for still-deciding students®, graphic design, health services administration, history, hospitality management, information systems, information technology, interior design, international area studies, international business, invasive cardiovascular technology, legal studies, management information systems, marketing, materials engineering, mathematics, mechanical engineering, media arts and design for still-deciding students®, music industry, nursing, nutrition and foods, operations management, pathway to health professions, philosophy, photography, physics, political science, product design, psychology, radiologic technology, science for still-deciding students®, screenwriting and playwriting, sociology, software engineering, sport management, and television.

Qualified Drexel applicants can also choose from several accelerated degree programs, including B.A./B.S./J.D. in law; B.S./D.P.T. in physical therapy; B.S./M.B.A. in business, design and merchandising, and music industry; B.S./M.D. in medicine; B.S./M.H.S. for physician assistant studies; B.S./M.S. programs in biomedical engineering, engineering, higher education, information systems, psychology, and science of instruction; or B.S./Ph.D. in engineering.

Academic Programs

Students with high ability can apply to the Pennoni Honors College, which is open to students in every major. Honors sections of general and required courses and honors colloquia and seminars are available. Special living communities designed for the exceptional student and independent projects characterize the program.

At Drexel, students have opportunities to conduct research. Students Tackling Advanced Research (STAR) allows students to participate in research projects in their field as early as the freshman year. Students who take part in these research opportunities may be eligible for stipends or academic credit for their work.

Off-Campus Programs

Drexel has an active study-abroad program that allows students to spend a term or several terms studying abroad, earning credits toward their degree and gaining valuable international experience. Since this is a Drexel-sponsored program, students pay their regular Drexel tuition and receive their regular Drexel financial aid while they are abroad.

Classroom study is essential, challenging, and inspiring. But experience makes all the difference. Drexel Co-op allows students to alternate periods of full-time work experience with periods of classroom study. With Drexel Co-op, students have the opportunity to explore how they will use their degree in a professional setting. Fortune 500 companies, major pharmaceutical companies, and top design firms are among the workplaces where students can gain up to eighteen months of experience before graduation. More than 2,200 employers from forty-one states and fifteen other countries participate in this program.

Academic Facilities

Drexel comprises three campuses in Philadelphia, as well as one campus in Sacramento, California. These locations include the University City Main Campus, Hahnemann Center City Campus, Queen Lane Medical Campus, and the Sacramento Center for Graduate Studies. Buildings contain dozens of state-of-the-art laboratories for classes and research. Drexel University's library system comprises a main library (W. W. Hagerty Library) on the University City Main Campus site as well as three health sciences libraries to serve the needs of students and faculty and staff members. The W. W. Hagerty Library, the University's central library, houses 1.4 million volumes and maintains subscriptions to nearly 12,000 electronic journals. The library provides access via its Web site to these journals and 200 databases from library computers or remotely through the Internet. The library circulates laptops for use with its wireless network. The additional libraries on the health sciences campuses provide study space, 75,000 books, and network access to the same set of online journals and databases.

As early as 1983, Drexel required incoming freshmen to have personal access to a microcomputer. By 2000, the University had created one of the nation's first fully wireless campuses, including all health sciences campuses. The University has most recently launched a new high-performance parallel computing facility available for faculty and student research. The parallel machine, an IBM RS/6000 S-80 Enterprise Server, offers high-speed performance and scalability. This server provides a shared memory computing environment with low latency, high bandwidth communication between processors.

The Edmund D. Bossone Research Enterprise Center, a $37-million, 155,000-square-foot, multistory facility, strengthens the research capabilities of faculty members and students in the engineering and biomedical engineering fields. Recently opened is the new School of Law building, a four-story facility in the heart of Drexel's campus.

Costs

Depending on the course of study, a student at Drexel may enroll in a four- or five-year degree program. Typically, students enroll in a five-year program, spending eighteen months of that time on co-op gaining valuable work experience; the income earned during co-op can help make the cost of education more affordable for Drexel students. The full-time undergraduate tuition for the 2010–11 academic year is $30,900 for a student in the five-year program and $38,000 for a student in the four-year program. Costs for on-campus housing and the campus meal plan average $13,125 per year. Fees are approximately $2130 per year, depending on the degree program.

Financial Aid

Approximately 90 percent of all freshmen receive financial aid. The aid package may contain academic, athletic, or performing arts scholarships; grants; loans; or part-time employment. Federal programs are also included. All students applying for aid must submit the Free Application for Federal Student Aid (FAFSA) by March 1. Notification to incoming freshmen and transfer students begins mid-March. Drexel offers a unique achievement-based award, the A. J. Drexel Scholarship, to all qualified incoming freshmen and transfer students. With an annual award value of up to $27,000, the A. J. Drexel Scholarship is renewable on a yearly basis, provided the student maintains at least a 3.0 GPA and full-time status. Criteria include a strong academic record and involvement in extracurricular and community service activities.

Faculty

Approximately 94 percent of Drexel's full-time faculty members hold a Ph.D. or the highest degree in their field. Many of the engineering faculty members are registered professional engineers. As a matter of policy, faculty members engaged in research and graduate teaching are also required to teach at the undergraduate level. Thus, the undergraduate student benefits from the research activities of the faculty. Specially selected faculty members serve as advisers for freshmen. The student-faculty ratio is 10:1.

Admission Requirements

All colleges within the University require completion of a college-preparatory program in high school that includes at least 3 years of mathematics and 1 year of laboratory science. Students applying to major in engineering, the sciences, and business and engineering are required to take 4 years of mathematics (through trigonometry) and 2 years of laboratory science. Engineering requires four years of mathematics (through trigonometry and precalculus), chemistry, and physics. The quality of academic performance is more important than merely meeting minimum requirements. The strength of preparation is judged primarily by rank in class or relative grade point average, by the degree of improvement in the quality of the academic record, and by the comments and recommendations from principals, guidance counselors, or teachers. Freshman applicants are required to take the SAT or the ACT. An essay or personal statement is required, with its subject dependent on the major and program. Transfer applicants must have a minimum 2.5 cumulative average (2.75 for engineering, information systems, information technology, and a 3.0 GPA for nursing) for consideration and generally are expected to complete at least 24 credits at a regionally accredited four-year college or two-year community college in a program of study comparable to the one being sought at Drexel.

Application and Information

Applications to Drexel are available online (http://www.drexel.edu/apply) or from the address listed. The Common Application and the Universal Application are accepted as well. Each application must be accompanied by a nonrefundable application fee of $75; however, the fee is waived for online applications or if submitted during a campus visit. Applications for regular full-time undergraduate status are accepted throughout the senior year until March 1. Applications for Drexel's premier scholarship program—the A. J. Drexel scholarship—are due on January 15. Applications for accelerated degree options are due on December 1. Drexel subscribes to the College Board's Candidates Reply Date of May 1. Transfer students should apply at least three months before the beginning of the term in which they wish to enroll.

Undergraduate Admissions
Drexel University
3141 Chestnut Street
Philadelphia, Pennsylvania 19104-2876
Phone: 215-895-2400
800-2-DREXEL (toll-free)
Web site: http://www.drexel.edu/em

Ms. Joan McDonald
Senior Vice President of Enrollment Management
Drexel University
Phone: 800-2-DREXEL (toll-free)
Fax: 215-895-1285
E-mail: enroll@drexel.edu

DUKE UNIVERSITY

DURHAM, NORTH CAROLINA

The University

Duke University is an independent, comprehensive, coeducational research university that traces its roots to 1838, when it was established as Union Institute in Randolph County, North Carolina. Renamed Trinity College twenty-one years later, the school moved to Durham in 1892. In recognition of its primary benefactors, the Duke family, Trinity College became Duke University in 1924.

Duke offers a variety of outstanding undergraduate programs in two schools—Trinity College of Arts and Sciences and the Pratt School of Engineering. At the graduate level, the master's and doctoral programs in these schools (as well as the University's professional schools in business administration, divinity, the environment, law, medicine, nursing, and public policy) consistently rank at or near the top of their fields.

With a limited enrollment of 13,457 full-time students, Duke is among the smallest of the nation's major universities. Of these, 6,340 are undergraduates—5,222 in arts and sciences and 1,118 in engineering. Because of its size and the emphasis on meeting the needs of a diverse student body, the University maintains a commitment to individual education. At Duke, learning is a priority and teaching is personal. As a result, the student body, as a whole, reflects a quality of creativity and mental restlessness that goes far beyond excellent grades and testing. The University attracts students from all fifty states as well as eighty-five other countries, and about 85 percent of Duke's undergraduates come from states other than North and South Carolina.

Duke believes that to build a strong community students must live together. For this reason, all undergraduates are guaranteed housing as long as space remains available and are required to live on campus for their first three years. To accommodate students' widely varying interests, the residence halls provide diverse living styles, including single-sex or coed dorms, unique academic environments, and theme houses or other selective living groups. About 85 percent of undergraduates live on campus. All first-year students live on East Campus in a community designed to support the academic, residential, and recreational needs and interests of new students, and all sophomores live on West Campus. About 36 percent of undergraduates belong to fraternities or sororities. In addition to a rich campus living environment, students can enjoy a full calendar of activities through the University Union, the University-sponsored Artists Series, the Broadway at Duke Series, and nearly 400 clubs and organizations based on diverse political, cultural, social, arts, health, recreational, service, academic, and religious interests as well as intramural sports.

Location

Durham, located about 450 miles from Atlanta and 250 miles from Washington, D.C., is a city of about 240,000 with active research, medical, and arts communities. Together, Durham and nearby Raleigh and Chapel Hill, with a combined population of around 1.5 million, compose the Research Triangle, one of the nation's foremost centers for research and high-tech industry. The Research Triangle has one of the highest concentrations of Ph.D.'s and M.D.'s in the world. Two interstates and the Raleigh-Durham International Airport, only 20 minutes from campus, make Durham easily accessible.

Majors and Degrees

Duke offers both a rigorous academic program and considerable flexibility in course selection and degree programs. Undergraduates can choose courses in nearly 100 different programs in the humanities, social sciences and natural sciences, mathematics, and engineering. Forty-four majors are offered in Trinity College of Arts and Sciences, and students with interests that cannot be met within an established major are able to design their own curriculum with the help of a faculty adviser. In addition, students may pursue dual degrees, minors in most fields, and any of the University's twenty-three certificate programs.

Trinity College of Arts and Sciences offers programs leading to the A.B. degree or the B.S. degree in African and African American studies, art history, Asian and Middle Eastern studies, biology, Canadian studies, chemistry, classical studies, computer science, cultural anthropology, dance, earth and ocean sciences, economics, English, environmental sciences, environmental science and policy, evolutionary anthropology,French studies, German, history, international comparative studies, Italian studies, linguistics, literature, mathematics, medieval and Renaissance studies, music, neuroscience, philosophy, physics, political science, psychology, public policy studies, religion, Russian, Slavic and Eurasian studies, sociology, Spanish, statistical science, theater studies, visual arts, and women's studies.

Interdisciplinary nonmajor certificate programs are available in aerospace engineering; architectural engineering; arts of the moving image; children in contemporary society; documentary studies; early childhood education studies; energy and the environment; genome sciences and policy; global health; health policy; human development; information sciences and information studies; Islamic studies; Jewish studies; Latino/Latina studies; marine science and conservation leadership; markets and management studies; modeling biological systems; neurosciences; policy journalism and media studies; politics, philosophy, and economics; study of ethics; and study of sexualities.

The Pratt School of Engineering offers accredited four-year programs leading to the B.S.E. in biomedical engineering, civil and environmental engineering, electrical and computer engineering, and mechanical engineering and materials science.

Academic Programs

The year is divided into two semesters with two optional summer terms; first-semester exams fall before the winter break. Students in the liberal arts plan their own courses of study, with the help of an adviser, according to guidelines rather than specific course requirements. Academic Writing, a one-semester class in expository writing, is the only course required of undergraduates. The Trinity College liberal arts curriculum of approximately 15 semester courses encompasses five areas of knowledge: arts, literatures, and performance; civilizations; social sciences; natural sciences; and quantitative studies. As students take courses in these areas, the curriculum provides significant exposure to cross-cultural and ethical inquiry, methods of analysis and reasoning, foreign language, writing, research, and the relationships between science, technology, and society. Thirty-four courses are required for graduation.

First-year students are encouraged to participate in the Focus Program, consisting of about a dozen clusters of interrelated seminars spanning topics such as Evolution and Humankind, Engineering Frontiers: Living Systems for a Living Planet, Exploring the Mind, The Faces of Science, The Power of Ideas, and Visions of Freedom. Students in each Focus Cluster live together to expand the opportunities for discussion and learning. Also, in more than forty-five first-year seminars, offered in nearly every department, professors chosen for their outstanding undergraduate teaching lead classes of 15 or fewer students. In general, other than the occasional large lecture hall, classes at Duke contain between 16 and 35 students.

When students declare a major—no later than the end of the sophomore year in Trinity College and the end of the first year in the Pratt School of Engineering—a faculty member from the major department becomes their adviser. Students who plan to continue their study in a professional school also work with career-specific advisers to plan a program of study that provides the appropriate foundation for advanced work and meets their unique interests.

Off-Campus Programs

Through internships and study-abroad programs, students are encouraged to take advantage of nearly 130 Duke-affiliated off-campus study opportunities. These range from oceanographic studies at the Duke Marine Laboratory in Beaufort, North Carolina, and arts programs in New York or Los Angeles to a variety of overseas programs. Through the Office of Study Abroad, students can choose international programs from four weeks to a full year in length. In most cases, scholarship aid can be applied to study abroad. Approximately 50 percent of each graduating class studies away from campus on nearly every continent in the world. DukeEngage provides funding and faculty support for any undergraduate student who wishes to pursue a summer or semester-long service project.

Academic Facilities

With more than 5 million volumes, 17 million manuscripts, 1.4 million public documents, 3.9 million microforms, and tens of thousands of films, video recordings, and serials, Duke University's library holdings are among the most extensive in the nation. The University's most sophisticated teaching and research facilities—including the Fitzpatrick Center for Interdisciplinary Engineering, Medicine, and Applied Sciences and the Bostock Library—are available to undergraduates as they work with faculty mentors on various research projects.

All students have access to extensive computing facilities and services supported by the Office of Information Technology. Services include free accounts on Duke's main computer system, which provide access to high-speed Internet and e-mail as well as access to the twenty-three campus computer labs, which provide computers, printers, and access to DukeNet, the campuswide fiber-optic network. All undergraduate residence hall rooms are wired for DukeNet access.

Costs

For 2009–10, a year in Trinity College or the Pratt School of Engineering cost $53,390, with $39,080 allotted for tuition and fees, and an average of $11,170 for room and board (although costs vary with accommodations). The total yearly estimate included $3140 for books and miscellaneous expenses. All fees are subject to change, and up-to-date information is available through the Office of Undergraduate Financial Aid.

Financial Aid

Duke University believes that access to a high-quality private education should depend on a student's qualifications, not his or her family's financial strength. Admission to Duke is need-blind for U.S. citizens and permanent residents. Ability to pay is not considered in the admission decision.

All admitted students who apply for financial aid receive 100 percent of their demonstrated financial need for all four years of undergraduate study.

With Duke's new financial aid initiatives, parents whose incomes total $60,000 or less no longer have to contribute financially to their child's education. In addition, student loans have been eliminated for families whose incomes total $40,000 or less, and reduced for families with incomes up to $100,000.

The University also makes need-based financial aid available for a limited number of students who are not U.S. citizens or permanent residents. Duke will also meet the full demonstrated financial need for these students; however, financial need is a factor in the admissions decision for foreign citizens applying for financial aid.

The aid program includes honorary and need-based scholarships, grants, federal and institutional college work-study program awards, Federal Perkins Loans and Stafford Student Loans, and University-sponsored internships. Limited merit, ROTC, and athletic scholarships are available, and all admitted students are automatically considered for all appropriate merit scholarships.

U.S. citizens and permanent residents applying for financial aid should submit the PROFILE application provided by the College Scholarship Service, the Free Application for Federal Student Aid (FAFSA), and a copy of their family's most recently filed tax forms. Financial aid applicants who are citizens of other countries should submit the College Board's International Student Financial Aid Application along with a copy of their family's most recent national tax forms. Also, their parents' employers must provide, in English, statements that outline annual income and benefits received in connection with their current employment. Further information is available through the Office of Undergraduate Financial Aid.

Faculty

Duke has a faculty of 2,877 full-time and part-time members in its undergraduate, graduate, and professional schools, 814 of whom teach undergraduates, making the student-faculty ratio 8:1. More importantly, people of national or international prominence, members of major academic societies, state and national advisers, and faculty chairs honoring professors of extraordinary ability are found in every department or division. About 90 percent of tenured or tenure-track faculty members teach undergraduates, and many serve as first-year student and departmental advisers.

Student Government

Students at Duke are considered mature individuals capable of governing their own actions, while furthering the best interests of the broader University community. The Duke Student Government and various student-faculty-administration committees provide diverse avenues for student interaction with professors and administrators. In addition, the Duke Student Government supports students who want to start their own campus organizations. Undergraduates also serve as voting members of the University's Board of Trustees.

Admission Requirements

The Committee on Admissions selects students on the basis of their academic record and quality of their secondary school program, recommendations from teachers and counselors, extracurricular activities and accomplishments, the application essay, and standardized test scores. The University does not discriminate on the basis of race, color, national or ethnic origin, gender, handicap, sexual orientation, or age in its admission policies. No geographic quotas are imposed. Applicants should have at least four years of English and at least three of mathematics, natural science, foreign language, and social studies. Engineering applicants are strongly advised to take four years of mathematics and four years of science, including physics and chemistry. Engineering applicants must have taken calculus before they enroll. Students are encouraged to enroll in advanced-level work as preparation for the Duke curriculum.

Duke accepts both ACT and SAT scores. Students should take either the ACT including writing or the three-part SAT Reasoning and SAT Subject Tests in two areas. Engineering applicants who submit SAT scores must take the SAT Subject Test in mathematics. Personal interviews in the applicants' local areas by members of the Alumni Admissions Advisory Committee are recommended but not required.

Application and Information

Application deadlines for first-year students are November 1 for early decision and January 2 for regular decision. Duke accepts the Common Application or the Universal College Application plus the Duke Student Supplement. Students who want to arrange an alumni interview should file either their application or the Duke Student Supplement of their application by October 19 for early decision or by December 10 for regular decision. For transfer students, the application deadline for fall admission is March 15. Students must apply either to Trinity College of Arts and Sciences or the Pratt School of Engineering at the time of application. Required tests should be taken by January of the senior year or by October for early decision applicants. For additional information, students should contact:

Office of Undergraduate Admissions
Duke University
2138 Campus Drive, Box 90586
Durham, North Carolina 27708-0586

Phone: 919-684-3214
Fax: 919-681-8941
Web site: http://www.admissions.duke.edu/

D'YOUVILLE COLLEGE

BUFFALO, NEW YORK

The College

D'Youville College is a private, coeducational, liberal arts and professional college that has offered students an education of high quality since 1908. The College was the first in western New York to offer baccalaureate degrees to women. Its current enrollment is 2,900 men and women. Students may choose from thirty undergraduate and graduate degree programs that are enhanced by a 14:1 student-faculty ratio. The College is committed to helping its students to grow not only in academics but in the social and personal areas of their college experience as well.

The multiple-option Nursing Degree Program is one of the largest four-year private-college nursing programs in the country. Available nursing programs include B.S.N., B.S.N./M.S. (five years), and RN to B.S.N. Of D'Youville's 2006 graduates, 94 percent are employed in their field or are in graduate school.

Students residing in Marguerite Hall or the new student apartment complex have a scenic view of the Niagara River and Lake Erie, which separate the U.S. and Canadian shorelines. The Koessler Administration Building, which once housed the entire college, now contains administrative offices, the chapel, Kavinoky Theatre, and the Learning Center. The Student Center, the focal point of leisure and extracurricular activities, has a new gymnasium, a swimming pool, fitness and wellness area, a training room, a dance studio, a general recreation center, and the main dining facilities. Student organizations and regularly scheduled activities, including intramural sports, NCAA Division III intercollegiate sports (baseball, basketball, crew, volleyball, golf, cross-country, soccer, and softball), a ski club, the College newspaper, the yearbook, and social organizations, as well as academic programs, all help to make up an active campus life.

Location

D'Youville is situated on Buffalo's residential west side. The College is within minutes of many local attractions, including the downtown shopping center, the Kleinhans Music Hall, the Albright-Knox Art Gallery, two museums, and several theaters that offer stage productions. Seasonal changes in the area offer a variety of recreational opportunities. Buffalo is only 90 miles from Toronto and 25 minutes from Niagara Falls, making it a gateway to recreation areas in western New York and Ontario. Holiday Valley, a skier's paradise, is an hour's drive away. The city is served by the New York State Thruway, Amtrak, Greyhound and Trailways bus lines, and most major airlines.

D'Youville enjoys a diversified interchange with the community due to its affiliations with schools, hospitals, and social agencies in the area. College students in the Buffalo area number more than 60,000.

Majors and Degrees

D'Youville offers the degrees of Bachelor of Arts (B.A.), Bachelor of Science (B.S.), and Bachelor of Science in Nursing (B.S.N.). Majors include accounting, biology, business management, chemistry, chiropractic, dietetics, education (elementary, secondary, and special), English, exercise and sports studies, global studies, health services management, history, information technology, international business, mathematics, nursing, occupational therapy, pharmacy, philosophy, physical therapy, physician assistant studies, preprofessional studies (dental, law, medicine, and veterinary studies), psychology, and sociology. Five-year combined bachelor's/master's (B.S./M.S.) programs are offered in accounting, dietetics, education, information technology (B.S.)/international business (M.S.), international business, nursing, occupational therapy, and physician assistant studies. A six-year B.S./D.P.T. program is offered in physical therapy. A seven-year B.S./D.C. program is offered in chiropractic.

Academic Programs

The area of concentration recognizes individual differences and varying interests but still provides sufficient specialization in one discipline to form a foundation for graduate studies and professional careers. Students attending D'Youville are expected to complete the requirements of their chosen concentration while earning a minimum of 120 credit hours. Core requirements include humanities, 24 hours; social science, 12 hours; science, 7 hours; mathematics/computer science, 6 hours; and electives, 9 hours. A cumulative average of at least 2.0 must be maintained to meet graduation requirements. Sixteen credit hours, or five or six courses per semester, are considered a normal workload. Internships to meet specific career goals may be arranged in any major.

The College offers a Career Discovery Program that was purposely designed for the undecided student. This program, which can last for two years, offers credit courses and internships meeting two years of study in any major.

The academic year is composed of two semesters, each lasting approximately fifteen weeks. The first semester, including final examinations, ends before the Christmas holidays. During the eight-week summer sessions, programs of selected courses are given at all levels on a daily basis.

Off-Campus Programs

The baccalaureate program in nursing is affiliated with thirteen area hospitals and public health agencies. The education program is affiliated with local elementary, junior high, and secondary schools and with special education centers in the area for purposes of student teaching. The occupational therapy, physical therapy, and physician assistant programs are affiliated with appropriate clinical settings throughout the United States.

Academic Facilities

D'Youville's modern Montante Family Library offers state-of-the-art computer reference capabilities for both in-house and off-site users, including access to over seventy online databases. The multimillion-dollar Alt Health Science Building houses laboratories, including those for anatomy, organic chemistry, and gross anatomy; activity and daily living labs for the health professions; and additional laboratories for physics, chemistry, quantitative analysis, and computer science. It also houses classrooms, faculty member offices, and development centers, including one for career development. This is augmented by the modern Bauer Family Academic Center, which provides state-of-the-art classrooms, laboratories, and faculty offices.

Costs

For 2010–11, tuition is $10,400 per semester, and room and board cost $4900 per semester. A general College fee is required and is based on credit hours taken; a Student Association fee of $40 per semester is applied toward concerts, yearbooks, activities, and guest lectures. A $100 deposit ($150 for dietetics, physician assistant studies, occupational therapy, and physical therapy programs), credited toward tuition, must be submitted by all candidates who accept an offer of admission.

Financial Aid

D'Youville attempts to provide financial aid for students who would not otherwise be able to attend. Determination of aid is based on the Free Application for Federal Student Aid. Aid is available in the form of grants, loans, and employment on campus. In addition, D'Youville automatically offers scholarships for academic achievement to all eligible incoming students.

All students may qualify for D'Youville's Academic Scholarship Program, which offers scholarships with total values up to $58,600. Students who apply, are accepted, and meet the criteria instantly qualify for one of these scholarships, all of which are renewable annually. These scholarships are not based on need. The three scholarship programs are the Honors Scholarship, the Academic Distinction Scholarship, and the Achievement Scholarship. The Honors Scholarship requires an 85 academic average, a minimum SAT score of 1100 (math and critical reading) or an ACT score of at least 24, and awards 50 percent of tuition and 25 percent of room and board costs. The Academic Distinction Scholarship requires SAT scores of at least 1000 (math and critical reading) or ACT scores of 21 to 23 and an academic average of at least 85. It awards 25 percent of tuition and 50 percent of room and board costs. The Achievement Scholarship criteria include SAT scores of 900 to 1090 (math and critical reading) or ACT scores of 19 to 23 and an academic average of 80 to 84. This scholarship awards $1000–$5000. The Transfer Honors Scholarship is based on a starting GPA of 2.75. This scholarship's award ranges from $1000 to $5000.

Faculty

The ratio of faculty members to students is 1:14. All members of the full-time instructional staff hold a doctorate or another advanced degree. Faculty members act as advisers and are available for consultation with students.

Student Government

The Student Association (SA), a representative form of student self-government, seeks to inspire in its members dedication to the intellectual, social, and moral ideals of the College and works closely with the administration and faculty. All students of D'Youville are considered members of the SA and may be elected to the executive council and the student senate. There are seventeen academic and social clubs affiliated with the SA.

Admission Requirements

An applicant must be a high school graduate or have a high school equivalency diploma before matriculating. The applicant should have a college-preparatory background, including required English and history courses and a sequence in either mathematics or science. Scores on the SAT or the ACT are also required for admission. High school advanced placement credit is acceptable and transferable. The admission decision is based on high school grade point average, rank in class, and scores on the SAT or ACT. Students who have difficulty meeting normal admission standards may be admitted with a reduced academic load.

The College Learning Center offers academic assistance to students whose education has been interrupted or has not prepared them adequately for college courses. The Tutor Bank, a system of peer tutoring, offers the assistance of qualified students to those who need help in specific academic disciplines.

Application and Information

D'Youville admits students on a rolling admission basis; therefore, applications are reviewed as they are received by the admissions office. Transfer students who have a quality point average of at least 2.0 are encouraged to apply by December 1 for the spring semester and by July 1 for the fall semester. A brochure listing course offerings and giving details about costs and room and board is available upon request.

Steve Smith
Director of Admissions
D'Youville College
One D'Youville Square
320 Porter Avenue
Buffalo, New York 14201-1084
Phone: 716-829-7600
800-777-3921 (toll-free)
Fax: 716-829-7900
E-mail: admissions@dyc.edu
Web site: http://www.dyc.edu

COLLEGE CLOSE-UPS

EASTERN CONNECTICUT STATE UNIVERSITY

WILLIMANTIC, CONNECTICUT

The University

Eastern Connecticut State University, Connecticut's public liberal arts university, offers thirty-one undergraduate majors and graduate degrees in education and organizational management. Eastern has all the advantages of a private liberal arts college combined with "public-university resources and cost." The University's public liberal arts focus and concern for the individual student, along with its small classes, personalized counseling, and independent-study opportunities, encourage involvement and engagement as well as intellectual and personal growth and development. The student body (4,124 full-time undergraduates) is remarkably diverse and includes students from various ethnic, geographic, and socioeconomic backgrounds. Students attending Eastern come from 163 of Connecticut's 169 towns, twenty-three states, and forty-two countries. Eastern is a residential liberal arts campus. The residence life component is considered integral to students' overall liberal arts education. Most full-time students, including 92 percent of the freshmen, reside on campus. There are seven residence halls and five apartment complexes on campus. Hurley Hall, the University's main food court-style dining area, offers unlimited dining during operational hours. On-campus parking is available to students, except incoming freshmen living on campus. There are more than sixty special interest clubs and organizations on campus, as well as a student newspaper, a yearbook, and a literary and arts magazine. Extracurricular events include concerts, an art and lecture series, dances, films, intramural sports, musical and dramatic productions, and bus trips to Boston and New York City. Varsity sports for men include baseball, basketball, cross-country, lacrosse, soccer, and track. Women participate in intercollegiate basketball, cross-country, field hockey, lacrosse, soccer, softball, swimming, track, and volleyball. Sports facilities include an athletic center with a 2,800-seat gymnasium for badminton, basketball, tennis, and volleyball; a six-lane swimming pool; handball and squash courts; saunas; a fitness center and rooms for physical conditioning, modern dance, and gymnastics; and an athletic complex that includes a state-of-the-art baseball field with a 1,500-seat grandstand as well as field hockey and multipurpose fields. The University's impressive Student Center includes ample meeting space, a theater, multipurpose room, game area, expansive food court, and a glass-enclosed exercise room.

Location

Willimantic, Connecticut, a small city of diversified interests and many styles of living, has a population of 22,000. It has convenient shopping centers and a growing community of ambitious and ecology-minded individuals who are concerned with the city's future. The eastern Connecticut region is famous for its rolling hills, forests, state recreational areas, nature trails, clear lakes and streams, and beaches. Skiing areas are nearby. Hartford is 40 minutes away, and New York City and Boston are both less than 2 hours from Willimantic by car.

Majors and Degrees

Eastern offers four undergraduate degrees: the Bachelor of Arts, the Bachelor of General Studies, the Bachelor of Science, and the Associate in Science. The Bachelor of Arts degree is awarded with majors in economics, English, history, history and social sciences, music, political science, psychology, social work, sociology, Spanish, theater, and visual arts (academic tracks in art history, digital art and design, printing and drawing, and sculpture). The Bachelor of Science degree programs include accounting, biochemistry, biology (academic tracks in premedicine, predentistry, pre–veterinary studies, and ecology), business administration (concentrations in the areas of finance, human resource management, international business, management, and marketing), business information systems, communication, computer science, early childhood education, elementary education, English, environmental earth science, mathematics, physical education, secondary education, and sport and leisure management. Certification in secondary education is available in biology, English, environmental earth science, history, and mathematics. The associate degree program is available in the arts and sciences. The Bachelor of General Studies is a flexible degree program for adults who are 25 or older. Students may design a program integrating life experience into major or minor concentrations through a learning contract developed with their academic adviser.

Academic Programs

The graduation requirements for a bachelor's degree embrace the University's liberal arts mission and require a minimum of 120 hours of credit and completion of a major program of study. All degree candidates must take a freshman English composition course and fulfill specified course requirements in a three-tier liberal arts core. The tier system includes study in methods and concepts, synthesis and application, and independent inquiry. The University operates on a two-semester system. The fall semester usually starts the first week in September and ends in mid-December; the spring semester, which includes a one-week break in March, runs from the third week of January to the middle of May. One 6-week and two 3-week sessions are offered during the summer. An Intersession program is offered in January of each year.

Eastern offers an Honors Program for academically talented students. This highly competitive program emphasizes scholarly activity, independent study, and special courses and offers tuition scholarships. The Contract Admissions Program (CAP) is an educational support service that offers counseling, tutoring, developmental courses, and financial assistance to highly motivated students who might otherwise have been denied admission on the basis of traditional criteria. Cooperative Education (Co-op) is an optional work-study program; students may choose to participate in the program for one or more periods.

The University grants credit for Advanced Placement Program examination in all the subject areas tested and accepts up to 60 credit hours earned through the College-Level Examination Program (CLEP). Persons with a minimum of five years of successful work experience in areas of specialization taught by the University may qualify for advanced placement through credit for life experience and learning.

U.S. Army and Air Force ROTC programs, which are offered by the University of Connecticut at Storrs, are available to qualified Eastern students.

Off-Campus Programs

Eastern offers a number of opportunities for off-campus study for college credit. These include off-campus internships, study abroad, and consortium arrangements. Internships are available in the academic areas of biology, business administration, communication, computer science, economics, education, environmental earth science, psychology, public policy and government, sociology, and Spanish. Biology majors may study in Belize or Bermuda through the tropical biology program. There are also opportunities to join international study groups for one semester, one academic year, or a summer session. Eastern also participates in the National Student Exchange (NSE) program, which allows students to attend other public colleges and universities across the United States while still paying tuition and fees to Eastern.

Academic Facilities

The J. Eugene Smith Library contains more than 500,000 volumes and 127,000 square feet of educational learning space. The Media Building contains a color television studio, a recording studio, an FM radio station, an electronic auditorium, a computer center, darkrooms, and graphic arts areas and serves as the hub of the audiovisual distribution system. The planetarium contains two electron microscopes and a geology laboratory. The new LEED-approved Science Building provides modern, well-equipped laboratories for biology, chemistry, and physics. A four-story, 72,000 square-foot classroom building and the library and clock tower serve as the main academic areas of the campus. The Childhood and Family Resource Center, with state-of-the-art classroom and teaching space, meeting facilities, and a full-service day-care center, serves as a model facility for its resources. A new Performing Arts Centers is in the planning stages.

Costs

For 2009–10, tuition and fees for a Connecticut resident are $7813, and nonresident tuition and fees are $17,505 on an annual basis. The fees include a required non-refundable tuition deposit of $200, which is required to secure a place in the University, and a non-refundable $250 housing deposit. Room was estimated at $5410 and board at $4170 for two semesters. Books and supplies average $1000 per year. Tuition and fees are subject to change as warranted and are itemized on the University's Web site.

Financial Aid

Financial aid includes grants and scholarships, low-interest loans, student employment opportunities, and special programs for veterans and their families. The University participates in the Federal Perkins Loan, Federal Pell Grant, Federal Supplemental Educational Opportunity Grant, and Federal Work-Study programs. In addition, it provides aid through alumni funds and other resources of its own. Approximately two thirds of all Eastern students receive financial aid. Awards are based primarily on demonstrated financial need. All students who wish to apply for financial assistance are required to complete the Free Application for Federal Student Aid (FAFSA) and send it to the processing agency by March 15 for the fall semester or by November 15 for the spring semester.

Faculty

The friendliness and approachability of the University's professors are usually noted by the students enrolled at Eastern. While faculty members are focused primarily on quality teaching and the full development of students enrolled, many write and conduct significant research. Faculty members hold advanced degrees from leading American and international colleges and universities; 95 percent hold terminal degrees. Faculty members serve as academic counselors and mentors for students. Full-time advisers and counseling services are available to assist students in matters of personal and academic concern. The student-faculty ratio at Eastern is 16:1. The average class size is 24.

Student Government

An organized plan of student government and student representation on University committees permits students to be actively involved with important issues and develop basic policies for student life. The Student Senate is the governing body; it supervises and coordinates all student activities and serves as a liaison with the faculty, administration, and Board of Trustees.

Admission Requirements

Eastern is considered to be selective in admission. Applicants are considered on an individual basis, with emphasis placed on the applicant's secondary school record, satisfactory SAT or ACT scores, rank in the high school graduating class, personal accomplishments and motivation, and teachers' or guidance counselors' recommendations. Applicants' complete requirements for secondary school graduation or its equivalent should include 16 academic units of college-preparatory work, with the following divisions: English, 4 years; mathematics, 3 years (4 years preferred); science, 2 years (including 1 year of laboratory science); social sciences, 2 years (including U.S. history); and foreign language, 2 years (3 years preferred). Students who are admitted without having fulfilled the language requirement must complete one year of a foreign language (6 credits) at Eastern. Deferred admission is also available. A campus visit is strongly suggested, although not required. A limited number of highly motivated students who do not qualify for admission if traditional criteria are used may be admitted to the University by successfully completing the Summer Transition Experience Program/Contract Admission Program or the Summer Proof of Ability Option. Students should contact the Office of Admissions for more information on special admission options.

Application and Information

Eastern reviews completed applications for admission on a rolling basis. Offers of admission are made and deposits accepted until the University reaches its enrollment capacity. Students are encouraged to apply early in their senior year. Tuition and housing deposits are due upon admission. Applications for the fall semester can be submitted after the first quarter of the senior year of high school. Freshman applicants must submit an admission application; a $50 nonrefundable application fee; a complete transcript of high school grades and rank in class; an essay explaining why Eastern, Connecticut's public liberal arts college, is the right college choice for the applicant; two recommendations from guidance counselors or teachers; and an official copy of their SAT or ACT score report. Applicants are usually notified of the admission decision within one month after the application is complete. Applicants are encouraged to apply online at http://www.easternct.edu. Application forms and information may be requested from:

Kimberly Crone
Director of Admissions and Enrollment Management
Eastern Connecticut State University
83 Windham Street
Willimantic, Connecticut 06226
Phone: 860-465-5286
Fax: 860-465-5544
E-mail: admissions@easternct.edu
Web site: http://www.easternct.edu

Eastern's J. Eugene Smith Library, with more than 500,000 volumes and 127,000 square feet of educational space, serves as the academic hub of the campus.

EASTERN NAZARENE COLLEGE

QUINCY, MASSACHUSETTS

The College

Eastern Nazarene College (ENC) is a Christian college of the liberal arts and sciences with an innovative curriculum, focused on global issues, at the intersection of faith and culture. Founded in 1900 as a preparatory academy and liberal arts college, ENC continues to award baccalaureate and graduate degrees in over fifty areas of academic study to students of all ages. Located just six miles from downtown Boston and half a mile from the nearest subway station, ENC students and faculty enjoy a beautiful South Shore residential campus with everyday access to the city known as America's college town.

With an idyllic 15-acre campus set in a safe, suburban, residential New England neighborhood and a total student population of just over 1,000, ENC's size is one of its greatest assets. The campus atmosphere fosters a sense of belonging, and long-lasting friendships are forged not just between classmates, but between all members of the ENC community. Class sizes also remain small, facilitating discussion among peers and allowing professors to engage their students more effectively.

The newest additions to the College footprint are the Cecil R. Paul Center for Business and the James R. Cameron Center for History, Law, and Government. Other facilities, such as the Mann Student Center, have recently undergone extensive renovations.

In addition to the curricular life of the College, Eastern Nazarene is home to over seventy-five student organizations, ranging from academic clubs to social justice-oriented ministries. The College also participates in NCAA athletics and hosts numerous intramural sports. Other extracurricular opportunities at ENC include a student-run literary magazine, the *Veritas News* campus newspaper, numerous theatrical productions, and several musical ensembles including the A Cappella Choir, Gospel Choir, Chamber Singers, Symphonic Winds, Jazz Band, Choral Union, Quincy Bay Chamber Orchestra, and others.

Location

Eastern Nazarene College is conveniently located in Quincy, Massachusetts, recently ranked as the second-safest city in the state. A suburb of Boston, Quincy was the birthplace of John Adams and John Quincy Adams, as well as John Hancock. The Wollaston Park campus was also once the summer home of Boston mayor Josiah Quincy Jr.

The College owns two campuses in Quincy. The main campus is located in Wollaston Park, six miles from downtown Boston and a quarter mile from beautiful Quincy Bay and Wollaston Beach, the largest of the Boston Harbor beaches. The Wollaston Park campus is home to administrative and classroom buildings, a fine arts center, a prayer chapel, a student center, a college library, a physical education center, athletic fields, tennis courts, five residence halls, and a college-owned apartment building.

The Old Colony Campus is home to the Campus Kinder Haus Early Childhood Education Center; the James R. Cameron Center for History, Law, and Government; the Cecil R. Paul Center for Business; and the Adams Executive Center. The Old Colony Campus also serves as the main classroom location for the College's Leadership Education for Adults (LEAD) program for working adults and graduate students.

Both campuses are conveniently located a half mile from Wollaston Station, on the Red Line of the Boston subway system.

Majors and Degrees

As a college of the liberal arts and sciences, Eastern Nazarene primarily awards Bachelor of Arts (B.A.) and Bachelor of Science (B.S.) degrees. Majors, minors, and concentrations are as follows: accounting, Biblical languages, Biblical literature, biochemistry, biology, business, chemistry, chemistry and business, child and adolescent developmental psychology, Christian ministry, clinical and research psychology, communication arts, computer engineering, computer science, contemporary music and recording, criminal justice, criminal justice and social relations psychology, early childhood education, electrical engineering, elementary education, engineering, English, environmental science, environmental studies, forensic science, general science, government, health science, history, history education, instrumental music performance, journalism, liberal arts, literature, management, marketing, mathematics, middle school education, missions, movement arts, music and business, music and communication arts, music business, music composition, music education, music history, music ministry, music performance, music recording, music theory, philosophy, physical education, physics, predentistry, prelaw, premedicine, prenursing, pre–occupational therapy, prepharmacy, pre–physical therapy, pre–veterinary science, religion, secondary education, social relations psychology, social welfare, social work, sociology, special education, sports management, theater arts, theology and philosophy, visual arts, vocal music performance, writing, and youth ministry. Dual-degree programs in cooperation with other Boston-area institutions are also offered in mechanical engineering, nursing, and pharmacy.

Academic Programs

Eastern Nazarene operates on a two-semester academic calendar from late August to early May. Bachelor's degrees are awarded upon successful completion of 130 credit hours, including the 52-credit liberal arts core and completion of a major course of study. Dual-degree programs leading to both a B.A. and a B.S. from ENC require 153 total credit hours. Students are also strongly encouraged to earn credits through study abroad and internships.

The Cultural Perspectives sequence has long been a distinctive feature of the core liberal arts curriculum at Eastern Nazarene. Originally conceived as a series of interdisciplinary courses that challenge students to ponder the tensions and possibilities between Christian values and modern society, the sequence has expanded beyond Western perspectives to embrace a global understanding of Christianity and culture. These courses integrate various disciplines in the liberal arts and present students with opportunities to engage the world by looking at all aspects of knowledge (philosophy, art, history, literature, science, music, religion, etc.) through a variety of cultural lenses, so that they may transcend their own cultural contexts and begin to see the world from the perspectives of others.

Off-Campus Programs

Students at Eastern Nazarene College are encouraged to take advantage of the numerous semester-long study-abroad opportunities available through the College. Programs in the United States and Canada include a Contemporary Music Center on Martha's Vineyard, a Film Studies Center in Los Angeles, both a Journalism Center and an American Studies Program in the District of Columbia, and exchange opportunities at any of the 109 members of the Council for Christian Colleges and Universities. ENC also offers study programs in several locations outside the United States, including Drummoyne, Australia; Beijing, Hong Kong, Xiamen, and Xian, China; San José, Costa Rica; Cairo, Egypt; Oxford, England; Nairobi, Kenya; Moscow, Nizhni Novgorod, and St. Petersburg, Russia; Sighisoara, Transylvania; and Mukono, Uganda.

Many ENC students also participate in various short-term trips abroad. Recently, students have studied the economy and politics of the European Union while traveling throughout Europe, studied field problems in ecology while in Belize, visited the Fiji and Hawaiian islands on an international choir tour, and participated in mission trips to Honduras, Mozambique, and Mexico.

Academic Facilities

The new Nease Library is a center for on-campus study. In addition to private study rooms, the library provides common space for collaborative work and the Instructional Resource Center offers a full range of media resources. The library houses approximately 118,500 volumes, more than 500 periodicals, and 13,000 online periodicals. Reference service is available for all materials. A 24-hour study room provides opportunity for late-night study, computer labs offer PC and Macintosh work environments for all students, and the campuswide wireless network gives students and visitors access to e-mail and the Internet. Nease Library is also home to the Café Savoie.

In addition to the educational resources provided by Nease Library and the academic facilities provided by Gardner, Angell, and Canterbury Halls, the College features a science center with state-of-the-art equipment; a fine arts center for music and theatrical practice and performance; and new centers for business, early childhood education, and history, law, and government.

Costs

Tuition for the 2010–11 academic year is $22,982 for 12–18 credit hours while room and board are $7250 and fees are $790. Tuition and fees at ENC are among the lowest for private colleges in New England.

Financial Aid

Eastern Nazarene College offers institutional aid to all incoming students, from first-time freshmen to transfer and international students. This aid comes in two forms: merit-based aid, which is determined by a student's academic qualifications; and need-based aid, which is determined by a student's financial need. These forms of aid can be combined with Federal Pell Grants, the FSEOG program, state grants, Federal Stafford Student Loans, Federal Perkins Loans, PLUS loans, and work-study programs. In 2009, Eastern Nazarene awarded approximately $11.5 million in aid, $4.7 million of which came from ENC scholarships and grants.

Faculty

Professors at Eastern Nazarene College are committed Christians who hold degrees from top-ranked research institutions, receive national recognition for their academic achievements, interact with students on an individual basis, and are professionally active in Boston and beyond. Of the 43 full-time faculty members who teach at the College, 75 percent hold an earned Ph.D. or other terminal degree. Professors, not teaching assistants, teach all the classes. While teaching is the primary focus, many of the professors at ENC are also involved in research and are experts in their field. The average class size is 15 and the overall student-to-faculty ratio is 13:1, allowing students and faculty members to get to know each other personally. These highly respected scholars are thereby able to provide guidance and mentoring opportunities that encourage students to grow intellectually, socially, and spiritually.

Student Government

The ENC Student Government Association (SGA) annually elects officers to represent the student body in working alongside the College administration in planning events and establishing new student organizations. Extracurricular activities at Eastern Nazarene are intended to develop character through a wide variety of activities that invite a rich tradition and a high degree of participation.

Admission Requirements

Admission to the College is selective, but very personal and interactive. The Office of Admissions employs an assessment method that evaluates all admission criteria equally. The College offers admission to qualified applicants who demonstrate academic achievement, extracurricular involvement, and community engagement. Notification of the admission decision is made on a case-by-case basis and as soon as possible after all the required materials have been received.

Application and Information

In addition to an online application form, first-time freshman applicants must submit a secondary school record and SAT/ACT scores, while transfer student applicants must submit transcripts from all colleges previously attended. International student applicants must also submit a Certification of Finances and have all transcripts evaluated by either WES or AACRAO. Non-native English speakers must submit TOEFL scores and all applicants must submit academic and character recommendations. A campus visit and interview are recommended.

For additional application information, or to arrange a campus visit, contact:

Office of Admissions
Eastern Nazarene College
23 East Elm Avenue
Quincy, Massachusetts 02170
Phone: 617-745-3711
800-88-ENC-88 (toll-free)
Fax: 617-745-3992
E-mail: admissions@enc.edu
Web site: http://www.enc.edu

Spring commencement takes place on the College green, between Gardner Hall, Munro Hall, and the Wollaston Church of the Nazarene.

EASTERN UNIVERSITY

ST. DAVIDS, PENNSYLVANIA

The University

Eastern University is a Christian university committed to the integration of faith, reason, and justice. In all of its undergraduate, graduate, professional, and international programs, the University's mission is to produce Christians who are capable of confronting injustice and indifference. Viewing education through the lens of a Christian worldview, Eastern challenges students to look outside themselves and strive to change the world that is into the world that ought to be.

Eastern University values its affiliation with the American Baptist Churches USA and also welcomes an interdenominational student body, faculty, and campus community. As a result, everyone at the University can actively pursue the full dynamic of abundant Christian life with freedom and confidence.

The academic curriculum at Eastern University emphasizes the liberal arts and sciences while helping a student pursue a major field of study. Classroom experience is intellectually rigorous and practical experience is gained through a variety of internships and practicums.

More than 1,700 full-time undergraduates are enrolled at Eastern in the College of the Arts and Sciences. The total enrollment at the University, including adult education, seminary, and graduate programs, is approximately 3,700 students. These programs take place in the Campolo College for Graduate and Professional Studies, Esperanza College, and Palmer Theological Seminary.

On-campus housing at the St. Davids campus accommodates more than 1,200 students in eight residence halls. Rooms are structured as singles, doubles, quads, suites, and apartments. The entire St. Davids campus is wireless, including dorms and living areas.

Athletics at Eastern University are NCAA Division III and the teams compete in the MAC Freedom Conference. Intercollegiate teams for men are fielded in baseball, basketball, cross-country, Frisbee (club), golf, lacrosse, soccer, swimming (club), tennis, and volleyball (club). The intercollegiate program for women offers basketball, cheerleading (club), cross-country, field hockey, Frisbee (club), lacrosse, soccer, softball, swimming (club), tennis, and volleyball. An intramural program also offers numerous opportunities for students to actively participate in sports.

Eastern provides students with a well-developed Student Ministry Program that challenges students and helps them grow in their faith. Student ministries include weekly chapel, "Sunday Night Live" worship led by students, grow groups, and student chaplains. Among the outreach opportunities available are Evangelicals for Social Action, Fellowship of Christian Athletes (FCA), Youth Against Complacency and Homelessness Today (YACHT), and Habitat for Humanity. Although it is an independent mission organization, the Evangelical Association for the Promotion of Education (EAPE) works closely with the Student Ministry Program and welcomes Eastern student volunteers to staff its programs in inner-city Philadelphia and Camden.

Location

Eastern University is located 25 minutes west of Philadelphia, Pennsylvania, and within 2½ hours of New York City; Washington, D.C.; and Baltimore, Maryland. Sitting in the historic Main Line in the town of Wayne, Eastern's convenient suburban setting provides easy access to Philadelphia via SEPTA trains that run every half hour from the St. Davids station.

Eastern University has one of the most picturesque campuses in America, with its three lakes, wooded walking trails, historic buildings, and working waterwheel. Besides major metropolitan centers, the campus is also within an hour of Lancaster, Pennsylvania, the Jersey Shore, and the Pocono Mountains and within 20 minutes of Valley Forge National Park.

Majors and Degrees

Undergraduate degrees include the Bachelor of Arts, Bachelor of Science, and Bachelor of Social Work degrees. Majors are offered in accounting and finance, athletic training, biblical studies (biblical languages/without biblical languages), biochemistry, biokinetics (exercise science, sports medicine, pre-occupational/pre–physical therapy), biological studies, biology, chemistry, chemistry business, communication studies (interpersonal/organizational, media, rhetoric), dance, economic development, elementary education (early childhood, special education), engineering (3+2 with Villanova), English (journalism, literature, writing), environmental studies, entrepreneurial studies, history, individualized, international area studies and business, management, marketing, mathematics, missions and anthropology, music (church music, composition/electronic music, performance, teaching), nursing, political science, psychology, secondary education (five-year M.Ed. option), social work, sociology, Spanish, theological studies, and youth ministry.

Minors are offered in accounting, American history, anthropology, astronomy, biblical studies, biology, chemistry, communication studies, dance, English (journalism, literature, writing), environmental studies, European history, finance, fine arts, French, gender studies, Latin American studies, legal studies, management, marketing, mathematics, missions, music, nonprofit administration, philosophy, political science, psychology, social welfare, sociology, Spanish, sport and coaching, and theological studies. Preprofessional programs are offered in dentistry, law, and medicine.

Academic Programs

In the core curriculum, students take courses designed to fulfill the basic mission of Eastern: to provide a biblical foundation for all learning and action, to ensure the acquisition of basic skills, and to broaden the student's view of the world. The central themes of the Christian faith are integrated into the course content of the core curriculum, which includes courses such as Justice and Diversity in a Pluralistic Society and Science, Technology and Values.

The Templeton Honors College, "a college within the University," offers a rigorous, classically oriented curriculum designed to challenge academically gifted students and prepare them for leadership and service in all areas of culture and society. The honors college includes special events and a required study-abroad, study-away semester. Enrollment in the honors college is highly competitive and limited to 24 to 35 new students each academic year. Students qualify to apply to the Templeton Honors College by achieving a combined score of 1350 or higher on the SAT or 30 or higher on the ACT or by ranking in the top 9 percent of their high school class.

Off-Campus Programs

Eastern students are encouraged to study abroad or participate in special programs recognized by the University. Academic study abroad is required of language majors. Non–language majors may select from many options, including (but not limited to) Austria, Canada, England, Israel, Kenya, Peru, South Africa, and Uganda. At the AuSable Institute in Michigan, students may apply for certificate programs leading to the designation of naturalist, land resources analyst, water resources analyst, or environmental analyst.

The American Studies Program, sponsored by the Coalition of Christian Colleges and Universities, provides an opportunity for students to study or serve as interns in Washington, D.C., with the nation's leaders. In the Latin American Studies Program, students live with native families; study Spanish and the local culture, history, politics, economics, and religious life; participate in service projects; and travel in Central America. The coalition also operates a film-study center in California and offers Russian and Middle East studies programs.

The Oregon Extension offers a semester of community living and liberal arts studies in the Cascade Mountains of southern Oregon. The Honors Research Program at the Argonne National Laboratory in Chicago provides junior and senior biology, chemistry, and math majors an opportunity for advanced research at a nationally recognized laboratory. Through the Goshen Study Service Trimester, students and faculty members study the history and culture of Caribbean nations and engage in a service project. Exchange programs with selected American Baptist colleges allow upperclass students to spend a semester or a year at another college. May Term opportunities include special courses, semesters, and study tours. Eastern Baptist Theological Seminary offers students the chance to take selected course work.

Academic Facilities

Of Eastern's twenty-six buildings, the primary academic facility is the McInnis Learning Center. In addition to classrooms and offices for faculty members and administrators, the main floor includes a 300-seat auditorium and several music practice rooms. Other features are the biology center; a highly regarded curriculum laboratory for those preparing to be teachers; a technology classroom for distance learning; the Julia Fowler Planetarium, containing a digital projector "Scidome" powered by Starry Night; a media services center; a computer-assisted language laboratory; fully equipped "smart" classrooms; and three student computer centers. The state-of-the-art Bradstreet Observatory is located on the roof of the McInnis Learning Center.

Heritage House offers an acoustically designed Great Room for music performances as well as smart classrooms with the latest computer technology.

The recently constructed Harold Howard Center is a 25,000-square-foot addition to the Warner Library. In addition to more space for the library, the addition features wireless technology, smart classrooms, and more study and office space. Eastern students have direct access to libraries throughout the region and around the world via the computer and more than fifty electronic databases.

Facilities for chemistry, physics, and computer science are located in Andrews Hall. In addition to offices and classroom space, Andrews houses six teaching laboratories, a computer center, and scientific equipment generally found only at larger colleges and universities. Instrumentation includes 300 MHz FT-NMR, FT-IR, GC-MS, AAS, Diode-array UV-Vis, HPLC, PCR, 96-well microplate reader, and molecular modeling.

Costs

For the academic year 2009–10, tuition was $23,770 and room and board were $8870. Total costs for the year were approximately $32,640.

Financial Aid

Eastern is committed to providing education to qualified students regardless of their means. The financial aid program offers scholarships, grants, loans, and employment. The University utilizes the Pennsylvania Higher Education Assistance Agency (PHEAA) for needs analysis forms processing. The student is required to complete the Free Application for Federal Student Aid (FAFSA) to determine financial aid eligibility.

Overall, the University views financial assistance to students as a cooperative investment. If parents contribute to the maximum of their ability and the student contributes a fair share through earnings and personal savings, the University attempts to complete the partnership.

Non-need academic scholarships ranging from $500 to full tuition are available. These scholarships are awarded on the basis of SAT or ACT scores and high school class rank information. Music, leadership, Templeton Honors College, FCA, Young Life, and church matching grants are other University-based grant programs.

Faculty

Eastern University employs more than 125 full- and part-time faculty members. Eighty-seven percent have earned doctorates. With an emphasis on teaching and a commitment to research, faculty members have authored more than 300 scholarly publications. Some faculty members teach both graduate and undergraduate courses, and almost all serve as academic advisers. Classes are kept small, with a student-faculty ratio of 14:1.

Admission Requirements

The University seeks applicants who present acceptable academic records. The average applicant has a GPA of 3.2 and a score of 1100 out of 1600 on the SAT. A campus visit and interview are recommended. Transfer applicants are welcome.

Application and Information

Applications are generally accepted until the beginning of each term. Admission decisions are made on a rolling basis. For more information, students should visit Eastern's Web site at http://www.eastern.edu. Students should contact:

Michael Dziedziak, M.B.A.
Director of Undergraduate Admissions
Eastern University
1300 Eagle Road
St. Davids, Pennsylvania 19087-3696
Phone: 800-452-0996 (toll-free)
E-mail: ugadm@eastern.edu
Web site: http://www.eastern.edu

EDINBORO UNIVERSITY

EDINBORO, PENNSYLVANIA

The University

Edinboro University, a part of the Pennsylvania State System of Higher Education, is located in the borough of Edinboro, Erie County, Pennsylvania. It is the oldest teacher-training institution in Pennsylvania west of the Allegheny Mountains and the second-oldest in the state. Edinboro Academy was chartered in 1856. After the passage of the State Normal Act in 1857, the school opened as Edinboro Normal School for the preparation of teachers. Under its original charter, the school was privately administered until 1861, when the commonwealth chartered it as a state normal school. The school was purchased by the commonwealth of Pennsylvania in 1914. The state recognized Edinboro State Teachers College as a four-year college in 1926 and granted it the right to offer a Bachelor of Science in Education degree in the areas of elementary, secondary, and art education. The name of the institution was changed to Edinboro State College in 1960. In 1983, university status was given to each of the state colleges, and a comprehensive commonwealth university system was established.

Edinboro's graduate school offers the Master of Arts, Master of Fine Arts, Master of Education, Master of Science, Master of Science in Nursing, Master of Social Work, and post-master's certifications.

The University is accredited by the Commission on Higher Education of the Middle States Association of Colleges and Schools (3624 Market Street, Philadelphia, Pennsylvania 19104; phone: 215-662-5606). The commission is an institutional accrediting agency that is recognized by the U.S. Secretary of Education and the Commission on Recognition of Postsecondary Accreditation. Other University accreditations and program approvals include the American Dietetic Association, the Council on Rehabilitation Education, the Council for Accreditation of Counseling and Related Educational Programs, the American Speech-Language-Hearing Association, the Council on Social Work Education, the National Association of Collegiate Business Schools and Programs, the Commission on Collegiate Nursing Education, the National League for Nursing Accrediting Commission, and the National Council for Accreditation of Teacher Education.

Of the 8,286 students at Edinboro, 6,417 are undergraduates. The University maintains on-campus residence. Each residence hall is wired for digital satellite cable television services, two high-speed data connections, and a telephone connection. Edinboro University has undertaken a $115-million housing project on campus that when finished in 2009 will provide suite- and semi-suite–style housing units as well as new dining facilities for students.

There are more than forty-three buildings situated on the spacious 585-acre campus, which includes open fields, a 5-acre lake, and many acres of woods.

Edinboro University in Erie–The Porreco Center and Edinboro University in Meadville offer classes and University services at convenient off-campus locations.

Location

Located adjacent to the business district of Edinboro, Pennsylvania, the University is accessible by automobile from all sections of the state and is near the intersection of Interstates 90 and 79. Passenger service of all kinds operates on frequent schedules, connecting Edinboro with nearby cities and towns, including Erie, Pennsylvania's fourth-largest city. The Erie Airport is approximately 15 miles to the north. Within walking distance of the campus, the community of Edinboro has eight churches of various denominations.

Majors and Degrees

The University awards the Associate of Arts, Associate of Engineering Technology, Associate of Science, Bachelor of Arts, Bachelor of Fine Arts, Bachelor of Science, Bachelor of Science in Education, and Bachelor of Science in Nursing. These degrees permit majors in the following areas: anthropology, applied media arts (with concentrations in animation, cinema, graphic design, and photography), fine arts/crafts (with concentrations in ceramics, drawing, jewelry/metalry, painting, printmaking, sculpture, and wood/furniture design), art education, art history, biology, biology/premedical, broadcast journalism, business administration/accounting, business administration/administration, business administration/financial services, business administration/forensic accounting, business administration/marketing, business administration/management information systems, chemistry, chemistry/forensic sciences, chemistry/industrial biochemistry, communication studies (with concentrations in broadcasting, organizational communication, and public relations/advertising), computer science, criminal justice, earth sciences, economics, elementary education, elementary/early childhood education, elementary/special education, English/literature, English/writing, environmental science/biology, environmental studies/geography, environmental science/geology, foreign language, general business administration, general studies, geography, geology, German, health and physical education (with concentrations in health promotion, recreation administration, sport administration, and teacher education), history, humanities, human services/developmental disabilities, human services/social services, innovative nursing, liberal studies, manufacturing engineering technology, mathematics, medical technology, music, music education, natural science and math, natural science and math/wildlife, nuclear medicine technology, nursing, philosophy, physics 3-2 engineering, physics/liberal arts, physics/theoretical, political science, preschool education, print journalism, psychology, secondary education (biology, chemistry, earth and space science, English, general science, German, mathematics, physics, social studies, and Spanish), social science, social work, sociology, Spanish, special education, special education/elementary education, specialized studies, speech and hearing sciences, and women's studies. Preprofessional programs are offered in dentistry, law, medicine, pharmacy, and veterinary science. Minors also exist in fifty-seven specializations.

Academic Programs

Associate degrees require a minimum of 60 semester hours of credit, including a general education component.

Baccalaureate degrees require a minimum of 120 semester hours of credit. A general education requirement of 60 semester hours is distributed among the arts, humanities, and science and technology to ensure a basic liberal arts foundation. The remaining 60 semester hours are devoted to specialization and may include major and professional courses, a minor, and other concomitant courses.

Advanced Placement credit and honors courses are available.

The Office of Adult Student Information Services enables nontraditional students to enroll for academic programs at convenient times and locations on a full- or part-time basis.

An Army Reserve Officers' Training Corps (ROTC) program is available.

The Office for Students with Disabilities provides services that are essential for physically disabled, hearing-impaired, visually impaired, and learning-disabled individuals. Edinboro University has one of the finest programs in the nation for students with disabilities.

Academic Facilities

The seven-story Baron-Forness Library is the focal point of the University campus. The library houses more than 500,000 bound volumes and more than 1.4 million microform units. Technology and Communications supports and manages thirty-seven computer labs.

Costs

For 2009–10, the tuition fee for a resident of Pennsylvania was $5554 per year; for nonresident students, the cost per year was $8332. Room rent per year was $4780 and meals were $2250. Additional annual fees included a student activity fee of $340, a University Center fee of $500, a health fee of $160, an instructional service fee of $555, and an instructional technology fee of $206. The cost of books and supplies varies with the academic major. Costs are subject to change.

Financial Aid

With more than $68 million in financial aid for eligible students, Edinboro offers student employment, loans, grants, and scholarships. In most cases, Pennsylvania State Grant and Free Application for Federal Student Aid forms are used to determine eligibility for these programs. Federal aid administered by the University is available for both the regular academic year and the summer sessions. The application deadline for upperclass students for these programs is normally May 1 for the following academic year. Freshmen may apply for aid upon acceptance by the University. Financial aid is also available through the University's ROTC program. For additional information, students should contact the Assistant Vice President for Student Financial Support and Services at 888-611-2680 (toll-free) or access the information online at http://www.edinboro.edu.

Faculty

Edinboro's student-faculty ratio of 18:1 makes it possible to maintain close interaction between students and the highly qualified faculty members. A large percentage of the faculty has completed terminal degrees in their area of specialization.

Student Government

The Student Government Association is a vital and active organization on the campus and serves as the official student voice in all University matters. Student Government Association representatives serve on nearly all University committees and participate in the University governance system. This organization sponsors special events, activities, and student clubs to satisfy a variety of student interests. The Student Government Association participates in the annual budget recommendations regarding the budgeting of the student activity fund.

Admission Requirements

Edinboro University grants admission on the basis of general scholarship, character, interest, and motivation as they may be determined by graduation from an approved high school, home school, or institution of equivalent grade or equivalent preparation, as determined by the Credentials Division of the Department of Education; official scholastic records; aptitude tests; recommendations; and interviews. To fully prepare for a University program of study and increase the probability for academic success, students should pursue a college-preparatory curriculum at the secondary level and provide evidence of scholastic aptitude, as measured by scores on the SAT or ACT. Submission of aptitude scores can be waived for nontraditional adult learners. An audition is required for all applicants to any music curriculum; music students are invited to participate in the audition some time after the application for admission is received by the Office of Undergraduate Admissions.

Application and Information

Students may apply for admission as early as July 1, after finishing the junior year of high school; the application can be found online at the University's Web site. Requests for application papers, viewbooks, financial aid forms, and further information should be addressed to:

Admissions Office
Academy Hall
200 East Normal Street
Edinboro University
Edinboro, Pennsylvania 16444
Phone: 814-732-2761
888-8GO-BORO (toll-free)
Fax: 814-732-2420
E-mail: eup_admissions@edinboro.edu
Web site: http://www.edinboro.edu

A view of the campus at Edinboro University.

COLLEGE CLOSE-UPS

ELIZABETHTOWN COLLEGE

ELIZABETHTOWN, PENNSYLVANIA

COLLEGE CLOSE-UPS

The College

Founded in 1899, Elizabethtown College is committed to an academic program of liberal arts and professional training built upon a core curriculum that focuses on teaching students to think, analyze, and communicate. The more than 1,900 students at Elizabethtown come from thirty states and forty countries, providing a diversity of backgrounds that enhances the College as a whole.

Elizabethtown is a residential college, where 85 percent of students live on the 195-acre campus in eight residence halls and senior town houses. Student-run residence hall councils plan programs and provide service and leadership opportunities. A wide variety of campus cultural events and other activities keep 80 percent of the students on campus throughout the weekends. The College maintains an active intramural sports program and fields ten NCAA Division III teams for men (baseball, basketball, cross-country, golf, lacrosse, soccer, swimming, tennis, track and field, and wrestling) and ten for women (basketball, cross-country, field hockey, lacrosse, soccer, softball, swimming, tennis, track and field, and volleyball), several of which contend for national titles each year.

The College offers effective academic, personal, and career counseling services through the Center for Student Success, which encourages students to make use of its office as early as their first year. Ninety-five percent of students who graduate from Elizabethtown are employed or enrolled in graduate school within eight months after graduation.

In addition to its undergraduate degree programs, Elizabethtown also offers a Master of Science degree in occupational therapy.

Location

Elizabethtown is a community of 20,000 people located in southeastern Pennsylvania, within 20 minutes of Harrisburg (the state capital), Hershey, and Lancaster. Philadelphia and Baltimore are within 1½ hours of Elizabethtown; New York and Washington are within 4 hours. Elizabethtown is easily accessible by Amtrak train service from New York, Philadelphia, and Pittsburgh, and the Harrisburg International Airport is 15 minutes away.

Majors and Degrees

Bachelor of Arts degrees are awarded in communications, criminal justice, economics, engineering, English, fine art, French, German, history, international business, Japanese, music, philosophy, political philosophy and legal studies, political science, psychology, religious studies, secondary education, social work, sociology-anthropology, Spanish, and theater.

Bachelor of Science degrees are offered in accounting, actuarial science, biochemistry, biology, biotechnology, business administration, chemistry, citizenship education, computer engineering, computer science, elementary education, engineering, environmental science, forestry and environmental management, general science education, health and occupation, industrial engineering management, information systems, mathematics, physics, secondary education, social sciences, and social studies.

Bachelor of Music degrees are offered in music education and music therapy. More than eighty minors and concentrations as well as seven certification programs in secondary education are available.

The College offers joint 3-2 programs with Duke University, leading to a Master of Forestry or Master of Environmental Management. A 3-2 program in engineering with Pennsylvania State University is also offered, leading to a Bachelor of Arts in engineering from Elizabethtown and a Bachelor of Science in engineering from Penn State.

Elizabethtown offers cooperative programs in biology and allied health with Thomas Jefferson University and Widener University. These programs lead to a Bachelor of Science degree from Elizabethtown and a master's or doctoral degree from the cooperating university. The College also participates in a Cardiovascular Invasive Specialty Program with Lancaster General College of Nursing and Health Sciences. Through articulation agreements, qualified Elizabethtown students may be admitted to the Philadelphia College of Osteopathic Medicine's Doctor of Osteopathic Medicine Program or to Temple University's School of Dentistry.

Preprofessional majors are also offered in law, medicine, the ministry, and veterinary medicine.

The Primary Care Pre-Admissions Program through the Pennsylvania State University College of Medicine at the Milton S. Hershey Medical Center provides options for Elizabethtown students who are Pennsylvania residents and are pursuing careers in internal medicine, family practice, and pediatrics.

Academic Programs

Through Elizabethtown's core program of traditional and innovative liberal arts, students develop skills for critical analysis, effective communication, and habits of mind that ensure adaptability in the ever-changing global job market. Independent and directed studies and extensive internship and externship possibilities are available.

The Elizabethtown College Honors Program offers top academic students a highly selective program of study with the opportunity for a stipend to fund professional development, research, or travel-related study.

The College operates on a semester calendar. First-year students arrive in the last week of August, and examinations are given prior to the winter break. The spring semester begins in the middle of January and runs through early May. Intensive summer-session courses are available for students who wish to accelerate their academic program. Students may earn credit toward graduation through Advanced Placement examinations, College-Level Examination Program tests, or tests administered by the individual departments.

Off-Campus Programs

Elizabethtown College students may study abroad in twenty-six different locations on all six continents through one of five affiliate partners: AustraLearn (Australia and New Zealand); Brethren Colleges Abroad (fifteen locations worldwide); Queen's University International Study Centre at Herstmonceux Castle,

United Kingdom; Nihon University, Japan; and School for Field Studies (Costa Rica, Kenya, and Turks and Caicos Islands).

A number of short-term opportunities are available as well, including two- to three-week study tours at England's Oxford University and in Beijing, China; Costa Rica; Ecuador; and Prague. In addition, students majoring in programs including occupational therapy, music therapy, and social work are required to complete extensive fieldwork in on- and off-campus facilities.

Academic Facilities

Academic buildings include the High Library; Zug Memorial Hall, home of Hess Gallery and the Department of Fine and Performing Arts; Wenger Center for the Humanities; Steinman Center for the Communications and Art; Nicarry Hall; and the James B. Hoover Center for Business. The Masters Center for Science, Mathematics and Engineering includes the Lyet Wing for Biological Sciences as well as classroom and lab space for the newly ABET-accredited engineering program. In addition, the student center, Brossman Commons, is the location for the Tempest Theatre and a dance studio.

Costs

For 2010–11, tuition is $33,250 and room and board are $8500, for a total comprehensive fee of $41,750. Students should also plan on an additional cost of about $1950 for books, transportation, and personal expenses, for a total cost of $43,700. Financial aid is based on this figure.

Financial Aid

Financial aid packages are typically a combination of scholarships, grants, loans, and student employment; 90 percent of the students receive some form of aid. To apply for financial aid, students must file the Free Application for Federal Student Aid (FAFSA) and the Elizabethtown College Verification Form. Estimated data should not be filed. Signed copies of the parent's (and student's, if applicable) most recent federal income tax form, including all schedules, must also be submitted to the financial aid office.

More than half of Elizabethtown's first-year students with the strongest academic credentials receive merit-based scholarships, which are awarded on a competitive basis and without regard to need.

Elizabethtown's deadline for financial consideration is March 15.

Faculty

Elizabethtown has a teaching faculty of 131 full-time professors. The student-faculty ratio is 11:1. More than 90 percent of the full-time faculty members hold a Ph.D. or the highest earned degree in their field. In addition to being assigned a faculty adviser through the First-Year Seminar program, when students declare a major, they are assigned a new faculty adviser within that department.

Student Government

Students play an active role in campus governance through the Student Senate, the Campus Residence Association, and other organizations. Members of the Student Senate are elected from each class to advocate for students, coordinate special events, and allocate funds for student activities and more than ninety student-run clubs and organizations. Students Working to Entertain E-town (SWEET) allocates funding for weekend programs, campus social activities, and entertainment for the College community.

Admission Requirements

Decisions about admission to Elizabethtown are made without regard to sex, sexual orientation, race, religion, physical handicap, or place of residence. On an average, 60 percent of all applicants are accepted. Students should have followed an academic curriculum, with the completion of at least 18 college-preparatory units recommended. The middle 50 percent of enrolled students scored between 1040 and 1240 on the critical reading and mathematics sections of the SAT, and 36 percent were in the top 10 percent of their high school class.

The College seeks diversity, and students who display leadership abilities or special talents are considered highly desirable. Campus interviews are highly recommended but not required for most students, although the College reserves the right to require interviews in special cases. Students applying to the Honors Program are required to interview, as are occupational therapy students. Auditions are required for music students.

Early admission is available for highly qualified high school juniors.

Application and Information

The College operates on a rolling admission basis—applications are processed as they are received—and the application deadline is March 1. Students can apply using the Common Application or online at the College's Web site. Applicants must submit a high school transcript, first-quarter grades, SAT or ACT scores, two letters of recommendation, and a personal statement, essay, or graded paper. Early application is strongly recommended. Accepted students should notify the College of their decision to attend by May 1; matriculation after that date is on a space-available basis. Students who are interested in the Elizabethtown College Honors Program must submit a completed application by January 15.

For more information, students should contact:

Debra Murray
Director of Admissions
Elizabethtown College
One Alpha Drive
Elizabethtown, Pennsylvania 17022-2298
Phone: 717-361-1400
Fax: 717-361-1365
E-mail: admissions@etown.edu
Web site: http://www.etown.edu

Elizabethtown offers more than 1,900 students liberal arts and professional programs through fifty-three majors and eighty minors and concentrations.

COLLEGE CLOSE-UPS

ELMHURST COLLEGE

ELMHURST, ILLINOIS

The College

Elmhurst is a four-year comprehensive college in the liberal arts tradition. Founded in 1871, the College has a long history of preparing students for lifetimes of professional and personal achievement. Elmhurst is affiliated with the United Church of Christ.

The College offers more than fifty majors, four accelerated majors for adults, fifteen preprofessional programs, and nine graduate programs. The honors program provides extra opportunities for students who are especially talented, curious, and motivated.

Elmhurst ranks in the top tier of Midwest colleges and universities with master's programs, according to *U.S. News & World Report*'s "America's Best Colleges" issue. *The Princeton Review* also lists Elmhurst among the region's premier institutions of higher learning. Students come to Elmhurst from many states and countries and from nearly every religious, racial, and ethnic background.

The student body comprises about 2,700 traditional undergraduate students, 350 adults pursuing an undergraduate degree, and nearly 300 graduate students. Students participate in more than 100 activities, including theater, intramurals, and student government. More than half play intramurals or participate in one of eighteen NCAA Division III varsity teams. Six residence halls and a variety of apartment-style housing options are available for students who want to live on campus.

Location

Elmhurst, Illinois, a quiet suburb of Chicago, is filled with family-owned stores and restaurants, as well as theater, music, art museums, and other recreational activities. In *Chicago* magazine's 2003 study of the "best places to live" among 192 Chicago suburbs, the city of Elmhurst ranked number 1.

The beautiful 38-acre campus looks like a college should look: big trees, broad lawns, and twenty-four stately redbrick buildings. With more than 600 varieties of trees and shrubs, the Elmhurst campus is an arboretum; with modern facilities, top-notch faculty members, and a great geographical location, it's an excellent place to get an education.

Just 16 miles away (30 minutes by train), Chicago has something for everyone. Sports fans can enjoy watching the Bears, Bulls, Cubs, or White Sox in action, or play sports in Millennium Park or along the waterfront. Students who are interested in art or culture can visit the Museum of Contemporary Art, the Art Institute of Chicago, or the 57-acre Museum Campus, featuring the Adler Planetarium and Astronomy Museum. Chicago also features lots of shopping, dining, and nightlife.

Majors and Degrees

The College offers bachelor's degrees in accounting, American studies, art, art business, art education, biology, business administration, chemistry, communication studies, computer game and entertainment technology, computer science, criminal justice, early childhood education, economics, elementary education, English, exercise science, finance, French, geography, German, history, information systems, interdisciplinary communication studies, international business, jazz studies, logistics and supply chain management, management, marketing, mathematics, multi-language, music, music business, music education, musical theater, nursing, organizational communication, philosophy, physical education, physics, political science, psychology, religion and service, religious studies, secondary education, sociology, Spanish, special education, speech-language pathology, theater, theater arts education, theological studies and Christian ministry, and urban studies. Students also may design their own interdepartmental major.

Preprofessional programs are available in actuarial science, allied health sciences, dentistry, engineering, law, library science, medicine, seminary studies, and veterinary medicine.

Academic Programs

Elmhurst College confers five undergraduate degrees: Bachelor of Arts, Bachelor of Fine Arts, Bachelor of Science, Bachelor of Music, and Bachelor of Liberal Studies. While requirements for each degree vary, all require a minimum of 128 semester hours of credit. The academic program consists of three interrelated parts: courses that meet the general education requirements, courses that fulfill requirements of the major, and elective courses that students select to satisfy intellectual curiosity or to enhance the breadth of their academic programs.

The General Education Program includes course work drawn from eleven categories of knowledge: fine arts; global society; human behavior; inquiry and issues in science and technology; Judeo-Christian heritage and religious faith; literature; the natural world; people, power, and politics; the search for humane values; Western culture; and writing and reasoning. An undergraduate student graduating from Elmhurst College completes at least one course, taken for a letter grade, in each of the eleven categories.

Beyond the general education requirements, major-course requirements, and courses taken to fulfill elective requirements, students earning the Bachelor of Science must complete an additional 8 semester hours in mathematics; students earning the Bachelor of Music must complete at least 64 semester hours in music (specific courses are determined by the Department of Music); and students earning the Bachelor of Liberal Studies must complete 32 to 48 semester hours in two areas of concentration (rather than a traditional major). Students are expected to declare their major field of study prior to completion of the sophomore year. Students may also select a maximum of two minors.

Off-Campus Programs

Elmhurst encourages first-, second-, and third-year students to pursue international education programs by going global for a month, a term, or a year. Through a wide range of opportunities to study and work abroad, students refine their language skills, challenge their cultural assumptions, grow as individuals, better understand themselves and their countries, and gain a greater respect for other cultures.

During the January and summer terms, Elmhurst faculty members teach in such places as Costa Rica, England, Germany, Jamaica, and Morocco through the Elmhurst College Abroad program.

In addition to sponsoring its own courses abroad, the College offers programs through a consortium of colleges and through two partnership programs. For example, students can combine classes with internships in Australia, Belgium, France (Paris), Germany, and Spain; students can earn academic credit for participating in service-learning and academic courses in the Czech Republic, Ecuador, India, Mexico, the Philippines, and Scotland; and other programs take students to Austria, China, England, Italy, Ireland, and New Zealand.

Academic Facilities

The A. C. Buehler Library provides a wide variety of services for Elmhurst students. Books, periodicals, and audiovisual materials are available, along with interlibrary loan services, databases, electronic journals, and other electronic resources.

The Elmhurst College Learning Center helps students succeed as independent learners. Students can receive one-on-one tutoring in math, reading, writing, and study-skills areas or attend test preparation workshops.

Daniels Hall has computer rooms for student use and features PCs, Macs, scanners, and laser printers. The Center for Professional Excellence offers opportunities for self-assessment, career guidance, graduate school preparation, internships, mentoring, and shadowing.

Costs

Full-time tuition for 2009–10 was $27,270. Part-time tuition was $3104 per full course ($776 per credit hour). Other costs included a matriculation fee of $125 ($50 for transfer students), an academic technology fee of $30 per term, and a residential network fee of $50 per term. Students living on campus can expect to pay $4720 for a double-occupancy room and $3154 for a standard meal plan.

Financial Aid

Financial aid is awarded to approximately 90 percent of entering students. Entering freshmen are eligible for renewable scholarships based on grade point average and composite ACT scores or combined SAT scores. Students should apply for admission by January 15 for scholarship consideration. Other Elmhurst scholarships are awarded based on grade point average, program of study, financial need, and other criteria. Awards range from $1000 to $19,000 per academic year. Elmhurst need-based grants are available for eligible full-time students.

The Illinois Student Assistance Commission administers grants of $496 to $4968 per year to eligible Illinois residents. The Department of Education awards Federal Pell Grants of $976 to $5350 per year. Pell recipients may also be eligible for Supplemental Educational Opportunity Grants of $100 to $4000 a year.

Student loans include the Federal Direct Loan, Federal Perkins Loan, and Federal PLUS Program. Alternative loans may be available from private lenders.

Faculty

Elmhurst provides superior teaching on a personal scale. All classes are taught by professors, not teaching assistants. About 84 percent of the College's 133 full-time faculty members hold a Ph.D. or other terminal degree in their field. The student-faculty ratio of 13:1 is among the best in higher education. The average class has 19 students.

Student Government

The Student Government Association (SGA) consists of 21 students elected by the student body, 3 members of the faculty elected by the faculty, and 3 administrators selected by the student members. The SGA serves as the major policy-recommending body to the President and Trustees on issues of student and campus life. The Elmhurst College Union Board and its committees serve as the primary student programming organization on campus.

Admission Requirements

Elmhurst seeks students who show evidence of their ability to complete college-level work based on high school performance. Preference is given to students who have completed 16 academic units, including 3 units of English; 2 units each of mathematics, laboratory science, and social studies; and 7 units in additional college-preparatory subjects.

Application and Information

In order to apply, prospective students are required to submit an application for admission. Applications may be completed online, or paper copies can be downloaded or requested from the Office of Admission and Financial Aid. Students must also submit official high school transcripts or GED results, official SAT or ACT scores, and a teacher recommendation. Elmhurst College's ACT code is 1020. An interview and essay are recommended but not required. Applications are accepted on a rolling basis. Application review begins October 1.

Prospective students can arrange an individual visit, which might include an overnight stay and meetings with faculty members, or come for a Preview Day.

Further information about the College, the application process, and campus visits can be obtained from:

Office of Admission
Elmhurst College
190 Prospect Avenue
Elmhurst, Illinois 60126-3296
Phone: 630-617-3400
800-697-1871 (toll-free)
E-mail: admit@elmhurst.edu
Web site: http://www.elmhurst.edu/

ELMIRA COLLEGE

ELMIRA, NEW YORK

COLLEGE CLOSE-UPS

The College

Elmira College is a small, private, coeducational college that is recognized for its emphasis on education of high quality in the liberal arts and preprofessional programs. One of the oldest colleges in the United States, Elmira was founded in 1855. The College has always produced graduates interested in both community service and successful careers. Friendliness, personal attention, strong college spirit, and support for learning beyond the classroom help to make Elmira a unique community. Elmira College is one of only 270 colleges in the nation to be granted a chapter of the prestigious Phi Beta Kappa honor society.

The full-time undergraduate enrollment is about 1,200 men and women. The students at Elmira represent more than thirty-five states, primarily those in the Northeast, with the highest representation coming from New York, New Jersey, Massachusetts, Connecticut, Maine, and Pennsylvania. International students from thirty-one countries were enrolled in 2008. Ninety percent of the full-time undergraduates live in College residence halls, and dormitory rooms are equipped to provide direct access to the Internet. Wireless access is also available in the Library and Campus Center.

The intercollegiate sports program includes men's and women's basketball, golf, ice hockey, lacrosse, soccer, and tennis and women's cheerleading, field hockey, softball, and volleyball. Intramural programs are also available. Emerson Hall houses the student fitness center, a pool, and a gym capable of seating 1,000, as well as the Gibson Theatre, which has a state-of-the-art sound and lighting system. Professional societies; clubs; music, dance, and drama groups; a student-operated FM radio station; and the student newspaper, yearbook, and literary magazine also provide numerous opportunities for extracurricular activity.

Location

Elmira College is located in the city of Elmira, which has a population of 35,000, in the Finger Lakes region of New York. The campus is a 10-minute walk from downtown Elmira. The relationship between the College and the local community is excellent, and numerous community activities and facilities are open to students, including the Elmira Symphony and Choral Society, the Elmira Little Theatre, clubs and civic groups, museums, movies, and a performing arts center. Excellent recreational areas are available in upstate New York and nearby Pennsylvania.

Majors and Degrees

Elmira College offers programs leading to the bachelor's degree in more than thirty-five majors, including accounting, American studies, art, art education, biology, biology-chemistry, business administration, chemistry, classical studies, criminal justice, economics, elementary education, English literature, environmental studies, French, history, human services, individualized studies, international business, international studies, mathematics, medical technology, music, nursing, philosophy and religion, political science, psychology, public affairs, secondary education, social studies, sociology and anthropology, Spanish, speech and hearing, and theater. Secondary teaching certification is offered in several areas. A 3-2 program in chemical engineering with Clarkson University is available, and 4-1 M.B.A. programs are available at Alfred University, Clarkson University, and Union College. Army and Air Force ROTC are available through respective units at Cornell University.

Preprofessional preparation is offered in education, medical technology, nursing, and speech pathology and audiology. Faculty advisers assist those who seek preparation for graduate study in dentistry, law, or medicine in choosing appropriate course work. Nearly 45 percent of Elmira graduates pursue graduate study.

Academic Programs

The College's calendar is composed of two 12-week terms followed by a six-week term in the spring. Students enroll for four subjects during the twelve-week terms, completing the first term by mid-December and the second during the first week of April. Term III, the six-week term, running from mid-April through May, may be devoted to a particular project involving travel, internship, research, or independent study. Students are required to participate in internships in order to gain practical and meaningful experience related to their program of study. Credit is awarded for these experiences. Forty percent of Elmira College students study abroad at some point during their four years of study.

Special opportunities for outstanding students include participation in thirteen national honorary societies on campus and a chance to assist faculty members in research. The College also offers an accelerated three-year graduation option for outstanding students, and an Advanced Placement Program is available.

Army ROTC and Air Force ROTC are available.

Off-Campus Programs

Through the study-abroad programs, students may study in the United Kingdom, France, Spain, and Japan, as well as in other countries throughout Europe and Asia. Elmira students may study at the Washington Center for Learning Alternatives. Students from Elmira may spend Term III studying marine biology or doing sociological research on the island of San Salvador in the Bahamas. The six-week Term III permits students in any major to study abroad, and students are able to participate in this program starting in their freshman year.

Academic Facilities

The Elmira campus offers exceptional academic facilities in a beautiful setting. The modern Gannett-Tripp Library houses more than 391,000 volumes, receives 2,500 periodicals, and includes a special Mark Twain collection room and photography and audiovisual facilities.

The College Computer Center offers four PC and Apple Macintosh microcomputer labs for student use.

A Center for Mark Twain Studies has been established at Quarry Farm, the author's summer home, which is located only a few miles from campus. The College also operates a Speech and Hearing Clinic on campus, which serves the public and provides valuable internship experience for students. Excellent facilities for drama and music are available.

Costs

Tuition for 2009–10 was $33,500, room was $6000, board was $4800, and fees were $1500.

Financial Aid

Financial aid is available for both freshmen and transfer students. Awards are based upon the Free Application for Federal Student Aid (FAFSA) as well as the student's past academic performance. Types of aid include grants, scholarships, loans, and work opportunities. Sources of aid include college, federal, state, and private dollars. In addition, superior students may qualify for non-need based Elmira College Honors Scholarships, which are available to both freshmen and transfer students and range from $6000 to full tuition per year, renewable throughout four years. For 2008–09, the average freshman aid package (including all types of aid) amounted to more than $25,000. About 75 percent of the full-time undergraduates receive need-based financial aid. Twenty percent of students receive non-need merit aid.

Faculty

Members of the faculty are chosen for their ability in and dedication to teaching. All full-time faculty members serve as advisers. Currently, the full-time faculty consists of 10 full professors, 28 associate professors, 30 assistant professors, and 12 instructors. Ninety-eight percent of the faculty hold the Ph.D. or highest degree necessary to teach undergraduate students in their field.

Student Government

Student government, an important part of the educational system at Elmira College, prepares students for active and responsible citizenship in society. Student government organizations include the Student Senate, the Judicial Board, and the Student Activities Board.

Admission Requirements

The Office of Admissions at Elmira College uses a rolling admission system. Each applicant is evaluated individually on the basis of his or her total application, including academic record, rank in class, SAT or ACT scores, essay, activities, references, and goals. The College strongly advises a personal interview. The recommendations of teachers and guidance counselors are also important. Special consideration is given to applicants from distant states and other countries, applicants with special skills, and applicants who are prepared to become actively involved in the campus community.

Elmira has two early decision programs available to students.

Application and Information

For further information, applicants should contact:

Director of Admissions
Elmira College
Elmira, New York 14901
Phone: 800-935-6472 (toll-free)
E-mail: admissions@elmira.edu
Web site: http://www.elmira.edu

COLLEGE CLOSE-UPS

The Mark Twain Study is one of the most famous literary landmarks in America.

EMBRY-RIDDLE AERONAUTICAL UNIVERSITY

EMBRY-RIDDLE
Aeronautical University

DAYTONA BEACH, FLORIDA

The University

Embry-Riddle Aeronautical University's reputation as the leader in aviation and aerospace education is recognized worldwide. The University's history and legacy date back almost to the time of the Wright brothers, and in 2009 the University introduced the nation's first and only Ph.D. program in aviation. Embry-Riddle is an independent, nonsectarian, not-for-profit, coeducational university serving culturally diverse students seeking careers in aviation, aerospace, engineering, business, and related fields. Residential campuses in Daytona Beach, Florida, and Prescott, Arizona, provide education in a traditional setting, while the Worldwide Campus provides instruction through more than 170 centers in the United States, Europe, Canada, and the Middle East and through online learning.

Approximately 4,500 undergraduate students and 500 graduate students are currently enrolled at the 185-acre Daytona Beach residential campus. Students come from all fifty states, and nearly 100 countries are represented, making Embry-Riddle truly an international university.

More than twenty undergraduate degree programs, six graduate programs, and two doctoral programs are offered at the Daytona Beach campus. Embry-Riddle's premier aeronautical science (professional pilot) program and award-winning aerospace engineering program are the largest on campus and among the largest of their type in the nation.

Embry-Riddle conducts applied research valued at approximately $10 million per year, and is leading the development of the Next Generation Air Transportation System along with the Federal Aviation Administration, Lockheed Martin, Boeing, and other high-tech organizations. Alumni are leaders in every facet of the aviation and aerospace industries and serve as a strong network and resource for students.

Students at the Daytona Beach campus enjoy a wide array of activities and clubs, many focused on aviation and aerospace, as well as fraternities, sororities, and recreational opportunities. Forty-three percent of students live on campus.

Embry-Riddle's award-winning precision flight demonstration teams offer students the opportunity to compete nationally in air and ground events. Embry-Riddle also has the largest all-volunteer Air Force ROTC detachment in the country and among the fastest-growing Navy ROTC units and Army ROTC battalions. Embry-Riddle athletes participate in intercollegiate and intramural competitions in many sports, including baseball, basketball, crew, cross-country, golf, soccer, tennis, volleyball, and ice hockey.

The 68,000-square-foot ICI Center contains two full-size NCAA basketball courts, a fitness center, and a weight room. The ICI Center provides a place to host sporting events and assemblies. The University sports complex also includes a soccer field, the Sliwa Stadium ballpark, the Ambassador William Crotty Tennis Center, and the Track and Field Complex. The Tine Davis Fitness Center is adjacent to the pool and features comprehensive fitness services and wellness programs.

The 5,300-square-foot interfaith chapel accommodates the variety of faiths represented by the student body of Embry-Riddle. It consists of a 140-seat nondenominational worship area, four prayer rooms (Catholic, Jewish, Muslim, and Protestant).

Location

The year-round clear flying weather and the resort communities surrounding Embry-Riddle's residential campus in Daytona Beach, Florida, offer students an excellent environment in which to study, fly, and enjoy recreational activities. The campus, which is located adjacent to the Daytona Beach International Airport, is only 3 miles from what is called the world's most famous beach. The high-technology industries located in nearby Orlando provide the University with an outstanding support base. In addition, the Kennedy Space Center is less than a 2-hour drive away.

Majors and Degrees

The Daytona Beach campus of Embry-Riddle awards undergraduate degrees at the baccalaureate and associate level. Bachelor of Science degrees are offered in a variety of areas, each with a focus on the aviation and aerospace industries. In engineering, students can pursue a Bachelor of Science degree in aerospace engineering, civil engineering, computer engineering, electrical engineering, engineering physics, mechanical engineering, and software engineering. Students who are interested in business administration may elect to major in management or air transportation. For those inclined toward technological pursuits, degrees are offered in aerospace electronics and aviation maintenance science. The College of Aviation awards degrees in aeronautical science (professional piloting), air traffic management, applied meteorology, and safety science. Other majors include interdisciplinary studies (design your own major), communication, computational mathematics, homeland security, human factors psychology, and space physics. Students entering Embry-Riddle with an undecided major have the opportunity to explore a variety of academic pursuits before making a commitment to a specific track.

Academic Programs

Even a field as specialized as aviation requires a broad background. General education courses required of all students who are pursuing a baccalaureate program include communication skills, such as English composition, literature, and technical report writing; humanities; social sciences; mathematics; physical science; economics; and computer science. To ensure academic success, Embry-Riddle provides free tutorial services.

The academic year is divided into two semesters of fifteen weeks each, with the summer session divided into two terms. The average course load for each fall or spring semester is 15 credit hours.

Academic Facilities

The College of Aviation building at the Daytona Beach campus provides an unsurpassed environment for aviation education and research. The multimillion-dollar simulation laboratories duplicate the components and functions in the national airspace system, including capabilities to replicate actual weather reporting, airports, airways, air traffic control, flow control, and pilot and aircraft performance as found in the national air transportation system. The simulator building, which is located in the greater College of Aviation complex, contains highly sophisticated flight training devices (FTD) that provide realistic training in aircraft used in flight training as well as the major airlines. Flight instruction is provided in the Embry-Riddle fleet of sixty-plus aircraft and a wide array of flight training devices. Aircraft are equipped with Automatic Dependent Surveillance-Broadcast (ADS-B) technology that decreases hazards associated with traffic, weather, and terrain.

The Advanced Flight Simulation Center gives Embry-Riddle students the opportunity to train in world-class simulators. The center, with more than 20,000 square feet of space and four high bays, currently houses eight Cessna 172S NAVIIIs (Skyhawk), one Piper PA44 (Seminole), four Diamond DA42s (Twinstar), and one Canadair Regional Jet (CRJ-200). These devices exactly duplicate the actual cockpit, adverse weather conditions, a full range of emergency situations, and virtually any flight pattern and complement flight training done in actual aircraft. Flight simulation enables students to learn aircraft performance, experience aerodynamic effects, and perform flight maneuvers immediately and without risk. Qualified to Level 6, the University's devices faithfully reproduce Embry-Riddle's fleet of single-engine and multiengine aircraft and are equipped with 220-degree panoramic visual theaters. In addition, the Aviation Building houses air traffic control and tower simulators, one motion-based disorientation trainer, and six Basic Aviation Training Devices (BATDs).

In 2009, construction of the James Hagedorn Aviation Complex began the expansion of the aviation complex. The 96,000-square-foot, three-building facility is planned to become the home of flight training operations, aircraft maintenance training, and a fleet maintenance hangar. The Emil Buehler Aviation Maintenance Science building is slated to house cutting-edge labs dedicated to aircraft systems, turbine engines, metallic and composite materials, avionics, and avionics electronics. The facility is designed to include classrooms, a licensed engine-repair station, a machine shop, offices, and a third-floor observation deck overlooking the Daytona Beach International Airport runways.

The facilities in the Lehman Engineering and Technology Center serve academic departments including Human Factors, Engineering Physics and Space Physics, Mathematics, and Computer Sciences and all the engineering disciplines. Labs include the Atmospheric Research Lab, Flight Dynamics & Simulation Lab, Materials Testing Lab, Structures Lab, Aerospace Composites Lab, Real Time Lab, Aerospace Engineering & Design Lab, Wind Tunnels, Airport Noise Abatement Lab, Electronic Communications & Microwave Lab, Microcomputer & Digital Lab, Circuits & Power Lab, Electricity & Magnetism Thermo Lab, Human Factors Research Lab, and many more. Students use the labs to work in teams to develop hands-on projects. Research is conducted by faculty members and graduate and undergraduate students.

The 18,500-square-foot Capt. Willie Miller Instructional Center, a lecture auditorium and classroom complex, provides space for large audience events, including presentations by distinguished lecturers and speakers.

New in 2008, the College of Business academic building features the Aviation Operations Simulation Lab, which is used to develop and evaluate aviation/airline operational strategies and processes. In addition, the College's Teaching Airport, a partnership between Embry-Riddle and Daytona Beach International Airport, is focused on teaching, research, and public outreach.

The Jack R. Hunt Memorial Library is a 49,000-square-foot facility with a seating capacity of 800. The library houses more than 230,000 volumes and book titles, and more than 340,000 items of microfiche, periodicals, documents, newspapers, and media programs. Among the library's resources is a historical aviation collection that includes materials dating from 1909 to the present. The library provides rapid interlibrary loan service and wireless access points as well as computer terminals for research.

Costs

The 2010–11 tuition is $14,280 per semester. Flight fees are charged in addition to tuition. On-campus room and board costs are approximately $4250 per semester. Personal expenses, books, and fees are in addition to the above. Costs are subject to change.

Financial Aid

Applicants for financial aid are required to complete the Department of Education's Free Application for Federal Student Aid (FAFSA) and any other documents requested by the University. Students are encouraged to apply early if they wish to be considered for all types of programs. Florida residents may also apply for several additional programs that are available through the state.

Faculty

The faculty members provide an excellent balance of professional experience and academic achievement. There is also a healthy balance between maturity and youth among the faculty. Faculty members who teach in the specialized and major programs have had professional experience in their areas of instruction. The student-faculty ratio is 14:1, and the average class size is 25. The primary concern of each faculty member is personalized teaching in classrooms and laboratories, on the flight line, and in student advising.

Student Government

The University places great emphasis on student self-government. The Student Government Association supports publication of the weekly newspaper and oversees the Touch 'n Go Office that organizes campus entertainment and broadcast of the student radio station, Eagles FM. In addition, the president of the Student Government Association is a voting member of the University's Board of Trustees.

Admission Requirements

Admission is open to any qualified applicant, regardless of creed, sex, race, national origin, handicap, or geographical location. Admission decisions are based on high school grades and course load, college courses attempted, SAT or ACT scores, and letters of recommendation. Embry-Riddle encourages every student to visit the campus before making the decision to attend the University.

Transfer students are required to submit transcripts from all colleges and universities attended. High school transcripts are not required if the student has earned 30 college credits or more.

Application and Information

Embry-Riddle requires each applicant to submit an application form and fee, SAT or ACT scores, two letters of recommendation, and an official high school/college transcript. Flight students must provide an FAA Class I or Class II medical certificate. When a student is accepted for admission, tuition and housing deposits are required by May 1.

University Admissions
Embry-Riddle Aeronautical University
P.O. Box 11767
Daytona Beach, Florida 32120-1767
Phone: 386-226-6100
800-862-2416 (toll-free nationwide)
E-mail: dbadmit@erau.edu
Web site: http://www.erau.edu/db

Embry-Riddle Aeronautical University's Daytona Beach, Florida, campus.

EMERSON COLLEGE

BOSTON, MASSACHUSETTS

The College

Founded in 1880, Emerson is one of the premier colleges in the United States for the study of communication and the arts. Students may choose from more than two-dozen undergraduate and graduate programs supported by state-of-the-art facilities and a nationally renowned faculty. The campus is home to WERS-FM, the oldest noncommercial radio station in Boston; the historic 1,200-seat Cutler Majestic Theatre; and *Ploughshares,* the award-winning literary journal for new writing.

A pioneer in the fields of communication and performing arts, Emerson was one of the first colleges in the nation to establish a program in children's theater (1919), an undergraduate program in broadcasting (1937), professional-level training in speech pathology and audiology (1935), educational FM radio (1949), closed-circuit television (1955), and a B.F.A. degree program in film as early as 1972. In 1980, the College created the country's first graduate program in professional writing and publishing.

Today, Emerson's 3,100 undergraduate and 900 graduate students come from across the country and more than forty other countries. Approximately 1,200 students live on campus, some in special learning communities, such as the Writers' Block and Digital Culture Floor. All of the College's residence halls are air conditioned with cable television and Internet access. Wireless service is available in several campus locations. There is a fitness center, athletic field, and a new fourteen-story campus center and residence hall that houses a gymnasium, student-services offices, and meeting space for student organizations.

Emerson College is fully accredited by the New England Association of Schools and Colleges.

In addition to its undergraduate programs, Emerson College offers more than a dozen master's degree programs for its graduate students.

Location

With dozens of institutions of higher learning, Boston is considered one of the country's best-known college towns. The city contains a wealth of diversions ranging from scenic harbor cruises and Boston Pops concerts to baseball's Fenway Park and the legendary Boston Marathon. Emerson's campus is located on Boston Common in the heart of the city's Theatre District—within sight of the Massachusetts State House and walking distance from the historic Freedom Trail, Boston Public Garden, Chinatown, financial district, and numerous restaurants and museums. Boston is also an international city with more than thirty foreign consulates, a busy international airport, and several multinational corporations.

Majors and Degrees

Emerson confers Bachelor of Arts, Bachelor of Fine Arts, and Bachelor of Science degrees. Students can major in acting; broadcast journalism; communication disorders; communication studies; marketing communication: advertising and public relations; media production (animation and motion media, digital postproduction, film, interactive media, radio, sound design, studio television production, writing for film and television); media studies; musical theater; political communication: leadership, politics, and social advocacy; print and multimedia journalism; stage/production management; theater design/technology; theater education; theater studies; and writing, literature, and publishing. Popular minors include business studies and entrepreneurship. Interdisciplinary and self-designed majors, as well as an honors program, are available through the College's Institute for Liberal Arts and Interdisciplinary Studies.

Academic Programs

Emerson's academic calendar consists of two fifteen-week semesters, plus two six-week sessions during the summer months. The requirements for graduation combine general education and liberal arts courses with advanced, specialized classes that are specific to individual departments and majors. Internships for academic credit are available in almost every major and the Institute for Liberal Arts and Interdisciplinary Studies offers exciting first-year seminars, independent study options, and innovative courses that cut across academic disciplines.

Off-Campus Programs

Internships are popular with Emerson students. Hundreds of placements exist throughout Boston and in major cities across the country, including the College's Los Angeles Center—a residential study and internship program in the heart of the world's entertainment capital.

Emerson also sponsors a semester-long study program in Washington, D.C., the Netherlands, and Taiwan. In addition, there is a summer film program in Prague and course cross-registration with the six-member Boston ProArts Consortium, whose members include the Berklee College of Music, the Boston Conservatory, Boston Architectural Center, Emerson, the School of the Museum of Fine Arts, and Massachusetts College of Art.

Academic Facilities

Emerson possesses the highest quality visual and media arts equipment, including sound-treated television studios, digital editing labs, audio postproduction suites with analog and digital peripherals, industry-standard software, and a professional marketing-research suite/focus room. In fact, more than half of Emerson's campus has been built new or completely refurbished since 2002. There are two radio stations, seven on-campus facilities and programs to observe speech and hearing therapy, and an integrated digital newsroom for aspiring journalists. The eleven-story Tufte Performance and Production Center houses expanded performance and rehearsal space, a theater design/technology center, makeup lab, and costume shop. Current on-campus projects include renovations to the historic Colonial Building and Paramount Theatre complex, which will house a cinema, scene shop, sound stage, and residence hall.

Emerson's Iwasaki Library houses more than 175,000 volumes and serial subscriptions, 11,000 microforms, 9,000 audio/visual materials, and 30,000 e-books. The library's Web pages are designed to serve as a gateway for research and can be accessed from the library's workstations, computers located throughout the campus, and dormitory rooms or off-campus apartments, using a student account. Emerson students can also access the resources of a dozen cooperating libraries through the College's membership in the Fenway Library Consortium.

Costs

The basic expenses related to attending Emerson College for the 2008–09 academic year were $28,352 for tuition and $11,832 for room and board. Approximately $2500 should be allotted for books and supplies, fees, health insurance, and personal expenses, including travel.

Financial Aid

Each year, more than two thirds of Emerson's student body receives some form of financial assistance, packaged in awards that typically combine grant and scholarship, loan, and College work-study. Academic scholarships ranging from $10,000 to half-tuition are awarded on a limited basis to students who meet high academic standards. Special performance-based scholarships, averaging $4000, are available to exceptional students in the performing arts.

In order to apply for financial assistance, students must complete the Free Application for Federal Student Assistance (FAFSA) and CSS PROFILE form. Deadlines are March 1 for September admission or November 15 for January admission. More information about financial assistance at Emerson can be found online at http://www.emerson.edu/financial_services or by contacting the Office of Student Financial Services at 617-824-8655 or finaid@emerson.edu.

Faculty

With classes that average between 20 and 25, students at Emerson develop close relationships with remarkably talented and active instructors. Faculty members are nationally recognized and award-winning authors, directors, producers, consultants, playwrights, and editors. The vast majority of the faculty have earned doctorates or the highest degree obtainable in their field. The student-teacher ratio is 14:1.

Student Government

Emerson has more than sixty student organizations and performance groups, fifteen NCAA intercollegiate teams, and several student publications and honor societies. The Student Government Association, in cooperation with the Office of Student Affairs staff, plans and executes student activities, allocates and supervises funding for clubs, and serves as a liaison between the student body and the College administration.

Admission Requirements

Emerson accepts the Common Application and Application Supplement. Students whose interests and abilities are compatible with the College's specialty in communication and the arts are welcome to apply. Admission is competitive. Each year, more than 5,000 applications are received for a class of 750. Selection is based on academic promise as indicated by secondary school performance, recommendations, writing competency, and SAT or ACT scores (or TOEFL if English is not the first language). The College also considers personal qualities as seen in extracurricular activities, community involvement, and demonstrated leadership.

The academic preparation for successful candidates should include 4 years of English and 3 years each of mathematics, science, social science, and a single foreign language. Candidates for programs offered by the Department of Performing Arts are asked to fulfill additional requirements (a theatrical resume and one of the following: audition, interview, portfolio, or essay) found on a dedicated Web site, http://stagedoor.emerson.edu. Applicants for the film program must submit a sample of creative work: either a 5–10 page script or 5–7 minute video.

Application and Information

First-year candidates for September admission should file their application by January 5. Early action applications are due November 1. The regular admission deadline for January admission is November 1.

Transfer students should submit their applications and supporting credentials by March 15 for September admission or November 1 for January admission.

Office of Undergraduate Admission
Emerson College
120 Bolyston Street
Boston, Massachusetts 02116-4624
Phone: 617-824-8600
Fax: 617-824-8609
E-mail: admission@emerson.edu
Web site: http://www.emerson.edu

COLLEGE CLOSE-UPS

Emerson College: Bringing Innovation to Communication and the Arts.

EMORY & HENRY COLLEGE

EMORY, VIRGINIA

The College

Emory & Henry College is a transformative academic community. The education it offers is distinguished by progress—sometimes sudden, sometimes gradual—toward an expanded sense of personal potential and an enlightened sense of civic responsibility. This transformation, this increase in excellence, is the foundation of the Emory & Henry campus culture. Its impact is lasting and profound.

The College supports a strong research program in the arts and sciences, explicitly designed to encourage student collaboration and initiative. The faculty is committed to teaching as a transformative practice, an opportunity to inspire students to reimagine the nature and purpose of their education.

Emory & Henry claims a proud heritage of enlightened civic activity. A hallmark of the College's civic engagement is its leadership in advancing a pragmatic understanding of sustainable communities and practices.

With an emphasis on service, excellence, and action, Emory & Henry encourages students to envision the world in which they would like to live and then challenges them to create it. Founded in 1836, the College is named for two men who symbolize this dual emphasis on thought and action—Bishop John Emory, an eminent Methodist church leader at the time the College was founded, and Patrick Henry, a famous orator of the American Revolution and Virginia's first governor.

Emory & Henry graduates have found tremendous personal success, which they have used to improve the world around them. Through its comprehensive, four-year liberal arts education, Emory & Henry has produced leading scientific researchers, NASA engineers, well-known writers, and successful physicians, ministers, lawyers, educators, and businesspeople. Emory & Henry provides innovative programs in public policy and community service as well as international studies and environmental science.

Students have opportunities for involvement in a variety of campus activities: service clubs, fraternities, sororities, sports clubs, honor groups, religious life, and multicultural groups. Student staffs produce a yearbook, an online magazine, and a literary magazine; others operate an educational FM radio station. Musically talented students have opportunities to participate in a choral program and a pep band. The prestigious Concert Choir has toured throughout the United States and in parts of Europe. The Barter Theatre, a professional theater in nearby Abingdon, works with Emory & Henry College to provide a theater education program that integrates college-level drama study with the benefits of experience on a professional stage. The Appalachian Center for Community Service is available for students committed to community service and integrates service learning into many classes. The King Health and Physical Education Center includes a state-of-the-art fitness center and enhances the College athletics program. Varsity sports for men are baseball, basketball, cross-country, football, golf, soccer, and tennis; women compete in basketball, cross-country, soccer, softball, swimming, tennis, and volleyball. Several sports are also played on either a club or an intramural basis.

Location

Emory & Henry is located in Emory, Virginia, which is approximately 25 miles north of Bristol, a city that offers large shopping areas, movies, and restaurants. The area surrounding Emory is known for its scenic beauty, recreational opportunities, and talented artisans. Within an hour's drive are slopes for snow skiing, lakes for waterskiing, the Appalachian Trail for hiking, and locations for horseback riding, canoeing, and many other sports. The historic town of Abingdon, Virginia, which lies just 7 miles south of Emory, is the home of the renowned Barter Theatre, the oldest professional theater in the United States. Abingdon's downtown district includes shopping areas, movie theaters, restaurants, and museums. The town also hosts the annual Virginia Highlands Festival, bringing together musicians, artists, and craftsmen for exhibitions and competition.

Majors and Degrees

Emory & Henry College offers programs of study in art, athletic training, biology, business administration, chemistry, computer information management, economics, education (early childhood through high school, including many subject-area options), English, environmental studies, geography, history, international studies (East Asia, European community, or Middle Eastern and Islamic studies), languages, mass communications, mathematics, music, philosophy, physical education, physics, political science, psychology, public policy and community service, religion, sociology, and theater. Preprofessional preparation in dentistry, law, medicine, and veterinary medicine may be completed within several of the programs.

The Bachelor of Arts degree is awarded in all programs of study and the Bachelor of Science degree in selected areas. Individualized programs of study may be developed in consultation with a faculty adviser.

Academic Programs

Emory & Henry offers a liberal arts program with an emphasis on writing, ethical reasoning, critical thinking, and knowledge of global concerns, as well as a broad introduction to liberal arts subjects. All students complete a core curriculum, which requires students to integrate their classroom work with study and research beyond the classroom and the campus, in order to acquire a deep understanding of regional and cultural differences and challenges. The new curriculum emphasizes foreign language and there are plans to eventually require students to spend time in locations throughout the United States and abroad.

Undergraduate programs of study include art, athletic training, biology, business administration, chemistry, computer information management, economics, education, English, geography, history, languages, mass communications, mathematics, music, philosophy, physical education, physics, political science, psychology, religion, sociology, and theater. Special and interdisciplinary programs of study offered are environmental studies, international studies, pre-engineering, prelaw, premedicine, and public policy and community service.

Emory & Henry operates on a semester calendar from late August to mid-December and from mid-January to mid-May. Two summer sessions run from late May to early July. First-year students typically carry a four-course load of 13 to 14 credit hours per semester, including the yearlong course on Western Tradition. Upperclass students carrying a full load complete five courses (14 to 15 credit hours) each semester. Classes meet on Monday-Wednesday-Friday or Tuesday-Thursday schedules.

One important feature of the Emory & Henry curriculum is the College's commitment to helping students achieve a smooth transition from high school to college. The Powell Resource Center provides academic support, advising, career services, and personal counseling. The Writing Center helps students in every department to use writing for effective communication.

Off-Campus Programs

Many faculty members encourage students to get involved in community projects or research that benefit the region. Internship opportunities are available for students in most of the College's programs, providing academic credit for off-campus work in community agencies and businesses. Many students have completed internships in the surrounding communities, while others have opted for internships outside the region, including several in Washington, D.C., in positions related to the Congress or the federal government.

Emory & Henry students participate in a wide variety of study-abroad programs. From Rome to Beijing and from Eastern Europe to East Asia, Emory & Henry students experience cultures and people in a way that enriches their perspective on their studies, their lives, and their futures. Emory & Henry helps students prepare for these experiences through language study and with courses offered through a comprehensive international studies program and an international studies and business program. The College has exchange agreements with colleges and universities in Asia, Europe, and Central and South America. Students who desire other types of travel/study are assisted by faculty and staff members in locating suitable programs.

Academic Facilities

McGlothlin-Street Hall is a 70,000-square-foot academic center that houses the Departments of Biology, Business, Chemistry, Education, Environmental Studies, Geography, International Studies, and Psychology, along with a 104-seat auditorium and a tiered sixty-seat auditorium. Classrooms and laboratories in McGlothlin-Street Hall are equipped with the most current technological equipment. Miller Hall contains computerized classrooms used for instruction in such fields as accounting and computer science. Science departments located in Miller and McGlothlin-Street Halls feature a variety of equipment, such as a microcomputer-based laboratory for physics students, computerized chromatography for chemistry students, a DNA sequencer in the biology department, and biofeedback equipment. Art students have access to studios, an exhibition area, and printing equipment, and music students make use of practice rooms and a recital hall.

The historic Byars Hall, which recently underwent massive renovations, is home to the College's Division of Visual and Performing Arts. The building includes choir and ensemble rehearsal halls, a digital art lab, two large art studios, practice rooms for instrumental music, a large piano lab, and a theater support room. In addition the College has renovated Wiley Hall, its historic administrative building and is in the midst of two major fund-raising projects that will increase and enhance student involvement within fine arts and athletics.

Costs

For 2009–10, resident students paid a comprehensive fee of $33,180, which included tuition, room, and board.

Financial Aid

Forms of aid include need-based and non-need-based scholarships, loans, and part-time jobs. A Bonner Scholars program provides substantial scholarships for selected students who do volunteer work in the surrounding region. Virginia residents are eligible for a special residency grant. Merit-based scholarships are awarded based on academic performance, and many can be renewed based on continued academic success. The average first-year student received an aid package (grants and scholarships) worth $23,469 in recent years. The priority application deadline for financial aid is April 1.

Faculty

Emory & Henry professors are among the best in the nation. Over the last seventeen years, Emory & Henry has received the Carnegie Foundation Virginia Professor of the Year Award six times—more than any other college or university in Virginia. The College's professors are also five-time recipients of the Virginia Outstanding Faculty Award, given by the State Council for Higher Education. Emory & Henry has 75 full-time faculty members, and the current faculty-student ratio is 1:11. The majority of the faculty members hold terminal degrees. Every student is provided with a faculty adviser, who assists in the selection of courses. While the faculty members are encouraged to continue study and research, their primary function is teaching. Many professors live near the campus, and they make their homes open to students for special events, informal class meetings, or other activities.

Student Government

Students at Emory & Henry are encouraged to take part in campus decision making. They have voting representatives on nearly every faculty committee and on the Board of Trustees. The central body in campus government is the Student Senate, which brings together representatives of the student body, faculty, and administration.

Admission Requirements

Admission to Emory & Henry is determined on the basis of both academic achievement and personal qualifications. An applicant's secondary school preparation must include the following: 4 years of English, 3 years of mathematics (algebra I, algebra II, and geometry), 2 years of laboratory sciences, 2 years of a single foreign language, and 2 years of social studies. Strong emphasis is also placed on involvement and leadership in extracurricular and community activities, in addition to consistency and improvement surrounding academic progress.

Application and Information

To apply for admission, students should submit the basic application form, a copy of the high school transcript, scores from either the SAT or the ACT, at least one recommendation letter, and a nonrefundable $30 application fee. While not required, an essay/personal statement is strongly recommended.

Transfer applicants must submit an application and a transcript from any college previously attended, along with a completed Dean's Certificate for Transfer Students. A rolling admissions policy allows notification of a decision within two to four weeks after a file has been completed.

In addition to its rolling admissions policy, Emory & Henry College also welcomes interested applicants under the Early Application program. This program offers a nonbinding decision made on completed applications and aforementioned materials received by December 1. Not only does the College guarantee a decision by December 15, but a tentative financial aid package (with necessary materials) is offered to these students prior to January 1. Like rolling admissions decisions, students receiving acceptance under Early Application have until May 1 to make their final decision.

Application forms and other information may be obtained by contacting:

Office of Admissions
Emory & Henry College
P.O. Box 10
Emory, Virginia 24327-0947
Phone: 276-944-6133
800-848-5493 (toll-free)
Fax: 276-944-6935
E-mail: ehadmiss@ehc.edu
Web site: http://www.ehc.edu

Wiley Hall.

COLLEGE CLOSE-UPS

EUGENE LANG COLLEGE THE NEW SCHOOL FOR LIBERAL ARTS

NEW YORK, NEW YORK

THE NEW SCHOOL
A UNIVERSITY

The College

Eugene Lang College is the undergraduate liberal arts division of The New School, a leading university in New York City with a tradition of innovative learning. Eugene Lang College offers all the benefits of a small and supportive college as well as the full range of opportunities found in a university setting. At Lang, rigorous academic programs are closely connected with all that New York City has to offer: its wealth of music, theater, and arts; its vibrant international community; its history; and its energy.

Eugene Lang students are encouraged to participate in the creation and direction of their education. The desire to explore and the freedom to imagine shared by students and faculty members contribute to a distinctive academic community.

Eugene Lang College students currently come from thirty-five states and ten countries. The ratio of men to women is approximately 2:3. About 45 percent of the College's 1,425 students come from outside the New York metropolitan area; 5 percent hold foreign citizenship and 27 percent are members of minority groups. The student body is composed of both residential and day students. The university operates residence halls within walking distance of classes; incoming freshmen and transfer students are given housing priority within these facilities, and housing is guaranteed for the first year for new students. Great diversity in interests and aspirations is found among the students. Through the Office of Student Services, students produce a student newspaper and an award-winning literary magazine. They organize and participate in dramatic, musical, and artistic events through the "Lang in the City Program," as well as numerous political, social, and cultural organizations at the university and throughout New York City.

The New School was founded in 1919 by such notable scholars and intellectuals as John Dewey, Alvin Johnson, and Thorstein Veblen. It has long been a home for leading artists, educators, and public figures. For example, the university was the first institution of higher learning to offer college-level courses in fields such as black culture and race, taught by W. E. B. DuBois, and psychoanalysis, taught by Freud's disciple Sandor Ferenczi. Among the world-famous artists and performers who have taught at The New School are Martha Graham, Aaron Copland, and Thomas Hart Benton. Today, noted scholars and artists are among the hundreds of university faculty members accessible to Eugene Lang College students.

The other divisions of the university are The New School for General Studies, which offers nearly 1,000 credit and noncredit courses to students each semester and awards the B.A., B.S., M.A., M.S., and M.F.A. degrees; The New School for Social Research, which grants M.A. and Ph.D. degrees; Milano The New School for Management and Urban Policy, which awards the M.S. and Ph.D. degrees; Parsons The New School for Design, one of the oldest and most influential art schools in the country; Mannes College The New School for Music, a renowned classical conservatory; The New School for Jazz and Contemporary Music; and The New School for Drama. The total university enrollment in 2009–10 was approximately 10,260 degree-seeking students.

Location

The university is located in New York City's Greenwich Village, which historically has been a center for intellectual and artistic life. This legendary New York City neighborhood of town houses and tree-lined streets offers students a friendly and stimulating environment. Over and above the resources of Greenwich Village, New York City offers virtually unlimited cultural, artistic, recreational, and intellectual resources that make it one of the world's great cities.

Majors and Degrees

Eugene Lang College awards the Bachelor of Arts degree in the arts (dance, music, theater, visual arts, and arts in context), culture and media, economics, environmental studies, history, interdisciplinary science, literary studies, philosophy, psychology, urban studies, and liberal arts. Within the liberal arts major, students may complete interdisciplinary programs of study in education studies, religious studies, and social inquiry. They may also elect a self-designed program of study. Students may supplement their course of study by taking advantage of Lang's new cluster offerings. These interdisciplinary options draw on courses offered across the university. Clustered courses, which may also be used as part of the self-designed liberal arts major, include civic engagement, gender studies, Jewish studies, ethnicity and race, and foreign languages. In addition, students are encouraged to pursue an internship, where appropriate.

Students may apply to a five-year, dual-degree B.A./B.F.A. program in conjunction with Parsons The New School for Design or The New School for Jazz and Contemporary Music. Students may also apply for the accelerated B.A./M.A. option offered in conjunction with the university's graduate divisions.

Academic Programs

By actively participating in the process of their education, Eugene Lang College students gain the knowledge to make informed choices about the direction of their studies with the help of their advisers and peers.

Small seminar classes serve as the focus of the academic program at the College. The maximum class size is 20 students. Classes are in-depth, interdisciplinary inquiries into topics or issues selected each semester by the College's outstanding faculty. Most important, the classes engage participants in the study of primary texts, rather than textbooks, and emphasize dialogue between teacher and student as a mode of learning. Here, not only is intellectual curiosity fostered by the small classes, but a genuine sense of community develops as well.

Freshmen are required to take one writing course and three other seminars of their choice in each of their first two semesters at the College. Upper-level students create their programs by selecting seminars from the College's curriculum, or they may combine offerings of the College with courses and workshops offered by The New School for General Study, The New School for Social Research, Milano The New School for Management and Urban Policy, and Parsons The New School for Design.

The College operates on a semester calendar; the first semester runs from September through mid-December, and the second runs from late January through mid-May. Students generally earn 16 credits per semester; a minimum of 120 credits is required for graduation.

Off-Campus Programs

Eugene Lang College recognizes the immense value of work undertaken beyond the classroom. The College arranges appropriate projects—internships with private and nonprofit organizations—that serve to strengthen the connection between theoretical work in the classroom and practical work on the job.

Sophomores and juniors have the option of spending a year on a sponsored exchange with Sarah Lawrence College and the University of Amsterdam. Other exchanges, both in the United States and abroad, are available.

Academic Facilities

Eugene Lang College is located on 11th Street between Fifth and Sixth Avenues in Greenwich Village. The university includes twelve academic buildings, including a student center, the University Computing Center with IBM and Macintosh stations, a 500-seat auditorium, art galleries, studios for the fine arts, classrooms, a writing center, and faculty offices. Eugene Lang College students have full and easy access to the Raymond Fogelman Library and the Adam and Sophie Gimbel Design Library. In addition, the university participates in the South Manhattan Library Consortium. Together, the libraries in the consortium house approximately 3 million volumes covering all the traditional liberal arts disciplines and the fine arts.

Costs

Tuition and fees for the 2009–10 academic year were $34,040 plus $1714 for student health insurance. Room and board cost approximately $15,260, depending upon the student's choice of specific meal plan and dormitory accommodations.

Financial Aid

Students are encouraged to apply for aid by filing the Free Application for Federal Student Aid (FAFSA) and requesting that a copy of the need analysis report be sent to The New School (FAFSA code number 002780). Qualified College students are eligible for all federal and state financial aid programs in addition to university gift aid. University aid is awarded on the basis of need and merit and is part of a package consisting of both gift aid (grants and/or scholarships) and a self-help component (loans and Federal Work-Study Program awards). Aid is renewable each year as long as need continues and students maintain satisfactory academic standing at the College. Special attention is given to continuing students who have done exceptionally well.

Faculty

At Eugene Lang College, the faculty-student ratio is 1:10. Class size ranges from 10 to 20 students. Faculty members are graduates of outstanding colleges and universities and represent a wide variety of academic disciplines; 95 percent hold Ph.D.'s. College faculty members also serve as academic advisers, who are selected carefully in order to ensure thoughtful supervision of students' programs and academic progress.

Well-known faculty members from other divisions of the university teach at the College on a regular basis. In addition, every semester, the College hosts distinguished scholars and writers as visiting faculty and guest lecturers who further enrich the academic program of the College and the university.

Student Government

There is a student union at the College, which is an organized vehicle for student expression and action as well as a means of funding student projects and events. Students are encouraged to express their views and concerns about academic policies and community life through regular student-faculty member meetings.

Admission Requirements

Eugene Lang College welcomes admission applications from students of diverse racial, ethnic, religious, and political backgrounds whose past performance and academic and personal promise make them likely to gain from and add to the College community. The College seeks students who combine inquisitiveness and seriousness of purpose with the ability to engage in a distinctive, rigorous liberal arts program. Each applicant to the College is judged individually; the Admissions Committee, which renders all admission decisions, considers both academic qualifications and the personal, creative, and intellectual qualities of each applicant. A strong academic background, including a college-preparatory program, is recommended. An applicant's transcript; teacher and counselor recommendations; SAT, ACT, or SAT Subject Test scores; and personal essays are all taken into consideration. In addition, an interview, a tour of university facilities, and a visit to Eugene Lang College seminars are optional but highly recommended.

High school students for whom the College is their first choice are strongly encouraged to apply as early decision candidates and are notified early of an admission decision. Early entrance is an option for qualified high school juniors who wish to enter college prior to high school graduation. Candidates for early entrance must submit two teacher recommendations.

Students who have successfully completed one full year or more at another accredited institution may apply as transfer candidates. If accepted, transfer students may enter upper-level seminars and pursue advanced work. International students may apply for admission as freshmen or transfers by submitting a regular application to the College. If English is spoken as a second language, TOEFL scores are required. The New York Connection Program invites students from other colleges to Eugene Lang College for a semester and incorporates an internship into their studies.

Students interested in applying for the combined B.A./B.F.A. degree program in fine arts or jazz studies are encouraged to apply for admission as freshmen to these special five-year programs. In addition to the admission requirements outlined above, a home exam and a portfolio are required for fine arts, and an audition is required for jazz studies.

Application and Information

Freshmen, transfers, and visiting students may apply for either the September (fall) or January (spring) semester. To apply for admission to the College, students must request an application packet and submit the required credentials and a $50 application fee by the appropriate deadline. The application fee may be waived in accordance with the College Board's Fee Waiver Service. For the semester beginning in January, the required credentials must be submitted by November 15, with notification by December 15. For the September semester, early decision candidates must submit the required credentials by November 15, with notification by December 15. For freshman candidates applying for general admission and freshman early entrants, the deadline is February 1, with notification by April 1. For transfers and visiting students, the deadline is rolling to May 15, with notification rolling until July 1. For further information, students should contact:

Karen Williams
Director of Admissions
Eugene Lang College The New School for Liberal Arts
72 Fifth Avenue, Second Floor
New York, New York 10011
Phone: 212-229-5665
Fax: 212-229-5355
E-mail: lang@newschool.edu
Web site: http://www.newschool.edu/lang

FAIRLEIGH DICKINSON UNIVERSITY

COLLEGE AT FLORHAM, MADISON, NEW JERSEY
METROPOLITAN CAMPUS, TEANECK, NEW JERSEY

The University

Founded in 1942, Fairleigh Dickinson University (FDU) is a center of academic excellence dedicated to the creation of world citizens through global education. It has two strategically located and uniquely different campuses in northern New Jersey—the College at Florham in Madison and the Metropolitan Campus in Teaneck—offering more than 100 career-oriented undergraduate and graduate programs. Building on its long history of international outreach and its proximity to New York City, the University strives to provide students with the multidisciplinary, intercultural, and ethical foundation needed to participate, lead, and prosper in the global marketplace of ideas, commerce, and culture. Fairleigh Dickinson was the first university in the nation to require that all undergraduates complete at least one distance-learning course a year as part of their educational requirements.

Location

Fairleigh Dickinson University's two campuses in northern New Jersey provide undergraduates with the choice of distinctively different living and learning environments.

The University's College at Florham is located on the former Vanderbilt-Twombly estate in suburban Madison, New Jersey (Morris County), about 45 minutes from New York City. Its focus is on providing outstanding on-campus and residential living opportunities, hands-on learning experiences, strong graduate and professional school preparation, and customized educational options—all framed by a global perspective.

The University's Metropolitan Campus is located in the dynamic New York–New Jersey corridor less than 10 miles from New York City in Teaneck, New Jersey (Bergen County). Its university atmosphere and international perspective attracts students from the U.S. and around the world. Undergraduates have access to the resources of a major graduate center, and nearby New York City is an integral part of their learning experience. Accelerated bachelor's/master's options are among its many professional preparation programs.

Residence halls and off-campus housing are available on both campuses. There are nearly 100 active academic, social, political, and professional student organizations; sororities and fraternities; and sports at the varsity, intramural, club, and intercampus levels. Lectures, seminars, concerts, performances, and special events are also an intrinsic part of University life.

The University also owns and operates two international campuses, Wroxton College in Oxfordshire, England, and FDU-Vancouver in British Columbia, Canada, which offer students outstanding study-abroad experiences.

Majors and Degrees

Bachelor of Arts degrees are offered in art, communication, communication studies, creative writing, criminal justice, criminology, economics, English language and literature, film and animation, fine arts, French language and literature, history, humanities, interdisciplinary studies, international studies, literature, mathematics, philosophy, political science, psychology, sociology, Spanish language and literature, and theater arts.

Bachelor of Science degrees are offered in accounting, allied health technologies, biochemistry, biology, business management, chemistry, civil engineering technology, clinical laboratory sciences, computer science, construction engineering technology, electrical engineering, electrical engineering technology, entrepreneurship, environmental science, finance, hotel and restaurant management, information technology, marine biology, marketing, mathematics, mechanical engineering technology, medical technology, nursing (including a one-year accelerated program), radiologic technology, and science.

The QUEST five-year teacher certification program allows students to earn a bachelor's degree in a field of their choosing in the liberal arts or sciences as well as dual teacher certification in one or two high-demand specifications and a Master of Arts in Teaching (M.A.T.) degree. Premed and prelaw programs are also available. In collaboration with leading professional schools, 6½- or 7-year combined bachelor's/doctoral programs are offered in chiropractic, dental medicine, optometry, pharmacy, physical therapy, podiatry, and veterinary medicine.

In addition, the University offers dozens of concentrations and minors in such marketable fields as actuarial science, biotechnology, computer engineering, cybersecurity, forensic psychology, gaming development, information systems, pharmaceutical biostatistics, toxicology, and visual communication. Fairleigh Dickinson also offers many combined degree programs, which enable students to earn both their undergraduate and graduate degrees in just five years in such fields as accounting, biology, business administration, chemistry, civil engineering or construction technology/systems science, communication/corporate and organizational communication, computer science, computer science/computer engineering, criminal justice/public administration, electrical engineering, electrical engineering/computer engineering, environmental science/systems science, hotel and restaurant management/hospitality management, political science, psychology, and public administration.

An Associate in Arts degree in liberal arts and an Associate in Science in radiography are also offered.

Academic Programs

Candidates for the degree of Bachelor of Arts or Bachelor of Science must complete a minimum of 128 credit-hours of course work, maintain a minimum 2.0 CGPR (individual colleges have minimum CGPRs for course work within their majors), and complete the University Core Curriculum—a sequence of four courses designed to provide all FDU undergraduates with a solid foundation in the liberal arts, sciences, and humanities. The core provides students with a common base of knowledge; improves skills in communications and analysis; promotes understanding of individual, societal, and international perspectives; and instills an appreciation for the interrelationship among bodies of knowledge. Candidates for the B.A. must take 30 to 44 credits in the major, 40 to 63 credits in distribution requirements (19 to 23 credits in foundation courses, 15 to 30 credits in humanities and social and behavioral sciences, and 6 to 10 credits in laboratory science), and the University Core; the remainder of credits may be taken as free electives. Candidates for the B.S. degree must complete 54 to 60 credits in the major and the University Core; the remaining credits are taken in foundation and free elective courses. The undergraduate program includes all courses needed to meet graduate and professional school requirements.

The University offers a variety of specialized honors programs and a cooperative education program, and many departments have internships and work-experience programs. Adult students may participate in a variety of specialized programs, including the Bachelor of Arts in individualized studies, that are offered on campus and at over fifty off-site locations. An all-online degree-completion program is also available for adult learners.

Through the University's Regional Center for College Students with Learning Disabilities, students can receive academic support within the regular college curriculum (enrollment is selective and limited). The Freshmen Intensive Studies and Enhanced

Freshman Experience programs are designed to assist a limited number of promising students who require focused support as they begin their college careers. The University also offers English Language Centers (a division of Berlitz, Inc.) at the Metropolitan Campus as a service to international students.

Off-Campus Programs

The University strongly encourages all students to incorporate an international learning experience into their education. For example, students can spend a semester or summer at FDU's Wroxton College, the historic British campus located 70 miles from London that Fairleigh Dickinson has owned and operated since 1965. Summer-study opportunities are also offered at FDU-Vancouver. A wide range of other international experiences are also available based on student interests and career goals. The University's requirements in distance learning further expand students' international learning experiences, enabling them to study with its Global Virtual Faculty™ of scholars and professionals around the world.

Domestic learning experiences available to students include the well-known Semester in Washington and internships with the United Nations. In addition, the marine biology curriculum includes laboratory field experiences at Samana Station, the University's own marine biology research and learning facility in the Dominican Republic.

Academic Facilities

The University maintains comprehensive libraries on each campus as well as a business reference library on the Metropolitan Campus. The libraries have combined holdings of 410,000 volumes and subscriptions to 1,160 periodicals. The University is a participating member of the Online Computer Library Center and maintains a University-wide online catalog. Each library has a number of distinguished special collections on subjects such as the Columbia film archives, the Kahn Memorial Collection on the History of Photography, and the Harry Chesler Collection of comic art, graphic satire, and illustration.

Students have ready access to minicomputers and microcomputers on campus as well as to programming languages and software. In addition, there are state-of-the-art computer graphics laboratories on both campuses. Computer, software, and Internet training are offered through the campus computer centers. Resident students with their own computers can link to the campus computer network from their rooms. Student e-mail and Internet access accounts are offered to all students. Nearly all buildings throughout the University offer wireless computer access.

Costs

Educational costs for 2009–10 for the College at Florham were $30,683 for tuition, a $680 technology fee, $6795 for residence (based on standard double occupancy), and $3722 for meals (based on an eleven-meal plan plus a $300 flex plan). For the Metropolitan Campus, costs included $29,998 for tuition, a $680 technology fee, $7244 for residence (based on standard double occupancy), and $3836 for meals (based on an eleven-meal plan plus a $300 flex plan).

Financial Aid

More than $56 million in University-funded financial aid is awarded annually, including a generous program offering annually renewable academic scholarships ranging from $3500 to $22,500 for academically outstanding students. To be considered for financial aid, students should file the Free Application for Federal Student Aid (FAFSA). Applications for aid should be filed by February 15 for priority consideration.

Faculty

There are 309 full-time and approximately 614 part-time faculty members at Fairleigh Dickinson University. Of the full-time faculty members, most hold a doctorate or the highest terminal degree in their field. The University's full-time undergraduate student-faculty ratio is 12:1. All courses are taught by faculty members, not graduate students or teaching assistants. All first-year students are assigned faculty mentors to help develop class schedules and assess their academic progress.

Student Government

Each campus has a student council that acts as the governing body to enforce student regulations and to plan social club activities. The student council serves as a liaison with the faculty and administration of both the campus and the University. It offers students' opinions as an aid in developing University curricular and extracurricular policies. The University Senate, which formulates University policies, includes voting representatives from the student body.

Admission Requirements

The University recommends at least 16 units of full-credit work from an accredited secondary school, including 4 years of English, 2 years of history, 2 years of laboratory sciences (3 years preferred), 3 years of college-preparatory mathematics, 4 elective units (at least 3 of which should be academic), and 2 years of a foreign language. Additional science and mathematics units are required for some majors. The criteria that are used for University-wide admission are the high school record, SAT or ACT scores, and counselor recommendations. SAT Subject Test scores are used for placement only. Campus visits are strongly recommended. Interviews are encouraged for all students and may be required in select cases.

Application and Information

Students must submit a completed and signed application form, a secondary school record form listing all courses and grades, SAT or ACT scores, and a nonrefundable $40 application fee (which can be waived in cases of hardship). The fee also is waived for students filing online. Freshmen and transfer students are admitted in September and January and during summer sessions. Applicants for regular admission are reviewed on a rolling basis and are notified after receipt of all credentials. Information on filing an online application can be found by visiting the University's Web site.

For application forms, financial aid information, and other materials, students should contact:

Office of University Admissions
Fairleigh Dickinson University
1000 River Road, H-DH3-10
Teaneck, New Jersey 07666
Phone: 800-338-8803 (toll-free)
E-mail: admissions@fdu.edu
Web site: http://www.fdu.edu

FAIRMONT STATE UNIVERSITY

FAIRMONT, WEST VIRGINIA

The University

Fairmont State University (FSU) has an enrollment of approximately 4,550 students. Founded as a private school in 1865, the University is located in Fairmont, West Virginia.

The mission of FSU is to provide opportunities for individuals to achieve their professional and personal goals and discover roles for responsible citizenship that promote the common good. FSU offers more than ninety baccalaureate programs/concentrations as well as graduate programs. Graduate programs are available in business, criminal justice, education, human services, and nursing.

The main campus, which FSU shares with Pierpont Community & Technical College, features twenty-two buildings on more than 90 acres. From the historic administration building, Hardway Hall, to the brand-new Bryant Place residence hall, the facilities are a blend of tradition and technology. Facilities also include the Gaston Caperton Center in Clarksburg, West Virginia.

The student center, called the Falcon Center, features 7,000 square feet of fitness equipment; five versatile courts for indoor sports; space for fitness classes; four-lane pool with a whirlpool, sauna, and outdoor sunning deck; four-lane cushioned jogging/walking track; game rooms; dining facilities; and more.

Fairmont State is a member of the NCAA Division II and the West Virginia Intercollegiate Athletic Conference. Varsity programs for men are offered in football, basketball, baseball, cross-country, golf, tennis, and swimming. The intercollegiate athletic programs for women include tennis, golf, basketball, volleyball, swimming, softball, and cross-country.

Fairmont State offers more than eighty clubs, organizations, student publications, honoraries, sororities, and fraternities, as well as wide range of intramural sports. Many fine arts performances and exhibits are planned each semester. Nationally prominent speakers are invited to the campus.

Location

Fairmont, a city of more than 19,000 in north central West Virginia, is the county seat of Marion County. Located along Interstate 79 approximately 90 miles south of Pittsburgh, Fairmont and the University are easily accessible to all travelers. Shopping malls, restaurants, cultural entertainment, and nightlife are easily found throughout the area.

West Virginia's natural treasures—mountains, rivers, waterfalls, wildlife, wildflowers, clean air, and vast tracts of national forest—are all close at hand. In and near Fairmont are popular trails for hiking and biking, rivers for white-water rafting, excellent spots for rock and mountain climbing, camping, fishing, and some of the best skiing in the East.

Majors and Degrees

FSU offers more than ninety baccalaureate programs/concentrations, as well as graduate programs. For a complete list of majors offered, students should visit the University's Web site (http://www.fairmontstate.edu).

Academic Programs

Programs are offered in the following areas: business, education, health, fine arts, language, nursing and allied health administration, science, mathematics, social science, and technology.

The Honors Program encourages and instructs highly motivated students through general honors classes, advanced seminars, and an interdisciplinary colloquium. Students conduct independent scholarship, research assignments, internships, and creative projects. Students have the opportunity for field trips, lectures, and cultural events.

Academic Facilities

The Ruth Ann Musick Library has a collection of more than 200,000 books and more than 15,000 bound periodicals, microfilms, and other materials, including a large collection of audiotapes and videotapes. The library also has sites at the Caperton Center and the National Aerospace Education Center.

FSU's state-of-the-art technology infrastructure includes thirty computer labs and high-speed network connections that are accessible from the library, classrooms, and every residence hall room, as well as the most up-to-date teaching software.

FSU is also home to the Frank and Jane Gabor West Virginia Folklife Center, which is dedicated to the identification, preservation, and perpetuation of the region's rich cultural heritage through academic studies, educational programs, festivals, performances, and publications. The center is part of the FSU Department of Language and Literature.

Costs

For the 2008–09 academic year, in-state students at Fairmont State paid $2512 in tuition and fees, $3326 for room and board, and $500 for books and supplies, for a total of $6338 each semester. For out-of-state students, tuition and fees were $5295, room and board were $3326, and books and supplies were $500, for a total of $9121 each semester.

Financial Aid

About 86 percent of students receive some form of aid. Guidelines and forms for West Virginia and out-of-state residents are available from high school guidance counselors or the Fairmont State Financial Aid Office. Fairmont State awards more than $40 million in financial assistance each year.

Faculty

FSU employs more than 200 full-time faculty members, ensuring a student-teacher ratio of 17:1. Dedicated academic advisers and faculty members work one-on-one with students to meet their individual needs.

Student Government

Student Government actively seeks to supplement the academic atmosphere with intellectual, cultural, and social activities. Student Government members are involved in all aspects of life on campus and work cooperatively with the administration.

Admission Requirements

First-time freshmen who wish to apply for admission to Fairmont State University must submit an application for admission; an official high school transcript or GED certificate (sent by the high school or the Department of Education), with a GPA of 2.0 or higher; ACT or SAT scores (at least 18 on the ACT or 870 on the SAT); a college transcript (if college credit was earned during high school); immunization records (if the applicant was born after January 1, 1957); and a statement of activities (if the applicant has been out of high school more than six months). Students applying for transfer admission must submit an application for admission; a college transcript from accredited institutions, showing a minimum GPA of 2.0; an official high school transcript and ACT/SAT scores if there are fewer than 24 earned credit hours being transferred; immunization records (if the applicant was born after January 1, 1957); and a statement of activities. Postbaccalaureate students who are seeking another degree must submit an application for admission, official college transcripts, a statement of activities, and immunization records (if the applicant was born after January 1, 1957).

Transient students (students enrolled at another school and returning to that institution) must submit an application for admission and a course approval form (from their Registrar's office).

Application and Information

On a Saturday each spring and fall, Fairmont State schedules a Campus Visitation Day so potential students and their family members and friends can visit the campus and attend information sessions on admissions, financial aid, and living on campus. An Academic Fair is also scheduled so students can meet with faculty members about the academic schools and departments.

Campus tours through the Office of Admissions are available Mondays through Fridays. To set up a tour, students should call 800-641-5678 (toll-free) or 304-367-4892. Tours can also be scheduled online at the University's Web site (http://www.fairmontstate.edu).

For further information, students may contact:

Office of Admissions
Fairmont State University
1201 Locust Avenue
Fairmont, West Virginia 26554
Phone: 304-367-4892 (admissions)
800-641-5678 (toll-free)
304-367-4213 (financial aid)
304-367-4216 (residence life)
304-367-4000 (campus operator)
304-367-4026 (Gaston Caperton Center)
304-842-8300 (Robert C. Byrd National Aerospace Education Center)
304-367-4200 (TDD)
Fax: 304-367-4789
E-mail: admit@fairmontstate.edu
Web site: http://www.fairmontstate.edu

The Falcon Center, centrally located on FSU's main campus, provides an environment where students and faculty and staff members can comfortably interact while enjoying a variety of fitness and wellness programs, eating areas, and places to take a break between classes. The campus bookstore, Aladdin food services, the Nickel (a convenience store and fast food restaurant), and game room are available. The building also features a pool and sauna, a large fitness area, an indoor track, and a conference center.

COLLEGE CLOSE-UPS

FASHION INSTITUTE OF TECHNOLOGY

State University of New York

NEW YORK, NEW YORK

COLLEGE CLOSE-UPS

The College

The Fashion Institute of Technology (FIT) is New York City's celebrated urban college for creative and business talent. A selective State University of New York (SUNY) college of art and design, business, and technology, FIT is a creative mix of innovative achievers, original thinkers, and industry pioneers, with nearly forty programs of study leading to the A.A.S., B.F.A., and B.S. degrees. The School of Graduate Studies offers six programs leading to either a Master of Arts (M.A.) or Master of Professional Studies (M.P.S.) degree. The college is accredited by the Middle States Association of Colleges and Schools, National Association of Schools of Art and Design, and Council for Interior Design Accreditation.

FIT serves approximately 10,000 students from the greater metropolitan area, New York State, across the country, and around the world, offering full- and part-time study options, evening/weekend degree programs, and online studies. The college provides a singular approach to higher education—balancing a real-world-based curriculum and hands-on instruction with a rigorous liberal arts foundation, marrying design and business, supporting individual creativity in a collaborative environment, and encouraging faculty members to match teaching expertise with professional experience. It offers a complete college experience with a vibrant student and residential life.

FIT's mission is to produce well-rounded graduates: doers and thinkers who raise the professional bar to become the next generation of business pacesetters and creative icons.

All full-time, matriculated students are eligible for FIT housing. Four residence halls house 2,300 in fully furnished single-, double-, triple-, and quad-occupancy rooms. Each residence hall has centrally located lounges and laundry facilities; George and Mariana Kaufman Residence Hall also provides an on-site fitness center. Students have the option of either traditional (meal plan included) or apartment-style accommodations. Counselors and student staff members live in the halls, helping students adjust to college life and living in New York City.

Throughout the David Dubinsky Student Center are lounges, a game room, a dining hall, a student radio station, the Style Shop (a FIT student-run boutique), student government and club offices, a comprehensive health center, two gyms, a dance studio, a weight room, and a counseling center.

Location

Occupying an entire block in Manhattan's Chelsea neighborhood, FIT's campus places students at the heart of the fashion, advertising, visual arts, design, business, and communications industries. Students gain unparalleled exposure to their field through internship opportunities and professional connections. A wide range of cultural and entertainment options—from dining to galleries to theater—are available within walking distance of the campus, as is convenient access to several subway and bus routes and the city's major rail and bus transportation hubs.

Majors and Degrees

FIT offers fifteen Associate in Applied Science (A.A.S.) and twenty-three baccalaureate programs. All students complete a two-year A.A.S. program in their major area of study and the liberal arts and then typically continue in a related, two-year Bachelor of Fine Arts (B.F.A.) or Bachelor of Science (B.S.) program. If students choose, they may begin their careers with the A.A.S. degree, which qualifies them for entry-level positions in their chosen field.

The School of Art and Design offers eleven A.A.S. and thirteen B.F.A. programs, the Jay and Patty Baker School of Business and Technology offers four A.A.S. and nine B.S. programs, and the School of Liberal Arts offers one B.S. program.

The fifteen A.A.S. programs, all of which provide the foundation for one or more corresponding baccalaureate-level programs, are accessories design*; advertising and marketing communications*; communication design*; fashion design*; fashion merchandising management* (with an online option); fine arts (with a career-exploration component); illustration; interior design; jewelry design*; menswear; photography; production management: fashion and related industries; textile development and marketing*; textile/surface design*; and visual presentation and exhibition design. Programs with an * are also available in a one-year format for students with acceptable transferable credits.

The thirteen B.F.A. programs are accessories design and fabrication; advertising design; computer animation and interactive media; fabric styling; fashion design (with specializations in children's wear, fashion design, intimate apparel, and knitwear); fine arts; graphic design; illustration; interior design; packaging design; photography and the digital image; textile/surface design; and toy design.

The ten B.S. programs are advertising and marketing communications; cosmetics and fragrance marketing; direct and interactive marketing; fashion merchandising management; home products development; international trade and marketing for the fashion industries; production management: fashion and related industries; technical design; textile development and marketing; and visual art management.

For those students looking to balance the demands of career or family with their education, FIT offers nine degree programs available through evening/weekend study that include advertising and marketing communications (A.A.S. and B.S.), communication design (A.A.S.), fashion design (A.A.S.), fashion merchandising management (A.A.S. and B.S.), graphic design (B.F.A.), illustration (B.F.A.), and international trade and marketing for the fashion industries (B.S.).

Academic Programs

Each undergraduate program includes a core of traditional liberal arts courses, providing students with a global perspective, critical-thinking skills, and the ability to communicate effectively. The School of Liberal Arts offers FIT students the opportunity to minor in a variety of liberal arts areas in two forms: traditional subject-based minors and interdisciplinary minors unique to the FIT liberal arts curriculum. Selected minors include film and media, economics, Latin American studies, and sustainability.

All degree programs are designed to prepare students for creative and business careers—the college's Career Services, which offers lifetime placement, reports a graduate employment rate of 90 percent—and to provide them with the prerequisite studies so that they may go on to graduate degree programs. Internships are a required element of most programs and are available to all students. More than one third of FIT student internships result in employment offers from the sponsoring organization.

The Presidential Scholars honors program, available to academically exceptional students in all disciplines, offers special liberal arts courses, projects, colloquiums, extracurricular activities, and off-campus visits designed to broaden horizons and stimulate discourse. Past areas of study have included cultural studies, Greek mythology, theories of public space, and urban archeology. Presidential Scholars are also awarded priority course registration and an annual merit stipend.

Precollege programs (Saturday and Sunday/Summer Live) are available to high school students during the fall, spring, and summer. More than sixty courses provide the chance to learn in an innovative environment, to develop art and design portfolios, to explore the business and technological sides of a wide range of creative careers, and to discover natural talents and abilities. Courses for middle school students are available in the summer.

The School of Continuing Education and Professional Studies provides convenient evening and weekend credit and noncredit classes to students and working professionals who are interested in pursuing a degree or certificate or furthering their knowledge and expertise in a particular industry.

Off-Campus Programs

The study-abroad experience provides students with the opportunity to immerse themselves in diverse cultures and prepares them to live and work in a global community. Australia, China, England, France, and Mexico are some of the countries where FIT semester study-abroad courses are offered. Students can also study in Italy during the winter or summer sessions, a semester, or a full academic year, concentrating in fashion design or fashion merchandising management.

Academic Facilities

FIT provides its students with an urban campus of classrooms, laboratories, and studios that reflects the most advanced educational and professional practices. The Fred P. Pomerantz Art and Design Center houses photography studios; drawing, painting, and sculpture studios; a printmaking room; display and exhibit design rooms; a model-making workshop; and a graphics printing service bureau. The Peter G. Scotese Computer-Aided Design and Communications Facility provides students with the opportunity to explore the latest advancements in technology and their integration in the design of textiles, toys, interiors, fashion, and advertising, as well as photography and computer graphics and animation. The Annette Green/Fragrance Foundation Studio, a professionally equipped fragrance development laboratory, is the only one of its kind on a U.S. college campus. Cutting and sewing laboratories for the production management program students offer the most advanced design and cutting machinery among educational facilities in the U.S. The Design/Research Lighting Laboratory, an educational and professional development facility for interior design and other disciplines, features more than 400 commercially available lighting fixtures. Other college facilities include a broadcasting studio, knitting and weaving labs, a multimedia foreign language laboratory, and twenty-three computer labs containing nearly 700 Mac and PC workstations, in addition to several additional labs with computers reserved for students in specific programs.

The renowned Museum at FIT is New York City's only museum dedicated to the art of fashion, and students, designers, and historians use it for research and inspiration. The museum operates year-round, and its exhibitions are free and open to the public. Recent exhibitions include Fashion and Politics; American Beauty: Aesthetics and Innovation in Fashion; and Night and Day. The Gladys Marcus Library provides more than 300,000 volumes of print, nonprint, and electronic materials. The newspaper and periodicals collection includes 500 current subscriptions, with a specialization in international design and trade publications; online resources include more than 90 searchable databases. The library also offers specialized resources, such as clipping files, fashion and trend forecasting services, sketch collections, and runway show DVDs.

Also on campus are three multimedia venues—the Katie Murphy Amphitheatre, the Morris W. and Fannie B. Haft Auditorium, and the John E. Reeves Great Hall—used for student presentations, industry panels, conferences, and special events.

Costs

The 2009–10 associate-level tuition per semester for New York State residents was $1857; for nonresidents, it was $5571. Baccalaureate-level tuition per semester was $2584 for residents and $6302 for nonresidents. For fall 2009, per-semester housing costs were $5435–$5590 for traditional residence hall accommodations with mandatory meal plan and $4580–$8325 for apartment-style accommodations. Meal plans ranged from $1510 to $1940 per semester. Textbook costs and other nominal fees, such as locker rental or laboratory use, vary per program of study. All costs are subject to change.

Financial Aid

FIT attempts to remove financial barriers to college entrance by providing scholarships, grants, loans, and work-study employment for students in financial need. Nearly all full-time, matriculated students who complete the financial aid application process receive some type of assistance. The college directly administers its own institutional grants and scholarships, which are provided by The Educational Foundation for the Fashion Industries.

College-administered federal funding includes Federal Pell Grants, Federal Perkins Loans, Federal Supplemental Educational Opportunity Grants, Federal Work-Study awards, and Federal Family Educational Loans, which include student and parent loans. New York State residents who meet state guidelines for eligibility may also receive Tuition Assistance Program (TAP) and/or Educational Opportunity Program (EOP) grants. Financial aid applicants must file the Free Application for Federal Student Aid (FAFSA), through which they apply for the Federal Pell Grant. They should also apply for all available outside sources of aid. Other documentation may be requested by the Financial Aid Office. Applications for financial aid should be completed prior to February 15 for fall admission or prior to November 1 for spring admission.

Faculty

FIT's faculty is drawn from top professionals in academia, art, and business who bring their experience to the classroom and introduce students to the real-life opportunities and challenges of their disciplines through field trips, guest lectures, and sponsored competitions. Academic departments consult with industry advisory boards of noted experts in their fields, ensuring that the curriculum and classroom technology reflect evolving industry practices. Student-instructor interaction is encouraged, with a maximum class size of 25, and courses are structured to foster participation, independent thinking, and self-expression.

Student Government

The Student Council, the governing body of the Student Association, gives all students the privileges and responsibilities of citizens in a self-governing college community. Many faculty committees include student representatives, and the president of the student government sits on FIT's Board of Trustees.

Admission Requirements

Applicants for admission must be either candidates for or recipients of a high school diploma or a General Educational Development (GED) certificate. Admission is based on class rank, strength and performance in college-preparatory course work, and the student essay. A portfolio evaluation is required for art and design majors. Specific portfolio requirements are explained on FIT's Web site. SAT and ACT scores are required for placement in math and English classes and they are required for students applying to the Presidential Scholars honors program. Letters of recommendation are not required.

Transfer students from regionally accredited colleges must submit official transcripts for credit evaluation. Students may qualify for the one-year A.A.S. option if they hold a baccalaureate degree from an accredited college or if they have a minimum of 30 transferable credits from an accredited college, including 24 credits that are equivalent to FIT's liberal arts requirements and at least one semester of physical education.

Students seeking admission to a B.F.A. or B.S. program must hold an A.A.S. degree from FIT or an equivalent degree from an accredited and approved college. They must also meet the appropriate prerequisites for the specific major and must have completed FIT's liberal arts requirements. Further requirements may include an individual interview with a departmental committee, review of academic standing, and a portfolio review (for applicants to B.F.A. programs). Any student who applies for transfer to FIT from a four-year program must have completed a minimum of 60 credits, including the requisite art or technical courses and the liberal arts requirements.

Application and Information

Students wishing to visit FIT are encouraged to attend a group information session. The visit schedule is available online at http://www.fitnyc.edu/visitfit.

Interested candidates may apply online at http://www.fitnyc.edu/admissions. For more information, students should contact:

Admissions
Fashion Institute of Technology
227 West 27th Street
New York, New York 10001-5992
Phone: 212-217-3760
800-GO-TO-FIT (toll-free)
E-mail: fitinfo@fitnyc.edu
Web site: http://www.fitnyc.edu

FELICIAN COLLEGE

LODI, NEW JERSEY

The College

Felician College is a Catholic/Franciscan college serving more than 2,000 men and women. Its mission is to create a close-knit nurturing community committed to putting students first and enabling every student's full potential. Felician provides a solid and supportive foundation within a liberal arts framework, which allows students to meet the challenges of the new century with informed minds and understanding hearts. The College is accredited by the Middle States Association of Colleges and Schools, and carries program accreditation from the Commission on Collegiate Nursing Education, Teacher Education Accreditation Council, and the International Assembly for Collegiate Business Education.

In addition to its undergraduate degree programs, Felician College offers the Master of Science in Nursing (M.S.N.), Master of Business Administration (M.B.A.), Master of Arts in Religious Education, and Master of Arts in Teacher Education.

Felician College competes in Division II of the National Collegiate Athletic Association (NCAA). The Felician teams, called the Golden Falcons, compete in men's baseball, men's and women's basketball, men's and women's soccer, men's and women's cross-country, men's golf, and women's softball and volleyball. The Athletic Department also sponsors numerous intramural sports activities, such as indoor soccer, faculty-student softball and volleyball games on the quad.

Students may elect to reside in one of the spacious suites in Elliott Hall or Milton Court Residence, both located on the Rutherford Campus, a 10-minute shuttle bus ride from the campus in Lodi. The campuses offer comfortable student lounge areas, student meeting rooms, dining halls, a gymnasium, a fitness center, and grassy areas for outdoor recreation.

Location

Felician College is located on two beautifully landscaped campuses in Lodi and Rutherford, in Bergen County, in northern New Jersey. Both campuses, nestled in suburban towns, are 12 miles from New York City and a few miles from the New Jersey Meadowlands sports complex.

Majors and Degrees

Felician College offers programs of study in the arts and sciences, business and management sciences, nursing and health management, and teacher education.

A liberal arts program leading to the Bachelor of Arts, Bachelor of Science, Bachelor of Science in Nursing, or Associate in Arts degree is designed to provide students with a broad general education and concentrated preparation in a major area. For the B.A. degree, a student may choose a departmental major in art, biology, communications, computer information systems, English, history, mathematics, music, philosophy, psychology, or religious studies. A student may choose an interdisciplinary major in one of three liberal arts areas: humanities, natural sciences and mathematics, or social and behavioral sciences. Concentrations are available in digital video production, fine arts, general science, global peace and justice, graphic design, international education and foreign languages, journalism, mathematical sciences, political science, sociology, and theater arts. Bachelor of Arts degree programs are available in elementary education (K–5), early childhood education (P–3 and K–5), elementary education with content area specializations (5–8), special education (K–5, dual certification), teacher of students with disabilities (K–12), and secondary education (art, English, history, math, and science).

The Bachelor of Science degree is offered in accounting, business administration, criminal justice, management, marketing, and nursing. A program leading to the Bachelor of Science degree in clinical laboratory science and eligibility for national certification is offered in collaboration with the University of Medicine and Dentistry of New Jersey's School of Health-Related Professions (UMDNJ–SHRP). For this degree, a student may concentrate in cytotechnology or medical technology. Also offered in conjunction with UMDNJ–SHRP is a Bachelor of Science program in allied-health technology. Students may study medical sonography, nuclear medicine technology, respiratory care, or vascular technology. Joint degree programs that lead to a master's or doctoral degree are offered for the following preprofessional programs: audiology, chiropractic studies, medicine, occupational therapy, optometry, physical therapy, physician assistant studies, and podiatry.

Two-year programs are offered leading to the Associate in Arts degree in liberal arts, with a concentration in business.

Academic Programs

A candidate for the B.A. in liberal arts is required to complete an organized program of study comprising a minimum of 120 semester hours distributed among prescribed and elective courses. Four interdisciplinary courses in the College's Core Curriculum are mandatory for all students. Each baccalaureate degree student in arts and sciences is required to prepare a written and oral senior research project. A minimum of 30 credit hours must be earned at the College. A student who pursues an A.A. degree is required to complete 64 to 66 credits in an approved program of study.

A candidate for the B.A. in elementary or special education is required to complete a program of 126 to 131 semester hours, including credits in general education, professional education, and a major in the arts and sciences. Field experience begins in the freshman year, students participate in a practicum in the junior year, and there is supervised teaching during the senior year in a public elementary school. The education programs are accredited by the Teacher Education Accreditation Council.

Evening and weekend classes provide adults with the opportunity to earn associate and baccalaureate degrees offered at Felician College. Students may take courses through the traditional semester format and through an accelerated trimester format. Distance learning courses are also offered.

The Honors Program, for students with strong academic records, provides an opportunity to conduct scholarly research and develop leadership skills through service learning. Upon successful completion of the program students graduate as Honors Scholars.

The Service Learning Program allows students to be of service to others while learning the value of citizenship and responsibility through action and reflection.

Academic Facilities

Seminar rooms, multimedia and learning resource centers, and laboratories in accounting, computers, psychology, science, and writing are updated annually the latest instructional technology. Through the Internet Laboratories, all students have access to e-mail and the World Wide Web. The College auditorium comfortably seats 1,500 people; its large stage with modern theatrical features hosts performing groups from all parts of the country. The College library has a selective collection of more than 110,000 volumes, as well as periodicals, cassettes, records, microfilms, and ultrafiche. A curriculum library serves as a resource center for the teacher education programs. The Nursing Skills Laboratory, located on the Lodi campus, furnishes convenient facilities for observation, application of learning, and field experiences.

Costs

Undergraduate tuition in 2009–10 is $23,650 per year for full-time students. The annual cost of room and board is $9700 (double occupancy). There are additional student fees, commuter fees, and resident fees.

Financial Aid

Felician College participates in federal, state, and institutional programs of financial assistance. To determine the amount and type of aid needed, applicants must file a Free Application for Federal Student Aid (FAFSA) with the Department of Education. The College participates in the Federal Work-Study, Federal Pell Grant, Academic Competitiveness Grant, and Federal Supplemental Educational Opportunity Grant programs. Students from New Jersey may be considered for New Jersey tuition aid grants. Through a state-guaranteed loan program, students may also take out low-interest bank loans. A number of institutional scholarships are available for qualified students in need of financial assistance. The Office of Undergraduate Admission also awards merit-based scholarships to those who are eligible, regardless of need. Monies range from $4000 to full tuition based on GPA and SAT scores. To take advantage of federal financial aid programs exclusively for veterans, a certificate of eligibility should be submitted to the director of financial aid at Felician College. More than half of the students attending Felician receive some form of financial aid.

Faculty

All courses are taught by fully qualified faculty members with advanced degrees, who are dedicated primarily to teaching, advising, and continued involvement in their disciplines. The student-faculty ratio of 10:1 facilitates a close working relationship, as well as individualized programs of instruction. The faculty members are dedicated to supporting student growth and development in a supportive, learner-centered environment designed to help students reach their highest potential.

Student Government

All students participate in the Student Government Organization (SGO). The governing body of the SGO, composed of elected representatives from various student groups, coordinates activities on and off campus, including community service, campus ministry, and social, cultural, civic, and athletic events. Student representatives also serve on College committees with faculty members and administrators.

Admission Requirements

Applicants must be graduates of an accredited high school or have the high school equivalency certificate and satisfactory SAT or ACT scores. A personal essay and interview are strongly recommended.

Students graduating with an associate degree from a recognized junior college are eligible for admission into the upper division of Felician College. Applications for transfer are considered for both fall and spring semesters. Admission requirements may be adjusted for adults on the basis of maturity and experience.

Felician College offers credit and advanced placement of up to 90 credits for coursework from accredited colleges as well as for acceptable scores on the College Board Advanced Placement tests and the College-Level Examination Program tests.

Application and Information

Applications, accompanied by a $30 fee, should be submitted during the fall of the senior year. The Office of Undergraduate Admission evaluates applicants' credentials on a rolling basis. However, applicants for the fall semester are strongly encouraged to apply before April 15.

Office of Undergraduate Admission
Felician College
262 South Main Street
Lodi, New Jersey 07644
Phone: 201-559-6131
Fax: 201-559-6138
Web site: http://www.felician.edu

On the Rutherford campus of Felician College.

COLLEGE CLOSE-UPS

FITCHBURG STATE COLLEGE

FITCHBURG, MASSACHUSETTS

The College

Fitchburg State College is a liberal arts institution where career-oriented and professional education programs thrive. The College guarantees that its graduates are qualified for jobs in their fields and continues to place more than 70 percent of its graduates in their chosen professions within six months of graduation.

Fitchburg State's excellent academic reputation and graduate placement can be attributed to a nationally recognized faculty and a strong commitment to teaching. The College enrolls approximately 3,500 undergraduate students in its day and evening divisions and another 3,000 students in its graduate programs. The average undergraduate class size is 25, and the overall student-teacher ratio remains low at 16:1. Each student is assigned to an academic adviser to assist with the planning of a program of study. In addition, each department has access to state-of-the-art equipment and an internship network that spreads throughout New England.

Student life at Fitchburg State is friendly and informal. There are numerous and varied opportunities for student leadership through the Student Government Association, the Student Athlete Advisory Committee, the All-College Committee, the Campus Center Advisory Committee, publications, and student-faculty-administration committees. More than sixty student-run clubs and organizations are open to all students, including the Dance Club, a student newspaper, the Falcon Players (theater), WXPL (student radio station), and the Black Student Union. Several sororities and fraternities contribute to the social and recreational life of the campus. Hundreds of popular and well-attended activities take place during the year, including films, lectures, concerts, seminars, coffeehouses, pub entertainment, recreational tournaments, a performing arts series, and visual arts exhibits.

In addition to B.A., B.S., and Bachelor of Science in Education degrees, Fitchburg State confers the Master of Arts, the Master of Arts in Teaching (M.A.T.), the Master in Business Administration (M.B.A.), the Master of Education (M.Ed.) in several disciplines, and the Master of Science (M.S.) in applied communication, computer science, counseling, and nursing. Several Certificate of Advanced Graduate Studies (C.A.G.S.) programs are available as well.

Location

The College is located in a residential area near the center of Fitchburg, a city with a population of 43,000, which serves as the hub of the commercial and industrial life of north-central Massachusetts. The Wallace Civic Center provides a variety of activities, such as exhibits, fairs, performances, ice skating, hockey, and lectures. Fitchburg offers many opportunities for study and practical experience in the areas of sociology, psychology, health, computer technology, business, industry, political organization, and community service. Outdoor activities, including skiing, camping, hiking, canoeing, and fishing, are just minutes from the campus.

The historic and literary centers of Lexington and Concord and the widely varied cultural advantages of Boston are approximately an hour's travel from the College. Worcester is a half hour to the south. Both commuter rail and bus service are available.

Majors and Degrees

Fitchburg State College confers the Bachelor of Arts, Bachelor of Science, and Bachelor of Science in Education degrees and offers the following undergraduate programs: accounting, architectural technology, biology, biotechnology, clinical exercise physiology, communication studies, computer information systems, computer science, construction technology, criminal justice, developmental psychology, earth science, economics, education (teacher education programs are available in early childhood education; elementary education; middle school education; secondary education, with emphases in biology, earth science, English, history, and mathematics; special education, with emphases in intensive severe disabilities (all levels), moderate disabilities (pre-K–8), and moderate disabilities (5–12); and technology education), electronics engineering technology, English, environmental biology, exercise and sport science, facilities management, film/video production, fitness management, geo/physical sciences, graphic design, history, human services, industrial and organizational psychology, interactive media, interdisciplinary studies–humanities, international business and economics, literature, management, manufacturing engineering technology, marketing, mathematics, nursing, photography, political science, professional communication, professional writing, psychology, sociology, technical theater arts, theater, and the following preprofessional programs: dentistry, law, medicine, and veterinary medicine.

Academic Programs

The College's undergraduate programs operate on a two-semester calendar. The first semester begins in early September and ends in mid-December, and the second semester begins in mid-January and ends in mid-May.

The curriculum has a strong liberal arts and sciences requirement, providing a solid foundation for either further academic study or a career. Students may obtain practical experience through numerous internships in social agencies, government offices, and businesses related to their interests. Some major programs require an extensive supervised practicum to complete degree requirements. For education and nursing majors, a broad spectrum of student-teaching and clinical experience is incorporated into their respective programs of study. The Leadership Academy (the College's four-year honors program) culminates in a senior thesis or project.

Off-Campus Programs

Fitchburg State is one of nine state colleges under the jurisdiction of the Massachusetts Department of Higher Education. Through this affiliation, students may participate in the College Academic Program Sharing program, which allows study for a semester or a year at another college. The Office of International Education at Fitchburg State provides undergraduate students with the opportunity to study abroad at a variety of colleges and universities overseas. Programs may vary in length from as short as a few weeks to as long as a semester or a year. Program locations include Australia, Canada, England, Finland, France, Ireland, Italy, New Zealand, Scotland, Spain, and Sweden.

Academic Facilities

The College has a number of special facilities. An unusually well-equipped Academic Success Center includes offices for academic advising, career services, disability services, math and writing centers, and peer tutoring. The McKay Campus School Teacher Education Center is specifically designed for observing pupil development and instructional techniques. An Instructional Media Center is located in the Conlon Building. Modern, well-equipped shops support the industrial education and industrial technology programs. The nursing program utilizes an on-campus clinical lab that simulates a hospital setting with computerized training models. The communication media program owns a full range of late-model equipment, such as a full-color dye-sublimation printer and CD recording and slide-scanning equipment, and supports multiple editing rooms, a production studio, darkrooms, and graphic design computer labs. Communication students at Fitchburg State have access to appropriate equipment and facilities as early as their freshman year.

Costs

Tuition for residents of Massachusetts was $970 per year in 2009–10; out-of-state students paid $7050. Required fees include the student activity fee, Campus Center fee, and athletic fee. Fees are subject to change.

Financial Aid

Many sources of financial aid are available to Fitchburg State students. The College participates in federal and state programs. Packages consisting of grants, loans, work-study awards, and scholarships are given to students demonstrating financial need and academic merit. Financial aid applications for the fall semester must be completed by the preceding March 1 to be given priority consideration.

Faculty

More than 90 percent of Fitchburg State's 184 full-time faculty members hold earned doctoral or other terminal degrees. Full professors teach freshman sections as well as advanced courses and serve as academic advisers to students majoring in their respective programs.

Student Government

All full-time undergraduate students are members of the Student Government Association (SGA). The purposes of the SGA are to encourage responsibility and cooperation in democratic self-government; to form an official body for expressing the judgments of students and fostering activities and matters of general student interest; and to promote full understanding and cooperation among the students, the faculty members, and the administration in order to further the welfare of the College.

The governing body of the SGA consists of 6 SGA officers and a General Council, which includes these officers and 55 elected representatives of classes and residence halls, as well as the commuter student body. The SGA operates through a number of standing and ad hoc committees, membership on which is open to all students.

A 14-member All-College Committee, representing students, the faculty, and the administration, makes recommendations to the president of the College concerning matters of campuswide policy.

Admission Requirements

The College seeks to admit, without regard to race, religion, or ethnic background, students who are capable of success. To this end, significant attention is given to the student's high school record and SAT or ACT scores. The record of achievement in high school is the single most important item in the applicant's academic credentials. Freshman applicants should have completed a college-preparatory program that includes 16 college-preparatory units, with 4 units in English, 2 units in the same foreign language, 2 units in social studies, 3 units in mathematics (algebra I and II and geometry), 3 units in the natural sciences (2 of which must be laboratory courses), and two college-preparatory electives.

An essay is required; however, interviews are not required. Applicants who have questions about the programs and admission procedures at the College are encouraged to request an interview through the Admissions Office.

Transfer students are welcome to apply to Fitchburg State. An official transcript from each college previously attended must be submitted.

International students are encouraged to apply. Scores on the Test of English as a Foreign Language (TOEFL), evaluations of all international transcripts, and translations of international transcripts must also be submitted. Additional information for international students is available on the College's Web site.

Application and Information

Fitchburg State College reviews applications on a rolling basis, sending its first set of admission decisions for the fall semester by mid-December. The priority deadline for applications is March 1. Applicants to the communications media and nursing programs are strongly encouraged to submit their applications by January 1. In addition, applicants who wish to be considered for merit scholarships and the Leadership Academy must complete their admission and financial aid application process (i.e., submit all required materials) by February 1.

Transfer applicants are encouraged to apply by April 15 for the fall and by December 1 for the spring semester. International applicants must complete the application process by June 1 for the fall semester and by October 1 for the spring.

For further information, students should contact:

Office of Admissions
Fitchburg State College
160 Pearl Street
Fitchburg, Massachusetts 01420
Phone: 800-705-9692 (toll-free)
Fax: 978-665-4540
E-mail: admissions@fsc.edu
Web site: http://www.fsc.edu

A student works on a laptop in Edgerly Hall at Fitchburg State College. The College began its laptop initiative, which requires all incoming freshmen to purchase laptops, in fall 2006.

FIVE TOWNS COLLEGE

DIX HILLS, NEW YORK

The College

Located on Long Island's North Shore, Five Towns College offers students the opportunity to study in a suburban environment that is close to New York City. Founded in 1972, Five Towns College is an independent, nonsectarian, coeducational institution that places its emphasis on the student as an individual. Many students are drawn to the College because of its strong reputation in music, media, education, and the performing arts. The College offers associate, bachelor's, master's, and doctoral degrees. The College also offers programs leading to the Master of Music (M.M.) degree in jazz/commercial music and in music education as well as a Master of Science in Education (M.S.Ed.) and a Doctor of Musical Arts (D.M.A.).

From as far away as England and South Korea and from as close as Long Island and New York City, the 1,100 undergraduate and graduate students reflect a rich cultural diversity. The College's enrollment is 55 percent men and 45 percent women, with a minority population of approximately 30 percent. The College's music programs are contemporary jazz in nature, although classical musicians are also part of this creative community. The most popular programs are audio recording technology, broadcasting, journalism, music performance, music business, music and elementary teacher education, theater, and film/video production.

Coeducational living accommodations are available on campus. The Five Towns College Living/Learning Center is a brand-new complex containing four modern life residence halls. Each residence hall contains single- and double-occupancy rooms equipped with private bathrooms, broadband Internet access, cable television, and other amenities.

Location

The College's beautiful 35-acre campus, located in the wooded countryside of Dix Hills, New York, provides students with a quiet college setting to pursue their studies. Just off campus is Long Island's bustling Route 110 corridor, home to numerous national and multinational corporations. New York City, with everything from Lincoln Center to Broadway, is just a train ride away and provides students with some of the best cultural advantages in the world.

Closer to the campus, the many communities of Long Island abound with cultural and recreational opportunities. The College is located within the historic town of Huntington, which is home to the Cinema Arts Center, Hecksher Museum, Vanderbilt Museum, and numerous restaurants, coffeehouses, and quaint shops. The nearby shores of Jones Beach State Park and the Fire Island National Seashore are world renowned for their white, sandy beaches.

Majors and Degrees

Five Towns College offers the Associate in Arts (A.A.) degree in liberal arts, with concentrations in teaching assistant studies and theater arts; the Associate in Science (A.S.) degree in business administration; and the Associate in Applied Science (A.A.S.) degree in business management and in jazz commercial music, with concentrations in accounting, audio recording technology, computer business applications, and music business.

The College offers the Bachelor of Music (Mus.B.) degree in music education and in jazz/commercial music, with concentrations in audio recording technology, composition/songwriting, music business, musical theater, and performance; the Bachelor of Fine Arts (B.F.A.) degree in theater or film/video arts; the Bachelor of Professional Studies (B.P.S.) degree in business management, with concentrations in audio recording technology and music business; the Bachelor of Science (B.S.) degree in childhood education; and the B.S. in mass communication, which features broadcasting and journalism concentrations.

Academic Programs

The following describes some of the more popular programs at Five Towns College. For a complete description of the College's academic program, students should visit the Five Towns College Web site at http://www.ftc.edu.

The music education program is designed for students interested in a career as a teacher of music in a public or private school. The undergraduate program leads to New York State provisional certification. The course work provides professional training and includes a student-teaching experience. The audio recording technology concentration is designed to provide students with the tools needed to succeed as professional studio engineers and producers in the music industry. The music business concentration is designed for students interested in a career in entertainment-related business fields. The course work includes the technical, legal, production, management, and merchandising aspects of the music business. The composition/songwriting concentration provides intensive instruction in a core of technical studies in harmony, orchestration, counterpoint, MIDI, songwriting, form and analysis, arranging, and composition for those who intend to pursue careers as composers, arrangers, and songwriters. The performance concentration includes a common core of technical studies and a foundation of specialized courses, such as music history, harmony, counterpoint, improvisation, ensemble performance, and private instruction. The theater arts program is designed for students interested in careers as actors, entertainers, scenic designers, directors, stage managers, and lighting or sound directors. The film/video program includes extensive technical preparation in videography, filmmaking, linear and nonlinear editing, storyboarding, scriptwriting, producing, and directing for filmmakers and videographers. Elementary education students are prepared as teachers for grades 1–6, while those interested in journalism and broadcasting are prepared for careers in radio, television, newspaper, or editorial writing.

To earn a bachelor's degree, students must accumulate between 122 and 130 credits, depending on the program of study, with a proper distribution of courses and a GPA of a minimum of 2.0. To earn an associate degree, students must accumulate between 62 and 66 credits.

Off-Campus Programs

Off-campus internship opportunities are available to Five Towns College students who have fulfilled the necessary prerequisites, including a cumulative grade point average of at least 2.5, with a 3.0 in their major. In recent semesters, students have interned for major corporations such as MTV, Atlantic Records, Polygram Records, CBS, ABC, EMI Records, MCA Records, Sony Records, The Power Station, Universal Mastering Studios, Channel 12 News, and many others.

Academic Facilities

Five Towns College occupies a multiwinged facility that comprises approximately 120,000 square feet and includes a 500-seat auditorium, production studios, athletic and dining facilities, classrooms, PC and Mac computer labs, and a student center. T-3 lines connect the College's completely fiber-optic computer network to the Internet. All students have access to this network and are provided with an e-mail account.

The Five Towns College Library has more than 35,000 print and nonprint materials. These include nearly 31,500 books and print items, 500 periodical subscriptions, and approximately 5,000 records, 2,500 videos and DVDs, and more than 2,000 CDs. Through its membership in the Long Island Library Resource Council (LILRC), students have access to other libraries around the country.

The Technical Wing at Five Towns College consists of many studio/control rooms. These facilities house the College's state-of-the-art 72-channel SSL9000J audio board, 24-track digital recording studios, Pro Tools HD 3, and the Electronic Music-MIDI Studio equipped with G5 iMacs and Korg M3 keyboards. The Film/Video Division utilizes high definition Sony SxS Pro memory cards and standard definition DVCAM/DVCPRO video as well as the Super 16mm film format. Nonlinear editing suites utilize Final Cut 7 and Adobe CS4 Production Suite on iMac and Mac Pro computers. Students utilize these facilities to develop their skills while creating professional-quality productions, both in the studio and on location under the supervision of industry professionals. Student productions include short films, music videos, documentaries, public service announcements, commercials, and live events, among many others.

The Dix Hills Center for Performing Arts at Five Towns College is an acoustically "perfect" venue, with digital lighting systems, digital sound reinforcement for concert production, and a Barco 6300 digital projection system for multimedia productions. The professional stage is 60 feet wide, with a proscenium opening of 16 feet and 32 feet of fly space. Students utilize this facility to produce live concerts, plays, musicals, and other performances and special presentations.

Costs

The tuition for 2010–11 is $19,400 per year. Miscellaneous fees total approximately $400, and books cost about $700. Private instruction fees for performing music students are $775 per semester.

Financial Aid

The annual tuition at Five Towns College is among the lowest of all the private colleges in the region. Nevertheless, approximately 78 percent of all students receive some form of financial assistance. Need-based and/or merit-based grants, scholarships, loans, and work-study programs are available to qualified recipients, including transfer students. Prospective students are urged to contact the Financial Aid Office as early as possible.

Faculty

The College's growing faculty consists of 120 full- and part-time members. The student-faculty ratio is 14:1. While the faculty is more strongly committed to teaching than to research, many members continue to be active in their respective areas of expertise.

Student Government

Student Government Association (SGA) serves as a voice of the students to the faculty and administration. Students can get involved through organizations and committees. All recognized organizations and committees fall under the jurisdiction of the SGA. The SGA is the elected representative student body of the campus and is responsible for creating many of the policy-making decisions that affect organizations and student life.

There are several media clubs and organizations for students. They include *Keynotes*, the College yearbook, *The Record*, the student newspaper, and WFTU, the College radio station.

Admission Requirements

The College encourages applications from students who will engage themselves in its creative community. Students applying to the College should have attained a minimum high school average grade of 78 percent. The SAT or ACT exam is required for all freshmen. Transfer students must also submit official transcripts of all college-level work as well as their high school transcripts. International students from non-English-speaking countries must submit a TOEFL paper score of at least 550 or its equivalent. The College does not accept students on an early admissions basis, although early decision is available. Candidates for admission must submit a completed Application for Undergraduate Admission, official high school transcripts, at least two letters of recommendation, and a personal statement. International students must submit their TOEFL scores, financial documentation and sponsor information.

Application and Information

Admission into any music program is contingent upon passing an audition demonstrating skill in performance on a major instrument or vocally. Admission into any theater program is also contingent upon passing an audition. In some cases, the Admissions Committee may request an on-campus interview with an applicant. Music, theater, and film/video students are encouraged to submit an electronic portfolio or DVD, if available.

Except for applicants applying on an early decision basis, new students are accepted on a rolling basis, with decisions for the fall and spring semesters mailed starting February 15 and December 1, respectively. There is an application fee of $35.

For further information, students should contact the Admissions Office at 631-656-2110 or admissions@ftc.edu.

Director of Admissions
Five Towns College
305 North Service Road
Dix Hills, New York 11746-5871

Phone: 631-656-2110
Fax: 631-656-3199
E-mail: admissions@ftc.edu
Web site: http://www.ftc.edu

COLLEGE CLOSE-UPS

FLORIDA ATLANTIC UNIVERSITY

BOCA RATON, FLORIDA

The University

Florida Atlantic University (FAU) is a midsize comprehensive university that serves more than 27,000 students on seven campuses throughout South Florida. FAU was established in 1961, making it the fifth-oldest university in the state system. As an upper-division and graduate state university, FAU admitted its first students in September 1964. In 1984, FAU admitted its first freshman class, instituting a comprehensive four-year undergraduate program. Enrollment has increased from 867 in the first year to more than 27,000 in the 2009–10 academic year.

FAU is located in a rapidly expanding metropolitan area encompassing cities and towns from Fort Lauderdale to Port St. Lucie. Since the original Boca Raton campus was founded in 1964, the University has expanded to six other campuses in South Florida: Dania Beach, Davie, Fort Lauderdale, Jupiter, and Port St. Lucie.

The Boca Raton campus provides an exciting and supportive learning environment for students. The University Center hosts student activities and meetings. In addition, its 2,400-seat auditorium enables students to enjoy performances ranging from rock groups to the Florida Philharmonic Orchestra. The Boca Raton campus is also the home of FAU's Division 1 intercollegiate athletics program and facilities. Its new recreation and fitness center includes an aquatic center, gymnasium, treadmill and elliptical area, and personal trainers. The recreation and wellness complex includes tennis courts, track, and a variety of fields for club and intramural sports competition. The five-story S. E. Wimberly Library houses a large collection of monographs, serials, and other academic resources. Computer labs, study lounges, a media center, and tutoring services also provide valuable academic support for students.

One of FAU's newest campuses is Dania Beach, also known as SeaTech. This is FAU's Institute for Ocean and Systems Engineering, located on eight acres between the Atlantic Ocean and the Intracoastal Waterway, with valuable access to the ocean and sea water. Established in 1997 as a state-funded Type II research center, the institute is part of FAU's Department of Ocean Engineering.

FAU's Davie campus is located on 38 acres in western Broward County and is FAU's second-largest campus after the Boca Raton campus. The Davie campus has served FAU students since 1990 with 2+2 programs in partnership with Broward Community College.

The Fort Lauderdale campus in downtown Fort Lauderdale takes advantage of its unique urban setting to serve as a center for FAU programs in creative industries and urban affairs. The campus is part of Fort Lauderdale's evolving, dynamic urban community and provides a laboratory for students in business, computer arts, graphic arts, multimedia communication, architecture, urban and regional planning, and public administration.

The John D. MacArthur Campus is conveniently located off I-95 and Donald Ross Road within Jupiter's Abacoa community. The campus offers a wide range of upper division and graduate programs from six of FAU's colleges, including seventeen bachelor's degrees and seven master's degrees. The MacArthur Campus is also home to FAU's Harriet L. Wilkes Honors College and the Scripps Research Institute.

In 2006, FAU opened the FAU/Harbor Branch Marine Sciences Building—a 40,000-square-foot, joint-use facility housing specially equipped marine science labs, classrooms and video-conferencing equipped meeting rooms—at the Harbor Branch Oceanographic Institution's 600-acre site in Fort Pierce.

The Treasure Coast campus is conveniently situated in St. Lucie West, part of the rapidly developing city of Port St. Lucie. The first-rate facilities are shared with Indian River State College in a unique 2+2 partnership. Located off I-95 and St. Lucie West Boulevard, the Treasure Coast campus is an easy commute for area students.

The FAU/Harbor Branch Oceanographic Institution Marine Science Partnership Building in Fort Pierce is a new FAU location on the Treasure Coast. This state-of-the-art facility provides an ideal setting for marine science research and teaching.

Through its partnerships with other educational institutions, local businesses, industries, and civic and cultural organizations, FAU enhances the economic, human, and cultural development of the surrounding communities and beyond. Students at Florida Atlantic University may participate in a work-study program that combines their classroom learning with hands-on experience. Many local businesses and government laboratories participate in the program each year.

FAU has developed a new program in medical sciences offered in cooperation with the University of Miami Miller School of Medicine. Students in this program complete all four years of their clinical studies at the FAU Boca Raton Campus.

Florida Atlantic University is accredited by the Commission on Colleges of the Southern Association of Colleges and Schools to award associate, bachelor's, master's, and doctoral degrees. In addition, it is accredited by fourteen professional agencies. FAU is also a member of the National Association of State Universities and Land-Grant Colleges and the Council of Graduate Schools in the United States.

Location

FAU campuses can be found throughout the southeast-Florida region. FAU's main campus in Boca Raton is on an 850-acre site located only 3 miles from the Atlantic Ocean. The campus is conveniently located halfway between Palm Beach and Fort Lauderdale and offers a broad range of academic programs, activities, and services.

Students attending FAU–Boca Raton have some honored guests: burrowing owls. In fact, the Audubon Society has named the site a burrowing owl sanctuary, and FAU varsity athletic teams are known as the Owls in their honor.

South Florida's climate is subtropical, with an average year-round temperature of 75 degrees. FAU's campuses are within easy driving distance of some of the most beautiful beaches and recreational facilities to be found anywhere.

Majors and Degrees

FAU offers programs leading to the Bachelor of Arts, Bachelor of Science, Associate of Arts, and specialized bachelor's degrees. A minimum of 120 credit hours is required for a bachelor's degree.

The College of Architecture, Urban and Public Affairs offers majors in architecture, criminal justice, public management, social work, and urban and regional planning. The Dorothy F. Schmidt College of Arts and Letters offers a general college major and majors in anthropology, art, Caribbean and Latin American studies, English, history, Jewish studies, languages and linguistics (French, German, Italian, Japanese, and Spanish), music, philosophy, political science, social science, sociology, and theater. The College of Business offers majors in accounting, economics, finance, hospitality and tourism management, industry studies, insurance, international business and trade, management, management information systems, and marketing. The Harriet L. Wilkes Honors College in Jupiter offers a liberal arts and sciences education in a highly selective environment. Majors include American studies, anthropology, biological sciences/pre-med, chemistry, economics, English literature, environmental studies, history, international studies, Latin American studies, law and society, marine biology, math and science, mathematics, philosophy, physics, political science, psychology, Spanish, and women's studies. The College of Education offers majors in elementary education, exceptional student education, and exercise science and wellness education. Secondary certification is also available. The College of Engineering and Computer Science offers majors in computer science as well as civil, computer, electrical, mechanical, and ocean engineering. The Christine E. Lynn College of Nursing offers the Bachelor of Science in Nursing degree. The Charles E. Schmidt College of Science has majors in biological science (biotechnology, ecology and organismic biology, marine biology, microbiology, and molecular biology), chemistry, geography, geology, mathematical sciences, physics, psychology, and social psychology.

Academic Programs

Florida Atlantic University prepares its undergraduate students to be productive and thoughtful citizens by offering a broad liberal education coupled with the development of competency in fields of special interest. FAU encourages students to think creatively and critically and provides the intellectual tools needed for lifelong learning.

Off-Campus Programs

FAU has established a work-study program between its colleges and cooperating businesses, industries, and government laboratories. FAU has exchange agreements with international schools in locations ranging from China to Germany. Arrangements must be made through the Office of International Programs (http://www.fau.edu/goabroad).

Academic Facilities

The Boca Raton campus resources feature the S. E. Wimberly Library, with more than 1 million holdings. The Dorothy F. Schmidt College of Arts and Letters features a 75,000-square-foot, three-building complex encompassing a performance arts center, an art gallery, an experimental theater, a visual arts center, lecture halls, classrooms, and offices. The College of Business occupies a four-story building including wireless classrooms with a simulated trading room floor. The College of Education's four-story, 90,000-square-foot facility houses its five academic departments and offers a teaching gymnasium, an early childhood center, and the A. D. Henderson University School, a public elementary, middle, and high school operated by the College of Education. The Science and Engineering and Social Science Buildings were joined by the Physical Science Building and the Charles E. Schmidt Biomedical Center. There is also a marine sciences center, Gumbo Limbo, located between the Intracoastal Waterway and the Atlantic Ocean; it provides teaching and research facilities. The Christine E. Lynn College of Nursing is housed in a state-of-the-art building which has received the Gold Medal for Leadership in Energy and Environmental Design (LEED).

FAU continues to enhance the campus environment with many new facilities in the planning and construction stages. Some recently completed projects on the Boca Raton campus include a gymnasium and arena renovation; a 600-bed residence hall; the College of Business Office Depot Center for Executive Development; a 45,000 square foot Student Recreation Center, and the Marleen and Harold Forkas Alumni Center. The new College of Engineering and Computer Science facility, which is designed to achieve LEED platinum certification, is under construction. The new classroom building and a Living Room Theater are scheduled to open in fall 2010. Plans for future development include an on-campus stadium, a new arena, and additional apartment-style resident halls.

Expansions are underway across all of FAU's seven campuses. On the Davie campus, a new student activity center was recently completed. The Treasure Coast campus has added additional classroom facilities to accommodate its growing student body.

Costs

For the 2009–10 academic year, in-state tuition was $139.55 per credit hour and out-of-state tuition was $584.41 per credit hour. A full-time course load is 24 to 50 credit hours per academic year. Average room and board costs are $9582. Additional expenses are $900 for books, $1608 for personal items, and $2744 for transportation for off-campus students. Fees are subject to change at any time by action of the Florida legislature.

Financial Aid

Approximately $60 million in financial aid is awarded each year. A comprehensive program of student financial aid includes scholarships, grants, loans, and employment that may provide assistance from initial enrollment through graduate study. Assistance is tailored to fit each student's requirements and may vary during his or her enrollment. As a member of the College Scholarship Service of the College Board, the University is guided by the principles and policies of that organization. Students who are interested in applying for need-based aid must complete the Free Application for Federal Student Aid (FAFSA), which is available online at http://www.fau.edu/finaid and at all U.S. high schools, colleges, and universities. Students are strongly encouraged to complete the FAFSA in January for fall admission. The process of applying for aid normally takes six to eight weeks. The priority deadline is March 1. Students must be notified of their acceptance to the University before award allocations can be made.

There is a variety of scholarships available for academic, athletic, or artistic talent. Students should visit the Admissions Web site at http://www.fau.edu/admissions and click on "Scholarships" for more information.

Faculty

Recognizing that the excellence of its faculty is the true measure of the worth of a university, FAU has brought together a distinguished group of scholars who hold a balanced dedication to both teaching and research. Faculty members come from more than thirty states and several countries. The majority hold a doctorate or professional degree. They all represent a high level of professional experience and academic attainment and are committed to the development of a vigorous educational program of high caliber. The University community has benefited from the presence of 12 Eminent Scholars, distributed over seven colleges. In addition, two Endowed Chairs have been fully funded and five others partially funded. The presence of these distinguished scholars and researchers has greatly enhanced the academic climate of the University and has provided focal points for the development of new programs, particularly at the graduate level.

Student Government

FAU gives students an active role on virtually all University and faculty committees, including the Curriculum Committee. They serve on the Board of Trustees and college advisory councils and operate the Student Government Association and Residence Hall Councils as well as the interclub, interfraternity, and Panhellenic groups. Students also serve on the University Senate along with faculty and staff members.

Admission Requirements

Admission to the University is limited to applicants who have graduated from regionally accredited high schools or who hold a GED certificate. Evaluation is based on the academic course grade point average combined with acceptable results on the SAT or ACT. Beginning in summer 2011, candidates for admission should have 18 academic high school units, including 4 units of English, 4 units of mathematics (algebra I and above), 3 units of natural science (2 with labs), 3 units of social science, 2 units of foreign language in sequence, and 2 academic electives. Score reports are accepted directly from the testing. Applicants who have completed the GED test should request official high school transcripts (if applicable) and an official GED score report from the Department of Education.

Admission for freshman students requires an application for admission, a nonrefundable $30 application fee, official transcripts from an accredited high school, and the official results of the SAT or ACT. Admitted freshmen must confirm their intention to enroll and secure their place with the freshman class by submitting a nonrefundable $200 admissions tuition deposit. The deposit will be applied to the student's tuition and other expenses for the term in which they have been admitted to FAU.

Admission into FAU as an undergraduate transfer requires students to be in good academic standing at their previous college or university and to have a minimum 2.5 GPA. Students with fewer than 60 transferable credits should submit an application for admission, a nonrefundable $30 application fee, official transcripts from high school and previously attended colleges or universities, and acceptable results of the SAT or ACT. Students with 60 or more transferable credits must submit an application for admission, a nonrefundable $30 application fee, and official transcripts from each previously attended college or university.

All freshmen, undergraduate transfer, and second-baccalaureate students who have completed all or part of their education abroad are required to have their foreign credentials evaluated by an independent evaluation service. International students must also furnish evidence of proficiency in English by submitting TOEFL scores. For additional international student requirements, students should visit http://www.fau.edu/admissions and click on "International Freshmen" or "International Transfer".

Application and Information

Office of Undergraduate Admissions
Florida Atlantic University
777 Glades Road
Boca Raton, Florida 33431
Phone: 561-297-3040
800-920-8705 (Honors College, toll-free)
E-mail: admissions@fau.edu
hcadmissions@fau.edu (Honors College)
Web site: http://www.fau.edu

COLLEGE CLOSE-UPS

FLORIDA INSTITUTE OF TECHNOLOGY

MELBOURNE, FLORIDA

The Institute

Founded in 1958 by visionary physicist Jerome P. Keuper to educate area professionals working on the U.S. space program, Florida Institute of Technology got its start with an initial donation of 37 cents. Today, Florida Tech is a fully accredited, coeducational, independent, privately supported university that offers more than 130 bachelor's, master's, and doctoral degree programs in science and engineering, aviation, business, humanities, psychology, education, and communication. The only independent technological university in the southeastern U.S., Florida Tech offers an excellent faculty, hands-on and technology-focused majors, a culturally diverse student body, and dynamic personal and professional growth opportunities.

Florida Tech has more than 2,600 undergraduate and 1,100 graduate students from all fifty states and more than 100 countries enrolled at its main campus in Melbourne, Florida. Additionally, over 4,500 students are enrolled in Florida Tech's extended campus and online programs. Over 100 student organizations represent the varied interests of Florida Tech's students and include student government; fraternities and sororities; political and religious groups; college-run radio and television; dance, music, science fiction, choral, and theater performance; and academic and honor organizations.

Florida Tech competes in fifteen NCAA Division II intercollegiate sports. Women's sports include basketball, cross-country, golf, rowing, soccer, softball, tennis, and volleyball. Men's sports include baseball, basketball, cross-country, golf, rowing, soccer, and tennis. Panther teams have earned regional titles in baseball, men's soccer, and women's basketball; and Sunshine State Conference championships in men's soccer, men's and women's cross-country, men's and women's basketball, and women's rowing.

Florida Tech is listed as a *Barron's Guide* "Best Buy" in college education. In addition, the University is ranked as a "Best Southeastern College" by the Princeton Review in 2009–10.

Responses to the last three alumni surveys of recent Florida Tech graduates report a 97 percent placement rate in jobs, graduate schools, or military service within six months of commencement. Of those employed, 99 percent are working in a field related to their major and 68 percent are earning starting salaries of over $50,000.

Location

Florida Tech is located along the Atlantic coastline of central Florida in Brevard County, better known as the Space Coast. Situated within Florida's High Tech Corridor, it is home to Kennedy Space Center, United Space Alliance, and many other government agencies and technology companies. The area has the nation's fourth-largest high-tech workforce and supports hundreds of high-tech companies.

The area's attractive business climate is matched only by its natural resources, many of them ideal for scientific study and research, including the estuarine habitats of the Indian River Lagoon, the Atlantic Ocean marine ecosystem, area beaches and wetlands, thousands of acres of protected wildlife habitats, and a variety of tropical/subtropical Gulf Stream weather phenomena.

With the Indian River Lagoon and the Atlantic Ocean less than 5 miles from the campus, water sports such as swimming, sailing, surfing, diving, fishing and boating are popular year-round activities. Central Florida attractions such as Walt Disney World, Sea World, and Universal Orlando are within a 1-hour drive, and Miami is only 3 hours south of the campus.

Majors and Degrees

Florida Tech offers bachelor's degrees in accounting, aeronautical science (flight option), aerospace engineering, applied mathematics, astronomy and astrophysics, aviation computer science, aviation management (flight option), aviation meteorology (flight option), aquaculture, biochemistry, biology, business administration, business and environmental studies, chemical engineering (biochemical engineering, business, petroleum engineering emphases), chemical management, chemistry (chemical management, research chemistry options), chemistry education, civil engineering, communication (business and marketing, scientific and technical emphases), computer engineering, computer science, construction, ecology, e-commerce technology, electrical engineering, environmental science, forensic psychology, humanities, information management, interdisciplinary science (military science option), international business, marine biology, marketing, mathematics education, mathematical sciences, mechanical engineering, meteorology, middle grades math and science education, molecular biology, ocean engineering, oceanography (biological oceanography, chemical oceanography, coastal zone management, marine environmental science, physical oceanography concentrations), physics, premedical studies, prelaw, psychology (animal learning and behavior, clinical/counseling psychology, industrial/organizational psychology, sport psychology concentrations), software engineering, science education (biology, chemistry, earth and space science, general science, physics options) and space sciences (astrobiology; astronomy and astrophysics; and solar, earth, and planetary science options). Engineering majors may select technical electives to build an emphasis in systems engineering, environmental engineering, nuclear technology, energy engineering, and materials science engineering.

The university also offers minors in seventeen areas: accounting, biology, business administration, chemistry, communication, computational mathematics, computer science, environmental science, forensic psychology, history, management, management information systems, meteorology, oceanography, physics, psychology, and science/math education.

Academic Programs

The University operates on a semester-based academic year. All majors incorporate some form of scholarly inquiry, such as research, cooperative education, internships, or interdisciplinary capstone design projects. Programs in the sciences prepare the student for graduate and professional work. Practical aspects of all engineering disciplines and the computer sciences may be combined with management science for the business minded. A wide variety of programs are available for the environmentalist.

College of Engineering students may enroll in the University's new ProTrack cooperative education program, a unique, hybrid on-campus/online/work program that allows students to build a year of relevant, hands-on, professional-level career experience within the four years it takes to complete their academic studies. Participants graduate on time and ready for the workforce.

In the College of Aeronautics, the bachelor's programs provide a strong business or science background in the first two years and concentrate on specialized knowledge in the aviation industry during the junior and senior years. For students interested in flight options, training begins immediately within the first week of classes. Flight students earn their FAA commercial, instrument, and multiengine flight certificates; and can earn their instructor, air taxi, and airline transport pilot ratings; and flight dispatcher certificate.

Students at Florida Tech may qualify for advanced placement through English and mathematics examinations administered by the University. Advanced credit is awarded for Advanced Placement (AP) exams and higher-level International Baccalaureate subjects.

The University offers a four-year Army ROTC program, and it rewards ROTC scholarship winners with a generous supplemental grant package. Prospective cadets should contact an ROTC representative at the University.

Academic Facilities

Florida Tech has more than 125 laboratories and state-of-the-art research facilities. Built into the University's largest academic buildings, the F. W. Olin Engineering Complex, F. W. Olin Physical Sciences Center, and F. W. Olin Life Sciences Building are some of the latest electronic and communications technology. Connected to a global network of space science facilities, the largest research-grade telescope in Florida operates in the dome of the F.W. Olin Physical Sciences Center.

The Harris Center for Science Engineering, home to the newly established Harris Institute for Assured Information, provides cutting-edge resources for cyber research aimed at designing innovative solutions to global information security problems. It also includes space for biological sciences and computer sciences.

Flight training is conducted at the brand new Emil Buehler Center for Aviation Education and Research at the Melbourne International Airport, a short drive from campus. The Florida Tech fleet consists of over forty aircraft, the majority of which are Piper aircraft; the Warrior for initial private pilot and instrument flight training; the Arrow for complex aircraft and commercial pilot training; and the Seminole for multi-engine and commercial pilot training. To accompany the FIT Aviation fleet, the Warriors and Seminoles are equipped with the Avidyne Integrated Flight Deck System. The Avidyne system features large format, flat panel, liquid crystal displays that integrate all flight instruments and engine gauges. Additionally, FIT Aviation recently received certification as a Cirrus Certified Training Center and can offer initial and recurrent training to owners and users of Cirrus aircraft and to university students. Cirrus aircraft are a new breed of technologically advanced planes with composite construction and fully electronic flight instrumentation.

Campuswide computer facilities include three technology-teaching laboratories, a network of Linux workstations, a National Science Foundation–funded computational physics laboratory, a variety of microcomputers and other types of hardware, and a large number of microcomputer periodicals and current software catalogs.

Evans Library houses an additional seventy-microcomputer laboratory with an extensive software library. Additional teaching labs, virtual-reality labs, and online interactive classes with the latest multimedia and information technology are available in the F. W. Olin Engineering Complex.

Costs

Tuition for the 2010–11 academic year is $32,294 for science and engineering majors and $29,470 for aeronautics, business, psychology, and liberal arts majors. Students pursuing aviation majors with flight training could expect an additional cost of $15,000 per year in flight fees. New student room and board costs for the year are $11,210.

Financial Aid

Florida Tech is committed to making a priceless education affordable for students and their families. Generous institutional grants, merit-based scholarships, school-year employment, and incentive opportunities as well as low-interest federal loan programs are available to all qualified applicants. Approximately 80 percent of Florida Tech students qualify for a combination. Financial aid packages are based on a combination of merit and financial need. Monthly payment plans are available for tuition and other expenses. Prospective students are encouraged to apply for admission by January 15 for priority scholarship consideration. Admitted students are encouraged to file the Free Application for Federal Student Aid by March 1. Students eligible for Veterans Administration benefits may contact the VA representative on the Melbourne campus.

Faculty

The student-faculty ratio is 9:1, and 88 percent of full-time faculty members have a Ph.D. or other terminal degree. The small average class size of 25 provides the opportunity to work one-on-one with some of the finest minds in education. In general, freshman- and sophomore-level instructors carry full-time teaching loads. They are closely involved with student life and serve as advisers and counselors. Upper-level and graduate instructors participate in teaching and research activities.

Student Government

Student government at Florida Tech is the vital link between the administration and the student body and functions as the liaison between the University and the community as well as a catalyst for social change. The organization promotes new ideas and encourages students to participate at all levels of university involvement.

Admission Requirements

Applicants to Florida Tech must demonstrate the readiness to succeed in a challenging academic curriculum. Admission decisions are based on: (1) the student's academic record (with an emphasis on strength of the curriculum); (2) performance on standardized tests (SAT or ACT); (3) teacher recommendations; and (4) participation in special classes, clubs, or teams that involve research and advanced problem-solving activities. The high school transcript is the most important element of the application. While no minimum grade point average, class rank, or standardized test score is specified, these measures must indicate a readiness for rigorous university study in the field of interest.

An applicant who is a U.S. citizen must have earned a high school diploma or high school equivalency credential by the date of first enrollment. Personal recommendations by counselors or faculty members are not required but are taken into consideration in certain circumstances. Transfer students are considered individually on the basis of transcripts and overall performance. Prospective applicants who do not meet the standardized admission requirements but are interested in attending Florida Tech are urged to arrange a personal interview with the admission counselor to receive individual attention.

Application and Information

Florida Tech encourages applicants from every social, ethnic, racial, and religious background. The University practices a rolling admission policy. Fees for applications are $50 when mailed or $40 when submitted online. Completed applications, high school and college transcripts, and standardized test results should be sent to the Office of Undergraduate Admission.

For further information, students may contact:

Office of Undergraduate Admission
Florida Institute of Technology
150 West University Boulevard
Melbourne, Florida 32901-6975
Phone: 321-674-8030
800-888-4348 (toll-free)
E-mail: admission@fit.edu
Web site: http://www.fit.edu/ugrad

Immersed in a thriving atmosphere of dedicated scientists, high-technology corporations, and natural habitats, Florida Tech responds to the educational and research challenges of the twenty-first century.

COLLEGE CLOSE-UPS

FLORIDA SOUTHERN COLLEGE

LAKELAND, FLORIDA

The College

The oldest private college in the state, Florida Southern College was chartered in 1885 and settled on the shores of spectacular Lake Hollingsworth in Lakeland in 1922.

Florida Southern today is a nationally ranked, residential, coeducational, and comprehensive college. Its 2,200 students represent forty-four states and thirty-one countries. Students choose Florida Southern because of its national reputation for dynamic, hands-on learning that features guaranteed internships and study abroad. The atmosphere is friendly and personal, fostering a close-knit student body and faculty.

All members of the academic community take pride in the beautiful campus, a historic landmark and home to the world's largest single-site collection of buildings designed by renowned architect Frank Lloyd Wright.

Students, whether members of fraternities and sororities or as independents, live in a variety of contemporary on-campus accommodations, including the new state-of-the-art Barnett Residential Life Center, which features stunning views of the lake, contemporary student lounges, modern kitchens and bathrooms, and wireless Internet access.

The George Jenkins Field House, which seats 3,000, includes a three-court gymnasium, a weight room, and an athletic training room. Facilities for tennis, racquetball, dance, swimming, and waterskiing are available at the popular Nina B. Hollis Wellness Center, which offers a fully equipped fitness center, an aerobics/dance studio, an intramural gymnasium, an Olympic swimming pool, and a wide-screen TV/lounge area.

There are branches of seven national Greek fraternities and seven national Greek sororities on campus. Popular student activities include intercollegiate and intramural sports, drama and music groups, publications, and more than seventy clubs and organizations related to academic, political, religious, and social interests. A high percentage of students are involved in volunteer programs and internships in the surrounding community, statewide, and internationally.

Location

Florida Southern's campus consists of approximately 100 acres on the shore of Lake Hollingsworth in Lakeland, Florida, a dynamic suburban community of about 120,000 residents in the heart of Florida's high-tech corridor. The campus is within walking or biking distance of Lakeland's historic downtown, and Lakeland is just 45 minutes from Tampa and an hour from Orlando. Within an hour's drive of the state's major recreational attractions, including Walt Disney World and award-winning beaches, the College is ideally situated for internships and job opportunities with leading corporations that tap into one of the largest markets in the U.S. Students enjoy Festival of Fine Arts series performances in music, dance, and drama; distinguished speakers; and exciting College and business symposiums. The Lakeland Center also offers many cultural and entertainment opportunities.

Majors and Degrees

Florida Southern College offers Bachelor of Arts, Bachelor of Fine Arts, Bachelor of Music, Bachelor of Music Education, Bachelor of Science, and Bachelor of Science in Nursing degrees in more than fifty majors including accounting, art (art education, art history, graphic design, and studio art), athletic training, biochemistry and molecular biology, biology, business administration (concentrations in finance, international business, management, and marketing), chemistry, citrus, communication (advertising, broadcast journalism, print journalism, and public relations), criminology, economics, education (elementary education), English, history, horticultural science, mathematics, mathematics/computer science, music (music composition, music education, and music performance), nursing, philosophy, physical education, political science, psychology, religion, sociology, Spanish, theater arts (performance and technical), and youth ministry. Divisional majors are available in humanities and social science.

Preprofessional programs are offered in dentistry, engineering, law, medicine, pharmacy, physical therapy, theology, and veterinary medicine. Interdisciplinary professional programs include music management and sport management. Programs in environmental horticulture include recreational turfgrass management as well as two tracks in production and landscape design. Students who wish to teach at the secondary level choose a major in a subject area and complete the requirements for secondary education certification by the state of Florida.

An honors program provides special opportunities for a select group of entering freshmen to explore topics of common interest in an integrated and interdisciplinary fashion.

Academic Programs

All degree programs require the satisfactory completion of a minimum of 128 semester hours with a minimum grade point average of 2.0. Students and professors work together in discussion-based classes featuring debate, collaborative projects, and other forms of engaged learning. The College operates on the semester system, with two 15-week semesters, a three-week May term, and three 4-week summer sessions. The average course load is 16 hours per semester. Students are required to complete a general education curriculum designed to help develop knowledge, skills, and attitudes for lifelong success, in addition to their major course work. Credit by examination is awarded on the basis of successful scores on Advanced Placement tests, the International Baccalaureate (I.B.), and College-Level Examination Program (CLEP) tests.

Florida Southern has a Career Center that assists students in clarifying their career and life goals and provides opportunities for them to explore these goals. Approximately 20 percent of Florida Southern graduates go immediately to graduate school, and some FSC signature programs, such as premedicine, have a 100 percent placement rate.

Florida Southern guarantees every student an internship, and those real-world experiences help to place the vast majority of graduates in jobs in their chosen fields. Ninety-four percent of graduates report having a great job or being enrolled in graduate school within three months of graduation.

Off-campus Programs

The College sponsors a number of popular study-abroad opportunities, including May Option experiences in Harlaxton Manor (England), Cuernavaca (Mexico), and Salamanca and Alicante (Spain). Beginning with students entering in fall 2010, all students will be guaranteed a domestic or international travel experience in their junior or senior year at no charge other than the usual course credit fees.

Other study-abroad options include Angers (France) and semester or yearlong programs in England, Northern Ireland, Central and South America, or a vast array of additional options through one of the College's consortium programs.

Florida Southern participates in the Washington Semester of American University in Washington, D.C., through which selected students spend a semester in Washington studying government and international relations. Selected students may also spend one semester at Drew University in Madison, New Jersey, studying various aspects of the United Nations through Drew's United Nations Semester.

Academic Facilities

The College recently opened the new Marshall and Vera Lea Rinker Technology Center, which is staffed 24 hours a day, seven days a week. The Rinker building is equipped with the latest technology and Wi-Fi, as are other computer labs on campus, such as the popular new TûTû's Cyber Café in the library.

There are several new academic buildings on campus, including the state-of-the-art Joe K. and Alberta Blanton Nursing Building, home to the College's growing School of Nursing; and the Dr. Marcene H. and

Robert E. Christoverson Humanities Building, which features contemporary classrooms, a modern language lab, film studies center, and art gallery.

Florida Southern's Roux Library houses a collection of 175,213 volumes; more than 650 periodical subscriptions; access to more than 2,000 full-text electronic periodicals and more than 72,000 electronic books; a 5,700-item media collection that includes videocassettes, CDs, DVDs, and CD-ROMs; a substantial microforms collection; and seating for more than 350 students. The new, adjacent Sarah D. and L. Kirk McKay Jr. Archives Center houses records from the Florida Conference of the United Methodist Church; Frank Lloyd Wright drawings and documents; the Lawton M. Chiles Center for Florida History; and the Florida Citrus Archives.

In addition, the Branscomb Memorial Auditorium seats 1,800 and is nationally known for its perfect acoustics. The Ludd M. Spivey Fine Arts Center comprises the Marjorie M. McKinley Music Building, the Melvin Art Gallery, and the Loca Lee Buckner Theater, which seats 350. The Polk Science Building houses the College's state-of-the-art science laboratories and planetarium. The Preschool and Kindergarten Lab School provides an opportunity for students majoring in elementary education to observe and teach preschoolers.

Costs

The comprehensive cost for 2010–11 is $32,972 ($24,662 for tuition and standard fees and $8310 for room and board). There are additional fees for individual music instruction and the use of practice rooms. FSC estimates that another $1000 is adequate for books and supplies, and $1500 should cover personal expenses, exclusive of travel to and from home.

Financial Aid

The Student Financial Aid Office offers students its counsel and assistance in meeting their educational expenses. Aid is awarded on the basis of an applicant's need, academic performance, and promise. Ninety-six percent of the students at Florida Southern receive financial assistance. To demonstrate need, an applicant is required to file the Free Application for Federal Student Aid (FAFSA). Various forms of aid, such as scholarships, grants, loans, and campus employment, are used to help meet students' needs. Merit scholarships are available, and awards are based on academic promise; performance ability in music, theater, or art; or athletic ability in baseball, basketball, cross-country, golf, soccer, softball, swimming, tennis, or volleyball. Applicants for aid must reapply each year. Florida Southern participates in the Federal Perkins Loan, Federal Supplemental Educational Opportunity Grant, and Federal Work-Study college-based programs. All applicants are expected to apply for any entitlement grant for which they are eligible, such as a Federal Pell Grant and, for Florida residents, the Florida Student Assistance Grant and the Florida Tuition Voucher. The Federal Stafford Student Loan Program is also available. There are extensive on-campus employment opportunities. The completed FAFSA and the College's financial aid application must be filed with the Student Financial Aid Office by April 1. Early application is encouraged for students seeking academic scholarships.

Faculty

Ninety percent of Florida Southern's faculty members have doctoral or other terminal degrees in their fields. The faculty is devoted to teaching and the success of students; all faculty members have posted office hours and are available for consultation and advising. Faculty members are selected not only for their teaching ability but also for their ability to relate to the needs and concerns of college students. The student-faculty ratio is 12:1.

Student Government

The Student Government Association represents the student body in matters involving the College administration, faculty, and student body and is responsible for coordinating student government. Each full-time student is a member of the association and has a vote in its affairs. The subsidiaries of the association are the Association of Campus Entertainment (ACE), the House of Representatives, the Student Senate, and the four classes: freshman, sophomore, junior, and senior.

Admission Requirements

Florida Southern looks for two things in applicants: performance and promise. The majority of applicants who have been admitted as freshmen have had a grade of B or better in college-preparatory courses (including four courses in English, three in mathematics, and the balance divided among science, foreign language, and social science); and have earned minimum scores of 500 on each of the verbal and math portions of the SAT or a composite score of at least 23 on the ACT. The Admissions Office is committed to reviewing individual applicants on their own merits, based on the level of challenge attempted, patterns of grades over time, recommendations from references, and an applicant's own assessment of the learning environment best suited to his or her needs. Evidence of leadership and community service also are typical attributes of a successful applicant.

Applicants must graduate from an accredited high school with a minimum of 19 credits, 16 of which must be academic. Qualified high school juniors may apply for early admission if they have the recommendation of their secondary school and have had a personal interview with the Director of Admissions. Applications from transfers are welcome, as are those from students resuming their education and from older students who have delayed their entrance into college. Transfer applicants should have a minimum 2.5 grade point average and be graduates of or be eligible to return to their former institutions. Transfer students with fewer than 25 semester hours must submit high school transcripts and standardized test scores. Applicants who hold Associate of Arts degrees from regionally accredited two-year institutions are typically granted junior standing. All applicants are encouraged to interview; an interview may be required for some candidates.

Application and Information

An application is considered by the Admissions Committee when it has been received with the $30 application fee, required test scores and references, and transcripts from each school attended. Because all students are required to live on campus unless they are seniors, married, or living with their parents, early application is desirable to ensure that housing is available. The freshman application priority date is March 1. The deadline for early decision applicants is December 1.

For more information about Florida Southern College, prospective students should contact:

Office of Admissions
Florida Southern College
111 Lake Hollingsworth Drive
Lakeland, Florida 33801-5698
Phone: 800-274-4131 (toll-free)
E-mail: fscadm@flsouthern.edu
Web site: http://www.flsouthern.edu

Students walk alongside the Frank Lloyd Wright Water Dome.

FORDHAM UNIVERSITY

NEW YORK, NEW YORK

The University

Fordham, the Jesuit University of New York, offers a distinctive educational experience that is rooted in the nearly 500-year-old Jesuit tradition of intellectual rigor and personal respect for the individual. A Fordham education blends a challenging curriculum with the resources, culture and energy of New York City—a unique combination by any measure.

The University enrolls approximately 14,600 students, of whom 7,950 are undergraduates. Fordham has four undergraduate colleges and six graduate and professional schools. In addition to its full-time undergraduate programs, the University offers part-time undergraduate study at Fordham College of Liberal Studies and through two summer sessions.

Fordham features two residential campuses: Rose Hill, on 85 green, leafy acres adjacent to the New York Botanical Garden and the Bronx Zoo; and Lincoln Center, a cosmopolitan campus in the cultural heart of Manhattan, which features a twenty-story complex that provides apartment-style living and great city views. Both campuses are easily accessible by public and private transportation. Enjoying the academic and student life of both is convenient with the University's Ram Van service, which operates between the two campuses.

The University has an extensive athletics program consisting of twenty-two varsity sports and numerous club and intramural sports. Murphy Field is the heart of intramural and recreational sports at Fordham, hosting softball, soccer, and flag football games. The Vincent T. Lombardi Memorial Center provides facilities for basketball, squash, swimming and diving, tennis, track, and water polo.

Location

As the Jesuit University of New York, Fordham offers its students the unparalleled academic, cultural, and recreational advantages of one of the world's great cities. Fordham draws students from across the country who want to live and learn while immersed in the diversity and opportunity of a global capital. More than 2,600 corporations and organizations—from the United Nations to Fortune 500 companies—offer valuable work experience to Fordham interns. New York City not only provides extraordinary internship possibilities and career advantages, but also a never-ending list of things to see and do—from Broadway theater, museums and music to major league sports or a bike ride through Central Park.

Majors and Degrees

Fordham offers undergraduates more than fifty majors. Fordham College at Rose Hill provides programs of study leading to the B.A. or B.S. in African and African American studies, American studies, anthropology, art history, biological sciences, chemistry, classical civilization, classical languages (Latin and Greek), communication and media studies, comparative literature, computer and information sciences, economics, engineering physics, English, French, French studies, general science, German, German studies, history, international political economy, Italian, Italian studies, Latin American and Latino studies, mathematics, mathematics/economics, medieval studies, Middle East studies, music, philosophy, physics, political science, psychology, religious studies, social work, sociology, Spanish, Spanish studies, theology, urban studies, visual arts, and women's studies.

Also located at the Rose Hill campus, the College of Business Administration offers programs leading to majors, minors, concentrations, or specializations in accounting, accounting information services, applied accounting and finance, business administration, business economics, business law and ethics, communication and media management, e-business, entrepreneurship, finance, human resource management, information systems, management of information and communication systems, management systems, marketing, and public accountancy. The G.L.O.B.E. Program (Global Learning Opportunities and Business Experiences) provides business students with an international study option that incorporates course offerings in language, culture, and history with business.

Special programs at Rose Hill include a cooperative engineering program, double majors or individualized majors, interdisciplinary studies, a B.S./M.B.A. program, numerous joint masters degree programs (dual degree), 3-3 law and honors programs. Preprofessional programs are offered in architecture, dentistry, law, medicine, and veterinary medicine, and a program for teacher certification is offered in elementary and secondary education.

At Fordham College at Lincoln Center students choose from the B.A. in African and African American studies, anthropology, art history, classical civilization, classical languages (Latin and Greek), communication and media studies, comparative literature, computer science, dance, economics, English, French, French studies, German, German studies, history, information science, international studies, Italian, Italian studies, Latin American and Latino studies, mathematics, mathematics/economics, medieval studies, Middle East studies, music, natural science, philosophy, political science, psychology, religious studies, social science, social work, sociology, Spanish, Spanish studies, theater, theology, urban studies, visual arts, and women's studies. Special programs at Fordham College at Lincoln Center include options in the performing arts (including a B.F.A. in dance with The Ailey School), creative writing, double majors or individualized majors, independent study, an honors program, and interdisciplinary studies. Preprofessional studies are offered in dentistry, health, and law. A teacher certification program is offered in elementary and secondary education.

Academic Programs

Students in all undergraduate colleges pursue a common core curriculum designed to provide them with the breadth of knowledge that marks the educated person. The core involves foundational courses chosen from groups of academic disciplines: history, philosophy, theology, natural sciences, social sciences, languages, and literature. In every core course, students think, speak, write, and act in fundamentally new ways, with a broadened appreciation of human values and a deepened commitment to the human community.

Off-Campus Programs

Reflecting the values-centered education that is a Fordham hallmark, more than 1,300 students engage in community service each year, locally and in distant corners of the world. The Global Outreach program is an ambitious international service program designed for students to live and work in communities of need. The University also provides access to yearlong, semester-long and summer study-abroad programs in more than fifty countries on six continents including La Sorbonne in Paris and American University in Cairo.

Academic Facilities

The outstanding libraries on the two campuses have combined holdings of more than 2.28 million volumes and more than 40,476 electronic and print periodicals. On the Rose Hill campus, the William D. Walsh Family Library, which serves the entire Fordham community, has seating for more than 1,500 and a state-of-the-art Electronic Information Center, as well as media production laboratories, studios, and auditoriums. Students also have access to the vast library facilities of New York City, neighboring universities, and the various specialized collections maintained by numerous local museums and other institutions. Among laboratory facilities utilized by undergraduates are Mulcahy Hall (chemistry), Larkin Hall (biology), and Freeman Hall (physics and biology). The University has more than forty buildings that provide ample space for smart classrooms, science laboratories, theaters, and athletic facilities.

Costs

At the Rose Hill and Lincoln Center campuses, undergraduate costs for the 2009–10 academic year were $35,825 for tuition and fees, and averaged $13,716 for room and board. Chemistry, physics, and biology fees were approximately $50 per laboratory course. Nominally priced meals are available in cafeterias on each campus. Such incidentals as transportation and laundry vary in cost. There is no difference in fees for out-of-state students.

Financial Aid

More than 90 percent of the entering students enroll with aid from Fordham as well as from outside sources. Among the major aid programs are Federal Pell Grants, Federal Supplemental Educational Opportunity Grants, Federal Perkins Loans, work grants sponsored by both the government and the University, and University grants-in-aid. Outside sources of aid include state scholarships, the New York State Tuition Assistance Program (TAP), privately sponsored scholarships, state government loan programs, and deferred-payment programs. The University also offers academic merit scholarships ranging from $10,000 to the full cost of tuition and room. Applicants for aid must submit the Free Application for Federal Student Aid (FAFSA) and the College Scholarship Service (CSS) PROFILE. Please direct inquiries to Fordham's Office of Undergraduate Admission or Office of Student Financial Services.

Faculty

The University has a full-time faculty of 699 and a student-faculty ratio of 13:1. Most members of the undergraduate faculty also teach at the graduate level, and 95 percent of the full-time faculty members hold doctoral or other terminal degrees.

Student Government

The traditional student governing body at Fordham has been the United Student Government, composed of undergraduates attending the University.

Admission Requirements

Admission is based on academic performance, class rank (if available), secondary school recommendations, and SAT or ACT scores. Extracurricular activities and essays are also factors in the evaluation process. Religious preference, physical handicap, race, or ethnic origin is not considered. Out-of-state students are encouraged to apply. More than 85 percent of the students accepted for the freshman class ranked in the top quarter of their secondary school class. The middle 50 percent combined SAT score for students entering in fall 2009 was 1200–1340. Recommended are 22 high school units, including 4 in English, 3 in mathematics, 3 in science, 2 in social studies, 2 in foreign language, 2 in history, and 6 electives. For regular admission, the SAT or the ACT should be taken no later than the January preceding entrance. Candidates for early action should complete the examinations by October of their senior year. The University participates in the College Board's Advanced Placement Program. Personal interviews are not required.

Application and Information

Application may be made for either September or January enrollment. The regular decision application deadline is January 15 for fall admission. The completed application, the secondary school report, the results of the SAT or ACT, and an application fee of $50 (check or money order made payable to Fordham University) should be submitted by this date. All financial aid forms are due by February 1. Students are notified on or about April 1. Candidates for Early Action should apply by November 1 and receive notification by December 25. Transfer students must apply by December 1 for spring admission or by June 1 for fall admission.

For additional details and application forms, students should contact:

Peter Farrell
Director of Admission
Fordham University
Duane Library
441 East Fordham Road
Bronx, New York 10458

Phone: 800-FORDHAM (367-3426)
E-mail: enroll@fordham.edu
Web site: http://www.fordham.edu

Members of the class of 2008 join Fordham's distinguished alumni family of more than 120,000.

FRAMINGHAM STATE COLLEGE

FRAMINGHAM, MASSACHUSETTS

The College

Framingham State College offers small, personalized classes to 6,000 undergraduate and graduate students on a traditional, New England campus. Student success is central to the mission of the College. Many options are available for student support, including programs to help freshmen transition to college. The College also has a robust honors program for exceptional students.

The breadth of programs offered by Framingham State College reflects the expertise of the faculty. Although the College's original focus was teacher education, the majority of students today major in fields ranging from business to the sciences to fashion design and retailing, along with a significant number who continue to major in education. The College offers twenty-six majors and many career-related concentrations.

In addition to its undergraduate program, Framingham State College graduates approximately 500 master's students each year. In 2008, the College added an M.S.N. program to its graduate program mix. In addition, the College is a pioneer in undergraduate and graduate online education, having offered online courses since 1998.

Traditional college-age students as well as nontraditional students seeking higher education on either a full- or part-time basis have opportunities to participate in campus life through a variety of cocurricular programs and activities and to develop the knowledge and skills needed to compete in a global and technological society.

Forty-four percent of Day Division students live on campus. Students of color represent 12 percent of the student body, while students over the age of 25 represent 17 percent of undergraduates.

Framingham State College offers residential housing to more than 1,500 students in six residence halls. Resident students are required to purchase a ten-, fourteen-, or nineteen-meal-per-week plan. Both the Dining Commons and the State Street Grille are located in the McCarthy College Center, the hub of all student activities. The newly renovated College Center is the home for the campus art gallery, game room, meeting rooms, radio station, college newspaper, club and organization offices, and offices for student services and student activities.

The Student Union Activities Board (SUAB), one of the largest and most active clubs on campus, plans the majority of campus events, including concerts, films, special social programs, travel, recreation, concerts, dances, lectures, films, spring break events, cultural activities, and much more. SUAB also sponsors the Annual Semi-Formal, Family Weekend, Spring Show, and the Sandbox Carnival.

The College competes in NCAA Division III athletics for men and women, including baseball, basketball, cross-country, field hockey, football, ice hockey, lacrosse, soccer, softball, and volleyball. Intramural sports are also offered, including cheerleading and rugby. A 65,000-square-foot athletic facility opened in 2001.

Location

The College is located just 20 miles west of Boston. It is the only public four-year college between Route 495 and Route 128, close to the heart of the high-technology industry and within reach of hundreds of professional companies and businesses. The 73-acre campus offers students a small- to medium-sized suburban campus with access to the cultural, recreational, educational, and career opportunities of Boston and New England.

Majors and Degrees

Framingham State College confers the Bachelor of Arts, Bachelor of Science, and Bachelor of Science in Education degrees. Undergraduate majors are offered in art history, biology, business administration, business and information technology, chemistry, communication arts, computer science, early childhood education, economics, elementary education, English, environmental science, fashion design and retailing, food and nutrition, food science, geography, health and consumer sciences, history, liberal studies, mathematics, modern languages, nursing (post-RN program), politics, psychology, sociology, and studio art. Within the twenty-six major programs are a variety of concentrations and minors. Pre-engineering, prelaw, and premedical professional programs are also offered.

Academic Programs

The mission of Framingham State College is to offer a dynamic and affordable program of educational excellence to its students. The College emphasizes a broad curriculum that blends liberal arts and sciences with several professional fields.

Each student must satisfy a thirty-two-course requirement for completion of any degree program. Up to twenty courses form the basis of a student's major area of study. The remaining twelve courses are used to fulfill the general education requirement, which encompasses writing, mathematics, humanities, social sciences, physical and life sciences, foreign language, and the study of federal and state constitutions. The general education requirement ensures that students experience the benefits of a liberal arts education through familiarity with a variety of curricula. Each student is assigned a faculty member in his or her major as an academic adviser. Undeclared students are assigned advisers through the Center for Academic Support and Advising (CASA). Selected students may participate in departmental and College-wide honors programs.

The College operates on the traditional two-semester calendar, with two optional summer sessions as well as a winter intersession.

Off-Campus Programs

Framingham State College students may choose to participate in one or several college-affiliated programs, allowing them to take credit-bearing courses outside of the College. Among the most popular are internships; the College Academic Program Sharing (CAPS) program; the Massachusetts Bay Marine Studies Consortium; the Washington, D.C., Internship; and study abroad.

Internships are available in most majors. Annually, hundreds of Framingham State College students serve as interns in the

Massachusetts State House, town and city governments, museums, and a variety of businesses and high-technology firms in the greater Boston area. Internships allow students the opportunity to gain direct, practical experience while applying the knowledge and skills they have acquired in the classroom.

Through the CAPS program, Framingham State College students may take up to 30 semester hours of college credit at one of the seven other Massachusetts state colleges. Students who participate in the Massachusetts Bay Marine Studies Consortium may also attend a variety of credit-bearing classes and symposia at other schools.

Students who seek an international dimension to enhance their undergraduate program can study abroad for a summer, semester, or academic year. In the past, students have studied in Australia, Canada, England, France, Ireland, Italy, Mexico, New Zealand, and Spain.

Academic Facilities

The Henry Whittemore Library houses more than 200,000 bound volumes, 600,000 volume equivalents in microforms, and 1,600 current periodicals in subscriptions. Electronic databases supplement the library's in-house journal collection, and students have access to a variety of materials shared within the Minuteman Library Network. The College provides extensive computing capabilities for its students, including a wireless network across the campus.

A child-development center, planetarium, and greenhouse provide students with the opportunity to gain practical experience in related studies. Likewise, the radio station and television studios serve as forums to apply textbook knowledge.

The Challenger Learning Center, established in memory of Christa Corrigan McAuliffe, the nation's first teacher astronaut and a 1970 graduate of the College, is located on campus. The center provides a unique hands-on learning experience designed to foster interest in mathematics, science, and technology.

Costs

Tuition and fees for the 2009–10 academic year were $6540 for in-state students and $12,620 for out-of-state students. Yearly residence hall charges were $5248, and the yearly meal plan was $2900. Students should anticipate additional expenses for books, a laptop computer, supplies, transportation, and personal items. All costs are subject to change.

Financial Aid

Sources of financial aid available to Framingham State College students include federal, state, and institutional programs. Framingham State College students were the recipients of more than $19 million last year in loans, scholarships, grants, and work-study.

Federal programs include the Federal Work-Study Program, the Federal Pell Grant, Federal Supplemental Educational Opportunity Grant, the Federal Perkins Loan, and both subsidized and unsubsidized Federal Stafford Student Loans. State-funded aid includes state scholarship grants and a no-interest loan program. Institutional funds mainly provide merit and need-based scholarships.

All students applying for financial aid must file the Free Application for Federal Student Aid (FAFSA), designating Framingham State College as the recipient. Transfer students must submit financial aid transcripts documenting all previous aid received. The priority filing deadline for fall entrance is March 1.

Faculty

One hundred sixty-four full-time faculty members are dedicated to upholding the undergraduate mission of the College. More than 83 percent of the faculty members hold the terminal degree in their field. The active involvement of many professors in research and writing complements their primary commitment and dedication to teaching excellence at the undergraduate level. With an impressive student-faculty ratio of 17:1, Framingham State College is able to offer a variety of programs in a challenging academic atmosphere.

Student Government

The Student Government Association (SGA) is the center of all political and social activity of the students of Framingham State College. The primary duties of SGA are to provide funding for more than fifty organizations through the student activity fee, to ensure representation of Framingham State College students in the state student organization, and to act on all other matters that concern the students of the College. SGA also plays a major role in the formulation of College policies that are of mutual concern to the students, the faculty, and the administration.

Admission Requirements

Framingham State College seeks to enroll students with a strong academic background who possess the necessary skills to succeed in college. Admission decisions are based primarily on the strength of the high school record and test scores. Secondary school students are required to pass 16 college-preparatory units: 4 years of English; 3 years of math, including algebra I and II and geometry; 3 years of science, including 2 years of laboratory science; 2 years of history/social science, including 1 year of U.S. history; 2 years of the same foreign language; and two college-preparatory-level electives. High school students are encouraged to elect additional courses in music, art, and computer science.

Students in the upper 50 percent of their class with a B average or higher are encouraged to apply. An essay and at least one recommendation are required as part of the application. International and transfer students, as well as adults returning to college, are also encouraged to apply.

Application and Information

To be considered for admission to a degree program at the College, all applicants must submit a completed application along with the application fee, an official high school transcript, and official complete SAT scores. Transfer students must submit official transcripts from all colleges previously attended.

It is recommended that students apply by the priority filing date of February 15 for fall admission and December 1 for spring admission. Students are encouraged to attend an admissions information session and tour. The information sessions are presented by a member of the admissions staff and are followed by a tour of the campus conducted by a student admissions representative. Students should call the Office of Undergraduate Admissions to arrange an appointment.

For further information and application materials or to schedule a campus visit, students should contact:

Office of Undergraduate Admissions
Framingham State College
100 State Street
P.O. Box 9101
Framingham, Massachusetts 01701-9101
Phone: 508-626-4500
E-mail: admissions@framingham.edu
Web site: http://www.framingham.edu

FRANKLIN COLLEGE

FRANKLIN, INDIANA

The College

As an innovative scientist, diplomat, thinker, writer, and leader, Benjamin Franklin's remarkable life and accomplishments left a mark on not only a young nation, but also the world. Named in the spirit of this extraordinary American icon, Franklin College continues his legacy of exploration and knowledge.

Since its founding in 1834, Franklin College has a long history of preparing students for lives committed to excellence, leadership, and service. With a comprehensive liberal arts curriculum combined with a leading edge Professional Development Program, Franklin College provides an education that blends thinking with doing, reasoning with acting, and discovering with challenging.

Small classes and dedicated faculty members ensure that students get the attention needed to succeed, and Franklin's career and graduate school admission rates prove this.

Franklin combines liberal arts training with preprofessional development like no other college. Students can develop the competencies and resources necessary to be successful in their personal and professional lives through Franklin's innovative Professional Development Program (PDP). This exciting program gives them the opportunity to dine with corporate executives, network with national and community leaders, learn the finer points of corporate communication, and develop a level of polish and sophistication that sets them apart from other college graduates.

Location

Located in the heart of the Midwest, Franklin College offers students the best of both a small community and a big city's excitement.

Franklin, Indiana, only 20 miles south of Indiana's capital city Indianapolis, is the thirteenth largest city in the U.S. It offers a wide variety of internship opportunities, as well as athletic, cultural, and entertainment events that appeal to all students.

Majors and Degrees

Flagship programs at Franklin College include athletic training, business, journalism, pre-med, and education. The Pulliam School of Journalism is one of a few comprehensive journalism schools housed at a small liberal arts institution. Student media opportunities include a student-run PR agency and a student newspaper, magazine, news show, radio show, and yearbook. After graduation, education majors are placed at 97 percent or higher in the classroom, while business students repeatedly score in the top 5 percent on the National College Business Examination. One hundred percent of athletic training majors are employed six months after graduation. Preparation for graduate school is exceptional, with 85 percent of students gaining admission to medical school and 90 percent of applicants accepted to law school.

Franklin College confers more than twenty-five Bachelor of Arts degrees in the following areas: accounting, American studies, art, biology, business (finance, general, international business, management/industrial relations, and marketing), Canadian studies, chemistry, computing/computer information systems, economics, education (elementary, middle school, and secondary), English, French, history, journalism (advertising/public relations, broadcasting, news-editorial, and visual communications), mathematics, music (piano and vocal), philosophy, physical education, political science, psychology, recreation, religious studies, sociology (criminal justice and social work), Spanish, and theater. Minors are also offered in many of these areas, including fine arts, leadership, and physics.

Engineering is offered as a 3+2 program. Students earn a Bachelor of Arts degree from Franklin College and a Bachelor of Science degree in one of the engineering disciplines from the Purdue School of Engineering and Technology (IUPUI).

Students considering a career in dentistry, forestry, medical technology, medicine, optometry, physical therapy, or veterinary medicine arrange their program with the advice of the preprofessional adviser of the science division. Students seeking a career in law plan their program in consultation with prelaw advisers. Students planning a career in secondary education may elect an academic area of concentration that will satisfy the state requirements for a teaching major. The education department is endorsed and approved by the Indiana Professional Standards Board and the National Council for Accreditation of Teacher Education (NCATE).

Academic Programs

The current academic program is the result of the faculty's plan to meet the express needs of students; the primary emphasis is on the unity of knowledge. Franklin believes in the importance of providing students with a liberal arts background while they develop talents for a particular professional career. Approximately one third of each student's total course work is composed of the prescribed and exploratory courses that make up the general education core curriculum.

All of Franklin's academic departments offer individualized study, allowing a student to pursue his or her field of interest in depth. Students interested in pursuing a major not offered at Franklin may submit a proposal for their individualized major.

As part of the 4-1-4 calendar, students complete up to 8 hours of credit in a special four-week winter-term program in January. The winter term is designed to allow students to study in areas of particular interest to them, either within or outside their major field of study. Some January classes offer students the opportunity to travel to locations such as Belize, England, France, Italy, and Mexico.

A large number of internships are available during the winter term and the summer, offering practical experience under the supervision of a professional. The fall semester ends before Christmas; the spring semester begins in February and ends in May. An eight-week summer session beginning in mid-June allows students to take up to 9 additional credit hours. Ninety-five percent of Franklin College students complete an internship prior to graduation.

Franklin gives credit in seventeen academic areas for successful scores on CLEP subject examinations; credit is also granted for successful scores on the Advanced Placement tests of the College Board. The Running Start Program enables talented high school students to get an early start on their college education.

Off-Campus Programs

Franklin College students participate in a variety of off-campus study experiences, including a year or a semester of study through Acadia University of Nova Scotia, Telemark University of Norway, and Hong Kong Baptist University. Other off-campus study programs include the American University Washington Semester; a junior year abroad; programs at Harlaxton College in

England, Franklin College of Switzerland, and Brethren Colleges Abroad; and specific exchange programs in Japan and Taiwan. Students may also participate in a Semester at Sea program sponsored by the University of Pittsburgh.

Academic Facilities

Franklin College has two campus buildings listed on the National Historic Register. Old Main, the original home of the College, and Shirk Hall, home of the Pulliam School of Journalism, are footholds of the rich past and recent renovation of the Franklin College campus. Classrooms and administrative, business, and professorial offices, along with computer laboratories, occupy Old Main; Shirk Hall also houses classrooms and the radio and television station.

A. A. Barnes Science Building houses all physics, biology, and chemistry department classrooms and laboratories. The Spurlock Center gymnasium and fitness center provides increased classroom and office space along with a weight room.

The Dietz Center for Professional Development is the home of the Professional Development Program. State-of-the-art conference rooms and computer facilities enhance Franklin's career programming commitment to its students.

The B. F. Hamilton Library, containing more than 117,000 volumes and collections of microfilm, slides, art reproductions, recordings, and periodicals, is a member of P.A.L.N.I. (Private Academic Library Network of Indiana). The Johnson Center for Fine Arts provides classrooms and practice and performance accommodations, and it houses the facilities and meeting rooms for the Leadership Program.

Costs

The direct cost for the 2010–11 academic year is $32,340. This amount is derived from tuition, which is $24,470; residence hall, which is $4330; student fees of $265; and Winter Term meal fees of $310 plus the meal plan, which is $2965.

Financial Aid

The Franklin College financial aid program assists students who might not otherwise be able to attend college and rewards applicants for excellent academic achievement in high school. Awards are based on scholarship, curricular and extracurricular activities, and financial need. Aid involving financial need includes Franklin College grants, loans, and employment. Franklin participates in the Federal Stafford Student Loan, Federal Perkins Loan, and Federal Work-Study programs. Ben Franklin Scholarships, President's Scholarships, Founders Scholarships, and Trustees Scholarships are awarded on academic performance, activities, and standardized test scores. The Ben Franklin Scholarship covers the full cost of tuition; the President's Scholarship is a $14,000 award; and Academic Excellence and Dean's Scholarships are awarded on specified criteria. In addition, students identified by the state of Indiana as 21st Century Scholars will be awarded full tuition scholarships. Scholarships are renewable for each of the recipient's four academic years at Franklin, provided students maintain a minimum GPA of 3.0 and advance in class status each year. The Free Application for Federal Student Aid (FAFSA) is required.

Faculty

The 12:1 student-faculty ratio allows Franklin faculty members to provide excellent instruction in small classes that promote participatory learning. Eighty percent of current faculty members have obtained the highest degree in their field. Faculty members serve as advisers and provide supplemental attention outside the classroom. While many faculty members carry on research and publish their work, their main emphasis is teaching. No classes are taught by graduate students or teaching assistants.

Student Government

The Student Congress is composed of representatives elected by the student body. The congress provides a forum for student concerns and is the most important governmental communication link among students, faculty members, and the administration. Student government also includes the Judicial Board and the Residence Hall Council. These groups have jurisdiction over certain questions concerning the social standards and regulations of the College.

Admission Requirements

Applications for admission to Franklin College are evaluated on an individual basis. A student's potential academic and personal contributions to the College, recommendations, school and community activities, academic record, and standardized test scores are taken into consideration by the Admissions Committee. A student should complete a strong college-preparatory program. Candidates for admission are urged to visit the campus in order to experience the College community.

Application and Information

To be considered for admission, an applicant must submit a completed application (paper or online), a transcript of all secondary school and college work attempted, and either SAT or ACT scores. A decision regarding acceptance is made after the College receives all necessary credentials. Notification is sent immediately after the Enrollment Committee has acted.

Office of Admission
Franklin College
101 Branigin Boulevard
Franklin, Indiana 46131
Phone: 317-738-8062
888-852-6471 (toll-free)
Fax: 317-738-8274
E-mail: admissions@franklincollege.edu
Web site: http://admissions.franklincollege.edu

The bell tower on top of Old Main on the Franklin College campus.

COLLEGE CLOSE-UPS

FRANKLIN COLLEGE SWITZERLAND

LUGANO, SWITZERLAND

The College

Franklin College Switzerland, named for the United States' first and most illustrious ambassador to Europe, was founded in 1969 as a nonprofit, independent, postsecondary institution. It takes as its cornerstone Benjamin Franklin's vigorous support of intellectual interchange between nations. An American liberal arts institution in an international environment, Franklin is fully accredited in the United States by the Commission on Higher Education of the Middle States Association of Colleges and Schools and in Switzerland by the Swiss University Conference.

Franklin College places a strong emphasis on cross-cultural perspectives, advocating that international studies should be an integral part of a college education, as a prelude to, and basis for, a student's commitment to a major field of study. Franklin defines higher education from its beginning as the experience of thinking internationally. Its emphasis, both academic and social, on global perspectives is designed to affect the direction and meaning of a student's college experience, life, and career.

The essence of a Franklin College education is the exposure of its students to cultures other than their own, providing them with a better understanding of others, the world, and their place in the world. The College's location in Lugano, a vibrant Swiss city that is part of the cultural milieu of northern Italy, ensures a constant commingling of cultures in a quadrilingual nation. Students and faculty members, many who have a cross-cultural background, come to Franklin College from every corner of the globe, further strengthening international study and international experiences.

Approximately 60 percent of the students come from the United States; 40 percent are from Europe, Asia, Africa, South America, and the Middle East. Bringing diverse experiences and perspectives to college life, they live in College residences both on and near the campus. These apartments all have kitchens available, and two campus dining facilities provide regular meal service and a meal plan. There are residence supervisors for each of the ten buildings.

Campus activities are varied. Franklin's Student Government Association (SGA) promotes a student newspaper; a literary magazine; a drama society; cultural, language, and sports clubs; and numerous social events that take advantage of southern Switzerland's extensive recreational resources. There are competitive College sports teams in men's and women's soccer, and intramural teams include basketball, soccer, and volleyball. In addition, the Athletic Director enrolls interested students in a considerable number of local Swiss clubs and teams that welcome newcomers—basketball, ice hockey, soccer, and volleyball teams, as well as clubs for crew, fencing, flying, golf, hang gliding, ice skating, judo, parachuting, riding, rock climbing, sailing, swimming, tennis, track, and windsurfing. By joining these local groups, Franklin students become part of the region's life; they are themselves essential to the cross-cultural learning the College promotes.

Location

Franklin College's campus is in the community of Sorengo, a section of the city of Lugano, southern Switzerland's principal business, banking, medical, and cultural center. Easily accessible from the campus either by public transportation or on foot, downtown Lugano and its surrounding lakeside villages are renowned for their scenic beauty and Mediterranean climate. Palm trees line lakefront piazzas, and an outdoor lifestyle is typical of Ticino, the Italian-speaking canton of Switzerland that best exemplifies Swiss versatility in all three of the national languages—Italian, German, and French.

Throughout the year, Lugano features outstanding cultural activities at the world-famous Thyssen art collection, the Swiss-Italian radio station with its own permanent symphony orchestra, and the International Convention Center, which attracts guest performers from around the world. Nine public museums, many art galleries, several movie houses, and a multitude of restaurants and discotheques make for a range of recreational choices normally found only in a large city. A covered ice rink, swimming pools, and a wide range of other sports facilities are maintained by local sports clubs; Lugano and the southern part of Switzerland offer access to an extraordinary variety of sports activities. In the spring and fall, Ticino's most popular recreation is hiking. In winter, skiing is available in San Bernardino and Andermatt, about an hour from the campus, or in the fabled St. Moritz, Davos, Klosters, and Zermatt.

Majors and Degrees

The Bachelor of Arts program offers majors in art history, comparative literary and cultural studies, environmental studies, history, international banking and finance, communication and media studies, international economics, international management, international relations, literature, French studies, Italian studies, and visual and communication arts, with combined and double majors in a number of study areas. The Associate in Arts degree program provides a strong liberal arts foundation for students who usually continue their education in a baccalaureate degree program.

Academic Programs

Franklin's curricula promote international awareness and critical thinking, while being interdisciplinary in the highest tradition of liberal education. The courses of study explore the diverse disciplines that enlighten an educated human being. Students must complete at least 126 credit hours to be eligible for the B.A. degree and 64 for the A.A. degree, while maintaining a minimum cumulative grade point average of 2.0 on a 4.0 scale.

As an integral credit-bearing part of the academic program, twice a year (in mid-October and mid-March) students participate in faculty-led academic travel programs to various destinations in Eastern and Western Europe, Africa, Asia, Latin America, and North America.

All degree candidates must demonstrate a foreign language proficiency in a language other than their mother tongue equivalent to three years of university-level instruction in one of the languages taught at Franklin. This requirement is met by successfully completing appropriate courses at Franklin or by passing an equivalency test administered by the language department.

In addition to their major field of study, students may add courses within another discipline to form a minor. The number of credit hours (12 to 15) and the program of courses are subject to departmental approval.

The College operates on a two-semester calendar, with classes starting in late August and mid-January; two 3-week summer sessions and one concurrent 6-week summer session are also available. A required orientation program for all new students is held in August and mid-January.

Off-Campus Programs

Franklin's renowned Academic Travel Program is a fully integrated part of the regular curriculum. Each semester, students participate in two weeks of faculty-led academic travel. More than any other program of study, it gives students an opportunity to learn through experience. Travel destinations for 2009–10 included Botswana, Croatia, the Czech Republic, Egypt, England, France, Germany, Greece, India, Ireland, Italy, Japan, Morocco, Scotland, Serbia, Slovakia, Slovenia, Spain, Thailand, Turkey, and the United States.

Internships are also available. Students with academic interest in any area may apply for an internship after two semesters of residence at Franklin, either by asking to be considered for one of the internships provided by the College or by arranging for an appointment themselves. The Dean of Intercultural Engagement and Learning coordinates the internship program; a student may earn a maximum of 3 credit hours in an assignment.

Students in good standing who major in modern languages are eligible for study in a country where the target language is spoken; such study is limited to one semester at an approved institution.

Academic Facilities

The Franklin College Library contains 38,000 volumes and offers numerous English and foreign-language periodicals. The library also participates in the Swiss interlibrary loan system linking major Swiss university libraries. In addition to the print and AV collections, the library subscribes to many indexes and full-text databases, including ProQuest resources, EBSCO resources, Lexis-Nexis Academic Universe, MarketWatch, Earthscape, Columbia International Affairs Online (CIAO), and National Bureau of Economic Research. Three computer labs with Internet access are available for student use.

Costs

The comprehensive fee for the 2009–10 academic year was $45,300. This figure includes the cost of tuition, room and board, academic travel, and student fees. The estimated cost of personal expenses and incidentals, including textbooks, is $6300 per year. The estimated cost range to fly round-trip from the United States is from $1000 to $1300.

Financial Aid

Franklin College offers academic merit awards and need-based financial aid to qualified students. U.S. applicants for financial aid must submit the FAFSA for evaluation. Veterans' and Social Security benefits are also available to eligible students. Federal Stafford Student Loans and PLUS loans may be obtained through local lenders. International students must submit the International Student Financial Aid Form. Campus internships are also available. Students interested in applying for one can do so by requesting information about available Life Long Learning Scholarships through the Center for Intercultural Engagement and Learning Opportunities (CIELO) at the beginning of each semester.

Faculty

Franklin College has 51 full-time and part-time professors, approximately half of whom are American or British; the other half are of various nationalities. The majority have advanced degrees from prestigious American universities, the others from highly recognized British and Continental universities; most have lived, studied, and taught in a variety of countries. The teaching staff characterizes the cross-cultural essence of the College. Professors are committed to both the European and global arenas of study; are knowledgeable about particular countries enough to organize and lead rewarding academic travels; are competent in more than one language; and are dedicated to the personal, discursive style of teaching required by a small liberal arts college with small classes. The faculty members also advise the various student activities, lead local excursions, and regularly contribute to the College's cocurricular program of lectures. In addition, each faculty member acts as academic counselor to a number of students. The faculty-conducted Academic Travel Program promotes the intellectual friendship between teacher and student essential to a liberal arts education. Franklin's student-faculty ratio is approximately 10:1.

Student Government

The student body elects the members of the Student Government Association (SGA). In addition to sponsoring interest groups and arranging social events, the SGA is actively involved in campus governance by appointing members to participate in meetings of the Curriculum Committee, Faculty Assembly, and the Appeals Board.

Admission Requirements

Franklin College seeks students who are eager to meet the challenge of studying and living in Europe, serious about undertaking college-level learning, and prepared to contribute positively to the intellectual life of the College. To identify such students, and also to ensure a diverse student population, the College Admissions Committee considers both academic and personal facts, including the student's academic record, evaluations by teachers and counselors, standardized test scores, extracurricular interests and talents, and academic distinctions. Admission to the College is limited and therefore competitive. To achieve the best match between the student and Franklin, a personal interview is strongly recommended; one can be arranged by contacting the Admissions Office in Lugano or New York. Applicants to the freshman class must submit a completed application form and a nonrefundable fee of $90; an official transcript of their secondary school record; SAT or ACT scores, either included on transcripts or forwarded by the testing service to Franklin College (CEEB code number 0922; ACT code number 5223); and three letters of academic evaluation. Applicants whose first language is not English must submit their score on the Test of English as a Foreign Language (TOEFL); a score of at least 79 iBT, 217 CBT, or 550 PBT is required. Transfer applicants and institute applicants are required to submit a completed application and a nonrefundable application fee of $90, an official transcript of their college record, a dean's report from the dean of students, and one letter of academic recommendation.

Application and Information

The priority application deadline for fall entry is March 15 for applicants to the freshman class and June 15 for transfer and institute applicants. The application deadline for the spring semester is November 15. Admission decisions are made on a rolling basis. Applicants can usually expect a decision within three weeks from the time their application is completed. All inquiries and applications should be directed to the nearest Admissions Office.

Franklin College Switzerland
US Office, Suite 2746
420 Lexington Avenue
New York, NY 10170

Phone: 212-922-9650
Fax: 212-922-9870
E-mail: info@fc.edu

Karen Ballard
Dean of Admissions
Franklin College Switzerland
Via Ponte Tresa, 29
6924 Sorengo/Lugano
Switzerland

Phone: 41-91-986-3613
Fax: 41-91-993-3906
E-mail: info@fc.edu
Web site: http://www.fc.edu

FRANKLIN PIERCE UNIVERSITY

RINDGE, NEW HAMPSHIRE

The University

Franklin Pierce University is a small, private, regionally accredited (NEASC) university grounded in the liberal arts, with a focus on personal attention and high-quality instruction. The University consists of the College at Rindge and the College of Graduate & Professional Studies. Degrees are offered through the doctoral level. The institutional mission focuses on preparing citizens and leaders of conscience for a new century who make significant contributions to their professions and communities, whether their aspirations are local or global.

The main campus in Rindge is located in the beautiful Monadnock region of New Hampshire and enrolls approximately 1,500 undergraduates. The College of Graduate & Professional Studies enrolls approximately 1,000 adult learners at its five graduate and professional studies campuses across the state, in Arizona, and through distance learning. The diverse student population represents thirty-two states and twenty-eight countries.

Physical facilities of the main campus include modern classroom buildings with state-of-the-art technology, a MAC computer lab, digital photo and print labs, the library, an academic services center, a campus center, residence halls and apartment houses, town-house complexes, a field house, an air frame recreation complex, a dance studio, a health center, a boat house, the Lakeside Educational Center, a glassblowing facility, and a theater. A wide range of services are offered to students, including health-care services, counseling, and career planning and placement assistance.

Campus activities include a number of academic and special interest clubs, such as the Campus Activities Board; groups centered around common political, arts, and academic interests; *Pierce Arrow* (newspaper); *Raven* (yearbook); *Nevermore* (literary magazine); the Student Government Association; and many others. Bus trips to special events are offered on weekends. The University's active Adventure Recreation and intramural programs offer a wide variety of activities on both the University's 1,200-acre campus and throughout the region's many natural recreational facilities.

The Franklin Pierce Ravens compete at the NCAA Division II level. Men compete in baseball, basketball, crew, golf, ice hockey, lacrosse, soccer, and tennis. Women compete in basketball, cross-country, rowing, lacrosse, field hockey, soccer, softball, tennis, and volleyball. The University has earned national championships in men's and women's soccer and achieved top regional honors in baseball and women's basketball.

Location

The main campus in Rindge, New Hampshire, is situated on 1,200 wooded acres on the shore of Pearly Pond near the base of Mount Monadnock. Rindge, which is in southwestern New Hampshire, is 65 miles from Boston, 112 miles from Hartford, and 236 miles from New York City. The area is an ideal setting for outdoor activities. There are many lakes and streams, including the Pearly Pond beach facility, which is ideal for fishing, swimming, and sailing, and there are also numerous trails for hiking, mountaineering, biking, and cross-country skiing.

Majors and Degrees

Franklin Pierce University offers Bachelor of Science and Bachelor of Arts degrees through five academic divisions. The Division of Behavioral Sciences offers majors in anthropology/archaeology, art education, criminal justice, elementary education, psychology, secondary education, and social work and counseling. In the Division of Business Administration, students can major in accounting-finance, arts management, management, marketing, and sports and recreation management. The Division of Natural Sciences offers majors in biology, computer information technology, environmental science, and mathematics. In the Division of Visual and Performing Arts, students major in fine arts, graphic communications, mass communication (journalism, media production, and media studies), music, and theater arts and dance. Majors in the Division of Humanities are American studies, English, history, and political science. The University also offers preprofessional programs in law, medicine, and allied health fields, such as physical therapy. In addition to a major, students may complete a minor area of study, and they also have the option of designing their own interdisciplinary majors.

Academic Programs

Franklin Pierce University's curriculum is a blend of traditional liberal arts, preprofessional study, teacher preparation programs, and a nationally recognized core curriculum, The Individual and Community. In 1997, the University was the recipient of the Templeton Award for Character Building Colleges. Students receive personal attention at Franklin Pierce University; the average class size is 16 and the student-faculty ratio is 14:1.

A total of 120 semester hours are required for graduation. These include the courses in the student's chosen major (generally 30 to 54 credits); and the required 38-credit Individual and Community Integrated Curriculum. The purpose of the Individual and Community program is to foster a common understanding of the questions and issues that lie at the heart of contemporary American life. The Integrated Curriculum begins with a one-semester freshman seminar called Individual and Community and continues with a sequence of courses culminating in the Senior Liberal Arts Seminar.

Three academic institutes are housed on campus. They are: The Fitzwater Center for Communication; The Monadnock Institute of Nature, Place, and Culture; and the New England Center for Civic Life. These institutes help students and faculty combine theory with practice and conduct research that enhances their careers and contributes to society.

Franklin Pierce offers an Honors Program, which was established to help provide challenge and intellectual community to participants. The program offers honors sections of core courses, occasional honors electives, and honors options in major courses designed to appeal to the more academically committed student. Students are invited to participate in the freshman honors program based on their high school academic records.

Off-Campus Programs

Credit-bearing internships are available for qualified upperclassmen in several academic divisions, and students may participate in the Washington Center for Internships and Academic Seminars, a comprehensive, credit-bearing learning experience in Washington, D.C.

Franklin Pierce University is one of sixteen member colleges of the New Hampshire College and University Council (NHCUC). The NHCUC Student Exchange Agreement allows students to take courses at other NHCUC colleges at no extra tuition cost. Students may take courses at Franklin Pierce University and another member college during the same semester, or they may spend up to two semesters in residence at a member school.

Franklin Pierce offers opportunities for academic programs abroad and international studies on campus. The Global Citizenship Program and the University's own programs in Vienna, Austria; Athens, Greece; and Lyon, France give students the chance to engage in studies with a global focus. In addition to its own programs abroad, Franklin Pierce has formed affiliations with a variety of institutions that allow students from any academic discipline to fulfill their program requirements while studying at an affiliated university or program abroad. Students have the opportunity to take part in programs in Australia, New Zealand, Spain, Belgrade, Scotland, England, and Ireland.

Another study-abroad opportunity is the Walk in Europe. This program is unique to Franklin Pierce University and has been part of the curriculum since 1969. Approximately 25 students are chosen to participate in the semester-long project: a long-distance walk through several European countries. The sheer adventure and vitality of the project profoundly changes the participants' outlook on the world. The Walk is structured to facilitate engagement with Europeans and their cultures and with each member of the group. Students who have participated have described the Walk as the single most valuable learning experience of their years at Franklin Pierce.

Academic Facilities

The Franklin Pierce University Library provides a comfortable, open-stack environment for study and research. The 137,500-volume collection includes books, microforms, CDs, DVDs, software, and audio and videocassettes. More than 30 licensed Web-based databases, including EBSCOhost and LexisNexis, provide full-text access to more than 37,518 electronic and print periodical titles. The Curriculum Library supports the education curriculum of the University and includes a wealth of resources related to K–12 teaching and learning, and children's literature.

Costs

Basic charges for the 2010–11 academic year are $27,700 for tuition, $5300 for a standard room, and $4700 for board. Other fees and deposits bring the total to $39,000 per year.

Financial Aid

Both need-based and merit-based financial aid is available in the forms of loans, grants, scholarships, and on-campus employment. Students should visit the University's Web site for details about the various aid programs. The University awards $18 million in institutional scholarships and grants each year. It is anticipated that 100 percent of students accepted to the College at Rindge for the 2010–11 academic year will receive financial aid.

Faculty

There are 110 full-time and 141 part-time professors at the undergraduate residential campus in Rindge, 68 percent of whom have terminal degrees in their field. All Franklin Pierce University students are taught by faculty members who are active professionally in organizations that span the academic disciplines. Over the years, their work has received the support of the Council for the International Exchange of Scholars (Fulbright Scholars), the Hewlett Foundation, the Whiting Foundation, the Lilly Endowment for the Arts, the National Endowment for the Humanities, the National Science Foundation, the Carnegie Foundation for the Advancement of Teaching, the Council for Advancement and Support of Education, and the Kettering Foundation. Faculty members regularly contribute their work as researchers, writers, presenters, editors of professional journals, and performing artists.

Student Government

The Franklin Pierce University Student Government Association (SGA) is made up of dedicated student representatives working to make positive change for the student body. In addition to being an advocate for the student body, the SGA also funds the various clubs and organizations that enrich campus life and the Pierce experience.

Admission Requirements

Applicants are evaluated on an individual basis, with the student's potential and seriousness of purpose of primary concern. The trend toward improved grades, more difficult course work, and greater school involvement are weighed heavily in the student's behalf. Counselor support and supplementary recommendations are valued and are given special consideration. Class size and the campus environment are such that SAT Reasoning Test or ACT results are generally a less valid predictor of success at Franklin Pierce University than ongoing classroom achievement.

Each entering student must submit evidence of adequate preparation for college. Sixteen credits of secondary school work are required of each candidate. The preferred distribution is English, 4 credits; mathematics, 3 credits; laboratory sciences, 2 credits; social sciences, 3 credits; and electives, 4 credits. Candidates deemed to have potential and motivation, yet not meeting all the admission requirements, may be accepted provisionally.

The application consists of the completed application form, official secondary school transcripts, official transcripts from each college attended, an official secondary school recommendation (guidance counselor, principal, or teacher), and SAT Reasoning Test or ACT scores. An on-campus interview is recommended. Students whose native language is not English must also submit the Certification of Finances and an acceptable TOEFL score.

Application and Information

Students may apply to enter in the fall, spring, or summer sessions. Applications are processed on a rolling basis, but students are encouraged to apply and have their transcripts and recommendations sent early in their senior year.

Franklin Pierce University
Department of Admissions
40 University Drive
Rindge, New Hampshire 03461-0060
Phone: 603-899-4050
800-437-0048 (toll-free)
Fax: 603-899-4394
E-mail: admissions@franklinpierce.edu
Web site: http://www.franklinpierce.edu

COLLEGE CLOSE-UPS

GANNON UNIVERSITY

ERIE, PENNSYLVANIA

The University

Gannon University, which is consistently named one of America's Best Colleges by *U.S. News & World Report,* is dedicated to excellence in holistic education. The oldest part of the University is Villa Maria College, which was founded in 1925 by the Sisters of St. Joseph. In 1933, Archbishop John Mark Gannon established Cathedral College, a two-year institution, which by 1941 had evolved into a four-year college, the Gannon School of Arts and Sciences. The name Gannon College was adopted in 1944, and Gannon achieved university status in 1979. Villa Maria College subsequently merged with Gannon University in 1989.

Gannon's campus is located in the heart of downtown Erie, giving students the benefit of internships with businesses, law and law-enforcement agencies, health-care facilities, industries, and social service organizations. It is also within walking distance of stores, shops, restaurants, and theaters. The campus consists of more than thirty buildings located within six city blocks. Among these buildings is the Carneval Athletic Pavilion, which has a pool; three gyms; a running track; a weight room; courts for racquetball, handball, volleyball and basketball; and other facilities. Also on campus are two residence halls, nine apartment buildings, classroom and faculty office buildings, an administration building, and a multipurpose chapel building. The Waldron Campus Center is a focal point that gives students the opportunity to meet and socialize between classes with faculty members and other students.

Gannon offers students a broad intramural sports program that runs throughout the entire year. In Division II intercollegiate athletics, Gannon offers men's baseball, basketball, cross-country, football, golf, soccer, water polo, and wrestling and women's basketball, cross-country, golf, lacrosse, soccer, softball, volleyball, and water polo. There is also an intercollegiate coed swimming and diving team. Gannon's athletes utilize the Gannon University Field, a multipurpose athletic facility that is conveniently located on campus.

There are approximately 4,200 students at Gannon, more than 2,700 of whom are undergraduates. The ratio of commuters to resident students is approximately 1:4. The University has a Career Development and Employment Services Office to aid students in locating internships and part-time work during school and full-time work after graduation.

Location

Erie is Pennsylvania's fourth-largest city and is located in the northwestern corner of the state on the shore of Lake Erie. Erie is approximately 120 miles north of Pittsburgh, Pennsylvania; 90 miles east of Cleveland, Ohio; and 90 miles southwest of Buffalo, New York. The campus is within 5 miles of Interstates 79 and 90 and 5 miles from Erie International Airport. Erie is also serviced by rail and bus transportation.

Majors and Degrees

The College of Humanities, Education, and Social Sciences awards the Bachelor of Arts and Bachelor of Science degrees.

In the College of Humanities, Education and Social Sciences, the areas of study from which students may select a major are communication arts, criminal justice, English (with concentrations in applied communications, literature, and writing), foreign language and international studies, foreign language and literature, foreign language teaching (Spanish only), history, journalism communications, legal studies, liberal arts, mortuary science, philosophy, political science, prelaw, a 3+3 prelaw program that includes early admission to Duquesne University, psychology, social work, theater, theater and communication arts, and theology.

In the School of Education, the areas of study from which students may select a major are early childhood education Pre-K–4, middle level education 4–8, secondary education (in biology, English, foreign language (Spanish only), mathematics, and social studies), and special education.

The Morosky College of Health Professions and Sciences offers degrees in the health professions and sciences. The degrees offered in the health professions include medical technology, nursing, nutrition and human performance, occupational therapy, physical therapy, physician assistant, radiologic sciences, respiratory care, sport and exercise science, and undecided health science.

The School of Sciences offers degrees in bioinformatics, biology, biotechnology, chemistry, environmental science, mathematics, science, scientific and technical sales, and sport and exercise science. Also offered are preprofessional programs for students who wish to enter medical, dental, or veterinary school, as well as accelerated and cooperative medical programs in allopathy, osteopathy, optometry, podiatry, and pharmacy.

The Morosky College of Health Professions and Sciences recently relocated to the Robert H. Morosky Academic Center. This 99,000-square-foot facility includes classrooms, labs, and faculty offices. It also includes a 5,800-square-foot state-of-the-art Patient Simulation Center.

The College of Engineering and Business offers degrees in a variety of areas. Students may choose from majors in bioinformatics, chemical engineering, computer science, electrical engineering, electrical engineering (five-year co-op program), environmental engineering, management information systems, mechanical engineering, mechanical engineering (five-year co-op program), and software engineering. Business majors include accounting, advertising communications, business administration, entrepreneurship, finance, international business, management, marketing, risk management and insurance, scientific and technical sales, and sports management and marketing. All business students are required to participate in an internship before graduation.

The associate degree program offers Associate of Science and Associate of Arts degrees. Areas of study in which students may major are accounting, business administration, criminal justice, early childhood education, legal studies, radiologic sciences, and respiratory care.

Academic Programs

Each undergraduate program has its own sequence of requirements. Students in all programs must complete credits in liberal studies. A faculty adviser is assigned to each student to assist with academic planning. A department chairperson and faculty adviser also assist each student in selecting courses that fulfill requirements and best meet the student's desired career objectives. The basic graduation requirements for bachelor's degree candidates are 128 credit hours, including completion of requirements for their major and the liberal studies program. To earn an associate degree, students must usually complete 60 to 68 credit hours, depending on the program. Students may receive credit through the Advanced Placement Program.

Gannon offers a program for students with learning disabilities (PSLD) and an Army ROTC program that is open to interested students.

Gannon's academic calendar consists of two full semesters, running from August to December and from January to May. There are also optional summer classes.

Academic Facilities

The Nash Library currently has more than 250,000 bound volumes. The library subscribes to more than 1,000 periodicals and has book and periodical materials on various forms of microfilms and microcards. The wireless library contains a personal computer lab; a lecture room; a curriculum library; the Founder's Room for fine and rare books; the Cyber Café, containing personal computers, laptop ports, and cappuccino and juice machines; lounges; study rooms; typing rooms; an information-retrieval system; a TV studio; the latest audiovisual and tape equipment; and a multimedia studio classroom. In addition, students may use the facilities and resources of the Erie County Law Library and the Erie County Library. For specialized research projects, an efficient interlibrary loan service is available.

The A. J. Palumbo Academic Center houses the College of Humanities, Education and Social Sciences. It offers some of the finest laboratories, technology, and classrooms available today. From education to criminal justice and foreign language programs, the faculty members and facilities in Palumbo provide high-quality education. The University's Honors Program also has a home in the Palumbo Center.

The Zurn Science Center has laboratories for research in biology, anatomy, physics, chemistry, and engineering. The building also houses an open engineering computer lab as well as additional computer labs for student use. There are numerous classrooms and two auditoriums in the building. Among other University facilities are additional classroom buildings, a radio station, and a theater. All academic buildings are wireless.

Costs

For 2009–10, full-time tuition was $11,525 per semester ($12,220 for engineering and health sciences), or $23,050 per academic year ($24,440 for engineering and health sciences). Tuition for part-time students was $715 per credit hour. Room and board were approximately $4545 per semester. The total cost for the academic year at Gannon was between $23,256 and $24,646 for commuting students and $32,345 and $33,530 for resident students, depending on the program of study.

Financial Aid

In order to bring a Gannon education to qualified students who could not otherwise afford it, the University offers an integrated financial aid program of scholarships, grants, loans, and employment. Gannon's financial aid program is open to all full-time students attending classes during the period from August to May. It is highly recommended that all students seeking financial aid should file the admissions and financial aid applications no later than March 15. Numerous scholarship opportunities are available including the full-tuition Valedictorian Award and the Founders Scholarship.

Faculty

Gannon's faculty consists of 200 lay and religious men and women, and 72 percent of the full-time faculty members have either doctoral or terminal degrees. The student-faculty ratio is about 14:1, and there are approximately 25 students in each class. Most faculty members assist in the faculty adviser program, giving each student individual attention and counseling on academic and personal matters.

Student Government

The Student Government Association (SGA) is composed of students elected by members of their class. Through the SGA, students can play a responsible role in the planning and working of the University. SGA has voting representatives on all of the standing committees of the University. Members of the SGA not only research existing policies and problems, they also look for new ways to improve the academic life of students. The SGA also plans social events for the student body.

Admission Requirements

Gannon University actively recruits students of all races, creeds, and ages from all geographic regions. Transfer and international students are encouraged to seek admission. Applicants are required to submit scores (including senior-year scores) on either the SAT or ACT; an up-to-date transcript of the high school record, showing rank in class (plus a college transcript for transfer applicants); a completed application form; and a nonrefundable $25 fee. Admission decisions are based upon numerous factors, central of which is the strength of the high school record, as demonstrated through grades and relative class standing and SAT and/or ACT scores and other test scores that may be available. Recommendations and personal statements also affect admission decisions. Transfer and international students should check with the admissions office for special application procedures.

Application and Information

Students applying for admission in the fall semester should start the application process at the beginning of their senior year in high school. Gannon operates on a rolling admissions basis, which means that there is no deadline for filing applications, with the exceptions of the LECOM (Lake Erie College of Osteopathic Medicine) and PCOM (Philadelphia College of Osteopathic Medicine) 4+4 Medical Programs and the accelerated pharmacy options, which have a deadline of January 15 for the fall semester. Due to the competitiveness of the program, students who are interested in the physician's assistant studies program are highly encouraged to file their applications in September. Early applications are recommended, as are enrollment deposits.

For further information, students should contact:

Office of Admissions
Gannon University
109 University Square
Erie, Pennsylvania 16541
Phone: 814-871-7240
800-GANNON-U (426-6668, toll-free)
Fax: 814-871-5803
E-mail: admissions@gannon.edu
Web site: http://www.gannon.edu

Gannon University's faculty advisers are always available to help students chart their personal, educational, and professional accomplishments and potential.

GARDNER-WEBB UNIVERSITY

BOILING SPRINGS, NORTH CAROLINA

Gardner-Webb University

The University

Gardner-Webb University was founded in 1905 as a private high school by a group of Baptist associations. It became a junior college in 1928, was renamed Gardner-Webb College in 1942 in honor of former governor O. Max Gardner, and became a fully accredited senior college in 1971. Gardner-Webb moved to university status in 1993. Gardner-Webb's mission is to provide a high-quality liberal arts education in a Christian environment while inspiring a love of learning, service, and leadership. The most outstanding characteristics of the University are its Christian environment, sense of community, and proven record of academic distinction. Its origins are obviously deep in Christian tradition, which is exemplified in the lives of staff and faculty members. Because the University is small, students can be well known by a large percentage of the faculty and administration members. The cosmopolitan student body (more than 3,800 men and women, of whom nearly 2,700 are undergraduates) represents thirty states and thirty other countries and gives an added, valuable dimension to a student's educational experience.

The heritage of the University is reflected in its beautiful landscape and stately brick buildings. However, the University is constantly forging ahead with advanced technology and state-of-the-art facilities. There are several social and service clubs on campus, including the Webb Spinners drama club, Fellowship of Christian Athletes (FCA), Campus Ministries United, student government, and various university and student committees. There are many extracurricular activities for those who are interested; an Army ROTC program, intramurals, and the GWU Marching Band provide strong outlets for student involvement on campus. The Student Entertainment Association offers a full program of social events and entertainment. The Gardner-Webb Theatre offers a full season of plays. There are a student newspaper, a literary magazine, a television studio, and a campus radio station. Students may also participate in community projects or in various kinds of off-campus ministries, including those to the deaf and to prison inmates.

The Master of Arts degree is awarded in elementary education, English, English education, mental health counseling, middle school education, school administration, school counseling, and sport and science pedagogy. Gardner-Webb also offers the following degrees: a Master of Business Administration, International Master of Business Administration, Master of Accounting, Master of Science in Nursing, Master of Divinity, Doctor of Ministry, and Doctor of Education.

There are over 20 intramural sports in which all students are urged to participate, including basketball, racquetball, softball, tennis, touch football, volleyball, and others. Intercollegiate sports include baseball, basketball, cross-country running, football, golf, soccer, softball, swimming, tennis, track and field, volleyball, and wrestling. A modern physical education building, an indoor heated pool, and an athletic field amply accommodate these programs. A wellness center and an Alpine Tower are available for student use.

The Program for the Blind at Gardner-Webb University has been developed to allow students with visual handicaps to receive a liberal arts education. Special support services and job opportunities are provided for every entering student who is visually impaired.

The Degree Program for the Deaf provides interpreters, note takers, and tutors who are skilled in sign language so that hearing-impaired students have full access to all University programs.

Location

The University is located at the foot of the beautiful Blue Ridge Mountains in Boiling Springs, North Carolina, a university town of about 3,000 people. The campus comprises 250 acres of land in an area of gently rolling, wooded hills. Nine miles away is Shelby, a town of about 30,000 people. There are a Greater Shelby Community Theatre and a Community Concert Series, and restaurants abound in the area. Charlotte, an area of about 400,000 people only 50 miles away, offers many other opportunities for cultural, social, and recreational activities. Several nearby lakes and Asheville and Beech Mountain, an hour and a half away in the heart of the mountains, provide facilities for summer and winter sports. Greenville, South Carolina, is 55 miles away and Spartanburg, 36 miles. Shelby is served by Greyhound-Trailways bus lines, and the Charlotte airport is served by major airlines. Interstate 85 is only 15 miles away, and Highway 74 runs through Shelby.

Majors and Degrees

The degrees of Bachelor of Arts, Bachelor of Fine Arts, Bachelor of Music, Bachelor of Science, and Associate in Arts are offered. Fields of concentration are available in the following subjects: accounting, American sign language, athletic training, biology, business administration, chemistry, communications, computer science, elementary education, English, environmental science, finance, French, health/wellness, history, international business, interpreter training, management information systems, mathematics, middle grades education, music, nursing, physical education, physician assistant studies, political science, psychology, public relations, religion, sacred music, social sciences, sociology, Spanish, sports management, theater arts, and visual arts.

Preprofessional programs are available in dentistry, law, medicine, ministry, pharmacy, and veterinary medicine.

Academic Programs

The total program is marked by flexibility for the student but encourages, through active faculty advisement, choosing a substantial course of study. Elements of the humanities, the social and physical sciences, and mathematics or related disciplines must be taken. A typical bachelor's degree program requires 128 semester hours for graduation: 59 to 63 in the core (humanities and social and physical sciences), 36 in the major, and 39 to 42 in supporting subjects and free electives. Requirements for science curricula vary somewhat. The associate degree requires the completion of 64 semester hours. A cumulative average of C (2.0 on a 4.0 scale) or better is required for graduation.

Gardner-Webb grants advanced placement and credit on the basis of the College-Level Examination Program (CLEP), the Advanced Placement (AP) tests of the College Board, and the International Baccalaureate Program.

Off-Campus Programs

Students in the Departments of Business, Fine Arts, Foreign Languages and Literature, and Religious Studies and Philosophy are given the opportunity to enrich their educational experiences through travel and study in Europe, Latin America, the Holy Land, and other destinations.

Academic Facilities

The University's library currently holds 250,000 volumes. There are fully equipped biology, chemistry, and physics laboratories as well as computer and learning-assistance laboratories. A special events/convocation center houses a theater and an athletics arena. The University also has a 50,000-watt FM stereo radio station.

Costs

Costs for the 2009–10 academic year are $20,780 for tuition and $6810 for room and board. Part-time tuition is $345 per semester hour for 1 to 9 hours. Books and supplies average $800 to $1000 per year.

Financial Aid

Gardner-Webb University makes available to its students a variety of scholarships, loans, grants-in-aid, and work-study awards. Prospective applicants with financial need should contact the financial aid director early in their senior year of high school for a financial need estimate. Applications received after April 1 can be considered only in terms of available funds. An applicant must be accepted for admission before being awarded aid. Students should file the Free Application for Federal Student Aid (FAFSA). Scholarships and other types of aid include academic awards, Christian service awards, endowed scholarships, and annual scholarships. There are several Gardner-Webb loan funds. The University also administers aid from the full range of federal programs: Federal Pell Grants, Federal Work-Study Program awards, Federal Perkins Loans, and federally guaranteed Federal Stafford Student Loans and Federal PLUS loans. North Carolina students have access to state grant funds administered by the University. Scholarships based on academic promise are also granted each year. Of all students, 90 percent receive aid in some form. The two criteria for receiving financial aid are financial need and academic promise.

Faculty

The faculty-student ratio is 1:13. Faculty members engage both formally and informally in student advising and counseling. A staff of professional counselors is also available. Faculty members teach at all class levels without regard to academic rank or length of service. Graduate assistants are not used to teach classes.

Student Government

The University has a student government whose members are elected by the student body. This organization, which is set up with executive, legislative, and judicial branches, is very influential in campus affairs. In addition, students have voting positions on all standing committees of the University.

Admission Requirements

Although a fixed pattern of high school credits is not prescribed, the following minimum course distribution is recommended: 4 units in English, 2 in a foreign language, 2 in social science, 2 in algebra, 1 in geometry, and 2 in natural science, plus electives. The University requires each applicant to submit an application form, a high school transcript, and SAT or ACT scores. Acceptance to Gardner-Webb is based on the applicant's high school record, rank in class, SAT or ACT scores, and extracurricular activities. Transfer students' course credits are evaluated on courses as credit only, not on grade point average. An interview is recommended but not mandatory.

Gardner-Webb admits students of any race, color, and national or ethnic origin to all the rights, privileges, programs, and activities generally accorded or made available to students at the University.

Application and Information

Applications, together with a nonrefundable $40 application fee, may be submitted for either semester. Students may also apply online at http://www.gardner-webb.edu. Early application is advised. Notification of the admission decision is given on a rolling basis upon receipt of all application data. A $150 room deposit for boarding students is due thirty days after acceptance and is refundable until May 1. A $50 deposit is required of commuting students.

For further information, students should contact:

Office of Undergraduate Admissions
Gardner-Webb University
Boiling Springs, North Carolina 28017
Phone: 704-406-4498
800-253-6472 (toll-free)
Web site: http://www.gardner-webb.edu

Gardner-Webb University seeks a higher ground in education—one that embraces faith and intellectual freedom, balances conviction with compassion, and inspires in students a love of learning, service, and leadership. Gardner-Webb University has great things in mind—for its students and the world.

COLLEGE CLOSE-UPS

THE GEORGE WASHINGTON UNIVERSITY

WASHINGTON, D.C.

THE GEORGE WASHINGTON UNIVERSITY WASHINGTON DC

The University

Located just four blocks from the White House, The George Washington University (GW) is the largest institution of higher education in the nation's capital. Founded in 1821 by an Act of Congress, GW is a private nonsectarian coeducational institution accredited by the Middle States Association of Colleges and Universities. GW prides itself in being at the forefront of major research endeavors, while providing a stimulating intellectual environment for its diverse students and faculty members.

The student population at GW consists of approximately 9,700 undergraduates and 10,000 graduates. Undergraduates hail from all fifty states, the District of Columbia, Puerto Rico, the Virgin Islands, and 125 countries. The undergraduate student body is 11 percent Asian American, 6 percent African American, 7 percent Hispanic American, and 6 percent international.

Both the Foggy Bottom and Mount Vernon campuses are located in historical and prestigious D.C. neighborhoods. The Foggy Bottom campus is situated in the heart of downtown D.C., neighbored by the Kennedy Center, the Watergate complex, the State Department, and the White House. The 26-acre Mount Vernon campus is home to athletic facilities and is surrounded by embassy and diplomatic residences. Both campus communities offer vibrant and distinctive residential options to freshmen and continuing students.

GW guarantees housing for entering freshmen and sophomores and houses approximately 70 percent of undergraduates in thirty-two residence halls. GW offers a number of living arrangements, including apartment-style living for upperclassmen and residential town houses. GW's community living and learning philosophy guarantees that residence hall life is a valuable extension of the undergraduate experience. With 100 percent of the entering class living in University housing, the atmosphere proves to be academically as well as socially stimulating.

GW hosts a strong intercollegiate varsity athletic program with twenty-two teams participating in the NCAA Division I and Atlantic 10 Conference. They include men's baseball, basketball, crew, cross-country, golf, soccer, swimming, tennis, and water polo, and women's basketball, crew, cross-country, gymnastics, soccer, swimming and diving, tennis, volleyball, and water polo. Students interested in playing sports, but not quite up to the varsity level, may join a number of University-supported club and intramural sports.

There are more than 350 student-created and student-run organizations at GW. These organizations run the spectrum from academic to cultural, spiritual to recreational, and political to artistic. In addition to these special-interest organizations, GW is home to twenty-eight national sororities and fraternities and nineteen honor societies, the Student Association (details in the Student Government section), the Program Board, the *Hatchet* (GW's independent newspaper), and WRGW (the campus radio station). The Student Activities Center plans large-scale events for students on campus, ranging from Welcome Week to Excellence in Student Life Awards to Fall Fest and Fountain Fling.

Location

Many students at GW also choose to immerse themselves in the excitement of Washington, which has been called the most livable city on the East Coast. Washington, D.C., offers an infinite array of internships and cooperative education experiences, allowing GW students to explore their career aspirations outside of the four walls of the classroom. GW students have interned at the White House, the World Bank, IBM, the U.S. House of Representatives and Senate, NASA, the National Zoo, and CNN, among many other world famous organizations.

The hordes of tourists that flock to Washington, D.C., every year experience the vibrant college town and young professional social scene in the nation's capital. There are more than 400,000 college students at forty-four colleges and universities concentrated in the metropolitan area.

Majors and Degrees

GW offers a wide range of undergraduate programs in six undergraduate schools: the Columbian College of Arts and Sciences, the Elliott School of International Affairs, the School of Business, the School of Engineering and Applied Science, the School of Medicine and Health Sciences, and the School of Public Health and Health Services.

GW offers eighty-seven majors, more than 1,000 courses, and yet, the average class size is only 28. Students may earn an undergraduate degree in a single field of study, or they may choose to double major, major in one field and minor in another, participate in an interdisciplinary program, or create their own individualized field of study.

The University awards an array of bachelor's degrees, including Bachelor of Arts (B.A.), Bachelor of Science (B.S.), Bachelor of Accountancy (B.Accy.), and Bachelor of Business Administration (B.B.A.).

Several joint-degree programs are available to undergraduates. In addition to a seven-year B.A/M.D. program, the University offers seventeen 5-year B.A./M.A. programs.

Academic Programs

Most undergraduate students must complete 120 credit hours to be eligible for graduation, which means that the average student carries 15 credit hours (five courses) per semester. All students at GW are required to participate in the University's writing program. In addition, each school has general curriculum requirements, ranging from 17 to 45 credit hours.

GW is home to nineteen honor societies, including Phi Beta Kappa and Golden Key National Honor Society. GW offers a variety of specialized academic programs. The University Honors Program, which does not replace a regular program of study but rather enhances it with intellectually challenging analysis and discussion, consists of approximately 500 undergraduates.

The seven-year Integrated B.A./M.D. Program is designed for students who wish to obtain a strong foundation in the liberal arts prior to becoming physicians, enabling them to accomplish that goal in a shorter amount of time than a traditional program of study. The Integrated Engineering and Law Program offers highly qualified high school students the opportunity to earn a B.S. degree in engineering or computer science, and a J.D. degree in order to launch successful careers in such fields as patent law, intellectual property rights, and environmental law.

Off-Campus Programs

GW students are encouraged to study abroad in order to expand their world view and their educational opportunities. GW offers study abroad centers in Madrid, Paris, and England, as well as affiliated and exchange programs. Each year, more than 1,000 GW undergraduates study abroad in nearly fifty countries.

Many GW students also take advantage of cooperative education (co-op), which provides students with an opportunity to gain valuable paid work experiences directly related to their major. The Career Center manages the program, in partnership with area employers, to ensure that co-op experiences are substantive and well-supervised. Similarly, most GW students engage in internships, which serve as a means for students to gain practical, professional experience and to augment their academic knowledge. Internships can be paid or unpaid, offered for academic credit, and can last for as long (or short) as the student and employer choose. The Career Center also acts as a clearinghouse for internship positions.

Academic Facilities

The Gelman Library houses more than 2 million volumes and, as a member of the Washington Research Library Consortium (WRLC), offers GW students access to more than 6 million volumes at eight area universities. Gelman Library is open 168 hours per week offering 24-hour study lounges, group discussion rooms, computer labs, walk-up reference consultation, and an interlibrary loan service. GW provides on-site and remote access to ALADIN, the shared online catalogue of WRLC libraries, plus databases indexing periodical articles and some full-text journals. GW is also home to the Eckles Library, the Jacob Burns Law Library, and the Himmelfarb Health Sciences Library.

GW is infused with the latest, state-of-the-art facilities enhancing campus life. Completed and planned projects include a new hospital, the Elliott School of International Affairs classroom and residential complex, the School of Business, the stunning 400-bed Ivory Tower residence hall, Potomac House, a 700-bed freshman residence hall, the Science and Engineering Complex, and Pelham Hall, a 287-bed suite-style residence hall for first-year and upperclass students with multimedia studios, a black box theater, and a fitness center.

Costs

In response to family concerns about paying for college, GW has instituted a fixed tuition plan. Under this plan, the tuition remains the same each year for students who remain enrolled in full-time status during their undergraduate programs. Therefore, except for marginal increases in housing costs, cost of attendance will not rise. Students who entered in fall 2009 have tuition costs of $41,610 per year for four years. Room and board costs are approximately $10,120.

Financial Aid

The ability to finance a GW education is a priority, so the Office of Student Financial Assistance seeks to assist students and their families in meeting the costs to attend the University. The University budgets more than $133 million for undergraduate financial assistance, which includes scholarships and need-based assistance. In addition, GW offers families the opportunity to participate in a number of payment plans.

By applying for admission, students with outstanding academic credentials are automatically considered for Presidential Academic Scholarships. Approximately 24 percent of freshmen receive merit-based financial assistance. In addition, approximately 60 percent of GW's students receive need-based assistance with an average package of over $27,000.

The Presidential Scholars in the Arts Program awards scholarships to, and encourages the work of, entering freshmen who have shown promise in the fine arts (ceramics, design, drawing, painting, photography, and sculpture), music, theater, technical theater, directing, dance, and choreography.

More information about financial aid at GW can be obtained online at http://www.gwu.edu. Both merit scholarships and a portion of need-based financial aid are guaranteed for all four years for students who remain enrolled in full-time status during their undergraduate program.

Faculty

There is 1 faculty member for every 14 students at GW. Ninety-two percent of GW's full-time faculty members hold a doctoral degree. Part-time and adjunct faculty members are often leaders in their fields of expertise. GW professors are engaging, eminently qualified, and well connected, which allows for a robust intellectual community.

Student Government

The Student Association (SA) is an organization chartered by GW's Board of Trustees to represent students and their concerns. Any person registered for any academic credit at GW is a member of the SA. The SA undertakes initiatives related to academics, community service, neighborhood relations, and student activities.

Admission Requirements

GW receives approximately 21,000 applications for freshman admission and aims to recruit a class of 2,350. Admitted students have strong academic records and the demonstrated ability to achieve success in their college endeavors. To be considered for admission, applicants must submit the following credentials: application and fee, high school transcripts, essay, letters of recommendation from a teacher and a guidance counselor, and either SAT or ACT scores. Details can be obtained online at http://www.gwu.edu. GW also accepts the Common Application, with the GW supplement to the Common Application. Freshman interviews are not required, but may be helpful.

Application and Information

GW has a number of application options: regular decision, early decision I, and early decision II. Prospective students should consult the Web site (http://www.gwu.edu) for the application and deadlines.

Office of Admissions
The George Washington University
2121 I Street, NW, Suite 201
Washington, D.C. 20052
Phone: 202-994-6040
E-mail: gwadm@gwu.edu
Web site: http://www.gwu.edu

Students on campus at The George Washington University.

COLLEGE CLOSE-UPS

GEORGIAN COURT UNIVERSITY

LAKEWOOD, NEW JERSEY

The University

Georgian Court University (GCU) was founded in 1908 by the Sisters of Mercy, and for more than 100 years has helped students of all faiths and backgrounds realize their dreams of a high-quality, affordable private education. Georgian Court, the only Mercy University in New Jersey and one of only two Catholic universities in the state, incorporates the Mercy core values of respect, integrity, compassion, service, and justice in every aspect of the student experience. Mercy values are a distinctive part of a Georgian Court University education.

Georgian Court University's strong liberal arts foundation offers students a personalized and supportive learning environment within a technologically advanced university setting. With a student body of 3,023 and an average class size of just 14, GCU students are able to work closely with faculty members who are leaders in their respective fields, including neurobiology, biochemistry, school administration, music, business and industry, criminal justice, and history.

A National Historic Landmark, the stunning 156-acre campus borders Lake Carasaljo in suburban Lakewood, New Jersey, and is distinguished by impressive Georgian architecture, prompting its name, Georgian Court. With magnificent statuary, lush gardens, and close proximity to the popular Jersey Shore, GCU is truly an inspiring place to learn, study, and live.

Georgian Court University students can choose from among thirty undergraduate programs—including four new majors in dance; exercise science, wellness, and sports; nursing; and tourism, hospitality, and recreation management—offered through GCU's two highly regarded colleges, the Women's College and University College.

The Women's College at Georgian Court University is dedicated to the success of women, both personally and professionally. The college offers a comprehensive liberal arts education with an emphasis on building strong women leaders who excel in their careers; contribute to the greater good of their communities, state, and nation; and can approach any obstacle with confidence. Studies show that students at women's colleges like GCU develop high self-esteem, participate fully in and out of the classroom, and enjoy success in their careers. The Women's College is open to both residential and commuter students.

The University College encompasses GCU's coeducational, nonresidential graduate programs and certificates, as well as over sixteen undergraduate programs geared to nontraditional learners—students whose family obligations, hectic employment schedules, and other commitments leave them limited time to attend class. University College features flexible scheduling, technology-enhanced courses, and convenient locations, while upholding the high caliber of education expected of GCU. University College programs are offered in the evening at the GCU main campus in Lakewood and during the day and evening at GCU at Woodbridge, GCU at Cumberland County College, and GCU at the New Jersey Coastal Communiversity in Wall.

Residents and commuters alike enjoy a variety of activities, including trips to museums, theater events, and concerts. GCU offers a wide variety of clubs and special interest organizations, in addition to the Student Government Association, and sixteen academic honor societies. GCU's Learning-Living Communities bring together students who are interested in a special topic—international cultures, the arts, outdoor adventures—for discussion groups, lectures, and off-campus experiences.

Committed to empowering students through education, GCU fosters academic leadership through the honors program, while professional growth is nurtured through Women in Leadership Development (WILD), an innovative program that cultivates the students' professional skills through hands-on workshops and seminars led by notable professional women who are leaders in business, education, and government.

The University also participates in eight NCAA Division II sports: basketball, cross-country, lacrosse, soccer, softball, tennis, track and field, and volleyball.

In fall 2008, Georgian Court debuted its highly anticipated $26-million Wellness Center. The 64,000-square-foot, eco-friendly building has a 1,200-seat arena to support the basketball, volleyball, and physical education programs; an exercise science laboratory and offices to support the new exercise science, wellness and sports major; professional dance studios to support the new dance major; a fitness center, a fifty-seat classroom, and the GCU bookstore. Outside the Wellness Center are state-of-the-art athletic fields for softball, soccer, and lacrosse, an eight-lane track, and tennis courts.

There are three residence halls on campus: Maria Hall, St. Joseph Hall, and St. Catherine Hall, as well as a new chapel, a residence hall for visiting faculty members and Sisters of Mercy, and the Gilded Age mansion, now home to a series of interactive history theater productions.

Location

Georgian Court University is located in Lakewood, New Jersey, a suburban town midway between the urban excitement of New York City and Philadelphia, and only minutes from the spectacular beaches of the Jersey Shore. The campus is easily accessible from Route 9, the Garden State Parkway, and Interstate 195. New Jersey Transit bus access is within walking distance, giving students quick, inexpensive transportation to points of interest throughout the tristate area.

Majors and Degrees

The three prestigious schools of Georgian Court University—the School of Arts and Sciences, the School of Business, and the School of Education—are seamlessly integrated into both the Women's College and University College. GCU regularly reviews its academic offerings, based on recommendations from faculty members, students, and industry and community leaders.

The Bachelor of Arts is awarded in applied arts and sciences, art, biology, chemistry, communications, criminal justice, dance, elementary education, English, history, humanities, mathematics, music, physics, psychology, sociology, and Spanish. The Bachelor of Science is awarded in accounting; allied health technologies; biochemistry; biology; business administration; chemistry; clinical laboratory sciences; exercise science, wellness, and sports; natural sciences; nursing; tourism, hospitality, and recreation management; and physics. Students planning a career in social work may earn a Bachelor of Social Work, and future fine and graphic artists may participate in the Bachelor of Fine Arts program.

There are more than fifty minor field sequences, certification programs, and concentrations available, including anthropology, bilingual/bicultural studies, coaching women athletes, communications, criminal justice, economics, English as a second language, general fine art, gerontology, graphic design/illustration, holistic health, human resource management, marketing, medical technology, nuclear medicine technology, philosophy, political science, pre–physical therapy, toxicology, and more. Preprofessional programs include chiropractic, dentistry, law, medicine, and veterinary medicine. Interdisciplinary minors are offered in international area studies, Latin American studies, and women's studies. Internships and practicums are offered in most majors, and independent study is available.

Academic Programs

A Georgian Court University education is holistic, developing students in mind, body, and spirit. A well-rounded, wide-ranging liberal arts education is intellectually rigorous, and participating in service learning develops the spirit. With this dual approach, GCU graduates become successful professionals as well as compassionate neighbors, concerned citizens, and ethical civic leaders.

The undergraduate curriculum is designed to capitalize on the student's college preparation as well as embrace the aptitudes, talents, and interests of the individual. Service learning opportunities, such as working hand in hand with Honduran villagers to build a new school or install clean water systems, or helping disadvantaged segments of society in Lakewood to access social services, challenge GCU students to put classroom learning into action.

Candidates for a bachelor's degree at Georgian Court must complete 120 credit hours. With departmental approval, students may elect a second major. Elementary education majors are required to choose a second liberal arts major. A minimum cumulative GPA of 2.0 and a minimum cumulative major GPA of 2.5 are required for graduation.

Georgian Court University hosts more than sixteen chapters of national honor societies in biology, business administration, chemistry, education, English, mathematics, physics, psychology, social work, and sociology.

Off-Campus Programs

In addition to offering students opportunities to study abroad, Georgian Court University offers joint-degree programs allowing students to take courses at GCU and at a partner institution, such as the University of Medicine and Dentistry of New Jersey.

Academic Facilities

The Arts and Science Center is Georgian Court's largest academic building, providing classrooms, seminar rooms, offices, art studios, and a computer lab. The state-of-the-art Audrey Birish George Science Center offers the latest laboratory and instruction space for scientific study.

Other campus buildings include the Sister Mary Joseph Cunningham Library, the Raymond Hall Complex, which houses the School of Education, the Raymond Hall Computer Center, and the GCU Dining Hall. The School of Business and the Department of Psychology reside in Farley Center, which includes a computer lab, student lounge, and conference center. The newest building on campus is the Wellness Center, which offers state-of-the-art spaces for hands-on learning.

Costs

Full-time tuition for the 2009–10 academic year was $23,246. Residence and board for the Women's College were $9386. Full-time undergraduate fees were $1244. Instructional materials (textbooks and other items) cost extra and vary depending on the course.

Financial Aid

As a private university, Georgian Court strives to keep the cost of attendance affordable. Ninety-nine percent of first-year, full-time students at GCU receive financial aid in the form of scholarships, grants, loans, and work-study. The average financial aid package for a first-year student is $25,240. GCU also offers the Women's Leadership Award, a $2500 grant given to qualified full-time resident students in recognition of outstanding leadership and service to school, community, or church. It also participates in the New Jersey Educational Opportunity Fund. To be considered for financial aid, candidates must submit a Free Application for Federal Student Aid (FAFSA) to the Office of Financial Aid online at http://www.fafsa.ed.gov.

Faculty

Eighty-seven percent of the full-time faculty members hold doctoral degrees. From the freshman year on, students have the opportunity to take classes taught by department chairs, even school deans. Georgian Court features a student-faculty ratio of 15:1 and an average class size of 14. This promotes individual attention and open, thoughtful discourse among students and professors. All students receive individual counseling by a faculty adviser.

Student Government

The Student Government Association, composed of elected students, organizes extracurricular activities, charity fund-raisers, and other events. Through the student government structure, students take leadership roles in shaping student life and participate in all major University committees, alongside members of the faculty and administration.

Admission Requirements

Georgian Court University welcomes applications from qualified students of all faiths and backgrounds who desire a liberal arts education. The University strives to enroll students who can benefit most from its academic program. Entrance is based on individual merit. The high school record of achievement is of primary importance and must reflect solid performance. Candidates for admission must have completed 16 academic (Carnegie) units. The majority of students at Georgian Court ranked in the upper half of their senior high school class.

Submission of SAT or ACT scores is optional. Further consideration is given to the applicant's extracurricular activities and the letters of recommendation submitted by teachers, counselors, employers, or similarly qualified people. A campus interview is highly recommended, and a guided tour of the campus is available at the interview.

Qualified applicants whose first choice is Georgian Court University and who apply no later than November 15 may be considered for early decision. A mature, well-qualified student who wishes to enter the University after three years of high school may apply for early entrance.

Transfer students are accepted into the freshman, sophomore, and junior classes for fall and spring semesters. All transfer applicants must be in good standing at their previous college. Applicants with fewer than 24 credits must fulfill all requirements for admission to the freshman class. International students in need of a student visa must present official documents at least six months prior to the semester start and must have a minimum TOEFL score of 550 on the paper-based test or 213 on the computer-based test. International students must also complete a GCU financial support form and should be prepared to assume full financial responsibility for their educational and personal expenses in the United States.

Application and Information

To apply for admission, first-time freshman applicants should send an application, high school transcript, and nonrefundable $40 application fee payable to Georgian Court University to the Office of Admissions. Transfer students should submit those materials as well as transcripts from all colleges previously attended. Freshman applicants are urged to submit an application as early as possible during their senior year of high school. Completed applications must be received by August 1 for the fall semester and December 15 for the spring semester. Printable and electronic applications are available at http://www.georgian.edu. Schedules and registration for campus visits are available at http://www.georgian.edu/admissions.

For further information, prospective students should contact:

Office of Admissions
Georgian Court University
900 Lakewood Avenue
Lakewood, New Jersey 08701-2697
Phone: 732-987-2760
800-458-8422 Ext. 2760 (toll-free)
Fax: 732-987-2000
E-mail: admissions@georgian.edu
Web site: http://www.georgian.edu/admissions

Georgian Court University students.

GONZAGA UNIVERSITY

SPOKANE, WASHINGTON

The University

Founded in 1887, Gonzaga is an independent, comprehensive university with a distinguished background in the Catholic, Jesuit, and humanistic tradition. Gonzaga emphasizes the moral and ethical implications of learning, living, and working in today's global society. As a testament to this educational approach, Gonzaga's first-to-second-year retention rate tops 90 percent. Through the University Core Curriculum, each student develops a strong liberal arts foundation, which many alumni cite as a valuable asset. In addition, students choose from more than seventy-five academic areas of study in which to specialize.

Gonzaga's 120-acre campus is characterized by sprawling green lawns and majestic evergreen trees. Towering above the campus are the stately spires of St. Aloysius Church, the well-recognized landmark featured in the University logo.

Because personal growth is as important as intellectual development, Gonzaga places great emphasis on student life outside the classroom. Ranging in population size from 35 to 361 students and offering both coed and single-sex living, Gonzaga's eighteen residence halls and seven apartment complexes offer an intimate atmosphere and a lively campus experience. Each hall has one or more Residence Assistants and a chaplain or a resident Jesuit. While freshmen and sophomores are required to live on campus, 40 percent of the upperclass students also reside in Gonzaga's halls and apartments. Campus-based activities ranging from residence hall government to current affairs symposiums to intramural sports keep students informed and entertained. Students in all academic majors integrate with the Spokane community through a variety of activities, such as volunteer opportunities and internships at numerous businesses and agencies. Gonzaga provides both career and counseling centers.

Gonzaga enrolls approximately 7,229 students, of whom about 4,517 are undergraduates. About 46 percent of the students come from Washington State, with forty-seven other states and fifty-four other countries also represented. In addition to its undergraduate colleges and schools, Gonzaga University offers about twenty master's programs, a doctoral program in leadership studies, and a School of Law.

Location

Located along the banks of the Spokane River in a quiet, turn-of-the-century neighborhood, Gonzaga University is just a 15-minute walk from downtown Spokane, a city with a metropolitan-area population of 462,677. Spokane's beautiful 125-acre Riverfront Park, in the heart of downtown, lies near the INB Performing Arts Center, Spokane Convention Center, and Spokane Arena. Fine restaurants, a twenty-screen AMC movie theater, and an assortment of shops and department stores, many of which can be reached through a convenient, weatherproof skywalk system, are also in the city's core. For mall shoppers, the Northtown Mall is a 10-minute drive from the campus. Easily accessible outdoor recreation activities, such as skiing, golfing, hiking, biking, camping, and rock climbing, add excitement for the avid outdoorsperson.

Majors and Degrees

Gonzaga's undergraduate school awards the B.A., B.B.A., B.E., B.Ed., B.S., B.S.C.E., B.S.Cp.E., B.S.G.E., B.S.E.E., B.S.M.E., and B.S.N. degrees. Majors offered in the College of Arts and Sciences are applied communication studies, art, biochemistry, biology (research option), broadcast and electronic media studies, chemistry, classical civilizations, criminal justice, economics, English (writing track option), environmental studies, French, history, integrated studies, international studies (including international relations and Asian, European, and Latin American studies), Italian studies, journalism, mathematics, mathematics/computer science, music (including composition, education, general studies, jazz, and performance), philosophy (Kossel track option), physics, political science, psychology, public relations, religious studies, sociology, Spanish, and theater arts.

The School of Business Administration, which is accredited by AACSB International–The Association to Advance Collegiate Schools of Business, offers a Bachelor of Business Administration degree with a major in accounting or a major in business administration, with concentrations in economics, entrepreneurship, finance, human resource management, individualized study, international business, law and public policy, management information systems, marketing, and operations and supply chain management.

As well as granting teacher certification on both the elementary and secondary levels, the School of Education offers degrees in physical education, special education, and sport management.

The School of Engineering and Applied Science awards Bachelor of Science degrees in civil, computer, electrical, and mechanical engineering, as well as computer science and engineering management. The engineering management program includes numerous business courses and also allows attainment of the M.B.A. in five years of study. The civil, computer, electrical, and mechanical programs are accredited by the Engineering Accreditation Commission of the Accreditation Board for Engineering and Technology, Inc. (EAC/ABET).

The School of Professional Studies offers degrees in human physiology and nursing.

Academic Programs

Gonzaga University believes that all students, regardless of their chosen major or profession, benefit from attaining an education that goes beyond specialization. Therefore, all students receive a strong liberal arts background as well as depth in their majors. The Core Curriculum is a very important component of the minimum 128 semester units a student must earn for graduation.

The Honors Program challenges exceptional students with an integrated curriculum that is compatible with any major and most double majors. Motivated and imaginative students in all majors create new ventures and seek to make a difference in the world through the Hogan Entrepreneurial Leadership Program. The Comprehensive Leadership Program, which is also open to students from all majors, allows students to fine-tune their leadership skills and knowledge while completing an academic leadership concentration. All three programs require separate applications. The Gonzaga University Summer Term (GUST) offers motivated high school students intensive course work in a variety of academic disciplines. Academic and co-curricular activities are included in the six-week session.

Credits earned through the Washington State Running Start Program or International Baccalaureate (I.B.) program are accepted on a class-by-class basis. College credit is given for certain test scores in most Advanced Placement (AP) subjects. (Please see Gonzaga's website for the most current policy.) The academic year follows a two-semester system, beginning in late August. Two summer sessions are also available.

Off-Campus Programs

Gonzaga University offers qualified students the opportunity to study abroad through programs in Australia, Benin, China, Costa Rica, Ecuador, El Salvador, England, France, Italy, Japan, Mexico, the Netherlands, Spain, Turks & Caicos, and Zambia (see http://www.GoAbroadZAGS.org for more details). As the largest and most popular program, Gonzaga-in-Florence allows approximately 100 students the opportunity to live in Italy for a year, a semester, or a summer; and to travel to many other countries and continents.

Academic Facilities

Gonzaga's "library of the future," the Ralph E. and Helen Higgins Foley Center, is a $20-million window to worldwide information resources. The library features more than 300 specialized databases, satellite capabilities, an advanced computer-controlled video editing system, a rare book room, computerized retrieval services, a wireless Internet connection, and beautiful views.

Foley Center holdings include 782,000 volumes and microform titles, with two special collections of materials that are especially rich in the areas of philosophy and classical civilization. The Foley Center also has the nation's most extensive collection of works by the famous

Jesuit poet Gerard Manley Hopkins. The School of Law maintains its own library of 130,000 volumes. The historic College Hall houses Harry & Colleen Magnuson Theatre, the computer center, a 24-hour computer lab, the University chapel, and the main administrative offices and classrooms. A student-operated FM radio station, a state-of-the-art television broadcasting studio, and the offices of the *Bulletin*, a weekly student-published newspaper, reside in the newly renovated Communications Building.

Campus computing services include more than 250 PC and Macintosh computers and Sun workstations dispersed throughout a dozen computer labs. An HP9000/K100 minicomputer provides central academic services and student electronic mail. Students have sculpted T-3 cable access to the Internet, library, and central academic services from their dorm rooms and other University facilities. All buildings on campus and open spaces are wireless-accessible. The Herak Center for Engineering and the PACCAR Center for Applied Science house a CAD/CAE center, general-purpose computer facilities, a computer cluster network array, electronics and mechanical calibration rooms, and laboratories for physics, electronics, digital electronics/circuits, microprocessors, communications/controls, computer analysis, automation and embedded systems, power, mechanical design, mechanical engineering, materials testing, manufacturing engineering, rapid prototyping, water/wastewater, geotechnical engineering, and hydrology/hydraulics. The centers also contain a large Fabrication Facility, extensive areas for the design and construction of student projects, a sensor networks and robotics lab, and a transmission and distribution electric utility lab.

Hughes Hall Life Sciences Building offers lab and classroom space for a program that is especially rich in environmental biology and student research opportunities. The Martin Athletic Centre provides a 13,000-square-foot fitness center, and the 6,000-seat McCarthey Athletic Center hosts basketball games and concerts. The Patterson Baseball Complex and Washington Trust Field is located on the south side of campus. A 23,000-square-foot addition to the Jepson Center for Business Administration houses additional classrooms, computer labs, the Ethics Institute, the Hogan Entrepreneurial Leadership Program, and a student lounge and café.

Costs

Tuition for the 2009–10 academic year was $29,200. Average room and board costs were $7976 for the year.

Financial Aid

Gonzaga University offers many different types of financial aid to qualified students, including scholarships, Federal Pell Grants, Federal Supplemental Educational Opportunity Grants, work-study jobs, Federal Perkins Loans, Federal Stafford Student Loans, and on- and off-campus employment. In order to apply for financial aid awards, a student must first be accepted by the University and must submit the Free Application for Federal Student Aid (FAFSA) by February 1. After this date, awards are made on a funds-available basis. Approximately 95 percent of the students at Gonzaga receive financial assistance, and the average award for this group (for the 2007–08 year) is $21,251 (includes all types of aid).

Faculty

The student-faculty ratio is 11:1, and the average class size is 22, allowing close, mentoring relationships to develop. All classes at Gonzaga are taught by faculty members, and faculty members also serve as academic advisers. Eight percent of the faculty members are Jesuits, and 83 percent of the 385 full-time faculty members hold the highest degree in their fields.

Student Government

The Gonzaga Student Body Association provides the means for students to participate in making decisions about student life at Gonzaga. The 5-member Executive Council, an elected board of students that administers and initiates programs, also serves as a liaison between the administration and the students. The Student Senate, a legislative body consisting of 26 senators, is responsible for sounding out the needs of the student body and directing this information to the Executive Council. Students also serve on the Board of Regents, search committees, the budget committee, and many other University committees.

Admission Requirements

Gonzaga expects freshman applicants to have taken a challenging college-preparatory curriculum and to submit strong test scores on the ACT or SAT. Transfer students who have earned at least 30 semester credits or 45 quarter credits do not need to submit a high school transcript or test scores. The admission process is selective, and applicants are considered through a pooling process. The Admissions Committee seeks motivated, well-rounded students and considers the rigor of academic study in high school in addition to grades and test scores, as well as personal characteristics, awards and activities, and an essay.

Application and Information

Gonzaga University's nonbinding Early Action deadline for admission applications is November 15. Students who meet this deadline with a complete application are notified of an admission decision by January 15. The final deadline for freshmen to apply for admission under Regular Decision is February 1. Regular Decision applicants receive an admission decision by the middle of March. Transfer students are admitted on a rolling admission basis. Transfer students seeking financial aid are encouraged to apply for admission by March 1. Otherwise, to ensure a smooth transition to Gonzaga, transfer students should apply by June 1. After June 1, the University accepts transfer applicants only if space is available. First-year students may apply by using the Common Application or Universal College Application. Transfer students can apply using the application on the Gonzaga Web site. For priority financial aid, all students are encouraged to submit the FAFSA by February 1.

All requests for further information or materials should be addressed to:

Julie McCulloh
Dean of Admission
Gonzaga University
502 E. Boone Ave.
Spokane, Washington 99258-0102
Phone: 800-322-2584 (toll-free)
E-mail: admissions@gonzaga.edu
Web site: http://www.gonzaga.edu

Gonzaga University: Education that inspires mind, body, and spirit.

GOUCHER COLLEGE

BALTIMORE, MARYLAND

The College

Goucher College is a small, private, coeducational liberal arts college, where all students are required to study abroad and where the academic program partners classroom learning with real, hands-on experience.

Since it was founded in 1885, Goucher has provided a truly global kind of education that puts learning in perspective against the events and developments of the entire world, encouraging students to test what they've learned against experience in service-learning, study-abroad, and internship programs around the nation and around the globe. It is a small college with a big view of the world—an educational community without boundaries. Goucher remains the first and only college to require each of its students to complete a study abroad requirement.

Goucher's more than 1,450 undergraduates come from forty-three states plus the District of Columbia, and ten other countries. They represent a tremendous variety of backgrounds, interests, and points of view. They live together in the center of the campus in six field-stone residence halls with living spaces designed to blur the lines between the students' educational, cultural, and social lives. Each of the residence halls is divided into "houses" of 40 to 50 students. Students can further tailor their residential experience by choosing to live in a healthy-living themed residence hall, on a foreign language floor, in a quiet area, or in a single-sex or coed house.

The residence hall buildings also house many of Goucher's academic and social resources, including the dining halls, the student union, a coffeehouse, health and counseling services, music practice rooms, and computer and language labs. Residence on campus is generally required of all first-year and sophomore students who do not live within 30 miles of the College.

The Goucher College Athenaeum is alive with the energy of the people—in and all around it—coming together at the intellectual, cultural, and social crossroads of the campus. It represents an important step forward in the evolution of Goucher College and an exciting new shape for the future of liberal arts education.

The newest building on campus, the Athenaeum has a high-tech four-level library, sixty computers, a public forum, various classrooms, a café, an art gallery, a radio station, a center for community service, a cardio workout area, places to meet and converse, and many other spaces.

Pearlstone Student Center houses a café, lounge, bookstore, post office, student activities office, game room, and the popular Gopher Hole, a coffeehouse offering space for casual conversations and featuring entertainment several nights a week. The Kraushaar Auditorium, with approximately 1,000 seats, is the campus cultural center; lectures and performances here by leading actors, actresses, dancers, musicians, writers, and political and cultural figures attract audiences from the Baltimore-Washington area, around the nation, and around the world.

Athletic facilities include a 50,000-square-foot Sports and Recreation Center, the Welsh Gymnasium, and the von Borries swimming pool. The sports center features a field house, sauna, wellness and cardio space, strength and conditioning space, squash and racquetball courts, lockers, and offices. There are five dance studios, 4 miles of wooded riding and jogging trails, six tennis courts, riding rings, and stables. Goucher belongs to NCAA Division III and competes in the Landmark Conference. Varsity sports include basketball, cross-country, equestrian events, field hockey, lacrosse, soccer, swimming, tennis, track and field, and volleyball.

Location

Ideally located on 287 wooded acres just a few miles north of downtown Baltimore, Maryland, and an hour's drive from Washington, D.C., Goucher takes full advantage of its environs with a curriculum and programs that engage students directly in the lives of the communities that surround them—local, national, and international—and bring the best of those communities to the Goucher campus to enrich the cultural and intellectual life of the College.

Majors and Degrees

Goucher awards the Bachelor of Arts degree. Areas of study and concentration include Africana studies, American studies, anthropology and sociology, art, arts administration, biochemistry, biological sciences, chemistry, cognitive studies, communication and media studies, computer science, dance, economics, elementary education, English, environmental studies, European studies, history, international business, international relations, jazz studies, Judaic studies, management, mathematics, modern languages (French, German, Russian, Spanish), music, peace studies, philosophy, physics, political science, prelaw studies, premedical studies, psychology, religion, sociology, special education, theater, and women's studies. Goucher students are encouraged to tailor their studies to their own goals and interests through traditional, double, or individualized majors or by taking a major and a minor. The College also offers a dual-degree program in engineering with Johns Hopkins University.

Academic Programs

Goucher encourages students to plot their own course, offering degrees in thirty-one different areas of study and enabling them to design their own majors. Thoroughly accomplished in all of the areas of study it has embraced, Goucher is particularly noted for its stellar programs in dance, the sciences, and creative writing. Goucher education takes an interdisciplinary perspective, encouraging students to assimilate the knowledge they gain throughout their academic careers into a cohesive whole.

Requirements for graduation include a demonstrated proficiency in a foreign language, completion of the study-abroad requirement, English composition, and computer technology and successful completion of liberal education core courses in the arts, natural sciences, humanities, social sciences, and mathematics. Degree requirements include 120 semester hours of credit. A departmental major consists of at least 30 credits (about ten courses); a double major requires 60 credits. Goucher's calendar is based on the semester system.

Off-Campus Programs

Education at Goucher extends far beyond the classroom walls. Students test the lessons they learn in class against firsthand experience through internships, service-learning programs, and other off-campus opportunities tailored precisely to their course of study.

More than 75 years old, Goucher's internship program provides students with a view into potential careers, opportunities to apply classroom theory to working reality, and the chance to network with professionals in the field. Supported by advisers who work to ensure a close fit between internships and academic interests, Goucher students have worked with organizations ranging from the *Baltimore Sun* to the European Parliament.

Study-abroad options range from three-week intensive courses to semester-long and yearlong programs. Many students build more than one complementary international experience into their course work. The international studies staff works with students to identify programs that neatly match their interests. Scholarship and other funds make study abroad possible even for students of limited financial means.

Through Goucher's student-founded Community Auxiliary for Service, students tutor at-risk students at area middle schools, serve meals at soup kitchens, and build houses with Habitat for Humanity, often for academic credit. The Hughes Field Politics Center offers high-quality internships in government, politics, and public service in Washington, D.C., and elsewhere, including recent placements with NATO in Brussels, the White House, CNN, and the Sierra Club.

The College has reciprocal agreements with the College of Notre Dame of Maryland, Johns Hopkins University, Loyola College, Maryland Institute College of Art, Morgan State University, and Towson University, to name a few, where qualified students at either institution may elect to take courses at no additional cost.

Academic Facilities

Goucher's campus is home to impressive facilities in technology, the sciences, and the arts, including a scientific visualization laboratory, a nuclear magnetic resonance spectrometer, and several computer, multimedia, and language labs. The campus is nearly completely wireless; it features more than a dozen smart classrooms and provides widespread access to the Internet, cable television, and internal networks. Students have access to well-equipped laboratories and research facilities, superb performance and studio art spaces (including the Meyerhoff Arts Center and the Kraushaar Auditorium), and the Hughes Field Politics Center. The library includes a collection of more than 295,500 volumes, audiovisual materials, and 1,200 periodical subscriptions, along with several special collections and extensive access to Web-based resources.

Costs

Tuition for 2010–11 is $34,626 for two semesters. The cost for a basic room for two semesters is $6278 and the cost for a 190-block meal plan is $4005. Fees total $516.

Financial Aid

Goucher's financial aid program is designed to put the College within reach of students with the desire and ability to pursue a rigorous academic program of study. Students and their families are expected to contribute to the financing of their education to the degree that they are able, but Goucher is committed to working with every qualified student to provide aid toward covering the difference between the limits of their financial resources and the total cost of their education.

The College awards financial aid in the form of packages based on results of needs analysis. Aid comes from a variety of resources that may include need-based grants, loans, and work-study opportunities. The College also offers merit-based scholarships.

Faculty

Goucher's faculty includes Danforth, Fulbright, Guggenheim, Newberry, and Woodrow Wilson fellows and a finalist for the National Book Award. All faculty members develop close, personal relationships with their students, often collaborating with them on nationally recognized, federally funded research projects of the kind most students at other colleges don't get to do until graduate school. With a student-faculty ratio of just 10:1 and 19 or fewer students in the vast majority (nearly 75 percent) of classes, nobody is ever just a face in the classroom at Goucher.

Student Government

The Student Government Association coordinates social activities, dispenses student activity funds, and formulates and enforces social regulations and the academic honor code. Students are represented on faculty and administrative committees. Students have founded a variety of departmental clubs in such fields as chemistry, computer science, French, history, math, political science, and Russian. Special interest groups include Community Auxiliary for Service (CAUSE), International Students' Club, and Environmental Concerns Organization (ECO). Student publications include a yearbook, literary magazine, and newspaper.

Admission Requirements

The Goucher Admissions Committee seeks to enroll students with strong academic ability who represent a variety of talents, ambitions, backgrounds, and experiences. Each candidate is considered individually. Goucher offers early decision, early action, and regular decision classifications for first-year applicants. A complete application, ready for review, consists of the following: a Common Application form and Goucher Supplement; one essay of at least 500 words; a nonrefundable $55 application fee (or fee waiver form); recommendations from 1 teacher who has taught the applicant in an academic subject and from a counselor or school principal; the official school transcript, including senior courses; and the TOEFL for students with less than three years of spoken English background. Goucher is a test-optional (SAT/ACT) institution. For more details, students should visit the College's Web site, http://www.goucher.edu. Goucher admits to the freshman class carefully selected students who have completed the eleventh grade and are ready to begin college a year early. Admission criteria are reviewed and weighed in the following order of importance: (1) the quality and level of secondary courses selected (a sound preparation includes at least 15 units of college-preparatory subjects; AP or IB classes are recognized as more rigorous); (2) grades received in grades 9–12; (3) the essay; (4) letters of recommendation; and (5) activities, special interests, and awards. Students should refer to the College Web site for specific application entrance plan deadlines. Applications are reviewed by the Admissions Committee, and the candidate is notified on or before April 1. The candidate reply date is May 1. Applications from transfer students filed by April 1 are given priority. Those filed after that date are considered on a rolling admissions basis.

Application and Information

Director of Admissions
Goucher College
1021 Dulaney Valley Road
Baltimore, Maryland 21204-2794
Phone: 410-337-6100
800-GOUCHER (toll-free)
E-mail: admissions@goucher.edu
Web site: http://www.goucher.edu

On the campus of Goucher College.

COLLEGE CLOSE-UPS

GRACELAND UNIVERSITY

LAMONI, IOWA

The University

Graceland University (GU) offers a strong academic program firmly rooted in the liberal arts tradition with an emphasis on career preparation. Since its founding in 1895 as a private, coeducational university, Graceland has maintained a tradition of academic excellence based on a commitment to the Christian view of the wholeness, worth, and dignity of every person. The University, sponsored by Community of Christ, is nonsectarian and offers a varied religious life program for those who wish to participate. Of Graceland's fall 2007 freshman class on the Lamoni campus, 17 percent came from Iowa. The remaining 83 percent represent twenty-six states and seventeen countries.

Graceland believes that an important part of a student's learning experience is achieved through association with other students in residence hall living. This belief is supported by an on-campus housing system that provides students with the camaraderie of a fraternity or sorority without the competition. Within the residence halls, there are men's and women's "houses." Members of each house elect a house council to plan social, intramural athletic, religious, and academic support activities. Residence halls are equipped with voice mail, e-mail, Internet connections, and cable TV.

Graceland University is a member of the North Central Association of Colleges and Schools (NCA) and is accredited by the Higher Learning Commission (30 North LaSalle Street, Suite 2400, Chicago, Illinois 60602-2504; 800-621-7440 (toll-free); http://www.ncahigherlearningcommission.org). All teacher-education programs at GU are approved by the Iowa Department of Education. The Bachelor of Arts (B.A.) in education and Master of Education (M.Ed.) programs in collaborative teaching and learning, quality education, and special education are accredited by the National Council for Accreditation of Teacher Education (NCATE; 2010 Massachusetts Avenue NW, Suite 500, Washington, D.C. 20036; 202-466-7496; http://www.ncate.org). All GU nursing programs are accredited by the Iowa and Missouri Departments of Education and the Commission on Collegiate Nursing Education (CCNE; One Dupont Circle NW, Suite 530, Washington, D.C. 20036; http://www.aacn.nche.edu). The athletic training program is accredited by the Commission on Accreditation of Athletic Training Education Programs (CAATE; 2201 Double Creek Drive, Suite 5006, Round Rock, Texas 78664; 512-733-9700; http://www.caate.net). These academic standards ensure that a degree from Graceland University is recognized by educational, business, and professional communities.

Graduate programs include the Master of Arts in Christian Ministries, Master of Arts in Religion, Master of Education, and Master of Science in Nursing. Certificates are offered in American humanics nonprofit management, post-master's family nurse practitioner, post-master's nurse educator, and post-master's health-care administration.

In addition to its traditional programs Graceland offers many options for distance learners. Programs offered online by the School of Nursing include the Bachelor in Healthcare Management, RN-B.S.N., RN-M.S.N., and M.S.N. programs. The M.S.N. program has three tracks: family nurse practitioner, nurse educator, and health-care administrator. The Graceland University School of Education offers a Master of Education with an emphasis in collaborative learning and teaching and special education. The Community of Christ Seminary also offers master's programs in religion and Christian ministries at a distance. The Master of Education program is offered in Cedar Rapids, Des Moines, and Lamoni, Iowa; Independence, Missouri; and online.

The Community of Christ Seminary offers a Master of Arts in Religion and a Master of Arts in Christian Ministries in blended delivery systems. The Community of Christ Seminary also offers master's programs in religion and Christian ministries at a distance.

Location

Lamoni, in south-central Iowa, is on Interstate 35. It is 3 miles north of the Missouri border, 1 hour from Des Moines, 2 hours from Kansas City, and 3 hours from Omaha. Lamoni is the home of Liberty Hall Historic Center, a 6-mile bike trail, an annual Civil War Days Re-Enactment and Living History Event, numerous hometown eateries, and several unique gift and antique shops. A county lake, Slip Bluff County Park, and Nine Eagles State Park are within 10 miles.

Majors and Degrees

Graceland awards the degrees of Bachelor of Arts, Bachelor of Science, and Bachelor of Science in Nursing. These degrees represent study in liberal arts with a concentration of courses in a major.

The majors and concentrations offered in the Bachelor of Arts programs are accounting, art (studio or visual communication), athletic training, business administration (emphases in entrepreneurship and free enterprise, finance, management, marketing, and pre-M.B.A.), chemistry, communications, economics, elementary education, English (concentrations in cinema studies, literature, and writing), fitness leadership, health, health-care administration, history, information technology, international business, international studies, liberal studies, mathematics, modern foreign language, music, music education, philosophy and religion, physical education and health, psychology, publications writing and design, recreation, religion, social science, sociology (concentrations in criminology, general sociology, and human services), Spanish, theater, visual communications (see: art), and wellness program management.

Bachelor of Science programs and majors are basic science, biology (concentrations in animal biology, ecology/environmental biology, molecular/cellular biology, preprofessional, and secondary school teaching), chemistry, clinical laboratory science/medical technology, and computer science.

The first two years of the Bachelor of Science in Nursing program are offered on the Lamoni campus, while the junior and senior years are on the Independence, Missouri, campus.

Graceland also offers degree programs at extended campus locations. Through a partnership with North Central Missouri College, Graceland offers undergraduate degrees in liberal studies and elementary education. Through a partnership with Indian Hills Community College, Graceland offers an undergraduate degree in elementary education. The undergraduate elementary education program is offered at the Graceland Independence campus location.

Academic Programs

Graceland is committed to helping develop the lives of its students—intellectually, socially, physically, and ethically—through a curriculum that is strongly rooted in the liberal arts. General education requirements are based on ten core competencies and can be satisfied by course selections, internships, portfolios, proficiency exams, work experience, independent studies, performance, and achievement. Graceland programs foster conceptual thinking, encourage team building, develop communication skills, and accommodate growth and enrichment.

Two programs at Graceland give attention to the special needs of students. The Honors Program is designed for highly motivated students wanting to expand their learning beyond the regular academic curriculum by developing and completing an honors thesis or project. Chance is a program for bright students who have the aptitude for university education but have experienced learning difficulties. The Lindamood and Bell clinical models are used for remediation in reading, spelling, and language comprehension.

The University operates on a 4-1-4 academic calendar. The regular semesters are separated by a one-month winter term in January. Full tuition for either the fall or the spring semester includes the winter term. This program is geared toward innovative and exceptional approaches and action-oriented learning experiences. On-campus programs vary from dance basics to science fiction to philosophy, and off-campus experiences range from scuba diving in Grand Cayman to touring Italy. Winter term is also the ideal time to explore career interests through an internship.

Off-Campus Programs

Many students see the world during the winter term by visiting such places as Australia, China, England, France, Grand Cayman Island in the British West Indies, Hungary, Italy, India, Israel, Japan, and Mexico. Students who major in a foreign language may study abroad during their junior or senior year under the auspices of a recognized study program. Graceland sponsors an International Health Center that provides opportunities for students to interact with health workers in villages in Africa and Asia.

Academic Facilities

The Helene Center for the Visual Arts includes 29,000 square feet for classrooms, studios, and exhibits. The large north-facing windows, an important feature, provide optimum light for artists.

The Shaw Center for the Performing Arts includes an 800-seat auditorium, a 150-seat studio theater, a 40-foot proscenium stage with orchestra pit, a Casavant pipe organ, a full fly gallery, a spacious scene shop, an art gallery, classrooms, rehearsal rooms, and faculty offices.

Computer facilities include three primary microcomputer laboratories with Macintosh and IBM-compatible computers. Students have access to equipment of commercial quality for desktop publishing and graphics design and to a music laboratory that provides computer-assisted tutoring, synthesis, and composition as well as professional-quality manuscript printing. The centerpiece of this laboratory is the Kurzweil synthesizer. Graceland's Enter.Net.C@fe provides 24-hour Internet access for student research and recreation.

The Frederick Madison Smith Library uses the latest technologies to provide the information services that students need. Ten fully networked computer workstations offer access to the Internet and many research databases, including 7 reference databases and more than 45 periodical databases, many providing access to full-text articles. Access to LIBBIE, the library's online catalog, and to the online reference sources is available to all patrons who use the library on the campus network as well as off-campus users via the Internet. Articles and books may be ordered from a worldwide network of research libraries. Students log on to the library's home page to ask reference questions. Holdings include 113,018 books and bound journals, 3,545 audiovisual materials, 72,866 government documents, 575 magazine and newspaper subscriptions, and 4,533 items in the Teacher Curriculum Lab. Three microcomputer labs and the Iowa Communications Network (ICN) classroom are located in the library.

The Dr. Charles Grabske, Sr. Library on the Independence campus provides resources for both on-campus and distance students in the nursing, education, and business departments. The library contains more than 3,000 nursing, education, and medical books; 250 audiovisual items, and approximately 1,000 journal titles. Grabske Library has one of the largest collections of nursing journals in the Kansas City area, with current subscriptions to more than 1,000 journals online and in print. Books, journal articles, and interlibrary loan services are available to on-campus and online students. Grabske Library is a member of the Health Sciences Library Network of Kansas City and a member library of the National Network for Libraries of Medicine. In 2006, Grabske Library received the award for Outstanding Academic Health Science Library from Health Sciences Library Network of Kansas City.

Students have the opportunity to use the ABT 52 scanning electron microscope, nuclear magnetic resonance spectroscope, Fourier-transform infrared spectroscope, and a computer lab with PCs that provide access to a multiple-operating system environment in the Platz-Mortimore Science Hall.

The Eugene E. and Julia Travis Closson Physical Education Center includes an indoor junior Olympic-size pool; an indoor track; a weight room; basketball, tennis, and volleyball courts; and a racquetball court. The Bruce Jenner Sports Complex contains the outdoor track, the football stadium, three soccer fields, five intramural fields, and eight tennis courts. The campus borders a nine-hole golf course and two small ponds for fishing and canoeing. Disc golf courses are located throughout the community.

Costs

Full-time tuition for 2010–11 is $20,680. Freshmen and sophomores are required to live on campus.

Financial Aid

Graceland's financial aid program is designed to assist qualified students attending the University. More than 90 percent of Graceland's students receive financial aid such as academic scholarships, performance grants, work-study, federal and state grants, and government loans. Academic scholarships are based on the high school GPA and composite ACT or combined SAT scores for entering freshmen and on cumulative GPA for transfer and continuing students. Grants are available for achievement in athletics and performing arts and for international students. The University matches a grant up to $1500 annually for a contribution made by a congregation and designated for a student attending Graceland. Some financial aid is available for distance learning programs; interested students should contact the Graceland University Financial Aid Services Office for specific information.

Faculty

The majority of faculty members have earned a doctorate or the highest degree in their field. Faculty members are active in their professional fields but consider teaching their primary responsibility. The student-faculty ratio is 15:1.

Student Government

Students are actively involved in the decision-making process of the University. Student-elected executive members of the Graceland Student Government attend faculty meetings and participate with voice and vote. Each academic department has student representatives who participate in business sessions and serve on faculty search committees. Students provide leadership for the housing system and for the campus social program. These and many other avenues are available allowing students to gain practical leadership experience.

Admission Requirements

Admission to Graceland is selective. To be considered, high school graduates must qualify in two of the following three areas: (1) rank in the upper 50 percent of their class; (2) have a minimum 2.5 GPA, based on a 4.0 system; and (3) have either a minimum composite ACT score of 21 or a minimum SAT combined score (Critical Reading and Math) of 960. Applicants who do not meet the above criteria may be considered individually. If accepted, they will be required to take developmental courses. Some applicants may be requested to test for the Chance Program prior to being considered for acceptance. Transfer, international, and home-schooled students should refer to the requirements listed in the catalog on the University's Web site. No one is denied admission to the University on the basis of race, color, religion, age, sex, national origin, disability, or sexual orientation. Prospective students and their families are encouraged to visit the campus.

Application and Information

Students are encouraged to apply as early as possible.

Admissions Office
Graceland University
1 University Place
Lamoni, Iowa 50140
Phone: 641-784-5196
866-GRACELAND (toll-free in the U.S. and Canada)
Fax: 641-784-5480
E-mail: admissions@graceland.edu
Web site: http://www.admissions.graceland.edu

Higdon Administration Building on Graceland's Lamoni Campus.

GRAND CANYON UNIVERSITY

PHOENIX, ARIZONA

The University

Founded in 1949, Grand Canyon University (GCU) is an accredited, private, Christian university located in Phoenix, Arizona. The University offers online and campus-based bachelor's, master's, and doctoral degree programs through the Ken Blanchard College of Business, College of Education, College of Nursing and Health Sciences, College of Liberal Arts, and College of Fine Arts and Production. GCU emphasizes individual attention for both traditional undergraduate students and working professionals. More than just a four-year education, Grand Canyon University (GCU) is a robust living and learning experience that nurtures students' growth physically, mentally, and spiritually.

While surrounding students with the social, cultural, and recreational opportunities of a lifetime, GCU enables them to build a solid academic foundation for a rich and rewarding life. A degree from Grand Canyon University represents a well-rounded education accomplished through a wide range of educational, artistic, social, and spiritual activities. Students enjoy small class sizes, hands-on learning opportunities, and stimulating courses; serve in student government; participate in "Adopt-a-Block," an outreach to the surrounding neighborhoods; become mentors and student counselors or serve in the on-campus ministry; take part in intercollegiate and intramural sports; and enjoy campuswide social events.

For GCU students, their future starts the day they move onto campus. Hegel Hall is a modern dormitory residence featuring all the amenities college students want. Spacious dorm suites include a furnished living room, a private bathroom, and two bedrooms, each equipped with a vanity sink and mirror, individual closets, beds, study desks, and chairs. Telephone, basic cable, and high-speed wireless Internet are also part of the resident's daily life. Designed to facilitate social interaction and serious study, the comfortably appointed suite becomes home to 4 GCU students.

Surrounding the GCU dorms and student apartments is a beautiful, parklike environment and an exciting campus lifestyle. This includes an active student center, complete with a fitness center, a copy center, an outstanding full-service cafeteria, and a gourmet coffee shop, Latté Dah. Students enjoy kicking back in big cushy chairs and catching up on their favorite shows on large-screen plasma TVs. They also enjoy student movie nights and other events on "The Slab," an outdoor gathering area that invites students to take a break and enjoy Arizona's wonderful weather.

While exploring a major field of study in depth at Grand Canyon University, students are exposed to a wide range of experiences both on and off the campus. This diversity is a key element of the University's vision of educating students for successful careers and lives. Even though fellow GCU students come from a wide variety of backgrounds, they all share the same commitment to academic excellence and intellectual growth; they are all pursuing the goal of a high-quality education. GCU students make friends quickly in the coed community, and they share a wealth of new and exciting experiences. Many of the alumni happily report their GCU college roommates and classmates have continued to be great friends and an integral part of their life after college.

Students who enjoy sports should consider GCU their playing field. From intramural athletics to pickup games of Ultimate Frisbee on Mariposa Lawn, they experience life at its fullest. The GCU Antelopes ("Lopes") compete in a variety of Division II intercollegiate sports as well as intramural sports. GCU offers a complete exercise facility outfitted with the finest equipment as well as tennis courts and two indoor basketball courts.

Beyond the fun, there's faith. GCU students can expect to be part of a student body that comes together to celebrate a mutual faith. Students see the celebration of that faith at the Gathering (a contemporary evening chapel), at the Grand Celebration (a weekly worship assembly), through GCU's campus and community ministries and mission trips. Chapel meetings, which feature music, drama, and speakers from various denominational backgrounds, offer the opportunity to become energized and inspired by a supportive Christian community.

To help prospective and current students achieve career goals, Grand Canyon University provides comprehensive guidance and resources for lifelong career development. GCU workshops provide students with valuable information on topics such as resume writing, interview preparation, developing job leads through networking, and adapting to changes associated with local business conditions.

GCU holds the following accreditations: the Higher Learning Commission of the North Central Association of Colleges and Schools (30 North LaSalle Street, Suite 2400, Chicago, Illinois 60602-2504; telephone: 800-621-7440 (toll-free); Web site: http://www.ncahigherlearningcommission.org/); the Association of Collegiate Business Schools and Programs (ACBSP), through the Ken Blanchard College of Business, for the following business degrees: Bachelor of Science (B.S.) with majors in accounting, business administration, and marketing and Master of Business Administration (M.B.A.); and the Commission on Collegiate Nursing Education (One Dupont Circle NW, Suite 530, Washington, D.C. 20036; telephone: 202-887-6791) and the Arizona State Board of Nursing for the Bachelor of Science in Nursing degree program.

The Arizona State Department of Education has given formal approval of the work done at the University for the certification of elementary and secondary teachers and for the renewal of certificates.

Location

New students quickly discover there is more to the Grand Canyon University experience than classroom learning and campus living. Grand Canyon University is located just minutes from downtown Phoenix, Arizona's state capital and one of the fastest-growing regions in the nation. The greater Phoenix metropolitan area, known as the "Valley of the Sun" for its more than 300 days of sunshine each year, offers numerous educational, social, cultural, and recreational activities that enhance university life. GCU is next door to myriad urban activities and attractions, including cultural and artistic centers, world-class concerts, five major professional sports teams, and expansive shopping malls plus all the outdoor attractions expected from a city famous for its year-round sunshine, including golf, hiking, biking, horseback riding, and water sports.

Within a 2-hour drive of Grand Canyon University's campus is some of the best snow skiing in the Western United States. GCU students flourish in the school's Southwestern environment. Surrounded by rugged mountains, lush valleys, and the arid beauty of the Sonoran Desert, Grand Canyon University students feel a part of the larger human experience.

Majors and Degrees

Grand Canyon University comprises five renowned institutes of education (Ken Blanchard College of Business, College of Liberal Arts, College of Education, College of Fine Arts and Production, and College of Nursing and Health Sciences) and more than 100 esteemed academic programs. Specific study areas include accounting, applied management, art (art education and graphic design), athletic training, biochemistry, biology (environmental, general, human, and secondary teaching), business administration, chemistry (general and secondary teaching), Christian studies (applied ministry: biblical and theological studies, applied ministry: pastoral, applied ministry: worship, and applied ministry: youth), communications (public relations and broadcasting), corporate fitness and wellness, elementary education, English literature, English teaching, history, history education, international studies, justice studies, marketing, mathematics, mathematics engineering, mathematics secondary teaching, music education (choral conducting and instrumental conducting), nursing, organizational sociology, philosophy, physical education, physical science, physics (secondary teaching), political science, psychology, public safety administration, recreation, science for elementary teachers, sociology, special education, and speech teaching.

Academic Programs

The Grand Canyon University curriculum is challenging and radiates from a strong core of liberal arts and sciences. The University provides both traditional and innovative programs that enable students to think critically and creatively, solve problems through open-minded analysis, and communicate effectively. Academic habits acquired at Grand Canyon University stay with Grand Canyon University graduates, enabling them to live flexible lives, to be open to new career opportunities, and to develop confidence in their ability to learn and adapt.

The curriculum at Grand Canyon University is not easy. It requires the highest levels of personal commitment, intellectual honesty, and academic diligence. The course work is rigorous but helps individuals discover their talents and perfect their skills.

Academic Facilities

Grand Canyon University consists of thirty-six buildings on a 90-acre campus. The campus features the Fleming Library, which houses a collection of more than 166,000 volumes, 700 periodicals, newspapers, microfilm, and audiovisual materials. Fleming Library is a member of the CCLC network and as a designated depository receives a variety of government documents. Library holdings are expanded by CD-ROM databases, computerized database searches, and interlibrary loans. Computers housed in the library have Internet access to assist students. Grand Canyon University also offers all students access to the Online Library.

There are two computer labs on campus, both outfitted with new Dell OptiPlex computers and 17-inch monitors. The computer labs offer Internet access and a host of applications for use outside of the classroom. Each student has an individual login ID and secured space on a server to store personal files. In addition to the lab computers, wireless access is available for students with laptops.

Costs

There is no application fee to apply. For the 2009–10 academic year, traditional undergraduate students taking 1–11 credits paid $687.50 per credit hour. Students carrying 12–18 credits paid block tuition of $8250 per semester; students carrying 19 or more credits paid block tuition plus $687.50 for each credit hour above 19.

Students living in University housing can expect to pay $1800 to $3600 per semester, depending on occupancy and individual desires. Various meal plans are available to students living on campus and range from $520 to $2040 per semester. Although phone service is the responsibility of the student, basic cable service is included in the rent. Grand Canyon University reserves the right to change all fees and charges, without notice, if necessary.

Financial Aid

Grand Canyon University has made a commitment to their students by keeping costs down year after year and focusing its dollars on what benefits students directly. This effort has fostered an educational experience that offers high value and quality for the educational investment made. GCU's Office of Finance and the Business Office are committed to working with the individual and their family to discuss various financial options and ensure every available resource is utilized to meet their personal financial needs.

More than 80 percent of Grand Canyon University students receive some form of financial assistance to help meet the cost of their education. In addition to federal and state financial aid, Grand Canyon University has academic and other specific-criteria scholarships and aid available. Grand Canyon University also offers Federal Work-Study programs, on-campus part-time jobs, connections to providers of off-campus jobs, and federal community service opportunities.

Faculty

Grand Canyon University's professors are highly qualified in their respective fields, having garnered many awards as authors, presenters, and teachers. They give individual attention to students, stress mutual interaction with others, and use cutting-edge, research-based pedagogy to convey the most current information. With a 13:1 student-teacher ratio, classes at GCU are small, so students enjoy the highest level of personal attention from professors who know them by name. Professors at GCU are at their student's side every step of the way, helping them explore their academic gifts. They are also spiritual visionaries who help learners incorporate their faith regardless of the discipline they pursue.

Student Government

The ASGCU is GCU's student-led government. The student-elect President is the direct link between the undergraduate student body and the GCU administration. The President advocates for the needs of the student body and is the person the administration looks to when seeking student opinion on decisions made by the University. The President oversees the cabinet, which includes the Vice President, Intramurals Coordinator, Marketing Director, Community Service Director, Events Coordinator, Communications Director, and the Student Voice Director.

Admission Requirements

For admission to Grand Canyon University, students should submit an application for admission and the application fee to the University's Office of Admission. Freshmen must submit their official high school transcript and/or GED scores and have their ACT or SAT scores submitted to Grand Canyon University. Transfer students must have their transcripts forwarded to Grand Canyon University.

Application and Information

Grand Canyon University operates on a rolling admission system. Applicants generally receive an admission decision within ten days after all required documents are on file in the Office of Admission. It is to the student's advantage to apply as early as possible. Applications for financial aid and housing cannot be completely processed and transcripts are not evaluated until the admission application is complete.

For further information and application materials, students should contact:

Office of Enrollment
Grand Canyon University
3300 West Camelback Road
Phoenix, Arizona 85017
Phone: 800-486-7085 (toll-free)
E-mail: admissionsground@gcu.edu
Web site: http://www.gcu.edu/petersons

GRAND VIEW UNIVERSITY

DES MOINES, IOWA

The University

Grand View is a liberal arts institution affiliated with the Evangelical Lutheran Church in America. Founded more than 100 years ago, Grand View offers a high-quality education to a diverse student body in a career-oriented, liberal arts–grounded curriculum at two campus locations in greater Des Moines. Grand View welcomes traditional students and adult learners representing a wide range of religious and cultural backgrounds.

At Grand View University, students find a winning combination of high-quality programs, experienced professors, and caring individuals. With 2,000 students and an average class size of 14, students get to know their professors and other students well. They learn independence and seek responsibility in Grand View's educational environment. Learning is an interactive process at Grand View—students engage in lively discussions, work on real-world projects, and participate in career-related work experiences.

Grand View University stands out from other colleges because of its partnerships with leading businesses and organizations in Des Moines, which has led to challenging internships and to nearly 100 percent of students finding jobs right after graduation or continuing their education every year for a decade and a half. Grand View is known for its ability to connect students with exciting and challenging career opportunities.

Students are encouraged to develop leadership and team skills through involvement in campus organizations, which include intercollegiate and intramural athletics, speech and theater groups, major department clubs, student government, and musical ensembles. Active honorary societies include Alpha Chi, Alpha Mu Gamma, Alpha Psi Omega, Alpha Sigma Lambda, Beta Beta Beta, Phi Eta Sigma, Sigma Theta Tau, and Theta Alpha Kappa. Grand View's student leadership program provides opportunities for students without leadership experience to seek and develop critical thinking, interpersonal, and networking skills.

Student athletes compete in men's baseball, basketball, bowling, cross-country, football, golf, soccer, track and field, and wrestling and women's basketball, bowling, competitive dance, cross-country, golf, soccer, softball, track and field, and volleyball. Grand View participates in the Midwest Collegiate Conference of the National Association of Intercollegiate Athletics. Athletic scholarships are available.

Two locations offer Grand View students convenient scheduling options for their program of study. Weekend and evening classes are offered at the main campus in Des Moines and at Grand View's campus in Johnston, Iowa. For motivated students seeking to complete their degree quickly, accelerated schedules are offered for several of fifteen evening majors.

Location

Grand View is located in Des Moines, a metropolitan area of more than half a million people in central Iowa. Des Moines is the state capital and serves as the communications hub for Iowa. Nationally recognized organizations that have their corporate offices in Des Moines include Pioneer Hi-Bred International, Inc.; the Principal Financial Group; Meredith Corporation; and the *Des Moines Register*.

Grand View's campus is Des Moines—and as part of the Grand View community, students are not limited by the confines of a small school or small town. In a given day, students can catch an Iowa Cubs professional baseball doubleheader, head down to the Court Avenue district for great food and nightlife, or take in a rock concert at Wells Fargo Arena.

A thriving arts program in Des Moines features the Des Moines Metro Opera, Ballet Iowa, the Des Moines Symphony, the Des Moines Art Center, and the Des Moines Playhouse. The summer Des Moines Art Festival is ranked third in the nation.

Des Moines features four distinct and beautiful seasons. Except for a month or so of bundle-up, see-your-breath weather, the climate is ideal for outdoor activities. Grand View students can take advantage of terrific recreational opportunities, including several golf courses, Saylorville Lake, and many city parks and state forests.

Easily accessible from Interstates 35 and 80, Grand View is 4 hours from Minneapolis, 6 hours from Chicago, and 3 hours from Kansas City.

Majors and Degrees

Grand View University grants the Bachelor of Arts degree and offers thirty-seven majors in areas such as accounting, art education, biology, broadcast, business administration (with concentrations in agricultural business, finance, human resource management, management, marketing, and real estate), computer science, criminal justice, elementary education, English, general studies–liberal arts, graphic design, graphic journalism, health promotion, history, human services, individualized major, journalism, management information systems, mass communication, math, music, music education, organizational studies, paralegal studies, physical science, political studies (prelaw or public administration), psychology, religion, secondary education, service management, sociology–liberal arts, Spanish for careers and professionals, theater arts, and visual arts. Grand View also offers a Bachelor of Science degree in nursing, as well as an RN to B.S.N. program. In addition, the University offers certificate programs in art therapy, entrepreneurship, human resource management, in-house communication, real estate, Spanish essentials, and sport management, as well as postbaccalaureate certificates in accounting and management in accounting.

The Master of Science in innovative leadership is an interdisciplinary advanced degree with tracks in business, education, and nursing. This cutting-edge, 40-credit-hour program qualifies graduates as organizational leaders, clinical nurse leaders, and teacher leaders.

Academic Programs

Grand View operates on a 4-4-1 academic calendar. The first semester runs from September to December. The second semester begins in early January and ends in late April. Three 1-month summer sessions are offered in May, June, and July, as is a summer trimester evening program.

Grand View University has adopted a competency-based General Education Core. Requirements for the core are defined in student learning goals. Completion of the educational core enables students to achieve a measurable level of competency in key skill and knowledge areas, such as writing, critical analysis, oral communication, and computer proficiency.

The Logos Honors Program provides an alternative to the General Education Core. By invitation, freshman and sophomore students enrolled in this program complete a series of courses designed to challenge exceptional students.

The Expressions Business Honors Program offers a three-year accelerated option. And the *ALT* honors magazine offers invited students an opportunity to design, write, and produce an award-winning publication.

The Grand View academic mission is to provide a diverse student body with an academically rigorous education. In order to meet this commitment, Grand View provides a variety of learning environments and teaching techniques. The University's academic support programs and services were lauded as a national model by the examining team from the North Central Association of Colleges and Schools during reaccreditation in 2005, when the University received complete ten-year accreditation with no follow-up required.

Costs

For 2009–10, the comprehensive cost for freshmen on campus is approximately $25,796, which includes tuition, an activity fee, a technology fee, and room and board. Students have several residential and meal plan options that affect cost. Health services and Internet access are also included in the comprehensive fee.

Financial Aid

Typically, most full-time Grand View students received financial assistance. The average freshman full-time award package is usually around $21,000 with about $11,500 in grants and scholarships and the remainder in work-study and student loans. The amount of aid is determined through a combination of merit and analysis of need as determined through the Free Application for Federal Student Aid. The priority deadline for financial aid is March 1. Students receive notification of financial aid packages following acceptance of admission to the University and receipt of their financial aid analysis of need.

Faculty

There are approximately 85 full-time faculty members and 111 part-time faculty members. More than fifty percent hold terminal degrees. All classes are taught by professors; no graduate or teaching assistants instruct Grand View classes.

Student Government

Students participate in University governance. The Student Activities Council and Viking Council plan student activities that promote educational, social, cultural, and recreational aspects of student life. Students serve as representatives on faculty and staff search committees, programming committees, and student life committees.

Admission Requirements

Applicants' files are reviewed to determine their preparedness for a Grand View education. Official high school transcripts and submission of ACT or SAT scores are required for applicants with less than 24 semester hours of college credit. Applicants transferring from another college are required to submit official transcripts from all colleges previously attended.

Application and Information

For more information about Grand View, students should contact:

Admissions Office
Grand View University
1200 Grandview Avenue
Des Moines, Iowa 50316
Phone: 515-263-2810
800-444-6083 (toll-free)
Fax: 515-263-2974
E-mail: admissions@grandview.edu
Web site: http://www.admissions.grandview.edu

Grand View students chat with a professor on their way to class.

COLLEGE CLOSE-UPS

GREENSBORO COLLEGE

GREENSBORO, NORTH CAROLINA

The College

Established in 1838, Greensboro College is a four-year coeducational liberal arts college affiliated with the United Methodist Church. It is located in the College Hill Historic District of Greensboro, North Carolina. With an enrollment of approximately 1,250 men and women, the College enjoys a small-community atmosphere and maintains a student-faculty ratio of 11:1.

The 60-acre campus is located in the College Hill Historic District, only six blocks from downtown Greensboro. Its architecture is in the traditional Georgian style. The buildings include an indoor athletic center, four residential halls, classroom buildings, a chapel, a performing arts center, a library, and a main administrative building.

At the Royce Reynolds Family Student Life Center, students enjoy squash, racquetball, and basketball courts; a fitness facility; an indoor pool; an aerobics room; a Jacuzzi; a steam room; and a sauna. Intercollegiate sports include baseball, basketball, cross-country, football, golf, lacrosse, soccer, and tennis for men as well as basketball, cross-country, lacrosse, soccer, softball, swimming, tennis, and volleyball for women. Greensboro College is a member of the NCAA Division III and competes in the U.S.A. South Athletic Conference. An intramural program is also offered for students.

There is cultural, religious, and ethnic diversity at Greensboro College, where students come from more than thirty states and twenty-four nations. Many graduates have earned distinction in graduate and professional schools in all parts of the United States and abroad. Recent Greensboro College graduates have been accepted into the graduate schools of the College of William and Mary as well as Duke, Emory, Georgetown, Johns Hopkins, North Carolina State, Princeton, St. Andrews (Scotland), Temple, Vanderbilt, and Wake Forest Universities and the Eastman School of Music. Most graduates pursue careers in business, education, health care, and the arts.

Extracurricular activities are designed to supplement and reinforce academic study at the College. More than 100 student leadership positions are available in more than sixty different student organizations, enabling most students to be as active in campus life as they wish.

In addition to its undergraduate programs, Greensboro College offers the Master of Education degree.

Location

The city of Greensboro, which is located near the center of North Carolina, offers major industries, including insurance companies and textile manufacturers, and many cultural, social, and athletic opportunities. With a population of more than 1 million people in the Triad region, the city is a thriving business center that offers excellent internship opportunities. More than 45,000 college students study at the six colleges and universities within the city. Greensboro College is at the heart of this community.

Majors and Degrees

Greensboro College awards the Bachelor of Arts (B.A.), Bachelor of Science (B.S.), and Bachelor of Business Administration degrees. Students can major in the following areas: accounting, art, athletic training, biology, birth-through-kindergarten teacher education, business administration and economics, chemistry, criminal justice, education or special education, English and communications, exercise and sport studies, French, history, history and political science, mathematics, middle school education, music, physical education, political science, psychology, religion and philosophy, secondary education, sociology, Spanish, theater, and urban ecology. Minors are available in child and family studies, Christian education, computer information systems, computer science, dance, ethics, interdisciplinary studies, international studies, legal administration, women's studies, and other areas in which majors are offered. Combined-degree programs are offered in medical technology and radiological technology.

Academic Programs

All students are required to take courses in the humanities, the natural sciences, the social sciences, and the arts. The general education requirements for both the B.A. and B.S. degrees total 52 semester hours. Graduation requires the completion of 124 semester hours.

Greensboro College offers an honors program for superior students who qualify on the basis of SAT or ACT scores, high school grade point averages, or AP examination results. Students enrolled in the program must complete requirements in addition to those expected of students in the regular B.A. and B.S. degree programs.

Because Greensboro College recognizes that people must learn not only how to live but also how to make a living, the liberal arts curriculum and setting provide the context for a variety of professional programs, including accounting, business, and legal administration, as well as preprofessional programs in law, medicine, and theology. Besides providing career and academic counseling, the College seeks to ensure that its graduates acquire the basic intellectual and communications capabilities to cope with the changing demands of any career. An internship program during the junior and senior years places students in business and agency settings that are related to their major and career aspirations. The College also seeks to develop in its graduates a philosophy of life and an appreciation of Judeo-Christian values that transcend particular vocational skills.

Off-Campus Programs

Greensboro College is a member of the Greater Greensboro Consortium and the Piedmont Independent Colleges Association, which provide for arrangements with Bennett College, Elon University, Guilford College, Guilford Technical Community College, High Point University, North Carolina Agricultural and Technical State University, Salem College, and the University of North Carolina at Greensboro. With permission from the academic dean, students at Greensboro College may take courses offered at any of the other campuses. Library resources are shared.

Academic Facilities

The James Addison Jones Library has approximately 110,000 volumes, periodicals, CD-ROMs, and microfilm reels. The computerized card catalog system allows students to access the holdings of other area colleges. Interlibrary loan among the colleges is permitted. There are reading rooms, periodical and browsing rooms, and a multipurpose meeting room.

One of the College's goals is to ensure that every student develops a broad range of technical skills in order to flourish in the twenty-first century. State-of-the-art computer labs are available for all students, and students can access the Internet and World Wide Web from most points on campus. All dorm rooms provide high-speed access to the Internet.

Other facilities include a computerized writing laboratory, natural science laboratories, the Annie Sellars Jordan Parlor Theater, and the Gail Brower Huggins Performance Center, one of the most elegant and state-of-the-art performance facilities in the area. Music facilities include a computerized music laboratory, practice rooms, two recital areas, thirty-nine pianos (including a 9-foot concert grand), and a concert stage. In addition, Greensboro College is one of only three colleges in the state to have a Fisk organ. There are two large art studios, one for the teaching of two-dimensional media and one for the teaching of three-dimensional media. Students in the education department are served by the Curriculum Materials Center, which contains audiovisual equipment, books, teaching kits, and a variety of other special supplies.

Costs

For 2009–10, the total cost of tuition, fees, room, and board was $32,070. A private room cost an additional $4500. Greensboro College estimates that $800 to $1600 is adequate for books, clothing, entertainment, and other incidental expenses.

Financial Aid

Greensboro College participates in many federal programs of student aid, including the Federal Pell Grant, Federal Work-Study, Federal Perkins Loan, Federal Supplemental Educational Opportunity Grant, Federal Parent Loan for Undergraduate Students, and Federal Stafford Student Loan programs. Authorized state programs include North Carolina Legislative Tuition Grants, the State Contractual Scholarship Fund, North Carolina Prospective Teacher's Scholarships/Loans, and North Carolina Student Incentive Grants. Institutional programs funded by Greensboro College include the College work-study program, grants, scholarships, and loans. Full- and partial-tuition scholarships are awarded to students based on merit. United Methodist Church scholarships and grants, which are based on both financial need and merit, are available. Full Tuition Presidential Scholarships, valued at more than $80,000 each, are available. Approximately 90 percent of the students at Greensboro College receive some form of financial assistance. All students are encouraged to apply for financial aid, and the College accepts the Free Application for Federal Student Aid (FAFSA). Applications for United Methodist Church scholarships and grants are available from the financial planning office. A career-development office on campus is available to aid all students seeking a part-time job, regardless of their financial need.

Faculty

Greensboro College has 85 full- and part-time faculty members. All of the full-time faculty members hold the highest degree in their areas of study. Although some faculty members have distinguished themselves by their research, scholarship, and creativity, all are deeply and primarily committed to undergraduate teaching and the personal welfare of the students. Every student has a faculty adviser; the average class size is 14, and there is a favorable student-faculty ratio of 11:1.

Student Government

The College's Student Government Association (SGA), acting within the policies and regulations of the College, is the main representative voice of the students. The SGA addresses various policy decisions that affect the students and acts as a sounding board for student opinions. The SGA is the communication link between student organizations, the student body, the administration, the staff, and the faculty. The Campus Activities Board plans and executes student events on campus.

Admission Requirements

Admission decisions are based on all available information. Although applicants are asked to submit scores from the SAT and/or ACT, the high school record is actually the most important single factor. No exact formula can be applied to all applications, but acceptable scores on the SAT or ACT, rank in class, grade point average, and high school program form the basis for evaluation. Candidates for admission should demonstrate academic achievement in a select academic program in high school, although completion of a given program of study is not as important as evidence of intellectual curiosity and emotional and social maturity. A curriculum that provides good preparation for Greensboro College might include 4 units of English, 3 units of college-preparatory math (algebra I and II and geometry), 2 units of science (including one laboratory science), 2 units of history, 2 units of the same foreign language, and electives chosen from art, music, physical education, and social science. An interview on campus is very helpful to the student and to the College. Arrangements may be made for the interview at the student's convenience.

Greensboro College accepts transfer credits on a case-by-case basis. Credit is given for courses that have been successfully completed at accredited universities, senior colleges, junior colleges, community colleges, and technical colleges.

Application and Information

Students should submit an application for admission and immediately ask high schools and any colleges they have attended to forward official transcripts to Greensboro College. SAT or ACT scores should be forwarded to the College by the testing agency or the student's high school. Reference letters may be requested by the Admissions Committee, which reviews all applications on a rolling basis. As soon as a decision is reached, the student is notified. Greensboro College has no closing date for applications, but those received before March 31 are given priority.

For inquiries and application materials, students should contact:

Office of Admissions
Greensboro College
815 West Market Street
Greensboro, North Carolina 27401-1875
Phone: 800-346-8226 (toll-free)
Fax: 336-378-0154
E-mail: admissions@greensborocollege.edu
Web site: http://www.greensborocollege.edu

Greensboro College students frequently gather near the historic Main Building.

GROVE CITY COLLEGE

GROVE CITY, PENNSYLVANIA

The College

The beautifully landscaped campus of Grove City College (GCC) stretches more than 150 acres and includes twenty-seven neo-Gothic buildings valued at more than $100 million. The campus is considered one of the loveliest in the nation. While the College has changed to meet the needs of the society it serves, its basic philosophy has remained unchanged since its founding in 1876. It is a Christian liberal arts and sciences institution of ideal size and dedicated to the principle of providing the highest-quality education at the lowest possible cost. Wishing to remain truly independent and to retain its distinctive qualities as a private school governed by private citizens (trustees), it is one of the very few colleges in the country that does not accept any state or federal monies. It is informally affiliated with the Presbyterian Church (U.S.A.) but not narrowly denominational; the College believes that to be well educated a student should be exposed to the central ideas of the Christian faith. A 20-minute chapel program offered Tuesday and Thursday mornings, along with a Sunday evening worship service, challenges students in their faith. Sixteen chapel services per semester are required out of fifty opportunities. Religious organizations and activities exist to provide fellowship and spiritual growth.

Grove City students generally come from middle-income families. The greatest number comes from Pennsylvania, Ohio, New Jersey, Virginia, and New York, although forty-three states and nine other countries were represented in 2009–10. Eighty-three percent of the women and 71 percent of the men in the most recent freshman class ranked in the top fifth of their high school class. Their average SAT combined score was 1259 (combining only the critical reading and math scores); the average ACT composite score was 28.

Ninety-three percent of the 2,500 students live in separate men's and women's residence halls. All others are regular commuters or married students. A full program of cultural, professional, athletic, and social activities is offered. An arena, Crawford Auditorium, and the J. Howard Pew Fine Arts Center are used for athletics, concerts, movies, plays, and lectures. The Physical Learning Center is one of the finest among the nation's small colleges and includes an eight-lane bowling alley, two swimming pools, handball/racquetball courts, playing surfaces, fitness rooms with free weights, aerobic equipment and Cybex machines, an indoor three-lane running track, and the basketball arena. The Breen Student Union provides an eatery; mailroom; bookstore; commuters' lounge; and a commons area for dining, studying, and socializing. The Ketler and South Hall Recreation Lounge are also available for cooking, games, and socializing. There are more than 130 organizations and special interest groups, including local fraternities and sororities. No alcohol or drugs are permitted on campus. The athletic activities include an extensive intramural, club, and varsity sports program that provides nineteen intercollegiate teams that compete at the NCAA Division III level for men and women.

The College's well-established placement services, ranked recently by *The Princeton Review* in the top 20 in the nation, are used constantly by students who are interested in business and industrial employment and by those seeking educational positions in the teaching field. A complete file of personal data, scholastic records, and recommendations is prepared for each registrant. These files are available to the scores of prospective employers who visit the campus annually to interview the graduating seniors. One of Grove City's strengths is placing students in business, industrial, and teaching positions, as well as in professional institutions such as medical schools.

Location

Grove City, a town of 8,000 people, is 60 miles north of Pittsburgh. Convenient to I-79 and I-80, Grove City is only a day's drive from Chicago, New York City, Toronto, and Washington, D.C. The municipal airport has a 3,500-foot runway, and there is bus service to Pittsburgh.

Majors and Degrees

Grove City College offers undergraduate degrees in liberal arts, sciences, engineering, and music. The Bachelor of Arts is offered with majors in Christian thought, communication studies, economics, English, history, modern language (French and Spanish), philosophy, political science, psychology, secondary education, and sociology. Preprofessional students in law or theology usually earn the B.A. degree. Interdisciplinary major programs are also available for qualified students.

The Bachelor of Science is granted with majors in accounting, applied physics, applied physics/computer, biochemistry, biology, business management, chemistry, computer information systems, computer science, early childhood education, elementary education, entrepreneurship, financial management, industrial management, international business, marketing management, mathematics, molecular biology, and psychology. Preprofessional students often select one of these majors for dentistry, medicine, or other health fields.

The Bachelor of Science in Electrical and Computer Engineering degree is also offered. The Bachelor of Science in Mechanical Engineering major provides for mechanical systems design and/or thermal systems design. The electrical and computer and mechanical engineering programs are accredited by the Engineering Accreditation Commission of the Accreditation Board for Engineering and Technology, Inc. (ABET).

The Bachelor of Music degree is awarded to those who major in music. Programs may also include concentrations in business, education, performing arts, or religion.

Academic Programs

Grove City College's goal is to assist young men and women in developing as complete individuals—academically, spiritually, and physically. The general education requirements provide all students with a high level of cultural literacy and communication skills. They include 46 semester hours of courses with emphases in the humanities, social sciences, and natural sciences; in quantitative and logical reasoning; and in science, faith, and technology, as well as a language requirement for nonengineering and science majors. Degree candidates must also complete the requirements in their field of concentration, physical education, electives, and convocation. To graduate, a student must have completed 128 semester hours (132 hours for electrical engineering) plus 4 convocation credits. Seventy-eight percent of those entering as freshmen stay and receive a diploma in four years.

A distinctive liberal arts–engineering program includes engineering courses plus courses in the humanities to provide students with a well-grounded preparation for entering the engineering field, as well as the civic and cultural life of society. The Austrian economics program exposes students to all economic philosophies, yet strongly advocates economic freedoms and free markets.

Grove City follows the early semester calendar plan. Academic credit may be granted to incoming freshmen on the basis of scores on appropriate Advanced Placement tests, International Baccalaureate tests, or College-Level Examination Program tests. Honors courses, independent study, seminars, and the opportunity for juniors to study abroad for credit are also offered.

Academic Facilities

The Hall of Arts and Letters opened in 2003. This state-of-the-art teaching facility features a 200-seat lecture hall, forty classrooms (including multimedia-equipped rooms and tiered "case study" rooms), eighty faculty offices, the Early Education Center, the Curriculum Library, and language, computer, and video production labs.

The College library houses 135,100 books and 13,250 microform units; 2,905 audio/video tapes, CDs, and DVDs; and 36,992 periodical subscriptions. Modern, well-equipped laboratories for biology, chemistry, engineering, and physics are available, as are facilities for language and piano studies.

The College recently acquired an observatory and the remote structure will be utilized for astronomy classes as well as faculty and student research.

The Weir C. Ketler Technological Learning Center consists of forty microcomputers and three big-screen projection systems and houses the help desk and repair center that support the student technology initiative. All freshmen receive their own tablet PC and color printer/scanner/copier.

The J. Howard Pew Fine Arts Center has art, photography, and music studios; a rehearsal hall; a little theater; a museum; an art gallery; music practice rooms; and an auditorium and stage large enough to accommodate the most elaborate drama productions and concerts. An addition completed in 2002 contains additional classrooms, practice rooms, and a 188-seat recital hall.

Costs

As a relatively small, financially sound college, Grove City is able to charge an unusually low tuition in comparison to other independent institutions of similar quality. The 2009–10 annual tuition charge is $12,590 for all degrees. The cost of a tablet PC for all freshmen is included in the tuition fees. There is no comprehensive fee. Part-time tuition is $395 per credit. Room and board are $6824. Expenses for books, laundry, transportation, and personal needs vary considerably with the lifestyle of the individual.

Financial Aid

Because the College's tuition charges are low, every student, in effect, receives significant financial assistance. Sixty-two percent of the freshmen receive additional aid from GCC. Students applying for financial assistance must complete Grove City College's financial aid form. Job opportunities are available both on and off campus.

Faculty

The focus of the Grove City faculty members is on teaching students, although many members are involved with research and writing. Ninety-two percent of the faculty members hold doctorates. Most of the administrative staff members also teach part-time in various departments. The student-faculty ratio is approximately 16:1. Faculty members emphasize teaching and attention to the students' individual needs; they also participate extensively in the College's extracurricular programs.

Student Government

The Student Government Association provides an opportunity for direct student interaction with the faculty members and administration in matters relating to campus activities. Students serve on regular College committees (library, publications, religious activities, and student activities) and also on the Men's and Women's Governing Board and the Discipline Committee.

Admission Requirements

The College seeks academically qualified students without regard to race, color, sex, religion, or national or ethnic origin. An applicant for admission should be a high school graduate with the following recommended units: English, 4; foreign language, 3; mathematics, 3; history, 2; and science, 2. Engineering, science, and mathematics majors should have 4 units each in both mathematics and science. Auditions are required for music majors. An interview is highly recommended, especially for those who live within a day's drive (400 miles).

Transfer students may receive advanced standing if they have been in good standing at their previous institutions and have maintained a minimum grade point average of 2.0 (on a 4.0 scale).

Application and Information

A regular admission applicant should take the SAT or ACT by October or November of the senior year in high school. The application should include scores on the SAT (preferred) or the ACT, a high school transcript, references, a recommendation from the student's principal or counselor, and a nonrefundable application fee of $50. An application may be submitted after the eleventh grade. An early decision applicant should take the entrance test in the eleventh grade, visit the College for an interview, and submit the application by November 15; notification of the admission decision is mailed on December 15. Approved early decision applicants must accept by January 15 and submit a nonrefundable deposit of $250.

Applicants seeking regular decision must submit the completed application and supporting documents by February 1 of their senior year. Notification of the admission decision is mailed on March 15. Students who are offered admission should reply as soon as possible, but no later than May 1, and include a nonrefundable deposit of $250. Applications received after February 1 are considered as space permits. The College receives three applications for every freshman vacancy.

Additional information may be obtained from:

Jeffrey C. Mincey
Director of Admissions
Grove City College
100 Campus Drive
Grove City, Pennsylvania 16127-2104

Phone: 724-458-2100
Fax: 724-458-3395
E-mail: admissions@gcc.edu
Web site: http://www.gcc.edu

A view of the campus at Grove City College.

GUILFORD COLLEGE

GREENSBORO, NORTH CAROLINA

The College

Founded in 1837 as the Quaker New Garden Boarding School, Guilford College, (www.guilford.edu) is located on 340 wooded acres in Greensboro, North Carolina. Guilford is among the oldest coeducational colleges in the nation and has a long-standing history of commitment to the individual student and to Quaker values. Guilford College draws on Quaker and liberal arts traditions to prepare men and women for a lifetime of learning, work, and social responsibility dedicated to the betterment of the world.

Guilford's 2,688 students, aged 16 to 72, come from more than forty-five states and nineteen countries. The College's size ensures the academic community's commitment to personalized education (95 percent of classes have fewer than 30 students) while embracing academic diversity. Students are encouraged to take an active part in extracurricular activities on campus, including seminars and lecture series, interest and service clubs, and wide-ranging cultural opportunities, as well as a program of intercollegiate athletics and intramurals for both men and women. The Student Union, a student organization, sponsors many of the social, recreational, and cultural programs offered at the College. Many students participate in a variety of community service projects and volunteer programs.

The Bryan Distinguished Visiting Professorship in the Arts, Humanities, and Public Affairs at Guilford College (www.guilford.edu/bryanseries) brings to campus individuals who are widely regarded as experts in their field. Past speakers include Mikhail Gorbachev, Madeleine Albright, Cokie Roberts, Archbishop Desmond Tutu, and Sidney Poitier, among others. Guilford College students attend Bryan Series lectures free of charge.

Guilford's intercollegiate athletic teams (www.guilford.edu/athletics) compete at the NCAA Division III level and in the Old Dominion Athletic Conference (ODAC). The sports include women's basketball, cross-country, lacrosse, soccer, softball, swimming, tennis, track, and volleyball, as well as men's baseball, basketball, cross-country, football, golf, lacrosse, soccer, tennis, and track. Sports programs are coupled with special academic opportunities in sports medicine, sport management, and physical education. Guilford's athletic facilities include basketball courts, cardio and weight-training facilities, racquetball courts, and additional multipurpose courts.

Location

A city of 245,000 people, Greensboro is located midway between Washington, D.C., and Atlanta, Georgia. The greater metropolitan area has a population of approximately 1.3 million. Greensboro is the home of six colleges and universities, with a total student enrollment of approximately 40,000. Guilford participates in an academic consortium with the other institutions. Two interstate highways serve the city, and the Piedmont Triad International Airport is less than 5 miles from campus. Numerous historic sites as well as local, state, and national parks are within day-trip distance of the College. Greensboro's central location in the state allows easy access to the state's beautiful beaches and to several major ski areas in the mountains. The amenities of life in the Southeast—climate, pace, and friendliness—coupled with rich cultural opportunities and sound economic growth make the Sun Belt an attractive area in which to study and live.

Majors and Degrees

Guilford College offers B.A. or B.S. degrees (www.guilford.edu/academics) in accounting, African-American studies, art, biology, business management, chemistry, community and justice studies, computer information systems, computing and information technology, criminal justice, economics, education studies, English, environmental studies, exercise and sports studies, forensic biology, French, forensic accounting, geology and earth sciences, German, German studies, health sciences, history, integrative studies, international studies, life sciences, mathematics, music, peace and conflict studies, philosophy, physics, political science, psychology, religious studies, sociology/anthropology, Spanish, sport management, sports medicine, theater studies, and women's studies. The B.F.A. degree is offered in art. Also offered is a Bachelor of Music degree.

Concentrations are available in accounting, African-American studies, African studies, anthropology, applied ethics, astronomy, business, business law, chemistry, communications, community studies, computing and information technology, criminal justice, dance, earth science, East Asian studies, economics, education studies, English, environmental studies, field biology, forensic science, French language and society, German language and society, history, human resource management, integrated science, international business management, international political economy, interpersonal communication, Japanese language and society, Latin American studies, mathematics for the sciences, medieval/early modern studies, money and finance, music, nonprofit management, organizational communication, peace and conflict studies, philosophy, philosophy of mathematics, physics, political science, psychology, Quaker studies, religious studies, sociology, Spanish language and society, sport administration, sport marketing, theater studies, visual arts, and women's studies.

Most recently, Guilford College has entered into an agreement with University of North Carolina at Greensboro to offer an accelerated Master of Business Administration (M.B.A.) degree. Preprofessional programs are offered in dentistry, law, medicine, ministry, and veterinary science.

Academic Programs

Each student works closely with a faculty adviser to select courses that meet individual educational and career goals. Thirty-two semester courses are required for graduation, eight of which are generally in the major field of study. Required courses are few but represent a distribution over the principal fields of the arts and sciences. Flexible requirements allow for interdisciplinary and double majors.

Incoming first-year students and transfer students participate in an orientation program that includes computer training, learning skills, academic advising, self-awareness workshops, and outdoor experiences.

Independent studies, off-campus internships, and off-campus seminars are open to all students. An expanded honors program includes a variety of honors courses for students with exceptional academic credentials and motivation. One pass/fail elective course may be taken each semester.

Entering students may waive courses through Advanced Placement (AP) examinations in English, history, laboratory science, mathematics, and foreign languages. Advanced placement requires an AP score of 3 or better or a general CLEP score of 500 or better; credit requires an AP score of 4 or better or a general CLEP score of 550 or better. Subject CLEP scores must be at least 50 for advanced placement and at least 55 for credit.

Guilford College has a two-semester calendar. The first semester ends before winter break and the second semester ends in early May.

Off-Campus Programs

Semester abroad programs (www.guilford.edu/studyabroad) enable students to study in China, England, France, Germany, Ghana, Greece, Ireland, Italy, Japan, Mexico, the Netherlands, Scotland, Spain, and Wales, as well as a variety of other locations. Students can choose Guilford-led programs or those managed by affiliated partners like the School for Field Studies, the Foundation for International Education, or the School for International Training. A full year of academic credit for study in Japan is available through a cooperative program with International Christian University in Tokyo.

Guilford participates in two consortia that allow open registration in eight area colleges and universities without additional fees. Other member schools are Bennett College, Elon University, Greensboro College, Guilford Technical Community College, High Point University, North Carolina A&T State University, and the University of North Carolina at Greensboro.

An on-campus programs director assists students who wish to study abroad. An internship director helps place students who wish to study elsewhere in the United States. Course credit is given for all approved off-campus study. The Washington Semester in Washington, D.C., supplements the academic program and helps students develop professional skills and career potential through internships with the federal government, lobbying organizations, or public agencies.

Internships may be done in any discipline. Locally, students may pursue internships as part of their academic and career development in business, education, government, health services, law, medicine, scientific research, and social services. In addition, the Guilford College Career and Community Learning Center sponsors a variety of community service activities, such as the Student Literacy Corps and Project Community.

Academic Facilities

Guilford's stately Georgian-style buildings house classrooms, a spacious auditorium, the library, student center, administrative offices, and residence halls. The state-of-the-art 65,000-square-foot Frank Family Science Center features fourteen laboratories (with twenty-four workstations each), 1,600 computer connections, a rooftop observatory with a computer-driven telescope, and a 150-seat multipurpose auditorium/planetarium. Multiple studio spaces are available to students in the fine arts.

Guilford's Hege Library is one of the three largest private libraries in North Carolina. The library contains 250,000 volumes and includes an art gallery, a media center, and the only Friends Historical Collection in the Southeast. Hege Library is fully automated and is linked to buildings across the entire campus. Students also have library privileges at six colleges within 20 miles that have an additional 1.3 million volumes.

Bauman Telecommunications Center houses two computer-equipped classrooms, faculty offices, and three computer labs with ninety-one personal computers. In addition, there are 200 public terminals in the Center and other terminals in academic buildings around the campus. Fiber-optic hookups link Bauman Telecommunications Center to most academic buildings on campus, and all students living on campus can access the facility from their residence hall rooms. In addition, satellite connections make it possible to bring in foreign language programming from around the world. Guilford offers state-of-the-art computers in its multimedia learning center for cultures and languages. Most residential students have PCs in their rooms connected to the College network, and the College has full Internet access. Wireless access is available in Hege Library, Founders Hall Terrace, and Community Center Terrace. All students have e-mail accounts, and through an interdisciplinary course, students can play an active role in developing the College's Web site.

Costs

Basic expenses for the 2009–10 academic year were $27,120 for tuition, with $7890 for room and board and fees. Personal expenses, book costs, and transportation expenses vary according to individual need.

Financial Aid

Guilford College tries to meet the demonstrated financial need (www.guilford.edu/finaid) of all students, as determined by the Free Application for Federal Student Aid (FAFSA). More than $22 million in scholarships, loans, grants, and work-study opportunities was awarded to students last year. Academic scholarships are awarded on a competitive basis. Guilford offers six merit-based and special interest scholarship programs. Approximately 86 percent of last year's student body received some form of merit-based or need-based assistance. The average need-based award was more than $19,052 a year per recipient. The average merit-based award was $6286.

Faculty

Guilford has 136 full-time faculty members. The College seeks faculty members who value the sense of community and concern for individuals that are part of Guilford's heritage. The student-faculty ratio is currently 16:1. The average class size is 19.

Student Government

Guilford entrusts its students with responsibility for governing their own actions and furthering the best interests of the entire College community. The student Community Senate is composed of representatives from residence halls and the day-student organization, a member of the administration, and 2 faculty members. Students serve on all faculty and administrative committees and on the College's Board of Trustees and Alumni Board.

Admission Requirements

As one of the oldest coeducational institutions in the nation, Guilford takes the commitment to academics and the liberal arts seriously. To that end, the Admission Committee (www.guilford.edu/admission) uses a holistic method of application evaluation. Each applicant is considered on an individual basis. Students are encouraged to challenge themselves within their high school environment, both in and out of the classroom. While the majority of applicants submit some form of standardized test scores (ACT or SAT), students have the option of submitting a portfolio of written work in lieu of standardized test scores. The Guilford College community is full of active and involved citizens. The evaluation process seeks to continue to admit students that bring a diverse variety of backgrounds and interests to the College. Interviews, although not required, are available so that the applicant can become better acquainted with Guilford and so that the admission staff can better evaluate the candidate. Guilford is competitive with respect to admissions.

Application and Information

Admission plans (www.guilford.edu/apply) include early action and regular decision. Early action applicants must apply by January 15 and are notified by February 15. The regular decision priority deadline is February 15, and applicants are notified by April 1. After February 15, applications are considered on a space-available basis. Candidates admitted for regular decision must reply to their offers of admission by May 1.

Early entrance applicants are considered after their junior year of high school. They must have an outstanding academic record and must be sufficiently mature socially to adjust to college life.

Transfer candidates should apply for admission by December 1 for the spring semester and by June 1 for the fall semester.

The priority deadline for applying for financial aid is March 1.

The Admission Office is open for visits (www.guilford.edu/visit) Monday through Saturday during the academic year. During the summer, the Admission Office is open for visits Monday through Friday. Guilford College encourages students to visit for a campus tour. More than a classroom education, the Guilford experience is designed to stimulate the whole person and provide the critical thinking that will help today's students take their place as leaders who will guide tomorrow.

For further information and application forms for admission and financial aid, students should contact:

Admission Office
Guilford College
5800 West Friendly Avenue
Greensboro, North Carolina 27410
Phone: 336-316-2100
800-992-7759 (toll-free)
E-mail: admission@guilford.edu
Web site: http://www.guilford.edu

GWYNEDD-MERCY COLLEGE

GWYNEDD VALLEY, PENNSYLVANIA

The College

Founded by the Sisters of Mercy, Gwynedd-Mercy College (GMC) is a Catholic college offering a strong foundation in the liberal arts. For sixty years, Gwynedd-Mercy College has been "Bringing Futures Into Focus" by preparing students to become top professionals in the fields of allied health professions, arts and sciences, business and computer information sciences, education, and nursing. GMC offers more than forty associate, bachelor's, and master's degree programs on a full- and part-time basis. GMC's academic distinction lies in the intersection of excellent programs in health care, education, and business administration, which prepare students to become leaders in the region's powerful and growing life sciences industry.

Located just 30 minutes from Philadelphia and with an enrollment of nearly 3,000 students, Gwynedd-Mercy College is large enough to offer a vibrant campus life but small enough that professors can develop mentoring relationships with students. The College educates students in the Mercy tradition of service to society, preparing graduates who not only are recruited for jobs but also create lives and careers with deep meaning. In the 2008 edition of *U.S. News & World Report*'s "America's Best Colleges," Gwynedd-Mercy College ranks among the top master's-level universities in the North.

Gwynedd-Mercy College has twenty NCAA Division III athletic teams, including baseball, basketball, cheerleading, cross-country, field hockey, golf, indoor/outdoor track and field, lacrosse, soccer, softball, tennis, and volleyball. The men's baseball and men's and women's basketball teams have won various championships. The College also offers a variety of intramural sports.

Students are encouraged to participate in activities and student government so that they can socialize with friends, develop talents, and build leadership skills. The College offers more than thirty clubs and organizations, including the drama club, campus ministry, a nationally renowned choir, the yearbook staff, and social committees. The first Catholic college chapter of Habitat for Humanity, which has been endorsed by former President Jimmy Carter, gives students the chance to help in the actual construction of homes for the less fortunate. Students can write for the College newspaper, the *Gwynmercian*, which has received a first-place rating with special merit from the American Scholastic Press Association. Through the on-campus chapter of the Mercy Works Program, students can help the poor with fund-raising efforts and adopt-a-family programs at the Thanksgiving and Christmas holidays. Some students decide to give a year of service after graduation to Mercy Volunteer Corps' nationwide outreach program.

A student lounge dedicated as an International Center for Understanding and Culture (ICUC) gives American students the opportunity to meet, socialize with, and get to know young people from other countries. The College's diversified international students come from many different countries. The ICUC is a popular campus meeting place for students to confide their hopes and dreams.

On the graduate level, Gwynedd-Mercy College offers a master's degree program in education (educational administration, reading, school counseling, special education, and a Master Teacher program) and nursing (geriatrics, oncology, and pediatrics).

Location

Gwynedd-Mercy's idyllic 160-acre campus is located in Gwynedd Valley, Pennsylvania, a suburb 20 miles from downtown Philadelphia. Old City, South Street, and sports arenas are a 25- to 30-minute car or train ride from the campus. The College is situated just minutes from several major highways, including the Pennsylvania Turnpike. The immediate area is rich in the history of Colonial America, and two of the oldest homes in Pennsylvania are located on the Gwynedd campus. In addition to the vibrant city life of Philadelphia, students can travel to the New Jersey beaches or the Pocono Mountains, which are only 2 hours from the campus.

Majors and Degrees

Gwynedd-Mercy offers baccalaureate degrees in accounting, behavioral/social gerontology, biology, business administration, business education, computer information technology, criminal justice, elementary education, English, history, human services, mathematics, nursing, psychology, sociology, and special education. Seven certification options are available through the School of Education.

Associate in Science degrees are awarded in the allied health fields of cardiovascular technology, health information technology, and respiratory care. Associate degrees are also granted in accounting, business administration, computer programming, liberal studies, natural science, and nursing.

Academic Programs

The school year is divided into two semesters, and most baccalaureate degree programs require the completion of a minimum of 125 credit hours. GMC maintains a strong liberal arts component in all of its degree programs. Whether the student chooses to major in one of the liberal arts or to pursue a professionally oriented degree, courses are required in language, literature and the fine arts, humanities, and behavioral, social, and natural sciences.

Individualized internships and work-experience programs are available and recommended in all majors to give students firsthand experience in their chosen major. Nearby Fortune 500 companies offer a variety of experiences to students in business and accounting. TAP, the Teacher Assistant Program, places every education major in the classroom one day a week beginning in the freshman year. All allied health and nursing programs require clinical experience. The 2-2 programs—those with an associate degree to bachelor's degree progression—offer allied health and nursing students the opportunity to gain employment in their field while continuing toward the baccalaureate degree. The School of Business and Computer and Information Sciences maintains a successful work-experience semester. Through this paid internship, students earn credit while gaining valuable experience in challenging positions.

Students have the opportunity to come to the Academic Resources Center for free class tutoring and to obtain help in improving their writing skills.

Off-Campus Programs

The excellent on-campus laboratory facilities are extended by affiliations with more than 200 hospitals and health-care agencies in Pennsylvania, New Jersey, and Delaware, where students may complete their clinical experience. Merck provides a one-semester industrial laboratory experience for qualified biology majors. Gwynedd-Mercy College maintains a close relationship with nearby companies, including Johnson & Johnson, McNeil, and Sun Company, for work-experience programs.

Academic Facilities

Gwynedd-Mercy has expanded its physical facilities as its student enrollment has increased. The Sister Isabelle Keiss Center for Health and Science opened in 1999 and houses the Schools of Nursing and Allied Health Professions and the Division of Natural Sciences. The 50,000-square-foot state-of-the-art facility offers laboratories for areas such as nursing skills, respiratory care, cardiovascular technology, radiation therapy, health information technology, organic chemistry, and microbiology. The College's Griffin Complex houses the College's Student Union—which is equipped with a game room, full gymnasium and track, racquetball court, and weight room. The College offers four residence halls that house 40 percent of the school population. Theaters include the Julia Ball Auditorium, a small in-the-round theater, and a TV production studio. One computer laboratory is reserved for computer majors. A separate facility is maintained for use by the general student body. Both are staffed and open at hours that are convenient to student use. The Valie Genuardi Hobbit House, a private school for preschoolers where students in the School of Education are trained, is situated on campus.

Costs

The 2009–10 academic-year tuition (two semesters) for full-time students (12 to 18 credits per semester) was $23,730. The tuition for allied health and nursing students was $25,230. Room and board were, on average, $9208. Professional liability fees for students enrolled in clinical components and lab fees are extra.

Financial Aid

Gwynedd-Mercy's financial aid program is designed to provide financial assistance to academically qualified students whose resources are inadequate to meet the costs of attending the College. The student Financial Aid Committee endeavors to assist as many students as possible, using Gwynedd-Mercy funds as well as federal, state, and other available funds. Aid is awarded on the basis of demonstrated financial need, academic proficiency, and responsible campus citizenship.

A financial aid packet is sent, with instructions, to those who request it on their application form. High school students should request the Free Application for Federal Student Aid (FAFSA) from their guidance office. In 2007–08, 91 percent of Gwynedd-Mercy College full-time students received some form of financial aid. March 15 is the deadline for freshmen entering in the fall semester. The deadline for Academic Scholarships is February 15.

Faculty

The student-faculty ratio is 13:1, allowing for personal contact, advising, and after-class instruction. This is a widely acknowledged strength of the GMC experience. For nursing students in the clinical setting, there are never more than 8 students to 1 clinical adviser; in the allied health programs, there often is one-to-one instruction. The quality of teaching is enhanced by the diversified interests of the faculty. The 181 faculty members teach both day and evening classes, allowing students the greatest flexibility in scheduling. Free tutoring is available in all disciplines.

Student Government

All students are encouraged to take part in the responsibilities of student government. This student participation and shared responsibility for the welfare of the College are promoted through a framework of committees. The student government president and 3 other students are members of the College Council, which is responsible for the continuing self-evaluation of the College and policy formation. In addition, students share membership in the Educational Planning Committee, Faculty/Student Committee, Financial Aid Committee, and Library Committee.

Admission Requirements

Admission to Gwynedd-Mercy College is based on a student's high school record, rank in class, SAT or ACT scores, counselor's recommendation, and choice of major. Entrance requirements vary with the program. For the fall 2008 entering class, the College based admission decisions on the critical reading and mathematics scores on the SAT. The rolling admission policy allows the student to be informed of the admission decision within two to three weeks after the file is complete.

GMC awards College credit for satisfactory completion of Advanced Placement courses. The exam score must be 3 or above.

A minimum 2.0 grade point average (on a 4.0 scale) is generally required to transfer from another college. Gwynedd-Mercy College does, however, retain the right to require a higher GPA for admission to some programs.

GMC selects all students on the basis of academic achievement and does not discriminate on the basis of race, religion, gender, handicap, or sexual orientation.

Application and Information

All prospective applicants are urged to visit the campus to meet and talk with an admission counselor, a dean, or a program director. To apply for admission, applicants should complete an application form and submit it to the admissions office along with the required nonrefundable $25 application fee. The fee is waived for students who apply online at http://gmc.edu. First-time freshmen must also submit an official high school transcript or equivalency certificate; a written recommendation from a principal, teacher, guidance counselor, or employer; and results of the SAT or ACT (for recent high school graduates). All applicants should verify that they meet the specific requirements and have the necessary high school prerequisites for admission.

Students who wish to transfer to Gwynedd-Mercy College should complete the application form and submit it to the admissions office along with the required nonrefundable $25 application fee, high school and college transcripts, and a letter of recommendation.

For additional information or to schedule campus tours and visits, students are encouraged to contact:

Office of Admissions
Gwynedd-Mercy College
1325 Sumneytown Pike
P.O. Box 901
Gwynedd Valley, Pennsylvania 19437-0901
Phone: 800-DIAL-GMC (toll-free)
E-mail: admissions@gmc.edu
Web site: http://www.gmc.edu

Gwynedd-Mercy College.

HAWAI'I PACIFIC UNIVERSITY

HONOLULU, HAWAI'I

The University

Hawai'i Pacific University (HPU) is a private, nonprofit university with an international student population of approximately 8,200 students. HPU is one of the most culturally diverse universities in America with students from all 50 U.S. states and more than 100 countries. Founded in 1965, HPU prides itself on maintaining strong academic programs, small class sizes, individual attention to students, and a diverse faculty and student population. HPU offers more than 50 acclaimed undergraduate programs and 12 distinguished graduate programs. HPU is recognized as a Best in the West college by the Princeton Review and a Best Buy by *Barron's* business magazine. HPU is accredited by the Western Association of Schools and Colleges, the National League for Nursing Accrediting Commission, and the Council on Social Work Education, to name a few.

The diversity of the HPU student body stimulates learning about other cultures firsthand, both inside and outside of the classroom. There is no majority population at HPU. Students are encouraged to examine the values, customs, traditions, and principles of others to gain a clearer understanding of their own perspectives. HPU students develop friendships with students from throughout the United States and the world and form important connections for success in the global economy of the twenty-first century.

HPU has NCAA Division II intercollegiate sports. Men's athletic programs include baseball, basketball, cross-country, golf, soccer, and tennis. Women's athletics include basketball, cross-country, soccer, softball, tennis, and volleyball.

The housing office at HPU offers many services and living options for students. Residence halls with cafeteria service are available on the windward Hawai'i Loa campus, while off-campus apartments are available in the Honolulu and Waikiki areas for those seeking more independent living arrangements.

Location

Hawai'i Pacific University's main campus in downtown Honolulu provides a fast-paced, exciting urban environment in the heart of the business community. The downtown campus comprises six buildings in the center of Honolulu's business district, and is home to the College of Business Administration and the College of Humanities and Social Sciences. The campus location makes it easy for students to commute to and also find and maintain internship opportunities at neighboring businesses.

Eight miles away, the 135-acre windward Hawai'i Loa campus, which is set in the lush foothills of the Ko'olau mountains, is home to the College of Nursing and Health Sciences and the College of Natural and Computational Sciences. The Hawai'i Loa campus has residence halls, dining commons, the Educational Technology Center, a student center, and outdoor recreational facilities, including a soccer field, tennis courts, a softball field, and an exercise room.

HPU is also affiliated with the Oceanic Institute, a 56-acre aquaculture research facility located at Makapu'u Point on the southeastern coast of O'ahu, Hawai'i. At the facility, undergraduate and graduate students are able to get hands-on experience in marine science. All three sites are conveniently linked by a free shuttle.

Majors and Degrees

Hawai'i Pacific University offers programs that lead to the undergraduate degrees of Bachelor of Arts (B.A.), Bachelor of Science (B.S.), Bachelor of Science in Business Administration (B.S.B.A.), Bachelor of Science in Nursing (B.S.N.), and Bachelor of Social Work (B.S.W.).

Undergraduate majors include the B.A. in anthropology, Asian studies, communication, East-West classical studies, economics, English, environmental studies, history, human resource development, human services (general and concentrations in nonprofit management and substance abuse counseling), international relations, international studies, journalism (concentrations in broadcast, design, photojournalism, and print), justice administration, multimedia (concentrations in digital media, media studies, video production, and Web design), political science, prelaw, psychology, social science, sociology, and teaching English as a second language. The B.S. is available in advertising/public relations (concentrations in strategic creative and strategic planning/account management), biochemistry, biology (concentrations in general biology and human and health sciences), computer science, diplomacy and military studies, environmental science, health science, marine biology, mathematics (concentrations in 3-2 engineering, applied math, math education, and pure math), oceanography, prechiropractic, pre–medical studies, and pre–physical therapy. The B.S.B.A. is available in accounting, business economics, computer information systems, entrepreneurial studies, finance, general business, human resource management, international business, management, marketing, public administration, and travel industry management. The Bachelor of Education (B.Ed.), Bachelor of Science in Nursing (B.S.N.) and Bachelor of Social Work (B.S.W.) are also available. Dual degrees, double majors, and minors are also offered.

In addition to the undergraduate programs, HPU offers twelve graduate programs. The Master of Arts (M.A.) is offered in communications, diplomacy and military studies, global leadership and sustainable development, human resource management, organizational change, and teaching English as a second language. The Master of Business Administration (M.B.A.) is available in accounting, e-business, economics, finance, human resource management, information systems, international business, management, marketing, and travel industry management. Other graduate programs include Master of Education in Secondary Education (M.Ed.), Master of Science in Information Systems (M.S.I.S.), Master of Science in Marine Science (M.S.M.S.), Master of Science in Nursing (M.S.N.), and Master of Social Work (M.S.W.)

Academic Programs

The baccalaureate student must complete at least 124 semester hours of credit. Forty-five of these credits provide the student with a strong foundation in the liberal arts, while the remaining credits are composed of appropriate upper-division classes in the student's major and related areas. The academic year operates on a semester system, with regular fall and spring semesters as well as shorter sessions, including one winter and three summer sessions. By attending the supplemental summer and winter sessions, a student may complete the baccalaureate degree program in three years. A five-year B.S.B.A./M.B.A. program is also available.

Off-Campus Programs

As part of its emphasis on international education and global citizenship, Hawai'i Pacific University offers study-abroad opportunities that complement and enhance students' academic experience. Study-abroad opportunities are available in Australia, Austria, Brazil, France, Germany, Great Britain, Japan, Korea, Mexico, Spain, Sweden, Taiwan, and Thailand. HPU undergraduates and graduates who have completed at least one semester of studies at HPU and intend to complete a degree at HPU are eligible to apply.

The Career Services Center offers a comprehensive education/internship program to further develop students' studies and elevate their career-related position through experience. HPU intertwines academic and cocurricular programs with the world of work so students gain academic credit, work experience, and a salary. HPU students have done co-ops and internships at some of the world's best-known companies and organizations, including American Express Financial Advisors; Deloitte & Touche, LLP; the FBI; Hilton Hotels; Microsoft; Oceanic Institute; Polo Ralph Lauren; and Walt Disney World. The staff at the Career Services Center continues to work with students before and after graduation, assisting with everything from resume writing to job interview preparation.

Academic Facilities

The downtown campus comprises six buildings in the center of Honolulu's business district. One of these buildings is the HPU Frear Center, which houses state-of-the-art classrooms, a communication lab, and a high-tech information systems classroom. HPU's Meader Library provides a multitude of general and specialized resources, including a business reference collection, a National Endowment for the Humanities (NEH) collection, and many online databases and journals. The circulating book collections support communications, computer studies, education, literature, social sciences, and other curriculum areas. Also available are study areas, group study rooms, computer work stations, and wireless Internet. The Tutoring and Testing Center provides free tutoring in all core subjects. The expanded downtown computer lab includes more than 420 computers for student use.

On the suburban and residential windward Hawai'i Loa campus, academic life revolves around the Amos N. Starr and Juliette Montague Cooke Academic Center (AC). The AC houses classrooms; organic chemistry, nuclear magnetic resonance, and regular laboratories; faculty and staff offices; a theater; an art gallery; and the Atherton Library, which includes circulating and reference book collections in the areas of art, history, marine science, nursing, and Hawai'i and the Pacific. Additionally, the library provides access to electronic books (e-books), databases, study rooms, IBM computers, and wireless Internet. Computers are also available for library research, e-mail, and word processing.

HPU is also affiliated with the Oceanic Institute, a major research center specializing in marine biology, marine aquaculture, biotechnology, and ocean resource management. It is located on a 56-acre site at Makapu'u Point on the windward coast of O'ahu, Hawai'i. Learning, internship, and research opportunities for graduates and undergraduates abound in this hands-on learning environment.

Costs

For the 2009–10 academic year, tuition was $14,860 for most majors, while books, supplies, and health insurance cost approximately $2610. Tuition for marine science majors was $17,540, and tuition for junior- or senior-year nursing majors was $21,760. The cost to live in on-campus residence halls or off-campus apartments is comparable; room and board were $11,094 for a double occupancy room. There is an additional $500 refundable security deposit required for residence halls and off-campus apartments.

Financial Aid

HPU offers most forms of federal financial aid, including student grant and loan programs, as well as loans for parents of dependent students. Over 60 percent of the University's students benefit from federal financial aid programs or a wide range of institutional scholarships. Students should complete the Free Application for Federal Student Aid (FAFSA) to be considered for federal aid programs. While aid can be awarded throughout the academic year, students should complete the application prior to the March 1 priority deadline to be considered for all available funding. Visit http://www.hpu.edu/financialaid for current financial aid and scholarship information.

Faculty

HPU faculty members are renowned for the personal interest they take in each of their students. HPU is proud to offer more than 500 full- and part-time faculty members with outstanding academic and business credentials from around the world, giving HPU students access to a world's worth of knowledge and experiences. A vast majority of HPU faculty members hold the highest degrees in their fields. The student-faculty ratio is 15:1, and the average class size is less than 20.

Student Government

HPU students can join one of the more than 70 student clubs; run for office in the Associated Students of Hawai'i Pacific University (ASHPU), the University's governing body; participate in Army or Air Force ROTC; write for the student newspaper, *Kalamalama*, edit the school's literary journal, *Hawai'i Pacific Review;* or join HPU's stage and pep band or international choral program.

A variety of on-campus activities and events are organized for students by the Student Life Office, including Movie on the Mall, Music on the Mall, intramural sports tournaments, and recreational activities. Annual events include Club Carnival, Welcome Week, Da Freakshow, Halloween Hoopla, and Pacific Bowl.

Admission Requirements

Hawai'i Pacific University seeks students who are motivated and show academic promise. The Admissions Office requires that applicants complete and forward the admission application and their high school transcripts. Transfer students should also submit college transcripts. SAT and/or ACT scores should be submitted if these scores are not posted in their transcripts. First-time freshmen are expected to have a minimum GPA of 2.5 (on a 4.0 scale) in college-preparatory courses. HPU recommends that students complete 4 years of English, 4 years of history or social science, 3 years of math, and 2 years of science. Transfer students with 24 or more postsecondary credits are required to have a GPA of 2.0 or above. For students with less than 24 credits, a combination of college and high school GPA is used.

The marine science and environmental science programs require a GPA of 3.0 or above and 3 years of science, including biology and chemistry (physics is recommended), as well as mathematics through trigonometry (calculus is recommended). Transfer students must demonstrate ability in science and math at the college level. Students not meeting the above criteria are encouraged to enroll at HPU without declaring a major to demonstrate the ability to do college-level work in science and math.

Application and Information

Candidates are notified of admission decisions on a rolling basis, usually within two weeks of receipt of application materials. Early entrance and deferred entrance are available.

For further information and for application materials, students should contact:

Office of Admissions
Hawai'i Pacific University
1164 Bishop Street, Suite 200
Honolulu, Hawai'i 96813

Phone: 808-544-0238
866-CALL-HPU (toll-free in U.S. and Canada)
Fax: 808-544-1136
E-mail: admissions@hpu.edu
Web site: http://www.hpu.edu/petersons

COLLEGE CLOSE-UPS

HESSER COLLEGE

MANCHESTER, NEW HAMPSHIRE

The College

The primary purpose of Hesser College is to provide a high-quality education that is personalized and employment oriented. Hesser College's approach to higher education provides students with increased flexibility. After two years of college, students earn an associate degree and are prepared to enter the workplace, or, if they prefer, students can continue their studies in one of Hesser College's bachelor's degree programs.

Hesser College was established in 1900 as Hesser Business College, a private, nonsectarian college. Since 1972, Hesser College has expanded and enriched its curriculum in keeping with its tradition of providing an affordable career education of high quality.

Hesser College is accredited by the New England Association of Schools and Colleges.

Many students work in the afternoons, evenings, or weekends while attending Hesser College. The men and women currently enrolled represent several states and more than fifteen countries. A large part of the student population is from the New England region.

Hesser College offers intercollegiate sports in men's and women's basketball and soccer, men's baseball, and women's softball. The basketball team has consistently been a major power in the Northern New England Small College Conference. Students also participate in a number of intramural sports programs. Extracurricular activities are varied and include social activities, clubs, trips, and programs in the residence halls.

Hesser College has developed a number of learning assistance programs to help students succeed in their studies. Tutoring and special classes are provided by the faculty throughout each semester. In addition, several departments offer honors programs and special opportunities for independent study. The College also sponsors an active chapter of the national honor society, Phi Theta Kappa, which promotes scholarship and service to the College and the community.

Location

Hesser College is located in Manchester, New Hampshire. With a population of more than 100,000, Manchester is a medium-sized city that offers many cultural, historical, and social events. Hesser's central location provides easy access to entertainment, shopping, and a variety of part-time jobs and academic work experiences.

Manchester was recently named by *Money* magazine as the number-one small city in the northeastern United States. In addition, Manchester was recently named one of the best cities in the United States for business. According to *U.S. News & World Report,* it is "at the hub of things" in the fast-growing high-technology and financial industries of southern New Hampshire.

Manchester has been called the "Gateway to Northern New England," and several major carriers serve the Manchester Airport. Manchester is within 1 hour of Boston, and the mountains and major ski resorts are within 1 to 2 hours of Hesser's campus.

Majors and Degrees

Hesser offers a wide range of programs that prepare students for high-demand careers. Associate degree programs include accounting, business administration, communications and public relations, criminal justice, early childhood education, graphic design, interior design, liberal studies, medical assistant studies, paralegal studies, physical therapist assistant studies, psychology, radio and video production and broadcasting, and small business and management/entrepreneurship.

In addition, Hesser College offers Bachelor of Science degree programs in accounting, business administration, and criminal justice.

Academic Programs

The primary goal of the curriculum is to prepare students for success in specific career areas. The general education requirements are designed to provide the skills necessary for career growth and lifelong learning. Externships, practicums, and opportunities for part-time work experience are available in all majors. An education from Hesser College provides a solid career foundation. Hesser College's goal is quite simple: to prepare people for careers and career advancement.

Many of Hesser College's programs are for the career-minded student who wants to concentrate on the skills required to be successful in the workplace. Most of the courses that students take are directly related to their career choices.

Hesser College follows a traditional semester calendar.

Off-Campus Programs

The College offers opportunities for cooperative education and externships in most of its academic programs. The early childhood education program includes practicums and supervised fieldwork in a variety of child-care facilities. In addition, the curricula of several programs may incorporate short-term study trips to places such as Walt Disney World and Washington, D.C.

Academic Facilities

The academic facilities include five computer labs, a Macintosh-based graphic design lab, medical assistant labs, physical therapist assistant labs, and a radio/video production lab. The

College library contains more than 30,000 titles. The Center for Teaching, Learning, and Assessment provides special tutoring and programs in study skills, reading, writing, math, and computer skills.

Costs

Costs vary by program. Students should contact Hesser College for more information.

Financial Aid

Hesser College offers financial assistance to students who qualify. Many students receive some form of aid. Scholarships are awarded each year to selected students based on academic and financial standing. Hesser College also offers loans and grants. Students should contact Hesser College for more information.

Faculty

The faculty members of Hesser College consistently receive high student evaluations for their interest in each student's success and for the high quality of their teaching. The majority of the faculty members have completed programs of advanced study; many hold doctoral degrees, and all have practical experience in business or other career fields.

Admission Requirements

Hesser College has a rolling admissions policy. Students may apply for admission at any time and should contact the Hesser College admissions team for more information.

Application and Information

Applicants must submit an application form with a $10 nonrefundable fee. Applications are reviewed on a first-come, first-served basis and normally take seven to fourteen days to be fully reviewed upon receipt of all required information.

Requests for additional information and application forms should be addressed to:

Director of Admissions
Hesser College
3 Sundial Avenue
Manchester, New Hampshire 03103
Phone: 800-994-8412 Dept. 266 (toll-free)
Web site: http://www.hesser.edu/

Students at Hesser College.

COLLEGE CLOSE-UPS

HIGH POINT UNIVERSITY

HIGH POINT, NORTH CAROLINA

HIGH POINT UNIVERSITY

The University

High Point University (HPU) is a dynamic private university related to the United Methodist Church. At High Point, every student receives an extraordinary education in a fun environment with caring people. With 3,700 students, the University is large enough to guarantee high quality and diversity in programs and services yet small enough to enable community among students and faculty and staff members. HPU has a beautiful, 170-acre campus with state-of-the-art facilities in a small, caring environment. In a typical year, students come from forty-four states and fifty countries, making the campus a microcosm of the nation and the world, thereby creating an ideal learning environment.

The University fully recognizes its responsibility to provide the best liberal arts education possible, but faculty and staff members recognize that education, as often defined, is not sufficient. Therefore, the University intentionally seeks to provide a holistic education and develop character by encouraging personal responsibility and by inculcating values through curricular and cocurricular programs and services, including a required ethics course, the President's Seminar on Life Skills, and the University chapel, where services are offered each week. Although attendance is voluntary, chapel services are packed each Wednesday.

In addition to the bachelor's degrees described below, the University offers four master's degrees: the Master of Business Administration (M.B.A.); the Master of Education (M.Ed.) in elementary education, educational leadership, and special education; the Master of Science (M.S.) in international management, management, and sport studies; and the Master of Arts (M.A.) in history and nonprofit management.

Location

Together, High Point, Greensboro, and Winston-Salem form the Piedmont Triad of North Carolina, a metropolitan area of approximately 1.5 million people, more than 90,000 of whom live within the city of High Point. Both Winston-Salem and Greensboro are 20 minutes from the campus, as is the Piedmont Triad (Greensboro–High Point) International Airport. Both Raleigh and Charlotte are 1½ hours away, the Appalachian Mountains are 2 hours away, and the Atlantic Ocean and beaches are 4 hours away.

The region is known nationally and internationally for the quality of its institutions of higher education. Within a 60-mile radius are Duke University, the University of North Carolina at Chapel Hill, and Wake Forest University, along with twenty-eight other colleges and universities. Obviously, such an area is replete with athletic, cultural, recreational, and social activities for young adults.

Majors and Degrees

High Point University awards the Bachelor of Arts degree in art, art education, criminal justice, elementary education, English: literature, English: writing, French, graphic design, history, human relations, international studies, middle grades education, music: general studies, music: organ or piano, music: voice, North American studies, philosophy, political science, religion, sociology, Spanish, special education, theater: performance, and theater: technical. The University awards the Bachelor of Science degree in accounting, actuarial science, athletic training, biology, biochemistry, business administration (accounting, economics, finance, information security and privacy, international management, management, and marketing), chemistry, chemistry: business, communication (electronic media–interactive communication and video gaming, journalism, media and popular culture, and strategic communication), computer science, entrepreneurship, exercise science, forestry, home furnishings marketing, interior design, international business, management information systems, mathematics, medical technology, physical education, psychology, recreation, and sport management. Within the liberal arts major, students can complete the requirements for admission to professional schools, including dentistry, engineering, forestry, law, medicine, pharmacy, physician assistant studies, and veterinary medicine.

Academic Programs

The academic program includes sixty-eight majors administered through the College of Arts and Science, the Phillips School of Business, the Qubein School of Communication, the Wilson School of Commerce, and the Brayton School of Education. In addition, the University allows students with well-defined objectives that cannot be satisfied within the regular curriculum to design their own individualized majors. An honors program recognizes and encourages creativity and academic achievement in top academic students.

The curriculum emphasizes the study of the liberal arts in the belief that there is no better way to encourage communication skills, critical thinking, and personal integrity and in the belief that in the process of acquiring these skills, students become self-learners who are equipped to succeed in life and work. Within the liberal arts framework, the University provides several professional programs, including athletic training, business administration, computer information systems, computer science, exercise science, home furnishings marketing, human relations (a program affiliated with American Humanics, Inc.), information security and privacy, international business, management information systems, and sport management. Cooperative baccalaureate programs are offered in engineering, environmental management, forestry, and medical technology.

The curriculum prepares students to pursue graduate programs consistent with the majors listed above and professional programs beyond the baccalaureate degree in areas that include, but are not limited to, business, dentistry, law, medicine, ministry, pharmacy, physical therapy, physician assistant studies, and sports medicine.

Through the Student Career Intern Program, juniors and seniors at High Point University are able to explore career opportunities outside the classroom. The program enables a student to assume the responsibilities of a regular employee in a local or national business or agency before graduating from High Point, thereby enabling the student to evaluate a career choice prior to graduation.

Students who have completed Advanced Placement courses in high school and who have achieved a score of 4 or 5 on the Advanced Placement tests administered by the College Board may receive credit at High Point University. Applicants may also receive credit for university-parallel courses successfully completed prior to enrollment at High Point, including courses completed while in high school through dual-enrollment or international baccalaureate programs.

Off-Campus Programs

Students may choose to study abroad for a year, a semester, or a summer through the High Point University in England program, which is offered in cooperation with the University of Leeds, or through the University's program at Oxford/Brookes University. The University's affiliation with international study programs administered by other institutions also makes it possible for students to study in Canada, France, Germany, Scotland, Spain, and Mexico. In addition, the University is now offering new venues in Swansea, Wales; Florence, Italy; and London, England. In spring 2007, students took advantage of the opportunity to choose from many of these study-abroad locations in a concentrated three- to four-week "Maymester" program. In addition to the countries listed above, Australia, China, Ireland, and Japan have been added to the "Maymester" program. Subject to prior approval, transfer credit may be awarded for university-parallel work offered by institutions other than those with which the University has formal affiliation.

Students enrolled at High Point University may cross-register on the campus of any other member institution in the Greater Greensboro Consortium, including two state institutions and a women's college.

Academic Facilities

Smith Library, a fully electronically integrated library system, supports sixty-eight undergraduate majors and seven graduate programs. The library contains more than 300,000 print volumes, including more than 50,000 electronic books, and more than 20,000 electronic journals. All electronic resources are accessible online by students and other patrons, both on and off campus.

The Learning Assistance Center, which is located in the library, provides tutoring and other programs designed to facilitate learning. Although 90 percent of enrolled students own personal computers, more than 500 computers are available for student use in classrooms, laboratories, the library, the University Center, and other locations. A roaming profile enables students to save and access their personal documents from any campus PC, including their personal computers and those provided by the University. Computer laboratories in computer science and mathematics are equipped with Linux-based PCs connected to a Linux computing cluster.

Phillips Hall, opened in August 2007, houses a state-of-the-art School of Business designed after the Harvard School of Business. The Congdon Hall of Science provides science laboratories and modern equipment. The James H. and Jessé E. Millis Athletic and Convocation Center houses a state-of-the-art sports medicine center, along with facilities for physical education that include, but are not limited to, the Aerobic Center, an Olympic-size pool, racquetball courts, and tennis courts. The Charles E. and Pauline Lewis Hayworth Fine Arts Center includes the Pauline Theatre, the Sechrest Art Gallery, galleries for student exhibits, a laboratory for computer graphics, and studios for design, drawing, music, painting, photography, printmaking, and theater. Norton Hall, which was built on campus by the international furnishings industry, is a state-of-the-art facility that houses the Knabusch-Shoemaker International School of Furnishings and Design. The Qubein School of Communication opened in fall 2009, with $5 million in television, radio, and video gaming studios. Also recently completed is the Plato Wilson School of Commerce, which includes a Wall Street–style ticker-tape trading room for finance and investing classes, an entrepreneurship center, and many other state-of-the-art amenities.

Costs

For 2009–10, High Point University's comprehensive fee (including tuition, room, board, and general fees) for full-time boarding students ranged from $33,400 to $36,900 for a super deluxe private room.

Financial Aid

Students who require financial assistance should complete the Free Application for Federal Student Aid (FAFSA). The FAFSA provides an estimate of how much the student and the parents/guardians of dependent students can contribute toward the cost of attending High Point University. The University's Office of Student Financial Services uses the results of the FAFSA to determine the types of assistance available to students. Scholarships, grants, loans, and college work-study are possible sources of support.

Presidential Fellowships, ranging from $9000 to $24,000 per year, are awarded on a competitive basis to academically talented entering freshmen through an application and interview process. The University awards up to 100 Leadership Fellowships and Scholarships in amounts ranging from $3000–$7000 to entering freshmen annually, also on a competitive basis.

Faculty

High Point University has a student-faculty ratio of 14:1 and an average class size of fewer than 20 students. More than 82 percent of faculty members have earned either the Ph.D. or another terminal degree. All classes are taught by full faculty members, and one of the professors in each student's major is his or her adviser. High Point University does not use any graduate students or assistants to teach class. Faculty members routinely interact with students outside of class.

Student Government

High Point University intentionally seeks to involve students in campus life through Student Government, service on University-wide committees, and student activities, including fourteen NCAA Division I athletic teams, twelve Greek organizations, and more than seventy other campus organizations. In addition, High Point University students provide more than 30,000 hours annually of voluntary service to the community of High Point.

Admission Requirements

Freshman applicants must be graduates of an accredited secondary school and must exhibit satisfactory performance in a college-preparatory curriculum of 18 units, distributed as follows: English, 4; foreign language, 2; mathematics, 3; history, 3; laboratory science, 3; and electives, 3. Every freshman applicant must submit their scores on the SAT or the ACT. International applicants should submit both TOEFL and SAT or ACT scores. Campus visits and personal interviews are strongly recommended.

Application and Information

Application forms must be completed online by the student and submitted to the Office of Admissions, along with a nonrefundable $40 processing fee. Official transcripts (high school and college, where applicable) and a Counselor Report Form must be sent directly to the University by the appropriate school official. Students should request that a copy of their SAT, ACT, or TOEFL scores be sent to the Office of Admissions at High Point University by the testing agency. High Point University operates under a deadline admission plan, including early decision and early action. Because enrollment is limited by available residential spaces, early application is encouraged. All requests for application materials and information should be directed to:

Office of Undergraduate Admissions
High Point University
833 Montlieu Avenue
High Point, North Carolina 27262-3598
Phone: 336-841-9216
800-345-6993 (toll-free)
E-mail: admiss@highpoint.edu
Web site: http://www.highpoint.edu

High Point University, which is located on a 170-acre campus, enrolls 3,700 students from forty-four states and fifty countries.

COLLEGE CLOSE-UPS

HILBERT COLLEGE

HAMBURG, NEW YORK

The College

Since its founding in 1957, Hilbert College has provided challenging academic programs and close personal attention to its students. The College is an independent, Catholic four-year institution that grants degrees on both the baccalaureate and associate levels. There is a strong commitment to the philosophy of a liberal arts education being the cornerstone of any Hilbert graduate's success. In harmony with its Franciscan spirit, the College provides individual counseling and support services for students whose diversified needs are best met in this small-college setting. Hilbert's campus currently consists of the following buildings: Bogel Hall, which is the academic building; the Francis J. and Marie McGrath Library; the Campus Center; six on-campus residence halls, one traditional-style, four apartment-style, and a suite-style residence hall that opened in fall 2009; a grounds and maintenance building; the Hafner Recreation Center, which hosts several athletic events and where the fitness center is located; Franciscan Hall, which is the student services and administration building; the William E. Swan Auditorium; and Paczesny Hall, the newest academic building on campus, that houses classrooms, faculty offices, and a communications lab and serves the region by hosting a number of cultural events. Hilbert is also the home of the Institute for Law and Justice, a local, regional, and national resource for law enforcement, crime prevention, and community well-being.

Hilbert College has a student body of approximately 1,100 students. About 35 percent of the full-time student body resides on campus. All students are offered myriad social activities, ranging from academic and student clubs to NCAA Division III athletics. Student government takes an active role in the planning and operation of most campus events. Hilbert also offers a select comprehensive Leadership Development Program as well as an honors program.

The College's NCAA Division III athletics program offers intercollegiate competition in men's baseball, basketball, cross-country, golf, lacrosse, soccer, and volleyball. Women's sports include basketball, cross-country, lacrosse, soccer, softball, and volleyball. Competitive lacrosse is new to the College in the 2010–11 school year. Hilbert College competes as a member of the Allegheny Mountain Collegiate Conference. Hockey is a club-level sport.

Location

Hilbert College's nearly 50-acre campus is located in the town of Hamburg in western New York State, on the shore of Lake Erie. The campus is approximately 10 minutes south of Buffalo, a city of 350,000 people, and just minutes from the shores of Lake Erie. Hilbert's proximity to Buffalo makes many cultural and recreational resources easily accessible to its students. Downtown attractions include Kleinhans Music Hall, Studio Arena Theatre, the Albright-Knox Art Gallery, the Museum of Science, and the Buffalo Zoo. The historic Shea's Theatre is also located downtown and is Buffalo's home to many concerts, operas, and Broadway shows. Niagara Falls, one of the nation's greatest natural attractions, is just a 30-minute drive from the campus. Buffalo also provides professional sports in football, hockey, lacrosse, and triple-A baseball. Hamburg also is located a short distance from several cross-country and downhill ski resorts.

Majors and Degrees

Hilbert College offers programs of study leading to a Bachelor of Arts (B.A.) degree in digital media and communication, English, and psychology. The Bachelor of Science (B.S.) degree is offered in accounting (including three separate tracks: commercial accounting, economic crime investigation, and a five-year master's degree track), business administration, computer security and information assurance, criminal justice, forensic science/crime scene investigation, human services, liberal studies (law and government), paralegal studies, political science, and rehabilitation services. The College also offers associate degree programs (A.A. and A.A.S.) in accounting, banking, business administration, criminal justice, human services, liberal arts, and paralegal studies.

Academic Programs

The Bachelor of Arts and Bachelor of Science degrees are granted upon completion of 120 credit hours.

The Associate in Arts, the Associate in Applied Science, and the Associate in Science degrees are all granted upon successful completion of 60 credit hours.

Common to all programs is the completion of the Liberal Learning Core Curriculum. The purpose of the Liberal Learning Core Curriculum is to provide students with a cumulative, holistic liberal arts education to complement and strengthen their professional training. The curriculum is designed to develop habits of critical examination, methods of critical investigation, and ethical perspectives that enable students to make sound judgments and increase their capacity for leading fuller lives. By studying the various liberal arts disciplines, students should achieve a greater awareness of their cultural and social identity while cultivating the intellectual skills and competence that allow them to perform successfully in their chosen careers.

Hilbert has developed a series of transfer articulation agreements with most two-year colleges in New York State. These agreements allow two-year college graduates to move directly into related four-year programs at Hilbert College as full juniors and with no course duplication. In addition, Hilbert is accredited by the Commission on Higher Education of the Middle States Association of Colleges and Schools. Therefore, its credits are readily transferable nationwide to other four-year colleges and universities.

Academic Facilities

Bogel Hall, the original academic building, underwent a massive expansion and renovation in 2007. It contains the Palisano Lecture Hall, faculty offices, computer labs, a hands-on economic crime investigation computer lab, a newly designed forensic science wing with labs, the Academic Services Center, the chapel, and classroom space.

McGrath Library, an expansive building consisting of a two-level core housing the library collection, a seminar wing, and a conference wing, maintains a collection approaching 45,000 volumes, more than 340 periodicals, and a large selection of microforms and audio and video materials. In addition, the McGrath Library supports a law collection for its criminal justice, paralegal studies, and law and government programs on the campus. This collection ranks as one of the largest academic law collections open to the public in western New York State. The library's seminar wing has video-equipped classrooms and a legal research lab. Ample study space is available throughout the library, with both private carrels and group-study tables available for student use.

Paczesny Hall, which opened in 2006, is an academic building that holds faculty offices, high-tech computer labs, smart classrooms, a digital media lab for digital media and communication, and the 435-seat William E. Swan Auditorium. Hilbert is a leader in integrating technology into the classroom. Hilbert's entire campus is wireless and 100 percent of the instructional space has SmartBoard technology.

Costs

For 2010–11, tuition and fees are $18,350, and room and board are $7900. The approximate cost for books and supplies is $700 and for travel and miscellaneous expenses, $1000.

Financial Aid

Ninety-two percent of the members of the current freshman class receive financial aid. Financial aid packages consist of loans, scholarships, grants, and jobs. Most awards are provided on the basis of need, as established by the Free Application for Federal Student Aid (FAFSA), and as funds are available. There are several merit-based scholarships for academic and leadership talents as well as transfer articulation and minority scholarships.

Faculty

Hilbert has a faculty of 91 men and women. Sixty-four percent of the full-time faculty members hold doctoral or terminal degrees. Faculty members play a primary role in the advisement of all students at Hilbert College. The student-faculty ratio is 14:1, with an average class size of 25. All classes are taught by professors.

Student Government

The largest student organization on campus is the Student Government Association (SGA). Headed by student-elected officers, this representative organization acts on the behalf of the entire student body. The SGA administers student funds to sponsor on-campus activities and events that range from intimate concerts to larger campuswide festivities. The SGA is composed of two bodies, the association and the student senate. The association comprises elected students who represent the needs of different classes, residents, and commuters. The student senate is a smaller group that consists of student government–elected officers and individual class representatives. The senate is responsible for the disbursement of funds to student-run clubs and organizations.

Admission Requirements

Hilbert College is open to men and women regardless of faith, race, age, physical handicap, or national origin. All students have an equal opportunity to pursue their educational goals through programs available at the College.

The College considers for admission to regular degree study those applicants who have been awarded a high school diploma or a New York State High School Equivalency Diploma.

Application and Information

The closing date for the receipt of applications is September 1. Admission decisions are made on a rolling basis.

For a catalog or an application, students should contact:

Office of Admissions
Hilbert College
5200 South Park Avenue
Hamburg, New York 14075
Phone: 716-649-7900
800-649-8003 (toll-free)
E-mail: admissions@hilbert.edu
Web site: http://www.hilbert.edu

Franciscan Hall, the Student Services Center.

COLLEGE CLOSE-UPS

HILLSDALE COLLEGE

HILLSDALE, MICHIGAN

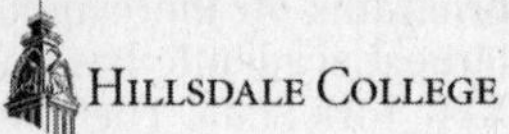

The College

Hillsdale College is a private, independent, nonsectarian institution of higher learning founded in 1844 by men and women who described themselves as "grateful to God for the inestimable blessings" resulting from civil and religious liberty and as "believing that the diffusion of learning is essential to the perpetuity of those blessings." The College has maintained institutional independence since its founding by refusing to accept aid from or control by federal authorities. Far-reaching private support from a national constituency has enabled Hillsdale to continue its trusteeship of the intellectual and spiritual inheritance derived from the Judeo-Christian faith and Greco-Roman culture.

The undergraduate enrollment for fall 2009 was 1,350, of whom 48 percent were men. The College draws students from forty-seven states and seven foreign countries. Approximately 40 percent of students are from Michigan. The entering freshman class in 2009 had an average high school grade point average of 3.75 and mean ACT (28) and SAT (1950) scores well above national averages. Hillsdale students are housed in dormitories, fraternity and sorority houses, and various off-campus dwellings. Single and double rooms are available on campus; there are no coed dormitories. Each College-owned residence hall is supervised by a resident director and resident advisers. All freshmen (except commuters) are required to live on campus; upperclass students seeking to live off campus must apply to the dean of men or dean of women for this privilege.

Hillsdale's Charger athletes compete in eleven intercollegiate NCAA Division II varsity sports as part of the Great Lakes Intercollegiate Athletic Conference (GLIAC). In the past 20 years, the College has produced 180 athletic and academic All-Americans, 24 conference champions, and seventeen teams that have finished tenth or better nationally. An active intramural program is also available. Four national fraternities, three national sororities, and more than seventy other social, academic, spiritual, and service organizations provide Hillsdale students with a diverse array of cocurricular opportunities. A resident drama troupe and dance company, a bagpipe and drum corps, a concert choir, and chamber chorale, a jazz program with big band and combos, instrumental chamber ensembles from string quartets to percussion ensemble, and a College-community orchestra and band constitute the College's performing arts organizations.

Special student services provided by the College include career planning and placement counseling, academic advising and tutoring, and a health service staffed by a physician and a resident nurse.

Location

Hillsdale College is located amidst the hills, dales, and lakes of south-central Michigan. The Indiana and Ohio turnpikes are each 30 minutes away, and the College is within close reach of such metropolitan areas as Detroit, Chicago, Cleveland, Toledo, Ft. Wayne, and Indianapolis. The town of Hillsdale is a county seat with a population of 10,000. Stores, churches, restaurants, and movie theaters are all within walking distance of the campus.

Majors and Degrees

Hillsdale awards Bachelor of Arts and Bachelor of Science degrees in accounting, art, biochemistry, biology, chemistry, classical studies, computational mathematics, economics, education, English, financial management, French, German, Greek, history, Latin, marketing/management, mathematics, music, philosophy, physical education, physics, political science, psychology, religion, Spanish, speech, and theater. Interdisciplinary majors in American studies, Christian studies, comparative literature, European studies, international studies in business and foreign language, political economy, and sociology and social thought are also available. Preprofessional programs are offered in allied health services (including optometry, physical therapy, nursing, and medical technology), dentistry, engineering, environmental sciences, forestry, law, medicine, osteopathy, theology, and veterinary medicine. Hillsdale also offers 2-2 and 3-2 cooperative programs in engineering.

Academic Programs

Hillsdale operates on a two-semester schedule, with the fall term beginning in late August and ending in mid-December and the spring term beginning in mid-January and ending in mid-May. Two 3-week summer sessions are also offered.

The College believes that a sound classical liberal arts education includes study in the humanities, natural sciences, and social sciences, and each student is required to complete a structured core of courses in these areas. All students declare a major by the end of the sophomore year. To graduate, students must complete a minimum 124 hours of course work and fulfill the requirements of at least one major field. It is not unusual for a student to complete two majors or a major and a minor. Each baccalaureate program is based on the completion of four years of study in the liberal arts. The B.A. program includes a foreign language proficiency requirement. The B.S. program requires additional studies in mathematics and the natural sciences.

The honors program enables exceptionally talented students interested in an interdisciplinary community of learning to develop their intellectual potential through an accelerated college core and honors seminars in the junior and senior years. Discussions, guest lectures, and travel opportunities contribute to the social cohesiveness of the group. All Honors students complete a senior thesis on an interdisciplinary topic of their choosing.

The Center for Constructive Alternatives conducts four weeklong symposia during the academic year and is one of the largest college lecture series in America. These programs, dealing with themes ranging from historical to political, business, science, and the arts, are of major importance in the intellectual life of the College. Each brings to the campus distinguished scholars and public figures of national and international renown. All students are required to enroll in two full seminars for credit prior to graduation, one in the first two years and one in the final two years of the curriculum.

Off-Campus Programs

For thirty-five years, the Washington Hillsdale Internship Program (WHIP) has provided students the opportunity to participate in full-time, academically intensive internships in the nation's capital. The program has been significantly bolstered with the 2008 establishment of the Hillsdale College Allan P. Kirby, Jr. Center for Constitutional Studies and Citizenship in Washington, D.C. Past interns and fellows have been placed in locations as challenging and rewarding as the U.S. House of Representatives, the U.S. Senate, the White House, various think tanks including the Heritage Foundation, news and media outlets, national security agencies, lobbying firms, international trade and relations organizations, and private sector companies.

Through the College's affiliations with the Center for Medieval and Renaissance Studies and the Oxford Study Abroad Program, Hillsdale students are able to study abroad for a summer or a year at one of the more than thirty colleges of Oxford University. Hillsdale offers a summer business program in cooperation with Regents College in London, England, and the opportunity to study subject areas ranging from ancient history to theoretical physics at the University of St. Andrews in St. Andrews, Scotland. Science students benefit from Hillsdale's 685-acre field research laboratory in northern Michigan, as well as from a marine biology program in the Florida Keys, internship opportunities with the Omaha Zoo, and a summer research program in South Africa. Foreign language students frequently study abroad in Argentina, France, Germany, and Spain. Qualified individual students who wish to study in another country for a semester or a year are assisted by their faculty adviser and the registrar in planning a program that enables them to gain academic credit as well as take full advantage of their experience.

Academic Facilities

The Hillsdale College Mossey Library is a three-floor facility with a collection of more than 300,000 volumes. In addition to the main study and research collections, the Library also contains a number of rare and special holdings, including the Ludwig von Mises, Russell Kirk,

Richardson Heritage, and Richard Weaver collections. Connected to other Michigan libraries through MelCat, and with college libraries nationwide via interlibrary loan, students have access to most any material necessary for on-campus research. Numerous individual study areas and group study rooms are available for students, as well as computer research terminals.

Lane and Kendall Halls at the front of campus serve as the primary academic facilities in the humanities and contain classroom space and faculty offices, as well as a special laboratory for experimental psychology. The Strosacker Science Center houses the departments of biology, chemistry, and physics. The Joseph H. Moss Family Laboratory Wing, completed in 2008, is a 17,000-square-foot addition that includes a microbiology/cell biology lab, anatomy/physiology lab with human cadaver access, conservation genetics lab, water lab, greenhouse, and organic/general chemistry labs. The 32,000-square-foot Herbert Henry Dow Science Building provides additional classrooms, research laboratories, animal rooms, and a computer lab. The Mary Randall Preschool is a circular laboratory school in which nursery school children are taught by students specializing in early childhood education and psychology. Experts in the field have called this building "a model for the nation." The Hillsdale Academy, a K–12 private model school, provides additional opportunities for classroom observation.

The Roche Sports Complex is a facility available to varsity athletes and the general student body alike. The building houses the 60,000-square-foot Jesse Philips Arena, which features a six-lane, 200-meter running track and basketball/volleyball court. The building also houses the John "Jack" McAvoy Natatorium for swimming and diving, an exercise physiology and sports medicine facility, three racquetball courts, extensive locker room space, and a weight/fitness room. Adjacent is the 7,000-seat capacity Frank "Muddy" Waters Stadium, which features an artificial surface football field; all-weather, Olympic-quality eight-lane running track; outdoor tennis courts; and fields for soccer, baseball, and women's softball.

The Sage Center for the Arts is home to the departments of art, theater, and speech. This 47,000-square-foot facility contains studios, classroom space, an exhibition gallery, a prop- and scene-construction shop, a sound studio, graphics lab, black box theatre, and the Markel Auditorium, a 353-seat performance hall (with orchestra pit). Completed in 2003, the 32,809-square-foot Howard Music Hall houses office, studio, classroom, rehearsal, and performance space for the John E. N. and Dede Howard Department of Music. Notable features include the McNamara Rehearsal Hall, Conrad Recital Hall, and studio space for percussion and jazz studies. Lower-level practice rooms are available to students during business hours without reservation.

Dedicated in January 2008, the 53,000-square-foot Grewcock Student Union is the center of student life. The two-story structure houses the cafeteria, bookstore, student mail center, offices for student activities and publications, a lounge with a 100-inch flat screen television, a formal lounge and conference room, AJ's Café, and a game area. The entire building is wireless, and any Hillsdale student can check out a laptop at the main desk. Couches around the massive two-story fireplace are popular study spots in the colder months.

Costs

Annual tuition for the 2009–10 academic year was $19,380, room was $3850, board was $3900, and mandatory fees were $540. Books, supplies, and personal expenses (including travel, recreation, and clothing) are estimated at $2800 per year.

Financial Aid

Financial aid at Hillsdale is available in many forms. Academic scholarships are awarded on a competitive basis, regardless of financial need, to students who rank in the top 10 percent of their high school class and have standardized test scores in the top 10 percent according to national test norms. The priority deadline for academic scholarship consideration is January 1. The application for admission also serves as the Hillsdale application for merit-based aid. Athletic scholarships are available on a competitive basis in men's baseball and football; men's and women's basketball, track, and cross-country; and women's swimming and volleyball. The departments of art and music also award a select number of scholarships based on strength of portfolio/audition. To apply for aid on the basis of financial need, students are required to file Hillsdale's Confidential Family Financial Statement (CFFS) in January or February of the year of prospective enrollment at Hillsdale. Grants and loans are available from the College. Students may defer payment of up to $500 per semester while working on campus.

Faculty

The faculty consists of 117 full-time members. No classes are taught by graduate students. The size and closeness of the College community enable personal attention and faculty mentorship inside the classroom and during office visits after class. Each student has a faculty adviser for core and major coursework who directs the program of study and provides academic and career counseling. Hillsdale's faculty considers teaching their first priority. Many faculty members also engage in research and scholarly writing, supported by summer and sabbatical leaves funded by the College, and are often invited to comment on the national scene in lecture programs and media outlets.

Student Government

Hillsdale's student government and campus organizations offer students special opportunities to develop leadership skills that enrich both their collegiate experience and lives after graduation. The governing organization of the student body is the Student Federation, which is composed of 18 elected representatives. This group funds student organizations, sponsors all-College entertainment, and acts upon matters of concern to the student community. The Men's Council and Women's Council serve as legislative and judicial bodies within their respective domains in cooperation with members of the administration. The Leadership Workshop, which works closely with the administration, faculty, and community organizations, provides an additional forum for students to cultivate and perfect their leadership skills.

Admission Requirements

Admission is a privilege extended to students who will benefit from, and contribute to, the academic, social, and spiritual environments of the College. Important determinants for admission are intellectual curiosity, ambition, leadership, and volunteerism. Accordingly, grade point average, test scores, class rank, strength of curriculum, extracurricular activities, interviews, self-evaluations, writing samples in the form of two essays, and recommendations are all reviewed carefully and are important in the evaluation process. Although some factors are necessarily more important than others, seldom is any single criterion, however important, decisive.

Transfer students must submit the standard application, including the high school record, SAT or ACT scores, transcripts from all colleges previously attended, and a transfer form from the dean of students of the most recent college attended. Applications by transfers are evaluated similarly to nontransfers.

Candidates for admission from other countries follow the regular entrance procedures. Students who come from a non-English-speaking country must demonstrate proficiency in English by satisfactory performance on the Test of English as a Foreign Language (TOEFL) or the Michigan Test of English Proficiency or at an ESL Center.

Application and Information

Students may apply to Hillsdale College any time after the completion of the junior year of high school. A formal application includes a completed application form accompanied by a nonrefundable fee of $35 (free if submitted online) and all required credentials. Application plans include Early Decision (November 15), Early Action (January 1), and Regular Decision (February 15). Hillsdale College has been distinguished since its founding in 1844 by voluntarily adhering to a nondiscriminatory policy regarding race, religion, sex, and national or ethnic origin—long before the government began regulating such matters.

All records and forms should be mailed to:

Office of Admissions
Hillsdale College
Hillsdale, Michigan 49242-1298
Phone: 517-607-2327
Fax: 517-607-2223
E-mail: admissions@hillsdale.edu
Web site: http://www.hillsdale.edu

HOBART AND WILLIAM SMITH COLLEGES

GENEVA, NEW YORK

The Colleges

Under the mentorship of dedicated faculty members and guided by a curriculum grounded in exploration and rigor, Hobart and William Smith (HWS) students are educated broadly and deeply, focusing on a specific discipline, while making connections between seemingly disparate fields through interdisciplinary study.

HWS students put their education into practice through internships at organizations across the globe and through extensive service-learning programs in the local community and beyond. They are at home on six continents, with 59 percent of students spending at least one semester experiencing life and studying in another country.

Through these carefully designed programs, HWS students develop confidence and gain the necessary clarity to be competitive when seeking employment. They win prestigious fellowships. They gain admittance into the best graduate programs in the world. They go on to lead lives of consequence.

Location

Hobart and William Smith are located on a spectacular 188-acre campus along the northern tip of Seneca Lake in the City of Geneva, New York. With a student body of just over 2,000, Hobart and William Smith are small, coordinate residential colleges where learning does not stop at the classroom door—or even at the boundaries of campus.

Majors and Degrees

Hobart and William Smith Colleges offer Bachelor of Arts, Bachelor of Science, and Master of Arts in Teaching degrees. Majors include Africana studies; American studies; anthropology; anthropology and sociology; architectural studies; art (history and studio); biochemistry; biology; chemistry; classics; comparative literature; computer science; critical social studies; dance; economics; English; environmental studies; European studies; French and Francophone studies; geosciences; Greek; history; international relations; Latin; Latin American studies; lesbian, gay, and bisexual studies; mathematics; media and society; music; philosophy; physics; political science; psychology; public policy studies; religious studies; Russian area studies; sociology; Spanish and Hispanic studies; urban studies; women's studies; and writing and rhetoric.

The Colleges offer dual-degree programs in engineering in cooperation with Columbia University, Dartmouth College, and Rensselaer Polytechnic Institute. A 4-1 M.B.A. program is offered in conjunction with Clarkson University and the Rochester Institute of Technology.

Academic Programs

At the heart of a Hobart and William Smith education is the requirement that each student complete a major and a minor or two majors, one of which must be disciplinary and the other interdisciplinary. The first option gives a student depth of knowledge in a discipline; the latter gives breadth and coherence in learning across traditional disciplines. Each student must also address the Colleges' educational goals and objectives.

The academic year is divided into two 14-week semesters. Students normally take four courses each semester.

Off-Campus Programs

Hobart and William Smith offer more than forty off-campus and international study programs on six continents. Most programs are a semester in length in the following locations: Australia, Argentina, Brazil, China, Denmark, Dominican Republic, Ecuador, England, France, Germany, Hungary, India, Ireland, Italy, Japan, Jordan, Netherlands, New Zealand, Peru, Romania, Russia, Senegal, South Africa, South Korea, Spain, Switzerland, Taiwan, Vietnam, Wales, and Washington, D.C. Many off-campus programs include internships as well as community service components.

Academic Facilities

Among the major academic and administrative buildings on the campus is the Warren Hunting Smith Library that includes the new Rosensweig Learning Commons. This space combines services as well as staff from the library, the Information Technology department, and the Center for Teaching and Learning to create a cohesive environment that enables complex learning, deep exploration, and rigorous intellectual pursuit. The Rosensweig Learning Commons has more than 130 computers, nine LCD screens, six copier/printer/scanner/fax capable machines, and SmartBoards.

Other recent additions to the campus include Stern Hall, housing the departments of economics, anthropology, sociology, political science, and Asian studies; the Elliot Studio Arts Center; and a major renovation and expansion of the Scandling Campus Center. The Colleges also own a 110-acre preserve for biological research and maintain a 65-foot research vessel, *The William Scandling*, which is used for studies on Seneca Lake.

Costs

For 2009–10, tuition was $39,144 and room and board totaled $10,024. Total costs of $50,245 included $1077 in student fees.

Financial Aid

More than 75 percent of Hobart and William Smith students receive some form of financial aid. Hobart and William Smith Colleges offer competitive scholarships recognizing academic achievement and artistic talent as well as excellence in leadership and service. HWS-funded grants as well as federal and state grant monies help support student accessibility, along with numerous loan and student-employment programs.

The Colleges require submission of the Free Application for Federal Student Aid (FAFSA) and the College Scholarship Service's Financial Aid PROFILE from all students who wish to be considered for need-based financial aid. Both forms should be filed before February 15.

Faculty

The full-time teaching faculty numbers 180 members, of whom more than 94 percent hold Ph.D. degrees. The student-faculty ratio is 11:1.

Student Government

Hobart and William Smith students gain leadership skills, express creative talents, develop social and political views, and embrace community citizenship through more than seventy student-run clubs and organizations. The Colleges sponsor twenty-two intercollegiate athletics programs and students regularly participate in both club and intramural sports. One Hobart and one William Smith student sit as voting members on the Colleges Board of Trustees.

Admission Requirements

Admission to the Colleges is based on demonstrated potential to undertake college-level work and to contribute to life on campus. The Committee on Admission is most interested in students with comprehensive high school programs. Applicants are expected to have had a minimum of 4 years of English, 3 years of math, 3 years of science (2 laboratory), and at least 2 years of a modern or classical language (3 years preferred). Other units could come from social studies and from additional work in mathematics, science, literature, and languages. One academic recommendation is required. Standardized test scores (SAT or ACT) are optional. Campus tours and personal interviews are available throughout the year and may be arranged by contacting the Office of Admissions.

Application and Information

Application should be made early in the senior year of high school and not later than February 1. A nonrefundable $45 fee must accompany each application, although this fee is waived for applications submitted electronically. A campus visit, which should include an interview, is strongly recommended. First-year candidates are notified of their application results by April 1 and must respond by the candidates reply date of May 1. Two binding early decision plans are offered to students who select Hobart and William Smith as their first-choice college. Under these plans, students must apply by November 15 of their senior year in high school and are notified of the admission decision by December 15; students applying by January 1 are notified by February 1.

For more information, students should contact:

John W. Young
Director of Admissions
Hobart and William Smith Colleges
629 South Main Street
Geneva, New York 14456
Phone: 315-781-3622
Phone: 800-852-2256 (toll-free)
E-mail: admissions@hws.edu
Web site: http://www.hws.edu

Coxe Hall, on the campus of Hobart and William Smith Colleges.

HOFSTRA UNIVERSITY
HEMPSTEAD, NEW YORK

The University

Hofstra University is a dynamic, private university where students find their edge to succeed in about 140 undergraduate and 150 graduate programs of study. With an outstanding faculty, advanced technological resources, and state-of-the-art facilities, Hofstra enjoys a growing national reputation. Professors teach small classes that emphasize interaction, critical thinking, and analysis. The average class size is just 22, and the student-to-faculty ratio is 14:1.

Five undergraduate colleges at Hofstra offer students a broad array of academic offerings. Major University divisions are the Hofstra College of Liberal Arts and Sciences; the School of Communication; the Frank G. Zarb School of Business; the School of Education, Health, and Human Services; and Honors College.

Hofstra's student body is diverse, with students on the main campus representing forty-seven states and territories, and sixty-seven countries. Total enrollment at Hofstra is about 12,100, with 7,327 full-time undergraduates.

Residential facilities accommodate more than 4,000 students in thirty-seven modern residence halls. Hofstra is 100 percent program accessible to persons with disabilities. Necessary services are provided for students with physical, learning, and/or psychological disabilities who meet the University's academic requirements for admission.

Hofstra has a vibrant campus life, with more than 170 student clubs and organizations, about thirty local and national fraternities and sororities, seventeen NCAA Division I athletic teams for men and women, and more than 500 cultural events on campus each year.

Recreational and athletic facilities include a 15,000-seat stadium, a 5,000-seat arena, a 1,600-seat field turf soccer stadium, and a new field hockey stadium. Students can also take advantage of a physical fitness center, a swim center with an indoor Olympic-sized swimming pool and high-dive area, a softball stadium, and a recreation center offering a multipurpose gymnasium, an indoor track, a fully equipped weight room, spacious locker rooms, a cardio area, and mirrored aerobics/martial arts room. Extensive recreational and intramural sports are also available.

Location

A nationally recognized arboretum, Hofstra's distinctive 240-acre campus is situated just 25 miles east of New York City. Students have easy access by train or car to the incredible cultural resources of New York City as well as the corporate headquarters of some of the world's leading companies, where many students secure internships that lead to future careers. The surrounding Long Island area offers excellent beaches and parks, golf courses, fine dining, and theaters. Long Island's Nassau Veterans Memorial Coliseum is just minutes from Hofstra's campus and hosts the NHL's New York Islanders and numerous concerts and cultural events each year.

Majors and Degrees

The Bachelor of Arts (B.A.) is awarded in African studies, American studies, anthropology, art history, Asian studies, audio/radio, biology, chemistry, Chinese, Chinese studies, classics, comparative literature and languages, computer science, creative arts, dance, drama, early childhood and childhood education (with dual major in another discipline), early childhood education (with dual major in another discipline), economics, elementary education (with dual major in another discipline), engineering science, English, English education, film studies and production, fine arts, foreign language education (French, German, Italian, Russian, Spanish), French, geography, geology, German, global studies, Hebrew, history, humanities, Ibero-American studies, Italian, Jewish studies, journalism, labor studies, Latin, Latin American and Caribbean studies, liberal arts, linguistics, mass media studies, math education, mathematical economics, mathematics, music, natural sciences, philosophy, physics, political science, psychology, public relations, religion, Russian, science education (biology, chemistry, Earth science, physics), social sciences, social studies education, sociology, Spanish, speech communication and rhetorical studies, speech-language-hearing sciences, urban ecology, video/television, and women's studies.

The Bachelor of Business Administration (B.B.A.) is awarded in accounting, business, business education, entrepreneurship, finance, information technology, international business, legal studies in business, management, and marketing.

The Bachelor of Science (B.S.) is offered in applied physics, athletic training, biochemistry, biology, business economics, chemistry, community health, computer engineering, computer science, computer science and mathematics, electrical engineering, environmental resources, exercise specialist studies, fine arts, forensic science, geology, health education, health science, industrial engineering, mathematical business economics, mathematics, mechanical engineering, music, physician assistant studies, physics, University Without Walls, technology and public policy, urban ecology, video/television, video/television and business, and video/television and film.

The Bachelor of Science in Education (B.S.Ed.) is offered with specializations in dance, fine arts, music, and physical education.

The Bachelor of Engineering (B.E.) is offered in engineering science with specializations in biomedical engineering and civil engineering.

The Bachelor of Fine Arts (B.F.A.) is awarded in theater arts with specializations in performance and production.

A combined Bachelor of Arts/Juris Doctor (B.A./J.D.) is awarded in engineering science/law.

Academic Programs

Requirements for graduation vary among schools and majors. A liberal arts core curriculum is an integral part of all areas of concentration. The University calendar is organized on a traditional semester system, including one January session and three summer sessions. Some divisions offer part-time programs during the day and evening and on weekends.

Hofstra offers innovative programs designed to meet the needs of its diverse student body. These include Honors College, Legal Education Accelerated Program (LEAP), Living/Learning Communities, and First-Year Connections.

Honors College provides a rich academic and extracurricular experience for students who show both the potential and the desire to excel. Honors students can elect to study in any of the University's undergraduate programs; these students are involved in all fields of advanced study, including premedicine, prelaw, engineering, business, communication and media arts, humanities, and social sciences.

The Legal Education Accelerated Program allows students to earn both a B.A. and a J.D. in just six years.

In the Living/Learning Communities, the learning experience is not limited to the four walls of the classroom, or even to the borders of the campus. In this program, Hofstra students are exposed to environments that are intellectually stimulating, supportive, and conducive to building lasting friendships and a memorable first-year college experience.

First-Year Connections, an integrated academic and social program, helps first-year students connect to each other and all the resources and opportunities of the University. This program is comprised of seminars and clusters. At the heart of the program are small classes taught by distinguished faculty in areas of interest ranging from architecture to writing. These courses introduce students to the intellectual and social life of the University and satisfy the general education requirements for all majors.

Off-Campus Programs

Hofstra extends learning beyond the classroom through an active internship program and many study-abroad opportunities. The internship program takes advantage of the proximity of New York City, allowing students to gain on-the-job experience in areas such as finance, business, media, advertising, and entertainment.

Hofstra sponsors study-abroad programs in the Czech Republic, England, France, Greece, Ireland, Italy, and Spain; as well as in Ecuador, Jamaica, Japan, and Mexico. Previous international locales have included Australia, Austria, Belgium, China, Germany, the Netherlands, Russia, Singapore, South Korea, Taiwan, Ukraine, and the West Indies. Students wishing to pursue such study should contact the appropriate program director or the International Off-Campus Education program. Other overseas opportunities are organized by faculty members as part of credit-bearing courses. Recent courses have been held in China, Egypt, Greece, and Mexico.

Academic Facilities

Hofstra's libraries contain more than 1.2 million print volumes and provide 24 hours a day, seven days a week electronic access to more than 49,000 full-text journals and 42,400 electronic books. There are special units for periodicals, reserve books, government documents, curriculum materials, special collections, and microfilm.

Hofstra University's Student Computing Services provides students with a multitude of resources and learning opportunities. The Hofstra computer network provides individual accounts for all students for Internet, e-mail, and about 200 networked software programs. Almost 1,600 PC, Macintosh, and UNIX workstations are available to students in the various labs and classrooms on campus. The labs are staffed, and one computer lab is open 24 hours a day, seven days a week. All campus workstations have high-speed Internet access, and there are numerous wireless hotspots on campus. All resident students are provided with Internet and e-mail access from their residence hall rooms.

Other facilities include art galleries, an arboretum, an accredited museum, bird sanctuary, writing center, career center, cultural center, language lab, technology lab, six theaters, dance studios and performing arts classrooms, and a rooftop observatory with powerful telescopes. The state-of-the-art facilities in Hofstra's School of Communication include a 24-hour, student-operated radio station, one of the largest noncommercial television broadcast facilities in the Northeast, audio production studios, a film/video screening room, film editing rooms, and a cutting-edge converged newsroom and multimedia classroom. C. V. Starr Hall, home to the Zarb School of Business, features one of the most advanced academic trading rooms in the nation, complete with Bloomberg terminals and Internet access at every student seat. The innovative School of Education, Health and Human Services building, Hagedorn Hall, is a completely wireless environment featuring assessment centers for child observation and mock counseling and interactive Smart Boards in many classrooms.

Costs

The annual cost of tuition and fees at Hofstra University for 2009–10 for a full-time undergraduate student was $29,980. The minimum housing and dining plan was $9890. Books and supplies cost approximately $1000; personal expenses and transportation generally amount to $2640. For the full tuition and fees schedule, students should visit http://www.hofstra.edu/tuition.

Financial Aid

To help students achieve their educational goals, Hofstra University offers several financial-aid options. For 2009–10, Hofstra awarded more than $65 million in merit- and need-based financial aid. The average award for first-year students with financial need was $15,176, while the average financial-aid package for first-year students who had no financial need was $12,633. Nearly 900 first-year students received merit-based scholarships from Hofstra University, ranging from $4500 to full-tuition scholarships. About 85 percent of all Hofstra students received some form of financial aid, including more than 90 percent of first-year students. For detailed information, students should visit http://www.hofstra.edu/FinancialAid.

Faculty

Hofstra has 1,180 faculty members, including 544 full-time members; 91 percent of the full-time faculty members hold the highest degree in their fields. The faculty is dedicated to excellence in teaching, scholarship, and research, and many have been recognized with the nation's highest academic honors, including membership in the American Academy of Arts and Sciences, Fulbright and Guggenheim Fellowships, and Emmy Awards. The student-faculty ratio is 14:1. The average class size is 22. All classes are taught by faculty members who are accessible to students outside the classroom; no courses are taught by graduate assistants.

Student Government

The Student Government Association is a student-run governing body that supervises and coordinates all student activities and serves as a liaison with the faculty and administration. The Student Government Association sends representatives to the committees of the University Senate. A judicial board has responsibility for promoting justice in the conduct of student affairs.

Admission Requirements

Hofstra is a competitive institution that seeks to enroll students who demonstrate academic ability, intellectual curiosity, and the motivation to be successful and contribute to the campus community. Careful consideration is given to a student's high school record, types of courses taken, SAT or ACT scores, letters of recommendation, extracurricular involvement, and the personal essay. The most competitive applicants will have followed a rigorous college preparatory curriculum within their high school and will have taken advantage of honors and advanced placement level courses where appropriate. The Office of Admission prefers to see a high school curriculum, which includes 4 years of English, 3 to 4 years of social studies, 2 to 3 years of foreign language, 3 years of mathematics, and 3 years of science. Prospective engineering majors need at least 4 years of mathematics, 1 year of chemistry, and 1 year of physics. Campus visits are strongly recommended. Hofstra accepts applications from first-year, transfer, and international students.

The University offers an early action plan for students whose first choice is Hofstra. There are two early action periods: when submitted by November 15, notification is made to the student by December 15; when submitted by December 15, notification is made to the student by January 15. Students applying for regular decision are considered on a rolling basis.

First-year applicants must submit an application, $70 application fee, high school transcript, SAT or ACT scores, personal essay, and letter of recommendation. Hofstra accepts applications via mail or online and participates in the Common Application; the online application fee is $50.

Application and Information

Hofstra University
Office of Admission
100 Hofstra University
Hempstead, New York 11549-1000
Phone: 516-463-6700
800-HOFSTRA (toll-free)
Fax: 516-463-5100
Web site: http://www.hofstra.edu/admission
E-mail: admission@hofstra.edu

HOLLINS UNIVERSITY

ROANOKE, VIRGINIA

The University

Hollins University was founded in 1842 as Virginia's first chartered women's college. Today, Hollins is an independent arts and sciences university that enrolls approximately 1,050 students in its undergraduate programs for women and its coed graduate programs. Hollins is proud of its creative writing program, career internships, leadership opportunities, small class size, and study-abroad opportunities. Hollins prepares its students for career excellence in the social sciences, sciences, humanities, fine arts, and business. An 11:1 student-faculty ratio enables students to work closely with their professors both inside and outside the classroom. In addition to the Bachelor of Arts degree in twenty-seven major fields, Hollins awards a Bachelor of Science degree in four major fields, a B.A./B.F.A. degree in dance, a Master of Arts degree in children's literature, liberal studies, screenwriting and film studies, and teaching and a Master of Fine Arts degree in creative writing, children's literature, dance, playwriting, and screenwriting. Hollins' coeducational graduate creative writing program has long been acknowledged as one of the best of its size in the country.

Hollins gives students the month of January to focus on an internship, innovative course work, senior thesis, independent study, or travel/study abroad.

The majority of Hollins students do at least one internship before graduation. Students have interned at the New York Stock Exchange, UBS Financial Services, Centers for Disease Control, ABC News, National Institute of Mental Health, Lincoln Center for the Performing Arts, the *London Times*, *Vanity Fair* magazine, and the Metropolitan Museum of Art, to name a few.

Through Hollins' innovative Batten Leadership Institute, undergraduates can earn a Certificate in Leadership Studies through a combination of classes, skills-building groups, seminars, and student-designed leadership projects. The 20-hour program gives students the opportunity to gain both practical and academic experience in leadership studies, serving as a perfect complement to any major field of study.

Situated on a 475-acre campus in the Shenandoah Valley of the Blue Ridge Mountains, Hollins is a quiet campus for the serious student looking to broaden her mind through a rigorous academic program. Students come to Hollins from forty-seven states and fourteen countries and bring with them cultural and ethnic diversity. Women returning to college can earn a bachelor's degree in the Horizon Program.

Because approximately 78 percent of Hollins women live on campus in dormitories, language houses, or University apartments, a large family of friends develops in the first year and replaces the need for sororities. For those interested in group activities, there are twenty-eight clubs and organizations, including a multicultural club, Black Student Alliance, literary societies, and political, environmental, women's, and volunteer organizations. Each year, many students volunteer in social service agencies locally and internationally, including a Hollins-directed Jamaica service project. The Wyndham Robertson Library features state-of-the-art technology, is a National Literary Landmark, and won the 2009 Excellence in Academic Libraries Award. The well-equipped athletic complex enables Hollins to compete and train its athletes effectively for NCAA Division III competition in basketball, golf, lacrosse, riding, soccer, swimming, tennis, and volleyball. Hollins' strong riding program offers top facilities, including stables where riders may board their horses. The academic program is enriched by guest lectures, dance and theater productions, and the annual Literary Festival. The Hollins Outdoor Program (HOP) provides outdoor adventure activities such as canoeing, hiking, rock climbing, and caving.

Location

Hollins is located on the outskirts of Roanoke, a cosmopolitan center with a population of approximately 250,000. Hollins is a 3½-hour drive from both Washington, D.C., and Richmond; 5 hours from Virginia Beach; and within easy driving distance of more than a dozen other colleges. The Roanoke Regional Airport is a 10-minute drive from the campus. The campus has been described as "achingly picturesque." The Front Quadrangle is listed on the National Register of Historic Places. The Blue Ridge Mountains are minutes from campus and ideal for hiking the Appalachian Trail, camping, caving, and skiing.

Majors and Degrees

Hollins grants the Bachelor of Arts degree in art history, biology, business, chemistry, classical studies, communication studies, dance, economics, English and creative writing, environmental studies, film, French, gender and women's studies, history, interdisciplinary studies, international studies, mathematics, music, philosophy, physics, political science, psychology, religious studies, sociology, Spanish, studio art, and theater; the B.A./B.F.A. degree in dance; and the B.S. degree in biology, chemistry, mathematics, and psychology. Minors are offered in most major areas, and preprofessional programs are offered in education, law, medicine, and veterinary science. Students can earn certificates in leadership and arts management.

Academic Programs

Candidates for the Bachelor of Arts degree normally follow a four-year program. They are required to complete 128 credits of academic work and 16 January Short Term credits.

Candidates for the degree of Bachelor of Arts and Bachelor of Fine Arts normally follow a four-year program. They are required to complete a minimum of 150 semester credits of academic work, 16 Short Term credits, and two physical education courses. Included in the 150 credits are 82 credits in dance and general education.

Candidates for the degree of Bachelor of Science normally follow a four-year program. They are required to complete a minimum of 140 semester credits of academic work, 16 Short Term credits, and two physical education courses. Included in the 140 credits are 60 credits in the major (biology, chemistry, mathematics, or psychology) and general education.

The University offers first-year seminars that focus on collaborative and active learning, critical thinking, creative problem solving, research, writing, and oral communication skills. Each seminar is limited to 15 students. Seminar instructors also serve as academic advisers who help students with both course selection and academic goal setting. Each seminar also has an upper-class peer mentor who attends seminars, helps students with advising, and answers academic questions.

First-year students are required to take a seminar on campus during Short Term. Students may spend subsequent Short Terms pursuing career internships, independent study, study-abroad experiences, or service projects. In Hollins' general education program, called Education through Skills and Perspectives, students choose from a wide variety of classes that reinforce the basics of a liberal arts education.

Students must choose a major by the end of their sophomore year and complete a minimum of 32 credits in the major field before graduation. Each first-year student must meet a writing requirement. Hollins grants 4 academic credits for Advanced Placement examination scores of 4 or 5 and in some cases for a score of 3. Hollins grants 8 academic credits for International Baccalaureate scores between 5 and 7 and up to 32 credits for an I.B. diploma with a score of 30 or higher.

Off-Campus Programs

For semester or full-year study, Hollins has its own programs in England and France and affiliated programs in Argentina, Germany, Ghana, Greece, Ireland, Italy, Japan, Mexico, South Africa, and Spain as well as with the School for Field Studies. About half of Hollins students have an international learning experience before graduation. Domestic exchange programs are possible with members of the six-college exchange.

Academic Facilities

The Wyndham Robertson Library's collections consist of more than a half-million titles, ranging from e-books to incunabula and from musical scores to manuscripts. Through a catalog shared with Roanoke College, students are offered access to the materials in the combined collections of both libraries. Access to a wide range of electronic databases enables students to locate articles and documents from more than 40,000 journals, magazines, newspapers, and other titles. Hollins houses a notable selection of children's books and the papers of former poet laureate William Jay Smith. The archives and special collections include books and manuscripts from many famous faculty members and alumni/alumnae of Hollins, including R. H. W. Dillard, George Garrett, Eudora Welty, Margaret Wise Brown, Lee Smith, and Annie Dillard.

Extensive media facilities include a television studio and control room, a video editing suite, viewing and listening booths, and a screening room. The building has 40 public computers and wireless access, ample study seating, group study rooms, and many comfortable reading spaces.

Windows XP/Professional– and Macintosh-based computers are available in dedicated computer labs as well as various common areas around the university—many open 24 hours a day. Wireless access is abundant on campus.

The Dana Science Building houses accessible labs and research facilities for computerized recording and analysis of physiological and behavioral data, plant and animal tissue culture, animal learning laboratories, photomicroscopy, biochemistry and molecular biology, chromatography, spectrophotometry, electrochemistry, gas kinetics, centrifugation, and EEG and biofeedback equipment.

The Richard Wetherill Visual Arts Center houses the Eleanor D. Wilson Museum, which features the work of internationally renowned artists and emerging and regional artists.

Hollins also has dance studios, a career center, center for learning excellence, theater, and health and counseling center.

Costs

The 2009–10 costs are $27,550 for tuition and $10,040 for room and board, which includes telephone, cable television, and computer network connections for each student's room. The Student Government Association fee is $275, student technology support fee is $280, and University green fee is $10. The University estimates a budget of $1000 for books, $800 for transportation, and $1000 for other expenses.

Financial Aid

Financial aid is awarded on the basis of both academic merit and need. Seventy percent receive need-based aid in the form of grants, merit scholarships, low-interest loans, and campus jobs. The average award in 2008 was $24,419. The types of scholarships and grants available to undergraduates are Federal Pell Grants, Federal Supplemental Educational Opportunity Grants (FSEOG), state grants, University scholarships and grants, private scholarships and grants, academic merit scholarships, and aid for undergraduate students who are members of a minority group. Federal Perkins Loans, Federal PLUS loans, and Federal Stafford Student Loans are also available, as well as a tuition payment plan with Sallie Mae. A financial aid form should be filed with the financial aid office by February 15. Notification of awards is on a rolling basis.

Faculty

Faculty members are committed to teaching and are dedicated to their students. Although scholarly research and writing are emphasized, primary attention is placed on teaching. There are 72 full-time and 26 part-time faculty members, of whom 51 percent are women; 97 percent of the full-time faculty members hold the doctoral or corresponding terminal degree in their fields. A few courses are taught by graduate assistants.

Student Government

Each year, students sign the honor code, pledging not to lie, cheat, or steal. Hollins is thereby able to conduct daily operations with a great deal of trust. Final exams are freely scheduled and administered by students under the Independent Exam System. The campus judicial system is run by the students. Students who are elected to the Student Government Association have the authority to administer all student-related activities. Weekly Senate meetings are open to the entire campus. Students are represented on policymaking faculty committees and the Board of Trustees.

Admission Requirements

To be considered for admission, a student must have completed a minimum of 16 secondary school units in English, mathematics, science, social studies, and foreign language. All students must take the SAT or the ACT. In addition to standardized test scores, the Admissions Committee takes into account an applicant's secondary school record, class rank, essay, recommendation, and personal interview. Transfer students are accepted in both semesters. International applicants can submit TOEFL scores in place of the SAT or ACT.

At Hollins, the application process is very personal. The admissions officers go to great lengths to ensure that Hollins and the applicant are a good match.

Application and Information

Hollins has a formal early decision plan. The early decision application deadline is December 1; the deadline is February 15 for regular admission. Notification of admission is on a rolling basis beginning December 15 for early decision candidates and late January for regular admission candidates. The application fee is $40. A $400 tuition deposit must be made by early January for early decision, May 1 for others. For more information, students should contact:

Office of Admissions
Hollins University
P.O. Box 9707
Roanoke, Virginia 24020
Phone: 540-362-6401
800-456-9595 (toll-free)
E-mail: huadm@hollins.edu
Web site: http://www.hollins.edu

Students enjoying Hollins' historic Front Quadrangle.

HOPE COLLEGE

HOLLAND, MICHIGAN

The College

Founded in 1862, Hope College has always promoted, in a liberal arts setting, the dual concept of preparation for life and vocation. The stimulating academic program is supported by an accepting Christian campus community. Students from all walks of life are welcomed, respected, and given freedom to grow in this vibrant environment. Preparation for a career and for life in general involves both classroom and extracurricular activities. Activities include student publications, musical groups, and political organizations. Students manage an FM radio station, and their cable TV shows are broadcast weekly to the Holland community. There are four major theater productions each year as well as a film series, a Great Performance Series, and lectures by outstanding speakers. Many Christian activities broaden the range of student involvement, including the Campus Ministries Office, the Crossroads Project, Fellowship of Christian Athletes, Intervarsity Christian Fellowship, and similar organizations. Voluntary chapel is offered Monday, Wednesday, and Friday, plus an extended service on Sunday evening, and is well attended. Intercollegiate sports include baseball, basketball, cross-country, football, golf, soccer, swimming, tennis, and track for men and basketball, cross-country, golf, soccer, softball, swimming, tennis, track, and volleyball for women. Club sports include lacrosse, ice hockey, sailing, men's volleyball, and Ultimate Frisbee. An extensive program of intramural sports is also very popular among Hope students. An excellent health and recreation facility is available for student use. As Hope is a residential college, 84 percent of the students reside on the campus. The College has eleven residence halls, with capacity ranging from 40 to 300 students. Styles include corridor, cluster, suite, coed, and single-sex residence halls. In addition, upperclass students have the option of living in one of fifteen apartment buildings or sixty-two cottages, which are houses on or near the campus that have been refurbished to accommodate students. The services of a well-developed Career Services Center are available to students and alumni for help with everything from assessing interests to arranging job interviews. The current enrollment is 3,238. Four percent of the students attend on a part-time basis. The student body represents forty-two states and thirty countries.

Location

Hope College's 77-acre wooded campus is in a residential area two blocks from the central business district of Holland, Michigan, a community that was founded by Dutch settlers and now has a population of 35,000 within city limits and a total area population of 100,000. The town is only a 30-minute drive from Grand Rapids and a 2-hour drive from Chicago and Detroit. An 85-acre biological field station is located on the shores of Lake Michigan, 5 miles from the campus. Holland has long been known as a summer resort area, but it is also a fine spot for winter sports. Excellent relations exist between Holland and the College.

Majors and Degrees

Hope College awards the Bachelor of Arts, Bachelor of Science, Bachelor of Music, and Bachelor of Science in Nursing degrees. Major programs include accounting (public accounting), ancient civilization, art** (studio art and art history concentrations), athletic training, biology*, chemistry* (biochemistry emphasis), communication, computer science, dance**, economics*, engineering (ABET-accredited biochemical, chemical, computer science, electrical, and mechanical emphases), engineering physics, engineering science, English** (literature, writing emphases), French*, geology* (environmental emphasis), German*, history*, Japanese, kinesiology* (physical education, exercise science, and athletic training), Latin*, management, mathematics**, music** (instrumental education, vocal education, jazz studies emphasis, performance), nursing, philosophy, physics*, political science*, psychology, religion*, social work (CSWE approved), sociology* (criminal justice emphasis), Spanish*, special education (emotional impairments and learning disabilities endorsements), and theater*. Hope is fully accredited for certification in elementary, secondary, and special (emotionally impaired and learning disabilities endorsements) education. Preprofessional programs are offered in dance therapy, dentistry, law, library science, medicine, optometry, physical therapy, seminary, and veterinary medicine.

Alternatives to departmental majors include the composite major and contract curriculum major. The composite major is concentrated study in any approved combination of majors related to a particular academic or vocational objective of the student. Some examples include fine arts, communication/English, international studies, and language arts. The contract curriculum major allows the student to develop a plan of study within the educational objectives of the College.

*Secondary teaching certification available; **secondary and/or elementary teaching certification available.

Academic Programs

To graduate, students must pass all College-required courses, earn at least 126 credit hours, and meet minimum GPA requirements. A Phi Beta Kappa institution, Hope is widely respected as a liberal arts college that balances academic excellence with a deep concern for the quality of life of its students and alumni. Hope's commitment to the Christian faith provides an incentive for academic excellence and rigorous inquiry and a perspective on the wholeness and value of life. A core curriculum brings teachers and students together for the purpose of facilitating student growth in seven areas: communication skills, social adaptation, an understanding of American heritage and society, a respect for science and discovery, an awareness of other cultures, an understanding and appreciation of the arts, and an understanding of religion and its impact on society. To accomplish this, students select course work in the following disciplines: English, fine arts, foreign language, kinesiology, mathematics, natural science, philosophy, religion, and social science.

Off-Campus Programs

Hope College participates in off-campus programs that are sponsored and supervised by the Associated Colleges of the Midwest (ACM), the Institute for Asian Studies (IAS), the Institute for European Studies (IES), and the Great Lakes Colleges Association (GLCA). Students may study for a semester or a year in more than sixty countries. Some continents and countries included are Africa, Austria, China, France, Germany, Great Britain, India, Japan, Latin America, Russia, Spain, the Middle East, and the Netherlands. Hope also runs a summer study-abroad program in Vienna, Austria. The College's director of international education assists students in arranging programs in other countries. Domestic programs include the Washington Semester, Urban Semester in Philadelphia, Semester at the Chicago Metropolitan Center, the Oregon Extension, Arts Program in New York City, the New York Center for Arts and Media Studies, Oak Ridge Science Semester, the Border Studies Program, and Newberry Library Program in the Humanities.

Academic Facilities

The campus library contains more than 350,000 volumes. The $36-million science facility contains the most modern laboratory equipment available and facilitates close working relationships between faculty members and students. The physics laboratories include an electron particle accelerator. Students from many academic disciplines take advantage of state-of-the-art computer facilities. The theater, music, dance, and art departments are proud to offer excellent facilities as well. The DePree Art Center is a $1.3-million facility that contains a major art gallery, classrooms, and studios. An $11-million center for communication and global studies and a $22-million athletic field house were dedicated in fall 2005. Lubbers Hall, one of the College's most venerable academic buildings, underwent a $3-million renovation project during the summer of 2006. Major renovations to the baseball and softball fields were completed for the spring 2008 seasons. Graves Hall, a centerpiece of the College's identity and early history, is currently undergoing a $5.7-million "adaptive restoration" planned to be completed in 2009. The $5.3 million Van Andel Soccer Stadium is set to be completed in fall 2009.

Costs

Annual charges for the 2009–10 academic year are tuition, $25,500; room, $3590; board (21 meals per week, reduced-cost meal plans are available), $4280; and activity fee, $160; for a total of $33,530.

Financial Aid

Types of aid include academic scholarships, grants, loans, and campus employment. Approximately 59 percent of Hope's students qualify for need-based aid. All accepted students may be considered for federal and Hope-funded assistance. Michigan residents may apply for state-funded programs. Applicants for aid should be accepted for admission and should submit the Free Application for Federal Student Aid (FAFSA) and a Hope institutional form by March 1 to receive priority consideration for need-based aid. Hope sponsors National Merit Scholars with a $17,000-per-year tuition scholarship. Other academic awards range from $3000 to $17,000. Talent awards of $2500 are also available in the fine arts and creative writing. Seventy-one percent of freshmen enrolling in fall 2008 received a merit award. Consideration for merit awards requires submission of a complete application for admission by February 15 of the application year.

Faculty

Hope has 230 full-time faculty members, and 77 percent hold a Ph.D. or terminal degree in their field. In addition, there are 98 part-time faculty members who teach in a broad range of disciplines, many of whom also teach, perform, and work outside the campus community. The student-faculty ratio is 12:1. Members of the faculty are dedicated to maintaining excellence in both teaching and scholarship and to taking a personal interest in students. Many conduct research programs in which students actively participate, sometimes as early as their freshman year. Faculty members also serve as academic advisers and frequently host student groups in their homes.

Student Government

Hope has an established community governance system. Decisions that concern the College community are made primarily by boards and committees composed of students, faculty members, and administrators. The Academic Affairs, Administrative Affairs, and Campus Life boards bear the major responsibility for policy decisions, while subcommittees of each deal with more specific areas. Residence hall units elect representatives to Student Congress; these representatives are then appointed to the major boards. A Judicial Board of 7 students, 2 faculty members, and 1 staff person is charged with maintaining high standards of student life.

Admission Requirements

Hope is interested in students who seek the rigors of a proven, demanding academic program and feel comfortable in an open, supportive, Christian campus community. A complete admission file includes the completed application form, the application fee, high school/college transcripts, and either ACT or SAT scores. Primary factors considered are the applicant's high school course selection, grades, rank, test scores, counselor's recommendation, essay, and involvement in extracurricular/leadership activities. The College prefers that its students enroll having completed at least four college-preparatory classes per semester in the ninth through twelfth grades, including a variety of subject areas. The minimum background includes 4 years of English, 2 years of mathematics, 2 years of foreign language, 2 years of history or social studies, and at least 1 year of laboratory science as well as five other college-preparatory classes. For fall 2009, freshmen had a mean GPA of 3.72 (on a 4.0 scale), the average SAT score (critical reading and math) was 1181, the average ACT composite score was 26, and their average rank was in the 78th percentile. Campus visits are not required but are strongly recommended for interested students and their parents.

Application and Information

Most students apply for the fall semester, but applications are accepted for the spring semester or other sessions. The first admission decisions are announced in mid-December. A traditional rolling admission process continues after mid-December until late spring for fall admission. Students must submit the application form, official high school transcript, results of the SAT or ACT, and $35 (online) or $50 (paper) application fee. Prospective freshmen are encouraged to submit applications during the first semester of their senior year in high school. Completed applications for admission must be on file by February 15 to ensure consideration for merit scholarships. A $300 enrollment deposit is requested by May 1. Prospective students may also apply online; application forms are available on the Web (http://www.hope.edu/admissions).

Hope College Admissions
69 East 10th Street
P.O. Box 9000
Holland, Michigan 49422-9000
Phone: 616-395-7850
800-968-7850 (toll-free)
E-mail: admissions@hope.edu
Web site: http://www.hope.edu

The Pull, an annual tug-of-war between freshmen and sophomores for the past 111 years, has been called "the most unique sporting event in the nation" by *Sports Illustrated*.

HUNTER COLLEGE OF THE CITY UNIVERSITY OF NEW YORK

NEW YORK, NEW YORK

HUNTER
www.hunter.cuny.edu

The College

In 1870, Thomas Hunter founded Hunter College to train young women to become school teachers. Their contributions helped make New York City's schools among the most highly regarded public school systems in the world. Today, Hunter College is a coeducational liberal arts college serving 21,000 undergraduate and graduate students of all racial, ethnic, and cultural backgrounds. Wide offerings in the liberal arts and sciences and three professional schools—education, health sciences, and social work—meet the highest academic standards. A distinguished faculty encourages intellectual and personal growth in each student.

Location

Hunter students study in the heart of Manhattan. Many of the world's finest museums, libraries, concert halls, cultural centers, and theaters are just a quick walk away.

Majors and Degrees

Hunter College offers bachelor's and master's degrees in the arts and sciences, education, health professions, nursing, and social work, along with several combined (B.A./M.A. or B.A./M.S.) degrees. The following programs of study are available: accounting, Africana and Puerto Rican/Latino studies, anthropology, archaeology, art history, biological sciences, chemistry, Chinese language and literature, classical studies, community health education, comparative literature, computer science, dance, economics, elementary education, environmental studies, English, English language arts, film, French, geography, German, Greek, Hebrew, history, honors curriculum, Italian, Jewish social studies, Latin, Latin American and Caribbean Studies, Latin and Greek, mathematics, media studies, medical laboratory sciences, music, nursing, nutrition and food science, philosophy, physics, political science, psychology, religion, Romance languages, Russian, secondary education, sociology, Spanish, statistics, studio art, theater, urban studies, and women's studies. Secondary education programs are for grades 7–12 unless otherwise noted and include biology, chemistry, Chinese, dance (pre-K–12), English, French, German, Hebrew, Italian, mathematics, music (pre-K–12, accelerated B.A./M.A. program only), physics, Russian, social studies, and Spanish.

Special programs in anthropology, biological sciences/environmental and occupational health sciences, biopharmacology, biotechnology, economics, English, history, mathematics, music, physics, sociology/social research, and statistics and applied mathematics lead to the combined bachelor's/master's degree, enabling highly qualified students to earn both degrees more quickly.

Hunter College also provides preprofessional advisement and preparation for advanced study in chiropractic, dentistry, engineering, law, medicine, optometry, osteopathy, pharmacy, podiatry, and veterinary medicine.

Academic Programs

Hunter instills a rich and informed sense of the possibilities of humanity in its students and expects them to carry their liberal arts education forward in their careers, their public responsibilities, and their personal lives.

The College trains its students in the sciences, the humanities, and a number of professional fields. As they strive to achieve their career goals, students are expected to perceive their chosen fields of study as only a part of a wider realm of knowledge. Undergraduate programs of study at Hunter consist of five parts, totaling 120 credits: a general education requirement, a pluralism and diversity requirement, a concentration of in-depth study (major), elective courses, and a minor.

Undergraduate students at Hunter who exhibit intellectual curiosity and exceptional ability may apply to the Thomas Hunter Scholars Program, an interdisciplinary program that individualizes study according to needs and interests and grants a Bachelor of Arts degree.

Students may earn sophomore standing (up to 30 credits) if they score well on the College-Level Examination Program (CLEP) subject tests, the Advanced Placement examinations of the College Board, and the Regents College Examination (RCE) Program of New York State.

Off-Campus Programs

Hunter College taps Manhattan to allow innumerable internships. Hosts have included Atlantic Records, CNN, the Council on Foreign Relations, DreamWorks SKG, Madison Square Garden, Metropolitan Museum of Art, New York City Council, Simon & Schuster, and many more. Interns perform curatorial and administrative work in museums, research and production work on TV news shows and newspapers, design work in commercial graphics, and booking, managing, and technical work in theaters.

Academic Facilities

The College is made up of five sites in Manhattan. The largest, a modern complex of buildings connected by skywalks at 68th Street and Lexington Avenue, sits above a convenient subway stop. This campus offers programs in the arts and sciences and in teacher education.

Downtown, the Brookdale Campus on East 25th Street houses the Division of the Schools of the Health Professions, which includes the Hunter-Bellevue School of Nursing, one of the nation's largest nursing programs, and the School of Health Sciences.

Uptown on East 79th Street is the Hunter College School of Social Work, which was recently listed among the top ten schools of its kind in the nation by *U.S. News & World Report*.

On Manhattan's West Side, Hunter's Studio Art Building houses an 8,000-square-foot gallery and provides M.F.A. students with individual studios that are among the best in the city.

At East 94th Street, the Campus Schools house an elementary school and a high school for the intellectually gifted that are renowned, as is the College itself, for a long tradition of academic excellence.

All locations are minutes from Grand Central Terminal, Penn Station, and the New York/New Jersey Port Authority Bus Terminal, making Hunter easily accessible from Connecticut, Westchester, New Jersey, and Long Island.

The collections of the Hunter College libraries are housed in the Jacqueline Grennan Wexler Library and the Art Slide Library (located at the main campus), as well as at the branch libraries at the Brookdale Campus and the School of Social Work. The libraries hold over 750,000 volumes, 2,300 periodicals, a nonprint collection of more than 1 million microforms, and 250,000 art slides in addition to records, tapes, scores, music CDs, and videos. Recently, Hunter installed new computer, multimedia, and Internet labs and its first CD-ROM network. The CD-ROM network provides access to indexes, abstracts, and complete texts and multimedia resources, and Internet labs make the World Wide Web accessible.

Costs

Hunter College is affordable. In 2009–10, New York State residents enrolled as full-time, matriculated students paid $2300 per semester ($195 per credit part-time). Nonresidents enrolled as full-time, matriculated students paid $415 per credit. All students paid a Student Activity Fee ($84.50 per semester for full-time students and $54.45 per semester for part-time students) and a $15-per-semester Consolidated Fee.

Financial Aid

Hunter College participates in all state and federal financial aid programs. Financial aid is available to matriculated students in the form of grants, loans, and work-study. Grants provide funds that do not have to be repaid. Loans must be repaid in regular installments over a prescribed period of time. Work-study consists of part-time employment, either on campus or in an outside agency. More information is available from the Office of Financial Aid at 212-772-4820.

Entering freshmen whose high school records indicate a high level of academic achievement may apply to the Macaulay Honors College at Hunter College. This prestigious program offers a generous financial aid package, including a full academic scholarship, as well as extensive benefits, including a free room at the Hunter College Residence Hall. In addition, Hunter College offers a wide array of other scholarships.

Faculty

Thanks to its location in the heart of New York City, Hunter College attracts a special kind of faculty member. Some are well-known scholars and researchers in their fields, such as biologists involved in advanced research on genetic structure. Others are professionals with active careers in the city, including well-known painters, sculptors, architects, and urban design experts. Hunter's faculty also includes environmental health scientists who work on occupational health and safety issues, nursing administrators who work in the country's leading hospitals, and film directors, theater critics, and musicians who are engaged in New York City's cultural milieu. Many members of the faculty are nationally renowned; they maintain Hunter's reputation for academic excellence through outstanding teaching and cutting-edge publications and by securing millions of dollars in annual grants for research.

Student Government

Several governing assemblies involve students in Hunter's governance. The College Senate, the legislative body of the College, includes faculty members, students, and administrators. Two Student Governments (undergraduate and graduate) also play essential roles in the life of the College. Students with voting power sit on faculty and administrative committees.

Admission Requirements

Candidates for freshman admission are considered based on the overall strength of their academic preparation, cumulative high school averages, and SAT or ACT scores. The College recommends 4 years of English, 4 years of social studies, 3 years of mathematics, 2 years of a foreign language, 2 years of laboratory sciences, and 1 year of performing or visual arts as the minimum academic preparation for success in college.

Transfer applicants with fewer than 24 credits must have a cumulative grade point average (GPA) of at least 2.3 and must meet the freshman criteria previously outlined. Those with 14 to 23.9 credits and a GPA of at least 2.5 as well as those with 24 or more credits and a GPA of at least 2.3 are eligible, regardless of high school average. For more information, applicants should visit Hunter College's Web site.

Application and Information

Applicants are considered for fall (September) and spring (February) admission. Applications for the fall must be filed no later than October 1 and for spring, no later than February 1. Applications can be filed from the CUNY Web site at http://www.cuny.edu.

Welcome Center
Hunter College
695 Park Avenue, Room 100N
New York, New York 10065
Phone: 212-772-4490
Fax: 212-650-3336
E-mail: WelcomeCenter@hunter.cuny.edu
Web site: http://www.hunter.cuny.edu

Students at Hunter College enjoy the convenience of skywalks that connect all four buildings at the 68th Street campus. Hunter's Upper East Side location provides easy access to some of New York's finest offerings; Central Park and the Metropolitan Museum of Art are just blocks away.

THE ILLINOIS INSTITUTE OF ART–CHICAGO

CHICAGO, ILLINOIS

The Illinois Institute of Art·Chicago

The Illinois Institute of Art–Chicago provides students with a creative educational environment. Offering twelve bachelor's degree programs and four associate degree programs, the school and its dedicated faculty members are committed to preparing students to pursue entry-level positions in the creative arts.

Under the guidance of industry professionals, students learn by doing the types of tasks they are likely to encounter in the workplace. In addition, assistance is available to help students with resume writing, networking, and keeping aware of what employers are looking for in job candidates.

The student population includes recent high school graduates, transfer students, and those who have left a previous employment situation to study and train for a new career. Students are creative, competitive, and open to new ideas. They place great value on an education that prepares them to pursue an exciting entry-level position in the arts.

The Illinois Institute of Art–Chicago places a high value on the quality of student life inside and outside the classroom. Students can take part in a wide variety of activities, clubs and organizations, community service opportunities, and various student life enhancing committees.

Instructors are encouraged to look for upcoming books and to advise the administration of any books that may prove useful to their students. Students also have access to the public libraries.

The Student Affairs Office helps students who need assistance in locating housing.

The Illinois Institute of Art–Chicago is accredited by the Higher Learning Commission and is a member of the North Central Association, 30 North LaSalle Street, Suite 2400, Chicago, Illinois, 60602; phone:800-621-7440; http://www.ncahlc.org.

The Illinois Institute of Art–Chicago is authorized by the Illinois Board of Higher Education, 431 East Adams, Second Floor, Springfield, Illinois 62701; phone: 217-782-2551; http://www.ibhe.state.il.us/default.htm.

The Associate of Applied Science degree program in culinary arts is accredited by the Accrediting Commission of the American Culinary Federation Education Foundation.

The interior design program leading to the Bachelor of Fine Arts degree is accredited by the Council for Interior Design Accreditation, 206 Grandville Avenue, Suite 350, Grand Rapids, Michigan 49503; http://www.accredit-id.org.

Location

The city of Chicago provides a backdrop like no other. With two locations downtown, the school offers students the opportunity to learn both in the classroom, and through the many events and experiences that come with being immersed in downtown Chicago.

Programs of Study and Degrees

Bachelor's degree programs are offered in advertising, audio production, culinary management, digital filmmaking and video production, digital photography, fashion design, fashion marketing and management, game art and design, hospitality management, interior design, media arts and animation, and visual communications.

Associate degree programs are offered in culinary arts, fashion merchandising, graphic design, and hospitality management.

The culinary arts, culinary management, graphic design, interior design, and visual communications programs are also available in an evening and weekend option format.

Certificate programs are offered in professional baking and pastry and professional cooking.

Academic Programs

The Illinois Institute of Art–Chicago operates on a year-round, four quarter system.

Academic Facilities

The Illinois Institute of Art–Chicago is home to classrooms, studios, offices, a student lounge, a supply store, and a learning resource center. Equipment provided at The Illinois Institute of Art–Chicago is specific to the program of study and may include projectors, editing decks, camcorders, PC and Macintosh computers, printers, drafting tables, and kitchen appliances.

Costs

Tuition cost varies by program. Prospective students should contact the school for current tuition costs. Other charges include a starting kit for all first quarter students. Kits vary in price depending on the program of study.

Financial Aid

Financial aid is available for those who qualify. Students who require financial assistance should first complete and submit a Free Application for Federal Student Aid (FAFSA) and meet with a financial aid officer.

Faculty

Faculty members at The Illinois Institute of Art–Chicago have professional knowledge that they bring into the classroom. The school's faculty members provide their students with a unique, relevant educational experience.

Admission Requirements

Applicants must provide proof of high school graduation or achievement of a General Educational Development (GED) certificate as a prerequisite for admission. In lieu of documenting high school graduation or a GED certificate, applicants may provide proof of attaining an associate degree or higher from an accredited institution. An official transcript indicating date of high school graduation, GED certificate (including test scores), or date of college graduation (including degree granted) is required as proof.

All individuals seeking admission to The Illinois Institute of Art–Chicago are interviewed in person or by phone by an assistant director of admissions, and each applicant must create an original essay of at least 150 words stating how an education at The Illinois Institute of Art–Chicago would help the student to achieve career goals. There is a $50 application fee.

For the most recent information regarding admission requirements, please refer to the current academic catalog.

Application and Information

To obtain an application, make arrangements for an interview, or tour the school, prospective students should contact:

The Illinois Institute of Art–Chicago
350 North Orleans Street
Chicago, Illinois 60654-1593
Phone: 312-280-3500
800-351-3450 (toll-free)
Fax: 312-280-8562
Web site: http://www.artinstitutes.edu/chicago

The Art Institute of Atlanta; The Art Institute of Atlanta–Decatur[1]; The Art Institute of Austin[2]; The Art Institute of California–Hollywood; The Art Institute of California–Inland Empire; The Art Institute of California–Los Angeles; The Art Institute of California–Orange County; The Art Institute of California–Sacramento; The Art Institute of California–San Diego; The Art Institute of California–San Francisco; The Art Institute of California–Sunnyvale; The Art Institute of Charleston[1]; The Art Institute of Charlotte; The Art Institute of Colorado; The Art Institute of Dallas; The Art Institute of Fort Lauderdale; The Art Institute of Fort Worth[3]; The Art Institute of Houston; The Art Institute of Houston–North[2]; The Art Institute of Indianapolis[4]; The Art Institute of Jacksonville[5]; The Art Institute of Las Vegas; The Art Institute of Michigan; The Art Institute of New York City; The Art Institute of Ohio–Cincinnati[6]; The Art Institute of Philadelphia; The Art Institute of Phoenix; The Art Institute of Pittsburgh; The Art Institute of Portland; The Art Institute of Raleigh–Durham; The Art Institute of Salt Lake City; The Art Institute of San Antonio[2];The Art Institute of Seattle; The Art Institute of Tampa[5]; The Art Institute of Tennessee–Nashville[1,7]; The Art Institute of Tucson; The Art Institute of Vancouver; The Art Institute of Virginia Beach[1,8]; The Art Institute of Washington[1,8]; The Art Institute of Washington–Northern Virginia[1,8]; The Art Institute of York–Pennsylvania; The Art Institutes International–Kansas City; The Art Institutes International Minnesota; The Illinois Institute of Art–Chicago; The Illinois Institute of Art–Schaumburg; Miami International University of Art & Design; The New England Institute of Art.

[1]A branch of The Art Institute of Atlanta
[2]A branch of The Art Institute of Houston
[3]A branch of The Art Institute of Dallas
[4]The Art Institute of Indianapolis is regulated by the Indiana Commission on Proprietary Education, 302 West Washington Street, Room E201, Indianapolis, Indiana 46204, AC-0080
[5]A branch of Miami International University of Art & Design
[6]The Art Institute of Ohio–Cincinnati, 8845 Governors Hill Drive, Suite 100, Cincinnati, Ohio 45249-3317, OH Reg. #04-01-1698B
[7]The Art Institute of Tennessee–Nashville is authorized for operation as a postsecondary educational institution by the Tennessee Higher Education Commission.
[8]Certified by the State Council of Higher Education to operate in Virginia

THE ILLINOIS INSTITUTE OF ART–SCHAUMBURG

SCHAUMBURG, ILLINOIS

The Illinois Institute of Art•Schaumburg

The Illinois Institute of Art–Schaumburg provides students with a creative educational environment. Offering twelve bachelor's degree programs and two associate degree programs, the school and its dedicated faculty members are committed to preparing students to pursue entry-level positions in the creative arts.

Under the guidance of industry professionals, students learn by doing the types of tasks they are likely to encounter in the workplace. In addition, assistance is available to help students with resume writing, networking, and keeping aware of what employers are looking for in job candidates.

The student population includes recent high school graduates, transfer students, and those who have left a previous employment situation to study and train for a new career. Students are creative, competitive, and open to new ideas. They place great value on an education that prepares them to pursue an exciting entry-level position in the arts.

The Illinois Institute of Art–Schaumburg places a high value on the quality of student life inside and outside the classroom. Students can take part in a wide variety of activities, clubs and organizations, community service opportunities, and various student life–enhancing committees.

The Student Affairs Office helps students who need assistance in locating housing.

The Illinois Institute of Art is accredited by the Higher Learning Commission and is a member of the North Central Association, 30 North LaSalle Street, Suite 2400, Chicago, Illinois 60602; http://www.ncahlc.org.

The Illinois Institute of Art–Schaumburg is authorized by the Illinois Board of Higher Education 431 East Adams, Second Floor, Springfield, Illinois 62701; phone: 217-782-2551; http://www.ibhe.state.il.us/default.htm.

The interior design program leading to the Bachelor of Fine Arts degree is accredited by the Council for Interior Design Accreditation, 206 Grandville Avenue, Suite 350, Grand Rapids, Michigan 49503; http://www.accredit-id.org.

Location

Located in suburban Chicago, in Schaumburg, the school provides easy access to the big city, while giving students a more suburban environment in which to live and learn.

Programs of Study and Degrees

Bachelor's degree programs are offered in advertising, audio production, digital filmmaking and video production, digital photography, fashion design, fashion marketing and management, game art and design, graphic design, interior design, media arts and animation, visual effects and motion graphics, and Web design and interactive media.

Associate degree programs are offered in graphic design and Web design and interactive media.

Diploma programs are offered in digital design, residential planning, and Web design.

The digital design, game art and design, graphic design, interior design, media arts and animation, residential planning, Web design, and Web design and interactive media programs are also available in an evening and weekend option format.

Academic Programs

The Illinois Institute of Art–Schaumburg operates on a year-round, four-quarter system.

Academic Facilities

The Illinois Institute of Art–Schaumburg is home to classrooms, studios, offices, a student lounge, a supply store, and a learning resource center. Equipment provided at The Illinois Institute of Art–Schaumburg is specific to the program of study and may include projectors, editing decks, camcorders, and PC and Macintosh computers.

Costs

Tuition cost varies by program. Prospective students should contact the school for current tuition costs. Other charges include a starting kit for all first-quarter students. Kits vary in price depending on the program of study.

Financial Aid

Financial aid is available for those who qualify. Students who require financial assistance should first complete and submit a Free Application for Federal Student Aid (FAFSA) and meet with a financial aid officer.

Faculty

Faculty members at The Illinois Institute of Art–Schaumburg have professional knowledge that they bring into the classroom. The School's faculty members provide their students with a unique, relevant educational experience.

Admission Requirements

Applicants must provide proof of high school graduation or achievement of a General Educational Development (GED) certificate as a prerequisite for admission. In lieu of documenting high school graduation or a GED certificate, applicants may provide proof of attaining an associate degree or higher from an accredited institution. An official transcript indicating date of high school graduation, GED certificate (including test scores), or date of college graduation (including degree granted) is required as proof.

All individuals seeking admission to The Illinois Institute of Art–Schaumburg are interviewed in person or by phone by an assistant director of admissions, and each applicant must create an original essay of at least 150 words stating how an education at The Illinois Institute of Art–Schaumburg would help the student to achieve career goals. There is a $50 application fee.

For the most recent information regarding admission requirements, please refer to the current academic catalog.

Application and Information

To obtain an application, make arrangements for an interview, or tour the school, prospective students should contact:

The Illinois Institute of Art–Schaumburg
1000 North Plaza Drive, Suite 100
Schaumburg, Illinois 60173-4990
Phone: 847-619-3450
800-314-3450 (toll-free)
Fax: 847-619-3064
Web site: http://www.artinstitutes.edu/schaumburg

The Art Institute of Atlanta; The Art Institute of Atlanta–Decatur[1]; The Art Institute of Austin[2]; The Art Institute of California–Hollywood; The Art Institute of California–Inland Empire; The Art Institute of California–Los Angeles; The Art Institute of California–Orange County; The Art Institute of California–Sacramento; The Art Institute of California–San Diego; The Art Institute of California–San Francisco; The Art Institute of California–Sunnyvale; The Art Institute of Charleston[1]; The Art Institute of Charlotte; The Art Institute of Colorado; The Art Institute of Dallas; The Art Institute of Fort Lauderdale; The Art Institute of Fort Worth[3]; The Art Institute of Houston; The Art Institute of Houston–North[2]; The Art Institute of Indianapolis[4]; The Art Institute of Jacksonville[5]; The Art Institute of Las Vegas; The Art Institute of Michigan; The Art Institute of New York City; The Art Institute of Ohio–Cincinnati[6]; The Art Institute of Philadelphia; The Art Institute of Phoenix; The Art Institute of Pittsburgh; The Art Institute of Portland; The Art Institute of Raleigh–Durham; The Art Institute of Salt Lake City; The Art Institute of San Antonio[2];The Art Institute of Seattle; The Art Institute of Tampa[5]; The Art Institute of Tennessee–Nashville[1,7]; The Art Institute of Tucson; The Art Institute of Vancouver; The Art Institute of Virginia Beach[1,8]; The Art Institute of Washington[1,8]; The Art Institute of Washington–Northern Virginia[1,8]; The Art Institute of York–Pennsylvania; The Art Institutes International–Kansas City; The Art Institutes International Minnesota; The Illinois Institute of Art–Chicago; The Illinois Institute of Art–Schaumburg; Miami International University of Art & Design; The New England Institute of Art.

[1]A branch of The Art Institute of Atlanta
[2]A branch of The Art Institute of Houston
[3]A branch of The Art Institute of Dallas
[4]The Art Institute of Indianapolis is regulated by the Indiana Commission on Proprietary Education, 302 West Washington Street, Room E201, Indianapolis, Indiana 46204, AC-0080
[5]A branch of Miami International University of Art & Design
[6]The Art Institute of Ohio–Cincinnati, 8845 Governors Hill Drive, Suite 100, Cincinnati, Ohio 45249-3317, OH Reg. #04-01-1698B
[7]The Art Institute of Tennessee–Nashville is authorized for operation as a postsecondary educational institution by the Tennessee Higher Education Commission.
[8]Certified by the State Council of Higher Education to operate in Virginia

IMMACULATA UNIVERSITY

IMMACULATA, PENNSYLVANIA

The University

Immaculata University (IU), a comprehensive Catholic liberal arts university for students of all faiths, offers a high-quality education that is firmly grounded in values and tradition. Immaculata graduates are known for their skills and knowledge and also for their desire to serve. The University was founded in 1920 and has since grown to enroll almost 4,000 students in bachelor's, master's, and doctoral degree programs and accelerated degree-completion programs.

Approximately 1,000 traditional-aged men and women attend the College of Undergraduate Studies, with 80 percent of them living in University-sponsored housing. The College of Lifelong Learning includes undergraduate programs that are open to adult men and women. Students represent seventeen states and seventeen countries, giving the campus both ethnic and geographic diversity. Resident students live in four residence halls containing double rooms. Both resident and nonresident students participate in more than sixty student clubs and organizations that represent interests in athletics, student government, academic disciplines, community action, music, dance, theater, and student publications.

Intercollegiate sports include women's basketball, cross-country, field hockey, golf, lacrosse, soccer, softball, tennis, and volleyball and men's baseball, basketball, cross-country, golf, lacrosse, soccer, and tennis. In 2010–11, track and field will become part of the athletic offerings. Immaculata competes in Division III athletics as part of the Colonial States Athletic Conference. A turf field, stadium, indoor batting cages, gymnasia, fitness room, and pool are available for student use and provide numerous opportunities for physical activities and wellness programs. The Student Association of Immaculata University provides the unity, enthusiasm, and leadership that are integral parts of the traditional undergraduate experience.

Immaculata University celebrates unique traditions as a part of the overall collegiate experience, such as Freshman Investiture, the academic capping of the newest members of the University community. Carol Night, one of Immaculata's best-loved traditions, involves students, faculty members, alumni, and families singing around the Christmas tree in the rotunda of Villa Maria Hall.

The main building, Villa Maria Hall, is of neo-Renaissance architecture in gray stone with a red tile roof. The other thirteen major campus buildings are also of gray stone with red tile roofs, unifying the aesthetic appearance of the campus.

Graduate degrees offered in the College of Graduate Studies include the Master of Arts in counseling psychology, cultural and linguistic diversity, educational leadership and administration, music therapy, nursing, nutrition education, and organization leadership. Doctoral degrees are offered in educational administration, clinical psychology, and school psychology. ACCEL, the accelerated degree-completion program, offers bachelor's degrees in financial management, human performance management, and information technology.

Location

Immaculata's 375-acre campus is located in historic Chester County, 20 miles west of Philadelphia and 10 miles south of Valley Forge. The area is primarily suburban, with numerous colleges and universities offering a wide range of cultural and social activities. Many places of interest in Philadelphia and Lancaster are easily reached by car, train, or bus. The campus is 15 minutes from the King of Prussia Mall, the second largest mall in the U.S. Southern New Jersey shore resorts and New York City are within 1½ hours by car, with Pocono Mountain ski resorts and Washington, D.C., only 2½ hours away by car or train. The University provides numerous opportunities for internships in the business, educational, and scientific communities throughout the area.

Majors and Degrees

The College of Undergraduate Studies at Immaculata offers the Bachelor of Arts, Bachelor of Music, Bachelor of Science, Associate of Arts, and Associate of Science degrees. Undergraduate major fields of study include accounting, allied health, biology, biology/psychology, business administration, chemistry, communication, criminology/sociology, education, English, exercise science, family and consumer sciences, fashion merchandising, finance, food service management, French, general science, health-care management, history, information technology, international business/foreign language, marketing management, mathematics, mathematics/computer science, music, music education, music performance, music therapy, nursing, nutrition/dietetics, political science/international relations, prelaw, premedicine, pre–physical therapy, pre–veterinary medicine, psychology, sociology, sociology/social work, Spanish, Spanish/psychology, Spanish/social work, theology, and undecided. Allied health concentrations include: clinical laboratory science, diagnostic medical sonography, invasive cardiovascular technology, nuclear medicine technology, and surgical technology. IU also offers partnership programs with Thomas Jefferson University (TJU) in physical therapy, occupational therapy, bioscience technologies, and radiologic sciences. These programs allow students to seamlessly matriculate into TJU after three years of study at IU.

Academic Programs

Two factors are emphasized in the educational program at Immaculata: a comprehensive liberal arts background and a major field of concentration that prepares students to begin a career or to attend graduate school. The honors program offers an array of courses designed to give those who participate a special involvement in the learning process.

The Mary Bruder Center houses the offices for personal, career, and graduate study counseling and for educational and career testing. Workshops and seminars in resume writing, interviewing, career options, internship opportunities, and graduate fellowships are offered at regular intervals.

Off-Campus Programs

Both summer-abroad and junior-year-abroad programs combine travel with academic study to heighten the experience of students who seek these opportunities. Students can study in England and Ireland through IU and in other countries through the University's collaboration with Arcadia University.

Every undergraduate major department offers numerous internship opportunities for students in agencies, businesses, institutions, or corporations related to their study. Some majors, such as nutrition, fashion merchandising, and music therapy, require a multiweek internship for the degree to be granted.

Academic Facilities

The Gabriele Library houses 130,000 volumes and offers 714 periodical subscriptions. In addition to the computer center, students have access to networked computers in the library, an interactive language lab with a video screen, and a multifaceted science lab with computer-simulated experiments; they also have Internet/Intranet access from their residence halls. Well-equipped laboratories, art studios, media centers, and a 1,150-seat theater give students a variety of settings in which to pursue their interests.

State-of-the-art computer labs include the Campus Learning and Language Laboratory, the Sister Maria Socorro Studio Laboratory for Mathematics and Science, a new Biology Laboratory, and the Loyola Executive Technology Center. Classrooms and the library utilize wireless technology in the smart classrooms.

Costs

For 2009–10, tuition and fees were $26,540 and room and board were $10,920. An additional $1000 is estimated to cover books and personal spending. Immaculata offers a Fixed Tuition program. This guarantees the same tuition cost for four years for all full-time students entering the College of Undergraduate Studies. Immaculata is the only college in the Commonwealth of Pennsylvania to offer this program.

Financial Aid

Financial aid is available in the form of scholarships, grants, loans, and part-time campus employment through the resources of Immaculata, federal and state governments, and private endowments. Scholarships are awarded for academic excellence. Approximately 90 percent of the students receive some form of aid, and all students who demonstrate need are offered financial aid packages. The University requires that students submit the Free Application for Federal Student Aid (FAFSA) to be considered for financial aid. The University sends financial aid packages to accepted students as their files are completed by the end of February. The FAFSA reporting code is 003276.

Faculty

The faculty has more than 90 full-time and 200 part-time members, more than half of whom hold doctorates. Several members of the Immaculata faculty conduct research and present papers in various disciplines, both nationally and internationally. High-quality teaching is of the greatest importance to Immaculata's academic program. Full-time faculty members serve as academic counselors and activity moderators. The student-faculty ratio is 11:1.

Student Government

The Student Association of Immaculata University (SAIU) governs most aspects of student life for both resident and commuter students. The resident assistant program moderates residence life by holding open meetings to discuss safety issues and to set residence hall regulations. Students serve on the various University policymaking committees and handle all student activity funds.

Admission Requirements

In order to be considered for admission to the College of Undergraduate Studies, students must submit an official secondary school transcript indicating course selection for the senior year and SAT or ACT scores. The reporting code for the SAT is 2320, and the reporting code for the ACT is 3596. An essay and recommendations are required. The Admission Committee requires 14 or more course units, as follows: 4 units of English, 2 units of social science, 2 units of mathematics, 2 units of science (1 lab), and 2 consecutive years of the same foreign language. Most candidates exceed this curriculum. The mid-range GPA for the past two years was 3.2.

All admission credentials should be sent to the College of Undergraduate Studies. Students can apply online at the University's Web site, http://www.immaculata.edu/admissions. The application fee of $35 is waived for students who apply online or who visit the campus and complete an application during their visit. Students also have the option to apply through the Common Application, http://www.commonapp.org, which is free as well.

Application and Information

Applications are accepted from prospective freshman and transfer students on a rolling admissions basis, and decisions are made three to four weeks after an applicant's file is complete. The only exceptions are those students applying for nursing and the Thomas Jefferson University programs. Those applications have a deadline date of December 15. All of the credentials required for admission must be received and the file completed by that date.

For further information, students should contact:

Rebecca H. Bowlby, Director of Admission
Immaculata University
P.O. Box 642
Immaculata, Pennsylvania 19345-0642
Phone: 610-647-4400 Ext. 3060
877-42-TODAY (toll-free)
Fax: 610-640-0836
E-mail: admis@immaculata.edu
Web site: http://www.immaculata.edu

Students at Immaculata University.

INDIANA UNIVERSITY OF PENNSYLVANIA

INDIANA, PENNSYLVANIA

The University

Founded in 1875, Indiana University of Pennsylvania (IUP) draws its enrollment of 14,638 students from nearly every state and from scores of other countries. With three campuses located in the foothills of the Allegheny Mountains, IUP is the largest of the fourteen universities in the Pennsylvania State System of Higher Education and the only one that grants doctoral degrees.

The University sustains a tradition of high academic quality at an affordable cost. In forty-five academic departments located within six colleges and two schools, IUP offers approximately 140 undergraduate and graduate major fields of study. Graduate programs in many professional and applied areas are available, as are ten doctoral programs. IUP has one of the largest internship programs in Pennsylvania, providing students with professional experience to supplement their classroom learning.

The following publications have recognized IUP for its high academic standards and competitive costs: *Consumers Digest* Top 50 Best Values for Public Colleges and Universities, *Kiplinger's Personal Finance* magazine's annual *100 Best Values in Public Colleges, Two Hundred Most Selective Colleges: The Definitive Guide to America's First-Choice Schools,* Princeton Review's *The Best 371 Colleges,* Princeton Review's *Best 296 Business Schools,* and *U.S. News & World Report.*

Location

Located 50 miles northeast of Pittsburgh in the borough of Indiana, the seat of Indiana County, the main campus of IUP is just three blocks from the town's business district. The University is easily accessible by automobile from all sections of the state. The campus's residential facilities are being transformed from traditional double rooms with communal bathrooms to multiroom suites and bathrooms shared by no more than 2 students. The community of Indiana has more than thirty churches that represent all major faiths. All churches are within walking distance of the campus.

Majors and Degrees

IUP awards B.A., B.S., B.F.A., B.S.Ed., and B.S.N. degrees in approximately 140 undergraduate and graduate majors in the areas of the arts and sciences, business, consumer services, elementary and secondary education, fine arts, food and nutrition, health and physical education, home economics, medical technology, nursing, respiratory therapy, and safety sciences. IUP also offers the Associate of Arts degree in business. Dual majors are available to students who wish to augment their academic background.

Academic Programs

IUP provides for the nourishment of the whole person through its Liberal Studies Program. In addition to fulfilling the minimum 48-semester-hour Liberal Studies Program requirement, each student must complete the necessary major and minor requirements to reach the minimum total of 120 credits necessary for graduation.

Courses taken by students under the Advanced Placement program of the College Board prior to admission may be recognized by the awarding of college credit or by the exemption of required subjects from the student's curriculum. For students who have acquired learning in nontraditional or other ways or who have advanced in a given field, an opportunity to gain exemption from a course is offered through examinations given at the discretion of each department.

The University offers an Army Reserve Officers' Training Corps (ROTC) program.

IUP operates on two 14-week semesters—September through December and January through May—plus two 5-week summer sessions. The University also offers a Pre-Summer Session.

Off-Campus Programs

The University participates in joint programs with other colleges and universities. Included in these cooperative programs are one in family medicine with Jefferson Medical College of Thomas Jefferson University, one in forestry with Duke University, two in engineering with Drexel University and the University of Pittsburgh, one in graphic arts with the Art Institute of Pittsburgh, one in jewelry with the Bowman Technical School, one in optometry with Pennsylvania College of Optometry, and one in podiatry with Philadelphia School of Podiatry.

The Office of International Education has arrangements for students to study in numerous countries. Each year, approximately 200 students study abroad. Other opportunities for off-campus study include the marine science consortium, the graphic arts exchange program, internships, and studies in the health services, which are offered through the University's affiliations with hospitals and other universities.

Academic Facilities

Information Technology Services provides computational support for undergraduate and graduate courses, faculty and student research, and the administrative requirements of the University. Terminals may be found in various locations on campus.

The University's campuswide cable system and fiber-optic backbone are fully connected to all academic buildings and each residence hall room, allowing immediate connection to the University's mainframe computer and access to the University's television station and educational programming.

The Stapleton-Stabley Library complex provides study space for about 1,200 students. The monograph holdings total more than 900,000 volumes. The general holdings are enhanced by the reference collection, which has more than 16,000 current serial titles and 16,000 electronic serial publications, 2.4 million items of microform materials, and an extensive media collection. IUP is a designated select depository for federal and state publications and is currently housing more than 37,000 volumes of governmental publications. The Special Collections and Archives collections highlight the labor history and industrial heritage of western Pennsylvania. Media Resources provides children's and curricular material to support the teacher preparation programs. The Cogswell Music Library houses approximately 10,000 books, 29,000 scores, 11,200 recordings, and 3,300 CDs.

There is a public computer lab in Stapleton and more than 118 public computers throughout the library. Increasing numbers of resources are available in full text electronically. The Instructional Design Center actively supports the growing distance-education courses.

Costs

The basic costs that in-state students incurred per year in 2009–10 included $7209 for tuition and fees, $8558 for room and board, and approximately $1000 for books and supplies. Additional costs included $2633 for personal expenses. Tuition and fees for out-of-state students were $15,645 per year. All costs are subject to change.

Financial Aid

More than 86 percent of IUP students received some type of financial assistance during the 2008–09 academic year. The types of financial aid offered by IUP include student employment, loans, grants, and scholarships. In most cases, the Free Application for Federal Student Aid (FAFSA) serves as the application used to determine eligibility for these programs. Federal student assistance is available during the fall, spring, and summer terms. The application deadline for all students for the FAFSA is April 15, with award notifications to accepted freshmen beginning on March 15. Financial assistance is also available through IUP's Army ROTC program.

Faculty

There are 678 full-time and 72 part-time faculty members. The student-faculty ratio is 18:1. While primarily serving as instructors, faculty members also aid students in course selections and career planning and advise student organizations and clubs.

Student Government

IUP students actively participate in the governance of the University through the Student Government Association, the elected members of which represent students in the University Senate.

Admission Requirements

Any graduate of an accredited four-year high school or holder of a high school equivalency diploma is qualified to apply for admission to IUP. Applicants are reviewed by the Admissions Committee on the basis of high school records, recommendations, and scores earned on the SAT or the ACT. Applicants are expected to name their major field upon application, but a change in major can be made prior to or during the freshman year.

Application and Information

Applications are accepted for consideration for the fall and spring semesters after August 1 of the preceding year. Applications are reviewed on a rolling basis beginning on September 15 until vacancies are filled. However, space in the incoming class and in the residence halls fills up quickly; prospective students are strongly encouraged to apply early in their senior year.

To request an application or further information, students should contact:

Office of Admissions
117 Sutton Hall
Indiana University of Pennsylvania
1011 South Drive
Indiana, Pennsylvania 15705-1046
Phone: 724-357-2230
800-442-6830 (toll-free)
Fax: 724-357-6281
E-mail: admissions-inquiry@iup.edu
Web site: http://www.iup.edu/admissions

COLLEGE CLOSE-UPS

INTERNATIONAL ACADEMY OF DESIGN & TECHNOLOGY

CHICAGO, ILLINOIS

The Academy

The International Academy of Design & Technology (IADT) locations in Chicago and Schaumburg offer educational programs in a variety of unique, diverse, energetic, and professional environments. Here students find the real-world guidance they want with the hands-on experience they need. They gain support from outstanding faculty members and fellow students and have the opportunity to cultivate career-building connections that may last a lifetime. The institution is filled with inspiration in the heart of Chicagoland's fashion, interior design, and advertising industries.

IADT is a postsecondary degree-granting institution with career-based curricula provided by professional staff members who contribute to students' development in their chosen fields. IADT provides a high-quality education, prepares students for positions in fields related to their area of study, and provides students with a professional environment that fosters cultural enrichment and personal development. The Academic Department at the school maintains high-quality curricula that are sensitive to industry needs, as defined by the IADT's Advisory Boards. The Career Services department offers career-planning services leading to employment opportunities for graduates to allow them to utilize their knowledge, skills, and talents.

There are ten IADT campuses nationwide and an online school that delivers a variety of creative design degrees in a virtual environment. Students at the ground campuses also have the opportunity to complete a portion of their program of study through online courses.

There are various associations and clubs for IADT students. These clubs include the Fashion Council (fashion design), Behind the Scene (merchandising management), the Information Technology Organization (IT), the Interior Design Student Association (interior design), Gamers Anonymous (game design), Anime Student Alliance, the Green Academy, the Book Club, and the American Institute of Graphic Arts (graphic design). GLBT@IADT Community is the Academy's outreach to gay, lesbian, bisexual, and transgender students. All of these clubs are organized by the students and for the students. In addition, the school hosts an annual fashion show, Imagine, bringing together students from various disciplines within the school to showcase their talent in a public arena.

IADT is incorporated under the laws of the state of Illinois and accredited by the Accrediting Council for Independent Colleges and Schools (ACICS). The interior design program is accredited by the Council for Interior Design Accreditation.

Location

The International Academy of Design & Technology is located in Chicago's Loop at historic One North State Street. The campus is close to some of Chicago's famous and world-renowned landmarks. Within walking distance of the campus are the Merchandise Mart and the Apparel Center complex in historic River North and the retail shops of North Michigan Avenue. Along the revitalized State Street are Macy's, Sears, and a multitude of nationally advertised retail outlets. More importantly, the school is conveniently located in a region known for its internationally prominent advertising, graphic design, and interior design firms.

Majors and Degrees

IADT is authorized by the Illinois Board of Higher Education to grant a Bachelor of Arts degree in merchandising management (tracks in fashion merchandising and retail operations management), a Bachelor of Applied Science degree in information technology, a Bachelor of Science degree in computer forensics, and a Bachelor of Fine Arts degree in fashion design, interior design, and visual communications (tracks in advertising communication, advertising design, game design, graphic design, multimedia and Web design, and video and animation production). IADT is also authorized to grant Associate of Applied Science degrees in fashion design, merchandising management (tracks in fashion merchandising and retail operations management), information technology, and visual communication (tracks in advertising communication, advertising design, graphic design, multimedia and Web design, and video and animation production).

All degree programs provide students with the opportunity for in-depth career preparation and a firm foundation in general education studies. In the bachelor's degree programs, students benefit from advanced career courses and have the option of choosing elective courses to complete their general education requirements.

Academic Programs

The programs of the Academy involve both classroom education and supervised activities off campus that are designed to prepare students for entry-level positions in their chosen field. Students must take a minimum of 180 quarter hours of study to earn the baccalaureate degree. Transfer credits are acceptable in all programs. Students must take a minimum of 96 quarter hours to earn the Associate of Applied Science degree and must complete all prescribed courses satisfactorily with a minimum grade point average of 2.0.

The curriculum for each program is reviewed periodically by faculty members, program chairs, and members of the program Advisory Boards. Members of the Advisory Boards are experienced professionals in their fields. The Advisory Boards provide the Academy with input on a variety of subjects related to their specific industry. These successful practitioners form an essential link between the academic world and the world that students enter upon graduation.

As a result of the career-oriented emphasis of IADT, course work is highly specialized and prepares students for entry into a career field. From the point at which they begin their studies at the Academy and continue through to graduation, students are given personal one-on-one academic guidance. Students are regularly advised by IADT's academic advisers regarding their progress in classes.

Academic Facilities

Classrooms are designed to facilitate learning and consist of lecture rooms, textile labs, drafting labs, design studios, and sewing and pattern-making rooms. Computer labs equipped with Macintosh and IBM-compatible personal computers are used for instruction and practice.

The CECybrary is an Internet-accessible information center committed to facilitating the lifelong learning and achievement of the Career Education Corporation community. This virtual library contains a collection of full-text journals, books, and reference materials, links to Web sites relevant to each curricular area, instructional guides for using electronic library resources, and much more.

The virtual collection is carefully selected to support students as they advance through their programs of study and includes quality, full-text, peer-reviewed articles from scholarly journals and full-text electronic books. Instructional materials for students and faculty are designed to enhance information literacy skills.

A full-time librarian located at corporate headquarters manages the CECybrary. The librarians at the various CEC colleges participate in selecting the electronic resources and Web site links, and help prepare the instructional materials that are on the Web site.

Students at all CEC colleges have access to the CECybrary from their campus location and from home, if they have an Internet service provider. Access to the Cybrary is password-controlled. The password is easily obtained from the campus library.

The bookstore sells books and supplies used in the courses taught at the Academy. The bookstore attempts to keep a balance of inventory between new and used books whenever possible. School-specific merchandise and clothing are also available for purchase. The bookstore coordinates book buy-back periods at the end of each quarter.

Costs

Tuition for the 2010–11 academic year for all programs is $405 per credit hour. Books and supplies are additional.

Financial Aid

IADT helps students find the financial resources they need to achieve their educational goals. Financial aid is available for those who qualify. The Academy participates in the Federal Pell Grant, Federal Supplemental Educational Opportunity Grant (FSEOG), Federal Stafford Student Loan, Federal Parent PLUS programs, Academic Competitiveness Grant, and the National Science and Mathematics Access to Retain Talent Grant. In addition to state and federal aid, IADT has its own scholarship programs.

Faculty

Faculty members of the school possess extensive academic and professional credentials. Their experience enables them to teach theoretical principles while emphasizing current practices in the field. Faculty members are sought and retained because they are committed to teaching at the undergraduate level. In and out of the classroom, the faculty is an integral part of the students' career preparation.

Admission Requirements

Pursuant to the mission of the institution, IADT desires to admit students who possess appropriate credentials and have demonstrated the capacity or potential for successfully completing the educational programs offered by the institution. To that end, the institution evaluates all students and makes admission decisions on an individual basis. To assist the admissions personnel in making informed decisions, an admissions interview is required.

Transfer students meeting admission requirements are accepted. Students must have an official transcript from postsecondary institutions previously attended forwarded to the school. Credit may be given for a course taken at the previous institution if it is comparable in scope and length to an International Academy course, as stated in the Academy's Transfer Credit Guidelines.

Application and Information

Prospective students should apply for admission as soon as possible in order to be officially accepted for a specific program and its starting date. Prospective students must have an admissions interview, during which they are given an opportunity to tour the school with their families to see its equipment and facilities. At this time, there is also an opportunity to ask questions relating to the school's curricula and a student's possible career goals.

At the time of application, the student must complete an enrollment agreement, pay a $20 application fee, and complete an attestation of high school graduation or its equivalency or provide proof of high school graduation or its equivalency. Once an applicant has completed and submitted the enrollment agreement, the school reviews the information and informs the applicant of its decision.

IADT Chicago does not guarantee employment or salary. CEC2356270

For further information, students should contact:

Ernest Cochran III, Vice President of Admissions
International Academy of Design & Technology
One North State Street
Chicago, Illinois 60602-3300
Phone: 888-803-2111 (toll-free)
Fax: 312-541-3929
E-mail: info@iadtchicago.com
Web site: http://www.iadtchicago.edu

COLLEGE CLOSE-UPS

IONA COLLEGE

NEW ROCHELLE, NEW YORK

The College

Iona College is a four-year, coed college in New Rochelle, a suburb of New York City. The 35-acre campus is located just 20 minutes by rail from the heart of Midtown Manhattan. A medium-size college, Iona offers more than forty majors and thirty minors in business and liberal arts. The most popular undergraduate majors are finance, mass communication, education, psychology, and criminal justice. Iona was founded in 1940 by the Congregation of Christian Brothers and is a diverse community of learners and scholars dedicated to academic excellence in the tradition of the Christian Brothers and American Catholic higher education.

Iona's overall enrollment is 4,500 students, of whom 3,000 are traditional undergraduate students. The student body is talented and diverse, with students coming from thirty-five states. Thirty-three percent of the students are members of minority groups, and contribute to a college environment that values diversity.

More than ninety clubs and over 100 activities are available for student participation, including student government, Greek organizations, intramural sports, community service, a student-run newspaper, radio and TV stations, the yearbook, theater groups, a pipe band, ethnic-affinity groups, various honor societies, and music groups.

Iona offers twenty-one NCAA Division I athletic teams. Men's sports include baseball, basketball, cross-country, rowing, soccer, swimming and diving, track (indoor and outdoor), and water polo. Women's sports include basketball, cross-country, lacrosse, rowing, soccer, softball, swimming and diving, track (indoor and outdoor), and water polo.

The Office of Student Development organizes many activities for students to participate in each week, including trips to nearby New York City for theater, sports, and museums; on-campus movie nights; parties and dances; karaoke nights; wellness workshops; and other activities.

The College offers students four-year housing in five residence halls. Sixty-seven percent of freshmen and over a third of the undergraduate population reside on campus. The residential experience includes living and learning environments, where students are housed together based on their academic and curricular interests. An off-campus housing office was recently established to work with nonresidential students and the local community. All students are offered a unique meal plan that enables them to dine at on- and off-campus locations. On-campus eateries include a food court, dining commons, Quiznos, and Starbucks café.

Location

Iona's campus is located in New Rochelle, New York, one of the oldest cities in the U.S. Founded in 1654, New Rochelle is a city of 70,000 on the shore of the Long Island Sound.

Majors and Degrees

Iona College offers Bachelor of Arts, Bachelor of Science, and Bachelor of Business Administration degrees through its School of Arts and Science and Hagan School of Business. Undergraduate majors include accounting, biochemistry, biology (general, pre-dental, pre–physical therapy, preprofessional, and premedicine), business administration, chemistry, computer science, criminal justice, economics, education (childhood and adolescence), English, environmental science, finance, foreign languages (French, Italian, and Spanish), history, information systems, interdisciplinary science, international business, international studies, management, marketing, mass communication (advertising, journalism, public relations, and television and video), mathematics, medical technology, philosophy, pre–physical therapy, physics, political science, psychology, religious studies, social work, sociology, speech communication studies, and speech/language pathology and audiology. Five-year combined bachelor's and master's degree programs are offered in computational/computer science, computer science, criminal justice, English, history, and psychology. A fast-track M.B.A. program is available to students after graduation.

There are also minors available in accounting, biology, business, chemistry, classical humanities, computer science, criminal justice, economics, English, film studies, finance, fine and performing arts, French, history, information systems, international business, Italian, management, marketing, mass communication, mathematics, peace and justice studies, philosophy, physics, political science, psychology, public policy, religious studies, sociology, Spanish, speech communication, sports and entertainment studies, women's studies, and writing. A number of programs offer a business minor in combination with a major or concentration.

An honors program is available for top students who desire additional enhancement to their academic program. Special courses, seminars, mentoring, advising, and off-campus opportunities are part of the honors students' curriculum.

Academic Programs

Many of Iona's programs are accredited by the highest specialized accrediting councils, including AACSB International–The Association to Advance Collegiate Schools of Business for the Hagan School of Business and the National Council for Accreditation of Teacher Education (NCATE) for the Department of Education. Mass communications (ACEJMC) is one of four accredited programs in the state of New York, and the Departments of Social Work (CSWE), Education, and Computer Science (ABET) boast the top accreditations available.

Off-Campus Programs

Iona College encourages students to broaden their educational experience through study and travel abroad. Iona sponsors summer, semester, and intersession programs in Australia, England, France, Ireland, Italy, and Spain. The College also offers a wide range of internships in most majors. In recent years, students have held internships at some of the best-known corporate names in New York City and the surrounding area.

Academic Facilities

To meet the demands of a new generation of students, Iona heavily invests in updating its campus and technology. The latest investment in campus infrastructure is the expansion and renovation of the main library. A new atrium and wing incorporate new study space; meeting rooms; classrooms with the latest technology, including Apple dual-boot iMacs; a digital archive room; and refurbished auditorium. The two campus libraries, Ryan Library and the Helen T. Arrigoni Library/Technology Center, house extensive collections and offer computer access to collections worldwide. The on-site collections, including more than 261,000 volumes, 687 periodical titles, audiovisual materials, and microforms, have been developed to support Iona's curriculum and special interests.

As part of a multimillion-dollar capital campaign, a student union was added and the athletic center was expanded and updated. The Robert V. LaPenta Student Union features a bookstore, commons/lounge areas, a food court, a bistro, a state-of-the-art media center, and offices for student services and campus organizations. The Hynes Athletics Center includes a multipurpose arena, an Olympic-size swimming pool, a Nautilus center, training facilities, and coaching offices. It is the home to the Iona College Gaels Division I teams that compete in the Metro Atlantic Athletic Conference (MAAC). Featuring a state-of-the-art cardiovascular center, three multipurpose courts, a rowing tank, and an aerobics/dance studio, the Hynes Center also allows Iona's nonathletes to participate in an intramural program that includes many various sports. Classes in Pilates, yoga, salsa dancing, and more are also be offered by qualified instructors.

The Arts Center on North Avenue provides space for the study of art, dance, and theater and includes the Brother Kenneth Chapman Gallery.

The College was one of the first wireless campuses in the region and was recognized by the Intel Corporation as a "Most Unwired" campus. Students can access the Internet and other online tools from anywhere on campus. The College's thirty-six computing facilities are kept updated with the latest hardware and software.

Costs

For the 2009–10 academic year, tuition and fees were $28,850; room and board costs were $12,100.

Financial Aid

Financial aid is critical to a student's decision to attend any college, and Iona College is no exception. Iona uses a system of academic scholarships in combination with need-based financial aid to help students enroll. For the 2009–10 academic year, 94 percent of undergraduates received some financial aid, with the average aid award near $21,751. To apply for financial aid, students should file the Free Application for Federal Student Aid (FAFSA) and the Iona College Financial Aid Application forms by February 15.

Faculty

Iona College has approximately 170 full-time and 80 part-time faculty members; 92 percent possess a terminal degree in their field. Faculty members conduct research and write books and articles, but their primary responsibility is teaching undergraduate students. All classes are taught by faculty members—there are no teaching assistants.

The student-faculty ratio is 13:1. Faculty members are readily available to meet for individual conferences. In addition, because of the College's proximity to New York City, many faculty members include regular excursions to Manhattan as part of their classes and invite guest speakers to lecture about special topics.

Student Government

The Student Government Association (SGA) is a service organization that coordinates, supervises, and promotes student activities. The Office of Student Activities hosts hundreds of on- and off-campus events throughout the year.

Admission Requirements

Admission decisions at Iona are based on a wide range of criteria. Most important is an applicant's academic record, including the level of curriculum taken and grades earned. Also considered are SAT or ACT scores, grade trends, a writing sample, activities, and recommendations.

For the class entering in September 2009, the average grade point average was 3.4 (89 percent); middle 50 percent on the SAT ranged from 1080 to 1300. Slightly over 7,300 applications were submitted and about 4,300 (59 percent) of the applications were accepted and offered admission.

Application and Information

The Office of Admissions at Iona College works with each applicant on an individual basis. While the outcome of the admission decision may not be what every applicant hopes, Iona tries to ensure that each applicant is treated with courtesy and dignity. In order to be considered for admission, Iona requires students to submit an application (paper or online), a $50 application fee, an official transcript, SAT or ACT scores, a counselor recommendation, and an essay. Transfer students must also submit official transcripts from all colleges and universities previously attended.

The deadline for submitting applications for regular admission is February 15; for early action, it is December 1. Decisions are mailed by April 1 for regular admission and late December for early action. Deposits for all accepted students are due on May 1.

Campus visits are available on most weekdays that classes are in session and on selected Saturdays; appointments are recommended. A visit can be scheduled by calling the Campus Visit Center at 914-633-2622 or by e-mail at eenglish@iona.edu.

For more information, students should contact:

Office of Admissions
Iona College
715 North Avenue
New Rochelle, New York 10801
Phone: 914-633-2502
800-231-IONA (toll-free)
Fax: 914-637-2778
E-mail: admissions@iona.edu
Web site: http://www.iona.edu

Iona students take a break from classes out on the lawn in front of the Robert V. LaPenta Student Union.

JOHN CABOT UNIVERSITY

ROME, ITALY

The University

John Cabot University (JCU) was founded in 1972 and is the first overseas American university in Italy with regional accreditation by the Middle States Commission of Higher Education. JCU is a four-year liberal arts college following the American system of education with a distinctive European and international character. Located in the historic center of Rome, the University has unparalleled access to history, culture, and the active diplomatic and international communities associated with both the United Nations organizations and embassies to Italy and the Holy See. JCU's international setting, commitment to a serious liberal arts education, and unique relationship with leading multinational corporations, media, cultural and other international organizations, provides degree-seeking students the academic training and opportunities to participate in exclusive internships and enter directly into demanding careers, or continue their studies at prestigious graduate programs.

The University has a diverse and unique student body, composed of American, Italian, and international degree-seeking students from more than forty countries. This group is complemented by visiting American students from major universities across the United States. The visiting American students bring to Rome their own regional diversity which complements the European diversity at JCU resulting in a dynamic and engaging student body. JCU's commitment to creating a student community of both four-year degree and visiting students provides degree students with the friendly, close community of a small campus, with the active and energetic networks that come from studying with a larger pool of students from across the U.S.

The average class size is 15 students, and there are approximately 100 full- and part-time faculty members holding advanced degrees from major universities all over the world. Working closely with professors and classmates, students receive the individual attention needed to fully develop their academic talents and abilities. With a student-centered approach to both education and human relationships, the University offers an active learning environment while also teaching the ethical standards that are essential for responsibility and leadership in today's world. JCU graduates are accepted into a wide array of graduate programs in the U.S., U.K., and Italy such as Columbia University, Johns Hopkins University, London School of Economics, and Università Bocconi.

The University is licensed by the Delaware Department of Education to award its degrees and is authorized by the Italian Ministry of Research and Instruction to operate as an institution of American higher education in Rome. John Cabot University was accredited in 2003 by the Middle States Commission on Higher Education (http://www.msche.org). Since 2000, the University has also had a validation agreement with the University of Wales allowing students to simultaneously earn both the American B.A. and the British B.A. Honors degree for JCU majors in business administration, international affairs, marketing, and political science.

Location

John Cabot University is located in Rome, Italy, in the picturesque Trastevere neighborhood, just down the river from St. Peter's Basilica and the Vatican and a short walk from the Roman Forum. John Cabot University has two campuses within a 5-minute walk of each other. The Frank J. Guarini Campus, a former convent, consists of a central main building of three floors and an adjacent wing connected by terraces and courtyards. The original separate chapel now serves as the student lounge. The property offers students a tranquil atmosphere in which to study and interact, while historic, bustling Rome is just a few steps away. Surrounded by the green gardens of the Accademia dei Lincei (the National Academy of Sciences, of which Galileo was an early member) and next door to the Villa Farnesina of Raphael's famous frescoes, the Guarini Campus is buttressed by the Aurelian Wall of the Roman Empire. The Guarini Campus is approached through the Porta Settimiana, which was built by Pope Alexander VI Borgia in 1498 and later restored by Pope Pius VI in 1798. John Cabot also has spacious classrooms in the Tiber Campus, which is along the banks of the famous Tiber River. Both campuses are equipped with Wi-Fi and classrooms furnished with multimedia equipment. The JCU Frohing Library is one of the most impressive English language libraries in Rome. JCU's fine arts and art history classes often meet at famous monuments such as the Colosseum and the Forum, which are within easy reach of JCU. In effect, all of Rome is John Cabot University's campus, and students take advantage of JCU's urban setting, meeting with friends and faculty at local cafés and trattorias as well as in many of the piazzas that are hidden within the small streets of Rome's historic center.

Majors and Degrees

John Cabot University offers the Bachelor of Arts degree in twelve majors: art history, business administration, classical studies, communications, economics and finance, English literature, history, humanistic studies, international affairs, Italian studies, marketing, and political science. The University of Wales, in the United Kingdom, has validated JCU degrees in business administration, international affairs, marketing, and political science since 2000. As a result of this validation, students in these programs may simultaneously work toward both an American degree from John Cabot University and a European degree (validated Honors) from the University of Wales. Students may select minors in all of the major areas, as well as in computer science, creative writing, religion, philosophy, and psychology.

John Cabot also offers the Associate of Arts degree in all major fields of study. Each of these programs is designed to develop the characteristics of the individual student by means of a unique learning and living experience in a setting rich in history, culture, and geopolitical interaction. All majors are complemented by internship opportunities at the United Nations, museums, and international firms in Rome. JCU's Career Services Center is dedicated to providing students with support for their preparation and transition into post-graduate activities. JCU's alumni network provides additional opportunities for graduates to continue their career development through international connections that have become more and more valued in today's global world.

Academic Programs

Unlike most European university systems, the American system of higher education encourages experimentation and breadth, particularly during the first two years of the university experience. The curricula of the University's programs are, therefore, divided into two basic categories: the general distribution requirements of the first two years of study, which give the student a broad exposure to the basic disciplines of the liberal arts educational experience, and the specific, additional requirements of each degree awarded by the University.

The general distribution and other introductory courses equip the student to select an area of specialization as a degree candidate. Within each degree program, there are specific requirements that must be met by the student who wishes to earn a degree at John Cabot. These requirements include ten to twelve core courses deemed by faculty members to be essential to the discipline of the degree and comparable to the requirements for the same degree at recognized and accredited colleges and universities in the American system of higher education. In addition to the core requirements, other requisites include electives that support the core program and offer opportunities to take courses in other discipline areas of particular interest or need.

The academic year is divided into two semesters of fifteen weeks each, beginning in September and January (students should see the academic calendar for more information). In one semester, a student normally enrolls in five courses, earning 15 credits in the semester and 30 credits in the year. A summer session of five weeks allows students to take one or two additional courses. To earn the Bachelor of Arts degree, a student must complete 120 credits (forty courses); to earn the Associate of Arts degree, a student must complete 60 credits (twenty courses).

Special programs include English language preparation for university study (ENLUS).

Off-Campus Programs

The Go Global program at JCU offers degree-seeking students the opportunity to study at universities in the United States as well as several international locations. This enriching opportunity contributes to educational growth and cultural awareness in general and helps prepare students for careers in international fields.

Academic Facilities

The Frohring Library, constructed in 1999, provides the latest in online access to academic journals and indexes and is the University center for research in support of the academic programs as well as a quiet place for study and pleasure reading. The computer laboratories contain desktop computers equipped with the latest software as well as high-speed printers and a full-color scanner. The Aula Magna Regina is the largest room in the University and serves as the theater for the drama club. The Aula Magna is also used for orientation, cultural and community events, concerts, and student activities.

Costs

Tuition is $9450 or €6650 per semester and housing costs begin at $4600 per semester.

Financial Aid

U.S. citizens attending a college or university outside the United States are eligible to apply for the Federal Family Education Loans (FFEL), including the Stafford Student Loan and PLUS loans. The Free Application for Federal Student Aid (FAFSA) form must be completed to apply for a Stafford Student Loan. Current U.S. government legislation prohibits U.S. citizens enrolled in colleges or universities outside the United States from receiving Federal Pell Grants, Federal Supplemental Educational Opportunity Grants (FSEOG), Federal Perkins Loans, and Federal Work-Study Program funds, even though they may be eligible for such assistance. Academic scholarships are awarded each year based on merit and need. John Cabot University is proud to participate in the Secchia Family Foundation's Secchia Scholars program. The four types of Secchia Scholarships are the Norman R. Peterson Scholarship, the Order Sons of Italy in America Scholarships, the Secchia–De Vos Merit Scholarships and the Economic Club of Grand Rapids–Secchia Scholarship. Other institutional scholarships include the Presidential Scholarships, the John Cabot University Alumni Matching Scholarship, the Italian Merit Scholarships, the 100/100 Italian Maturità Scholarships, and the Maxwell Rabb Scholarship. A number of work-study assistantships are available for students who are interested in and capable of assisting the various administrative offices and academic departments of the University.

Faculty

The University has a distinguished faculty of approximately 100 part- and full-time professors from around the world who are actively engaged in research. In addition to teaching, the faculty members take part in academic advising, the careful planning and monitoring of a student's progress through the academic program; and extracurricular activities, such as academic field trips, student fund-raising events, and lectures and seminars.

Student Government

Student government at John Cabot University contributes significantly to the quality of student life. A Student Senate is elected each year to coordinate activities. During the year, the Student Government sponsors a number of programs, such as the International Student Government Conference, which brings together student leaders from Italy, Europe, and the Middle East. The Student Government works with a faculty adviser and staff adviser in planning social, cultural, intellectual, and sports activities to respond to students' interests and needs. Student Government also sponsors social events to raise funds for charitable activities.

Admission Requirements

Admission to John Cabot University is selective. Successful applicants must have maintained a scholastic record demonstrating a serious commitment to their studies and the ability to succeed at college-level work.

Each applicant is considered as an individual, and no single factor can guarantee acceptance to the University. The previous school's documentation of the applicant's academic ability, motivation, character, and contribution to school life is very important. This information should be reflected in the student's academic record and letters of recommendation. The University does not prescribe a fixed secondary school course of study but considers both the quality and breadth of the student's record. The University is open to all applicants without regard to race, national origin, religion, or gender. For applicants coming from the U.S. secondary school system, a standard college-preparatory program is expected. For applicants from other national systems, an essential requirement is successful completion of a secondary school program permitting university admission in the respective system. Students holding the Italian Diploma di Maturità, the International Baccalaureate, or other equivalent academic credentials may be granted advanced standing. Results of the SAT or the ACT are required for high school students graduating from an American secondary school. Applicants whose first language is not English or who did not attend a secondary school where classes were taught in English must demonstrate sufficient preparation in the English language. Standardized test scores, such as the Test of English as a Foreign Language (TOEFL) or the International English Language Testing System (IELTS), are useful in assessing a student's language capability. A minimum score of 550 on the TOEFL (213 on the computer-based exam or 85 on the Internet-based test), a minimum score of 6.5 on the IELTS, or an equivalent passing score on the John Cabot English Proficiency Test are accepted as evidence of sufficient preparation in the English language.

Application and Information

Admissions decisions are based on the review of official transcripts, results of standardized tests, the student's GPA, final examination results, a personal statement, and letters of recommendation from teachers or professors. Transfer students from another university must be in good academic standing. An application form completed in its entirety must be accompanied by two recent passport-size photographs and a nonrefundable application fee of $50 or €50. Students may complete the application online or use the printable application. The University deadline is June 1 for fall admission and November 15 for the spring semester. Candidates are urged to submit their application and supporting documents as early as possible.

Students may apply online or obtain an application by contacting:

Admissions Office
John Cabot University
Via della Lungara, 233
00165 Rome
Italy
Phone: 39-06-681-9121
Fax: 39-06-683-2088
E-mail: admissions@johncabot.edu
Web site: http://www.johncabot.edu

U.S. Admissions Office
Karen Altieri
Manager, U.S. Office
14100 Walsingham Road, Suite 36, #10
Largo, Florida 33774
Phone: 866-457-6160 (toll free)
E-mail: kaltieri@johncabot.edu

Student on studying on one of John Cabot University's many terrazzos.

John Cabot University student on terrazzo.

JOHN CARROLL UNIVERSITY

UNIVERSITY HEIGHTS, OHIO

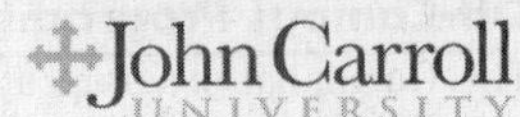

COLLEGE CLOSE-UPS

The University

In the Jesuit tradition of leadership, faith, and service, John Carroll University provides its students with a rigorous education, rooted in the liberal arts and focused on questions of moral and ethical value. The University wants its graduates to make a difference in their chosen careers and in bettering their communities. One of twenty-eight Jesuit colleges and universities in the United States, John Carroll offers degree programs at the undergraduate and graduate levels in fifty-four arts and sciences, business, and preprofessional fields.

John Carroll was founded in 1886 as St. Ignatius College. In 1923, its name was changed to Cleveland College briefly. Later it became John Carroll University, named after the first Catholic bishop of the United States. In 1934, the University moved from its original location on Cleveland's near west side to its current location in University Heights. Originally a men's college, the University and all its programs officially became coeducational in 1968.

In 2009–10, the enrollment was 3,600, with 3,100 students enrolled in full-time undergraduate programs and 500 in graduate programs. Students come from thirty-eight states, the Virgin Islands, Puerto Rico, and twenty other countries. The student body, including graduate students, is 46 percent men, 54 percent women, and 12 percent students of color. The University's eight residence halls house 1,860 students.

A well-rounded education includes learning and leadership activities outside the classroom. The University owns Thorn Acres, a 30-acre recreational facility used for fishing, canoeing, retreats, and student-group meetings. John Carroll offers more than 100 student organizations and clubs, as well as community volunteer service opportunities, men's and women's varsity and intramural sports, and academic honor societies. A natatorium, racquetball and tennis courts, two gymnasiums, and weight-training and fitness facilities are located in the Student Center. Office space is set aside for a host of student activities, including the newspaper, radio station, yearbook, Student Union, fraternities and sororities, and various other organizations. University Counseling Services provides free personal and psychological counseling, therapy, and testing. In addition, the Center for Career Services offers resources for students looking to choose a major or trying to land their first job.

Students at John Carroll, in the Jesuit spirit of "making a difference," take advantage of the numerous opportunities and programs offered to volunteer to help improve the local community as well as communities across the country and around the globe.

The Graduate School at John Carroll offers Master of Science degree programs in accountancy, biology, and mathematics; Master of Arts degree programs in biology, communications management, community counseling, education, English, history, humanities, integrated science, mathematics, nonprofit administration, and religious studies; the Master of Education; and Master of Business Administration degree programs. In addition, Economics America (the Cleveland Center for Economic Education), a nonprofit educational organization located on John Carroll's campus, provides advanced course work in economics for educators.

Location

Just 20 minutes from downtown Cleveland, John Carroll is located in the quiet, residential Heights neighborhood; it is surrounded by Shaker Heights, University Heights, and Cleveland Heights. The graceful walkways, rich landscape, and Gothic and contemporary architecture of the campus complement the surrounding community beautifully. The campus is easily accessible by bus, rapid transit, and car. Three shopping centers are within walking distance, so restaurants, theaters, banks, department stores, grocery stores, and specialty shops are all nearby. University Circle, 10 minutes from the campus, is the home of the Cleveland Symphony Orchestra; Cleveland Museums of Art, Natural History, and Health Education; and Garden Center of Greater Cleveland. Downtown Cleveland offers comedy clubs; world-class shopping; theater at the Cleveland Play House; the Warehouse District, an extensive entertainment district located near the Cuyahoga River; the Rock and Roll Hall of Fame; the Great Lakes Science Center; Progressive Field, home to the Cleveland Indians; Quicken Loans Arena, home to the Cleveland Cavaliers; and Cleveland Browns Stadium.

Majors and Degrees

There is a wide range of programs of study available to John Carroll University students. The School offers degree programs in over forty fields of study, including majors in the College of Arts and Sciences and the John M. and Mary Jo Boler School of Business. The University is expanding its undergraduate programs to meet new interests of students. This includes the Dolan Center for Science and Technology, which is home to several departments in the natural sciences.

In 2009, the University renamed its Department of Communication and Theatre Arts in memory of alumnus Tim Russert and also established the Tim Russert Endowed Scholarship and a Meet the Press fellowship in partnership with NBC.

In terms of academics, JCU has consistently received high rankings from independent college profiling organizations. In 2009, JCU was named the seventh best among master's granting colleges and universities in the Midwest. The University's four-year graduation rates exceed U.S. and Ohio averages.

Information on all our academic programs can be found at http://www.jcu.edu/academics/.

Academic Programs

In keeping with the Jesuit tradition of liberal arts education, every undergraduate takes a core curriculum that includes a single-theme first-year seminar course, three courses in humanities, three in science and mathematics, three in philosophy, two in social sciences, two in religious studies, one in English composition and rhetoric, and one in speech communication. Therefore, all students enroll in the College of Arts and Sciences for their first two years. After the first two years, students select a major and are admitted to their respective degree programs.

To earn a degree, a student must complete a minimum of 128 credit hours with a grade point average of at least 2.0 (C) for all course work. The last 30 hours of instruction must be completed at John Carroll. Candidates for graduation must complete all the courses and proficiency requirements for the degree, and they must complete all the major requirements with an average of at least 2.0. All course work required for a declared minor or concentration must be completed with a GPA of at least 2.0.

The University operates on a semester calendar, with three 5-week summer sessions offered between academic years.

Off-Campus Programs

John Carroll offers many special educational opportunities, including programs in London, Vatican City, China, and Japan. The Center for Global Education works with students who hope to study abroad. Explore their Web site (http://www.jcu.edu/global/) for more information.

John Carroll University is a member of the Northeast Ohio Commission on Higher Education and offers students the opportunity to take one course per semester at one of the other sixteen area universities while enrolled full-time at John Carroll. There is no additional charge for tuition; the only stipulation is that the course may not be offered at the home institution. Students often take courses in the performance-based arts or in specific engineering fields through this cross-registration program.

Academic Facilities

The Administration Building was built in 1935 and is John Carroll's oldest building. Along with administrative and faculty offices, Kulas Auditorium is located inside the Ad Building. A $7-million renovation of the Administration Building took place during the winter of 2002, when most of the spaces on the first two levels were renovated. During the renovation, a Student Service Center and an Einstein Bros. Bagel restaurant were incorporated into the basement level.

The Dolan Center for Science and Technology, a $66.4-million, 265,000-square-foot building, opened with a grand celebration on September 6, 2003. This facility houses the biology, chemistry, psychology, physics, mathematics, and computer science departments. With the Dolan Center, the University has advanced its science and mathematics curriculum, upgraded instructional technology, and expanded partnerships with area schools and employers. A number of years ago, a $6.8-million expansion of the Grasselli Library doubled the capacity of the building; it has also enhanced accessibility of electronic databases. The O'Malley Center for Communications and Language Arts features an electronic newsroom, computer-assisted and audio language laboratories, and a center for writing instruction. The Tim Russert Department of Communication and Theatre Arts features the Vincent Klein Television Studio, which recently received an over $500,000 facelift.

Costs

Tuition and fees are $30,250 for the 2010–11 academic year. Room and board are $8750. The average cost for books and supplies is $1200 per year.

Financial Aid

John Carroll works closely with families to lay out a reasonable financial plan to make private education at John Carroll an affordable opportunity. The financial aid process strikes a balance between scholarships and need-based assistance. Competitive merit awards that recognize significant academic, leadership, and service accomplishments are offered, but not at the expense of keeping John Carroll affordable for all students. Every year, students from across the economic spectrum enroll at John Carroll and go on to graduate.

In 2009–10, more than 80 percent of the student body received some type of need-based financial assistance. Merit-based scholarships are awarded to approximately half of the freshman class. Most students apply for need-based aid by completing the Free Application for Federal Student Aid (FAFSA). The financial aid application deadline is March 1.

For more information about JCU's scholarships and grants, please go to http://www.jcu.edu/aidjcu/.

Faculty

The majority of John Carroll's 240 faculty members teach undergraduate classes, although some teach graduate programs as well. Of the full-time faculty members, 94 percent hold doctorates or the appropriate terminal degree in their field, and 75.6 percent are tenured. The faculty's primary focus is teaching and scholarship. Counseling of students, research and publication, and community service are also important pursuits. John Carroll's faculty includes 8 resident Jesuit priests. The student-faculty ratio is 14:1.

Student Government

The John Carroll student body is self-governed, with the elected Student Union officers actively representing all students—undergraduate, graduate, full- and part-time, and day and evening—in all academic, social, religious, and disciplinary matters. Fifty-six men and women are elected to Student Union service for one-year terms.

Admission Requirements

Applications for admission from all serious candidates are welcome. John Carroll has a holistic review process for admission. Each applicant to the institution is reviewed individually, and all information is considered carefully to determine if the student will be able to succeed in the curriculum and what the student would contribute to the University community.

Admission criteria, in descending order of importance, are the quality of the high school curriculum, grade point average, extracurricular activities, test scores on either the SAT or ACT, the essay, and the recommendation of a high school counselor or teacher.

The deadline for applications to John Carroll is February 1. The priority scholarship deadline is December 1. Admission decisions are mailed to candidates approximately twice a month, starting in December. Please visit http://www.jcu.edu/admission/apply/ for more information.

Application and Information

John Carroll is a member of the Common Application group, and there is no fee to apply. John Carroll subscribes to the Candidates Reply Date of May 1. Accepted students who wish to reserve their place in the freshman class must submit their enrollment reservation form and $300 enrollment deposit by May 1 to ensure their place in the class. All deposits are refundable by written request up to the May 1 deadline.

To request more information, students are encouraged to contact:

Steve Vitatoe
Executive Director of Enrollment
John Carroll University
University Heights, Ohio 44118-4581
Phone: 888-335-6800
E-mail: admission@jcu.edu
Web site: http://www.jcu.edu/admission

Grasselli Tower stands behind the bust of Archbishop John Carroll, the University's namesake, along the main quadrangle.

THE JOHNS HOPKINS UNIVERSITY
Krieger School of Arts and Sciences and Whiting School of Engineering
BALTIMORE, MARYLAND

The University

Privately endowed, the Johns Hopkins University (JHU) was founded in 1876 as the first American university committed to the idea that knowledge should be discovered, rather than merely transmitted. Daniel Coit Gilman, the first president of Johns Hopkins, stated that the object of the University was "not so much to impart knowledge as to whet the appetite, exhibit methods, develop powers, strengthen judgment, and invigorate the intellectual and moral forces." Today, Johns Hopkins continues to stress creative scholarship by providing research-oriented education for undergraduates. Students in all disciplines are encouraged to explore intellectual questions and discover new ideas within a supportive environment.

Johns Hopkins seeks diversity in its students, who come from all fifty states and from seventy-one other countries. Of the total undergraduate enrollment of approximately 4,800 students, about 48 percent are women and 52 percent are men. All out-of-town freshmen and sophomores must live in campus residence halls. In addition, University-owned housing, located directly across from the University on North Charles Street, is available for juniors and seniors. Upperclassmen may also live in private housing or in Greek housing. Johns Hopkins has thirteen fraternities and seven sororities in the Inter-Fraternity Council and the Panhellenic Council.

Films, concerts, seminars, and athletic events are regularly offered on campus. The Student Council runs a number of activities, including an annual Spring Fair featuring outdoor concerts, arts and crafts booths, food, carnival rides, and exhibits. Men's varsity teams compete in twelve sports. In the fall, men's teams compete in cross-country, football, soccer, and water polo. In the winter, basketball, fencing, swimming, and wrestling are offered. The big sports season at Johns Hopkins is spring, with baseball, lacrosse, tennis, and track and field. The men's and women's lacrosse teams compete at the Division I level, and the men have won forty-four national championships. Women's varsity sports also include basketball, cross-country, fencing, field hockey, soccer, swimming, tennis, track and field, and volleyball. An extensive intramural program is also available. The O'Connor Recreation Center contains basketball and volleyball courts, a running track, racquetball courts, a rock-climbing wall, a weight room, and fitness and aerobic areas. In addition to the athletic programs, there are over 320 student-run clubs that hold events throughout the year. From the performing arts to hobby-centered clubs, there are many options for students of all interests.

Location

Johns Hopkins University's Homewood campus is on 140 acres of lush greenery, bounded on all sides by residential areas. Johns Hopkins offers the best of both worlds—the tranquil seclusion of the campus plus the adjacent urban environment. Two museums are owned by the University: Homewood Museum, on campus, and Evergreen Museum & Library, located nearby on North Charles Street, both of which provide academic opportunities for students. The Baltimore Museum of Art is on the southwest corner of the campus. The Walters Art Museum, a 10-minute drive away, has a collection that spans civilization from Egypt to the nineteenth century, and many smaller museums, galleries, and outdoor showings feature local artists. The University is located just three miles from the heart of downtown Baltimore; the theater, symphony, and opera are 10 minutes away, as are Oriole Park at Camden Yards and M&T Bank Stadium. Weekend activities include shopping at Harborplace, visiting the National Aquarium, enjoying an ethnic festival by the water, sailing on the Chesapeake Bay, and hiking around the Maryland countryside. Washington, D.C., is a 50-minute drive by car or a 1-hour train ride. Opportunities abound for on- and off-campus entertainment.

Majors and Degrees

Bachelor of Arts degrees are awarded in Africana studies, anthropology, archaeology, behavioral biology, biology, biophysics, chemistry, classics, cognitive science, earth and planetary sciences, East Asian studies, economics, English, film and media studies, French, German, global environmental change and sustainability, history, history of art, history of science and technology, interdisciplinary studies, international studies, Italian, Latin American studies, mathematics, natural sciences, Near Eastern studies, neuroscience, philosophy, physics, political science, psychology, public health studies, Romance languages, sociology, Spanish, and the Writing Seminars. A Bachelor of Arts degree in engineering is available for students who seek preparation for professional careers (such as law or business) with a technological orientation. The B.A. in engineering is awarded in applied mathematics and statistics, biomedical engineering, computer science, electrical engineering, general engineering, and geography. Bachelor of Science degrees are awarded in applied mathematics and statistics, biomedical engineering, chemical and biomolecular engineering, civil engineering, computer engineering, computer science, electrical engineering, environmental engineering, materials science and engineering, mechanical engineering, molecular and cellular biology, and physics.

Accelerated bachelor's/master's degree programs are offered in biology, biophysics, German, history, international studies, mathematics, neuroscience, policy studies, psychology, public health studies, and Spanish. Accelerated B.S./M.S.E. programs are offered in most engineering departments. A dual-degree program leading to a Bachelor of Arts or Bachelor of Science degree and a Bachelor of Music degree is available in cooperation with the University's Peabody Institute and Conservatory of Music.

Academic Programs

The departments in the Krieger School of Arts and Sciences and the Whiting School of Engineering comprise four general areas for undergraduate programs: engineering, humanities, natural sciences, and social sciences. If a student has special interests that fall outside the bounds of the departmental majors, an individual program can be devised, or a student may study independently with the guidance of a faculty member. Qualified students may complete their degree requirements in fewer than four years. In a number of departments, undergraduates of exceptional ability and motivation may in some cases engage in graduate work with the object of qualifying for the simultaneous award of the bachelor's and master's degrees at the end of four years.

Johns Hopkins has an extremely flexible program. There are no required freshman courses. All students must fulfill distribution requirements as well as the requirements for their major; the distribution requirements include a writing element. In most majors, 120 credits are required for graduation. Johns Hopkins has a 4-1-4 calendar.

The University offers the Army ROTC program on campus and the Air Force ROTC program in cooperation with the University of Maryland College Park.

Off-Campus Programs

If qualified, a student may undertake a program for study abroad, normally during the junior year. Programs are offered at Johns Hopkins' international center in Bologna, Italy, as well as in Paris, France; Madrid, Spain; Berlin, Germany; and Latin America and through independent study-abroad programs with Johns Hopkins credit. The University participates in a cooperative program with the following colleges in the Baltimore area: Goucher College, Loyola College, Morgan State University, College of Notre Dame of Maryland, Towson State University, Baltimore Hebrew University, and Maryland Institute, College of Art. Undergraduates may also take courses at the other divisions of Johns Hopkins University, including the Peabody Conservatory, the School of Nursing, the Bloomberg School of Public Health, the Nitze School of Advanced International Studies, the School of Education, the Carey Business School, and the School of Medicine.

Academic Facilities

The Milton S. Eisenhower Library on the Homewood campus—housing more than 2.9 million volumes—is part of the University's Sheridan Libraries, which comprise the Milton S. Eisenhower Library, the John Work Garrett Library, the Albert D. Hutzler Undergraduate Reading Room, and the George Peabody Library. Together, these libraries provide one of the most comprehensive learning resources in the world, containing more than 3.5 million books, more than 55,000 print and electronic journals, more than 700,000 electronic books, more than 10,000 videos and DVDs, more than 216,000 maps, and significant rare books, manuscripts, and archival resources. The University's other libraries are the Welch Medical Library at the School of Medicine (encompassing the Lilienfeld Library at the Bloomberg School of Public Health), the Arthur Friedhem Library at the Peabody Institute, the Mason Library at the School of Advanced International Studies in Washington, D.C., the Montgomery County Campus Library, the Bologna Center Library in Italy, the Hopkins-Nanjing Center for Chinese and American Studies Library in China, and the R. E. Gibson Library at the Applied Physics Laboratory.

The Mattin Student Arts Center contains the Swirnow Theater, a dance studio, music practice rooms, film and digital labs, darkrooms, a café, art studios, and spaces for students to gather. Hodson Hall includes classrooms, a meeting room for the Board of Trustees, the archives of the Hodson Trust, and a 500-seat auditorium, in which every seat is wired to the Internet. Clark Hall houses a state-of-the-art research and teaching facility for biomedical engineering. Charles Commons, a 618-person residential complex and dining facility, also houses the University's two-story Barnes and Noble bookstore.

Host systems, an academic computer lab, and user support are provided by Information Technology@Johns Hopkins (IT@JH). Students living in University residence halls and apartments can connect directly to the Internet and the Johns Hopkins network via a high-speed data jack. Wireless network coverage is also available throughout most areas of the campus with the use of a supported wireless LAN card. Those living off campus can remotely access University systems and library resources. The Homewood Academic Computing Lab is open 24 hours a day, has more than 115 computers, and provides student consultants who can assist with problems that arise. The Brown Foundation Digital Media Center offers an environment where students can bring artistic inspiration to life using digital tools. It features twelve high-end computers that enable digital and audio composition and editing, animation, virtual painting, and 3-D modeling. All campus buildings are networked with each other and the other Johns Hopkins campuses.

Costs

Costs for 2009–10 were $39,150 for tuition, $12,040 for room and board, and $2200 for books and personal expenses. Travel expenses vary.

Financial Aid

Financial aid is based on demonstrated eligibility, as determined by the Free Application for Federal Student Aid (FAFSA) at the time of acceptance. Approximately 45 percent of students receive financial assistance. Students must reapply for financial aid each year with the FAFSA and the College Scholarship Service (CSS) Financial Aid PROFILE. Johns Hopkins offers several merit-based scholarships, including the Hodson Trust Scholarship. Johns Hopkins also offers Army ROTC scholarships worth up to full tuition. The Baltimore Scholars Program provides full-tuition scholarships to eligible Baltimore City public high school graduates.

Faculty

The University's intellectual reputation is based on the strength of its faculty, of whom 95 percent hold a doctorate. The student-faculty ratio is 12:1. The well-known professors at Johns Hopkins teach both undergraduate and graduate students, which means that students receive a great deal of personal attention both in and out of the classroom. Johns Hopkins has a large number of notable professors, including Alice McDermott (professor of the Writing Seminars), winner of the 1998 National Book Award for Fiction; Saul Roseman (professor of biology), a molecular biologist who is a principal authority on the biochemistry of complex carbohydrates and on cell membrane functioning and serves as a consultant to the American Cancer Society and the National Academy of Science; and Charles O'Melia (professor of geography and environmental engineering), who specializes in aquatic chemistry, water and wastewater treatment, and modeling of natural surfaces and subsurface waters and is a member of the National Academy of Engineers. The faculty includes 45 American Academy of Arts & Sciences fellows, 3 National Medal of Science winners, 2 Presidential Medal of Freedom winners, and 7 MacArthur Fellows. Faculty members are always accessible to advise and assist students and to work with them on research projects.

Student Government

Johns Hopkins students enjoy the benefits of a well organized and far-reaching student government, which is led by a powerful Student Council. The council is composed of elected class representatives and officers, but it relies on the active participation of many students in its numerous committees, boards, and commissions. Through the Student Activities Commission, the University encourages initiative and independence by giving students full responsibility and control of funds for various clubs and organizations.

Admission Requirements

In choosing from a large number of applicants, the University selects those men and women who will benefit from a Johns Hopkins education. A student's intellectual interests and accomplishments are of primary importance, and the Admissions Committee carefully examines each applicant's scholastic record, standardized test results, essays, and recommendations from secondary school officials and other sources about the student's character, intellectual curiosity, seriousness of purpose, and range of extracurricular involvement. The application essays are an important part of how the Admissions Committee learns more about students during the application review process. Two essays must be submitted, as well as counselor and teacher recommendations. In addition, the SAT or the ACT with Writing Test is required. For students submitting SAT scores, Johns Hopkins recommends the submission of SAT Subject Tests, and if submitted, requests results from three tests. Students should consult the Web site for additional details on test requirements. Every year, the University enrolls a first-year class of approximately 1,200 men and women from all parts of the U.S. and a number of other countries. In addition, transfer students from other colleges and universities are admitted to the sophomore and junior classes. Advanced-standing credit is granted from college-level work completed at an accredited college or through the Advanced Placement and International Baccalaureate programs.

Application and Information

Johns Hopkins accepts the Common Application and the Universal College Application, both with a Johns Hopkins supplement. The application deadline is January 1. If applicants consider Johns Hopkins to be their first choice, they may apply under the Early Decision Plan. This requires that the application be filed by November 1. Notification is given by April 1 for regular decision students and by December 15 for those applying under the Early Decision Plan. Students wishing to enroll in the biomedical engineering (BME) program must indicate BME as their first choice of major on their application. Freshmen who are BME majors are admitted specifically as such. Accepted students who wish to postpone their college studies for one or two years after graduation from high school may do so provided that they notify the dean of admissions and submit the nonrefundable enrollment deposit by May 1.

Office of Undergraduate Admissions
The Johns Hopkins University
Mason Hall
3400 North Charles Street
Baltimore, Maryland 21218-2683
Phone: 410-516-8171
Fax: 410-516-6025
E-mail: gotojhu@jhu.edu
Internet: http://apply.jhu.edu

THE JOHNS HOPKINS UNIVERSITY
School of Nursing
BALTIMORE, MARYLAND

The University

Since its founding in 1876, The Johns Hopkins University has been in the forefront of higher education. Originally established as an institution oriented toward graduate study and research, it is often called America's first true university. Today, Johns Hopkins' commitment to academic excellence continues in its nine academic divisions: Nursing, Medicine, Public Health, Arts and Sciences, Engineering, Education, Business, Advanced International Studies, and the Peabody Conservatory of Music. With a full-time enrollment of approximately 7,000 students, it is the smallest of the top-ranked universities in the United States and, by its own choice, remains small. The School of Nursing attracts a national and international student body of 622 students.

The School of Nursing was established in 1983 by Johns Hopkins University. By choosing to attend Johns Hopkins University School of Nursing, students can become leaders in the nursing profession. A Hopkins education can provide a solid foundation on which to base a lifelong career in the ever-growing field of nursing. Hopkins students enjoy the advantages of an education at an institution with a worldwide reputation and an outstanding network of alumni who are willing to serve as guides and mentors. Students at the School of Nursing are given the opportunity to participate in designing an educational program tailored to their individual needs. A rigorous academic curriculum, which includes a strong scientific orientation, gives students the background to understand the health-care decisions they are likely to make as professionals. Students learn in an atmosphere where excellence is expected, valued, and reinforced.

The School of Nursing is one of only a few in the country that emphasize baccalaureate-level research. Its graduates are prepared for professional practice through an educational process that emphasizes clinical excellence, critical thinking, and intellectual curiosity. Hopkins is also one of a few schools of nursing that offer resources from four health-related institutions: Johns Hopkins Hospital and the Schools of Nursing, Medicine, and Public Health.

In addition to the baccalaureate program, master's and doctoral programs and postdegree options are also offered. The Ph.D. program in nursing prepares nurse scholars to conduct original research that advances the theoretical foundation of nursing practice and health-care delivery. The School of Nursing has also launched a Doctor of Nursing Practice (D.N.P.) program that is a practice-focused doctoral program designed to prepare expert nurse clinicians, administrators, and executive leaders to improve health and health-care outcomes.

Location

The School of Nursing is located on the campus of Johns Hopkins Medical Institutions, including the School of Medicine, the Bloomberg School of Public Health, and Johns Hopkins Hospital. Located 10 minutes away is the Homewood Campus of Johns Hopkins University, which is accessible to students via a free shuttle service.

Often referred to as "the biggest small town in America," Baltimore has undergone one of the most successful transformations of any city in the nation. Baltimore's famous Inner Harbor and the National Aquarium are focal points of this revitalization. Washington, D.C., is less than an hour away by car or train.

Major and Degrees

The School of Nursing offers an NLNAC-accredited upper-division program that leads to a Bachelor of Science degree with a major in nursing. A 13½-month accelerated option of study makes it possible for students who hold a bachelor's degree in another discipline to receive a bachelor's degree in nursing. Students who hold a bachelor's degree in another discipline are also eligible to apply to the Direct Entry Combined B.S. to M.S.N. option. In addition, students who do not hold a bachelor's degree may consider a traditional twenty-one-month program that leads the B.S. with a major nursing. Students may transfer to the School of Nursing after successful completion of the 60 semester hours of prerequisite course work from any accredited college or university. Those students who hold a previous bachelor's degree may also consider the twenty-one-month option.

Students interested in pursuing the B.S. to M.S.N. option of study may select from a number of master's options, including clinical nurse specialist (in an area of interest, such as, but not limited to, forensic, geriatric, infectious disease, adult or pediatric health, or woman's health), M.S.N./M.P.H., M.S.N./M.B.A., nurse practitioner, public health, and, in collaboration with Shenandoah University Divison of Nursing, a clinical nurse specialist in women's health and a certificate of completion in midwifery.

Academic Programs

Johns Hopkins University School of Nursing prepares students for professional nursing practice through an educational process that combines a strong academic curriculum with intensive clinical experience. The program is built on the University's commitment to research, teaching, patient service, and educational innovation and the consortium hospitals' commitment to excellence in clinical practice. The School's mission is to prepare its students academically and technologically for challenges of the future and to graduate professional nurses who can participate in all aspects of modern health care.

The upper-division courses in the baccalaureate nursing program are planned to meet the nursing needs of people in a complex and rapidly changing health-care system. The program is built on the liberal and general education prerequisites. The curriculum is planned to provide a balance among technologies, the theories of nursing, and the caring functions of the nurse. A high priority is placed on educating the nurse to practice in a variety of health-care settings, including overseas, as they exist today and in the future.

Johns Hopkins University School of Nursing is the first school of nursing in the country to offer a Peace Corps Fellows Program. The School of Nursing is world known for the Community Outreach Program, which offers students opportunities to gain additional clinical experiences with underserved populations in East Baltimore. Students may also enroll in the Birth Companions Program—another opportunity to work with underserved populations.

The Army Reserve Officers' Training Corps (ROTC) is the principal source of commissioned officers for the Active Army, Army Reserve, and Army National Guard. All Army nurses are officers. Johns Hopkins University offers two- and three-year scholarships to students enrolled in Army ROTC, which is located on the Homewood Campus of Johns Hopkins University.

Academic Facilities

The William H. Welch Medical Library is the central resource library serving Johns Hopkins Medical Institutions. Students have free 24-hour-per-day access to the Welch Library Gateway, which leads users to local and remote bibliographic databases, full-text journals, and other resources available locally and on the Internet. The Nursing Information Resource Center (NIRC), located in the School of Nursing, is managed by the Welch Library. In addition, the University's Milton S. Eisenhower Library, on the Homewood Campus, is available to School of Nursing students.

Three computer laboratories are equipped with a computer network and printers. Several classrooms and the auditorium have PC hookup and distance learning capabilities. Additional computer resources are available throughout the University.

Nursing practice and simulation labs are available to provide students with an opportunity to gain experience and confidence in performing a wide variety of nursing technologies. Students practice basic nursing technologies at numerous patient care stations designed to closely approximate hospital inpatient areas. Practice using actual medical equipment is an integral part of the laboratory experience, and patient simulators are provided to facilitate clinical skill mastery.

Clinical facilities throughout the Baltimore/Washington metropolitan area serve as clinical sites during student clinical rotations. These include the famed Johns Hopkins Hospital as well as a variety of other acute, research, long-term community and specialty health-care institutions. Students also have opportunities with international clinical experiences in locations such as Haiti, Singapore, South Africa, Dubai, and Uganda, to name a few.

Costs

For the 2009–10 academic year, baccalaureate tuition was $31,920.

Financial Aid

Johns Hopkins University School of Nursing attempts to provide financial assistance to all eligible accepted students. The School of Nursing will assist those students who qualify for need-based aid. Such assistance is usually in the form of loans, grants, scholarships, and work-study programs. While most of the financial aid received by students is based on financial need, many students also benefit from awards based on academic merit and achievement.

Faculty

The faculty members view professional nursing as a unique health service offering effective, humane, and competent care to individuals, families, groups, and communities. Nurses function in independent, interdependent, and dependent roles to promote and improve delivery of health care. The faculty members view education as a process and as an enriching interaction in which both the teacher and learner must actively participate in an atmosphere of mutual trust. They believe that it is the responsibility of the teacher to guide the teaching-learning process and to develop the potential of each individual student to the highest level possible. The student-faculty ratio is 9:1.

Student Government

Each class within the School of Nursing has a government board and a president. There is also the Student Government Association (SGA), which includes all divisions of the entire University. Each class has representatives to the SGA, and anyone may attend the meetings. There are also a number of University and School of Nursing student organizations.

Admission Requirements

The School seeks individuals who will bring to the student body the qualities of scholarship, motivation, and commitment. The Admissions Committee is interested in each applicant as an individual and considers both academic potential and personal qualities. Therefore, academic records, test scores, recommendations, and a personal statement about goals and interests are all important. Interviews may be requested.

A complete application consists of an application form and nonrefundable $75 application fee; recommendations from 3 persons, 2 of whom must be instructors in current or recent courses and 1 from professional or volunteer experience; official college/university transcripts; an official high school transcript (unless the applicant has already completed a college degree or has been out of high school for over five years); and SAT or ACT scores, if they are not more than five years old and the student does not already hold a bachelor's degree. Applicants should have a GPA greater than 3.0 (on a 4.0 scale).

First-degree students are required to complete 60 semester hours of prerequisite course work essential for entry into the upper-division nursing curriculum. This course work may be completed at any accredited college or university and includes the natural sciences, humanities, social sciences, statistics, and electives. Students who possess a bachelor's degree must complete prerequisite course work in anatomy and physiology, microbiology, nutrition, human growth and development across the lifespan, and statistics. In addition, the School of Nursing has articulation agreements for direct transfer with the College of Notre Dame of Maryland; Dickinson University, Pennsylvania; Gettysburg College, Pennsylvania; Johns Hopkins University, Maryland; Juniata College, Pennsylvania; Loyola University of Maryland; Mount Holyoke College, Massachusetts; Mount St. Mary's University, Maryland; Randolph College, Virginia; Virginia Polytechnic Institute and State University; Washington College, Maryland; Wheaton College, Illinois; Wittenberg University, Ohio; Stern College of Yeshiva University, New York; State University of New York College at Geneseo; and St. Mary's College of Maryland.

International students must submit official test score reports of the Test of English as a Foreign Language (TOEFL) unless they have received a prior bachelor's degree in the U.S. or they have lived in the U.S. for more than five years. In order to be considered for admission, nonpermanent residents must establish their ability to finance their education in the U.S. International students must have their academic transcripts evaluated course-by-course by World Education Service (WES) or by the American Association of College Registrars and Admissions Officers (AACRAO). International registered nurses may have their transcripts evaluated course-by-course through the Commission on Graduates of Foreign Nursing Schools (CGFNS). Official results from WES, AACRAO, and CGFNS must be sent directly to Johns Hopkins University School of Nursing.

Johns Hopkins University is an affirmative action/equal opportunity institution.

Application and Information

All inquiries concerning the School of Nursing should be directed to:

Office of Admissions and Student Services
The Johns Hopkins University
School of Nursing
Suite 113
525 North Wolfe Street
Baltimore, Maryland 21205-2110

Phone: 410-955-7548
Fax: 410-614-7086
E-mail: jhuson@son.jhmi.edu
Web site: www.nursing.jhu.edu

JOHNSON & WALES UNIVERSITY

PROVIDENCE, RHODE ISLAND

The University

Johnson & Wales University (JWU), founded in 1914, is a nonprofit, private institution. A recognized leader in career education, the University offers accredited degrees to more than 16,000 graduate and undergraduate students, representing all fifty states and ninety-six countries. By integrating academics and professional skills, related work experiences, leadership opportunities, and career services, JWU prepares students who are seeking a competitive advantage in the global economy. The University's 80,000 alumni, from 140 countries, pursue careers around the world. The University is committed to urban revitalization and thoughtful historic renovation. Through active civic participation and unique learning opportunities, JWU seeks to improve the quality of life in its campus communities in Providence, Rhode Island; North Miami, Florida; Denver, Colorado; and Charlotte, North Carolina.

JWU is a career-oriented institution offering programs that are geared to the success of a range of students. Most students are recent graduates of high school business, college-preparatory, and vocational/technical programs. The academic focus of the University is on degree programs in business, culinary arts, education, hospitality, and technology. M.B.A. programs include global business leadership (with concentrations in accounting, financial management, international trade, organizational leadership, or marketing) and hospitality and tourism global business leadership (with concentrations in finance and marketing). M.A. programs in teaching (with or without certification) include business, food service, and special education. The Alan Shawn Feinstein Graduate School also offers the Certificate of Advanced Graduate Study (CAGS) in finance, human resources management, and hospitality. The University also offers a doctoral program in educational leadership.

Students are involved in a variety of extracurricular activities. Nearly 20 percent of the students at the University are members of national student organizations such as Business Professionals of America; DECA (Delta Epsilon Chi), Future Business Leaders of America (Phi Beta Lambda); Family, Career, Community Leaders of America (FCCLA); National FFA; Junior Achievement; SkillsUSA; and Technology Association of America. The Office of Student Activities (OSA) and fraternities and sororities are among the many groups that schedule social functions throughout the academic year. Sports and fitness programs include aerobics, baseball, basketball, golf, ice hockey, sailing, soccer, tennis, volleyball, and wrestling.

The University maintains twenty-four residence halls throughout its four campuses. In addition, City View Towers, which is independently owned and operated, offers housing near the Charlotte campus for upperclassmen. Student services include academic counseling and testing, a tutorial center, and health services. The University's Experiential Education and Career Services office provides extensive career planning and placement services.

Johnson & Wales is accredited by the New England Association of Schools and Colleges. The hospitality programs in Providence are accredited by the Accreditation Commission for Programs in Hospitality Administration.

Location

The location of each of the University's campuses enables students to take advantage of internship and part-time work activities offered by many nearby businesses, community groups, and government agencies. All of Johnson & Wales' city campuses retain a small-town feel and easy accessibility to students. The urban setting of the Providence campus provides students proximity to the city's many cultural and recreational facilities. The North Miami campus is a short trip from the sun and fun of Fort Lauderdale and the culture and diversity of Miami. The Denver campus offers students great opportunities as the nation's sixth-leading tourist destination and *Fortune* magazine's "second best city in America to work and live." The Charlotte campus is located in a vibrant urban setting that combines commercial and residential life. More than 300 Fortune 500 companies have offices in Charlotte, which is known as the second-largest financial center in the U.S.

Majors and Degrees

The degree programs described in this section are for the 2010–11 academic year and are subject to change. Students may pursue concentrations related to their program of study to further tailor their degrees to their specific interests and career goals. They also have the opportunity to take concentrations through the School of Arts and Sciences.

Johnson & Wales University's Providence campus offers degree programs in accounting; baking and pastry arts; baking and pastry arts and food service management; business administration; business/information systems analysis; creative advertising; criminal justice; culinary arts; culinary arts and food service management; culinary nutrition; electronics engineering; engineering design and configuration management; entrepreneurship; equine business management; equine business management/riding; fashion merchandising and retail marketing; finance; food service entrepreneurship; graphic design and digital media; hotel and lodging management; international business; international hotel and tourism management; management; management accounting; marketing; network engineering; restaurant, food, and beverage management; software engineering; sports/entertainment/event management; strategic advertising; technology services management; and travel, tourism, and hospitality management.

In its Continuing Education division, Johnson & Wales' Providence campus offers associate and bachelor's degrees in business, culinary arts, hospitality, and technology. JWU also offers diploma programs in baking and pastry arts and culinary arts; certificate programs are offered in computer-aided drafting, legal nurse studies, and paralegal studies.

The North Miami campus offers degree programs in baking and pastry arts; business administration; criminal justice; culinary arts; culinary arts and food service management; fashion merchandising and retail marketing; hotel and lodging management; management; marketing; pastry arts and food service management; restaurant, food, and beverage management; sports/entertainment/event management; and travel, tourism, and hospitality management.

The Denver campus offers degree programs in baking and pastry arts; baking and pastry arts and food service management; business administration; criminal justice; culinary arts; culinary arts and food service management; culinary nutrition; entrepreneurship; fashion merchandising and retail marketing; hotel and lodging management; international business; management; marketing; restaurant, food, and beverage management; sports/entertainment/event management; and strategic advertising.

The Charlotte campus offers degree programs in baking and pastry arts; baking & pastry arts and food service management; business administration; culinary arts; culinary arts and food service management; fashion merchandising and retail marketing; hotel and lodging management; international hotel and tourism management; management; management accounting; marketing; restaurant, food, and beverage management; and sports/entertainment/event management.

Academic Programs

Johnson & Wales University offers programs in business, culinary arts, food service, hospitality, and technology within an academic

COLLEGE CLOSE-UPS

structure of three 11-week terms. The "upside-down" curriculum of the University provides immediate concentration in the student's chosen major.

Learning by doing is an important part of career training at JWU, and many programs include laboratory studies as well as formal internship requirements. Special advanced-placement programs are featured for high school seniors with exceptional skills in culinary arts or baking and pastry arts. In addition, the University awards credit for certain courses based on the successful completion of Challenge, CLEP, or Portfolio Assessments. All degree candidates must successfully complete the required number of courses and/or quarter credit hours, as prescribed in the various curricula, with a minimum average of 2.0 or higher, depending on the program.

Off-Campus Programs

Learning at Johnson & Wales is not limited to the classroom. Many of the majors offer internships at University-owned facilities. The hotel-restaurant management program features an internship at the Johnson & Wales Inn, Radisson Airport Hotel, or DoubleTree Hotel; all are full-service hotel complexes that are owned and/or operated by the University (the Radisson and DoubleTree are corporate franchises). For all majors, optional selective career internships are available with cooperating businesses throughout the U.S. and worldwide, such as Marriott International, Compass Group NAD, Foxwoods Resort and Casino, and Putnam Investments. Most internships are one term in duration and carry 13.5 quarter hours of credit. International exchange and term-abroad programs are also offered.

Academic Facilities

The facilities of the Providence campus are located throughout the intimate state of Rhode Island and in nearby Massachusetts. The Downcity campus in Providence is home to the University's College of Business, The Hospitality College, and the School of Technology. A number of academic and residential facilities are located at this campus, as are several training facilities. The Harborside campus, also in Providence but located a short distance away from the Downcity campus, houses the University's College of Culinary Arts. This campus has five student residence halls as well as specialized classrooms and laboratories, production kitchens, bakeshops, dining rooms, a storeroom, and meat-cutting facilities. This campus is also home to the Alan Shawn Feinstein Graduate School, the School of Education, the University Recreation and Athletic Center, a student activities office, a bookstore, a gymnasium, a dining center, a snack bar, and an arcade.

JWU's North Miami campus is located in the heart of North Miami, between Miami and Fort Lauderdale. Facilities include academic classrooms, production/demonstration kitchens, a bakeshop, residence halls, and a specially designed conference center.

The Denver campus, which is located in the Park Hill neighborhood, combines old-world charm with the latest technological resources, including stately turn-of-the-century buildings and newer student centers in a quiet park landscape. The traditional residential campus is fully wired, with computers in every classroom and laboratory.

The Charlotte campus is located in the heart of Gateway Village in Uptown Charlotte. The academic center is home to a 200-seat auditorium, a production kitchen, state-of-the-art culinary laboratories, classrooms, seminar rooms, and computer labs.

Costs

Tuition at all campuses for 2010–11 is $23,034. Room and board plans range from $8274 to $10,383. There is also a general fee of $1107 charged to all students and an orientation fee of $288 for new students. Books and supplies are estimated at $800 to $900 per year, depending on the program. A weekend meal plan is also available for $1068 per year.

Room and board fees vary at each campus. Students should consult the respective campus catalogs for further details.

Financial Aid

Johnson & Wales students are eligible to apply for a variety of financial aid programs, including the Federal Pell Grant, Federal Supplemental Educational Opportunity Grant, Federal Work-Study, and Federal Perkins Loan programs. They are also eligible for University-based student scholarship programs and state-supported grants and scholarships. In the past, approximately 90 percent of the University's entering students have received some sort of financial assistance. Students must submit the Free Application for Federal Student Aid (FAFSA) to the Federal Student Aid Processor to be considered for financial aid. Early application is strongly suggested for full consideration.

Faculty

The University's 475 full-time and 242 part-time faculty members (all campuses) are oriented toward instruction rather than research. Many are chosen for their professional experience in business, culinary arts, hospitality services, or technology. The student-faculty ratio is 28:1.

Student Government

Student Government Association (SGA) is the voice of students on campus and serves as the governing student organization on campus. Students are elected to major leadership positions in the spring, and senator positions are available to any interested student in the fall. SGA is responsible for allocating student funds, recognizing new organizations, and addressing student concerns on campus.

Admission Requirements

Johnson & Wales University seeks students who are career-focused and have a true desire to succeed. Academic qualifications are important, but an applicant's motivation and interest in doing well are given special consideration. Graduation from high school or the equivalent credentials are required for admission. It is recommended that students applying for admission into the culinary arts and baking and pastry arts programs have some prior education or experience in food service. Although tests are not required for most programs, all applicants are encouraged to submit scores from the SAT or ACT. Students who wish to apply for the honors program must have either a score of at least 500 math and 500 critical reading on the SAT or a score of at least 21 math and 21 verbal on the ACT. High school juniors may apply for early admission under the Early Enrollment Program (EEP). Transfer students are required to submit official high school and college transcripts and to have a minimum GPA of 2.0. Credits to be transferred from other institutions are evaluated on the basis of their equivalent at Johnson & Wales.

Application and Information

Johnson & Wales does not require an application fee. After submitting the application, the student is responsible for requesting that appropriate transcripts be forwarded to JWU's Admissions Office. While there is no deadline, students are advised to apply as early as possible before the intended date of enrollment to ensure full consideration of their application. Applications are accepted for terms beginning in September, December, and March and for the summer sessions (for most programs).

Inquiries and applications should be addressed to:

Kenneth DiSaia
Vice President of Enrollment Management
Johnson & Wales University
8 Abbott Park Place
Providence, Rhode Island 02903
Phone: 401-598-1000
800-DIAL-JWU (toll-free)
Fax: 401-598-4901
E-mail: jwu@admissions.jwu.edu
Web site: http://www.jwu.edu

COLLEGE CLOSE-UPS

JUNIATA COLLEGE

HUNTINGDON, PENNSYLVANIA

The College

Juniata College is an independent, coeducational college of liberal arts and sciences, founded in 1876 by members of the Church of the Brethren to prepare individuals "for the useful occupations of life." Juniata holds a place of national prominence in higher education. Recent studies rank the College highly in the percentage of graduates that eventually earn doctoral degrees; one, in fact, ranked Juniata in the top 10 percent in the nation among all four-year private undergraduate institutions. Juniata's national reputation is strongest in several fields, including biology, chemistry, environmental science and education, health sciences, peace and conflict studies, and prelaw. The College is known for the personal attention it gives to students. Each student is assigned 2 faculty advisers, and the average student-faculty ratio is 13:1.

Juniata is a very strong community where student involvement is paramount. There are no fraternities or sororities so the entire campus gets involved. School spirit and campus activities are the heart and soul of the institution. The 100 clubs and organizations not only have a positive impact on the Juniata campus but also on the community of Huntingdon and the surrounding area.

Location

Juniata is located in Huntingdon, a community of 10,000 people, in the scenic Allegheny Mountains of central Pennsylvania. It is 30 minutes from the cities of Altoona (population 65,000) and State College (population 55,000), Pennsylvania. The 110 acres on College Hill overlook the historic architecture of a classic river town. Juniata's campus also consists of a 365-acre field station and a 315-acre nature preserve. The surrounding area is suited for many outdoor activities, including swimming, fishing, hunting, rock climbing, and hiking. Raystown Lake, the largest recreational lake wholly in Pennsylvania, is 15 minutes from Juniata. Several major cities lie within a short drive of the campus—3 hours to Pittsburgh, Baltimore, and Washington, D.C.; 4 hours to Philadelphia; and 5 hours to New York City. The nearest commercial airport is in State College, the location of Penn State University. In addition, Huntingdon is on the main U.S. east-west railway line, with travel by train to East and West Coast cities available.

Majors and Degrees

Juniata awards B.A. and B.S. degrees in the arts, humanities, natural sciences, and social sciences. Rather than complete a traditional major, each Juniata student designs a Program of Emphasis (POE) tailored to the student's own goals and often crossing departmental lines. Working closely with 2 academic advisers, students select courses for either a designated or an individualized POE.

Current areas of study include accounting; anthropology; art (art history; museum studies, with an art history focus; and studio art); arts production; biochemistry, biology; chemistry; communication; communication and conflict resolution; computer science; digital media; earth and space science; English; entrepreneurship; environmental science; environmental studies; finance; geology; health communication; history; human resource management; information technology; international business; international politics; international studies; languages (French, German, Russian, and Spanish/ Hispanic cultures); management; marine science; marketing; mathematics; peace and conflict studies; performing arts management; philosophy, politics, and economics; philosophy and religious studies; physics (engineering physics and physics); politics; prehealth (art therapy, audiology, biotechnology, cytotechnology, genetic counseling, health administration, medical social work, medical technology, naturopathic medicine, nursing, occupational therapy, physical therapy, physician's assistant studies, and radiological sciences); pre-health professions (chiropractic, dentistry, medicine, optometry, pharmacy, podiatric medicine, public health, and veterinary medicine); pre-K–4 education; professional writing; psychology; religious studies; secondary education (biology, chemistry, earth and space science, English, French, general science, German, mathematics, physics, social studies, and Spanish); social work; sociology; theater performance; and wildlife conservation.Secondary emphases are available in most majors and in accounting, business, and economics; communication and theater arts; fine arts; and women and gender studies.

Academic Programs

Designed to foster individual responsibility, Juniata's flexible and academically rigorous program allows both acquisition of a broad range of knowledge and in-depth examination of a particular field. Almost 50 percent of the students attending Juniata develop their own program through a flexible program of emphasis (POE).

Students must satisfactorily complete 120 semester credit hours. Writing, computer and bibliographic skills, and the transition to college are addressed in the freshman year. Graduation requirements also include a two-course cultural analysis sequence, advanced communication/writing skills, quantitative studies, social sciences, humanities, international, fine arts, and natural sciences and an optional service learning component. In addition, all students complete a 45–60 credit POE, and many choose to complete an integrative senior project to graduate with distinction.

Many students include independent study and independent research in their POEs. Although not required, 85 percent of students participate in internships. The Juniata College Center for International Education provides excellent study-abroad opportunities that are taken advantage of by approximately 44 percent of the junior class. Experiences include summer, semester, and year-long opportunities.

Academic Facilities

Juniata's academic programs are complemented by up-to-date technology, labs, and bibliographic resources. In addition to the College's academic computer center, the campus has high-tech classroom/laboratory and computer labs devoted specifically to business, education, psychology, and world languages. The College supports the Juniata Center for Entrepreneurial Leadership (JCEL), a unique opportunity for students of all academic areas to pursue developing their own business. JCEL provides students with hands-on experience in every aspect of entrepreneurial endeavors. A human interaction lab offers students the opportunity to study communication and group interaction. In addition, the College has a distance learning and teleconferencing facility, multimedia classrooms, and a teaching and learning technology center (Solutions Center) for both student and faculty member use. The Solutions Center was designed to give faculty members and students the resources for utilizing advanced technology in their course work and presentations. The William J. von Liebig Center for Science is a $20-million facility that provides state-of-the-art facilities for teaching and learning in chemistry and biology. The Brumbaugh Academic Center houses the business, communications, computer science, environmental sciences, information technology, mathematics, and physical sciences departments as well as a digital media studio.

For research projects, students in the natural sciences use laboratories equipped with sophisticated instrumentation typically reserved for graduate students. Juniata's Raystown Field Station serves as an ecology, zoology, and environmental science laboratory. The field station recently expanded facilities to allow students to live and learn at an on-site field laboratory. Juniata's Beeghly Library provides the College with an online public-access catalog that is accessible campuswide and an extensive CD-ROM network.

Costs

For 2009–10, the general fee was approximately $40,200, with tuition costs of $30,880, and room, board, and fee costs of $9320. Several special and occasional fees of $30–$300 for laboratory or studio use are also required.

Financial Aid

The Juniata College Office of Student Financial Planning is committed to building relationships with families striving to meet the long-term investment needs associated with quality education. Juniata succeeds by maximizing available assistance opportunities from Juniata programs as well as state and federal government programs in the form of grants, loans, and work-study initiatives. The College's commitment includes scholarship and loan programs. Juniata's Academic Scholarship Program offers aggressive scholarship programs designed to recognize and reward academic achievement. Students who exhibit promise of future success may be eligible for academic awards ranging from $10,000 to full tuition, room, and board. Students who wish to be considered for Nomination Scholarships should have their admission applications postmarked no later than January 4 of their senior year.

Juniata representatives work with each family, matching their individual circumstances to all applicable aid programs. For need-based aid, individual plans are developed using the Free Application for Federal Student Aid (FAFSA) as the basis for determining need. The results of the FAFSA needs analysis should reach Juniata by March 1.

Faculty

Juniata has 100 full-time and 40 part-time faculty members, of whom 94 percent hold a doctoral or terminal degree in their field. The student-faculty ratio is 13:1. Although faculty members engage in numerous scholarly pursuits and maintain professional ties to their academic fields, they consider teaching and advising their primary functions.

Student Government

Juniata seeks to provide an environment within which students can mature intellectually, socially, and personally in a manner consistent with academic programs. In campus life as well as in the classroom, many opportunities for growth and self-exploration exist. Students have a voice—and in most cases a vote—in all essential areas of campus governance.

Admission Requirements

Juniata seeks students who show strong academic promise, motivation, and maturity. The College seeks a wide geographic representation and a variety of cultural, social, and economic backgrounds. Selection is made without regard to race, sex, religion, creed, color, handicap, or the ability to afford a private college education. Careful consideration is given to the academic record, test results, and personal qualities of applicants. Applicants should have completed a minimum of sixteen college-preparatory courses in mathematics, social studies, world language, and laboratory science. International student candidates may be required to submit TOEFL scores. Interviews and campus visits are strongly recommended.

Transfer students who have completed A.A. or A.S. requirements in an approved collegiate transfer program at an accredited community or junior college may enter Juniata with junior-class standing and receive transfer credit for two years of course work. Students who transfer without a degree receive credit on a course-by-course basis. Students whose college has a formal transfer agreement with Juniata College should consult with their transfer coordinator to review requirements for that agreement. It is strongly recommended that transfer students have an interview.

Application and Information

Students may apply to Juniata after completion of their junior year in secondary school. A nonrefundable $30 fee must accompany the application (waived for students who visit campus or apply online). A complete secondary school transcript that indicates courses and grades (with a list of senior courses, if required) must be sent from the applicant's guidance office along with SAT or ACT scores or SAT Alternative Program, an essay, and a letter of recommendation. An on-campus interview is highly recommended but not required. Transfer students must complete the normal application requirements and submit an official transcript from each college previously attended.

Candidates for freshman admission can choose from three application deadlines: Early Decision, Early Action, and Regular Decision.

Early Decision is designed for students who believe that Juniata College is their first choice. The early decision application deadline is December 1 of the student's senior year in secondary school, with notification no later than December 31. The student is asked to complete Juniata's institutional aid form in order to receive an early financial planning award. Students are required to submit a nonrefundable $400 matriculation deposit by February 25.

Early Action allows students to apply and get a response earlier than Regular Decision while still adhering to the May 1 deposit deadline. The Early Action application deadline is January 1 of the student's senior year, with notification of a decision by January 31. Financial aid award packages are determined after the Free Application for Federal Student Aid (FAFSA) has been completed. (Juniata's FAFSA Code is 003279.) Students should fill out the FAFSA form as soon as possible after January 1 of their senior year in order to have it completed by the March 1 deadline.

The Regular Decision application deadline is March 15 of the student's senior year. First notification for Regular Decision begins February 28. As with Early Action applicants, financial award packages are determined after the FAFSA has been completed. Students should fill out the FAFSA form as soon as possible after January 1 of their senior year in order to have it completed by the March 1 deadline.

Juniata accepts applications for transfer admission for either the spring or fall semesters. The application due date for fall applicants is June 1; the due date for spring applicants is December 1. It is to the student's benefit to submit all application materials before the due date. Juniata's transfer admission policy is rolling. In most cases, transfer students receive an admission decision within one month of receipt of all credentials. Necessary credentials include an essay, a statement of interest, a secondary school transcript, SAT or ACT scores, and college transcripts.

Application forms and additional information may be obtained from:

Enrollment Center
Juniata College
1700 Moore Street
Huntingdon, Pennsylvania 16652
Phone: 814-641-3420
877-JUNIATA (877-586-4282, toll-free)
Fax: 814-641-3100
E-mail: admissions@juniata.edu
Web site: http://www.juniata.edu/

On the campus of Juniata College.

KEENE STATE COLLEGE

KEENE, NEW HAMPSHIRE

The College

The public liberal arts college of New Hampshire, Keene State College (KSC) is a vibrant educational community that provides an extensive range of opportunities, awarding bachelor's and master's degrees. Students come to Keene State College for small classes, engaged faculty, integrative learning, the choice of forty major programs, a location in the heart of New England, and a private feeling at a public price.

A member of the University System of New Hampshire, Keene State College is a coeducational, residential college with an enrollment of approximately 4,900 full-time, undergraduate students and 600 part-time and graduate students. Founded in 1909 as a normal school for teacher education, the College enrolled 27 students in its first year. From its original 20 acres, the campus has expanded to 170 acres and more than seventy-six buildings that feature a remarkable blend of traditional and contemporary architecture.

The superb physical facilities on campus include living accommodations ranging from traditional older residence halls to apartments and suites. The College has three buildings that are registered as National Historic Landmarks and numerous recently completed facilities, including an expansive Recreation Center, the Thorne-Sagendorph Art Gallery, and a new Media Arts Center housing the departments of communication, journalism, film studies, and graphic design. KSC's most ambitious building project ever—the David F. Putnam Science Center—opened in 2004, and the $20-million Zorn Dining Commons was completed in 2005. The College's newest residence hall, Pondside III, was awarded LEED "silver" certification in 2008 and hosts several living/learning student communities.

Keene State is affiliated with CoPLAC (the Council for Public Liberal Arts Colleges) and Campus Compact: The Project for Public and Community Service. Community service, a core value, is integrated into the curriculum to prepare students for service and leadership on all levels. In 2006, the College received a prestigious Carnegie Foundation Award for community engagement. In 2007, Keene State received a Carter Partnership Award for community service. In 2008, students contributed more than 15,000 hours of noncredit service to the local community and more than 400,000 hours of credited service learning.

Location

Keene, New Hampshire, which is located at the geographic center of New England—only 84 miles from Boston and 200 miles from New York City—is a thriving, prosperous city of 23,000. The Keene State campus is bordered by Main Street on one side and the Ashuelot River on another. The campus is only four blocks from the historic downtown district, which offers a variety of shops, restaurants, and theaters. The surrounding New England landscape includes Mount Monadnock (the most-climbed mountain in the world), which is only 18 miles to the southeast of Keene. Opportunities for camping, hiking, mountain climbing, skiing, and swimming are all within a short drive of the campus.

Majors and Degrees

Bachelor of Arts, Fine Arts, Music, and Science degrees are granted. Majors are available in American studies, applied computer science, architecture, art, athletic training, biology, chemistry, chemistry-physics, communication, computer mathematics, economics, education, English, engineering (transfer program), environmental studies, film studies, French, general science, geography, geology, graphic design, health science, history, Holocaust and genocide studies, journalism, management, mathematics, mathematics-physics, music, physical education, political science, psychology, safety studies, social science, sociology, Spanish, sustainable product design and innovation, technology studies, and theater and dance. An individualized B.A. or B.S. major is available for students who wish to design their own interdisciplinary program. Music education and music performance students are awarded the Bachelor of Music degree. Minors in thirty-seven areas, including Holocaust and genocide studies and women's studies, make it possible for students to supplement and strengthen their program. A strong cooperative education program provides work/credit opportunities in many majors.

The College also offers a master's degree in education and post-master's certification programs.

Academic Programs

Education in the liberal arts and sciences and in several professional fields is provided through baccalaureate degree programs. The College recently implemented three major curricular initiatives: the move from a 3-credit to a 4-credit curriculum, a new Integrative Studies Program (ISP) to replace the general education requirements, and an honors program for incoming freshmen. In addition, a comprehensive academic plan, ratified in 2009, reflects the College's dedication to academic excellence and service, and enhances the breadth and balance of scholarship and learning at the school. All entering freshmen enroll in ISP courses on thinking and writing and quantitative literacy. The College's areas of emphasis include teacher education, science and technology, safety studies, psychology, management, communication, and the fine and performing arts.

All baccalaureate programs have ISP requirements, which broaden, deepen, and integrate the student's understanding of the most significant aspects of humanity's heritage. These studies also enhance the capacity for aesthetic enjoyment, critical thinking, creativity, abstract and logical reasoning, and oral and written communication.

A total of at least 120 credit hours is required to graduate, including courses in English composition, arts and humanities, social sciences, and science/mathematics.

The academic year at Keene State consists of fall and spring semesters, plus two optional summer sessions.

Off-Campus Programs

Students are encouraged to study for a semester or a year in national and international exchange programs, facilitated by the Global Education Office (GEO), or consider a domestic alternative to study abroad, with programs at 175 colleges and universities in the U.S., Guam, the Virgin Islands, and Puerto Rico. Keene State has eleven Direct Exchange Programs with institutions in Ecuador, England, France, Ireland, and Russia and more than sixty consortium programs in such popular destinations as China, Costa Rica, Greece, Italy, Scotland, and Spain.

Academic Facilities

The Wallace E. Mason Library houses more than 300,000 paper volumes; has active subscriptions to more than 1,200 periodicals, newspapers, and annual publications; and has a microform collection of more than 550,000 items. Students also have access to the 100,000 volumes that are available nearby at Keene Public

Library. Mason Library has direct online access to thousands of other libraries and also subscribes to EBSCOhost, FirstSearch, and JSTOR for access to additional online resources. Mason Library houses the Cohen Center for Holocaust and Genocide Studies, with resources for scholars and teachers; it also houses the Curriculum Materials Library, which is used by student and classroom teachers across the state.

The library is also home to the Orang Asli Archive, with materials from the indigenous peoples of peninsular Malaysia.

Keene State's new David F. Putnam Science Center prepares graduates for professional life in business, industry, and the public sector and trains science teachers on all levels. The $23-million, state-of-the-art building is a center for interactive learning and research in science and mathematics.

Other academic resources include the Media Arts Center, the BodyWorks Fitness Center, the Film Studies Center, the Language Learning Center, and the Writing and Math Centers.

The Redfern Arts Center on Brickyard Pond, which serves as a major regional performing arts center, houses classrooms and performance spaces for the art, dance, music, and theater programs. The Thorne-Sagendorph Art Gallery hosts exhibits by KSC students and faculty members as well as regional, national, and international artists.

Computer equipment, both wired and wireless, is available in all academic areas. A network connects student rooms and the offices of full-time faculty members and administrative personnel to the online library catalog, e-mail, and the Web.

Costs

Tuition for the 2009–10 academic year was $7000 for New Hampshire residents and $15,170 for out-of-state students. Room and board cost $8174, and mandatory fees totaled $2334. Books and supplies cost about $800 per year.

Financial Aid

Financial assistance is available in three basic forms: grants and scholarships, loans, and part-time employment. Grants and scholarships do not have to be repaid. Educational loans must be repaid, but such loans are made on a long-term, low-interest basis. Additional aid consists of part-time, on-campus employment. At Keene State, aid can be based on merit or need or a combination of both. Matriculated students are eligible to apply for assistance if they are enrolled in at least 6 credits per semester. Currently, approximately 70 percent of Keene State students receive some sort of financial aid. Interested students should write to Student Financial Services for more information.

Faculty

The resident faculty numbers 415 men and women (185 full-time and 230 part-time), who value personal attention to students and a commitment to academic advising. They are also active in their academic fields—writing books and articles, serving as consultants, presenting papers and seminars, participating in exhibits, and performing in concerts. The full-time student-faculty ratio is 18:1.

Student Government

The 27-member Student Assembly is the official student government organization of Keene State College. Its members are elected by the student body, with representatives for each academic class, off-campus students, and adult learners. A student body president and vice president are elected by the entire student body, while the chair of the Student Assembly, the secretary, and the treasurer are elected by Student Assembly members. Members of the Student Assembly serve on student committees and College Senate committees. The Student Assembly allocates student activity fee money and recognizes and sets policies for official student organizations.

Admission Requirements

The following requirements apply to all undergraduate programs. Keene State uses the Common Application and a KSC Supplement, available online or by request. Applicants should provide the application fee, an official high school transcript and evidence of high school graduation or a satisfactory high school equivalency certificate, SAT or ACT scores (applicants are responsible for making arrangements to take the test and for having the results forwarded to Keene State College), and a satisfactory evaluation from a high school guidance counselor, principal, or teacher. Applicants who have been out of high school for several years do not need to submit the evaluation; questions regarding this requirement should be addressed to the Director of Admissions.

Applicants should have completed college-preparatory course work, ensuring competence in English grammar and composition, college-level reading speed and comprehension, and a distribution of courses in the humanities (including 4 units in English literature), the social sciences (2 units required), the sciences (3 units required, 1 of which must be a lab), and mathematics (algebra I, algebra II, and geometry at minimum).

A personal interview is not required, although all applicants are encouraged to visit the campus. Visits are arranged through the Admissions Office.

Application and Information

To receive an application form and additional information, students should contact:

Peggy Richmond
Director of Admissions
Elliot Hall
Keene State College
Keene, New Hampshire 03435-2604
Phone: 603-358-2276
800-KSC-1909 (toll-free)
Fax: 603-358-2767
E-mail: admissions@keene.edu
Web site: http://www.keene.edu

Appian Gateway serves as a gathering place for students and welcomes visitors to Keene State College's traditional New England campus.

KEISER UNIVERSITY

FORT LAUDERDALE, FLORIDA

The University

In 1977, Keiser University was founded by the Keiser family in recognition of a need in the community for high-quality career education with a hands-on orientation. This philosophy, combined with solid academics, provides Keiser University graduates with a competitive edge when entering the workforce. With multiple locations throughout Florida, Keiser University offers small class sizes for individualized attention. The University's state-of-the-practice facilities help students gain hands-on experience in career-specific areas. Day, evening, and online classes with course materials that are relevant to current workforce needs ensure that students get the most from their education.

At Keiser, students receive an education one class at a time. Students take just one course for four weeks, then take a final exam before moving on to the next class. This schedule eliminates juggling several classes or multiple assignments and exams simultaneously. The focused approach on a single class, combined with small class size, ensures easy access to faculty and hands-on education to better meet student needs.

Keiser University helps students succeed by providing the professional and academic foundation to meet their educational goals and objectives. The University serves as a partner to employers, the community, and, above all, a valued choice for students serious about their education and career.

Keiser University is accredited by the Commission on Colleges of the Southern Association of Colleges and Schools to award associate, baccalaureate, master's, and doctoral certificates and degrees. Contact the Commission on Colleges at 1866 Southern Lane, Decatur, Georgia 30033-4097 or call 404-679-4500 for questions regarding the accreditation of Keiser University.

Location

Keiser University has campus locations throughout sunny Florida, with the main campus and the Graduate School in Fort Lauderdale. The other locations are in Daytona Beach, Jacksonville, Kendall, Lakeland, Melbourne, Orlando, Pembroke Pines, Port St. Lucie, Sarasota, Tallahassee, Tampa, and West Palm Beach. Keiser University eCampus is the online division of the Fort Lauderdale campus.

Majors and Degrees

Associate, bachelor's, master's, and Ph.D. degrees are offered at Keiser University, both on campus and online. Not all programs are offered at each campus.

Undergraduate programs are offered in accounting, baking and pastry arts, biotechnology, business administration (with concentrations in finance, human resource management, international business, management, and marketing), business administration (online in Spanish, with concentrations in international business, leadership for managers, and marketing), computer-aided drafting, computer graphics and design, computer programming, crime scene technology, criminal justice, culinary arts, diagnostic medical sonography, diagnostic vascular sonography, elementary education, fashion design and merchandising, fire science, golf management, health science, health information management, health services administration, histotechnology, homeland security, information technology, information technology management, interdisciplinary studies, legal studies, management information systems, massage therapy, medical assisting, medical laboratory technician studies, nuclear medicine technology, nursing, occupational therapy assistant studies, paralegal studies, physical therapist assistant studies, professional accounting, public safety, radiologic technology, sports medicine and fitness technology, surgical technology, technology integration, video game design, and Web design and development.

Graduate programs offered are the M.B.A. program, master's in criminal justice, master's in physician assistant, and master's in education which has specializations in college administration, leadership, teaching, and learning. A Ph.D. program is offered in educational leadership.

Academic Programs

Students take one course at a time for four weeks, which enhances opportunities for practical hands-on learning and helps with the retention of information. Students complete one class before moving to the next class. This promotes focus on each subject and eliminates juggling assignments, projects, and exams for multiple courses at the same time.

Day, evening, or online classes are available to help accommodate each student's schedule. The University understands that today's students have many responsibilities and obligations in their lives, and delivers the same quality education through different options. Students can choose day, evening, or online classes to efficiently and conveniently help them fulfill their commitment to higher education.

Students also benefit from small class sizes. The school was founded when the Keiser family recognized a need for hands-on career education in small classes. This student-friendly concept has remained at the foundation of the Keiser mission and continues to attract students who desire a more personal learning environment.

Keiser University offers students hands-on learning experiences. Students do more than just learn classroom theory—they gain valuable experience using the equipment utilized in their future professions. The technology and resources that are used prepare students for the challenges of the workplace.

Academic Facilities

At Keiser University, students gain valuable experience on equipment used in their professions. Computer students have labs that are equipped with the computers, programs, and technology used in some of the most advanced companies in the field. Students majoring in nursing and medical assisting work in the classroom with equipment to familiarize them with real-world medical settings. Keiser University is a member of five regional library cooperatives throughout Florida, which give students unparalleled access to millions of library resources. Keiser University also offers student housing facilities at the Fort Lauderdale campus.

Costs

Tuition varies by program, and students should contact the campus that they wish to attend for specific cost figures.

Financial Aid

For current information about financial aid available to students attending Keiser University, interested students can visit the University's Web site where admissions department contact information is provided for each campus.

Faculty

Qualified instructors with real-world experience compose the Keiser University faculty. Curricula taught by professionals who have faced workplace challenges prepare students to compete and overcome obstacles when they enter their chosen professions. Keiser University faculty members embrace a student-centered approach, which helps students develop the skills and qualifications necessary to succeed in today's competitive job market.

Student Government

Keiser students have an opportunity to contribute to their campus and community by becoming part of the Student Government Association (SGA). The purpose of the SGA is to foster student learning, professional development, social awareness, leadership skills, and provide campus enhancement to all its members. SGA schedules periodic meetings as well as special promotions and activities. SGA representatives give a brief presentation at all student orientations. The student government assists in the planning of social, fund-raising, sporting, and community-service activities.

Admission Requirements

For information about the current requirements for admission to the various programs offered by Keiser University, interested students should visit the University's Web site.

Application and Information

Applications are accepted on a rolling basis. Applications may be submitted online at: https://secure.ecollege.com/keiser/D1index.real?area=31

Fort Lauderdale Admissions Office
Keiser University
1500 West Commercial Boulevard
Fort Lauderdale, Florida 33309
Phone: 954-776-4456
888-534-7379 (toll-free)
E-mail: admissions-ftl@keiseruniversity.edu
Web site: http://www.keiseruniversity.edu

KENDALL COLLEGE

CHICAGO, ILLINOIS

The College

For 75 years, Kendall College has offered engaging, specialized fields of study with a strong emphasis on immersive learning that is geared to a student's academic, personal, and professional success.

Whether choosing Kendall's acclaimed School of Culinary Arts, distinctive School of Hospitality Management, innovative School of Business, or well-established School of Education, students are encouraged to explore their talents, interests, and passions—and to discover a wealth of exciting opportunities.

Kendall's School of Culinary Arts has prepared outstanding culinary professionals for twenty-five years. Its bachelor's and associate degree programs are intensive, hands-on, and cutting-edge, utilizing twelve commercial-grade kitchens, an exclusive onsite fine-dining restaurant, and an equally well-regarded cafeteria. The programs are designed to successfully launch students' careers in the vast foodservice industry, equipped with superb culinary skills, and the equally critical business management and communication skills. Students intern locally, nationally, and internationally at top-notch hospitality and culinary venues. Instructors have strong professional and academic credentials, formal culinary training, and at least ten years of professional experience.

Kendall's School of Hospitality Management combines European customer-focused competencies with American management skills. The B.A. program offers a variety of concentrations: asset management, casino management, club management, events management, hotel and lodging management, restaurant and foodservice management, and sports and leisure management. Students intern locally, nationally, and internationally at leading hospitality and culinary venues.

Kendall's School of Business prepares graduates to succeed in today's global workforce by focusing on the service industries. The program offers a Bachelor of Arts in Business with five concentration options: baking and pastry, food service management, management, personal chef and catering, and professional cookery. The curriculum is taught by an accomplished, multinational faculty of industry experts and uses situation-based challenges, actual case studies, management simulations, and integrative projects to produce employment-ready graduates. The School of Business also offers a B.A. in psychology with three concentrations—advanced studies in psychology, organizational psychology, and human resources management. This program provides a foundation for understanding the many realms of human behavior to increase success in a variety of careers from sales to human services.

Kendall's School of Education is designed specifically for working adults. Courses are offered on campus and online, allowing students the flexibility to work full-time but also the benefit of interacting with classmates and faculty in small-class environments. For those pursuing their bachelor's degree in early childhood education, Kendall provides two concentration options: special education, and infants and toddlers.

Kendall College is a member of the Laureate International Universities, a global network of more than fifty institutions of higher learning with more than 100 campuses in twenty countries. Through this partnership, students have unprecedented access to study-abroad programs, internships, and professional opportunities in Asia, Australia, Europe, and Latin America.

Kendall College is accredited by the Higher Learning Commission and a member of the North Central Association (http://www.ncahlc.org/). The A.A.S. in culinary arts and the A.A.S. in baking and pastry in the School of Culinary Arts are accredited by the American Culinary Federation Education Foundation Accrediting Commission. Kendall College's teacher certification program in early childhood education (birth through age 8) is approved by the Illinois State Board of Education for licensure in Illinois.

Location

Kendall College's campus, located near the heart of downtown Chicago, prepares its graduates for the newest leading-edge opportunities in the culinary, hospitality, and business industries. The school is minutes from some of the country's best restaurants, hotels, and companies, providing students prime access to internships and work experiences. The facility offers sweeping views of the Chicago skyline, access to newly developed areas on the Chicago River, and all the cultural and social benefits of the third-largest city in the United States. Kendall College's residence hall is Presidential Towers, located at 555 West Madison Avenue, just steps away from renowned museums, shopping, and entertainment.

Majors and Degrees

Kendall College awards Bachelor of Arts (B.A.) degrees in business, culinary arts, early childhood education, hospitality management, and psychology. The College also awards the Associate of Applied Science (A.A.S.) degree in baking and pastry, and culinary arts.

The culinary arts program offers certificates in baking and pastry, personal chef and catering, and professional cookery.

Academic Programs

Kendall College operates on a quarter system. The first quarter term extends from October to mid-December, the second term extends from January to March, and the third term extends from April to June. Summer sessions are offered from July to September.

Academic Facilities

The Chicago Riverworks campus provides wireless Internet access, computer labs, and two distance-learning videoconference facilities. Classrooms and study environments are designed to give students an effective setting in which to learn. There are student lounges, twelve commercial grade kitchens, an academic success center, secure parking spaces, and a number of nearby health clubs.

Costs

In 2009–10, full-time (12–19 credit hours/term) tuition in the School of Culinary Arts was $21,450 for three quarters.

Full-time tuition for the School of Hospitality Management was $18,675 for three quarters.

Full-time tuition in the School of Business was $12,600 for three quarters.

Full-time tuition for the psychology program in the School of Business was $12,600 for three quarters.

Full-time tuition in the School of Education was $250 per credit hour for in-classroom courses and $200 per credit hour for online courses.

Housing is located at Presidential Towers, located at 555 West Madison Avenue in Chicago. Students may lease double-occupancy one-bedroom apartments for $11,980 per twelve-month lease. Single-occupancy one-bedroom apartments are leased to students for $23,940 per twelve-month lease. Quad-occupancy two-bedroom apartments are leased to students for $9600 per twelve-month lease.

Financial Aid

Kendall College administers federal, state, and institutional aid for undergraduates. The College works with each student to help file required applications leading to the awarding of financial aid. The College's goal is to assist students to receive all funding for which they are eligible. The financial aid packaging process ensures effective use of available funds, providing fair and equitable treatment of all applicants.

Faculty

The student-faculty ratio is approximately 19:1, providing students the benefit of small classes and the ability to engage one-on-one with the faculty and the material. Faculty members at Kendall College believe students work best when they are actively involved in making choices about their own learning.

Student Government

Kendall College's Student Government Federation (SGF) is the students' organization. It provides students with a leadership role, a voice within Kendall College, and access to improving the campus community. SGF represents the student body on various committees and boards within the College, such as the Board of Trustees, Student Affairs Committee, and Faculty Senate. SGF also oversees all student clubs and organizations, along with program activities for students. SGF is elected at the beginning of the fall quarter with the term of service extending for three academic quarters.

Admission Requirements

Students who apply to Kendall College are evaluated on individual merit. Each applicant is evaluated on the basis of probable success at Kendall College. Cumulative grade point average(s) (GPAs), standardized test scores, personal statements, and admissions interviews are among the methods of evaluation. Special consideration is given to adult students who are returning to school. To determine official GPAs, the College must receive an official institution transcript directly from the institution or the organization housing the institution's records. Admissions interviews are required either via a face-to-face tour of the campus or on the phone to help determine the admission decision. An official high school transcript with graduation date and unweighted final GPA of at least 2.0 (on a 4.0 scale) are required for acceptance.

Students whose academic record does not meet Kendall admission standards in one or more admission categories (high school GPA, transfer GPA), but who demonstrate the potential for success at Kendall may be admitted with provisions.

Application and Information

Prospective students may obtain applications from the Office of Admissions or via the College's Web site. Students may submit the admission application at any time. The Office of Admissions must be sent an official transcript.

For further information, students should contact:

Office of Admissions
Kendall College
900 N. North Branch Street
Chicago, Illinois 60622
Phone: 312-752-2020
888-905-3632 (toll-free)
Fax: 312-752-2021
E-mail: admissions@kendall.edu
Web site: http://www.kendall.edu

A view of Kendall College's Riverworks campus in Chicago.

COLLEGE CLOSE-UPS

KENT STATE UNIVERSITY

KENT, OHIO

The University

Kent State University has experienced tremendous growth since its founding in 1910. Today, Kent State is a multicampus network serving more than 38,000 students at eight locations throughout northeastern Ohio. The eight-campus network is anchored by a classic residential campus in Kent, Ohio. Throughout the network, students can pursue certificate, associate, bachelor's, master's, and doctoral degrees. The Kent Campus, serving more than 18,500 undergraduates and more than 4,500 graduates, offers 281 undergraduate study areas and numerous graduate degrees. Kent State's seven regional campuses are located in Ashtabula, Geauga (including the Twinsburg Center in Twinsburg, Ohio), Stark, Trumbull, and Tuscarawas counties, and the cities of Salem and East Liverpool.

As a residential campus, Kent State requires students to reside in one of the twenty-four residence halls until junior academic standing is achieved. Exceptions include commuting and nontraditional students. Students can easily walk to any of the more than 100 academic, residential, administrative, and recreational buildings. The University has an eighteen-hole golf course, a 291-acre airport, a two-rink indoor ice arena, three on-campus theaters, and a student recreation and wellness center. There are more than 200 student organizations, seventeen fraternities, seven sororities, and eighteen varsity sports. The Career Services Center provides career counseling and job placement assistance for students and alumni.

Location

Kent, Ohio, a city with a population of 28,000, is within easy traveling distance of the major metropolitan areas of northeastern Ohio. Within a 40-mile radius are concerts, cultural events, museums, nature preserves, recreational areas, and year-round sports.

Majors and Degrees

The College of Architecture and Environmental Design offers the Bachelor of Science and Master of Architecture degrees. The School of Interior Design offers a Bachelor of Arts in interior design.

The College of the Arts offers the Bachelor of Arts, Bachelor of Fine Arts, Bachelor of Music, and Bachelor of Science degrees. The college also offers multiple-degree programs. The academic divisions are the Schools of Art, Fashion Design and Merchandising, Music, and Theatre and Dance.

The College of Arts and Sciences awards Bachelor of Arts, Bachelor of Science, and Bachelor of General Studies degrees. Major fields of concentration are American Sign Language, American studies, anthropology, applied conflict management, applied mathematics, biology, biological chemistry, biology, biotechnology, botany, chemistry, classics, computer science, conservation, criminal justice studies, earth science, economics, English, French, French translation, geography, geology, German, German translation, history, international relations, Latin, Latin American studies, mathematics, medical technology, Pan-African studies, paralegal studies, philosophy, physics, political science, psychology, Russian, Russian translation, sociology, Soviet and East European studies, Spanish, Spanish translation, and zoology. Numerous interdisciplinary and preprofessional programs are available, including general studies, integrated life sciences, pre-dentistry, pre-engineering, prelaw, premedicine, pre-osteopathy, prepharmacy, and pre–veterinary medicine. Students may also design their own individualized major.

The College of Business Administration awards the Bachelor of Business Administration degree. Major fields of concentration are accounting, business management, computer information systems, economics, entrepreneurship, finance, managerial marketing, marketing, and operations management. Students can choose a minor in any of these programs as well as international business.

The College of Communication and Information offers the Bachelor of Arts, Bachelor of Fine Arts, and the Bachelor of Science degrees. Major fields of concentration are advertising, communication studies, electronic media, news, photo illustration, public relations, radio-television, visual communication design, and visual journalism.

The College of Education, Health, and Human Services offers the Bachelor of Science in Education, Bachelor of Arts, Bachelor of Science degrees, and Master of Arts degrees, with licensure programs available in adolescence/young adult education, early childhood education, intervention specialist studies (majors include deaf education, educational interpreter studies, gifted education, mild/moderate educational needs, and moderate/intensive educational needs), middle childhood education, multiage education, and career technical teacher education (vocational education). In addition, separate degree programs are offered in the Schools of Health Sciences; Foundations, Leadership, and Administration; Lifespan Development and Educational Sciences; and Teaching, Learning, and Curriculum Studies.

The College of Nursing awards the Bachelor of Science in Nursing degree. The four-year program includes clinical practicums in the Cleveland-Akron-Warren-Youngstown areas.

The College of Public Health offers a baccalaureate program called the Bachelor of Science in Public Health degree. This academic degree addresses the health of populations and communities through instruction, service, and community-based research. A Master of Public Health degree is also offered.

The College of Technology offers associate, bachelor's, and master's degree programs throughout Kent State's eight-campus system. Students can select from a number of specialized academic programs in aeronautics, industrial, electrical, manufacturing, or educational technologies. Construction management and air traffic control are two new undergraduate programs.

Academic Programs

Kent State's colleges and schools all maintain separate academic programs; completion of about 36 credits of liberal education course work (known as the Kent Core) is a University requirement for all students. The number of credit hours required for graduation varies but is generally 121 semester hours. Credits can be transferred from previous college work satisfactorily completed or earned through courses taken at one of Kent State's regional campuses. Credit by examination is available. Generally, to earn a degree, students must earn 30 semester hours in residence.

The Honors College provides opportunities for students and faculty members to develop and implement special learning experiences. It offers four-year programs of undergraduate study with concurrent enrollment in one of the University's degree-granting programs. In addition, the Honors College awards Advanced Placement and International Baccalaureate credit and specialized academic advising. Its Experimental and Integrative Studies Division offers nontraditional learning experiences for students and faculty members of the entire University community.

Support services are available for students needing assistance to ensure a successful college experience. The Academic Success Center program offers tutoring, and Student Accessibility Services assists students with various physical disabilities and specific learning disabilities.

Army and Air Force ROTC programs are offered on campus.

Off-Campus Programs

Through the Office of International Affairs, Kent State offers students a variety of overseas academic programs that provide a balance of academic, linguistic, and cross-cultural experiences and learning opportunities. Credit is granted toward degrees.

Academic Facilities

The collections of the University libraries total more than 2.9 million bound volumes and 54,637 electronic and 3,180 print subscriptions. The Honors Center is a living-learning residential complex that houses undergraduate students as well as staff offices, a library-seminar room, a student computer facility, and an audiovisual center. The Center for Applied Conflict Management is an academic unit offering programs of study, research, and service activities that focus on the dynamics of change in human systems. The Instructional Television Service operates a closed-circuit, campuswide network and a production center for NETO, Inc., Channels 45 and 49, northeastern Ohio's public television stations. Audiovisual services support regularly scheduled classes with films and other educational materials. The Instructional Resources Center assists students in the production of educational media materials. The Language Laboratory provides tapes and other tools to assist students in foreign language studies. The Academic Testing Services Office offers test administration, test scoring, and research activities. The School of Fashion Design and Merchandising sponsors a working museum of fashion for students and the public. This school houses classrooms, labs, a library, and a collection of costumes donated from the Silverman-Rogers estate for hands-on study.

As a recognized leader in liquid crystal technology, Kent State's Glenn H. Brown Liquid Crystal Institute is the nation's only center devoted solely to liquid crystal research. With a recent grant from the National Science Foundation, Kent State became the home of Ohio's first Science and Technology Research Center for the Study of Advanced Liquid Crystalline Optical Materials.

Costs

Instructional and other fees for Ohio residents for 2009–10 were $8730 per year. For students residing outside Ohio, instructional and other fees were $16,418 per year. Although room rates vary, costs for board and a double room averaged $7940 per year. The average student spends $1030 per year for books and supplies and should budget extra money for personal needs and expenses. All fees and charges are subject to change.

Financial Aid

More than 80 percent of Kent State's freshmen receive assistance through scholarships, grants, loans, or employment opportunities. To be considered for financial aid awards, students must be admitted to the University and must submit the Free Application for Federal Student Aid (FAFSA) online. Ohio students should also check the Ohio College Opportunity Grant (OCOG) box on the FAFSA if they are interested in being considered. Students planning to attend the fall semester as freshmen should apply for financial aid online after January 1 and before March 1 of the same year. In order to meet the March 1 priority deadline, it is recommended that all financial aid forms be completed no later than February 1. Applications received after March 1 are considered, but sufficient funds to assist all late applicants may be lacking. Additional information is available from the Student Financial Aid Office at http://www.sfa.kent.edu.

First-time freshmen and incoming transfer students from forty-nine states outside of Ohio are eligible for a $3846 University Award. For eligibility requirements, students should visit http://www.sfa.kent.edu.

Kent State's Honors College awards merit scholarships to selected individuals who have the potential for superior scholarly and creative work at the University as determined by academic performance and creative artist competitions. For additional information, students should visit the Honors College Web site at http://www.kent.edu/honors.

The Student Financial Aid Office also administers numerous scholarships, including the Founder's Scholarship, the Trustee Scholarship, the Oscar Ritchie Memorial Scholarship, the President's Scholarship for out-of-state students, the President's Grant for out-of-state students who are children of alumni, and various departmental scholarships.

To be considered for freshman scholarships at the Kent Campus, students must complete an application for admission by January 15 for priority consideration. Scholarships range from $1000 to full tuition and fees. Freshmen applying after this date are considered for scholarships if funds are available.

Faculty

The University's commitment to scholarship and teaching excellence is enhanced by a full-time faculty of approximately 2,100 members. Some of the faculty members are research oriented, and others publish widely.

Student Government

Students have leadership opportunities through residence hall and Greek organizations and the Undergraduate Student Senate. The senate is responsible for allocating student activity fees to registered undergraduate organizations, appointing undergraduates to all University committees and to other positions, conducting elections, and polling student opinion. Two students serve on Kent State's Board of Trustees.

Admission Requirements

Kent State's freshman admission policy differs for students with varying degrees of preparation for college studies. The students most likely to be admitted and to succeed at the Kent campus are those who have graduated with at least 16 units of the recommended college-preparatory curriculum in high school, achieved a high school grade point average of 2.5 or higher, and acquired an ACT score of 21 or better (or a combined SAT critical reading and math score of 980 or better).

For freshmen, selective admission requirements apply to aeronautics flight technology, architecture, dance, education, fashion design and merchandising, interior design, music, nursing, sport administration, theater, and the six-year B.S./M.D. medical program with the Northeastern Ohio Universities College of Medicine (NEOUCOM). For transfer students, selective requirements apply to all of the preceding and to art and business. Students should refer to http://www.kent.edu/admissions for information.

Application and Information

Students are strongly encouraged to apply for admission online at http://www.admissions.kent.edu/apply. A $40 nonrefundable application fee is required. Application early in the senior year helps ensure priority consideration for fall registration, residence hall preference, and financial aid. Applications are processed on a rolling basis.

Nancy J. DellaVecchia
Director, Admissions Office
Kent State University
P.O. Box 5190
Kent, Ohio 44242-0001
Phone: 330-672-2444
800-988-KENT (toll-free)
E-mail: kentadm@kent.edu
Web site: http://www.kent.edu
http://www.kent.edu/admissions

COLLEGE CLOSE-UPS

KETTERING UNIVERSITY

FLINT, MICHIGAN

The University

Founded in 1919, Kettering University is a private university specializing in technical degrees. The school enrolls about 1,900 undergraduate students and offers a 12:1 student-faculty ratio. Most classes have fewer than 20 students and are taught by Ph.D.-level professors, not teaching assistants. This combination of small class size and highly qualified teaching staff ensures students a much more personalized learning experience.

Kettering is a highly acclaimed university with the one of the country's most modern cooperative education programs. Whatever major is chosen, students alternate between study terms and full-time work terms—otherwise known as co-op. During study terms, students learn material in small, intense classes taught by University professors. During co-op terms, students work as paid professionals at corporations related to their studies and interests. Kettering co-op students have done everything from testing ballistic systems for the U.S. government to reengineering crowd management at Disney World. Kettering has the only cooperative program of its kind where students begin working as early as their freshman year. By graduation from Kettering, students have up to 2½ years of professional experience and an impressive resume. Traditionally, nearly all of Kettering students graduate with job offers or graduate school acceptances in hand.

Kettering University's cooperative education program pairs hands-on education with real-world experience—all undergraduate students alternate between on-campus study terms and full-time terms of cooperative employment with one of more than 500 corporate partners. This unique system of education prepares students to be technology innovators—professionals with cutting-edge skills who are ready to compete in tomorrow's business environment.

Kettering University is accredited by the North Central Association of Colleges and Schools, the Accreditation Board for Engineering and Technology (ABET), and the Association of Collegiate Business Schools and Programs (ACBSP). Kettering is also a member of the National Commission of Cooperative Education (NCCE) and the Association of Independent Technological Universities.

Besides being academically ahead of the game, Kettering students bring a wide range of skills and interests with them to campus. To make sure that students get a life along with an education, Kettering offers more than fifty student organizations, including thirteen fraternities and six sororities, an active student government, a state-of-the-art recreation and fitness facility, and very competitive intramural sports. Recreation facilities include athletic fields, tennis courts, and a recreation center with an Olympic-size, six-lane swimming pool; aerobic fitness rooms; a full line of Nautilus equipment; and basketball, tennis, and racquetball courts. A public golf course is adjacent to the campus.

Professional counseling, support services, and health-care services are available.

Kettering also offers Master of Science degree programs in engineering, engineering management, information technology, manufacturing management, manufacturing operations, and operations management, in addition to an M.B.A. program.

Location

Kettering University is located in Flint, Michigan, which is 60 miles west of Lake Huron and 60 miles north of Detroit. Flint has approximately 115,000 residents and a metropolitan area population of 450,000.

Flint is particularly proud of its Cultural Center, which is only 10 minutes from Kettering's campus. Built and endowed entirely by the gifts of private citizens, the Cultural Center includes the Alfred P. Sloan Museum, the Whiting Auditorium (home of the Flint Symphony and host to leading stage shows and entertainers), the Robert T. Longway Planetarium (Michigan's largest and best-equipped sky show facility), the Flint Institute of Arts, the F. A. Bower Theater, the Dort Institute of Music, Mott Community College, and the Flint Public Library. Nearby is the University of Michigan–Flint campus.

The area also offers numerous outdoor and indoor recreational opportunities. Within a few minutes' drive are downhill and cross-country skiing facilities, lakes for the entire range of water sports, a wide selection of good public golf courses, excellent indoor and outdoor skating rinks, and plentiful shopping facilities and restaurants

Majors and Degrees

Kettering University offers a 4½-year, professional, cooperative education program with Bachelor of Science degrees in applied mathematics, applied physics, biochemistry, business administration, chemical engineering, chemistry, computer engineering, computer science, electrical engineering, engineering physics, industrial engineering, and mechanical engineering. Kettering also offers a Bachelor of Business Administration degree.

Kettering also offers a variety of dual-degree programs and enough minors, specialties, and concentrations to ensure that students' degrees are custom-fit to their interests and career goals. Examples include computer gaming, fuel cells and hybrid technology, system and data security, premedicine, and prelaw.

Academic Programs

Although each program at Kettering University has its own requirements, 160 credit hours are generally required for graduation. The program involves nine academic terms and nine co-op terms, two of which are focused on the capstone thesis project, which is a major work project assigned by the co-op employer. Students alternate between eleven-week periods of academic study on the campus in Flint and twelve-week periods of related work experience with their corporate employer. The academic year consists of two 3-month academic terms on campus and two 3-month terms of paid work experience.

Academic Facilities

Kettering University offers some of the best facilities, labs, and educational resources in the world, and students start using them as early as their freshman year. The Crash Safety Center, for example, is the only one of its kind in the nation used in an undergraduate program. The University also offers labs in areas such as fuel-cell research, polymer optimization, machining, acoustics, and more.

Kettering is fully networked and allows 24-hour access to computer resources and the Internet from dorms and labs. A 445-student residence hall and an apartment complex are located on the campus for student housing. The library offers more than 94,000 cataloged volumes and 540 periodicals. And through online resources like Kettering Connect and Blackboard, students can always be in touch with professors and University staff members.

Costs

For 2009–10, tuition costs were $27,584, and room and board cost $6390.

Financial Aid

Kettering University wants to invest in its students, so it does what it takes to help finance education through scholarships, loans, and work-study opportunities. In fact, more than 92 percent of the students receive some sort of financial aid. Pair that with co-op earnings—between $40,000 and $65,000 over the course of the college career—and students are looking at one of the best values in education today. In addition, Kettering's Merit Scholarship program awards students with scholarships up to $67,500 for 4½ years.

Students should fill out the Free Application for Federal Student Aid (FAFSA) and request a copy of the analysis to be sent to Kettering University. The University works to create a financial aid package for based on those results.

Faculty

Kettering University's 144 full-time faculty members have teaching as their main responsibility. Most professors have industrial experience in addition to academic credentials and maintain contact with industry through consulting, sponsored research, and advising on student thesis projects. More than 80 percent of faculty members hold a doctorate. Because only half of the students are on campus at any one time, class sizes are small, and opportunities for enrichment and extra help are readily available.

Admission Requirements

Admission to Kettering University is competitive and based on scholastic achievement and extracurricular interests, activities, and achievements. Applicants are required to have earned the following: 3 years of English, 2 years algebra, 1 year of geometry, 1 semester of trigonometry, 2 years of lab science (1 must be physics or chemistry; both are recommended). Applicants must submit results of the SAT or ACT (Kettering's ACT code number is 1998 and the SAT code number is 1246).

Most Kettering University students are in the top 10 percent of their graduating class. Kettering University also welcomes students wishing to transfer from other colleges and universities. The transfer alternative is an excellent way to gain admission for students who do not enroll as freshmen.

Application and Information

There is more than one way to apply to Kettering. Students can apply online at http://www.admissions.kettering.edu or print an application and send it by mail. Students should call 800-955-4464 Ext. 7865 for assistance.

Kettering officials review applications and let students know if they have been accepted. Although Kettering accepts and processes applications throughout the year, it is best to apply as early as possible. Once accepted, students receive information on programs and the professional co-op program, which are only available to admitted students. Students should complete the co-op registration (resume) online and pay a $300 tuition deposit (to be credited to the first-semester tuition). The deposit shows that a student is as serious about Kettering as Kettering is about the student and ensures a place in the entering class and eligibility to begin the co-op employment search process.

Admissions Office
Kettering University
1700 University Avenue
Flint, Michigan 48504
Phone: 810-762-7865
800-955-4464 (toll-free in the United States and Canada)
E-mail: admissions@kettering.edu
Web site: http://www.admissions.kettering.edu

Kettering has the experts, the labs, and the programs that bring theory and practice together.

KEYSTONE COLLEGE

LA PLUME, PENNSYLVANIA

The College

Keystone College was founded in 1868 as Keystone Academy in La Plume, Pennsylvania. Initially opened as the only high school between Binghamton, New York, and Scranton, Pennsylvania, Keystone flourished as a secondary school for more than sixty-five years. Rechartered as Scranton-Keystone Junior College in 1934 and then Keystone Junior College in 1944, the College served as one of the premier two-year institutions in the Northeast until 1995. In this year the school was again renamed, as Keystone College, and began its tenure as an "ideal" four-year degree-granting college. Keystone College has a current enrollment of 1,700, including students from fourteen states and seven countries. Students can choose from over forty programs of study.

Location

Located at the foot of the Endless Mountains in northeastern Pennsylvania, the 270-acre campus is both scenic and historic, with buildings dating back to 1870. Located 13 miles from Scranton, Pennsylvania, the campus offers easy access to major East Coast cities, including New York, Philadelphia, and Baltimore.

Majors and Degrees

The Bachelor of Arts degree is offered in communications and visual arts. The Bachelor of Science degree is offered in accounting; biology, with tracks in the medical professions; business; criminal justice, with a track in prelaw; early childhood education; elementary education, with a special education certification option; environmental biology; environmental resource management; forensic biology; information technology; organizational leadership; social sciences; sport and recreation management; teaching: art education; teaching: child and society; teaching: math education; and teaching: social studies education.

Postbaccalaureate certification is available in elementary education, early childhood education, teaching: art education (K–12), teaching: math education, and teaching: social studies education.

Associate of Applied Science degrees are offered in accounting, culinary arts, and information technology. The Associate in Fine Arts is offered in art. The Associate in Arts is offered in communications, environmental studies, forest/resource management, landscape architecture, liberal studies, liberal studies–education emphasis, and wildlife biology. The Associate in Science is offered in biology; business; criminal justice; early childhood education; health sciences with emphasis in medical technology, nursing/cytotechnology, occupational therapy/respiratory care, and radiotherapy/medical imaging/cardiac perfusion; and sport and recreation management. In addition, there are one-year programs in culinary arts, forestry technology, Microsoft Certified Systems Administrator, Microsoft Certified Systems Engineer, and pre–major studies (undeclared major).

Academic Programs

The College runs on a two-semester schedule (fall and spring) and has night, online, and weekend classes available. The number of credit hours required to earn a degree is dependent upon the field of study chosen, and students must have attained a minimum cumulative GPA of 2.0. Every student must complete a set of general core curriculum requirements as well as the courses specific to his or her major course of study. Depending on their course of study, students may be required to complete an internship or co-op before graduation.

Students have the opportunity to participate in both the Army and Navy ROTC programs in conjunction with other local participating institutions. There are opportunities for double majors as well as minors in various fields of study.

Academic Facilities

The Harry K. Miller Library is available on campus to all students. This facility offers standard print and online research opportunities. The Hibbard Campus Center is the setting for the student cafeteria, a full-service restaurant, The Chef's Table (a student-run restaurant), as well as a U.S. post office, a print shop, a student-run radio station (WKCV), and reception halls. The campus also boasts an art gallery, a celestial observatory, early childhood center, career development center, theater, and the Poinsard Greenhouse. Keystone College also serves as the home for the Urban Forestry Center, Willary Water Resource Center, and the Countryside Conservancy.

There are more than 120 computers available on campus for general student use, and both the Internet and campus network can be accessed from all residence halls and most buildings on campus.

Costs

Tuition and fees for Keystone College for the 2008–09 academic year are $18,224, while room and board costs are $8,880. Books and general supplies average $500 per semester and vary according to major.

Financial Aid

The Financial Aid Office provides adequate funds and resources to meet the financial needs of students from all income categories. In fact, 90 percent of incoming freshmen receive financial aid. Scholarships are awarded based on merit, academic performance, and extracurricular involvement. Keystone College also participates in the following federally sponsored programs: Federal Perkins Loan, Federal Pell Grant, Federal Supplemental Educational Opportunity Grant (FSEOG), Federal PLUS Loan, and Federal Stafford Student Loan. The College also offers college employment programs to students and alternative loans as well as state grants and Keystone grants. In order to be considered for financial aid, students must complete the Free Application for Federal Student Aid (FAFSA). Keystone's financial aid code is 003280.

Faculty

The student-faculty ratio is 13:1, and the average class size is 15 students. Counseling is available for academic, personal, and vocational issues. Keystone College is supported by strong interpersonal relationships among its students and faculty and staff members. All faculty members post regular office hours and are generally available outside of these hours.

Student Government

Student Senate is the central governing body of all student government organizations on the campus. It serves as the liaison between the student body and the College administration. Members of Student Senate are chosen by their peers and are responsible for improving and maintaining student life both on and off campus. Students may choose from more than twenty-five different clubs and organizations, including those with academic, service-oriented, and social interests.

Admission Requirements

Keystone accepts qualified students regardless of race, religion, handicap, or national origin, and admissions are on a rolling basis. Admission is based on prior academic performance and the ability of the applicant to profit from and contribute to the academic, interpersonal, and extracurricular life of the College. Keystone considers applicants who meet the following criteria: graduation from an approved secondary school or the equivalent (with official transcripts), satisfactory scores on the SAT or ACT, one teacher evaluation, essay, and evidence of potential for successful college achievement. All students are strongly encouraged to visit the campus for a personal interview with the admissions staff and a member of the faculty from the student's area of interest. Students applying to the art and teaching–art education programs are required to participate in a portfolio interview.

Transfer students in good academic and financial standing at their current institution are also encouraged to apply to Keystone. Transfer students should contact the Office of Admissions and may be required to submit high school transcripts or transcripts from each college attended or both.

Admissions decisions are made within two weeks from the day all required materials are received in the Office of Admissions.

Application and Information

Students wishing to be considered for admission must submit an application and a $30 processing fee, along with official high school transcripts, college transcripts (if applicable), a teacher evaluation, essay, and scores from either the SAT or ACT (submitted directly to the Office of Admissions; Keystone's CEEB code numbers are 2351 for the SAT, 3602 for the ACT).

Applications and any additional information about Keystone College may be obtained by contacting:

Office of Admissions
Keystone College
One College Green
La Plume, Pennsylvania 18440
Phone: 570-945-8111
800-824-2764 (toll-free), Option 1
E-mail: admissions@keystone.edu
Web site: http://www.keystone.edu

Students on the campus of Keystone College.

COLLEGE CLOSE-UPS

KING'S COLLEGE

WILKES-BARRE, PENNSYLVANIA

The College

King's College is an independent, coed, four-year Catholic college with 2,700 students. Founded by the Holy Cross Fathers and Brothers of the University of Notre Dame in 1946, King's prepares students for a purposeful life with an education that integrates the human values inherent in a broadly based liberal arts curriculum. The College encourages the religious, moral, personal, and social development of its students.

In addition to the undergraduate degrees, King's College offers a Master of Science (M.S.) degree in health-care administration, a Master of Education (M.Ed.) degree (with a concentration in reading), and a five-year physician assistant studies program leading to a master's degree.

Academic advising begins before students enroll and continues with an innovative program of career development across the curriculum. King's Academic Skills Center includes a nationally certified tutoring program and a faculty-staffed writing center. More than 80 percent of King's first-year students return for their sophomore year. Over 70 percent of students who attend King's graduate from the College, which is well above the national average, and 99 percent are employed or attend graduate school within six months of graduation.

Campus features include the Charles E. and Mary Parente Life Sciences Center, the Mulligan Physical Sciences Center, the William G. McGowan School of Business, and Robert L. Betzler Fields at McCarthy Stadium, a 33.5-acre athletic complex that includes a field house and fields for baseball, softball, men's and women's soccer, football, and field hockey. The 15-acre campus also includes Monarch Court; the Sheehy-Farmer Campus Center, which includes an art gallery, an outdoor waterfall, a student restaurant, and marketplace dining; the J. Carroll McCormick Campus Ministry Center; and the William S. Scandlon Physical Education Center, which includes a 3,200-seat basketball arena, wrestling facilities, racquetball and handball courts, an Olympic-size swimming pool, a Wellness Center, and a state-of-the-art sports medicine facility. The Student Health Center is located in Hafey-Marian Hall, a modern six-story building housing classrooms and faculty offices, and a consulting physician is on call at all times. The six-story administration and science buildings form a unit that houses the College's theater, the newly renovated Susquehanna Room dining hall and coffee bar, administrative offices, science laboratories, and classrooms. Residence halls have cable television, Internet access, and 24-hour computer labs.

More than forty student organizations provide King's students with the opportunity to explore interests outside the classroom. Student athletics include intercollegiate competition in men's baseball, basketball, football, golf, lacrosse, soccer, swimming, tennis, and wrestling; women's basketball, field hockey, lacrosse, soccer, softball, swimming, tennis, and volleyball; and coed cross-country. Club sports include cheerleading and ice hockey. Intramural sports include basketball, bowling, field hockey, flag football, racquetball, softball, street hockey, and volleyball. Other cocurricular activities include academic clubs in almost every department, the King's Players (theater), the nationally ranked debate team, Cantores Christi Regis, Campus Ministry, the Experiencing the Arts Series, *The Crown* (student newspaper), the *Regis* (yearbook), and *SCOP* (literary magazine).

Location

The King's campus is located in a residential area near downtown Wilkes-Barre, Pennsylvania, a city of approximately 50,000 on the banks of the Susquehanna River. A growing city, Wilkes-Barre has developed both economically and culturally, yet it has avoided many typical urban problems. The crime rate in the city is one of the lowest in the nation. Local events include the Cherry Blossom Festival, a national ice carving competition, and the Fine Arts Fiesta. Shopping malls, multiplex theaters, a brand new riverfront park, art galleries, and restaurants are nearby. Two blocks from King's is the F. M. Kirby Center, which has hosted national performances, music groups, traveling theater, and more. National recording acts regularly perform in nearby venues.

King's is a short drive from several ski resorts, state parks, and major lakes, as well as the stadium of the New York Yankees' AAA baseball team, the Pocono International Raceway, and the Mohegan Sun Arena, which is home to the Pittsburgh Penguins' minor-league ice hockey team and features regular concerts and is the site of the King's commencement. New York City and Philadelphia are within a 2½-hour drive; Harrisburg, Pennsylvania, and Morristown, New Jersey, are within 2 hours; and New England and Washington, D.C., are within 4 hours.

Majors and Degrees

King's awards Bachelor of Arts, Bachelor of Science, Associate of Arts, and Associate of Science degrees. The College's thirty-five major programs are offered in the arts and sciences and the William G. McGowan School of Business, which is accredited by AACSB International—The Association to Advance Collegiate Schools of Business.

Arts and sciences include the humanities and social sciences division (computers and information systems, criminal justice, economics, English–literature, English–professional writing, French, history, mass communications, philosophy, political science, psychology, sociology, Spanish, theater, and theology); the education division, which recently received NCATE accreditation (preschool–grade 4, secondary certification, and special education); the science division (biology, chemistry, computer science, environmental science, environmental studies, general science, mathematics, and neuroscience); and the allied health division (clinical lab science, physician assistant studies, and athletics training education/sports medicine accredited by CAAHEP). Available majors in the William G. McGowan School of Business are accounting, business administration, finance, human resources management, international business, and marketing. King's offers preprofessional programs in chiropractic, dentistry, law, medicine, optometry, pharmacy, and veterinary science.

Academic Programs

The general education program at King's is recognized nationwide by its peers. King's is included in *Barron's Best Buys in College Education* and has been honored in sixteen consecutive issues of *U.S. News & World Report*'s *Best Colleges Guide.* The College was also recognized by the John Templeton Foundation Honor Roll for Character-Building Colleges, the Forbes/CCAP list of America's best colleges, and is one of sixteen institutions nationwide named to the Greater Expectations initiative. The core curriculum is recognized as a model curriculum. It incorporates traditional and new concepts in liberal arts education, develops competence in such areas as communications and problem solving, and measures students' progress throughout the program.

The honors program offers highly motivated students the challenge of learning in discussion-centered courses that explore distinctive subject matter with exciting and innovative approaches. Sixteen honor societies encourage students to excel in their chosen fields and recognize students for their academic distinction; members are honored each year at the All-College Honors Convocation. Science students receive hands-on lab training much earlier than students at other institutions and work together with faculty members on real-world research projects.

Off-Campus Programs

Experiential learning (via internships) is available in conjunction with almost every major. Placement possibilities include CNN, the New York Stock Exchange, PricewaterhouseCoopers, the Pennsylvania Department of Education, the Pennsylvania State House of Representatives, the U.S. House of Representatives, U.S. Senators' offices, the U.S. Department of Energy, Walt Disney World, and Xerox Corporation. Every year, students are placed with local, regional, and national companies around the globe.

The International Internship Program and the study-abroad program are also options for King's students who work in a variety of professions. Many of King's students have studied on campuses throughout Europe, Thailand, China, and Australia.

Academic Facilities

King's facilities include the 51,000-square-foot, three-story D. Leonard Corgan Library, which contains several study rooms, a 100-seat auditorium, and a 160,000-volume collection accessed by a computerized catalog. The library uses its affiliation with the Online Computer Library Center to provide students and faculty members with access to college and research libraries throughout the United States. The library provides full-text databases from every computer on campus. Students and faculty members have direct access to more than 1 million volumes through the local library cooperative (NEPBC).

King's features computer labs with more than 440 PCs; 24-hour labs in residence halls; e-mail accounts for all students; computerized library databases; multimedia classrooms with a variety of instructional aids; course discussions on electronic bulletin boards and chats via e-mail outside of the traditional classroom; a technology component of the core curriculum that requires all students to learn to access, process, and develop their own computer and information presentation skills; distance learning facilities for teleconferencing; satellite down-link capabilities in the 220-seat Burke Auditorium of the William G. McGowan School of Business; and cross-registration with area colleges that enables students to take courses complementary to their majors.

The $6.4-million Charles E. and Mary Parente Life Sciences Center, which contains a molecular biology laboratory and a genomics center, includes computer facilities, instrumentation rooms, a rooftop greenhouse, and environmental chambers. The $6-million Mulligan Physical Sciences Center includes modern research laboratories, computer facilities, and state-of-the-art instrumentation used for molecular identification.

Costs

For the 2009–10 academic year, tuition for full-time students was $25,644. Room and board totaled $10,138.

Financial Aid

King's assists all qualified students through its financial aid programs. Currently, more than 95 percent of King's students currently receive financial aid in the form of scholarships, grants, work-study, or loans. Aid is awarded on the basis of demonstrated financial need, the difference between the total cost of education and the expected family contribution. Usually, a combination of financial aid sources and types are used in a student's financial aid package. Of all financial aid awarded to its students, grants and scholarships funded by King's comprise approximately 40 percent of the total aid awarded.

In addition to financial aid programs, installment payment plans are available, offering students and/or their families the ability to make monthly payments throughout the academic year. Students who wish to be considered for financial aid must fill out the Free Application for Federal Student Aid (FAFSA) and the King's College Financial Aid Application. The preferred filing deadline for new freshmen is February 15. Forms are mailed to students accepted for admission but can be completed prior to acceptance.

Faculty

King's College has 125 full-time and 83 part-time faculty members. Eighty-one percent of the full-time faculty members have a Ph.D. or an equivalent terminal degree. Graduate assistants do not teach courses. The student-faculty ratio is 13:1.

Student Government

The student government coordinates and participates in numerous activities for both the student body and the surrounding community. It regularly holds open forums for students and senior administrators at the College, coordinates informal socials for the students with the College president, and makes presentations at each meeting of the Board of Directors. In addition, the student government sponsors events that foster awareness for social and justice issues and a celebration of cultural diversity. Community projects, which incorporate a strong service component, include CitySERVE, National Collegiate Alcohol Awareness Week, and fund-raisers for the United Way. The Association for Campus Events, a student-operated organization, also sponsors comedians, movies, and performers throughout the year.

Admission Requirements

King's encourages applications from qualified high school students and those who wish to transfer from another institution. To be considered for admission, students must be prepared to successfully pursue a program of study at the College, as evidenced by the quality of previous academic and extracurricular performance, the recommendation of school officials and character references, and the student's display of personal promise, maturity, and motivation. King's admits students of any race, sex, color, creed, or national or ethnic origin.

Admission decisions are made for both high school students and transfer students with the understanding that all current courses and examinations will be completed satisfactorily. Candidates should complete 4 years of mathematics (through trigonometry or precalculus). One year each of high school chemistry, biology, and physics is also strongly recommended.

The Office of Admission offers two methods for candidates to apply for admission: the SAT/ACT Traditional Choice and the Standardized Test Option/Essay Choice. Applicants are required to state their preference prior to the application review, and the decision is nonreversible. Students who select the SAT/ACT Traditional Choice must submit a completed application, official high school transcripts, SAT or ACT scores, guidance counselor recommendation, an essay, and the $30 application fee, which is waived if students apply online. Students who choose the Standardized Test Option/Essay Choice must submit a completed application, official high school transcripts, an official graded writing sample from either their junior or senior year—submitted and notarized by the high school guidance office, guidance counselor recommendation, an essay, and the $30 application fee, which is waived if students apply online.

Application and Information

Applicants should forward a completed application and the $30 fee to the Office of Admission or apply online at http://www.kings.edu in order to waive the application fee. Secondary and postsecondary (if applicable) transcripts must be sent. Admission decisions are not made until all credentials are received. King's subscribes to a rolling admission policy. Decisions are announced within two weeks from the date of application. Upon notification of acceptance, a $200 nonrefundable deposit is requested to reserve a place in the class. The deposit deadline is May 1 but may be extended upon request. To schedule an interview, obtain an application form, or for more information, students should contact:

Office of Admission
King's College
133 North River Street
Wilkes-Barre, Pennsylvania 18711
Phone: 570-208-5858
888-KINGS-PA (toll-free)
E-mail: admissions@kings.edu
Web site: http://www.kings.edu

KUTZTOWN UNIVERSITY OF PENNSYLVANIA

KUTZTOWN, PENNSYLVANIA

The University

In an independent survey, 93 percent of students and recent alumni rated their education at Kutztown University (KU) as excellent or good in regard to their overall college experience, the quality of instruction they received, and the quality of the faculty. KU offers excellent academic programs through its undergraduate Colleges of Liberal Arts and Sciences, Visual and Performing Arts, Business, and Education and through its graduate studies program. A wide range of student support services complements the high-quality classroom instruction.

Students have the advantage of a well-rounded program of athletic, cultural, and social events at KU. There are clubs, organizations, and activities to satisfy nearly every taste. Currently, more than 10,000 full- and part-time students are enrolled at the University. About 4,400 undergraduates live in residence halls, more than a third live nearby off campus, and the remainder commute.

Kutztown University's attractive 330-acre campus includes a mix of old and new buildings, including stately Old Main, the historic building known to generations of Kutztown's students; University Place, a modern residence hall in a courtyard setting; and the McFarland Student Union. The Student Recreation Center opened in fall 2006, and the state-of-the-art Academic Forum opened in January 2007. Renovations of the Sharadin Arts Building and a new 865-bed suite-style residence hall were completed for fall 2008. All residence hall rooms are wired for Internet usage, and multistation computer labs are available in buildings across the campus.

In addition to its undergraduate program, the University's graduate program awards master's degrees in a number of fields. The Master of Science is awarded in computer and information science and electronic media. The Master of Arts is awarded in counseling psychology and English. The Master of Education is awarded in art education, elementary education, elementary school counseling (certification and licensure), instructional technology, reading specialist, secondary education (with specializations), secondary school counseling (certification and licensure), and student affairs in higher education (administration and college counseling licensure). The Master of Library Science, Master of Business Administration, Master of Public Administration, and Master of Social Work are also awarded.

Location

The University is located in a beautiful, rural Pennsylvania Dutch community, midway between the cities of Allentown and Reading. Both cities are a short drive from the campus and have major shopping and recreational facilities. Kutztown borough, an easy walk from the campus, has ample stores and shops to meet the needs of students. Philadelphia is about 1½ hours away and New York City, about 2½ hours.

Majors and Degrees

Undergraduate degrees are offered in a wide variety of fields. The Bachelor of Arts is awarded in anthropology, English, French, German studies, geography, history, music, philosophy, political science, sociology, Spanish, speech communication, and theater. The Bachelor of Fine Arts is awarded in communication design, crafts, and studio art. The Bachelor of Science is awarded in art education, biology, biochemistry, chemistry, computer science, criminal justice, electronic media, environmental science, geology, leisure and sport studies, library science, marine science, mathematics, medical technology, music education, physics, psychology, and public administration. The Bachelor of Science in Business Administration is awarded in accounting, finance, general business, international business, management, and marketing. The Bachelor of Science in Education is awarded in elementary education, with concentrations in coaching education, early childhood development, English, French, German, instructional technology, mathematics, psychology, reading, science, social studies, Spanish, and urban education; in secondary education, with specializations in biology, chemistry, citizenship education, communications, earth-space science, English, French, German, general science, mathematics, physics, physics and mathematics, social sciences, social studies, and Spanish; in special education, with concentrations in mentally/physically handicapped and visually impaired; and in library science. The Bachelor of Social Work also is awarded, and there is a B.S.N. completion program for registered nurses. The four most popular majors are criminal justice, communication design, psychology, and elementary education. The most popular minors are psychology and public relations.

Academic Programs

The University observes a two-semester calendar, and first-semester examinations are completed by mid-December. A minimum of 120 semester hours and a cumulative quality point average (QPA) of at least 2.0 are required for graduation. In the College of Liberal Arts and Sciences and College of Business, a quality point average of at least 2.0 in the major is also required.

Students seeking admission to teacher education must complete a three-stage process. (1) Applicants must have a projected grade point average (PGPA) of at least 2.2; art education requires a 2.30. Students with less than a 2.2 PGPA may be granted admission to their second-choice major and can reapply to the education program once they earn a minimum QPA of 3.0. (2) Once admitted to the major and by the fourth semester (or after completing 64 semester hours), applicants must present evidence of 30 hours of classroom observation. They must also achieve at least a 3.0 overall average, pass a speech screening test, and complete basic speech, mathematics, English composition and literature, EDU 100, student teaching, and professional education courses, as determined by each major, with a minimum grade of C. (3) Prior to student teaching, applicants must complete a professional semester or early field experience, have achieved at least a 3.0 GPA as well as a 3.0 QPA in all courses in the major required for student teaching, and be recommended by the department screening committee. Students are required to pass the National Teachers Examination (three core batteries and a specialty area) at the end of their academic program before the Pennsylvania Department of Education will issue an Instructional I (Probationary) Certificate.

The distinctive University Honors Program is available to qualified students in all areas of study. Freshmen who have been identified as potential honors students based on their high school records and SAT scores, transfer students from other honors programs, and incumbent students who have at least a 3.25 GPA are invited to enroll in the program. The 21 semester hours in honors work, which include a senior thesis project, count toward the 120 hours required for graduation. Honors students select specially designed courses, independent study, and internships. The honors program awards several merit-based scholarships, and students who complete the program receive an honors diploma upon graduation.

Kutztown University provides an opportunity for higher education for students who, because of economic need, cultural disadvantage, or inadequate preparation, have previously been unable to attend college. Students admitted to the University under the Summer Start Program attend a one-week program designed to introduce them to university study and to provide supportive services as well as instruction in study skills, reading strategies, college issues, and critical thinking.

Off-Campus Programs

Students majoring in education spend one semester of their senior year student teaching in area schools under the guidance of an experienced teacher. Additional teaching field experiences are available in the junior year during the "professional semester." Internships in other programs provide students with one semester of practical experience in their specialty. For example, political science students may work in local, state, or federal government agencies; psychology students in area psychiatric hospitals, clinics, and rehabilitation centers; social welfare and criminal justice students in various social agencies; electronic media students in commercial or public broadcasting, cable television, and industrial, medical, or institutional television; and medical technology students in area hospitals.

The University has exchange and study-abroad programs with colleges and universities in thirteen countries. KU participates in the College Consortium for International Studies, which administers seventy-five study-abroad programs. In addition, through the International Student Exchange Program, KU students may study for a year in any of sixty institutions in twenty-seven countries. Kutztown participates in a cooperative program with the Diplomatic Academy of the Russian Foreign Ministry, Moscow, in which prominent Russian scholars and foreign affairs experts visit KU to meet with classes and give public lectures. KU also has cooperative programs with institutions in England, Germany, the Netherlands, Hungary, Italy, Spain, and China.

Through consortium arrangements with colleges and universities in three states, Kutztown participates in the operation of a marine science research center at Wallops Island, Virginia, which has laboratories, research equipment, and coastal research ships. Through this facility, students in marine science classes are able to gain firsthand knowledge of the ocean environment. The University's participation in the Pennsylvania Consortium for International Education provides opportunities for study abroad during the summer.

Academic Facilities

The Rohrbach Library is a modern facility that provides many attractive and functional areas that greatly enhance the learning environment for all students. Its technologies are state of the art, and it was the first completely wireless building on campus. In addition to the 527 computer connection points that were installed when the building was expanded in 1998, students may bring their own laptops to access the Web or use one of the 100 that are available for circulation. The library has both Macintosh and PC public-access computers throughout the building. The library has more than 517,000 books and bound periodicals, subscriptions to nearly 42,000 print and electronic periodicals, access to 95 electronic databases, and more than 1.32 million microforms. Electronic access to these library materials is provided through the online catalog and the library's Web page, which provides students with easy access to all of its resources and links them to electronic resources available throughout the world. The map collection is one of the finest in Pennsylvania, with 40,400 sheets, and includes Braille maps, city plans, geographic maps, and raised-relief maps.

The Audiovisual Center maintains a comprehensive collection of more than 15,000 items, including microcomputer software, films, filmstrips, videocassettes, records, audiocassettes, digital cameras, projectors, and laptops, that circulate to students. The Curriculum Materials Center provides preservice and in-service teachers with current teaching and learning resources and includes one of the most coveted collections of children's literature in the country. Supplementing this collection is the Dornish Collection, which features first-edition signed books from top writers in the children's literature field. Kutztown's resources are supplemented by a traditional interlibrary loan service, a rapid document delivery service, and a direct borrowing system that links students with the collections of additional academic libraries in the state of Pennsylvania.

Other resources include a modern science complex, an astronomical observatory and planetarium, a seismic observatory, the Sharadin Art Gallery, a television studio, a modern language laboratory, and a speech clinic.

Costs

In 2009–10, tuition was $5554 for Pennsylvania residents and $13,886 for out-of-state residents. The average cost of room and board for an incoming freshman was $7200. Fees were $1844 for Pennsylvania residents and $1948 for out-of-state residents. Books, travel expenses, and other supplies are additional.

Financial Aid

KU believes that no student who is eligible to enroll at the University should be denied the opportunity for an education solely because of lack of funds. Financial assistance is available through grants, private and institutional scholarships, military officer training programs, on-campus part-time employment, and loans. A booklet describing financial aid opportunities may be obtained by writing to the Director of Financial Aid. Any student wishing to investigate financial aid opportunities should do so when applying for admission, as most programs have application deadlines. The only form needed to apply for financial aid is the FAFSA. KU has a priority filing date of March 1. Pennsylvania residents should file the FAFSA no later than May 1 to qualify for Pennsylvania state grants.

Faculty

Although many professors at KU are involved in important research and are leaders in their fields, their primary interest is in the classroom. The University has more than 320 full-time instructors and a favorable 20:1 student-faculty ratio. The average class size is 29. Approximately 82 percent of the faculty members hold terminal degrees in their field of study. Upon enrollment in the University, each student is assigned a faculty adviser to help plan his or her academic career. Many faculty members are active in campus groups as members or advisers, creating a close and friendly working relationship with students.

Student Government

All students are members of the Student Government Association and elect representatives who form the Student Government Board (SGB). Students at Kutztown are regarded as mature individuals who can be, in great measure, responsible for the control of their own environment. For that reason, the SGB exercises considerable discretion in coordinating and funding student organizations. Most University committees, including the Council of Trustees, have student members with full voting rights.

Admission Requirements

The main criteria for admission are achievement as indicated on scholastic records and standardized tests. Candidates must have graduated from an approved secondary school or demonstrate equivalent preparation. Scores on either the SAT or the ACT are required and are regarded as evidence of ability to do university-level work. It is the responsibility of the applicant to request that his or her scores be forwarded to the Admissions Office. Either test should be taken no later than the fall of the senior year; sitting for these exams during the junior year is encouraged. For admission to special programs, the candidate may be required to supply additional evidence of ability to succeed in the given field. Specific requirements and instructions are included in the admission application materials.

Application and Information

The completed application and all other required materials must be mailed to the Director of Admissions. No action is taken by the Admission Committee until all necessary steps have been completed. For additional information and application forms, students should contact:

Dr. William Stahler
Director of Admissions
Kutztown University of Pennsylvania
Kutztown, Pennsylvania 19530
Phone: 610-683-4060
E-mail: admission@kutztown.edu
Web site: http://www.kutztown.edu/admissions

LAFAYETTE COLLEGE

EASTON, PENNSYLVANIA

The College

Classified as one of the nation's most academically competitive colleges, Lafayette focuses exclusively on undergraduates, offering a wide variety of academic choices in the humanities, social sciences, natural sciences, and engineering. The College is committed to providing the best education for men and women who possess the ability to benefit from the Lafayette experience, and the capacity to contribute to a vibrant campus community with no graduate programs and no graduate students.

The breadth and depth of Lafayette's curriculum are unusual and unexpected in a college of its size. One of just a few undergraduate colleges with fully accredited programs in engineering, Lafayette enrolls 2,400 students from more than forty U.S. states and territories, and more than 50 other countries. The College draws strength from the diversity of its students, who represent a wide range of interests, special talents, and aspirations.

Lafayette is a residential college where learning continues outside the classroom. Living in college housing is guaranteed and required for all four years. More than 95 percent of students live in College-owned residence halls, apartments, special-interest houses, fraternities, or sororities. An array of student organizations, cultural events, social opportunities, and varsity and intramural sports programs are available to all students.

Recent trends indicate that approximately two thirds of Lafayette graduates obtain a graduate or professional degree. A large and growing number obtain practical experience through employment, and then undertake full-time study for an advanced degree, often with an employer's financial support. Others continue academic pursuits on a part-time basis. A strong internship program with alumni and parent mentors helps pave the way to fulfilling careers for Lafayette graduates.

Location

Lafayette is located in a picturesque setting atop a hill overlooking the Delaware and Lehigh rivers and the progressive city of Easton, population 30,000, located 70 miles from New York City, and 60 miles from Philadelphia.

Easton, Allentown, and Bethlehem are the principal cities of the Lehigh Valley, Pennsylvania's third-largest metropolitan area, which has a population of about 800,000.

Shops, restaurants, and other business establishments that serve the needs of Lafayette students are located adjacent to the campus, and in nearby downtown Easton. Beyond Easton to the west and north are great ski slopes, top fishing rivers, and challenging hiking trails.

Majors and Degrees

Lafayette awards the Bachelor of Science (B.S.) degree in biochemistry, biology, chemical engineering, chemistry, civil engineering, computer science, electrical and computer engineering, geology, mathematics, mechanical engineering, neuroscience, physics, and psychology.

The Bachelor of Arts (A.B.) degree is awarded with the following majors: Africana studies; American studies; anthropology and sociology; art; Asian studies; biochemistry; biology; chemistry; computer science; economics; engineering studies; English; French; geology; German; government and law; government and law and foreign language; history; international affairs; international economics and commerce; mathematics; mathematics-economics; music; philosophy; physics; policy studies; psychology; religion and politics; religious studies; Russian and East European studies; and Spanish.

In addition, Lafayette offers a two-degree program leading to an A.B. in international studies and a B.S. in one of four engineering disciplines.

Academic Programs

Students are engaged, active learners taught to think critically and to connect ideas with students and faculty from different majors to solve real-world problems. They say that extensive course offerings, personal attention from faculty members, and a personal approach to learning are what make Lafayette special. The emphasis on small-group and team-based learning is part of an educational philosophy that places the highest value on giving students the greatest possible access to an exceptionally qualified and dedicated faculty—in the classroom, in research projects, and in social settings.

Interdisciplinary programs are offered in Africana studies; architectural studies; biotechnology/bioengineering; classical civilization; computational methods; drama/theater; environmental science; film; health and life science; health care and society; Jewish studies; Latin American and Caribbean studies; medieval, Renaissance, and early modern studies; Russian; women's and gender studies, and writing.

The Dean of the College's staff mentors students in their academic development, provides support for students interested in careers in law and the health professions, and works with students to pursue prestigious undergraduate and post-graduate fellowships and awards.

The academic year is divided into two semesters with a January interim session, where courses are offered on and off campus, including study overseas.

Off-Campus Programs

Lafayette recognizes that we live in an increasingly complex and interrelated global environment, and connecting the classroom to the world outside our walls is at the core of the College's mission. Off-campus study combines academic rigor with experiential learning through immersion in an international or culturally significant domestic setting.

Semester-long programs led by Lafayette professors are offered at Jacobs University Bremen; Saint Louis University in Madrid; Goldsmith's College at the University of London; and the University of Ghana. Lafayette students also choose from semester-long and yearlong programs, coordinated by affiliated institutions, in many countries.

During interim session, Lafayette faculty lead distinctive three-week courses around the world. Courses have been offered in Australia, China, East Africa, England, Guatemala, Italy, Japan, New Zealand, Russia, Scandinavia, Spain, South Africa, Thailand, Turkey, and the West Indies, among many other locations.

Academic Facilities

With an endowment per student that typically ranks among the top 2 percent of private colleges and universities nationally, the College has invested more than $200 million in new academic, residential, and recreational facilities recently, including a science center, a center for psychology and neuroscience, a center for the visual arts, and a center for intramural and recreational sports. Improvements also include an expansion and transformation of the main library, a thorough modernization of the engineering complex, and new and renovated residence halls.

Costs

The tuition for 2010–11 is $38,810. Additional costs include a standard room fee of $7265, board fee of $4694 (20 meals/week), activity/technology fee of $305, matriculation fee of $700 (for new students only), and an estimated $2000 for books, travel, and miscellaneous expenses.

Financial Aid

An education that is personal—featuring faculty time with students on-task in the classroom and in student-faculty research—and emphasizes teams of students learning together across different majors will always be more costly to deliver than the traditional large, lecture-based classes taught by graduate students at large public or private research universities.

Lafayette is committed to providing need-based scholarships and grants to meet the full need of every admitted student. In addition, the College provides the Marquis Scholarship, worth $20,000 per year to applicants whose grades, high school curriculum, SAT scores, and activity leadership put them in the top 10 percent of the pool of accepted students. Students with financial need above $20,000, who are awarded a Marquis Scholarship, will have their full need (minus a small loan and work opportunity) met with a grant.

In 2009–10, Lafayette provided more than $34 million in scholarship and need-based grant assistance to more than half of enrolled students. Detailed information regarding financial assistance is available from the Office of Student Financial Aid, Lafayette College, Easton, Pennsylvania 18042-1777 (phone: 610-330-5055).

Faculty

Lafayette is committed to reducing the student-to-faculty ratio from the current 10.6:1 to below 10:1. All of the College's 206 full-time faculty members hold the doctorate or other terminal degree in their field. All faculty members—full professors and heads of departments as well as junior faculty members—teach courses and serve as academic advisers to students. Many have earned wide recognition for their research and scholarship and won awards for superior teaching.

Admission Requirements

Lafayette seeks to enroll students who can benefit from and contribute to the Lafayette experience. To maintain a student body that reflects society and to enhance every student's educational experience, the College seeks to enroll students from diverse backgrounds—from different cultures and ethnicities, from different parts of the country and the world, and from across the socioeconomic spectrum. The Admissions Office selects students with a wide variety of academic and extracurricular interests and talents, using a holistic evaluation process that employs no formulas. The most important aspect of the College's evaluation of applicants' ability to succeed academically at Lafayette is a review of the quality of the courses taken in high school, grades in academic courses, and, when available, class rank.

Applicants are required to submit scores from either the SAT reasoning test or ACT (with writing). SAT subject test results are recommended but not required. Prospective math, science, or engineering majors are encouraged to take subject tests in mathematics and science. Students are strongly encouraged to visit the Lafayette campus for an admission interview and student-guided tour.

Application and Information

The application deadline is January 1. Applicants are notified about admission decisions on or about April 1. May 1 is the Common Candidates' Reply Date, by which admitted students must reply to the College's offer of admission.

Students who have decided that Lafayette is their first choice may request consideration of their applications under early decision. The deadline for early decision applications is November 15, with notification by December 15.

Regular decision applicants who meet the January 1 application deadline have until February 15 to convert their applications to early decision, with notification within 30 days of conversion.

To be considered for early decision admission, students must sign and submit the early decision plan agreement. Applicants admitted under early decision must withdraw their applications to other institutions.

Office of Admissions
Lafayette College
Easton, Pennsylvania 18042-1770
Phone: 610-330-5100
Web site: http://www.lafayette.edu

A view of Lafayette College's campus.

LAWRENCE TECHNOLOGICAL UNIVERSITY

SOUTHFIELD, MICHIGAN

COLLEGE CLOSE-UPS

The University

Lawrence Technological University is a premier private university offering over 100 undergraduate and graduate degrees in architecture and design, arts and sciences, engineering, and management. The University's Leadership Program, integrated into all bachelor's degrees, helps students gain critical thinking, teamwork, and communication skills. An honors program is available to highly qualified students, as well as Quest, which encourages students to explore their interests on a deeper level. Lawrence Tech is known for cutting-edge technology, small class sizes, and a commitment to theory and practice. The 102-acre campus features state-of-the-art learning facilities and many housing, recreation, and meal service options.

The University, including its graduate programs, is accredited by the Higher Learning Commission and is a member of the North Central Association of Colleges and Schools. Appropriate national professional agencies provide additional accreditation to various programs in architecture, interior architecture/design, imaging, administration and management, chemistry, and engineering.

Approximately 4,500 students attend Lawrence Tech; more than 500 live in on-campus housing. Women make up 26 percent of the student body, and twenty-nine states and forty countries are represented on campus.

Numerous fraternities, sororities, and social and professional organizations sponsor a variety of activities during the year. Recreational facilities include the Don Ridler Field House, which features a fitness track, gymnasium, racquetball courts, game room, saunas, and a weight and conditioning room. Intramural and club sports teams in badminton, basketball, billiards, curling, flag football, golf, hockey, racquetball, soccer, softball, table tennis, tennis, volleyball, and wallyball are active throughout the academic year.

Location

Southfield is a dynamic suburb that provides a pleasant balance between big-city entertainment opportunities and a quiet residential atmosphere. Lawrence Tech's campus is about a 30-minute drive north of downtown Detroit, which offers a rich variety of recreational and cultural activities.

Within a few miles of the campus, students can find many restaurants, parks, shopping areas, and recreational facilities. Research, manufacturing, scientific, and business enterprises are also nearby, aiding students in co-op and internship programs as well as those who work full- or part-time while attending classes. More than 200 Fortune 500 companies have headquarters or business operations in the Detroit metropolitan area.

Majors and Degrees

Most Lawrence Tech programs are available days or evenings; some are offered online and on weekends. Dual majors and customized degree programs are available. Preprofessional programs are offered in dentistry, law, and medicine.

The College of Architecture and Design offers bachelor's degrees in architecture, game art, imaging (digital arts and digital design), industrial design, interior architecture, and transportation design. Certificates are available in animation and visual effects for film; building information modeling and computer visualization; and set design. Lawrence Tech enrolls more architectural students than any other school in Michigan, and is one of the top 10 largest architecture schools in the nation.

The College of Arts and Sciences awards bachelor's degrees in chemical biology, chemistry, computer science (business software development, game software development, network software development, and scientific software development), English and communication arts, environmental chemistry, humanities, mathematics, mathematics and computer science, media communication, molecular and cell biology, physics, physics and computer science, and psychology (clinical psychology, industrial/organizational psychology, and premedical/biobehavioral psychology). Associate degrees are offered in chemical technology, general studies, and radio and television broadcasting. Minors offered are business management, chemistry, computer science, economics, English, general sciences, history, mathematics, philosophy, physics, psychology, Spanish, technical and professional communication, and television and video production. Certificates can be earned in computer science, entrepreneurial strategy, film and audio technique, film and production techniques, industrial/organizational psychology, technical and professional communication, television and video production, and video and audio technique.

The College of Engineering offers bachelor's degrees in architectural engineering (combining bachelor's and master's studies), audio engineering technology, biomedical engineering, civil engineering, computer engineering, construction management, electrical engineering (computer engineering, electronic engineering, and energy engineering), engineering technology, industrial operations engineering, and mechanical engineering (alternative energy, automotive engineering, manufacturing, mechanical system design, and thermal system design). The College offers evening associate programs in communications engineering technology, construction engineering technology, manufacturing engineering technology, and mechanical engineering technology. Also available are minors in aeronautical engineering and energy engineering, and certificates in alternative energy engineering technology, biochemical engineering, bioelectronics, biomechanics, electrical power systems, embedded systems, and entrepreneurial engineering.

The College of Management awards bachelor's degrees in business management and information technology.

Academic Programs

Graduation from Lawrence Tech's undergraduate programs requires completion with an overall GPA of at least 2.0. Most disciplines combine a strong concentration in the major with a core curriculum of natural science, social science, humanities, and mathematics requirements.

Off-Campus Programs

Lawrence Tech students have the opportunity to participate in co-op programs, alternating semesters of classes and work. Internships are also available.

The University offers programs at Education Centers in southeastern and northern Michigan as well as international programs in Asia, Canada, Europe, Mexico, and the Middle East.

Lawrence Tech's Detroit Studio and Innovation Center gives architecture students the opportunity to explore community-based architectural, urban design, and community development projects. Architecture students also regularly build homes for Habitat for Humanity.

The Global Engineering Program arranges for Lawrence Tech engineering students to work and study abroad and brings international engineering students to campus for further study.

Lawrence Tech also offers a study-abroad program, open to all students.

Academic Facilities

Lawrence Tech is Michigan's first wireless laptop campus and all undergraduates are provided laptop or tablet computers customized with specialized software.

The library houses a wide selection of print and electronic materials, including numerous online databases and full-text periodical titles accessible on or off campus.

Lawrence Tech's modern facilities include architectural and design studios; senior project lab and studio space; fabrication labs; wind tunnel; wood, metal, and model shops; dedicated labs for constructing Baja- and Formula-style competition vehicles; physics, chemistry, biology, and tissue labs; bioengineering lab; anechoic chamber for sound studies; structural testing center; alternative energy, mechanical, and electrical labs; thermal science lab; graphics lab; clay modeling studio; and the DENSO Instructional Technology Lab.

Lawrence Tech also owns a nearby Frank Lloyd Wright–designed home that is used as a study center.

The A. Alfred Taubman Student Services Center consolidates all student support services—from admissions through career services—into a convenient one-stop center. This innovative 42,000-square-foot center utilizes energy-efficient and environmentally friendly features and technologies, serving as a living laboratory for students to study.

The Center for Innovative Materials Research is a state-of-the-art laboratory for the research, development, and testing of composite materials for defense and infrastructure applications. Students participate in related research projects as part of their academic programs.

The Automotive Engineering Institute provides students opportunities to conduct sponsored research on a unique 4 x 4 vehicle chassis dynamometer, which measures many areas of vehicle performance.

Costs

Tuition for all undergrads includes a laptop or tablet computer. The 2009–10 tuition for students majoring in arts and sciences and management was $686 per credit hour for freshmen and $734 per credit hour for sophomores. The tuition for juniors and seniors majoring in arts and sciences and management was $767 per credit hour. In architecture and design and engineering, tuition for freshmen and sophomores was $767 to $774 per credit hour; for juniors and seniors, it was $792 to $799 per credit hour.

A normal course load is 12–17 credit hours per semester. The undergraduate registration fee is $115 each semester. International students on temporary visas must have sufficient funds to pay for an entire year of tuition, room and board, and books at the time of first registration. Additional fees for specific labs and studio courses vary.

Financial Aid

Approximately 70 percent of full-time students receive financial assistance, and the University awards nearly $40 million in scholarships, grants, loans, and work-study funds each academic year. Many privately funded scholarships are awarded to qualified students, based on need and/or scholastic performance. Part-time employment is available at the University for full-time students. Student loans are also available.

Faculty

Approximately 430 full- and part-time faculty members teach at Lawrence Tech. Many part-time faculty members hold full-time jobs in industry and bring their real-world perspective to the classroom. More than 70 percent of the full-time faculty members hold a doctoral or terminal degree in their field. Faculty involvement is extensive in student chapters of professional associations that meet on campus. Many faculty members are active and/or registered professionals in their fields. Lawrence Tech's student-faculty ratio is 12:1. Most classes average 19 or fewer students, and less than 1 percent of the classes have more than 50.

Student Government

The Student Government sponsors and supports a variety of campus activities. More than fifty student clubs and organizations, including fraternities, sororities, honor societies, and student chapters of professional groups, are also active on campus.

Admission Requirements

A high school diploma or the equivalent is required of all students applying to baccalaureate or associate degree programs. Most baccalaureate applicants must have a minimum 2.5 overall GPA in academic subjects; architecture students must have a minimum 2.75 overall GPA. ACT or SAT results are required of all entering freshmen. Required high school courses vary with the curriculum, and Lawrence Tech offers a number of basic studies courses designed to augment incoming students' backgrounds if deficiencies exist.

Application and Information

Programs start in August and January. An optional summer semester begins in May. Students must submit transcripts from all schools attended, along with a nonrefundable $30 application fee. To obtain a University catalog and an application form, visit ltu.edu or contact:

Office of Admissions
Lawrence Technological University
21000 West Ten Mile Road
Southfield, Michigan 48075-1058
Phone: 800-CALL-LTU or 248-204-3160
Fax: 248-204-2228
E-mail: admissions@ltu.edu
Web site: http://www.ltu.edu

Below Lawrence Tech's new campus quadrangle are eighty-eight geothermal wells sunk 300 feet deep, which heat and cool the adjacent A. Alfred Taubman Student Services Center. *Lawrence Technological University Photo/Justin Munter.*

LEBANON VALLEY COLLEGE

ANNVILLE, PENNSYLVANIA

The College

Founded in 1866, Lebanon Valley College (LVC) was the first college east of the Alleghenies to offer higher education to both men and women. Now, 143 years later, the College remains a leader—enjoying the number two ranking on *U.S. News & World Report*'s Great Schools, Great Prices list, and for the fourteenth consecutive year, ranking among the top baccalaureate colleges in the North. A remarkable student body, an exceptional faculty, academic programs that stress experience-based education, and a groundbreaking merit-based scholarship program distinguish this private liberal arts college. Students who graduate in the top 30 percent of their high school class can receive an automatic LVC scholarship equivalent to one-quarter to one-half of the cost of tuition.

Lebanon Valley aims to educate its 1,600 students to become people of broad vision, capable of making informed decisions and prepared for a life of service to others. To that end, the College provides an education that imparts the knowledge, skills, and values necessary to live and work in a changing, diverse, and fragile world. Students obtain a solid foundation in a major of their choosing as well as wide exposure to a variety of disciplines and intellectual tools. In the process, they develop the desire and ability to think deeply, ask critical questions, solve complex problems, and communicate effectively, preparing themselves to be competitive and flexible in whatever career they pursue or challenge they encounter.

Lebanon Valley College professors strive to continue the College's proud tradition of inspired teaching with a dedication and commitment to community that has long been an LVC hallmark. A supportive intellectual community and a 13:1 student-faculty ratio ensure that students have direct access to the men and women who teach and guide them; relationships beyond the classroom are common.

One of the most significant aspects of teaching and learning at LVC comes in the form of collaborative research. Each summer, dozens of LVC students work alongside their professors as funded research assistants, contributing to important discoveries while gaining invaluable skills and experiences. Many LVC students coauthor articles in scientific journals or present their work at professional conferences while they're still in college. The College's Pleet Initiative grants support student/faculty collaboration in the humanities and social sciences, an opportunity seldom found at the undergraduate level.

LVC's strong advising, straightforward requirements, and outstanding student support services mean that almost every student is able to graduate in four years. If a student is not able to earn the LVC bachelor's degree in four years because of a course scheduling problem, the college will cover the costs of any additional course work the student needs.

LVC's fifty-five buildings provide for every aspect of college life. The College's thirty-three student residences include four apartment-style halls. Academic buildings feature enhanced classrooms with the latest technology for teaching and learning. Two student centers support community gatherings, group study, and extracurricular interests. Students enjoy a recreational sports center; a new varsity gymnasium; soccer, baseball, field hockey, and softball parks; and a state-of-the-art physical therapy facility. The baseball and soccer fields were each named National Collegiate Athletic Association (NCAA) field of the year in their respective categories, and the softball park has twice been recognized as regional field of the year.

LVC's Career Services staff helps students research careers and establish contacts with potential employers, and offers seminars on resume writing and interviewing skills. The Career Connections alumni database provides students direct access to successful alumni in their fields—men and women who have volunteered to mentor, advise, or otherwise assist LVC students or recent graduates. In an average year, approximately 80 percent of graduates who respond to an annual survey are employed, and approximately 26 percent are in graduate or professional school within six months of graduation.

Location

Annville is a small town of approximately 5,000 residents located near Pennsylvania Dutch country, just 10 minutes east of Hershey and within a 2- to 3-hour drive of Philadelphia, Baltimore, New York, and Washington, D.C. Nestled in a beautiful valley, the College is located on a 365-acre site. A wide variety of internship opportunities, potential employment options, cultural events, and other activities are available on campus and within the surrounding communities.

Majors and Degrees

The College confers five baccalaureate degrees. The Bachelor of Arts is available in American studies, art and art history, criminal justice, economics, English, French, German, historical communications, history, international studies, music, music business, philosophy, political science, religion, sociology, Spanish, and certain individualized majors.

The Bachelor of Science is available in accounting, actuarial science, biochemistry and molecular biology, biology, business administration, chemistry, computer science, cooperative engineering, cooperative forestry, digital communications, early childhood education, health-care management, health science, mathematics, music education, physics, psychobiology, psychology, and certain individualized majors.

The Bachelor of Science in Chemistry, Bachelor of Science in Medical Technology, and Bachelor of Music (with an emphasis in music recording technology) are also available.

Lebanon Valley offers master's degree programs in business, music education, and science education; a doctoral program in physical therapy; and preprofessional programs in dentistry, law, medicine, ministry, pharmacy, and veterinary medicine.

Academic Programs

Lebanon Valley has long been known for the strength of its academic programs and the achievement of its faculty members and alumni. The sciences are a particular strength, with well-equipped and up-to-date laboratories. For the past ten years, the National Science Foundation has recognized LVC among the top 15 percent of the nation's private, predominantly undergraduate institutions for producing the most Ph.D. students in biology, biochemistry, and chemistry.

Other particularly well-known and respected LVC programs include actuarial science (nearly 100 percent of graduates land high-paying jobs), physical therapy (which offers a six-year doctoral program), music (the music recording technology major is especially popular), business (which provides the fundamentals of accounting and business administration within a strong liberal arts context), and education (alumni of which are in high demand throughout the region).

Each student's academic program is complemented by a wide range of extracurricular activities. The College's more than eighty-five clubs, organizations, and other student-run initiatives mean ample opportunities for leadership. Many students choose to participate in community outreach, often by volunteering with children from surrounding communities. More than 25 percent of students play on one or more of LVC's Division III athletics teams, and many more play club or intramural sports. All students benefit from extensive campus programming that includes guest lectures, concerts, conferences, symposia, and a variety of cultural activities.

Off-Campus Programs

Students are encouraged to take advantage of numerous off-campus study opportunities offered by the College. Options abroad include programs in Argentina, Australia, England, France, Germany, Greece, Italy, the Netherlands, New Zealand, Northern Ireland, Spain, and Sweden. Internship-based programs in Washington, D.C., and Philadelphia are also popular options. A student's scholarship funding and financial aid can be transferred to any of the programs, making study abroad available to all students, regardless of their family's financial situation.

Internships are another important aspect of experience-based learning at LVC. With guidance from professors and help from professional counselors, students in every major find internship placements, gain professional experiences, and build confidence, all of which helps when it comes time to apply for a job.

Academic Facilities

While Lebanon Valley's tree-lined walkways and beautiful gardens recall campuses of yesteryear, the College teems with twenty-first-century technologies. The Bishop Library print collection contains more than 220,000 volumes and 700 periodical subscriptions. More than 7,000 popular DVDs/videos and 6,500 music CDs are available to be checked out. The library, residence halls, smart classrooms, and administrative offices are all linked to the campus wireless network, maximizing the effectiveness and mobility of learning. Well-equipped, up-to-date laboratories provide students with the tools and technologies they need to conduct cutting-edge research—independently, or in partnership with faculty.

Costs

Annual tuition for the 2010–11 school year is $30,910. Room and board charges are $8365 and fees are $710.

Financial Aid

Committed to helping all families afford the first-rate education it offers, LVC has received national recognition for its generous and distinctive merit-based scholarship program, which rewards strong high school performance with automatic merit scholarships. Students who graduate in the top 30 percent of their high school class receive an automatic LVC scholarship equivalent to one-quarter to one-half the cost of tuition.

Need-based financial assistance is also available. Last year, the College committed more than $18.5 million in merit- and need-based aid. Overall, 98 percent of LVC students receive some form of financial assistance from the College. Students and their families should complete Free Application for Federal Student Aid (FAFSA) and the LVC Financial Aid Institutional Data Form to determine eligibility. The priority deadline for filing for financial aid is March 1.

Faculty

The LVC faculty includes scientists, scholars, artists, and professionals in a wide range of fields, many of whom are respected contributors to their disciplines. LVC professors are dedicated to teaching and are drawn to the College for its close-knit community and for the opportunity to be actively involved in the students' educational growth. Most faculty members are involved in research, scholarship, and professional organizations and play an active role in helping students find internships and get started with their own research. Of LVC's 99 professors, 86 percent have earned a Ph.D. or equivalent terminal degree. The College is committed to maintaining a low student-teacher ratio of 13:1 (FTE). The average class size is 20, and all courses are taught by professors, not graduate students.

Student Government

Lebanon Valley students participate in the College's governing system through Student Government and the Student Programming Board. Student Government fosters understanding, communication, and cooperation among students, faculty, and administration. The Student Government president meets every other week with LVC president Stephen MacDonald, ensuring that there is a clear line of communication between the student body and the administration. The Student Programming Board organizes off-campus trips and schedules comedians, musicians, and other on-campus entertainment.

Admission Requirements

The LVC admission process is selective, and the applicant's academic record is the most important factor in admission decisions. The College seeks students from a variety of backgrounds as well as those who display leadership abilities, a commitment to community involvement, and special talents or interests that might benefit or enrich the LVC community. Competitive applicants will have pursued a challenging high school course of study that includes at least 4 courses in English, 2 in foreign language, 3 in mathematics, 2 in science, and 1 in social studies. Additional course work in math and science is strongly recommended. More than 70 percent of recent incoming LVC students rank among the top 30 percent of their high school class. Submission of SAT or ACT scores is optional. Advanced standing is offered through CLEP and AP examinations.

Application and Information

To apply, students should submit a completed application, a $30 application fee, and official copies of their high school transcript. Although Lebanon Valley has a rolling admission process, students are encouraged to apply during the fall of their senior year. Personal visits to campus are encouraged.

For more information, applicants should contact:

Susan Jones
Director of Admission
Lebanon Valley College
101 North College Avenue
Annville, Pennsylvania 17003-1400
Phone: 866-LVC-4ADM (866-582-423, toll-free)
Fax: 717-867-6026
E-mail: admission@lvc.edu
Web site: http://www.lvc.edu

LVC students gather for an afternoon class on the College's Academic Quad.

LE MOYNE COLLEGE

SYRACUSE, NEW YORK

The College

Le Moyne College is a four-year, coeducational Jesuit college of approximately 2,500 undergraduate students that uniquely balances a comprehensive liberal arts education with preparation for specific career paths or graduate study. Founded by the Society of Jesus in 1946, Le Moyne is the second youngest of the twenty-eight Jesuit colleges and universities in the United States. Its emphasis is on the education of the whole person and on the search for meaning and value as integral parts of an intellectual life. Le Moyne's personal approach to education is reflected in the quality of contact between students and faculty members. A wide range of student-directed activities, athletics, clubs, and service organizations complement the academic experience. Intramural sports are very popular with Le Moyne students; nearly 85 percent of the students participate. Le Moyne also has sixteen NCAA intercollegiate teams (eight for men and eight for women). Athletic facilities include soccer/lacrosse, softball, and baseball fields; tennis, basketball, and racquetball courts; a weight-training and fitness center; practice fields; and two gymnasiums. A recreation center houses an Olympic-size indoor swimming pool, jogging track, indoor tennis and volleyball courts, and additional basketball, racquetball, and fitness areas. Nearly 80 percent of students live in residence halls, apartments, and town houses on campus. The Residence Hall Councils and the Le Moyne Student Programming Board organize a variety of campus activities, including concerts, dances, a weekly film series, student talent programs, and special lectures as well as off-campus trips and skiing excursions.

Location

Le Moyne's 160-acre, tree-lined campus is located in a residential setting 10 minutes from downtown Syracuse, the heart of New York State, whose metropolitan population is about 700,000. Syracuse is convenient to most major cities throughout the Northeast, New England, and Canada and offers a wide array of shopping centers and restaurants, many near Le Moyne. Syracuse offers year-round entertainment in the form of rock concerts at the Landmark Theatre, professional baseball and hockey, Bristol Omnitheatre, the Syracuse Symphony Orchestra, Syracuse Stage, Everson Museum of Art, and the Armory Square district downtown, which offers one-of-a-kind eateries, pubs, and coffeehouses in addition to a wide variety of social and cultural events. All are easily accessible via the excellent public transportation service, which schedules regular stops on Le Moyne's campus. Just a few miles outside the city are the rolling hills, picturesque lakes, and miles of open country for which central New York is renowned. An extensive network of state and county parks, recreational areas, and other facilities offer an abundance of recreational opportunities, including swimming, boating, hiking, downhill and cross-country skiing, snowboarding, and golf.

Majors and Degrees

Le Moyne College awards the Bachelor of Arts degree in biological sciences, communication (advertising, filmmaking, print journalism, public relations, television/radio), computer science, criminology (human services, international affairs, law enforcement, research), economics, English (creative writing, literature), French, history, mathematics (actuarial science, pure mathematics, statistics), peace and global studies, philosophy, physics, political science, psychology, religious studies, sociology (anthropology, criminology and criminal justice, human services, research and theory), Spanish, and theater arts. The Bachelor of Science degree is awarded in biochemistry, biological sciences (health professions, molecular biology, neurobiology), chemistry, economics, general science, natural systems science, physics, psychology, and work and employment relations. The Bachelor of Science in business is awarded in accounting, applied management analysis, finance, information systems, management and leadership, and marketing. A Bachelor of Science in Nursing is also offered.

Students may minor in Catholic studies, classical humanities, film, gender and women's studies, Irish literature, Italian, Latin, management information systems, music, urban and regional studies, or visual arts as well as most of the major fields of study offered. Preprofessional programs are offered in dentistry, law, medicine, occupational therapy, optometry, physical therapy, physician assistant studies, podiatry, and veterinary science. Students may prepare for teaching careers through certification programs in adolescent education, dual adolescent/special education, dual childhood/special education, middle childhood specialist studies, and TESOL.

Le Moyne College and the L. C. Smith College of Engineering and Computer Science at Syracuse University offer a dual-degree program in which students may earn a bachelor's degree from Le Moyne and a master's degree in engineering from Syracuse University in as few as five years. Concentrations include aerospace; chemical, electrical, and mechanical engineering; computer science; and other fields of engineering.

Formal accelerated 3-4 programs are offered in dentistry, optometry, and podiatry in cooperation with the State University of New York at Buffalo School of Dental Medicine, Pennsylvania College of Optometry at Salus University, and the New York College of Podiatric Medicine. Predental students may also participate in an early assurance program with the State University of New York at Buffalo School of Dental Medicine. Cooperative 3-2 dual-degree programs in engineering are available with Clarkson University, Manhattan College, and University of Detroit Mercy.

SUNY Upstate Medical University in Syracuse offers students pursuing careers in the health-related professions an accelerated 3-3 doctoral-level transfer program in physical therapy as well as two-year cooperative transfer programs in medical technology, and respiratory care. Premedical students at Le Moyne are also offered the opportunity to participate in a medical school early assurance program. An early assurance program for premedical students is also available through the State University of New York at Buffalo School of Medicine.

Academic Programs

While each major department has its own sequence requirements for the minimum 120 credit hours needed for the Le Moyne degree, the College is convinced that there is a fundamental intellectual discipline that should characterize the graduate of a superior liberal arts college. Le Moyne's core curriculum provides this foundation by including studies of English language and literature, philosophy, history, religious studies, natural sciences, and social sciences.

For exceptional students, Le Moyne offers an integral honors program that includes an interdisciplinary humanities sequence as well as departmental honors courses. Le Moyne also offers a part-time course of study during evening hours through its Center for Continuing Education.

Le Moyne students may enroll in Army and Air Force ROTC programs in conjunction with Syracuse University.

Off-Campus Programs

The study-abroad program allows qualified students to spend a semester or year in almost any country throughout the world. Le Moyne College has study-abroad programs or affiliations in China, Czech Republic, Dominican Republic, Germany, Italy, Spain, and the United Kingdom. Students can also use partner programs to study in locations such as Australia, Costa Rica, Egypt, France, Ireland, Japan, and South Africa. Le Moyne is a participant in the sixty-member New York State Visiting Student Program. As part of the mission of preparing future leaders, Le Moyne College places a strong emphasis on career preparation through internships and other forms of experiential education. Academic departments and the Office of Career Services both provide programs and services for students interested in interning part-time and full-time, both locally and in major cities such as New York and Washington, D.C. The Offices of Service Learning and the Academic Deans are also involved in experiential education to promote learning outside the classroom. In the sciences, students take part in campus research with mentor faculty members. Others receive assistance in pursuing outstanding opportunities off campus in leading research laboratories and health-care settings. The College has maintained a long-standing relationship with the "Washington center" internship programs, where students from all majors complete full-time semester-long internships in Washington, D.C., with government, business, or major nonprofit organizations. Faculty members in the Political Science Department assist students interested in opportunities in Albany, New York State's seat of government, with either the New York State Senate or Assembly. Finally, the education programs at Le Moyne put students into school classrooms starting immediately as freshmen and continuing each year until graduation.

Academic Facilities

Le Moyne students benefit from an ongoing commitment to technological excellence. The College's thirty-four buildings are equipped with accounting, biology, chemistry, computer science, physics, psychology, and statistics laboratories. The W. Carroll Coyne Center for the Performing Arts houses generous production, performance, and classroom space; the latest light and sound technology; scene and costume shops; an aerobics and dance studio; and rehearsal rooms for instrumental and choral music. Academic facilities also include an extensively renovated color television studio; a radio/recording studio; a receiver-antenna satellite dish; transmission and scanning electron microscopes; a nuclear magnetic resonance spectrometer; a gas chromatograph/mass spectrophotometer; a 230,000-volume, open-stack library; and extensive on-site computer facilities. A fiber-optic network enables students to access the library system, the campus network, and the Internet from several computer labs around the campus or from their personal computers in their rooms. All classrooms have been converted to smart classrooms, with multimedia capabilities that expand and enrich the learning process. Le Moyne students have access to other libraries through the Central New York Library Resources Council, and the campus Academic Support Center is available to students for instructional support.

Costs

For 2009–10, Le Moyne's tuition was $25,110. Room and board charges were $9990. Additional fees amounted to approximately $700, and books and supplies cost approximately $700.

Financial Aid

Financial aid is offered to a large percentage of Le Moyne's students through scholarships, grants, loans, and work-study assignments. Le Moyne offers a generous program of merit-based academic and athletic scholarships as well as financial aid based on a student's need and academic promise. Federal funds are available through the Federal Pell Grant, Federal Work-Study, Federal Supplemental Educational Opportunity Grant, and Federal Perkins Loan programs. A student's eligibility for need-based financial aid is determined from both the Free Application for Federal Student Aid (FAFSA) and the Le Moyne Financial Aid Application Form. It is recommended that these forms be mailed by February 1.

Faculty

The Le Moyne full-time faculty numbers 158 men and women; 94 percent have earned the highest degree in their field. With an average class size of 20, a student-faculty ratio of 13:1, and private offices for all full-time faculty members, the College promotes a personal as well as an academic relationship between students and faculty members. All classroom instruction is done by faculty members, and they are happy to assist and encourage students who wish to pursue undergraduate research through tutorials or senior research projects. These projects are carried out in an atmosphere free of competition from graduate students for books, laboratories, or professors' time. Le Moyne emphasizes advising and academic counseling for students throughout their four years.

Student Government

The College encourages student leadership in all activities. Positions of leadership are open to students in all class years. Students are represented by a Student Senate and have formal representation through the senate on most College-wide committees involved in decision making and policy formation.

Admission Requirements

Le Moyne seeks qualified students who are well prepared for serious academic study. Secondary school preparation must have included at least 17 college-preparatory high school units, 4 of which must be in English, 4 in social studies, 3–4 in mathematics, 3–4 in foreign language, and 3–4 in science. It is also recommended that prospective science and mathematics majors complete 4 units of mathematics and science. The SAT or ACT is required and should be taken by December or January of the senior year in high school. Campus visits are strongly recommended, as the admission process is a personal one. As bases for selection, academic achievement and secondary school recommendations are of primary importance. SAT or ACT scores are important as they relate to the record of achievement and to recommendations. Out-of-state students are encouraged to apply.

Application and Information

The Admission Committee reviews applications and mails decisions on a rolling admission cycle beginning January 1. The priority deadline for applications is February 1; all students who wish to be considered for academic merit scholarships should have a completed application on file in the Office of Admission before this date. Students who wish to be considered under the early-decision program must have a completed application submitted by December 1. Early-decision applicants are notified by December 15. Transfer students are encouraged to apply before June 1 for the fall semester and December 1 for the spring semester. Orientation programs for incoming freshmen and transfer students take place in midsummer.

Dennis J. Nicholson
Director of Admission
Le Moyne College
Syracuse, New York 13214-1399
Phone: 315-445-4300
800-333-4733 (toll-free)
E-mail: admission@lemoyne.edu
Web site: http://www.lemoyne.edu

Grewen Hall, the oldest building on campus, overlooks Le Moyne's beautiful 160-acre campus.

COLLEGE CLOSE-UPS

LESLEY UNIVERSITY

CAMBRIDGE, MASSACHUSETTS

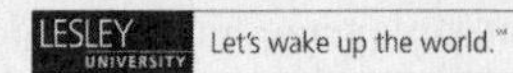

The College

Lesley College prepares young men and women for careers that matter and lives that make a difference. The combination of expert faculty, stimulating classes, hands-on learning, career-focused internships, and exciting cocurricular activities transform, inspire, and prepare students to become catalysts and leaders of social change in their careers and in their communities. Whether embarking on their first professional position—95 percent of Lesley students have jobs within six months of graduation—or pursuing graduate study, students leave Lesley ready to make a difference in the world around them.

As one of four colleges that comprise Lesley University, Lesley College integrates the advantages of a small learning community with the academic and cocurricular resources of a large university. Students are able to cross-register for courses in the other schools at Lesley University, including The Art Institute of Boston. Five- and six-year Accelerated Bachelor's/Master's programs have been developed in conjunction with the School of Education and the Graduate School of Arts and Social Sciences. In addition, the Lesley Dividend offers qualified Lesley College students up to 12 free credits of graduate study in one of Lesley's on-campus master's degree programs.

Located steps from Harvard Square and minutes from downtown Boston, Lesley College offers the University's more than 1,400 undergraduates small classes taught by accomplished University faculty members (not graduate students); more than fifty majors, minors, and specializations in the liberal arts and the professions (art therapy, communications, counseling, education, expressive arts therapy, human services, management, the environment, and the arts), including an honors program; and the opportunity to design their own program of study. Most importantly, Lesley students participate in field-based internships that begin freshman year, and complete between 450 and 600 hours of significant career-related experience.

The University is accredited by the New England Association of Schools and Colleges. The teacher certification programs have been approved by the National Association of State Directors of Teacher Education and Certification (NASDTEC), which offers a reciprocity agreement in which more than forty states and other organizations have established standards for granting certification.

Location

The Lesley campus is a mix of modern and Victorian-era buildings, located in Cambridge, right next to Harvard Law School, a quick walk from Harvard Square, and a short subway ride from Boston. The Boston/Cambridge area has everything: bookstores, cafés, theaters, concert halls, parks, festivals, professional sports teams, and students. In fact, nearly 230,000 students live in the "neighborhood," making it America's ultimate college town. Because of their educational, scientific, and business resources, a global political lens, and an outstanding cultural scene, both cities aptly support the many and varied internships in which our students are engaged. Additionally, the "T", or subway system, takes people wherever they need to go including the airport and train stations, providing connections to all regions of the United States and the world.

Majors and Degrees

Lesley College offers Bachelor of Science and Bachelor of Arts degrees in the following liberal arts and professional areas: art–studio (design, illustration, photography), art history, art therapy, business management (marketing, not-for-profit, sport management, arts management), child and family studies, communication (integrated business, technology, visual), counseling, creative writing, education, English (drama, literature), environmental science, environmental studies, expressive arts therapy, global studies, health, history (American studies, European and world studies), holistic psychology, honors program, human services, mathematics, natural science, political science, psychology, sociology, and undecided, as well as self-designed programs of study in such areas as foreign language, health studies, intercultural relations, international management, leadership and social policy, and prelaw. All undergraduate students at The Art Institute of Boston at Lesley University earn Bachelor of Fine Arts degrees.

Students who are interested in teaching major in one of the following areas: early childhood education, early learning (not a licensure program), elementary education, middle school education, secondary education, or special education. These students are also required to elect a double major in one of nine liberal arts areas. Completion of a major in education qualifies a student to be recommended for initial licensure in Massachusetts and the other states that are members of NASDTEC and have signed the Interstate Contract.

In conjunction with Lesley's graduate programs, the following accelerated bachelor's/master's degree programs are offered: a B.S./M.A. in art therapy, clinical mental health counseling, counseling psychology, or expressive arts therapy, and a B.A./M.Ed. in early childhood education, elementary education, and middle school education.

Academic Programs

All of Lesley's academic programs are designed to integrate study in the liberal arts with professional course work and significant hands-on internship experience.

Internship experiences begin in the freshman year and are developmentally sequenced to complement classroom instruction throughout the undergraduate program. Internships are designed to show students what the workplace is like, challenge assumptions they may have about themselves and the world, and give the kind of experience that creates exceptional resumes. The internships are linked with seminar classes in which students discuss and evaluate their fieldwork, learning also from fellow students' experiences about workplace issues and emerging trends. It is this careful integration of theory and practice that distinguishes Lesley's curriculum from those at other colleges, providing students with a critical understanding of the real-world demands of their profession and the leadership skills necessary to succeed.

Through a comprehensive general education program, students also build a strong liberal arts foundation by taking courses in the arts, humanities, sciences, and social sciences. It is through their liberal arts coursework that students develop their ability to think critically and analytically, become creative problem solvers and strengthen their writing skills. Lesley's goal is to build a culture of life-long learning.

Off-Campus Programs

Lesley University offers students the opportunity to participate in a number of Lesley-affiliated programs of off-campus study, in the United States and abroad.

Lesley students have studied in Florence, Hong Kong, Madrid, Prague, and Washington, D.C., as well as francophone Africa, China, Costa Rica, England, Ireland, and Sweden. In addition, planned travel study tours led by distinguished members of the faculty offer students the chance to discover the history, culture, and art of various regions or gain an in-depth understanding of significant world events. Previous tours have included Bali; the British Experience; the Cuban Experience in Education and the Arts; Ecuador: Wisdom of Indigenous Peoples; Learning from the Holocaust; Morocco; People and Culture of Mexico; Tibet; Traditions and Cultures of the Southwest, and the sacred spaces of India.

Academic Facilities

Sherrill Library houses more than 225,000 items and offers access to over 95 databases and more than 50,000 e-books. Study space, information literacy instruction, and technical support are available for all members of the Lesley community. The Teaching Resources Center, in the lower level of the library building, houses both a unique collection of teaching resource materials and an excellent juvenile literature collection.

Lesley is a member of the Fenway Library Consortium (FLC), a cooperating group of sixteen libraries in the Boston area that allows students and faculty access to all collections. Lesley is also affiliated with the Fenway Libraries Online, which allows direct online borrowing privileges and book delivery from additional Boston art libraries.

Lesley's state-of-the-art science labs are housed at University Hall. Their unique design emphasizes the integration of theory and practice.

Costs

Fees in 2010–11 for enrollment in Lesley College include tuition, $29,150; room and board, $12,800; a health services fee, $800 (estimate); and a student activity fee, $250. Costs are subject to change without prior notice. Students should call the University to confirm current expense figures.

Financial Aid

No student should fail to consider Lesley because of financial concerns. More than 80 percent of Lesley College students receive financial aid from one or more sources. The average financial aid package for last year's entering class, not including loans and work-study, was over $17,000.

The University participates in all federal aid programs, including the Federal Pell Grant, Federal Supplemental Educational Opportunity Grant, Federal Perkins Loan, and Federal Work-Study programs. Lesley also offers its own grants and need-based scholarships, as well as guaranteed merit scholarships, ranging from $13,000 to full tuition.

Students applying for financial aid must submit the Free Application for Federal Student Aid (FAFSA) and request that copies of the analyses be sent to Lesley University. Students applying for the fall term are advised to file the FAFSA by February 1.

Faculty

Lesley College faculty members hold the teaching of undergraduates as their highest priority. Even more important to a student's classroom experience, however, is the fact that many members of the faculty are trained practitioners, classroom educators, counselors, social workers, and business professionals. In fact, many continue to work in the field or as consultants and bring a wealth of real-world experience into their classroom teaching.

Of the 245 full- and part-time faculty members, more than two thirds hold a doctorate or other terminal degree. Faculty members serve as academic advisers for students, and the student-faculty ratio of 13:1 allows for a close relationship to develop between students and their professors.

Student Government

The Student Government is the representative governing body of the Lesley College student population. Through its sponsorship, numerous organizations, activities, seminars, and conferences are brought to the Lesley campus.

Admission Requirements

Lesley College has designed the admission process to be reflective of the institution and its values. Lesley is an institution that values community and service to the community. Therefore, the College is interested in students who value making a difference in the lives of others and who have shown a commitment to community service. Lesley also seeks students who, through a strong college-preparatory curriculum, have gained the knowledge and skills that allow them to thrive and be successful in the academic programs. Graduates of accredited secondary schools with a total of 20 college-preparatory units of study are encouraged to apply for admission. Included in the 20 units are the following: English, 4 units; mathematics, at least 3 units (including algebra II); science, at least 3 units (including at least one lab course); and U.S. history, 1 unit. Please refer to the Lesley Web site for a full list of required admission credentials.

Students who have been fully matriculated in a degree program at another college or university may apply for admission as transfers. Transfer applicants must present a minimum cumulative grade point average of 2.5. The maximum number of credit hours that may be transferred is 65. Advanced standing is determined by the nature and quality of the work offered for credit.

Application and Information

Applications are reviewed on a rolling basis beginning December 1, with a first-year early action deadline of December 1, a regular admission deadline of February 15, and a transfer application deadline of May 1 for the fall semester. All applications for the spring semester are due by December 1. A $50 application fee must accompany all freshman and transfer applications. Apply online and Lesley will waive the $50 application fee.

For further information about Lesley, students should contact:

Office of Admissions
Lesley College
29 Everett Street
Cambridge, Massachusetts 02138-2790
Phone: 617-349-8800
800-999-1959 Ext. 8800 (toll-free)
E-mail: lcadmissions@lesley.edu
Web site: http://www.lesley.edu/lc/college

LEWIS & CLARK COLLEGE

PORTLAND, OREGON

The College

Founded in 1867 in a small town south of Portland, Lewis & Clark College moved to its present location in Portland's southwest hills in 1942. The 137-acre campus is situated in a wooded residential area 6 miles from the center of the city and overlooks the lush Willamette Valley and Mount Hood in the distance.

The student body is known for its geographic diversity. In fall 2008, of the 1,921 undergraduates, 16 percent were from Oregon, and 84 percent came from forty-six other states plus the District of Columbia and fifty-eight countries. Approximately 65 percent live in housing on campus, most of which is coed (91 percent). There are no fraternities or sororities.

The College offers numerous co-curricular activities, including twelve music groups; nine media organizations; ten religious/spiritual life groups; eighteen international, cultural, and diversity groups; and more than fifty student organizations. Cultural events such as lectures, symposia, art exhibits, theater productions, concerts, recitals, and dance performances occur on a regular basis. Currently, there are nineteen NCAA Division III varsity athletic teams, nine club teams, and numerous intramural sports. Athletic facilities include three basketball courts, a competition-size swimming pool, a weight-training room, a stadium, a baseball/softball complex, and six tennis courts, three of which are covered by an airdome. The renowned College Outdoors Program offers adventures such as backpacking, rafting, skiing, snowshoeing, caving, winter camping, sea kayaking, and environmental service projects in Oregon's and Washington's nearby wilderness areas.

Location

Portland has long been known for its livability and its excellent transportation system. Public buses and a free College shuttle run from the Lewis & Clark campus to the center of Portland, 6 miles away. The metropolitan area (population 2 million) is bisected by the Willamette River. Mount Hood, offering skiing ten months per year, is 50 miles away, and Oregon's rugged coastline lies 90 miles to the west. The city has 10,447 acres of parks, thirty-three music associations, thirty-five theater and dance companies, more than ninety galleries and museums, and more than 1,000 restaurants. Professional sports teams compete in baseball, hockey, and NBA basketball.

Majors and Degrees

Lewis & Clark offers programs leading to the Bachelor of Arts degree. Academic majors include art (art history and studio art), biochemistry and molecular biology, biology, chemistry, communications, computer science, computer science and mathematics, East Asian studies, economics, English, environmental studies, foreign languages, French studies, German studies, Hispanic studies, history, international affairs, mathematics, music, philosophy, physics, political science, psychology, religious studies, sociology/anthropology, and theater. Students may also design a major or pursue a double major and numerous minors. Preprofessional programs are available in education, health sciences, and law.

Dual-degree (3-2 and 4-2) programs in engineering are offered in cooperation with Columbia University, Washington University (St. Louis), the University of Southern California, and the Oregon Graduate Institute. A 4-2 B.A./M.B.A. program is offered in cooperation with the University of Rochester's Simon Graduate School of Business Administration. A 4-1 B.A./M.A.T. program is offered through Lewis & Clark's Graduate School of Education and Counseling.

Academic Programs

The liberal arts curriculum offers sufficient structure to ensure depth and breadth of study, but it also incorporates a high degree of freedom in order to promote creative and critical thinking. In the four-year plan of study, approximately one third of a student's time is devoted to general education, one third to a major program, and one third to elective courses. Students are also encouraged to participate in departmental honors programs, undergraduate research, independent study, and internships.

The academic calendar consists of two 15-week semesters. A normal load is four 4-semester-hour academic courses, plus one or more activity courses. By graduation a student is expected to have earned at least 128 semester hours—equivalent, roughly, to eight different classes a year. The fall semester begins early in September and ends before Christmas, and the spring semester begins in mid-January and ends in early May. There are also a limited number of courses offered during two summer sessions.

The community of scholars at Lewis & Clark College is dedicated to personal and academic excellence. Joining the Lewis & Clark community obligates each member to observe the principles of mutual respect, academic integrity, civil discourse, and responsible decision making.

Off-Campus Programs

Lewis & Clark offers nationally recognized international and off-campus study opportunities that have been in existence for more than forty-seven years. Approximately twenty-five different overseas study programs and two domestic programs are available annually. Usually, 20 to 24 students plus a faculty leader participate in each program. More than half of the College's graduates have taken advantage of these outstanding programs, often satisfying General Education or major requirements at the same time.

Overseas study may have either a general-culture focus or a specialized academic focus. On general-culture programs, students become immersed in the everyday life of the host country by living with local families, traveling, studying in classes and seminars, and working on independent projects. Programs with a more specific academic focus may include studying German language and literature in Munich; perfecting language skills in France, Ecuador, Russia, Japan, or China; or studying literature in England. Sites for overseas study programs from 2010 through 2013 are Australia, Chile, China, Cuba, Dominican Republic, Ecuador, England, France, Germany, Ghana, Greece, India, Italy, Japan, Kenya/Tanzania, Morocco, New Zealand, Russia, Scotland, Senegal, Spain, and Vietnam. Domestic programs are available in the Arizona borderlands, New York, and Washington, D.C., for those interested in immigration, economics, political science, sociology, theater, or art. Students receive academic credit on all programs, both overseas and domestic.

Academic Facilities

The Aubrey R. Watzek Library (open 24 hours per day when school is in session) houses more than 300,000 volumes and includes electronic access to thousands of periodical titles. Its mission is to provide a solid core of materials designed to support the curriculum and the research needs of the Lewis & Clark community. The library offers individualized reference assistance in the use of both print and electronic resources. The library's Web site provides access to its catalog as well as to a full range of electronic databases and links to useful Internet resources. The library is a member of Summit, a consortium of thirty-six academic libraries that have a unified catalog that enables students to request and receive materials from member libraries within two days.

Music department facilities include Evans Auditorium, a 400-seat recital hall equipped with an orchestra pit and stage elevator; an extensive (more than 4,000) record, CD, and tape collection; twenty-two practice rooms; forty-three pianos, including several 6- and 7-foot concert grands and a 9-foot Steinway concert grand; two harpsichords; a Baroque organ; an electronic music studio with CD production capability; Zimbabwe marimbas; and an Indonesian gamelan orchestra. The 600-seat chapel houses an 85-rank Casavant organ.

The Fields Center for the Visual Arts is equipped with studio space for painting, drawing, ceramics, sculpture, design, and printmaking as well as a photography lab. The department also has a Visual Resources Collection of 50,000 slides and several thousand digital images representing artwork from a wide range of media, time periods, world regions, and cultures. The collection exists to support instruction in the art department as well as historical and cultural studies campuswide. The arts center contains gallery and classroom space as well. The humanities and social sciences also enjoy state-of-the-art classroom and lab facilities.

The natural sciences are housed in the Biology/Psychology, BoDine, and Olin Buildings, which are well equipped with modern instrumentation to support the College's emphasis on collaborative student-faculty research. These buildings contain numerous research laboratories and equipment, used by students in classes or research projects, in addition to teaching labs and classrooms. Among the notable facilities are a laboratory for the study of human-computer interactions, a scanning electron microscope, a modern greenhouse, an astronomical observatory with several telescopes, a molecular modeling laboratory equipped with high-speed computers, a laboratory for the study of parallel computing, a laboratory for studying the biomechanics of animal locomotion, and an astrophysics laboratory that is equipped to remotely operate and acquire data from a specialized telescope at Kitts Peak, Arizona. All labs are computerized for acquiring and analyzing data and are networked to allow sharing and acquisition of data remotely. Ecological investigations and studies of the environmental impacts of human activity can be conducted both on the College's heavily wooded campus and at the nearby Tryon Creek State Park.

Computer facilities include several computer laboratories in academic buildings that are for student use. More than 130 Macintosh, IBM, and compatible computers are available for student use, along with peripherals such as color scanners, color printers, digital cameras, and digital video editing. All residence halls have direct Internet access. Parts of the campus also have wireless network capability.

Costs

Tuition and fees for 2009–10 are $35,233. The room and board charge is $9006 for fourteen (flex) meals per week; other meal plans are also available. The estimate for books and personal expenses is $2040.

Financial Aid

In 2008–09, 69 percent of the College's students received some form of financial assistance. Institutional, state, and federal resources, including Federal Pell Grants, Federal Supplemental Educational Opportunity Grants, Federal Perkins Loans, and Federal Work-Study awards, may be part of an aid award. Other options include low-interest Federal Stafford Student Loans and opportunities to work on and off campus. To receive priority consideration for need-based financial aid, students must meet appropriate deadlines for admission and should submit the Free Application for Federal Student Aid (FAFSA) and the CSS/Financial Aid PROFILE application by February 15.

Merit-based awards are offered to exceptional students who are selected as Neely Scholars (up to ten full-tuition scholarships), Trustee Scholars (up to ten half-tuition scholarships), Dean's Scholars (one-quarter tuition), and Leadership and Service Award recipients (one-quarter tuition). Students designated as National Merit finalists with Lewis & Clark officially named as their first choice receive $1000.

Faculty

The 139 full-time members of the faculty are committed to undergraduate teaching and advising and are also active in research, writing, and publishing. Involving students in the research process is of high priority. Ninety-seven percent of the full-time faculty members hold a Ph.D. or the highest advanced degree in their discipline. The student-faculty ratio is 12:1. The average class size is 19, with 86 percent of classes having 29 or fewer students.

Student Government

The Associated Students of Lewis & Clark (ASLC) has a decentralized structure that encourages co-curricular participation by students and places a high priority on participation with faculty and staff in the process of enriching the academic environment. ASLC consists of a Student Senate, governing boards, and appointed students who serve on faculty constitutional, standing, and special committees. The 33 members of the Student Academic Affairs Board (SAAB) are appointed on a departmental basis to solicit, evaluate, and support undergraduate and faculty research, instruction, curriculum, and program enhancement. One quarter of the total ASLC budget of more than $400,000 is used by SAAB in support of undergraduate research grants and speakers.

Admission Requirements

Lewis & Clark College seeks first-year and transfer applicants who are committed to academic excellence and personal growth. Admission is competitive. Applications are carefully reviewed and examined for degree of academic preparation, ability to express ideas in essay form, participation in activities, citizenship and community service, and support given by the school through recommendations. Campus visits are encouraged. Interviews are available but not required. Recommended high school preparation includes 4 years of English, 4 years of history or social science, 4 years of mathematics, 3 years of laboratory science, 2 to 3 years of foreign language, and 1 year of fine arts. The SAT or ACT is required, unless the student is applying via the Portfolio Path.

Application and Information

First-year applicants should submit the Common Application (online or paper); the required Common Application Supplement; a personal essay; an official academic transcript, including senior grades from the first marking period; one recommendation from a counselor; and at least one reference from an academic teacher. The application fee is waived if the applicant uses the online Common Application. Application deadlines for the fall semester are November 1 for nonbinding Early Action (notification by January 1) and February 1 for Regular Decision (notification by April 1).

Transfer applicants are evaluated on a rolling basis. To ensure full consideration, the College strongly recommends that transfer students submit all credentials before the end of March.

The application deadline for first-year and transfer students for the spring semester is November 1 (notification within three weeks of file completion). The optional Portfolio Path admissions program provides an opportunity for applicants who have shown exceptional academic initiative to demonstrate the full extent of their pursuits by presenting a portfolio of their academic work. Under this plan, SAT or ACT scores are optional.

For more information about Lewis & Clark College or to arrange a visit, students should contact:

Office of Admissions
Lewis & Clark College
0615 Southwest Palatine Hill Road
Portland, Oregon 97219-7899
Phone: 503-768-7040
800-444-4111 (toll-free)
Fax: 503-768-7055
E-mail: admissions@lclark.edu
Web site: http://www.lclark.edu

LEWIS UNIVERSITY

ROMEOVILLE, ILLINOIS

The University

Lewis University is a coeducational, comprehensive, Catholic, and Lasallian university located in the Midwest, 30 minutes from Chicago, Illinois. Lewis shows its commitment to high-quality, mission-based education by providing approximately 85 percent of its new incoming students with some form of financial aid. The main campus is a picturesque 376-acre setting with twelve residence halls that house 1,300 students within walking distance of all campus buildings.

Lewis has been strengthened by the educational mission of the De La Salle Christian Brothers and their colleagues. Since arriving on the campus in 1960, the Christian Brothers have been the providers of a high-quality education and personal attention based on the heritage of their founder, Saint John Baptist de La Salle. The student-faculty ratio of 13:1 ensures that students interact with their instructors. Lewis is large enough to offer the resources of a university while maintaining personal contact with each student. It is now the ninth largest private, not-for-profit university in Illinois, with 5,900 students.

The Lewis education includes small classes, service-learning opportunities, a beautiful and safe campus environment, an ideal location, and an active campus life. These elements combine to provide an educational experience that focuses on career preparation, academic choices, community service, and lifelong learning. Lewis has positioned itself as an academic leader and is recognized for its commitment to mission effectiveness.

The majority of Lewis students are Illinois residents, but students represent more than thirty-six states and twenty-five countries. Campus residence halls allow for various living styles, including apartment and suite arrangements. More than thirty clubs and organizations offer students opportunities for a variety of social, athletic, academic, career, or hobby-related interests. Eighteen intercollegiate sports include men's and women's basketball, cross-country, golf, soccer, swimming, track, tennis, and volleyball plus men's baseball and women's softball. All teams compete in NCAA Division II. Lewis teams have captured the Great Lakes Valley Conference (GLVC) All-Sports Trophy twelve times, more than any other conference member. Lewis student-athletes also excel in the classroom; the University produced another Academic All-American in 2008–09, giving it 9 recipients of that prestigious award in the past seven years, and was second in GLVC in the number of Academic All-GLVC honorees (113).

On the graduate level, the University offers programs leading to the Master of Business Administration (M.B.A.); the Master of Arts (M.A.) in counseling psychology, education, organizational leadership, and school counseling and guidance; the Master of Education (M.Ed.); the Master of Science (M.S.) in aviation and transportation, criminal/social justice, information security, management, and public safety administration; and the Master of Science in Nursing (M.S.N.). An M.S.N./M.B.A. option is also available. A Certificate of Advanced Study (C.A.S.) leading to a superintendent endorsement or a general administrative endorsement is available as is a Doctor of Education (Ed.D.) in educational leadership for teaching and learning.

Location

Located in Romeoville, Illinois, Lewis is only 30 minutes southwest of Chicago. This allows students to take advantage of the resources of one of the nation's largest cities while enjoying the beautiful suburban campus. Shopping and recreational facilities are located nearby.

Majors and Degrees

Lewis University offers programs leading to the Bachelor of Arts (B.A.) degree in art studio, athletic training, biochemistry, biology, broadcast journalism, business studies, chemistry, communication studies, communication technology, computer graphic design, computer science, contemporary global studies, criminal/social justice, drawing, education, English, environmental science, fire service administration, forensic criminal investigation, history, human resource management, illustration, international business, liberal arts, mathematics, multimedia journalism, multimedia production, music, music merchandising, painting, paralegal studies, philosophy, philosophy of law, physics, print journalism, private security/loss prevention management, psychology, public relations, radio and television broadcasting, social work, sociology, special education, sport management, theater, and theology.

Programs leading to a Bachelor of Science (B.S.) degree include accountancy, biochemistry, business administration, chemistry, chemical physics, computer information systems, computer science, dental hygiene, diagnostic medical sonography, economics, environmental science, finance, information security and risk management, marketing, mathematics, nuclear medicine technology, physics, political science, public administration, radiation therapy, and vascular ultrasound technology.

Preprofessional programs are offered in chiropractic medicine, dentistry, engineering, law, medicine, optometry, pharmacy, physical therapy, physician assistant studies, and veterinary medicine.

To prepare students for careers in aviation, the University offers B.S. degree programs in aviation administration, aviation flight management, aviation maintenance management, aviation security, avionics, and a new program in air traffic control, as well as Associate of Science (A.S.) degree programs in air traffic control, aviation flight management, and aviation maintenance technology. Certificate programs are offered in aircraft dispatch and aviation maintenance technology.

The Bachelor of Science in Nursing (B.S.N.) degree is offered in the College of Nursing and Health Professions.

The Bachelor of Elected Studies (B.E.S.) degree and a liberal arts degree may be pursued by students whose educational and career goals lead them to combine course work from several areas. The B.E.S. degree allows students to develop their own major by choosing a concentration from any area of the University. The liberal arts degree permits them to combine two minors into a major.

In addition to its nearly eighty undergraduate majors and programs of study, Lewis offers interdisciplinary courses in women's studies and ethnic and cultural studies. Accelerated programs for working adults are available in applied sociology and political science, business administration, fire service administration, health-care leadership, human resource management, information technology management, management, organizational leadership, and RN/B.S.N. completion.

Lewis University's Scholars Academy allows eligible students in every major to enhance their educational opportunities through intensive projects that are arranged by contract with faculty members. Open to all undergraduates, membership in the Scholars Academy requires an ACT score of 24 or higher or a grade point average of 3.25 (B) or better. Members of the Scholars Academy who successfully complete Scholars Activities are awarded a Scholars Diploma upon graduation.

Academic Programs

The undergraduate curriculum has three parts: general education, major required courses, and elective courses. The general education requirements include courses in the humanities and the social or natural sciences that are designed to introduce the student to liberal culture. Requirements for the student's chosen major provide the opportunity for a greater depth of study in one academic field. Electives allow the student to select additional courses that are suited to his or her educational needs. The emphasis on humanities and communication arts in the undergraduate curriculum provides students with the knowledge of history and of the human experience necessary to develop an awareness of and responsiveness to contemporary social issues. Qualified students may receive academic credit through Advanced Placement and CLEP testing and for prior learning.

Students selecting majors in the College of Arts and Sciences discover that course work has been developed to foster critical thinking, open inquiry, precision in thought and expression, and familiarity with a broad range of knowledge. The College of Business seeks to educate individuals who are competent in the functional areas of business and who can recognize the responsibilities of business to the political, social, and economic segments of society. Many of the courses taken by business students are selected from the liberal arts area.

Similarly, the College of Nursing and Health Professions and the College of Education build on a foundation of liberal education. Nursing students take a concentration of natural and behavioral sciences, humanities, and electives during the first two years. The nursing major course work is taken primarily at the upper-division level, with clinical experience acquired in hospitals and other health-care facilities. The nursing program prepares nursing practitioners who are competent to deliver health-care services in many situations.

The College of Education prepares future and current teachers and administrators to meet the diverse needs of all students. Students can major in elementary education, special education, or secondary education. The college offers teacher education programs for secondary certification in English/language arts, mathematics, science (designation in biology, chemistry, or physics), and social science (designation in history or psychology). A combined certification in elementary education and special education also is offered.

The University operates on a semester system. The fall semester begins the Monday before Labor Day, and the spring semester starts in early January. Summer school sessions are six, eight, or ten weeks in length. A May term offers students the option of taking a four-week class at the end of the spring semester. Accelerated programs offer nine sessions per year in five-week and eight-week formats.

Academic Facilities

Lewis is committed to providing learners with access to modern educational technology, including computer labs, networks, Internet access, e-mail, classroom media, and distributed learning resources. Lewis is connected to the Illinois Century Network (ICN), which provides Internet access to schools and other educational entities in the state. The campus network includes a high-speed, fiber-optic backbone to all buildings. The main campus is entirely wireless.

All students receive a campus e-mail address. Staffed computer labs are available during generous hours in all major classroom buildings and provide access to a host of campus resources, including software applications, Web support for classes, library materials, and Internet searching. Lewis also provides specialized computer labs, which are supported for digital music, journalism, writing, graphic arts, nursing, aviation, computer science, and tutoring.

The University Library houses nearly 150,000 volumes and an extensive microfiche and microfilm collection and is a depository for U.S. government documents. Besides housing a specialized music collection and an art-print collection, the library is home to the Archives of the Illinois and Michigan Canal Heritage Corridor. Online public-access terminals are available for use in the Lewis library. Patrons may access the University's card catalog as well as the holdings of more than sixty other academic libraries in Illinois through this computerized system. More than 80 different periodical databases are also available through computer access; many of these full-text and more specialized databases are added each semester.

The Department of Aviation is housed in the $2.5-million Harold E. White Aviation Center, which is located next to the Lewis University Airport. The airport, which houses more than 300 aircraft, is the site of flight-training and management programs.

Costs

Tuition for 2009–10 full-time students (12 to 18 semester hours) was $22,990, while yearly room and board costs averaged $8350, depending on room size and the meal plan chosen. General service fees and student activity fees are included in the tuition.

Financial Aid

Lewis University is committed to helping all students who need financial assistance. Besides assisting students in obtaining federal and state grants, Federal Work-Study Program jobs, or loans (repayable after graduation), the University offers academic and athletic scholarships as well as additional Lewis grants to students with demonstrated financial needs. To be considered for any financial assistance, a student must apply for federal, state, and Lewis aid, using the appropriate forms. Additional information is available from the University's Office of Admission or the Office of Financial Aid Services.

Faculty

The Lewis University faculty places a strong emphasis on scholarship and personal contact. The greater majority of the general faculty members hold doctoral degrees, and 100 percent of the members of the aviation faculty hold FAA-approved licenses. In addition, because the student-faculty ratio is 13:1, classes tend to be close-knit, enhancing the opportunities for extensive interaction between faculty members and students, both in class and through office hours.

Student Government

The Student Governing Board (SGB), which has 11 student members, consists of the Presidents of each of the seven councils: the Commuter Council, the Cultural Awareness Council, the Honorary Organization Council, the Interfratority Council, the Interorganizational Council, the Pan Hellenic Council, and the Residence Hall Council. Four at-large members are appointed by the Office of Student Services. The SGB works to develop an effective activity program, reviews the quality of student life, oversees the effective functioning and financing of student organizations, represents student needs and concerns to the University's administration, and serves as the judicial body in overseeing organizational conduct.

Admission Requirements

Lewis University welcomes candidates for admission who present a strong record of academic success and high motivation. Freshman candidates are required to present ACT or SAT results as well as a record of high school work. Students whose main language is not English also must present a score of at least 500 on the Test of English as a Foreign Language (TOEFL). Applicants for the nursing program also must have taken one year of chemistry, one year of biology, and at least one year of algebra.

Transfer students with fewer than 12 semester hours should apply in the same manner as freshman applicants. Transfer students with 12 or more college credits may be admitted to the College of Arts and Sciences if they have maintained an overall GPA of 2.0 or higher. (The College of Education, the College of Nursing and Health Professions, and the College of Business have additional transfer requirements. For more information, students should contact the transfer coordinator in the Office of Admission.) Most transfer students have all college credits accepted. However, for the Lewis degree, a maximum of 72 credit hours may be transferred from community colleges.

Application and Information

Application forms for admission and financial aid may be obtained online at http://www.lewisu.edu/apply or from the Office of Admission. Freshman applicants should submit the application for admission, ACT or SAT scores, and high school transcripts. Transfer applicants who have earned 12 or more credit hours should submit transcripts from each college or university attended and the completed admission application.

Dean of Admission
Lewis University
One University Parkway
Romeoville, Illinois 60446-2200
Phone: 800-897-9000 (toll-free)
E-mail: admissions@lewisu.edu
Web site: http://www.lewisu.edu

Lewis University offers a sprawling campus of more than 376 acres, including twelve residence halls. All campus buildings are within easy walking distance. Pictured is the Brother Paul French, FSC, Learning Resource Center, which houses the Lewis University Library, classrooms, and administrative and faculty offices.

LIM COLLEGE

NEW YORK, NEW YORK

The College

With its flagship location situated in a lovely town house in the center of the fashion capital of the world, LIM College has been a major force in fashion and business education for almost seven decades. Its graduates can be found throughout all aspects of the industry, and its high standards of education have earned LIM College accreditation from the Middle States Association of Colleges and Schools.

LIM College is a highly personal school where students learn about the business of fashion, with an emphasis on academic and professional study. Lifelong friends are made at LIM College, as well as lifelong careers. Although most students come to the College directly from high school or transfer from other colleges, there are also those of nontraditional college age who enroll. Students come to LIM College from many parts of the country and the world. The current enrollment is approximately 1,350 undergraduates.

LIM College prides itself on its placement record. Prior to graduation, the Center for Career Development undertakes the important task of counseling each student with regard to her or his career. The office has had outstanding success in helping both four-year and two-year graduates obtain positions relevant to their studies. More than 90 percent of the graduates available for placement have been placed in positions related to their studies within six months of graduation.

The unique nature of LIM College's curriculum provides students with a foundation of core courses in liberal arts and business while offering diverse and intensive hands-on preparation in the fashion industry. This affords graduates the opportunity to accept executive training, merchandising, management, marketing, and communications positions in a wide variety of areas within the fashion and business worlds.

Support services are important at LIM College. In addition to academic and career advising, personal counseling is available. Because of the College's small size and the close relationships between students and staff members, any faculty member or administrator, including the president, is readily accessible to help and advise all students. LIM College's Advisory Board members, all successful fashion industry executives, may also serve as mentors to students, offering additional guidance and advice.

LIM College has a very dynamic student life. Active clubs include the Fashion Club, SIFE, Student Life Activities Board, Student Council, and many more. There are also student publications including the *LIMLIGHT* yearbook and *Fashion Sense* magazine.

LIM College proudly opened a new residence hall in fall 2008. Located at 1760 Third Avenue, this state-of-the-art facility boasts a plethora of modern amenities. All rooms have private bathrooms, free wireless Internet access, free phone service, and 130 free cable channels. Rooms are also equipped with full refrigerators and 25-inch flat-screen televisions. The facility also contains a private gym, game room, computer lab, and three full-service kitchens.

LIM College's unique Open House Program offers students and their families the opportunity to tour the school's campus and learn not only of LIM College's unique academic programs, but also of the vast array of careers found in the fashion industry. The day also includes a special presentation on financial aid information on a group or individual level. Current LIM College students assist in hosting the event and are available to answer questions.

Location

LIM College is situated in four buildings—on East 53rd, East 54th, and East 45th Streets; and on Fifth Avenue, one of the most fashionable locales in the world. A whole world of fashion is at the College's doorstep and includes such famous stores as Saks Fifth Avenue, Bloomingdale's, Henri Bendel, Armani, and Ralph Lauren. New York City is the headquarters for the garment, cosmetics, advertising, publishing, and textile industries, all of which are essential to the fashion industry and are visited regularly by LIM College students. The College incorporates all of these resources into the curriculum. For example, the Fashion Magazines course includes trips to photography studios and modeling agencies as well as tours of magazine offices and advertising firms. New York City offers LIM College students an unparalleled learning experience.

Majors and Degrees

LIM College offers four-year programs in fashion merchandising, management, marketing, and visual merchandising, leading to a Bachelor of Business Administration (B.B.A.) or a Bachelor of Professional Studies (B.P.S.) degree, and a two-year program in fashion merchandising leading to the Associate in Applied Sciences (A.A.S.) degree. Qualified students with a bachelor's degree may also apply to a one-year program (ACCESS) leading to the associate degree. LIM College has recently added a Master of Business Administration (M.B.A.) to its curriculum in March 2009. The program features two exciting courses of study in either entrepreneurship or fashion management.

Academic Programs

LIM College offers a combination of classroom education and supervised practical fieldwork that has been designed to prepare students for executive training programs and other entry-level executive positions in various areas of the fashion industry. Classroom study is supplemented by weekly field trips into the heart of the fashion industry and guest lectures by luminaries from the fashion world.

Work experience is an integral part of a LIM College education. During the four-year bachelor's degree program, a student enters the fashion industry three times for internships. Each of the first two years of study contains a five-week, 3-credit work project. During Work Project I, freshmen are placed in paid, full-time positions in order to learn the basics of retailing. Work Project II, sophomore year, allows qualified students to choose an internship in more specialized areas, such as cosmetics, magazines, designer showrooms, and fashion forecasting companies.

The third and most significant work experience is the Senior Co-op. Students spend one semester working full-time in the fashion industry in an area relevant to their career goals and ambitions. This is required for graduation from the bachelor's degree program. The responsibility, challenge, and fun of this semester prepare students for their next step—the business world.

Students who are applying to the associate degree program follow the first two years of the bachelor's degree program, including the required Work Projects.

To graduate, students must complete 128 credits for the bachelor's degree (130 for visual merchandising). Associate degree candidates must earn 66 credits (34 for one-year ACCESS students). All students must maintain a grade point average of at least 2.0, and satisfactorily complete the cooperative work assignments.

LIM College accepts qualified students as transfers throughout the four years. The maximum number of credits that LIM will accept is 70. Transfer students must complete a minimum of 33 semester hours in addition to the co-op semester at LIM College.

The College calendar runs on a traditional semester format, offering both fall and spring start dates. Also offered are summer and Saturday Fashion Lab programs for high school students. The specially selected courses, such as Fashion Buying and Fashion Magazines, blend academics with hands-on experience. The Fashion U program allows visiting transfer students to take up to 9 credits at LIM College over the summer and gain valuable experience in New York City.

Off-Campus Programs

Study-abroad options are available, including study in places such as London, Paris, Milan, Barcelona, and China.

Academic Facilities

The 5,000-square-foot Adrian G. Marcuse library contains 9,000 volumes pertaining to fashion, management, marketing, and the liberal arts, as well as 110 professional and academic journals. The library has more than forty computer terminals that connect to the Internet and provide access to online databases through the library's subscriptions. DVDs and VHS cassettes useful for fashion-related studies are also at students' disposal. Personal computers are available for use in the library, lounges, and classrooms. The student-to-computer ratio is 4:1. The Math Center and Writing Centers offer one-on-one tutoring for all students.

LIM College's brand-new facility on Fifth Avenue is equipped with two fashion merchandising studios, one of which has a laboratory area for cosmetics. There are also two new 1,100-square-foot visual merchandising studios, as well as a state-of-the-art Color and Materials Laboratory at the new location.

Costs

Tuition for the 2009–10 school year was $19,900 with additional mandatory fees of $525. Housing charges for the 2009–10 year were $15,400. Students who commute spend from $700 to $2000 for transportation, depending on distance. The estimated cost of books and supplies are $1100. The personal expense allowance is $2000.

Financial Aid

LIM College believes that lack of funds should not keep students from attaining a degree; thus, admissions decisions and financial aid are totally separate, and a request for aid has no effect on admissions. About 80 percent of LIM College's students receive some form of financial aid. Institutional scholarships, Federal Pell Grants, Federal Supplemental Educational Opportunity Grants, and New York State TAP grants are all available for eligible students. In addition, the College participates in the Federal Stafford Loan program for students and Federal PLUS Loan program for parents. The College also works with several private lenders to offer alternative education loans for students to supplement their federal loans. International students are eligible to apply for alternative loans with a credit-worthy U.S.-based co-signer. The Free Application for Federal Student Aid (FAFSA) should be filed by all applicants by March 1 for priority consideration. Aid is granted on the basis of financial need and scholarships are merit based, although some awards take need into consideration. Details of the financial aid programs are available on the LIM College Web site or are available directly from the Office of Student Financial Services.

LIM College features a Merit Scholarship Program for incoming freshmen and transfer students. These scholarship monies are awarded for academic achievement in high school or college. Students can remain eligible for their scholarship throughout their stay at the College by maintaining a GPA of 3.0 or above. LIM College's nonprofit Fashion Education Foundation also administers a number of merit scholarships (both need and non-need based) other than direct institutional awards.

Faculty

LIM College prides itself on its faculty members. More than a third of the teaching staff, including all members of the liberal arts faculty, has advanced degrees; all professional subject faculty members have wide business and professional experience. Many, through their business contacts, bring guests to class to share in the lectures and discussions. The student-faculty ratio is 8:1.

Each student is assigned an academic adviser. Work-study and career guidance is given to students by the Center for Career Development, with conferences held before, during, and after the cooperative work assignments and prior to permanent placement interviews. Students are always welcome to discuss career options at any other time as well.

Student Government

The Office of Student Life is the center of all student activities at LIM College. This department supports student government, approves other student organizations, and establishes operating budgets. One of LIM College's more popular clubs is the Fashion Club which plans an annual fashion show that recently hosted over 1,000 people. Another popular activity is the student-run *Fashion Sense* magazine. LIM College's Office of Student Life plans many other activities including diversity programming, philanthropic service, and new student orientation.

Admission Requirements

All applicants are required to submit high school transcripts, SAT or ACT scores, two letters of recommendation, an essay, and the completed application with the application fee. Transfer students must also submit their college transcripts. The College will waive the standardized test requirement if the student has earned 30 credit hours. International students should have their transcripts evaluated by World Education Services and submit TOEFL, IETLS, or PTE test scores. It is also strongly suggested that all applicants create an activity sheet or resume highlighting their experience, with emphasis on business and fashion activities.

Application and Information

LIM College's Admissions Committee recognizes that many intangibles go into the making of a successful student, and it evaluates each applicant individually and holistically. The College uses a rolling admission policy. Applicants are informed of the admission decision within approximately four to six weeks after all admission requirements have been fulfilled. An application may be obtained from the LIM College Web site or by contacting the Admissions Office.

Kristina Gibson
Assistant Dean of Admissions
LIM College
12 East 53rd Street
New York, New York 10022-5268
Phone: 212-752-1530
800-677-1323 (toll-free outside New York City)
Fax: 212-750-3432
E-mail: admissions@limcollege.edu
Web site: http://www.limcollege.edu

COLLEGE CLOSE-UPS

LIMESTONE COLLEGE

GAFFNEY, SOUTH CAROLINA

The College

Founded in 1845, Limestone is a fully accredited, private, coeducational liberal arts college. The College maintains a small student body and a well-qualified faculty in order to create an atmosphere in which each student develops intellectually, physically, and socially. The College endeavors to help students prepare for a satisfying, useful life through effective communication skills, responsible decision-making abilities, meaningful leisure-time activities, and lifelong aspirations. In addition to its programs on campus, Limestone offers several of its academic majors in an accelerated format called The Block Program at several locations throughout South Carolina. These programs are intended primarily for working adults. The College also has an impressive Virtual Campus Program on the Internet with many majors offered. The two programs were combined in 2005 to be the Extended Campus.

Extracurricular activities play a vital part in the development of all students at Limestone College. Among these activities are intercollegiate athletics in men's baseball, basketball, cross-country, golf, lacrosse, soccer, swimming, tennis, track and field, volleyball, and wrestling and in women's basketball, cross-country, golf, field hockey, lacrosse, soccer, softball, swimming, tennis, track and field, and volleyball. Students who are interested in music have the opportunity to participate in several instrumental and choral ensembles. A theater program is also available.

The 115-acre Limestone campus is well laid out for pleasant college living. The classrooms, library, laboratories, auditorium, bookstore, post office, and administrative offices are housed in buildings that border the central and circular drives, making each easily accessible to the others. The back campus has a plaza of five dormitories, and a dining hall is located nearby. The Timken LYFE Center is a physical education complex that houses the gymnasium, an AAU-size swimming pool, and athletic training facilities. The Walt Griffin Physical Education Center, named for the current Limestone College president, offers three classrooms, nine offices, locker rooms, athletic training and education facilities, a state-of-the-art fitness center, and a wrestling practice facility. The College also has eight lighted tennis courts, a baseball field, a softball field, a soccer/lacrosse field, field hockey field, and several practice fields.

Location

Gaffney, a small city with a population of 25,000, provides an ideal setting for a college campus. Whereas the distractions associated with a large city are absent from daily life, the cultural programs and services offered in Charlotte, North Carolina, and Spartanburg and Greenville, South Carolina, are all within a 50-mile radius of the campus. All are connected to Gaffney by Interstate 85.

The climate is free from extreme heat or cold. The well-known resort areas of the Blue Ridge Mountains, the Great Smoky Mountains, and the beaches of the Atlantic Coast are accessible for weekend visits. In the immediate area, facilities are available for all water sports, horseback riding, golf, tennis, and skiing.

Majors and Degrees

Limestone College offers the Bachelor of Arts, Bachelor of Science, and Bachelor of Social Work degrees with majors in art (concentrations in studio art and graphic design); athletic training, strength, and conditioning; biology; business administration (concentrations in accounting, computer science, e-business, economics, general business, human resource management, health care administration, management, and marketing); chemistry; computer science (concentrations in Internet management, management information systems, and programming); criminal justice; English; history; liberal studies; mathematics; music; physical education (concentrations in athletic training and strength/conditioning); prelaw; premedical; predental; prechiropractic; preveterinary; prenursing; prepharmacy; pre–physical therapy; psychology; social work; sports management; and theater. Majors approved for South Carolina teacher certification are elementary education, English education, mathematics education, music education, and secondary education.

The Associate of Arts degree is offered with majors in business administration (concentrations in general business), computer science (majors in Internet management, management information systems, and programming), and liberal studies.

Academic Programs

The course of study leading to the B.A., B.S., B.S.W., or A.A. degree consists of four elements: requirements in communication and quantitative skills; a general liberal arts program, involving five different subject groups; courses in the major; and appropriate electives. The baccalaureate degree programs require the completion of a minimum of 123 semester hours. The associate degree programs require the completion of a minimum of 62 semester hours.

Advanced placement and credit are given for scores of 3 or higher on the Advanced Placement examinations of the College Board.

An Honors Program involving special courses, seminars, and lectures is available for exceptional students. Admission to this program is contingent upon outstanding high school grades and scores on the SAT of the College Board, the completion of a special application, and an interview. Almost 10 percent of all Limestone students are enrolled in this rigorous academic program.

A Program for Alternative Learning Styles (PALS) is available for qualified students with certified learning disabilities who might not otherwise succeed at the college level.

Academic Facilities

Limestone has outstanding computer facilities, including free e-mail accounts for all main campus students, residence hall high-speed Internet connections, and several well-equipped, state-of-the-art computer labs. There are also well-equipped science labs. The modern A. J. Eastwood Library houses approximately 112,976 volumes and is fully computerized, including student Internet access. Fullerton Auditorium, with a seating capacity of 975, serves for drama and musical productions and is one of the finest such facilities in the state of South Carolina.

Costs

The direct cost for a student at Limestone College for the 2010–11 school year is $26,200; the tuition is $19,200, and room and board costs are $7000. In addition, the cost of books, supplies, laundry, travel, and personal expenses are estimated at $4000 per year.

Financial Aid

Limestone College, one of the least costly private colleges in South Carolina, endeavors to meet the financial need of any qualified student through scholarships, grants, loans, work-study opportunities, or a combination of these. Limestone offers merit scholarships to students with outstanding academic, leadership, or athletic abilities as well as to those who have exceptional talents in such areas as art, music, and theater.

More than 90 percent of Limestone College day students receive some type of financial aid. Because institutional financial aid is limited, students are urged to submit their applications for admission and financial aid as early as possible.

Faculty

Personal attention to students and high-quality instruction characterize the faculty at Limestone College. Three quarters of the faculty members hold Ph.D.'s or other terminal degrees in their fields. The student-faculty ratio is 12:1. Students and instructors work closely together in both learning and counseling situations. Each student has an assigned faculty adviser for assistance in course selection and for personal counseling.

Student Government

The Student Government Association exemplifies the College's democratic tradition and the principles of honor and individual responsibility. It is every student's privilege to participate in the government of the learning community of which he or she is a member. The more highly organized activities, including student organizations and social events, are coordinated through the Student Government Association. The College also has a literary magazine and a yearbook.

Admission Requirements

Limestone College does not discriminate on the basis of race, color, creed, national origin, financial need, or physical handicap. Each candidate for admission is evaluated as an individual. The College recommends that applicants have the following high school preparation: English, 4 units; social science, 3 units; mathematics, 3 units; and science, 2 units.

Applicants must submit an official transcript of the secondary school record, scores on the SAT, and a nonrefundable $25 application fee. The application fee is waived if the student applies online at the College's Web site. Transfer applications are encouraged.

Application and Information

Completed application forms for admission and for financial aid should be sent to the Office of Admissions at Limestone College. It is recommended that applications be submitted by May 1. Any admission applications received after that date are considered on a space-available basis. The College practices a rolling admissions policy. As soon as the application, high school transcript, and test scores have been received, the applicant is notified of his or her status. Upon acceptance, a student is required to submit a $100 tuition deposit.

Vice President of Enrollment Services
Limestone College
1115 College Drive
Gaffney, South Carolina 29340-3799
Phone: 864-488-4554
Fax: 864-488-8206
E-mail: admiss@limestone.edu
Web site: http://www.limestone.edu

COLLEGE CLOSE-UPS

The Winnie Davis Hall of History, named in honor of the daughter of Jefferson Davis, was completed about 1904 and is listed on the National Register of Historic Places.

LINDENWOOD UNIVERSITY

ST. CHARLES, MISSOURI

The University

An independent teaching university founded in 1827, Lindenwood is the oldest university west of the Missouri River. Lindenwood is a dynamic four-year liberal arts institution dedicated to excellence, delivering a high-quality education that leads to the development of the whole person and preparation for life and work after graduation, through more than eighty values-centered programs.

Lindenwood University (LU) is accredited by the Higher Learning Commission of the North Central Association of Colleges and Schools and the Missouri Department of Elementary and Secondary Education and is a member of the Teacher Education Accreditation Council. Lindenwood University is authorized to grant associate, bachelor's, master's, Education Specialist, and Doctor of Education degrees. Lindenwood is an independent, public-serving, liberal arts university that has a historical relationship with the Presbyterian Church and is committed to the values inherent in the Judeo-Christian tradition. Lindenwood welcomes students from all religious denominations.

The University's athletic teams compete in the Heart of America Athletic Conference and the National Association of Intercollegiate Athletics (NAIA). Lindenwood's men and women athletes participate in forty-six sport programs. Over the last eight years, Lindenwood athletic teams have won forty national championships. The teams use the Robert F. Hyland Performance Arena, Harlen C. Hunter Stadium, baseball and softball fields, and a new eight-lane all-weather track. Students also participate in an assortment of intramural sports at the University's Fitness Center.

Student organizations and clubs provide avenues for extended personal growth, leadership, and community service. The University radio station, 35,000-watt KCLC-FM, and LUTV, Lindenwood's new television station, are staffed by students.

Students wishing to live on campus may choose from residence halls, houses, and apartment-style living. Six new residence halls have opened since 2000. Sibley Hall, named in honor of founders Mary Easton and Major George C. Sibley, was built in 1856 to replace the original log cabin that served as the first University building. It is listed on the National Register of Historic Places and is now a women's residence hall. All residential buildings have easy access to University facilities.

Location

The 500-acre campus is located in St. Charles, Missouri, a city of about 55,000 people, situated 20 miles from downtown St. Louis. Resting on the banks of the Missouri River, just south of the Mississippi, St. Charles is the site of Missouri's first state capital. The area offers a wide range of opportunities for all types of interests and is particularly rich in state heritage and attractions associated with the history of America's westward expansion. Lindenwood's proximity to a major city allows students to enjoy theme parks, a delightful zoo, professional sporting events, Broadway plays and theater, performances of a world-renowned symphony orchestra, state parks, and lakes. St. Louis–Lambert International Airport is located just 5 miles from Lindenwood University on Interstate 70.

Majors and Degrees

With a foundation as solid as the campus' century-old linden trees, the academic programs of Lindenwood University have a tradition of excellence and innovation. Lindenwood awards Bachelor of Arts, Bachelor of Fine Arts, and Bachelor of Science degrees with majors in accounting, agribusiness, art history, art management, art (studio), athletic training, biology, business administration, chemistry, computer science, corporate communications, criminal justice, dance, early childhood education, elementary education, English, fashion design, fashion merchandising, finance, French, general studies, history, human resource management, human service agency management, information technology, international studies, management, management information systems, marketing, mass communication, mathematics, medical technology, music, nonprofit administration, performing arts, physical education, political science, psychology, public administration, religion, retail marketing, secondary education, social work, sociology, Spanish, special education, theater, theater management, and writing.

Preprofessional courses are offered in dentistry, engineering, law, medicine, and veterinary medicine. In addition, programs in engineering are available in conjunction with Washington University in St. Louis, the University of Missouri–Columbia, and the University of Missouri–Rolla.

Academic Programs

The emphasis at Lindenwood University is on an individualized liberal arts education with career-oriented preparation. Students fulfill general education requirements, participate in the University's Work and Learn Program when qualified, and acquire an in-depth knowledge of at least one area of study as a major. Lindenwood requires the completion of 128 credit hours to earn a bachelor's degree.

Academic Facilities

The newly renovated Margaret Leggat Butler Library houses volumes, microfilm items, and a computer lab and subscribes to 450 periodicals. Roemer Hall serves as the main administration building and has classrooms and faculty offices on the upper floors. Roemer Hall is also home to the 450-seat Jelkyl Theatre. Young Science Hall houses an auditorium, laboratories, and classrooms for natural science, mathematics, and computer science, as well as a state-of-the-art television studio. Harmon Hall provides students with art, photography, dance, music, and performing arts studios; classrooms; practice rooms; a recital and lecture hall; the Harmon Theatre; and the Harry D. Hendren Gallery, which attracts local and national art exhibits. The Lindenwood University Cultural Center provides a 750-seat auditorium, classrooms, meeting rooms, and offices. It is home to the University's music department and is the site of theatrical productions, concerts, convocations, and lectures. In addition, the Spellmann Campus Center opened in 2002. The Campus Center serves as a student union and houses a state-of-the-art cafeteria, Macintosh and PC computer labs, conference rooms, networking and campus life offices, and career planning and placement services. The 132,000-square-foot J. Scheidegger Center for Fine and Performing Arts, completed in 2008, is home to Lindenwood's Theatre, Dance, and Music Departments, as well as the 1,200-seat Bezemes Family Theater, the

Emerson Black Box Theater, the Boyle Family Gallery, and the Charter Communications LUTV HD Studio.

Costs

For the academic year 2010–11, tuition is $13,260. Students who choose to live on campus pay $6850 for room and board, plus $360 for communications service and $240 for an activity fee. There is a refundable $300 room deposit. Books and other supplies are extra.

Financial Aid

Financial aid is available to all qualified students. A student must submit the Free Application for Federal Student Aid (FAFSA). To qualify for the full amount of financial aid, students must submit their federal financial aid forms before April 1. As determined by the evaluation, a student's financial need may be met with a combination of federal, state, and institutional sources of aid. In addition, institutional awards are available in the areas of academics, leadership, athletics, drama, yearbook/newspaper, and music. Resident students may earn $2400 toward their expenses by working on campus.

Faculty

Lindenwood has 228 full-time faculty members, who serve as teachers, mentors, and advisers to their students. Faculty members advise students regarding majors and other matters to help them succeed academically.

Student Government

The Lindenwood Student Government Association (LSGA) is made up of representatives elected by the student body. LSGA has the responsibility of providing a balanced program of cultural, social, and recreational events and activities throughout the year.

Admission Requirements

To apply for admission, a student should submit a completed application form with a nonrefundable $30 application fee, a transcript of high school and/or college work, and ACT or SAT scores.

Applicants are evaluated on an individual basis, and admission is based on an analysis of the student's grade point average, ACT or SAT scores, extracurricular activities, recommendations, and personal qualifications. Students are admitted without regard to race, sex, or national origin.

Application and Information

Although admission to Lindenwood is on a rolling basis, students are encouraged to apply by April 15 for the fall semester and by December 1 for the spring semester. Notification of the admission decision is mailed soon after all required materials are received and evaluated by the Director of Undergraduate Admissions.

Applications for admission, financial aid, and scholarships and other information about Lindenwood University can be obtained by contacting:

Undergraduate Admissions
Lindenwood University
209 South Kingshighway
St. Charles, Missouri 63301-1695
Phone: 636-949-4949
Fax: 636-949-4989
Web site: http://www.lindenwood.edu

Student life at Lindenwood University.

COLLEGE CLOSE-UPS

LINFIELD COLLEGE

MCMINNVILLE, OREGON

The College

Linfield College (1858) is an independent, coeducational, residential, comprehensive liberal arts and sciences college dedicated to providing an educational environment conducive to learning and participation. There are 1,700 full-time students on the McMinnville campus. These students come primarily from the thirteen Western states (twenty-seven states overall) but also from twenty-four other countries. Students of color make up 16 percent of the student body, and 5 percent of students are international. Most students are between 18 and 22. Linfield is primarily residential, with one residence hall for men, three for women, and thirteen that are coeducational, each accommodating between 10 and 100 residents. There are also four fraternity houses. Each hall establishes its own calendar of social, educational, and recreational events throughout the year. Students who reside on campus eat their meals in the College dining hall. Houses and apartments are available for upper-division students. Social clubs, professional organizations, sororities (one local: Sigma Kappa Phi; three national: Alpha Phi, Phi Sigma Sigma, and Zeta Tau Alpha) and fraternities (one local: Delta Psi Delta; three national: Kappa Sigma, Pi Kappa Alpha, and Theta Chi), service clubs, and almost forty other organizations play an important role in the daily life of a Linfield student. Linfield's winning athletics tradition fosters participation at all levels of competition. Women compete in intercollegiate basketball, cross-country, golf, lacrosse, soccer, softball, swimming, tennis, track and field, and volleyball. Men compete in intercollegiate baseball, basketball, cross-country, football, golf, soccer, swimming, tennis, and track and field. Water polo, Ultimate Frisbee, and men's lacrosse are club sports. Linfield also has an extensive and active year-round intramural program.

Linfield hosts the Oregon Nobel Laureate Symposium. (There are only five such symposiums worldwide.) At each symposium, several Nobel laureates come to share their backgrounds and expertise within the context of a basic theme.

The Linfield–Good Samaritan School of Nursing, an academic unit of the College at its Portland campus, prepares students for the B.S.N. or a degree in health science. This campus, at the Good Samaritan Hospital and Medical Center, has residence facilities, food service options, and a residence life program. In 2006, the College decided to make the Portland campus programs open only to transfer admission. The Portland campus median age is 26.

Location

Located in McMinnville, 40 miles southwest of Portland, Linfield College is a leader in the cultural, educational, and recreational events of the fast-growing community of 32,000. The seat of county government, McMinnville provides Linfield faculty and students with many opportunities to participate in community service activities. Cinemas, a community theater, bowling alleys, coffeehouses, and a wide variety of restaurants welcome Linfield students. Shopping is within walking distance. The central Oregon coast is an hour to the west, and the outdoor activity areas of the Oregon Cascade Range, including year-round skiing at Mt. Hood, are 2 hours to the east. Salem, the state capital of Oregon, is 25 miles to the southeast, and Eugene is 80 miles south. Rainfall in western Oregon averages 42 inches annually, and the winter temperature averages 41°F.

Majors and Degrees

Linfield offers the Bachelor of Arts degree in art, communication, creative writing, electronic arts, English, Francophone and African Studies, French, German, German studies, history, Japanese, music, philosophy, political science, religious studies, sociology, Spanish, and theater arts. The Bachelor of Arts or Bachelor of Science degree is offered in accounting, anthropology, applied physics, athletic training, biology, business, chemistry, computing science, economics, elementary education, environmental studies, exercise science, finance, general science, health education, health sciences, international business, mathematics, nursing, physical education, physics, and psychology. The College has programs to prepare students for advanced study in dentistry, law, and medicine. The education department offers a strong program of teacher certification at the secondary and elementary levels. A 3-2 engineering program is available in cooperation with Oregon State University, Washington State University, and the University of Southern California.

Academic Programs

The academic year is divided into two 15-week semesters (fall and spring) and an optional four-week winter term in January. The January Term offers regular departmental courses and off-campus and international study. Academic courses are assigned 1–5 semester credit hours each; 125 credits are required for a B.A. or a B.S. degree. Students divide their time equally among required general education courses, a major area of study, and elective subjects. The Linfield Curriculum courses, selected to provide a solid foundation in the liberal arts, require students to take 3 semester hours in each of the six modes of inquiry as well as one upper-division course in one of these areas. These modes of inquiry are as follows: the Vital Past; Ultimate Questions; Individuals, Systems, and Societies; the Natural World; Creative Studies; and Quantitative Reasoning. In addition, students are required to take a writing-intensive course, a course addressing global pluralisms, and a course dealing with United States pluralism. Major requirements differ from department to department. Individually designed majors are available with faculty approval. Students majoring in a foreign language spend an academic year in a country in which the language being studied is the native tongue. Language majors have recently studied in such cities as Avignon, Guadalajara, Nantes, Munich, Quebec, and Valencia. The Advanced Placement (AP) Program of the College Board is recognized, and up to 5 semester hours of credit are granted for a score of 4 or 5 on an AP test. AP examinations do not satisfy general education requirements. The College recognizes the International Baccalaureate (IB) Diploma and awards up to 30 semester hours of credit for higher-level courses on a course-by-course basis. Total credit awarded by AP or IB may not exceed 30 semester hours.

The College offers courses in English with the English Language and Culture program. These courses are designed to help international students whose native language is not English to achieve competence in academic and social English skills, so that they may work effectively in their undergraduate classes at Linfield.

Off-Campus Programs

Off-campus educational experiences include the Semester Abroad Program, involving four months of study in San Ramon, Costa Rica; Aix, Angers, or Avignon, France; Vienna, Austria; Tokyo or Yokohama, Japan; Oaxaca, Mexico; Oslo, Norway; Beijing or Hong Kong, China; Seoul, South Korea; Galway, Ireland; Nottingham, England; Quito and Galapagos, Ecuador; Christchurch, Dunedin, and Hamilton, New Zealand; and Cairns, Townsville, Melbourne, Warrnambool, and Geelong, Australia. Sophomores, juniors, and seniors are encouraged to participate, and approximately 20 students are selected for each country each year. The program is designed to serve students who have successfully completed one year of study at Linfield in the appropriate language and who will return to the campus to share their international experiences with the College community. Transportation for the first round trip is included in the cost of tuition, and most of these study programs cost the same as a semester on campus. January Term study-abroad programs for four weeks are also offered. Recent offerings included the Emergence of Modern Ghana (West Africa); Mainland Southeast Asia History (Cambodia, Vietnam, and China); American Expatriate Writers in

Europe: The Lost Generation Tour (nine European cities); and Australia: From Colony to Asian Power.

Academic Facilities

Murdock Hall houses the biology and chemistry departments and up-to-date laboratories and equipment. Laboratory and research space is provided for general and advanced chemistry and biology, organic chemistry, biochemistry, microbiology, bacteriology, immunology, ecology, botany, physiology, embryology, and gross and microscopic anatomy. There are approximately 200 IBM and Macintosh computers on campus available for student use. Services on the network that students can use include the two UNIX hosts (available for programming, e-mail, and other communication services), a connection to the Internet, file servers, and both laser and dot-matrix printers. Linfield students benefit from a communications and technology network, including phone service, voice mail, e-mail, and wireless Internet connections in each residence hall room. In addition, there is wireless access in the library and other academic areas of the campus.

The Health and Physical Education/Recreation Complex houses three gymnasiums; weight rooms; fitness laboratories with a hydrostatic weighing tank, a metabolic and pulmonary measuring system, and an electrocardiovascular exercise ECG system; an eight-lane, 25-yard indoor pool; handball and racquetball courts; classrooms; offices; and a 28,000-square-foot field house.

Linfield boasts seventeen beautiful new or recently renovated buildings, including residence halls and apartments, a state-of-the-art library (containing $1 million worth of technology), two art buildings, a theatre building, and a music building, all completed since 2000. New and old buildings alike contain up-to-date teaching tools, computer labs, and science labs. The College has wireless Internet access in 90 percent of the classrooms and lots of other hot spots on campus. Other facilities include art galleries and studios, a 250-watt FM radio station, an experimental psychology laboratory, dance and music studios, a preschool, and a 425-seat auditorium that houses a three-manual, 48-rank Casavant pipe organ.

Costs

For 2009–10, tuition and fees were $28,760 per two-semester year, board was $3710, and a double room was $4480. There was a $170-per-credit fee for on-campus January Term classes.

Financial Aid

Eligibility for most of Linfield's assistance programs is based on need as determined by a federally approved needs analysis processor. The only form required for need-based programs is the Free Application for Federal Student Aid (FAFSA). Linfield participates in the Federal Perkins and Federal Stafford Student Loan programs, Federal Supplemental Educational Opportunity Grants, Federal Work-Study, and other forms of financial assistance on the basis of demonstrated need.

The College awards a number of scholarships to full-time students based on scholastic achievement, independent of financial need. These academic scholarships vary from 20 to 75 percent of tuition. To be considered, students must have a minimum GPA of 3.4. A number of other criteria are used when determining scholarships. Linfield sponsors special scholarships for National Merit finalists. The minimum award is 50 percent of tuition. Awards can range to full tuition, depending on financial need, provided the student has indicated that Linfield is his or her first-choice college. The College also sponsors the annual Academic Competitive Scholarship Day in early spring each year. Participation is limited to high school seniors who meet particular academic requirements and apply by December 1. Each academic department offers prizes ranging from $10,000 to $16,000, divided over the student's four years at Linfield, provided the student maintains a grade point average of at least 3.0. Scholarships of varying amounts are awarded to entering students who are particularly talented in music performance. Amounts range from $1500 to $2500 annually. Interested students are required to audition either in person or by cassette tape by February 15. Financial assistance for non-U.S. citizens is limited to partial tuition scholarships and the opportunity to work part-time on campus. Other scholarships are available for students who demonstrate outstanding leadership and community service.

Faculty

There are 114 full-time and 64 part-time faculty members, each of whom is committed to undergraduate teaching and scholarship. Ninety-four percent have doctoral or other terminal degrees within their field. The student-faculty ratio is 12:1, and faculty members serve as academic advisers. There are no teaching assistants.

Student Government

Students have a significant voice in establishing and changing College policies and regulations. The Student Senate, chosen through campus elections, is the focus of student opinion and debate. Students are represented on most College governing councils and committees with faculty members and trustees, and they are encouraged to express and implement their ideas on academic or extracurricular matters.

Admission Requirements

Admission to Linfield College is selective. Admission is granted to students who are likely to grow and succeed in a personal and challenging liberal arts environment. Each applicant is judged on individual merit. A faculty admission committee evaluates candidates in a number of areas that commonly indicate academic potential. These include high school performance, a writing sample, recommendations from teachers and counselors, and precollege standardized test results (ACT or SAT). The committee also considers the depth and quality of an applicant's involvement in community and school activities. It reviews all applications as a group, selecting those students who show the greatest likelihood of benefiting from and contributing to the Linfield community. Linfield is a member of the Common Application Association.

International students whose education has been in a language other than English must submit certified English translations of their academic work. Proficiency in English is required, as demonstrated by an official TOEFL score report.

Application and Information

Early action applicants must apply by November 15, and notification is made by January 15. The priority application deadline for regular admission is February 15, with notification made on or before April 1. Admitted international students must show evidence of financial responsibility and submit a $2000 deposit.

Interviews are not required, but students are encouraged to visit. Appointments should be made in advance and can be requested online at http://www.linfield.edu/stopby. The Office of Admission is open Monday through Friday, 7:30 a.m. to 5:30 p.m., and on Saturdays during the school year from 9 a.m. to 2 p.m. The Linfield Web site provides students with information on student life, academic programs, and athletics. Students may also complete their application for admission online or ask for additional information. Interested students are encouraged to contact:

Director of Admission
Linfield College
McMinnville, Oregon 97128
Phone: 503-883-2213
800-640-2287 (toll-free)
Fax: 503-883-2472
E-mail: admission@linfield.edu
Web site: http://www.linfield.edu

LOYOLA MARYMOUNT UNIVERSITY

LOS ANGELES, CALIFORNIA

The University

Loyola Marymount University (LMU), situated on a picturesque campus, offers competitive students an education of high quality in a friendly and relaxed atmosphere. As successor to the oldest institution of learning in southern California, St. Vincent's College, the University is steeped in a tradition and history of dedication to academic excellence and the total development of its students. Although the emphasis is within the undergraduate school (full-time enrollment is approximately 5,600 and part-time enrollment is approximately 145), approximately 1,800 students attend the Graduate Division, primarily in the evening hours, working toward master's degrees in the fields of arts, arts in teaching, business administration, education, and science (including engineering). The Ed.D. in educational leadership for social justice is offered by the School of Education. The School of Law, situated at a separate campus, has both day and evening divisions and offers the Juris Doctor degree. Law school enrollment is approximately 1,300.

Sixty-one percent of the undergraduate students live on campus and are able to choose accommodations in one of eleven residential halls or six apartment complexes. Students have access to a sports pavilion, one swimming pool, baseball and soccer fields, tennis and volleyball courts, and four indoor racquetball courts. A new recreation center includes three additional courts and a fitness center. LMU fields teams in thirteen intercollegiate sports (baseball, basketball, cheer, crew, cross-country, golf, soccer, softball, swimming, tennis, track, women's volleyball, and water polo) and has club teams in lacrosse, rugby, men's volleyball, and more. Over 2,000 undergraduate students participate in the active intramural program, which includes coed sports. Student organizations include the AM/FM radio station (KXLU), Chemistry Society, Black Students Union, Han Tao Chinese Cultural Club, MEChA, Business Law Society, Student-Athlete Advisory Committee, University choruses, fraternities and sororities, and various honor and service groups. LMU's Debate Team and Air Force ROTC detachment have received national recognition in their respective areas.

Location

LMU is ideally located on a 152-acre mesa that overlooks the southwest section of Los Angeles and the Pacific Ocean from Malibu to Santa Monica. The campus is close to the beach, and the University community enjoys a cool, clean coastal climate. LMU is near the metropolitan complex, but it has the benefits of the slower pace of its residential community, Westchester. Los Angeles International Airport is 10 minutes away, and nearby freeways provide easy access to the city and its cultural and recreational activities.

Majors and Degrees

Loyola Marymount University offers the B.A. in the fields of African American studies, animation, art history, Asian Pacific studies, biology, Chicano studies, classical civilizations, classics, communication studies, dance, economics, English, European studies, film and television production, French, Greek, history, humanities, Latin, liberal studies (elementary education), mathematics, music, philosophy, political science, psychology, recording arts, screenwriting, sociology, Spanish, studio arts, theater arts, theology, urban studies, and women's studies. The College of Business Administration offers the Bachelor of Science degree in accounting and applied information management and the Bachelor of Business Administration degree with majors in entrepreneurship, finance, management, and marketing. The College of Science and Engineering offers bachelor's degrees in applied mathematics, athletic training, biochemistry, biology, chemistry, computer science, engineering (civil, electrical, and mechanical), engineering physics, environmental science, mathematics, natural science, and physics. Areas of emphasis can include such fields as computer engineering and marine biology.

Academic Programs

While pre-major and major requirements differ with each area of study, a core curriculum is maintained as a degree requirement in the fields of American cultures, college writing, communication skills, creative and critical arts, history, literature, mathematics/science/technology, philosophy, social science, and theology, thus ensuring each student a balanced education. The maximum requirement in each of the core fields is 6 units of academic work. The interdepartmental honors program provides challenges for the exceptional student.

The academic calendar consists of two semesters and two 6-week optional summer sessions. The fall semester begins in late August and ends before Christmas. The spring semester usually begins in mid-January and ends in mid-May. Students may earn credit when receiving scores of 4 or 5 through Advanced Placement (AP) examinations. In addition, it is possible for students to earn credit by examination for any course offered by LMU.

Off-Campus Programs

Students who are interested in studying abroad have a choice of several University-sponsored programs. LMU offers programs in Africa, Australia, China, England, France, Germany, Greece, Guatemala, Honduras, India, Ireland, Italy, Japan, Mexico, New Zealand, the Philippines, South Korea, and Spain. The University also has numerous affiliated programs, including the Rome Center of Loyola University Chicago and the American Institute for Foreign Study. Choice of programs is made on the basis of the student's interest and ability or skill. Courses may be conducted in English, the language of the country in which the student elects to study, or both. In addition, LMU offers internship programs through which students can earn course credit for independent study that has been approved by the dean of the college in which the student is enrolled. The programs range from student involvement in political campaigns to the counseling of underrepresented youths to professional work at film/TV studios.

Academic Facilities

The William H. Hannon Library is the newest and most sophisticated library facility in Los Angeles. The new, state-of-the-art 88,000-square-foot library is expected to become the cultural and intellectual hub of the Loyola Marymount University campus. Its three above-ground stories and two basement levels have space for more than 1 million volumes, and the more than 100 computer workstations, four classrooms, and dozens of group study rooms will facilitate all forms of learning. The Law School Library, located within the School of Law in downtown Los Angeles, contains more than 560,000 volumes and microforms and is a depository for government documents of the state of California and the United States. It also has complete holdings of all publications relating to California law. All students have at their disposal an IBM 360/30 computer that is equipped to program five languages. The communication arts complex houses the Louis B. Mayer Motion Picture Theatre, a full-size color-television studio, a motion-picture soundstage, and state-of-the-art industry equipment. Strub Theatre offers excellent theatrical facilities for the performing arts of drama and dance.

Costs

Tuition for the 2009–10 academic year was $35,378. The cost of room and board varies with options that students select—for example, a full- or partial-meal plan, an apartment on campus, or a residence hall. However, the average yearly cost is approximately $12,000. Students should expect to spend about $1638 for books and supplies and $2250 for additional miscellaneous expenses.

Financial Aid

Approximately 75 percent of the University's undergraduate students receive some type of financial assistance. The total amount of financial aid awarded to students for the 2008–09 academic year was approximately $112 million. Students applying for aid must file the Free Application for Federal Student Aid (FAFSA). The CSS Financial Aid PROFILE is no longer required, starting with the 2010–11 academic year. All students are expected to apply for the Federal Pell Grant, and California residents must apply for the California grants. Most aid is awarded on the basis of need, but the University does offer merit scholarships (including full-tuition scholarships). The priority date for financial aid is February 1. Aid is awarded after that date on a funds-available basis.

Faculty

LMU's faculty is dedicated to undergraduate teaching and is easily accessible to students. Ninety percent of the faculty members hold a Ph.D. in their area of instruction.

Student Government

The University believes that active student input is an essential part of the undergraduate years. Students sit on every University committee, including the Board of Trustees, with full voting rights. Students operate the campus recreation centers, manage the dormitories as resident advisers, operate a used-book store, and serve as advisers to their academic departments. Student actions have resulted in the development of such things as a campus recreation center, the water polo team, and the complete semester calendar.

Admission Requirements

Admission to LMU is selective, and a candidate is expected to present a strong record in college-preparatory courses. In determining an applicant's eligibility, the University gives careful consideration to the student's academic preparation, national test scores, letters of recommendation, extracurricular activities, and family relationships to the University. A personal interview is not required for admission. Prospective candidates are always welcome to visit the campus, and personal tours can be arranged on request. Students who, for academic reasons, were not accepted for admission as freshmen may be considered for admission to advanced standing if they have completed at least the equivalent of 30 semester hours of transferable college work with at least a B average.

Application and Information

Applicants must submit official transcripts from the last high school attended and from each college attended, arrange for SAT or ACT scores to be sent to the Office of Admission, submit a recommendation form from an official of the last school attended, and file the Common Application with the $60 nonrefundable fee. Applications are considered when all necessary documents have been received prior to the deadline of the semester for which application is made. The priority deadline for freshman applicants for the fall semester is November 1 for Early Notification and January 15 for Regular Decision. Early Notification applicants receive a decision by December 20. The deadline for transfer applicants for the fall semester is March 15. For the spring semester for both freshman and transfer students, the priority deadline is October 15.

International students are welcome to apply to LMU and follow the same admission procedure. They are also required to submit scores of 80 minimum from the Test of English as a Foreign Language (TOEFL) or an IELTS exam of 6.5 overall bandwidth. LMU also offers conditional admission through ELS language centers. International students must also provide a statement of financial responsibility for all obligations covering the full period of time for which the student is making application. All records of previous academic training must be original or authentic copies with notarization and have notarized English translations.

For more information about Loyola Marymount University, prospective students should contact:

Matthew X. Fissinger
Director of Admission
Loyola Marymount University
1 LMU Drive
Los Angeles, California 90045
Phone: 310-338-2750
800-LMU-INFO (toll-free)
Fax: 310-338-2797
E-mail: admissions@lmu.edu
Web site: http://www.lmu.edu/

Between classes at Loyola Marymount University.

LOYOLA UNIVERSITY MARYLAND

BALTIMORE, MARYLAND

The University

Loyola University Maryland (formerly Loyola College in Maryland) is a private liberal arts school with the Catholic traditions of the Jesuits and the Sisters of Mercy. It is an educational community of students and faculty members cooperating for the intellectual, spiritual, and professional enrichment of all its members and for the improvement of the local community and society in general. The intellectual enterprise is a joint creation of the faculty members and the students. Loyola's current full-time undergraduate enrollment is 3,500 men and women; more than 80 percent of the student body lives on campus.

Loyola encourages cocurricular activities that contribute to the academic, social, and spiritual growth of the student. These include social and cultural organizations, Student Government activities, military science activities, national honor societies, and Division I athletic programs such as basketball, crew, cross-country, golf, lacrosse, soccer, swimming and diving, tennis, track, and volleyball. The majority of the student body participates in the wide variety of club and intramural sports offered.

In recent years, Loyola's campus has undergone significant expansion. Thirteen apartment complexes and four freshman residence halls provide Loyola students with on-campus housing. The Andrew White Student Center offers several dining choices, and spacious meeting and recreational space. The Student Center also provides facilities for athletics and the fine arts, including the McManus Theatre and the 4,000-seat Reitz Arena. The Center also has an art gallery, classrooms, and music, photography, and studio art labs. A popular addition to Loyola's sports facilities is the Fitness and Aquatic Center. This 110,000-square-foot athletic facility provides an indoor pool, basketball courts, squash courts, a climbing wall, fitness equipment, tracks, and outdoor playing fields. The Ridley Athletic Complex, completed in spring 2010, is a 6,000-seat grandstand stadium with locker rooms, a weight-training suite, an expertly staffed first aid suite, concession areas, and memorabilia for sale on-site.

Location

The Loyola campus is located in a lovely residential area of north Baltimore, 5 miles from the Inner Harbor area. This location offers the student the advantages of quiet residential living with the attractions of city life. The metropolitan area has a wide variety of theaters, museums, professional and intercollegiate sports events, and historical points of interest. Other colleges and universities in the vicinity help to expand the social calendar and academic life.

Majors and Degrees

Loyola offers programs in thirty-six majors. The Bachelor of Arts degree is awarded in art history, classical civilization, classics, communication, computer science, economics, elementary education, English, fine arts, global studies, history, modern languages and literatures, philosophy, political science, psychology, sociology, speech pathology/audiology, theology, and writing. The Bachelor of Business Administration degree is awarded in accounting, business economics, finance, general business, information systems, international business, management, and marketing. The Bachelor of Science degree is awarded in biology, chemistry, computer science, engineering science, mathematical science, and physics.

Academic Programs

The curriculum at Loyola is divided into three parts: the core, the major, and electives. The core contains those courses that Loyola considers essential to the liberal arts curriculum. These courses, which are required of all students regardless of major, are completed during the four years. The core consists of a classical or modern language, English literature, writing, mathematics and natural science, social science, fine arts, history, philosophy, ethics, and theology. The major enables students to pursue in depth their specialized area of study. Electives give students the opportunity to broaden their intellectual and cultural background in areas of special interest. To prepare for graduate study, students may enroll in one of the four preprofessional programs: dental, law, medical, or veterinary.

An honors program and honors housing are available to outstanding students. The honors program stresses independent work by specially grouped students in many of the core courses. Honors housing provides an environment that is conducive to study and close social interaction.

Off-Campus Programs

Loyola University Maryland participates in a cooperative program with the College of Notre Dame of Maryland, Johns Hopkins University, Goucher College, Morgan State University, Towson University, the Peabody Conservatory of Music, and the Maryland College Institute of Art. Loyola students may cross-register at any of these area colleges and universities.

Students in good academic standing may pursue studies abroad through Loyola's programs in Leuven, Belgium; Bangkok, Thailand; Alcalá, Spain; Melbourne, Australia; Newcastle, England; Auckland, New Zealand; Beijing, China; Cork, Ireland; Rome, Italy; Paris, France; and San Salvador, El Salvador. Loyola has programs available in twenty-eight other countries in conjunction with other schools.

Academic Facilities

The Donnelly Science Center has recently been expanded, making it the largest academic building on the Evergreen campus. It features state-of-the-art laboratories for tomorrow's scientists and health-care professionals; and new classrooms and offices that give faculty members even more space for instruction and research.

In the spring 2000 semester, Loyola welcomed the Sellinger School of Business. For the first time since its formation in 1980, the School of Business and Management is headquartered in one central location on the Evergreen campus. Highlights of this newest academic addition include eleven classrooms, five seminar rooms, fifty-two faculty and departmental offices, and an information center. In addition, 90 percent of Sellinger classes are taught in Internet-linked, multimedia classrooms.

Costs

For 2010–11, tuition for all undergraduate students is $37,950 per year. Room for freshmen is $8550. Student fees are estimated at $1400.

Financial Aid

It is the intent of Loyola to assist qualified students who might not otherwise be able to provide for themselves an opportunity for higher education. Financial aid is awarded on academic ability and financial need. Two thirds of the student body receive financial assistance in the forms of Loyola University Maryland scholarships, state scholarships, Federal Pell Grants, Federal Supplemental Educational Opportunity Grants, Federal Perkins Loans, and Federal Work-Study Program opportunities. To apply for financial assistance, students must submit the Free Application for Federal Student Aid and the Financial Aid PROFILE through the College Scholarship Service in Princeton, New Jersey. The financial aid application deadline is February 15.

Faculty

Loyola intends to maintain its faculty-student ratio of approximately 1:12 and an average class size of 25 students to ensure interest in the individual student. Of the 410 faculty members, 81 percent are full-time and 81 percent hold a doctoral or terminal degree in their field. No classes are taught by graduate students.

Student Government

The Student Government serves three chief functions, which make its existence not only valuable but also necessary. These functions are to represent the student body outside the University, to provide leadership within the student body, and to perform services, both social and academic, for the students. Responsibility for budgeting activities also rests with the Student Government. The president of the Student Government is a member of the College Academic Council.

Admission Requirements

Applicants for admission to Loyola University Maryland are evaluated according to their academic qualifications. The most important academic criteria include the secondary school record and recommendations from an academic source. Submission of SAT and ACT scores is optional for first-year applicants, excluding home-schooled students and NCAA athletic recruits. SAT and ACT scores will be reviewed as a core component, if submitted. Students who choose not to submit standardized test scores must submit an additional letter of recommendation or personal essay. The University welcomes applications from men and women of character, intelligence, and motivation, without discrimination on the grounds of race or religious belief.

Application and Information

Interested students seeking to enroll at Loyola may apply online using the Loyola Application or the Common Application. Each applicant must submit a counselor letter of recommendation, a teacher letter of recommendation, and a personal statement. Applicants for all forms of financial aid must submit the Financial Aid PROFILE of the College Scholarship Service and the Free Application for Federal Student Aid. A $50 application fee must accompany the application for admission.

For additional information, students are encouraged to contact:

Undergraduate Admission Office
Loyola University Maryland
4501 North Charles Street
Baltimore, Maryland 21210-2699
Phone: 410-617-5012
800-221-9107 (toll-free)
Web site: http://www.loyola.edu

Loyola's campus offers the freedom of a residential setting, yet it is only minutes from the resources of a major metropolitan area.

LOYOLA UNIVERSITY NEW ORLEANS

NEW ORLEANS, LOUISIANA

The University

Founded by the Jesuits in 1912, Loyola University's more than 35,000 graduates have excelled in innumerable professional fields for over ninety years. The 3,000 undergraduate students (5,000 students total) enjoy the individual attention of a caring faculty in a university dedicated to creating community and fostering individualism while educating the whole person, not only intellectually, but spiritually, socially, and athletically. Loyola students represent all fifty states and forty-eight countries. This diversity is found in a setting where the average class size is 17–24 students. Almost 70 percent of the students permanently reside outside Louisiana, and 37 percent belong to minority groups.

Loyola's 20-acre main campus and 4-acre Broadway campus are located in the historic uptown area of New Orleans and are hubs of student activity. The University's residence halls, equipped with computer labs, kitchen, laundry, and study facilities, are home to nearly 75 percent of the freshmen who reside on campus. The Joseph A. Danna Center, the student center, houses six food venues, including the Orleans Room, Flambeaux's, Fresh Market, Smoothie King, and Satchmo's, Loyola's own jazz hall. An art gallery and post office can also be found in the Danna Center. Nationally affiliated fraternities and sororities are among Loyola's more than 120 student organizations. During the fall's Organizational Fair, students can join the 2006 Pacemaker Award–winning newspaper, the Loyola University Community Action Program (a volunteer community service organization, the largest organization on campus), or one of the many special interest groups. Students can also take this opportunity to sign up for one of Loyola's club sports. Every year, approximately one third of the student body participates in club sports, such as cheerleading, crew, cycling, dance, golf, swimming, and volleyball, as well as in men's lacrosse, rugby, and soccer. Loyola participates in the National Association of Intercollegiate Athletics (NAIA) men's baseball, basketball, cross-country, and track (distance) and women's basketball, cross-country, and volleyball. The University Sports Complex offers six multipurpose courts, an elevated running track, an Olympic-size swimming pool, weight rooms, and aerobics and combat-sports facilities.

The career services offered by the Career Development Center include career counseling and testing, assistance with choosing a course of study, recommendations about graduate and professional school, and assistance in securing internships and jobs.

Career development services include individualized consultation and counseling (with personality and career-interest testing), a career exploration course, career-related speakers, and a career information library. Publications include information on a wide range of career choices, graduate school directories, scholarship and financial aid directories, and field-specific directories of employers.

The Joseph A. Butt, S.J., College of Business is fully accredited at both the undergraduate and graduate levels by the Association to Advance Collegiate Schools of Business–AACSB International, and houses the Mildred Soule and Clarence A. Lengendre Chair in Business Ethics. The College of Music and Fine Arts offers students opportunities in music industry studies and music performance areas as well as visual and theater arts. This college also hosts the Thelonious Monk Institute of Jazz Performance. Students in the College of Humanities and Natural Sciences might choose premed preparation, psychology, or areas in the humanities, such as history or modern foreign languages. The College of Social Sciences houses a School of Mass Communication that offers award winning programs in advertising, journalism, and public relations.

Location

Loyola's main campus fronts oak-lined St. Charles Avenue in uptown New Orleans. Its red-brick, Tudor-Gothic buildings overlook Audubon Park, home of the famous Audubon Zoo. The downtown area is a 20-minute streetcar ride away, allowing students to take advantage of the city's broad cultural and artistic environment. Considering that New Orleans enjoys an average temperature of 70 degrees, students can enjoy year-round outdoor activities in a city famous for its food, music, and cultural festivals. Lake Pontchartrain is within the city limits and provides facilities for water sports.

Majors and Degrees

Loyola University grants degrees in four-year undergraduate programs. The College of Humanities and Natural Sciences grants the B.A. degree in classical studies, English, English writing, French, history, philosophy, psychology, psychology (premed), religious studies (Christianity and world religions), and Spanish. It grants the B.S. in biology (predentistry, premedicine, and pre–veterinary studies), chemistry (premedicine), chemistry–forensic science, mathematics, and physics. The College of Business awards the B.B.A. degree in economics, finance, international business, management, marketing, and music industry studies, as well as the Bachelor of Accountancy. The College of Music and Fine Arts grants the B.M. in composition, jazz studies, music education, music industry studies, music therapy and performance (instrumental and vocal), and grants the B.S. in music industry studies. The College also grants a B.A. in graphic arts, theater arts, theater arts–communications, theater arts (with a minor in business administration), and visual arts and a B.F.A. in visual arts. The College of Social Sciences offers the B.A. in criminal justice, political science, and sociology, and the School of Mass Communication offers the B.A. in advertising, journalism, and public relations. Minors are available in all disciplines offered as majors. Africana, African American, American, environmental, film studies, Latin American, medieval, and women's studies are offered as interdisciplinary minors addressing important areas of national and international concern.

Academic Programs

Once enrolled at Loyola, students are introduced to the Common Curriculum, designed to give them a well-rounded preparation in their major field of concentration, as well as the ability to understand and reflect on disciplines allied to or outside their major. The curriculum is divided into four categories: major, minor, Common Curriculum, and elective courses. Students must meet the requirements of their degree program as specified by their particular college; the minimum four-year program requires 120 hours. Common Curriculum courses include seven introductory courses in English composition, math, science, philosophy, religion, literature, and history and nine upper-division courses in humanities, social science, and natural science. The College of Business requires that all students with junior or senior standing complete a 3-credit-hour internship prior to graduation. Internships provide professional-level experience in area business firms and not-for-profit organizations, along with college credit for semester-long participation. The College of Humanities and Natural Sciences also requires a minimum of one year of study in a modern foreign language. The honors program and independent studies provide special opportunities for qualified students.

Off-Campus Programs

Through the Center for International Education, students may spend their junior year in Rome. Summer programs in Germany, Greece, Ireland, London, and Mexico are also available, as well as opportunities to study in Belgium, France, Japan, and Spain. Through consortium arrangements, students may cross-register for courses for credit at Xavier University, Tulane University, and Notre Dame Seminary and participate with these institutions in joint social-cultural events. In addition, the University offers a rigorous internship program in New Orleans at businesses, institutions, and schools to give students practical experience in their fields, including business, communications, modern foreign languages, music, and writing. Loyola offers a 3-3 program with the Loyola College of Law for students interested in pursuing a prelaw track, an early acceptance program with Tulane University Medical School, and a five-year M.B.A. program through the College of Business.

Academic Facilities

A $13-million Communications/Music Complex includes classrooms, offices, specialized instructional facilities for the College of Music and

Fine Arts and the School of Mass Communication, and a 600-seat performing arts facility for the College of Music and Fine Arts.

Computing is an integral part of campus life at Loyola. The University provides more than 450 computers in seventeen computer labs throughout the campus. These labs consist of Windows- and Macintosh-based computers with a wide variety of application software and access to the Internet. Loyola's high-speed Ethernet network can also be accessed from locations such as residence halls, the library, and other public areas. A noteworthy characteristic of Loyola's computing resources is its student-centered emphasis. For example, specialized computer labs exist in the Writing Across the Curriculum Center, English and Math Basic Skills Labs, Poverty Law Clinic, and Business Solutions Center.

The Broadway campus, approximately two blocks down St. Charles Avenue, houses the Loyola College of Law, the visual arts department, the Division of Institutional Advancement, and a residence hall.

Other facilities on campus include the J. Edgar and Louise S. Monroe Library, the region's most technologically advanced facility and the 2003 recipient of the Association of College and Research Libraries' Excellence in Academic Libraries Award, which contains more than 367,000 volumes and provides access to over 27,000 electronic books and more than 23,000 electronic journals. The Monroe Library also offers more than 660,000 microform units and 2,500 media titles. There are also specialized libraries for music and law. The 150,000-square-foot Monroe Library contains 1,800 computer links, media/instructional technology services, a visual arts center, and the Lindy Boggs National Center for Community Literacy. The library also offers three 24-hour microcomputer labs, two multimedia classrooms, and sixteen group-study rooms.

Costs

For the full-time undergraduate student attending during 2010–11, tuition is $30,468 for the year. The cost of residence halls (double occupancy) and a complete meal plan is $10,188 for the year. This does not include a $1346 University fee.

Financial Aid

Loyola University's endowment provides money for financial aid in addition to that provided by federal funding. Assistance in the forms of merit- and talent-based scholarships, loans, work-study program awards, and grants is awarded on the basis of academic achievement and need. More than 450 scholarships are awarded annually to students with competitive grades and test scores. To apply for one of the scholarships, students must have a GPA of at least 3.2 and competitive standardized test scores. Offers of financial aid are not made until after admission. Notifications of awards are sent in early February. Awards of need-based financial aid packages are made on a first-come, first-served basis and are announced in mid-March. Eighty-four percent of Loyola students receive some form of financial aid.

Faculty

Behind every program at Loyola is a faculty of Jesuit and lay professors who are especially well qualified in their particular fields. The Jesuit Order, recognized throughout the world for its educational contributions over the centuries, administers the University's faculty of 258 full-time professors, of whom 91 percent hold the terminal degree in their field. Loyola also employs 148 part-time instructors. No graduate assistants teach classes. The student-faculty ratio of 11:1 emphasizes the University's special quality of personal involvement and concern for each student and his or her particular needs.

Student Government

Loyola's Student Government Association consists of representatives elected by the student body from each of the four colleges and the law school. The association conducts general meetings, elections, and student activities. Student representatives sit on nearly all University committees.

Admission Requirements

Prospective students must submit an application, resume, and essay; have a high school transcript or GED test results sent; submit ACT or SAT scores; and have their counselor or teacher send a recommendation. Individual attention is given to each application form. Final selection is based on high school grades, test scores, and counselor or teacher recommendations. Significant community involvement and demonstrated leadership abilities are recommended. Auditions are required for final acceptance to the College of Music and Fine Arts, which includes the Department of Theatre Arts and Dance. Portfolios are required for final acceptance to the Department of Visual Arts.

December 1 is the priority deadline for freshman admission and scholarship consideration. January 15 is the regular deadline for freshman scholarship consideration. February 15 is the regular deadline for freshman admission consideration.

Transfer students are required to submit an official transcript for each institution previously attended along with their transfer application. Transfer scholarships are available only to students entering in the fall. Transfer students interested in competing for a scholarship should apply by March 1 if possible, and no later than April 15. For nonscholarship admission consideration, transfer students should apply no later than May 15 for the fall semester and no later than December 1 for the spring semester.

Application and Information

Interested students are encouraged to contact:

Office of Admissions
Loyola University New Orleans
6363 St. Charles Avenue, Box 18
New Orleans, Louisiana 70118
Phone: 504-865-3240
800-4-LOYOLA (toll-free)
Fax: 504-865-3383
E-mail: admit@loyno.edu
Web site: http://www.loyno.edu

Loyola is located on beautiful, oak-lined St. Charles Avenue adjacent to Audubon Park.

LUTHER COLLEGE

DECORAH, IOWA

The College

Luther College, which was founded in 1861, is a four-year residential liberal arts college of the Evangelical Lutheran Church in America (ELCA). The College, which was founded by Norwegian immigrants, is an academic community of faith and learning where students of promise from all beliefs and backgrounds have the freedom to learn, to express themselves, to perform, to compete, and to grow. The College, which is located in Decorah, Iowa, is home to 2,500 students from forty-one states and forty-seven countries. Thirty-two percent of the students are from Iowa; 87 percent come from the four-state area of Iowa, Minnesota, Wisconsin, and Illinois. Each year, over 125 international students choose to study at Luther.

In keeping with its liberal arts tradition, the College requires students to develop a depth of knowledge in their chosen major and a breadth of knowledge through exposure to a wide range of subjects and intellectual approaches (general requirements). Learning at Luther is about engagement: faculty members who are passionate in their teaching and scholarship, students who are active and involved, and a College community characterized by personal attention, hands-on experiences, academic challenge, and community support. At Luther, all students become immersed in the liberal arts through the College's common year-long course for first-year students called Paideia. The course, which is uncommon in its approach, helps train students' minds and develop their research and writing skills as they explore human cultures and history. In addition, Luther offers a Phi Beta Kappa chapter and several departmental honor societies, evidence of the quality of teaching and learning on campus.

At Luther, students are encouraged to seek out connections between their lives in the classroom and their lives outside the classroom. The College provides a stimulating cultural and educational atmosphere by bringing distinguished public figures, theater groups, musicians, and educators to the campus. Cocurricular activities are an important part of College life. The College sponsors seven choirs, three orchestras, three bands, two jazz bands, and a full theater and dance program. Numerous student organizations and societies provide ample opportunities for student involvement in meaningful activities. As a community of faith, students can participate in daily chapel, weekly Sunday worship, outreach teams, and midweek Eucharist.

Nineteen intercollegiate sports are offered. Men may participate in ten sports: baseball, basketball, cross-country, football, golf, soccer, swimming, tennis, track and field, and wrestling. Women compete in nine intercollegiate sports: basketball, cross-country, golf, soccer, softball, swimming, tennis, track and field, and volleyball. Club sports include Ultimate Frisbee, rugby, and men's volleyball. Sixty-four percent of the student body is involved in an extensive intramural and recreational sports program. Available for recreational use and for the physical education program are twelve outdoor tennis courts, an eight-lane polyurethane 400-meter track, numerous cross-country running and ski trails, and 15 acres of intramural fields. The well-equipped field house contains a 25-yard indoor pool, three racquetball courts, four hardwood basketball courts, a wrestling complex, and a 3,000-seat gymnasium. A sports forum houses a six-lane, 200-meter indoor track; six indoor tennis courts; locker rooms; and athletic training facilities. The Legends Fitness for Life Center provides the latest fitness equipment and a 30-foot-high rock-climbing wall.

Location

The College is located in Decorah, a city of 8,500 people in the scenic bluff country of northeast Iowa. The Upper Iowa River, which runs through the campus, is designated as a National Scenic and Recreational River. Rich in Scandinavian heritage, Decorah is a popular recreation area, providing opportunities for canoeing, fishing, hunting, cross-country skiing, camping, hiking, cycling, and spelunking. Three airports are located within a 75-mile radius of Decorah: in Rochester, Minnesota; Waterloo, Iowa; and La Crosse, Wisconsin.

Majors and Degrees

Luther College grants the Bachelor of Arts (B.A.) degree and offers majors in accounting, Africana studies, anthropology, art, athletic training, biblical languages, biology, business, chemistry, classical languages (Greek and Latin), classics, communication studies, computer science, economics, elementary education, English, environmental studies, health, history, management, management information systems, mathematics, mathematics/statistics, modern languages (Chinese, French, German, Norwegian, and Spanish), music, nursing, philosophy, physical education, physics, political science, psychology, religion, Scandinavian studies, secondary education, social work, sociology, sociology/political science, speech and theater, theater/dance, and women and gender studies. Interdisciplinary programs are available in arts management, international management, international studies, museum studies, music management, Russian studies, Scandinavian studies, sports management, and theater/dance management. Preprofessional preparation is offered in dentistry, engineering, environmental management, forestry, law, medical technology, medicine, music therapy, optometry, pharmacy, physical therapy, sports management, theology, and veterinary medicine.

Academic Programs

Luther operates on a 4-1-4 academic calendar. The first semester runs from September to December, followed by a three-week January Term and the second semester, which runs from February to May. Two 4-week summer sessions are offered in June and July. Each candidate is required to complete a total of 128 semester hours of credit with a C average or better. At least 76 of the required 128 semester hours must be earned outside the major discipline. Each senior writes a research paper in his or her major. Students are required to complete the following number of semester hours of credit in designated areas: 12 of Paideia, an interdisciplinary course; 9–12 of religion/philosophy; 7–8 of natural science; 6–8 of social science; 3–9 of foreign language (proficiency based); 3–4 of fine arts; 3–4 of global studies; 3–4 of quantitative or symbolic reasoning; and 2 of physical education. Advanced placement and credit by examination are available. A qualified student may develop an interdisciplinary major with a faculty adviser.

Off-Campus Programs

Students may participate in off-campus programs during the fall and spring semesters, the January Term, and summer sessions. All of the programs carry academic credit. Luther participates in the Iowa General Assembly Legislative Intern Program during the spring semester of each year. Urban studies semesters may be arranged in conjunction with other colleges. The Washington Semester gives qualified juniors the opportunity to study at American University and work within one department of the federal government. Luther College also cosponsors a semester program in Washington, D.C., through the Lutheran College Washington Consortium. Students may elect to be exchange students at other colleges for one semester or a January Term.

Luther is an affiliate of the Institute of European Studies, which has centers in more than twenty European and Asian countries; students studying at one of these centers receive credit in accordance with the provisions for transfer credit for study abroad under the Junior Year Abroad programs. A community studies program in Nottingham, England, is staffed by a Luther professor each year. In alternate years, a Luther professor directs on-site programs in Münster, Germany; Lillehammer, Norway; and Sliema, Malta. In addition, opportunities for study are available in a variety of settings, such as the Bahamas, China, Russia, Tanzania, and Norway.

Academic Facilities

The 1,000-acre campus includes the Preus Library, housing 350,000 volumes, 1,100 periodicals, and the College art collection. The library offers five online indexes and ten commercial online services and provides access to more than 480 other libraries. Modern, well-equipped laboratories in the Valders Hall of Science are supplemented by several other science-teaching facilities on campus: a planetarium, a greenhouse, an herbarium, a live-animal center, a human anatomy laboratory, a natural history museum, and a psychology sleep laboratory. Sampson Hoffland, a dynamic new 58,000-square-foot science and research center, was completed in fall 2008. The science facilities also include an extensive field study area and two electron microscopes. Within easy walking distance of the campus, the field study area offers an ideal setting for studies in aquatic biology, ecology, and field biology. Five ponds, two reestablished prairies, marshes, wooded areas, and agricultural lands are available for classwork and independent study. The College has a fiber-based campus network connecting a variety of PC and Macintosh computers (in several environments) to shared computing resources and to the Internet. More than 400 microcomputers and terminals are available for student use throughout the campus.

Luther College maintains radio station KWLC-AM, and the College's affiliate station, KLSE-FM, is part of the Minnesota Public Radio network. Luther also maintains the largest archaeological research center in Iowa. The Norwegian American Museum in Decorah, one of the finest ethnic museums in the country, provides an invaluable resource for museum and Scandinavian studies. The foreign language departments maintain a twenty-five-station electronic classroom, and the psychology department houses a twenty-station IBM interactive computer network.

The impressive F. W. Olin Building houses the economics and business, mathematics, and computer science departments. Among its technological wonders is the Luther Round Table Room, where students experience simultaneous decision making via a computer network.

The award-winning Jenson Hall of Music contains state-of-the-art computer facilities, a recording studio, and four pipe organs: 23-stop/34-rank and 42-stop/61-rank tracker organs for practice and performing and two Schlicker practice organs of 8 and 5 ranks, respectively. Jenson Hall of Music also contains 32,000 square feet of classrooms, studios, practice rooms, and rehearsal rooms for keyboard, vocal, and instrumental music. The Center for Faith and Life (CFL) houses a 42-stop/62-rank organ in the 1,600-seat auditorium for the performing arts. The CFL also houses the offices of the campus ministry, a 24-hour meditation chapel, a 200-seat recital hall, and one of four campus art galleries.

The Center for the Arts serves as the home for theater, dance, and the arts.

Costs

For 2010–11, the comprehensive fee is $39,265, which includes tuition, general fees, facilities fees, room, board, subscription to student publications, and admission to College-supported concerts, lectures, and other events. A room telephone, cable TV, computer access from residence hall rooms, and a health-service program are also included. Private music lessons are $350 per semester. It is estimated that an additional $3000 is adequate for books, clothing, entertainment, and other personal expenses.

Financial Aid

More than 97 percent of all Luther students receive financial aid in the form of grants, such as the Federal Pell Grant; scholarships from Luther and other sources; loans; and jobs on campus. Luther awards Regent and Presidential Scholarships to those demonstrating superior academic achievement. The amount of aid given is determined by the College's analysis of the Free Application for Federal Student Aid (FAFSA). The priority deadline for a financial aid application is March 1. Students receive notification of financial aid awards after their acceptance for admission.

Faculty

There are 177 full-time and 74 part-time faculty members; 89 percent hold a Ph.D., first professional, or other terminal degree. The student-faculty ratio is 12:1.

Student Government

Students share in the governance of the College and participate in social and cultural programming. They have full membership on most College committees, majority representation in the Community Assembly, and nonvoting representation on the Board of Regents.

Admission Requirements

Admission is selective. An applicant must be a graduate of an accredited high school and have completed at least 4 units of English, 3 units of mathematics, 3 units of social science, and 2 units of natural science. It is strongly recommended that the applicant have at least two years of a foreign language. Seventy percent of entering students rank in the top quarter of their high school class. Transfer students may enroll in either semester. Early admission and admission with honors are available. The priority deadline is March 1.

Application and Information

An application, SAT or ACT scores, an educator's reference, and a transcript of previous academic work are required for admission. On-campus interviews are recommended but not required. For more information about Luther, students should contact:

Admissions Office
Luther College
Decorah, Iowa 52101-1042
Phone: 563-387-1287
800-458-8437 (toll-free)
Fax: 563-387-2159
563-387-1062 (international)
E-mail: admissions@luther.edu (admissions)
finaid@luther.edu (financial aid)
intladmissions@luther.edu (international)
Web site: http://www.luther.edu

Luther College's spacious 1,000-acre campus in the scenic bluff country of northeast Iowa.

LYNCHBURG COLLEGE

LYNCHBURG, VIRGINIA

The College

Lynchburg College is a fully accredited, coeducational, nonsectarian liberal arts college related to the Christian Church (Disciples of Christ). It offers undergraduate programs in the liberal arts, sciences, and professional disciplines (including business, communications, education, and nursing) and graduate programs in art, business, education, and nursing. A Doctorate of Physical Therapy program will begin in the fall of 2010. The College is committed to the principle that every individual is of infinite worth, and it endeavors to provide a program of liberal education consistent with the needs of contemporary society. It draws its undergraduate student body of approximately 2,100 men and women from thirty-five states and fourteen countries. The College community is largely residential, with approximately 92 percent of the full-time undergraduate student body living on campus. Approximately 40 percent of the undergraduates are from out of state.

The 214-acre campus has long been considered one of the most beautiful in the South. Thirty-seven buildings of mostly Georgian Colonial design have the majestic Blue Ridge Mountains as a backdrop. The Claytor Nature Study Center, a 470-acre farm in nearby Bedford County, is utilized for environmental and educational purposes as a learning laboratory to promote the property as a model of environmental management in cooperation with various organizations locally and nationally. Claytor Nature Center is also home to the Belk Astronomical Observatory, a 700-square-foot facility that boasts an RC Optical Systems 20-inch (0.51 meter) Truss Ritchey-Chrétien telescope. The facility also includes a 384-square-foot observation deck equipped with twelve piers for mounting smaller telescopes. An observatory control room is equipped with instrumentation that will allow LC to pursue astronomical research in conjunction with other regional colleges and universities.

A wide variety of activities are available in the Lynchburg College community: service and honor organizations, including the national Bonner Leader Program; more than 100 clubs and organizations; five fraternities; and six sororities as well as opportunities to participate in dramatic productions, student publications, religious activities, and musical performances. New Horizons provides adventure-based leadership and team-building opportunities for individuals and groups. Community service is a distinguishing feature of the Lynchburg College students, staff, and faculty, who annually contribute more than 48,000 volunteer hours to the community through such projects as Habitat for Humanity, Camp Jaycees, Special Olympics, and other programs.

The varsity athletic program is diverse and includes baseball, basketball, cheerleading, cross-country, equestrian sports, golf, indoor and outdoor track and field, lacrosse, soccer, and tennis for men and basketball, cheerleading, cross-country, equestrian sports, field hockey, lacrosse, soccer, softball, tennis, indoor and outdoor track and field, and volleyball for women. The College participates in NCAA Division III and is a charter member of the Old Dominion Athletic Conference, which includes Bridgewater, Eastern Mennonite, Emory & Henry, Guilford, Hampden-Sydney, Hollins, Lynchburg, Randolph-Macon, Randolph, Roanoke, Sweet Briar, Virginia Wesleyan, and Washington and Lee. In addition, the College supports several club sports, including men's and women's lacrosse, men's and women's soccer, cycling, skiing, snowboarding, and shotokan karate. An intramural program exists for interested men and women as well. The Turner Athletic Facility includes state-of-the-art exercise and fitness areas, a dance studio, and one of the top exercise physiology labs in Virginia. The gymnasium seats 1,500.

Shellenberger Field is a state-of-the-art athletic facility with a brand new artificial turf field and eight-lane track. With a 3,000-spectator capacity including chair and bleacher seating and night lighting, it is a formidable venue for opponents who compete with the home team in men's and women's soccer, lacrosse, track and field, and field hockey. Intramural and club sports take advantage of this facility. Also included are Moon Field upgrades—a permanent softball outfield fence and new areas for the track and field events of javelin, hammer, shot put, and discus. The baseball field, Fox Field, was updated recently to include seating for up to 1,000 fans, batting cages, and a press box. These improvements allow students to enjoy many more recreational opportunities in varsity, intramural, and club sports and general activities.

Location

Lynchburg College is located in central Virginia, 100 miles from Richmond, 180 miles southwest of Washington, D.C., and 50 miles east of Roanoke. Greater Lynchburg is a growing business and industrial center with a population of more than 240,000. The city is noted for its climate, culture, and historic landmarks. It is within an easy drive of the Blue Ridge Mountains, where many popular lakes and resorts are located. Air, bus, and railroad transportation place Lynchburg within easy reach of any urban center.

Majors and Degrees

Lynchburg College offers the Bachelor of Arts in the following fields: accounting, art (graphic design or studio art), business administration, communication studies (journalism or speech communication), economics (financial or general), English (literature or writing), French, history, international relations, management, marketing, music, philosophy, political science, religious studies, sociology (criminology or general), Spanish, sports management, and theater. The degree of Bachelor of Science is offered in the following fields: athletic training, biology, biomedical science, chemistry, computer science, environmental science, exercise physiology, health and physical education, health promotion, human development and learning (elementary education or special education), mathematics, nursing, physics, and psychology.

A candidate for a B.A. degree may elect to take a joint major in foreign language–business management, philosophy–political science, philosophy–religious studies, psychology–special education, religious studies–sociology, or religious studies and another major. Double majors and minors may also be taken in many areas of study. Advanced undergraduates may also take some graduate courses.

Preprofessional and professional courses are available for students who want preparation for careers in art therapy, dentistry, engineering, forestry and wildlife management, law, library science, medicine, ministry and ministry-related occupations, occupational therapy, optometry, pharmacy, physical therapy, and veterinary medicine.

Academic Programs

To be eligible for a degree, a student must complete at least 124 semester hours of college-level academic work. In addition, a degree candidate must have a grade point average of at least 2.0 on all work undertaken, plus an average of at least 2.0 or higher depending on the program on all work undertaken in the major field.

The curriculum at Lynchburg College is divided into two general areas; some additional hours are available for students to explore course work in free elective areas of their choice. The first of the two areas of study consists of General Education Requirements (GERs) selected from the broad disciplines of world literature, fine arts, philosophy, religious studies, mathematics, history, social science, laboratory science, foreign languages, and health and movement science. All students are exposed to each of these academic areas. The second of the two general areas is the major. The College offers thirty-eight majors, ranging from education and business to the sciences and the humanities, forty-six minors, as well as thirteen preprofessional programs. This curriculum offers students breadth (GERs) as well as depth (the major). Students may devote their free elective hours to a minor to further enhance their education.

Outstanding students may be selected to participate in the College's Westover Honors Program, the purpose of which is to attract, stimulate, challenge, and fulfill academically gifted students. The program offers a challenging curriculum that promotes intellectual curiosity and independent thinking and places strong emphasis on creative problem solving.

The College operates on an early semester calendar. The first semester begins in late August and ends before Christmas, and the second semester runs from mid-January to early May. An optional winter term abroad is also offered. An Advanced Placement Scholars Program permits some students to enter with advanced standing, credit, or both. Credit is also awarded on the basis of satisfactory scores on the CLEP subject exams. Early admission is available for the talented student. Eligible students who want to accelerate their program may meet degree requirements in three years.

Lynchburg offers entry-level computer courses to all students, and students are strongly encouraged to become computer literate. New students may bring a computer of their own or utilize one of the many available on campus. All students are assigned an e-mail account and have access to the Internet. In addition, all students are allowed to develop their own home pages on the World Wide Web, which they have access to through the computer resources provided by the College. All residence hall rooms are wired for network access and the Intranet, which serves the College community. Wireless Internet access is available in most areas of the campus.

Off-Campus Programs

Various agency and intercollegiate exchange programs are available for interested students. Language students may engage in foreign-study programs and are encouraged to do so. In addition, any student who wishes to study abroad may do so as part of the College's study-abroad program.

Internships, organized through the Academic and Career Services Office, are available locally, nationally, and internationally. More than 1,000 internships are already established, and new sites are developed each year. Specific guidelines for these programs are set forth by each department. In addition, Lynchburg College, Randolph College, and Sweet Briar College, as members of the Tri-College Consortium of Virginia, maintain cooperative relationships for the sharing of facilities and offerings. Students at each of the colleges have access to the libraries of the other two and may enroll in a course on either of the other campuses without payment of additional tuition.

Academic Facilities

The Hobbs Science Center provides an outstanding learning environment for students pursuing studies in biology, chemistry, physics, biomedical sciences, environmental science, psychology, mathematics, and computer science. In addition to state-of-the-art research labs, including a cadaver lab, students studying environmental science can utilize the online weather station, GIS and remote sensing software, and digitizer. This modern facility is also used during the summer by the Virginia Governor's School for Math and Science to provide programming for selected high school students. Extending over 470 acres, the Claytor Nature Study Center is a hands-on learning environment with natural woodlands, grasslands, two lakes, wetlands, and a mile-long stretch of the Big Otter River, and an 8,000-square-foot education/research facility.

Schewel Hall is Lynchburg College's newest, state-of-the-art, $12-million classroom and laboratory facility, which houses the School of Business and Economics, the Communication Studies program, foreign languages, performing arts, and multiple venues for students to congregate and study. This 67,000-square-foot facility includes technology-based classrooms, computer laboratories, and specialized teaching-learning settings, including a model stock exchange room, a digital darkroom, and a multimedia development center with television and recording studios.

The regional community can also enjoy a variety of special events in the 250-seat Sydnor Performance Hall.

The Daura Art Gallery is the major repository of more than 1,000 works of the Catalan-American artist, Pierre Daura. The expansion of this facility makes the Daura Gallery the largest visual art exhibit center in the city of Lynchburg. Each year, it is the site for the Senior Art Show in which chosen student works are exhibited.

Costs

For resident students who enter in the 2010–11 session, total charges are $37,125; this includes $28,960 for tuition, $7220 for room and board, and $945 for student fees.

Financial Aid

Lynchburg College administers a financial aid program of more than $20 million. These resources are awarded to students for meritorious achievement and/or for demonstrated need. Lynchburg College offers academic and achievement scholarships that range from $3000 to $14,000 and are based on performance and accomplishments at the high school or community college level. These awards are renewable each year until the student graduates, as long as the recipient maintains a qualifying minimum academic average each year. Students are identified to receive these scholarships through the admission application; no separate application is necessary. Free early aid estimates are available for students. More than 96 percent of last year's entering class received academic and/or need-based financial aid. The average amount of aid received was $18,000.

To determine eligibility for need-based financial aid, the student should complete the Free Application for Federal Student Aid (FAFSA), which may be obtained at most high schools and at Lynchburg College. The FAFSA results determine the student's eligibility for federally funded grants and loans and other support such as work-study opportunities. In addition, students from Virginia are eligible to apply for the Virginia Tuition Assistance grant.

Faculty

The Lynchburg College faculty has 135 full-time members, 80 percent of whom hold the doctorate or terminal degree in their field. The student-faculty ratio is 12:1. While many faculty members are involved in research projects, it is a College policy that the faculty's top priorities must be in the classroom.

Student Government

The student government of Lynchburg College is regulated by agreements determined by the students, faculty, and administration. It is felt that the College should not be run by the faculty alone or by students alone, but through the cooperative interest of all. Campus government is vested in the Student Government Association, the Judicial Boards, the Campus Life Policies Committee, and the Office of the Dean of Student Development. The Student Government Association is also responsible for the Academic Honor Code, a prominent part of campus life.

Admission Requirements

A candidate for admission to Lynchburg College should be a graduate of an approved secondary school with a minimum of 16 academic units or the equivalent, as shown by examination. It is required that the academic work include major emphases in the areas of English, foreign language, social science, natural sciences, and mathematics. An applicant must demonstrate above-average academic ability in all areas of study, as admission is competitive. In support of the record, a student must present satisfactory scores on the ACT or SAT (critical reading and math scores are used to determine admission decisions and merit scholarship awards). It is recommended that all students have a personal interview and visit the campus beginning the spring semester of their junior year or during their senior year. Enrollment Office hours during the academic year are 9 to 5 Monday through Friday and 9 to noon on Saturday during the academic year.

Application and Information

Early decision admission applications must be received by November 15; notification of acceptance is made by December 15. All other applications are processed on a rolling admissions basis. Applicants are notified of the status of their application usually within two to four weeks of the date their application file is completed.

For information, students should contact:

Sharon Walters-Bower, Director of Admissions
Lynchburg College
1501 Lakeside Drive
Lynchburg, Virginia 24501
Phone: 434-544-8300
800-426-8101 (toll-free)
Fax: 434-544-8653
E-mail: admissions@lynchburg.edu
Web site: http://www.lynchburg.edu

COLLEGE CLOSE-UPS

LYNN UNIVERSITY

BOCA RATON, FLORIDA

The University

Lynn University in Boca Raton is a private, coeducational, liberal arts university awarding bachelor's and master's degrees in the liberal arts and sciences and professional education. Founded in 1962 and accredited by the Southern Association of Colleges and Schools, Lynn offers a distinctive, innovative, and individualized approach to learning within an international community. The University currently enrolls more than 2,300 students, representing forty states and eighty-four nations. Specialized programs include a Conservatory of Music, a School of Aeronautics, and the Institute for Achievement and Learning, which is an international pioneer in developing successful teaching strategies for students with learning differences.

Although grounded in the liberal arts, Lynn has a collection of colleges and majors oriented toward emerging professional opportunities. The University's five colleges and two schools offer twenty-eight undergraduate majors as well as four master's degrees representing eight majors. A doctoral program in educational leadership began in fall 2009.

About 60 percent of Lynn's undergraduate students live in the five residence halls. The campus offers wireless coverage for classrooms, labs, residence halls, the library, and other public spaces. All residence halls include study and computer lounges.

Campus recreation areas include two pools, athletic fields, tennis and basketball courts, outdoor grills, a sand volleyball court, and a newly remodeled fitness center. The Lynn Student Center houses the cafeteria, an auditorium, student activities offices, and a snack bar with flat screen TVs and pool tables. Christine's, an on-campus coffee bar, serves a variety of Starbucks coffee drinks, smoothies, snacks, and sandwiches. Campus facilities also include laundry and mail rooms, bookstore, classroom buildings, newly renovated library, small concert hall, international student center, and a gymnasium. The new 750-seat Keith C. and Elaine Johnson Wold Performing Arts Center opened in spring 2010 and is the main performance venue for the world-renowned Lynn University Conservatory of Music.

University life is designed to create learning opportunities both within and outside the classroom. As a learning-centered community, Lynn University expects students to embrace decision-making and leadership. Lynn's student involvement program offers myriad ways to develop leadership talents and skills that will translate into the workplace. Lynn has more than thirty-five campus organizations and activities covering a variety of special interests, including student government, multicultural organizations, and Greek life as well as a Leadership Academy. The career center's comprehensive services include workshops, vocational and personality testing, a mentoring program, career fairs, and extensive internship placements. Alumni receive lifetime job placement assistance.

Lynn also has a top-ranked NCAA athletic program, which has earned nineteen national championships, twenty-five Sunshine State Conference championships, and three NCAA coaches of the year. Lynn University has had ninety-five Academic/Scholar All-America honors in its history. The Fighting Knights intercollegiate athletic program includes men's and women's basketball, golf, soccer, and tennis; men's baseball; and women's softball and volleyball.

Location

Located in Boca Raton on Florida's southeastern coast, the Lynn campus is only 50 minutes from Miami, 30 minutes from West Palm Beach, and 30 minutes from Fort Lauderdale and is easily accessed from the international airports of West Palm Beach, Fort Lauderdale, and Miami. Because of its location in the heart of one of the world's leading business, sports, media, and hospitality industry centers, Lynn students benefit from a wide variety of internship as well as cultural and recreational opportunities. The safe, beautiful 123-acre campus is in a residential area, three miles from the beaches of the Atlantic Ocean, two miles from Boca Raton's city center, and only a few minutes from first-class shopping and restaurants.

Majors and Degrees

The College of Liberal Education offers the Bachelor of Arts and Bachelor of Science degree with majors in natural science (biology, environmental studies); law, justice, and public policy (criminal justice); American studies; and global studies. Students may design a customized major with guidance from a faculty adviser.

Lynn's renowned Conservatory of Music awards the Bachelor of Music in composition and in music performance, with specializations in bass trombone, bassoon, cello, clarinet, double bass, flute, French horn, oboe, percussion, piano, trombone, trumpet, tuba, viola, and violin.

The College of Business and Management offers the Bachelor of Science in business administration, with specializations in aviation management, fashion management, general management, finance, and marketing.

The College of Hospitality Management offers a Bachelor of Science in hospitality management, with specializations in hospitality and resort management and sports management.

The Eugene M. and Christine E. Lynn College of International Communication offers the Bachelor of Arts or Bachelor of Science degree with majors in advertising; computer animation; drama; film; graphic design; illustration; multimedia journalism; photography; public relations; and radio, television, and Internet media.

The Donald E. and Helen L. Ross College of Education offers the Bachelor of Science in elementary education, with specializations in exceptional student education, grades K–6, and grades K–6 plus pre-K/primary (age 3–grade 3).

Academic Programs

Lynn University follows a semester calendar, and offers a summer session and January term. All classes are taught by faculty members, not graduate assistants or teaching assistants. The University embraces students who have varying levels of academic abilities and learning styles along with a strong motivation to excel. Average class size is 17 students.

The University's innovative curriculum challenges students to build increasing competencies not only in their chosen field of study, but in every area of life. Dialogues of Learning, the core curriculum, offers a strong foundation in liberal arts for all students. In their majors, students put theory into practice through internships, partnerships with businesses, and community service projects. Lynn has a January term that lasts two to three weeks and is based on experiential learning opportunities, giving students the chance to select a course outside the realm of their major. First-year students who have excelled academically may apply for a special three-year degree program called Lynn Degree 3.0 that enables the selected students to complete all academic credits and requirements in three years.

Lynn students also benefit from an exceptionally strong advising program that pairs each incoming student with a faculty member in the student's chosen major field. Faculty advisers become mentors throughout each student's academic career and beyond. All faculty members are committed to great teaching and challenge students to become active, intentional, and purposeful learners.

The honors program at Lynn provides a unique opportunity for select students to test themselves academically, and achieve special recognition for their efforts. Honors classes are smaller than regular classes and offer close-knit, seminar-style learning, and more direct interaction with professors. Students have increased opportunities to participate in customized research and experiential learning, and to have their work recognized publicly. Honors students present their projects every year at state, regional, and national Collegiate Honors Council conferences, and may publish their work in the Lynn scholarly journal, *The Scholar*. Students with appropriate academic standing will be invited to join the honors program.

Lynn University's Institute for Achievement and Learning is a model for higher education. Led by a nationally recognized learning specialist, the institute brings together an array of services and professionals that help support students, regardless of their learning style. All Lynn students have access to the institute, which offers a variety of services: academic coaching, diagnostic testing and recommendations for students struggling academically, tutoring, group sessions to help students prevent anxiety related to test-taking and learning challenges, and individual and group content-area tutoring. The institute also has a distraction-reduced testing environment and offers specialized Dialogues of Learning classes taught by Institute Fellows who are trained in learning differences and who use a variety of teaching and learning strategies. The institute also houses Lynn University's ADA Office.

Off-Campus Programs

Lynn University's international programs are among the best in higher education. For the last four years, *U.S. News & World Report* has ranked Lynn first in number of international students among universities its size in the Southeast. At Lynn, every student is encouraged to complete study-abroad academic credits in his or her major, by either participating in a faculty-led short-term program during semester breaks, or studying abroad for a semester or a full academic year. Recently students have studied in Australia, New Zealand, China, Hong Kong, Cambodia, Singapore, Thailand, South Africa, Morocco, Puerto Rico, Costa Rica, Argentina, Ireland, Scotland, England, Belgium, Luxembourg, Germany, Switzerland, Italy, France, Spain, and Portugal.

Academic Facilities

Over several years Lynn has invested in extensive technological enhancements, including interactive whiteboards and document projectors in 70 percent of classrooms and labs. Computer labs are available in five buildings across the campus, and computer stations offer the latest versions of popular software applications. In addition, the campus wireless network reaches classrooms and residential buildings, as well as outdoor gathering places.

Specialized academic facilities include a fully equipped television studio and radio station, along with video editing and production facilities, a demonstration kitchen, and biology and chemistry laboratories. Performing arts spaces include ample practice rooms and two auditoriums, including a new state-of-the-art performing arts center. The Lynn University School of Aeronautics' airport location offers flight simulators, and is home to the University's fleet of Cessna 172 and Cirrus SR-20 aircraft. The facility also houses a first-class flight academy for individuals interested in becoming a pilot.

Costs

Undergraduate tuition for the 2010–11 academic year is $29,400, with room and board fees beginning at $10,900, depending on meal plan and room type. Additional student fees vary depending on whether students live on or off campus. Books are purchased separately.

Financial Aid

Lynn is committed to making the University affordable for every student. Sixty-two percent of students receive some form of financial assistance and scholarships. The University's broad program of student financial aid includes scholarships, grants, work-study, and loans. Academic, athletic, and need-based scholarships are awarded. For complete information on the financial-aid process and available programs, along with a financial-aid calculator, students should visit the Lynn Web site at http://www.lynn.edu.

Faculty

Faculty members are thoroughly committed to teaching and are readily accessible to students. The University has a very favorable student to faculty ratio of 17:1. Seventy percent of full-time faculty members hold doctoral degrees, and the vast majority bring real-world experience in their field—many in some of the world's most prestigious companies and industries—to the classroom. Lynn has four Fulbright Scholars on its faculty and many of its professors are actively engaged in research. Among them is a chemistry professor who invented a newly patented process for screening cough syrup for the presence of a dangerous ingredient—a discovery that might help save lives in Third World countries that don't have sophisticated laboratory equipment; an international expert on sexual offenders and public policy; and a three-time Grammy award nominee. Several other faculty members are editors of prestigious international journals.

Student Government

The Student Government Association represents all Lynn students and elects its officers annually. The SGA provides a voice for representation of and advocacy for students and serves as a liaison among the student body, faculty, staff, and administration, while promoting scholastic pride and ethical integrity.

Admission Requirements

Lynn encourages high school students to apply during the fall of their senior year. Prospective students are encouraged to visit the campus. Applicants must submit a completed application form, including the personal statement and any required supplements (for Common Application or Universal College Application); official transcripts indicating all secondary school course work and graduation dates (or GED score report); and official SAT or ACT scores. Students must also include a letter of recommendation from a school guidance counselor or teacher commenting on the student's determination and motivation, in addition to academic performance. Conservatory students have additional application requirements, including an audition; specific instructions can be found online at http://www.lynn.edu/admissions/applying-to-lynn/guide-for-conservatory-students.

International applicants for whom English is not a first language are required to submit results from the TOEFL/IELTS. Applicants with at least a 525 (paper-based), 213 (computer-based), or 71 (Internet-based) or with IELTS scores of 6.0 will be considered for admission. All transcripts of previous academic work must be accompanied by certified English translations. Additional requirements for international applicants can be found online at http://www.lynn.edu.

Transfer students who have completed a minimum of 12 academic college credits should submit an application form and official transcripts from the current college and all previous colleges attended, along with a recommendation from the dean of students at the candidate's current or last school attended. Transfer students with fewer than 12 credits must submit high school transcripts and ACT or SAT scores. Every effort is made to facilitate the transfer of credit from other institutions, and a credit evaluation is provided upon admission.

Application and Information

Lynn University welcomes and evaluates applications on a rolling basis. For fall term admission, the priority deadline is March 1. The application fee is $35. For additional information about admission, to obtain an application packet, or to arrange for an interview and tour of the campus, prospective students should contact:

Office of Admission
Lynn University
3601 North Military Trail
Boca Raton, Florida 33431-5507
Phone: 561-237-7900
800-888-5966 (toll-free)
Fax: 561-237-7100
E-mail: admission@lynn.edu
Web site: http://www.lynn.edu/admission

On the campus of Lynn University.

Lynn University does not discriminate on the basis of race, color, gender, religion, nationality, ethnic origin, disability, and/or age in its administration of its educational and admission policies, scholarship and loan programs, and athletic, and/or other school-administered programs.

MANCHESTER COLLEGE

NORTH MANCHESTER, INDIANA

The College

At Manchester College, students find academics that matter. They find their place among students who are motivated to learn and faculty members with top degrees who know what it takes to succeed.

With a rich social life, students become part of the Manchester family that covers the globe. With lasting relationships, their college years will last a lifetime.

Manchester students learn how to give meaning to success. They get the most from their college experience so they can get the most out of life.

Tim Polakowski, a recent graduate from Illinois, now teaching English in South Korea as a Fulbright scholar, says he found success at Manchester College. "In high school, I knew I wanted to make a difference. Today, I feel that Manchester College has not only prepared me to make that difference, but also made a difference in me. The professors want you to succeed and the challenges in and out of the classroom prepare you for a life outside the norm. After a year studying in Spain, a semester south of the border, and working with on-campus groups like Habitat for Humanity, I'm more convinced than ever that Manchester was the right place for me."

The undergraduate enrollment is 1,145. Most students are between the ages of 18 and 22. Approximately 85 percent of the full-time students are from Indiana. Students from twenty-five states and twenty-five countries are being enrolled during 2008–09. Six percent of the students are members of the Church of the Brethren. Many different religious backgrounds are represented, and all are welcomed.

Manchester is a member of the National Collegiate Athletic Association Division III and offers nine men's and eight women's sports. The Physical Education and Recreation Center houses physical education classes, a fitness center, intercollegiate and intramural sports, and recreational activities. The College has a very strong intramural program that involves about 80 percent of its students.

Location

Located in the heart of Indiana's beautiful lake country, North Manchester is a thriving community of 6,000 people. It is within a half hour's drive of Indiana's second-largest city, Fort Wayne, and is only 3½ hours from Chicago. Wide streets with large shade trees, graceful homes, and a beautiful park combine to provide a classic setting for college living.

Majors and Degrees

Manchester College grants Bachelor of Arts and Bachelor of Science degrees. Areas of study include accounting, adapted physical education, art, athletic training, biochemistry, biology, biotechnology, business, chemistry, coaching, communication studies, computer science, corporate finance, criminal justice, early childhood education, economics, elementary education, engineering science, English, environmental studies, exercise science, finance, fitness and sport management, French, gender studies, gerontology, history, journalism, management, marketing, mathematics, media studies, medical technology, music, peace studies, philosophy, physical education, physics, political science, prelaw, premedicine, prenursing, pre–occupational therapy, pre–physical therapy, psychology, public relations, religion, secondary education, social work, sociology, Spanish, and sports management. Individualized interdisciplinary majors can also be arranged to meet a student's particular goals.

Academic Programs

The curriculum reflects a commitment to sound training in a specific area of study, the major and broad development of skills and understanding through the liberal arts. In addition, students may explore interests different from specific career or professional areas through elective courses. This combination prepares students for careers or graduate school immediately after graduation and equips them for the challenges and changes of the future.

Manchester College operates on a 4-1-4 calendar and offers online courses during two summer sessions. The College's innovative Fast Forward program allows students to complete a four-year degree in three years on campus and two summers online. Students save as much as $25,000 and enter graduate school or their careers a year earlier than their classmates.

Off-Campus Programs

Manchester College students may study abroad for a semester or year in ten countries: Philipps-Universität Marburg in Marburg/Lahn (Germany), the Institut International d'Études Françaises of the University of Strasbourg (France), the University of Nancy (France), the University of Barcelona (Spain), St. Mary's College in Cheltenham (England), Hokkai Gakuen University in Sapporo (Japan), the Dalian Institute of Foreign Languages in Dalian (People's Republic of China), the Athens Center (Greece), the Catholic University of Ecuador, Cochin (India), and Universidad Veracruzana (Mexico).

During January session, numerous classes are held off campus. In recent years, professors have taken classes to India, Kenya, England, Mexico, Russia, France, Jamaica, Ghana, Vietnam, Nicaragua, Haiti, Germany, Costa Rica, Cuba, and Hawaii as well as destinations in the continental United States.

Field experiences and internships are offered for credit in accounting, broadcasting, business, criminal justice, early childhood education, elementary education, forensic chemistry, gerontology, health sciences practicum, journalism, peace studies, physical education, political science, psychology, secondary education, and social work.

Academic Facilities

Manchester College has more than 160 personal computers in student labs, one for every 6 students. In addition, the Clark Computer Center houses file servers, three computer labs, and an AS400 for student use. PC labs tied to the network are located in each residence hall and the library. A 45-Mbs DS3 line provides high-speed Internet access.

The $17-million Science Center, opened in fall 2005, provides extraordinary laboratories and fully wired classrooms. Students in astronomy use the 10-inch Newtonian reflector telescope in the Charles S. Morris Observatory.

The College Union, which was completely renovated in 2007, houses the Success Center, campus store, art gallery, dining facilities, and Oaks coffee bar.

The Funderburg Library is a recently renovated, three-story building that houses more than 170,000 books, 800 periodicals, and 4,500 audio recordings available for student use. Computer connections and interlibrary loan allow access to major library collections across the country.

Costs

Tuition and fees for 2010–11 are $24,100 for full-time students. Room and board costs for the residence halls (double occupancy) are $8860. The total charges with fees are $33,780 for the academic year.

Financial Aid

Manchester offers extensive scholarship and grant assistance through institutional resources. Academic awards include Honors, Trustee, Presidential, and Dean's Scholarships. Special scholarships based on academic merit and interest are awarded in music and entrepreneurship. International students can receive scholarships based on academic accomplishments and financial need. Manchester awards significant need-based grants. More than $11 million in College funds have been awarded in 2008–09.

Ninety-eight percent of Manchester's students have some type of financial assistance, whether it is a scholarship, a grant, a loan, or campus employment. Questions about financial aid should be referred to the Office of Admissions.

Faculty

Manchester's faculty consists of 71 full-time and 32 part-time members. Nearly 90 percent of full-time faculty members hold the highest degree in their field, and 94 percent of all courses are taught by full-time faculty members. The primary emphasis of the faculty members is teaching, but many are actively engaged in research as well. Faculty members serve as academic advisers, with a specially trained group of faculty members acting as primary advisers for new students. There is a 13.3:1 student-faculty ratio.

Student Government

Students at Manchester assume responsibility for the governmental and judicial activities of the College. The Student Government Association provides a forum for discussion and investigation of community concerns and a channel for evaluating and solving community problems.

Each of the College's five residence halls elects a governing body, which is responsible for providing leadership.

The Manchester Activities Council organizes programming of student events. Students are offered a wide variety of leadership and participation opportunities as part of the College's student development program.

Admission Requirements

Manchester College seeks to enroll students whose scholastic record, test scores, and personality give promise of success in college. Graduation from an accredited high school or its equivalent is required.

The College recommends that students take 4 years of English, 3 years of laboratory science, 3 years of mathematics, 2 years of foreign language, and 2 years of social studies in high school. Students may take either the ACT or the SAT, and personal recommendations from a high school principal or guidance counselor are required.

For transfer students, transcripts of all previous college work are required.

Application and Information

Students may apply for admission prior to each term. Applications are accepted on a rolling basis. There is a nonrefundable $25 application fee. Online applications are free.

Interested students and their parents are encouraged to visit Manchester College and meet faculty members, coaches, and current students; sit in on classes; and take a campus tour. Arrangements can be made by writing or calling the Office of Admissions.

For application forms and further information, students may contact:

Office of Admissions
Manchester College
North Manchester, Indiana 46962-0365
Phone: 800-852-3648 (toll-free)
E-mail: admitinfo@manchester.edu
Web site: http://www.manchester.edu

Students on the campus of Manchester College.

COLLEGE CLOSE-UPS

MANHATTAN COLLEGE

RIVERDALE, NEW YORK

MANHATTAN COLLEGE

The College

With over 155 years of history as a Lasallian institution, Manhattan College maintains its fine reputation as an outstanding Catholic college, dedicated to educating students with strong moral values, a concern for the community, and a love of independent and critical thinking. Since its inception in 1853, Manhattan College has never wavered from its principal goal—to ensure that its students fulfill their potential and are well prepared to take their places as contributing members of society.

The College has an enrollment of some 3,500 students, of whom 3,000 are undergraduates. Approximately 70 percent of Manhattan's students come from New York State; the remaining 30 percent represent thirty-nine other states and sixty other countries. Approximately 2,100 housing units are available, consisting of on-campus residence halls and off-campus apartments. Nearly 80 percent of undergraduates are resident students. Manhattan offers seventy extracurricular organizations and five student publications and fields twenty varsity and club sports teams. Of Manhattan's 40,000 active alumni, a large number are prominent leaders in business, government, education, the arts, the sciences, and engineering.

Location

The main campus of the College is located 10 miles north of midtown Manhattan in the suburban Riverdale section of the Bronx, about a mile from Westchester County. It is an area that offers the calm and quiet of a residential, suburban setting as well as easy access to the many cultural and educational advantages of New York City. The College is easily accessible by subway, bus, or highway; three airports are also nearby.

Majors and Degrees

The liberal arts curriculum of the School of Arts provides programs that lead to a Bachelor of Arts or Bachelor of Science with majors in the humanities and the social sciences, including communication, economics, English, French, government, history, modern foreign languages, philosophy, psychology, religious studies, and sociology. Interdisciplinary majors include international studies, peace studies, and urban affairs.

In the School of Science, programs lead to a Bachelor of Science or Bachelor of Arts with majors in biochemistry, biology, chemistry, computer science, mathematics, and physics. Premedical, predental, and pre–veterinary studies programs are also available.

The School of Engineering has a well-deserved reputation as one of the best small-college engineering schools in the nation and offers programs leading to a Bachelor of Science in chemical, civil, computer, electrical, and mechanical engineering. The program is fully accredited by the Educational Accreditation Commission of ABET.

The School of Business, accredited by AACSB International, has programs leading to a Bachelor of Science in Business Administration with majors in accounting, computer information systems, economics, finance, global business studies, management, and marketing.

The School of Education offers a curriculum leading to a Bachelor of Arts in childhood education, childhood/special education (dual program), and adolescent education. The physical education curriculum leads to a Bachelor of Science in physical education and exercise science. The health education curriculum leads to a Bachelor of Science in allied health, with a concentration in health-care administration, health counseling, or scientific foundations. Curricula in radiological and health sciences lead to a Bachelor of Science in radiation therapy or nuclear medicine technology. All programs are approved by the New York State Education Department and accredited by the Teacher Education Accreditation Council.

Academic Programs

The core curriculum shared by the School of Arts and the School of Science studies some of the vital works of humankind, explores new ideas, examines the meaning of scientific experimentation, and encourages a student to develop his or her thinking and leadership abilities. The major programs offer advanced work in specific humanistic and scientific disciplines and opportunities to work on research projects in collaboration with faculty scholars.

In the School of Engineering, all engineering students follow a common core curriculum during the first two years and choose a major at the beginning of the junior year. Each curriculum includes a generous selection of courses in basic sciences, the engineering sciences, humanistic studies, and mathematics.

The School of Business prepares students for positions of executive responsibility in business, government, and nonprofit organizations. The business curriculum is based on a strong commitment to liberal education and is well balanced between professional business courses, humanities, sciences, and social sciences. This is a reflection of the school's belief that executives should be broadly educated and should involve themselves, as well as their organizations, in efforts to solve social problems.

The School of Education prepares students for teaching, counseling, and health professions. Students complete the College's core curriculum in liberal arts and sciences and then complete a major in various programs in the school's three departments: Education, Physical Education and Exercise Science, and Radiological and Health Professions. All programs include internships/practicums in schools, hospitals, or other institutions. Graduates of the school's teacher-preparation programs receive New York State provisional teaching certification. The school also offers a five-year B.A./M.S. program in childhood/special education and special education.

Off-Campus Programs

Students in the liberal arts curricula who have demonstrated superior achievement in their first two years are encouraged to spend their junior year studying abroad. Manhattan College also offers summer study-abroad programs in many countries; arrangements can be made to study in a country of choice. Students in the School of Business may participate in the International Field Studies Seminar. As participants, they spend time in another country studying the effect of that environment on international firms. Career services and co-op education integrate classroom theory with the practical experience of a job in industry, business, the social services, the arts, or government. Portions of the education courses are conducted in New York City schools, so that student teachers may gain experience in urban education at an early stage.

Academic Facilities

There are more than forty scientific and engineering laboratories at Manhattan, including the Research and Learning Center, as well as a modern language laboratory and a computer information systems laboratory. Manhattan's newly built O'Malley

Library is a state-of-the-art facility featuring modern accommodations for study and research. It is connected to the renovated and updated Cardinal Hayes Pavilion (formerly the Cardinal Hayes Library). The library combines Hayes' traditional neo-Georgian accents with strong contemporary lines. The five-story addition to the original building doubles the original square footage and connects the current library to the upper campus. Students and faculty members are able to enter directly from a brick walkway that starts at the Quadrangle.

Costs

For 2009–10, the tuition for Manhattan College was $23,900 per year plus program fees. The cost of room and board for the year was $10,160.

Financial Aid

Manhattan grants or administers financial assistance in the form of tuition awards to students on the basis of need and/or ability. Need is evaluated by submitting the FAFSA. In addition to a merit scholarship fund, Manhattan offers endowed scholarships, special-category scholarships and grants, student athletic grants, Federal Pell Grants, Federal Supplemental Educational Opportunity Grants, student loans, Federal Work-Study Program awards, and New York State financial assistance are also available to students who qualify. A total of 1,650 students receive financial aid from Manhattan College, and approximately 87 percent receive financial aid from government or private agencies.

Faculty

Manhattan's faculty has about 185 full-time and about 100 part-time teachers. The faculty-student ratio is approximately 1:13. Nearly 95 percent of the faculty members hold doctorates. The maximum teaching load on the undergraduate level is 9 credit hours per semester. Faculty members serve on the College Senate, the Council for Faculty Affairs, and numerous faculty and campus committees. In addition, they are available to students for informal guidance and counseling and also serve as official moderators of many campus organizations.

Student Government

The Manhattan Student Government is composed of students elected annually by their peers to fill posts outlined in the Student Government Constitution. The Student Government allocates funds to all student organizations. Members are also full voting members of the College Senate.

Admission Requirements

Manhattan has a long-standing policy of nondiscrimination. No applicant is refused admission because of race, color, religion, age, national origin, sex, or disability. All applicants must present an academic diploma from an accredited high school and must offer a minimum of 16 credits in academic subjects. Liberal arts candidates must be proficient in at least one foreign language. At the discretion of the Committee on Admissions, quantitative requirements may be modified for applicants with especially strong records who show promise of doing well in college. In the selection process, attention is given to scholastic ability, as indicated by grades and rank in class, as well as to standardized test scores and recommendations from teachers and counselors. All candidates must submit either SAT or ACT results. An interview with a member of the admission staff can be arranged but is not required. Applicants may submit scores on the General Educational Development test in lieu of a formal high school diploma; however, all such applicants must submit the results of the appropriate College Board tests. Manhattan College offers early acceptance for high school seniors, admission to advanced standing, advanced placement, and credit by examination. Junior college or other transfer students are welcome. Manhattan College requires applicants whose native language is not English to take the Test of English as a Foreign Language (TOEFL), the SAT, or ACT exam. The average SAT scores of entering freshmen in 2009 were 575 in mathematics and 555 in the verbal portion.

Application and Information

Application forms are furnished by the Admission Office on request and available on the Manhattan College Web site. The Common Application Form, which is available in many high school guidance offices and online, may also be used. After supplying the information required, students must send the application to the Admission Office at Manhattan College. The high school report, recommendation letters, and transcript must be submitted by the high school guidance counselor. This should be done after six terms of high school or right after the seventh term. There is a rolling admissions policy and a March 1 deadline for financial aid applications. A nonrefundable application fee of $60 is required.

William J. Bisset
Vice President for Enrollment Management
Manhattan College
Riverdale, New York 10471
Phone: 718-862-7200
800-MC2-XCEL (toll-free)
E-mail: admit@manhattan.edu
Web site: http://www.manhattan.edu

Students walking in the Quadrangle of the Manhattan College campus.

MANHATTANVILLE COLLEGE

PURCHASE, NEW YORK

The College

On its 100-acre campus 30 minutes north of New York City, Manhattanville College has created a small global village. The private coeducational college founded in 1841 draws its 1,600 students from seventy-six different countries and forty states. This richly diverse community embodies the College's mission: to educate ethically and socially responsible leaders for the global community.

Manhattanville's proximity to New York City creates a constant flow of opportunity that brings learning to life. Many students choose to spend a "semester abroad" living, interning, and studying in the city. Manhattanville students know how to have fun, but they also have a sense of purpose. The College's social conscience is informed by a commitment to serving the community—whether it is defined as the surrounding geographic area, where undergraduates logged 23,000 hours of service in a year, or as the global community. Manhattanville students actively seek opportunities to serve humanitarian causes in the developing world.

Manhattanville's global perspective is enriched by its role as a Non-Government Organization of the United Nations. Select students have an opportunity to intern at the UN and to study with an ambassador on Manhattanville's faculty. In addition, the College offers a Meet the Ambassadors Series on campus, where students attend lectures by leading ambassadors, followed by dinner at the home of the College's president.

Location

Manhattanville's campus lies in the heart of Westchester County, bordered on the east by Long Island Sound and on the west by the Hudson River. From the roof of the castle that serves as the campus' main hall, the skyline of Manhattan is clearly visible. This proximity to the city that calls itself the "Capital of the World" is one of Manhattanville's many assets. The College provides transportation to the city on weekends and to Manhattan-bound commuter trains during the week so students can take advantage of all New York City has to offer.

Majors and Degrees

Manhattanville College offers undergraduate degrees in more than fifty academic concentrations in the arts and sciences, including Bachelor of Arts (B.A.), Bachelor of Science (B.S.), Bachelor of Fine Arts (B.F.A.), and Bachelor of Music (B.Mus.) degrees; a self-designed major; a double major with teacher certification; and preparation for professional and graduate study (prelaw, premed, prehealth, and predentistry).

Students may choose from the following areas of study: African studies, American literature, American studies, art history, art (studio), Asian studies, biochemistry, biology, British literature, chemistry, communications studies, computer science, creative writing, criminal justice, dance and theater, dance therapy, economics, education (five-year M.A.T. program offered), English, environmental studies, film studies, finance, French, German, history, Holocaust and genocide studies, human resource management, international management, international studies, Irish studies, Italian, Latin American studies, legal studies, management, mathematics, music, music management, musical theater, neuroscience, philosophy, physics, political science, psychology, Romance languages, self-designed major, social justice, sociology and anthropology, Spanish, theater education, women's studies, world literature, and world religions.

Manhattanville also offers undergraduate certification programs in computer science, finance management, and teaching.

Academic Programs

Manhattanville College offers full-time, part-time, and accelerated opportunities for study as well as dual-degree programs. The Manhattanville curriculum nurtures intellectual curiosity and independent thinking. Students and professors form close collaborative relationships beginning with the Preceptorial, an interdisciplinary survey of the liberal arts that is required of all freshmen.

The core of the Manhattanville curriculum is the Portfolio System, which provides for a level of flexibility that is unusual in traditional liberal arts education. Under the guidance of a faculty adviser, the student maps an academic and cocurricular program, establishing a major and minor from different branches of the liberal arts. The student may begin studies in the chosen field as early as the freshman year. Over the course of four years of study, the student assembles a portfolio consisting of study plans, evidence of academic proficiency in written critical analysis and qualitative research, annual evaluations, transcripts, and examples of the student's best work. A College-wide review board evaluates the portfolio.

A special option for B.A. candidates is the self-designed major. If a student's interests direct them beyond existing departmental majors, they may propose a program of study to the Board of Academic Standards. Manhattanville students also have the opportunity to earn academic credit for internships in New York City.

Manhattanville College offers college credit for A-level exams, International Baccalaureates, and Advanced Placement examinations.

Off-Campus Programs

Manhattanville offers more than two dozen study-abroad opportunities at various levels of language proficiency, including Argentina, Belgium (internship at the European Union), Chile, Czech Republic, England, France, Germany, Ireland, Italy, Japan, Kenya, and Spain, among others, as well as a semester in New York City or a semester at sea.

Academic Facilities

Manhattanville has been named one of the "Top 100 Wired Colleges in the U.S." The Manhattanville Library capitalizes on the power of the Internet to connect students with information and analysis found in powerful subscription databases, electronic journals, and electronic books. Manhattanville is one of the first colleges in the U.S. to outsource a service that enables students to interact online with experienced reference librarians at any time of the day or night from anywhere in the world. The virtual research service, "Ask a Librarian 24/7," uses cobrowsing to connect students with professional librarians who can answer questions about research and help students navigate the College's extensive array of subscription databases and other library resources. Manhattanville's teaching library, which supports the School of Education, ranks among the foremost undergraduate teaching libraries in the country. The Menendez Language Laboratory includes tapes and record libraries that provide materials for class instruction and individual practice in French, Spanish, Russian, Italian, German, Chinese, Japanese, Hindi, Marathi, modern Hebrew, and English as a second language. The College provides a writing clinic, a reading clinic, audiovisual facilities, and a bibliographic instruction program. The library building is open 24 hours a day, seven days a week through most of the fall and spring semesters, and it has computer labs, quiet study areas, group-study rooms, and a café where students and faculty members can meet informally.

The College has state-of-the-art computers, computer labs, and campus networking for student use and instruction. In addition, advanced music technology systems offer performing arts students limitless opportunities for creativity.

Costs

For the 2009–10 academic year, tuition and fees were $32,125. Average room and board costs were $13,500.

Financial Aid

Manhattanville College offers both merit scholarships and need-based financial aid. Nearly 80 percent of students receive financial awards. The institutional form and the Free Application for Federal Student Aid (FAFSA) are required. The types of awards available are honors, merit, arts, and community service scholarships; Manhattanville grants and scholarships; Federal Perkins Loans; Federal Stafford Student Loans; Federal Pell Grants; Federal Supplemental Educational Opportunity Grants; Federal Work-Study Program awards; and Tuition Assistance Program awards.

Faculty

Nearly 90 percent of faculty members have Ph.D. or terminal degrees in their fields, and the vast majority serve full-time. Many faculty members live on the campus. The Manhattanville curriculum nurtures intellectual curiosity and independent thinking. The student-faculty ratio of 12:1 promotes close and collaborative relationships between faculty members and students, aided by the structure of the curriculum and the Portfolio System, which fosters collaboration between student and faculty adviser. Faculty members, not teaching assistants, teach all Manhattanville classes, and 80 percent of the classes have 20 or fewer students.

Student Government

Students in large measure shape the quality of life on the Manhattanville campus. Elected representatives of the student body run the student government, which serves as a principal means of communication among the administration, faculty members, and students. Its board of directors is responsible for formulating policy on student life and for implementing this policy through various committees. Student government members also serve on the College's policymaking and ad hoc committees.

Admission Requirements

Manhattanville College admits men and women as candidates for undergraduate degrees if their academic records indicate a competence to engage in a challenging liberal arts curriculum. Admission to the College is selective, and the most important consideration is the student's secondary school performance. When weighing this aspect, the admissions committee evaluates the quality of the school, the strength of the student's program, and success in those studies. Next, the committee considers the various recommendations that are submitted on behalf of the student, along with scores on required standardized tests and the student's personal statement. The SAT or the ACT is required. A campus interview is strongly recommended. Students who plan to specialize in music or musical theater should come to Manhattanville for an audition or should secure permission to submit a tape. Students who plan to apply for the B.F.A. degree program should present portfolios to the art department for evaluation. The portfolios are not required for admission to the College. Students who plan to study dance and theater may audition for scholarships.

Application and Information

The deadline for early decision applications is December 1, 2007, and the deadline for rolling admission is March 1, 2008. The College subscribes to the Candidates Reply Date. Applications should be submitted as early in the senior year as possible. The application fee of $65 is waived for online applications. All application decisions are made without regard to race, religion, sex, national or ethnic origin, or handicap. Candidates may apply online at http://www.manhattanville.edu.

For further information, students should contact:

Office of Undergraduate Admissions
Manhattanville College
2900 Purchase Street
Purchase, New York 10577
Phone: 914-323-5464
800-32-VILLE (toll-free)
Web site: http://www.manhattanville.edu

Reid Hall ("The Castle") is the centerpiece of the Manhattanville College campus.

MANNES COLLEGE THE NEW SCHOOL FOR MUSIC

THE NEW SCHOOL
A UNIVERSITY

NEW YORK, NEW YORK

The College

Mannes College The New School for Music in New York City is one of the world's preeminent conservatories of classical music. The Mannes community is made up of students and a faculty of professional musicians from every corner of the world. Here, aspiring artists learn and play music with scholars, composers, conductors, and performing artists from some of the world's most revered orchestras, ensembles, and opera companies. Most of the more than 400 concerts produced by the School each year at its two concert halls or at venues throughout the New York metropolitan region feature Mannes students. With only 319 college students, Mannes provides an intimate, supportive atmosphere that allows for close and constructive relationships among students, faculty members, and administrators.

Part of The New School, a leading urban university, Mannes offers its own undergraduate academic curriculum focused on areas most pertinent to classical music. Students may choose to supplement this curriculum by taking courses at the other divisions of The New School. In addition, throughout their studies, students follow a program of instruction in the techniques of music. This program includes studies in ear training, sight singing, keyboard skills, theory, analysis, and dictation that are among the best in the world, all helping to train students to meet the unique challenges faced by musicians in the twenty-first century.

Graduate degrees offered include the Master of Music (M.M.), a two-year degree program offered in all orchestral instruments (violin, viola, cello, bass, flute, oboe, clarinet, bassoon, saxophone, horn, trumpet, trombone, tuba, harp, and percussion), piano, harpsichord, guitar, vocal accompaniment for pianists, voice, composition, conducting, and theory. Students receive private lessons in their major field and take performance classes (such as orchestra, opera, and chamber music), courses in the techniques of music, and chosen electives that focus on specialized topics of the student's interest.

Mannes also offers the Professional Studies Diploma (PSD), an advanced course of study designed to enhance performance or compositional skills. The PSD is generally pursued following a master's degree or the equivalent. Individual programs are designed in coordination with the associate/assistant dean. Orchestral instrument majors participate in the Mannes Orchestra, which performs at Lincoln Center and other major venues, during each semester of residency. Additionally, chamber music is a curricular component of some instrumental majors. All Mannes and some New School courses are available to qualified students; however, only graduate-level courses apply toward the Professional Studies Diploma.

Total enrollment is 319, 49 percent of whom are international students. There are 156 faculty members, and the student-teacher ratio is less than 2:1. The average class size is 10–12 students.

Through The New School, Mannes is proud to offer housing facilities that include apartment-style dormitory suites equipped with full kitchens, full bathrooms, air conditioning, Internet service, and other amenities. Residences available to Mannes students are located in Chelsea, Greenwich Village, Union Square, and lower Manhattan. All dormitories are equipped with a 24-hour security guard and resident advisers on every floor. All incoming freshman are offered on-campus housing, but it is not a requirement for admission. The housing office offers assistance with off-campus housing.

Location

Mannes is located in Manhattan's Upper West Side, one of the finest residential areas of New York City. It is within walking distance of the Museum of Natural History and Lincoln Center for the Performing Arts (home to the New York Philharmonic, the Metropolitan Opera, and other world-renowned performing arts organizations). Mannes students benefit from and contribute to New York City's rich musical and cultural life.

Majors and Degrees

Undergraduate degrees offered include the Bachelor of Music (B.M.) in all orchestral instruments (bass, bassoon, cello, clarinet, flute, harp, horn, oboe, percussion, saxophone, trombone, trumpet, tuba, viola, and violin), composition, conducting, guitar, harpsichord, piano, theory, and voice. Students receive private lessons in their major field and take performance classes (such as chamber music, orchestra, or opera) and courses in the techniques of music and liberal arts, as well as electives.

A Bachelor of Science (B.S.) is offered in all majors by completing the Bachelor of Music curriculum and taking or transferring from another institution an additional 30 academic credits.

The Undergraduate Diploma (UDPL) is offered in all majors and is equivalent to the Bachelor of Music degree minus the liberal arts courses.

Academic Programs

Some outstanding performance opportunities include the Mannes Orchestra, led by David Hayes; the Mannes Opera Program, led by Joseph Colaneri; the Mannes Chorus; the Mannes Baroque Chamber Players; the Percussion Ensemble; NewMusicMannes; and numerous chamber music ensembles that perform year-round.

The Mannes Community Services Office employs students to perform in the widest range of New York settings, such as official receptions, galas, and public and private settings, and also encourages them to perform with many of New York's orchestras, choruses, and opera companies.

Mannes also offers concerto competitions for all performance majors, an audio recording facility, and career development advisement.

Academic Facilities

Degree candidates have access to the university's broad liberal arts curriculum, with offerings in the humanities, fine arts, and the social sciences. Mannes students share resources with The New School's other divisions, which include Parsons The New School for Design, Eugene Lang College The New School for Liberal Arts, The New School for General Studies, The New School for Drama, The New School for Social Research, Milano The New School for Management and Urban Policy, and The New School for Jazz and Contemporary Music.

Mannes' home is a Federal-style building on Manhattan's Upper West Side. The building houses classrooms, practice rooms, a state-of-the art computer lab, and the Harry Sherman Library, which offers access to more than 3 million books, 25,000 journals, a complete music and listening library, and study carrels. The New School also offers the facilities of the Bobst Library at New York University through a consortium known as the Research Library Association of South Manhattan. The consortium's online catalog, Bobcat, is accessible over the Internet.

Mannes' two concert halls, seating 250 and 75 people, are the venues for hundreds of performances each year by students, faculty members, and artists-in-residence, as well as for master classes. The John Goldmark Practice Center, adjacent to Lincoln Center, provides additional practice rooms and an opera rehearsal room.

Costs

Tuition for the 2009–10 school year was as follows: for the B.M., B.S., M.M., and UDPL programs, $32,860; for the Professional Studies Diploma, $23,310; and for the ESL course work program, $3860. Fees totaled $1944 per academic year (university services $200, student health insurance $1714, divisional fee $30). Room and board cost approximately $15,260 in 2009–10, depending upon a student's choice of specific meal plan and dormitory accommodations. A small percentage increase in costs is expected for the 2010–11 school year.

Financial Aid

Scholarships are available on the basis of merit and are determined at the time of the audition. Approximately 75 percent of Mannes students receive some form of scholarship. The average award ranges from 25 percent to 50 percent of tuition. In certain majors, opportunities exist for further assistance up to full tuition. Loans, grants, and work-study programs are available to students who fill out the Free Application for Federal Student Aid, the filing of which is required for U.S. citizens and permanent residents seeking financial aid of any type. A package of loans and information is sent along with the acceptance letter.

Faculty

Mannes is committed to providing broad and rigorous musical training in a friendly and supportive community that encourages artistic growth. The distinguished faculty includes some of New York City's most prominent musicians, including members of the Metropolitan Opera Orchestra and New York Philharmonic, as well as internationally known artists and ensembles. All students receive private lessons and participate in ensembles, and the 2:1 student-faculty ratio ensures personalized instruction and close interaction among, students, faculty and staff members, and administrators.

Admission Requirements

An application for admission to Mannes College The New School for Music consists of a completed Unified Application for Conservatory Admission–Mannes Edition (available online at http://www.unifiedapps.org), a $100 nonrefundable application fee, official high school or college academic transcripts for all schools attended (graduate degree applicants need only send college transcripts), and one letter of recommendation from a recent music teacher or an evaluation from a professional musician. International students must submit a recent TOEFL score. Mannes' school code is 2398. A minimum computer-based TOEFL score of 213 and a successful English test taken at the audition is required. A minimum computer-based TOEFL score of 250 is required for all graduate theory, composition, and conducting majors.

Audition requirements vary by field of study and program sought, outlines of which can be found in the Mannes College catalog. During the audition period, musicianship skills are tested for all degree and UDPL applicants. These tests in dictation, ear training, piano, and theory are required in order to complete the application for entrance to the undergraduate and master's degree programs. English language testing is required of applicants whose first language is not English.

Application and Information

The application deadline for the main March entrance auditions is December 1. The application deadline for the late auditions in May is April 1.For more information, students should contact:

Office of Admissions
Mannes College The New School for Music
150 West 85th Street
New York, New York 10024
Phone: 212-580-0210 Ext. 4862
800-292-3040 (toll-free)
E-mail: mannesadmissions@newschool.edu
Web site: http://www.newschool.edu/mannes

Mannes College The New School for Music.

COLLEGE CLOSE-UPS

MARIETTA COLLEGE

MARIETTA, OHIO

The College

Founded in 1835, Marietta College traces its roots to the Muskingum Academy, which was founded in 1797 as the first institution of higher learning in the Northwest Territory. Marietta's chapter of Phi Beta Kappa was the sixteenth in the nation, showing the College's early dedication to scholarship. Women were first admitted in 1897. About half of Marietta's 1,400 students come from a variety of states along the Eastern Seaboard, the South, and the Midwest; the rest come primarily from Ohio, the surrounding states, and twenty other countries. More than forty states are represented in the Marietta student body. Situated on 120 acres within a block of downtown Marietta, the College has a number of academic and extracurricular facilities. Highlights of the campus include the McDonough Leadership Center, home to the most comprehensive program in leadership studies in the country; the McKinney Media Center, which houses two radio stations, a cable television station, and an award-winning student newspaper; and a pedestrian mall that enhances the central campus. A new recreation center features a 200-meter competition track, performance gymnasium, indoor rowing training room, and more. The new Rickey Science Center opened in spring 2003, and it offers state-of-the-art science labs to house biology, chemistry, biochemistry, environmental science, math, computer science, and physics.

Marietta is one of the few colleges in Ohio with intercollegiate crew, a sport in which it has excelled. In 2006, Marietta crew captured the Dad Vail national title in Philadelphia. Marietta's premier men's baseball program has earned twenty-eight conference championships, nineteen World Series appearances, and four World Series titles for NCAA Division III. Students become involved with the campus radio and television stations, the student newspaper, the literary magazine, the yearbook, drama productions, and musical groups, plus service and special interest clubs. National invitational art exhibits are sponsored annually by the College for the educational and cultural enrichment of students.

Location

Historic Marietta, Ohio, was the first permanent settlement in the Northwest Territory, settled by New Englanders in 1787. The city of 17,000 people retains a New England flavor with its wide, tree-lined brick streets, Colonial architecture, and large parks. Marietta is readily accessible by car via Interstate 77 (2 miles from campus) or by air from Wood County/Parkersburg Airport in West Virginia (6 miles from campus). The Ohio and Muskingum Rivers meet in Marietta, contributing to the economic, cultural, and recreational vitality of the area.

Majors and Degrees

Marietta offers all students foundation study in the liberal arts and sciences and the opportunity to gain concentrated study in either the traditional liberal arts disciplines or a number of preprofessional programs. Among the liberal arts are strong programs in biochemistry, biology, chemistry, English, physics, and psychology. Preprofessional programs include accounting, computer science, education, environmental science, graphic design, journalism, musical theater, petroleum engineering, radio/television studies, and a nationally renowned program in sports medicine.

Marietta College grants four baccalaureate degrees: the Bachelor of Arts, the Bachelor of Fine Arts, the Bachelor of Science, and the Bachelor of Science in Petroleum Engineering. Marietta is the only liberal arts college in the nation offering the petroleum engineering degree, which is accredited by the Accreditation Board for Engineering and Technology. Marietta also offers a major in athletic training, the first such program at a small college to be accredited by the National Athletic Trainers Association. Students have the opportunity to be involved in the Bernard McDonough Leadership Program. The program, known as "the Marietta Model," allows students to study leadership through a multidisciplinary liberal arts perspective. Students involved in the McDonough Leadership Program have the option of completing a minor in leadership or receiving a certificate. In addition, students have the opportunity to major in international leadership studies—the only undergraduate program in the nation. Along with the core courses of problem solving, critical thinking, and leadership, the program also requires an internship and community service involvement at one of the many organizations in the Marietta area or throughout the world.

"Binary" programs—cooperative study programs with other institutions—enable qualified Marietta students to earn two degrees in such fields as engineering, forestry, and natural resources. Preprofessional programs are offered in dentistry, law, medicine, physical therapy, and veterinary medicine.

The College's Education Department is accredited by NCATE and the state of Ohio Department of Education and offers programs leading to licensure in early childhood, middle childhood, and secondary school education. Ohio has reciprocity with many other states. In addition, the College's programs are accredited by the North Central Association of Colleges and Schools.

Academic Programs

Marietta students are known for both their breadth and depth of study. Freshmen take a special first-year program that begins with the College Experience Seminar and includes courses in composition (English 101), oral presentation (Speech 101), and mathematics. Every student also completes a liberal arts core of sequence courses in the humanities, social sciences, science, and the fine arts. There is an honors program for students who are prepared for and desire an extra challenge and who wish to graduate with honors.

Off-Campus Programs

Students seeking international study experience may make use of Marietta's association with the Institute for the International Education of Students (IES), the international study program of Central College of Iowa, or the programs of the East Central College Exchange. The programs have centers in Austria, the British Isles, France, Germany, Mexico, and Spain and in Asia. Students may also choose other accredited international-study programs. Finally, the College has numerous exchange programs with the People's Republic of China and annually has both faculty members and students teaching and studying in China.

Students whose interests range from economics to government and politics may take advantage of programs offered through the College's affiliation with two institutions located in the nation's capital. Courses are offered through the Washington Semester program of American University, and internships are available through the Washington Center for Learning Alternatives.

Academic Facilities

A new learning and library/resource center opened in January 2009. The $20-million project houses 250,000 volumes, 6,700 periodicals, and an online card catalog. As a member of OhioLINK, the Library provides access to a substantial number of books, materials, and databases. Among the special collections are the Rodney M. Stimson Collection of Americana, a collection of rare fifteenth- through nineteenth-century books, and an extraordinary collection of historic documents pertaining to the Northwest Territory and early Ohio. The card catalog and database are computerized through OCLC (Online Computer Library Center). The Anderson Hancock Planetarium also opened in January of 2009 and is 40 feet in diameter with an additional 3-foot-wide perimeter aisle with reclining theater seats that will accommodate 85 to 100 people. The projection system will combine an optical-mechanical star-field projector with a powerful full-dome digital video projector. The optical-mechanical projector will have the capabilities of accurately charting the night skies from thousands of years ago to thousands of years in the future. The Hermann Fine Arts Center includes a laboratory theater, providing study and performance facilities for the College's art, drama, and music departments. Modern computing facilities include 200 personal computers connected by campus network. The campuswide network provides e-mail, Internet, and World Wide Web access. Students can work in computer labs, the library, and the student center, as well as in five academic buildings. The College has well-equipped science labs and its own astronomical observatory and a state-of-the-art computer lab for graphic design students. For instructional and communications purposes, the College operates a media center with a 9,200-watt stereo FM station, a 10-watt FM station, and a television station that reaches more than 12,000 homes via a community cable system. All programs are run by students.

Costs

The total two-semester cost for 2009–10 for a student residing on campus was $35,112. This figure includes $4400 for room, $3646 for board, and $680 for fees, but does not include the cost of books (approximately $500 per year) and personal expenses.

Financial Aid

About 90 percent of current Marietta students receive financial aid based on need. The average award for 2008–09 was over $20,000. A number of merit-based scholarships are available in addition to funds allocated through College grants and federal and state sources. Qualified students can also compete in the annual Pioneer Scholars Competition. Pioneer Scholars are a select cadre of students who rank among the best college bound seniors in the nation based on their high school academic record and test scores. Base scholarships begin at $8000 with the opportunity to increase the value of the scholarship up to full tuition. Fine Arts Scholarships are awarded annually to winners of an art, music, and drama competition. Numerous work-study jobs are available to students in many campus departments. Grants are available for children and grandchildren of alumni.

Faculty

Close personal contact between students and professors is one of Marietta's primary features. All departmental faculty members, regardless of rank, teach courses. Full professors teach freshman courses. Ninety-two percent of the College's full-time faculty members hold doctorates or other terminal degrees. Professors share their homes, outside interests, and hobbies with students. A 12:1 student-faculty ratio makes this possible.

Student Government

Through the Student Senate and its committee system, students have responsibility for the cocurricular aspects of College life. Students hold memberships on most faculty and trustee committees, as well as on various departmental committees. Housing boards in both men's and women's residence halls provide programming and dormitory governance. In addition, there are more than 100 active clubs and organizations on campus.

Admission Requirements

Admission decisions are based upon the high school record, scores on national exams (SAT or ACT), an essay, extracurricular involvement, and recommendations from guidance counselors or teachers. While admission is selective and competitive, individual consideration is given to each application. The admission committee seeks a cross section of students whose ability and past performance indicate that they can compete successfully. Credit is granted for Advanced Placement and International Baccalaureate higher-level 1B exams.

Application and Information

Students should apply late in their junior year or early in their senior year of high school to guarantee a place in the fall. Marietta operates on a rolling admission plan, and students are notified of acceptance within one month after all application materials are complete. Students applying for financial aid should apply before March 1 of their senior year to be considered for merit scholarships.

To receive information about Marietta or to apply for admission, students should contact:

Office of Admission
Marietta College
Marietta, Ohio 45750-4005
Phone: 800-331-7896 (toll-free)
E-mail: admit@marietta.edu
Web site: http://www.marietta.edu

Erwin Hall (1850), the oldest building on the Marietta campus, is listed on the National Register of Historic Places.

MARLBORO COLLEGE

MARLBORO, VERMONT

The College

Students come to Marlboro College with a passion for learning and a desire to create a course of study tailored to their own interests. Tucked away in the foothills of Vermont's Green Mountains, Marlboro offers a rigorous liberal arts curriculum that is taught in small classes and advanced one-to-one instruction, called tutorials. Marlboro's goal is to teach students to think clearly and learn independently, develop a command of concise and correct writing, and aspire to academic excellence, all while participating responsibly in a self-governing community. The College's 8:1 student-faculty ratio sparks dynamic exchanges between students and faculty members both in and out of the classroom and fosters a close-knit community in which asking the right questions is more important than knowing the right answers. Two thirds of all Marlboro students go on to graduate study.

Marlboro opened in fall 1947. The campus was originally a cluster of barns and other farm buildings that the first students converted into classrooms and dormitories. The fields and woodlands that make up its rural 350-acre campus are ideal for cross-country skiing and other outdoor activities. The Outdoor Program offers instruction and equipment for canoeing, kayaking, rock climbing, backpacking, and other sports that bring students in touch with the surrounding environment. The soccer team competes with other colleges, and more impromptu volleyball, basketball, softball, and Ultimate Frisbee teams compete intramurally. In addition, Marlboro's broomball (a game akin to hockey) tournament takes place each winter, with prizes for the winning teams and those with the best costumes. Campus committees organize many events both on and off campus, including concerts, lectures, poetry and fiction readings, art shows, and trips to Boston, Montreal, and New York for museum visits, shopping, and baseball games. Other activities that enrich campus life include parties, dances, plays, and film screenings.

Marlboro is—and intends to remain—one of the nation's smallest liberal arts colleges, with some 330 students. Students come from nearly forty states and approximately six other countries. Transfer students—who make up one quarter of each incoming class—bring an important perspective to the campus community. More than 80 percent of all students live in campus housing, which consists of small dormitories (both single-sex and coed), several four-bedroom cottages, and a renovated country inn.

Location

The village of Marlboro, which is 2 miles from the College, consists of a post office, a town clerk's office, and an inn. About 1,200 residents live within the 36-square-mile township. During the summer, the village swells to accommodate the famous Marlboro Music Festival. The town of Brattleboro, 12 miles away, is a lively cultural and commercial center located on the first Vermont exit off Interstate 91. The College is 2 hours by car from Boston and 4 hours from New York City and Montreal.

Majors and Degrees

Marlboro confers the Bachelor of Arts and Bachelor of Science degrees in more than thirty areas of study, which can be combined in an almost limitless number of ways. Students have the license to design their own majors, which allows them to make interdisciplinary connections and pursue individualized research. The College also offers Bachelor of Arts and Bachelor of Science degrees in international studies through its World Studies Program (WSP).

Areas of study offered at Marlboro include American studies, anthropology, art history, Asian studies, astronomy, biochemistry, biology, ceramics, chemistry, classics, computer science, cultural history, dance, development studies (in the WSP), economics, environmental studies, film/video studies, history, international studies, languages, literature, mathematics, music, painting, philosophy, photography, physics, political science, psychology, religion, sculpture, sociology, theater, visual arts, and writing.

Academic Programs

In the first two years, Marlboro students study broadly, discover new interests, and begin to see the connections that lead many to pursue interdisciplinary work. Each new student is paired with a faculty adviser and joins an advising group of sophomores, juniors, and seniors as well as freshmen. Students learn from each other at Marlboro in seminar-style classes.

Marlboro believes that clear writing both reflects and engenders clear thinking. The College, therefore, requires each new student to pass a Clear Writing Requirement within three semesters of enrolling at the College. Designated writing courses, faculty advisers, and student writing tutors all help new students meet the requirement.

Marlboro's Plan of Concentration, more than any other academic component, sets the College apart from other undergraduate programs. Undertaken by all Marlboro students in their junior and senior years, the plan is the collection of related projects and papers that form the final product of the student's academic work at Marlboro. It is an individualized program of classes, research, experiences, one-to-one study, and original thought, driven by the student's interests and academic goals and designed in close collaboration with faculty sponsors. Final evaluation of the student's plan is conducted by her or his faculty advisers and an outside examiner who is a recognized expert in the student's field.

Off-Campus Programs

The College sponsors multiple academic, adventure, and humanitarian trips each year, ranging from community service work in South Carolina and Costa Rica to interdisciplinary research in Cuba, Vietnam, and China. Students working on their Plan of Concentration often travel abroad or attend other institutions for a period of time to augment their academic work. Marlboro faculty members may help plan these pursuits and frequently aid students in securing internships in academic fields.

The World Studies Program is a four-year program leading to a Bachelor of Arts or Bachelor of Science degree in international studies. The program involves intensive study on campus as well as a six- to eight-month internship abroad. In addition, WSP sponsors regular International Nights, which generally include a themed dinner, music from other countries, and lectures or films.

Academic Facilities

Marlboro's academic facilities offer small classrooms and oversized faculty offices for students to meet in small groups and individually with their professors. Facilities are open 24 hours a day, supporting student research and creative explorations include a DNA lab, a state-of-the-art black-and-white/ digital darkroom, a digital film-editing studio, two pottery studios, and an astronomical observatory. In the last five years, Marlboro's ongoing campus renewal project has doubled the size of the library and added a suite-style dorm. The new Rudolf and Irene Serkin Performing Arts Center has been added to offer more than 10,000 square feet for music, dance, and drama rehearsals and performances. In 2008, the campus added a new Total Health Center to provide additional space for medical and psychological counseling services and a fitness room.

Costs

Tuition and fees at Marlboro were $32,550 for the 2009–10 academic year. Room and board costs were $9220.

Financial Aid

No one should refrain from applying to Marlboro because of perceived inability to meet costs. More than 80 percent of all Marlboro students receive financial help. The College is committed to helping any student who qualifies for admission assemble the financial resources necessary to attend, and need is not a factor in the admission decision. Merit scholarships are also available.

Faculty

Marlboro's 40 full-time faculty members are committed first and foremost to teaching, rather than to publishing or research. The lively exchange of ideas between teachers and students is the cornerstone of the Marlboro curriculum.

Student Government

All students and faculty and staff members are equal members of the College Town Meeting. Since the opening of the College in 1947, the community has come together every few weeks to debate and decide budget initiatives, College policies, and other issues. A board of Selectpersons, elected by the College community, serves the College's interests and is responsible for drafting Town Meeting rules and regulations. Students serve with faculty and staff members on more than thirty College committees, including those that make admissions and faculty-hiring decisions. Other important committees include the social committee and the Community Court, which is responsible for enforcing campus regulations.

Admission Requirements

The Admissions Committee seeks students with intellectual promise; a high degree of motivation, self-discipline, personal stability, and social concern; and the ability and desire to contribute to the College community. All applicants are considered without regard to race, creed, sex, sexual orientation, gender identity or its expression, national or ethnic origin, age, or disability. Transfers and older or returning students are encouraged to apply.

Like most colleges, Marlboro requires students to submit a variety of documentation, from high school transcripts to teacher recommendations. Unlike most colleges, however, current students, faculty, and staff members provide input into the review process. The Admissions Committee evaluates each applicant as a unique individual who possesses qualities that are not necessarily quantifiable.

A campus visit is strongly recommended for all applicants, and interviews are encouraged. Many campus interviews are conducted by faculty members in the applicant's area of interest. Marlboro does not use a formulaic approach in making admission decisions. Applicants are encouraged to demonstrate their particular strengths; the goal is a successful match between the student and the College.

Application and Information

New students and transfers are admitted for either the spring or fall semester. Applicants for the fall semester have a choice of three admission plans. The early decision plan is for those students who have thoroughly researched Marlboro and for whom Marlboro is the first choice. Applicants should be aware that early decision is binding. The deadline for first-year students to submit application materials is December 1, and applicants are notified by December 15. Early action, a nonbinding plan, has a deadline of February 1. These applicants are notified of a decision on February 15. The regular admission deadline is March 1. The deadline for transfer students to submit applications materials for the fall semester is April 15, and for the spring semester it is December 1.

An application for admission must include a completed Common Application form and a Marlboro College Supplement Form with a "Why Marlboro" personal statement, a $50 fee, complete transcripts from all secondary schools and colleges, an analytical writing sample, and two letters of recommendation. SAT or ACT are not required, but will be taken into consideration if submitted by the prospective student. The Admissions Committee welcomes applications from home-schooled students. In lieu of a high school transcript, home-schooled students must submit a detailed description of their curriculum.

Office of Admissions
Marlboro College, 2582 South Road
Marlboro, Vermont 05344-0300
Phone: 802-257-4333
800-343-0049 (toll-free)
Fax: 802-451-7555
E-mail: admissions@marlboro.edu
Web site: http://www.marlboro.edu

The center of the campus at Marlboro College.

MARYLAND INSTITUTE COLLEGE OF ART

BALTIMORE, MARYLAND

The College

Established in 1826, the Maryland Institute College of Art (MICA) is the oldest independent, fully accredited art college in the nation. Because of its belief in the vital role of art in society, MICA is dedicated to the education of professional artists and to the development of an environment conducive to the creation of art. MICA has a well-equipped network of studio facilities, an exceptional faculty, extensive exhibition space, and an impressive art college library. A unique on-campus residential environment is provided, designed with the artist in mind.

The College offers many options not fully available at a liberal arts college, including a visiting artists program that welcomes more than 100 artists a year to the campus; seven-days-a-week access to some of the most outstanding facilities and best equipped studios in the country; the opportunity to exhibit work in numerous galleries, starting in the freshman year; the opportunity to study, through College-sponsored programs, art and design at colleges throughout the United States and abroad; a challenging liberal arts program that is integrated into and expands upon the studio program; and the advantage of studying with other talented students in a rigorous program of art.

In addition to its undergraduate degrees, MICA offers the Master of Fine Arts in sculpture, painting, multidisciplinary fine arts, graphic design, and photographic and electronic media; Master of Arts in Teaching; Master of Arts in Art Education; and Master of Arts in Community Arts degree programs.

The faculty is composed of 270 professional artists, designers, art historians, writers, and scholars—an assemblage of dedicated, working professionals who share the insights and experiences they have gained as practicing artists and scholars.

The College's 1,900 students represent forty-seven states and forty-eight other countries. They are marked by their intellectual curiosity, creativity, motivation, and self-discipline. Students develop a body of work that prepares them for a variety of career paths. The MICA experience, which includes internship programs and other reality-based opportunities, develops a firm base upon which students can launch and build their careers.

MICA is a residential campus providing apartment-style housing that includes dining, laundry, and fitness facilities and is wired for high-speed Internet access. Additional benefits include many private rooms and studio spaces that are incorporated into the residences. MICA housing offers independence, privacy, and a lively sense of activity generated by a community focused on art. Student life is also focused at the Meyerhoff House, which houses the Center Café and meeting rooms for student organizations, and in the Gateway Building, which houses the BBOX Theater and the Meyerhoff Center for Career Development.

The College is accredited by the Middle States Association of Colleges and Schools and the National Association of Schools of Art and Design.

Location

MICA is an urban campus of twenty-eight buildings that is located in a historic and beautiful neighborhood, surrounded by many cultural and educational institutions. These include the Meyerhoff Symphony Hall, the Lyric Opera House, and the Theatre Project. Baltimore has been cited as a city especially attractive to artists because of its vibrant and supportive atmosphere and its low cost of living. In addition to four world-class museums—the Contemporary Museum, the Walters Art Museum, the Baltimore Museum of Art, and the American Visionary Art Museum—Baltimore features a wide range of alternative art spaces and galleries that present works by acclaimed and emerging artists. It is also ideally situated for an artist because it is at the center of the Washington–New York art corridor. By train, Washington, D.C., is 40 minutes to the south; New York City, less than 3 hours to the north. The College offers inexpensive bus trips to New York studios, galleries, and museums every other week during the academic year.

Majors and Degrees

MICA offers the Bachelor of Fine Arts degree in the following majors: animation, art history, ceramics, drawing, environmental design, fibers, general fine arts, graphic design, illustration, interaction design and art, painting, photography, printmaking, sculpture, and video and film arts. Additional studio concentrations are offered in ten areas, including book arts, curatorial studies, and fashion design. The Division of Liberal Arts offers minors in art history, literature, and writing. Students may also pursue double majors. A five-year combined Bachelor of Fine Arts/Master of Arts degree is offered in teaching.

Academic Programs

To receive the Bachelor of Fine Arts degree, students must complete a minimum of 126 credits, including 42 liberal arts credits. Students participate in a foundation program during their freshman year and then select a studio major. During the first year, the curriculum is well structured to provide the conceptual and technical skills necessary for further specialized study. By the end of four years, students are expected to be able to work independently in their chosen medium. The program integrates writing and academic inquiry with studio practice. This combination reflects the need for artists to pursue intellectual concepts as well as aesthetic principles.

Off-Campus Programs

MICA participates in a cooperative exchange program with thirteen colleges, including Goucher College, the Johns Hopkins University, Loyola College, the Peabody Conservatory of Music, and the University of Baltimore. This program makes it possible for full-time students at the College to enroll in one course per semester at one of the cooperating institutions without incurring an additional tuition charge. This option has proved to be exceptionally useful in offering studies not available at MICA, such as languages, the sciences, and business.

The Maryland Institute is a member of the Alliance of Independent Colleges of Art and Design (AICAD), which has cooperatively developed a program of study in New York City for eligible second-semester juniors and first-semester seniors. The New York Studio Program's center, a loft facility in the Tribeca area of lower Manhattan, is home base for the semester-long program. Students may pursue either an independent study or, as apprenticeship students, they may work with a professional artist, museum, gallery, or an art-related business.

MICA encourages young artists to work and live in other cultural settings so that they will better understand the universality of the language of art. MICA offers an honors program for juniors in Florence as well as other study-abroad opportunities in England, France, Ireland, Italy, Japan, Korea, the Netherlands, and Scotland that allow third-year students to study for one semester at colleges and universities noted for their strength in the visual arts. Summer study abroad in specialized subjects has been designed to provide students an opportunity to work closely with senior faculty members in locations that offer diverse cultural, environmental, and philosophical experiences. France, Italy, Jamaica, Korea, Spain, and Turkey are the current sites for two- and four-week programs. Exchange programs in twenty countries are also options for students.

The director of career development arranges job internships for juniors and seniors. These internships provide educational experiences that bridge the worlds of academics and work. There are more than 800 local and national listings.

Academic Facilities

The campus includes twenty-eight buildings with 430,706 square feet of studio and classroom space, creating a coherent and unified urban campus. The studios are fully furnished with state-of-the-art equipment for each area of concentration. The Decker Library includes more than 50,000 volumes, 300 current periodical subscriptions, and 250,000 slides of artwork. It is one of the largest art college libraries in the country.

MICA has taken a leadership role in integrating new technologies into its programs of study. Within a very short time, the oldest degree-granting college of art in the United States has developed its facilities to provide more than one computer and/or video workstation for approximately every 4 students. The College's faculty has introduced computer-based courses in all of the professional studio majors, and the computer is also an important resource in the liberal arts area, whether as a tool for word processing or as a research medium for accessing images and information in a variety of forms. In some departments, such as environmental design, graphic design, animation, interactive media, or photography, competency in the creative use of digital technologies is considered fundamental to the curriculum.

MICA has outstanding instructional facilities with specialized equipment for both traditional and new media. Independent and/or dedicated studio space is provided for seniors. Seven-days-a-week access is provided in all departments. Liberal Arts classrooms and lecture halls are intimately sized. A 550-seat auditorium and a 200-seat black box theater provide programming for a full schedule of visiting artists and lecturers as well as for film, video, and performing arts.

The Meyerhoff Career Development Center houses a full staff of counselors providing services related to internships, job listings, alumni networking, corporate recruitment, and career development skills.

Exhibitions play a major role in the artistic and intellectual life at the Institute. Each year, more than ninety public exhibitions are featured in the Institute galleries, which are unrivaled by any art college. They bring the work of regional, national, and international artists, as well as faculty members and students, to the public year-round.

Costs

For the 2009–10 academic year, tuition was $33,000. Room was $7100 and board, $1990. Mandatory fees totaled $1230.

Financial Aid

Each year approximately 85 percent of the full-time students receive $18 million in financial assistance. The College administers a variety of programs, including need-based grants and scholarships, government-related loans, and college work-study programs. The College also awards more than $520,000 through competitive, merit-based scholarship programs. Students who are not U.S. citizens or permanent residents are not eligible for financial aid.

Faculty

The faculty consists of 140 full-time and 130 part-time professional artists, designers, art historians, writers, and poets. Their work is represented in more than 250 public and private collections from the Museum of Modern Art to the Stedelijk Museum in Amsterdam and the Victoria and Albert Museum in London. They have won individual honors and awards from notable foundations, such as the National Endowment for the Arts and the Guggenheim Foundation. They are Fulbright Scholars and recipients of the Prix de Rome, the Louis Comfort Tiffany Award, and the MacArthur Fellowships. The faculty-student ratio is 1:9.6.

Student Government

The Student Voice Association represents the interests and viewpoints of students to the faculty, administration, and board of trustees.

Admission Requirements

Students applying to the Maryland Institute must have made a serious commitment to art; therefore, a portfolio of artwork that demonstrates talent, ability, and experience is required for admission to the College. The portfolio is very important; however, evidence of academic ability as determined by level of course work, grades, test scores, and class rank are also weighted heavily in the admission decision. Individual interests and accomplishments, revealed in the personal statement, letters of recommendation, and lists of extracurricular and volunteer activities beyond classroom instruction, strengthen the application. The required personal essay is seriously considered. A minimum TOEFL score of 550 (paper-based test), 213 (computer-based test), or 80 (Internet-based test) is required of students whose native language is not English.

Application and Information

Students interested in early decision must complete all requirements for admission by November 15. Freshmen applicants for the fall term should complete the application process by February 15 for priority admission and to be considered for merit-based scholarships. Transfer students have a March 1 deadline. Applicants for admission to the spring term are asked to complete the application process prior to December 1. For an application, catalog, and further information, students should contact:

Office of Undergraduate Admission
Maryland Institute College of Art
1300 Mount Royal Avenue
Baltimore, Maryland 21217

Phone: 410-225-2222
Fax: 410-225-2337
E-mail: admissions@mica.edu
Web site: http://www.mica.edu

MARYMOUNT MANHATTAN COLLEGE

MarymountManhattan
a college of the liberal arts

NEW YORK, NEW YORK

The College

Marymount Manhattan College (MMC) is an urban, independent, coeducational, undergraduate liberal arts college. The mission of the College is to educate a socially and economically diverse population by fostering intellectual achievement and personal growth and by providing opportunities for career development. Inherent in this mission is the intent to develop an awareness of social, political, cultural, and ethical issues in the belief that this awareness will lead to concern for, participation in, and the improvement of society. To accomplish this mission, the College offers a strong program in the arts and sciences to students of all ages—as well as substantial preprofessional preparation. Central to these efforts is the particular attention given to the individual student. Marymount Manhattan College also seeks to be a resource and learning center for the metropolitan community.

The social and extracurricular life of the student body of approximately 2,000 students centers on more than forty clubs and organizations sponsored through the Student Affairs Office, including the International Students Club, Psychology Club, French Club, Philosophy Club, Science Society, Black and Latino Student Organization, the student newspaper and yearbook, WMMC Radio, Student Government Association, intramural sports, and other special interest organizations. Students attend musical events, and MMC's own off-Broadway theater, the only one on the Upper East Side of Manhattan, offers students an opportunity to participate in student productions.

The Residence Life Office at Marymount Manhattan College is committed to providing residents with numerous opportunities and experiences that foster intellectual achievement and social and personal growth. Students are encouraged to become involved in the many activities that are sponsored by Residence Life and are assisted with assuming responsibility for their own lives and living environment. The College provides housing for approximately 800 students at various locations in Manhattan. The buildings offer suite-style, traditional dormitories, or apartment-style living, with classrooms, lounges, a laundry room, and rehearsal space. Additional off-campus facilities are obtained as needed.

The Office of Career Development and Internships serves the entire College community by providing an integrated program of academic and career counseling. The office helps students by offering internship opportunities and workshops in job placement, resume writing, and graduate school preparation. For the past five years, 90 percent of biology majors who apply are accepted to advanced professional schools, including Mt. Sinai School of Medicine and Cornell Medical College. Other College services include personal and financial aid counseling and campus ministry.

Location

Marymount Manhattan College is centrally located on Manhattan's Upper East Side at 221 East 71st Street between Second and Third avenues. Within walking distance of the campus are the Frick, Metropolitan, Whitney, and Guggenheim museums; the Asian Society, French Institute, and National Audubon Society; Central Park; New York Hospital and Sloan-Kettering Research Center; and public libraries. All forms of public transportation are easily accessible. Within minutes of the College are shops, restaurants, and movie theaters. This location gives students the opportunity to take advantage of New York City's rich culture and to explore a variety of neighborhoods.

Majors and Degrees

Marymount Manhattan College offers programs leading to the Bachelor of Arts, Bachelor of Science, and Bachelor of Fine Arts degrees. Majors are offered in accounting, acting, art (concentrations in art history, graphic design, photography, and studio art), biology, business management, communication arts, dance, English, history, humanities, international studies, philosophy and religious studies, political science, psychology, sociology, speech-language pathology and audiology, and theater arts (B.A., B.S., and B.F.A. degrees). Minors offered are business, creative writing, economics, education, forensic psychology, French, Hispanic studies, interdisciplinary writing, mathematics, media studies, neuroscience, philosophy, religious studies, and social work. Certificate programs are offered in industrial organizational psychology and teacher certification.

Academic Programs

Marymount Manhattan College has designed its programs to enable students to meet the challenges of contemporary society. MMC is committed to the belief that a liberal arts education provides students with the ability and the flexibility to manage change and with broad understanding and the communication and problem-solving skills that are essential for success in any career and in life. To accomplish its goals, the College offers a liberal arts education, integrated with preprofessional training opportunities and individualized attention. The curricula are organized into five divisions: humanities, fine and performing arts, sciences, social sciences, and business management. Also offered are special-interest sequences that complement the student's major and minor, with added concentration in such areas as art history, creative writing, finance and investments, international business, marketing, photography, predentistry, prelaw, premedicine, pre–veterinary science, and social work. The College's small size provides students with an individually planned academic career, reflects students' academic needs and interests, and supports their career goals.

Candidates for the Bachelor of Arts, Bachelor of Science, and Bachelor of Fine Arts degrees must complete 120 credits. To qualify for a degree, a student must maintain an overall scholastic average of at least 2.0. Requirements for certificate programs vary.

The College recognizes various types of nontraditional credit, including credit for acceptable scores on the Advanced Placement (AP), International Baccalaureate (IB), College-Level Examination Program (CLEP), and New York State College Proficiency Examination (CPE) tests and credit for life experience.

MMC encourages its students to participate in internship programs in New York City that range from work at hospitals, financial institutions, magazines, publishing houses, and off-Broadway theaters to HBO and CBS.

Off-Campus Programs

The College's Academic Year Abroad offers an opportunity for students to broaden their educational experience and to gain cultural perspectives through study at other colleges in the Americas and overseas. Students may spend one or both semesters of their junior year in this program. MMC summer sessions and January intersessions also offer students opportunities in travel/study-abroad courses in Egypt, France, Great Britain, Greece, Eastern Europe, Ireland, Italy, Russia, and Spain.

Academic Facilities

The Thomas J. Shanahan Library at MMC is a library/learning center. It contains more than 100,000 volumes in open stacks and maintains an extensive periodical collection. The media center, on the main library floor, houses nonprint materials, microfiche, microfilm, filmstrips, slides, tapes, videotapes, DVDs, and records. Through the library's affiliation with the New York Metropolitan Reference and Research Library Agency, MMC faculty members and students have access to the materials of the member libraries. The library also participates in the Online Computer Library Center (OCLC), a computerized database of the holdings of some 4,000 libraries that is currently being used for cataloging and reference purposes.

The modern 250-seat Theresa Lang Theatre is equipped with an orchestra pit capable of accommodating 40 musicians. The theater has a special acoustical design, a sprung dance floor, a full technical balcony with equipment for lighting and sound, thirty-five counter-weighted-line sets in the fly system, dressing rooms with showers, and a scene shop. Students benefit from exposure to the numerous professional dance, opera, and theatrical groups that perform at the College.

Recently, two completely remodeled laboratory facilities were opened to strengthen education in two areas in which MMC has always excelled—science and communication arts.

MMC's science facilities in biology, chemistry, and physics underwent a total reconstruction valued at close to $1 million, thanks to the generosity of the Samuel Freeman Charitable Trust and the Ira De Camp Foundation. The Samuel Freeman Science Center opens many new doors of opportunity to students who are biology/premedicine majors or who are interested in pursuing careers in other science or health-related fields.

The College's Theresa Lang Center for Producing features the latest in digital computer technology and is one of the most advanced facilities of its kind in New York City. With digital multimedia capability, a decor inspired by top television postproduction houses, and access to the public library's B. Altman Advanced Learning Superblock, the center further enhances students' skills in traditional video and television production and allows them to develop, design, and evaluate cutting-edge multimedia projects. In conjunction with the Communication Arts Department, the College offers students the Media Library, where many videos and screening computers are available to students.

The Writing Center at MMC provides a range of services and activities, including career-based courses, personal critiques and one-on-one assistance, lectures, workshops, and special events such as the Best-Selling Author Series and Annual Writers' Conference, as well as a minor in creative writing. This enables students to be a part of the highly respected New York City writing community.

The College recently opened the Lowerre Family Terrace. It is a 5,000-square-foot rooftop garden—complete with a stone waterwall, a deck, and WiFi service—that connects the two main campus buildings. Another new facility opened in fall 2009—the Commons, a two-tiered dining/student lounge that flows out to the Lowerre Family Terrace, providing an outdoor dining option for MMC students.

Costs

For the 2009–10 academic year, full-time tuition and fees are $22,656. Room and board costs are $12,874 per year. For part-time students, tuition is $689 per credit. Additional fees are applicable for various laboratory and studio classes.

Financial Aid

The College administers a variety of financial aid programs, including scholarships sponsored by the College. Some of the awards are based on academic achievement; others are based on financial need. Students are also eligible for aid through a wide variety of state and federal programs. In addition, a number of jobs are available for students on campus, and the Offices of Financial Aid and Academic and Career Advisement can help students locate part-time off-campus jobs to help finance their education. More than 85 percent of MMC students receive some form of financial assistance. Therefore, limited finances alone need not prevent any student from attending the College. Priority consideration for merit- and need-based financial aid is November 15 for spring admission and March 15 for fall admission.

Faculty

Marymount Manhattan College's student-faculty ratio is 11:1. In addition to the staff of the advisement office, faculty members act as advisers to students. Full-time faculty members teach in all sessions and divisions (days, evenings, and some weekends). Part-time instructors, who are drawn from the wealth of experienced teaching professionals in New York City, supplement the full-time faculty.

Student Government

The Student Government Association responds to three areas of concern at MMC. The association primarily serves the needs of its constituents by managing the student government budget, planning and publicizing events, and establishing organizations that reflect the interests of the students. In addition, the association assists faculty and administrative groups and committees in their policy and procedural tasks and communicates the results of committee work to the student body. Finally, the Student Government Association provides special representatives for students' rights and freedoms through established and clearly defined channels of authority.

Admission Requirements

Marymount Manhattan College seeks candidates with qualities that indicate potential for success in higher education and the ability to contribute to the College community. Admission is based on a combination of factors: the student's academic program, including scholastic average; two recommendations (judicial form required for transfer students in lieu of one recommendation) from teachers, counselors, or employers; an essay; and SAT or ACT scores. TOEFL scores are required for international student applicants.

Each year the College enrolls an increasing number of transfer students. Transfer students may receive up to 90 credits for course work completed at a regionally accredited postsecondary institution with a grade of C- or better. Transcripts are evaluated on a course-by-course basis.

Application and Information

The admissions application must be received by March 15 (fall entry) and November 15 (spring entry) for priority consideration for MMC scholarships. Students may apply online. For application forms and for more information about Marymount Manhattan College, students should contact:

Office of Admissions
Marymount Manhattan College
221 East 71st Street
New York, New York 10021
Phone: 212-517-0430
800-MARYMOUNT (toll-free)
Fax: 212-517-0448
E-mail: admissions@mmm.edu
Web site: http://www.mmm.edu

Marymount Manhattan College, in the heart of Manhattan.

MARYWOOD UNIVERSITY

SCRANTON, PENNSYLVANIA

The University

Marywood University is coeducational, comprehensive, residential, and Catholic. Founded in 1915 by the Sisters, Servants of the Immaculate Heart of Mary, the University serves men and women from a variety of backgrounds and religions. The University enrolls more than 3,400 students in an array of undergraduate and graduate programs. Motivated by a pioneering, progressive spirit, Marywood provides a framework for educational excellence that enables students to develop fully as persons and to master professional and leadership skills that are necessary for meeting human needs.

Students at Marywood have the opportunity to build on their academic interests and proactively shape their educational experience. Students' energy and intellectual curiosity guides their work, growth, and success. Marywood believes in the power of the individual and in the premise that education is the most empowering tool.

Marywood is fully accredited by the Commission on Higher Education of the Middle States Association of Colleges and Schools. Accreditations/approvals have been granted by Accreditation Review Committee on Education for the Physician Assistant, American Psychological Association, American Art Therapy Association, American Music Therapy Association, Commission on Accreditation for Dietetics Education, American Dietetic Association, Council on Academic Accreditation, American Speech-Language-Hearing Association, Association of Collegiate Business Schools and Programs, Commission on Accreditation of Athletic Training Education, Council for Accreditation of Counseling and Related Educational Programs, Council on Social Work Education, National Association of Schools of Art and Design, National Association of Schools of Music, National Council for Accreditation of Teacher Education, and National League for Nursing Accrediting Commission.

The athletic program for women and men at Marywood provides students with opportunities to play on competitive intercollegiate, club, and intramural teams. Students compete on an intercollegiate basis in baseball, basketball, cross-country, field hockey, lacrosse, soccer, softball, swimming/diving, tennis, and volleyball. Marywood is a member of NCAA Division III and the Colonial States Athletic Conference (CSAC). Marywood's teams have been successful, winning titles in basketball, field hockey, lacrosse, soccer, softball, tennis, and volleyball. In addition, Marywood teams and individuals have participated in tournaments at the national level.

Location

Situated on a hilltop, Marywood's scenic 115-acre campus is part of an attractive residential area of the city of Scranton, in northeastern Pennsylvania. With a population of 78,000, Scranton is the fifth-largest city in Pennsylvania and is the county seat of Lackawanna County (the county population is approximately 213,000). Marywood is relatively close to many major cities of the Northeast; traveling by car, it is 1 hour to Binghamton; 2½ hours to New York and Philadelphia; 4 hours to Washington, D.C.; and 5½ hours to Boston. Several airlines serve the Wilkes-Barre/Scranton International Airport, which is 20 minutes from the campus. The Pocono Mountains, offering spectacular scenery and an abundance of outdoor recreational opportunities, including downhill skiing, are a short distance from the campus.

Majors and Degrees

Marywood University offers a variety of majors and minors at the undergraduate level. Individually designed majors, developed with faculty guidance, and double and interdisciplinary majors are also available. Several five-year bachelor's/master's degree programs are offered.

At the undergraduate level, Marywood University awards the Bachelor of Arts (B.A.), Bachelor of Architecture (B.Arch.), Bachelor of Business Administration (B.B.A.), Bachelor of Environmental Design in Architecture (B.E.D.A.), Bachelor of Fine Arts (B.F.A.), Bachelor of Music (B.M.), Bachelor of Science (B.S.), Bachelor of Science in Nursing (B.S.N.), and Bachelor of Social Work (B.S.W.).

Marywood offers majors and minors in the following areas of study: accounting, ad hoc (self-designed), advertising and public relations, architecture and interior architecture/design, art (studio: ceramics, painting, sculpture; design: graphic design, illustration, photography), art education, art therapy, arts administration (art, music, theater), aviation management, biology, biotechnology, communication sciences and disorders (audiology, deaf studies, speech-language pathology), comprehensive social sciences (general, history, sociology), computer information and telecommunications systems, computer science (minor), criminal justice, dance/movement (minor), digital media and broadcast production (broadcast, corporate), early childhood special education, education (elementary, secondary), English, environmental science, family and consumer sciences education, financial planning, French, general science education, health and physical education (athletic training, education, physical activity), health services administration, history/political science, hospitality management, industrial/organizational psychology, international business, journalism (minor), management, marketing, mathematics, medical technology/clinical laboratory science, multimedia (minor), music, music education, music therapy, nursing (preservice, post-RN), nutrition and dietetics (coordinated program, didactic program), performance, performing arts, philosophy, physician assistant studies, psychology, psychology/clinical practice, public administration, religious studies, retail business management, science, social sciences secondary education, social work, Spanish, special education/elementary education (dual certification), theater, and women's studies (minor).

Preprofessional programs are offered in chiropractic, communication sciences and disorders, dentistry, law, medicine, physician assistant studies, and veterinary medicine. A joint seven-year bachelor's/doctoral program in chiropractic involves three years of study on the Marywood campus and additional work at New York Chiropractic College, which is located in Seneca Falls, New York.

Academic Programs

Undergraduate degrees are offered in more than sixty academic programs, including the arts, sciences, music, fine arts, social work, and nursing. All students are required to complete a core curriculum in the liberal arts in addition to the courses in their major. Opportunities for undergraduates abound through double majors, honors and independent-study programs, practicums, internships, and study abroad. Army and Air Force ROTC programs are available.

Off-Campus Programs

Study-abroad opportunities are available in countries such as Australia, Canada, England, France, Mexico, and Spain. Through Studio Art Centers International (SACI), art students may study in Florence, Italy. Students can also earn credits toward a degree through the distance learning program.

Academic Facilities

In recent years, the University has made $100 million in improvements to the campus, including new athletic, residence hall, and dining facilities, and one of the finest studio arts facilities in the northeast. The Insalaco Center for Studio Arts features 60,000 square feet of fully equipped studios, labs, and classroom spaces for a broad variety of artistic disciplines. The O'Neill Center for Healthy Families gives students an opportunity to study and perform research in a first-rate human performance laboratory.

Costs

Tuition for full-time students (12–18 credits per semester) for the 2009–10 academic year was a flat fee of $25,150. There is also a general fee of $920 for full-time students. Costs for room and board for a full academic year are approximately $11,498, depending on which meal plan is selected and the desired room occupancy. Costs of books and supplies are estimated at $900.

Financial Aid

Marywood offers a comprehensive program of financial aid to assist students in meeting educational costs. Eligibility for federal and state programs is based on demonstrated financial need, as determined by a federal eligibility formula that analyzes family income and assets. In addition, approximately $22 million in institutional aid is awarded annually to Marywood students. Applicants to Marywood are considered for all financial assistance programs for which they qualify. Candidates are required to submit the Free Application for Federal Student Aid (FAFSA) and the Marywood application form, preferably by February 15.

Faculty

Among faculty members at Marywood, 144 are full-time, and 84 percent of these hold the Ph.D. or the highest degree in their field. The student-faculty ratio is 14:1. Faculty members are evaluated on their teaching and on their scholarly and artistic activities.

Student Government

All matriculated students in the undergraduate school are members of the Student Government Association (SGA). The SGA operates with a number of committees, including the Student Council, the Resident Committee, and the Commuter Committee. The association plays a key role in establishing a positive campus environment.

Admission Requirements

Candidates for admission should demonstrate reasonable progress toward graduation in an accredited secondary school, have graduated from a secondary school, or offer evidence of an equivalent secondary education. Each candidate should show satisfactory academic preparation in 16 units of subject matter, including 4 units of English, 3 units of social studies, 2 units of mathematics, 1 unit of science with laboratory, and 6 additional units. Either SAT or ACT scores are required for those who wish to enter as freshmen.

In addition to fulfilling general admission requirements, candidates for admission to a degree program in architecture, art, education, music, nursing, and pre–physician assistant studies must meet special standards established by the department. Prior to enrollment, music, theater, and art candidates are required to audition or to present an art portfolio.

For certain programs, candidates without the recommended distribution of units may be eligible for admission if their course work as a whole and the results of their tests offer evidence of a strong foundation for college work. Candidates who are deficient in required course work may complete the appropriate work during the summer or the first year in college.

A student who demonstrates satisfactory academic performance at another college may apply for admission as a transfer student. Academic courses presented for transfer should be equivalents of courses required by the programs of study at Marywood. Students should have earned a grade of C or higher in their course work; C– will not transfer. A student should expect to earn a minimum of 60 credits at Marywood University; ordinarily, at least one half of the credits required for a major must also be earned at Marywood.

International candidates are required to meet the academic standards for admission, demonstrate proficiency in the use of the English language, and submit documentation of having sufficient funds to cover educational and living expenses for the duration of study. To certify proficiency in the use of English, international applicants whose primary language is not English must submit scores from the Test of English as a Foreign Language (TOEFL).

Application and Information

Applications for admission are considered on a rolling basis; however, candidates are strongly encouraged to submit applications by March 1. Applications received after March 1 are considered on the basis of available space in particular programs. To be considered for admission, freshman applicants must submit to the Office of Admissions a completed application (paper or online), a nonrefundable $35 application fee (waived if applying online), an official high school transcript with an indication of class rank, an official report of scores from the SAT or ACT, and at least one letter of recommendation. Students can apply online at http://www.mymarywood.com/home/apply.html.

Transfer students must submit a completed application, a nonrefundable $35 application fee (waived if applying online), an official high school transcript, official academic transcript(s) reflecting all college course work for which the candidate has enrolled, and at least one letter of recommendation.

All submitted credentials become the property of Marywood and are not returnable to the applicant. Admission standards and policies are free of discrimination on grounds of race, color, national origin, sex, age, or disability.

For further information, interested students should contact:

Christian DiGregorio, Director
University Admissions
Marywood University
2300 Adams Avenue
Scranton, Pennsylvania 18509
Phone: 570-348-6234
TO-MARYWOOD (866-279-9663, toll-free)
Fax: 570-961-4763
E-mail: yourfuture@marywood.edu
Web site: http://www.mymarywood.com

The rotunda in the Liberal Arts Center on Marywood's campus.

MASSACHUSETTS COLLEGE OF PHARMACY AND HEALTH SCIENCES

BOSTON, MASSACHUSETTS

The College

Founded in 1823, the Massachusetts College of Pharmacy and Health Sciences (MCPHS) is the oldest institution of higher education in Boston and the second-oldest college of pharmacy in the United States. As a private independent institution with a prominent history of specializing in health sciences education, the College offers traditional and nontraditional programs that combine in-depth knowledge with hands-on practice.

MCPHS has a distinguished history and international reputation in pharmacy and health-care programs. With a background of liberal arts, general education, and other courses, graduates are compassionate as well as competent practitioners. MCPHS graduates are in great demand, even before they graduate. Most are employed at or soon after graduation, with 100 percent employment in two years. Salaries exceed those of most other new college graduates, beginning at $50,000 to $100,000.

The curriculum is designed to develop active thinkers and learners who are prepared for changing professions and a complex world. Developed by educators and working professionals, these courses are often tailored to give students practical information and valuable insights into today's health-care concerns. Students benefit from hands-on learning in the College's state-of-the-art laboratories and computer centers. Ultimately, the programs, which combine the basic sciences with the humanities, provide an education for lifelong enrichment.

The Department of Recreation and Wellness offers opportunities for all students to participate in club sports, intramurals, wellness classes, and the Wellness Center. The intramural program is open to all MCPHS students, faculty and staff members and is an ideal way for students to be involved with the College community. Baseball, basketball, cross-country, golf, soccer, softball, and volleyball operate as Student Government Association (SGA) clubs on campus. Other student activities include the Academy of Students of Pharmacy, the Black Student Union, the Indian Student Organization, the International Student Association, the Republic of China Student Association, the Vietnamese Student Association, the College yearbook, and the *Dispenser* (student newspaper). There are also four professional fraternities—one men's, two women's, and one coed.

In September 2000, MCPHS opened a second campus in Worcester, Massachusetts. The College offers an innovative, accelerated PharmD program for transfer students and a sixteen-month B.S.N. for students who already hold a bachelor's degree in another major, an RN to M.S.N. program for practicing RNs who have only an associate or bachelor's degree, and a twenty-four month master of physician assistant studies. MCPHS opened a third campus in 2003, in Manchester, New Hampshire, where it offers a Master of Physician Assistant Studies program, a B.S.N. program, and a PharmD program, each following the Worcester model. Programs on these two newer campuses are designed specifically for students holding a bachelor's degree in another field looking to transition into the health-care field.

MCPHS Boston is a member of the Colleges of the Fenway (COF). Other participating members are Wentworth Institute of Technology, Wheelock College, Simmons College, Emmanuel, and Massachusetts College of Art and Design. Students can take courses and participate in numerous extracurricular activities at the other institutions in the consortium.

Location

Dedicated solely to health sciences education, MCPHS Boston is a highly respected institution in the world-renowned Longwood Medical and Academic Area. Its location alone gives students resources for enriching their education. The area is home to the nation's premier medical centers and educational and research institutions—a highly stimulating and inspiring environment in which to learn.

Boston is "America's College Town"—it is highly cultural, accessible, and a vibrant mecca for students. They can experience Boston's history along the Freedom Trail, enjoy its seafood on the waterfront, or explore its ethnic neighborhoods. Favorite spots include Faneuil Hall Marketplace; the Esplanade along the Charles River, for outdoor concerts and movies, biking, jogging, and in-line skating; and the Public Gardens and Boston Common, for walks, picnics, and just relaxing. The city's elaborate public transportation network (the "T") connects students to all these places and many more, such as Cambridge and Harvard Square, where students might browse in bookstores and enjoy a sidewalk performance; Newbury Street, for shopping and distinctive galleries; TD Banknorth Garden, where the Celtics and Bruins play; Fenway Park, a 5-minute walk for baseball fans; and Symphony Hall, home of the Boston Symphony Orchestra and the famed Boston Pops.

Majors and Degrees

Massachusetts College of Pharmacy and Health Sciences is the oldest college in the City of Boston and offers innovative and cutting-edge academic programs that respond to the ever-changing needs of the health-care field. Programs at the College are designed to actively engage students in the learning process and to educate students to become skilled, compassionate, health-care workers who are committed to their own lifelong learning.

MCPHS offers undergraduate and professional degrees in chemistry, health psychology, pharmaceutical marketing and management, pharmaceutical sciences, pharmacy, physician assistant studies, and premedical and health studies with professional pathway opportunities. The College also offers accelerated three-year programs in dental hygiene as part of the renowned Forsyth School of Dental Hygiene program, as well as, radiologic sciences, and nursing.

The College offers a distinct advantage over other schools by accepting students directly into the dental hygiene, nursing, pharmacy, and radiologic sciences programs, known as "direct-entry."

Academic Programs

Students in each of the undergraduate programs begin their studies in the basic sciences, humanities, and social sciences. First-year classes include two semesters of English, math, biology or anatomy and physiology, and chemistry. After completing basic science courses, Bachelor of Science degree candidates progress to advanced courses in chemistry, psychology, pharmaceutics, and pharmacology. Students are also required to complete professional development courses, such as interpersonal communications, ethics, and law courses. In addition, students must complete 12 semester hours of elective courses in the humanities, social sciences, and behavioral sciences, as well as 12 semester hours of general elective course work.

Off-Campus Programs

The externship/clinical experience is a very important part of an MCPHS education and is built into most programs. The programs place students in professional settings for firsthand learning and guidance as they work with mentors from a sponsoring institution's staff. Students may choose experiences at more than fifty-five hospitals, 100 community-practice sites, and various research centers throughout New England.

Because the College is located in the heart of Boston's world-renowned Longwood Medical and Academic Area and has affiliations with Boston's high-caliber medical centers, top teaching hospitals, and pharmacies, students are ensured the highest-quality experience. Affiliates include such well-known institutions as Boston Medical Center, Massachusetts General Hospital, Harvard-affiliated hospitals, Dana Farber Cancer Institute, Children's Hospital, Joslin Diabetes Center, Brigham and Women's Hospital, and Genzyme.

Academic Facilities

MCPHS dedicated a new, architecturally arresting, academic building on Huntington Avenue in April 2009. The Richard E. Griffin Academic Center houses 49,700-square-feet of classrooms, teaching laboratories, a technology center, and a 2,300-seat auditorium. The Boston campus also features the $30-million Ronald A. Matricaria Academic and Student Center. The six-story, 93,000-square-foot building houses a state-of-the art library and chemistry, pharmacy, and computer laboratories. The building also houses four floors of beautiful apartment-style residences for 230 students.

Significant renovations in the White Building in 2005 included state-of-the-art clinics and laboratories for students enrolled in the dental hygiene, nursing, and physician assistant studies programs.

Costs

Tuition and fees for two semesters in 2009–10 were $23,800 for undergraduate students. For two semesters and a summer session (accelerated dental hygiene, nursing, and radiologic sciences students), tuition was $34,500, and room and board (two semesters only) ranged from $10,200 to $12,390. Additional fees may apply for years two and three. Worcester and Manchester tuition and fees vary—please check http://www.mcphs.edu.

Financial Aid

The College offers a variety of scholarships, grants, loans, and employment opportunities to assist students in meeting costs of education that cannot be met through the family's own resources. The College is committed to making MCPHS an affordable option and in recent years has awarded more than $10 million annually to eligible students. It participates in all federal and state college funding programs. Priority consideration is given to students who meet the March 15 financial aid application deadline for all available funds.

MCPHS offers incoming freshman students several merit scholarships. All awards are based on academics, regardless of financial need. There is no separate application for these awards; merit scholarships are automatically awarded at the time of admission. In addition, these awards automatically renew each year provided students maintain continuous full-time enrollment and meet a specified grade point average. Students should contact the Admission Office at admissions@mcphs.edu for the specific requirements of the merit scholarships.

Faculty

MCPHS has around 200 outstanding full-time faculty members, with 500-plus adjunct and clinical faculty members who support the programs. Almost 85 percent of the faculty members hold the highest degree possible in their fields. Classes and laboratories are taught by regular and adjunct faculty members, not teaching assistants.

Student Government

The Student Government Association is an elective body charged with appropriating funds for and monitoring student activities, overseeing class elections, and functioning as the voice of the students and their interests. Its membership includes the Dean of Students, 18 student representatives, and 2 faculty representatives.

Admission Requirements

First-year applicants should have a high school diploma or GED credential or have fewer than 12 college credits. In addition, they should have a minimum of 16 units of course work in a challenging college-preparatory program and good to excellent grades in the following subject areas: 4 units of English, 3 in mathematics (algebra 1, algebra 2, and trigonometry), 2 in laboratory science (1 each in biology and chemistry), 2 in social sciences (including 1 in history), and 5 in additional college-prep courses. Advanced Placement (AP), International Baccalaureate (IB), and honors-level courses are highly desired. Additional science and mathematics courses are highly recommended.

Freshman applicants must provide SAT (all three sections) and/or ACT scores; a personal essay that cites reasons for choosing the academic program marked on the application, selecting the specific health career to be pursued after graduation, and applying to MCPHS; at least two letters of recommendation, one from a guidance or college counselor and one from a mathematics or science teacher; and a description of extracurricular activities to show a genuine interest, commitment, and involvement in activities outside of the classroom that demonstrate leadership, compassion and dedication—especially activities that are related to health care, including community service positions of leadership, musical instruments played, athletic participation, and any other significant accomplishments.

Transfer applicants are those who have completed 12 or more college credits, with strong performance in math and science courses. They must have a cumulative grade point average of at least 2.5 on a 4.0 scale (depending on program of study) attained at an accredited college or university and evidence of being able to handle a full-time course load (12–15 credits) at the four-year college or university level. SAT and/or ACT scores are required for transfer candidates with fewer than 30 college or university credits at the time of application. Transfer students must also submit the personal essay and description of extracurricular activities.

Application and Information

For early action admission, freshman candidates with solid academic records who have decided that MCPHS is their top-choice college are encouraged to apply. Applicants must submit the application and supplement (through the Common Application) by November 15. The Admission Office makes decisions on early action applications by mid-December. Early action is only open to prospective freshmen and is nonbinding. Accepted students have until May 1 to respond to the College's offer of admission.

For regular admission, the priority application date is February 1, but students should apply as soon as possible. The Admission Office replies on a rolling basis once applications are complete and evaluated by the review committee and faculty members. Review for fall-entry candidates typically begins in early January. Accepted students have until May 1 to respond to offers of admission. Although there are priority filing dates for all programs, MCPHS continues to welcome applications received after these dates until all spaces are filled.

For transfer students, the priority application date is February 1, but students are encouraged to apply as soon as possible. The Admission Office replies on a rolling basis once applications are complete and reviewed by admission counselors and faculty members.

MCPHS is a member of the Common Application (http://www.commonapp.org). Applicants can visit their Web site to submit or download and print an application

For more information, students should contact:

Office of Admission
Massachusetts College of Pharmacy and Health Sciences
179 Longwood Avenue
Boston, Massachusetts 02115
Phone: 617-732-2850
800-225-5506 (toll-free outside Massachusetts)
Fax: 617-732-2118
E-mail: admissions@mcphs.edu
Web site: http://www.mcphs.edu

The Massachusetts College of Pharmacy and Health Sciences Ronald A. Matricaria Academic and Student Center.

MENLO COLLEGE

ATHERTON, CALIFORNIA

COLLEGE CLOSE-UPS

The College

Menlo College, an independent, coeducational, nonsectarian institution, stands out among institutions of higher education in five exciting ways: programs, location, small size, sports, and alumni. Rather than offer a traditional set of majors as many institutions do, Menlo concentrates on providing excellent programs in business management with a strong foundation in the liberal arts. Menlo's location in the heart of the Silicon Valley allows the College to train tomorrow's leaders in an intimate, student-centered, academically challenging environment. The College is small enough to be a real community but large enough to support a wide array of intercollegiate sports, student organizations, and internship opportunities, giving students the confidence and breadth of experience to flourish after graduation. The College's distinguished alumni provide a strong base of support for graduates, which helps students make the transition from college to career with great success.

A Menlo education is a process that trains and cultivates leaders. This process begins with a broad-based liberal arts foundation in the humanities, mathematics, sciences, and social sciences. At the same time, students are also challenged to enrich and develop their writing, critical-thinking, and decision-making skills. Next, students enter rich major programs staffed with seasoned practitioners who are experts in their respective fields. The advantage is a cutting-edge curriculum that equips students to succeed. Menlo's superior business program is renowned throughout the world and has produced generations of dynamic and successful business, industrial, and civic leaders around the globe.

The learning process does not end in the classroom. Students are encouraged to participate in internships and study programs that bridge the gap between theory and practice. These opportunities range from Fortune 500 companies to innovative start-up enterprises, from San Francisco to South America, Asia, and Europe. Not only do participants gain hands-on experience, but also they grow personally as they encounter diverse peoples, cultures, and values.

As a whole, College-sponsored activities promote self-exploration and often lead to the discovery of hidden talents. Students can participate in a variety of clubs or organizations, ranging from the Alpha Chi National Honor Society and the Poetry, Art, and Music Society to the Menlo Oak Newspaper and the Outdoor Club. Leadership skills are cultivated through an activist student government and student life positions and special workshops that tackle pressing contemporary issues. In addition, Menlo's international exchange programs offer students opportunities to expand their horizons and bring global awareness to their futures.

This commitment to personal and intellectual growth, coupled with Menlo's ideal location in the heart of the Silicon Valley, draws students from all across the United States and around the world. The global village is a reality at Menlo, given the broad social, religious, cultural, and national makeup of the student body. The appreciation of different cultures that results becomes a tremendous advantage in the marketplace.

Menlo's warm, friendly atmosphere is enhanced by its residential status. Nearly two thirds of all students live in one of five residence halls. Nearby off-campus apartments (for students who are older than 21 or married) are also an option.

For those who enjoy the exhilaration of intercollegiate competition, Menlo offers men's baseball, basketball, cross-country, football, golf, soccer, and wrestling, and women's sports include basketball, cross-country, soccer, softball, volleyball, and wrestling. The College competes in the NAIA Pacific Conference and the NCAA Division III. Intramural sports are also popular, and altogether almost 40 percent of students participate in sports.

To meet students' health needs, the College provides care via the Menlo Medical Clinic. Counseling services are offered by faculty and resident life staff members.

Whether in the classroom, in the laboratory, or on the playing field, Menlo College nurtures students by creating programs, activities, and services that foster individual success.

Location

Menlo College is located on the San Francisco peninsula in the town of Atherton, a residential community near the cities of Menlo Park and Palo Alto. Major freeways do not pass near the campus, nor is heavy industry nearby. The area ranks among the most attractive and exciting in the world, with numerous cultural resources and a temperate climate. San Francisco lies 30 miles to the north. Many other important educational centers are within an hour's drive of Menlo, making the area an exciting place in which to study and live. The campus is in the heart of Silicon Valley, where high-tech companies in the electronics, computer, aerospace, biotechnology, and pharmaceutical industries are literally transforming the world in which we live and work. Surrounding the San Francisco Bay Area is the great natural beauty of northern California, extending from the spectacular California coast to the majestic Sierra Nevada Mountains. Favorite spots such as Big Sur, Monterey Bay, Lake Tahoe, Napa Valley, and Yosemite National Park are just a few hours' drive from Menlo.

Majors and Degrees

Menlo College offers the following fields of study: accounting, finance, general business management, international management, management information systems, marketing, marketing communication, media management, psychology, sports management, real estate, and an individually designed major where students can combine existing programs to create their own major.

Academic Programs

Menlo College operates on a semester calendar. To earn a bachelor's degree, students must complete 124 units of credit and maintain good academic standing.

Menlo's renowned Academic Success Center provides dynamic resources for increasing students' academic ability and morale. Included are innovative approaches to counseling and tutoring. The goal is to develop strong self-advocacy and to assist faculty members in meeting the needs of a varied student population using an assortment of individualized, small-group, and computer-based instruction. This method facilitates study and discussion of course material, tutoring, and test preparation.

Off-Campus Programs

The difference between obtaining an exciting professional position with opportunity for advancement and growth and settling for second best often comes down to experience. Internships enable students to apply theory to practice—to take classroom knowledge and test its relevancy. Through the Career Services

Office and each academic department, qualified students are urged to participate in local, national, or international internships. Students spend one or more semesters working on or off campus in their fields of study obtaining academic credit and/or financial compensation and valuable insight. Menlo also has exchange agreements with Francisco de Vitoria University in Madrid, Spain; Peking University, in Beijing, China; Anáhuac University, in Mexico City; Universidad Adolfo Ibanez in Chile; Guangdong College of Business in Guangzhou, China; and with Kansai Gaidai University in Japan.

Academic Facilities

Bowman Library maintains a strong collection of books and periodicals, including electronic journals, books, and AV materials. The Bowman Library's Electronic Information Gateway provides access to general and specialized online research databases, including full-text periodicals and reference resources as well as high-speed access to the Internet and World Wide Web. The Bowman Library contains rooms for group study, viewing AV materials, and photocopying. In addition, wireless access to the campus network resources is available through the library's laptop computer checkout program.

The Resource for Online Services and Information Electronically (ROSIE) is Menlo College's electronic information gateway, providing access 24 hours a day, seven days a week through the Web from the library, dorms, and off-campus sites to the online catalog, electronic research databases, and reference assistance. For more information, students should visit http://www.menlo.edu/library. ROSIE also provides access to WOODIE, the online research-skills tutorial required of all students through the Menlo College General Education curriculum.

Menlo College's four computer labs provide students with access to state-of-the-art PC and Macintosh hardware, software, and networking capabilities. All computer-lab equipment is connected to the campus network as well as the Internet and World Wide Web. Classroom labs include both individual workstations and presentation facilities. The Open Access lab is open daily and is staffed by experienced monitors who are familiar with all lab equipment and applications and are able to provide students with the best possible technical and instructional services. With a 5:1 student-computer ratio, Menlo College offers students ample access to a wide range of computing resources for both classroom assignments and personal use.

Costs

Tuition and fees for 2009–10 are $32,150. Residence costs, including room and board, are $11,330.

Financial Aid

Menlo is noted for a strong program of merit and need-based aid. Approximately 80 percent of Menlo's students enroll with financial assistance, including Menlo scholarships, achievement awards, and on-campus employment as well as Federal Pell Grants, Federal Stafford Student Loans, State of California Grants, Federal PLUS loans, and others. Students transferring to Menlo are fully eligible to be considered for financial aid. Merit scholarships of up to $12,000 per year are available for both domestic and international students.

Faculty

Menlo's faculty members devote their full attention to teaching. The College faculty is composed of approximately 60 members, both full- and part-time. Guest lecturers from business, industry, and other professions add to the breadth of instruction. Faculty members are readily available to give students personal help and counseling. A student-teacher ratio of 15:1 allows for small classes and individual attention to students' progress.

Student Government

Students elect their own representatives to student government, which is responsible for legislative and executive decisions affecting student activities and the coordination of student affairs. At Menlo, students take the lead in shaping their education and the future of their College.

Admission Requirements

The Admissions Committee considers each candidate individually, through the assessment of academic achievement and personal qualities, talents, and interests. There is an early action plan for entering freshmen, and transfer students are welcome. Applicants are evaluated on the basis of their academic record, course of study, personal recommendations, school activities, essay, and scores on either the SAT or ACT. A personal visit is strongly recommended but not required. The College looks for freshmen with both breadth and depth of academic background in college preparatory subjects. Transfer students are evaluated on the strength of their college programs. Applicants are considered without regard to age, race, color, creed, gender, sexual orientation, national origin, marital status, disability, or any other characteristic protected by law.

Application and Information

Students may enter Menlo College at the opening of the fall or spring semester. Application deadlines are: early action deadline, December 1; priority deadline for freshmen, February 1 for fall and November 1 for spring; and priority deadline for transfers, April 1. For further information concerning admission, students should contact:

Office of Admissions
Menlo College
1000 El Camino Real
Atherton, California 94027-4301
Phone: 650-543-3753
800-55-MENLO (toll-free)
Fax: 650-543-4496
E-mail: admissions@menlo.edu
Web site: http://www.menlo.edu

COLLEGE CLOSE-UPS

MEREDITH COLLEGE

RALEIGH, NORTH CAROLINA

COLLEGE CLOSE-UPS

The College

Meredith College, chartered in 1891, is today the largest private women's college in the Southeast. Even as the College has grown to more than 2,200 undergraduate degree candidates, the student-faculty ratio of 10:1 offers students individualized attention in all aspects of their experience at Meredith College. With a focus on the liberal arts, students are encouraged in all areas from career preparation to personal development. Degree candidates choose from more than forty fields, including preprofessional studies.

The faculty is dedicated to teaching, advising, and challenging the students to meet their academic and personal goals. Undergraduate students pursue programs leading to Bachelor of Arts, Science, Music, and Social Work degrees; the College also offers Master of Business Administration, Master of Education, Master of Arts in Teaching, and Master of Science in nutrition degrees. College programs are accredited by the Southern Association of Colleges and Schools, the National Council for the Accreditation of Teacher Education, the Association to Advance Collegiate Schools of Business International (AACSB), the Council on Social Work Education, the Council for Interior Design Accreditation (formerly FIDER), and the National Association of Schools of Music. The College has an approved American Dietetic Association Plan V Program.

The College focuses heavily on leadership development for women. Students are encouraged to participate in a wide variety of campus activities, including performing groups, sports, publications, academic and personal interest clubs, and student government. More than 500 leadership positions are available for women to fill. Rich with diversity with students from thirty states and sixteen countries, Meredith celebrates its students' uniqueness and potential to return to their communities as active participants in whatever capacity that they choose. A member of NCAA Division III, Meredith fields intercollegiate teams in six sports: basketball, cross-country, softball, soccer, tennis, and volleyball. The College joined the USA South Athletic Conference in 2007.

Location

Meredith's beautiful 225-acre campus is on the western edge of Raleigh, North Carolina's capital city, and is adjacent to the booming Research Triangle area of Raleigh, Durham, and Chapel Hill. A total of eleven colleges and universities that serve approximately 108,000 students can be found here. Raleigh, a city of 350,000 people, is centrally located between the North Carolina coast and the mountain ranges of the western part of the state. Two interstates and the Raleigh-Durham International Airport (15 minutes from the campus) make Raleigh easily accessible.

Majors and Degrees

Meredith confers four baccalaureate degrees. A candidate for the Bachelor of Arts degree can select her major from art, biology, chemistry, communication, dance, economics, English, environmental studies, history, international studies, mathematics, music, political science, psychology, religion, sociology, Spanish, and theater. The Bachelor of Science degree is available in accounting, biology, business administration, chemistry, child development, computer information systems, computer science, exercise and sports science, family and consumer science, fashion merchandising and design, foods and nutrition, interior design, and mathematics. The Bachelor of Music degree candidate can major in music education or performance. The Bachelor of Social Work degree is available in social work. In addition, a student may work with the faculty to create a self-designed major.

Licensure programs taken in addition to a major are offered in birth to kindergarten (B–K), elementary (K–6), middle grades (6–9), secondary (9–12), and special subject areas (K–12).

Preprofessional preparation is available in dentistry, law, medicine, pharmacy, physical therapy, physician assistant studies, and veterinary medicine. Minors are offered in most major fields and in some other areas, such as communication, criminal justice, ethics, philosophy, and physical education. Concentrations are also available within most departments. A five-year dual-degree program with North Carolina State University is available in engineering.

Academic Programs

Meredith's academic program blends a strong liberal arts foundation with opportunities for career and preprofessional preparation. To achieve breadth in her education, each student must fulfill general education requirements in humanities and arts, social and behavioral sciences, mathematics and natural sciences, and health and physical education. By the end of her sophomore year, she declares a major and begins to study her chosen field in depth. She may round out her program by completing options such as a second major, a minor or a concentration, a teacher education program, an experiential learning component (an internship, co-op, or fieldwork), or a study-abroad program.

There are opportunities for advanced placement with credit for those who show by examination (AP, I.B., CLEP, and/or departmental examinations) that they have mastered the material for any college-level course. Each year approximately 25 entering students are invited to participate in the Honors Program. Nearly 30 entering students participate in the Teaching Fellows Program, which provides special seminars, mentors, honors classes, and cultural opportunities for the winners of the prestigious North Carolina Teaching Fellows Scholarship/Loan.

Off-Campus Programs

Through the Cooperating Raleigh Colleges consortium, students may take courses with typically no extra cost at North Carolina State and Shaw Universities and at Peace and St. Augustine's Colleges.

Women who are interested in expanding their international horizons can participate in either summer or academic-year intercultural programs in almost any country. Every summer, students and faculty members travel to England, Italy, and Switzerland for five or eleven weeks of study. It is possible to earn an entire semester of credit through this summer study at approximately the same price as a regular semester on campus in Raleigh. Meredith's newest study abroad program is a semester-long program in Sansepolcro, Italy. Those seeking a less traditional venue can work with the Office of Study Abroad to find a program appropriate to their academic or travel interests. Recent study abroad locations include Denmark, Iceland, Costa Rica, Kenya, and Morocco.

Students may take advantage of opportunities within the United States by completing a United Nations Semester at Drew University, a federal government semester through the Washington Semester program at American University, a semester at Marymount College in New York City, and a capital city semester in state government through Meredith's own program in Raleigh.

Academic Facilities

The Carlyle Campbell Library contains more than 190,000 volumes, 16,000 microforms, and over 3,000 newspaper and journal subscriptions with access to articles from more than 27,000 journals, magazines, and newspapers online. As part of its academic department facilities, the campus also houses a music library, art galleries, a research greenhouse, music practice rooms, a state-of-the-art language lab, an autism lab, computer labs, a child-care lab, an indoor swimming pool, lighted outdoor tennis courts, a putting green, a soccer field, and track. The campus is also cabled to provide network and e-mail access in classrooms, computer labs, and residence halls as well as wireless Internet access throughout much of the campus.

Costs

For 2009–10, tuition and fees were $24,490, and room and board were $7020.

Financial Aid

Meredith's financial aid program is designed to meet a high percentage of the analyzed need of the student. Approximately 65 percent of undergraduate students receive need-based assistance; when competitive scholarships and state entitlement grants are added, over 95 percent of Meredith students receive some form of financial assistance. The Free Application for Federal Student Aid (FAFSA) is used to determine eligibility for need-based federal, state, and institutional funds that include grants and scholarships, loans, and work-study. A freshman candidate may also file special application forms for the competitive scholarships that recognize students for superior academic ability and talent in art, music, or interior design. A North Carolina Teaching Fellow who is selected for Meredith's program may use her scholarship at the College and will have other gift assistance coordinated to match the stipend provided by the state.

Faculty

The College has 147 full-time faculty members. Ninety percent of the full-time faculty members have earned terminal degrees. The student-faculty ratio is 10:1, and the average class size is 16. Sixty-seven percent of the full-time faculty members are women.

Student Government

Meredith has one of the oldest student government associations in the South and has an honor code that is a key ingredient of the Meredith community. All students assume primary responsibility for making and enforcing regulations; therefore, every student is a member of the Student Government Association (SGA). As members, students are encouraged to actively participate in branches of the SGA, such as the Association for Meredith Commuters, Elections Board, Honor Council, Residence Hall Board, Senate, Student Life, and Women in New Goal Settings.

Admission Requirements

Along with academic achievement, Meredith values individuality, integrity, and diversity. Each application is evaluated to determine how the student's academic preparation and ability match Meredith's requirements and challenges and to assess motivation, special talents, and commitment to learning. A freshman candidate is expected to have at least 16 units of academic credit earned in grades 9–12. Her program should include English (4 units), history/social studies (3 units), mathematics (3 units in algebra I, algebra II, and geometry or a higher level course), science (3 units), foreign language (2 units), and electives (1 unit from the academic subjects). Careful attention is given to an unweighted grade average on the academic subjects and to class rank; test scores (SAT or ACT) are reviewed in relation to the high school record; recommendations from a school official and a teacher are also required. Applicants must also complete an essay of at least 250 words on a topic of their choice. An interview may be requested in some instances, and students are encouraged to visit for an admissions conference and campus tour.

For transfer admission from an accredited college or university, the student needs at least an overall C average in transferable courses, must be eligible to return to the last institution regularly attended, and must be recommended by college officials. If the student has fewer than 30 semester hours of transferable work, she must also meet Meredith's freshman admission requirements.

International students must also provide proof of English proficiency (if English is not their first language) via the TOEFL or IELTS exams. Results of national or external exams must be provided, along with original transcripts from any secondary and post-secondary institutions attended. If the student is receiving secondary instruction in English, they must also submit results from either the SAT or the ACT. Recommendations from a school counselor and academic teacher are also required, in addition to an essay. International applicants are encouraged to meet the same 16 academic unit requirements as domestic applicants, as their curriculum allows.

Nontraditional age students are also welcome at Meredith College. Any prospective student of age 23 or older is encouraged to contact the Office of Admissions to learn about Meredith's conditional admissions program.

Application and Information

An application for admission should be sent to the Office of Admissions along with a nonrefundable $40 processing fee (or acceptable fee-waiver request). The student is responsible for requesting that her official high school transcript, SAT or ACT scores, and recommendations be sent to the admissions office. A transfer student must file an official transcript from each postsecondary institution attended.

Meredith has two freshman admission plans: early decision and rolling admission. An early decision candidate must apply by October 30; this "first choice" plan means that if accepted under early decision, the student fully expects to enroll and will withdraw any other pending applications. The student is notified by November 15. A candidate under the rolling plan is encouraged to file early in the senior year, with February 15 as the recommended deadline. Notifications under this plan begin in mid-November. The candidates' reply dates are December 15 for early decision and May 1 for rolling admission candidates.

Transfer applicants are encouraged to apply by February 15. Notifications begin in late January, and May 1 is the candidates' reply date. For admission to the spring semester, a freshman or transfer student should apply by December 1.

For additional information and for planning a campus visit, students should visit http://www.meredith.edu/admissions or contact the College by e-mail at admissions@meredith.edu or by phone at 800-MEREDITH (toll-free).

Office of Admissions
Meredith College
3800 Hillsborough Street
Raleigh, North Carolina 27607-5298
Phone: 919-760-8581
800-MEREDITH (toll-free)
Fax: 919-760-2348
E-mail: admissions@meredith.edu
Web site: http://www.meredith.edu

Meredith College's beautiful 225-acre campus is located on the edge of North Carolina's capital city near urban activity and eleven other colleges and universities.

MESSIAH COLLEGE

GRANTHAM, PENNSYLVANIA

The College

Sharpening intellect, deepening faith, and inspiring action—since 1909, this has been Messiah College's goal for its students. Messiah College is an independent, nationally-ranked, private Christian college with a socially, denominationally, and politically diverse undergraduate student body.

There are 2,766 undergraduate students attending Messiah from thirty-seven U.S. states and thirty other countries. Nearly 8 percent of students are from underrepresented racial, ethnic, and cultural populations and 2.6 percent are international students. Messiah has a distinctive residential atmosphere and a strong sense of community; 88 percent of students live on campus.

Messiah College competes in twenty-two intercollegiate sports and maintains one of the most successful NCAA Division III athletics programs in the nation. Messiah athletic teams have garnered eleven national championships and regularly achieve national rankings and conference titles. Messiah athletes have been recognized as all-Americans and have featured in *Sports Illustrated*, *USA Today*, and on national network television. Several coaches have received national coaching awards.

Messiah students participate in more than sixty student groups and organizations, including theater and music groups, a campus newspaper, and a student-operated radio station. The College's Student Government Association (SGA) represents the student body and develops students' leadership skills.

Students have many opportunities to grow in faith and fellowship at Messiah College, including chapel and worship services, discipleship groups, ministry outreach teams, community service, mission trips, and a variety of other special programs. In April 2008 Messiah College was selected to host "The Compassion Forum," an unprecedented, nationally televised conversation with presidential candidates speaking on the integration of faith and public policy.

The College has been widely recognized for its commitment to service-learning and civic engagement, and teaches students to engage their Christian faith to build community, to serve as agents for peace and reconciliation, and to champion the rights of the poor and the dispossessed. In 2009, Messiah was named to the President's Higher Education Community Service Honor Roll, a distinction granted to only seven colleges in Pennsylvania; the College's service-learning program was nationally recognized by *U.S. News & World Report* as a 2010 "Program to Look For;" and in 2008, the College was awarded the Carnegie Foundation's prestigious Community Engagement Classification for curricular engagement and outreach and partnership. Opportunities for community engagement at Messiah include the College's Agapé Center for Service and Learning, Collaboratory for Strategic Partnerships and Applied Research, Harrisburg Institute, Philadelphia campus, Ernest L. Boyer Center, Center for Public Humanities, School of the Arts, and Oakes Museum.

The College offers both traditional residence halls and apartment-style residences on campus. Staffed by trained, full-time professional Residence Directors, student Assistant Residence Directors, and Student Resident Assistants, these facilities provide an environment that fosters personal growth and responsibility, as students experience living in an intentional Christian community. All residence halls offer carpeting, air conditioning, cable television, Internet, and laundry facilities. Messiah does not have any fraternities or sororities at either the national or local level.

The College operates a number of campus safety services for students, such as an after-hours transport and accompaniment service; sixteen 24-hour emergency telephone alarm devices; a 24-hour, unarmed, professional security patrol; and student security patrols. In addition, all entrances to the residence halls are electronically operated. A crisis management and response team, emergency text-messaging system, and emergency evacuation plan are also in place on the campus.

Location

Messiah College, named a 2008 Green College by the National Association of Independent Colleges and Universities, is situated on 471 scenic wooded acres, just 12 miles from Harrisburg, Pennsylvania's capital. The College is approximately 2 hours from the major urban centers of Philadelphia, Baltimore, and Washington, D.C. There are many recreational and outdoor activities in the immediate vicinity, including the Yellow Breeches Creek, which flows through the campus, the nearby Susquehanna River, and the Appalachian Trail. The College also operates a satellite campus in Philadelphia in conjunction with Temple University.

Majors and Degrees

Messiah College awards Bachelor of Arts and Bachelor of Science degrees in more than fifty-five academic majors. It also offers six preprofessional programs and two graduate programs: a Master of Arts in counseling and a master of music conducting. Teacher certification is also available in many disciplines. Students must complete 123 units to graduate, except as noted in the requirements for selected majors. In addition to courses required by their major field, all students must complete core general educational requirements that include writing and oral communication, the arts and sciences, language and culture, Christian faith, social responsibility, and physical education. Students fulfill the remaining required units through elective courses.

Academic Programs

The College operates on a two-semester academic calendar, with a January term between the fall and spring terms. During January term, students take one intensive, three-week course of study with transcultural travel programs among the innovative courses offered during this term. A three-week May term immediately follows the spring term and is exclusively for cross-cultural studies.

Messiah's Internship Center is nationally recognized for excellence in training students for today's workforce. Last year, the Center celebrated an all-time high of 188 students completing internships in 157 locations. In addition, Messiah's Internship Center has been instrumental in the consistently high post-graduation placement rate of graduates. Ninety-nine percent of Messiah's past-year graduates surveyed reported securing full-time employment, or acceptance into graduate school, or were serving as volunteers within six months of graduation.

Off-Campus Programs

Messiah offers study-abroad opportunities in more than 40 countries and is ranked fourteenth in the U.S. by the Institute of International Education among institutions sending students to study abroad. Qualified students may also participate in the Honors Program or design an individual major or an independent study program. Many students also participate in a variety of local, regional, and international service-learning programs and internships.

Academic Facilities

Messiah's outstanding academic facilities include Murray Library, a research library with more than 300,000 volumes; the Jordan Science Center, a state-of-the-art science facility providing technically advanced science laboratories and equipment as well as housing the College's Oakes Museum of Natural History that includes a unique treasury of large mammal, insect, seashell, and bird egg collections; Frey Hall, primarily an engineering, mathematics, and business building with engineering and physics labs, but also housing a variety of art studios; Climenhaga Fine Arts Center, complete with a

400-seat performance auditorium, a recital hall, and an art gallery; and Boyer Hall, a state-of-the-art academic facility that opened in 2003.

Students have access to hundreds of computers in general computer labs conveniently located across campus (including several in residence halls), as well as computers in department labs. All student rooms on campus are set up for both wired and wireless access to the campus network. In addition, wireless connections to the campus network are available in all major campus buildings and all academic halls.

Athletic and recreational facilities include the 90,000-square-foot Sollenberger Sports Center with an indoor track, wrestling and gymnastics areas, a natatorium including an eight-lane pool with separate diving well, racquetball and basketball courts, and exercise and fitness equipment; and the Starry Athletic Complex with a lighted artificial turf field for field hockey and lacrosse, lighted soccer stadium, eight-lane all-weather track, ten tennis courts, baseball and softball fields, and practice field space.

Costs

Messiah College is ranked third in its region in *U.S. News & World Report's* listing of "Great Schools at a Great Price." For the 2009–10 academic year, tuition was $25,900, room and board averaged $7880, and average basic fees were $800.

Financial Aid

In 2006, the College announced an initiative to raise an additional $20 million in financial aid in five years. The percentage of first-year students receiving financial aid in the 2009–10 academic year was 100 percent. The average first-year student aid package was $18,402.

Faculty

Messiah College selects its educators for their Christian commitment as well as their proven teaching ability. They are practicing Christians who serve as role models for integrating a life of faith with intellectual pursuits. Every Messiah professor signs a statement of faith as an indication of his or her commitment to the mission of the College.

Messiah professors are also dedicated scholars and accomplished professionals, who have been educated at top universities all over the world. Eighty-two percent of the College's 170 full-time faculty members have earned the terminal degree in their field. Collectively, they hold degrees from more than 150 graduate schools in five countries.

Messiah professors are often sought after by local, regional, and national journalists for their commentary, insight, and expertise. They are not only experts in their fields, but also accomplished scholars, who have authored or published more than 90 works in the past two years.

All classes at Messiah College are taught by professors rather than teaching assistants. The student-to-faculty ratio at the College is 13:1.

Admission Requirements

Messiah seeks students with demonstrated academic promise who wish to share in the College's multidenominational, multicultural Christian community. Messiah encourages transfer, home-schooled, international, and minority students to apply. The College provides two methods for candidates to apply for admission: Standard Choice and Write Choice. Both options require the submission of the application form, high school transcript, application essay, and one Christian life recommendation. In addition, the following materials or activities are required to complete an application for admission. Standard Choice: applicant must submit the new SAT or ACT score results. Write Choice: applicant must rank in the top 20 percent of their class, participate in an admissions interview, and submit an additional graded writing sample.

Selective in its admission policy, the College considers academic achievement, extracurricular involvement, leadership skills, and Christian service. Thirty-four percent of the first year students in 2009–10 ranked in the top 10 percent of their high school class. Their average SAT composite score was 1145 and their average ACT score was 25. Within the past 12 years, Messiah has produced graduates who have distinguished themselves as Rhodes, Fulbright, Carnegie, and Truman scholars.

Application and Information

Messiah College operates on a rolling admission basis beginning September 15 of the student's senior year in high school. The Admissions Office is open weekdays from 8 a.m. to 5 p.m. Appointments can be made Monday through Friday, and on some selected Saturdays by contacting the Visit Coordinator at 800-233-4220 or by e-mail at visitmessiah@messiah.edu. (A two-week notice is suggested.)

Admissions Office
Box 3005
Messiah College
One College Avenue
Grantham, Pennsylvania 17027
Phone: 717-691-6000
800-233-4220 (toll-free)
Fax: 717-691-2307
E-mail: admiss@messiah.edu
Web site: http://www.messiah.edu

At Messiah College, Christian faith and intellect are intertwined, so students are equipped to see the world's realities in deeper ways and may bring a discerning spirit to all they do.

COLLEGE CLOSE-UPS

MIAMI INTERNATIONAL UNIVERSITY OF ART & DESIGN

MIAMI, FLORIDA

Miami International University of Art & Design

Miami International University of Art & Design provides programs that prepare graduates to pursue entry-level employment in the creative arts. Programs are developed with and taught by experienced educators. The School offers twelve bachelor's degree programs, three associate degree programs, and five master's degree programs.

The Career Services Department works with students to refine their presentations to potential employers. The Department also helps provide student advisers with insight into each student's specialized skills and interests. Specific career advising occurs during the last two quarters of a student's education. Interviewing techniques and resume-writing skills are taught, and students receive portfolio advising from faculty members.

Students come to Miami International University of Art & Design from throughout the United States and abroad.

The student population includes recent high school graduates, transfer students, and those who have left a previous employment situation to study and train for a new career. Students are creative, competitive, and open to new ideas. They place great value on an education that prepares them to pursue an exciting entry-level position in the arts.

Miami International University of Art & Design places high importance on student life, both inside and outside the classroom. The School provides an environment that encourages involvement in a wide variety of activities, including clubs and organizations, community service opportunities, and various committees designed to enhance the quality of student life. Numerous all-school programs and events are planned throughout the year to meet students' needs.

The Student Affairs Department offers a variety of services to students to help them make the most of their educational experience. These services include both school-sponsored and independent housing options.

Miami International University of Art & Design and its branch campuses, The Art Institute of Jacksonville and The Art Institute of Tampa, are accredited by the Commission on Colleges of the Southern Association of Colleges and Schools to award the associate, baccalaureate, and master's degrees. Contact the Commission on Colleges at 1866 Southern Lane, Decatur, Georgia 30033-4097 or call 404-679-4500 for questions about the accreditation of Miami International University of Art & Design.

Miami International University of Art & Design is licensed by the Commission for Independent Education, Florida Department of Education. Additional information regarding this institution may be obtained by contacting the commission at 325 West Gaines Street, Suite 1414, Tallahassee, Florida 32399-0400; phone: 888-224-6684 (toll-free).

The interior design program leading to the Bachelor of Fine Arts is accredited by the Council for Interior Design Accreditation, 206 Grandville Avenue, Suite 350, Grand Rapids, Michigan 49503; http://www.accredit-id.org.

Location

Miami is a culturally rich region that celebrates events year-round, including the African-American Heritage Festival, Haitian Heritage Week, the Viva Mexico Celebration, the Israel Independence Celebration, and Asian Cultural Week. The city is home to professional sports teams, and residents enjoy the sandy beaches, international cuisine, local clubs, the historic Art Deco District, Coral Gables, and Key Biscayne. The Florida Keys, Disney World, and the Bahamas are all just a short trip away.

Programs of Study and Degrees

Bachelor's degree programs are available in advertising, audio production, computer animation, fashion design, fashion merchandising, film and digital production, graphic design, interior design, photography, visual and entertainment arts, visual effects and motion graphics, and Web design and interactive media.

Associate degrees are available in accessory design, fashion design, and fashion merchandising.

Master's degree programs are offered in film, graphic design (Master of Arts or Master of Fine Arts), interior design, and visual arts.

Academic Programs

Miami International University of Art & Design operates on a year-round, quarterly basis. Each quarter totals eleven weeks. Bachelor's degree programs are twelve quarters in length.

Academic Facilities

Miami International University of Art & Design is located within a 60,000-square-foot academic and administration building. The facility includes industry-related equipment, a painting and sculpture studio, a production facility, and an editing facility. There are also interior design and fashion resource rooms.

Costs

Tuition cost varies by program. Prospective students should contact the School for current tuition costs. Other charges include a starting kit for all first-quarter students. Kits vary in price, depending on the program of study.

Financial Aid

Financial aid is available for those who qualify. Students who require financial assistance should first complete and submit a Free Application for Federal Student Aid (FAFSA) and meet with a financial aid officer.

Faculty

Faculty members at Miami International University of Art & Design are experienced professionals, many of whom bring real-world knowledge into the classroom. There are full-time and part-time faculty members.

Admission Requirements

Applicants must provide proof of high school graduation or achievement of a General Educational Development (GED) certificate as a prerequisite for admission. In lieu of documenting high school graduation or a GED certificate, applicants may provide proof of attaining an associate degree or higher from an accredited institution. An official transcript indicating date of high school graduation, GED certificate (including test scores), or date of college graduation (including degree granted) is required as proof.

All individuals seeking admission to the School are interviewed in person or by phone by an assistant director of admissions, and each applicant must create an original essay of at least 150 words stating how an education at Miami International University of Art & Design would help the student to achieve career goals. There is a $50 application fee.

For the most recent information regarding admission requirements, please refer to the current academic catalog.

Application and Information

To obtain an application, arrange for an interview, or tour the school, prospective students should contact:

Miami International University of Art & Design
1501 Biscayne Boulevard, Suite 100
Miami, Florida 33132-1418
Phone: 305-428-5700
800-225-9023 (toll-free)
Fax: 305-374-5933
Web site: http://www.artinstitutes.edu/miami

COLLEGE CLOSE-UPS

The Art Institute of Atlanta; The Art Institute of Atlanta–Decatur[1]; The Art Institute of Austin[2]; The Art Institute of California–Hollywood; The Art Institute of California–Inland Empire; The Art Institute of California–Los Angeles; The Art Institute of California–Orange County; The Art Institute of California–Sacramento; The Art Institute of California–San Diego; The Art Institute of California–San Francisco; The Art Institute of California–Sunnyvale; The Art Institute of Charleston[1]; The Art Institute of Charlotte; The Art Institute of Colorado; The Art Institute of Dallas; The Art Institute of Fort Lauderdale; The Art Institute of Fort Worth[3]; The Art Institute of Houston; The Art Institute of Houston–North[2]; The Art Institute of Indianapolis[4]; The Art Institute of Jacksonville[5]; The Art Institute of Las Vegas; The Art Institute of Michigan; The Art Institute of New York City; The Art Institute of Ohio–Cincinnati[6]; The Art Institute of Philadelphia; The Art Institute of Phoenix; The Art Institute of Pittsburgh; The Art Institute of Portland; The Art Institute of Raleigh–Durham; The Art Institute of Salt Lake City; The Art Institute of San Antonio[2];The Art Institute of Seattle; The Art Institute of Tampa[5]; The Art Institute of Tennessee–Nashville[1,7]; The Art Institute of Tucson; The Art Institute of Vancouver; The Art Institute of Virginia Beach[1,8]; The Art Institute of Washington[1,8]; The Art Institute of Washington–Northern Virginia[1,8]; The Art Institute of York–Pennsylvania; The Art Institutes International–Kansas City; The Art Institutes International Minnesota; The Illinois Institute of Art–Chicago; The Illinois Institute of Art–Schaumburg; Miami International University of Art & Design; The New England Institute of Art.

[1]A branch of The Art Institute of Atlanta
[2]A branch of The Art Institute of Houston
[3]A branch of The Art Institute of Dallas
[4]The Art Institute of Indianapolis is regulated by the Indiana Commission on Proprietary Education, 302 West Washington Street, Room E201, Indianapolis, Indiana 46204, AC-0080
[5]A branch of Miami International University of Art & Design
[6]The Art Institute of Ohio–Cincinnati, 8845 Governors Hill Drive, Suite 100, Cincinnati, Ohio 45249-3317, OH Reg. #04-01-1698B
[7]The Art Institute of Tennessee–Nashville is authorized for operation as a postsecondary educational institution by the Tennessee Higher Education Commission.
[8]Certified by the State Council of Higher Education to operate in Virginia

MICHIGAN TECHNOLOGICAL UNIVERSITY

MichiganTech

HOUGHTON, MICHIGAN

The University

Michigan Technological University students create the future in engineering; forest resources; computing; technology; business; economics; natural, physical and environmental sciences; arts; humanities; and social sciences.

More than 7,100 students from all fifty states and more than eighty nations enjoy beautiful Upper Michigan while pursuing associate, bachelor's, master's, and Ph.D. degrees. Michigan Tech is ranked in the top tier of national universities, and its environmental engineering program is ranked thirteenth in the nation, according to the *U.S. News & World Report*'s "America's Best Colleges 2010." Tech is also rated highly for academics, career preparation, and quality of life in the Princeton Review's *Best 371 Colleges, 2010 Edition*. The University is also cited by the Princeton Review for its great athletic facilities and good town-gown relations, and Michigan Tech's excellent academics are reflected in student comments: the University "offers a real hands-on learning experience, not only in the classroom but in life." Students from many majors work together on real-world industry projects as part of the Enterprise program, from video games and nanosatellites to forest management and the EcoCAR challenge. Michigan Tech has one of the nation's largest programs in scientific and technical communication and has top-ten enrollments in environmental and mechanical engineering programs.

The latest improvements to the campus include a new apartment complex for upperclassmen and beautiful new suites in the John MacInnes Student Ice Arena. On the lakefront adjacent to campus, a new $25-million Great Lakes Research Center is planned, including aquatic laboratories, a hydraulics lab, coastal research instrumentation, boathouse, and offices and conference rooms in order to provide a home for interdisciplinary research and education related to the Great Lakes.

More than 56 percent of students are enrolled in the College of Engineering. The College of Sciences and Arts (CSA) accounts for 24 percent; Graduate School, 16.7 percent; the School of Business and Economics, 7 percent; the School of Technology, 6 percent; and the School of Forest Resources and Environmental Science, 3.5 percent. Overall enrollment increased in fall 2009, and while students gain access to the latest theories, equipment, and scholarship, they work closely with faculty members who are acknowledged leaders in their fields.

Michigan Tech is accredited by the North Central Association of Colleges and Schools. Engineering programs are accredited by the Engineering Accreditation Commission of the Accreditation Board for Engineering and Technology (ABET), Inc.; technology programs are accredited by the Technology Accreditation Commission of ABET; and the surveying program is accredited by the Related Accreditation Commission of ABET. The forestry program is accredited by the Society of American Foresters, the chemistry program offers American Chemical Society–approved options, and the secondary teacher certification programs are approved by the Michigan Board of Education. The School of Business and Economics is accredited by AACSB International–The Association to Advance Collegiate Schools of Business. Only about 400 U.S. business programs have earned this distinction.

Residence halls are close to classrooms and well connected. They feature ultrafast Ethernet lines, and wireless zones abound across the campus. Residence halls also feature Finnish saunas, cable TV, lounges, and weight-lifting and laundry facilities. First-year students must live in the residence halls; they can choose from numerous meal plan and food options and eat at the cafeterias in Wadsworth, McNair, or Douglass Houghton Halls. Some cafeterias are open later, especially during exam weeks, and students can also eat, relax, and study at the Memorial Union, the center of campus life and home to many student organization offices, the bookstore, billiards, and a bowling alley. Guides to off-campus housing are available.

In athletics, the hockey Huskies have been national champions three times and compete in the Western Collegiate Hockey Association, which has produced more NCAA Division I National Champions than any other conference. Football, men's and women's basketball, tennis, cross-country, track, and women's soccer and volleyball teams compete in the Division II Great Lakes Intercollegiate Athletic Conference against teams from Michigan, Wisconsin, Ohio, Pennsylvania, Indiana, and Illinois. The men's and women's basketball teams have been rated number one in NCAA Division II, and the football team hosted an NCAA Division II playoff game in 2004. Most Michigan Tech students compete in intramural sports in everything from Ultimate (Frisbee) and wrestling to water polo and floor hockey. Club sports include lacrosse, women's hockey, and paintball. The biggest game on campus, however, is broomball, where students slide around on ice and hit a volleyball using a broom. The Student Development Complex includes a health center, swimming and diving pools, two gyms (one with a running track), a rifle range, an ice arena, a weight room, and more. A new child-care center is located nearby.

Traditions include K-Day, which is an afternoon to enjoy McLain State Park on the shores of Lake Superior. The Parade of Nations is a celebration of the eighty nations of the world that have students, faculty, and staff members at Michigan Tech. At homecoming, students dress in their worst attire and parade through the campus in autos that barely run. During homecoming weekend, students enjoy a football game and other special activities. The biggest event is Winter Carnival, when massive snow statues emerge on campus and in the towns. Skits, queen competitions, first-class entertainment, ice hockey, and tourists everywhere make this a great experience. Before finals, students take a break for Spring Fling and celebrate with games, food booths, music, and more.

Location

Michigan Tech is situated on the Keweenaw Waterway in the hills of Houghton, a friendly, safe environment. The area offers abundant opportunities for outdoor recreation, including the University's own ski hill; cross-country skiing, running, and biking trails; and golf course. A waterfront jogging and biking trail cuts through the campus. Houghton is about 4 hours' drive from Green Bay and Duluth, 7 hours from Minneapolis, and 10 hours from Detroit. The Houghton County Memorial Airport has daily flights to Chicago that connect to other major cities; bus service to Houghton is also available.

Majors and Degrees

The School of Technology awards Bachelor of Science degrees in computer network and system administration, construction management, electrical engineering technology, industrial technology, mechanical engineering technology, and surveying engineering.

The College of Engineering offers Bachelor of Science degrees in applied geophysics, biomedical engineering, chemical engineering, civil engineering, computer engineering, electrical engineering, engineering (mechanical design or manufacturing), environmental engineering, geological engineering, geology, materials science and engineering, and mechanical engineering.

The School of Business and Economics awards Bachelor of Science degrees in accounting, economics, finance, management, management information systems, marketing, and operations and systems management.

The School of Forest Resources and Environmental Science awards Bachelor of Science degrees in applied ecology and environmental sciences, forestry, and wildlife ecology and management.

The College of Sciences and Arts awards Bachelor of Science degrees in anthropology, applied physics, audio production and technology, biochemistry and molecular biology, bioinformatics, biological sciences, cheminformatics, chemistry, clinical laboratory science, communication and cultural studies, computer science, computer systems science, exercise science, health and physical education, mathematics, pharmaceutical chemistry, physics, preprofessional programs (medicine, dentistry, pharmacy, and law), psychology, scientific and technical communication, social sciences, software engineering, and theater and entertainment technology. The CSA awards the Bachelor of Arts degree in communication and culture studies, liberal arts, scientific and technical communication, sound design, theater and electronic media performance, and theater and entertainment technology. The College of Sciences and Arts also awards a two-year associate degree in humanities.

The secondary education program offers certification in biology, business education, chemistry, computer science, earth science, economics, English, mathematics, physics, social studies, and technology and design.

Michigan Tech offers certificate programs in design engineering, industrial forestry, international business, media, mine environmental engineering, modern language and area study, and writing. An advanced certificate in modern language and area study and a graduate certificate in sustainability are also offered.

Michigan Tech's minors are aerospace studies, American studies, applied geophysics, art, astrophysics, biochemistry, biological sciences, chemistry, communication studies, computer science, diversity studies, earth sciences, ecology, economics, electronic materials, engineered wood products, enterprise, environmental studies, ethics and philosophy, geological engineering, historical studies, international modern languages (French, German, or Spanish), international studies, journalism, law and society, manufacturing, mathematical sciences, microbiology, military arts and science, mineral processing, mining, modern languages (French, German, or Spanish), municipal engineering, music, nanoscale science and engineering, pharmaceutical chemistry, physics, plant biotechnology, plant sciences, polymer science and engineering, product design, psychology, remote sensing, social and behavioral studies, state of Michigan secondary teacher certification (see options above), structural materials, technical theater, and theater arts.

Academic Programs

Michigan Tech operates on a fifteen-week fall and spring semester system with three options available for summer: two 7-week tracks and one 14-week track. Typically, it takes 130 credits to graduate, but that varies by department. Students must also complete general education requirements to help develop fundamental scholastic habits of careful reading, communication, critical reasoning, and balanced analysis and argument; the habit of applying multi-disciplinary perspectives in interpretation, analysis, and creative problem solving; respect for diversity; awareness of complex contexts of their study and their work; and knowledge of a broad range of topics and disciplines complementary to the major. Some graduate courses are open to undergraduates with faculty approval. The International Programs and Services Office helps international students adjust to life in Houghton. Nearly 900 students come from approximately eighty other nations to study at Michigan Tech. Students may also study abroad in one of thirty nations, improving their global perspective.

Off-Campus Programs

The Career Center works with more than 200 industries, businesses, and organizations to help students find co-op, internship, and summer employment opportunities. Job fairs are held on campus and in the region. Co-op assignments earn academic credits; internships do not. Students average seven job interviews before they graduate.

Academic Facilities

The J. R. Van Pelt and John and Ruanne Opie Library contains more than 800,000 volumes and regularly receives approximately 10,000 serials and periodicals. The library is a designated depository for official international, U.S. government, and Michigan state documents and for the U.S. Army Map Service. The archives maintain a collection of original materials concerning the history of the Keweenaw region, including the records of various copper-mining companies. The Rozsa Center for the Performing Arts is within walking distance of all residence halls and features nationally known lecturers, musicians, comedians, and theatrical performers as well as Michigan Tech's own productions. The student-run newspaper, the *Lode,* has won national and state awards, and the campus radio station, WMTU, allows students to be disc jockeys. The A. E. Seaman Mineral Museum, the official "Mineralogical Museum of Michigan," is the home of one of the nation's premier collections of crystals, minerals, and ores. The collection contains more than 30,000 specimens, including the world's finest display from Michigan's copper- and iron-mining districts.

Costs

Tuition is $10,500 for Michigan residents and $22,770 for out-of-state students for an academic year; room and board are $8121. Computer and other fees total approximately $1200; books and supplies are approximately $1200.

Financial Aid

Currently, 87 percent of Michigan Tech's students receive financial aid, totaling nearly $50 million annually. Four kinds of assistance are available to Michigan Tech students, including scholarships, which are awarded on the basis of student potential and, in some cases, financial need; grants, which are provided by the federal or state government or by Michigan Tech and do not need to be repaid; student loans, in which the interest charged is below regular interest rates (payment of the interest and principal on need-based loans does not begin until after students leave Michigan Tech); and part-time employment, which consists of on-campus student employment opportunities. The financial aid process begins with filing an application for admission. Students should apply for admission by January 15 of the year in which they plan to enroll. Michigan Tech students rank in the top twenty-five nationally in the least amount of debt owed when they graduate, according to *U.S. News & World Report.*

Faculty

Most of the 445 faculty members possess terminal degrees. Ninety-five percent of undergraduate classes are taught by faculty members, and the student-faculty ratio is 12:1. Faculty members at Michigan Tech balance teaching and research and have long been known for their student guidance.

Student Government

Undergraduate Student Government and the Graduate Student Council are the two agencies of student involvement in University governance. Fraternities and sororities maintain a strong presence on campus, and there are more than 180 student organizations, including academic/professional, ethnic/cultural, service, religious, sporting, governmental, media, and honor societies. It is a great way for students to get involved and gain teamwork and leadership experience.

Admission Requirements

Michigan Tech has a selective admissions policy. The University admits only those applicants who give definite evidence that they are qualified through education, academic capability, aptitudes, interests, and character to complete the University's requirements. Once students are accepted for admission, every effort is made by the faculty and staff members to help students realize their potential.

Application and Information

Applications received by January 15 are given priority consideration for admission and merit-based scholarships. Undergraduate and graduate applications are free. First-year applicants are required to submit official ACT or SAT test scores. An information page must also be completed by a high school counselor or principal and sent to the admissions office with an official high school transcript. Transfer students must have official college transcripts sent directly to Michigan Tech. An official high school transcript and ACT/SAT scores may also be required. International students should contact the International Programs and Services office. Following acceptance, students receive a packet containing information regarding on-campus housing and various University deadlines.

Admissions Office
Michigan Technological University
1400 Townsend Drive
Houghton, Michigan 49931-1295
Phone: 888-688-1885 (toll-free)
Web site: http://admissions.mtu.edu

Overlooking the campus of Michigan Tech.

COLLEGE CLOSE-UPS

MILLERSVILLE UNIVERSITY OF PENNSYLVANIA

Millersville University
SEIZE THE OPPORTUNITY

MILLERSVILLE, PENNSYLVANIA

The University

Millersville University is a multifaceted public institution with a wide range of programs and a commitment to high-quality undergraduate instruction. Millersville's student body of approximately 8,300, including 7,200 undergraduates, is large enough for the University to offer a wide variety of programs. The University is small enough, however, to provide friendly service and individual attention. Students report that the relaxed, friendly campus atmosphere is one of the things they like best. The Millersville campus features a beautiful green and flowered landscape, a lake with resident swans, and clean, well-maintained facilities.

Millersville University was established more than 150 years ago, in 1855, as a normal school, the first one in Pennsylvania. It remained a teachers' college until 1962, when it was authorized to offer liberal arts degrees. It has been Millersville University of Pennsylvania since 1983.

The two reasons students most frequently cite for choosing Millersville are its excellent academic reputation and affordable tuition. The most popular majors are education, business administration, biology, psychology, and speech communication/theater. Millersville's undergraduates are diverse; 1 in 8 students attends part-time, 12 percent are members of a racial/ethnic minority group, and 12 percent are more than 25 years old. Thirty-five percent of Millersville undergraduates are from Lancaster County, 60 percent from elsewhere in Pennsylvania, 4 percent from out of state, and 1 percent from other countries.

The University offers a wide range of intercollegiate varsity, intramural, and club sports; special interest clubs; fraternities and sororities; musical organizations; and publications. A broad program of cultural events is offered, with alcohol-free nightclubs particularly popular.

Thirty-five percent of undergraduates live in campus residence halls, with the rest commuting from home or living nearby. Coed dormitories are provided. University-affiliated apartments are adjacent to campus. Freshmen and sophomores not commuting from home are required to live on campus. The possession, use, or sale of alcoholic beverages and illegal drugs is prohibited on the University campus. Smoking is prohibited in all academic and residential buildings on campus. Freshmen and sophomores living on campus are not permitted to have motor vehicles.

Special services provided for students include free tutoring, academic advisement, career planning and placement, personal counseling, health services, wellness activities, fee-for-service child care, and special facilities for commuters.

Location

Millersville, in the heart of Pennsylvania Dutch country, is 3 miles from Lancaster city, a growing metropolitan area. Lancaster County is an exceptionally friendly and beautiful area with a large number of stores, restaurants, theaters, parks, and tourist attractions. The campus is served by the area bus system, and Lancaster has train and air service.

Lancaster County is one of the fastest-growing counties in Pennsylvania and has one of the lowest unemployment rates in the state. The local economy is unusually sound and diverse. Sixty percent of Millersville graduates settle within the county.

Majors and Degrees

Millersville offers the Bachelor of Arts degree in anthropology, art, biology, chemistry, earth sciences, economics, English, French, geography, German, government and political affairs, history, international studies, mathematics, music, philosophy, physics, psychology, social work, sociology, and Spanish.

The Bachelor of Science degree is offered in biology, business administration, chemistry, communications and theater, computer science, earth sciences, geology, industrial technology, mathematics, meteorology, occupational safety and environmental health, oceanography, and physics.

The Bachelor of Science in Education degree with teaching certification is offered in art education, biology, chemistry, earth sciences, Pre-K–4 education, English, French, German, mathematics, middle level education, music education, physics, social studies, Spanish, and technology education.

The University also offers the Bachelor of Fine Arts degree in art, the Bachelor of Science in Nursing degree for RNs only, the Associate of Science degree in chemistry and in computer science, and the Associate of Technology degree in industrial technology.

Most majors offer several options that permit specialization, including accounting, finance, international business, management, and marketing in business. Students should refer to the Web site for a complete listing. More than thirty minors are offered along with 3-2 engineering programs for chemistry and physics majors. Special advisement is available for students interested in premedicine and prelaw.

Academic Programs

Millersville University places a strong emphasis on the liberal arts. Nearly half of the courses required for all its undergraduate degrees, including those with technical or professional majors, are in the liberal arts. This prepares students for a lifetime of learning and gives them a background in writing, speaking, analysis, and critical thinking across a broad range of subjects.

Millersville's baccalaureate degree programs have four common curricular elements: proficiency requirements in English composition and speech; the general education program, which constitutes about half the curriculum; the major field of study; and elective courses, if needed, to meet the minimum of 120 credits required for graduation. Within this framework, students have many choices in developing programs of study.

The general education program has requirements in writing, speaking, humanities, natural sciences and mathematics, social sciences, and interdisciplinary and/or multicultural study. There is also a health and physical education requirement.

Millersville offers a University Honors College, departmental honors programs, independent study, a pass/fail option, remedial courses, and special advisement to students who are undecided about a major.

The University operates on a 4-1-4 academic calendar with summer sessions.

Off-Campus Programs

An exchange agreement with Franklin and Marshall College allows Millersville students to take Franklin and Marshall courses not offered at Millersville. Cooperative education internships are available to students in most majors, and some majors offer or require specialized internships. Millersville has study-abroad programs in Australia, Chile, England, France, Germany, Ireland, Japan, Peru, Scotland, South Africa, and Spain. Qualified students who wish to study abroad elsewhere may do so through the University's cooperative arrangements with other colleges and universities.

Academic Facilities

Ganser Library houses more than 495,000 books and more than 558,000 other items and subscribes to more than 4,000 periodicals. Materials from other libraries are available through interlibrary loan. The library also houses computerized database-searching facilities, a curriculum center, a listening room, and archives.

Millersville's computing facilities include IBM and VAX mainframes and SUN Workstations. There are 450 terminals and microcomputers available, including IBM and Macintosh models. Users with their own microcomputers can access University mainframes through telephone lines. On-campus access to the Internet is available for all faculty members and students. Wireless access is available in the library, the Student Center, and the cybercafé in Roddy Science Center.

Other University facilities include an extensive scientific instrumentation inventory, industry and technology laboratories, a variety of art studios and galleries, a large auditorium and a small theater, two gymnasiums and swimming pools, radio and television production facilities, soundproof music practice modules, and a language laboratory. The University's day-care center and prekindergarten provide field experiences in early childhood education.

Costs

Annual tuition and fees in 2009–10 were $7147 for Pennsylvania residents and $15,583 for out-of-state students. Annual room and board charges for 2009–10 were $7766. Students paid approximately $900 for books and incidentals.

Financial Aid

Approximately 82 percent of Millersville undergraduates receive financial aid through grants, scholarships, employment, and loans. Scholarships are available on the basis of academic performance. Federal Pell and Federal Supplemental Educational Opportunity grants and Pennsylvania Higher Education Assistance Agency (PHEAA) grants are awarded on the basis of need. Students may also qualify for Federal Perkins Loans and Federal Stafford Student Loans. On-campus and off-campus job opportunities are plentiful.

Students applying for a federal or state grant, Federal Work-Study, or a Federal Perkins Loan must complete the Free Application for Federal Student Aid. The forms are available from high school guidance offices, from the Financial Aid Office, or online at http://www.fafsa.ed.gov. Deadlines are given in the forms' instructions.

Faculty

Millersville University faculty members are dedicated to teaching and to offering individual attention. They take a personal interest in their students' lives and careers and are solely responsible for providing academic advisement. The University keeps a relatively low student-faculty ratio of 18:1 and an average class size of 25. No classes are taught by graduate assistants. Ninety-six percent of the 325 full-time faculty members hold a doctorate or the terminal degree in their field.

Student Government

Millersville University students participate in University governance through the Student Senate, faculty-student committees, and representation on the Faculty Senate, the Council of Trustees, and the Millersville Borough Council. The Student Senate works with faculty members and the administration on major University policies.

Admission Requirements

Millersville University admits approximately half its applicants. More than 80 percent of its full-time freshmen rank in the top 40 percent of their high school class. Academic records are the most important factor in admission decisions. Applicants must have successfully completed at least 4 years of high school English, 3 years of social studies, 3 years of mathematics (including a minimum of algebra I and II and geometry), and 3 years of science (2 units must be labs). In addition, 2 years of foreign language and 1 additional year each of math and science are strongly recommended.

Because an important part of the college experience is meeting people with backgrounds and interests different from one's own, Millersville University is committed to recruiting a diversified student body. SAT or ACT scores are required. Interviews, recommendations, and essays are not required. Out-of-state, international, and transfer applicants are welcome. Exceptional high school students may apply for early admission at the end of their junior year. Admitted applicants may request to defer their admission for one semester. Advanced standing is offered through CLEP and AP examinations.

Application and Information

To apply, students should submit a completed application along with a $50 processing fee and official copies of the high school record and SAT or ACT scores. The online application fee is $35. The University has a rolling admission policy, and students are encouraged to apply early (by mid-November) in their senior year for fall admission. Applicants are usually notified of a decision within a month after a completed application is received.

For application forms and additional information, students should contact:

Office of Admissions
Millersville University of Pennsylvania
P.O. Box 1002
Millersville, Pennsylvania 17551-0302
Phone: 717-872-3371
800-MU-ADMIT (toll-free)
E-mail: admissions@millersville.edu
Web site: http://www.millersville.edu

Millersville University's campus includes shaded areas that invite students to study or relax with friends.

MILLIGAN COLLEGE

MILLIGAN COLLEGE, TENNESSEE

The College

Milligan College is a four-year private Christian liberal arts college in northeast Tennessee. From its beginning in 1866, Milligan College has integrated academic excellence with a Christian worldview, and its mission is to educate men and women as Christian servant-leaders. A comprehensive humanities program and a core curriculum are complemented by specialized training in more than twenty-five majors and several master's degrees. Christian perspectives are integrated throughout the curriculum and student life activities as students are prepared intellectually and spiritually to change lives and shape culture.

Milligan's student body of 1,000 comes from more than forty states and ten nations. Eighty percent of traditional students live on the campus in one of six residence halls. More than forty clubs and organizations provide opportunities to develop leadership skills. A wide variety of activities and campus events encourage social, cultural, and spiritual growth. Milligan College is affiliated with the Christian Churches/Churches of Christ, but the interdenominational student body is diverse.

All campus facilities are networked with fiber optics. Every residence hall room and apartment features a high-speed data connection to the campus network and the Internet as well as telephone service, voice mail, and cable TV.

Milligan is well recognized as an NAIA athletic powerhouse with a highly competitive athletic program in twenty varsity sports. In the past ten years, Milligan has won more than fifty conference titles and made over fifty-seven national tournament appearances. Men's varsity teams include baseball, basketball, cross-country, golf, mountain biking, soccer, swimming, tennis, and track and field. Women's varsity teams include basketball, cheerleading, cross-country, golf, mountain biking, soccer, softball, swimming, tennis, track and field, and volleyball.

Milligan is accredited by the Commission on Colleges of the Southern Association of Colleges and Schools (1866 Southern Lane, Decatur, Georgia 30033-4097; phone: 404-679-4501) to award bachelor's and master's degrees. Milligan offers a Master of Education degree, a Master of Science in Occupational Therapy degree, and a Master of Business Administration degree.

Milligan continues to be named among Southern colleges and universities in *U.S. News & World Report's* America's Best Colleges issue. More than 90 percent of its graduates are employed full-time, attending graduate school, or in voluntary service within six months after graduation, and more than 75 percent of premed students who take the MCAT are accepted to medical school.

Location

Milligan's picturesque 181-acre campus, which comprises more than twenty buildings of Colonial architecture, is located in the beautiful mountains of northeast Tennessee, just minutes from Johnson City and the dynamic Tri-Cities region. Students enjoy historical locations, theaters, parks, restaurants, and shops; explore the breathtaking Appalachian Mountains by hiking or camping in state parks near the campus; visit local lakes and rivers for outdoor recreation; or ski the nearby North Carolina slopes. Because Milligan believes leadership is about service, students are encouraged to be active in the local community. Many are employed in internships or part-time work in area businesses.

Majors and Degrees

The Bachelor of Science, Bachelor of Arts, and Bachelor of Science in Nursing degrees are offered. Undergraduate majors include accounting, applied finance and accounting, Bible (children's ministry, general studies, missions, pastoral ministry, youth ministry), biology, business administration (accounting, economics, general, health-care administration, international business, legal studies, management, marketing, sports management), chemistry, child and youth development, child life, communications (broadcasting, digital media studies, film studies, interpersonal and public communication, journalism, public relations), computer information systems, education (professional teacher licensure), English, fine arts (art, music, photography, theater arts), history, human performance and exercise science (exercise science, fitness and wellness, physical education, sports management), humanities, language arts, mathematics, music (general music studies–applied study, jazz studies), music education (vocal, instrumental), nursing, psychology (general, preprofessional), public leadership and service, sociology, and worship leadership.

Professional teacher licensure areas include early childhood, elementary education, K–12, middle grades, secondary, and special education. Preprofessional programs are available in dentistry, law, medicine, occupational therapy, optometry, pharmacy, and physical therapy. An adult degree completion program allows adults who have completed 60 or more semester hours of college credit to complete a business administration or early childhood education major in about eighteen months.

Academic Programs

Milligan College offers students a liberal arts education taught from a perspective of God's activity with humanity. The College's strong core curriculum educates students toward the world in an open and constructive way. The candidate for the bachelor's degree must have completed a major and electives to total 128 semester hours of credit, with at least a 2.0 GPA. Core curriculum requirements include courses in humanities, the Bible, social sciences, ethnic studies, laboratory science, speech communication, mathematics, and health/fitness.

Realizing that not all college-level learning occurs in a college classroom, Prior Learning Assessment programs provide a method by which other modes of learning can be evaluated for college credit. The Advanced Placement (AP) program, the College-Level Examination Program (CLEP), Defense Activity for Non-Traditional Educational Support (DANTES) programs, and the International Baccalaureate (IB) program are available to all students interested in receiving college credit for studies or work experience already completed.

Milligan College operates on a semester system (semesters begin in August and January) with two 4-week summer sessions in June and July or one 8-week term. Also available are short-term classes during January term (one week before the onset of the spring semester) and May term (the weeks between the spring semester and the summer sessions).

Rising juniors are required to take a test covering general knowledge, and graduating seniors are required to take a test to demonstrate knowledge in their major field of study.

Off-Campus Programs

Students can go beyond geographical and cultural boundaries and earn up to 16 hours of credit with Milligan's Study Abroad Program or with the many off-campus learning opportunities sponsored by the Council for Christian Colleges & Universities. These include an American Studies Program in Washington, D.C.; Australia Studies Centre; China Studies Program; Contemporary Music Center near Martha's Vineyard; Latin American Studies Program in Costa Rica; Los Angeles Film Studies Center; Middle East Studies Program in Cairo; Oxford Summer Programme; Russian

Studies Program; Scholars' Semester in Oxford; Summer Institute of Journalism in Washington, D.C.; and Uganda Studies Program. Through an affiliation with the International Business Institute, business majors can earn college credit through an intensive ten-week summer program in Europe. Milligan also offers a four-week summer Humanities Tour in Europe, during which students explore the origins of Western civilization. In addition, internship opportunities offer students college credit and work experience in their field of interest.

Academic Facilities

Milligan College's library has extensive holdings and online access to other major libraries and databases. Special collections within the library contain materials on the history of the College, the Restoration Movement, and the local area. The library also participates in resource-sharing agreements with Emmanuel School of Religion and East Tennessee State University. A Writing and Study Skills Center offers access to resources, instruction, and tutoring for academic success. Television and radio production studios and an FM radio station provide on-site training for communication students. A darkroom and art gallery feature works by fine arts students. Standardized laboratory facilities, including a gross anatomy lab, are available for general and advanced work in the sciences.

Recent on-campus projects include a new state-of-the-art theater and convocation facility; renovation of the College's main classroom building and several other lecture halls and labs; the addition of a new education center, a new tennis complex, and a new physical plant facility; and a 30-acre land acquisition. Construction recently began on a new wellness facility.

Costs

Tuition for 2009–10 was $21,200. Room and board were $5650. Additional fees are approximately $660. Typical annual miscellaneous costs (books, supplies, etc.) were approximately $1000. As a private institution, Milligan supplements student fees with income from endowments and gifts from alumni, friends, and churches in order to keep tuition below the national average of similar four-year private institutions.

Financial Aid

Approximately 96 percent of all students at Milligan College receive federal, state, institutional, and/or outside (such as from a church or private foundation) aid, including both academic scholarships and need-based grants. Each year, Milligan budgets more than $5 million in institutional scholarships, grants, and work-study opportunities. Financial assistance is allocated on the basis of need demonstrated by information supplied on the Free Application for Federal Student Aid (FAFSA), which should be completed by January 1 for priority consideration. Returning students must complete and submit a Milligan College Financial Aid Scholarship/Renewal Application. The Milligan College Office of Financial Aid begins mailing award letters between March 1 and March 15.

Faculty

More than 75 percent of Milligan's faculty members have earned the highest degree in their field from well-respected colleges and universities in the U.S. and abroad. Professors integrate biblical truths into their classes and are active leaders both on and off the campus. The low student-faculty ratio and small classes put the student at the center of attention and allow faculty members to cultivate special mentoring relationships with students. Professors serve as advisers to students from registration to graduation and are often instrumental in helping students find employment or gain admission to graduate school following graduation. Milligan's faculty members are mature and caring scholars who are committed to world-class scholarship, excellence in teaching, and their students.

Student Government

The Student Government Association (SGA) serves as the official representative voice of Milligan students and promotes academic, social, and spiritual activities for the campus community. SGA operates under a constitution approved and supported by the administration of the College, promotes well-ordered conduct among students, and enforces the regulations of the College. SGA leadership is provided by an executive council and representatives from throughout the campus. As a Christian college, Milligan adopts basic moral and social principles and expects students to serve Christ in an atmosphere of trust, encouragement, and respect for one another.

Admission Requirements

Character, ability, preparation, and seriousness of purpose are the qualities emphasized in considering applicants for acceptance to Milligan College. Overall excellence of performance in high school subjects as well as evidence of Christian commitment and academic potential provide the basis for admission to Milligan College. These qualities are evaluated by consideration of each applicant's academic record (based on transcripts), two personal references, ACT or SAT scores, and participation in extracurricular activities. Some majors, such as music and theater, may require auditions and interviews. All applicants should have a high school diploma or the equivalent and have completed a college-preparatory curriculum with course work in English, math, science, history and/or social sciences, foreign language, and some work in speech, music, or art in preparation for study in a liberal arts curriculum. Satisfactory scores on the ACT or SAT are required of all applicants to the freshman class. The average ACT score for the current first-year class is 23. Transfer students should have a grade point average of 2.5 or above and must follow the same application procedures as first-time students, with the addition of providing official transcripts of all previous college work. ACT or SAT scores and high school transcripts are not required for transfer students with at least 24 earned semester hours.

Application and Information

Applications are processed on a rolling basis, and early application is encouraged. Notification is also given on a rolling basis. An application packet, complete with detailed instructions and requirements, can be obtained from the Admissions Office.

For further information, students should contact:

Admissions Office
Milligan College
P.O. Box 210
Milligan College, Tennessee 37682
Phone: 423-461-8730
800-262-8337 (toll-free)
Fax: 423-461-8982
E-mail: admissions@milligan.edu (general)
visits@milligan.edu (visits)
Web site: http://www.milligan.edu

Milligan College is a Christian liberal arts college that unites humanities, sciences, and fine arts with a Christian worldview.

MILLS COLLEGE

OAKLAND, CALIFORNIA

COLLEGE CLOSE-UPS

The College

For more than 150 years, Mills College has shaped women's lives. Offering a progressive liberal arts curriculum taught by nationally renowned faculty, Mills gives students the personal attention that leads to extraordinary learning. At Mills, students gain the ability to make their voices heard, the strength to risk bold visions, an eagerness to experiment, and a desire to change the world.

Nestled on 135 lush acres in the heart of the San Francisco Bay Area, Mills College is a hidden gem. The idyllic setting, combined with the College's community of forward-thinking individuals, makes Mills home to one of the most dynamic, creative liberal arts educations available to women today.

Historically a college for women only, Mills continues that proud tradition today at the undergraduate level. To provide enhanced professional opportunities for all students, Mills also offers renowned graduate programs that are open to both women and men. Ranked one of the top colleges in the West by *U.S. News & World Report*, Mills has also been named one of the greenest colleges in the nation by the Princeton Review.

Mills provides a collaborative, interactive learning environment that encourages intellectual exploration and self-discovery. The faculty of distinguished scholars and artists is dedicated to developing the strengths of every student, preparing them for lifelong intellectual, personal, and professional growth. With an impressive student-teacher ratio of 12:1, Mills women are assured of access to and support from these inspiring professors. The hallmark of a Mills education is the collaboration between students and faculty members that goes beyond the classroom and into innovative research.

Mills students also compete in seven intercollegiate sports—cross-country, rowing, soccer, swimming, tennis, track and field, and volleyball—as members of the National Collegiate Athletic Association (NCAA) Division III. Students may also participate in recreational activity courses for credit or take advantage of the on-campus fitness facilities and off-campus excursions.

Location

Located in the foothills of Oakland, California, Mills offers students access to the diverse metropolitan centers that make up the greater San Francisco Bay Area. Amid the rolling hills and the century-old eucalyptus trees of the Mills campus, students find a welcoming place to live and learn, with new friends and new ideas at every turn. The campus is heavily accented with Mediterranean-style buildings, many designed by architectural innovator Julia Morgan. Paths and streams wind their way through groves and meadows that pervade the 135-acre wooded campus.

Outside the campus gates, students have access to the dynamic Bay Area, with Berkeley, San Francisco, Napa, and Silicon Valley nearby. The close proximity allows Mills students to connect with centers of learning, business, and technology; pursue research and internship opportunities; and explore the Bay Area's many sources of cultural, social, and recreational enrichment.

Majors and Degrees

With more than forty different majors to choose from at Mills, students find themselves active, engaged participants in their own learning. Students have the chance to work directly with nationally renowned faculty members and get involved in their innovative work and research.

Mills offers the Bachelor of Arts (B.A.) degree in American studies; anthropology and sociology; art (history and studio); biochemistry and molecular biology; biology; biopsychology; business economics; chemistry; child development; comparative literature; computer science; dance; economics; English (creative writing and literature); environmental science; environmental studies; ethnic studies; French and Francophone studies; government; history; intermedia arts; international relations; Latin American studies; literary and cultural studies; mathematics; music; philosophy; political, legal, and economic analysis; psychology; public policy; sociology; Spanish and Spanish-American studies; and women's studies. The major in child development meets the requirements for a state child development permit for teaching in preschool and day-care centers and provides a strong basis for graduate school and for many other careers. Special prelaw and premedical advising is available.

Mills offers the Bachelor of Science (B.S.) degree in biochemistry and molecular biology, biology, biopsychology, chemistry, environmental science, and mathematics. Mills also provides the first two years of courses leading to a Bachelor of Science in Nursing degree from Samuel Merritt University.

Students can also choose to create their own major, working with 3 faculty advisers to plan an individual program that draws courses from across the curriculum and creates an integrated and unique educational experience.

Mills offers seven dual-degree programs that enable undergraduates with clear career goals in certain fields to streamline their college and graduate school programs. These dual degrees are the 4+1 B.A./M.B.A. Business Administration Program, the 4+1 B.A./M.P.P. Public Policy Program, the 4+1 B.A./M.A. Infant Mental Health Program, the 4+1 B.A./M.A. Interdisciplinary Computer Science Program, the 4+1 B.A./M.A. Mathematics Program, the 3+2 B.A./B.S. Engineering Program, and the newest program, the 4+1 B.A./M.A./Credential Program in Teacher Education.

Academic Programs

To earn a Mills bachelor's degree, students complete 34 semester course credits (usually four courses each semester). Grading is traditional, and a pass-fail option is available outside the major.

The innovative general education program is guided by a thoughtfully constructed set of learning outcomes, instead of a list of required courses. Each student designs her own program with the guidance of her faculty adviser, tailoring it to the student's specific needs and interests. The program places the work a student does in her major in a larger context and ensures that she explores and appreciates realms of knowledge beyond her field. The general education requirements fall into three outcome categories: skills (written communication, quantitative and computational reasoning, and information literacy/information technology skills), perspectives (interdisciplinary, women and gender, and multicultural), and disciplinary experiences (creation and criticism in the arts, historical perspectives, natural sciences, and human institutions and behavior).

Career Services offers a comprehensive career counseling and coaching program to assist students in clarifying their goals. Workshops, individual counseling sessions, an extensive internship program, a strong alumnae network, and special opportunities to meet Bay Area business leaders and top professional women in every field all help students to focus their interests and plan career goals.

Off-Campus Programs

Mills has exchange or visiting programs with eleven American colleges and universities, including American, Barnard, Manhattanville, Mount Holyoke, Simmons, Spelman, Swarthmore, Wellesley, and Wheaton.

Adventurous students with a minimum 3.0 GPA may study abroad. With programs in Europe, Africa, South America, Asia, and Australia—in nearly every country in the world—Mills encourages students to study abroad. Students receiving financial aid may continue to do so while studying with an approved program. Mills also has exchange programs with universities in Hong Kong and South Korea.

Sophomores, juniors, and seniors may cross-register for one course per semester at the following schools: Berkeley City College; California College of the Arts; California State University, East Bay; Chabot College; City College of San Francisco; College of Alameda; Contra Costa College; Diablo Valley College; Graduate Theological Union; Holy Names University; Laney College; Merritt College; St. Mary's College of California; Skyline College; Sonoma State University; and University of California, Berkeley.

Academic Facilities

Mills' commitment to providing students with exceptional academic resources is underscored by the two new environmentally friendly buildings on campus. The new home of the Lokey Graduate School of Business hosts both undergraduate and graduate classes and is designed to meet the high standards required to attain Gold-level LEED certification. Students enjoy smart classrooms and lecture halls with the latest educational technology and light-filled community areas that encourage student collaboration. Opened in 2007, the Moore Natural Sciences Building provides students with a state-of-the-art learning environment that is also a model of green construction. The Platinum LEED-certified facility features high-tech classrooms, multiple teaching laboratories, and a research lab.

Newly renovated Littlefield Concert Hall reopened in 2009. The venue features an expanded stage area for larger performances and enhanced acoustic features for improved performing and recording quality. Nearby Lisser Hall contains a flexible proscenium stage as well as a small experimental theater.

The open-stack, computerized F. W. Olin Library provides students with access to more than 235,000 volumes in addition to more than 22,000 rare books and manuscripts. A Web-based catalog and more than 60 databases, including Academic Search, LexisNexis, PsycINFO, and Britannica Online are available 24 hours a day via the library's Web site.

The Mills College Art Museum houses the largest permanent collection of any liberal arts college on the West Coast and presents a changing array of innovative exhibitions. The highly regarded Children's School at Mills College provides hands-on experience for students preparing for careers in early childhood education.

Costs

In 2009–10, tuition was $35,196 and room and board were $11,480. Health insurance, a comprehensive fee covering such items as van shuttle service, a discounted area bus pass, technology, and associated student fees totaled $3156 for resident and commuting students. Students should calculate the costs of travel, books, and personal expenses on an individual basis.

Financial Aid

Mills College is committed to ensuring that a Mills education is within reach for those who have the desire and the qualifications to attend. Financial aid options at Mills include grants and scholarships, loans, and student employment. Some are funded by Mills directly, and others are state and federal programs.

In fall 2009, more than 80 percent of undergraduates at the College received some type of financial assistance in the form of grants, scholarships, loans, or on-campus employment. Ninety-one percent of Mills students received some portion of their aid directly from Mills. Awards are based on need and academic merit. Scholarship amounts range from $1000 per year to full tuition. Mills makes a special effort to provide financial aid to all students who demonstrate need.

All first-year students and transfer candidates must file the Free Application for Federal Student Aid (FAFSA) and the Mills College Financial Aid Form to be considered for government aid and need-based Mills scholarship funds. The FAFSA is required for non-Mills aid, such as the Federal Pell Grant, Federal Supplemental Educational Opportunity Grant, Federal Academic Competitiveness Grant, and the National SMART Grant. California residents must also file the Cal Grant GPA Verification Form to be considered for a Cal Grant. More than 40 percent of Mills students have some of their determined need offset by such non-Mills awards.

Faculty

More than 60 percent of the Mills faculty members are women, enabling students to work with professional women mentors in every academic area. Faculty members are selected for their teaching ability and scholarly achievement; 88 percent of full-time faculty members hold the highest degrees in their fields. Twenty-five percent of the full- and part-time faculty members are members of minority groups.

Student Government

An important goal of an education at Mills is to develop leadership skills, and participating in student government can be instrumental in furthering this goal. The Associated Students of Mills College (ASMC) is run by an executive board of 15 elected or appointed positions. Following a student-drafted Constitution, the board supports student organizations, student publications, campuswide events, and various student initiatives. From academic issues to social events to honor code concerns, the ASMC is the voice of the student body to the College administration.

Admission Requirements

Most first-year students admitted to Mills have a strong B average and have followed a full college-preparatory course in their secondary school, including 4 years of English, 3 to 4 years of mathematics, 2 to 4 years of foreign languages, 2 to 4 years of social sciences, and 2 to 4 years of a laboratory science. Additional course work in fine arts is given positive consideration, as is evidence of special talents or interests. Mills is interested in individuals, not statistical averages, so each application is carefully reviewed. Credit may be awarded for the College Board Advanced Placement tests and the International Baccalaureate program's higher level examinations.

Applications from transfers are welcome, as are those from students resuming their education or women who have delayed their entrance to college or who wish to continue work on their B.A. degrees. The SAT or ACT requirement is waived if 24 or more transferable semester hours are presented. For international applications, both the SAT and TOEFL are required. Applications should be accompanied by transcripts, letters of recommendation, and SAT/ACT scores. An interview, either on campus or with an alumna representative, is strongly recommended for all applicants. International students are required to interview if English is not their primary language.

Application and Information

The priority scholarship deadline for admission applications is February 1 for first-year students. All students are encouraged to meet this deadline; however, merit scholarship applicants (including international students) must apply and submit all required materials by February 1. The regular decision deadline date is March 1 for first-year applicants. The priority scholarship deadline for transfer students is March 1, and the regular decision deadline is April 1. Admission decisions for first-years and transfer students are mailed on a rolling basis.

For admission to the spring term, the deadline for both first-year and transfer applicants is November 1.

For more information, students should contact:

Office of Undergraduate Admission
Mills College
5000 MacArthur Boulevard
Oakland, California 94613
Phone: 510-430-2135
800-87-MILLS (toll-free)
Fax: 510-430-3298
E-mail: admission@mills.edu
Web site: http://www.mills.edu

Mills women discover their best selves—and prepare to change the world.

COLLEGE CLOSE-UPS

MILWAUKEE SCHOOL OF ENGINEERING

MILWAUKEE, WISCONSIN

The School

Ambitious students who want personal and professional success find a home at Milwaukee School of Engineering (MSOE). For more than 107 years, top students choose a rigorous and collaborative education and the supportive guidance of expert faculty members who are dedicated to student success. The university is fully dedicated to every student who is willing to be challenged and work hard to become a better person as a successful MSOE graduate. The close-knit campus is nestled in a vibrant downtown Milwaukee neighborhood, and offers students an engaging learning and living environment.

Advancing beyond acquisition to the highly sophisticated application of knowledge is the foundation of MSOE's educational philosophy. This approach, which is the university's educational niche, produces graduates who are well-rounded, technologically experienced, and highly productive professionals and leaders. Graduates begin their careers as work-ready problem solvers and develop into leaders: creating new products, starting or heading companies, and working to better their communities.

For the past five years, MSOE's average graduate placement rate is 95 percent. The average starting salary for graduates is more than $53,300. Representatives from hundreds of firms from throughout the country, including Fortune 500 companies, visit MSOE during the academic year to interview graduating students for employment and discuss career opportunities. MSOE's long-standing ties with business, industry, and health care are represented by the Board of Regents, with more than 50 members, and the MSOE Corporation, with more than 200 members, who are elected from leaders in business and industry nationwide.

The student body of more than 2,600 men and women comes from throughout the United States and numerous countries. Since its founding, the university has encouraged the enrollment of students of any race, color, creed, or gender. Approximately half of the full-time students live in three high-rise residence halls.

MSOE's Counseling Services Office provides individual assistance for students with educational, personal, or vocational concerns. Free on-campus tutoring is provided by the Learning Resource Center and Tau Omega Mu, an honorary fraternity founded in 1953 for the purpose of aiding students who need extra help with their studies.

The Student Life and Campus Center provides on-campus recreational activities. This facility houses student activity rooms, student organization offices, a TV viewing area, a marketplace eatery, and a game room. Additional recreation areas can be found in the residence halls. The Kern Center is a 210,000-square-foot health, wellness, fitness, and recreation facility that houses a 1,600-seat ice arena, a fitness center, a 1,200-seat basketball arena, a field house, a recreational running track, and a wrestling area.

More than seventy professional societies, fraternities, and other special-interest groups serve the campus. MSOE's students also participate in intramural sports programs. MSOE is a member of the National Collegiate Athletic Association (NCAA) Division III and the Northern Athletics Conference (NAC). The Athletic Department sponsors NCAA varsity teams in men's baseball, basketball, cross-country, golf, ice hockey, indoor and outdoor track and field, lacrosse, rowing, soccer, tennis, volleyball, and wrestling and women's basketball, cross-country, golf, indoor and outdoor track and field, soccer, softball, tennis, and volleyball that compete with teams from other private colleges and universities in the Midwest.

MSOE's (and one of Milwaukee's) newest attraction and home to the world's most comprehensive art collection dedicated to the evolution of human work opened in October 2007. The Grohmann Museum welcomes visitors to three floors of galleries where the Eckhart G. Grohmann Collection "Man at Work" is housed. The collection comprises more than 800 paintings and sculptures from 1580 to the present, reflecting a variety of artistic styles and subjects that depict organized work from farming to mining to trades to more unusual occupations such as seaweed gathering.

In addition to its seventeen undergraduate degree programs in the fields of engineering, architectural engineering and building construction, engineering technology, computers, business, nursing, and health-related areas, MSOE offers nine Master of Science degree programs: cardiovascular studies, engineering, engineering management (accelerated option available), environmental engineering, marketing and export management, medical informatics (jointly offered with the Medical College of Wisconsin), new product management, perfusion, and structural engineering.

MSOE is a member of, and accredited by, the North Central Association of Colleges and Schools. Program-specific accrediting agencies are identified in the MSOE academic catalogs.

Location

The MSOE campus is located in the vibrant neighborhood of East Town in downtown Milwaukee. Nearby are the Bradley Center sports arena, the Midwest Airlines Center, the Marcus Center for the Performing Arts, the theater district, churches of most denominations, major hotels and office buildings, restaurants, and department stores. Famous for its friendly atmosphere, Milwaukee offers students many opportunities for educational, cultural, and professional growth as well as ample employment opportunities. The metropolitan area has more than 15,000 acres of parks and river parkways and miles of bike trails. A few blocks east of the MSOE campus is Lake Michigan, which offers year-round natural beauty. MSOE also offers classes in other locations in Wisconsin for students who wish to pursue select programs in the evening on a part-time basis.

Majors and Degrees

Four-year programs are offered that lead to Bachelor of Science degrees in business management, construction management, engineering, and specific areas of engineering (architectural, biomedical, biomolecular, computer, electrical, industrial, mechanical, and software), engineering technology—transfer programs only (electrical and mechanical), international business, management information systems, and nursing. A Bachelor of Science or Bachelor of Arts degree is offered in technical communication. A five-year, double-major option is available in a combination of business, construction management, engineering, and technical communication programs. An engineering/environmental or structural engineering dual degree (B.S./M.S. combination) also is available. Study-abroad opportunities and many double majors also exist.

Academic Programs

MSOE guarantees that the classes needed to graduate in four years will be available for full-time undergraduate students who start and stay on track and meet academic requirements.

The degree programs at MSOE combine study in degree specialty courses with basic study in sciences, communication, mathematics, and humanities in a high-technology, applications-oriented atmosphere. Students who are admitted with advanced credit to a program leading to a bachelor's degree must complete at least 50 percent of the curriculum in residence at MSOE. MSOE operates on a quarter system. Students average between 16 and 19 credits per quarter, which represent a combination of lecture and laboratory courses. Undergraduate students average 600 hours of laboratory experience.

MSOE offers students the opportunity to participate in the Air Force Reserve Officer Training Corps (AFROTC) program, the Army ROTC program, or the Navy ROTC program.

Academic Facilities

The Fred Loock Engineering Center adjoins the Allen-Bradley Hall of Science, forming a prime technical education and applied research complex. Rosenberg Hall houses the Rader School of Business, technology-integrated classrooms, and the U.S. Export Service Center for Milwaukee.

The Walter Schroeder Library is a popular meeting place on campus that houses more than 60,000 volumes, with collections that represent the specialized curricula of the university. The library offers Web-based access to more than 70,000 e-journals, 25,000 e-books, hundreds of specialized databases, unique collections, government agencies, and other sources of information throughout the world.

All students participate in a Technology Package program that includes a notebook computer and affiliated services. A full range of software is available on these systems and via the local area network linked by a fiber-optic ring around the campus. Most areas also have wireless capability for laptop use. State-of-the-art architectural, computer, electrical, mechanical, industrial, nursing, science, and software laboratories complement the respective areas of study.

The Applied Technology Center™ (ATC) utilizes faculty and student expertise to solve technological problems confronting business and industry. The ATC is heavily involved in the transferring of new technologies into real business practice through the Rapid Prototyping Center (MSOE is the only university in the world to possess the five leading rapid prototyping technologies), the Fluid Power Institute™, the NanoEngineering Laboratory, the Photonics and Applied Optics Center, the Construction Science and Engineering Center, and the Center for BioMolecular Modeling.

There are more laboratories than classrooms at MSOE, many with industrial sponsorship from such companies as Johnson Controls, Harley-Davidson, Rockwell Automation/Allen-Bradley, Master Lock, Snap-on, General Electric and Outboard Marine Corp. Undergraduates average an amazing 600 hours of laboratory experience.

Costs

For 2009–10, tuition was $28,665 per year plus $1140 for the Technology Package (notebook computer, software, insurance, maintenance, Internet access, and user services). The cost of room and board in the residence halls was approximately $7164 per year. Books and supplies average $400 per quarter but may be somewhat higher for the first quarter.

Financial Aid

Qualified students are assisted by a comprehensive financial aid program, including MSOE and industry-supported scholarships, student loans, and part-time employment; Federal Perkins Loan, Federal Stafford Student Loan, Federal Work-Study, Federal Pell Grant, and Federal Supplemental Educational Opportunity Grant Programs; and state-supported grant programs. Ninety-nine percent of full-time students receive financial aid. Students can also visit MSOE's Web site for a financial aid estimate.

Faculty

MSOE faculty members engage and challenge students, with individual attention and practical perspectives gained from an average of seven years of professional employment experience in their area of expertise. They are at MSOE because they love to teach—there is no "publish or perish" tenure system. There are more than 200 men and women on the MSOE faculty (full-time and part-time). Many are registered professional engineers, architects, and/or nurses. They and their colleagues in nontechnical academic areas are active in related professional societies. The student-faculty ratio is 14:1. MSOE does not use teaching assistants.

Student Government

The MSOE Student Government Association (SGA) represents clubs and fraternities as well as residence halls and commuting students. SGA appoints representatives to the Campus Security and Disciplinary Hearing committees, the Executive Educational Council, and the Alumni Association's Board of Directors.

Admission Requirements

Each applicant to MSOE is reviewed individually on the basis of potential for success as determined by academic preparation. Admission may be gained by submitting an application for admission and the appropriate transcripts. High school students are encouraged to complete math through precalculus (including algebra and geometry), chemistry, biology (nursing), physics, and four years of English. All entering freshmen are also required to provide results from the ACT or the SAT.

Transfer opportunities exist into the junior year of the Bachelor of Science in business management, electrical engineering technology, mechanical engineering technology, and technical communication programs with the appropriate associate degree or equivalent credits.

Application and Information

Classes start in September, November, March, and late May. Freshmen and transfer students may enter at the beginning of any quarter; however, entry in the fall quarter is recommended. An application for admission may be obtained by contacting the address below or by visiting MSOE's Web site. Applicants are encouraged to visit MSOE and have a preadmission counseling interview. Transfer students are required to submit transcripts from all prior institutions attended. An applicant's prior course work is reviewed to determine eligibility for admission. Required course work varies depending on the desired course of study.

Admission Office
Milwaukee School of Engineering
1025 North Broadway
Milwaukee, Wisconsin 53202-3109
Phone: 414-277-6763
800-332-6763 (toll-free)
E-mail: explore@msoe.edu
Web site: http://www.msoe.edu

MSOE's undergraduate students average 600 hours of laboratory experience—just one more advantage to an MSOE education.

MISERICORDIA UNIVERSITY

DALLAS, PENNSYLVANIA

The University

Misericordia University is a high-quality liberal arts and professional studies institution rooted in a foundation of service to others and committed to providing the challenging academics and personal attention students need to learn in order to succeed both professionally and personally. Founded by the Religious Sisters of Mercy, Misericordia offers undergraduate and graduate programs to resident and commuter students, as well as adult students. Current enrollment is more than 2,700 men and women.

Misericordia provides an academic atmosphere designed to stimulate critical thinking, independent judgment, and creativity, as well as encourage the development of curiosity, good study habits, and personal values. The University also cultivates a spirit of community service and a lifelong love of learning in its students through extracurricular activities, experiential learning, and challenging academic programs. In the National Survey of Student Engagement, Misericordia students say they are more involved in learning and have better relationships with faculty members and peers than students at other similar institutions. Misericordia is also recommended by the Princeton Review and ranked in the top tier of *U.S. News & World Report*'s "America's Best Colleges 2010" in the Master's North category.

The University is fully accredited by the Middle States Association of Colleges and Schools. Its programs in nursing, social work, medical imaging, occupational therapy, physical therapy, and speech-language pathology are accredited by the National League for Nursing Accrediting Commission, the Council on Social Work Education, the Joint Review Committee on Education in Radiologic Technology, the American Occupational Therapy Association, the American Physical Therapy Association, and the American Speech-Language and Hearing Association, respectively.

Misericordia operates four residential facilities and eighteen townhouse units, with a total capacity for 850 students. The new McGowan Residence Hall opened to students in 2008. A nearby home is reserved for upper-level students. Residents have a number of options, including single rooms and wellness housing. On average, students living in campus housing hold GPAs of more than 3.2. Each residence hall offers study rooms, laundry facilities, and recreational lounges. The new dining hall is located in the Banks Student Life Center, which also houses the Cougar's Den coffeehouse, snack bar, and the newly renovated Student Union, which features big flat-screen televisions, and pool and foosball tables.

There are numerous campus activities for students. Besides Student Government, there are forty-one chartered student clubs and organizations. Cultural events, Campus Ministry, intramural and intercollegiate athletic programs for men and women, performing arts shows, art exhibits in the Pauly Friedman Art Gallery, and many other social activities complement and reinforce the academic experience. In keeping with the University's tradition of mercy, justice, service, and hospitality, students also have opportunities to develop leadership potential through a variety of volunteer service projects that benefit the surrounding communities. The University's Service Leadership Center engages students in the development of lifelong civic responsibility through academic course work.

Campus Ministry provides opportunities to participate in campus and community programs. These programs are designed to promote social awareness in students. On spring break, students have elected to serve those most in need in rural Appalachia, the storm-ravaged Gulf Coast, Texas, California, and the South Bronx. A six-week summer Cross-Cultural Ministry Experience in Guyana, South America, awaits selected participants, while students have also volunteered abroad in Jamaica and Romania.

Personalized attention is the key to the support available in the Student Success Center. A psychologist, counselors, therapists, and peer counselors form a dedicated team of professionals who conduct workshops each semester on a variety of topics, including test anxiety, stress management, time management, and goal setting. Many services are free of charge to students, and contacts are strictly confidential.

First-year students may join the Guaranteed Placement Program (GPP) through the Insalaco Center for Career Development. Misericordia was named a "Best School for Standing by Grads" in *Kiplinger's Personal Finance Magazine*'s December 2009 special edition, "The Best of Everything 2009." The GPP program includes academic standards; cocurricular activities, such as leadership and service projects; internships; resume development; and interviewing skills. If a student fulfills the requirements of the program and is not employed in his or her field or enrolled in graduate or professional school within six months of graduation, a paid internship is assured. The center also copresents the Choice Program, offering special guidance for students who have not chosen a major. Opportunities for career exploration, cooperative education, and internships are available for students to develop the knowledge and skills they need to enter the working world.

Student Health Services occupies a convenient facility near campus housing. Health-care staff members provide first aid, assessment and treatment of common illnesses, and referrals for more serious health conditions. Health center activities are directed by a registered nurse with a master's degree in nursing administration, under the guidance of a physician. A nurse practitioner is also available. A self-care room offers reference materials and up-to-date information on personal health concerns. All services are confidential.

A rapidly evolving world and development of new technologies have increased the number of adults who seek higher education. Misericordia offers special bachelor's, master's, and doctoral programs for adults, including the Expressway Program, an accelerated bachelor's degree program; Women with Children, which provides housing and support services for single women with children; and evening, online, and weekend formats for people with families and full-time jobs.

At Misericordia University, students can earn master's and/or doctoral degrees by attending classes online, in the evening, and/or on weekends. The small-class format enhances critical thinking and decision-making skills and draws out a variety of viewpoints that help broaden the perspectives of the student. Master's degrees are available in education, nursing, occupational therapy, physical therapy, speech-language pathology, business administration, and organizational management. A doctoral program in physical therapy is available to students entering in a full-time and part-time format, and a doctoral program in occupational therapy is available for graduate students via part-time study, including online and in-class components.

Location

Located on a 124-acre campus in northeastern Pennsylvania, Misericordia University is the oldest institution of higher education in Luzerne County. Expansive lawns and thick stands of trees dominate the campus. It is 9 miles from the city of Wilkes-Barre. The area offers shopping centers, malls, cinemas, skiing, professional sporting events, and a variety of cultural activities. Pennsylvania's largest natural lake and two state parks are nearby, as are Pocono ski resorts. Metropolitan New York and Philadelphia are each within a 3-hour drive. Public and college-sponsored transportation serves the campus.

Majors and Degrees

Misericordia University awards the Bachelor of Arts (B.A.) degree in English, history, communications, government, liberal studies, and philosophy. The Bachelor of Science (B.S.) degree is awarded in accounting, biochemistry, biology, business administration, chemistry, clinical laboratory science, communications, computer science, diagnostic medial sonography, elementary education, health-care management, information technology, interdisciplinary studies, management, marketing, mathematics, math/computer science, medical imaging, professional studies, psychology, secondary education, special education, and sport management. A Bachelor of Science in Nursing (B.S.N.) is awarded to nursing majors, and a Bachelor of Science in Social Work (B.S.W.) is awarded to social work majors. Specializations in accounting, early childhood education, prelaw, special education, and preprofessional occupations are also available. Certification programs include addictions counseling, child welfare services, diagnostic medical sonography, geriatric care management, gerontology, health-care informatics, and secondary education and may be taken in support of several degrees offered by Misericordia or as stand-alone programs.

The University offers five-year entry-level graduate majors in occupational therapy and speech-language pathology. Students graduate with a master's degree in speech-language pathology or occupational therapy and a bachelor's degree in health sciences. The physical therapy program is a 6½-year doctoral program. Students graduate with a bachelor's degree in one of several areas and a Doctor of Physical Therapy (D.P.T.) degree.

Academic Programs

Candidates for the B.A., B.S., B.S.N., or B.S.W. must fulfill a 48-credit liberal arts core curriculum in addition to the requirements of their chosen major to graduate. They must earn at least 36 credit hours in a chosen field. For regularly enrolled students, the average requirement for a baccalaureate degree is a total of 126 credits. Other options include minors, specializations, certifications, and electives.

Courses are offered on a semester basis, beginning in August and January and ending in December and May. Summer, weekend, and accelerated courses are also available.

Academic Facilities

The chemistry, physics, and biology departments all have modern, fully equipped research laboratories available to students in these fields of concentration. State-of-the-art equipment includes high-performance liquid chromatography (HPLC), a rotary evaporator, an infrared spectrophotometer, and gas chromatography. The University also houses an energized radiation laboratory for the medical imaging program. The College of Health Sciences provides classrooms and high-technology laboratories for the occupational therapy, physical therapy, speech-language pathology, and nursing programs.

In addition to the four main computer labs, the Banks Student Life Center and Bevevino Library offer wireless Internet access. The University operates e-MU, a secure online portal where students can access e-mail, course schedules, group and chat functions, and student account and registration information from a single sign-on. The Munson Center for Communications features the area's only all-digital television control room and editing bays

Mercy Hall, the University's original administrative building, underwent extensive renovations in 2002, with new multipurpose academic classrooms and facilities. In addition, many key student service departments, including the registrar, student accounts, and financial aid are now centralized in one area in Mercy Hall. Insalaco Hall, a new state-of-the-art classroom and conference building, provides a modern art gallery, café, computer labs, an ensemble room, fine arts classroom, several music teaching and practice areas, and the Assistive Technology Research Institute.

The three-story Bevevino Library covers 37,500 square feet and houses stacks for 90,000 volumes. Materials include information and communication technology and a reference section that offers books, serials, and a variety of periodicals as well as reference search tools, CD-ROMs, and multiple online databases and microfilm. The Bevevino Library is a member of the Northeastern Pennsylvania Library Network, which provides users access to the 1.5-million-volume collections of participating libraries via its new virtual online catalog.

Costs

Tuition for 2009–10 was $22,850 per year. The general fee is $1200. Housing options include traditional rooms, suites, town houses, and wellness housing. The median room cost was $5930. All resident students must participate in a ten-, fourteen-, or nineteen- meal plan. In addition, town-house residents are eligible to choose a five-meal plan. The median board cost was $3595.

Financial Aid

All students applying for financial aid must complete the Free Application for Federal Student Aid (FAFSA) by May 1. The application is used for Federal Pell Grants, Federal Supplemental Educational Opportunity Grants (FSEOG), subsidized and unsubsidized Federal Stafford Student Loans, Federal Perkins Loans, nursing loans, and Federal Work-Study Program awards. This application is also the basis upon which state and institutional aid is awarded. The University also offers a no-interest monthly payment plan. In addition, many scholarships are available for qualified students, including $6.7 million in honors and presidential scholarships based on academic abilities and $2.3 million in McAuley Awards for students who have experience in leadership roles and volunteer service.

Faculty

There are 96 full-time faculty members. A student-faculty ratio of 13:1 results in students receiving a great deal of individual attention from a highly qualified faculty; 79 percent of the faculty members hold doctorates. Besides student academic advising, the faculty members also serve as advisers to clubs.

Student Government

An active student government organization serves as a liaison between the students and the faculty and staff members. The administration enables students to become involved by serving as student representatives on various University committees.

Admission Requirements

Misericordia University admits applicants based on their secondary school record, high school recommendation, extracurricular activities, and personal promise. The University requires SAT or ACT scores. Although a personal interview is highly recommended, it is not necessary for all majors. Misericordia offers both early decision and early admissions programs.

Transfer students with a cumulative average of at least 2.0 (on a 4.0 scale) may be considered for admission and may receive advanced standing. Some majors require a 2.5 or higher cumulative average. Transfer students must submit official high school transcripts. A transcript of work completed at other colleges and universities and proof of honorable dismissal are also required.

Application and Information

Applicants must submit an official application form (available upon request), transcripts, and SAT or ACT scores. Applicants may also apply for admission online at the University's Web address. There is a nonrefundable application fee of $25, which is waived for students who visit the campus.

The University considers applications on a rolling basis. Usually, candidates are notified of the admission decision within three weeks of receipt of all required materials.

Office of Admissions
Misericordia University
301 Lake Street
Dallas, Pennsylvania 18612-1090
Phone: 570-674-6461
866-262-6363 (toll free)
Fax: 570-675-2441
E-mail: admiss@misericordia.edu
Web site: http://admissions.misericordia.edu

Students at Misericordia University pursue their studies with an emphasis on academic excellence, service leadership, and professional preparation.

MITCHELL COLLEGE

NEW LONDON, CONNECTICUT

The College

Mitchell is a private, coeducational four-year residential college. With 961 students and a 12:1 student-faculty ratio, the College provides a supportive student-centered learning environment that addresses the educational needs of all students, including those with learning disabilities. Mitchell is especially proud of its success in working with students who have yet to reach their full academic potential. To that end, the College maintains access for students with varied academic abilities who are highly motivated to succeed.

To help guide students, Mitchell College's mission is connected to five distinctive values: Character, Achievement, Respect, Engagement, and Self-Discovery (CARES). The CARES model provides a learning foundation that emphasizes character development, personal and social responsibility, respect for others, and community service. CARES is a comprehensive hands-on partnership that keeps students on course toward their goal of graduation and beyond.

Mitchell College's innovative PG year program, Thames Academy, continues to grow and strengthen. Launched in 2006, Thames Academy is a postgraduate/precollege program—a year of academic preparation for students between the end of their secondary school/high school education and the start of their college studies. As one of the country's foremost colleges in promoting student academic success, Mitchell provides a challenging education in a caring and supportive environment, focusing on student asset development, rather than deficit management.

Nearly all full-time students are of traditional college age, 18 to 22, and come from throughout the country and around the globe. Most students come from New England states, with about 60 percent from Connecticut, 30 percent from other New England states, and the remaining 10 percent from throughout United States and other countries. International students and representatives of multicultural groups make up approximately 32 percent of the student population. About 150 part-time students, many of whom are adult commuters, enhance the classroom experience.

Nearly 80 percent of full-time students live in three traditional residence halls, each housing 100 students. Each building has three floors with double rooms and common baths. The College also offers four historic Victorian and Colonial waterfront residence halls accommodating between 20 and 35 students each. One waterfront residence is dedicated to Thames Academy, the postgraduate/precollege transitional program. In addition to the traditional resident halls, Mitchell has themed, apartment-style living, accommodating 16 students. A new suite-style, 120-bed residence hall opened in fall 2008. Facilities include a fully equipped gymnasium, a new fitness center, new dining hall and café, athletic fields, a sailing dock, and indoor recreation areas.

Biking, business, communications, community service, choir, Hillel, music, the newspaper, the yearbook, skiing, multicultural affairs, psychology, and history are among the clubs that bring together students with similar interests. Weekends are filled with guest comedians, bands, formal and casual dances, lectures, and organized trips to Boston and New York City.

The tradition of the scholar-athlete is strong at Mitchell. A provisional member of the NCAA Division III, Mitchell College recently joined the New England Collegiate Conference. Other colleges in this conference include Wheelock College, Newbury College, Lesley University, Elms College, Bay Path College, Becker College, Southern Vermont College, and Daniel Webster College.

Mitchell College fields ten intercollegiate teams. Men play baseball, basketball, cross-country, golf, lacrosse, sailing, soccer, and tennis; women play basketball, cross-country, golf, sailing, soccer, softball, tennis, and volleyball. The College has a history of athletic excellence, winning many national and New England championships. A full schedule of intramural sports is organized for students of all athletic experience and ability.

Location

New London, Connecticut, where Mitchell College makes its home, is a major center of activity in southeastern Connecticut, a region rich in historic significance. This small but sophisticated city, also home to Connecticut College and the U.S. Coast Guard Academy, is a maritime and resort center located midway between Boston and New York City on the main rail line.

The campus is situated in the city's most scenic residential section. Bordered by a long stretch of sandy beach, the campus consists of 68 acres of gently sloping hillside and forest. Places for shopping, banking, dining, and fun are within easy walking distance or can be accessed by buses that pass the College entrance. Major shopping malls, factory outlets, and fine and casual dining are minutes from the campus. The region is also home to major tourist attractions, such as the U.S.S. Nautilus and Submarine Museum, Mystic Marinelife Aquarium, Mystic Seaport, Olde Mystic Village, Ocean Beach Park, Stonington Vineyards, Foxwoods Resort and Casino, the Mohegan Sun Casino, and the Essex Steam Train.

Majors and Degrees

Baccalaureate degrees are offered in business administration, communication, criminal justice, early childhood education, environmental studies, homeland security, global studies, hospitality and tourism, human development and family studies, liberal and professional studies, psychology, and sport management. Associate degrees are offered in early childhood education, graphic design, and liberal arts.

Students undecided about their academic majors are enrolled in the Discovery Program, which is specially designed to provide special courses, additional advising, and services to explore their full potential and assistance in choosing a major.

Academic Programs

The academic calendar consists of two full semesters that run from September to December and from January to May. In addition to five summer sessions, Mitchell College also offers STEP, a five-week bridging program for incoming freshmen.

All first-year freshman students participate in the First Year College. This comprehensive program is designed to ease the transition from high school to college and establish the foundation for academic success. Students are clustered into freshman interest groups based on a common interest in a theme of their choosing. Courses within the freshman college include expository writing, college writing and research, presentations, and information technology literacy. These courses are linked within a collaborative format consisting of a common theme, a team of instructors, and ability-based assessment.

If a student is having difficulty, it is recognized early. Mitchell grades at four, seven, and fifteen-week intervals. If a student is experiencing a problem, faculty members and the student's academic adviser work with the student to get back on course. Mitchell's Tutoring Center provides free, unlimited individualized tutoring by trained professionals (not peer tutors) in almost every academic discipline. It also offers assistance in improving writing, research, and computer skills as well as test and exam preparation and study skills development. Some of Mitchell's most successful students are regular users of the Tutoring Center, and they attribute much of their success to its programs.

Students with diagnosed learning disabilities may enroll in the College's nationally recognized Learning Resource Center, which provides instruction and support to complement a student's regular academic program. Each student is assigned two learning specialists to work one-on-one with the student and in small-group settings. The program is designed to teach the learning strategies a student needs to gain independence.

Off-Campus Programs

When not in class, Mitchell students gain the skills and experience they need to succeed in their careers and to make a difference in their communities. Nearly all academic programs require or encourage students to participate in volunteer opportunities, internships, or practical experiences as part of their curriculum.

Some of the opportunities include exploring the seacoast with a nationally recognized scientist, teaching at a local elementary school, partnering with a local police officer, helping to negotiate a bill through the state legislature, assisting with advertising campaigns, coaching developmentally challenged athletes and practicing the skills of injury prevention, and sparking the imagination of local school children through storytelling sessions.

Academic Facilities

Mitchell's unique 68-acre waterfront campus includes a 73,590-volume library, classroom buildings, and the Duques Academic Success Center. Located in the center of campus, the Duques Academic Success Center houses academic advising, the Career Center, the Learning Resource Center, tutoring, and classrooms.

Students have full use of Mitchell's state-of-the-art computing facilities with high-speed Internet access. The Mitchell College Library, dining hall, residence hall lounges, and most classrooms are equipped with wireless network and Internet access. Computer access is also available seven days a week in the library and computer labs. Campus computers are fully equipped for e-mail, scanning, network printing, and secure access to each student's individual network server storage. Students have access to extensive online information resources (including journal databases, music databases, and eBooks) via the library Web site. High-speed Internet is also available to each student living in the residence halls and most of the campus buildings have wireless Internet access. For those who do not own a computer, Mitchell offers a computer purchasing plan through Dell and additional service agreements through a local authorized Dell service provider.

Costs

Tuition, room and board, and fees for the 2009–10 year were $37,176. Additional annual miscellaneous expenses, including books, were estimated at $1500 per year. Students enrolled in the Learning Resource Center paid an additional $6500 per year.

Financial Aid

Mitchell annually awards more than $4 million in financial aid, both in need-based and merit-based scholarships and in grant programs designed to recognize academic and leadership abilities. Accepted students may qualify for grants and scholarships that do not need to be repaid. They include the Connecticut Independent College Student Grant Program, Federal Pell Grants, Federal Supplemental Educational Opportunity Grants, and Mitchell Scholarships. Self-help aid in the form of loans is also available. They include Federal Stafford Student Loans (subsidized and unsubsidized), Federal PLUS Loans, and Federal Perkins Loan programs. On-campus job opportunities are plentiful for students regardless of their financial aid status.

Mitchell Valued Potential (MVP) scholarships are awarded based on an individual student's ability to contribute to the College. They may be given to students who demonstrate potential in leadership, volunteerism, and involvement in school activities. Various payment plans are available.

Faculty

Thirty-four full-time and 58 part-time faculty members teach in Mitchell's classrooms. The student-faculty ratio is 12:1.

Student Government

The Student Government Association (SGA) is made up of officers and senators who represent the residents and commuters. It addresses issues with campus administration, organizes community projects, serves as the active voice for the student body, and sponsors at least one campuswide program each semester. The SGA also works in tandem with the Student Activities Office concerning club funding and overall programming.

Student involvement is not only encouraged but also expected of all Mitchell students. An active student leads to a well-rounded person. Students enhance their life with self-discipline skills, demonstrate selfless service, and become happier members of the College family through involvement in student activities, athletics, campus employment, and community service opportunities.

Admission Requirements

Each student is evaluated individually as soon as the completed application, along with the official transcript, is received. Admission is based on academic preparation, scholastic aptitude, personal character, and potential for academic success. Other important factors taken into consideration include the student's motivation, initiative, maturity, seriousness of purpose, and leadership potential. SAT or ACT test scores are optional. Campus visit and admissions interviews are required. Open houses and interview days are held in October, November, February, March, and April, and throughout the summer.

Application and Information

Mitchell uses a rolling admission policy. Students can expect to be notified of decisions within weeks of the College's receipt of completed applications and official transcripts sent directly from the students' high schools.

For more information, students should contact:

Kimberly S. Hodges
Director of Enrollment Management and Marketing
Mitchell College
437 Pequot Avenue
New London, Connecticut 06320-4498
Phone: 800-443-2811 (toll-free)
Fax: 860-444-1209
E-mail: admissions@mitchell.edu
Web site: http://www.mitchell.edu

Mitchell is known for its sense of community and commitment to students' academic success.

MOLLOY COLLEGE

ROCKVILLE CENTRE, NEW YORK

The College

In 1955, 44 students became part of an exciting new tradition in higher education on Long Island. As the first freshman class of Molloy College, located in Rockville Centre, New York, these young students made a commitment to academic excellence. So did the College, which had a distinguished faculty of 15 and a library containing 5,000 books.

Today, Molloy offers students a rich and multidimensional education experience. The Long Island school encourages critical thinking and creative exploration in a personal community setting. Molloy combines the strengths of academic excellence and leadership with personal, compassionate mentoring to bring out the best in every student.

For over fifty years, Molloy College has evolved to become a dynamic learning institution with outstanding faculty, advanced technology, and a wide range of academic programs. In addition, Molloy has expanded its reach, offering graduate level courses at its Suffolk Center in East Farmingdale, New York, along with a number of on-site opportunities at area hospitals and school districts.

Molloy College students possess the confidence needed to live and work in this fast-paced, ever-changing world. The college has expanded its global learning program, where students travel from Rockville Centre and study abroad in Belgium, India, Italy, France, Spain, Thailand, and Australia. By traveling from Long Island and immersing themselves in cultures in other parts of the world, students gain knowledge while learning acceptance and understanding.

Closer to home, Molloy College students make a difference in Rockville Centre as well as other nearby local communities. For example, as part of Molloy's tradition of service, students become involved in a number of service projects that include BoxTown, a program to raise social consciousness about the issue of homelessness.

Athletics and academics go hand-in-hand at Molloy College, where students are known for both their athletic and scholastic success. The Long Island school has a winning tradition in a number of athletic programs, and recently won conference championships in women's basketball and men's soccer. Molloy College athletes compete in the East Coast Conference, NCAA Division II.

Campus life in Rockville Centre, New York, is alive and vibrant, with more than forty student clubs and honor societies. Whether it is writing for a campus publication or serving as a student government representative, Molloy has something for each student.

In recent years, Molloy College has become a focal point for civic discourse with key community forums. Top regional, national, and international leaders (including former Secretary of State Colin Powell and *Newsweek International* editor Fareed Zakaria) have come to Rockville Centre to visit the College in order to address critical and timely issues.

The college launched two new initiatives recently to enhance students' experience. The Sustainability Institute at Molloy College is Long Island's first-ever venture combining environmental advocacy and sustainability education within an academic institution. Molloy started its new Irish Studies Institute recently with a presentation from Bertie Ahern, the former prime minister of Ireland.

Through Molloy College's diversity of programs, personal attention from faculty, and commitment to improving both Long Island and the world, students develop an "I will" attitude that prepares them to enter the professional world—ready and able to make a difference.

Location

Located on a 30-acre campus in Rockville Centre, Long Island, Molloy College is close to metropolitan New York and all its diverse and rich resources. The College is easily accessible from all parts of Nassau, Suffolk, and Queens counties.

Majors and Degrees

Molloy College offers the A.A. degree in liberal arts; the A.A.S. degree in nuclear medicine technology, respiratory therapy, and cardiovascular technology; and B.A., B.S., B.F.A., or B.S.W. degrees in accounting, art, biology, business management, communication arts, computer information systems, computer science, criminal justice, English, environmental studies, history, interdisciplinary studies, international peace and justice studies, mathematics, modern languages, music, music therapy, nursing, philosophy, political science, psychology, social work, sociology, speech-language pathology/audiology, and theology. Teacher certification programs are available in childhood (1–6), adolescence (7–12), and special education. Dual certification is available for birth–grade 2/childhood 1–6.

Special advisement is offered for students interested in predental, prelaw, premedical, or pre–veterinary programs.

On the graduate level, Molloy College offers a Master of Science degree as well as post-master's certification in nursing and education. M.B.A. programs are available in business, accounting, and personal financial planning. A Master of Social Work is offered through Molloy's partnership with Fordham University.

The internship program at the College offers students the opportunity for on-the-job experience along with the classroom exposure so essential to the completely educated person. Internships are available in all areas of study.

Academic Programs

Advanced Placement credit is granted for a score of 3 or better on the AP exam. CLEP and CPE credit is also given. Molloy has a 4-1-4 academic calendar.

Academic Facilities

The James E. Tobin Library houses a collection of 110,000 volumes, along with hundreds of subscriptions to print journals and periodicals. Students and faculty members have access to the library's databases on campus and off campus as well as through the College's Web site. The library also houses a library instruction room, where librarians meet with professors and individual classes for instruction on the use of the databases and related research methods. The Tobin Library is a wireless facility. In the Media Center, over 3,000 DVDs and VHS tapes support the curriculum.

Students may use more than 300 computers located in nineteen labs and open space areas. The College has 100 percent wireless coverage for portable devices.

The Wilbur Arts Center features numerous art studios, music studios, a cable television studio, and the Lucille B. Hays Theatre.

Kellenberg Hall houses six science labs, a language lab, and the education resource center. The Casey Center houses two nursing labs, and the behavioral sciences research facility is located in Siena Hall.

Costs

For 2009–10, tuition and fees were $19,970. The cost per credit for part-time students was $660.

Financial Aid

More than 85 percent of the student body of Molloy College is awarded financial aid in the form of scholarships, grants, loans, and Federal Work-Study Program employment. Financial aid awards are based on academic achievement and financial need. Completion of the Molloy College Application for Financial Aid/Scholarship and the Free Application for Federal Student Aid (FAFSA) is required. No-need scholarships and grants are also available.

Students who have attained a 95 percent or better high school average and a minimum combined score of 1280 on the SAT (composite math and verbal scores) are considered for the Molloy Scholars' Program, which awards full-tuition scholarships. Partial scholarships are available under Dominican, Community Service, and Fine Arts Scholarships. The Transfer Scholarship Program grants partial-tuition scholarships to students transferring into Molloy College with at least a 3.0 cumulative average. Athletic grants (Division II only) are awarded to full-time students based on athletic ability in a variety of sports. The Community Service Award is awarded to full-time freshmen demonstrating a commitment to their community and their school.

Faculty

The over 500 full-time and part-time faculty members at Molloy are dedicated as much to the students as to their respective fields. The 9:1 student-faculty ratio allows for small classes where students can receive the individual attention they deserve.

In addition to their teaching responsibilities, faculty members advise students in their fields to help them select courses that both satisfy major course requirements and lead to the attainment of career goals.

Student Government

Every member of the Molloy College student body belongs to the Molloy Student Association, whose elected leaders form the Molloy Student Government. This group of students provides the leadership necessary to keep extracurricular life at Molloy College alive, productive, and practical.

Admission Requirements

Recommended admission qualifications include graduation from a four-year public or private high school or equivalent (GED test) with a minimum of 18.5 units, including 4 in English, 4 in social studies, 3 in a foreign language, 3 in mathematics, and 3 in science. Nursing applicants must have taken courses in biology and chemistry. Mathematics applicants must have taken 4 units of math and 3 of science (including chemistry or physics). Biology applicants must have credits in biology, chemistry, and physics and 4 units of math. A portfolio is required of art applicants, and music students must audition. Social work applicants must file a special application with the director of the social work program.

The admissions committee bases its selection of candidates on the secondary school record, SAT or ACT scores, class rank, and the school's recommendation. A particular talent or ability can be important. Character and personality, extracurricular participation, and alumni relationships are all considered. On-campus interviews are recommended but not required.

The St. Thomas Aquinas Program, which houses both HEOP and the Albertus Magnus Program, may be an option for students not normally eligible for admission.

Molloy College offers an honors program, and an early admission plan is available.

Application and Information

To apply to Molloy College, students should submit the following credentials to the Admissions Office: a completed application for admission, a nonrefundable $30 application fee, an official high school transcript or GED score report, official results of the SAT or ACT, and official college transcripts (transfer students only).

The College uses a rolling admission system. Students are advised of an admission decision within a few weeks after the application filing process is complete.

For further information, prospective students should contact:

Director of Admissions
Molloy College
1000 Hempstead Avenue
P.O. Box 5002
Rockville Centre, New York 11571-5002
Phone: 888-4-MOLLOY (toll-free)
Web site: http://www.molloy.edu

On the campus of Molloy College.

MONMOUTH UNIVERSITY

WEST LONG BRANCH, NEW JERSEY

The University

Monmouth University is a private, moderate-sized coeducational school committed to providing a learning environment that enables men and women to pursue their educational goals and realize their full potential for making significant contributions to their community and society. Small classes, which allow for individual attention and student-faculty dialogue, together with careful academic advising and career counseling, are hallmarks of a Monmouth education.

The student body is diverse, with a population of more than 4,700 undergraduates and 1,730 graduate students. Although most are from the Northeast, twenty-five states and twenty-eight nations are represented. Of the nearly 4,300 full-time undergraduate students enrolled, approximately 1,600 live on campus in traditional residence halls and garden apartment complexes. Both resident and commuting students have a wide variety of extracurricular activities to choose from: an active Student Government Association; the campus newspaper *(Outlook)*, FM radio station (WMCX), and television station (Hawk TV); the yearbook *(Shadows)* and the literary magazine *(Monmouth Review)*; the African American Student Union; Hillel; a vast array of special-interest groups; theater; intramurals; and sororities and fraternities that engage in service work both on behalf of the University and the community. Many special events are planned each year including art exhibits, concerts, lectures, sightseeing trips, and more.

The University's NCAA Division I intercollegiate athletics program includes nine men's teams—baseball, basketball, cross-country, football (FCS), golf, indoor track, outdoor track and field, soccer, and tennis—and ten women's teams—basketball, cross-country, field hockey, golf, indoor track, lacrosse, outdoor track and field, soccer, softball, and tennis. The new, 153,200-square-foot Multipurpose Activity Center (MAC) opened in fall 2009 and features a 4,100-seat arena with premium suites; a 200-meter, six-lane indoor track; locker rooms; a fitness center; educational and conference space; Champions' Hall; the University Store; and more. Boylan Gymnasium has an indoor pool, regulation-size basketball courts, a training room, and a fitness center. Outdoor facilities include tennis courts; an all-weather track; and baseball, football, soccer, and softball fields.

Monmouth students are accorded many special services, including the full resources of the First Year at Monmouth Office and the Center for Student Success, which offers academic advising and individual personal and career counseling. Academic skills services, including the Math Center, the Writing Center, and the Peer Tutoring Office, provide personalized academic assistance. Employment counseling is available through Career Services.

In addition to its undergraduate degree programs, Monmouth offers numerous graduate degree programs in business administration, computer science, corporate and public communication, criminal justice, education, English, financial mathematics, health-care management, history, liberal arts, mental health counseling, nursing, psychological counseling, public policy, social work, and software engineering. There are also graduate certificate programs in numerous areas of academic interest.

Location

The University is located in a residential area of an attractive community near the Atlantic Ocean, slightly more than a 1-hour drive from the metropolitan attractions of New York City and Philadelphia. The University's safe and secure 156-acre campus, considered to be one of the most beautiful in New Jersey, includes among its fifty-four buildings a harmonious blending of traditional and contemporary architectural styles.

The centerpiece building is Woodrow Wilson Hall, a National Historic Landmark that houses humanities classrooms and administrative offices. The Jules L. Plangere Jr. Center for Communication and Instructional Technology provides state-of-the-art facilities for students. Restaurants, shops, and theaters are within easy reach, and several large shopping malls and the PNC Bank Arts Center (an entertainment hub) are only a few miles away.

Another advantage is proximity to many high-technology firms, financial institutions, and a thriving business-industrial sector. These provide not only employment possibilities for graduates but also the opportunity for undergraduates to gain practical experience through various internships and the cooperative education program conducted by the University.

Majors and Degrees

Monmouth University offers thirty-one baccalaureate degree programs within six schools. The Leon Hess Business School awards bachelor's degrees in business administration with concentrations in accounting, economics, finance, management, marketing, and real estate. The School of Education awards bachelor's degrees that allow students to earn certification as elementary teachers, as P-3 with teacher of students with disabilities endorsement, as secondary teachers, or with K-12 endorsement. The Wayne D. McMurray School of Humanities and Social Sciences awards bachelor's degrees in the areas of anthropology, art, communication, criminal justice, English, fine arts, foreign language, graphic design, history, history/political science, music, political science, psychology, and theater. A Spanish and international business bachelor's degree is awarded jointly through the Leon Hess Business School and the School of Humanities and Social Sciences. The School of Science awards bachelor's degrees in biology, chemistry, clinical laboratory sciences, computer science, marine and environmental biology and policy, mathematics, medical technology, and software engineering. The School of Social Work awards the Bachelor of Social Work degree. The Marjorie K. Unterberg School of Nursing and Health Studies awards the Bachelor of Science in health studies and the Bachelor of Science in Nursing, the latter of which is available to upper-division transfer students. A preprofessional advising program is available for students who intend to pursue careers in medicine, dentistry, or other health-care fields. Monmouth also offers the Five-Year Baccalaureate/Master's Program, which enables students to achieve both a bachelor's and a master's degree in just five years in the areas of business, computer science, criminal justice, education, English, history, public policy, social work, or software engineering.

Academic Programs

The curriculum is attuned to today's globally oriented, technological society while retaining a strong grounding in the liberal arts. Under the general education curriculum, students in all degree programs acquire a breadth of knowledge beyond their major fields of study, including an appreciation of world culture. Monmouth University also emphasizes writing, speaking, and other interpersonal skills that are critical to personal and professional success. Monmouth requires all students to fulfill a technology literacy component and an experiential education component that is a real-world experience related to the student's academic major.

Monmouth University believes that in addition to providing sound preparation for successful careers, a major goal of higher education is to help students develop values. These include a keen sense of citizenship and social responsibility and the leadership qualities that equip graduates to contribute actively to the democratic society in which they live. Academic programs at Monmouth prepare students for life in an increasingly complex, multicultural world.

The Honors School at Monmouth University allows qualified students to participate in an educational environment that encourages and supports intellectual and personal excellence. Courses are clustered, with professors developing common themes and assignments. Honors classes are distinguished by in-depth coverage of material through discussion and writing, smaller class size, and a heightened student/faculty rapport. Extracurricular activities like cultural excursions to New York City are scheduled to reinforce the themes of the program.

Cooperative education is available to students, enabling them to gain practical experience in jobs related to their majors while completing their studies. All education majors are required to complete a semester of student teaching. The University also participates in the Washington Center, which is a partnership through which students may earn credit for experiential learning gained through internships and symposia in the nation's capital.

Genuine concern for the individual student characterizes the Monmouth University educational program. Professors—not teaching assistants—conduct all courses and supervise all laboratories. Students benefit from direct interaction with professors who are recognized for their scholarly expertise.

Academic Facilities

The Monmouth University Library holds approximately 260,000 volumes and more than 31,000 electronic and print journal subscriptions. Academic programs are amply supported by state-of-the-art computer hardware and software and classroom/laboratory facilities. The major components supporting Monmouth's academic programs include UNIX and Windows 2008 server systems connected by a sophisticated campus Ethernet network spanning twenty-three buildings and encompassing more than 2,400 workstations campuswide. Workstations that are specifically dedicated to student use are distributed among many instructional and open-use laboratories and include PC workstations and Macintosh workstations. Laptop plug-in ports and wireless connectivity are available throughout the campus. A campus communications network (HawkNet) connects all Monmouth University computing resources to the Internet. All students receive a computer account that provides them with e-mail, World Wide Web browsing and authoring tools, and electronic access to the Monmouth University Library catalog.

The Lauren K. Woods Theatre offers students an opportunity to experience all phases of the theater arts, from acting to lighting. Control of all aspects of a theatrical performance is maintained by students. The University supports communications facilities for both radio and television, a student-run FM radio station, a student-run greenhouse, and studios for art and music majors.

Costs

For 2009–10, tuition and fees were approximately $25,013 per year. Room and board costs were approximately $9554 per year; actual costs are determined by the type of room and meal plan selected. Costs are subject to change for 2010–11.

Financial Aid

Monmouth University believes that qualified students should not be denied an educational opportunity due to lack of financial resources. The financial aid staff counsels students and their families and assists them in obtaining the maximum financial aid to which they are entitled. In a cooperative effort, the University utilizes institutional, federal, and state resources and expects a reasonable family contribution toward the student's cost of attendance. In developing each student's award package, all resources available are utilized to address individual circumstances and to provide equitable treatment for all applicants.

A wide range of University scholarships and grants is offered to the incoming class each year. These scholarship and grant programs are available to all prospective full-time, first-year and transfer students and are offered without regard to financial need. Eligibility for University scholarship and grant funding varies according to the quality of the student's previous academic record. Award amounts range from $3000 to $16,500. Scholarships and grants are renewed at the same amount for each year of the student's undergraduate career, provided the student maintains satisfactory levels of academic performance. Scholarship recipients are required to maintain a minimum 3.0 cumulative GPA; academic excellence grant recipients must maintain a minimum 2.5 cumulative GPA; incentive grant recipients must maintain a minimum 2.0 cumulative GPA. The University also participates in all federal and state grant and loan programs. To establish eligibility for these programs and capitalize on the assistance available to them, students must complete the Free Application for Federal Student Aid (FAFSA) and are encouraged to do so as soon after January 1 as possible. Students and their families are invited to call 732-571-3463, send e-mail to finaid@monmouth.edu, or visit the Financial Aid Office for assistance.

Faculty

The University's professors are leaders in their fields and contribute through research, publishing, and consulting to their respective academic areas. There are 249 full-time and 326 part-time faculty members. Approximately 84 percent of the full-time instructional faculty members have doctorates or other terminal degrees in their fields. The average class size is 21, and the student-faculty ratio is 15:1. Professors often know each student by name, and faculty members are available to students for office consultation and extra help.

Student Government

Monmouth's Student Government Association is an important and necessary voice in the University community. Six senators from each class, 2 commuter senators, 4 senators-at-large, and members who have been installed by the executive leadership express clear and definite opinions and cast votes on University policy as it affects the student community. Senators actively meet with campus administrators and faculty members in an effort to present the opinions of the student body and take part in resolution-adopting events. The Student Government Association also hosts a number of events annually, including Homecoming; the SGA Giving Trees; the Big Event/Day of Community Service; Springfest; the SGA Auction to benefit Michael's Feat, a local charity; and the Student Awards Ceremony. All students are strongly encouraged to participate in these activities.

Admission Requirements

Many factors are considered when candidates are evaluated for admission. For freshman applicants, the committee evaluates grades and test scores. High school transcripts, a resume of activities including leadership positions held, and SAT or ACT scores are required. Counselor recommendations and other information supporting the application are welcome. Campus tours and information sessions with admission counselors are available. Transfer students must submit official transcripts from all colleges attended. If they have earned fewer than 24 transferable credits, they must fulfill freshman admission requirements as well.

Application and Information

The early action option is a non-binding option for students with a strong desire to enroll at Monmouth. The application deadline for early action is December 1. The admission decision notification date is January 15. The application deadline for regular decision is March 1. The admission decision notification date is prior to April 1. Applications received after March 1 are considered on a space-available basis. Freshman housing is guaranteed for students who submit the required enrollment deposit, housing deposit, and housing contract by May 1. Students who submit their deposits and housing contract after May 1 will be placed on a housing wait list.

For further information, students should contact:

Office of Undergraduate Admission
Monmouth University
400 Cedar Avenue
West Long Branch, New Jersey 07764-1898
Phone: 732-571-3456
800-543-9671 (toll-free)
Fax: 732-263-5166
E-mail: admission@monmouth.edu
Web site: http://www.monmouth.edu

MONTCLAIR STATE UNIVERSITY

MONTCLAIR, NEW JERSEY

The University

For over 100 years, students have come to Montclair State University to fulfill their potential and reach for their dreams. Montclair State University is a four-year comprehensive public university that offers a broad range of educational and cultural opportunities. The second largest university in New Jersey, Montclair State is comprised of the College of the Arts, the College of Education and Human Services, the College of Humanities and Social Sciences, the College of Science and Mathematics, the School of Business, and the Graduate School. The University offers 250 undergraduate majors, minors, and concentrations, and graduate programs in 100 fields of study.

Montclair State has been designated a Center of Excellence in the fine and performing arts in New Jersey. It is accredited by the Middle States Association of Colleges and Schools, and its teacher education, administrative, and school service personnel programs are approved by the National Council for Accreditation of Teacher Education. The School of Business is also accredited by AACSB International—The Association to Advance Collegiate Schools of Business.

The total enrollment was 18,171 in fall 2009, 14,139 of whom were enrolled as undergraduates. The University is focused on the overall development and the well-being of its students. Believing that small class environments are more conducive to learning, the student-faculty ratio is 17:1, with professors interacting personally with their students to help further the learning process.

There are 3,500 resident students living on campus. Special interest living communities enable residential students to live among people with whom they share interests. For example, the First Year Connections living community puts incoming freshmen together in a residence hall that has common areas where new students can meet and mingle. Whether it's the international living community—in a residence hall that has cooking facilities and is open all year to host international students—or living communities for arts students or students majoring in science and mathematics, Montclair State wants its students' residence experience to be enjoyable as they learn and build lifelong friendships.

The University's Center for Student Involvement provides clubs, organizations, activities, and events to meet the needs of all students, including intramural sports, Student Government Association, cultural organizations, religious organizations, service- and volunteer-based organizations, commuter association resources and services, diversity retreats, and Greek organizations.

With seventeen varsity sports for men and women, Montclair State University athletics has one of the most competitive programs around. To date, Montclair State has captured five NCAA Division III national championships and had over 260 of its athletes honored as all-Americans. Montclair State competes in the highest of Division III conferences, including the New Jersey Athletic Conference (NJAC), Eastern College Athletic Conference (ECAC), Skyline, and Knickerbocker conferences.

Location

Montclair State is situated on a beautiful 246-acre suburban campus only 14 miles west of New York City. There are two New Jersey Transit train stations right on campus that provide easy access to Penn Station in New York City. This proximity to the city gives students the opportunity to take advantage of the unusually rich cultural, social, and educational environment of the metropolitan area, while Montclair's suburban setting offers a nice contrast to city life. Convenient access to all major New Jersey highways makes day trips to nearby mountain resorts and ocean beaches an easy option.

Majors and Degrees

Montclair State offers programs of study leading to the Bachelor of Arts degree in anthropology, broadcasting, child advocacy, classics, communication studies, economics, English, family and child studies, fine arts, French, general humanities, geography, history, Italian, jurisprudence, justice and families, justice studies, Latin, linguistics, music, music therapy, philosophy, political science, psychology, religious studies, sociology, Spanish, theater studies, and women's and gender studies. The Bachelor of Science degree is offered in athletic training, biochemistry, biology, business administration, chemistry, computer science, geosciences, health education, information technology, mathematics, molecular biology, nutrition and food science, physical education, physics, and science informatics. The Bachelor of Fine Arts degree is awarded in dance, fine arts, and theater. The Bachelor of Music is awarded in music, and there is a five-year combined B.A./B.Mus. program. There is a four-year/five-year combined B.S./M.S. program in aquatic and coastal sciences, biology, chemistry, and mathematics. Combined Bachelor of Science/Doctor of Dental Medicine and Bachelor of Science/Doctor of Medicine degrees are also offered with the University of Medicine and Dentistry of New Jersey–New Jersey Dental School, and University of Medicine and Dentistry of New Jersey–New Jersey Medical School, respectively. Articulated programs in physical therapy and physician assistant studies with the University of Medicine and Dentistry of New Jersey are offered, as is an articulation leading to a Pharm.D. with Rutgers.

The Family and Child Studies major offers concentrations in child life specialist, early and middle childhood for elementary school certification K–5, and early childhood for preschool through third grade certification. In addition, teacher certification programs are offered in many of the subject areas mentioned for grades through 12.

Minors and interdisciplinary academic programs are available in many of the majors listed, as well as in areas such as African American studies; Arabic; art and design; Asian studies; archeology; cognitive science; criminal justice; environmental policy studies; film; gay, lesbian, bisexual, transgender, and queer studies; German; international studies; Jewish American studies; journalism; Latin American and Latino studies; microtonal music studies; musical theater; paralegal studies; prelaw studies; public administration; Portuguese; Russian; Russian area studies, and urban studies. Part-time bachelor's degree programs are available.

The University offers robust career services and community-based learning programs that help students discover their aptitudes and uncover future career possibilities.

Academic Programs

Successful completion of a minimum of 120 semester hours is necessary for graduation. Course requirements include general education (34–58 semester hours), comprising communication, humanities and the arts, pure and applied sciences, social and behavioral sciences, a physical education requirement, a multicultural awareness requirement, and courses in the major field of study (32–82 semester hours).

The academic calendar is organized into two semesters (fall and spring) and summer sessions.

Off-Campus Programs

Through the Cooperative Education Program, a student may receive academic credit for a full-time job and earn a full-time salary. This program gives a student the opportunity to receive on-the-job training in his or her prospective career area. Internships—work for credit, not pay—are available through many major departments.

Through programs offered by the New Jersey State College Council for International Education, the International Student Exchange Program, and the College Consortium for International Studies, students have the opportunity to study abroad in the continent of Australia and such countries as Argentina, Australia, Austria, Belgium, Brazil, Chile, China, Costa Rica, Czech Republic, Denmark, Dominican Republic, Egypt, England, France, Germany, India, Ireland, Italy, Japan, Mexico, Morocco, Norway, Peru, Russia, South Africa, South Korea, and Spain. In addition, foreign language majors may spend a year, a semester, or a summer in French-, German-, Italian-, or Spanish-speaking countries.

The University is a charter member of the New Jersey Marine Sciences Consortium, through which students may take field-oriented courses in the marine sciences. Montclair State University's School of Conservation, located in Stokes State Forest, is the largest university-operated environmental education center in the world. Through this facility, students may take courses relating to the environment in the humanities, social sciences, and natural and physical sciences and in outdoor pursuits.

Academic Facilities

University Hall is the largest and most sophisticated building in Montclair State University's history. It houses more than sixty instructional spaces for use by all of the University's colleges and schools, including one 200-seat and six 100-seat lecture halls, thirty-nine general classrooms, eleven specialized classrooms and laboratories, and a number of student study lounges and gathering spaces, including a Mission-style outdoor courtyard.

The south wing of University Hall provides a state-of-the-art home for the University's nationally recognized College of Education and Human Services, including the ADP Center for Teacher Preparation and Learning Technologies, the Center of Pedagogy, the Literacy Enrichment Center, the Institute for the Advancement of Philosophy for Children, and offices and conference rooms for the more than 150 faculty and staff members in the College of Education and Human Services.

Two floors of the north wing of the building are dedicated to the University's information technology services and house the University's Information Commons and Technology Solutions Center for students and faculty members. Located on the seventh floor of University Hall is the region's newest and most sophisticated conference center, with meeting, conference, and event space for groups of up to 500.

The holdings of the Harry A. Sprague Library include more than 430,000 monographs as well as materials in diverse formats such as DVDs, CDs, videocassettes, audiocassettes, and microforms. The library subscribes to over 70 online index/abstract databases that give access to over 30,000 online journals and magazines available through computers in the library, and on and off campus. The University also subscribes to over 2,000 serials (magazines, journals, newspapers, annuals, and yearbooks) in print format. It serves as a depository for United States and New Jersey government publications that are available in print, microform, CD-ROM, and online formats.

Café Diem, a sleek and modern 4,300-square-foot Internet café at Sprague Library, offers food, beverages, and wireless access to the Internet for students and staff members. The Library and Café Diem are open 24/7.

The state-of-the-art, 78,000-square-foot Student Recreation Center features a six-lane swimming pool; a two-court gymnasium with an elevated running track; two racquetball courts; fitness, strength, and cardio training areas; space for aerobics and other fitness activities; locker rooms; and a snack bar.

The completely renovated and vastly expanded Chapin Hall is the new home to the John J. Cali School of Music, the only university-based school of music in the state of New Jersey.

Costs

In 2009–10, full-time tuition and fees were assessed at a yearly rate of $9800 for New Jersey residents and $17,800 for out-of-state students. Approximate annual room and board for dormitory students were $10,100 (costs are subject to change).

Financial Aid

Four major types of financial aid programs are available at Montclair State: loans, grants, scholarships, and employment. Within each of these categories, funding may be available through federal, state, and/or institutional sources. State aid programs include Tuition Aid Grants, Educational Opportunity Fund Grants, Bloustein Distinguished Scholars, state-funded scholarships, and NJCLASS Loans. Federal sources of aid include Federal Pell Grants, Federal Supplemental Educational Opportunity Grants, the Federal Work-Study Program, Federal Stafford Student Loans, Federal PLUS Program loans, and programs for veterans. Over 70 percent of undergraduates receive financial aid. Students should contact the Financial Aid Office regarding application materials and deadline dates.

Faculty

Faculty members teach both graduate and undergraduate courses, with few departments employing graduate assistants. Approximately 94 percent of the faculty members hold doctorates or the appropriate terminal degree in their disciplines. A faculty-student ratio of 1:17 permits considerable interaction between students and professors. All faculty members have posted office hours in order to provide students with assistance in course material and in planning a program of study. In addition, faculty members participate actively in student-oriented activities, serve as advisers to student clubs, and conduct extracurricular workshops and field trips.

Student Government

The Student Government Association (SGA), a parent corporation that includes within its structure various class organizations and services for the student body, is composed of all undergraduates. The substantial budget of the SGA allows for the development and financing of student activities and services. The Student Government Association Legislature acts as the final representative for the entire undergraduate student body and is composed of elected representatives from each class and major curriculum.

Admission Requirements

Montclair State is an Equal Opportunity/Affirmative Action institution and does not discriminate on the basis of sex, race, color, national origin, age, or physical handicap in providing access to its benefits and services, in compliance with relevant federal and state legislation.

Montclair State University considers a number of factors during the admission process. These factors include the rigor of high school curriculum, the overall grade point average (GPA), standardized test scores, and additional factors that contribute to successful degree attainment. These standards are subject to change depending on the demand for programs and the number of students that can be accommodated.

In preparation for the academic rigor of Montclair State University, students should have followed a challenging high school curriculum. Freshman applicants are required to have completed the following high school courses with satisfactory grades: 4 units of English, 3 units of math (in the algebra, geometry, algebra II sequence), 2 units of the same foreign language, 2 units of lab sciences, 2 units of social sciences, and 3 units of academic electives (which may include additional units of math, languages, sciences or social sciences).

Montclair State University reviews each application individually; however, when considering an applicant for freshman admission, certain minimum standards are followed. Strong candidates for admission generally meet the following criteria: a GPA of 3.0 or greater in the required curriculum, a combined SAT score of 1425 (math, critical reading, and writing), or ACT composite score of 20.

Application and Information

Applicants must submit a completed application form, a nonrefundable application fee, a copy of their official high school transcript, and copies of their SAT or ACT scores. Admission decisions are announced on a rolling basis until all spaces are filled.

For application forms and additional admission information, students should contact:

Office of Undergraduate Admissions
Montclair State University
1 Normal Avenue
Montclair, New Jersey 07043-1624
Phone: 973-655-4444
E-mail: undergraduate.admissions@montclair.edu
Web site: http://www.montclair.edu

COLLEGE CLOSE-UPS

MOORE COLLEGE OF ART & DESIGN

PHILADELPHIA, PENNSYLVANIA

The College

Moore College of Art & Design sets the standard of excellence in educating women for careers in the visual arts. It is the only women's college for the visual arts in the nation, and students enjoy Moore's accessible, supportive, small-college community and are taught by a dedicated faculty of award-winning artists, designers, and scholars.

Moore offers nine Bachelor of Fine Arts (B.F.A.) degree majors, emphasizing career and leadership throughout the academic programs. Each major provides strong career preparation for its field and requires internships that are funded through internship fellowships for all students. The Locks Career Center also provides extensive career resources for students and alumnae, including internship support, one-on-one career counseling, mentoring, job bulletins, and workshops on topics ranging from networking to resume writing.

On-campus leadership organizations provide the opportunity to learn about and utilize leadership skills and to develop self-confidence. Leadership fellowships provide financial support for students to work either with an individual leader in the arts community or within an innovative organization. Other experiences are available through community service or study abroad.

Approximately 65 percent of first-year students live in College housing, which includes Louise Zimmerman Stahl Residence Hall and Sartain Hall. Some students choose to rent apartments near the campus or in one of Philadelphia's many residential neighborhoods.

Moore alumnae are accomplished artists and designers who use their creativity, skills, and talent to excel in a wide variety of industries. Among Moore's notable graduates are fashion designer and business icon, Adrienne Vittadini; renowned twentieth-century portraitist, Alice Neel; award-winning interior designer, Karen Daroff; and Pulitzer Prize-winning photojournalist, Sharon J. Wohlmuth.

Moore is accredited by the Commission on Higher Education of the Middle States Association of Colleges and Schools (3624 Market Street, Philadelphia, Pennsylvania 19104-2680, phone: 215-662-5606). The Commission on Higher Education is an institutional accrediting agency recognized by the U.S. Secretary of Education and the Commission on Recognition of Postsecondary Accreditation; by the National Association of Schools of Art and Design (11250 Roger Bacon Drive, Suite 21, Reston, Virginia 20190, phone: 703-437-0700); by the Commonwealth of Pennsylvania, Department of Education (333 Market Street, Harrisburg, Pennsylvania 17126-0333, phone: 717-787-5820); and by the Council for Interior Design Accreditation (formerly FIDER) (146 Monroe Center NW, #1318, Grand Rapids, Michigan 49503-2822, phone: 616-458-0400).

Location

Moore is ideally located on the Benjamin Franklin Parkway in the scenic Museums District of Center City, Philadelphia. Neighbors on The Parkway include the Philadelphia Museum of Art, the Rodin Museum, the Academy of Natural Sciences, the Franklin Institute, and the Free Library of Philadelphia. The Parkway is also the future site of the new Barnes Foundation, which has one of the largest collections of impressionist and post-impressionist art in the world.

Philadelphia is also the home of Independence National Historical Park and to dozens of art galleries, diverse neighborhoods, and shops and restaurants of every variety. This artistic and cultural vitality provides Moore students with a multitude of resources and recreation in a stimulating urban setting. Nearly eighty nearby colleges and universities form one of the largest higher-education communities in the nation, second only to New York City.

Philadelphia is 100 miles south of New York City and 133 miles north of Washington, D.C., a short journey by car, bus, or train. Faculty members regularly organize classroom trips to take advantage of these cities' additional galleries, museums, and designer showrooms.

Majors and Degrees

Moore College of Art & Design offers a four-year program leading to a Bachelor of Fine Arts degree, with majors in art education, art history, curatorial studies, fashion design, fine arts (with 2-D and/or 3-D emphasis), graphic design, illustration, interior design, and photography and digital arts. Students can minor in business and any major offered except art education.

In all majors, students are required to participate in an internship to acquire practical experience in their chosen field. In addition to Bachelor of Fine Arts degree programs, Moore also offers postbaccalaureate certificate in art education.

Three coeducational graduate programs include an M.F.A. in studio art, M.A. in art education with an emphasis in special populations, and an M.F.A. in interior design for students with an undergraduate degree in a field other than interior design. Moore's graduate programs are summer-intensive, low-residency programs designed for working adults.

Academic Programs

The College operates on a two-semester academic year. In B.F.A. programs, approximately two thirds of the required credits are in studio courses. One third of the credits are in academic courses.

A student's first year includes a broadly based core of studies in art history, two- and three-dimensional basic design, color, drawing, computer applications, figure drawing, and the humanities. Introductory courses to the fine and design arts are also offered.

Tutorial support is available for all students. At the end of the first semester of their first year, the student declares her major.

While instruction in the core studies is highly directive, advanced studio courses require more initiative and self-discipline, because the College provides each student with an increasingly personal program of study and assistance. Seniors in both the fine arts and design arts acquire practical experience in their fields through internships, apprenticeships, and the College's cooperative education program.

The College participates in the Association of Independent Colleges of Art and Design (AICAD) Student Mobility Exchange Program. A student who meets eligibility requirements may apply for one semester's study at an AICAD member school's program.

In addition to Bachelor of Fine Arts programs, Moore also offers leading continuing education (CE) programs. Moore's adult CE courses for men and women, offered mainly in the evening and on weekends, include certificate programs in digital media and decorative arts for interiors. The 86-year-old Young Artists Workshop (YAW) provides art education opportunities for girls and boys in grades 1–12. The Summer Fine Arts Institute is a four-week summer residency program that offers high school–age women a program that earns 3 college credits. For CE information, students should call 215-965-4030 or contact CE via e-mail at ce@moore.edu.

Academic Facilities

The main campus is a complex of interconnected buildings that includes Wilson Hall, Sarah Peter Hall, and the Stahl Residence Hall. Sartain Residence Hall is located two blocks from the main campus.

Main campus includes expansive studios and classrooms, technology centers, MAC and PC computer labs, a professional woodshop, ferrous and nonferrous metal workshops, ceramic studios with indoor and outdoor kilns, abundant student exhibition space, two contemporary art galleries, several outdoor courtyards and student lounges, a sculpture park, The Art Shop, a dining café, and two auditoriums.

The Connolly Library's extensive holdings include 40,000 volumes reflecting subjects in the curriculum, artists' books, rare design folios, a slide collection of more than 123,000 images, reference materials, exhibition catalogs and annuals, and subscriptions to 185 local, national, and international periodicals.

The Galleries at Moore are internationally known and present a wide range of exhibitions and educational programs of both established and emerging artists. The Paley Gallery exhibits challenging and innovative work by national and international artists, while the Levy Gallery displays artists from the Philadelphia area. The galleries also provide a professional exhibition space for shows by Moore students, faculty members, and alumnae.

In addition, Moore has two galleries showing student, alumnae, and faculty work at Philadelphia's landmark Kimmel Center for the Performing Arts as well as exhibition space in the CBS 3 and CW Philly offices.

Costs

Tuition and fees for 2009–10 were $28,140. Room and board for students living in College residence halls were $10,930. Books, supplies, and personal expenses (excluding transportation) are estimated to be approximately $3500 per year for most students.

Financial Aid

Moore offers financial aid based on financial need as established by information provided on the Free Application for Federal Student Aid (FAFSA).

The principal forms of financial aid are Federal Pell Grants, Federal Supplemental Educational Opportunity Grants, Federal Perkins Loans, and Moore College of Art & Design scholarships and grants. Assistance is also available through the Federal Work-Study program. For full consideration, students are encouraged to apply for financial aid by March 1.

Moore College annually grants $3.5 million in scholarship aid to students who demonstrate excellence both academically and artistically. Awards are granted based on the portfolio review and academic merit.

Faculty

Moore College of Art & Design has 121 undergraduate faculty members, 24 in academic, and 97 in studio areas. All studio classes are taught by practicing professionals. The student-faculty ratio is approximately 9:1.

Student Government

On-campus leadership organizations provide the chance to learn about and utilize leadership skills and to develop self-confidence participating in groups such as Student Government, Student Mentors, Residence Life Staff, and the Student Judiciary Committee. Students are trained in areas such as teambuilding, presentation skills, ethics, diversity, time management, and creating community on campus.

Admission Requirements

The admission decision is based on an evaluation of the following required materials: transcripts from high schools and any colleges attended, SAT or ACT scores, and a portfolio of between twelve and twenty pieces of original artwork. (International students may submit TOEFL or IELTS scores instead of SAT or ACT scores.) First-year students may enter in the fall and spring semesters.

Transfer students are encouraged to apply for advanced class standing at Moore. Class standing is determined based on acceptable transfer credits and an evaluation of the applicant's portfolio. All transfers who are applying for advanced standing must submit their portfolio in slide or digital form, accompanied by a detailed description letter. Upper-level transfer students may enter in the fall or spring semester.

Application and Information

Although Moore has a rolling admissions policy and therefore no application deadline, students seeking admission in the fall semester are encouraged to submit applications to the Admissions Office by March 1. For application forms, catalogs, and additional information, students should contact:

Office of Admissions
Moore College of Art & Design
20th Street and The Parkway
Philadelphia, Pennsylvania 19103-1179
Phone: 215-965-4015
800-523-2025 (toll-free)
Fax: 215-568-3547
E-mail: enroll@moore.edu
Web site: http://www.moore.edu

Moore College of Art & Design sets the standard for educating women for careers in the visual arts as the first and only art college for women in the United States.

COLLEGE CLOSE-UPS

MORNINGSIDE COLLEGE

SIOUX CITY, IOWA

The College

The Morningside College experience cultivates a passion for lifelong learning and a dedication to ethical leadership and civic responsibility. For more than 115 years, the goal of Morningside College has been to provide students with an education of the highest quality. Morningside is rooted in a strong church-related, liberal arts tradition, and its challenge is to prepare students to be flexible in thought, open in attitude, and confident in themselves.

Founded in 1894, Morningside College is a private, four-year, coeducational, liberal arts institution affiliated with the United Methodist Church. The College seeks both students and faculty members representing diverse social, cultural, ethnic, racial, and national backgrounds.

At the graduate level, Morningside confers a Master of Arts in Teaching, with professional educator or special education tracks.

Morningside College's 1,200 full-time undergraduate students are encouraged to participate in a wide variety of activities, including departmental, professional, and religious organizations; honor societies; and sororities and fraternities. A newspaper, literary magazine, and campus radio station are all student directed. These activities provide students with many opportunities to develop leadership, interpersonal, and social skills. Since nearly all activities on campus are student initiated and student directed, ample opportunities for leadership development exist. Music recitals and concerts, theater productions, and an academic and cultural arts and lecture series are held each semester. Intercollegiate athletics are available for men in baseball, basketball, cross-country, football, golf, soccer, swimming, tennis, track and field, and wrestling and for women in basketball, cross-country, golf, soccer, softball, swimming, tennis, track, and volleyball. A variety of intramural activities are available.

The Hindman-Hobbs Center includes a pool, saunas, racquetball courts, a weight room, basketball courts, a wrestling room, and a jogging track as well as classroom facilities and offices.

Location

Morningside College is located on a 68-acre campus in Sioux City, the fourth-largest city in Iowa. The campus is based in a residential section of the community, adjacent to a city park, swimming pool, and tennis courts and within 5 minutes of a major regional shopping mall and a new shopping center. The Sioux City metropolitan area offers a blend of urban shopping, commerce, and recreation in a scenic setting. Students find Morningside's Sioux City location to be advantageous in seeking internship opportunities and full- or part-time employment.

Majors and Degrees

The five undergraduate degrees conferred by Morningside College are the Bachelor of Arts, Bachelor of Science, Bachelor of Science in Nursing, Bachelor of Music, and Bachelor of Music Education. Career programs consist of accounting, advertising, art, biology, business administration, chemistry, computer science, corporate communications, elementary education, engineering physics, English, graphic arts, history, interdisciplinary studies, marketing, mass communications, mathematics, music, nursing, philosophy, photography, political science, psychology, religious studies, Spanish, special education, and theater. Students choosing to teach in secondary school may be certified in most academic majors.

In cooperation with other institutions, Morningside offers preprofessional programs in dentistry, engineering, law, medical technology, medicine, the ministry, optometry, pharmacy, physical therapy, physician assistant studies, and veterinary medicine.

Academic Programs

Morningside operates on a two-semester system; sessions are held from late August to December and from January to early May. Evening classes are offered each semester. A three-week May Term and a six-week summer session are also available.

The Morningside College experience provides an education that develops the whole person through an emphasis on critical thinking, effective communication, cultural understanding, practical wisdom, spiritual discernment, and ethical action. By working with talented faculty members in a large number of majors, caring college staff members who provide numerous opportunities for valuable cocurricular experiences, and other exceptional and interesting students with whom they will form lifelong connections, Morningside students gain the knowledge, skills, and personal dispositions that will ensure their success.

Special opportunities include a voluntary Interdepartmental Honors Program, in which students meet weekly to discuss ideas that have shaped history from the ancient world into the future. Friday Is Writing Day, offered in a weekly discussion format, allows students and faculty members to read aloud and react to one another's writing.

Every entering full-time student is provided with a notebook computer that is used in classroom work. Student technology services include high-speed Internet connection, ports in all residence halls and classrooms, Web-accessible personal e-mail accounts, a digital library accessible day and night, specialized computer labs to support academic programs, and wireless network access points across campus.

Off-Campus Programs

Morningside students who qualify have the opportunity to take advantage of special programs for off-campus study. Programs are available for a semester or the entire school year. The College has agreements with schools in England, Japan, and Northern Ireland.

Students participate in exchange programs with Kansai Gaidai University in Japan; Queen's University, the University of Ulster, Belfast Institute for Further and Higher Education, Stranmillis University College, and St. Mary's University College in Northern Ireland; and Edge Hill University and the Centre for Medieval and Renaissance Studies in England.

In addition, Morningside has opportunities for students to enroll for a semester at American University in Washington, D.C., to study the U.S. government in action. Students may also be nominated for a semester at Drew University in New Jersey to study the United Nations. Students who participate in these programs maintain their enrollment at Morningside College.

Academic Facilities

The Hickman-Johnson-Furrow Learning Center is the home of the library and the Academic Support Services Center. The library has more than 99,000 volumes, nearly 3,000 audio recordings and video materials, and nearly 440 current print periodical subscriptions. Online accessibility includes student/faculty access to more than 18,000 full-text journals. The library's Web-based, integrated online system allows seamless access to numerous subscription databases as well as other online catalogs and Web sites. The library building also houses the Spoonholder Café, classrooms, the Mass Communication Department, and a computer lab.

Charles City College Hall is listed individually on the National Register of Historic Places and houses classrooms and offices for the History and Political Science, Philosophy, Religious Studies, and Theatre Departments.

The Eugene C. Eppley Fine Arts Building is one of the finest music and art facilities in the Midwest. The auditorium seats 1,400 and is noted for its acoustical qualities and the majestic Sanford Memorial Organ. The MacCollin Classroom Building, adjoining the auditorium, houses offices, art studios, practice rooms, and classrooms for music and art students.

The Helen Levitt Art Gallery adjoins the Eppley Auditorium and is home to the Levitt art collection, which includes work by internationally famous artists.

Lewis Hall, the second-oldest building on campus, is the site of the Education, English, Modern Languages, and Nursing Departments as well as administrative offices and Student Services.

The Robert M. Lincoln Center houses the College's division of business administration and economics and contains a library, auditorium, a conference room, several classrooms, and the newly remodeled Center for Entrepreneurship Education.

The James and Sharon Walker Science Center, completely renovated in 2001, features up-to-date laboratories and classrooms and houses offices for the Natural Sciences and Mathematics Division.

Costs

Tuition and fees for 2009–10 were $22,020, and room and board were $6740. These figures do not include books and personal expenses.

Financial Aid

In 2008–09, more than $27.6 million was awarded in financial aid to Morningside students, with an average financial aid package of $22,800. The financial aid resources of federal, state, and College programs are available to Morningside students through a combination of scholarships, grants, loans, and work-study employment. Morningside values students who achieve both in and out of the classroom—people who are thinkers and doers. Morningside Celebration of Excellence Scholarships recognize academic excellence and outstanding service, and awards of up to $10,000 per year are renewable for four years. Morningside also values its ties with alumni and the United Methodist Church, and those awards are also renewable for four years.

Students are encouraged to submit the Free Application for Federal Student Aid (FAFSA) as early as possible. The College's code number is 001879. The annual priority deadline for need-based financial aid is March 1.

Faculty

Seventy-one percent of Morningside College's 70 full-time faculty members have earned the terminal degree in their chosen field. The College also employs 103 part-time instructors and has a 17:1 student-faculty ratio.

Student Government

Student government is directly responsible for regulation, supervision, and coordination of student campus activities. The president of the student body is a voting member of the Board of Directors, allowing for student input in decisions facing the Board.

Admission Requirements

Morningside College selects students for admission whose scholastic achievement and personal abilities provide a foundation for success at the college level. While the College seeks students who rank in the upper half of their graduating class, each application is considered on an individual basis. The student's academic record, class rank, and test scores are considered. Transfer students must have earned 24 transferable semester hours of a 2.25 or better cumulative GPA on previous college work to qualify for automatic admission. It is the policy and practice of Morningside College to not discriminate against persons on the basis of age, sex, religion, creed, race, color, national or ethnic origin, sexual orientation, or physical or mental disability.

Application and Information

Rolling admission allows for flexibility; however, prospective students are encouraged to apply as early as possible before the semester in which they wish to enroll. Transfer and international students are welcome. Catalogs, application forms, and financial aid forms are available from the Office of Admissions.

For further information, students should contact:

Office of Admissions
Morningside College
1501 Morningside Avenue
Sioux City, Iowa 51106
Phone: 712-274-5111
800-831-0806 (toll-free)
E-mail: mscadm@morningside.edu
Web site: http://www.morningside.edu

Morningside College students enjoy small class sizes and one of the most attractive campuses in the Midwest.

MOUNTAIN STATE UNIVERSITY

BECKLEY, WEST VIRGINIA

COLLEGE CLOSE-UPS

The University

Mountain State University (MSU) is a private not-for-profit university whose main campus is located in the scenic highlands of southern West Virginia. MSU is dedicated to providing students with an outstanding professionally oriented education in a relaxed environment that promotes academic excellence. With six campuses, dozens of educational sites, and distance learning options, Mountain State University serves more than 8,000 students a year from across the United States and around the world with degree programs offered at the associate, bachelor's, and graduate levels. It is accredited by the Higher Learning Commission of the North Central Association of Colleges and Schools (phone: 312-263-0456; Web site: http://www.ncahigherlearningcommission.org).

The School of Arts and Sciences offers degrees in a wide range of professional fields, including criminal justice, forensic investigation, and psychology. It also offers degrees in general studies and liberal studies.

The School of Business and Technology prepares students for careers in traditional areas of business administration and accounting and in specialized fields, including computer science and information technology, culinary arts, legal studies, office administration, and paralegal studies. These programs help students develop the managerial and technical skills they need to identify and respond to complex challenges in business.

The Patsy H. Haslam School of Health Sciences prepares students for a wide range of health-care professions, including nursing, occupational therapy assistant studies, physical therapist assistant studies, and health studies. A prerequisite physician assistant studies curriculum prepares undergraduate students for the University's entry-level master's program. These health sciences programs prepare students to apply for certifications and licensures required for clinical practice and qualify them to pursue more advanced degrees in their specific field or a related discipline. The social work program is also housed within this school.

The School of Leadership and Professional Development offers a bachelor's degree completion program in organizational leadership, a master's degree program in strategic leadership, and a doctoral program in executive leadership. All three are available in a format that requires one evening a week in a classroom or online meeting, with individual assignments and group projects between meetings. Optional undergraduate concentrations in criminal justice leadership and hospitality leadership are available.

At the graduate level, MSU offers degree programs in criminal justice administration, health science, interdisciplinary studies, nursing, physician assistant studies, and psychology in addition to the previously discussed leadership programs. Some graduate programs provide for flexible study and distance learning with no residency requirement.

Student services include orientation, academic advising, tutoring, and a testing center. A variety of student organizations and activities are based on campus, and a student union is centrally located on campus.

All Mountain State University students receive a complimentary membership to the Beckley–Raleigh County YMCA, located within easy walking distance of the campus, which provides an indoor pool and track, racquetball and basketball courts, a newly renovated fitness center with Nautilus equipment, and a variety of classes, including spinning and Pilates. In intercollegiate competition, the men's basketball team regularly appears in NAIA Division I tournament play and won the 2004 national championship. MSU's other intercollegiate teams—men's and women's soccer, track and field, and cross-country, as well as women's volleyball—compete in NAIA Division II.

Hogan Hall, a 192-bed residence hall, provides two-bedroom suites and apartment-style living in a central campus location. Accommodations include high-speed Internet connections, lounges, study rooms, and laundry facilities. Meal plans are available for students to take advantage of campus dining facilities, including the primary dining hall, which was completely renovated in 2009.

Location

Mountain State University's main campus is located in Beckley, West Virginia, a small metropolitan area in the heart of the southern West Virginia highlands. The campus is within walking distance of downtown restaurants, retail stores, and services. Beckley is about an hour away by car from the state capital of Charleston; most major cities in the eastern United States are within a day's drive.

City, state, and national parks provide breathtaking panoramas as well as perfect settings for outdoor activities that range from mountain biking and rock climbing to hiking, picnicking, and swimming. In season, outdoor enthusiasts enjoy white-water rafting on the famed Gauley and New Rivers or hit the slopes of nearby ski areas. All are within a 20-minute drive of the campus.

Selected degree programs and courses are available through MSU's branch campuses, located in Center Township, Pennsylvania; Martinsburg, West Virginia; Mooresville, North Carolina; Orlando, Florida; and Washington, D.C. Selected programs and courses are also available in Hickory, North Carolina; at educational sites throughout West Virginia; and through online study and other distance learning options.

Majors and Degrees

Bachelor's and associate degrees are offered in accounting; allied health imaging; aviation; biology; business administration (concentrations in finance, health care management, hospitality, human resource management, management, and marketing); business studies; computer science; criminal justice (concentrations in corrections management, homeland security, and police science); culinary arts; diagnostic medical sonography; elementary and secondary teacher preparation; emergency medical services; environmental studies; fire science; forensic investigation; general engineering; general studies; graphic design; health science; health science education; health studies; human resource management; information technology; information technology/Web site design; legal studies; legal studies/paralegal; legal studies /prelaw; liberal studies; medical assisting; mining and environmental engineering; nursing; occupational therapy assistant studies; office administration (medical and secretarial concentrations); organizational leadership (optional concentrations in criminal justice leadership and hospitality leadership); physical therapist assistant studies; psychology; psychology of early childhood development; radiologic technology; religious studies; social work; and wildlife management.

Academic Programs

To earn a bachelor's degree, students must complete a minimum of 120 semester hours, including 36 hours of general studies, and meet all program requirements. Degree requirements vary on some branch campuses in compliance with state regulations. Many programs include an internship or practicum that provides hands-on experience and employment credentials.

Students in associate degree programs must complete a minimum of 64 hours, including 24 hours of general studies, and meet all program requirements.

MSU grants credit for nontraditional course work and demonstrated college-level learning. Students gain credit through transfer; proficiency examinations, including the College-Level Examination Program (CLEP) and Advanced Placement exams; demonstration of prior experiential learning; and online and individualized study. Degree completion programs allow adult students who have already earned at least 40 credit hours to earn a bachelor's degree in an adult-friendly format in the classroom or online, and the Spectrum option for integrated general education, as well as an online general education option, allows students to complete general education requirements conveniently.

Academic Facilities

Mountain State University's rapidly growing main campus currently encompasses ten main structures and four smaller buildings. The newest, Wisemen Hall, opened in fall 2007 and houses health sciences classrooms and lab space in addition to the University's testing center.

Academic facilities housed within the University's Robert C. Byrd Learning Resource Center, or LRC, include a library and media center. The library has holdings of more than 95,500 titles and networked access to more than one million titles. The core collection is supported by an online catalog and supplemented by electronic resources that include ProQuest, Cumulative Index to Nursing and Allied Health Literature (CINAHL), Social Issues Resources Index (SIRS), EBSCOhost, Westlaw, Wilson Web, NewsBank, and MEDLINE.

Computer stations include current software and broadband Internet access. Specialized learning resources include multimedia classrooms, a video lab, computer-assisted instruction, and science laboratories.

Costs

Mountain State University provides the educational advantages of a private institution at a financially accessible cost. Full-time tuition and fees for the 2009–10 academic year were $8700, or $290 for each credit hour. Tuition varies for some programs, and additional laboratory and clinical fees are sometimes required.

Financial Aid

Eligible students receive Federal Pell Grants, Federal Supplemental Educational Opportunity Grants, state grants, Federal Work-Study, and Federal Stafford Student Loans. Students must submit the Free Application for Federal Student Aid (FAFSA) for determination of eligibility. A number of scholarships based on academic merit and/or financial need are available to students. Available state loan programs vary for branch campus students outside West Virginia.

Faculty

More than 450 full- and part-time faculty members provide students with personalized, high-quality instruction.

Student Government

The Student Government Association (SGA) links students with the University's administration and faculty. Governed by student-elected officers, the SGA works to improve the quality of student life, develops leadership skills in students, and provides representation of student views and opinions on University issues.

Admission Requirements

The University's overall admissions policy is open, although some programs have more competitive requirements. Prospective students who have graduated from an accredited high school or received a General Educational Development (GED) certificate are eligible to apply. Applications are welcome from all qualified students regardless of age, sex, religion, race, color, creed, national origin, or disability.

Application and Information

Students apply for undergraduate admission by submitting an application; an official high school transcript, home schooling document, or GED certificate; and a housing application or exemption form with the $25 application fee. Transfer applicants must also submit official transcripts for previous college-level course work. Applications are accepted on a rolling basis, and applicants are notified of their acceptance status as soon as the application process is completed. ACT or SAT scores are not required for University admission but are recommended for placement purposes. Competitive programs or courses may have minimum ACT or SAT scores, placement tests, recommended application dates, or other requirements. Additional processes and an application fee of $50 are required for international applicants.

Mountain State University encourages prospective students and their families to arrange a campus visit. Campus tours and individual meetings are available.

For an application or more information, students should contact:

Mountain State University Information Center
Box 9003
Beckley, West Virginia 25802-9003
Phone: 304-929-INFO (4636)
866-FOR-MSU1 (866-766-6067) (toll-free)
Web site: http://www.mountainstate.edu

MOUNT ALOYSIUS COLLEGE

CRESSON, PENNSYLVANIA

The College

Mount Aloysius College is a private, comprehensive, Catholic liberal arts college sponsored by the Sisters of Mercy. Established in 1853, the College today specializes in both undergraduate and graduate education. Since the founding of the College, more than 12,000 students have become proud Mount Aloysius College graduates. The College is committed to providing a small classroom size and a highly structured environment. Mount Aloysius College students come from the commonwealth of Pennsylvania, but many other states are represented on campus, including Connecticut, Delaware, Maine, Maryland, Missouri, New Jersey, New York, Vermont, Virginia, and West Virginia. Approximately 65 percent of the College's students are women. There are approximately 2,000 students enrolled (unduplicated headcount).

Mount Aloysius College is one of sixteen Mercy Colleges nationwide. As part of the Mercy College curriculum, students are encouraged to evaluate ethical issues and form a sound character consistent with traditional, Judeo-Christian values. Social growth is seen as a vital element of a complete liberal arts education, encompassing the important ability to relate closely to people.

The College recognizes that student activities play a distinctive role in the total campus educational program. There are approximately 100 organized clubs, groups, honor societies, and intramural sports programs, including a newspaper, residence hall associations, student government, cheerleading, dance team, scholarship-funded theater and choir programs, and a student activities planning board. Student activities include many social events, intramural sports programs, NCAA Division III athletic events, comedians, cultural and educational events, campus forums, and lectures by guest speakers.

Mount Aloysius College is a member of NCAA Division III. The following athletic programs are available to both women and men: basketball, cross-country, golf, soccer, and tennis. Men's baseball and women's softball and volleyball are also offered. Both intercollegiate and intramural athletes benefit from the Ray S. and Louise S. Walker Athletic Field Complex, which includes a softball field, one of the finest soccer fields in the area, and the Calandra-Smith baseball field.

Many buildings make up the 193-acre campus. The main building is a picturesque structure dating to 1897; it houses the admissions, financial aid, security, health, and academic offices, along with the Office of the President, classrooms, telenursing research facilities, and the Wolf-Kuhn art gallery. Cosgrave Center is the main hub on campus, serving as the Student Union. The building contains the dining hall, snack bar, bookstore, child-care center (part of the elementary education/early childhood program at the College), lounges, recreational rooms, student affairs offices, and meeting rooms. The College's Health and Physical Fitness Center is adjacent to Cosgrave Center. Its main athletic arena has a seating capacity of approximately 2,000 and serves as the home to all Mounties fans. The facility provides space for three basketball courts, three volleyball courts, a tennis court, a weight and exercise room equipped with a sauna, two locker rooms, office areas, changing rooms for sports officials, public restrooms, a lobby, and a vestibule. Ihmsen Halls are key housing facilities for residential students. Misciagna Residence is a state-of-the-art residence hall, providing twenty-five suites and private bathrooms. Opened in fall 2009, McAuley Hall features both double and single rooms, a large multipurpose room, and study lounges on each of its three floors. Alumni Hall is a historic, multipurpose room that is used for College drama, musicals, and many performing arts events. This hall is scheduled for renovation during the fall 2010 semester, with performances slated to resume there in spring 2011. The College operates twelve months per year and opens its facilities to the outside community as well.

The campus offers 100 percent wireless Internet access for laptops and PDAs. Wireless access points are installed in all buildings throughout the campus. In addition, several smart classrooms are located around campus.

Mount Aloysius is a comprehensive college that is fully accredited by the Middle States Association of Colleges and Schools and approved by the Pennsylvania Department of Education. All nursing programs and health studies programs are fully accredited by their professional accrediting bodies, including the National League for Nursing Accrediting Commission, the Commission on Accreditation in Physical Therapy Education, the American Association of Medical Assistants, and the Joint Commission on Accreditation for Programs of Surgical Technology.

In addition to its undergraduate programs, Mount Aloysius offers master's degrees in business administration, community counseling, criminal justice management in correctional administration, education, and psychology.

Location

Mount Aloysius College is located in the scenic southern Allegheny Mountains of west-central Pennsylvania, in the small town of Cresson, which is adjacent to U.S. Route 22. The College's setting is rural, with two midsized cities, Altoona and Johnstown, within a very short distance. The area has warm, beautiful summers; brisk, breathtaking autumns; invigorating, snowy winters; and cool, blooming springs. Facilities in the area are available for outdoor activities, including biking, golfing, swimming, horseback riding, waterskiing and water activities, hiking, spelunking, picnicking, and amusement and water parks.

Majors and Degrees

Mount Aloysius College awards bachelor's and associate degrees in the arts, sciences, and health studies fields in both career-oriented and traditional liberal arts programs. Baccalaureate degrees are available in accounting, behavioral and social science, biology and general science, business administration, computer science, criminology, elementary/early childhood education and secondary education (with certifications), English, general science, history/political science, humanities, information technology, math/science, medical imaging, nursing (RN-B.S.N. program), nursing (2+2), occupational therapy (3-2), physical therapy (4-2), physician assistant studies (3-2), prelaw, psychology, sign language/interpreter education, and undecided/exploratory. Associate degrees are offered in applied technology, business administration, criminology, early childhood studies, general studies, legal studies, liberal arts, medical assistant studies, nursing, nursing (LPN to RN), physical therapist assistant studies, prenursing, radiography/medical imaging, sign language/deaf studies, and surgical technology.

Academic Programs

Whether preparing students for careers upon graduation or for graduate school, Mount Aloysius recognizes the importance of a broad and liberal education. Thus, in addition to receiving solid preparation for a chosen career, every student at the College receives a foundation in the arts, sciences, and humanities through an outstanding core curriculum. Strong emphasis is placed on the specialized courses within each program of study, and many academic programs combine classroom experience with internships and related training at area clinical sites, agencies, and institutions. In addition to its regular academic programs, Mount Aloysius offers independent and directed study with a commitment to service, which is a key ingredient in a Mercy education. The College has an excellent honors program and academic services area. The academic calendar has two traditional semesters and two or three optional summer sessions.

Off-Campus Programs

An important feature of many academic programs is off-campus training. The majority of the College's programs of study require credit-yielding practicums, through which students work and receive training at local and regional hospitals, public and private schools, or health or human service agencies. Students in all health programs participate in required on-the-job training during their time at the College.

Academic Facilities

In 1995, Mount Aloysius College opened both a new library and a new era, signifying greater access to information for the College community. This state-of-the-art facility is the campus hub for technology and studying. With a Buhl Electronic Classroom and more than 80,000 print and nonprint titles, the library is an impressive, 31,000-square-foot facility with ample seating space, four group-study rooms, a reading lounge, a law library and classroom, an unparalleled 18,000-volume ecumenical collection that was donated by Pastor Gerald Myers, and additional room for future expansion. This facility is completely automated, with an online catalog and access to remote libraries and the World Wide Web at more than thirty public workstations. Also located in the library is the Information Technology Center, home to fifteen multimedia computer workstations and some of the latest offerings in educational software.

Pierce Hall serves as the science center on campus and is a state-of-the-art, 31,000-square-foot facility that was completed in 1997 and houses all science laboratories, health science centers, and offices of faculty members in the health studies programs. Academic Hall is an impressive facility that is home to the College Honors Program. It also has classrooms, labs, seminar rooms, faculty offices, and electronic rooms. The College is proud of its bridge to the past and its progress in providing twenty-first-century buildings.

Costs

Annual tuition and fees for the 2009–10 academic year for full-time students were $16,580, and room and board were $7260.

Financial Aid

Mount Aloysius recognizes the expense involved in acquiring a liberal arts education and encourages all students to apply for all available aid. Through the Office of Financial Aid, the College assists students in applying for state and federal grants, loans, work-study awards, and College merit scholarships and grants. The College awards academic monies based on GPA and SAT or ACT scores; these awards are renewable over a four-year period and range from $1000 to $10,000 per year. Mount Aloysius College participates in all federal and state programs; 90 percent of the College's students receive some form of financial aid. *U.S. News & World Report* has ranked Mount Aloysius College as one of the best-priced private liberal arts colleges in the U.S.

Faculty

The Mount Aloysius faculty consists of approximately 60 full-time members, whose primary responsibility is teaching and advising students. Most full-time faculty members hold advanced or terminal degrees and are expected to maintain close instructional ties with students. Many professors hold national professional certificates in such disciplines as criminology, education, law, and nursing. The Mount Aloysius student-faculty ratio of 14:1 allows close contact between students and faculty members, providing personal attention in a highly structured environment—a key ingredient in the College's academic philosophy.

Student Government

The Student Government Association (SGA) represents students on all issues that concern the College. The SGA appoints student representatives to all student-oriented College committees. The College encourages active student participation in the general governance structure and in other matters concerning the development and implementation of policies on residential student life.

Admission Requirements

The College admits a freshman class of approximately 350 students, which amounts to a total class of 500 with transfer students. Admission is selective and is based on academic promise, as indicated by a student's secondary school performance and activities, standardized test scores, and special experience and talents. Applicants are required to have, or expect to earn, a diploma from an approved secondary school or a GED diploma. Submission of official transcripts and SAT or ACT scores is required. In addition to the general admission requirements, specific admission requirements exist for the health programs; students should visit the College's Web site (http://www.mtaloy.edu) for further information. Prospective students are highly encouraged to visit the scenic 193-acre campus. The College is open Monday to Friday from 8:30 to 5 and on select Saturdays.

Application and Information

To apply for admission to Mount Aloysius College, candidates are encouraged to submit their application and $30 application fee to the Office of Undergraduate and Graduate Admissions. In addition, students may apply online. For further information, students should contact:

Office of Undergraduate and Graduate Admissions
Mount Aloysius College
7373 Admiral Peary Highway
Cresson, Pennsylvania 16630
Phone: 814-886-6383
888-823-2220 (toll-free)
Fax: 814-886-6441
E-mail: admissions@mtaloy.edu
Web site: http://www.mtaloy.edu

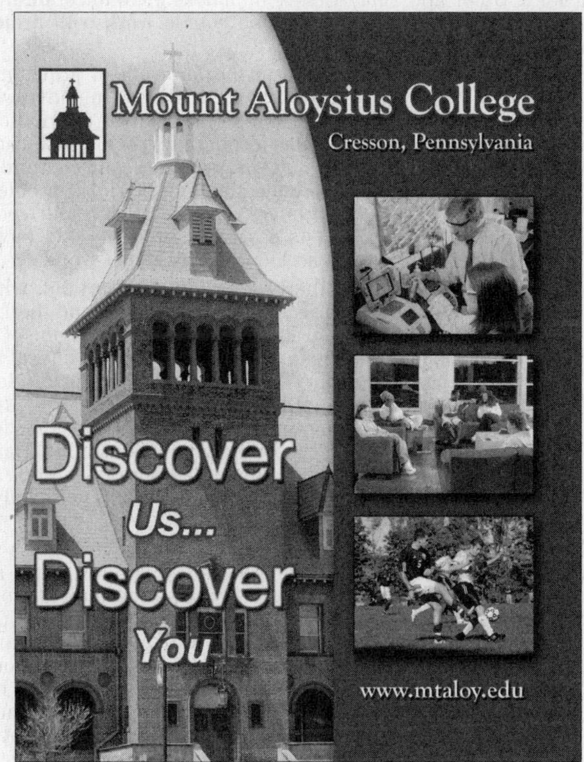

Student activities abound on the Mount Aloysius College campus.

MOUNT HOLYOKE COLLEGE

SOUTH HADLEY, MASSACHUSETTS

The College

Long distinguished for the quality of its curricular and cocurricular life as well as for the diversity of its student body and the success of its alumnae, Mount Holyoke is an independent college of liberal arts and sciences for women. The student body, numbering 2,200, represents forty-eight states and nearly seventy countries. More than 1 out of every 3 students is an international student or an African American, Latina, Asian, or Native American. Ninety-two percent of all graduates are either employed or in graduate/professional school within six months of graduation. Of those who choose to pursue an advanced degree, 20 to 25 percent enroll within five years of graduation.

Mount Holyoke is committed to maintaining small classes and individualized academic advising. The College's student-faculty ratio is 10:1. Half of Mount Holyoke's classes enroll 15 or fewer students, and 28 percent enroll fewer than 10. All students are advised by faculty members. Non-Western cultures are a focus of the College's curricular life. Most students pursue interdisciplinary courses, some taught by teams of faculty members from different fields. Use of computers, proficiency in foreign languages, and development of speaking and writing skills are stressed throughout the curriculum. The College offers first-year students the opportunity to enroll in first-year seminars—small classes designed to introduce first-year students to Mount Holyoke's intellectual community and to help them develop essential skills in writing, speaking, and analytic and critical inquiry.

The College is distinguished in developing women leaders. The Weissman Center for Leadership and the Liberal Arts is devoted to increasing students' understanding of public policy issues and giving them the tools to create change. The work of the center focuses on enhancing students' ability to frame, articulate, and advocate positions constructively and effectively. A major component is the Speaking, Arguing, and Writing Program, which is a nationally recognized model among liberal arts colleges for training students to be powerful communicators. Other Weissman Center initiatives include community-based learning courses, which combine course work with project-based fieldwork in the community.

Mount Holyoke also has long been at the forefront of providing a global education. The McCulloch Center for Global Initiatives was founded in 2004 to unite Mount Holyoke's wealth of international programs and people, and implement a coherent vision for education for global citizenship. The center initiates, promotes, and coordinates educational activities to advance understanding of global problems and solutions from cross-disciplinary, cross-cultural, and cross-national perspectives. Through its programs, students and faculty members engage critically with an increasingly global world.

Mount Holyoke participates in the Five College Consortium, which also includes Amherst, Hampshire, and Smith Colleges and the University of Massachusetts Amherst. Students enrolled at any one of the Five Colleges can take the courses and participate in the cultural and social offerings of the other four. In addition, the five institutions' faculty and classes are coordinated in areas of common interest, such as African studies, Asian/Pacific/American studies, Latin American studies, Middle Eastern studies, and international relations. Dance and astronomy—the two Five College majors—both rank among the largest and most distinguished undergraduate programs nationally in their respective fields.

Forming a vital part of Mount Holyoke's offerings are diverse cocurricular opportunities—concerts, conferences, exhibitions, films, and social events. Noted actors, dancers, and musicians perform at Mount Holyoke and within the Five College area. In addition, there are performance opportunities through instrumental ensembles, dance groups, theater productions, and an active choral program. Groups such as the Five College Dance Department, the Five College Jazz Improvisation Orchestra, and the New World Theatre supplement these opportunities. More than 150 clubs and organizations provide creative outlets, leadership experiences, and service opportunities.

The residence halls complement the liberal arts experience, coordinating cultural and social events and providing a home away from home for all students. Almost all students live on campus in the residence halls, each of which accommodates between 65 and 130 students. All four classes are mixed in each hall, and housing is guaranteed for all four years. A new, 175-bed residence hall offering a variety of living options opened in 2008. Dining options available across campus include a full-service café and several coffee shops. A kosher/halal dining room serves the dietary needs of observant Jews and observant Muslims and is open to the entire campus community.

Other facilities include five cultural houses, a Japanese teahouse and meditation garden, a health clinic and counseling center, and a center for spiritual life and community service. Students of all religious traditions and spiritual paths are made welcome at Mount Holyoke. Four chaplains—Catholic, Jewish, Protestant, and Muslim—and a number of faculty advisers respond to the pastoral and liturgical needs of the College's diverse religious community.

Recent renovation to the Blanchard Campus Center has transformed the building's interior into a center for dining, entertainment, and social activity. Highlights include a cyber café, coffee bar, art gallery, game room, performance space, and campus store. The radio station, student programs offices, and meeting rooms are also located here.

The College recently invested $15 million in updating the sports and dance facilities. A comprehensive sports and dance complex has 130,000 square feet of facilities. The field house includes basketball, tennis, volleyball, squash, and racquetball courts; a 200-meter track; and an eight-lane swimming pool with a separate diving tank. The field house adjoins the gymnasium and dance studios. There are also twelve outdoor tennis courts, a new eight-lane outdoor track, a synthetic multipurpose turf field with lights, and several grass playing fields. An equestrian center provides a sixty-stall barn and large indoor and outdoor riding arenas as well as three cross-country show courses. This center is widely considered one of nation's finest riding facilities. The College's eighteen-hole golf course, designed by Donald Ross, was the site of the 2004 USGA Women's Open. Mount Holyoke is an NCAA Division III school and offers thirteen intercollegiate teams as well as intramural and club sports.

Location

South Hadley, Massachusetts, is about 20 minutes from Springfield, 1½ hours from Boston, and 3 hours from New York City by car. Convenient bus, plane, and train service to the College is available. Bradley International Airport, 40 minutes away by car, serves Hartford and Springfield; Amtrak train stations are located in Amherst and Springfield. Bookstores, coffee shops, and restaurants are within walking distance of campus, and the nearby towns of Northampton and Amherst are easily reached via the free Five College bus service.

Majors and Degrees

Mount Holyoke offers the Bachelor of Arts degree. Majors include African and African American studies, American studies, ancient studies, anthropology, architectural studies, art (history and studio), Asian studies, astronomy, biochemistry, biological sciences, chemistry, classics, computer science, critical social thought, dance, economics, engineering, English, environmental studies, European studies, film studies, French, gender studies, geography, geology, German studies, Greek, history, international relations, Italian, Latin, Latin American studies, mathematics, medieval studies, music, neuroscience and behavior, philosophy, physics, politics, psychology, psychology and education, religion, Romance languages and literatures, Russian and Eurasian studies, self-designed studies, sociology, Spanish, statistics, and theater arts. Students may also follow prelaw and premedical courses of study. In addition, students can earn both an A.B. from Mount Holyoke and a B.S. in engineering from Caltech, UMass' College of Engineering, or Dartmouth's Thayer School of Engineering in a five-year period.

Academic Programs

Within the framework of the liberal arts and sciences, Mount Holyoke offers students considerable freedom of choice in the academic program. The basic plan of study includes a distribution of courses among at least seven disciplines, courses in language, courses in a major and minor field, and at least one course dealing with an aspect of Africa,

Asia, Latin America, the Middle East, or the nonwhite peoples of North America. A normal schedule is four 4-credit courses per semester, each meeting one to four times per week. By graduation, a student has completed 128 credits of academic work in courses that provide exposure to a variety of disciplines, as well as specialization in a major and a minor field. Independent study, honors work, and self-scheduled examinations are among the options available. The Frances Perkins Program is designed for women beyond the traditional undergraduate age who wish to initiate, continue, or enrich their undergraduate education.

The academic calendar consists of two semesters separated by an active January Term program. During January Term, students may take a single intensive course, pursue an independent project, engage in volunteer work, or complete a three-week internship.

Off-Campus Programs

The Mount Holyoke student lives and studies in an area where four independent colleges and a large university enroll more than 30,000 students. Amherst, Hampshire, Mount Holyoke, and Smith Colleges and the University of Massachusetts Amherst participate in an extensive Five College cooperative exchange program. Free buses run among the institutions (all within a 12-mile radius) every 20 minutes from morning to late evening, seven days a week, during the school year.

Mount Holyoke is a member of the Twelve College Exchange, and students can spend a year or semester at any of the other participating institutions (Amherst, Bowdoin, Connecticut, Dartmouth, Smith, Trinity, Vassar, Wellesley, Wheaton, and Williams Colleges and Wesleyan University). The exchange also includes the Williams/Mystic Seaport Program in American Maritime Studies and the O'Neill National Theater Institute Program. Mount Holyoke also has its own exchange programs with Mills College in Oakland, California, and Spelman College in Atlanta, Georgia. Semester programs include the American University Washington Semester and the Semester in Environmental Science at the Marine Biological Laboratory, Woods Hole. Each year, 40 percent of the junior class studies abroad for a semester or a year in such countries as Argentina, Australia, Chile, China, Costa Rica, Denmark, France, Germany, Italy, Japan, Kenya, Korea, Republic of Georgia, Russia, Senegal, and the United Kingdom.

The College's Career Development Center assists students in developing both summer and January internships, which involve full-time work for six to twelve weeks over the summer or for three weeks during January Term. Internships have been undertaken in the fields of the arts, business and banking, communications, education, government, health, public policy, sciences, social services, and technology. Reflecting the College's internationalism and building on the College's extensive overseas ties, Mount Holyoke has a strong network of international internship opportunities around the world. Sponsoring organizations typically include the World Bank, UNESCO, and the United Nations.

Academic Facilities

In recent years, the College has invested $75 million in the renovation and expansion of facilities and technology. The music and art buildings have been fully updated and expanded, including the Mount Holyoke College Art Museum, one of the nation's leading collegiate art museums with an active teaching collection. The new Science Center advances the College's international reputation as a leader in scientific education for women. A multistory, 40,000-square-foot environmentally sound building, Kendade Hall, connects three other science buildings and features a four-story atrium that provides a gathering place for all members of the community. The Science Center houses eight departments—astronomy, biochemistry, biological sciences, chemistry, computer science, earth and environment, mathematics, and physics—and offers classrooms, adjacent labs and offices, common spaces, and shared equipment for students and faculty members with overlapping research interests.

The 800-acre campus includes two lakes, wooded bridle trails, lawns, and forests. An undeveloped nature preserve covers 330 of these acres and serves as an environmental classroom for students and faculty members. Taking advantage of this "outdoor classroom," the Center for the Environment is a resource for students interested in using the campus and surrounding community to advance their studies of ecology and environmental studies.

The College's 740,000-volume library incorporates dedicated science and music libraries and computerized access to 8 million volumes through the Five College Consortium. Within the main library, the Information Commons has forty high-end computers and a Help Desk. The Mediated Educational Work Space (MEWS) has flexible work areas, 52-inch plasma screens, and dual-boot Intel Macs to support multimedia teaching and collaborative projects. The computer and language learning center uses state-of-the-art methods for teaching languages. Technology tools currently in use include wireless networking, video conferencing, and interactive, multimedia-based, curriculum-enhancing Web software. There are ongoing training opportunities for students to learn emerging technologies.

An extensive Career Development Center assists students in clarifying their goals and in identifying internships, jobs, graduate schools, and fellowships.

Costs

For 2010–11, tuition is $40,070, and room and board are $11,780, with a student activity fee of $186 for a total of $52,036.

Financial Aid

Financial need should not discourage any student from applying to Mount Holyoke. Aid (grants, loans, and campus employment) is based on financial-aid eligibility as determined by the College. Mount Holyoke also offers a limited number of competitive merit aid awards.

Faculty

Mount Holyoke's 200 faculty members are dedicated teachers as well as active scholars, research scientists, and creative artists. Fifty percent are women, and 25 percent are persons of color. All courses are taught by faculty members; professors are also active in advising students about classes, cocurricular opportunities, and careers. Mount Holyoke professors have won numerous awards, including National Science Foundation CAREER awards, MacArthur and Carnegie Corporation fellowships, Guggenheims, Fulbrights, the Pulitzer Prize, the Rome Prize, and the National Book Award.

Student Government

Mount Holyoke students, together with the faculty and administrators, have a strong hand in shaping campus life. Students sit on several committees, including the President's Commission on Diversity, the Academic Policy Committee, and the Board of Admissions. The Student Government Association allows students to govern their cocurricular lives and maintain communication with the faculty and administration. Students have an effective honor code of long standing.

Admission Requirements

Mount Holyoke seeks smart, ambitious students who value a liberal arts education and who are fired by a love of learning. Students who do well here tend to demonstrate a high level of maturity and independence. Mount Holyoke welcomes students of all economic, ethnic, geographic, religious, and social backgrounds. A high school program providing a good preparation for Mount Holyoke includes 4 years of English, 3 years of a foreign language, 3 years each of mathematics and laboratory sciences, and 2 years of history. SAT or ACT scores are optional. The Test of English as a Foreign Language (TOEFL) or the International English Language Testing System (IELTS) is required for students for whom English is not a primary language. Personal interviews are highly recommended for all candidates either on campus or with an alumna admissions representative.

Application and Information

Two rounds of early decision are available: the deadline for Round I is November 15, with notification by January 1; the deadline for Round II is January 1, with notification by February 1. The deadline for regular admission is January 15, with notification by April 1. Other admission options, such as early entrance, deferred entrance, and advanced standing, are available.

The admission office is open all year, Monday through Friday, from 9 a.m. to 5 p.m., and Saturday mornings from 9 a.m. to noon. Visitors may come to the admission office to attend an information session, take a campus tour, obtain admission materials, or meet with a staff member. For more information, students should contact:

Office of Admission
Mount Holyoke College
50 College Street
South Hadley, Massachusetts 01075-1488

Phone: 413-538-2023
Fax: 413-538-2409
E-mail: admission@mtholyoke.edu
Web site: http://www.mtholyoke.edu

MOUNT MARY COLLEGE

MILWAUKEE, WISCONSIN

The College

Mount Mary College, one of only 65 women's colleges in the nation, is home to nearly 1,800 undergraduate and graduate students. Located on a beautiful 80-acre wooded campus, only 15 minutes from downtown Milwaukee, students at Mount Mary are fully engaged in and outside of the classroom, learning not just the subject matter but also how to express opinions and develop leadership skills. Through exciting internships, club activities, community service, and campus ministry programs, students explore their interests and discover their skills. Special and professional interests are served by affiliates of national societies.

Caroline Hall, the student residence hall, provides accommodations for private occupancy and single and double suites. Over 90% of the rooms feature walk in closets and over two thirds have private bathrooms. Every floor in Caroline Hall has a kitchen, lounge area and a mini–computer lab. All residence hall rooms have wireless computer access and are wired for cable television and telephone service. Mount Mary College sponsors many social activities including performances by comedians, holiday dances and campus picnics.

Physical fitness and an interest in athletics are fostered through various activities, fitness programs, health and dance courses, and intramural and intercollegiate athletics. Mount Mary College is a provisional member of the NCAA Division III. The Blue Angels compete in basketball, cross-country, soccer, softball, tennis, and volleyball. Facilities on campus and in the Bloechl Recreation Center, which opened in 2006, include a gymnasium, an indoor swimming pool, outdoor soccer fields and a fitness center. Bordering the campus is the Menomonee River Parkway, ideal for biking, jogging, cross-country skiing, and much more.

Academic and professional student services are available to all Mount Mary students, including free tutoring and assistance with tests through the Academic Resource Center; advising, resume writing, and career planning through the Advising and Career Development Center; and personal counseling through the Counseling Center.

Location

Mount Mary College is located in a residential area in northwestern Milwaukee, just 20 minutes from downtown and less than 5 minutes from a major shopping mall. Students can access public transportation right in front of the campus. Several other private and public universities call Milwaukee home, making it a great environment to meet students from other colleges.

Majors and Degrees

Mount Mary offers over sixty areas of academic study including accounting, art, art therapy, behavioral science, biology, business administration, chemistry, communication arts, diagnostic medical sonography, dietetics, education, English (literature, professional writing, and education), fashion (apparel product development and: merchandise management), graphic design, health sciences (preprofessional programs), history, interior design, international studies, justice, mathematics, nursing, occupational therapy, philosophy, psychology/behavioral science, public relations, radiologic technology, social work, Spanish, student designed, and theology. Columbia College of Nursing and Mount Mary College jointly offer a Bachelor of Science in Nursing (B.S.N.) degree. Special services for undeclared students help them find and focus on a major suited to their interests and talents.

In addition to undergraduate programs, Mount Mary also offers graduate programs in art therapy, business administration (M.B.A.), counseling (community, pastoral, and school), dietetics, education, English, and occupational therapy.

Academic Programs

Mount Mary's curriculum integrates leadership skills into each student's educational experience, developing leaders who take individual responsibility for social justice. The curriculum and co-curricular activities promote self-knowledge and competence, an entrepreneurial sense of vision, effective oral and written communication skills, and the ability to strengthen leadership in others. In their professions, churches, and communities, Mount Mary students model collaborative leadership, enabling them to work effectively both in leadership positions and as supportive team members.

Many academic programs at Mount Mary College offer internships, which allow students to relate theory to practice and interact with professionals while learning life skills. The process encourages students to reflect on the skills and knowledge they hope to gain and allows them to tailor their practical experience to the career goals they have set for the future. Many of the programs incorporate a work experience into the curriculum. Work experience includes student teaching, clinicals, fieldwork, practicum, and internships. Several majors also offer study abroad components allowing students to gain hands on experience in their major along with learning about another culture.

Off-Campus Programs

Mount Mary encourages its students to take advantage of a variety of study abroad opportunities. Accordingly, Mount Mary College sponsors trips to a variety of countries including China, England, France, Guatemala, Ireland, Italy, Nicaragua, and Peru. In addition to these study-abroad programs, the College maintains affiliate relationships with numerous international colleges and universities, including the American College, Dublin, Ireland; the American Intercontinental University, London and Dubai; Nanzan College, Japan; Universidad Cathólica de Santa Maria (UCSM), Arequipa, Peru; and Notre Dame College, Kyoto, Japan.

The Office of International Studies also aids students in finding an accredited program that meets their individual needs.

Academic Facilities

Located on 80 beautiful acres, Mount Mary offers students unlimited space to grow.

Costs

For the 2009–10 academic year, undergraduate tuition is $20,736 for full-time students and $596 per credit for part-time students. The undergraduate fee is $430 per year for full-time students and $220 per year for part-time students and includes counseling services (academic and personal); disability services; career services and advising (mock interviews, resume writing workshops, and interest inventories); parking pass; e-mail account; attendance at athletic, campus ministry, and student activities events; and use of the academic resource center, library, computer lab and printers, fitness center, and swimming pool. Room and board costs averaged $7280. All costs are subject to change.

Financial Aid

The financial aid office at Mount Mary College develops a financial package on an individual basis for qualified students. All students are automatically awarded an academic scholarship upon acceptance ranging from $5000 to $9000 per year. Additional scholarships are available. More than 95 percent of Mount Mary's full-time students receive some form of financial assistance. Students filing for financial aid should complete the Free Application for Federal Student Aid (FAFSA) by March 1.

Faculty

Faculty members holding advanced degrees do all the teaching; no classes are taught by teaching assistants. In addition, every student is assigned a faculty advisor with whom they meet with prior to registering each semester. With a total enrollment of nearly 1,800, Mount Mary offers a low faculty-to-student ratio with an average of 25 students per class and no large lecture halls.

Student Government

Students are encouraged to participate in the governance of the College. Student Government makes recommendations about College policies and other matters of importance to students and serves as a liaison to the Mount Mary administration, faculty, and staff.

Admission Requirements

Candidates for admission are considered on the basis of academic preparation, scholarship, and evidence of the ability to do college work and benefit from it. Sixteen secondary school units are required; of these, 11 must be academic (3 in English, 2 in college-preparatory mathematics, 2 in science, 4 in history, language, or social science) and 4 in electives. Students must have achieved a minimum composite score of 18 on the ACT (870 on the SAT) and rank in the top 40 percent of their high school graduating class or have a minimum GPA of 2.5 (on a 4.0 scale). Students who do not meet the admission requirements are reviewed by an admission committee. International students must take the Test of English as a Foreign Language (TOEFL) and achieve a minimum score of 500. Mount Mary does not discriminate against any individual for reasons of race, color, religion, age, national or ethnic origin, or disability.

Application and Information

Mount Mary has a rolling admission policy. Early acceptance is available, and advanced placement and IB credits are honored. Interested students should submit an admission application, official high school transcripts, ACT or SAT scores and a $25 application fee. After notification of acceptance, students wishing to enroll need to submit the $200 nonrefundable tuition deposit.

For further information, students should contact:

The Admission Office
Mount Mary College
2900 North Menomonee River Parkway
Milwaukee, Wisconsin 53222-4597
Phone: 414-256-1219
800-321-6265 (toll-free)
Fax: 414-256-0180
E-mail: admiss@mtmary.edu
Web site: http://www.mtmary.edu

Mount Mary College is located on 80 acres in a convenient Milwaukee neighborhood. Students have a safe, secure environment in which to live and learn.

MUHLENBERG COLLEGE

ALLENTOWN, PENNSYLVANIA

The College

Founded in 1848, Muhlenberg College aims to develop independent critical thinkers who are intellectually agile, characterized by a zeal for reasoned and civil debate, knowledgeable about the achievements and traditions of diverse civilizations and cultures, able to express ideas with clarity and grace, committed to lifelong learning, equipped with ethical values, and prepared for lives of leadership and service.

Muhlenberg students achieve the College's goals by assuming strong individual responsibility for intense involvement in vigorous academic work and for personal involvement within the College community. The more than 100 student organizations provide outlets for the diversified cultural, athletic, religious, social, leadership, and service interests of the students. The campus is primarily residential; more than 90 percent of the 2,150 students live on campus. A close sense of community develops naturally, one in which their diversified academic and personal interests enable students to contribute positively to the intellectual and personal growth of their peers.

Students are aided by an active Career Planning and Placement Service in relating academic and personal knowledge and skills to appropriate career goals and in obtaining positions upon graduation. About one third of a typical graduating class proceeds immediately to graduate or professional school.

Location

Muhlenberg College is located in suburban west Allentown, an area made up primarily of attractive family homes and parks. The downtown area of Allentown, a city of approximately 104,000 people, is a 10-minute ride from the campus. The College is located 90 miles west of New York City and 60 miles north of Philadelphia.

Majors and Degrees

Muhlenberg offers the Bachelor of Arts (A.B.) degree in the following fields: accounting, American studies, anthropology, art, business, communication, dance, economics, English, film studies, finance, French, German, history, history/government, international studies, music, philosophy, philosophy/political thought, political economy, political science, psychology, religious studies, Russian studies, social science, sociology, Spanish, and theater arts. The Bachelor of Science (B.S.) degree is offered in the following fields: biochemistry, biology, chemistry, computer science, environmental science, mathematics, natural sciences, neuroscience, and physics. Students may also design their own major.

In addition, students may receive certification to teach at the elementary and secondary levels. Other opportunities include a 4-4 guaranteed-admission program with Drexel University College of Medicine; a 3-4 dental program with the University of Pennsylvania; a 3-3 B.S./Ph.D. program in physical therapy with Thomas Jefferson University; a 3-2½ B.S./M.S. program in occupational therapy with Thomas Jefferson University; a 3-2/4-2 combined program in engineering, offered in cooperation with Columbia University; and a 3-2 combined program in forestry, offered in cooperation with Duke University.

Academic Programs

The A.B. and B.S. programs emphasize breadth of study in the liberal arts as well as in-depth study of a particular academic major. All students must fulfill requirements in foreign culture, the humanities, social sciences, and natural sciences. Strong achievement on Advanced Placement examinations may enable a student to receive advanced placement, possibly with credit. Scores of 4 or 5 earn automatic credit. Scores of 3 are evaluated by the appropriate department.

Students work closely with academic advisers to formulate programs well suited to their individual interests, abilities, needs, and goals. Generally, students are expected to declare their major at the end of the freshman year; however, many students later change their academic major with no difficulty. A double major is possible, and several fields are available as minor programs. These minor fields are accounting, African American studies, anthropology, business, chemistry, computer science, economics, English, French, German, history, Jewish studies, mathematics, music, philosophy, physics, political science, public health, religion, sociology, Spanish, and women's studies. In addition, independent study and research are available. The College also enriches the freshman-year experience through more than thirty special-focus Freshman Seminars.

Off-Campus Programs

Study abroad is available through Muhlenberg's Semester-in-London Program, Netherlands Semester, or more than sixty affiliate agreements with international universities all over the world. In addition, the Lehigh Valley Association of Independent Colleges sponsors summer study-abroad options in England, France, Germany, Israel, and Spain. Credit for study-abroad programs sponsored by other institutions or by private agencies may also be transferred to Muhlenberg by special arrangement.

Students may participate in a variety of internships in local businesses, health-care facilities, schools, public agencies, theaters, broadcasting stations, and magazines. Government internships in Harrisburg, Pennsylvania, and Washington, D.C., and an Ethics and Public Affairs semester in Washington, D.C., are also available.

Students may enroll in courses offered at any of the five other member institutions of the Lehigh Valley Association of Independent Colleges: Lafayette College, Lehigh University, Cedar Crest College, DeSales University, and Moravian College.

Academic Facilities

Muhlenberg's library collection contains more than 200,000 volumes as well as numerous government documents, periodicals, and microforms. The $12-million Harry C. Trexler Library, a state-of-the-art library facility, opened in 1988. Students may also use library materials owned by the other institutions participating in the Lehigh Valley Association of Independent Colleges.

The Baker Center for the Arts was designed for Muhlenberg by the well-known architect Philip Johnson. It houses a modern theater complex, a recital hall, classrooms, art studios, and a fine arts gallery. The Trexler Performing Arts Pavilion opened in 2000 and provides dance performance and studio space, a new theater, a Black Box, and additional arts spaces.

Life science facilities include numerous laboratories, classrooms, two electron microscopes, a DNA sequencer, an isolation room used for growing and studying viruses, and a museum of natural history. Facilities supporting students in the physical sciences include equipment for optics, electronics, and atomic, nuclear, and solid-state physics. A new 40,000-square-foot addition to the science facilities opened in fall 2006. The College uses a UNIX/Windows computer system with Novell software.

Costs

The comprehensive tuition fee for the 2009–10 academic year was $36,990. The room and board fee averaged $8060. The total cost for a resident student was approximately $45,050.

Financial Aid

Muhlenberg College endeavors to make its educational opportunities available to all qualified students regardless of their financial circumstances. While most financial aid at Muhlenberg is based on financial need as demonstrated by the College Scholarship Service Financial Aid PROFILE, there is also significant merit aid available. Typically, about 70 percent of Muhlenberg's students qualify for and receive financial aid.

Faculty

The Muhlenberg faculty consists of 170 full-time and 113 part-time members. Ninety percent of full-time faculty members hold doctoral or terminal degrees. While many faculty members are distinguished for their scholarly research, teaching is the main emphasis of their work. Professors at all levels work closely with students both inside and outside of the classroom. Most department heads teach introductory courses.

Student Government

Muhlenberg students are expected to demonstrate a high level of responsibility with regard to their own governance and to participate extensively in internal decision-making and communication processes throughout the campus. These responsibilities are coordinated by the Student Council, which transacts all business pertaining to the student body. This organization is in charge of a student activities budget of more than $350,000. In addition, 2 students serve as representatives to the Board of Trustees, and students hold full voting privileges on many faculty committees.

Admission Requirements

The College selects students who give evidence of ability and scholastic achievement, seriousness of purpose, and the capacity to make constructive contributions to the College community. Approximately 70 percent of a typical freshman class ranked in the top fifth of their secondary school class. SAT scores for entering freshmen average approximately 606 verbal, 612 math, and 612 writing.

Submission of SAT or ACT scores is optional. An on-campus interview is strongly recommended for all applicants and required for students who choose not to submit standardized test scores.

Application and Information

Students who wish to be considered for admission should submit a completed application form as early as possible during their senior year of secondary school and no later than February 15. Candidates receive notice of admission decisions in late March. Early decision plans and transfer admission are possible.

For further information, interested students should contact:

Christopher Hooker-Haring
Dean of Admission and Financial Aid
Muhlenberg College
Allentown, Pennsylvania 18104-5586
Phone: 484-664-3200
E-mail: admissions@muhlenberg.edu
Web site: http://www.muhlenberg.edu

The Bell Tower of the Haas College Center stands as the focal point of the Muhlenberg College campus.

MULTNOMAH UNIVERSITY

PORTLAND, OREGON

The College

Multnomah Bible College and Biblical Seminary—together Multnomah University—has been devoted to teaching the Bible to men and women since the 1930s. The mission of Multnomah University is to produce, through collegiate education, biblically competent, culturally aware, maturing servants of Jesus Christ, whose love for God, His Word, and people shapes their lives into a transforming force in the church and world. Multnomah's education is more than time in the classroom—it's learning through hands-on ministry, late-night talks with friends in the coffee shop, and discovering the heart of God through prayer. At Multnomah, the Bible is central to everything students learn. Whether majoring in journalism or pastoral ministry, students are challenged at the end of the day to think and live biblically. Multnomah offers one of the most comprehensive Bible programs in the nation, requiring each student to complete a comprehensive Bible and theology major. Multnomah also offers a Master of Arts in Teaching and a Master of Arts in Teaching English to Speakers of Other Languages (TESOL). The University is accredited by the Northwest Commission on Colleges and Universities (NWCCU) and the Association of Biblical Higher Education (ABHE) and is recognized by the state of Oregon to award bachelor's degrees.

Effective education teaches the whole person. Community life presents challenges but provides tremendous opportunities to build lifelong friendships and to make service to others a lifelong habit. It allows faculty and staff members to give each student the individual attention befitting one created in God's image. But Multnomah does not leave its populace unprepared for the world's harsh realities. Rather, the University continually seeks ways to train students to have the greatest possible impact on the world today. Students are instructed in and saturated with a biblical, Christian worldview designed to prepare them for any situation encountered. Opportunities to make the world the classroom are offered through cross-cultural experiences and internships in the community. Students can work side-by-side with their instructors as they share the gospel in the community or minister in a home for abused women, or even bring young people to Christ. The opportunities are endless.

Something is always happening on Multnomah's campus. Opportunities abound for students to get involved in a variety of activities, each designed to cultivate life skills that enhance their college experience. Students can join the student government, intramural sports, the Ambassador Choir, or various chapel worship bands, among other activities.

Multnomah Biblical Seminary was launched to provide a complementary, nonrepetitive seminary option for the Bible college graduate, although many professionals from other walks of life enroll to earn their seminary degree. Programs include the graduate certificate, the Master of Arts in biblical studies or in pastoral studies (emphases in family ministry, intercultural studies, ministry management, spiritual formation, and women's ministry), the Master of Divinity, and the Master of Theology. The seminary is accredited by the Association of Theological Schools and the Northwest Commission on Colleges and Universities.

Location

The city of Portland offers an endless supply of adventure and excitement. The campus is only 15 minutes from downtown. On weekends, the Saturday Market offers a huge collection of handmade crafts, art, and ethnic food. Waterfront Park hosts the Rose Festival in late May, and many shops and restaurants overlook the Willamette River. The eclectic Hawthorne, Hollywood, Pearl, and northwest Portland districts have unique shopping, arts, and restaurants—all within 5 miles of campus. Portland is home to museums, concert venues, and the Trail Blazer basketball team. Less than 2 hours from Multnomah are Oregon's sandy beaches. The slopes of Mt. Hood, a favorite for skiers and snowboarders throughout the world, are just an hour east. Portland International Airport (PDX) is less than 10 minutes from campus, and Portland has an excellent public transportation system that includes a world-class light rail system.

Majors and Degrees

In addition to the undergraduate Bible and theology major all students earn, students may select a second major or minor in one of sixteen areas of study. The Bachelor of Arts degree program provides students with more exposure to languages and humanities, while the Bachelor of Science degree program focuses more on social sciences. Areas of study include biblical Hebrew, education, educational ministries, history, intercultural studies, journalism, missionary aviation, music ministry, New Testament Greek, pastoral ministry, speech communication, and youth ministry. Minors are now available in English, psychology, and TESOL. Students may also opt to study Bible and theology alone as a double-major, choosing from one of three concentrations—biblical language, biblical studies, or theological studies—to enhance their biblical education.

Academic Programs

Multnomah University believes that there is no substitute for a thorough knowledge of the Word of God and that it is basic to all successful Christian service. For that reason, the College has made teaching the Bible its primary objective and enrolls all bachelor's students in the Bible major. As a result of the large proportion of Bible in the curriculum, students are able to obtain a sound and thorough training in the Word of God. A varied program of second majors and minors enables students to specialize in a particular area of interest for more effective Christian service and professional competency. General education provides learning experiences that enhance and complement the academic majors, giving the student an integrated Christian worldview. Students gain an understanding and awareness of broad areas of language, history, philosophy, communication, science, and human development.

Off-Campus Programs

Multnomah offers a South American Studies program through a cooperative program with George Fox University and Bolivian Evangelical University in Santa Cruz, Bolivia's second-largest city. Alternative study-abroad options are available though the Council of Christian Colleges and Universities (CCCU), of which Multnomah University is an affiliate campus.

Academic Facilities

The John and Mary Mitchell Library has a rich and developing collection of conventional and electronic resources to support the programs of study at Multnomah University. Multnomah is a member of a consortium of five libraries with a union database of more than 400,000 library holdings. The library has more than 100,000 volumes, nearly 15,000 e-books, over 10,000 periodicals in bound and microform formats, 2,400 videos and DVDs, and access to 30 online databases to assist scholarly research. The library staff is pleased to assist patrons in locating materials and answer any questions about the library, its resources, and its use.

The upper floor comprises stacks filled with a wide variety of books and a large study area for student and guest use. The lower floor has four classrooms, with seating capacities ranging from 38 to 55. A fifth classroom with auditorium-style seating accommodates 186 people. This classroom also has modern audiovisual computer capabilities. Two outside classrooms can seat 24 people. The Travis-Lovitt seminary building houses seven classrooms able to seat from 20 to 60 students. Each classroom is equipped with state-of-the-art audiovisual and networked computer equipment.

Costs

In 2010–11, tuition and fees are $14,280 per year, and room and board averages $5960, for a total of approximately $20,240. Multnomah strives to keep costs manageable for students so that they will be better able to go into ministry or professional life with as little academic debt as possible. Most students find their Multnomah education reasonably priced when compared to other similar institutions. Adult degree completion, graduate, and seminary program prices are even more competitive and can be found on Multnomah's Web site.

Financial Aid

Multnomah provides a variety of aid through many sources, including federal and institutional aid. A variety of scholarships based on academics and experience are awarded. Some examples include the President's Scholarship, Multnomah's most prestigious award, which provides $5000, and the Academic Dean's Scholarship, a second-tier scholarship providing $2500 toward the cost of tuition. Multnomah offers a variety of leadership opportunities on campus that include financial assistance. Each student can apply for leadership opportunities after his or her first year at Multnomah. In addition to this, there is a strong commitment to on-campus student jobs and a student employment office that assists in finding work off-campus when needed.

Faculty

The faculty members are the foundation upon which programs of academic excellence are built. Though highly educated and respected as scholars, faculty members do not promote "ivory tower" scholarship in their classrooms. Faculty members are skilled communicators who make the ideas and principles they teach relevant to their students' lives. While the faculty members love to teach, they also consistently broaden their knowledge base—indicated by their ongoing pursuit of advanced degrees, publishing of books and journal articles, and their involvement in various scholarly societies. They serve the church as pastors, church planters, counselors, and conference speakers. The content of their classroom instruction has been tested in the laboratory of experience, allowing them to teach with confidence. In fact, Portland, Oregon has been called a "living laboratory" for those pursuing ministry training.

Student Government

STUGO, the student government organization, advocates on behalf of student needs and organizes social events and ministries to help students become mature, Christ-like individuals. STUGO's Multnomah Community Outreach (MCO) provides opportunities for students to serve the surrounding community in after-school programs, workdays, and individual-care services. The Student World Outreach Team (SWOT) facilitates a world missionary vision through Monday chapels and missions-related events throughout the school year. All STUGO activities are designed to enrich the students' lives and contribute to their educational experience.

Admission Requirements

Because the academic load at Multnomah is rigorous, applicants should have a minimum 2.5 GPA. Students must complete the full application packet, which includes a personal statement and two reference forms (one pastoral, and one other reference). Applicants must also submit official transcripts (from high school or community college), SAT or ACT scores, and the $40 application fee. There are also ample admission opportunities for homeschooled students. The admissions committee also examines an applicant's character and his or her demonstrated commitment to Jesus Christ through service, leadership, and other factors.

Application and Information

Applicants should file admission forms well in advance of the enrollment date. Applications must arrive by July 15 for August admission (fall semester) or by November 15 for January admission (spring semester).

Admissions Office
Multnomah University
8435 Northeast Glisan Street
Portland, Oregon 97220
Phone: 503-251-6485
800-275-4672 (toll-free)
E-mail: admiss@multnomah.edu
Web site: http://www.multnomah.edu/

MUSKINGUM COLLEGE

NEW CONCORD, OHIO

The College

Since its founding in 1837, Muskingum has been a community of people learning from and with each other. Its mission is to offer high-quality academic programs in the liberal arts and sciences that educate the whole person intellectually, spiritually, socially, and physically. Muskingum's programs foster critical thinking, positive action, ethical sensitivity, and spiritual growth so that students may lead vocationally productive, personally satisfying, and socially responsible lives. Muskingum College is accredited by the North Central Association of Colleges and Schools and receives periodic reauthorization from the Ohio Board of Regents.

The College's proud heritage reaches back to the first half of the nineteenth century, when settlers were traveling westward over the newly completed National Road. During its first half-century, Muskingum adhered to the educational patterns of the classical college of the period. In 1877, Muskingum became associated with the Synod of Ohio of the United Presbyterian Church. Today, approximately 1,700 undergraduate students are enrolled at Muskingum; 90 percent of these students live on campus, representing twenty-eight states and fifteen other countries.

One of Muskingum's longest traditions is its affiliation with the Presbyterian Church. The Center for Church Life—a joint venture of Muskingum College, the Presbyterian Church Bicentennial Fund, and the Presbytery of Muskingum Valley—provides programs and services to support the ministries and missions of local congregations. On campus, the Office of the College Minister has created a multidimensional, unified campus ministry that allows students to worship and celebrate their faith.

While worship is important at Muskingum, students participate in other activities as well. More than ninety campus groups operate at the College, including varsity athletics, honor societies, music and religious organizations, and FM radio and cable TV stations. The residence halls are another center of student activity; living options range from traditional residence halls and sorority/fraternity houses to special program houses and College-owned apartments. Each residence hall provides lounges, computer labs, and television, kitchen, and laundry facilities.

Location

The village of New Concord, one of the many attractions along National Road, is a 1-hour drive from Columbus and a 2-hour drive from Pittsburgh and Cleveland. New Concord is surrounded by venues for boating, golfing, trail biking, skiing, hiking, camping, and rock climbing, all of which can be enjoyed in the town's temperate climate. New Concord is perhaps best known for its most famous resident—former astronaut and senator (and Muskingum alumnus) John Glenn, whose childhood home has become a museum.

Majors and Degrees

Bachelor's degrees are offered in the following areas: accounting, anthropology, art, biology, business, chemistry, Christian education, computer science, earth science, economics, early childhood education, English, French, geology, German, health education, history, mathematics, middle childhood education, music, philosophy, physical education, physics, political science, psychology, religion, religion and philosophy, sociology, Spanish, special education, speech communication, and theater. Interdisciplinary majors include American studies, child and family studies, conservation science, criminal justice, environmental science, humanities, international affairs, international business, journalism, molecular biology, neuroscience, and public affairs. Students may also design their own interdisciplinary program. Preprofessional programs are available in Christian ministry, dentistry, engineering, law, medical technology, medicine, physical therapy, and veterinary medicine. Teacher licensure programs are available in the following areas: adolescent/young adult, art, early childhood, foreign language (French, German, or Spanish), middle childhood, music, physical education, and special education. A nursing major will be offered in fall 2008.

Academic Programs

Undergraduate programs combine solid classroom curricula with a level of field work and independent study that is rarely encountered in an undergraduate setting. The bachelor's degree requires completion of at least 124 credit hours with a minimum GPA of 2.0. The curriculum includes Liberal Arts Essentials, a series of courses that ensure the breadth that is inherent in a liberal arts education. This core requires 21–24 hours in core courses, including one English course, two writing courses, one speech course, one mathematics course, one art and humanities course, and one physical education course. Another 35–37 hours are completed in area requirements such as religious understanding, moral inquiry, Western civilization, foreign languages, social sciences, global studies, and other subjects. Students are also required to complete 15 credits in their major area of study, 12 of which must be completed at the College. Credit by examination allows students to earn credit for a course by passing a proficiency examination. A student earns credit for the course by scoring a C or better on the exam.

Off-Campus Programs

Selected students may spend one semester at American University in Washington, D.C., studying the American governmental system in action. Assignments may include the State Department, lobbying groups, or Capitol Hill. Students majoring in art may be able to spend their junior year studying at one of seventeen Art Institutes locations. Commercial art programs are available in the areas of fashion merchandising, industrial design technology, interior design, photography/multimedia, and visual communications. United Nations Semester is a program under which Muskingum students may apply for one semester of study at Drew University, during which time they take two courses involving on-site study at the United Nations headquarters in New York. International study provides the opportunity for sophomores, juniors, and seniors to study for one or two semesters at an international university in Asia, Canada, Europe, Latin America, or Puerto Rico.

Academic Facilities

The library contains 215,000 volumes, 574 print journals, and an extensive microfilm collection, plus access to more than 16,500 online journals, 17,000 electronic books, 1,200 electronic videos, and 110 research databases. The library is a member of the OPAL and OhioLINK consortia, thus giving students and faculty and staff members borrowing privileges at eighty-four academic libraries throughout the state. Brown Chapel serves as church, chapel, and auditorium for the College. Its main auditorium seats nearly 500, and the basement contains a lounge area, music practice rooms, and a small chapel. The John Glenn Physical Education Building houses two gymnasiums, a swimming pool, recreation and intramural equipment, and coaches' offices, while the Physical Education and Recreation Center holds a 2,800-seat gymnasium, four handball/racquetball courts, a baseball/softball hitting area, a weight room, and an athletic training room.

Costs

In the 2009–10 academic year, tuition was $9595 per semester. Other costs per semester included a student activity fee of $115 and a technology fee of $175. Students living on campus could expect to pay $3870 per semester for room and board, as well as $55 for laundry services. Books and supplies, transportation, and other miscellaneous costs vary according to the student's specific needs.

Financial Aid

A small number of entering students receive the John Glenn Scholarship, a full-tuition award, while other students may receive academic scholarships ranging from $1000 to $12,000 per year. These awards are renewable with a GPA of 3.0 or higher. Other scholarships are available in the performing arts. These awards range from $500 to $2000 per year and are renewable with a satisfactory GPA. The College also offers Awards of Circumstance to students who meet the eligibility requirements. These awards range from $500 to $5000 per year. The limit on non-need assistance is $13,500 for recipients of Presidential Scholarships and $12,000 for all other students. Students may also be eligible for federal and state grants, including Federal Pell Grants of up to $4050, Federal Supplemental Educational Opportunity Grants of up to $2000 per year, Ohio College Opportunity Grants of up to $4992 per year, and Federal PLUS loans of up to $2000 annually.

Federal Stafford Student Loans are available to all students who are enrolled at least half-time at a 6.8 percent interest rate. Federal Perkins Loans are available at an interest rate of 5 percent and are repayable after completion of studies. Federal PLUS loans are loans to parents of dependent students. The interest rate is 8.5 percent, and repayment begins within sixty days of disbursement. The College has a limited amount of funding available to be used as loan assistance to students. Repayment with 8 percent interest begins upon the student's departure from Muskingum. Students may also borrow from other lenders. Campus job opportunities are available to students under the Federal Work-Study Program or the Muskingum Work Program. Most students are paid minimum wage and work 5–10 hours per week; students are limited to a total of 20 hours per week for all jobs combined.

Faculty

Of the more than 100 faculty members at the College, more than 90 percent hold a doctorate or the highest degree in their fields; 25 percent of them are full professors, while another 70 percent are associate and assistant professors. A student-faculty ratio of 16:1 allows for greater classroom participation.

Student Government

The Student Senate includes members elected from classes, social clubs, and residence areas. The Executive Board includes a president, vice president, secretary, and treasurer, all of whom are elected each spring, and four independent representatives. In addition, the sophomore, junior, and senior classes each elect a president, vice president, secretary, and treasurer. Student Senate meetings are held biweekly and are open to all members of the College community.

Admission Requirements

Prospective students must submit an application form, a Secondary School Report Form that has been completed and signed by a guidance counselor, official high school transcripts, official ACT or SAT scores, and, optionally, letters of recommendation, a personal written statement, and a recent photo. The admission decision is based on an evaluation of the student's overall background, including extracurricular activities, community service, and volunteerism. However, students who have completed a college-preparatory curriculum with a C+ average or better and scored 18 or higher on the ACT (860 or higher on the SAT) may be qualified for admission. The college-preparatory curriculum includes 4 years of English, 3 years of college-prep math, and at least 2 years each of laboratory science, social sciences, and foreign language.

Application and Information

Admission is made on a rolling basis, so prospective students may apply any time after the end of their senior year. After all application materials are received, the Admission Committee notifies the applicant of their decision within a few weeks. Interested students may request applications from:

Office of Admission
Muskingum College
163 Stormont Street
New Concord, Ohio 43762
Phone: 740-826-8137
800-752-6082 (toll-free)
Fax: 740-826-8100
E-mail: adminfo@muskingum.edu
Web site: http://muskingum.edu/home/index.html

NAROPA UNIVERSITY

BOULDER, COLORADO

The College

Naropa University is a private, nonprofit, nonsectarian liberal arts institution with a core mission of contemplative education. This approach to learning integrates the best of Eastern and Western educational traditions, creating a complementary relationship between rigorous academic study and self-exploration at the deepest intuitive level.

Contemplative education offers students a highly experiential and transformative learning path that brings a spiritual component to the student's educational experience while sharpening skills crucial to critical thinking: reading, writing, speaking, and listening. This experience lets students be who they are while exploring who they want to be.

The curriculum integrates academic, artistic, and traditional Eastern awareness practices to enhance students' understanding of themselves, their field of study, and the world. As a result, Naropa students are better prepared for the constant challenges and rapid change of modern society. Through disciplines such as sitting meditation, yoga, and t'ai-chi ch'uan, students develop mindfulness and are trained to acknowledge the direct experience of learning, moment by moment. This process brings precision, openness, and kindness to oneself and others; it teaches students how to integrate intellect and intuition; and it amplifies the confidence and desire required to work for the benefit of others. This initiates a lifelong process of creative personal development that goes well beyond the college experience.

Students enjoy an environment of discovery and learning shared between themselves and the faculty. With a dual legacy from both the liberal arts and contemplative practice, a Naropa education offers dynamic, unpredictable, and engaging classes, where real learning and growth take place. Naropa undergraduates are independent thinkers, intellectually curious, civic-minded, adventurous, spiritual, and caring. They come from forty-five states and territories and eight countries, representing a wide range of life experiences, backgrounds, and ages. Of the 1,049 degree-seeking students at Naropa University, 444 are undergraduate students.

Naropa University was founded thirty-five years ago by Chögyam Trungpa Rinpoche, a Tibetan meditation master and scholar, who envisioned a liberal arts institution that would honor and respect the importance of various world wisdom traditions, including his own, and offer an educational experience that integrated knowledge of oneself with knowledge of the external world for a transformative learning path.

Accredited by the Higher Learning Commission of the North Central Association of Colleges and Schools, Naropa University offers B.A. and B.F.A. degrees through its four-year undergraduate program as well as M.A., M.Div., and M.F.A. degrees through its graduate school.

Location

Naropa University is located in Boulder, Colorado, at the base of the Rocky Mountain foothills and 25 miles northwest of Denver. Boulder offers something for everyone and has earned a well-deserved reputation for a great quality of life with a dynamic arts community, excellent music venues, and many cultural events. Hiking, skiing, and snowboarding enthusiasts have ample opportunity to pursue their sport and recreation activities. Boulder has bike paths all over town, and Boulder public transportation provides a frequent and comprehensive bus schedule throughout the day.

Naropa University has three campuses in Boulder, two of which serve undergraduate programs. The Arapahoe Campus is home to classrooms for most undergraduate classes, undergraduate advising, university administration, a performing arts center, a meditation hall, the Allen Ginsberg Library, a computer center, an art gallery, student lounges, the bookstore, and the Naropa Café. The Nalanda Campus, approximately 3½ miles from the Arapahoe Campus, is home to Naropa's performing and visual arts programs.

Majors and Degrees

Naropa University offers a B.F.A. in performance and ten B.A. degree programs: contemplative psychology, early childhood education, environmental studies, interdisciplinary studies, music, peace studies, religious studies, traditional Eastern arts, visual arts, and writing and literature.

The contemplative psychology major integrates Western psychology and Eastern approaches to healing mind and body. Students choose a concentration in psychological science, psychology of health and healing, somatic psychology, or transpersonal and humanistic psychology.

Nurturing the genuine and compassionate nature of teachers, the early childhood education major applies teaching methods drawn from Waldorf, Montessori, and Buddhist traditions. The major offers apprentice-style internships with master teachers from these traditions in a variety of contemplative preschool settings.

The environmental studies major empowers students to develop the knowledge base and skill set needed to address complex environmental issues. Core courses emphasize field science, sacred ecology, sustainability, horticulture, environmental history and justice, and learning community.

Interdisciplinary studies invites students to design a major by selecting courses from two or three disciplines at Naropa. Recent examples of senior work include Documentary Poetics, The Embodied Teacher, and Shambhala Path of Hip-Hop Warriorship.

Naropa's music major gives students fundamental training in musicianship that includes harmonic analysis, ear training, rhythmic acuity, music theory, improvisation, composition, history, and multicultural perspectives.

The peace studies major focuses on the study of peace and explores the causes of violence and war through four related areas of inquiry: history and politics of social change, theory and practice of peacemaking, the arts in peacemaking, and engaged learning.

The major in religious studies emphasizes the role of contemplative practice in the world's great religions, especially Buddhism, and uses present traditions from perspectives sympathetic to the living religious communities themselves.

The traditional Eastern arts major is the only degree program of its kind in the country, combining the practice of sitting meditation with an in-depth study of the philosophy, history, and culture of a body-mind awareness discipline. Concentrations are offered in aikido, t'ai-chi ch'uan, or yoga teacher training.

The visual arts major blends traditional and contemporary visual arts study with contemplative practice while offering courses in photography, calligraphy, sculpture, pottery, and several painting media.

Writing and literature offers intensive training in the practice and study of writing through small writing workshops, literary studies courses, and exposure to a range of contemporary writing offered through the Summer Writing Program.

The B.F.A. in performance offers rigorous technical training, an emphasis on student-centered creative process, and a contemplative approach to performance and performance studies.

Academic Programs

Undergraduate students develop competencies in college-level academic studies and are exposed to a breadth of knowledge, practice, and experience necessary for success in their major and minor fields of study. Core course work is designed to help students think and read critically, write effectively, identify and understand multicultural issues, and cultivate awareness and compassion for others. Naropa's core requirements include the humanities, the arts, cultural and historical studies, diversity, world wisdom traditions, contemplative practice, body/mind practice, writing skills, and scientific inquiry. Students explore the meaning of effective citizenship through the integration of classroom learning and community engagement.

Upon completion of 30 semester credits, students may declare a major. Students must complete a total of 120 semester credits to earn an undergraduate degree.

Off-Campus Programs

Community-based learning is offered through Naropa University's Community Studies Center and provides opportunities for students and faculty members to develop skills for participating in the public life of their communities. Through its emphasis on applied, experiential projects, community-based learning offers Naropa University faculty members and students innovative tools to forward the knowledge of their academic and artistic disciplines, augment student learning, and educate a citizenry to perform the public work of a democracy. The Community Studies Center also provides AmeriCorps scholarship funds for Naropa students involved in community work.

Costs

Undergraduate tuition for the 2009–10 academic year is $23,420. The on-campus room and board costs are $7758.

Financial Aid

Naropa University makes every attempt to assist students who do not have the financial resources to accomplish their educational objectives. Naropa offers institutional grants and scholarships as well as all types of federal student aid. Some financial aid for international students is also available. Approximately 67 percent of Naropa degree-seeking undergraduate students receive financial assistance in the form of loans, student employment, scholarships, and grants.

Faculty

The Naropa University faculty is distinguished by a wealth of experience in the professional, artistic, and scholastic applications of their disciplines. In addition to the outstanding core faculty, an international community of scholars and artists is consistently drawn to Naropa because of its strong vision and leadership in education. The average class size is 14, and Naropa's student-faculty ratio is 10:1.

Student Government

The Student Union of Naropa (SUN) consists of two active branches: United Naropa (UN) and Student Life Programming (SLP). Both groups share an overarching purpose: to represent the student voice, to empower student engagement, and to provide opportunities for student leadership.

United Naropa (UN) is comprised of students representing their academic departments with a focus on student action, connections, and communication among the departments, to ensure student input in decision making.

Student Life Programming (SLP) is a committee of students that organizes and supports student life beyond the classroom through planning various campus activities, overseeing the student lounges, and supervising student organizations. Both bodies of SUN have adopted a nonhierarchical structure for conducting their business.

Admission Requirements

Naropa University seeks students who have a strong appetite for learning and who enjoy experiential education in an academic setting. The Admissions Committee considers academic background, connection to Naropa's unique mission, and readiness to engage in contemplative, experiential college work when making admission decisions. A student's transcript, essays, interview, and letters of recommendation play important roles in the admissions process. SAT and ACT scores are optional.

Application and Information

A completed application for admission to Naropa University includes a $50 nonrefundable application fee, three essays, two letters of recommendation, official high school transcripts for first-year applicants (0 to 30 credits), and official transcripts from all previous college-level study. Many departments also require supplemental application materials. An interview, either in person or by telephone, is required for all programs, with the exception of writing and literature.

Prospective students are strongly encouraged to visit the University. The Office of Admissions hosts a preview weekend each semester, and guided campus tours are offered throughout the year.

The suggested deadline for receiving completed applications for the fall semester is January 15 and for the spring semester, October 15. Any applications received after the suggested deadline are reviewed on a space-available basis. For additional information, prospective students should contact:

Admissions Office
Naropa University
2130 Arapahoe Avenue
Boulder, Colorado 80302-6697
Phone: 303-546-3572
800-772-6951 (toll-free)
Fax: 303-546-3583
E-mail: admissions@naropa.edu
Web site: http://www.naropa.edu

The Lincoln Building at Naropa University.

NAZARETH COLLEGE OF ROCHESTER

ROCHESTER, NEW YORK

The College

Nazareth College is an independent, coeducational, comprehensive college that offers career programs solidly based in the liberal arts. Its suburban campus is located in Pittsford in western upstate New York, approximately 7 miles from the city of Rochester. Founded in 1924, the College has conferred more than 27,000 baccalaureate and master's degrees. Of the more than 3,200 men and women enrolled at Nazareth, more than 2,000 are undergraduates.

Twenty-two buildings of traditional and contemporary design are conveniently situated on the College's 150-acre campus. The Otto A. Shults Community Center, housing a 20,000-square-foot gymnasium, the student union, a multi-faith religious center, a 25-meter swimming pool, the fitness center, and student personnel offices, is the hub of on-campus student life. The resident students, constituting two-thirds of the undergraduate population, are housed in eleven separate residence halls. As an alternative to traditional campus housing, foreign language majors may live in La Maison Française, which is maintained by the language department. The Casa Italiana, Casa Hispana, and German Cultural Center serve as facilities for social, cultural, and academic programs reflecting Italian, Spanish, and German heritages, respectively.

Intercollegiate athletics are available in the areas of men's and women's basketball, equestrian, golf, lacrosse, soccer, swimming and diving, tennis, track and field and cross-country, volleyball, and women's field hockey and softball.

Location

Rochester, a city of more than 300,000 people, is the third-largest city in New York State and the site of cultural, educational, and industrial centers. Located on the shore of Lake Ontario, the city is noted for the Eastman Theatre, the Strasenburg Planetarium, and the International Museum of Photography at the George Eastman House. Rochester is the world headquarters of Eastman Kodak and Bausch & Lomb and the site of a major Xerox facility. It is only 20 minutes from beautiful mountains, lakes, and recreational areas, where students can enjoy various outdoor activities, including skiing, hiking, water sports, and camping. The city supports professional sports teams in baseball, hockey, lacrosse, and soccer.

Majors and Degrees

Nazareth College awards the Bachelor of Music degree and Bachelor of Arts and Bachelor of Science degrees in accounting, American studies, anthropology, art (studio), art education, art history, biochemistry, biology, business administration, business and marketing education, chemistry, communication and rhetoric, communication sciences and disorders, economics, English, environmental science, foreign languages (French, German, Italian, Spanish, and modern foreign languages), health science/physical therapy, history, human resource management, information technology, international business, international studies, mathematics, marketing, music, music business, music education, music performance, music theater, music theory, music therapy, nursing, peace and justice studies, philosophy, political science, psychology, religious studies, social science, social work, sociology, and theater arts.

Preprofessional programs are available in dentistry, law, and medicine. Teacher certification (grades 1–9 and 7–12) is offered with many majors. Certification in learning disabilities is available through an undergraduate program in inclusive education (grades 1–9 and 7–12). Certification for birth–12 is offered in art education, business education, music education, and speech pathology (communication sciences and disorders).

Academic Programs

To qualify for a degree, a candidate must fulfill the core curriculum requirements of the College as well as those of the major department or area of concentration. The candidate must also earn a minimum of 120 semester credits and satisfy a comprehensive test requirement in the major field during the senior year.

Off-Campus Programs

Nazareth College offers Study Abroad programs in affiliation with the Université de Haute Bretagne in Rennes, France; the Institute of Spanish Students in Valencia, Spain; and the Universita degli G. D'Annunzio in Pescara, Italy. Students need not be language majors to take advantage of this exceptional program. Language students taking German or Japanese have the opportunity to study at the Studienforum in Berlin and Osaka University in Japan, respectively. Nursing students have opportunities to study in Finland and Hungary. Education students can do student teaching in Wales.

Nazareth College is a member of the Rochester Area Colleges, a consortium that includes Rochester Institute of Technology, the State University of New York College at Geneseo, and the University of Rochester, among others. Through this consortium, Nazareth College students can cross-register for credit in up to two courses per semester at any of the member institutions on a space-available basis.

Academic Facilities

Nazareth's classrooms, laboratories, and studios are located in Smyth Hall, Carroll Hall, the Golisano Academic Center, and the award-winning Arts Center, which houses art, music, and theater facilities as well as a 1,000-seat auditorium. The Golisano Academic Center and Carroll Hall houses speech pathology, physical therapy, counseling, and health services. Lorette Wilmot Library houses 248,000 volumes and has extensive resources in such areas as women's studies, education, minority issues, and religions in America. The library subscribes to approximately 1,900 periodicals and other serials. The building has seating for 450 students and includes a large number of individual carrels. The library also has a fine collection of lecture tapes and a growing collection of musical and spoken-word disks and tapes. The Rare Book Room is distinguished by special collections of works by Maurice Baring, Hilaire Belloc, Gilbert Keith Chesterton, and the Sitwells. The library is currently enlarging its resources and services in the nonprint media. In addition, the College's membership in the regional consortium and the Online Computer Library Center provides students with access to the resources of 1,300 other academic and research libraries.

Costs

Total estimated costs for 2010–11 are $36,860. This included $25,045 for tuition, $10,715 for room and board, and $1100 for the required fees. The total does not include books, personal expenses, or transportation (if applicable). All fees are subject to change; up-to-date information can be obtained from the Admissions Office.

Financial Aid

Nazareth College endeavors to meet financial need as demonstrated on the Free Application for Federal Student Aid (FAFSA). The FAFSA should be submitted by February 15 of the year in which the student intends to enroll. The CSS PROFILE is required of early decision applicants only and should be submitted by November 15. Financial assistance is available through grants, loans, employment, and scholarships. Sources of aid include the Federal Pell Grant, New York Tuition Assistance Program, Federal Perkins Loan, and Federal Work-Study programs; the New York State Higher Education Services Corporation; and Nazareth College merit scholarships and grants.

Faculty

The full-time faculty members in the various academic departments hold advanced degrees from more than 100 institutions throughout the United States and abroad. Ninety-four percent of the faculty members hold the highest degree offered in their field of study. The student-faculty ratio of approximately 12:1 and an average class size of 19 ensure that students receive the individual attention that only a small college can offer.

Student Government

The Undergraduate Association of Nazareth College is the vehicle through which students can express the need for and initiate change within the College community. It is also responsible for the disbursement of funds, generated from the undergraduate activities fee, to various activities and social/cultural clubs.

Admission Requirements

Nazareth College welcomes applicants of all ages and educational backgrounds. Students of any race, color, sex, or national or ethnic origin are admitted to all of the rights, privileges, programs, and activities generally accorded or made available to students at the College. Nazareth College does not discriminate on the basis of race, color, sex, or national or ethnic origin in the administration of its educational policies, scholarship and loan programs, and sports and other school-administered programs.

Recommended academic preparation includes courses in English, college-preparatory mathematics, social studies, a foreign language, and science. Although the Admissions Committee considers academic achievement and potential for collegiate success, it also considers talent in art, drama, or music and involvement in cocurricular activities. A personal interview, although not required, is strongly recommended, as it allows the applicant to view the campus and facilities, talk with students and faculty members, and meet with an admissions counselor.

Nazareth College is pleased to consider applications from students in good standing at accredited two- and four-year colleges and universities. A minimum GPA of 2.5 or better is expected. Transfer applicants who hold, or will hold prior to registration, the Associate in Arts (A.A.) or the Associate in Science (A.S.) degree from a fully accredited college may transfer a maximum of 60 semester hours of credit and enter with full junior status. Transfer applicants who hold, or will hold prior to registration, the Associate in Applied Science (A.A.S.) degree, or the Associate of Occupational Studies (A.O.S.) degree from a fully accredited college or institute will have these credits evaluated on a course-by-course basis. Careful advisement on tailoring programs for holders of these degrees is offered by Nazareth College.

Application and Information

Regular decision applicants for the fall semester should submit the application form, transcripts, standardized test scores, an essay, recommendations, and a $40 application fee by February 15 (November 15 for early decision and December 15 for early action). Notification for regular decision begins March 1 (December 15 for early decision and January 15 for early action). For more information regarding the different application options, students should contact the Admissions Office.

For an application packet or information about a campus tour and interview, applicants should contact:

Vice President for Enrollment Management
Nazareth College
4245 East Avenue
Rochester, New York 14618-3790
Phone: 585-389-2860
800-462-3944 (toll-free)

NEUMANN UNIVERSITY

ASTON, PENNSYLVANIA

The University

Neumann University (formerly Neumann College), a Catholic coeducational institution in the Franciscan tradition, recognizes the value of developing intellectual excellence, professional competence, and strong community life. As a university that balances the liberal arts with the professions, Neumann was founded to meet and expand the educational and professional horizons of men and women through instruction that is based on values, ethical behavior, and service to others. With the addition of the Living and Learning Center (multimedia-capable residences), Neumann University serves a diverse geographic and demographic population.

Founded and sponsored by the Sisters of St. Francis of Philadelphia, the University is committed to a varied student body and welcomes students of all denominations. Current enrollment is 3,084.

The Life Center houses the Meagher Theatre, the Bruder Athletic Center, and the Crossroads Cafe dining facility. Intercollegiate sports include women's basketball, field hockey, ice hockey, lacrosse, soccer, softball, tennis, and volleyball and men's baseball, basketball, golf, ice hockey, lacrosse, soccer, and tennis. Neumann University competes as a member of the National Collegiate Athletic Association (NCAA) Division III, the Pennsylvania Athletic Conference (PAC), and the Eastern Collegiate Athletic Conference (ECAC). Intramural sports are available to all members of the campus community.

The Living and Learning Center is designed to provide a state-of-the-art residential experience, with a focus on education within a real-world living environment. Technologically smart, the center connects students to both faculty members and friends via the Internet, which is available in every suite and apartment. The system provides full access to campus resources and activities, as well as activities and resources worldwide. The center also houses a separate computer lab, a fitness center, a reflection room, various study rooms with warming kitchens for group study or meetings, and a laundry.

The University provides a full range of services to students, including career placement, which averages above 95 percent within six months of graduation; career and personal counseling; a tutoring program; and health services.

Neumann students are involved in a wide variety of campus and community activities. Major and special interest clubs are available for student participation. Clubs bring together students who share common interests and help foster new friendships.

At Neumann, the spiritual dimension of one's life is recognized as integral to total human development. The Ministry Team provides a pastoral presence on campus and promotes a sense of community. The entire University community is invited to serve the needs of the poor and neglected in society through various outreach programs, with special attention to the need for peace and justice in the world today.

Neumann is well positioned to respond to the academic and extracurricular needs of students who are of traditional or nontraditional age, commuters or residents, and full-time or part-time.

In addition to undergraduate programs, Neumann confers master's degrees in education, nursing, pastoral counseling, sport management, and strategic leadership as well as doctoral degrees in education (Ed.D.) and physical therapy (D.P.T.).

Location

Neumann, with a beautiful 63-acre suburban campus in Aston, Delaware County, Pennsylvania, is a short distance from Philadelphia; Wilmington, Delaware; southern New Jersey; and Maryland. It is easily accessible from major arteries such as I-95, Route 476, Route 1, and the Pennsylvania Turnpike.

Majors and Degrees

Neumann offers strong academic majors leading to a Bachelor of Arts degree or a Bachelor of Science degree in accounting, arts production and performance, athletic training, biology, business administration, communication and media arts, computer and information management, criminal justice, education, English, environmental studies, international business, liberal arts, marketing, nursing, political science, psychology, and sport management. The education programs lead to teacher certification in Pennsylvania and reciprocating states, with secondary certification in biology/general science, English, social studies, and special education. Preprofessional programs in law and medicine are also available. An accelerated evening program for adults using a 6-credit seminar format leads to an Associate of Arts, Bachelor of Arts, or Bachelor of Science degree in liberal studies.

Academic Programs

The academic program at Neumann University is composed of a core curriculum (required of all students), a major area of study (chosen by each student), and a wide range of elective offerings. Students may also choose a minor area of study. The University's broad base of liberal arts offerings prepares students for the intellectual and social challenges they will face in the employment marketplace and throughout their lives. The core is intended to provide basic knowledge of the liberal arts and sciences; develop verbal, written, and symbolic communication skills; and stimulate interest in a broad range of topics for the purpose of enhancing the individual's contributions to society, thereby enabling the individual to realize full human potential.

Classroom instruction is supplemented by cooperative education and internships, through which students can earn credit and gain experience by working in a job related to their career interest. Fieldwork and student teaching are required of all education majors. Clinical practice for the nursing major occurs in a variety of health-care facilities in the tristate area.

The honors program is an opportunity for academically talented students to explore imaginative and innovative perspectives on learning. It is also an opportunity to stimulate and motivate students to expand their knowledge and interest and to strive for greater excellence. Moreover, it is a reward for prior perseverance and dedication as well as an obligation to use skills and abilities in service to others. Admission to the honors program is by invitation.

Neumann University has transfer articulation agreements with numerous schools throughout the area.

Academic Facilities

The Child Development Center is a state-of-the-art, octagonal-shaped building, specifically designed to house an educational program for preschoolers. As a state-licensed day-care facility, it enrolls children of Neumann students, the faculty, and the community. The Child Development Center is part of the Division of Education and Human Services. Students enrolled in education courses use the center for observation, practical experience, and student teaching.

The Academic Computer Center is located on the ground floor of the University. The computers are viewed as tools to support all fields of study and all students and faculty members. Neumann University has installed a wireless Local Area Network (LAN) that connects various computers and provides shared services such as printing, e-mail, and support for the instructional use of computers by providing for the sharing of files. Computers are available to all students, as is software related to various academic disciplines. Access to the Web and the Internet is available.

The Academic Resource Center is a service that enables students to meet Neumann's academic standards and successfully attain their personal educational goals.

The University library contains a balanced collection of more than 70,000 volumes, 95,000 microfilm units, 2,000 videos, and 400 periodical subscriptions. Private study rooms and conference rooms are available for both student and faculty use. In addition to traditional media services support, a full-color video studio and a graphics production area are available. Serving as a comprehensive resource for students, other holdings include Neumann's online catalog system, Francis, which is accessible via the Web. The library is a member of the Tri-State College Library Cooperative, the Consortium for Health Information and Library Services, SEPCHE, and the Online Computer Library Center, which provide additional convenient resources for students. The library subscribes to various online research services.

Costs

Tuition for full-time students (12 to 18 credits per semester) in 2009–10 was $20,580. Room and board were $9906 (full meal plan).

Financial Aid

Typically, about 95 percent of Neumann undergraduate students receive some form of financial aid (scholarships, grants, and student loans).

Neumann offers a variety of renewable scholarships each year to entering full-time freshmen. Interested applicants should contact the Office of Admissions and Financial Aid as soon as possible to determine eligibility.

In addition to Neumann scholarships, funds are available through the Federal Pell Grant, Federal Supplemental Educational Opportunity Grant, and Federal Work-Study Programs. Many states provide grant money to attend Neumann (non-Pennsylvania residents should check with their state's higher education agency for details). Veterans Administration benefits can be received by qualified veterans or their dependents. Federal Stafford Student Loans and Federal PLUS Program loans are available and can be applied for through Neumann's preferred lender or any participating bank. Neumann also offers institutional need-based grants. All students requesting financial aid must complete the Free Application for Federal Student Aid (FAFSA) each year to determine eligibility. In order to expedite processing, the FAFSA should be submitted by March 15 for the following school year. Financial aid funds are renewable annually based on need, as determined by the FAFSA results.

Faculty

Neumann students describe faculty members as sincere, hard working, determined, and energetic. Faculty members view themselves, first and foremost, as teachers and are proud partners in their students' journeys toward professional careers. Each student has a faculty adviser, who assists in arranging a program designed to meet the student's educational goals. Many faculty members serve as moderators of student clubs. The student-faculty ratio is 14:1.

Student Government

The Student Government Association (SGA) is the representative body for all students. Its function is to implement the aims and purposes of the University, foster cooperation in student relationships, assist the University in being responsive to the needs of the student body, and encourage personal responsibility for an intelligent system of student self-government. Through the Student Activities Board, social functions are planned throughout the year. Students serve on various University committees, including the Student Affairs Committee of the Board, Academic Advising Committee, Honors Program Committee, Registration/Orientation Task Force, and Student Judicial Board. For full-time students, a Student Government Association fee of $60 per semester is required.

Admission Requirements

Neumann has a rolling admission policy and accepts applications throughout the year. Applicants are considered on the basis of high school record, SAT or ACT scores, recommendations, class rank, and other indicators of potential to succeed in university-level studies. Applications for admission are reviewed without regard to sex, race, creed, color, national origin, age, sexual orientation, pregnancy, military status, religion, or disability. Applicants should be graduates of an accredited high school (or present equivalent credentials) and have a recommended curriculum of 16 units of high school course work, distributed as follows: 4 in English, 2 to 3 in science, 2 in mathematics, 2 in social studies, 2 in foreign language, and 4 in electives. Students intending to pursue a major in biology or clinical laboratory science must have at least 1 year of high school biology and chemistry, and high school physics is also highly recommended.

Neumann participates in the Advanced Placement (AP) Program and the College-Level Examination Program (CLEP). Students with superior ability and a sound academic background may begin University studies at the end of the junior year in high school.

An interview and tour of the campus are highly recommended for all prospective students and parents. Visits can be arranged by contacting the Office of Admissions.

Application and Information

Applicants for freshman admission are requested to have SAT or ACT scores and high school transcripts sent to the Office of Admissions. A nonrefundable $35 application fee should accompany the completed application. A free application is available online at http://www.neumann.edu.

Neumann University welcomes applications from students who have attended or are currently attending either two-year or four-year regionally accredited institutions of higher learning.

For further information, students should contact:

Office of Admissions
Neumann University
One Neumann Drive
Aston, Pennsylvania 19014-1298
Phone: 610-558-5616
800-9NEUMANN (toll-free)
E-mail: neumann@neumann.edu

NEW COLLEGE OF FLORIDA

SARASOTA, FLORIDA

COLLEGE CLOSE-UPS

The College

New College of Florida offers serious students the opportunity to pursue rigorous academic study in an environment designed to promote depth in thinking, free exchange of ideas, and highly individualized interaction with faculty members.

Study is focused in the arts and sciences and is highly accelerated and independent. Nearly two thirds of the College's graduates pursue graduate or professional study, gaining admission to Harvard, Yale, MIT, Brown, Georgetown, Berkeley, and other leading graduate programs. New College is competitive with other top schools in the nation when it comes to the percentage of graduates who go on to earn the Ph.D., especially in the sciences.

New College was founded as a private institution in 1960 with a devotion to the values implicit in a liberal arts education and a dedication to creating an innovative academic program where talented students and outstanding faculty members could come together and pursue learning through small classes, seminars, and individual tutorials to pursue advanced undergraduate research. Entry into Florida's public university system in 1975 served to strengthen and perpetuate the idealistic vision and academic mission of the College's founders. These qualities, as well as the College's national reputation, were enhanced further in 2001 when New College was designated as the official honors college in the arts and sciences for the State University System of Florida. A public-private funding arrangement provides students at New College with a private honors college experience at a public college cost. As a result, the College is regularly featured in guidebooks as being among the nation's leading educational values and as one of the country's top small, public colleges.

New College's student population is 825, of whom approximately 60 percent are women. Approximately 20 percent of students are out-of-state or overseas residents. Through active recruitment of out-of-state students, the College plans to increase its percentage of non-Florida residents in the years ahead. First-year and second-year students must live on campus, but many continuing students choose to live on campus as well. In fact, five new, state-of-the-art residence halls opened at the start of the 2007–08 academic year, allowing New College to house nearly 80 percent of students on campus. The new residence halls include a variety of accommodation options to match student lifestyle interests and incorporate the latest in green building technology. Architecture for the new buildings complements existing campus dormitories, such as the College's historic Pei Residence Halls, which were designed by the eminent architect I. M. Pei in the 1960s. The historic, 131-room Pei complex provides rooms with individual entrances, private baths, central air-conditioning, and various combinations of large picture windows, sliding glass doors, and/or balconies. Two other campus dorms, Dort and Goldstein Residence Halls, provide apartment-style housing with four single rooms, two bathrooms, and a common living room and kitchenette in each unit. Dining facilities on campus include a campus dining hall with full meal plans available for both on- and off-campus students, a snack bar and deli, and the student-owned and -operated Four Winds Café. The College's Counseling and Wellness Center offers basic health care and personal counseling, as well as a variety of related services.

New College student life is informal. Activities are largely student initiated and include academic, artistic, religious, political, and recreational pursuits. The College's 110-acre bay front location on the Gulf of Mexico includes basketball, racquetball, tennis, and volleyball courts; a multipurpose soccer and athletic field; a running trail; a 25-meter swimming pool; and a comprehensive fitness center. Sailboats, sailboards, and canoes are also available for use by students and faculty members free of charge.

Location

Situated along the coastline of the Gulf of Mexico in southwest Florida, New College serves as the northern gateway to Sarasota, a bustling city with more than 250,000 residents. Located 50 miles south of Tampa, Sarasota is noted for its recreational, cultural, and artistic attractions, including beautiful white-sand beaches and an abundance of professional theater, art, and music venues. Notably, New College sits adjacent to the world-famous John and Mable Ringling Museum of Art, which offers students free entry to view its Baroque and Renaissance art collections.

The climate is semitropical, consisting of long, warm springs and autumns plus mild winters. Transportation from throughout the nation and within the city is readily accessible. Many major airlines serve Sarasota-Bradenton International Airport, which is proximate to the College. Within the city, buses link the campus to downtown, shopping malls, parks, and beaches. While mass transit is available, bicycling is the favored means of transportation among students. The College's Office of Student Affairs offers group outings on a regular basis to the Sarasota Downtown Farmers Market, grocery stores and other venues around town.

Majors and Degrees

New College awards the Bachelor of Arts degree in liberal arts and sciences. Each of the College's more than thirty different areas of concentration (majors) is an individualized program of study that students design in consultation with, and with the approval of, faculty members. These include anthropology, art history, biology, chemistry, Chinese language and culture, classics, economics, English, environmental studies, French language and literature, German language and literature, history, humanities, international and area studies, literature, mathematics, medieval and Renaissance studies, music, natural sciences, philosophy, physics, political science, psychology, public policy, religion, Russian language and literature, social sciences, sociology, Spanish language and literature, and urban studies. Partial areas of concentration include computational science, gender studies, and theater. Students may also pursue self-designed concentrations, with faculty permission. Premed, prelaw, and prebusiness advising and guidelines are provided by faculty members and by the Office of Career Education and Off-Campus Study.

Academic Programs

New College of Florida's academic program aims to encourage academic excellence, creativity, and personal initiative and to provide essential tools for lifelong intellectual, personal, and professional growth. The College's distinctive curriculum enables students, in close consultation with faculty members, to develop programs of seminars, tutorials, independent research, and off-campus experiences that meet each student's personal academic interests and goals.

At the end of each semester, rather than grades, students receive detailed narrative evaluations of their work from individual faculty members along with satisfactory/unsatisfactory assessments. In order to graduate, students must satisfactorily complete seven academic contracts (one per semester), three independent-study projects, a senior project, and an oral baccalaureate examination. In addition to the requirements for individual majors, students must complete eight courses within the liberal arts curriculum, with at least one course each in the humanities, social sciences, and natural sciences. All students must meet basic mathematics and computer literacy requirements, and pass or be exempted from Florida's College-Level Academic Skills Test.

The College operates on a 4-1-4 calendar year. The College offers a January interterm when students undertake independent-study projects, which they design and complete under faculty sponsorship.

Off-Campus Programs

Internships, fieldwork, and independent research away from the campus offer New College students the opportunity to gain new skills and test career interests. Because off-campus study can make a major contribution to an undergraduate education, New College facilitates such study through its flexible, individualized curriculum and special support services. New College is a member of the National Student Exchange, which provides access to more than 180 universities with programs in the U.S. and abroad (many with comparable tuition costs). Students may also participate in programs offered by independent providers, such as the School for International Training and

AustraLearn, as well as international programs available through the State University System of Florida and Center for Cross Cultural Studies. With faculty approval, students may pursue off-campus independent study or participate in programs including Living Routes, which offers nontraditional venues for study abroad.

Academic Facilities

New College's wireless-equipped Jane Bancroft Cook Library is befitting of one of the country's leading colleges for the liberal arts and has an open stack arrangement that allows free access to most materials. Administration, trustees, faculty members, and the New College Library Association have implemented an ambitious acquisition program to expand the current holdings of approximately 274,000 volumes. An expansion of the library's visual image collection is also in the works. In total, the library subscribes to more than 900 serial titles, including 700 magazines and journals and many state, national, and international newspapers. In addition, through computer networks and other cooperative programs, New College students and faculty members have access to hundreds of online databases and electronic journals and newspapers, as well as numerous online document delivery services. Through a comprehensive online interlibrary loan system, New College students also have ready access to holdings throughout Florida's public university libraries.

The Sudakoff Conference Center on campus hosts visiting lecturers, meetings of campus and community organizations, and an assortment of diverse special events. The Caples Fine Arts Complex includes the 264-seat Mildred Sainer Music and Arts Pavilion, which features student, local, and national performances; the Lota Mundy Music Building, which houses eight music practice rooms, plus the Benjamin and Barbara Slavin Electronic Music Studio; the Christianne Felsmann Fine Arts Building; the Betty Isermann Fine Arts Gallery and Studio; and a sculpture studio. Science facilities include the R. V. Heiser Natural Sciences Complex, which houses laboratories, classrooms, offices, a computer lab, two electron microscopes, and an auditorium, plus the $2.5-million Rhoda and Jack Pritzker Marine Biology Research Center. The marine center, one of the leading marine research centers in southwest Florida, features state-of-the-art culture rooms, laboratories, and aquariums with water drawn from Sarasota Bay. Saltwater effluent from the tanks is cleaned by means of a wetland constructed in 2001 as part of a New College senior thesis project. In January 2010, the College broke ground on the new 35,000-square-foot, LEED-certified Academic Center, featuring 10 new classrooms, 45 faculty offices, an on-site café, and a central plaza, that is expected to become a hub of student activity. The new Academic Center is scheduled to open in early 2011.

Costs

For the 2009–10 academic year, in-state tuition and fees at New College of Florida were $4784 and out-of-state tuition and fees were $26,386. Room and board costs were $7783.

Financial Aid

The actual cost of providing New College of Florida's highly individualized honors college experience is far greater than the state funding appropriated for support of the College. The New College Foundation secures independent funding to provide the difference. Part of the foundation's endowment produces income for scholarships.

Approximately 98 percent of New College students receive some form of financial assistance, including merit-based scholarships and need-based financial aid. To apply for financial aid, students should file the Free Application for Federal Student Aid (FAFSA). March 1 is the priority date for need-based financial aid. All first-time college students who complete applications by February 15 and who are admitted to New College are guaranteed merit scholarship funding. No additional scholarship application is necessary.

Faculty

Of New College's permanent faculty members, 100 percent hold the Ph.D. or terminal degree in their fields. They have come to New College from the finest universities nationally and abroad, drawn by an environment that emphasizes excellence in teaching and fosters a close-knit community of scholars. Faculty members sponsor individual students in the formulation of their academic programs, gradually moving toward a form of mentorship through which joint research is sometimes pursued. A 10:1 student-faculty ratio is a key factor in the College's individualized approach to education. At New College, all classes are taught by faculty, not by teaching assistants.

Student Government

Student input is a decisive factor in campus governance. Elected student representatives serve on the Board of Trustees, most major policymaking committees, and are voting participants in divisional and campuswide faculty meetings. The New College Student Alliance, the College's student government, has authority over funding for recreation, social events, and student organizations on campus.

Admission Requirements

New College of Florida seeks highly capable students eager to take responsibility for their own education. The admissions staff reviews each candidate individually, assessing his or her potential for success within, and contribution to, the College's unique environment. Writing ability, academic record, and course selection are focal points of the committee's review. The majority of first-year students entering in fall 2009 ranked in the top 10 percent of their high school class. The middle 50 percent of SAT takers scored 1220–1400. The middle 50 percent of ACT takers scored 27–30.

All prospective students may apply for entrance to either the fall or the spring term. However, the College reserves the right to cancel the spring admission cycle if its enrollment goals have been met. Candidates must submit an admission application and fee/fee waiver, official transcript(s), SAT or ACT scores, and a letter of recommendation. Thorough research into the College and a campus visit are recommended for all those with serious interest in applying.

Application and Information

Admissions application materials and descriptive literature are available through the New College Office of Admissions and Financial Aid. The College has two application deadlines for the fall class: February 15 (the priority deadline) and April 15. Notification of the admissions decision occurs by April 1 and April 25, respectively. A completed application and all supporting documents must be submitted to the Admissions Office before a candidate is considered for admission.

Inquiries and application requests should be directed to:

Kathleen M. Killion
Dean of Admissions and Financial Aid
New College of Florida
5800 Bay Shore Road
Sarasota, Florida 34243-2109
Phone: 941-487-5000
Fax: 941-487-5010
E-mail: admissions@ncf.edu
Web site: http://www.ncf.edu

College Hall, former home of circus magnate Charles Ringling, helps form the picture-perfect setting for New College of Florida.

NEW ENGLAND COLLEGE

HENNIKER, NEW HAMPSHIRE

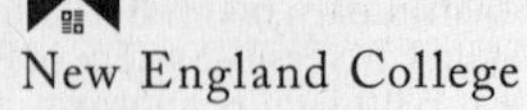

The College

New England College (NEC) is a place where students amaze themselves with what they learn and with what they can accomplish. A college that prepares students for the professional world, NEC also empowers its graduates with a broad knowledge base that results from a focus on the liberal arts and hands-on learning. In addition, students develop strong analytical and communication skills that are vital to success in any career. The College's current enrollment stands at about 2,477 students (1,219 are undergraduates). The diverse student body, which represents thirty-one states and twenty other countries, enriches the College curriculum's multicultural focus and global perspective. New England College prides itself on its commitment to each individual student and provides a strong support network to assist students with a variety of learning styles. The Pathways Center plays a key role in the academic and professional achievements of all students. It is an innovative combination of academic advising, study skills and support services, and career planning and placement. The Pathways Center is an integral part of academic life at NEC; students begin honing their academic and professional skills, planning for their future, and building their resumes from the moment they arrive on campus. Thus, NEC graduates are extremely successful in finding employment upon graduation. As an example, education majors have enjoyed 100 percent job placement over the last twelve years.

The campus, which is nestled in the center of Henniker, a classic small New England town, consists of thirty-two buildings. Students take advantage of the many extracurricular activities available at NEC, ranging from outdoor recreation to theater productions and the student newspaper. There are thirteen Division III intercollegiate sports teams at NEC in addition to numerous club and recreational sports options. The campus offers 26 acres of playing fields, a fitness center with the latest exercise and strength-building equipment, a gymnasium, and an indoor field house for student athletic activities. The Lee Clement Ice Arena, home to the NEC Pilgrims, provides some of the best hockey games in the region. The College's new state-of-the-art outdoor artificial turf field is scheduled to be ready for use in spring 2010.

Location

New England College's location offers students the best of all worlds. Students have easy access to vibrant cities and the incomparable recreation and wilderness regions of New Hampshire. The College is located a short drive from the state capital, Concord, and about 30 minutes from the state's largest city, Manchester, and its airport. Portsmouth, Boston, and some of the best ocean beaches in New England can be reached in just 90 minutes. Alpine and Nordic skiing opportunities abound. Pats Peak, located only 3 miles from the campus, provides free skiing and snowboarding to all NEC students. The College's 225-acre campus offers excellent trails for cross-country skiing and hiking. The Contoocook River flows through the center of the campus, spanned by the College's historic covered bridge, a popular subject for photographers, especially during autumn. Almost all NEC students reside on campus in the six residence halls located adjacent to classroom buildings and the student center.

Majors and Degrees

The College offers thirty-one majors, a remarkable number for a small college. Such variety permits students to consider a number of options before selecting a major, which is encouraged. Graduates of the undergraduate program are awarded the Bachelor of Arts or the Bachelor of Science, depending upon their major. A number of concentrations are offered within the majors, further permitting students to develop expertise based upon their specific career goals. For instance, a student can major in art with a concentration in photography.

Majors available at NEC include accounting, art, art history, biological studies, biology, business administration, communication, comparative literature, creative writing, criminal justice, educational studies, elementary education, engineering (3+2 program with Clarkson University), English, environmental chemistry, environmental science, environmental studies, environmental sustainability, health sciences, history, kinesiology, mathematics, outdoor leadership, philosophy, physical education, political science, psychology, secondary education, sociology, special education, sport and recreation management, theater, and theater education.

In addition, New England College offers a 3+3 program in conjunction with New York Law School that allows students to obtain their undergraduate and law degrees in six years. There are also a 4+1 M.B.A. program with Union University and a 4+3 Doctor of Physical Therapy program with Franklin Pierce University, giving students postgraduate opportunities to look forward to. In conjunction with Massachusetts College of Pharmacy and Health Sciences, NEC also offers Bachelor of Science in Nursing (B.S.N.), Master of Physician Assistant, and Doctor of Pharmacy programs.

Students may elect an individually designed major, combining elements from several majors, subject to faculty approval. Many students pursue internship options (required for 75 percent of majors) in a wide range of disciplines, including business, fine and performing arts, government, health care and human services, law, media and communications, professional sports, and many others. Recent internship sites have included National Public Radio, Disney World, the Verizon Wireless Center, the Army Corps of Engineers, the Manchester Monarchs, and Edge Sports. In addition, a joint venture between Edge Sports and the College has allowed students to manage the Edge Sports Magazine and Web site (http://www.edgesportsonline.com). This cross-curriculum project has provided students hands-on experience in the full production of these publications, from sales calls to marketing to layout and print.

Education majors have many opportunities to interact with children and adolescents, from the first year in their program to their capstone student-teaching experience.

Academic Programs

A comprehensive liberal arts college that also offers professional programs, NEC aims for its students to develop certain abilities: to think and communicate effectively, to understand the methods of the broad academic disciplines, to develop a strong sense of ethics, to respect other identities and cultures, and to develop a lifelong love of learning.

The First-Year Experience at NEC introduces students to college-level learning. It includes two writing courses, a computer technology course, seminars on what it means to be human and cultural diversity, a course in science, and a course in basic mathematics. The New England College curriculum is rooted in the belief that students learn best when actively involved with their subject matter; thus, NEC courses focus on learning by doing. Students may also apply to the honors program, where they can explore an academic discipline in more depth and graduate with either an honors certificate or honors diploma, depending on the tier in which the student enrolls. The academic year is divided into two main semesters, fall and spring. Additional sessions during January and the summer months offer students opportunities to take courses online or on campus. To graduate, students are required to complete a minimum of 120 credits as part of an approved program of study. CLEP and AP credits are accepted.

Off-Campus Programs

New England College encourages students to consider study-abroad options available to them via consortia agreements with a wide range of institutions located throughout the world. Students generally spend one semester when studying abroad, although some opt for a year-long program. Some of the participating institutions are located in Australia, Canada, England, France, Japan, and South Africa. Students may also choose to participate in travel courses, which are generally offered during the January term.

NEC's membership in the New Hampshire College and University Consortium (NHCUC) enables NEC students to take courses at any of the NHCUC member institutions and apply these credits to their degree program at the College.

Academic Facilities

The College's Center for Educational Innovation (CEI) was opened in 2001. A state-of-the art facility, the CEI provides networked data ports, Internet access, videoconferencing, and the full range of electronic and broadcast media access that enables professors to enhance their teaching by connecting to today's global network of information. The Simon Center, at the heart of the NEC campus, serves as the student center for the College. The entire campus is wireless, enabling students to access the College's network and the Internet from laptop computers at any location on campus. The H. Raymond Danforth Library provides a comprehensive research facility in addition to housing the Academic Support Center, where students may receive comprehensive subject tutoring and organizational and time management skill training from professional tutors. The library holds more than 100,000 volumes as well as a new thirty-three-station computer laboratory with Internet access. The science building serves as the home of the science departments, although classes for many other disciplines are scheduled in this large facility. Also located in the science building is the newly renovated Mainstage Theatre, where a number of plays are presented each year by NEC's outstanding Theatre Department.

Costs

For the 2009–10 year, tuition and fees were $27,450. Room and board were $9626.

Financial Aid

New England College offers a wide range of scholarships and grants for incoming students, ranging from $1500 to $18,000. The majority of these awards are merit-based, taking into account the student's academic achievement or other talents and accomplishments, such as participation in the arts, community service, and student government. Some need-based grants are available as well and are awarded to students based upon information provided on the Free Application for Federal Student Aid (FAFSA), and the NEC financial aid application. All awards are renewable on an annual basis, depending upon the student's academic record and/or documented financial need.

Faculty

There are 62 full-time faculty members at New England College. More than 76 percent hold terminal degrees in their fields. The NEC faculty is highly accomplished and active professionally, publishing books and articles, participating in national conferences, conducting scientific research, and creating works of art. The main focus of the NEC faculty members is teaching. They understand that students learn best by doing and so incorporate practical projects and activities into their course syllabi. The low student-teacher ratio (13:1) contributes to the friendly, highly personalized classroom experience. Students benefit from regular, personalized interaction with their professors, which helps them develop their knowledge and abilities beyond what they had ever thought possible.

Student Government

New England College's student government is actively involved in the academic, cultural, social, and organizational life of the institution. The Student Senate functions as a liaison between students and the NEC faculty, administration, alumni, and trustees. The Student Senate is responsible for its own budget, which funds numerous student-run clubs, organizations, social events, and recreational activities.

Admission Requirements

Freshman applicants must have received their high school diplomas (or equivalent) before attending New England College. A basic college-preparatory program is recommended, with course work in English, mathematics, science, social studies, and other academic electives. The Office of Admission takes into account the student's academic record, extracurricular activities and achievements, personal statement, and letters of recommendation, as well as the student's maturity and determination to succeed. Standardized tests (SAT or ACT) are not required, although most students submit scores. Students are encouraged to arrange an interview, conducted either in person or via telephone, with an admission counselor.

Application and Information

New England College has a rolling admission system; applications are reviewed as they become complete. All applicants must submit a completed application form, a $30 application fee, official high school transcripts covering at least the first marking period of the senior year, a personal essay, and two letters of recommendation from high school teachers or guidance counselors. Most students receive decisions within two weeks of their file's completion. Students are encouraged to apply early, as scholarship decisions are made shortly after admission, and they are considered for the full range of scholarship opportunities at the early part of the application cycle. Students whose native language is not English must submit TOEFL scores. Those students who do not meet TOEFL score minimums may participate in the English language learner (ELL) program at NEC. Transfer students must also provide official college transcripts and a supporting letter from their college's dean of students.

Application forms may be obtained from the Office of Admission or at the New England College Web site. Students may submit their applications online. For further information, interested students should contact:

Diane Raymond
Director of Admission
New England College
102 Bridge Street
Henniker, New Hampshire 03242-3297
Phone: 800-521-7642 (toll-free)
Fax: 603-428-3155
E-mail: admission@nec.edu
Web site: http://www.nec.edu/

Students enjoying a beautiful autumn day on the Gilmore Dining Hall deck.

COLLEGE CLOSE-UPS

THE NEW ENGLAND INSTITUTE OF ART

BROOKLINE, MASSACHUSETTS

The New England Institute of Art provides students with a creative educational environment and dedicated faculty members committed to preparing students to pursue entry-level positions in the creative arts. The New England Institute of Art offers ten bachelor's degree programs and three associate degree programs.

Under the guidance of industry professionals, students learn by doing the types of tasks they are likely to encounter in the workplace. In addition, assistance is available to help students with resume writing, networking, and keeping aware of what employers are looking for in job candidates.

The student population includes recent high school graduates, transfer students, and those who have left a previous employment situation to study and train for a new career. Students are creative, competitive, and open to new ideas. They place great value on an education that prepares them to pursue an exciting entry-level position in the arts.

The New England Institute of Art places a high value on the quality of student life inside and outside the classroom. Students can take part in a wide variety of activities, clubs and organizations, community service opportunities, and various student life enhancing committees.

Instructors are encouraged to look for upcoming books and to advise the administration of any books that may prove useful to their students. Students also have access to the public libraries.

The Student Affairs Office helps students who need assistance in locating housing.

The New England Institute of Art is accredited by the New England Association of Schools and Colleges (NEASC) through its Commission on Institutions of Higher Education (CIHE), 209 Burlington Road, Suite 201, Bedford, Massachusetts 02730-1433; phone: 781-271-0022.

The New England Institute of Art is authorized to award Associate in Science and Bachelor of Science degrees by the Commonwealth of Massachusetts, Massachusetts Department of Higher Education, One Ashburton Place, Room 1401, Boston, Massachusetts 02108-1696; phone: 617-994-6950.

Location

The New England Institute of Art is located in the heart of the Boston area, the home to more colleges and universities than any other city in North America. Museums and sporting events, theater, and a top 10 media market, are all easily accessible from the school.

Programs of Study and Degrees

Bachelor's degree programs are offered in advertising, audio and media technology, digital filmmaking and video production, fashion and retail management, graphic design, interior design, media arts and animation, photography, sound and motion picture technical arts, and Web design and interactive media.

Associate degree programs are offered in audio production, broadcasting, and photography.

The graphic design program is available in an evening and weekend option.

Academic Programs

The New England Institute of Art operates on a year-round, four-quarter system.

Academic Facilities

The New England Institute of Art is home to classrooms, studios, offices, a student lounge, a supply store, and a learning resource center. Equipment provided at The New England Institute of Art is specific to the program of study and may include projectors, editing decks, camcorders, PC and Macintosh computers, printers, drafting tables, and kitchen appliances.

Costs

Tuition cost varies by program. Prospective students should contact the school for current tuition costs. Other charges include a starting kit for all first-quarter students. Kits vary in price, depending on the program of study.

Financial Aid

Financial aid is available for those who qualify. Students who require financial assistance should first complete and submit a Free Application for Federal Student Aid (FAFSA) and meet with a financial aid officer.

Faculty

Faculty members at The New England Institute of Art have professional knowledge that they bring into the classroom. The school's faculty members provide their students with a unique, relevant educational experience. Faculty members are employed on a part-time and full-time basis.

Admission Requirements

Applicants must provide proof of high school graduation or achievement of a General Educational Development (GED) certificate as a prerequisite for admission. In lieu of documenting high school graduation or a GED certificate, applicants may provide proof of attaining an associate degree or higher from an accredited institution. An official transcript indicating date of high school graduation, GED certificate (including test scores), or date of college graduation (including degree granted) is required as proof.

All individuals seeking admission to The New England Institute of Art are interviewed in person or by phone by an assistant director of admissions, and each applicant must create an original essay of at least 150 words stating how an education at The New England Institute of Art would help the student to achieve career goals. There is a $50 application fee.

For the most recent information regarding admission requirements, please refer to the current academic catalog.

Application and Information

To obtain an application, make arrangements for an interview, or tour the school, prospective students should contact:

The New England Institute of Art
10 Brookline Place West
Brookline, MA 02445-7295
Phone: 617-739-1700
800-903-4425 (toll-free)
Fax: 617-582-4500
Web site: http://www.artinstitutes.edu/boston

The Art Institute of Atlanta; The Art Institute of Atlanta–Decatur[1]; The Art Institute of Austin[2]; The Art Institute of California–Hollywood; The Art Institute of California–Inland Empire; The Art Institute of California–Los Angeles; The Art Institute of California–Orange County; The Art Institute of California–Sacramento; The Art Institute of California–San Diego; The Art Institute of California–San Francisco; The Art Institute of California–Sunnyvale; The Art Institute of Charleston[1]; The Art Institute of Charlotte; The Art Institute of Colorado; The Art Institute of Dallas; The Art Institute of Fort Lauderdale; The Art Institute of Fort Worth[3]; The Art Institute of Houston; The Art Institute of Houston–North[2]; The Art Institute of Indianapolis[4]; The Art Institute of Jacksonville[5]; The Art Institute of Las Vegas; The Art Institute of Michigan; The Art Institute of New York City; The Art Institute of Ohio–Cincinnati[6]; The Art Institute of Philadelphia; The Art Institute of Phoenix; The Art Institute of Pittsburgh; The Art Institute of Portland; The Art Institute of Raleigh–Durham; The Art Institute of Salt Lake City; The Art Institute of San Antonio[2];The Art Institute of Seattle; The Art Institute of Tampa[5]; The Art Institute of Tennessee–Nashville[1,7]; The Art Institute of Tucson; The Art Institute of Vancouver; The Art Institute of Virginia Beach[1,8]; The Art Institute of Washington[1,8]; The Art Institute of Washington–Northern Virginia[1,8]; The Art Institute of York–Pennsylvania; The Art Institutes International–Kansas City; The Art Institutes International Minnesota; The Illinois Institute of Art–Chicago; The Illinois Institute of Art–Schaumburg; Miami International University of Art & Design; The New England Institute of Art.

[1]A branch of The Art Institute of Atlanta
[2]A branch of The Art Institute of Houston
[3]A branch of The Art Institute of Dallas
[4]The Art Institute of Indianapolis is regulated by the Indiana Commission on Proprietary Education, 302 West Washington Street, Room E201, Indianapolis, Indiana 46204, AC-0080
[5]A branch of Miami International University of Art & Design
[6]The Art Institute of Ohio–Cincinnati, 8845 Governors Hill Drive, Suite 100, Cincinnati, Ohio 45249-3317, OH Reg. #04-01-1698B
[7]The Art Institute of Tennessee–Nashville is authorized for operation as a postsecondary educational institution by the Tennessee Higher Education Commission.
[8]Certified by the State Council of Higher Education to operate in Virginia

THE NEW SCHOOL FOR JAZZ AND CONTEMPORARY MUSIC

NEW YORK, NEW YORK

THE NEW SCHOOL
A UNIVERSITY

The School

Part of The New School, a leading university in New York City, The New School for Jazz and Contemporary Music offers a unique course of study in which a passionately engaged faculty of professional artists, drawn from New York's renowned jazz community, guides serious, talented students toward high standards of achievement and the ongoing development of the individual creative voice. The School's curriculum is based on the tradition of artist-as-mentor and is taught by accomplished, active musicians with significant links to the history and evolution of jazz, blues, pop, and new genres.

Recognized as a leading center of arts education, The New School for Jazz and Contemporary Music is known for its curricular depth and the widely varied backgrounds of both students and instructors. Students do their core work in classrooms and private studios with exceptional musician-educators, gaining direct exposure to modern music's traditions and practices in an intellectual context that encourages exploration and innovation. Students have numerous opportunities for cross-registration in classes ranging from classical theory, composition, counterpoint, and musicology to music therapy, management, and liberal arts. The opportunity to take courses at Mannes College The New School for Music, a classical music conservatory, adds greater depth and provides an additional standard of professionalism against which students can measure their achievements and progress.

The School's primary goal is to provide students with a thorough technical, conceptual, and historical grasp of jazz and contemporary music, employing a comprehensive curricular structure in which teaching takes place in three environments: in the classroom, where students are instructed in ensemble playing, instrumental music, music history, and related topics; in traditional, tutorial instrumental study, where students meet one-on-one with great jazz and classical performers who live, work, and teach in New York City; and in master classes. These scheduled lectures/performances/workshops have featured such artists as Jon Faddis, Jim Hall, Barry Harris, Lee Konitz, Wynton Marsalis, and Jimmy McGriff.

There are a variety of activities in which students can become involved at New School Jazz and throughout the university. Interested students may serve on most New School committees, including Student Life, Libraries, Diversity, Food Services, and the Student Advisory Council. Jazz students have opportunities for involvement on the Executive Committee, the Curriculum Committee, the Student Advisory Council, and in the Pan-African Cultural Organization. The New School is also home to a wide variety of student organizations and clubs. Students are encouraged to form new student groups by contacting the Office of Student Life.

All first-time freshmen are guaranteed dormitory housing for their first year. The New School maintains several residence halls as well as university-leased apartments, most located within six blocks of the Greenwich Village campus. Through the enthusiasm and creativity of the resident advisers, students are exposed to diverse programs that take advantage of the rich traditions of The New School and the cultural opportunities of New York City. For additional information, students should contact the Office of University Housing at universityhousing@newschool.edu or 212-229-5459 or visit the Web site at http://www.newschool.edu/studentaffairs/housing/.

Location

The New School is located in Greenwich Village, home to many of the city's fabled jazz nightclubs, such as the Village Vanguard, Blue Note, Smalls, and Jazz Standard. The area is also home to design and art studios, galleries, shops, and restaurants as well as avant-garde artists, musicians, and writers. World-famous performance venues such as Carnegie Hall and Lincoln Center are just a short subway ride away. With its rich cultural resources, international sophistication, and cutting-edge attitude, New York City is a vibrant environment that has inspired and challenged artists throughout its history.

Majors and Degrees

The New School for Jazz and Contemporary Music offers the Bachelor of Fine Arts (B.F.A.) for instrumentalists and for vocalists. A five-year combined Bachelor of Arts/Bachelor of Fine Arts (B.A./B.F.A.) program is also available in conjunction with Eugene Lang College The New School for Liberal Arts.

Academic Programs

The B.F.A. degree is granted upon completion of at least 134 credits and must include 90 credits of applied music, along with the required liberal studies and music history distribution. The B.A./B.F.A. degrees are granted upon completion of at least 90 credits of applied music, along with 90 credits of liberal arts, which includes the required Lang seminars and senior work and can also include music history or other liberal arts credits.

Student progress is monitored on the basis of entrance evaluations, ensemble work, student juries (normally in the second half of the sophomore year), successful completion of the core curriculum, and the normal accumulation of course credits. In addition to course work within The New School for Jazz and Contemporary Music, students take some classes at Mannes College. Once this foundation is acquired, students experiment with a large number of theory and performance electives to define personal goals.

Off-Campus Programs

The New School's proximity to several major jazz record labels and performance venues offers significant opportunities for students. Music industry internships, such as those at Blue Note Records, Verve Records, BMG Records, Jazz at Lincoln Center, the Blue Note Jazz Club, and the Knitting Factory, provide hands-on experience, develop networking skills, and create potential job opportunities.

Students appear weekly on stages and in clubs throughout the city and the greater metropolitan area. Performances include weekly professional sessions at the Fat Cat jazz club, and the Jazz Presents series showcasing faculty with alumni or current students. New School Jazz musicians have also appeared at a number of high-visibility venues, including Jazz at Lincoln Center's Dizzy's Club Coca-Cola, and performed live at radio stations WBGO and WBAI. Students have access to the Gig Office, which connects them to professional performance opportunities.

The New School for Jazz and Contemporary Music and Veneto Jazz offer a two-week workshop in Bassano del Grappa, Italy. The workshop is taught by 8 of the finest New York musicians and faculty members from The New School. Courses are divided into various levels and include master classes, theory, arranging, combos, and Big Band, and public performances take place in the city theaters. This workshop is part of the Veneto Jazz Festival, one of the most important European jazz festivals.

Academic Facilities

The New School for Jazz and Contemporary Music is located on the fifth and sixth floors of 55 West 13th Street, the university's primary building for technology services. The School's 20,000-square-foot, state-of-the-art facility was designed specifically to help young artists realize their goal of becoming effective music professionals. The facility offers administrative, classroom, practice, and rehearsal space, all constructed with attention to acoustics, soundproofing, and aesthetics. All classrooms are fully dedicated with Yamaha grand pianos, drum kits, amplifiers, vocal PA systems, and full-component stereo systems. Specialized instrumental practice and teaching rooms are offered, as well as a listening library and piano/MIDI labs.

Performance and recording needs are served in an intimate 120-seat performance space, with full capacity for professional sound, lighting, and recording. A second studio is used for recording and engineering. Both studios are connected to the university's server and Internet sites, with the possibility for both posted archival recordings and live streaming performance. Additional university performance facilities within a two-block radius of the Greenwich Village campus include a 170-seat performance auditorium and an excellent and acoustically balanced concert hall with an audience capacity of 500.

A library consortium links the libraries at The New School with those at New York University and Cooper Union, making library privileges available reciprocally to matriculated students. This constitutes a resource of more than 3 million volumes and includes the Avery Fisher Center for Music and Media, which provides access to the most up-to-date electronic media, records, tapes, video, and a library of music materials. In addition, New School students have access to a wealth of public library resources throughout the five boroughs of New York City, including the New York Public Library for the Performing Arts, which is located in Manhattan at Lincoln Center.

The Office of Academic Computing operates three general-access laboratories; each offers a wide variety of software, including word processing, spreadsheets, databases, e-mail, music notation, and graphics and statistical packages. Students using the centers are supported by a full-time staff and assisted by lab aides. Training seminars and documentation are available on supported software and hardware. The Knowledge Union is a state-of-the-art film, video, and multimedia production facility located on the eighth and ninth floors of 55 West 13th Street. Among its studios is a dedicated music lab where many New School Jazz music technology courses are held.

Costs

Tuition for all full-time (12–18 credits) students was $16,430 each semester for 2009–10 ($32,860 for the year). B.A./B.F.A. students paid $16,905 (12–21 credits) per term ($33,810 for the year). Fees totaled $120 per semester (university services $100, divisional fee $15, student senate fee $5), plus $1714 for student health insurance during the academic year. Although housing costs vary depending on accommodations and meal plan selected, room and board average about $15,260 per year.

Financial Aid

Students may receive a merit scholarship award, which is determined at the initial audition as part of the acceptance package. Students are encouraged to apply during Audition Period 1, as scholarships are available on a limited basis to students auditioning during Audition Period 2 (late auditions). Students are encouraged to file the FAFSA form (online at http://www.fafsa.ed.gov) to determine eligibility for federal grants and loans. Almost 75 percent of students receive some kind of financial aid, awarded on the basis of financial need and merit. The university's financial aid office is open year-round to assist students and their families with the task of meeting educational costs. For information on specific kinds of assistance, amounts of funding, loan repayment, and scholarships for students meeting certain criteria, students should contact the financial aid office at 212-229-8930 or financialaid@newschool.edu.

Faculty

The faculty members of The New School for Jazz and Contemporary Music are drawn from the top ranks of professional musicians in the New York area. This unique artist-as-faculty concept offers extraordinary resources for weekly classes, individual private lessons, special performance events, and master classes. The key to the success of the School lies in its use of experienced professionals to guide the intense involvement of students in the challenges of small-group playing. Students work with the creators, not just the interpreters, of jazz and its offshoots.

Admission Requirements

An applicant must submit the completed application, the nonrefundable $100 application fee, a personal statement, official high school/secondary school transcript or school records, and one letter of recommendation from a teacher, counselor, or professional who can comment on the applicant's qualifications for study at The New School for Jazz and Contemporary Music. International applicants should supply official English translations of all documents and credentials and scores from the TOEFL (minimum 550 on the paper-based exam is preferred).

A performance audition is required of all students. A prescreen tape or CD is required for all applicants on drums, guitar, and voice. Vocalists who pass the prescreen must audition live; drummers and guitarists may audition live or online, or submit an audition tape or CD. Live auditions are held in February, March, and April.

Prospective students and their parents are welcome to tour the facilities of The New School for Jazz and Contemporary Music. Tours are offered Tuesday, Wednesday, and Thursday at 3 p.m. while school is in session. Students also have the opportunity to observe one of the improvisation ensembles. Students interested in scheduling a tour should call the Jazz office at 212-229-5896 Ext. 4589 or schedule online at http://www.newschool.edu/jazz at least one week in advance.

Application and Information

Applications are available online at http://www.newschool.edu/jazz. The priority deadline for fall admission is January 1 (the latest application deadline is March 15); the priority deadline for spring is September 15 (the latest deadline is November 1). Applicants are notified by April 1 and November 15, respectively. For more information, students should contact:

Teri Lucas, Director of Admissions
The New School for Jazz and Contemporary Music
55 West 13th Street, 5th floor
New York, New York 10011
Phone: 212-229-5896 Ext. 4584
Fax: 212-229-8936
E-mail: jazzadm@newschool.edu
Web site: http://www.newschool.edu/jazz

COLLEGE CLOSE-UPS

NEW YORK SCHOOL OF INTERIOR DESIGN

NEW YORK, NEW YORK

New York School of Interior Design
founded 1916

The School

The New York School of Interior Design (NYSID) is a nationally ranked, independent, nonprofit college accredited by National Association of Schools of Art and Design (NASAD). It was established in 1916 by architect Sherrill Whiton and chartered by the Board of Regents of the University of the State of New York in 1924. Throughout its history, the School has devoted all of its resources to a single field of study—interior design—and has played a significant role in the development of the interior design profession. Enrollment is approximately 750.

NYSID's curriculum is a reflection of the complex yet sophisticated profession of interior design. Courses stress the discipline's call to protect the health, safety, and welfare of the public while being functional and aesthetically pleasing. Today's students learn not only the colors and materials appropriate to residential interiors, but also how to design environmentally sound and accessible hospitals, offices, schools, restaurants, and more. Whether learning the importance of sustainability and historic preservation or the latest programs in computer-aided design, NYSID students learn a wide range of skills and techniques taught by faculty members who work in the field. The area's art and antique shops, museums, professional design studios, and showrooms are all an exciting part of the college's "campus."

The atmosphere of the college is cosmopolitan, not only because of its excellent location but also because it attracts students from all areas of the United States and abroad. International students make up approximately 10 percent of the student population. Students also transfer from other colleges in order to obtain a more professional, career-directed education.

Because of its select faculty and established reputation, the School continues to maintain a close relationship with the interior design industry. This provides an excellent means for students to develop associations that offer opportunities to move into the profession after completing their degree program at NYSID.

In addition to the four programs in interior design listed below, NYSID also offers three graduate programs: a professional-level Master of Fine Arts (M.F.A.) degree in interior design, a post–professional-level M.F.A. degree in interior design, and a Master of Professional Studies (M.P.S.) degree in sustainable interior environments.

Location

The New York School of Interior Design is located on Manhattan's Upper East Side, where many of the major interior design studios are located. Many of the world's most important galleries, museums, and showrooms are close by, most within walking distance. The city is world-renowned for its architecture, cosmopolitan urban experience, cultural activities, and historic districts. The college can be reached easily by bus, car, subway, and train.

Majors and Degrees

The New York School of Interior Design offers four programs in interior design: a four-year Bachelor of Fine Arts (B.F.A.) degree accredited by the Council for Interior Design Accreditation (CIDA), a two-year Associate in Applied Science (A.A.S.) degree, a 24-credit nondegree Basic Interior Design certificate, and a four-year Bachelor of Arts (B.A.) degree in the History of the Interior and the Decorative Arts.

Academic Programs

The New York School of Interior Design is devoted exclusively to the design of the interior environment. The various academic programs make up an integrated curriculum covering interior design concepts; history of art, architecture, furniture, and interiors; technical and communication skills, materials and methods, and philosophy and theory; and professional design procedures and design problem solving.

The Basic Interior Design program consists of a 24-credit required sequence of foundation courses in which all design students enroll. These courses provide a cultural, general, and professional introduction to the field of interior design. Although completion of the Basic Interior Design program may be the major goal for some, for most students it serves as the foundation for matriculation into the degree programs.

The A.A.S. degree program provides the minimum educational requirement to become a certified interior designer in New York State. The 66-credit program includes design, liberal arts, and professional courses.

The 132-credit Bachelor of Fine Arts degree program provides the education that, with practical experience, enables the graduate to take qualifying exams for interior design certification in many states and to join national and local professional associations. Studies focus on the development of a broad array of conceptual analysis, creative problem-solving, relevant cultural development, and technical skills. Students are required to take 32 credits of liberal arts courses in addition to 100 credits of professional design-related courses.

The 120-credit Bachelor of Arts in the History of the Interior and the Decorative Arts program provides students with an undergraduate liberal arts degree in art history with a special focus on the interior environment and the objects it contains. Graduates of the program have the opportunity to apply to NYSID's professional-level graduate program with one year of advanced standing, allowing the student to complete the three-year program in just two years.

NYSID's curriculum is flexible and permits students to take courses on a full- or part-time basis during the day or evening and on weekends. The college maintains an active job placement service. Students may be placed in a wide variety of positions that reflect the full spectrum of job opportunities in the interior design profession.

Academic Facilities

The NYSID campus occupies two buildings on Manhattan's Upper East Side. The college has a first-rate physical plant with light-filled studios; a unique lighting laboratory; a centralized computer facility for computer-aided design (CAD); a large atelier for independent work furnished with drafting tables, computers, and a materials collection for use in projects; a lecture hall and seminar rooms; a well-stocked bookstore; and a handsome auditorium. The library's collection includes more than 12,000 books on design, architecture, and allied disciplines; over 100 periodical subscriptions; a product literature collection; and an electronic image database for the study of the history of interior design and the decorative arts.

Costs

Tuition for B.I.D., A.A.S., and B.F.A. programs for 2010–11 will be $765 per credit, plus a $280 registration/technology/activities fee each semester. Typical expenses for the first year are projected to be $25,245 for tuition and $560 in registration fees. Students entering the B.A. program in fall 2010 will pay $11,500 per semester plus $280 in fees. NYSID room-only housing costs are approximately $15,600 for nine months.

Financial Aid

Financial assistance is available to students who are matriculated and in good academic standing. Both need- and merit-based scholarships are offered, and there are financial aid programs for both full- and part-time study. An applicant is considered for financial assistance upon completion of the Free Application for Federal Student Aid (FAFSA). This single application will be reviewed to determine a student's eligibility for Federal Pell Grants, Federal Supplemental Educational Opportunity Grants, Federal Work-Study Program, NYSID scholarships, and New York State aid, if applicable.

Faculty

Since New York City is a world-class design center, many top designers, art historians, architects, and authorities on the decorative arts teach and lecture at the college. NYSID faculty work as practicing designers in addition to being educators, authors, and active members of professional design organizations, and as such, give NYSID students special insight into the practice of their chosen field.

Student Government

The Student Council of the New York School of Interior Design is the elected voice of the student body in academic, administrative, residential, and leisure matters at the college. It is the representative forum through which student concerns are brought to the attention of the administration. It also organizes and sponsors a number of social events throughout the academic year.

In addition, the college has an active student chapter of the American Society of Interior Designers (ASID). ASID organizes lectures, tours, workshops, and other events providing an inside view of the interior design industry. The Contract Club arranges visits to top commercial interior design firms providing the opportunity to see actual projects being designed, ask questions of senior designers, and tour professional working offices.

Admission Requirements

All applicants must submit an application, an official secondary school transcript, SAT or ACT scores, and two letters of recommendation. Applicants to the A.A.S. and B.F.A. degree programs must meet the visual requirements by providing a portfolio or sketchbook, as described in the catalog and Web site; transfer students must also submit college transcripts.

International applicants should contact the college's International Student Adviser for assistance in applying.

Application and Information

Admission decisions are made on a rolling basis. However, for processing purposes, it is recommended that the Admissions Office receive an application for fall admission by March 1. An application for spring admission should be received by October 1. Applicants are notified of the Admission Committee's decision by mail shortly after all required documents have been received and visual requirements fulfilled.

Inquiries and applications should be directed to:

Director of Admissions
New York School of Interior Design
170 East 70th Street
New York, New York 10021-5110
Phone: 212-472-1500 Ext. 204
800-33NYSID (toll-free)
Fax: 212-472-1867
E-mail: admissions@nysid.edu
Web site: http://www.nysid.edu

The campus of the New York School of Interior Design is centered on its building at 170 East 70th Street in the Upper East Side Historic District.

NEW YORK UNIVERSITY

NEW YORK, NEW YORK

The University

New York University (NYU) is one of the foremost private research universities in the United States and the world. At its campus in downtown Manhattan, NYU offers over 230 undergraduate programs of study that match almost every professional interest. In addition, NYU's new campus and honors college in Abu Dhabi, the United Arab Emirates, is set to welcome its first class in fall 2010 and blends a global academic opportunity with a liberal arts, science, and engineering curriculum. No matter where in the world NYU students choose to study, the goal for educating undergraduates is lofty: to help them become confident, global citizens and tomorrow's leaders by cultivating a spirit of inquiry, creativity, and independent ambition.

NYU is a member of the prestigious Association of American Universities. Full professors teach at both the graduate and undergraduate levels. Eleven total undergraduate schools, colleges, and programs provide offerings in a wide range of subjects: more than 4,500 courses in over 230 major fields are available to full-time undergraduates. The average class size is under 30, and the faculty-student ratio is 1:12—benefits generally associated with a much smaller institution.

NYU's residence hall program is an important aspect of the total educational experience. Approximately 12,500 undergraduate students live in twenty-one University residence halls, seven of which are reserved exclusively for freshmen. All freshmen who request housing on their admission application and meet all deadlines are guaranteed housing during all their years of undergraduate study. Freshmen are not required to live on campus, and many students live in private apartments off campus.

The traditions of campus life—nearly 400 clubs, eighteen fraternities and ten sororities, and athletics and other activities—are very much a part of the University. Students have the opportunity to write for the campus newspaper and to work with the University's radio station, WNYU-FM. The Jerome S. Coles Sports and Recreation Center and the Palladium Athletic Facility serve all student recreational needs. Coles provides the setting for over 275 intramural sports teams and is home to NYU's twenty-one varsity teams. NYU and seven other private, urban research universities comprise the University Athletic Association (UAA). The athletic program includes men's basketball, fencing, golf, soccer, swimming and diving, tennis, track and cross-country, volleyball, and wrestling and women's basketball, cross-country, fencing, golf, soccer, swimming and diving, tennis, track, and volleyball.

Location

Located in Greenwich Village, NYU's New York City campus is unlike any other institution of higher education in the United States. When students enter, they become part of a community that combines the nurturing atmosphere of a small- to medium-sized college with the myriad offerings and research opportunities of a global, urban university. The energy and resources of the city serve as an extension of the campus, providing opportunities for research, internships, and job placement. On campus, NYU's intellectual climate is fostered by a faculty of world-famous scholars, researchers, and artists.

Additionally, in fall 2010, NYU is scheduled to open NYU Abu Dhabi in the United Arab Emirates, a highly selective liberal arts, sciences, and engineering college. As the first such campus operated by an American university outside of the United States and the only comprehensive liberal arts college in the Middle East that is fully integrated into a major research university, NYU Abu Dhabi is ready to welcome students with top qualifications from around the globe. Like NYU's campus at Washington Square in New York City, it will be a portal campus within NYU's extensive global network, offering a complete residential college education as well as access to NYU's international academic centers on five continents.

At NYU Abu Dhabi, students will be able to receive a four-year undergraduate education that begins with a curriculum incorporating the humanities, science, and technology, and moves into specialized courses in a chosen area of study, culminating with a capstone project. They will also have the opportunity to study abroad at NYU's academic centers around the world or at NYU in New York City.

Together, NYU's campus in New York City and the new Abu Dhabi campus form the backbone of a uniquely interconnected global network university. Faculty and students from either New York or Abu Dhabi may spend semesters abroad at one or more of NYU's numerous academic centers in Ghana, Germany, Argentina, Italy, England, Spain, France, the Czech Republic, China, and Israel—or in any of the 15 exchange programs the University has established with outstanding urban research universities around the world. NYU's individual schools and colleges also offer international intersession programming and major-specific, semester-long, and summer-long study abroad programs.

Majors and Degrees

NYU Abu Dhabi is slated to award B.A. and B.S. degrees in biology, brain and cognitive science, chemistry and biochemistry, computer science, economics and finance, engineering, film and media, history, literature, mathematics, music, philosophy, physics, political science, psychology, theater, and visual arts.

The College of Arts and Science awards B.A. and B.S. degrees in Africana studies, anthropology, anthropology-linguistics, art history, biochemistry, biology, chemistry, cinema studies (in conjunction with Tisch School of the Arts), classical civilization and Hellenic studies, classical civilization-anthropology, classics, classics-art history, comparative literature, computer science, dramatic literature, East Asian studies, economics, economics and computer science, economics and mathematics, engineering (chemical and biological, civil, computer, electrical, and mechanical, in a dual-degree program with Polytechnic Institute of NYU), English, English and American literature, environmental studies, European and Mediterranean studies, French, French and linguistics, gender and sexuality studies, German, German and linguistics, Greek, Hebrew language and literature, Hellenic studies, history, Iberian studies, international relations, Italian, Italian and linguistics, Jewish history and civilization, journalism, language and mind, Latin, Latin American studies, Latino studies, linguistics, Luso-Brazilian language and literature, mathematics, mathematics and computer science, medieval and Renaissance studies, metropolitan studies, Middle Eastern and Islamic studies, music, neural science, philosophy, physics, politics, psychology, religious studies, Romance languages, Russian and Slavic studies, self-designed honors major, social and cultural analysis, sociology, Spanish, Spanish and linguistics, and urban design and architecture studies. Preprofessional programs are available in dentistry, law, medicine, optometry, and podiatry. A seven-year B.A./D.D.S. program is also available.

The Leonard N. Stern School of Business awards the B.S. degree in accounting, actuarial science, business and political economy, economics, finance, information systems, management and organizations, marketing, and statistics.

The Steinhardt School of Culture, Education, and Human Development awards the B.S. in applied psychology, communication (with a major in media, culture, and communications), communicative sciences and disorders, education (with majors in childhood education/childhood special education; early childhood education/early childhood special education; and secondary education with teaching specializations in English, foreign languages, mathematics, science, or social studies), health (with a major in nutrition and food studies with specializations in food and restaurant management, food studies, and nutrition and dietetics), and public health. In arts professions, Steinhardt offers the B.F.A. in studio art, the B.S. in educational theater, and the B.Mus. in instrumental, music business, music education, music technology, music theory and composition, piano (classical and jazz), and voice (classical voice and music theater).

Tisch School of the Arts awards the B.A. in cinema studies (film history, theory, and criticism) and the B.F.A. in dance, dramatic writing, film and television (animation, film, television, and video), photography and imaging, recorded music, and theater (acting, directing, music theater, and technical production and design).

The Silver School of Social Work awards the B.S. degree in social work.

At the Gallatin School of Individualized Study, students under the mentorship of faculty advisers create and refine their own plans of study by combining Gallatin courses with courses at other schools within NYU, independent studies, and internships and, upon completion, receive a B.A. degree.

The Preston Robert Tisch Center for Hospitality, Tourism, and Sports Management at the School of Continuing and Professional Studies offers the B.S. in sports management and the B.S. in hotel and tourism management.

The College of Nursing awards the B.S. degree in nursing.

The Liberal Studies Program is a two-year course of study in the liberal arts that is offered to a select group of students chosen by the NYU Admissions Committee. After successful completion of this program, students move on as juniors into the school or college to which they originally applied.

The Global Liberal Studies Program is a B.A degree program in the liberal arts with a strong global component including international study.

Academic Programs

Requirements for graduation vary among departments and schools. A liberal arts core curriculum is an integral part of all majors. The baccalaureate degree requires completion of at least 128 credits. The University calendar is organized on the traditional semester system, including two 6-week summer sessions. Some divisions offer part-time programs during the day and evening and on weekends.

Off-Campus Programs

NYU's global network includes the NYU campus in New York City and the new portal campus in Abu Dhabi, United Arab Emirates, along with ten international academic centers in Accra, Ghana; Berlin, Germany; Buenos Aires, Argentina; Florence, Italy; London, England; Madrid, Spain; Paris, France; Prague, the Czech Republic; Shanghai, China; and Tel Aviv, Israel. Additionally, NYU has exchange agreements with fifteen outstanding urban research universities around the world. The individual NYU schools and colleges also offer international intersession programming and major-specific, semester-long, and summer-long study-abroad programs.

Students move with ease between locations within NYU's global network. They may find themselves spending a fall semester in Buenos Aires and a spring semester in Abu Dhabi, all the while taking major courses and electives that will keep them on track to graduate with their class. Through international study, students develop the ability to see opportunities where others cannot, overcome cultural barriers, and become confident world citizens.

Academic Facilities

NYU offers an exceptional range of facilities and student services and a diverse program of clubs and activities, residence halls, meal plans, and dining locations. Academic facilities include nine libraries and centers and institutes renowned for their research in applied mathematics, physics, neural science, and fine arts. Foreign language and cultural centers offer lectures, films, and concerts. In addition, students have access to the award-winning NYU Wasserman Center for Career Development, advanced computer and multimedia resources, and specialized offices that address almost every student need, from medical attention to discount theatre tickets. The Kimmel Center for Student Life houses dining facilities, lounges, computers, student club spaces, and the Skirball Center for the Performing Arts, the largest performance space in lower Manhattan.

Costs

For 2009–10, tuition and fees were $38,765, and average room and board costs were $13,226. Books and supplies cost about $950, and personal expenses total between $500 and $1000.

Financial Aid

NYU believes that students should be able to choose a college that offers the best range of educational opportunities. To make this choice possible, the University attempts to aid students in need of financial assistance. There are many financial aid sources at NYU, and all students are invited to apply for financial aid or one of NYU's financing plans. Sixty-seven percent of full-time NYU undergraduates receive some form of financial aid.

Scholarships take into account both financial need and academic merit; however, while merit-based scholarships are available, NYU is committed to using the vast majority of its scholarship funds to assist students whose families are unable to pay the full cost of an NYU education. Low-interest education loans are available for both students and parents. Part-time employment, on and off campus, is another source of funding.

NYU also offers or participates in a variety of payment plans, ranging from interest-free prepayment plans to extensive loan programs that allow financing of a college education over many years.

A financial aid package might include any combination of scholarships, loans, or work-study programs. Students wishing to be considered for aid must submit the Free Application for Federal Student Aid (FAFSA). The FAFSA submission deadline is February 15 for the fall semester and November 1 for the spring semester.

Faculty

NYU faculty members are among the country's leading intellectuals, including world-famous scholars and researchers who have received Nobel, Crafoord, and Pulitzer Prizes; MacArthur, Guggenheim, and Fulbright Fellowships; and Oscars and Emmy Awards. Faculty members teach both graduate and undergraduate courses, making it possible for undergraduates to become involved in research projects with internationally known scholars.

Student Government

Each of NYU's schools and colleges has a student council, organized by its respective students, that represents those students. The University Senate, the major policymaking body for all matters relating to academic concerns not delegated to the separate schools and colleges, has 22 student members.

Admission Requirements

Undergraduate admission to NYU is highly selective. The process involves a comprehensive review of the applicant's academic background, standardized test scores, extracurricular activities, an essay, personal statements, and recommendation letters. Several programs also require the applicant to audition or submit creative materials. Applicants who have successfully completed a broad range of challenging course work throughout high school are the most desirable candidates. Also considered are students' unique talents, personal attributes, and future goals.

Applicants must submit official score reports for standardized tests, and may choose from one of the following options: SAT Reasoning Test and two SAT Subject Tests, ACT (with Writing Test), SAT Reasoning Test and two Advanced Placement (AP) exam scores, three SAT Subject Test scores (one in literature or the humanities, one in math or science, and one nonlanguage of the student's choice), or three AP exam scores (one in literature or the humanities, one in math or science, and one nonlanguage of the student's choice).

Students who demonstrate evidence of an extraordinary accomplishment outside of normal classroom or scholastic activity, such as publication in a major national or international journal, a published book, a film or other outstanding visual or performing artistic accomplishment, a scientific or other remarkable discovery, winning a national competition, or the equivalent are required to provide only an SAT score, or two SAT Subject Test scores, or two AP exam scores.

Application and Information

For entrance in the fall term, the application for admission—including all supporting credentials—must be received by November 1 (early decision freshman candidates), January 1 (freshmen), or April 1 (transfer students). For entrance in the spring term (transfer students only), application materials must be received by November 1. For entrance in the summer (transfer students only), application materials should be received by April 1. Applications for admission received after these dates are considered only if space remains. Official notification of fall admission is made on or around April 1.

The admissions staff also visits high schools and hosts receptions throughout the country. Visit the Admissions Web site at http://admissions.nyu.edu for dates and times.

For a campus tour or an information session appointment, call 212-998-4524 or visit http://events.embark.com/event/nyu/on_campus/.

Office of Undergraduate Admissions
New York University
Phone: 212-998-4500
Web site: http://admissions.nyu.edu

NIAGARA UNIVERSITY

NIAGARA UNIVERSITY, NEW YORK

COLLEGE CLOSE-UPS

The University

Niagara University (NU), founded in 1856, is a private, independent university rooted in a Catholic and Vincentian tradition. The suburban 160-acre campus combines the old and new; both ivy-covered buildings and modern architectural structures are among its thirty-three buildings. The University is easily accessible from every major city in the eastern and midwestern United States via the New York State Thruway, Buffalo International Airport, and rail and bus service.

There are more than 3,000 undergraduate and 950 graduate students enrolled at Niagara. A large percentage of these students take advantage of the more than eighty extracurricular and cocurricular activities offered. Volunteer work in the community is popular among the students and enhances community relations. Students work with numerous organizations, including Habitat for Humanity, Big Brothers/Big Sisters, and the Skating Association for the Blind and Handicapped.

University teams compete on the Division I level and are members of the NCAA, the Eastern College Athletic Conference, and the Metro Atlantic Athletic Conference. Intercollegiate sports for men include baseball, basketball, cross-country, golf, ice hockey, soccer, swimming and diving, and tennis. Intercollegiate sports for women include basketball, cross-country, golf, ice hockey, lacrosse, soccer, softball, swimming and diving, tennis, and volleyball. Club sports include cheerleading, danceline, hockey, martial arts, rugby, and skiing. The Kiernan Center offers a variety of sports and recreational facilities, including a multipurpose gymnasium, a swimming and diving pool, an indoor track, racquetball courts, free-weight and Nautilus rooms, and aerobics rooms. There are several outdoor athletic fields and basketball and tennis courts.

Additional student services include the Health Center, which provides inpatient and outpatient care during the day; the Learning Center, which provides free tutoring services; and the Career Development Office, which offers professional and career counseling. Other services include counseling, orientation, academic planning, career planning, and job placement.

Niagara University's housing accommodations include five residence halls, a grouping of five small cottages, and a student apartment complex. Both coed and single-gender accommodations are available.

The University offers graduate studies in business, counseling, criminal justice, education, and interdisciplinary studies.

Location

Niagara University's picturesque 160-acre campus is located in the town of Lewiston, New York, 2 minutes off I-190 on Route 104. The campus is situated on Monteagle Ridge overlooking the lower Niagara River, which connects the two Great Lakes of Erie and Ontario. The University's suburban campus setting is just a few miles from the world-famous Niagara Falls, 20 minutes from Buffalo, which offers a variety of cultural events, sports, and entertainment opportunities, and just 90 minutes from Toronto, Canada's largest metropolitan area. In addition, the University is minutes away from the quaint village of Lewiston, New York, and the city of Niagara Falls, New York.

Majors and Degrees

The College of Arts and Sciences offers the Bachelor of Arts degree in chemistry, communication studies, English, French, history, international studies, liberal arts, life sciences, mathematics, philosophy, political science, psychology, religious studies, social sciences, sociology, and Spanish. The Bachelor of Science degree is awarded in biochemistry (with a concentration in bioinformatics), biology (with concentrations in bioinformatics and biotechnology), chemistry (with a concentration in computational chemistry), computer and information sciences, criminal justice and criminology, mathematics, nursing (completion program for students who are registered nurses), and social work. This division also offers the Bachelor of Fine Arts degree in theater studies (with concentrations in design technology, general theater, and performance). Preprofessional programs are offered in dentistry, law, medicine, pharmacy, veterinary medicine, and Army-ROTC. An Associate of Arts degree is available in general studies. In addition, Niagara offers an environmental studies concentration to supplement a degree in biology, chemistry, or political science. Enrichment courses in fine arts and languages are also available.

In addition to the programs listed above NU offers a number of preprofessional partnerships. These include a 3+4 partnership in pharmacy with the State University of New York at Buffalo (SUNY), a 2+3 partnership in pharmacy with Lake Erie College of Osteopathic Medicine (LECOM), a 3+4 partnership in medicine with LECOM, and a 3+4 partnership in dentistry with SUNY at Buffalo. Qualified premedical Niagara students are eligible to apply for the early assurance program sponsored by the SUNY at Buffalo.

Niagara University's College of Business Administration is accredited by AACSB International—The Association to Advance Collegiate Schools of Business and offers a B.B.A. and a combination B.B.A./M.B.A. degree (five-year program) in accounting. This division offers B.S. degrees in economics, finance, management (with concentrations in human resources, international business, and supply chain management), and marketing. In addition, an A.A.S. degree can be earned in business.

Real-world learning occurs through internships, study abroad, and cooperative education programs as well as research being conducted in several business-focused campus centers. These centers include the Family Business Center, the Center for Supply Chain Management, and the Center for International Accounting.

Holding the highest accreditations possible in both the United States and Canada—the United States National Council for Teacher Education (NCATE) and Canada's Ontario College of Teachers—Niagara University's College of Education provides students with an option of earning dual certification to teach in both countries. The College of Education offers bachelor's degree programs leading to New York State initial certification in early childhood (birth–grade 6), childhood (grades 1–6), childhood and middle childhood (grades 1–9), middle childhood and adolescence (grades 5–12), adolescence (grades 7–12), certification for teaching students with disabilities (grades 1–6 childhood and grades 7–12 adolescence), and in Teaching English to Speakers of Other Languages (TESOL). All education majors pursue an academic concentration to establish expertise in one of the following subject areas: biology, business, chemistry, English, French, liberal arts, mathematics, social studies, and Spanish. Business education is offered only at grades 5–12. The academic concentration in liberal arts can only be pursued in the early childhood and childhood (birth–grade 6), and special education and childhood (grades 1–6). Most other states, and Puerto Rico, have reciprocity agreements with New York, meaning that an NU education would qualify education majors to teach in those states as well. In addition, the Canadian province of Ontario recognizes Niagara graduates as qualified for the Letter of Eligibility to teach in that province.

The College of Hospitality and Tourism Management provides a career-oriented curriculum leading to a B.S. degree in three specific areas: hotel and restaurant management (with concentrations in hotel and restaurant planning and control, foodservice management, and restaurant entrepreneurship), sport management (with a concentration in sport operations), and tourism and recreation management (with concentrations in special events and conference management and tourism destination management). The College of Hospitality and Tourism Management offered the world's first bachelor's degree in tourism. NU's hotel and restaurant program, the second oldest in New York State, has the distinction of being the seventh program nationally to be accredited by the Accreditation Commission for Programs in Hospitality Administration by the Council of Hotel, Restaurant, and Institutional Education. The College introduces students to a comprehensive body of knowledge about the hotel, restaurant, tourism, and recreational areas and applies this knowledge to current industry challenges. The College requires that its students accumulate 800 hours of industry-related experience. These and other practical experiences offer NU students the knowledge necessary to advance in the field. Students work with industry leaders in classroom projects, join academic clubs and professional organizations, and participate in special trips to trade shows and conventions and specially designed study-abroad experiences, making NU a national leader in the area.

For students who are undecided about which major to choose, Niagara University offers an award-winning Academic Exploration Program (AEP). AEP provides a structured opportunity for students to participate in a thorough, organized process of selecting a major that meets their academic talents and career goals.

Academic Programs

Niagara University's curricula enable students to pursue their academic preferences and to complete courses that lead to proficiency in other academic areas. Courses that have been considered upper-division courses are available to all students. This provides students with the opportunity to avoid introductory and survey courses and permits motivated students to take advantage of more challenging courses early in their collegiate career. The honors program provides special academic opportunities that stimulate, encourage, and challenge participants. In addition, an accelerated three-year degree program is offered to qualified students.

Students pursuing a bachelor's degree must complete a total of 40 or 42 course units (120 or 126 hours) to meet graduation requirements. Niagara grants credit for successful scores on the Advanced Placement and College-Level Examination Program tests.

Internships, research, independent study, and cooperative education are available in many academic programs. An Army ROTC program is also offered.

The University operates on a two-semester plan (fall and spring). A comprehensive summer session offers a variety of courses.

NU is fully accredited by the Middle States Association of Colleges and Schools. Its programs in the respective areas are accredited by the National Council for Accreditation of Teacher Education, AACSB International–The Association to Advance Collegiate Schools of Business, and the Council on Social Work Education, and the chemistry department has the approval of the American Chemical Society. The travel, hotel, and restaurant administration program is accredited by the Commission for Programs in Hospitality Administration.

Off-Campus Programs

For those students who wish to study abroad, the University offers semester and summer programs in Chile, England, France, Mexico, Netherlands, Spain, Switzerland, Thailand, and many other countries. Upon request, programs may be offered in other countries. NU is also affiliated with Western New York Consortium. Through this program, students may take courses at other colleges and universities and apply the credits to Niagara's graduation requirements.

Academic Facilities

The University's open-stack library exceeds 200,000 books and has more than 21,000 periodical titles as well as reference databases accessible through the Web. The library is housed in a modern facility that includes seating for 500 people, including individual study carrels. The library is affiliated with the Online Computer Library Center (OCLC) network.

The Academic Complex, the home to the College of Education and the College of Business Administration (Bisgrove Hall), is a state-of-the-art learning facility. Dunleavy Hall, outstanding both educationally and architecturally, includes a behavioral science laboratory, a computerized lecture hall, and TV production rooms. The University's facilities also include the Computer Center; DePaul Hall of Science; St. Vincent's Hall; the Kiernan Center, NU's athletic and recreation center; the Leary Theatre; the Castellani Art Museum; Bailo Hall, which houses the Office of Admissions; and the Dwyer Arena, a dual-rink ice hockey complex.

Costs

Tuition for 2009–10 was $23,700. Room and board (with a choice of meal plans) cost an additional $10,250 per year. Fees were estimated at $1000 per year. Niagara estimates that an additional $2500 to $3050 per year is adequate for books, laundry, and other essentials, such as travel to and from home.

Financial Aid

Ninety-eight percent of the incoming students who enrolled at NU received a financial aid package averaging more than $18,000 per year. They receive assistance in the form of merit scholarships, loans, grants, or campus employment. Students seeking financial aid should file the Free Application for Federal Student Aid (FAFSA). New York State residents should also file a Tuition Assistance Program (TAP) application.

Faculty

Niagara University has a dedicated, accessible faculty who genuinely cares about the academic and personal growth of their students. Their commitment to teaching is their primary concern. A student-faculty ratio of 14:1 and an average class size of 25 allow personal attention and classroom interaction.

Student Government

The Student Government represents all parts of the student body equally. It coordinates and legislates all student activities, serving as both liaison to and a participating member of the University. In addition, students serve on all major departmental committees and on the University Senate, which is the major advisory committee to the president and Board of Trustees.

Admission Requirements

The University welcomes men and women who have demonstrated aptitude and academic achievement at the high school level. Either SAT or ACT test scores are required. International students are required to submit the results of their TOEFL examination. Interviews are recommended. Transfer students are accepted in any semester. (Transfer credit is evaluated individually by the dean of each division.) Students who complete high school in less than four years are eligible for early admission. Students may also apply under an early action program. Economically and educationally disadvantaged students from New York State are eligible to apply for admission through the Higher Educational Opportunity Program (HEOP).

Application and Information

Niagara operates on a rolling admission basis and adheres to the College Board Candidates Reply Date. A visit to the campus is encouraged, and overnight accommodations in a residence hall are available through the Niagara Nights program.

Information on all aspects of the University can be obtained by contacting the Office of Admissions.

Harry Gong
Director of Admissions
630 Bailo Hall
Niagara University
Niagara University, New York 14109-2011
Phone: 716-286-8700
800-462-2111 (toll-free)
Fax: 716-286-8710
E-mail: admissions@niagara.edu
Web site: http://www.niagara.edu

The main campus of Niagara University.

NORTHERN KENTUCKY UNIVERSITY

HIGHLAND HEIGHTS, KENTUCKY

ESTABLISHED 1968

The University

Northern Kentucky University (NKU) was founded in 1968 and is the newest of Kentucky's eight state universities. The atmosphere of the campus is futuristic, emphasizing a high-quality education by supporting the liberal arts. Major buildings are of modern, contemporary architectural design and are set on 300 acres of rolling countryside. NKU has an enrollment of approximately 15,000 students from forty-one states and eighty-two countries and is accredited by the Southern Association of Colleges and Schools. The Salmon P. Chase College of Law is accredited by both the American Bar Association and the Association of American Law Schools.

There are more than 200 student organizations. NKU competes in the NCAA Division II Great Lakes Valley Conference. Intercollegiate sports are offered for men and women in basketball, cheerleading, cross-country, golf, soccer, and tennis; for men in baseball; and for women in fast-pitch softball and volleyball. Intramural activities vary by semester, but include basketball, dodgeball, field hockey, flag football, ice hockey, racquetball, soccer, softball, Tae Kwan Do, volleyball, and many others. Students should visit the University's Web site for a complete listing at http://www.nku.edu/~camprec/index.htm.

Location

NKU is located in the largest metropolitan area of any state university in Kentucky. It is located at the junction of U.S. Highway 27 and Interstates 275 and 471 in Highland Heights, Kentucky, 8 miles southeast of Cincinnati, Ohio. NKU is only 60 miles from Dayton, 79 miles from Lexington, 93 miles from Louisville, and 114 miles from Indianapolis. While the immediate surroundings are suburban, NKU is part of the metropolitan area of greater Cincinnati.

Majors and Degrees

Northern Kentucky University awards the Bachelor of Arts, Bachelor of Fine Arts, Bachelor of Music, Bachelor of Science, Bachelor of Science in Nursing, and Bachelor of Social Work degrees. NKU also offers preprofessional programs, secondary education teacher certification, certificates, and the Associate of Applied Science degree.

The B.A. and B.S. degrees are offered in accounting, anthropology, athletic training, art (teaching), biological sciences, business administration, business education, business informatics, chemistry, chemistry/biology, computer education technology, computer information technology, computer science, criminal justice, early childhood education, economics, electronic engineering technology, electronic media and broadcasting, elementary education, English, entrepreneurship, environmental science, finance, French, geography, geology, German, graphic design, health science, history, industrial education, human resources, construction management, international studies, journalism, liberal studies, management, mechanical and manufacturing engineering, marketing, mathematics, media informatics, mental health–human services, middle grades education, organizational leadership, organizational systems technology, organizational systems technology management, philosophy, photography, physical education, physical education recreation, physics, political science, psychology, public relations, radio-TV, recreation-fitness, social studies (teaching), sociology, Spanish, special education, speech communication, sports business, and theater.

The B.F.A. degree is granted in art and in theater arts. The B.Mus. degree is offered in music. The B.S.N. degree is offered in the nursing major and the B.S.W. degree in the social work major.

Preprofessional programs are available in dentistry, engineering, forestry, human resources, law, medicine, optometry, pharmacy, physician assistant studies, physical therapy, veterinary medicine, and wildlife management. In addition, the University offers majors, minors, and areas of discipline for secondary education teacher certification.

The University also awards the A.A.S. degree in construction technology, criminal justice, human services, liberal studies, prebusiness studies, radiologic technology, and respiratory care.

Certificates are also available at the University in architectural drafting, automated manufacturing processes, entrepreneurship, information systems development, information systems management, organizational systems, piano pedagogy, and training and organizational development.

Academic Programs

NKU operates on a semester calendar. To receive a bachelor's degree, students must complete a minimum of 128 credit hours. At least 64 credit hours are required for the associate degree.

The University offers a variety of career planning and placement, internship, independent study, work-study, and cooperative-education programs. There is also an Advising, Counseling, and Testing Center available. Other programs include an honors program, a program that allows for the dual enrollment of high school students, a program where students can combine their career interests in the liberal arts and engineering fields, and University 101, an orientation program for freshmen and transfer students.

NKU recognizes credit earned through the Advanced Placement (AP) Program and the general, subject, and institutional tests of specific College-Level Examination Program (CLEP). A maximum of 45 credit hours may be applied toward the bachelor's degree from the AP and CLEP examinations. The International Baccalaureate Program allows students to earn credit in science, mathematics, psychology, and languages.

Off-Campus Programs

A variety of study-abroad opportunities are available to NKU students through membership in several consortia, through NKU exchange agreements with international universities, and through independent NKU professor-led trips.

Study in Australia, Belize, England, Ghana, Hong Kong, India, Ireland, Jamaica, and Scotland is possible in a wide range of courses and programs available through NKU's membership in the Cooperative Center for Study Abroad (CCSA), which is headquartered at NKU.

The Kentucky Institute for International Studies (KIIS) offers students academic language programs in Argentina, Austria, Brazil, China, Costa Rica, Czech Republic, Denmark, Ecuador, France, Germany, Greece, Italy, Japan, Mexico, Poland, Spain, Turkey, and Ukraine.

The NKU Office of International Programs has student and faculty exchanges with universities in Costa Rica, Denmark, France, Germany, Japan, Korea, Mexico, Russia, Scotland, and Spain.

Academic Facilities

Among the academic facilities at NKU are an anthropology museum, a biology museum, and an art gallery with rotating exhibits. NKU also has a new laser projection planetarium. NKU becomes only the seventh institution worldwide to boast such equipment, joining six major planetariums in cities such as Tokyo, Los Angeles, and London. Additionally, the University has nursing, respiratory care, and radiologic technology laboratories. In spring of 2008, NKU opened a 9000-seat arena called the Bank of Kentucky Center. In fall of 2008, NKU's brand-new Student Union, a student-centered facility, which is a focal point for campus programs and student organizations, opened. The W. Frank Steely Library at NKU contains 311,155 book titles and maintains 1,729 paper periodical subscriptions (additional periodicals are available in electronic format). Computer laboratories offer students opportunities to learn and utilize a variety of software programs. The Computer Science Department and Criminal Justice Department have collaborated to offer students a computer forensics minor to teach students how to handle digital evidence and how to present such evidence in court.

Costs

Tuition and fees for 2009–10 were $12,792. Other costs were $10,750 for room and meals, the cost of books, supplies amounted to about $850, and miscellaneous expenses were $2773.

Financial Aid

Last year, 80 percent of undergraduates received some form of financial assistance. To receive financial aid, applicants must complete the Free Application for Federal Student Aid (FAFSA). Academic, athletic, music-drama, and art scholarships and scholarships for members of minority groups are available at Northern Kentucky University.

The application deadline for all academic scholarships is February 1. There is no deadline for the University's financial aid application; however, students who wish to receive institutional aid must apply by March 1 for priority consideration. Applicants are notified of acceptance on a rolling basis.

Faculty

More than 82 percent of the faculty members at NKU hold a doctoral degree or the terminal degree in their field. Classes are small, with an average class size of 24 and a student-faculty ratio of 14:1. All classes are taught by faculty members; no classes are taught by graduate assistants.

Student Government

Student Government (SG) is the elected student assembly at Northern Kentucky University. It is the official student voice on campus and represents the student viewpoint on University committees. All SG meetings are open, and students are encouraged to attend.

Admission Requirements

Incoming freshmen must submit an application for admission; arrange for the official ACT, SAT, or COMPASS score report to be sent; and request that the high school send an official transcript. In order to be considered for regular admission, a student must meet precollege curriculum requirements for Kentucky and institutional admission standards. Out-of-state applicants must also meet the Kentucky precollege curriculum requirements.

Based on the review of official test results and the precollege curriculum, students are admitted into one of two categories: regular admission or admission with conditions. Students who are found to have three or more deficiencies are referred to the NKU Academy, which is a five-week, intensive summer remediation program. Some degree programs require that students meet additional criteria; students should refer to the current catalog for more information (http://www.nku.edu).

Application and Information

The $40 paper application fee or $25 online application fee may be waived for applicants with demonstrated need. The fall semester early action and scholarship deadline is January 15, the priority application deadline is May 1, assured consideration deadline is June 1, and the final deadline is August 1. The priority application deadline for the nursing program is January 31. The priority application deadline for the respiratory care program is February 15.

For more information, students should contact:

Office of Admissions
Northern Kentucky University
Highland Heights, Kentucky 41099
Phone: 859-572-5220
800-637-9948 (toll-free)
E-mail: admitnku@nku.edu
Web site: http://www.nku.edu

Northern Kentucky University's modern campus is set in Highland Heights, just minutes from downtown Cincinnati.

NORWICH UNIVERSITY

NORTHFIELD, VERMONT

The University

Norwich University was established in 1819 as the first private military college in America. It was at Norwich that the idea of the citizen-soldier developed and eventually evolved into the Reserve Officer Training Corps (ROTC) program. Norwich was the first private college to offer civil engineering, and many University alumni were involved in the construction of the nation's continental railway system. In 1974, Norwich became one of the first military colleges to admit women into its Corps of Cadets, preceding the federal academies.

Norwich University offers a diverse blend of disciplines, teaching styles, and viewpoints. Students enrolled in the Corps of Cadets have a more disciplined, challenging, and structured path through college, while their civilian student classmates lead a more traditional collegiate lifestyle. However, both groups are coeducational and attend classes and participate in sports and other activities together.

In keeping with its mission, Norwich provides opportunities for all of its students to develop leadership skills with a strong commitment to community service. Both groups gain skills such as leadership, honor, and integrity, which are required to be successful in today's job market. These two diverse groups of students are very different and yet have much in common—they are Norwich.

Norwich University has an enrollment of 2,000 students from more than forty states and twenty countries. The University's minority enrollment is consistently higher (by percentage) than that of any other Vermont university or college.

The athletic facilities at Norwich are comparable to the best at any of New England's Division III universities. The main athletic complex, Andrews Hall, features a gymnasium, a modernized athletic training room, an equipment room, laundry facilities, five racquetball courts, and locker rooms. Kreitzberg Arena is a multipurpose facility with a seating capacity of 1,500 and a fully equipped weight room. It was here that the University's men's hockey team won the Division III National Championship in 2003. Plumley Armory has a huge gym as well as an indoor track, weight and aerobics rooms, a wrestling room, and an indoor swimming pool. Shapiro Field House has 50,000 square feet of floor space and includes a 200-meter indoor track, tennis courts, and a climbing wall. The 1,200-acre campus includes numerous playing fields for baseball, football, rugby, soccer, and softball. Norwich also has a paintball course, a rappel tower, an obstacle and confidence course.

Norwich has the only professional five-year Master of Architecture program in northern New England. The University also offers online graduate degrees in business administration, diplomacy, information security assurance, and justice administration.

Location

Norwich University is located in the heart of the Green Mountains of Vermont, right in the middle of ski country. Some of the nation's most popular resorts, such as Stowe, Sugarbush, and Killington, are located within an hour's drive. Vermont is world renowned as one of America's most beautiful states. Nature's playground is just outside the dorm room—skiing, snowboarding, telemark skiing, cross-country skiing, snowshoeing, rock climbing, hiking, mountain biking, canoeing, kayaking, and more are available.

The University campus is located in the small town of Northfield, Vermont. Northfield is 10 miles south of the state capital of Montpelier and is 50 miles from Burlington, the largest city in Vermont. Both Montpelier and Burlington are cultural centers for the arts. Burlington International Airport is within an hour's drive. In addition, the cities of Boston and Montreal are only a 3-hour drive from the campus.

Majors and Degrees

Norwich offers students more than thirty academic majors from which to choose. The Bachelor of Arts degree is awarded in communications; criminal justice; English; history; international studies; peace, war, and diplomacy studies; political science; psychology; and Spanish. The Bachelor of Science degree is awarded in accounting, architecture, athletic training, biochemistry, biology, chemistry, civil/environmental engineering, communications, computer/electrical engineering, computer information systems, computer science, computer security and information assurance, economics, engineering management, environmental science, geology, international studies, management, mathematics, mechanical engineering, physical education, physics, sports medicine and health studies, strategic studies and defense analysis, and studies in war and peace. Teacher licensure, prelaw, premedical, and predental programs are also available.

Academic Programs

Norwich University is dedicated to the discovery, preservation, and dissemination of knowledge and the search for truth. Norwich is distinctive in that it maintains a strong emphasis on the development of leadership in both military and civilian pursuits and in providing for the educational needs of students. The University's mission is to foster in each student the growth of self-discipline, personal integrity, social responsibility, physical fitness, respect for law, and intellectual ability essential for full and effective participation in a free society.

For students enrolling in the Corps of Cadets, six semesters of Reserve Officer Training Corps are required. Norwich is considered the birthplace of ROTC; therefore, all four service branches can be found on campus. Prior to their junior year, cadets may elect to contract with their ROTC program and be considered upon graduation for a commission as officers in the Army, Navy, Air Force, or Marine Corps. Cadets not on an ROTC scholarship are not required to join the military.

Students typically take an average of five classes per semester. Each semester is sixteen weeks long, with holiday breaks at Thanksgiving, Christmas, and New Year's and in March during spring break. The academic year normally begins the last week in August and ends after the first week in May.

Academic Facilities

The academic facilities at Norwich are among the finest in New England. Completed in 1997, the math and science building was designed to keep classes small. Its labs hold no more than 16 students, and all of the classrooms are hard-wired to allow for multimedia presentations. Students can find numerous computer labs across the campus, and the Kreitzberg Library offers students plenty of resources, space, and technology. Students may research Norwich's facilities on the University's Web site.

Costs

For 2009–10, tuition and fees were $13,628 per semester. The cost of room and board was $4979 per semester. Books and personal expenses averaged $1200 per semester. Cadets pay a uniform fee of $1630.

Financial Aid

Most families assume they cannot afford a private college education and fall victim to "sticker shock," but a Norwich education is often as affordable as a local state college. Last year, 92 percent of Norwich students, with an average family income of $44,000, shared in more than $35 million of financial aid from all sources, including ROTC scholarships. This included an aggressive need-based financial aid program that enabled deserving students to secure a private education at Norwich.

Norwich awards academic scholarships on a competitive basis to students who are placed in the top 10 or 20 percent of their high school class. These scholarships may pay from $8000 to $12,500 of the student's tuition for four years. Students are required to maintain a specified GPA in order to renew the scholarship each year. Students whose high schools do not rank academic standing should contact the University admissions office and ask to speak with a counselor.

Norwich also offers a vast array of leadership and merit scholarships based on a student's record of demonstrated leadership as well as their participation in sports, community and school organizations, employment, volunteer work, and other extracurricular activities. Students who bring a three- or four-year ROTC scholarship to Norwich are eligible for the General I. D. White Scholarship, which covers the cost of room and board. Students who are interested in applying for an ROTC scholarship should visit the individual ROTC detachment's Web page on the Norwich University Web site.

Faculty

The student-faculty ratio is 14:1. Faculty members are full-time instructors with advanced degrees; 80 percent hold a doctorate. Small classes help promote a close relationship between faculty members and students. Students are assigned faculty advisers within each academic division.

Student Government

The Norwich University Corps of Cadets is a military organization made up of and led by cadets under the supervision of the Commandant of Cadets. Members of the Corps and student body preside over the University Honor Council. The University's honor code binds all Norwich students. Members of the Corps and student body also participate on the Student Affairs Committee, whose members include the Dean of Students, members of the faculty, and the Senior Vice President and Commandant of Cadets. This committee serves as the voice of the Norwich community and provides a channel of communication for change.

Admission Requirements

Admission to Norwich is based on a review of the applicant's academic record, personal essay, letters of recommendation, and extracurricular activities. Students at Norwich are heavily involved in community service and leadership development activities. Applicants should be able to demonstrate participation in activities both inside and outside of their high school.

Norwich is looking for students who want to become leaders, serve others, and give back to their communities. While the admissions office uses a rolling admissions system (meaning applications may be submitted at any time), there is a priority deadline of March 1. Students applying for admission or financial aid after March 1 are admitted on a space-available basis.

Application and Information

Students can visit the University's Web site or contact the University for more information.

Dean of Enrollment Management
Norwich University
27 I. D. White Avenue
Northfield, Vermont 05663
Phone: 800-468-6679 (toll-free)
Fax: 802-485-2032
E-mail: nuadm@norwich.edu
Web site: http://www.norwich.edu

A view of Norwich University's campus.

COLLEGE CLOSE-UPS

NOTRE DAME COLLEGE

SOUTH EUCLID, OHIO

The College

Notre Dame College was established in 1922. A Catholic institution in the tradition of the Sisters of Notre Dame, the College educates a diverse population in the liberal arts for personal, professional, and global responsibility. The College believes that truly progressive education selectively blends traditional values with new ideas that represent real growth. Within the scope of a career-oriented liberal arts education, students can grow to meet the challenges of the present and the future. The College is accredited by the North Central Association of Colleges and Schools and is registered for the awarding of State Teachers' Licenses by the State of Ohio Department of Education.

A variety of clubs and activities enrich the educational experiences of the College's 1,900 students. The Campus Ministry program promotes the spiritual growth of the Notre Dame College community and facilitates community service, retreats, liturgy, and more. The Masquers promote talent in the performing arts and provide entertainment for the College community and general public. Campus publications include the *Notre Dame News* and *PIVOT,* the literary magazine. Faculty members and students schedule and coordinate lectures, plays, performances, and concerts. Most on-campus events are free, and students may purchase tickets at reduced rates for off-campus programs such as performances of the world-famous Cleveland Orchestra, the Cleveland Opera, and road shows of Broadway productions at the Palace Theatre, State Theatre, and Ohio Theatre at Playhouse Square. Performances at the Cleveland Play House are also available.

Notre Dame College is a member of the National Association of Intercollegiate Athletics (NAIA) and competes in the American Mideast Conference. Notre Dame College fields twenty-one scholarship athletic teams, including men's and women's intercollegiate basketball, bowling, cross-country, golf, soccer, swimming and diving, and track and field; men's baseball, football, tennis, and wrestling; and women's lacrosse, softball, and volleyball. In July 2009, NDC announced that a membership application for NCAA Division II had been approved. Notre Dame began the 2009–10 academic year as a candidacy-year-one institution in the NCAA Division II membership process.

Location

The College is located in South Euclid, 25 minutes from downtown Cleveland and only 5 minutes from Legacy Village, Cleveland's lifestyle retail center. The area combines the excitement and cultural wealth of a major urban and educational center with the relaxed atmosphere of a suburban setting. University Circle in Cleveland, a 500-acre complex containing an unusual blend of cultural, educational, medical, religious, and social service institutions, is easily accessible from the College.

Situated on the shores of Lake Erie, Cleveland is the home of the Rock and Roll Hall of Fame and several professional sports teams. The Cleveland Metroparks offer a variety of activities and recreational opportunities. Snowy winters provide abundant opportunities for skiing and tobogganing, and popular ski areas are located a short distance from the city.

The beautiful 53-acre wooded campus provides the perfect setting for the Clara Fritzsche Library; the Administration Building, housing all of the classrooms and offices; Connelly Center, the cafeteria and student center; the Keller Center, the recreational and fitness facility; and five residence halls, including two brand new apartment-style facilities housing 288 upperclass students.

Majors and Degrees

The College awards the Bachelor of Arts degree in accounting (business administration); biology; chemistry; communication; education, including early childhood (pre-K–3), middle childhood (4–9), and young adult education and mild-moderate intervention specialist studies; English; graphic design; history/political science; information systems; international business; management; marketing; mathematics; psychology; public administration; sports management; studio art; and theology. The Bachelor of Science is awarded in biology, chemistry, and mathematics. A student can also design his or her own major that leads to a Bachelor of Arts or Bachelor of Science degree by combining two or three academic areas, such as graphic design, human resource management, and public relations.

Notre Dame College also offers a Bachelor of Science in Nursing program. An RN to B.S.N. completion program is also available.

A Master of Education (M.Ed.) degree, which is designed for classroom teachers, is offered, with concentrations available in special education, reading, and critical and creative thinking.

Teacher licensure is available in early childhood education, middle childhood education, adolescent/young adult education, and multiage for mild/moderate intervention specialist studies.

The Associate in Arts degree is awarded at the completion of two-year programs in business management, education paraprofessional studies, and pastoral ministry.

The Center for Pastoral Theology and Ministry grants a two-year catechetical diploma and the Bachelor of Arts degree.

Academic Programs

All students pursue a career-oriented liberal arts education. For the bachelor's degree, students must earn 128 semester hours of credit, with a minimum cumulative grade point average of 2.0. From 36 to 68 semester hours of credit are required in the major field of study.

Through a cooperative education program, students can earn a maximum of 6 credit hours for paid or volunteer work experience related to their academic field of study.

Advanced Placement credit is awarded to students who have demonstrated the ability to pursue course work beyond the level of entering freshmen, as indicated by their scores on the Advanced Placement (AP) or College-Level Examination Program (CLEP) tests of the College Board. College credit is given on the basis of a decision made jointly by the academic dean and the department involved.

Academic Facilities

The Clara Fritzsche Library, housing the modern Media Center, has a capacity for 100,000 volumes. As a member of Ohiolink, the College also has online access to members throughout the state, with access to more than 31 million library items and more than 90 research databases. The library also houses the smart classroom, a state-of-the-art classroom equipped with laptops for each student and two SmartBoards.

The Dwyer Learning Center consists of an electronic classroom, a student computer lab, a writing lab, a test proctoring room, and a tutoring room. The writing lab is staffed by English faculty members who provide professional writing assistance to students free of charge. The tutoring room is staffed with graduate assistants and upperclass peer tutors for one-on-one study skills and subject specific assistance.

The Academic Support Center for Students with Learning Differences (ASC) was designed to support students with disabilities such as Attention Deficit Disorder (ADD), Attention Deficit Hyperactivity Disorder (ADHD), dyslexia, Asperger's Syndrome, and SLD. In order to be accepted into the Learning Differences Program, students must meet the admission requirements of Notre Dame College. To participate in the Academic Support Center, students must submit documentation of a learning disability. Among its services, the ASC provides professional tutoring, advising, and lessons on adaptive equipment.

The multimedia lab for graphic design majors offers PC and Macintosh technology for advanced multimedia production capabilities.

The Center for Continuing and Professional Development offers course work for working adults on a variety of topics. The center offers seminars and short, flexibly scheduled courses for professionals throughout the year, along with certificate programs in athletic coaching, business intelligence, and intelligence for homeland security.

Costs

For the 2009–10 academic year, tuition charges were $22,742. Room and board costs were $7588 for double occupancy. Student fees were $550.

Financial Aid

A comprehensive financial assistance program of more than $25 million assists nearly 93 percent of all full-time students. Students applying for aid must submit the Free Application for Federal Student Aid (FAFSA).

Faculty

The faculty has 54 full-time members. The faculty is augmented by highly qualified instructors in special areas. Faculty members hold advanced degrees from more than thirty universities in the United States, Canada, and Europe.

Student Government

The Undergraduate Student Government (USG) is the central coordinating group for all student organizations. In addition, students have representation on various College committees.

Admission Requirements

In fulfilling its mission, Notre Dame College seeks to attract students of diverse religious, racial, and economic backgrounds. Candidates for admission as first-time, full-time freshmen are reviewed on an individual basis, and decisions are based on a broad range of criteria. The most important consideration is the candidate's high school performance, as demonstrated by her/his overall grade average, class rank, grade trends, and level of courses completed. Aptitude for verbal and mathematical reasoning, as measured by performance on standardized tests, is also considered. In addition, counselor and teacher recommendations are reviewed.

Notre Dame College recommends that students complete at least 16 units of high school credit in academic subjects as a prerequisite for matriculation in the College. The distribution of these subject areas and the units are as follows: English, 4; mathematics, 3 (to include algebra I, geometry, and algebra II); science, 3 (with laboratory experience); social studies, 3; foreign language, 2 (from the same language); and fine arts, 1. Applicants should generally rank in the upper half of their high school graduating class and have a minimum average of C+. Either ACT or SAT scores are accepted.

Students wishing to transfer from other regionally accredited colleges and universities are admitted to advanced standing upon presentation of satisfactory evidence of scholarship and character.

Special consideration may be granted to an applicant whose academic preparation is not consistent with the requirements stated above.

Notre Dame College strongly recommends that prospective students schedule an appointment to visit the campus and talk with an admissions counselor.

Application and Information

The College maintains a rolling admission policy. To apply, students should submit the completed application for undergraduate admission, an official transcript of their high school record, results of the ACT or SAT, and a nonrefundable $30 application fee to:

Office of Admissions
Notre Dame College
4545 College Road
South Euclid, Ohio 44121
Phone: 216-373-5355
877-NDC-OHIO Ext. 5355 (toll-free)
Fax: 216-373-5278
E-mail: admissions@ndc.edu
Web site: http://www.NotreDameCollege.edu

NOVA SOUTHEASTERN UNIVERSITY

FORT LAUDERDALE, FLORIDA

The University

Years from now, historians will look back and discover that the future officially began in 1964. The Beatles arrived and changed the face of music. The first Ford Mustang rolled out of Detroit. And, in Fort Lauderdale, Florida, a tiny college was born with a handful of students and some revolutionary ideas. That college grew up to become Nova Southeastern University (NSU), and the rest is history.

Today, NSU is the nation's seventh-largest independent university, with more than 28,000 students; 100,000 alumni; a sprawling, 300-acre Fort Lauderdale main campus; and a presence in nine countries around the world. Through five decades of explosive growth, NSU's reputation for academic excellence and innovation continues to flourish.

So what exactly is NSU? NSU is a small, nurturing, private undergraduate college. It is an exciting, multifaceted university. NSU is young and agile, fearless, and forward thinking. And it's traditional. NSU does not fit easily within a standardized niche, because neither do its students.

The traditional undergraduate student population is approximately 5,700 students from all fifty states and forty-two other countries. About 1,200 students live on campus in six residential halls. With more than 190 on-campus student organizations, a powerful student government, socially active fraternities and sororities, intramural sports, and NCAA Division II athletics, NSU has all the elements of a classic, traditional college.

Unusual among institutions of higher education, NSU is truly an institution for all ages. From the University School, for children pre-K through grade 12, to numerous undergraduate and graduate degree programs in a variety of fields and nondegree continuing education programs for retired professionals, all are available at NSU.

Location

Between the undergraduate and graduate programs, NSU offers more than 120 degrees. But for some people, the degrees that matter most are found on a thermometer, and 77°F sounds very good. That is the average temperature in South Florida. So, when students are not in class, they can be outdoors all year round—and they will need that time to experience everything South Florida has to offer.

There is hiking, biking, fishing, boating, and windsurfing and endless open-air festivals and concerts. Fort Lauderdale Beach is 15 minutes to the east and the Everglades are 15 minutes in the other direction. Students can be on South Beach in about half an hour; in 3 hours, they can be screaming their lungs out at one of Orlando's theme parks or chilling in the Florida Keys. For sports fans, there are professional baseball, basketball, hockey, and football. For foodies, there is everything from casual waterfront dives to world-class gourmet cuisine. And for students who view shopping as a competitive sport, South Florida is the Olympics, with everything from funky flea markets to some the world's most exclusive shopping malls and boutiques, all just minutes from campus.

Majors and Degrees

Nova Southeastern University offers bachelor's degrees in accounting, American studies, anthropology, applied professional studies, art, arts administration, athletic training, biology (premedical), business administration, child development, communication studies, computer information systems, computer science, criminal justice, dance, elementary education, English, environmental science/studies, exceptional student education, finance, general studies, health science (completion program), health science: vascular sonography, history, humanities, international studies, legal studies, management, marine biology, marketing, middle grades English with ESOL endorsement, middle grades general science, middle grades social studies, music, nursing, nursing: entry level, nursing: RN-BSN, nursing: RN-MSN, paralegal studies, prekindergarten/primary education, psychology, secondary English education with ESOL endorsement, secondary biology education, secondary mathematics education, secondary social studies, sociology, sport and recreation management, and theater.

NSU pioneered the Dual Admission Program for a select group of highly motivated students who have maintained a laser focus on their career goals from an early age. Qualified students in the Dual Admission Program are automatically reserved a seat in one of NSU's graduate or professional schools while they earn their bachelor's degree. In today's competitive world, that is like getting a head start on the rest of their life. Dual-admission programs are offered in accounting, audiology, business administration, clinical psychology (Psy.D.), computer information systems, computer sciences, conflict analysis and resolution, criminal justice, dental medicine, doctoral psychology (Ph.D.), education, family therapy, human resource management, international business administration, law, leadership, marine biology, mental health counseling, nursing, occupational therapy, optometry, osteopathic medicine, pharmacy, physical therapy, physician assistant studies, psychology: clinically based, psychology: research-based, public administration, school psychology, speech-language pathology, and taxation.

Academic Programs

The undergraduate program at NSU combines a general education curriculum with a set of majors designed to prepare students for their future, whether that is starting a graduate school degree or a professional career. With the incredible personal attention and intimate class sizes of a small, private college and the powerful academic resources of a well-rounded university, students are able to explore an almost limitless range of career paths.

NSU's open-door policy helps build strong connections between faculty members and students. Since classes are taught by professors who are still actively engaged in their professions outside the classroom, students are better prepared for real life.

NSU created the Honors Program for students who have demonstrated a passion for learning and crave more from their college experience. The program is intensely personal, offering broader, richer, and deeper insights into topics that are pleasing to each individual student. The goal is not to make students work harder but to help them get more from the work they do. Carefully selected faculty members and course work ensure that the program is engaging and involving, and emphasis is placed on achieving great understanding of concepts. The program fosters powerful mentoring relationships between students and their professors and provides life-changing learning opportunities through research, social activities, real-world encounters, and study abroad.

Academic Facilities

A tour of the NSU campus is an architectural and intellectual feast, with cutting-edge research and learning facilities at every turn. As a leader in technology and innovation, NSU has been named one of America's Top 20 Cyber Universities by *Forbes* magazine. It has also been designated a National Center of Academic Excellence in Information Assistance Education by the National Security Agency and the Department of Homeland Security. Wireless access and computer micro labs throughout the campus make it possible to connect to the world from virtually anywhere. In fact, NSU is so firmly connected to the real world that it may actually be the only college in America with a professional football team. The Miami Dolphins' headquarters and training camp are located right on campus; the Bubble, a 2-acre, inflatable dome, houses one of the team's three practice fields.

The tour would not be complete without mention of three other NSU showcases: The Oceanographic Center, which sits on 10 acres of Atlantic oceanfront and serves as home to the National Coral Reef Institute; the 325,000-square-foot Alvin Sherman Library, Research, and Information Technology Center, the largest library in the state of Florida; and the Don Taft University Center, which houses a 4,500-seat arena designed to host everything from NSU's NCAA Division II Shark athletics to concerts, a two-story rock-climbing wall, three multipurpose studios for group exercise, a state-of-the-art recreation complex, and a performing arts center with a theater, dressing rooms, costume and scenery shops, and art gallery. A spectacular outdoor pool area, where students can worship the Florida sun, and the Flight Deck, NSU's popular student lounge, are also at the UC.

Costs

Tuition for undergraduate students at Nova Southeastern University varies according to the academic program. For the 2009–10 academic year, tuition for the full-time day program is $20,550, and the double-occupancy room rate is $2757 per semester. The declining meal plan is $1200 per semester, and textbooks cost $75–$100 per course.

Financial Aid

Nova Southeastern University offers a comprehensive program of financial aid to assist students in meeting their educational expenses. Financial aid packages are available that include scholarships, grants, and loans.

Applicants for financial aid are required to submit the Free Application for Federal Student Aid (FAFSA) to be considered for all campus-based aid programs. Students who apply before April 1 are given priority consideration for funds; however, applications are accepted all year.

Faculty

The undergraduate faculty at Nova Southeastern University is full-time and resident. In addition, faculty members are drawn from qualified professionals in the community as well as from other centers and programs within the University. Most of the faculty members have backgrounds in professional, industrial, managerial, civic, educational, or other private and public sectors of the community. For example, lawyers and judges teach criminal justice courses; accountants, personnel managers, and others teach in their respective fields; and principals and curriculum specialists teach education courses. All faculty members are dedicated to the philosophy that contemporary higher education combines theory and practice and that the education of working professionals and adult students requires the active participation of both the student and the instructor.

Admission Requirements

Admission requirements vary according to the program. A counseling session is recommended. Freshman applicants must submit official high school transcripts and SAT or ACT scores.

Transfer applicants must submit official college transcripts. Each student's record is evaluated individually to determine the number of transferable credits. There is a maximum of 90 transferable credits, and students must complete 30 semester hours at Nova Southeastern University.

Application and Information

The application should be submitted with a nonrefundable $50 application fee. There is no closing date for applications for the fall term. Applicants are notified of the admission decision on a rolling basis.

For further information, prospective applicants are invited to contact:

Office of Undergraduate Admissions
Nova Southeastern University
3301 College Avenue
Fort Lauderdale, Florida 33314
Phone: 954-262-8000
800-338-4723 (toll-free)
E-mail: admissions@nova.edu
Web site: http://www.nova.edu/admissions

Nova Southeastern University's Library, Research, and Information Technology Center is Florida's largest library.

OBERLIN COLLEGE

OBERLIN, OHIO

The College

Oberlin College, which was founded in 1833, is an independent, coeducational liberal arts college dedicated to recruiting students from diverse backgrounds. Oberlin comprises two divisions: the College of Arts and Sciences, with roughly 2,200 students, and the Conservatory of Music, with about 600 students. Students in both divisions share one campus; they also share residence and dining halls as part of one academic community. Many students take courses in both divisions. Oberlin awards the Bachelor of Arts (B.A.) and the Bachelor of Music (B.Mus.) degrees. In Oberlin's distinctive double-degree program, students pursue the B.A. and the B.Mus. degrees in a unified, five-year program. Selected master's degrees are offered in the Conservatory.

Oberlin made interracial education central to its mission in 1835; by 1900, nearly half of all the black college graduates in the country—128 to be exact—had graduated from Oberlin. This core of Oberlin-educated men and women formed the first black professional class in the country. In 1837, Oberlin became the first consistently coeducational school in the United States. This legacy continues today in a strong sense of community—one that celebrates differences and recognizes them as opportunities for learning.

Today, Oberlin is a community of thinkers, scholars, scientists, musicians, athletes, activists, and artists—all of whom seek to make the world a better place. Students are united by a commitment to social justice and a willingness to confront social issues that many would prefer to ignore. As the *New York Times* noted in an article marking Oberlin's 150th anniversary, "In its century and a half, while Harvard worried about the classics and Yale about God, Oberlin worried about the state of America and the world beyond."

Recognizing that interaction with others of widely different backgrounds and experiences fosters the effective and concerned participation in the larger society so characteristic of Oberlin graduates, Oberlin is dedicated to recruiting a culturally, economically, geographically, and racially diverse group of students. Students from every walk of life and from around the world seek pathways of individual expression inside Oberlin's tight-knit community of learners, doers, and volunteers. More Oberlin graduates have gone on to earn Ph.D.'s than at any other American college. Its alumni, who include 3 Nobel laureates and 7 MacArthur "Genius" award recipients, are leaders in law, scientific and scholarly research, medicine, the arts, theology, communications, business, and government.

Oberlin has several distinctive academic programs. During the four-week Winter Term, students focus on career aspirations or explore new interests on or off campus. Past projects have taken students to every corner of the globe, from a geology department expedition to Java to a group of students working in a Russian orphanage. Oberlin's Experimental College, a student-run program, offers courses for limited academic credit taught by Oberlin students, townspeople, administrators, and faculty members. Oberlin's First Year Seminar Program is a series of small discussion-based seminars designed to hone students' writing and critical-thinking skills while establishing a context and direction for their personal development.

Oberlin offers a small-town atmosphere and is located not far from Cleveland. There is never a lack of something to do. More than 500 concerts and recitals take place on campus annually, from ticketed events like the Cleveland Orchestra to free student and faculty recitals. Each year, the Conservatory stages two operas, and the theater and dance programs present more than fifty productions. Numerous lectures and readings feature guests prominent in a variety of disciplines. Over 140 student organizations exist, from the Bike Co-op to the Forensic Team. The College allows students to launch new clubs.

Location

Oberlin College is an integral part of the city of Oberlin, a town of about 8,100 residents located 35 miles southwest of Cleveland. The town is primarily residential, with tree-lined streets and fine old clapboard houses. The College is located in the center of town, close to the business district, and virtually everything a student needs is within walking or biking distance.

Majors and Degrees

Oberlin offers the Bachelor of Arts degree (awarded by the College of Arts and Sciences) and the Bachelor of Music degree (awarded by the Conservatory of Music). Oberlin also offers a distinctive double-degree program, a five-year course of study leading to the B.A. and B.Mus. degrees. Students wishing to enter the double-degree program must be accepted by both the College of Arts and Sciences and the Conservatory of Music.

The B.A. is awarded in African American studies; anthropology; archaeological studies; art (history, studio, and visual); biology; chemistry; cinema studies; classics (Greek, Latin, and classical civilization); comparative American studies; comparative literature; computer science; creative writing; dance; East Asian studies; economics; English; environmental studies; French; gender, sexuality, and feminist studies; geology; German; Hispanic studies; history; Jewish studies; Latin American studies; law and society; mathematics; music; neuroscience; philosophy; physics; politics; psychology; religion; Russian; Russian and East European studies; sociology; theater; Third World studies; and 3/2 engineering. In addition, many students pursue interdisciplinary individual majors as well as preprofessional studies in law and medicine.

The B.Mus. is awarded in composition, electronic and computer music, historical performance, jazz studies (performance or composition), music history, and performance (baroque cello/viola da gamba, baroque flute, baroque oboe, baroque violin, bassoon, clarinet, classical guitar, double bass, flute, harp, harpsichord, horn, lute, oboe, organ, percussion, piano, recorder, saxophone, trombone, trumpet, tuba, viola, violin, violoncello, and voice). A major in music theory is only offered as part of a double major.

The Conservatory of Music also offers combined five-year B.Mus. and M.Mus. degrees in opera theater, conducting, and music education and teaching, as well as an M.Mus. in historical performance and a four-semester Artist Diploma.

Academic Programs

To receive the B.A. or the B.Mus. degree, students must complete a major; 9 credit hours in each of Oberlin's three divisions: humanities, natural sciences, and social sciences, as well as 9 hours in courses dealing with cultural diversity; and three Winter Term projects. Students must also demonstrate quantitative proficiency and writing proficiency. For the B.A., 112 credit hours are required for graduation; for the B.Mus., 124 hours are required. The recommended semester course load is 14 credit hours for students in the College of Arts and Sciences and 15 or 16 credit hours for students in the Conservatory of Music.

Academic Facilities

Oberlin's four libraries contain more than 2.4 million items, including 1.1 million catalogued volumes—an unusually large collection for a college of Oberlin's size. Other features include an online catalog, connections to several networks, access to numerous online and CD-ROM databases, and access to an additional 45 million volumes via OhioLINK. The College's Allen Memorial Art Museum is considered one of the top college or university art museums in the nation. Seventeenth-century Dutch and Flemish painting, European art of the late nineteenth and twentieth centuries, and contemporary art are especially well represented among the more than 14,000 objects spanning the range of art history in the museum. The one-of-a-kind art-rental program allows students to rent original works of art each semester for only $5, including works by such artists as Picasso, Rembrandt, and Toulouse-Lautrec.

The Conservatory of Music contains 153 practice rooms—all with windows—and houses 168 Steinway grand pianos and eighteen uprights (there are 207 Steinways on campus). The Conservatory also has two concert halls, numerous instrument collections, state-of-the-art electronic music studios, and recording facilities. A state-of-the-art jazz studies facility opens in spring 2010, the result of what is believed to be the largest private gift in support of jazz education at a U.S. college and the first music facility in the world to achieve a gold LEED rating.

Oberlin's Irvin E. Houck Computing Center provides more than 250 Macintosh and Dell computers for student use in several locations on campus. In all of the residence hall rooms, students have direct access to the Internet and the campus network from their personal computers. Computer accounts are automatically given to all students at no charge.

Oberlin's Science Center was designed to accommodate contemporary methods in science education. Everything is interconnected, promoting communication across disciplines and the collaborative research relationships for which Oberlin is so well known. The strength of Oberlin's science program and its supercomputer capability make Oberlin one of the leading undergraduate colleges in computational modeling. The Science Center complex is a testament to Oberlin's long-held belief that the best liberal arts education has a strong science component and that the best science education occurs in a liberal arts environment.

The Adam Joseph Lewis Center for Environmental Studies is the largest photovoltaic-run building among colleges and universities in the country. The Lewis Center is a living laboratory for the emerging field of ecological design. The center is a classroom, a case study, and a stunning example of how environmental commitment, the latest technologies, and life-cycle thinking can come together to create living and working spaces that minimize the negative impact on the world. Oberlin has been invited to become the eighteenth city in the world to join the Clinton Climate Initiative along with cities such as London, Seoul, Stockholm, Sydney, and Toronto.

Costs

Tuition for the 2009–10 academic year was $39,686. Double-room and board fees were an additional $10,480. The student activity fee was $318.

Financial Aid

In an average year, Oberlin commits more than $49 million, more than one fifth of the College budget, to financial aid. The Office of Financial Aid works to develop financial aid packages that meet the demonstrated financial need of all regularly admitted students who comply with the filing deadlines. Canadian citizens are treated as U.S. citizens for financial aid purposes. Limited financial aid is also available for other international students.

To apply for assistance, students must submit the Financial Aid PROFILE of the College Scholarship Service and the Free Application for Federal Student Aid (FAFSA).

Faculty

Of Oberlin's 339 faculty members, 253 teach in the College of Arts and Sciences and 86 teach in the Conservatory of Music. They are eminently qualified for their positions, with more than 97 percent having earned doctoral or terminal degrees in their field, many from the world's finest graduate institutions. The student-faculty ratio is 11:1 in the College and 8:1 in the Conservatory.

Student Government

By serving on Oberlin's Student Senate and in other ways, Oberlin College students have the opportunity to influence College policy on academic and student-life issues. Student representatives sit on nearly every faculty committee, and allocation of the student activity fee is determined by a committee composed solely of students.

Admission Requirements

Admission to both the College of Arts and Sciences and the Conservatory of Music is highly selective. Candidates for admission must submit the results of the SAT or ACT with writing. The College also recommends that two SAT Subject Tests be taken. For the class of 2013, the median 50 percent of SAT scores were 660–750 critical reading, 630–720 math, and 650–740 writing. The median 50 percent of ACT scores was 28–32. Of those students who attend high schools that rank their students, 81 percent were in the top tenth of their high school class, and 97 percent were in the top fifth. For admission to the Conservatory of Music, the most important factor is the performance audition or, in the case of composition and electronic and computer music applicants, the compositions, tapes, and supporting materials submitted.

Application and Information

For more information, students should write to:

Office of Admissions, College of Arts and Sciences
Oberlin College
Oberlin, Ohio 44074
Phone: 440-775-8411
800-622-OBIE (toll-free)
E-mail: college.admissions@oberlin.edu

Office of Admissions, Conservatory of Music
Oberlin College
Oberlin, Ohio 44074
Phone: 440-775-8413
E-mail: conservatory.admissions@oberlin.edu
Web site: http://www.oberlin.edu

Office of Financial Aid
Carnegie Building
Oberlin College
52 West Lorain Street
Oberlin, Ohio 44074
Phone: 440-775-8142
800-693-3173 (toll-free)
E-mail: financial.aid@oberlin.edu

OHIO NORTHERN UNIVERSITY

ADA, OHIO

The University

Ohio Northern University (ONU) is a selective, comprehensive University with an enrollment of more than 3,600 students from 43 states and 23 countries. ONU is one of the few private universities to offer a distinctive blend of nationally ranked liberal arts and professional programs in its five colleges: Arts & Sciences, Business Administration, Engineering, Pharmacy, and Law.

At the turn of the twentieth century, Ohio Northern became affiliated with the United Methodist Church. While no longer owned and operated by the UMC, the University continues to cherish this heritage by welcoming, serving, and supporting students of all faiths. The University's motto *Ex diversitate vires* (Out of diversity, strength) illustrates ONU's mission to provide experiences and programs that prepare graduates to live in an inclusive world characterized by difference.

Ohio Northern is a student-centered, service-oriented, values-based institution of higher learning committed to a rigorous pursuit of academic inquiry and achievement. Education is a collaborative process at Ohio Northern. Students work side-by-side with accomplished faculty members in a constant pursuit of new knowledge. The result is serious research, real collaboration, and meaningful learning experiences that extend to both sides of the classroom.

Students can choose from a variety of campus activities including nearly 200 student organizations, four national sororities and six national fraternities, music and theatrical events, and intramural and club sports. Residence hall living is an integral part of the educational program, and the residence halls' staff, facilities, and programs contribute to students' personal development. There are ten residence halls on campus as well as seven campus apartment complexes and an Affinity Housing complex, which typically houses juniors and seniors. The dining hall is located in the student union.

The University is Division III and a member of the Ohio Athletic Conference with teams in eleven men's teams: baseball, basketball, cross-country, football, golf, soccer, swimming and diving, tennis, indoor and outdoor track, and wrestling; and ten women's teams: basketball, cross-country, fast-pitch softball, golf, soccer, swimming and diving, tennis, indoor and outdoor track, and volleyball.

Ohio Northern is strongly committed to developing policies and practices that are environmentally friendly. The use of geothermal technology to heat and cool recently built or renovated residential facilities is just the most recent example of this commitment.

Guests of the University, as well as the public, enjoy the luxury and comfort of The Inn at Ohio Northern, which offers deluxe accommodations, fine dining and a pub, and meeting and conference space. For more information, visit http://www.onu.edu/inn.

Location

The campus of Ohio Northern University is located on 342 beautiful acres in the safe, friendly, rural village of Ada, a community of 5,000 residents. Located in northwestern Ohio, ONU is easily accessible by major highways. Students also have convenient access to Columbus, Dayton, Toledo, and Fort Wayne, Indiana.

Majors and Degrees

Ohio Northern University offers the undergraduate degrees of Bachelor of Arts, Bachelor of Fine Arts, Bachelor of Music, Bachelor of Science, Bachelor of Science in Business Administration, Bachelor of Science in Civil Engineering, Bachelor of Science in Clinical Laboratory Science, Bachelor of Science in Computer Engineering, Bachelor of Science in Electrical Engineering, Bachelor of Science in Mechanical Engineering, and Bachelor of Science in Nursing.

Majors are offered in advertising design, applied mathematics, art education, athletic training, biochemistry, biology, chemistry, clinical laboratory sciences, communication studies, construction management, creative writing, criminal justice, early childhood education, education studies, environmental and field biology, exercise physiology (clinical/research, corporate fitness/personal training), forensic biology, French, geography–area studies, geography–geographic information systems, German, graphic design, health education, history, international theater production, journalism, language arts education, literature, manufacturing technology, mathematics, mathematics/statistics, middle childhood education, molecular biology, music (music history and literature, music theory and composition), music education, music performance, musical theater, nursing, philosophy, physical education, physics (physics, applied physics, astronomy), political science (American politics, international relations–comparative politics), professional writing, psychology (behavioral neuroscience, clinical and counseling, psychology), public relations, philosophy (religion, Eastern, Western), social studies, sociology, Spanish, sport management, statistics, studio arts (2D, 3D), technology education, theatre, and youth ministry.

Special preprofessional programs are available in art therapy, dentistry, medicine, occupational therapy, optometry, physical therapy, physician assistant studies, seminary, and veterinary medicine. Interdisciplinary degree programs are available in arts/engineering and arts–business/pharmacy. Additional programs are offered in athletic coaching certification. Teacher licensure programs are offered at the adolescent, early childhood, middle childhood, and multiage levels and in sixteen program areas.

In addition to the undergraduate programs, ONU offers a Juris Doctor, a Doctor of Pharmacy (Pharm.D.), and a Doctor of Pharmacy/Law.

(Changes in programs of study are updated at http://www.onu.edu)

Academic Programs

The Getty College of Arts and Sciences creatively combines a traditional liberal arts education with cutting-edge professional studies. The college offers more than fifty majors in sixteen academic departments, and students can earn a Bachelor of Arts, Bachelor of Fine Arts, Bachelor of Music, Bachelor of Science, Bachelor of Science in Clinical Laboratory Science, or Bachelor of Nursing degrees. Working closely with dedicated faculty, students complete the general education requirements, delve deeply into advanced courses, and engage in research, internships, practicum experiences, study abroad, and more.

The James F. Dicke College of Business Administration at Ohio Northern is focused on creating entrepreneurial, ethical, and engaged business and civic leaders. The College offers a rigorous academic curriculum with signature programs in pharmaceutical business and forensic accounting. Internships are required by the College and available year-round as well as international programs including study abroad, work abroad, and study tours. An office of experiential learning supports students looking for these opportunities.

The first two years of study are devoted to general education courses plus introductory courses in several of the business disciplines. To graduate, a student must satisfactorily complete a minimum of 182 quarter hours of appropriate course work for the specific major(s) and maintain at least a 2.0 grade point average.

Personal attention and mentoring from faculty, small intimate classes, and active student organizations combine with an emphasis on experiential learning, technological proficiency, global awareness, and the entrepreneurial spirit. The college is accredited by the AACSB International—The Association to Advance Collegiate Schools of Business, making it one of the best business colleges in the world.

The College of Engineering at Ohio Northern University is focused on providing a premier undergraduate experience that inspires creativity and supports innovation. The college features five accredited, disciplinary majors in civil, computer, electrical, and mechanical engineering and computer science.

The courses for the first academic year are essentially the same for each degree program, offering students an easy track to move from one program to another if they are initially uncertain which disciplines they prefer to study. Students are required to maintain a minimum cumulative grade point average of 2.0 as well as a minimum GPA of 2.0 for all engineering and computer science courses.

An optional five-year co-op program is available for students in each program, provided they maintain a minimum 2.5 GPA. A minor in computer science and options in environmental studies, business administration, and entrepreneurship are available to the College's students provided they maintain at least a 2.5 GPA.

There is an emphasis on team projects and students participate in many design competitions such as the ASCE Concrete Canoe, the Baja SAE off-road vehicle and the AIAA Design Build Fly competitions.

Many opportunities are available for valuable work experience through the co-op, internship and Engineer-in-Residence programs, with an overall 98 percent job placement rate for graduates.

For more than 125 years the College of Pharmacy has offered distinctive, challenging, and comprehensive training for some of the nation's most talented pharmacists. This University signature program features a six-year Doctor of Pharmacy (Pharm.D.) degree accredited by the American Council on Pharmaceutical Education.

Ohio Northern's program is direct-entry—admitting students immediately from high school into the College's professional program. This approach is unique as the program enables students to take pharmacy courses from the very first day. A rigorous curriculum utilizes an innovative modular format to organize learning around the human body systems and disease types and implement pharmaceutical science and patient care. Students complete a minimum of 324 credit hours and follow a prescribed curriculum and requirements, all while earning a grade of C or better in any course.

Leading-edge clinical facilities include the Pharmacy Skills Center, where students access state-of-the-art compound/counseling pods with portable OTC simulation stations. Students gain considerable experience through a strong undergraduate research program and may pursue minors or dual majors in biochemistry and medicinal chemistry. Faculty members are teaching-focused, but remain current in their research disciplines. Upon graduation, students are well schooled in every aspect of pharmacy and have a 100 percent placement rate.

Off-Campus Programs

Many majors may take part in study-abroad programs developed in consultation with faculty members. Field experiences and internships are available in most majors. Externships are required of all pharmacy majors and place students in retail and clinical experiences. Teacher licensure requires one quarter of primary or secondary classroom teaching experience under the supervision of practicing teachers. Additional opportunities include computer science and mathematics co-op programs (professional practice), engineering co-op programs (professional practice, domestic and international), and an honors program. All of these off-campus learning experiences carry credit.

Academic Facilities

Among the 31 modern buildings on campus, the newest is the Mathile Center for the Natural Sciences that expands the science-learning environment. The 95,145-square-foot structure is a student-centered academic research and learning facility that blends hands-on teaching excellence with advanced technology in a functional modern environment. The building connects the Meyer Hall of Science with the Robertson-Evans Pharmacy building. Features include classrooms and offices for mathematics and statistics; biology and chemistry laboratories for student-faculty research; and classrooms and laboratories for the clinical laboratory sciences, forensic science, and the new baccalaureate nursing programs.

The College of Business offers students a modern setting for high-tech classrooms, meeting rooms and a 150-seat lecture forum, as well as a real-time digital stock ticker.

ONU's Heterick Memorial Library and the Taggart Law Library provide information resources and services to support course offerings and foster independent study.

The Freed Center for the Performing Arts features a 550-seat theater/concert hall, a 120-seat studio theater, and TV and radio production facilities. WONB-FM is the commercial-free voice of ONU.

The campus network is available in every academic building and residence hall room. In addition, wireless networking is available in most academic and administrative buildings. More than 580 computers are available to students in academic areas.

Costs

Charges for the 2010–11 year are $41,793 for tuition, room, and board for the Colleges of Arts & Sciences and Business Administration, $44,031 for the College of Engineering, and $45,870 for the College of Pharmacy. The cost of books and supplies is approximately $1500 per year.

Financial Aid

Ohio Northern University makes every effort to ensure that no qualified applicant is denied admission because of inability to pay the total cost. More than 90 percent of the student body receives some type of financial assistance. To be considered, the student should submit the FAFSA to the University along with the admission application. Both merit and need-based aid are available to students.

Faculty

More than 200 full-time faculty members bring extensive academic, work, travel, and life experience to their classrooms. Ohio Northern values excellence, innovation, technology, diversity, and its people. Many faculty members live near the campus and participate in some area of co-curricular student activities. With a 12:1 student-to-faculty ratio, students get lots of personal attention from professors who are passionate about teaching and mentoring.

Student Government

The Student Senate provides self-government in many areas of student life and seeks to further ideals of character and service to the University. Officers of the Student Senate are elected by the students, and the group meets on a weekly basis. The Student Senate serves as the official representative group of the student body to the University administration and agencies in matters pertaining to the student body.

Admission Requirements

High school students applying for admission to the University should present an official transcript indicating at least 16 total units, including work in the academic areas indicated by each college, as follows: College of Arts & Sciences, 12 units—4 in English, 2 in mathematics (algebra and geometry), and 6 in history, social studies, language, or natural science; College of Business Administration, 13 units—4 in English, 3 in mathematics (including algebra and geometry), and 6 in history, social studies, language, or natural sciences; College of Engineering, 16 units—4 in English, 4 in mathematics (including geometry, trigonometry, and 2 of algebra), 2 in science (including physics and, preferably, chemistry), and 6 in history, social studies, language, or natural sciences; and College of Pharmacy, 20 units—4 in English, 4 in mathematics (algebra I and II, plane geometry, trigonometry, precalculus, or calculus), 4 in science (including biology and chemistry), and 6 of history, social studies, languages, or any combination thereof. Applicants are also required to submit scores on the ACT and/or SAT. Ohio Northern University recommends that students take the writing section of the ACT. For scholarship purposes, the traditional sections of the ACT and the SAT are considered. An interview on campus is recommended.

Application and Information

Completed applications should be sent along with a $30 nonrefundable application fee. It is recommended that students apply for admission at the end of their junior year in high school or early in the senior year. Students are encouraged to apply no later than December 1 of their senior year for maximum scholarship consideration (November 1 for pharmacy).

The Colleges of Arts & Sciences, Business Administration, and Engineering operate on a rolling admission basis, and applications are processed immediately upon receipt of all necessary information (application, application fee, high school transcript, letter of recommendation, and ACT and/or SAT scores).

The College of Pharmacy application deadline is November 1 for entering freshmen. A student file is considered complete when it contains the application, application fee, high school transcript, and ACT and/or SAT scores. A campus visit is strongly encouraged for consideration for admittance into the College of Pharmacy.

Requests for catalogs, application forms, or additional information should be directed to:

Office of Admissions
Ohio Northern University
Ada, Ohio 45810
Phone: 888-408-4668 (toll-free)
Fax: 419-772-2821
E-mail: admissions-ug@onu.edu
Web site: http://www.onu.edu

OHIO WESLEYAN UNIVERSITY

DELAWARE, OHIO

The University

A unique blend of liberal arts learning, preprofessional preparation, internships, research opportunities, study-travel, and study abroad sets Ohio Wesleyan University (OWU) apart. Founded by the United Methodist Church in 1842, the University is strongly committed to education for leadership and service, to fusing theory and practice, and to preparing students to succeed in a global community.

A selective residential institution, Ohio Wesleyan is home to approximately 1,850 undergraduates, with a nearly equal number of men and women. Students come to Ohio Wesleyan from forty-seven states and fifty-seven countries; most live on the attractive 200-acre campus. Housing options include six large residence halls; several small living units (SLUs), such as the Creative Arts House, the Modern Foreign Languages House, and the Peace and Justice House; and seven fraternity houses. The five sorority houses are nonresidential.

Ohio Wesleyan has long been committed to education for a global society. The curriculum has an international perspective, and a significant portion of the student body is drawn from other countries. OWU has the highest percentage of international students among undergraduate, bachelor's degree-granting colleges in the state of Ohio and the fourteenth-highest percentage among similar colleges in the United States.

One of the richest of OWU's cocurricular traditions is service. The University sends as many as ten mission teams throughout the world each year. Nearly the entire student body participates in at least one community service or philanthropic project each year. The University has been recognized on the President's Honor Roll for its breadth and depth of community service.

Students publish the nation's oldest independent student newspaper. They also participate in cultural- and ethnic-interest groups such as the Student Union on Black Awareness (SUBA) and SANGAM and VIVA (which promote an understanding of the cultures of South Asia and Latin America, respectively), the College Republicans and College Democrats, and prelaw and premed clubs. In the course of a year, students may enjoy more than 100 concerts, plays, dance programs, films, exhibits, and speakers. The Department of Theatre & Dance stages four major productions and much additional studio work each year, while the Music Department sponsors four large performance groups and a variety of smaller ensembles. The impressive Hamilton-Williams Campus Center is the hub of cocurricular life on campus.

OWU is home to twenty-two Division III varsity athletic teams—eleven for men and eleven for women. In 2009, the University won the North Coast Athletic Conference (NACA) All-Sports Trophy for the third consecutive year and the ninth time overall. In 2010, Ohio Wesleyan is scheduled to open the Meek Aquatics and Recreation Center, which will feature a ten-lane pool, 1- and 3-meter diving boards, and a 13-foot-deep diving well. The entire building and pool is to be heated and cooled by ninety geothermal wells.

Intramural and club sports programs are extensive, and all students have access to racquet sports, and weight-lifting facilities in the Branch Rickey Physical Education Center. Fitness equipment and health services are housed in the 7,000-square-foot Health and Wellness Center. Off-campus opportunities for backpacking, boating, camping, golf, skiing, and swimming are abundant.

Location

Delaware combines the small-town pace and maple-lined streets of the county seat (population 34,000) with easy access to the state capital, Columbus, the sixteenth-largest city in America. Thirty minutes south of the campus, Columbus provides rich internship opportunities, international research centers, fine dining and shopping, and cultural events that complement those on campus.

Majors and Degrees

With more than ninety majors, sequences, and courses of study, Ohio Wesleyan offers the Bachelor of Arts in accounting; ancient, medieval, and Renaissance studies; astronomy; biological sciences (botany, genetics, microbiology, and zoology); chemistry; computer science; economics (including accounting, international business, and management); education (elementary and secondary licensure in seventeen areas); English literature and writing; fine arts; French; geography; geology; German; history; humanities-classics; journalism; mathematics; music (applied or history/literature); philosophy; physical education; physics; planetary science; politics and government; psychology; religion; sociology/anthropology; Spanish; and theater and dance. Interdisciplinary majors include Black world studies, East Asian studies, environmental studies, international studies, Latin American studies, neuroscience, urban studies, and women's and gender studies. Preprofessional studies include prelaw, premedicine, pre-engineering, predentistry, pre–veterinary medicine, pre–public administration, preoptometry, pretheology, and pre–physical therapy. Students also may design majors in topical, period, or regional studies.

Two professional degrees are awarded: the Bachelor of Fine Arts in art history, arts education, and studio art, and the Bachelor of Music in music education and performance. Combined-degree (generally 3-2) programs are offered in engineering, medical technology, optometry, and physical therapy. Ohio Wesleyan is one of only eleven colleges in the United States that has a 3-2 engineering program with the California Institute of Technology.

Academic Programs

Ohio Wesleyan provides opportunities for students to acquire not only depth in a major area but also knowledge about their cultural past through the insight provided by a broad liberal arts curriculum. At Ohio Wesleyan, education is placed in a context of values, and students are encouraged to develop the intellectual skills of effective communication, independent and logical thought, and creative problem solving. To these ends, students are required to demonstrate competence in English composition and a foreign language (often through placement testing) and to complete distributional study in the natural and social sciences, the humanities, and the arts. With few exceptions, the major requires the completion of eight to fifteen courses. Many students double major or take more than one minor in addition to their major, and self-designed majors are not uncommon. Thirty-four courses are required for graduation.

Advanced placement is available with or without credit. Under the four-year honors program, even first-year students may be named Merit Scholars and work individually with faculty mentors on research, directed readings, or original creative work. Undergraduate students frequently present their research to prestigious societies such as the American Society for Microbiology, the American Microscopy Society, the American Chemical Society, the American Physical Society, the American Ornithologists' Union, and other nationally recognized professional organizations. Upperclass students also are encouraged to participate in independent study. One of the twenty-six scholastic honorary societies with chapters on campus, Ohio Wesleyan's chapter of Phi Beta Kappa is 103 years old.

The objectives of an Ohio Wesleyan education are crystallized in the distinctive Sagan National Colloquium, a program focused annually on one issue of compelling public importance. Through speakers, seminars, and student-led initiatives, the colloquium stimulates campuswide dialogue; and encourages students to discover not only what they think about the issue but why they think as they do, and how to make important decisions based on their beliefs. In 2009, Sagan Fellows courses were added to the program. These courses, many of which involve international travel and study, are developed and taught by selected faculty designated as Sagan Fellows. Also in 2009, the University instituted a series of Theory into Practice Grants to foster original research by students and faculty.

Off-Campus Programs

Full-semester internships and apprenticeships, as well as programs of advanced research, are available to students. Many are approved by the Great Lakes Colleges Association, Inc. (GLCA), a highly regarded academic consortium of thirteen independent institutions. Programs are available at the Philadelphia Center, the GLCA New York Arts

Program, and the Oak Ridge Science Semester. Other cooperative arrangements include the Newberry Library Program, Wesleyan in Washington, and the Drew University United Nations Semester. Students also conduct research locally at the U.S. Department of Agriculture (USDA) Laboratories in Delaware, the nearby Columbus Zoo, The Wilds, and several other sites. The Summer Science Research Program offers selected students the opportunity for an intensive, ten-week, one-to-one research experience with a faculty mentor. The program concludes with a symposium at which research results are presented to the entire campus.

Ohio Wesleyan has been long committed to education for a global society. The curriculum has an international perspective, and a significant portion of the student body is drawn from other countries. In fact, OWU has the highest percentage of international students among undergraduate, bachelor's-degree-granting colleges in the state of Ohio and the fourteenth-highest percentage among similar colleges in the United States. Students are offered a wide variety of opportunities to study abroad. Students can arrange individual projects, but formal programs are offered in more than twenty countries. These include Ohio Wesleyan's affiliation with the University of Salamanca in Spain as well as programs in Mexico, Ireland, Central Europe, Turkey, Africa, China, England, India/Nepal, Japan, Russia, and others.

Academic Facilities

The Beeghly Library houses more than 550,000 holdings, one of the largest collections in the country for a private university of Ohio Wesleyan's size. The library's federal documents depository is among the nation's oldest and largest, providing an additional 200,000 reference publications. Beeghly Library also offers the Online Computer Library Center's most advanced cataloging system. The collection is enhanced by OhioLINK and CONSORT membership. An Internet Café within the Beeghly Library provides students with a 24-hour study area. The café has eight computer workstations and wireless capabilities and serves Starbucks coffee and assorted snacks.

The comprehensive academic computing system is accessible to students 24 hours per day, and all residence hall rooms are wired for campus network and global Internet access. The latest generation of wireless communication allows students to work online anywhere on the campus.

The Conrades-Wetherell Science Center includes a 145,000-square-foot three-level building that houses state-of-the-art instrumentation, including a scanning electron microscope and scanning and transmission electron microscopes, all for undergraduate use. Located in the Science Center is the Hobson Science Library, which consolidates all of OWU's science holdings. The University has a state-of-the-art Geographic Information Systems Computer Laboratory.

The R.W. Corns Building houses the Woltemade Center for Economics, Business, and Entrepreneurship; the Department of Economics; the Sagan Academic Resource Center, which includes the Writing Resource Center, the Academic Skills Center, and the Quantitative Skills Center; and Information Systems.

Perkins Observatory features a 32-inch reflecting telescope and two smaller instruments, while an on-campus student observatory includes a 9.5-in refracting telescope. Two University wilderness preserves cover a total of 100 acres. Other special facilities include the multi-stage Chappelear Drama Center; Sanborn Hall, home to the Music Department, Jemison Auditorium, and the Kinnison Music Library; and the 1,100-seat Gray Chapel, which houses the largest of only six Klais concert organs in the United States.

Costs

The general fee for 2010–11 is $45,674. This amount covers tuition and fees ($36,398) and room and board ($9276). Books and personal expenses average $1100. Nominal fees are charged for some studio art courses, off-campus study, private music lessons for students who are not majoring in music, and student teaching.

Financial Aid

OWU awards financial assistance to almost every entering freshman who demonstrates need. Aid packages include a combination of grants, loans, and employment. Federal and state aid are often part of an aid package. Nearly 70 percent of all undergraduates receive need-based financial assistance; another 25 percent are granted merit-based aid. More than three-quarters of all aid is awarded in the form of grants and scholarships.

The University awards several merit scholarship programs, ranging from $5000 to full tuition. The school awarded more than 2,000 scholarships to new and prospective students for 2010–11. Private loan programs and flexible payment plans are available to all students, regardless of demonstrated financial need.

Faculty

The full-time faculty numbers 137, providing a student-faculty ratio of approximately 12:1. One hundred percent of the full-time tenure-track faculty members hold the highest degree in their fields. Although committed first to teaching and advising, most faculty members maintain active research programs and publish important articles and books. Some members of the faculty are artists whose contributions include the exhibition of works of art and theater.

Student Government

Students have a significant voice in the government of campus life. The Wesleyan Council on Student Affairs formulates basic policy. Students also sit on judicial boards, individual department student boards, and nine faculty committees. They are represented at all meetings of the Board of Trustees.

Admission Requirements

The admission process is competitive. Each student's application is individually reviewed. Although the applicant's academic record and strength of academic program are the most important factors, followed closely by teacher and counselor evaluations and SAT or ACT scores, many other aspects are considered, such as evidence of creativity, community service, and leadership. A minimum sixteen-course preparatory program is required. Four units of English and 3 each of mathematics, social studies, science, and foreign language are recommended, but variations of this program are considered. SAT Subject Tests are not required but may qualify students for advanced placement. Candidates for the Bachelor of Music degree must audition (tapes are accepted). Early action and transfer admission are offered. Campus interviews are strongly recommended but not required. For the 2009–10 school year, approximately 4,200 applications were received; 65 percent of the applicants gained admission.

Application and Information

Students are urged to complete the application as early as possible in the senior year, especially if they are applying for merit- or need-based financial aid. Once complete credentials (application, transcript, recommendations, and SAT or ACT scores) are received, decisions are made on a rolling basis after January 1. The student's response is required by May 1. The deadline for Early Action I application is November 30; the deadline for Early Action II application is January 15. Notification is given within four weeks after application is complete. After April 1, students are admitted on a space-available, rolling admission basis. For further information, students should contact:

Office of Admission
Ohio Wesleyan University
Delaware, Ohio 43015
Phone: 740-368-3020
800-922-8953 (toll-free)
Fax: 740-368-3314
E-mail: owuadmit@owu.edu
Web site: http://www.owu.edu

The Hamilton-Williams Campus Center is a magnificent meeting place for the campus community.

COLLEGE CLOSE-UPS

OLIVET NAZARENE UNIVERSITY

BOURBONNAIS, ILLINOIS

The University

Olivet Nazarene University (ONU) is a private, Christian liberal arts university with a strong emphasis on both academic excellence and Christ-centered living. ONU offers one of the finest liberal arts educations in the Midwest, world-class facilities for learning and entertainment, and an atmosphere that promotes fun, relationship building, and spiritual growth.

Olivet's high retention, graduation, and employment/placement rates demonstrate the University's commitment to students' success. The members of the faculty, staff, and administration are dedicated to teaching, encouraging, and mentoring each student as a whole person—academically, socially, and spiritually.

With 4,600 students (2,600 undergraduates), Olivet offers an ideal student population for a private institution, maintaining diversity without sacrificing personalized attention. Nearly half the student body comes from the Nazarene denomination, and the rest come from some thirty other denominations. Most U.S. states are represented, as are more than twenty countries.

The campus offers a championship-caliber athletics department (eighteen intercollegiate men's and women's sports in all) and a large intramural sports program. Music and drama groups involve hundreds of students, and many clubs are organized for a wide variety of interests. Olivet students are also heavily involved in dozens of ministry groups and volunteer efforts, small-group Bible studies, and weekly student-led services.

The University recently completed a number of campus improvements, including the renovation of the lower level of Ludwig Center, the student union, to include a glass-enclosed gaming room featuring plasma TV screens, a convenience store, and new student leadership offices. In addition, the Department of Communication moved to a new, technologically advanced facility in Benner Library, which also houses some of the University's art programs, representing a partnership between the Departments of Communication and Art. A new 3,059-seat chapel is under construction.

The University is home to the Chicago Bears' summer training camp and Shine.FM, a 35,000-watt station ranked among the top stations in the nation and staffed by Olivet's broadcasting students.

In addition to its traditional undergraduate programs, Olivet offers six degree-completion and continuing-studies programs, more than twenty master's degrees, and a Doctor of Education in ethical leadership. The School of Graduate and Continuing Studies strives to meet the needs of the ever-expanding number of adults returning to school. Adult degree-completion programs are designed to assist working adults so they can complete their degree requirements without an interruption to their employment. The school serves as a resource for adults striving to enhance their personal and professional lives in a constantly changing world.

In addition to the classes held on the main campus, the School of Graduate and Continuing Studies offers courses for students throughout the Chicago area. Numerous students gather with other working adults for classes in churches, schools, hospitals, and other convenient locations near their home or workplace.

Location

The main University campus is located just 50 miles south of Chicago's Loop in the historic village of Bourbonnais. The area includes malls, restaurants, entertainment, and natural recreation centered on the Kankakee River State Park system. Olivet students enjoy many activities nearby and often make the quick trip north for the limitless offerings of Chicago and its surroundings.

In addition to recreation, students find numerous opportunities for employment and internships in the area, which is ranked as one of the top locations in the nation for small businesses, and the vast professional resources of Chicago. Students, faculty members, and staff members also find themselves working side by side in local and regional ministry projects. Olivet students are recognized professionally and ministerially as a valuable commodity by area businesses, churches, and parachurch organizations.

Majors and Degrees

Olivet confers Bachelor of Arts (B.A.) and/or Bachelor of Science (B.S.) degrees in the following fields of study (includes all majors, minors, and concentrations): accounting, actuarial science, art, art (education), athletic training, biblical languages, biblical studies, biochemistry, biology, business administration, business information systems, chemistry, child development, children's ministry, Christian education, church music, coaching, commercial graphics, communication studies, computer engineering, computer science, corporate communication, criminal justice, dietetics, digital media (graphics), digital media (photography), drawing/illustration, early childhood education, earth and space science, economics, economics/finance, electrical engineering, elementary education, engineering, English, English as a second language, English (education), environmental science, exercise science, family and consumer sciences, family and consumer sciences (education), fashion merchandising, film studies, finance, forensics, French, general studies, geology, geography, geological engineering, Greek, health education, history, hospitality, housing and environmental design, industrial technology management, information technology, information systems, intercultural studies, international business, international marketing, journalism, literature, management, marketing, mass communication, mathematics, mathematics (education), mechanical engineering, media production, military affairs, military science, missions, music, music composition, music (education), music performance, nursing, painting, pastoral ministry, philosophy and religion, photography, physical education/health, physical science, political science, practical ministries, predentistry, prelaw, premedicine, preoptometry, prepharmacy, pre–physical therapy, pre-physician's assistant studies, pre–veterinary studies, psychology, public policy, public relations, radio, recreation and leisure studies, religion, religious studies, science (education), social science, social science (education), social work, sociology, Spanish, Spanish (education), sports management, television/video production, theater, writing, youth ministry, and zoology.

Academic Programs

Olivet seeks to offer an "Education with a Christian Purpose." The University believes that this commitment to Christ mandates nothing less than the highest-quality academic programs. Olivet's liberal arts curriculum requires that students complete 45 to 58 hours of general education courses. With the addition of major and minor programs of study, students must complete a minimum of 128 credit hours to obtain a bachelor's degree. Credit may be earned through AP and CLEP tests. Students may also participate in ROTC.

Olivet operates on a two-semester schedule, from August to May. Two summer sessions are also available.

Off-Campus Programs

Olivet students are encouraged to participate in the various off-campus study programs offered each semester. International locations include Xiamen, China; San José, Costa Rica; Cairo, Egypt; Sydney, Australia; Oxford, England; Moscow, Nizhni Novgorod, and St. Petersburg, Russia; and Mukono, Uganda. Domestic opportunities include the American Studies Program in Washington, D.C.; the Los Angeles Film Studies Program in Los Angeles, California; the Focus on the Family Institute in Colorado Springs, Colorado; and the Contemporary Music Center on Martha's Vineyard. Costs are usually comparable to a semester at Olivet, and credit is given for these programs. In addition, some sources of financial aid are applicable.

Many Olivet students participate in numerous educational and missions-oriented short-term trips that are available during the Christmas, spring, and summer breaks.

Academic Facilities

Olivet's 250-acre campus offers leading-edge academic facilities. These include high-quality performance halls and athletic venues; excellent natural science, engineering, and nursing laboratories; smart classrooms; and an observatory. It is one of only a handful of small college campuses in the nation to have a planetarium, which was completely renovated in 2008 with the same technology used in Chicago's Adler Planetarium. Each department uses the top software in its field. More than a dozen campus computer labs are available for student use, and two network ports in each dorm room and the campuswide wireless network give students access to e-mail, the Internet, and classroom applications 24 hours a day.

Benner Library and Resource Center provides unlimited access to any material a student needs, either on-site or through the interlibrary loan system. Benner Library offers more than 170,000 books, 350,000 other items in various formats, 700 periodicals, more than 15,000 full-text electronic journals, and more than 30,410 electronic books.

Costs

Tuition, based on 12 to 18 credit hours, will be $24,750 per year in 2010–11. Room and board, based on double occupancy and the fourteen-meals-per-week plan, will cost $6400 per year. Additional fees will be $840 per year.

Financial Aid

Approximately 99 percent of traditional undergraduates receive a total of $27.7 million in federal and state grants and institutional scholarships.

Olivet's cost is below average for private colleges nationwide. The University also participates in all federal and state financial aid programs. The priority deadline for filing the Free Application for Federal Student Aid (FAFSA) is March 1. To apply for aid, students must fill out the FAFSA as well as Olivet's application for financial aid. The student must be an accepted applicant before a financial aid package can be created. Olivet offers a monthly installment plan in addition to the traditional three-payment plan. Olivet believes funding a student's education is a partnership between each family, Olivet, and the state and federal governments. The friendly staff is committed to making an Olivet education affordable to every young person.

Faculty

Olivet's more than 100 full-time faculty members are the key to excellence in and out of the classroom. Teaching is a ministry for these dedicated Christian individuals, and Olivet's student-faculty ratio gives them an opportunity to teach, mentor, and encourage students on a personal level. To that end, the faculty is heavily involved in campus life, whether sponsoring social organizations or participating in talent shows.

Student Government

The Associated Student Council is the student government organization on campus. Its executive council consists of a president, vice president of finance, vice president of spiritual life, vice president of social affairs, vice president of publicity, vice president of women's residential life, vice president of men's residential life, vice president of office management, the *GlimmerGlass* (student newspaper) editor, and the *Aurora* (yearbook) editor. They work alongside the University's administrative team to ensure the health and promotion of campus activities and organizations.

Admission Requirements

Admission to the University is moderately difficult. Students are considered for admission on the basis of their high school GPA and ACT or SAT scores. An ACT score is required for placement in courses. For international students, TOEFL results are an additional factor in the admission decision. Students with low test scores and GPAs may be admitted on a provisional basis. A campus visit and interview are strongly recommended for all prospective students.

Application and Information

Admission is on a rolling basis until the application deadline of May 1. An early decision is required for some scholarships. Students may apply via Olivet's home page online or in print. The application process includes the written (or electronic) application, high school transcripts, ACT or SAT scores, and a health form. An enrollment deposit is collected to prioritize both student housing and class registration.

For more information or to arrange a campus visit, students should contact:

Office of Admissions
Olivet Nazarene University
One University Avenue
Bourbonnais, Illinois 60914
Phone: 800-648-1463 (toll-free)
E-mail: admissions@olivet.edu
Web site: http://www.olivet.edu

Olivet's 250-acre, parklike campus is just 50 minutes south of Chicago's Loop, with additional locations in Rolling Meadows, Illinois; the Greater Chicago area; and Hong Kong.

COLLEGE CLOSE-UPS

OREGON STATE UNIVERSITY

CORVALLIS, OREGON

The University

Exceptional students, an outstanding faculty, and a challenging curriculum combine to make Oregon State University (OSU) a nationally and internationally recognized comprehensive university.

OSU has earned the Carnegie Foundation's "Very High Research Activity" designation for commitment to education and research. Widely recognized research programs add to the quality of teaching by bringing new knowledge into the classroom and by encouraging undergraduate students to work with faculty members on research projects in many fields. As a member of the non-tiered Oregon University System, OSU is the premier research university in the state of Oregon. In fact, OSU's economic impact to the state of Oregon exceeds $1.5 billion.

The University's 20,320 students come from all fifty states and more than eighty-nine countries around the world to pursue a wide choice of undergraduate programs that prepare them for careers and leadership positions in science, engineering and computer-related fields, natural resources, government, teaching and social service, pharmacy, and other professions. Employers from across the nation recognize the value of an OSU degree, and more of them recruit at Oregon State University each year than at any other university in the state.

OSU is committed to offering students the resources they need to be successful in their education. In addition to utilizing Blackboard™ as an electronic tool to assist students with class materials, interactive topic conversations, and resources, OSU continues to innovate by systematically adding wireless networks to classrooms, libraries, and common areas on campus. Students also have access to one of the largest open-source software labs in the world, where new shareware is developed, housed, and distributed.

Students also benefit from more than 300 cocurricular activities on campus. These include student government, student media, theater and music, intramural and club sports, and numerous social, academic, cultural, and professional clubs and organizations. In addition, Dixon Recreation Center offers opportunities for swimming and diving, weight training, aerobic exercise, and the largest collegiate rock-climbing center in the Northwest. Two campus child-care facilities offer educationally oriented day-care programs for children of students and faculty and staff members.

OSU offers a wide range of housing and dining options, including special-program residence halls, cooperative houses, student family housing, and fraternity and sorority housing. Many apartments and houses are available within biking or walking distance of OSU for students who choose to live off campus. There are twenty-eight restaurants on campus.

Graduate degrees are offered through the Colleges of Agricultural Sciences, Business, Engineering, Forestry, Health and Human Sciences, Liberal Arts, and Science. Graduate and professional degrees are also offered through the Colleges of Oceanic and Atmospheric Sciences, Pharmacy, and Veterinary Medicine, and through the School of Education.

Location

The OSU main campus is in Corvallis, which is consistently ranked as one of the safest university communities on the West Coast. Farmers Insurance named Corvallis the "Most Secure" city in the U.S. for 2007 and 2008. With about 55,000 residents, Corvallis offers a friendly, university-oriented atmosphere. In fact, students rated OSU as the fifth-friendliest campus in the United States, according to CampusDirt.com. *Forbes* magazine also rated Corvallis as one of the top 5 smartest cities. Miles of bike lanes and free city bus service make it easy for students to get around town. Within a couple hours of Corvallis are the Oregon Coast; the Cascade Mountains, with skiing, hiking, camping, and snowboarding; and Portland, Oregon's largest city. The OSU Cascades Campus in Bend, Oregon, represents a unique educational partnership involving four distinguished institutions, creating an innovative and collaborative university to serve the needs of central Oregon.

Majors and Degrees

Oregon State is a comprehensive university, with more than 200 academic programs. Undergraduate degrees are offered through the Colleges of Agricultural Sciences, Business, Education, Engineering, Forestry, Health and Human Sciences, Liberal Arts, and Science.

Students in any undergraduate major can strengthen their transcripts by earning an Honors Degree or an International Degree. Almost 600 top students are enrolled in the University Honors College, which offers a small-college atmosphere within the larger University. The University also offers twenty-eight preprofessional programs that prepare students for graduate programs and careers in fields such as health sciences, law, and education.

Academic Programs

All undergraduate students at Oregon State complete the Baccalaureate Core, which helps develop skills and knowledge in writing, critical thinking, cultural diversity, the arts, science, literature, lifelong fitness, and global awareness, ensuring that as graduates they will be well prepared for life as well as a career.

Many students take advantage of OSU's first-year experience program, called U-Engage, which offers opportunities for new students to interact with faculty members and other students throughout the year, thus easing the transition to college life. The year begins with a five-day "Connect" orientation that features Convocation (the official kickoff to the school year), small-group meetings between faculty members and students, a barbecue, outdoor movies, open houses, and more.

Undergraduate research is an important component of many academic programs, and more than 2,000 OSU undergraduates participate with faculty members and graduate students on research projects each year. One example is the Howard Hughes Medical Institute Summer Research Program, which funds undergraduate researchers to the tune of $1.9 million.

OSU has more majors, minors, and special programs than any other college in Oregon and offers a University Exploratory Studies Program for students who want to try various options before choosing a major field. Oregon State uses the quarter system for its academic year. Most majors require between 180 and 192 credit hours for a bachelor's degree. There are no impacted majors at Oregon State University.

The Academic Success Center helps OSU students deal with problems and develop the skills they need in college and beyond. The Center for Writing and Learning, the Math Learning Center, and departmental resource centers assist students in preparing for assignments in specific areas, while the African American, Hispanic American, Asian American, and Native American education offices, along with the Educational Opportunities Program, help mentor students throughout their college careers. University Counseling and Psychological Services offers learning resource materials and professional assistance to help students deal with problems, both in and out of the classroom. Career Services assists students in locating internships and in finding jobs when they graduate.

Off-Campus Programs

Through the International Degree, study-abroad, and international internship programs, OSU students can study, work, or conduct research almost anywhere in the world. Programs, which range from a term to a full year, are offered in Australia, Canada, China, Denmark, Ecuador, England, France, Germany, Hungary, Italy, Japan, Korea, Mexico, New Zealand, Norway, Russia, Spain, Thailand, Tunisia, and Vietnam.

OSU also participates in the National Student Exchange Program, allowing students to spend up to a year at one of more than 160 colleges and universities in the U.S. and its possessions, while paying in-state tuition and fees.

Academic Facilities

OSU's Valley Library is a state-of-the-art facility that offers modern electronic services, including a wireless computer network, and unique special collections as well as traditional library services to students and the community. The OSU library is the first academic library to be named "Library of the Year" by *Library Journal* (1999). Library holdings include more than 2.5 million books, periodicals, and government documents on paper or microform. A reciprocal agreement makes more than 5 million additional volumes in the Oregon University System available to OSU students and faculty members. OSU's special collections include the papers and memorabilia of Linus Pauling, the only winner of two unshared Nobel Prizes, and the Atomic Energy Collection. The Valley Library is an official depository for U.S. government and state of Oregon publications.

Students at OSU have access to more than 2,200 computers at labs around the campus, including some that are available 24 hours per day. In addition, all rooms in campus residence facilities are wired for high-speed access to the Internet, and wireless networks are located across the campus. Special research facilities include OSU's Mark O. Hatfield Marine Science Center, Oregon Nanoscience and Microtechnologies Institute (ONAMI), Center for Gene Research and Biotechnology, Forest Research Laboratory, Radiation Center, and Hinsdale Wave Research Lab.

Costs

In-state undergraduate tuition and fees are approximately $6725 for the 2009–10 academic year, while nonresident charges are about $19,417. The average cost for a residence hall double room and meal plan is approximately $8352.

Financial Aid

OSU offers the full range of scholarships, grants, work-study, and loans from federal, state, and University sources, investing more than $130 million in student aid annually. Some form of financial assistance is received by 70 percent of the students at OSU. To qualify, students must have applied for admission and must submit the Free Application for Federal Student Aid (FAFSA), listing OSU as one of their top six choices (Title IV code: 003210). Some students help meet educational expenses with one of the many part-time jobs available on or near the campus. For financial aid information, interested students should contact the Office of Financial Aid and Scholarships, 218 Kerr Administration Building, Corvallis, Oregon 97331 (phone: 541-737-2241, Web site: http://oregonstate.edu/financialaid).

Through the University Scholars Program, OSU offers a variety of scholarships and additional scholarship search assistance for new students who have strong academic records. University scholarships range from $500 to $6000 annually for up to four years. In 2008, Oregon State University was first on the awards list of the Oregon Student Assistance Commission with 451 scholarship students receiving a total of $1,696,455. In addition, many OSU colleges offer scholarships to new students, and the OSU Foundation has a number of University-wide scholarships.

Faculty

Undergraduate education is a priority at OSU, and nationally prominent scholars and scientists regularly teach undergraduate courses at all levels. Students receive individual attention and the chance to know their professors both in and out of the classroom. Faculty members consistently receive awards for teaching and research, and many of them are nationally and internationally renowned. For example, Jane Lubchenco, marine biology professor, was chosen by President Obama to lead the National Oceanic and Atmospheric Administration (NOAA). The more than $206 million in external research funds received annually by OSU faculty exceeds that of all other Oregon public universities combined.

Student Government

The Associated Students of Oregon State University (ASOSU) plays a major role in making policy and regulating activities for students and in governing the University through student participation on more than fifty University-wide committees. In recent years, ASOSU has become more involved with local, state, and national issues that affect the welfare of students.

Admission Requirements

A minimum 3.0 high school GPA (on a 4.0 scale) qualifies students for freshman admission to OSU when all subject requirements are met. Applicants for undergraduate admission are required to complete an "Insight Resume," a written assessment designed to evaluate students' noncognitive attributes. These attributes include self-concept, realistic self-appraisal, handling the system, ability to set long-range goals, leadership, connections with a strong support person, community engagement, and nontraditional learning. High school subject requirements are 4 years of English, 3 years each of mathematics and social studies, and 2 years each of science and of the same foreign language. Students who do not meet the subject requirements may be considered for admission by earning a total score of at least 1410 on three SAT Subject Tests or by successfully completing course work to make up specific deficiencies. The alternatives must be completed by the time of high school graduation.

Transfer admission requires successful completion of at least 36 graded, transferable credits (24 semester credits) from accredited U.S. institutions, with a minimum GPA of 2.25. Grades of C- or better are required in college-level writing and mathematics. Students with less than 36 transferable credits are considered for admission on the basis of their high school records.

Application and Information

Applicants are required to complete OSU's online application, which can be found at the Web site. An *OSU Viewbook*, with information on specific academic programs, housing, financial aid, scholarships, and activities, is sent to students upon request.

Prospective students are encouraged to visit OSU to determine in person whether the University meets their needs. A visit, including a campus tour and an opportunity to talk to faculty members in the student's area of interest, can be arranged by calling the Office of Admissions.

To request more information, students should contact:

Office of Admissions
104 Kerr Administration Building
Oregon State University
Corvallis, Oregon 97331-2106
Phone: 800-291-4192 (toll-free)
Fax: 541-737-2482
E-mail: osuadmit@oregonstate.edu
Web site: http://oregonstate.edu/admissions

PACE UNIVERSITY

NEW YORK CITY AND WESTCHESTER, NEW YORK

The University

Founded in 1906, Pace University is a leading private metropolitan university that offers an exceptional liberal arts education combined with superior career preparation, two strategic undergraduate New York locations, and robust financial aid. The diverse student population of 7,800 undergraduates (4,800 in New York City and 3,000 in Westchester) is enrolled in more than 3,000 courses across 100-plus majors and combined degree programs. These are offered through five undergraduate schools and colleges: the Lubin School of Business, the Dyson College of Arts and Sciences, the Seidenberg School of Computer Science and Information Systems, the School of Education, and the Lienhard School of Nursing. Pace University offers career preparation through one of the largest internship programs in New York. Each year, over 1,200 students intern at more than 500 partner companies throughout metropolitan New York, Westchester County, and southern Connecticut.

Many student-led clubs and organizations are active on the campus, including the Pace Advertising Club, African Students Association, the Pace Press, the Student Government Association, and the Collegiate Italian American Organization. Pace also offers many campus activities, including student government associations, fraternities, sororities, two campus newspapers, two literary magazines, two yearbooks, and two campus broadcasting systems. Athletic facilities are available for students, and intercollegiate sports include baseball, basketball, cross-country, cheerleading, equestrian, football, golf, lacrosse, women's soccer, women's softball, swimming and diving, tennis, and track and field.

The student body is diverse, representing forty-eight states, five U.S. territories, and more than 100 countries.

Location

Pace University is a multicampus institution with campuses in both New York City and Westchester, New York. Both locations are within reach of cultural, business, and social resources and opportunities. The New York City campus is located in the heart of the Financial District in lower Manhattan, and within a short walking distance of Wall Street and the South Street Seaport. Lincoln Center, Broadway theaters, museums, and many world-famous attractions are minutes away by public transportation. Located 35 miles north of New York City, the Westchester campus offers a traditional college experience: state-of-the-art science and video production labs, competitive athletics, fraternities and sororities, and access to internship opportunities at many Fortune 500 companies. Both campuses are accessible by car and public transportation.

Students can take courses at either campus, and housing is available in both New York City and Westchester. Residence facilities feature Internet connectivity, voicemail, and cable TV access.

Majors and Degrees

The following programs are offered at both the New York City and Westchester campuses. The Bachelor of Business Administration (B.B.A.) is offered with majors in accounting–general, accounting–public, finance, information systems, international management, management (with concentrations in business, entrepreneurship, and human resources management), and marketing (with concentrations in advertising and promotion, e-business and interactive media, international marketing, and marketing management). In addition, five-year combined B.B.A./M.B.A and B.B.A./M.S. programs in public accounting are available for qualified students. The Bachelor of Arts (B.A.) degree is granted in American studies, applied psychology and human relations, economics, environmental studies, film and screen studies, history, liberal studies, mathematics, modern languages and cultures, philosophy and religious studies, political science, and psychology. The Bachelor of Science (B.S.) degree is offered in biochemistry, biology, biology–preprofessional (occupational therapy, optometry, physical therapy, and podiatry), chemistry, clinical laboratory science, computer science, criminal justice, environmental science, information systems, information technology, mathematics, professional communication studies, professional computer studies, professional studies, professional technology studies, and technology systems.

Certain programs are available only on one campus. The B.S. programs in business economics and forensic science; the B.B.A. programs in hospitality and tourism management, and management science major/mathematics minor; the B.F.A. programs in acting, fine arts, and musical theater; and the B.A. programs in art history; communication science and disorders; communication studies; language, culture, and world trade; Latin American studies; sociology-anthropology; Spanish; teaching students with speech and language disabilities; theater arts; and women's and gender studies are offered only at the New York City campus. The B.A. programs in art, biological psychology, communications, communication arts and journalism, English, English and communications, education, personality and social psychology, and social science; and the B.S. programs in art, education, and nursing are available at the Westchester campus only.

Pace University offers two 5-year engineering programs in cooperation with Manhattan College and Rensselaer Polytechnic Institute. In one program, students attend Pace for three years and Manhattan College for two years, leading to a B.S. degree in science with a concentration in physics from Pace and a B.S. degree in electrical engineering from Manhattan. In the other program, students attend Pace for three years and either Manhattan College or Rensselaer for two years. Upon successful completion, students receive a B.S. degree in chemistry from Pace and either a Bachelor of Chemical Engineering (B.C.E.) in chemical engineering from Manhattan or a B.S. degree in engineering from Rensselaer.

Academic Programs

At Pace University, an innovative core curriculum allows students to develop critical thinking and communication skills by studying subject areas that are integrated around a theme. Students can choose from civic engagement and public values, critical writing, world traditions and cultures, and public speaking. Students also participate in community-based learning where they are given opportunities to practice their skills in real-life settings. Selective academic programs in the University are preparatory for professional training in dentistry, law, medicine, and veterinary science.

The Pforzheimer Honors College is a highly esteemed opportunity at Pace—a community of talented undergraduate scholars studying under the distinguished faculty of the University's five undergraduate schools and colleges. It is a place to excel and realize potential.

The Cooperative Education Program is nationally recognized and offers qualified students the opportunity to gain experience in their field of study while earning a four-year degree. Students can choose full-time, part-time, or summer positions working in an area directly related to their major course of study.

Academic Facilities

The Pace University Library is a comprehensive teaching library and student learning center, a virtual library that combines strong core collections with ubiquitous access to global Internet resources to support broad and diversified curricula. Reciprocal borrowing and access accords, traditional interlibrary loan services, and commercial document delivery options supplement the aggregate library. Pace offers Instructional Services librarians, a state-of-the-art electronic classroom, digital reference services, and multimedia applications. Pace's computer resource centers are linked to high-speed data networks and feature sophisticated hardware and software to facilitate active learning. Pace supports high-speed Internet and Internet2 access on every campus—residence facilities are wired, and most public areas are enabled for wireless connectivity. Full-motion videoconference facilities enable remote delivery of instruction between campus sites for synchronous learning applications.

Costs

For the 2009–10 academic year, undergraduate tuition was $31,860 per year for full-time study. The cost for an on-campus double-occupancy room and board is $10,000–$12,000, with different housing options available.

Financial Aid

Pace University strives to provide opportunities to students of diverse backgrounds and varied circumstances and is committed to offering financial aid to students to the fullest extent of its resources. University-sponsored scholarships are awarded to students on the basis of academic merit, service to the community, and financial need. The goal is to offer every student as much financial assistance as possible, based upon availability and need. Last year, students at Pace received more than $201 million. Pace's comprehensive student financial aid assistance program includes scholarships, grants, on-campus employment, student loans (federal and alternative plans), and tuition payment plans. Pace participates in all federal financial aid programs and the New York State Tuition Assistance Program (TAP) and honors awards from other states' incentive grant programs.

Students should submit the Free Application for Federal Student Aid (FAFSA) by February 15 for priority consideration for the fall semester. Further information about any financial aid programs can be obtained by contacting the Office of Financial Aid at any campus location.

Faculty

First and foremost, Pace University professors are dedicated teachers. All Pace classes are taught by professors. Students will never take a course taught by a teaching assistant. Faculty members also bring real-world experience and scholarship into the classroom through their work with outside companies and organizations and by leading cutting-edge research projects. Faculty members come from the best graduate and doctoral programs in the country. Professors—75 percent of whom hold Ph.D.'s—have earned degrees from the University of Pennsylvania, Harvard, Brown, Columbia, and Yale. Pace professors work closely with students to not only broaden their academic horizons, but to show how their work in the classroom is applicable to their future careers.

Admission Requirements

A minimum of 16 units from an accredited secondary school, or equivalent, are required. Academic subjects in high school should be distributed as follows: 4 units of English, 3–4 units of college-preparatory mathematics, 2 units of foreign language, 4 units of history/social science, 2 units of laboratory science, and 4–5 units of academic electives. It is recommended that students applying to the Lubin School of Business complete 4 units of preparatory mathematics. Applicants to the Lienhard School of Nursing should complete 3–4 units of science (2 of which should be laboratory science) and 3–4 units of college-preparatory mathematics. All applicants are required to take either the SAT or ACT examination and have results forwarded to the University. International students are required to take the TOEFL.

Application and Information

The freshman application deadline is February 15. Transfer applications are reviewed on a rolling basis. Requests for application forms and information for both the New York City and Westchester campuses should be addressed to:

Enrollment Information Center
Pace University
One Pace Plaza
New York, New York 10038
Phone: 800-874-7223 (toll-free)
E-mail: infoctr@pace.edu
Web site: http://www.pace.edu

PACIFIC UNIVERSITY

FOREST GROVE, OREGON

The University

Pacific University is a private, fully accredited four-year liberal arts university encompassing the undergraduate College of Arts and Sciences and nine graduate programs: seven in the health professions, an M.F.A. in writing, and one in teacher education. Founded in 1849 by Congregational pioneers, Pacific is still a frontier institution, proud of its tradition in liberal arts and sciences and innovative in its programs.

Pacific's 3,000 students come from all over the United States and twenty-eight countries, creating a diverse and dynamic student body. Students are taught by the University's full-time faculty members, each of whom is chosen for his or her distinctive devotion to teaching and an emphasis on individual mentoring.

The College of Arts and Sciences is noted for its exceptionally personalized approach to education that is grounded in a philosophy of service. It is recognized for outstanding programs in the natural sciences, education, business, psychology, world languages, and the humanities. Pacific's select group of graduate health profession programs includes the Pacific Northwest's only College of Optometry, as well as the School of Professional Psychology, School of Occupational Therapy, School of Physical Therapy, School of Dental Health Sciences, School of Pharmacy, and School of Physician's Assistant Studies. In addition, the College of Education offers undergraduate and master's-level programs leading to teacher licensure. Graduate programs in the college include the fifth-year M.A.T., M.A.T. Flex, M.Ed., and M.Ed. in visual function and learning (in conjunction with the optometry program).

The lively and vigorous campus springs from the college's residential nature. Freshmen and sophomores under 21 are required to live in one of the University's coed residence facilities. Students living on campus reside in one of five residence halls or Vandervelden Apartments. All on-campus rooms are connected to the campus computer network, which is linked to the Internet. Students who choose to live off campus may live in University-owned housing units or other nearby apartment complexes. Pacific is also the home of an active Greek system, including three fraternities and four sororities.

On campus, the University Center is a hub of activity, housing the dining commons, a new lounge, student government offices, Macintosh and PC lab facilities, the campus radio station, and the newspaper office. The Pacific Undergraduate Community Council (PUCC) provides funding to more than sixty student interest groups, ranging from the Outback program to the Hawaiian Club to the Politics and Law Forum. Pacific Outback provides a multitude of outdoor activities for interested students, such as kayaking, hiking, cross-country and downhill skiing trips, camping, and outings to Portland-area events.

In athletics, Pacific is a member of the NCAA Division III Northwest Conference. Men's intercollegiate sports are baseball, basketball, cross-country, golf, soccer, swimming, tennis, track and field, and wrestling. Women compete in basketball, cross-country, golf, lacrosse, soccer, softball, swimming, tennis, track and field, volleyball, and wrestling. Pacific athletes train and compete in the Pacific Athletic Center, which houses a gymnasium (with three basketball courts), a state-of-the-art fitness center, a versatile field house, three handball/racquetball courts, a dance studio, a wrestling room, and a complete sports medicine training facility.

Pacific and the city of Forest Grove have also partnered to build another outstanding athletic facility for the University and the community. This new facility features a 1,100-seat stadium with a nine-lane, 400-meter track and a FieldTurf soccer and lacrosse field; a brand-new Bond baseball field with a permanent grandstand; a new varsity softball field with permanent grandstand seating; and other new park amenities. The Lincoln Park Athletic Complex is one of the best outdoor facilities of any small college in the Northwest.

In addition to the Forest Grove campus, the University has a campus in Eugene, Oregon, serving the needs of the College of Education and another in Hillsboro, Oregon, serving the needs of the College of Health Professions, and it operates facilities in Portland that support the academic and clinical programs of the College of Optometry and the School of Professional Psychology.

Pacific offers seven graduate programs in the College of Health Professions: professional psychology (M.A. and Psy.D.), Doctor of Physical Therapy (D.P.T.), Master of Occupational Therapy (M.O.T.), dental health science (B.S. and M.S.), Doctor of Pharmacy, Doctor of Optometry, and a physician's assistant studies program (M.S.P.A.). Physical therapy students must have completed a bachelor's degree program with specific course work before applying to the program. The physician's assistant studies master's program is a twenty-eight-month consecutive program. Through the College of Optometry, students receive a degree (O.D.) with four years of graduate work. Optometry students can be admitted into the College of Optometry's four-year doctoral graduate program after completing three years of undergraduate prerequisite work.

Location

Situated in the northwest corner of Oregon between metropolitan Portland and the Pacific Ocean, the College of Arts and Sciences, College of Education, and College of Optometry are located in Forest Grove (population 18,000), about 35 minutes from the heart of Portland, a vibrant metropolitan area. The 55-acre, oak-covered campus is surrounded by green countryside and the foothills of the Coast Range Mountains, beyond which is the 300-mile stretch of Oregon coast. Opportunities abound in Oregon for hiking, skiing, camping, fishing, beachcombing, and bicycling. The climate is temperate throughout the year, with winter rainfall tapering off to a pleasant spring and sunny summer.

Majors and Degrees

Major programs leading to the B.A. or B.S. degree are offered through the College of Arts and Sciences in anthropology/sociology, applied science, art, bioinformatics, biology (with an emphasis in ecology and evolution or in molecular and cellular), business administration (with an emphasis in accounting, finance, management, or marketing), chemistry (with an emphasis in biological chemistry or chemical physics), computer science, coordinated studies in humanities, creative writing, economics, education and learning, environmental science (with an emphasis in biology or chemistry), exercise science (with an emphasis in human performance), French studies, German studies, history, international studies, Japanese studies, literature, mathematics, media arts and communications (with an emphasis in film production, film studies, integrated media, journalism, or video production), modern languages (with an emphasis in Chinese, French, German, Japanese, or Spanish), music (with an emphasis in education or performance), philosophy (with an emphasis in bioethics), social work, sociology, Spanish, and theater. A B.M. degree is offered in music. Secondary education certification is available in art, biology, English, French, German, health education (combined endorsement only), integrated science, Japanese, mathematics, music, reading (combined endorsement only), social studies (secondary education students only), and Spanish.

Pacific offers a 3-2 program in engineering, which is designed as a transfer program in which students spend three years at Pacific studying physics, chemistry, mathematics, and computer science (as well as electives in other areas of the liberal arts) and then transfer to an engineering school for their final two years of professional training in engineering. At the end of this period, students receive a B.S. degree in engineering from the engineering school and a B.S. in applied science, physics, chemistry, mathematics, or computer science from Pacific University. Pacific's program currently involves transfer agreements with Washington University in St. Louis, Oregon State University, and Washington State University. However, students can (and do) transfer to other engineering schools of their choice. There is also a 4-1 cooperative program with Oregon Health & Science University (OHSU) that awards a B.S. in environmental science from Pacific and an M.S. degree in environmental science and engineering from OHSU.

Academic Programs

Pacific provides an excellent education in the liberal arts and sciences. The core curriculum in the College of Arts and Sciences emphasizes writing, reasoning, and communication skills, with attention given to cross-cultural education and work in the natural sciences and the fine arts. All freshmen participate in a semester-long first-year seminar program designed to introduce students to college-level writing and research expectations. Pacific has a long tradition of ethical concern that is reflected in its undergraduate courses and its many opportunities for service both on campus and within the broader community. Pacific maintains small classes to ensure close contact among students and faculty members.

Special programs in the College of Arts and Sciences include the interdisciplinary Peace and Conflict Studies Program as well as minors in dance, disabilities studies, and feminist studies.

Basic requirements for the B.A. or B.S. degree are 120 semester hours of credit, completion of a major, and completion of the core requirements in the College of Arts and Sciences. The year is divided into two semesters, with a three-week winter term between the two semesters. Students typically take 15 credit hours during each semester and 3 credit hours during the winter term.

Pacific grants credit for both subject and general CLEP examinations. Each department or school at Pacific University determines whether or not a specific examination may substitute for a specific course. Students who score 4 or better on the Advanced Placement examinations of the College Board are given advanced placement and credit toward graduation. Pacific recognizes the International Baccalaureate program as providing college-level work. Six credit hours are awarded for each higher examination passed at a score of 5 or higher.

Off-Campus Programs

Pacific offers study-abroad programs in twelve different countries, as well as an agreement with the Oregon University System (OUS) giving Pacific students additional study-abroad sites. Foreign language and international studies majors are required to spend at least one semester studying abroad and may use financial aid toward their international study. Pacific also emphasizes internships, which are regularly arranged for students in business, communications, political science, psychology, sociology, and other fields. The internships, which may be arranged for periods lasting from fourteen weeks to an entire academic year, offer students the opportunity to become thoroughly acquainted with professional work and often lead to employment upon graduation.

Academic Facilities

The 55-acre Forest Grove campus contains buildings in a picturesque setting with green lawns and tall shade trees. Architecture at Pacific is a pleasant blend of the old and new. Representing the long history of Pacific University, Old College Hall was the first permanent structure; built in 1850, it contains museum galleries and historic exhibits. Recent construction includes five LEED certified buildings: the university library, Berglund Hall, Burlingham Hall, Gilbert Hall, and the Pacific University Health Professions Campus. Also included are a 90,000-square-foot Pacific Athletic Center and the Lincoln Park Athletic Complex. Historical Marsh Hall, which was originally constructed in 1893 and completely refurbished in 1977, holds classrooms, professors' offices, and administration facilities.

Wireless Internet can be accessed throughout the campus. Built in 2005, the new library houses superior technology, large study areas, and a collection of materials to support the curriculum and student and faculty research in a variety of formats, both traditional and electronic. While the library strives to build a strong core collection, it also participates in SUMMIT, a regional library consortium meeting the considerable research needs of Pacific's students and faculty members by allowing them access to the collections of sixty-two other northwest college and university libraries. Through computer technology, courier services, and interlibrary loans, students and faculty members can efficiently tap the research resources of the region and beyond.

Encompassing the Schools of Dental Health Science, Occupational Therapy, Pharmacy, Physical Therapy, Physician Assistant Studies, and Professional Psychology, Pacific University's College of Health Professions prepares its students through interdisciplinary activities to provide compassionate delivery of exemplary health care for a diverse population in a changing health-care environment. The Pacific University Health Professions Campus opened in fall 2006 and is located on a half-acre site on the Tuality Hospital Hillsboro campus. This location will also be the site of phase two, which will be built in the next five years.

Costs

Tuition and fees for the 2009–10 school year are $29,966. Room and board are approximately $8118 for a double room and include a University meal plan. Books and supplies are estimated at approximately $950. Total direct cost is $39,034. Pacific has consistently been named one of the best values west of the Mississippi by several national publications, including *U.S. News & World Report.*

Financial Aid

Financial assistance at Pacific is awarded on the basis of demonstrated need, academic merit, and talent. The Free Application for Federal Student Aid (FAFSA) is used in evaluating need. Prospective students are encouraged to apply for financial assistance by submitting the FAFSA to the federal processor as soon after January 1 as possible. Pacific provides financial assistance through grants, scholarships, loans, and part-time employment. Further information is available via e-mail at financialaid@pacificu.edu.

Faculty

Pacific's outstanding faculty members provide the foundation for the University's academic program. A student-faculty ratio of 13:1 allows for personal attention by the professors. Pacific's faculty is made up of 147 dedicated educators, of whom 96 percent hold terminal degrees in their field. As professionals, they uphold the University's standard of academic excellence and work closely with students. Pacific does not use graduate or teaching assistants; all faculty members teach their own courses.

Student Government

Participatory government at Pacific enables students to help shape the campus community in which they live and work. Students are encouraged to voice their opinions and to pursue new ideas that further not only personal growth but also the overall growth and development of the University. Pacific Undergraduate Community Council (PUCC), the official student government body, manages activity funds, reviews and supports student issues, and coordinates student participation within the system.

Admission Requirements

Pacific University is selective in considering new students. Primary consideration is given to a candidate's academic preparation and potential for successful study at the college level, as assessed by evaluating the student's transcripts of college-preparatory work, counselor and teacher recommendations, personal essay, SAT and/or ACT scores, and other student-submitted information. Transfer students must submit high school records and test scores if they have completed less than 30 semester hours, plus official transcripts from any institution previously attended.

Application and Information

Students may apply early and may be notified early through the modified rolling admissions plan. The regular priority deadline for admission is February 15. For additional information, interested students should contact:

Office of Admissions
Pacific University
2043 College Way
Forest Grove, Oregon 97116
Phone: 503-352-2218
800-677-6712 (toll-free)
E-mail: admissions@pacificu.edu
Web site: http://www.pacificu.edu

PARSONS THE NEW SCHOOL FOR DESIGN

NEW YORK, NEW YORK

THE NEW SCHOOL
A UNIVERSITY

The University

Parsons The New School for Design in New York City is one of the premier degree-granting colleges of art and design in the nation. A pioneer in art and design education since its founding in 1894, Parsons has cultivated outstanding artists, designers, scholars, businesspeople, and community leaders for more than a century. Today, when design thinking is increasingly being employed to solve complex global problems, Parsons is leading new approaches to art and design education.

Parsons comprises five schools—Art, Media, and Technology; Fashion; Constructed Environments; Art and Design History and Theory; and Design Strategies—and the programs within each span contemporary art and design practices. As part of The New School, a leading university in New York City, Parsons students also weave the liberal arts, social sciences, performance, management, and urban policy into a comprehensive education.

Parsons embraces curricular innovation, pioneering uses of technology, collaborative methods, and global perspectives on the future of design. Parsons graduates and faculty members appear on the short list of outstanding practitioners in every realm of art and design—creative, management, and scholarly. Responsive to societal needs and predictive of cultural trends, Parsons makes tangible, usable, and beautiful The New School's mission of bringing positive, innovative change to the world.

Approximately 4,100 undergraduate students and 490 graduate students are enrolled in Parsons The New School for Design. Nearly a third of all degree-seeking students are international, coming from sixty-eight countries. Some 2,000 continuing education students take individual courses or are enrolled in certificate programs. More than 700 children and young people attend weekend and summer precollege programs.

More than 1,100 students live in the university's residence halls in the Greenwich Village and Wall Street areas and take part in the social and educational programs and activities provided there. Through programming that addresses students' intellectual, artistic, and creative efforts, the residence life program fosters the development of the whole student. The University endeavors to provide comfortable and inclusive communities where students and staff members promote cultural awareness and academic success and develop new ideas and diverse experiences. For more information, students should contact the Office of University Housing at universityhousing@newschool.edu or 212-229-5459 or visit the Web site at http://www.newschool.edu/studentaffairs/housing/.

Parsons and The New School are fully accredited by the Commission on Higher Education of the Middle States Association of Colleges and Schools. Its credits and degrees are recognized and accepted by other accredited colleges, universities, and professional schools throughout the United States. The New School, a privately supported institution, is chartered as a university by the Regents of the State of New York.

Location

Parsons' main campus is located downtown in Greenwich Village, a historic neighborhood with a style and atmosphere found nowhere else in New York City. The area is home to design and art studios, galleries, shops, and restaurants as well as avant-garde artists, musicians, and writers. With its rich cultural resources, international sophistication, and cutting-edge attitude, New York City is a vibrant environment that has inspired and challenged artists and designers throughout its history. Not surprisingly, Parsons faculty members use New York City as an urban design laboratory. The city offers more than eighty museums, such as the Metropolitan Museum of Art, the Museum of Modern Art, and Cooper-Hewitt, National Design Museum.

Majors and Degrees

Undergraduate degrees offered are an Associate in Applied Science (A.A.S.), a Bachelor of Business Administration (B.B.A.), a Bachelor of Fine Arts (B.F.A.), a Bachelor of Arts (B.A.), and a Bachelor of Science (B.S.). Students may also earn a Bachelor of Arts and a Bachelor of Fine Arts (B.A./B.F.A.) through a five-year, dual-degree program offered in conjunction with Eugene Lang College The New School for Liberal Arts, with classes and studios located conveniently on one campus.

Associate degrees are available in fashion marketing (available online and on campus), fashion studies, graphic design, and interior design. Bachelor's degrees are offered in architectural design, communication design, design and management, design and technology, environmental studies, fashion design, fine arts, illustration, integrated design, interior design, photography, product design, and urban design.

Academic Programs

The degree programs at Parsons are academically challenging, demanding, and, ultimately, professionally rewarding for emerging designers. On average, students register for 16 to 18 credits (six classes) per semester. Most students are in class for 20 to 30 hours per week and spend an equivalent amount of time in preparation. Studio critique sessions and critical studies seminars depend on thoughtful student input and discussion. All courses require active attendance and regular participation.

The A.A.S. degree requires 65 credits; the B.B.A. and B.F.A., 134 credits each; the B.S. and B.A. in Environmental Studies, 120 credits; and the B.A./B.F.A., 180 credits. The five-year B.A./B.F.A. program is offered in conjunction with Eugene Lang College The New School for Liberal Arts.

Off-Campus Programs

In 1920, Parsons School of Design, as it was known then, was the first art and design school in America to found a campus abroad. Today, the school offers its students the possibility to expand their horizons by studying at art and design schools around the world. During their junior year, bachelor's degree students may enroll for one or two semesters in another school in the United States or abroad. Several departments assist students in securing noncredit internships that provide valuable work experience and professional contacts. Current and past internships include Marc Jacobs, Polo-Ralph Lauren, HBO, MTV, the *New York Times, Rolling Stone* magazine, Marvel Comics, and the Museum of Modern Art.

Academic Facilities

Students at Parsons have access to extensive studio facilities and professionally staffed model, fabrication, and print shops, including rapid prototyping, photography, and imaging labs; and metalworking, jewelry, and woodworking facilities. Visit Parsons' individual program listings online to learn more. In addition to the facilities and services at specific academic programs, Parsons also offers resources for all students that provide optimal conditions for learning.

The Sheila C. Johnson Design Center is a new, award-winning campus center for Parsons that combines spaces for learning with galleries and meeting places at the intersection of Fifth Avenue and 13th Street. Features include the Anna-Maria and Stephen Kellen Gallery and Auditorium, and the Arnold and Sheila Aronson Galleries. The Center also provides a new home for the Anna-Maria and Stephen Kellen Archives, a significant collection of drawings, photographs, letters, and objects documenting twentieth-century design. An innovative and highly visible student critique area enables the public to observe the design dialogue that is central to a Parsons education.

The Angelo Donghia Materials Library and Study Center is composed of a library, a gallery, a computer lab, and a lecture hall. The library allows students and faculty members to review and check out state-of-the-art resources, putting the latest and most exclusive materials at their fingertips. Regular exhibitions at the gallery run by a full-time curator are open to the public, creating an open forum and dialogue with the larger interior design community.

Over the past several years, The New School has invested more than $30 million in a series of extensive labs. The Knowledge Union consists of state-of-the-art technology spread over four floors; the 600 networked workstations include all relevant platforms. Servers support work that ranges from traditional print output to online projects using webcasting and secure transaction technology. Specialty work—whether audio or video production, MIDI, recording, or physical computing installation—takes place in private studios spread across the campus. Portable production equipment, including digital still, video, and audio, is readily available. Digital projectors, surround sound, and active white boards feed into equipment racks that enable presentation of all media types.

The University Computing Center, on the third and fourth floors at 55 West 13th Street, is a central hub of technologies. Computers and hands-on classrooms support multimedia, Web design, and desktop publishing as well as word processing and research. The Fashion Computing Center at 560 Seventh Avenue provides computing support for the Parsons B.F.A. program in fashion design. It has more than forty UNIX, Macintosh, and Windows workstations and color and black-and-white printers. Software includes high-end graphic and three-dimensional modeling applications.

Costs

For 2009–10, full-time (12–19 credits) undergraduate students paid $16,905 or $17,610 in tuition, depending on their program of study, and approximately $290 in fees per semester plus $1714 for student health insurance. Although housing costs vary depending on accommodations and meal plan selected, room and board averaged about $15,260 per year. Additional fees may apply.

Financial Aid

Almost 75 percent of Parsons students receive some kind of financial aid, awarded on the basis of financial need and merit. The University's financial aid office is open year-round to assist students and their families with the task of meeting educational costs. For information on specific kinds of assistance, amounts of funding, loan repayment, and scholarships for students meeting certain criteria, students should visit Student Financial Services' Web site at http://www.newschool.edu/studentservices/financialaid/.

Faculty

More than 1,150 full- and part-time faculty members teach at Parsons. All of them are successful professionals in the design, art, and business fields. The student-faculty ratio is 9:1. Faculty members and visiting critics are principals in their own design firms, hold key positions in the art and design community, and frequently have their work published. Parsons' strong ties to industry bring numerous guest lecturers and critics into forums and classrooms. Visiting critics have included Richard Meier, Donna Karan, Mayer Rus, Arthur Corwin, and Paula Scher.

Admission Requirements

Parsons seeks serious, responsible, and highly motivated applicants. Each applicant is reviewed individually with regard to experience, achievements, and potential for artistic growth. While Parsons recognizes the benefits of strong artistic preparation, some applicants are admitted based on their academic strengths more than their visual material. For B.F.A. applicants, a large part of the Admissions Committee's decision is based on portfolio evaluations and the Parsons Challenge, as well as academic achievement. For B.B.A., B.S., and B.A. applicants, academic achievement is weighted heavily along with the Parsons Challenge. The A.A.S. program is best suited to students who have had some prior college experience, are clear about their interests within the world of design, and are prepared for rapid immersion in a professional course of study.

All applicants must submit the completed application, the nonrefundable $50 application fee, and original copies of official high school and/or college transcripts. Bachelor's applicants who are residents of the United States must also submit SAT or ACT scores; international students must send in their TOEFL scores (minimum of 580 on the paper-based exam or 237 on the computerized exam). All applicants must submit the multipart Parsons Challenge exercise. A portfolio is required of all B.F.A. applicants (except those applying to study design and management). This must consist of eight to twelve pieces of work, including, but not limited to, drawings, paintings, photographs, digital media, or design. A personal interview is recommended for all applicants.

Application and Information

The admission and financial aid deadline for the fall semester is February 1, and the deadline for spring admission is October 15. The Admissions Committee reviews applications and sends students its decision a few weeks after all materials are received.

Admissions Office
Parsons The New School for Design
72 Fifth Avenue, Second Floor
New York, New York 10011
Phone: 212-229-8989
Fax: 212-229-8975
E-mail: thinkparsons@newschool.edu
Web site: http://www.newschool.edu/parsons

Part of the Parsons experience—taking part in critiquing student assignments.

PENN STATE ERIE, THE BEHREND COLLEGE

ERIE, PENNSYLVANIA

The College

Penn State Erie, The Behrend College, is committed to providing a high-quality, comprehensive education in business, engineering, the humanities and social sciences, science, and nursing. Students benefit from the resources and opportunities provided by a major research university in a welcoming, student-centered learning environment. The College offers thirty-four bachelor's degree programs, six associate degree programs, and two graduate degree programs—a Master of Business Administration (M.B.A.) and a Master of Project Management (M.P.M.).

Among all public colleges and universities in Pennsylvania, Penn State Behrend ranks in the top five in student-to-faculty ratio, SAT scores, first-year student retention, and graduation rate.

The historic core of Penn State Behrend's picturesque, wooded hilltop campus features the original Glenhill Farmhouse given to Penn State by the Behrend family, founders of Hammermill Paper Company in Erie. More recent additions to the College's campus include an athletics and recreation complex, a research and development center, a chapel and carillon, an observatory, numerous residence halls, and the new Metzgar Admissions and Alumni Center, a one-stop shop of services for incoming and current students. The campus and its environs offer extensive woodlands, deep gorges, beautiful streams, and cross-country skiing and fitness trails.

More than 4,700 students attend classes in modern academic buildings and labs, and 1,650 students live on campus in traditional student housing, four-bedroom suites, and two-bedroom apartments.

A member of NCAA Division III and the Allegheny Mountain Collegiate Conference, Penn State Behrend fields twenty-two varsity sports: eleven teams for men (baseball, basketball, cross-country, golf, indoor track, soccer, swimming and diving, tennis, track and field, volleyball, and water polo) and eleven for women (basketball, cross-country, golf, indoor track, soccer, softball, swimming and diving, tennis, track and field, volleyball, and water polo). More than 65 percent of students participate in a comprehensive intramural program.

Location

Penn State Behrend students benefit from the college's convenient location near I-90 (and close to I-79 and I-86) in a suburb of Erie, Pennsylvania. Situated along Lake Erie's beautiful Presque Isle Bay, Erie is the fourth-largest city in Pennsylvania, with a regional population of more than 280,000. The region has a variety of cultural, sports, and recreational resources, including Presque Isle State Park, the Commonwealth's most popular park, offering 7 miles of sandy beaches, boating, and trails for walking, jogging, biking, and more.

Public transportation departs from campus every half hour to points throughout the Erie area, including movie theaters, restaurants, a philharmonic orchestra, museums, performing arts venues, and a zoo. A convention center in downtown Erie features Broadway plays and top-name performers in rock, classical, and country music. Erie is located within 2 hours of Buffalo, Cleveland, and Pittsburgh and is a comfortable 4-hour drive from Toronto.

Majors and Degrees

Penn State Behrend confers the Bachelor of Arts degree in communication, economics, English, general arts and sciences, history, political science, psychology, and science. The Bachelor of Fine Arts degree is offered in creative writing. The Bachelor of Science degree is offered in accounting; biology; business economics; business, liberal arts, and science; chemistry; computer engineering; computer science; electrical engineering; electrical and computer engineering technology; finance; interdisciplinary business with engineering studies; international business; management; management information systems; marketing; mathematics; mechanical engineering; mechanical engineering technology; physics; plastics engineering technology; psychology; science; secondary education in mathematics teaching, and software engineering. An RN to B.S. program in nursing is also offered.

The Associate in Arts degree is awarded in one major—letters, arts, and sciences. The Associate in Science degree is offered in general business, and the Associate in Engineering degree is offered in electrical engineering technology, mechanical engineering technology, and plastics engineering technology. The College also offers an associate degree in nursing.

Academic Programs

Each bachelor's degree program has two components: at least 46 credits in general education and at least 78 credits in specific requirements for the major. Students must complete a minimum of 124 semester hours to earn a bachelor's degree; the exact number depends on the program. Associate degrees require a minimum of 60 semester hours. All Penn State Behrend majors require an overall grade point average of at least 2.0 and a grade of C or better in all upper-level courses in the major. An honors program and the Schreyer Scholars Program are available to students who show exceptional promise. Several majors serve as excellent preparation for law or medical school. Special prelaw and premed advisers assist students in planning their programs. The College's Academic and Career Planning Center helps students who have not yet decided on an academic major to explore areas of study before selecting a specific program.

The Bachelor of Fine Arts degree in creative writing is one of only a few such programs in the country. It is an intensive course of study in poetry and prose writing. Students have the opportunity to serve on the editorial staff of the national literary journal, *Lake Effect*.

Penn State Behrend's School of Engineering is the largest undergraduate-only engineering program in the country. The plastics engineering technology program is one of only four accredited plastics programs in the country. The School of Engineering's ten engineering degrees are accredited by the Accreditation Board for Engineering and Technology (ABET).

Penn State Behrend's chemistry program is approved by the American Chemical Society and annually produces more ACS-certified graduates than other comparably-sized institutions.

The Sam and Irene Black School of Business is the only school of business in the Erie region to receive accreditation from AACSB International, the premier accrediting agency for schools of business worldwide. The school was named for Sam and Irene Black following a $20-million endowment bequest.

The fall and spring semesters are each fifteen weeks in length. Registration and advising take place before the first week of classes, and final examinations are given after the last week. Three summer sessions are also offered. The Academic and Career Planning Center provides a summer preregistration and counseling service for all first-year students and their parents.

The College annually awards more than $250,000 in undergraduate research opportunities each year. Many students present their research at regional and national conferences, and others publish in refereed journals. This provides Penn State Behrend students with an advantage when looking for a job or applying to professional or graduate school. The Academic and Career Planning Center works closely with employers and each fall hosts recruiters on campus at its successful engineering and business career fairs.

Academic Facilities

Penn State Behrend features a mix of contemporary and traditional buildings in a parklike setting. Among the most impressive facilities on campus is the $30-million Research and Economic Development

Center (REDC), home to the college's colocated schools of engineering and business. The REDC features state-of-the-art teaching and research labs, including the largest academic plastics lab in the country. Knowledge Park, on the eastern edge of campus, gives companies housed there access to the College's strengths in applied research and technology transfer, while providing internship and job opportunities for students and graduates.

In addition to using Penn State Behrend's library collection, students can draw on the resources of the entire Penn State University Libraries collection through the computerized Library Information Access System. The collection, one of the largest in the country, comprises more than 5 million cataloged items, 38,500 serial titles, and 2.5 million government documents. Computers connect students to major databases throughout the world.

Costs

Educational costs at Penn State Behrend vary depending on whether the student is a resident of Pennsylvania, whether enrollment is in the upper or lower division, and whether he or she lives off campus or in a residence hall. The 2009–10 tuition for Pennsylvania residents (lower division) was $11,942 for the academic year. For out-of-state students, the tuition was $18,270 for the academic year. On-campus rooms are a fixed cost, but board and all other costs are variable according to each student's spending habits. These variable costs are approximately $8170 for room and board, $1360 for books and supplies, and $1200 to $2400 for personal expenses, including clothing, laundry, travel, and miscellaneous items. Other costs are a nonrefundable $50 application fee, a nonrefundable $200 enrollment fee and general fee, and a $100 housing fee for students living in on-campus residences.

Financial Aid

More than 80 percent of students receive some form of aid, and students benefit from more than $1 million in annual Penn State Behrend scholarships. Awards are based on an analysis of the student's financial need. Students should file the Free Application for Federal Student Aid (FAFSA) by February 15 of their senior year of high school. Penn State's school code is 003329. Students are encouraged to seek grant assistance from their home state. Financial aid applications are available from high school counselors and financial aid offices at colleges and other institutions. These forms and the application for admission are the only forms that first-year students need to complete to be considered for federal, state, and University aid. Aid includes Federal Pell Grants, Pennsylvania Higher Education Assistance Agency Grants, Federal Work-Study Program awards, Federal Perkins Loans, Federal Supplemental Educational Opportunity Grants, Federal Stafford Student Loans, and Penn State awards and scholarships.

Faculty

A first-rate faculty is at the heart of the Penn State Behrend experience. More than 325 faculty members, almost all of whom have earned terminal degrees in their major fields, teach both undergraduate and graduate students. There are no graduate teaching assistants, and the use of part-time professors is limited. The faculty members are distinguished scholars and superb teachers. They are extensively involved in research and publishing, and they are caring people with a record of excellence in advising students. Professors and students get to know one another, and such close relationships generate many educational and career advantages.

Student Government

The Student Government Association is the official representative of the student body of Penn State Behrend. In addition to representing students to the administration and faculty, the Student Government Association charters all student organizations and allocates funds to support and promote student activities. The association also appoints student representatives to serve on key administrative and faculty committees and the appropriate adjudicatory boards.

Admission Requirements

As part of Penn State University, and in compliance with federal and state laws, Penn State Behrend is committed to the policy that all persons shall have equal access to admission without regard to race, religion, sex, national origin, ancestry, color, sexual orientation, handicap, age, or status as a disabled or Vietnam veteran. Each applicant is evaluated on the basis of his or her high school record and the results of the SAT or scores from the ACT. The high school grade point average, when combined with the SAT score, produces an evaluation index, and students are admitted on the basis of that index.

Application and Information

Students interested in freshman admission to Penn State Behrend may obtain a Web application at http://www.admissions.psu.edu. Students who do not wish to file a Web application can obtain an admission application form from any Penn State campus or by writing to Penn State Behrend. Application forms are available in late summer. The recommended deadline for submitting an application is November 30. Applicants admitted to Penn State Behrend are notified approximately four to six weeks after the application and credentials are received. The student must make certain that the Educational Testing Service forwards the SAT scores to the Undergraduate Admissions Office, Pennsylvania State University, University Park, Pennsylvania 16802.

This description is available in alternative media upon request. For application forms, more information, or a campus visit, interested students should contact:

Office of Admissions
Penn State Erie, The Behrend College
4701 College Drive
Erie, Pennsylvania 16563-0105
Phone: 814-898-6100
866-374-3378 (toll-free)
E-mail: behrend.admissions@psu.edu
Web site: www.behrend.psu.edu

Penn State Behrend was one of the first academic institutions in the country to bring its schools of business and engineering together under a single roof in the College's Research and Economic Development Center.

PENNSYLVANIA COLLEGE OF TECHNOLOGY
An Affiliate of The Pennsylvania State University
WILLIAMSPORT, PENNSYLVANIA

Pennsylvania College of Technology
PENNSTATE

COLLEGE CLOSE-UPS

The College

Pennsylvania College of Technology (Penn College) is a special-mission affiliate of Penn State committed to applied technology education. The College has a national reputation for "degrees that work" in the high quality and diversity of its traditional and advanced technology majors. Partnerships with industry leaders, including Honda, Ford, and Caterpillar, provide students unique opportunities to build relationships that can advance their careers.

Excellent graduate placement rates exceed 95 percent annually (100 percent in some majors). Among the keys to graduate success are Penn College's emphasis on small classes, personal attention, and hands-on experience using the latest technology. State-of-the-art classrooms and laboratories reflect the expectations of the modern workforce. A number of campus buildings, including a conference center, a Victorian guest house, an athletic field house, and a rustic retreat used for professional gatherings, have been designed, constructed, and maintained by students.

More than 6,400 students attend Penn College. More than 5,000 additional men and women take part in noncredit classes, including customized business and industry courses offered through Workforce Development and Continuing Education.

Most Penn College Wildcat sports teams compete regionally in the Penn State University Athletic Conference (PSUAC) and nationally in the United States Collegiate Athletic Association (USCAA). Varsity sports include archery, baseball, basketball, bowling, cross-country, dance team, golf, soccer, softball, team tennis, and volleyball.

Location

Penn College is located in north-central Pennsylvania. The main campus is in Williamsport, a city known around the world as the home of the Little League Baseball World Series. Penn College offers credit classes at three other locations: the Advanced Automotive Technology Center in the Wahoo Drive Industrial Park in Williamsport, the Aviation Center at the Williamsport Regional Airport in Montoursville, and the Earth Science Center, 10 miles south of Williamsport near Allenwood. Noncredit classes are offered from locations in Williamsport and Wellsboro.

Majors and Degrees

Bachelor of Science (B.S.) degrees focus on applied technology in traditional and emerging career fields. Majors include accounting; applied health studies; applied human services; automotive technology management; aviation maintenance technology; building automation technology; building science and sustainable design (concentrations in architectural technology and building construction technology); business administration (concentrations in banking and finance, human resource management, management, marketing, and small business and entrepreneurship); civil engineering technology; computer-aided product design; construction management; culinary arts and systems; dental hygiene (concentrations in health policy and administration and special-population care); electronics and computer engineering technology; graphic communications management; graphic design; health information management; heating, ventilation, and air conditioning (HVAC) technology; industrial and human factors design; information technology (concentrations in IT security specialist studies, network specialist studies, and Web and applications development); legal assistant/paralegal studies; manufacturing engineering technology; nursing; physician assistant; plastics and polymer engineering technology; residential construction technology and management; technology management; Web design and multimedia; and welding and fabrication engineering technology.

Associate degrees (A.A.S., A.A.A., or A.A.) are offered in accounting; advertising art; architectural technology; automated manufacturing technology; automotive service sales and marketing; automotive technology (including Ford ASSET and Honda PACT industry-sponsored majors); aviation technology; baking and pastry arts; building construction technology; building construction technology/masonry; business management; civil engineering technology; collision repair technology; computer-aided drafting technology; culinary arts technology; dental hygiene; diesel technology; early childhood education; electric power generation technology; electrical technology; electromechanical maintenance technology; electronics and computer engineering technology (emphases in communications and fiber optics, nanofabrication technology, and robotics and automation); emergency medical services; forest technology; general studies; graphic communications technology; health arts; health arts/practical nursing; health information technology; heating, ventilation, and air conditioning (HVAC) technology; heavy construction equipment technology (emphases in Caterpillar equipment industry-sponsored, operator, and technician); hospitality management; human services; individual studies; information technology (emphases in network administration, network technology, technical support technology, and Web and applications technology); landscape/nursery technology/turfgrass management; legal assistant/paralegal studies; machine tool technology; mass media communication; nursing; occupational therapy assistant studies; ornamental horticulture (emphases in landscape technology and plant production); physical fitness specialist studies; plastics and polymer technology; radiography; renewable energy technologies; studio arts; surgical technology; surveying technology; and welding technology.

Certificate majors are offered in automotive service technician studies, aviation maintenance technician studies, collision repair technician studies, construction carpentry, diesel technician studies, electrical occupations, health information coding specialist studies, machinist general, nurse/health-care paralegal studies; paramedic technician studies, plumbing, practical nursing, and welding.

Academic Programs

Penn College offers unique bachelor's degrees that are designed to prepare students for employment or serve as the basis for additional educational opportunities. The bachelor's degree offerings either parallel or build upon two-year majors or stand as their own unique majors. Seven B.S. degrees are offered via distance learning: applied health studies, automotive technology management, dental hygiene, health information management, nursing, technology management, and Web design and multimedia.

While associate degrees primarily emphasize practical applications, the bachelor's degree curricula complete a larger educational base by adding advanced practical applications, broader liberal arts study, systematic problem solving, writing-enriched courses, cultural diversity, senior-year capstone projects, and interdisciplinary courses that develop appreciation for the relationships between science, technology, and society.

Off-Campus Programs

Penn College students earn academic credit for real work experience if they choose to participate in an internship. Many majors require internships. Penn College students have worked throughout Pennsylvania and the United States and around the world.

Academic Facilities

The hands-on experience offered at Penn College creates a need for a variety of special academic facilities. Campus computers are very accessible. Wireless zones and networked on-campus residences make study across campus very convenient. Besides extensive, accessible computer labs, the main campus has an automated manufacturing center, a plastics manufacturing center, a printing and publishing facility, a dental hygiene clinic, automotive and collision repair centers, a machine shop, a welding shop, a building technologies center, an architectural studio, computer-aided drafting labs, a broadcast studio, a video production studio, modern science laboratories, a fine-dining restaurant and campus guest house, an aviation and avionics instructional facility located at the regional airport, greenhouses, a working sawmill, a diesel center, and a heavy-equipment training site.

Off-campus sites include the Aviation Center, one of the nation's finest aviation instructional facilities, located at the regional airport; the

Earth Science Center, located on 378 acres of wooded land and featuring greenhouses, a working sawmill, a diesel center, and a heavy-equipment training site; and an Advanced Automotive Technology Center, with motorsports and other advanced laboratories.

The Madigan Library on the main campus is open every day during the academic semesters and offers an impressive selection of print and electronic resources. Services available include a professional reference staff, a well-developed instructional program, reciprocal borrowing with regional libraries, interlibrary loans, and paper and electronic reserves. The library also houses fourteen study areas, two computer laboratories, a 100-seat open computer lab complex, a café, and the art gallery.

Costs

Tuition and related fees are based on a per-credit-hour charge. Pennsylvania residents attending Penn College in 2009–10 paid approximately $21,530 per year, and out-of-state residents paid approximately $24,680 per year. These estimated costs are based on tuition and fees for an average 15 credits per semester plus estimated expenses for housing, meals, books, and supplies. Rates vary according to specific choices for classes, housing, meal plans, and other costs.

On-campus housing offers apartment-style and lodge-style living options. On-campus housing is alcohol free, drug free, noise controlled, and secure. Students are offered a variety of meal plans, which are accepted in the College's dining facilities, including the main dining hall, an all-you-can-eat buffet, a gourmet restaurant, a convenience store, snack bars, and a café.

Financial Aid

Approximately 4 out of 5 Penn College students receive some form of financial assistance. Types of aid available include Federal Pell Grants, Pennsylvania Higher Education Assistance Agency Grants, Federal Supplemental Educational Opportunity Grants, Federal Work-Study Program awards, Federal Stafford Student Loans, Federal PLUS Loans, veterans' benefits, and Bureau of Vocational Rehabilitation benefits. A deferred-payment plan allows students to spread their tuition over two payments each semester. Penn College offers a variety of academic, need-based, and technical scholarships to qualified students. Detailed information on scholarships can be obtained from the Financial Aid Office or on the Web at http://www.pct.edu/finaid.

Faculty

Penn College's faculty members (308 full-time and 199 part-time) provide the kind of individual attention students need to be successful in the classroom and in the workplace. Faculty members are both educated and experienced in their field. Penn College recognizes excellence among the faculty members through distinguished faculty award programs. Small class sizes (fewer than 20 students in most classes) provide individual attention and promote student success. In addition, advisory committees of business and industry leaders and faculty and staff members work together to ensure that programs of study meet current workplace needs.

Student Government

Student Government Association (SGA) and Wildcat Events Board (WEB) represent the student body in matters related to College policy and social activities. All enrolled students are members of SGA and WEB. Active participation offers the opportunity to develop leadership skills while contributing to the well-being of the College and the student body. In addition, Greek Life (four fraternities and two sororities) and more than fifty student organizations, including the Residence Hall Association, which represents all on-campus student residents, offer opportunities for organized campus activity and leadership experiences.

Admission Requirements

The application deadline for fall is July 1. Students may submit applications and the $50 application fee online at http://www.pct.edu or they may contact the Admissions Office for an application form. Applicants for bachelor's degree majors must submit SAT/ACT scores in addition to high school transcripts to be considered for admission. Applicants must satisfactorily complete placement testing and satisfy other major-specific admission criteria in order to be offered acceptance into a major program of study.

Penn College offers educational opportunities to anyone who has the interest, desire, and ability to pursue advanced study. Due to the wide variety of majors, admission criteria vary according to the major. At a minimum, applicants must have a high school diploma or its equivalent. Some majors are restricted to people who meet certain academic skills and prerequisites, who have attained high levels of academic achievement, and who have achieved acceptable scores on the SAT or ACT. Questions regarding the admission standards for specific majors should be directed to the Admissions Office.

To ensure that applicants have the entry-level skills needed for success in Penn College majors, all students are required to take placement examinations, which are used to assess skills in math, English, and reading. The College provides opportunities for students to develop the basic skills necessary for enrollment in associate degree and certificate programs when the placement tests indicate that such help is needed. International students whose native language is not English are required to take the TOEFL, submit an affidavit of support, and comply with test regulations of the Immigration and Naturalization Service, along with meeting all other admission requirements.

Penn College offers opportunities for students to transfer course credit earned at other institutions, college credit earned before high school graduation, service credit, DANTES credit, and credit earned through the College-Level Examination Program (CLEP). The College offers equal opportunity for admission without regard to age, race, color, creed, sex, national origin, handicap, veteran status, or political affiliation.

Application and Information

Viewbooks, financial aid information, and other informative brochures as well as applications for admission are available from the Admissions Office. The College invites prospective students and their families to contact the Admissions Office to arrange a personal interview or campus tour. Annual fall and spring open house events offer the best opportunity to see the entire campus in action. Interested students should visit the College's Web site or contact the Admissions Office for dates or to schedule a tour at any time.

All inquiries should be addressed to:

Admissions Office
Pennsylvania College of Technology
One College Avenue
Williamsport, Pennsylvania 17701-5799
Phone: 570-327-4761
800-367-9222 (toll-free)
E-mail: PCTinfo@pct.edu
Web site: http://www.pct.edu/peter4

Banners representing each of the eight academic schools at Penn College adorn lampposts on the road leading from the main entrance to the heart of the campus.

PHILADELPHIA UNIVERSITY

PHILADELPHIA, PENNSYLVANIA

The University

Founded in 1884, Philadelphia University is a private institution of higher learning for students with high motivation and academic ability. Philadelphia University is professionally oriented and offers undergraduate and graduate degree programs in the areas of architecture, business, design, engineering, fashion, general sciences, health sciences, and textile engineering technology. The University's enrollment of approximately 2,500 undergraduates represents a diverse and talented group of students from forty states and twenty-five countries. With an average class size of 18 and a 14:1 student-faculty ratio, students receive the personal attention so important to social and professional growth.

Through a unique blend of liberal and specialized education with an interdisciplinary focus, the University prepares students for today's complex, global workplace. Recognized as a premier professional university, Philadelphia University has established a phenomenal record of career success for its graduates. The University is committed to a technologically advanced approach to career planning, and students have full access to the Career Services Center's CareerLink, an Internet-based resume and job-listing management system that electronically stores resumes, job listings, and employer information. Students have access to job-search resources, including ReferenceUSA, a database of 1.5 million companies nationwide. Prospective employers gain access to students through the various career fairs and industry spotlights hosted by the center annually. The University's innovative academic programs that meet emerging needs in the marketplace, extensive networking with prospective employers (connecting students with 150 employers on campus and 1,200 employers electronically last year), and extensive career and professional development opportunities for students all add up to a nearly 90 percent placement rate within just a few months of graduation.

Philadelphia University believes the college experience of every student should extend well beyond the classroom. The Student Life Programs at Philadelphia University build bridges between the classroom and out-of-class experiences to create a dynamic learning community for students. Fifteen varsity teams compose the intercollegiate athletics program. Men participate in baseball, basketball, cross-country, golf, rowing, soccer, and tennis. Women's teams include basketball, cross-country, lacrosse, rowing, soccer, softball, tennis, and volleyball. An extensive intramural sports program is available to all students. Students are actively engaged in campus life, whether through one of the nationally ranked athletic teams, events sponsored by Student Government, a wide array of community service opportunities, an extensive intramural program, or participation in the more than thirty student clubs and organizations.

More than 1,200 students live on campus in residence halls, apartments, and townhouses. Professional and paraprofessional staff members live within each residential area to assist students with daily concerns and program activities to enhance residential living.

The University holds accreditation from the Middle States Association of Colleges and Schools, the National Architectural Accrediting Board (NAAB), Council for Interior Design Accreditation (CIDA), the American Chemical Society (ACS), Accreditation Review Commission on Education for the Physician Assistant (ARC-PA), National Association of Schools of Art and Design (NASAD), the Landscape Architecture Accreditation Board (LAAB), and the Engineering Accreditation Commission of the Accreditation Board for Engineering and Technology (ABET), Inc., as well as certification from the International College Reading and Learning Center Association.

Location

The University's sprawling, 100-acre campus is adjacent to Fairmount Park, the largest urban park system in the country. Students enjoy the best of both worlds—a beautiful campus with tree-lined walkways, spacious lawns, and classical architecture, and easy access to Philadelphia (just minutes away) for entertainment, cultural events, great night spots, and more than 300 years of American history.

Philadelphia also serves as a "living lab" where students frequently interact with area professionals for class projects, internships, and off-campus jobs.

Majors and Degrees

Philadelphia University offers the Bachelor of Science in more than thirty areas, including accounting, architectural engineering, architectural studies, architecture, biochemistry, biology, biopsychology, chemistry, digital animation, digital design, engineering (with minor tracks in architectural, environmental, industrial, mechanical, and textile), environmental and conservation biology, environmental sustainability, fashion design, fashion industry management, fashion merchandising, finance, financial information systems, graphic design communication, health sciences, industrial and systems engineering, industrial design, interior design, international business, landscape architecture, law and society, management, management information systems, marketing, mechanical engineering, physician assistant studies, premedical studies, professional communication, psychology, public health, textile design, and textile engineering technology.

The University also offers several five-year B.S./M.B.A. joint-degree programs and a five-year B.S./M.S. physician assistant studies program. The five-year architecture program leads to a Bachelor of Architecture (B.Arch.), and the five-year landscape architecture program leads to the Bachelor of Landscape Architecture (B.L.A.). For students wishing to keep their choices open, an undeclared option offers an introduction to college courses in preparation for entering a specific major in the sophomore year.

Academic Programs

Philadelphia University's commitment to quality professional education is realized in curricula that combine a solid foundation in liberal studies with career preparation. These curricula are designed to enhance students' ability and desire to learn; to ensure them an understanding of the ideas, traditions, and values of their own and other cultures; and to prepare them to apply the concepts and techniques of both general and specialized learning to their lives as citizens with productive careers. Degree requirements include successful completion of 121 to 138 credits (depending upon the major chosen), successful completion of both major and general education programs, and the satisfactory completion of at least 60 credits in residence at the University. All students have the option to participate in the University's Internship Program, through which they earn both academic credit and a salary.

As a rule, the University grants credit to students who obtain satisfactory grades in subject examinations developed by the Advanced Placement Program, the College-Level Examination

Program, and the Proficiency Examination Program. Students may, by invitation, participate in the honors program, which offers a number of courses expressly for honors students.

The University's academic calendar consists of two semesters and two summer sessions.

Off-Campus Programs

Internships are available, and the University's Internship Office has affiliations with a wide variety of organizations, such as L. L. Bean, Isdaner & Company, the Hillier Group, Citizens Bank, Burlington Industries, J. Crew, and Federated Department Stores.

Study abroad at Philadelphia University prepares students for successful participation and competition in an increasingly interdependent world and to perform with distinction in the international and multicultural contexts that are increasingly shaping professional life. Students at Philadelphia University may study abroad and receive credit for courses that apply directly to their challenging, professions-oriented curricula. Opportunities are available for fall, spring, and summer semesters. The University has its own programs in Rome and Milan, Italy, and affiliations with more than twenty-five programs all over the world and in most majors.

Academic Facilities

In fall 2006, the University opened the Kanbar Campus Center, a 72,000-square-foot building with an open design, featuring walls of windows to optimize the spectacular natural setting. In addition, the University opened The Gallagher Athletic, Recreation, and Convocation Center.

The Tuttleman Center at Philadelphia University, a 31,500-square-foot academic building, provides students and faculty members with access to the most sophisticated technologies for teaching and learning.

Many major labs and studios enable students to gain practical experience in engineering, design, textiles, apparel manufacturing, foreign languages, the sciences, computer technologies, and physician assistant studies. The University's Paul J. Gutman Library is a state-of-the-art information center. Through the contemporary information system, students can search the library's collections, as well as major indexes and full-text journals, from on or off campus. An international computer network links Philadelphia University to the resources of more than 14,000 libraries worldwide. With more than 400 study spaces and nine group study rooms, the library provides an ideal environment for reading and research. The Architecture and Design Center houses studio space, a photo lab, and computer-aided design labs. The Design Center at Philadelphia University houses an extensive collection of textile artifacts and hosts changing exhibits in its galleries.

General-purpose and departmental computing labs are updated using a multiyear migration strategy as changes in technology dictate. The labs are currently equipped with Pentium PCs and Macintoshes running at speeds from 1.0 to 1.8 MHz. The University operates a switched, 100-megabit network with building-to-building gigabit (1000-megabit) connections in high-traffic areas. The network provides students with access to the Internet, e-mail service, network storage (300 MB per student), digital library resources, online databases, and the Blackboard course management system.

Costs

The University's 2009–10 cost for regular tuition was $27,428. Room was $4540 and board was $4642.

Financial Aid

Philadelphia University's total financial aid program has amounted to more than $65 million annually. About $22.8 million came from the University itself and the remainder from federal, state, and private sources. While 96 percent of the University's full-time day students receive direct institutional scholarship assistance, 98 percent receive some form of aid each year (e.g., other scholarships, loans, and job opportunities). Candidates for aid should complete the Free Application for Federal Student Aid by April 15. The University offers a wide range of institutional scholarships and grants to incoming students each year. Award amounts vary according to the quality of each student's academic record. The University's scholarship program is available to all prospective students (freshmen and transfer students). Scholarships are awarded regardless of financial need. Students and parents are strongly encouraged to call the admissions or financial aid offices for further information.

Faculty

Primarily a teaching institution, the University encourages close connections between the faculty and students. Classes intentionally are kept small, and faculty members make a practice of being available to students outside the classroom. Often, students can partner with faculty members to pursue joint research interests and gain career experience. The University's faculty is composed of a diverse group of professionals who not only hold strong academic credentials but also frequently possess impressive work experience. They are often sought out as consultants in their fields.

Student Government

The Student Government Association (SGA) is an independent, self-governing student group. In addition to the basic responsibility of protecting students' rights, SGA recommends students to University-wide committees, addresses student grievances, and sponsors campuswide events. The Campus Activities Board is the major programming organization on campus. Its primary responsibility is to provide a wide variety of cultural, scholastic, social, educational, and recreational programs.

Admission Requirements

The University evaluates applicants on the basis of their high school record (including GPA and quality of courses taken), scores on either the SAT or the ACT, and extracurricular activities. Normally, 15 units of secondary school preparation are required for admission. Three units of mathematics (including algebra II and geometry) are required for admission. Students who wish to enter a science curriculum are strongly encouraged to take 4 units of mathematics and 4 units of science. The University actively recruits qualified transfer students, who represent approximately one fifth of the incoming class each fall. The University also has a large international student population. These students must score at least 170 (computer-based) on the TOEFL in order to be considered for admission.

Application and Information

The University maintains a rolling admission plan. Applications are reviewed and decisions are made soon after an application, academic credentials, and standardized test scores are received. Students are encouraged to submit applications early in the senior year; applications received after March 1 are considered on a space-available basis. All applicants are encouraged to come to the campus for an interview with a member of the professional admission staff.

Greg Potts
Director of Admissions
Philadelphia University
School House Lane and Henry Avenue
Philadelphia, Pennsylvania 19144
Phone: 215-951-2800
800-951-7287 (toll-free)
Fax: 215-951-2907
E-mail: admissions@PhilaU.edu
Web site: http://www.PhilaU.edu

COLLEGE CLOSE-UPS

PITZER COLLEGE

CLAREMONT, CALIFORNIA

The College

Pitzer is a nationally recognized independent, residential liberal arts college. The College's emphasis on interdisciplinary studies, intercultural understanding, and social responsibility sets it apart from most other colleges in the country. The College believes students should take an active part in formulating their individualized plans of study, bringing a spirit of inquiry and adventure to the planning process. Because there are fewer required general education courses, Pitzer gives its students more freedom to choose the courses they want to take.

Pitzer offers the best of both worlds: membership in a small, close-knit academic community and access to the resources of a midsize university through Pitzer's partnership with The Claremont Colleges. The Claremont Colleges are a consortium of five distinct undergraduate colleges (Pitzer, Claremont McKenna, Harvey Mudd, Pomona, and Scripps) and two graduate institutions (Claremont Graduate University and the Keck Institute for Applied Biological Sciences). Each college has its own personality, but all share major facilities, such as the library, bookstore, campus security, health services, counseling center, ethnic study centers, and chaplains' offices. The total enrollment of all of the colleges is nearly 7,300 students. Students at Pitzer may enroll in courses offered by the other colleges and may consult with professors on all of the adjoining campuses.

The College was founded in 1963. Today, Pitzer offers forty-three majors in the arts, humanities, sciences, and social sciences. Majors currently with the largest enrollments include anthropology, art, biology, economics, English, environmental studies, history, organizational studies, political studies, psychology, and sociology.

In 2008, the first-year class of 257 students represented thirty different states and five other countries. About 52 percent of the first-year students came from outside of California.

Pitzer has a deep commitment to welcoming members of underrepresented groups since its founding. In 2008, members of underrepresented groups made up approximately 33 percent of the entering class: 17 percent Chicano/Latino, 7 percent Asian American and Pacific Islander, 6 percent African American, and 3 percent multiracial.

Residential life plays a significant role in a student's educational experience. Each of Pitzer's residence halls establishes its own Hall Council to serve as a forum for addressing and meeting the needs of the community. Pitzer students have a long tradition of arranging their living communities based on common interests. All rooms are wired for Internet access, television, and phone service. Three new Gold Lead Certified residence halls opened in fall 2007.

Opportunities abound at Pitzer and the other Claremont Colleges. Students may participate in a wide variety of sports, clubs, community service programs, and social activities. Currently, more than 150 student organizations allow students to get involved in a wide variety of activities. Pitzer partners with Pomona College to field NCAA Division III teams in baseball, basketball, cross-country, football, golf, soccer, softball, swimming and diving, tennis, track and field, volleyball, and water polo. Club sports for men include crew, cycling, lacrosse, rugby, ultimate frisbee, and volleyball. Club sports for women include crew, cycling, lacrosse, rugby, and Ultimate Frisbee.

Location

Pitzer is located in the city of Claremont (population 35,000) at the base of the San Gabriel Mountains, about 35 miles east of Los Angeles and 78 miles west of Palm Springs. Pitzer is a short drive away from rock climbing at Joshua Tree National Park, ski resorts, the beaches of southern California, and the Getty, Norton Simon, and other Los Angeles County museums.

Majors and Degrees

Pitzer offers the Bachelor of Arts degree in American studies; anthropology; art; art history; Asian American studies; biology; biology-chemistry; black studies; chemistry; Chicano studies; classics; dance; economics; English and world literature; environmental science; environmental studies; gender and feminist studies; history; human biology; international and intercultural studies (African studies, Asian studies, European studies, Latin American and Caribbean studies, Third World studies); linguistics; management engineering; mathematical economics; mathematics; media studies; molecular biology; music; neuroscience; organismal biology; organizational studies; philosophy; physics; political economy; political studies; psychology; religious studies; science and management; science, technology, and society; sociology; Spanish; and theater.

Minors are available in anthropology, art, art history, Asian American studies, biology, black studies, classics, dance, economics, English and world literature, environmental studies, gender and feminist studies, history, linguistics, mathematics, media studies, music, philosophy, science, technology and society, sociology, Spanish, and theater.

Academic Programs

To earn the Bachelor of Arts degree, students are required to complete thirty-two courses, about one third of which are in the major. Students work with faculty advisers to organize a curriculum that meets the educational objectives of the College: breadth of knowledge, understanding in depth, written expression, interdisciplinary and intercultural exploration, and social responsibility and the ethical implications of knowledge and action. Specific course requirements depend on the student's academic interests. Certain concentrations require a senior thesis.

The system of cross-registration at the Claremont Colleges provides Pitzer students with the opportunity to take advantage of the wide range of courses available at each of the other colleges. Advanced students may also enroll in certain courses at Claremont Graduate University with the instructor's approval.

The College observes a semester calendar; classes begin in early September and end in mid-May. There is a study break near the middle of each semester and another break between semesters from mid-December through mid-January.

Off-Campus Programs

Nearly 72 percent of students participate in study-abroad programs. Pitzer approves thirty-five international study options in Argentina, Australia, Botswana, Bulgaria, Canada, China, Costa Rica, Denmark, Ecuador, England, Finland, France, Germany, Ghana, Hungary, India, Ireland, Japan, Korea, Latvia, Mexico, Morocco, Nepal, South Africa, Spain, Thailand, Turkey, and fourteen exchanges with U.S. institutions.

Academic Facilities

The central services of the Claremont Colleges include the Honnold-Mudd Library, which houses more than 2 million volumes and more than 6,000 serial subscriptions. Other shared facilities include theaters, music halls, music and dance studios, the Keck Joint Science Center (shared with Claremont McKenna and Scripps Colleges), and a wellness center that includes counseling and health services.

Specialized facilities at Pitzer include a television studio, film editing suites, art galleries, social science laboratories, an arboretum, a reading library, and several computing facilities, including a 24-hour computer center.

Costs

Expenses for 2008–09 were as follows: tuition and fees, $37,870; room and board, $10,930; and books and personal expenses, $2000. Travel expenses vary. Costs are subject to change for 2009–10.

Financial Aid

Nearly 44 percent of Pitzer's students receive aid in the forms of grants, loans, and work-study. To apply for aid, students must complete the Free Application for Federal Student Aid (FAFSA) and the CSS PROFILE. California residents should also apply for California state grants. Students must reapply for aid each spring.

Faculty

One hundred percent of Pitzer's faculty members hold a Ph.D. or the terminal degree in their fields. All courses are taught by the faculty members. The student-faculty ratio is 12:1, and faculty members are readily available for academic advising. Most faculty members are conversant with at least one other field of study in addition to the area of their degrees and may teach in more than one area.

Student Government

Pitzer's governmental structure is distinctive among American colleges. Instead of the traditional student government that restricts student participation to limited areas, students are represented on all standing committees of the College, including those that deal with the most vital and sensitive issues of the College community. Though it demands a serious time commitment from those who choose to participate, it offers interested students an active educational experience and the opportunity to make a genuine impact on the life of the College and its students, faculty, and staff.

Admission Requirements

Pitzer has developed a highly personalized admission process. Each applicant is considered on the basis of his or her own strengths. In general, the College seeks students who have performed well in high school, have shown a significant amount of involvement in activities outside of the classroom, are motivated to learn, and are interested in the opportunity to take an active role in planning their education in a liberal arts framework. The selection process is designed to help achieve a diverse and energetic class. Selection is based on high school transcripts, rigor of curriculum, recommendations, essays, extracurricular activities, and other special talents. Applicants are encouraged to visit the campus and arrange for an interview.

Application and Information

Pitzer College offers both early decision and regular decision for prospective applicants. Students interested in applying early must submit a completed application by November 15 and are notified late December. Interviews for early decision are required by December 1. Regular decision candidates must submit their applications for admission by January 1 and are notified by April 1. Applicants must supply an official transcript of grades, two teacher evaluations, one counselor or school official recommendation, and the application fee of $50 by the necessary deadline. Pitzer accepts the Common Application as the only application for admission for first-year students. When submitting the Common Application, students must complete a supplemental form, which is available on the Common Application Web site at http://www.commonapp.org. Pitzer College is test optional in the admission process. Students should contact the College for further details.

For additional information, students should contact:

Office of Admission
Pitzer College
1050 North Mills Avenue
Claremont, California 91711-6101
Phone: 909-621-8129
800-PITZER1 (800-748-9371, toll-free)
Fax: 909-621-8770
E-mail: admission@pitzer.edu
Web site: http://www.pitzer.edu

Students on the campus of Pitzer College.

POLYTECHNIC INSTITUTE OF NYU

BROOKLYN, NEW YORK

The Institute

Long recognized as a leading technological university and research center, Polytechnic Institute of NYU offers degrees in computer science, digital media, engineering, humanities, the sciences, and technology management. The core feature of the Institution's research and education programs focuses on i2e–invention, innovation, and entrepreneurship. Founded in 1854 as Polytechnic Institute of Brooklyn (Brooklyn Poly), it is the second-oldest independent technological university in the United States. Polytechnic has a main campus in the MetroTech Center in downtown Brooklyn, New York, and graduate centers in Long Island, Manhattan, and Westchester. Polytechnic has an undergraduate student body of approximately 1,700 students.

Polytechnic Institute of NYU is a microcosm of greater New York. Undergraduates come from forty states and fifty-five countries. The students represent a mosaic of racial, ethnic, religious, and cultural backgrounds, all working together to achieve common goals. A student-faculty ratio of 15:1 enables students to work closely with professors in both the classroom and the research lab. Located at Polytechnic are a variety of research centers where students and world-renowned faculty members are involved in innovative fields of study and research, including telecommunications, electronics, robotics, digital systems, wireless communications, and integrative digital media, among others. Although it emphasizes science and engineering, Polytechnic has long recognized the importance of tempering technology with humanistic understanding.

The Institute offers a wide variety of student activities, as it ranks among the top 5 universities in the nation in social diversity. The Student Council and a school newspaper are just two of the many options available. A number of academic organizations, many with national affiliations, host programs, lectures, and discussion groups for students majoring in the various disciplines. Athletics for both men and women—from basketball to lacrosse to volleyball—are popular and widely available at Polytechnic on both intercollegiate and intramural levels.

Polytechnic offers on-campus housing in the Othmer Residence Hall. The residence hall is located across the street from the MetroTech campus in downtown Brooklyn. It features 4-student, two-bedroom suites for underclassmen and two-bedroom apartments for upperclassmen. Amenities include rooms that are fully wired for personal computers, laptops, cable TV, and telephone access; study rooms; student lounges; 24-hour security; a laundry room; and a modern dining hall.

Students can use the central computer labs and various specialized labs, connect wirelessly with a laptop, or dial in from home.

Location

Polytechnic is located in the heart of historic downtown Brooklyn in MetroTech Center, a 16-acre, $1-billion academic/professional park in New York City. Situated at the foot of the famous Brooklyn Bridge, the campus is the gateway to such places as Wall Street, Broadway, and the South Street Seaport on one side of the river and the Brooklyn Museum and Prospect Park on the other. All of these attractions are readily accessible via public transportation and a network of modern highways. Polytechnic is just a 10-minute subway ride from Manhattan.

Exceptional careers begin with exceptional locations, and Polytechnic has an unrivaled one in the greater New York area. Serving students with a dynamic range of experiences and powerful examples of excellence, New York City gives a unique context to their studies. In addition, it places them in the middle of an international capital with diverse surroundings, unique perspectives, vibrant cultures, and thriving enterprises. The career opportunities are virtually everywhere—from Wall Street to New York's new media industry, affectionately dubbed "Silicon Alley."

Majors and Degrees

Polytechnic Institute of NYU offers the Bachelor of Science degree. The undergraduate majors include biomolecular science (premed), chemical and biological engineering, civil engineering, computer engineering, computer science, construction management, digital media studies, electrical engineering, liberal studies, mathematics, mechanical engineering, physics, technical and professional communications, and technology management. Five-year B.S./M.S. programs are also available.

Academic Programs

While requirements vary according to the major, students must complete an average of 128 credits with an average of at least 2.0 (on a 4.0 scale) to earn the Bachelor of Science degree. Science and engineering students begin fundamental courses in their specialties during their second year and concentrate on advanced courses in their last two years.

Recent academic initiatives include an Honors College and an admission assurance program with the State University of New York Health Science Center at Brooklyn for outstanding premed students.

Academic Facilities

The Bern Dibner Library of Science and Technology houses one of the finest collections of technical and scientific literature in the metropolitan area. In addition, the library hosts a massive collection of online reference databases to assist in classwork and scholarly research. A $130-million upgrade to the MetroTech campus is reflected in an academic building, a modern residence hall, an athletic facility, labs, and a state-of-the-art computing infrastructure. Wireless networking is available, allowing students to connect to the Institute's network and the Internet from virtually anywhere on campus. Computer labs feature high-end workstations for research, 3-D modeling, and dynamic simulation. As an affiliate of NYU, students also have access to the Bobst Library on NYU's Greenwich Village campus.

Well-known for scientific and technological discovery, Polytechnic sponsors a number of important research centers that typically involve multidisciplinary teams of Polytechnic faculty members, research staff members, and students. Included among these centers are the Institute for Mathematics and Advanced Supercomputing, the Transportation Research Institute, the Othmer Institute for Interdisciplinary Studies, and the Polymer Research Institute, the oldest academic center of polymer (plastics) investigation in the United States. In 1983,

Polytechnic was designated a Center for Advanced Technology in Telecommunications in New York State.

Costs

Tuition for 2009–10 was $33,274. Estimates of other expenses are $1146 for fees, $1000 for books, $2925 for personal expenses, and $9044 for room and board.

Financial Aid

Scholarships and loans are the principal sources of financial aid for full-time undergraduates. Federal sources of funds include Federal Pell Grants, Federal Supplemental Educational Opportunity Grants, Federal Stafford Student Loans, Federal Perkins Loans, and Federal Work-Study Program awards. New York State residents may be eligible for assistance under the New York State Tuition Assistance Program. In addition to the usual financial aid programs, Polytechnic offers a large number of scholarships, including several full-tuition, four-year scholarships that are awarded to students admitted to the Honors College. Approximately 75 percent of all undergraduates at the Institute receive some financial aid. Opportunities for student employment are good. Students desiring financial assistance should submit the Free Application for Federal Student Aid. For more detailed information about financial aid, students should contact the Office of Financial Aid at Polytechnic or visit http://www.poly.edu/admissions.

Faculty

Polytechnic has 138 full-time faculty members, 90 percent of whom have doctoral degrees. Most of the faculty members teach both graduate and undergraduate courses. The Institute's faculty is world renowned for the research, inventions, and scholarly publications of its members. Several are members of the National Academy of Engineering, and many are frequent recipients of both national and international awards for excellence. Recent examples include the Institute of Electrical and Electronics Engineers' Educational Medal for Excellence, the President's Medal of Sciences, and the prestigious Humboldt Award. The American Society for Engineering Education recently ranked the graduate electrical engineering faculty among the top 10 in the nation for scholarly activity; many of its members also teach on the undergraduate level.

Student Government

The Student Council is important on the Polytechnic campus. In working with the Student Leadership Office and administration, it directs the activities of the undergraduate student body and represents student interests. As the administrating agency for student fees, the council allocates money to student organizations, publications, and activities. Student representatives also serve on many faculty and administrative committees dealing with all phases of academic and student life.

Admission Requirements

Admission to Polytechnic is competitive. Candidates must submit a formal application for admission, a secondary school transcript, an essay, two academic recommendations, and standardized test scores (SAT or ACT). The Committee on Admissions evaluates each applicant on an individual basis regardless of financial need and seeks students who rank in the top 25 percent of their graduating class, have taken 3 to 4 years of college-preparatory math and science, and have achieved a grade average of B+ or higher.

Students whose first language is not English are advised to submit scores on the Test of English as a Foreign Language (TOEFL). This test must be taken by all international applicants whose native language is not English regardless of whether or not their previous education was conducted in English. Advanced placement is awarded to students whose scores on the Advanced Placement tests indicate proficiency in a given subject.

Application and Information

A completed application form, $50 application fee, and supporting documents are required for evaluation of prospective students. Applications should be submitted as early as possible, preferably by January 15 for admission in the fall and December 1 for admission in the spring. Admission decisions are made on a rolling basis. For application forms and additional information, students should contact:

Ms. Joy Colelli
Dean of Undergraduate Admissions
Wunsch Building
Polytechnic Institute of NYU
6 MetroTech Center
Brooklyn, New York 11201
Phone: 718-637-5955
800-POLY-TECH (toll-free)
Web site: http://www.poly.edu/admit

A view of the campus at Polytechnic Institute of NYU.

POST UNIVERSITY

WATERBURY, CONNECTICUT

The University

Founded in 1890, Post University is a student-focused, career-driven university committed to providing students with the knowledge, personal skills, and experience required to be leaders in their chosen fields. Located in Waterbury, Connecticut, Post University is known for its quality academic programs, small classes, award-winning student activities, and competitive NCAA Division II athletics. In 2009, it added a Collegiate Sprint Football team and extended its commitment to serving military students by adding an ROTC program. Its students come from the United States and abroad and are supported by faculty whose mission is to prepare students to compete and succeed in today's global workplace.

Post University attracts students from all races, cultures, geographies, and socio-economic backgrounds. This array of diverse viewpoints and experiences gives students many opportunities to learn about others and themselves.

Students enjoy all the benefits of a small, close-knit New England campus community, including the ability to form lifelong friendships with their peers, receive one-on-one attention from professors, and more personal interaction with other faculty members, students, and staff. They can also participate in a wide array of on-campus activities and have nearby access to two of the nation's most vibrant cities, New York and Boston. The smaller campus also means more opportunities to take on leadership roles within and beyond the classroom. Post University also has an Honors College designed to meet the needs of highly motivated and academically accomplished students.

Approximately two thirds of Post University's students live on campus in one of six residence halls. The residence halls range from single rooms to suites consisting of private rooms around a shared living and eating facility. This is in addition to the campus's large dining rooms.

Post students participate in a year-round schedule of intercollegiate and intramural athletic activities. The Post University Eagles compete in the National Collegiate Athletic Association (NCAA) Division II and the Central Atlantic Collegiate Conference (CACC). Men's intercollegiate sports teams include baseball, basketball, cross-country, golf, soccer, swimming, and tennis. In 2010, Post University will compete in the Collegiate Sprint Football League against well-known universities such as Army, Navy, Princeton, and Cornell. Women's teams include basketball, cross-country, lacrosse, soccer, softball, swimming, tennis, and volleyball. The University also sponsors an active coeducational equestrian team and an International Dressage team. Intramural sports are diverse, ranging from softball and volleyball to basketball and flag football. Students enjoy the facilities of the Drubner Fitness Center, including a gymnasium, swimming pool, tennis and racquetball courts, fitness club, and weight-training rooms.

Location

Post University offers students the best of both worlds. Located midway between New York City and Boston, Post University occupies a 58-acre hilltop residential campus in the suburbs of Waterbury, Connecticut. Post's campus and the surrounding community offer a safe, scenic, friendly, and convenient home for students. Its location in the heart of Connecticut provides convenient service from Amtrak's Northeast Corridor as well as airline service to Hartford.

Majors and Degrees

Students enrolled at Post University may earn an undergraduate in accounting, biology, business administration, child studies, computer information systems, criminal justice, environmental sciences/studies, equine business management, finance, human services, legal studies, management, marketing, psychology, sociology, sport management, and early childhood education. In addition, Post University has a number of certificate programs that prepare students for the practice of specific specialties and which can be integrated into either an associate or baccalaureate degree.

The academic programs at Post University are accredited by the New England Association of Schools and Colleges (NEASC) using the same standards that are applied to other well-known New England universities.

Academic Programs

For the bachelor's degree, students must complete a minimum of 120 credit hours. To receive an associate degree from Post, students must complete a minimum of 60 credit hours. All programs offer opportunities for cooperative education. The University has a two-semester calendar.

Off-Campus Programs

Post University offers students the opportunity to study abroad through a University-sponsored program and/or an approved study/internship-abroad program at another institution. The equine business management program offers a study-abroad option in England. Through these programs, students have an opportunity to broaden their perspectives and experiences. Courses taken abroad are accepted for degree credit at Post University.

To qualify for study abroad, a student must have a cumulative grade point average of 2.5 or better at the time of attendance.

Academic Facilities

Post University's campus offers wireless Internet access inside and outside. It includes a new computer lab; recently renovated dining hall; classrooms that are equipped with needed technology; and a gymnasium, pool and fitness center. Residence halls include single-room and suite options. The University also includes a Writing Center and a Tutoring Center that are available for student use at no additional charge. The University's library has more than 84,000 volumes and a growing media collection. As a government document depository, the library houses an extensive government publications collection. Post University also has reciprocal borrowing agreements with academic libraries throughout the state.

Costs

For 2009–10, full-time Main Campus students paid $33,600, which covered tuition, technology, room, and board. For commuting students, the comprehensive fee was $24,100 per year. Equine and laboratory fees, the paper application fee, and an estimated $1000 to $1500 per year for books and supplies are not included in this total.

Financial Aid

Post University offers financial assistance through the Federal Work-Study, Federal Supplemental Educational Opportunity Grant, Federal Stafford Student Loan, and Federal Perkins Loan programs. Aid is awarded upon evidence of financial need, as determined by the Free Application for Federal Student Aid

(FAFSA). In addition, the University has its own academic and athletic scholarship and grant programs, and participates in all applicable state programs. In order to apply for financial assistance, a student must apply for admission and be accepted to Post University, and then submit the FAFSA.

Faculty

Post University has 40 full-time and 122 part-time faculty members, who hold advanced degrees and bring relevant work experience in the fields they teach. All full-time faculty members serve as academic advisers and maintain weekly office hours for student consultation. The student-faculty ratio is 15:1, and students are never in classes with hundreds of students or taught by teaching assistants.

Student Government

Students play active roles in the day-to-day functioning of Post University. The students' official voice at the University is the Student Government Association (SGA), which expresses recommendations pertaining to student life, oversees the operations of each active student group, and decides on funding for each group. Students participate in a wide array of campus activities, programs, and athletics.

Admission Requirements

Post University welcomes applicants who are motivated to succeed academically and in their careers. Admission to Post University is based upon an evaluation of the candidate's qualifications and the recommendation of an admissions representative. All decisions are made without regard to race, creed, color, religion, national origin, handicap, or sexual orientation.

The applicant's academic experience, standardized test scores, personal qualities, recommendations, and individual characteristics are considered. Post University has a rolling admissions policy. The Admissions Committee makes a decision with respect to a candidate's admission to the University as soon as the candidate's file is complete. The minimum requirements to make an admissions decision include the submission of an application, official high school transcripts, and standardized test scores. International students are required to earn a minimum score of 500 on the paper-based version or 173 on the computer-based version of the TOEFL and adhere to the above requirements.

Campus visit appointments may be scheduled Monday through Friday at 11, 1, and 3 and on select Saturdays from 10 to 2. Post periodically offers Group Information Sessions, on-site and off-site Open Houses, and live Internet chats. To schedule a campus visit, students should call the Office of Admission at 800-345-2562 (toll-free) or send an e-mail message to admissions@post.edu.

Post University welcomes transfer students and has a flexible credit transfer policy. Transfer candidates must have a minimum GPA of 2.0 and must provide transcripts from all other colleges and universities attended. Grades of C or higher may receive transfer credits. The maximum number of transfer credits allowed for bachelor's candidates is 90; the maximum for associate candidates is 30.

Application and Information

To apply, students should submit the application form, the nonrefundable $40 application fee, a recommendation, SAT or ACT scores, and high school or college transcripts. Online applications are available through the University's Web site at http://www.post.edu.

For additional information, students should contact:

Office of Admissions
Post University
800 Country Club Road
P.O. Box 2540
Waterbury, Connecticut 06723-2540
Phone: 203-596-4520
800-345-2562 (toll-free)
Fax: 203-756-5810
E-mail: admissions@post.edu
Web site: http://www.Post.edu

The Post University campus is lovely year-round.

PRATT INSTITUTE

BROOKLYN, NEW YORK

The Institute

Industrialist and philanthropist Charles Pratt founded Pratt Institute in 1887 to educate students for various professions on a non-degree level. As the educational preparation necessary for various professions expanded, Pratt Institute moved to offer baccalaureate degrees with its first granted in 1938 and its first graduate degree granted in 1950.

With a wide variety of highly ranked programs in art, design, and architecture, Pratt has continued to add programs at all educational levels, including undergraduate programs in creative writing and critical and visual studies, undergraduate and graduate programs in art history and art education, and graduate programs in arts and cultural management, historic preservation, and design management.

Although the characteristics and educational requirements of the professions for which Pratt prepares people have changed over the course of a century, the Institute has succeeded in pursuing its abiding purpose—to blend theoretical learning with professional and humanistic development—and has kept its curricula current by hiring practicing professionals to teach. Standards are high, modeled after the professional world.

Pratt offers four-year bachelor's, two-year associate, and master's degrees. In educating more than five generations of students to be creative, technically skilled, and adaptable professionals as well as responsible citizens, Pratt has gained a national and international reputation that attracts undergraduate and graduate students from more than forty-nine states, the District of Columbia, Puerto Rico, the Virgin Islands, and sixty countries. Unlike the typical American college student, most students who choose Pratt already have career objectives, or at least they know they want to study art, design, architecture, or creative writing.

A short subway or bus ride from the museums, galleries, and design centers of both Manhattan and Brooklyn, Pratt Institute has twenty-four buildings of differing architectural styles spread about a 25-acre campus. Eighteen of the buildings house studios, classrooms, laboratories, administrative offices, auditoria, sports facilities, food services, and student centers. Six buildings are student residences, including the Stabile Hall freshman residence, which provides studio space on each floor. There are adequate parking facilities for residents and commuters. Student services include career planning and placement, health and counseling, and student development. The more than sixty student organizations include fraternities and sororities, honorary societies, professional societies, and clubs.

Location

Pratt Institute, the country's premier college of art, design, writing, and architecture, is located in the Clinton Hill section of Brooklyn, just minutes from downtown Manhattan. Eighty-eight percent of Pratt's freshmen and over half of its undergraduates live on the school's beautifully landscaped 25-acre, tree-lined Brooklyn campus. The campus includes a contemporary sculpture garden (ranked among the top ten campus art collections by *Public Art Review*), an athletic center, residence halls, dining halls, outstanding studio facilities, and historic buildings. Students find a green oasis just minutes from the art capital of the world, Manhattan.

Majors and Degrees

Pratt Institute offers the Bachelor of Architecture, Bachelor of Fine Arts, Bachelor of Art, Bachelor of Industrial Design, Bachelor of Professional Studies, Bachelor of Science, Associate of Occupational Studies, and Associate of Applied Science degrees.

The Bachelor of Architecture degree program is a five-year, accredited program. For the Bachelor of Fine Arts degree, a candidate may choose to major in art and design education (teacher certification), art history, communications design (advertising, graphic design, illustration), digital arts (traditional and digital animation, interactive arts), fashion design, film/video, fine arts (ceramics, drawing, jewelry, painting, printmaking, sculpture), interior design, photography, or writing. The Bachelor of Arts is offered in critical and visual studies and art history. The Bachelor of Industrial Design is offered for students interested in car, product, and furniture design. In the Bachelor of Professional Studies degree program, the major is in construction management. Students seeking the Bachelor of Science degree can major in construction management.

The two-year Associate of Occupational Studies degree is offered in digital design and interactive media, graphic design, and illustration. The Associate of Applied Science is offered in painting/drawing and graphic design/illustration. The two-year Associate of Applied Science degree is transferable to a four-year program.

Students may also earn combined bachelor's/master's degrees. Programs include the B.F.A./M.S. in art and design education as well as art history.

Academic Programs

Educating artists and creative professionals to be responsible contributors to society has been the mission of Pratt Institute since it assembled its first group of students in 1887. Within the structure of that professional education, Pratt students are encouraged to acquire the diverse knowledge that is necessary for them to succeed in their chosen fields including sustainability. In addition to the professional studies, the curriculum in each of Pratt's schools includes a broad range of liberal arts courses. Students from all schools take these courses together and have the opportunity to examine the interrelationships of art, science, technology, and human need.

At the time of graduation, students in the associate degree programs have completed 67 credit hours of course work. In the bachelor's programs, credit-hour requirements range from 132 to 135 credits, depending on the particular program. For the Bachelor of Architecture degree, 170 credits are required.

Pratt's academic calendar consists of two semesters plus optional summer terms that allow students to choose alternative courses or various options usually not offered during the fall or spring semester. Two summer sessions are offered.

Off-Campus Programs

Pratt Institute offers credit for a wide variety of off-campus study programs. The Internship Program offers qualified students challenging on-the-job experience related to their major fields of interest; this extension of the classroom and laboratory into the professional world adds a practical dimension to periods of on-campus study.

International programs, available during all academic sessions, have included art and design offerings in the cities of Copenhagen and Rome and in the countries of England, France, Italy, and South Africa. Architecture programs have been held in Italy, Finland, and Japan. New programs are developed regularly in these and other countries. A semester-long program is offered in Rome each year.

Academic Facilities

Founded as the first free library in Brooklyn, the Pratt Institute Library now has more than 186,589 bound volumes, serial backfiles, and other material, including government documents; 251,603 audiovisual materials; and 3,996 microforms and subscribes to 925 periodicals—the largest collection of any independent art school. With their ID cards, Pratt students also have access to numerous college libraries in the metropolitan area. The Multi-Media Center has been developed to facilitate and improve the educational communication process by providing materials in multimedia formats to support and enrich the Institute's curricula. These include slides, ¾-inch videotapes, 16-mm films, audiocassettes, and other formats appropriate for group use.

Extensive studio and state-of-the-art computer lab facilities are provided for all Pratt students. In the School of Art and Design, these include studio, shop, and technical facilities for work in all media, from the traditional to the most experimental. Gallery space, both on campus and at Pratt Manhattan, is extensive, showing the work of students, alumni, faculty members, staff members, and other well-known artists, architects, and designers. The Pratt Center for Community Development functions as a laboratory for the study of planning and advocacy issues in real-world situations including sustainable planning.

Costs

Tuition for the 2009–10 academic year was $33,500. Room charges were $6156 per academic year. A meal plan is available, and cost about $3600 for the year. The fees were approximately $1380. The estimated cost of books and supplies is $3000 per academic year. Students should allow an additional $1000 for transportation and personal expenses. For an updated list of tuition and fees, prospective students should visit http://www.pratt.edu/admissions/financing_your_education/costs_and_budgeting.

Financial Aid

Pratt Institute offers a large number of merit-based scholarships, need-based grants, loans, and awards based on academic achievement, talent, financial need, or all three. More than 75 percent of Pratt students receive financial assistance through one or more of these kinds of aid. Through funds from the federal and state governments, contributions from Pratt alumni, and industry scholarships, Pratt is able to maintain generous financial aid program in a time of escalating costs.

Faculty

The faculty at Pratt Institute is exceptional in that a large number of practicing professionals augment the regular full-time faculty. There are 120 full-time and 877 part-time faculty members; there are no graduate teaching assistants. In small classes and studios, students have easy access to professors whose natural environment is the design studio, the architectural office, or the industrial research department. Faculty members often connect students with internships and eventually jobs.

Student Government

The Student Government Association (SGA) maintains primary responsibility for all student interests and involvement at Pratt. The SGA structure includes the Executive Committee, Senate, Finance Committee, Buildings and Grounds Committee, Academic and Administrative Affairs Committee, and Program Board. Student representatives serve on the Board of Trustees and on its various committees. All undergraduate students are encouraged to become involved in the SGA, whose main functions are allocating and administering funds collected through the student activities fee, scheduling student activities, and representing the student viewpoint to the rest of the Pratt community.

Admission Requirements

Pratt Institute attracts and enrolls highly motivated and talented students from diverse backgrounds. Applications are welcome from all qualified students, regardless of age, sex, race, color, religion, national origin, or handicap. Admission standards at Pratt are high. One of the major components for admission consideration in art, design, or architecture is the evaluation of a student's art or writing portfolio, which must be submitted along with the other required documents.

All applicants must submit transcripts and letters of recommendation from any high schools and colleges attended. Additional professional requirements are specific to each school or major. Instructions can be found at http://www.pratt.edu/apply.

The admission committee bases its decisions on careful reviews of all credentials submitted by applicants in relation to the requirements of the program to which students seek admission. The SAT or ACT and a strong college-preparatory background are required of all applicants for four-year programs. International students must submit TOEFL or IELTS scores or SAT scores, but not both. In certain cases, an extraordinary talent may offset a low grade or a test score.

Application and Information

Pratt has two admissions deadlines: November 1 for early action and January 5 for regular admissions. To receive full consideration, students must submit applications by January 5 for anticipated entrance in the fall semester and by October 1 for anticipated entrance in the spring semester.

For more information about Pratt Institute, students should contact:

Office of Admissions
Pratt Institute
200 Willoughby Avenue
Brooklyn, New York 11205
Phone: 718-636-3514
800-331-0834 (toll-free)
E-mail: admissions@pratt.edu
Web site: http://www.pratt.edu
http://www.pratt.edu/request (to request a catalog)

COLLEGE CLOSE-UPS

PROVIDENCE COLLEGE

PROVIDENCE, RHODE ISLAND

The College

Under the auspices of the Order of Preachers of the Province of St. Joseph, commonly known as the Dominicans, Providence College (PC) was established in 1917. Originally a college for men, it became coeducational in 1971. The College's full-time undergraduate enrollment is 3,850 students. Approximately 1,800 students live in nine residential halls and a suite-style residence facility, and an additional 900 upperclass students are housed in one of the five College apartment complexes. The remainder of the students live in apartments directly off campus or commute from home. At the graduate level, the College offers M.A., M.S., M.Ed., and M.B.A. degree programs.

The newly renovated Slavin Center, as the nucleus of student, social, cultural, and recreational activity, provides space for programs, informal social gatherings, and numerous facilities, available 24/7. It offers lounges; McPhail's Entertainment Facility; a dining facility; club offices; an ATM machine; a bookstore/gift shop; the Student Activities, Involvement, and Leadership Office (SAIL); and offices for the Student Congress, the Board of Programmers, student publications, and the Career Services Office.

The Concannon Fitness Center, a 23,000-square-foot, two-level, state-of-the-art facility, opened in September 2007. Emphasizing the College's commitment to health and fitness, the center offers sixty-two cardiovascular machines; all but six are equipped with cable TV. There are eight types of cardiovascular machines, including eighteen treadmills, twelve cross-trainers, twelve arc-trainers, six upright bikes, and six recumbent bikes. The center also offers fitness options, from selectorized strength pieces and cable motion pieces to numerous workout benches and free weights.

The Peterson Recreation Center is the site of intramural athletic activities on campus, which have one of the highest participation rates in the country. The center has five convertible basketball, tennis, and volleyball courts; a 220-yard track; three racquetball courts; a 25-meter pool; and an aerobics room. Providence College has a fine tradition of competition in intercollegiate athletics, and it continues to play an active role through its membership in the NCAA, Hockey East Conference, and the Big East Conference. Additional on-campus sports facilities include Alumni Hall, Schneider Arena, three large fields and recreational areas, and a new artificial-turf field for varsity, club, and intramural sports.

Location

The College is situated on a 105-acre campus in the city of Providence, Rhode Island. It has the advantages of an atmosphere that is far removed from the traffic and commerce of the metropolitan area but is also conveniently located near the many cultural attractions of a vibrant city that is not only the capital of a historic state but also the center of a variety of institutions of higher learning. Providence College has an established relationship with the Tony Award–winning Trinity Square Repertory Company, which is located in downtown Providence. Trinity provides special discount rates for students for the full spectrum of its programs. The Providence Performing Arts Center, which was originally a movie palace, has been restored to its former baroque splendor and now serves as the site of symphony concerts, opera, ballet, and road shows of Broadway musicals. In addition, the Dunkin' Donuts Civic Center attracts well-known performers and rock groups, trade shows, and sports events. The center is also the home court of the Friars, PC's basketball team. A Providence College ID enables students to travel free on any RIPTA bus route throughout Rhode Island.

Majors and Degrees

Providence College offers the B.A. degree, with major programs of study in American studies, art and art history, biology, business economics, chemistry, economics, education (elementary/special and secondary), English, global studies, history, humanities, mathematics, modern languages, music/music education (K–12), philosophy, political science, psychology, public and community service studies, social science, social work, sociology, theater arts, theology, and writing. The B.S. degree is offered, with major programs of study in applied physics, biochemistry, biology, chemistry, combined biology/optometry (3+4 program), computer science, engineering (3+2 program), health policy, and management. The School of Business offers the B.S. degree, with major programs of study in accountancy, finance, management, and marketing. A 4+1 B.A./B.S./M.B.A. program is also offered for qualified students.

Academic Programs

The primary objective of Providence College is to further the intellectual development of its students through the disciplines of the sciences and the humanities. The liberal education provided by the College gives students the chance to increase their ability to formulate their thoughts and communicate them to others, evaluate their varied experiences, and achieve insight into the past, present, and future of civilization. All dimensions of the student experience are deeply rooted in the Dominican value of dynamic spirituality, with its concern for the whole person—mind and body, heart and soul—and respect for the gifts and uniqueness of every person. The College's programs are also designed to help students discover their particular aptitude and prepare them to undertake specialized studies leading to careers.

The rigorous core curriculum at Providence College, a values-centered examination of the traditional humanities curriculum, provides students of all majors with a well-balanced academic program. Through an in-depth immersion in the fundamental concepts and issues addressed by the social and natural sciences, literature, history, philosophy, mathematics, the fine arts, and theology, students learn to think critically and reason well. Demanding, exhilarating and memorable, the Development of Western Civilization program is the cornerstone of our core curriculum. It is one of the nation's most academically ambitious interdisciplinary programs which integrates the study of literature, history philosophy, theology, and the fine arts. Special academic programs are offered to enhance the educational experience and allow for a variety of interests, including double majors, individualized programs, nondepartmental courses, liberal arts honors, preprofessional medical and legal programs, the Early Identification Program (offered to Rhode Island residents in cooperation with Brown University Medical School), and Army ROTC.

The College participates in the Advanced Placement (AP) Program, which is administered by the College Board. Students who demonstrate superior performance (a score of 4 or 5) on any of the Advanced Placement examinations are considered for advanced-placement credit.

Providence College recognizes credit earned through the International Baccalaureate (I.B.), an internationally recognized curriculum and examination program. The College recognizes the Higher Level examinations when a score of 5, 6, or 7 has been achieved. Each examination that is successfully passed in the Higher Level of the I.B. program earns 3 credits.

Students who are granted AP or I.B. credit are still required to complete the College's full-time, eight-semester requirement.

PC operates on a two-semester calendar. Fall-semester classes begin in early September, and spring-semester classes begin in mid-January.

Off-Campus Programs

Providence College recognizes that a liberal arts education can be enriched through diverse intellectual and social experiences and encourages all of its students to study abroad. With a new Center for International Studies, there is renewed energy in the opportunities available for students to gain an international academic experience. Providence College is one of the few institutions to have study-abroad arrangements with both Oxford University and Cambridge University in England. Students may also study in Africa, Asia, Australia, New Zealand, Central and Latin America, Europe, and Russia. A few of the countries that are most popular among PC students are Spain, Italy, Ireland, and England. The Washington Semester is also an option for students, allowing them to enrich their education by spending one semester of academic study and experiential learning at American University in Washington, D.C.

Academic Facilities

The Phillips Memorial Library, which has received two national architectural awards for its design, is the center of intellectual activity at the College. PC's library is an electronic resource complete with radio-frequency technology, a wireless network, electronic classrooms, and the second-largest electronic database access in the state. The library has current holdings of 366,000 volumes in open stacks and seating accommodations for 750 students. Phillips Library also houses various faculty offices, reading and rare book rooms, archives, the Department of English, and the Office of Academic Services. The library is a member of the Consortium of Rhode Island Academic and Research Libraries, through which the resources of most of the libraries in the state are accessible to Providence College students. Located in Accinno Hall and Koffler Hall are the College's academic microcomputer laboratories, which serve the computer instruction and research needs of faculty members and students. The College's state-of-the-art science laboratories, computer workstations, and research facilities are located in the Albertus Magnus–Sowa–Hickey Science Complex. The Feinstein Academic Center is a newly renovated academic facility that is home to the Feinstein Institute for Public Service Program, the Liberal Arts Honors Program, and the Center for Teaching Excellence. The comprehensive new Smith Center for the Arts features a theater, a concert hall, a dance studio, a black-box theater, music practice rooms, and scenery and costume shops.

Costs

The total costs for the 2009–10 academic year are tuition, $32,320, and room and board, $11,360 (seven-day plan). Books, travel, and personal supplies are estimated to cost $800.

Financial Aid

Providence College's financial aid is distributed on the basis of demonstrated need and the student's ability to benefit from the educational opportunity the assistance offers. To apply for financial aid, candidates who are applying for Early Action must submit a College Scholarship Service PROFILE application by December 1 and the Free Application for Federal Student Aid (FAFSA) by February 1. Students applying for Regular Decision must submit both the College Scholarship Service PROFILE application and the FAFSA by February 1. Upon final determination of students' need, the Office of Financial Aid constructs aid packages consisting of work, loan, and grant assistance in accordance with federal regulations, the availability of funds, and institutional policy, as approved by the College's Financial Aid Advisory Committee. Sources of financial aid include Federal Work-Study Program awards, Federal Perkins Loans, Federal Pell Grants, Federal Supplemental Educational Opportunity Grants (FSEOG), Providence College grants-in-aid, Providence College Achievement Scholarships, and Merit Scholarships for highly qualified students who are invited into the Liberal Arts Honors Program.

Faculty

The faculty consists of 295 full-time professors and 96 special lecturers. The majority of PC instructors teach both undergraduate- and graduate-level courses; no graduate students or student assistants teach at either level. About 92 percent of the faculty members hold terminal degrees. Professors engage in advanced research, and frequently publish books and articles, but they are focused primarily on teaching and advising undergraduates; all students are assigned a faculty adviser in their major area. The student-faculty ratio is 12:1.

Student Government

The Student Congress represents the students in its emphasis upon lifestyles and student prerogatives. Its officers are elected annually by the entire student community, and representatives are elected by each class. The Student Congress has created the Providence College Bill of Rights, the most significant of its legislative actions. Student representatives are appointed annually by the Student Congress to all standing committees of the College. The Student Congress has primary responsibility for the allocation of $125,500 in student activity funds to support most student-run organizations.

Admission Requirements

The admission committee gives recognition to students with various talents, backgrounds, and geographic origins. Admission decisions are made without regard to race, color, sex, handicap, age, or national or ethnic origin. An estimate of the applicant's character and accomplishments by his or her college adviser in secondary school and an official transcript of the secondary school record should be sent to the College no later than November 1 for Early Action and January 15 for Regular Decision. The secondary school transcript should consist of courses of a substantially college-preparatory nature. Although individual cases may vary, the College highly recommends that a student complete 4 years of English; 4 of mathematics; 3 of one foreign language; 3 of science, with at least two laboratory courses; and 2 of social sciences. However, students who have been most competitive for admission in recent years have taken 4 years in all academic subject areas, taking advantage of honors or advanced-level courses that are available at their high school. Applicants are encouraged to submit letters of recommendation and evaluation from their secondary school teachers, especially from English teachers. Letters of recommendation from people who know the applicant personally and who have been involved in his or her scholastic development are most valuable.

Submission of standardized test scores is optional for students applying for admission. The academic review for admission at Providence College has always focused on each student's high school performance rather than standardized test results. This policy change allows each student to decide whether they wish to have their standardized test results considered as part of their application for admission. Students who choose not to submit SAT or ACT test scores are not penalized in the review for admission. Additional details about the test-optional policy can be found online at http://www.providence.edu/testoptionalpolicy.

Application and Information

Providence College accepts the Common Application. The deadline for receiving freshman applications for the September term is November 1 for Early Action and January 15 for Regular Decision. The deadline for receiving transfer applications is April 1 for the fall term and December 1 for the spring term. Further information may be obtained by contacting:

Providence College
549 River Avenue
Providence, Rhode Island 02918-0001
Phone: 401-865-2535
800-721-6444 (toll-free)
Fax: 401-865-2826
E-mail: pcadmiss@providence.edu
Web site: http://www.providence.edu

Harkins Hall, the administration building at Providence College.

PURCHASE COLLEGE, STATE UNIVERSITY OF NEW YORK

PURCHASE, NEW YORK

The College

Enrolling just over 4,000 students, Purchase College is a selective public coeducational college that serves both residential and commuter students. A Purchase College education is founded upon a unique vision that combines the energy and excitement of professional training in the performing and the visual arts with the intellectual traditions and spirit of discovery of the sciences and the humanities. The College emphasizes creativity, individual accomplishment, openness, and exploration of the world. A student's education at Purchase College culminates in a senior project that serves as an excellent springboard to a career or advanced academic study.

Purchase students come from around the world, and nearly all of them share a love of imagination, originality, and new experiences. The mix of students in the liberal arts and sciences and the performing and visual arts contributes to a campus that is wide open to diversity in perspectives and ambitions. The intersection of the arts and liberal arts and sciences also fosters an appreciation of the contributions of both scholarly and artistic achievement to make a humane culture.

The youngest of the SUNY system's sixty-four campuses, Purchase College has rapidly emerged and is increasingly recognized as a distinguished, imaginative, and dynamic institution for the study of the liberal arts and sciences and the visual and performing arts and for its service to the region and the state.

Purchase is primarily a full-time undergraduate institution, but as a public institution, Purchase College also promotes lifelong learning for students of all ages, backgrounds, and incomes through its School of Liberal Studies and Continuing Education, which offers a Bachelor of Arts in liberal studies as well as various credit and noncredit courses, certificate programs, and part-time degree programs.

In addition to its baccalaureate degrees, Purchase College also offers an M.F.A. in theater arts/stage design, visual arts, and dance and an M.A. in art history. The College also offers three postgraduate programs in music: Music Performance Certificate (one to two years of postbaccalaureate study), Master of Music, and Music Artist Diploma (one to two years of post-master's study).

Location

Built in the early 1970s on the 500-acre estate that was settled in 1734 by Judge Thomas Thomas, the Purchase campus combines the advantages of a semirural setting with proximity to the educational and cultural opportunities of Westchester County and New York City. As the only four-year public institution in Westchester, Purchase College is a cultural resource for the entire community. Approximately 250,000 people visit the campus each year to take advantage of its many programs and activities, including exhibits at the Neuberger Museum of Art, world-class performances at the Performing Arts Center, and public programs and lectures, such as the Royal and Shirley Durst Chair Lecture Series.

Majors and Degrees

Purchase College's liberal arts and sciences programs lead to Bachelor of Arts (B.A.) and Bachelor of Science (B.S.) degrees. The College offers a full range of disciplines through its two liberal arts schools: Humanities (art history, cinema studies, creative writing, drama studies, history, journalism, language and culture, literature, and philosophy) and Natural and Social Sciences (anthropology; biochemistry; biology; chemistry; economics; environmental studies; mathematics/computer science; media, society, and the arts; political science; psychology; and sociology). Students may also pursue premedicine or prelaw tracks. There are interdisciplinary programs in Asian studies, global black studies, Latin American studies, lesbian and gay studies, new media, and women's studies.

Purchase College offers professional conservatory training that leads to a Bachelor of Music degree; a Bachelor of Fine Arts (B.F.A.) degree in acting, dance, dramatic writing, film, stage design/technology, or visual arts; and a B.A. in arts management.

Academic Programs

Purchase College operates on a semester calendar. Students typically take 16 credits per semester in order to fulfill the minimum requirement of 120 hours for a bachelor's degree as well as the SUNY-mandated general education requirements. Most courses in liberal arts are 4 credits, as the College specializes in intensive study within the majors, and many courses include scheduled classwork in the arts, fieldwork, plenary sessions, and intensive tutorials.

Students in the liberal arts and sciences declare their major concentrations by the junior year, electing intensive course work that builds toward their senior projects. The senior project represents a culmination of their four years at Purchase and can take the form of a research paper, presentation, or original expression of thought and research (e.g., a work of fiction, poetry, or art or a multimedia presentation). The curriculum in each major is organized to build on disciplinary expertise, research, and writing skills, starting with the freshman year and culminating in the senior project. Senior projects in natural sciences are often published or copublished with a faculty member.

The senior project is a solid foundation for graduate study, professional school, or a career. For many Purchase students, internships in agencies, businesses, and corporations are also an important part of their educational experience that often leads to full-time employment.

Purchase College has some of the few conservatory training programs for the arts within the State University of New York System. Much of this training is provided by instructors who are also practicing professionals. Proximity to New York City gives access to these professionals and their respective art worlds, establishing a valuable network of contacts for undergraduate students. Professional job placement begins at an early stage, with special assistance from the active career development office. For example, some students occasionally interrupt their study program to work with a professional dance company or with a professional filmmaker.

Academic Facilities

The College's extraordinary facilities include the first building in the United States designed exclusively for the study and performance of dance; a large science research center; The

Performing Arts Center and its five theaters; and the Neuberger Museum, which has an outstanding collection of modern American art. Both the center and the museum play central roles in the curriculum and the student experience. There is also an exceptionally well-equipped physical education building; an increasing number of multimedia and computer classrooms; and a 160,000-square-foot visual arts building.

Costs

For 2008–09, tuition for undergraduate in-state residents was $4660 for the academic year; it was $10,920 for out-of-state students. Room and board (dormitory double room and full meal plan) were about $10,000. Books and supplies were estimated at $2300. There was also an applied music fee of $2312 per year for music majors. Costs are subject to change.

Financial Aid

Purchase College participates in all federal and state financial aid programs. All students who complete the Free Application for Federal Student Aid (FAFSA) receive some form of financial assistance, which may include low-interest student loans. It is strongly recommended that students file the FAFSA prior to April 1 in order to receive the maximum amount of financial aid for which they are eligible. Approximately 70 percent of all Purchase College undergraduates receive some type of financial assistance.

Scholarships based on merit only and scholarships based on both merit and need are available to qualified students.

Faculty

The Purchase College faculty is distinguished by depth of specialized knowledge as well as broad interdisciplinary interests, scholarly and professional activity, and dedication to undergraduate teaching. The liberal arts and sciences faculty includes prominent scholars in a variety of fields. More than 95 percent hold doctorates from prestigious schools, and several have won Guggenheim, Fulbright, NEH, and NEA awards, among others. The visual and performance arts faculty consists of leading teachers and practicing professionals in dance, film, music, theater, and visual arts.

Student Government

The Student Government Association, a campuswide organization, is made up of students elected by their peers. The organization is responsible for campus activities, sends representatives to faculty and administrative councils, and administers its own budget.

Admission Requirements

Applicants are considered by the Office of Admissions on an individual basis without regard to race, religion, geographic origin, or handicap. Major factors for admission consideration in the liberal arts and sciences programs are the high school and the academic records, including subjects studied, proficiency in English, test scores (SAT or ACT), and recommendations. All students write an application essay to demonstrate an appropriate fit with Purchase. The liberal arts program has become increasingly selective, and early application is encouraged. A rolling admission system is used, with selective deadlines in some programs.

In the visual and performing arts, students must demonstrate talent by means of an audition, interview, or portfolio review in addition to an assessment of their academic credentials. Because these programs are very competitive, early application is encouraged for both freshmen and transfers. Typically, auditions of conservatory candidates are completed by the end of March.

Application and Information

Students are urged to visit the campus for information sessions and open houses. For further information, students should contact:

Ms. Stephanie McCaine
Director of Admissions
Purchase College, State University of New York
735 Anderson Hill Road
Purchase, New York 10577-1400
Phone: 914-251-6300
Fax: 914-251-6314
E-mail: admission@purchase.edu
Web site: http://www.purchase.edu

A reason to cheer—graduation day at Purchase College.

QUEENS COLLEGE OF THE CITY UNIVERSITY OF NEW YORK

FLUSHING, NEW YORK

The College

Queens College (QC), with more than 15,500 undergraduates, is one of the largest of the four-year colleges in the City University of New York (CUNY) system. The College opened its doors in 1937 with the goal of offering a first-rate education to talented people of all backgrounds and financial means. Often referred to as "the jewel of the CUNY system," Queens College enjoys a national reputation for its liberal arts and sciences and preprofessional programs. Students come from more than 140 different nations; the result is an unusually rich education that gives Queens College graduates a competitive edge in today's global society.

The 77-acre campus is lined with trees surrounding grassy open spaces and a traditional quad. Some of the original Spanish-style stucco and tile buildings from the early 1900s still stand, including Jefferson Hall, which houses the beautiful Welcome Center. Powdermaker Hall, the major classroom building, has state-of-the-art technology throughout, and a $30-million renovation of the College's science labs is nearing completion. The entire campus has Wi-Fi capability and students may relax and meet friends in the spacious Student Union and the College's many cafés, lounges, and dining areas.

With the opening of the College's first residence hall, The Summit, in August 2009, Queens College shed its commuter school identity. It now offers students the option of enjoying all the benefits of living on campus. The low-rise facility provides individually climate-controlled single- and double-room accommodations arranged in suites with shared kitchen and lounge areas. It also has its own exercise facility.

The administration remains dedicated to making its many commuter students feel that QC is their home away from home. A Child Development Center, staffed by professionals, offers inexpensive child-care services to students with children. There are more than 100 clubs on campus, from the Accounting Honors Society and Alliance of Latin American Students to clubs for theater, fencing, environmental science, science fiction, and the fine arts. Queens, the only CUNY college that participates in Division II sports, sponsors twenty men's and women's teams and has some of the finest athletics facilities in the metropolitan area. Ongoing cultural events include readings by renowned authors such as Margaret Atwood, Toni Morrison, and Salman Rushdie; concerts by world-famous artists; and theater and dance performances. QC is home to the Godwin-Ternbach Museum, the only comprehensive museum in the borough of Queens, with art from antiquity to the present.

The College's centers and institutes serve students and the larger urban community by addressing society's most important challenges—such as cancer, AIDS, pollution, and racism—and exploring the heritages of the borough's many ethnic communities, including Asians, Greeks, Italians, and Jews.

Queens College has had a chapter of Phi Beta Kappa since 1950 (less than 10 percent of U.S. liberal arts colleges are members of Phi Beta Kappa, the nation's oldest and most respected undergraduate honors organization). In 1968, Queens College became a member of Sigma Xi, the national science honor society. The American Association of University Women includes Queens College in its list of approved colleges for membership.

Location

Queens College, located off Exit 24 of the Long Island Expressway, is in a residential area of Flushing and is easily accessible by public transportation. It is only 20 minutes from Manhattan, whose magnificent skyline overlooks the campus quad.

Majors and Degrees

The Bachelor of Arts degree is awarded in accounting, Africana studies, American studies, anthropology, art, art history, biology, Byzantine and modern Greek studies, chemistry, Chinese, communication arts and media, communication sciences and disorders, comparative literature, computer science, drama and theater, East Asian studies, economics, education (early childhood and elementary), English, environmental sciences, environmental studies, film studies, French, geology, German, Greek, Hebrew, history, home economics, Italian, Jewish studies, labor studies, Latin, Latin American area studies, linguistics, mathematics, music, neuroscience, philosophy, physics, political science and government, psychology, Russian, sociology, Spanish, studio art, theater-dance, urban studies, and women's studies.

The Bachelor of Arts program in secondary school teaching includes the following subject areas: Africana studies, anthropology, biology, chemistry, economics, English, French, geology, German, history, Italian, Latin American area studies, mathematics, physics, political science and government, sociology, Spanish, and urban studies.

The College also awards the Bachelor of Arts in interdisciplinary studies; an individualized Bachelor of Arts program; the Bachelor of Business Administration; the Bachelor of Fine Arts in studio art; the Bachelor of Music in instrumental or vocal performance studies; and the Bachelor of Science in applied social science, computer science, environmental sciences, geology, graphic design, nutrition and exercise sciences, and physical education.

The Departments of Chemistry, Computer Science, Philosophy, Physics, and Political Science and the Aaron Copland School of Music offer qualified undergraduates the opportunity to take combined bachelor's and master's degree programs.

Pre-engineering students can take advantage of a 3-2 transfer program through the physics department that offers admission to Columbia University after three years at QC. Following two years at Columbia, students graduate with a B.A. in physics from Queens and an engineering B.A. from Columbia.

Special interdisciplinary programs include Africana studies, American studies, business and liberal arts, business administration, Byzantine and modern Greek studies, Honors in Mathematics and Natural Sciences, Honors in the Humanities, Honors in the Social Sciences, Irish studies, Italian American studies, journalism, Latin American and Latino studies, and religious studies. Special programs and advisement are also available in accounting, pre-engineering, prelaw, and the pre–health professions.

Academic Programs

Queens College awards bachelor's and master's degrees in the arts and humanities, education, mathematics and the natural sciences, and social sciences. Certificate programs provide additional training in specialties in education, library science, and psychology. QC also participates in doctoral programs overseen by CUNY's graduate center; many of these programs involve lab work or clinical studies conducted on the Flushing campus.

Honors programs are central to the College's tradition of value and excellence, enhancing education by providing opportunities for faculty mentorship, advanced research, or other individualized projects. These programs create a community of learners in which students enjoy small classes, while still having access to QC's many resources and diverse student body. The emphasis is on discussion and projects rather than lectures.

Queens College is the only CUNY institution in the borough participating in the Macaulay Honors College, which supports gifted students with full tuition, a textbook allowance, free laptop, a $7500 grant over four years, and other benefits. A flagship program of the University, it provides an enhanced undergraduate education to academically gifted students. Since its inauguration in 2001, the Honors College has grown rapidly, drawing on the unique resources of CUNY and New York's cultural, scientific, government, and business communities to provide its students with a broad-based and challenging liberal arts education.

In addition, QC has its own multidisciplinary Freshman Honors Program and divisional honors programs in the humanities, math and natural sciences, and social sciences. Outstanding high school seniors may apply to become Queens College scholars. Prospective math teachers may qualify for scholarships and other incentives through QC's innovative math education program, TIME 2000. Business and Liberal Arts—designed for top-performing underclassmen regardless of their major—familiarizes students with basic business disciplines and offers internships sponsored by participating corporations.

The wide range of majors and interdisciplinary studies, combined with the award-winning Freshman Year Initiative program, encourages students to explore their interests and abilities to the fullest. In most cases, degree programs require the completion of 120 credits.

The Bachelor of Business Administration (B.B.A.) degree provides a solid business education that responds to the demand of employers for specific quantitative and technological skills. Students may choose from three majors: finance, international business, and actuarial studies. The B.B.A. also has an investments/chartered financial analyst track to prepare students for the CFA examination, the only such undergraduate program in New York.

The Adult Collegiate Education program, offered to students 25 and older, includes the option of obtaining college credit for life achievement. The Weekend College allows busy students to pursue their degrees by taking classes on Saturdays and Sundays.

Academic Facilities

Among the many centers where research and creativity are joined in the pursuit of knowledge is the Kupferberg Center for the Visual and Performing Arts, which brings together the College's academic departments in the arts (music, drama, art, and media studies), and its museums (the Godwin-Ternbach, the Queens College Art Center, and the Louis Armstrong House Museum). The center's venues include the 2,200-seat Colden Auditorium; the Goldstein Theatre, designed especially for the staging of experimental student productions; and the Aaron Copland School of Music facility, which includes thirty-five practice rooms and the 491-seat LeFrak Concert Hall. The College is also home to the Institute for Low-Temperature Physics, and the Speech and Hearing Center, which investigates communication disabilities and provides clinical experience for students of speech and hearing therapy.

Queens College administers the historic Louis Armstrong House Museum in Corona with its vast personal collection of Armstrong photographs, papers, recordings, and memorabilia that draws scholars and jazz fans from around the world. The Benjamin Rosenthal Library, with its soaring, light-filled atrium and art center, has more than 1 million print and electronic volumes.

Costs

For New York State residents, undergraduate tuition is $2300 per semester. For out-of-state and international students, undergraduate tuition is $415 per credit. In addition to tuition, there are various expenses each semester, such as student activity and technology fees.

Financial Aid

More than 50 percent of Queens College students receive need-based financial aid. The aid may include state and federal loans and grants, Tuition Assistance Program awards, Regents Scholarships, Federal Direct Student Loans, Federal Pell Grants, State Aid for Native Americans, and Federal Work-Study Program awards.

The Queens College Scholars Program offers a variety of merit-based scholarships to full-time freshmen, with awards of $2300 per year. Selection is competitive, and scholarships are awarded on the basis of the high school record, test scores (SAT and SAT Subject Tests), writing ability, letters of recommendation, and extracurricular activities. Scholarships are renewable with continued high academic achievement. Applicants who rank in or near the top 10 percent of their class and have a rigorous academic program, excellent grades, and minimum combined SAT (critical reading and math) scores of 1250 are encouraged to apply. The application deadline is December 15.

Faculty

The Queens College faculty consists of top scholars who are dedicated to teaching and research, and enjoy working in a diverse urban environment. Many are relatively new to campus; half were hired between 2002 and 2008.There are 637 full-time professors, almost 90 percent of whom have the terminal degree in their fields (not all fields offer doctorates); 64 percent have tenure. Many also teach in the doctoral programs at the CUNY Graduate Center. Faculty members have received numerous fellowships, awards, and research grants from such prestigious organizations as the National Science Foundation and the National Institutes of Health. In recent years, faculty members received two Guggenheim awards and two Fulbright grants. CUNY has recognized the excellence of the faculty by honoring 11 members with the title of Distinguished Professor in fields as diverse as chemistry, economics, English, history, and physics. Among the more widely known faculty members are scientist Steven Markowitz; historian Morris Rossabi; sociologist Stephen Steinberg; and poets Jeffrey Renard Allen, Nicole Cooley, and Kimiko Hahn.

Student Government

Through the Student Association, students at Queens run many services and activities that influence the daily operations of the College. Its elected officers and senators poll students regularly about relevant topics and sponsor such services as free legal advice, apartment and tutor referral, and voter registration. In addition, students constitute one third of the College's Academic Senate.

Admission Requirements

Queens College seeks to admit freshmen who have completed a strong college-preparatory program in high school with at least a B+ average. Admission is based on a variety of factors, including the applicant's high school grades, academic program, and SAT or ACT scores. Successful candidates have chosen a well-rounded program of study that includes academic course work in English (4 years), foreign language (3 years), math (3 years), lab science (2 years), and social studies (4 years).

The Search for Education, Elevation & Knowledge Program (SEEK) offers academic support, counseling, and financial assistance to motivated students who would not otherwise qualify for admission. The SEEK Program has its own admissions criteria, including financial need.

For earliest consideration, students should apply by January 1 for fall admission and by October 15 for spring admission.

Application and Information

The staff of the Undergraduate Office of Admissions is available to answer questions and give more information. To make an appointment for a tour or to meet with a counselor, students should contact:

Office of Admissions
Jefferson Hall
Queens College of the City University of New York
65-30 Kissena Boulevard
Flushing, New York 11367-1597
Phone: 718-997-5600
E-mail: admissions@qc.cuny.edu
Web site: http://www.qc.cuny.edu

A view of the Queens College quad, part of a 77-acre campus in New York City, where students from 140 nations receive a solid education for today's global society.

QUINNIPIAC UNIVERSITY

HAMDEN, CONNECTICUT

QUINNIPIAC
UNIVERSITY

The University

Quinnipiac offers four-year and graduate-level degree programs leading to careers in health sciences, business, communications, natural sciences, education, liberal arts, and law. A curriculum that combines a career focus with a globally oriented liberal arts background prepares graduates for the future, whether they start their careers right after commencement or opt to pursue advanced study.

Quinnipiac is coeducational and nonsectarian and currently enrolls 5,686 full-time undergraduates, 1101 full-time graduate and law students, and 971 part-time students in its undergraduate, graduate, professional, and continuing education programs. Twenty-five percent of the students are residents of Connecticut; the rest represent primarily the northeast corridor, in all a total of twenty-eight states and several countries. Quinnipiac is big enough to sustain a wide variety of people and programs but small enough to keep students from getting lost in the shuffle. Life on campus emphasizes students' personal, as well as academic, growth. The approximately seventy-five student organizations and extracurricular activities, including intramural and intercollegiate (NCAA Division I) athletics, give students a chance to exercise their talents, muscles, and leadership skills. The University has a student newspaper, TV station, and an FM radio station (WQAQ) and nineteen intercollegiate teams in men's baseball, basketball, cross-country, ice hockey, lacrosse, soccer, and tennis, and in women's basketball, competitive cheer, cross-country, field hockey, ice hockey, lacrosse, soccer, softball, tennis, track (indoor and outdoor), and volleyball. Teams compete in the Northeast Conference (NEC); men's and women's ice hockey teams are members in the ECAC.

The University has three distinct campus settings. The 250-acre Mount Carmel campus has fifty buildings including the Arnold Bernhard Library, academic facilities, an athletic and recreation center, and twenty-five residence halls of different styles, mainly for freshmen and sophomores, with traditional double and quad (4-person) rooms, suites, and multilevel suites with kitchens. About 95 percent of all freshmen and 75 percent of the total undergraduate population live in Quinnipiac housing. The nearby 250-acre York Hill campus includes the TD Bank Sports Center with twin 3,500-seat arenas for ice hockey and basketball; a new suite-style 1,800-bed residence halls for juniors and seniors; student center; and multilevel parking garage for 2,000 vehicles. Seniors may also live in University-owned houses or apartments. Just 4 miles away is the 104-acre North Haven campus with state-of-the-art facilities for graduate and upper division programs in the School of Health Sciences. All four buildings in the facility have been acquired from Anthem Blue Cross and there are plans for phased expansion for additional graduate programs as well as a proposed medical school.

The Athletic and Recreation Center includes a 24,000-square-foot recreation/fitness facility with a large free-weight room; an exercise machine center; aerobics studios; basketball, volleyball, and tennis courts; and a suspended indoor track. There are also lighted tennis courts, playing fields, and miles of scenic routes for running and biking.

Career Planning takes place in each of the schools with assistance from the deans' offices in health sciences, communications, education, business, and the college of arts and sciences. It begins with faculty advisement, along with career exploration, a strong focus on internships and clinical placements, exploration of various major and job fields, and exposure to prospective employers and job preparation. Approximately 30 percent of the undergraduate student population remains at Quinnipiac for their graduate degree in combined or direct entry majors, particularly in education, business, physical and occupational therapy, and physician assistant programs.

Graduate programs lead to the Master of Science degree in accounting, computer information systems, interactive communications, journalism, molecular and cell biology, and organizational leadership; the Master of Health Science in medical lab sciences, cardiovascular perfusion, pathologist assistant studies, and physician assistant studies; the Master of Science in Nursing in nurse practitioner studies; the Master of Business Administration; the Master of Business Administration in Health Care Management, the Master of Business Administration–Chartered Financial Analyst, and the Master of Arts in Teaching. The Quinnipiac University School of Law offers full-time and part-time programs leading to a J.D. degree or J.D./M.B.A. degree in combination with the School of Business. Several of the graduate degree programs are offered online or in a hybrid format.

Location

Situated at the foot of Sleeping Giant Mountain in Hamden, Connecticut, Quinnipiac provides the best of the suburbs and the city. The University is only 8 miles from New Haven, 30 minutes from Hartford (the state capital), and less than 2 hours from New York City and Boston. Bordering the campus is the 1700-acre Sleeping Giant State Park, for walking and hiking. The free campus shuttle takes students to shopping and restaurants in nearby Hamden and North Haven, plus to New Haven, where they can visit the acclaimed Yale Center for British Art, attend a performance at the Schubert or Long Wharf Theater (which hosts productions by Quinnipiac's Theater Department), find great restaurants, and have easy access to Metro North and Amtrak at the New Haven train station.

Majors and Degrees

The School of Health Sciences grants bachelor's degrees in athletic training/sports medicine, biomedical science, diagnostic imaging, microbiology/molecular biology, nursing, occupational therapy (5½-year entry-level master's), physical therapy (6- or 7-year entry-level doctorate), and physician assistant studies (6-year freshman entry-level master's). Students who wish to prepare for entry into medical, dental, chiropractic, veterinary, or other medical schools work with a premed adviser and take classes that prepare them to sit for the various entrance exams.

The School of Business (accredited by AACSB International) offers bachelor's degree programs in accounting, advertising, biomedical marketing, entrepreneurship, finance, information systems management, international business, management, and marketing. The school also offers a five-year combined-degree program in which students may be awarded the B.S. degree in business and a graduate degree in accounting, business administration, or computer information systems (M.S. or M.B.A.).

The College of Arts and Sciences offers bachelor's degree programs in biochemistry, biology, chemistry, computer science, criminal justice, English, gerontology, history, interactive digital design, legal studies (paralegal), liberal studies, mathematics, political science, psychobiology, psychology, social services, sociology, Spanish, and theater. Students can also design their own majors. Students can also continue their study in graduate programs in business, law, journalism, or interactive communications.

The School of Communications offers undergraduate majors in communications; film, video, and interactive media; journalism; and public relations; and graduate programs in journalism and interactive communications.

The School of Education's five-year program for undergraduates provides certification for teaching elementary and secondary grades through a B.A./Master of Arts in Teaching (M.A.T.) program (accredited by NCATE).

Academic Programs

All degree programs at Quinnipiac University are offered through one of the five academic schools. The academic year consists of two 15-week fall and spring semesters and two summer sessions. All baccalaureate candidates are required to complete the University Curriculum, which consists of up to 46 of the 120 semester hours of credit generally needed for graduation at the bachelor's degree level. The foundation of the University Curriculum is three university seminars, which focus on the broad theme of community: individual, national, and global in scope. The Writing Across the Curriculum initiative (WAC) stresses the improvement in writing skills in all subject areas. The University honors program addresses the needs and interests of the most academically talented and committed students. Academically talented students are identified during the admission process and are invited to participate in the University honors program. Approximately 60 full-time freshmen enter the honors program each fall.

Advanced placement, credit, or both are given for appropriate scores on Advanced Placement tests and CLEP general and subject examinations as well as for scores of 4 or higher in the International Baccalaureate higher-level subjects.

Off-Campus Programs

Students can study abroad in a variety of countries. Most students choose a study-abroad option in their sophomore year. Students in any of the five undergraduate schools can also get hands-on experience in their field through off-campus internships. Academic credit is available for internships and affiliations, which are often part of degree requirements.

Academic Facilities

Academic life focuses on the Bernhard Library. This attractive facility provides individual carrels and small rooms for group study and is open 24/7 during the fall and spring semesters. A wireless network provides access to automated library systems and extensive Web-based resources.

Quinnipiac University was identified as one of the top ten most-wired campuses in the country by *PC Magazine* in January 2007. All incoming students must purchase a University-recommended laptop. A help desk offers support to the laptop program.

The multimedia and video laboratories in the Ed McMahon Mass Communications Center each have the latest Mac workstations and software. The computer cluster in the Financial Technology Center at the School of Business is a high-tech, simulated trading floor providing students with the opportunity to access real-time financial data, conduct interactive trading simulations, and develop financial models in preparation for careers in finance.

The Lender School of Business has satellite capabilities and the Ed McMahon Mass Communications Center, which contains a state-of-the-art, fully digital, high-definition TV production studio; audio production, print journalism, and desktop publishing laboratories; and a news technology center.

The Graduate and Health Sciences Center on the North Haven campus provides state-of-the-art facilities for the health sciences programs in diagnostic imaging, nursing, occupational therapy, physical therapy, physician assistant studies, and radiologist assistant studies. In addition to a breathtaking location and expansive exterior and interior spaces, there are specialized facilities and equipment for the various health sciences disciplines, such as movement study/motion analysis and biomechanics labs; the ergonomics and assistive technology lab; a model adaptive apartment; orthopedics lab; several rehabilitative sciences labs; CT scan, MRI, radiography, ultrasound, and mammography facilities; and the latest clinical skills simulation labs for adults and pediatric/neonatal patients including an intensive care unit, physical diagnosis lab, physical exam suite, and health assessment labs, which duplicate care in an outpatient primary care setting.

Costs

The basic 2009–10 cost was $44,780, of which tuition and fees (12–16 credits per semester) were $32,400, and room and board averaged $12,380. Other expenses, estimated at $1200 per year, included books, laboratory, and course fees associated with specific courses, and personal travel expenses.

Financial Aid

Quinnipiac designs financial aid packages to include need-based grants and merit-based scholarships that do not have to be repaid, plus self-help financial aid programs such as federal and University-based work study, and loans. Beginning with students applying for fall 2011, Quinnipiac will use the CSS Profile form plus the Free Application for Federal Student Aid (FAFSA) to determine need. Transfer students are eligible for the same need-based financial aid consideration as first-time freshmen.

Faculty

The faculty is characterized by its teaching competence and outstanding academic qualifications. Of the 290 full-time faculty members, 75 percent have earned a Ph.D. or the appropriate terminal degree in their field. The faculty also includes a number of part-time teachers who are practicing professionals and experts in their fields. Classes are taught by these scholars and professionals and not by student instructors, and a low student-faculty ratio promotes close associations among faculty members and students.

Student Government

The Student Government is the student legislative body of Quinnipiac. It represents student opinion, promotes student welfare, supervises student organizations, appropriates funds for student groups, and provides voting student representation on the Board of Trustees.

Admission Requirements

Quinnipiac seeks students from a broad range of backgrounds. On average, freshman students have a 3.4 GPA or better average in college preparatory courses (transfer students generally have a 2.5 GPA or better), rank in the top 25 percent of their high school class, and have an average combined score of 1120 on the SAT (critical reading plus math). Visits to the campus for either an interview, open house, group information session, or a campus tour are strongly encouraged. Transfer students are welcome to make an appointment to discuss requirements and the transfer of credit from previous institutions. Quinnipiac sponsors four open house programs during the year and several Saturday morning information sessions followed by a campus tour.

Application and Information

Quinnipiac generally receives between 14,000 and 15,000 applications for admission and admits about 60 percent, to enroll an incoming class of 1,600 freshmen and 200 transfer students. Quinnipiac has a rolling admission policy for its undergraduate programs and therefore recommends that freshman applicants submit their application materials starting early in the fall of their senior year and well before the deadline of February 1. Students applying to the physical therapy, nursing, and physician assistant studies programs should submit their applications by November 1. Applications begin to be reviewed as soon as they are complete, and the University begins notifying students of decisions in early January. For most programs, a completed application consists of a Quinnipiac application form; a transcript of completed high school courses, including grades for the first quarter of the senior year; a score report for either the SAT or ACT; a personal statement (250-word minimum essay); letter(s) of recommendation; and the application fee: $45. Quinnipiac is a member of the Common Application and recommends that applications be submitted online. Students placed on a waiting list are notified of any openings by June 1. When reviewing applications, the University uses the results of the critical reading and the mathematics sections of the SAT and/or the composite score on the ACT for admission and scholarship purposes. Transfer students must forward a transcript of college course work undertaken. Quinnipiac subscribes to the May 1 Candidates Reply Date Agreement. For information about full-time undergraduate study, students should contact:

Office of Undergraduate Admissions
Quinnipiac University
Hamden, Connecticut 06518-1940
Phone: 203-582-8600
800-462-1944 (toll-free)
Fax: 203-582-8906
E-mail: admissions@quinnipiac.edu
Web site: http://www.quinnipiac.edu

For information regarding transfer and part-time study:

Office of Transfer and Part-time Admissions
Quinnipiac University
Hamden, Connecticut 06518-1940
Phone: 203-582-8612
Fax: 203-582-8906
E-mail: transferadmissions@quinnipiac.edu

RAMAPO COLLEGE OF NEW JERSEY

MAHWAH, NEW JERSEY

The College

Ramapo College of New Jersey has been recognized by the State Legislature as New Jersey's "public liberal arts college." Offering a diverse student body and the educational ambience associated with liberal arts colleges, Ramapo has fulfilled its promise as one of the more distinguished institutions of moderate size. In recognition of Ramapo College of New Jersey's strong commitment to character-building programs, the John Templeton Foundation, which publishes a reference guide for students, families, and high schools, named Ramapo to its Honor Roll. The Honor Roll program recognizes and promotes colleges and universities that emphasize character building as an integral part of the college experience.

Ramapo offers bachelor's degrees in the arts, business, humanities, social sciences, and sciences as well as in professional studies that include nursing and social work. In addition, Ramapo offers programs leading to teacher certification at the elementary, middle school, and secondary levels. The student body reflects the diversity of the regions served by the College, including eighteen states and fifty-two countries as of fall 2009. This diversity, the talents of the faculty, the expectations the College has of its students, and the proximity of the College to some of the world's major multinational organizations give Ramapo an edge in meeting its objective of preparing students of all ages for an increasingly interdependent and multicultural world.

Ramapo College takes pride in four distinctive features that enhance each student's education: concern for student development in and out of the classroom, an exemplary faculty committed to a curricular emphasis on the international and multicultural dimensions of all fields of study, an interdisciplinary orientation in its philosophy and programs, and a collaborative association with local corporations, communities, and educational institutions in the development of experiential educational opportunities and other new ventures both nationally and globally.

The fall 2009 undergraduate enrollment was 5,353 men and women. During the academic year, the campus is alive with exciting cultural events, such as music festivals, plays, art exhibits, and film and lecture series. The Robert A. Scott Student Center, with recreation rooms, lounges, and club offices, is the hub of on-campus activity. Students take an active part in planning the calendar of events for the College community. The campus contains attractive residential units housing more than 2,900 students. An 116,684-square-foot sports and recreation center opened in fall 2004, and Laurel Hall, a new 432-bed dormitory, opened in fall 2006. In addition, a sports complex has twelve lighted tennis courts; baseball, soccer, and softball fields; and a track. The gym is equipped with a full-size basketball court, an indoor pool, and a fitness center. At Ramapo, sports facilities are available for all students, not just the varsity athletes, who participate in twenty-two intercollegiate sports in one of the most challenging NCAA Division III conferences in the country. The College offers a rewarding blend of academic, social, and cultural experiences in the students' daily routine.

In addition to bachelor's degrees, the College offers the Master of Arts in Liberal Studies, the Master of Science in Educational Technology, and the Master of Science in Nursing.

Location

Ramapo College's barrier-free campus, more than 300 acres in size, is located in the foothills of the Ramapo Mountains in Mahwah, New Jersey, just 25 miles from New York City and all of its cultural advantages.

Majors and Degrees

Ramapo College offers programs of study leading to the Bachelor of Arts degree in American studies, communication arts, contemporary arts, economics, environmental studies, history, international business, international studies, law and society, literature, music, political science, psychology, social science, sociology, Spanish language studies, theater, and visual arts. The Bachelor of Science degree is awarded in accounting, allied health, biochemistry, bioinformatics, biology, biology/physical therapy track, biology/physician assistant track, business administration (including finance, management, and marketing), chemistry, clinical laboratory sciences, computer science, engineering physics, environmental science, information systems, integrated science studies, mathematics, and psychology. The Bachelor of Social Work and Bachelor of Science in Nursing degrees are also offered.

Ramapo also offers state-approved teacher education programs to train and certify teachers. Students seeking teacher certification take a sequence of professional education courses in subjects relating to elementary, middle school, junior high, and senior high curricula. Subjects include, but are not limited to, art, biology, business, chemistry, drama, earth science, elementary education, English, foreign languages, mathematics, music, physical science, physics, and social studies.

Academic Programs

Each course at Ramapo is offered through one of five academic schools. These schools are relatively small groupings of faculty members, organized around individual themes considered to be important and useful areas of study.

The five schools include the Anisfield School of Business, American and International Studies, Contemporary Arts, Social Science and Human Services, and Theoretical and Applied Science. Each student is associated with one of these schools while at Ramapo. This association brings the student in contact with others who have the same or similar academic interests and provides the student with easy access to academic advisement and to the courses needed to satisfy degree requirements.

Academic Facilities

A construction boom during recent years has resulted in the completion of the Bill Bradley Sports and Recreation Center, with a main arena of 1,516 bleacher seats and 914 floor seats, a skybox, a fitness center, a jogging track, and a climbing wall; the Angelica and Russ Berrie Center for Performing and Visual Arts that houses performance theaters, art galleries, and specialized spaces devoted to fine arts, computer art, photography, theater, dance, and music; residence facilities that include a suite-style residence hall, a townhouse-style apartment complex, and two traditional-style residence halls; and newly renovated classrooms and computer labs. A five-story academic facility to house the Anisfield School of Business opened in the fall 2007 semester. Groundbreaking for a new 1,787-square-foot Sustainability Education Center commenced in October 2007, with completion targeted for the fall 2009 semester.

Costs

Full-time tuition and fees in 2009–10 were $11,416 for New Jersey residents and $19,098 for out-of-state students. The combined cost of tuition and fees was $356.75 per credit for New Jersey residents and $5496.85 for out-of-state students. Other charges, depending on circumstances, included $10,590 per year for room and board, and a parking fee of $200 per year. Books and supplies cost about $1200 per year.

Financial Aid

Most financial aid is awarded on the basis of a student's financial need. To qualify for aid at Ramapo, students must complete the Free Application for Federal Student Aid (FAFSA). A student should apply for financial aid prior to March 1 to receive preferential consideration. Federal Perkins Loans, Federal Pell Grants, and Federal Work-Study Program funds are vital parts of the College financial aid program. New Jersey residents should also apply for a state-supported tuition-aid grant. In addition, Ramapo College offers scholarships for high-achieving incoming freshman students. Merit awards are offered for eight semesters as long as the student maintains the required grade point average. New student applicants are automatically considered for these scholarships provided they apply by December 15. Continuing students not receiving an initial scholarship award may apply for additional merit awards based on their academic achievement at the College through the Ramapo College Foundation.

Faculty

Ramapo College has 434 full- and part-time faculty members as of fall 2009. Most have been at the College for a number of years and have played a significant role in shaping the College and building strong academic programs. Faculty members have been recruited principally for their effectiveness as teachers of undergraduate students. The College believes it has a distinguished faculty in this regard. Of the full-time faculty members teaching academic courses, 95 percent have a doctoral or equivalent final degree. Their graduate research training—from Ivy League institutions, from the great state universities of the nation, and from universities abroad—as well as their professional experience indicate that faculty members possess high quality and diverse experience in the subject matter of their courses.

Student Government

There is an active student government. Each spring, students are elected to this body. The group meets on a weekly basis to discuss any issues that it feels affect the welfare of the student body. Executive officers of the student government meet regularly with the College president and participate actively on committees of the Board of Trustees. Each year students elect a student trustee and student trustee alternate. A member of the Faculty Assembly is designated as liaison to the group so students and others are aware of issues being discussed by the faculty. The president of the Student Government Association makes presentations to both the Faculty Assembly and the trustees at their regular meetings. Students also participate actively in the governance of the College's schools as members of the unit councils. It is here that students have the greatest opportunity to influence decisions on personnel and academic programs.

Admission Requirements

High school seniors generally are expected to have completed a minimum of 18 academic units (although most have more), distributed as follows: 4 units of English, 3 units of social studies/history, 3 units of mathematics (including algebra, algebra II, and geometry), 3 units of science (including 3 of laboratory science), 2 units of a foreign language, and 3 units of academic electives. In addition, students applying from high school must take the SAT or the ACT and have their test scores sent to Ramapo.

Admission of candidates is made on the basis of the academic record, SAT or ACT scores, a school counselor's evaluation, and evidence of motivation and community and school contributions. Rank in the top quarter of the student's secondary school class is expected. Transfer students are also admitted. Deferred admission is possible.

Immediate Decision Day (IDD), Ramapo College of New Jersey's antidote to the stress of the college selection and application process, is an opportunity to apply and receive a notice of acceptance in just one day. At least two weeks before the appointed day, high school seniors submit their applications and supporting materials, then at IDD they have an admissions interview and receive a decision notice, all on the same day.

On the day of their visit, students and their families receive information about the College, tour the campus (including the residence halls), attend a class, and then have lunch in the student dining hall. They also interview individually with an admissions officer. At the end of the day, students receive the College's decision regarding their application. Immediate Decision Days are scheduled in the fall semester.

The College hosts open house programs during the fall and spring that give students and their families the opportunity to learn about academic programs, admissions, and financial aid; to meet faculty and staff members and students; and to tour the campus. Students are encouraged to visit during these special events. Weekday tours of the campus are available as well and personal interviews are available during the Immediate Decision Days in the fall. Interested students should contact the Office of Admissions at 201-684-7300 or 7301, or visit http://www.ramapo.edu for further details about campus visits.

Application and Information

Students may enter in September or January. Freshmen are encouraged to apply during the fall of their senior year. Applications for the freshman year are accepted until March 1. Applications from transfer students are accepted until May 1. Applying for admission as a matriculating (degree-seeking) student involves completing an application, having the high school and college (if a transfer student) forward transcripts, and submitting a $60 nonrefundable application fee to the admissions office. Students are encouraged to apply online at http://www.ramapo.edu. Admission decisions are made on a rolling basis. The College Board Candidates Reply Date of May 1 is used for confirming an offer of admission.

For a viewbook, application forms, and additional information, including current costs, students should contact:

Director of Admissions
Ramapo College of New Jersey
505 Ramapo Valley Road
Mahwah, New Jersey 07430
Phone: 201-684-7300 or 7301
E-mail: admissions@ramapo.edu
Web site: http://www.ramapo.edu

The Russ and Angelica Berrie Center for the Performing and Visual Arts on the campus of Ramapo College of New Jersey.

REED COLLEGE

PORTLAND, OREGON

The College

For its 1,481 students and 133 faculty members, Reed College is foremost an intellectual community. Since classes began in 1911, Reed has attracted students with a high degree of self-discipline and a genuine enthusiasm for academic work and intellectual challenge. Reed comprises a diverse student body; more than four fifths of Reed's students come from outside the Northwest, with 25 percent from the Northeast and 8 percent from outside the United States. A quarter of Reed's incoming students are members of historically underrepresented ethnic groups.

Campus social opportunities are open to all, with no closed clubs or organizations; there are no sororities or fraternities at Reed. Community life is full of activity and variety with more than seventy student organizations. Although there are competitive club sports at Reed, such as rugby, soccer, and Ultimate (Frisbee), there are no varsity athletic teams. Fitness and the development of lifelong skills take precedence over competition.

Location

Reed's 119-acre wooded campus is located in a quiet, residential section of southeast Portland. The nearby ocean and mountains of the Pacific Northwest provide a balance to the social and cultural offerings of the greater Portland metropolitan area.

Majors and Degrees

Reed awards the Bachelor of Arts degree in a wide variety of fields, based on work in traditional departments or in interdisciplinary combinations. Students may select from the following majors: American studies, anthropology, art, biochemistry and molecular biology, biology, chemistry, chemistry-physics, Chinese literature, Chinese studies, classics, classics-religion, dance-theater, economics, English literature, environmental studies, French literature, general literature, German literature, history, history-literature, international and comparative policy studies, linguistics, literature-theater, mathematics, mathematics-economics, mathematics-physics, music, philosophy, physics, political science, psychology, religion, Russian literature, sociology, Spanish literature, and theater.

Students may also design additional interdisciplinary majors. The approval of such special programs, which link two or more disciplines, is reviewed by the student's adviser and the departments concerned.

Reed offers several combined 3-2 programs, which allow the student to earn both a bachelor's degree from Reed and a professional degree from the cooperating institution. Science programs and institutions include engineering (California Institute of Technology, Columbia University, and Rensselaer Polytechnic Institute), computer science (University of Washington), and environmental sciences (Duke University). The College also has a combined program in fine arts (Pacific Northwest College of Art).

Academic Programs

Hallmarks of academic life at Reed include the small-group conference method of teaching and its reliance on active student participation, a de-emphasis of grades, a yearlong interdisciplinary humanities program, and an integrated academic program that balances the breadth of traditional course content and distribution requirements with flexibility in designing an in-depth senior thesis. The development of skills in preparation for a life of learning takes precedence over the mere memorization of facts. In addition to fulfilling the requirements for the major, taking the humanities course, and writing the senior thesis, students must satisfy a distributional requirement, consisting of two core classes from each of the following academic groups: literature, philosophy, and the arts; history, social sciences, and psychology; the natural sciences; and math, foreign language, logic, and linguistics. Students must also take two classes from one other department outside their major course of study.

Off-Campus Programs

Reed participates in domestic exchange programs with Howard University in Washington, D.C.; Sarah Lawrence College in New York; and Sea Education Association in Massachusetts. In addition, Reed provides study-abroad opportunities for students in Germany (University of Munich, Tübingen University, Freie University), Russia (ACTR Russian Language, Middlebury School in Russia, National Theater Institute of Moscow, Smolny College at St. Petersburg University), Hungary (Budapest Semester in Mathematics), France (Université de Rennes II Haute Bretagne, Université de Paris), Spain (Hamilton College's Madrid Center, Middlebury School in Spain, University of Santiago de Compostela, University of Barcelona), Greece (College Year in Athens), Italy (Intercollegiate Centers for Classical Studies in Rome and Sicily, Florence Center of Syracuse University, Sarah Lawrence College Foreign Program in Florence), England (Sarah Lawrence College Foreign Programs in London Theater and at Wadham College at Oxford University, University of East Anglia, Sussex University, University of Nottingham), Ireland (Trinity College at the University of Dublin, University College Cork), Israel (Hebrew University), Egypt (American University in Cairo), Morocco (Al Akhawayn University), China (East China Normal University in Shanghai, Capital Normal University in Beijing, Fujian Normal University in Fuzhou), Costa Rica (Organization for Tropical Studies, University of Costa Rica), South Africa (Organization for Tropical Studies), Ecuador (Ecuador Program), and Argentina (University of Buenos Aires/FLASCO). Students may also arrange independent study plans in consultation with appropriate faculty members, the director for off-campus studies, and the registrar.

Academic Facilities

Students have access to Reed's substantial library collection (600,967 volumes, 2,700 periodicals, and 340,000 government documents) by searching the online catalog in the library or from any computer on the campus network. Through its participation in PORTALS (Portland Area Library System) and Summit, a union catalog of Oregon and Washington academic libraries, Reed provides online access to other library catalogs and databases. Students may borrow materials directly from academic libraries in the Portland area, and they have access to collections worldwide through interlibrary loan. In addition, the Reed library accommodates a first-rate art gallery, a language lab, and a music listening facility. The Reed library is open 18 hours most days and 24 hours a day during examinations.

Computer technology is highly developed at Reed and widely used for instruction, research, and communication by all members of the College community. A state-of-the-art campus network links all residence halls, classrooms, laboratories, offices, and the library to one another and to the global Internet. The Educational Technology Center houses more than 100 computers and a variety of other teaching and technology resources that are used by students and faculty and staff members. The science laboratories at Reed are among the best equipped of any undergraduate college in the United States. These include the A. A. Knowlton Laboratory of Physics, the Arthur F. Scott Laboratory of Chemistry, and the L. E. Griffin Memorial Biology Building, where a recent $10-million renovation includes improved student thesis space, a tiered-seating classroom, and new teaching labs. Reed's research nuclear reactor (the only such reactor in the country that is staffed primarily by undergraduates) and radiochemistry lab are actively used for student research, instruction, and training. For those interested in the arts, the campus houses studio art facilities that recently saw a $2-million expansion, performing arts facilities, twenty instrumental practice rooms, a computer music laboratory, a recording system, and an 800-seat auditorium. Other popular facilities include a radio station and a modern sports center. In fall 2008, Reed opened five new residence halls, which enable 75 percent of students to live on campus.

Costs

Tuition for 2009–10 was $39,440, and room and board were $10,250. The student body fee was $260, bringing the yearly total cost to approximately $49,950. The cost of books and incidental expenses averages $2000.

Financial Aid

About half of the Reed student body receives financial assistance from the College. A full need-based financial aid program makes Reed accessible to students from a wide range of economic backgrounds. The College guarantees to meet the full demonstrated need of all continuing students in good academic standing who complete their financial aid applications on time. Reed's own funds are the primary source of grants to students. The College budgeted more than $18 million for this purpose in 2009–10. Reed also administers federal and state grants as well as federally subsidized loan programs. Campus employment and work-study programs are available. The size of a financial aid award is based solely upon analysis of the student's need. The average amount awarded to students receiving financial aid in 2009–10 was $33,090, which includes grants, loans, and work opportunities.

Faculty

All classes at Reed are taught by professors, about 90 percent of whom hold the highest degree in their field. The average class has 15 students. Reed students point to the opportunity to work closely with faculty members as one of the great benefits of a Reed education. Reed faculty members point to the opportunity to work with students who are serious scholars as one of the great benefits of teaching at Reed. Faculty members commit themselves primarily to teaching, with scholarly and scientific research furthering this primary goal; they view students as partners in learning, often serving as coauthors and coinvestigators on professional papers and research projects. This close association is due, in large part, to a 10:1 student-faculty ratio and the one-on-one relationship between thesis adviser (a professor) and student during the senior year.

Student Government

The Student Senate is the central body in student governance. The Senate consists of the student body president, vice president, and 8 student representatives, all elected by the students. Its two primary functions are to allocate student body funds and to represent student interests and concerns to the faculty, administration, and Board of Trustees. The Senate distributes approximately $40,000 each semester to the many student organizations on campus. As agreed under the community constitution, students participate fully in discussions and decisions on a wide variety of issues. The Student Committee on Academic Policy and Planning participates in debate about the curriculum at Reed; many other committees, from the Library Board to the Reactor Committee, have substantial student input. The Senate and student body president make all student appointments to such committees.

Admission Requirements

Reed welcomes applications from freshman and transfer candidates who are genuinely committed to the pursuit of a liberal arts education and a rigorous academic program. Those applicants are admitted who, in the view of the Admission Committee, are most likely to become successful members of and contribute significantly to the Reed community. The College is committed to maintaining a student body distinguished by its intellectual passion, yet diversified in its range of backgrounds, interests, and talents.

Admission decisions are based on many integrated factors, but academic accomplishments and talents are given the greatest weight in the selection process. A strong secondary school preparation, including honors and advanced courses where available, improves a student's chances for admission. Such a program usually includes 4 years of English and 3 to 4 years of mathematics (through precalculus), science, foreign language, and history or social studies. Given the wide variation in high school programs and quality, however, there are no fixed requirements for secondary school courses. Applicants are expected to have obtained a secondary school diploma prior to enrollment, although exceptions are occasionally made. There are no "cutoff points" for high school or college grades or for test scores.

Reed recognizes the qualities of character—in particular, motivation, intellectual curiosity, individual responsibility, and social consciousness—as important considerations in the selection process, beyond a demonstrated commitment to academic excellence. Thus, the Admission Committee looks for students whose accomplishments and interests in various fields of endeavor will contribute to the overall liveliness of the Reed community. Personal interviews, either on or off campus, are not a requirement in the admission process but are strongly recommended whenever possible. Applications for early decision should be submitted by November 15 (Option I) or December 20 (Option II), regular freshman admission by January 15, and transfer candidates by March 1.

Application and Information

The Office of Admission is open Monday through Friday from 8:30 a.m. until 5 p.m. (Pacific time) all year, except for major holidays. Students may apply online at http://www.reed.edu/apply/apply_reed.html. For further information or to arrange a campus tour, overnight stay, information session, or interview, students should contact:

Office of Admission
Reed College
3203 Southeast Woodstock Boulevard
Portland, Oregon 97202-8199
Phone: 503-777-7511
800-547-4750 (toll-free)
Fax: 503-777-7553
E-mail: admission@reed.edu
Web site: http://www.reed.edu/

Shooting pool in the Pool Hall.

THE RESTAURANT SCHOOL AT WALNUT HILL COLLEGE

PHILADELPHIA, PENNSYLVANIA

The School

The Restaurant School at Walnut Hill College was established in 1974 and is dedicated to inspiring the future of the restaurant and hotel industry through training that is dynamic, timely, and insightful, with a commitment of service to its students. The Restaurant School at Walnut Hill College combines both intensive classroom training and practical experience: students use their knowledge while they learn.

A student's education is cultivated by the College's philosophy that hands-on training is an essential part of education. This approach has multiple benefits—it enhances learning abilities, creates marketable skills and experience for a resume, brings education to life, and, most importantly, puts the student at the center of it all.

The Restaurant School at Walnut Hill College is accredited by the Accrediting Commission of Career Schools and Colleges of Technology, certified for veteran's training by the Veterans Administration, approved by the United States Department of Justice to grant student visas, and recognized as a Professional Management Development Partner of the Educational Foundation of the National Restaurant Association.

There is a diverse population at the Restaurant School at Walnut Hill College, with students coming from throughout the United States and abroad and ranging in age from the high school graduate to the adult who wants to change careers.

Whether it is a celebrity chef's cooking demonstration, dinner and a tour at a notable restaurant or hotel, or a winery tour and tasting, students at the Restaurant School are exposed to the very best Philadelphia has to offer. There are activities and weekly special events that are sponsored by student clubs. The Student Culinary Team has been the winner of several major competitions in recent years—both nationally and internationally. Activities are both educational and fun, combining opportunities to learn and to establish camaraderie and professional development. Events are listed in the student newsletter and monthly calendar.

Location

Philadelphia is a great place to live and learn. As the fourth-largest city in the United States, Philadelphia has much to offer and is a city of firsts—the first public library, the first college, and the first zoo—all in a first-class city.

The Restaurant School at Walnut Hill College is located in the University City section of Philadelphia, neighboring both the University of Pennsylvania and Drexel University. Located just across the Schuylkill River from Center City, University City has a wonderful college-town ambiance. Restaurants, museums, shops, and theaters abound, with local merchants offering discounts to students. The Amtrak train station is within walking distance of the campus, and the airport is 20 minutes away by car.

Center City is located just minutes from campus. Here, students find a bustling shopping and business district, complete with an award-winning restaurant row, luxury hotels, and exclusive boutiques.

Diversity abounds in this city of neighborhoods, including Chinatown, complete with exotic restaurants and shops; South Philadelphia, with its famed Italian market; and the ever-eclectic South Street, with blocks of restaurants, galleries, shops, and entertainment—not to mention the Historic District, which was the birthplace of the nation, and a waterfront that features an exciting nightlife.

Philadelphia is rich in culture and heritage. Students find world-class art and science museums, theaters that feature major Broadway shows and renowned regional production, and music, which includes everything from jazz to pop to the internationally acclaimed Philadelphia Orchestra.

Majors and Degrees

The College offers associate and bachelor's degrees in four program majors: hotel management (101 A.S. and 202 B.S. credits), restaurant management (101 A.S. and 202 B.S. credits), culinary arts (103 A.S. and 201 B.S. credits), and pastry arts (106 A.S. and 199 B.S. credits). Each major provides students with a broad-based knowledge of the overall workings of a fine restaurant or hotel. Beyond that, the programs prepare students with the day-to-day skills and specific knowledge required as they develop careers as restaurant managers, chefs, pastry chefs, hotel managers, or restaurateurs. In partnership with the Educational Foundation of the National Restaurant Association, the College's curriculum includes up to twelve nationally recognized food-service and hospitality-management courses. Upon successful completion of the courses and the certification exam, students receive national certification.

Academic Programs

All students must successfully complete twelve 10-week terms to be awarded a Bachelor of Science degree or six 10-week terms to be awarded an Associate of Science degree in their field of study. Each academic year consists of three terms. A student must fulfill the required term hours in a major as well as the basic requirements of the core curriculum. All students are required to participate in special service programs prior to graduating.

Off-Campus Programs

The Restaurant School at Walnut Hill College was one of the first schools in the country to offer a travel experience as part of a curriculum. Culinary and pastry students participate in an eight-day tour of France, and hotel and restaurant management students participate in an eight-day Orlando resort and cruise tour. This travel experience enhances both training and resumes.

A capstone program to England is in place for all baccalaureate students. Students may contact the College for detailed information.

Academic Facilities

Recently completing a yearlong renovation, the Restaurant School at Walnut Hill College is poised to offer one of the most dynamic hands-on learning opportunities in the country. The dining experience, situated in the breathtakingly restored 1855 Allison Mansion, turns into a dining event, with the addition of three theme restaurants, including the Italian Trattoria, which is a casual Italian restaurant that features classic pasta presentations set amidst an Italian terrace. Guests are invited to sit inside the restaurant, where they can enjoy homemade pasta or dine outside among the twinkling lights in the European courtyard.

American cuisine is presented in an innovative new style of the American Heartland. Depicting a country farm with a painted blue sky and cornfields, this restaurant allows students to explore some of America's best cooking while guests enjoy the comfort of a country dining or veranda setting.

Most notable is the elegant Great Chefs of Philadelphia restaurant. Amidst glittering crystal chandeliers and a rich tapestry motif, guests enjoy wonderful cuisine and service designed by some of Philadelphia and America's top chefs.

Also in the mansion is the Student Resource Center, featuring state-of-the-art computer lab stations as well as the Alumni Library, which encompasses thousands of books, magazines, and videotapes on cooking, management, and wine. The building also houses a student conference room and a wine lab.

The Pastry Shop and Café is filled each morning with buttery croissants, crisp French baguettes, and glistening pastries that are prepared by the pastry arts students. Also available is a selection of pastas, salads, soups, and entrees for an informal café lunch, prepared by the culinary arts students.

The education and the Center for Hospitality Studies buildings are the focal points of the student's training. They house six modern classroom kitchens, four lecture halls, and the College's purchasing center and school store.

Hunter Hall is a turn-of-the-century masterpiece that features magnificent carved mahogany, marble, and fireplaces. The College's Offices of Admissions, Financial Aid, and Independent Student Housing are located in this building.

Costs

Tuition for students who start September 2010 is $36,900 ($18,450 per academic year) for the two-year Associate of Science degree program or $73,000 ($18,450 per academic year) for the four-year Bachelor of Science degree program. Equipment, activity fees, culinary whites, and management dining room attire cost approximately $825. Students may contact the College for information on on-campus housing.

Financial Aid

Financial aid programs are available for those who qualify. It is recommended that students apply early. The College participates in the Federal Pell Grant, the Pennsylvania PHEAA State Grant, the subsidized Federal Stafford Student Loan, and parents' Federal PLUS Loan, in addition to other alternative loans. The financial aid officers assist students and their families with the creation of a personal plan that outlines expenses and identifies financial resources available to incoming students. For more specific information, students may contact the College.

Faculty

Learning comes to life under the guiding hands and encouragement of the highly trained, technically skilled faculty. The faculty members are seasoned professionals, having logged many years of experience in restaurants and food service. Through their instruction, students gain professional insight that gives them a competitive edge on entering the hospitality field. The chefs and instructors are committed to helping students achieve success. As professionals, they continuously keep pace with current trends in the hospitality industry and convey their professional dedication and work ethic to their students.

Admission Requirements

Typically, the admissions procedure begins with a visit to the College. At that time, prospective students and their families tour the campus, watch hands-on classes in action, and get a feel for campus life. Application for admission to the College is available to any individual with a high school diploma or its equivalent and an interest in developing a career or ownership options in the fine restaurant, food service, or hospitality field. Applicants are evaluated on their educational background and demonstrated or stated interest in their chosen field. Two references are required, as are high school transcripts and an essay.

Students may contact the College for information on the early decision program for high school juniors and seniors.

Application and Information

The Restaurant School at Walnut Hill College practices rolling admission; qualified applicants are accepted at any time. Applications for admission are submitted with a $50 application fee and a $150 registration fee. Prospective students should contact:

Office of Admissions
The Restaurant School at Walnut Hill College
4207 Walnut Street
Philadelphia, Pennsylvania 19104
Phone: 215-222-4200 Ext. 3011
877-925-6884 Ext. 3011 (toll-free)
Fax: 215-222-4219
E-mail: info@walnuthillcollege.edu
Web site: http://www.walnuthillcollege.edu

The Restaurant School at Walnut Hill College.

THE RICHARD STOCKTON COLLEGE OF NEW JERSEY

POMONA, NEW JERSEY

STOCKTON COLLEGE
THE RICHARD STOCKTON COLLEGE OF NEW JERSEY

The College

The Richard Stockton College of New Jersey (RSCNJ) is a selective, medium-sized, highly ranked, public liberal arts college within the New Jersey system of higher education, offering programs in the arts and humanities; business; education; health sciences; and social, behavioral, and natural sciences. Students enjoy small class sizes, modern facilities, exceptional educational experiences, an environmentally friendly campus, a great location, and reasonable tuition.

Founded in 1969, the College was named for Richard Stockton, one of the New Jersey signers of the Declaration of Independence.

Stockton enrolls more than 7,000 students from New Jersey, the surrounding mid-Atlantic states, and many other countries, providing distinctive traditional educational programs and alternative educational experiences that extend learning beyond the classroom. Stockton looks to develop students' analytic and creative capabilities and encourages individually planned courses of study that promote self-reliance, acceptance of change, and an educated response to change.

The College's campus provides an excellent natural setting for a wide range of outdoor recreational activities, including sailing, canoeing, hiking, jogging, and fishing. Students and faculty and staff members participate together in an extensive intramural and club sports program that includes aikido, crew, flag football, golf, ice hockey, soccer, softball, street hockey, swimming, and volleyball. At the intercollegiate level, Stockton fields NCAA Division III sports teams in men's baseball, basketball, lacrosse, and soccer; women's basketball, crew, field hockey, soccer, softball, tennis, and volleyball; and men's and women's cross-country and track and field. The new multipurpose Sports and Recreation Center has fitness facilities, racquetball courts, weight rooms, a gymnasium, and outdoor recreational facilities that include a field house, NCAA track, field-event venues, and four playing fields for soccer and lacrosse.

College Center I is the hub for social, recreational, cultural, and leisure activities. Many clubs and organizations have their offices in the center: social clubs, such as the Film Committee, Concert Committee, and Performing Arts Committee; service clubs, including the Social Work Club, Speech and Hearing Association, and Unified Black Students' Society; special interest clubs, such as the Accounting and Finance Society, Dance Club, and Photography Club; and independent organizations, including the Jewish Student Union, New Life Christian Fellowship, and twenty-one sororities and fraternities. Participation in cocurricular activities can be documented through the College's student development program, ULTRA (Undergraduate Learning, Training and Awareness), culminating in a cocurricular transcript issued to students.

College Center II, which is connected to the main academic complex, is an open living room–type area featuring a dining facility for students and staff members, a wide-screen television, a game room, lounge areas, and several conference rooms.

A new Campus Center currently under construction will include student services, student meeting rooms, classrooms, computer labs, dining services, and large meeting and conference facilities.

The Residential Life Center provides a curricular/cocurricular facility within two student housing areas. With its large and small meeting rooms, convenience store, and computer lab, the center encourages activities and programs for both organized and informal student groups.

Lakeside Center, located in the garden apartment housing area, contains a convenience store, snack bar, outdoor concert area, computer lab, multipurpose room for large programs, and a small meeting room for student groups.

Stockton provides on-campus housing for almost 2,500 students in traditional residence hall–style arrangements and apartment-style living. All complexes are completely furnished and air conditioned, with cable TV, telephone service, and Internet access (port-per-pillow) provided. Residence Life will assist students choosing to live off campus by providing a listing of suitable off-campus availabilities. Choices range from new townhouse complexes near campus to winter rentals in one of the local seashore towns.

The Richard Stockton College of New Jersey is accredited by the Commission on Higher Education of the Middle States Association of Colleges and Schools. In addition, the social work program is accredited by the Council on Social Work Education; the teacher education sequence is approved by the New Jersey Department of Education, the National Association of State Directors of Teacher Education and Certification, and the Teacher Education Accreditation Council; the nursing program is accredited by the New Jersey Board of Nursing and the Commission on Collegiate Nursing Education; the chemistry program (B.S.) is accredited by the American Chemical Society; the physical therapy program is accredited by the Commission on Accreditation in Physical Therapy Education (CAPTE) of the American Physical Therapy Association; the environmental health/public health program is accredited by the National Environmental Health Sciences and Protection Accreditation Council; the health administration/public health program is accredited by the Association of University Programs in Health Administration; and the occupational therapy program is accredited by the Accreditation Council for Occupational Therapy Education (ACOTE) of the American Occupational Therapy Association (AOTA).

In addition to undergraduate bachelor's degrees, Stockton offers graduate studies in Doctor of Physical Therapy; Master of Arts in criminal justice, Holocaust and genocide studies, education, and instructional technology; Master of Business Administration; and Master of Science in computational science, nursing, occupational therapy, and social work; a Professional Science Master in environmental science, as well as certificate programs in education, ESL (English as a second language), NJ Standard Supervisor Endorsement, and paralegal studies.

Location

The Richard Stockton College of New Jersey is located on a stunning 1,600-acre campus in Pomona, New Jersey, nestled in the Pinelands National Reserve 12 miles from Atlantic City, with easy access to Philadelphia and New York City. The environmentally friendly campus has a rural parklike setting, yet is close to a variety of cultural and recreational activities with nearby opportunity for shopping and dining.

A full schedule of concerts, art exhibitions, lectures, recreation, and sports on campus is complemented by the nearby Jersey Shore resort destinations. Within a 15-minute drive, students find fishing, boating, swimming, and cultural attractions, as well as the entertainment of Atlantic City.

Majors and Degrees

The Bachelor of Arts degree is offered in studies in the arts, applied physics, biology, business studies, chemistry, communication, computer science and information systems, criminal justice (forensic science), economics, education, environmental studies, geology, historical studies, languages and culture studies, liberal studies, literature, marine science, mathematics, philosophy and religion, political science, psychology, and sociology and anthropology.

A Bachelor of Fine Arts degree is offered in visual arts.

The Bachelor of Science degree is offered in applied physics, biochemistry/molecular biology, biology, business studies (accounting, finance, hospitality and tourism management, international business, management, marketing), chemistry, computational science, computer science and information systems, environmental studies, geology, marine science, mathematics, nursing, psychology, public health, social work, and speech pathology and audiology.

Stockton's flexible curriculum allows students to prepare for professional careers, such as dentistry, law, medicine, and veterinary medicine, while pursuing a traditional major. The College also offers preprofessional preparation in occupational therapy, optometry, pharmacy, physical therapy, and podiatry, with the master's in occupational therapy and the doctorate in physical therapy completed at Stockton.

Stockton has accelerated seven-year dual-degree articulation agreements with the University of Medicine and Dentistry of New Jersey (Robert Wood Johnson Medical School, New Jersey Medical School, School of Osteopathic Medicine, New Jersey Dental School), the

Pennsylvania College of Podiatric Medicine, the New York College of Podiatric Medicine, the New York State College of Optometry, and Rutgers School of Pharmacy. Stockton also has an articulation program with Cornell University for veterinary medicine as well as five-year, dual-degree programs with New Jersey Institute of Technology (NJIT) and Rutgers University for students interested in engineering. Students participating in the engineering program earn a Bachelor of Science degree in chemistry, physics, or math from Stockton and a Bachelor of Science degree in engineering from NJIT or Rutgers. A dual degree in pharmacy allows students to graduate from Stockton with a Bachelor of Science degree in biochemistry/molecular biology and finish their Doctor of Pharmacy degree at the Ernest Mario School of Pharmacy at Rutgers University.

Academic Programs

To earn a baccalaureate degree at Stockton, a student must satisfactorily complete a minimum of 128 semester credits. Degree programs include a combination of general studies and program (major field) studies. The Bachelor of Arts student must earn 64 credits in general studies; the Bachelor of Science student must earn 48. General studies courses are broad cross-disciplinary courses designed to introduce students to all major areas of the curriculum and to the broadly applicable intellectual skills necessary for success in college. Students must select some courses from each major curricular area. The only required courses within general studies are the basic studies courses (up to three), but students may be exempt from these courses based on diagnostic testing. The Bachelor of Arts student must earn 64 credits in program studies; the Bachelor of Science student must earn 80. Program studies requirements are carefully structured and emphasize sequences of specific courses.

Stockton students have special opportunities to influence what and how they learn by participating in the major decisions that shape their academic lives. The opportunities of the preceptorial system enable students to work on a personalized basis with an assigned faculty-staff preceptor in planning and evaluating individual courses of study and in exploring various career alternatives. Stockton's academic programs emphasize curricular organization and methods of instruction that promote independent learning and research, cross-disciplinary study, problem solving, and decision making through analysis and synthesis.

Off-Campus Programs

Off-campus educational experiences for credit are a key feature of most degree programs at Stockton. Internships, research projects, and field studies extend the principles and methods learned beyond the classroom. Study abroad, Semester at Sea, and four-year independent study with the One-on-One Connect mentor/scholar program are also available.

The Washington, D.C., Internship Program gives students the opportunity to gain professional work experience. Stockton sends more students to the program than any other college or university outside the Washington, D.C., area.

Coordination of off-campus internship programs is provided by the academic divisional offices; coordination of foreign study is provided by the coordinator of international education.

Academic Facilities

Stockton's award-winning academic complex serves as a living-learning center. Academic, recreational, and living spaces are mixed to promote interaction among students and faculty and staff members. The facilities, all constructed since 1971, include several large classroom/office buildings, a library, a lecture hall/auditorium, and the 550-seat Performing Arts Center.

The library contains more than 300,000 volumes, more than 2,600 periodical subscriptions, 280,000 government documents, more than 19,000 reels of microfilm, and about 68,000 other units of microtext. The media collection includes films, slides, videotapes, audiotapes, compact discs, and phonograph records. The library also houses a special collection on the New Jersey Pine Barrens and is a depository for federal, state, and Atlantic City documents.

Costs

Costs for the 2009–10 academic year, including flat-rate tuition and fees based on up to 40 credits per year, were $10,940 for in-state students and $16,624 for out-of-state students; on-campus housing and board was $10,286 (double-occupancy residence room and Ultimate 19 meal plan). Books, supplies, transportation, and personal items are extra. All costs are subject to change.

Financial Aid

Financial aid is available in the form of scholarships, grants, loans, and work-study. Need-based financial aid is awarded according to student and family need. Students seeking financial aid should file the Free Application for Federal Student Aid (FAFSA) by March 1. Merit-based aid is awarded to recognize academic excellence. Stockton offers aggressive and generous scholarship opportunities for academically talented freshmen and transfer students based on standardized test scores, grade point average, high school class rank, and college-level performance.

Faculty

Stockton's 265 full-time and 80 part-time and adjunct faculty members represent highly diverse academic, training, and social backgrounds, with 95 percent holding the terminal degree in their field. Faculty members work closely with students through small class sizes and individual research opportunities and share with students and staff members the initiative and responsibility for the College's social, recreational, athletic, and cultural programs and activities. This arrangement supports the exceptional rapport and learning relationships among students and faculty members.

Student Government

The RSCNJ Student Senate consists of 25 student members. The advisory council is made up of 1 faculty member and 2 staff members. Student senators hold office for one year, with elections held every spring. Among other duties, the Student Senate reviews and makes recommendations on budgets of funded student organizations and acts as the official representative of the student body.

Admission Requirements

Stockton operates on a rolling admission basis. For most freshman majors, the deadline for fall admission is May 1. Students should check the Web site for special program deadlines. Transfer student deadline for fall admission is June 1. Spring term (January) admission deadline for all students is December 1. Students may apply for admission to the fall or spring term and are notified of the admission decision as soon as their application file has been completed and reviewed. Freshman applicants must submit ACT and/or SAT scores. All students must submit official transcripts from all educational institutions attended. Admission is selective.

Stockton offers early acceptance programs for high school students in their junior year. Armed Services veterans and those who have been away from formal education for some time are also invited to apply for admission. Stockton makes no distinction between part- and full-time students in offering admission.

Stockton offers special admission access to a limited number of New Jersey students from educationally and financially disadvantaged backgrounds. Students wishing to explore this opportunity should contact the Admissions Office.

Application and Information

For more information, prospective students should contact:

Dean of Enrollment Management
The Richard Stockton College of New Jersey
P.O. Box 195
Pomona, New Jersey 08240-0195
Phone: 609-652-4261
866-RSC-2885 (toll-free)
Fax: 609-626-5541
E-mail: admissions@stockton.edu
Web site: http://www.stockton.edu

COLLEGE CLOSE-UPS

RICHMOND, THE AMERICAN INTERNATIONAL UNIVERSITY IN LONDON

LONDON, ENGLAND

The University

Richmond, The American International University in London, prepares men and women to serve with purpose and generosity in an interdependent and multicultural world. Richmond offers a strong academic program with many choices of fields of study, an exceptional faculty, superb campus life, and fellow students from all over the world. In the United States, Richmond is accredited by the Commission on Higher Education of the Middle States Association of Colleges and Schools, a regional accrediting body recognized by the U.S. Department of Education. Richmond is accredited in the United Kingdom by the Open University and holds related degree validation. The University's undergraduate and graduate degrees are designated by the United Kingdom's Department of Education and Employment. The University is a comprehensive American liberal arts and professional university. In addition to the undergraduate degree programs described below, Richmond offers Master of Arts degrees in art history and international relations.

Freshmen and sophomores study and live at the Richmond campus, 7 miles from central London. Junior and senior years are spent at the Kensington campus in one of London's most beautiful residential and historic districts. As part of their four-year B.A. degree program, students may spend a semester or a year studying at one of the University's two international study centers in Florence and Rome, Italy. Richmond currently enrolls 1,000 students from more than 100 countries. Approximately 21 percent of the degree students are from Europe and the United Kingdom, 13 percent are from Asia, and 18 percent are from the Middle East. Fifteen percent of the student body represents the continent of Africa, and 3 percent are from South America. The remaining students are from North America. About 350 study-abroad students from various universities are enrolled for a semester or a year at Richmond.

Small classes, averaging 17 students, enable students to receive personal attention from professors in a supportive environment. The curriculum and academic advising system are structured to enable students to choose courses that provide broad knowledge, relevant skills, and an understanding of the world's many cultures and nations.

Richmond students supplement academic programs with activities that complement and balance the classroom experience. Many extracurricular and cocurricular programs are available to students, including student government, the Green Project, Model United Nations, Gay Straight Alliance, RTV (Richmond Television), and sports and business clubs.

Location

The Richmond Hill campus in the London suburb of Richmond offers a variety of entertainment, shopping, cultural, and recreational opportunities. Only yards from the University campus is Richmond Park, more than 2,200 acres of rolling hills and lush woodland, where one can ride horses, play tennis, jog, or simply relax. The journey from Richmond into Central London takes about 30 minutes.

The Kensington campus is located in the heart of London's Borough of Kensington, which has fine museums, libraries, theatres, concert halls, historic buildings, and well-known cultural and educational resources. The University takes full advantage of London's cultural and social resources through selected academic courses, work experience placements with multinational corporations, and special visits to museums, art galleries, theatres, and concert halls.

Majors and Degrees

Richmond operates its academic program on the American system. The University offers the four-year Bachelor of Arts (B.A.) degree in eleven majors, with a further choice of sixteen minors. Majors offered by the University are art, design, and media; business administration (finance, international business, marketing); communications; economics; history; international journalism and media; international relations; political science; and psychology.

Academic Programs

In order to graduate with the dual-validated U.S. and U.K. degree [B.A./B.A. (Honors)], students must earn a minimum of 120 credits. Usually, this means taking a full load for four years, or eight semesters. Within these 120 credits, students must complete all course requirements for their majors. Students must also meet the University's Language Proficiency and General Education requirements. In addition, valuable work experience for credit is offered through the International Internship program. Recent placements have been at the International Herald Tribune, General Electric, The House of Commons, CNN, the United Nations, Lloyds Bank, the Museum of London, and Sony Music Corporation.

Credit is also awarded for Advanced Placement tests (6 credits for each subject grade of 3, 4, or 5); a grade of A, B, or C on the "A" Level exams is awarded 9 credits (6 for D or E). Credit is also awarded for the International Baccalaureate, the Baccalauréat de l'Enseignement du Second Degré (France), the Abitur/Reifzuegnis (Germany), the Diploma di Maturità (Italy), and the School Leaving Diploma (Denmark, Finland, Norway, and Sweden).

The fall semester begins in late August and ends in mid-December. The spring semester begins in mid-January and runs through mid-May. Two sessions of summer school run from mid-May to mid-June and mid-June to mid-July.

Off-Campus Programs

Students may complement their studies in London with a semester, year, or summer at one of two international study centers. The centers, each offering intensive study of the language and culture of the country, are in Florence and Rome, Italy. The Florence Study Center emphasizes studio and fine arts. The Rome Center offers study in the Italian language and culture, art history, economics, and political science.

Academic Facilities

Information technology is integrated into the curriculum in ways that are natural to the discipline under study. Supporting this are nine student computer laboratories with 300 PCs and Macintosh computers, which connect to the Internet and are networked for student, faculty, and administrative use. Wireless network access is also available.

Richmond's libraries support the courses taught at each campus. Students may use either campus library. The libraries house 75,000 volumes and add approximately 4,000 new titles each year. In addition, the libraries have subscriptions to approximately 250 periodicals. Computers are available in both libraries for CD-ROM data searches and access to online databases through the network. Richmond students also have access to thirty-seven of the best libraries in London.

Costs

Tuition for the 2009–10 academic year was $27,000. Room and board were $12,900. Personal expenses, books and supplies, clothing, recreation, and travel costs also need to be factored in.

Financial Aid

Scholarships are awarded annually to students of high academic ability. Financial aid for U.S. citizens includes Federal Stafford Student Loans and Federal PLUS loans. All U.S. citizens must file the Free Application for Federal Student Aid (FAFSA) to qualify. Students should contact the admissions office for details regarding application procedures for scholarships and financial aid.

Faculty

The student-faculty ratio of 12:1 enables optimum interaction and individualized instructional assistance. The 94 faculty members (43 full-time, 51 part-time) have professional degrees from top European and American universities such as Harvard, the University of California (Berkeley), the University of Michigan, Cambridge, Oxford, the London School of Economics, the Royal College of Art, and the University of Bonn.

Student Government

The Richmond Student Union acts as a resource for all students, student organizations, and clubs to voice their opinions and ideas. The Student Union functions as a network between the student body and the administration. Using student ideas, it holds events and seeks to feature student talent while enhancing the overall University experience. The Student Union is ongoing in its development and thus offers possibilities for students to shape and change it. It is an organization directed by students for students and is structured to provide flexibility as well as the opportunity for all students to become involved.

Admission Requirements

Applicants are admitted on the basis of academic performance, references, intended major, and career interests. The required autobiographical essay is of paramount importance. Applicants to Richmond have usually completed a total of twelve years of primary and secondary school with a minimum grade of C+ (2.5 out of 4.0) in the American high school grading system, or its equivalent. British system students should have attained a minimum of five GCSE passes (grades of A, B, or C) in acceptable academic subjects, one of which must be mathematics or science. Equivalent qualifications gained under other educational systems are also considered for the purpose of admission.

Students must submit a completed application form, an essay, transcripts of all secondary and postsecondary school work, and one letter of recommendation. SAT or ACT scores are optional. The ATP code for Richmond is 0823L. The ACT code is 5244. Evidence of proficiency in the English language is required from students whose first language is not English or who did not attend English-speaking schools. Standardized test scores, such as the TOEFL or the ALIGU, or completion of recognized examinations, such as GCSE, Pitman, RSA, or lower Cambridge, are considered in assessing students' language capability.

Richmond admits students on a rolling basis, and applicants are encouraged to submit their application at the earliest opportunity. All documents in languages other than English must be accompanied by official translations. Applicants are usually notified of a decision within two to three weeks.

Application and Information

An application for admission and further information may be obtained by contacting the appropriate admissions office.

Applicants residing in the United States should contact:

Director of U.S. Admissions
U.S. Office of Admissions
Richmond, The American International University in London
343 Congress Street, Suite 3100
Boston, Massachusetts 02210-1214
Phone: 617-450-5617
Fax: 617-450-5601
E-mail: us_admissions@richmond.ac.uk
Web site: http://www.richmond.ac.uk

Applicants residing in all other countries should contact:

Director of Admissions
Office of Admissions
Richmond, The American International University in London
Queens Road, Richmond
Surrey TW10 6JP
England
Phone: 44-20-8332-9000
Fax: 44-20-8332-1596
E-mail: enroll@richmond.ac.uk
Web site: http://www.richmond.ac.uk

The Richmond Hill campus is situated near the River Thames in one of London's most attractive and secure areas. The impressive neo-Gothic structure was constructed in 1843.

RIDER UNIVERSITY

LAWRENCEVILLE AND PRINCETON, NEW JERSEY

The University

Founded in 1865, Rider University is an independent, coeducational, nonsectarian institution accredited by the Middle States Association of Colleges and Schools. Rider's business programs are accredited by AACSB International–The Association to Advance Collegiate Schools of Business, and its education programs are recognized by the National Council for the Accreditation of Teacher Education (NCATE). Westminster Choir College is accredited by the National Association of Schools of Music (NASM). Rider has campuses in Lawrenceville and Princeton, New Jersey.

Rider comprises four academic schools and colleges: the College of Business Administration; the College of Liberal Arts, Education, and Sciences; the College of Continuing Studies; and Westminster College of the Arts.

Ninety-seven percent of Rider's faculty members hold a doctorate or other appropriate advanced degree. Primarily a teaching institution, Rider University selects instructors who are committed to imparting the knowledge and skills of a particular discipline. Full professors teach at all levels. There are no teaching assistants in the classrooms or laboratories.

Rider University's Lawrenceville campus is home to academic, recreational, and housing facilities. A state-of-the-art recreational facility features an indoor track, basketball courts, and exercise equipment. Approximately 64 percent of the 4,900 undergraduates live in University residence halls or in fraternities or sororities on the campus.

Rider participates in NCAA Division I in all of its intercollegiate sports. Women's sports are basketball, cross-country, field hockey, soccer, softball, swimming and diving, tennis, track and field, and volleyball. Men's sports are baseball, basketball, cross-country, golf, soccer, swimming and diving, tennis, track and field, and wrestling.

Preparation for career success goes beyond the classroom at Rider. The Office of Career Services enables students and alumni to increase career awareness through assessment, research, experiential learning, and the development of job-search competencies, resulting in informed decision making. Career Services encourages the ongoing documentation of acquired skills, experiences, achievements, and leadership development and is committed to building partnerships with students, alumni, faculty members, administrators, and employers.

Location

Rider University is located in New Jersey, with suburban campuses in Lawrenceville and Princeton. It is approximately 35 miles northeast of Philadelphia and 65 miles southwest of New York City. The location combines the advantages of accessibility to the cultural and recreational facilities of major urban areas and to the peaceful surroundings of a suburban community.

Westminster Choir College, a subsidiary of Westminster College of the Arts, is ideally located in picturesque Princeton, within walking distance of Princeton's Palmer Square, and is an outstanding atmosphere for living, performing, and learning.

All students have full access to the academic and recreational services available on both campuses.

Majors and Degrees

The College of Business Administration awards the Bachelor of Science in Business Administration (B.S.B.A.) degree in accounting, advertising, business administration, business economics, computer information systems, entrepreneurial studies, finance, global supply chain management, human resource management, international business, management and leadership, and marketing.

The College of Liberal Arts, Education, and Sciences (CLAES) awards the Bachelor of Arts (B.A.) degree in elementary education and secondary education and the Bachelor of Science (B.S.) degree in business education.

The CLAES also awards the B.A. degree in American studies, communication, economics, English, French, German, global and multinational studies, history, journalism, mathematics, philosophy, political science, psychology, Russian, sociology, and Spanish. It offers the B.S. degree in biochemistry, biology, behavioral neuroscience, chemistry, environmental science, geosciences, integrated sciences and math, and marine sciences.

The Westminster College of the Arts is composed of two divisions: Westminster Choir College and the School of Fine and Performing Arts. Westminster Choir College, located on the Princeton campus, awards the Bachelor of Music degrees in sacred music, music education, theory/composition, voice performance, piano, and organ performance.

Located on Rider's Lawrenceville campus, the School of Fine and Performing Arts currently offers a Bachelor of Arts in Fine Arts with tracks in dance, music, theater, and art; a Bachelor of Arts in Music; a Bachelor of Music in Music Theater; and the Bachelor of Arts in Arts Administration. Students accepted into these programs will live and study on the Lawrenceville campus.

Rider's postbaccalaureate premedical studies program is geared toward career changers who have not taken the undergraduate course prerequisites for admission to medical, dental, and veterinary schools.

Academic Programs

Rider University operates on the semester system. Each college requires a minimum of 120 semester hours of credit for graduation; the last 30 semester hours of credit must be earned at Rider University. The College of Business Administration requires that a student earn at least 45 semester hours, including the last 30, at Rider University.

The Baccalaureate Honors Program is available to students in all programs. Selection in Rider's honors program is competitive. The recommended criteria are a 1230 or higher SAT score (combined critical reading and math); applicants must have a minimum of 600 of each of the critical reading and math sections and a minimum score of 530 on the writing portion. Students submitting ACT scores should have a minimum score of 27, with a minimum score of 26 on the English and math components and a minimum score of 27 on the writing portion. All applicants must have a minimum 3.25 high school grade point average to qualify for this program.

Rider University recognizes the Advanced Placement (AP) Program and offers credit and placement for scores of 3, 4, or 5 on most AP tests. Credit is awarded for the College-Level Examination Program (CLEP) tests, provided that the minimum required score is obtained. The minimum score varies according to the specific area covered by the examination.

Off-Campus Programs

Rider University offers semester-long and academic-year programs at a variety of international sites through an extensive study-abroad program. Popular sites include Austria, Australia, England, France, Greece, Italy, Ireland, Mexico, and Spain. Short-term, faculty-led study abroad programs are available in January and during the summer months. Summer study-abroad programs are also available in selected countries.

Academic Facilities

The Franklin F. Moore Library contains 481,958 volumes and 648,418 microforms, among many other resources. The library is automated with an integrated library system, sophisticated website, and other tools. To complement its on-campus holdings, the library offers 134 online databases for finding journal articles and other scholarly information. The Talbott Library on the Princeton campus houses 74,790 scores and music-related books and journals, and over 31,000 sound and video recordings. Talbott Library's Performance Collection comprises approximately 5,425 choral music titles in performance quantities. Special collections at Talbott include significant reference collections of choral octavos (more than 80,000 titles), organ music, hymnals, nineteenth-century American choral music, music education materials, and the Westminster Archives. In addition, the American Organ Archives of the Organ Historical Society are housed at Talbott Library.

The Office of Information Technology (OIT) is to ensure a pervasive, state-of-the-art, and well-utilized environment for the University. OIT is responsible for all university technology services including but not limited to computing, voice network, cable television, electronic classrooms, and instructional technology. There are two general access computer labs and computer kiosks for Internet access. Teaching computer labs are located on both campuses.

Other academic facilities include well-equipped laboratories for biochemistry, biology, biopsychology, chemistry, communications, environmental sciences, geology, physics, and psychology and performance facilities.

Costs

The total annual tuition charge for new students who began their studies in 2009–10 was $28,470, plus applicable mandatory fees. Room (standard double room) and board charges totaled $10,720 for the academic year.

Financial Aid

Rider University offers merit-based scholarships for qualified applicants. These scholarships are renewable for up to four years of study if the student maintains the minimum grade point average specified by the Scholarship Committee. Scholarships range from $8000 to $20,000 annually.

Other financial aid is based on demonstrated financial need. Students and their parents are required to file the Free Application for Federal Student Aid (FAFSA) prior to March 1 to be considered for financial assistance administered by Rider University. Students are eligible for consideration for Federal Pell Grants, Federal Supplemental Educational Opportunity Grants, Federal Work-Study Program awards, Federal Perkins Loans, New Jersey Tuition Aid Grants, New Jersey Distinguished Scholar Scholarships, Rider University grants, Trustee Scholarships, Alumni Scholarships, and other forms of institutional aid.

Faculty

There are 243 full-time and 383 part-time faculty members, 97 percent of whom hold a doctorate or terminal degree in their field. The same faculty members teach both graduate and undergraduate courses; graduate assistants do not teach classes at Rider University. The student-faculty ratio is approximately 13:1. Faculty members serve on student affairs committees and as faculty advisers to all student organizations.

Student Government

The active Student Government Association (SGA) sponsors concerts, lectures, plays, and other events. All social rules and regulations are made, enforced, and adjudicated by students. Each class, each residence hall, and many other student organizations are represented in the Student Government Association.

Admission Requirements

Students applying for admission to Rider University are expected to have completed a minimum of 16 acceptable college-preparatory units of study by the end of their senior year in high school. These 16 units must include 4 in English and 3 in mathematics, including algebra I, algebra II, and geometry. The other 9 units should be selected from traditional academic areas, including history, mathematics, science, social studies, foreign languages, and literature. Business or vocational courses completed in high school are not considered college-preparatory units. Students are required to submit official SAT or ACT results, a personal statement, and two letters of recommendation in support of their application. Most successful applicants rank in the upper half of their high school senior class.

Rider University seeks a diverse student body and encourages applications from students from varied ethnic, economic, and geographic backgrounds. Campus interviews are strongly recommended but not required for most candidates.

Application and Information

Rider University works on a rolling admissions basis, but it encourages applications for the fall semester to be submitted by January 15. Applications for the spring semester should be submitted by December 1. The application fee is $50. The early decision option is available for freshmen applying for the fall semester. The application deadline for early decision is November 15, and students are notified of a decision by December 15. Early decision is a binding option. The early action option is available for fall applicants. Students interested in the early action option must submit all necessary documentation by November 15 and are notified of an admissions decision by December 15. Early action is a non-binding option. All other applicants are notified of the admission decision approximately three to four weeks after the completed application is received. Transfer applicants receive the same priority for admission, housing, and financial aid as freshman applicants. More information can be found at http://www.rider.edu/admissions. Apply at http://www.rider.edu/applynow.

Interested students are encouraged to contact:

Director of Undergraduate Admissions
Rider University
2083 Lawrenceville Road
Lawrenceville, New Jersey 08648-3099
Phone: 609-896-5042
800-257-9026 (toll-free)
E-mail: admissions@rider.edu
Web site: http://www.rider.edu/admissions

Rider students on the Lawrenceville campus.

RIPON COLLEGE

RIPON, WISCONSIN

The College

Together with the other members of its tightly knit learning community, Ripon students often feel as if they learn more deeply, live more fully, and achieve more success. There are more opportunities to be involved, lead, speak out, make a difference, and explore new interests than at many colleges many times its size. Through collaborative learning, group living, teamwork, and networking, students tap into the power of a community where all work together to ensure their success, at Ripon and beyond. The best residential liberal arts colleges strive to be true learning communities like Ripon. Ripon succeeds better than most, because the enrollment of just over 1,000 students is perfect for fostering connections inside and outside the classroom. Students flourish in this environment of mutual respect, where shared values are elevated and diverse ideas are valued. Students who are seeking academic challenge and want to benefit from an environment of personal attention and support should take a closer look at Ripon. In classes that average 20 students, professors are able to know the students and their strengths and capabilities extraordinarily well. They tailor course work to make sure students are always challenged to perform at the top of their game, yet they are always ready to provide extra support when needed. Faculty members collaborate with students on research projects, suggest independent-study topics, and connect them with internships and other active learning experiences.

A Ripon education can take graduates anywhere. A student could study psychology and play basketball and then become a seven-time Grammy winner like jazz singer Al Jarreau, '62; guide the space shuttle into orbit like Jeff Bantle, '80, a chief flight director with NASA; or become an international opera star like Gail Dobish, '76. A student could set records in medical science like neonatologist Dr. John Muraskas, '78, who is on record for saving the world's smallest premature baby, or cover world events like Richard Threlkeld, '59, former Moscow correspondent for CBS News, or a student might end up in Donald Trump's inner circle like Ashley Cooper, '82, a former senior manager of Trump National Golf Club, who has served as an adviser to "The Donald" on *The Apprentice.*

The list of student clubs and organizations is ever changing, reflecting students' ever-changing interests. A recent addition is FUERZA Alliance, designed to educate students about Latino cultures and to provide services to the Spanish-speaking community of Ripon.

Every day at Ripon is packed with a host of activities such as concerts (there are eight vocal and instrumental groups that perform regularly on campus, as well as many individual student and faculty recitals). The Caestecker Fine Arts Series and the Chamber Music at Ripon Series annually bring national performers to the campus. The Ethical Leadership Program sponsors an annual ethics conference that has included nationally known personalities Tim Russert, Miles Brand, and Bud Selig. The Theatre Department sponsors two major productions annually, plus a series of student-directed one-act plays. The most recent Ripon Film Festival (an annual showcase for independent films from around the country) included the premiere of a feature-length horror film written, directed by, and starring a Ripon student.

Ripon's NCAA Division III intercollegiate teams compete in the Midwest Conference. Men's varsity sports include baseball, basketball, cross-country, cycling, football, golf, indoor and outdoor track and field, soccer, swimming and diving, and tennis. Women's varsity sports include basketball, cross-country, cycling, dance, golf, indoor and outdoor track and field, soccer, softball, swimming and diving, and tennis.

Location

Located on 250 tree-lined, rolling acres adjacent to downtown Ripon, the campus looks and feels like a college should. Ripon's twenty-six first-rate buildings are a striking combination of historic (ten campus structures listed on the National Register of Historic Places) and modern architecture.

Majors and Degrees

Majors include anthropology, art, art history, biology, business administration, chemistry, chemistry/biology, communication, computer science, economics, educational studies, English, environmental sciences, exercise science, foreign languages, French, German, global studies, history, Latin American area studies, mathematics, music, philosophy, physics, politics and government, psychobiology, psychology, religion, sociology/anthropology, Spanish, and theater. Programs are also available in leadership studies, sports medicine/athletic training, and women's studies.

Preprofessional programs include dentistry, journalism, law and government, library and information science, medicine, ministry, optometry, physical therapy, and veterinary medicine.

Dual-degree programs include allied health sciences/medical technology, engineering, forestry, and social welfare.

Certification programs include education certification, early childhood, elementary, elementary/middle school, secondary, secondary/middle, music K–12, and physical education K–12.

Academic Programs

Ripon's liberal arts curriculum is designed to introduce students to a wide variety of disciplines. About 40 percent of the students complete double or triple majors, whereas some create special self-designed majors. Excellent communications skills—written and oral—as well as critical-thinking and problem-solving skills are the hallmark of a Ripon education, regardless of major. In addition, the leadership studies program and the newly established ethical leadership program provide a strong foundation for leadership skills. An Army ROTC program is also available.

Off-Campus Programs

Ripon offers more than forty different off-campus programs of varying lengths to choose from, each one officially sanctioned by and affiliated with Ripon. Although most programs are connected with a major or minor program, all are open to every Ripon student, regardless of major.

U.S. programs include Chicago Urban Studies Semester, Fisk University–Ripon Exchange Program, Newberry Seminar in the Humanities, Oak Ridge Science Semester, Washington Semester, and Woods Hole Marine Biology.

International programs include Bonn, Germany, Program; Budapest Semester; Central European Studies Program in the Czech Republic; Costa Rica; Cross-Cultural Study Center in Seville, Spain; Florence Program; France and Spain; Global Studies Program in Turkey; India Studies; Japan Study; London and Florence Program in the Arts; Madrid Program; Montpellier, France; Paris, France; Ripon and York St. John Exchange; Russia Program; Sea Education Association (marine biology abroad); Sea Semester at Woods Hole; Swansea Program; Tanzania; Toledo, Spain; and University of Wales in Bangor.

Academic Facilities

Constant additions and improvements, like a recent multimillion-dollar apartment-style residence hall, the renovation and classroom expansion of Todd Wehr Hall, and upgrades to upperclass residence halls, the library, the bookstore, dining facilities, and a coffee shop, maintain Ripon's ability to meet the needs of today and tomorrow. Technology services include high-speed Internet and e-mail, telephone, and video communication. Intranet and Internet services are accessible from systems located throughout the College. The campuswide network provides access from every room, and several wireless hot spots in key areas let students access the world without being tied down.

The library staff provides friendly, efficient circulation, reference, instruction, and interlibrary loan services that aid in research. The library also houses the College archives, a computer lab, and more than a dozen online databases. Library holdings include 164,000 volumes, 800 current periodicals, and microfilms.

The C. J. Rodman Center for the Arts is home to a theater with a state-of-the-art computerized lighting system, a recital hall with one of only fifty existing Bedient organs, an art gallery, and a sculpture garden.

The J. M. Storzer Center includes an Olympic-size pool, a first-class gymnasium, tennis and racquetball courts, a dance studio, training facilities, and a weight room. The outdoor playing fields and courts are among the best in their class. In addition, a large, modern exercise facility was recently added in the main student residence area.

Costs

Tuition is $25,170, room and board are $7270, and fees are $275, for a total cost of $32,715.

Financial Aid

Ripon is one of just eighty-one colleges and universities in the country recognized as a best value by the Princeton Review in the 2009 edition of *America's Best Value Colleges,* which noted, "Best of all, Ripon strives to provide aid in a form that reduces your long-term debt." More than 90 percent of Ripon students receive some form of merit-based scholarship and/or need-based grants and loans.

Ripon recognizes and rewards students' success in high school with its institutionally funded scholarships, based not only on academic merit but also on special achievements in other areas, such as the creative arts. The scholarships range from $1000 to full tuition. Ripon participates in all federal and state need-based financial aid programs. The financial aid counselors work individually with students and their families to investigate every possible financial resource for which they are eligible.

Faculty

Ripon has 57 full-time and 25 part-time faculty members. Ninety-seven percent of the full-time faculty members have Ph.D.s.

Admission Requirements

Ripon enrolls students who are expected to contribute to and benefit from the academic and residential programs provided. Ripon does not discriminate on the basis of gender, sexual orientation, race, color, age, religion, national or ethnic origin, or disability in the administration of its educational policies, admission practices, scholarship and loan programs, and athletic and other College-administered programs.

Application and Information

The faculty committee on academic standards establishes the criteria for admission. The school considers a variety of factors, including secondary school record, standardized test scores (SAT or ACT), recommendations, a written essay, and extracurricular or community service activities. Ripon's admission process reflects the personal attention students can expect to receive during their college careers, and applicants are encouraged to provide any additional information they consider helpful.

For further information, students should contact:

Steven M. Schuetz
Dean of Admission
Ripon College
300 Seward Street
P.O. Box 248
Ripon, Wisconsin 54971-0248
Phone: 800-947-4766 (toll-free)
E-mail: adminfo@ripon.edu
Web site: http://www.ripon.edu

Ripon College students and their families celebrate commencement on the lawn of Harwood Memorial Union.

COLLEGE CLOSE-UPS

RIVIER COLLEGE

NASHUA, NEW HAMPSHIRE

The College

Rivier College, a private Catholic college founded in 1933, has gained a reputation for academic excellence in more than forty programs. The College has adapted to changing needs by developing liberal arts/career-oriented programs designed to prepare graduates in many fields.

Rivier's School of Undergraduate Studies enrolls approximately 1,500 students, including 900 full-time day students. With a 15:1 student-faculty ratio, day students have plenty of opportunities to connect with faculty and become active members of the academic community.

Most full-time undergraduate day students are of traditional age: between 18 and 22 years old. Though the majority comes from New England, Rivier attracts students from states around the country, including Florida, California, and Delaware. International students represent countries in Africa, Asia, Europe, the Middle East, and South America. Students who live on campus reside in four modern residence halls. Most rooms are doubles, with some triples, quads, and singles available. Rivier also provides substance-free housing in Presentation Hall. The newest hall offers suite-style living, with several double and triple rooms sharing a kitchenette and common area. The Dion Center houses the dining room, the commuter lounge, the mail room, a campus store, student development offices, and meeting rooms. All students are permitted to have cars on the campus.

The Office of Student Development, the Student Government Association, and more than twenty-five student clubs and organizations provide a calendar of social, cultural, and recreational activities, including concerts, live entertainment, films, and sporting events. The College and student organizations frequently organize outings, including trips to Boston and New York. Students also enjoy a variety of performances by the Rivier Theater Company.

Rivier offers an orientation for new students to introduce them to the College's wide array of services. Academic advisers, staff at the Writing and Resource Center, and peer tutors help students meet their academic goals. The Health Services Center and Counseling Center ensure students' physical and emotional well-being. A full-time chaplain and Campus Ministry team coordinate spiritual activities and service opportunities, while a comprehensive career development service helps students prepare for employment after graduation.

Rivier offers a variety of team and individual sports, including NCAA Division III men's baseball, basketball, cross-country, lacrosse, soccer, and volleyball; and women's basketball, cross-country, field hockey, lacrosse, soccer, softball, and volleyball. The men's volleyball team has been nationally ranked every year since 2001. The Muldoon Health and Fitness Center is home to Rivier's varsity athletics and to many intramural sports and fitness activities, including volleyball, floor hockey, basketball, weight training, aerobics, self-defense, and more. The campus also has soccer and softball fields, as well as a beach volleyball court and cross-country trail. Student athletes and others can take advantage of an on-campus rehabilitation clinic offering free injury assessment, physical and occupational therapy, and athletic training.

Location

Nashua (population 87,000) is located in southern New Hampshire. The city of Boston lies within easy access 40 miles to the south. Local access to public transportation provides for easy travel to and from the campus. Recreational activities abound year-round at nearby lakes and ski areas, in the White Mountains to the north, and at the seacoast, just an hour's drive to the east.

Majors and Degrees

Rivier College awards Bachelor of Arts and Bachelor of Science degrees in the following areas of concentration: art (studio art, graphic design, and photography and digital media), biology (allied health and environmental science) and biology education, business, communications (advertising/public relations, journalism, photojournalism, scriptwriting, video production, and Web design/online publishing), criminal justice, education (early childhood/special education, elementary education/special education, and human development/interdisciplinary), English and English education, finance, history, human development, international studies, liberal studies, marketing, mathematics and mathematics education, modern languages (modern languages education and Spanish), nursing, political science, psychology, social studies education, and sociology. Five-year combined bachelor's/master's degree programs are available in business, English (teacher certification), and psychology. The College offers preprofessional programs in law, dentistry, medicine, and veterinary medicine. Associate degrees are offered in art, business management, early childhood education, liberal studies, and nursing.

Academic Programs

Rivier College takes special pride in its curriculum, which offers both professional studies and liberal arts to prepare students for a fast-changing, highly technological society. The broad-based curriculum focuses on preparing students for challenging and rewarding careers and furthering their personal growth. Core curriculum requirements vary slightly depending on the degree to be obtained, but generally include courses in English, mathematics and/or natural sciences, modern language and literature, philosophy, religious studies, social science, and Western civilization. No fewer than ten courses must be taken in the major field. Students may choose electives that suit their personal interests and professional goals. The bachelor's degree requires a minimum of 120 credits with a grade point average of at least 2.0. For the associate degree, the student must complete a minimum of 60 credits with a grade point average of at least 2.0.

All departments encourage qualified students to pursue internships in their field of study during their junior or senior year. Education specialists student teach in local schools. Nursing majors complete clinical rotations in health-care facilities throughout southern New Hampshire and northern Massachusetts. History, law, and political science majors may work in a law office, business, legal-assistance agency, or government agency. Sociology and psychology majors work with local social service agencies. English and communications majors work in public relations, broadcasting, or corporate communications positions. Art majors work in advertising or graphic design or at local galleries. Business majors work in marketing, management, and technology.

Honors awards include placement on the dean's list, membership in Kappa Gamma Pi, listing in *Who's Who Among Students in American Universities and Colleges,* listing in *The National Dean's List,* and degrees with honors. Academically talented students may also apply to the four-year honors program.

The college year is divided into two 15-week semesters, with first-semester examinations held before Christmas recess. Students usually take five courses each semester. Academic credit may be granted to incoming freshmen on the basis of scores on Advanced Placement tests and CLEP examinations. Students may also "challenge" courses and receive credit by special examination.

Off-Campus Programs

Through Rivier College's membership in the New Hampshire College and University Council, a sixteen-member consortium of senior and two-year colleges, Rivier students may register for courses at any of the member colleges and receive transfer credits.

Academic Facilities

Academic facilities include Memorial Hall, which houses fourteen classrooms, faculty offices, a lecture hall, a fully equipped digital imaging studio, a communications lab offering the most recent software and video/sound editing equipment, a behavioral science lab, the studio of community television station tv13 Nashua (WYCN), and art department facilities that include a gallery, a slide library, and studios. The Academic Computer Center features up to sixty-eight workstations with a full range of cutting-edge software and Internet/e-mail access. Regina Library houses more than 100,000 volumes and provides access to more than 3 million volumes in twelve area libraries, as well as online access to licensed databases in virtually every academic subject. The Writing and Resource Center offers assistance from professional writing consultants as well as student tutors. Other academic facilities include nursing and science laboratories; a physical assessment lab and nursing skills simulation lab, which provide nursing students with practical experience using blood pressure cuffs, ophthalmoscopes, IV pumps, patient simulators, and more; the McLean Center for Finance and Economics; the BAE Student Research Lab; a clinical psychology lab; electronic classrooms offering multimedia learning tools; and the Education Center, which houses an eight-classroom Early Childhood Center, observation rooms, and an educational resource center.

Costs

Tuition and fees for the academic year 2009–10 were $23,490; room and board, $9154; and books and supplies, approximately $700. Students should expect to pay a $100 activities fee and a $25 registration fee each semester.

Financial Aid

Financial aid is awarded on the basis of the financial need of the student and family. Approximately 98 percent of Rivier's full-time undergraduate students receive financial aid from the College or from government or private sources. Federal aid includes Federal Pell Grants, Federal Supplemental Educational Opportunity Grants, Federal Perkins Loans, Federal Stafford Student Loans, the Federal PLUS loan program, and the Federal Work-Study Program. To be considered for financial aid, a student must file the Free Application for Federal Student Aid (FAFSA) with the federal government as soon as possible after January 1 for the coming year. FAFSA results should be on file with the College Financial Aid Office prior to March 1 for the following academic year. Each applicant is assessed individually to determine the best combination of grant, work, scholarship, and loan amounts to meet the need of the student. The College awards more than $6 million in merit-based scholarships and grants annually, ranging in value from $1000 to full tuition. For more information, students should contact the Office of Financial Aid.

Faculty

The College employs 71 full-time faculty members. The full-time student–faculty ratio is 15:1. Part-time instructors in specialized areas are working professionals who bring current knowledge and expertise in their field to their classes. All classes are taught by faculty members, and department chairs serve as academic advisers to students in their major programs.

Student Government

Every full-time day student automatically becomes a member of the Student Government Association (SGA) upon registration and payment of the student activity fee. The main goals of the SGA are to stimulate active participation in all College functions, to establish and maintain effective channels of communication among members of the College community and the community at large, and to foster a mutual trust, encourage a spirit of cooperation, and initiate new endeavors. The SGA also supervises student clubs and organizations and oversees their finances. The SGA Executive Board serves as the channel of communication through which the views of the students on institutional policies reach the College administration.

Admission Requirements

Applicants for admission should ordinarily have completed, in an accredited high school, a minimum of 16 academic units, including 4 in English, 2 in a modern foreign language, 3 in mathematics, 2 in social science, 2 in science, and 3 in electives. The most successful candidates are in the upper half of their class, with at least a B average. Combined SAT scores average 1410–1500. A personal interview is strongly recommended but not required.

Rivier welcomes applications from qualified transfer candidates from accredited institutions, as well as applications from international students. Transfer students must forward transcripts of all previous college work and a high school transcript. International students must fulfill the requirements for general admission; they may also be required to submit Test of English as a Foreign Language (TOEFL) scores. Deferred admission may be granted to students who wish to postpone entrance for up to one year, provided they have not been enrolled full-time at another postsecondary institution.

Application and Information

Applications must be accompanied by a nonrefundable $25 application fee, SAT scores, one letter of recommendation, and a high school transcript. The School of Undergraduate Studies employs a system of rolling admission that allows qualified students to be admitted approximately one month after their application is completed. Transfers should apply by June 1 for fall admission and by December 1 for spring admission. Those applying for financial aid should observe the March 1 deadline. Interviews are arranged through the Admissions Office. Students may apply online at the College's Web site.

For an application or additional information, please contact:

Office of Undergraduate Admissions
Rivier College
420 South Main Street
Nashua, New Hampshire 03060
Phone: 603-897-8507
800-44-RIVIER (toll-free)
Fax: 603-891-1799
E-mail: admissions@rivier.edu
Web site: http://www.rivier.edu

Students enjoy Rivier's great location in the heart of New England—approximately an hour's drive from Boston, the mountains, and the seacoast.

ROBERT MORRIS UNIVERSITY

PITTSBURGH AND MOON TOWNSHIP, PENNSYLVANIA

The University

Robert Morris University (RMU), founded in 1921, is one of the leading universities in the Pittsburgh region. RMU built its reputation by offering strong academic programs in traditional business fields such as accounting, finance, marketing, and management. To prepare students for success in a changing and competitive workforce, the University has created undergraduate programs in communications, information systems, engineering, mathematics, science, education, social sciences, and nursing during the past decade. The University also offers students the opportunity to gain a global perspective by studying abroad.

Because Robert Morris University is a teaching-centered institution, classes are small and are taught by faculty members, not teaching assistants. The student-faculty ratio is 15:1, and the University has an average class size of 24. More than 4,800 full- and part-time undergraduate and graduate students from forty states and thirty-seven countries are enrolled at Robert Morris University.

The 78,000-square-foot Nicholson Center, which opened in 1999, is located at the heart of the campus and provides a gathering place for students, alumni, and faculty and staff members. The center is the hub for student activities and programs, and it houses a food court, a café, a bookstore, and administrative offices.

Nearly 100 activities and organizations help students to develop leadership skills, network professionally, and meet new friends. Student activities include varsity, club, and intramural sports; fraternities and sororities; student government; and community service projects. RMU offers twenty-three NCAA Division I men's and women's varsity sports, including the only Division I men's and women's ice hockey programs in Pittsburgh. In 2003, the University purchased the Island Sports Center, a 32-acre sports and recreation complex with two ice rinks, two multipurpose rinks, an indoor golf driving range, a miniature golf course, batting cages, a fitness center, a pro shop, and a bistro.

The Student Life Office organizes dances, parties, movie screenings, comedy acts, health and wellness fairs, educational programs, and day trips. Business organizations, professional clubs, and honor societies provide students with career preparation opportunities. RMU students also get involved in the community, organizing Habitat for Humanity projects, coordinating blood drives, collecting food donations, and organizing holiday parties for needy youngsters.

Robert Morris University offers eighteen graduate degree programs including the Master of Science (M.S.) in business education, communications and information systems, competitive intelligence systems, engineering management, human resource management, information security and assurance, information systems management, information technology project management, instructional leadership, Internet information systems, nonprofit management, nursing, organizational studies, and taxation; the Master of Business Administration (M.B.A.); the Doctor of Nursing Practice (D.N.P.); the Doctor of Science (D.Sc.) in information systems and communications; and the Doctor of Philosophy (Ph.D.) in instructional management and leadership.

Location

The 230-acre main campus is located in Moon Township, Pennsylvania, just 15 minutes from Pittsburgh International Airport and 17 miles from downtown Pittsburgh. The RMU Island Sports Center, a 32-acre sports and recreation complex, is located 15 minutes from campus on Neville Island, while the University's Center for Adult and Continuing Education is located in downtown Pittsburgh.

Majors and Degrees

Robert Morris University offers sixty undergraduate degree programs, many of which offer multiple specializations. Bachelor's degree programs include the Bachelor of Arts (B.A.) in applied mathematics, communications, English, environmental science, media arts, and social science; the Bachelor of Fine Arts (B.F.A.) in media arts; the Bachelor of Science (B.S.) in actuarial science, applied mathematics, applied psychology, biology, business education, competitive intelligence systems, computer information systems, elementary education, engineering (industrial, mechanical, and software), environmental science, health services administration, information sciences, manufacturing engineering, nuclear medicine technology, nursing, organizational studies, professional communications and information systems, and social science; and the Bachelor of Science in Business Administration (B.S.B.A.) in accounting, economics, finance, hospitality and tourism management, management, marketing, and sport management. In addition, RMU offers preparation for secondary teacher certification in biology, business, communication, English, mathematics, and social studies education.

Academic Programs

Robert Morris is on a two-semester schedule with various summer sessions. A total of 126 credits are required for the bachelor's degree. Internship or co-op credits of 3 to 12 hours may be used toward degree requirements. The University participates in a cross-registration program with nine local colleges through the Pittsburgh Council on Higher Education consortium.

Academic Facilities

Learning resources include a traditional library with more than 137,000 bound volumes, more than 100 reference databases, and nearly 600 periodical subscriptions.

The Academic Media Center, with full production facilities, provides students with opportunities to collaborate on projects in all areas of media, including television/video production, audio production, and photography.

State-of-the-art laboratory facilities were recently opened to support the engineering, mathematics, science, and nursing programs. Graphic and Web design students benefit from a cutting-edge design studio.

Costs

Annual tuition for the 2009–10 year was $19,950 flat rate, based on a 24- to 36-credit, two-semester schedule. Room and board fees were $10,370 based on double occupancy and a full meal plan.

Financial Aid

More than 90 percent of RMU undergraduates receive some sort of financial aid, including scholarships, grants, loans, and work-study programs. Both need-based and achievement-based awards are available. All applicants must complete the admissions application, the Free Application for Federal Student Aid, and the grant forms from their own state.

Faculty

The University has nearly 400 full- and part-time faculty members; 81 percent of full-time faculty holds terminal degrees in their fields. The student-faculty ratio is 15:1 and the average class size is 24. Students may take advantage of the expertise offered by the faculty in academic advisement and counseling, as well as counseling from the staff at the Center for Student Success.

Student Government

The Student Government Association represents all student organizations, including fraternities and sororities. Members participate in the planning of all social and cultural events on campus.

Admission Requirements

First-time freshmen must submit an application for admission with a $30 application fee (waived for online applicants), official high school transcripts or GED credential, and official SAT or ACT scores. Preference is given to applicants with a minimum 3.0 high school GPA and a combined SAT score of 1000 or a composite ACT score of 22.

Transfer students who have earned credits from another regionally accredited institution must submit transcripts from all postsecondary institutions attended and must have a minimum 2.0 GPA. Students with less than 30 college credits must also submit high school transcripts or GED credential.

Interviews are not required for admission except for students interested in the engineering, elementary education, and nursing programs. Students are encouraged to arrange for a campus visit with an enrollment manager.

Robert Morris University is committed to a policy of nondiscrimination on the basis of race, sex, color, religion, national origin, or handicap.

Application and Information

Students are encouraged to submit applications in the fall of their senior year of high school. Official transcripts and counselor recommendations should accompany the application; there is a $30 application processing fee that is waived for online applicants.

Robert Morris uses a rolling admission system; students are considered for acceptance as soon as all application materials have been received and evaluated.

For additional information and application materials, students should contact:

Office of Admissions
Robert Morris University
6001 University Boulevard
Moon Township, Pennsylvania 15108
Phone: 800-762-0097 (toll-free)
Web site: http://www.rmu.edu

Robert Morris University's Nicholson Center.

ROBERTS WESLEYAN COLLEGE

ROCHESTER, NEW YORK

The College

Roberts Wesleyan College (RWC) is characterized by its mission: scholarship, spiritual formation, and service. RWC was founded in 1866 as the first Free Methodist academic institution in North America. Since then, the institution has continually adapted its programs to meet the current academic, professional, and personal needs of its students. The integration of broad-based intellectual thought with the Judeo-Christian heritage continues to be the motivation for Roberts Wesleyan's existence. The College fosters wholesome principles by setting standards for student life, requiring regular chapel attendance, and maintaining a perspective rich in values within the classroom.

The current enrollment is 1,928: 1,382 women and 546 men. Although students come primarily from New York State, twenty-seven other states and eighteen other countries are represented. The majority of students are between 18 and 25 years of age, but there is a growing population of married and older students. The traditional undergraduate population is primarily residential, with approximately 65 percent of students living on campus.

RWC offers a broad selection of student activities. Student leaders, in cooperation with the Assistant Dean for Student Programming, plan a calendar of numerous events each year, including social, cultural, and religious programs. The College's suburban Rochester location also allows students to take advantage of cultural and academic opportunities within the community. The College's intramural program complements the intercollegiate sports program. There are six varsity sports for men: basketball, cross-country, golf, soccer, tennis, and track and field; there are seven varsity sports for women: basketball, cross-country, golf, soccer, tennis, track and field, and volleyball. Students may take advantage of the Voller Athletic Center, which includes a pool, four basketball courts, an indoor track, racquetball courts, a weight room, saunas, a student center, BT's Café, and a bookstore. The Career Services Office provides numerous services for students. Other College services available to students include academic advisement, counseling, and assistance from the Learning Center.

The College is a member of the Middle States Association of Colleges and Schools, the Association of Colleges and Universities of the State of New York, Rochester Area Colleges, the Association of Free Methodist Educational Institutions, the Council of Independent Colleges and Universities, and the Council for Christian Colleges & Universities. The programs in accounting, art, business, education, management, marketing, music, nursing, and social work are professionally accredited. The Art Department is accredited by the National Association of Schools of Art and Design. The Music Department is accredited by the National Association of Schools of Music. The Division of Nursing is accredited by the Commission on Collegiate Nursing Education. The Division of Social Work is accredited by the Council on Social Work Education. The Division of Business and Management is accredited by the International Assembly for Collegiate Business Education. The Division of Teacher Education is accredited by New York State Regents Accreditation of Teacher Education.

In addition to undergraduate programs, RWC offers the Master of Education, Master of Music in Education, Master of Science in Health Administration, Master of Science in Nursing Education, Master of Science in Nursing Leadership and Administration, Master of Science in School Counseling, Master of Science in School Psychology, Master of Science in Strategic Leadership, Master of Science in Strategic Marketing, and Master of Social Work degree programs. Northeastern Seminary at Roberts Wesleyan College offers the Master of Arts in Theological Studies, Master of Divinity, Master of Divinity/Master of Social Work (with RWC), and Doctor of Ministry degree programs.

Location

Roberts Wesleyan College is located 8 miles southwest of Rochester, New York, in the suburb of North Chili. Rochester, with a metropolitan-area population of more than 1 million, is a thriving cultural and corporate area. Eastman School of Music, the Rochester Philharmonic Orchestra, and several leading corporations, such as Eastman Kodak, Xerox, Paychex, Bausch & Lomb, and PAETEC are based there.

The College seeks a strong relationship with the community, and the resulting internships and opportunities for practical work are particularly advantageous for RWC students. Students and graduates benefit from the employment opportunities that result from Rochester's economy. Lake Ontario, Niagara Falls, Watkins Glen, Letchworth Park, and the Finger Lakes are all nearby.

Majors and Degrees

Baccalaureate degrees are offered in accounting and information management, adolescence education (biology, chemistry, English, mathematics, physics, social studies, and Spanish), art education, art-graphic design, art—studio art, biblical studies, biochemistry, biology, biology with concentration in medical technology, business administration, chemistry, childhood education and special education (elementary education), communication, comprehensive science, comprehensive social studies, computer science, contemporary ministries, criminal justice, cross-disciplinary studies, early childhood education and special education, economic crime investigation, elementary education (childhood education and special education), engineering (with RIT, RPI, or Clarkson), English, forensic science, health administration, history, humanities, information systems management, international business, liberal arts, management and social entrepreneurship, marketing, mathematics, middle childhood education and special education, music, music education, music performance (instrument, piano, and voice), nursing, organizational management, pharmacy (with University at Buffalo), physical education, physics, psychology, religion/philosophy, religious studies, secondary education (adolescence education), social work, Spanish, special education and childhood education (elementary education), time-based media, and visual art education (art education).

A 3-2 program in engineering is offered in cooperation with Clarkson University, Rensselaer Polytechnic Institute (RPI), and Rochester Institute of Technology (RIT). The program leads to a B.S. in mathematics, chemistry, or physics from RWC and a B.S. in engineering from Clarkson, RPI, or RIT. A B.S./M.S. program is also available with RIT.

Secondary (grades 5–12) teaching certification may be earned in biology, chemistry, English, mathematics, physics, social studies, and Spanish. Preprofessional programs include dentistry, law, medicine, pharmacy, physical therapy, and veterinary medicine.

Other areas of preparation include library science and medical technology.

Academic Programs

RWC endeavors to involve each student in learning experiences that promote commitment to Christian stewardship and service to society. Approximately 45 semester hours of core courses are required of each baccalaureate degree candidate. These liberal arts survey courses introduce four main fields of knowledge: biological science, physical science, and mathematics; history and the behavioral sciences; language, literature, and the fine arts; and biblical studies and philosophy. A minimum of 124 semester hours is required for graduation with a baccalaureate degree, including a minimum of 30 to 81 semester hours within the student's major discipline.

Many academic programs at Roberts Wesleyan include internships or practical work experiences. Independent study and cross-cultural study opportunities are also available. Students may receive credit through the Advanced Placement Program, the International Baccalaureate Program, or the College-Level Examination Program. The Learning Center provides assistance for students possessing exceptional skills or a deficiency in any area.

The College calendar consists of two 15-week semesters scheduled from September to December and from January to May. Three sessions are held in the summer.

Off-Campus Programs

Various off-campus opportunities exist for which credit is awarded. These include the Appalachian Semester in Kentucky, Focus on the Family Institute in Colorado, Spanish language studies at the University of Murcia in Spain, EDUVenture in Irian Jaya, and a semester or full year of study at Richmond College in London, England. Under the direction of an RWC professor, students may also participate in a short-term exchange study program with Osaka Christian College and Seminary in Osaka, Japan. There are also opportunities for off-campus experiences through the Council for Christian Colleges & Universities. These include the American Studies Program, Australia Studies Centre, China Studies Program, Contemporary Music Center, Latin American Studies Program, Los Angeles Film Studies Center, Middle East Studies Program, Programmes in Oxford, Uganda Studies Program, and Washington Journalism Center. The January Experience Program offers transcultural and enrichment courses in this country or abroad. In addition, through RWC's membership in the Rochester Area Colleges consortium, students may cross-register to take courses at other member institutions.

Academic Facilities

The 43,000-square-foot B. Thomas Golisano Library is a LEED-certified building with a geothermal heating and cooling system. The Golisano Library includes a 24-hour computer lab and study café, two smart classrooms for bibliographic instruction (including forty computer stations), two fireplaces for comfortable study areas, 375 student stations, and a graduate study room. The library holds 132,000 volumes (with room for 300,000), 1,100 periodicals, more than 100 online databases (most with full text, including JSTOR), Internet access, and 171,000 microforms, recordings, and filmstrips. Also included in the library are the Learning Center, the Historical Center, and Archives. Through its participation in the Rochester Regional Research Library Council, the library provides access to extensive interlibrary loan resources.

Well-equipped science laboratories, a lecture auditorium, and computer laboratories connected to the campus network are included in the Merlin G. Smith Science Center. The new Hastings Center for Academics houses the undergraduate divisions of business and teacher education. Other facilities include the music studios, practice rooms, and recital auditorium of Cox Hall; the newly renovated Carpenter Hall which includes classrooms and offices for the social science and social work divisions; the Cultural Life Center, which houses Shewan Recital Hall, Hale Auditorium, and Davison Art Gallery; the Rinker Community Service Center; and the soccer stadium and Mondo track. High-speed Internet connections for each student are available in all residence halls. The academic areas of campus are wireless.

Costs

Tuition for full-time study for the 2010–11 academic year is $23,460 but varies if a student's course load is fewer than 12 or more than 18 credit hours. There are additional fees for music and laboratory courses. Room and board is $8826; miscellaneous fees are $900. Book costs and personal expenses vary with individual needs.

Financial Aid

Roberts Wesleyan College offers a complete financial aid program, consisting of grants, scholarships, loans, and employment. Filing the Free Application for Federal Student Aid (FAFSA) is a prerequisite for determining eligibility for most financial aid programs. Sources of aid include Federal Pell Grants, Federal Supplemental Educational Opportunity Grants, Federal Perkins Loans, and Federal Stafford Student Loans; New York State Tuition Assistance Program awards; and institutional resources. Numerous on-campus employment opportunities are available. Institutional aid is also available in recognition of academic, athletic, artistic, and musical achievement. More than 94 percent of the student body receives financial aid each year. In 2007 RWC was ranked third in the Princeton Review's Top 10 Best Value Colleges. In 2009, RWC was ranked as a top tier Northern master's university by *U.S. News & World Report* and is also listed by the Princeton Review as one of 2010's Best Northern Colleges.

Faculty

The primary concern of the faculty at RWC is to provide an educational experience of high-quality. Sixty-seven percent of the professors hold the doctoral or terminal degree, and all are well respected within their specific discipline. The 102 full-time and 146 part-time faculty members are committed to Christian higher education and are genuinely interested in each student's development. A 14:1 student-faculty ratio allows for much individualized attention, and most professors go well beyond their tasks of teaching and advising to participate in campus activities.

Student Government

All students belong to the Student Association and have the freedom to express their opinions to the staff, faculty, and administration. There are also elected senators and officers, under the direction of the Office of Student Services, who act as liaisons between the student body and administration in areas concerning academics and student activities.

Admission Requirements

Because the type of student a college enrolls significantly determines the personality of the institution, Roberts Wesleyan seeks students whose personal lives are characterized by honesty, integrity, and devotion to high moral and ethical standards. Admission consideration is given to applicants who rank in the upper third of their graduating class and have earned a minimum of 12 academic units of high school credit, with no fewer than 4 units in English, 2 units in algebra (or 1 in algebra and 1 in geometry), and 1 unit in biology, chemistry, or physics. Three years each of social studies, a foreign language, and science are strongly recommended. Further preparation in mathematics and science is required of applicants who wish to enter degree programs in nursing, mathematics, or science. Scores on the SAT or ACT and a formal recommendation are required. Special talents are considered an asset for applicants but are not required. An on-campus admission interview is strongly recommended. In admitting students, the College does not discriminate on the basis of race, age, color, sex, handicap, creed, or national or ethnic origin. Children of alumni and staff members are considered on the same basis as other applicants.

Transfer students must fulfill the same admission requirements as first-time students and must also have transcripts forwarded to the College from all the institutions they have attended. Credit is usually accepted from regionally accredited institutions for any course in which a grade of C– or above has been earned if the course parallels a course given at RWC.

Application and Information

Applicants should submit an application form (or apply online), the $35 application fee, a completed recommendation form, SAT or ACT scores, and transcripts from all schools previously attended. Art students should prepare a portfolio for review by the art faculty, and music students should schedule an audition with the Music Department. Students are encouraged to submit an application prior to the February 1 priority deadline. Admission decisions are made on a rolling basis, and students are notified of the admission decision as soon as all of their credentials have been received and evaluated.

For more information and application forms, students should contact:

Kirk Kettinger
Director of Admissions
Roberts Wesleyan College
2301 Westside Drive
Rochester, New York 14624-1997
Phone: 585-594-6400
800-777-4RWC (toll-free)
Fax: 585-594-6371
E-mail: admissions@roberts.edu
Web site: http://www.roberts.edu

The B. Thomas Golisano Library.

ROCHESTER INSTITUTE OF TECHNOLOGY

R·I·T

ROCHESTER, NEW YORK

The Institute

Rochester Institute of Technology (RIT) is one of the world's leading career-oriented, technological universities. RIT's eight colleges offer more than ninety undergraduate programs in areas such as engineering, computing, information technology, engineering technology, business, hospitality, science, art, design, photography, biomedical sciences, game design and development, and the liberal arts including psychology, advertising and public relations, and public policy. Students may choose from more than ninety different minors to develop personal and professional interests that complement their academic program. Experiential education is integrated into many programs through cooperative education, internships, study abroad, and undergraduate research. As home to the National Technical Institute for the Deaf (NTID), RIT is a leader in providing access services for deaf and hard-of-hearing students. RIT enrolls students from every state and more than ninety countries.

Close to 70 percent of RIT's approximately 11,300 full-time undergraduate students live on the campus in residence halls or campus apartments. The residence halls have eight special-interest houses where students with shared interests live and learn together. Park Point is located on the northeast corner of the campus and consists of more than 100 residential units and approximately 80,000 square feet of retail space, including a mix of restaurants and shops.

Because RIT's student body is so diverse, there are many different activities, clubs, organizations, and sports in which students may participate. There are seventeen fraternities and twelve sororities, representing approximately 5 percent of the student population. A radio station and a biweekly student magazine allow those interested in media to gain experience on campus. A number of special interest clubs and career organizations are also available, and RIT offers twenty-three varsity sports, including Division I men's hockey. Recreational facilities include an ice rink, an aquatics center, a field house with an indoor track, and fitness facilities.

Location

The greater Rochester area has a population of about 745,000. Per-capita income is among the highest in the nation for metropolitan centers. The area's many internationally known industries employ a high proportion of scientists, technologists, and skilled workers. Rochester is the world center of photography, the largest producer of optical goods in the United States, and among the leaders in graphic arts and reproduction and in production of electronic equipment and precision instruments. Rochester's industries have always been closely associated with RIT's programs and progress.

Majors and Degrees

The College of Applied Science and Technology offers the Bachelor of Science in civil engineering technology, computer engineering technology, electrical engineering technology, electrical/mechanical engineering technology, manufacturing engineering technology, mechanical engineering technology, and telecommunications engineering technology. It also grants the Bachelor of Science in environmental management and technology, hospitality and service management, nutrition management, packaging science, and safety technology. An undeclared option allowing freshmen to delay selecting a major for up to a year is available in the School of Engineering Technology.

The E. Philip Saunders College of Business offers the Bachelor of Science in accounting, consumer finance, finance, graphic media marketing, international business, management, management information systems, and marketing. An accelerated B.S./M.B.A. option is available, as is a minor in entrepreneurship. An undeclared option allowing freshmen to delay the selection of their major for up to one year is also available.

The B. Thomas Golisano College of Computing and Information Sciences offers the Bachelor of Science degree in applied networking and systems administration, computer science, game design and development, information technology, medical informatics, new media interactive development, and software engineering.

The Kate Gleason College of Engineering grants the Bachelor of Science in biomedical engineering, chemical engineering, computer engineering, electrical engineering, industrial and systems engineering, mechanical engineering, and microelectronic engineering. Degree options in aerospace, automotive, bioengineering, biomedical, energy and environment, ergonomics, information systems, manufacturing, and software engineering are also offered within the college. Accelerated B.S./M.S. options are available. The Engineering Exploration Program, which allows freshmen to delay the selection of their major for up to one year, is also available.

The College of Imaging Arts and Sciences offers the Bachelor of Fine Arts in advertising photography; ceramics and ceramic sculpture; digital cinema; film, video, and animation; fine art photography; fine arts studio, glass and glass sculpture; graphic design; illustration; industrial design; interior design; medical illustration; metals and jewelry design; new media design and imaging; photojournalism; 3D digital graphics; visual media; and woodworking and furniture design. The college also offers the Bachelor of Science in biomedical photographic communications, digital media, graphic media, imaging and photographic technology, and new media/publishing. An undeclared option allowing freshmen to delay the selection of their major for up to one year is also available in the School of Art, the School of Design, and the School for American Crafts.

The College of Liberal Arts confers the Bachelor of Science in advertising and public relations, criminal justice, economics, journalism, international studies, philosophy, professional and technical communication, psychology, public policy, and urban and community studies. The Liberal Arts Exploration Program is designed to help undecided students formulate education and career plans.

The College of Science offers the Bachelor of Science in applied mathematics, applied statistics, biology, biochemistry, bioinformatics, biomedical sciences, biotechnology, chemistry, computational mathematics, diagnostic medical sonography (ultrasound), environmental chemistry, environmental science, imaging science, physician assistant studies, physics, and polymer chemistry. Special options are available in premedical studies (medicine, dentistry, veterinary medicine). Minors are available in astronomy, exercise science, imaging science, mathematics, physics, and statistics. Accelerated B.S./M.S. and B.S./M.B.A. programs are available. The General Science Exploration Program, which allows freshmen to delay the selection of their major for up to one year, is also available.

As home of the National Technical Institute for the Deaf, RIT is a leader in providing educational opportunities and access services for deaf and hard-of-hearing students. NTID awards associate degree programs and offers a prebaccalaureate studies program for the deaf and hard-of-hearing. The associate degree programs prepare students for immediate employment after graduation or transfer into one of RIT's bachelor's degree programs. The prebaccalaureate studies program prepares students, who may not qualify initially, for entry into a bachelor's degree program. Nearly 50 percent of the 1,300 deaf and hard-of-hearing students at RIT are enrolled directly into one of the bachelor's degree programs in the other seven colleges.

Academic Programs

Most students entering RIT enroll directly in the college and academic program of their choice; specialization is spread over the duration of their study. Options for undeclared students are available in several colleges and a University Studies program is available for students who wish to explore programs in two or more colleges. Approximately one third of the program of each professional curriculum consists of general education courses in the humanities, math and science, and social sciences. Students may choose from more than ninety different minors to develop personal and professional interests that complement their academic program. Double-major and accelerated dual-degree (combined bachelor's/masters) options are available. An honors program admits approximately 180 students each year. Air Force and

Army ROTC programs are available on the campus. A Naval ROTC program is offered jointly with the University of Rochester.

Every academic program at RIT offers some form of experiential education opportunity. This takes many forms, including cooperative education, internships, study abroad, undergraduate research, and industry-sponsored project work. Notable among these programs is cooperative education (co-op). The College of Applied Science and Technology, the E. Philip Saunders College of Business, the B. Thomas Golisano College of Computing and Information Sciences, and the Kate Gleason College of Engineering all require co-op for undergraduate students. It is available on an optional basis in other RIT colleges. Co-op students alternate periods of full-time study with periods of full-time paid work experience in business and industry directly related to their field of study and career interests. Last year more than 3,500 students completed work assignments with nearly 1,900 employers, earning collectively in excess of $30 million.

Off-Campus Programs

RIT has three international branch campuses. The American College of Management and Technology is a branch campus in Croatia, offering an associate degree and a Bachelor of Science degree in hospitality and service management, a Master of Science degree in service management, and several certificate programs to serve the local tourism industries. The American University of Kosovo provides a career-oriented education that fosters the links between the university, industry, and government necessary to support the workforce development needs of Kosovo. RIT Dubai offers graduate and undergraduate programs for students from the Middle East, North Africa and Southeast Asia. RIT has a growing study-abroad program. Through affiliations with other institutions, RIT offers more than 150 study-abroad programs in twenty countries.

Academic Facilities

Excellent facilities add to the quality of academic life. Students have access to a laser-optics laboratory, an observatory, an animal-care facility, more than 100 color and black-and-white photography darkrooms, electronic prepress and publishing equipment, ceramic kilns, glass furnaces, a blacksmithing area, a student-operated restaurant, computer graphics and robotic labs, and some of the most up-to-date microelectronic, telecommunications, and computer engineering facilities in the U.S. Wallace Memorial Library is a true multimedia learning center. Its collections are exceptionally extensive in the areas of art and design, education for the deaf, photography, and printing.

RIT is a leader in academic computing, and students use state-of-the-art computer equipment regardless of their major. Central computer systems can be accessed via a high-speed data network connecting the library, academic facilities, residence hall rooms, and on-campus apartments. There are more than sixty locations campuswide, with wireless networking connectivity utilizing 802.11b technology. The RIT campus network is served by two OC3 connections, each operating at a data rate of 155 Mbps, and one T3 connection operating at 45 Mbps. RIT is among a select group of institutions with access to the Internet2 research network, a collaborative research and development effort led by more than 170 U.S. universities working in partnership with industry and government. Its goal is to develop a new family of advanced Internet applications and technologies.

Costs

For 2008–09, tuition for the normal academic year (three academic quarters) was $27,624. Students on the cooperative education plan pay tuition only for the quarters they are at RIT. Fees, including the activities and health fees, are $411 for the academic year. Room and board (twenty meals per week) cost $9381.

Financial Aid

Approximately 77 percent of the full-time undergraduates receive some form of financial aid that includes RIT scholarships, alumni or industry-supported scholarships, and state and federal government grants. A variety of loans and part-time work positions are also available. The FAFSA must be submitted by March 1. Giving full recognition to scholarship apart from financial need, RIT awards a number of academic scholarships based on grades, test scores, and activities. Freshmen applying by February 1 and transfers applying as juniors by April 1 are considered for these scholarships.

Faculty

There are 798 full-time faculty members, 406 part-time faculty members, and an administrative and supporting staff of more than 1,800. Approximately 80 percent of the faculty members have earned a Ph.D. or the terminal degree in their field.

Student Government

The Student Government is the representative body for students. It works with RIT administration and faculty and staff members to communicate the needs and desires of the student body and to communicate the decisions of the administration to the students. Fraternity and sorority members, off-campus and hearing-impaired students, and students from minority groups elect special representative bodies. All full-time and part-time undergraduate and graduate students become members of the Student Government when they pay the student activities fee.

Admission Requirements

The general requirements for freshman entrance are a high school diploma (an equivalency diploma is considered), high school grades that give evidence of the ability to complete college work successfully, satisfactory scores on the SAT or ACT, and completion of prerequisite high school–level math and science courses indicated in the college catalog. An important factor for admission is the record of academic achievement in high school (or in another college in the case of transfer students). The results of standardized tests are supplementary. Students applying for programs in the fine and applied arts must submit a portfolio of original artwork.

Rochester Institute of Technology admits qualified men and women of any race, color, national or ethnic origin, religion, sexual orientation, gender identity, gender expression, or marital status. RIT does not discriminate on the basis of handicap in the recruitment or admission of students or in the operation of any of its programs or activities, as specified by federal laws and regulations.

Application and Information

An application, a nonrefundable processing fee of $50, official transcripts of all high school or college records, and SAT or ACT scores (for prospective freshmen) should be forwarded to RIT. Freshman applicants who provide all required materials for entry in the fall quarter by February 1 receive admission notification by March 15. Prospective freshmen who apply after February 1 and all transfer students are notified of the admission decision by mail on a rolling basis four to six weeks after their application is complete. RIT also offers an early decision plan; prospective freshmen must have their completed application and credentials on file in the Admissions Office by December 1 to receive notification by January 15.

For application forms, students should contact:

Director of Undergraduate Admissions
Rochester Institute of Technology
60 Lomb Memorial Drive
Rochester, New York 14623-5604
Phone: 585-475-6631
Fax: 585-475-7424
E-mail: admissions@rit.edu
Web site: http://www.rit.edu

A view of the campus.

ROCKY MOUNTAIN COLLEGE OF ART + DESIGN

DENVER, COLORADO

The College

When Philip J. Steele founded Rocky Mountain College of Art + Design (RMCAD) in 1963, his dream was to provide students with an education based on traditional art and design principles in an environment that fostered personal meaning and growth. From years of working as an artist and teacher, he understood that in order to provide a high-quality education, it was essential that students have the opportunity to study with professional artists and designers who could both teach the courses and guide students as they sought to push the boundaries of creativity and innovation. The College continues to reflect this vision today.

As a privately owned institution, RMCAD is regionally accredited by the Higher Learning Commission of the North Central Association of Colleges and Schools and by the National Association of Schools of Art and Design (NASAD). The interior design program is accredited by the Council for Interior Design Accreditation.

RMCAD's long history of successful alumni is its testimony to an educational philosophy that works. The RMCAD curriculum is specifically designed to facilitate each student's transition from the classroom to employment within their chosen profession. In fact, more than 86 percent of RMCAD graduates report they are working in their field of study.

Location

RMCAD is located on twenty-three wooded acres at the foot of the Rocky Mountains in Lakewood, Colorado, in the west-central part of metropolitan Denver. Looking east from the campus, students can see downtown Denver's skyline; looking west, the beautiful Rocky Mountains. Whether they are into skiing, snowboarding, hiking, or just soaking up Denver's more than 300 days of sunshine each year, students find the Rocky Mountain Front Range is a great place to live. With a population of more than 2 million people, Denver offers students a multitude of ways to spend their free time—from museums to concert halls to shopping centers and entertainment districts.

Majors and Degrees

RMCAD offers a Bachelor of Fine Arts degree in seven different areas of study: animation (2-D or 3-D), art education, fine arts, game art, graphic design and interactive media, illustration, and interior design.

Academic Programs

While traditional educational approaches of lecture, demonstration, teaching by example, and presentation of studio technique are utilized, RMCAD is extremely responsive to the contemporary climate of all of the art and design disciplines. Classroom methods incorporate the newest equipment, processes, and ideas to further challenge students in an atmosphere that encourages experimentation with media not yet established as art materials. As a result, graduates are both versatile and qualified to produce complete, professional-quality work.

The strength of all of RMCAD's art and design programs is realized in the development of each student's perceptual, technical, and creative abilities to the highest level. This rigor enables students to realize success in a challenging and competitive marketplace and helps ensure professional opportunities for each student after graduation. Emphasis is placed on skills that include consolidating ideas into visual form, rendering artwork, sharpening communication skills, developing creative concepts, and improving career skills.

The College operates on a trimester system. Students who take a full-time course load can complete their program in a minimum of eight semesters. Students who maintain continuous enrollment each term, including the summer, do not experience tuition increases.

Academic Facilities

RMCAD's campus includes eighteen historical buildings built in a variety of twentieth-century architectural styles. All of the buildings have been modernized to create a wireless campus with state-of-the-art classrooms. The campus has six Macintosh and Windows NT computer labs that are connected to print centers and are designed for multiuse by all departments. Specific labs are designated for 3-D computer animation, video and sound, multimedia, computer-aided drafting, and advanced special effects. Special learning facilities include a woodshop, ceramics studio, photography lab, professional sound studio, 283-seat theater, 35-seat audiovisual theater, large meeting rooms, and a library/resource center.

The Philip J. Steele Gallery features a rotating schedule of exhibitions that includes a mix of student, faculty, and alumni work as well as displays by community groups and exhibitions by well-known visiting artists. Students can relax or study in the student lounge, take a break between classes on the grassy lawns under 100-year-old trees, shop in the College bookstore, or grab an espresso and a bite to eat at the Underground Café.

Costs

Tuition and fees at Rocky Mountain College of Art + Design for the 2010–11 academic year are $13,416 per semester. Housing costs average $7500 per year, depending on accommodations. Books and supplies are approximately $600 per semester. Costs are subject to change.

Financial Aid

A variety of financial aid programs are available to students attending RMCAD. These programs are designed to assist students in meeting their educational expenses. Some financial aid funds are limited, so students are encouraged to apply early. A number of scholarships are awarded annually to RMCAD students who have proven themselves through outstanding work and effort during the academic year. Rocky Mountain

College of Art + Design awards artist merit-based scholarships to incoming freshmen and transfer students. Prospective students should contact the Office of Admission or visit RMCAD's Web site for details.

Faculty

Rocky Mountain College of Art + Design employs approximately 25 full-time and 45 part-time or adjunct faculty members. Because RMCAD instructors are working artists, they possess a wide variety of educational and professional backgrounds. A trait they all share, however, is a dedication to the philosophy of integrating real-life experience with academic excellence.

Student Government

All current RMCAD students belong to the Student Government Association (SGA), a group formed to represent the student body to the college and outside community. The SGA coordinates activities, communication, and services of general benefit to RMCAD students. SGA seeks to enhance involvement in curricular, cocurricular, and extracurricular activities. Each spring, representatives are elected to serve as the voting membership of the SGA. The elected students represent their peers on matters that are brought to the attention of the SGA, including proposed programs and policies. The SGA encourages all current RMCAD students to attend meetings and to bring ideas and concerns to the attention of the SGA.

Admission Requirements

Rocky Mountain College of Art + Design admits students who have a desire to explore new possibilities, work hard to realize their personal best, and who are eager to produce original, innovative works. Although a variety of evaluation criteria are necessary for a sound admission decision, evidence of potential in the fine and applied art disciplines is the primary consideration in the admissions process. A degree candidate must either be a graduate of an accredited high school and possess a minimum cumulative grade point average of 2.0 or possess a high school equivalency diploma with satisfactory GED scores. Applicants who do not possess a cumulative grade point average of 2.0 or higher may be admitted with a provisional status. Applicants must also present a portfolio of recent work, unless they are declaring interior design as their intended area of study. Students without a portfolio should ask an admissions counselor about substitute arrangements that may include alternative experiences or examples that illustrate an individual's interest and potential in professional art and design education. An interview with an admissions counselor, either in person or by telephone, is also required. Through the personal interview, applicants gain a better understanding of the visual arts education at Rocky Mountain College of Art + Design.

In addition to the above requirements, transfer students must arrange to have copies of official transcripts from all postsecondary institutions they have attended sent to the Admissions Department for review. Official transcripts for courses completed at colleges outside of the United States must be submitted to the College and to an approved evaluation agency before transfer credit can be evaluated by RMCAD.

Application and Information

Students are accepted to Rocky Mountain College of Art + Design on a rolling basis. Students are encouraged to apply as early as possible, however, in order to be considered for portfolio merit scholarships. Interested students should visit the Rocky Mountain College of Art + Design Web site for more details.

An application and additional information may be obtained by contacting:

Office of Admission
Rocky Mountain College of Art + Design
1600 Pierce Street
Denver, Colorado 80214
Phone: 800-888-2787 (toll-free)
E-mail: admissions@rmcad.edu
Web site: http://www.rmcad.edu

ROSEMONT COLLEGE

ROSEMONT, PENNSYLVANIA

The College

Founded in 1921, Rosemont College is an independent liberal arts institution in the Catholic tradition. Rosemont's reputation for academic excellence in an intimate setting is its hallmark. Rosemont College offers students an exceptional and comprehensive coeducational learning experience.

Rosemont College works to recognize and develop every student's unique talents. It believes that a student's educational experience should incorporate their goals, their strengths, and their efforts to make positive changes to the world. Students at Rosemont gain knowledge, develop critical skills, and grow as persons of character.

Rosemont is consistently highly ranked by *U.S. News & World Report*. It has been named to the John Templeton Foundation Honor Roll for Character-Building Colleges, a designation that recognizes colleges and universities that emphasize character building as an integral part of the college experience.

Rosemont is one college with three schools: the Undergraduate College, the School of Graduate Studies, and the School of Professional Studies. The nationally acclaimed, traditional Undergraduate College confers the Bachelor of Arts, the Bachelor of Fine Arts, and the Bachelor of Science degrees in twenty-three majors. Rosemont has approximately 7,000 living alumni, many of whom have been in the vanguard of expanding career and professional opportunities. They can be found in high-ranking positions in science and medicine, law, business, education, the social sciences, publishing, and the arts.

Building on its historic commitment to education, Rosemont also includes the Schools of Graduate Studies and Professional Studies, which are open to working people. The School of Professional Studies confers the Bachelor of Science and the Bachelor of Arts in three majors, while the School of Graduate Studies offers seven graduate degrees, including Master of Arts in education, English literature, and publishing programs, as well as a Master of Fine Arts degree in creative writing, a Master of Science in management, and a Master of Business Administration.

From the institution's early days through the present Cornelia Connelly, founder of the Society of the Holy Child Jesus, has been a driving force behind Rosemont's charge to educate students "to meet the wants of the age." Rosemont knows that students come to college with their eyes on their future. At Rosemont, their dreams are the starting point for an education that is truly their own. While at Rosemont, students will carve a unique path that leads from their dreams to the rest of their lives and all its rich possibilities.

Rosemont participates in NCAA Division III varsity teams for men's basketball, cross-country, golf, lacrosse, soccer, and tennis; and women's basketball, cross-country, field hockey, lacrosse, softball, tennis, and volleyball.

Location

Rosemont's 56-acre campus is located in the town of Rosemont, a historic suburban community with many shops, movie theaters, restaurants, and bookstores. The city of Philadelphia is 11 miles east of Rosemont and just a 20-minute train ride from the campus. The College's proximity to Philadelphia provides students with a vast array of cultural and social opportunities, such as the Philadelphia Museum of Art, the Philadelphia Orchestra, the Pennsylvania Ballet, and various professional sports events, including Phillies, Flyers, and Eagles games. Within the Philadelphia area there are approximately eighty other colleges and universities. Rosemont is ideally located for recreational activities; it is only a short distance from both the Pocono Mountains and the New Jersey shore.

Majors and Degrees

Rosemont College awards the Bachelor of Arts, the Bachelor of Fine Arts, and the Bachelor of Science degrees. Majors are offered in accounting, biology, business, chemistry, communication, education, economics, English, environmental studies, French, history, history of art, humanities, international business, philosophy, political science, psychology, religious studies, sociology, social science, Spanish, studio art and design, and women's studies. In addition, Rosemont offers ten preprofessional, certification, and dual-degree programs.

Academic Programs

To earn a Rosemont undergraduate degree, each candidate must complete 120 credits. In addition to the requirements of a major concentration, all students must complete general requirements. An internship, service-learning, or study-abroad experience is required prior to graduation. During their senior year, all students must successfully complete a comprehensive exam, exhibiting competency in their declared major.

Rosemont College offers dual-admission medical programs with the Drexel University College of Medicine, Temple University, and Villanova University.

For students interested in a French and business major, Rosemont offers specialized courses in business French to prepare students for the examination of the Chambre de Commerce et d'Industrie de Paris. The Certificat Pratique de Français Commercial et Économique is awarded to students who successfully complete this exam.

Rosemont offers programs granting certification in the following teaching areas: art education, early childhood education/elementary education, elementary education, secondary education, and special education with a concentration in hearing impaired.

Off-Campus Programs

Through academic exchange programs that expand course offerings, students may take courses at neighboring Villanova University, Eastern University, Arcadia University, Cabrini College, Chestnut Hill College, Gwynedd-Mercy College, Holy Family College, Immaculata University, and Neumann College.

Rosemont students may participate in any of a variety of study-abroad programs. These programs give students the opportunity to combine travel with academic and cultural study. Students receive full credit at Rosemont for course work successfully completed on an approved program.

There are many opportunities for full-semester internships in various fields of study. Each candidate must be academically qualified and meet the approval of the appropriate faculty member. Fieldwork and practicums, as well as summer internships, are also available.

Academic Facilities

The Student Academic Support Center, located in the Brown Science Building, is the comprehensive source for academic assistance. The center offers a wide range of advising, experiential learning, and learning support services to enhance students' educational experiences at the College. All services are offered to all students at no cost.

The Gertrude Kistler Memorial Library creates a setting that is conducive to study and research. The library was the first academic building erected on the campus. It houses more than 170,000 volumes, approximately 563 current periodicals, and numerous electronic indexes and databases as well as access to the Internet. The library also houses a 10,000-volume collection of children's literature. The online catalog, the Rosemont Electronic Learning and Library System (TRELLIS), is the basic index to the library's collections. TRELLIS includes a number of computerized periodical indexes and encyclopedias and provides access to the Internet's World Wide Web.

The science building is composed of the Dorothy McKenna Brown Science Building and the McShain Performing Arts Center. The Brown Science Building provides laboratory facilities and lecture rooms for the natural sciences. State-of-the-art equipment includes a phase microscope with video camera and color TV monitor, physiographs, spectrophotometers, and an environment chamber. The building also houses two electronic classrooms equipped with the latest in Windows PC and Macintosh technology. Students have access to laser and full-color printers, and scanners, as well as numerous software resources for word processing, desktop publishing, indexing, and graphic arts. A mobile cart containing eleven wireless laptop computers is also housed in the Brown Science Building and is available for use throughout the building. The McShain Performing Arts Center is a 300-seat auditorium used for special forums, theatrical performances, and ceremonies.

The Global Curriculum Classroom located in Good Counsel Hall, houses a sympodium, an interactive smart computer/touch screen; integrated projector DVD/VCR; and sound system. A mobile cart equipped with twenty-four wireless laptop computers is also located in the Global Curriculum Classroom.

Costs

For 2009–10, tuition for full-time students was $26,230; room and board were $10,580.

Financial Aid

Many Rosemont students receive some form of financial aid. Financial aid includes scholarships, grants, loans, and work-study awards. Most financial packages are a combination of various forms of aid. To apply for aid, students should submit the Free Application for Federal Student Aid (FAFSA) by February 15.

Faculty

The faculty is one of Rosemont's most important assets. The faculty members are dedicated individuals who believe the student must be engaged to learn; therefore, all classes at Rosemont are small, which lends to the discussion or seminar format. Approximately 84 percent of the faculty members hold either the Ph.D. or the highest degree in their field.

Student Government

The student government at Rosemont coordinates the ongoing governing processes to be responsive to the needs and opinions of students, to stimulate change as needed, to provide a range of programs and activities, and to represent students to Rosemont College as a whole.

Admission Requirements

Rosemont College seeks to enroll men and women interested in the liberal arts and who have the capacity and the desire to pursue a rigorous academic program. Students are considered without regard to race, religion, disability, or ethnic or national origin. A candidate for admission must present a satisfactory record of scholastic ability and personal integrity from an accredited high school as well as acceptable scores on the SAT or ACT. Applicants' records are reviewed by the Admissions Committee. The student must have an official copy of their high school transcript sent to Rosemont's Office of Admissions. An applicant's secondary school preparation should include sixteen college-preparatory courses. For admission to the traditional college program, all applicants are advised to include in their high school program a minimum of 4 units of English, 2 units of foreign language, 2 units of social studies, 2 units of college-preparatory math, and 2 units of laboratory science, one of which must be a lab science. Prospective business majors must present additional units of college-preparatory math. Applicants are expected to carry a full academic program during their senior year of high school.

Two recommendations are required in support of the student's application. The applicant should ask their guidance counselor or other adult who knows the student well (coach, mentor, etc.) and a teacher who has taught the student an academic subject to submit recommendations on their behalf and forward them to Rosemont's Office of Admissions. All applicants are required to submit results of the SAT. Students may also submit ACT scores. The code for Rosemont College is 3676. More information can be obtained by writing to ACT Registration–81, Box 414, Iowa City, Iowa 53343-0414. A personal interview with a member of the admissions staff is strongly recommended as an important part of the application process. Students who are seriously considering Rosemont should visit the campus to enhance their understanding of the academic and social atmosphere. Arrangements can be made by calling the Office of Admissions.

Application and Information

Applications are accepted on a rolling basis. Those interested in scholarships should apply no later than February 15. To arrange for an interview and a tour, or to receive additional information, students should contact:

Office of Admissions
Rosemont College
1400 Montgomery Avenue
Rosemont, Pennsylvania 19010-1699
Phone: 610-526-2966
888-2ROSEMONT (toll-free)
E-mail: admissions@rosemont.edu
Web site: http://www.rosemont.edu

Rosemont College offers students academic excellence, character building, and a unique educational experience.

COLLEGE CLOSE-UPS

RYERSON UNIVERSITY

TORONTO, CANADA

The University

Founded in 1948, Ryerson University is Canada's leader in providing a high standard of professionally relevant education that combines the traditional university focus on theory with a career-oriented emphasis on professional practice and application.

Ryerson offers close to 100 undergraduate, master's, and Ph.D. programs. Undergraduate degree programs are offered through the University's five faculties: the Faculty of Arts; the Faculty of Engineering, Architecture, and Science; the Faculty of Community Services; the Ted Rogers School of Management; and the Faculty of Communications and Design. Known for attracting people with motivation, direction, and drive, Ryerson offers professionally targeted programs as well as contemporary arts and science degrees. Professional relevance is the essence of Ryerson, characterizing the people, curricula, and facilities that serve Ryerson's more than 25,000 undergraduate and graduate students. This special combination has earned Ryerson its reputation for excellence.

A vibrant and energetic campus community is characterized by on-campus residences, state-of-the-art athletic facilities, and numerous cultural, political, and recreational clubs. The University's location enables students to pursue their education in the financial, industrial, and cultural centre of Canada—the nation's largest city, Toronto.

Ryerson houses 840 students in three residences: Pitman Hall, O'Keefe House, and the International Living Learning Centre. Each residence has its own unique features and attributes. For more information, prospective students should visit http://www.ryerson.ca/housing.

Ryerson operates fourteen men's and women's varsity teams that continually qualify for postseason playoffs. Ryerson student athletes travel throughout Ontario, across Canada, and south to the United States to represent the University. Ryerson's intramural program is open to all students regardless of their skill level in sports and offers students the opportunity to meet people and get some exercise at the same time. More than twenty-five different leagues run throughout the academic year.

The Recreation and Athletics Centre (RAC) at Ryerson offers an extensive fitness centre with free weights and weight machines; a large cardio room with treadmills, elliptical trainers, stationary bicycles, recumbent bikes, and rowing machines; a three-lane, 160-yard, banked indoor running track; two sprung hardwood-floor dance studios; four international squash courts; six gymnasiums; a pool; spacious locker rooms with saunas; and helpful staff members.

Location

Ryerson University is located right in the heart of downtown Toronto. Recognized internationally for its high quality of life, Toronto is a major cultural center and Canada's hub for business and finance providing students with exciting learning opportunities. Ryerson's campus lies within walking distance of music, movies, theaters, and great food and shopping, and it is a short distance from professional sports complexes and international attractions. One of North America's cleanest, safest, and most ethnically diverse cities, Toronto offers many neighborhoods to explore, such as Chinatown, the Beaches, and the Danforth. Other attractions include Ontario Place, the Canadian National Exhibition (CNE), the Ontario Science Centre, and the Royal Ontario Museum (ROM).

Majors and Degrees

Ryerson offers the following undergraduate degrees: Bachelor of Arts, Bachelor of Applied Science, Bachelor of Architectural Science, Bachelor of Commerce, Bachelor of Design, Bachelor of Engineering, Bachelor of Fine Arts, Bachelor of Health Administration, Bachelor of Health Sciences, Bachelor of Interior Design, Bachelor of Journalism, Bachelor of Science, Bachelor of Science in Nursing, Bachelor of Social Work, Bachelor of Technology, and Bachelor of Urban and Regional Planning.

The full-time undergraduate programs available in Ryerson's five faculties are Faculty of Arts: arts and contemporary studies, arts undeclared, criminal justice, geographic analysis, international economics and finance, politics and governance, psychology, and sociology; Ted Rogers School of Management: business management (accounting, economics and management science, entrepreneurship, finance, human resource management, management, marketing management), hospitality and tourism management, information technology management, and retail management; Faculty of Communications and Design: fashion (communication, design), graphic communications management, image arts (film studies, new media, photography studies), journalism, radio and television, and theater (performance acting, performance dance, performance production); Faculty of Community Services: child and youth care, early childhood education, midwifery, nursing, nutrition and food, occupational health and safety, public health and safety, social work, and urban and regional planning; and Faculty of Engineering, Architecture, and Science: architectural science, biology, chemistry, computer science, contemporary science, mathematics and its applications, medical physics, and undeclared, as well as several engineering programs (aerospace, biomedical, chemical, civil, computer, electrical, industrial, mechanical, and undeclared).

Academic Programs

Relevant curricula—a unique mix of professional, professionally related, and liberal studies course work—enable students to practice while they learn; students are well prepared with the skills necessary to enter their chosen career or profession upon graduation. In professional and professionally related courses, theory and practice are viewed as partners in the learning process. Lecture material is translated into practice through cooperative education and internship options, laboratory work, field trips, off-campus project work, and regular contact with business and industry. Liberal studies courses enhance the students' capacity to understand the social and cultural environment in which they will function, both as professionals and as educated citizens. With an education of this scope and rigor, graduates are uniquely adaptable to the challenges and opportunities in their professional fields.

Academic Facilities

Ryerson has recently completed a $210-million expansion, transforming the University campus with the addition of six new buildings. The new buildings include the 30,000-square-foot Heidelberg Centre–School of Graphic Communications Management and the Sally Horsfall Eaton Centre for Studies in Community Health, both adding specialized classroom and laboratory space, and the Centre for Computing and Engineering, featuring state-of-the-art lecture theaters and classrooms, high-tech labs, and specialized applied research facilities. Other new buildings include the Ted Rogers School of Management building on Bay Street—the street that defines business in Canada—housing the Ted Rogers Schools of Business Management, Information Technology Management, Retail Management, and Hospitality and Tourism Management.

The Ryerson Library has an extensive collection of print titles, print and electronic journal titles, and audiovisual materials. The library's Ronald D. Besse Information and Learning Commons combines the expertise of student services and new technologies to equip students with the academic skills needed to access and analyze information effectively. A campuswide network can be accessed from student residence rooms and from off campus. The Rogers Communications Centre (RCC) is the University's flagship building for studies in converging communications and interactive media and is one of Canada's premier facilities for education in digital media communications. As an integral part of Ryerson University, the RCC houses and supports the Schools of Journalism and Radio and Television Arts.

Costs

Tuition for full-time international students for the 2009–10 academic year is Can$15,390 to Can$16,471. The average cost for room and board is Can$8565. Expenses vary according to the student's choice of board plan and housing facility.

Financial Aid

Various scholarships and bursaries and a dedicated series of financial-planning services are available. Every year, the University offers more than Can$10 million in scholarships, awards, and bursaries. All international students are automatically considered for an International Student Merit Scholarship when they apply to Ryerson. The University has been authorized by the U.S. Department of Education to administer Federal Stafford Student Loans and the Federal PLUS Program.

Faculty

In addition to holding advanced degrees, many of Ryerson's professors are professionals who either are currently working in the industry or have worked in the industry in the past. They bring their expertise and up-to-date knowledge or even internship opportunities for students. Ryerson's relatively small class sizes enhance the learning process by maximizing student contact with faculty members.

Student Government

The Ryerson Student Union (RSU) is the student government. RSU's Board of Directors is an elected representative body of full-time students. Terms for those elected begin in May and run through the next academic year, ending in April. The board comprises a number of different types of directors. As defined in the bylaws, the RSU empowers an executive team to be responsible for the day-to-day operations of the organization and to carry the directions of the Board of Directors. These 4 individuals act as officers of the corporation. The president and 3 vice presidents are elected annually by Ryerson's full-time students.

Admission Requirements

To be eligible for admission to a Ryerson program, students must meet Ryerson's admission requirements from the jurisdiction or country from which the student is applying and hold the prerequisites for the specific program of interest. Individual programs may stipulate specific subject prerequisites for admission, including specific courses and minimum grades. Due to competition, candidates may be required to present averages/grades above the minimum. It is essential that the required subject prerequisites and grades for specific programs form part of an applicant's academic background, especially in the last two years of secondary and/or postsecondary studies. Programs may also stipulate nonacademic requirements for admission, such as a portfolio, an admission essay, an interview, or an audition. Students are strongly encouraged to check the requirements before applying to any programs at Ryerson.

Proof of English proficiency at a satisfactory level is required from all students, except those whose first language is English or who have four years of full-time study in an English-language school in a country where the primary language is English. For more details about the English proficiency requirement, students should check the English Language Requirements page on Ryerson's Web site.

Application and Information

Ryerson programs begin only in September of each year. Ryerson generally does not grant admission in the winter (January) or spring (May) terms. Application for admission should be made as early as possible.

All students must apply to Ryerson through the Ontario Universities' Application Centre (OUAC) at http://www.ouac.on.ca. Undergraduate Admissions and Recruitment must receive all officially certified academic transcripts that include promotion/graduation status. The date for guaranteed consideration for the fall 2010 semester for grades-plus-selective-admission programs (those that select students on the basis of grades plus auditions, interviews, portfolios, essays, etc.) is February 1 and March 1 for programs that select on the basis of grades.

Ryerson offers general walking tours of the campus, guided by current students representing a variety of the full-time undergraduate degree programs. These tours run Monday to Friday at 10 a.m. and 1 p.m. Visitors can register for campus tours online through the Undergraduate Admissions and Recruitment Web site.

Undergraduate Admissions and Recruitment
Ryerson University
350 Victoria Street
Toronto, Ontario M5B 2K3
Canada
Phone: 416-979-5036
Fax: 416-979-5067
E-mail: international@ryerson.ca
Web site: http://www.ryerson.ca/undergraduate/admission/

SACRED HEART UNIVERSITY

FAIRFIELD, CONNECTICUT

The University

Distinguished by the personal attention it provides its students, Sacred Heart University in Fairfield, Connecticut is known for its commitment to academic excellence, cutting-edge technology, career preparation, and community service. Founded in 1963 by the Most Reverend Walter W. Curtis, Bishop of the Diocese of Bridgeport, Sacred Heart University (SHU) is the second-largest Catholic university in New England and the first in America to be led and staffed by lay people.

Characterized by its mission and the Catholic intellectual tradition, Sacred Heart University is committed to the holistic development of its students. With endless opportunities for hands-on education through research, internships, clinical placements, independent study, service learning, work-study, and study abroad programs worldwide, Sacred Heart University students are consistently challenged to apply their skills and knowledge outside the classroom.

Nearly 6,000 students are enrolled in over 40 undergraduate, master's, and doctoral programs in the College of Arts and Sciences, College of Education and Health Professions, and the AACSB-accredited John F. Welch College of Business. Experiential and classroom learning opportunities are complemented by a vibrant residential and student life program that includes 31 Division I athletic teams and more than 80 student organizations. Drawing on the rich resources of New England and New York City, students are immersed in personal and professional growth experiences both on campus and within the greater Fairfield County and New York metro areas.

The current undergraduate enrollment includes over 3,500 full-time students. Extracurricular activities include national and local fraternities and sororities, student government, the student newspaper, the student yearbook, a student radio station, a student television station, academic clubs, political organizations, recreational organizations, community service organizations, multicultural organizations, the performing arts, intramural programs, and eighteen competitive club sports programs. Sacred Heart University has thirty-one NCAA Division I men's and women's sports, placing it among the largest Divison I programs in the country. Varsity teams include: baseball, basketball, bowling, crew, cross-country, equestrian, fencing, field hockey, football, golf, ice hockey, lacrosse, soccer, softball, swimming and diving, tennis, track and field (indoor and outdoor), volleyball, and wrestling. Over 500 students also participate in the University's twenty-five intercollegiate club sport teams, competing in leagues against junior varsity and club teams from some of the top schools in the Northeast, including Ivy League institutions.

In addition to more than 30 degree programs at the undergraduate level, the University offers several graduate degree programs: Master of Arts in Criminal Justice (M.A.C.J.), Master of Arts in Religious Studies (M.A.R.S.), Master of Arts in Teaching (M.A.T.), Master of Business Administration (M.B.A.), Master of Science in Nursing (M.S.N.), Master of Science (M.S.) in chemistry, Master of Science (M.S.) in computer science and information science (including a new concentration in computer game design and development), a nationally ranked Master of Science in Occupational Therapy (M.S.O.T.), Master of Science (M.S.) in geriatric rehabilitation and wellness, a new Master of Science (M.S.) in exercise science and nutrition, and a Doctor of Physical Therapy (D.P.T.) program ranked first in the State of Connecticut and among the five best in the Northeast according to *U.S. News & World Report.* Many of these programs are combined undergraduate and graduate programs.

Location

Situated on 67 picturesque acres in coastal Fairfield, Connecticut, Sacred Heart University is ideally located 1 hour north of New York City and 2½ hours south of Boston with international campuses in County Kerry, Ireland and Luxembourg. Rated ninth in the nation and best in the Northeast on a recent *Money Magazine* list of "Best Places to Live," Fairfield is an ideal location for study, work, and recreation.

SHU students are exposed to a multitude of cultural and professional opportunities within and outside the campus gates, including the many multistate and multinational companies headquartered in Connecticut, with Fairfield County playing an integral role in the state's impressive twelfth-place national ranking in number of Fortune 500 company headquarters. Sacred Heart University's neighbors include the world headquarters for General Electric as well as the Discovery Museum of Science and Industry.

Majors and Degrees

At the undergraduate level, Sacred Heart University offers Bachelor of Arts (B.A.) and Bachelor of Science (B.S.) degrees as well as a Bachelor of Social Work (B.S.W.) degree. Programs of study in education and allied health include athletic training, education (elementary and secondary certification), exercise science, nursing, occupational therapy, and physical therapy. In the arts and sciences, the following areas of study are available: art, biology, Catholic studies (minor only), chemistry, communications/media studies, communications technology, computer science (game design concentration available), criminal justice, English, French (minor only), history, Italian (minor only), information technology, mathematics, Middle Eastern studies (minor only), music (minor only), philosophy, political science, psychology, religious studies, social work, sociology, Spanish, and women's studies (minor only). In business, the University offers accounting, business administration, business economics, finance, marketing (fashion marketing and merchandising concentration available) and sport management. Preprofessional programs are available in dentistry, law, medicine, optometry, osteopathy, physician's assistant, pharmacy, podiatry, and veterinary.

Special programs include the Honors Program, internships, legislative internships, and study abroad. The University has its own study-abroad programs in Australia, Bahamas, Bermuda, Luxembourg (SHU satellite campus), Ireland (SHU satellite campus), Italy, and Spain, and facilitates study-abroad opportunities worldwide.

Academic Programs

Academic programs are divided into four colleges—the College of Arts and Sciences, the AACSB-accredited John F. Welch College of Business, the College of Education and Health Professions, and University College. The academic year consists of two 15-week semesters.

Candidates for the bachelor's degree must complete a minimum of 120 credits, with a minimum of 30 credits including half of the academic major credits taken at the University. The baccalaureate curriculum is made up of several components: the required core (12 credits), the elective core (33–35 credits), the major field (30–58 credits), and the new Core Curriculum (15 credits), introduced in September 2007. The innovative undergraduate Core Curriculum features an academically rigorous, multidisciplinary centerpiece known as "The Common Core: The Human Journey." The Core exemplifies distinctiveness in its emphasis on cocurricular activities including collaborative, team-taught classes, capstone experiences, and cultural learning opportunities beyond the customary classroom environment.

Off-Campus Programs

Through the Internship Program, students combine employment in business, industry, government, education, and/or social service agencies with classroom work and receive academic credit and/or compensation for learning derived from the work experience. Students in all majors and intended career fields have opportunities to intern in professional settings throughout their undergraduate experiences, with some majors requiring one or more internship experiences off-campus. The Career Development Center facilitates professional preparation including career counseling and major declaration assistance, resume writing, interviewing and job-search skills, graduate school preparation assistance, and access to job and internship listings for roughly 4,000 employers. The University's emphasis on career preparation has led to a post-graduate placement rate of 95 percent over the past five years. The Career Center's popular "Major in Success" program also facilitates career decision-making and major declaration for undecided students. Several hundred undergraduate students benefit from the personalized career counseling they receive through this program each year.

Academic Facilities

The Sacred Heart University campus is fully wireless, indoors and out, allowing students to utilize their required laptop computers in the residence halls, classroom buildings, grounds, and all other campus locations. The University's library contains nearly 150,000 volumes, including 67,000 periodical titles, and provides online database searching services. The new Cambridge Campus housing the College of Education and Health Professions is a state-of-the-art, 50,000-square-foot facility with its own library, laboratories, and specialized learning environments. The Art Department includes studios for graphic design. Science facilities include newly renovated laboratories, a climate-controlled greenhouse, a microbiology preparation lab, and a neuroscience lab. The Media Studies and Digital Culture facilities include a studio for beginning and advanced television production courses and a state-of-the-art media lab equipped with DVD authoring and multimedia production workstations. The campus also houses an 850-seat theater, an art gallery, student radio station, professional radio station (WSHU, National Public Radio), and a new, first-rate University chapel (Chapel of the Holy Spirit) which opened in fall 2009.

Costs

2009–10 full-time undergraduate tuition and fees is $30,298 and $11,684 for room and board. The cost of books was estimated to be $1000 per year.

Financial Aid

Sacred Heart University maintains a strong commitment to provide higher education to as many students as possible by making available scholarships, grants, loans, and part-time employment. Financial aid packages are developed by combining Sacred Heart University's own resources with a variety of federal and state financial aid programs. Eighty-five percent of all students receive some form of financial assistance.

Any undergraduate or graduate student who is enrolled in the University on at least a part-time basis (6 credits per semester) is eligible for consideration. Emphasis is placed on students who are enrolled in a full-time degree program; part-time awards are limited. Applicants for aid must submit the Free Application for Federal Student Aid (FAFSA) and the CSS PROFILE to the College Scholarship Service on or before February 15.

The University offers several sources of financial aid, including academic, athletic, and special program scholarships, state loan programs, and Federal Supplemental Educational Opportunity Grants. A Family Allowance is available when 2 or more members of the same family attend the University. Deferred-payment plans and endowed scholarships are also awarded. Employment within the University is awarded under the terms of the Federal Work-Study Program. The Office of Career Development maintains a list of part-time jobs in the local area. Further information can be obtained from the Dean of University Student Financial Assistance.

Faculty

The student-faculty ratio is 13:1. There are 567 faculty members, over 90 percent of whom teach at the undergraduate level. Of those members, 204 are full-time, and over 75 percent have terminal degrees in their field. Faculty members are involved in research, writing, and production, with their primary focus on teaching students. Close communication between students and faculty members is facilitated and encouraged; all students are assigned a faculty adviser within their major field of study.

Student Government

Students play a major role in planning and decision-making at Sacred Heart University. Student Government representatives and class officers are concerned with continuously enhancing the University and working for the needs of their classmates. In addition to sponsoring many events, the Student Government serves as a liaison between the administration/staff and the student body.

Admission Requirements

Undergraduate admission staff members execute a holistic application review process to carefully evaluate each student's unique qualifications, strengths, and interests. The University is committed to enrolling a diverse, highly qualified, and well-motivated student body. Candidates for admission must demonstrate their ability to perform academically and contribute significantly to the life of the University. High school seniors should submit an official high school transcript, one letter of recommendation, an essay, and a completed application. Submission of SAT/ACT scores is optional for all first-year student candidates.

Transfer students should submit an official transcript from all previously attended colleges, a high school transcript, one letter of recommendation, an essay, and a completed application.

Application and Information

Full-time students may enroll in either the fall or the spring semester. All applicants must submit a completed application, all necessary credentials, and an application fee of $50. Applications for the Early Decision Program must be received by December 1. Applications for priority admissions must be received by February 1 for an April 1 notification date. All other applications are considered on a rolling admission basis; candidates are notified of the admission decision as soon as all credentials have been received and reviewed.

Inquiries or application materials should be sent to:

Dean of Undergraduate Admissions
Sacred Heart University
5151 Park Avenue
Fairfield, Connecticut 06825-1000
Phone: 203-371-7880
E-mail: guastellek@sacredheart.edu
Web site: http://www.sacredheart.edu

SAINT ANSELM COLLEGE

MANCHESTER, NEW HAMPSHIRE

The College

Saint Anselm is a small liberal arts college of 2,000 undergraduates in the hills of southern New Hampshire, less than an hour north of Boston. Founded in 1889 by the Catholic Order of Saint Benedict, it maintains a strong sense of community that is characteristic of a Benedictine institution. The College has earned a national reputation for high academic standards. It prides itself on offering a challenging intellectual environment while encouraging the students' intellectual, social, spiritual, and physical development. Saint Anselm's extraordinary commitment to community engagement, evidenced by the involvement of students, faculty, and staff in projects that impact the local community and our world, has earned the College a new and special designation by the Carnegie Foundation for the Advancement of Teaching. Saint Anselm takes pride in being one of seventeen liberal arts colleges nationwide cited as an "institution of community engagement."

All Saint Anselm College students pursue specialized major courses of study in such areas as liberal arts, business, the sciences, nursing, and preprofessional preparation. A curriculum that emphasizes critical thinking, communication, research, and analysis skills leads to strong placement in graduate and professional schools. The College's primary goal, however, is to offer an educational experience that produces well-rounded graduates with a creative and open-minded spirit.

The beauty of Saint Anselm College's 400-acre campus changes with the seasons. Buildings surrounding the "quad" range from original ivy-covered brick to contemporary architecture, and the grounds include The New Hampshire Institute of Politics at Saint Anselm College and a church with an abbey. In addition to student housing, administration, and academic facilities, the campus includes a multipurpose activities center with a new fitness center; Davison Hall dining commons; Stoutenburgh Gymnasium, home of Saint Anselm varsity athletics; the Thomas F. Sullivan hockey arena; and Cushing Student Center, which houses academic and career counseling offices, student organizations, health services, and an academic resource center. A short drive away is a 100-acre tract used for retreats and environmental study and research.

Saint Anselm College has students from thirty-one states and twelve countries, more than 88 percent of whom live on campus in traditional dormitories and modern apartments. The list of more than eighty clubs and organizations that match the students' diverse interests is constantly evolving and includes music, community service, theater, outdoor recreation, debating, prelaw and premedicine, and a local chapter of the Knights of Columbus. Intercollegiate sports are offered for men in baseball, basketball, cross-country, football, golf, hockey, lacrosse, skiing, soccer, and tennis. For women, teams are organized in basketball, cross-country, field hockey, lacrosse, skiing, soccer, softball, tennis, and volleyball. There are nearly twenty club sports, including cheerleading, cycling, ice skating, rugby, and soccer.

Location

Less than an hour from Boston, Saint Anselm offers easy access to the cultural attractions of a large city, yet it is equally close to ski slopes, the Appalachian Trail, and the Atlantic coast. It has the feel of a rural campus, but is only minutes from downtown Manchester, the largest city in New Hampshire. In Manchester, students find excellent restaurants, galleries, shopping malls, and theaters as well as professional offices with internship and employment opportunities.

Majors and Degrees

Saint Anselm awards the Bachelor of Arts degree in the following academic programs and majors: accounting, biochemistry, biology, business, chemistry, classics, communication, computer science, computer science with business, computer science with mathematics, criminal justice, education (secondary and elementary), economics, English, environmental science, financial economics, fine arts, French, history, international business, international relations, liberal studies in the great books, mathematics, mathematics with economics, natural science, nursing, philosophy, physics, politics, psychology, sociology, Spanish, and theology. It also offers a program leading to the Bachelor of Science in Nursing (B.S.N.) degree.

The College offers preprofessional programs in dentistry, law, medicine, and theology.

A 3-2 program in engineering is available in cooperation with the University of Notre Dame, Catholic University of America, Manhattan College, and the University of Massachusetts Lowell.

Academic Programs

Saint Anselm College provides students with a strong liberal arts background, including required courses in philosophy, theology, and foreign language. Students generally take ten to fifteen courses in their majors, while the liberal arts core courses and a wide range of electives make up the remainder of the forty courses required for graduation. Honors program participants distinguish themselves by taking additional courses in order to graduate with honors.

All Saint Anselm students participate in a nationally recognized humanities program, Portraits in Human Greatness, during their freshman and sophomore years. The program's nondisciplinary approach to Western culture integrates science, sociology, history, philosophy, and the arts. The heart of the program is its seminar component, which strengthens skills in reasoning, articulating ideas, and debating.

Saint Anselm College participates in the Advanced Placement Program of the College Board. Students who receive a score of 3 or better on the Advanced Placement examinations may obtain advanced placement and credit in the pertinent subject matter. Applicants who have completed examinations under the College-Level Examination Program may receive advanced placement and credit if the scores they receive are acceptable.

Off-Campus Programs

More than 40 percent of Saint Anselm students complete an internship related to their major field of study, usually during their junior or senior year. Internships help students apply theoretical knowledge, explore careers and graduate school choices, and improve employment prospects. Internships are arranged locally and in major cities such as Boston, New York, and Washington, D.C.

The College provides access to several approved semester-long study-abroad programs, and Saint Anselm faculty members often lead summer study trips abroad. The College has an archeological dig site in Umbria, Italy. Students of all academic majors can participate in fieldwork at the dig site. Service trips sponsored by the Office of Campus Ministry take place from Arizona to Maine as well as in Latin America.

Academic Facilities

Among the College's sixty buildings are facilities for classes, research, arts performances and exhibits, and campus events. Geisel Library holds 230,000 bound volumes and 68,000 microform titles and maintains a collection of 4,000 periodical titles and 1,700 video recordings, as well as CDs and audiotapes. Goulet Science Center has been expanded and renovated to meet the students' needs, and contains its own library. The 20,000-square-foot New Hampshire Institute of Politics is a center for civic education and engagement: It attracts diplomats, candidates, and political experts throughout the year and is in the national and international spotlight during presidential primary and election seasons. The Charles A. Dana Center houses a 700-seat theater and serves as the home of the humanities program. Poisson Computer Science Center contains more than 200 PCs and specially equipped classrooms and offices. Fine arts studios and a small theater are located in the Comiskey Center.

Costs

Tuition for the 2009–10 school year was $29,720, and room and board charges were $11,240. Books and other miscellaneous fees cost approximately $1850.

Financial Aid

Saint Anselm College offers financial aid through various federal and private programs. Assistance is awarded as a supplement to the reasonable financial sacrifice that the College expects will be made by the interested student and his or her parents. Eighty-eight percent of Saint Anselm's students receive some form of financial assistance to help defray the cost of their education. Financial aid packages consist of scholarships, grants, loans, and work opportunities. Merit awards (Presidential Scholarships) of up to $16,000 are awarded to outstanding students.

Two forms are required in applying for aid. The student must submit the CSS Financial Aid PROFILE and the Free Application for Federal Student Aid (FAFSA) to the College Scholarship Service by March 1.

Faculty

The College's faculty consists of full-time and part-time members. Ninety-six percent of the faculty members have earned doctorates or the appropriate terminal degrees in their fields. With a student-teacher ratio of 12:1, professors are extremely accessible. In addition to teaching, the faculty members serve as advisers to students in their departments. No classes are taught by graduate students or teaching assistants.

Student Government

Students participate in the affairs of the college in a variety of ways. Students are elected to positions as class officers and serve on the Student Senate and Campus Activities Board. They serve as student body representatives on the Board of Trustees and on administrative committees, including the college judiciary board, curriculum committee, and health committee. Saint Anselm encourages students to express their opinions and take active roles in shaping the life of their college and to be aware of their potential as active and engaged citizens to effect change in the world around them.

Admission Requirements

In selecting a freshman class, the admission committee considers each candidate personally and thoroughly, evaluating their high school record, SAT scores, letters of recommendation, and essay (part of the application). Of greatest importance is the student's high school transcript, in terms of both the quality of courses taken and the grades earned.

Transfer and international students are welcome to apply. The same general admission procedures are required, along with at least a C average in all transferable courses and, for international students, a satisfactory score on the TOEFL.

Application and Information

The Office of Admission is open from 8:30 to 4:30 on weekdays and is open for Saturday Visit program in the fall. Please go to www.anselm.edu for a list of current visit programs and admission application deadlines. The College strongly recommends a campus visit and an interview in order to discover the many benefits of Saint Anselm.

For more information, students should contact:

Office of Admission
Saint Anselm College
100 Saint Anselm Drive
Manchester, New Hampshire 03102
Phone: 603-641-7500
888-426-7356 (toll-free)
E-mail: admission@anselm.edu
Web site: http://www.anselm.edu

Saint Anselm College Alumni Hall.

ST. BONAVENTURE UNIVERSITY

ST. BONAVENTURE, NEW YORK

The University

St. Bonaventure University provides a values-based education with individual attention from professors, a beautiful residential setting, and a friendly, close-knit atmosphere. Of the 2,500 students enrolled, 2,000 are undergraduates. More than 74 percent of the undergraduates are full-time residents. Complementing St. Bonaventure's traditions are innovative degree programs, computerized career placement aids, comprehensive student life activities, and modern academic facilities. Among major campus events during the academic year are concerts and coffeehouse acts, indoor and outdoor recreational programs, current and classic film offerings, and dramatic and musical plays. Aspiring writers and broadcasters from all academic majors—Bonaventure has produced 5 Pulitzer Prize winners—find challenging and plentiful opportunities working with one of the four University media: WSBU-88.3 FM-The Buzz, the nationally ranked campus radio station; *The Bona Venture,* the award-winning weekly newspaper; *The Bonadieu,* the yearbook; and *The Laurel,* the nation's oldest student literary publication, which marked its 100th anniversary in 1999. Other organizations on campus include academic fraternities, academic honor societies, a variety of club and intramural sports, and arts organizations that include choral, instrumental, dance, and drama ensembles. The Thomas Merton Ministry Center is open 24 hours a day and aims to foster a community of friendship and mutual service. Many students take the opportunity to serve as Bona Buddies to area children or senior citizens; help with the national award-winning soup kitchen The Warming House; or volunteer in one of many service organizations, including SIFE and BonaResponds, one of the most active collegiate disaster relief organizations in the nation. Volunteer opportunities include immersion experiences and service opportunities with the poor, both in the U.S. and abroad.

St. Bonaventure University students enjoy two athletic facilities: the new $6.2-million Richter Center, which is open 24 hours a day, features three basketball courts, a running/walking track, racquetball/squash/wallyball courts, an aerobics room, a recreational area for roller hockey, a weight room, a cardiovascular fitness room, locker rooms, an equipment check-out, a reception area, and a climbing wall; and the Reilly Center, housing a 5,780-seat sports arena, swimming pool, and weight room. Also available are outdoor tennis and basketball courts and a nine-hole golf course. NCAA Division I athletics for men are baseball, basketball, cross-country, golf, soccer, swimming, and tennis. Division I competition for women includes basketball, cross-country, lacrosse, soccer, softball, swimming, and tennis.

In addition to its undergraduate programs, St. Bonaventure offers the Master of Arts degree in English and in Franciscan studies. A Master of Science in Education program includes adolescence education, advanced inclusive processes, counselor education, differentiated instruction, educational leadership, literacy, school building leader, and school district leader. A Master of Business Administration program and a Master of Arts program in integrated marketing communications are also offered.

Location

St. Bonaventure is located on Route 417 between Olean, a city of approximately 17,000 residents, and Allegany, a village with about 2,000 residents. Shops, restaurants, and movie theaters are all within walking distance. The campus is spread over 500 acres in a valley surrounded by the Allegheny Mountains. The free Bona Bus connects the campus with Olean and Allegany, carrying students to and from the area attractions. The region around St. Bonaventure provides a beautiful setting for many outdoor activities. A renowned ski resort is just 20 miles away, and nearby Allegany State Park offers excellent facilities for swimming, boating, and hiking. St. Bonaventure is accessible by car, bus, and commercial air transportation, with Buffalo/Niagara International the nearest major airport.

Majors and Degrees

St. Bonaventure University grants the Bachelor of Arts degree with majors in art, art history, classical languages, English, gerontology, history, interdisciplinary studies, international studies, journalism and mass communication, modern languages (French and Spanish), music, philosophy, political science, psychology, sociology, theater, theology, and women's studies. The Bachelor of Science is granted with majors in biochemistry, bioinformatics, biology, chemistry, childhood studies, computer science, early childhood education, economics, elementary/special education (dual certification), environmental science, interdisciplinary studies, mathematics, physical education, physics, psychology, and sport studies. The Bachelor of Business Administration is granted with majors in accounting, finance, management sciences, and marketing. Popular five-year master's programs are also available in business, English, integrated marketing communications, and inclusion, and dual-admission/dual-degree programs offer unique opportunities for students pursuing careers in medicine, dentistry, pharmacy, and physical therapy.

Academic Programs

Students in all majors begin their intellectual journey in Clare College, St. Bonaventure's nationally acclaimed core curriculum, which offers a values-based education grounded in the vision of St. Francis and St. Bonaventure.

A candidate for a bachelor's degree must complete at least 120 credit hours, with a cumulative index of 2.0 or better in the major field and the overall program. A pass/fail grade option, available to all upperclass students, may be elected for one course per semester, but not for courses in a student's major field.

Advanced credit is granted for grades of C or better on either the College Proficiency Examination or the College-Level Examination Program (CLEP) tests. Advanced placement is granted on the basis of scores obtained on the College Board's Advanced Placement (AP) examinations.

Men and women may also elect to participate in the University's Army ROTC program, MacArthur Award winner as best small unit in the nation in 1998.

Off-Campus Programs

Through St. Bonaventure's membership in the College Consortium for International Studies (CCIS), St. Bonaventure students have access to six continents. More than sixty semester-long international study programs, including St. Bonaventure–sponsored study in Italy, Spain, Ireland, and Australia, are available to students in good academic standing in their junior year. Faculty-directed, short-term opportunities include a three-week intersession in China, the Francis E. Kelly Oxford summer program, and a three-week travel study program to Mexico. For further information, students should contact the Office of International Studies. Fieldwork or internships are available in several major programs.

Academic Facilities

Friedsam Memorial Library houses more than 250,000 volumes and includes a trilevel resource center with a curriculum center, the University archives, and digital media and conferencing centers, as well as world-class special collections. An automated online card catalog greatly improves research capabilities.

The William F. Walsh Science Center opened in 2008 and doubled the space for science studies. The center houses state-of-the-art computer science, laboratory and classroom space, biology labs, organic and general chemistry labs, a Natural World lab, a 150-seat indoor amphitheater, and faculty offices integrated with lab space for better student-teacher accessibility. It is attached to historic De La Roche Hall, which received a major face-lift in 2008.

The John J. Murphy Professional Building provides the most up-to-date equipment for the School of Business and the School of Journalism and Mass Communication. The Bob Koop Broadcast Journalism Laboratory features a television studio with an anchor desk, digital and videotape editing bays, while a remote TV production studio allows for live broadcasting of athletic events. A fiber-optic network connects microcomputers in academic and administrative areas. There are seven labs for student use containing more than 100 Macintosh systems. St. Bonaventure students also have wireless Internet access across campus.

An annex to Plassmann Hall houses computer-adaptable education classrooms, seminar rooms, and offices for the education faculty. An observatory allows students access to three compact telescopes, two 8-inch Celestron telescopes, and one 11-inch Schmidt-Cassegrain telescope, along with a heated classroom.

The Regina A. Quick Center for the Arts provides acoustically designed classroom space for music courses and painting and drawing studios. The center also includes a musical instrument digital interface lab, a 325-seat theater, and an atrium that is often used for receptions and impromptu musical performances. The F. Donald Kenney Museum and Art Study Wing includes four climate-controlled galleries offering nationally acclaimed traveling exhibits, works from the University's permanent collections, and student exhibits.

Historic Hickey Dining Hall received a spectacular makeover in 2006, and a 5,500-square-foot coffee café and gourmet deli opened in spring 2007. Some residence halls were overhauled in 2006, while the new science center and a $2.2-million library addition opened in 2008.

Costs

For 2009–10, the annual costs were $24,920 for tuition and $965 for fees. Room and meal plans averaged $9200 per year.

Financial Aid

Students who qualify for financial aid normally receive a package consisting of a combination of scholarships, grants, loans, and work-study awards. An average financial aid package for an incoming freshman is more than $22,000. Athletic Grants-in-Aid are available for men in baseball, basketball, golf, soccer, swimming, and tennis; and for women in basketball, lacrosse, soccer, softball, swimming, and tennis. Music scholarships are also available. Students must file the Free Application for Federal Student Aid (FAFSA) in order to be considered for financial assistance. For more complete details, a student should contact the director of financial aid at the University.

Faculty

Like the student body, the 155 full-time and 67 part-time faculty members at St. Bonaventure come from a wide range of geographic, ethnic, and religious backgrounds. The student-faculty ratio of 14:1 allows faculty members the time to help each student to understand different modes of thinking, develop as a person, and lay a foundation for lifelong learning. Eighty-four percent of the faculty members hold the terminal degree in their field. Friars, many of whom teach and live on campus, add to the unique atmosphere of St. Bonaventure.

Student Government

Life at St. Bonaventure is centered on the residence halls, and the foundation of student government begins in the dormitories with the Residence Hall Councils. The elected council members determine the norms by which the residents are guided in their daily lives. The Student Government, whose members are elected from the student body, serves as the general student-governing unit, and its members serve on every major University board and committee.

Admission Requirements

St. Bonaventure University welcomes applications for admission from all serious candidates from a variety of backgrounds. St. Bonaventure University provides equal opportunity without regard to race, creed, color, gender, age, national or ethnic origin, marital status, veteran status, or disability in admission, employment, and in all of its educational programs and activities. Applicants, who are welcome to apply online, must show evidence of academic achievement to be selected for admission. The criteria used in making admission decisions, in order of importance, are quality of the high school curriculum, grade point average in college-preparatory courses, ACT (preferred) or SAT scores, class rank, recommendations from high school teachers and counselors, and extracurricular activities.

Application and Information

For more information about St. Bonaventure University, prospective students should contact:

Director of Admissions
St. Bonaventure University
P.O. Box D
St. Bonaventure, New York 14778
Phone: 716-375-2400
800-462-5050 (toll-free)
E-mail: admissions@sbu.edu
Web site: http://www.sbu.edu

Built in 1928 and renovated in 1999, Devereux Hall is an example of the beautiful Florentine architecture found at St. Bonaventure University.

ST. EDWARD'S UNIVERSITY

AUSTIN, TEXAS

The University

St. Edward's University offers students the best of both worlds—small classes and a supportive community in the midst of one of the most exciting cities in the country. Located 10 minutes from downtown Austin, the 160-acre campus featuring hills, trees, and historic architecture offers one of the best views of the Austin skyline. But it is the University's vision, more than the view, which makes it distinctive. A St. Edward's University education combines the critical-thinking skills of a liberal arts curriculum with hands-on experience in internships, service learning, and study abroad. Its Catholic character gives students a foundation in ethics and encourages them to strive for justice.

It is an exciting time to be a student at St. Edward's. The total student population has grown to 5,350, including 3,505 undergraduates. The University has built nine new buildings since 2000, including a 65,000-square-foot science building with state-of-the-art labs and a rooftop greenhouse. Three new residence halls that opened in 2009 showcase urban living with suite-style rooms above a dining facility, coffeehouse, and wellness resources on the ground floor. In addition to the new facilities, St. Edward's has added eleven new majors, including forensic science, graphic design, and entrepreneurship.

Founded by the Congregation of Holy Cross in 1885, the University teaches its students to think creatively and with integrity, to build a more just world, and to develop a global perspective. The St. Edward's mission statement is lived each day as students connect their education to the Austin community and the larger world. The University values diversity in all its forms—ethnic, religious, socioeconomic, geographic—and supports programs and events that help expand students' worldviews.

The most popular majors at St. Edward's are psychology, communication, biology, and business. The unique theater arts program allows students to earn points toward their Actors' Equity membership card while working with professional mentors. The Academic Exploration Program guides students who have not chosen a major, offering a class designed to help freshmen find their strengths and interests. All students are paired with faculty advisers who assist them in planning degree programs and who provide academic counseling throughout the students' college careers.

An essential part of the academic experience at St. Edward's is preparing for life after earning an undergraduate degree. The Career Planning Office helps students explore careers, secure internship opportunities, and prepare for graduate school and employment.

Outside of class, opportunities abound for recreation and cultural enrichment. The more than ninety student organizations include intramural sports, Student Government Association, political groups, honor societies, spirit groups, and cultural organizations. Campus Ministry offers retreats, volunteer projects, interfaith dialogue, opportunities to grow in the Catholic faith, and support for the campus Hillel group and the Muslim student organization. Athletic events, theater productions, concerts, and campus traditions give students a chance to relax and have fun.

Students have many choices in on-campus housing, from apartments for upper-level students to traditional residence halls to house-style living in the Casitas. Freshmen are required to live in the residence halls unless they are living with their parents while attending the University.

St. Edward's is a member of the NCAA Division II Heartland Conference, and in the past three years, its teams have won nineteen conference championships. Men compete in baseball, basketball, golf, soccer, and tennis. Women compete in basketball, golf, soccer, softball, tennis, and volleyball.

Location

St. Edward's University is located in Austin, the capital of Texas and one of the most vibrant educational and political centers in the United States. Along with its internationally known film festival and music scene, Austin also offers local theaters, galleries, and museums. Students at St. Edward's enjoy year-round use of Austin's three major lakes and nearly 200 parks, such as nearby Zilker Park with its natural, spring-fed swimming pool, canoe rentals for use on Lady Bird Lake, a hike-and-bike trail, a botanical garden, and playing fields.

Majors and Degrees

St. Edward's University confers four undergraduate degrees—Bachelor of Arts, Bachelor of Arts in Applied Science, Bachelor of Business Administration, and Bachelor of Science—and offers more than fifty areas of study through the Schools of Behavioral and Social Sciences, Management and Business, Natural Sciences, Humanities, and Education. Majors offered are accounting, accounting information technology, art, biochemistry, bioinformatics, biology, business administration, chemistry, communication, computer information science, computer science, criminal justice, criminology, digital media management, economics, English literature, English writing and rhetoric, entrepreneurship, environmental chemistry, environmental science and policy, finance, forensic chemistry, forensic science, global studies, graphic design, history, international business, kinesiology, Latin American studies, liberal studies, management, marketing, mathematics, philosophy, photocommunications, political science, psychology, religious studies, social work, sociology, Spanish, and theater arts. Minors are offered in many of the above subjects and art history, Catholic studies, French, German, Jewish studies, journalism, multimedia, music, professional ethics, teacher education, and women's studies.

The School of Education also offers teacher certification programs for early childhood–grade 6, grades 4–8, grades 8–12, early childhood–grade 12 (in art, kinesiology, and theater arts), and secondary religious education. Supplemental certification is available in bilingual education and ESL.

Many students choose to pursue a preprofessional program in conjunction with their established majors. St. Edward's offers preprofessional programs in dentistry, engineering, law, medicine, and physical therapy. In addition, St. Edward's offers eleven master's degrees.

Academic Programs

All students share an intensive general education requirement of 57 credit hours spanning all four years. The requirements are split into three areas: foundational skills (English writing, college math, computational skills, oral communication, and foreign language), cultural foundations (six courses including American Dilemmas, Literature and Human Experience, and Contemporary World Issues), and foundations for values and decisions (five courses including Ethics and Science in Perspective). The general education curriculum culminates with Capstone, a writing course in which students investigate a controversial issue, analyze it, and propose a resolution, both orally and in a major paper. The reasoning and communication skills and the understanding of society that these general studies develop are reinforced in each student's in-depth study of a major discipline.

Graduation is based on the successful completion of 120 semester hours of study. St. Edward's observes a two-semester academic calendar, and the University's flexible summer course schedule offers day and evening classes.

Off-Campus Programs

Hands-on experiential learning is a central component of a St. Edward's University education. Students conduct research and complete internships on and off campus, including work for businesses, nonprofit organizations, and political groups (the campus is located 10 minutes from the Texas State Capitol).

St. Edward's offers study-abroad opportunities in reciprocal exchange programs with universities in Germany, Mexico, Scotland, and Argentina. The University recently established a campus in Angers, France, a 90-minute train ride from Paris. In Angers, students can participate in a six-week summer program, a semester, or a year-long program to develop French fluency and learn about politics, philosophy, art, and literature. Tuition at the Angers campus is the same as in Austin.

Students can also participate in study-abroad activities sponsored by other U.S. universities through the International Student Exchange

Program and in community service programs offered by the International Partnership for Service Learning.

Academic Facilities

St. Edward's provides facilities that support every aspect of the student experience—academic, residential, and social—because learning can happen in many places and situations. Main Building, named a Texas Historic Landmark for its architectural significance, is a landmark visible from many parts of the city of Austin. Trustee Hall, the award-winning academic building, enhances the University's outstanding record as a technologically sophisticated institution. The biology and chemistry programs are housed in the new John Brooks Williams Natural Sciences Center, with state-of-the-art laboratories, classrooms, and meeting and study spaces. The new residential village consists of three student residences built above a dining hall and the Health and Counseling Center and surrounding a pedestrian street.

The Robert and Pearle Ragsdale Center is home to everything from dining services and a coffeehouse to parties, concerts, lectures, and conferences. The Recreation and Convocation Center offers a fitness center, a swimming pool, and courts for basketball, racquetball/handball, and volleyball. Students also have access to on-campus 24-hour computer labs.

Costs

The 2010–11 costs for full-time undergraduate students are $26,484 for tuition and fees and $8816 for room and board. The latter figure varies with the choice of residence hall and meal plan.

Financial Aid

St. Edward's has a strong track record of awarding financial assistance. In fall 2009, the average freshman grant package was $14,447, and 89 percent of freshmen received merit- or need-based grant assistance. St. Edward's University administers several financial assistance programs funded by federal, institutional, and state resources. These programs help students meet college expenses through grants, scholarships, low-interest loans, and work-study programs. To qualify for financial assistance, accepted students should submit the Free Application for Federal Student Aid (FAFSA) online at http://www.fafsa.ed.gov.

All students are automatically reviewed for academic scholar awards when they apply for admission. The priority deadline for fall semester applications is February 1, and students are strongly encouraged to apply by this date. The regular admission deadline for fall is May 1.

Faculty

Faculty members at St. Edward's do much more than teach students. From working together in service projects and research projects, students get to know faculty members inside and outside the classroom, often forming lifelong friendships. The University's 14:1 student–faculty ratio fosters collaboration between students and faculty members.

Student Government

The Student Government Association (SGA), composed of elected student officers, has campuswide representation. The executive board and senate meet weekly to plan and direct activities that involve the entire St. Edward's community. In addition, the SGA president acts as the voice of the student body and regularly attends Board of Trustees meetings and the Austin mayor's Council on Student Affairs.

Admission Requirements

Students who apply for admission to St. Edward's are evaluated individually on the basis of their academic performance in high school; rank in class; essay; SAT or ACT scores, including the writing section; and rigor of high school curriculum. To be considered for admission, qualified applicants should rank in the top half of their class and have test scores of at least 500 on each section of the SAT or 21 composite on the ACT. The average SAT score for the fall 2009 freshman class was 1131 on the combined critical reading and math sections, and the average ACT was 24.

Application and Information

St. Edward's University employs a rolling admission policy. The Admission Committee makes decisions on applications within a few weeks of when a student's file becomes complete. A completed file consists of an application, an essay, a $45 nonrefundable application fee, SAT or ACT scores, official high school transcripts, and a recommendation from a teacher or counselor. St. Edward's is a member of the Common Application.

All admission credentials should be mailed to:

Office of Undergraduate Admission
St. Edward's University
3001 South Congress Avenue
Austin, Texas 78704-6489
Phone: 512-448-8500
800-555-0164 (toll-free)
Fax: 512-464-8877
E-mail: seu.admit@stedwards.edu
Web site: http://www.gotostedwards.com

Main Building, designated a Texas Historic Landmark in 1973, is the center of the St. Edward's community.

SAINT FRANCIS UNIVERSITY

LORETTO, PENNSYLVANIA

The University

Saint Francis University is a small, coeducational, liberal arts university. The University was founded in 1847 and conducted under the tradition of the Franciscan Friars of the Third Order Regular. The University is concerned with the development of each student for the world of today. For more than 150 years, the University's philosophy of education and student life has continued to emphasize two values: instruction of high quality and respect for the student as an individual. The University believes that a liberal arts education, encompassing a major field of study, is the soundest kind of preparation a student can have for a productive life. In recent years, Saint Francis University has garnered recognition for advances in study abroad and outreach in health care. Additionally, *U.S. News & World Report* has named Saint Francis as a Best Value institution. The University is accredited by the Middle States Association of Colleges and Schools. Departmental accreditations include the Accreditation Review Commission on Education for the Physician Assistant, Inc., Commission on Collegiate Nursing Education, Council on Social Work Education, and others. A complete list of accreditations may be found in the University catalog.

Students at Saint Francis University can find a number of outlets for their talents, interests, and abilities. Departmental clubs; volunteer organizations; social, business, and service fraternities; social sororities; and a service sorority are part of campus life. Athletics have played a major role in the University's history, and the athletics program offers twenty-two NCAA Division I sports for men and women as well as intramural sports. The Student Activities Organization sponsors an impressive program of lectures, films, and concerts. The Southern Alleghenies Museum of Art, separately chartered, is located on the campus as well.

The full-time undergraduate enrollment is 635 men and 931 women; the University as a whole enrolls 2,300 students. Saint Francis University offers Associate of Science degrees in business administration, and religious education. On the graduate level, Saint Francis grants a Master of Arts degree in human resource management and industrial relations. The University also offers the Master of Business Administration, Master of Education, Master of Medical Science, Master of Science in physician assistant sciences, and Master of Science in Occupational Therapy degrees. A doctoral degree in physical therapy is also available.

Location

Saint Francis University is situated on 600 acres in the heart of the Allegheny Mountains. The campus is located in the borough of Loretto, which has a population of approximately 1,400. The campus is 6 miles from the county seat of Ebensburg, which has a population of 4,000. The cities of Johnstown and Altoona are within 25 miles of Loretto and have populations of 35,000 and 55,000, respectively. The University is a 90-minute drive east of Pittsburgh.

Majors and Degrees

Saint Francis University grants the Bachelor of Arts degree and offers majors in American studies, biology, computer science, engineering (3-2 program), English, English/communications, history, mathematics, philosophy, political science, psychology, public administration/government service, religious studies, and sociology. The Bachelor of Science degree is also granted, with majors in accounting, biology, chemistry, computer science, economics and finance, elementary education/special education, environmental management (3-2 program), environmental studies (interdisciplinary), exercise physiology, management information systems, marketing, mathematics, medical technology, nursing, occupational therapy (five-year master's), pharmacy (3+2 or 3+3), physical therapy (six-year doctoral degree), physician assistant science (five-year master's), podiatric science, psychology, public administration/government service, social work, and sociology.

Areas of preprofessional study include dentistry, engineering (3-2 program), law, medicine, optometry, podiatry, and veterinary medicine. Areas of concentration within majors include anthropology, biochemistry, bioinformatics, communications, computer science, criminal justice, environmental politics, environmental science, forensics, information and network security, international studies, management information systems, marine and environmental education specialties, marine biology, molecular biology, political communications, public management, public relations, software development, and Web application development. The University also grants secondary education certification in the areas of biology, chemistry, English, general science, mathematics, and social studies. A 3-2 cooperative program with Duke University in forestry and environmental management, a 3+4 accelerated program in primary care, a 2+3 accelerated program and a 3+3 program in pharmacy with Lake Erie College of Osteopathic Medicine, and a 3+4 accelerated program leading to the baccalaureate and Doctor of Dental Medicine degrees with Temple University are also offered.

It is possible for students to major in one area and minor in another or to have a double major. A self-designed major program is available as well. The University offers an honors program to challenge intellectually ambitious students from all disciplines. While pursuing their major field of study, students enroll in the full four-year curriculum, which allows in-depth, creative study in a variety of subject areas.

A continuing education program provides credit and noncredit courses on campus as well as in the communities surrounding Loretto. The Office of Continuing Education offers Associate of Science degrees in business administration and religious education and Bachelor of Science degrees in accounting and management.

Academic Programs

The program of study leading to a bachelor's degree is usually completed in eight semesters. To qualify for graduation, a student must follow a program of study approved by the Office of the Provost that totals at least 128 credits distributed among liberal arts courses, major requirements, collateral requirements, and general electives. All students, regardless of major, are required to complete the University's general education program of 58 credits.

The academic calendar is divided into two semesters and three summer sessions.

Electronic capabilities at Saint Francis University enable students to access library holdings and communicate with professors, fellow students, and the world through the use of personal computers via e-mail and the Internet. Every classroom and residence hall room is wired for Internet access or can be accessed through the wireless network. The University has several classrooms equipped with state-of-the-art equipment that allows videoconferencing. All incoming freshmen receive a laptop computer as part of their tuition.

Off-Campus Programs

Students at Saint Francis University may, with permission of the University's administration, spend their junior year of study abroad or may earn credit for participation in summer programs conducted in Canada, France, Germany, Spain, and other countries by accredited American colleges and universities.

Students are encouraged to take advantage of the University's study abroad facility in Ambialet, France.

A number of departments offer students the opportunity for off-campus study. For some majors, such as nursing, occupational therapy, physical therapy, physician assistant science, education, medical technology, and social work, off-campus study is required;

in all other majors, an internship is available as an elective. Such an internship can be a meaningful experience and can significantly enhance a student's career preparation.

Academic Facilities

The six-story Pasquerilla Library contains more than 176,000 volumes, 582 periodicals, and a substantial microfilm collection. Other features of the library are typing areas, seminar rooms, reading rooms, microfilm reading rooms, several multimedia classrooms, technologically equipped study rooms, and a collection of study items and educational materials for elementary and secondary education majors. Special features of the library include an automated card catalog, periodical search systems, and a satellite hookup.

Scotus and Padua halls contain modern classroom facilities, language laboratories, two computer laboratories, a recording studio for radio and television, and lecture facilities (halls and an amphitheater). Sullivan Science Hall contains twelve well-equipped biology, chemistry, and physics laboratories; fully equipped electronic classrooms; a greenhouse for botanical research; an examining room for use in the physician assistant science program; and other facilities.

The recently completed DiSepio Institute for Rural Health and Wellness includes a human performance lab, a state-of-the-art fitness facility, conference space, and rehabilitation facilities. The focus of the Institute is delivering health and wellness programming and services to the campus community as well as the local population.

Costs

For 2009–10, tuition was $24,504, room and board were $8716, and technology program was $1050, for a total of $34,270.

Financial Aid

Approximately 90 percent of the Saint Francis University student body receives financial aid. In addition to participating in federal and state need-based student aid programs, Saint Francis University offers its own substantial grant program and a generous scholarship program that is based on SAT or ACT scores, high school average, and class rank. Academic awards range from $1000 to $15,500.

Faculty

Faculty members are chosen for their knowledge of subject matter, as well as for their ability to communicate. Of the teaching faculty at Saint Francis University, 79 percent hold a doctorate or the highest degree attainable in their specific field of expertise. No graduate students teach classes at Saint Francis University.

Student Government

The Student Government Association's Steering Committee involves students who are interested in self-government. Students also serve on a number of committees in the Faculty Senate. The Student Government offices are located in the John F. Kennedy Student Center, which also houses a 600-seat auditorium, a campus bookstore and post office, a study lounge, and a café.

Admission Requirements

The admission committee considers applicants and renders decisions on the basis of the secondary school record, the recommendation of the secondary school principal or counselor, and the results of the SAT or ACT. Applicants to the School of Health Science should be aware of application requirements and deadlines. Applicants should have a minimum of 16 academic units and are strongly encouraged to visit the University campus for an admission interview and tour. Interviews and campus tours are available Monday through Friday throughout the year and select Saturday mornings while classes are in session.

Transfer students must submit a formal transfer application and a college clearance form in addition to official transcripts from each high school and college previously attended. Transfer students receive an advanced standing evaluation after an offer of admission has been made.

Saint Francis University, an equal opportunity/affirmative action employer, complies with applicable federal and state laws regarding nondiscrimination and affirmative action, including Title IX of the Educational Amendments of 1972, Titles VI and VII of the Civil Rights Act of 1964, and Section 504 of the Rehabilitation Act of 1973. Saint Francis University is committed to a policy of nondiscrimination and equal opportunity in employment, education programs and activities, and admissions that includes all persons regardless of race, gender, color, religion, national origin or ancestry, age, marital status, disability, or Vietnam-era veteran status. Inquiries or complaints may be addressed to the University's Director of Human Resources/Affirmative Action/Title IX Coordinator, Saint Francis University, Loretto, Pennsylvania 15940; telephone: 814-472-3264. For other University information, students should call 814-472-3000.

Application and Information

The University operates under a rolling admission policy. The application deadline for the physical therapy, occupational therapy, and physician assistant programs is January 15. For more information about Saint Francis University, students should contact:

Vice President for Enrollment Management
Saint Francis University
P.O. Box 600
Loretto, Pennsylvania 15940
Phone: 814-472-3100
866-342-5738 (toll-free)
E-mail: admissions@francis.edu
Web site: http://www.francis.edu

Christian Hall.

COLLEGE CLOSE-UPS

ST. JOHN FISHER COLLEGE

ROCHESTER, NEW YORK

The College

Founded in 1948 by the Basilian fathers, St. John Fisher College is dedicated to serving the individual needs of its students. Originally a Catholic college for men, Fisher is now an independent, coeducational college with 58 percent women and 52 percent resident students. The College offers thirty-one undergraduate programs in business, the humanities, nursing, natural sciences, and social sciences, and is accredited by the Middle States Association of Colleges and Schools. The College also offers eleven master's programs and three doctoral programs leading to the Master of Business Administration, the Master of Science, the Master of Science in Education, the Doctor of Education, the Doctor of Nursing Practice, and the Doctor of Pharmacy.

Fisher's unique First-Year Program reaches beyond the transition to college to focus on developing responsible campus citizens with independent learning skills, who fully explore educational and career aspirations. The Learning Community Program gives first-year students the opportunity to take courses in clusters that focus on a central theme. Through this approach to learning, students and faculty members examine a complex topic from multiple perspectives and discover connections among various disciplines. Fisher's Learning Communities also enable students to learn cooperatively and develop close working relationships with other students and faculty members.

All of the residence halls have been renovated, giving all students access to the Internet and cable TV in their rooms. Keough Hall, the College's newest residence, opened in September 2005 and added more than 200 beds.

Fisher offers a full range of extracurricular activities designed to cater to the diverse interests of the 2,600 full-time and 220 part-time undergraduate students, nearly 700 master's students, and over 350 doctoral students. Such activities include a student newspaper, a campus radio station, a complete intramural program, and more than seventy student organizations. In addition, the Student Activities Board sponsors appearances by on-campus lecturers and entertainers.

Fisher is a member of NCAA Division III, ECAC, and the Empire 8. Men's intercollegiate sports are baseball, basketball, football, golf, lacrosse, soccer, and tennis. Women's intercollegiate sports are basketball, golf, lacrosse, soccer, softball, tennis, and volleyball. Club sports include cross-country, ice hockey and men's and women's rugby. The Student Life Center, which is the hub of the athletic activities, includes courts for basketball, racquetball, squash, tennis, and volleyball; a sauna; a lounge; and a fitness area. Growney Stadium, complete with 2,100 bleacher seats and a press box, is equipped with an all-weather synthetic playing field to allow for all-season and nighttime play. Other on-campus athletics facilities include a nine-hole golf course, a softball field, a baseball complex, four outdoor tennis courts, and two grass practice fields. In the summer, Fisher is proud to host the Buffalo Bills training camp on campus. In fall 2010, the College is scheduled to begin construction of a new track and field complex. As a result, in fall 2011, Fisher plans to add men's and women's indoor and outdoor track, men's and women's cross-country, and field hockey.

Location

Located on 154 parklike acres, Fisher offers a balance of city activity and suburban tranquility. Just 10 minutes from the Fisher campus, Rochester, the "World's Image Centre," offers many cultural attractions, including the Eastman Theater, the Rochester Philharmonic Orchestra, the International Museum of Photography at George Eastman House, the Rochester Museum and Science Center, the Memorial Art Gallery, and the Strasenburgh Planetarium. Home to a number of Fortune 500 companies, such as Eastman Kodak Company, Xerox Corporation, and Bausch and Lomb, the city of Rochester offers Fisher students opportunities for internships and employment after graduation.

Majors and Degrees

St. John Fisher College offers courses leading to the Bachelor of Arts and Bachelor of Science degrees. Undergraduate majors are offered in accounting, adolescence education, American studies, anthropology, applied information technology, biology, chemistry, childhood education, communication/journalism, computer science, corporate finance, economics, English, French, history, interdisciplinary studies, international studies, management, mathematics, nursing, philosophy, physics, political science, psychology, religious studies, sociology, Spanish, special education, sport management, and statistics. The areas of concentration available in the management major include corporate finance, financial planning, general business management, human resource management, and marketing.

Fisher offers an RN to B.S. degree-completion program in nursing and a fast track to the B.S/M.S. in advanced practice nursing. The College also offers a cooperative engineering program with the University of Detroit, Clarkson University, Manhattan College, Columbia University, and the University at Buffalo, the State University of New York.

Academic Programs

The bachelor's degree is conferred upon those who complete a minimum of 120 semester hours of credit with a cumulative GPA of at least 2.0. Thirty hours of credit and half of the requirements for the major must be earned at St. John Fisher College. Graduates of the accounting program are eligible to sit for the CPA exam in New York State.

Off-Campus Programs

Fisher offers a multitude of special programs that are designed to complement its academic programs. Students in various disciplines can take advantage of an internship program, Albany and Washington Semesters, and cross-registration with fourteen member colleges of the Rochester Area College Consortium. Study-abroad opportunities throughout the world are also available to students.

Academic Facilities

Over the last ten years, most of the academic and athletic facilities on campus have been upgraded and enhanced. Classrooms have been modernized and outfitted with state-of-the-art media facilities. Laboratory space has been upgraded with state-of-the-market educational technology. The Golisano Academic Gateway, complete with the Frontier Cyber Café and the learning resource center, opened in January 2001. The Ralph C. Wilson, Jr. Building opened in September 2003, expanding classroom capacity by 20 percent and providing additional faculty offices, seminar rooms, and meeting spaces.

The Campus Center opened in fall 2005 and serves as the hub and central gathering place of student activity on campus. This two-story facility supports general student gathering spaces, which include a performance space, recreational area, offices for student clubs and organizations, and the College Store (bookstore), all located on the first floor. The second floor of the Campus Center houses the Offices of the Dean of Students, Residential Life, Campus Life, and Campus Ministry, as well as additional student organization offices and meeting spaces.

The Charles J. Lavery Library meets the information needs of twenty-first-century students. A blend of traditional and electronic resources covering a broad range of subjects is available to the Fisher community. The library's print collection is supplemented by an extensive offering of online scholarly resources. Information resources include 162,300 volumes, 7,836 audiovisual items, 484 print periodical subscriptions, and 33,442 electronic periodical titles in 72 databases.

Professional librarians welcome students to the library reference desk during day and evening hours. There is also a 24/7 online-chat reference service. The librarians are information specialists committed to the academic success of all students. Individual research guidance is available by appointment. Librarians also teach classes in information literacy and subject-specific research to all levels of students.

Lavery Library is a member of the Rochester Regional Library Council, representing a regional collection of more than 3,400,000 titles. Interlibrary loan staff can obtain resources not owned by Lavery Library from regional, national, and international libraries.

Costs

Tuition for 2009–10 was $23,850. Room and board costs were $10,090 with a meal plan and a room in one of Fisher's residence halls, and fees were $470.

Financial Aid

Committed to helping students meet the cost of their education, Fisher works to assess each individual's financial need. Financial aid is provided through scholarships, grants, loans, and work-study arrangements and is awarded by Fisher, the state, and the federal government. In 2009–10, the average financial aid package for incoming Fisher students was $20,445.

St. John Fisher College offers a generous academic scholarship program that is based on high school average, strength of curriculum, and SAT or ACT scores. Students eligible for academic scholarships are automatically notified by the Office of Freshman Admissions. Scholarship award amounts are $9500 to $12,500 per year. The College also offers an honors program and a science scholars program. The award in each of these programs is $3000, in addition to any academic scholarships for which the student qualifies.

Fourteen years ago, the College introduced the Service Scholars Program. This program is designed to recognize and reward high school seniors who demonstrate an ongoing interest in serving the needs of others through a commitment to community service. Scholarship awards equal one third of the total yearly cost of tuition, and room and board for four years. St. John Fisher College was recently named to the President's Higher Education Community Service Honor Roll for exemplary service efforts and service to disadvantaged youth.

In 1998, the College announced the creation of the Fannie and Sam Constantino First Generation Scholarship Program, designed to provide financial and academic assistance to high school students whose parents did not graduate from a postsecondary institution—much like the pioneer classes of St. John Fisher College. Recipients receive annual scholarships ranging from $5000 to one half of the total cost of Fisher's tuition, room, and board.

Faculty

Fisher's 199 full-time faculty members are dedicated to helping students, both in and out of the classroom, as they strive to achieve their goals. Eighty-five percent of full-time faculty members hold doctoral or terminal degrees. The student-teacher ratio of 14:1 offers a personal approach to education; 75 percent of all classes have fewer than 30 students. Fisher's Office of Academic Affairs and an outstanding faculty share responsibility for academic advising, helping students to explore the thirty-one majors that are available to them.

Student Government

Student leadership skills are developed through the Student Government Association, which is responsible for the social, cultural, and judicial areas of student life. Resident students elect a Resident Student Association, while commuting students elect a Commuter Council to represent them in planning special activities. The Student Activities Board is responsible for social activities and cultural events throughout the academic year.

Admission Requirements

Admission to St. John Fisher College is based primarily on the following: grade point average, strength of curriculum, scores on standardized tests (SAT/ACT); a personal statement, essay, or graded paper; extracurricular activities and/or work experience, and the counselor/teacher recommendation.

A candidate for admission to the freshman class must be a graduate of an approved secondary school and present a minimum of 16 units of college-preparatory course work in English, foreign languages, mathematics, and natural and social sciences. An applicant should present a secondary school average of 85 percent or above in these academic subjects.

Fisher welcomes qualified transfer students from two- and four-year colleges for both the fall and spring terms. To be considered for admission, transfer students must have a cumulative grade point average of 2.0 or better. If the student has obtained an A.A., A.S., or A.A.S. degree, 60 to 66 credit hours are transferred. All transfer applicants should consult the Undergraduate Bulletin for details.

The College has various special admission programs, including early decision, abbreviated procedures for veterans and other military personnel, and admission for part-time study.

The College offers the Arthur O. Eve Higher Education Opportunity Program (HEOP) for students who need special academic and financial assistance. The program provides academic support services, counseling, and financial aid for qualified students to help them achieve academic success.

Fisher grants college credit for satisfactory grades on the Advanced Placement test, the International Baccalaureate (I.B.) Program exams, and the College-Level Examination Program (CLEP). Only students who receive a 3 or higher in all AP subjects and a 4 or higher on the AP science and language exams are granted Advanced Placement credit. CLEP and I.B. scoring guidelines are available through the Office of Freshman Admissions. Credit is only granted for subject-specific CLEP exams. In addition, recognizing the college-level course work being completed at the high school level, St. John Fisher College will consider granting credit for any college course work in which a student earns a grade of "C" or better.

Application and Information

Applications are accepted on a rolling basis. Early-decision applications are due December 1. The admissions application deadline for merit scholarship consideration is January 15.

Although a personal interview is not required for admission, all applicants are encouraged to visit the College. Interviews and campus tours are available weekdays from 8:30 to 4:30 and on selected Saturdays throughout the academic year.

For additional information or an application, students should contact:

Office of Freshman Admissions
St. John Fisher College
3690 East Avenue
Rochester, New York 14618
Phone: 585-385-8064
800-444-4640 (toll-free)
Fax: 585-385-8386
E-mail: admissions@sjfc.edu
Web site: http://www.sjfc.edu/admissions/freshman

Kearney Hall, Fisher's main administration building.

ST. JOHN'S COLLEGE

ANNAPOLIS, MARYLAND, AND SANTA FE, NEW MEXICO

The College

St. John's College maintains two widely separated campuses, one in Annapolis, Maryland, and another in Santa Fe, New Mexico. Each has its own admissions and financial aid offices. A common curriculum, however, enables students and faculty members to move from one campus to the other. Both campuses are cohesive intellectual communities in which students are eagerly responsive to one another. Students also pursue interests in such activities as publications, dance, dramatics, photography, art, wilderness exploration, and sailing. The social climate is informal and lively, and students enjoy many celebrations each year. Facilities are available for almost any intramural sport; most students participate. There is a bookstore on each campus. In fall 2008, opening enrollment at the Annapolis campus was 231 women and 261 men, for a total of 492 students. The opening enrollment of 440 at the Santa Fe campus consisted of 172 women and 268 men.

The students on both campuses are outstanding, yet they fit no pattern. Though their backgrounds are varied geographically, academically, and otherwise, they are, most typically, young people who habitually read books and value good conversation. Their commitment to ideas and their enthusiasm for the St. John's program are well illustrated by the fact that about one fifth of them on each campus have transferred to St. John's as freshmen after a year or more of college elsewhere.

Location

St. John's is the third-oldest college in the United States. It has been located since 1696 in the Colonial seaport city of Annapolis, the capital of Maryland, 30 miles from Washington, D.C. In 1964, a second campus was opened at the foot of the mountains surrounding Santa Fe, a cultural center and the capital of New Mexico. The campuses are alike in curriculum and methods, but their settings and moods are as different as sailing on the Chesapeake Bay and skiing in the Sangre de Cristo Mountains, as Georgian and Spanish Colonial architecture. St. John's students participate in a number of activities of benefit to their communities at large.

Majors and Degrees

St. John's College is committed to liberal education in the most traditional and yet radical way. It accomplishes this through direct engagement with the books in which the greatest minds of Western civilization have expressed themselves and through translation, mathematical demonstration, musical analysis, and laboratory experimentation. Whether in Annapolis or in Santa Fe, all St. John's students follow the same course of study leading to the B.A. degree. One of the purposes of this program is to emphasize the unity of knowledge; thus, the faculty is not divided into departments and there are no majors.

Academic Programs

The academic program is a unified, cohesive whole; instruction takes the form of annual sequences of related seminars, tutorials, and laboratories, in each of which the books that form the core of the curriculum are the basis of study and discussion. To ensure that the intellectual life of the College extends beyond the classroom and that students bring a common frame of reference to the continuing discussion, this academic program is required of everyone, but no two students are expected to approach any subject in the same way or to reach the same conclusions about it. A central purpose of the St. John's program is to give students both the opportunity and the obligation to think for themselves. The books at the heart of the program serve to foster that thinking. They not only illuminate the enduring questions of human existence but also have great relevance to contemporary problems. They can change minds, move hearts, and touch spirits. They help all students to arrive independently at rational opinions and conclusions of their own. From this common curriculum, about 70 percent of the students go on to graduate and professional study in a wide range of fields.

There are two semesters a year. All classes are small discussion groups and range in size from between 12 and 16 students in tutorials to between 18 and 20 in seminars and laboratories. Final examinations are oral and individual. Students are not routinely informed of their grades. Instead, a student's tutors, as members of the faculty are called, evaluate the student's intellectual performance twice a year in his or her presence and with his or her help. St. John's students are participants in their own education. Annual essays and shorter papers, prepared by students without recourse to secondary sources, are based directly on the books of the program.

Seminars are devoted to reading works of the greatest minds and engaging in thoughtful discussion about them. The first-year seminar focuses on Greek authors; the second on the works of the Roman, medieval, and early Renaissance periods; the third on books of the seventeenth and eighteenth centuries; and the fourth on writings from the nineteenth and twentieth centuries. The seminar consists almost exclusively of student conversation. The aim of the discussions is to ascertain not how things were but how things are. Everyone's opinion must be heard and must also be supported by argument and evidence. The role of the tutors is not to give information or to produce the "right" interpretation; it is to guide the discussion, to aid in defining the issues, and to help the students to understand the authors, the issues, and themselves. If tutors do take a definite stand and enter the argument, they are expected to defend their positions just as students do. Reason is the only recognized authority.

Preceptorials replace seminars for eight weeks of the junior and senior years. In the preceptorial, students and tutors gather in groups of 8 or 9 to discuss, with more leisure than the pace and discipline of the seminar permit, books or topics of particular interest to them.

In the language tutorial, Greek is studied in the first two years and French in the last two. By translating works written in Greek and French into English and comparing those languages with each other as well as with English, the student gains an appreciation of all three and learns something of the nature of language in general.

The language of number and figure does not require a special aptitude. Rather, mathematics is an integral and necessary part of comprehending the world. The mathematics tutorial seeks to affect an understanding of the fundamental nature and intention of mathematics. Throughout the four years, the student is in contact not only with the pure science of mathematics but also with the foundations of mathematical physics and astronomy. The blackboard becomes an arena of logical struggle, which brings the imagination constantly into play.

The music tutorial aims at understanding music through study of musical theory and analysis of significant works. Students investigate rhythm, the diatonic system, ratios of musical intervals, melody, counterpoint, and harmony.

In the modern world, the liberal arts are practiced at their best and fullest in the laboratory. This practice puts into serious question the common distinction between the "natural sciences" and the "humanities." The laboratory is a part of the program in all years but the second. It weaves together the main themes of physics, biology, and chemistry with careful scrutiny of the interplay of hypothesis, theory, and observed fact.

On Friday evenings, the College community assembles for a formal lecture or concert by a tutor or visitor. It is the only time the students are lectured to. Afterward, interested students and faculty members engage the speaker or performer in questions and discussion.

Academic Facilities

The library on each campus—about 100,000 volumes in Annapolis, nearly 60,000 in Santa Fe—emphasizes material appropriate to the nature of the academic program, supplemented by a more general collection and by a variety of special collections. Recordings and representative periodicals and newspapers are included. Academic facilities on each campus also include the resources and equipment necessary for study and experimentation in physics, chemistry, and biology (including a planetarium in Annapolis); for audition and performance of music; for display and studio work in art, photography, and other crafts; and for drama productions.

Costs

For 2009–10, annual tuition and fees total $39,992. Room and board are $9600. Books and supplies range in cost from $250 to $300. Personal expenses depend on the student's habits and tastes.

Financial Aid

The criterion for financial assistance is need. On both campuses the application for financial aid is the CSS PROFILE, supplemented by the Free Application for Federal Student Aid (FAFSA) and an institutional aid application. More than half of all St. John's students receive aid, usually in a combination of grants, loans, and employment. Federal Perkins Loans, Federal Pell Grants, Federal Supplemental Educational Opportunity Grants, Federal Work-Study Program employment, and College grants and jobs are available.

Faculty

The faculty-student ratio is 1:8 on each campus. Faculty members all hold the same rank. Their intellectual range and vitality come from teaching throughout the curriculum. This breadth and tension and the fact that St. John's is an intellectual community in which all teach and all learn are distinctive characteristics of the St. John's faculty.

Student Government

Inside the classroom and out, the dignity of the students as adults is respected. On both campuses, student government is part of the general College pattern. A Delegate Council and Student Committee on Instruction work with the faculty members and administrators on matters of mutual concern.

Admission Requirements

Criteria for admission to either campus are intellectual and academic, though any accomplishment showing initiative and drive may strengthen an application. The written application consists of a series of reflective essays. The academic record and recommendations are considered supplements to it. SAT or ACT scores are optional but may prove helpful. There are no minimums for grades or test scores; both may be made irrelevant by what the candidate writes. On each campus, applicants are judged on their own merits. Although interviews are not required except in special cases, interested students are urged to visit either campus for several days to sit in on seminars and tutorials.

Application and Information

Students may be admitted to either campus for the fall term or, if they are prepared to continue their studies through the following summer, in January. Application must be made to one campus or the other, not to both. Early application is advisable. Each campus seeks to complete its class by mid-May. All applications for admission and financial aid are acted on as soon as they are complete, and the candidate is notified of the decision within two weeks.

In response to inquiries, the College sends a catalog, information on financial aid, an application form, and forms for the school report and for recommendations. Students should contact:

John Christensen
Director of Admissions
St. John's College
Annapolis, Maryland 21404
Phone: 800-727-9238 (toll-free)
E-mail: admissions@sjca.edu
Web site: http://www.stjohnscollege.edu

Larry Clendenin
Director of Admissions
St. John's College
Santa Fe, New Mexico 87501
Phone: 800-331-5232 (toll-free)
E-mail: admissions@sjcsf.edu
Web site: http://www.stjohnscollege.edu

St. John's College at Annapolis.

SAINT JOSEPH COLLEGE

WEST HARTFORD, CONNECTICUT

The College

Saint Joseph College is focused on helping students fulfill their potential by combining excellence in liberal arts with a career-focused, professional education for women. Since the College's founding in 1932, the vision of the Sisters of Mercy has continued to shape the way Saint Joseph College (SJC) has grown. SJC now offers students the opportunity to study in competitive undergraduate and graduate degree programs, including the College's first doctoral program in pharmacy (pending accreditation). With an emphasis on offering an academically rigorous education framed within a commitment to service in the community, Saint Joseph College is a place the student can quickly call home.

The core values of compassionate service, Catholic identity, commitment to women through academic excellence, and diversity are evident in the College's curriculum and daily life. Students from a multitude of faith traditions and backgrounds are empowered for success.

There are 1,062 undergraduates in The Women's College. Faculty members and students emphasize leadership in academics, career, and community. Drawing on its Mercy heritage, the College is a community that promotes the growth of the whole person. This is accomplished in a caring environment that encourages strong ethical values, personal integrity, and a sense of responsibility to the needs of society. Women lead every organization on campus, from the Business Society and Student Government to Campus Ministry and honors societies. Saint Joseph College students shine in artistic performances, as coordinators of community service projects, and on the athletic fields. Students also serve with faculty members and administrators on College-wide committees. In the field of athletics, the College's women compete in eight NCAA Division III sports: basketball, cross-country, lacrosse, softball, soccer, swimming/diving, tennis, and volleyball. The O'Connell Athletic Center features a six-lane pool, gymnasium, suspended jogging track, dance studio, fitness center, outdoor track, softball field, and tennis courts for all students' recreational purposes.

Saint Joseph College has a beautiful residential campus in the bustling town of West Hartford. Approximately 75 percent of the first-year students in The Women's College live on campus. Special student services include career planning, alumni mentoring, internship placement, counseling, health services, academic advisement, and campus ministry.

Saint Joseph College alumni have considerable impact on the welfare of their communities. They are leaders in many fields, including aerospace research, business, education, environmental science, law, medicine, and politics. Recent graduates enjoy successful careers in accounting, the arts, business, education, government, health care, human services, industry, the sciences, and nonprofit organizations.

Saint Joseph College is accredited by the New England Association of Schools and Colleges. The chemistry program is accredited by the American Chemical Society, and the social work program is accredited by the Council on Social Work Education. The coordinated undergraduate program in dietetics is accredited by the American Dietetic Association. The nursing program is accredited by the Commission on Collegiate Nursing Education.

Location

The College is located in suburban West Hartford, 4 miles from the state capitol and the city of Hartford's arts and entertainment district. Among the nearby attractions are the XL Center and Coliseum, Bushnell Performing Arts Center, where the latest Broadway musicals are performed, and the Wadsworth Atheneum, the oldest public art gallery in the United States. Hartford is a cosmopolitan city with diverse ethnic flavors. It is also the home of the Tony Award–winning Hartford Stage Company, the Hartford Symphony Orchestra, the Connecticut Opera Company, the Hartford Ballet, and the Dodge Music Center, which features indoor and outdoor concerts. West Hartford Center, just minutes from campus, offers an array of coffee bars, boutiques, restaurants, and a beautiful movie theater in the newly completed Blue Back Square.

Majors and Degrees

Saint Joseph College has always enjoyed a strong academic reputation based on a combination of liberal arts and career-focused, professional majors. The College awards the B.A. or B.S. in accounting, American studies, art history, biochemistry, biology, chemistry, child study, English (literature, writing), family studies (family and consumer science, contemporary family issues), history (archives and museum skills), international studies, liberal studies, management, mathematics, nursing, nutrition and dietetics, philosophy, psychology, religious studies, social work, Spanish, special education, and women's studies. Preprofessional programs are offered in conjunction with an academic major and include prepharmacy, predentistry, prelaw, premedicine, pre–physical therapy, and pre–veterinary studies.

Teaching certification is offered in early childhood education, elementary education, secondary education, and special education.

Research, clinical, and work placements are important components of all academic programs.

Academic Programs

Each student must complete a minimum of 120 credits to obtain a baccalaureate degree, and 47 of those credits must be distributed among the general education/liberal arts courses at the College. Specifically, students must take courses in the humanities, social sciences, natural sciences, philosophy, religious studies, and physical education. An academic advisement counselor assists each student in planning her program of study.

Many unique facets to the academic programs offered increase students' propensity for success. An honors program and several dual degree programs are offered. The Center for Academic Excellence manages the College's award-winning Writing Portfolio Program, which enhances students' writing skills. The center also provides tutoring and other academic support services. Students may design their own major or may develop an interdisciplinary major or minor around a particular theme or problem related to their special talents, personal interests, or career goals. An exciting component of most majors at Saint Joseph College is the internship. Students earn credit for internships at a variety of sites, including the state capitol, the Bushnell Performing Arts Center, Aetna, Legislative Office, the Connecticut Department of Economic Development, WVIT-TV, Connecticut Children's Medical Center, the Science Center of Connecticut, and numerous other businesses.

Off-Campus Programs

Students at Saint Joseph College may take courses at cooperating institutions through the Hartford Consortium for Higher Education. This is a special arrangement among five Hartford-area colleges—Saint Joseph College, Trinity College, University of Connecticut Greater Hartford Branch, Central Connecticut State University, and the University of Hartford—through which students are able to cross register for courses. No additional tuition is charged, and all credits are transferable.

Students at Saint Joseph College have countless opportunities for global study experiences through our many study abroad programs. Students are assisted by the Director of International Studies and Programs in planning for an international-study experience during a semester, winter recess, or even over spring break. Saint Joseph College also offers a specialized program in Guyana, South America, through the College's sister hospital. Students in the education and health science fields are encouraged to participate in this program for a work abroad experience at the end of the spring semester during their junior or senior years.

Those students majoring in nursing, social work, and nutrition, and those in the graduate counseling program, may gain practical experience providing community-based, accessible health screenings and referrals; health and nutrition education; counseling services; and social work case management services at The Wellness Center on Church Street in Hartford. The College has also established a partnership with the Franciscan Center for Urban Ministry in order to reach out to its neighboring city and enhance the quality of life of its residents in need.

Academic Facilities

The Pope Pius XII Library has a collection of more than 134,000 volumes, including computer databases, periodicals, microforms, audiovisuals, a Sirsi online catalog, and OCLC interlibrary loans. A collection of materials used in elementary and secondary education is featured in the Curriculum Materials Center.

The College uses laboratory schools with several of its academic programs. The renowned School for Young Children, located one block from the campus, and its counterpart, the School for Young Children at Asylum Hill, in Hartford, are operating preschools that provide child study majors with training and experience. The College also recently opened a Charter School in Hartford to enhance the diversity of classroom experiences available to students while serving the community. The Gengras Center, located on the campus, is a special education school serving children and young adults (ages 4–21) from approximately fifty area cities and towns in Connecticut and Massachusetts. It provides for special education needs and also helps to prepare special education teachers.

The College's primary technology centers are located in McDonough Hall; Internet access is available throughout campus including many WiFi hotspots. Additional facilities and services include a media center that provides production materials, expertise, and equipment for making and using a number of media instructional aids; science and nursing labs; and the Carol Autorino Center for the Arts and Humanities. The center includes Lynch Hall, which houses humanities, faculty offices, and classrooms; the Bruyette Athenaeum, featuring the 365-seat Hoffman Auditorium; the Saint Joseph College Art Gallery; a print study room; large lecture hall; reception room; and music practice rooms. The building also houses the College's archives.

Costs

The tuition and fees for full-time freshmen entering in 2010 are $27,580. Room and board cost is approximately $11,680. The cost per credit for part-time students is $625.

Financial Aid

The goal of the Saint Joseph College Financial Aid Program is to place a high-quality, private education within the reach of as many qualified students as possible. This goal is achieved by offering need- and merit-based financial aid that includes a combination of grants, loans, and on-campus employment opportunities. More than 85 percent of full-time undergraduate students receive some form of financial assistance. Merit-based scholarship awards are available to all eligible first-year, transfer and international students.

Faculty

Saint Joseph College's faculty consists of 85 full-time faculty members and 4 librarians. Of the total faculty, 68.8 percent are women. Of the full-time faculty, 90 percent hold the highest possible degrees in their fields. Small classes benefit both students and professors. The student-faculty ratio is 11:1. The faculty and all members of the College community promote the welfare of students and help them attain the objectives set forth by the College's mission. Faculty members also serve as advisers to many extracurricular activities, including sports, campus ministry, and community service; direct students in independent study; involve students in scholarly research; and act as mentors before and after graduation.

Student Government

The Student Government Association works for effective communication among students, faculty members, and administrators. Students are encouraged to voice their opinions and concerns to the association for consideration and action. In addition, student representatives sit as voting members with faculty members and administrators on major College-wide committees. The Student Government Association encourages the development of leadership skills and provides funds annually for several of its members to attend leadership workshops and conferences.

Admission Requirements

Saint Joseph College seeks women who are anxious to accept the challenge of rigorous academic programs while pursuing the interests and careers that will help them achieve their goals. Applications are encouraged from interested students of every race, age, and religious affiliation. In accordance with Section 504 of the Rehabilitation Act of 1973, which prohibits discrimination on the basis of disability, and the Americans with Disabilities Act of 1990, Saint Joseph College is committed to the goal of achieving equal educational opportunities and full participation for people with disabilities in higher education.

Candidates for first-year admission should complete a four-year course of study in a regionally accredited secondary school or have equivalent homeschooling preparation. The program should include 16 academic units in college-preparatory courses distributed among the areas of English, mathematics, natural sciences, social studies, and foreign languages. Applicants are required to submit scores of the SAT or ACT tests. A personal interview is a highly recommended part of the admission procedure, since it offers a mutual opportunity for the student and Admissions Counselors to discuss educational and professional goals.

The Committee on Admissions operates on the principle that a student's ability, motivation, and maturity should be determined by a careful individual review of all the applicant's credentials, including the academic record, standardized test scores, written personal statement, and letter(s) of recommendation. Special consideration may be given to some applicants whose preparation varies from the recommended pattern but whose record gives evidence of genuine intellectual ability and interest. International students should contact the Office of Admissions for further information. Additional information is available online at http://www.sjc.edu/admissions.

Saint Joseph College admits qualified students for transfer in both fall and spring semesters.

Application and Information

The Committee on Admissions recommends that application for first-year admission be made in the first semester of the senior year in secondary school. All applications should be completed by April 1. A nonrefundable $50 fee must be sent with paper applications; the application fee is waived for students who apply online at http://www.sjc.edu/admissions. Students are encouraged to begin the financial aid process by completing the FAFSA form online at http://www.fafsa.ed.gov as soon as possible after January 1 of the year they are applying for admission. The priority deadline for completing the FAFSA is February 15. Students should complete the FAFSA using estimated income information if they or their families will not have completed their tax returns prior to February 15. Financial aid counselors are available to assist prospective students and families with the financial aid process.

Transfer applicants for the spring semester should apply by December 1; applicants for the fall semester, by June 1. Students applying to the nursing program should contact the College to learn about special deadlines. Transfer candidates who wish to apply for financial aid should complete or update the FAFSA online by November 15 if applying for the spring semester or by August 15 if applying for the fall semester.

For further information about admission to Saint Joseph College, students should contact:

Nancy D. Wunderly
Director of Admissions
Saint Joseph College
1678 Asylum Avenue
West Hartford, Connecticut 06117

Phone: 860-231-5216
866-44-CTSJC (toll-free)
Fax: 860-231-5744
E-mail: admissions@sjc.edu
Web site: http://www.sjc.edu/admissions

COLLEGE CLOSE-UPS

ST. JOSEPH'S COLLEGE

BROOKLYN AND PATCHOGUE, NEW YORK

The College

Since 1916, St. Joseph's College has been inspiring students to transform their lives. A private coeducational institution with campuses in Brooklyn and Patchogue, Long Island, the College enrolls nearly 5,000 undergraduates and over 600 graduate students in its School of Arts and Sciences and School of Professional and Graduate Studies.

St. Joseph's helps students turn aspirations into accomplishments. In addition to offering a liberal arts education of the highest quality, St. Joseph's offers students an unrivaled degree of personal attention, encouraging them to lead lives characterized by integrity, a commitment to upholding intellectual and spiritual values, social responsibility, and service to others.

St. Joseph's students immerse themselves in learning in ways that go far beyond the classroom, through independent projects, team-building assignments, internships, community service opportunities, and study-abroad programs designed to suit every schedule. Moreover, with just 15 students for every professor on campus, St. Joseph's students easily find mentors to guide them in everything from academics to focusing on future career and life goals.

Although most of St. Joseph's students commute at both campuses, the Brooklyn campus offers student housing through Educational Housing Services at the nearby St. George Residence. Each of the campuses offers a lively atmosphere enriched by social events, athletic competitions, and a Common Hour to encourage students to explore new possibilities for fun, leadership, and connections. On any given day at St. Joseph's, students might come to campus to hear a Pulitzer Prize–winning author, enjoy a jazz concert, join a community service effort, view an art exhibit, attend an athletic event, or engage in a political debate over dinner with other students and professors. Each campus supports over thirty student clubs and activities, including intercollegiate basketball; women's softball, swimming, tennis, and volleyball; men's baseball, basketball, tennis, and volleyball; and coed cross-country. The Long Island campus also offers men's soccer, and a coed equestrian team.

For undergraduates, St. Joseph's offers fast tracks to advanced degrees through special affiliated programs in accounting, podiatry, and computer science. The School of Professional and Graduate Studies at St. Joseph's College offers a wide range of graduate programs in education, human services, management, and nursing, including the Executive M.B.A., an M.B.A. in accounting, an M.B.A. in health care management, and the M.S. in nursing, to name a few.

Location

The Brooklyn campus is located in the Clinton Hill Historic District, a neighborhood where so many of New York's wealthiest citizens once lived that it was dubbed Brooklyn's "Gold Coast" in the 1920s. Today this area is home to several prestigious schools, including the Pratt Institute of Art and the Brooklyn Academy of Music, and serves as a hub of cultural and intellectual activity. This convenient location allows students to enjoy the freedom of a safe, well-landscaped campus easily accessible to New York City by car or public transportation.

St. Joseph's Long Island campus is located in the village of Patchogue on Great South Bay, about 50 miles from Manhattan and 60 miles from Montauk Point. Patchogue offers plenty to do, with fine harbors, shops, restaurants, athletic fields, and tennis courts right in the village. There are lovely parks nearby as well as museums, golf courses, hiking and ski trails, and beaches. Patchogue is easily accessible via Long Island Rail Road, bus service, or ferry. A major regional airport, McArthur Airport, is just minutes away.

Majors and Degrees

Through individual attention, interactive teaching, and intensive advising, St. Joseph's meets students where they are academically, then guides them through the essential next steps to help them stretch intellectually, personally, and professionally. St. Joseph's offers four-year programs leading to B.A. and B.S. degrees at both the Brooklyn and Patchogue campuses, with majors in accounting, business administration, biology, chemistry, child study, computer information systems, criminal justice, English, history, human relations, marketing, mathematics, recreation, psychology, social sciences: economics, sociology and political science, Spanish, and speech communication. Among these majors are a variety of minors and certificate programs from which students can choose.

No matter what major students choose, they can also earn additional certificates designed to help them delve deeper into specific interests and give them a head start when entering the workforce. Certificate programs include criminology/criminal justice; gerontology; information technology; leadership and supervision; management, marketing, advertising, and public relations; and religious studies.

For students interested in a fast track to an advanced degree after completing their undergraduate studies, St. Joseph's offers special affiliated programs. Through a partnership between St. Joseph's College and Polytechnic Institute of NYU, students at the Brooklyn campus can pursue a bachelor's degree in any field and a master's degree in computer science in a combined B.A./B.S. plus M.S. program. The Brooklyn campus also offers an accelerated biomedical program in cooperation with the New York College of Podiatric Medicine. This program allows students to receive a B.S. in biology and a doctorate in podiatric medicine within six years. Students at both the Brooklyn and Patchogue campuses can earn B.S./M.B.A. degrees in accounting within five years or can choose to pursue preprofessional programs in law, teaching, and numerous health fields, including dentistry, medicine, and optometry.

Those with nontraditional academic backgrounds or with professional training and experience can pursue degrees in community health, general studies, health administration, nursing, and organizational management through St. Joseph's School of Professional and Graduate Studies at either campus.

Academic Programs

The School of Arts and Sciences at each campus operates on the semester system, with additional courses offered in January and during the summer. St. Joseph's students take a core curriculum of 128 credits to graduate; a wide range of choices allows students to tailor their academic programs to their personal and professional needs. The College recognizes the Advanced

Placement (AP) Program and offers credit and placement for scores of 3 or above on AP tests. In each case, the score is reviewed by the registrar and/or department chairperson to determine credit and placement.

The School of Professional and Graduate Studies on each campus offers flexible schedules, summer programs, and online courses to meet the needs of working students. Courses may meet for a semester or for six- or twelve-week sessions.

Academic Facilities

The Brooklyn campus is composed of eight buildings, including historic landmark buildings. Students majoring in the widely recognized child-study program use the Dillon Child Study Center, which is a laboratory preschool enrolling approximately 100 hundred students and a teaching and observation resource right on campus. McEntegart Hall, a modern five-level structure, houses the library, audiovisual resource center, curriculum library, archives, and computer labs. Other academic facilities include top-notch biology, chemistry, computer, physics, and psychology research laboratories.

At the Long Island campus, students enjoy 28 acres of well-landscaped grounds and athletic fields. The main building houses administrative and faculty offices; laboratories for biology, chemistry, physics, and psychology; the computer center; art and music studios; the Local History Center; and the Office of Counseling. The library building houses a curriculum library, seminar rooms, administrative offices, and classrooms. This campus also features the John A. Danzi Recreation/Fitness Center, which includes a competition-sized swimming pool, fitness rooms, and a full-sized gym with an elevated track. The 33,000-square-foot Business and Technology Center allows St. Joseph's students to integrate technology into their studies. The Clare Rose Playhouse serves as a cultural center where students and local communities can explore theater production and performance.

A high-speed fiber-optic network connects all offices, institutional facilities, computer laboratories, and libraries on both the Brooklyn and Long Island campuses. Direct Internet access is available to all students and faculty and staff members through the College's server. The integrated online library system enables students to locate and check out books at either campus and provides links to online databases and other electronic information sources.

Costs

The 2009–10 annual full-time tuition rate for undergraduates was $17,000, or $555 per credit.

Financial Aid

St. Joseph's offers scholarships and grants-in-aid. Students who wish to apply for either form of assistance must file the Free Application for Federal Student Aid (FAFSA) and a state aid form. After a student has been accepted to the College and all financial aid forms are processed, the Financial Aid Office prepares aid packages that usually consist of federal, state, and College funds. St. Joseph's is fully approved for veterans. Campus work-study programs are also available.

Faculty

With nearly 500 faculty members who are widely respected scholars in their fields and a student-faculty ratio of 15:1, St. Joseph's students benefit from close professional and personal working relationships with their professors. Faculty members serve as academic advisers, are active on student affairs committees, and act as moderators in student organizations.

Admission Requirements

St. Joseph's College seeks a diverse student body and welcomes applications from high school students, transfer students, and those students who may have a nontraditional academic background. The College offers programs to serve all of these groups.

Students who wish to enter as freshmen are expected to have completed at least 18 units of college-preparatory work by the end of their senior year. This should include the following distribution: 4 years of English, 2 years of foreign language, 3 years of mathematics, 2 years of science, and 4 years of social studies. Applicants interested in accounting, allied health fields, biology, business administration, chemistry, or mathematics should have more extensive backgrounds in mathematics and science. In addition, the College requires the submission of official results from the critical reading and math sections of the SAT.

St. Joseph's College accepts a block transfer of credits from students holding an A.A. or A.S. degree in certain majors from an accredited junior or community college. All other transfers are considered on an individual basis.

Application and Information

Admission is offered on a rolling basis. Applications and supporting documents should be submitted online or to the appropriate school. The College reviews each application carefully and usually sends a decision one month after receiving all necessary credentials. For more information and an online application, students can access the Web site at http://www.sjcny.edu.

Brooklyn Campus:
Director of Admissions
St. Joseph's College
245 Clinton Avenue
Brooklyn, New York 11205
Phone: 718-940-5800

Long Island Campus:
Director of Admissions
St. Joseph's College
155 West Roe Boulevard
Patchogue, New York 11772
Phone: 631-687-4500
Web site: http://www.sjcny.edu

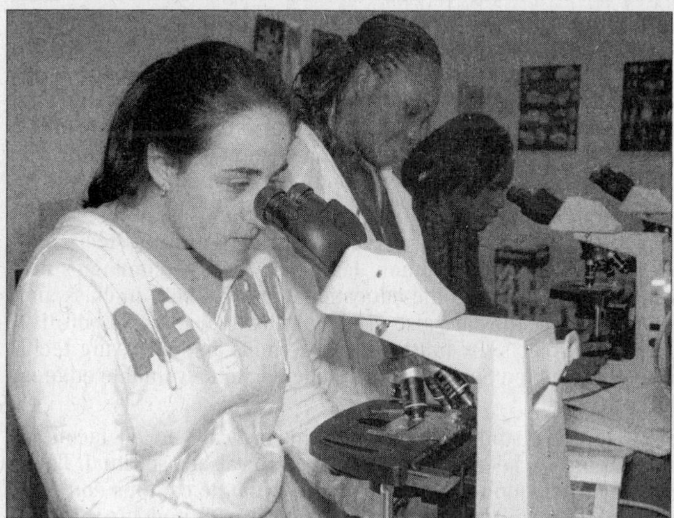

Both campuses of St. Joseph's College provide up-to-date science, computer, and psychology laboratories.

SAINT JOSEPH'S UNIVERSITY

PHILADELPHIA, PENNSYLVANIA

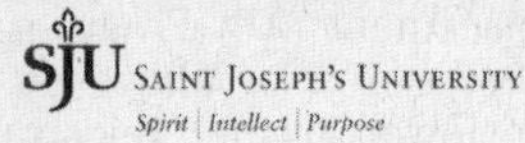

The University

Saint Joseph's University is a nationally recognized, Catholic, Jesuit university. For more than 150 years, Saint Joseph's has advanced the professional and personal ambitions of men and women by providing a rigorous Jesuit education—one that demands high achievement, expands knowledge, deepens understanding, stresses effective reasoning and communication, develops moral and spiritual character, and imparts enduring pride. One of only 142 schools with a Phi Beta Kappa chapter and business school accreditation by AACSB International–The Association to Advance Collegiate Schools of Business, Saint Joseph's is the home of 4,200 full-time undergraduates and 2,600 graduate, part-time, and doctoral students.

As a Jesuit university, Saint Joseph's believes each student realizes his or her fullest potential through challenging classroom study, hands-on learning opportunities, and a commitment to excellence in all endeavors. The University also reinforces the individual's lifelong engagement with the wider world. Graduates of Saint Joseph's attain success in their careers with the help of an extensive network of alumni who have become leading figures in business, law, medicine, education, the arts, technology, government, and public service.

A Saint Joseph's education encompasses all aspects of personal growth and development, reflecting the Ignatian credo of *cura personalis.* Guided by a faculty that is committed to both teaching and scholarship, students develop intellectually through an intense Jesuit liberal arts curriculum and advanced study in a chosen discipline. Students mature socially by participating in Saint Joseph's campus life, noted for its rich variety of activities, infectious enthusiasm, and mutual respect. Students grow ethically and spiritually by living their own values in the larger society beyond the campus.

Steeped in the Jesuit, Catholic tradition, Saint Joseph's provides a rigorous, intensive education that both disciplines and expands the mind. Students develop a lifelong desire to learn and grow while also acquiring the skills and knowledge necessary for success in their professional lives. At the core of this education is a general education requirement, which exposes students to primary fields of inquiry and the cultural values that shape their world. A Jesuit emphasis on engaged teaching and mentoring permeates the university. Faculty members at Saint Joseph's, many of whom are leading scholars in their disciplines, expect students to perform at the highest level and set demanding standards in the classroom.

Saint Joseph's is at the forefront of utilizing innovative technologies to enhance and promote learning. These technologies are widely integrated into the educational process both in class and beyond, where they are also used for individual and collaborative research projects. By mastering these tools and achieving technological fluency, Saint Joseph's students gain a valuable edge in their careers.

Saint Joseph's students engage enthusiastically in all facets of campus life—academic, social, athletic, ethical, and spiritual. Their active participation creates a vibrant, dynamic campus community, one that embraces a "not for spectators" attitude. In all their activities, students emphasize personal integrity as well as a respect and concern for others. This produces a mutually supportive, humane, and tolerant environment for individual success and service to others.

Location

Located on the edge of metropolitan Philadelphia, Saint Joseph's provides ready access to the vast career opportunities and cultural resources of America's sixth-largest city, while affording students a cohesive and intimate campus experience.

Because of its location, Saint Joseph's has close ties to the people, professional opportunities, and cultural life of Philadelphia. Students enjoy direct access to internships, cooperative programs, and positions in virtually all careers, most of which have a major presence in the Philadelphia area. Saint Joseph's location also offers ample outlets for community involvement and service, and students can easily take advantage of Philadelphia's professional sports, entertainment, and cultural events.

Majors and Degrees

Saint Joseph's offers full-time baccalaureate degree programs in more than forty major fields of study and numerous specialty programs, which are administered by two separate colleges.

The College of Arts and Sciences awards the Bachelor of Arts degree in art education, classics, economics, English, fine and performing arts, French, French studies, German, history, international relations, Italian, Latin, philosophy, political science, Spanish, and theology and the Bachelor of Science degree in actuarial science, biology, chemical biology, chemistry, computer science, criminal justice, education, environmental science, interdisciplinary health services, labor studies, mathematics, physics, psychology, public administration, and sociology.

The Erivan K. Haub School of Business awards the Bachelor of Science degree in accounting, decision and system sciences, finance, food marketing, information systems, international business, international marketing, management, marketing, and pharmaceutical marketing. A co-op program is available for all business majors.

Five-year B.S./M.S. programs are offered in education, international marketing, psychology, and writing studies. The University also offers special academic programs in aerospace studies (Air Force ROTC); Africana; allied health (bioscience technologies, nursing, occupational therapy, physical therapy (D.P.T.), and radiologic sciences); American, Asian, business ethics, European, faith-justice, gender, Latin American, medieval, Renaissance, and Russian and East Central European studies; writing studies; and teacher certification at the elementary and secondary levels. Preprofessional study is available in most major fields.

Academic Programs

At Saint Joseph's University, the aim of providing the student with the qualities of a liberally educated individual is pursued through a threefold plan encompassing 120 academic credits. The major concentration (30–45 credits) is intended to provide students with depth in a given field in order to prepare them for effective work in that field or graduate study. The general education requirement (60 credits) is intended to ensure that students have mastered basic skills necessary for further work, have been exposed to the main divisions of learning, and have been introduced to several new fields of study. Languages and literature, mathematics, natural sciences, history, social sciences, philosophy, and theology are among the areas of study included in the general education requirement. Free electives (15–30 credits) are intended to provide flexibility by encouraging students to pursue studies in areas they have found interesting, to test their interest in an unexplored area, or to deepen their knowledge in the major field.

A competitive honors program is available for qualified students, as are independent and interdisciplinary study options. Claver

House provides a place for honors students to have meetings, take classes, study, and conduct research.

Off-Campus Programs

Saint Joseph's offers to an increasing number of students the opportunity to study abroad and directly sponsors programs each year in Europe, Africa, Asia, Australia, Latin America, and the UK. International study tours have been made to Africa, Australia, Brazil, Canada, Greece, Ireland, Italy, Japan, Scotland, and Spain.

Students may take advantage of an arrangement with the Washington Center for Internships and Academic Seminars, which allows for a one-semester internship in the nation's capital.

Fieldwork experiences are required in several majors, and the University's location provides for internship opportunities to support virtually all other disciplines. The Career Development Center has a full-time internship coordinator and provides opportunities for on-campus interviews. The Alumni Mentor Alliance matches students with alumni in their fields of interest to gain real-world perspectives.

Academic Facilities

The facilities at Saint Joseph's are a blend of the old and the new. Barbelin/Lonergan Hall is a fine example of collegiate Gothic architecture. Its spired carillon tower rises above the campus and is easily the most recognizable landmark at Saint Joseph's. Mandeville Hall, a modern international academic center, opened in 1998. Home of the Erivan K. Haub School of Business, Mandeville offers distance learning technology and unique learning environments. The Francis A. Drexel Library and the Campbell Collection in Food Marketing house a collection of approximately 352,500 volumes, 1,450 print journals, 7,500 full-text electronic journals, 2,700 online books, and 848,000 microforms.

Costs

Tuition for the 2009–10 academic year was $33,940. Room and board were $11,800. These costs do not include student fees associated with specific majors or residence halls.

Financial Aid

The majority of Saint Joseph's students receive merit and/or federal financial assistance. In the 2008–09 academic year, approximately 85 percent of the University's student body received assistance in the form of academic and athletic scholarships, grants, loans, and work-study funds, either singly or in combination.

Students are automatically considered for merit scholarships upon application to the University. Students who wish to be considered for federal financial assistance should submit the Free Application for Federal Student Aid (FAFSA). Residents from states other than Pennsylvania should file the FAFSA and the proper state grant application from the Education Assistance Agency of their resident state. The preferred deadline is February 15.

Faculty

Saint Joseph's possesses an esteemed research faculty that is committed to undergraduate teaching. A student-faculty ratio of 15:1 and an average class size of 25 offer excellent opportunities for student–faculty member exchange, both inside and outside the classroom. Approximately 98 percent of the full-time faculty members hold a doctorate or terminal degree in their field.

Student Government

The Office of Student Leadership and Activities is dedicated to enhancing the educational development of students by providing opportunities for involvement in cocurricular programs and services. These include leadership programs, student clubs and organizations, Greek life, event programming and planning, and the University Student Senate. Through innovative programming that complements academic and personal development, the University nurtures the mind, body, and spirit of each individual student while enhancing the Jesuit mission of the University.

The University Student Senate, the governing board for the student body, is dedicated to addressing student issues through advocacy and policy recommendations. The Senate consists of an executive board that includes the president, executive vice president, speaker of the Senate, vice president for financial affairs, vice president for student life, four elected representatives from each class, and five appointed at-large members. The Senate has four standing committees: Academic Affairs, Student Budget Allocations, Campus Life, and Administrative Services. Elections for the Senate take place in December. Freshman representatives are elected in September.

The Student Union Board, known as SUB, is a student-run organization that encourages the development of student leadership, responsibility, and social competency by planning and participating in campus programs. These activities are designed to enhance the educational, recreational, cultural, and social aspects of the collegiate experience. All registered undergraduate students are welcome to take part in the activities and to be a part of the standing committees that are responsible for the programming.

Admission Requirements

Candidates for admission to the freshman class must submit evidence of academic achievement in a college-preparatory program, which should emphasize study in English, mathematics, foreign languages (classical or modern), science, history, and social studies. Successful candidates have traditionally completed a secondary school background that included the following: English, 4 units; foreign languages, 2 units; history and social studies, 3 units; mathematics, 3 units (4 units for students interested in the natural sciences or math); and science, 2 units. Applicants are required to submit scores on the SAT or the ACT.

Application and Information

A completed application form may be submitted with the $60 application fee at any time after the student's junior year. Students are accepted to the University and merit scholarships are awarded within the context of a deadline admissions policy with an early action date of November 15 and a regular decision deadline of February 1. Students should visit the admissions Web site at http://www.sju.edu/admissions for current admission information.

Office of Undergraduate Admissions
Saint Joseph's University
5600 City Avenue
Philadelphia, Pennsylvania 19131-1395
Phone: 610-660-1300
888-BE-A-HAWK (232-4295) (toll-free)
Fax: 610-660-1314
E-mail: admit@sju.edu
Web site: http://www.sju.edu/admissions/

Mandeville Hall, Saint Joseph's international academic center and home of the Haub School of Business.

ST. LAWRENCE UNIVERSITY

CANTON, NEW YORK

The University

St. Lawrence University invites students to learn new ways of seeing the world, voicing ideas, and connecting with others. Graduates have the tools with which to think clearly, express themselves persuasively, and step into the world community with an understanding of their responsibility to all people and to the planet.

Founded in 1856, St. Lawrence is the oldest continuously coeducational degree-granting institution of higher learning in New York State. Initially established as a theology school for the Universalist Church, it quickly evolved into the liberal arts college that it is today. St. Lawrence is a private, nonsectarian university of approximately 2,100 undergraduate men and women, with a small graduate program in education. St. Lawrence is known for its residential/academic First-Year Program, its international study opportunities and area studies programs, its students' strong interest in the environment and the outdoors, and its friendliness.

St. Lawrence students are self-starters. The self-designed major is popular, intramural sports leagues are always full, and more than 100 student organizations serve broad interests, from communication to community service and creativity to social action. The University routinely hosts well-known speakers, and concerts, plays, and films are regulars on the weekly events calendar. A 60,000-square-foot Student Center opened in winter 2004.

St. Lawrence students have historically placed high value on athletic activity, and a large number participate in varsity, intramural, or club sports. The thirty-two varsity men's and women's teams compete at the Division III level of the NCAA, with the exception of men's and women's ice hockey, which compete in Division I. Recreational facilities include cross-country ski and running trails, indoor and outdoor tennis courts, an athletic complex with a gymnasium, two field houses, a 133-station fitness center, a three-story climbing wall, a pool, an ice rink, an equestrian center, a boathouse, a golf course, a nine-lane all-weather track, an artificial-turf field for lacrosse and field hockey, ten squash courts, and newly renovated performance fields for soccer, football, baseball, and softball.

Residential life is an important aspect of the St. Lawrence experience. The University's innovative and highly regarded First-Year Program creates communities where groups of approximately 30–35 first-year students live and learn together. In the upperclass years, students can choose from traditional dormitories, Greek chapter houses, and suites and theme cottages that focus on student interests such as low-impact living and community service. Seniors may also choose town houses. St. Lawrence sponsors a full range of student services, from counseling to career planning.

Location

St. Lawrence is situated on a 1,000-acre campus on the edge of the village of Canton, New York (population 6,400), the seat of St. Lawrence County. Canton, with its Victorian homes, tree-lined streets, village green, and small shops, is typical of college towns throughout the Northeast. Students and residents often mix in stores, at athletic events, and in community projects. Ottawa, Canada's capital, is 75 minutes to the north, while Lake Placid, one of America's hiking and skiing meccas, is 90 minutes to the southeast.

Majors and Degrees

St. Lawrence offers the Bachelor of Arts and Bachelor of Science degrees; students can choose from thirty-six majors and have the option of picking one of thirty-seven minors. Combined five-year programs with other institutions are in place in engineering and management, and specialized advising is offered in preparation for postgraduate work in dentistry, law, medicine, and veterinary medicine.

Academic Programs

St. Lawrence's foremost mission is to provide its students with a liberal arts education. Students complete requirements in six areas and concentrated work in a major field as well as demonstrating competence in writing. Close faculty-student interaction is a hallmark of a St. Lawrence education. Every semester, many students engage in independent or honors projects, often working with professors on joint research projects that lead to publication in leading scholarly journals. A senior project is required in most majors.

Off-Campus Programs

Nearly 50 percent of St. Lawrence students study in one of the University's international programs during their collegiate careers. St. Lawrence operates programs in Australia, Austria, Canada, China, Costa Rica, Denmark, England, France, India, Italy, Japan, Kenya, Spain, Thailand, and Trinidad and Tobago. In addition, the University's membership in the International Student Exchange Program permits students to directly enroll in universities in more than thirty-five additional countries. St. Lawrence also operates programs at two other campuses in the U.S.: Fisk University in Nashville, Tennessee, and American University in Washington, D.C. St. Lawrence also administers its own Adirondack Semester Program.

Academic Facilities

Owen D. Young Library and Launders Science Library contain more than half a million volumes as well as electronic resources and ample space for reading and research. Griffiths Arts Center is the home of the University's fine arts and performance and communication studies programs as well as two theaters and an art gallery in which selections from St. Lawrence's 7,000-piece collection are frequently shown. Facilities for the arts have undergone expansion into the building that was formerly the student center, and the Newell Center for Arts Technology opened in spring 2007. A unified science complex houses the Departments of Biology, Chemistry, Physics, Psychology, Geology, and Mathematics, Computer Science and Statistics and is connected via a covered hallway to the science library and computing center. The new 120,000-square-foot Johnson Hall of Science, the first gold LEED science building in New York State, opened in fall 2007. Richardson Hall, St. Lawrence's oldest building and on the National Register of Historic Places, is home to the English and religious studies departments. Other departments can be found in academic buildings clustered on one part of the campus, so classrooms are not a long walk apart.

Costs

The comprehensive fee for 2009–10 is $49,925, including tuition, fees, and average room and board. Students should allow approximately $1450 for books and personal expenses.

Financial Aid

St. Lawrence awards both merit scholarships and need-based financial aid. More than 80 percent of the University's students receive some form of financial assistance, including scholarships, grants, student loans, and campus jobs. St. Lawrence is committed to assisting as many students as possible and recognizes academic and personal achievement in making financial aid decisions. To apply for need-based financial aid, students must file the Free Application for Federal Student Aid (FAFSA) and the CSS Profile form between January 1 and February 1 and request that the results be sent directly to St. Lawrence.

Faculty

The 190 members of St. Lawrence's faculty are teachers and scholars. While teaching and advising are their primary responsibilities, they are also active researchers, artists, performers, and regular contributors in their academic disciplines. Faculty members teach all courses at St. Lawrence; no undergraduate courses are taught by graduate students. Active teaching assistants and tutoring programs, involving qualified upperclass students, are closely supervised by faculty members. The student-faculty ratio is about 11:1. Faculty members hold regular office hours, serve as academic advisers to students, and frequently take part in extracurricular activities on campus.

Student Government

The Thelomathesian Society, comprising all students on campus, is governed by a senate of elected representatives. The senate distributes funds in support of student activities and provides 2 student delegates to the University's Board of Trustees.

Admission Requirements

St. Lawrence seeks students who can be successful in a demanding academic program and who can contribute to the quality of life of the community. The University is committed to enrolling students who represent the widest possible diversity of economic, social, ethnic, and geographic backgrounds. Academic preparation and ability are the most important criteria, but demonstrated ability in the creative arts, athletics, or social service is also a measure of a student's potential to benefit St. Lawrence. Candidates may choose whether or not they submit standardized test scores (SAT or ACT). A campus visit is strongly encouraged, and interviews may be scheduled on campus or off campus in certain areas.

Although there is no set distribution of required high school courses, successful applicants typically show strong preparation in the humanities, the social sciences, mathematics, and the natural sciences. Honors, Advanced Placement, and International Baccalaureate courses are opportunities for applicants to demonstrate intellectual maturity and curiosity, qualities highly valued in the admission process.

Application and Information

St. Lawrence uses the Common Application, with the St. Lawrence Supplement, as its sole application form. The application is available on the University's Web site. The application processing fee is $60. Regular decision applications should be submitted by February 1, with notification by late March. Students who decide that St. Lawrence is their first choice may apply under one of the early decision deadlines, November 15 or January 15. In each case, notification is one month after the deadline. Transfer candidates should submit applications no later than November 1 for the spring semester or March 1 for the fall semester.

To request an application or for more information, students should contact:

Office of Admissions and Financial Aid
St. Lawrence University
Canton, New York 13617
Phone: 315-229-5261
800-285-1856 (toll-free)
E-mail: admissions@stlawu.edu
Web site: http://www.stlawu.edu

The St. Lawrence University Student Center.

SAINT LEO UNIVERSITY

SAINT LEO, FLORIDA

The University

Founded in 1889, Saint Leo University is now recognized as one of the nation's leading Catholic teaching universities and a school of international consequence. The main campus in Saint Leo, Florida, is home to the vibrant University College, serving the education needs of nearly 1,750 traditional-age undergraduate students. The University also offers a variety of dynamic graduate programs, a weekend and evening program for working adults, and both undergraduate and graduate degree programs through seventeen education centers in seven states and through the Center for Online Learning, which houses the University's cutting-edge online degree programs.

The University College student body represents forty states and territories, as well as forty-two countries. International students make up 11 percent of the student population. Minority students represent 30 percent of the University College enrollment. Approximately 71 percent of traditional full-time students live in one of thirteen residence halls.

Students can participate in the nationally recognized honors program and the more than fifty different clubs and organizations on campus, including national fraternities and sororities. The Student Government Union and various campus organizations also sponsor movies, concerts, art exhibits, lectures, dances, and other special events throughout the academic year.

Saint Leo is a member of the Sunshine State Conference and competes in NCAA Division II intercollegiate athletics for men and women. Men's sports include baseball, basketball, cross-country, golf, lacrosse, soccer, swimming, and tennis. Women compete in basketball, cross-country, golf, soccer, softball, swimming, tennis, and volleyball. Cheerleading is offered as a club sport. Students can also participate in a wide variety of intramurals. Campus recreational facilities include lighted racquetball and tennis courts; soccer, baseball, and softball fields; a weight room/fitness center; and a heated outdoor Olympic-size swimming pool. The campus is bordered by a 154-acre lake and an eighteen-hole golf course.

Saint Leo is committed to giving its students an education that prepares them for the future. The goal of the University is to develop the whole person, both academically and personally, by providing a values-based education in the Benedictine tradition. In a recent satisfaction survey, 95 percent of respondents said they would recommend Saint Leo to a friend.

Saint Leo University is accredited by the Commission on Colleges of the Southern Association of Colleges and Schools to award the associate, bachelor's, and master's degrees. Saint Leo University's degree program in social work is accredited by the Commission on Accreditation of the Council on Social Work Education (B.S.W. level). The School of Business is accredited by the International Assembly for Collegiate Business Education (IACBE).The University's undergraduate sport business program is nationally approved by the Sport Management Program Review Council (SMPRC). Saint Leo University also has Teacher Education Programs approval by the State of Florida Department of Education.

In addition to associate and bachelor's degrees, Saint Leo University offers a Master of Business Administration (M.B.A.) degree, a Master of Education (M.Ed.) degree, a Master of Science (M.S.) degree in criminal justice, critical incident management, and instructional design, a Master of Arts (M.A.) degree in theology, a Master of Social Work (M.S.W.), and an education specialist degree.

Location

Saint Leo is located 35 minutes north of Tampa and 90 minutes west of Orlando. The lakeside campus occupies 186 acres of rolling hills and wooded grounds. The rural setting is conducive to academic success, but the University is located near enough to metropolitan areas to give the students the advantage of a wide variety of social and professional opportunities.

Majors and Degrees

Saint Leo University offers over forty traditional majors, preprofessional studies, specializations, endorsements, and programs. Degrees offered are the Bachelor of Arts, Bachelor of Science, and Bachelor of Social Work.

The School of Business offers degrees in accounting, business administration (specialization in international business), communication management, computer information systems, international hospitality and tourism management, management, marketing, and sport business. The School of Arts and Sciences offers majors in biology, English, environmental science, history, international studies, mathematics, medical technology, political science, psychology, religion, and sociology. The School of Education and Social Services offers majors in criminal justice, elementary education, middle grades education, human services administration, and social work.

Preprofessional studies programs in chiropractic, dentistry, law, medicine, and veterinary science are also offered, including 4+4 medical school and 3+4 dental and chiropractic school programs.

Academic Programs

Saint Leo's LINK (Learning Interdisciplinary Knowledge) general education program ensures that all graduates have a solid grounding in theories, issues, and knowledge to prepare them for successful careers and graduate work. The program develops the skills that are the foundation of a liberal arts education and that today's employers demand. Students learn to communicate effectively; function at a high level, both alone and as a part of a team; develop a general knowledge base in many different areas; and analyze and solve problems effectively.

Students complete foundation courses of core requirements (writing, computer literacy, math, and wellness), Perspectives courses (liberal arts, fine arts, humanities, and physical, social, and behavioral sciences), and a senior capstone course that connects all prior course work in the major and leads to research and independent projects demonstrating mastery of the field.

Saint Leo has an academic skills program to assist first-year students in their adjustment to university life. Included in this program are freshman studies, tutoring, and advising. All first-year students at Saint Leo are assigned faculty advisers, who act as mentors from the first day that the student arrives on campus through the time when the student selects a major.

Students who demonstrate course mastery for any course listed in the catalog have the opportunity to receive up to 40 hours of credit through examination. Detailed information about credit by examination is available through the Registrar's Office.

Most students at Saint Leo earn the credits needed for their bachelor's degree through a four-year program of study. All major programs require a 2.0 minimum grade point average for graduation.

Off-Campus Programs

Saint Leo University is committed to helping students expand their horizons through study-abroad programs. Saint Leo University students have the opportunity to spend a semester studying in London, Madrid, Paris, Rome, Singapore, Australia, Ecuador, Germany, Greece, Ireland, Scotland, and various cities within the United Kingdom. Articulation agreements also afford study opportunities throughout Asia and the Pacific Rim. The University continues to add new programs and partnerships in order to provide students with a wide variety of educational and cultural experiences.

Students are also able to work with their professors and academic advisers to identify and pursue a wide variety of internship options, further enhancing the real-world experience component of their education.

Academic Facilities

The Cannon Memorial Library contains 169,623 volumes, and provides access to 66,519 e-books, 56,502 current periodical subscriptions (including 581 print and 55,758 e-journals), and 63 online databases. Also located in the library are the Hugh Culverhouse Computer Instruction Center classrooms, a student computer lab, and two VTT-equipped instruction/conference rooms.

Campus laboratories have all been renovated and feature state-of-the-art equipment. Lab facilities include three teaching labs and one research lab for biology; two teaching labs, one research lab, and an instrumentation room for chemistry; and one physics lab. The bulk of general classroom space is contained in Crawford Hall and Lewis Hall. Plans are underway for the construction of a new state-of-the-art classroom building to house the School of Business. Additional classrooms are located in Saint Edward and Saint Francis Halls as well as in the Bowman Activity Center.

All students are encouraged to utilize the University's Learning Resource Center (LRC). The LRC features study and meeting space for small groups as well as such technology as high-speed laser printers. Tutoring services are available to students and may be scheduled through the LRC.

The University's exciting new Student Community Center opened in late fall 2007; it includes substantial meeting space for groups of various sizes.

The University's campus is a mostly wireless environment. All students who reside in campus housing receive a state-of-the-art laptop computer. For students living off campus, laptops are available for use through the library.

Costs

For the 2010–11 school year, tuition is $17,500; freshman room and board costs are $8848, and mandatory fees are $650. Miscellaneous indirect costs for the year (such as books, personal living expenses, insurance, and travel) are estimated at $4242.

Financial Aid

Financial aid, both federally funded and awarded by the University, is available in the form of scholarships, grants, and loans. Financial aid is allocated on the basis of academic performance and need, as determined by the federal government from the financial information provided on the Free Application for Federal Student Aid (FAFSA). On-campus jobs are available for students, with priority given to students with demonstrated financial need. Ninety-two percent of students receive some form of financial aid.

Faculty

At Saint Leo University, outstanding teaching and active learning go hand in hand. Caring and capable faculty members provide students with knowledge, guidance, academic support, and a broad range of learning opportunities both in and outside the classroom. Students enjoy small classes (average class size is 18) and develop close relationships with experienced, well-qualified professors. At Saint Leo, 87 percent of full-time instructional faculty members hold the terminal degree in their field.

Student Government

A significant contribution to the University comes from the activities initiated by the Student Government Union (SGU). The SGU is an annually elected body organized and conducted in accordance with democratic procedures. This organization strives to foster leadership and loyalty among the students, to formulate recommendations for student life, and to recognize all extracurricular activities.

Admission Requirements

All candidates for admission should be, or expect to be, graduates of secondary schools accredited by a regional or state accrediting agency. Applicants should show successful progress toward graduation with a minimum of 16 academic units of course work: 4 units of English, 3 units of mathematics (algebra I and II and geometry), 3 units of social studies, 2 units of science, and 4 units of electives, preferably to include 2 units of a foreign language. All domestic applicants are required to take the SAT or the ACT examination. A letter of recommendation from the student's guidance counselor is also required. Preferred candidates are students with a GPA of B or better and an average SAT combined score (critical reading and math) of 1030 or an average ACT score of 22. The records of students who do not meet these criteria are also reviewed by the Admission Committee and considered for the Learning Enhancement for Academic Progress (LEAP) program, a preparatory program that has a summer attendance component.

Once the applicant has submitted the application with the $35 application fee (fee is waived if application is submitted online), high school transcripts, test scores, and letter of recommendation, the file is reviewed and a decision is rendered. Notification is on a rolling basis and generally takes two weeks. The priority application deadline is March 1, but all applicants are encouraged to apply early.

Transfer and international students are also encouraged to apply. The same general admission procedures are required, along with at least a C average for all college work (for transfer students) and a score of at least 550 (paper-based test), 213 (computer-based test), or 75 (Internet-based test) on the TOEFL (for international students for whom English is not the primary language of instruction).

Campus visits and interviews are recommended but not required. The Office of Admission is open from Monday through Friday from 8 a.m. to 5 p.m. and on select Saturdays during the academic year from 9:00 a.m. to noon. Appointments are preferred. Campus tours are available Monday through Friday at 10 a.m., 11 a.m., 2 p.m., and 3 p.m., as well as at 10 a.m. on select Saturdays during the academic year. Summer tours are available Monday through Friday at 10 a.m. and 2 p.m. only. The Office of Admission is closed on Sunday.

Application and Information

Additional information and application forms can be obtained by contacting the Office of Admission.

Gary Bracken
Vice President for Enrollment
Office of Admission—MC2008
Saint Leo University
P.O. Box 6665
Saint Leo, Florida 33574-6665
Phone: 352-588-8283
800-334-5532 (toll-free)
Fax: 352-588-8257
E-mail: admission@saintleo.edu
Web site: http://www.saintleo.edu

The Saint Leo University campus.

ST. LOUIS COLLEGE OF PHARMACY

ST. LOUIS, MISSOURI

The College

Founded in 1864, St. Louis College of Pharmacy is one of the oldest and largest colleges of pharmacy in the nation and one of the very few that are not part of a larger university. Members of the first board of trustees included pharmacists, physicians, and business leaders, such as Henry Shaw, founder of Missouri Botanical Garden, and John O'Fallon, nephew of explorer William Clark. St. Louis College of Pharmacy consistently graduates one of the top 20 largest classes of pharmacists in the nation. The College admits students directly from high school and integrates the liberal arts and sciences with a six-year professional curriculum leading to a Doctor of Pharmacy (Pharm.D.) degree.

The 1,176 students at the College are among the best prepared in Missouri. The average ACT score of a recent freshman class, at 28, was the second highest in the state. The average class rank for incoming freshmen was in the top 15 percent, and the average high school grade point average was 3.88. Total enrollment for the 2007–08 academic year was 684 women and 492 men. Graduates have an enormous impact on the pharmacy profession and health of people nationwide. Nearly 3 out of 4 practicing pharmacists in the St. Louis region are graduates of St. Louis College of Pharmacy, providing current students with local mentors.

In addition to a well-rounded pharmaceutical curriculum, the College offers a full student-life experience with on-campus housing and more than forty clubs, athletic teams, fraternities, service and religious groups, a theater, a chorale group, and social organizations. An eight-story residence hall features suite- and efficiency-style units and is connected to a spacious dining facility that serves both fast food and plate meals. Upper-level students may elect to live on campus in Rabe Hall, a fifty-seven-unit apartment building featuring studios and one- and two-bedroom units.

St. Louis College of Pharmacy offers an athletic program for both intercollegiate and intramural sports. The College is a member of NAIA Division II in five competitive sports: men's and women's cross-country, men's and women's basketball, and women's volleyball.

Location

Only a few miles from the Gateway Arch, St. Louis College of Pharmacy is located in the city's Central West End, surrounded by the nationally recognized medical community of Barnes-Jewish Hospital, Washington University School of Medicine, Siteman Cancer Center, and St. Louis Children's Hospital. The campus is one block from Forest Park, with its 1,300 acres of green space, tennis courts, ice-skating rink, golf course, and world-class museums, zoo, outdoor opera theater, and science center. Students at the College are near the cultural and entertainment scene of St. Louis on a safe, 5-acre campus within walking distance of public transportation.

Majors and Degrees

The College offers a six-year professional program leading to a Doctor of Pharmacy (Pharm.D.) degree.

Academic Programs

The Doctor of Pharmacy program includes intensive courses in biology, chemistry, mathematics, and physics, as well as electives in literature, humanities, and social and behavioral sciences. Introductory practice experiences throughout the curriculum give students the opportunity to apply their education and enable students to develop knowledge, communication skills, and professional values through interaction with other health-care practitioners and patients. The six-year Pharm.D. program is comprised of specialized didactic courses and includes a calendar year of clinical rotations.

Off-Campus Programs

The College offers advanced-practice experiences in fourteen states at more than 400 community, government, and hospital settings, including the U.S. Food and Drug Administration, Barnes-Jewish Hospital, Lindenwood Drug, Pfizer, Walgreens, St. Luke's Hospital, Copper Bend Pharmacy, Bristol-Myers Squibb, North Texas Medical Center, and Tampa General Hospital.

Academic Facilities

The O. J. Cloughly Alumni Library, located in Jones Hall, is an integral part of the Pharm.D. program at the College and houses a number of volumes covering the fields of pharmacy, allied sciences, and the liberal arts. The library also archives a variety of leading pharmaceutical and scientific periodicals, journals, bulletins, and reports. Jones Hall contains the majority of College classrooms, lecture halls, laboratories, and faculty/administrative offices. Whelpley Hall features a 300-seat auditorium in addition to small- and medium-size classrooms.

Costs

For 2007–08, tuition and fees for students in years one and two were $19,710, years three through five were $21,470, and year six was $21,730. A notebook computer (issued to all new students) and lab fees are included in tuition costs. Room and board costs were $7650 for the academic year. Additional costs, including books, vary each year but average $500 per semester.

Financial Aid

Financial aid is awarded based on merit, need, and availability of funds. The College participates in all applicable federal and state financial aid programs. Scholarships, grants, loans, and student employment are offered to help qualified students pay for college expenses. Financial aid may be funded by the federal or state government, the College, benefactors and friends of the College, or other sponsoring organizations or agencies. Merit-based scholarships are offered to qualified students regardless of need.

Students planning to attend the College in the fall semester should submit the Free Application for Federal Student Aid (FAFSA) along with signed copies of student and parent federal tax returns as early as possible during the previous spring semester. The College begins awarding financial aid in February and continues until all funds are exhausted. Further information on student financial aid may be obtained from the College's Financial Aid Office.

Faculty

The College's student-faculty ratio of 18:1 overall and 14:1 in the professional years ensures that learning is interactive and student focused. No classes are taught by graduate students. Of the 73 full-time faculty members, 92 percent hold a Ph.D. or the highest degree in their field. More than 200 pharmacists serve as adjunct instructors in the advanced-practice experiences program.

Admission Requirements

All students applying for admission to St. Louis College of Pharmacy must present evidence of the satisfactory completion of a four-year course of study in, and graduation from, a high school approved by a recognized accrediting body. A high school transcript, including class standing, should be sent by the high school directly to the Director of Admissions. The high school course of study should include 4 units of English; 4 units of math, including algebra 1 and 2 and geometry; and at least 3 units of science, including biology/lab and chemistry lab. The College also requires that the SAT or ACT examination be completed.

Advanced credit may be earned through Advanced Placement examinations. Further details are available from the Office of Admissions.

Students transferring into St. Louis College of Pharmacy must submit transcripts of their college records and are required to have taken the PCAT. Transfer students must apply for admission through the Pharmacy College Application Service (PharmCAS) at http://www.pharmcas.org. Applications and admission materials sent to St. Louis College of Pharmacy will not be accepted—all materials for admission must be submitted directly to PharmCAS. For more information, students should visit the PharmCAS Web site.

Application and Information

Application deadlines can be found at http://www.stlcop.edu. The College offers an early decision selection process as well as a regular decision process for prospective students.

The application deadline for transfer students is March 1. However, the PharmCAS deadline for submission of all admission materials is February 1. Very few transfer students are accepted into the College, and as a result, admission is extremely competitive. Transfer students are only accepted into the third year of the six-year program.

For additional information or to apply, students should contact:

Registrar/Director of Admissions
St. Louis College of Pharmacy
4588 Parkview Place
St. Louis, Missouri 63110
Phone: 314-367-8700 Ext. 8313
800-278-5267 (toll-free)
E-mail: pbryant@stlcop.edu
Web site: http://www.stlcop.edu

SAINT LOUIS UNIVERSITY–MADRID CAMPUS

MADRID, SPAIN

Saint Louis University
Madrid Campus

The University

Saint Louis University is a Jesuit, Catholic university ranked among the top research institutions in the United States. The University fosters the intellectual and character development of more than 13,000 students, over 650 of whom pursue their studies in Madrid, Spain. Through teaching, research, health care and community service, Saint Louis University has provided one-of-a-kind education, leadership and service for 190 years.

Founded in 1818, Saint Louis University is the oldest university west of the Mississippi River and the second oldest Jesuit university in the United States. Its campus in Madrid (SLU–Madrid), originally established in the 1960s as a study-abroad destination, is the first free-standing campus in Europe operated by a U.S.-based university and is recognized by Spain's higher education authority as an official foreign university, the first U.S. institution to hold this endorsement. Today, students from more than sixty-five countries earn either U.S. four-year undergraduate degrees, graduate degrees or, in the case of study-abroad students, credits towards their degrees from their home campuses.

About 25 percent of the University's students come from Spain, 40 percent from the United States (all fifty states), and 35 percent from over sixty-five countries around the world.

Academic and social orientation is held at the beginning of the fall and spring semesters for all students. The University offers several day trips at the beginning of each term in order to give new students the opportunity to make friends and settle into life in Spain before the start of classes. The Office of Student Life arranges many opportunities for students to participate in cocurricular activities. Students can participate in up to nineteen different sports at varying levels as well as join local gyms or take a scuba diving course. Basketball, football, volleyball, lacrosse, soccer, Ultimate (Frisbee), squash, American football, and field hockey are just some of the sports that students may participate in while at SLU–Madrid.

The Office of Student Life charters all student-led organizations and welcomes students to start clubs that align with the University mission. The Student Government Association represents the student body at SLU–Madrid. *La Voz*, the student-led newspaper, and the Campus Ambassador group are two popular activities on campus. Campus Ambassadors, a select group of student leaders who are committed to upholding the mission of Saint Louis University, collaborate within the Madrid and St. Louis Campuses to help organize important events.

Campus Ministry offers many volunteer opportunities which include helping in a soup kitchen, Christian Life Community groups, day retreats, and a retreat to Loyola in the Basque country in order to learn more about the founder of the Jesuits, Saint Ignatius of Loyola. SLU–Madrid students also collaborate with La Universidad de Comillas in a program to feed the homeless.

Each semester SLU–Madrid presents a dance performance as well as a theater production in English.

While SLU–Madrid does not have a housing requirement, it is happy to facilitate the placement of students in University-sponsored housing, as well as provide valuable information for those seeking housing elsewhere. As a further service to its students, the Office of Student Life provides guidance and selective referrals to students who are seeking housing outside of the University system. SLU–Madrid strongly encourages those seeking housing to take advantage of the host family option through which students who wish to experience Spanish society to the fullest can be part of a Spanish household. One of the most rewarding and culturally integrating experiences a student can have is to be part of a Spanish household, offering the opportunity to learn and experience day-to-day life in urban Madrid.

Location

Spain's capital, Madrid, with a population of more than 4 million, is politically, culturally, and geographically the heart of Spain. From the Prado Museum to the Royal Palace, the city's spectacular cultural offerings are surpassed only by its vibrant nightlife. SLU–Madrid is located in the city, amidst many Spanish public and private universities with easy access to the historic city center.

Majors and Degrees

Saint Louis University degree programs in Madrid include the B.A. in communication, B.A. in economics, B.A. in English (one-semester requirement in St. Louis), B.S. in business administration with a concentration in international business, B.A. in political science with a concentration in international relations (one summer-session requirement at SLU–Madrid), and B.A. in Spanish. SLU–Madrid also offers the first two years of more than eighty-five undergraduate degree programs, including engineering, nursing and health science, humanities, social sciences, and business, all of which are fully integrated with programs at the St. Louis Campus.

All degree programs are accredited by the Higher Learning Commission of the North Central Association of Colleges and Schools. Individual schools and programs on the St. Louis Campus also maintain separate accreditations (e.g., business, engineering, nursing) with their respective professional organizations.

Academic Programs

SLU–Madrid follows the U.S. academic calendar, consisting of two semesters; the campus also holds intensive summer sessions. Undergraduate programs are completed in four years.

In keeping with the Jesuit tradition of promoting the development of the whole person, undergraduate students complete, in addition to their major field of study, a set of courses that provides a framework for acquiring a broad foundation of knowledge in the humanities, natural sciences, and social sciences called the Liberal Arts Core Curriculum. The core fosters intellectual inquiry, ethical decision making, and effective communication across the disciplines.

Degree requirements for the B.A. programs in communication, economics, English, political science, and Spanish, offered in conjunction with the College of Arts and Sciences, consist of completing the core (48–63 hours), completing the major requirements as listed in the undergraduate catalog (30–36 hours), and completing a second major (30–36 hours), a certificate (18–30 hours), or minor (15–21 hours).

Degree requirements for the B.S. in business administration/international business, offered through Saint Louis University's John Cook School of Business, consist of four groups of classes: arts and sciences core requirements (48 hours), business common body of knowledge (CBK) requirements (42 hours), courses specific to the international business concentration (15 hours), and elective courses. Electives are not limited to business courses and may be chosen from any area of study within the University, thus giving the student the opportunity to diversify his/her background. A minimum of 120 hours is required for the degree. In addition, a minimum of 48 credits of arts and sciences courses must be taken.

The master's degree in English (30 hours) is a dual-degree program offered year-round with the Universidad Autónoma de Madrid and requires one 6-week summer session on the St. Louis Campus. The master's degree in Spanish (30 hours), offered on both a year-round and summer-only basis, can be completed in its entirety at SLU–Madrid.

SLU–Madrid offers minors and certificates in art history, business administration, communication, computer science, economics, English, history, philosophy, political science, psychology, Spanish, and Ibero-American Studies; students who start their studies in Madrid and then transfer to St. Louis have additional minors and certificate programs from which to choose. Unique to SLU–Madrid, the Ibero-American certificate program offers students an interdisciplinary approach to the history, politics, and culture of Spain, Portugal, and Latin America, drawing from the arts, history, culture, economics, and politics.

SLU–Madrid places a strong emphasis on language acquisition and fluency. Arabic, Chinese, Classical Greek, French, German, Latin, and Portuguese are offered in addition to the obvious offerings in English and Spanish. Furthermore, while the language of instruction is English, a number of courses across disciplines in are taught in Spanish—an exceptional opportunity to develop fluency.

Off-Campus Programs

SLU–Madrid offers a wealth of opportunities for students to enhance their classroom experiences through volunteer service or internships, academic trips or day-excursions and seminars, among others.

Recognizing travel as an integral part of the academic program, the University organizes trips each semester as experiential components of course work. These experiences not only provide the connections necessary to enhance learning, but are also a unique opportunity to learn and explore course content in a dynamic and hands-on manner. Travel opportunities span several continents and are integrated into a wide range of disciplines: sciences, economics, politics, history, languages, art, theology, etc. In addition, in coordination with the Association of American International Colleges and Universities, students can pursue study-abroad opportunities at partner schools in Europe, Africa, and the Middle East.

The Office of Career Services provides a full range of resources to assist students in career exploration and job placement. Some of the services provided include resume and cover letter writing workshops, career decision-making programs, and an extensive job bank. In addition, students are encouraged to pursue internships in the offices of multinational corporations. SLU–Madrid works with over 100 companies in Madrid including the Banco Santander, France Telecom, and BMW, as well as the American embassy,

The Saint Louis University Alumni Association actively collaborates with the Office of Career Services to provide internship and job opportunities for past and present students. University alumni living in Spain, the United States, and abroad, share in an international network of professionals who have reached high levels in their fields. Alumni benefit from sharing in a community that provides social and professional networking opportunities, and a lifelong affiliation to Saint Louis University, along with many additional University benefits.

Academic Facilities

The Madrid Campus comprises five buildings: Padre Rubio Hall, Padre Arrupe Hall, Loyola Hall, Manresa Hall, and the Manresa Annex. Padre Arrupe Hall, a restored eighteenth-century chalet, contains administrative offices and faculty member offices; three classrooms; two computer labs; and the biology, chemistry, and physics labs. Padre Rubio Hall, also dating to the eighteenth century, houses the Offices of Student Life, the Campus Ministry, Career Development offices, various faculty offices, a computer lab, the bookstore, and the copy center. The University library and cafeteria are located in Loyola Hall. Manresa Hall is the location of the Counseling Services Department, the Rector's Office, the Registrar, and various faculty member offices. Manresa Annex houses the art studio.

Costs

Tuition and fees are competitive—about 33 to 50 percent lower than at comparable universities in North America. Tuition and fees for permanent students at the SLU–Madrid campus for 2010–11 are €7830 per semester. Room and board costs range from €2300 to €4040 per semester, depending on accommodations. Books and supplies cost approximately €500 per semester. Students should budget €500 per month for travel and activities. Costs are subject to change.

Financial Aid

Getting a college degree is an investment; it requires effort and perseverance, as well as financial planning. In addition to the services and offerings provided to assist students in their academic and personal journey to graduation, SLU–Madrid offers an array of scholarship and financial-aid opportunities. Significant scholarship, grant, loan, and work opportunities are available to qualified students.

All new degree-seeking and transfer students are automatically considered for SLU–Madrid merit-based scholarships ranging from €2000 to €8000 per year. All admitted students are eligible to apply for a work-grant position and families with more than one dependent child enrolled may apply for the Family Award. Other scholarship awards include the Madrid Campus Jesuit High School scholarship for permanent students as well as the Robert Tieken and Cristina Acosta and Amy King scholarships for visiting students. U.S. students also have access to all federal, state, and privately funded student-aid programs by submitting the Free Application for Federal Student Aid (FAFSA).

Faculty

SLU–Madrid faculty consists of recognized academics and practitioners in their fields of study and represents a wide range of backgrounds, adding to the cultural richness of the University's international campus. Over 110 full- and part-time faculty members deliver the courses in the four-year programs, certificates, and minors, with a dynamic team of research scholars and professionals teaching courses that complement both these programs and the study-abroad experience. SLU–Madrid's student to faculty ratio is 7:1 and the average class size is 15 students.

Admission Requirements

The programs of SLU–Madrid are open to all without regard to race, color, sex, age, national origin, religion, sexual orientation, disability, or veteran status. All University policies, practices, and procedures are administrated in a manner consistent with its Catholic, Jesuit identity. Students who have demonstrated past academic achievement and who show promise and aptitude for successful performance in an international-university environment are encouraged to apply for admission. SLU–Madrid welcomes students from diverse school systems around the world.

A student's potential for success in college studies at SLU–Madrid is judged by the student's high school grades, aptitude test scores, personal statement, and letters of recommendation.

Transfer students in good academic standing are invited to apply. Students who transfer to SLU–Madrid are typically interested in majoring in Spanish, communication, political science/international relations, economics, and business administration/international business. Transfer students from other disciplines are welcome to apply, but will ultimately have to transfer to the St. Louis campus (or another American university) to finish their degree program.

Students from universities and colleges are invited to spend a semester, summer, or year on the Madrid campus. SLU–Madrid specializes in semester programs for students from academic disciplines such as engineering and premedicine, who traditionally have a difficult time enrolling in a study-abroad program.

Admissions decisions are made on a rolling basis.

Application and Information

To be considered for admission, a student should complete the online application found on the University's Web site. The application deadlines for the fall 2011 semester are May 31, 2011 (non-European Union students) and August 1, 2011 (Spanish and European Union students); however, applicants are encouraged to apply early.

Office of Admissions
Saint Louis University–Madrid Campus
Avenida del Valle, 34
28003 Madrid
Spain
Phone: 34-91-554-58-58
E-mail: admissions@madrid.slu.edu
Internet: http://spain.slu.edu

Saint Louis University–Madrid Campus students visit the home of St. Francis Xavier on a trip organized by Campus Ministry.

SAINT MARY'S COLLEGE

NOTRE DAME, INDIANA

The College

She's a staff nurse in a Chicago neurology intensive care unit or a Peace Corps volunteer in Uganda. She's studied abroad in Rome or been a student teacher at Marquette School in South Bend. She's received a first place award in the North Central Sociological Association's National Student Competition or danced the entire night to help raise over $90,000 to benefit Riley's Children's Hospital. She's a woman using her talents to make a difference in our world—she's a Saint Mary's woman.

A Saint Mary's education will challenge students to reach beyond the ordinary and reach for new academic heights. Every area of study emphasizes the exceptional writing and critical thinking skills needed to become a confident leader, well-prepared for an ever-changing world. St. Mary's offers professional programs such as accounting, education, nursing, social work, and communicative disorders. Nearly half of the students will complete a minimum of a semester-long study aboard experience in one of over thirty locations across the globe. There are established study-abroad programs in Italy, Ireland, Spain, and France; or students can seek a location a bit out of the ordinary like China, Honduras, or Argentina. And all Saint Mary's students complete a senior comprehensive, a graduate-quality project that is the capstone of their educational experience.

Founded by the Sisters of the Holy Cross in 1844, Saint Mary's is a nationally recognized Catholic college that empowers women by providing a strong liberal arts education foundation, leadership development, and attention to social responsibility.

With more than 1,650 students from forty-two states and seven countries, Saint Mary's brings together women from a wide range of geographical areas, social backgrounds, and educational experiences. International and diverse students comprise 10 percent of the student body.

Saint Mary's has a unique co-exchange program with the University of Notre Dame that encompasses both academics and extracurricular activities. Saint Mary's and Notre Dame's students can take courses and be part of the study-abroad programs at both institutions. Saint Mary's students can try out for Notre Dame's legendary marching band (10 percent of its members are Saint Mary's students); work for *The Observer*, the daily newspaper published jointed by Notre Dame/ Saint Mary's; or gain broadcast experience on WVFI, the Notre Dame/ Saint Mary's radio station. In addition, dances, concerts, lectures, and social organizations open to students on both campuses create a fluid social life between Saint Mary's and Notre Dame.

One of the distinctive features of Saint Mary's is its campus life. There are over sixty clubs and organizations, eight varsity athletic teams, over twenty community service organizations, and numerous other opportunities to help develop leadership skills and abilities, with all these groups lead and organized by women. Most students choose to live on campus for a minimum of six semesters and many seniors opt to remain on campus their final year. Saint Mary's has five residence halls, each with its own distinctive character. Seniors may choose to live in Opus Hall, which offers apartment-style living on campus. Residence halls offer a full calendar of activities, from twice-yearly dances to coffee nights with the College President, intramural athletic events, and a full array of activities designed involve students in campus life. The College has a new student center, a dining hall, and a clubhouse for extracurricular activities. All residence halls have chapels, and the Church of Loretto, the main chapel, offers mass on a daily basis.

As an NCAA Division III school and a member of the Michigan Intercollegiate Athletic Association, Saint Mary's sponsors varsity teams in basketball, cross-country, golf, soccer, softball, swimming and diving, tennis, and volleyball. Club sports, cosponsored with Notre Dame, include equestrian, gymnastics, lacrosse, and figure ice skating. In addition, Saint Mary's offers many intramural sports.

The College's Angela Athletic Facility contains multipurpose courts for tennis, volleyball, and basketball; a training and fitness center; and racquetball courts. The campus has tennis courts and athletic fields for both soccer and softball.

Location

Saint Mary's 75-acre campus, set alongside the Saint Joseph River, has great natural beauty. The College is located just across the street from the University of Notre Dame, minutes north of the city of South Bend (with a population of more than 200,000), and only 90 miles from Chicago. Students from Saint Mary's and Notre Dame form a dynamic intercollegiate community. South Bend provides sites for internships and practicums and opportunities for volunteer service. One of the hallmarks of a Saint Mary's education is the way students use their God-given talents to enrich their community; annually, 75 percent of St. Mary's students commit time to a variety of community service organizations.

Majors and Degrees

Saint Mary's College offers programs leading to the Bachelor of Arts, Bachelor of Science, Bachelor of Fine Arts, Bachelor of Business Administration, and Bachelor of Music degrees.

For a Bachelor of Arts degree, students may choose majors in art, biology, chemistry, communication studies, communicative disorders, economics, elementary education, English literature, English writing, French, history, humanistic studies, Italian, mathematics, music, philosophy, political science, psychology, religious studies, social work, sociology, Spanish, statistics and actuarial mathematics, and theater.

A Bachelor of Science degree may be obtained in biology (with concentrations in cellular/molecular biology, environmental biology, and general biology), chemistry, computational mathematics, mathematics, nursing, and statistics and actuarial mathematics.

The Bachelor of Music degree program, which is a member of the National Association of Schools of Music, offers concentrations in music education and music performance. For talented art students, Saint Mary's offers a Bachelor of Fine Arts degree with concentrations in several media.

The Bachelor of Business Administration degree program offers majors in accounting, business administration (with concentrations in accounting, finance, international business, management, and marketing), and management information systems.

Superior students who are candidates for either a Bachelor of Arts or a Bachelor of Science degree may design a program of study outside the traditional department structure, called a Student Designed Major.

For women interested in engineering fields, a five-year, dual-degree program offered in cooperation with the University of Notre Dame leads to a bachelor's degree from Saint Mary's College and a Bachelor of Science in Engineering degree from Notre Dame in aerospace, chemical, civil, computer, electrical, environmental, or mechanical engineering.

Saint Mary's education department, accredited by the National Council for Accreditation of Teacher Education, offers certification in elementary and secondary education. Secondary Education Certification is available in art, biology, business administration, chemistry, English literature, English writing, French, history, mathematics, music, music education, political science, psychology, sociology, and Spanish.

In addition, the College offers more than forty minors in a variety of fields, including American history, communicative disorders, information science, justice studies, Latin American studies, and women's studies.

Academic Programs

Graduation from Saint Mary's College requires successful completion of at least 128 semester hours of credit. Every student must also complete a comprehensive examination in her major, which may take the form of a thesis, a research or creative project, or a written or oral examination, depending on the discipline. All students must also demonstrate writing proficiency by satisfactorily completing a writing-intensive "W" course, usually in the first year, and an advanced portfolio of writings in the major discipline, usually in the senior year.

Off-Campus Programs

Through Saint Mary's international study programs, students can study with Irish students at the National University of Ireland Maynooth, just outside Dublin. They can absorb Italian art and culture on Saint Mary's campus in the center of Rome or experience Southeast Asia with the India-based program in Mumbai.

Saint Mary's students may also enroll in the Spanish language programs of the Center for Cross-Cultural Study in Seville, Spain, or in the French language and culture study in Dijon, France. An exchange program with the Australian University of Notre Dame based in Freemantle is also available, as is a program based in Pietermaritzburg, South Africa. A summer study program in China was recently added.

Saint Mary's students may study in Austria and other countries through a cooperative program with the University of Notre Dame.

A student majoring in political science has the opportunity to spend a semester at the American University in Washington, D.C. Saint Mary's also participates in student and faculty member exchange programs with the University of Notre Dame and members of the Northern Indiana Consortium for Education.

Academic Facilities

Students have abundant access to technology systems, software, and services. Residence halls are wired for network access, and secure wireless network access is available in most public areas on campus, including many classrooms in the new Spes Unica academic building. Computer labs for students are available in several campus buildings as well as computer "collaboratories," where students and faculty members can conduct online research in groups in classroom settings. Extensive support services are available to students and faculty and staff members for instructional, administrative, and network systems. Faculty members make significant use of information technology resources for teaching, research, and scholarship.

The modern Cushwa-Leighton Library houses an outstanding collection of more than 228,000 volumes, and it includes the Trumper Computer Center, the Instructional Technology Resource Center, the College archives, and a rare book room.

In addition to extensive biology, chemistry, and physics lab facilities, laboratories for psychology research and for foreign language study and practice are available to students. Art studios, music practice rooms, the O'Laughlin Auditorium, and Moreau's Little Theatre provide ample space for fine arts creation, practice, and performance. The new Spes Unica academic building opened in August 2008, providing students with state-of-the-art classrooms and gathering places.

The professionally staffed Early Childhood Development Center provides education and psychology majors with an unusual on-campus opportunity to work with young children. Other facilities include the Madeleva classroom building, Science Hall, Havican nursing facility, and Moreau Art Galleries.

Costs

Expenses for the 2009–10 academic year include tuition and fees, $29,616; room and board, $9206 (double occupancy); and miscellaneous expenses (books, transportation, and living costs), $2700.

Financial Aid

The College strives to make a Saint Mary's education available for every admitted student by offering eligible students financial aid packages that may include grants, scholarships, work-study, and loans. Competitive scholarships, awarded solely on academic merit, as well as grants determined by financial need are available. Last year, more than 90 percent of Saint Mary's students received more than $25 million in financial assistance, more than $18 million from the College alone.

All applicants for financial assistance must complete the College Board PROFILE and the Free Application for Federal Student Aid (FAFSA) each year that they desire assistance. Applications for assistance must be received at the processing center by March 1 to be given priority consideration. For non–early decision candidates, decisions concerning financial aid are made in mid-March, as soon as possible after a student has been accepted and upon receipt of the College Board PROFILE and FAFSA forms.

Faculty

Saint Mary's has 137 full-time and 81 part-time faculty members. About 98 percent of full-time faculty members hold earned doctorates or other terminal degrees; of these, most teach first-year students as well as upper-division students. Faculty members work with students in all phases of college life, including academic counseling. All classes are taught by faculty members, not by teaching assistants.

Student Government

Students are active at every level of campus governance and share in community decision making. There are voting representatives on the president's two highest advisory boards, the Student Affairs Council and the Academic Affairs Council. A student is also a voting member of the College Board of Trustees. Student government sponsors many extracurricular and cocurricular activities.

Admission Requirements

Applicants for admission to Saint Mary's College should be graduates of an accredited high school and have completed a four-year program of 16 or more academic units. These academic units must include four units of English, three units of college-preparatory mathematics, two units of the same foreign language, two units of social science, and two units of laboratory science. The remaining units should be completed in college-preparatory courses in the previously mentioned areas. An applicant's credentials should include an academic transcript showing current rank and senior-year subjects, a counselor/administrator recommendation, SAT or ACT scores (at least one test should include the writing exam), and an essay. There is no application fee for students who apply online at http://www.saintmarys.edu or by completing the Common Application.

Home-schooled students are encouraged to apply for admission and should contact the Office of Admission for specific details.

An interview with an admission officer is recommended. Saint Mary's encourages students to visit the campus. The Office of Admission can make arrangements for students who wish to attend classes or stay overnight.

Mature, well-qualified students who graduated from high school after three years and who wish to enter college immediately upon graduation may apply for early admission. Saint Mary's College also grants deferred admission upon request to candidates who are accepted in the normal application process.

Application and Information

Saint Mary's has two application and notification programs: Early Decision and modified rolling admission. Highly qualified students who have selected Saint Mary's as their first choice for admission may apply under the Early Decision program. The application deadline is November 15, and the notification date is December 15. Students who apply for modified rolling admission and whose application files are complete on or before December 1 are notified of the admission decision in mid-January. Candidates are encouraged to apply by early fall of their senior year. The priority application deadline for regular admission is February 15. Applications are accepted, however, as long as space is available.

Interested students are encouraged to contact:

Director of Admission
Saint Mary's College
Notre Dame, Indiana 46556-5001
Phone: 574-284-4587
800-551-7621 (toll-free)
Fax: 574-284-4841
E-mail: admission@saintmarys.edu
Web site: http://www.saintmarys.edu

ST. MARY'S COLLEGE OF MARYLAND

The Public Honors College

ST. MARY'S CITY, MARYLAND

The College

St. Mary's College of Maryland (SMCM) is a public, state-supported, coeducational college dedicated to providing an excellent education in the liberal arts tradition. There are 1,978 full-time students, of whom 851 are men and 1,127 are women. Almost 85 percent of the students live on campus in dorms, suites, apartments, and town houses. Housing on campus is guaranteed for eight semesters for all full-time students.

In 1992, St. Mary's was designated the State of Maryland's Public Honors College in recognition of the academic excellence of its faculty and students. Every student participates in the intellectual and social life of the College. St. Mary's combines the educational and personal advantages of a small private college with the affordability of a public institution. Active learning and the development of critical thinking are encouraged in the discussion-oriented format made possible by modest class sizes. Student leadership in academic, cultural, and social spheres is aided by the community atmosphere, and opportunities are greater than at larger schools.

The campus covers 361 acres of riverfront, open space, and woodland. Among the waterfront facilities are a boathouse, river center, ocean kayaks, rowing shells, and a fleet of sailboats. Other facilities include a field house, lighted tennis courts, a baseball field, an outdoor track, and a stadium for field hockey, soccer, and lacrosse. The athletic facility includes an aquatic center with two indoor swimming pools including an Olympic-sized pool, a basketball stadium, a fitness center, an aerobic center, additional team rooms, and a rock-climbing wall. The College's teams compete in NCAA Division III and the Intercollegiate Sailing Association. Varsity sports for men are baseball, basketball, lacrosse, sailing, soccer, swimming, and tennis. For women, sports include basketball, field hockey, lacrosse, sailing, soccer, swimming, tennis, and volleyball. The College's sailing teams have earned national recognitions. Club sports available for both men and women include cross-country and track, equestrian, fencing, golf, rowing, rugby, sailing, soccer, and Ultimate (Frisbee).

The College is accredited by the Middle States Commission on Higher Education.

Location

St. Mary's College of Maryland is situated along the banks of the St. Mary's River. It is tidewater country, still inhabited by people who make their living from the land and water. Watermen harvest oysters and crabs from the St. Mary's, Potomac, and Patuxent rivers and the Chesapeake Bay; wild swans, ducks, and Canada geese winter in the creeks of St. Mary's County.

The Patuxent River Naval Air Station, the county's largest employer, is a naval aircraft testing facility, attracting over 100 contractors that sponsor internships for SMCM students. It is an environment that is alive, providing fresh air and space, conveniently located just 75 miles south of Washington, D.C.

Majors and Degrees

St. Mary's College offers the Bachelor of Arts degree in anthropology; art and art history; Asian studies; biochemistry; biology; chemistry; computer science; economics; engineering (dual degree program); English; history; human studies; international languages and cultures (Chinese, French, German, Latin American studies, Spanish, and courses in translation); mathematics; music; natural science; philosophy; physics; political science; psychology; public policy studies; religious studies; sociology; theater, film, and media studies; and student-designed majors.

Minors are available in African and African diaspora studies; anthropology; art history; art studio; Asian studies; biology; computer science; democracy studies; economics; educational studies; environmental studies; film and media studies; history; international languages and cultures (Chinese, French, German, Latin American studies, Spanish, and courses in translation); mathematics; museum studies; music; the neurosciences; philosophy; physics; political science; religious studies; sociology; theater studies; and women, gender, and sexuality studies.

Preprofessional sequences are offered in dentistry, law, medicine, and veterinary medicine.

St. Mary's also offers teaching certification through a one-year, full-time Master of Arts in Teaching program. This program requires participation in the county school system, aiding in the transition from theory to practice. Certificates can be obtained for grades 1 through 6 and middle school, Secondary education certificates for grades 7 through 12 are offered in English, math, social studies, biology, chemistry, physics, and modern languages. Certificate programs for K–12 in art, music, and theater, and an early childhood education certificate to supplement the elementary certificate are also offered. All certificate programs have been approved through the Maryland State Department of Education and may be eligible for reciprocity with other states.

Academic Programs

The undergraduate course of study at the College provides both diversity and depth, leading to a broad understanding of the humanities, arts, and sciences. All students must complete the core curriculum requirements in addition to the requirements for a major field of study.

The core curriculum requirements are designed to develop skills in critical thinking, information literacy, written communication and oral communication, as well as promote the capacity for integration and synthesis of knowledge across disciplines. The core curriculum begins with first-year students completing a seminar of unique topics in every discipline, designed by the faculty members. In addition, students will fulfill the experiential component of the core by completing an internship, taking a service-learning course, or studying abroad.

History, anthropology, and archaeology students can take advantage of the College's relationship with historic St. Mary's City, the fourth permanent English settlement in the New World and Maryland's first capital. Many experts consider this area to contain the most abundant and earliest undisturbed artifacts of any American seventeenth-century town.

St. Mary's College offers several courses in aquatic biology as an option within the biology major program. The College's location on the St. Mary's River, a tributary of the Potomac near the mouth of the Chesapeake Bay, is ideal for the study of estuarine ecology.

A strong music program provides advanced training in composition and piano performance and a jazz ensemble, percussion ensemble, choir, chamber vocal group, wind ensemble, and chamber orchestra for classical performances.

Independent study for credit is possible in every major, allowing students to investigate subjects not covered in normal course offerings. There is also an opportunity for students to design their own majors using components from several majors to create an interdisciplinary, individualized program of study.

Off-Campus Programs

Internship programs for academic credit are available for junior- and senior-level students. Within these semester-long internships, students find ways to explore their career and scholarly interests. In recent years, St. Mary's interns have worked in state and federal government offices and laboratories, in the news media, in museums and art galleries, in commercial organizations, and in positions abroad. In a number of cases, internships have led to either full-time employment after graduation or to graduate or professional study.

Opportunities to study abroad include: The Centre for Medieval and Renaissance Studies in Oxford, England; Fudan University in China; Heidelberg University in Germany, University of The Gambia in The Gambia; the Alba Program in Italy; Akita University in Japan; Lingnan University in Hong Kong; Payap University in Thailand; Université Michel de Montaigne and Sciences Po in France; Institute for Central American Development Studies in Costa Rica; the Buenos Aires Program in Argentina; George Washington University Partnership in Santiago, Chile; and other study-abroad programs are available for qualified St. Mary's students. St. Mary's also participates in the National Student Exchange Program with other colleges throughout the United States.

Academic Facilities

The College's laboratories are equipped for course work in anthropology, biology, chemistry, physics, psychology, and the neurosciences. There are also several smart classrooms and discipline-specific labs in Goodpaster, Kent, Montgomery, and Schaefer Halls. All of the computer labs have access to the library system, e-mail, the student portal, and the Internet. There is 24-hour access to College computers in Baltimore Hall and Lewis Quad. Upon enrollment, every student is given a network account that provides access to e-mail, the student portal, shared file systems, and other resources.

Students are encouraged but not required to own a computer, since they have access to computers in the College's general purpose and departmental computer labs. However, many students find it more convenient to own a computer so they can complete assignments in their rooms. Each residence hall room has high-speed Internet 1 and 2 access (ResNet).The College offers wireless access in all academic buildings of the campus for those with laptop computers.

The College library provides access to locally held resources and participates in a statewide consortium of academic libraries that supports intercampus borrowing (interlibrary loan) for books and access to more than 70 research databases. Students have access to a writing center, located in the library, which provides assistance in writing and researching papers.

The Media Services Department, through its editing lab and loans of video equipment, supports students pursuing multimedia and video projects. The College Archives house documents, photographs, and objects of significance to the history of the College and Southern Maryland.

The Montgomery Fine Arts Center includes facilities for practice and performance in music and theater and also houses the Boyden Gallery. Auerbach Auditorium, located in St. Mary's Hall, is also a popular venue for public lectures, concerts, and other events.

Costs

Annual costs for 2010–11 include tuition and fees of $13,630 for Maryland residents and $25,023 for nonresidents. The most typical residence hall rooms are available for $5745 per year, and the most typical cost for board is $4505 per year. Costs for books and supplies are estimated at $1000 per year. Semester charges for tuition, room, board, and other fees are payable at or prior to registration in the fall and in the spring.

Financial Aid

The Office of Financial Aid provides advice and assistance to students in need of financial aid and joins other College offices in awarding scholarships and loans and in offering part-time employment under the work-study program. Various scholarships are awarded to students on a merit basis, and other scholarships, loans, and grants for students are awarded on ability and need as determined by the federal government's Free Application for Federal Student Aid, which should be filed no later than March 1.

Faculty

Faculty appointments and promotions are made on the basis of commitment to undergraduate teaching, an interest in new approaches to education, and academic and scholarly achievement. The faculty members have experience in a wide range of activities, including government, business, research, environmental studies, civil rights, theater, musical performance, and writing. Since 1982, St. Mary's College has had 23 Fulbright Scholars on its faculty and staff. Ninety-nine percent of the regular full-time faculty members hold a doctorate or other terminal degree in their field.

A student-faculty ratio of 12:1, average class size of 16, the relatively small size of the College, and the informal atmosphere all encourage close and personal relationships between students and faculty members. Faculty members serve as academic advisers and provide much informal counseling and individual attention to students' academic and personal development outside of the formal structure.

Student Government

Student Government Association (SGA) is the center of many activities and sponsors a variety of social and cultural events, including campus movies, speakers, dances, concerts, and excursions to cultural centers such as Annapolis, Baltimore, and Washington, D.C. The SGA also sponsors over 100 student-run clubs and organizations. Opportunities exist for students to serve as voting members on several faculty committees.

Admission Requirements

The application deadline for freshman admissions is January 1. Strong high school preparation usually includes 4 units of English, 3 units of social science (including U.S. history), 3 units of laboratory science (exclusive of ninth-grade general courses in science), 3 units of mathematics, and 7 units of other academic electives. Upon entrance, the student should have obtained a high school diploma with a minimum of 22 units or should present evidence of equivalent achievement (e.g., a passing score on the high school equivalency examination administered by the student's state department of education). The applicant must present scores on the SAT and/or the ACT examination, which should be taken by the fall of the senior year. In addition, any student whose native language is not English must obtain a minimum score of 550 (paper-based) on the TOEFL. St. Mary's College is interested in evidence of talent and ability as demonstrated in a variety of ways by each student. While the most emphasis is placed on the student's academic record, SAT scores, essay, resume, and letters of recommendation are all considered in the admissions process.

Students enrolled in Advanced Placement courses may receive credit for scores of 4 or 5 on the examinations. In addition, St. Mary's may also award credit to students who receive a score of 5, 6, or 7 on the International Baccalaureate Higher Level examinations.

Transfer applicants with at least 24 semester hours of credit are evaluated on their college transcripts. Students who have earned fewer than 24 semester hours of credit must submit their high school records and SAT or ACT scores. Standardized test scores are required only for individuals who have graduated from high school within the past three years.

St. Mary's College of Maryland does not discriminate for reasons of age, citizenship, color, disability, gender/gender identity and expression, national origin, race, religion, sex, sexual orientation, or special disabled veteran and Vietnam-era veteran status in the admission of students. The College complies with the Title IX of the Education Amendments of 1972.

Application and Information

An application form, financial aid information, and other materials are available by contacting:

Office of Admissions
St. Mary's College of Maryland
18952 East Fisher Road
St. Mary's City, Maryland 20686
Phone: 240-895-5000
800-492-7181 (toll-free)
Fax: 240-895-5001
E-mail: admissions@smcm.edu
Web site: http://www.smcm.edu/admissions

A bird's-eye view of St. Mary's College of Maryland.

SAINT MICHAEL'S COLLEGE

COLCHESTER, VERMONT

The College

Saint Michael's College is a residential, Catholic liberal arts college in Vermont where 2,000 undergraduates learn to make the world a better place.

Saint Michael's is among the 270 colleges and universities nationwide allowed to host a prestigious Phi Beta Kappa chapter on campus. The superb faculty members are committed first and foremost to teaching and are known for challenging students to reach higher than they ever thought possible. With a student-faculty ratio of just 12:1, students are ensured personal attention from their professors both in class (lively First-Year Seminars set the interactive tone) and out of class. Because of the holistic approach, Saint Michael's graduates are the beneficiaries of an education that prepares them not only for their first jobs, but also for entire careers.

Service to the community and to all humankind is a vibrant part of student life, reflecting the heritage of service of the Edmundite priests who founded Saint Michael's—the one and only Edmundite college in the world—in 1904. Today, more than 70 percent of the student body actively pursues community service projects through Mobilization of Volunteer Efforts (M.O.V.E.), reflecting a unique passion for social justice issues on campus. In the classroom, ethical and moral considerations always complement intellectual discourse. In addition, students can find spiritual engagement through the extensive programming offered by the Office of Edmundite Campus Ministry.

With nearly 100 percent of the students living on campus (with guaranteed housing for four years), the 24/7 living and learning environment means that exceptional teaching extends beyond the classroom, building lifelong bonds among the College's students and faculty and staff members. The remarkable sense of community on campus is fueled by the size of the student body and the supportive learning environment, which compels students to get involved in campus organizations, take risks, and think differently. Global perspectives enrich the atmosphere through the thriving study-abroad programs and the presence of the Applied Linguistics Department, one of the nation's oldest English language institutes.

Location

Saint Michael's is situated less than 3 miles from Burlington, Vermont's largest city and a vibrant college town that is home to the 14,000 students enrolled in five local colleges and universities. In addition to the shops, restaurants, and cafés of the Church Street Marketplace and a lively local music scene, Burlington offers great opportunities for hands-on learning through internships. Vermont, known for its natural beauty, environmentalism, and year-round recreational activities, inspires many students to take advantage of some of the best skiing in the East through a relationship with Smugglers' Notch ski resort—a program that provides an all-access season pass to any Saint Michael's student in good academic standing—and through the College's renowned Wilderness Program.

Saint Michael's enjoys a uniquely accessible location. Burlington International Airport is only a 10-minute drive from the campus. In addition, an Amtrak station is in nearby Essex Junction and a Greyhound bus station is in Burlington; both are within a 15-minute drive of the campus.

Majors and Degrees

Saint Michael's College offers bachelor's degrees in the following areas: accounting, American studies, art, biochemistry, biology, business administration, chemistry, classics, computer science, economics, elementary education, engineering, English, environmental science, French, gender/women's studies, history, information systems, journalism, mathematics, modern languages and literature, music, philosophy, physical science, physics, political science, psychology, religious studies, sociology, Spanish, and theater. In addition, advising programs for premedicine, prelaw, predentistry, and pre–veterinary studies are available. Secondary education licensure is also available in several subject areas.

A special 3+2 engineering program is offered in conjunction with Clarkson University (Potsdam, New York) and the University of Vermont (Burlington, Vermont) for students interested in combining a liberal arts background with engineering. A 4+1 M.B.A. program is offered in conjunction with Clarkson University. An English as a second language program is available for international students. Saint Michael's also offers minors in many subject areas, some of which are interdisciplinary. Environmental studies, global studies, marketing, and peace and justice are just some of the minors offered.

Academic Programs

Saint Michael's academic year consists of two semesters and a summer session. The College's focus is on undergraduate instruction, and its small classes support this primary emphasis. All students must complete a liberal studies core curriculum, which includes course work in the following areas: social sciences, organizational studies, natural and mathematical sciences, humanities, religious studies, philosophy, and an artistic experience. Students must also demonstrate writing and foreign language proficiency. In addition to fulfilling these requirements, students must complete the degree requirements for one of the majors listed above or for an approved combination of those majors.

Off-Campus Programs

Many students enhance their academic work with an internship related to their career goals and major. Internships are available both locally and in other selected areas around the U.S. and abroad. Sites have included scientific research laboratories, brokerage houses, hospitals, schools, newspapers, and accounting firms.

Study-abroad programs are available to students in all majors. Programs and locations are selected by the student in consultation with the Director of Study Abroad.

Unique Saint Michael's programs include study-abroad experiences at University of the Americas, Mexico; College of Ripon and York St. John, England; Kansai Gaidai University, Japan; and a Washington, D.C., semester program. In recent years, many students have studied abroad in locations such as Australia, Botswana, China, France, Ghana, Ireland, Italy, Nepal, Samoa, and Spain.

Academic Facilities

The Jeremiah Durick Library holds 227,000 volumes, 110 research databases, access to articles from more than 25,000 online journals, and 10,000 electronic books, maps, videos, and other items. Students in all majors are able to take short courses in computer applications. Although most students bring their own computers, students have access to more than 120 computers connected to the College's campuswide information technology network. This network provides access to PC applications, including Microsoft Windows XP Professional, the Internet, e-mail, and the College library. Computer hookups are available in all residence hall rooms. Wireless access is available in the Durick Library, Alliot Student Center, and all academic buildings.

Cheray Science Center has facilities for the study of biochemistry, biology, chemistry, environmental science, and physics. Generous grants in recent years have provided state-of-the-art research equipment that is always available to undergraduates.

Saint Edmund's Hall, an impressive academic complex, includes media labs, psychology labs, computer facilities, and language labs, in addition to traditional classroom and lecture hall space.

Costs

The 2010–11 tuition and residence fee is $43,530. The residence fee includes housing and meals and is based on a standard double room and a standard meal plan. Housing options on campus include traditional residence halls, apartment-style housing, theme housing, and suite-style housing. Some science, journalism, language, and art courses require laboratory fees. Book, personal, and travel expenses vary according to course selection and individual needs.

Financial Aid

Approximately 90 percent of admitted students receive financial aid in the form of loans, grants, and work-study dollars. Students must file the FAFSA by February 15 for fall-semester enrollment.

Faculty

The undergraduate faculty at Saint Michael's consists of 150 full-time professors. Ninety-four percent of tenured and tenure-track faculty members have the doctoral or terminal degree in their field, and many have been recipients of grants, awards, and honors in recent years. While undergraduate instruction is the focus of the College, faculty members are encouraged to remain abreast of developments in their field through research and publication, often facilitated through sabbaticals.

Student Government

The Student Association (SA), an active and important part of campus life, is an elected body of students that authorizes and funds most other student activities and organizations. Representatives from the SA sit on many campuswide committees, including the Curriculum Committee and various committees of the Board of Trustees.

Admission Requirements

Successful applicants to Saint Michael's typically rank in the top 25 percent of their high school class and have a strong college-preparatory background. Students should have completed 16 units of courses in English, foreign language, mathematics, science, and social science. SAT or ACT scores are required. For reference, the average SAT score last year ranged between 1590 and 1890, and the average ACT score ranged between 25 and 26. In addition, students should submit a counselor recommendation and any teacher recommendations they choose. Transfer applicants must submit transcripts of all college work in addition to the information required of first-year applicants.

Application and Information

Saint Michael's offers an Early Action admission program deadline of either November 1 or December 1, as well as a Regular Action deadline of February 1. Students should consult the Web site for application deadlines and information. Candidates for the fall semester are notified of their admission decision on or before April 1. A limited number of students may be admitted to the spring semester and should have their applications in by November 1. The College adheres to the Candidates Reply Date of May 1 for the fall semester.

For further information, students should contact:

Office of Admission
Saint Michael's College
One Winooski Park, Box 7
Colchester, Vermont 05439
Phone: 800-762-8000 (toll-free)
Fax: 802-654-2906
E-mail: admission@smcvt.edu
Web site: http://www.smcvt.edu

COLLEGE CLOSE-UPS

Students enjoy a sunny day on campus, with the Durick Library in the background.

ST. NORBERT COLLEGE

DE PERE, WISCONSIN

The College

New national rankings, a new state-of-the-art library, a new apartment-style residence hall, a new athletics facility ,and plans for newly remodeled science facilities—these are just a few of the exciting things happening at St. Norbert College. The riverfront campus is part of the thriving corporate, entertainment, educational, arts, and cultural environment of northeastern Wisconsin. Learning takes place in residence halls and classrooms, on campus, and, literally, around the world.

The St. Norbert learning community helps students becomes critical thinkers, strong writers, and able communicators, in a setting that encourages student-faculty collaborative research. The graduate-level work done by St. Norbert undergraduates, even as freshmen, is surprising and puts them ahead of their peers when heading to graduate school or the workforce.

St. Norbert seeks to challenge student viewpoints and encourage exploration of new or different ideas, in an environment where students from around the world come together in exploration of local and global perspectives.

Faculty members at St. Norbert are active researchers and creators who make ongoing contributions to their fields. They're also compassionate individuals who care not only about their students' grades, but also about their growth, making time for one-on-one conversations with students on a daily basis. Student success is their top priority, and they regularly give out even their home phone number for easy student access.

St. Norbert College offers more than forty programs of study, including several preprofessional programs. Students can also design their own major, unique to their aspirations. Opportunities to study abroad abound, with seventy-five program sites in thirty-seven countries on six continents. There are also numerous service opportunities for students locally, nationally, and internationally.

Each St. Norbert student is paired with an adviser who helps ensure that the student is on track with classes and will graduate in four years. St. Norbert's innovative career services office provides service through the college years and beyond; the alumni career network can help students find their first job as well as their last one. When St. Norbert students are surveyed nine months after graduation, 95 percent of them are typically employed or attending graduate school.

Student life offers a blend of learning and fun. Students flourish within the academically challenging environment, but with more than sixty-five clubs and organizations on campus, there's no shortage of ways to become involved outside the classroom. Extracurricular activities can also complement classroom learning.

Students frequently comment on the sense of community and worldwide opportunities available at St. Norbert. They talk about the challenges of the classroom and the heartfelt rewards of the service opportunities. Graduates value the friendships with peers and faculty members that started at St. Norbert and may last a lifetime. Some students love the campus so much they refer to St. Norbert as their "home."

Location

The St. Norbert campus, approximately 93 acres, is located on the banks of the Fox River in De Pere, Wisconsin, just minutes south of Green Bay, a metropolitan area of about 230,000 people and home to the world-famous Green Bay Packers football team. Rich culture, arts, and entertainment are present in historic De Pere and Green Bay, which is recognized as a "Best City." Located near the gateway to Door County, one of Wisconsin's favorite vacation spots, the campus is part of a vibrant eighteen-county region of 1.2 million people.

Majors and Degrees

St. Norbert offers programs leading to the Bachelor of Arts, Bachelor of Science, Bachelor of Music, and Bachelor of Business Administration degrees. Students also have the opportunity of applying their education at St. Norbert toward any of three master's degree programs: the Master of Science in Education, Master of Arts in Liberal Studies, and Master of Theological Studies.

St. Norbert College has partnered with several other institutions to further extend its offerings. Students can earn a nursing degree through a partnership with Bellin College in Green Bay; complete an engineering degree in four years through a partnership with Michigan Tech; or earn a master's degree in applied economics in just one additional year, rather than two, through a partnership with Marquette University.

Programs of study at St. Norbert include: accounting, American studies, anthropology, art–fine arts, art–graphic design, biology–biomedical, biology–organismal, business administration, chemistry, chemistry–biochemistry, classical studies, communications and media studies, computer science, computer science–business information systems, computer science–graphic design and implementation, economics, education, English, English–creative writing, environmental science, French, geography, geology, German, history, human services (social work), international business and language area studies, international studies, Japanese, leadership studies, mathematics, military science/ROTC, music, natural sciences, nursing, peace and justice, Philippine studies, philosophy, physics, political science, predental, pre-engineering, prelaw, premedical, prepharmacy, pre-veterinary, psychology, religious studies, religious studies–youth ministry, sociology, Spanish, teacher education, theater studies, and women's and gender studies.

Academic Programs

Degrees are awarded upon the successful completion of thirty-two courses (128 semester hours) that include an approved major sequence, course work in general education, and either an academic minor or electives. Academic majors can be started as early as the first semester of the freshman year. Early selection of a major is encouraged but not required in most majors. Students are not required to officially declare a major until the end of the sophomore year. The College offers a four-year graduation guarantee in all but two academic programs.

The College's goal is to educate students broadly, regardless of major. Competence in writing and quantitative skills is required of all graduates. An honors program offers additional challenge in areas of general education to those of superior ability, and an honors degree is awarded to those who successfully complete the program.

Army ROTC is available and several St. Norbert students are recipients of full Army ROTC scholarships each year. Among the College's alumni are 11 Army generals who completed ROTC at the College—the highest total of any college (with the exception of West Point).

Off-Campus Programs

St. Norbert students, regardless of major, can spend a summer, a semester, or a year abroad. The College has more than seventy-five study-abroad program sites in thirty-seven countries on six continents. Students completing liberal arts majors are encouraged to spend at least a semester abroad. An international study component is a part of majors in French, Spanish, and German, and both the international business program and the international studies major. All approved international study carries regular academic credit. St. Norbert scholarship assistance and other financial aid carry over to overseas study.

St. Norbert considers international experience vital to today's graduates and it is a key component of the college's educational mission.

Study-abroad opportunities include a Third World science field trip; exchange programs in Australia, France, Japan, Germany, the Philippines, Spain, and Ukraine; student teaching in Europe, Africa, Australia, and Latin America; and other study sites throughout Europe, South America, and Egypt. St. Norbert's international curriculum, taught by a faculty committed to global learning, prepares students to live in a global society. A Washington semester is also available through American University.

Additional service-learning opportunities are available throughout the year. Students can participate in the TRIPS (Turning Responsibility into Powerful Service) program in local, national, and international locations, or participate in a variety of other off-campus service opportunities.

Academic Facilities

A new $20-million state-of-the-art library opened in the fall of 2009. It houses more than 247,000 volumes, including books, journals and other serials, microforms, maps, and charts. More than 3,000 volumes are added to the collection each year. The 80,000-square-foot library features enhanced technology, flexible study and classroom spaces, and a welcome center with computers, media players, and a 24-hour computer study area.

The F. K. Bemis International Center provides students with opportunities to prepare for careers with greater international emphasis. Students from more than thirty countries attend St. Norbert College annually and 32 percent of each class studies abroad. The center also serves as a resource for K–12 schools and Wisconsin businesses for language instruction, translation, and interpretation.

The John Minahan Science Hall houses the science programs and thirty-eight laboratories. Planning is underway for renovation and expansion of this building to facilitate current and future research and education in the natural sciences.

Austin E. Cofrin Hall houses the business administration, computer science, mathematics, and economics programs. It also holds the campus' computing resources.

Residence halls provide the link between living and learning at St. Norbert. Some residence halls focus on community service or feature campus programs, such as the Women's Center in Sensenbrenner Hall or the honors program in Bergstrom Hall. Many halls have chapels for students to reflect and pray.

A new outdoor athletics complex, scheduled to open in fall 2010, will provide the practice and competition venue for football, soccer, and track and field.

Costs

For 2009–10, tuition and required fees for full-time students totaled $26,972. Room costs averaged $3700 per year, and the average meal plan for full-time students cost $3358 per year.

Financial Aid

Students share in more than $47 million of financial aid each year, including scholarships and grants, campus jobs, and educational loans. St. Norbert awards $22 million of its own scholarships and grants annually. There are both need-based and merit-based awards.

Wisconsin residents who show need can qualify for assistance provided by the state through the Wisconsin Tuition Grant Program. The College participates in the Federal Supplemental Educational Opportunity Grant, Federal Perkins Loan, and Federal Work-Study programs.

Need-based awards are made on the basis of the Free Application for Federal Student Aid (FAFSA; St. Norbert College's code is 003892) and the St. Norbert College institutional application for financial aid. Freshman applicants should submit these forms by March of their senior year of high school.

Faculty

The St. Norbert faculty is comprised of 182 men and women, 134 of whom are full-time. At least 87 percent of the full-time faculty members hold the doctoral or other terminal degree in their field. The student-faculty ratio is approximately 14:1, and student success is a top priority of the faculty. They work closely with students in their major area of study, help students prepare for graduate school, write letters of recommendation, and work with those who seek independent study and research opportunities. Two-year research fellowships with faculty members are available to first-year students, who may ultimately have the opportunity to present their research findings collaboratively with faculty members at national conferences. Faculty members also work with Career Services in its professional practice program.

Student Government

The College's Student Government Association (SGA) is active on campus, with representation extending as far as the college's board of trustees. The president of the College and his cabinet respect the voice of the student body, and openly discuss issues that impact students and the college community. The SGA meets regularly and holds town-hall meetings for the campus community. Its goal is to serve as a representative governing body and to create an environment conducive to intellectual, spiritual, and personal growth throughout the campus community.

Admission Requirements

The College welcomes enrollment from a diverse group of students who are prepared academically and who will make a contribution to the St. Norbert living and learning community. Every completed application is considered carefully and students who are likely to succeed in this environment are accepted. In 2009, more than 85 percent of the freshman class ranked in the top half of their high school senior class, the average GPA was 3.42, and the average ACT composite score was 24.16. Students with superior scores and grades are invited to enroll in the honors program.

Application and Information

Because the College gives preference to students according to the date of admission and enrollment deposit, it benefits students to apply as early as possible in their senior year. Notification of the admission decision is made on a rolling basis beginning in late September. A $350 deposit is required to confirm enrollment. For more information about St. Norbert College, students should contact:

Executive Director of Enrollment
St. Norbert College
100 Grant Street
De Pere, Wisconsin 54115
Phone: 920-403-3005
800-236-4878 (toll-free)
E-mail: admit@snc.edu
Web site: http://www.snc.edu

The riverfront Campus Center is a favorite place for students to hang out, grab a bite to eat, study, work out, or relax on the St. Norbert campus.

SAINT PETER'S COLLEGE

JERSEY CITY, NEW JERSEY

The College

Saint Peter's College (SPC) offers a strong liberal arts education focused on the holistic, personal development of the individual student; the advantages of its international, New York City metropolitan location; and affordable tuition. Located within minutes of New York City and the Statue of Liberty, the College has offered academic excellence in the Jesuit, Catholic tradition since its founding in 1872. Saint Peter's students can participate in class, internship, and cooperative education experiences in a variety of international, cultural, business, and communication institutions and corporations. Saint Peter's participates in NCAA Division I athletics, with strongly competitive teams in both men's and women's sports. The diverse, international student body is composed of students from throughout the Northeast, America, and the world.

Saint Peter's offers a curriculum based on students' developing a breadth of knowledge in the core curriculum of the liberal arts and sciences and depth of knowledge, skills, and proficiencies within the major area of study. The College seeks to develop graduates of competence and conscience by emphasizing ethical and moral decision making throughout the entire course of study. Students may choose to prepare for positions in professional fields such as business or education; preprofessional programs in fields such as medicine and dentistry; or graduate study in many disciplines.

The goal of a Saint Peter's College education is to equip students to succeed in learning, leadership, and service. The *ethos* of the College is reflected in the motto of the twenty-eight American Jesuit colleges and universities, which is to develop "men and women for others." The College serves as a significant educational, religious, cultural, social, and economic resource for Jersey City and the surrounding area. Its main campus is located in Jersey City, New Jersey, with additional branch campuses in Englewood Cliffs and South Amboy, New Jersey. Total enrollment is 3,000, including 2,200 full-time undergraduates in the College of Arts and Sciences and the School of Business Administration, 500 adult undergraduates in the School for Professional and Continuing Studies, and 700 graduate students. SPC alumni, over 32,000 strong, are successful professionals in the arts, business, humanities, law, medicine, education, politics, public service, and the sciences.

The College offers more than fifty major programs leading to the baccalaureate degree as well as graduate programs in accountancy, business, education, and nursing.

Location

Saint Peter's College is easily accessible by all major forms of transportation. Midtown Manhattan is a short ride on the PATH subway system from Journal Square. Liberty International Airport is only 20 minutes away, and there are numerous trains (including Amtrak) and Greyhound buses leaving from Penn Station in Newark and New York City, the Erie-Lackawanna Railroad Terminal in Hoboken, and Port Authority and Grand Central Station in New York City. SPC is also accessible from the New Jersey Turnpike and other major highways.

Majors and Degrees

Saint Peter's College offers baccalaureate degrees in accountancy, American studies, art history, Asian studies, biological chemistry, biology, biotechnology, business management, chemistry, classical civilizations, classical languages and literature, communications, computer science, computer science/CIS, computer science/MIS, criminal justice, economics and finance, elementary and secondary education, English literature, fine arts, graphic arts, health and physical education, history, humanities*, international business and trade, Latin American studies, marketing management, mathematical economics, mathematics, modern languages and literature, natural sciences, nursing, philosophy, physics, physics/electrical engineering, political science, prelaw, psychology, social sciences*, sociology, Spanish, theology, urban studies, and visual arts. Five-year bachelor's degree programs in cytotechnology and medical technology are offered in affiliation with the University of Medicine and Dentistry of New Jersey (UMDNJ). Preprofessional programs in accountancy (3-3 at SPC), dentistry (3-4 with UMDNJ), law (3-3 with Seton Hall), medicine (3-4 with UMDNJ), occupational therapy (3-3 with Seton Hall), pharmacy (3-4 with the Rutgers School of Pharmacy), physician assistant studies (3-3 with UMDNJ and 3-3 with Seton Hall), and physical therapy (3-3 with UMDNJ) are available. Associate degrees are offered in banking*, business management, finance, humanities, information systems, international business and trade, marketing management, public policy*, social sciences, and theater arts. (*School for Professional and Continuing Studies only.)

Academic Programs

The liberal arts core curriculum, required for all degrees, comprises 60 semester hours and includes study in composition and fine arts (a minimum of 3 semester hours each), history, literature, mathematics (6–8 semester hours), modern language, natural sciences (9 semester hours), philosophy, social sciences, theology (6 semester hours each), and a core elective in ethical values (3 semester hours). The baccalaureate degree requires the completion of 120 semester hours. Approximately half of the courses required for the degree are in the core curriculum, one quarter are in the major area of study, and one quarter are in elective courses. Students may complete majors in two areas by meeting all degree requirements or design a composite major to meet individual interests following consultation with and approval from the academic dean. Summer sessions are available on both campuses. Sessions for full-time undergraduates are based on a semester system.

The honors program provides an opportunity for academically talented students to participate in challenging classes and to do research with a faculty mentor. Students who complete the entire honors program successfully are awarded degrees *in cursu honorum.* The College recognizes the Advanced Placement (AP) Program as well as the College-Level Examination Program (CLEP).

Under the direction of the freshman dean, the College offers a number of summer and freshman-year programs in order to foster the successful transition of students to college life. All freshmen are assigned faculty advisers. SPC participates in the Educational Opportunity Fund (EOF) program in partnership with the state of New Jersey. This program offers a six-week summer study program and individual support and guidance throughout the entire College experience. The Summer Academy is offered to all students who would benefit from structure and directed study in order to successfully acclimate to the demands of college-level study. During the year, the Academic Success Program fosters student success through individual attention and mentoring. Additional resources are available to meet students' needs, such as the Center for the Advancement of

Learning and Language (C.A.L.L.), Center for Personal Advisement, Campus Ministry, Residence Life, and Freshman Seminar.

Off-Campus Programs

Supervised, off-campus cooperative education opportunities and internships are available in all fields. Students in SPC's nationally ranked Cooperative Education Program may earn a maximum of 9 academic credits and up to $10,000. Up to 15 credits are awarded through the Washington Center Program in Washington, D.C., which provides experience working in the nation's capital in a wide range of internship positions. Study abroad is arranged through the International Student Exchange Program (ISEP), which conducts programs in more than sixty universities in Europe, Asia, Africa, and Latin America.

Academic Facilities

The Edward and Theresa O'Toole Library houses a large collection of volumes, periodicals, and information databases. Students also benefit from interlibrary loan arrangements as well as access to the New Jersey state-supported university library system. Students may obtain referral cards to other metropolitan-area libraries, including the New York Public Library and the Science, Industry, and Business Library, both located in midtown Manhattan, minutes from the campus.

Saint Peter's was one of the first colleges in the nation to adopt a wireless Ethernet throughout the campus. Wireless access is available to all students free of charge. The College is also implementing a new information infrastructure that supports the Student Information System, instruction in the classrooms, student computer labs, and faculty and student research. Students are offered individual e-mail accounts and Internet connectivity through the campus local area network (LAN).

Costs

Annual tuition and student fees for 2009–10 were $26,825 for full-time study (12–18 semester hours each semester). Typical housing costs for room and board were $10,900. Personal expenses, books, supplies, and transportation were estimated to be $3850 for residential students and $2200 for commuter students.

Financial Aid

Saint Peter's College admits students without regard to financial status. Ninety percent of SPC students receive financial assistance. For the 2009–10 academic year, the average award was more than $21,000. The only form required is the Free Application for Federal Student Aid (FAFSA). It is recommended that students file the FAFSA by March 15 for full consideration for all federal, state, and institutional funds available.

Federal sources include Federal Pell Grants, Federal Supplemental Educational Opportunity Grants (FSEOG), the Federal Work-Study Program (FWS), Federal Stafford Student Loans, and Parent Loans for Undergraduate Students (PLUS). New Jersey state sources include Tuition Aid Grants (TAG) and the Educational Opportunity Fund (EOF). All applications for admission are reviewed for academic scholarships, grants, athletic scholarships, and need-based grants. Prospective students should call the Student Financial Aid Office at 201-761-6060 for more information.

Faculty

All classes at Saint Peter's are taught by faculty members rather than graduate students or teaching assistants. Faculty members in every discipline are expected to meet high standards for teaching. Faculty members work with students as advisers and mentors in the classroom and in supervised areas of study, such as research or internships and cooperative education experiences. Faculty members are expected to maintain currency in their fields of instruction through a scholarly agenda of research and/or through continued development as active professionals. Saint Peter's offers small classes so that students can obtain the maximum benefit from their interaction with the faculty members. The 118 full-time faculty members have completed advanced degrees at some of the nation's finest institutions of higher learning. All of Saint Peter's faculty members are committed to *cura personalis,* or personal attention, and to the success of each student individually.

Student Government

The Student Senate consists of an elected executive committee and 5 elected student senators from each class. The objectives of the Student Senate are to coordinate student activities, provide effective means of communication between the student body and the College administration, and strive to maintain and further the spirit and ideals of Saint Peter's College.

Admission Requirements

Admission to Saint Peter's College is based upon a student's demonstrated academic performance, academic preparation, and potential for success in college-level study. Each application is reviewed on an individual basis, and SAT/ACT scores, class rank, high school record, personal statement, letters of recommendation, part-time employment, leadership positions, athletics/extracurricular activities, and community service are all considered. Interviews are not required but are strongly recommended for all applicants. Students are expected to have a solid preparation for college. Saint Peter's requires a minimum of 16 units of high school academic courses for admission: 4 units in English, 2 units in history, 2 units in a modern language, 3 units of college-preparatory mathematics, and 2 units of science (including at least 1 unit of a laboratory science). In addition to these 13 basic units, students must have completed at least 3 more units in any combination of the subject areas listed above. One unit is the equivalent of one year of study in a high school subject.

Application and Information

Students are encouraged to submit their applications in the fall of their senior year of high school. Admission is on a rolling basis. Students who wish to be considered for an academic scholarship should apply by February 15. When a student's completed application and records are on file, they are reviewed by the committee. Students are ordinarily notified of the admission decision within two weeks of receipt of the complete admission file, which must include the completed application form, a personal statement, a high school transcript with official SAT scores, and recommendations. Transfer students should submit official copies of all college transcripts by December 1 for admission to the spring semester and before August 1 for admission to the fall semester.

To complete their admission file, international students should submit the results of the Test of English as a Foreign Language (TOEFL) or the equivalent, all official documents of education, an affidavit of financial support, and the completed application form, including a personal statement. International students are encouraged to apply before March 1 for the fall term and before October 1 for the spring term.

For more information, students should contact:

Office of Admission
Saint Peter's College
2641 Kennedy Boulevard
Jersey City, New Jersey 07306-5944
Phone: 201-761-7100
888-SPC-9933 (toll-free)
Fax: 201-761-7105
E-mail: admissions@spc.edu
Web site: http://www.spc.edu

ST. THOMAS AQUINAS COLLEGE

SPARKILL, NEW YORK

The College

St. Thomas Aquinas College (STAC) was founded in 1952 as a three-year teacher-training college with 30 students. Today, the College offers over 100 different majors, minors, specializations, and dual degree programs and has a total student body of 2,700 in all programs, on and off campus. Much growth and development has taken place over the College's history. The College offers a Master of Science in Education, with concentrations in literacy education, special education, and educational leadership as well as postgraduate certificate programs in literacy and special education. The College also offers a Master of Business Administration (M.B.A.) program with concentrations in finance, management, and marketing; and an online M.B.A. in general studies. St. Thomas offers a Master of Science in Teaching program for individuals without a background in teacher education who are seeking a career change. Certification is offered in childhood education, grades 1–6; childhood education and special education, grades 1–6; and adolescence education, grades 7–12. The College is home to New York University's Master in Social Work program.

The College's most dramatic growth has occurred to meet the challenges of the twenty-first century. Capital improvements continue to be made and new facilities added, so that the main campus now consists of twenty-one buildings on 48 acres. The suburban campus includes two residential complexes: Aquinas Village, which consists of self-contained townhouse units that house 300 students, and the McNelis Commons, which consists of townhouse residential units that house 375 students and a common dining hall and laundry building. Approximately 40 percent of the College's full-time student population resides on campus.

Extracurricular activities are provided through thirty-five different organizations, including the Spartan Volunteers, a community service program; a student-run radio station (WSTK); and the student-edited campus newspaper and yearbook. The College has excellent sports facilities, and several of its athletic teams have competed in national championships. The College fields NCAA Division II teams in men's and women's cross-country, golf, indoor track and field, and tennis; women's basketball, lacrosse, soccer, and softball; and men's baseball, basketball, and soccer. Intramural athletics are also available.

The College has a campus ministry office, a health office, and residence life, career placement, and counseling services.

Location

The College is located in Sparkill, a hamlet in southern Rockland County, New York, 16 miles north of New York City and adjacent to Bergen County, New Jersey. Rockland County, a sprawling suburban area of about 300,000 people, is rich in history and convenient to the vast cultural and educational resources of New York City.

Majors and Degrees

St. Thomas Aquinas College's Business Administration division awards Bachelor of Science (B.S.) degrees in accounting (and accounting as a dual degree with a Master of Business Administration degree), business administration, finance, and marketing. Minors are offered in business administration, international business, and management information systems. Specializations are offered in management relations/industrial and organizational psychology. The Humanities division awards Bachelor of Arts (B.A.) degrees in art therapy and fine arts and a B.S. in graphic design, which are all also offered as minors. B.A. degrees include communication arts, English, philosophy and religious studies, Romance languages, and Spanish. Communication arts, journalism, performing arts, public relations, Spanish, and writing are also offered as minors. The Natural Sciences and Mathematics division offers B.S. degrees in applied mathematics, computer and information sciences, and mathematics. B.S. degrees are offered in biology, forensic science, medical technology, and natural sciences. There are specializations in biology, chemistry, and physics. Dual-degree options are also offered and are described below. The Social Sciences division awards B.S. degrees in criminal justice, psychology, recreation and leisure studies, and social science and a B.A. in history. The division of teacher education offers programs in grades 1–6 childhood education, the same plus special education, and grades 7–12 adolescence education, the latter offering certification in biology, English, mathematics, natural science with either biology or chemistry, social sciences, and Spanish.

The College offers a five-year dual-degree program in mathematics/engineering with the George Washington University (GWU) or Manhattan College. Students study at St. Thomas for three years. After completion of their final two years at either GWU or Manhattan, they earn a B.S. in mathematics from STAC and a B.S. in engineering from one of the other two institutions. The College also offers several dual-degree options in biology: a dual degree in biology (B.S. from STAC) and biomedical engineering (M.S. from Polytechnic University), a dual degree in biology (B.S. from STAC) and physical therapy (D.P.T. from New York Medical College), a dual degree in biology (B.S. from STAC) and chiropractic (D.C. from New York Chiropractic College), and a dual degree in biology (B.S. from STAC) and podiatry (D.P.M. from New York College of Podiatric Medicine). There are several other strategic alliances, such as preferred admission to St. John's University School of Law in New York and a similar program with Barry University School of Law in Florida that includes scholarship funds. St. Thomas seeks out additional strategic opportunities for its undergraduate and graduate students on a regular basis; students should contact the College for information about new alliances.

Academic Programs

The College maintains academic flexibility and is committed to responding to the needs of individual students. The College strives to develop students who are not only generally educated but also possess advanced knowledge in specialized areas, are prepared for further study, and have the background to undertake fulfilling careers. To earn a bachelor's degree, students must complete a total of 120 semester hours, including a minimum of 51 credits in a core curriculum; complete all requirements for the specific major; and complete the final 30 hours at St. Thomas. The College awards up to 30 credits for life experience and up to 30 credits for achievement on the College-Level Examination Program (CLEP). The College operates on a semester calendar (quarterly on the M.B.A. level). Students may enroll in classes in the fall, winter (a one-month session), spring, and summer (three separate sessions). Classes are scheduled during the day and evening, and students are permitted considerable academic flexibility in planning their programs.

Students can pursue independent study and internships, and many majors require a field practicum. The College maintains an active Center for Academic Excellence as a resource for enhancing academic performance, and students are encouraged to meet regularly with faculty advisers for academic guidance and career direction.

Several unusual programs supplement the traditional academic areas. The College has a widely recognized program for college-age learning-disabled students, called the Pathways Program (at an additional cost). The College also participates in the New York State Higher Education Opportunity Program for economically and academically disadvantaged students and provides an Honors Program for exceptionally qualified students. The full-tuition-scholarship Honors Program includes summer study at Oxford University.

Off-Campus Programs

The College offers a campus interchange program involving three other fully accredited colleges (Barry University in Miami Shores, Florida; Dominican College of San Rafael in San Rafael, California; and Aquinas College in Grand Rapids, Michigan) through which a student may attend a semester at one of the participating colleges during the junior year.

The College offers courses at local businesses and industries and an associate degree program at West Point for eligible students at the United States Military Academy.

A study-abroad program is offered through the College, providing students with the opportunity to study at colleges and universities in such places as Brazil, Canada, England, France, Hungary, Ireland, Italy, Morocco, and Spain. Several other locations are available.

Academic Facilities

The College's most dramatic growth occurred during the last decade as it modernized to meet the challenges of the twenty-first century. Costello Hall houses the science laboratories, technology theaters, and Azarian-McCullough Art Gallery. Spellman Hall houses a multiroom technology corridor with a state-of-the-art communication studio, and technology and language labs. Lougheed Library provides a variety of online research opportunities for students. Aquinas Hall houses athletic facilities and a new fitness center. Maguire Hall is home to classrooms, art studios, and the Sullivan Theater, and Marian Hall houses accounting labs. Additional meeting areas are provided in the Romano Student-Alumni Center and in the two residence complexes, McNelis Commons and Aquinas Village.

Costs

For 2010–11, the tuition for full-time study (12 to 16 credits per semester) is $21,910. Room and board at the College Commons is expected to cost $10,300. Certain studio, laboratory, and computer courses carry fees.

Financial Aid

In 2009–10, 80 percent of the student body received financial aid. The College is committed to providing competent but needy students with the resources necessary to continue their education. Students who lack adequate financial resources should submit the Financial Aid Form to the College Scholarship Service and to the College. Financial aid is usually granted in a package of awards. Financial aid programs include Presidential Grants, special scholarships, athletic grants, Federal Pell Grants, Federal Supplemental Educational Opportunity Grants, New York State Tuition Assistance Program (TAP) grants, Federal Perkins Loans, Federal Stafford Student Loans, Federal PLUS loans, and Federal Work-Study Program awards.

St. Thomas rewards academic excellence with several scholarship tiers—from full tuition scholarships for its honors students, to partial academic and athletic scholarships, and need-based awards. It strives to partner with the student to make college education affordable. The College has one of the lowest private college tuition rates in New York State, and scholarships make it even more affordable. The College is also a member of the Yellow Ribbon program for veterans.

Faculty

The faculty has 70 full-time and 55 part-time members; 80 percent have terminal degrees. The student-faculty ratio is 18:1. All faculty members participate in the academic advising of students and serve on College committees. Many serve as advisers to extracurricular activities.

Student Government

The Student Government consists of elected members who officially represent the student body, are responsible for planning and implementing student-originated programs, and coordinate and oversee all extracurricular organizations. Through its various offices, students play a vital part in offering consultation on new policies, planning social and cultural events, managing student funds, and operating the judicial system. In addition, the All-College Forum, which is composed of elected students, faculty members, alumni, administrators, and trustees, meets regularly to discuss policies, procedures, long-range plans, and any problems affecting the College.

Admission Requirements

All applicants must have successfully completed an approved secondary school program or the equivalent, including 4 years in English, 3 years in mathematics, 3 years in science, 3 years of foreign language, and 4 years of social studies. Applicants whose high school background varies from the recommended pattern are considered if they demonstrate interest and ability. Freshman applicants must submit the application for admission, including an essay, high school transcripts, SAT or ACT scores, and their guidance counselor's recommendation. Transfer students must submit the application and official transcripts of all previous college work. An academic evaluation is prepared for every matriculant.

Application and Information

Candidates should submit completed application forms to the Admissions and Financial Aid Office and must request that their official transcripts be sent to the Admissions Office from their school. Students are notified of the admission decision on a rolling basis upon receipt of all the necessary credentials.

The College does not discriminate against students, faculty and staff members, and other beneficiaries on the basis of race, color, national origin, gender, age, sexual orientation, disability, marital status, genetic predisposition, carrier status, veteran status, or religious affiliation in admission to or in the provision of its programs and services. The Section 504 Coordinator, the Title IX Coordinator, and the Age Act Coordinator is the Executive Director of Human Resources, Marian Hall, 845-398-4038.

For more information or an application, students should contact:

Admissions and Financial Aid Office
St. Thomas Aquinas College
125 Route 340
Sparkill, New York 10976-1050
Phone: 800-999-STAC (toll-free)
Web site: http://www.stac.edu

A view of the campus at St.Thomas Aquinas College.

ST. THOMAS UNIVERSITY

MIAMI, FLORIDA

The University

Founded in 1961 by the Augustinian Order of Villanova, Pennsylvania, at the invitation of the late Most Reverend Coleman F. Carroll, the Archbishop of Miami, St. Thomas University has grown from an institution with an initial enrollment of 45 students to become one of Florida's most comprehensive Catholic coeducational universities, with more than 2,600 students in all programs of study. Founded originally as Biscayne College, the institution achieved university status in 1984 and changed its name to St. Thomas University. The University is sponsored by the Archdiocese of Miami and is accredited by the Southern Association of Colleges and Schools. At present, the undergraduate student population represents thirty-five states, the District of Columbia, Puerto Rico, the Virgin Islands, and sixty-five countries. Fifty-nine percent of the undergraduates are women; 20 percent of the undergraduates reside on campus.

The University is located in northwest Miami on a 140-acre campus with fifteen major buildings. The Student Center contains a student lounge, a bookstore, the rathskeller, and other facilities. Adjacent to the University's two dormitories are the dining hall and the University Inn.

Sports facilities include six tennis courts, a recreational swimming pool, two basketball courts, four baseball fields, a soccer field, and two football fields. As a member of the NAIA, St. Thomas supports men's varsity teams in baseball, golf, soccer, and tennis and women's varsity teams in fast-pitch softball, golf, soccer, tennis, and volleyball and men's and women's cross-country. In fall 2009, St. Thomas University will move to NCAA Division II, and it has added both men's and women's basketball.

The University offers a full range of cultural, governmental, and social activities, including publications and clubs. The Office of Campus Ministry provides liturgical celebrations in the University chapel and sponsors social justice and community service activities.

St. Thomas University offers a Master of Business Administration (M.B.A.); Master of International Business; Master of Science (M.S.) in educational administration, guidance and counseling, management, marriage and family therapy, mental health counseling, special education, and sports administration; Master of Accounting (M.Acc.); and Master of Arts (M.A.) degrees in communication arts and pastoral ministry. In addition, St. Thomas offers a Ph.D. in practical theology and an Ed.D. in educational leadership. The Ambassador Nicholas H. Morley Law Center was established in 1984 with a charter class of 160 students. St. Thomas University School of Law offers the Juris Doctor degree (J.D.) and is the only accredited Catholic law school south of Georgetown University's law school in Washington, D.C. The School of Law and the Graduate Studies Office offer four joint degree programs, including an M.B.A./J.D. in accounting and international business and an M.S./J.D. in marriage and family counseling and sports administration.

Location

Located midway between Fort Lauderdale and downtown Miami, the University is near numerous cultural and recreational facilities. In fact, St. Thomas is located approximately 1½ miles south of Pro Player Stadium, which is home to the Miami Dolphins. The area's subtropical climate allows students to enjoy the nearby Atlantic Ocean beaches and many other natural attractions, such as the Florida Keys, Everglades National Park, and state and county parks, throughout the year. A short drive from campus are Key Biscayne, Bal Harbour, Miami Beach, Fort Lauderdale, and other cities of Florida's Gold Coast. The city of Miami and surrounding Dade County, known as the "Gateway to South America," house an international banking and trade center and offer a truly cosmopolitan atmosphere.

Majors and Degrees

St. Thomas University awards the Bachelor of Arts (B.A.) or Bachelor of Business Administration (B.B.A.) degree through day and evening programs in twenty-eight major fields of study: accounting, biology, business management, communication arts, computer information systems, computer science, criminal justice, elementary education, English, environmental justice, finance, forensic science, global leadership, history, human services, international business, liberal studies, marketing, nursing (a 2+2 program with the University of Miami), pre-engineering (a 2+2 program with the Florida International University), political science, psychology, religious studies, secondary education (social studies), sports administration, and tourism and hospitality management. St. Thomas also offers a minor in environmental studies; preprofessional programs, which include dentistry, law, medicine, and veterinary studies; a joint B.A./J.D. program with the School of Law; and courses in French, humanities, Italian, philosophy, and South Florida regional studies.

Academic Programs

The University's academic calendar consists of two 15-week semesters, beginning in early September and in mid-January, along with two 6-week summer sessions.

To receive a bachelor's degree, students must complete at least 120 semester credits with a minimum grade point average of 2.0 overall and an average of at least 2.25 in their academic major; 30 of the last 36 semester credit hours must be earned and at least half of a student's academic major courses must be taken at St. Thomas University. All students must fulfill the general core education requirements of 42 semester credits, which include courses in English, humanities/foreign language, history, social science, mathematics/physical science, philosophy, and religious studies. An honors program is offered to qualified students to provide them with an interesting, stimulating, alternative way of fulfilling some or all of the University's general education requirements. The normal full-time academic load is 15 semester credit hours, but the load may range between 12 and 18 credit hours per semester. To graduate, all students must take an area of concentration or an academic major. A student may enter as an exploratory or undecided student but, with the assistance of a faculty adviser or a division chairperson, must declare his or her academic major by the second semester of the sophomore year.

Special academic features at the University include the Academic Support Center, Institute for Pastoral Ministries, summer school, and study abroad.

Off-Campus Programs

Internships are offered in nearly every academic major. A cooperative education program is also available. In addition, qualified students may participate in the Semester Abroad Program in Spain.

Academic Facilities

The 50,000-square-foot library houses a 145,000-volume book collection, 850 periodicals, a reference room, a technical processing area, a convocation hall that seats 600 people, four seminar rooms for small classes and group study, and a Media Center with two screening rooms, a video studio, and an audiovisual laboratory with individually wired carrels. Kennedy Hall, the University's main academic center, includes administrative offices, classrooms, science laboratories, the Academic Support Center, the chapel, and a computer lab.

Costs

Tuition for the 2009–10 academic year was $21,690 ($723 per undergraduate semester credit hour), and room and board costs were $6516 for a double room and $10154 for a single room. Insurance, which is mandatory for all resident students, was estimated at $925 for the year. These costs do not include books, supplies, travel, and personal expenses and are subject to change.

Financial Aid

The University has established a financial aid program to assist as many students as possible. University scholarships and grants, along with federally funded scholarships, grants, loans, and work-study awards, are allocated in a financial aid package according to a student's financial need. Currently, about 92 percent of the University's students receive financial aid. Of all financial aid recipients, 90 percent receive University scholarships and grants. To be eligible for any scholarship or financial aid program, an applicant should complete a Free Application for Federal Student Aid (FAFSA) with the Department of Education. The filing deadline for University financial aid funds is April 1. Applicants should indicate affirmatively on the FAFSA that their information may be forwarded from the U.S. Department of Education in order to be considered for any state grants for which they may be eligible. The application deadline for need-based state financial aid programs is April 1.

Florida applicants who have resided in Florida for the prior twelve consecutive months are eligible to be awarded a Florida Resident Access Grant to attend a private four-year college or university in Florida. The funds for the Florida Resident Grant Program are dependent upon yearly appropriations from the Florida legislature. These funds are outright grants and are not based on financial need.

Faculty

The St. Thomas University faculty is a teaching faculty that is dedicated to furthering the academic and personal growth of students. The undergraduate student-faculty ratio is 14:1. Faculty-student interaction is a hallmark of the University because classes are small and because members of the faculty are available outside the classroom. Faculty members also participate in the academic advisement program to give students individual academic guidance, and they serve as advisers to student clubs and organizations.

Student Government

The Undergraduate Student Government Association, of which all full-time undergraduates are members, provides students with the opportunity to become involved in representative government. This democratic body is governed by elected student officers who serve on the Administrative Council and by representatives from each class who compose the Student Assembly. The association also assists in planning a varied program of social and cultural activities. In addition, students are represented on key committees throughout the University community. The Resident Council, consisting of representatives from each of the four dormitories, voices the concerns of residential students and is involved in the planning and implementation of University policies regarding residential life.

Admission Requirements

St. Thomas University seeks academically prepared students who are eager to improve themselves intellectually, socially, and spiritually within the University community. The Admissions Committee evaluates applicants individually in light of personal accomplishments, motivation, and the academic major selected. The committee places primary emphasis on the secondary school record, SAT or ACT scores, class rank, a personal interview, a recommended 250- to 300-word personal essay, and a teacher's or guidance counselor's recommendation. The committee does not discriminate against applicants on the basis of race, sex, religion, or national origin; in fact, the University welcomes diversity. Applicants for most divisions must have earned 16 units from an accredited high school in a college-preparatory program that included 4 years of English, 2 years of mathematics, 2 years of social studies, 1 year of science, 1 year of a foreign language or computer elective, and six electives; applicants for the Division of Science must have earned 17 units, including 3 years of mathematics (including trigonometry) and 3 years of science, but they need have only four electives. All international applicants for either freshman or transfer entrance must also submit letters of financial guarantee.

The University offers deferred admission and dual enrollment. It also gives credit and advanced placement for scores of 3 or better on the Advanced Placement examinations of the College Board. Credit is also awarded for successful scores on both the general and subject tests of the College Board's College-Level Examination Program.

Transfer applicants should be in good academic standing with a GPA of at least 2.5 and not be on disciplinary or academic probation at their former college. The University grants junior-year status to any admitted transfer student graduating from a Florida community college with an Associate of Arts degree. Transfer applicants must submit official transcripts from each of their previous colleges.

Application and Information

To facilitate the admission and financial aid processes, students should submit applications during the fall or winter of their senior year in high school and have all supporting material forwarded directly to the University's Undergraduate Admissions Office. Application for entrance as a resident student for the fall semester should be filed by May 15; for entrance as a commuting student, by August 1. Application for the spring semester should be made by December 15. The University operates with a policy of rolling admissions; beginning December 15, applicants for the fall semester are notified of the admission decision within a three-week period provided that all appropriate information has been received. The University adheres to the College Board's Candidates Reply Date of May 1 and does not require a tuition deposit or a room reservation deposit until May 1 in order to allow students ample opportunity to select the college or university of their choice. Dormitory space, however, is limited and is assigned in the order that room reservation deposits are received.

For further information, students should contact:

St. Thomas University
Office of Admissions
Kennedy Hall
16401 Northwest 37th Avenue
Miami Gardens, Florida 33054
Phone: 305-628-6546
800-367-9010 (toll-free outside Florida)
800-367-9006 (toll-free in Florida)
Fax: 305-628-6591
E-mail: signup@stu.edu
Web site: http://www.stu.edu

SALISBURY UNIVERSITY

SALISBURY, MARYLAND

The University

A Maryland University of National Distinction, Salisbury University (SU) consistently ranks in the top 10 percent of public and private institutions in national guidebooks and magazines. A member of the University System of Maryland (USM), SU emphasizes undergraduate research, study abroad, professional internships, and community engagement as pillars of its academic programs.

A midsize university of over 7,500 undergraduates and 380 full-time faculty on a 182-acre campus, SU provides a private college feel with the opportunities and affordability of a public institution. This distinct combination is why 98 percent of recent graduates say they would recommend SU based on their experience. The foundation of SU's success is the relationship between students and professors. Full professors serve as undergraduate advisers, and routinely lead students on trips and retreats, from exploring the Chesapeake Bay to touring Europe and beyond. Their professional concern for educating the whole student has had measurable results. According to the latest figures, SU has the fastest time-to-degree average and the highest four-year graduation rate of all comprehensive institutions in the USM. This success has not gone unnoticed. For the thirteenth consecutive year, SU is one of *U.S. News & World Report*'s "Top Public Universities–Master's category (North)," the highest-placing public master's-level university in Maryland. Similar kudos comes from the Princeton Review's guides and *Kiplinger's Personal Finance* magazine which, respectively, have again named SU among the top 50 and top 100 "Best Value" public colleges in the nation.

Salisbury students come from thirty states, the District of Columbia, and fifty-four other countries. Some 56 percent are from Maryland's western shore (which contains the Metropolitan Baltimore-Washington corridor). Many of SU's 100-plus student organizations and clubs find a home in the Guerrieri University Center. An NCAA Division III member of intercollegiate athletics, SU has twenty-one varsity sports that compete in the Capital Athletic Conference and in the Atlantic Central Football Conference. Women's sports are basketball, cross-country, field hockey, lacrosse, soccer, softball, swimming, tennis, track and field, and volleyball. Men's sports are baseball, basketball, cross-country, football, lacrosse, soccer, swimming, tennis, and track and field. The Sea Gulls have won thirteen national championships, eight in men's lacrosse and five in field hockey. One of the leading Division III programs, for the eighth time in school history, Salisbury athletics have been ranked in the top 25 of the national Directors' Cup standings. Nearly half of the student body participates in twenty-two intramural programs and thirteen additional sports clubs.

The University has three art galleries; supports film and distinguished lecture series and artist-in-residence programs; maintains WSCL/WSDL-FM (national public radio affiliates) and WXSU-FM (a student-run radio station); offers performing arts disciplines in music, theater, and dance; and serves as the home of the Salisbury Symphony Orchestra. Beyond the campus are Maryland's scenic Eastern Shore, the pleasures of Ocean City, Maryland (a nearby popular beach resort), and the activities of an energetic Outdoor Club. Faculty members lead trips abroad during winter and summer terms.

The University also offers thirteen graduate programs.

Location

With a population of 89,000, metropolitan Salisbury is the cultural and economic hub of Delmarva (containing portions of Delaware, Maryland, and Virginia), a historically and ecologically rich peninsula located between the Atlantic Ocean and Chesapeake Bay. The city is 30 minutes west of the white beaches of Assateague and Ocean City, Maryland; approximately 2 hours from Baltimore, Wilmington, Norfolk, and Washington, D.C.; and 4½ hours from New York City.

Majors and Degrees

Three undergraduate degrees are offered in addition to the Bachelor of Arts and Bachelor of Science: the Bachelor of Arts in Social Work (B.A.S.W.), the Bachelor of Science in Nursing (B.S.N.), and the Bachelor of Fine Arts (B.F.A.) in art. B.A. degrees are awarded in art, communication arts, conflict analysis and dispute resolution, economics, English, English for speakers of other languages, environmental issues, fine arts, French, history, interdisciplinary studies, international studies, music, philosophy, political science, psychology, sociology, Spanish, and theater. Bachelor of Science degrees are awarded in accounting, athletic training, biology, business administration, chemistry, clinical laboratory science/medical technology, computer science, early childhood education, elementary education, exercise science, finance, geography and geosciences, health education, interdisciplinary studies, management, management information systems, marketing, mathematics, nursing, physical education, physics, and respiratory therapy.

Academic Programs

At Salisbury University, majors are designed to educate the whole student. No false distinctions are made between the liberal arts and the professions. While gaining a liberal education, for example, students in preprofessional programs prepare for careers in dentistry, law, medicine, optometry, pharmacy, physical therapy, podiatry, and veterinary science. Certification programs train educators for both elementary and secondary teaching. Dual-degree programs with the University of Maryland Eastern Shore (UMES) enable students to earn two bachelor's degrees in four years in biology/environmental marine science and social work/sociology. SU, UMES, and the University of Maryland College Park also collaborate on an electrical engineering degree. In addition, SU supports an Army Reserve Officers' Training Corps (ROTC) program on campus. Both the graduate and the undergraduate programs of SU's business school are accredited by The Association to Advance Collegiate Schools of Business and the Network of International Business Schools. Other national accreditations are in chemistry, education, allied health (respiratory therapy, exercise science, and athletic training programs), social work, clinical laboratory science (medical technology program), music, and nursing and through the Middle States Commission on Higher Education.

SU's fifty-five academic programs are administered through four schools: the Franklin P. Perdue School of Business, the Samuel W. and Marilyn C. Seidel School of Education and Professional Studies, the Charles R. and Martha N. Fulton School of Liberal Arts, and the Richard A. Henson School of Science and Technology. All four schools are endowed, a rarity among public institutions nationwide. These endowments have enriched the scholastic climate of the campus, providing expanded scholarships, resources, and opportunities.

University planning encourages interdisciplinary study. Students in all majors must take a minimum of nine courses in three disciplines: history, humanities and social sciences, and mathematical and natural sciences. Two courses are required in English composition and literature. All courses, from science to business to music, require written assignments in analysis/criticism, research, or creative writing.

SU's advising system has been praised by students in a Maryland Higher Education Commission survey as one of the best in the state. Exceptional orientation programs for students and parents help freshmen make a successful transition from home to college. For example, SU's New Student Seminars offer an orientation-in-the-wilderness experience, which won the Maryland Association for Higher Education Distinguished Program Award. Orientation options include cycling in Maine and canoeing in Canada.

Incoming students may earn credit through Advanced Placement and departmental challenge examinations and the College-Level Examination Program (CLEP) for nontraditional educational experiences. Internships have included work abroad; legislative service in Washington, D.C., and Annapolis; and media experience in fields from fine arts to television. Students who relish intellectual challenge are invited to join the honors program housed in the Thomas E. Bellavance Honors Center. Others present research at national and international conferences. SU is also the only university in Maryland to twice host some 2,800 of the country's top scholars for the National Conference on Undergraduate Research. Study-abroad programs are popular. For example, business majors study economics in China and France, education students teach elementary children in New Zealand, and nursing students provide aid in Africa.

Academic Facilities

The SU campus is in the midst of an extensive transformation. In addition to a recent 19-acre land acquisition, construction is underway for a new 600-bed residence hall and commercial complex, scheduled to open in 2011, the same year as a new home for the Perdue School of Business. SU has also initiated a multimillion-dollar renovation program for its older residence halls. The campus' first parking garage opened in fall 2009. SU is pursuing the U.S. Green Building Council's LEED Silver certification, at a minimum, for all construction projects. New in 2008 was the University Fitness Center and SU's new $65-million, 165,000-square-foot Teacher Education and Technology Center, lauded as a showcase facility for education in the mid-Atlantic region. The building, with its award-winning design, was the first on Maryland's Eastern Shore to earn LEED Silver certification. With $5.3 million in new technology equipment, it features Smart classrooms and an Integrated Media Center with a 24-track audio recording studio, 15 editing suites, a cutting-edge digital exhibition gallery, a digital photography lab and one of the few campus-based high-definition digital video production studios in the nation.

In 2002, classes began in Henson Science Hall, SU's $42-million science education and research building, one of the largest in Maryland. Blackwell Library is the main research center on campus, with more than a quarter of a million books and bound periodicals and computers with access to databases, such as FirstSearch. Twelve computer labs are part of the campus Novell network, which provides students with various software applications, e-mail, and the Internet. Resident students have network connections in their rooms and all academic and administrative buildings now offer wireless Internet access. Fulton Hall is home to the fine and performing arts, and the Center for Conflict Resolution engages students in mediation efforts at home and abroad. The only institution in the USM with an endowed theater program, SU boasts three theaters for performing arts, including the acoustically lauded Holloway Hall Auditorium. Off the main campus, the Edward H. Nabb Research Center for Delmarva History and Culture is a treasure trove of information for students and visitors. SU's Ward Museum of Wildfowl Art was named one of the "10 Great Places to See American Folk Art" by *USA Today*.

Costs

Maryland residents paid undergraduate tuition and fees of $6618 for the academic year. Tuition for out-of-state undergraduates was $15,114. Students living on campus paid about $7800 for room and board; the figure varies, depending on the residence hall and meal plan.

Financial Aid

Financial assistance is available to students through loans, grants, scholarships, and on- and off-campus employment. The University participates in the Federal Perkins Loan, Federal Pell Grant, Federal Supplemental Educational Opportunity Grant, and Federal Work-Study and Direct Loan Programs. Numerous other forms of financial aid on the state and local levels are based exclusively on demonstrated financial need. All students who wish to apply for financial assistance must complete the Free Application for Federal Student Aid (FAFSA) by February 15. Complete details are available through the University's Admissions and Financial Aid Offices.

Through the University's Work Experience Program, which has a budget in excess of $2 million and provides employment for one quarter of the student body, students may be assigned to jobs related to their academic interest. They can earn approximately $1500 to $2000 per semester by working 10 to 20 hours a week. Non-need academic scholarships for incoming freshmen are awarded on the basis of high school performance and SAT scores. Application for admission to the University is the initial step in applying for these scholarships.

Faculty

Faculty members at Salisbury have won national teaching, research, and leadership awards. Ninety-two percent of the tenure-track faculty members, many of whom are National Endowment for the Humanities and Fulbright professors, have the Ph.D. or other highest degree in their field. Professors not only publish but also donate countless hours to community service, thus teaching by deed as well as word. The student-professor ratio is 17:1; smaller classes are not unusual.

Student Government

Shared governance is a hallmark of campus life, and students are actively involved in all its aspects. The Student Government Association (SGA) serves as a liaison between the faculty and administration for students. SGA officers serve on many University committees, both administrative and academic, including the President's Advisory Team. The all-student Appropriations Board budgets student activity fees to clubs and organizations. Students are encouraged to participate in a full complement of events, many sponsored by the Student Organization for Activity Planning.

Admission Requirements

The University seeks to admit outstanding students who bring diverse talents, experiences, and points of view to campus. Most successful candidates for admission have earned above-average high school grades in a strong academic program and a score above the national average on the SAT or ACT. The high school record, test scores, essay, and recommendations of the high school principal and guidance counselors are considered. Interviews are not required, but applicants are encouraged to discuss programs and procedures for housing and financial aid with the staff of the Admissions and Financial Aid Offices.

The University has introduced an SAT/ACT optional admissions policy. Applicants who have earned a weighted grade point average of 3.5 or higher on a 4.0 scale have the choice of submitting a standardized test score. The SAT or ACT is required for applicants with a weighted grade point average below 3.5 or who wish to be considered for University scholarships.

Transfer students must have earned at least 24 semester hours at an accredited community college or four-year college or university and have a minimum 2.0 average (on a 4.0 scale). For transfer students who have attempted fewer than 24 hours at another institution, the University's admission policy for entering freshmen applies.

Application and Information

Applications are accepted beginning September 1 for the spring and fall semesters. Applications received by November 1 for the spring semester and by January 15 for the fall semester are given the fullest attention. The University reserves the right to close admissions when the projected enrollment is met. The application is available online at http://www.salisbury.edu/apply. For further information, students should contact:

Admissions Office
Salisbury University
1200 Camden Avenue
Salisbury, Maryland 21801-6862
Phone: 410-543-6161
888-543-0148 (toll-free)
Fax: 410-546-6016
E-mail: admissions@salisbury.edu
Web site: http://www.salisbury.edu

Salisbury University's Teacher Education and Technology Center opened in fall 2008.

COLLEGE CLOSE-UPS

SAMFORD UNIVERSITY

BIRMINGHAM, ALABAMA

The University

Samford University is a private, comprehensive liberal arts university with high academic standards. The University's well-prepared, accessible faculty members who take time to know and interact with students are responsible for its academic reputation. Samford, which has some 4,500 students, offers a wide range of extracurricular activities diverse enough to satisfy the social, cultural, physical, and spiritual needs of all of its students. A lively Greek system; an honors program; men's and women's intramural and varsity athletics, including seventeen NCAA Division I sports; music and drama groups; an award-winning debate program; and more than 100 other interest groups bond the students and faculty members into a community of friends and scholars. Students annually come from about forty-five states and more than thirty countries. A majority of undergraduate students live on campus, enhancing the sense of school spirit and involvement. Students enjoy modern recreational facilities, including a fitness/wellness center, concert and recital halls, a theater, an indoor pool, racquetball and tennis courts, and an indoor track. Comfortable housing, including modern apartment-style units and fraternity/sorority residence facilities, is available.

Samford University is in the top tier of the 262 national institutions in the doctoral research university category, as published by *U.S. News & World Report;* was marked as "very competitive" by *Barron's Profiles of American Colleges;* and has been selected for *Peterson's Competitive Colleges.* Samford was ranked twenty-seventh among national universities by *Forbes* in a study conducted by the Center for College Affordability and Productivity. Its programs are also included in *The Templeton Guide: Colleges that Encourage Character Development.*

Special student services include an active Career Development Center, which offers guidance in career exploration as well as ample opportunities for placement interviews, and an Academic Success Center for first-year students. Externship programs add work experience and business contacts to the rewards of achievement and income for the participants. The externship program can be an excellent source of financial assistance that complements the scholarship and federal aid programs available to Samford students.

In addition to its extensive undergraduate program, Samford University grants the following graduate degrees: Doctor of Education in educational leadership, Doctor of Ministry, Doctor of Pharmacy, Doctor of Nursing Practice, Educational Specialist, Juris Doctor, Master of Accountancy, Master of Business Administration, Master of Comparative Law, Master of Divinity, Master of Science in Environmental Management, Master of Music, Master of Music Education, Master of Science in Education, Master of Science in Nursing, and Master of Theological Studies. Several joint graduate degree programs are also available.

Location

Samford's wooded 180-acre campus, with its Georgian architecture, is one of the most beautiful in the nation. Located in the picturesque, mountainous area of Shades Valley, the campus is less than 6 miles from the heart of Birmingham, Alabama's largest city and the state's industrial, business, and cultural center. Birmingham annually hosts the Regions Charity Classic Professional Golf Association Champions Tournament and other major sports events. The city attracts national entertainment acts to its civic center, historic Alabama Theater, and Oak Mountain Outdoor Amphitheater. Gulf Coast beaches to the south and ski slopes to the north can be reached within 4½ hours by car. The world's largest space and rocket museum, located in Huntsville, Alabama, is also only a short drive away. Alabama's abundant freshwater lakes and rivers are sites for enjoyable outings. One of the South's largest shopping centers, the Riverchase Galleria, is only 7 miles from the Samford campus. Samford students enjoy the best of two worlds: a suburban setting for study, contemplation, and social enjoyment and easy access to the varied offerings of a metropolitan area.

Majors and Degrees

Samford University offers an Associate of Science (A.S.) degree in the following concentrations: administrative/community services and natural/environmental sciences.

The Bachelor of Arts (B.A.) degree is attained through the following majors: classics, communication studies, English, English (with a concentration in film studies), family studies, fine arts, fine arts (with a concentration in graphic design), French, German, Greek, history, interior design, journalism and mass communication, Latin, music, musical theater, philosophy, philosophy and religion, physics, political science, psychology, religion, religion (with a concentration in congregational studies), sociology, Spanish, and theater. The interdisciplinary concentrations offered in the Bachelor of Arts degree are Asian studies, international relations, language and world trade (with a specialty in French, German, Spanish, or world languages), Latin American studies, and public administration.

The University's evening degree program offers the Bachelor of Science in Interdisciplinary Studies (B.S.I.S.) degree in the following concentrations: administrative/community services, counseling foundations, manager and leadership development, and liberal studies.

The Bachelor of Music (B.M.) degree is offered in the following majors: church music, music, music education (instrumental, vocal, and choral), music theory/composition, musical theater, performance (instrumental, organ, piano, and voice), and performance with a pedagogy emphasis (piano).

Students can earn a Bachelor of Science (B.S.) degree through the following majors: athletic training, biochemistry, biology, biology (with an emphasis in marine science), chemistry, computer science, engineering and mathematics (dual degree), engineering and physics (dual degree), engineering physics, environmental science, exercise science, fine arts, fine arts (with a concentration in graphic design), fitness and health promotion, fitness and health promotion/nutrition and dietetics (dual major), geography, mathematics, music, nutrition and dietetics, physics, and sports medicine (premedicine). The interdisciplinary concentrations offered in the B.S. degree are biochemistry and environmental science/geographic information science.

The University offers the Bachelor of Science in Business Administration (B.S.B.A.) in the following majors: accounting, economics, entrepreneurship, finance, management, and marketing.

The Bachelor of Science in Education (B.S.E.) is attained through the following majors: early childhood/special education/elementary/collaborative teacher education, English/language arts education, history/social science education, physical education, physical education (with athletic training option), P–12 education, secondary education, and teacher education.

The University offers the Bachelor of Science in Nursing (B.S.N.) in the nursing major.

Various preprofessional programs are offered, including dentistry, engineering, law, medicine, optometry, pharmacy, and veterinary medicine.

The Degree with Honors is available to students whose academic achievement is remarkable.

Academic Programs

In order to graduate, students must complete a minimum of 128 semester credits with an average grade of C or better. Six courses make up the core curriculum: Cultural Perspectives I and II, Communication Arts I and II, Biblical Perspectives, and Concepts of Fitness and Health. The curriculum is designed to address ideas and issues that cross the usual disciplinary boundaries and to help students actively engage in learning rather than simply memorizing notes for an exam. The core is also designed to promote a global perspective, recognizing the influence and achievement of many cultures.

Students also complete several education courses to prepare them for work in a major field and/or to help them experience the sciences, the social sciences, the humanities, and the fine arts.

At least 40 credits must be earned in junior- and senior-level courses. At least 50 percent of credits must be earned at Samford University. Between the end of the sophomore year and graduation, undergraduate students (including transfer students) must pass a writing proficiency test.

The new University Fellows program is a highly selective, academically rigorous, honors program that includes a focus on great texts and a study abroad opportunity in the sophomore year.

Off-Campus Programs

The international studies program at Samford's Daniel House Study Centre in London, England, or a variety of other locations (Austria, Canada, China, Costa Rica, Ecuador, France, Germany, Greece, Italy, Japan, Mexico, Peru, Portugal, Russia, Spain, and Switzerland) offers opportunities to develop a broad worldview.

Academic Facilities

The Harwell Goodwin Davis Library furnishes the facilities and materials necessary for reference, research, and independent study. Its reading areas with individual carrels provide ideal working conditions for Samford students. The open-stack system allows students easy access to a collection of more than 1 million volumes of books, periodicals, microfilm and microfiche, records, and tape. The library annually adds 7,000 volumes and 2,600 government documents. The library's Multimedia Collection houses the Religious Education Curriculum Laboratory and provides audiovisual aids and hardware, computers, and computer software. A staff of professional librarians guides students in the use of the fully equipped library. The Alabama Baptist Historical Commission's collection of Baptist church records and other important historical materials is located in the library and maintained by the Special Collection Department. Historical documents are also preserved through an active microfilming program. The Samford library system includes the Lucille Stewart Beeson Law Library, which has more than 232,850 volumes; the Education Curriculum Laboratory; the Global Drug Information Center; the Global Center; and the Music Library, which has more than 8,000 CDs, records, scores, and audiocassettes. University library holdings are accessed through a state-of-the-art library system. Other libraries in the Birmingham area cooperate with Samford on a reciprocal basis.

Costs

The cost of attending Samford is significantly lower than that of many institutions of comparable size and commitment to quality. The basic charge for 2009–10, including tuition ($20,200), room, and board, is about $27,600. The typical student spends about $750 per year for books and supplies.

Financial Aid

At Samford University, a student's educational costs are frequently offset by scholarship and other financial assistance programs, which annually total more than $20 million. The application for admission also serves as the application for merit-based scholarships. Students interested in need-based opportunities should complete the Free Application for Federal Student Aid (FAFSA) by the March 1 priority filing date. In addition, non-need-based scholarship awards, usually based on academic merit, range up to full tuition.

Faculty

Samford's faculty consists of 275 full-time and about 160 part-time members, who have earned academic degrees from universities throughout the world. All classes are taught by members of the faculty; the faculty-student ratio is 1:11. Faculty members serve as academic advisers and also serve on many University committees.

Student Government

The Student Government Association (SGA) provides an excellent opportunity for students to participate in and influence governance. The SGA has autonomy in many programs, activities, and budgetary decisions; through the Student Senate, proposals related to improving campus life are sent to the University administration for consideration. The largest SGA organization is the Student Activities Council. Its committees provide a variety of activities, including concerts, lectures, dances, and outdoor recreation. The largest student-run activity is Step Sing, an annual variety show involving several hundred students that fills the 2,700-seat concert hall for three consecutive nights. Students are also involved in disciplining students who do not live up to University values. Alcohol is not permitted on campus.

Admission Requirements

Samford University seeks to enroll students capable of success in a challenging academic environment. Every applicant is evaluated individually on the basis of academic preparedness and potential, as well as personal fit with the mission and purpose of the University. The Admission Committee considers factors such as the strength of the high school curriculum, grade point average, standardized test scores, demonstrated leadership skills, and recommendations. The freshman class that entered in 2007 possessed an ACT composite middle 50 percent range of 22 to 28; the SAT middle 50 percent range was 1010 to 1230. The average high school grade point average of the entering class was 3.61. These statistics continue to demonstrate the competitive environment of Samford. International students must also demonstrate proficiency on the Test of English as a Foreign Language (TOEFL). Transfer students should have completed at least 24 semester hours or 36 quarter hours and maintained at least a 2.5 cumulative grade point average. Early admission is available to high school juniors who present an outstanding academic record and the recommendations of their parents and principal. Credit can be earned through I.B. and Advanced Placement tests. One school recommendation and an essay are required of every applicant, and a campus visit is strongly recommended.

Application and Information

Applications are received and notifications processed on a monthly rolling basis beginning in October. Students may also apply online by visiting the University's Web site. Applications are accepted until the class is filled.

Application inquiries should be addressed to:

Jason E. Black
Acting Dean of Admission
Samford University
800 Lakeshore Dr.
Birmingham, Alabama 35229
Phone: 205-726-3673
800-888-7218 (toll-free)
Web site: http://www.samford.edu/admission

The Harwell G. Davis Library on the campus of Samford University.

SARAH LAWRENCE COLLEGE

BRONXVILLE, NEW YORK

The College

Sarah Lawrence College is a model for individualized education among liberal arts colleges. It offers an innovative program of study that encourages students to take intellectual risks and explore highly challenging topics as they take an active role in the planning and pursuit of their education.

The College's forty-six buildings are set on a 44-acre campus combining the charm of a rural English village with award-winning contemporary buildings. There are 1,367 undergraduates and 334 graduate students. Approximately 40 students attend the Center for Continuing Education, which is a flexible, supportive program for returning adult students. The College draws its students from across the country and around the world. Nearly 90 percent live on campus. Sarah Lawrence has an active campus, offering opportunities for involvement in clubs, student organizations, dramatic productions, musical performances, literary societies, student publications, student government, and athletics. There are no sororities or fraternities.

The College is accredited by the Middle States Association of Colleges and Schools and approved by the New York State Education Department.

On the graduate level, the College offers programs in writing, theater, dance, human genetics, health advocacy, art of teaching, child development, and women's history. A dual degree in child development and social work is offered with the New York University School of Social Work, and a joint degree in women's history and law is offered in cooperation with Pace University Law School. The College also offers a 3-2 program in which the student receives a Bachelor of Arts in the Liberal Arts from Sarah Lawrence College and a Bachelor of Science in Engineering from Columbia University. There are also 3-2 master's programs with the College's Art of Teaching and Women's History graduate departments.

Location

Sarah Lawrence is located in southern Westchester County, 15 miles north of midtown Manhattan. Highways and the railroad make it possible to reach the city in 30 minutes, enabling students to take advantage of a wide range of social and cultural riches as well as internship possibilities in New York City. Students obtain internships in the arts, business, communications, law, medicine, publishing, social services, theater, and the non-profit sector.

Majors and Degrees

Sarah Lawrence grants the Bachelor of Arts in liberal arts degree to undergraduate students. The academic program is divided into four divisions: history and the social sciences, consisting of anthropology, economics, history, political science, psychology, public policy, science technology and society, and sociology; humanities, consisting of art history, Asian studies, film history, languages, literature, music history, philosophy, and religion; natural sciences and mathematics, consisting of biology, chemistry, mathematics, physics, and computer science; and creative and performing arts, consisting of dance, music, theater, writing, and visual arts (drawing, filmmaking, painting, photography, printmaking, and sculpture). There are no majors or required courses, but students are expected to work in at least three of the four divisions.

Academic Programs

Each student works with his or her faculty adviser, called a don after the Oxford and Cambridge tradition, to plan a course of study. Most courses consist of two parts: the seminar, limited to 15 students, and the conference, a private, biweekly meeting with the seminar professor. In conference, students create individual projects that extend the material assigned in the seminar and connect it to their academic and career goals. In the performing arts—dance, music, and theater—students' work makes up several components that together constitute a full course. Although transcripts of official grades are available, written evaluations that more clearly define strengths, weaknesses, and progress are provided to each student.

The College operates on the semester system, with terms beginning in early September and late January.

Off-Campus Programs

Within the U.S., Sarah Lawrence College has established exchange programs with Reed College in Portland, Oregon; Spelman College in Atlanta, Georgia; Pitzer College in Claremont, California; California Institute of the Arts in Valencia, California; and Eugene Lang College, the undergraduate division of New School University in New York City's historic Greenwich Village. Outside the United States, the College sponsors academic programs in Florence, Catania (Sicily), Havana, Oxford, and Paris as well as a program in cooperation with the British American Drama Academy in London and Dartington College of Art at the University of Falmouth, England. Students may also study in other countries around the world. Students can combine on-campus study with off-campus fieldwork and internships at a variety of places, including art museums, theaters, and hospitals and with orchestras, dance companies, publications, social action programs, government agencies, and businesses.

Academic Facilities

The College's facilities include classrooms, laboratories, and computer centers; a collegewide academic network to which all students' rooms are fully wired; wireless access points to the Internet throughout the entire campus; a library with 283,000 volumes and 916 periodicals, which is linked by computer to more than 6,000 other libraries; the Performing Arts Center, consisting of four theaters, a dance studio, and a concert hall; a music building, including a music library; a Sports Center with a competition pool, basketball and squash courts, a fitness center, an aerobics room, and a rowing tank; a laboratory preschool; a science center; and the Center for Continuing Education. A 60,000-square-foot visual arts center includes a 200-seat lecture hall/film theater, a café, new media facilities, a sound stage, darkrooms, workshops, printmaking facilities, and eight studios—each with individual work areas for sculpture, painting, and visual fundamentals.

Costs

Tuition for the 2009–10 academic year was $41,040. The costs of room and the average meal plan were $13,370. The College fee was $928.

Financial Aid

All applicants with financial need are considered for Sarah Lawrence College aid programs and all federal campus-based programs. Over half of the students receive financial aid. The awarding of institutional funds is based on a determination of the student's financial need. Students are expected to apply for financial aid from the Federal Pell Grant Program and from their state scholarship and grant programs. Students must submit the Financial Aid PROFILE and the Free Application for Federal Student Aid (FAFSA) by February 1.

Faculty

Sarah Lawrence's student-faculty ratio is 9:1, one of the lowest in the country. Students work closely with an exceptional faculty of respected scholars, writers, artists, scientists, historians, and social scientists. Each faculty member is a committed teacher who attaches great importance to individual work with students. Ninety percent of Sarah Lawrence's faculty members in the sciences, social sciences, and the humanities hold a Ph.D. or terminal degree. Faculty members in the arts have achieved demonstrable excellence in the fields of music, dance, theater, the visual arts, and writing; many of them are acclaimed in their respective fields and include published authors and practicing professionals.

Student Government

The Sarah Lawrence College student body is self-governed by the Student Senate and the Student Life Committee. The Student Senate is the principal policymaking and legislative body for matters concerning student affairs.

Admission Requirements

Sarah Lawrence College accepts first-year students for the fall semester and transfer applicants for both the fall and spring semesters. The College recognizes that intelligence and creativity can be expressed in many different ways and is willing to look at both traditional and nontraditional criteria in assessing applicants. The completion of 16 units of secondary school work or the equivalent is the standard academic requirement for first-year admission. The College specifies these units as follows: 4 units required of English; a minimum of 2 units required (3–4 units recommended) each of mathematics, science, foreign language, and history; and 3–4 units recommended of social studies.

High school seniors who consider Sarah Lawrence their first-choice college and who wish to be informed of an admission decision early in their senior year may apply as early decision candidates. The Admission Committee also considers as early admission applicants those students with very strong academic qualifications and personal maturity who have completed three years of high school and who wish to apply after their junior year of high school.

The College welcomes transfer applications from students who have completed at least one full year of college and from students who expect, in qualifying for the Bachelor of Arts degree, to spend at least two consecutive years at Sarah Lawrence College. (Students with less than one full year of credits who have matriculated at another college may apply for first-year admission with possible advanced standing.) Approximately 50 transfers matriculate each year from a wide range of postsecondary institutions.

Sophomores, juniors, and seniors enrolled at other institutions may apply to the Sarah Lawrence Guest Year Program for one semester or a complete year of full-time study at the College. Guests attend Sarah Lawrence to concentrate in a particular discipline not offered at their home institution, work with respected teachers one-on-one in conferences, and take advantage of the facilities of New York City in conjunction with rigorous academic study. Students who have not matriculated elsewhere but wish to enroll in one or two specific courses for credit may apply as nonmatriculated students.

Sarah Lawrence does not consider the SAT or ACT scores in the application process. The Test of English as a Foreign Language (TOEFL) must be taken by students who speak English as a second language and who have not been educated in an English-language medium. A personal interview on campus or with a local alumna/alumnus is strongly recommended for all applicants.

Sarah Lawrence College admits students regardless of race, color, sex, sexual orientation, disability, or national origin and thereafter accords them all the rights and privileges generally made available to students at the College. The College is strongly committed to basing judgments about individuals upon their qualifications and abilities and to protecting individual rights of privacy, association, belief, and expression.

Application and Information

Students interested in attending Sarah Lawrence College should request application materials from the Office of Admission. The application deadline for first-year students for the fall semester is January 1. Financial Aid applications are due February 1. The notification date is early April, and the reply date is May 1. The College has two early decision programs. The fall early decision deadline is November 1, and notification is made on December 15. The winter early decision deadline is January 1, and notification is made on February 15.

The application deadline for transfer students for fall semester is March 1. Notification is May 1 and the reply date is May 15. The application deadline for transfer students for spring semester is November 1. Notification and reply are in late November or early December.

Office of Admission
Sarah Lawrence College
Bronxville, New York 10708
Phone: 914-395-2510
800-888-2858 (toll-free)
Fax: 914-395-2515
E-mail: slcadmit@sarahlawrence.edu
Web site: http://www.sarahlawrence.edu

Students relax on Westland's lawn.

COLLEGE CLOSE-UPS

SCHOOL OF THE ART INSTITUTE OF CHICAGO

CHICAGO, ILLINOIS

The School

Since its founding in 1866, the School of the Art Institute of Chicago (SAIC) has been providing a leading global vision for the education of artists, designers, and others who shape contemporary art practice. The School of the Art Institute of Chicago's primary purpose is to foster the conceptual and technical education of artists, designers, and scholars in a highly professional, studio-oriented, and academically rigorous environment, encouraging excellence, critical inquiry, and experimentation. SAIC was recognized as "the most influential art school in the nation" by a poll conducted by Columbia University and a panel of national art critics. *U.S. News & World Report* has consistently ranked SAIC's Master of Fine Arts program as number one of the top three in the nation.

SAIC's 2,379 undergraduate and 719 graduate students and a faculty of artists, designers, and scholars work in an environment that facilitates the exchange of ideas, the sharing of resources, and the critiquing and refining of technical abilities and conceptual concerns.

The School of the Art Institute of Chicago is distinguished from other art and design schools in the breadth and depth of its curriculum in both studio and academic areas, with more than 900 courses offered each semester. SAIC is committed to interdisciplinary exploration and the awareness that the boundaries between artistic fields are not always easily defined. Students are encouraged to experience the full range of studio practices and academic approaches; they do not declare a major but are free to design a path of study that best suits their creative development. A student may choose to do all their course work in one area of study or among multiple department areas. SAIC's credit/no-credit grading system encourages students to investigate, develop, or resolve a creative problem by exploring new approaches and to develop the self-motivation and discipline necessary for life as a practicing artist, designer, and scholar in the twenty-first century.

Liberal arts and art history are central to the life of the School of the Art Institute of Chicago and underscore one of SAIC's primary commitments: to enrich a strong studio program with a first-rate, nationally and regionally accredited liberal arts education. SAIC has one of the largest art history departments in the nation and is the only college in the country that offers a systematic series of courses on the history, theory, and philosophical bases of art criticism, taught by contemporary critics and scholars.

Students may live in one of two distinctive residence halls with loft-style rooms, each with their own bathroom, kitchen, voice mail, and Internet access. The residence halls have 24-hour security and controlled access as well as spacious, well-lit studios, lounge rooms with big screen TVs, computer labs, and laundry facilities. Students can immerse themselves in a community of fellow artists, live in the heart of Chicago's loop, and enjoy conveniences unavailable in most student apartments.

Students have access to a wide variety of unique resources, beginning with the premiere collection of SAIC's sister institution, the Art Institute of Chicago with its new Modern Wing, and the Ryerson & Burnham Libraries, the largest art and architecture research libraries in the country. The Gene Siskel Film Center, located in the same building as the 162 North State Street Residences, presents significant programs of world cinema and presentations by an international array of film and video artists. SAIC's Video Data Bank houses more than 1,600 titles and is the leading resource in the United States for videotapes by and about contemporary artists. The Poetry Center brings renowned poets and writers to Chicago to share their work with the public.

The School of the Art Institute of Chicago offers a broad spectrum of services to accommodate its diverse population, including an international student office, multicultural affairs office, health and counseling services, Disability and Learning Resource Center, an extensive program for academic advising, and a career development department.

The School of the Art Institute of Chicago is accredited by the Higher Learning Commission of the North Central Association of Colleges and Schools and by the National Association of Schools of Art and Design.

Location

The School of the Art Institute of Chicago is located in the heart of downtown Chicago, home to the nation's second-largest art scene that includes world-class museums, numerous galleries, alternative spaces, and organizations that support the arts. Chicago is a city of diverse neighborhoods, each with its own atmosphere, customs, and cuisine. Students have a wide variety of cultural and recreational resources from which to choose: ballet, opera, theater, orchestra halls, cinemas, libraries, architecture, blues and jazz clubs, parks, ethnic restaurants, a variety of world-class sports venues, and street festivals.

Chicago itself is a vital part of the campus, as a source of social and cultural activities and the stimulus for ideas and attitudes ultimately expressed through art. Peter Frank, art critic and curator says, "Of all American cities, Chicago has contributed the most solid and distinctive artwork and art thinking. The School of the Art Institute of Chicago is at the nucleus of this longstanding distinction."

The School of the Art Institute of Chicago is located across the street from an extraordinary space that rivals the quads of any other big-city college or university. Millennium Park is a twenty-first-century marvel, and SAIC, its faculty members, and students played a key role in its realization. One of the signature pieces of public art at the park, the Crown Fountain by Spanish artist Jaume Plensa, was created with the assistance of both SAIC students and faculty members, who collaborated with Plensa in producing the 1,000 video portraits that are screened continuously on the fountain's twin video towers. The park, with its unique mix of art, architecture, and nature, has become an urban oasis for SAIC students.

Majors and Degrees

Students do not declare majors but are free to concentrate in one or any combination of the following areas: animation, architecture, art and technology, art education, art history, ceramics, designed objects, drawing, fashion design, fiber, filmmaking, interior architecture, new media, painting, performance, photography, print media, sculpture, sound, video, visual communication, visual and critical studies, and writing.

The Bachelor of Fine Arts (B.F.A.) degree in studio allows students to develop a particularized course of study in the visual arts. The openness of the curriculum allows for creative, idiosyncratic, and tailored programs, thereby emulating the very process of art making. Academic advising, provided by the Office of Student Affairs, helps students in determining their particular path of study. The School of the Art Institute of Chicago offers Illinois teacher certification (K–12) through its B.F.A. with an emphasis in art education, with a goal of graduating artists and teachers who are informed and engaged citizens, creators and critics of visual culture. The B.F.A. with an emphasis in art history, theory, and criticism emphasizes art history, theory, and criticism, while allowing students the ability to develop their own studio practice. The B.F.A. with an emphasis in writing offers a solid grounding in literary conventions, a practical exposure to form in fiction and poetry, and an enhanced ability to read and critique peers' work, while encouraging students to openly explore what "writing" is.

The Bachelor of Arts in visual and critical studies allows students to pursue in-depth academic study in the creative environment of an art school, sharing classes with students in the B.F.A. programs. Core courses provide students with diverse critical methods for exploring the cultural meanings of visual phenomena as they relate to social, economic, and material circumstances.

The Bachelor of Interior Architecture (B.I.A.) is intended for students interested in interdisciplinary study and a focus in contemporary, professional design practices, such as sustainability, embedded and emerging technologies, and designed objects.

Academic Programs

Completion of 132 hours is required for the B.F.A. and B.A. degrees; approximately two thirds is in studio areas and one third is in academic course work. All entering students who have completed fewer than 15 credit hours of college-level studio art must enroll in the First Year Experience. Students take liberal arts courses in the humanities, natural sciences, mathematics, and social sciences and are required to complete an art history requirement.

Off-Campus Arrangements

The off-campus study requirement is an opportunity for students to gain practical experience at the same time as they gain a broader sense of society and the world.

Students can choose from a wide variety of off-campus programs. The Mobility program allows students to attend partner schools within the United States and Canada and includes the New York Studio semester. SAIC also maintains semester exchange agreements with more than twenty schools in Europe, Asia, and South America. The Off-Campus Programs Office works closely with students to help them develop their individual programs. SAIC faculty members lead study trips during each summer and winter interim session to such destinations as Cuba, New York, Puerto Rico, Venice, and Vietnam.

SAIC is home to the largest and most successful arts-related cooperative education program in the country, providing employment opportunities throughout Chicago and worldwide with individual artists; museums; galleries; multimedia firms; film, video, and animation production houses; interior architecture firms; fashion designers; and community service organizations.

Academic Facilities

SAIC's campus encompasses six buildings in downtown Chicago. There are fully equipped studios for each area of concentration, and the School's policy allows 24-hour access to facilities.

The School of the Art Institute of Chicago is committed to new technologies and the integration of computer-based resources throughout the curriculum. Currently, more than sixty digital technology courses are taught each semester in nearly all departmental areas. An aggressive laptop program coupled with state-of-the-art facilities and accessible resources provides cutting-edge capability in every corner of the School. Facilities available to all students include general-access computer labs equipped with the latest-model Apple computers and high-end peripherals; a Service Bureau, providing professional digital output, including laser cutting and 3-D printing; a Media Center, offering a wide variety of equipment for student loan; wood and metal shops; and fabrication studios.

The John M. Flaxman Library's 120,000 items—books, magazines, movies, and special collections—support the entire SAIC curriculum in the arts, liberal arts, and sciences. Web-accessible resources include the School's own growing digital library, a traditional online library catalog, e-reserves, and a rich assortment of full-text licensed databases. The Joan Flasch Artists' Book Collection contains more than 3,000 artists' books along with a research collection of exhibition catalogs and other related material. The MacLean Visual Resource Center maintains a noncirculating collection of more than 500,000 slides.

Exhibition spaces include new and acclaimed Sullivan Galleries offering 32,000 square feet of exhibition space—the only single contemporary exhibition site of its size in the Chicago Loop, and the Betty Rymer Gallery, which highlights work from departments and presents special exhibitions. In addition, Gallery X and the Lounge Gallery, sponsored by the Student Union Galleries, provide exhibition space for currently enrolled students.

Costs

Tuition for the 2009–10 academic year was $34,200 for full-time undergraduate students or $1140 per credit hour. For 2009–10, student housing cost $9800 per academic year for a double room.

Financial Aid

The School of the Art Institute of Chicago makes every effort to assist students who need help in financing their education. Through an extensive financial aid program, a substantial amount of gift aid funding from private, institutional, state, and federal sources is distributed annually. In addition to scholarships and grants, the School grants merit scholarships and offers an extensive college work-study program. To apply for financial aid, students should complete the FAFSA. To receive priority consideration, students should submit completed forms to the Financial Aid Office no later than March 1. All awards are made on a first-come, first-served basis to students in good standing who demonstrate need.

Faculty

Faculty members are selected for their skills, insight, and dedication as teachers and for their professional accomplishments as artists, designers, and scholars. There are currently more than 600 full- and part-time faculty members, among them NEA grant recipients, Louis Comfort Tiffany Foundation Fellowship recipients, and Rockefeller Foundation grant recipients. SAIC's faculty members have their work exhibited in museums, galleries, and festivals nationally and internationally. They publish books, plays, poetry, and criticism; organize and curate exhibitions; and design, build, and preserve buildings throughout the world. Each year, 100 or more well-known visiting artists, including poets, political activists, and visual artists, present workshops and provide individual student critiques through the Visiting Artists Program. Notable alumni include Claes Oldenburg, Ivan Albright, Georgia O'Keeffde, David Sedaris, Cynthia Rowley, and Vincente Minnelli.

Student Government

Student Government officers are elected each spring, and their mission is to promote student interests and concerns to the broader School community by serving on a variety of faculty and administrative staff committees. Student Government also provides funds for the more than forty student groups on campus. All students are encouraged to attend the weekly open Student Government meetings.

Admission Requirements

To be considered for the undergraduate program, applicants are required to submit an electronic application; a nonrefundable application fee of $65 for domestic students ($85 for international students); a portfolio consisting of ten to fifteen examples of recent work, a minimum of 5 minutes of time-based work, or an "alternative" portfolio submission that demonstrates the applicant's creative intent; a statement of purpose; transcript(s) from high school(s) or an official copy of the high school equivalency certificate; transcripts from any college previously attended; and one letter of recommendation. Domestic applicants must submit either scores from the SAT or the ACT. Any transfer applicant who has successfully completed the School of the Art Institute of Chicago's English requirements and/or other liberal arts course work at another accredited college may be exempt from standardized test requirements for admission. All international undergraduate students who are not U.S. citizens or permanent residents or are nonnative English speakers are required to take either the TOEFL or the IELTS.

Application and Information

Prospective students may apply to the School of the Art Institute of Chicago through the Immediate Decision Option (IDO) or the traditional admission procedure. IDO Days allows prospective students who have submitted all their application materials an opportunity to receive an admissions decision by the end of the day while on the SAIC campus.

Those students applying through the traditional admission procedure are required to submit their applications electronically at http://www.artic.edu/saic/ugapp. The applicant's portfolio and academic credentials are reviewed and evaluated by the Admissions Office. Students are admitted on a rolling basis and are informed of the committee's decision by mail. Students who anticipate a need for financial assistance are urged to complete their applications for admission and financial aid by February 15 for the fall semester and November 15 for the spring semester in order to receive priority consideration. These dates are also the final deadlines for applicants who wish to be considered for the School of the Art Institute of Chicago's Merit Scholarship Program.

Admissions Office
School of the Art Institute of Chicago
36 South Wabash
Chicago, Illinois 60603
Phone: 312-629-6100
800-232-7242 (toll-free)
Fax: 312-629-6101
E-mail: admiss@saic.edu
Web site: http://www.saic.edu

SCHOOL OF THE MUSEUM OF FINE ARTS, BOSTON

BOSTON, MASSACHUSETTS

The School

The School of the Museum of Fine Arts, Boston (SMFA), or Museum School, is a division of the Museum of Fine Arts, Boston (MFA), and affiliated with Tufts and Northeastern Universities. In partnership with Tufts, the School offers the following degree programs: the Bachelor of Fine Arts, the five-year Combined-Degree program (B.A./B.F.A. or B.S./B.F.A.), the Master of Fine Arts, and the Master of Arts in Teaching in Art Education. In partnership with Northeastern, the School offers a Bachelor of Fine Arts and a Master of Fine Arts in Studio Art. All students in degree programs are fully enrolled at the School of the Museum of Fine Arts and Tufts or Northeastern University and graduate with a Tufts or Northeastern degree. The School also offers the all-studio Diploma program and the one-year Fifth Year and Post-Baccalaureate Certificate programs.

As in an artists' colony, the Museum School's focus is on creative investigation, risk taking, and the exploration of an individual vision. A truly interdisciplinary institution, the School does not have a mandatory foundations program nor does it have majors. Students are given the freedom to design a program of study that best suits their needs and goals. This freedom comes with strong support and guidance from faculty advisers.

The School's studio curriculum is developed continually in order to incorporate new media and new approaches, concepts, and theories. Dynamic exhibition and visiting artists programs complement the curriculum.

Student Affairs has a knowledgeable staff that is available to assist students in finding living accommodations and to answer questions. A limited amount of residence hall housing is available at a state-of-the-art dormitory, built exclusively for artists. The office also provides a comprehensive guide to housing in the city and listings of local realtors, studio contacts, and currently available apartments and roommates.

Location

The School of the Museum of Fine Arts, Boston, is tucked among many of Boston's finest academic and cultural institutions, thriving commercial and business centers, and a world of diverse people. The campus is within walking distance of numerous other colleges and major art museums. In addition to the Museum of Fine Arts, Boston, students soon discover the Isabella Stewart Gardner Museum and the Museum of the National Center of Afro-American Artists in the campus neighborhood. The Institute of Contemporary Art and galleries on Newbury Street, the South End, and Fort Point are easily accessible by T, Boston's public transportation. Students also may take the T to Cambridge to explore the museums of Harvard University and the List Visual Arts Center at MIT. SMFA's campus is also bordered on one side by parkland that invites long walks or jogs, picnics, or an afternoon of sketching.

The city responds to and reflects the culture and interests of its residents with venues featuring a world's view of music: alternative, hip-hop, jazz, folk, blues, and Latin. Harvard Square's eclectic range of restaurants, shops, theaters, and street performers are just across the Charles River. The Back Bay boasts a dizzying range of shops and eateries. And the Fenway and Jamaica Plain offer parks, gardens, and quiet spots. Students find a mix of theater—classical and experimental—some of the best independent movie houses around, comedy clubs, people-watching spots, poetry slams, lectures, and great bookstores.

Majors and Degrees

In partnership with Tufts, the School offers the following undergraduate degree programs: the Bachelor of Fine Arts and the five-year Combined-Degree program (B.A./B.F.A. or B.S./B.F.A.). In partnership with Northeastern, the School offers the Bachelor of Fine Arts at the undergraduate level. All students in degree programs are fully enrolled at the School of the Museum of Fine Arts and Tufts or Northeastern University and graduate with a Tufts or Northeastern degree. The School also offers the all-studio Diploma program and the one-year Fifth Year and Post-Baccalaureate Certificate programs. The School offers courses in the following areas: ceramics, core, drawing, film and animation, glass, metals, painting, performance, photography, print and paper, professional practices, sculpture, sound, text and image arts, video, and visual and critical studies.

Academic Programs

All students in the degree programs are enrolled at both the Museum School and Tufts or Northeastern University and graduate with a degree from Tufts or Northeastern. While the academic curriculum is set by Tufts and Northeastern, students design their own programs of studio art study.

The only limitations on this elective system in studio art are the prerequisites stipulated for some courses. The School recommends basic courses for students who need foundation work in any studio area.

Teaching methods range from structured classes, requiring regular attendance, to individual instruction for work done independently outside the School.

Students' studio art work is evaluated at the end of every semester by a review board made up of teachers and students; the student being reviewed participates in this evaluation. Letter grades are not given for studio courses. Students advance on an individual basis. Academic courses are graded in the traditional manner.

Students in the degree programs take courses in studio art at the School and courses in academic areas of study at Tufts or Northeastern.

The School is also a member of the Pro Arts Consortium, which allows students to take classes on a space-available basis at Berklee College of Music, the Boston Architectural Center, Emerson College, the Boston Conservatory, and Massachusetts College of Art and Design. The Museum School also offers selective cross-registration with MIT.

Academic Facilities

The School is a division of the Museum of Fine Arts, Boston. Students and faculty members have special privileges of access to the museum's curatorial departments and library. The collection of the School's W. Van Alan Clark Jr. Library, which is the circulating branch of the Museum of Fine Arts, Boston's William Morris Hunt Memorial Library, includes books, periodicals, DVDs, slides, ephemeral materials, and artists' books and focuses on contemporary to late-twentieth- and twenty-first-century art. This encyclopedic collection of more than 200,000 volumes comprises the largest art library in Boston and supports research on collections, exhibitions, studio practice, and interpretation.

Students may also use the collections of the Fenway Libraries Consortium, which consists of nine local academic libraries plus an inter-library loan system, the Virtual Catalog, involving 300 lending libraries throughout Massachusetts. Degree students and those taking a class through the Pro Arts Consortium, an association of six schools in Boston, have access to the Tufts and

Northeastern University libraries and libraries of Pro Arts member institutions (Berklee College of Music, Boston Architectural Center, The Boston Conservatory, Emerson College, Massachusetts College of Art, and the Museum School).

The Exhibitions Office plans a program of shows covering work accomplished during the entire academic year. Work by students in each area of the School is represented on a rotating basis in the lobby, corridor, and student galleries.

Computers are available throughout the Museum School—including classrooms, print shops, painting and sculpture studios, and hallways. The School also provides computer labs with high-speed T3 Internet connections for all Diploma, Certificate, Degree, and Graduate program students. Each student gets an e-mail account. The Macintosh Lab includes a thirty-six-seat lab with Intel Core 2 Duo iMacs and PowerMac G5s. Labs have flatbed and film scanners for flat originals and small, medium, and large-format films. The lab also has various DVD and CD writers and printers, including an Epson 9900, which can print up to 44 inches by 100 inches. Two black-and-white laser writers allow page sizes of up to 11-by-17 inches.

Costs

For 2009–10, the full-year tuition for studio courses was $29,540. Therefore, students enrolled only in studio art courses pay this amount. Tuition for degree-program students in any one semester varies individually with the ratio of academic to studio courses taken in that semester. More information about tuition and fees can be found at http://www.smfa.edu.

Financial Aid

Financial aid is awarded on the basis of demonstrated financial need; approximately 73 percent of students receive some sort of financial aid. Merit scholarships range from $3000 to full tuition scholarships. Students are eligible to apply for Federal Pell Grants, Federal Supplemental Educational Opportunity Grants, Federal Work-Study Program awards, Federal Stafford Student Loans, and SMFA Scholarships. The priority deadline for receipt of completed application forms is March 15. Students should contact the Financial Aid Office to request the necessary forms.

Faculty

All faculty members who teach studio courses are practicing professional artists who have regional, national, and international reputations in their fields. There are approximately 50 full-time and 50 part-time faculty members. Selected members of the undergraduate faculty also work with graduate students. The student-faculty ratio is approximately 10:1.

Student Government

The standing committees of the School, made up of administrative staff members, students, and faculty members, meet regularly to review the School's goals, curriculum, and problems. Each student, teacher, or member of the administration has an equal opportunity to join committees and the Student Government Association.

Admission Requirements

The Admissions Committee endeavors to select for entrance those applicants who appear highly motivated and best suited by apparent creative potential and background to benefit from the professional education offered by the School.

Diploma evaluation criteria are based primarily on the strength of the applicant's portfolio. Degree program evaluation criteria consist of a review of the applicant's portfolio as well as the strength of his or her academic records. The School strongly recommends that prospective students arrange to tour the School or have an interview before a formal application is filed. Qualified secondary school students in their junior year are encouraged to apply at that time for early acceptance for the term beginning in the September following their senior year.

Application and Information

Applicants should arrange for all of the following to be delivered to the School: transcripts from the secondary school and any institution of higher education attended, official SAT or ACT scores (optional), an application form and the $65 nonrefundable application fee, and a portfolio. The portfolio of work must be sent to the School to be reviewed by the Admissions Committee. The School intentionally does not designate any specific composition or number of pieces for the portfolio; however a minimum of twenty pieces is recommended. Portfolios should be made up of what the applicant—rather than an art teacher, counselor, or relative—feels best shows a potential for development in visual art.

The admission deadline for the Diploma program is on a rolling basis. Portfolios received from September to May are reviewed within ten days, and diploma applicants are notified of the Admissions Committee's decision by mail within three weeks. Portfolios received from June through August are reviewed on a weekly basis. Students may be accepted to the Diploma program for the second semester beginning in January. The regular procedure is followed, and all application materials should be delivered to the School by October 1. The deadline for application to B.F.A. program is February 1 for first-time freshmen; the deadline for spring admission is October 1 for first-time freshmen. The deadline for application to the combined B.A./B.S. and B.F.A. programs is January 1 for first-time freshmen.

Applications from international students are welcome. Applicants from countries other than the United States should offer documentary evidence of financial resources sufficient to satisfy all educational and living expenses for one year of study at the School. Applicants whose native language is not English should also submit scores on the Test of English as a Foreign Language (TOEFL).

For further information, students should contact:

Admissions Office
School of the Museum of Fine Arts, Boston
230 The Fenway
Boston, Massachusetts 02115
Phone: 617-369-3626
800-643-6078 (toll-free)
E-mail: admissions@smfa.edu
Web site: http://www.smfa.edu

The Review Board system, in which students are awarded credit based on a semester's worth of artwork by a panel of faculty members and students, is a hallmark of the SMFA education.

SEATTLE PACIFIC UNIVERSITY

SEATTLE, WASHINGTON

The University

With a long and distinguished history in Christian higher education, Seattle Pacific University (SPU) entered the new century positioned to engage the culture and influence the world for good. At a time when the legacy of the secularized modern university is under scrutiny, Seattle Pacific provides 4,000 students with a high-quality, comprehensive education grounded on the gospel of Jesus Christ. This combination of vital scholarship and thoughtful faith is a powerful one that brings about lasting change in the lives of graduates and in the people and communities they serve.

Founded in 1891, SPU has been designated one of "America's Best Colleges" by *U.S. News & World Report* and has been acknowledged as one of the country's character-building institutions. Located just minutes from downtown Seattle, the leading urban center in the Pacific Northwest, SPU is committed to engaging and serving in the modern city, cultivating a global consciousness, supporting the church, and addressing the crisis of meaning in modern culture. SPU believes these are some of the Christian university's most important contributions in this century.

SPU students come from forty-three states and forty-six countries, representing more than thirty-six different Christian denominations. More than half of Seattle Pacific's undergraduate students live on the campus in four residence halls and several apartment complexes. All residence facilities are wired to allow dedicated online connections to e-mail, the Internet, and the campus computer network.

Seattle Pacific University celebrates diversity and learning to live together in Christian community. In 2004, civil rights leader John Perkins and SPU President Philip Eaton founded the John Perkins Center on campus. The first of its kind in the nation, the Perkins Center helps SPU become a more diverse campus, practice reconciliation, build new relationships in the city, and bring about positive change in the world. The Ames Minority Leadership Scholarships support high school graduates who come from minority groups and have leadership potential. Prospective students from urban areas and diverse backgrounds annually visit the campus for Urban Youth Preview.

Seattle Pacific's intercollegiate athletic program fields NCAA Division II teams in men's and women's basketball, crew, cross-country, soccer, and track and field and women's gymnastics and volleyball. All students have access to thirty-two intramural sports as well as extramurals, special events, and health and fitness activities.

The University's unique leadership program encourages students to cultivate their individual talents through opportunities in student government, ministries, performing groups, publications, clubs, and organizations.

In addition to its bachelor's degrees, SPU awards M.A., M.B.A., M.Ed., M.F.A., M.S., M.A. (TESOL), M.S.N., Ed.D., and Ph.D. degrees.

Seattle Pacific University is accredited by the Washington State Board of Education, the Northwest Commission on Colleges and Universities, AACSB International–the Association to Advance Collegiate Schools of Business, the National Council for Accreditation of Teacher Education, the Washington State Board of Education for the preparation of elementary and secondary teachers, the Commission on Collegiate Nursing Education, the Washington State Nursing Care Quality Assurance Commission, the Accreditation Board for Engineering and Technology, the Commission on Accreditation/Approval for Dietetics Education of the American Dietetics Association, and the Commission on Accreditation for Marriage and Family Therapy Education. The doctoral degree program in clinical psychology is accredited by the American Psychological Association. SPU is approved by the American Council on Education, the Board of Regents of the State of New York, the Commission on Christian Education of the Free Methodist Church for preparation of ministers and missionaries, and the Department of Christian Education of the Free Methodist Church. SPU is a member of the Christian College Consortium, the Council for Christian Colleges and Universities, the American Association of Colleges for Teacher Education, and the National Association of Schools of Music.

Location

Seattle Pacific's beautiful 43-acre, tree-lined city campus lies in a residential area just 10 minutes from downtown Seattle, the business and cultural heart of the Pacific Northwest. A gateway to Canada and the Pacific Rim, Seattle offers easy access to a wide variety of outdoor recreation such as sailing, skiing, hiking, and camping. The city also offers world-class fine arts, including opera, theater, symphony, and ballet. Seattle Pacific takes advantage of its urban setting by providing hundreds of internship and service experiences in the city's hospitals, schools, businesses, and churches.

Majors and Degrees

An array of academic options in the arts, sciences, and professions allows Seattle Pacific students to specialize in one discipline while exploring many others. The University awards B.A. and B.S. degrees and offers sixty undergraduate majors.

The College of Arts and Sciences offers the following undergraduate majors: art; biochemistry; biology; biology education; biotechnology; chemistry; classics; communication; computational mathematics; computer engineering; computer science; electrical engineering; engineering and applied science; English; European studies (Europe, French, German, Latin, Russian, Spanish, and classics); exercise science; family and consumer sciences; fine and applied arts education; food and nutritional sciences; general studies; history; language arts education; Latin American studies (Spanish); mathematics; mathematics education; music; music education; philosophy; physical education; physics; political science; science education; social science education; sociology; textiles, clothing, and interiors; theater; and visual communication.

The School of Business and Economics offers undergraduate majors in accounting, business administration, and economics. The School of Education offers elementary certification with any major of the University, secondary certification with endorsements in most Washington state–approved areas, and a major in special education. The School of Health Sciences offers an undergraduate nursing degree. The School of Psychology, Family, and Community offers undergraduate majors in organizational behavior and psychology. The School of Theology offers majors in Christian theology, Christian scriptures, educational ministries, global and urban ministry, and youth ministry. Preprofessional programs are available in dentistry, law, medicine, optometry, pharmacy, physical therapy, and veterinary medicine.

Academic Programs

Seattle Pacific's academic disciplines set high standards for students. Undergraduate students are taught not by graduate assistants but by experienced professors who are recognized locally and nationally for the quality of their scholarship. Small class sizes mean students actively participate in their own education, gaining the confidence to achieve their goals. In addition, SPU's clear Christian commitment gives depth and perspective to classroom learning, balancing knowledge with values.

The Common Curriculum, which includes seven required courses spread out over four years, is at the heart of an undergraduate liberal arts education at Seattle Pacific. Very few comprehensive universities in an urban setting with an equal mix of residential and commuter students require participation in common learning over four years.

SPU students begin in the first quarter of their freshman year with University Seminar, a focused exploration of a special interdisciplinary topic. The fewer than 25 students enrolled in each course form a "cohort" and attend other freshman classes in the Common Curriculum together, with their University Seminar professor serving as their academic adviser. In their freshman, sophomore, and junior years, students participate in two parallel sequences of required courses that address key human questions from the perspective of various disciplines and the foundations of Christian faith. Cumulative and developmental in nature, these classes are designed to support and enhance students' learning in the majors.

Off-Campus Programs

Seattle Pacific students have many opportunities to enhance their education with off-campus study. The Pacific Northwest itself provides a living laboratory for academic pursuits in all disciplines. SPU's own campuses on Whidbey Island and Blakely Island in Puget Sound are ideal for research and field study in areas such as marine biology and environmental science.

From summer 2009 to summer 2010, more than 200 students are slated to participate in SPU's faculty-led programs to Europe, South Africa, Belize, Galapagos, Vietnam, Japan and China. Students can also choose to study with many other approved programs around the world. During quarter and summer breaks, students have the opportunity to join Seattle Pacific Reachout International (SPRINT) teams that travel to Camden, New Jersey, and countries such as China, Russia, India, Rwanda, and Vietnam for a short-term mission experience.

Students may apply to take one or two quarters of study at one of the twelve other Christian College Consortium campuses, or they may enroll in programs sponsored by the Council for Christian Colleges and Universities, including American Studies in Washington, D.C.; Latin American Studies in Costa Rica; Film Studies in Los Angeles; Australian Studies Center in Sydney; Contemporary Music Center in Martha's Vineyard; Middle East Studies in Cairo; China Studies; Oxford Program in Oxford, United Kingdom; Ugandan Studies or Journalism in Washington, D.C.

Academic Facilities

At the heart of the Seattle Pacific campus is the 62,000-square-foot library. This spacious, four-level facility serves as the center for academic endeavors outside the classroom. It provides learning resource services, the latest technology, space for study and research, and approximately 200,000 volumes. The library also has seventy networked computers, and the building is one of the University "hotspots" for wireless connections. Students also have access to 28 million items held in thirty-six Washington and Oregon academic libraries through the Orbis Cascade Alliance and Summit. SPU's Center for Scholarship and Faculty Development is located in the library, and it includes Instructional Technology Services, which offers media production, satellite downlink, and duplication services.

Other educational facilities at SPU include a $24-million science facility for biology, chemistry, and related sciences. Otto Miller Hall, which houses computer science, electrical engineering, mathematics, and physics, has undergone a $5.4-million renovation. The University's flexible-forestage performing arts facility, E. E. Bach Theatre, is one of the city's finest, and the Royal Brougham Pavilion is one of the premier sports and recreation arenas in the Puget Sound area.

Costs

Tuition and fees for the 2009–10 academic year were $27,450; annual room and board were $8544 (based on 2 people in a room, full meal plan). Individualized meal plans are available. Book costs and personal expenses vary, depending on personal needs.

Financial Aid

Seattle Pacific expects to award nearly $70 million in scholarships and financial aid in 2010–11. Need-based financial aid is available in the form of scholarships, grants, loans, and employment. To be considered for maximum aid, students must submit the Free Application for Federal Student Aid (FAFSA) as soon as possible after January 1 and be admitted to the University by March 1. SPU participates in various federal aid programs, including the Federal Pell Grant, Federal Supplemental Educational Opportunity Grant, Federal Perkins Loan, Federal Work-Study Program, and Federal Stafford Student Loan. SPU also participates in the Federal Academic Competitiveness Grant, Federal SMART Grant, Federal TEACH Grant, Federal Parent PLUS Loan, Federal Graduate Student PLUS Loan, and Federal Nursing Student Loan.

Merit-based University scholarships are given annually to students who exhibit academic excellence and exemplify the ideals of the institution. Merit scholarships are available in amounts ranging from $1500 to full tuition. The Division of Fine Arts offers renewable scholarships (up to $3000) regardless of major. The Athletic Department awards scholarship aid to qualified athletes.

Faculty

The faculty at Seattle Pacific is composed of 187 full-time faculty members and 150 adjunct and other faculty members, who are committed to the highest academic standards. Eighty-four percent of SPU's full-time faculty members hold the Ph.D. or an equivalent terminal degree. Seattle Pacific professors are experts in their fields; they publish, speak, and conduct research throughout the world. Their first priority, however, is teaching. SPU faculty members also make themselves available to students outside the classroom and act as models of compassionate, educated Christians.

Student Government

All full-time students are members of the Associated Students of Seattle Pacific (ASSP). Each spring, students elect 5 ASSP executive officers, along with representatives to the ASSP Senate, the student governing body. ASSP provides services to students in the areas of campus activities, campus ministries, leadership development, and student publications.

Admission Requirements

Admission to Seattle Pacific is offered on the basis of academic credentials and personal qualifications. SPU selects those students who will benefit most from a Christian university education. Factors in the admission decision include high school or college grades, academic and personal recommendations, the application essays, and scores on the SAT or ACT. An applicant is also evaluated in terms of leadership potential, church and community activities, special talents, and personal responsibility. Prospective students are encouraged to visit the campus at any time.

Application and Information

Prospective students may visit the Seattle Pacific University Web site to apply online or request application materials. High school students should request these materials early in their senior year. While applications for autumn quarter are accepted until June 1, prospective students must be admitted by February 1 to be considered for scholarships and the best financial aid, housing, and course registration opportunities.

Applications are reviewed in the order they are received. Beginning December 1, decisions regarding admission are announced after all application materials have been received. If an interview is required, students are contacted by telephone.

Forms may be requested from:

Jobe Korb-Nice, Director of Undergraduate Admissions
Seattle Pacific University
3307 Third Avenue West, Suite 115
Seattle, Washington 98119-1922
Phone: 206-281-2021
800-366-3344 (toll-free)
E-mail: admissions@spu.edu
Web site: http://www.spu.edu

Alexander Hall, built in 1904, was Seattle Pacific University's first building.

SEATTLE UNIVERSITY

SEATTLE, WASHINGTON

COLLEGE CLOSE-UPS

The University

Seattle University provides an ideal environment for motivated students interested in self-reliance, awareness of different cultures, social justice, and the fulfillment that comes from making a difference in the world. Its location in the center of one of the nation's most diverse and progressive cities attracts a varied student body, faculty, and staff. Its urban setting promotes the development of leadership skills and independence and provides a variety of opportunities for students to apply what they learn through internships, clinical experiences, and volunteer work.

As a Jesuit institution, Seattle University is part of a network of twenty-eight colleges and universities and forty-six high schools across the United States noted for both academic strength and commitment to social justice. Seattle University's core curriculum provides a rigorous liberal arts and sciences foundation designed to develop leadership skills, enhance global awareness, and enable graduates to serve others. In the Jesuit educational tradition, students are taught how to think, not what to think. Professional undergraduate offerings include highly respected Colleges of Business, Nursing, and Science and Engineering and career-oriented liberal arts programs such as communication, criminal justice, journalism, public affairs, and social work. The Albers School of Business and Economics and the University's Colleges of Education, Law, and Theology and Ministry offer graduate-level opportunities.

Seattle University is noted for its focus on the individual through small, faculty-taught classes and an engaging student life program. The result is graduates who enjoy successful and fulfilling lives. Seattle University is recognized as one of the leading institutions in the Pacific Northwest in producing Truman and Wilson scholars.

The Seattle University campus has undergone more than $200 million in recent improvements. Although its First Hill location is in the heart of the city, the 48-acre campus has been designated by the state as an official Backyard Wildlife Sanctuary for its distinctive landscaping and environmentally conscious practices.

Fall quarter 2008 had a freshman class of 888, with 52 percent coming from outside Washington State. The ethnic breakdown for the class was 52 percent white, 20 percent Asian American, and 15 percent African American, Latino, and American Indian. The 4,253 undergraduate students represent fifty-five states and eighty nations. International students make up approximately 8 percent of the student body.

Approximately 1,600 students in total, and 88 percent of freshman, live on campus in four residence halls and an apartment complex. Students are required to live on campus for both their freshman and sophomore years unless able to commute from home.

Seattle University has more than 130 extracurricular clubs and organizations and has seven varsity teams for men (baseball, basketball, cross-country, golf, soccer, swimming, tennis, and track) and nine for women (basketball, cross-country, golf, soccer, softball, swimming, tennis, track, and volleyball). Seattle University is a member of NCAA Division I. The student life program includes 100 extracurricular clubs and organizations, including the Hui O Nani Hawaiian Club, Associated Students of African Descent, Outdoor Adventure and Recreation, Beta Alpha Psi (national accounting honorary), and other professional honoraries and clubs.

The Connolly Athletic Center serves as the major facility for varsity and intramural athletics and recreation. The center features two swimming pools, two full-size gymnasiums, and locker room saunas. A 6-acre complex provides fields for outdoor sports.

Seattle University receives the highest professional accreditation from the Accreditation Board for Engineering and Technology, AACSB International–The Association to Advance Collegiate Schools of Business, American Bar Association, American Chemical Society, Association of Theological Schools, Commission on Accreditation of Allied Health Education Programs, National Association of Schools of Public Affairs and Administration, National Council for Accreditation of Teacher Education, Commission on Collegiate Nursing Education, Council on Social Work Education, and Northwest Commission on Colleges and Universities.

Location

Nestled between two mountain ranges, containing three lakes, and situated along Puget Sound, Seattle is a magnificent setting for a university. The city pulses with music, art, and culture. Seattle is the Pacific Northwest's center for legal, medical, business, and high-tech industries, and Seattle University students supplement their studies through internships, research, volunteer projects, mentors, and meeting alumni in their fields.

Seattle's residents love the outdoors, and areas for skiing, hiking, backpacking, and climbing are within an hour of campus. Biking, walking, and jogging are also popular, with paths and trails throughout the city.

Seattle's sights and sounds, rich ethnic diversity, celebrated restaurants, eclectic entertainment, major-league athletics, theater, opera, and ballet are within walking distance, and are a central part of the Seattle University experience.

Majors and Degrees

Seattle University offers the following undergraduate degrees: Bachelor of Arts, Bachelor of Fine Arts, Bachelor of Music, Bachelor of Science, Bachelor of Science in Nursing, Bachelor of Social Work, Bachelor of Criminal Justice, Bachelor of Public Affairs, and the Bachelor of Arts in Business Administration.

The University offers programs in six major academic units. The Albers School of Business and Economics awards degrees in accounting, business administration, business economics, e-commerce/information systems, economics, finance, international business, international economic development, management, and marketing. The College of Arts and Sciences grants degrees in art history, Asian studies, communication studies, creative writing, criminal justice, cultural anthropology, drama, environmental studies, English, film studies, fine arts, French, history, international studies, journalism, liberal studies, military science/ROTC, philosophy, photography, political science, psychology, public affairs, social work, sociology, Spanish, sport and exercise science, strategic communication, string performance, theology/religious studies, visual art, and women studies. The College of Nursing offers a Bachelor of Science in Nursing degree. Matteo Ricci College awards degrees in humanities and humanities for teaching. The College of Science and Engineering offers degree programs in biochemistry, biology, chemistry, civil engineering, clinical laboratory science, computer engineering, computer science, diagnostic ultrasound, electrical engineering, environmental engineering, environmental science, general science, mathematics, mechanical engineering, and physics. Preprofessional programs include dentistry, law, medicine, optometry, and veterinary medicine.

Academic Programs

The Core Curriculum has several distinguishing characteristics in keeping with the Jesuit educational tradition: it provides an integrated freshman year; gives order and sequence to student learning; provides experience in the methods and content of the range of liberal arts, sciences, philosophy, and theology; calls for active learning in all classes, for practice in writing and thinking, and for an awareness of values; and it fosters a global perspective and a sense of social and personal responsibility.

Seattle University offers two honors program options for students seeking rigorous academic challenge. The University Honors Program is a small, humanities-focused learning community with a curriculum that examines the most significant texts and ideas of Western culture. The Core Honors Program involves seminar sections of nine required courses in English, history, philosophy, social science, and theology/religious studies; this option is particularly suited to students in professional degree programs, for whom participation in University Honors is less feasible due to specific major requirements and scheduling conflicts.

Seattle University operates on a quarter calendar. The fall quarter begins in mid-September; the winter quarter in early January; the spring quarter in late March; and the summer quarter in mid-June. Undergraduates typically take 15 credit hours per quarter for the fall, winter, and spring quarters.

Off-Campus Programs

Seattle University offers a diverse array of short- and long-term international study programs. Some are appropriate for any student interested in study of a particular culture or language, while others are designed to complement specific majors. Short-term programs include opportunities in Brazil, Costa Rica, France, India, Ireland, Italy, Japan, Korea, Mexico, South Africa, and Sweden. Long-term programs, which last an entire academic quarter or more, are available for Austria, Belize, China, Denmark, Ecuador, France, Ghana, Ireland, Japan, Mexico, and Spain. Students also have the opportunity to intern with non-governmental organizations in Asia, Africa, and Latin America through the unique International Development Internship Program (IDIP), which embodies the Jesuit emphasis on social justice and global awareness. Additional study-abroad programs in other nations, in conjunction with other colleges' overseas programs, are also offered. Arrangements are made through the Education Abroad Office.

Academic Facilities

Twelve academic buildings house classrooms, thirty-four instructional laboratories, twenty-five specialized laboratories, computer facilities, and other instructional equipment to support state-of-the-art instruction.

The Lemieux Library has nearly 300,000 volumes and 2,700 current serial subscriptions, 1,300 online databases, and microforms periodicals. Study carrels provide quiet study space while lounges accommodate study groups.

The Albers School of Business and Economics features classrooms designed to enhance student interaction and access to high-tech teaching equipment.

The College of Nursing's new 20,000-square-foot clinical performance laboratory is among the most technically advanced clinical laboratories in the country. It joins two clinical practice rooms and a suite of laboratories.

The Lee Center for the Arts is a showcase for theater and musical performances. This modern building seats 135 and includes a prop room, dressing room, costume shop, and professional lighting and sound booths that give students career-building technical skills.

The Chapel of St. Ignatius is Seattle University's spiritual center. This award-winning structure is recognized as a place of beauty, contemplation, and worship.

Costs

In 2009–10, tuition is $29,340; room and meals are $8805. The estimate for books, fees, and personal expenses is $3693. Costs are subject to change.

Financial Aid

Seattle University awarded $10.8 million in its own financial aid to fall 2008 freshmen, including 240 scholarships ranging from $11,000 to $36,600. Ninety-four percent of freshmen received University aid. Students are required to apply for financial aid by February 1, as awards are made early each spring for the following fall quarter. Applications received after this deadline are evaluated in order received for any remaining aid. Students must submit the Free Application for Federal Student Aid (FAFSA) and be accepted for admission to be considered for financial assistance. Scholarships are awarded on the basis of academic achievement, extracurricular involvement, and community service.

Faculty

There are 663 faculty members, 80 percent of whom possess doctoral or terminal degrees. All classes are taught by faculty. With an average class size of 20 and a faculty-to-student ratio of 1:13, the primary responsibility of Seattle University professors is the success of their students. Faculty members are available to provide assistance outside of class, to help students with research, and to assist in arranging internships. Faculty advisers provide guidance, direction, and encouragement throughout a student's academic career. New students are assigned faculty advisers prior to registration according to their major.

Student Government

All undergraduates belong to the Associated Students of Seattle University (ASSU), the central student organization on campus. ASSU is organized around an elected president, an executive vice president, and an activities vice president. A 12-member representative council oversees every facet of the student body and is responsible for policymaking and providing a diverse activities program to meet the needs of Seattle University's student body. In addition, ASSU communicates student needs to the administration and faculty. ASSU oversees over 120 clubs and organizations.

Admission Requirements

Freshman applicants are required to have completed a college-preparatory program upon high school graduation, including 4 years of English, 3 years of social studies/history, 3 years of mathematics, 2 years of laboratory science, and 2 years of a foreign language. Applicants to the College of Science and Engineering must complete 4 units of college-preparatory mathematics for admission to any of its specific majors; laboratory chemistry and laboratory physics are prerequisites for engineering program consideration. Applicants to the nursing major must complete laboratory biology and chemistry to be considered for admission.

ACT or SAT scores, an official high school transcript, a counselor recommendation, a teacher recommendation, and an essay are also required for freshman admission consideration. The middle 50 percent of 2008 freshman had GPAs between 3.3 and 3.8 on a 4.0 scale and ACT scores between 22 and 28 or SAT scores between 520 and 630 (critical reading), 520 and 620 (math), and 510 and 610 (writing).

College credit is awarded to those who have successfully completed Advanced Placement or International Baccalaureate examinations. Qualifying scores can be obtained by contacting the Office of the Registrar.

Application and Information

Seattle University is an exclusive member of the Common Application. A Seattle University Supplemental Application is also required. The application essay and the Supplemental Application's personal statement are carefully considered during application review.

Students can apply directly online at commonapp.org; the forms can also be downloaded from the Seattle University Web site (seattleu.edu). Hard copies can be requested from the Admissions Office.

High school students applying for early action consideration must apply by November 15 of their senior year. Those applying for regular admission consideration must apply by January 15. The priority application deadline for fall transfer applicants is March 1. Transfer students must submit official transcripts from all postsecondary institutions attended, regardless of whether course work was completed. Please note that applications will be accepted after these dates on a space available basis, but funds for financial aid may no longer be available.

Campus visits can be scheduled Monday through Friday and many Saturdays. (Please contact Admissions for availability). With two weeks' notice, visitors can be scheduled to attend a class, meet with a faculty adviser, participate in a campus tour, and speak individually with an Admissions representative. For additional information students should contact:

Admissions Office
Seattle University
901 12th Avenue
Seattle, Washington 98122-1090
Phone: 206-296-2000
800-426-7123 (toll-free)
E-mail: admissions@seattleu.edu
Web site: http://www.seattleu.edu

SETON HALL UNIVERSITY

SOUTH ORANGE, NEW JERSEY

The University

Seton Hall University has been preparing students to assume leadership roles for over 150 years. A Catholic university founded with the purpose of becoming "a home for the mind, the heart and the spirit," Seton Hall offers more than sixty majors and concentrations, as well as honors and leadership programs. With a 14:1 student-faculty ratio and an average class size of 25, Seton Hall offers all the advantages of a large university; however, with just 5,300 undergraduate students, the University also provides the personal attention of a small college. Seton Hall's mission of "preparing student leaders for a global society" is evident through its high academic standards, values-centered curriculum, and cutting-edge technology. Recently cited by the Intercollegiate Studies Institute's critically acclaimed college guide *Choosing the Right College* as "a Catholic university evolving from being a regional treasure to a national resource," Seton Hall was listed among 110 of the nation's top colleges.

The University comprises eight schools and colleges: the College of Arts and Sciences, the Stillman School of Business, the College of Education and Human Services, the College of Nursing, the Whitehead School of Diplomacy and International Relations, the Immaculate Conception Seminary School of Theology, and the School of Health and Medical Sciences, all on the South Orange campus. The School of Law is in nearby Newark.

Emphasizing Judeo-Christian intellectual traditions and values, the University was founded by Bishop James Roosevelt Bayley, the first Catholic bishop of Newark. Seton Hall was named after Bishop Bayley's aunt, St. Elizabeth Ann Seton, the founder of the first American community of the Sisters of Charity. Established as the first diocesan college in the United States in 1856 and organized into a University in 1950, Seton Hall continues to operate under the auspices of the Roman Catholic Diocese of Newark. As such, Seton Hall is both a Catholic university and a catholic university—meaning that the school fosters the values and traditions of the Catholic faith while also universally welcoming students of all denominations.

At Seton Hall, technology is integrated into the curriculum. Every undergraduate is issued a laptop computer with wireless connectivity to facilitate learning through technology both inside and outside the classroom. Seton Hall has integrated technology into course work by including the use of streaming video to increase learning, note-taking, and collaborative work online. The state-of-the-art laptop is upgraded after two years, and students who graduate in four years keep their laptops after graduation.

Seton Hall's on-campus recruiting events and career fairs help students find paid internships at companies like CNN, Prudential, AT&T, Pfizer, Johnson & Johnson, the United Nations, the FBI, ESPN, and the New Jersey Devils. More than 600 employers and alumni come to the campus each year to mentor and recruit students for internships and employment after graduation. Seton Hall interns earned more than $870,000 in 2008.

The relationships forged with these companies are so solid that more than 90 percent of the University's employers report that they would hire their Seton Hall interns after graduation if they had appropriate openings. Graduates of Seton Hall University join the ranks of the more than 70,000 alumni who work in leadership positions in business, industry, law, health care, and education nationally and internationally. Overall average starting salary for 2009 graduates was $45,000, with Seton Hall nursing students averaging almost $60,000 and accounting students averaging more than $52,000.

Unique opportunities with the School of Health and Medical Sciences allow students to enter dual-degree programs to earn advanced degrees in athletic training, physical therapy, occupational therapy, and physician assistant studies.

Six months after graduation 64 percent of Seton Hall students have career-related employment, 26 percent have been accepted to graduate school, and 7 percent are interviewing or awaiting graduate school acceptance.

Location

The suburban village of South Orange, New Jersey, is home to the University's 58-acre parklike campus. With the village center a short walk away, students find practically anything they need. Just beyond the border of the suburban residential community is New York City—the Big Apple—the capital of finance, fashion, art, theater, and international relations. Travel to New York is convenient via a midtown direct train from the village center. Just 14 miles away, New York City provides students with opportunities for cultural exploration and internships. Career opportunities also abound throughout northern New Jersey, which is the site of an extensive pharmaceutical, chemical, and financial center. Social, cultural, and recreational opportunities are available throughout the area, with the New Jersey Performing Arts Center, the Meadowlands sports complex, numerous state parks, and the beautiful New Jersey shore all close by.

Majors and Degrees

The College of Arts and Sciences offers the Bachelor of Arts (B.A.) in Africana and Diaspora studies, anthropology, art (art history, fine art, graphic design and advertising art, theater), Asian studies, athletic training, broadcasting and visual media, Catholic studies, classical studies, communication studies, creative writing, criminal justice, economics, English, environmental studies, French, history, Italian, journalism and public relations, liberal studies, Latin America and Latino/Latina studies, modern languages, music, occupational therapy, philosophy, physical therapy, physician assistant studies, political science, psychology, religious studies, social and behavioral sciences, social work, sociology, Spanish, and theater studies and performance. It offers the Bachelor of Science (B.S.) in biochemistry, biology, chemistry, computer science, mathematics, and physics.

The College of Education and Human Services offers the B.S. in a unique integrated early childhood, elementary, and special education program and in secondary education.

The College of Nursing offers the Bachelor of Science in Nursing (B.S.N.).

The Stillman School of Business offers the B.S. in accounting, economics, finance, information technology management, management, marketing, and sport management. It also offers the B.A. in business administration with concentrations in arts and sciences, diplomacy, international studies, and occupational therapy.

The Whitehead School of Diplomacy and International Relations offers the B.S. in diplomacy and international relations.

Preprofessional programs are available in dentistry, law, medicine, optometry, seminary, and veterinary science. A dual-admission program with Seton Hall University School of Law is offered to qualified undergraduates. Engineering students participate in a five-year program (chemical, civil, computer, electrical, industrial, or mechanical) offered jointly with New Jersey Institute of Technology. Combination undergraduate and postgraduate programs in athletic training, occupational therapy, physical therapy, physician assistant studies, and speech-language pathology are also offered.

Academic Programs

The University uses a semester calendar. It also offers day, evening, and summer sessions.

Select students are invited to participate in the University Honors Program, which consists of four semester-long colloquia devoted to the history of civilization, from ancient through medieval and early modern cultures to contemporary civilization.

With the oldest college of nursing in New Jersey, Seton Hall provides nursing education that prepares its graduates for a variety of health-care settings. Clinical experience is provided in hospitals, public health agencies, schools, nursing homes, industrial organizations, and other community agencies. More than 97 percent of Seton Hall nursing students pass the national nursing exam. Graduates of Seton Hall hold leadership positions in nursing throughout the state.

Seton Hall's Stillman School of Business is accredited by AACSB International—The Association to Advance Collegiate Schools of Business, which puts it among the most rigorous business programs in the United States. Founded on a background of liberal arts courses, the Stillman School offers specialized programs in leadership studies, international business, and sport management.

The Whitehead School of Diplomacy and International Relations is the only school affiliated with the United Nations Association of the United States of America and offers a Bachelor of Science degree in international relations. This program emphasizes ethno political studies or world cultures and the development of management and leadership skills, as well as a high degree of competency in a second language. Requirements include study abroad and internships.

The University offers an Army ROTC program on campus.

Off-Campus Programs

Seton Hall offers study-abroad programs in more than forty countries including the Dominican Republic, England, France, Germany Japan, Korea, and the People's Republic of China. Seton Hall offers semester or yearlong exchange programs with colleges and universities in Austria, China, Germany, Ireland, Japan, Puerto Rico, South Korea, and the United Kingdom. Through the international student exchange program, students may study at any of the 101 universities in thirty-five countries for one academic year. Students have several opportunities for cooperative learning and internships in the metropolitan area. Many co-op positions are with Fortune 500 companies, while others are with leading government, cultural, charitable, and scientific organizations. A semester in Washington, D.C., is also available for students to obtain internships and to take classes at exchange universities.

Academic Facilities

At Seton Hall, there is an emphasis on the use of state-of-the-art technology and available facilities to aid in the overall development and college experience for all students. Seton Hall's award-winning Mobile Computing Program provides all incoming, full-time freshmen with a brand-new, fully loaded laptop. The Department of Information Technology also supports and maintains numerous public computer labs around campus. The Richie Regan Recreation Center serves the recreational and fitness needs of the Seton Hall community with cardio machines, an Olympic-sized pool, an indoor track, and six indoor basketball courts. The brand-new fitness center features a free-weight center, new cardiovascular equipment, plasma screen televisions, and wireless headsets to listen to the TVs.

The University's Walsh library is a twenty-first-century research center with a computerized card catalog, four electronic multimedia rooms, ten CD-ROM information search and retrieval stations, 200 computer workstations for students, nearly 1 million holdings, and the University Gallery. The University Center houses most of Seton Hall's cultural, social, and recreational activities. The University Center is the hub of student activity and includes the Galleon Dining Room/food court, the Pirate's Cove (lounge and coffee house), Theatre-in-the-Round, an art gallery, a study lounge, and the student government office as well as a wide variety of student clubs and organizations. Services such as aptitude testing, career counseling, career services, health services, and personal counseling are also provided for all Seton Hall students. Fahy Hall contains classrooms and offices, a TV studio, two classroom amphitheaters, and language and journalism laboratories. McNulty Hall, renovated in October 2007, is a state-of-the-future science and technology center. The new center is home to more than thirty research and teaching laboratories, a confocal microscope laboratory, a computational chemistry laboratory, a radiochemistry laboratory, and a rooftop observatory and greenhouse. The Art Center (a registered National Historic landmark) houses an art gallery, studios, classrooms, and offices of the Department of Art and Music. The College of Nursing has multipurpose and audiovisual laboratories. Jubilee Hall, completed in 1997, contains state-of-the-art lecture halls, computer rooms, faculty offices, a 300-seat auditorium, conference rooms, and the University's new Trading Room, where students learn about stocks, bonds, and trading. There are also microcomputer laboratories in several locations on campus, and a large University-operated mainframe computer is located in the Computer Center. The University also has various centers and research institutes, including the Center for Catholic Studies, the G.K. Chesterton Institute, the Center for Jewish Christian Studies, and the 50-year-old Asia Center.

Costs

For the 2009–10 academic year, tuition and fees were $30,770 per year. This amount covered 36 credits and all fees, including a mobile-computing and orientation fee. The charge for room and board was $11,700.

Financial Aid

The University offers federal, state, and institutional aid. Most aid is based on need, but many scholarships are based on outstanding scholastic ability and achievement. Athletic grants are also available. Currently, about 90 percent of the students receive financial aid, with 75 percent receiving aid directly from Seton Hall. All applicants for aid are required to file the Free Application for Federal Student Aid (FAFSA) by March 1 for the fall semester and by October 1 for the spring semester.

Faculty

The University has 860 faculty members, and 92 percent of the full-time faculty members have doctoral degrees. The ratio of full-time students to full-time faculty members is 14:1. Faculty members serve as advisers to students in their respective departments.

Student Government

The Student Government Association consists of students who make up two legislative bodies that have the responsibility of representing their fellow students and providing programs of interest to the campus community. Students are elected to seats on the University Senate, which deals with all legislative matters pertinent to the University. In addition, the Resident Student Association represents the interests of resident students, and the Commuter Council represents the interests of commuter students.

Admission Requirements

Applicants are selected on their school achievement record, SAT or ACT scores, personal essay, and teacher and counselor recommendations. Students must graduate from an accredited high school or have passing scores on the GED test. Sixteen high school units are required: 4 in English, 3 in mathematics, 2 in social studies, 2 in a foreign language (taken consecutively), 1 in a laboratory science, and 4 in approved academic electives. Special admission policies exist for students who have been out of high school for an extended period. There is also a $55 application fee. The application fee may be waived for applicants with financial need.

Transfer applicants must have a minimum 2.5 grade point average and must be in good standing at the last institution attended. Applicants must submit transcripts from all colleges and universities attended. Credit is usually given for grades of 2.0 or higher in University-equivalent courses taken at approved institutions; a maximum of 100 semester hours of transferable credit are allowed toward a bachelor's degree.

Application and Information

The University offers a non-binding early action deadline of November 15. Those meeting the deadline will receive their admissions decision by December 30. The University also offers rolling admissions. The preferred application deadlines are March 1 for freshman and June 1 for transfers.

Office of Admissions
Seton Hall University
400 South Orange Avenue
South Orange, New Jersey 07079-2680
Phone: 800-THE-HALL (toll-free)
E-mail: thehall@shu.edu
Web site: http://www.shu.edu

SETON HILL UNIVERSITY

GREENSBURG, PENNSYLVANIA

The University

Seton Hill was founded by the Sisters of Charity in 1883 and chartered as a college by the commonwealth of Pennsylvania in 1918. In 2002, it became Seton Hill University.

Seton Hill, a coeducational liberal arts and sciences institution, is situated in the Laurel Highlands, an area of southwestern Pennsylvania known for its beautiful scenery and wealth of outdoor activities such as skiing, cycling, hiking, and white-water rafting. Recreational opportunities include on-campus lectures, theater productions, a fitness center, and aerobics classes, as well as University-sponsored trips to Pittsburgh for cultural and sports events. A new performing arts venue is in the works, and recently constructed are two new residence halls and a new recreation facility that includes new athletic fields.

Seton Hill has varsity teams for women in basketball, cross-country, equestrian competition, field hockey, golf, lacrosse, soccer, softball, tennis, track and field, and volleyball and for men in baseball, basketball, cross-country, equestrian competition, football, golf, lacrosse, soccer, tennis, track and field, and wrestling, as well as a variety of intramural teams.

At the graduate level, Seton Hill grants the Master of Arts degree in art therapy, elementary education, inclusive education (online), marriage and family therapy, special education, and writing popular fiction; a Master of Business Administration; and a Master of Science in physician assistant studies. Seton Hill has graduate certificate programs in entrepreneurship, genocide and holocaust studies (online), and writing popular fiction.

Location

Seton Hill University's beautiful 200-acre campus is located in Greensburg, Pennsylvania. As a private university, Seton Hill is able to maintain a safe, secure environment that allows students to concentrate on academics.

Seton Hill is easily accessible by car, train, or plane. Just 35 miles east of Pittsburgh, Greensburg enjoys all the advantages of a large city while maintaining a small-town atmosphere. The seat of Westmoreland County, Greensburg is home to the Westmoreland Museum of Art, the Westmoreland Symphony Orchestra, a large mall, several shopping centers, and a hospital.

Majors and Degrees

The University grants the Bachelor of Arts, Bachelor of Fine Arts, Bachelor of Science, Bachelor of Music, and Bachelor of Social Work degrees. Students choose from the following programs: accounting; art, including art and technology, art education, art history, art therapy, arts administration, fine arts studio–3D or 2D, graphic design, and studio art; biochemistry; biology; business, including entrepreneurial studies, human resources, information management, international organization, and marketing; chemistry; communication, including political communication; computer science; criminal justice; dietetics; education, including art; biology; business, computer, and information technology; chemistry; dual elementary/special; early childhood; elementary; English; family and consumer sciences; French; mathematics; music; social studies; Spanish; and special education; engineering (3+2); English, including creative writing, journalism/new media, and literature; family and consumer sciences, including child care administration and education; forensic science; history; hospitality and tourism; international studies; mathematics, including actuary science; medical technology; music, including music education, music therapy, performance, and sacred music; physicians assistant studies; political science; prelaw, preprofessional health; psychology; religious studies/theology; social work; sociology; Spanish; sports management; and theater, including music theater, theater design and technology, theater arts, theater business, and theater performance.

The University offers osteopathic medicine through a (3+3 or 3+4) and pharmacy (3+3 or 3+4) cooperative program with Lake Erie College of Osteopathic Medicine.

The University also offers adult degree programs.

Academic Programs

Seton Hill offers five academic divisions, with the opportunity to self-design a major, all enhanced by the University's award-winning liberal arts core curriculum. Special programs are available for students who are undecided about their major.

The Seton Hill University Honors Program is available for students who have distinguished themselves academically in high school. It includes scholarship money as well as housing for qualified candidates.

Prior to graduation, all undergraduate students complete a portfolio, a four-year compilation of their academic, professional, and personal achievements at Seton Hill. Portfolios allow students to showcase their learning and assist them in documenting their accomplishments as they transition from students to practicing professionals.

Students hoping to one day own a business may be interested in Seton Hill University's E-Magnify, a center for entrepreneurs. The center is the first organization of its kind in the United States to offer courses in business ownership and entrepreneurial activities to students in any major.

Off-Campus Programs

Seton Hill University recognizes that important learning experiences occur in nonacademic settings. For this reason, the University offers a variety of internships, fieldwork experiences, and cooperative education opportunities. The Office of Career Development and University faculty members assist students in finding an off-campus placement where practical experience related to the major and valuable job contacts for the future may be gained.

In addition, students may opt to spend a semester or year studying abroad. Seton Hill also offers many travel-abroad opportunities during J-term and M-term semesters.

Academic Facilities

While all of Seton Hill's facilities feature modern technology, the University continues to add new classrooms, buildings, and centers that feature the very best in adaptable learning spaces that facilitate the incorporation of current interactive and assistive technologies into Seton Hill's teaching and learning environment. Seton Hill's new Technology Learning Commons includes the ultramodern MediaSphere and Inquiry Zone classroom/labs which include everything students need (from specially designed furniture to wall-sized monitors and SmartBoards) to create virtual worlds, teach online courses, or work on group projects with students or faculty members in other parts of the campus—or the globe. The new Performing Arts Center incorporates the very best design and technology into its performance venues, classrooms, technical areas, and studios—from Steinway pianos to the latest in lighting, sound, video, and acoustics. Seton Hill's twenty-one academic and residence facilities have been specifically designed to provide a seamless, supportive learning environment for students.

Costs

For full-time students, approximate costs for the 2009–10 academic year included tuition of $26,322, approximate room and board fees of $8550, and books and personal expenses amounting to $1000 to $2000.

Financial Aid

Seton Hill's Financial Aid Office works with each student to develop an aid package from the wide variety of scholarships, grants, loans, and work-study programs available.

Seton Hill Presidential Scholarships are awarded to incoming freshman who have attained a cumulative high school grade point of average of a 3.3 or higher. SAT/ACT Seton Hill University Scholarships are awarded to students who achieve SAT scores of 900 or higher and ACT scores of 19 or higher. The SAT/ACT scholarship is to be added to the presidential scholarship amounts if the student meets both criteria. These scholarships are renewable for a total of 8 semesters as long as the student maintains a minimum cumulative GPA of 3.3 at the end of each academic year. Seton Hill provides eight full-tuition scholarships each year (two natural health sciences, two humanities, two social sciences, and two visual and performing arts). Honors Program Scholarships are available, if students have at least a 1200 on SAT's math and verbal or a 26 on the ACT composite score, and a cumulative high school GPA of a 3.5. Rising Star Scholarships are available to graduates from a Catholic high school. Division Scholarships are based on the student's academic excellence in their specific division of study. Selection for these scholarships is based on the SAT score and the student's GPA. In addition, Seton Hill offers Alumni and Sibling scholarships.

Faculty

With a student-faculty ratio of 15:1, Seton Hill faculty members can explore the needs of each student and offer individual attention. The low student-faculty ratio allows each student to become personally acquainted with the instructor. In addition, Seton Hill faculty members understand the importance of being accessible to their students.

The Seton Hill faculty consists of 70 full-time professors, 81 percent of whom have doctoral or terminal degrees.

Student Government

Through the Seton Hill Government Association, students participate in the government of the University and enjoy voting representation on a number of faculty committees. Each residence hall floor is represented by a senator, who acts as a liaison between the student senate and the student body. Participation in student government is a valuable experience that develops leadership skills and a working understanding of government.

In addition, the student government helps to sponsor numerous on-campus political, cultural, and social events. Off-campus activities include trips to Pittsburgh, New York City, and Washington, D.C.

Admission Requirements

Acceptance to the University is based on the successful completion of a college-preparatory curriculum in high school. Applicants should have completed at least 15 secondary school academic units. These units should include 4 units of English, 2 units of college-preparatory mathematics, 2 units of social science, 2 units of the same foreign language, 1 unit of laboratory science, and 4 academic electives.

Students who wish to transfer credits to Seton Hill from another college or university must present their transcripts for evaluation on a course-by-course basis. A transfer student will receive a credit evaluation upon admission to the University.

Application and Information

Seton Hill University has a rolling admissions policy. Decisions of the Admissions Committee are rendered shortly after all application materials have been submitted.

The first-time freshman applicant should submit a completed application form, a $35 nonrefundable application fee, an official secondary school transcript that includes the applicant's rank and cumulative grade point average, official score reports from either the SAT or ACT, an essay, and a recommendation form or letter from a guidance counselor or teacher.

Prospective students who do not have SAT or ACT scores may submit two graded written assignments from their junior or senior year for consideration.

For more information, students should contact:

Sherri Bett
Director of Admissions
One Seton Hill Drive
Box 991
Seton Hill University
Greensburg, Pennsylvania 15601
Phone: 800-826-6234 (toll-free)
Fax: 724-830-1294
E-mail: admit@setonhill.edu
Web site: http://www.setonhill.edu

The Administration Building is a picturesque focal point on the Seton Hill campus.

SHIPPENSBURG UNIVERSITY OF PENNSYLVANIA

SHIPPENSBURG, PENNSYLVANIA

The University

Shippensburg University, founded in 1871, is a comprehensive public institution in south-central Pennsylvania enrolling more than 6,700 undergraduate students and approximately 1,100 graduate students. Of the undergraduates, 52 percent are women and 48 percent are men. The University is divided into the College of Arts and Sciences, the College of Education and Human Services, the John L. Grove College of Business, and the School of Graduate Studies. There is also a School of Academic Programs and Services, which includes the Office of Undeclared Students.

Shippensburg University is a member of the Pennsylvania State System of Higher Education and is accredited by the Middle States Association of Colleges and Schools. The University's programs are also accredited by AACSB International (business); ABET, Inc. (computer science); the American Chemical Society; the Council on Social Work Education; the Council for the Accreditation of Counseling and Related Educational Programs; the International Association of Counseling Services; the Council for Exceptional Children; the National Council for the Accreditation of Coaching Education; and the National Council for the Accreditation of Teachers. Shippensburg University is a member of the Council of Graduate Schools.

Graduate degrees conferred are the Master of Arts, Master of Business Administration, Master of Education, Master of Science, Master of Social Work, and Master of Public Administration. Programs are as follows: Master of Arts in applied history; Master of Science in administration of justice, biology, communication studies, computer science, counseling (college, community, mental health, student personnel), geoenvironmental studies, organizational development and leadership (business, communication, education, environmental management, higher education, historical management, individual and organizational development, modern languages, public organizations, social structure and organization), and psychology; Master of Business Administration; Master of Public Administration; Master of Social Work; and Master of Education in counseling (elementary and secondary), curriculum and instruction (biology, early childhood education, elementary education, English, geography/earth science, history, mathematics, middle-level education), reading, school administration, and special education (comprehensive, mental retardation, learning disabilities, behavior disorders). The School of Graduate Studies also offers post-master's degree curricula leading to various types of education certification, including supervisory certification, and is one of twenty-two national sites for a post-graduate academic training program in Reading Recovery.

More than 200 student clubs, organizations, and activity groups, resulting in nearly 600 leadership opportunities, are available. Organizations include academic clubs, community service groups, special interest organizations, media organizations, musical groups, performing arts troupes, and national or local fraternities and sororities.

Student activities are complemented by programs that bring nationally and internationally known figures to campus. Pulitzer Prize–winning author David McCullough, Nobel Peace Prize recipient Archbishop Desmond Tutu, Rev. Jesse Jackson, actor Danny Glover, actor Sidney Poitier, author and poet Maya Angelou, Vice President Dick Cheney, jazz musician Wynton Marsalis, and astronaut Buzz Aldrin have all appeared on campus.

Each of the eight residence halls is equipped with lounges, exercise rooms, music practice rooms, study rooms, and computer connections to the online library catalog system. Each residence hall room has one cable television and two direct computer network connections. Most residence hall rooms are double occupancy; some single rooms are available. Seavers Complex houses six students in each unit. Student safety is emphasized through controlled access to the residence halls, trained supervisory personnel, and a keycard entry system. There is also an apartment-style student housing facility with one, two, or four bedrooms, living room, bathroom, and full kitchen.

The University offers a variety of athletic facilities for both intercollegiate and intramural sports. These include a 2,768-seat field house, an 8,000-seat stadium, a gymnasium, outdoor tennis courts, indoor and outdoor tracks, an indoor swimming pool, squash and handball courts, a rehabilitation center, and sand volleyball courts. The 62,000-square-foot student recreation center includes a cardio/strength area with thirty-nine cardiovascular machines with individual televisions, four multipurpose courts, a group fitness studio, and an elevated running track. The University is a member of the Pennsylvania State Athletic Conference and NCAA Division II. Men's intercollegiate sports include baseball, basketball, cross-country, football, soccer, swimming, track and field, and wrestling. Women's intercollegiate sports include basketball, cross-country, field hockey, lacrosse, soccer, softball, swimming, tennis, track and field, and volleyball. There are ten intramural sports, which include street hockey, and thirteen club sports, which include men's and women's rugby.

Etter Health Center provides 24-hour access to medical services. The eight-bed infirmary is staffed by a team of physicians and nurses. Chambersburg Hospital is only 20 minutes from campus.

Students have access to comprehensive counseling services on request in academic, career, psychological, social, personal growth, and religious areas. The Career Development Center offers career counseling, workshops in resume preparation, job interview techniques, and job search assistance.

Location

Shippensburg University is on 200 acres overlooking its namesake community, a borough of approximately 6,700 people in the Cumberland Valley. The University is about 40 minutes southwest of Harrisburg, 2 hours from both Baltimore and Washington, D.C., and 2½ hours from Philadelphia. The campus is within easy walking distance of the center of town.

Majors and Degrees

Undergraduate degrees conferred are the Bachelor of Arts (B.A.), Bachelor of Science (B.S.), Bachelor of Science in Business Administration (B.S.B.A.), Bachelor of Science in Education (B.S.Ed.), and Bachelor of Social Work (B.S.W.). The College of Arts and Sciences awards the B.A. degree in art (computer graphics); communication/journalism (electronic media, print media, public relations); English (writing); French; history (public history); human communication studies; interdisciplinary arts; political science; psychology; secondary certification (art, English, French, and Spanish); sociology; and Spanish. The B.S. degree is awarded in applied physics (nanofabrication); biology (biotechnology, ecology and environment, health professions, medical technology); chemistry (biochemistry, health professions, medical technology); computer science (computer graphics, embedded programming, related discipline, software engineering, systems programming); economics (business, mathematics, political science, public administration, social studies); geoenvironmental studies; geography (geographic information systems, land use, human-environmental); health-care administration; mathematics (applied, statistics); physics (nanofabrication); public administration; secondary education (biology, biology/environmental education, chemistry, mathematics); and technical management. The B.S.Ed. degree is awarded in earth science, physics, social studies/economics, social studies/geography, social studies/history, and social studies/political science.

The John L. Grove College of Business awards the B.S.B.A. degree in accounting, finance (personal financial planning), information technology for business education, management (entrepreneurship, general, human resource, international), management information systems, marketing, and supply chain management (logistics).

The College of Education and Human Services awards the B.S. degree in criminal justice and exercise science; the B.S.W. degree in social work; and the B.S.Ed. degree in elementary education K–4, and mid-level education 4–8, (biology, chemistry, environmental education, mathematics, multicultural education, sociology, TESOL).

Preprofessional preparation is available for admission to schools of chiropractic, dentistry, engineering, forensic science, law, medicine, optometry, pharmacy, physical therapy, podiatry, and veterinary medicine.

Shippensburg University offers 2+2 transfer programs in the allied health fields of biotechnology, nursing, occupational therapy (2+3), P.A.C.E. Program (2+2, 3+3), and radiologic sciences.

Academic Programs

The University is on the semester system with a fall semester beginning in late August and a spring semester beginning in mid-January. Three terms, one of three weeks and two of five weeks, comprise the summer program.

The general education program, which comprises one half of the credits required for graduation, is the core of the undergraduate curriculum. It includes courses to develop competence in writing, speaking, mathematics, and reading. The program ensures exposure to history; language and numbers; literary, artistic, and cultural traditions; laboratory science; biological and physical sciences; political, economic, and geographic sciences; and social and behavioral sciences. Ample elective opportunities are available.

The University requires students to take one approved diversity course for a total of 3 credit hours.

Academic options include an honors program, independent study and research, internships, field experience (mandatory in such areas as teacher education, social work, and medical technology), the Marine Science Consortium Program at Wallops Island, a 3+2 engineering program, and Army ROTC.

Academic Facilities

Ezra Lehman Memorial Library has a computerized library system that includes access to full-text journal articles and electronic indexes to journal literature. The library also provides access to the Internet and many CD-ROM databases. The library's collection of more than 2 million items includes books, journals, government documents, maps, and audiovisual material. The library participates in several consortia that have reciprocal borrowing privileges for students.

Student instruction is supported by multiple computer systems for student e-mail and computer network connections to the Internet. Several hundred terminals or personal computers for student use are available in residence halls, the library, academic buildings, microcomputer labs, and the Computing Technologies Center. Students with their own computers also have access to the systems. All students can use the systems 24 hours a day and have unlimited computer time at no additional expense. Most buildings have wireless network capabilities and several have satellite capability for distance education. The University also has its own campuswide information system available on and off campus.

Costs

For Pennsylvania residents, the cost per semester in 2008–09 included tuition of $2679; room and board, $3126; educational services fee, $267; technology fee, $90.50; student activities fee, $145; student union fee, $113; health services fee, $93; and recreation center fee, $162. Nonresidents paid tuition of $6698 per semester and a technology fee of $136.50; the remaining fees were the same. Maryland residents paid tuition of $6028.

Financial Aid

The University's extensive financial aid program helps students who deserve a college education but who cannot afford to pay the full cost themselves. Shippensburg offers a wide range of aid in the form of grants, scholarships, loans, and campus employment. Most aid is awarded as a package consisting of all types for which the applicant is qualified. Nearly 80 percent of undergraduates receive some form of financial assistance.

Faculty

The University has 404 full- and part-time faculty members. The undergraduate student-faculty ratio is 19:1. Nearly 90 percent of the full-time instructional faculty members hold a doctorate or other terminal degree in their field. Each student has a faculty adviser.

Student Government

Shippensburg's strong student organization, built around a Student Senate, standing committees, and an Activities Program Board, provides a highly diversified program of student activities. Students sit on many policymaking administration-faculty committees and administer their own budget for the Student Services, Inc.

Admission Requirements

Shippensburg University, in compliance with federal and state laws and University policy, is committed to human understanding and provides equal educational, employment, and economic opportunities for all people without regard to race, color, sex, age, creed, national origin, religion, veteran status, or disability. A student's potential for success is judged by the high school average, rank in class, aptitude test scores (SAT or ACT), and recommendations. The high school record is generally considered the most important factor. A college-preparatory program, consisting of 4 units of English, at least 3 units of math, 3 units in the sciences, 2 units of social studies, and 2 units in the same foreign language, is strongly recommended. A campus interview and visit are encouraged. Transfer students in good standing are welcome.

Application and Information

To be considered for admission, a student should submit the application form with a $30 application fee. The high school transcript, recommendations, and aptitude test results should be sent by the high school. Transfer students must submit college transcripts. The Admissions Office operates on a rolling basis.

For application materials and additional information, students should contact:

Dean of Enrollment Services
Shippensburg University of Pennsylvania
1871 Old Main Drive
Shippensburg, Pennsylvania 17257
Phone: 717-477-1231
800-822-8028 (toll-free)
Fax: 717-477-4016
E-mail: admiss@ship.edu
Web site: http://www.ship.edu

The 200-acre Shippensburg University campus is located 40 miles southwest of Harrisburg, Pennsylvania.

COLLEGE CLOSE-UPS

SHORTER UNIVERSITY

ROME, GEORGIA

The University

Since 1873, Shorter University has been combining academic excellence with a caring Christian commitment. The University was established through the generosity of a Baptist layman, Alfred Shorter, and the vision of his pastor. They led a group of northwestern Georgia Baptists in founding the school, which was originally named Cherokee Baptist Female College. The name was changed to Shorter Female College in 1878 and to Shorter College in 1923. The College became coeducational in 1951. On June 1, 2010, the College changed its name to Shorter University. Shorter's enrollment of 3,200 includes students in both traditional semester programs and innovative continuous programs for working adults. Approximately 1200 of these students are located on the main campus in Rome, Georgia. Students come from all parts of the United States and from other countries around the world. Shorter University has an overall graduate school acceptance rate of 80 percent and an impressive 82 percent acceptance rate to medical colleges over the past twenty-one years. Shorter University is very committed to providing a high-quality education in an intentionally Christian atmosphere. Each year, the campus is visited by noted Christian leaders, scholars, and outstanding musical performers. The dean of the chapel and the campus minister work together to provide a wide range of opportunities for spiritual growth. The largest religious organization on campus is the Baptist Collegiate Ministries (BCM), which includes Christians of many denominations. Student publications include a newspaper, a yearbook, and a literary magazine. Highly skilled music and drama groups include the Shorter Chorale, the Shorter Chorus, the Shorter Theater Company, the Opera Workshop, and the Shorter Marching Band. The Shorter Chorale was selected to represent the United States in choral festivals held in Yugoslavia, France, and Austria and represented the University in St. Petersburg, Russia. The Chorale was also selected in 2008 to perform mass at the Vatican during a tour of Italy. Shorter has also been the home of numerous National Metropolitan Opera Audition winners and finalists. The University has three fraternities and three sororities as well as chapters of two national music fraternities and honor societies for majors in biology, communication, English, music, religion, and social sciences. Shorter University is a member of the Southern States Athletic Conference of the NAIA. The University also has a competitive cheerleading program and competes in the Mid-South Conference of the NAIA in football and track and field. Varsity teams compete in men's baseball, basketball, cross-country, football, golf, soccer, tennis, and track and field and in women's basketball, cheerleading, cross-country, fast-pitch softball, golf, soccer, tennis, track and field, and volleyball. Wrestling and men's and women's lacrosse are scheduled to be added in fall 2010.

Location

The University is situated on 150 acres atop Shorter Hill, in Rome, Georgia (area population 93,000). Rome is located just 65 miles northwest of Atlanta and 65 miles south of Chattanooga, Tennessee, and cultural opportunities abound. The city of Rome offers the Symphony Orchestra, Rome Little Theatre, Rome Area Council for the Arts events, popular concerts and attractions at The Forum, and the 334,859-volume modern city library. The University sponsors numerous events, including faculty, alumni, student, and guest musical recitals; four guest lecture series; recitals; drama and opera productions; art exhibits; and athletic events.

Majors and Degrees

Shorter University offers seven baccalaureate and three master's degrees: the Bachelor of Arts, the Bachelor of Science, the Bachelor of Science in Nursing, the Bachelor of Business Administration, the Bachelor of Science in Education, the Bachelor of Fine Arts, the Bachelor of Music, the Master of Education, the Master of Arts, and the Master of Business Administration.

The Bachelor of Arts is offered in art, communication arts (with concentrations in electronic media and journalism), English, French, health science and counseling, history and political science, international studies, liberal arts, mathematics, music, psychology, public relations, religion and philosophy, sociology, and Spanish. The Bachelor of Science is offered in biology, chemistry, Christian ministries, computer information systems, communication leadership, economics, ecology and field biology, general studies, history and political science, mathematics, mathematics education, ministry studies, psychology, religious studies, sociology, and sports studies. The Bachelor of Business Administration is offered in accounting, accounting–CPA track, business administration, and sports management. The Bachelor of Science in Education is offered in early childhood education (K–4) and middle grades (4–8). Programs leading to certification in secondary school teaching are available in English, general science, history, mathematics, and social science. Certification is also offered in music for grades K–12. The Bachelor of Fine Arts is offered in art, musical theater, and theater. The Bachelor of Music is offered in church music, music education, organ performance, piano pedagogy, piano performance, and voice performance. Preprofessional programs are available in allied health, dentistry, law, medicine, pharmacy, physical therapy, physician's assistant studies, and veterinary medicine. Courses are also available in German, health and physical education, and interdisciplinary studies.

Academic Programs

Shorter is accredited by the Southern Association of Colleges and Schools and the National Association of Schools of Music and strives to provide an academic environment of high quality. Teacher programs are approved by the Georgia Professional Standards Commission. Small classes (freshman lecture courses average 22 students) taught by dedicated and highly qualified professors (71 percent of freshman lecture courses are taught by full-time faculty members, 26 percent by full professors) ensure that each student receives an education that is both challenging and personally rewarding. For any degree, a candidate must have earned a minimum of 126 semester hours; some degrees require a greater number of hours. As part of the orientation program at the beginning of the fall semester, each new student is assigned to one of several small orientation groups that assist the student in adjusting to University life; the student is also assigned to an academic adviser, who assists in the selection and scheduling of courses. Early registration sessions are available in the summer. Freshman advisers are specially trained faculty and staff members. The academic calendar is divided into two semesters from September to May, with two "mini" sessions offered during the summer. On-campus evening classes are available in selected disciplines. Shorter offers an honors program that spans all four years and provides students with learning opportunities that are not generally available to undergraduates.

Off-Campus Programs

Shorter's School of Business and School of Education and Social Sciences offer the Professional Studies Programs, which are specifically designed for working adults, on campus and in Lawrenceville, Riverdale, and Marietta, Georgia. Majors are business, education, and human resources. Classes meet one evening or weekend per week, year-round, with a required weekly study group.

Shorter University offers several monthlong study-abroad programs immediately following the end of the second semester in May, including MAYTERM (in Europe), the Asia Program, and the Americas Program. Students earn 12 semester hours of credit through travel, study, and classroom experiences. Students are housed in student residences or college dormitories, and the cost of most meals is usually included. Shorter University faculty members accompany the students and teach the courses that are offered. MAYTERM is usually based at British American College London and includes visits to England and to one other European country. The Asia Program is generally based at Zhengzhou University in China or at Mahidol University in Thailand. The Americas Program includes two weeks in Ecuador and the Galapagos Islands and two weeks in another Central or South American country. Studies in other countries can be arranged on an individual basis through the Office of International Programs.

Academic Facilities

Livingston Library, which was dedicated in 1976 as a memorial to Ray Livingston, houses more than 213,297 books, 582 periodical subscriptions, 8,099 microform materials, 12,134 audio/video items, 38,312 e-books, and 7,000 e-journals. The library also contains conference rooms (for both individual and group study), projection rooms, a graphics preparation room, computer terminals, typewriters, and music listening facilities for student use. The Alice Allgood Cooper Fine Arts Building and the Randall H. Minor Fine Arts Building are connected to form an outstanding fine arts complex, providing up-to-date facilities for the departments of music, communication arts, and art. The Cooper Building contains classrooms, music faculty offices, the art department's drawing and painting studio, and Brookes Chapel, the meeting place for convocations, concerts, recitals, and lectures. A renovated home adjacent to the campus houses expanded art facilities. The Minor Building contains classrooms, twenty-five music practice rooms (with a baby grand piano in each), a choral rehearsal room, faculty offices, photography facilities, a theater, a desktop publishing lab, a radio studio, and an art gallery. Rome Hall was named in honor of the citizens of Rome in appreciation of their generous support of the University. It contains classrooms, science laboratories (including the Stergus Collection of Internal Organs, one of the most complete pathology collections in the United States), faculty offices, lounges, and the Robert T. Connor exhibit of some 150 African and North American animals and skins. Alumni Hall houses the educational materials center and faculty offices. The Winthrop-King Centre houses classrooms, offices for coaches, a basketball gym, a dance and aerobic studio, two racquetball courts, a fitness center, and an indoor jogging track. The Fitton Student Union contains the campus bookstore, a 24-hour study room, a 24-hour game room, and an indoor swimming pool. Two computer labs are available for general student use. Computer labs for business and communication arts are also available. Smaller computer labs are available for art, music, and recreation. All residence halls have computer and Internet access. The Robert H. Ledbetter College of Business is located adjacent to the main campus in a newly renovated facility that offers seven academic classrooms, three computer labs, faculty offices, and student lounges. The College of Nursing is located in the heart of Rome's medical community and provides state-of-the-art lab equipment, simulators, computer labs, and classroom facilities.

Costs

Tuition for the 2010–11 academic year is $16,700 and fees are $350. Room and board charges are $8200.

Financial Aid

Shorter University offers aid through each of the five federal programs: the Federal Pell Grant, Federal Supplemental Educational Opportunity Grant, Federal Work-Study Program, Federal Perkins Loan, and Federal Stafford Student Loan. Full-time students who are Georgia residents are eligible to receive the Georgia Tuition Equalization Grant and may be eligible to receive the HOPE Scholarship. Scholarships are offered for achievement in academics, music, art, theater, humanities, and athletics. Awards range from $500 to full tuition, room, and board. Academic scholarships are renewable each year, provided the student maintains at least the required grade point average. Special grants and scholarships are available to students who plan to enter church-related vocations or who are dependents of full-time employees of a Southern Baptist church, institution, or agency. Shorter University offers need-based aid to students with demonstrated financial need as determined by the Free Application for Federal Student Aid (FAFSA).

Faculty

The Shorter faculty is composed of 97 full-time, highly qualified professors, of whom 67 percent hold doctoral degrees. The University also employs 50 part-time faculty members. A favorable student-teacher ratio of 11:1 in traditional programs ensures that each student receives individual attention.

Student Government

One of Shorter's truly distinctive features is that students may participate in a wide variety of significant extracurricular activities, each of which affords a chance to develop social and leadership skills that prepare a student to win in a competitive world. The Student Government Association (SGA) is the official voice of the students. Through SGA's Executive Council, Senate, judicial boards, and special committees, students are directly involved in the life of the University.

Admission Requirements

Students are admitted into the freshman class based on their academic grade point average, SAT or ACT scores, and required essay. A review of the student's goals and their compatibility with the purpose of the University are also determining factors. The University requires 4 years of English, 4 years of mathematics (including 2 years of algebra), 3 years of history/social science, 3 years of science, and 2 units of foreign language. In addition to the general requirements for admission to the University, students majoring in music must meet the following requirements: each student must perform in an audition of approximately 10 minutes in his or her major medium, and each student must take a series of music placement tests. Students must successfully fulfill these requirements prior to the beginning of classes in August of their freshman year, since the music curriculum requires at least four years for completion. An audition is also required for students majoring in theater, and an art portfolio review is required for students majoring in art. High school students who have completed their junior year, have an outstanding academic record, and have completed the units outlined above may be considered for early admission. High school seniors entering their senior year may be admitted on a joint-enrollment basis. Such students should have above-average grades and SAT or ACT scores. Transfer and international students are also welcome to apply. For international students, a minimum paper-based TOEFL score of 500, Internet-based score of 61, or computer-based score of 173 is required. All international students must have their academic credentials evaluated by WES or another transcript evaluation service affiliated with the National Association of Credential Evaluation Services (NACES). For all transfer students, credit for college work below a C cannot be transferred. Homeschooled students should contact the Office of Admissions directly for requirements.

Application and Information

Shorter accepts students on a rolling basis. Campus visits are highly recommended through a personal campus tour or one of three Open Houses.

Director of Admissions
Shorter University
315 Shorter Avenue
Rome, Georgia 30165-4298
Phone: 706-233-7319
800-868-6980 Ext. 7319 (toll-free)
Fax: 706-233-7224
E-mail: admissions@shorter.edu
Web site: http://www.shorter.edu

SIENA COLLEGE

LOUDONVILLE, NEW YORK

The College

Siena College is a four-year liberal arts college with a Franciscan and Catholic tradition. The College's 3,000 students pursue degrees in business, liberal arts, and the sciences. Siena's wide range of academic programs provides more than 1,200 combinations and the foundation for students' successful careers and lives after graduation.

Siena offers a welcoming, student-centered environment with an emphasis on community. The College integrates Franciscan values such as diversity, respect, and service into everyday life. Siena seeks to instill in students a desire to always seek better for themselves and others, and to measure success by personal growth and integrity, not just achievement.

Small classes and involved professors help students grow both academically and personally. Siena's faculty members, 90 percent of whom hold the highest degree in their fields, are committed first and foremost to teaching. The student-faculty ratio of 14:1 helps to develop interaction between students and faculty members, including research projects, which often lead to student presentations at national conferences and published, peer-reviewed articles.

Eighty-five percent of Siena's students live on campus in traditional residence hall rooms, suites, and townhouse units. More than sixty clubs and organizations provide something of interest for everyone. The College offers eighteen Division I intercollegiate sports, plus many club teams and intramurals.

The Franciscan Center for Service and Advocacy is the College's primary vehicle for service. From serving meals to the poor, teaching adults and teenagers how to read, or assisting at a homeless shelter, to mentoring a child as a big brother or sister, there are many opportunities for improving the world. In return, Siena students learn understanding, respect, and dignity.

Siena also provides numerous student support services, including counseling, tutoring, health services, peer counseling, and a career center.

Location

Siena's 166-acre campus is ideally located in Loudonville, New York, a residential community 2 miles north of Albany, the state capital. The Capital Region is also referred to as New York's Tech Valley, one of the country's foremost regions for innovation and technology.

Albany is a college town with a wide variety of educational and social activities off campus. The Times Union Center hosts performances by major concert artists and professional sporting events. Siena is close to a number of theaters, museums, shopping centers, and restaurants. The nearby Adirondacks, Berkshires, and Catskill Mountains provide numerous outdoor activities including hiking, skiing, and snowboarding. Boston, Montreal, and New York City are less than 3 hours away. The alumni network in the Capital Region is a strong one, supporting numerous Siena interns and hiring Siena graduates.

Majors and Degrees

The College offers bachelor's degrees in the following areas: accounting, actuarial studies, American studies, biochemistry, biology, chemistry, classics, computational science, computer science, economics, English, environmental studies, finance, French, history, marketing and management, mathematics, philosophy, physics, political science, psychology, religious studies, social work, sociology, and Spanish. In addition, the College offers thirty-eight minors and nine certificate programs.

Academic Programs

A strong liberal arts core forms the basis for all of Siena's programs. The Core Curriculum, consisting of 42 credits from fourteen courses, provides every Siena student with a common, coherent educational experience. Through the core, students pursue courses in the traditional liberal arts and sciences. Core courses engage students in critical thinking and dialogue, stress effective communication, and introduce students to the perspectives and modes of knowing specific to the arts and sciences.

ROTC affiliation is available at Siena in a U.S. Army unit, and two partnership programs are available at nearby colleges.

Off-Campus Programs

Siena students are encouraged to study abroad. Programs directly affiliated with the College include Siena at Regent's College, London; the Siena in London Internship Experience; the Siena semester at the Centre d'Études Franco-Américain de Management in Lyon, France; and the Center for Cross-Cultural Studies in Seville, Spain. However, programs are available for all majors virtually anywhere in the world.

Locally, internships are available through government, business, and nonprofit organizations. More than 400 students work as interns at nearly 300 different organizations each year. Those organizations sometimes offer jobs to Siena student interns upon graduation.

Within six months of graduation, 96 present of Siena students have started either their career or graduate school. Siena graduates are hired because companies know and recognize the value of the College's education.

Academic Facilities

The Standish Library collection of more than 321,000 volumes consists of books, journals, microforms, compact discs, videocassettes, and a growing number of electronic information sources. More than 6,000 volumes are added annually, and 1,600 serial subscriptions are currently maintained, with electronic access to thousands of additional journals. Siena Hall, a high-technology teaching and learning center is also home to Siena's Hickey Financial Technology Center. The Hickey Center provides Siena's students the opportunity to trade stocks, bonds, cash, and currency in a virtual environment and provides students with access to leading sources of financial data.

All academic and residential buildings are interconnected with a high-speed Ethernet network connected via fiber optics. Every student residence space includes a connection point to access the College's network and the Internet. The network includes more than 2,500 ports. The computer facilities are accessible 24 hours a day, seven days a week. Numerous computers are available throughout the campus for student use.

Costs

Tuition at Siena remains on average $7000 lower than its top ten private competitors, allowing the College to provide a rigorous education at a moderate cost. In 2008, *Business Week* cited Siena College as having one of the biggest returns on investment. For 2009–10, tuition was $25,350 and room and board were $9930.

Financial Aid

More than 86 percent of students receive financial aid. Siena is committed to providing personal attention to every student's financial needs, recognizing that each situation is different. Aid packages are awarded in a layered approach, combining scholarships, grants, and loans.

Faculty

Siena's faculty members are committed to teaching. Student concerns and development are at the heart of the curriculum. The student-faculty ratio of 14:1 helps to develop interaction with students, as does the fact that Siena professors teach labs. Students are assigned a faculty adviser to help in the planning of their course of study.

Student Government

The Student Senate oversees student involvement in academic and social life and interprets students' attitudes, opinions, and rights for the faculty and administration. It charters all student organizations and provides funds for many through fees collected by the College. The governing board is made up of officers and representatives of all four classes and of the commuting students.

Admission Requirements

Siena seeks bright, articulate people who will take advantage of the opportunities available at the College. The average SAT score of accepted freshman students is 1160. The high school curriculum, activities, recommendations, and campus visit all affect the final decision. Students seeking degrees in the science or business division should be well versed in mathematics. Those interested in American studies, English, history, or philosophy are likely to find a working knowledge of a foreign language very helpful.

Application and Information

The deadline for the submission of a regular application is March 1 of a student's senior year in high school. Decisions are sent starting in mid-March. Siena also offers an early decision and an early action program.

For more information, students should contact:

Admissions Office
Siena College
515 Loudon Road
Loudonville, New York 12211
Phone: 518-783-2423
888-AT-SIENA (toll-free)
E-mail: admit@siena.edu
Web site: http://www.siena.edu

SIMMONS COLLEGE

BOSTON, MASSACHUSETTS

The College

Decades before women gained the right to vote, Boston businessman John Simmons had a revolutionary idea: women should be able to earn independent livelihoods and lead meaningful lives. Simmons College was the result.

Founded in 1899, Simmons was the first college in the nation to offer women a liberal arts education integrated with professional preparation. Today, Simmons provides a strong liberal arts education for undergraduate women that is integrated with professional career preparation, interdisciplinary study, and global perspectives. Simmons offers the many benefits of a small university: an innovative undergraduate women's college, renowned coeducational graduate programs and the world's first MBA program designed for women. Exceptional internship and research opportunities provide hands-on experience and career exposure. It is the Simmons faculty that makes the educational experience unique by challenging students to reach their full potential while providing individual support and mentoring. Furthermore, the Simmons community encourages dialogue, respect and collaboration—making the Simmons experience as thoughtful as it is thought-provoking.

Simmons's interdisciplinary approach offers great advantages: a broader education and view of the world; personalized plans of study; and a chance to develop a range of professional skills and strengths needed for graduate school and an increasingly competitive job market. This is reflected by the large percentage of students employed or attending graduate school shortly after graduation. Every student explores a variety of subjects while gaining an in-depth theoretical and practical understanding of her major. First-year core courses emphasize critical thinking and writing skills, while integrating two or more subjects—ranging from bioethics and Buddhist studies to computational linguistics and visual communication.

Students fulfill their independent learning requirement through internships, fieldwork, and research projects. In doing so, they develop skills, confidence, impressive resumes, and a network of professional contacts. Some students co-publish research with faculty in nationally recognized academic journals as undergraduate students. Many students spend one or more semesters interning for businesses and organizations, ranging from Boston Public Schools and *The Boston Globe* to the Museum of Fine Arts, Smash Advertising, and the World Affairs Council. Simmons's Longwood Medical Area partnerships provide outstanding clinical opportunities at Boston's world-renowned hospitals. On campus, students conduct research using state-of-the-art equipment in areas such as materials science, gene splicing, and computer modeling. In addition, professors frequently invite undergraduates to collaborate on professional research projects, articles, and presentations.

Acquiring a global outlook is integral at Simmons—including an understanding of languages, cultures, and international politics. Programs such as Africana studies, East Asian studies, international relations, and modern languages offer a direct route to cross-cultural immersion. Simmons encourages students to spend an entire semester or year abroad. Short-term international courses provide unique opportunities to study topics such as journalism in South Africa, music in Austria, or history and civilization in Japan. Students also take part in local and international service-learning projects, ranging from education initiatives in Boston to health care in Nicaragua.

Approximately 55 percent of Simmons undergraduates live in college housing two blocks from the main campus. The "quintessential New England" residence campus features nine brick residence halls and a private, landscaped quad, as well as Bartol Dining Hall, the state-of-the-art Holmes Sports Center, a student-run cafe, and the campus health center.

Students say that Simmons's location offers the best of both words—an intimate college experience in the heart of a vibrant city. Simmons's 2,060 undergraduates love the fact that they can easily access the city's rich social and cultural resources but also come home to a safe, friendly campus.

Location

Considered by many to be the best college town in the nation, Boston has more than fifty colleges and universities and approximately 300,000 students. Boston is big league in every sense but size—just like Simmons. The historic, tree-lined Simmons campus is located in Boston's eclectic Fenway neighborhood, which is alive with music and fine arts, medical care and research, action and activism, and the resounding cheers of baseball fans at legendary Fenway Park. From campus, it's a safe, easy stroll to other colleges and universities as well as shops, cafes, clubs, museums, movie theaters, parks, and public transportation. Students hop aboard the "T" (Boston's public transportation system) and head to destinations such as Downtown Crossing, the Italian North End, Chinatown, Harvard Square, and Greater Boston's many other diverse neighborhoods.

Majors and Degrees

Simmons offers more than 40 majors and programs. Popular majors include psychology, nursing, biology, political science, and communications. Faculty advisors help each student create a plan that fulfills requirements and satisfies her personal and professional goals. A number of integrated degrees and accelerated programs allow students to go directly from an undergraduate program to earning a graduate degree in areas such as education, health care, liberal arts, physical therapy, and science information technology. Simmons also offers individually designed preprofessional programs for dentistry, law, medicine, and veterinary medicine. Simmons students typically declare a major by the end of their sophomore year, and nearly a third choose to double major.

Academic Programs

Simmons offers a strong liberal arts education integrated with professional preparation, interdisciplinary study, and global perspectives. A minimum of 128 semester hours is required for graduation. Students must demonstrate competence in math and foreign language, complete a core curriculum in the liberal arts and sciences (40 semester hours), complete the courses required for the selected major(s) (20 to 40 semester hours for each major), fulfill an independent learning requirement (8 to 16 semester hours), and round out their program with appropriate electives. Other special academic opportunities include Simmons' outstanding honors, service-learning, and study-abroad programs. The Dorothea Lynde Dix Scholars option is available for women who are 24 years or older, or who hold a previous bachelor's degree.

Off-Campus Programs

Simmons is a member of the Colleges of the Fenway consortium, which allows students to cross-register with neighboring colleges, including Emmanuel College, Massachusetts College of

Art, Massachusetts College of Pharmacy and Allied Health Sciences, Wentworth Institute of Technology, and Wheelock College. A domestic exchange program allows juniors to spend a semester at Belmont University, Mills College, Spelman College, or Fisk University. Students interested in international study may elect to spend one semester or one year at an approved university exchange or participate in intensive study-abroad programs during the spring semester. Many students take advantage of the over 20 short term study abroad programs which bring students to another location for three weeks, typically following the spring semester.

Qualified students, usually juniors, also may apply for the Washington Semester at American University in Washington, D.C. Other opportunities include Success Connection, a mentoring program that matches select seniors with highly successful Simmons alumnae, and the Barbara Lee Internship Fellows program, which places students in Massachusetts legislators' offices and policy advocacy groups for one semester.

Academic Facilities

The beautiful Simmons campus offers an attractive, practical mix of historic and modern architecture, including state-of-the-art facilities and conveniences. The Main College Building houses a dining area and coffee bar, lecture halls and classrooms, administrative and faculty offices, the bookstore, the Student Activities Center, art studios, music practice rooms, and the Trustman Art Gallery.

Park Science Center offers technologically advanced learning environments, including faculty and student research facilities, fully equipped science laboratories, environmental rooms, observation rooms for psychological testing, and food science kitchens.

One Palace Road, the home of Simmons's School of Social Work and Graduate School of Library and Information Science, features electronic classrooms and also houses the centers for academic support, counseling, career education and resources, media, and technology. The newly renovated Beatley Library offers a number of high-tech services, including a wireless network, laptop loans, sophisticated online library service, technology-equipped group study rooms, and more. In January 2009, Simmons will open a state-of-the-art LEED-certified 'green' building to house the School of Management.

Costs

Undergraduate tuition and fees for the 2008–09 academic year were $14,560 per semester; room and board charges were $5750 per semester. Total costs, not including books, supplies, and personal expenses, were $41,490.

Financial Aid

More than 90 percent of Simmons students receive some form of financial aid. Scholarships, grants, loans, and federal work-study are determined by the Free Application for Federal Student Aid (FAFSA). Simmons also awards academic merit scholarships, ranging from $2000 to $15,000 awards, renewable for four years.

Faculty

Simmons offers a learning experience that is highly collaborative and much more personal than that of large universities. The Simmons faculty includes noted researchers, authors, and experts in their respective fields — yet professors passionately uphold their primary obligation to teach. Students say the small classes, intellectual focus, and welcoming environment contribute to their confidence and success. Simmons has 206 full-time and 340 part-time faculty members; 72 percent are women. A 13:1 student-teacher ratio ensures that every student receives individual attention, and reinforces the strong tie between students and professors.

Student Government

The Student Government Association (SGA) coordinates the policies and activities of various student organizations, allocates the student activities funds, and promotes the interests of the student body by working closely with the Simmons faculty and administration. In addition, every academic department has a student liaison that participates in department evaluations and helps promote educational and social activities for students, faculty members, and staff members. Simmons has more than 50 student organizations, clubs and academic liaisons, including 10 NCAA Division III varsity teams, honor societies, cultural organizations, volunteer programs, and a literary magazine.

Admission Requirements

There isn't one "type" of Simmons student, but there are common qualities. Simmons women are intellectually motivated and open-minded. They are serious about their personal and professional goals, and they are determined to make a difference in the world. With this in mind, the Simmons admission team reviews applications to see not only what applicants have accomplished, but also who they are and what kind of person they hope to become.

The admission team also evaluates high school performance, SAT or ACT scores, recommendations, and the application essay. If English is not the applicant's first language, the TOEFL, IELTS, or a comparable exam score is required. Additional English language proficiency exams are accepted on a case by case basis.

Simmons welcomes applications from prospective freshmen, transfer students, international students, and students who are beyond the traditional college age.

Although not required, an interview is highly recommended. This gives admission officers better perspective about an applicant's abilities, interests, and personality—and at the same time, allows the applicant to evaluate Simmons and decide if it's the right place for her.

Application and Information

Students may apply online at www.Simmons.edu, use the Common Application, or submit a print application, along with the $55 fee and all supporting credentials. Simmons waives the application fee for students who apply online. The Early Action deadline is December 1 and is a nonbinding deadline. The deadline for freshman applicants is February 1. Transfer students are evaluated on a continual basis; the preferred filing date for applications is April 1. Students applying for the semester beginning in January should apply by December 1.

Simmons encourages prospective students and their families to attend an admission event or request an individual visit. They are welcome to tour the campus, sit in on a class, talk to current students, and interview a professor, department chair, or program director.

For further information, interested students should contact:

Office of Undergraduate Admission
Simmons College
300 The Fenway
Boston, Massachusetts 02115
Phone: 800-345-8468 (toll-free)
Fax: 617-521-3190
E-mail: ugadm@simmons.edu
Web site: http://www.simmons.edu

SIMPSON COLLEGE

INDIANOLA, IOWA

The College

Founded in 1860, Simpson College is a private liberal arts college affiliated with the United Methodist Church. Simpson combines the best of a liberal arts education with outstanding career preparation and extracurricular programs. With a student to faculty ratio of 14:1, students have the opportunity to work closely with their professors. Simpson professors are as dedicated to their fields of study as they are to teaching—and it shows in the classroom. When this type of dedication and passion is combined with well-prepared and motivated students, the potential for success is virtually unlimited.

Extracurricular activities at Simpson are designed to supplement and reinforce the academic program and contribute toward a total learning experience. Activities range from an award-winning music program to nationally recognized NCAA Division III teams. Students may participate in student government, campus publications, religious life, music, theater, residence hall organizations, departmental clubs, and various other organizations. Simpson has seven Greek chapters on campus, including three national fraternities, one local fraternity, and three national sororities. Simpson competes in nineteen intercollegiate sports and has an extensive intramural program.

Outstanding facilities are continually enhanced and updated, including the state-of-the-art Carver Science Center, named after Simpson's most distinguished alumnus, George Washington Carver. The 4-4-1 academic calendar includes a May Term that provides students with unique learning opportunities in the classroom, internship settings, or while studying abroad. Simpson's beautiful 85-acre, tree-lined campus provides a setting that nurtures creativity, energy, and productivity.

Location

Simpson is located in Indianola, a residential community with a population of 14,400. Indianola is just 12 miles south of Des Moines, Iowa's capital city, with easy access to Interstates 35 and 80. The Des Moines International Airport is 20 minutes from campus. Indianola is host to nationally known events including the Des Moines Metropolitan Opera and the National Balloon Classic. The vibrant, small-town community has many choices for entertainment and recreation including Lake Ahquabi State Park, Summerset Trail, and unique restaurants and shops within walking distance of campus on the town square. Indianola's proximity to Des Moines gives students plenty of distinct advantages. Within minutes, students are right in the heart of some of the best entertainment and employment options Iowa and the Midwest have to offer.

Majors and Degrees

Simpson College grants Bachelor of Arts and Bachelor of Music degrees. Majors include accounting, applied philosophy, art, athletic training, biochemistry, biology, chemistry, computer information systems, computer science, criminal justice, economics, education (elementary and secondary), English, environmental science, exercise science, forensic science/biochemistry, French, German, history, integrated marketing communication, interdisciplinary studies, international management, international relations, management, marketing, mathematics, multimedia journalism, music, music education, music performance, philosophy, physical education, physics, political science, psychology, religion, sociology, Spanish, sports administration, and theater arts.

Simpson also offers preprofessional programs in dentistry, engineering, law, medicine, optometry, pharmacy, physical therapy, theology/ministry, and veterinary medicine. Concentrations areas such as early childhood education and ethics are available, as well as many additional minors, including women's studies, social work, human resources management, Latin American studies, and coaching endorsements.

Academic Programs

Simpson College operates on a 4-4-1 academic calendar. The first semester starts in late August and ends in mid-December; the second semester starts in mid-January and ends in late April. A three-week session takes place during the month of May. During this period, students have three options: take one class on campus with a hands-on focus, participate in a field experience/internship, or study abroad.

The First Year Program is an extensive program of orientation, team-building, mentoring, community service, advising, and course work structured to help new students adapt to their first year of college. The program begins with summer orientation and continues throughout the academic year. College and Character, a national initiative of the John Templeton Foundation, named Simpson College one of the 60 colleges in the nation that offer students an exemplary program in their first year to develop moral character.

The academic component of the First Year Program is the Liberal Arts Seminar, a joint classroom and advising concept that is unique among first-year programs. The seminars are small in size—no more than 18 first-year students each—and all are taught by each student's faculty adviser.

All students must complete the requirements of the Cornerstone Studies in liberal arts and competencies in foreign language, math, and writing. To earn the Bachelor of Arts degree, students take a maximum of 42 hours in their major department (excluding May Term programs) and 84 hours in the division of the major (including May Term programs). At least 128 semester hours of course work with a grade point average of C (2.0) or better must be accumulated for graduation.

For a Bachelor of Music degree, the same requirements apply—except 84 hours must be earned in the major (excluding May Terms) and the candidate is limited to 12 additional hours in the division of fine arts. A minimum of 132 hours of course work must be completed with a cumulative grade point average of C (2.0) or better to meet graduation requirements.

Off-Campus Programs

Simpson provides many opportunities for studying abroad, with the choice of a semester-long program or a three-week May Term. Simpson's semester-long, faculty-led study-abroad programs include London, England; Schorndorf, Germany; Pathom, Thailand; Tahiti, French Polynesia; and Rosario, Argentina. Students also have the opportunity for semester study-abroad programs in France, Spain, Italy, Australia, and more locations.

Additionally, ten to fifteen travel courses are offered each May Term. Recent destinations include Africa, Central America, Great Britain, France, Greece, Ireland, New Zealand, the Galapagos Islands, Brazil, Argentina, and Scandinavia. May Term study abroad courses are led by Simpson faculty members and give students the opportunity to experience a different culture while gaining a stronger global perspective. Simpson has been recognized as one of the top 100 colleges in the nation for the highest percentage of students who study abroad—43 percent of Simpson students will travel abroad by the time they graduate.

The Capitol Hill Internship Program (CHIP) provides students with the opportunity to spend either the fall or spring semester in Washington, D.C. Past participants have had various experiences including interning for members of Congress, the Smithsonian Institution, the Republican National Committee, the Justice Department, CNN, the Australian Embassy, and FOX News. In addition, students participate in two seminars for course credit.

Academic Facilities

The George Washington Carver Science Center provides state-of-the-art research facilities, computer labs, a cadaver lab, and many classrooms.

Simpson has a wireless campus network with high-speed Internet access. There are numerous computer labs throughout campus where students can use standard office suite applications or specialized, discipline-specific applications.

The Henry H. and Thomas H. McNeill Hall houses classrooms for management, accounting, economics, and communication studies. In addition, the hall houses a seminar room and the Pioneer Hi-Bred International Conference Center.

The Amy Robertson Music Center houses the music department and contains the Sven and Mildred Lekberg Recital Hall, ten studios, twenty-two practice rooms, a music computer lab, and the band rehearsal room. The Salsbury Wing includes a choral rehearsal room, a classroom, and studios.

Dunn Library, a modern academic learning resource center, contains approximately 154,710 volumes, 335 current periodicals, 28,328 electronic journals, 3,126 DVDs and videotapes, 2,274 music CDs, and access to more than 7,480 e-books. Additional materials for research can be obtained through a national interlibrary loan network. The library also provides media equipment and services to classrooms and the entire campus. Hawley Academic Resource Center, which provides free academic support services to all students, is located within Dunn Library.

The A. H. and Theo Blank Performing Arts Center accommodates Simpson's well-known programs in theater arts and opera and includes the magnificent 500-seat Pote Theatre, with both proscenium and hydraulically controlled thrust stages, a studio theater, the Barborka Gallery, technical facilities and shops, and classrooms.

Wallace Hall, named to the National Register of Historic Places in 1991, contains facilities for education, sociology, and applied social science.

Mary Berry Hall, renovated during the summer of 2008, houses the psychology department as well as faculty offices, six new labs, a control room for observation and data processing, and an animal care space. There are several remodeled classrooms, a language lab, and the building is home to the Iowa History Center.

Costs

Tuition and fees for 2009–10 were $25,733; room charges were $3485; and board was $3776. These figures do not include books, music fees, or personal expenses.

Financial Aid

Simpson College seeks to make it financially possible for qualified students to experience the advantages of a Simpson education. Generous gifts from alumni, trustees, and friends of the College—in addition to state and federal student aid programs—make this opportunity possible. Simpson offers financial aid on both a need and non-need basis. Need is determined by filing the Free Application for Federal Student Aid.

Financial aid granted on a non-need basis includes generous academic scholarships (awarded on the basis of prior academic records) and talent scholarships (available in theater, music, and art). The talent scholarships are determined by audition/portfolio.

Also, specific scholarships such as Great Ape Trust, Earth Corps, United Methodist Community to Service Grant, the John C. Culver Fellowship Program, and George Washington Carver Scholarship can be obtained through application.

Faculty

Eighty-eight percent of Simpson's 99 full-time faculty members have earned their terminal degrees. At Simpson, faculty members serve as academic advisers as well as teachers and often attend College plays, operas, and athletic events, reinforcing their sincere interest in the lives of the students.

Student Government

Each year students elect a president and vice president of the Student Government Association. In addition, students elect representatives to the Student Senate. The Student Senate appoints student members to all campus organizations in which students may hold membership. The senate also appoints 3 at-large students to attend plenary sessions of the Simpson College Board of Trustees.

Admission Requirements

Admission to Simpson College is selective and competitive. A strong academic record is essential. Applications are acted upon by an admissions committee, which is elected by the faculty and represents the five academic divisions of the College. These faculty members consider the college-preparatory courses taken and the grades received in those courses, rank in class, and standardized test scores (ACT and/or SAT), including test subscores, as well as a guidance counselor recommendation form.

Transfer applicants are accepted on the basis of successful completion of academic work at an accredited college or university. In addition, transfer applicants are required to submit official high school transcripts and ACT/SAT results.

Application and Information

Simpson's rolling admission policy allows flexibility; however, early application is recommended. Transfer and international students are welcome to apply. Students are strongly encouraged to visit the campus.

For additional information or to obtain application materials, students should contact:

Office of Admissions
Simpson College
701 North C Street
Indianola, Iowa 50125
Phone: 515-961-1624
800-362-2454 Ext. 1624 (toll-free)
E-mail: admiss@simpson.edu
Web site: http://www.simpson.edu

The George Washington Carver Science Center provides Simpson students with state-of-the-art labs and research facilities.

SKIDMORE COLLEGE

SARATOGA SPRINGS, NEW YORK

The College

Skidmore College is an independent liberal arts college of 2,300 men and women with a creative spirit that has been evident since its beginnings. Founded by Lucy Skidmore Scribner as the Skidmore School of Arts in 1911, it became Skidmore College in 1922. In addition to being accredited by the Middle States Association of Colleges and Schools, the College has a chapter of Phi Beta Kappa and has program accreditation with the Council on Social Work Education and the National Association of Schools of Art and Design.

Throughout its history, Skidmore has steadily reflected a spirit of innovation and imagination in response to need. In the 1960s, the College built an entirely new campus; in 1971, it became coeducational; in 1983, it completely revised its curriculum to emphasize interdisciplinarity through a comprehensive liberal studies program; and in 1993, it installed the Master of Arts in Liberal Studies program. Skidmore has embraced change, seeing in it the opportunity to serve the needs and realize the potential of its students. By expanding and refining its programs, the College has broadened its educational mission to reflect the evolving opportunities and challenges of a global society.

Students enjoy a full schedule of cultural, intellectual, and social activities, including lectures, art exhibits, concerts, opera, dance, and theater. There are more than 100 student organizations, such as a weekly newspaper, a radio station, an Asian cultural association, an art and literary journal, and a student-volunteer network. There are no fraternities or sororities. A strong intercollegiate sports program for men and women—nineteen teams in all—includes baseball, basketball, field hockey, golf, ice hockey, lacrosse, riding, rowing, soccer, softball, swimming and diving, tennis, and volleyball. The College has a vigorous intramural program, supports team activities of club status, and provides a growing health, fitness, and wellness program.

Skidmore's campus includes forty-nine buildings. The sports and recreation complex includes a pool, racquet-sport courts, basketball and volleyball courts, a small stadium with artificial turf field and a 400-meter all-weather track, three dance studios, a weight room, a fitness center, a human performance laboratory, and other recreational and competitive sport facilities. The Frances Young Tang Teaching Museum and Art Gallery, unique in its interdisciplinary approach, opened in fall 2000, and renovations to the student center include a cyber café and an intercultural center.

September 2006 saw two major additions to the campus. The Northwoods Apartments opened with 380 single-room units across ten new buildings. A brand new dining hall also opened, offering extensive vegetarian options, fresh-made pasta, locally grown organic items, and a broad range of daily choices. The Arthur Zankel Music Center, a state-of-the-art music building with a 700-seat auditorium opened in January 2010.

Location

Set on 850 acres in the historic destination city of Saratoga Springs, New York, the College offers students the advantage of a beautiful, wooded campus setting and the benefits of a city of 30,000 residents that balloons in size during the summer months. Saratoga Springs has long been famous as a resort and as a horse-racing and cultural center. The city is located 30 miles north of Albany, the capital of New York State, and is cosmopolitan in character. Skidmore is within an hour of major ski areas, state parks, large lakes, and mountainous regions of eastern New York, Vermont, and western Massachusetts. During the summer, groups such as the New York City Ballet and the Philadelphia Orchestra are in residence at the Saratoga Performing Arts Center as are top jazz and rock performers.

Bus service is available from Saratoga Springs to New York City, Montreal, Boston, and other major cities. There are daily trains to and from New York City and Montreal. Rental cars are available at the Albany International Airport, which is served by major airlines. The College is located near Exit 15 of I-87 (the Northway).

Majors and Degrees

Skidmore College grants a Bachelor of Arts degree in the following liberal arts subjects: American studies, anthropology, Asian studies, biology, chemistry, classical studies, computer science, economics, English, environmental studies, foreign languages and literatures (French, German, and Spanish), geosciences, government, history, history of art, international affairs, mathematics, music, neuroscience, philosophy, physics, political economy, psychology, religious studies, sociology, and women's studies. The Bachelor of Science degree is granted in areas of a more professional nature, including business, dance, education studies, exercise science, social work, studio art, and theater. There are twenty-seven interdepartmental majors, biology-philosophy major being just one example. Self-determined majors, double majors, and minors are also available. Almost half of Skidmore students choose a second major or minor.

The College offers 3-2 programs in engineering with Dartmouth College and Clarkson University. Also available is a 4-1 M.B.A. program offered with Clarkson and a 4+1 Master of Arts in Teaching program with Union College. Through a cooperative program with the Cardozo Law School of Yeshiva University, Skidmore students may obtain a bachelor's degree and a law degree in six years. In addition, Skidmore has certification programs in teaching and social work and preprofessional programs in law and medicine.

Academic Programs

Skidmore College is known for its unusual blend of courses in the traditional liberal arts with opportunities in preprofessional disciplines, the combination of which often creates interesting and unexpected courses of study and career directions. It is also recognized for its interdisciplinary approach, which starts with a required first-year seminar. Students choose from a myriad of topics. Faculty seminar leaders function as their students' first-year advisers. Additional core requirements include one lab course in science, one in the social sciences, one in the humanities, one in the arts, one in a foreign language, and one in non-Western culture. All students choose a major at the end of their sophomore year from among sixty-four options, some of which include interdepartmental concentrations, self-determined majors, and minors.

The College operates on a two-semester system with opportunities for internships directly following the end of the second semester in May. Students normally carry four or five courses during each semester.

The College offers a six-week residential academic summer program (PASS) enabling high school students to take two courses for college credit.

Off-Campus Programs

Skidmore's membership in the Hudson-Mohawk Association of Colleges and Universities enables students to cross-register at any of fourteen other colleges and universities in the area. The Washington Semester, conducted through American University in Washington, D.C., offers an intensive, twelve-week workshop experience through course work, seminars, research projects, and internships with government committees. Skidmore's Office of Off-Campus Study and Exchanges enables students to study in China, England, France, and Spain. Skidmore is also affiliated with other study-abroad programs, facilitating study for a semester or a year in many locations in Asia, Australia, Europe, and Latin America. Approximately 55 percent of Skidmore students study abroad for a year or a semester.

Arrangements for credit-bearing internships are made through academic departments or through the Office of Career Services. Internships are available in such diverse fields as government, social work, the arts (dance, theater, and museum work), business, scientific research, and medicine.

Academic Facilities

Scribner Library, housing approximately 400,000 volumes, numerous online publications, and advanced information technology, has been designated a depository for U.S. government documents. Students have access to forty libraries in the region through the College's membership in an area council. Skidmore also participates in the Lockheed/Dialog system for information search and retrieval. Dana Science Center has laboratories and sophisticated university-like equipment for the biology, chemistry, environmental studies, physics, and geology departments/programs.

The new Arthur Zankel Music Center contains a large recital hall, practice and listening rooms, state-of-the-art recording facilities, and an electronic and a music library. Other special facilities include a language laboratory in Bolton Hall; the Saisselin Art Building, with drawing, painting, ceramics, sculpture, weaving, and jewelry-making studios—in addition to a state-of-the art digital photography lab and the Schick Art Gallery; the Skidmore Theatre; dance studios; and the Tang Teaching Museum and Art Gallery at the center of the campus.

Students have access to ample computer resources, including 350 MAC and Windows PCs in general-purpose rooms, eight Linux workstations, twelve Silicon Graphics workstations, network connections in all residence hall rooms, and nearly 650 computers in public areas and academic departments.

Costs

In 2009–10, tuition and fees for all students were $40,420; room and board cost $10,776.

Financial Aid

Skidmore awards financial aid based on demonstrated need. The Free Application for Federal Student Aid (FAFSA), a copy of the federal income tax form, and the CSS PROFILE must be filed each year. The application date is January 15 for entering freshmen. The College hosts an annual Filene Music Scholarship Competition to award four $40,000 ($10,000 per year) scholarships on the basis of musical ability without regard to financial need. Five $10,000 scholarships in math and science are also awarded annually. Other grants are available for superior math and science students, including the new S3M (Skidmore Scholars in Science & Math). Detailed information concerning scholarships, grants, loans, and/or work awards can be obtained through the Office of Student Aid and Family Finance.

Faculty

Skidmore College has 229 full-time teaching faculty members and 68 part-time members, including those with special appointments. Ninety-four percent of the liberal arts and sciences faculty members hold the doctoral degree or the highest degree in their field. The student-to-faculty ratio is about 9:1, and the average class size is 16. Although actively engaged in research and publication in their individual fields, the Skidmore faculty members regard teaching as their primary commitment. All students have faculty advisers who assist them in selecting courses and in designing individual academic programs.

Student Government

Students at Skidmore play an active role in College governance. Through the Student Government Association (SGA) and by membership on a number of major College committees, they participate in all phases of academic and social life. The SGA operates under the authority granted by the Board of Trustees and is dedicated to the principles of democratic self-government and responsible citizenship. Within the association, elected faculty members and student representatives serve on the All-College Council, the Academic Integrity Board, and the Social Integrity Board. The broad concerns of the SGA include educational policy, elections, social and student events, freshman orientation, student publications, and student clubs and organizations.

Admission Requirements

Applicants for admission to the freshman class are expected to complete a secondary school program with a minimum of 16 college-preparatory credits. The Admissions Committee also considers applications from qualified high school juniors who plan to accelerate and enter college early. Typical preparation for entrance includes 4 years of English, 4 years of a foreign language, 4 years of mathematics, 4 years of social studies, and 3–4 years of laboratory science. Among the required credentials are a secondary school transcript, a report from the school guidance counselor, and assessments from 2 teachers. Skidmore also requires applicants to take the SAT or ACT (with writing test) examination and recommends that two SAT Subject Tests be taken. A campus interview is strongly recommended.

Through the Higher Education Opportunity Program (HEOP) and the Academic Opportunity Program (AOP), Skidmore enrolls talented, energetic, and motivated students who have been economically and educationally disadvantaged and who otherwise would be unable to attend the College.

Application and Information

An applicant for admission registers by completing the Common Application and submitting it with a $65 fee. All information should be postmarked by January 15. Applications from early decision candidates may be submitted by November 15 for the Round I early decision plan or by January 15 for the Round II early decision plan. Transfer candidates are urged to apply by April 1 for the next fall term and by November 15 for the next spring term. Interested freshmen and transfer students are strongly urged to visit the campus for interviews and guided tours.

Mary Lou W. Bates
Dean of Admissions and Financial Aid
Skidmore College
Saratoga Springs, New York 12866
Phone: 518-580-5570
800-867-6007 (toll-free)
E-mail: admissions@skidmore.edu
Web site: http://www.skidmore.edu

Aerial view of the Skidmore College campus.

SOUTHERN CONNECTICUT STATE UNIVERSITY

NEW HAVEN, CONNECTICUT

The University

The rich academic and social environment at Southern Connecticut State University encourages students to discover who they are, who they want to be, and how to realize their dreams. A public coeducational university founded in 1893, Southern offers 117 undergraduate and graduate programs. Fascinating internships, unique research opportunities, a challenging faculty, and a dynamic campus enrich every program. Southern is located in New Haven, the heart of "academic Connecticut."

Southern has six academic schools: Arts and Sciences; Business; Education; Communication, Information, and Library Sciences; Health and Human Services, including nursing, public health, recreation and leisure studies, and social work; and Graduate Studies. Southern offers several honors programs, including the Honors College, for highly motivated students. The Honors College is a four-year alternative program featuring team-taught interdisciplinary courses, symposia, and a written thesis. The Office of Student Supportive Services provides tutorial support and includes services and programs for veterans, international students, and students with learning, physical, and emotional/psychiatric disabilities.

The student body represents diverse ethnic and socioeconomic groups. Although most students reside in Connecticut, students from thirty-eight states and thirty-nine countries also enroll at Southern. Approximately 12,000 students attend Southern, including about 9,000 undergraduates. Of the 7,200 full-time undergraduates, 2,700 live on campus in eight modern residence halls and town houses. Other students commute or reside in off-campus housing in the Southern neighborhood.

Competitive athletes and eager amateurs enjoy multifaceted intramural and intercollegiate sports programs at Southern. Intramural and club sports include coed three-on-three and five-on-five basketball, cheerleading, flag football, coed floor hockey, a golf tournament, ice hockey (men), karate, rugby (men and women), skiing and snowboarding, coed softball, Ultimate Frisbee, coed soccer, a tennis tournament, Wiffle ball, and coed volleyball. A member of the National Collegiate Athletic Association (NCAA), the Eastern College Athletic Conference, and the Northeast-10 Conference, Southern offers student athletes competitive opportunities in several intercollegiate sports. A university with a long tradition of athletic excellence, Southern ranks among the top ten NCAA Division II colleges and universities, with nine NCAA team championships and sixty-seven individual championships. Southern offers intercollegiate competition in men's baseball, basketball, cross-country, football, soccer, swimming, and track and field. Southern holds six national championships in men's soccer and three in men's gymnastics. Southern offers intercollegiate programs for women in basketball, cross-country, field hockey, gymnastics, lacrosse, soccer, softball, swimming, track and field, and volleyball. Outstanding facilities are available to all athletes in Moore Fieldhouse, Pelz Gymnasium, and the Jess Dow Field outdoor sports complex.

Location

New Haven, Connecticut, is a sophisticated city of 130,000 people on picturesque Long Island Sound. Southern is located in the city's Westville section, near historic West Rock Park. Rich in tradition, New Haven is a classic college town; about 35,000 students attend its half-dozen fine universities and colleges. Only 75 miles from New York City and 3 hours from Boston, New Haven is an integral part of the economic, cultural, and social life of the Northeast. Students enjoy easy access to outstanding cultural opportunities, including movies, restaurants, clubs, concerts, seaside activities, sports, museums, and world-famous theater at the Yale Repertory, the Shubert, and Long Wharf.

Majors and Degrees

Southern offers the Bachelor of Arts (B.A.) and the Bachelor of Science (B.S.) degrees. The Bachelor of Arts degree is awarded in anthropology, art (art history and studio art), biology, chemistry (biochemistry), communication (communication disorders and media studies), earth science, economics, English, French, geography, German, history, Italian, journalism, liberal studies, mathematics, media studies, music, philosophy, physics, political science, psychology, sociology, Spanish, and theater.

The Bachelor of Science degree is awarded in anthropology (archeology, cultural, general, linguistics, and physical), art (ceramics, graphic design, jewelry making, painting, photography, printmaking, and sculpture), athletic training, biology, business (accounting, business economics, finance, international business, management, managing information systems, and marketing), chemistry and biochemistry, communication (creative message construction, interpersonal/relational, organizational communication, and video production), computer science (information systems), earth science (environmental, geology, and oceanography), exercise science (human performance and teacher education), geography, information and library science, journalism, mathematics, nursing, physics, political science, psychology (research), public health (environmental and health promotion), recreation and leisure (community, outdoor, and therapeutic), social work, and sociology.

The Bachelor of Science degree with teaching certification is offered in art education, early childhood education, and elementary education.

The Bachelor of Science degree with certification for secondary education is offered in biology, chemistry, earth science, English, exercise science, French, geography, German, history and social science, Italian, mathematics, physics, political science, Spanish, sociology, and special education.

Southern also offers preprofessional study in dentistry, engineering, law, medicine, and veterinary medicine.

Academic Programs

The University operates on a two-semester calendar. The fall semester usually begins the first week in September and ends in mid-December. The spring semester, which includes a one-week spring recess in March, begins the third week of January and ends in mid-May. Southern also offers several summer session programs and a three-week intersession program in January.

Southern maintains a strong commitment to the liberal arts and sciences as fundamental elements of a high-quality education. To ensure all students acquire the best education possible, Southern offers a strong yet flexible program that underscores the basics while encouraging individual choice. All baccalaureate degree candidates must complete a minimum of 122 hours of credit. Majors consist of at least 30 prescribed hours of credit in one specific, approved field. Degree candidates also must fulfill the All-University Requirements, a common core of courses ranging from 41 to 54 credits in liberal studies. In addition, candidates for the B.A. degree must meet a foreign language requirement plus 28 credits of electives from areas of interest. Candidates for the B.S. degree must also satisfy the foreign language requirement and meet certain distribution requirements. Some professional B.S. degree programs enable students to develop a minor or a concentration in addition to the major with 12 credits in electives.

Off-Campus Programs

Southern's location in the heart of a major urban area enables the University to cultivate a growing list of meaningful regional internships. Aspiring social workers enjoy learning opportunities that extend beyond the classroom into New Haven's dynamic urban environment. Students in the B.S. nursing degree program acquire clinical experience at Yale–New Haven Hospital, the Hospital of Saint Raphael, and other sites that are linked by distance learning programs. Internships also are available for journalism students in city newsrooms and local TV stations. The University also offers internships at Long Wharf Theatre; ESPN Broadcasting; the Circle in the Square Theatre in New York City; MTV; Shearson Lehman Brothers, Inc.; and others.

Academic Facilities

A $260-million building program is rapidly transforming Southern campus life. The evolving landscape features a new West Campus Residence Complex and parking garage, a new baseball field, and the expansion of Engleman Hall, the University's main administration and classroom building. Renovations have begun that will double the size of the Hilton C. Buley Library. The new Michael J. Adanti Student Center opened in early 2006. The 125,000-square-foot facility includes a ballroom, a 200-seat movie theater, a fitness center, and an expansive bookstore. A focal point for campus life, the center is also home to Southern's student newspaper, the radio station, a modern cafeteria, a bookstore, a TV lounge, a copy center, and other facilities. Southern supports more than ninety campus clubs and organizations, ranging from academic and career groups, such as the marketing club and the literary magazine, to religious, theatrical, and political clubs. Southern's campus groups sponsor popular extracurricular activities such as film festivals, concerts, and art exhibits.

Southern continues to provide students with a full range of facilities and services throughout the multiphase building project. Operations continue without interruption at the Hilton C. Buley Library, which houses 125,000 electronic databases and academic resources. Seventy Macintosh terminals, laser printers, scanners, and twenty PC compatibles are available in a Macintosh lab in the library's lower level. The library also houses the Learning Resources Center, a well-equipped multimedia education curriculum laboratory. Manson Van B. Jennings Hall contains sixty-six science laboratories, a large amphitheater, classrooms, and the University's Academic Computer Center, with more than 100 workstations for student and faculty research. Additional computer centers are available in residence halls. All on-campus housing includes high-speed Internet service via RESNET. Other campus facilities include a satellite-equipped journalism lab; a modern television studio in Ralph Earl Hall of Fine Arts; the John Lyman Center for the Performing Arts, a 1,650-seat theater for major productions; the Robert Kendall Drama Lab for experimental theater; the Center for the Environment; the Multicultural Center; the Communication Disorders Center; the Adaptive Technology Lab; and the Disability Resources Center.

Costs

Annual tuition and fees for 2009–10 for Connecticut residents are $7578. Tuition and fees for out-of-state residents are $17,270. On-campus room and board fees for the year are $8161. Student books, supplies, and personal expenses average $2000 per year. All costs are subject to change. Prospective students should contact the Office of Financial Aid and Scholarships for current information.

Financial Aid

The Office of Financial Aid and Scholarships coordinates grants, scholarships, long-term low-interest loans, and part-time student employment for students and families who demonstrate financial need. The University offers the Federal Perkins Loan, the Federal Pell Grant, the Federal Supplemental Educational Opportunity Grant, the Federal Stafford Student Loan, the Federal PLUS loan, and the Federal Work-Study Program. Southern also provides alumni scholarships. Southern's Tuition Installment Plan enables matriculated students to make monthly tuition payments throughout the academic year. More than 60 percent of Southern's undergraduates receive financial aid. Students who seek assistance must complete the Free Application for Federal Student Aid (FAFSA) and send it to the central processor for receipt by March 5, 2010. Prospective students can file the FAFSA form on paper or on the Web at http://www.fafsa.ed.gov.

Faculty

Like the University's student body, Southern's faculty members represent a broad spectrum of backgrounds, interests, and scholarly achievements. Southern's more than 700 faculty members share a deep commitment to teaching, writing, and research. More than 90 percent of the 402 full-time faculty members hold Ph.D.'s from major colleges and universities around the world. Many faculty members serve as academic advisers. In addition, the University offers counseling to help students with academic, personal, and career decisions. The student-faculty ratio is 17:1.

Student Government

The Student Government is the voice of the undergraduate student body at Southern. The Student Government's 24 voting members meet regularly to discuss students' interests in several areas, from funding to academic policies. Student Government members also serve with administrators and faculty members on key University committees. Resident students govern themselves through their respective residence hall councils and the Inter-Residence Council.

Admission Requirements

Southern's selective admission policy considers each student as an individual, with particular consideration given to personal accomplishments and motivation. Southern seeks students with diverse cultural values and backgrounds; no applicant is accepted or rejected because of race, color, gender, sexual orientation, age, disability, religion, or national origin. Candidates must be high school graduates or hold an equivalency diploma. Their secondary school program should include at least 13 academic units of college-preparatory work, including 4 years of English, 3 years of mathematics (algebra 1, geometry, and algebra 2), 2 years of foreign language, 2 years of science (including 1 year of laboratory science), and 2 years of social sciences (including U.S. history). Other factors include the student's high school record, class rank (preferably in the upper 50 percent), and competitive SAT or ACT scores.

Application and Information

Candidates for admission should apply early in the fall of their high school senior year. The Admissions Office mails its first acceptance notice in early December. Early applicants have priority for housing and financial aid. Applicants must submit academic records, including a complete transcript of high school grades and class rank; an online admission application; a $50 nonrefundable fee; a written recommendation from a high school principal, teacher, or school guidance counselor; and a copy of the SAT or ACT score report. For additional information, students should contact the Undergraduate Admission Office, Southern Connecticut State University, 131 Farnham Avenue, New Haven, Connecticut 06515. Students are encouraged to apply online by visiting the University's Web site and clicking on admissions.

Paula Kenned
Associate Director of Admissions
Admissions House
Southern Connecticut State University
131 Farnham Avenue
New Haven, Connecticut 06515-1355
Phone: 203-392-SCSU
888-500-SCSU (toll-free)
Web site: http://www.SouthernCT.edu

Southern's "Serie Metafisica XVIII" (1983), an outdoor sculpture by Herk Van Tongeren, provides the ideal setting for study in the sunshine.

COLLEGE CLOSE-UPS

SOUTHERN ILLINOIS UNIVERSITY CARBONDALE

CARBONDALE, ILLINOIS

The University

Southern Illinois University Carbondale (SIUC), chartered in 1869, is a comprehensive state-supported institution with nationally and internationally recognized instructional, research, and service programs. SIUC is fully accredited by the North Central Association of Colleges and Schools.

SIUC offers more than 150 undergraduate majors, specializations, and minors; two associate degree programs; 101 baccalaureate degree programs; seventy-four master's degree programs; thirty-two doctoral programs; and professional degrees in law and medicine. SIUC is a multicampus university and includes the Carbondale campus as well as the SIUC School of Medicine at Springfield.

During the 2009 academic year, SIUC's enrollment reached 20,350, which included 15,551 undergraduate students, 4,113 graduate students, and 686 professional students. The average age of undergraduates is 23. International students account for 5.8 percent of SIUC's enrollment. Of U.S. undergraduate students, 19.5 percent are African American, 0.4 percent are American Indian/Alaskan, 2.3 percent are Asian or Pacific Islander, and 4.6 percent are Hispanic.

Students who are ready to start college but not ready to commit to a specific major can enroll in SIUC's Pre-Major Program. Premajor advisers and career counselors help premajor students plan their education and careers. SIUC faculty members, staff members, and alumni help students arrange internships, cooperative education programs, and work-study programs.

All single students under the age of 21, not residing with their parents or legal guardians, and with fewer than 26 credit hours earned after high school, are required to live in University-owned and operated residence halls. SIUC offers four on-campus residential areas for single students, each with a dining hall, post office, and laundry facilities. Learning Resource Centers are available on both sides of campus and offer writing centers, computer labs, and student lounges. University Housing Residence Hall Dining provides a variety of meal plans, with all-you-care-to-eat meals and late-night dining. Residence Hall Dining offers a variety of menus, vegetarian and light entrees, display cooking, and a full-time dietitian to help students with special dietary needs. Apartment housing is available for upperclass undergraduates, graduate students, and students with families.

SIUC intercollegiate sports teams compete at the NCAA Division I level (football is Division I-FCS). Conference affiliations include the Missouri Valley Conference and the Missouri Valley Football Conference. Intercollegiate sports teams include men's and women's basketball, cross-country, diving, golf, swimming, tennis, and track and field; men's baseball and football; and women's softball and volleyball. The campus has various playfields, several tennis courts, and a campus lake with a beach and boat dock. SIUC's Student Recreation Center offers an Olympic-size pool; indoor tracks; handball/racquetball and squash courts; a climbing wall; weight rooms; and basketball, volleyball, and tennis courts; outdoor equipment rental; an aerobic area; walleyball; martial arts; and dance and cardio studios.

The Student Center is one of the largest in the U.S. without a hotel. It holds a bookstore, several restaurants, a craft shop, a bakery, facilities for bowling and billiards, headquarters for 400 active student organizations and the student government office, four ballrooms, and an auditorium. On-campus events throughout the year include concerts, plays, festivals, guest speakers, and musicals.

Location

Carbondale is 6 hours south of Chicago, 2 hours southeast of St. Louis, and 3 hours north of Nashville. Four large recreational lakes, the two great rivers (the Mississippi and the Ohio), and the spectacular 270,000-acre Shawnee National Forest are within minutes of the campus. The mid-South climate is ideal for year-round outdoor activities.

Carbondale is a city of 26,000 people that supports one large enclosed mall, several mini-malls, theaters, and restaurants. Students frequent the shops and restaurants that line Illinois and Grand Avenues.

Majors and Degrees

The University offers associate in applied science degree programs at the College of Applied Sciences and Arts in aviation flight and physical therapist assistant studies.

The College of Applied Sciences and Arts offers bachelor's degree programs in architectural studies, automotive technology, aviation management, aviation technologies, dental hygiene, electronic systems technologies, fashion design and merchandising, fire service management (off campus only), health care management, information systems technologies, interior design, mortuary science and funeral service, radiologic sciences, and technical resources management.

The College of Agriculture offers bachelor's degree programs in agribusiness economics, agricultural systems, animal science, forestry, hospitality and tourism administration, human nutrition and dietetics, and plant and soil science.

The College of Business and Administration offers bachelor's degree programs in accounting, business and administration, business economics, finance, management, and marketing.

The College of Education and Human Services offers bachelor's degree programs in athletic training, communication disorders and sciences, early childhood education, elementary education, exercise science, health education, physical education teacher education, recreation, rehabilitation services, social work, special education, sport administration, and workforce education and development. Teacher preparation is available in art, biological sciences, English, French, German, health education, mathematics, physical education, secondary education, social sciences with designations in history and social studies, Spanish, and special education.

The College of Engineering offers bachelor's degree programs in civil engineering, computer engineering, electrical engineering, engineering technology, industrial technology, mechanical engineering, and mining engineering.

The College of Liberal Arts offers bachelor's degrees in anthropology, art, classics, criminology and criminal justice, design, economics, English, foreign language and international trade, French, geography and environmental resources, German, history, linguistics, mathematics, music, musical theater, paralegal studies, philosophy, political science, psychology, sociology, Spanish, speech communication, theater, and university studies.

The College of Mass Communication and Media Arts offers bachelor's degrees in cinema and photography, journalism, and radio-television.

The College of Science offers bachelor's degree programs in biological sciences, chemistry and biochemistry, computer science, geology, mathematics, microbiology, physics, physiology, plant biology, zoology, and preprofessional programs in dentistry, medicine, nursing, optometry, pharmacy, physical therapy, physician assistant studies, podiatry, and veterinary medicine.

In addition to many majors offered at SIUC, specializations are offered in all colleges in many areas.

Academic Programs

Each bachelor's degree candidate must earn a minimum of 120 semester hours of credit, including at least 60 at a senior-level institution and the last 30 at SIUC. Each student must maintain at least a C average in all course work at SIUC, fulfill the University core curriculum, and the specific requirements of their degree programs. SIUC awards credit through qualifying extension and correspondence programs, military experience, the High School Advanced Placement Program, the College-Level Examination Program (CLEP), SIUC's proficiency examination program, and work experience.

SIUC offers honors course work and special recognition for students who demonstrate exceptional academic achievement. The Air Force and Army offer ROTC programs at SIUC. SIUC offers fall and spring semesters, and a summer term.

Off-Campus Programs

At Southern Illinois University Carbondale, distance education courses are offered in interactive, print-based and Web-based formats. Print-based (correspondence) and Web-based courses are offered by the Individualized Learning Program (ILP). Web-based courses and Two-Way Interactive Video courses are offered through the Office of Distance Education. Many of the courses offered through the ILP and other distance education courses can be taken to complete the University Studies Degree (B.A.) in the College of Liberal Arts.

Off-campus credit programs are designed to meet the educational needs of adults wishing to pursue a degree but who are unable to travel to the Carbondale campus. Faculty members who teach off-campus courses travel to distant sites to teach SIUC courses.

Contractual services are provided and include specialized educational services to groups, organizations, governmental agencies, and businesses on a cost-recovery basis. These services are provided regionally, nationally, and internationally.

All credit courses offered through these programs carry full SIUC academic credit and are taught by faculty members appointed by the academic departments of the University. Additional information can be found on the Web (http://www.dce.siu.edu/siuconnected).

Academic Facilities

In addition to the 2.8 million volumes, 3.6 million microfilms, and more than 12,500 periodicals currently available in Morris Library, students and faculty members have access to more than 27,000 full-text electronic journals. SIUC students have access to several computer learning centers that are equipped, in all, with more than 1,600 microcomputers. Additional information can be found on the Web (http://www.lib.siu.edu).

Students learn and practice in the Southern Illinois Airport, outdoor laboratories, the student-run *Daily Egyptian* newspaper, WSIU-TV, WSIU-FM, art and natural history museums, a literary magazine, McCleod Theater, Memorial Hospital, a vivarium, the plant biology greenhouses, the University Farms, and the Touch of Nature Environmental Center.

Costs

Tuition and fee charges for the 2009–10 academic year (fall and spring) for students enrolled in 15 or more semester hours were $10,411 for Illinois residents and $21,795 for out-of-state residents, including international students. Room and board were $8082. All costs are subject to change. Beginning fall 2009, new freshman, transfer, and graduate students from Arkansas, Indiana, Kentucky, Missouri, and Tennessee will qualify for a reduced tuition rate equal to the Illinois in-state rate. The cost of books and school supplies varies among programs. The average cost is $900 per academic year. Some courses require that students purchase special materials.

Financial Aid

More than $223 million in financial aid was distributed to more than 79 percent of SIUC students in fiscal year 2009 through federal, state, and institutionally funded financial aid programs.

To apply for financial aid at SIUC, students should complete a Free Application for Federal Student Aid (FAFSA). Applications that are filed before April 1 receive priority consideration for campus-based aid. The FAFSA can be completed electronically at the U.S. Department of Education's Web site (http://www.fafsa.ed.gov). When completing the FAFSA, students should list Southern Illinois University Carbondale (Federal School Code 001758) as a school of choice.

SIUC has one of the largest student employment programs in the country, with approximately 5,000 students employed each year in a wide variety of job classifications. SIUC offers competitive scholarships based on talent and academic achievement.

Faculty

Faculty members are dedicated to excellence in teaching and to their advancement of knowledge in a wide variety of disciplines and professions. Many faculty members are well-known both nationally and internationally for their varied research contributions. The student-faculty ratio is 15.7:1. There are 1,392 full-time and 250 part-time instructional faculty members.

Teaching assistants at SIUC are graduate students who assist faculty members in teaching. While some teach introductory undergraduate classes, others provide support to faculty members by assisting in laboratories, monitoring tests, and helping students.

Student Government

The undergraduate student government consists of a president, vice president, executive assistant, and chief of staff. Under the vice president, there are 43 senators: 1 senator per 388 students. Each student has at least 2 representatives: 1–6 for their residential area, and 1–6 for the college in which they are enrolled. Under the 6 commissioners are a list of committees on which a varying number of students sit to represent the student body. The student government writes and passes legislation on University policies, funding, student organizations, and other matters that affect the students and the University.

Admission Requirements

Freshman applicants whose ACT or SAT scores are at or above the 66th percentile and class rank is in the upper three quarters are admitted to the University. Applicants can also be admitted with an ACT or SAT score at or above the 50th percentile and class rank in the upper half. Finally, applicants can be admitted with an ACT or SAT score at or above the 33rd percentile and class rank in the top quarter. Admission standards are subject to change. Freshman applicants must meet course pattern requirements: 4 years of English, 3 years of mathematics, 3 years of laboratory science, 3 years of social science, and 2 years of electives.

Transfer applicants must have an overall grade point average of at least 2.0 on a 4.0 scale, based on work attempted at all institutions and calculated by SIUC grading policies. Transfer applicants must also be eligible to continue at the last institution attended.

Some programs have higher admission requirements or require additional screening for admission. Undergraduates can apply online (http://www.admissions.siuc.edu).

Application and Information

Admission is granted on a rolling basis. Application priority deadlines for freshmen are: June 1 for the summer 2010 term; May 1 for the fall 2010 semester; and December 1, 2010, for the spring 2011 semester. Application priority deadlines for transfer students are: June 1 for the summer 2010 term; July 1 for the fall 2010 semester; and December 1, 2010, for the spring 2011 semester. The application fee is $30.

Undergraduate Admissions MC 4710
425 Clocktower Drive
Southern Illinois University Carbondale
Carbondale, Illinois 62901
Phone: 618-536-4405
Fax: 618-453-4609
E-mail: joinsiuc@siu.edu
Web site: http://www.siuc.edu

SIUC's Pulliam Hall.

COLLEGE CLOSE-UPS

SOUTHERN NEW HAMPSHIRE UNIVERSITY

MANCHESTER, NEW HAMPSHIRE

The University

At Southern New Hampshire University (SNHU), there are no limits to what students can achieve. Academic programs are created with the real world in mind, so students are prepared to launch successful careers when they graduate. Classes are taught by highly credentialed faculty who have professional experience and remain current in their fields. Academic and personal support is readily available, both inside and outside the classroom. If students need help, faculty and staff will rally around them quickly.

The University operates on the belief that college should change students' lives, not break the bank—a private university education should be affordable. That's why financial aid has been increased. Students with high school GPAs of 2.5 and higher can receive up to $18,000 in grants and scholarships. About 90 percent of the students receive some kind of financial aid.

The University has approximately 1,900 traditional, full-time undergraduate day students, with a total enrollment in all divisions (day, evening, weekend, and online undergraduate and graduate students) of about 9,400. Programs are offered on campus, on location at the University's centers in New Hampshire and Maine, and online. SNHU offers undergraduate programs in business, culinary arts, education, hospitality management, and liberal arts and graduate programs in business, community economic development, education, and hospitality.

SNHU is the first carbon-neutral school in New Hampshire. The wireless campus features a new academic center (opened fall 2009), a new dining hall (opened January 2010), new dorms and apartment buildings, a simulated stock trading room, multimedia classrooms, an auditorium, the museum-quality McIninch Art Gallery, virtual science labs, technology-ready buildings, a library with resources that can be accessed via the Internet, a fitness center that rivals members-only gyms, athletic fields, cooking labs, a bakery, and an award-winning, student-run restaurant.

Students can participate in one of the University's more than forty student clubs or start new ones. Intercollegiate teams compete in Division II of the NCAA, the Eastern College Athletic Conference, and the Northeast-10 Conference. Sports include baseball, men's and women's basketball, cheerleading, men's and women's cross-country, golf, ice hockey, men's and women's lacrosse, men's and women's soccer, softball, men's and women's tennis, and volleyball. Intramural sports, including basketball, flag football, cricket, and volleyball, also are extremely popular. SNHU's powerful athletic teams dominate on the field—and in the classroom. The University's student-athletes earned honors from the NCAA and *USA Today* for high grades and 100 percent graduation rates.

Athletic facilities include an indoor, 25-meter, competition-size swimming pool; a racquetball court; an aerobic studio; cardiovascular equipment; four outdoor lighted tennis courts; a soccer/lacrosse turf field; baseball and softball fields; and two indoor gymnasiums with four basketball courts and areas for indoor soccer, indoor tennis, volleyball, and many other activities. The fitness center features 4,000 square feet of strength equipment and a 1,500-square-foot cardio deck.

The Wellness Center provides short-term health care, health education, and counseling services for students, and the buildings and facilities are accessible to the physically handicapped. A well-qualified student-services staff provides personal, career, and academic counseling; counselors are available on campus. Lifetime career services and counseling are available to all current students and to alumni.

Location

The University is ideally located, with easy access to downtown Manchester, New Hampshire's largest city and the most livable city in the East, according to *Money* magazine. It has also been named one of the top college towns in the country. Public transportation is available, and students may keep cars on campus. The mountains, beaches, and Boston are only an hour away. Morgan Quitno Press has repeatedly named New Hampshire the nation's most livable state.

Majors and Degrees

The University has four schools: the School of Business, the School of Community Economic Development, the School of Education, and the School of Liberal Arts. The University offers associate, bachelor's, master's, and doctoral degrees. Undergraduate programs provide students with a strong liberal arts foundation and the knowledge and skills they need to succeed in their careers.

The School of Business majors include accounting, accounting/finance, accounting/information systems, advertising (B.S. option), business administration, business studies, computer information technology (B.S. option), fashion merchandising, finance, finance/economics, game design and development (B.S. option), hospitality business, international business, management advisory services, marketing, retailing, sport management, technical management, and the unique 3-Year Honors Program in Business Administration—the only three-year program of its kind in the country. Students save a full year of tuition by acquiring a bachelor's degree in just three years. Customized and outcomes-based, it is not a condensed four-year degree program and does not require night, weekend, or summer course work. The six-semester, 120-credit program features an interdisciplinary course of study. Students can start their careers earlier or use the fourth year to complete a master's degree.

The School of Education majors include child development, early childhood education, elementary education, English education, and social studies education.

The School of Liberal Arts offers degrees in advertising (B.A. option); communication; computer information technology (B.A. option); creative writing (three-year option available); digital media; English language and literature; environment, ethics, and public policy; game design and development (B.A. option); graphic design; history; justice studies (three-year option available); liberal arts; political science; psychology; psychology/child and adolescent development; public service; and social science. Students in any major within the School of Liberal Arts may participate in the prelaw program.

Other programs include baking and culinary arts.

An honors program, a prelaw program, and a pre-M.B.A. program are also available for students seeking additional challenges.

Academic Programs

At Southern New Hampshire University, undergraduate students receive a broad education in the liberal arts and intense practice in oral and written communication, coupled with the specific knowledge and skills they need to succeed in their chosen fields.

Recognizing that successful leaders must be able to view problems from a variety of perspectives, the University mandates that all students complete courses in writing, the fine arts, the social sciences, mathematics, science, and public speaking. First-year students must take SNHU 101, a critical-thinking seminar to help them make the transition to University life. Students also have the opportunity to take elective courses in whatever areas capture their curiosity and may elect to concentrate their electives to earn a minor. The University curriculum offers both structure and flexibility.

Off-Campus Programs

Southern New Hampshire University is adept at mixing academic theory with practical experience inside and outside the classroom. Half of the undergraduates participate in off-campus cooperative education experiences/internships, earning 3 to 12 academic credits. Such opportunities are based on a student's major and career goals and typically are taken during a student's junior or senior year. Students work with faculty members and the Career Development Office to find appropriate assignments. About 70 percent of those who complete co-ops/internships are offered positions by their employers.

The University has established relationships with a number of respected, high-profile employers who provide internship and job opportunities, including Fidelity Investments, New York Life, Walt Disney World, LEGO Systems, the Boston Celtics, the Boston Red Sox, and Marriott International.

Students also work with real-world off-campus partners in their courses. For example, advertising students have created media campaigns for area businesses, marketing students have conducted market research for external groups, and education students assist local teachers in their classrooms. The University's graduates are in demand because businesses know they have been prepared to contribute both on the job and in their communities.

Opportunities for studying abroad are available at a number of partnering institutions in thirty-two countries around the world.

Academic Facilities

The main campus features a new academic center, a new dining hall, new dormitory and apartment buildings, state-of-the-art classrooms, wireless Internet access, auditoriums, technology labs, multimedia rooms, computer labs, a graphic arts lab, a student-run gourmet restaurant, a student-run bakery, a simulated stock trading room, a museum-quality art gallery, and more.

The Harry A. B. and Gertrude C. Shapiro Library features the Education Resource Center, networked computers, conference rooms, a career and placement resource center, and a growing collection of bound volumes, microfilm, microfiche, and ultrafiche; materials are available online as well. A recording studio, a listening room, and a closed-circuit television network that covers the entire campus are among the school's audiovisual assets.

Costs

Undergraduate tuition for the 2009–10 academic year was $26,112. Typical room and board charges were an additional $10,176. Students must pay $330 in student activity fees each year and should plan to budget funds for books, supplies, travel, and personal expenses.

All students are required to bring wireless laptop computers. Culinary arts students are required to purchase uniforms and knife sets.

Financial Aid

More than 90 percent of the University's students receive some form of financial aid, which may include need-based grants, academic and commuter scholarships, work-study funds, and loans. The average aid package has a value of more than $17,500 and includes a combination of scholarships, grants, loans, and employment sources.

The University participates in the Federal Work-Study Program, the Federal Perkins Loan Program, and the Federal Supplemental Educational Opportunity Grant Program. The school is also eligible under the Federal Stafford Student Loan Program and the Federal Pell Grant Program. Aid applicants must complete the Free Application for Federal Student Aid (FAFSA). The Office of Financial Aid can provide the appropriate forms, or students can go online to http://www.fafsa.ed.gov. Academic, athletic, and leadership scholarships are available for students who qualify.

Faculty

The University has more than 128 full-time faculty members and more than 200 part-time instructors. The student-faculty ratio is 15:1. Nearly 75 percent of the full-time faculty members hold Ph.D.'s or the equivalent in their areas of expertise.

The instructional programs blend theory with practice to stimulate students' professional development and personal growth. Faculty members bring extensive academic, work, travel, and life experiences to their classrooms. Although their primary goal is teaching, faculty members remain current in their disciplines. Outside the classroom, faculty members are management consultants, CPAs, analysts, small-business owners, economists, accountants, marketing professionals, entrepreneurs, innkeepers, chefs, world travelers, artists, poets, novelists, and much more.

Student Government

The Student Government Association is led by 25 students, including 5 officers, who represent all the students at the University. Its primary function is to represent the student body in campus affairs and to dispense student activity funds. One student is appointed to represent the student body on the Board of Trustees. Students are also appointed to most other standing committees, including the Financial Aid Advisory Committee, the Curriculum Advisory Committee, the Library Committee, and judiciary committees.

Admission Requirements

Applicants for admission are evaluated individually on the basis of academic credentials and personal characteristics. When reviewing applicants, primary emphasis is placed on a student's academic record, as demonstrated by the quality and level of college-preparatory course work and achievement attained. Most successful candidates admitted to SNHU present a program of study consisting of sixteen college-preparatory courses, including 4 years of English, 3 or more years of mathematics, 2 or more years of science, and 2 or more years of social science. Separate consideration is given to admission decisions for freshman, transfer, culinary arts, 3-Year Honors Program, nontraditional, and international applicants. Students may complete a paper application for admission or apply online.

Application and Information

Applicants for undergraduate day programs must submit an application for admission, an up-to-date official high school transcript, a personal essay, and high school recommendations. SAT or ACT scores are required of freshman applicants. Test scores are optional for students applying to the culinary arts programs. Candidates for the 3-Year Honors Program are also required to have an interview. Transfer students must also submit official transcripts from all schools previously attended. International students whose native language is other than English must prove proficiency in the English language through the TOEFL examination. Admission decisions are based on the quality of academic performance, but a campus visit and interview are strongly recommended for all candidates. The University operates on a rolling admission basis, and applicants can expect a decision within one month of the receipt of their complete credentials. Applicants may also apply as Early Action candidates by submitting their application prior to November 15. SNHU is a member of the Common Application. There is a $40 application fee.

For more information about Southern New Hampshire University, students should contact:

Office of Admission
Southern New Hampshire University
2500 North River Road
Manchester, New Hampshire 03106-1045
Phone: 603-645-9611
800-642-4968 (toll-free)
Fax: 603-645-9693
Web site: http://www.snhu.edu

Students on the campus of Southern New Hampshire University.

SOUTH UNIVERSITY

MONTGOMERY, ALABAMA

SouthUniversity℠

The University

Established in 1899, South University is a private academic institution dedicated to providing educational opportunities for the intellectual, social, and professional development of a diverse student population. To achieve this, the University offers focused and balanced curricula at the associate, bachelor's, and master's degree levels in the areas of business, criminal justice, health-care management, health science, information technology, legal studies, nursing, and psychology. In addition, the University offers a Master of Arts degree in professional counseling, a Master of Business Administration, and a Master of Business Administration in health-care administration.

South University in Montgomery became part of South University in 1997 and has been part of the postsecondary education community in Alabama since 1887.

South University in Montgomery has a diverse student body enrolled in day, evening, weekend, and online classes. South University is designed to accommodate the range of needs of its student body. Students are primarily commuters who live within 50 miles of the city. They include men and women who have enrolled directly after completing high school, who have transferred from another college or university, or who have experience in the workforce and are pursuing an education that will prepare them to expand their current position or help them take a new professional direction.

South University in Montgomery is located in two buildings on a 3.75-acre campus. The facilities house computer, health science, and nursing labs; classrooms; a library; a student lounge; a bookstore; and faculty and administrative offices. Since most students live within driving distance of the campus, the campus does not currently offer or operate student housing. However, housing is planned in the near future. If housing is needed, prospective students should contact the Admissions Office.

South University is accredited by the Commission on Colleges of the Southern Association of Colleges and Schools (SACS, 1866 Southern Lane, Decatur, Georgia 30033-4097; 404-679-4501) to award associate, bachelor's, master's, and doctoral degrees. South University in Montgomery is authorized as an educational institution under Act No. 2004-282, Regular Session, Alabama Legislature, 2004, to conduct programs within the state of Alabama. The institution is also authorized by the State Approving Agency for the training of veterans under chapters 31, 34, and 35.

Certain programs offered at South University in Montgomery have earned programmatic accreditation. The Alabama Board of Nursing has granted provisional approval for the Bachelor of Science in Nursing degree program. The Associate of Science degree program in medical assisting is accredited by the Commission on Accreditation of Allied Health Education Programs (CAAHEP, 1361 Park Street, Clearwater, Florida 33756; 727-210-2350) on recommendation of the Curriculum Review Board of the American Association of Medical Assistants Endowment (AAMAE). The Bachelor of Science in legal studies and Associate of Science in paralegal studies degree programs are approved by the American Bar Association (321 North Clark Street, Chicago, Illinois 60610; 312-988-5617). The Associate of Science in physical therapist assisting degree program is an expansion program accredited by the Commission on Accreditation in Physical Therapy Education of the American Physical Therapy Association (1111 North Fairfax Street, Alexandria, Virginia 22314; 703-684-2782).

Location

The campus is located on the rapidly growing east side of Alabama's capital city. As the state capital, Montgomery is a hub of government, banking, and law as well as a state center for culture and entertainment. Montgomery is situated in the middle of the southeastern U.S. and is less than a 3-hour drive from Atlanta and the Gulf of Mexico.

Majors and Degrees

South University in Montgomery awards the following two-year degrees: Associate of Science in business administration, Associate of Science in information technology, Associate of Science in medical assisting, Associate of Science in paralegal studies, and Associate of Science in physical therapist assisting.

The following four-year bachelor's degrees are awarded: Bachelor of Business Administration, Bachelor of Science in criminal justice, Bachelor of Science in health-care management, Bachelor of Science in information technology, Bachelor of Science in legal studies, Bachelor of Science in health science, Bachelor of Science in Nursing, and Bachelor of Arts in psychology. A Bachelor of Science in Nursing completion program (RN to B.S.N.) for current registered nurses is also available.

Academic Programs

South University offers degree programs that are designed to meet the needs and objectives of students. Each curriculum combines didactic and practical educational experiences that provide students with the academic background needed to pursue the professions of their choice. In addition, faculty members strive to instill the value not only of education and professionalism but also of contribution and commitment to the advancement of community.

South University operates on a quarter academic calendar, and each University quarter comprises eleven weeks. Associate degree programs require a minimum of eight quarters to complete, and bachelor's degree programs require a minimum of twelve quarters for completion. Programs are offered on a year-round basis, providing students with the ability to work uninterrupted toward their degrees. More importantly, students have the opportunity to take classes on campus, online, or a combination of both through South University's unique Plus+ program. Combining campus and online classes provides students with maximum flexibility, allowing them to organize their college education around their work and/or family commitments.

Academic Facilities

The library has wireless technology throughout, comfortable seating, and quiet study space. The collection includes books, print and online periodicals, CDs, videos, and numerous online proprietary databases. Materials are housed in circulating, reference, and reserve collections and have been selected to support the academic programs. Also for student use, the library has a modern computer lab with ten workstations, each with Internet access, online database services, an office suite, tutorials, and class-support software.

Costs

For information about tuition and fees, prospective students should contact the South University Admissions Office.

Financial Aid

South University's Student Financial Services Office helps qualified students secure financial assistance to complete their studies.

The University participates in several student aid programs. Forms of federal financial aid available to qualified students include the Federal Pell Grant Program, Federal Supplemental Educational Opportunity Grant (FSEOG) Program, Federal Work-Study Program, Federal Perkins Loan Program, Federal Stafford Student Loan Program (subsidized and unsubsidized), and Federal PLUS Loan Program. South University employs the Federal Methodology of Need Analysis, approved by the U.S. Department of Education, as a fair and equitable means of determining a family's ability to contribute to the student's educational expenses, as well as eligibility for other financial aid programs. Qualified students may apply for veterans' educational benefits. Students also are encouraged to investigate the availability of grants and scholarships through community resources.

Faculty

The South University in Montgomery faculty includes individuals of high academic distinction. Of the more than 40 instructors, 38 percent hold terminal degrees within their fields of expertise. In addition to teaching, faculty members strive to help students develop the requisites to appreciate knowledge and understand how experiences in the classroom and laboratory relate to professional performance in the workplace. The average student-faculty ratio per class is 13:1. Each student is assigned a faculty adviser, who oversees the student's progress and can answer questions about academic and career concerns. Students are encouraged to discuss program-related issues with and seek academic and career advice from their faculty advisers.

Admission Requirements

To be admitted to South University, prospective undergraduate students must be high school graduates or hold a GED certificate and submit an SAT or ACT score or a satisfactory score on the University-administered admissions examination. Transfer students must meet University-established criteria for acceptance as a transfer student.

All applicants must demonstrate English as a first language through submission of a diploma from a secondary school (or above) in which English is the official language of instruction. Applicants whose first language is not English must submit a Test of English as a Foreign Language (TOEFL) score. Applicants should contact the Admissions Office to determine other examinations/scores that are acceptable as an alternative to the TOEFL.

Applicants not meeting the entrance testing standards for general admission may be accepted under academic support admission.

Application and Information

Applicants must complete and submit an application form along with transcripts from high school and all colleges attended. Applicants must also complete all tests administered by the University or submit their SAT or ACT scores to the Registrar's Office. Applications are accepted on a rolling basis and should be made as far in advance as possible. Admissions officers are available weekdays, Saturdays, and by appointment. An appointment for an admissions interview or tour of the campus should be made in advance.

All international (nonimmigrant) applicants to South University must meet the same admissions standards as all other students. In addition, international applicants must have official educational records prepared in English, verify sufficient funds to cover the cost of the educational program, and meet certain other immigration-mandated criteria. South University in Montgomery is authorized under federal law to admit nonimmigrant students.

For additional information, prospective students should contact:

Anna Pearson
Director of Admissions
South University
5355 Vaughn Road
Montgomery, Alabama 36116-1120
Phone: 334-395-8800
866-629-2962 (toll-free)
Fax: 334-395-8859
Web site: http://www.southuniversity.edu

South University in Montgomery, Alabama, has a diverse student body enrolled in day, evening, weekend, and online classes.

COLLEGE CLOSE-UPS

SOUTH UNIVERSITY

TAMPA, FLORIDA

SouthUniversity℠

The University

Established in 1899, South University is a private academic institution dedicated to providing educational opportunities for the intellectual, social, and professional development of a diverse student population.

The Tampa, Florida campus offers focused and balanced curricula at the associate and bachelor's degree levels in the areas of business, health-care management, health science, nursing, nursing completion (RN to B.S.N.), physical therapist assisting, and psychology. The University also offers a Master of Science in physician assistant studies.

In addition, the Tampa campus offers students flexible scheduling with the choice of pursuing many of its courses on campus, online, or a combination of both through South University's unique Plus+ program. Combining campus and online classes provides students with maximum flexibility, allowing them to organize their college education around their work and/or family commitments.

The Tampa campus affords students the opportunity to learn in a modern facility based in a central location near Raymond James Stadium. Most students live within driving distance of the campus, but the Admissions Office does maintain information on various housing options should students relocate to the Tampa area for their education.

South University has a diverse student body enrolled in day, evening, and weekend classes. A sizeable portion of students have experience in the workforce and are pursuing an education that will prepare them to expand on their current career or take them in a new professional direction.

South University is accredited by the Commission on Colleges of the Southern Association of Colleges and Schools to award associate, bachelor's, master's, and doctoral degrees. The Commission on Colleges can be contacted at 1866 Southern Lane, Decatur, Georgia 30033; phone: 404-679-4500; for questions regarding the accreditation of South University. South University's Tampa campus is licensed to confer associate, bachelor's, and master's degrees through the Commission for Independent Education, Florida Department of Education, 325 West Gaines Street, Suite 1414, Tallahassee, Florida 32399; phone: 850-245-3200; Web site: http://www.fldoe.org/cie. The Tampa campus is approved for training veterans and other eligible individuals by the State of Florida Department of Veterans' Affairs, Division of Veterans' Benefits and Assistance, Bureau of State Approving for Veterans' Training.

Certain programs offered at South University in Tampa have earned programmatic accreditation. The physical therapist assisting program on the Tampa campus has been approved as a Candidate for Accreditation by the Commission on Accreditation in Physical Therapy Education (CAPTE). The Bachelor of Science in Nursing program at the Tampa campus is accredited by the Commission on Collegiate Nursing Education (CCNE), One DuPont Circle NW, Suite 530, Washington, D.C. 20036-1120; phone: 202-887-6791; Web site: http://www.aacn.nche.edu. The Bachelor of Science in Nursing program at South University is also authorized to operate by the Florida State Board of Nursing.

Location

Located on North Himes Avenue, South University's Tampa campus affords students the opportunity to enjoy all the culture and excitement a large city has to offer. Major league sporting events, major concerts, theater, world-renowned restaurants, and a cosmopolitan social scene are all within easy reach.

Majors and Degrees

South University in Tampa awards a two-year Associate of Science degree in physical therapist assisting.

The following four-year bachelor's degrees are awarded: Bachelor of Business Administration, Bachelor of Science in health-care management, Bachelor of Science in health science, Bachelor of Science in Nursing, Bachelor of Science in Nursing completion program (RN to B.S.N.), and Bachelor of Arts in psychology.

Academic Programs

South University in Tampa offers degree programs that are designed to meet the needs and objectives of students. Some curricula combine didactic and practical educational experiences that provide students with the academic background needed to pursue the professions of their choice. In addition, faculty members strive to instill the value not only of education and professionalism but also of contribution and commitment to the advancement of community.

Each University quarter comprises eleven weeks. Associate degree programs require a minimum of eight quarters to complete, and bachelor's degree programs a minimum of twelve quarters to complete. Programs are offered on a year-round basis, providing students with the ability to work uninterrupted toward their degrees.

Academic Facilities

South University's Tampa campus provides ample classroom and student service areas and features several smart classrooms with audiovisual technology. The campus also contains a fully equipped medical lab, multiple computer labs featuring PC and Mac computers, and more. The library maintains a highly focused collection of resource materials, including current books, journals, and related materials. In addition, students have access to WebVoyager, an online catalog of holdings; the Internet; various bibliographic databases; and subject-specific software programs. Interlibrary loans are available through the Tampa Bay Library Consortium (TBLC), and OCLC, an organization serving 43,559 libraries in eighty-six countries and territories around the world.

Costs

Information about tuition and fees can be obtained by contacting the South University Admissions Office.

Financial Aid

South University's Office of Student Financial Services helps qualified students secure financial assistance to complete their studies. The University participates in several student aid programs. Forms of financial aid available to qualified students through federal resources include the Federal Pell Grant Program, Federal Supplemental Educational Opportunity Grant

(FSEOG) Program, Federal Work-Study Program, Federal Perkins Loan Program, Federal Stafford Student Loan Program (subsidized and unsubsidized), and Federal PLUS Loan Program. South University employs the Federal Need Analysis Methodology, approved by the U.S. Department of Education, as a fair and equitable means of determining a family's ability to contribute to the student's educational expenses, as well as eligibility for other financial aid programs. Qualified students may also apply for the Florida State Assistance Grant (FSAG), Florida Bright Futures Scholarship Program, and veterans' educational benefits. Students also are encouraged to investigate the availability of grants and scholarships through community resources.

Faculty

The South University faculty includes individuals of high academic distinction. Of the more than 50 instructors on the campus, 46 percent hold terminal degrees in their fields of expertise. In addition to teaching, faculty members strive to help students develop the requisites to appreciate knowledge and understand how experiences in the classroom and laboratory relate to professional performance in the workplace. The average student-faculty ratio per class is 14:1. Each student is assigned a faculty adviser, who oversees the student's progress and can answer questions about academic and career concerns. Students are encouraged to discuss program-related issues with and seek academic and career advice from their faculty adviser.

Admission Requirements

To be admitted to South University, prospective students must be high school graduates or hold a GED certificate and submit SAT or ACT scores or achieve a satisfactory score on the University-administered admissions examination. Students who wish to transfer must meet the criteria established for acceptance as a transfer student.

All applicants to South University in Tampa must demonstrate English as a first language through submission of a diploma from a secondary school (or above) in which English is the official language of instruction. Applicants whose first language is not English must submit a Test of English as a Foreign Language (TOEFL) score. Applicants should contact the Admissions Office to determine other examinations/scores that are acceptable as an alternative to the TOEFL.

Application and Information

Applicants must complete and submit an application form, along with the general application fee, and official transcripts from all high schools and colleges attended. Applicants must also complete all tests administered by the University or submit their SAT or ACT scores to the Registrar's Office. Applications are accepted on a rolling basis and should be made as far in advance as possible.

All international (nonimmigrant) applicants to South University must meet the same admissions standards as all other students. In addition, international applicants must have official education records prepared in English, verify sufficient funds to cover the cost of the educational program, and meet certain other immigration-mandated criteria. South University in Tampa is authorized under federal law to admit nonimmigrant students.

Admissions officers are available weekdays, Saturdays, and by appointment. An appointment for an admissions interview or a tour of the campus should be made in advance. For additional information, all prospective students should contact:

Michele D'Alessio
Director of Admissions
South University
4401 North Himes Avenue, Suite 175
Tampa, Florida 33614-7095
Phone: 813-393-3800
800-846-1472 (toll-free)
Fax: 813-393-3814
Web site: http://www.southuniversity.edu

South University offers students a flexible education and all the excitement and activites of Tampa, Florida.

SOUTH UNIVERSITY

WEST PALM BEACH, FLORIDA

SouthUniversity℠

The University

Established in 1899, South University is a private academic institution dedicated to providing educational opportunities for the intellectual, social, and professional development of a diverse student population. To achieve this, South University in West Palm Beach offers focused and balanced curricula at the associate and bachelor's degree levels in the areas of business, criminal justice, health-care management, health science, legal studies, nursing, nursing completion (RN to B.S.N.), physical therapy assisting, and psychology. Other degree programs offered by the University include a Master of Arts degree in professional counseling, a Master of Business Administration (M.B.A.) in both traditional and twelve-month accelerated programs, and a Master of Business Administration in health-care administration.

The West Palm Beach location of South University, established in 1974, strives to maintain small class sizes that permit students to receive more individualized instruction and interaction with faculty and staff members.

South University in West Palm Beach has a diverse student body enrolled in both day and evening classes. Students are primarily commuters who live within 50 miles of Palm Beach County. They include men and women who have enrolled directly after completing high school, who have transferred from another college or university, or who have experience in the workforce and are pursuing an education that will prepare them to grow in their current role or take a new professional direction.

In addition to classrooms and administrative offices, the campus includes a bookstore, student lounge, career services center, and ample parking. Since most students live within driving distance of the campus, the campus does not offer or operate student housing. If housing is needed, students should contact the Admissions Department.

South University is accredited by the Commission on Colleges of the Southern Association of Colleges and Schools to award associate, bachelor's, master's, and doctoral degrees. The Commission on Colleges can be contacted at 1866 Southern Lane, Decatur, Georgia 30033; phone: 404-679-4500; for questions regarding the accreditation of South University. South University's West Palm Beach campus is licensed to confer associate, bachelor's, and master's degrees by the Commission for Independent Education, Florida Department of Education, 325 West Gaines Street, Suite 1414, Tallahassee, Florida 32399; phone 850-245-3200; Web site: http://www.fldoe.org/cie. The campus is approved for training veterans and other eligible individuals by the State of Florida Department of Veterans' Affairs, Division of Veterans' Benefits and Assistance, Bureau of State Approving for Veterans' Training.

Certain programs offered at the campus have earned programmatic accreditation. The Associate of Science in physical therapist assisting degree program is accredited by the Commission on Accreditation in Physical Therapy Education of the American Physical Therapy Association, 1111 North Fairfax Street, Alexandria, Virginia 22314; phone: 703-684-2782. The Bachelor of Science in legal studies and Associate of Science in paralegal studies degree programs are approved by the American Bar Association, 321 North Clark Street Court, Chicago, Illinois 60610; phone: 312-988-5617. The Bachelor of Science in Nursing program at the Tampa campus is accredited by the Commission on Collegiate Nursing Education (CCNE), One DuPont Circle, NW, Suite 530, Washington, D.C. 20036-1120; phone: 202-887-6791; Web site: http://www.aacn.nche.edu. The Bachelor of Science in Nursing program at South University is also authorized to operate by the Florida State Board of Nursing.

Location

South University West Palm Beach recently moved to a new 40,000-square-foot campus in the University Centre complex, located in Royal Palm Beach.

Majors and Degrees

The West Palm Beach campus of South University awards the following two-year degrees: Associate of Science in paralegal studies, and Associate of Science in physical therapist assisting.

The following four-year bachelor's degrees are awarded: Bachelor of Business Administration, Bachelor of Science in criminal justice, Bachelor of Science in health-care management, Bachelor of Science in health science, Bachelor of Science in legal studies, Bachelor of Science in Nursing, and Bachelor of Arts in psychology. A Bachelor of Science in Nursing completion program (RN to B.S.N.) for current registered nurses is also available.

Academic Programs

The West Palm Beach campus of South University offers degree programs that are designed to meet the needs and objectives of students. Each curriculum combines didactic and practical educational experiences that provide students with the academic background needed to pursue the professions of their choice. In addition, faculty members strive to instill the value not only of education and professionalism but also of contribution and commitment to the advancement of community.

Each University quarter comprises eleven weeks. Associate degree programs require a minimum of eight quarters to complete, and bachelor's degree programs require a minimum of twelve quarters for completion. Programs at the West Palm Beach campus are offered on a year-round basis, providing students with the ability to work uninterrupted toward their degrees.

Academic Facilities

In January 2010, South University West Palm Beach relocated to a new facility at University Centre in Royal Palm Beach, Florida, to better serve students and the broader Palm Beach County community. The facility features a hurricane-resistant infrastructure and includes several large labs, lecture halls, a library, and seminar rooms.

The West Palm Beach campus library houses a large collection that includes extensive law resources. Students may retrieve periodicals in paper or electronic form. Library-based computers provide access to several commercial online services, including Westlaw, the computerized legal research service; and the Southeastern Library Network (SOLINET). CD-ROM resources include the Grolier's Multimedia Encyclopedia and the EBSCO magazine full-text database. Internet access is available in the library.

Costs

For information on South University's tuition and fees, prospective students should contact the campus Admissions Office.

Financial Aid

South University's Office of Student Financial Services helps qualified students secure financial assistance to complete their studies. The University participates in several student aid programs. Forms of financial aid available to qualified students through federal resources include the Federal Pell Grant Program, Federal Supplemental Educational Opportunity Grant (FSEOG) Program, Federal Work-Study Program, Federal Perkins Loan Program, Federal Stafford Loan Program (subsidized and unsubsidized), and Federal PLUS Loan Program. Qualified students may also apply for the Florida State Assistance Grant (FSAG), Florida Bright Futures Scholarship Program, and veterans' educational benefits. Students also are encouraged to investigate the availability of grants and scholarships through community resources.

Faculty

The South University faculty includes individuals of high academic distinction. Of the more than 60 instructors on the West Palm Beach campus, 37 percent hold terminal degrees in their fields of expertise. In addition to teaching, faculty members strive to help students develop the requisites to appreciate knowledge and understand how experiences in the classroom and laboratory relate to professional performance in the workplace. The average student-faculty ratio is 16:1. Each student is assigned a faculty adviser, who oversees the student's progress and can answer questions about academic and career concerns. Students are encouraged to discuss program-related issues with and seek academic and career advice from their faculty advisers.

Admission Requirements

To be admitted to South University, prospective students must be high school graduates or hold a GED certificate and submit an SAT or ACT score or a satisfactory score on the University-administered admissions examination. Students who wish to transfer must meet the criteria established for acceptance as a transfer student.

All applicants to South University must demonstrate English as a first language through submission of a diploma from a secondary school (or above) in which English is the official language of instruction. Applicants whose first language is not English must submit a Test of English as a Foreign Language (TOEFL) score. Applicants should contact the Admissions Office to determine other examinations/scores that are acceptable as an alternative to the TOEFL.

Applicants not meeting the testing standards for general admission may be accepted under academic support admission. General admission to the University does not guarantee admission to the nursing program. To obtain specific entrance requirements for the nursing program, prospective students should contact the campus Admissions Office or visit the South University Web site.

Application and Information

Applicants must complete and submit an application form, along with the general application fee, and official transcripts from all high schools and colleges attended. Faxed documents are not considered official. Applicants must also complete all tests administered by the University or submit their SAT or ACT scores to the Registrar's Office. Applications are accepted on a rolling basis and should be made as far in advance as possible.

All international (nonimmigrant) applicants to South University's West Palm Beach campus must meet the same admissions standards as all other students. In addition, international applicants must have official education records prepared in English, verify sufficient funds to cover the cost of the educational program, and meet certain other immigration-mandated criteria. South University in West Palm Beach is authorized under federal law to admit nonimmigrant students.

Admissions officers are available weekdays, Saturdays, and weekends. An appointment for an admissions interview or tour of the campus should be made in advance. For additional information, all prospective students should contact:

Gary Malisos
Director of Admissions
South University
University Centre
9801 Belvedere Road
Royal Palm Beach, Florida 33411
Phone: 561-273-6500
866-629-2902 (toll-free)
Fax: 561-273-6420
Web site: http://www.southuniversity.edu

South University in West Palm Beach, Florida, relocated in 2010 to a new facility with classroom and lab space for its arts and sciences, business, health professions, and nursing programs.

SOUTH UNIVERSITY

SAVANNAH, GEORGIA

SouthUniversity℠

The University

South University is a private academic institution dedicated to providing educational opportunities for the intellectual, social, and professional development of a diverse student population. To achieve this, the Savannah campus offers focused and balanced curricula at the associate and bachelor's degree levels in the areas of business, health sciences, information technology, and legal studies. The University also offers master's degree programs in anesthesiology assistant studies and physician assistant studies. In addition, the campus offers a Master of Arts in professional counseling, a Master of Business Administration (M.B.A.) in both traditional and twelve-month accelerated programs, and a Doctor of Pharmacy degree through its School of Pharmacy—one of only three programs in the state of Georgia and the only one in the state that is currently available in an accelerated three-year format. South University is the first university or college in Savannah to offer a health professions doctoral degree program.

South University traces its heritage back to 1899 and today has grown into a multicampus system with locations in Columbia, South Carolina; Montgomery, Alabama; Richmond and Virginia Beach, Virginia; Savannah, Georgia; and Tampa and West Palm Beach, Florida.

Students can also pursue degrees through a combination of on-campus and online classes as part of the University's unique Plus+ program, which provides maximum scheduling flexibility. This flexibility allows students to organize their college education around work and family commitments. For those who choose to take on-site courses, Savannah campus facilities and amenities include a bookstore, student lounges, a career services center, wireless Internet access, and ample parking in addition to classrooms and offices.

The cornerstone of the Savannah campus is the School of Pharmacy building, which joins the College of Business and College of Health Professions buildings. The University strives to maintain small class sizes that permit students to receive individualized instruction and interaction with faculty and staff members.

The Savannah campus of South University has a diverse student body enrolled in day, evening, and weekend classes. Undergraduate students are primarily commuters who live within 60 miles of the city. Graduate students come from all of the United States and as far away as California and Alaska. They include men and women who have enrolled directly after completing high school, who have transferred from another college or university, or who have experience in the workforce and are pursuing an education that will prepare them to grow in their current position or enable them to take a new professional direction. The University offers a school-sponsored housing option in conjunction with local apartment communities for students who are relocating to Savannah to pursue their degrees.

South University is accredited by the Commission on Colleges of the Southern Association of Colleges and Schools to award associate, bachelor's, master's, and doctoral degrees. The Commission on Colleges can be contacted at 1866 Southern Lane, Decatur, Georgia 30033; phone: 404-679-4500; for questions regarding the accreditation of South University. The Savannah campus is also authorized under the Georgia Non-public Postsecondary Educational Institutions Act of 1990 to confer those degrees. In addition, the campus is approved for training military veterans and other individuals by the State of Georgia Department of Veterans' Services, State Approving Agency, in Atlanta, Georgia.

Certain programs offered at the Savannah campus have earned programmatic accreditation. The South University Associate of Science degree in medical assisting is accredited by the Commission on Accreditation of Allied Health Education Programs (http://www.caahep.org) on recommendation of the Curriculum Review Board of the American Association of Medical Assistants Endowment (AAMEA). The Associate of Science in physical therapist assisting program is accredited by the Commission on Accreditation in Physical Therapy Education of the American Physical Therapy Association (CAPTE), 1111 North Fairfax Street, Alexandria, Virginia 22314; phone: 703-706-3425; e-mail: accreditation@apta.org; Web site: http://www.capteonline.org.

South University's Doctor of Pharmacy program is accredited by the Accreditation Council for Pharmacy Education, 20 North Clark Street, Suite 2500, Chicago, Illinois 60602-5109; phone: 312-664-3575; fax: 312-664-4652; Web site: http://www.acpeaccredit.org. The school is a member of the American Association of Colleges of Pharmacy (AACP).

The anesthesiologist assistant program has received accreditation from the Commission on Accreditation of Allied Health Educational Programs (CAAHEP) through its Accreditation Review Committee for Anesthesiologist Assistant Programs (ARC-AA). Contact ARC-AA in care of CAAHEP, 35 East Wacker Drive, Suite 1970, Chicago, Illinois 60601; 312-553-9355. The Master of Science in physician assistant studies program on the Savannah campus is accredited by the Accreditation Review Commission on Education for Physician Assistant Programs (ARC-PA), 1000 North Oak Avenue, Marshfield, Wisconsin 54449-5788; phone: 715-389-3785; or 12000 Findley Road, Suite 240, Johns Creek, Georgia 30097; phone: 770-476-1224; fax: 770-476-1738; Web site: http://www.arc-pa.org. This accreditation status qualifies graduating students to take the national certifying examination administered by the National Commission on Certification of Physician Assistants (NCCPA). The physician assistant studies program is a member of the Association of Physician Assistants Programs, the national organization representing physician assistant education programs. The Bachelor of Science in legal studies and Associate of Science in paralegal studies programs are approved by the American Bar Association, 321 North Clark Street, Chicago, Illinois 60610; phone: 312-988-5617.

Location

This campus, the largest among South University's locations, is located in the midtown section of historic Savannah, Georgia, minutes from downtown, cultural activities, and the beach. The buildings are situated on 9 acres of land and are easily accessible from any section of Savannah, the surrounding region, and coastal South Carolina.

Majors and Degrees

The Savannah campus of South University awards the following two-year degrees: Associate of Science in accounting, Associate of Science in business administration, Associate of Science in information technology, Associate of Science in medical assisting, Associate of Science in paralegal studies, and Associate of Science in physical therapist assisting.

Four-year degree programs include a Bachelor of Business Administration, Bachelor of Science in criminal justice, Bachelor of Science in health-care management, Bachelor of Science in information technology, Bachelor of Science in legal studies, and Bachelor of Arts in psychology.

Academic Programs

The Savannah campus of South University offers degree programs that are designed to meet the needs and objectives of students. Each curriculum combines classroom and practical educational experiences that provide students with the academic background needed to pursue the professions of their choice. In addition, faculty members strive to instill the value not only of education and professionalism but also of contribution and commitment to the advancement of community.

South University operates on a quarter system, with each quarter comprising eleven weeks. Associate degree programs require a minimum of eight quarters to complete, and bachelor's degree programs require a minimum of twelve quarters for completion. Undergraduate programs are offered on a year-round basis, providing students with the ability to work uninterrupted toward their degrees.

Academic Facilities

The Savannah campus library has a large collection that includes an extensive law and health professions library. Students may retrieve periodicals in paper or electronic form. Library-based computers provide access to several commercial online services, including Westlaw, the computerized legal research service; GALILEO, the Georgia network of databases; and MEDLINE, for health sciences students. CD-ROM resources include the Encyclopedia Britannica, the Official Code of Georgia Annotated, ADAM, and the EBSCO magazine full-text database. Internet access is available on all computers throughout the campus, and the University offers wireless Internet access through an on-campus Wi-Fi network.

Costs

Tuition information is available by contacting the South University Admissions Department.

Financial Aid

South University's Student Financial Services Office helps qualified students secure financial assistance to complete their studies. The University participates in several student aid programs. Forms of financial aid available to qualified students through federal resources include the Federal Pell Grant Program, Federal Supplemental Educational Opportunity Grant (FSEOG) Program, Federal Work-Study Program, Federal Perkins Loan Program, Federal Stafford Loan Program (subsidized and unsubsidized), and Federal PLUS Loan Program. Qualified students may apply for the Georgia HOPE Scholarship, Georgia Tuition Equalization Grant, Georgia LEAP Grant Program, and veterans' educational benefits. Students are also encouraged to investigate the availability of grants and scholarships through community resources.

Faculty

The South University faculty includes individuals of high academic distinction. Of the more than 80 instructors on the Savannah campus, 40 percent hold terminal degrees. In addition to teaching, faculty members strive to help students develop the requisites to appreciate knowledge and understand how experiences in the classroom and laboratory relate to professional performance in the workplace. The average student-faculty ratio is 14:1. Each student is assigned a faculty adviser who oversees the student's progress and can answer questions about academic and career concerns. Students are encouraged to discuss program-related issues with and seek academic and career advice from their faculty advisers.

Admission Requirements

To be admitted to South University, prospective students must be high school graduates or hold a GED certificate and submit an appropriate SAT or ACT score (students should contact the Admissions Office) or a satisfactory score on the University-administered placement examination. Students who wish to transfer must meet the criteria established for acceptance as a transfer student.

All applicants to South University must demonstrate English proficiency. Students may furnish proof of English as a first language competency through submission of a diploma from a secondary school (or higher level) in which English is the official language of instruction. Applicants whose first language is not English must submit Test of English as a Foreign Language (TOEFL) scores. Applicants should contact the Admissions Office to determine other examinations/scores that are acceptable as an alternative to the TOEFL.

Applicants not meeting the testing standards for general admission may be accepted under academic support admission.

Application and Information

Applicants must complete an application form and submit it along with the general application fee as well as official transcripts from all high schools and colleges attended. Faxed documents are not considered official. Applicants must also complete all tests administered by the University or submit their SAT or ACT scores to the Registrar's Office. Applications are accepted on a rolling basis and should be made as far in advance as possible.

All international (nonimmigrant) applicants to South University must meet the same admissions standards as all other students. In addition, international applicants must have official educational records prepared in English, verify sufficient funds to cover the cost of the educational program, and meet certain other immigration-mandated criteria. South University in Savannah is authorized under federal law to admit nonimmigrant students.

Admissions officers are available weekdays, Saturdays, and by appointment. An appointment for an admissions interview or tour of the campus should be made in advance. For additional information, all prospective students should contact:

Marie Neal
Director of Admissions
South University
709 Mall Boulevard
Savannah, Georgia 31406-4805
Phone: 912-201-8000
866-629-2901 (toll-free)
Fax: 912-201-8070
Web site: http://www.southuniversity.edu

South University is located on the south side of historic Savannah, Georgia.

SOUTH UNIVERSITY

COLUMBIA, SOUTH CAROLINA

SouthUniversity℠

The University

Established in 1899, South University is a private academic institution dedicated to providing educational opportunities for the intellectual, social, and professional development of a diverse student population. The Columbia, South Carolina campus offers focused and balanced curricula at the associate and bachelor's degree levels in the areas of business, criminal justice, graphic design, health-care management, health science, information technology, legal studies, nursing, and psychology. Other degree programs offered at South University in Columbia include a Master of Arts in professional counseling, a Master of Business Administration, a Master of Business Administration in health-care administration, and a Doctor of Pharmacy.

In addition, the Columbia campus offers students flexible scheduling with the choice of pursuing many of its courses on campus, online, or a combination of both through South University's unique Plus+ program. Combining campus and online classes provides students with maximum flexibility, allowing them to organize their college education around their work and/or family commitments. Most students live within driving distance of the campus, but the Admissions Office does maintain information on various housing options should students relocate to the Columbia area for their education.

South University has a diverse student body enrolled in day, evening, and weekend classes. A sizeable portion of students have experience in the workforce and are pursuing an education that will prepare them to expand on their current career or take them in a new professional direction.

South University is accredited by the Commission on Colleges of the Southern Association of Colleges and Schools to award associate, bachelor's, master's, and doctoral degrees. For questions about the accreditation of South University, contact the Commission on Colleges at 1866 Southern Lane, Decatur, Georgia 30033-4097; phone: 404-679-4501.

South University in Columbia is licensed to award associate, bachelor's, and master's degrees and certificates by the South Carolina Commission on Higher Education, 1333 Main Street, Suite 200, Columbia, South Carolina 29201; phone: 803-737-2260. The Columbia campus is also chartered by the state of South Carolina and approved by the South Carolina Commission on Higher Education (Veterans' Education Section) for the training of veterans and other eligible persons.

Certain programs offered at South University in Columbia have earned programmatic accreditation. South University's Doctor of Pharmacy program is accredited by the Accreditation Council for Pharmacy Education, 20 North Clark Street, Suite 2500, Chicago, Illinois 60602-5109; phone: 312-664-3575; fax: 312-664-4652; Web site: http://www.acpeaccredit.org. The school is a member of the American Association of Colleges of Pharmacy (AACP). The South University Associate of Science degree in medical assisting is accredited by the Commission on Accreditation of Allied Health Education Programs (http://www.caahep.org) upon the recommendation of the Curriculum Review Board of the American Association of Medical Assistants Endowment (AAMAE). The South Carolina State Board of Nursing has granted South University approval to accept qualified applicants for admission into the nursing program.

The Bachelor of Science in legal studies and Associate of Science in paralegal studies are both approved by the American Bar Association, 321 North Clark Street, Chicago, Illinois 60610; phone: 312-988-5617.

Location

South University's Columbia campus relocated to the Carolina Research Park in northeast Columbia in fall 2006. The campus features spacious classrooms, multiple computer labs, a fully equipped medical lab, and a student lounge. The campus is located just minutes from downtown in the Carolina Research Park off I-77 at Farrow Road and Park Lane.

The campus surroundings are highlighted by a natural wooded landscape and vast green space featuring a tranquil campus courtyard. Convenient to malls, shopping, and the growing northeast side of Columbia, the new campus location provides easier access to students from throughout the greater Columbia area.

Majors and Degrees

South University in Columbia awards the following two-year degrees: Associate of Science in business administration, Associate of Science in graphic design, Associate of Science in information technology, Associate of Science in medical assisting, and Associate of Science in paralegal studies.

The following four-year bachelor's degrees are awarded: Bachelor of Business Administration, Bachelor of Science in criminal justice, Bachelor of Science in graphic design, Bachelor of Science in health-care management, Bachelor of Science in health science, Bachelor of Science in information technology, Bachelor of Science in legal studies, Bachelor of Science in Nursing, and Bachelor of Arts in psychology.

Academic Programs

South University in Columbia offers degree programs that are designed to meet the needs and objectives of students. Some curricula combine didactic and practical educational experiences that provide students with the academic background needed to pursue the professions of their choice. In addition, faculty members strive to instill the value not only of education and professionalism but also of contribution and commitment to the advancement of community.

Each University quarter comprises eleven weeks. Associate degree programs require a minimum of eight quarters to complete, and bachelor's degree programs require a minimum of twelve quarters to complete. Programs are offered on a year-round basis, providing students with the ability to work uninterrupted toward their degrees.

Academic Facilities

South University's multimillion-dollar Columbia campus provides ample classroom and student service areas and features several smart classrooms with audiovisual technology. The campus also contains a tiered lecture hall with videoconferencing capability, a fully equipped medical lab, multiple computer labs featuring PC and Mac computers, and more.

The library houses a large collection that includes an extensive legal library. Students may retrieve periodicals in paper or electronic form. Students may also access several commercial online services, including Westlaw, the computerized legal research service; LIRN; SearchBank; Infotract; UMI ProQuest; and the Electronic Library. Internet access is available on all computers throughout the campus.

Costs

Information about tuition and fees can be obtained by contacting the South University Admissions Office.

Financial Aid

South University's Office of Student Financial Services helps qualified students secure financial assistance to complete their studies. The University participates in several student aid programs. Forms of financial aid available to qualified students through federal resources include the Federal Pell Grant Program, Federal Supplemental Educational Opportunity Grant (FSEOG) Program, Federal Work-Study Program, Federal Perkins Loan Program, Federal Stafford Student Loan Program (subsidized and unsubsidized), and Federal PLUS Loan Program. South University employs the Federal Need Analysis Methodology, approved by the U.S. Department of Education, as a fair and equitable means of determining a family's ability to contribute to the student's educational expenses, as well as eligibility for other financial aid programs. Qualified students may apply for the South Carolina HOPE Scholarship, LIFE Scholarship, and veterans' educational benefits. Students also are encouraged to investigate the availability of grants and scholarships through community resources.

Faculty

The South University faculty includes individuals of high academic distinction. Of the nearly 60 instructors on the campus, 46 percent hold terminal degrees in their fields of expertise. In addition to teaching, faculty members strive to help students develop the requisites to appreciate knowledge and understand how experiences in the classroom and laboratory relate to professional performance in the workplace. The average student-faculty ratio per class is 14:1. Each student is assigned a faculty adviser, who oversees the student's progress and can answer questions about academic and career concerns. Students are encouraged to discuss program-related issues with and seek academic and career advice from their faculty adviser.

Admission Requirements

To be admitted to South University, prospective students must be high school graduates or hold a GED certificate and submit SAT or ACT scores or achieve a satisfactory score on the University-administered admissions examination. Students who wish to transfer must meet the criteria established for acceptance as a transfer student.

All applicants to South University in Columbia must demonstrate English as a first language through submission of a diploma from a secondary school (or above) in which English is the official language of instruction. Applicants whose first language is not English must submit a Test of English as a Foreign Language (TOEFL) score. Applicants should contact the Admissions Office to determine other examinations/scores that are acceptable as an alternative to the TOEFL.

Application and Information

Applicants must complete and submit an application form, along with the general application fee, and official transcripts from all high schools and colleges attended. Applicants must also complete all tests administered by the University or submit their SAT or ACT scores to the Registrar's Office. Applications are accepted on a rolling basis and should be made as far in advance as possible.

All international (nonimmigrant) applicants to South University must meet the same admissions standards as all other students. In addition, international applicants must have official education records prepared in English, verify sufficient funds to cover the cost of the educational program, and meet certain other immigration-mandated criteria. South University in Columbia is authorized under federal law to admit nonimmigrant students.

Admissions officers are available weekdays, Saturdays, and by appointment. An appointment for an admissions interview or a tour of the campus should be made in advance. For additional information, all prospective students should contact:

Trisha Wade
Director of Admissions
South University
9 Science Court
Columbia, South Carolina 29203-6443
Phone: 803-799-9082
866-629-3031 (toll-free)
Fax: 803-935-4382
E-mail: twade@southuniversity.edu
Web site: http://www.southuniversity.edu

South University is located on the fast-growing northeast side of Columbia, South Carolina.

SOUTH UNIVERSITY

RICHMOND, VIRGINIA

SouthUniversity℠

The University

South University is a private academic institution dedicated to providing educational opportunities for the intellectual, social, and professional development of a diverse student population. To achieve this, the Richmond campus offers focused and balanced curricula at the associate and bachelor's degree levels in the areas of business, health science, health-care management, nursing degree completion, and legal studies. In addition, the campus offers a Master of Arts in professional counseling and a Master of Business Administration (M.B.A.) program.

South University traces its heritage back to 1899 and today has grown into a multicampus system with locations in Columbia, South Carolina; Montgomery, Alabama; Savannah, Georgia; Richmond and Virginia Beach, Virginia; and Tampa and West Palm Beach, Florida.

Students can also pursue degrees through a combination of on-campus and online classes as part of the University's unique Plus+ program, which provides maximum scheduling flexibility. This flexibility allows students to organize their college education around work and family commitments. For those who choose to take on-site courses, Richmond campus facilities and amenities include a bookstore, student lounge, wireless Internet access, and ample parking in addition to classrooms, labs, and offices.

The University strives to maintain small class sizes that permit students to receive individualized instruction and interaction with faculty and staff members.

The Richmond campus of South University has a diverse student body enrolled in day, evening, and weekend classes. Most students live within driving distance of the campus, but the Admissions Office does maintain information on various housing options should students relocate to the Richmond area for their education. The student body includes men and women who have enrolled directly after completing high school, who have transferred from another college or university, or who have experience in the workforce and are pursuing an education that will prepare them to grow in their current position or enable them to take a new professional direction.

South University is accredited by the Commission on Colleges of the Southern Association of Colleges and Schools to award associate, bachelor's, master's, and doctorate degrees. The Commission on Colleges can be contacted at 1866 Southern Lane, Decatur, Georgia 30033; phone: 404-679-4500; for questions regarding the accreditation of South University. South University's Richmond campus is certified to operate in Virginia by the State Council for Higher Education in Virginia, James Monroe Building, 101 North Fourteenth Street, Richmond, Virginia 23219; phone: 804-225-2600.

Location

South University Richmond is located in the West Broad Development in Glen Allen, Virginia, minutes from downtown Richmond and the area's cultural activities. The campus is situated in a vibrant and convenient community of mixed-use living space with shopping and restaurants within a short walk.

Majors and Degrees

The Richmond campus of South University offers a two-year Associate of Science in paralegal studies degree program.

Four-year degree programs include a Bachelor of Business Administration, Bachelor of Science in criminal justice, Bachelor of Science in health-care management, Bachelor of Science in health science, and Bachelor of Arts in psychology. A Bachelor of Science in Nursing completion program (RN to B.S.N.) for current registered nurses is also available.

Academic Programs

The Richmond campus of South University offers degree programs that are designed to meet the needs and objectives of students. Each curriculum combines classroom and practical educational experiences that provide students with the academic background needed to pursue the professions of their choice. In addition, faculty members strive to instill the value not only of education and professionalism but also of contribution and commitment to the advancement of community.

South University operates on a quarter system, with each quarter comprising eleven weeks. Associate degree programs require a minimum of eight quarters to complete, and bachelor's degree programs require a minimum of twelve quarters for completion. Undergraduate programs are offered on a year-round basis, providing students with the ability to work uninterrupted toward their degrees.

Academic Facilities

The Richmond campus library provides individual and group study areas, a computer lab, and a diversified collection of online, audiovisual, and printed materials. Professional librarians are available during all hours of operation to provide assistance in locating information and materials at South University libraries and at other libraries. The collections include books, magazines, audiovisual, and digital sources that support class assignments, tutorial needs, current events, and recreational reading. The computer lab offers Internet access, online databases with indexing and full text access to thousands of journals, tutorial programs, and an office suite of software programs. Internet access is available on all computers throughout the campus and the University offers wireless Internet access through an on-campus Wi-Fi network.

Costs

Tuition information is available by contacting the South University Admissions Department.

Financial Aid

South University's Student Financial Services Office helps qualified students secure financial assistance to complete their studies. The University participates in several student aid programs. Forms of financial aid available to qualified students through federal resources include the Federal Pell Grant Program, Federal Supplemental Educational Opportunity Grant (FSEOG) Program, Federal Work-Study Program, Federal Perkins Loan Program, Federal Stafford Loan Program (subsidized and unsubsidized), and Federal PLUS Loan Program. Students are also encouraged to investigate the availability of grants and scholarships through community resources.

Faculty

The South University faculty includes individuals of high academic distinction. In addition to teaching, faculty members strive to help students develop the requisites to appreciate knowledge and understand how experiences in the classroom and laboratory relate to professional performance in the workplace. The average student-faculty ratio is 14:1. Each student is assigned a faculty adviser who oversees the student's progress and can answer questions about academic and career concerns. Students are encouraged to discuss program-related issues with and seek academic and career advice from their faculty advisers.

Admission Requirements

To be admitted to South University, prospective students must be high school graduates or hold a GED certificate and submit an appropriate SAT or ACT score (students should contact the Admissions Office) or a satisfactory score on the University-administered placement examination. Students who wish to transfer must meet the criteria established for acceptance as a transfer student.

All applicants to South University must demonstrate English proficiency. Students may furnish proof of English as a first language competency through submission of a diploma from a secondary school (or higher level) in which English is the official language of instruction. Applicants whose first language is not English must submit Test of English as a Foreign Language (TOEFL) scores. Applicants should contact the Admissions Office to determine other examinations/scores that are acceptable as an alternative to the TOEFL.

Applicants not meeting the testing standards for general admission may be accepted under academic support admission.

Application and Information

Applicants must complete an application form and submit it along with the general application fee as well as official transcripts from all high schools and colleges attended. Faxed documents are not considered official. Applicants must also complete all tests administered by the University or submit their SAT or ACT scores to the Registrar's Office. Applications are accepted on a rolling basis and should be made as far in advance as possible.

All international (nonimmigrant) applicants to South University must meet the same admissions standards as all other students. In addition, international applicants must have official educational records prepared in English, verify sufficient funds to cover the cost of the educational program, and meet certain other immigration-mandated criteria. South University in Richmond is authorized under federal law to admit nonimmigrant students.

Admissions officers are available weekdays, Saturdays, and by appointment. An appointment for an admissions interview or tour of the campus should be made in advance. For additional information, all prospective students should contact:

Patrick Riley
Director of Admissions
South University
2151 Old Brick Road
Glen Allen, Virginia 23060
Phone: 804-727-6800
888-422-5076 (toll-free)
Fax: 804-727-6790
Web site: http://www.southuniversity.edu

South University at Richmond is located in Glen Allen, Virginia, at West Broad Village, a mixed-use area of residents, shopping, and restaurants.

COLLEGE CLOSE-UPS

SOUTH UNIVERSITY

VIRGINIA BEACH, VIRGINIA

SouthUniversity℠

The University

South University is a private academic institution dedicated to providing educational opportunities for the intellectual, social, and professional development of a diverse student population. To achieve this, the Virginia Beach campus offers focused and balanced curricula at the associate and bachelor's degree levels in the areas of business, health professions, health care management, nursing degree completion, and legal studies. In addition, the campus offers a Master of Arts in Professional Counseling and a Master of Business Administration (M.B.A.) program.

South University traces its heritage back to 1899 and today has grown into a multicampus system with locations in Columbia, South Carolina; Montgomery, Alabama; Savannah, Georgia; Richmond and Virginia Beach, Virginia; and Tampa and West Palm Beach, Florida.

Students can also pursue degrees through a combination of on-campus and online classes as part of the University's unique Plus+ program, which provides maximum scheduling flexibility. This flexibility allows students to organize their college education around work and family commitments. For those who choose to take on-site courses, Virginia Beach campus facilities and amenities include a bookstore, student lounge, wireless Internet access, and ample parking in addition to classrooms, labs and offices.

The University strives to maintain small class sizes that permit students to receive individualized instruction and interaction with faculty and staff members.

The Virginia Beach campus of South University has a diverse student body enrolled in day, evening, and weekend classes. Most students live within driving distance of the campus, but the Admissions Office does maintain information on various housing options should students relocate to the Virginia Beach area for their education. The student body includes men and women who have enrolled directly after completing high school, who have transferred from another college or university, or who have experience in the workforce and are pursuing an education that will prepare them to grow in their current position or enable them to take a new professional direction.

South University is accredited by the Commission on Colleges of the Southern Association of Colleges and Schools to award associate, bachelor's, master's, and doctorate degrees. The Commission on Colleges can be contacted at 1866 Southern Lane, Decatur, Georgia 30033; phone: 404-679-4500; for questions regarding the accreditation of South University. South University's Virginia Beach campus is certified to operate in Virginia by the State Council for Higher Education in Virginia, James Monroe Building, 101 North Fourteenth Street, Richmond, Virginia 23219; phone: 804-225-2600.

Location

The campus, located in the Convergence Center Business Park in Virginia Beach, is just minutes from shopping and outdoor and cultural activities.

Majors and Degrees

The Virginia Beach campus of South University awards a two-year Associate of Science degree in paralegal studies.

The following four-year bachelor's degrees are awarded: Bachelor of Business Administration, Bachelor of Science in criminal justice, Bachelor of Science in health-care management, Bachelor of Science in legal studies, and Bachelor of Arts in psychology. A Bachelor of Science in Nursing completion program (RN to B.S.N.) for current registered nurses is also available.

Academic Programs

The Virginia Beach campus of South University offers degree programs that are designed to meet the needs and objectives of students. Each curriculum combines classroom and practical educational experiences that provide students with the academic background needed to pursue the professions of their choice. In addition, faculty members strive to instill the value not only of education and professionalism but also of contribution and commitment to the advancement of community.

South University operates on a quarter system, with each quarter comprising eleven weeks. Associate degree programs require a minimum of eight quarters to complete, and bachelor's degree programs require a minimum of twelve quarters for completion. Undergraduate programs are offered on a year-round basis, providing students with the ability to work uninterrupted toward their degrees.

Academic Facilities

The Virginia Beach campus library provides individual and group study areas, a computer lab, and a diversified collection of online, audiovisual, and printed materials. Professional librarians are available during all hours of operation to provide assistance in locating information and materials at South University libraries and at other libraries. The collections include books, magazines, audiovisual, and digital sources that support class assignments, tutorial needs, current events, and recreational reading. The computer lab offers Internet access, online databases with indexing and full text access to thousands of journals, tutorial programs, and an office suite of software programs. Internet access is available on all computers throughout the campus, and the University offers wireless Internet access through an on-campus Wi-Fi network.

Costs

Tuition information is available by contacting the South University Admissions Department.

Financial Aid

South University's Student Financial Services Office helps qualified students secure financial assistance to complete their studies. The University participates in several student aid programs. Forms of financial aid available to qualified students through federal resources include the Federal Pell Grant Program, Federal Supplemental Educational Opportunity Grant (FSEOG) Program, Federal Work-Study Program, Federal Perkins Loan Program, Federal Stafford Loan Program (subsidized and unsubsidized), and Federal PLUS Loan Program. Students are also encouraged to investigate the availability of grants and scholarships through community resources.

Faculty

The South University faculty includes individuals of high academic distinction. In addition to teaching, faculty members strive to help students develop the requisites to appreciate knowledge and understand how experiences in the classroom and laboratory relate to professional performance in the workplace. The average student-faculty ratio is 14:1. Each student is assigned a faculty adviser who oversees the student's progress and can answer questions about academic and career concerns. Students are encouraged to discuss program-related issues with and seek academic and career advice from their faculty advisers.

Admission Requirements

To be admitted to South University, prospective students must be high school graduates or hold a GED certificate and submit an appropriate SAT or ACT score (students should contact the Admissions Office) or a satisfactory score on the University-administered placement examination. Students who wish to transfer must meet the criteria established for acceptance as a transfer student.

All applicants to South University must demonstrate English proficiency. Students may furnish proof of English as a first language competency through submission of a diploma from a secondary school (or higher level) in which English is the official language of instruction. Applicants whose first language is not English must submit Test of English as a Foreign Language (TOEFL) scores. Applicants should contact the Admissions Office to determine other examinations/scores that are acceptable as an alternative to the TOEFL.

Applicants not meeting the testing standards for general admission may be accepted under academic support admission.

Application and Information

Applicants must complete an application form and submit it along with the general application fee as well as official transcripts from all high schools and colleges attended. Faxed documents are not considered official. Applicants must also complete all tests administered by the University or submit their SAT or ACT scores to the Registrar's Office. Applications are accepted on a rolling basis and should be made as far in advance as possible.

All international (nonimmigrant) applicants to South University must meet the same admissions standards as all other students. In addition, international applicants must have official educational records prepared in English, verify sufficient funds to cover the cost of the educational program, and meet certain other immigration-mandated criteria. South University in Virginia Beach is authorized under federal law to admit nonimmigrant students.

Admissions officers are available weekdays, Saturdays, and by appointment. An appointment for an admissions interview or tour of the campus should be made in advance. For additional information, all prospective students should contact:

Richard Kriofsky
Director of Admissions
South University
301 Bendix Road
Virginia Beach, Virginia 23452
Phone: 757-493-6900
877-206-1845 (toll-free)
Fax: 757-493-6990
Web site: http://www.southuniversity.edu

South University in Virginia Beach, Virginia, is conveniently located for day, evening, and weekend students.

SPRINGFIELD COLLEGE

SPRINGFIELD, MASSACHUSETTS

The College

Springfield College graduates enter the workforce or advanced education with a competitive advantage—top-quality academic preparation and real-world experience.

Founded in 1885, Springfield College has an international reputation for educating leaders in health sciences, human and social services, sport and movement studies, education, business, and the arts and sciences. Accredited by the New England Association of Schools and Colleges, it is a private coeducational institution offering bachelor's, master's, and doctoral degree programs. It is designated by the YMCA of the U.S.A. as a premier leadership development center. Students perform fieldwork, internships, or service learning as early as their first year, gaining real-world experience while serving the community. It's a learning advantage based in the College's mission: education in spirit, mind, and body for leadership in service to others. Springfield has been named to the President's Higher Education Community Service Honor Roll, has received Carnegie Foundation Community Engagement classification, and has won the Jostens/NADIIIAA Award of Merit for community service by student athletes. The Institute for International Sport named it one of the fifteen most influential educators through sport in America.

An ethnically diverse student body of 3,200 undergraduate and graduate students at the main campus represents many U.S. states and other countries, with the majority from the northeastern U.S.

Springfield College is a vibrant living and learning environment. The picturesque, 180-acre lakeside campus is technologically up-to-date. Several new and newly renovated state-of-the-art facilities, including the new Richard B. Flynn Campus Union, blend with traditional campus architecture.

Ten campus residence halls provide guaranteed on-campus housing. Options include traditional residence halls and suite-style accommodations with private rooms for 2 to 4 students sharing a lounge, kitchen, and bathrooms. There are single-sex and coeducational residence halls. Seniors may elect to live off campus. The main student dining facility features a range of fresh food options. There are snack and other light-fare services around the campus, including a food court with a two-story atrium in the new campus union.

Enriching the undergraduate experience is a wide array of cocurricular activities, health and wellness programs, arts and cultural events, an extensive campus recreation program, and one of the largest athletics programs in the nation for a midsized college. There are more than 100 organizations and opportunities for involvement. More than 80 percent of undergraduates participate in some form of athletics, including varsity teams, intramurals, or club sports. There are men's and women's teams in basketball, cross-country, gymnastics, lacrosse, soccer, swimming and diving, tennis, track, and volleyball. Women's teams also include field hockey and softball, and there are additional men's teams in baseball, football, golf, and wrestling.

Location

On Lake Massasoit in the Pioneer Valley, Springfield College is located in Springfield, the fourth-largest city in Massachusetts. A wide range of social, cultural, and athletic activities enhance the valley, as well as twelve other colleges and universities. For example, Springfield Symphony Hall is the site of concerts, plays, musicals, and dance performances; the Springfield Armor is an NBA development league team; the Springfield Civic Center is home to the American Hockey League's Springfield Falcons; and the Basketball Hall of Fame is an international attraction.

Nearby cities and towns offer many additional attractions. Northampton bustles with trendy shops, coffeehouses, galleries, theater productions, health food stores, nightclubs, and restaurants. The Berkshire Hills offer hiking, skiing, biking, and other outdoor activities. Boston lies 90 miles to the east, New York City is less than a 3-hour drive away, Vermont is 1 hour away, and Bradley International Airport is 20 miles to the south.

Majors and Degrees

Springfield College offers Bachelor of Science or Bachelor of Arts degrees in American studies, applied exercise science, art, art therapy, athletic training, biology, business administration, communication disorders, communications/sports journalism, computer and information sciences, computer graphics/digital arts, criminal justice, dance, early childhood education, elementary education, emergency medical services management, English, general studies, health science/general studies, health services administration, health education (health studies), history, human services, mathematics, mathematics and computer technology, occupational therapy, physical education (movement and sport studies), physical therapy (entry-level six-and-a-half year program culminating in a Doctor of Physical Therapy degree), physician assistant studies (entry-level five-year program culminating in a Master of Science degree), psychology, recreation management, rehabilitation and disability studies, secondary education, applied sociology, sport management, sports biology, teacher preparation, youth development, and an undeclared major.

Academic Programs

Consistent with Springfield College's humanics philosophy, undergraduate education is designed to promote an understanding of how the spirit, mind, and body work together in preparing students for a life of leadership in service to others.

The College has a two-semester academic calendar. To graduate, students must complete 120 credits, including required courses for the major field of study, electives, and required courses for all students (writing, computer applications, arts and humanities, analytical and natural sciences, social sciences, international/multicultural studies, social justice, and physical education). Students may also earn credit for successful completion of Advanced Placement (AP) high school courses, and through the DANTES subject standard test, and the College-Level Examination Program (CLEP) administered by the College Board.

Springfield College has agreements with several medical schools that guarantee acceptance of its qualified students. In addition, many Springfield College programs allow undergraduates to take graduate-level courses.

There are campus chapters of the following honor societies: Beta Beta Beta (biology), Kappa Delta Pi (education), Phi Alpha (social work), Phi Epsilon Kappa (health, physical education, recreation, or safety), and Psi Chi (psychology).

Off-Campus Programs

For fieldwork, internships, and service learning, the College maintains relationships with businesses, not-for-profit organizations, public and private agencies, and schools. Sites have included the Basketball Hall of Fame, American Hockey League, the *Boston Globe*, YMCAs, American Heart Association, MassMutual,

Children's Hospital, Hilton Head Crowne Plaza, Reebok Health and Fitness Center, Baystate Medical Center, parks and recreation departments, and many other venues.

The cooperative education program links students with work experiences in their fields of study. It is open to second-, third-, and fourth-year students, who average 15 to 20 hours per week of study-related work.

Extensive study-abroad programs are available. Students may also enroll in courses at some of the other colleges in the Springfield area.

Academic Facilities

Technologically up-to-date, the campus has wireless zones, smart classrooms, computer labs, a videoconferencing facility, conference center, language laboratory, and more. There is a new television studio and journalism laboratory and a radio station.

The new Athletic Training/Exercise Science Complex and the new Wellness and Recreation Complex have been cited as among the most outstanding facilities of their kind in the nation. Science facilities include the newly renovated Schoo-Bemis Science Center with state-of-the-art equipment and the Allied Health Sciences Center with a human anatomy laboratory and sophisticated equipment for physical testing, analysis, and treatment. Herbert P. Blake Hall contains labs, testing, and treatment facilities. Locklin Hall contains a well-equipped rehabilitation, assessment, and counseling services center.

For arts studies and programs, the newly renovated Fuller Arts Center and Appleton Auditorium is the site for performances, while the Visual Arts Center contains studio work space and a public exhibition center.

The 82-acre East Campus comprises a forest ecosystem with camping facilities and lake shoreline. It is a training ground for students in several academic programs. The Springfield College Child Development Center is an exceptional fieldwork facility for students of education and psychology.

Babson Library, well known for its resources in physical education, psychology, education, health, and human services contains a rich collection of full-text print and digital materials. Library staff members assist with access to a full range of information sources.

Costs

For 2009–10, tuition and fees were $26,480 and room and board were $9510.

Financial Aid

Students are encouraged to apply for grants, loans, and student employment. Springfield College financial aid is based on need, intellectual promise, leadership, and character. The College gives full consideration to students who submit the Free Application for Federal Student Aid and the Springfield College Financial Aid Application by March 15, 2010 for first-year students and May 1, 2010 for transfer students. Students not eligible for financial aid may be considered for campus employment.

Faculty

Most of the 211 faculty members hold doctorates or other terminal degrees. The student-teacher ratio is 12:1.

Student Government

The Student Government Association, managed by elected students, promotes students' interests and welfare. It guides and finances more than thirty student organizations, adopts policies affecting students, and is a liaison between students and the College administration.

Admission Requirements

Springfield College evaluates applicants on the basis of academic and personal factors. Applications for regular admission or early decision must be submitted to the Office of Undergraduate Admissions and include a completed application form, a high school transcript, one personal reference, and SAT or ACT scores. Transfer students must also submit a transcript and a dean's report from each college attended.

Springfield College is interested in meeting each applicant and encourages candidates to visit the College and experience campus life. The College offers personal interviews, campus tours, and open-house programs and will also facilitate contact with alumni and current students.

Application and Information

Application due dates for the 2010–11 academic year are April 1, 2010 for undergraduate applicants and August 1, 2010 for transfer students. Application due dates for the 2011–12 academic year are December 1, 2010 for athletic training and physical therapy applicants; January 15, 2011 for physician assistant studies and occupational therapy applicants; April 1, 2011 for undergraduate applicants; and August 1, 2011 for transfer students.

Springfield College's Admissions Committee reviews applications upon receiving them. Application forms and information may be obtained from:

Office of Admissions
Springfield College
263 Alden Street
Springfield, Massachusetts 01109
Phone: 413-748-3136
800-343-1257 (toll-free)
E-mail: admissions@spfldcol.edu
Web site: http://www.springfieldcollege.edu (online application)

Students pass the Marsh Memorial building on Naismith Green at Springfield College.

STATE UNIVERSITY OF NEW YORK AT OSWEGO

OSWEGO, NEW YORK

The University

Founded in 1861, SUNY Oswego is well into its second century of meeting the needs of today's students. Although its origins were in teacher education, the University expanded its curriculum in 1962 to include the arts and sciences and professional studies. Today, Oswego is a comprehensive college with an excellent academic reputation and commitment to undergraduate education. Approximately 3,150 men and 3,560 women are currently enrolled as full-time undergraduates. More than 110 liberal arts and career-oriented programs are offered through the College of Liberal Arts and Sciences, the School of Business, the School of Communication, Media, and the Arts, and the School of Education. The School of Education is nationally accredited by the National Council for the Accreditation of Teacher Education (NCATE), and the School of Business is accredited by AACSB International–The Association to Advance Collegiate Schools of Business. Other individual programs within the College of Liberal Arts and Sciences and the School of Communication, Media, and the Arts are accredited by specific discipline-oriented accrediting organizations.

Located on 696 acres on the southern shore of Lake Ontario, the spacious tree-lined campus consists of forty-five buildings. Eleven residence halls offer a variety of on-campus housing opportunities to all degree-seeking students. The campus is alive with more than 150 extracurricular organizations covering a wide range of social, academic, cultural, and intellectual interests. Theater, art, film, music, dance, and discussion events fill the campus cultural calendar. SUNY Oswego also offers a full slate of twenty-four NCAA Division III intercollegiate sports for men and women, along with a full complement of club sports and intramural athletics.

Oswego, a selective college, receives over 13,000 applications for some 2,000 freshman and transfer openings each fall. Accredited by the Middle States Association of Colleges and Schools, it has been recognized by a number of authoritative guides as a college with outstanding academic opportunities and high academic standards. During the last several years, SUNY Oswego has been cited for excellence and selectivity in *Princeton Review's Best Northeastern Colleges* and *U.S. News & World Report's Best Colleges Guide*. Oswego was also honored as one of the top Up-and-Coming Schools *in America's Best Colleges 2010*.

Oswego is taking part in a comprehensive renewal project involving more than $400 million in recently completed projects, including the $56-million campus and convocation center, and over $300 million in current and planned construction and renovations. This includes developing a $35-million, on-campus townhouse village for 350 students (opening fall 2010); renovating several academic buildings and residence halls; and investing more than $110 million in new and renovated science facilities.

Location

With a population of nearly 20,000, the city of Oswego is a modest-sized, friendly upstate New York community. It is the country's oldest freshwater port and one of the leading ports on the Great Lakes and St. Lawrence Seaway. The city and its surrounding area are well known for all kinds of summer and winter recreation, including camping, boating, sailing, fishing, tennis, and golf and, in the winter months, ice skating, cross-country skiing, and sledding. It is at the heart of the booming sports fishing industry, with a thriving tourism scene. The campus is conveniently located 35 miles northwest of Syracuse and 65 miles east of Rochester. Students traveling by rail or air may utilize bus service to Oswego through the Regional Transportation Center located adjacent to the Carousel Mall in Syracuse.

Majors and Degrees

SUNY Oswego awards the Bachelor of Arts (B.A.), Bachelor of Science (B.S.), and Bachelor of Fine Arts (B.F.A.) degrees.

Through the College of Liberal Arts and Sciences, students can earn a baccalaureate degree in American studies, anthropology, applied mathematics, applied mathematical economics, biochemistry, biology, chemistry, cinema and screen studies, cognitive science, computer science, creative writing, economics, English, French, geochemistry, geology, German, global and international studies, history, human development, information science, language and international trade, linguistics, mathematics, meteorology, philosophy, philosophy-psychology, physics, political science, psychology, public justice, sociology, software engineering, Spanish, women's studies, and zoology.

The School of Business offers Bachelor of Science degree programs in accounting, business administration, finance, human resource management, management accounting, marketing, operations management and information systems, and risk management and insurance.

The School of Communication, Media, and the Arts offers baccalaureate degree programs in art, broadcasting and mass communication, communication, graphic design, journalism, music, public relations, and theater.

The School of Education offers Bachelor of Science degree programs in adolescence education, childhood education, teaching English to speakers of other languages (TESOL), technology education, technology management, vocational-teacher preparation, and wellness management.

In addition, three innovative five-year combined bachelor's and master's programs are available: a bachelor's degree in accounting with a master's in business administration, a bachelor's in psychology with an M.B.A., and a bachelor's in psychology with a master's in human computer interaction.

Cooperative programs include a 3+2 zoo technology program, resulting in a bachelor's degree in zoology at Oswego and an associate degree in zoo technology from Santa Fe Community College (Florida) or Niagara Community College; 3+2 engineering programs leading to a bachelor's degree from Oswego in chemistry or physics and a B.S. in engineering from Case Western Reserve, Clarkson, or SUNY Binghamton; 2+2 programs leading to a B.S. in cardiovascular perfusion, medical imaging sciences, medical technology, radiation therapy, or respiratory care from SUNY Upstate Medical University in Syracuse; a 3+3 program leading to a B.S./D.P.T. in physical therapy from SUNY Upstate Medical University; and a 3+4 preoptometry program leading to a bachelor's in chemistry from Oswego and an O.D. in optometry from SUNY College of Optometry.

Academic Programs

Oswego offers students a broad range of courses in the liberal arts and in preprofessional and professional studies. In addition to core courses within a major, all students must satisfy general education requirements designed to strengthen basic writing and analytical proficiency, give students awareness of their cultural heritage, and provide a level of literacy in the social and behavioral sciences, natural sciences, and humanities. By completing these general education requirements during their first two years of study, Oswego students are able to select a major with a sense of confidence and purpose. However, students who are certain of their academic interest may begin working on their major program in their first year.

Before arriving on campus, students are assigned an adviser from either their major area or the college's Student Advisement Center. Advisers assist students who have not declared a major; help with academic, personal, and career concerns; and collaborate in scheduling courses needed for graduation. In addition, most students are matched with a first-year peer adviser, an older student, to help them face the challenges of their first year. The college has more than 500 undeclared students; many drawn by Oswego's reputation for helping learners find their way in education and life.

Students may consider applying for the college's Honors Program, which provides a challenging academic experience for high achievers regardless of major. Students also have the option of receiving credit through proficiency CLEP and Advanced Placement examinations.

Off-Campus Programs

Opportunities exist for students to broaden their knowledge of other countries by participating in one of forty different summer or semester overseas academic programs offered. Programs are available throughout the world, and costs are held as close as possible to the cost of an average semester on the Oswego campus. A newer option is short study-abroad quarter courses offering an intensive curriculum followed by a one-to-two-week experience in a foreign country. Through cooperative arrangements, Oswego also participates in semester programs in Albany and Washington.

Internships and other field experiences are available for students from all disciplines through the Experience-Based Education Office. Each year, more than 1,000 Oswego students participate in internships and career-awareness activities on the Oswego campus, in the local area, and throughout the Northeast, the country, and the world.

Academic Facilities

Penfield Library is a high-tech information center supporting the curriculum, teaching, and research of SUNY Oswego. The library houses a collection of over 475,000 bound volumes, including partial U.S. and New York State government documents depositories, and provides access to nearly 26,000 print and/or electronic journals, magazines, and newspapers. Through InterLibrary Loan, Penfield can provide additional materials from libraries all over the world. The library's listening area has more than 12,000 recordings, cassettes, and CDs, ranging from classical to rock. Additional facilities include the Lake Effect Café, an online catalog, a 24-hour study room with computers, study carrels, wireless Internet access, and computer labs with word processing.

Campuswide computer technology services for student use include instructional and administrative technologies as well as network and telecommunications. The campus maintains several Sun servers, providing e-mail and Web publishing support. In addition, the campus has hundreds of Macintosh and Windows-based computers in ten public-access labs. Students also have access to more than 500 computers and numerous Sun workstations in forty specialized departmental labs. Students receive an account that can be activated online to use the time-sharing computers and to access e-mail, the Web, and other Internet services. High-speed Internet service is also available from all residence hall rooms via Ethernet. Wireless network access is available in an ever-increasing number of locations throughout the campus, including many academic buildings, the Campus Center complex, Hewitt Union, Penfield Library, and all resident dining centers.

Adjacent to the campus, the college maintains Rice Creek Field Station, including the 26-acre Rice Pond, surrounded by 350 acres of natural habitat. The facility contains two lab/classrooms, a lecture room, and exhibit areas with an indoor viewing gallery, providing a unique vista of the creek and pond. College classes and community education programs are regularly held at the field station, which ranks among the five most extensively used facilities of its kind in the country.

Tyler Hall, Oswego's fine arts center, hosts two art galleries that feature annual traveling exhibitions, locally produced theme exhibitions, and the best work of students and faculty members. Tyler Hall's Waterman Theatre hosts a variety of student plays, musical performances, and productions by internationally renowned traveling artists.

The WRVO Stations, the college's 50,000-watt public radio outlet, provides outstanding on-campus internship opportunities. Communication department facilities also include two new all-digital television studios, a modern radio lab, and two new journalism labs in Lanigan Hall. Student-run TV and radio stations and the college newspaper are located in the new Campus Center facilities.

Costs

Tuition for 2009–10 was $2485 per semester for New York State residents and $6405 per semester for nonresidents. Room and board charges were approximately $5435 per semester for entering students, depending on the meal plan selected, and additional fees totaled approximately $700 per semester. SUNY Oswego guarantees that a student's initial first-year costs for room and board will be frozen for up to four consecutive years. Although many activities on campus are free of charge, students need to budget for personal expenses.

Financial Aid

Need-based financial assistance consists of grants, loans, and part-time employment. Oswego offers approximately $66 million in aid to its student body annually. Students interested in financial aid must file a Free Application for Federal Student Aid (FAFSA). New York State residents also need to file an application for the state's Tuition Assistance Program. Priority is given to those applications on file by March 1 for the fall term and November 15 for the spring term.

Oswego offers a very generous merit scholarship program, with more than 35 percent of the entering freshman class receiving an Oswego merit scholarship. Students receive over $2.5 million annually in merit scholarships; the average four-year renewable scholarship is more than $2300 per year. For scholarship qualifications and details, students should visit http://www.oswego.edu/admissions/scholarships.

Faculty

Oswego's faculty, consisting of more than 300 full-time educators, is dedicated to teaching undergraduate students. With 83 percent of teachers holding doctoral or other terminal degrees from many of the finest institutions in the country, students can be assured of the opportunity for an outstanding undergraduate education. The student-faculty ratio is approximately 18:1. While the Oswego faculty is first and foremost dedicated to teaching, faculty members are also actively engaged in research—often in partnership with undergraduate students—as well as publications and public service.

Student Government

Students at SUNY Oswego are represented by the Student Association, which has as its aim the efficient and intelligent governance of a democratic student body. The functions of the Student Association are divided among various committees that allocate funds to student organizations, intercollegiate and intramural athletics, the student newspaper, and the student literary magazine, along with various campus social, cultural, and intellectual activities.

Admission Requirements

Admission to Oswego is competitive, with high school average, academic program, and standardized test scores being the most important criteria for applicants. Special talents such as artistic, musical, athletic, and creative writing skills are also considered. The Committee on Admissions accepts results on either the ACT or the SAT. Although not required, a campus admissions visit is encouraged.

Transfer students in good standing are encouraged to apply for admission. The average GPA for entering transfer students is 3.0.

Application and Information

Oswego accepts both The Common Application and the SUNY Application for admission. Both applications are available online at http://www.oswego.edu/apply or at high school guidance offices and college transfer offices. Oswego evaluates applications as they are completed and as space remains available. Applications completed by January 15 for the fall term or October 15 for the spring term are ensured equal consideration. Applications received after those dates are considered as space remains available.

Prospective students and their parents are encouraged to visit the campus to participate in a student-guided tour and speak with an admissions counselor. Visits can be scheduled online through the college's Web site (http://www.oswego.edu/visit). Interested candidates can also call the Office of Admissions in advance to schedule a visit. For further information, students should contact:

Office of Admissions
229 Sheldon Hall
SUNY Oswego
Oswego, New York 13126
Phone: 315-312-2250
Fax: 315-312-3260
E-mail: admiss@oswego.edu
Web site: http://www.oswego.edu

SUNY Oswego is located on 696 acres on the southern shore of Lake Ontario.

STATE UNIVERSITY OF NEW YORK COLLEGE OF ENVIRONMENTAL SCIENCE AND FORESTRY

SYRACUSE, NEW YORK

The College

Since it was founded in 1911 as the New York State College of Forestry, the SUNY College of Environmental Science and Forestry (ESF) has expanded both its role in education and its physical boundaries. The College has expanded its initial emphasis on forestry to include professional education in environmental science, landscape architecture, environmental studies, and engineering in addition to distinguished programs in the biological and physical sciences. Throughout its history, the College has focused on the environmental issues of the time in each of its three mission areas—instruction, research, and public service. The College is dedicated to educating future scientists and managers who, through specialized skills, will be able to use a holistic approach to solving the environmental and resource problems facing society.

A leader in its field, ESF is one of the doctoral degree–granting colleges in the State University of New York System. The College currently supports undergraduate and graduate degree programs in several disciplinary areas and in its broad program in environmental science. (Undergraduate programs are described in the Majors and Degrees section below.) Graduate programs lead to the Master of Science (M.S.), Master of Landscape Architecture (M.L.A.), Master of Professional Studies (M.P.S.), and Doctor of Philosophy (Ph.D.) degrees. ESF's research program has attracted a worldwide clientele, and support currently amounts to $14.5 million per year.

ESF's main campus is located on 12 acres adjacent to Syracuse University and the SUNY Upstate Medical University in an urban residential setting. There are 1,500 full-time and 300 part-time undergraduates enrolled (40 percent are women); the College's traditional affiliation with Syracuse University offers ESF students the opportunity for academic diversity and depth, as well as participation in cultural events, honorary societies, social fraternities and sororities, and professional and academic organizations.

Location

Syracuse, a metropolitan area of more than 730,000 people, is a leader in the manufacture of china, air-conditioning equipment, medical diagnostic equipment, drugs, automotive parts, and lighting equipment. It offers many cultural, recreational, and educational opportunities, including a symphony orchestra, museums, live theater, and historic points of interest. Syracuse is one of the few cities in the nation situated at the crossing point of two superhighways. The driving time to Syracuse from New York City, Philadelphia, Boston, Toronto, and Montreal is about 5 hours; from Buffalo and Albany, about 3 hours. The city is served by a modern international airport and major bus and rail lines.

Majors and Degrees

The SUNY College of Environmental Science and Forestry offers three undergraduate degrees: the Bachelor of Science (B.S.), the Bachelor of Landscape Architecture (B.L.A.), and the Associate in Applied Science (A.A.S.). The B.S. degree is awarded in aquatic and fisheries science, bioprocess engineering, biotechnology, chemistry, conservation biology, construction management, environmental biology, environmental resources and forest engineering, environmental science, environmental studies, forest ecosystem science, forest health, forest resources management, natural history and interpretation, natural resources management, paper engineering, paper science, wildlife science, wood products engineering, and an undeclared option. A number of options and concentrations are offered within specific curricula. The B.L.A. degree, which requires an additional year of study, is awarded in landscape architecture. A.A.S. degrees are awarded in forest technology and land surveying technology at the Ranger School campus in Wanakena, New York.

Academic Programs

Students at ESF all have opportunities for additional specialized study as well as research and field experience. The Department of Environmental and Forest Biology is the largest department on campus and encompasses seven different majors, including studies in biotechnology, conservation, wildlife, aquatic and fisheries science, forest health, and natural history and interpretation. With the exception of biotechnology students, biology students are required to complete a four-week period of summer field study, usually at ESF's Cranberry Lake Biological Station, after the junior year. Options for specialization within the chemistry program include biochemistry, environmental chemistry, and natural and synthetic polymer chemistry. Biology and chemistry students can also earn their secondary science teacher certification through Syracuse University.

The construction management program teaches management, analysis, and design of the construction process, with an emphasis on environmental and engineering issues. Wood products engineering students focus on marketing and production of forest products, wood science and technology, and building construction and renovation.

Environmental resources and forest engineering students learn skills in such areas as biological, environmental, and water resources engineering; mapping science; and geographic information systems. The closely related environmental science program also deals with engineering science, along with areas of focus in watershed science, health and the environment, earth and atmospheric systems science, environmental analysis, and renewable energy.

Bioprocess engineering students focus on the engineering, biology, and chemistry of ecologically sound industrial technologies and processes, giving students career opportunities in areas such as chemical engineering and bioengineering, pharmaceuticals, renewable energy, and environmental engineering. The forest resources management curriculum offers areas of focus in forest management, measurement, and policy, along with forest ecology and biology. The program also includes a minor in management in conjunction with Syracuse University. Natural resources management students can concentrate in either recreation or water resources management. Forest and natural resources management students are required to participate in a four-week period of summer field study, which is usually taken at ESF's Wanakena campus prior to the junior year.

Environmental studies offers specializations in environmental communication and culture, policy and management, and biological science applications. The landscape architecture program is a five-year bachelor's degree with options in site design, urban and regional planning, historic preservation, community and environmental design, and computer applications. During the first semester of the fifth year, the landscape architecture curriculum requires participation in off-campus independent study. Paper engineering students can study process and product design and environmental engineering applied to pulp, paper, and other related chemical industries, while paper science students focus on a variety of industry-related areas, including management and computer systems. In addition, ESF offers preparation for graduate study in dentistry, law, veterinary science, and medicine, and the College has a transfer articulation agreement with the College of Health Professions at nearby SUNY Upstate Medical University.

Academic Facilities

Specialized facilities and equipment include electron microscopes, plant-growth chambers, climate-controlled greenhouses, an animal environmental simulation chamber, a bioacoustical laboratory, a radioisotope laboratory, numerous computer labs, nuclear magnetic resonance spectrometers, gas chromatography apparatus, a mass spectrometer, ultracentrifuges, and X-ray and infrared spectrophotometers. The photogrammetric and geodetic facilities of the environmental resources and forest engineering department are among the most extensive available in the United States. The paper science and engineering laboratory has a semicommercial paper mill with accessory equipment. The construction management and wood products engineering faculty has a complete strength-of-materials laboratory, a pilot-scale plywood laboratory, and a machining laboratory. The landscape architecture faculty has a one-of-a-kind environmental simulation laboratory with a visual simulator. The greenhouses and forest insectary are used to produce plant and insect materials for the classroom and laboratory. Extensive collections are available, including wood samples from all over the world, botanical materials, insects, birds, mammals, and fishes. The Theodore Roosevelt Wildlife Collection contains more than 10,000 species of well-preserved vertebrate and invertebrate animals.

A complete renovation to the F. Franklin Moon Library was completed in 2007 with the addition of an Academic Success Center for tutorial support in mathematics and other SUNY ESF courses. A Writing Center is also located in Moon Library. Moon Library contains 106,000 cataloged items, and more than 1,800 journals and their corresponding indexes are currently received. The library also provides comprehensive abstract and indexing services that are relevant to the College's programs. These facilities and services are supplemented by the collections of Syracuse University and the SUNY Upstate Medical University, both of which are within easy walking distance.

ESF's regional campuses in Tully, Warrensburg, Cranberry Lake, Newcomb, and Wanakena, New York, have a great diversity of forest sites that are used as outdoor teaching laboratories and for intensive research. ESF also operates several field stations to support its instruction, research, and public service programs.

Costs

Estimated costs for the 2008–09 academic year included resident tuition and fees of $5100 and out-of-state tuition and fees of $11,400. Room and board, which are provided for ESF students by Syracuse University, were $11,920. Books, personal expenses, and travel were estimated at $2250.

Financial Aid

A wide variety of financial aid is available for ESF students, and more than 85 percent of the students receive some type of support. The forms of financial aid include merit- and need-based scholarships, grants, low-interest student loans, and student employment programs. All students are encouraged to apply for financial aid by completing the Free Application for Federal Student Aid (FAFSA).

Faculty

The members of the faculty at ESF are highly trained and are dedicated to the College's teaching, research, and public-service missions. There are 136 regular faculty members and 46 adjunct members. Many are nationally and internationally recognized for their expertise in specialized fields. Nearly all regular faculty members serve full-time, and most hold twelve-month appointments. Just over 80 percent are tenured, and more than half are full professors, of whom 93 percent have earned doctorates. There is no distinction between the undergraduate and graduate faculty. Faculty members teach at both levels, and no courses are taught by teaching assistants. Faculty members serve as advisers to students and student groups and encourage excellence in scholarship and research. The student-faculty ratio is about 12:1.

Student Government

The College has a representative Undergraduate Student Association, and student representatives also participate in a counterpart association at Syracuse University. The ESF student government body organizes and presents student social activities, and its representatives attend College administrative meetings, communicate students' concerns and ideas to the administration, and serve as a conduit of information back to the student body. A formal set of student rules and regulations has been established. In addition, ESF students are obligated to abide by Syracuse University's general rules and regulations.

Admission Requirements

Students who are interested in the academic programs offered at ESF have four enrollment options: Early Action, Regular Freshman Entry, Guaranteed Transfer Admission, and Transfer Admission.

Outstanding high school seniors who have selected SUNY-ESF as a top choice may apply for Early Action, a nonbinding early application/early notification program for fall-entry freshmen. Early Action allows students to apply to as many institutions as they wish and, if admitted, make their final college choice no later than May 1. Students filing an application for Early Action must meet the SUNY application filing deadline date of November 15 and have supporting credentials to SUNY-ESF by December 1. Students applying for Early Action are notified by January 1.

Regular Freshman Entry is for applicants who want to enroll immediately following high school. These candidates should demonstrate strong academic performance in a college-preparatory program, with emphasis on mathematics and science preparation. Freshman candidates must apply to their intended programs of study.

Guaranteed Transfer Admission (GTA) candidates apply to ESF as high school seniors but are offered admission to either their sophomore or junior year. Students who plan to attend another college prior to transferring to ESF select this option to ensure a place at ESF for their chosen entry date. This option may also be offered to students who do not meet the freshman admission criteria. Those who are accepted for Guaranteed Transfer Admission receive a letter of acceptance for their sophomore or junior year of college, contingent upon the successful completion of all the prerequisite courses required for the curriculum they have selected. The prerequisite courses are outlined and described in an enclosure with the student's acceptance letter and can also be found on the College's Web site at http://www.esf.edu.

Students not applying or not accepted under these programs are considered for admission to ESF on the basis of their previous college course work, overall academic aptitude, and interest in the College's programs. Consideration is given to both the quality and the appropriateness of each student's prior academic experience. Students may spend one or two years at any accredited college of their choice. The College has developed Cooperative Transfer Programs with other four-year and two-year colleges in New York, Connecticut, Maryland, Massachusetts, New Jersey, and Pennsylvania. All admission acceptances are conditional upon satisfactory completion of course work in progress.

Application and Information

Students may apply for fall or spring admission. Admission decisions are made on a rolling basis until the class is filled. Decisions for the fall semester are made beginning on or around December 15, and decisions for the spring semester are made beginning on or around October 15. Application forms are available for New York State residents at New York State high schools and at all SUNY two- and four-year colleges. Out-of-state students should request an application form directly from the Office of Undergraduate Admissions at ESF. Both parts of the application can also be found online at the College Web site. Requests for more information should be directed to:

Office of Undergraduate Admissions
106 Bray Hall
State University of New York College of Environmental Science and Forestry
1 Forestry Drive
Syracuse, New York 13210-2779

Phone: 315-470-6600
Fax: 315-470-6933
E-mail: esfinfo@esf.edu
Web site: http://www.esf.edu

STATE UNIVERSITY OF NEW YORK INSTITUTE OF TECHNOLOGY

UTICA, NEW YORK

COLLEGE CLOSE-UPS

The College

The State University of New York Institute of Technology (SUNYIT) offers undergraduate degree programs in technology, professional studies, and the liberal arts. SUNYIT's broad curriculum embraces the humanities, communications, math, and science. Students enjoy close contact with faculty members in small classes, many with fewer than 20 students.

Founded in 1966, SUNYIT offers twenty-two bachelor's degree programs for freshmen and undergraduate transfer students and thirteen graduate degrees, including the Master of Business Administration in technology management.

SUNYIT enrolled 2,300 undergraduate and 600 graduate students on both a full-time and part-time basis in fall 2009. The men-women ratio was approximately 1:1. International students comprise approximately 3 percent of the student body, representing over twenty nations, and 12.5 percent of students were members of minority groups.

In addition to its academic facilities, SUNYIT provides student services through the Campus Life, Career Services, Health, and Counseling Center Offices. Town-house-style residence halls provide on-campus housing to 584 students. The Campus Center provides health, physical education, and recreation facilities as well as a dining hall and student services offices. In addition to providing a wide variety of intramural sports for students, SUNYIT has competitive intercollegiate teams in men's and women's basketball, bowling, cross-country, golf, soccer, swimming, and volleyball; men's baseball; and women's softball.

Location

SUNYIT is located in Marcy, New York, a few minutes from Utica. The city of Utica, which has a population of 60,000, is situated in the geographic center of New York State, approximately 220 miles from New York City and 190 miles from Buffalo on the New York State Thruway. Utica, a cultural and recreational center for this area of New York State, has a variety of recreational and educational opportunities. Museums, theaters, restaurants, and professional sports events are available either within walking distance of the campus or a short bus ride away. As a natural gateway to the Adirondack Mountains, Utica provides its residents with access to hiking, boating, skiing, and other outdoor activities. Served by buses, Amtrak, and airlines, the city is easily reached from locations throughout the eastern United States.

Majors and Degrees

SUNYIT awards the following baccalaureate degrees: Bachelor of Professional Studies (B.P.S.), Bachelor of Science (B.S.), Bachelor of Arts (B.A.), and Bachelor of Business Administration (B.B.A.). At the graduate level, the Master of Science (M.S.) and Master of Business Administration (M.B.A.) degrees are awarded.

Academic majors available to undergraduate students include accounting, applied mathematics, business administration, civil engineering technology, communication and information design, computer and information science, computer engineering technology, computer information systems, criminal justice, electrical engineering, electrical engineering technology, finance, general studies, health-information management, health services management, industrial engineering technology, mechanical engineering technology, nursing, psychology, sociology, and telecommunications.

A number of options and concentrations within specific curricula are also available, as are minors in accounting; anthropology; communication and information design; computer information systems; computer science; criminal justice; finance; health services management; human resources management; marketing; mathematics; nanotechnology; physics; psychology; quality engineering and system technology; science, technology, and society; sociology; and telecommunications.

Academic Programs

SUNYIT's academic year is divided into two semesters and runs from September through May. Summer sessions are also available.

Baccalaureate degree requirements vary from program to program but usually consist of a combination of specific major courses and liberal arts studies. Specializations and other options exist within the Schools of Arts and Sciences, Business, Information Systems and Engineering Technology, and Nursing and Health Systems. Specializations are developed through the use of electives and individual advisement.

Off-Campus Programs

Internship and cooperative education experiences are integral to effective career planning and job search strategies. These experiences can influence career plans by providing an opportunity for occupational exploration, developing marketable career-related skills and characteristics, and establishing a network of contacts that can provide relevant and timely information critical to the career decision-making process. In addition, employers are increasingly using internships and cooperative education programs as training opportunities leading to full-time permanent employment. All students, regardless of major, are encouraged to consider gaining experience in their chosen field that complements classroom learning. For additional information, students should contact the academic department or the Office of Career Services.

Academic Facilities

SUNYIT's academic facilities are located on its scenic 800-acre campus just north of the city of Utica, easily accessible by municipal bus service. The campus consists of four building complexes, a facilities building, and residence halls. Four new buildings are in varying phases of construction: a $20-million sports complex, a $13-million student center, a $23-million first-year residence hall, and a $27-million advanced technology center.

The Peter J. Cayan Library, with 68,000 square feet of space, provides group and individual study rooms, and has an advanced computerized library instruction room.

Kunsela Hall contains administrative offices, classrooms, a bookstore, and laboratories for the telecommunications, electrical engineering, electrical engineering technology, and computer science programs. Donovan Hall—the academic complex—houses classrooms, faculty offices, and laboratory facilities for all other programs, including business, industrial engineering technology, mechanical engineering technology, communication and information design, nursing, and arts and sciences. The Campus Center contains a cafeteria, gymnasium, recreational facilities, student services offices, a swimming pool, and meeting rooms for clubs, special activities, and student government.

Costs

Costs for the 2009–10 academic year included state resident tuition and fees of $6070. Out-of-state tuition and fees were $13,970. Room and board costs were $9400; personal expenses, books, supplies, and travel cost approximately $2950. The total expenses were about $18,570 for New York State residents and $26,470 for out-of-state students. Costs may be subject to change. Graduate student costs will vary; more information is available on the SUNYIT Web site.

Financial Aid

A wide variety of financial aid is available to students at SUNYIT. Academic scholarships are awarded for the entering fall class, and are based on merit, personal achievement, and other factors. Additional financial aid is awarded on the basis of need, as determined by an assessment of the Free Application for Federal Student Aid. At present, approximately 85 percent of the students receive financial assistance. The forms of financial aid available include Tuition Assistance Program awards (for New York State residents only), Federal Supplemental Educational Opportunity Grants, Federal Pell Grants, Federal Work-Study Program employment, Federal Perkins Loans, federal Nursing Student Loans, Federal Direct Student Loans, a variety of state-sponsored loans, and a broad range of private scholarships and grants. Students with a cumulative transfer GPA of 3.25 or better or a high school average of 90 are automatically considered for merit scholarships at the time of their application.

Faculty

SUNYIT faculty members come from all over the world and are committed to teaching, research, and service to the community. Among the faculty members are a Distinguished Service Professor, a Fulbright Scholar, and numerous recipients of the Chancellor's Award for Excellence in Teaching. More than 80 percent of SUNYIT's full-time faculty members have doctoral or terminal degrees. The faculty members are fully engaged in academic orientation and advisement, individualized instruction, cooperative faculty-student efforts in research projects, and concern for students as individuals. In the classroom, the average student-faculty ratio is 19:1.

Student Government

All full-time undergraduates are members of the SUNYIT Student Association. Its primary functions are to develop and monitor the student-activity-fee budget, to approve and oversee all student organizations, to debate issues of concern to students and take action as needed, and to develop programs of interest to all students. Student government consists of a 7-person executive committee and 11 senators. Students are encouraged to take an active role in the governance process, and many opportunities for involvement, in addition to those listed above, are available for interested students.

Admission Requirements

Generally, freshman applicants should carry a B/B+ average in a college-preparatory program and have achieved an SAT score in the 1000–1100 range (or approximately 22–24 composite ACT score). Admission is based on high school average, SAT or ACT scores, strength of course work, and other relevant information.

For transfer students, most programs require a minimum GPA of 2.5 for guaranteed admission; some programs require a higher GPA or additional application materials. Transfer students below a 2.5 GPA but above a 2.0 GPA may be admitted under special circumstances. Transfer students are required to furnish an official transcript from all previous colleges they attended.

Students with a cumulative GPA of at least 3.25 are automatically considered for merit scholarships; no separate application is required.

Application and Information

The deadline for all applications is August 1 for fall entry and December 1 for spring entry. Prospective students are encouraged to apply early as programs may close prior to application deadlines.

All applications are reviewed on an individual basis. All EOP applicants are also required to complete a supplemental application and are encouraged to apply for fall semester by December 1. The recommended application deadline for EOP and regular admission is February 15. However, applications received after that date will be considered on a rolling basis. Notification of admissions decisions begins on December 15.

SUNYIT participates in the SUNY Early Action program. Early action students must submit their application by November 1 and complete their application by November 15; applications are reviewed and students are notified of admission by December 15. Students admitted under early action are required to submit a deposit by May 1.

Students who wish to apply should apply online through the SUNYIT Web site. A copy of the State University of New York application booklet can also be obtained from a two-year college, a local high school, or the Admissions Office. Application forms for international students may also be obtained through the SUNYIT Web site or the Admissions Office.

SUNYIT adheres to the principle that all persons should have equal opportunity and access to its educational facilities without regard to race, creed, sex, or national origin.

Official transcripts from all previously attended high schools and colleges should be sent to the Director of Admissions. All communications and requests for additional information should also be directed to:

Director of Admissions
SUNY Institute of Technology
100 Seymour Road
Utica, New York 13502
Phone: 315-792-7500
866-2SUNYIT (toll-free)
Fax: 315-792-7837
E-mail: admissions@sunyit.edu
Web site: http://www.sunyit.edu

SUNYIT student-athletes with the Wildcat mascot.

STATE UNIVERSITY OF NEW YORK MARITIME COLLEGE

FORT SCHUYLER, THROGGS NECK, NEW YORK

The College

Founded in 1874, the State University of New York Maritime College is the original, federally approved, commercial nautical institution in the United States. The primary mission of Maritime College is the preparation of men and women for a full spectrum of professional careers by providing high-quality undergraduate programs in international business, engineering, science, and technology, with particular emphasis on the marine industry. Most of the degree programs may be completed while concurrently preparing for the U.S. Merchant Marine officer's license as a third mate or third assistant engineer.

Maritime College graduates receive a well-rounded education that enables them to pursue career options in engineering or business, in private industry or government service, or at sea as civilian officers of merchant ships, research ships, and other U.S. vessels. In addition, while there is no military obligation, commissioning options exist for those seeking careers as officers in the U.S. Navy, Marine Corps, Coast Guard, or Air Force or in the National Oceanographic and Atmospheric Administration (NOAA). Maritime College is the only college that hosts a Naval ROTC program in the greater New York metropolitan area. The College has a consistent record of 100 percent career placement upon graduation.

Maritime College fields twenty-one varsity sports and is nationally known for its sailing and crew teams.

Location

The scenic 56-acre campus is located at historic Fort Schuyler on the Throggs Neck peninsula, where the East River meets Long Island Sound. The College campus has a suburban setting yet is a short bus ride from midtown Manhattan. The peninsula offers panoramic views of the East River and Long Island Sound, with impressive sights of coastal Connecticut, the North Shore of Long Island, and the Manhattan skyline.

The College's extensive waterfront property allows berthing of the College's training ship, the Empire State VI, as well as research craft and a training coastal tanker. The waterfront activities center/boathouse is home to a fleet of 420s, Lasers, FJ's, and offshore racing yachts.

Majors and Degrees

The College offers Bachelor of Engineering (B.E.) degrees in electrical, facilities, marine, and mechanical engineering; marine electrical and electronic systems; and naval architecture. It offers the Bachelor of Science (B.S.) degree in general marine business and commerce (with a humanities concentration), international transportation and trade, marine environmental science (with a marine biology or oceanography and meteorology minor), marine operations, marine transportation, and maritime studies. With the exception of international transportation and trade and maritime studies, all degree programs may be combined with preparation for the professional license as a U.S. Merchant Marine officer through participation in Maritime's Regiment of Cadets. Students pursue the deck license option to qualify as a third mate, and the engine license option to qualify as a third assistant engineer.

The marine transportation program couples the nautical education and training required of a ship's deck officer with the business administration academic core (liberal arts and sciences, accounting, economics, and marketing and management). Students may concentrate in the areas of management, logistics, international business, vessel operations, or port security.

Graduates of this degree/license program are qualified to sail as third mates aboard oceangoing ships, on the Great Lakes, and on all types of inland and near-coastal vessels. In addition to careers at sea, the federal license enhances graduates' opportunities to find exciting positions in virtually all aspects of global transportation, from marine insurance to management of import/export industries and terminal operations. A related program, international transportation and trade, does not require license preparation. Also available is a major in general marine business and commerce, which includes deck license preparation and a humanities study area concentration. A B.S. in marine operations combines a deck license with a technical background and a limited horsepower engineering license.

Maritime's Accreditation Board for Engineering and Technology (ABET)–accredited engineering programs include a marine engineering program, which provides graduates with a broad understanding of the energy and power industries and includes preparation for a third assistant engineer's license. The electrical, facilities, and mechanical engineering programs offer specialization within some of the areas covered by the marine engineering discipline, and students may pursue the license option or internship option. Naval architecture, offered with either a deck or engine license option or the intern option, is a challenging enterprise, demanding imagination and technical expertise in the design of seaborne structures from ultralarge tankers to high-speed recreational craft. Engine license candidates operate a live power plant aboard the training ship, while intern option students utilize an industrial co-op experience to gain the hands-on component for which Maritime graduates are renowned.

The marine environmental science program offers undergraduate study in the ocean and atmospheric sciences, with a strong emphasis on environmental chemistry, ecology, and environmental protection. Students choose a minor in either marine biology or meteorology and oceanography. Marine environmental science students may elect the deck, license, or intern options.

Maritime offers a two-year Associate in Applied Sciences (A.A.S.) degree program in marine technology/small-vessel operations (MTSVO) and is the only school in the country to offer an assistant engineer (limited oceans) associate degree. MTSVO qualifies graduates for a 200-ton U.S. Coast Guard mate's license, and the assistant engineer (limited oceans) program qualifies graduates to work as an officer in charge of an engineering watch or a designated duty engineer.

Academic Programs

The deck or engine license, issued by the Coast Guard qualifies graduates to sail on oceangoing vessels engaged in international commerce or coastal, Great Lakes, or inland waterway shipping. License candidates are required to be members of the Regiment of Cadets. This structured, military-style program emphasizes leadership, self-discipline, and individual responsibility. All programs include hands-on, professional experience, either during Summer Sea Terms aboard the training ship Empire State VI or through industrial co-ops/internships.

The annual Summer Sea Term, which is an important part of Maritime College curricula, takes place aboard the 565-foot training ship, the Empire State VI, the largest and best-equipped training ship in the United States. Summer Sea Term provides a leadership laboratory in which cadets assume responsibility for the operation of the ship under the supervision of licensed officers and staff. The Empire State VI visits at least three international ports throughout the course of the Sea Term. Recent ports of call include the Bahamas, England, France, Gibraltar, Greece, Iceland, and Italy.

Academic Facilities

Pre–Civil War Fort Schuyler houses the Stephen B. Luce Library with its more than 80,000 volumes and 375 periodical subscriptions, accessed through an online catalog. Full-text CD-ROM databases and online searches are also available. A $1.5-million Center for Simulation and Marine Operations is also housed in the fort. It contains a state-of-the-art full bridge simulator, a liquid cargo simulator, an electronic navigation simulator, ten Automatic Radar Plotting Aid (ARPA)–equipped radar simulators, and Global Maritime Distress and Safety System (GMDSS) simulators.

The Science and Engineering Building contains a marine diesel simulator; a ship model basin (towing tank); and five computer classroom/laboratories; as well as advanced electrical and mechanical engineering laboratories; physics, chemistry, and meteorology laboratories; and smart classrooms.

Floating laboratories include the training ship Empire State VI, a coastal tanker used for liquid cargo training, and several marine research craft, including a 147-foot buoy tender.

Costs

For 2009–10, tuition for New York State residents was $4970. Since the Maritime College has been designated as a regional maritime college, students from East and Gulf Coast states (Alabama, Connecticut, Delaware, Florida, Georgia, Louisiana, Maryland, Mississippi, New Jersey, North Carolina, Pennsylvania, Rhode Island, South Carolina, and Virginia) and the District of Columbia also pay the New York State tuition rate of $4970 per year. In addition, students from any state who apply for and are qualified to enroll in the federally funded Student Incentive Program (SIP) are charged New York State tuition.

For students who did not participate in SIP and were not residents of New York or any of the regional states, tuition was $11,740 per year in 2009–10. This rate also applied to international students.

Additional costs in the 2009–10 school year totaled approximately $17,000. This fee includes room and board, Summer Sea Term, uniform fees, and other costs.

Financial Aid

Maritime College students have access to several special forms of aid. Cadets who apply for and are selected for the federal Student Incentive Program receive $3000 per year. SIP participants pay New York State tuition rates regardless of residence and agree to complete one of the license programs at the College and serve in the U.S. Naval Reserve (inactive duty, including the Merchant Marine Reserve). Full-tuition scholarships are also available through Naval ROTC. Four-year NROTC scholarship winners are also offered free room at the College, and the Maritime Academy Graduate Program (MARGRAD), a Coast Guard Commissioning Program, provides generous compensation to select Maritime College cadets beginning their sophomore year.

A variety of privately funded scholarships, including full-tuition Cadet Appointment Program (CAP) scholarships, are available to qualified students. Need-based aid, including Federal Pell Grants, TAP grants, Federal Perkins Loans, Federal Stafford Student Loans, and Federal Work-Study awards, is available and requires the Free Application for Federal Student Aid (FAFSA) as well as the Maritime College financial aid form.

New York State residents who are in great financial need and who have not been able to achieve up to their academic potential because of factors beyond their control may apply for assistance through the Educational Opportunity Program (EOP) when they apply for admission.

Faculty

Maritime College prides itself on an innovative, hands-on approach to instruction, directed by a dedicated faculty who are experts in their fields. The faculty members involved with license preparation course work have the appropriate United States Coast Guard licenses and professional credentials. Faculty members teaching in traditional academic disciplines possess appropriate credentials, with 35 holding the doctorate or other terminal degree in their field. Many faculty members, recognized as experts within the maritime industry, are involved with consulting work. A student-to-faculty ratio of 17:1 is maintained.

Student Government

The College has an active student government association. It oversees College-wide activities, over thirty clubs and organizations, and a diverse athletic program. Students are also represented on various faculty committees.

Admission Requirements

Admission is competitive and is based strictly on the applicant's abilities. Political nomination is not required. Decisions are based on strength of academic preparation, grades, SAT and/or ACT scores, outside activities and achievements, and trends in performance. Transfer students are welcome. Math, through at least intermediate algebra and trigonometry, and a year of either chemistry or physics are required. Four years of math and science are strongly recommended.

Application and Information

Applications (the SUNY Application for Admission and Maritime supplemental form) and additional information are available from the Office of Admissions. Prospective students are encouraged to schedule an interview and guided tour (arranged with the admissions office). Students may apply online through the College's Web page.

Office of Admissions
State University of New York Maritime College
6 Pennyfield Avenue
Throggs Neck, New York 10465
Phone: 718-409-7221
E-mail: admissions@sunymaritime.edu
Web site: http://www.sunymaritime.edu

Maritime College—a degree and more!

STEPHEN F. AUSTIN STATE UNIVERSITY

NACOGDOCHES, TEXAS

The University

Stephen F. Austin State University (SFA) is a public four-year university located in the heart of Texas Forest Country, only a few hours' drive from Houston or Dallas. Established as a teachers' college that first held classes in 1923, the University today is perfectly sized. Enrolling nearly 12,000 students, SFA offers a wide variety of high-quality academic programs with the personalization one would expect to find at a private college.

SFA offers an array of strong undergraduate and graduate programs through its six colleges: Business, Education, Fine Arts, Forestry and Agriculture, Liberal and Applied Arts, and Sciences and Mathematics. Students can choose from more than eighty undergraduate majors, more than 120 study areas, and nearly fifty graduate degrees, including three doctoral programs. SFA is accredited by the Commission on Colleges of the Southern Association of Colleges and Schools (1866 Southern Lane, Decatur, Georgia 30033-4097; phone: 404-679-4500) to award degrees at the bachelor's, master's, and doctoral levels.

Students study, live, and thrive on SFA's beautiful campus, with an impressive setting among towering pines that has led many groups to name it one of the most beautiful in the state. In fact, Kaplan Publishing has called SFA a "hidden treasure." The main campus encompasses 412 acres, part of the original homestead of Thomas J. Rusk, early Texas patriot and United States senator. In addition, SFA maintains a 728-acre agricultural research center that includes beef, poultry, and swine production and an equine center; an experimental forest; and a forestry field station on Lake Sam Rayburn.

Because living on campus is one of the best and most memorable experiences of one's college career, the campus offers numerous residence halls. Students who are younger than 21 with fewer than 60 semester hours live on campus and have the opportunity to enjoy the full college experience.

Recent progress at the University has been marked and continues at an unprecedented pace. Recently completed construction totals approximately $170 million, and additional improvements valued at more than $51 million are underway.

In September 2007 the University opened a $24-million student recreation center, which features a large cardio-fitness and weight area; an indoor elevated walking and jogging track; aerobics and dance rooms; a climbing rock; a pool with a lazy river, diving well, and 30-seat spa; glass-backed racquetball courts; outdoor adventure center; indoor and outdoor basketball courts; sand volleyball courts; and a picnic area.

In April 2007, the University completed a $30-million student center renovation and expansion that features a three-story atrium, a movie theater, a food court, retail shops, and more.

Lumberjack Lodge, a four-story apartment-style facility that houses approximately 315 students, opened in January 2006. A 550-space detached parking garage accommodates students living in this residential facility. Lumberjack Village, a 610-bed, four-building student housing complex, and a 750-space parking garage also opened in 2006. A new, multi-story freshman residence hall is slated to open in fall 2011.

Outside of class, students have numerous opportunities to make friends or develop leadership skills through SFA's thriving Greek community and more than 200 student organizations. The University competes in intercollegiate varsity sports including men's baseball, basketball, cross-country, football, golf, and track and field; and women's basketball, bowling, cross-country, golf, soccer, softball, tennis, track and field, and volleyball. With campus activities from movies to intramurals, there is always something to do.

Location

SFA is located in historic Nacogdoches. With a population of approximately 30,000, Nacogdoches offers the friendliness and hospitality of a small town with the conveniences of a city. A popular tourist destination, downtown Nacogdoches entices visitors with its charming brick streets and its many unique shops and dining opportunities. The city is steeped in history and offers a number of museums, including the Stone Fort Museum on the SFA campus. Recreational opportunities, including water skiing and fishing at Lake Nacogdoches, abound. Nacogdoches is 140 miles from Houston; 180 miles from Dallas; 80 miles from Shreveport, Louisiana; and 260 miles from Austin.

Majors and Degrees

The University offers more than 1,800 undergraduate courses as part of its curriculum. Bachelor's degrees are offered in accounting, agribusiness, agricultural machinery, agriculture development, general agriculture, agronomy, animal science, applied arts and sciences, art, art history, biochemistry, biology, business economics, chemistry, child development and family living, communication (journalism, radio/television), communication disorders, communication studies, computer information systems, computer science, creative writing, criminal justice (corrections, law enforcement, legal assistant studies), dance, deaf and hard of hearing, economics, English, environmental science, family and consumer sciences, fashion merchandising, finance, foods and nutrition/dietetics, forestry (management, recreation, wildlife), French, general business, geography, geology, health science, history, horticulture, hospitality administration, interdisciplinary studies (teacher education), interior design, interior merchandising, international business, kinesiology, liberal studies, management, marketing, mathematics, music, nursing, orientation and mobility, philosophy, physics, political science, poultry science, psychology, public administration, rehabilitation services, social work, sociology, Spanish, spatial science, and theater.

Preprofessional programs include predentistry, pre-engineering, prelaw, premedicine, pre–occupational therapy, preoptometry, prepharmacy, pre–physical therapy, pre–physician's assistant, preseminary, and pre–veterinary medicine.

The five most popular areas of undergraduate study at the University are interdisciplinary studies (teacher education), nursing, kinesiology, general business, and psychology. Other popular majors include biology, music, and marketing.

Academic Programs

At SFA, career preparation is a top priority. In addition to the academic education one should expect to receive in college, internships, hands-on study, and research opportunities are an important part of preparing students for rewarding careers and fulfilling lives. Through opportunities like these, SFA's students hone critical-thinking and communication skills and discover their calling, their world, and their future.

The Nelson Rusche College of Business awards 15 percent of the top ten bachelor's degrees at SFA through majors in general business and management. The James I. Perkins College of Education is one of the largest, most comprehensive producers of Texas educators and routinely achieves one of the highest educator certification pass rates in the state. The College of Fine Arts has embraced increased societal globalization by developing international initiatives, including School of Art summer course offerings in Italy; School of Music performance tours to England, Austria, and Italy; and School of Theatre academic exchanges with institutions in London, Barcelona, and Tallinn, Estonia. The Arthur Temple College of Forestry and Agriculture fulfills vital Texas needs through rural economic development and enhanced educational research opportunities with unique programs such as the Columbia Regional Geospatial Service Center, the National Center for Pharmaceutical Crops, and the Poultry Science Center. The College of Liberal and Applied Arts provides a solid, diverse educational foundation by teaching nearly half of all core curriculum courses and strives to offer service-learning opportunities and promote development of skills with real-life applications. The Richard and Lucille Dewitt School of Nursing achieves one of the highest licensure pass rates and graduation/persistence rates in Texas. The College of Sciences and Mathematics is also home to the second-largest observatory in the Central Time Zone and the William W. Gibson Entomarium, one of the largest public insect collections in the state.

The School of Honors provides exceptional intellectual challenge and stimulation for academically talented students. All qualified students, regardless of their major, are eligible to apply for admission to the program, which offers scholarships, specialized classes, and access to laptop computers.

Off-Campus Programs

The Office of International Studies and Programs coordinates international enrollment and exchanges at SFA. Since the creation of the office, study groups have traveled to Austria, China, Costa Rica, England, Germany, Ireland, Italy, Mexico, Spain, and a number of other places. Students may choose to study abroad for a single semester or longer, depending on the number of credits desired and the availability of appropriate courses. SFA is a member of the International Student Exchange Program, which allows SFA students to study abroad at the University's regular cost for tuition and fees.

Academic Facilities

The University has forty-nine academic buildings with modern classrooms and laboratories. State-of-the-art facilities include a $16.6-million Human Services Building that opened in 2004. The building contains classrooms with the latest technology and excellent clinics and research facilities, including a groundbreaking Human Neuroscience Laboratory. Other recent construction has included a facility that provides academic space for an athletic training program, as well as four new broiler houses operated by the University's respected Center for Applied Poultry Studies and Research. The new $30.8-million Early Childhood Research Center opened in July 2009 and a new School of Nursing facility will open in 2010.

The Ralph W. Steen Library is one of the largest academic library facilities in the state. The library contains extensive electronic resources that are available to students both in-house and from remote locations. Three general-purpose student microlabs collectively house approximately 200 public-access workstations. Campus computing and instructional technology services are supported by three main offices and by laboratories and technology centers in various departments and colleges, with twenty computer labs and approximately 800 workstations.

The library houses the award-winning Academic Assistance and Resource Center, which provides one-on-one peer tutoring and student-led study groups to improve intellectual development and ensure student success. It is the only learning center in the nation to achieve distinguished certification from the National Association for Developmental Education. The Texas Higher Education Coordinating Board has recognized the center's success and its contribution to higher education with a prestigious Star Award.

Costs

SFA is a tremendous value in education, in comparison with other state universities and with private institutions. Tuition and room-and-board fees are competitive with other Texas public universities. Annual tuition and fees for 2009–10 for full-time undergraduates is approximately $5520 for Texas residents, $6240 for border state residents, and $12,168 for out-of-state residents. Room and board rates will average $7496 for the academic year.

Financial Aid

SFA awarded approximately $98.1 million in scholarships, grants, work-study, educational loans, waivers, and exemptions during 2007–08. Financial aid programs in which the University participates include the Federal Pell Grant, Federal Supplemental Educational Opportunity Grant, Texas Grant Program, Texas Public Educational Grant, Federal Work-Study Program, Federal Perkins Loan, Federal Family Educational Loan Program (Stafford Loan), and Hinson-Hazelwood Student Loan Program.

SFA has hundreds of scholarships available to new and returning students. Scholarships are based on need, merit, or athletic and special skills. Selection criteria may include, but are not limited to, an applicant's academic record, degree goals, financial status, and performance on a standardized test. Prospective students can search scholarships at http://www.sfascholarships.sfasu.edu. The application deadline for most is February 1 for the fall semester. Included are scholarships offered by Office of Admissions, Office of Student Financial Assistance, Alumni Foundation, SFASU Foundation, Intercollegiate Athletics, and various academic departments and organizations. Amounts vary, with some as much as $10,000 per year.

Faculty

In the 2008–09 academic year, the faculty numbered 621 members, of whom 511 were full-time. More than 80 percent of professors and instructors hold the highest degrees in their field. SFA has a student-faculty ratio of 20:1 and an average class size of 27.

Student Government

The Student Government Association serves as the representative voice of the student body to the faculty and administration. Concerns and issues that are important to students can be made known through legislation passed by the SGA. A three-branch system, consisting of the executive, legislative, and judicial branches, is used.

Admission Requirements

Applicants for admission must meet the following high school class rank and minimum test scores: first quarter, no minimum score; second quarter, 850 SAT/18 ACT; third quarter, 1050 SAT/23 ACT; fourth quarter, 1250 SAT/28 ACT. First-time freshman applicants are required to have completed the Recommended High School Program or the Distinguished Achievement Program or demonstrate they have completed a high school curriculum more rigorous than what is required of the Minimum Graduation Plan.

Application and Information

All new undergraduate applicants for admission must complete the Texas Common Application and submit it with a $35 nonrefundable application fee. For additional information, prospective students should contact:

Office of Admissions
Stephen F. Austin State University
P.O. Box 13051, SFA Station
Nacogdoches, Texas 75962-3051
Phone: 936-468-2504
E-mail: admissions@sfasu.edu
Web site: http://www.gosfa.com

Stephen F. Austin State University campus.

COLLEGE CLOSE-UPS

STEPHENS COLLEGE

COLUMBIA, MISSOURI

The College

Stephens College was founded in 1833 as the nation's second-oldest women's college. Stephens is ranked nationally in *U.S. News & World Report* and has repeatedly been selected to the *Princeton Review's* list of the best colleges in the country (listed one of the Best in the Midwest, 2009, and seventh on the list of best college theater programs in the nation).

Students from around the globe enrich Stephens with their varied talents, interests, and backgrounds. Stephens students may choose to join one of ten honorary societies on campus, including Psi Chi, Alpha Epsilon Rho, and Mortar Board, or become involved in student government. Leadership experience is emphasized in all aspects of life at Stephens.

Stephens' residence halls provide much of the focus for campus activity. The Honors House Plan offers a living/learning environment in the humanities to a select group of freshmen each year. Since it began in the 1960s as an experiment funded by the Ford Foundation, the program has served as a model for similar living/learning communities in colleges and universities across the nation.

In addition to undergraduate degrees, Stephens offers master's degrees.

Location

Stephens College is located in Columbia, Missouri. Situated halfway between Kansas City and St. Louis, Columbia is the cultural, medical, and business center of mid-Missouri. Often called "College Town, USA," Columbia is also the home of Columbia College and the University of Missouri. Stephens students have easy access to Columbia's shopping, dining, and entertainment offerings.

Majors and Degrees

Stephens College awards the Associate in Arts, Bachelor of Arts, Bachelor of Fine Arts, and Bachelor of Science. Majors include accounting; biology; creative writing; dance; digital filmmaking; education; English; entrepreneurship and business management; equestrian business management; equestrian instruction and training; fashion communication; fashion design and product development; fashion marketing and management; graphic design; human development; interior design; legal studies; liberal studies; marketing: public relations and advertising; mass media (journalism, public relations, or TV and radio); psychology; student-initiated majors; theater arts; theater management; and theatrical costume design. The B.F.A. program includes professional-level work in the fine or performing arts plus a strong component in liberal arts.

Academic Programs

The bachelor's degree is generally completed in four years. Students pursue depth of study in an academic area, breadth in liberal arts study, and elective course work with guidance from faculty advisers. Academic departments require relevant internships and often provide opportunities for research projects in field settings. Stephens has introduced many innovative educational concepts into its programs. Stephens emphasizes personalized teaching and development of the individual. Small classes are offered, and most departments offer tutorial projects and readings.

Students in the bachelor's degree programs—B.A., B.F.A., or B.S.—must complete the residency requirement of seven semesters. Students take a total of 30 hours in the liberal arts program throughout their three or four years at the College. These courses provide an interdisciplinary platform of study with a global focus in behavioral/social sciences, literature, cultural studies, history, natural science, math, and ethics. All liberal arts courses, regardless of the topics they cover, provide opportunities for students to sharpen their critical thinking and communication skills.

Degree requirements for the Bachelor of Arts include completion of at least 24 semester hours in a department. At least 15 of these hours must be at or above the 300 level. As many as 45 semester hours may be required in the major, but no more than 45 may count toward a 120-semester-hour degree program. Students also may elect to design an interdisciplinary student-initiated Bachelor of Arts major.

The Bachelor of Science degree program requires completion of 45 to 57 hours, including a minimum of 15 hours at or above the 300 level. Bachelor of Science candidates may elect additional courses in the major, but no more than 60 hours may count toward a 120-semester-hour degree program. Students also may elect to design an interdisciplinary student-initiated Bachelor of Science major.

Degree requirements for the Bachelor of Fine Arts include completion of 60 to 75 semester hours, including at least 15 hours at or above the 300 level. B.F.A. candidates may elect additional courses in their major, up to a maximum of 78 hours within a 120-semester-hour degree program. The B.F.A. degree programs in theater and in dance are completed in three years and two summers. Students also may elect to design an interdisciplinary student-initiated Bachelor of Fine Arts major.

Through the Stephens College Division of Graduate & Continuing Studies, nontraditional students have the opportunity to earn degrees through programs that build on prior and current learning. The Division of Graduate & Continuing Studies offers an online-based degree completion program with several options for concentrations; an undergraduate program in health information administration (the first accredited external degree program in medical record administration in the country); and postbachelor's certificate programs in health information administration, business, event planning, human behavioral studies, and nonprofit management.

In addition, Stephens offers a Master of Business Administration (M.B.A.); a Master of Education (M.Ed.) in counseling, with three emphasis areas; and a Master of Education in curriculum and instruction. Undergraduates in entrepreneurship and business management, creative writing, education, equestrian business management, equestrian instruction and training, fashion marketing man management, filmmaking, and marketing: public relations and advertising, psychology, and theater management may continue immediately into a master's program through the College's "Plus One" master's program. Students earn a bachelor's degree followed by a M.B.A. or M.Ed. in as little as one additional year. Certain requirements apply.

Stephens also offers numerous partnerships with other institutions wherein students may earn a bachelor's degree from

Stephens in three years and a master's degree from another college or university after two or three additional years. Partnerships currently exist in occupational therapy, physical therapy, physician assistant studies, accounting, and law. Training in Avid and Final Cut Pro is available to film students in a cross-training agreement with the University of Missouri-Columbia.

Off-Campus Programs

Stephens sponsors summer seminars in several countries, including France, Italy, and Japan, as extensions of courses that are regularly offered at the College. Summer-study programs include drama and musical theater at Okoboji Summer Theatre in Spirit Lake, Iowa. Stephens also offers international study opportunities in Korea, India, South America, and Spain.

Many other study opportunities are available through global partnerships with other universities.

Academic Facilities

The Hugh Stephens Resources Library contains more than 135,000 volumes. The library is the central building of a quadrangle that includes the Helis Communication Center and the Patricia Barry Television Studio. The E. S. Pillsbury Science Center houses science and mathematics classrooms and laboratories. Other working laboratories include the digital film G5 Mac lab, student-run Warehouse Theatre, the Johnson Plant Laboratory, and the Audrey Webb Child Study Center, which has an enrollment of approximately 100 children in preschool through fifth grade who interact with Stephens' college students.

Costs

For 2010–11, tuition is $25,400. Room costs range from $4770 to $7470 and prices for meal plans range from $2400 to $3300, which brings total direct costs for the year to $33,470–$36,170. Students should also plan for indirect costs such as books, supplies, and personal expenses. The enrollment deposit is $100.

Financial Aid

More than 95 percent students receive some form of assistance through scholarships, grants, loans, or employment. Stephens participates in the Federal Pell Grant, Federal Supplemental Educational Opportunity Grant, Federal Perkins Loan, Federal Stafford Student Loan, and Federal Work-Study programs. Missouri residents are encouraged to apply for aid under the Missouri Student Grant Program. The Free Application for Federal Student Aid (FAFSA) is required for financial aid consideration. Applications for financial aid should be received by March 15. Stephens also offers an early financial aid estimate service.

Faculty

Though most faculty members have come to college teaching via the recognized route of graduate study and scholarship, some have prepared for teaching through work experience, particularly those in applied and performing arts with careers as actors, dancers, musicians, and artists. The faculty is primarily a teaching faculty, and many of the instructors include students in independent scholarly research. Men and women join the Stephens faculty with a commitment to individualized education. They are actively engaged in academic advising and tutorial relationships and frequently spend many more hours working with students outside the classroom than in formal teaching situations. The student-faculty ratio is 12:1.

Student Government

Each student is a member of the Student Government Association (SGA). Working in the SGA provides women with experience in planning and administering cultural, social, and recreational activities and in dealing with academic, residential, and community concerns. SGA recently founded an environmental awareness initiative, Stephens College Going Green (SCG^2), to encourage recycling and energy conservation by the entire campus community. The association has executive and legislative powers to govern student activities and to develop and maintain group-living standards. Students also serve as voting members of established faculty committees and in advisory capacities to committees of the Board of Trustees. Stephens has been nationally recognized for the many leadership opportunities it provides students.

Admission Requirements

Applicants are considered by the Admissions Committee on an individual basis without regard to race, religion, geographic origin, or handicap. Major factors for admission consideration are the recommendations and academic record, including rank in class, subjects studied, grade point average, proficiency in English, and test scores (SAT and ACT).

Application and Information

Candidates for admission should submit the application with the $25 application fee and arrange to have transcripts and recommendations mailed to the Office of Admissions. Students who visit campus or apply online at http://www.stephens.edu/admission/apply can waive the application fee. Upon receipt of the application, any additional material is mailed to the student. Qualified students are accepted on a rolling admissions basis upon receipt of all necessary credentials.

Office of Admission
Campus Box 2121
Stephens College
Columbia, Missouri 65215
Phone: 573-876-7207
800-876-7207 (toll-free)
Fax: 573-876-7237
E-mail: apply@stephens.edu
Web site: http://www.stephens.edu

On the Stephens College campus.

COLLEGE CLOSE-UPS

STEVENSON UNIVERSITY

STEVENSON AND OWINGS MILLS, MARYLAND

The University

Stevenson University (SU), formerly Villa Julie College, is a coeducational, independent institution dedicated to providing its 3,400 undergraduate and graduate students with a career-focused liberal arts education. Individual attention from faculty members, extensive career preparation gained through real-world training, and two ideal locations just north of Baltimore, Maryland, in Stevenson and Owings Mills, make the University truly unique.

At SU, academic quality is viewed as a personalized education that fosters intellectual growth and prepares students to thrive in the working world after graduation. With a student-faculty ratio of 13:1, it is easy to understand why students often cite the congenial rapport with faculty members as one of the University's strong points.

Through Stevenson University's concept of Learning Beyond, students step outside of the classroom to take their learning to the next level. Experiential learning opportunities include study abroad, service learning, field placements, and independent research. In addition, through an approach known as Career Architecture[SM], each student develops a professional career plan based on their values, skills, and strengths.

Stevenson's graduates maintain a placement rate that tops 95 percent each year, with students acquiring jobs or going on to further their education within six months of graduation.

At SU, students enjoy more than forty-five clubs and organizations, multiple honor societies, and NCAA Division III athletics. The following sports are offered: men's and women's basketball, cross-country, golf, lacrosse, soccer, tennis, and volleyball; men's baseball; and women's field hockey and softball. Cheerleading, dance, and intramural sports are also extremely popular. Stevenson will add football in 2010 and will compete as a member of the NCAA in Division III in 2011.

In addition to its undergraduate programs, the University offers the following master's degree programs: business and technology management, forensic science, and forensic studies.

Location

Stevenson University has two beautiful campuses in the heart of Maryland, in Stevenson and Owings Mills. SU students truly appreciate the beauty of a rural campus as well as the convenience and appeal of a more urban setting.

The original 60-acre Greenspring Campus is nestled among the rolling hills in Stevenson, Maryland. The Owings Mills Campus is a thriving center of student activity and offers both academic and residential facilities. Classes are held on both campuses, and the University provides a free shuttle service that runs between these locations.

Majors and Degrees

Stevenson University offers the following bachelor's degree programs: accounting; applied mathematics; biology; biotechnology; business administration; business communication; business information systems; chemistry; computer information systems; criminal justice; early childhood education: liberal arts and technology; elementary education: liberal arts and technology; English language and literature; fashion merchandising; film, video, and theater; human services; interdisciplinary studies; medical technology; middle school education; nursing; nursing: RN to B.S.; paralegal studies; psychology; public history; and visual communication design.

Stevenson's B.S. to M.S. degree programs give students the option of earning both a bachelor's and a master's degree in as few as five years. Graduate study begins in the spring semester of the junior year and runs concurrently with undergraduate work until the end of the spring semester of the senior year. All subsequent course work is at the graduate level.

Academic Programs

At SU, academic quality is regarded as a personalized curriculum that prepares students to enter the working world with the knowledge and skills that employers value. SU infuses the traditional liberal arts education with a distinct career focus. The University's goal is to prepare students for employment, graduate study, and productive involvement in today's world.

Academic Facilities

From recent enhancements to the Greenspring Campus to brand-new facilities at the Owings Mills Campus, the University provides modern facilities that serve the needs of all students.

The University's Greenspring Campus includes a 350-seat theater, multiple computer labs and classrooms, video and graphic studios, science laboratories, a student union, and athletic facilities. Each classroom and laboratory on the campus is capable of multimedia projection and computer-assisted learning.

Also at the Greenspring Campus is the Verizon Center for Excellence in Teaching and Learning. The center comprises classrooms equipped with technology that accommodates distance learning.

The Owings Mills Campus hosts the University's newest facilities, including an expansive student center and dining hall, a 10,000-square-foot community center, a newly renovated athletic complex with a new gymnasium slated to open in 2010, multiple classrooms and study spaces, a fitness center, and additional athletic fields.

The Howard S. Brown School of Business and Leadership offers state-of-the-art technology housed in twelve traditional classrooms and seven seminar halls. The facility also includes two distance learning labs where students are able to interact with other learners worldwide, six computer labs utilizing the most up-to-date equipment, a student lounge, a law library, and a high-tech digital mock trial courtroom.

The University's library, located on the Greenspring Campus, has an extensive collection of more than 100,000 printed volumes, periodicals, videotapes and audiotapes, CDs, and microfilm and microfiche selections and an interlibrary loan consortium. In addition to the electronic databases it owns, the library has access to thousands of outside databases, such as LexisNexis Academic Universe, WESTLAW, Dialog, and Dow Jones News Retrieval.

Costs

Stevenson is among the most affordable universities in the state of Maryland. For the 2009–10 academic year, tuition and fees for full-time students were $20,644. Part-time tuition and fees were $487 per credit hour, plus a $75 registration and technology fee per semester. Room and board for the 2009–10 year were $10,296.

Financial Aid

Stevenson University offers financial assistance to qualified students in the form of grants, scholarships, loans, student employment, and a special payment plan. On average, approximately 90 percent of the University's students receive some form of financial assistance. The University has a generous scholarship program that grants awards based on academic merit. SU participates in all major federal aid programs as well as all Maryland state programs. Applicants are required to file the Free Application for Federal Student Aid (FAFSA). The priority deadline for filing is February 15.

Faculty

The faculty at Stevenson University is primarily a teaching faculty. The University's 13:1 student-teacher ratio demonstrates the institution's dedication to personalized education. A majority of the full-time faculty members have the doctoral or terminal degree offered in their field, and a significant number are widely published. In addition, many are concurrently employed as professional specialists in their fields.

Student Government

The Student Government Association (SGA) facilitates an environment that encourages students to express their thoughts and opinions concerning Stevenson University, its policies, and sponsored activities. The SGA serves as the principal governing body of all campus clubs and activities. In conjunction with the Office of Student Affairs, the SGA organizes an array of campuswide events that promote the social aspects of college life. Each student at Stevenson is welcome and encouraged to participate in all SGA functions.

Admission Requirements

Applications for admission to Stevenson University are reviewed on a rolling basis. In evaluating each applicant, the University considers the applicant's high school academic record, SAT or ACT scores, recommendations, writing sample, and any other special talents or personal interests. Admission to the University is determined without regard for race, color, sex, religion, national or ethnic origin, or handicap. SU complies with all applicable laws and federal regulations regarding discrimination and accessibility on the condition of handicap, age, veteran status, or otherwise.

Application and Information

Applications for admission to undergraduate programs should be received by March 1 for fall-semester entry and October 15 for spring-semester entry. Scholarship consideration adheres to earlier deadlines. Applications received after these dates are reviewed on a space-available basis. Students applying to the University as freshmen must submit official high school transcripts, standardized test scores, the Counselor Recommendation Form, typed responses to the essay questions listed on the application, and a $40 nonrefundable application fee. The application fee is waived for all students who apply online (http://www.stevenson.edu). Transfer students must submit official transcripts from all colleges or universities they have attended and should contact the Transfer Admissions Counselor to discuss additional credential requirements.

For further information and application forms, students should contact:

Admissions Office
Garrison Hall, Suite 200
Stevenson University
100 Campus Circle
Garrison Hall
Owings Mills, Maryland 21117-7804
Phone: 410-486-7001
877-468-6852 (toll-free)
Fax: 443-352-4440
E-mail: admissions@stevenson.edu
Web site: http://www.stevenson.edu

The residences at Stevenson University offer spacious apartments and suites with extensive amenities.

STONEHILL COLLEGE

EASTON, MASSACHUSETTS

The College

Stonehill College is a selective, coed Catholic college with a welcoming, academically challenging community of 2,400 students on a beautiful, active campus located 22 miles south of Boston. Stonehill offers more than 80 diverse majors and minors in the liberal arts, sciences, and business to prepare students for a life of learning, leadership, and responsible citizenship. Over 80 percent of Stonehill students complete an internship, study abroad, practicum, or field experience by the time they graduate.

More than 80 percent of Stonehill students participate in at least one sport on campus. Stonehill competes in the Northeast-10 Conference, the largest NCAA Division II conference in the country, and offers twenty different varsity sports, including baseball, lacrosse, football, basketball, and soccer. Over 60 percent of all Stonehill students participate in the extensive intramural program, which offers two different levels of competition in basketball, dodgeball, field hockey, kickball, softball, and more. Club sports such as rugby and volleyball are yet another option, offering a spirited, fun experience without the demands of more competitive athletics.

Founded by the Congregation of Holy Cross in 1948, Stonehill's mission is "to educate the whole person so that each graduate thinks, acts, and leads with courage toward the creation of a more just and compassionate world." The idea of making the world a better place is part of the Catholic faith and an intrinsic element of the Stonehill experience. Each year, approximately 1,400 Stonehill students (more than 50 percent of the student body) participate in community service. Last year, Stonehill students provided more than 41,000 hours of service.

Stonehill consistently receives nationwide recognition as one of the country's top colleges. Recently, *U.S. News and World Report's* "America's Best Colleges" guide singled out Stonehill as a top up-and-coming school. The Princeton Review recently chose Stonehill as one of the best in the nation for in-depth student engagement, beautiful campus, career services, study abroad program, and more. The Princeton Review's "The Best 371 Colleges" ranked Stonehill seventh on their list of institutions with the happiest students.

Location

Stonehill is located in Easton, Massachusetts, a friendly residential community nestled between New England's largest capital cities. Just 22 miles from Boston, America's number-one college town, and 37 miles from Providence, it is perfectly situated for internships, service opportunities, job prospects, museums, professional sports games, cultural events, and more.

Whether the countless trees are in full bloom in the spring or the leaves are bursting into reds and golds in the fall, Stonehill is beautiful every season of the year. Encompassing 384 acres, Stonehill's New England college campus features traditional landscaping, ponds, wooded trails, and Georgian-style architecture.

Majors and Degrees

Students may receive Bachelor of Arts degrees in American studies, art history, Catholic studies, chemistry, communication, computer science, criminology, economics, education (early childhood/elementary and secondary education minors), English, environmental studies, foreign languages, French, gender studies, graphic design, health-care administration, history, international studies, mathematics, multidisciplinary studies, philosophy, physics, political science, psychology, public administration, religious studies, sociology, Spanish, studio arts, and visual and performing arts (music and theater arts concentrations).

Bachelor of Science degrees are offered in biochemistry, biology, chemistry, computer science, mathematics, neuroscience, and physics. Bachelor of Science in Business Administration degrees are offered in accounting, finance, international business, management, and marketing. In addition, Stonehill College partners with the University of Notre Dame to offer a combination 3+2 program in engineering with concentrations in aeronautical, chemical, civil, computer, electrical, environmental geosciences, and mechanical engineering.

Preprofessional advising programs are offered in dentistry, education, law, medicine, veterinary science, and medical technology. Students interested in the field of education can receive early childhood, elementary, middle, and secondary school teacher certification. Students may pursue a double major as well as design their own major by combining various departmental courses into a comprehensive multidisciplinary program.

Academic Programs

The core of Stonehill's liberal arts curriculum is the Cornerstone Program, which leads students to examine themselves, society, culture, and the natural world through courses in ethics, sciences, language, and more.

Stonehill's students and alumni succeed because the entire college community collaborates to help them develop the knowledge, skills, and character to meet their professional goals and live lives of purpose and integrity. Its graduates can be found around the world enrolled in top graduate programs, enjoying meaningful careers, and working to improve their communities.

Among the members of a recent Stonehill graduating class, 92 percent were employed within one year of graduation at organizations such as Goldman Sachs, the New England Patriots, and Brigham and Women's Hospital; 38 percent attended medical, law, or other graduate programs at top schools like Brown, Georgetown, NYU, and Tufts within a year of graduation; and 8 percent joined or applied for a year-long volunteer service program such as the Peace Corps, Teach for America, Americorps, and World Teach.

On average, Stonehill students graduate at a higher rate and in less time than students at many other colleges and universities. About 82 percent of Stonehill students graduate within four years, which is more than double the national average. And Stonehill's four-year graduation rate is 40 percent higher than at public institutions where the national average is five years.

Off-Campus Programs

At Stonehill, students are given experiential learning opportunities that allow them in-depth exploration of what they learn in the classroom and the opportunity to apply it in the real world. The National Survey of Student Engagement ranks Stonehill in the top 10 percent of colleges nationwide for its enriching educational experiences such as competitive internships, nationally ranked study-abroad opportunities, and cocurricular programs.

Students take part in interdisciplinary Learning Communities (LCs), which combine two academic courses from different disciplines with a team-taught seminar that explores an interrelated topic. Some LCs even incorporate travel to places like Ireland, Italy, the Florida Everglades, and the deserts of the Southwest.

In addition, the Institute of International Education (IIE) ranks Stonehill thirteenth in the country among colleges for semester study-abroad programs. Nearly 50 percent of Stonehill students study abroad before graduation in programs located in dozens of countries, including Argentina, Australia, China, Greece, Morocco, and South Africa.

Academic Facilities

Stonehill is dedicated to developing programs and projects that will continually improve quality of life for everyone on campus. For example, its new, multimillion dollar science center provides state-of the-art facilities to faculty, staff, and students of all majors, such as labs, observation rooms, research areas, and a café.

Kaplan's *Insiders Guide to the 320 Most Interesting Colleges* ranked Stonehill among the colleges with the "Best Freshman Housing." No wonder nearly 90 percent of Stonehill's students live on campus—plus, all resident students are guaranteed housing for all four years. Students can choose from a variety of living options, including suites, townhouses, and double- and triple-occupancy rooms, and take advantage of amenities such as communal TV lounges, kitchen and laundry facilities, recreation rooms, pool tables, basketball courts, beach volleyball courts, and outdoor grills for barbeques.

Costs

For the 2009–10 academic year, Stonehill's costs were $31,210 for tuition and $12,240 for room and board.

Financial Aid

Stonehill is committed to helping each qualified student find the resources to make the dream of a Stonehill education become reality. Stonehill offers loans, grants, scholarships, employment programs, and tuition payment plans to help students become a part of the community here. In the 2009–10 academic year Stonehill distributed $47.5 million in financial aid to a student body of 2,417. On average, students received $20,150 each in scholarships, grants, loans, and work-study. A wide range of competitive merit-based scholarships is also available to outstanding students who do not demonstrate a financial need.

To file for Stonehill scholarship and/or financial aid consideration, students should complete the online CSS PROFILE form at https://profileonline.collegeboard.com. Stonehill's CSS PROFILE code is 3770. In addition, students must file the Free Application for Federal Student Aid (FAFSA) online at http://www.fafsa.ed.gov to be considered for government funds. Stonehill's FAFSA code is 002217.

Faculty

With a student-faculty ratio of 13:1 and an average class size of 20, Stonehill sees individual attention as a key component of our academic programs. Stonehill's accomplished faculty champions its students throughout all four years and is dedicated to teaching and frequently conducting publishable research with students to help with their integrated learning process. Students benefit from graduate-level access to high-tech equipment, attend professional academic conferences, and coauthor in-depth papers, while guided by faculty mentors. Stonehill students take advantage of collaborating one-on-one with their professors on a regular basis and they will always be taught by a faculty member, not a teaching assistant or graduate student.

Student Government

From enjoying on-campus activities to just hanging out with friends, students have plenty of opportunities for fun at Stonehill. The Student Government Association (SGA) is one of the country's most active—its programming won an award from the National Association of Campus Activities—so there's always something happening, from concerts and guest speakers to contests and game shows. More than seventy clubs and organizations are available, including the College's literary magazine *Rolling Stonehill,* the Ski/Snowboard Club, and the Neuroscience Society.

Stonehill also offers free transportation to Boston's public subway system, allowing easy access to the excitement of the city. And with Stonehill's unique Fun Fund, students can get up to $200 to pay for entertainment with friends, such as a show in New York City, a pottery class, or a Red Sox game.

Admission Requirements

Admission to Stonehill is selective. Annually, more than 6,000 high school students apply for 630 first-year places. Stonehill actively seeks an academically strong and geographically, culturally, and ethnically diverse student body. In the admissions process, all information on each applicant is carefully considered, but academic performance and high school curriculum are given the greatest weight. The Admissions Committee evaluates the depth and strength of each applicant's course selection and the consistency of their grades. Competitive students should have completed a strong academic program from among their high school's most challenging offerings. Stonehill admission is test optional, but students may choose to submit scores from either the SAT or ACT. The Admissions Committee also evaluates extracurricular activities, work, volunteer and community activities, recommendations, and writing samples. Stonehill awards credit for strong scores on AP, CLEP, and higher-level International Baccalaureate exams.

Application and Information

Students wishing to apply to Stonehill as a first-year, transfer, or international student may apply online at https://www.commonapp.org. The Common Application is also available in paper form at high school guidance offices.

Stonehill offers three admissions plans for first-year candidates: early decision (binding), early action (nonbinding), and regular decision. November 1 is the deadline for early acceptance and January 15 is the deadline for regular decision.

Dean of Admissions and Enrollment
Stonehill College
320 Washington Street
Easton, Massachusetts 02357-5610
Phone: 508-565-1373
Fax: 508-565-1545
E-mail: admissions@stonehill.edu
Web site: http://www.stonehill.edu

The MacPhaidin Library is a high-tech learning center, with fully networked seating areas for individual and collaborative study.

STRATFORD UNIVERSITY

FALLS CHURCH AND WOODBRIDGE, VIRGINIA

The University

Stratford University was founded in 1976 and has undergone constant changes as it has continued to expand and adapt to changing employer demands. Stratford is a small, private institution with a personalized approach to student needs. The Stratford community includes two campuses in northern Virginia just a short distance from Washington, D.C. and offers over thirty programs of study. The Stratford philosophy is to provide professional competencies that satisfy employer needs, utilizing a teaching method that accommodates a variety of different learning styles.

Stratford enrolls more than 2,000 students in its programs, offering small classes to ensure personal attention to each student. Stratford students represent a diverse population, from recent high school graduates to adult learners seeking to make a career change. The friendly and supportive environment at Stratford University ensures that students feel comfortable and well supported.

The University offers programs in technology, business, health sciences, hospitality, and culinary arts at both the undergraduate and graduate levels. The University is located in the heart of Fairfax County, Virginia, home of the Internet and numerous businesses that support the Internet, telecommunications, and information. User groups, national societies, and various technology councils provide networking avenues for Stratford students. Hospitality-related businesses abound in the Washington area, from world-class restaurants to boutique hotels; career opportunities are numerous. In addition, the business of government provides varied career paths for Stratford graduates.

The University provides a full array of career development and placement services. Students attend workshops on academic planning, resume writing, and effective interviewing skills. Career Services strives to help students make the contacts that lead to internships or permanent positions.

Stratford University partners with Collegiate Housing Services to offer comfortable and affordable dormitory-style apartments near both campuses. The typical housing configuration is a furnished, two-bedroom, two-bathroom apartment shared by up to 4 Stratford students of the same gender.

Location

Stratford University has two campuses in the greater Washington, D.C., region. Washington has much to offer. From politics to urban events, culture to recreation, the capital region is a great place to live, work, and study. Local sights include Mount Vernon, Old Town Alexandria, the White House, Capitol Hill, the Mall, and the Smithsonian Institute. Most of the sights are easily accessible by public transportation.

The prosperous D.C. job market is a draw for Stratford students. For both working students looking to upgrade skills and full-time students concerned with finding a job quickly after graduation, the region offers a wealth of jobs for graduates of all of Stratford's programs. As the nation's capital and a major tourist center, the metropolitan Washington area is a center for business, finance, industry, and entertainment.

Majors and Degrees

The School of Business Administration offers Associate of Applied Science (A.A.S.) and Bachelor of Science (B.S.) degrees in business administration. The School of Computer Information Systems offers A.A.S. degrees in digital design and in network management and security and four different B.S. degrees in information technology. The School of Culinary Arts and Hospitality confers A.A.S. degrees in advanced culinary arts, baking and pastry arts, and hotel and restaurant management; and a B.A. degree in hospitality management. The School of Health Sciences confers an A.A.S. degree in allied health with concentrations in medical assisting, clinical hemodialysis, phlebotomy technician, medical insurance billing and coding, and pharmacy technician. The School of Nursing offers the B.S. in Nursing degree. The business administration, hotel and restaurant management, and hospitality management programs are also offered online.

Academic Programs

Stratford University delivers competency-based educational programs that prepare individuals for employment in specific career areas. These competencies are employer centered. The curriculum in each program is designed to ensure that students have the required competencies demanded in their fields of endeavor. The instructional techniques at Stratford are student centered. At the beginning of each program, students are tested for both learning styles and learning modes, and instruction in all classes is individualized based on the results of this assessment. This dual emphasis results in student academic success, without lowering required employer-based standards. As a result, students who graduate enjoy a high placement rate.

The A.A.S. and the B.S. degree programs include core requirements, elective requirements, and general education arts and sciences requirements. The total requirement for the A.A.S. programs is 90 quarter credits. This normally takes approximately sixty weeks to complete. The total requirement for the B.S. degree programs is 180 quarter credits. The first 90 quarter credits are generally completed prior to beginning the 90 credits of junior- or senior-level courses. The B.S. programs take approximately 120 weeks to complete.

The diploma programs include core and elective requirements. The total requirement for these programs is 60 quarter credits, and they normally take fifty weeks to complete.

Students may receive transfer credit for courses transferred from accredited institutions. Also, certain training received from prior military schools, military service, or prior work experiences may be awarded as transfer credit. Stratford is approved for the training of veterans.

The course calendar is divided into five sessions, each of which is ten weeks in length. With start dates in January, March, May, August, and October, Stratford's flexible scheduling accommodates its busy students.

Academic Facilities

Stratford's libraries are located at the Falls Church and Woodbridge campuses, but all 2,400 titles are available online. In addition, the library subscribes to OCLC FirstSearch, ProQuest, Global Road Warrior, and EBSCOhost research database.

Both campuses have state-of-the-art facilities equipped with the latest technology and resources. All information systems classrooms are equipped with one computer for every student. Students may also access one of several computers for general use in the library/learning resource center. Culinary arts students at both campuses are trained in fully equipped professional kitchens.

Costs

Tuition is $355 per credit hour plus fees where applicable.

Financial Aid

Financial aid officers at Stratford are trained to guide students through the financial aid process to ensure that all available financial aid has been explored. Federal loans and grants (including PLUS, PELL, FSEOG, FWS) are applicable toward tuition at Stratford. The University is also approved for Veterans Association benefits, Vocational Rehabilitation benefits, and private institutional financing.

Stratford offers the Graduating High School Senior Scholarship Program and the Culinary Scholarship Programs. Stratford University also accepts private scholarships from foundations, service clubs, and other organizations.

Faculty

Stratford University's faculty members have been hand-chosen for their teaching ability, personality traits, and experience in their fields. The entire Stratford University staff works as a team to help students succeed.

Admission Requirements

Graduation from a secondary school or equivalent education as certified by the state department of education is normally required for admission.

Stratford is approved to offer I-20 certification for F1 visas for international students. Students for whom English is a second language are required to demonstrate English proficiency through a TOEFL or IELTS score.

Application and Information

Students must submit a completed application for admission and a $50 nonrefundable application fee. Applicants must also schedule an interview with admissions to complete the application process. Students may bring or have the registrar from their high school, college, or state GED office forward a copy of their transcripts to Stratford University. Student-issued copies of transcripts or diplomas can be submitted directly to the University.

Students interested in applying should contact:

Stratford University
7777 Leesburg Pike
Falls Church, Virginia 22043
Phone: 703-821-8570
800-444-0804 (toll-free)
Fax: 703-734-5339

Stratford University
14349 Gideon Drive
Woodbridge, Virginia 22192
Phone: 703-897-1982
888-546-1250 (toll-free)
Fax: 571-408-2499
E-mail: admissions@stratford.edu
Web site: http://www.stratford.edu

SUSQUEHANNA UNIVERSITY

SELINSGROVE, PENNSYLVANIA

The University

By nearly every indicator, Susquehanna University excels at preparing its graduates to achieve, lead, and serve in a diverse, interconnected world. Students benefit from more than fifty majors and minors encompassing a balance of liberal arts and professional studies programs, a devoted and passionate faculty, and state-of-the-art facilities that support intellectual and personal growth.

With more than 100 student organizations, twenty-three NCAA Division III varsity sports, and nationally recognized volunteer programs, students find opportunities to learn and grow well beyond the classroom.

A Susquehanna education is a proven advantage. Graduates consistently say their Susquehanna experiences have given them a competitive edge over other recent graduates entering the workplace. Ninety-five percent of students are employed full-time or enrolled in graduate school within six months of graduation—an exceptionally high percentage compared with other institutions. Susquehanna's four-year graduation rate is 80 percent, among the best in the country.

Location

Students find themselves at home in the eclectic town of Selinsgrove, Pennsylvania, nestled between the banks of the Susquehanna River and the foothills of the Appalachian Mountains. Favorite activities include checking out the shops on Market Street; enjoying the local flavor of downtown restaurants; kayaking, floating, or tubing down the Susquehanna River; or hiking, caving, and camping in nearby state parks and forests.

Selinsgrove is a 3-hour drive from New York City, Philadelphia, Baltimore, and Washington, D.C. Pennsylvania's capital of Harrisburg is approximately 60 miles from the campus, and the Harrisburg International Airport is served by American, United, Delta, Northwest, US Airways, several commuter airlines, and major rental-car agencies. The Penn Valley Airport in Selinsgrove provides facilities for private and charter aircraft.

Majors and Degrees

Susquehanna students pursue a Bachelor of Arts, Bachelor of Music, or Bachelor of Science degree in the following areas: accounting, art history, biochemistry, biology, business administration (emphasis in entrepreneurship, finance, global management, information systems, or marketing), chemistry, communications (emphasis in broadcasting, communication studies, corporate communications, journalism, mass communications, public relations, or speech communications), computer science, creative writing, earth and environmental sciences, ecology, economics (emphasis in financial economics, general economics, global economy, or financial markets), education (certification in early childhood, elementary, or secondary), English, French, German, graphic design, history, information systems, international studies (emphasis in Asian studies, comparative cultural studies, developing world studies, diplomacy, European studies, international trade and development, or sustainable development), liberal studies, mathematics, music, music education, music performance, philosophy, physics, political science, psychology, religion, sociology, Spanish, studio art (emphasis in painting and drawing or photography), and theater (emphasis in performance, production, or design).

Preprofessional programs are offered in dentistry, law, medicine, ministry, teaching, and veterinary medicine and include one-on-one advising, related internships, and test preparation for the MCAT and LSAT. Cooperative programs in allied health are offered with Thomas Jefferson University in Philadelphia, in dentistry with Temple University School of Dental Medicine in Philadelphia, and in forestry and environmental management with Duke University in Durham, North Carolina.

Minors are available in almost every major area and in the following additional areas: actuarial science, advertising, anthropology, Asian studies, dance, diversity studies, film studies, Greek, health-care studies, international business and foreign language, international relations, Jewish studies, legal studies, literature, music technology, music theory, and women's studies.

Academic Programs

Susquehanna's Central Curriculum is a hybrid model of liberal arts and practical education that emphasizes critical-thinking skills and ethics, and teaches students to put those skills to work in today's world. Throughout their four years at Susquehanna, students develop intellectual skills through courses of their choosing that study the richness of thought, human interaction, human connections, and the natural world.

Susquehanna's campus community explores a university theme each academic year. The theme is intended to focus classroom discussion, lectures, artistic performances, and student activities around a central idea for in-depth exploration. Past themes include Life on the Fringes, Water, Religion in the Public Square, and What Does It Mean to Be Educated? Reflecting the theme, the Common Reading Program asks Susquehanna faculty, staff, and incoming students to read a related common text every summer. The class of 2013 will explore What Does It Mean to Be Educated? by reading an anthology composed of community submissions, *Will This Be on the Test?*

Susquehanna houses the Arlin M. Adams Center for Law and Society as a complementary program to the Central Curriculum. The Adams Center explores the rich intersections between law and various other disciplines. It provides a forum and research opportunities for examining issues affecting human rights and social responsibility, involving science and technology, and requiring constitutional interpretation. The Adams Center provides several venues for student learning, including internships and field experiences, networking, professional seminars, independent study, research projects, enhanced library resources, symposia, dialogue series, and the *Justice for All?* radio program. Guest speakers for the Adams Center have included nationally known experts and a Supreme Court justice.

Off-Campus Programs

Susquehanna's Central Curriculum includes a unique Global Opportunities (GO) program. This distinctive program allows every student to have a cross-cultural experience away from campus, either in the United States or abroad, taking students out of their everyday environment. It might include a traditional semester study-abroad program (GO Long), a short-term faculty/staff-led program (GO Short), a self-designed experience proposed and accepted in advance, or service in a cross-cultural setting.

GO is flexible and affordable. Susquehanna currently offers thirty-six GO Long programs that cost approximately the same as, or less than, a semester on campus. GO Short programs are even more affordable, because they involve a shorter stay away from campus. Most forms of financial aid, including scholarships, are available during GO Long or GO Short experiences

About two thirds of Susquehanna's students participate in nationally recognized community service projects, with an annual average of more than 20,000 hours of community service delivered to the Susquehanna Valley and beyond.

Academic Facilities

Susquehanna's facilities include a rich mix of historic and new buildings. Two buildings are on the National Register of Historic Places and others, completed in recent years, have won architectural and design awards.

In fall 2010, a new science facility will transform teaching and learning for all Susquehanna students. With a prominent spot on the 306-acre campus, the 75,000-square-foot science facility will be the school's largest academic building. The facility will house Susquehanna's biology, chemistry, and earth and environmental sciences programs.

Plans for the new science building demonstrate Susquehanna's strong commitment to sustainability and environmental responsibility. The building will meet or exceed the U.S. Green Building Council's Leadership in Energy and Environmental Design (LEED) certification criteria. The investment will benefit all students, because science education is a part of the Central Curriculum. The initiative will advance other programs at Susquehanna, with the renovation of the current science building, Fisher Hall, planned to accommodate anticipated enrollment gains to 2,200 students. More than two thirds of Fisher Hall will be available after the new building opens, offering a number of academic programs larger, more modern spaces.

Susquehanna's new science facility will complement the already outstanding academic facilities available to students. Apfelbaum Hall, completed in 1999, is home to the Sigmund Weis School of Business and the Department of Communications. Apfelbaum houses two television studios, multimedia classrooms, a presentation room, and numerous small-group study rooms. Bogar Hall, renovated in 2007, includes a language lab for students studying modern languages and the Writers Institute's Editing and Publishing Center. Cunningham Center for Music and Art, renovated and expanded in 2002, offers contemporary art and music teaching facilities and flexible practice and performance space, including Stretansky Concert Hall, a 320-seat venue designed to optimize choral and instrumental music. Weber Chapel Auditorium is home to a classic, 1,500-seat theater, with a revolving stage and recording studio for students studying music technology. Additional performance space for theater students is available in the Degenstein Center Theater, which houses a modern 450-seat proscenium teaching theater with a counterweight fly system and an intimate, black-box studio theater.

Every student takes full advantage of the Blough-Weis Library. The fully automated library offers more than 253,000 volumes, 32,000 microforms, 5,000 DVDs, 3,000 CDs, and subscriptions to more than 50,000 periodicals. Students and faculty members have online access from any computer connected to the Internet. The library also houses Susquehanna's Media Center and Tutorial Services.

Costs

Tuition and fees for 2009–10 were $32,050. Room and board costs were $8800. A student's personal expenses, including books, travel, and other costs, are estimated at $1600 to $1900 per year.

Financial Aid

Ninety-two percent of Susquehanna students receive some form of financial aid. All students are encouraged to apply for need-based financial aid by filing both the FAFSA and PROFILE forms. Every applicant for admission to Susquehanna also is considered for merit awards regardless of financial need. Renewable for four years, Susquehanna's merit scholarships are awarded based on a student's academic achievement, talent in a particular area of University interest, or community involvement. Susquehanna is a participant in the Tuition Exchange program for children of employees at participating institutions. The University also participates in the Yellow Ribbon Program for veterans of the wars in Iraq and Afghanistan.

Faculty

Susquehanna's faculty members serve as advisers and creative mentors to their students both in the classroom and beyond. Whether meeting one-on-one with a student for more in-depth instruction after class or making their homes available for barbecues, faculty members make themselves accessible to students in a variety of formal and informal settings. Professors who seek employment at Susquehanna value the opportunity to live and learn alongside their students. By graduation, many Susquehanna students have shared a stage with faculty members, whether through a recital or a national conference presentation.

Of Susquehanna's 128 full-time professors, 93 percent hold a doctorate or terminal degree in their field. The student-faculty ratio is 13:1.

Student Government

Susquehanna's Student Government Association is a self-governing organization providing representation of the student body in University affairs. The main function of the legislative body is the allocation of student activities fees to recognized clubs, student groups, campus projects, and University activities. Senators are elected each year and serve as student representatives to various offices and groups on campus.

Admission Requirements

Susquehanna's average accepted student earns a GPA of 3.5 in a competitive college-prep curriculum. For those students who choose to submit test scores, the midrange SAT score is 1020–1210, and the midrange ACT score is 21–26.

Susquehanna looks for exceptional students who are attracted by its academic challenges and extracurricular opportunities. Admission is competitive. The University considers what it can do for students and how students might contribute to Susquehanna. It assesses applications based on course selections, grades, and class rank as well as factors such as motivation, creativity, and leadership. About 60 percent of students rank in the top quarter of their high school class. Honors Program students typically rank in the top 10 percent.

Students may choose to apply under the Write Option, which allows two graded, critical writing samples to serve as a substitute for SAT/ACT scores.

Susquehanna strongly encourages prospective students to visit the campus and interview with a member of the admissions staff. Counselors are happy to answer questions and explain programs firsthand. Students can see the facilities and perhaps meet with faculty members, coaches, and students. Susquehanna can usually arrange for class visits or overnight stays in residence halls.

Application and Information

Susquehanna accepts the Susquehanna Application as well as the Common Application or Universal Application, with no preference given to one over the other. All applications are free to file online.

Students applying to the Bachelor of Music degree program are required to audition. Students applying to major in graphic design or creative writing are required to submit a portfolio of their work.

Office of Admissions
Susquehanna University
514 University Avenue
Selinsgrove, Pennsylvania 17870-1164
Phone: 570-372-4260
800-326-9672 (toll-free)
Fax: 570-372-2722
E-mail: suadmiss@susqu.edu
Web site: www.susqu.edu

Historic Seibert Hall at Susquehanna University.

SWEET BRIAR COLLEGE

SWEET BRIAR, VIRGINIA

The College

Deeply committed to the education of women since its founding in 1901, Sweet Briar College is consistently ranked as one of the top national liberal arts and sciences colleges in the country. Its excellent academic reputation, beautiful campus, and attention to the individual attract ambitious, intellectually self-confident women who want to excel. Students can expect their Sweet Briar experience to allow them to fulfill their promise as scholars and leaders, while enjoying the close-knit friendships and camaraderie that come with a personal, residential community.

A Sweet Briar education sets in motion the conviction that any goal is achievable. Small classes (averaging 12 students per class) and a student-faculty ratio of 9:1 ensure personal attention and academic interaction. Students work one-on-one with faculty members who are committed to each student's academic success. The College has a wide geographic, ethnic, and socioeconomic representation. About 700 women from more than forty states and nineteen countries are enrolled at Sweet Briar's Virginia campus; another 120 students are enrolled in Sweet Briar's coed Junior Year in France and Junior Year in Spain programs. Any student may have a car.

Students who derive the most from the Sweet Briar experience are those who participate in and contribute to community life, striking a good balance between academic work and the rest of life. They recognize that one of the advantages of the College is the unlimited opportunities for women to participate and assume leadership roles in many types of organizations and activities. More than fifty campus organizations are available, including honor societies, a literary journal, community service groups, a multicultural club, political groups, a student newspaper, drama and dance clubs, a radio station, and singing groups. Students plan and participate in an extensive array of concerts, films, and dance and theater productions as well as workshops and master classes by visiting scholars and performers. Recent speakers on campus include the author Salman Rushdie, environmental attorney Robert F. Kennedy Jr., Olympic swimmer Maddy Crippen, *USA Today* sports columnist Christine Brennan, and civil rights pioneer Elaine Jones.

Twenty-one campus buildings, the work of renowned American architect Ralph Adams Cram, are on the National Register of Historic Places. In 2006, Sweet Briar opened a beautiful new studio arts facility. Sweet Briar is the only college in the United States with a residential artists' colony on its campus. Known as the Virginia Center for the Creative Arts, the colony is a working retreat for international writers, visual artists, and composers. In 2008, the College began construction of a 53,000 square foot fitness and athletic center addition to the existing gymnasium, and a sixty-bed apartment-style residence facility for upper class students. Both new projects will be ready for use in August 2009. The on-campus equestrian center, one of the largest and best college facilities in the country, attracts both competitive and recreational riders. Sweet Briar's equestrian program, both competitive and instructional, has consistently garnered national recognition. The 100-acre Rogers Riding Center has a 120-foot by 300-foot indoor arena with Perma-Flex footing, well-appointed stables for approximately 90 horses, several outdoor rings, numerous paddocks, and miles of hacking trails—all within walking distance of the main campus.

A fiber-optic backbone allows high-speed Ethernet communication among all academic and administrative buildings, as well as in residence hall rooms. Many of the academic buildings and student common spaces are equipped for wireless connection to the campus network.

In 2004, Sweet Briar launched two graduate degree programs: the Master of Arts in Teaching and the Master of Education. These programs are rooted in the teaching philosophy of differentiated curriculum and instruction. Sweet Briar also established a new degree program in engineering, only the second such undergraduate program at a women's college.

Varsity athletes compete in NCAA Division III field hockey, lacrosse, soccer, softball, swimming, tennis, and volleyball. Club sports include cross-country, fencing, and riding.

Location

Sweet Briar's 3,250-acre campus in the foothills of the Blue Ridge Mountains includes hiking, biking, and riding trails and two lakes that provide spectacular venues for outdoor recreational activities. The College is centrally located on the outskirts of Lynchburg, Virginia, southwest of Washington, D.C., and Charlottesville. Students also enjoy activities in nearby Roanoke and Richmond.

Majors and Degrees

Sweet Briar awards the Bachelor of Arts, Bachelor of Science, and Bachelor of Fine Arts degrees. The College offers thirty-five majors: anthropology, art history, biochemistry and molecular biology, biology, business management, chemistry, classics, dance, economics, education, engineering and management, engineering science, English, English and creative writing, environmental science, environmental studies, French, German, German studies, government, history, international affairs, Italian studies, mathematics, mathematics-physics, modern languages and literatures, music, philosophy, physics, psychology, religion, sociology, Spanish, studio art, and theater.

Additional area studies, minors, and certificate programs include arts management, equine studies, engineering (3-2 dual degree), film studies, Italian, Latin American studies, law and society, musical theater, prelaw, premed, pre–veterinary science, and gender studies. Students may design an interdisciplinary major focused on a topic of special interest or may construct personalized majors.

Academic Programs

Sweet Briar's mission is to prepare women to be active, responsible members of a world community. Underscoring every one of the thirty-five major fields of study is the idea that the best way to learn about the world is to experience it. The curriculum emphasizes hands-on learning, comprehensive understanding, analysis, reflection, creativity, and communication across disciplines. The academic programs are nationally celebrated. To add to this, the College recently launched the Sweet Briar Promise, a distinctive program that provides six guarantees to ensure every student has the opportunity for an academic experience that prepares her for a lifetime of success. Every qualified student is guaranteed an internship, study-abroad experience, and leadership and research opportunities. The Sweet Briar Promise also allows students who have an interest in an area not covered by one of the thirty-five majors, or who would like to focus on more than one area, the opportunity to create, with the help of a faculty mentor, a personalized program of study. The final component of the Sweet Briar Promise goes a step further than most and makes a team of advisers, including alumnae, staff members, and professors, available to assist every student with academic and career planning.

The general education program has four components—English 104, skills requirements, experiences requirements, and knowledge areas requirements—that work together to ensure the development of strong communication and quantitative reasoning skills. Independent studies and seminars are included in most majors, with a culminating senior course or exercise required in most majors. Sweet Briar has a chapter of Phi Beta Kappa and was the first women's college to establish a chapter of the prelaw honorary society Phi Alpha Delta. It also has a four-year honors program that is nationally recognized for its innovative partnering of interdisciplinary academic and cocurricular programs. Honors students may take special tutorials and seminars as well as complete a yearlong research project culminating in an honors thesis on an original topic.

Sweet Briar's two-semester calendar allows students to participate in intensive courses, independent research projects, or internships on campus or throughout the world.

Off-Campus Programs

By the time they graduate, more than a third of Sweet Briar students have studied abroad. The Sweet Briar Junior Year in France, the first program in Paris for American students, is considered the most academically rigorous program available today. Students from 258 colleges and universities have participated in the coed program. The successful Junior Year in Spain is recognized as the premier program in Seville. The College has special relationships with the University of St. Andrews in Scotland, Heidelberg University in Germany, Doshisha Women's College in Japan, and the University of Urbino in Italy. In recent years, Sweet Briar students have also chosen the following destinations for study abroad: Australia, China, the Czech Republic, Denmark, Greece, Holland, Ireland, Jamaica, Korea, Mongolia, Morocco, New Zealand, and Thailand. Off-campus study may also include an Environmental Junior Year, the Washington Semester at American University, and summer programs at St. Anne's College in Oxford, England. In addition, summer programs are offered in Australia; Central America, including Costa Rica; Münster, Germany; Rome and Urbino, Italy; Nepal; and Spain.

Sweet Briar participates in the Tri-College Consortium, which also includes Randolph College and Lynchburg College. In addition to taking courses at the other colleges, students can participate in combined social and cultural activities on those campuses.

Academic Facilities

Sweet Briar has the largest private undergraduate library collection in the state of Virginia, with resources of more than 240,000 volumes, 1,000 journal subscriptions, 430,000 microforms, 6,800 audiovisual materials, and special libraries in art, music, and the sciences. Some of the notable special holdings include Virginia Woolf, T. E. Lawrence, George Meredith, W. H. Auden, and a rare collection of twentieth-century Chinese works. Three computer labs with Macintosh and Windows/Intel Pentium computers are open free of charge 24 hours a day. The student-computer ratio is 6:1. A lab for Sweet Briar's new engineering department includes a 5-Kip-capacity Universal Test Machine; a United Tru-Blue Rockwell hardness tester; a set of gauged beams and test fixtures for mechanics experiments; eight new computers, each with NI ELVIS and Labview with Protoboards; and a well-equipped machine shop. Students studying science use state-of-the-art equipment that enhances faculty-student collaborative research. Biology equipment includes a scanning electron microscope with digital imaging system, equipment for plant and animal tissue culture, and DNA sequencing equipment. Chemistry students have access to two nuclear magnetic resonance spectrometers (NMR; 400 MHz and 60 MHz), an atomic absorption spectrometer (AAS), a diode array UV/Vis spectrometer, a Fourier-transform infrared spectrometer (FT-IR), a modular LASER laboratory, a gas chromatograph/mass spectrograph (GC/MS), a high-pressure liquid chromatograph (HPLC), and a differential scanning calorimeter (DSC). Physics equipment includes a scanning tunneling microscope, an X-ray crystallography system, a 10-inch-diameter reflecting telescope, and holographic instrumentation.

The environmental studies program occupies two sites. A renovated train station provides classroom and laboratory space equipped with a Rigaku Miniflex powder X-ray diffraction system for mineralogical analysis, a Rocklabs bench-top ring mill for grinding rock and soil samples, a drying oven and a high-temperature muffle furnace, and much more. An adjacent caboose car provides office space for faculty members. A water treatment plant was also converted to an environmental education/nature center and environmental lab; equipment includes water, soil, wastewater, and sediment sampling instrumentation, including N-Con composite samplers, macroinvertebrate samplers, and specialized water-collection devices.

The Babcock Fine Arts Center includes individual practice rooms, an electronic piano lab, dance studios, theaters, and Murchison Lane Auditorium for lectures and performing arts. Two former dairy barns were recently renovated for classroom and office space to house studio arts, including a ceramics and sculpture studio; four large studios for painting, drawing, and printmaking; and a photo studio and darkroom.

The Academic Resource Center (ARC) provides free of charge to all students academic support services that include assistance with papers and study strategies, a personalized time management system, stress management advice, tutoring information, and one-on-one peer mentoring. The ARC also provides support and learning strategies for students with diagnosed learning differences.

Costs

For 2009–10, tuition and fees were $29,335. Books and supplies are estimated to be $1500 and personal expenses average $1000.

Financial Aid

A family's financial circumstance does not limit a student's choices at Sweet Briar because of the College's generous financial aid program. More than 90 percent of enrolling students receive financial assistance from the College, including merit scholarships, need-based grants, loans, and work-study awards. Scholarships for international students are also available on a competitive basis.

Faculty

Sweet Briar's faculty members have been commended by numerous regional and national educational groups for their excellence in teaching. Faculty members are actively engaged in teaching, research, publication, and other forms of creative activity. More than 95 percent of full-time faculty members have a doctorate or the highest professional degree in his or her field. All classes are taught by a faculty member. About half of the faculty members are women.

Student Government

The Student Government Association (SGA) is founded upon a highly developed concept of honor and student ownership and involvement. The Honor System applies to all phases of academic and social life. Each entering student becomes a full member of the Student Government Association upon taking the Honor Pledge, which states that Sweet Briar women do not lie, cheat, steal, or violate the rights of others. Students participate in the governance of the College through the many offices and committee positions of the Student Government Association. SGA and its committees are largely responsible for the self-governance of the student body.

Admission Requirements

Sweet Briar seeks talented women who are adventurous, are enthusiastic about learning, and want to take an active part in their education. The Admissions Committee looks for qualities such as independent thinking, ethical principles, assertiveness, and an appreciation of diversity. Sweet Briar welcomes students of all economic, ethnic, geographic, religious, and social backgrounds.

Requirements normally include a minimum of 4 units in English, 3 in mathematics, 3 in social studies, 2 sequential years in a foreign language, and 3 units in science, as well as additional units in these subjects to total 16. Most candidates have 20 such academic units. Special attention is given to the difficulty of the applicant's curriculum and her academic achievement in the classroom; scores on the SAT or ACT are required. An interview at the College is strongly encouraged but not required. Candidates who are unable to visit the campus are invited to meet with staff members or to talk with alumnae in their hometowns.

Application and Information

Early decision applications are due by December 1 of the senior year, and notifications are sent December 15. The enrollment deposit is due January 15. Regular decision applications are due by February 1, and notifications are mailed by March 15. Students who are regular decision applicants have until the National Candidate's Reply Date of May 1 to submit the enrollment deposit. Transfer applications are due by May 1 for the fall semester and by November 1 for the spring semester. A completed application includes a transcript of the candidate's academic work, scores on the required test, recommendations from the guidance counselor and a teacher, and an essay written by the candidate. There is a $40 application fee, which may be waived at the request of the student's guidance counselor if it is deemed to be a financial burden. Sweet Briar also accepts the Common Application (paper or online; a supplement is required). All materials should be sent to the admissions office at the address listed in this description. Information may be requested from the same office.

Dean of Admissions
Sweet Briar College
P.O. Box B
Sweet Briar, Virginia 24595
Phone: 434-381-6142
800-381-6142 (toll-free)
Fax: 434-381-6152
E-mail: admissions@sbc.edu
Web site: http://www.sbc.edu

COLLEGE CLOSE-UPS

SYRACUSE UNIVERSITY

SYRACUSE, NEW YORK

The University

Syracuse University (SU), which was founded in 1870, is an independent, privately endowed university with an international reputation. Students attend from all over the United States and from more than 100 other countries. There are about 17,300 students enrolled; 12,600 are undergraduates. Approximately 65 percent of the students live in University housing, which includes modern residence halls, apartments, and town houses. The 200-acre campus features a main grassy quadrangle surrounded by academic buildings, with residential facilities nearby. The campus is situated on a hill overlooking the downtown area of Syracuse. Social life is centered on the campus, and there are innumerable recreational, athletic, and academic activities. The 50,000-seat Carrier Dome is the site of concerts, sports events, and Commencement. All of campus is connected to the University's high-speed wired or wireless networks.

Location

The city of Syracuse (metropolitan-area population of 700,000) is the business, educational, and cultural hub of central New York. The city offers professional theater and opera, as well as visiting artists and performers. Highlights of the downtown area include the Everson Museum of Art, the Milton J. Rubenstein Museum of Science and Technology (MOST), the impressive Civic Center, and the Armory Square shopping area. Central New York has many lakes, parks, mountains, and outstanding recreational opportunities.

Majors and Degrees

Syracuse University awards B.A., B.S., B.Arch., B.I.D., B.Mus., and B.F.A. degrees.

The School of Architecture offers a five-year baccalaureate program leading to the first professional degree of B.Arch.

Departmental and interdisciplinary majors in the College of Arts and Sciences are African-American studies, American studies, anthropology, art, art history, biochemistry, biology, biophysical science, chemistry, classical civilization, classics (Greek and Latin), communication sciences and disorders, economics, English and textual studies, European literature, fine arts, French, geography, geology (Earth sciences), German, Greek, history, history of architecture, international relations, Italian, Latin, Latino–Latin American studies, linguistic studies, mathematics, Middle Eastern studies, modern foreign languages, music, music history and cultures, philosophy, physics, policy studies (public affairs), political philosophy, political science, psychology, religion, religion and society, Russian, Russian and Central European studies, sociology, Spanish, women's studies, and writing and rhetoric.

The College of Human Ecology majors include child and family studies, hospitality, nutrition/dietetics, nutrition science, public health, social work, and sport management.

The School of Education offers majors in art education, elementary education (inclusive with special education), health and exercise science (including pre–physical therapy and 3+3 D.P.T.), music education, physical education, secondary education, selected studies in education, and special education (inclusive with elementary education and with early childhood education).

The L. C. Smith College of Engineering and Computer Science majors include aerospace, chemical, civil, computer, electrical, environmental, and mechanical engineering; bioengineering; and computer science.

The School of Information Studies offers a four-year bachelor's degree program in information management and technology.

The Martin J. Whitman School of Management majors include accounting, entrepreneurship and emerging enterprises, finance, management, marketing management, real estate, retail management, and supply chain management.

The S. I. Newhouse School of Public Communications majors are in the following areas: advertising, broadcast journalism, graphic design, magazine, newspaper, photography, public relations, and television/radio/film.

The College of Visual and Performing Arts majors are in the following areas: art and design, communication and rhetorical studies, drama, music, and transmedia. Art majors offered are advertising design, ceramics, communications design, fashion design, fiber and textile arts, history of art, illustration, industrial and interaction design, interior design, jewelry and metalsmithing, painting, printmaking, and sculpture. Transmedia majors include art photography, art video, computer art, and film. Drama majors include theater design and technology, drama (acting), musical theater, and stage management. Music majors include the Bandier Program for Music and the Entertainment Industries, music composition, music industry, performance organ, performance percussion, performance piano, performance strings, performance voice, and performance wind instruments. The Department of Communication and Rhetorical Studies offers a Bachelor of Science degree.

Academic Programs

The University operates on a two-semester calendar with two 6-week summer sessions. Students generally take five 3-credit-hour courses each semester. A minimum of 120 credit hours is required for graduation. Special programs include dual and combined enrollment, selected studies, internships, an honors program, ROTC, and preprofessional advising for students going on to study dentistry, law, medicine, or veterinary science.

Off-Campus Programs

The Syracuse University Abroad program operates campuses in London, Madrid, Hong Kong, Beijing, Florence, Santiago (Chile), and Strasbourg. SU Abroad also offers opportunities at thirty universities in many other countries, including Australia, Costa Rica, Ecuador, Egypt, India, Ireland, Japan, Korea, Poland, and Russia.

Academic Facilities

The academic buildings at Syracuse University span the century, with fifteen listed in the National Register of Historic Places and others representative of some of the most modern and technologically sophisticated architecture in the country. The Ernest Stevenson Bird Library houses approximately 3.1 million printed volumes, more than 16,000 online and print journals, and extensive collections of microforms, maps, images, music scores, sound recordings, video, rare books, and manuscripts. The University has computer facilities with laboratories and a data communications network that links computers to hundreds of terminals. The $107 million, 230,000-square-foot Life Sciences Complex combines research and teaching wings for biology, chemistry, and biochemistry. The Newhouse Communications Center has some of the finest facilities available for journalism and telecommunications. Slocum Hall, home to the School of Architecture, includes a new auditorium, gallery, and space for studio and research. The Center for Science and Technology is a state-of-the-art facility uniting research and academic programs in computer science and technology. It also houses the CASE Center for research in computer applications and software engineering. The new five-story addition to Link Hall, home of the L.C. Smith College of Engineering and Computer Science, features a three-story, high bay lab that houses a crane and space for civil engineering students to build and test structures. The high-tech Melvin A. Eggers Hall offers superior facilities for the University's social science programs. The new multimillion-dollar Whitman School of Management building provides students with access to the latest educational technologies and plenty of space for team meetings and work.

Costs

Tuition for 2009–10 was $33,630. The costs for housing and meals averaged $12,374, and fees were $1298. Books and supplies averaged $1306; travel expenses, $6006; and personal expenses, $892. Therefore, the total cost of attendance was approximately $50,100.

Financial Aid

About 80 percent of all entering first-year and transfer students receive some form of financial aid. By filing the Free Application for Federal Student Aid (FAFSA) and the CSS Financial Aid PROFILE, students are automatically considered for all financial aid programs administered by Syracuse University, including federal financial aid, Syracuse University Grants, and Federal Work-Study Program awards. Merit-based scholarships are available to both first-year and transfer students, based solely on their academic record. Syracuse University evaluates candidates for admission without respect to financial need. Information on financial aid policies, procedures, and deadlines can be obtained from the Office of Financial Aid and Scholarship Programs.

Faculty

The majority of faculty members hold the highest degree in their professional field. There are nearly 900 full-time faculty members, including recognized experts in their fields who teach at both the graduate and undergraduate levels.

Student Government

The Syracuse University Student Association works to protect students' rights and offers services through its three branches—the executive, the legislative, and the judicial.

Admission Requirements

Syracuse University seeks a diverse student body from all social, cultural, and educational backgrounds. Each candidate is evaluated individually, based on the requirements of the college of the University to which he or she has applied. Emphasis is placed on students' high school performance, standardized test scores (SAT or ACT), an essay, recommendations, extracurricular activities and community service, and portfolios or auditions, when required. Special admission requirements and deadlines for some programs are described on the University's Web site and in the Undergraduate Application for Admission.

Syracuse University is an Equal Opportunity/Affirmative Action institution and does not discriminate on the basis of race, creed, color, gender, national origin, religion, marital status, age, disability, sexual orientation, or gender identity or expression.

Application and Information

Regular Decision applicants for the fall semester should submit their completed application along with transcripts, standardized test scores, the essay, teacher recommendations, and the counselor evaluation by January 1 (postmarked deadline). Notification begins in mid-March. Completed applications for Early Decision applicants must be postmarked by November 1. Notification begins in mid-December.

Detailed information may be obtained by contacting:

Office of Admissions
100 Crouse-Hinds Hall
900 South Crouse Avenue
Syracuse University
Syracuse, New York 13244-2130
Phone: 315-443-3611
Web site: http://admissions.syr.edu

The historic buildings that make up the SU campus stand in testimony to the many years of distinction that are at the foundation of Syracuse University.

TEMPLE UNIVERSITY

PHILADELPHIA, PENNSYLVANIA

The University

Students who visit Temple University's Main Campus find they are quite impressed. Cutting-edge facilities and great faculty members create a dynamic academic environment that draws students from around the world. But what can transform a student's life at Temple happens outside the classroom as well. Temple is located in Philadelphia, a dynamic, world-class city with a diverse ethnic mix, a robust economy, and a thriving music and art scene. It is the perfect place to live and study. Two spectacular new academic buildings opened on Main Campus in January 2009—the Tyler School of Art and the Fox School of Business and Management's Alter Hall.

Students who prefer not to attend college in the city should take a look at the Ambler campus, Temple's 187-acre suburban home. Just about all undergraduate programs can be started there, and eighteen can be fully completed there. Ambler's $17-million Learning Center includes smart classrooms; fully integrated technology, including wireless access throughout the building; five computer lab/classrooms; a math, science, and writing center; a video editing lab; a café; and a 300-seat auditorium.

Temple's other local campus is the Health Sciences Center, where the College of Health Professions, Temple University Hospital, Temple University School of Medicine, and Temple Dental School are located.

Temple is in the city, but it has a large residential student population—about 11,000 students living on and around Main Campus. The calendar is crammed with theater, dance, and music performances. The Liacouras Center, Temple's 10,200-seat entertainment complex, hosts the University's NCAA Division I basketball games (free tickets for students!) as well as concerts. Great performers like Kanye West, Green Day, Maroon 5, John Mayer, Counting Crows, Rusted Root, Alicia Keys, and Bob Dylan have performed at the Liacouras Center. Temple has every type of student doing every type of activity. Beyond sports, students can join one of 100 or so clubs and organizations and take full advantage of the rich resources and recreation activities offered by Philadelphia and the surrounding area.

Location

Philadelphia has a lot more than juicy sandwiches and cream cheese. With more than 100 museums, 700 Zagat-rated restaurants, and the largest landscaped park in the country—Fairmount Park at 4,180 acres—Philly has a lot to offer. It is a walkable, manageable city that is just 1.5 miles from Temple's Main Campus. Just four stops on a quick subway ride and students are in Center City—or what most would call downtown. Shop, eat, play, or just chill. In addition, students can find a variety of internships in all fields in the Philadelphia area, and Temple has more than 100,000 alumni in the region who love to hire Temple students.

Majors and Degrees

The Tyler School of Art offers the Bachelor of Fine Arts with concentrations in ceramics/glass, fibers, graphic and interactive design, metals/jewelry/CAD-CAM, painting, photography, printmaking, and sculpture; the Bachelor of Arts in art history and art; and the Bachelor of Science in art education. Tyler's Architecture Program confers the Bachelor of Science in architecture (preprofessional), architectural preservation, and facilities management.

The Fox School of Business and Management offers the Bachelor of Business Administration in accounting, actuarial science, business management, economics, entrepreneurship, finance, human resource management, international business administration, law and business, management information systems, marketing, real estate, and risk management and insurance.

The School of Communications and Theater offers the Bachelor of Arts in advertising; American culture and media arts; broadcasting, telecommunications, and mass media; communication; film and media arts; journalism; strategic and organizational communications; and theater.

The College of Education offers the Bachelor of Science in applied communications, career and technical education, elementary education, and secondary education.

The College of Engineering offers the Bachelor of Science in Engineering in civil engineering, electrical engineering, and mechanical engineering. The Bachelor of Science is offered in construction management technology and general engineering technology.

The College of Health Professions offers the Bachelor of Science in communication sciences; health information management; linguistics; nursing; public health; speech, language, and hearing; therapeutic recreation, and kinesiology.

The College of Liberal Arts offers the Bachelor of Arts in African American studies, American studies, anthropology, Asian studies, classics, criminal justice, economics, English, French, geography and urban studies, German, Hebrew, history, Italian, neuroscience (systems, behavior, and plasticity), philosophy, political science, psychology, religion, Russian, sociology, Spanish, and women's studies.

The Boyer College of Music and Dance offers the Bachelor of Music in composition, dance, jazz studies, music education, music history, music therapy, performance (specific instrument or voice), and theory; the Bachelor of Fine Arts is offered in dance.

The College of Science and Technology offers the Bachelor of Science in biochemistry, biology, biophysics, chemistry, computer science, environmental studies, geology, mathematical economics, mathematics, physics, neuroscience (cell and molecular), and prepharmacy.

The School of Social Administration offers the Bachelor of Social Work degree.

The School of Tourism and Hospitality Management offers the Bachelor of Science in sport and recreation management and in tourism and hospitality management.

In addition, Ambler College offers Bachelor of Science degree programs in horticulture and landscape architecture and in community and regional planning.

Academic Programs

Temple provides an excellent and affordable education, which not only prepares the student for the specific demands of a career, but also enhances an understanding of the world and the ability to continue learning throughout life.

All students are required to complete our General Education curriculum, a cross-section of courses that form the intellectual foundation of a Temple education, which includes a "Philadelphia Experience" theme. Many first-year students take advantage of Learning Communities—groups of 20 to 30 participants who pursue common studies under the direction of a faculty team. They spend a semester together, taking a few common courses, participating in faculty-led discussion groups, studying together, and taking field trips related to their studies.

University Studies is a home for the many students who have not declared a major and for students interested in graduate or professional programs in health fields. Academically qualified students may seek extra intellectual challenge through the honors program, taking about a quarter of their course work in the program's smaller, more demanding classes.

After graduation, students are well-prepared for the job world. Temple's Career Development Services arranges cooperative education assignments, schedules on-campus interviews with employers and graduate schools, offers employment skills workshops, provides career and graduate school advisement, and maintains a network of thousands of successful Temple alumni.

Academic Facilities

With more than fifty computer labs and a 90 percent wireless campus, information is more accessible than ever. An exciting new addition to the Main Campus is the Teaching, Education, Collaboration and Help (TECH) Center. With up to 700 computers (600 fixed workstations and up to 100 laptop loaners), the TECH Center is one of the largest of its kind in the nation; thirteen breakout rooms where students can work on group projects and practice presentations; six specialized labs within the primary center, including video editing, graphic design/CAD, music composition, language/interactive audio, "quiet" zone, and software development facility; a 24-hour computer help desk for students and faculty and staff members; a 4,260-square-foot Temple Welcome Center (run by the Admissions Office) to host visits to the University by prospective students and their families; and a Starbucks café.

Costs

Tuition and fees for the 2008–09 academic year were $11,448 for Pennsylvania residents and $20,468 for out-of-state residents. Room and board for the academic year were about $9300.

Financial Aid

Scholarships, grants, loans, and work-study programs are available; 2 out of every 3 Temple students receive financial aid. Four-year academic merit scholarships for talented entering freshmen begin at $1000. Students need only apply for admission to be eligible for these scholarships. Applicants for need-based aid must file the Free Application for Federal Student Aid (FAFSA). Transfer students must file a financial aid transcript, even if they have received no aid from their previous school.

Faculty

At Temple, faculty members are valued not only for their ability to pursue knowledge, but also to share that knowledge with students. Full-time faculty members teach many introductory courses, and often act as academic advisers; from their first semester students can expect to have contact with the people at the forefront of their fields, winners of prestigious teaching and research awards such as the Lindback, the Golden Apple, the Sowell, the Fulbright, the Guggenheim, the Carnegie, and the National Endowment.

In 2007, Temple officially welcomed the largest group of new tenured and tenure-track faculty members in recent history. Faculty members were hired away from leading universities and research centers, including Princeton University, Brown University, the University of Wisconsin–Madison, the University of Maryland, Wellesley College, and the Cleveland Clinic. Nearly every college at Temple has been joined by at least one new presidential faculty recruit.

In addition to being superlative teachers and researchers, Temple faculty members are also known for their practical experience. For example, a marketing class may be led by a successful entrepreneur, or music lessons given by a member of the Philadelphia Orchestra. Marine biologists, newspaper editors, published authors, practicing architects, and health-care professionals all bring their expertise to the classroom to enhance students' education.

Admission Requirements

For freshman admissions, high school grades (quality of courses, grade trends), standardized test scores, and other factors (the required essay, recommendations, extracurricular activities, work or leadership experience, and other personal circumstances) are considered. Temple uses a sliding scale rather than absolute cutoffs for GPA and test scores. SAT Subject Tests and personal interviews are not required. The deadline for freshman admission is March 1; however, students should apply in the fall of their senior year. Official copies of high school transcripts and standardized test scores must be sent directly to the admissions office. Counselor forms are not required. The deadline for spring admission is November 1.

Temple has rolling admissions. Freshman decisions begin in early fall, and letters are sent four to six weeks after that point. Temple's admissions process is holistic; every aspect of the student's academic history is considered. Typically, students with a B average or better in a strong, college-prep curriculum in grades 9–12 and in the top 30 percent of their graduating classes are accepted. The SAT is required with all three sections considered—admitted students average 500–600 on each section. If students opt to take the ACT, they must also complete the writing section.

Freshman students who apply are automatically considered for merit-based scholarships and honors. Recommendations are not required but are accepted and considered. There is no recommendation form. The best way to apply is online. The application fee is $40—most students apply online.

Temple University welcomes transfer applicants from both two-year and four-year colleges and universities around the country and the world. Transfer students comprise more than half of each entering class and are a vital part of the vibrant campus community. Applicants are considered transfer students if they will have attempted 15 or more college-level credits by the time they apply. If this is not the case, they should apply as freshman students. In making admissions decisions, careful consideration is given to the quality of a student's program and the number of credits earned and the grade point average achieved. A cumulative GPA of at least 2.5 (on a 4.0 scale) and academic progress is required for consideration, but is not a guarantee of admission. The following programs have higher minimum grade point average requirements: architecture, nursing, pharmacy, and film and media arts. For most programs, transfer students must complete the application process by June 1 for the fall semester or by November 1 for the spring semester. The fall semester transfer application deadline for music is March 1. The fall priority deadline for nursing is February 15. Transfer applicants must request that all high schools and colleges that they previously attended send official transcripts to the Office of Undergraduate Admissions at Temple University by these deadlines. SAT or ACT scores are not required if an applicant has earned at least 15 college-level credits.

Application and Information

A completed file should contain an application form accompanied by a nonrefundable application fee, a secondary school transcript (sent by the student's school), and SAT or ACT scores. The University has a rolling admission policy; applicants are notified of the admission decision as soon as possible after all credentials have been received and reviewed.

For additional information, students may contact:

Office of Undergraduate Admissions
Temple University (041-09)
Philadelphia, Pennsylvania 19122-6096
Phone: 215-204-7200
888-340-2222 (toll-free)
E-mail: tuadm@temple.edu
Web site: http://www.temple.edu/undergrad

TENNESSEE STATE UNIVERSITY

NASHVILLE, TENNESSEE

The University

Tennessee State University (TSU), founded in 1912, is a multiracial, urban, land-grant university that fulfills its mission of providing education, research, and public service for residents of central Tennessee through myriad academic, cultural, research, service, and professional activities. Students can pursue degrees during the day or in evening courses. The Center for Extended Education and Public Service offers a wide variety of off-campus credit programs, contract credit classes with local employers, noncredit courses, and seminars to serve the expanding educational needs of local business and the professional community. The University also offers graduate programs and is dedicated to providing all students with a strong academic background. The Graduate School offers programs leading to the master's, Educational Specialist, and doctoral degrees. (Information on graduate programs is available from Graduate Admissions at the address given at the end of this description.) It is hoped that students will take full advantage of the University's offerings, use the experiences to serve themselves and society, and continue the institution's tradition of excellence.

The 9,065 students (7,112 undergraduates) currently enrolled at Tennessee State University come from a variety of cultural backgrounds and geographical areas. The campus has six residence halls (three for women, two for men, and one coed), although a large percentage of students live off campus. Easily accessible public transportation facilitates the commute to either campus. Extracurricular activities include Greek fraternities and sororities, academic societies, drama and dance groups, a concert choir, and marching, jazz, and concert bands. The University has competitive intercollegiate athletic programs in football as well as men's and women's basketball, cross-country, golf, tennis, and track and women's softball and volleyball. Intramural sports are also offered. An athletic and convocation complex seats 10,000 for basketball games and assemblies; it also contains a 220-yard indoor track, dance studios, racquetball courts, and a 35-meter swimming pool. The football team won the Ohio Valley Conference Championships two consecutive years, in 1998 and 1999. In addition, the women's track team won the Ohio Valley Conference Championship in 2001–02 and 2002–03, and the women's volleyball team was co-champion of the conference in 2005–06 and champion in 2007–08.

Special student services are offered through such resources as a counseling center, reading center, health service center, and career placement center. Tennessee State University is in the midst of a $112-million capital improvement project. The capital project includes seven new buildings and a completely landscaped campus with courtyards, plazas, and a state-of-the-art utility tunnel. The three-story campus center houses student services facilities, including offices for student organizations, admissions and records, and financial aid, and a bookstore and additional recreational facilities.

Location

Nashville is the state capital and the second-largest city in Tennessee. More than 600,000 people live in this thriving center of government, business, industry, and education. Known internationally as "Music City USA," it is the hub of the nation's country music industry. The entertainment and cultural scene does not stop there, however. A performing arts center offers an active schedule of Broadway plays, community theater, films, and performances by professional dance troupes, the Nashville Symphony, and a variety of vocal and instrumental musicians. Nashville also has three professional sports teams. Night spots and restaurants cater to a variety of cultural and ethnic tastes. Nashville's 6,000 acres of public parks and recreational facilities allow for the pursuit of many sports and leisure activities. As the city's only public four-year institution, Tennessee State University occupies an important place in Nashville. Its Main Campus is located in a residential area of the city, providing students with the atmosphere of a neighborly community. The Avon Williams Campus is located in the heart of downtown Nashville, within walking distance of the capitol and the central business district. TSU students and graduates are involved in a wide variety of academic and employment activities throughout the city.

Majors and Degrees

The College of Arts and Sciences offers majors in Africana studies, art, biological sciences, chemistry, criminal justice, English, foreign languages (French and Spanish), history, mathematics, music, physics, political science, social work, sociology, and speech communications and theater. The College also offers an interdisciplinary degree with concentrations in the humanities, the sciences, and the social sciences. Teacher certification in art, biological sciences, chemistry, elementary education, English, foreign languages, history, mathematics, music, political science, and speech communications and theater is also available. The College awards Bachelor of Science degrees.

The College of Business offers majors in accounting, business administration, business information systems, and economics and finance and grants the Bachelor of Business Administration degree.

The College of Education certifies students in elementary, special, and secondary education and awards the Bachelor of Science degree to students majoring in human performance and sports sciences and in psychology.

The College of Engineering, Technology, and Computer Sciences offers Bachelor of Science degree programs in aeronautical and industrial technology, architectural engineering, civil engineering, computer science, electrical engineering, and mechanical engineering.

The College of Health Sciences offers an Associate of Applied Science degree in dental hygiene and a Bachelor of Science degree to students who major in cardiorespiratory therapy, dental hygiene, health information management, health-care administration and planning, medical technology, or speech pathology and audiology. The School of Agriculture and Consumer Sciences offers undergraduate programs leading to the Bachelor of Science degree in agricultural sciences, early childhood education, and family and consumer sciences. The Department of Agricultural Sciences offers a bachelor's degree in agricultural sciences with options in agricultural education, agricultural statistics, agronomy, animal science and pre–veterinary medicine, food technology, ornamental horticulture, and resource economics. The Department of Family and Consumer Sciences offers bachelor's degrees in early childhood education and family and consumer sciences, with options in child development and family relationships, clothing and textiles, design, fashion merchandising, foods and nutrition, and food service management. The School of Nursing grants the two-year Associate of Science and four-year Bachelor of Science degrees in nursing. The College of Public Service and Urban Affairs offers a Bachelor of

Science degree in urban studies, with three concentrations—community leadership and public service, urban policy and planning, and urban diversity.

Academic Programs

Tennessee State University operates on a semester calendar and conducts two sessions during the summer. A minimum of 120 credit hours and a 2.0 or higher cumulative GPA are required for graduation. Individual departments may have additional requirements. An honors program, independent study, cooperative education, teacher certification, and the Air Force ROTC program are available. Early admission and advanced standing are offered to qualified students, and credit is given for satisfactory scores on the College-Level Examination Program tests.

The University honors program is designed to provide the challenge and opportunity for the academically superior student to achieve academic excellence. Honors courses require a higher level of achievement than those in the regular curriculum and are restricted to students in the honors program and to those with a B average who are recommended by an adviser or a teacher. Other courses from the regular curriculum may be taken for honors credit.

Off-Campus Programs

So that students can receive the practical training necessary for some professions, Tennessee State University has affiliations with several public and private institutions and agencies. The opportunities include a joint-degree program in allied health with Meharry Medical College, clinical training for nursing students through contractual arrangements with local hospitals, student teaching programs with the Metropolitan-Davidson County Public Schools, and field training programs with government agencies for students in social welfare and criminal justice. Students who participate in these programs earn credit toward their degree. The College of Arts and Sciences offers a dual degree in chemistry and pharmacy with Howard University and a dual degree in biology and medicine with Meharry Medical College, as well as co-op and internship experiences.

Academic Facilities

Tennessee State University has two campuses, the Main Campus and the Avon Williams Campus. The Main Campus, located on 450 acres, consists of sixty-five buildings, farmlands, and pastures. The Tennessee State University libraries house 463,621 volumes, 1,446 current periodical subscriptions, 78,185 bound periodicals, 816,934 microfiche, and 14,748 microfilm reels. A CD-ROM LAN serves both libraries with eleven CD databases; additional CD-ROM databases and Dialog services are also available. The Avon Williams Campus is housed in a large, modern building containing a library, a cafeteria, and ample meeting rooms. Parking facilities are adjacent to the building. A full curriculum is offered at this campus during evening hours.

A Learning Resource Center provides multimedia support for both campuses. Students pursuing programs in agriculture, engineering, biological sciences, chemistry, physics, dental hygiene, and nursing have access to fully equipped laboratories. Students also have access to advanced computer equipment and software.

Costs

Costs fall into four areas—maintenance, tuition, room and board, and special fees. In 2008–09, the maintenance fee for in-state students was $2566 (12 hours). Board plans ranged from $570 to $1240 per semester, and room rental costs ranged from $980 to $2840 per semester. The average total cost for a full-time, in-state undergraduate was $2566 per semester ($5132 per year). Out-of-state undergraduates paid tuition of $8012 per semester (including maintenance and special fees) in addition to room and board. Out-of-state students paid an average tuition of $16,024 per year. Average expenses for books, supplies, and personal items are $900 per semester ($1800 per year) for most students.

Financial Aid

The University has a strong commitment to assist students seeking financial aid. The types of aid available include grants, scholarships, loans, and employment. The University participates in the Federal Pell Grant, FSEOG, Federal Perkins Loan, Federal Stafford Student Loan, Federal PLUS loan, Federal Work-Study, and Tennessee Student Assistance Grant programs. Presidential Scholarships, Academic Work Scholarships, University Scholarships, Departmental Scholarships, and several private scholarship programs are also available. Approximately 80 percent of freshmen receive some type of financial assistance. Students who have a high school GPA of 3.0 or above (on a 4.0 scale) and an ACT score of 21 or above may apply for scholarships.

Prospective students must file the Free Application for Federal Student Aid by April 1 in order to be considered for financial aid. Students are also required to submit a processed Student Aid Report to the Financial Aid Office. All students are urged to start filing for financial aid January 1 to receive the maximum eligibility. All files must be complete by April 1 each year.

Faculty

Tennessee State University has a 434-member full-time faculty and a part-time faculty of 169, some of whom teach at both the undergraduate and graduate levels. Eighty percent of the faculty members hold doctoral degrees. The student-faculty ratio is 17:1. Some faculty members, particularly in the areas of agriculture, biological sciences, history, and psychology, are actively involved in research. Faculty members serve as advisers for students majoring in their discipline, and some also serve as advisers for student organizations.

Student Government

The Student Government Association consists of a president, a vice president, class officers, representatives-at-large, and organization representatives, all elected by student vote. The association operates under a formal constitution and is recognized by University administrators as the official voice of students.

Admission Requirements

In-state residents must pass the High School Proficiency Exam and have a high school GPA of 2.25 or better, an ACT score of at least 19, or a minimum SAT score of 900. Out-of-state residents must have a GPA of 2.5 or better, an ACT score of at least 19, or an SAT score of at least 900. In addition, students must pass fourteen State Board of Regents high school unit requirements. Scores on the TOEFL are required of international students.

Transfer applicants must submit a high school transcript, a transcript from every college attended, and must present a minimum grade point average of 2.0. Transfer students usually receive credit for grades of 2.0 and higher in Tennessee State University-equivalent courses taken at approved institutions. At least 30 hours must be completed in residence at Tennessee State University.

Application and Information

Applications should be received by July 1; the fee is $25. Additional information is available from:

Office of Admissions and Records
Tennessee State University
3500 John A. Merritt Boulevard
P.O. Box 9609
Nashville, Tennessee 37209-1561
Phone: 615-963-5052
888-463-6878 (toll-free)
Web site: http://www.tnstate.edu

TEXAS CHRISTIAN UNIVERSITY

FORT WORTH, TEXAS

COLLEGE CLOSE-UPS

The University

The mission of Texas Christian University (TCU) is to educate individuals to think and act as ethical leaders and responsible citizens in the global community, an idea that influences every area of the University.

Founded in 1873, TCU defied the American frontier status quo and offered an education grounded in values, innovation, and creativity. It was the first college in the Southwest to educate both men and women.

Today, TCU is a major teaching and research institution balanced by student-centered warmth typical of a smaller liberal arts college. The University rolls across some 269 picturesque tree-lined acres and within sixty buildings, from the traditional yellow-bricked neo-Georgians to a few angular ultramodern creations. Students find a diverse learning community offering over 100 undergraduate areas of study across seven colleges: business, communication, education, fine arts, health and human sciences, humanities and social sciences, and science and engineering. Approximately ninety percent of TCU's professors hold the highest degrees in their fields. It is also common to find qualified undergraduates assisting professors in the latest research activities.

TCU enrolls about 7,326 full-time undergraduate men and women from nearly every state and over eighty countries. The University competes in the nation's top collegiate athletics tier, Division I-A, offering more than twenty sports. TCU is also a member of leading education organizations such as Phi Beta Kappa, Sigma Xi, and Mortar Board. Research-oriented Ph.D. programs are offered in chemistry, divinity, education, English, history, physics, and psychology. Facilities and services include twenty residence halls, each with telephone, cable, and high-speed Internet connections. Upperclassmen have the option of living in fully furnished apartments complete with full kitchens. Sophomores may live in fully furnished, newly built lofts. Other campus amenities include nine eateries—one being an all-you-can-eat buffet—a bistro in the library; a store; a post office; thirty-one tennis courts; and the University Recreation Center with five basketball courts, a climbing wall, six racquetball courts, an elevated running track, pool and game tables, video arcade, outdoor pool and patio, and a floor full of the latest in cardio-fitness equipment. Students publish an award-winning newspaper and magazine and operate a top Dallas–Fort Worth radio station featuring alternative music and campus sports coverage.

Location

Fort Worth is home to some of the finest museums in the Southwest, including the Kimbell Art Museum. In fact, its cultural district also includes Casa Mañana, the Amon Carter Museum, the Modern Art Museum of Fort Worth, and the Fort Worth Museum of Science and Natural History. Downtown, one finds the Texas Ballet Theater, the Fort Worth Opera, the Fort Worth Symphony, and the world-class Bass Performance Hall, called one of the top ten opera houses in the world by *Travel and Leisure* magazine.

While the TCU Horned Frogs are considered the home team of Fort Worth, other nearby sports teams include the Texas Rangers, Dallas Cowboys, Dallas Stars, and Dallas Mavericks. The Texas Motor Speedway, which features NASCAR auto racing, is located north of Fort Worth. Those looking for other entertainment won't be disappointed, either. The Fort Worth Zoo is 1 minute from the campus, and the world-famous Stockyards are just a bit farther. Six Flags Over Texas is only a short drive away, as is Hurricane Harbor.

Fort Worth is also home to some of America's greatest corporations, including Burlington Northern Santa Fe (BNSF), RadioShack, Bell Helicopter-Textron, American Airlines, Pier 1 Imports, and Lockheed Martin. Other companies that look to TCU for employees are Accenture, Intel, Frito-Lay, and Electronic Data Systems.

Majors and Degrees

Programs lead to bachelor's degrees in more than eighty major areas: allied-health professions (athletic training, pre–occupational therapy*, pre–physical therapy*, and pre–physician assistant studies*), anthropology, art (art education, art history, and studio, with concentrations in ceramics, painting, photography, and sculpture), art administration (minor), astronomy, ballet, ballet and modern dance, biochemistry, biology, British and colonial/postcolonial studies (minor), broadcast journalism, business (with concentrations in accounting, electronic business, finance, finance/real estate, entrepreneurial management, marketing, and supply and value chain management, all of which are available with an international emphasis), chemistry, child development, classical studies (minor), communication sciences and disorders (speech-language pathology and habilitation of the deaf), communication studies, computer information technology, computer science, coordinated program in dietetics, criminal justice, dietetics, economics, education (early childhood, exceptional children, middle school, secondary, all-level certification, and endorsement in English as a second language), energy technology and management (minor), engineering (electrical and mechanical), English, environmental earth resources, environmental science, fashion merchandising (fashion merchandising, merchandising and textiles), film-television-digital media (criticism, industry, and production), food management, foreign languages, general studies, geography, geology, graphic design, habilitation of the deaf, health and fitness, healthy aging (minor), history, interior design, international communications (emphasizing advertising/public relations and news), international economics, international relations, journalism (broadcast and news-editorial), Latino/Latina studies (minor), liberal studies, lighting (minor), mathematics, modern dance, modern languages and literature (majors in Spanish and French, and minors in German, Italian, and Japanese), movement science, music (church music, music education, music history, performance, piano pedagogy, and theory/composition), neuroscience, nursing, nutritional sciences, philosophy, physical education, physics, political science, prehealth professions (dentistry, medicine, optometry, and veterinary), prelaw, psychology, psychosocial kinesiology, ranch management, religion, Reserve Officers' Training Corps (ROTC; aerospace studies or military science), social work, sociology, Spanish (fluency and teaching), speech-language pathology, strategic communication, theater (performance, production, and education), women's studies (minor), and writing. Programs that are indicated by an asterisk (*) begin at TCU and finish elsewhere.

Preprofessional programs are available in dentistry, law, and medicine. A certificate in ranch management is available; other certificate programs are offered by the Office of Extended Education.

Academic Programs

TCU specializes in a liberal arts and sciences education that strives to expose students to the world around them. Within the University core curriculum requirements, students have wide choices in the humanities, natural sciences, social sciences, fine arts, religion, and communication. Emphasis is placed on writing skills and critical and evaluative thinking. Freshmen are also given the opportunity to take part in Freshman Seminars, which are small classes taught by top professors.

The Center for Academic Services provides full-time advisers for students who choose to postpone the choice of a major. During the first four semesters of study, such students can satisfy University requirements while investigating potential majors. The Writing Center, also provided by the Center for Academic Services, is available to all students and faculty members who wish to refine or improve their writing skills. A full-time professional writing staff conducts individual consultation and group workshops.

Most TCU programs include internships, practicums, or other field experiences with organizations in the Dallas–Fort Worth area.

In addition, TCU's Honors College challenges students to pursue high intellectual goals. It joins interdisciplinary colloquiums and independent research with dedicated faculty members and motivated students in all fields of study.

Off-Campus Programs

Across the academic disciplines, TCU has a global perspective. Students can study abroad for a summer experience or a whole semester. Usually experiences will count toward a major or minor. Scholarships and financial aid that are awarded upon applying to the University may be used towards the cost of studying abroad. Other financial aid is also available. TCU's semester programs in London, Seville, and Florence offer classes at local universities and a variety of opportunities for immersion, cultural enrichment, and travel.

Academic Facilities

The library, open 24 hours a day, houses more than 2 million volumes, as well as an Internet collection that links students to hundreds of thousands of other periodicals and resources. It also has special collections in music, theology, government documents, and rare books. More than fifteen spacious computer labs are open to fit students' schedules, with a few open 24 hours a day. Of two concert halls, one is rated among the nation's best acoustically. The Neeley School of Business, geared toward e-business and entrepreneurship, is equipped with a trading room with stock market quote machines and newswire services, presentation rooms with videotape equipment, board rooms, a staffed computer resource center, and classrooms with a computer at every desk. Theater students enjoy the Walsh Center for Performing Arts, which includes the Pepsico Recital Hall, a theater, an all-Steinway piano wing, and two large rehearsal rooms.

Costs

For 2010–11, tuition and fees are $15,024 per semester, or $30,048 per academic year. Residence hall costs average $6370 per academic year. Board fees, which average $3742 per academic year, cover the cost of all meals in the primary, all-you-can-eat cafeteria. The board fee also includes a declining balance for other on-campus eateries, as well as many off-campus restaurants. Books and supplies average $1000 per year. The total annual cost for a resident student is $41,160.

Financial Aid

Approximately 78 percent of last year's freshman class received aid. Academic scholarships are based on the student's SAT or ACT scores, rank in class, and overall application. Awards range from $5500 to full tuition and include the Chancellor, Dean, Faculty, and TCU scholarships. National Merit Finalists who name TCU as their first choice receive a basic scholarship of $2000 and may be eligible for higher awards. Students with demonstrated financial need are eligible for federal-, state-, and University-funded awards, which include grants, loans, and work-study programs.

Faculty

The 465 full-time faculty members hold their highest degrees from more than 125 different institutions; 90 percent have the Ph.D. or other appropriate terminal degree. The University has kept classes comparatively small, with fewer than 4 percent of all classes having more than 50 students. Most instructors have an open-door policy for students, and all instructors post regular office hours. Some departments enlist part-time faculty members from the Dallas–Fort Worth professional community to augment their programs.

Student Government

The Student Government Association, composed of elected members, serves as the basis for student government. Its officers and programming council direct a varied program of entertainment, speakers, films, and social and cultural events. The House of Student Representatives makes many of its own policies within broad University guidelines. Residence halls form student councils to recommend policies and to provide activities for the hall. Students are voting members of all University-wide committees that recommend policy changes.

Admission Requirements

TCU evaluates applications by using broad criteria. Emphasis is placed on both test scores and on individual character. While academic credentials are most important, TCU also looks for talent, leadership potential, and personal determination to make a difference. Admitted students show above-average academic ability. Applicants are expected to have completed a college-preparatory curriculum during high school. A campus visit and interview are recommended before a decision is reached; admitted students are required to take part in an orientation session on campus before enrolling officially. Qualified students are admitted without regard to race, color, creed, age, sex, or ethnic or national origin, in accordance with Title IX and other government regulations.

Application and Information

Information about application deadlines and notification dates may be obtained from:

Raymond A. Brown
Dean of Admission
TCU Box 297013
Texas Christian University
2800 South University Drive, #112
Fort Worth, Texas 76129
Phone: 817-257-7490
800-TCU-FROG (828-3764; toll-free)
Fax: 817-257-7268
E-mail: frogmail@tcu.edu
Web site: http://www.tcu.edu

TCU graduates earn more than degrees that will improve their lives. They learn to change their world.

COLLEGE CLOSE-UPS

TEXAS WOMAN'S UNIVERSITY

DENTON, TEXAS

The University

Texas Woman's University (TWU) is a public university offering bachelor's, master's, and doctoral degree programs. A teaching and research institution, TWU emphasizes the health sciences, education, and the liberal arts. With an enrollment of more than 13,300 students in fall 2009, the University enrolls 8 percent men and welcomes all qualified students.

Established in 1901 by the Texas Legislature, Texas Woman's University is organized into three major academic divisions: the University General Divisions, the Institute of Health Sciences, and the Graduate School. Included in the University General Divisions are the College of Arts and Sciences, College of Professional Education, and School of Library and Information Studies. The Institute of Health Sciences includes the College of Health Sciences, College of Nursing, School of Occupational Therapy, and School of Physical Therapy. The Graduate School coordinates advanced degree programs across the University.

Old Main, the University's first building, still stands amid high-rise buildings and other modern facilities that distinguish the beautiful 270-acre wooded campus in Denton. Residence halls, recreational facilities, the library, and classroom buildings are conveniently located throughout the campus. Special campus landmarks include the statue of the Pioneer Woman and the historic Little Chapel in the Woods.

Location

TWU's main campus is in Denton, Texas (population 80,000+), just 35 miles north of Dallas and Fort Worth—the nation's ninth-largest urban center. Clinical centers, offering upper-level and graduate studies in the health sciences, are located in Dallas near the Parkland and Presbyterian hospitals and in Houston in the Texas Medical Center.

Majors and Degrees

Undergraduate programs lead to the Bachelor of Arts, Bachelor of Business Administration, Bachelor of Fine Arts, Bachelor of Science, and Bachelor of Social Work degrees. Baccalaureate degrees are offered in art (with concentrations in art history, ceramics, graphic design, painting, photography, and sculpture), biology (including a concentration in human biology), business administration (with concentrations in accounting, finance, human resources management, and marketing), biochemistry, chemistry, child development, communication science, computer science, criminal justice, culinary science and food service management, dance, dental hygiene, dietetics, drama, English, family studies, fashion design, fashion merchandising, general studies, government (with concentrations in public affairs, politics, and legal studies), health studies, history, kinesiology, mathematics, medical technology, music, music therapy, nursing, nutrition, pre–dental science, prelaw, premedicine, pre–occupational therapy, pre–physical therapy, psychology, social work, sociology, and teacher preparation for elementary, reading and bilingual, secondary, and special education.

Academic Programs

TWU is accredited by the Commission on Colleges of the Southern Association of Colleges and Schools to award bachelor's, master's, and doctoral degrees. Various programs are also accredited by appropriate state, regional, and national agencies. The University emphasizes the importance of a liberal arts education and specialized or professional study, especially in the health sciences.

The University's requirement for all bachelor's degrees includes the successful completion of a minimum of 120 credit hours, with at least 42 semester credit hours of core curriculum requirements plus additional hours specified for each degree. The University calendar consists of two semesters of approximately four months each, one minimester, two summer terms of five weeks each, and one summer session of ten weeks. Most degree programs are designed to allow students who carry a normal course load to complete degree requirements in eight semesters.

In accordance with the Texas Success Initiative, all undergraduate students must prove academic readiness prior to enrollment in a college or university by passing the Texas Higher Education Assessment (THEA). Students are exempt from taking the THEA if a qualifying score has been met on the TAKS, the SAT, or the ACT; there are other exemptions as well. More information about the THEA and the Texas Success Initiative can be found at http://www.twu.edu/aac/tests.asp.

Off-Campus Programs

Programs in each of the University's colleges and schools include clinical and practicum experiences that give students access to outstanding facilities of major health-care, business, and other institutions located in major metropolitan centers. Programs are offered annually to provide study-travel opportunities in the United States and abroad. A diverse cooperative education program integrates classroom study with planned and supervised work experience in educational activities outside the formal classroom.

Academic Facilities

The University library has holdings of 534,103 print volumes and 87,310 e-book volumes, 2,720 current periodical and serial publications, 959,750 microforms, and 87,310 audiovisual titles to support all major areas of study at TWU. In addition to the standard printed bibliographies, indexes, and abstracts, the library offers Web-based and local access to literature searches from 180 computer databases with access to 35,026 electronic journals. Special resources include the Woman's Collection, the largest depository in the South and Southwest of research materials about women. Other materials include a rare book collection as well as a departmental children's library in the School of Library and Information Studies.

Students have access to Texas academic and public library collections through TexShare, and, through membership in Amigos Library Services (the OCLC regional network), the TWU Library has access to collections in libraries throughout the United States. The Dallas Center maintains a special collection for students in the health sciences. Through a consortia membership, the students at the Houston Center have access to printed and online database collections and full library services in the Houston Academy of Medicine–Texas Medical Center Library as well as to an in-house TWU librarian for assistance with accessing and using all TWU Library resources.

Numerous classroom and laboratory buildings, including an undergraduate science laboratory building, are conveniently located on the Denton campus to meet specific needs of the individual components of the University. Special facilities on the Denton campus include honors and international programs with special housing facilities, Margo Jones Performance Hall, Redbud Theater Complex, an auditorium, dance studios, a television studio, numerous art and music studios and practice rooms, science laboratories, a computer center and several computer laboratories, a writing laboratory, laboratory facilities for programs related to therapy, and the Institute for Women's Health. Clinics are provided for speech and hearing, dental hygiene, occupational therapy, and reading. Also included are tennis courts, a golf course, an indoor track, indoor and outdoor pools, a Wellness Center and fitness room, and other facilities that support programs in physical education and human movement. Residence hall rooms are linked to the campus computer network.

The Dallas Center includes a campus in the Parkland Memorial Hospital complex and a campus adjacent to Presbyterian Hospital of Dallas. The Houston Center is located at the entrance of the Texas Medical Center. Both centers offer outstanding instructional facilities, including excellent library holdings, clinical learning resources, simulation and research laboratories, laboratories for occupational and physical therapy, and anatomy laboratories. The Dallas Center has renovated nursing skills laboratories, and the new Houston Center, opened in 2006, has research laboratories in biochemistry and nutrition.

Costs

The average cost for in-state resident students in 2009–10 for one semester of 15 semester hours was $3066 plus course fees and $990 for books and supplies. For out-of-state residents, the average cost of tuition for 15 semester hours was $7221. Residence hall rates, meals, and personal expenses vary. All rates are subject to change. Scholarship programs for honors students, class valedictorians from Texas, new freshmen, new transfer students, and international students are available.

Financial Aid

More than 70 percent of TWU's students receive financial aid in the form of scholarships, grants, loans, or on-campus employment. In addition to offering numerous scholarships and grants funded by the state and by friends of the University, TWU participates in many federally funded programs. Federal Pell Grants, Federal Supplemental Educational Opportunity Grants, Federal Perkins Loans, Federal Nursing Student Loans, Federal Stafford Loans, Federal Parent Loans, and Federal Work-Study Program awards are available. Suggested filing dates for financial aid applicants are April 1 for the fall and spring terms and March 1 for summer sessions. Applications for academic scholarships for both the fall and spring semesters should be made by March 1.

Faculty

A faculty of approximately 500 guides the academic program at TWU and gives careful attention to student needs. Faculty members hold the doctoral degree or another terminal or graduate degree in their field.

Student Government

All students are members of the United Student Association, which enables them to participate in a wide variety of activities. Students work with the faculty and administrators to develop University policies and programs of special interest and concern to the student body. Students also serve on various University committees. Leadership development is a special focus.

Admission Requirements

First-time freshman applicants are assured admission to Texas Woman's University if they have graduated from a regionally accredited high school in Texas within the last two years and have a class ranking that places them in the top 25 percent of their high school graduating class. Regular admission to the University is based on graduation from an accredited high school, a grade point average of at least 2.0 on a 4.0 scale, a score of at least 1000 (critical reading and math combined) on the SAT or a composite score of at least 21 on the ACT, and completion of at least 22 academic credits of the new recommended Texas high school graduation program. Transfer students must submit an official transcript from each college previously attended. They must have obtained a GPA of 2.0 or higher on a 4.0 scale when transferring to the University. Students holding an Associate of Arts or Associate of Science degree are assured admission.

Application and Information

Applicants should submit a completed application for admission and their official transcripts to the Office of Admissions. The fall and spring priority deadlines are March 1 and November 1, respectively. There is a $30 application fee for all new students ($50 for international students).

Additional information about the University and its programs is available from:

Office of Admissions
Texas Woman's University
P.O. Box 425589
Denton, Texas 76204-5589
Phone: 940-898-3188
866-809-6130 (toll-free)
E-mail: admissions@twu.edu
Web site: http://www.twu.edu

TWU welcomes women and men and traditional and nontraditional students to its campuses in Denton, Dallas, and Houston. TWU offers more than 100 degree programs and awards bachelor's, master's, and doctoral degrees.

THOMAS EDISON STATE COLLEGE

TRENTON, NEW JERSEY

The College

Thomas Edison State College provides flexible, high-quality, collegiate learning opportunities for self-directed adults. Identified by *Forbes* magazine as one of the top twenty colleges and universities in the nation in the use of technology to create learning opportunities for adults, Thomas Edison State College is a national leader in the assessment of adult learning and a pioneer in the use of educational technologies. Founded in 1972, Thomas Edison State College enables adults to complete associate, bachelor's, and master's degrees through a wide variety of rigorous and high-quality academic methods that can be customized to meet their individual needs.

The College's convenient programs are designed to help students pursue their educational goals while attending to the challenges and priorities of adult life. Accredited by the Commission on Higher Education of the Middle States Association of Colleges and Schools, Thomas Edison State College offers a distinguished academic program for the self-motivated adult learner. The College has approximately 34,500 alumni worldwide.

Academic advisement is provided to enrolled students by the College's Advisement Center, which assists students in integrating their learning style, background, and educational goals with the credit-earning methods and programs available. Students may access advisement through telephone and in-person appointments through the Advisement Phone Center, and they have 24-hour-a-day access through fax and e-mail.

In addition to the undergraduate programs highlighted in this description, the College offers five online master's programs. These online degrees are designed to have broad appeal for those who are not served by conventional graduate study programs.

The Master of Science in Human Resources Management (M.S.H.R.M.) degree serves human resources professionals who wish to become strategic partners in their organizations. This online program uses a cohort model and is designed to position human resources professionals as leaders within their organizations. The 36-semester-hour program provides practitioners with technical human resources skills in staffing, providing professional development, managing organizational culture, and measuring and rewarding performance.

The Master of Science in Management (M.S.M.) degree serves employed adults who have had professional experience in the management field. The M.S.M. program integrates the theory and practice of management as it applies to diverse organizations, educational institutions, and nonprofit agencies. The emphasis is on theory and practice in the management of organizations.

The Master of Arts in Liberal Studies (M.A.L.S.) degree enables students to study and apply the liberal arts to their professional lives. The M.A.L.S. program serves practitioners who are interested in broadening and deepening their professional skills, knowledge, and competencies through an intensive exposure to the liberal arts. The focus is on a deeper appreciation of the value and relevance of the arts, sciences, and humanities to the practical concerns of the workplace.

The Master of Arts in Educational Leadership (M.A.Ed.L.) degree is designed to prepare teachers and administrators to become educational leaders serving in the complex environment of elementary and secondary education. The 36-credit M.A.Ed.L. program is designed to present a coherent set of learning experiences that build and deepen students' understanding of educational leadership.

The Master of Science in Nursing (M.S.N.) degree in nurse education serves registered nurses (with current RN licenses that are valid in the United States) who have completed a Bachelor of Science in Nursing degree. Graduates of the 36-credit M.S.N. degree program are awarded a Nurse Educator Certificate in addition to the diploma and are prepared for teaching positions in schools of nursing and health-care settings. Furthermore, the School of Nursing at Thomas Edison State College offers an RN-B.S.N./M.S.N. degree program that is designed for experienced RNs who want a high-quality education with the convenience and flexibility that an online program can provide.

Location

Thomas Edison State College is located in Trenton, New Jersey.

Majors and Degrees

Thomas Edison State College offers twenty associate, bachelor's, and master's degree programs in more than 100 areas of study. Undergraduate degrees offered include Associate in Applied Science, Associate in Science, Associate in Science in Business Administration, Associate in Science in Applied Science and Technology, Associate in Arts, Associate in Science in Natural Sciences and Mathematics, Associate in Science in Public and Social Services, Bachelor of Arts, Bachelor of Science, Bachelor of Science in Applied Science and Technology, Bachelor of Science in Business Administration, Bachelor of Science in Health Information Management, Bachelor of Science in Health Sciences (a joint-degree program with the University of Medicine and Dentistry of New Jersey [UMDNJ] School of Health Related Professions [SHRP]), Bachelor of Science in Human Services, and Bachelor of Science in Nursing. The College's *Undergraduate Prospectus* contains a list of the more than 100 areas of study available within these degrees. To obtain the *Undergraduate Prospectus*, students should contact the College at its toll-free number or by e-mail.

Academic Programs

At Thomas Edison State College, students have the opportunity to earn degrees through traditional and nontraditional methods. These methods take into consideration personal needs and interests, while ensuring both breadth and depth of knowledge within the degree program. Thomas Edison State College offers one of the most highly regarded, comprehensive distance learning programs in the United States. Students at Thomas Edison State College may use several convenient methods of meeting degree requirements, depending upon their individual learning styles and preferences. Thomas Edison State College courses, examinations, Prior Learning Assessment, corporate or military education, and credits earned at other accredited colleges may be combined in a number of ways to earn credits toward an undergraduate degree.

Each undergraduate degree requires work in general education, a major area of study, and elective subjects. Students are encouraged to familiarize themselves with the requirements of their chosen degree and work in conjunction with one of the College's knowledgeable program advisers to develop a program plan that best meets their individual needs, goals, and interests.

Thomas Edison State College's Military Degree Completion Program (MDCP) serves military personnel worldwide. The MDCP was developed to accommodate the special needs of military personnel, whose location, relocation, and time constraints make traditional college attendance difficult, if not impossible. The program allows students to engage in a degree program wherever they may be stationed. The program allows maximum credit for military training and education. As a result of its long-standing commitment to providing access to educational options for military personnel, Thomas Edison State College participates in the Navy College Program Distance Learning Partnership (NCPDLP) and the Navy College Program for Afloat College Education (NCPACE) and is a participant in the Army University Access Online (eArmyU) program. The College is also honored to have been selected by the U.S. Department of Veterans Affairs (VA) as a participating institution of the Yellow Ribbon GI Education Enhancement Program. The Yellow Ribbon program, a provision of the Post-9/11 Veterans Educational Assistance Act of 2008, allows colleges and universities in the United States to voluntarily enter into an agreement with the VA to fund tuition expenses that exceed the highest public in-state undergraduate tuition rate. The College's participation in the Yellow Ribbon program can be especially beneficial for veterans interested in earning a master's degree and will enable some veterans, depending on the type and amount of their GI bill education benefits, to earn a college degree with little or no out-of-pocket expenses.

In addition, the College welcomes community and county college students and graduates and values their educational experience. Thomas Edison State College works closely with community and county colleges to assure maximum credit transfer for students. Up to 80 credits from a community or county college may be transferred to Thomas Edison State College toward the 120 credits needed for a bachelor's degree. Furthermore, the College accepts an unlimited number of four-year college credits toward degree requirements.

In addition, students are able to take distance learning courses through Thomas Edison State College, and they may earn credit for what they already know through testing, Prior Learning Assessment, and other methods of earning credit that are available through the College.

Thomas Edison State College also provides services for individuals who are not seeking a degree. These are credit-earning options for non-degree-seeking students, including Credit Banking and credit for licenses and certificates.

Credit-earning options for non-degree-seeking students benefit individuals who would like to earn credits through examinations, Prior Learning Assessment, Guided Study, and online courses. They may do so by paying the appropriate fee for these programs. An application to Thomas Edison State College is not required to take advantage of these credit-earning options.

Credit Banking is for students who wish to document college-level learning gained through military experience, professional licenses, college proficiency examinations, college-level corporate training programs, or American Council on Education (ACE) recommendations. Thomas Edison State College's Credit Banking is for individuals who wish to consolidate college-level work into a Thomas Edison State College transcript. Credits transcripted under the Credit Banking program may or may not apply to a degree program at Thomas Edison State College.

Thomas Edison State College grants credit for current professional licenses or certificates that have been approved for credit by ACE and the College's Academic Council. Students who have earned one of these licenses or certificates must submit notarized copies of the license or certificate and a current renewal card, if appropriate, to receive credit. A list of licenses and certificates approved for credit may be found in the College's *Undergraduate Prospectus*.

Academic Facilities

Distance education courses are provided through several venues, including Internet-based online courses via myEdison®, print-based Guided Study courses, standardized TECEP® examinations, *e*-Pack® courses, and assessment of prior learning through the College's unique Prior Learning Assessment (PLA) program. The College's distance learning program is administered through its Center for Directed Independent Adult Learning (DIAL).

Thomas Edison State College students utilize the rich library research facilities of the New Jersey State Library, which is an affiliate of Thomas Edison State College. Students have access to the Virtual Academic Libraries Environment (VALE), a system that provides access to a network of research libraries.

Costs

Tuition is payment for all costs that are directly associated with the academic delivery of a Thomas Edison State College education to registered students. Fees are designated as payment for administrative services associated with other activities in support of that educational process and for materials used by students for courses and other activities undertaken by them. Thomas Edison State College offers one annual tuition plan, the Comprehensive Tuition Plan, for students who want access to all components of the tuition package. Students who determine that they require only some components of the Comprehensive Tuition Plan are offered the Enrolled Options Plan. A complete listing of tuition and fees is included in the College's information packet, which may be obtained by calling the toll-free number or visiting the College Web site.

Financial Aid

Thomas Edison State College participates in a number of federal and state aid programs. Eligible students may receive Federal Pell Grants or federal education loans, such as the Federal Stafford Student Loan (subsidized and unsubsidized), for courses offered by the College. Eligible New Jersey residents may also tap a variety of state grant and loan programs. Students may use state aid to meet all or part of their College costs, provided they are taking at least 12 credits per semester.

Students interested in using financial assistance, including student loans, should file an application as well as the Free Application for Federal Student Aid (FAFSA) and submit all required documentation at least two months prior to the start of the first semester for which they plan to enroll in the College. Once a student's financial aid file is complete, a letter is sent to the student indicating what aid has been awarded.

Detailed information about the financial aid process may be found on the College's Web site. Students may also call the toll-free number listed in this description or send e-mail to the Office of Financial Aid at finaid@tesc.edu to obtain information.

Faculty

There are approximately 610 mentors at Thomas Edison State College. Drawn from other highly regarded colleges and universities, mentors provide many services to Thomas Edison State College, including assessment of knowledge adults already have, advisement, and other special assignments.

Admission Requirements

Adults seeking an associate or bachelor's degree who are high school graduates and at least 21 years of age are eligible to become Thomas Edison State College students. Adults seeking a graduate degree must have a bachelor's degree from a regionally accredited college or university, and must submit a current resume, provide two letters of recommendation, and complete and submit all appropriate essay questions. Because Thomas Edison State College delivers high-quality education directly to students wherever they live or work, students may complete degree requirements at their convenience. A computer is required to complete graduate degrees and to take online courses. Once a student has applied for a specific degree program, an evaluator determines the number of credits the student has already earned and fits those into the degree program requirements.

Application and Information

Students may apply to Thomas Edison State College any day of the year by mail or fax or through the College Web site. The Office of Admissions assists potential applicants in determining whether Thomas Edison State College suits their particular academic goals. For more information, students should contact:

David Hoftiezer
Director of Admissions
Thomas Edison State College
101 West State Street
Trenton, New Jersey 08608-1176
Phone: 888-442-8372 (toll-free)
Fax: 609-984-8447
E-mail: info@tesc.edu
Web site: http://www.tesc.edu

THOMAS JEFFERSON UNIVERSITY

PHILADELPHIA, PENNSYLVANIA

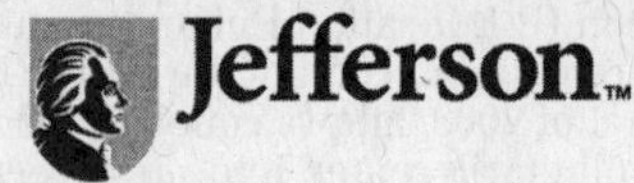

The University

Thomas Jefferson University (TJU) includes Jefferson School of Health Professions (consisting of Departments of Bioscience Technologies, Couple and Family Therapy, General Studies, Occupational Therapy, Physical Therapy, and Radiologic Sciences), Jefferson School of Nursing, Jefferson School of Pharmacy, Jefferson School of Population Health, Jefferson Medical College, and Jefferson College of Graduate Studies.

Jefferson has a campuswide commitment to excellence in educating health-care professionals and discovering knowledge to define the future of clinical care. Scholarship and applied, collaborative, and interdisciplinary research are integral to generating this new health-care knowledge.

Jefferson is mostly an upper-division and graduate university. For undergraduate programs, students generally transfer into Jefferson in their junior year. High school students can reserve a seat in a future class by applying to Jefferson through the PACE (Plan a College Education) program and attending an affiliated school for two years. Those interested in physical therapy, occupational therapy, radiologic sciences, or bioscience technologies can take advantage of special agreements with Elizabethtown College, Immaculata University, Juniata College, Muhlenberg College, Penn State Abington, Saint Joseph's University, University of Delaware, and Villanova University. An associate degree program in nursing is also available for high school graduates.

The University shares its campus with Thomas Jefferson University Hospital, one of the nation's premier health-care facilities. It is also the primary academic affiliate of the Jefferson Health System, a regional, integrated health-care delivery system.

Most Jefferson students come from the Middle Atlantic states. In 2007–08, there were 1,063 undergraduate students and 586 graduate students.

In addition to its undergraduate degree programs, Jefferson offers numerous graduate degree programs, many of which students can enter in their third year of undergraduate school. The School of Health Professions offers master's degrees in bioscience technologies (3+2 entry-level master's, accelerated professional master's, and advanced master's degrees), couple and family therapy, occupational therapy (entry-level master's, advanced master's, and doctorate in occupational therapy), and radiologic sciences (executive-style master's degree and a certificate in PET/CT) and a Doctor of Physical Therapy (D.P.T.) degree. The School of Nursing offers master's degrees in nursing, post-master's certificates, and a Doctor of Nursing Practice (D.N.P.). The School of Pharmacy offers the Doctor of Pharmacy degree. The School of Population Health offers master's degrees and certificates in health policy, public health, and healthcare quality and safety. The Master's in Family Therapy (M.F.T.) program is a collaboration between Jefferson and the Council for Relationships, a pioneering institution in the field of couple and family therapy treatment and training.

Location

Jefferson is in Center City, Philadelphia, stretching from 8th to 11th streets and from Chestnut to Locust streets. In this prime location, a short walk can take students almost anywhere they need to go. Students can walk four blocks to Independence Hall and the Liberty Bell, three blocks to Chinatown, seven blocks to South Street's funky shops and restaurants, and eight blocks to Rittenhouse Square's popular park and shopping area. In addition, students can easily catch a bus (several lines run through campus) or subway (only two blocks away) to get across town. Getting out of town is a breeze—the Market East regional rail station is two blocks away, Amtrak's 30th Street Station is less than a mile away, and the Philadelphia International Airport is a 30-minute train ride.

Living on campus means that classes, the hospital, and the library are within easy walking distance. From studios to luxury three-bedroom apartments, Jefferson Housing offers something to match almost any budget. The on-campus community includes students from the four Jefferson schools, Jefferson Medical College, and Jefferson College of Graduate Studies as well as postdoctoral fellows and medical residents.

Majors and Degrees

Two of Jefferson's schools offer undergraduate degrees: the Jefferson School of Health Professions and the Jefferson School of Nursing. The School of Health Professions offers baccalaureate degrees in bioscience technologies (biotechnology, cytotechnology, medical technology) and radiologic sciences. It also offers a combined B.S./M.S. degree in occupational therapy. The School of Nursing offers associate and baccalaureate degrees in nursing.

Academic Programs

The Department of Bioscience Technologies offers B.S., and B.S./M.S. undergraduate degrees in three programs: biotechnology/molecular sciences, cytotechnology/cell sciences, and medical technology/clinical laboratory sciences. The biotechnology/molecular sciences program educates students for health-care-related laboratory careers in the development of products using biologic and engineering principles. Through a combination of classroom and laboratory experiences, students are prepared to work with DNA, molecular modeling, and related areas.

In the cytotechnology/cell sciences program, students learn the specific microscopy skills necessary to study slides for evidence of normality or disease. Electron microscopy, cytogenetics, and the preparation and study of tissues prepare the student for further study, research, or teaching.

The medical technology/clinical laboratory sciences curriculum provides a thorough background in the physical and biological sciences, culminating in the application of research, theory, and principles to the performance of clinical laboratory procedures. The curriculum provides a firm foundation for teaching, supervisory functions, or graduate study. Jefferson offers one- or two-year baccalaureate degree programs. Postbaccalaureate specialty-track certificate programs are available in molecular biology, immunohematology, clinical chemistry, microbiology, and hematology. A master's degree is also available in all three bioscience technologies programs.

The radiologic sciences program prepares students for the expanding and multifaceted role of diagnostic imager. Recent trends in the delivery of health care indicate that the radiologic sciences curriculum must provide students with opportunities to develop skills in more than one modality. Multicompetency students earn a B.S. in radiologic sciences while studying their choice of two modalities from a total of ten: cardiac sonography, computed tomography, general sonography, invasive cardiovascular technology, magnetic resonance imaging, medical dosimetry, nuclear medicine, radiography, radiation therapy, and vascular sonography. Students may also choose education, health management, or health information systems in place of one modality. A one-year Advanced Placement baccalaureate program is available for students with a bachelor's degree in another field. A master's degree is also available in radiologic and imaging sciences.

The occupational therapy program provides students with an understanding of treatment that helps people achieve independence in their lives. Emphasis is placed on a bio-psycho-social approach to health care that concentrates on an individual's ability to perform daily-living activities, including self-care, work, and leisure. Course work is supplemented by six to nine months of supervised fieldwork. The program gives students the foundation necessary to successfully complete the national certification examination after graduation and develop skills in the areas of clinical practice, teaching, administration, or research. Degree programs include the combined B.S./M.S., as well as an entry-level M.S., post-professional M.S., and Doctorate in Occupational Therapy (O.T.D.).

The Doctor of Physical Therapy program's curriculum integrates lecture and laboratory classwork with carefully supervised clinical practice. It also provides a firm foundation in administration, research, consultation, planning, and education.

The Couple and Family Therapy program offers a master's degree in family therapy. This program is a collaboration with the renowned Council for Relationships.

Jefferson's Department of General Studies offers general courses in arts, humanities, and sciences as well as certificate programs in medical coding, medical practice management, human resources management, professional communication, and health-care information systems; associate degrees in EMS, business, information systems, and medical practice management; and bachelor's degrees in health services management, health professions management, and health services management information systems.

The Jefferson School of Nursing prepares men and women to become effective professional nurses with the background necessary to be responsible, self-directed practitioners of nursing. Jefferson provides a continuum of nursing education, offering degrees at the associate (A.S.N.), bachelor's (B.S.N.), master's (M.S.N.), and Doctor of Nursing Practice (D.N.P) levels, as well as post-master's certificates. There are no prerequisites to enter the A.S.N. to B.S.N. program, which prepares students for bedside nursing. The B.S.N. offers a background in nursing theory in addition to hands-on practice. Both programs provide students with the knowledge and clinical skills necessary to plan, implement, and evaluate nursing care for individuals, families, and communities. Degrees for RNs, master's degrees, and a clinical doctorate are also available.

The Jefferson School of Pharmacy offers the doctorate in pharmacy (Pharm.D.). After completing two years of prerequisite undergraduate work, students will come to Jefferson to complete the degree in four years.

The Jefferson School of Population Health offers the Master of Science in Health Policy (MS-HP), Master of Public Health (M.P.H.), and Master of Science in Healthcare Quality and Safety (MS-HQS) programs. Post-master's certificates are also available in these disciplines. The School also offers several dual degree programs: J.D./M.P.H., M.J./M.P.H. and M.D./M.P.H.

Academic Facilities

Administrative and academic offices, classrooms, laboratories, and a Learning Resource Center, including a computer laboratory, are located in Jefferson's Edison Building. Jefferson Alumni Hall, a basic medical science/student commons building, houses Jefferson College of Graduate Studies, basic science departments, classrooms, and research laboratories. The state-of-the-art Dorrance H. Hamilton building brings future nurses, pharmacists, physicians, therapists, and technologists into the same classrooms and simulated clinical settings. The University library and administrative offices are located in the Scott Building. Clinical experience is acquired at Thomas Jefferson University Hospital or at more than 1,800 clinical affiliate sites.

Professional counseling services are available for all students who need assistance in resolving academic, vocational, and personal concerns.

Costs

Tuition for 2009–10 varies by program, but starts at $25,372 for full-time baccalaureate degree students. Fees for associate and advanced placement programs vary. On-campus housing costs range from $427.50 to $1830 per month for one-, two-, and three-bedroom accommodations.

Financial Aid

About 72 percent of current Jefferson students receive financial assistance. Aid includes Federal Pell Grants, Federal Perkins Loans, Federal Work-Study Program awards, Air Force ROTC scholarships, Nursing Scholarships, Nursing Loans, state grants or scholarships, and state-guaranteed loans. To apply for aid, students must submit the Free Application for Federal Student Aid (FAFSA) as well as a Thomas Jefferson University application. Completed applications must be received by the Financial Aid Office no later than May 1.

Faculty

Jefferson School of Health Professions has 37 full-time and 162 part-time faculty members, Jefferson School of Nursing has 52 full-time and 134 part-time faculty members, Jefferson School of Pharmacy has 8 full-time faculty members, and Jefferson School of Population Health has 17 full-time faculty members. Most of the part-time faculty members serve in clinical teaching positions.

Student Government

Students are free to express their views on issues of institutional policy and on matters of student interest. Active membership on faculty and administrative committees enables students to participate in the formulation and application of University and School policy.

Admission Requirements

Admission for high school students is available three ways: through PACE (Plan A College Education), a program in which talented and ambitious high school seniors can reserve a seat in a future class; through the associate degree program in nursing; or through special physical therapy, occupational therapy, radiologic sciences, and bioscience technologies agreements with Elizabethtown College, Immaculata University, Juniata College, Muhlenberg College, Penn State Abington, Saint Joseph's University, University of Delaware, and Villanova University. Approximately two years of college-level course work are required for transfer admission. For a list of specific prerequisite courses and application deadlines for each program, prospective students should contact the Office of Admissions.

Interviews are required for all academically eligible applicants. An evaluation of foreign transcripts by the World Education Service (WES) is required. All international students and U.S. permanent residents must demonstrate English language proficiency as outlined by the Office of Admissions. The nonrefundable application fee is $50 (reduced to $25 for online applications).

Jefferson offers an equal opportunity for admission to all candidates who meet the admission requirements, without regard to race, color, national or ethnic origin, marital status, religion, sex, sexual orientation, gender identity, age, disability, or veteran's status.

Application and Information

Jefferson uses the self-managed application process. The application, fee, recommendation letters, transcripts, and other documents must be returned to the Office of Admission in a single envelope and at the same time. Admission and financial aid application forms and further information can be obtained by contacting:

Jefferson Schools Office of Admissions
Thomas Jefferson University
Edison Building, Suite 100
130 South 9th Street
Philadelphia, Pennsylvania 19107-5233
Phone: 215-503-8890
877-JEFF-247 (toll-free)
Web site: http://www.jefferson.edu/schools

Thomas Jefferson University is located within walking distance of many places of cultural inter est.

THOMAS MORE COLLEGE

CRESTVIEW HILLS, KENTUCKY

The College

Thomas More College features a very strong academic reputation, small class sizes, and an ongoing dedication to scholarly pursuits based on the foundation of a Catholic liberal arts curriculum. Located in northern Kentucky, just minutes from Cincinnati, Ohio, the college provides vibrant on-campus residential life in close proximity to a major metropolitan area. The result is an outstanding location offering all of the activities and resources of a major city with a suburban setting. With small class sizes and engaged faculty dedicated to teaching, the academic experience is one of personal attention and a hands-on approach to learning that forms the basis of a Thomas More education.

The student population includes 1,900 undergraduates and graduates. There are 900 traditional undergraduates attending classes full-time, of whom 320 are resident students. The student body is drawn primarily from the states of Kentucky, Ohio, and Indiana, but many other states and a number of countries are also represented. In addition to its undergraduate programs, Thomas More College offers graduate programs in business administration (M.B.A.) and teaching (M.A.T.). Students who choose to live on campus reside in either a suite-style residence hall or one of three town-house-style residence halls. All residence halls offer comfortable, air-conditioned rooms; Internet and cable TV access; and free laundry facilities. The 27,000-square-foot Holbrook Student Center contains a spacious bookstore, computer and study lounges, campus life offices, a café, and a dance rehearsal studio.

The college experience is enhanced through participation in many academic, social, and sports organizations. Intercollegiate athletics are part of the Presidents' Athletic Conference governed by NCAA Division III. Thomas More College competes in men's baseball, basketball, cross-country, football, golf, soccer, and tennis and women's basketball, cross-country, fast-pitch softball, golf, soccer, tennis, and volleyball. Track and field was added as a club sport in 2009 and will become competitive in 2011. Intramural sports offered include, among others, coed flag football, basketball, cornhole, dodgeball, softball, and volleyball. Thomas More College was proud to open a new on-campus athletic complex in fall 2008 for football and soccer, in addition to the Connor Convocation Center which houses basketball and volleyball facilities, and the College's baseball and softball fields. Students can also enjoy beautiful facilities for swimming, tennis, racquetball, and basketball and a complete fitness area at the Five Seasons Sports Club, adjacent to the campus.

Location

Thomas More College is located in northern Kentucky, 10 minutes south of Cincinnati, Ohio. The campus is convenient to major highways, and the Greater Cincinnati/Northern Kentucky International Airport is just 10 minutes from the College. Thomas More's suburban setting provides a safe environment for students and numerous opportunities for employment and internships. All students are permitted to have cars on campus.

The College's location offers a wide array of cultural and sporting events. Local attractions include the Broadway Series, the Cincinnati Pops, the Cincinnati Zoo, the Newport Aquarium, the Riverbend Music Center, and the Cincinnati Reds and Bengals. Numerous shopping areas and restaurants are also available, including the new Crestview Hills Town Center, located across the street from the College.

Majors and Degrees

Thomas More College offers bachelor's degrees in accounting, art, biology, business administration, chemistry, computer information systems, communications, criminal justice, economics, education, English, environmental science, forensic science, history, humanities, international studies, mathematics, medical technology, nursing, philosophy, physics, political science, psychology, Spanish, sports and entertainment marketing, sociology, speech and theater, and theology. Associate degrees are available in each of these content areas as well as art history, exercise science, French, pre–legal studies, and Web design.

Preprofessional programs are available in dentistry, engineering, law, medicine, occupational therapy, optometry, pharmacy, physical therapy, and veterinary science.

Academic Programs

To earn the Bachelor of Arts, Bachelor of Science, or Bachelor of Science in Nursing degree, a student must complete 128 credit hours, including 61 credit hours in liberal arts courses. The Associate of Arts degree requires the completion of 64 credit hours, including a liberal arts component. In addition to the traditional format, the College's TAP program offers associate, bachelor's, and master's degrees in business administration that are provided in an accelerated format for working adults.

The academic calendar for traditional students is composed of a fall and a spring semester and two summer sessions. The accelerated format includes classes year-round.

The Cooperative Education program enables students to gain hands-on professional experience in their field of interest. All students are eligible for this program after the completion of their freshman year. Cooperative Air Force and Army ROTC programs are available in conjunction with nearby universities. The nursing and sociology departments have excellent working relationships with nearby hospitals and social service agencies.

Off-Campus Programs

Nineteen area colleges, including Thomas More College, form the Greater Cincinnati Consortium of Colleges and Universities, through which all students at the local member colleges may take courses not available at their home institution. Thomas More encourages full-time students to take advantage of this opportunity for curriculum enrichment through cross-registration. In addition, students who wish to study abroad as part of their undergraduate education have a number of possibilities open to them.

Academic Facilities

The newly renovated library has a collection of more than 129,000 volumes of books, periodicals, and audiovisual materials; as a selective depository, it houses more than 8,400 volumes of U.S. government documents. In addition, the library's membership in the Southwest Ohio and Neighboring Libraries gives Thomas More students access to more than 15 million books and more than 75,000 periodicals held by seventy-five other libraries in the region.

Thomas More's computer facilities include computer classrooms and six labs for student use. Student computers are also available in some academic departments and in the library. All PCs are connected to a campuswide Novell network, with wireless access to e-mail, the Internet, and an on-campus Intranet server.

Students in the science programs receive hands-on experience through the use of the newly remodeled classrooms and labs and biology field station. These facilities allow students to participate in undergraduate research programs in such areas as immunology, forestry, environmental studies, astronomy, trace analysis, and synthesis. Research projects have been funded by the National Science Foundation and the National Institutes of Health.

Costs

The 2009–10 annual cost for Thomas More College was $22,500 for tuition and $6050 for room (double occupancy) and board. There is a differential fee of $30 per semester hour for all nursing courses. The Student Government fee is $60 per semester and the computer fee is $360 per semester for full-time students. The cost of books is estimated at $800 per year.

Financial Aid

Thomas More College is an excellent educational value offering a wide range of financial aid opportunities, assisting more than 90 percent of its full-time students in meeting college costs. Awards are determined on a rolling basis, with priority consideration given to applications filed by March 15. Financial aid awards are based on economic need, merit, scholastic achievement, and extracurricular activities. ROTC scholarships are also available. The filing of the Free Application for Federal Student Aid (FAFSA) and the Thomas More College Application for Financial Aid and Scholarship is required before any awards are determined. Other Thomas More College awards may require additional applications.

An extensive Federal Work-Study Program is in place, and there are excellent opportunities for outside employment in the immediate area.

Faculty

The faculty is committed to the ideals of a Catholic liberal arts education, with the main focus on teaching. The faculty has 135 members, including 71 who are full-time; 66 percent hold tenure and 69 percent hold doctoral or other terminal degrees. Faculty members serve as academic advisers to students in their disciplines. The student-faculty ratio is 16:1.

Student Government

The purpose of the Student Government Association is to serve as the official representative organization of the Thomas More College student body; to serve as the liaison between the student body and the faculty, administration, and Board of Trustees; to promote student projects and activities and improve the quality of student life; to assist the Dean of Students in supervising student organizations and student activities on campus; to protect the rights of the individual; and to preserve the general welfare of the student body of Thomas More College.

Admission Requirements

The admission criteria are as follows: an applicant should have a high school grade point average (based on college-preparatory courses) of 85 percent or better (2.5 on 4.0 scale), and a minimum composite score of 20 on the ACT Assessment, with a minimum of 20 in English, or a minimum combined score of 1010 on the SAT, with a minimum of 480 on the verbal portion. If the applicant does not meet all the admission criteria, the file is forwarded to the Admissions Committee for individual consideration.

Transfer students with 24 or more semester hours of transferable credit and an overall grade point average of at least 2.0 on a 4.0 scale are automatically accepted. Transfer students with fewer than 24 transferable hours must meet the general admission criteria outlined above.

The applicant must provide a completed application with a nonrefundable $25 fee (waived for online applicants), high school transcripts, college transcripts (if applicable), and ACT or SAT score reports.

Application and Information

Thomas More College operates under a rolling admission policy, with a final application deadline of August 15. Admission decisions are usually made within two weeks of receiving all application materials. Students can apply online at the College's Web site. The $25 application fee is waived for online applications.

For further information or to schedule a campus visit, students should contact:

Billy Sarge
Assistant Director of Admissions and Director of Recruitment
Thomas More College
333 Thomas More Parkway
Crestview Hills, Kentucky 41017-3495
Phone: 859-344-3332
800-825-4557 (toll-free)
E-mail: billy.sarge@thomasmore.edu
Web site: http://www.thomasmore.edu

Students on the Thomas More College campus.

TOCCOA FALLS COLLEGE

TOCCOA FALLS, GEORGIA

The College

Toccoa Falls College (TFC) provides the benefits of a Bible college and the strengths of a Christian liberal arts college in an authentic evangelical Christian environment. TFC was founded in 1907 and moved to its current campus location in 1911 for the young people of the South who had no access to a Christian education to prepare them for Christian service. Despite seemingly impossible obstacles, God has led and sustained the College through severe testing—including fire and flood. Throughout its history, the College has consistently transmitted to its students, along with their other studies, a practical knowledge of the Word of God. TFC is a four-year, independent, interdenominational Christian college that is affiliated with the Christian and Missionary Alliance. It offers a wide array of four-year, ministry-related, liberal arts and professional majors, as well as professional development and continuing education opportunities.

TFC remains committed to the challenge of preparing men and women to proclaim the gospel of Jesus Christ around the world. Along with their studies, students attend chapel four days per week, participate in student ministry assignments, and enjoy other spiritual formation opportunities as part of the extracurricular program.

TFC is committed to maintaining the highest standards of Christian scholarship. The College is accredited to award associate and bachelor's degrees by the Commission on Colleges of the Southern Association of Colleges and Schools (1866 Southern Lane, Decatur, Georgia 30033-4097; 404-679-4501) and by the Association of Biblical Higher Education (5575 South Semoran Boulevard, Suite 26, Orlando, Florida 32822-1781; 407-207-0808). TFC holds teacher education approval by the Professional Standards Commission of the state of Georgia (1452 Twin Towers East, Atlanta, Georgia 30334; 404-657-9000) and membership in the National Association of Schools of Music (11250 Roger Bacon Drive, Suite 21, Reston, Virginia 22090; 703-437-0700).

Toccoa Falls College enrolls about 800 students each year who are serious about impacting the world with the love and message of Jesus Christ. The majority of the student body consists of traditional residential students. Students at the College come from thirty-eight states, twelve countries, and represent twenty-eight evangelical denominations. On-campus housing is required for single students. TFC does not offer mixed-gender housing options. Single-gender housing options include residence halls, cottages, mobile housing, and apartments. Married students (13 percent of the TFC student population) can rent apartments from TFC or in the community. Campus dining facilities include a cafeteria, snack shop, and pizzeria.

Information about student activities can also be found online. The social calendar has something enjoyable to offer, including formal and informal dinners, social events, musical performances, and athletic events. Varsity sports include men's baseball, basketball, golf, and soccer, along with women's basketball, cross-country, soccer, and volleyball. Intramural sports offer TFC students and staff members the chance to enjoy additional sports, such as coed soccer, volleyball, flag football, Ultimate Frisbee, men's and women's basketball, indoor soccer, and coed softball.

Location

The Toccoa Falls College campus is located on a 1,000-acre tract holding natural forest, mountain streams, and a breathtaking 186-foot waterfall. The thirty-six major campus buildings currently utilize only about 100 acres, leaving the other 900 acres for outdoor recreation and future development. In northeast Georgia, students have immediate access to lakes, rivers, caving, hiking, fishing, waterskiing, boating, river rafting, rappelling, golf, and camping. The city of Toccoa offers a variety of choices for dining, entertainment, and employment for TFC students. The cities of Athens, Buford, and Gainesville, Georgia, and Seneca, South Carolina, are within an hour's drive of the campus. The Atlanta metropolitan area is 90 miles from TFC, and the Atlanta airport is about 105 miles away. Atlanta offers a full range of cultural opportunities, including entertainment of all kinds, restaurants, parks, professional athletics (Atlanta Braves, Atlanta Falcons, Atlanta Hawks, and Atlanta Thrashers), shopping, and various other historic charms of the state capital. Students at Toccoa Falls College enjoy big-city advantages and small-town hospitality.

Majors and Degrees

Toccoa Falls College offers students the Bachelor of Science and Bachelor of Arts degrees in the following majors: biblical studies, biology, business administration, Christian education, church music, communications, counseling psychology, cross-cultural adult education, cross-cultural business administration, cross-cultural studies, early childhood education, English, English education (6–12), family and children's ministries, history, history education (6–12), middle grades education, ministry leadership, music, music education, music performance, outdoor leadership and education, pastoral ministries, philosophy and religion, prelaw, science education (6–12), and youth ministries. Toccoa Falls College offers an Associate of Arts degree in general studies.

Academic Programs

Toccoa Falls College operates under a semester calendar with two summer sessions and a two-week session in January. A minimum of 126 credit hours is required for the bachelor's degree. Core courses in humanities, social sciences, computers/mathematics, and general education are required, as are 42 major-specific credit hours. Students are encouraged to take advantage of CLEP tests and AP courses. Toccoa Falls College recognizes that complete academic preparation for the Christian comes through advanced knowledge of a specific field of study and the integration of faith in learning. Every major includes a minimum of 30 hours of Bible credit to provide a biblical understanding and stimulate spiritual growth along with academic and professional development. Also required is the satisfactory completion of four semesters of student ministry, which gives students the opportunity for a practical ministry outlet.

Academic Facilities

Academic life centers on the Seby Jones Library, which currently houses a total of more than 151,499 holdings, including books, bound volumes, scores, vertical files, audiovisuals, and microfiche, with 300 periodical subscriptions in print and thousands of full-text journals available online. The Seby Jones Library also contains a full-service media center and curriculum labs for the School of Teacher Education. Other resources include the Interlibrary Loan Service, GALILEO (Georgia's statewide resource-sharing project), and direct access to the Internet. Other academic facilities include the computer lab, the Clary Science Building (including chemistry and biology labs), McCarthy Hall (home of the School of Teacher Education), the Woerner World Missions Building, and the White Memorial Photo Lab, complete with photo labs and curriculum labs for the School of Christian Education. The Grace Chapel and Performing Arts Center is used for artists' series and concerts, while also providing classroom space and practice rooms for the School of Music.

Costs

Tuition for 2010–11 full-time students (12 or more semester hours) is $15,700. Students are charged $5950 for room and meals. A student fee of $125 is charged to the student annually. Students should estimate $800 per year for books.

Financial Aid

Toccoa Falls College seeks to assist every qualified student who demonstrates financial need with one or more of the following types of aid: grants, loans, scholarships, work-study programs, and on- or off-campus employment. Funds come from federal, state, private, and school resources. Currently, 95 percent of Toccoa Falls College students receive some type of aid. All students must submit the Free Application for Federal Student Aid (FAFSA) to apply for specific programs. To receive priority consideration for maximum financial aid, students must submit all paperwork by May 1 for the fall semester and November 1 for the spring semester.

Faculty

Students at Toccoa Falls College benefit from professors who are academically qualified and experienced in their field and take a personal interest in their students. While their main responsibility is teaching students, many faculty members are recognized nationally and publish books, write for major magazines, serve in national organizations, or are featured guest speakers and lecturers. Their primary role on campus is active involvement in the interests of the students and as faculty advisers to assist in the course selection and academic counseling needs of the students. All courses at TFC are taught by degree-holding faculty members. Fifty-eight percent of full-time teaching faculty members hold earned doctoral degrees or the highest degree in their field. There are 68 faculty members; 45 are full-time and 23 are part-time. The student-faculty ratio is 15:1.

Student Government

The Student Government Association (SGA) acts as the umbrella organization over all student groups at Toccoa Falls College. SGA is the legislative and governing organization of the student body and the official representative of the student body to the TFC administration. The purpose of the SGA is to serve the student body, promote unity and spiritual growth, and control the student activity budget. SGA plays a vital role in organizing social events, activities, and spiritual meetings. SGA also stimulates communication between faculty and staff members and students and represents the needs of students to various official administrative committees.

Admission Requirements

TFC encourages applications from students who are interested in studying in a rigorous evangelical Christian environment. In selecting students for admission, Toccoa Falls College seeks evidence of Christian commitment and character, as well as the capacity and desire to learn. The Office of Admissions considers applications for admission after the applicant file is complete. A completed admissions file includes a completed and signed application, a $25 nonrefundable application fee, an official high school transcript or GED certificate, official transcripts from all colleges attended, an official SAT or ACT score report, a 250-word testimony, and a pastoral reference. In addition, Toccoa Falls College has the following spiritual requirements: students must have accepted the Lord Jesus Christ as Savior at least six months prior to enrollment; have evidence of good Christian character; have abstained from the use of tobacco, alcohol, and illegal drugs for at least six months prior to enrollment; have regular attendance in an evangelical church; and be in agreement with the College's doctrinal statement and policies, as printed in the current catalog and student handbook. All new freshmen, transfer, international, former, joint-enrolled, transient, and audit-only students from both in and out of state are considered on an equal basis. Campus visits and personal interviews with admissions counselors are highly encouraged. Toccoa Falls College reserves the right to examine further an applicant via psychological, achievement, and aptitude tests or personal interview. Toccoa Falls College admits qualified students without regard to race, age, color, gender, physical handicap, or national or ethnic origin.

Application and Information

Qualified students are encouraged to apply as early as possible after the final semester of their junior year in high school. Toccoa Falls College makes admissions decisions on a rolling basis and notifies applicants of their admission status via e-mail, mail, and phone within one week after all materials are received.

For more information, students should contact:

Office of Admissions
Toccoa Falls College
P.O. Box 800–899
Toccoa Falls, Georgia 30598
Phone: 706-886-7299 Ext. 5380
888-785-5624 (toll-free)
Fax: 706-282-6012
E-mail: admissions@tfc.edu
Web site: http://www.tfc.edu

The Toccoa Falls College campus has a beautiful 186-foot waterfall.

TRANSYLVANIA UNIVERSITY

LEXINGTON, KENTUCKY

COLLEGE CLOSE-UPS

The University

Transylvania, a small, private liberal arts college of about 1,100 men and women, is consistently ranked among the best small colleges in the nation. The name, from the Latin that means "across the woods", refers to the heavily forested Transylvania settlement in which the University was founded in 1780. Transylvania was the first college west of the Allegheny Mountains and the sixteenth in the nation. The University established the first schools of medicine and law in what was then the West and educated the doctors, lawyers, ministers, political leaders, and others who helped shape the young nation. Transylvania also founded the first college literary magazine in the West, *The Transylvanian*, still published by students today.

Transylvania continues as a pioneer in higher education, preparing future leaders in business, government, education, the sciences, and the arts. While professors engage in research and other scholarly activities, they never lose sight of their primary role, being great teachers. With their dedication to students, it is not surprising that Transylvania faculty members have dominated Kentucky Professor of the Year awards, winning six times in the last nine years. Students work closely with professors in small classes, many with fewer than 10 students. Due in large part to these close collaborations with faculty members, a high percentage of graduates attend selective medical, law, and other graduate and professional programs.

Transylvania students are an active and involved group, and they benefit from tremendous opportunities for learning outside the classroom and off-campus. Transylvania has over sixty active student organizations, covering a range of student interests. Over two thirds of students study abroad and many participate in internships, research projects, and volunteer activities.

Location

Transylvania is located in Lexington, Kentucky, a city of 270,000 and a growing center of commerce, culture, research, and education. Known as the horse capital of the world, Lexington is surrounded by the rolling green pastures of the famous Bluegrass region of central Kentucky. The area is home to over 30,000 college students, and Transylvania's parklike campus is just a 5-minute walk from downtown, with easy access to restaurants, shops, and entertainment. The proximity to downtown is an advantage for students who want convenient part-time jobs and internship opportunities in law offices, financial firms, hospitals, non-profits, and other organizations. Transylvania offers its students a shuttle service between the Transylvania library and the University of Kentucky libraries, and the main branch of the Lexington Public Library is only a few blocks from campus. Lexington is served by major airlines, and is only 80 miles away from both Louisville and Cincinnati.

Majors and Degrees

The Bachelor of Arts degree is awarded in the following majors: accounting; anthropology; art history; art studio; biology; business administration (concentrations in finance, hospitality management, management, and marketing); chemistry (concentrations in chemistry and biochemistry); classics; computer science; drama; economics; education; English; exercise science; French; German; history; mathematics; music; music technology; philosophy; physical education; physics; political science; psychology; religion; sociology; Spanish; and writing, rhetoric, and communication. Individually designed majors also may be arranged. Minors are available in most majors and in classical studies, communication, environmental studies, German, hospitality management, international affairs, multicultural studies, and women's studies. Advising and undergraduate preparation are provided for preprofessional programs in dentistry, engineering, law, medicine, ministry, pharmacy, physical therapy, and veterinary medicine. A cooperative program in engineering allows students to earn a B.A. in physics or math from Transylvania in three years and a B.S. in engineering from the University of Kentucky or Vanderbilt University in two years. A cooperative program in accounting allows students to earn a B.A. in accounting from Transylvania in four years and an M.S. in accounting from the University of Kentucky in one year; graduates qualify to take the CPA exam after the completion of the B.A.

Academic Programs

The academic year is based on a 4-4-1 academic calendar, with two 14-week terms (fall and winter) and a one-month May term. The fall term begins in early September and ends in mid-December. The winter term begins in mid-January and ends in late April. During the May term, students may participate in a variety of programs on or off campus. Students normally take four courses in each of the fall and winter terms and one course in the May term. Thirty-six courses are required to graduate. First-year students participate in a two-term program called Foundations of the Liberal Arts, which features small-group discussions with a faculty leader; lectures, films, concerts, and other presentations; and a tutorial program in basic communication, critical thinking, and study skills. Special study-skills clinics and workshops are offered on an optional basis. Students must complete requirements designed to ensure broad familiarity with the major areas of learning and human endeavor in the humanities and fine arts, social sciences, natural sciences and mathematics, logic, and languages.

Transylvania grants credit for scores of 4 or 5 on the Advanced Placement examinations of the College Board and at least 5 on the International Baccalaureate higher level exams. Detailed information may be obtained from the Office of the Registrar.

Off-Campus Programs

Experiencing diverse cultures through international study is a vital part of a Transylvania education, with over two thirds of students participating in study abroad. It is common for Transylvania students to study abroad for a summer, a semester, or during May Term. In recent years, Transylvania students have studied in fifty-two different countries. Scholarships are available for both semester-long and summer study abroad. Summer study programs, including those in Austria, Brazil, China, Costa Rica, Ecuador, France, Germany, Italy, Japan, Mexico, and Spain, are available through Transylvania's affiliation with the Kentucky Institute for International Studies. Transylvania also cooperates with the English-Speaking Union to offer advanced students scholarships for summer study at Cambridge and Oxford Universities. Students may participate in seminars or internships in Washington, D.C., through the Washington Center and in the Canadian Parliamentary Internship Program in Ottawa. Internships with congressional offices, Kentucky state government, city government, and local firms are easily arranged. Participation in Reserve Officers' Training Corps (Air Force and Army ROTC) is offered in cooperation with the University of Kentucky.

Academic Facilities

Two Georgian-style buildings combine elegance with high-tech facilities to offer the latest advances in teaching and learning. The Cowgill Center for Business, Economics, and Education includes a multimedia classroom where professors from any discipline can use a large display screen to show the entire class information from one of the twenty-five networked computers. A specialized area for education majors includes a laboratory classroom for teacher training. The Lucille C. Little Theater, used for faculty- and student-directed productions and drama classes, is a technically innovative facility that includes computerized lighting and sound, flexible staging options, and movable seating. The Frances Carrick Thomas/J. Douglas Gay, Jr. Library offers sophisticated computerized databases, which are invaluable for research and can be accessed from any computer connected to Transylvania's server. The Mitchell Fine Arts Center provides music program facilities, including practice rooms, a recital hall, and an auditorium. It also houses the Career Development Center, which helps students explore career options, improve job search skills, arrange internships and part-time jobs, and apply to graduate schools and to professional positions. The new, state-of-the-art fine arts technology lab can also be found in Mitchell. The Shearer Art Building is dedicated to instructional space, student and faculty studios, and a student gallery. Other modern facilities include the newly renovated L. A. Brown Science Center, the Haupt Humanities Building, and the Clive M. Beck Athletic and Recreation Center, which includes a state-of-the-art fitness center. About 80 percent of students live on campus in seven residence halls—two for men, one for women, and four for men and women. These include traditional-style accommodations, apartment-style living for upperclass students, and suite-style rooms. All rooms are air-conditioned and offer access to Transylvania's free cable television and computer networks. Thomson Hall, a new suite-style hall, opened in fall 2008, and became only the second residence hall in the southeast to earn the EPA's Energy Star certification. Each residence hall has ample lounge and study space and easy access to computer labs and recreational facilities. The William T. Young Campus Center offers a competition-size indoor pool, a gymnasium, and other meeting and recreational facilities.

Costs

Transylvania charges an annual tuition that covers fall, winter, and May terms for a normal full-time schedule of courses. Additional special instruction fees are charged for certain designated courses such as applied music and May Term travel courses. For 2009–10, tuition and fees were $25,280 and room and board (double occupancy) were $7770.

Financial Aid

Transylvania is committed to providing financial aid to students and their families. Four types of financial assistance are available. Scholarships are based on academic performance, and leadership. Grants, loans, and work-study are based on financial need. About 90 percent of Transylvania students receive some form of financial assistance, and many receive more than one type of aid. Outstanding entering freshmen may qualify for one of twenty William T. Young Scholarships—each worth more than $100,000 over four years—that cover tuition and fees. Submission of Transylvania's Application for Admission and Scholarships by the appropriate deadline is all that is necessary to be considered for academic scholarships at Transylvania. Students who are interested in need-based aid must file the Free Application for Federal Student Aid (FAFSA).

Faculty

Transylvania's relatively small size and low student-faculty ratio of 12:1 allow for close, personal attention in teaching and advising. Ninety-seven percent of full-time faculty members hold a doctorate or the highest degree in their fields, and they have come to Transylvania from a variety of graduate and professional schools. Many faculty members are recognized for their scholarship and professional activities, but their central concern is teaching and advising students. Transylvania professors have won six top professor awards over the past nine years from the Carnegie Foundation for the Advancement of Teaching and the Council for Advancement and Support of Education and from the Kentucky Advocates for Higher Education.

Transylvania's commitment to outstanding teaching is also reflected in its nationally recognized Bingham Program for Excellence in Teaching, the first of its type in the nation to attract and retain gifted teachers through an external evaluation process and financial incentives.

Student Government

Students at Transylvania have a high degree of access to the administration and governing board of the University. The Student Government Association serves as a representative government, and students hold positions on standing committees of the faculty and the Board of Trustees.

Admission Requirements

Each applicant is considered individually on academic records, SAT/ACT scores, activities, interests, essays, and recommendations. Admission is also offered to transfer students, international students, and nontraditional students.

Transylvania enrolled 297 new students for the 2009–10 academic year. The middle 50 percent composite ACT score for the freshman class was 23 to 29. Nearly 50 percent were in the top 10 percent of their high school class.

Application and Information

Submission of a Transylvania Application for Admission and Scholarships or submission of the Common Application is all that is necessary to be considered for admission and most merit scholarships at Transylvania.

The early action deadline is December 1 for applicants who wish to learn of their admission by January 15 and who want to be considered for all Transylvania scholarships. February 1 is the regular admission and scholarships deadline for applicants who wish to be considered for all Transylvania scholarships except the William T. Young Scholarship. Applicants who apply after February 1 are considered on a space-available basis. The deadline for applications for the winter term, which begins in January, is December 1.

Students considering Transylvania are urged to visit the campus, and high school seniors are encouraged to stay overnight in a dorm with a student admissions assistant.

Weekday visits may include a customized campus tour and opportunities to attend classes; talk with professors, coaches, students, and admissions and financial aid counselors; and enjoy meals on campus. Visits should be arranged through the Office of Admissions, preferably one to two weeks in advance. Open houses are held in the fall and winter, and a college planning workshop for high school juniors and sophomores is held in the spring.

For more information and application materials, students should contact:

Office of Admissions
Transylvania University
300 North Broadway
Lexington, Kentucky 40508-1797
Phone: 859-233-8242
800-872-6798 (toll-free)
E-mail: admissions@transy.edu
Web site: http://www.transy.edu

Small class sizes at Transylvania give professors and students the opportunity to work closely together, and many are directly involved in student research projects.

TRINE UNIVERSITY

ANGOLA, INDIANA

The University

Trine University is a private, independent, coeducational institution offering associate and baccalaureate degrees in more than thirty-five programs to students in engineering, mathematics, science, computer science, business administration, teacher education, communications, and criminal justice. In 2002, Trine was elevated to a graduate-degree-granting institution and now offers five-year Bachelor of Science/Master of Engineering dual-degree programs. In fall 2006, Trine introduced an interdisciplinary major in entrepreneurship. Majors in informatics and hospitality and tourism management have since been added.

Since its founding in 1884, Trine has focused on providing an affordable, comprehensive, career-oriented, hands-on education. With a worldwide reputation for being "job-ready," Trine graduates are in demand. That is why each year more than 94 percent of Trine graduates are employed in major-related positions within six months of graduation.

Trine's current main campus undergraduate enrollment is approximately 1,450. Nearly 1,000 of these students live on campus in one of sixteen residence halls, apartment buildings, or villas. The University's 400-acre campus includes an eighteen-hole championship golf course. In 2009, Trine's Golf Course Village, four student apartment buildings, opened on Zollner Golf Course. In August 2007, Trine opened its new $15.5-million University Center and Center for Technology and Online Resources, which houses a new dining hall, deli, bakery, bookstore, climbing wall, sports and wellness center, movie theater, post office, radio station, and library. Three new fully furnished student apartment buildings also opened in August 2007, providing suite-style housing options to freshmen and upperclassmen.

The University's campus offers an informal and friendly atmosphere, which complements the seriousness and determination with which Trine students pursue their academic goals. However, Trine students enjoy many opportunities to develop friendships and to build leadership and teamwork skills through their participation in athletics and a range of campus organizations.

Trine is a member of National Collegiate Athletic Association Division III and the Michigan Intercollegiate Athletic Association (MIAA), the nation's oldest athletic conference. Men's sports include baseball, basketball, cross-country, football, golf, lacrosse, soccer, tennis, track, and wrestling. Women's sports include basketball, cross-country, golf, lacrosse, soccer, softball, tennis, track, and volleyball. Women's field hockey is slated to be added in fall 2010. Intramural sports are also a big part of recreational life at Trine.

Trine's football team, the Thunder, is a two-time consecutive MIAA champion and advanced to round two of NCAA post-season play in 2009. Its softball team also notched consecutive MIAA championships in 2008 and 2009. Its wresting team is nationally ranked, and a cross-country runner also contended nationally in 2008. The Athletic and Recreation Center (ARC), which contains a 200-meter indoor track and training and practice facilities for other sports, opened in 2009 to develop Trine's track and field program year-round, and support tennis, intramurals, and other sports. Artificial turf has been installed on the main athletic field, and the Fred Zollner Athletic Stadium is scheduled to be completed in summer 2010.

Student organizations include the student senate, honor societies, professional organizations, the campus newspaper, the FM radio station, the yearbook, the drama club, music ensembles, pep and marching band, and more. Additionally, a total of fourteen social fraternities and sororities provide on-campus opportunities for service and camaraderie for 20 percent of the upperclassmen. Academic organizations such as Trine's student chapters of the American Institute for Chemical Engineering and American Criminal Justice Association allow students opportunities to claim regional and national awards.

Trine is accredited by the Higher Learning Commission and a member of the North Central Association of Colleges and Schools (Web site: http://www.ncahigherlearningcommission.org; phone: 312-263-0456). Trine's programs in chemical, civil, computer, electrical, and mechanical engineering are accredited by the Engineering Accreditation Commission of ABET, 111 Market Place, Suite 1050, Baltimore, Maryland 21202-4012; phone: 410-347-7700. All teacher preparation programs are accredited by the National Council for Accreditation of Teacher Education (NCATE) and the Indiana Department of Education/Office of Licensing and Development.

In addition to its undergraduate programs, Trine offers the Master of Engineering degree with majors in civil and mechanical engineering.

Location

Trine is located in Angola, Indiana, in the heart of northeast Indiana's scenic lake resort region and about halfway between the metropolitan areas of Chicago, Illinois, and Cleveland, Ohio. Just a 45-minute drive from Fort Wayne, Indiana, Trine offers the safety and ease of a small-town environment, located near some of the nation's most vital cities. Pokagon State Park provides year-round recreational opportunities for the community and is just 5 miles north of Trine's campus.

Majors and Degrees

The Allen School of Engineering & Technology awards Bachelor of Science degrees in chemical engineering, civil engineering, computer engineering, electrical engineering, and mechanical engineering; computer science; and design engineering technology.

Well-qualified high school graduates may be admitted directly into a five-year dual-degree mechanical or civil engineering program. Mechanical and civil engineers with the skills necessary to design complex systems are highly sought by industry professionals; therefore, the degree is a practice-oriented degree with a heavy design emphasis, as opposed to the research emphasis of a traditional Master of Science degree. On completion of this program, both the Bachelor of Science in mechanical or civil engineering and the Master of Engineering degree are awarded.

The Ketner School of Business awards the Bachelor of Science in Business Administration degree in accounting, entrepreneurship, finance, golf management, hospitality and tourism management, management, marketing, and sport management and the Bachelor of Science degree in fitness and recreational programming. Associate degrees are awarded in accounting and business administration.

The Franks School of Education awards Bachelor of Science degrees in elementary education, health and physical education, mathematics education, science education, and social studies education.

The Jannen School of Arts & Sciences awards Bachelor of Arts degrees with majors in communication, general studies, and psychology; and Bachelor of Science degrees in biology, chemistry, criminal justice, forensic science, informatics, and mathematics. A Bachelor of Science degree in criminal justice is also awarded. A premedical professional track is also available. Associate degrees are offered in arts, criminal justice, and science.

The Trine Virtual Campus makes Trine's excellent academic programs available anywhere, anytime, on the World Wide Web. With over 100 courses from which to choose, students can pursue an online degree program in business administration, with majors in health-care management and accounting, among others.

Academic Programs

Trine's engineering programs concentrate on providing a fundamental, application-oriented engineering education. In addition to concentrated studies in a specialized area, students are required to complete courses in communication skills, sociohumanistic studies, and analysis and design.

The University's business programs include a broad range of hands-on practical experience to acquaint the student with the practices, procedures, and problems of the contemporary business professional. Guest lecturers are frequent visitors to the campus, and field trips are considered vital to the total educational experience.

Off-Campus Programs

Co-op and internship opportunities are available. Semesters of classroom study are alternated with professional work experience, giving students the opportunity to integrate theory with practice and gain a competitive edge in the job market. The length of a co-op program depends upon the student's class status when entering the program. Work-study schedules require from three to six semesters on work assignments. During the semesters worked, students are paid directly by the employer.

Academic Facilities

Fawick Hall of Engineering reopened in 1997 after a yearlong $5-million full renovation to house the University's Departments of Chemical Engineering, Civil and Environmental Engineering, Electrical and Computer Engineering, Mechanical and Aerospace Engineering, and Technology. Because of the University's commitment to a high-quality education, Trine students use sophisticated equipment such as a scanning electron microscope in their cast metals laboratories and in projects related to industrial consulting. Each department has a computer lab with pertinent software.

Named in honor of John G. Best, a distinguished alumnus and former member of the Board of Trustees, the Best Hall of Science contains classrooms and science laboratories. Best Hall also houses the Fairfield Lecture Room, the Department of Mathematics, the Department of Science, the science laboratories, and the Department of Criminal Justice, Psychology and Social Sciences.

Planned renovations to the Ketner School of Business and Franks School of Education include new infrastructure and technology, including a fiber-optic network, a wireless environment, and shared multimedia access to resources for teaching (SMART) classrooms. The new T. Furth Center for Performing Arts will preserve a landmark church while providing classrooms for choral and instrumental music and an auditorium for drama and music productions.

The University has recently channeled $2 million into campus-wide technology upgrades. The University Center's Center for Technology and Online Resources houses a digital classroom with thirty desktop computers, a "my office" area with another twenty computers, and a global workspace with three videoconferencing stations to facilitate learning.

There are more than 200 computers dedicated to student access in labs across the campus. Every room in the student residences is wired to the University network and the Internet, and residential common areas are fitted with wireless Internet access.

Costs

Tuition for the academic year (two semesters) in 2009–10 was $24,100. Room and standard meal plan (19 meals per week) for the academic year were $8300 (double occupancy).

Financial Aid

Financial aid may be awarded in the form of scholarships, grants, loans, or employment. Any of these aids or any combination may be necessary to supplement family and student resources to meet basic educational expenses. Trine requires the Free Application for Federal Student Aid (FAFSA) and recommends its submission by March 10.

Faculty

Trine has a full-time faculty of 80 members. Most have doctoral degrees and/or are registered professional engineers. The central mission of the faculty members is teaching. The student-faculty ratio is 17:1.

Student Government

The student senate is organized for the purpose of promoting and coordinating campus activities for students. Representatives elected from campus organizations form the senate, which sponsors social activities and campus projects and aids in formulating policies for student organizations.

Admission Requirements

Graduation from an approved high school or equivalent preparation is required for admission. Trine gives careful consideration to the caliber of the academic records. Selection is made without regard to race, religion, or gender. The University requires that applicants for admission take the ACT or SAT prior to approval for admission (writing sections are optional).

Admission requirements for engineering include 4 years of English, 1 year of chemistry, 1 year of physics, 1 year of social studies, 2 years of algebra, 1 year of geometry, and ½ year of trigonometry. All other applicants must have the following high school credits: 4 years of English, 3 years of mathematics, 3 years of science, and 3 years of social studies.

Graduates of preprofessional or college-parallel programs at approved community or junior colleges are eligible for transfer into Trine's baccalaureate programs. Qualified graduates of these programs may be granted junior standing upon transfer. In general, credit may be allowed in subjects that parallel Trine programs, provided the student earned a grade of C or better in the course.

Application and Information

Trine University's online application is available at http://www.trine.edu; there is no application fee. The University admits applicants on the basis of scholastic achievement and academic potential. Admission decisions are made on a rolling basis, without regard to race, religion, color, gender, sexual orientation, or age. Applicants are notified of their status within two weeks after the online application and high school record have been received. Transfer students must also submit an official copy of their college transcript(s).

Interested students and their parents are encouraged to visit the campus. Arrangements can be made by writing or calling the Office of Admission.

For additional information, students should call or write:

Office of Admission
Trine University
One University Avenue
Angola, Indiana 46703-1764
Phone: 260-665-4100
800-347-4878 (toll-free within continental U.S.)
E-mail: admit@trine.edu
Internet: http://trine.edu

TRINITY COLLEGE

HARTFORD, CONNECTICUT

The College

Since its founding in 1823, Trinity has provided an undergraduate education of uncommon quality. Widely acknowledged as one of the top liberal arts colleges in the country, Trinity has been recognized by a panel of national education editors for its bold and innovative ideas to advance the cause of higher education and ensure greater access.

In its commitment to the rigorous pursuit of the liberal arts and to instruction that is personal and conversational, Trinity is an ideal college. At the same time, Trinity is in close touch with the world beyond its campus. In that respect and in terms of the outstanding opportunities Trinity's capital city location offers students, a Trinity education is indeed a real education.

While remaining faithful to the classic liberal arts tradition, Trinity offers a distinctive educational experience that prepares students for the challenges and opportunities of the twenty-first century. Building on its traditional strengths in arts and humanities and exceptional offerings in science and engineering, Trinity engages students in a conversation with the world through its study-abroad programs, interdisciplinary programs, and innovative, rigorous programs that draw on the rich cultural, educational, and professional assets of Hartford. State-of-the-art electronic facilities support Trinity's pioneering use of information technology in classrooms. The heart of a Trinity education, however, remains the personal encounter between professor and student, the intellectual partnership that discovers a world of ideas and ignites a passion for learning.

Trinity's students come from forty-three states and thirty countries. The College believes that a diverse community makes learning flourish. Trinity's undergraduate enrollment of more than 2,200 students is about equally composed of men and women. More than 90 percent of undergraduates live on campus in College housing. Trinity is engaged in continuing campus revitalization programs that preserve its impressive Gothic buildings as it also develops a campus for the twenty-first century.

Trinity offers a rich array of extracurricular activities—films, plays, concerts, musical theater, sports, academic symposia, and visits by nationally and internationally known writers, speakers, and performers. Participation is an important word on campus, and Trinity students have abundant opportunities to lead and to be involved in numerous student clubs; special interest groups; theater, dance, and music groups; debate; academic programs; campus cinema; Trinity's radio station; and many student publications. With 19 acres of playing fields, Trinity also offers an extensive athletic program. About 40 percent of the student body participate on twenty-nine men's and women's varsity teams (Division III) and even more participate in twelve intramural sports. The Ferris Athletic Center features a swimming pool, a fully equipped fitness center, crew tanks, eight international-size squash courts, basketball courts, and an indoor track.

Location

Situated on a beautiful 100-acre campus in the center of Hartford, the capital of Connecticut, Trinity offers the best of both worlds—a supportive and active campus community located in a city that provides students with myriad opportunities for internships, community service, and cultural exploration. Hartford's businesses, governmental agencies, cultural organizations, and nonprofit institutions offer Trinity students hundreds of opportunities to explore careers through the College's extensive internship program. Hartford has a number of cultural institutions, including the Wadsworth Atheneum (the oldest public art museum in the nation), Mark Twain House, Harriet Beecher Stowe Center, Connecticut Opera, Hartford Symphony, Hartford Stage, and a number of smaller theaters and clubs that provide a cultural stew of dance, theater, and music. The shopping districts of Hartford and surrounding suburbs are nearby. The impressive Connecticut coast is easily accessible, and Boston and New York are each about 2 hours from campus. Off campus, Trinity students have access to a field station in Ashford, Connecticut, dedicated to research in the natural sciences and a wide range of environmental educational endeavors.

Majors and Degrees

The College offers a Bachelor of Arts degree and a Bachelor of Science degree. Majors offered include American studies; anthropology; art history; biochemistry; biology; chemistry; classical civilization; classics; computer science; economics; educational studies; engineering; English; environmental science; history; international studies; Jewish studies; mathematics; modern languages: Chinese, French, German, Italian, Japanese, Russian, and Spanish; music; neuroscience; philosophy; physics; political science; psychology; public policy and law; religion; sociology; studio arts; theater and dance; and women, gender, and sexuality. Trinity also offers a computer coordinate major, and interdisciplinary majors may be individually constructed. Trinity offers a five-year program in engineering and computer science, which leads to a bachelor's degree from Trinity and a master's degree from Rensselaer Polytechnic Institute through Rensselaer at Hartford.

Academic Programs

Featuring more than 900 courses, Trinity's curriculum provides a framework within which students may explore the many dimensions of an undergraduate education. At the same time, the curriculum offers each student flexibility to experiment, to deepen old interests and develop new ones, and to acquire specialized training in a major field. Students must demonstrate proficiency in writing, mathematics, and a second language and fulfill a five-part distribution requirement that consists of at least one course in each of the following categories: arts, humanities, natural sciences, numerical and symbolic reasoning, and social sciences. They must also take a first-year seminar and at least one course that focuses on global engagement.

Off-Campus Programs

More than 50 percent of Trinity students study abroad for a semester or a year at Trinity's Rome Campus, at Trinity in Spain, or in other approved study programs in more than forty countries on six continents. Several Trinity-sponsored global learning sites operate in Austria, Chile, France, Spain, South Africa (Cape Town), and Trinidad. Through the theater and dance department, Trinity offers the Trinity/La MaMa Performing Arts Program in New York City, an extraordinary program that provides intensive study in theater, dance, and performance.

Academic Facilities

The Raether Library and Information Technology Center is home to the Raether and Watkinson Libraries, as well as the Computing Center. It is a place where students and faculty members come together for the serious work of scholarship, where researchers can pore over a book or conduct investigations through a wide selection of online databases. The Raether Library houses nearly 1 million print volumes and approximately 700,000 nonprint materials, including slides, microforms, sound recordings, and other materials in audiovisual and electronic formats. In addition, an online catalog linked with Wesleyan University and Connecticut College provides access to more than 2 million titles. The Watkinson Library, with its impressive collection of rare books, manuscripts, and other unique resources, supports a broad range of research interests.

The campus is fully wired, with every student room connected to the College network and the Web. Public access computers are also available 24 hours a day in select facilities.

Costs

Costs for the 2009–10 academic year were $38,900 for tuition, $10,560 for room and board, and $1940 for fees.

Financial Aid

Each student admitted to Trinity who qualifies for aid receives a package that fully meets his or her demonstrated need. While need status is occasionally a factor, the vast majority of admissions decisions are made on a need-blind basis. Students must file the Free Application for Federal Student Aid (FAFSA) as well as the Financial Aid PROFILE of the College Scholarship Service. Admissions applications are due by January 1; FAFSA and PROFILE applications are due by February 1. Students are notified of admission and aid decisions by the first week of April. Normally, need is met with a financial aid package that includes grant assistance, work-study, and federal student loans. Federal funds for which accepted students are eligible include Pell Grants, Federal Supplemental Educational Opportunity Grants (FSEOG), Perkins Loans, Stafford Loans, and PLUS Loans. The College administers a large student employment program, and most students who demonstrate need are granted an on-campus job as part of their financial aid package. The ratio of grant assistance to loans and work-study aid is sometimes affected by the academic strength of the student's record. Trinity continues to expand its aid budget to keep pace with the College's goal to increase the socioeconomic and ethnic diversity on campus. Forty percent of the students receive financial aid.

Faculty

The distinctive strength of a Trinity education has always been the close interaction between students and a faculty of devoted teacher-scholars. A student-faculty ratio of 11:1 enables supportive yet challenging educational experiences that establish a foundation for lifetime learning and enables students to pursue academic interests with passion. Students have numerous opportunities to collaborate with faculty members in conducting research; many students have made joint presentations at international, national, or local symposia or have published jointly prepared papers. All courses are taught by Trinity faculty members and not by graduate assistants.

Although the first calling of Trinity's professors is teaching, they are also active publishing scholars of national and international distinction. History professor Joan Hedrick, for example, won the Pulitzer Prize for her biography of Harriet Beecher Stowe. Other notable professors include Henry DePhillips, distinguished chemist and researcher on art restoration; Dan Lloyd, acclaimed philosopher and author of *Radiant Cool;* Lesley Farlow, accomplished dancer and choreographer; Samuel Kassow, distinguished historian; and Joseph Bronzino, an authority on biomedical engineering. Trinity professors pride themselves on their accessibility and keen interest in helping students.

Student Government

Trinity fosters the growth of future leaders by providing students with many opportunities to exercise and test their leadership skills. The Student Government Association (SGA), for example, provides students a strong voice in social, cultural, and—through membership on faculty committees—academic matters. Composed of elected class representatives, the SGA constantly seeks the expertise and insights of all interested students, and its committees offer enterprising students many chances to participate and to develop leadership skills.

Admission Requirements

Trinity seeks an ethnically and geographically diverse group of highly motivated students who have completed a rigorous course of study in secondary school and have demonstrated energy, talent, and leadership in a variety of extracurricular activities. Trinity has no specific GPA minimums or test-score cutoffs. The College is highly selective, and its candidates typically have an A– high school average. At least 16 academic units of college-preparatory course work are recommended, including a minimum of 4 years of English, 3 years of foreign language, 2 years of laboratory science, 2 years of algebra, 1 year of geometry, and 2 years of history. Last year, over 5,000 men and women from all over the nation and world applied for admission to the College, which enrolls an entering class of 575 students. Transfer students with a 3.0 GPA in a strong course of study at another accredited college or university are considered for admission to the sophomore or junior classes.

Admissions officers review each application individually; decisions are based on each candidate's academic record (course of study and GPA), recommendations from secondary school teachers and counselors, test scores, personal strengths, talents, activities, and application and supplemental essays.

Application and Information

Students must submit completed applications to the Admissions Office. Application deadlines are November 15 for early decision I applicants (with notification by December 15), January 1 for early decision II applicants (with notification by February 15), and January 1 for regular decision applicants (with notification by April 1). Transfer applicants must submit applications by April 1 for admission in the following fall semester (with notification by early June) and by November 15 for admission in the following spring semester (with notification by early January). Students may submit an electronic Common Application at http://www.commonapp.org.

Inquiries should be made to:

Larry Dow
Dean of Admissions and Financial Aid
Admissions Office
Trinity College
Hartford, Connecticut 06106-3100
Phone: 860-297-2180
Fax: 860-297-2287
E-mail: admissions.office@trincoll.edu
Web site: http://www.trincoll.edu/admissions

The Long Walk at Trinity Colleg

TRUMAN STATE UNIVERSITY

KIRKSVILLE, MISSOURI

The University

Truman has forged a national reputation for offering an exceptionally high-quality undergraduate education at a competitive price. For the thirteenth consecutive year, *U.S. News & World Report* has ranked Truman as the number one public institution in the Midwest offering bachelor's and master's degrees. In addition, Truman is ranked in the top fifty best values in higher education by Princeton Review's 2010 edition of *America's Best Value Colleges.*

A commitment to student achievement and learning is at the core of everything Truman does. This commitment is evidenced by faculty and staff members who recognize the importance of providing students with the opportunity to interact with their professors both in and out of the classroom. With class sizes averaging only 24 students and 93 percent of freshman-level academic courses being taught by instructional faculty members, students find many opportunities to ask questions of professors as well as interact with their multitalented peers. Truman's academic environment is enhanced by a student body that achieves at remarkable levels. The 2009 freshman class had an ACT midrange of 25 to 30 and an average GPA of 3.75 on a 4.0 scale. In addition, numerous opportunities exist for students to engage in undergraduate research. Each year, approximately 1,200 students work side by side with professors on University research projects, gaining greater confidence, knowledge, and skill in their chosen disciplines. The University offers these students the opportunity to present the results of their research at the annual Student Research Conference. In addition, selected students travel to the National Undergraduate Research Symposium to present their research findings. Undergraduate research stipends are also available.

Students wishing to attend Truman to become a teacher must first complete a bachelor's degree in an academic discipline and then apply for admission into professional study at the master's level to obtain a Master of Arts in Education (M.A.E.). Through this program, certification can be achieved for elementary education, middle school education, secondary education, and special education.

With more than 250 University organizations available to students, encompassing service, Greek, honorary, professional, religious, social, political, and recreational influences, Truman students have tremendous opportunities to become involved while enrolled at the University. Truman's Student Activities Board provides special events such as CSI Writers, comic acts such as Demetri Martin and Jen Koper, and musical artists like Cake, Dashboard Confessional, and Regina Spektor. In addition, adm[illegible]ll varsity athletic events, Truman theater prod[illegible] Series events is free to Truman stud[illegible]s have included *Jekyll and* [illegible] *Columbinus.*

[illegible] pproximately 17,000 [illegible] he town square, lo- [illegible] campus, provides a [illegible] e theater is located [illegible] cialized gift, book, [illegible] wide selection of

[illegible] ve fun and stay [illegible] a variety of ac- [illegible] o people of all [illegible] ing pool, per- [illegible] er-basketball. [illegible] y, a 1-meter [illegible] as a 20-foot

The northeast region of Missouri is also home to Thousand Hills State Park. A 3,252-acre state park and 573-acre lake for camping, hiking, biking, fishing, swimming, boating, and waterskiing is located within 10 minutes of the Truman campus.

Majors and Degrees

Undergraduate degrees offered by Truman include the Bachelor of Arts (B.A.), Bachelor of Science (B.S.), Bachelor of Music: Performance (B.M.), Bachelor of Fine Arts (B.F.A.), and Bachelor of Science in Nursing (B.S.N.). Truman offers more than forty areas of study in the following disciplines: accounting, agricultural science, athletic training, art, art history, biology, business administration, chemistry, classics, communication, communication disorders, computer science, creative writing, economics, English, exercise science, French, German, health science, history, interdisciplinary studies, justice systems, linguistics, mathematics, music, music: performance, nursing, philosophy and religion, physics, political science, psychology, Romance languages, Russian, sociology/anthropology, Spanish, and theater.

Professional paths include but are not limited to dentistry, engineering, law, medicine, optometry, pharmacy, physical therapy, and veterinary medicine.

Academic Programs

Truman is Missouri's premier liberal arts and sciences university and the only highly selective public institution in the state. The Liberal Studies Program is the heart of Truman's curriculum and is intended to serve as a foundation for all major programs of study offered by the University. Truman's mission is to "offer an exemplary undergraduate education, grounded in the liberal arts and sciences, in the context of a public institution of higher learning." Therefore, Truman is providing the kind of education in the liberal arts and sciences that has historically been offered only at private colleges. The program is a blend of two intellectual traditions in higher education, one that emphasizes the traditional thought and learning of the culture, as reflected in the classical works produced by it and the other that emphasizes personal investigation and freedom of discovery. The philosophy behind the Liberal Studies Program is based upon a commitment that Truman has made to provide students with essential skills needed for lifelong learning, breadth across the traditional liberal arts and sciences through exposure to various discipline-based modes of inquiry, and interconnecting perspectives that stress interdisciplinary thinking and integration as well as linkage to other cultures and experiences. All students graduating from Truman must complete 63 or more credit hours in liberal arts and sciences courses.

Truman also offers an especially challenging Honors Scholar Program. This program provides students with the opportunity to select the most rigorous honors courses to satisfy the liberal arts component of their respective programs. Students who successfully complete this program not only benefit from an even richer academic experience at Truman but also receive special recognition at graduation and distinction on their academic transcripts. Departmental honors are also available in several disciplines.

Off-Campus Programs

Each year, approximately 500 Truman students participate in enriching and life-changing study-abroad experiences. Truman's own study-abroad programs, combined with programs offered through Truman's membership in the College Consortium for International Studies, International Student Exchange Program, AustraLearn, and the Council on International Educational Exchange, provide students with study-abroad opportunities in more than forty countries worldwide, including Australia, China, England, Finland, France, Italy, Russia, Spain, and Thailand.

In addition, there are two cooperative programs affiliated with biology. Truman is affiliated with the Gulf Coast Research Laboratory at Ocean Springs, Mississippi. Marine biology courses may be taken at the laboratory during the summer, with credit awarded at Truman. In-depth study of the Ozark habitats is also available through Truman's affiliation with Reis Biological Station located near Steelville, Missouri.

In cooperation with the Washington Center for Internships and Academic Seminars, Truman offers a wide variety of experiential internships in Washington, D.C. Included are work-experience opportunities in such areas as public administration, the fine and performing arts, foreign affairs/diplomacy, government affairs, criminal justice, international relations, health and human services, environmental policy, business administration, and communications as well as other areas. Placement sites include nonprofit groups, media organizations, the State Department, Congress, museums, and much more.

Truman requires internships in education, health science, and exercise science and annually offers internship opportunities with the Missouri State Legislature. In recent years, students have completed internships with United States senators, the governor of Missouri, business and industry managers, zoos, broadcast and print media professionals, accountants, advertising agencies, physical therapists, musicians, artists, and the United States Supreme Court.

Academic Facilities

The Truman campus is beautifully situated on an expanse of 140 acres near downtown Kirksville. Featured among the forty facilities on campus is Pickler Memorial Library. This 460,116-volume facility provides a state-of-the-art library resource for students and faculty members alike. Materials not available in Pickler Memorial Library can be obtained through the Interlibrary Loan Office and MOBIUS.

Recent improvements to campus facilities include the $20-million renovation and expansion of Truman's science facility, Magruder Hall, which was completed for the spring 2006 semester and included new research labs, a greenhouse, classrooms, meeting areas, and a cyber café. The renovations of the Student Union Building were completed in 2008 with an expanded Center for Student Involvement, new technology, mural restoration, and a completely renovated university bookstore.

The West Campus Suites opened to students in fall 2006. Each suite is equipped with a living room, two bedrooms housing 2 students each, closet space, a large bathroom, and central air conditioning. Renovations have been completed on Missouri Hall. Improvements included a 2,500-square-foot addition, laundry facilities on every floor, and individually controlled heating and cooling in each room. Renovations are also complete on Blanton/Nason/Brewer and Dobson Hall and have begun on Ryle Hall, which will be finished for the fall 2011 semester.

Additional campus facilities include a student media center with a TV studio, a radio station, print media production facilities, a speech-and-hearing clinic for students in communication disorders, a biofeedback laboratory, an organic chemistry lab, an analytical chemistry lab, an independent learning center for nursing students, an observatory, a greenhouse, a 5,000-seat football stadium, a soccer field, tennis and racquetball courts, softball and baseball diamonds, a 3,000-seat arena with three basketball courts, an Olympic-size swimming pool, a multicultural affairs center, a writing center, a student success center, and a career center.

Costs

Tuition for Missouri residents for the 2009–10 academic year was $6458; out-of-state tuition was $11,309. Room and board totals for both Missouri residents and nonresidents start at $6340. Additional fees include a $305 freshman orientation fee, an annual $71 activities fee, a $4 student government fee, a $52 Student Health Center fee, an annual $100 athletic fee, a $100 parking fee for those with a vehicle, and the costs of books and personal expenses.

Financial Aid

Truman offers automatic scholarships ranging from $1000 to $3000. Competitive scholarship awards vary from $500 up to full tuition, room, and board plus a $4000 study-abroad stipend. The application for admission also serves as the application for the automatic and competitive scholarship programs.

Several scholarships are awarded to students for excellence in music, theater, debate/forensics, or art. These scholarships are available for instrumental, strings, or vocal music; acting or dramatic production; speech or debate; and studio art or art history. Of special interest to piano students is the Truman Piano Fellowship Competition.

The National Collegiate Athletic Association and the University authorize a limited number of grants to outstanding athletes. The value of this aid may vary with each individual recipient.

Truman accepts the Free Application for Federal Student Aid (FAFSA) and participates in all Federal Title IV financial aid programs. Financial aid estimates are available upon request.

Faculty

Truman State University is committed to teaching the academically talented undergraduate student. The University has 344 full-time faculty members and 27 part-time faculty members. Of these, 98 percent teach undergraduates and 80 percent hold a doctoral degree or the highest terminal degree in their discipline. Most major graduate institutions are represented among the Truman faculty, including Harvard, Princeton, Yale, Brown, Cornell, Oxford, and the Sorbonne. The student-faculty ratio at Truman is 16:1.

Student Government

Student Senate is the official elected governing body of the Student Association, representing approximately 5,800 students. Its mission is to represent the views of the Student Association in the formulation of the University policy through legislation and membership on all University committees; to facilitate communication and mutual understanding among the Student Association, faculty and staff members, and administration; to maintain a cohesive vision for the future of the University; and to actively participate in the fulfillment of the University's mission as an exemplary public liberal arts and sciences university.

Admission Requirements

Admission to Truman is competitive. Each applicant is evaluated for admission based upon academic and cocurricular record, ACT or SAT results, and the admission essay. Truman requires the following high school core: 4 units of English, 3 units of mathematics (4 recommended), 3 units of social studies/history, 3 units of natural science, 1 unit of fine arts, and 2 units of the same foreign language.

Application and Information

The priority deadline for admission is December 15. Students who have applied by this date are considered for all applicable competitive scholarships. Applications are processed on a rolling basis. There is no application fee. Students may apply online at the University's Web site. For further information or to schedule a campus visit, students should contact:

Admission Office
Ruth W. Towne Museum and Visitors Center
Truman State University
100 East Normal
Kirksville, Missouri 63501
Phone: 660-785-4114
800-892-7792
Fax: 660-785-7456
E-mail: admissions@truman.edu
Web site: http://admissions.truman.edu

COLLEGE CLOSE-UPS

UNION COLLEGE

SCHENECTADY, NEW YORK

The College

Chartered by the state of New York in 1795, Union College is one of the nation's oldest and most distinguished liberal arts colleges. A four-year, independent residential college serving approximately 2,100 undergraduate men and women, Union is known for its academic rigor, flexible programs, and close-knit community.

True to its 200-year tradition of innovation, the Union curriculum offers a multitude of academic and intellectual options. There is an increasing emphasis on interdepartmental and interdisciplinary programs that blend liberal arts with science and technology in a way that encourages students to think creatively, ethically, and entrepreneurially. Approximately half of Union students major in the arts, humanities, and social sciences, with an equal number majoring in the sciences and engineering.

Originally all-male, the College became coeducational in 1970; today, half of Union's students are women. The 2009–10 freshman class is the most diverse in Union history, with 21 percent multicultural students and 4 percent international students. Students come from thirty-nine states and thirty-five countries.

The international experience is a hallmark of a Union education, with more than 60 percent of students pursuing studies abroad. On campus, opportunities for leadership, discussion, and community abound in the Minerva system, offering residential, academic, and social programs. Every incoming student is assigned to one of seven Minerva Houses, which also involve faculty and staff.

There are about 100 student organizations, seventeen Greek organizations, and more than a dozen theme houses. Cultural events include concerts, theater, dance, film, and art exhibits at the Mandeville Gallery. About 90 percent of all students live in residence halls or college-owned houses, including traditional dorms, Minerva Houses, fraternity and sorority houses, townhouses, and College Park Hall, a renovated hotel. The Kenney Community Center connects students with Big Brothers Big Sisters, Habitat for Humanity, tutoring programs, and civic projects.

Union's comprehensive athletics program offers twenty-five varsity intercollegiate sports, organized intramurals, club sports, and recreational and fitness activities. Union is a member of the NCAA, Liberty League, and ECAC Hockey. Men's and women's ice hockey compete in NCAA Division I programs; other teams are Division III.

The Becker Career Center helps students with career planning, internships, and the graduate school and job search. Recent trends show that about a third of graduating seniors go directly to graduate or professional schools, and Union has earned an excellent reputation for placing graduates in medical, law, and business schools. Union's more than 22,000 alumni include U.S. President Chester A. Arthur (Class of 1848); Nobel Prize, National Book Award, and MacArthur "genius" award winners; Olympic medalists; and pioneers in business, engineering, entertainment, journalism, and medicine.

Location

Union is set on 100 acres in Schenectady, an historic city of 62,000 founded by the Dutch. Union became the first unified campus in America in 1813 with a distinctive design by noted French architect Joseph Ramée. Its centerpiece is the sixteen-sided Nott Memorial, a National Historic Landmark used for study, symposia, exhibits, and special events. Union is part of Upstate New York's picturesque Capital-Saratoga Region, with nearly 1 million residents. The region has a burgeoning high-tech industry and rich cultural heritage. A 15-minute drive from Albany International Airport, the College is 3 hours by car from New York City and Boston, 4 hours from Montreal, and close to East Coast ski slopes and the Adirondack Mountains.

Majors and Degrees

Union offers thirty-six majors; double majors; combined majors and minors; interdepartmental and multidisciplinary concentrations; and area, ethnic, and cultural studies programs. The self-designed Organizing Theme Major is for the student with intellectual curiosity in a particular topic involving multiple disciplines. Most students take three courses in each of the three 10-week terms that comprise Union's trimester system. The average introductory class has 20 students; the average upper level class, 12.

Most of Union's newest majors—such as bioengineering, neuroscience, and religious studies—encourage learning at the intersection of the liberal arts and sciences. Among the courses that cross traditional disciplinary boundaries are The Illustrated Organism, a class for artists and scientists, and The Business of Visual Art and Contemporary Entrepreneurship, which explores the economics of the art market. Union's Internal Education Foundation provides funding for special, innovative projects.

Union offers Bachelor of Arts (B.A.) and Bachelor of Science (B.S.) degrees. Students may declare up to two minors. Union also offers a leadership in medicine program with Albany Medical College and Union Graduate College; the law and public policy program with Albany Law School; and five-year bachelor's/M.B.A. or bachelor's/M.A.T. programs with Union Graduate College. The fourteen academic honor societies include Phi Beta Kappa, the first chapter established in New York (1817).

Academic Programs

Nearly every academic department requires students to complete some form of research in their subject area, and students have opportunities to work one-on-one with their professors. They often coauthor publications and present at conferences, such as the National Conference on Undergraduate Research (NCUR). Many participate in internships at businesses, hospitals, and social service organizations. The Steinmetz Symposium showcases the work of hundreds of student researchers through oral, dance, music, art, and poster sessions each spring.

The Campus Wide Computation Initiative, part of a National Science Foundation grant, helps students integrate computation into various fields of study. Through the Michael Rapaport ('59) Ethics Across the Curriculum initiative, faculty members from different departments offer courses that provide extensive training in everyday ethics. Writing Across the Curriculum requires all students to take five designated courses from at least two divisions and one Senior Writing Experience. The Freshman Year Preceptorial (FYP), a mandatory interdisciplinary course for first-year students, emphasizes critical reading and analytic writing. The Sophomore Research Seminar (SRS), also required, promotes research and writing skills.

Off-Campus Programs

More than 60 percent of all Union students go abroad. Most programs are led by Union faculty. Many programs combine elements of entrepreneurship, research, or community service. There are also opportunities for extended terms, formal exchanges, research trips, and independent study. Three-week mini-terms, for 1 credit, are offered during winter break in various U.S. cities and countries. Many students get involved in continuing hurricane relief efforts in New Orleans. The new Civil Rights Public History Mini-Term explores the American Civil Rights Movement in key cities and states. Union's innovative Minerva Fellows program sends graduating seniors to developing countries to work with welfare and anti-poverty initiatives. All programs are central to Union's mission of educating engaged, ethical contributors to a global society.

Academic Facilities

Union's nearly 100 buildings include the F. W. Olin Center, which features interactive computerization capabilities that make the building adaptable for use by nearly every academic department. The Science and Engineering Center houses the Center for Bioengineering and Computational Biology. Here, students can use sophisticated research tools such as a nuclear magnetic resonance spectrometer, a Pelletron accelerator, a centrifuge, and a scanning electron microscope.

Schaffer Library has 600,000 volumes, 1,600 journals and 2 online databases that provide access to a quarter-million printed books, documents, and musical scores. Flanking the library are the Humanities and Social Sciences Buildings. The Arts Building, located in North Colonnade, includes the Burns Atrium, where work by students, faculty, and alumni is exhibited. The Taylor Music Center includes the Fred L. Emerson Auditorium, an all-Steinway performance and teaching space with state-of-the-art recording technology. The Yulman Theater is the College's major performance space.

Currently under construction is the $18-million Peter Irving Wold Science and Engineering Center, which will provide a home for interdisciplinary studies across departments. It is slated for completion in 2011.

Costs

Tuition, room and board, and student fees cost $50,439 for the 2009–10 academic year. Estimated cost for books and personal expenses is $1,621.

Financial Aid

Union is committed to admitting an economically diverse student body and to meeting the full demonstrated need of all admitted students. The College offers more than $32 million annually in aid. The average Union need-based scholarship is $27,000; the average merit scholarship is $10,000. The average financial aid package for the 2009–10 freshman class exceeded $29,000. Those families who are unable to pay full tuition and fees are typically covered by a financial aid package consisting of a grant, loan, and work opportunity. About half of all applicants apply for financial aid; more than 60 percent of all students receive assistance.

Candidates for aid should complete the Free Application for Federal Student Aid (FAFSA) and the College Scholarship Service's PROFILE form and mail them directly to the appropriate agencies by February 1. For more information, visit http://www.union.edu/Admissions/.

Faculty

Close student-faculty interaction and small classes are a hallmark of the Union experience. The close relationship between students and faculty motivates students to learn through inquiry and discourse. Excluding library staff, 96 percent of the faculty members hold the doctorate, first professional, or terminal degree. Class size is generally small, with a 10:1 student-faculty ratio. Many upper-level courses function as seminars.

Student Government

Students play an integral role in directing the present and future of Union. With full voting rights on the two councils that recommend changes to educational policy and student life, students are engaged and active leaders on campus. Students also participate in groups that advise the president on matters like budgetary planning and long-range needs. Each year, two students are elected to membership on the College's Board of Trustees. Opportunities for leadership also abound with the Minerva houses, theme houses, Kenney Community Center, and other clubs.

Admission Requirements

Some 5,000 applicants seek freshman class positions; about half are in the top 10 percent of their secondary school class. In evaluating each application, admissions counselors look at the prospective student's grades, rigor of courses taken, class rank, teacher recommendations, and extracurricular involvement. Typically, 16 units of secondary school preparation are required for admission. These should include credits in certain fundamental subjects, such as English, a foreign language, mathematics, social studies, and science. It is strongly recommended that students visit Union for an admission interview and a student-guided tour. Alumni interviews may be requested online.

A student can choose not to submit his or her SAT or ACT scores for review, except for accelerated programs. Those interested in accelerated programs must submit the SAT and two SAT Subject Tests.

Application and Information

Early decision candidates have two options. The application deadline (including all supporting credentials) for Option I is November 15, with notification by December 15. Option II has a January 15 deadline (including all supporting credentials) and February 15 notification. Applications for regular decision admission must be filed by January 15, with decisions mailed by April 1.

Applications to the leadership in medicine program are due no later than December 15. Those for the law and public policy program must be filed no later than January 1. Those deferred under early decision and all regular applicants are given a final decision by April 1. Union adheres to the Candidates Reply Date of May 1.

Office of Admissions
Grant Hall
Union College
Schenectady, New York 12308
Phone: 518-388-6112
888-843-6688 (toll-free)
Fax: 518-388-6986
E-mail: admissions@union.edu
Web site: http://www.union.edu

The sixteen-sided Nott Memorial is Union College's centerpiece.

UNION UNIVERSITY

JACKSON, TENNESSEE

The University

Union University believes that today's world is in need of great thinkers, a new generation of serious-minded intellects, who will engage the culture with the truths of Christian faith. That's why this private, four-year, liberal arts–based university is committed to readying this generation of change agents. Founded in 1823 and affiliated with the Tennessee Baptist Convention, Union critically and creatively builds upon the tradition of thought and inquiry, so carefully shaped by the great Christian scholars who have preceded them. Union is committed to its four core values of being excellence driven, Christ centered, people focused, and future directed.

Union has consistently received national recognition for academic excellence and value. *U.S. News & World Report* has ranked Union sixteenth among master's universities in the South, which means Union has been classified as a top tier institution every year since 1997. Independent research by *America's 100 Best College Buys* ranks Union among the nation's best for combining academic quality and affordable price.

More than 4,000 undergraduate and graduate students from about forty states and thirty-five countries are represented in the student body.

On its Jackson campus, the University provides each resident student with a private bedroom within apartment-style complexes, most of which were built in 2008. The new units have four bedrooms with Internet connection, a kitchen, living room, washer/dryer unit, and two bathrooms.

A new student commons building features two fireplaces, TV and multi-purpose rooms, piano and band practice rooms, two kitchens, a gymnasium, a walking track, and outdoor grills and patios. The University coffeehouse is another favorite student destination for concerts, conversation, and study. Meals are served daily in the student dining hall as well as the Lexington Inn grill.

Union offers more than fifty major student-produced music and theater events each year. The University has seventy campus clubs, societies, fraternities, sororities, and other organizations. Students enjoy varsity and intramural sports and community service activities. In addition, students and faculty set aside one day a year to serve the local community though more than fifty different volunteer projects.

Union graduates enjoy a high acceptance rate at top graduate and law schools. Nearly 100 percent of faculty-recommended health science students have been accepted to medical school or professional graduate study. More than 80 percent of all graduates are accepted by graduate schools or employed, many with Fortune 500 companies, within a month of receiving their degrees. Nearly 77 percent of Union seniors plan to complete postgraduate work.

Location

The 290-acre campus is located in suburban Jackson, Tennessee, a growing community; the area's population is about 100,000. Jackson is located 80 miles east of Memphis and 120 miles west of Nashville along the I-40 corridor. Students find convenient access to entertainment, shopping, and many other services. Jackson hosts many cultural, recreational, and sporting events. Daily commercial flights are available at airports in Jackson, Memphis, and Nashville.

Majors and Degrees

Undergraduate students choose majors from among more than 100 programs of study.

Majors offered in the College of Arts and Sciences include applied linguistics, art (ceramics/sculpture, drawing/painting, graphic design, and photography), biology (cell biology, conservation biology, general biology, and zoology), broadcasting, chemical physics, chemistry, church history, church music, computer information systems, computer science, criminal justice, digital media studies (art, communication arts, and computer science), engineering (electrical and mechanical), engineering physics, English (literature and writing), film studies, French (languages and culture or literature), history, honors studies, intercultural studies, journalism, mathematics, medical technology, music, music education, music management, music marketing, music performance, music theory, physical science, physics, political science, psychology, public relations/advertising, social work, sociology and family studies, Spanish (languages and culture or literature), sport ministry, teaching English as a second language, and theater/speech.

Majors offered in the School of Christian Studies include biblical studies, biblical languages, Christian ethics, Christian studies, church history, philosophy, sport management with sport ministry emphasis, theology, and youth ministry.

Majors offered in the McAfee School of Business Administration include accounting, business administration, economics, general business, international business, management, and marketing.

Majors offered in the School of Education and Human Studies include athletic training, early childhood education (learning foundations pre-K–3), elementary education (learning foundations K–6), middle school education (liberal studies 4–8), modified and comprehensive special education (K–12), physical education, physical education and health/teacher licensure, sport communication, sport management, sport marketing, sport ministry, sports medicine/exercise science, and teacher licensure for secondary areas.

The School of Nursing offers a Bachelor of Science in nursing, the accelerated B.S.N., the RN-B.S.N. completion program, and the nurse anesthesia track.

Preprofessional programs include chiropractics, cytotechnology, dental hygiene, dentistry, health information management, medicine, occupational therapy, optometry, pharmacy, physical therapy, physician assistant studies, podiatry, and veterinary medicine.

Academic Programs

Union University requires those seeking a bachelor's degree to complete 46 hours of general core curriculum, 18 to 21 hours of specific core curriculum, a minimum of 30 hours in the major academic program, and 18 hours in the minor academic program. The completion of the required 128 hours usually requires four years, with 32 hours per year.

For each undergraduate degree granted, at least 25 percent of the required semester hours must be earned through instruction at Union University. The last 56 semester hours of credit for a bachelor's degree must be earned at an accredited senior college.

The academic calendar is divided into fall (August to December) and spring (February to May) semesters, January term, and three summer terms. Evening accelerated courses are available each term.

Off-Campus Programs

Students from a variety of academic areas participate in internships with regional and national companies. Study abroad includes destinations such as Belgium, China, France, Italy, Jordan, Mexico, Oxford University, Poland, and Spain. Union students also have the opportunity to go on short-term mission Global Outreach trips to locations in the Africa, Asia, Central America, Europe, and the United States.

Academic Facilities

The new student commons and Providence Hall, a three-story pharmacy and nursing building, are scheduled to open in 2010. Recent additions also include fifteen residence life buildings, a conference and banquet facility, an athletic fieldhouse, and a 64,000-square-foot science building.

Union provides three large computer labs on the Jackson campus for student use, with full access to e-mail and the Internet. Each residential student has a port for the campus network and Internet access in their private bedroom. Wireless access is available in many areas. Additional computer labs are specialized for use by various departments.

The Emma Waters Summar Library houses open stacks of books for student use, as well as periodicals, microfilm and microfiche, archives, and electronic resources. Through its membership in cooperatives, there is easy access to the combined collections of more than 41,000 libraries worldwide. The Stephen Olford Center Library houses more than 32,000 volumes, including several unique collections. The R. C. Ryan Center for Biblical Studies Library is also available to students.

Pharmacy, science, and nursing students benefit from state-of-the-art laboratories and simulation environments. Communication students produce a daily live news program in the University's HD television studio.

Other academic amenities include top-quality lecture facilities, fine and performing arts practice rooms, theaters, broadcast studios, digital media labs, and science and engineering laboratories.

Costs

The cost for a typical student for the 2009–10 academic year was $20,280 in tuition (up to 16 hours per semester), $5340 for housing in an apartment-style residence hall, $1590 for meals (100 meals per semester), and $660 for the student services fee. These costs, excluding books, total $27,870 per academic year. Prices for housing and meals may vary slightly according to a student's preferences.

Financial Aid

More than 90 percent of Union students receive some financial aid based on need or merit. Union commits very competitive scholarships and grants to qualified students. The University helps connect students with other financial resources such as loans, student-work programs, privately funded scholarships, and a host of state and federal assistance programs.

Faculty

Union University invests in faculty members who are experts in their fields and committed to excellence in teaching, advising, and mentoring. *U.S. News & World Report* named Union one of only eighty schools nationally where faculty members have an unusual commitment to undergraduate teaching. The faculty members at Union put a priority on classroom teaching, but also join students in the pursuit of significant research, especially at the undergraduate level. Among full-time faculty members, more than 84 percent hold doctorates or the highest degree offered in their field of study. The student-faculty ratio is 12:1, and all classes are taught by faculty members.

Student Government

Union's Student Government Association functions through its executive, legislative, and judicial branches. Its elected officers and representatives serve as the official voice of the students in institutional affairs.

Admission Requirements

Applicants must graduate from an accredited high school with at least 20 units in the areas of English, foreign language, mathematics, social and natural sciences, and approved electives. In addition, students who qualify for unconditional admission must meet or exceed two of the following three admissions criteria: a 2.5 core GPA, a composite score of 22 on the ACT or 1020 (math and critical reading combined) on the SAT, and a ranking in the top 50 percent of their high school class. Union also actively admits home-schooled students. A state high school equivalency diploma is accepted in lieu of a high school diploma.

Transfer students who have completed at least 24 semester hours of transferable credit at an accredited college may also apply. Transfer students with less than 24 semester hours must meet freshman and transfer admission requirements. Transfer students must have at least a 2.3 cumulative GPA to qualify for unconditional admission.

Application and Information

Applicants must complete and return the Union University applications for undergraduate admission along with the $35 application fee. All official transcripts and results of either the ACT or SAT must be requested and mailed directly to the Office of Undergraduate Admissions. Applications are accepted and decisions rendered on a rolling basis.

For more information or to request an application, students should contact:

Office of Undergraduate Admissions
Union University
1050 Union University Drive
Jackson, Tennessee 38305-3697
Phone: 731-661-5100
800-33-UNION (toll-free)
E-mail: info@uu.edu
Web site: http://www.uu.edu

The University is committed to its core values of being excellence driven, Christ centered, people focused, and future directed.

UNITED STATES AIR FORCE ACADEMY

COLORADO SPRINGS, COLORADO

The Academy

Established in 1954, the Air Force Academy prepares and motivates cadets for careers as Air Force officers. The Academy stresses character development, military training, and physical fitness as well as academics, emphasizing leadership in all areas.

The total enrollment is approximately 4,000; nearly 1,300 fourth class (freshman) students enter each year. The composition of the student body mirrors that of the Air Force officer corps: about 21 percent women and 23 percent minorities. Students come from all fifty states and several other countries. Their common bond is the desire to be military officers. All cadets must live in on-campus dormitories and wear uniforms.

The Academy is accredited by the North Central Association of Colleges and Schools. Its engineering programs are approved by the Engineering Accreditation Commission of the Accreditation Board for Engineering and Technology, and its computer courses are approved by the Computing Sciences Accreditation Board. The chemistry and biochemistry majors fulfill the requirements of the Commission on Professional Training of the American Chemical Society.

All cadets must participate in intramural, club, or intercollegiate athletics every semester. The intramural sports include basketball, boxing (men's), cross-country, flag football, flickerball, mountain biking, racquetball, rugby (men's and women's), soccer, softball, team handball, tennis, Ultimate Frisbee, volleyball, and wallyball. The intercollegiate teams compete in Division I of the NCAA regionally and nationally. The men's teams include baseball, basketball, boxing, cheerleading, cross-country, diving, fencing, football, golf, gymnastics, hockey, indoor and outdoor track, lacrosse, rifle, soccer, swimming, tennis, water polo, and wrestling. The women's teams include basketball, cross-country, cheerleading, diving, fencing, gymnastics, indoor and outdoor track, rifle, soccer, swimming, tennis, and volleyball. Cadets may also choose from more than eighty extracurricular activities, which include professional organizations, mission support, competitive and recreational clubs, sports groups, and hobby clubs.

Qualified Academy graduates may enter flight training upon graduation, and approximately 75 percent of the students in each graduating class pursue graduate education at other institutions within ten years of their graduation. Each year, numerous Academy graduates receive graduate scholarships and fellowships, such as the Marshall, Rhodes, National Science Foundation, National Collegiate Athletic Association, and Guggenheim awards.

Location

The Academy campus sits in the foothills of the Rampart Range of the Rocky Mountains in a setting of natural beauty. Built on a mesa at 7,000 feet, it is one of Colorado's top tourist attractions. The Cadet Chapel, with its seventeen aluminum spires towering 150 feet into the air, highlights the contemporary architecture of the buildings in the cadet area. The space-age effect reflects the Academy's mission of preparing cadets to become officers and leaders in the Air Force of the future. The Academy borders the northern edge of Colorado Springs, which lies at the foot of the famous 14,100-foot Pikes Peak. Colorado Springs has a metropolitan population of more than 500,000. Denver, the state's capital, has a population of almost 2.5 million in its greater metropolitan area and is located 55 miles north of the Academy. In addition to the social, sports, and cultural activities available in these cities, cadets enjoy skiing, hunting, horseback riding, white-water rafting, and other activities in the Colorado Rocky Mountains and nearby resorts.

Majors and Degrees

Graduates of the four-year service academy receive the Bachelor of Science (B.S.) degree and a commission as second lieutenants in the Air Force. The B.S. is granted in thirty-two majors: aeronautical engineering, astronautical engineering, basic sciences, behavioral sciences, biology, chemistry, civil engineering, computer engineering, computer science, economics, electrical engineering, engineering mechanics, English, environmental engineering, foreign area studies, general engineering, geospatial science, history, humanities, legal studies, management, mathematical sciences, mechanical engineering, meteorology, military strategic studies, operations research, physics, political science, social sciences, space operations, systems engineering, and systems engineering management. The Academy also offers minors in foreign languages and philosophy.

Academic Programs

A class enters the Academy during the last week in June or the first week in July. Incoming cadets undergo a strenuous thirty-eight-day summer training program that tests both their mental and physical abilities. Upperclass cadets conduct basic cadet training; commissioned officers serve as advisers. Basic cadets who complete this program are accepted into the Cadet Wing as fourth-class cadets. The academic year starts in early August and continues through May. During the first two years, cadets concentrate on core courses in engineering, humanities, science, and social science. During the last two years, they specialize in an academic major.

The required core courses prepare cadets for a broad scope of activity as Air Force officers. The core curriculum embraces courses in academic subjects, leadership and military training, and physical education and athletics. In addition, cadets complete the requirements for any of the thirty-two academic majors. To be eligible for graduation, cadets must also demonstrate an aptitude for commissioned service and leadership, demonstrate character consistent with professional military service, maintain a minimum cumulative grade point average and core grade point average of 2.0, and complete a minimum of 141 credit hours. The curriculum includes many elective courses.

All students must begin as freshmen; however, cadets who have taken some of the core course material prior to entry into the Academy may receive transfer or validation credit for this work. They may then substitute other courses for those granted transfer credit. Cadets who maintain the required grade point average may take advanced study classes.

The Academy aviation program familiarizes all cadets with operational activities of the Air Force. Optional courses provide instruction in soaring, parachuting, navigation, and basic flying. Those who take these courses may fulfill the requirements for

Federal Aviation Administration pilot or glider certificates. Cadets who qualify and are selected for pilot or navigator training may enter Air Education and Training Command flight programs following graduation from the Academy. Diversified summer programs in aviation and military training prepare cadets for officer responsibilities in the Air Force. Cadets may select their programs from several optional assignments at the Air Force Academy and other military installations.

Off-Campus Programs

Selected cadets may exchange visits with cadets from the Military Academy, Naval Academy, Coast Guard Academy, or one of fifteen international Air Force academies. The exchange program varies from one to two weeks for most of the international programs to a semester for the other U.S. service academies and the Canadian, Chilean, French, German, and Spanish Air Force academies, to name a few.

Academic Facilities

The Air Force Academy's excellent facilities support the academic, military, and athletics programs. Most classrooms accommodate small class sessions, averaging 17 students. Several classes and assemblies meet in larger lecture halls. Well-equipped laboratories supplement classroom instruction. Cadets conduct experiments using the Aeronautics Laboratory's wind tunnels, shock tubes, and rocket engines. A local network connects every dorm room, faculty and staff office, classroom, and laboratory at the Academy, and all entering cadets purchase notebook computers for academic and personal use. The Academy library, with more than 1.5 million volumes, supports all educational programs and maintains a collection of historical materials concerning aeronautics.

Costs

There are no tuition charges; the cost, including room, board, and medical and dental care, is borne entirely by the U.S. government. In addition, cadets receive a monthly salary to pay for supplies, clothing, and personal expenses. Careful management of the money covers obligations, with a small amount remaining for personal use.

Financial Aid

All cadets are on full scholarship at the Air Force Academy, as described above.

Faculty

The Academy's faculty is composed of Air Force officers and civilian professors. A few officers from other branches of the U.S. Armed Forces, those from allied nations, and distinguished civilian visiting professors supplement the faculty. There are no graduate student instructors. Faculty members must have a master's degree, and many have earned doctorates. Their educational backgrounds represent many outstanding colleges and universities in the United States, as well as some international institutions of higher education. Faculty members sponsor, coach, and referee extracurricular activities and athletics; adopt squadrons and attend their special events; and provide academic, career, and personal counseling.

Student Government

The Air Force Academy trains cadets for future leadership by allowing them to hold positions of responsibility in the Cadet Wing, the organization to which all cadets are assigned. The wing is under the operational supervision of first-class cadets (seniors). They hold cadet officer rank and command the wing and the subordinate units of groups, squadrons, flights, and elements. Through this organization, upperclass cadets are responsible for military training of the underclasses, the honor education and honor system, character development, and ethics and human relations programs.

Admission Requirements

Each year, young men and women who are U.S. citizens may be appointed from all states and territories of the nation. Citizens of other countries are admitted in limited numbers. Applicants must be at least 17 and not yet 23 years of age on July 1 of the year in which they desire to be admitted, be unmarried, have no dependents, and be of high moral character. They must be in good physical health.

Applicants must receive an official nomination. Members of Congress make the majority of the nominations for residents of their states and districts. Senators and representatives nominate young men and women who have excelled academically in high school, have demonstrated leadership potential through school activities, are physically fit, are respected by associates, and want to pursue military careers. Applicants need not know their member of Congress personally. Students may be eligible in nomination categories other than congressional. Students should ask high school counselors or Air Force Admissions Liaison Officers about other categories and apply for nominations in all categories for which they are eligible.

To enter the Academy upon graduation from high school, students should apply as soon as possible after January 31 of their junior year. If successful in receiving a nomination, they must take a physical fitness test, a medical exam, and either the SAT or the ACT.

Application and Information

High school juniors may obtain the application online at http://www.academyadmissions.com. Applicants should study the instructions and follow the proper application procedures. Air Force Admissions Liaison Officers, located in all states, assist students and counselors with the application and testing requirements.

HQ USAFA/RRS
2304 Cadet Drive, Suite 2300
USAF Academy, Colorado 80840-5025
Phone: 719-333-2520
800-443-9266 (toll-free)
Web site: http://www.academyadmissions.com

The Cadet Color Guard is the centerpiece of a Cadet Parade.

UNITED STATES MERCHANT MARINE ACADEMY

KINGS POINT, NEW YORK

COLLEGE CLOSE-UPS

The Academy

The United States Merchant Marine Academy is a four-year, tuition-free federal service academy that was founded in 1943 to educate and train maritime shipping industry (merchant marine) officers, officers on active duty in the armed forces, and leaders in the maritime and intermodal transportation industry. It is an accredited, degree-granting college whose students are commissioned as Ensigns in the Navy Reserve upon graduation. The Academy is one of the world's foremost institutions in the field of maritime education and is operated under the Maritime Administration (MARAD) of the U.S. Department of Transportation.

There are approximately 975 men and women enrolled as midshipmen at the Academy. Their daily routine at Kings Point is very demanding. The academic day begins at 8 a.m. and concludes at 4 p.m. After classes, midshipmen are free to participate in recreational activities until dinnertime. After dinner, they are required to devote their time to study and academic preparation.

The extracurricular program is broad and varied. In addition to varsity athletics in twenty-five intercollegiate sports, the Academy has an extensive intramural program that permits all students to enjoy physical activity and competition.

The nonathletic activities are also wide ranging and abundant, falling into as many categories as there are individual interests. Publications and the Drill Team, Glee Club, Regimental Band, Scuba-Diving Club, Eagle Scout Association, International Relations Club, and Fencing Club are but a few of the pursuits available to the midshipmen. Regimental and class dances and informal mixers provide the midshipmen with an interesting social program.

Midshipmen are granted liberty on weekends and leave at Thanksgiving, Winter Holidays (December), and fall and spring trimester breaks as well as annual leave during the period in June–July after graduation and before the next academic term begins. Perhaps the most unusual and exciting part of the Academy curriculum is the Shipboard Training Program. Each midshipman, during three trimesters of the sophomore and junior years, serves 300–360 days at sea aboard commercially operated American-flag merchant ships. This exceptional work-study program takes the midshipmen to many parts of the world and provides them with practical experience on several different types of vessels. It can be said that the world is their campus during their three trimesters of sea service.

Location

The Academy is located on 80.5 acres of land at Kings Point, on the North Shore of Long Island. Kings Point is a suburban residential community only 20 miles east of midtown New York City, close to various cultural and recreational facilities.

Majors and Degrees

A graduate of the U.S. Merchant Marine Academy receives a Bachelor of Science degree, a merchant marine license as a third mate or third assistant engineer, and a commission as an Ensign in the U.S. Navy Reserve. Graduates may apply to the Army, Navy, Air Force, Marine Corps, Coast Guard, or National Oceanic and Atmospheric Administration (NOAA) to serve on active duty. Six major programs are offered: marine transportation for the preparation of deck officers; maritime operations and technology (a marine transportation program enhanced with marine engineering studies); marine engineering for students interested in becoming engineering officers; marine engineering systems, which, in addition to leading to a license as a third assistant engineer, is accredited by the Accreditation Board for Engineering and Technology (ABET) and includes a curriculum with greater depth in mathematics and a significant component of engineering design, as compared to the marine engineering curriculum; marine engineering and shipyard management, which is also accredited by ABET; and logistics and intermodal transportation, a marine transportation program focusing on logistics and intermodal systems management.

Academic Programs

During the first trimester of the plebe (or freshman) year, all students take a common program of mathematics, science, English, and professional courses. This background enables midshipmen to determine intelligently the area of their special interest. After the first trimester, midshipmen select their major and from then on concentrate on a program aligned with their career choice. The professional majors each consist of required core courses in technical and general education areas as well as selected electives. The option program consists of six courses for marine transportation and marine engineering majors, who have a choice of taking a series of related elective courses in a specific area of concentration or any individual elective course for which they qualify. These courses include such specialized fields as nuclear engineering, management science, computer science, mathematics, chemistry, and naval architecture. By choosing to take the series of related courses, midshipmen can develop a proficiency in a subspecialty, supplementing their major field of study. Students in the marine engineering systems majors are not offered the choice of electives because of the required course load in their programs. General education courses make up about one third of each of the professional curriculums, and all midshipmen are required to take naval science courses prescribed by the Department of the Navy.

Thus, the Academy provides a balanced program of theoretical and practical study designed to provide the undergraduate with technical competence, leadership skills, and the well-rounded general education so essential for responsible citizenship in contemporary society.

Exemption credit may be awarded for college-level work completed at an accredited college if the course is equivalent to a course offered at the Academy.

Academic Facilities

With the exception of Wiley Hall, the former residence of Walter P. Chrysler and now an administration building, all the buildings of the Academy have been constructed since 1942. The Inter-Faith Chapel was dedicated in 1961, a three-story library was completed in 1968, and an indoor swimming pool and an engineering and science wing have been added since 1972. A modernization of all other academic buildings was completed in 1982. The Dean ('45) & Barbara White Admissions Center was dedicated in 2004. Upgrades to the dormitories and other facilities are currently under way.

Costs

Tuition, room and board, and medical and dental care are provided by the U.S. government. In addition, the government pays for books and the initial issue of uniforms. Each midshipman also receives $820 per month during periods when they are assigned aboard ship for training. Entering plebes are required to pay a little more than $7000 to cover the initial cost of a laptop computer as well as lab fees, equipment, and service, license, and activity fees. Upperclass members are also charged for service, license, and activity fees for the trimesters they are on campus (when they are not at sea).

Financial Aid

In effect, each midshipman receives a four-year scholarship from the U.S. government. Financial assistance is also available through the Federal Pell Grant Program, the Federal Stafford Student Loan Program, the Federal PLUS (parent loan) Program, the Federal Academic Competitiveness Grant, and the National Science and Mathematics Access to Retain Talent (SMART) Grant. A very limited number of need-based scholarships are also offered, and students may use outside scholarships to defray their costs.

Faculty

The Academy has 84 full-time faculty members and a student-faculty ratio of approximately 11:1. One third of the faculty members are licensed deck or engineering officers. Most hold advanced degrees in an academic discipline: 90 percent of the total faculty members hold master's degrees or higher; 50 percent have earned doctorates.

Student Government

The student body at the Academy is organized along military lines as a regiment, consisting of two battalions. Regimental life at the Academy is a form of student government and is an important part of the midshipman's total educational experience. The first classmen, or seniors, under the direction of the Commandant of Midshipmen, are responsible for exercising military command of the regiment and for administering the daily routine of the midshipmen. The military program is designed to develop leadership ability, self-discipline, and a sense of responsibility—attributes that are essential for effective citizenship as well as for a successful career as an officer.

Admission Requirements

Candidates for admission must be American citizens, be at least 17 years of age, must not have passed their twenty-fifth birthday by July 1 of the year of entry into the Academy, and be of good moral character. Candidates must be nominated by a U.S. representative or senator and must compete for vacancies allocated to their state in proportion to its representation in Congress. Candidates must achieve qualifying scores on the standard administration (timed) SAT or ACT. Candidates must have successfully completed chemistry or physics (including lab), as well as mathematics up to and including one semester of trigonometry or precalculus. Candidates' competitive standing is determined by their College Board score, their high school academic record and extracurricular participation, and their overall leadership potential. All candidates must meet the physical requirements for appointment as a midshipman in the Navy Reserve. Although not required, all applicants are strongly encouraged to perform a day or overnight visit to learn firsthand about midshipman life and academics. Visits are arranged through the Admissions Office when classes are in session, which is from mid-August to May.

Application and Information

Prospective candidates should write to the Admissions Office. They are sent detailed information on the nomination procedure, required tests, application procedures, and specific requirements. It is advisable to apply for a nomination during the late spring of the junior year in high school. The deadline for applications is March 1 of the year of desired entry.

Further information may be obtained by contacting:

Director of Admissions
U.S. Merchant Marine Academy
300 Steamboat Road
Kings Point, New York 11024-1699
Phone: 516-773-5391
866-546-4778 (toll-free)
Fax: 516-773-5390
E-mail: admissions@usmma.edu
Web site: http://www.usmma.edu

An aerial view of the 80.5-acre "sea campus" of the U.S. Merchant Marine Academy at Kings Point, Long Island, on the shores of Long Island Sound.

UNIVERSITY AT BUFFALO, THE STATE UNIVERSITY OF NEW YORK

BUFFALO, NEW YORK

The University

The University at Buffalo (UB) is a major public research university where undergraduate education is enriched and intensified by its close association with graduate programs and cutting-edge scholarship. With more than 100 bachelor's degree programs and minors, 184 master's programs, and ninety doctoral degree programs, UB offers more academic choices than any other public university in New York and New England. In addition to twenty-nine departments in the College of Arts and Sciences, the University has schools of architecture and planning, dental medicine, education, engineering and applied sciences, law, management, medicine and biomedical sciences, nursing, pharmacy, public health and health professions, and social work.

Because the University at Buffalo is a research-intensive university, undergraduates study and work with faculty members who are leaders in their fields in academic and research facilities that support work at the most advanced levels of knowledge. Through the University's Center for Undergraduate Research and Creative Activities, Discovery Seminars, and Undergraduate Academies, UB undergraduates have the opportunity to collaborate with faculty members on groundbreaking research and creative projects. This environment immerses students in the discovery process and encourages them to develop the kind of critical thinking required in the creation of new knowledge. UB's undergraduates have an opportunity to combine elements from several fields of knowledge or to design their own bachelor's degree programs. UB's Honors College enrolls more than 200 freshmen every year with SAT scores ranging from 1300 to 1600 (combined critical reading and math). Graduates of the honors program have won Fulbright, Marshall, Guggenheim, and other distinguished awards.

As a large university with more than 28,000 students, of whom more than 18,000 are undergraduates, the University at Buffalo can sustain a rich and varied student life. UB is home to a culturally diverse student body and ranks among the nation's leaders in international enrollment, with more than 4,000 students from 110 countries. The University has men's and women's sports programs at both the intramural and NCAA Division I levels, extensive recreational and entertainment facilities, more than 200 student organizations, and a busy calendar of general interest lectures, concerts, and films.

UB's North Campus, the seat of most of the undergraduate academic programs, occupies 2 square miles in suburban Amherst. It is one of the most modern university campuses in the nation, with more than 5 million square feet of academic space, laboratories, libraries, residence halls, and recreation facilities. A mathematics building and a state-of-the-art earthquake engineering simulation laboratory were completed in recent years. The University's commitment to adding apartment-style living space has resulted in five apartment complexes on or adjacent to campus, providing attractive living options for more than 1,900 students. Creekside, Flickinger Court, Flint Village, Hadley Village, and South Lake Village apartments have opened during the past decade.

The South Campus, 3 miles away in the residential northeast corner of Buffalo, is largely devoted to the health sciences and architecture. Buffalo's rapid transit line connects that campus with the city center and the waterfront. The South Campus also has residence halls for undergraduates. Many students who live off campus find apartments in the surrounding area.

Recently, UB has expanded its presence in downtown Buffalo. The area is already home to the New York State Center for Excellence in Bioinformatics and Life Sciences, the Ross Eye Institute, and the Jacobs Executive Development Center. The campus will include a range of programs that directly serve and work with the community's residents in the areas of education, information, job training, and health care.

Location

Buffalo is a Great Lakes city on an international border with a metropolitan area population of more than 1 million. It is a city of friendly neighborhoods with big-city recreation for all tastes: professional sports teams, the Buffalo Philharmonic Orchestra, the renowned twentieth-century art collection in the Albright-Knox Art Gallery, and a lively club scene. It also has a dramatic setting on Lake Erie and the Niagara River. Buffalo has abundant outdoor recreation in all four seasons. Skiing, hiking, camping, Lake Erie beaches, and the natural wonder of Niagara Falls are all nearby.

Majors and Degrees

The University is organized into one college and seven schools that serve undergraduates. The College of Arts and Sciences offers academic majors in African American studies, American studies, anthropology, art, art history, Asian studies, bioinformatics and computational biology, biological sciences, chemistry, classics, communication, computational physics, dance, economics, English, film studies, fine arts, geography, geological sciences, global gender studies, history, informatics, linguistics, mathematical physics, mathematics, mathematics-economics, media study, medicinal chemistry, modern languages and literatures (French, German, Italian, and Spanish), music, music performance, music theater, philosophy, physics, political science, psychology, sociology, speech and hearing science, studio art, and theater. An interdisciplinary degree program in the social sciences, with concentrations in cognitive science, environmental studies, health and human services, international studies, legal studies, and urban and public policy studies, is also offered. The School of Architecture and Planning offers majors in architecture and environmental design. The School of Engineering and Applied Sciences offers academic majors in computer science and engineering physics and in aerospace, chemical, civil, computer, electrical, environmental, industrial, and mechanical engineering. The School of Management offers a major in business administration, with concentrations in accounting, financial analysis, human resources management, internal auditing, international business, management information systems, and marketing. The School of Medicine and Biomedical Sciences offers academic majors in biochemistry, biomedical sciences, biophysics, biotechnology, medical technology, nuclear medicine technology, and pharmacology and toxicology,. The School of Nursing offers an academic major in nursing. The School of Pharmacy and Pharmaceutical Sciences offers academic majors in pharmaceutical sciences and a six-year Pharm.D. pharmacy program. The School of Public Health and Health Professions offers academic majors in exercise science and occupational therapy. Physical therapy is offered as a six-year doctorate; undergraduates major in exercise science. The University has approximately thirty combined-degree programs (B.A./M.A. and B.S./M.B.A., for example) that can be completed in five years. Students whose objectives cannot be met through existing programs can formulate their own degree programs through double-degree or double-, joint-, or special-major options and an extensive minors program.

Academic Programs

Candidates for a baccalaureate degree are required to complete a minimum of 120 semester hours, 30 of which must be completed in residence, and earn a minimum grade point average of 2.0. Students have great flexibility in planning their academic programs. All students must fulfill a University general education requirement. They must also complete an academic major, which is selected, with the advice of an academic adviser, usually by the end of the sophomore year. Students also have ample opportunity for independent study under departmental or faculty auspices. Placement and credit are granted on the basis of Advanced Placement or College-Level Examination Program scores. The academic year has two semesters, one beginning in late August, and the other in mid-January. An extensive summer session is also offered.

Off-Campus Programs

Full-time undergraduates may cross-register for a maximum of two courses per term at other colleges in Western New York. Many students take advantage of study-abroad programs. The University administers overseas programs in thirty countries for full academic years or fall, spring, or summer sessions. Students who wish to study abroad in locations not offered by the University may take advantage of nearly 300 programs offered by other colleges in the SUNY system.

Academic Facilities

The University at Buffalo's academic library collections are the largest in the SUNY system; in addition to more than 3.6 million bound volumes, they include more than 30,000 serials and periodicals, 5.4 million microforms, specialized holdings including the world's largest collection of James Joyce manuscripts, and a renowned collection of twentieth-century poetry in manuscript. All library holdings are digitally cataloged and accessible from terminals and computers on and off campus. The University is among the first to have software that makes the entire SUNY library system—more than 18 million volumes—available to students. State-of-the-art computer workstations for student use are located at public sites in the University's libraries.

Costs

In 2007–08, tuition for New York State residents was $4350 and for out-of-state residents, $10,610. For all students, fees were $1867, and room and board costs were $9132. Students should expect additional expenses for books and supplies, transportation, and personal expenses. Costs are subject to change.

Financial Aid

The University participates in all New York State and federal financial aid programs, including the Tuition Assistance Program (available only to New York State residents) and the Federal Pell Grant, Federal Work-Study, Federal Direct Student Loan, and Federal Perkins Loan programs. The recommended deadline for completing the Free Application for Federal Student Aid is February 1 for fall semester entry. All inquiries concerning financial aid should be addressed to the Student Response Center, 232 Capen Hall (telephone: 866-838-7257 (toll-free)). The University awards more merit-based scholarships than any other public university in New York State. In fall 2007, UB awarded more than $4 million in merit scholarship support to incoming freshmen. UB's top incoming freshmen receive the Presidential Scholarship, which covers the full cost of attendance, for all four years, and are invited to join the Honors College. Provost Scholarships range from $2500 to the full cost of tuition, depending on academic achievement, talent in the creative or performing arts, and the cost of attendance. The Daniel Acker Scholarship is for talented students who are traditionally underrepresented in higher education. Acker Scholars receive full tuition aid and participate in a comprehensive program of support services and activities. Athletic grants-in-aid are awarded to students recruited to participate in the University's NCAA Division I athletics program.

Faculty

The University's nationally renowned faculty includes winners of the National Medal of Science, the Nobel Prize, the Pulitzer Prize, and other awards. Of the 1,901 faculty members, 97 percent hold the doctorate or other terminal degree. A large number have published books or scholarly articles. Many have held major national or international fellowships; conducted research funded by government agencies or national foundations; served as consultants to business, education, and government; or otherwise demonstrated professional expertise. More than 100 have won the SUNY Chancellor's Award for Excellence in Teaching, the largest number of recipients on any SUNY campus.

Student Government

All daytime undergraduate students are members of the Student Association and are entitled to participate in its activities. The Student Association is involved at every level of student life, from freshman orientation to commencement. By their membership on many University-wide policy committees, representatives of the association are given a legitimate, permanent voice in the policies and direction of the University.

Admission Requirements

Applicants are required to submit their high school record; the results of the ACT or SAT critical reading and math sections; a Part II Supplemental Application, which includes an essay; and at least one recommendation from a high school counselor or teacher. Applicants should plan to take the SAT or ACT no later than November. Application review and notification begins in early February and continues until the freshman class is filled. Most freshmen admitted to the University make application to the major of their choice during the sophomore year. However, architecture, business administration, engineering and applied sciences, exercise science, nuclear medicine technology, nursing, and occupational therapy may offer departmental admission to freshman applicants.

Admission to programs in dance, music, music theater, and theater requires an audition.

Admission is competitive. Most successful students at the University have come with a strong level of academic preparation in basic academic areas. Among accepted freshmen in fall 2007, the mean high school average was 92 percent, 87 percent were in the top third of their high school class, and 81 percent scored at or above 1100 on the SAT (critical reading and math).

The University enrolls and provides specialized advisement and support to a limited number of freshmen who demonstrate academic potential through means other than quantitative measures. Creative talent, athletics, special academic achievement, demonstrated leadership, community service, and personal circumstances are examples of areas that the University may consider. These non-academic factors must be documented by submission of the supplemental application, which includes an essay section.

Transfer applicants must have completed a minimum of 12 semester hours at a regionally accredited college prior to application. Students with fewer than 24 semester hours are evaluated on the basis of their college and high school credentials in combination with standardized test score results. Admission of transfer students is based on the quality of previous academic performance and space availability. In order to receive consideration for transfer admission to SUNY at Buffalo, it is recommended that students present a strong record of college study, earning a minimum cumulative grade point average of 2.5 on a 4.0 scale. It should be noted, however, that requirements may vary depending on the academic program.

Admission to an academic department may occur concurrently with University admission if the applicant has fulfilled prerequisite requirements. These requirements include completed courses, but may also comprise essay, portfolio, exam, or audition requirements. Some departments have significantly higher GPA standards and early deadlines for application.

Application and Information

Students can apply online at http://www.suny.edu/student/apply_online.cfm or http://www.commonapp.org. Or they can visit http://www.admissions.buffalo.edu/apply for more information on applying to UB. Paper applications are available by contacting:

Office of Admissions
12 Capen Hall
University at Buffalo, the State University of New York
Buffalo, New York 14260-1660
Phone: 716-645-6900
888-UB-ADMIT (toll-free)
E-mail: ub-admissions@buffalo.edu
Web site: http://www.admissions.buffalo.edu

UNIVERSITY OF ADVANCING TECHNOLOGY

TEMPE, ARIZONA

The University

The University of Advancing Technology (UAT) is a unique, technology-infused private college founded by a techno-geek for techno-geeks. Its mission is to educate students in the fields of advancing technology to become innovators of the future. UAT's campus culture is devoted to continually nurturing a thriving geek community where everyone's personal lives and professional aspirations revolve around technology. UAT offers students a well-rounded education in a nontraditional setting. Students who are seeking a strictly career-oriented technical college experience will not find it here. Because of UAT's dedication to both scholastic excellence and technological innovation, it stands apart in academia as an ideal destination for the geeks of the world who feel disenfranchised by conventional institutions of higher learning. For the student who is looking at the future of technology and wishes to become a vital part of it, UAT beckons.

The beginning of the twenty-first century is an exciting time to be in the technology community, and UAT is serious about technology. As the twenty-first century unfolds, it is becoming more and more apparent how technology in all its manifestations profoundly alters how people work, live, play, and interact with each other. UAT students benefit from their fundamental understanding of both theoretical and applied aspects of technology. As technologists, UAT students see that there will always be newer and newer tools created to address mankind's emergent needs and desires. Changing the world through technology is inherent in UAT's mission. Current subjects of ongoing research and scholarship at UAT include robotics and embedded systems, artificial life programming, network security, game development, and other areas of advanced technology.

UAT has always devoted all of its resources to creating a vital academic environment where students are challenged to achieve, explore new and traditional concepts, and practice what they learn in real-world situations. This combination of research, scholarship, and application creates technically adept graduates who are equally at home in academia and the working world and valued by both. UAT graduates thrive in the digital age and meet and surpass every expectation of their high-technology employers and peers. They enter the professional world with accredited associate and bachelor's degrees, and many return to pursue a master's degree in the Graduate College of Applied Technology.

When the University of Advancing Technology was founded in 1983 (as the CAD Institute), it was conceived as a small school for training engineers and architects in the completely new field of computer-aided engineering. Its original students came to the CAD Institute seeking professional development training and certifications. From this beginning as a technical school, the institution became involved with advances in computer graphics and unique approaches to technology education. In 1998, the school moved to the new campus in Tempe, which was designed in accordance with Feng Shui principles. In 2002, the school changed its name to University of Advancing Technology to reflect its current broad technology focus.

UAT's 1,200 students (from all fifty states and many other countries) still find plenty of time to time to participate in clubs and other activities that enhance UAT's geek-friendly environment, such as ancient games, anime, technology philosophy, Yu-Gi-Oh, game developers, Web development, biking, C++, and photography. Special on-campus events include live-action games, Oktoberfest, LAN parties, Guitar Hero tournaments, and Thanksgiving dinner.

At any time, day or night, there are groups of students pounding coffee while working on course work and projects, looking to create the next big thing. It is not uncommon to see students burning the midnight oil, pulling all-nighters, exchanging ideas, and searching for solutions to perfect their creative innovations. There are students on their own laptops and PDAs, interacting and creating. There are also gatherings of students and instructors engaged in discussions of the latest technology developments and how they can make them better. UAT has an academic and social environment that integrates the contemporary and advancing principles of education and technology with its Year-Round Balanced Learning (YRBL) teaching model to create a unique collaborative educational environment.

Location

Located in sunny Tempe, Arizona, near the heart of downtown Phoenix, a booming urban center in the Sonoran desert, the University of Advancing Technology is 4 hours from Mexico and 2 hours from snowboarding. The campus is accessible from all parts of the Phoenix metropolitan region by public transportation, bicycle, or automobile. Students live on campus in Founder's Hall, the resident student complex, or off campus in nearby neighborhoods. The University is close to major freeways, bus lines, and Sky Harbor Airport, which is a major international airport that serves the entire Phoenix metropolitan area. Other local amenities include shopping, arts districts, and other attractions associated with a dynamic urban center.

Arizona is a land of incredible beauty, contrast, and opportunity. Tempe is located in the "Valley of the Sun", which is surrounded by beautiful mountain ranges. Within a short drive are attractions like the Grand Canyon (4½ hours), a variety of lakes and rivers (30–90 minutes), the red rocks of Sedona (2 hours), and the exquisite Sonoran Desert, just outside of town. UAT is close to every desert sport imaginable—golf, mountain biking, hiking, swimming, rollerblading, and skateboarding.

Majors and Degrees

UAT offers Bachelor of Arts, Bachelor of Science, Associate of Arts, and Associate of Science degrees in several advancing technology disciplines, including artificial life programming, advancing computer science, virtual modeling and design, game art and animation, game design, game programming, network security, and robotics and embedded systems.

Academic Programs

The Bachelor of Arts and Bachelor of Science programs require a minimum of 120 semester credits, including 84 core credits, forty 300/400–level credits, and 36 general education credits. The Associate of Arts and Associate of Science programs require a minimum of 60 semester credits: 45 core credits, and 15 general education credits.

Academic Facilities

The University is open 24/7. In just about every corner of campus, there are hundreds of computers, including Macs and state-of-the-art video game consoles. Students at UAT are immersed in a world of technology. From the miles of cables and walls of servers in the open-viewed server rooms to the vast array of industry technology in the NT lab, students who love technology feel right at home.

As an institution, UAT is dedicated to planning, implementing, and sharing its research with others in technology and academia. The UAT research centers operate within the University to further knowledge creation, foster institutional and community awareness, and improve initiatives in their focal areas. In addition, each research center publishes works to the broader community through a variety of channels (technology journals, online journals, and conference papers. In 1992, the University founded its first research center, the Computer Reality Center. It performed research primarily for the computer graphics industry, with specific emphasis on the field of virtual reality. The center adopted the Hyperlearning model and developed UAT's current teaching model, Year-Round Balanced Learning. YRBL combines lecture, tutorial teaching, group recollection, student teachback, and discovery learning. Year-round classes are available both on the campus and online, and students produce projects for a graduation portfolio to demonstrate an understanding of what they are learning.

Through research of learning and teaching methodologies, the Center for Learning Excellence develops and supports educational models that enable the University to build innovative and balanced learning experiences. Its main goal is to apply its research toward developing the UAT Faculty Certification Program. This program ensures baseline effective teaching preparation within UAT's learning model for all faculty members before they are assigned to the classroom. The center routinely assesses instruction at UAT in relation to student learning outcomes.

The Center for Institutional Research is the center for ongoing institutional research that accumulates, generates, maintains, communicates, and disseminates institutional information to support assessment and general awareness of student learning. The center also evaluates and reviews the efficacy of institutional policies.

The Center for Technology Studies conducts original research and produces works published in the broader community and furthers community understanding of technology disciplines, their applications, and their relevance in the global society. Within the center is the Center for Information Assurance, which produces knowledge solely within the information assurance disciplines at UAT: computer forensics and network security at the undergraduate level and information security at the graduate level.

Whenever and wherever possible, the campus and technology resources are open to allow students and professionals alike to participate collaboratively in this endeavor, whether as team members on a student project, speaking at Technology Forum, or submitting work to the University's *Journal of Advancing Technology*.

Costs

Undergraduate tuition for 2008–09 was $8400 per semester. Tuition for UAT-Online students was $4900 per semester. Housing costs were about $6615 per year.

Financial Aid

Average aid per academic year for first-academic-year freshmen is $11,784. The percentage of freshmen who receive aid is 84 percent. The percentage of freshmen who receive UAT academic scholarships is 26 percent. The average amount of scholarships received per freshman student per academic year is $1200.

Faculty

UAT's faculty comprises members who are thinkers, teachers, technological gurus, industry experts, and student mentors. They garner their skills, knowledge, and expertise from a range of experiences—from the classrooms of academe to the boardrooms of industry, from community meeting halls to international conferences. They are a group governed by their passion for technology, their students, and their own academic and professional growth. Sixty-four faculty members, distinguished by their academic abilities and accomplishments within their respective fields, serve as both instructors and mentors.

Student Government

The University-sanctioned student government was formed to give the student body at UAT a collective voice and set traditions within the University. University Student Government (USG) performs important roles in encouraging self-directed Student Life organizations, coordinating student community service activities, and providing a venue for feedback between students and staff members. Students are encouraged to participate in the Student Government, which holds monthly open meetings.

Admission Requirements

The University of Advancing Technology strives to admit undergraduate students who embody its passion for technology, are a cultural match to the University, demonstrate adequate academic achievement, and have a dedication to lifelong learning. All undergraduate applicants are evaluated based on these criteria: academic history and achievements; personal expression; desire to attend UAT; how they might fit with UAT's geek-friendly culture, passion, and aptitude for technology; and the supportiveness of the applicant's network of family, friends, and peers to achieve their educational goals (for UAT-Online applicants, employer support is also evaluated). All applicants are encouraged to submit high school transcripts, ACT and/or SAT scores, Advanced Placement scores, and college transcripts, so UAT's Admissions Office may thoroughly review the applicant's academic history.

In addition to the standard admission requirements, non-U.S. citizens applying for admission to the University of Advancing Technology must provide proof of English proficiency in one of the following ways: Test of English as a Foreign Language (TOEFL) with a score of 550 or higher on the paper-based test, 79 or higher on the Internet-based test, or 213 or higher on the computer-based test; successful completion of Level 108 from an ELS Center; ASPECT English Language Proficiency Level 5; or attendance for one year at a regionally accredited U.S. college or university and completion of English 101 (or equivalent) with grade C or better. Proof of English proficiency is not required if English is the applicant's native language. Official transcripts must be submitted with an English translation and be evaluated as a U.S. high school equivalent by Educational Credential Evaluators, Inc., P.O. Box 17499, Milwaukee, Wisconsin 53217-0499, U.S.A. (http://www.ece.org).

Application and Information

UAT has an admissions application that helps both the student and the admissions staff determine if the applicant and UAT are a good match. Students should complete and submit the application to the UAT Admissions Office prior to consideration. Students may apply online at http://www.uat.edu/admissions. To request an application, students should either e-mail admissions@uat.edu or call 877-UAT-GEEK (toll-free).

UAT Admissions
University of Advancing Technology
2625 West Baseline Road
Tempe, Arizona 85283-1056
Phone: 602-383-8228
800-658-5744 (toll-free)
E-mail: admission@uat.edu
Web site: http://www.uat.edu

THE UNIVERSITY OF ALABAMA AT BIRMINGHAM

UAB

BIRMINGHAM, ALABAMA

The University

The University of Alabama at Birmingham (UAB) is a fully accredited research university and academic health center with an annual enrollment of more than 16,000 students. In a short time, UAB has established outstanding programs through six liberal arts and professional schools, six health professional schools, and graduate programs serving all major units. As the University has grown, so have its contributions to the state, the nation, and the world. UAB is committed to education, research, and service programs of excellent quality and far-reaching scope. In terms of federal research and development funding, UAB ranks twenty-sixth nationally and first in the state of Alabama, receiving more funding than all Alabama universities combined. In such an environment, undergraduate students can pursue a wide array of research opportunities and gain valuable experience that pays off later in graduate studies or career development.

Part of the UAB experience is student life, consisting of a rich mix of academic organizations, honor clubs, social fraternities and sororities, volunteer groups, and activities ranging from intramural sports and SGA (Student Government Association) to supporting Blazer sports as a member of the "Gang-Green" spirit group. With more than 150 campus organizations to keep students involved, UAB offers the chance to make lifelong friendships while assisting in the development of skills essential to leadership and teamwork. The South is the place for sports year-round, and UAB is no exception. The athletic program is a Division I member of the NCAA and a founding member of Conference USA. UAB has seventeen intercollegiate teams, including men's and women's basketball, golf, rifle, soccer, and tennis; men's baseball and football; and women's cross-country, track, softball, synchronized swimming, and volleyball. Students enjoy a new Campus Recreation Center offering free weights, court sports, swimming pools/lazy river, fitness classes, nutrition education, fitness areas, a climbing wall, and a juice bar, as well as a new state-of-the-art "Commons on the Green" dining facility.

Location

Birmingham earned the name "The Magic City" during its first boom days. The expression still rings true as the metropolitan area continues to mirror UAB's phenomenal growth and reflects the many cultural opportunities available within the city. Birmingham is easily reached from major national routes (Interstates 20, 59, and 65), and UAB is only minutes away from the Birmingham International Airport.

Majors and Degrees

UAB's degree programs offer strong career preparation. With fifty majors from which to choose, UAB's broad curriculum allows students to explore new interests while receiving specialized training. Students may also integrate different areas of knowledge by choosing a minor in an additional field of study or by exploring the possibilities for developing an individually designed major.

The School of Arts and Humanities offers the Bachelor of Arts degree in African-American studies, art (concentrations in art education, art history, ceramic sculpture, drawing, graphic design, painting, photography, printmaking, and sculpture), communication studies (concentrations in broadcasting, communication arts, journalism, mass communication, and public relations), English (concentration in creative writing), foreign languages (tracks in French and Spanish), music (concentration in music education and music technology), philosophy, and theater.

The School of Business offers the Bachelor of Science degree in accounting (concentrations in forensic accounting and information technology auditing), economics (concentrations in economic analysis and policy and quantitative methods), finance (concentrations in financial investments and institutions and financial management), industrial distribution (concentrations in e-business engineering and medical equipment and supplies marketing), information systems, management (concentrations in general management, human resource management, management information systems, and operations management), and marketing.

The School of Education offers the Bachelor of Science degree in early childhood education, elementary education, health education, high school education, physical education, and special education.

The School of Engineering offers the Bachelor of Science degree in biomedical engineering, civil engineering, electrical engineering, materials engineering, and mechanical engineering.

The School of Health Related Professions offers the Bachelor of Science degree in cytotechnology, health information management, health sciences, medical technology, nuclear medicine technology, and respiratory therapy.

The School of Natural Sciences and Mathematics offers the Bachelor of Science degree in biology, chemistry, computer and information sciences, mathematics (concentrations in applied math and scientific computation), natural science, and physics.

The School of Nursing awards the Bachelor of Science degree. Students interested in pursuing the nursing degree and who meet the University's admission requirements are admitted to UAB as prenursing students. To be eligible for admission in good standing to the School of Nursing, students must successfully complete a prescribed set of courses with an acceptable grade point average.

The School of Social and Behavioral Sciences offers the Bachelor of Arts degree in anthropology, economics, history, international studies, political science, and sociology and the Bachelor of Science degree in criminal justice, neuroscience, psychology, and social work.

Academic Programs

UAB's undergraduate instructional programs are broad based and designed to serve the needs of its diverse student body while providing a strong general education foundation. All programs of study leading to the baccalaureate degree have as an essential component a common core curriculum. The minimum total credit hours required for a baccalaureate degree is 120 semester hours with a cumulative grade point average of at least 2.0 (C) in all credit hours attempted. A student may obtain a certain number of semester hours of academic credit for knowledge acquired independently through Advanced

Placement (AP), International Baccalaureate (I.B.), College-Level Examination Program (CLEP), Credit by Examination (CBE), evaluation of noncollegiate-sponsored courses, armed services courses, and prior learning.

The UAB Honors Academy offers rare and valuable opportunities to explore knowledge from new angles, enriching the overall educational experience for future success. The University Honors Program concentrates on the vast resources of a major research university in a small, liberal arts setting; the Science and Technology Honors Program offers students interested in a science or technology career the opportunity to work closely with world-renowned researchers; the Global and Community Leadership Honors Program draws from a community-based and cross-cultural perspective that prepares students for leadership roles on community and worldwide levels; and qualified students interested in a career in medicine, optometry, or dentistry may be accepted to professional school at UAB before they begin college through the Early Admission to Medical Professional Schools Program.

There are two academic semesters and a summer term during a calendar year. The fall and spring semesters each consist of approximately sixteen weeks of classes. Summer term offers several options, including twelve-week, nine-week, three-week, and 4½-week terms.

Academic Facilities

The UAB campus occupies more than 100 major buildings, more than 11 million gross square feet, and almost 90 square blocks near downtown Birmingham. The undergraduate area of campus is concentrated within an eight-square-block area, however, giving students the convenience and togetherness that is so important to the college experience.

The Mervyn H. Sterne Library houses a collection of more than 1.5 million items selected to support teaching and research at UAB. In addition, the collection consists of microforms and other print and nonprint materials. The Lister Hill Library of the Health Sciences is also available and provides a comprehensive collection of materials for medical study and research. Between the two, there are 26,000 periodicals available either in print or online.

UAB is the home of the Alys Robinson Stephens Performing Arts Center, with state-of-the-art concert halls and practice facilities. This beautiful facility draws national and international performers, enhancing the strong cultural opportunities in Birmingham.

A new 95,000-square-foot academic building, Heritage Hall, opened in January 2008. The new facility houses the School of Social and Behavioral Sciences, providing additional classroom space as well as a 200-station computer mathematics laboratory.

Costs

For the 2009–10 academic year, tuition was $176 per semester hour for in-state students and $440 per semester hour for out-of-state students. Based on a full (12 hours per semester) load of course work for the academic year, tuition and fees for Alabama residents are estimated at $5144 and $11,480 for nonresidents. A typical amount for books and supplies total approximately $900 per academic year. On-campus housing for freshmen is $4600 for the academic year.

Financial Aid

UAB's financial aid package consists of loans, employment, and grants and scholarships, enabling students from all economic backgrounds to attend UAB. Financial aid applications are available in early January for the following academic year, with a priority packaging deadline of April 1.

UAB awards over 1,500 scholarships each year. Students admitted by November 1 are automatically considered for all academic scholarships for which they are qualified. Awards are distributed on a first-come, first-served basis, so students are encouraged to apply and be admitted to the University as early as possible. Students admitted after November 1 will be considered for scholarships on a funds-available basis.

Faculty

UAB has 2,049 full-time faculty members, with more than 90 percent holding doctoral degrees. The student-faculty ratio is 18:1, with the vast majority of freshman- and sophomore-level courses taught by full-time faculty members.

Student Government

In addition to eight student government associations, the Office of Student Life offers many student-run committees and programs that are open to all students. These committees provide entertainment through comedy, music, movies, lectures, and multicultural programming. Other opportunities to lead and serve include social fraternities and sororities, a student leadership program, an ambassador program, a volunteer program, a scholarship pageant, and three award-winning student publications.

Admission Requirements

UAB is an equal educational opportunity institution. The requirements for regular admission for entering freshmen include a minimum high school GPA of 2.25 on a 4.0 scale, a minimum ACT score of 20 or SAT score of 950, and completion of a precollege curriculum (4 years of English, 3 years of math (algebra I and higher), 3 years of social sciences, 3 years of science (2 with lab components), 1 year of foreign language, and 2 additional core courses to total 17). For tentative action, a transcript may be sent during the student's senior year in high school. A final transcript must be sent upon graduation.

Transfer students must have a minimum cumulative GPA of 2.0 on a 4.0 scale after completing 24 semester hours (or 36 quarter hours) of college-level work. Students with previous college work must submit an official transcript from each institution attended and must be eligible to enroll at the last institution attended. UAB also encourages international students who have academic, linguistic, and financial capabilities to apply for admission.

Application and Information

All students who wish to attend UAB must complete an application for admission and submit proof of immunization against measles. An application may be submitted as early as one year prior to admission. A completed application, a nonrefundable $35 application fee ($30 for online applications), and all supporting documentation must be received by the Office of Undergraduate Admission by the priority deadline for the term for which admission is requested. The application priority deadline for fall term is March 1. For an application and further information, students should contact:

UAB Undergraduate Admission
Hill University Center, Room 260
1530 3rd Avenue, South
Birmingham, Alabama 35294-1150
Phone: 205-934-8221
800-421-8473 (toll-free)
E-mail: undergradadmit@uab.edu
Internet: http://www.uab.edu/apply

THE UNIVERSITY OF ALABAMA IN HUNTSVILLE

UAHuntsville
THE UNIVERSITY OF ALABAMA IN HUNTSVILLE

HUNTSVILLE, ALABAMA

The University

The University of Alabama in Huntsville (UAHuntsville) is a public, four-year, coeducational national research university and is a member of the University of Alabama System. UAHuntsville was founded in 1950 as an extension center of the University of Alabama and became an autonomous campus in 1969. UAHuntsville has earned national recognition in engineering and the sciences, and its programs in the humanities, fine arts, social sciences, business, and nursing are outstanding. Students interact with some of the most productive researchers in their respective disciplines. Close ties with business, industry, and government give students real-world opportunities and experience. UAHuntsville partners with more than 100 high-tech industries as well as major federal laboratories such as NASA's Marshall Space Flight Center, the National Space Science and Technology Center, and the U.S. Army's Redstone Arsenal. Its unique location provides many unparalleled career development opportunities for students to earn a significant portion of their college costs and maximize their employment potential. Students have unusual opportunities to work with some of the top scientists in the country. UAHuntsville is accredited by the Southern Association of Colleges and Schools' Commission on Colleges. UAHuntsville also holds professional accreditation from the American Chemical Society; the Computing Sciences Accreditation Board; the Accreditation Board for Engineering and Technology, Inc.; the Commission on Collegiate Nursing Education; the National Association of Schools of Art and Design; the National Association of Schools of Music; the National Council for Accreditation of Teacher Education; the Accreditation Council for Cooperative Education; and AACSB International–The Association to Advance Collegiate Schools of Business.

The fall 2009 enrollment consisted of 5,893 undergraduate and 1,538 graduate students. Eighty-six percent are from Alabama, 6 percent are from other countries, 52 percent are men, and 48 percent are women. UAHuntsville students represent more than forty-five states and eighty-six countries. Of the total undergraduate enrollment, 21 percent are members of ethnic minority groups. 50 percent of the entering freshman class had ACT scores between 23 and 28; the median GPA was 3.4.

Postbaccalaureate certificates are available in accounting, environmental science, human resource management, nursing education, software engineering, teaching of English to speakers of other languages, and technical communications for individuals. Through the School of Graduate Studies, students may earn the master's degree in accounting, aerospace engineering, atmospheric science, biological science, chemical engineering, chemistry, civil engineering, computer engineering, computer science, electrical engineering, English, history, industrial and systems engineering, management, management information systems, materials science, mathematics, mechanical engineering, nursing, operations research, physics, psychology, public affairs, and software engineering. The Master of Business Administration (M.B.A.) is also offered. The Ph.D. degree is awarded in applied mathematics, atmospheric science, biotechnology, civil engineering, computer engineering, computer science, electrical engineering, industrial and systems engineering, materials science, mechanical engineering, optical science and engineering, and physics.

UAHuntsville has more than 65 active student groups and organizations, including national fraternities and sororities, honor societies, special interest groups, religious organizations, the Student Government Association (SGA), the student-run newspaper, the student-run literary magazine, minority student organizations, international student organizations, the choir, the chorus, a film and lecture series, service organizations, professional interest groups, and intramural athletics. The University is a member of the NCAA Division II and the Gulf South Conference and competes in the following intercollegiate sports: men's baseball, basketball, cross-country, soccer, tennis, and track and field and women's basketball, cross-country, soccer, softball, tennis, track and field, and volleyball. UAHuntsville also competes at the NCAA Division I level in men's ice hockey.

On-campus housing is available for undergraduate and graduate students and consists of three traditional residence halls and one apartment-style complex, with a fourth residence hall under construction, with opening set for fall 2010. The Central Campus Residence Hall, a seven-story residence hall, is the designated freshmen housing facility that offers private bedrooms, kitchen-living room combos, and semiprivate baths. This hall is located in the center of campus and is connected to the University Center by an enclosed walkway. The University Center offers most student services and houses the Charger Café. The Frank Franz Residence Hall, assigned to freshmen, opened in 2002, and North Campus Residence Hall, assigned to athletes and upperclassmen, opened in 2005. Both offer private bedrooms and semiprivate baths.

In fall 2010 a new residence hall facility will open for current sophomores and upperclassmen. It will be attached to both a dining hall and an auditorium. Student apartments in Southeast Housing are reserved for upperclassmen and graduate students. Private apartments are available for married students and students with children. Handicapped-accessible apartments are available. In addition, five on-campus fraternity and sorority houses with private bedrooms opened in 2006. Each fraternity and sorority house serves 50 students. Starting in fall 2010, all UAHuntsville freshmen will be required to live on campus for both their freshmen and sophomore years.

Location

The University of Alabama in Huntsville is located in the Tennessee River Valley of north-central Alabama, 100 miles north of Birmingham and 100 miles south of Nashville, Tennessee. Huntsville is the home of more than fifty Fortune 500 companies that specialize in high technology, including aerospace engineering, rocket propulsion, computer technology, weapons systems, telecommunications, software engineering, information systems design, and engineering services. Most of these companies, as well as the UAHuntsville campus, are located in Cummings Research Park, one of the top ten research parks in the world and the second-largest research park in the United States.

Majors and Degrees

The Colleges of Business Administration, Engineering, Liberal Arts, Nursing, and Science and the School of Graduate Studies administer the degree programs of the University. The College of Business Administration awards the Bachelor of Science in Business Administration (B.S.B.A.) degree in the fields of accounting, finance, management, management information systems, and marketing. The College of Engineering awards the Bachelor of Science in Engineering (B.S.E.) degree in chemical, civil, computer, electrical, industrial and systems, mechanical and aerospace, and optical engineering. The College of Nursing awards the Bachelor of Science in Nursing (B.S.N.) degree. The Bachelor of Arts (B.A.) degree is awarded by the College of Liberal Arts in the fields of art, communication arts, education, English, foreign languages (French, German, Russian, Spanish), foreign languages/international trade, history, music, philosophy, political science, psychology, and sociology. In the College of Science, the Bachelor of Science (B.S.) degree is available in biological science, chemistry, computer science, Earth systems science, mathematics, and physics. A Bachelor of Arts degree is available in biological science and mathematics.

Undergraduate teacher certification programs are offered in collaborative teaching endorsement (K–6 or 6–12), elementary education (K–6), middle school (4–8), music education (P–12), or secondary/high school education (6–12), with majors in biology, chemistry, English, language arts, foreign language (French, German, Russian, and Spanish), general science, history, mathematics, physics, social science, and sociology.

Academic Programs

The general education course work is designed to broaden intellectual awareness and enhance cultural literacy and analytical thinking. All undergraduates are required to complete course work in English composition, humanities and fine arts, history, social and behavioral sciences, natural and physical sciences, and mathematics. B.A., B.S., B.S.B.A., and B.S.N. degrees require the completion of at least 128 total semester hours; B.S.E. degrees in computer, electrical, and optical engineering require 128; B.S.E. degrees in industrial and systems engineering, 130; B.S.E in chemical engineering, 131; and B.S.E. in mechanical, mechanical with aerospace, and civil engineering, 132. A variety of special academic programs and options are available, including cooperative education, cross-registration with other institutions, distance learning, double majors, dual enrollment, intensive English program, honors program, independent study, internships, and learning disabilities services. Credit is awarded for appropriate scores on CLEP and AP examinations. UAHuntsville offers Army ROTC jointly at a participating institution off campus. Special services are available for students with disabilities, including note-taking, readers, tape recorders, tutors, interpreters for the hearing impaired, special transportation, special housing, adaptive equipment, and Braille services. The fall 2010 semester begins August 18 and ends December 9; spring semester 2010 begins January 11 and ends May 5. Two summer sessions are offered beginning May 24 and June 28, 2010.

Academic Facilities

The 400-acre campus is in northwest Huntsville. All academic buildings have been constructed since 1960 and exemplify modern functional design. The UAHuntsville library houses a collection of more than 336,000 print volumes, a selective collection of over 500,000 U.S. government publications, more than 600,000 materials in microform and manuscript collections, approximately 52,000 electronic periodicals, more than 58,000 electronic books, and over 350 databases. The UAHuntsville Art Gallery hosts art exhibits by local, regional, and national artists as well as by students and faculty members. More than 1,100 personal computers are available across the campus for student use. Computer labs, one of which is open 24 hours a day, are located in several buildings and staffed to provide assistance. Access to the University fiber-optic network is available in all buildings, including all residence halls as well as wireless Internet in several buildings. Internet access and e-mail are available to all students. UAHuntsville has a number of state-of-the-art research labs accessible to undergraduates.

Costs

In 2009–10, tuition for undergraduate Alabama residents was $6150 (15 credits each semester) for the academic year. Out-of-state students paid $15,628 (15 credits each semester) for the academic year. Undergraduates can expect to spend approximately $1200 on books and supplies for the academic year. Undergraduate students pay an estimated $4600 for housing and $2124 for a meal plan.

Financial Aid

UAHuntsville awards nearly $32 million annually in need-based and non-need-based financial aid in the form of scholarships, grants, loans, and campus jobs. Financial aid programs available include veterans' educational benefits, Federal Work Study, Federal Stafford Student Loans (subsidized and unsubsidized), Federal PLUS Loans, Consolidation Loans, Federal Pell Grants, Federal SMART Grants, Academic Competitiveness Grants, Federal Supplemental Educational Opportunity Grants (FSEOG), state scholarships and grants, private scholarships, and institutional scholarships. Non-need-based scholarships are available for athletics, ROTC, academic merit, creative and performing arts, special achievement, leadership skills, and minority status. Students should submit the Free Application for Federal Student Aid (FAFSA) before April 1 for priority consideration and no later than the final closing date of July 31. Award notifications are made on a rolling basis. The priority date for scholarship application is December 1.

Faculty

Of the 289 full-time instructional faculty members, 91 percent hold the Ph.D. or other terminal degree in their field. The student-faculty ratio is 16:1. Graduate students teach less than 5 percent of introductory undergraduate courses. The average class size is 25.

Student Government

The primary purpose of the Student Government Association is to improve the educational environment and promote the welfare of students in all areas of University life. The SGA is responsible for developing and sponsoring programs that enrich the students' cultural, intellectual, and social life. An executive branch, a 15-member legislature, and a 5-member arbitration board are responsible for carrying out the official business of the organization. The SGA sponsors more than 65 clubs and organizations in addition to providing many student services, such as health insurance, special rates for community cultural events, and a student directory.

Admission Requirements

High school graduates may be admitted as regular freshmen based on acceptable high school achievement and standardized test scores (SAT or ACT), which are considered together. A higher result in one area offsets a lower performance in the other. For example, a minimum high school GPA of 2.5 is required if the ACT composite score is 23 or the combined SAT score is 1060. A high school GPA of 2.0 requires an ACT composite score of 25 or higher or a combined SAT score of 1140 or higher. Applicants should present a minimum of 20 Carnegie high school units, including 4 of English; 4 of social studies and history; 3 of mathematics, including 1 of algebra, 1 of geometry, and 1 of algebra II/trigonometry (recommended by all Colleges); 3 of science, including 1 of biology (recommended), 1 of chemistry or physics (recommended by all Colleges), and sufficient academic electives to meet the required 20 units. First-time freshmen and transfer students are admitted every academic term. Transfer students with fewer than 24 hours of earned college credit are admitted based on high school transcripts, test scores, and college course work. Transfer students are required to submit transcripts of all university work and have at least a 2.0 average on all work attempted to qualify for regular admission.

Application and Information

Completed applications and a nonrefundable $30 application fee must be received no later than August 1 for priority admission in the fall semester and by December 15 for priority admission in the spring semester. Admission notifications are sent on a rolling basis. Online applications are encouraged and can be accessed at http://apply.uah.edu. For a paper application form and more information, students should contact:

Office of Admissions
The University of Alabama in Huntsville
301 Sparkman Drive
Huntsville, Alabama 35899
Phone: 256-824-2773
800-UAH-CALL (toll-free)
Fax: 256-824-6073
E-mail: admitme@uah.edu
Web site: http://www.uah.edu

UNIVERSITY OF ALASKA FAIRBANKS

FAIRBANKS, ALASKA

The University

Founded in 1917, the University provides education, research, and service in the "last frontier." The Fairbanks campus, one of three in the statewide system of higher education, is the primary administrative and research center, with branches in Bethel, Dillingham, Kotzebue, and Nome, along with rural centers throughout the state.

The total University of Alaska Fairbanks (UAF) enrollment is close to 10,000 students. Eighty-five percent of the students are from Alaska. The other fifteen percent are students from the rest of the U.S. and thirty-eight other countries. The eight residence halls on campus are renovated and are capable of lodging 1,020 students. The Student Apartment Complex houses 234 sophomore and upperclass students in furnished two-bedroom units. The Eileen Panigeo MacLean House, housing for rural students, holds 22 students. The University also manages 153 furnished apartments for students with families.

The main campus contains a core of academic buildings and residences, as well as miles of trails, two lakes, and a boreal forest research and recreational area. Most of the University's research institutes, including the noted Geophysical Institute and the International Arctic Research Center, are clustered on the West Ridge—with incredible views of the Tanana Valley and Alaska Range. The University's Agricultural and Forestry Experiment Station is on campus, as are a Cooperative Fish and Wildlife Research Unit and various state and federal agencies and laboratories. The University awards graduate degrees in many of the same areas as the undergraduate studies, often in conjunction with one of its research institutes. The University has added or expanded several new buildings in the last five years, increasing research capabilities related to the biological sciences, cold-climate housing, and circumpolar studies. The North is a theme found in many other academic programs, including Alaska Native studies, anthropology, the arts, engineering, and the social sciences.

Intercollegiate athletics include men's and women's basketball, cross-country running and skiing, intercollegiate ice hockey (CCHA), and women's volleyball and swim teams. The University also has an outstanding rifle team which has produced several Olympic athletes—including a gold medalist—and has earned ten national championships. The Student Recreation Complex houses a variety of sports and physical activities facilities, including multipurpose areas for basketball, volleyball, badminton, tennis, calisthenics, dance, gymnastics, judo, and karate; a rifle and pistol range; courts for handball, racquetball, and squash; an elevated 200-meter, three-lane jogging track; a swimming pool; weight-training and modern fitness equipment areas; an ice arena for recreational skating and hockey; a special aerobics area; and a three-story climbing wall.

The cheery and roomy student union, the William Ransom Wood Center, is the focus of various out-of-class activities for students and faculty members. The center houses meeting and exhibit rooms, lounges and television areas, the student government offices, campus information, a pub, bowling alley, games room, cafeteria, snack bar, and an espresso bar.

Location

The campus of the University of Alaska Fairbanks is situated on a ridge overlooking the valley of the Tanana River and the city of Fairbanks. Serving a population of more than 85,000 within the 7,561-square-mile North Star Borough, Fairbanks is a major trade center for outlying villages in Interior Alaska. The city is connected with the rest of the state and the lower forty-eight states by air and highway. Municipal bus service is available between downtown Fairbanks, the surrounding area, and the campus. Shuttle bus service is available around the UAF campus.

Fairbanks offers the sophistication of larger cities through such luxuries as first-run movies and fine restaurants while maintaining the atmosphere of smaller, more personal towns. Denali National Park and Preserve and other vast wilderness areas are close at hand, and Anchorage is 350 miles south via the Parks Highway. Members of the Fairbanks community and the University join together in the Fairbanks Symphony, Arctic Chamber Orchestra, and in many other musical and theatrical enterprises.

Majors and Degrees

The University of Alaska Fairbanks awards occupational endorsements, certificates, A.A., A.S., and A.A.S. degrees, and B.A., B.A.S., B.S., B.B.A., B.E.M., B.M., B.T., and B.F.A. degrees in accounting; administrative assistant; airframe studies; Alaska Native studies; anthropology; applied accounting; applied business; applied physics; apprenticeship technology; art; arts and sciences; aviation maintenance technology; automotive technology; aviation technology; biological sciences; bookkeeping technician; business administration; chemistry; child development; civil engineering; communication; community health; computer science; culinary arts; diesel/heavy equipment; dental assistant studies; drafting technology; early childhood; earth science; economics; electrical engineering; elementary education; emergency services; English; entry-level welder; Eskimo (Inupiaq and Yup'ik); financial services representative; fisheries; food science and nutrition; foreign languages; general science; geography; geological engineering; geology; health-care reimbursement; health technology; high-latitude range management; history; human services; information technology specialist; instrumentation technology; interdisciplinary studies; Japanese studies; journalism; justice; law enforcement academy; linguistics; mathematics; mechanical engineering; medical assistant; medical office technologies; microcomputer support specialist; mining applications and technologies; mining engineering; music; Native language education; natural resources management (including forestry); Northern studies; nurse aide; paralegal studies; paramedic academy; petroleum engineering; philosophy; phlebotomy; physics; political science; powerplant; power generation; process technology; professional piloting; psychology; renewable resources; rural development; rural human services; rural utilities business management; Russian studies; safety, health, and environmental awareness technology; social work; sociology; statistics; technology; theater; tribal management; veterinary science; welding and materials technology; and wildlife biology and conservation. Preprofessional advising is available in dentistry, law, library science, medicine, pharmacy, physical therapy, physician assistant, and veterinary medicine.

Academic Programs

The academic year is divided into two semesters; registration begins in early April for the fall semester and in November for the spring semester. Preregistration is available for returning students. In addition, there are three-week, six-week, and twelve-week summer sessions. UAF offers an early orientation for new students in the fall and spring semesters. The University is organized into four colleges and four professional schools: the College of Liberal Arts, the College of Natural Science and Mathematics, the College of Engineering and Mines, the College of Rural and Community Development, and the Schools of Natural Resources and Agricultural Sciences, Education, Fisheries and Ocean Sciences, and Management. A minimum of 120 credits must be completed for the four-year baccalaureate degree programs.

Students who receive scores of 3 or higher on the College Board's Advanced Placement tests may be awarded credit by the University. Currently enrolled students may challenge courses for credit by successfully completing College-Level Examination Program (CLEP) examinations or by completing locally prepared examinations. Requests for advanced-placement credit and credit by examination are coordinated through the Office of Admissions.

The honors program is designed for highly motivated undergraduate students who wish to acquire a superior understanding of the natural and social sciences, the arts, and the humanities. Prospective honors students need a minimum ACT composite score of 29 or a minimum combined SAT score of 1875, with a minimum 3.6 high school GPA.

Off-Campus Programs

The University maintains exchange programs with various universities in Canada, Australia, Austria, Chile, Denmark, Finland, France, Germany, Iceland, Japan, Mexico, Norway, Russia, Sweden, and Switzerland; and multiple other universities through the North2North Exchange program. The University also participates in the Northwest Council on Study Abroad (NCSA), in cooperation with the American Heritage Association International (AHA), providing students with an opportunity to enroll in liberal arts programs in Argentina, Austria, England, France, Fiji, Greece, Ireland, Italy, Mexico, New Zealand, and Spain. UAF is also a member of the National Student Exchange, participating with more than 180 colleges and universities throughout the United States, in U.S. territories, and at nine locations in Canada.

Academic Facilities

The Fine Arts Complex features a 480-seat theater, a 1,072-seat concert hall, FM public radio (KUAC) and educational-television (PBS) studios, an art gallery, and the Elmer E. Rasmuson Library. The library collection contains more than 1.1 million volumes, including the prestigious Alaska and Polar Regions Collection. Electronic catalogs provide access to collections in 11,000 libraries nationwide.

Students have free use of the University's academic computing facilities which are accessible from Windows and Macintosh computer labs and via remote access. Various schools and colleges have their own special-purpose computer labs.

The University of Alaska Museum of the North attracts nearly 100,000 visitors each year to Interior Alaska and is located on the UAF campus. The museum collects, preserves, and exhibits materials from Alaska and the North.

Costs

In 2009–10, tuition and fees are $2569 per semester for full-time (15 credits) students. Nonresident students pay an additional $5040 for 15 credits of tuition each semester. Residents of Alaska, and cities having sister city agreements with any Alaskan city, are eligible for resident tuition rates. Generally, to qualify as a resident, a student must show proof they have been living in Alaska for two years. The approximate cost per semester for books and supplies is $1300. A double-occupancy residence hall room on campus costs $1805 per semester. Meal plans cost approximately $1595–$1875 per semester. These costs are subject to change. Married student housing on campus is also available.

Financial Aid

A large portion of financial aid is derived from the Alaska Supplemental Education Loan Program, which is available to all students attending UAF, regardless of residency. Three kinds of aid are available: grants and scholarships (which need not be repaid), loans, and part-time employment. Inquiries should be addressed to the Financial Aid Office, University of Alaska Fairbanks, P.O. Box 756560, Fairbanks, Alaska 99775-6560 or by e-mail to financialaid@uaf.edu.

The Chancellor's Scholarship, a one-year tuition waiver awarded by the Office of Admissions, is available to entering freshmen with a minimum 3.0 GPA and 1650 SAT combined score or 25 ACT composite score. To apply, students should submit a scholarship application, an application for admission, a high school transcript, and test scores for review. Questions about this scholarship should be directed to the Office of Admissions. The deadline for University of Alaska and UAF-funded scholarships is February 15. Check the financial aid Web site for other aid and applicable due dates at http://www.uaf.edu/finaid/.

Faculty

Fifty-two percent of full-time faculty members and thirty-two percent of part-time faculty members hold doctoral, professional, or terminal degrees, and many are actively engaged in research. In keeping with University policy, faculty members provide academic counseling for students. The combination of a student-faculty ratio of 11:1 and easy access to instructors for help outside of class produces a maximum educational benefit for students.

Student Government

The Associated Students of the University of Alaska Fairbanks (ASUAF) protects students' rights through its various governmental functions and also offers educational, social, recreational, and service activities. The school newspaper, *Sun Star*, is published weekly with the sponsorship of ASUAF, which also supports KSUA, the campus radio station; the international cinema and weekly movie series; and dances, concerts, and other entertainment. ASUAF publishes the results of its faculty evaluations and sends several student lobbyists to the Alaska state legislature in Juneau each spring. There is a student member seat on the Board of Regents of the University.

Admission Requirements

For admission to a baccalaureate program, applicants must be high school graduates with a GPA of at least 2.5 in a high school core curriculum of 16 credits and a cumulative grade point average of at least 3.0, or 2.5 plus an ACT score of 18 or SAT score of 1290 (including writing skills section). Transfer students must also have a minimum grade point average of 2.0 in all previous college work. Applicants for a major in a scientific or technical field may be required to present a higher grade point average and to have completed specific background courses before being accepted into the major department. All entering freshmen are required to submit scores from the ACT or SAT examination prior to registration for placement in English and math courses.

Application and Information

The application deadlines are July 1 for the fall semester and November 1 for the spring semester. Applications are processed after the deadlines only as long as space is available. Applicants are notified of the admission decision as soon as all application material has been received. Only accepted students are allowed to apply for campus housing. Students who desire campus housing should apply for admission as early as possible.

For further information, applicants should contact:

Office of Admissions
University of Alaska Fairbanks
P.O. Box 757480
Fairbanks, Alaska 99775-7480
Phone: 907-474-7500
800-478-1UAF (toll-free)
E-mail: admissions@uaf.edu
Web site: http://www.uaf.edu/admissions
http://www.uaonline.alaska.edu (To apply)

Constitution Park, located between the Rasmuson Library, Gruening Building, Constitution Hall, and Fine Arts Complex, is just one of the popular hangouts between classes.

UNIVERSITY OF CENTRAL FLORIDA

ORLANDO, FLORIDA

The University

The University of Central Florida (UCF) is a comprehensive research university with approximately 50,000 students. As one of the nation's fastest-growing universities in the South and the fifth-largest in the nation, UCF enrolls an academically talented and diverse student body representing all fifty states and more than 120 countries. The University offers educational and research programs that complement the regional economy, with strong components in aerospace engineering, business, education, film, health, hospitality management, medicine, nursing, and social sciences. UCF's programs in communication and the fine arts help to meet the cultural and recreational needs of a growing metropolitan area. The University also offers many graduate programs leading to master's and doctoral degrees, including a doctorate of physical therapy. The UCF College of Medicine was opened in the fall of 2009 which offers the M.D. degree.

UCF is accredited by the Commission on Colleges of the Southern Association of Colleges and Schools. In addition, a number of scientific, professional, and academic bodies confer accreditation in specific disciplines and groups of disciplines. In the College of Arts and Humanities, accreditation is conferred in music by the National Association of Schools of Music. In the College of Sciences, accreditation is conferred in chemistry by the American Chemical Society. The programs in the College of Business Administration are accredited at the undergraduate and graduate levels by AACSB International–The Association to Advance Collegiate Schools of Business. In the College of Engineering and Computer Science, programs are accredited by the Engineering Accreditation Commission of the Accreditation Board for Engineering and Technology (ABET). Also, engineering technology programs are accredited by the Technology Accreditation Commission of ABET. The program in computer science is accredited by the Computing Accreditation Commission of ABET. In the College of Health and Public Affairs, programs have been approved by the following agencies: health information management by the Commission on Accreditation of Health Informatics and Information Management Education, cardiopulmonary sciences by the Committee on Accreditation for Respiratory Care, athletic training by the Committee on Accreditation of Athletic Training Education, radiologic sciences by the Joint Review Committee on Education in Radiologic Technology, and social work by the Council of Social Work Education. In the College of Medicine, medical laboratory sciences programs have been accredited by the National Accrediting Agency for Clinical Laboratory Services. All teacher education programs are fully accredited by the Florida State Department of Education and by the National Council for Accreditation of Teacher Education. In the College of Nursing, the program has been approved by the Commission on Collegiate Nursing Education and the Florida Board of Nursing. In the Rosen College of Hospitality Management, the hospitality management program has been accredited by the Accreditation Commission for Programs in Hospitality Management.

UCF has established extensive partnerships with businesses and industries in the central Florida area that provide students with exceptional research and learning experiences. These partnerships bring practical learning environments to UCF students through co-op, internship programs, and joint curriculum development strategies.

The on-campus and campus-affiliated housing facilities include traditional residence halls, apartment-style options, and Greek housing that accommodate approximately 10,000 students. Several thousand students live in apartments located within walking distance of the campus. Approximately 400 students live in on-campus Greek housing.

Students participate in more than 350 student organizations, including special-interest clubs, multicultural organizations, fraternities and sororities, honor societies, and academic and preprofessional organizations. The Office of Student Involvement schedules a wide array of extracurricular programs, including concerts, movies, and guest speakers.

The University of Central Florida is a member of the NCAA and Conference USA. All teams compete on the NCAA Division I level. UCF's men's teams compete in intercollegiate baseball, basketball, cross-country, football, golf, soccer, and tennis. Women's teams compete in basketball, cross-country, golf, rowing, soccer, softball, tennis, track and field, and volleyball. Intercollegiate coed club activities include championship cheerleading, crew, and waterskiing teams. The University intramural sports program offers disc golf, flag football, floor hockey, racquetball, soccer, softball, tennis, and volleyball.

Location

The University of Central Florida is located on 1,415 acres approximately 13 miles east of downtown Orlando. Regional campuses are located in Daytona Beach, Cocoa, and South Lake.

Majors and Degrees

The University offers the degrees of Bachelor of Applied Science, Bachelor of Arts, Bachelor of Arts in Business Administration, Bachelor of Engineering Technology, Bachelor of Fine Arts, Bachelor of Science, Bachelor of Science in Business Administration, Bachelor of Science in Education, Bachelor of Science Engineering, Bachelor of Science in Nursing, and Bachelor of Science in Social Sciences. These degrees are available in the colleges listed below, with majors or areas of specialization as indicated.

The College of Arts and Humanities offers degrees in art, digital media, English, film, French, history, humanities, modern language combination, music, philosophy, photography, religious studies, Spanish, and theater.

The College of Business Administration offers degrees in accounting, economics, finance, general business administration, management, management information systems, marketing, and real estate. The College also offers a minor in international business.

The College of Education offers degrees in art education, early childhood education, elementary education, English language arts education, exceptional student education, foreign language education, mathematics education, science education, social science education, sports and fitness, and technical education and industry training.

The College of Engineering and Computer Science offers degrees in aerospace engineering, civil engineering, computer engineering, computer science, construction engineering, electrical engineering, electrical engineering technology, engineering technology, environmental engineering, industrial engineering, information systems technology, information technology, and mechanical engineering.

The College of Health and Public Affairs offers degrees in cardiopulmonary sciences, communication sciences and disorders, criminal justice, health information management, health sciences–athletic training, health sciences–preclinical allied health track, health services administration, legal studies, public administration, radiologic sciences, and social work.

The College of Medicine and the Burnett School of Biomedical Sciences offers degrees in molecular biology and microbiology, biotechnology, and medical laboratory sciences.

The College of Nursing offers degrees in nursing.

The College of Sciences offers degrees in actuarial science, advertising/public relations, anthropology, biology, chemistry, forensic science, interpersonal and organizational communications, international and global studies, journalism, mathematics, physics, political science, psychology, radio/television, sociology, social sciences, and statistics.

The Rosen College of Hospitality Management offers degrees in event management, hospitality management, and restaurant and foodservice management.

Preprofessional programs are offered in chiropractic, dentistry, medicine, optometry, pharmacy, physical assistant studies, physical therapy, podiatry, and veterinary medicine.

A degree in interdisciplinary studies is available through the Office of Undergraduate Studies.

Academic Programs

UCF provides a total education through a core curriculum of 36 hours of general education courses. In addition to fulfilling the general education requirement, each student must complete the necessary major and/or minor requirements to reach the minimum of 120 semester hours necessary for graduation.

Several special programs help students reach their academic and leadership potential. The Burnett Honors College at UCF encourages students to achieve academic excellence through small classes and interactive symposia. The innovative Leadership Enrichment and Academic Development (LEAD) Scholars Program fosters leadership and service commitment through a comprehensive student development program for freshmen. The Academic Exploration Program (AEP) helps entering freshmen define their career goals and develop an academic strategy to reach those goals. The University also offers an increasing number of Web-based courses and degree programs.

UCF offers Air Force and Army ROTC programs.

Off-Campus Programs

Career Services and Experiential Learning offers programs in which students alternate semesters of classroom study with equal periods of paid employment in government, industry, or business. The Department of Modern Languages offers summer study-abroad programs in Canada, Eastern Europe, France, Germany, Italy, Japan, Poland, Spain, Sweden, and Russia. Courses are available in the subject areas of language (all levels), art, and civilization. UCF is also a participant in the National Student Exchange Consortium.

Academic Facilities

In addition to the academic programs offered on the Orlando campus, upper division students can work toward a degree at eleven campuses located throughout Central Florida. These regional campuses work cooperatively with local community colleges to provide all four years of course work in many academic areas. The library houses nearly 1.4 million volumes and subscribes to more than 10,000 periodicals and journals. In addition, students have access to an online computer catalog that provides information on the collections of the State University System libraries. An extensive online network of more than 500 computer terminals and a network of nearly 1,000 IBM PCs cover the campus. The Institute for Simulation and Training gives students the opportunity to pursue undergraduate research. The College of Optics and Photonics allows faculty members and students to work directly with industry personnel in conducting basic and applied research at the regional and national levels. The Central Florida Research Park, located adjacent to the UCF campus, houses more than ninety important high-technology firms and agencies. This proximity fosters relationships between industry and the University, which strengthens the academic programs at UCF.

Costs

For Florida residents, the cost of tuition and fees in 2008–09, based on a full-time course load, was $3614 for the year; for out-of-state residents, the cost was $17,530. Room and board were approximately $8140 per year, and costs for books and supplies were approximately $925.

Financial Aid

Financial aid is awarded according to each student's demonstrated financial need in relation to college costs and may include grants, loans, scholarships, and part-time employment. Programs based upon need include the Federal Perkins Loan, Federal Pell Grant, Florida Student Assistance Grant, Federal Work-Study, Florida College Career Work-Study Program, and Federal Stafford Student Loan. To qualify for these programs, students must complete the Free Application for Federal Student Aid (FAFSA). The priority application deadline is March 1. Sixty-seven percent of UCF students receive some form of financial assistance.

Faculty

The University's teaching faculty consists of 1,258 full-time members and 498 adjunct members. Seventy percent of the full-time faculty members hold a doctoral degree. Undergraduate instruction is given primarily by the full-time and adjunct faculty members; graduate students play a very minor role in undergraduate instruction. Students are assigned to a faculty adviser in their area of specialization for assistance in academic matters. The student-faculty ratio is 23:1.

Student Government

UCF's Student Government Association provides an opportunity for students to become involved at UCF. Every UCF student is encouraged to voice his or her opinion through senate representatives. Student Government is divided into three branches—the student-elected executive branch, the student-elected legislative branch, and the appointed judicial branch. Student Government is responsible for the allocation of all activity and service fees paid by students as a part of their tuition. This money goes toward student services, including the online Macintosh lab, homecoming activities, campus activities board, legal services, and funding for clubs and organizations. Admission is free to all events directly sponsored by the Student Government.

Admission Requirements

A freshman applicant is a student with fewer than 12 hours of college course work after high school graduation. The most important criteria in the admission decision for these applicants are the high school academic record, quality and level of difficulty of courses, grade point average, grade trends, and SAT or ACT test scores. UCF operates on a rolling admission basis. Students are generally notified of their initial admission decision within two to three weeks after receipt of the application and all official supporting documents. If the number of qualified applicants exceeds the number that the University is permitted to enroll, a waiting list is established.

All applicants must have earned a minimum of 18 high school academic units (yearlong courses that are not remedial in nature). These include 4 units of English (3 must include substantial writing), 3 units of mathematics at or above algebra I, 3 units of natural science (2 must include a laboratory), 3 units of social science, 2 units of one foreign language, and 3 units of academic electives. Grades in honors, International Baccalaureate, Advanced Placement, AICE, dual-enrollment, pre-AP, pre-IB, and pre-AICE courses are given additional weight in the GPA computation. Students must meet the Florida Department of Education minimum eligibility to be considered for admission. Applicants should understand that the satisfaction of minimum requirements does not guarantee admission to UCF.

Transfer applicants with fewer than 60 semester hours of college course work must submit official high school transcripts, SAT or ACT test scores, and all official college transcripts. Transfer students with more than 60 semester hours or who have earned an Associate in Arts degree or a statewide articulated Associate in Science degree from a Florida public community college need only submit all official college transcripts. A transfer credit summary evaluation is provided to students once they are offered admission to UCF.

Application and Information

Students are encouraged to apply several months in advance and can apply online at http://www.admissions.ucf.edu. It is recommended that freshman students apply early during the fall semester of their senior year. Applications are accepted up to one year prior to the start of the term for which enrollment is desired. Priority application deadlines are May 1 for the fall term (July 1 for transfers), November 1 for the spring term, and March 1 for the summer term.

The Campus Visit Experience, which includes an information session and a campus tour, is offered Monday through Friday at 10 and 2 (except holidays). Students can sign up for a campus visit online at http://www.admissions.ucf.edu.

Office of Undergraduate Admissions
University of Central Florida
P.O. Box 160111
Orlando, Florida 32816-0111
Phone: 407-823-3000
E-mail: admission@mail.ucf.edu
Web site: http://www.ucf.edu

UNIVERSITY OF CHARLESTON

CHARLESTON, WEST VIRGINIA

The University

The University of Charleston (UC) strives to educate each student for a life of productive work, enlightened living, and community involvement. The University is very serious about its responsibility to provide students with the knowledge, abilities, and character necessary for them to have successful careers and to be productive and active citizens.

Founded in 1888 and formerly known as Morris Harvey College, the University of Charleston acquired its new name in 1979 to signify its importance as the leading higher education opportunity in the capital. Today, UC proudly represents the capital city of Charleston and the surrounding Kanawha Valley. Currently, approximately 1,400 students representing thirty-five states and twenty countries enjoy the University's 40-acre riverfront campus overlooking the State Capitol Complex and the beautiful city of Charleston.

The University has received numerous national accolades for its outstanding quality and educational approach. In September 2007, the University of Charleston was recognized as the national leader in outcomes-based learning and student assessment by the *New York Times Magazine.* The University also was ranked number 1 in the nation for 2007 by the Collegiate Learning Assessment (CLA), which also showed that UC students show the largest learning gain from freshman to sophomore year among all schools in the CLA report. The University of Charleston has been recognized as a national model for the Freshman-Year Experience, which includes faculty mentoring, university transitions, and living/learning communities. In addition, *U.S. News & World Report* placed UC in the top 20 in the Baccalaureate Colleges in the South category and as the Top Ranked Comprehensive College in West Virginia in its "Best Colleges for 2007" rankings. Students at UC also score among the highest in the country on the National Survey of Student Engagement.

The UC educational program focuses on "Learning Your Way." Students are the focus at UC. The academic program allows them to demonstrate what they have learned in order to earn the credits necessary for graduation. Students are expected to demonstrate knowledge and skills in the areas of communication, critical thinking, citizenship, ethical practice, science, and creativity. These attributes are integrated with knowledge and skills in a chosen field of study. Future employers and graduate schools consistently seek and employ college graduates with these abilities, and it is imperative that all University graduates have a strong foundation in these skills. Therefore, the University of Charleston has designed this program to help students master the knowledge and skills that are necessary for success.

Students are also encouraged to demonstrate mastery and earn credits at their own pace. Many students earn more than the traditional 15–18 credits per semester and graduate within three years, double major, or earn a master's degree quicker than at other schools.

Housing facilities for residential students are very modern and student friendly. Brotherton Hall was built in 2000 and houses 220 students; New Hall, built in 2003, houses 183 students; and Middle Hall, built in 2005 and 2006, houses 240 students. An expansion was completed for Middle Hall in August 2006 to accommodate increased student housing numbers, allowing the campus to house approximately 700 students.

Because the University believes that students learn from their involvement in community and campus activities, students are strongly encouraged to participate in one or more of the forty cocurricular organizations found at the University. There are academic clubs, publications, fraternities, sororities, religious organizations, intramural sports, honorary societies, drama clubs, cheerleading, chorus and band programs, and many student leadership organizations. The new Morrison Fitness Center opened in January 2007 and houses modern exercise equipment, weight systems, and classrooms for dance, yoga, Tae Kwon Do, or other activities. The University's Welch Colleague program integrates student involvement, the academic curriculum, community service, and leadership. The Community Service program provides opportunities for students to participate both on campus and in the Charleston area through opportunities like Habitat for Humanity. In addition, there are numerous civic, political, social, and charitable organizations easily accessible in the community.

The varsity sports program for men and women has become one of the University's most valuable assets. Men and women may participate in basketball, cheerleading, soccer, and tennis. Men may also participate in baseball, football, and golf and women in crew, cross-country, softball, track and field, and volleyball. The University's athletic teams compete in Division II of the NCAA. In recent years, men's and women's teams have been contenders in the WVIAC tournaments, with several teams winning conference championships and attending national championship tournaments. The women's basketball team participated in the Elite 8 in 2005 and 2006, and the men's football team had the largest one-season turnaround in conference history in 2005. UC athletics won the President's and Commissioner's Cups in 2006–07, signifying the top athletic teams in the WVIAC Conference.

The University of Charleston is accredited by the North Central Association of Colleges and Schools, National Council for Accreditation of Teacher Education, National Athletic Trainers Association, Commission on the Accreditation of Allied Health Education Programs–Athletic Training, Joint Review Committee on Education in Radiological Technology, and the National League for Nursing Accrediting Commission. The University holds a variety of professional recognitions, approvals, and memberships, including the International Assembly of Collegiate Business Education, West Virginia Academy of Sciences, Interior Design Educator's Council, and the American Council on Education.

The University offers master's degrees in business administration: an Executive M.B.A. and a plus-one M.B.A. for full-time study, one year beyond the bachelor's degree. A new Graduate School of Business is scheduled to open in fall 2008 with an emphasis on experiential learning and an enhanced master's program for outstanding students. The University of Charleston School of Pharmacy, which offers the University's first doctoral-level program, opened in fall 2006.

Location

Charleston, West Virginia's vibrant state capital, is a cultural, social, political, and economic hub. Located in the Kanawha Valley near the foothills of the Appalachian Mountains, it offers scenic tranquility as well as the convenience and excitement of a modern city. With a metropolitan population of 200,000, Charleston has grown to be West Virginia's finest city. Accessibility to the city is quite easy via plane, car, bus, and train. A large civic center, historic sites, libraries, movie theaters, shopping malls, and a symphony orchestra are all highlights of the Charleston business district. The rapport between the University and the community is excellent, and many events are cosponsored annually.

Downtown Charleston, just a short ride from the campus by campus shuttle or city bus, offers the kind of social and cultural opportunities that can be found only in a large city. In addition, fishing, hunting, horseback riding, waterskiing, snow skiing, mountain biking, and white-water rafting are just a few of the many recreational activities to be found within a short distance of the campus.

Majors and Degrees

The University of Charleston offers undergraduate degree programs through its various divisions: the Morris Harvey Division of Arts and Sciences, the Herbert Jones Division of Business, and the Bert Bradford Division of Health Sciences.

The Morris Harvey Division of Arts and Sciences offers the Bachelor of Arts degree with the following majors: art, communications, education (various certifications), general studies, interior design, political science, and psychology. The Bachelor of Science degree is offered with majors in biology, chemistry, and a biology/chemistry preprofessional program focused on the health sciences. The Division of Arts and Sciences is also home to the popular Pre-Pharmacy program. This program is segmented into the Pre-Pharmacy Scholars track and the Traditional Pre-Pharmacy track. Students who excel in this unique program have preferential entry into the Pharm.D. program.

The Jones Division of Business offers Bachelor of Science degree programs in accounting, sports administration, business administration, and finance.

The Division of Health Sciences offers the Bachelor of Science degree in athletic training, nursing, and radiologic science. An Associate of Arts degree in nursing is also offered at the University.

Students may pursue directed independent study and internships in most majors. Army ROTC is offered to interested men and women.

Academic Programs

Candidates for a bachelor's degree from UC are required to complete a minimum of 120 semester hours and have a cumulative grade point average of at least 2.0 on all college work attempted. This must include 30 hours in upper division courses; demonstration of learning in the required outcomes of communication, critical thinking, ethical practice, creativity, science, and citizenship; and advanced work leading to a major in a department or a division. The minimum requirement for an associate degree is 60 semester hours and a cumulative grade point average of at least a 2.0 on all college work attempted, including completion of a prescribed program of general education and specialized work in a department.

The University follows a semester academic calendar and offers summer terms for students who wish to accelerate their college program.

Academic Facilities

A large number of support facilities and programs supplement the various academic opportunities at the University of Charleston. The Schoenbaum Library serves as the center of the learning experience. Located in the technologically advanced Clay Tower Building, the library has a collection of more than 120,000 books, 200,000 microforms, and 3,600 audiovisual items. More than 8,000 journal titles are available either in print or electronically and are accessible from any Web-enabled computer, on or off campus. In addition, numerous specialized collections, CD-ROM-based electronic indexes, and online electronic search services are at the students' disposal for specialized research and study. The library also offers wireless technology and laptop computer check-out.

The University has numerous computer labs for student and faculty use: the Cabot Apple Lab, the IBM-PC combination classroom labs, an IBM-PC network lab, and an IBM-PC open lab. Wireless access is also available on much of the campus, including the scenic riverbank. The Learning Support Center provides a variety of services and classes to help students achieve academic, personal, and professional success. The Communication Resource Center provides support for students and faculty members through consultation services, workshops, and electronic access to a variety of writing resources.

The Clay Tower Building houses state-of-the-art science, technology, and information resource facilities. Riggleman Hall, the main college building, houses classrooms, a 976-seat auditorium and stage, education and language laboratories, the Carleton Varney Department of Art and Design, and administrative offices.

Costs

For the 2009–10 academic year, tuition was $12,000 per semester. Other costs associated with attending can be found on the University's Web site.

Financial Aid

The University of Charleston provides generous financial assistance that may include a combination of scholarships, grants, loans, and work-study. In 2007–08, more than 90 percent of full-time students received some form of financial aid. Special academic scholarships and grants are awarded to outstanding full-time students. The University also offers grants to qualified athletes and to students who are involved in leadership, community service, band, school newspaper, or vocal music.

Faculty

The University has 61 full-time and 38 part-time undergraduate faculty members. At the University of Charleston, faculty members provide academic, career, and in some cases, personal advice to students. They encourage active learning through collaborative projects and faculty/student research. Small classes through a 13:1 faculty-student ratio allow for individual attention for students.

Student Government

The Student Government Association is a policymaking body composed of students representing most campus organizations and student classes. Both the Student Government Association and the University believe that students should have the privilege, along with the faculty and administration, of participating in the governance of the University.

Admission Requirements

Admission to the University of Charleston is based on the academic records and potential for leadership and involvement. A qualified applicant's credentials must strongly suggest ability and motivation to succeed in higher education and in the University community. Candidates for admission must present a transcript of work from an accredited secondary school showing at least 16 academic units, grades indicating intellectual ability and promise, and proof of graduation or a GED. The pattern of courses should show purpose and continuity and furnish a background for the liberal learning outcomes curriculum offered by the University.

Since the unique and student-friendly curriculum emphasizes communication, critical thinking, and citizenship, secondary school courses should emphasize courses in English, mathematics, sciences, and social sciences. Candidates are also required to submit scores on the ACT or SAT. Students must have an above-average academic profile that includes a minimum 2.25 academic grade point average and a minimum ACT composite score of 19 or SAT score (combined math and critical reading) of 900. Applicants for admission are considered on an individual basis without regard to race, religion, geographic origin, or handicap. Letters of recommendation and a personal visit to the campus scheduled with the Office of Admissions are highly recommended.

Application and Information

For more information, interested students should contact:

Office of Admissions
University of Charleston
2300 MacCorkle Avenue, SE
Charleston, West Virginia 25304
Phone: 304-357-4750
800-995-GO UC (4682) (toll-free)
Fax: 304-357-4781
E-mail: admissions@ucwv.edu
Web site: http://www.ucwv.edu

The Clay Tower Building houses state-of-the-art science facilities and a library with lounges overlooking the Kanawha River. The campus is directly across the river from the State Capitol.

UNIVERSITY OF COLORADO AT BOULDER

BOULDER, COLORADO

The University

The University of Colorado at Boulder (CU-Boulder) is a dynamic community of scholars and learners situated on one of the most spectacular college campuses in the country. CU-Boulder is one of thirty-four U.S. public institutions belonging to the prestigious Association of American Universities (AAU) and the only member in the Rocky Mountain region. The university has a proud tradition of academic excellence, with four Nobel laureates and more than fifty members of prestigious academic societies. CU-Boulder was ranked the top green university in the nation in *Sierra* magazine's 2009 listing of greenest colleges, and was one of only three U.S. colleges and universities to receive a 2007 Presidential Award for General Community Service.

The campus offers more than 3,400 courses each year in approximately 150 areas of study. There are seventy-eight academic majors available at the bachelor's level, seventy at the master's level, and fifty-one at the doctoral level. Outstanding academic departments and programs include astrophysical and planetary sciences, biochemistry, biology, chemistry, engineering, English, entrepreneurial business, geography, integrative physiology, music, physics, and psychology. Talented undergraduate students may participate in honors programs, the Undergraduate Research Opportunities Program, and eleven residential academic programs or living and learning communities featuring small-class environments.

Total enrollment for fall 2009 at the Boulder campus was 30,196, including 25,408 undergraduate students. Students come from every state in the nation and about 100 countries. Approximately two thirds of the students come from Colorado. Many ethnic, religious, academic, and social backgrounds are represented, fostering the development of a multicultural community that enriches each student's educational experience.

Undergraduate students may apply to the following colleges and schools: Architecture and Planning, Arts and Sciences, Leeds School of Business, Engineering and Applied Science, Music, Journalism and Mass Communication, and Education. Students are admitted to Journalism and Mass Communication only after completing one or two years at CU-Boulder, with exceptions for highly qualified new freshmen. The School of Education accepts applications from students after they are enrolled in an approved degree program at CU-Boulder.

CU-Boulder offers a wide variety of campus activities. Students may participate in student government; clubs and organizations; intramural, club, and intercollegiate sports; and fraternities and sororities. An extensive calendar of cultural events is available.

Location

CU-Boulder is located in a scenic valley at the foot of the Rocky Mountains, 1 mile above sea level. With a population of approximately 100,000, Boulder is among the most dynamic, progressive, and attractive cities of its size in the United States. The Colorado state capital, Denver, is a 30-mile drive or bus ride (free for students) from Boulder. Boulder is surrounded by a greenbelt of more than 20,000 acres of open space. Much of the open space and nearby mountains are crisscrossed by an extensive system of hiking, biking, and riding trails. Many CU-Boulder students enjoy skiing, hiking, backpacking, rock climbing, white-water rafting, or mountain biking.

CU-Boulder is listed as one of the "most artistically successful campuses in the country" in *The Campus as a Work of Art* by Thomas Gaines. The 600-acre main campus, in the heart of Boulder, is distinguished by buildings featuring native sandstone walls and red-tiled roofs inspired by the rural Italian architectural style.

Majors and Degrees

CU-Boulder offers the following undergraduate majors: aerospace engineering; anthropology; applied mathematics; architectural engineering; art and art history–art history; art and art history–studio arts; Asian studies; astronomy; biochemistry; business-accounting; business-finance; business-management; business-marketing; business-operations and information management; chemical and biological engineering; chemical engineering; chemistry; Chinese; civil engineering; classics; communication; computer science; dance; ecology and evolutionary biology; economics; electrical and computer engineering; electrical engineering; engineering physics; English; environmental design–architecture; environmental design–design studies; environmental design–planning; environmental engineering; environmental studies; ethnic studies; film studies; French; geography; geology; Germanic studies; history; humanities; integrative physiology; international affairs; Italian; Japanese; journalism-advertising; journalism–broadcast news; journalism–broadcast production; journalism–media studies; journalism-news/editorial; linguistics; mathematics; mechanical engineering; molecular, cellular, and developmental biology; music; music–arts in music; music education; philosophy; physics; political science; psychology; religious studies; Russian studies; sociology; Spanish; speech, language, and hearing sciences; theater; and women's studies.

The following bachelor's degrees are offered: B.A., B.Envd., B.F.A., B.Mus., B.Mus.Ed., and B.S.

Concurrent bachelor's and master's degree programs are available in the following areas: applied mathematics, business (accounting, finance/accounting, operations and information management/accounting, operations and information management/telecommunications), classics, cognitive psychology, East Asian languages and civilizations (Chinese, Japanese), ecology and evolutionary biology, engineering physics/physics, film studies/art history, French, Germanic studies/German, integrative physiology, linguistics, mathematics, physics, religious studies, and in all engineering departments, including aerospace, architectural, chemical, civil, computer science, electrical, electrical and computer, environmental, and mechanical.

Academic Programs

The mission of the University of Colorado at Boulder is to educate undergraduate and graduate students in the accumulated knowledge of humankind, discover new knowledge through research and creative work, and foster critical thought, artistic creativity, professional competence, and responsible citizenship. Depending on their degree program, students may be required to complete 120 or 128 (engineering) semester hours for graduation. CU-Boulder offers a very flexible curriculum. Students may graduate with more than one major and with two different degrees from different colleges. Minors also are offered in arts and sciences, business, and engineering. The College of Arts and Sciences and the College of Engineering and Applied Science offer a four-year graduation guarantee, providing specific requirements are met. Advising for preprofessional study in health sciences (e.g., medicine, dentistry, pharmacy) and law is available through the PreProfessional Advising Center. Students can receive information about course requirements, test deadlines, enrollment limitations, and discuss other concerns about professional study.

CU-Boulder operates on a two-semester academic calendar. The fall semester begins in late August, and the spring semester begins in early January. Summer Session lasts ten weeks; courses meeting for shorter periods (one to four, five, or eight weeks) are scheduled during the ten-week session.

Off-Campus Programs

CU-Boulder sponsors more than 270 study-abroad programs each year. Programs are offered on six continents in seventy countries, including Australia, Costa Rica, Denmark, Egypt, England, France, Germany, Hungary, Japan, Mexico, and the Russian Federation. About twenty-five percent of CU-Boulder students have studied abroad by the time they graduate.

Academic Facilities

The University library system consists of more than 3.9 million volumes, nearly 7 million titles on microform, more than 55,000 periodical subscriptions, and more than a million video, graphic, and audio titles. The libraries system includes a main library and five branch libraries: business, earth sciences, engineering, math-physics, and music. There is also a law library.

Other facilities and resources include a planetarium and observatory, a natural history museum, extensive computing resources, a state-of-the-art foreign language technology center, a concert hall, four indoor theaters, and one outdoor theater. The Integrated Teaching and Learning Laboratory and the Discovery Learning Center provide hands-on, real-world experience to engineering undergraduates.

Recent additions to the campus include a new humanities building, equipped with smart classrooms; a new visual arts facility; and the Alliance for Technology, Learning, and Society (ATLAS) Center. ATLAS was established in 1997 with the goal of integrating information technology with all disciplines, people, and communities. The new Center for Community (C4C) building is under construction and due to be completed in late 2010. It will be home to a dining center and a student center featuring eleven core programs and services, including the Office of International Education, Disability Services, Counseling and Psychological Services, and the Center for Multicultural Affairs.

Costs

Tuition rates vary by school and college. For 2009–10, annual expenses for Colorado residents who were undergraduate students in the College of Arts and Sciences totaled $20,059 ($7932 for tuition and fees, $10,378 for room and board, and an estimated $1749 for books and supplies). Nonresident tuition and fees were $28,186.

Financial Aid

More than half of Boulder undergraduate students receive some type of financial assistance, totaling more than $200 million in awards. Students receive aid in the form of grants, loans, work-study awards, and scholarships. Funding is provided from federal, state, University, and private sources. All students applying for need-based financial aid are required to submit the Free Application for Federal Student Aid (FAFSA). Application forms are available from high school and community college counselors, the CU-Boulder Office of Financial Aid, and online. The priority processing date is April 1. Students may apply for CU-Boulder scholarships online by March 1. For students applying for scholarships that have a financial need requirement, results of the FAFSA must be on file in the financial aid office on March 1. Students may also obtain loans directly from the Office of Financial Aid rather than from a private lender.

Faculty

Approximately 1,400 full-time instructional faculty members teach undergraduate and graduate courses. The faculty includes nationally and internationally recognized scholars with many academic honors and awards. Tom Cech, distinguished professor of chemistry and biochemistry, shared the 1989 Nobel Prize in chemistry with Sidney Altman of Yale University. Carl Wieman (also U.S. 2004 Professor of the Year) and Eric Cornell won the 2001 Nobel Prize in physics for their creation of a new state of matter, just above absolute zero. John Hall shared the 2005 Nobel Prize in physics with Theodor W. Hänsch of the Max Planck Institute for Quantum Optics and the Ludwig Maximilians University in Munich, Germany and Roy J. Glauber of Harvard University. Kristi Anseth, professor of chemical and biological engineering, is a national leader in the study of biomaterials and is considered by many to be the pioneer in the field of tissue engineering. Her work includes developing new techniques and materials that aid in the healing of bones and cartilage. Seven faculty members have received MacArthur Fellowships, known as the "genius grant," the most recent two being in linguistics (2002) and physics (2003).

Student Government

One of the most influential student governments in the nation, the University of Colorado Student Union (UCSU) administers an operating budget of $30 million. UCSU student leaders and volunteers, working with the University staff, make policy decisions concerning the operation of the University Memorial Center, Student Recreation Center, Wardenburg Health Center, cultural events, the campus radio station, and other programs. Student fees and student-generated revenue support all of these activities. The student government also takes an active role in advocating student concerns.

Admission Requirements

Many factors are considered by the University in making admission decisions. Previous academic achievement, the quality of courses taken, GPA, college entrance test scores, the trend in grades, the extent to which the applicant has completed the recommended high school curriculum, the two required personal essays, and letters of recommendation are all considered. About 25 percent of the freshman class typically ranks in the top 10 percent of their high school graduating class. In fall 2009, 59 percent of the freshmen were Colorado residents. The University seeks to enroll students from a wide range of ethnic, cultural, economic, geographic, and educational backgrounds. The application is available online, either as an interactive Web application or as a downloadable, printable PDF.

Application and Information

Beginning in September, students may submit an application for admission to the spring, summer, or fall term.Spring applicants are processed on a rolling basis. CU-Boulder begins notifying applicants about admission decisions in October. Decisions are made approximately four to six weeks after an application is complete. Full consideration is given to applications that are complete (including the application fee and all required credentials) by the October 1 deadline.

Freshman applications for summer and fall terms are processed as either early notification applications or as regular decision applications.

Applicants who submit the online application and postmark all supporting credentials by the December 1 deadline are considered early notification applicants. Early notification applicants will be reviewed first and are notified of their initial decision on or before January 15. Early notification candidates may be offered admission, denied admission, or deferred to the regular decision process for further consideration. Applicants who are deferred to the regular decision applicant pool should submit mid-year senior grades and any new test scores and will be notified of a final admission decision on or before April 1. Applicants denied through early notification may not submit additional information and may not reapply under the regular decision process. Early notification applicants are not required to enroll at CU-Boulder if they are admitted. Admitted students who choose to attend must confirm their intent to enroll by May 1.

Freshman summer and fall applicants who do not complete their applications by the December 1 early notification deadline must submit the online application and postmark all supporting documents by the January 15 regular decision deadline. Regular decision applicants will be notified of their admission decision by April 1 and must, if they choose to attend, confirm their intent to enroll by May 1.

Summer and fall applications for transfer students are processed on a rolling basis, with full consideration given to transfer applications completed by the April 1 deadline.

For information and applications, students should contact:

Office of Admissions
University of Colorado at Boulder
552 UCB
Boulder, Colorado 80309-0552
Phone: 303-492-6301
303-492-5998 (TTY)
Web site: http://www.colorado.edu

The University of Colorado at Boulder is a major research and teaching university located in one of the most spectacular environments in the country, at the foot of the Rocky Mountains.

UNIVERSITY OF DALLAS

IRVING, TEXAS, AND ROME, ITALY

The University

In 1955, the Roman Catholic Diocese of Dallas/Fort Worth purchased land for a university on a 1,000-acre tract of rolling hills northwest of Dallas, and in 1956, the University of Dallas (UD) opened. His Excellency Bishop Thomas K. Gorman, Chancellor of the new university, announced that it would be a coeducational institution, welcoming students of all faiths and ethnic backgrounds. Headed by a lay president and a lay academic dean, the faculty was composed of laymen, diocesan and Cistercian priests, and sisters of the Order of St. Mary of Namur.

Current undergraduate enrollment is about 1,300 men and women. Undergraduates come from all fifty states and thirty-three other countries. Although approximately 75 percent are Catholic, twenty faiths are represented on campus.

The University of Dallas was the first Catholic institution to have a board of trustees made up of both lay and religious members. Since its founding, many other universities and colleges have followed its example. The first class, a group of individuals who won significant honors, such as Fulbright and Woodrow Wilson fellowships, graduated in 1960. There is a Phi Beta Kappa chapter on campus. In fact, UD is the youngest university in the twentieth century to have been awarded a Phi Beta Kappa chapter.

Through a $6-million endowment provided by the Blakley-Braniff Foundation, the Braniff Graduate School was established in 1966. Twelve graduate programs are now in existence, including doctoral programs in philosophy, politics, and literature and the M.F.A. program in art. The College of Business houses the Graduate School of Management, which is distinguished by its practice-oriented education, close ties with leading companies and professionals, and a global student body. In addition to its undergraduate programs, the College of Business offers Master of Business Administration (M.B.A.) and Master of Management degrees. The M.B.A. includes sixteen concentrations in the areas of finance, health care, information technology, management, marketing, and telecommunications.

The University of Dallas is a center of learning, and the experience on campus is intensive and highly directed. People choose to come to the University because they are serious students. While they engage in a full complement of extracurricular activities and independent study, it is the act of learning in association with their professors that shapes their college years. Because the undergraduate college is small and largely residential, it forms a close-knit community. Over 60 percent of UD's students come from outside of the state of Texas, a statistic shared by only one other Texas university; so UD is a constant bustle of activities, rarely emptying on the weekends. The University sponsors a number of lectures, concerts, and art exhibits, ranging from the old masters to the UD international printmaking invitational. The Student Government sponsors weekly events and current and classic films. The *University News* has consistently won awards for excellence in writing and design. Collegium Cantorum, the a cappella liturgical choir, performs both nationally and internationally. Intercollegiate NCAA Division III sports include baseball, basketball, cross-country, golf, lacrosse, soccer, softball, track, and volleyball. Rugby is very popular at the club level. Eighty-five percent of the on-campus students are involved in intramurals: basketball, flag football, soccer, softball, paintball, and other sports. Traditional events include coffeehouses featuring student entertainment, Charity Week, Mallapalooza, Oktoberfest, Spring Olympics, and Groundhog. UD boasts the second largest Groundhog Day celebration outside of Punxsutawney, Pennsylvania.

For Catholic students, daily and weekly Mass, Reconciliation, and rosary are held in the 500-seat Church of the Incarnation. Transportation is arranged for students of other faiths to attend services nearby. Campus Ministry provides numerous volunteer opportunities, including annual service projects in Appalachia and Ecuador.

Location

Irving, Texas, a city of 210,000 on the northwest side of the city of Dallas, is about 15 minutes from downtown Dallas, 10 minutes from Love Field airport, and 15 minutes from DFW airport. The Dallas–Fort Worth Metroplex, the fourth largest metroplex in the country, offers a diverse mix of cultural and entertainment attractions, including the Dallas Museum of Modern Art, the new Nasher Sculpture Center, and the Kimball Museum in Fort Worth. The Dallas Theater Center and Stage One have built reputations as top-notch theaters and as proving grounds for Broadway-bound productions. Dallas is home to professional sports teams in hockey, soccer, and basketball. Nearby Arlington is home to the Texas Rangers and the new Dallas Cowboys stadium.

Majors and Degrees

The Constantin College of Liberal Arts offers programs leading to the Bachelor of Arts (B.A.) degree in art and art history, biology, business, chemistry, classics, drama, economics, economics and finance, education, English, history, mathematics, modern languages (French, German, and Spanish), philosophy, physics, politics, psychology, and theology. The Bachelor of Science degree is awarded in biochemistry, biology, chemistry, mathematics, and physics.

The College of Business offers Bachelor of Arts degrees in business.

The University offers twenty-seven concentrations, or minors, including applied math, applied physics, art history, business, Christian contemplative studies, computer science, entrepreneurship, environmental science, international studies, journalism, math, medieval and Renaissance studies, modern language, music, and pure math.

Preprofessional programs in architecture, business, dentistry, engineering, law, medicine, and physical therapy are carefully integrated with the undergraduate Core Curriculum. The rate of acceptance and enrollment of the college's students by professional schools is exceptional. More than 80 percent eventually go on to graduate school, and the rate of acceptance to first-choice programs for medical and law school applicants is more than 90 percent.

Academic Programs

The undergraduate Core Curriculum is a shared series of specific courses, based on the great books of Western civilization that outline the development of Western thought and culture from classical to modern times. Every student becomes familiar with the same works of literature and the same great books and concepts, fostering a natural understanding and exchange of ideas. All students then go on to pursue their chosen major discipline, reaching a level of maturity and competence in the discipline that they could not have attained in the absence of a strong foundation shared among all students entering the major. The student body has an active and personal involvement with the Core Curriculum.

The University observes a two-semester calendar, with the semester examinations occurring before the month-long Christmas break. An interterm session and three summer sessions are also offered.

Off-Campus Programs

All undergraduates, regardless of major, are encouraged to spend one semester on the University's campus in Rome. While not compulsory, the Rome experience is an important part of the undergraduate education; to seek one's heritage in the liberal arts and to be a student of the Western world is, in a sense, to be a citizen of Rome. Courses offered in Rome are from the Core Curriculum and are taught by professors from the Texas campus. The Rome campus is located just outside of downtown Rome. Transfer students who need courses offered on the Rome campus may participate after one semester on the main campus. The cost for tuition, room, and board for all participants is roughly equivalent to that on the main campus. More than 85 percent of University of Dallas graduates have participated in the Rome program.

Academic Facilities

The Science Center, a $6-million, state-of-the-art facility, houses some of the most advanced tools for scientific research available, including a working observatory. The Haggerty Arts Village has established the University as a leading center for ceramics and fine arts in the Southwest. Drama productions are staged in the Margaret Jonsson Theater. Blakely Library holds more than 275,000 volumes, including the personal library of the late political philosopher Wilmoore Kendall.

Costs

Annual tuition and fees for 2009–10 are $24,645; room and board costs average $8220. Costs are the same for in-state and out-of-state students.

Financial Aid

Tuition, fees, room, and board are substantially lower at the University of Dallas than at many other nationally recognized universities. In addition, all high school seniors who apply for admission by the freshman scholarship priority deadline of January 15 receive priority consideration for all of the University's achievement-based awards. The University currently offers three types of achievement-based awards: academic achievements, co-curricular achievements, and departmental awards. Departments currently offering awards include art, chemistry, classics (Latin and Greek), German, French, math, physics, and Spanish. Students who apply for admission between January 16 and March 1 receive regular consideration for achievement-based awards. Those who apply for admission after March 1 are considered for achievement-based awards dependent on the availability of funding.

All students who submit a Free Application for Federal Student Aid (FAFSA) are considered for all forms of financial assistance based on their family's finances. These forms of assistance include scholarships, grants, loans, and work-study programs. Priority is given to applicants whose FAFSA is received by the University of Dallas on or before March 1. The school code for sending a FAFSA to the University of Dallas is 003651.

Faculty

The University prides itself on its teaching faculty. Ninety-two percent hold terminal degrees. With a faculty-student ratio of 1:13, extensive consultation and direction are possible. The average class size is 20. The faculty is characterized by authority in the various disciplines, and its members have published more than 1,000 books and articles and secured major research grants.

Student Government

The Student Government Association and various departmental and special clubs, such as the social, film, lecture, and fine arts committees, encourage an extracurricular life created by the students themselves.

Admission Requirements

Although no rigid cutoff point is adhered to in admission, 52 percent of the students who enter as freshmen rank in the top 10 percent of their high school class. General admission requirements include SAT or ACT scores, rank in the upper third of the high school class, and 16 college-preparatory units, including 4 in English, 3 in mathematics, 2 in the same foreign language, 2 in social science, and 2 in a laboratory science. Interviews are not required but are strongly recommended. Through the Office of Undergraduate Admission, counseling appointments, tours, and overnight accommodations on campus may be arranged. Transfer students are welcome.

Application and Information

A transcript and SAT or ACT scores must be submitted along with letters of recommendation from a teacher and a counselor. A completed application and completed supplement, both of which are obtainable online, must be submitted as well. Transfer students should submit all transcripts from colleges previously attended. A $40 application fee should accompany the application; the other material may follow as ready. The Early Action I deadline is November 1; the Early Action II deadline is December 1. The freshman priority scholarship deadline is January 15. The regular admission deadline is March 1. Rolling admission is March 2–August 1.

Transfer students should apply by December 1 for spring entry and by July 1 for fall entry.

For applications or further information, students should contact:

Office of Undergraduate Admission and Financial Aid
University of Dallas
1845 East Northgate Drive
Irving, Texas 75062
Phone: 972-721-5266
800-628-6999 (toll-free)
Web site: http://www.udallas.edu

University of Dallas students learning on-site at Sicily, Italy.

UNIVERSITY OF DENVER

DENVER, COLORADO

The University

Since its founding in 1864, the University of Denver (DU) has grown into one of the West's premier private universities, blending the friendliness and personal attention of a small college with the resources and intellectual diversity of an advanced research institution.

As the oldest private university in the Rocky Mountain region, the University is home not only to a top-ranked undergraduate program but also to a number of world-renowned research centers and professional programs, including the Josef Korbel School of International Studies, the Sturm College of Law, and the Graduate School of Professional Psychology.

The 125-acre campus brings together 4,884 traditional undergraduate students and 6,004 graduate students from fifty states and seventy-four countries. In an environment that prizes innovation, cross-disciplinary exploration, and adventurous learning partnerships between students and faculty, DU students prepare to excel in their life's work and to confront the great issues of the day.

Whatever their backgrounds and majors, DU students are engaged and active, taking advantage of the region's many recreation and cultural opportunities—everything from world-class skiing and white-water rafting to award-winning professional theater and alternative music. On campus, students attend performances at the three-venue Newman Center for the Performing Arts and cheer for the seventeen varsity teams that compete in NCAA Division I at the Ritchie Center for Sports & Wellness.

The University of Denver is accredited by the North Central Association of Colleges and Schools. The Carnegie Foundation classifies the University of Denver as a Doctoral/Research University–Extensive.

Location

Located just 8 miles from bustling downtown Denver and mere minutes from the Rocky Mountain foothills, the University of Denver's tree-shaded campus is surrounded by pleasant urban neighborhoods offering coffee shops, retail stores, and ethnic restaurants. The institution is located along a light rail line and major bus lines, providing access to the city's arts districts, shopping centers, sports arenas, and an extensive network of parks. DU students can ride all public transportation for free, using their University-supplied Eco-passes.

Majors and Degrees

The University of Denver offers twelve bachelor's degrees in over 100 programs of study, including the arts, business, computer science, engineering, humanities, international studies, mathematics, natural sciences, and social sciences. Students who are interested in preprofessional programs can choose from law, medical, dental, and veterinary programs that prepare them for professional study beyond their undergraduate degree.

In addition, the University offers 4+1 and 3+2 dual-degree programs that allow students to complete both a bachelor's and master's degree in five years or less. These dual-degree programs are offered in business, art history, international studies, public policy, and natural sciences, among others. Students in dual-degree programs maintain any financial aid and scholarships through their fifth year.

Academic Programs

Undergraduate programs at the University—which operates on the quarter system—emphasize experiential, active, and cross-disciplinary learning. All first-year undergraduate students are required to have laptop computers, which are used extensively in the classroom. DU students use their laptops as portable libraries and laboratories, extending their educational reach well beyond the classroom walls. The entire campus provides wireless Internet access through a secure connection. This includes classrooms, social areas, and even the campus greens.

First-year students enroll in a first-year seminar. Generally limited to 15 students, these seminars focus on a topic that reflects the professor's research interests. The professor, who serves as a mentor throughout the student's first year, introduces the class to university-level work and inquiry, while also advising students on everything from time management to university procedures. The seminar is complemented by a two-quarter writing sequence that trains students to conduct research, construct arguments, and write persuasively for the academic setting. The university's emphasis on writing continues throughout the next three years, with upper-division writing-intensive classes across the disciplines. By the time they graduate, DU students have developed the communication skills that are essential for career success.

Undergraduate students also complete foundations courses in mathematics and computer science, the arts and humanities, natural sciences, and social sciences. The core curriculum requires that students complete one class from each of three themes: communities and environments, self and identities, and change and continuity.

Because the university believes in the value of hands-on learning, students are encouraged to collaborate with faculty members and peers on research projects and creative endeavors. Through the Partners in Scholarship (PinS) program, the University sponsors student work through grants that fund field studies, research trips, and special materials. At year's end, students share their research and findings at a special symposium for their peers.

Thanks to opportunities like these, the University's academic programs earn high marks from students. In the 2008 National Survey of Student Engagement, a study of student satisfaction at 774 colleges and universities nationwide, first-year students and seniors at DU ranked it significantly higher than other participating doctoral-extensive schools in their appraisal of their level of academic challenge, their involvement in active and collaborative learning, their interaction with faculty members, and their enriching educational experiences.

Off-Campus Programs

To groom students for the challenges of global citizenship, the University of Denver sponsors Cherrington Global Scholars, a for-credit program that aims to send every eligible junior and senior abroad for at least a quarter of study. The University believes so strongly in this opportunity to expand understanding and foster connections that it ensures that qualifying students pay no more for the experience than they would for a quarter spent on campus. Nearly 75 percent of all students participate in study-abroad programs. The University budgets about $10 million each year in support of this outstanding program, which ranks DU second nationally for the percentage of students who study abroad.

Academic Facilities

In the last decade, the University has invested nearly $500 million in new buildings and learning centers to ensure that students can prepare for the challenges awaiting them after graduation. These include the Robert and Judi Newman Center for the Performing Arts, home to the University's celebrated Lamont School of Music and host to a performing arts series known for its adventurous offerings; the Daniels College of Business, which houses eleven case-style meeting rooms, nine seminar classrooms, and an Advanced Technology Center; the School of Hotel, Restaurant and Tourism Management, home to a full-production kitchen, a beverage-management center, a 120-person dining hall, a student-run coffee shop, and a student-faculty-staff commons; F. W. Olin Hall, which houses ten teaching labs, a greenhouse, and a full complement of classrooms and group study rooms; and the recently remodeled Sturm Hall, complete with multimedia labs and smart-to-the-seat classrooms, which serves as the headquarters for the humanities and social sciences.

Other new facilities support the University's commitment to community living and wellness. These include the Nelson Residence Hall, which features suites, common kitchens on each floor, a central courtyard, a grand dining hall, and an outdoor dining patio and the Ritchie Center for Sports & Wellness, where students of all majors and members of the Denver community come together to work out, try new sports, and watch the Pioneer athletics teams. With a state-of-the-art fitness center, a natatorium, a field house, two ice arenas, a gymnastics venue, a lacrosse stadium, and a tennis pavilion, the Ritchie Center complex supports the active lifestyle that DU students value.

Nagel Residence Hall, which opened in August 2008, serves as a campus gathering place, welcoming students and faculty at its food court, providing numerous locations for group study sessions, and offering studio space for students wanting to explore their artistic side. In keeping with the university's far-reaching sustainability initiative, the green building is LEED certified, meaning it uses key resources more efficiently than conventional buildings.

The University is committing $21.4 million to construct a new building that will house both the Morgridge College of Education and the Marsico Institute for Early Learning and Literacy. The influential institute serves as a regional and national hub for research and policy analysis on issues related to improving learning environments for young children.

The University is also home to the full-service Penrose Library whose special collections contain rare books and manuscripts as well as the Beck Archives of the Rocky Mountain Jewish Historical Society and the Carson-Brierly Dance Library.

Costs

For the 2009–10 academic year, tuition was $34,596, fees were estimated at $885, and on-campus room and board costs amounted to $9496—for a total cost of $44,977. Because the University of Denver is a private institution, costs are the same for in-state and out-of-state students.

Financial Aid

The University of Denver offers two types of financial assistance to students: need-based aid, which includes scholarships, grants, loans, and work-study based on financial need, and merit-based awards, which include scholarships based on merit or special talent. Each year, the financial aid office awards $80 million in need- and merit-based assistance to undergraduate students. About 40 percent of full-time DU undergraduates demonstrate financial need and receive some form of need-based assistance.

To recognize achievement in the classroom, the sports arena, leadership, and in music, theater, and art, the University sponsors a number of merit-based scholarships—several of which cover full tuition. Although the requirements vary from scholarship to scholarship, most are renewable each year if the student maintains a specified minimum GPA. A complete listing of scholarships is posted at http://www.du.edu/finaid/.

Need-based financial aid is computed using a number of factors, including family income, assets, size, and the number of family members attending college at the same time. DU utilizes both the CSS Profile and the Free Application for Federal Student Aid (FAFSA) to determine need-based aid. Need-based awards generally combine scholarships, grants, loans, and work-study opportunities from a variety of federal, state, and institutional sources. The financial aid offer may also include any competitive scholarships the student has been awarded at the point of admission.

The priority deadline for applying for financial aid is March 1. Because financial aid funds are limited, students who complete their financial aid applications in a timely manner are more likely to maximize financial aid resources. Funding for certain awards may not be available as time passes. The student's financial aid package cannot be determined until he or she is officially admitted to DU.

For more information on applying for financial aid at DU, students should visit http://www.du.edu/finaid.

Faculty

DU professors teach 95 percent of undergraduate courses, ensuring that students work closely with the faculty members and that the intensity of the learning environment is maximized. The average class size is 20 students, and 63 percent of undergraduate classes have fewer than 20 students.

Committed teachers, innovative researchers, and prolific publishers, University of Denver professors often include undergraduate students in their research projects and fieldwork. It is not uncommon for an undergraduate student to share publication credit with a professor or to participate in groundbreaking research with tangible benefits for humankind.

Student Government

At the University of Denver, the student population is represented by the All Undergraduate Student Association (AUSA) Senate, whose elected representatives participate in the University's legislative process and communicate student issues to the administration. In addition, the AUSA Senate oversees the allocation of the student activities fee and the licensing of DU's 100-plus student organizations.

The AUSA Senate includes senators from each major, each geographic area (on-campus, off-campus), and each class (senior, junior, etc.). The AUSA Executive Board includes an adviser, graduate adviser, president, vice president, and a cabinet of members.

Admission Requirements

Admission to the University of Denver is selective. Students are evaluated individually on the basis of their academic record, test scores, essay, and recommendations.

In making its admission decisions, the University seeks to foster an academic community of geographically, ethnically, and economically diverse learners. The admission committee looks for students who, for all their differences, are committed to integrity, innovation, inclusiveness, excellence, and community engagement.

Applicants are required to submit either the Common Application or the DU Pioneer Application, both of which are posted on the DU Web site. In addition, applicants are also required to submit their high school transcripts, scores from either the SAT or ACT, an essay, and a high school counselor recommendation. Students may also submit a teacher recommendation, although it is not required.

Applicants also are strongly encouraged to participate in the Ammi Hyde Interview, a face-to-face 20-minute conversation with as many as three members of the University community. Interviews are conducted in over 30 major cities across the country in November and February, and on campus throughout the year.

Application and Information

The University of Denver offers two application programs for first-year domestic students seeking fall-quarter admission. Early Action (postmarked by November 1) is a nonbinding program leading to an admission decision in early January. Hyde Interviews for Early Action applicants are conducted in November. Regular Decision (postmarked by January 15) is the final admission deadline for fall-quarter consideration. Hyde Interviews are conducted in February. Admission decisions are mailed in mid-March.

To learn more about the University of Denver, students should contact:

Office of Admission
University of Denver
2197 South University Boulevard
Denver, Colorado 80208

Phone: 303-871-2036
800-525-9495 (toll-free)
E-mail: admission@du.edu
Web site: http://www.du.edu/admission

UNIVERSITY OF DUBUQUE

DUBUQUE, IOWA

The University

The University of Dubuque (UD) is a private, Presbyterian, professional university with a focus in the liberal arts, as well as a theological seminary located in Iowa's first city—Dubuque. The Key City is on the Mississippi River at the point where the borders of Wisconsin, Illinois, and Iowa meet. Founded in 1852, the University is an institution in three parts: the undergraduate college, the graduate theological seminary, and the graduate institute. The University's mission of encouraging intellectual, moral, and spiritual development dates back to its founding.

Throughout its history, the University has been known as a place of educational opportunity. Even today, a large portion of its students are from first-generation or underrepresented populations. The University of Dubuque's welcoming interfaith community of approximately 1,600 students comes from across the country and around the globe.

Because students from many nations attend the University of Dubuque, UD offers students a cosmopolitan atmosphere. The school is convinced that students living in today's world are better prepared for life if they have a global perspective. American and international student interaction on campus, as well as the movement of faculty members and students across international boundaries, is essential for a meaningful education, human enrichment, and intercultural global awareness.

Location

The University of Dubuque, located in eastern Iowa, is in the heart of the Midwest. Dubuque is a city for all seasons. From bluffs blazing with autumn oranges and reds to the river sparkling with summer's blues and greens, the area scenery is spectacular year-round. Dubuque, the oldest city in Iowa, is a dynamic community built along the majestic Mississippi River and surrounded by dramatic bluffs. The setting is ideal for outdoor enthusiasts, with four seasons of ample outlets for recreation, including hiking, biking, boating, skiing, camping, golfing, climbing, and caving.

Dubuque offers the amenities of a larger city with the security and comfort of a smaller town. A lively cultural scene includes the Grand Opera House, the Dubuque Symphony Orchestra, and the Dubuque Museum of Art. The National Farm Toy Museum and the National Mississippi River Museum provide glimpses of the area's past. The city's theater productions, boutiques, and restaurants are wonderful ways to take a study break.

Nearby are some of the Midwest's most interesting cities, an easy drive for a weekend road trip. Historic Galena offers quaint shops and period architecture, while vibrant Chicago is famous for its museums and night life. Madison, Milwaukee, and Minneapolis–St. Paul are only hours away.

Majors and Degrees

With nineteen undergraduate majors, the University prepares students for careers in a variety of fields. From future teachers to corporate leaders to aspiring pilots, the University of Dubuque helps students achieve their career goals. The University's education department has the most majors, and its future teachers graduate with twice as many field-experience hours as required by the state of Iowa.

The University' Nursing Program was reinstated in the fall 2004 semester. The program offers a Bachelor of Science in Nursing (B.S.N.) degree. Nursing began at University of Dubuque in 1976 and, until 1997, the program offered fully accredited RN-to-B.S.N., B.S.N., and M.S.N. nursing preparation. The University has been granted interim approval by the Iowa Board of Nursing and is accredited by the American Association of Colleges of Nursing.

Academic departments encourage internships as an experiential component to complement classroom learning. For example, environmental science majors take advantage of the natural classroom of the Mississippi River, where students study the interaction between people and the environment. Aviation majors complete internships at the Dubuque Regional Airport or major airlines in addition to flying state-of-the-art equipment from UD's Garlick Flight Operations Center.

Academic Programs

The University of Dubuque education aims at helping students develop patterns of scholarship that make them effective learners throughout life. UD students are nurtured in the virtues of scholarship: the desire for understanding different peoples and cultures, an interest in learning, the skills to use multiple resources to explore ideas and find answers for life's questions, an understanding of conceptual connections, and the ability to reason and communicate effectively. Each graduate develops depth of knowledge in a particular field of study based on an integration of this field, the liberal arts, and his or her values.

University of Dubuque students begin to understand their chosen field of study by experiencing how it relates to other areas of knowledge. The process of exploring a variety of interests and possibilities in course work and in University activities results in the choice of a major. Current trends indicate that today's graduates change jobs and/or careers several times during their lifetimes. Therefore, professional preparation is more than a narrow, vocationally oriented process through which students prepare for one specific job. Rather, it is the development of transferable skills and attributes that allow students to succeed in a changing job market.

In the University of Dubuque community, the arts foster intellectual, emotional, and spiritual development. In literature, the visual arts, dance, drama, and music, students not only find aesthetic pleasure but also learn about other people's ideas, beliefs, and experiences and come to deeper understandings of their own.

Because of the University's location near the Mississippi—one of the world's great river systems—students have an appreciation of environmental issues. Through academic endeavors involving formal and experiential learning, students develop an understanding of the basic processes that underpin various ecological communities and of the complex interaction of human activities on the environment. The University of Dubuque encourages individuals to integrate their knowledge of the environment into personal, ethical, and spiritual guidelines, which can be used to improve their lives, their communities, and society.

The Lester G. and Michael Lester Wendt Character Initiative, supported by a substantial endowment, integrates virtues and values such as truthfulness, honesty, fairness, and the Golden Rule across the curriculum and throughout the University.

The University's Learning Institute for Fulfillment and Engagement (LIFE) offers an accelerated baccalaureate degree program for adult learners. Geared to adult learners age 23 and over, the UD LIFE program is designed to offer a flexible format, allowing students to earn a bachelor's degree in as few as three years. Offering classes on weekday evenings as well as online, the program helps adults balance their studies, career, and family life.

Off-Campus Programs

As a member of the Dubuque Tri-College Cooperative Effort, the University of Dubuque offers its students the opportunity to attend and receive credit for courses at Clarke College and Loras College, also in the city, thus providing access to the many different faculty members, professional societies, educational opportunities, and social activities of combined campuses of more than 3,500 students.

The University of Dubuque affirms the value of an international/intercultural experience and considers it to be an important component of any student's education. Overseas travel, exchanges, and study programs are available to help increase the global perspective of the students and to promote cross-cultural education.

Academic Facilities

The expanded and renovated University Science Center opened for classes in January 2007. With an additional 21,000 square feet of space, the University can devote the proper resources to its growing science programs. The new facility accommodates efficient laboratories, including state-of-the-art equipment and safety measures, bringing the science programs to the forefront of current teaching methods. Laboratory spaces include geology, zoology, general biology, cell/microbiology, science education, nursing, general chemistry, organic chemistry, geographic information systems (GIS), and five research labs to accommodate student-faculty collaborative research projects.

The Charles and Romona Myers Center, completed in September 2006, has added much-needed classroom and office space to the campus. Designed to be light, airy, and conducive to teaching and learning, the 44,000-square-foot facility houses classrooms, group study rooms, a seminar room, informal study nooks, and a 132-seat auditorium as well as administrative and faculty offices. The President's Office and the Wendt Center for Character Development are located in the building.

The Chlapaty Recreation and Wellness Center, which opened in October 2008, is an 87,000-square-foot facility enveloping the existing football stadium as well as additional construction looking west. Features include a 6,900-square-foot, two-level fitness center, including areas for cardiovascular workout and free weights/machines, as well as a room for activities such as pilates, yoga, etc.; a 200-meter, six-lane indoor track with synthetic flooring for fitness walking and performance; four multiuse courts nested in the center of the track for intramurals and indoor practices; a training room and examination rooms; home, visitor, officials, and faculty/staff locker rooms; a juice bar and lounge area; a 3,000-seat football stadium, including east side visitor seating for 1,000 and an expanded concessions area; and a lighted field, synthetic field turf surface, and new eight-lane outdoor track.

Costs

Tuition costs for the 2009–10 academic year were $20,758. Average room and board costs were $6990. These costs do not include books, supplies, personal expenses, and travel.

Financial Aid

Eighty-five percent of the University of Dubuque's students receive financial assistance through scholarships, awards and grants, loans, or work-study programs. The average financial assistance package for 2008–09 was $19,118. All levels of household incomes receive financial assistance.

To apply for financial assistance, applicants must submit a completed application package for admission to the University of Dubuque, file a FAFSA after January 1 and before April 1 (the priority deadline), and send or fax a copy of the completed FAFSA to the University of Dubuque Office of Student Financial Planning. Institutional, federal, state, and alternative loan programs are all available as forms of financial assistance.

Faculty

Seventy percent of University of Dubuque faculty members have earned a Ph.D. or other terminal degree. The student-faculty ratio is 15:1.

Student Government

The Student Government Association (SGA) represents the student body through general election of individual student representatives. The SGA sponsors four campus organizations, the University Program Council (UPC), the Spartan Spirit Club, *Under The Bell Tower* (student newspaper), and *The Key* (student yearbook). SGA provides student representatives for a number of key administrative committees.

Admission Requirements

An applicant for admission to the University of Dubuque undergraduate program is a graduate of a high school or equivalent (GED) and presents a minimum of 15 high school units, of which 10 are from academic fields (English, social studies, natural science, mathematics, foreign language). Either ACT or SAT scores are required. The admission committee looks at the application and transcript for indications of school achievement as well as aspiration, creativity, and adventurousness. Applicants to the University are usually active in cocurricular activities and these, as well as leadership qualities and character, are considered. An on-campus visit is encouraged. Two recommendations and an essay are requested and read with care.

Application and Information

First-year students are admitted to the University on a rolling basis. When the application and all supporting materials (e.g., transcripts and teacher and counselor recommendations) have been received, admission decisions are made by the admission committee and students are advised of the University's decision.

Transfer students who are enrolled or who were previously enrolled at another college or university may apply for transfer to the University of Dubuque. The University considers transfer applications for fall and spring semesters.

In addition to completing the application materials required for first-year applicants, transfer applicants must submit a complete official transcript for all college courses taken and grades received and a complete official transcript for all secondary school courses taken and grades received.

For further information, students should contact:

Office of Admission
University of Dubuque
2000 University Avenue
Dubuque, Iowa 52001
Phone: 563-589-3000
800-722-5583 (toll-free)
E-mail: admssns@dbq.edu
Web site: http://www.dbq.edu

Chalmers Field at the newly constructed Chlapaty Recreation and Wellness Center.

THE UNIVERSITY OF FINDLAY

FINDLAY, OHIO

The University

The University of Findlay (UF) is a private coeducational institution with more than 4,100 full- and part-time students. Founded in 1882 by the Churches of God, General Conference, and the citizens of Findlay, it emphasizes preparation for careers and professions in an educational program that blends liberal arts and career education. Students of many denominations attend Findlay, and religious participation is a matter of personal choice.

Bachelor's degree programs are available in nearly sixty different majors. Master's degrees are offered in athletic training; business administration; education; environmental, safety, and health management; occupational therapy; physician assistant studies; and teaching English to speakers of other languages (TESOL) and bilingual education. A Doctor of Pharmacy (Pharm.D.) degree program graduates its first class in 2010, and a Doctor of Physical Therapy program will graduate its first students in 2011.

The largest programs at Findlay are animal science/pre–veterinary medicine, equestrian studies, business, pharmacy, and education. Majors in the sciences and health professions include athletic training, chemistry, computer science, equestrian studies (English, Western, and equine management), nuclear medicine, occupational therapy, physical therapy, premedicine, and animal science/pre–veterinary medicine. Business degrees are founded in a comprehensive core program with eleven different majors.

Opportunities for internships and work-related experiences are available in most major fields.

Most of Findlay's students come from Ohio and the surrounding states of Michigan, Indiana, and Pennsylvania. More than thirty other states are also represented. UF also has a strong international-student population, with more than 500 international students from twenty-five countries and territories.

Resident students live in eight modern residence halls and several town-house-style apartments. Social life at Findlay centers on student organizations, fraternities, and sororities. Findlay has three officially recognized fraternities: Alpha Sigma Phi, Tau Kappa Epsilon, and Theta Chi; there are two sororities: Phi Sigma Sigma and Sigma Kappa. Organizations include department and special interest clubs, the newspaper, musical groups, a radio and TV station, Circle K, and Aristos Eklektos (honors).

Athletic programs are affiliated with NCAA Division II and the Great Lakes Intercollegiate Athletic Conference, with the exception of the equestrian teams, which have won national championships in the Intercollegiate Horse Show Association. Findlay offers twelve intercollegiate sports for men: baseball, basketball, cross-country, equestrian, football, golf, indoor track and field, outdoor track and field, soccer, swimming and diving, tennis, and wrestling. It has eleven varsity sports for women: basketball, cross-country, equestrian, golf, indoor track and field, outdoor track and field, soccer, softball, swimming and diving, tennis, and volleyball. Athletic scholarships are available.

Croy Physical Education Center has a 25-meter swimming pool, a gymnasium, offices, and classrooms. The Gardner Fitness Center is a state-of-the-art facility. The 130,000-square-foot Koehler Recreation and Fitness Complex, opened in 1999, contains the Malcolm Athletic Center, with a six-lane, NCAA-regulation track; sand pits for long jump; state-of-the-art timing system; wrestling room; four multipurpose courts; locker rooms; a cardio center; and offices for the athletic department. Also under the same roof are a cardio center, which serves an average of 500 patrons a day during the winter months, and as of August 2010, a new student recreation center with basketball, volleyball, and tennis courts, a rock climbing wall, a game room, and more.

Student services include career and placement counseling, the Cosiano Health Center, academic tutoring and personal counseling, and study skills assistance through the Academic Support Center.

Location

Findlay was voted the most livable micropolitan city in Ohio and scored among the top twelve in the United States. It is within easy driving distance of Toledo, Columbus, Detroit, and Fort Wayne. Interstate 75 and the Ohio Turnpike (Interstates 80 and 90) are major highways serving the area. Airports in Toledo, Columbus, and Detroit are convenient. The town of Findlay has more than 37,000 residents and is home to Marathon Oil Corporation and Cooper Tire and Rubber Company. The Findlay campus consists of more than 385 acres on several sites. A 152-acre campus-owned farm houses the pre–veterinary medicine and Western equestrian studies programs, including a 31,000-square-foot animal science center dedicated in 2009 with two 50-seat classrooms, a laboratory, a pharmacy, a student lounge, locker rooms, offices, instructional demonstration areas, holding pens, and other animal servicing areas. A second 52-acre facility houses the English riding program. Approximately 450 horses are stabled and trained at the equestrian facilities, which offer barns and indoor and outdoor riding arenas.

Many opportunities exist for students who want business-related and social service agency experience. The University has established strong relationships with the community, which supports athletic and cultural events on the campus. Besides the full program of on-campus activities, off-campus trips to cultural and entertainment events are scheduled. The city of Findlay, which has an excellent business climate, offers part-time job opportunities, volunteer service organizations, and the chance to be involved with the larger civic community. Findlay's campus is attractive, safe, comfortable, and friendly.

Majors and Degrees

The Bachelor of Arts (B.A.) degree is awarded in the following majors: adolescent/young adult/integrated English/language arts, adolescent/young adult/integrated social studies, art, art management, children's book illustration, criminal justice administration, digital media, English, English as an international language, graphic design, health communication, history, Japanese, journalism, law and the liberal arts, middle childhood/language arts and social studies, multiage/drama/theater, multiage/Japanese, multiage/Spanish, multiage/visual arts, organizational communication, philosophy/applied philosophy, political science, psychology, public relations, religious studies, social work, sociology, Spanish, studio art, teaching English to speakers of other languages, and theater. Minors are offered in numerous areas.

The Bachelor of Science (B.S.) degree is granted in accounting; adolescent/young adult/earth science; adolescent/young adult/integrated mathematics; adolescent/young adult/life science; animal science; biology (recommended for premedicine); business administration; business management; chemistry (recommended for premedicine); computer science; early childhood; economics; entrepreneurship; environmental, safety, and occupational health management; equestrian studies (English and Western emphases); equine business management; finance; forensic science; health education; health science (in preparation for occupational therapy, physical therapy, or physician assistant graduate study); health studies; hospitality management; human resource management; international business; intervention specialist/mild to moderate disabilities; marketing; mathematics; medical technology; middle childhood/language arts/math; middle childhood/language arts/science; middle childhood/math/science; middle childhood/math/social studies; middle childhood/science/social studies; multiage/health education;

multiage/physical education; nuclear medicine technology; operations and logistics; physical education; and strength and conditioning.

The Associate of Arts degree is available in accounting, computer science, criminal justice administration (corrections or law enforcement emphases), English as an international language, equestrian studies (English and Western riding), financial management, general social studies, human resource management, humanities, management information systems, massage therapy, nuclear medicine technology, personal training, religious studies, sales/retail management, and small business/entrepreneurship. Certificate programs are available in a variety of areas.

Academic Programs

Findlay operates on the semester system. Students must complete at least 124 semester hours with a minimum overall grade point average of 2.0 to earn a bachelor's degree. General education requirements and competency requirements in English, computer literacy, and speech must be fulfilled. The Oiler Experience is intended to introduce all freshmen to college life at UF. The course is designed and taught by a cadre of student services professionals whose educational backgrounds and specialized training are focused on assisting students to succeed, both in and out of the classroom. The Gateway Program offers students the chance to develop those skills in writing, reading, and thinking needed for their success as college students. Study skills, time management, and academic advising are included. Students are selected for this program at the time of admission. The Honors Program provides additional challenge to those students who qualify on the basis of academic credentials. Study- and travel-abroad programs are offered by various departments. Credit and/or placement can be earned through Advanced Placement (AP) exams.

The Equestrian Program is a well-recognized program of its kind and serves approximately 280 students from throughout the United States and abroad. Majors in equine business management and in English and Western riding are offered. The instruction, both in the classroom and on horseback, makes use of the expertise of recognized national equestrian champions. The pre–veterinary medicine program, using the farm facilities, offers the advantages of hands-on experience with livestock and an internship program in a distinctive curriculum. Graduates of the pre–veterinary program have been accepted to all twenty-eight veterinary schools in the United States, and several internationally.

The Nuclear Medicine Institute provides the training necessary to qualify students for careers in nuclear medicine technology, a growing health-related career field.

Academic Facilities

The focal point of the Findlay campus is Old Main, which houses classrooms, faculty and administrative offices, the computer center, facilities for various student activities, and the Ritz Auditorium. Shafer Library is a member of a consortium that provides extensive resources to students. The Gardner Fine Arts Pavilion, dedicated in 1994, houses the Mazza Museum of International Art from Children's Books, the first and largest teaching museum in the world dedicated to literacy and children's book art. The University has numerous computer labs. In 2006, the University acquired and renovated a building at 300 Davis St., with its 62,000 square feet comprising the largest addition of academic space since the construction of Old Main. Other academic buildings include the Frost Science Center, with the Newhard Planetarium, and the Egner Center for the Performing Arts, which houses a 200-seat theater.

Costs

Tuition for the 2009–10 academic year totaled $25,016 for most programs. Room and board cost $8554. The estimated cost for transportation, books, fees, and supplies was $2496. There are additional tuition charges for equestrian studies and pre–veterinary medicine.

Financial Aid

Assistance is based on need as well as scholastic achievement. In 2009–10, 80 percent of UF students received institutional financial aid from the University. The average financial aid award for students with need in fall 2009 was $19,944. Merit scholarships at UF range from $9000 to $14,000 a year. Notification of aid awards is made on a rolling basis. Work-study jobs are available. Scholarships for high-achieving students and student athletes are offered.

Faculty

The 16:1 student-faculty ratio results in small classes—with an average class size of 18 students. Professors know their students, and every student has a faculty adviser.

Student Government

The Student Government Association (SGA) and the Campus Program Board are involved in planning and implementing student activities. SGA provides leadership experience for students and enhances cooperation among faculty members, the administration, and students. A representative from SGA sits on the Board of Trustees. The Campus Program Board plans activities for recreation and cultural enrichment.

Admission Requirements

The University of Findlay considers each applicant on an individualized basis. The University accepts applications on a rolling basis, but it encourages students to complete applications by January 15, as the class fills rapidly. Application deadlines are August 1 for the fall semester and December 15 for the spring semester. Major factors associated with rendering a decision include GPA, standardized test scores, and strength of curriculum. Although it is not required, a campus admission visit is encouraged. Applicants to Findlay should have a college-preparatory high school background, including 4 years of English, 3 to 4 years of mathematics, 2 to 3 years of social studies, and 2 years of science. A foreign language is recommended but not required. Results of the ACT or SAT should be submitted with the application for admission. Transfer students must be eligible to return to the institution last attended and must submit transcripts of all college work. For students not meeting regular minimum admission requirements, Findlay has a Gateway Program, which provides skill building and academic support during the first semester of the freshman year. Findlay is an equal opportunity institution in admission and employment.

Application and Information

For application forms and other information, students may contact:

Office of Undergraduate Admissions
The University of Findlay
1000 North Main Street
Findlay, Ohio 45840
Phone: 419-434-4732
800-548-0932 (toll-free)
E-mail: admissions@findlay.edu
Web site: http://www.findlay.edu

Old Main.

UNIVERSITY OF GREAT FALLS

GREAT FALLS, MONTANA

The University

The University of Great Falls (UGF) is a private, Catholic liberal arts university sponsored by the Sisters of Providence within the jurisdiction of the Catholic Bishop of Great Falls–Billings. UGF is open to qualified men and women of every race and creed. UGF offers the Corps of Discovery, a distinctive, outside-of-the-classroom, personal-formation program. Students develop their leadership and team abilities through a variety of physical challenges, collaborative efforts, artistic endeavors, and spiritual and service activities.

UGF's academic programs are designed to educate students through curricula featuring liberal arts courses combined with career and professional preparation. The University's mission is to provide students with the opportunity to obtain a liberal arts education for lifelong learning and a successful career or profession. The faculty and staff members of the University join with students in a cooperative and enthusiastic search for truth, meaning, and the analytical skills to resolve moral and ethical dilemmas. The low student-faculty ratio (12:1) equates to more individual attention and help with both academic and personal development. Although faculty members participate in applied research, the focus is on teaching. Because teaching students is the primary concern of faculty members, they combine traditional classroom instruction with education using multimedia computer technology and learning through internships, field experiences, and community service.

The University was founded in 1932 by Bishop Edwin V. O'Hara to fill the need for an institution of higher education in Great Falls and the central Montana area. The present campus opened in 1960. Providence Tower, the main campus landmark, was constructed in 1964, and McLaughlin Memorial Center, a spacious physical education and recreation facility, was added in 1965. The campus consists of more than a dozen buildings, including Sullivan Hall, Emilie Hall, the DiRocco-Peressini Science Center, a theater/music building, an art building, Galerie Trinitas, Trinitas Chapel, and the library. The library, which was doubled in size in 1999, provides additional study room for students. The University of Great Falls has been accredited by the Northwest Association of Schools and Colleges since 1935.

The University's athletic programs include men's and women's basketball, cross-country, golf, soccer, and track; men's wrestling; and softball and volleyball. Playing in the Frontier Conference, the Argonauts enhance the community's quality of life and offer student athletes opportunities to be a part of a highly competitive, nationally recognized program. "Jason the Argonaut" has been the school's mascot since UGF started athletic programs in 1967. UGF's chosen mascot stems from Greek mythology and the story of Jason and his band of courageous men, called the Argonauts, in their quest for the Golden Fleece.

Student-life activities abound in the UGF community. The Argo Café and lounge in the Student Center are a popular socializing and studying place that is central to the campus. The spacious campus offers a year-round setting for student-initiated activities. On a winter day, it is quite common to see students snowboarding on the large hill next to Emilie Hall. On fall and spring days, many students enjoy flag football, Frisbee, FOLF, and, of course, the seasonal water fights and Slip 'N' Slide. Students also have opportunities throughout the semester to participate in intramural sports, attend community events, and engage in a wide variety of outdoor recreation.

Location

The city of Great Falls is located in north-central Montana. Situated next to the five waterfalls of the Missouri River at an elevation of 3,300 feet, the city lies between the Rocky Mountains and Great Plains. The river, a historically significant waterway explored by the Lewis and Clark Expedition in 1805, provides abundant recreational opportunities such as boating, canoeing, and fishing its blue-ribbon trout waters. Great Falls is also home to the Lewis and Clark National Historic Trail Interpretive Center and the Charlie Russell Museum, which displays the treasured works of the famous Western artist Charles M. Russell. On the museum grounds, sit the Russell home and the artist's log studio. Great Falls exemplifies the Western heritage and ethos of the Big Sky Country of Montana.

Nestled near the Big Belt, Little Belt, and Highwood Mountain Ranges, Great Falls is centrally located in one of the nation's most scenic regions. For skiing enthusiasts, the Little Belt Mountains, an hour south of Great Falls, offer excellent downhill skiing at Showdown Ski Area and 17 miles of groomed cross-country trails at Silver Crest. In addition to skiing, the surrounding area provides extensive outdoor recreational activities, including biking, hiking, camping, technical rock climbing, white-water rafting, archaeological exploration, fishing, and hunting. About an hour west of the city lies the Rocky Mountain Front Range, which extends northward to one of the country's crown jewels, Glacier National Park. The majestic peaks of this area provide outdoor enthusiasts with hundreds of miles of trails and pristine lakes and streams. Four hours to the south of Great Falls is Yellowstone National Park, where abundant herds of bison and elk roam the vast spaces. Many other species of wildlife call Yellowstone home, including the reintroduced wolf.

The central location of Great Falls gives students the opportunity to explore numerous surrounding communities with local attractions and shops.

Majors and Degrees

At the undergraduate level, the University of Great Falls offers curricular programs in thirty-five areas, including bachelor's degrees in twenty-three majors and associate degrees in three majors. Through the integration of liberal arts and professional preparation, the University helps students prepare for lifelong learning and rewarding careers.

Academic Programs

The University develops professional/career programs designed to meet society's present and future needs, as well as traditional academic degrees in appropriate fields. As part of the undergraduate core curriculum, students acquire fundamental skills and experiences that facilitate comprehension, information processing, and communication within particular disciplines. Beyond the learning required for their chosen majors, students embark on a path of self-discovery and learn to apply meaning to the world around them from historical, contemporary, and future perspectives. All students are required to complete courses in communications, composition, computer science, fine arts, history, literature, mathematics, natural science, social sciences, and theology and religion.

As part of the Freshman Experience, the University of Great Falls introduces its Corps of Discovery Program. Like the 1804 adventure lead by Captains William Clark and Meriwether Lewis, the Corps of Discovery at the University takes students on an extraordinary journey of adventure, discovery, and accomplishments. The Corps of Discovery at UGF is an opportunity for students to learn outside of the classroom while gaining the skills necessary to be successful academically and professionally. It is a life experience where lessons are learned from the desktop to the mountaintop.

UGF serves students of all beliefs while offering a foundation for actively implementing spiritual values and a variety of religious teachings that are rooted in the Catholic tradition. Students are strongly encouraged to complement classroom learning with nonacademic learning in the areas of community service, wellness activities, and cultural arts.

Off-Campus Programs

The Distance Learning Program provides instruction to students throughout the country and around the world, enabling them to complete four undergraduate degrees and one master's degree from their home or work. Many students choose to begin their lower-division course work at home and then move to the campus to complete their degree. Distance learning students receive instruction through a variety of media technologies, such as videotapes, e-mail, and Internet conferencing. Students benefit from a mix of self-study and live Internet classroom sessions for a uniquely personal distance learning environment. The UGF Distance Learning Program offers high-quality educational opportunities to students who would not otherwise have access to the campus.

Academic Facilities

The University library provides informational resources for students and faculty and staff members. The collection contains more than 106,000 books and 400 journal subscriptions. Services include access to reference materials, interlibrary loan, and more than 50 online databases from InfoTrac, ProQuest, OCLC First Search, and LexisNexis. In addition, fax services, copiers, and workstations for the disabled are available for student use. Special collections include the McDonald Collection of Business Resources, the Bertsche Collection of Montana History, and the Korontzos Law Library. An audiovisual collection with videocassettes, records, CDs, scores, and other media can be used in the library.

The main computer lab, which is centrally located in Sullivan Hall, houses more than forty personal computers, while other labs on campus house more than thirty-five additional personal computers. These computers are upgraded yearly and are available for use by all students. UGF students take advantage of the wireless Internet connection in the student center, Sullivan Hall, and the library. Students can access the Internet and e-mail through the UGFNET from on-campus residence halls. The lab supports one of the most widely used Windows-based software suites, and peripheral equipment is always available.

The University offers student support services to help students achieve academic success. The Center for Academic Excellence serves first-generation students, students with limited income, and students with disabilities and is strongly committed to both their academic success and personal growth. To accomplish this goal, the center provides a wide range of services and activities to all eligible students, including academic support, personal counseling, minority student support, and support for students with disabilities. Tutoring, academic support, and personal counseling are also available in the Grandma Rice Retention Center.

The University collaborated with the Montana State University–Bozeman College of Nursing to establish a student health center. The center offers limited primary care to UGF students and faculty and staff members. It is staffed by an advanced-practice registered nurse/family practitioner with prescriptive authority. The clinic focuses on treating acute illnesses as well as promoting wellness and education about at-risk behaviors.

The McLaughlin Memorial Center is a site used for health and physical education classes, as well as athletic competition. Facilities include a large gymnasium, a state-of-the-art wellness exercise center, a large conference room, and academic classrooms. In the fall of 2007, the McLaughlin Memorial Center began a huge transformation. It now houses a state-of-the-art fitness and recreation area and includes a juice bar, café, and comfortable fireside study and TV lounge areas for late night study sessions.

With seating for 357 people, the University Theater is used frequently by the campus and the community. Theater students produce one play per semester as part of their course requirement. Musicians, comedians, and local groups also perform regularly in the building.

Costs

Undergraduate tuition for the 2009–10 school year was $17,170. Room and board for students living in University housing were $6270. Books and supplies were estimated to cost $900 per year. Emilie Hall, a newly renovated residence hall on campus, is designated for first year students. A growing university population has opened the door for new student housing options. Most notable is the conversion of Providence Hall to student living quarters. A scenic courtyard, large kitchen facility, recently renovated lounge, and free wireless Internet access in rooms are just a few of the amenities Providence Hall has to offer. The on-campus location offers security and extreme proximity to important student services. Providence Hall is handicapped accessible and many of the rooms have sinks. The Villa, an off-campus apartment complex, is designated for students age 21 and older, married students, or students with children. The Lincoln Heights apartments are new housing units available to upperclass students.

Financial Aid

Approximately 95 percent of students at UGF receive some form of financial assistance. The University offers more than $2 million annually in merit-based, athletic, and need-based Courage awards. Information on need-based financial assistance programs is available from the Financial Aid Office. Scholarship information for new students is available from the Admissions Office. To be considered for financial aid, students should submit a Free Application for Federal Student Aid (FAFSA) form electronically at http://www.fafsa.ed.gov with UGF's school code of 002527. To be considered for scholarships, students should submit an application for admission along with academic transcripts.

Faculty

UGF has a student-faculty ratio of 12:1 and features faculty members who possess personal philosophies that are compatible with a Catholic learning environment. These experienced teachers, of whom 57 percent possess terminal degrees, are not only highly competent in their academic fields but also persons of integrity to whom students can look for example, inspiration, and information. Since a faculty member's influence is of paramount significance in education, an ability and willingness to mentor students about academic concerns and lifelong goals are traits that are expected of each teacher.

Student Government

The University's students are represented by the Associated Students of the University of Great Falls. The governing body is an elected Student Senate. The University student government was the first in Montana to eliminate the class structure in favor of giving greater representation to all students. One student is a full voting member of the Board of Trustees.

Admission Requirements

The University of Great Falls Admissions Office accepts applicants on a rolling basis. Students are encouraged to submit their test scores from the ACT or the SAT. The scores from these tests are used in scholarship consideration, academic counseling, and course placement. The University also has an early admission program for students in high school. The University of Great Falls grants advanced standing credit for AP, CLEP, and ACE military programs.

Application and Information

The University of Great Falls is committed to a program of equal opportunity for education, employment, and participation in University activities without regard to race, color, gender, age, religion, marital status, sexual orientation, physical handicap, national origin, or mental handicap. For additional information about the University of Great Falls, including an admission packet, students should contact:

Office of Admissions
University of Great Falls
1301 20th Street South
Great Falls, Montana 59405
Phone: 406-791-5202
800-856-9544 (toll-free)
Fax: 406-791-5209
E-mail: enroll@ugf.edu
Web site: http://www.ugf.edu

Why is courage our guiding light? Because the University of Great Falls was built on it.

COLLEGE CLOSE-UPS

UNIVERSITY OF GUELPH

GUELPH, ONTARIO, CANADA

The University

The University of Guelph is a high quality, student-focused, residential college that is committed to innovative programs, dynamic student-faculty interaction, and an integration of learning and research. It offers a wide range of undergraduate and graduate programs in the arts, humanities, social sciences, engineering, and natural sciences. Building on these core disciplines, Guelph also has a strong commitment to interdisciplinary programs, to a selected range of professional and applied programs, and to agriculture and veterinary medicine as areas of special responsibility.

Established in 1964 when three century-old founding colleges joined with a new college of arts and science, the University of Guelph is a vital community of more than 18,000 students on a campus of historical and modern buildings and redbrick walkways. By Canadian standards, Guelph is of medium size, offering a wide range of academic programs while providing a safe, accommodating environment for learning. On-campus living is available for more than 5,200 students, with all new first-semester students guaranteed on-campus housing if they apply by the deadline.

Guelph features state-of-the-art athletic facilities that include a double arena with an Olympic-size ice surface, two pools, a field house and indoor track, aerobic and weight-training gymnasiums, six squash courts, and a climbing wall. Guelph offers thirty varsity sports teams and in recent years has fielded national and provincial championship football, hockey, track and field, and rugby teams.

With 70 percent of Guelph's undergraduate classes consisting of fewer than 30 students, Guelph ensures a personal approach to learning with a 1:22 faculty-student ratio. The success of the Center for New Students, which assists new students with the transition from secondary school to university, is reflected in Guelph's 90.5 percent student retention rate and a 96.6 percent graduate employment rate, both well above the Canadian national average.

The University of Guelph offers a Doctor of Veterinary Medicine degree as well as several diploma programs and more than eighty master's and doctoral degree programs. The graduate calendar is available on the Web at http://www.uoguelph.ca/GraduateStudies.

Location

The University of Guelph's main campus is located in the southwestern Ontario region the *New York Times* calls "Canada's Technology Triangle," a locale known for its high-caliber educational institutions and innovative companies. This city of more than 118,000 features internationally recognized folk, jazz, and writers' festivals as well as a multipurpose performing arts center and a sports and entertainment center. Positioned within an hour's drive of Toronto, Canada's largest city, Guelph offers the comfort of small-community living with the excitement of an international metropolis at its doorstep. In addition to the main campus, the University of Guelph offers degrees in Toronto at the University of Guelph–Humber and regional campuses throughout Ontario in Alfred, Kemptville, and Ridgetown.

Majors and Degrees

The University of Guelph offers a number of undergraduate degree programs. Programs followed by an asterisk (*) indicate degrees that students can pursue in a traditional four-year or in a five-year co-op format. Co-ops offer students the opportunity to work in three to five different companies in paid work placements that result in one year of full-time work as a part of the degree experience.

The University of Guelph offers Bachelor of Arts degrees in anthropology; applied mathematics and statistics (co-op only); art history; classical studies; criminal justice and public policy; economics*; English; environmental governance; European studies; French studies; food, agriculture, and resource economics; geography; Hispanic studies; history; information systems and human behavior; international development; major to be determined; mathematical economics; mathematics; music; philosophy; political science; psychology*; rural and development sociology; sociology; statistics; studio art; and theater studies. In addition, a Bachelor of Arts and Sciences degree is available to students who excel in both arts/social sciences and sciences.

Bachelor of Applied Science degrees are available in applied human nutrition; child, youth, and family*; and adult development, families, and well-being*.

Bachelor of Commerce degrees are available in accounting, agricultural business*, hotel and food administration*, human resources management, management economics (industry and finance)*, marketing management*, public management*, real estate and housing*, tourism management, and undeclared (first year only).

Bachelor of Bio-Resource Management degrees are available in environmental management and equine management. Students in these programs begin their studies in the regional campuses and finish the final two years in Guelph.

The Bachelor of Computing degrees are available in computer science* and software engineering*.

Bachelor of Engineering degrees are available in biological engineering*, biomedical engineering*, computer engineering*, environmental engineering*, engineering systems and computing*, mechanical engineering*, water resources engineering*, and undeclared (first year only).

Bachelor of Science degrees are available in animal biology, applied mathematics and statistics*, biological and pharmaceutical chemistry, biomedical science, biochemistry*, biological science, biophysics*, chemical physics*, chemistry*, earth surface science, ecology, environmental biology, environmental toxicology*, food science*, human kinetics, marine and freshwater biology, mathematics, microbiology*, molecular biology and genetics, nanoscience, nutritional and nutraceutical sciences, physical sciences, physics*, plant science, psychology (brain and cognition), statistics, theoretical physics, toxicology*, wildlife biology, and zoology.

Bachelor of Science in Agriculture degrees are available in animal science; crop, horticulture, and turfgrass sciences; honors agriculture; and organic agriculture.

Bachelor of Science in Environmental Sciences degrees are available in earth and atmospheric science*, ecology*, environmental biology*, environmental economics and policy*, environmental geography*, and natural resources management*.

The University of Guelph also offers a Bachelor of Landscape Architecture degree and a Doctor of Veterinary Medicine degree.

University of Guelph–Humber programs include honors degrees in business administration (accounting, finance, not-for-profit enterprises, marketing, and small business management and entrepreneurship); applied science (early childhood services, family and community social services, justice studies, kinesiology, or psychology); and applied arts in media studies (journalism, public relations, digital communications, and image arts).

Academic Programs

The academic year is divided into three semesters: fall (September through December), winter (January through April), and summer (May through August), with the majority of students in attendance during the fall and winter semesters. Fall is the normal entry point for all semester one students. However, transfer students who apply by deadlines are considered for many programs at all entry points.

Four-year honors degrees require the completion of eight semesters. Three-year general degrees require the completion of six semesters. A typical full-time semester totals 2.5 credits.

Off-Campus Programs

An important part of Guelph's mission is to attract students from around the world and develop a global perspective in its students. The campus attracts more than 700 international students from over 100 countries, maintains fifty-four exchange programs with thirty-two countries, and offers five semester-abroad options. In addition, approximately 500 Guelph students study, research, or work each year in Africa, Australia, Europe, and South and Central America.

More than 2,500 students participate in co-op work semesters, making the co-op program at the University of Guelph one of the highest in co-op student enrollments among Ontario universities. Guelph also offers more than 100 distance degree credit courses to nearly 8,000 Open Learning course registrants.

Academic Facilities

Guelph's two libraries are linked with libraries at two other universities in the region, providing students with access to 7.5 million items through a new, state-of-the-art automated library system. Guelph's library holdings include Canada's largest collection of theater archives, extensive Scottish study materials, and one of the best collections of postcolonial African literature in Canada.

A 30-acre research park adjacent to the campus is home to a growing number of research-intensive industries. Industry and government trust Guelph's faculty members to meet their research needs, offering approximately Can$138 million annually for research that ranges from workplace efficiency to developing better approaches to food packaging and marketing to ensuring the availability of clean water.

All students receive free central computing accounts, which allow access to the University's integrated electronic services from on or off campus. These services include e-mail, access to the Internet, computer-assisted instruction, conferencing, course selection, and high-quality laser printing. All student residences are directly connected to the Internet via the campus high-speed network. Off-campus students have access to chargeable high-speed Internet providers.

The campus also features two art galleries, a Sculpture Park, two performance stages, a covered field house, a Can$144-million Science Complex, the new Guelph Institute for the Environment, as well as the Biodiversity Institute, which is the world's first center for high-volume DNA barcoding. The 408-acre Arboretum on the west side of the campus has nearly 5 miles of jogging trails and nature paths.

Costs

Full-time tuition for the 2010 academic year ranged from Can$2494 to Can$3922 per semester for Canadian residents and from Can$8097 to Can$10,715 per semester for international students. Mandatory fees totaled approximately Can$520 per semester, with slight variations according to each college. International students are obliged to purchase health-care coverage through the University. The cost for international students to attend Guelph for two semesters, including tuition and academic fees, health coverage, housing, clothing, food, and books, totaled between Can$26,000 and Can$32,000.

Financial Aid

The University of Guelph is committed to ensuring that a university education remains an attainable goal. In total, Can$14.3 million in annual student financial aid is given in the form of scholarships, awards, bursaries, and work-study opportunities. There are scholarships (ranging from Can$500 to Can$6000) and bursaries specifically designed for international students who are allowed to work on and off campus.

Faculty

The percentage of Guelph's 855 full-time professors who hold the Ph.D. degree or its equivalent is 99.9 percent, and all strive to bring the excitement and process of research into the learning environment. More than 100 professors have been recognized for excellence in teaching by external agencies, their peers, and students. No comparably sized university in the country has more 3M awards, Canada's most prestigious university teaching honor. Guelph has 19 Fellows of the Royal Society of Canada among its researchers.

Student Government

Students are involved at all levels of University government, from the residence council to the Senate and the Board of Governors. The Central Student Association (CSA), which represents all undergraduate students, oversees more than fifty student clubs that range from political to recreational. In addition, there are more than fifty academic and other student-government organizations located on campus. Students also have access to a number of service groups on campus, which range from the Ontario Public Interest Research Group to a community radio station and Habitat for Humanity.

Admission Requirements

Ontario applicants must present the Ontario Secondary School Diploma (OSSD), with a minimum of six 4U or 4M courses and specific subject requirements for the degree program desired. English 4U is required for all degree programs. For those outside Ontario, the secondary graduation certificate that would admit a student to a university in his or her home country is normally acceptable. Applicants must also satisfy the specific subject requirements for the program desired. Applicants who have completed the International Baccalaureate (I.B.) are granted credit for higher-level courses with grades of 5 or better. Applicants who have completed Advanced Placement (AP) exams with a minimum grade of 4 are eligible to receive University credit to a maximum of 2 credits, which is subject to the discretion of the appropriate faculty. United States applicants are required to have a minimum grade point average of 3.0 and a combined SAT score of at least 1100 (critical reading and math components) or an ACT score of at least 24. Applicants should include specific subject requirements at the highest secondary school level offered.

Interested students should call Admission Services or refer to its Web site at http://uoguelph.ca/admissions for application and deadline dates, detailed admission information, and downloadable application forms. Students interested in University of Guelph–Humber programs should contact Admission Services at http://www.guelphhumber.ca.

Application and Information

For additional information about admissions, academic programs, or University visits and tours, students should contact:

Admission Services
Office of Registrarial Services
Third Floor, University Centre
University of Guelph
Guelph, Ontario N1G 2W1
Canada
Phone: 519-821-2130 or 824-4120 Ext. 58721
Fax: 519-766-9481
E-mail: International inquiries: internat@registrar.uoguelph.ca
U.S. inquiries: usa@registrar.uoguelph.ca
Canadian inquiries: admission@registrar.uoguelph.ca
Web site: http://admission.uoguelph.ca
http://www.guelphhumber.ca

Students on the campus of the University of Guelph.

UNIVERSITY OF HARTFORD

WEST HARTFORD, CONNECTICUT

The University

The University of Hartford is a fully accredited, independent, nonsectarian institution. The University is composed of seven degree-granting schools and colleges: the College of Arts and Sciences; College of Engineering, Technology, and Architecture; College of Education, Nursing, and Health Professions; Hillyer College; the Barney School of Business; the Hartford Art School; and The Hartt School.

The current full-time undergraduate enrollment is more than 4,700 men and women. A wide range of interests, goals, and backgrounds is found among the students, who represent forty-six states and fifty-three countries. There are about 100 organized student groups, including clubs devoted to special interests or to political, professional, religious, or civic activities as well as service learning and community service activities and groups. Intercollegiate (NCAA Division I) and intramural athletics, student publications, and AM and FM radio stations provide further opportunities for extracurricular involvement. In addition, The Hartt School, the Hartford Art School, and the University Players present a variety of concerts, exhibitions, and theatrical productions each year. Recreational and fitness needs of the University community as well as intramural and intercollegiate sports are served by a well-equipped 130,000-square-foot Sports Center and outdoor athletic facilities.

More than 66 percent of all full-time undergraduates reside on campus. The University offers a wide array of types of residence halls, from traditional dormitory-style to fully equipped town house–style apartments.

Location

The University is located in the residential suburb of West Hartford. The area provides an environment conducive to the development of the student's cultural and intellectual pursuits. There are many area facilities that students can take advantage of including libraries, museums, theaters, the Hartford Civic Center and Convention Center, a symphony orchestra, several other colleges, modern shopping centers, fine restaurants, an international airport, surface transportation, and intercity highway systems.

Majors and Degrees

The College of Arts and Sciences offers majors in art history, biology, chemistry, chemistry-biology, cinema, communication, computer science, criminal justice, economics, English, foreign languages and cultures, history, international studies, Judaic studies, legal studies, mathematics, philosophy, physics, political economy, politics and government, psychology, rhetoric and professional writing, and sociology.

Within the College of Education, Nursing and Health Professions, there are majors in early childhood education, elementary education, integrated special education/elementary education, secondary education with a concentration in English or mathematics, human services, health sciences, nursing (for registered nurses only), radiologic technology, respiratory therapy, clinical lab science and a combined B.S. in health science, and doctorate in physical therapy (B.S./D.P.T.) program.

The Hartford Art School offers Bachelor of Fine Arts degrees in ceramics, design, drawing, illustration, media arts, painting, photography, printmaking, sculpture, and visual communication.

At the Hartt School, students can major in actor training, applied music (guitar, orchestral instrument, organ, piano, pre–cantorial studies, and voice), composition, dance (ballet pedagogy or performance emphases), jazz studies, music, music education, music history, music management, music production and technology, music theater, music theory, and performing arts management (interdisciplinary program offered in conjunction with the Barney School of Business). There are also 5-year double majors offered within the Hartt School.

Majors for the Bachelor of Science in Business Administration (B.S.B.A.) degree in the Barney School of Business are accounting, economics and finance, entrepreneurial studies, finance and insurance, management, and marketing.

Additional B.S. programs, offered by the College of Engineering, Technology, and Architecture include ABET-accredited programs in electrical, mechanical, civil, computer, and biomedical engineering as well as interdisciplinary B.S.E. options. The most popular B.S.E. options are acoustics and music (interdisciplinary program in conjunction with the Hartt School), biomedical engineering, and environmental engineering. Technology programs include the Bachelor of Science in architectural engineering technology, audio engineering technology, computer engineering technology, electronic engineering technology, and mechanical engineering technology as well as the Associate in Applied Science in electronic engineering technology (A.S.) and the Associate in Applied Science in computer engineering technology (A.S.).

Hillyer College offers the Associate of Arts and provides the general education course work required to complete most of the University's baccalaureate programs. Particular emphasis is placed on the development of academic skills through small classes and close faculty-student interaction.

University Studies offers the Bachelor of University Studies, a B.A. degree program created for the part-time adult student who typically has previous college experience and seeks to complete a baccalaureate degree. Also offered is a B.A. degree program in multimedia Web design and development for full-time undergraduates. Created for students who want to learn how to use and develop multimedia technologies that fit into today's wired world, this program combines courses across several disciplines where students create and use technology with user interaction in mind.

Academic Programs

The University of Hartford enjoys a national reputation for the breadth and depth of its academic programs. As highlighted above, more than seventy undergraduate majors are offered through seven schools and colleges. Students are encouraged to sample a variety of academic areas. Those who have special interests can develop interdisciplinary majors that combine courses from the different schools within the University. Academic advisers are assigned to all students to help guide them in curriculum choices, career exploration, and the transition to University life. In order to help students learn more about how different academic disciplines approach related problems, the All-University Curriculum was developed. Courses are often team taught from different fields of expertise, and topics are examined from the perspective of several academic disciplines. The University also has a special program to assist students who may be undecided about a major. A reading and writing center, where students on an individual basis are helped to increase their proficiency in writing, research, reading comprehension, and speed as well as study and test-taking skills, is available to the entire student body. Further help in math is given through the Math Tutoring Lab, which is staffed by full-time faculty members and math majors. Career Services provides vocational counseling and information on occupations, employers, testing, and graduate schools; serves as a reference and credential source; and provides an on-campus recruiting program for graduating students. University College addresses the needs of the part-time adult learner through courses, programs, and educational counseling. A trained counseling staff is available to assist part-time students in planning their education and resolving their special concerns and needs. Selected students are encouraged to participate in the Honors Program. Honors students have the opportunity to graduate with an Honors Degree.

Off-Campus Programs

Intercampus registration through the Hartford Consortium for Higher Education permits University of Hartford students to take certain courses at the School of the Hartford Ballet, Saint Joseph College, and Trinity College. Teaching and human services majors in the College of Education, Nursing, and Health Professions have opportunities for field and/or clinical experiences where applicable. A central internship and cooperative education office is available to custom-tailor work experiences within many of the University's programs.

Academic Facilities

Seven schools and colleges are housed on the main campus. The Harry Jack Gray Center houses the William H. Mortensen Library; the Mildred P. Allen Memorial Library; the Museum of American Political Life; the Harry J. Gray Conference Center; the Joseloff Gallery; the University Bookstore; studios for architecture, art, radio, and television; and the Communication Department. The library has approximately 583,000 items, including books, musical scores, recordings, periodicals, journals, and microfilm units as well as the latest in computer technology, including high-speed and wireless Internet access. Extensive resources are also available through the Hartford Consortium for Higher Education, the Hartford Library, and the Inter-Library-Loan systems.

The new state-of-the-art Mort and Irma Handel Performing Arts Center, located 5 minutes from the main campus, is a 55,000-square-foot facility that houses five dance studios, four theater rehearsal studios, two black box theaters, a small dining facility, and faculty and staff offices. The Handel Performing Arts Center provides a rehearsal and performance environment for the Hartt School's dancers.

The Asylum Avenue campus is listed on the National Register of Historic Places. The 13-acre wooded campus contains beautiful examples of traditional ivy-covered Georgian architecture.

The University of Hartford Computer Center houses the central computer systems and operates a high-performance campus-wide network, which connects all student residential housing, all academic buildings on campus, and the University's remote locations. The University's network is connected via a high-speed telecommunication link to the Internet and the World Wide Web. The residential network gives each student resident his or her own high-speed Ethernet connection to the campus network and the Internet. The library is connected to the campus network and provides network access through computers in study carrels and study rooms and through wireless access. The online systems of the library include the online catalog for book, audio, and video collections; CD-ROM databases; and easy-to-use Web access for many of the library's online resources and electronic reserves. All of the University network resources may be accessed on campus in any University facility and off campus by using computers with network connectivity.

Public access computing labs, used by all students of the University, are provided at various locations around the campus. In addition, college-specific labs are available to students. All labs are equipped with microcomputers (both PCs and Macs) and are connected to the campus network and the Internet. Typical microcomputer software includes word processing, spreadsheet, database management, and graphics programs; programming languages; and Web browsers for accessing the Internet. Help is available from on-duty lab assistants. In addition to these computer labs, there are specialized computer facilities for instruction and learning. Wireless Internet access is available in all academic buildings, libraries, and dining facilities.

Costs

Tuition for incoming students was $26,942 for the 2009–10 academic year; student service fees, $1230; on-campus room costs, $6706; and board, $4172. A variety of on-campus housing accommodates 3,400 students.

Financial Aid

Financial aid for University of Hartford students totals approximately $98 million annually, including student loans. Scholarships, grants, loans, and work-study opportunities are provided through the federal government, private agencies, interested individuals, and University funds. University funds are disbursed based upon the college or school in which the student is enrolled, availability of funds, applicant pool, and competition for funds. More than 85 percent of all full-time undergraduate students receive some type of University assistance; the average out-of-pocket expense is $18,100 (estimate) per year. Partial-tuition scholarships are awarded to entering students who have demonstrated outstanding academic achievement or talent.

Faculty

There are 787 full-time and adjunct faculty members. The undergraduate and graduate faculties are essentially the same group, and 82 percent of the members hold the terminal degree in their field. Academic and personal advisory service is readily available. Each new student is assigned to a faculty adviser during summer orientation.

Student Government

The student governing body that represents all full-time students is the Student Government Association, through which students and faculty join in developing and coordinating the cocurricular activities of the University. Students are also represented on all major administrative committees, including the Board of Regents.

Admission Requirements

The Office of Admission considers the quality of the secondary school curriculum, academic performance in secondary school, ACT or SAT results, evidence of a desire to succeed, and leadership qualities shown by academic and extracurricular activities. Auditions, portfolios, and other tests are required of music and art applicants.

Application and Information

The University employs a rolling admission policy. For further information, students should visit the University on the Web at http://admission.hartford.edu or contact:

Office of Admission
University of Hartford
West Hartford, Connecticut 06117
Phone: 860-768-4296
800-947-4303 (toll-free)
Fax: 860-768-4961
E-mail: admission@hartford.edu
Web site: http://admission.hartford.edu

UNIVERSITY OF INDIANAPOLIS

INDIANAPOLIS, INDIANA

The University

The University of Indianapolis is inspiring excellence with a personal approach to education and a commitment to academic quality. Outstanding faculty members inspire students in small classes that allow individual attention, and students are encouraged to apply their knowledge to real-world situations through internships, active learning in the classroom, and community service. A private, residential, comprehensive university founded in 1902 and affiliated with the United Methodist Church, the University of Indianapolis welcomes students of many nations and faiths from around the world. Every year, more than 4,900 full-time and part-time students, both undergraduate and graduate, benefit from the University's commitment to offering outstanding academic programs in more than sixty-five major fields or study. The University of Indianapolis accepts qualified applicants for admission without regard to race, color, sex, sexual orientation, age, religion, creed, marital status, or ethnic or national origin.

Students indicate that they choose the University because of its challenging, yet supportive, atmosphere and relatively small size, combined with the advantages of its location in the southern suburbs of a thriving state capital. As a result, there is a great sense of community and pride on the campus. The University helps students to determine and achieve their individual academic goals. The University has experienced much growth and has instituted many enhancements recently, including the renovation and addition to Esch Hall, which houses a new facility for the communication department.

More than 2,900 Day Division students are enrolled. There are students from sixty countries and thirty-five states. Approximately 82 percent of freshmen live in on-campus housing. The warmth and sensitivity of the faculty and staff members and students alike enable those who are a part of the campus to feel a strong sense of community.

In addition to the undergraduate division, the University is composed of the Graduate and Doctoral Division, including the nationally recognized Krannert School of Physical Therapy. The University of Indianapolis offers twenty-two graduate programs and four doctoral programs, including those in the Schools of Occupational and Physical Therapy, which rank among the finest in the nation. The most popular programs in the undergraduate division include pre–physical therapy, business, athletic training, communication, nursing, education, premedicine, psychology, and music.

Social life is organized through the Campus Program Board, Indianapolis Student Government, and Residence Hall Association, student organizations that plan weekly activities for all students. There are numerous social clubs and interest groups available for students who wish to become involved in extracurricular activities. Five residence halls house students; four house both men and women, and one is only for women. Students must be admitted on a full-time basis in order to be assigned housing. NCAA Division II sports for men include baseball, basketball, cross-country, football, golf, soccer, swimming and diving, tennis, track and field (indoor and outdoor), and wrestling. NCAA Division II sports for women include basketball, cross-country, fast-pitch softball, golf, soccer, swimming and diving, tennis, track and field (indoor and outdoor), and volleyball. Intramural sports are offered for men and women in flag football, basketball, softball, soccer, volleyball, indoor soccer, Ultimate Frisbee, and racquetball.

Location

The University is located in the southern neighborhoods of Indianapolis, the nation's third-largest capital city. Indianapolis and the surrounding area constitute a metropolitan area of nearly 2 million people. As a result, the city offers students valuable internship and service-learning experiences as well as recreational and cultural opportunities too numerous to mention. The campus is extremely accessible, just a few blocks from two major interstate highways (I-65 and I-465). The campus is served by Indygo bus, and Amtrak trains arrive daily at historic Union Station, just 10 minutes from the campus. Indianapolis International Airport is about 15 minutes away.

Majors and Degrees

The undergraduate programs are offered through the College of Arts and Sciences, the School of Business, the School of Nursing, the School of Education, the Krannert School of Physical Therapy, the School of Occupational Therapy, and the School of Psychological Sciences. The degrees awarded are the Associate in Arts, Associate in Science, Associate in Science in Nursing, Bachelor of Arts, Bachelor of Science, and Bachelor of Science in Nursing.

Baccalaureate and preprofessional fields of study include accounting (CMA/CPA), actuarial science, anthropology, archeology, art, athletic training, biology, business administration, chemistry, communication studies, computer engineering (dual degree), computer science, corporate communication, corrections, earth-space sciences, economics, electrical engineering (dual degree), electronic media, elementary education, English, entrepreneurship, environmental science, exercise science, experiential learning (concentrations in applied anthropology, applied history, and applied theater), finance, French, German, history, human biology, human communication, information systems, international business, international relations, journalism, law enforcement, management, marketing, mathematics, mechanical engineering (dual degree), medical technology, music, music performance, nursing, philosophy, physics, political science, pre–art therapy, predentistry, prelaw, premedicine, pre–occupational therapy, pre–physical therapy, pretheology, pre–veterinary science, psychology, public relations, religion, respiratory therapy, secondary education, social work, sociology, Spanish, sports administration, sports information, sports marketing, studio art, theater, youth ministry, and visual communication design.

Teaching majors are offered in business education (all grades), chemistry, earth-space science, English, French, life science, mathematics, music (all grades), physical education (all grades), physics, social studies, Spanish, speech communication, theater, and visual arts (grades 5–12).

Associate degrees are awarded in business administration, chemistry, corrections, information systems, law enforcement, liberal arts, nursing, and physical therapist assistant studies.

Academic Programs

The University of Indianapolis starts with a top-notch education that combines a liberal arts– and career-oriented curriculum that graduates call life-changing. Students find a powerful combination of features designed to inspire them to excellence. Faculty and staff members take a personal interest in students, encouraging them to explore their interests and apply what they learn, so they can excel when it comes time to make their place in the world.

Students can choose from more than sixty-five undergraduate academic programs. The goal of the liberal arts core classes is to provide learning above and beyond the student's major field, so students study topics and cultures that pique their interest in unexpected ways.

Students appreciate the curriculum because they don't have to wait to apply what they learn. At the University of Indianapolis, students have time—before they graduate—to practice what they learn. Most majors offer practical experiences, which give students an edge in the job market. The Indianapolis location is an excellent resource when it comes to finding internships, field experiences, service-learning opportunities, or part-time employment. Internships let students sample their future careers and gain some of the knowledge and experience they admire in their professors. At the University of Indianapolis, there's a host of possibilities for virtually any major.

Off-Campus Programs

The University operates a fully owned branch campus in Athens, Greece, that offers students a unique exchange program. Located within walking distance of the storied Acropolis, the Plaka, Constitution Square, and other historic landmarks, the University of Indianapolis–Athens offers students the opportunity to explore and experience Greece both inside and outside the classroom. Currently, the Athens campus offers thirty-two undergraduate programs in the arts and sciences, business, and psychology. Short-term study trips, as well as full-semester study-abroad programs, are available to students through the Odyssey Program. In addition, students at the main campus have many opportunities to travel to Athens on shorter trips during vacations or during the Spring Term in May. Other partnerships and extension sites for direct credit include Israel, Belize, and the People's Republic of China. Other off-campus study opportunities take place during the Spring Term, including assorted overseas travel openings. The University also has an Office of Career Services, which arranges off-campus internships related to one's field of study.

Academic Facilities

Krannert Memorial Library, which operates an online card catalog, houses more than 175,000 volumes, more than 1,000 periodicals, and more than 19,000 microfilm/microform/microfiche records. The library is home to a full media center. The communication department, with new state-of-the-art equipment for its radio station and television studio, is located in Esch Hall. Martin Hall contains outstanding resources for the Schools of Nursing, Physical Therapy, and Occupational Therapy and is connected to Lilly Science Hall, which recently underwent a major upgrade to all its science labs. Access to computers is available in all of the academic buildings and residence halls. Students have access to the campuswide information system from their rooms in the residence halls, and the whole campus is wireless. Ransburg Auditorium, with seating for nearly 800, is the setting for concerts, recitals, and theatrical productions. The $10-million Christel DeHaan Fine Arts Center features state-of-the-art music and art facilities, an art gallery, and a 450-seat, Viennese-style concert hall.

Costs

Directly billed expenses for the 2009–10 academic year were $22,020 for tuition and $7990 for room and board. Nonbilled indirect expenses were estimated at $800 for books and supplies, an average of $630 for transportation, and $1370 to $1830 for miscellaneous and personal expenses.

Financial Aid

All applicants for admission are eligible to apply for financial aid. Indiana residents should file the Free Application for Federal Student Aid (FAFSA) by March 1 to qualify for state of Indiana financial aid programs. All students should file the FAFSA along with the University of Indianapolis Application for Financial Aid by March 10 for priority consideration. For the 2008–09 academic year, about 88 percent of the enrolled full-time students received financial aid with an average financial aid package of $21,392 for entering students.

Faculty

All Day Division faculty members are assigned teaching (not research) duties, including many administrators and some professional staff personnel. Graduate students do not teach any undergraduate classes. Currently, the student-faculty ratio is 12:1, and the average class size is 18.

Student Government

The Indianapolis Student Government (ISG) consists of students elected to officer positions plus student representatives from each class, chosen for a one-year term in an annual student body election. ISG's main focus is to pass resolutions regarding student concerns.

Admission Requirements

Applicants for admission must be high school graduates or have a GED certificate and are expected to have taken a college-preparatory curriculum in high school. Applicants for regular admission should have completed a minimum of 4 years of English, 3 years of mathematics, 3 years of laboratory science, 2 years of social science (U.S. history, government, and economics), and 2 years of any foreign language. In addition, applicants for full-time admission without restrictions should rank in the upper half of their class and have average to above-average SAT or ACT scores. Essays are not required for admission. For immediate consideration, transfer applicants must have achieved a good overall record and have earned at least a C average in previous college or university work. An on-campus interview is recommended anytime after the junior year of high school. To apply for admission, the Application for Admission, official high school transcript, official college transcript (if applicable), and official SAT or ACT scores should be forwarded to the Office of Admissions.

Application and Information

All applications are reviewed on a rolling basis—an admission decision is made as soon as all documents are received, and notifications are mailed immediately thereafter. There is no deadline for applications, but high school seniors are encouraged to apply during the fall semester of their senior year. Scholarships are also awarded on a rolling basis. Admitted students are notified of scholarships they have been awarded shortly after they have been accepted.

Requests for appointments and information about the University should be directed to:

University of Indianapolis
1400 East Hanna Avenue
Indianapolis, Indiana 46227-3697
Phone: 317-STUDENT
317-788-3216
800-232-8634 (toll-free)
Fax: 317-788-3300
E-mail: admissions@uindy.edu
Web site: http://www.uindy.edu/

Smith Mall, the centerpiece of the University of Indianapolis campus, features a beautifully landscaped water garden canal.

COLLEGE CLOSE-UPS

UNIVERSITY OF MAINE

ORONO, MAINE

The University

The University of Maine, the land-grant university and sea-grant college of the state of Maine, has a mission to provide teaching and public service and to carry out research for the state of Maine and the country. The University was established in 1865 as the Maine State College of Agriculture and the Mechanic Arts. When the institution opened its doors in 1868, it had 12 students and 2 faculty members. Today, the University of Maine has approximately 798 faculty members and almost 12,000 students who represent forty-eight states and sixty-five countries. The University of Maine is a participant in the New England Regional Program sponsored by the New England Board of Higher Education.

The University of Maine is the flagship institution of the seven-member University of Maine System. Two hundred four buildings sit on the University of Maine's 660-acre central campus. Forests, botanical gardens, and other "green" spaces make up the rest of the 5,500-acre campus, overlooking the Stillwater River. Ivy-covered buildings and pathways shaded by evergreens create a campus that is inviting and picturesque during all four seasons. Students living on campus may select from a variety of housing options, from residence halls to apartment-style complexes to fraternity and sorority houses.

The University has more than 235 student organizations, including honor and professional societies, fraternities, and sororities. Eight women's and seven men's intercollegiate NCAA Division I athletic programs are part of the campus community. Numerous intramural and club sports give all students an opportunity to be physically active. Two gymnasiums, a field house, an indoor pool, a sports arena, a domed field, and a 10,000-seat athletic stadium are used for NCAA Division I athletics. A 14,000-square-foot recreation center, which opened in fall 2007, and the Maine Bound Center, with a climbing wall, provide opportunities for recreational sports. For students' creative interests, there are two theaters, excellent music facilities, recital halls, and studios for dance and the visual arts. Community services include a newspaper, a radio station, a police and safety department, and a health facility.

Location

The town of Orono is in central Maine, 8 miles north of Bangor, Maine's third-largest city. The University of Maine is 240 miles north of Boston and 306 miles from Montreal. The area is served by daily air and bus transportation. The local area offers many opportunities for a wide range of recreational activities. Within an easy drive of the campus are many sites of great natural beauty such as Acadia National Park, Mount Katahdin and Baxter State Park, as well as several ski resorts, including Sugarloaf/USA and Sunday River.

Majors and Degrees

The University of Maine offers more than eighty baccalaureate degree programs through five colleges: the College of Business, Public Policy, and Health; the College of Education and Human Development; the College of Engineering; the College of Liberal Arts and Sciences; and the College of Natural Sciences, Forestry, and Agriculture. The Division of Lifelong Learning also offers a Bachelor of University Studies degree for part-time adult learners.

Academic Programs

The University of Maine is a year-round educational institution. The academic year is divided into two 15-week semesters, from early September to early May; a three-week May term; a summer session with two- to eight-week sessions; and a summer field session. The University offers evening as well as day classes.

All students in baccalaureate degree programs must meet the University's General Education requirements. In addition, each academic college sets its own requirements in terms of grades and the number of credits and specific courses required for graduation. Information concerning specific graduation requirements can be found in the undergraduate catalog (http://catalog.umaine.edu). Academic advisers assist all students with completing their degree requirements and fulfilling their personal educational objectives.

The University of Maine provides many opportunities that encourage intellectual curiosity and recognize exceptional achievement. Outstanding entering first-year students are offered the opportunity to participate in the Honors College, one of the country's oldest. The Honors College provides a unique opportunity for students of all majors to be challenged in a supportive intellectual environment and to engage fellow students and enthusiastic faculty members in thoughtful provocative discussion. In addition, many academic colleges and majors also offer membership in various honor societies. Students and faculty members on campus are members of thirty-nine such societies, including Phi Beta Kappa, Phi Kappa Phi, Tau Beta Pi, Xi Sigma Pi, Kappa Delta Pi, Beta Gamma Sigma, and Alpha Zeta.

ROTC programs are available in the Army and Navy/Marine Corps.

Off-Campus Programs

At least forty departments of the University offer field-based learning programs, including internships, travel study, cooperative education programs, and field experience. Students are given academic credit and/or compensation for on-the-job experience in their major field.

The University of Maine offers a number of international student exchanges through the Council on International Education Exchange (CIEE), the College Consortium for International Studies (CCIS), and the International Student Exchange Program (ISEP). The University also sponsors reciprocal exchanges between the University of Maine and such countries as Australia, France, Germany, Ireland, and Japan and sponsors a Junior Year Abroad Program in Salzburg, Austria. The Canada Year program, which is coordinated by the University's Canadian-American Center, offers students the opportunity to study at various Canadian universities.

Academic Facilities

Fogler Library, which is located at the center of the campus, contains Maine's largest library collection and is the eighteenth-largest library in New England. It contains 1,148,891 volumes and more than 1.65 million microforms, subscribes to 16,988 periodicals, and is a regional depository for more than 2.34 million government documents.

All departments on campus provide the necessary laboratories and equipment to support student and faculty research. Undergraduates have access to computer facilities through the University's widespread wireless network as well as through computers located throughout the campus. All classroom buildings are wireless and all residence halls are connected to the University's computer system, which provides access to a variety of software programs and network services.

Among the other facilities on campus are the newly renovated Collins Center for the Arts, which includes the Hutchins Concert Hall (seating capacity of 1,435) and the Hudson Museum, an ethnographic and archeological museum with a permanent collection of 8,000 pieces of pre-Hispanic Mexican, Central American, and Native American artifacts. The University of Maine Museum of Art, located in downtown Bangor, is the only museum owned by the citizens of the state of Maine housing a permanent fine arts collection. Art Department Galleries, a public observatory, a planetarium, and the Page Home and Farm Museum are all part of the University of Maine campus community. Recently completed or renovated buildings include the Advanced Engineered Wood Composites Building, the Wes Jordan Athletic Training Center, and art galleries and studios in Lord Hall. Renovations on the Collins Center for the Arts were completed in February of 2009.

Costs

The University of Maine System Board of Trustees adjusts costs annually. For the 2009–10 academic year, tuition for undergraduate state residents was $253 per credit hour; for nonresident students, it was $728 per credit hour. (The average credit load for full-time students is 15 credit hours per semester or 30 credit hours for the academic year.) Canadian and nonresident students who qualify for the New England Regional Program pay $381 per credit hour. Required University fees ($1900 per year for a full-time student) include the Unified Fee, which provides a variety of health-care services and admission to cultural, recreational, and athletic events. Books and supplies averaged about $1200 for the academic year. Room and board (nineteen meals per week) charges for the academic year were $8008. These costs are subject to change.

Financial Aid

The University requires all financial aid applicants to file the Free Application for Federal Student Aid (FAFSA) and encourages students to file online. The priority deadline to apply for aid is March 1. Awards usually consist of a combination of several types of aid, ranging from grants and scholarships to work-study jobs and student loans.

Faculty

The University of Maine has approximately 798 full- and part-time faculty members and a student-faculty ratio of 15:1. A number of faculty members teach both undergraduate and graduate courses. Graduate students serve as teaching assistants in some departments. Faculty members are involved in both teaching and research, and also serve as academic advisers to undergraduate students. In addition, the faculty takes an active part in the education of students outside of the classroom through seminars, workshops, and discussion groups and by serving as advisers to student organizations. Many faculty members also serve on the Student Advisory Committee, the Student Conduct Committee, and other organizations on campus that serve the needs of students.

Student Government

An elected president, vice president, and vice president of financial affairs direct and coordinate Student Government programs at the University of Maine. Student Government works closely with the Office of the Vice President for Student Affairs and appoints 200 student representatives to the various University committees. These committees are involved with the planning and implementation of residence hall programs, student discipline, athletics, and cultural activities on campus. The work of the executive budgetary committee of Student Government includes the budgeting of approximately $400,000 in student activity fees. Student Government comprises five governing boards and the General Student Senate.

Admission Requirements

Admission to the University of Maine is a selective process. Successful applicants are those whose scholastic achievement, intellectual curiosity, and established study habits promise success in a comprehensive university environment. The admission committee reviews the strength of the high school curriculum, the grades received, the counselor recommendation, and either SAT or ACT scores as the primary criteria for admission. Essays and information regarding school and community activities provide additional information that may help the committee evaluate potential for success.

The University recognizes advanced work completed in secondary schools by means of Advanced Placement tests. In addition, students who demonstrate advanced knowledge may be exempted from certain courses and requirements if they pass examinations specially developed by the University's academic departments.

Application and Information

The University of Maine accepts three different application forms. Applicants may submit either electronic or paper versions of the Common Application or the University of Maine System application. The University of Maine also accepts the online-only Universal College Application. The University requires a supplement for the Common Application and the Universal College Application. Additional required documents for all applicants include official high school transcripts and counselor recommendations. Traditional-age applicants are required to submit scores from either the SAT or ACT.

Applicants are notified by rolling admission and they are encouraged to submit their applications and all supporting documents by February 1. The University of Maine also has an early action deadline of December 15. Students whose complete applications are postmarked by December 15 are reviewed by the end of January. Early action candidates are given first consideration for merit scholarships awarded by the Admissions Office. Students applying for the spring semester are encouraged to submit applications by December 1. Applications after these dates are processed on a space-available basis. Applications and all supporting documents should be sent to UMS Processing, P.O. Box 412, Bangor, Maine 04402-0412.

Office of Admission
5713 Chadbourne Hall
University of Maine
Orono, Maine 04469-5713
Phone: 207-581-1561
877-486-2364 (toll-free)
Fax: 207-581-1213
E-mail: um-admit@maine.edu
Web site: http://www.go.umaine.edu/

COLLEGE CLOSE-UPS

UNIVERSITY OF MAINE AT MACHIAS

MACHIAS, MAINE

The University

Located on the spectacular coast of Downeast Maine, the University of Maine at Machias (UMM) is a small, residential, undergraduate environmental liberal arts university of more than 1,000 students. The college was incorporated in 1909 and is a member of the University of Maine system. Small classes (the average is 17 students) and a faculty-student ratio of 1:13 contribute to an academic atmosphere that is intimate and intense and where independent thinking is encouraged.

Although many UMM students are from the state of Maine, the University's environmental emphasis, distinctive programs, and location attract many others from the New England, mid-Atlantic, and Midwest regions of the country.

Location

Machias, Maine, is a classic small New England town located on the tidal Machias River, with a town center that includes a number of retail stores, restaurants (including fast food), a supermarket, a natural foods store, and churches of various denominations. The greater Machias–area population is 5,000. The region is a popular outdoor recreation destination, with ocean beaches, inland lakes and streams, and miles of mountains, forests, and trails.

Downeast Maine has been a source of inspiration for generations of artists, outdoorsmen, mariners, and environmentalists. UMM's coastal location provides a unique learning environment, with excellent opportunities for fieldwork, hands-on learning, and cooperative education and internship experiences.

Majors and Degrees

The University of Maine at Machias awards Bachelor of Arts and Bachelor of Science degrees in behavioral science and community studies (applied psychology concentration); biology (concentrations in fisheries biology, wildlife biology, and preprofessional preparation in dentistry, medicine, optometry, pharmacy, and veterinary medicine); business and entrepreneurial studies; college studies; elementary teacher education (concentrations in coaching, early childhood, history/social studies, humanities, science/mathematics, special education, and teacher certification); English and book arts (concentrations in book arts, creative writing, and literary studies); environmental recreation and tourism management (concentrations in environmental recreation and recreation management); environmental studies (self-designed concentration); history; interdisciplinary fine arts (concentrations in book arts, creative writing, music, and visual arts); interdisciplinary studies; marine biology (concentrations in biological science, mariculture, and marine ecology); middle level teacher education (concentrations in English, history/social science, science, teacher certification); and secondary teacher education (concentrations in art, mathematics, English, social studies, life science, physical science, and teacher certification).

Academic Programs

Bachelor's degree candidates must complete at least 120 credit hours with a minimum cumulative grade point average of 2.0 and must also complete the core requirements in business studies, fine arts, humanities, physical education, science/mathematics, and social sciences.

Academic Facilities

All of the University's academic buildings are of modern construction and include a well-equipped science building with laboratories, a greenhouse, marine science aquariums, and a marine teaching and research laboratory. A Geographic Information Systems Laboratory and Service Center is located in Torrey Hall. Computer labs, some of which are open 24 hours a day, seven days a week for student use, house the latest in technology hardware and software. Located off-campus, UMM has an ongoing partnership with the Downeast Institute for Applied Marine Research and Education, where students conduct shellfish and finfish research.

Merrill Library provides a 24-hour study center with computer workstations for students, houses a collection of more than 100,000 volumes, and is linked to other libraries and educational resources throughout the state. A computer center with cross-campus networking and multiple computer labs enhances all of UMM's programs and provides access to the Internet and the Web. Individual computer access is also available in every residence hall room. The University of Maine at Machias Student Support Center provides faculty, peer, and professional assistance as well as computer and audiovisual aids for all students. A residence facility with contemporary suites and single rooms was completed in 2003.

The Reynolds Athletic Center includes a large gymnasium, an aquatics center with a competition-size pool, a state-of-the-art fitness center, racquetball/handball courts, and a recreational equipment center, in which students may check out canoes, kayaks, snowshoes, cross-country skis, bicycles, and camping equipment. The Flaherty Early Care and Education Center provides child-care facilities for the community and the University; it also provides an on-campus site for UMM elementary teacher education students to participate in field studies.

A wide variety of student activities, from meetings to coffeehouses and other social events, are accommodated in the Student Center. Located in the same building, the campus radio station, WUMM, is run entirely by students. The Performing Arts Center, a 358-seat amphitheater auditorium, is host to numerous campus and community meetings, seminars, festivals, and performing arts and theatrical presentations.

Costs

The basic expenses for the 2009–10 academic year (based on a 15-credit-hour load per semester) were $6030 per year for in-state tuition and $16,770 per year for out-of-state tuition. The

University of Maine at Machias participates in the New England Board of Higher Education Regional Student program, which allows reduced tuition ($9060 per year) for students from the other New England states who are enrolled in specific academic programs.

Financial Aid

The University of Maine at Machias administers scholarships, loans, grants, and work-study awards. The Presidential Scholarship is awarded to students who have a 3.0 GPA, or a score of 1000 on the SAT (critical reading and math parts combined), or a 22 composite score on the ACT. This award is $5500 for out-of-state students, and $2000 for in-state students. Transfer students receive a $1000 Presidential Scholarship if they have a 2.75 GPA. Transfer students from out-of-state receive a $2000 travel grant. Students living on campus receive a Campus Housing Award of $1500. Financial aid awards are made on the basis of need, and students must submit the Free Application for Federal Student Aid (FAFSA) to the College Scholarship Service. March 15 is the University's financial aid priority deadline.

Faculty

Nearly all University of Maine at Machias faculty members hold the highest degree in their professional field. The faculty-student ratio is 1:13. All faculty members work as advisers and mentors to students within their areas of academic expertise. Usually on a first-name basis, faculty members develop a close relationship with students during their years of study at UMM and beyond.

Student Government

The University of Maine at Machias is a member of the University of Maine Organization of Student Governments and operates its own Student Senate. Students are encouraged to become involved and participate.

Admission Requirements

Graduation from secondary school or a high school equivalency diploma is the basic requirement for admission. Applicants to the University should have followed a college-preparatory high school program with 4 years of English, 3 years of math, 3 lab sciences, 2 social sciences, a foreign language, and computer utilization. If a student is entering one of the business programs, consideration is given to business courses taken in high school. However, college-preparatory English, math, science, and social science courses are still necessary. Scores from the SAT or ACT are also required. Applicants should rank in the top half of their high school class and have an overall grade average of B or better.

The University of Maine at Machias does not discriminate on the basis of race, creed, color, sex, or national origin and is an Equal Opportunity/Affirmative Action Employer.

Application and Information

The University of Maine at Machias operates on a rolling admission system. Candidates should complete their applications as early as possible. Students may apply for early admission, through which they may be admitted directly into the University after completing three years of secondary school. Candidates for this program must have recommendations of support from their guidance counselor, principal, superintendent, and/or school board. Their high school grades should place them in the top 15 percent of their class. UMM accepts applications from transfer students. Transfer applicants should complete their applications by June 1 for the fall term or by December 1 for the spring term.

Application materials and additional information may be obtained by contacting:

Director of Admissions
University of Maine at Machias
116 O'Brien Avenue
Machias, Maine 04654
Phone: 207-255-1318
888-468-6866 (toll-free)
Fax: 207-255-1363
E-mail: ummadmissions@maine.edu
Web site: http://www.umm.maine.edu

Students at the University of Maine at Machias engaged in experiential learning on the coast of Maine.

UNIVERSITY OF MASSACHUSETTS BOSTON

BOSTON, MASSACHUSETTS

The University

Since 1964 the University of Massachusetts Boston (UMass Boston) has provided the opportunity to access superior public education at a moderate cost in the state's capital city of Boston. With more than 14,500 commuting students in its undergraduate, graduate, and continuing education programs, UMass Boston is the second-largest campus of the University of Massachusetts system. UMass Boston is a community of scholars who take pride in academic excellence, diversity, research, and service. The fabric of the school's academic research and scholarship is tightly woven into the public and community service needs of Boston and the modern metropolitan center.

The University's students represent an extraordinary range of backgrounds, talents, and interests. Many come straight from high school, while others transfer from two- and four-year colleges. Although the majority of students come from the Commonwealth of Massachusetts, many grew up in other states and countries and come from all levels of the economic, political, spiritual, and ethnic spectra.

UMass Boston has a vibrant student life. No matter what a student's interest, he or she can find activities to engage in—socially and intellectually. From student government to student literary endeavors; from a championship chess team to working with inner-city youth; from academically affiliated clubs and athletic opportunities to a unique course-credit-based leadership-development program, students are sure to find just the right activity to complement their own classroom experience.

The UMass Boston student body shares a strong motivation to succeed academically and relate their classroom pursuits to career aspirations. The University Advising Center provides comprehensive academic support, planning, and career advising services. A team of professional counselors provides personalized assistance for students to design their course of study, utilize tutorial and mentoring services, choose a major and career path, and develop interviewing, resume writing, and job-search skills.

Location

From its beautiful landscaped peninsula on Boston Harbor, just south of downtown Boston, the University overlooks Dorchester Bay and the harbor islands. Its neighbors are the John F. Kennedy Presidential Library and the Massachusetts State Archives and Commonwealth Museum.

Located just a half mile off Interstate Route 93, its entrance along a seaside promenade drive, the campus is easily accessed by both motor vehicle and public transportation. The Office of Undergraduate Admissions provides a number of free parking spaces for visitors in the campus's North Parking Lot. A free shuttle bus runs every few minutes for the half-mile ride from the Massachusetts Bay Transit Authority's (MBTA) JFK/UMass Red Line "T" stop to the front door of the campus. Student MBTA discount "T" passes are available for frequent users.

Many students commute from their home communities, while others utilize the Office of Student Housing for free, personalized help with finding a rental property and/or roommates. The University wants all its students to be at home at UMass Boston.

Boston itself, with its worldwide standing as a cultural center and well-earned reputation as America's favorite college town, offers UMass Boston students a wealth of resources for exploration and entertainment. Everything from Fenway Park and the Bank of America Garden to Symphony Hall and the Museum of Fine Arts is easily accessible from UMass Boston.

Majors and Degrees

Five undergraduate colleges award bachelor's degrees: the College of Liberal Arts and the College of Science and Mathematics (with thirty-three majors, twenty minors and programs of study, and six certificate programs between them), the College of Management (with two majors and thirteen concentrations), the College of Nursing and Health Sciences (with a B.S.N., an online RN-to-B.S.N., and an accelerated B.S.N. program, as well as the B.S. in Exercise and Health Sciences program), and the College of Public and Community Service (with five majors and three career concentrations). Also offered are premed, prelaw, and teacher licensure for undergraduates programs, along with programs for honors study, credit by examination, and advanced placement. Students are encouraged to participate fully in designing their own academic plan.

A joint Bachelor of Arts or Science/master's degree program in business is available for high academic achievers as well as a liberal arts or science degree with a minor in management.

Academic Programs

The academic calendar runs from early September through the end of May. There is also a one-month optional winter session in January, and summer school is available in June, July, and August. Matriculating students may choose to attend full- or part-time and may adjust their schedules from semester to semester. A minimum of 30 credits must be earned at UMass Boston as a residency requirement for graduation.

For the College of Liberal Arts and the College of Science and Mathematics, 120 credits are required to graduate. The general education curriculum comprises three elements: the distribution requirement, the core curriculum requirement, and the writing requirement. In addition, the requirements of the major must be fulfilled. The Colleges offer both an honors program and an individual major option.

In the College of Management, the 120-credit undergraduate program leads to a B.S. degree in management or information technology. By fulfilling the general education, management, and elective course work requirements, graduates build a liberal arts foundation and receive the theoretical, technical, and functional training needed to succeed in the business world. An honors program is also offered.

The College of Nursing and Health Science's B.S. program in nursing requires 123 credits for graduation, including general education courses and 63 credits of intensive study in the principles and practices of nursing. The Exercise and Health Sciences program prepares graduates for the technical aspects of a professional discipline and a solid foundation in liberal arts. Students may also elect to enter the Honors Program in Nursing.

The College of Public and Community Service (CPCS) is a nationally recognized model for competency-based education. It offers an innovative curriculum with strong emphasis on social justice. The completion of a total of 40 competencies is required for graduation. Students may draw upon a variety of learning options in pursuit of their degree, including classroom study, self-directed study, project-based learning, and the demonstration of competence gained through relevant prior experience. The University's Honors Program is also open to CPCS students.

Off-Campus Programs

The National Student Exchange Program offers UMass Boston students the opportunity to study at one of more than seventy participating colleges and universities in forty states at a cost comparable to what they pay to attend UMass Boston. The study-abroad program is available for students with a 3.0 GPA or better who seek international travel and academic experiences as well as summer and winter session programs. UMass Boston also participates in the New England Regional Student Program and the Boston Five-College Exchange Program.

The Cooperative Education and Internship programs place students in work assignments related directly to their fields of study so that they may apply what they learn in the classroom to practical work settings. Under the Co-Op Program, students are placed in full-time, paid positions for six-month work periods. Under the Internship Program, students are placed on a part-time basis, usually 15 to 20 hours per week, during a semester or over the summer months. Some are paid internships; others are volunteer opportunities. Both co-op and internship placements combine relevant practical learning, valuable work experience, career awareness, resume enhancement, personal and professional growth, and, in many instances, opportunities for academic credit, good pay, and a permanent job after graduation.

Academic Facilities

The Joseph P. Healey Library holds a collection of more than 600,000 volumes, 60,000 electronic and print journals and newspapers, 40,000 electronic books, 100 databases, and more than 5,000 videos, DVDs, and films in the fields of study on the campus. The library's electronic resources are available on and off campus, 24/7. UMass Boston is a member of three important library consortia, including the Boston Library Consortium, and is a member of nationwide resource sharing networks of scholarly and study resources. These offer over 10-million book titles and a total of nearly 30-million volumes available point-and-click. Students may obtain a library consortium card to check out books from any of the consortia libraries. Healey Library and the division of Information Technology offer graduate students many services through the Commons at Healey. The Commons has a media center, media viewing room, the IT Service Desk, the Graduate Resource Center, and many other facilities in the building, including reference assistance from expert librarians who specialize in different fields.

The Information Technology Services Division (ITSD) provides seven-day-a-week access to general-use computer labs, with more than 200 Dell Pentium Dual Core PCs, 17 Macintosh G5s, and 41 IMacs, as well as other specialized, course-related facilities, including an Adaptive Computing Lab, Graduate Research Center, media and language labs, and a media viewing center, all located within the Healey Library Information Commons, which also houses the IT Service Desk. ITSD supports equipment from Dell, Sun, and Apple, and operating systems include Windows XP, Unix, Linux, and Apple OS. The campus has over ninety technology enhanced classrooms and auditoria that are equipped with state of the art audiovisual equipment and network connections. ITSD also provides wireless access in the Healey Library and the campus center and other public spaces, as well as ensuring that a wide variety of information technology and data communications resources are available to students. The campus uses the Blackboard Vista learning management system in conjunction with the Wimba synchronous meeting tool. ITSD also provides support for a digital signage and Ethernet TV network and IP- and ISDN-based videoconferencing. The campus has a fiber-optic infrastructure with gigabit backbone and 100 MB switched connectivity.

The Kennedy Presidential Library is linked to the University by a variety of educational programs, enabling students to conduct research utilizing the more than 28 million pages of documents, 6.5 million feet of film, and more than 100,000 still photographs in the library's archives. Next door, the Archives of the Commonwealth of Massachusetts are a rich depository, covering more than 5½ centuries of Massachusetts history.

The state-of-the-art Campus Center provides easy access to student services, dining services, and spectacular meeting spaces, along with computer terminals and wireless Internet access.

Costs

Tuition and fees for the fall 2009 semester were $5315.50 for Massachusetts residents studying full-time (12 or more credits) or $11,408 for out-of-state students. Students enrolling part-time were charged tuition according to the number of credits taken, with Massachusetts residents paying tuition at $71.50 per credit; out-of-state residents paid tuition of $406.50 per credit. Annual mandatory fees for in-state residents ranged up to $8917 and up to $13,059 for out-of-state students.

Financial Aid

Financial aid is based on need and/or merit. Applicants must complete the Free Application for Federal Student Aid (FAFSA), keeping in mind a priority deadline of March 1 for fall semester and November 1 for spring semester. Need-based aid is awarded to students who demonstrate financial need, as determined by federal methodology. Aid consists of grants, waivers, and merit scholarships as well as self-help in the form of loans and work-study employment. An on-time applicant is automatically considered for all financial aid programs administered by the University's Office of Financial Aid Services.

Faculty

UMass Boston is proud of its distinguished faculty of 913 members, some 90 percent of whom have terminal degrees in their field. UMass Boston has a student-faculty ratio of about 15:1 and a small class size that averages only 28 students. The faculty's top priority is teaching and advising students, although they also conduct research, publish materials, and participate in grant activities and professional organizations. Faculty members maintain office hours for students and make themselves accessible as mentors. Faculty and academic issues are governed by the Faculty Council.

Student Government

The undergraduate Student Senate consists of elected members from the undergraduate colleges and programs, and it participates fully in matters related to the quality of student life and the allocation of the student activities trust fund. Students are also represented on numerous University- and college-based committees and councils that initiate major policy and procedural recommendations, forwarding those recommendations to governance bodies and the administration for enactment.

Admission Requirements

A freshman candidate for admission to the University should have earned a minimum of 16 academic units in high school that include 4 years of English, 3 years of mathematics, 3 years of science (including 2 with laboratory requirements), 2 years of social science (including 1 of U.S. history), 2 years of a single foreign language, and 2 years of electives in the arts or computer science (excluding vocational training). The student must also present satisfactory scores on either the SAT or ACT. The University looks for students with a strong academic background, as determined by a recalculated grade point average, and each candidate's academic program choices, motivation, achievement, and annual progress are closely scrutinized.

UMass Boston encourages qualified international students to apply for admission. A separate international application is required. The Test of English as a Foreign Language (TOEFL) is required of all students educated in a non-English language educational system.

Transfer students are considered based on a review of all college academic credentials. Several academic majors and programs have specific higher requirements for transfer students, but, in general, a minimum 2.5 GPA is required.

Participation in a campus visit and group informational session with an admissions counselor is strongly encouraged.

Application and Information

For informational materials and an application for admission, students should contact:

Enrollment Information Services
University of Massachusetts Boston
100 Morrissey Boulevard
Boston, Massachusetts 02125-3393
Phone: 617-287-6000
617-287-6010 (TTY/TDD)
Fax: 617-287-6040
E-mail: enrollment.info@umb.edu
Web site: http://www.umb.edu

UMass Boston students in conversation.

COLLEGE CLOSE-UPS

UNIVERSITY OF MEMPHIS

MEMPHIS, TENNESSEE

The University

Located on a beautifully landscaped campus in the heart of one of the South's largest and most progressive cities, the University of Memphis (U of M) is the flagship institution of the Tennessee Board of Regents System. Since its beginning in 1912, the University of Memphis has matured into a major public, metropolitan university recognized regionally and nationally for its academic, research, and athletic programs. The University offers more than 254 areas of study from which to choose.

The University campus comprises 1,160 acres at eight sites. In addition to the main campus, the Park Avenue campus contains spacious living accommodations for married students, a research park, and outstanding varsity athletic training facilities. The University of Memphis also owns the Meeman Biological Field Station, a 623-acre tract used for biological and ecological studies. The Chucalissa Archaeological Museum in southwest Memphis is frequently used as a research and training facility in archaeology and anthropology.

The University of Memphis is an Equal Opportunity/Affirmative Action institution committed to the education of a diverse student body. It has a total enrollment of 21,424 students, including 16,719 undergraduates, from almost every state and many other countries. Approximately 57 percent of University of Memphis students are between the ages of 18 and 22, and members of minority groups account for 43 percent of the enrollment.

Location

The greater Memphis area has a population of approximately 1.1 million, which makes the city the eighteenth largest in the country. Centrally located on the Mississippi River, Memphis is an active hub for business, agriculture, and the transportation industry. The city has the Mid-South's largest medical center and offers many cultural and entertainment opportunities. Major museum exhibits, sporting events, concerts, art shows, lectures, and even barbecue contests take place throughout the year. The AAA baseball team, the Redbirds, and the NBA team, the Grizzlies, both make their homes in Memphis. With its many businesses, industries, and schools, Memphis provides students with employment opportunities in a variety of fields during and after their college careers.

Majors and Degrees

The College of Arts and Sciences offers undergraduate majors organized into three concentration groups: the humanities, the natural and mathematical sciences, and the social sciences. Three degree programs are offered: the Bachelor of Arts, the Bachelor of Science, and the Bachelor of Science in Chemistry. Majors include African and African American studies, anthropology, biology, chemistry, computer science, criminology and criminal justice, earth sciences, economics, English, foreign languages and literatures, history, international studies, mathematical sciences, philosophy, physics, political science, psychology, social work, and sociology. Minors are available in each of those areas—as well as interdisciplinary minors in aerospace studies, Asian studies, environmental studies, Judaic studies, legal thought and liberal studies, military science, naval science, nonprofit management studies, public administration, and women's studies.

The Fogelman College of Business & Economics offers programs of study leading to the Bachelor of Business Administration degree. Majors include accounting, business economics, finance, hospitality and resort management, international business, management, management information systems, marketing management, and logistics/ supply chain management. The programs of the College of Business & Economics are fully accredited by AACSB International—The Association to Advance Collegiate Schools of Business.

The College of Communication and Fine Arts is made up of the Departments of Architecture, Art, Communication, Journalism, Interior Design, Theatre and Dance, and the Rudi E. Scheidt School of Music. Majors include architecture, art, art history, communication, journalism, music, music industry, and theater. The college offers three undergraduate degrees: the Bachelor of Arts, the Bachelor of Fine Arts, and the Bachelor of Music.

The College of Education at the University of Memphis is among a select few institutions nationwide to meet, without a weakness, National Council for the Accreditation of Teacher Education standards. It is home to more nationally recognized educator programs than any other public university in Tennessee. In addition to teacher education, the College offers accredited degree programs in counseling, health and sport sciences, and leadership. College of Education faculty members serve the community through more than 1,000 days of direct service annually and a rigorous research agenda.

The Herff College of Engineering offers undergraduate programs in biomedical, civil, computer, electrical, and mechanical engineering and in engineering technology. High-ability students have the opportunity to work with faculty members on world-class research for global companies such as FedEx, for governmental organizations such as the U.S. Army Corp of Engineers, or for other premier organizations such as St. Jude Children's Research Hospital.

The University College offers two nontraditional degrees: the Bachelor of Liberal Studies and the Bachelor of Professional Studies, for students with experience, talents, and interests served through personally designed or multidisciplinary programs. Examples of programs that have been developed include alcohol and drug abuse services, biomedical illustration, commercial aviation, correctional administration, family and consumer studies, fire administration and fire prevention technology, health services administration, human services, merchandising (fashion and home furnishings), organizational leadership, law enforcement administration, paralegal studies, preschool and child-care administration, religion in society, and technology and management services.

The University of Memphis also offers specialized degree programs. The Loewenberg School of Nursing offers a Bachelor of Science in Nursing degree. The program is accredited by the National League for Nursing Accrediting Commission and the Commission on Collegiate Education in Nursing. Students benefit from exceptional learning opportunities at health-care agencies in the Memphis area, including ten major hospitals.

Preprofessional training is offered for students who intend to enter law school or a college of dentistry, medicine, nursing, optometry, pharmacy, physical therapy, or veterinary medicine. The University also offers Air Force, Army, and Navy ROTC programs.

The University of Memphis has joined forty-five Tennessee Board of Regents institutions in offering Regents Online Degree Programs. The U of M offers three degree programs: the Bachelor of Liberal Studies in interdisciplinary studies, the Bachelor of Professional Studies in information technology, and the Bachelor of Professional Studies in organizational leadership. These degree programs are entirely online and are transferable among the participating institutions.

Academic Programs

Freshmen who have not declared a major are advised through the Academic Counseling Center in preparation for formal enrollment in one of the degree-granting colleges. Those freshmen who have chosen a major are assigned to their degree-granting college immediately for academic advising. Each student initially selects courses from the General Education Program, which offers classes in the areas of communication skills, sciences, humanities, and social sciences, thereby ensuring the acquisition of breadth as well as depth of knowledge in various fields. In addition to meeting the requirements of the General Education Program, all students must meet the requirements for their specific degree, as established by the appropriate college or department. The University-wide Helen Hardin Honors Program, now in its thirty-seventh year, is available for academically talented students, and there is an active Emerging Leaders program.

The academic year begins in late August and is divided into two semesters and a summer session. The fall semester ends in mid-December, and the spring semester begins in mid-January. There are also courses offered during shorter sessions within the semesters.

Off-Campus Programs

The University of Memphis participates in both the International and National Student Exchange Programs, allowing students to study in more than fifty other countries as well as in other areas in the continental United States. The University also offers credit and noncredit courses at various locations throughout west Tennessee.

Academic Facilities

The University Libraries of the University of Memphis comprises the Ned R. McWherter Library and four branch libraries: Audiology and Speech-Language Pathology, Chemistry, Mathematics and Music. The McWherter Library has 360,000 square feet of space on four floors. The University Libraries' collections include more than 1 million bound volumes, 9 million manuscripts, 3.5 million microfilms and fiches, and 11,850 compact discs. The mission of the University Libraries is to provide access to and management of information services and resources to support teaching, learning, and research for U of M students, faculty, and staff. The library also accommodates the general public. The Library maintains a library- and database-use instruction program which reached 8,500 students in 400 class sessions during 2008–09. The Learning Commons extends throughout the McWherter Library, with a Commons Room on the first floor where the Research and Information Services desk is located. All floors of the McWherter Library have wireless capabilities supporting the 168 public-use computers that give users access to all University-provided software applications. Laptop computers are available for loan to students. The library's Preservation and Special Collections Department has holdings on the history and culture of the South, the lower Mississippi River valley, the Mid-South region, Tennessee, the American Civil War and African-American history, including the Civil Rights Movement.

The Department of Theatre and Dance and the Rudi E. Scheidt School of Music, in their adjoining facilities, make an appreciable contribution to campus activities with live drama and concert series, films, and programming over WUMR, the student-staffed campus radio station.

Included among the many research facilities at the University of Memphis are the Benjamin L. Hooks Institute for Social Change, the Integrated Microscopy Center, the FedEx Center for Supply Chain Management, the Institute for Artificial Intelligence, the Ground Water Institute, and the Barbara K. Lipman Early Childhood School and Research Institute. The FedEx Institute of Technology, which opened in 2003, is a cutting-edge facility that brings together students, professors, researchers, and the global business community to formulate the ideas and products of tomorrow.

The state of Tennessee has designated five Centers of Excellence at the University: the Center for Applied Psychological Research, the Center for Research Initiatives and Strategies for the Communicatively Impaired, the Center for Research in Educational Policy, the Institute of Egyptian Art and Archaeology, and the Center for Earthquake Research and Information. In addition, the University houses twenty-five endowed Chairs of Excellence.

Costs

In 2009–10, in-state students paid a maintenance fee of $2652 per semester for full-time study or $221 per semester hour for part-time study. Out-of-state students were assessed fees of $9012 per semester (full-time) or $751 per semester hour (part-time). On-campus residence hall rates ranged from $3690 to $5950 for an academic year. All part-time students pay an additional program service fee of $78 per hour for part-time study or $577 per semester.

Financial Aid

Financial assistance is provided through four basic sources: scholarships, grants, loans, and employment. Scholarships are offered through the Scholarship Office as well as through various academic, performance, and athletic departments. Residents of Tennessee may be eligible for the state's HOPE Scholarship. An application for admission is required to be considered for general and distinguished academic scholarship programs. Applicants for financial aid must submit the completed Free Application for Federal Student Aid (FAFSA) to the Financial Aid Office, which places the student under consideration for all financial aid programs. The priority deadline for filing the FAFSA is February 15. More than $200 million is awarded annually. The University operates two programs of student employment: the Federal Work-Study Program and a regular work program.

Faculty

The University of Memphis has 870 ranked faculty members. In addition, many adjunct professors are hired from the community to teach in their fields of expertise.

Student Government

The Student Government Association consists of officers, a senate, a cabinet, and a judiciary elected annually by the student body. Its goals are to present the opinions of the student body to the administration, to enact legislation beneficial to the students, and to promote a broad range of student activities.

Admission Requirements

The admission of entering freshmen is based on the transcript of a four-year course of study at an approved or accredited high school that includes prescribed units of English, mathematics, natural/physical sciences, U.S. history, social studies, foreign language, and visual/performing arts. The General Educational Development test and high school equivalency diploma are accepted when applicable. The admissions process is a competitive one and is based on a student's cumulative high school grade point average and ACT or SAT scores. The average ACT for the fall 2009 freshman class was 22, and the average GPA was 3.2.The admission of transfer students is based on the applicant's grade point average, academic standing at a former institution, and scores on the approved admission tests. Transfer students will often be required to provide a high school transcript.

Application and Information

Inquiries about admission and requests for information about any undergraduate college of the University should be addressed to the Office of Admissions. Applications and supporting credentials must be submitted to the Office of Admissions before the beginning of the intended term of entry. While the established application deadlines are July 1 for the fall semester, December 1 for the spring semester, and May 1 for the summer session, early application is strongly encouraged so applicants can be considered for scholarship opportunities and take advantage of early registration. A student must apply and be accepted by March 1 to be considered for academic merit scholarships. Additional scholarships may have earlier deadlines. Registration for fall classes occurs at New Student Orientation. Prospective students are encouraged to visit the University for a campus tour, which can be arranged by contacting the Office of Admissions.

Office of Admissions
Recruitment and Orientation Services
University of Memphis
101 John Wilder Tower
Memphis, Tennessee 38152-3520
Phone: 901-678-2169
800-669-2678 (toll-free)
Web site: http://www.memphis.edu

The McWherter Library.

UNIVERSITY OF MOUNT UNION

ALLIANCE, OHIO

The University

The University of Mount Union was established in 1846 as a select school to meet the educational demands of a small community. Mount Union offers a liberal arts education grounded in the Judeo-Christian tradition. The University affirms the importance of reason, open inquiry, living faith, and individual worth. Mount Union's mission is to prepare students for meaningful work, fulfilling lives, and responsible citizenship.

Mount Union is primarily a residential campus, and its residence halls mirror the variety of lifestyles and diversity of interests of the students. Students have the opportunity to select from large residence halls housing from 70 to 175, suite-style halls, small houses, or fraternity houses. New apartment-style residences opened on campus in fall 2007. Upperclass students in good academic standing may be permitted to live off campus.

Student activities are an important complement to the academic program. From clubs allied with academic interests to those that are purely social, Mount Union has more than eighty student organizations in its cocurricular program, including chapters of one local sorority, three national sororities, and four national fraternities. Nearly 85 percent of Mount Union students participate in the cocurricular program either on or off campus. There are facilities on campus for basketball, dance, racquetball, swimming, tennis, track, volleyball, and wrestling. The University also has a newly renovated wellness and recreation facility, the McPherson Academic and Athletic Center, which includes the McPherson Center for Human Health and Well-Being, the Peterson Field House, and the Timken Physical Education Building. Nearly 65 percent of Mount Union students participate in organized intramural or intercollegiate sports. Mount Union competes in twenty-one intercollegiate sports: baseball, basketball, cross-country, football, golf, indoor track, outdoor track, soccer, swimming, tennis, and wrestling for men and basketball, cross-country, golf, indoor track, outdoor track, soccer, softball, swimming, tennis, and volleyball for women.

Location

Mount Union is located in Alliance, Ohio, a town of approximately 25,000 people. Alliance is situated 55 miles southeast of Cleveland, 75 miles northwest of Pittsburgh, 35 miles southeast of Akron, 40 miles west of Youngstown, and 15 miles northeast of Canton.

Majors and Degrees

The Bachelor of Arts is offered in accounting, American studies, art, Asian studies, business administration, cognitive and behavioral neuroscience, communication, criminal justice, early childhood education, economics, English, French, German, health, history, international business and economics, international studies, intervention specialist (special education), Japanese, media computing, middle childhood education, music, philosophy, physical education, political science, psychology, religious studies, sociology, Spanish, sport business, theater, and writing.

The Bachelor of Science is offered in athletic training, biochemistry, biology, chemistry, civil engineering, computer science, environmental science, exercise science, geology, information systems, mathematics, mechanical engineering, medical technology, and physics-astronomy.

Mount Union offers three degrees in music: the Bachelor of Music in performance, which is a professional degree; the Bachelor of Music Education, which is a professional degree; and the Bachelor of Arts in music, which is a liberal arts degree.

Preprofessional programs are available in engineering, health professions (including premedicine), law, and the ministry.

Academic Programs

The Mount Union education program is based on an academic year divided into two semesters of fifteen weeks each. The regular academic load is 12 to 19 semester hours per semester.

The Mount Union curriculum is designed with considerable flexibility to meet the needs of students who enter with widely varying educational backgrounds and objectives. The University has five basic educational plans: (1) a program geared toward specialization, with the student taking as many as sixteen courses in one department; (2) a program with a lesser degree of specialization, in which the student takes the minimum number of courses required for a major; (3) a program that permits concentration in interdepartmental areas, such as American studies and Asian studies; (4) a preprofessional program that prepares students for entry into professional degree programs in engineering, health professions (including premedicine), law, and the ministry; and (5) an interdisciplinary, individualized program, which students design in conjunction with a committee of faculty advisers to meet particular interests. While students have considerable latitude in determining their individual programs, the all-University comprehensive requirements ensure exposure to the fine arts, the humanities, the social sciences, the physical sciences, and mathematics. In addition, each student must complete a major requirement and a senior-year culminating experience.

Advanced placement, involving the awarding of credit or the waiving of certain prerequisites or requirements, is based on high school records, scores on College Board examinations or similar tests, scores and school reports on College Board Advanced Placement Program examinations, and tests devised and administered by departments within the University. Entering students are encouraged to take placement tests in applicable areas in order to begin course work at the proper level.

Academic Facilities

The library contains more than 230,000 volumes, receives more than 900 periodicals, and provides seating for 350 persons. The computer center, housed in the library, is equipped with the latest in computer and communications technology. The Kolenbrander-Harter Information Center houses two PC computer labs, a Macintosh computer lab, a language lab, several multimedia classrooms, and 24-hour access to study space. There also is a PC lab with thirty-six stations in Tolerton and Hood Hall and a twenty-station PC lab in the Hoover-Price Campus Center. All residence halls are wired for computers and closed-circuit television.

The Fine Arts Complex includes a 290-seat theater, an art gallery, a music library, an outdoor Greek theater, a large rehearsal hall, and a recital hall with a three-manual organ. The Eells Art Center contains classrooms, a printmaking area, a drawing and design studio, a kiln room, a sculpture and woodworking area, and a drama rehearsal hall.

Bracy Hall, a natural sciences facility that opened in 2003, houses the departments of biology, chemistry, geology, and physics as well as Mount Union's new master's-level Physician Assistant Studies Program. The 87,000-square-foot, $23-million structure has four floors and includes twenty-two laboratories of various types and sizes, three lecture halls, two classrooms, and twenty-one faculty offices.

The Clarke Astronomical Observatory is located on the roof of Bracy Hall, and a nearby private observatory is also used by the University. Mount Union has a 142-acre nature center, located 6 miles from the campus, for biology, chemistry, and ecology studies.

Costs

For 2009–10, the cost of a year at the University of Mount Union was $31,300, including $23,120 for tuition and fees and $7420 for room and board. This figure may vary slightly, depending upon the type of on-campus housing selected by the student. An additional $1000 should cover such expenses as books and transportation.

Financial Aid

Mount Union believes that no student should fail to apply for admission to the University purely for financial reasons. Approximately 73 percent of students receive some financial assistance based on demonstrated need. The University also offers allocated institutional dollars to students as merit-based awards. In 2009–10, Mount Union students received financial aid in excess of $48.7 million. More than $22.5 million of that total was awarded in the form of institutional grants and scholarships.

Faculty

Mount Union employs 123 full-time faculty members, nearly 85 percent of whom hold a terminal degree. The student-faculty ratio is 14:1.

Student Government

Student government is a significant part of Mount Union's decision-making process. Students are represented on all major campus committees that discuss matters affecting student life, and they serve as representatives at meetings of the administration, faculty, and trustees.

Admission Requirements

It is the policy of the University of Mount Union not to discriminate on the basis of race, sex, sexual orientation, religion, age, color, creed, national or ethnic origin, marital or parental status, or disability in student admissions, financial aid, educational or athletic programs, or employment as now or may hereafter be required by Title VII of the Civil Rights Act of 1964, Title IX of the Educational Amendments of 1972, Section 504 of the Rehabilitation Act of 1973, the Americans with Disabilities Act of 1990, regulations of the Internal Revenue Service, and all other applicable federal, state, and local statutes, ordinances, and regulations.

The qualifications of each candidate are evaluated on the basis of academic background, class rank, references, a required essay, recommendations, and entrance examinations. Applicants should have pursued a strong college-preparatory course in high school. All candidates are required to submit either SAT or ACT scores.

Mount Union welcomes applications from students wishing to transfer from other institutions.

Application and Information

Admission decisions are made on a rolling basis throughout the year. The first admission decisions are made in October. Students can apply for admission for free using either the online application on the University's Web site at http://www.mountunion.edu, or by submitting a paper application. The admission packet contains instructions, an application form, a secondary school transcript form, and a reference request form.

The Office of Admission is located in the Gartner Welcome Center and is open throughout the year from 8 a.m. until 4:30 p.m. on weekdays and from 9 a.m. until noon on Saturdays throughout the academic year. Candidates who find it possible to visit the campus are encouraged to schedule an interview, although this is not a requirement.

Applicants may obtain further information by contacting:

Director of Admission
University of Mount Union
1972 Clark Avenue
Alliance, Ohio 44601
Phone: 330-823-2590
800-334-6682 (toll-free)
E-mail: admission@mountunion.edu
Web site: http://www.mountunion.edu

Chapman Hall, built in 1864, serves as one of the main classroom buildings at the University of Mount Union.

UNIVERSITY OF NEW ENGLAND

BIDDEFORD AND PORTLAND, MAINE

The University

The University of New England (UNE) is an independent, coeducational, comprehensive university committed to academic excellence and the enhancement of the quality of life for the people, organizations, and communities it serves. The University fosters critical inquiry through a student-centered academic environment rich in research, scholarship, creative activity, and service while providing opportunities for acquiring and applying knowledge in selected clinical, professional, and community settings.

UNE's student body of 4,493 includes 2,059 full-time undergraduates, 282 part-time undergraduates, 733 doctor's degree–professional practice students, 1,058 full-time graduate students, and 261 part-time graduate students. Students are enrolled in a wide variety of academic programs in UNE's four colleges: the College of Arts and Sciences, the Westbrook College of Health Professions, the College of Pharmacy, and the College of Osteopathic Medicine (housing Maine's only medical school). At the undergraduate level students represent thirty-five different states and several other countries in over forty undergraduate degree programs.

UNE traces its history to 1831 with the founding of Westbrook College, one of Maine's oldest institutions of learning. Today's university represents the joining of three unique higher education institutions through the combining of St. Francis College and the New England College of Osteopathic Medicine in 1978 and Westbrook College in 1996.

The University has chosen as its primary fields of education business management, education, health sciences (both mental and physical), the humanities, the natural sciences, and social sciences. The University of New England's philosophy of education and student life places emphasis on the quality of instruction and the practical application of academic material.

Each program includes the opportunity for learning in a community-based setting. Internships, co-ops, clinicals, and student teaching add up to the practical experience that allows students at UNE to apply the skills learned in the classroom to real job situations.

The University of New England has two campuses. The Biddeford Campus is located on the southern coast of Maine, in Biddeford, 90 miles north of Boston and 20 miles south of Portland, Maine's largest city. UNE's Portland Campus is located in Portland, Maine. As both campuses are geographically placed in areas that afford a high-quality lifestyle, it is only natural that the University of New England consistently engages itself in providing its students with high-quality programming and high-quality education.

The University encourages students to become involved in activities, clubs, and sports. Popular interests include scuba diving, skiing, hiking, biking, varsity and intramural sports, swimming, community service programs, and photography. The University of New England offers a wide range of services on both campuses. Special features include a full health clinic, a dental hygiene clinic, career counseling, personal counseling, learning support services, and an extensive student leadership development program.

Student Support Services provides a wide-range of services to assist students with psychological and emotional health, academic support, educational and career planning, and equal opportunities during their academic experience. The Office of Career Services provides academic and career exploration assistance, assistance in applying to graduate schools, self-assessment and personal interest exploration, resume help, job listings, and job fairs. Learning Assistance Services, another department within Student Support Services, offers a comprehensive array of academic support, including placement testing, courses, workshops, tutoring, and individual consultations.

Both campuses offer a variety of cultural and social events. The Campus Center at the Biddeford Campus and the Finley Recreation Center on the Portland Campus provide a setting for many recreational and sports activities. The University of New England Athletic Department operates an NCAA Division III varsity athletics program. Varsity sports for men are basketball, cross-country, golf, lacrosse, soccer, and ice hockey. Varsity sports for women are basketball, cross-country, field hockey, lacrosse, soccer, softball, swimming, and volleyball. Intramural teams in basketball, floor hockey, softball, skiing, and volleyball are popular. The University also has a number of club sports teams.

On the Biddeford Campus, Decary Hall houses a cafeteria, classrooms, meeting rooms, and faculty and administrative offices. The Campus Center contains a fitness center, bookstore, gym, pool, student union, racquetball courts, an indoor track, a variety of multipurpose rooms, and administrative offices. The University maintains ten dormitories on campus. Marcil Hall houses a variety of classrooms, and faculty offices. The Harold Alfond Center for Health Sciences houses biology and chemistry labs as well as lecture halls, classrooms, a gross anatomy lab, and UNE's medical school facilities. The Marine Science Education and Research Center has classrooms, wet labs, aquaculture labs, and a marine mammal rehabilitation wing. There are three major recent additions to the Biddeford campus. The Pickus Center for Biomedical Research is a state-of-the-art facility; the Peter and Cecile Morgane Hall is a science center providing additional classrooms and laboratories for biology, chemistry, and physics; and the George and Barbara Bush Center houses the offices of UNE's president and provost and the ground-floor Windward Café with outdoor terraces and flexible areas for students to study, meet, and socialize.

On the University of New England's Portland Campus, there are two residence halls and the Alexander Hall Student Union, which houses the dining hall, bookstore, the Wing Lounge, and a variety of meeting rooms. The Finley Recreation Center has a gym and fitness facilities. Ludcke Auditorium, whose main structure was built in 1887, is home to concerts, plays, and a number of workshops and meetings. The new College of Pharmacy building welcomed the first professional pharmacy class in September of 2009.

Location

The University of New England's two campuses are located in the picturesque southern coastal beach communities of Maine. The 540-acre Biddeford Campus in Biddeford, home to the College of Arts and Sciences and the College of Osteopathic Medicine, is situated on a beautiful coastal site where the Saco River flows into the Atlantic Ocean and includes more than 4,000 feet of water frontage. Located 20 miles to the north is the Portland Campus, home to the Westbrook College of Health Professions and the College of Pharmacy. It is set on 41 acres in a quiet residential setting in Portland. Students at both campuses can enjoy the vibrant social life offered in nearby metropolitan Boston (located 90 miles to the south of Biddeford) or Portland and the dynamic outdoor recreational activities that have made Maine a prime tourist destination. Southern Maine is conveniently serviced by a number of airlines at the Portland International Jetport and by bus and train service with stations in Biddeford/Saco and Portland, making the University's campuses very accessible to all areas of the Northeastern United States and beyond.

Majors and Degrees

UNE offers highly competitive undergraduate and graduate programs in a variety of areas. On the undergraduate level, the University confers Bachelor of Arts and Bachelor of Science degrees.

Bachelor's degrees are offered in animal behavior, applied exercise science, aquaculture and aquarium science, art education, athletic training, biochemistry, biological sciences, business, chemistry, communications, dental hygiene, elementary education, English, environmental science, environmental studies, health sciences (for occupational therapy five-year entry-level master's degree), history, liberal studies (including prelaw), marine biology, mathematics, medical biology (health and medical sciences tracks for predental, premedicine, and pre–veterinary studies), neuroscience, nursing, political science, psychology, psychology and social relations, sociology, secondary education (science, English, social sciences, mathematics) and sport management.

Individualized majors, various minors, the pre–physical therapy designation, an accelerated pre–physician assistant studies programs, prepharmacy with a path to UNE's Pharm.D. program, a five-year entry-level master's degree program in occupational therapy, and a secondary education certification (Teacher Certification Program) are also available at the undergraduate level.

Academic Programs

All undergraduate programs at UNE have a core curriculum as a common thread. Designed to provide a foundation in the liberal arts, the core reflects the values of the college and is designed to prepare students for living informed, thoughtful, and active lives in a complex and changing society. It provides an innovative common learning experience for all UNE undergraduates. It invites students to explore four college-wide themes: Environmental Awareness, Social and Global Awareness, Critical Thinking: Human Responses to Problems and Challenges, and Citizenship. Skills of communications, mathematics, and critical thinking are taught throughout the core.

A bachelor's degree is awarded upon successful completion of at least 120 credit hours and fulfillment of specific program and University requirements.

The University academic year consists of two semesters.

Off-Campus Programs

UNE is committed to supplementing the traditional learning process with practical applications. All students are encouraged to participate in cooperative education programs, field placements, and practicums. These experiences provide valuable learning situations and increase a student's exposure to job-related opportunities, and they are required for graduation by most majors. Students also have the opportunity to arrange a study-abroad experience. The Office of International Education promotes the goals of international cooperation and understanding through rigorous academic programs, overseas study opportunities, student-faculty research projects, and a host of special programs designed to address current issues in international relations and cultural studies.

Academic Facilities

On the Biddeford Campus, Decary Hall houses classrooms, laboratories, and faculty and administrative offices. The Jack Ketchum Library has been expanded to provide more library and classroom space as well as a media center and special event space. Marcil Hall houses classrooms, faculty offices, and the facility for the occupational therapy program. The Harold Alfond Center for Health Sciences houses labs and classrooms for the medical school, undergraduate health and life science programs, and graduate health programs. The Marine Science Education and Research Center is a $7.5-million facility featuring a marine mammal rehab center as well as classrooms, wet and dry laboratories, and research areas. The marine mammal rehabilitation center works primarily with seals, porpoise, and sea turtles. The Department of Creative and Fine Arts has moved to a new building which provides faculty offices and more studio space for drawing, painting, printmaking, sculpting, and photography. The new Peter and Ceceile Morgane Hall houses biology and chemistry laboratories, undergraduate classrooms, and faculty office space. Two other new facilities have opened recently: the Pickus Center for Biomedical Research, and the George and Barbara Bush Center.

On the University's Portland Campus, Ludcke Auditorium is used for a variety of academic programs. Coleman Dental Hygiene Building houses classroom, clinic, and faculty space. The Blewett Science Center, home of UNE nursing programs, consists of science labs and classrooms. The University created a Performance Enhancement and Evaluation Center (PEEC) that is an entire center devoted to learning and assessment of patient evaluation skills. The equipment includes two METI Human Patient Simulators and two Laerdal SimMan simulators. Proctor Hall is also a classroom building and is home to the Proctor Learning and Career Center. Josephine S. Abplanalp Library houses study space and computer terminals, along with an outstanding collection of books and periodicals and the Maine Women Writers Collection. The University of New England libraries have over 150,000 volumes and print journals, over 22,000 print and electronic full-text journal titles, and 6,000 electronic books. The new building for the College of Pharmacy opened in the summer of 2009.

Costs

The costs per academic year for 2010–11 are tuition, $28,300; room and board, $11,410; and fees, $1030.

Financial Aid

In 2009–10, approximately 99.1 percent of all full-time students received some form of financial assistance. The average package was $25,268. Financial award packages include scholarships, grants, loans, and employment. The University of New England has an extensive scholarship program that is based on academic performance. These scholarships can range from $3000 to $16,000.

Faculty

The men and women who teach at the University of New England are an experienced group of people with more than 85 percent having earned the highest degree in their fields, and they bring to the University varied backgrounds as teachers and practitioners of their disciplines. They are highly competent, demanding, concerned, accessible, and willing to give individual attention to students. Most important, they have come to the University for many of the same reasons that prompt their students to attend. The match between what the faculty has to offer and what the students need and expect is the key to the rare educational environment at the University of New England.

Student Government

The Student Senate is a vital part of the student life at both campuses of the University of New England. The student government has its own operating budget, which is derived from the student fees. The organization covers student services and public relations.

Admission Requirements

The University welcomes applications from students who are seriously pursuing an education of high quality. Candidates can file their admission application after the completion of their junior year of high school. All applicants are considered on an individual basis.

Students applying for admission are expected to submit a completed application, a $40 nonrefundable application fee, transcripts of all academic work (high school and college), and scores on either the ACT or SAT. Students who do not use English as their primary language must submit TOEFL scores. Students applying for admission should have completed a curriculum that includes English, mathematics, science, and social sciences. International students must also complete the International Student Supplemental Application. Applicants who are considering majors in the life or health sciences should show strength and preparation in mathematics and science. All prospective students are strongly encouraged to visit the campuses of the University of New England for an information session and tour. Information sessions and tours are held weekdays from 10 a.m. to 4 p.m. An appointment should be requested by letter, telephone, or via the Web site at https://www.une.edu/admissions/visit/visit.asp.

Application and Information

The undergraduate freshman admission application deadline is February 15; applications received after that date are reviewed on a space-available basis. There is a December 1 priority application deadline with a December 31 notification date. Applications for the spring term are accepted through December 15.

For application information, students should contact:

Office of Admissions
University Campus
University of New England
Hills Beach Road
Biddeford, Maine 04005
Phone: 207-283-0171
800-477-4863 Ext. 2297 (toll-free)
Fax: 207-602-5900
E-mail: admissions@une.edu
Web site: http://www.une.edu/

UNIVERSITY OF NEW HAMPSHIRE

DURHAM, NEW HAMPSHIRE

The University

The University of New Hampshire (UNH) is a rising star among American research universities, a community of exceptional faculty members and talented and energetic students from forty-five states and twenty-four countries. The University has a sizeable undergraduate population of approximately 12,200 but still feels cozy and intimate. This is due in part to a campus layout that is manageable and beautiful—with college greens, water, and a pleasing mix of classic and modern buildings that gradually give way to 2,600 acres of woods, fields, and farms. It is also due to the school's traditions of strong student-faculty interaction and active student culture. As one student put it, "It's easy to meet people and get involved in campus activities here. You need to have some initiative, but student leaders, residence hall staff, and others also seek you out."

The University offers students a variety of housing options, including halls of 100 to 600 students and two on-campus apartment complexes. Themed housing, such as honors, first-year experience, or international, is offered by dorm or floor. Holloway Commons, a spectacular dining and conference facility with seating for 850 and an after-hours café, opened in fall 2003, and Southeast Residential Community (SERC) Buildings A & B, 326- and 227-bed residence halls, opened last fall. Kingsbury Hall, the home of the engineering school, underwent a $50-million renovation in 2007.

The Memorial Union Building (MUB) is the University's community center. Housed in the MUB are two movie theaters, the UNH Copy Center, the UNH Bookstore, the Ticket Office, specific lounge/study space for both nontraditional and graduate students, and Granite Square Station, the undergraduate mail center. Computing and Information Services provides a computer cluster and a help desk with walk-in service. The MUB Food Court offers expanded dining options, and food service is also available in the Coffee Office. The Student Senate Office; Office of Multicultural Student Affairs; WUNH-radio; *The New Hampshire,* the student newspaper; and nearly 160 other student organizations originate in the MUB. Students at the University can participate in a rich cultural life. Numerous lectures, films, concerts, exhibitions, meet-the-artist receptions, master classes, dance performances, and theatrical productions are offered throughout the year. The UNH Celebrity Series, the Art Gallery, and the Departments of Music, Theater and Dance, and Art and Art History bring artists of international stature to campus. Most events are free for students.

Many opportunities for athletics and recreation, regardless of skill or ability, are offered through Campus Recreation. The Hamel Student Recreation Center is available to all full-time matriculating students. The center offers participants two multipurpose courts, a group exercise studio, a club/martial art studio, an 8,000-square-foot fitness center with more than 100 exercise stations, three basketball/volleyball courts, an indoor track, a lounge, several classrooms, locker rooms, towel and lock service at the equipment room, and saunas. Campus Recreation offers a variety of activities designed to make it easier to reach personal fitness goals and have fun. Participants may take part in one of the many group exercise classes, such as step aerobics, Reebok cycling, or cardio kickboxing. Other opportunities include Pilates, yoga, tai chi, a climbing wall, racquetball, personal training, or massage therapy. Noncredit courses are also offered, including CPR and first aid. The intramural sports program consists of more than twenty different sports and activities offered to men's, women's, and co-rec teams. Campus Recreation forms and assists special interest groups or sport club teams to reflect the varied recreation and cultural preferences of campus community members. Some clubs are intensely competitive, requiring a daily commitment to workouts and conditioning. They compete either on an inter-collegiate basis with New England teams or sponsor University tournaments. Other clubs meet on a casual come-when-you-can basis. In addition, Campus Recreation offers ice skating, manages a large outdoor recreation facility with its own sailing and canoe center, runs a children's camp (Camp Wildcat) in the summer, and supports the men's and women's sport club crew boat house.

Location

Nestled in New Hampshire's seacoast region, the town of Durham is an outdoor-lover's dream, with ocean, ski and hiking mountains, and charming working-port cities nearby. Popular road trips for students include Boston (about an hour), Portsmouth (about 20 minutes), and the White Mountains (about an hour). With a nonstudent population of 8,000, Durham is a classic college town that caters to the student clientele. Durham's Main Street includes restaurants, coffeehouses, a bookstore, pizza shops, and other student hangouts.

Majors and Degrees

The University of New Hampshire comprises seven colleges and schools: College of Liberal Arts, College of Engineering and Physical Sciences, College of Health and Human Services, College of Life Sciences and Agriculture, Whittemore School of Business and Economics, Thompson School of Applied Science (which offers two-year associate degree programs), and the University of New Hampshire at Manchester, the University's urban campus. The University offers more than 100 majors through these fully accredited academic divisions. New Hampshire enjoys a strong reputation in a wide range of academic fields, with biology, business administration, English, communication, engineering, environmental studies, history, hospitality management, kinesiology, marine and animal sciences, performing arts, political science, and psychology among those topping the list. The business school offers several options under the business administration major that include accounting, entrepreneurial venture creation, information systems, international business and economics, management, and a student-designed track.

Academic Programs

The University's general education requirements provide students with a broad foundation in the liberal arts and an introduction to the methods of inquiry needed for academic success. All students must complete ten courses from eight categories: writing skills; quantitative reasoning; biological, physical, and technological sciences; historical perspectives; foreign culture; fine arts; social science; and works of philosophy, literature, and ideas. Four intensive writing courses are required but are usually satisfied by completing the ten core courses. Depending on their academic program, students may begin course work in their major as early as their first year.

A major research university, UNH prides itself on producing students who have had meaningful research experiences with a world-class faculty. Programs such as the Undergraduate Research Opportunities Program and International Research Opportunities Program provide research grants each year for undergraduates to work closely with faculty members, on campus or abroad, on original projects. Students majoring in a wide range of subjects can access a wealth of research centers and facilities, some on the campus itself, others in surrounding towns. As New Hampshire's major public institution, the University is involved in a wide range of outreach programs with state and industry groups. These partnerships provide abundant opportunities for students interested in internships.

Academic Facilities

The Dimond Library is the state's only public university research library. The library offers three grand reading rooms, seating for 1,200 students, and state-of-the-art technology, including wireless and Internet. The Parker Adaptive Technology Room provides an array of technological options for patrons who have learning, mobility, or vision disabilities. Through ResNet, students who live on-campus have high-speed Internet access to UNH library resources, class software and information, e-mail, and other services. The Environmental Technology Building is a multidisciplinary science and engineering research facility with a focus on environmental technology development. Most of the University's cultural events take place in the Paul Creative Arts Center, which houses two theaters, dressing rooms, a well-equipped scene shop, a costume shop, a green room, storage facilities, classrooms, and the faculty and staff offices. New Hampshire Hall contains the Newman Dance Studio and a smaller stage studio.

Costs

The 2009–10 tuition and fees for undergraduate in-state students were $12,743. For out-of-state students, tuition was $26,713. Room (double) and board (unlimited meal plan) cost $8874.

Financial Aid

Approximately 70 percent of students receive some form of financial assistance from UNH. University scholarships ranging from $1000 to $10,000 are awarded automatically to qualified first-year students who apply for admission. Amounts are subject to change. Other scholarships are awarded by individual academic departments. The average student's financial aid package, including gift, loan, and employment assistance, is $9717 for New Hampshire residents and $14,638 for nonresidents. The University participates in the Federal Pell Grant program, the Federal Supplemental Educational Opportunity Grant program, the Federal Perkins Loan program, the Federal Work-Study Program, and the Federal Stafford Student Loan program. Students are required to submit the Free Application for Federal Student Aid (FAFSA) by March 1.

Faculty

The University of New Hampshire has 708 full-time and 377 part-time faculty members, 83 percent of whom hold doctoral degrees, with 5 percent at the master's level. The student-faculty ratio is 18:1. The UNH faculty includes winners of the Pulitzer Prize, Guggenheim awards, and many other prestigious awards and honors, while the University ranks among the top campuses in the nation in the percentage of faculty members who have won Fulbright scholarships. This research productivity has a powerful effect on students, who can share the experience of discovery.

Student Government

The Student Senate comprises a governing body of student officers and senators. They are the voice of the student body, representing student opinion to members of the faculty, staff, and administration as well as the University community and the state legislature. The Senate believes that all students have the right to participate in University decisions and policy making. Committees of the Senate include areas in academics, residential life, commuters, health and human services, judicial affairs, and community change. They also approve and monitor the rates and uses of all mandatory student fees.

Admission Requirements

Admission to a bachelor's degree program is based upon successful completion of a strong secondary school program of college-preparatory course work. Primary consideration is given to the academic record, as demonstrated by the quality of the candidate's secondary school course selection and achievement, recommendation, and SAT or ACT with writing component results. Consideration is also given to character, initiative, leadership, and special talents. Most successful candidates present at least four years of English and mathematics and three or more years of laboratory science, social science, and foreign language. Recommended mathematics preparation includes the equivalent of algebra I, geometry, algebra II, and trigonometry or advanced math. Students who plan to specialize in health, physical sciences, life sciences, engineering, or mathematics should present at least four years of mathematics, including trigonometry as well as laboratory course work in chemistry and/or physics. Students pursuing business-related studies should also have completed four years of mathematics, including trigonometry.

All candidates for admission to bachelor's degree programs are required to submit SAT or ACT scores with writing component results. SAT Subject Tests are not required. A foreign language SAT Subject Test may satisfy the foreign language requirement of the Bachelor of Arts degree programs. Required scores vary by test. International students whose primary language is not English must submit TOEFL results. The recommended minimum TOEFL score is 213 (computer-based) or 550 (paper-based) or 80 (Internet-based).

Candidates applying for programs in the Department of Music must make arrangements with the department chairperson for an audition (603-862-2404).

Application and Information

High school students who seek fall-semester admission may apply anytime after the start of the senior year and before the February 1 regular decision deadline. Admission notifications are provided on a continuous basis through April 15. Admitted first-year students have until May 1 to confirm their intent to enroll at the University. The review of candidates begins with the receipt of all required application materials. The Early Action (EA) Program allows candidates to receive a response by mid-January of their senior year; EA candidates must submit admission applications by November 15. In some cases, the Admission Committee requests senior mid-year grade reports in order to make a final admission decision. All positive admission decisions made prior to the completion of a candidate's course work in progress are considered provisional and are subject to the verification of satisfactory senior-year achievement when final high school transcripts are reviewed.

Office of Admissions
University of New Hampshire
4 Garrison Avenue
Durham, New Hampshire 03824-3501
Phone: 603-862-1360
Fax: 603-862-0077
Web site: http://www.unh.edu/admissions

UNIVERSITY OF NEW HAVEN

WEST HAVEN, CONNECTICUT

The University

The University of New Haven's (UNH) mission is to prepare career-ready graduates for meaningful roles in today's global economy and to nurture pursuit of lifelong learning. Founded in 1920, the University of New Haven is a private, independent institution focused on combining professional education with liberal arts and sciences. UNH is committed to educational innovation, continuous improvement in career and professional education, and support of scholarship and professional development. UNH became a four-year college in 1958. Moving to its present location in West Haven in 1960, UNH rapidly expanded its programs, facilities, and faculty, attracting a student body that now stands at more than 5,200—including the current enrollment of 3,079 full-time day students among its undergraduates.

The University is fully accredited by the New England Association of Schools and Colleges (NEASC). Individual programs, departments, and schools hold various forms of national professional accreditation. Four of the University of New Haven's bachelor's degree programs—chemical, civil, electrical, and mechanical engineering—are fully accredited by the Engineering Accreditation Commission of the Accreditation Board for Engineering and Technology, Inc. (EAC/ABET). The computer science program is fully accredited by the Computing Accreditation Commission of the Accreditation Board for Engineering and Technology, Inc. (CAC/ABET).

Despite a broad academic program, UNH is small enough to accommodate individualized educational needs. Programs evolve and adapt to meet changing career interests as well as the requirements of business, industry, and professional fields. Small classes foster close student-faculty relationships. Accelerated weekend and evening programs in business and convenient evening hours provide access for part-time students in engineering, computers, public safety, and the arts and sciences.

The main campus is in West Haven, Connecticut, on a hillside close to Long Island Sound. UNH also operates a satellite branch, the Southeastern Center in New London, Connecticut. Main campus administrative and classroom buildings support the University's four academic colleges: the College of Arts and Sciences, the College of Business, the Tagliatela College of Engineering, and the Henry C. Lee College of Criminal Justice and Forensic Sciences. Following the addition of the Graduate School in 1969, New Haven College was designated a university. Twenty-nine master's degree programs attract full- and part-time graduate students, while nearly 100 associate and bachelor's degree programs are available to entering freshmen and transfer students in a great variety of academic disciplines. In 2007, UNH established University College to oversee the graduate school admissions process as well as its evening, accelerated, cohort, and executive degree programs.

Other main campus buildings include the Marvin K. Peterson Library, Echlin Hall, the Bayer Hall admissions building, the Campus Bookstore, new residence halls and apartments, and Bartels Hall, the campus center, which houses dining facilities and student activities. The Charger Gymnasium and athletic fields are located on the North Campus, just two short blocks from Maxcy Hall, the main administration building. The David A. Beckerman Recreational Center, a new state-of-the-art athletic facility for the benefit of all students, opened in fall 2007.

UNH is currently an NCAA Division II school and offers seventeen intercollegiate varsity athletic programs as well as an extensive intramural program for both men and women. Varsity teams for men include baseball, basketball, cross-country, golf, indoor track, outdoor track and field, soccer, and volleyball. Women's varsity sports are basketball, cross-country, indoor and outdoor track, lacrosse, soccer, softball, tennis, and volleyball. UNH Charger teams have earned national top-twenty rankings in a variety of sports. The University currently competes in the East Coast Conference (ECC); however, in fall 2009, UNH will move from the ECC to the Northeast 10 Conference. Considering a move to NCAA Division I, the University officially entered an exploratory year in June 2007. During this year, UNH continues to compete as a Division II school.

Approximately two thirds of the full-time undergraduate day students live on campus in the eleven residence halls. More than eighty clubs and organizations are open to students. Included are student chapters of professional societies, religious organizations, social groups, special-interest clubs, student councils, cultural groups, and fraternities and sororities.

Location

West Haven is contiguous to New Haven. There are theaters that attract star performers from the entertainment world, a deep-water harbor and beaches, fine restaurants, museums, and galleries in the area. Numerous social and cultural programs are presented by the many colleges and universities in the area. New Haven is served by a local airport and major railroads, and its location at the junction of two interstate highways places the University of New Haven within easy driving distance of New York, Boston, Cape Cod, and the ski areas of New England.

Majors and Degrees

The College of Arts and Sciences offers the Bachelor of Arts degree in art, chemistry, communication, English, global studies, graphic design, history, interior design, liberal studies, mathematics, music, music and sound recording, music industry, political science, and psychology; the Bachelor of Science degree in biology, biotechnology, dental hygiene, environmental science, marine biology, mathematics, music and sound recording, and nutrition and dietetics; and the Associate in Science degree in dental hygiene, graphic design, and interior design.

The College of Business offers the Bachelor of Science degree in accounting, business administration, finance, management of sport industries, and marketing and electronic commerce, as well as the Associate in Science degree in business administration. The College of Business also offers the Bachelor of Science degree in hotel and restaurant management and in tourism and hospitality administration.

The Tagliatela College of Engineering offers the Bachelor of Science degree in chemical engineering, chemistry, civil engineering, computer engineering, computer science, electrical engineering, general engineering, information technology, mechanical engineering, and system engineering and the Associate in Science degree in computer science.

The Henry C. Lee College of Criminal Justice and Forensic Sciences offers the Bachelor of Science degree in criminal justice, fire protection engineering, fire science, forensic science, and legal studies and the Associate in Science degree in criminal justice, fire and occupational safety, and legal studies.

Academic Programs

The University of New Haven offers a broad range of programs in both liberal arts and professional areas. Experiential learning is emphasized, and there are diverse and numerous opportunities for career-oriented internships, cooperative education, independent study, and industrial projects. Certain types of professional experience are required in a number of degree programs. The Center for Learning Resources offers a tutoring service that is open to all students.

The undergraduate division operates on a 4-1-4 calendar. Credit is given for successful scores on the CLEP and Advanced Placement examinations. A University honors program provides outstanding study opportunities in most undergraduate disciplines. The residence requirement for all degrees is 30 credit hours.

UNH believes that all students pursuing a bachelor's degree should develop a common set of skills; the University's goal is to prepare all graduates for the complex lives they will lead in a changing world. This can best be done through the University Core Curriculum, which consists of a minimum of 40 credit hours in six basic competencies.

An available option at the University is cooperative education, an academic program that offers students the opportunity to combine career-oriented, compensated, full-time work with their education.

Academic Facilities

The Marvin K. Peterson Library contains more than 400,000 volumes in hard copy and provides access to about 20,000 electronic books and 20,000 e-journals from the library Web site and Voyager online catalog. Databases are available on a wide variety of subjects, with a focus on business, criminal justice/forensic science, engineering, and psychology, as well as general arts and sciences. Through interlibrary loan services, the University community has access to the holdings of more than 8,650 libraries.

Communication majors participate in workshops along with studying sound, film, and television production and radio broadcasting techniques in well-equipped radio/television studios and laboratories. The Tagliatela College of Engineering has modern laboratories and equipment to support its programs. The College of Arts and Sciences maintains art studios, state-of-the-art recording studios, music practice rooms, and science, psychology, and language labs. Hands-on instruction and demonstrations are available in kitchen facilities for students in the hospitality and tourism and nutrition and dietetics programs. Dental hygiene students gain experience in the Dental Hygiene Clinic.

There are more than a dozen computer labs for student use and teaching on campus. One of these is devoted to forensic computing instruction for the Henry C. Lee College of Criminal Justice and Forensic Sciences.

Costs

Full-time undergraduate tuition for the 2009–10 academic year, including the activity and health fees, was $28,250; room and board cost $12,204.

Financial Aid

UNH offers a comprehensive financial aid program that includes University resources as well as state, federal, and private aid programs. Approximately 80 percent of full-time undergraduate students receive some form of assistance. Students receive federal aid through the Federal Pell Grant, Federal Supplemental Educational Opportunity Grant, Federal Work-Study, Federal Perkins Loan, Federal Stafford Student Loan, and Federal PLUS loan programs. The University also administers programs sponsored by the state of Connecticut for Connecticut residents attending the University. Some students also qualify for financial aid from other states and from private companies, organizations, and foundations.

Faculty

It is a long-standing University policy that the faculty members teach a mix of undergraduate and graduate courses in order to preserve academic quality at all levels. Faculty members are selected and promoted primarily on the basis of teaching effectiveness, professional qualifications and performance, and contributions to the academic community. No classes are taught by teaching assistants. Some faculty members hold administrative positions and continue to teach. There are 183 full-time and 320 part-time faculty members, making the student-faculty ratio 15:1. The majority of full-time faculty members (more than 80 percent) hold terminal degrees in their disciplines.

Student Government

The Undergraduate Student Government Association supervises annual expenditures by undergraduate clubs and organizations, directs liaison committees, supports student publications and the student-operated FM radio station, and schedules cultural and social events. Student representatives are elected annually to the University's Board of Governors.

Admission Requirements

To be eligible for admission, one must be a high school graduate or present evidence of equivalent preparation. Scores from the SAT or the ACT are required. The admission decision is based on the student's overall high school record, SAT or ACT results, letters of recommendation, and personal essay.

Prospective students are encouraged to visit the campus for an information session and tour. Out-of-state residents are considered for admission on the same basis as state residents.

Application and Information

To apply to the University of New Haven, a student must submit the completed application form, a nonrefundable $75 fee for paper submission ($25 for online submission), official records of all academic work completed, SAT or ACT results, a letter of recommendation, and a personal essay. International students are required to demonstrate proficiency in English as well as provide documentation of financial support. The University of New Haven does not discriminate on the basis of age, color, sex, religion, race, sexual orientation, national origin, or disability in admission or treatment of students, in administration or distribution of financial aid, or in recruitment or treatment of employees. The University is authorized under federal law to enroll nonimmigrant alien students who meet the University's academic and English proficiency standards. The admissions office employs a rolling admissions system.

Undergraduate Admissions
University of New Haven
300 Boston Post Road
West Haven, Connecticut 06516
Phone: 203-932-7319
800-DIAL-UNH (342-5864) Ext. 7319 (toll-free)
E-mail: adminfo@newhaven.edu
Web site: http://www.newhaven.edu

THE UNIVERSITY OF NORTH CAROLINA AT PEMBROKE

PEMBROKE, NORTH CAROLINA

The University

The University of North Carolina at Pembroke (UNCP), a constituent institution of the University of North Carolina, serves as a comprehensive university committed to academic excellence in a balanced program of teaching, research, and service. Combining the opportunities available at a large university with the personal attention characteristic of a small college, the University provides an intellectually challenging environment created by a faculty that is dedicated to effective teaching, to interactions with students, and to scholarship. Graduates are academically and personally prepared for rewarding careers, postgraduate education, and community leadership.

UNC Pembroke is a coeducational institution that enrolls approximately 6,300 students in undergraduate and graduate programs. The average class size is 23, and the student-faculty ratio is 14:1. Freshmen are guaranteed housing and are allowed to have cars. UNC Pembroke offers more than 100 clubs and organizations, including fraternities and sororities, professional honor societies, and ethnic and religious groups. UNCP offers special programs, such as the North Carolina Teaching Fellows, Esther G. Maynor Honors College, and North Carolina Health Careers Access Program, as well as various research and internship opportunities. UNC Pembroke also has strong student ensembles in the performing and dramatic arts.

UNCP is a member of the Peach Belt Athletic Conference of the National Collegiate Athletic Association Division II and fields teams in men's and women's basketball, cross-country, soccer, and track; men's baseball, football, golf, and wrestling; and women's golf, softball, tennis, and volleyball. The University also offers a full range of intramural sports programs.

Founded in 1887 to educate Native Americans, the University now serves a student body reflective of the rich cultural diversity of American society. *U.S. News & World Report* ranks UNCP first in campus diversity among Southern universities that grant master's degrees. According to *The Princeton Review*, the University of North Carolina at Pembroke is one of the nation's "best value" undergraduate institutions. As it stimulates interaction within and among its cultural groups, the University enables students to become informed, principled, and tolerant citizens with a global perspective. Drawing strength from its heritage, UNCP continues to expand its leadership role in enriching the intellectual, economic, social, and cultural life of the region, the state, and the nation.

Location

UNCP is located in the sandhills of North Carolina, an area famous for its temperate climate, natural scenic beauty, golf resorts, and Southern hospitality, in the historic town of Pembroke. Easily accessible from Interstate 95 and U.S. 74, North and South Carolina beaches are within a 1½-hour drive, and campus is within a 2-hour drive of the cities of the Research Triangle Park, Fayetteville, and Charlotte.

Majors and Degrees

UNC Pembroke offers a broad range of degrees and nationally accredited professional programs at the bachelor's and master's levels. The University is organized into the College of Arts and Sciences, School of Mass Communications and Business, School of Education, and School of Graduate Studies. UNCP confers five undergraduate degrees: the Bachelor of Arts, Bachelor of Music, Bachelor of Science, Bachelor of Science in Nursing, and Bachelor of Social Work.

Majors, minors, and/or concentrations are offered in African American studies; American Indian studies; art (art education, arts management, studio art—ceramics, digital arts, painting, print making, and sculpture); biology (biology education, biomedical emphasis, biotechnology, botany, environmental biology, environmental science, medical technology, molecular biology, premed, zoology); business administration (accounting, applied science, economics, finance, information technology management, international business, management, marketing); chemistry and physics (applied physics; chemistry—biomedical emphasis, environmental chemistry, forensic chemistry, medical technology, molecular biotechnology, prepharmacy, professional emphasis, premed, and science education); education (birth–kindergarten, elementary, middle grades (language arts, mathematics, science, social science), special education–learning disabilities and mental retardation); English, theater, and foreign languages (English, English education, Spanish, theater arts); health, physical education, and recreation (athletic training, community health education, exercise and sports management, health and physical education, health promotion, physical education, recreational management/administration); history (American studies, social studies education); mass communications (broadcasting, journalism, public relations); mathematics and computer science (computer science, mathematics—mathematics education); music (elective studies in business/music industry option, music education (instrumental emphasis, keyboard emphasis/instrumental, keyboard emphasis/vocal, and vocal emphasis), music theater); nursing (B.S.N. and RN to B.S.N. programs); philosophy and religion; political science (international studies, prelaw, public policy and administration); psychology; social work and criminal justice; and sociology (medical sociology).

Preprofessional programs are offered in dentistry, law, medicine, optometry, pharmacy, public health, and veterinary medicine. A candidate for a degree in medical technology completes a three-year program at UNC Pembroke and an additional year at one of several cooperating hospitals. The student receives a Bachelor of Science in either biology or chemistry upon completion of the year's hospital work.

Academic Programs

UNC Pembroke seeks to produce graduates with broad vision, who are sensitive to values, who recognize the complexity of social problems, and who will be contributing citizens with an international perspective and an appreciation for the achievements of diverse civilizations. To earn a degree, students must earn at least 120 to 128 semester hours of credit in a program of study. In addition to meeting all major program requirements, students seeking baccalaureate degrees are required to complete a 44-hour General Education program, which provides students with an understanding of the fundamental principles and contributions of a variety of disciplines. Moreover, the program fosters the ability to analyze and weigh evidence, exercise quantitative and scientific skills, make informed decisions, write and speak clearly, and think critically and creatively.

Academic Facilities

The Mary Livermore Library houses more than 200,000 books, 1,300 periodicals, and local historical materials and serves as the depository for selected state and federal documents. The School of Education's Education Center maintains a curriculum laboratory and test review resource center. The Department of English, Theatre, and Languages maintains a library of books, journals, and media resources for English education and foreign languages. Moreover, the Department of Music's library is home to various recordings and music scores by regional artists.

The Native American Resource Center offers a rich collection of authentic American Indian artifacts, handicrafts, and art as well as books, cassettes, record albums, and filmstrips about Native Americans, with emphasis on the Lumbee Indians of Robeson County. The center's exhibits include prehistoric tools and weapons, nineteenth-century household and farm equipment, and contemporary Indian art. Artifacts from Indian cultures of Canada and Central and South America as well as from other sections of the United States are also on display.

Each academic building houses at least one microcomputer laboratory. Additional computers are located in the Computer Center, Chavis University Center, and the Mary Livermore Library. The University's computer network is connected to LINC NET, a statewide data network, and the Internet, which provides worldwide computer access.

Costs

The 2009–10 cost, including tuition and fees, for in-state students residing on campus was $9962, and out-of-state students residing on campus paid $19,169.

Financial Aid

U.S. News & World Report listed UNC Pembroke as one of the most affordable universities in the South. UNC Pembroke makes every effort to assist students in securing the financial means necessary to attend the University. Aid is available to eligible students through scholarships, state and federal grants, loans, and college work-study. To apply for financial aid, students must complete the Free Application for Federal Student Aid (FAFSA), which is available from high school guidance offices and online. A variety of scholarships are available to students who demonstrate superior academic ability. Scholarships are awarded on the basis of personal and academic merit; some, however, are also based on financial need. The deadline for scholarship applications is March 1 for fall admission. Students applying for financial aid should complete the FAFSA by March 15.

Faculty

UNC Pembroke's teaching faculty numbers 311 full-time members, 80 percent of whom have doctoral or terminal degrees. The University has long valued personal attention within the classroom. With that in mind, all classes are taught by faculty members, not graduate assistants.

Student Government

The Student Government Association (SGA) represents and safeguards the interests of the student body. Once a student enrolls at UNCP, he or she becomes a member of the SGA. Officers and class representatives are elected by the student body each spring. The Student Senate is the legislative branch and policymaking body of the SGA. The senate recommends policies and regulations necessary for the general welfare of the student body.

Admission Requirements

Applicants for freshman admission must provide evidence (high school transcript) of graduation from high school, satisfactory class rank and GPA, and scores from either the SAT or the ACT (with the writing component). First-year students are expected to have completed: 4 course units in English (the courses should emphasize grammar, composition, and literature); 4 course units in mathematics, including algebra I, algebra II, geometry, and a higher-level mathematics course for which algebra II is a prerequisite; 3 course units in science, including a life or biological science, a physical science, and a laboratory science; 2 course units in social studies, including 1 unit in United States history; and 2 years of the same foreign language. It is recommended that students take mathematics in their senior year. Transfer students are evaluated for admission based on college work. For those students who have fewer than 24 semester credit hours, admissions decisions may be based on freshman criteria.

Application and Information

Applications should be submitted by December 1 for the spring semester and by July 15 for the fall semester. Students are encouraged to apply earlier if they wish to be considered for financial aid and scholarships. In addition, applications are accepted for both summer sessions. The priority deadlines are May 15 for summer session I and June 15 for summer session II. Applications and additional information are available from:

Director of Admissions
The University of North Carolina at Pembroke
One University Drive
P.O. Box 1510
Pembroke, North Carolina 28372-1510
Phone: 910-521-6262
800-949-UNCP (toll-free)
Fax: 910-521-6497
E-mail: admissions@uncp.edu
Web site: http://www.uncp.edu/admissions

UNIVERSITY OF OREGON

EUGENE, OREGON

The University

At the University of Oregon (UO), students are part of a community dedicated to making a difference in the world. Whether changing a community, a law, or someone else's mindset, the UO can give students the inspiration and resources needed to succeed.

The University offers 271 comprehensive academic programs (including new programs in African studies, cinema studies, Latin American studies, and queer studies) and more than 250 student organizations. The architecture, biochemistry, chemistry, economics, English, entrepreneurship, molecular biology, neuroscience, physics, psychology, special education, sports business, and sustainable design programs all rank among the top 10 in the U.S. Programs in comparative literature, finance, historic preservation, and mathematics rank in the top 20 in the U.S.

At the UO, students attend classes alongside students from all fifty states, three U.S. territories, and eighty-five countries—people with religious, cultural, and ethnic heritages different from their own. Global degree options include twenty-eight languages, as well as international, ethnic, religious, African, Asian, Latin American, Judaic, and Russian and East European studies. The UO offers 165 study programs and internships in ninety-five countries.

Campus buildings date from 1876, when Deady Hall opened, to 2010, when the Jacqua Center for Student Athletes was completed.

The Associated Students of the University of Oregon offers more than 250 student organizations, including cultural organizations, fraternities and sororities, student government, campus ministries, political groups, performing arts groups, international student clubs, and honor societies. More details can be found at http://asuo.uoregon.edu/. The University is among the top universities in the U.S. for Peace Corps volunteers, student voter registration, and the number of graduates who hold high-ranking military offices.

With nineteen NCAA Division I teams, as well as forty-four club sports, students have a wide variety of sports to play or teams to cheer for. In fall, students root for the Ducks' football team at Autzen Stadium. In the winter, the men's and women's basketball teams thrill the crowds at the state-of-the-art Matthew Knight Arena. In the spring, UO track stars compete at the world-famous Hayward Field.

Location

The UO is located in the center of Eugene (metropolitan area population 343,140), a classic college town small enough to bike across but large enough to offer diverse art, music, and social venues. The Oregon Bach Festival and numerous music venues lure a variety of nationally acclaimed musical acts. *Rolling Stone* magazine included Eugene in its list of top 10 College Towns that Rock.

The city of Eugene offers more than 100 city parks, 250 miles of bicycle trails, rock climbing areas, and beautiful public gardens, all within the city limits. Eugene is easy to reach, with service from several major airlines and a stop on the main north-south Amtrak artery connecting Seattle and San Diego.

Majors and Degrees

The UO offers academic majors, minors, certificates, and preparatory programs in a wide range of disciplines.

The School of Architecture and Allied Arts offers programs in architecture; art; art history; ceramics; community arts; digital arts; fibers; historic preservation; interior architecture; landscape architecture; material and product studies; metalsmithing and jewelry; multimedia; nonprofit administration; painting; photography; planning, public policy, and management; printmaking; product design; sculpture; and visual design.

The College of Arts and Sciences offers programs in African studies; anthropology; Asian studies; biochemistry; biology; chemistry; Chinese; cinema studies; classical civilization; classics; clinical laboratory science–medical technology*; comparative literature; computer and information science; computer information technology; dentistry*; East Asian studies; economics; engineering*; English; environmental science; environmental studies; ethnic studies; European studies; folklore; forensic science*; French; general science; geography; geological sciences; German; German studies; Greek; health sciences*; history; humanities; human physiology; independent study; international studies; Italian; Japanese; Judaic studies; Latin; Latin American studies; law*; linguistics; marine biology; mathematics; mathematics and computer science; medicine*; medieval studies; nursing*; occupational therapy*; optometry*; peace studies; pharmacy*; philosophy; physical therapy*; physician assistant*; physics; podiatry*; political science; psychology; queer studies; religious studies; Romance languages; Russian and East European studies; Scandinavian; second-language acquisition and teaching; social work*; sociology; Southeast Asian studies; Spanish; theater arts; veterinary medicine*; women's and gender studies; and writing, speaking, and critical reasoning.

The Charles H. Lundquist College of Business offers programs in accounting; business administration (with concentrations in entrepreneurship, finance, information systems and operations management, marketing, and sports business); and global management.

The College of Education offers programs in communication disorders and sciences, educational foundations, educational studies, family and human services, special education, and teacher education.*

The School of Journalism and Communication offers programs in communication studies, journalism, journalism: advertising, journalism: communication studies, journalism: electronic media, journalism: magazine, journalism: news-editorial, and journalism: public relations.

The School of Music and Dance offers programs in dance, music, music composition, music education, music education: elementary education, music: jazz studies, and music performance.

An * denotes preparatory programs.

Academic Programs

The UO follows a quarter system, and students spend about one third of their education on each of three areas: the general education requirements, major requirements, and elective credit. General education requirements include courses in the natural sciences, social sciences, and humanities, as well as multicultural course work.

Freshman Interest Groups bring together a small group of first-year students interested in the same academic area in three related interdisciplinary courses. Freshman Seminars are small-group discussion courses taught by some of the UO's most outstanding faculty members. These academically rigorous programs provide a helpful transition to college-level course work.

The Robert D. Clark Honors College offers the academic rigor of a small liberal arts college with the resources of a major research university. The Clark Honors College (CHC) is a community of scholars—exceptional students and premier resident faculty members—who are actively engaged in the life of the mind. Courses in the CHC include 21 or fewer students, and complement any major. The application process is competitive.

Upon acceptance to the UO, qualified students will be invited to join the College Scholars program, which provides access to specialized courses, internship opportunities, and special scholarships.

Off-Campus Programs

The Career Center offers off-campus internships in fields related to students' academic majors or extracurricular interests. Both paid and volunteer internships are widely available to all majors. The Global Graduates international program provides academic credit through overseas internships.

Pine Mountain Observatory, near Bend, Oregon, offers study options in physics and astronomy. Students can participate in an annual Archaeology Field School in central Oregon's Northern Great Basin. The Oregon Institute of Marine Biology on the Pacific coast provides access to deep sea, coastal watershed, and estuary habitat.

Cooperatively run by students, the top-ranked Outdoor Program offers skiing, rock climbing, and kayaking.

Academic Facilities

The UO Libraries, an Association of Research Libraries member, houses the largest research collection in the state, including 3 million volumes and 46,000 journal subscriptions, both print and electronic.

Two campus museums and multiple theaters are valuable resources in the sciences and visual arts. The Jordan Schnitzer Museum of Art offers exhibitions of classical and contemporary art. The Museum of Natural and Cultural History features Native American artifacts and archaeological finds. Students appear in music, dance, and theater performances in newly refurbished facilities.

Science facilities are among the best in the nation. Research and laboratory courses offer students firsthand experience with electron microscopes and microprobes, advanced optical microscopy, seismic array, atomic absorption and emissions, and one of the few MRI units in the country in an educational setting. The new Lokey Laboratories offer advanced nanotechnology facilities.

Costs

Resident undergraduate tuition and fees for the 2009–10 academic year were $7428. Room and board (on-campus residence hall, double occupancy) cost $8640 per academic year, books and supplies cost $1050, and personal expenses were estimated at $2412, for a total of $19,530.

Nonresident undergraduate tuition and fees for the 2009–10 academic year were $23,718. Room and board (on-campus residence hall, double occupancy) cost $8640 per academic year, books and supplies cost $1050, and personal expenses were estimated at $2412, for a total of $35,820.

Financial Aid

The UO makes a concerted effort to enable students to attend, regardless of family income. Financial aid in the form of grants, loans, and employment is available to qualifying students. Sixty-three percent of UO students receive scholarships and financial aid that are awarded through the federal government, University, and academic departments. To apply for financial aid, students must file the Free Application for Federal Student Aid (FAFSA) in early February. The UO's federal school code is 003223.

Incoming freshmen will be considered automatically for Dean's scholarships, Staton scholarships, Laurel scholarships, and General University scholarships by completing the UO admission application by January 15. The Presidential scholarship and Diversity Excellence scholarship require separate applications due January 15. For more information, visit http://financialaid.uoregon.edu/.

Dean's scholarships are awarded each year to academically successful entering freshmen and range from $1000 to $7000 per year. General University and Laurel scholarships are awarded each year and range from $1000 to $2000 per year. Presidential scholarships of $7800 per year, renewable for up to four years of study, are awarded each year to UO's brightest incoming freshmen. Diversity Excellence scholarships (DES) are tuition-remission awards in amounts ranging from partial to full tuition and fee waivers. Staton scholarships of $5500 are awarded each year to incoming Oregon students with extraordinary financial need, and are renewable for up to four years. Students must apply for admission by January 15, 2011 and complete the FAFSA to receive consideration. Western Undergraduate Exchange (WUE) offers selected freshmen from certain western states the opportunity to study at the University of Oregon for 150 percent of UO resident tuition.

Faculty

With a student-teacher ratio of 19:1 and an average class size of 22, students find it easy to connect with faculty members and peers. UO faculty members are recognized for their outstanding teaching skills and renowned for their original research. Among them are winners of every major recognition for research and scholarship, including the Fulbright, Rhodes, Woodrow Wilson, Guggenheim, MacArthur, National Science Foundation, American Council of Learned Societies, and National Endowment for the Humanities awards, as well as membership in the National Academy of Sciences.

Student Government

The Associated Students of the University of Oregon (ASUO) administers a budget of more than $11.5 million, financing a broad range of academic, political, ethnic, religious, and recreational programs. The ASUO is part of the governing body of the University and also works as a lobbying organization at the state and national levels.

Admission Requirements

To be considered for admission, students must have a minimum high school GPA of 3.0 on a 4.0 scale, complete at least fourteen college-preparatory units, be a graduate of a standard or accredited high school, and submit SAT or ACT scores. Students with a GPA below 3.4 on a 4.0 scale, or who have fewer than 16 total academic units, must submit a one-page application essay with their application.

For students who meet the minimum admission standards, the UO next looks at such factors as the strength of academic course work, senior year course work, grade trend, class rank, standardized test scores, academic motivation as demonstrated in the application essay, extracurricular activities including community service, or the need to work to assist one's family, and ability to enhance the diversity of the university. Academic potential and special talents are also considered. Extracurricular activities will not compensate for low grades or weak course schedules.

The UO requires the following college-preparatory courses: 4 years of English in preparatory composition and literature; 3 years of mathematics, including 1 year of algebra and 2 additional years of college-preparatory mathematics; 2 years of science in biology, chemistry or physics; and 3 years of social science that could include 1 year of U.S. history, 1 year of global studies such as world history or geography, and one elective. Two years of the same second language in high school or two college terms of the same second language are also required.

A student who does not meet one or more of the admission requirements should visit http://admissions.uoregon.edu/freshmen/alternativeadmission for more information on alternative admission.

For automatic admission, students must have a minimum high school GPA of 3.4 on a 4.0 scale, have at least 16 total college-preparatory units, and meet the other admission requirements. Test scores are required for all freshman applicants, regardless of whether or not they meet the automatic admission requirements.

To be considered as a transfer student, a student must have earned 36 or more quarter hours (24 semester hours) of college transfer credit and have a minimum GPA of 2.25 if an Oregon resident, or 2.5 if a nonresident. Transfer students must have completed one college-level English composition course and one college-level math course (with a prerequisite of intermediate algebra or above) with a grade of C or better.

Applicants must submit an application with a $50 nonrefundable application fee, transcripts from each high school and/or college or university attended, and, for freshmen, SAT or ACT scores.

A campus visit is the best way to decide whether the University of Oregon is the right choice. Tours and information sessions are offered twice daily, Monday through Friday, and once on Saturday mornings. Prospective students should go to http://admissions.uoregon.edu/visit for more information.

Application and Information

Students may apply any time after September 1 for the following academic year. The early notification freshman application deadline is November 1 and is non-binding. The standard freshman application deadline is January 15. The early notification transfer application deadline is March 15 and is non-binding. The standard transfer application deadline is May 15. Students planning to enter programs in architecture, interior architecture, landscape architecture, music, educational foundations, or family and human services, should visit the college Web site for additional application materials. Those who plan to major in Asian studies, business administration, communication disorders and sciences, computer and information science, international studies, mathematics and computer science, planning, public policy and management, or journalism and communication, should submit their application for admission and the Office of Admissions will then contact the academic department for departmental approval.

For information and an application, students should contact:

Office of Admissions
1217 University of Oregon
Eugene, Oregon 97403-1217

Phone: 541-346-3201
800-BE-A-DUCK (toll-free)
Web site: http://admissions.uoregon.edu
http://admissions.uoregon.edu/virtualtour (Virtual Tour)

UNIVERSITY OF PITTSBURGH AT BRADFORD

BRADFORD, PENNSYLVANIA

The University

The University of Pittsburgh at Bradford (Pitt-Bradford) can take students beyond—beyond the classroom by offering internships and research opportunities; beyond the degree by providing a robust Career Services Office and an informal alumni network; beyond 9 to 5 by offering an active student life, a friendly residence-life environment, excellent athletic and cultural facilities, and a wide range of recreational opportunities; beyond place by exposing students to the world and offering many study-abroad opportunities; and beyond students' expectations by giving them a college experience that can transform them.

At Pitt-Bradford, students live and learn on a safe, intimate campus, where they receive individual and personalized attention from committed professors who work at their side. In addition, students earn a degree from the University of Pittsburgh, which commands respect around the world.

Students can work out in a state-of-the-art fitness center or swim in the six-lane swimming pool in the Sport and Fitness Center. The building also houses facilities for intercollegiate and intramural athletic events.

The Frame-Westerberg Commons offers students a place to eat, gather, and participate in campus life. The building houses the dining hall, where students can help themselves to a wide assortment of meals; a bookstore, which features an after-hours convenience store; offices for many student clubs and organizations; and areas to read or relax.

There are more than forty clubs and organizations, varying from the campus radio station and newspaper to academic clubs, honor societies, and fraternities and sororities. Pitt-Bradford competes in Division III of the NCAA and fields seven men's teams in baseball, basketball, cross-country, golf, soccer, swimming, and tennis and eight women's teams in basketball, cross-country, golf, soccer, softball, swimming, tennis, and volleyball.

Location

Pitt-Bradford encompasses 317 acres in the foothills of the Allegheny Mountains, only steps from the Allegheny National Forest. Pitt-Bradford also is a short drive from larger cities such as Buffalo, New York (80 miles north); Pittsburgh (160 miles southeast); and Erie, Pennsylvania (90 miles west). Pitt-Bradford can also be reached easily by car and plane.

At Pitt-Bradford, students have many opportunities to participate in cocurricular opportunities in the region, including cross-country and downhill skiing, snowboarding, snowshoeing, ice skating, biking, fishing, hiking, and hunting.

Majors and Degrees

Students may pursue four-year degrees in accounting, applied mathematics, athletic training, biology, biology education 7–12, broadcast communications, business education K–12, business management, chemistry, chemistry education 7–12, computer information systems and technology, criminal justice, economics, elementary education, English, English education 7–12, entrepreneurship, environmental studies, environmental education K–12, health and physical education, history/political science, hospitality management, human relations, interdisciplinary arts, mathematics education 7–12, nursing, physical sciences, psychology, public relations, radiological science, social sciences, social studies education 7–12, sociology, sport and recreation management, sports medicine, and writing.

Pitt-Bradford also offers associate degrees in engineering science, information systems, liberal studies, nursing (RN), and petroleum technology.

Students may also study engineering for up to two years at Pitt-Bradford and then complete a program at the Oakland campus in bioengineering, chemical and petroleum engineering, civil and environmental engineering, electrical and computer engineering, industrial engineering, materials science and engineering, or mechanical engineering.

Pitt-Bradford also provides programs offered in conjunction with the University of Pittsburgh School of Dental Medicine and the Pennsylvania College of Optometry. Students begin their studies at Pitt-Bradford and, after three years, transfer to the appropriate graduate school to complete four more years of study.

Pitt-Bradford also offers the first two years of study leading to the doctorate in pharmacy. Students must complete the program at the Oakland campus, where admission is competitive. The Pittsburgh School of Pharmacy preadmits some qualified high school seniors, pending completion of the first two years of the preprofessional program at Pitt-Bradford.

The University also has an agreement with Lake Erie College of Osteopathic Medicine (LECOM), which allows qualifying students to continue their education in medicine at LECOM after their third year at Pitt-Bradford. Students who have successfully completed their first year of medical school classes at LECOM will receive their bachelor's degree from Pitt-Bradford. They will then continue at LECOM to finish their medical studies.

Academic Programs

The academic programs stress critical-thinking and communication skills and encourage hands-on learning through field experience, internships, and faculty-student collaboration on research. A Pitt-Bradford bachelor's degree requires 120–128 credit hours (requirements differ slightly among programs). Students need to complete between 60 and 70 credit hours to earn an associate degree.

The accounting major prepares students for the workplace, which has a growing need for accountants. The major also prepares students to earn a master's degree in either professional accountancy or business administration.

The biology program prepares students for careers in health-related professions, education, and research; technical positions in governmental agencies; and careers with food, pharmaceutical, chemical, and biotechnology companies. Most students interested in medicine, dentistry, optometry, pharmacy, osteopathy, physical therapy, occupational therapy, podiatry, chiropractic medicine, veterinary medicine, preclinical dietetics and nutrition, and a variety of careers in health and rehabilitation sciences are biology majors.

Students who choose to major in broadcast communications, English, public relations, or writing are able to work on the award-winning student newspaper, *The Source;* broadcast over the college radio station, WDRQ; and publish original works in the award-winning student literary magazine, *Baily's Beads.* Students also have access to an all-digital television studio and two digital radio facilities.

The business management program places a strong emphasis on teaching practical applications; courses often focus on cases taken from real business situations. Students may concentrate in accounting, finance, international business, or management information systems.

In the criminal justice program, students are able to intern with local and regional police departments, county court and probation offices, and a federal prison. New, state-of-the-art crime-scene investigatory tools enable students to "work a crime scene" using many of the same tools as professional law enforcement agents. In 2008, the University opened a Crime Scene Investigation (CSI) House, which enables students to process simulated crime scenes and collect "evidence" just like the pros.

An education major prepares a student for a career as a teacher in a world of rapid political, economic, scientific, and cultural change. The Education Department seeks to graduate students who have general knowledge and specific content knowledge, as well as sound theory and practice.

Students who graduate from the hospitality management program are prepared to work in a large hotel or resort, in a convention bureau or center, in the areas of event or banquet management, or on a cruise ship. As part of the program, students complete 800 hours of field work at such places as the ski resort in nearby Ellicottville, New York, and Glendorn, a luxurious mountain resort in Bradford.

The nursing program at Pitt-Bradford offers an Associate of Science degree that can be completed in two years and a Bachelor of Science in Nursing degree that requires two additional years. Students may commence this program upon completion of the associate degree. The University also offers a School Nurse Certification program for registered nurses who wish to work in the school system.

In psychology, students gain knowledge in the scientific and theoretical aspects of psychology as well as the application of this knowledge. The major prepares students for graduate work in psychology and related disciplines and for employment in social service agencies, mental health centers, industries, and not-for-profit and governmental agencies.

Students may relocate to another University of Pittsburgh campus to complete academic programs not offered at Pitt-Bradford, but they may earn no more than 70 credits before transferring. All students in the arts and sciences may relocate, provided they are in good standing. Engineering students may relocate if they maintain a grade point average of at least 2.5.

Academic Facilities

In addition to the T. Edward and Tullah Hanley Library on campus, Pitt-Bradford students have online access to the entire University of Pittsburgh library system.

Blaisdell Hall, the fine arts and communication arts building, houses the art, communication arts, theater, and music programs and features state-of-the-art equipment. Students can find a computer-graphics lab, two art studios, a music/theater rehearsal hall, and a radio and television studio. The building also houses a multipurpose theater and serves as the cultural center for the region by housing plays, concerts, lectures, and other arts-related events.

Fisher Hall houses the science programs, such as biology, chemistry, engineering, petroleum technology, and physics. The science labs are filled with up-to-date scientific equipment, enabling students to perform a variety of experiments. The building also has two computer-aided learning centers and, on the roof, a campus greenhouse.

In Swarts Hall, students take courses in business, education, sociology, anthropology, psychology, history/political science, languages, English, writing, and criminal justice. The building also houses a brand new nursing suite and multimedia classrooms that can turn a typical class into an audio and visual experience.

There is more to the Sport and Fitness Center than sports. The building also houses the athletic training, sports medicine, and sport and recreation management programs. The building houses a human performance lab and an athletic training room.

In the Ceramic Studio, students get their hands dirty—literally. In the building, students will find sixteen motorized pottery wheels, a manual kick wheel, a work table, and a kiln to help them take slabs of clay and create art.

Costs

For 2008–09, tuition for full-time students was $5506 per fifteen-week term for Pennsylvania residents and $10,286 for out-of-state students. Nursing tuition was $7050 per term for Pennsylvania residents and $13,118 for out-of-state students. Room and board expenses were $3740 per term. Other costs include an activity fee of $85 per term, a health fee of $50 per term, and a computer fee of $150 per term. Books and supplies cost approximately $500 per term.

Financial Aid

Pitt-Bradford believes that the cost of a college education should not be a deterrent to any student regardless of family financial circumstances. A variety of grants, scholarships, loans, and work-study opportunities are administered through the Financial Aid Office. All aid applicants must submit the Free Application for Federal Student Aid (FAFSA) by March 1 to receive priority consideration. Pennsylvania residents who complete the FAFSA by March 1 are also eligible for Pennsylvania Higher Education Assistance Agency (PHEAA) grants. Students who live outside of Pennsylvania should contact their state agency to learn more about the prerequisites for grants.

The University awards merit-based scholarships upon entry to those who demonstrate exceptional academic achievement. The University ROTC program is another possible source of financial aid. The University encourages veterans to contact the VA about educational benefits.

To learn more about financial assistance, students should contact the Financial Aid Office or visit the financial aid Web site at http://www.upb.pitt.edu/financialaid.aspx.

Faculty

Pitt-Bradford's 78 full-time faculty members hold doctorates and master's degrees from some of the most prestigious universities in the nation, including Cornell, Harvard, Stanford, and the University of Pittsburgh. Teaching is the primary activity of the faculty, and personal attention is emphasized in the classroom. Faculty members welcome the chance to meet with their students and know them by name. The student-faculty ratio is 18:1.

Student Government

Because Pitt-Bradford is a personalized campus, opportunities for leadership abound. Many students become campus leaders as early as their sophomore year. Regardless of students' background or interests, most find many places to become involved at Pitt-Bradford.

The Student Activities Council schedules comedy performances, lectures, art exhibits, movies, and trips to such places as Toronto, Canada; Niagara Falls, New York; Cooperstown, New York; and New York City.

Admission Requirements

In reviewing applications, the Admissions Committee considers three primary factors in evaluating an applicant's ability to succeed in college work: the high school record, the results of standardized tests (SAT or ACT), and the high school's recommendations. In addition, personal qualifications, extracurricular activities, and potential to contribute to the college community may be taken into consideration.

Application and Information

Pitt-Bradford has a rolling admissions program, and students may apply at any time. All candidates are notified as soon as action is taken on their application.

Candidates for admission should complete and return the application with a nonrefundable $45 fee. Students must also submit an official copy of their high school record and scores from either the SAT or ACT. In addition to fulfilling the above requirements, transfer applicants must submit all official college transcripts and must have a minimum cumulative grade point average of 2.0.

The Office of Admissions welcomes campus visits by students and their families; such visits help students arrive at a final decision about Pitt-Bradford. Interviews and tours are scheduled Monday through Friday, 9 a.m. to 3 p.m., and on selected Saturdays. Arrangements for these visits can be made by contacting the Office of Admissions or by going online to http://www.upb.pitt.edu/visit.aspx.

For application forms, catalogs, and further information, students should contact:

Office of Admissions
University of Pittsburgh at Bradford
300 Campus Drive
Bradford, Pennsylvania 16701-2898
Phone: 814-362-7555
800-872-1787 (toll-free)
Web site: http://www.upb.pitt.edu

The University of Pittsburgh at Bradford.

UNIVERSITY OF REDLANDS

REDLANDS, CALIFORNIA

The University

The University of Redlands has, for more than 100 years, offered its select student body a tradition of superior liberal arts education. While students may select from a variety of programs that prepare them for professional or graduate school, the heart and foundation of Redlands is in liberal studies. Its outstanding faculty, educated in the world's finest colleges and universities, provides students with extraordinary opportunities for learning and growth through excellent teaching and close, informal interaction. Intense intellectual activity is balanced by opportunities for quiet reflection, fun, and recreation.

The University College of Arts and Sciences enrolls more than 2,300 students. Sixty percent of the freshman class comes from California and the remainder from forty-two other states and ten countries. In addition to a strong academic program in the liberal arts, the sciences, preprofessional programs, and the arts, many extracurricular programs are available to the student, including debate, music, drama, dance, and athletics. Internships are available for students in many academic programs. The School of Music and the Department of Theatre Arts provide a rich selection of cultural events throughout the year. Prominent speakers are invited to the campus each year to give major addresses and participate in classes and public discussion groups, and many social functions are organized by the Student Life Office and individual residence halls. Additional social opportunities are provided for interested students by local nonresidential fraternities and sororities. The student services center provides assistance in the areas of career and personal counseling and academic support.

Seventy percent of the students live on campus in residence halls that offer a variety of accommodations, including single gender, coed by separate wings, and coed by alternate suites.

The University of Redlands is one of a select number of schools that have a chapter of Phi Beta Kappa, the nation's oldest and most prestigious academic honor society. In addition, 6 Redlands students have been awarded Fulbright awards within the past two years.

The University of Redlands offers master's programs in the fields of business, communicative disorders, education, geographic information systems, and music. The School of Education offers a Doctorate in Leadership for Educational Justice Ed.D. program.

Location

The University is located in the city of Redlands within the San Bernardino Valley. Overlooking the 160-acre campus are the two highest mountains in southern California, Mt. San Gorgonio and Mt. San Bernardino, each more than 10,000 feet high. Redlands has a population of 70,000 and is situated at an elevation of 1,500 feet. Metropolitan Los Angeles to the west and Palm Springs to the east are both about an hour's drive away by freeway.

Majors and Degrees

The B.A. degree is offered in the academic areas of art history, Asian studies, biology, business administration, communicative disorders, creative writing, economics, English literature, environmental studies, French, German, government, history, international relations, music, philosophy, psychology, race and ethnic studies, religion, sociology/anthropology, Spanish, studio art, theater arts, and women's and gender studies. The B.S. degree is offered in accounting, biology, business administration, chemistry, computer science, economics, environmental management, environmental science, mathematics, and physics. The professional degree of Bachelor of Music (B.M.) is offered by the School of Music. Primary and secondary credentials are granted by the School of Education. Strong interdisciplinary programs in Latin American studies, prelaw, and premedicine are also available.

Academic Programs

Academic majors are offered in the spirit of a liberal arts program, with emphasis on developing the whole student. In addition to the standard academic program, international-study programs, independent study, and an honors program are offered to provide greater diversity.

A liberal arts education, by definition, is an exposure to a wide variety of academic disciplines. Typically, such exposure carries no underlying theme but is distributed among broad categories such as the humanities, arts, social sciences, and natural sciences. The University of Redlands has never considered itself typical and, as a result, has developed an unusual approach to the implementation of its liberal arts philosophy by restructuring the general education requirements to provide a contemporary curriculum. This common experience emphasizes competence in writing, computing, problem solving, and creative skills, all of which are fundamental to a lifetime of learning and career development. In addition, the requirements include a first-year seminar that integrates the academic program and close personal relationships between students and faculty members. The overriding emphasis of this innovative curriculum is on a thorough investigation of human values as they affect the individual and society. An examination of the worth of the individual, respect for nature and life, free inquiry, and the understanding of other cultures are a few of the topics covered through various courses. The University hopes that this experience will broaden each student's understanding and better equip them to deal with today's dynamic society.

The Johnston Center for Integrative Studies provides a nontraditional approach for a select group of highly motivated students. Johnston Center students are exempted from most of the academic structure of Redlands and instead negotiate their entire course of study with a faculty/peer committee. Drawing from the Redlands curriculum as well as from courses created each semester by the Johnston community, each student proposes an individually designed general studies program and an area of concentration. Course performance is evaluated in a narrative format rather than with letter grades. These students live in the Johnston Center Complex, a living/learning community that includes student rooms, faculty offices, classrooms, and space for weekly community meetings. Students who are enrolled in the Johnston Center are expected to contribute to the life of the center's community.

The academic calendar divides the school year into a 4-4-1 plan, providing a fall semester, a spring semester, and a May term. The four classes taken in the fall semester are completed prior to the third Friday in December. The spring semester begins in January and runs through April. The four-week May term offers students the chance to pursue one subject in depth. Extensive off-campus opportunities, including internships, international study, and on-campus independent study, are available.

Academic Facilities

The institution has facilities with a mix of Greek, Spanish, and modern California architecture. The newly renovated ground floor of the Armacost Library includes rooms for collaboration and learning, the Fletcher Jones Computing Center, a student study area, the Bulldog café, and an Internet lounge. Other facilities include the Stauffer Complex for Science, Mathematics, and Environmental Studies; and a brand-new Center for the Arts, featuring the Glen Wallichs Theatre, Frederick Loewe Performance Hall, and an art gallery. The library houses 400,000 publications and online databases such as Dialog, ABI/INFORM, PsychLIT, ERIC, Wilson Indexes, and the Music Index. These facilities and surrounding common spaces also have access to a wireless network.

Costs

Tuition for 2010–11 is $35,240, and room and board costs are $10,832.

Financial Aid

Recognizing that many worthy and capable students find it impossible to obtain a college education without financial assistance, the University has established a program of aid. Most aid is need-based, but no-need scholarships based on academic achievement in high school and/or college are available. Presidential Scholarships are also available, based on grades and test scores, as are Achievement Awards. Talent Awards, ranging from $500 to $8000 each, are available in art, creative writing, debate, music, and theater.

Students seeking financial assistance should inquire through the Office of Admissions when applying for admission. The Free Application for Federal Student Aid (FAFSA) should be submitted by February 15. FAFSA forms received after this date are evaluated subject to the availability of funding. Forms may be obtained most conveniently from high school counselors' offices and college financial aid offices, as well as online at http://www.fafsa.gov.

Faculty

The highly qualified full-time faculty numbers 167 men and women, 90 percent of whom hold doctorates or other terminal degrees in their field. The wide variety of academic backgrounds represented in the faculty provides students with an excellent opportunity to live and work in an atmosphere of intellectual inquiry. Academic advising is handled by faculty members, and all students are assigned an adviser in the area of their major interest.

Student Government

Authority and responsibility for student government is delegated to the Associated Students of the University by the president and the faculty to make possible genuine participation by students in the governance of the University. The organization is composed of all students in the college, and its officers are chosen by the student body. More than sixty positions of representation are open to students on faculty, administrative, trustee, and alumni committees. Among other activities and responsibilities, the student government finances and operates a student-union complex, on-campus shuttle, information center, vending program, convocation series, Internet radio station, and weekly newspaper.

Admission Requirements

Graduation from an accredited high school or the equivalent is necessary for admission. No set pattern of courses in high school is required, but applicants should have had 4 years of work in English and should have completed an academic program strongly emphasizing such studies as foreign language, science, mathematics (including algebra II), and social science. An average grade of at least B should have been maintained in the high school program. Applicants are requested to submit the results of the SAT I or the ACT. The writing portion is used for placement in English classes. SAT Subject Tests are not required. Standardized test scores are not required of transfers who bring at least 24 transferable units to the University.

Transfer students should have maintained a minimum 2.8 grade point average and may transfer up to 66 units of credit from a community college. There is a 24-unit residence requirement for transfers from other four-year institutions.

Application and Information

Applications are processed on a rolling basis. Those wishing to be considered for an academic or merit scholarship should apply by November 15. Those applying for need-based financial aid should apply by January 15. Transfer and late applicants should apply by March 1. Applications made after this date are considered on a space-available basis.

Further inquiries should be addressed to:

Dean of Admissions
University of Redlands
P.O. Box 3080
Redlands, California 92373-0999
Phone: 800-455-5064 (toll-free)
Fax: 909-335-4089
E-mail: admissions@redlands.edu
Web site: http://www.redlands.edu

The University of Redlands stands out brilliantly against the majestic San Bernardino Mountains.

UNIVERSITY OF RHODE ISLAND

KINGSTON, RHODE ISLAND

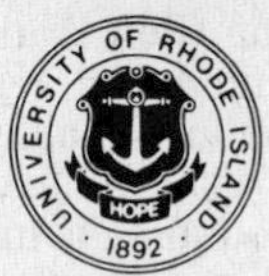

The University

As a land-grant college since its founding in 1892, the University of Rhode Island provides its students with an outstanding education and prepares them for responsible citizenship. The University also fosters significant research and takes its expertise to the community through a variety of extension and outreach programs. The current undergraduate enrollment is about 13,000 men and women. The center of the spacious country campus is a quadrangle of handsome, old granite buildings surrounded by other, newer academic buildings, student residence halls, and fraternity and sorority houses. On the plain below Kingston Hill are gymnasiums, athletic fields, tennis courts, a freshwater pond, agricultural fields, greenhouses, and a large convocation center. There are twenty-one residence halls on campus, offering a variety of living accommodations, including several new residence halls and apartment buildings for upperclass students. A variety of dining centers and meal plans are offered to all students. There are approximately 1,000 fraternity and sorority members living in nationally affiliated houses that are privately owned by alumni corporations. Some students commute from home, and other students commute from houses or apartments in the local and surrounding beach communities. Approximately 50 percent of the undergraduate students come from outside Rhode Island.

Lectures, art programs, music and dance concerts, film programs, and theater presentations are available. An extensive program of intercollegiate and intramural athletics is offered and is sufficiently varied to provide an opportunity for every student to participate. The Mackal Field House, Tootell Physical Education Center and the Keaney Gymnasium provide excellent facilities, including three pools, four gymnasiums, weight-training rooms, a dance studio, and a modern athletic training room. The Mackal Field House provides gymnasium space for a variety of recreational uses as well as an indoor track. In addition to a football stadium, there are twelve tennis courts, two softball diamonds, a baseball field, a lighted lacrosse/soccer field, a hockey field, and numerous practice fields for recreation and competition. The 8,000-seat Ryan Center houses the men's and women's basketball programs in addition to concerts and other large events. The Boss Ice Arena houses the club hockey teams and is also available for student skating. A sailing pavilion and rowing facility are located near campus. The Memorial Union Building houses a wide variety of educational, social, cultural, and recreational services, including lounges, study rooms, a radio station, the campus newspaper, a game room, dining facilities, a bookstore, a coffee shop, a restaurant, a ballroom, and a special events room.

Location

The University's 1,200-acre campus is located in the historic village of Kingston, 30 miles south of Providence. Bus transportation is available from the campus to most locations in the area, including Wakefield, where the nearest shopping facilities are located. The Kingston Amtrak train station is 1 mile from campus, and the T. F. Green Airport in Warwick, Rhode Island, is only 25 miles from campus. The campus is 6 miles from the ocean, and weekend ski trips to the mountains are easily managed in the winter season.

Majors and Degrees

The College of Arts and Sciences offers the Bachelor of Arts, Bachelor of Science, Bachelor of Fine Arts, and Bachelor of Music degrees. The Bachelor of Arts degree is offered in African and African American studies, anthropology, art history, art studio, chemistry, classical studies, communication studies, comparative literature, computer science, economics, English, film media, French, German, history, Italian, journalism, Latin American studies, mathematics, music, music history, philosophy, physics, political science, psychology, public relations, sociology, Spanish, women's studies, and writing and rhetoric. The Bachelor of Science degree is available in applied sociology, chemistry, chemistry and chemical oceanography, computer science, economics, mathematics, physics, and physics and physical oceanography. The Bachelor of Fine Arts degree is offered in art and theater, and the Bachelor of Music degree is available in music education and music theory, performance, and composition.

The College of Business Administration offers the Bachelor of Science degree in accounting, entrepreneurial management, finance, general business administration, global business management, marketing, and supply chain management. Business degree programs are accredited by the Association to Advance Collegiate Schools of Business. A five-year International Business Program is also offered.

The College of Engineering offers the Bachelor of Science degree in biomedical, chemical, chemical and ocean, civil, computer, electrical, industrial, mechanical, and ocean engineering. A five-year International Engineering Program is also offered, as is an Engineering/M.B.A. Program. Engineering degree programs are accredited by the Accreditation Board for Engineering and Technology, Inc.

The College of the Environment and Life Sciences offers the Bachelor of Science degree in animal science and technology, aquaculture and fishery technology, biological sciences, biology, clinical laboratory science, environmental economics and management, environmental horticulture and turfgrass management, environmental science and management, geology and geological oceanography, geosciences, marine affairs, marine biology, microbiology, nutrition and dietetics, resource economics and commerce, and wildlife and conservation biology. The Bachelor of Landscape Architecture degree is awarded in landscape architecture and is accredited by the American Society of Landscape Architects.

The College of Human Science and Services offers the Bachelor of Science degree in communicative disorders, early childhood education, elementary and secondary education, human development and family studies, kinesiology, textile marketing, and textiles, fashion merchandising, and design.

The College of Nursing offers the Bachelor of Science degree in nursing, which is approved by the Commission on Collegiate Nursing Education and the Rhode Island Board of Nurse Registration and Nursing Education.

The College of Pharmacy offers a six-year Doctor of Pharmacy degree, which is accredited by the American Council on Pharmaceutical Education.

Preprofessional preparation is available in dentistry, law, medicine, physical therapy, and veterinary studies.

Academic Programs

All programs of study aim for a balance of the natural and social sciences, the humanities, and professional subjects. All freshmen who enter the University to earn a bachelor's degree are first enrolled in University College; its advising program helps students choose a concentration and appropriate courses. A student must meet the curricular requirements of the college in which the degree is to be earned. As a general rule, 120 credits are required for a Bachelor of Arts degree and 130 for a Bachelor of Science degree, including the specified general education requirements. The University of Rhode Island operates on a two-semester calendar, with semesters beginning in September and January. Two 5-week summer sessions are also available. Credit is granted to students who have passed a College Board Advanced Placement examination with a grade of 3 or better. In addition, credit may be given for satisfactory scores on departmental proficiency examinations or College-Level Examination Program (CLEP) subject examinations and for the International Baccalaureate Program exam (IB Higher Level Tests). The University Honors Program offers academically talented students opportunities to broaden their intellectual development and to strengthen their preparation in their major fields of study.

Off-Campus Programs

The Office of Internships and Experiential Education offers internships for academic credit, including one-semester and one-year programs. Additionally, the University has exchange agreements with universities in England, France, Germany, Japan, and Spain. Other off-campus study and exchange programs are also available.

Academic Facilities

The University library has more than 1 million bound volumes and 1.5 million titles available electronically. Active research programs are carried on in all seven colleges. The Graduate School of Oceanography, located on the Narragansett Bay Campus, provides undergraduates with a living research lab for science-related courses. The University houses a large collection of American historic textiles, a center for robotics research, a planetarium, the Watson House Museum, a Confucius Institute, two animal science farms, and the state Crime Lab for forensic study.

Costs

The comprehensive cost for 2009–10 is estimated at $36,664 for out-of-state students and $20,166 for Rhode Islanders. This covers tuition, fees, and room and board. Books, travel, and personal expenses are not included in these figures. Laboratory fees are extra. The University participates in the cooperative plan of the New England Board of Higher Education, whereby students from other New England states are able to enroll in certain degree programs that are not offered in their own states and pay reduced tuition.

Financial Aid

To be considered for financial aid at the University, students must submit the Free Application for Federal Student Aid (FAFSA). Although there is no deadline for applying, priority is given to applications received by March 1. Most students receive notification of admission decisions on or about April 1. Merit scholarships are available to incoming freshmen with superior academic credentials. Consideration for these scholarships is given to freshmen who apply by the December 1 early action deadline. For 2009–10, 75 percent of new students who completed applications were awarded some form of aid. In addition, students have opportunities for employment through work-study programs that use federal, state, and institutional funds.

Faculty

The faculty consists of 817 full-time equivalent members, or 1 professor for every 16.5 students. Approximately 88 percent of the full-time faculty members hold doctoral degrees. Faculty members serve both the graduate and undergraduate populations and have wide-ranging interests and responsibilities. In addition to teaching and research, they serve as student advisers.

Student Government

The Student Senate is a legislative body that represents the students to the administration and faculty and supervises extracurricular activities. It also distributes the activities funds among the various student organizations through its funding committee. Individual residence halls form their own governments. The Interfraternity Council supervises fraternity affairs, and the Panhellenic Association governs sorority life. The Commuter Association provides social activities and other assistance for commuter students.

Admission Requirements

Admission to the University is competitive. Applicants are given individual consideration, but it is expected that all candidates have completed at least 18 units of college-preparatory work; specific unit requirements vary for each of the seven colleges of the University. Academic achievement in a challenging high school program receives the strongest consideration in the review of an applicant's credentials. An audition is required for the Bachelor of Music degree. All freshman candidates must submit a high school transcript and scores on the SAT or the ACT examination, which should be taken no later than January 1 of the senior year. International students for whom English is not the primary language must take the Test of English as a Foreign Language (TOEFL). Scores on equivalency examinations may be presented by applicants who have not been able to complete formal high school studies. Transfer students may enter in either semester (although some degree programs admit students only in the fall semester) and must submit transcripts of all previous work at both the high school and college levels. Early admission is available to high school juniors with superior records.

Students are selected primarily on the basis of academic competence and without regard to age, race, religion, color, sex, creed, national origin, disability, or sexual orientation.

Application and Information

Visits to the campus are encouraged. Information sessions and tours are scheduled daily during the week and on many Saturdays throughout the year. Students should visit the Admission Web site (http://www.uri.edu/admission) for details about these sessions as well as open house programs and directions to the campus. Admission representatives attend college fairs in Rhode Island and throughout the Northeast during the academic year.

Students are encouraged to submit applications early in their final year of high school, as the University subscribes to a rolling admission policy and reviews applications as they become complete. The early action deadline is December 1, and students receive notification by January 31. The regular deadline for fall term freshman applications is February 1, and the deadline for transfer applications is May 1. Most decisions are reported in March. The closing date for spring-term applications is November 1. Applications are available online. Requests for information should be directed to:

Office of Admission
University of Rhode Island
14 Upper College Road
Kingston, Rhode Island 02881
Phone: 401-874-7000
E-mail: admission@uri.edu
Web site: http://www.uri.edu/admission

UNIVERSITY OF ROCHESTER

ROCHESTER, NEW YORK

The University

Founded in 1850, Rochester is one of the leading private universities in the country, one of sixty-two members of the prestigious Association of American Universities, and one of eight national private research institutions in the premier University Athletic Association. Including the Eastman School of Music, the University has a full-time enrollment of 4,839 undergraduates and 2,900 graduate students. Rochester's personal scale and the breadth of its research and academic programs permit both attention to the individual and unusual flexibility in planning undergraduate studies.

Along with the distinctive Rochester Curriculum to help make the most of the undergraduate years, students in the College of Arts, Sciences, and Engineering (the College) also have access to resources at the Eastman School of Music, the William E. Simon Graduate School of Business Administration, the Margaret Warner Graduate School of Education and Human Development, the School of Medicine and Dentistry, and the School of Nursing. Special opportunities include the Take Five program, which allows selected undergraduates a tuition-free fifth year or semester of academic study; Rochester Early Medical Scholars (REMS), an eight-year combined B.A. or B.S./M.D. program; Rochester Early Business Scholars (REBS), a six-year combined B.A. or B.S./M.B.A program; Graduate Engineering at Rochester (GEAR), a 3-2 B.S./M.S. program; Guaranteed Rochester Accelerated Degree in Education (GRADE), a five-year B.A. or B.S./M.S. program; study abroad; Quest courses, first-year classes designed to allow collaborative research between faculty and students; seven certificate programs; Senior Scholars Program; and employment opportunities that include a national summer jobs program and paid internships.

Set on a bend in the Genesee River, the River Campus is home to almost all undergraduates who live in a variety of residence halls, fraternity houses, and special-interest housing. Most of the campus is built in a consistent neoclassical architecture, yet all academic buildings are wireless, and all residence halls are wired for the Internet and cable television. Facilities include Wilson Commons, the student union; the multipurpose Goergen Athletic Center; and a new research facility, the Goergen Hall of Biomedical Engineering and Optics.

Rochester students participate in more than 220 organizations, including twenty-two varsity teams, thirty-six intramural and club sports, eighteen fraternities and thirteen sororities, performing arts groups, musical ensembles, WRUR radio, URTV, and campus publications.

Location

With Lake Ontario on its northern border, the scenic Finger Lakes to the south, and more than a million people, Rochester is rated among the most livable cities in the United States. Cultural and recreational opportunities include museums, parks, orchestras, planetarium, theater companies, and professional sports teams.

Majors and Degrees

The University offers a Bachelor of Arts program through the College, with majors in African and African-American studies; American Sign Language; anthropology; archaeology, engineering, and architecture; art history; astronomy; bioethics; biology; brain and cognitive sciences; chemistry; classics; comparative literature; computer science; economics; English; environmental studies; epidemiology; film and media studies; financial economics; French; geological sciences; German; health, behavior and society; health policy; history; interdepartmental studies; international relations; Japanese; linguistics; mathematics; mathematics/statistics; music; philosophy; physics; political science; psychology; religion; Russian; Russian studies; Spanish; statistics; studio arts; and women's studies.

Bachelor of Science programs are offered in the College, with majors in applied mathematics; biological sciences (biochemistry, cell and developmental biology, ecology and evolutionary biology, microbiology, molecular genetics, or neuroscience); brain and cognitive sciences; chemistry; environmental science; geological sciences; geomechanics; physics; and physics and astronomy.

The College also offers certificate programs in actuarial studies, Asian studies, biophysics, biotechnology, literary translation studies, mathematical modeling in political science and economics, medphysics, and Polish and Central European studies.

The Hajim School of Engineering and Applied Sciences—part of the College—offers Bachelor of Science programs in biomedical, chemical, computer science; electrical and computer, and mechanical engineering; geomechanics; optics; and engineering and applied science, an interdepartmental program with specializations in a variety of areas. A B.A. program in engineering science is also offered.

In addition to the College's Bachelor of Arts in Music, a Bachelor of Music degree is offered through the Eastman School, with majors in applied music, composition, jazz studies and contemporary media, music education, musical arts, and music theory. Students may pursue a double-degree in Eastman and the College.

A Bachelor of Science degree is offered through the School of Nursing for those who already have their RN certification.

Additional opportunities include 3-2 or guaranteed 4-2 admissions programs offered through the William E. Simon Graduate School of Business Administration, in which students earn both a B.A. or B.S. from the College and an M.B.A. from the Simon School; 3-2 B.S./M.S. programs in biological sciences—biomedical engineering, chemical engineering, electrical and computer engineering, mechanical engineering, neuroscience, and optics; a program leading to a B.A. or B.S. and a master's in public health; and a guaranteed admission program leading to a B.A. or B.S. in an undergraduate major and an M.S. from the Margaret Warner Graduate School of Education and Human Development. Transfer students can pursue a 3-2 program that combines a B.A. and a B.S. in an engineering concentration.

Academic Programs

The University's calendar includes two regular semesters. The distinctive Rochester Curriculum allows students to select their major from one of the three branches of learning (the humanities, the natural sciences, and the social sciences). In each of the two branches outside their major, students choose a cluster of three courses that allows them to dig deeply in an area that particularly interests them. For most students, there are no other distribution requirements, except choosing one of seventy freshman writing classes.

The Take Five program lets selected students take a tuition-free fifth year or semester in order to pursue their varied interests.

The Quest program offers first-year students the advantages of small classes, student/teacher collaboration, and original research. Quest courses teach students how to learn, as undergraduates and beyond.

Students may arrange independent study courses or pursue research in all departments. Those whose interests may not be fully realized through a traditional major, double major, or major/minor, may work with faculty advisers to design an interdepartmental concentration.

Undergraduates from any academic discipline may devote their senior year to a self-designed creative project in the form of scholarly research, a scientific experiment, or a literary or artistic work through the Senior Scholars Program.

Undergraduates enrolled in the College may take private instruction at the Eastman School of Music. A double-degree program leading to the Bachelor of Music degree from Eastman and a bachelor's degree from the College is also available.

The Rochester Early Medical Scholars program is an eight-year B.A. or B.S./M.D. program for exceptionally talented undergraduates. Students enrolled in this program enter the University of Rochester with assurance of admission to the University's medical school upon successful completion of their undergraduate degree program.

The Graduate Engineering at Rochester (GEAR) program provides selected students with an assurance of admission into one of seven engineering master's programs at the Hajim School of Engineering and Applied Sciences: biomedical engineering, chemical engineering, computer science, electrical and computer engineering, material science, mechanical engineering, or optics. GEAR students receive a 50 percent tuition award in their fifth year of study in the form of a teaching assistantship.

The University's research centers include the Frederick Douglass Institute for African and African-American Studies, the Susan B. Anthony Institute for Gender and Women's Studies, the Center for Future Health, the Center for Judaic Studies, the W. Allen Wallis Institute of Political Economy, the Center for Visual Science, the Sign Language Research Center, the Skalny Center for Polish and Central European Studies, the Center for Optics Manufacturing, the Laboratory of Laser Energetics, the Center for Electronic Imaging Systems, and the Center for Biomedical Ultrasound, and many others in the School of Medicine and Dentistry and Strong Medicine.

Off-Campus Programs

Full-year and semester-long study-abroad opportunities and special summer and winter trips are offered through seventy different study-abroad programs. Semester and full-year destinations include Argentina, Australia, Austria, Belgium, Chile, China, Czech Republic, Egypt, England, France, Germany, Ghana, Hungary, Ireland, Israel, Italy, Japan, Jordan, Mexico, Netherlands, New Zealand, Peru, Poland, Russia, Senegal, Spain, Sweden, and Taiwan. International internships are offered in Berlin, Bonn, Brussels, London, Madrid, and Paris.

Academic Facilities

As one of the smallest of the 151 American universities classified by the Carnegie Foundation for the Advancement of Teaching as offering an extensive range of doctoral programs, Rochester offers an environment that combines the vast learning resources of a national university with the intensive personalized attention of a private college. Research opportunities for undergraduates are available in every field. Major research facilities include a comprehensive Medical Center; an extensive on-campus computer system; direct access to the CYBER 205 Supercomputer in Princeton, New Jersey; fifteen electron microscopes; a 12-trillion watt, 24-beam laser fusion laboratory; and a 3-million-volume library system, including the Eastman School's Sibley Music Library, the largest collection of any music school in the Western Hemisphere. The University is widely known as the nation's premier institution for the study of optics and is home to the Omega, the world's most powerful ultraviolet laser.

Costs

In 2008–09, tuition and fees cost $37,250, room and board averaged $10,810, and books, transportation, and other expenses averaged $2490. Part-time study is offered on a per-course basis.

Financial Aid

The University offers a strong program of financial assistance, including academic merit scholarships, grants, loans, tuition payment plans, and part-time jobs. Applicants should submit the CSS PROFILE application and the Free Application for Federal Student Aid (FAFSA). Special awards include full-tuition Renaissance Scholarships, Bausch & Lomb Honorary Science Scholarships, Frederick Douglass and Susan B. Anthony Scholarships, George Eastman Young Leaders Scholarships, Xerox Scholarships for Innovation and Information Technology, International Baccalaureate Scholarships, Seventh Generation Scholarships, FIRST Scholarships, National Merit Scholarships, National Achievement Scholarships, Urban League Scholarships, AHORA Scholarships, and other merit-based awards. In 2009, the University joined the Yellow Ribbon program and created the Rochester Pledge Scholarship, guaranteeing coverage of full tuition and mandatory fees for qualified U.S. Armed Forces veterans who enroll in undergraduate studies at the College or the Eastman School of Music. The University also awards room and board grants to selected Naval ROTC scholars and Phi Theta Kappa Scholarships for transfer students. Special applications are not required for merit scholarship consideration.

Faculty

Students work closely with a faculty of internationally renowned scholars, all of whom engage both in advanced research and in teaching at the undergraduate level. The University's faculty is held in high regard by colleagues at sister institutions, and many of its departments are widely recognized as among the best in the country.

Student Government

All undergraduates are members of the Students' Association, which has an annually elected president and a student Senate; there is also a Judicial Council, whose members are appointed by the Senate. The Students' Association in the College strives to coordinate student activities; protect academic freedom; improve students' cultural, social, and physical welfare; develop educational standards and facilities; and provide a forum for the expression of student views and interests.

Admission Requirements

The University of Rochester seeks to admit students who will take advantage of its resources, be strongly motivated to do their best, and contribute to the life of the University community. An applicant's character, extracurricular activities, job experience, academic accomplishments, and career goals are considered. More than three quarters of last year's enrolled students ranked in the top tenth of their secondary school classes. The middle 50 percent of admitted freshmen scored between 620 and 730 on the SAT critical reading exam and 670 and 760 on the SAT math and between 30 and 32 on the ACT.

The recommended application filing date for freshman applicants is January 1 for fall admission and October 1 for spring admission. An early decision plan is available. Transfer students can enter in the fall and spring semesters. Transfer applications are due by June 1 for fall enrollment and November 1 for spring. The University accepts the Common Application and the Universal College Application. An electronic online application is available on the University's Web site. Applicants for freshman admission are required to submit scores from either the SAT or ACT. SAT Subject Test results are reviewed but are not required. An interview is recommended. Candidates for admission from lower-income groups are encouraged to investigate the Higher Education Opportunity Program (New York State residents only), for supportive services and financial aid.

The University of Rochester provides equal opportunity in admissions and student aid regardless of sex, age, race, color, creed, disability, sexual orientation, and national or ethnic origin and complies with all applicable nondiscrimination laws. Questions on compliance should be directed to the particular school or department and/or to the University's Intercessor at University of Rochester, P.O. Box 270039, Rochester, New York 14627-0039; phone: 585-275-9125.

Application and Information

To obtain application forms and further information on admission and financial aid, students should contact:

Dean of Admissions and Financial Aid
University of Rochester
P.O. Box 270251
Rochester, New York 14627-0251
Phone: 585-275-3221
888-822-2256 (toll-free)
Web site: http://www.enrollment.rochester.edu/admissions

Director of Admissions
Eastman School of Music
26 Gibbs Street
Rochester, New York 14604
Phone: 585-274-1060
800-388-9695 (toll-free)
Web site: http://www.rochester.edu/eastman

Rush Rhees Library on the University of Rochester's Eastman Quadrangle.

UNIVERSITY OF ST. THOMAS

ST. PAUL, MINNESOTA

The University

The University of St. Thomas, founded in 1885, is a Catholic, independent, liberal arts university that emphasizes values-centered and career-oriented education. With 10,851 students (6,146 undergraduate and 4,705 graduate), it is Minnesota's largest independent college or university. St. Thomas has been coeducational at the undergraduate level since 1977; today enrollment is 49.5 percent women. St. Thomas welcomes students of all ages, nations, and religions and from a broad range of racial and socioeconomic backgrounds. During the 2009–10 academic year the University enrolled undergraduate students from forty-six states and sixty-three other countries.

St. Thomas has both undergraduate and graduate seminaries, and its Center for Catholic Studies is home to the nation's oldest and largest undergraduate program in Catholic studies.

At the undergraduate level, St. Thomas offers ninety-six majors and five bachelor's degrees. At the graduate level, St. Thomas offers forty-eight degree programs; forty-three master's, two education specialist, one juris doctor, and four doctorates. It also offers six joint- or dual-degree programs that combine a degree in law with degrees in business, psychology, education, or social work. The University offers its degree programs through seven academic divisions: College of Applied Professional Studies (School of Education and Graduate School of Professional Psychology), College of Arts and Sciences, Opus College of Business, School of Engineering, St. Paul Seminary School of Divinity, School of Law, and School of Social Work.

Entrepreneurship programs at St. Thomas' Opus College of Business are ranked among the top 50 in the nation, according to *Entrepreneur* magazine. St. Thomas was the only Minnesota college or university named to the magazine's top 50 national list. The Opus College of Business is housed in a $22-million facility for the Schulze School of Entrepreneurship and the $25-million McNeely Hall for business education. St. Thomas has won both the National Model Undergraduate Program of the Year and the National Model M.B.A. Program of the Year awards of the U.S. Association for Small Business and Entrepreneurship.

Murray-Herrick Campus Center, the center of student life, contains the University's post office; bookstore and dining facilities; student-life offices, such as Campus Ministry, Multicultural Student Services, and the Career Development Center and Personal Counseling and Testing; and the student government, student media, yearbook, and club and student organization offices. More than 100 clubs and professional and social groups thrive on campus. Students produce a multimedia news portal, tommiemedia.com; the *Aquinas* yearbook; a literary magazine, *Summit Avenue Review;* and on-campus television and radio programs. Students with musical talent choose from about twenty vocal and instrumental groups. Numerous events, such as homecoming, keep the campus calendar full.

St. Thomas has an extensive intramural sports program and is home to eleven men's and eleven women's varsity teams that compete in the Minnesota Intercollegiate Athletic Conference and the National Collegiate Athletic Association (NCAA) Division III. Over the last 30 years, St. Thomas teams have won 240 men's and women's titles in MIAC play and have taken home the all-sports conference trophy 40 times. A new athletic and recreation complex is due to open in fall 2010. The Anderson Athletic and Recreation Complex will feature a 2,000-seat basketball and volleyball arena; an aquatic center containing an eight-lane, 25-meter swimming pool and diving area; and a new field house with a 200-meter track, locker rooms, meeting rooms, and training rooms. The west wing will include a fitness center, weight room, and aerobic rooms.

The historic Chapel of St. Thomas Aquinas houses the magnificent 2,787-pipe Gabriel Kney organ. The Chapel of St. Thomas Aquinas and the St. Mary's Chapel on the School of Divinity campus are the University's main worship centers. Masses are celebrated daily during the academic year; ecumenical prayer services also are offered.

Ninety-one percent of freshmen live on campus. The date of application and class year are among the criteria considered for on-campus housing. Handicapped-accessible facilities are available.

Location

St. Thomas' main campus is located in St. Paul, where the city's historic Summit Avenue meets the Mississippi River. While situated in a quiet, residential neighborhood, the 78-acre parklike campus is only minutes from the downtowns of Minnesota's Twin Cities, St. Paul and Minneapolis. Its three-block downtown Minneapolis campus is home to the University's business law, psychology, and education divisions. St. Thomas' Gainey Conference Center is located in Owatonna, Minnesota. The Bernardi Campus in Rome, Italy, is located on the Tiber River. The Twin Cities are known for a high quality of life.

St. Paul is a winner of a "Most Livable City" award and is the home of the acclaimed Ordway Music Center for the Performing Arts and the Science Museum of Minnesota. Minneapolis, the "City of Lakes," has the renowned Guthrie Theater, Walker Art Center, and Nicollet Mall. The cities also are home to scores of lakes, professional sports teams, and companies with worldwide reputations, such as 3M, Best Buy, General Mills, and Medtronic.

Majors and Degrees

St. Thomas offers ninety-six undergraduate majors and awards the Bachelor of Arts, Bachelor of Science, Bachelor of Science in Mechanical Engineering, Bachelor of Science in Electrical Engineering, and Bachelor of Music degrees. The majors are available in actuarial science, art history, biochemistry, biology, business administration (accounting, business communication, entrepreneurship, financial management, general business management, human resources management, international business, leadership and management, legal studies in business, marketing management, operations management, and real estate studies), Catholic studies, chemistry, classical civilization, classical languages, communication and journalism (advertising, broadcast journalism, communication studies, media studies, print journalism, and public relations), community health education, computer and information sciences, criminal justice, economics, education (elementary education, physical education, science and mathematics for elementary education and secondary education) electrical engineering, English, English (writing), environmental science, environmental studies, French, geographic information systems, geography, geology, German, health education, health promotion, health promotion (science emphasis), history, international studies, justice and peace studies, Latin, literary studies, mathematics, music (liturgical music, music business, music education—instrumental, music education—vocal, music performance), neuroscience, philosophy, physics, political science, psychology, social sciences, social work, sociology, Spanish, theology, and women's studies.

Students may take courses or choose a major field, if not offered at St. Thomas, through the Associated Colleges of the Twin Cities, a consortium of St. Thomas and four other nearby private colleges and universities. Free intercampus bus transportation and a common class schedule make access to other colleges convenient.

St. Thomas undergraduates may elect minors from sixty fields of study. Additional study and licensure programs are offered in Air Force, Army, and Navy ROTC; elementary and secondary school teacher licensure programs; individualized majors; predentistry; pre-engineering; prelaw; premedicine; prepharmacy; pre–physical therapy; pre–veterinary medicine; social work licensure; and school social worker licensure programs.

Academic Programs

The undergraduate program has two components: core curriculum requirements (in literature and writing, fine arts, social analysis, human diversity, historical studies, moral and philosophical reasoning, faith and the Catholic tradition, natural science and mathematical and quantitative reasoning, and language and culture) and course requirements for completion of a major concentration. A total of 132 semester credits is required for a degree. The University operates on a 4-1-4 calendar, with spring and fall semesters and a four-week January Term. St. Thomas also offers summer sessions.

Special programs include the First-Year Experience, designed to promote student achievement in college; the Aquinas Scholars Honors Program; study-abroad programs; and internships. In most academic areas, credit is granted to students who have a score of at least 3 or 4, depending on the discipline, on Advanced Placement examinations sponsored by the College Board. Students also may receive credit through qualifying scores on the College-Level Examination Program (CLEP). It is possible to earn credit for scores of 4 or higher on the International Baccalaureate Diploma examination in subjects included in the St. Thomas curriculum.

Off-Campus Programs

St. Thomas is ranked by the Institute of International Education in the top five nationally for the percent of undergraduates studying abroad (61.1 percent in 2008) in the doctoral category. Each year more than 1,000 St. Thomas students travel to some 40 countries all around the world.

Academic Facilities

The University has eighty-six buildings on four campuses.

St. Thomas is home to four libraries. Three of them—the O'Shaughnessy-Frey Library Center on the main campus, the John Ireland Memorial Library on the St. Paul south campus, and the Charles J. Keffer Library on the Minneapolis campus—collectively house 615,000 volumes and have seating for 2,630 readers. The newest of the four, the Schoenecker Law Library, contains 165,000 volumes in print and microform and provides access to 62,000 electronic books and journals. Library users have access to hundreds of electronic databases and thousands of online resources, including electronic books, newspapers, and journals. CLICNet, the libraries' online catalog, is searchable via the Internet. It serves as the catalog of the holdings of the St. Thomas libraries as well as the collections of an eight-library consortium in the Twin Cities, with a combined collection of 2 million volumes.

Four auditoriums provide facilities for speakers, forums, and concerts. State-of-the-art equipment in the Frey Science and Engineering Center includes a Fourier-transform infrared spectrometer. A wide range of computing and telecommunication services is available, including several computer labs for student use, wireless Internet access in all residence hall rooms and public spaces on campus, e-mail accounts and server space for all students, and class registration via the Web.

Costs

Tuition for the 2009–10 academic year was $28,944 for full-time students carrying 32 credits a year. The average combined room and board rate was $8042. Student fees (student activities and technology) were $523.

Financial Aid

Federal, state, and institutional aid programs are available for students who demonstrate need. St. Thomas is committed to students who demonstrate academic achievement and who have contributed to their community, school, or church. The University makes that commitment by offering merit scholarships to outstanding students. For fall 2009, more than 90 percent of freshmen received some form of aid.

Faculty

St. Thomas' 865 faculty members make teaching their highest priority. Many involve students in their research efforts as well. Eighty-seven percent of full-time St. Thomas faculty members have the highest degree in their field. A low undergraduate student-faculty ratio allows for personal interaction between professors and students both inside and outside the classroom. All classes are taught by professors, not by teaching assistants.

Student Government

The Undergraduate Student Government (USG) is the main student government board at St. Thomas. It represents student views and interests in academic, financial, and social affairs. The ACC plans numerous campus events, provides a variety of student services, and communicates regularly with the University's administrators and faculty members.

Admission Requirements

Applicants are considered on an individual basis. They are typically in the top 40 percent of their high school class, have a minimum cumulative high school grade point average of 3.0, and have earned an ACT composite score of 20 or higher or an SAT combined math and verbal score of 970 or higher. A GPA of 2.3 or better in transferable credits is required of transfer students. A rolling admission system, which begins October 1, enables applicants to learn of their admission status within one to three weeks after their applications are reviewed.

Application and Information

A completed application, a writing sample, an official high school transcript, and standardized test scores are required. The application fee is waived. Students may request a paper application or download an application from the Web site; completed applications can be sent by mail or submitted electronically. Transfer students are encouraged to contact the Office of Admissions for deadlines and details.

For information and an application form, students should contact:

Office of Admissions
University of St. Thomas
Mail 32F
2115 Summit Avenue
St. Paul, Minnesota 55105-1096
Phone: 651-962-6150
800-328-6819 Ext. 2-6150 (toll-free)
Fax: 651-962-6160
E-mail: admissions@stthomas.edu
Web site: http://www.stthomas.edu/admissions/undergraduate

UNIVERSITY OF SAN FRANCISCO

SAN FRANCISCO, CALIFORNIA

COLLEGE CLOSE-UPS

The University

From its beginnings as a one-room schoolhouse, founded in 1855 by the Jesuits, the University of San Francisco (USF) has developed into one of the premier Catholic universities on the West Coast. Throughout its history, USF has been committed to preparing students to improve the world in which they live. With more than 8,000 undergraduate and graduate students, the University has remained faithful to the Jesuit tradition and has maintained its small class size and low student-faculty ratio. Its programs in the arts, the sciences, business, education, nursing, and law foster a love of learning grounded by the challenge to serve society. The University's foundation encompasses academic excellence; the Jesuit, Catholic learning tradition; a multicultural, diverse community; and a global perspective that begins in San Francisco, which offers unparalleled opportunities for internships, service, and connections.

USF is one of the most diverse university campuses in the United States. Living and learning with a student body that consists of students from all fifty states and sixty-nine other countries is a unique opportunity. All new incoming freshman and sophomore students under the age of 21 are required to live on the campus, unless living with their parents. More than 90 percent of the incoming freshmen and 55 percent of all undergraduates live on-campus.

The University offers five on-campus residence halls, two on-campus apartment-style residences, and one off-campus traditional residence hall. Gillson and Hayes-Healy house freshmen, while Phelan and Lone Mountain are for sophomores and upperclass students. Fromm Hall is the only all-female residence hall. Located just twelve blocks from the USF campus, Pedro Arrupe Hall is the off-campus traditional residence hall offered to sophomore and upperclass students. Loyola Village is a student residential community that features apartment-style living for students who are 21 or over or in their junior year. Most rooms in residence halls are doubles, with some single rooms available for upperclass students. Each residence hall has laundry facilities, study/computer rooms, television lounges, and 24-hour front desks.

On the campus, students have access to various University facilities. The Koret Health and Recreation Center is an exciting complex that provides facilities for exercise, racquetball, court games, weight training, personal training, and various aquatic activities in an Olympic-size pool. Tai Chi, yoga, hip-hop, and spinning are just some of the classes offered at Koret. Outdoor adventures include horseback riding, sailing, and sea kayaking. Intramural and club sports are offered in the fall and spring semesters and include basketball, boxing, flag football, fencing, karate, lacrosse, rugby, and co-ed volleyball. NCAA Division I sports include baseball, basketball, cross-country, golf, soccer, tennis, track and field, and women's volleyball.

Dining facilities are located all over campus and are within walking distance of the residence halls and classrooms. Located on the main campus, The Market Café offers a food court experience with a variety of choices, including global, vegan, homestyle classics, and vegetarian options. Other dining options include Outtakes Café, Crossroads coffeehouse, Club Ed, and Kendrick Café at the Law School.

Undergraduates keep busy by participating in nearly 100 on-campus, student-run associations, fraternities and sororities, honor societies, and clubs, such as the USF Rugby Club and Los Locos, a club that supports USF athletics. Among these clubs are the oldest continuously performing theater group west of the Mississippi River, an award-winning FM radio station, an award-winning weekly newspaper, and a literary magazine.

For students interested in giving back to the community, the Office of Service-Learning and Community Action forms a partnership between the local community and USF. Students may participate in community service activities that include preparing meals for the homeless, tutoring underprivileged children, habitat restoration, and annual events such as AIDS Walk San Francisco.

Location

The University of San Francisco is located on a stunning 58-acre campus in a residential neighborhood just minutes from downtown San Francisco, the Financial District, Fisherman's Wharf, and the Pacific Ocean. The hilltop campus, renowned for its beautiful landscaping, borders the 1,000-acre Golden Gate Park and offers spectacular panoramic views of the city. The dynamic city of San Francisco keeps students entertained with concerts, the ballet, opera, museum exhibits, theater, and sporting events. Because of the diversity and geographical compactness of San Francisco, students find research facilities, opportunities for community involvement, and employment experiences that cannot be matched by most cities.

Majors and Degrees

The College of Arts and Sciences offers both B.A. and B.S. degrees. Majors include advertising, architecture and community design, art history/art management, biology, chemistry, communication studies, comparative literature and culture, computer science, design, economics, economics B.A.-M.A. (five-year program), English, environmental science, environmental studies, exercise and sports science, fine arts, French studies, history, international and development economics B.A.-M.A. (five-year program), Japanese studies, Latin American studies, mathematics, media studies, performing arts and social justice, philosophy, physics, physics/engineering, politics, psychology, sociology, Spanish, theology/religious studies, undeclared arts, undeclared science, and visual arts. The McLaren College of Business offers Bachelor of Business Administration degrees in accounting, business administration, entrepreneurship, finance, hospitality industry management, international business, management, and marketing, as well as a 3+1 bachelor's degree in business administration and a joint Master of Global Entrepreneurship and Management program. The School of Nursing offers a four-year Bachelor of Science in Nursing for qualified high school graduates and for second-baccalaureate candidates.

USF has sixty minors and offers unique programs that enhance the learning experience at USF. Special programs include the Catholic Studies interdisciplinary minor, Asia Pacific Studies B.A.-M.A. (five-year program); ethnic studies; film studies; Honors Program in the Humanities; Intensive English Program; journalism; Judaic studies; Middle East studies; neuroscience; 4+3 dual degrees in law, military science, premedical, and other pre-professional health studies; Saint Ignatius Institute Program; a five-year dual degree Teacher Preparation Program that results in teacher certification at the elementary or secondary level; and the McLaren College of Business Honors Cohort program.

Academic Programs

The University of San Francisco is committed to providing students with the essentials of a well-rounded education. A baccalaureate degree is issued upon the successful completion of a 128-unit curriculum. The curriculum consists of 44 units of core courses chosen from six specified categories in addition to 80–85 units that are divided among departmental major requirements and electives. An honors program is available for selected superior students seeking a strong academic challenge. The academic year is based on the two-semester system, with a summer session and a winter intersession also available.

In an effort to encourage high school students to move rapidly into the study of subjects now customarily reserved for colleges, the University of San Francisco honors advanced placement credits, as certified by the College Board's Advanced Placement Program tests and the International Baccalaureate program. The University also cooperates with the College-Level Examination Program (CLEP). Students intending to earn such credit must take the CLEP examinations prior to registering at the University for their freshman courses.

The USF Pre-Professional Health Committee serves to guide and recommend students to medical and dental professional health schools as well as to schools for pharmacy, optometry, veterinary medicine, and podiatry. A student may complete the premedical or other pre-health science requirements as part of, or in addition to, the requirements of an academic major. The Pre-Professional Health Committee assists students with the application process, develops a professional file for each student, collects and mails recommendations to professional schools, conducts interviews in preparation for application, and endorses approved candidates via a committee letter of recommendation sent to all professional schools selected by the student.

The St. Ignatius Institute has an integrated core curriculum based on the great books of Western civilization and an emphasis upon the great works of Christianity. Any undergraduate student at the University, regardless of major, may take courses through the Institute to meet general education requirements. The University also offers Army ROTC. ROTC scholarships are available for qualified applicants and continuing students.

Off-Campus Programs

The University of San Francisco's Center for Global Education has numerous study-abroad programs available to students with junior standing and a cumulative minimum GPA of 3.0. Exchanges with Jesuit universities include locations in Japan, Mexico, China, Spain, Philippines, El Salvador, and Chile. USF's St. Ignatius Institute program includes an exchange with Oxford University in England. Affiliations with other Jesuit universities make travel to other countries possible, e.g., Gonzaga University's study-abroad program in Florence, Italy, and Loyola University of Chicago's program in Rome. USF is also an associate member of the Institute of European and Asian Studies, which offers programs in Durham and London, England; Paris, Dijon, and Nantes, France; Berlin and Freiburg, Germany; Vienna, Austria; Madrid and Salamanca, Spain; Milan, Italy; Tokyo and Nagoya, Japan; Moscow, Russia; Adelaide and Canberra, Australia; Beijing, China; and Singapore. Numerous other study-abroad opportunities are also available. USF assists students in selecting a location, applying to programs, making financial arrangements, registering for academic credit, securing a passport and visa, and making travel plans.

Academic Facilities

University of San Francisco students have access to Gleeson Library's more than 1.8 million holdings and Harney Science Center, which houses the Computer Center, Applied Math Laboratory, the Institute of Chemical Biology, and the Physics Research Laboratories. Cowell Hall, the base for nursing classes and the Nursing Skills Laboratory, also includes the Instructional Media Center. Students also have access to Phelan Hall, the home of KUSF, the University's FM radio station, and *The Foghorn*, the official campus newspaper. Malloy Hall, headquarters for the McLaren College of Business, houses an additional computer laboratory and special seminar rooms. Kalmanovitz Hall, the new home for humanities and social sciences, features state-of-the-art classrooms, a rooftop sculpture garden, and seventeen laboratories for language, writing, media, and psychology.

Costs

Tuition for the 2008–09 school year was $34,519. Room and board were $11,130 for the academic year. Books, travel, and other expenses are about $4200 per year.

Financial Aid

A wide variety of scholarships, grants, loans, and work-study programs are available at the University. Domestic students who wish to be considered for financial aid must submit the Free Application for Federal Student Aid (FAFSA) by February 1. More than two thirds of all USF students receive some type of financial aid. There are also many on- and off-campus jobs available.

The University Scholars Program is available to new domestic freshman applicants who have an exceptional cumulative GPA, SAT combined score, or ACT composite score. Scholars are awarded a nonneed-based scholarship that pays a significant percentage of the cost of tuition for four years of undergraduate study. To remain eligible, University Scholars are expected to maintain a minimum GPA of 3.25. Eligible students are identified during the admission process and must apply under early action by the November 15 deadline.

Faculty

The University has a faculty of 371 full-time and 526 part-time members; 92 percent of the full-time faculty members hold doctoral degrees. The University of San Francisco fosters a close relationship between students and faculty members. This is reflected in the small size of classes, the low student-faculty ratio, and the faculty members' availability for advising. Classes are not taught by student teachers or teachers' assistants.

Student Government

All undergraduates are members of the Associated Students of the University of San Francisco (ASUSF). ASUSF is the official representative body of undergraduate students at USF. The ASUSF government has three functions: to represent the official student viewpoint, to recommend policies, and to fund activities and services. ASUSF consists of three branches: the executive branch, the Student Senate, and the Student Court. The Senate comprises an executive board and student senators.

Admission Requirements

The University seeks students who are sincerely interested in pursuing a well-rounded education. The admission process is selective, and each application is reviewed individually. To enhance the quality and diversity of its student body, the University of San Francisco encourages men and women of all races, nationalities, and religious beliefs to apply. Eligibility is based on high school course work and GPA, the application essay, an academic and personal recommendation, and satisfactory test scores. Domestic applicants are required to submit SAT or ACT test scores with writing. International applicants are required to submit TOEFL or IELTS test scores; however, if an international applicant submits sufficient SAT or ACT test scores, the TOEFL or IELTS may be waived.

Application and Information

A completed application includes the application form, the application fee, a personal essay, all academic transcripts, test scores, and one letter of recommendation. For the fall semester, the application deadlines are November 15 for early action and January 15 for regular action.

Inquiries should be addressed to:

Office of Undergraduate Admission
University of San Francisco
2130 Fulton Street
San Francisco, California 94117-1046
Phone: 415-422-6563
800-CALL-USF (toll-free outside California)
Fax: 415-422-2217
E-mail: admission@usfca.edu
Web site: http://www.usfca.edu

St. Ignatius Church, where freshman convocation and all graduation ceremonies are performed by each college.

THE UNIVERSITY OF TAMPA

TAMPA, FLORIDA

The University

The University of Tampa (UT) is a private comprehensive university that offers challenging learning experiences in four colleges and the John H. Sykes College of Business. Together, they offer hundreds of courses in more than 200 fields of study. In all colleges, students work with experts in their fields, and there is a shared belief in the value of a liberal arts–centered education, practical work experience, and the ability to communicate effectively, all of which are trademarks of a University of Tampa education.

Situated on a beautiful, parklike campus on the Hillsborough River, the University is just two blocks from downtown Tampa. At the center of campus is Plant Hall, once a luxurious 511-room hotel for the rich and famous. Its ornate Victorian gingerbread and Moorish minarets, domes, and cupolas remain a symbol of the city and one of the finest examples of Moorish architecture in the Western Hemisphere. Although Plant Hall receives most of the attention, the campus has forty-eight other buildings, including a student center, a library, modern art galleries and studios, state-of-the-art science labs, a computer resource center, a television studio, a theater, ten residence halls, and complete athletic facilities. Eighty percent of all residence hall space is new since 1998. Representing fifty states and more than 100 countries, 5,800 students, including 4,800 full-time undergraduates, are enrolled. All students may have cars on campus.

The environment outside the classroom is supportive, stimulating, and fun. Students choose from more than 120 student organizations, including honor societies, social clubs, fraternities, and sororities. The University of Tampa has one of the best NCAA Division II sports programs in the nation. Spartan athletes have won ten national championships, including four in baseball, three in men's soccer, and one in women's volleyball. Intercollegiate sports for men and women include basketball, cross-country, soccer, swimming, and track. Men's baseball and golf and women's crew, softball, tennis, and volleyball are also offered.

The University is accredited by the Southern Association of Colleges and Schools (SACS). The John H. Sykes College of Business is accredited by AACSB International–The Association to Advance Collegiate Schools of Business. The music program is accredited by the National Association of Schools of Music, and all nursing programs are accredited by the National League for Nursing Accrediting Commission. In addition, the University is accredited for teacher education by the Florida State Board of Education and the athletic training program is accredited by the Joint Review Committee on Educational Programs in Athletic Training of the Commission on Accreditation of Allied Health Education Programs (CAAHEP).

On the graduate level, the University offers the Master of Arts in Teaching (M.A.T.), Master of Education (M.Ed.), Master of Business Administration (M.B.A.), Master of Science (M.S.) in accounting, Master of Science in Finance (M.S.F.), Master of Science in Innovation Management (M.S.I.M.), Master of Science in Marketing (M.S.M.), and Master of Science in Nursing (M.S.N.).

Location

There is much more to Tampa's location than beautiful beaches and pleasant year-round temperatures. Home to 3.2 million people, Tampa Bay is one of the fastest-growing areas in the United States. The city is the commercial and cultural center of Florida's west coast.

Students attend concerts, art exhibitions, theater productions, dance performances, and special lectures on campus and nearby. Just across the river are the Museum of Art, the St. Pete Times Forum, the Performing Arts Center, the Convention Center, the Aquarium, and a public library. Busch Gardens is just a few miles from campus. Within 1 hour are Disney World and Universal Studios in Orlando. Tampa International Airport, which is just 15 minutes from campus, conveniently connects students with every major city in the United States and around the globe.

Majors and Degrees

The University of Tampa offers bachelor's degrees in accounting, advertising and public relations, art, athletic training, biochemistry, biology, chemistry, communication, criminology, digital arts, economics, education, electronic media and arts technology, English, entrepreneurship, environmental science, exercise science and sport studies, film and media arts, finance, financial services and operations, forensic science, government and world affairs, graphic design, history, international business, international and cultural studies, liberal studies, management, management information systems, marine science (biology and chemistry), marketing, mathematical programming, mathematics, music, nursing, performing arts, philosophy, psychology, public health, social sciences, sociology, Spanish, sport management, theater, and writing.

Certificate programs include early childhood education, European studies, French, German, gerontology, Italian, Latin American studies, and Spanish.

Preprofessional programs include allied health, art therapy, dentistry, law, medicine, and veterinary science.

Minors and concentrations are offered in accounting, advertising, adult fitness, aerospace studies, applied dance, arts administration and management, art history, business administration, chemistry, criminology, dance/theater, economics, English, entrepreneurship, environmental science, exercise science and sports studies, finance, French, government and world affairs, history, humanities, international studies, law and justice, management information systems, marketing, military science, molecular biology, music, philosophy, physical education, psychology, recreation, sociology, theater and speech, Spanish, urban studies, women's studies, and writing.

Academic Programs

The curriculum is designed to give students a broad academic and cultural background as well as concentrated study in a major. Hundreds of internships are available in many areas of study. The baccalaureate experience begins with a special freshman seminar program designed to help students assess their skills and research their interests. Students participate in a special Gateways orientation program during the freshman year. During the first two years, students pursue an integrated core program of thirteen courses consisting of two in English, one in math, one in computer science, two in natural sciences, three in social science, and three in humanities. Prior to graduation, students are also required to take three writing-intensive courses, one course that deals with non-Western/Third World concerns, an international/global awareness course, and an aesthetics course.

Transfer students who have an associate degree may be given full junior status. Students receive advanced placement by earning acceptable scores on Advanced Placement exams, the College-

Level Examination Program (CLEP) tests, or by completing the International Baccalaureate Diploma. As much as one year's credit may be awarded.

For qualifying students, the University offers an honors program of expanded instruction and student research. The program features honors classes, honors floors in residence halls, a senior thesis, and study in London or at Oxford University.

From basic tutoring to graduate school placement test practice, the Academic Center for Excellence helps students stay on track academically. The center is one of the few facilities internationally certified by the College Reading and Learning Association. The Saunders Writing Center also offers free tutorial assistance to students working on writing projects. Other academic support offices include the Academic Advising and Career Services Offices.

Army, Navy, and Air Force ROTC programs are offered.

Off-Campus Programs

One-year study-abroad programs are available during the sophomore and junior years. Programs of shorter duration are also offered such as the Oxford Program in England; the Washington Center in Washington, D.C.; and the Model United Nations Program in Cambridge, Massachusetts.

Academic Facilities

The University has recently completed $201 million in construction and technology improvements. These include six new residence halls, a new student center, and the John H. Sykes College of Business building. A high-speed computer network connects the entire campus, and many areas are wireless. Every student has free access to the Internet and e-mail, either from their residence hall room or from one of the convenient computer labs located on campus.

The library is computerized and well equipped to meet the diversified needs of the students. It is also a depository for United States and state government publications.

The University has a fully equipped marine science research center and three boats located on Tampa Bay, which is near the Gulf of Mexico and numerous freshwater lakes, rivers, and cypress swamps. Other facilities include the Ferman Music Center, the Jaeb Computer Center, the R. K. Bailey art studios, and Falk Theatre. There are also a public-access cable television station and a radio station on campus.

Costs

The total estimated cost for the 2009–10 academic year, excluding summer sessions, was $30,778. This figure includes tuition, fees, and average room and board costs of $8296.

Financial Aid

A high-quality, private education at the University of Tampa is not as difficult to finance as students may think. Each family's situation is evaluated individually for need-based assistance. Academic achievements, leadership potential, athletic skills, and other special talents are recognized, regardless of need. ROTC scholarships are also available. The Free Application for Federal Student Aid (FAFSA) is required to determine eligibility for need-based funds. Early estimates of aid are available October through January.

Faculty

UT faculty members hold degrees from the most prestigious universities. Ninety percent have Ph.D.'s, and many are Fulbright Scholars and recipients of teaching awards. All classes are taught by professors and not by graduate assistants. Faculty members prize the relationships they are able to cultivate with students in classes where enrollment averages 21. The student-faculty ratio is 15:1. Faculty members also pursue scores of research projects each year, often with students as assistants. The College of Business provides cutting-edge opportunities for practical experience through its Strategic Analysis Program.

Student Government

Student Government is the principal avenue for student participation in campus governance. It also provides leadership and serves as the major coordinating body for more than 120 recognized student organizations, interest groups, fraternities and sororities, residence halls, and student productions.

Admission Requirements

Eighteen high school units are required from the following areas: 4 units in English, 3 units in college-preparatory mathematics, 3 units in science (at least two lab courses), 3 units in social studies, 2 units in foreign language, and 4 units of academic electives. The results of the SAT or the ACT are required. A personal essay and at least one recommendation from a high school counselor are requested.

Early admission may be granted to students who have completed 16 academic units by the end of their junior year and who have a minimum 3.2 average (on a 4.0 scale), good SAT or ACT scores, and their counselor's or principal's recommendation. Transfer students should have an overall 2.8 average or better (on a 4.0 scale) for college or university work attempted.

All international students for whom English is not a native or first language should take the Test of English as a Foreign Language (TOEFL); minimum scores of 550 (PBT), 312 (CBT), or 79–80 (iBT) are required. An IELTS score of at least 6.5 is also acceptable.

Application and Information

The University requires a $40 application fee. For more information or to apply online, students may contact:

Office of Admissions
The University of Tampa
401 West Kennedy Boulevard
Tampa, Florida 33606-1490
Phone: 813-253-6211
888-MINARET (toll-free)
Fax: 813-254-4955
E-mail: admissions@ut.edu
Web site: http://www.ut.edu

The University of Tampa's Plant Hall was once a luxury hotel.

THE UNIVERSITY OF TEXAS AT DALLAS

RICHARDSON, TEXAS

The University

The University of Texas at Dallas (UT Dallas) attracts an extraordinary combination of student and faculty resources to the vibrant, dynamic, and globally connected Dallas/Fort Worth area. Students seeking the close-knit community of a liberal arts college and the reputation and resources of a research university find the perfect balance at UT Dallas.

UT Dallas provides a high-quality education. Students enjoy many benefits, including apartment-style living and easy access to a first-rate faculty and research team that has included Nobel laureates and members of the National Academies of Sciences and Engineering. The cultural and recreational opportunities of the Dallas metropolitan area provide many advantages. Students enjoy unique academic opportunities with UT Dallas's emphasis on innovative, multidisciplinary degree programs. Collegium V—the UT Dallas honors program—features an enriched curriculum, special seminars, and research opportunities with faculty.

UT Dallas students excel in national and international competitions of the mind. Its chess team is ranked among the top intercollegiate chess teams in the nation, and its debate team has qualified for the National Debate Tournament for the past three years. Other mind-game endeavors include creative problem solving (formerly Odyssey of the Mind), medical computation, moot court, legal mediation, model United Nations, College Bowl, and world-level computer programming competitions.

UT Dallas consistently ranks among the top 100 colleges and universities in the United States in number of freshmen National Merit Scholars and is ranked as one of the Top 100 best values among public universities by *Kiplinger* magazine. The average SAT score of incoming freshmen, above 1200 out of 1600 (critical reading and math), is among the highest of any public university in the state. Students who take a college-prep high school curriculum and graduate in good standing and who possess an SAT score of 1200 or greater out of 1600 (critical reading and math), or an ACT composite score of at least 26 or rank within the top 15 percent of their high school graduating class in an accredited high school are typically admitted.

Also of interest is the fact that 56.5 percent of UT Dallas undergrads are transfer students. Special programs for transfers include the Comet Connection, a program offering transfer students from select community colleges the opportunity to lock in a money-saving fixed tuition rate by declaring their intention to attend UT Dallas early in their community college careers.

UT Dallas has more than 125 degree programs and has a national and international reputation in such areas as audiology, telecommunications, arts and technology, brain health, digital forensics and cybercrime prevention, nanotechnology, sickle-cell disease research, and space science. UT Dallas launched the first accredited telecommunications engineering degree in the United States, and it is one of only a handful of institutions that offers a software engineering degree.

Exciting research in next-generation technology and biotechnology is at the crux of many collaborative efforts at such UT Dallas centers as NanoTech Institute, Digital Forensics and Emergency Preparedness Institute, Callier Center for Communications Disorders, Center for BrainHealth, and the Institute for Interactive Arts and Engineering. The University provides outstanding education and research programs from the freshman through Ph.D. levels. Qualified undergraduates benefit from having access to research opportunities with faculty members, employment at the many nearby companies, and participation in fast-track academic programs offering the option of a dual bachelor's and master's degree in five years, depending on the discipline. UT Dallas graduates are routinely recruited by major corporations, continue their studies at top-ranked graduate schools, and are admitted to medical and law schools at rates far higher than the national averages.

UT Dallas offers an outstanding quality of life. Freshmen who choose to live on campus may reside in either a four-bedroom apartment inside University Village or in a new, 144,000-square-foot residence hall that opened in fall 2009. Located on campus, within easy walking distance to class, University Village offers students the convenience and comforts of home. The four-bedroom plans feature a balcony, washer/dryer, refrigerator/freezer, stove/oven, and dishwasher. Apartment amenities include a swimming pool, outdoor grills, volleyball, study centers, and a clubhouse. Billiards and Ping-Pong tables are located in the clubhouse. The new suite-style residence hall, also located on campus, will include a mix of three-bedroom suites with a living area and will offer large, open communal spaces, numerous study areas, and living-learning communities, which group students with similar interests and majors. The campus Activities Center houses basketball courts, a 25-meter pool, a fitness/weight room, racquetball and squash courts, locker rooms, and an auxiliary gym for indoor soccer. The more than 160 organizations on campus are a testament to UT Dallas' students' strong tradition of creating new organizations that uniquely suit them. Students pursue extracurricular interests in professional organizations; student government; ethnic and honor societies; Greek letter fraternities and sororities; political, religious, and service groups; music; theater; and debate.

UT Dallas' intercollegiate athletic program, the Comets, is one of the most successful in the NCAA Division III American Southwest Conference (ASC). UT Dallas teams perennially challenge for conference championships in almost every sport. The University has both men's and women's teams in basketball, cross-country, golf, soccer, and tennis as well as men's baseball and women's softball and volleyball teams.

Location

Located on 500 acres in the Dallas suburb of Richardson, UT Dallas is next door to one of the largest concentrations of corporate headquarters in the nation. Many alumni work in the area, and the University actively maintains relationships with corporate partners through alumni groups and by working with companies to provide employment opportunities, internships, and co-op programs for UT Dallas students.

While the rolling, creek-lined campus offers a quiet setting for study, off-campus, the Dallas-Fort Worth Metroplex is one of the nation's largest urban areas, with shopping and a wide variety of restaurants and entertainment venues that include five major sports teams, live bands, numerous museums, and theme parks. A convenient on-campus bus—the Comet Cruiser—provides free transportation to local shopping centers and DART rail lines. All UT Dallas students are eligible to register for a free DART pass that provides a gateway to exploring downtown Dallas or the adjoining suburbs.

Majors and Degrees

UT Dallas offers Bachelor of Arts and Bachelor of Science degrees in a wide range of academic programs. Majors include accounting and information management, American studies, art and performance, arts and humanities, arts and technology, biochemistry, biology, biology and crime and justice studies, business administration, business administration and biology, chemistry, child learning and development, cognitive science, computer engineering, computer science, criminology, economics, electrical engineering, emerging media and communication, gender studies, geography, geosciences, historical studies, interdisciplinary studies, international political economy, literary studies, materials sciences and engineering, mathematical sciences, mechanical engineering, microelectronics, molecular biology, molecular biology-business administration, molecular biology and crime and justice studies, neuroscience, physics, political science, psychology, public affairs, sociology, software engineering, speech-language pathology and audiology, teacher certification (secondary and elementary), and telecommunications engineering. Many offer the option of a master's degree through a five-year program.

Academic Programs

Undergraduate education at UT Dallas is designed to provide students with a breadth of knowledge in natural sciences, mathematics, arts, humanities, and social and behavioral sciences through a general education core of 42 semester credit hours in addition to depth in a major field of study. A total of at least 120 semester credit hours are required for graduation, with at least 51 junior- and senior-level semester credit hours.

UT Dallas students have an impressive 58 percent graduation rate, which ranks above the national average. Transfer students who join UT Dallas after 30 semester credit hours elsewhere have a graduation rate of nearly 62 percent, which ranks The University of Texas at Dallas as one of the top three public universities in Texas in terms of graduation rates for transfer students and almost 10 percent above the state average of 52.5 percent.

Academic Facilities

UT Dallas has a well-equipped, modern campus and thirty-six research centers, including student labs in natural sciences, engineering, computer science, and rhetoric.

The Natural Science and Engineering Research Laboratory—one of the most revolutionary research facilities in the nation—is a four-story 192,000-square-foot facility that supports interdisciplinary collaborations among researchers in disciplines as diverse as chemistry, biology, physics, electrical engineering, and materials science.

The Eugene McDermott Library houses a collection of 1.4 million volumes and 2.8 million units of microform and provides access to a wide range of journals and newspapers through its Electronic Reference Center.

Costs

UT Dallas' Guaranteed Tuition Plan guarantees locked-in, fixed tuition and mandatory fees for four full years. As a further financial incentive, all courses beyond 15 credit hours incur no additional basic tuition or mandatory fee charges. The following costs are what students might expect to pay for one year at UT Dallas, taking 15 semester-credit-hours in fall and spring semesters for a total of 30 semester credit hours. Texas residents can expect total costs of $22,602. This total includes $10,340 for guaranteed fixed tuition and mandatory fees, $1200 for books, and—though the cost-of-living expense varies from student to student—typical students can estimate $7733 for housing and meals and $3324 in miscellaneous and transportation expenses. Nonresidents who earn a merit-based competitive scholarship of $1000 or more may be granted a waiver of nonresident tuition for the period of time covered by the scholarship, not to exceed twelve months. Oklahoma residents pursuing their first undergraduate degree pay the Texas resident tuition rate plus $30 per credit hour.

Financial Aid

Every undergraduate student who applies to UT Dallas is considered an applicant to the Academic Excellence Scholarship (AES) program. This merit-based program offers a variety of generous awards to outstanding students. Scholarship programs range from $1000 per semester (for eight semesters) to cash awards, tuition, fees, and housing allowance for up to four years. Last year, more than 50 percent of first-time-in-college freshmen received AES scholarships. In addition, UT Dallas is a sponsor of the National Merit Scholarship program.

The Financial Aid Office provides a comprehensive program of need-based grants and scholarships, loans, and job opportunities. To apply for need-based financial aid, students should complete the Free Application for Federal Student Aid (FAFSA) using UT Dallas FAFSA code 009741. The FAFSA is available from high school counselors and online. Students can visit the Financial Aid Office Web site at http://financial-aid.utdallas.edu, select Applying for Financial Aid, and access the FAFSA. To receive priority consideration for the fall semester, students should submit all financial aid application materials prior to March 31.

Faculty

UT Dallas has a world-class faculty and one of the best research faculties in the Southwest. Since most of the undergraduate courses are taught by full-time faculty members, students learn from leaders in their fields. Students regularly praise the availability of faculty members to answer questions, give advice, and provide mentoring.

Student Government

Students play a critical role in shaping UT Dallas. Student Government Association leaders are instrumental in advocacy for policy changes and facility expansion. The University administration seeks student input on a wide range of issues, including sports, recreation, entertainment, and other University programs affecting students.

Admission Requirements

Students who take a college-prep high school curriculum and graduate in good standing and who possess an SAT score of 1200 (critical reading and math) or greater or a composite ACT score of at least 26 or rank within the top 15 percent of their high school graduating class in an accredited high school are typically assured admission. Entering freshmen should have successfully completed a full, college-track high school curriculum, including language arts (4 units), mathematics (3.5 units), science (3 units of laboratory science, excluding physical science), social sciences (3 units), foreign language (2 units in a single foreign language), fine arts (.5 unit in music, art, or drama), and general education electives (1.5 units).

All students who do not meet the assured admission criteria are reviewed by the UT Dallas Admissions Committee. The UT Dallas Admissions Committee considers the applicant's achievements in work experiences, community service, extracurricular activities, and surmounting obstacles to pursue higher education. Letters of reference from high school teachers, counselors, supervisors, and activity leaders are appropriate in such instances. Students seeking such consideration should respond to essay topic C on the Texas Common Application. Students may refer to the UT Dallas catalog on the University's Web site at http://utdallas.edu/student/catalog/ or contact a UT Dallas admission counselor for further clarification.

Application and Information

To apply for admission to UT Dallas, students should submit a completed application; one current high school transcript sent directly in a sealed school envelope (one official final high school transcript that reflects graduation date, class rank, and national test scores must be sent upon graduation from high school); SAT or ACT scores (if test scores are not on the high school transcript, they must be submitted by the testing agency by using UT Dallas code 6897 for the SAT and UT Dallas code 4243 for the ACT); and a $50 nonrefundable application fee. Students should use the electronic application available at http://www.applytexas.org.

Permanent residents and United States citizens should submit applications, including all necessary supporting documents, prior to the following dates to ensure timely processing: fall semester, July 1; spring semester, November 1; and summer semester, April 1. Application deadlines for international students are: fall semester, May 1; spring semester, September 1; and summer semester, March 1. International applicants also must submit a financial affidavit of support, TOEFL score (minimum score 550 paper-based, 213 computer-based, or 80 Internet-based test) or IELTS score (minimum 6.5), and an additional $50 fee for evaluation of international documents.

For further information, students should contact:

Office of Admission and Enrollment Services
Hoblitzelle Hall, HH10
800 West Campbell Road
The University of Texas at Dallas
P.O. Box 830688, HH10
Richardson, Texas 75080-3021
Phone: 972-883-2270
800-889-2443 (toll-free)
E-mail: interest@utdallas.edu
Web site: http://utdallas.edu/enroll

With more than 160 student organizations on campus, The University of Texas at Dallas provides a wide range of student pursuits, from academic to social as well as special career interests.

THE UNIVERSITY OF THE ARTS
College of Art and Design, College of Performing Arts, College of Media and Communication
PHILADELPHIA, PENNSYLVANIA

UArts
The University of the Arts

COLLEGE CLOSE-UPS

The University

The only university in the nation devoted exclusively to educating creative individuals in art and design, the performing arts, and media and communication, The University of the Arts (UArts) is located in the heart of Philadelphia's vibrant professional arts community. More than 2,300 students from forty states and thirty countries are enrolled in the undergraduate and graduate programs. For more than 135 years, UArts has defined creativity. Composed of the College of Art and Design, the College of Performing Arts, and the College of Media and Communication, the University offers intensive concentration within a major field as well as creative challenges in multidisciplinary exploration. Founded in 1876, the College of Art and Design is one of the country's leading art colleges, with nationally renowned design, fine arts, and crafts departments. Since its founding in 1870 as the Philadelphia Musical Academy, the College of Performing Arts has expanded to include a School of Dance, with programs in ballet, modern, jazz, and tap, as well as a School of Theater Arts, with acting, applied theater arts, theater design and technology, and musical theater. In 1996, the University inaugurated the College of Media and Communication to prepare students for careers in emerging fields, such as multimedia design, electronic communication, information architecture, computer-generated design, electronic arts and performance, and writing for film/TV.

The University sponsors a variety of activities and regular gallery and museum trips to New York City and Washington, D.C. One fourth of the students live in University housing, which provides coed apartment-style accommodations with complete kitchen and bath facilities and laundry rooms on the premises. Resident advisers live on each floor, and there is 24-hour security. Out-of-town freshmen are guaranteed housing if their contracts are received by June 1. The University also assists students in finding off-campus residences.

The graduate programs of the University of the Arts offer an impressive combination of strengths: exceptionally accomplished faculty members, a remarkably individualized and interactive learning environment, access to outstanding facilities and resources, specialized studios, and programs of study that are both highly focused and highly flexible. UArts offers graduate degrees in art education; book arts/printmaking; ceramics, painting and sculpture; industrial design; jazz studies; museum communication; museum education; museum exhibition, planning and design; music education; and teaching visual arts. A postbaccalaureate certificate in crafts is also offered.

Location

The UArts campus spans the Avenue of the Arts from South Street to Walnut Street and is part of the business and cultural hub of Center City Philadelphia. Next door to the University's historic Hamilton Hall is the city's magnificent Kimmel Regional Performing Art Center; in adjacent blocks are the famous Academy of Music, Wilma Theater, and the University's Merriam Theater, which books touring Broadway shows for the public and hosts UArts student performances. The area also has excellent museums (Philadelphia Museum of Art and Barnes Museum), galleries, music and dance facilities, superb restaurants, and retail stores. Of historic importance, but also modern and sophisticated, the city is at the same time a series of small, close-knit neighborhoods with verdant squares. Fairmount Park provides facilities for sports activities and picnicking. UArts has the reputation of being the safest campus in the city.

Majors and Degrees

The College of Art and Design confers the B.F.A. degree in animation, crafts, film/animation, film/digital video, graphic design, illustration, multidisciplinary fine arts, painting/drawing, photography, printmaking, and sculpture and the B.S. in industrial design. It also offers a certificate program in art education and a concentration in art therapy. The School of Music confers the B.M. in composition, instrumental performance (with a jazz/contemporary focus), and vocal performance. A four-year diploma in music is also available. The School of Dance offers the B.F.A. in ballet, dance education, jazz dance, and modern dance. The School of Theater Arts offers the B.F.A. in acting, musical theater, theater design and technology, and theater management and production. A two-year certificate is available in dance and music. The College of Media and Communication also confers the B.F.A. in multimedia and in writing for film and television and the B.S. in communication.

Academic Programs

Students are attracted to UArts because of its dynamic, creative atmosphere. Whether majoring in dance, sculpture, graphic design, or multimedia, they enjoy interacting with their talented peers in other disciplines. The Freshman Project, the culmination of the required first-year writing course in liberal arts, provides the first opportunity for freshmen to work with students in other majors on a cross-disciplinary creative project. Students are further encouraged, to the extent that their busy schedules allow, to take elective courses outside their chosen major. All students take 42 credits in liberal arts, which gives them vital exposure to humanities, social science, and science and provides them with the historical and theoretical framework of their major field.

The freshman year in the College of Art and Design is devoted to the Foundation Program; its focus is exploratory, allowing students to investigate various disciplines before deciding on a specific major. Students are assigned to small sections, each with a team of 3 instructors. In the fall, students take two-dimensional design, three-dimensional design, and drawing; in the spring, they may substitute a Time and Motion course for one of these. General program requirements vary from department to department. At the end of the freshman year, students select a major in animation, crafts, film/animation, film/digital video, graphic design, illustration, painting/drawing, photography, printmaking/book arts, or sculpture, and they may add a concentration in art education or art therapy. A wide variety of internship experiences is available to qualified students. A minimum of 123 credits is required for graduation, including 18 credits in the Foundation Program, 42 credits in the major, 42 credits in liberal arts, 15 credits in electives (9 credits of which must be taken in a department other than the major), and 6 credits in other areas outside the major. Students may request credit by exam in liberal arts subjects and by portfolio exam in studio art subjects.

In the College of Performing Arts, the School of Music program stresses individualized training, with a performance emphasis. Students undergo intensive training in theory and musicianship. Private lessons are supplemented by master classes and ensemble work. In the School of Dance, two years of ballet, modern, and jazz dance are required before students choose a major in the junior year. Electives include improvisation, repertory, partnering, Spanish dance, ethnic dance, character, and mime. In the School of Theater Arts students can choose one of three majors. Acting majors focus on developing a strong rehearsal and performance process through a wide range of acting, speech, and movement techniques. Musical theater majors train in a similar foundation technique while strengthening their skills in music and dance. Theater management and production majors study a range of disciplines, such as stage management, directing, playwriting, dramaturgy, production and arts administration, and mask and stage combat, preparing for careers or graduate study in these or related fields. The design and technology major explores the full spectrum of theatrical design and technical production. In the College of Performing Arts, a minimum of 126 to 130 credits is required for graduation, 42 of which must be in liberal arts. Participation in the 17-credit MATPREP Program enables students to complete bachelor's and master's degrees in teaching music in five years. The University has close working relationships, including internships, with professional theater, dance, and music groups in Philadelphia and elsewhere. Students are also encouraged to seek professional roles.

The College of Media and Communication was inaugurated in 1996 in recognition of new artistic opportunities that have arisen from advances in digital technology. In the College's B.F.A. program, Writing for Film and Television, students learn to create feature length screenplays, episodic television series, and movies for television. In addition, students take courses in film history, history of television, video production, and cinema arts. In the B.F.A. program in multimedia students receive a broad education that focuses on the integration of image, sound, text, and interactivity into works that tell stories. The program is designed to prepare students to work in fields in which close interaction among arts disciplines, digital fluency, collaboration, and effective communication are key components. The B.S. in communication is for students who wish to work in media related industries—television, documentary, Web-based, advertising, and writing. It is designed to be flexible, allowing students to create their own areas of emphasis, working both collaboratively and individually in the studio and on location. Students choose skills drawn from areas ranging from sound and video editing to photography, writing for film, producing streaming media, and visual and Web design. They take two application areas drawn from documentary video, narrative video, screenwriting, strategic advertising, digital journalism, Web design, and game design. By their senior year, students produce portfolio quality work and learn to collaborate as well as to combine different application areas. Internships in professional settings provide students with real-life experience in the field. In short, the program provides the skills, the applications, the theory, and the experience required to succeed in media and communication.

Students who want to learn more about the world of media and communication before choosing a major can enroll in the CMAC Discovery Year. This is a 30-credit program offered to entering freshmen. It was created for students who have not yet decided on a major focus but are certain that their interests lie within the fields of media and communication. The program provides students an overview of media and communication and gives them an opportunity to take courses in the college's three majors—communication, multimedia, and writing for film and television—before they finally decide on a major. Students also take foundation courses in liberal arts to satisfy their general education requirements.

Academic Facilities

The University facilities are composed of numerous buildings, with studios, classrooms, galleries, theaters, lounges, cafes, dormitories, and administrative offices. The Terra Building provides seventeen floors of studios, computer labs, classrooms, performing spaces, and TV and video production and recording studios. All design departments provide individual workstations for seniors and exhibition spaces that feature student and faculty work throughout the year. The University also maintains several public galleries, where students may exhibit their work along with curator-managed exhibitions of the work of distinguished guest artists. These include the Rosenwald-Wolf Gallery, the Arronson and Great Hall Galleries, and the Mednick Gallery. Student performances are held in the University's formal theaters, such as the 200-seat Dance Theater, the historic 1,800-seat Merriam Theater, the black box theater, the music recital hall, the Arts Bank, and a 239-seat state-of-the-art theater and rehearsal hall, and in the many informal spaces on campus.

As part of a multimillion-dollar telecommunications project, the campus has installed a multifunctional telephone system and a campus-wide data network, which provides Internet access for every computer attached to the network. Academic computing resources include more than twenty labs on Macintosh and PC platforms that are used for special applications, such as animation, digital imaging, 3-D modeling, multimedia, music, CAD, Web page design, and more, as well as some for word processing and general purposes. Several "smart" classrooms enable faculty members to use computer applications and Internet access in their presentations; smart studios allow students to function as they would in the professional world, with a computer in the studio or office.

Students work in a large number and variety of specialized facilities—both high and low technology—throughout the campus that support the learning of their craft. Among these are the Typography Lab, the Borowsky Center for Publication Arts, digital video editing suites, photo/film/animation labs and darkrooms, a scanner lab, an SGI lab, a bronze foundry and plaster workshop, and crafts studios and workshops for ceramics, metals, wood, glassblowing, papermaking, and fibers. The performing arts facilities include a recording studio; music technology (MIDI) studios; editing suites; chamber music studios and practice rooms; computer labs; dance and movement studios, with barres, mirrors, and resilient floors; and acting studios.

Library facilities include Albert M. Greenfield Library, which contains an extensive collection of books, journals, photographs, and videotapes devoted to the arts; a Picture Resource File; Special Collections, with special strengths in book arts and textiles; a slide library with a collection of more than 140,000 slides of art works and historical images; and a music library with manuscripts, journals, scores, and listening and viewing facilities. Holdings include books and periodicals, music scores, mounted pictures, slides, music recorded in LP and CD formats, videocassettes, videodiscs, and multimedia formats.

Costs

Tuition for the 2009–10 academic year was $30,700 plus a general student fee of $950. Accommodations in 3- or 4-person apartment-style dormitory units averaged $7350.

Financial Aid

Last year, UArts provided $8 million in scholarships and grants to new students, alone. About one third went to those demonstrating financial need; the balance was awarded in talent- or merit-based scholarships. Overall, UArts students receive over $30 million in scholarships, grants, loans, and part-time employment each year. Typically, 80 percent of the students enrolled on a full-time basis are eligible for some type of need-based aid. All students should apply. Financial need is defined as the difference between the cost of education and the family's federally calculated contribution to those costs, called the Expected Family Contribution (ECF). Where need exists, UArts assists in meeting costs within its available resources.

The University funds Presidential Scholarships, based on artistic potential and academic achievement. Financial aid is also available on the applicant's demonstrated financial need. Applicants must submit the Free Application for Federal Student Aid (FAFSA). March 1 is the suggested filing date. The University administers the following federal, campus-based student assistance programs: Federal Perkins Loans, Federal Work-Study, and Federal Supplemental Educational Opportunity Grants. Applicants who wish to be considered for scholarships should complete applications for admission and financial aid prior to March 31. Families from many different income levels can qualify for some type of financial assistance. In addition, the University's location in a large, active city provides students with diverse opportunities for part-time employment.

Faculty

Faculty members are practicing professionals who are deeply committed to the development of their students. As active participants in the arts, they have successfully achieved recognition in their specific fields of study. This real-world experience gives them the knowledge and understanding so vital in the training of young, emerging artists, not just professionally but also in terms of personal growth. The faculty consists of 381 full- and part-time members; the majority hold advanced degrees. The faculty-student ratio is about 1:9.

Student Government

Student Council serves as the voice of the students from all three colleges within the University. It also supports a variety of arts-oriented student organizations, including a dance/step troupe, a Web radio station, and a student-run gallery, among many others.

Admission Requirements

In addition to submitting a portfolio or auditioning, applicants should submit their high school transcript, SAT or ACT scores, one letter of recommendation, and a personal statement of purpose.

The placement of transfer students is made after an evaluation of their portfolio or audition and a determination of their approved credits. Transfer students may be given advanced standing.

International applicants are required to submit scores on the Test of English as a Foreign Language (TOEFL); a minimum score of 550 on the paper-based TOEFL or 213 on the computer-based TOEFL is required. Early entrance and deferred entrance are possible.

Application and Information

The University of the Arts follows a system of rolling admission. All students are notified within two weeks of the receipt of all required materials. Students are encouraged to submit applications by March 15 for fall admission and December 1 for spring admission. For additional information, students should contact:

Office of Admission
University of the Arts
320 South Broad Street
Philadelphia, Pennsylvania 19102
Phone: 215-717-6030
800-616-ARTS (toll-free)
Fax: 215-717-6045
Web site: http://www.uarts.edu

UNIVERSITY OF THE SCIENCES IN PHILADELPHIA

PHILADELPHIA, PENNSYLVANIA

University of the Sciences

The University

The University of the Sciences in Philadelphia was founded in 1821 as the Philadelphia College of Pharmacy, America's first college of pharmacy. The University of the Sciences in Philadelphia is located on a 35-acre campus in the academic section of historic Philadelphia known as University City. Besides University of the Sciences, the University of Pennsylvania and Drexel University also call University City home. The University currently enrolls more than 2,600 undergraduate students in twenty-five majors and over 300 students in thirteen graduate programs. The campus consists of nineteen buildings. The University offers a wide variety of cocurricular activities that include intercollegiate and intramural athletics; literary publications; social, professional, religious, and honors organizations; and musical and drama groups. University of the Sciences competes athletically at the NCAA Division II level and is a member of the Central Atlantic Collegiate Conference.

Location

The University's location in the University City section of Philadelphia offers considerable advantage and appeal. It not only offers a wide variety of educational opportunities, it also is a culturally, architecturally, and socially diverse community that caters to the local college student population. The University of the Sciences is also actively involved with a number of local community organizations that are designed to foster improvement, development, and unity in the University City community. The Philadelphia metropolitan area is the home of more than forty other colleges and universities. University of the Sciences students realize that Philadelphia and its immediate region provide abundant off-campus clinical and scientific opportunities, which are required in a number of programs. Within a short 10-minute trolley ride to the Center City area are the vast cultural, historical, and shopping attractions of the sixth-largest city in the United States.

Majors and Degrees

The University of the Sciences in Philadelphia includes four undergraduate colleges: the Philadelphia College of Pharmacy, which offers programs in pharmacy, pharmaceutical sciences, and pharmacology and toxicology; the Samson College of Health Sciences, which offers programs in exercise science and wellness management, health science, medical technology, occupational therapy, physical therapy, and physician assistant studies; the Misher College of Arts and Sciences, which offers majors in biochemistry, bioinformatics, biology, computer science, chemistry, environmental science, humanities and science, microbiology, pharmaceutical chemistry, and psychology; and the newest college, Mayes College of Healthcare Business and Policy, which offers a number of graduate programs as well as a bachelor's degree in pharmaceutical and health-care business. Students with strong academic interests in multiple areas may pursue double degrees, including two B.S. degrees or one B.S. degree and one entry-level professional degree.

Academic Programs

Four majors are offered in the Philadelphia College of Pharmacy: a six-year Doctor of Pharmacy (Pharm.D.) program and four-year B.S. degree programs in pharmacy and toxicology and in pharmaceutical sciences. In the Doctor of Pharmacy program, students are guaranteed a seat in the professional phase (years 3–6) as long as the preprofessional phase (years 1–2) is successfully completed and an acceptable academic record is maintained. The pharmacy program at the University is recognized worldwide and prepares students for the increasingly clinical nature of pharmacy practice.

Pharmacology and toxicology, pharmaceutical sciences, and pharmaceutical and health-care business are unique B.S. degree programs that provide excellent career opportunities and address specific manpower needs within the pharmaceutical and health-care industries. Many graduates pursue postgraduate study as well as enter careers in research, manufacturing, and business.

Six programs of study are available in the Samson College of Health Sciences: exercise science and wellness management, health science, medical technology, occupational therapy, physical therapy, and physician assistant studies. Both physical therapy and occupational therapy programs are direct-entry, integrated undergraduate/professional degree programs that lead to the Doctor of Physical Therapy (D.P.T.) and Master of Occupational Therapy (M.O.T.), respectively. The physical therapy program was one of America's first programs to receive approval to offer the six-year, direct-entry D.P.T. In both the physical therapy and occupational therapy programs, students are admitted as first-year students and are guaranteed a professional-phase seat, provided an acceptable academic record is maintained. In the newest major in the Samson College of Health Sciences, the B.S. degree in exercise science and wellness management, students learn about healthy lifestyles and living as well as how sports and leisure activities improve community well-being.

The physician assistant studies program at the University of the Sciences in Philadelphia is a five-year program that leads to the Bachelor of Science and Master of Science degrees in health science and is in partnership with the Philadelphia College of Osteopathic Medicine (PCOM). Students enrolled in the physician assistant studies program complete their preprofessional component (years 1–3) in the natural sciences, social sciences, and humanities at University of the Sciences. The professional component of the program (years 4–5) is completed at PCOM. A four-year B.S. degree in health science for students who want to focus on general health care and community service is also available.

Medical technology students at the University of the Sciences receive an excellent three-year academic foundation in preparation for their fourth year, which is spent in a clinical setting at an approved hospital school of medical technology.

Ten different four-year Bachelor of Science degree programs are offered in the Misher College of Arts and Sciences. They include biochemistry, bioinformatics, biology, computer science, chemistry, environmental science, humanities and science, microbiology, and pharmaceutical chemistry. Psychology students may elect to remain at the University for an additional year and qualify for the M.S. in health psychology program. The College of Arts and Sciences combines the expertise of an outstanding group of scientists, researchers, and educators with academic facilities that are not often found at an institution the size of University of the Sciences. This combination creates an academic atmosphere of especially high quality. The newest major in the Misher College of Arts and Sciences is the B.S. in humanities and science. This major provides a unique combination of scientific and humanistic study, which is particularly attractive to students who want to pursue medical, dental, or veterinary studies.

The University of the Sciences in Philadelphia's strong tradition of excellence prepares graduates to enter postbaccalaureate degrees in medicine, dentistry, veterinary medicine, and other health professions. Traditionally, premed students choose to major in chemistry, biochemistry, biology, microbiology, pharmacology and toxicology, or psychology. The curricula in these and most of the other programs include the basic courses required for admission to medical school. Beginning with the first year, premed students receive individualized counseling by the Pre-Professional Advisor and their faculty adviser in selecting courses to meet their career goals. Premed students may also elect to take advantage of the University's agreement with Philadelphia College of Osteopathic Medicine, which reserves five seats each year for University of the Sciences students.

Students may enroll at the University of the Sciences in the one-year undeclared program and select from premedical, predental, preveterinarian, science and technology, or pre–health professional options. Through a special orientation program, undeclared students are introduced to the various academic disciplines and career opportunities available to them. Undeclared students formally declare a major during the spring semester of the first year.

Academic Facilities

Classes and laboratory course work are conducted in ten academic buildings on the University of the Sciences in Philadelphia's campus, while the remaining buildings serve as residence halls or support-service facilities. University of the Sciences houses more than 100 scientific laboratories and many computer terminals for student use. The Joseph W. England Library contains more than 84,000 volumes and 8,400 periodicals in addition to numerous electronic information programs.

Costs

Tuition for the 2009–10 academic year was $28,190; room and board were $11,600. Costs are subject to change.

Financial Aid

Currently, 98 percent of the undergraduates at University of the Sciences receive financial assistance, amounting in the aggregate to more than $8 million. Types and sources of aid include Federal Perkins Loans; Health Professions Loans; Federal Work-Study Program; USP Merit Scholarships, Athletic Scholarships, Grants, student employment, and institutional loan funds; deferred tuition payment plans; student loans; and scholarships received from states, municipalities, and service clubs or other organizations. All applicants who seek financial assistance must complete the Free Application for Federal Student Aid (FAFSA). The University's merit scholarship and grant program provides awards for both first-year and transfer candidates.

Faculty

There are 160 full-time faculty members. Of these, more than 100 have doctoral degrees. All full-time faculty members teach undergraduates, and many also teach graduate students and conduct research. Graduate assistants do not teach but serve as laboratory aides.

Student Government

Student government is composed of representatives from all undergraduate classes and class officers. It takes an active part in governance through participation in faculty and administrative committees and sponsors a number of campus activities and functions.

Admission Requirements

The University of the Sciences in Philadelphia seeks students whose aptitudes and achievements are in the areas of science, mathematics, and humanities. Sixteen total high school credits are required and must include English (4 credits), mathematics (3 credits, including algebra I and II and plane geometry), and science (3 credits of laboratory science, including at least two of the following: biology, chemistry, and physics). Physical science, IPS, general science, or similar courses do not fulfill the laboratory science requirement. Class rank, if provided by the applicant's high school, and grade point average are also considered in the admission decision process. Candidates are required to submit the results of their SAT and/or ACT examinations. Supplemental testing or an interview may be requested to clarify a specific aspect of a candidate's record. For students whose first language is not English, the Test of English as a Foreign Language (TOEFL) is suggested. Applications for transfer are welcome, although the number of seats available each year is less than that for first-year students, since all students admitted to University of the Sciences are admitted for the entire program length. Advanced standing may be achieved through the College Board's Advanced Placement Program, the International Baccalaureate Program, or earned college credit.

The University of the Sciences in Philadelphia does not discriminate in the administration of its educational policies, admission policies, scholarship and loan programs, or athletic and other University-administered programs on the basis of sex, age, handicap, race, creed, color, or national origin. All students are entitled to all of the rights, privileges, programs, and activities generally accorded or made available to students at the University. This institutional policy complies with the requirements of Title IX of the Education Amendments of 1972 (45 CRF 86), Section 504 of the Rehabilitation Act of 1973, and other applicable statutes and regulations.

Application and Information

An Admission Application Booklet may be obtained by calling the Admission Office. Applicants may submit an online application at http://www.usp.edu/applying. Each paper application must be accompanied by a nonrefundable $45 application fee. However, there is no fee for an online application. First-year applications for admission are considered until the entering class roster has been completed. University of the Sciences follows a rolling admission policy, and applicants are notified of the admission decision after the University has received all required data. Students accepted into any of the programs have until May 1 to submit a nonrefundable enrollment reservation deposit of $300 for non-pharmacy candidates and $500 for pharmacy candidates to hold a place in the class. Applicants accepted after May 1 have two weeks to submit a tuition deposit.

Applicants for transfer to the professional programs should submit completed applications no later than the following dates: physical therapy (December 1), pharmacy (December 1), occupational therapy (March 1), and physician assistant studies (March 15). All transfer applications are reviewed on a rolling basis except for physical therapy and pharmacy, which are reviewed during the spring semester.

Executive Director of Admission and Enrollment Services
University of the Sciences in Philadelphia
600 South 43rd Street
Philadelphia, Pennsylvania 19104-4495
Phone: 215-596-8810
888-996-8747 (toll-free)
Fax: 215-596-8821
E-mail: admit@usp.edu
Web site: http://www.usp.edu

COLLEGE CLOSE-UPS

UNIVERSITY OF THE WEST

ROSEMEAD, CALIFORNIA

The University

University of the West (UWest) is a Buddhist-founded campus open to students of all backgrounds who are interested in gaining cultural competency as well as a solid undergraduate or advanced education in religious studies, business administration, psychology, or languages. UWest is accredited by the Western Association of Schools and Colleges (WASC).

Founded in 1991 by Buddhist Venerable Master Hsing Yun, who is one of the earliest promoters of Humanistic Buddhism, University of the West's stated goals are to deliver an education informed by Buddhist wisdom and values as well as to serve as a bridge between East and West.

UWest welcomes students of all beliefs and backgrounds. Outside the well-known Buddhist studies programs, Buddhist knowledge is available to students of all programs on a voluntary basis through workshops and other campus activities.

Students and faculty members come together as a community of scholars to participate in an ongoing dialogue to advance knowledge, address societal and cultural issues, and promote education and understanding across cultures. At UWest, creativity, adaptability, and leadership are fostered together with tolerance, ethical commitment, and social consciousness.

A range of activities that enhance learning and physical and mental well-being, such as yoga, martial arts, music, meditation, and travel, are available to students outside of the classroom.

The Student Recreation Center is equipped with fitness and weight-training equipment, table tennis, billiards, and a student lounge with a kitchen. The two residential halls each have a 24-hour study room, a multipurpose student lounge on each floor, and a laundry facility. Each room is furnished and has its own air-conditioning unit, private bathroom, telephone, and high-speed Internet access. Recreational facilities include a swimming pool, a spa, and exercise and game rooms.

UWest is a member of NAFSA: Association of International Educators and the American Association of Collegiate Registrars and Admissions Officers.

Location

UWest is located in the city of Rosemead in Los Angeles County. It occupies 10 acres of beautifully landscaped grounds and has modern, well-equipped facilities. The campus sits on a hillside overlooking the verdant Whittier Narrows nature preserve with an unobstructed view of the San Gabriel Mountain range and the Puente Hills range. UWest is about 10 minutes by car from downtown Los Angeles, which a Harvard scholar called "the most complex Buddhist city in the world."

Majors and Degrees

Undergraduate programs at UWest include accounting, Buddhist studies, comparative religious studies, computer information systems, English (language track and literature track), international business, marketing, psychology, general education, and English as a second language.

Graduate programs offered at the University are the Executive Master of Business Administration (E.M.B.A.); Master of Business Administration (M.B.A.) with concentrations in computer information systems, finance, international business, or nonprofit management and organization; Master of Arts (M.A.) in psychology with concentrations in multicultural counseling generalist (marriage and family therapist track) or Buddhist psychology (marriage and family therapist track); M.A. in religious studies with concentrations in Buddhist studies or comparative religious studies; and the Master of Divinity (M.Div.) in Buddhist chaplaincy.

UWest also offers an advanced degree program for the Doctor of Religious Studies (Ph.D.) with specializations in Buddhist studies or comparative religious studies.

Academic Programs

The business administration program offers deep perspectives on Eastern and Western business theory and practice. Students are educated in small, interactive classes with an average faculty-student ratio of 1:8.

The Department of Religious Studies' programs in Buddhist studies and comparative religious studies offer students the unique opportunity to study religion in a setting that is informed by Buddhist wisdom and values, and dedicated to furthering religious and cultural understanding between East and West, and among religions in general. All Buddhist traditions are covered, and students can choose to study any of the Buddhist canonical languages, i.e., Canonical Chinese, Pali, Sanskrit, or Tibetan. The library contains one of the best American collections of writing from all the major Buddhist traditions, including the largest set of Dunhuang Cave manuscript reproductions in the U.S.

The major in English explores the dynamic and reciprocal relationship between language, literature, and culture. Course work is designed to help students develop superior communication skills, understand the nature of language and the way it can be described and analyzed, appreciate the esthetic and intellectual enjoyments of literature, and recognize the cultural values reflected in literature. The major imparts knowledge and skills that are foundational to pursuing a graduate degree in English literature, linguistics, or a related field, such as teaching English as a second language.

UWest's undergraduate major in psychology prepares students as competitive graduate school candidates in the particular fields of research psychology, applied counseling psychology, clinical psychology, school psychology, Buddhist psychology, and social work. The M.A. in psychology with a concentration in multicultural counseling generalist (marriage and family therapist track) and the M.A. in psychology with a concentration in Buddhist psychology (marriage and family therapist track) prepares students to pass California's rigorous Marriage and Family Therapist licensure exam.

All of the bachelor's programs require the completion of a minimum of 120 semester units.

The ESL program provides a variety of instructional formats to improve students' command of the English language and familiarize them with American life and culture, including a residential English program and the Program in American Cultural Education (PACE), which provides short-term immersive experiences in the classroom, combined with travel and cultural experiences in the Los Angeles region.

Academic Facilities

The library provides access to the University's collection as well as Internet access to several major databases including LexisNexis, ProQuest, and JSTOR.

Three research centers are located on campus. The Center for the Study of Minority and Small Business helps the Department of Business reach out to minority-owned and small businesses and provides resources and support so students at UWest are exposed to and become familiar with business realities and the existing business environment.

The Institute of Chinese Buddhist Studies develops interdisciplinary research, teaching, and other scholarly activities relating to Chinese Buddhism.

The Digital Sanskrit Buddhist Canon is a joint research project by the University of the West and the Nagarjuna Institute of Exact Methods (NIEM) in Nepal for the purpose of researching the vast corpus of Sanskrit Buddhist texts.

Costs

Undergraduate tuition for the 2009–10 academic year was $320 for the business administration and psychology programs; $300 per unit for religious studies and languages; and $625 per unit for nursing. Graduate tuition is $330 per unit for the business administration, psychology, and Buddhist chaplain programs; and $310 for religious studies.

Room and board with meal plan are $4692 for single occupancy, $3145 for double occupancy, $2710 for triple occupancy, and $2440 for quadruple occupancy. Further details of costs and fees are available at http://www.uwest.edu under Admissions/Admissions Procedures/Tuition and Fees.

Financial Aid

Financial aid is available in the form of federal aid, a work-study program, private scholarships, and grants (both need- and merit-based). UWest offers full- and half-tuition fellowships, scholarships for room and board, and the UWest Scholarship of $2000 per academic year. The International Buddhist Education Foundation scholarship provides 50 students in the religious studies program with scholarships of $2000 to $4000 depending on academic level. UWest also offers private scholarships ranging from $500 to $2000 per semester.

Faculty

Among full-time faculty members, 82 percent have doctoral degrees. Adjunct faculty members are required to have a minimum of a master's degree and at least ten years of experience working in the fields relevant to the subjects they teach. UWest has a total of 70 faculty members.

Student Government

The UWest Student Association acts as a liaison between the University and the students to provide services, programs, and facilities that enhance the quality of education by extending the learning environment beyond the classroom into the extracurricular lives of UWest students. It also provides a forum for student expression and interests. All students who are enrolled at the University are included as members of the Student Association.

Admission Requirements

Applicants are required to supply accurate and complete information on the application for admission form and to submit official transcripts from each school or college attended. Other application requirements and documentation can be found on the University's Web site. Student selection is based on academic achievement and potential, irrespective of ethnicity, gender, disability, or religion. A minimum GPA of 2.0 is required of undergraduate applicants. Graduate applicants must have a minimum GPA of 2.5. A 500-word personal essay and three letters of recommendation are required of all applicants. International students must meet the minimum TOEFL or IELTS requirement as published in the UWest catalog.

Application and Information

Application deadlines for domestic applicants are June 1 for fall, September 2 for spring, and April 2 for summer. There is a $50 nonrefundable application fee for domestic applicants and a $100 nonrefundable application fee for international applicants ($50 for all ESL applicants).

Ms. Grace Hsiao
Admissions Officer
University of the West
1409 North Walnut Grove Avenue
Rosemead, California 91770
Phone: 626-571-8811 Ext. 120
Fax: 626-571-1413
E-mail: info@uwest.edu
Web site: http://www.uwest.edu

COLLEGE CLOSE-UPS

A panoramic view of UWest's campus.

UNIVERSITY OF TULSA

TULSA, OKLAHOMA

The University

The University of Tulsa (TU) is a four-year, private, liberal arts university featuring highly personalized study in engineering, natural sciences, business, health professions, the humanities, and fine and performing arts. TU features three undergraduate colleges: the Henry Kendall College of Arts and Sciences, the Collins College of Business, and the College of Engineering and Natural Sciences.

The University is fully accredited by the North Central Association of Colleges and Universities and is an NCAA Division I participant in Conference USA. TU maintains an affiliation with the Presbyterian Church (USA).

A customizable array of majors, minors, concentrations within majors, and certificate programs allows undergraduates to assemble a personalized education, which can include a self-designed major. TU's low 10:1 student-faculty ratio, average class size of 19, and emphasis on individual attention anchor an educational culture where students are rigorously challenged and comprehensively supported.

Long regarded for programs that include accounting; petroleum, mechanical, and chemical engineering; English; environmental law; MIS; and psychology, TU is also emerging as a leader in computer science and information security. TU was the first institution selected by the National Science Foundation for the Federal Cyber Service Initiative (Cyber Corps).

A joint bachelor's/master of science in finance and a highly selective six-year joint bachelor's and J.D. (law degree) program are available.

The University's 34-acre sports and recreation complex features a student fitness facility, competition-grade tennis complex, NCAA soccer and softball fields, multiuse recreational fields, and an NCAA track and field. TU offers ample extracurricular opportunities through 160 campus-based organizations, including intramural sports, special interest clubs, preprofessional organizations, fraternities and sororities, and campus ministry groups. Residence life offers a variety of living arrangements, including traditional residence halls, suite-style halls, premium-style student apartments, and special living communities.

Fall 2008 enrollment was 4,192, with 3,049 undergraduates and 1,143 graduate and law students and a 53:47 ratio of men and women. International and multicultural students made up 29 percent of the student population, with fifty-seven countries represented.

Based on academic reputation and other factors, *U.S. News & World Report* ranks TU 83rd among doctoral/research universities in the U.S.

Location

The University of Tulsa features a residential campus in midtown Tulsa, Oklahoma. Tulsa's prominent industries include energy, telecommunications and data, finance, medicine, aerospace, transportation, and education—all of which present rich internship opportunities for students and employment opportunities for graduates. *Newsweek* has named Tulsa one of ten "New Frontier" technology cities, and the *New York Times* declared Tulsa "a new economy hotbed." *Southern Living* magazine named Tulsa one of its five favorite Southern cities. Tulsa has more than 400,000 residents and features cultural assets including the Performing Arts Center, ballet, theater, symphony, opera, two nationally renowned museums, and cultural festivals such as Jazzfest, Mayfest, and Oktoberfest. Professional sports in Tulsa include baseball, basketball, golf, hockey, arena football, and horse racing. The extensive River Parks development, 3 miles from the campus, has facilities for outdoor activities, jogging and bicycle trails, and an outdoor floating amphitheater.

Majors and Degrees

The Henry Kendall College of Arts and Sciences grants the Bachelor of Arts, Bachelor of Fine Arts, Bachelor of Music, Bachelor of Music Education, or Bachelor of Science degrees in anthropology, art, art history, arts management, communication, deaf education, economics, education, English, environmental policy, film studies, French, German, history, music, music education, musical theater, organizational studies, philosophy, political science, psychology, religion, Russian studies, sociology, Spanish, speech/language pathology, and theater. Students can create their own designated area of concentration with the approval of the dean of the college. Teacher certification at the elementary and secondary levels is available through the college.

The Collins College of Business awards the Bachelor of Science in athletic training, business administration (majors in accounting, economics, finance, management, management information systems, and marketing), energy management, exercise and sports science, (with tracks available in physical education and preprofessional tracks for physical therapy and physician's assistant), international business and language (with emphases in Chinese, French, German, Russian, and Spanish), and nursing. The college offers minors in accounting, business administration, coaching, finance, international business studies, management information systems, and marketing communication. Management majors may choose concentrations in business law, entrepreneurship and family business management, and human resource management. Marketing majors may choose an emphasis in integrated marketing communication. The college is home to several specialized centers, including the Energy Management Program, Family Owned Business Institute, the Genave King Rogers Center for Business Law, and the Williams Risk Management Center.

The College of Engineering and Natural Sciences offers the Bachelor of Science degree in applied mathematics, biochemistry, biogeosciences, biology, chemical engineering, chemistry, computer science, electrical engineering, engineering physics, geosciences (options in earth and environmental science, environmental sciences, geology, and geophysics), information systems technology, mathematics, mechanical engineering, petroleum engineering, and physics. The college also offers a B.A. in chemistry, earth and environmental science, and geology. The college features state-of-the-art research facilities, including the Center for Information Security and the Williams Communications Fiber Optic Networking Laboratory. From 1995 to 2009, 44 TU engineering students received the prestigious Barry M. Goldwater Scholarship, the nation's premier award for undergraduate students in engineering, math, or science, while 28 students received National Science Fellowships.

Academic Programs

A TU education links a broad, humanities-based core curriculum for all majors and a highly flexible group of majors, minors, concentrations, and certificate programs. With so many program options and a high level of faculty support, TU students can receive an education that is well-rounded, in-depth, and uniquely personalized. Candidates for graduation must complete at least 124 semester hours of course work, with more hours required of students majoring in engineering and business administration.

The University offers a number of special academic programs. The Honors Program engages students in intensive multidisciplinary work and in specialized study culminating in a major research or creative project during the senior year. Honors freshmen may live in the Honors House. The Tulsa Undergraduate Research Challenge program (TURC) combines advanced research, scholarship, and community service. The Federal Cyber Service Initiative (Cyber Corps) prepares students for advanced federal careers in computer security. In the spring of 2007, TU's Office of Research and Sponsored Programs funded five Interdisciplinary Institutes to research alternative energy; individual differences determined by biochemical and psychological factors; bioinformatics and computational biology; nanotechnology; and trauma, abuse, and neglect. Other special programs include internships, study abroad, Air Force ROTC, a six-year accelerated law degree, and a five-year M.B.A. program.

Qualified students may receive advanced standing or credit for scores on the tests of the Advanced Placement and College-Level Examination programs. Students who complete the International Baccalaureate diploma with a score of 28 or above receive at least 30 college credits, the equivalent of one year in college.

The University of Tulsa operates on a semester calendar. The fall term begins in late August, the spring term in early January, and the summer session in mid-May.

Off-Campus Programs

TU students can choose from several study-abroad options, including summer, semester, and yearlong programs. TU has direct international exchange partnerships with universities in Australia, Austria, Finland, France, Germany, England, Spain, Switzerland, and New Zealand and is part of the ISEP Exchange Program Network. TU also offers a wide selection of international study options through consortia and study-abroad affiliate programs. All approved study-abroad programs allow students to choose courses in various disciplines, and with their college's approval, apply those courses towards their majors or other graduation requirements. Federal financial aid and scholarships are portable with TU's study-abroad programs.

The city of Tulsa and TU have agreed to a historic public-private partnership whereby TU will manage operations at the city's Gilcrease Museum, home to the world's most comprehensive collection of art and artifacts of the American West. The partnership provides strategic opportunities for the museum and unparalleled opportunities for academic research of the museum's extensive holdings.

Academic Facilities

The University's McFarlin Library and Mabee Legal Information Center house about 4 million items, including periodical subscriptions to scholarly and popular journals. The Mabee Legal Information Center has almost 408,000 total volumes. McFarlin holdings include more than 900,000 print volumes, 120,000 electronic book titles, and 37,000 journal titles. McFarlin's Department of Special Collections is internationally recognized, particularly for holdings in Native American history and nineteenth- and twentieth-century Irish, English, and American literature. McFarlin is home to the papers of Nobel Laureate V. S. Naipaul. McFarlin is also developing a specialization in World War I literature, correspondence, and artifacts. Special Collections rare book holdings currently number about 130,000 volumes.

Keplinger Hall is the $15-million home to the College of Engineering and Natural Sciences. Equipment here includes a comprehensive multimillion-dollar telecommunications networking laboratory developed with Williams Communications and other industry partners.

The TU Center for Information Security is developing defenses against cyberterrorist attacks and information warfare and supports the University's National Security Agency (NSA)–accredited certificate program in information assurance, a curriculum that integrates information security with computer law and policy issues. TU is designated a Center of Excellence in Information Assurance by the NSA and is one of the original six institutions selected by the National Science Foundation for the Federal Cyber Service Initiative (Cyber Corps).

The Mary K. Chapman Center for Communicative Disorders links the University to the community with its clinical facility and its curricula in education of the deaf and speech/language pathology. The Tulsa Center for the Study of Women's Literature offers concentrated studies in women's literature and in feminist literary critical theory. The National Energy-Environment Law and Policy Institute researches energy, natural resource, and environmental law and policy development. TU's engineering students have the opportunity to participate in research projects through ten consortia funded by the petroleum industry. The Family-Owned Business Institute provides a forum for the development and dissemination of information relevant to the succession and stability of the family business. The TU Innovation Institute combines research and interdisciplinary programs in innovation, product development, and entrepreneurship.

Other facilities include the Genave King Rogers Center for Business Law, which supports the business law specialization within the management major, and the Williams Risk Management Center in the Collins College of Business, an advanced learning environment that combines the latest in trading floor technology and advanced study in risk-management theories and techniques. The performing arts utilize Chapman Theatre, the home of TU's symphony orchestra, concert band, wind ensemble, jazz workshop, modern choir, theater, and opera productions. Other facilities include the Allen Chapman Activity Center, which features student organization offices, the Great Hall for lectures and entertainment, a food court, and the University bookstore. The Donald W. Reynolds Center serves as the campus arena and convocation center. This $28-million facility is the site for several intercollegiate athletic programs, student concerts, facilities for video editing and strength training, and the state's only accredited academic program in athletic/sports medicine. Collins Hall, which houses administrative, alumni, and admission offices, opened in 2007.

Costs

For 2008–09, the typical cost for students living on campus was $32,241, including $23,860 for tuition, $7776 for room and board, and fees of $605. Expenses for books average about $1200 per year.

Financial Aid

In 2008, more than 90 percent of entering full-time freshmen received some form of financial aid (including grants, scholarships, work-study, and loans). Academic, athletic, and performance scholarships are available, as well as federally funded grants, loans, and Federal Work-Study awards. The University of Tulsa participates in the National Merit program and offers full-tuition, room, and board scholarships for selected National Merit Finalists. University Scholarships are also awarded to qualified students. Performance scholarships are available in music, theater, and athletics. Applicants for aid should submit the Free Application for Federal Student Aid (FAFSA) and the TU Financial Aid Application by March 1 for priority consideration.

Faculty

The University has 309 full-time faculty members, with 96 percent having earned the highest degree in their field of study. The faculty is primarily a teaching faculty, although most of its members are also involved in funded research or publishing activities. Many faculty members serve as student advisers and work collaboratively with students in and outside the classroom. The faculty includes a number of distinguished scholars, with 30 endowed chairs, 2 visiting endowed chairs, 3 endowed professorships, 2 fellows, and 9 Wellspring chairs.

Student Government

All full-time students are members of the Student Association, which consists of legislative, executive, and judicial branches. Regular elections are held for representatives from each college, who appropriate nearly $500,000 annually for student organizations and special events. The executive cabinet's main function is to schedule speakers, artists, and events on campus that are sponsored by the Student Association.

Admission Requirements

TU seeks students who demonstrate intellectual promise in a challenging curriculum and are committed to the liberal education reflected in the University's mission. TU uses an individualized and holistic approach in evaluating candidates for admission.

Performance in high school college-preparatory subjects and scores on the SAT or ACT are the primary criteria considered in the admission evaluation. Academic and extracurricular achievement, school records, and personal qualities are also carefully considered. The counselor recommendation and information about the applicants' extracurricular activities and job experience are also considered. Campus visits and interviews are highly recommended but not required.

The recommended high school curriculum consists of four years of English and math, three years of science and social science, and a solid foundation in a foreign language and computer science. In addition, students are encouraged to take an active part in their school and community or hone special talents that demonstrate traits such as leadership, initiative, maturity, and creativity.

Application and Information

Students are encouraged to complete an application for admission and scholarships by the priority date of February 1. The admission process is rolling, and applicants are reviewed and notified as their admission files are completed. The reply date for students is May 1. An application, accompanied by a six-semester secondary school transcript, ACT or SAT scores, and a guidance counselor's recommendation are required when applying for admission. Completed applications should be sent to the Office of Admission. For additional information, students should view the online tour (http://www.utulsa.edu/virtualtour), or contact:

John C. Corso
Associate Vice President for Enrollment and Student Services
University of Tulsa
800 South Tucker Drive
Tulsa, Oklahoma 74104-3189
Phone: 918-631-2307 (in Tulsa)
800-331-3050 (toll-free)
Fax: 918-631-5003
E-mail: admission@utulsa.edu
Web site: http://www.utulsa.edu/admission

UNIVERSITY OF WINDSOR

WINDSOR, ONTARIO, CANADA

The University

The University of Windsor offers a very broad range of programs—its 16,000 full- and part-time students are enrolled in some 150 bachelor's, master's, and doctoral degree programs. Academic disciplines range from humanities and liberal arts to science. Professional studies are offered in business, engineering, education, law, computer science, creative writing, kinesiology, nursing, social work, clinical psychology, music, dramatic art, and visual arts.

The University has an impressive commitment to research in a richly diverse community, with a special focus on automotive-, environmental-, and social justice–oriented interdisciplinary research. It is also firmly committed to providing increased opportunities for students to participate in research at the undergraduate level.

Community and business partnerships have helped to establish research institutions at the University of Windsor that are unmatched in Canada. The University's Great Lakes Institute for Environmental Research is the world's leading institution in large lakes research, attracting top students from around the world.

The University of Windsor is Canada's most international campus—10 percent of its population comes from eighty countries outside of Canada. This sharing of international experiences helps prepare Windsor graduates for the global workforce.

The University began as Assumption College in 1857, affiliated with the University of Western Ontario. In 1954, it was admitted to full membership in the National Conference of Canadian Universities and Colleges, the University Articulation Board of Ontario, and the Association of the British Commonwealth. The University became the University of Windsor in 1963, and, a year later, it became a member of the International Association of Universities. In recent years, the University has spent millions of dollars in new buildings, classroom upgrades, and lab renovations, including a new residence hall and facilities for health education, dramatic arts, and a medical education building. The Centre for Engineering Innovation is also in the process of being built.

Today, the campus offers more than 150 undergraduate and graduate programs across nine faculties for 16,000 full- and part-time students. It offers nine cooperative education programs for approximately 1,100 students. Most come from the Ontario region, but some come from other regions of Canada; 10 percent of students are international students. More than 95 percent of graduates find employment within six months.

The University operates several residences on or adjacent to the campus, offering many accommodation choices from traditional residence rooms to suite-style accommodations. All residences are coed, with some single-gender floors. Most rooms are double rooms, but some single-occupancy spaces are available throughout the residence halls. Each residence hall includes wireless Internet, laundry rooms, common lounge areas for watching TV or relaxing, vending machines, kitchen areas, and other amenities. Residence life staff members are available at each residence hall to assist students. A variety of meal plans are available for students, allowing them to eat at one of the University's dining facilities or off campus at partnering restaurants.

Location

The tree-lined campus of the University of Windsor is in the midst of Windsor, Ontario. Windsor is Canada's southernmost city and is located just across the river from Detroit. The city is bordered by Lake Erie, Lake St. Clair, and the Detroit River. Its temperate climate makes it ideal for recreational activities, such as biking, golfing, hiking, and swimming, and it makes it possible to enjoy such outdoor attractions as Dieppe Gardens, Jackson Park, and the Odette Sculpture Park. Windsor also offers restaurants, shopping venues, museums, and galleries as well as performances in dance, music, and theatre.

Majors and Degrees

Students may earn a Bachelor of Arts degree in anthropology, art history, classical civilization, communication studies, criminology, developmental psychology, diaspora studies, drama, drama and communication studies, drama in education and community, economics, English language and literature, English literature and creative writing, family and social relations, forensics, French studies, history, interdisciplinary studies (Lambton College), international relations and development studies, labor studies, liberal and professional studies, modern languages (German, Italian, Spanish), modern languages and second language education, music, philosophy, political science, psychology, social justice, sociology, sociology and criminology, visual arts, visual arts and art history, visual arts and communication studies, or women's studies.

Bachelor of Commerce degrees are available in business administration, business administration co-op, business and computer science, business and computer science co-op, business and economics, and international business.

Bachelor of Computer Science degrees are available, including computer science, computer science co-op, and computer science (honours applied computing) which is also available with co-op.

The Bachelor of Education is available as a consecutive program; it is also available in concurrent programs that include the Bachelor of Arts/Bachelor of Education/Early Childhood Education Diploma; Bachelor of Arts-French/Bachelor of Education; Bachelor of Math/Bachelor of Education; Bachelor of Science (chemistry or biological sciences)/Bachelor of Education; and Bachelor of Computer Science/Bachelor of Education.

Bachelor's degrees in engineering can be obtained in automotive, civil, civil (environmental engineering option), electrical and computer, industrial, industrial (with a minor in business administration), industrial (automotive manufacturing systems option), industrial (supply chain option), mechanical, mechanical (automotive option), mechanical (materials option), and mechanical (environmental option).

Bachelor of Fine Arts degrees are available in acting and in visual arts.

Bachelor of Mathematics degrees are available in mathematics, general mathematics, mathematics and statistics, and mathematics and computer science.

The Bachelor of Music, Bachelor of Music Therapy, and Bachelor of Arts in Music are available.

Bachelor of Science degrees are offered in behavior, cognition, and neuroscience; biochemistry; biochemistry and biotechnology; biology; biology and biotechnology; chemistry; chemistry and physics; computer information systems (co-op); computer science with software engineering specialization (co-op); environmental geoscience (co-op); environmental science; general science; and physics and high technology (co-op).

The Bachelor of Social Work degree is available in social work, social work and diaspora studies, and social work and women's studies.

Other degrees offered include a Bachelor of Arts and Science; Bachelor of Environmental Studies; Bachelor of Forensic Science;

Bachelor of Human Kinetics; Bachelor of Laws; combined Bachelor of Laws and Doctor of Jurisprudence; and Bachelor of Nursing.

There are also many programs in Science and in Arts and Social Sciences that combine two or more majors.

Academic Programs

During each regular academic year, the fall term runs from early September to early December, and the winter term runs from early January to mid-April. In addition, the University schedules courses during a summer term, which includes Intersession (May–June) and Summer Session (July–August), each of which is approximately six weeks in duration. Some courses run from May through August (twelve weeks). Bachelor's degrees typically require the completion of thirty courses, including ten to sixteen courses within the major program of study; six to eight courses in arts, languages, sciences, or social sciences; and ten to twelve courses in any area within or outside the major program of study. Honours programs of study require the completion of forty courses.

Academic Facilities

The Leddy Library, the main campus library for the University, has a collection that consists of more than 3 million items, including electronic resource holdings of more than 23,000 digital journal titles and several hundred thousand digital monographs and data sets. The University of Windsor campus offers wireless Internet and also has more than 350 hard-wired computer workstations that provide access to library resources and the Internet and run Microsoft, Adobe, SPSS, and other programs.

The Academic Writing Centre provides writing assistance to University students through individualized writing programs, small group workshops, and classroom presentations. The Computer Literacy Skills (CLS) program provides all members of the University community with the tools necessary to gain the confidence and experience to effectively use campus computer systems and productivity software. This is achieved through both e-learning and instructor-led workshops. Academic resource centers are available for mathematics and statistics and chemistry and physics.

Costs

For 2009–10, annual full-time tuition (in Canadian dollars) ranges from $5663 to $7592 for Canadian students and $15,199 to $19,152 for international students, depending on the program of study. Residence fees are $4834 to $5337 per year for a double room or $5809 to $6857 per year for a single room. These rates include activity fees, wireless Internet, refrigerator rental, cable TV, and laundry and telephone fees. Meal plans cost an additional $3350–$3900 per year, depending on the meal plan selected. Books and other materials typically cost approximately $800 to $1000 per year.

Financial Aid

U.S./Mexico Entrance Scholarships: For newly admitted students with U.S./Mexican citizenship or permanent resident status, an entrance scholarship is available. A renewable scholarship (for up to eight terms) valued at $3000 per term is offered to engineering, education, and nursing students. A renewable scholarship of $1500 per term is offered to students in other programs of study (except for law).

Entrance Scholarships: Outstanding Scholars Awards of $10,000 to $16,000 (over four years) are given to students entering the University directly from high school who demonstrate and maintain outstanding academic achievement. The candidate must be entering one of the selected academic programs supported by the Outstanding Scholars Award.

In-Course Scholarships and Awards: The University of Windsor also offers a variety of awards for students in their second, third, and fourth years of study through In-Course Scholarships and Awards.

For further information, students should visit the Scholarship and Bursary section of the University's Web site

Faculty

There are approximately 524 faculty members at the University, with a fairly equal number of full, associate, and assistant professors and many lecturers. The ratio of men to women faculty members is approximately 3:2. Faculty members are from around the world and have won numerous awards, earning national and international acclaim.

Student Government

The University of Windsor Student Alliance (UWSA) represents all full-time undergraduate students who pay fees to the organization on a semester basis and are considered members of the organization. The UWSA strives to enhance student life through advocacy, representation, and services, such as the used book store and the student health and dental plan, and it works to ensure that all qualified students are able to obtain a university education, regardless of their financial situation. The UWSA also provides students with an element of campus life outside of the classroom. Events are organized on and off campus, and students can get involved through clubs, committees, and all aspects of the community.

Admission Requirements

Admission is competitive for many of the University's programs. Direct entry is available to most programs within the Faculty of Arts and Social Sciences, although some require specific grade 12 U prerequisites. Auditions are required in acting and music programs. Programs within the Faculties of Science, Engineering, Human Kinetics, and Nursing and the Odette School of Business Administration require prerequisite courses at the grade 12 U level and fulfillment of minimum average requirements in these prerequisite courses. Admission to the University requires a GPA of at least 70 percent (some programs require 75 to 80 percent); specific departments may require completion of certain high school courses in English, math, and sciences for admission. Applicants from the United States must submit ACT or SAT test scores with their applications; other international students must submit certification in compliance with their country's requirements. Application requirements vary depending on the program of study.

Application and Information

Applications must be submitted online through the Ontario Universities' Application Centre (OUAC), 170 Research Lane, Guelph, Ontario N1G 5E2; http://www.ouac.on.ca.

For more information, students should contact:

Office of Liaison and Student Recruitment
University of Windsor
401 Sunset Avenue
Windsor, Ontario N9B 3P4
Canada
Phone: 519-973-7014
800-864-2860 (toll-free in Canada and the U.S.)
Fax: 519-561-1428
Web site: http://www.uwindsor.ca

COLLEGE CLOSE-UPS

UNIVERSITY OF WYOMING

LARAMIE, WYOMING

UNIVERSITY OF WYOMING
New Thinking

The University

Being a student at the University of Wyoming (UW) means more than just a first-rate education, it also the opportunity for adventure and challenge. The University of Wyoming is a welcoming community of 13,000 students with the benefits of a larger university; such as awesome research opportunities and NCAA Division I-A athletics while still having the individual feel of a small school with reasonable class sizes and individual attention.

The University of Wyoming, a public land-grant institution founded in 1886, is a reflection of the global community it serves. The extensive range of academic programs offered at UW, as the school is affectionately known, inspires the development of new thinking and promotes fulfilling careers throughout the rapidly evolving world.

The research done by the professors and students of the University of Wyoming pushes the boundaries of modern science and technology, and has resulted in UW's classification as a Carnegie Doctoral/Research University–Extensive.

It is this academic ambition that has allowed UW to provide high-quality undergraduate and graduate education, research, and service since its inception.

Wyoming, unique among the fifty states, has only one university. UW enjoys tremendous support from within its state as well as from an alumni network that spans the globe. More than 12,538 students from all fifty states of the U.S., and seventy-seven other countries attend UW classes in Laramie and at outreach sites around the state. The variety of students at UW enriches the educational experience for all by fostering a multicultural environment that encourages sharing and learning about those with different heritages and cultural backgrounds. It is this dialogue that continues to promote respect and appreciation for diversity.

UW offers bachelor's degree programs in six undergraduate colleges: the Colleges of Agriculture, Arts and Sciences, Business, Education, Engineering and Applied Science, and Health Sciences. Undergraduate education is a high priority at UW. More than 91 percent of the undergraduate courses are taught by professors, and the average class size is 29 students. UW also offers graduate and professional programs, including the Doctor of Pharmacy and the Juris Doctor.

There are more than 200 recognized campus clubs and organizations, including fifteen national fraternities and sororities, honor and professional societies, political and religious organizations, and special interest groups. Students also have the opportunity to participate in more than sixty different intramural and club sports. UW is a Division I member of the NCAA and competes in the Mountain West Conference in seventeen men's and women's sports. Campus recreational facilities include the Wyoming Union, which includes the UW bookstore, eating establishments, student computers, study areas, and a variety of services and resources for students. Additional facilities on campus include Half Acre Gym, an indoor climbing wall, an eighteen-hole golf course, tennis and racquetball courts, weight rooms, two swimming pools, rifle and archery ranges, indoor and outdoor tracks, softball and baseball fields, and a hockey rink.

UW houses 2,400 students in six residence halls, and freshmen are required to live on campus during their first year. While primarily coed, the residence halls offer a number of unique living environments, including quiet/study floors, special interest floors, honors floors, single-sex floors, and other academic living environments. UW also offers fourteen different Freshman Interest Groups, which are learning communities that offer common living areas and clustered classes to students with similar academic areas of interest.

Location

UW's 785-acre campus is located at the foot of the Rocky Mountains in Laramie, a scenic town of 30,000 people in southeastern Wyoming. Many UW students enjoy the easy access to Alpine and Nordic skiing, snowboarding, snowmobiling, hiking, backpacking, camping, hunting, fishing, rock climbing, and mountain biking. Laramie—with its blue skies, clean air, and 320 days of sunshine a year—is a friendly and supportive university town, conveniently located 45 miles west of Wyoming's capital, Cheyenne, and only 130 miles northwest of Denver, Colorado.

Majors and Degrees

UW offers more than eighty undergraduate programs within its six colleges, leading to B.A., B.S., B.F.A., and B.S.N. degrees.

The College of Agriculture offers undergraduate majors in agricultural business (with options in agribusiness management, farm and ranch management, and international agriculture), agricultural communications, agroecology, animal and veterinary sciences (with options in animal biology, business, communication, meat science and food technology, pre–veterinary science, production, and range livestock), family and consumer science (with options in child development, dietetics, family services, human nutrition and food, and textiles and merchandising), microbiology, molecular biology, and rangeland ecology and watershed management.

The College of Arts and Sciences offers undergraduate majors in American studies, anthropology, art, astronomy/astrophysics, biology, botany, chemistry, communication, criminal justice, English, earth system science, French, geography, geology (with options in earth science and environment/natural resources), German, history, humanities/fine arts, international studies, journalism, management, mathematical sciences, mathematics, microbiology, music (with options in education, performance, and theory and composition), philosophy, physics, political science, psychology, Russian, social science, sociology, Spanish, statistics, theater and dance, wildlife/fisheries, women's studies, and zoology and physiology as well as the option of a self-designed major.

The College of Business offers undergraduate majors in accounting, business administration, business economics, economics, finance, management, and marketing.

The College of Education offers undergraduate majors in elementary education, industrial technology education, and secondary education (with options in agriculture, art, business, English, family and consumer sciences, industrial technology, mathematics, modern languages, sciences, and social studies).

The College of Engineering and Applied Science offers undergraduate majors in architectural engineering, chemical engineering (with environmental and petroleum options), civil engineering, computer engineering, computer science, electrical engineering (with a bioengineering option), mechanical engineering, petroleum engineering, and earth system science (with an atmospheric science option).

The College of Health Sciences offers majors in dental hygiene, kinesiology and health promotion (athletic training option), nursing, pharmacy, physical education teaching, social work, and speech-language and hearing sciences.

UW offers preprofessional programs in dentistry, law, medicine, nursing, occupational therapy, optometry, pharmacy, physical therapy, and veterinary medicine.

The School of Environment and Natural Resources also offers interdisciplinary studies that can be combined with course work in seven other fields of study, including the humanities, physical sciences, and social sciences.

The School of Energy Resources offers a diverse curriculum that combines engineering, science, business, law, and natural resources content to build a fundamental understanding of interaction and trade-offs between energy, environment, policy, and the economy.

Academic Programs

The UW academic calendar consists of two semesters and a complete summer session. Depending on their degree program, students are required to complete 120 to 164 credit hours for graduation. Undergraduate programs for most majors can be completed in four years. Students may choose to double major within the same college, or they may pursue majors in two separate colleges for a cross-college major. Minors are also available in many areas. All students are required to complete the University Studies Program, which is a core curriculum that assists students in developing their knowledge of oral and written communication, mathematics, science, diversity, global awareness, government, and culture.

The University Honors Program provides academically ambitious undergraduates innovative and intellectual learning opportunities. Award-winning faculty members, unique and challenging course work, and senior research projects are the hallmarks of this program.

Off-Campus Programs

UW has approximately 641 international students and close to 100 international researchers/scholars during any given academic year. This diverse community represents some seventy-seven countries. The International Students and Scholars Office provides support to this population through an extensive orientation program, the Friendship Families program, the International Student Association, International Education Week, and the weekly International Coffee Hour.

International Student Services coordinates the National Student Exchange (NSE), which is a domestic student exchange consortium of more than 180 colleges and universities throughout the U.S. In addition, NSE host sites are available in Canada, Puerto Rico, the Virgin Islands, and Guam. Membership in the NSE provides UW students with access to thousands of unique academic programs, classes, and faculty members on host campuses for either a semester or an academic year.

The UW Outreach School extends the university learning experience to Wyoming and the nation through credit and noncredit programs, University of Wyoming Television, Wyoming Public Radio, and the UW/Casper College Center. Credit programs are delivered via Internet/Web-based instruction, compressed video, audio teleconferencing, flexible enrollment (correspondence study), and on-site instruction. Select programs are offered, and degree availability may be limited.

Academic Facilities

The University libraries' collections number nearly 1.3 million volumes and offer links to a variety of library service collections. The William Robertson Coe Library houses materials in the social sciences, humanities, visual and performing arts, business, education, and health sciences as well as more than 2 million federal publications and the Audio Visual Library, a collection of 4,000 video and film titles. Other libraries include the Science Library, the Brinkerhoff Earth Resources Information Center (geology library), and the Rocky Mountain Herbarium Research Collection. Additional collections are housed in the American Heritage Center and the George W. Hooper Law Library. A branch library is located at the National Park Service Research Center in Jackson, Wyoming. UW libraries participate in the Colorado Alliance of Research Libraries and in Region Four of the National Network of Libraries of Medicine. In addition, FERRET provides high-speed access to UW's online library catalogs.

Costs

UW tuition and fees for full-time undergraduates in the 2010–11 academic year are $3927 for Wyoming residents and $12,237 for nonresidents (based on an average class load of 15 credit hours). Room and board (double occupancy, unlimited meal plan) costs are $8360. Estimated expenses include $1200 for books and supplies, $892 for travel costs, and $2200 for personal expenses.

Financial Aid

Nearly 90 percent of all UW students receive financial assistance. More than $85 million is available in the form of scholarships, loans, grants, and work-study opportunities. The Free Application for Federal Student Aid (FAFSA) is required for need-based assistance (loans, grants, work-study) and for many scholarships. The priority deadline for FAFSA is March 1. Most scholarships at UW are based on academic merit. UW participates in the Western Undergraduate Exchange (WUE) program. The Rocky Mountain Scholars Award is available to nonresident students.

Faculty

More than 700 professors from the world's most respected colleges and universities have come to teach at UW. Recognized nationally and internationally as experts, almost 90 percent of the professors hold the highest degrees in their fields. UW professors are deeply committed to the success of their students. Only a small number of undergraduate courses are taught by graduate assistants, and many of the most distinguished and accomplished professors at UW teach first-year courses. UW maintains a low student-faculty ratio (14:1), which allows for individualized attention, instruction, and academic advising, as well as the inclusion of undergraduates in cutting-edge research projects.

Student Government

The Associated Students of the University of Wyoming (ASUW) is composed all students at UW. ASUW serves as the voice of the students, and its legislation impacts many aspects of student life. The ASUW Senate acts as a liaison between the student body and the administration as well as the UW Board of Trustees and local and state governments. The student body president also sits as an *ex officio* member of the UW Board of Trustees. UW encourages all students to actively participate in ASUW.

Admission Requirements

To ensure admission, high school graduates and new first-year students with fewer than 30 transferable college credit hours should have a cumulative high school GPA of 3.0 or above. Students should have a composite ACT score of 20 or greater or an SAT verbal/math score of 960 or greater. In addition, all students should complete 4 units of English, 3 units of mathematics, 3 units of science (including a physical science), and 3 units of cultural context courses (behavioral or social sciences, visual arts, performing arts, humanities, or foreign languages). Admission with conditions can be granted to students who do not meet these standards but have a minimum 2.5 GPA or a 2.25 GPA with a composite ACT score of at least 20 or an SAT score of at least 960. Transfer students with 30 or more transferable semester credit hours must have a minimum cumulative college GPA of 2.0.

Application and Information

Students must submit a completed UW Application for Admission, official high school or college transcripts, ACT or SAT scores, and a $40 nonrefundable application fee. Students may apply and pay the application fee online at www.uwyo.edu/apply. UW strongly encourages all prospective students and their parents to visit the campus.

Admissions Office
Department 3435
University of Wyoming
1000 East University Avenue
Laramie, Wyoming 82071-3435

Phone: 307-766-5160
800-DIAL-WYO (342-5996; toll-free)
E-mail: why-wyo@uwyo.edu
Web site: http://www.uwyo.edu

UTICA COLLEGE
UTICA, NEW YORK

The College

A private, independent college founded in 1946, Utica College (UC) is known for its excellent academic programs, outstanding faculty members, personal attention, and diversity among students. The hallmarks of Utica College's academic programs are the integration of liberal and professional studies and a strong emphasis on internships, research, and other experiential learning opportunities, but UC is best known for the close, personal relationship students have with both faculty and staff members. Approximately 3,000 undergraduate and graduate students attend UC, including men and women from a wide variety of socioeconomic and cultural backgrounds as well as older students, veterans, and students with disabilities. While most students come from New York, New England, and the Middle Atlantic States, students are drawn to UC from all parts of the United States, and there is a growing international student population.

Academic programs of note include accounting, construction management, economic crime investigation, education, geoscience, journalism, management, nursing, occupational therapy, physical therapy, psych–child life, risk management and insurance, and public relations. Utica College also offers a robust study-abroad program as well as an honors program.

Utica College is located on a modern, 128-acre campus on the southwestern edge of Utica, New York. Its facilities include a recently completed science and technology complex comprised of state-of-the-art learning and research facilities for health professions and justice studies, the Frank E. Gannett Memorial Library, a fully equipped high-definition television studio and convergence media center, the Ralph F. Strebel Student Center, seven residence halls, an athletic center, a 1,200-seat stadium, and numerous athletic fields.

Half of UC's students live on campus in residence halls that feature a variety of housing options, modern amenities, and lounges for studying or relaxing with friends. Freshmen primarily live in North and South Halls, which offer mostly double-occupancy rooms. Campus dining services provide a wide variety of options, including American and international cuisines, vegetarian meals, a large salad bar, and lighter fare such as burgers and pizza. Students enjoy a range of dining venues, from the main dining commons in Strebel Student Center to a student-run coffeehouse, convenient cafés in the Library and academic buildings, and a Subway sandwich shop on campus.

Whether students live on or off campus, they can take advantage of more than eighty student organizations, focusing on community service, music, theater, and politics as well as fraternities, sororities, and major-related clubs that provide opportunities for students to organize career-related events. Students can write for the student newspaper, work at the College's radio station, submit entries for the literary magazine, or work on the yearbook. Students also have the opportunity to enjoy lectures, concerts, poetry readings, art exhibits, plays, and nationally recognized speakers.

Utica College offers twenty-five NCAA Division III varsity sports, including men's baseball, basketball, cross-country, football, ice hockey, lacrosse, soccer, swimming and diving, tennis, and track and field; women's basketball, cross-country, field hockey, ice hockey, lacrosse, soccer, softball, swimming and diving, tennis, track and field, volleyball, and water polo; and coed golf. UC also offers club sports and a wide variety of intramural opportunities. Utica College is a member of the Empire 8 Athletic Conference, the Eastern College Athletic Conference, and the New York State Women's Collegiate Athletic Association. Nearly a third of all UC students participate in at least one Division III intercollegiate sport, and more than 45 percent are active in intramural or nonvarsity club sports.

Athletic facilities include a 1,200-seat multisport stadium with a state-of-the-art field turf synthetic grass playing surface; the Clark Athletic Center, which contains a large gymnasium, racquetball courts, a swimming pool, saunas, a recently renovated 6,400-square-foot free-weight room and fully equipped fitness facility, and numerous outdoor fields and courts. Ice hockey games are played at the downtown Utica Memorial Auditorium, which features pro-style hockey locker rooms and training facilities.

Graduate degrees are available in business administration, criminal justice administration, economic crime management, education, health-care administration, liberal studies, occupational therapy, and physical therapy.

Location

The city of Utica is located in the heart of the historic Mohawk Valley in the center of New York State. Just 90 miles west of Albany and 50 miles east of Syracuse, Utica has a thriving arts community, beautiful parks, and expanding shopping centers featuring national retailers. There are numerous recreational facilities, including a municipal ski slope and an excellent golf course less than a mile from the Utica College campus. Other nearby recreational opportunities include tennis, swimming, boating, fishing, hiking, and camping.

Majors and Degrees

Utica College offers undergraduate degree programs in accounting, accounting-CPA, biochemistry, biology, business economics, chemistry, communication arts, computer science, construction management, criminal justice, criminal justice–economic crime investigation, cybersecurity and information assurance, economics, English, foreign language, geoscience, gerontology, government and politics, health studies, health studies–human behavior, health studies–management, history, international studies, journalism studies, liberal studies, management, mathematics, nursing, occupational therapy, philosophy, physical therapy, physics, psychology, psychology–child life, public relations, public relations/journalism studies, risk management and insurance, sociology and anthropology, and therapeutic recreation.

Students interested in the occupational therapy or physical therapy major earn a bachelor's degree in health studies with direct entry into UC's graduate programs, as long as academic requirements are met. Utica College offers a master's degree in occupational therapy and a doctorate in physical therapy (D.P.T.).

Students may minor in anthropology, chemistry, communication arts, computer science, creative writing, economics, English language, film studies, French, gender studies, geoscience, gerontology, government, history, human rights advocacy, literature, management, mathematics, philosophy, psychology, recreation leadership, sociology, Spanish, theater, and writing.

Preprofessional programs include dentistry, law, medicine, optometry, podiatry, and veterinary medicine. Special programs are available in teacher education, gerontology, engineering, and joint health professions.

Academic Programs

Students may choose from thirty-seven undergraduate majors and twenty-seven minors in a wide variety of fields as well as accelerated programs, independent study, cooperative education, field placements, and internships. Utica College also offers a rapidly growing education program; students wishing to pursue a career in teaching choose either a liberal arts major (to teach elementary education) or a major in their intended field (to teach at the secondary level).

For those students who are undecided, the Academic Support Services Center provides academic advising and career counseling, and Career Services offers students opportunities to explore career options.

To earn a bachelor's degree, students must complete a minimum of 120 to 128 credits, satisfy major and major-related requirements, and complete any special program requirements. In addition, all Utica College students, regardless of their major, must complete a liberal arts core program as part of the degree requirements.

Utica College's ground programs operate on a semester system, with the fall term beginning in late August and ending shortly before Christmas, and the spring term beginning in late January and ending in early May. Summer and winter sessions offer students opportunities to accelerate their studies or take classes for which they have no time during the regular academic year.

First-year seminar offers freshmen and transfer students opportunities to earn academic credit while learning how to make the transition to college. Utica College offers the Higher Education Opportunity Program (HEOP), the Collegiate Science and Technology Entry Program (CSTEP), and a Summer Institute, which serves as an academic bridge between high school and college.

Off-Campus Programs

UC's Study Abroad program gives students opportunities to widen their global perspectives through exchange programs with universities in Spain, Italy, Poland, Finland, Hungary, Peru, Scotland, and Wales, as well as American College in Dublin, Ireland. UC students are also eligible to participate in Syracuse University's Division of International Programs Abroad in Madrid, Strasbourg, Florence, London, and Hong Kong. Special study-abroad opportunities include the College's annual forensic anthropology field school in Albania as well as learning experiences in London, Mexico, the Dominican Republic, and elsewhere.

Students are encouraged to complete internships and field placements to gain professional experience with businesses and organizations while they are earning college credit. Utica College's cooperative education program allows students to earn money while gaining professional experience.

Academic Facilities

The Frank E. Gannett Memorial Library includes a collection of some 200,000 volumes, 1,200 serial subscriptions, hundreds of online journals, and a microform collection of more than 60,000 journals, newspapers, and books. Located on the lower level of the library are the Media Center, computer labs, the Edith Langley Barrett Fine Art Gallery, and a large concourse—the site of special events, such as musical recitals, receptions, and guest lectures.

Classes, laboratories, and faculty offices are located in the main academic complex and within UC's new science and technology complex. F. Eugene Romano Hall, phase one of the new science and technology complex, opened in summer 2007 and provides state-of-the-art classroom, laboratory, and clinical space, as well as learning technology for students in the health sciences. The second phase, Utica College's innovative Economic Crime and Justice Studies building, opened in November 2008 and provides an appropriate platform for cutting-edge research and learning initiatives.

Named in honor of one of UC's most celebrated faculty members, Professor Emeritus of Public Relations Raymond Simon, UC's state-of-the-art high-definition broadcast facility provides a hands-on learning environment for the next generation of media professionals.

Utica College maintains eight academic computer laboratories with both IBM-compatible and Macintosh computers, including two portable wireless laptop laboratories. Students have additional Internet access in the Pioneer Café and in all student residence hall rooms. Other resources include the Academic Support Services Center, the Math/Science Center, and the Writing Center.

Costs

For 2009–10, tuition was $26,764; room and board costs were $10,850. Student activity and technology fees total $520. Books and supplies average $900 per year.

Financial Aid

The College has been recognized as a best buy in education and works to control costs and keep its education affordable. The average financial aid package for 2007–08 freshmen was $24,802. About two thirds of that aid came from grants and a third from loans and/or jobs. More than 90 percent of the freshmen received a financial aid package. At the same time, UC awarded numerous merit scholarships to students with outstanding grades and test scores.

Almost every federal and state financial aid program is available through Utica College. Students apply for institutional and governmental financial aid by filing the Free Application for Federal Student Aid (FAFSA) by February 15. UC offers three different deferred-payment programs that spread payments over the academic year.

Faculty

Utica College's faculty is diverse, energetic, accomplished, and devoted to their students. The vast majority have earned their Ph.D. or other terminal degree, and while many are involved in research, the primary focus of faculty members is teaching. The typical class size is 20 students, the student-faculty ratio is 15:1, and all faculty members are involved in assisting students with their academic planning.

Student Government

One of Utica College's strongest traditions is student participation in the College's governance structure. Students may serve on a number of student governing bodies, and students also serve on all standing committees of the College.

Admission Requirements

Utica College admits students who can best benefit from the educational opportunities the College offers. The Admission Committee gives each application individual attention, and the potential for a student's success at UC is measured primarily by an evaluation of past academic performance, scholastic ability, and personal characteristics. Freshman applicants must have completed 16 academic units, including 4 years of English. Students should follow a college-preparatory program, including 3 units of mathematics, 3 units of science, 2 units of foreign language, and 3 units of social studies.

Application and Information

Students may apply for fall, spring, or summer admission. Materials required include a completed Utica College application form, official high school or college transcripts, and a $40 application fee. Utica College prefers, but does not require, SAT or ACT scores, with the exception of the programs listed below. A personal interview for all applications is strongly suggested.

Occupational therapy, physical therapy, nursing, and joint health professions program applicants must submit SAT or ACT scores, a preferred letter of clinical recommendation if applicable, and a personal statement. International students must complete the international student application form. The application fee is waived for students who apply to HEOP or CSTEP; however, SAT or ACT scores are required to be considered for either program.

The College conducts a rolling admissions program; however certain programs do have application deadlines. For students applying to the occupational therapy or physical therapy programs, the joint health professions program, or for academic achievement awards, the application deadline is January 15. For students applying to the nursing program, the preferred application deadline is February 1. The application deadline for the HEOP program is January 15. Students should note that a tuition deposit of $200 is required by April 1 to secure a place in the HEOP program.

Additional admissions information can be found online at http://www.utica.edu/admissions.

Inquiries should be sent to:

Director of Enrollment Management
Utica College
1600 Burrstone Road
Utica, New York 13502-4892
Phone: 315-792-3006
800-782-8884 (toll-free)
E-mail: admiss@utica.edu
Web site: http://www.utica.edu

The Addison Miller White Hall Plaza.

VALPARAISO UNIVERSITY

VALPARAISO, INDIANA

The University

Valparaiso University (Valpo) was founded in 1859 by the citizens of Valparaiso, Indiana, but its recent history dates from 1925, when it was purchased by the Lutheran University Association. Valpo is one of the nation's largest Lutheran-affiliated universities, yet it remains independent and is open to individuals of all faiths. The University's 4,000 students represent most states and more than fifty countries; 64 percent come from outside of Indiana. Valparaiso University is a residential community in which activities outside the classroom form an important part of campus life; 66 percent of its students live on campus. Nearly 100 extracurricular and cocurricular programs are open to all, including NCAA Division I intercollegiate and intramural sports teams for men and women. Approximately 35 percent of the students are members of the University's nine national fraternities and seven national sororities. Both in and out of the classroom, students and professors operate a student-initiated honor code in which integrity is assumed to be the norm. If violations occur, they are handled by peers through a student-composed Honor Council. Because of these structures and the University philosophy as a whole, relationships among students, faculty, and administration are remarkably collaborative.

Major academic divisions at Valparaiso University include the Colleges of Arts and Sciences, Business Administration, Engineering, and Nursing; Christ College (the honors college); the School of Law; and the Graduate School. Over the past three years, graduates earned an average 93 percent job or graduate school placement rate within six months of graduation.

Location

Valparaiso University is located in Valparaiso, a community of 31,000 in Indiana. Only 1 hour west, Chicago and its theaters, museums, restaurants, and cultural and sports offerings are accessible by auto, train, or bus. The campus is within walking distance of a vibrant town square and commercial/entertainment center with national chain stores and restaurants. Just 15 miles north is the Indiana Dunes National Lakeshore on Lake Michigan, a famous recreational area and home of the finest ecological laboratory in the nation. Air service is available from Chicago's O'Hare and Midway International Airports and South Bend's Michiana Regional Airport.

Majors and Degrees

Valparaiso University offers the following undergraduate degrees: Associate of Arts, Associate in Science, Bachelor of Arts (B.A.), Bachelor of Liberal and Professional Studies, Bachelor of Music, Bachelor of Music Education, Bachelor of Science (B.S.), Bachelor of Science in Accounting, Bachelor of Science in Business Administration, Bachelor of Science in Civil Engineering, Bachelor of Science in Computer Engineering, Bachelor of Science in Education, Bachelor of Science in Electrical Engineering, Bachelor of Science in Fine Arts, Bachelor of Science in Mechanical Engineering, Bachelor of Science in Nursing, Bachelor of Science in Physical Education, and Bachelor of Social Work. The B.A. or B.S. degree may be earned in accounting, actuarial science, American studies, art, astronomy, biochemistry, biology, business administration, chemistry, Chinese and Japanese studies, church music, civil engineering, classics, communication, communication law, computer engineering, computer science, creative writing, economics, economics and computer analysis, education (elementary, middle, or secondary), electrical engineering, engineering, English, environmental science, exercise science, finance, French, geography, geoscience, German, history, international business, international economics and cultural affairs, international service, management, marketing, mathematics, mechanical engineering, meteorology, modern European studies, music, music composition, music education, music performance, new media–journalism, nursing, philosophy, physical education, physical education teacher education, physics, physics and astronomy teaching, political science, professional writing, psychology, public and corporate communication, public relations, social work, sociology, Spanish, sports management, television-radio, theater, theology, and youth, family, and education ministry.

Academic Programs

Valparaiso University has a long tradition of combining professional colleges with a strong commitment to the values and broadening experiences of the liberal arts. The University helps students of varied interests and objectives to clarify their goals and explore new possibilities. Connections between students' lives and the classroom are encouraged through an emphasis on hands-on learning programs, including the Valpo Core. Programs are structured to provide a solid base for exploration in various fields, while offering students the freedom to develop depth in a specific interest. This philosophy is extended through the upper division, where students have three options when completing a degree: an individual plan of study involving the major and complementary courses from related fields of study, the election of a second academic major in addition to the first, or a special minor in connection with the major. Career planning is aided through the professional programs and the University's Career Center. Many students also gain professional work experience in their chosen field before graduation by participating in the cooperative education program and internships.

Valparaiso operates on the semester system; the fall semester begins in late August and ends before Christmas, and the spring semester starts in early January and ends during the second week in May. Valpo also has two summer terms that further extend opportunities for study on campus or at various off-campus locations.

The University participates in the Advanced Placement Program, the College-Level Examination Program, and the International Baccalaureate Program. In addition, Valparaiso provides its own placement testing in several academic areas.

All departments of the University offer opportunities for honors work through independent study, seminars, and research. Christ College, the Honors College of Valparaiso University, has a well-established but continuously evolving program designed to challenge gifted students. Christ College students enroll concurrently in any other Valpo college.

Off-Campus Programs

Valparaiso University sponsors study-abroad programs in Reutlingen and Tübingen, Germany; Puebla, Mexico; Paris, France; Hangzhou, China; Granada, Spain; and Cambridge, England. Valparaiso also sponsors semester-long study opportunities at two universities in Japan, one in Namibia, and another in Greece. Valpo students may study at other overseas locations through Valparaiso's membership in the New American Colleges and Universities consortium. In addition, Valpo grants credit for the following cooperative programs: Urban Studies Semester (Chicago), Urban Affairs Semester and Washington Semester (Washington, D.C.), and Semester on the United Nations (Madison, New Jersey).

Academic Facilities

The Christopher Center for Library Information Resources is a state-of-the-art facility, which offers a robotic book-retrieval system. In addition to library resources, the four-story structure houses a ninety-one-seat tiered classroom; three fireplace lounges; a sixty-seat computer lab; a snack bar; twenty-four stations for listening to, viewing, and developing multimedia projects; reading rooms; a writing center; electronic information services; and much more. The Neils Science Center houses an astronomical observatory, a greenhouse, and other facilities that have earned the University a citation from the Atomic Energy Commission for having a model undergraduate physics laboratory. The Kade-Duesenberg German House and Cultural Center, Virtual Nursing Learning Center, weather station (which includes Doppler radar), Center for the Arts, VisBox 3-D scientific learning system, and nonlinear (digital) video editing lab are state-of-the-art facilities. The 202,000-square-foot Harre Union opened in spring 2009 and features a variety of dining options, a games and recreation center, study lounges, meeting rooms, a computer lab, and ballroom.

Costs

Tuition for the 2009–10 academic year at Valparaiso University is $27,360, room is $4910, and board is $3050. General fees are $960. The total cost of tuition, room, board, and fees is $39,120. Students spend approximately $2840 per year for books, supplies, and miscellaneous expenses such as laundry and travel.

Financial Aid

Ninety-four percent of Valparaiso's undergraduate students receive financial aid, totaling more than $60 million. Many scholarships and awards are determined by the admissions application. Students also are encouraged to file the Free Application for Federal Student Aid (FAFSA) to apply for need-based grants, loans, and employment. Valpo awards federal, state, and University need-based aid based on FAFSA results, attempting to make up the difference between the cost of attending Valpo and the amount a family can afford. Early application is recommended for Valpo assistance, since the awarding of aid begins in January of the year of enrollment.

Faculty

Valpo's full-time faculty members share a common interest—teaching in ways that encourage students and faculty members to get to know one another. The majority of the faculty members are full-time instructors, and a considerable number serve as advisers to the various academic and social organizations on campus. Classes are led by professors, not teaching assistants. Almost 91 percent of the full-time professors have terminal degrees, and this figure reaches 100 percent in many departments. Each department has a full advising system to help students with course and program selection.

Student Government

Students and faculty members alike are involved in the internal governance of the institution. House Councils in each of the residence halls are composed of representatives elected by the residents. Each council makes decisions and sets standards within the guidelines established by the University. Students in the living units and off-campus students elect representatives to the Student Senate (composed entirely of students) and the University Senate (made up of an equal number of representatives from the student body, faculty, and administration). The functions of these two separate bodies cover most phases of student life.

Admission Requirements

Valparaiso admits candidates who exhibit the potential for academic success at the University. The freshman retention rate averaged 85 percent over the past five years, reflecting in part the high quality of the admission program. Qualified students are admitted without regard to race, color, gender, disability, national origin, or ancestry. The credentials of each applicant are individually and personally evaluated, and consideration is given not only to ACT or SAT scores, but also to grades and trends in the student's record, the nature of the high school and the program followed, outside interests, and recommendations. A campus visit and an interview with an admission counselor are recommended but not required. Students who have taken the ACT or SAT in their junior year and have submitted their high school transcripts, complete through the eleventh grade, may be considered for admission.

Application and Information

An applicant must complete a formal University admission application or the Common Application to be considered for admission. In addition, Valpo requires a high school transcript (complete through the junior year), ACT or SAT scores, a counselor evaluation form, and college transcripts (when applicable). Valpo's nonbinding early action option requires applicants to submit their applications no later than November 1. Regular admission notification begins on a rolling basis after December 1. First priority for scholarship consideration is given to those who apply for admission by the early action deadline; preference is then given to those who apply by January 15.

Information and application forms for admission and financial aid may be obtained from:

Office of Admission
Kretzmann Hall
1700 Chapel Drive
Valparaiso University
Valparaiso, Indiana 46383-6493
Phone: 219-464-5011
888-GO-VALPO (toll-free)
Fax: 219-464-6898
E-mail: undergrad.admissions@valpo.edu
Web site: http://www.valpo.edu

Students on the campus of Valparaiso University.

COLLEGE CLOSE-UPS

VANDERBILT UNIVERSITY
NASHVILLE, TENNESSEE

The University

In 1873, on the heels of the Civil War, Commodore Cornelius Vanderbilt gave a million dollars to the university that now bears his name, with the hope that it would "contribute to strengthening the ties which should exist between all sections of our common country." Today, Vanderbilt enrolls America's most talented students and challenges them daily to expand their intellectual horizons and to free their imaginations. Vanderbilt's comprehensive interdisciplinary approach to education allows students to pursue a wide array of academic and cocurricular interests outside of their main focus of study.

Vanderbilt is a medium-sized university that includes four undergraduate schools and six graduate and professional schools. Each year, 1,550 first-year students join the University, bringing the total undergraduate population to approximately 6,800 students. The total enrollment at Vanderbilt is 12,506.

Known for the Southern splendor of its 330-acre, national arboretum campus, Vanderbilt provides a variety of housing options for its undergraduates, who live on campus all four years. First-year students live in The Commons, a collection of new and newly renovated residence halls, or Houses, clustered along one side of campus. Each House includes a faculty apartment. The Commons Center includes a new dining center with study space, a post office, and an exercise facility. One of Vanderbilt's unique housing options is the McTyeire International House, which is designed for students who are interested in a range of foreign languages, such as Chinese, French, German, Japanese, and Spanish. Other on-campus options include traditional dormitories, apartments, and suites.

The Sarratt Student Center houses a cinema, pub, art gallery, craft and darkroom facilities, an FM radio station, and plenty of meeting space. Facilities at the Student Recreation Center include gymnasiums, an indoor swimming pool, squash and racquetball courts, a rock climbing wall, an indoor suspended track, and a weight room. Other recreational facilities include indoor and outdoor tennis courts, baseball and softball diamonds, and a sand volleyball court.

Location

Vanderbilt University is located in Nashville, the capital of Tennessee. Known as Music City, USA, Nashville is a vibrant city of more than 1 million residents. The greater Nashville area is home to two major-league professional sports teams, eighty-one parks, and more than 30,000 acres of lakes. Three interstate highways intersect the city, and its international airport is a short cab ride from campus.

Majors and Degrees

The B.A., B.S., B.E., or B.M. degree is offered in African American and Diaspora studies; American studies; Ancient Mediterranean studies; anthropology; art; Asian studies; biological sciences; biomedical engineering; chemical engineering; chemistry; child development; child studies; civil engineering; classical languages; classics; cognitive studies; communication of science and technology; communication studies; computer engineering; computer science; early childhood education; earth and environmental sciences; ecology, evolution, and organismal biology; economics; economics and history; electrical engineering; elementary education; engineering science; English; English and history; European studies; film studies; French; French and European studies; German; German and European studies; history; history of art; human and organizational development; Italian and European studies; Jewish studies; Latin American and Iberian studies; mathematics; mechanical engineering; medicine, health, and society; modern European studies; molecular and cellular biology; musical arts; musical arts/teacher education track; music composition and theory; music performance; neuroscience; philosophy; physics and astronomy; political science; psychology; public policy studies; religious studies; Russian; Russian and European studies; secondary education; sociology; Spanish; Spanish and European studies; Spanish and Portuguese; Spanish, Portuguese, and European studies; special education; theater; women's and gender studies; and individually designed majors.

Academic Programs

Students apply directly to one of the four schools that offer undergraduate programs: the College of Arts and Science, the School of Engineering, Peabody College (education and human development), or the Blair School of Music. In all four schools, honors programs and opportunities for independent study and internships are available. Vanderbilt University operates on a two-semester calendar, and classes begin in late August. First-semester examinations take place prior to the winter holidays, and the second semester ends in early May. A variety of courses are offered during Maymester and two summer sessions.

The College of Arts and Science provides many opportunities to experience a wide range of academic disciplines and subjects. Within the requirements of the AXLE (Achieving eXcellence in Liberal Education) curriculum, students refine their skills in writing, mathematics, foreign language, the humanities, natural sciences, social sciences, history, and culture.

The Blair School of Music offers the Bachelor of Music degree in composition and theory, musical arts, musical arts/teacher education, and performance. Instruction is available in every instrument of the orchestra as well as piano, organ, euphonium, multiple woodwinds, saxophone, classical guitar, and voice. Unlike many schools of music, Blair has no graduate students. The curriculum combines intensive musical training with liberal arts studies. Approximately one third of a student's work is outside of music. The Blair School also offers a music minor and a wide variety of courses, private instruction, and performing organizations for nonmajors.

For more than 125 years, the School of Engineering has educated engineers for practice in industry, government, consulting, teaching, and research careers. In addition to technical courses, each student's program includes a rich complement of course work in the humanities and social sciences, resulting in a balanced foundation for future achievement and the assumption of leadership roles in their chosen fields. All programs leading to a Bachelor of Engineering degree are ABET-accredited, and students can earn the Bachelor of Science degree while majoring in Computer Science or Engineering Science.

Peabody College offers degree programs leading to teacher certification and to careers in other areas of education, child development, child studies, cognitive studies, and human and organizational development. The degree reflects a strong liberal arts foundation combined with a solid program of preprofessional courses and a multitude of internship and practicum opportunities. All undergraduates must complete requirements in communication, the humanities, mathematics, the natural sciences, and the social sciences. Students have an abundance of field experiences throughout their four years.

Off-Campus Programs

Study-abroad programs allow students to immerse themselves in languages and cultures around the world. More than seventy programs are offered in Argentina, Australia, Austria, Brazil, Chile, China, Costa Rica, the Czech Republic, Denmark, the Dominican Republic, Egypt, England, France, Germany, Greece, Ireland, Israel, Italy, Japan, Mexico, the Netherlands, New Zealand, Nicaragua, Russia, Senegal, South Africa, South Korea, Spain, and Sweden. Vanderbilt students receive direct credit for their courses, and the cost of tuition is usually the same as for study on campus in Nashville. In addition, any scholarships, grants, or loans a student has been awarded apply to Vanderbilt study-abroad programs. Students may also participate in programs sponsored by other universities by working with their adviser.

Academic Facilities

Students and faculty members take advantage of Vanderbilt's extensive library resources, obtaining easy access to books, periodicals, documents, microforms, and reference materials. The Jean and Alexander Heard Library is supported by nine major resource centers, which include special collections, University Archives, and more than 3.2 million volumes.

Costs

The costs for 2009–10 were: tuition, $37,632; room and board, $12,650; books and supplies, $1292; and the student activities and recreation fee, $946. All costs are subject to change. They are slightly higher for students in the School of Engineering.

Financial Aid

Approximately 60 percent of the University's undergraduate students receive some type of financial aid. Need-based aid is awarded according to the evaluation of the FAFSA and the CSS/Financial Aid PROFILE. Vanderbilt no longer includes need-based loans in financial aid packages. Need-based loans have been replaced with a combination of grant, scholarship, and work-study assistance from various sources including Vanderbilt, federal, state, and private entities. Under certain conditions and based upon individual family circumstances, loans from federal and other sources may be made available to students upon their request. Information on these and other programs can be obtained from the Office of Student Financial Aid and Undergraduate Scholarships, 2309 West End Avenue, Nashville, Tennessee 37203-1725. In addition, approximately 3 percent of freshmen applicants are awarded an honor scholarship based on academic merit.

Faculty

Vanderbilt has 3,309 full-time faculty members and a part-time faculty of 424. All undergraduate faculty members, many of whom hold awards for distinguished scholarship, are required to teach undergraduates. A low student-faculty ratio of 8:1 provides for an intimate academic experience between students and professors who are recognized nationally and worldwide for their research. Ninety-two percent of classes have fewer than 50 students.

Student Government

The Vanderbilt Student Government provides students with an opportunity to participate actively in maintaining a high quality of life on campus. It works with many of the more than 350 student organizations to bring nationally prominent speakers to campus and provide an interesting and diverse array of programming throughout the year. A vital part of life at Vanderbilt is the honor system, which is governed entirely by students through representatives on the Honor Council. Each year, a senior is selected as a Young Alumni Trustee of the University's Board of Trust.

Admission Requirements

Vanderbilt seeks students with high standards of scholarship and character. Admission is based on a thorough and holistic review of academic and personal credentials.

The typical applicant will have completed 20 or more units in a challenging high school curriculum, including at least 2 years of foreign language study. Applicants to the School of Engineering must complete at least 4 units of mathematics; calculus and physics are strongly recommended. The Admissions Committee evaluates each student's secondary school academic record, extracurricular involvement, counselor and teacher recommendations, and personal essay. Students must also submit scores (including the writing subscore) from either the SAT Reasoning Test or the ACT. Applicants to the Blair School of Music are required to audition on their primary instrument. A personal audition is preferred, but applicants may audition by videotape with permission from the Blair School of Music.

Campus visits are recommended, though student interest is not used as a measure of admissibility. In addition to daily information sessions and campus tours, the Admissions Office offers a number of different half-day and full-day visit programs for prospective students. All programs require reservations, so students are encouraged to call or visit http://admissions.vanderbilt.edu in advance of their visit for information about group information sessions, campus tours, and opportunities to attend classes.

Application and Information

Students whose first choice is Vanderbilt may apply under one of Vanderbilt's early decision plans. Applications and all supporting materials must be postmarked by November 1 for early decision I and by January 3 for early decision II; notification is made by December 15 for early decision I and by February 15 for early decision II. The deadline for applying under the regular decision plan is January 3. Students are informed of the admission decision by April 1. Personal auditions are scheduled in December, January, and February for students applying to the Blair School of Music. Students seeking transfer admission should submit an application and all supporting materials by March 1; Vanderbilt offers only fall semester entry for transfer students.

Office of Undergraduate Admissions
Vanderbilt University
2305 West End Avenue
Nashville, Tennessee 37203-1727
Phone: 615-322-2561
800-288-0432 (toll-free)
E-mail: admissions@vanderbilt.edu
Web site: http://admissions.vanderbilt.edu

VAUGHN COLLEGE OF AERONAUTICS AND TECHNOLOGY

FLUSHING, NEW YORK

The College

Vaughn College of Aeronautics and Technology is a private, four-year college committed to providing its students with the excellent education and skills needed to achieve professional success in engineering, technology, management, and aviation. Founded in 1932, the College, adjacent to LaGuardia Airport, is a small, high-quality institution where students can experience personal attention as they progress through their academic course work. The College fosters a culture of excellence in which rigorous degree, professional, technical, and certification programs are offered. These programs, built upon the College's aeronautical heritage, incorporate the latest technology and meet the universal needs of the industries they serve. The result is well-educated graduates who are successful in their fields. The College's student body of nearly 1,100 and its low 14:1 student-faculty ratio ensure a highly personalized learning environment. More than 93 percent of Vaughn College graduates are employed within six months of obtaining their degrees, and they work in twenty countries and in all fifty states.

On September 1, 2004, the College of Aeronautics became Vaughn College of Aeronautics and Technology. The name reflects the College's aviation heritage as well as its future as a greatly expanded academic institution, with new programs including a Bachelor of Science in mechatronic engineering and a master's-level management offering in fall. The name change is part of the College's five-year strategic plan and includes plans for a new library, additional degree programs, and other improvements to the campus.

Location

Located in New York City, the College offers numerous internship opportunities with a vast array of technology, manufacturing, and aviation companies. The cultural, spiritual, and physical needs of the students are met by the outstanding facilities of New York City. Restaurants are easily accessible, and hospitals and other medical facilities are among the best in the world. Various museums focus on arts, natural history, science, and world civilization.

Majors and Degrees

The College awards the Associate of Applied Science (A.A.S.) degree in aeronautical engineering technology, airport management, aviation maintenance, computerized design and animated graphics, electronic engineering technology–avionics, and flight.

The Bachelor of Science (B.S.) degree is available in general management, airline management, airport management, aviation maintenance, aviation maintenance management, electronic engineering technology–avionics, electronic technology-general electronics, electronic technology–optical communications (fiber optics), flight, mechatronics engineering, mechanical engineering technology–aeronautical option, and mechanical engineering technology–computer-aided design option. A non-degree course of study in air traffic control, a Federal Aviation Administration Collegiate Training Initiative program, is also available. The College is one of thirty-one institutions nationwide to offer this program. There is also an aircraft dispatch program offered.

Academic Programs

All students in associate and baccalaureate degree programs complete a core curriculum as part of their degree requirements. The core curriculum is derived from the mission of the College and reflects what the institution believes is important and elemental to students' education and development. In general, the core instills in students critical-thinking skills, values appropriate to an educated person, and the ability to communicate, and the curriculum provides context for advanced learning. The baccalaureate core consists of three components—academic skills (13 credits, including a year of English composition, a course in oral communication, and precalculus), the liberal arts (12 credits, including a year of world and American literature), and math and science (15 credits).

Off-Campus Programs

Internships are an important part of a student's learning experience at Vaughn College, and they often lead to job offers upon graduation. The Office of Career Development and faculty chair members arrange for internships with top U.S. corporations. As a Hispanic-serving institution, the College participates with the Hispanic Association of Colleges and Universities (HACU) to place students in internships with various federal agencies year-round. Some of the other active internships and cooperatives include the Boeing Company, Federal Aviation Administration (FAA), Federal Express, Global Air Dispatch, HACU, jetBlue, Lockheed Martin, the Metropolitan Transportation Authority (MTA), the National Broadcasting Company, the Northrop Grumman Corporation, Northwest Airlines, ORBIS, the Port Authority of New York and New Jersey, and Teterboro Airport.

Academic Facilities

Each laboratory provides the work/study environment suited to the requirements of each program. Students experience the technology that they will ultimately use once employed. This practical, hands-on experience helps qualify students for immediate employment upon graduation. From the new photonics laboratory to the CATIA/NASTRAN computer center, the College's faculty members are committed to providing students with the knowledge and tools they are likely to find in today's businesses. The FRASCA 142 flight simulator is a major component of the flight students on campus.

Over the last several years, the College has installed a \$1-million computer network, which allows a common interface for a number of operating systems, including Novell and Microsoft Windows. The system also supports other operating systems, including Windows NT, Windows 2000, Windows 2003,

Windows XP, Macintosh OSX, and UNIX as well as all of the previous server versions of Windows Operating Systems. More than 300 computers are connected through fiber-optic cables to allow sharing of more than thirty of the most up-to-date applications, including desktop publishing, CATIA, Autocad, Mechanical Desktop, mathematics, word processing, spread sheets, databases, shared print services, and file and scanning services. Four T1 lines give each workstation access to the Internet and full e-mail and messaging services on and off campus. In addition to the T1 lines, the College also has added wireless Internet access that is available across the campus. Registered students also have access to Vaughn's student information through the "Vaughn Portal." More information can be found on the College's Web site at http://www.vaughn.edu.

The College's library offers extensive general, technical, resource, and periodical material totaling more than 42,000 volumes. The real and virtual resources include books, periodicals, videos, and research databases. There are more than 150 periodical titles in the library's collection. The video collection consists of subject videos to support the College's curriculum, general interest videos, and movies. The library houses almost 2,000 VHS tapes and DVDs. In addition, there are research databases available that contain more than 8,000 full-text periodicals and newspapers. Ten personal computers are available for student use in the reference area. The library, which occupies more than 4,500 square feet, offers seating for 100 students and has an attached computer lab with twenty computer stations.

Costs

In 2009–10, full-time tuition (12 to 18 credits per semester) was $8150. Students taking fewer than 11 credits paid $550 per credit. The semester fee, which covers the cost of orientation courses, Internet and computer usage, and student-support services, activities, and leadership programs, was $200.

For the 2009–10 academic year, rooms in Vaughn's new residence hall were $3990 for a double room and $4575 for a single room, per semester. A $250 housing deposit is required. Residents live in either a two-person or a four-person suite with a semi-private bath. The residence hall has laundry, study, and kitchen facilities in a common area within the building. Residence hall rooms are supplied with a bed, dresser, closet, desk, chair, and wastebasket for each student. Each room is also equipped with phone and cable TV hookup, and computer port.

Financial Aid

Vaughn College of Aeronautics and Technology offers federal, state, and institutional funds to help students pay for their education. More than 85 percent of students are eligible for some type of financial aid. The first step is to file the Free Application for Federal Student Aid (FAFSA) and, if appropriate, the New York State Tuition Assistance Program (TAP) application. Applications for the fall semester should be filed by March 1. The College recognizes academic excellence by awarding scholarships to high-achieving students pursuing Bachelor of Science degree programs. In order to be eligible, all applicants must file the FAFSA. Awards for new students include Founders' Scholarships, which are merit-based and range from $500 to $6000 per year, and the need-based Vaughn College financial grants, which range from $250 to $2200.

Faculty

What separates Vaughn College of Aeronautics and Technology from other institutions is its uniquely committed faculty, whose members come to the classroom with extensive experience in such fields as engineering, manufacturing, management, and communications. Working closely with industry, the College has developed rigorous curricula that incorporate the latest technology and the knowledge students need for that all-important first professional position. The small student-faculty ratio of 14:1 enables students to work closely with faculty members in the classroom and laboratory settings.

Student Government

The Student Government Association (SGA) is primarily concerned with the quality of student life on campus. SGA carries the concerns of its constituency, the student body, to the administration and is the voice of the student body. Serving students as the liaison to the administration, SGA coordinates social programming and provides a system for cocurricular involvement through many clubs and organizations. SGA meets on a regular basis and encourages all students to attend meetings and become involved.

Admission Requirements

High school graduates must submit the completed application; the $40 application fee; SAT or ACT scores; an official copy of the high school transcript and any college transcripts (if applicable); a copy of the high school diploma (or GED), complete with scores; and immunizations records. Some students may need to take a placement exam, while flight operations applicants must pass the FAA Class II physical examination. An interview with an admissions counselor and a financial aid counselor is required for all flight operations applicants and recommended for all others.

Students who have lived in the United States for less than three years and for whom English is a second language, or international applicants from countries where English is not an official language, may substitute results of the TOEFL exam. Students who have completed 24 or more college credits are exempt from the SAT/ACT requirement.

Application and Information

The admissions office reviews applications on a rolling basis. All applicants are encouraged to file by March 1 for the fall semester and November 15 for the spring semester in order to take advantage of scholarship opportunities.

Vaughn College of Aeronautics and Technology
86-01 23rd Avenue
Flushing, New York 11369
Phone: 718-429-6600
866-6VAUGHN (toll-free)
Fax: 718-779-2231
E-mail: admitme@vaughn.edu
Web site: http://www.vaughn.edu

VILLANOVA UNIVERSITY

VILLANOVA, PENNSYLVANIA

The University

Villanova is the oldest and largest Catholic university in Pennsylvania, founded in 1842 by the Order of Saint Augustine. The Augustinian values of Veritas, Unitas, Caritas (translated as truth, unity, and love) guide academic and social life at Villanova to this day. Students of all faiths are welcome. The University tends to attract students who are interested in volunteerism. Each year, Villanovans provide more than 64,000 hours of service to communities locally, regionally, and nationally.

Villanova offers more than forty rigorous academic programs through four undergraduate colleges: the College of Liberal Arts and Sciences, the Villanova School of Business, the College of Engineering, and the College of Nursing. Total undergraduate full-time enrollment is 6,342. Total University enrollment is 10,172. There are more than 250 student organizations and thirty-two National Honor Societies at Villanova.

Located 12 miles west of Philadelphia, Villanova's picturesque 254-acre campus houses sixty buildings—including twenty-six residence halls. Villanova students can choose from a range of opportunities to study abroad. Incoming freshmen can opt to be part of a Villanova Learning Community. Through Learning Communities, students form close friendships as they live together in specially-designated residence halls and learn together in courses and cocurricular programs.

Location

Philadelphia offers endless opportunities for students to supplement campus life with cultural, recreational, and social service activities in the city. Whether it's going out for a world-famous Philly cheese-steak sandwich, visiting art, history, and science museums, shopping, or cheering for local sports teams at a game, there is something for everyone to enjoy in Philadelphia.

Majors and Degrees

Through the College of Liberal Arts and Sciences, Villanova grants the Bachelor of Arts degree in: art history, classical studies, communication, criminal justice, economics, secondary education, English, environmental studies, French and Francophone studies, geography, global interdisciplinary studies, history, honors, humanities, human services, Italian, liberal arts, philosophy, physics, political science, psychology, sociology, Spanish studies, and theology and religious studies. The college grants the Bachelor of Science degree in: astronomy and astrophysics, biology, biochemistry, chemistry, comprehensive science, computer science, environmental science, honors, mathematics, and physics.

Accelerated Bachelor/Master's degrees are also available to students in the areas of classical studies, criminal justice, political science, psychology, Spanish studies, theology and religious studies, biology, chemistry, computer science, and mathematics.

Interdisciplinary concentrations are offered by the college in: Africana studies, Arab and Islamic studies, Augustine in dialogue with faith and culture, cognitive science, East Asian studies, elementary education (in conjunction with Rosemont College), environmental studies, ethics, Irish studies, Latin American studies, military science, naval science, peace and justice, Russian area studies, women's studies, and writing and rhetoric.

Through the Villanova School of Business, the University grants the Bachelor of Science degree in accountancy, in business honors, and in business administration with the following majors: economics, finance, management, management information systems, and marketing. Villanova also offers an international business co-major and the following business minors: business law and corporate governance, entrepreneurship, and real estate.

Through the College of Engineering, Villanova grants the Bachelor of Science degree (with accelerated Bachelor/Master's degree options also available) in chemical engineering, civil engineering, computer engineering, electrical engineering, and mechanical engineering. The College of Engineering offers a concentration in business and a dual degree with the College of Liberal Arts and Sciences.

Through the College of Nursing, the University grants the Bachelor of Science degree in nursing.

Villanova offers the following Health Science Affiliation Programs: Drexel University School of Medicine, Doctor of Medicine; University of Pennsylvania School of Dental Medicine, Doctor of Medical Dentistry; Pennsylvania College of Optometry, Doctor of Optometry; and Jefferson College of Health Professions of Thomas Jefferson University, Doctorate of Physical Therapy, Masters in Occupational Therapy, Bioscience Technologies, and Radiologic Technologies.

An honors concentration is available to students in all four colleges.

Academic Programs

The College of Liberal Arts and Sciences provides a wide array of rigorous degree programs in the arts, the humanities, and the physical and social sciences. Required components of the curriculum include ethics, arts, and courses designed to develop students' writing abilities. Villanova is one of only eighteen Catholic universities in the nation to have a chapter of Phi Beta Kappa, the prestigious liberal arts honor society.

The College recently celebrated the "Year of Mendel" in honor of the scientist Gregor Johann Mendel—one of history's most famous Augustinians—whose experiments with the hybridization of pea plants led him to discover the laws of heredity.

The Villanova School of Business (VSB), consistently ranked as one of the top undergraduate business schools in the United States, is home to faculty research centers including the Center for Global Leadership, the Center for Marketing and Public Policy Research, the Daniel M. DiLella Center for Real Estate, the Center for the Study of Church Management, the Center for Entrepreneurship, and the Institute for Research in Advanced Financial Technology. VSB is located in Bartley Hall, with a light-filled, three-story atrium, the VSB Applied Finance Lab, class and study rooms, and common areas including the Bartley Exchange dining hall and the Holy Grounds coffee shop. The Clay Center at VSB, located at the heart of the school, provides program services to undergraduate business students.

The College of Engineering, ranked among the best engineering programs in the nation, is home to three research units: the Center for Advanced Communications, the Center for Nonlinear Dynamics and Control, and the Villanova Center for the Environment—a joint effort with the College of Liberal Arts and Sciences. The college's home, the Villanova Center for Engineering Education and Research, houses state-of-the-art instructional and research labs. Additional engineering-related facilities can be found on campus in White Hall, John Barry Hall, Tolentine Hall, and the 10,000-square-foot Structural Engineering Teaching and Research Laboratory.

A small and special group within the Villanova community is the student body of the College of Nursing. A manifestation of the Augustinian spirit of caring in action, Villanova nursing students have opportunities to work with community members in need while completing rigorous coursework. The College of Nursing is housed in Driscoll Hall. Unveiled in 2008, this 75,500-square-foot building offers resources including a 200-seat auditorium and a 200-seat lecture hall; clinical simulation labs for health assessment, adult health, maternal/child health, anesthesia, and critical care; simulation labs for standardized patient observation and testing; and a center for nursing research and scholarship.

Naval and Marine Reserve Officers Training Corps (ROTC) programs are available on the Villanova campus. The University has had a long and cherished relationship with its NROTC unit for over fifty years. The NROTC program at Villanova is structured to complement a normal college lifestyle. Midshipmen are encouraged to participate fully in their academic programs as well as in extracurricular activities.

Off-Campus Programs

Villanova's study-abroad programs are affiliated with an overseas four-year college or university, have overseas faculty members, and provide bicultural experiences such as homestays. Summer programs support language and area studies in locations including Chile, China, England, France, Germany, Greece, Ireland, Israel, Italy, Jordan, Palestine, Russia, and Spain.

Academic Facilities

Falvey Memorial holdings include more than 800,000 volumes, 5,400 serial subscriptions, and more than a million microform items.

Villanova's Office of Learning Support Services serves students with learning disabilities, other neurologically-based disorders, and those disabled by chronic illnesses.

With the help of the Career Services Office, students develop professional skills and learn about career options. Over 1,700 companies post on Villanova's job boards, and the average starting salary for Villanova graduates is $50,000. Ninety-seven percent of Villanova graduates are employed or enrolled in graduate school within six months of their degree completion. Internships are also an important source of professional development opportunities for students. Over 400 internships are posted on campus each year, and internships often lead to full-time job offers.

The technological resources on Villanova's campus are consistently recognized among the best in the nation. All undergraduates receive laptops with a full suite of office productivity tools and access to an Internet-based backup and vaulting product (U-Vault). Students have access to premium cable channels, HD broadcasts, and optional phone service in the residence halls. The university has a "Nova Alert" emergency system, web-based laundry reservation system, campus card-based student print system and off-campus merchant purchasing program, and basketball lottery system.

Costs

Tuition costs, including fees, were $37,210 for the 2009–10 academic year. Room and board costs for the full academic year were approximately $10,000.

Financial Aid

At Villanova, 98.5 percent of first-year students who apply for need-based aid are eligible to receive some type of assistance, and 79.6 percent of those eligible for need-based assistance receive Villanova Grants. The average grant award is $20,000. The average assistance package for students with demonstrated financial need (combining grants, scholarships, loans and student employment) is $29,446.

Villanova offers a Presidential Scholarship Program, through which it seeks to attract student leaders who represent diverse backgrounds, including those from families in which few or no members have attended college. Through this program, students are awarded scholarships that cover full tuition for eight consecutive semesters.

Faculty

Villanova has 570 full-time faculty members, nearly 90 percent of whom hold doctoral degrees. The student-to-faculty ratio is 11:1 and the average class size is 22.

Student Government

Empowering the Villanova student body since 1925, the Student Government Association (SGA) has three branches (administrative, community, and student relations) and twelve committees. The SGA provides opportunities for students leaders to serve the Villanova community as liaisons, representatives, and student senators.

Admission Requirements

Admission to Villanova is challenging. In addition to looking for academically-talented, well-rounded students, Villanova looks for applicants who have "compassionate minds"—those who want to make the world a better place. Villanova is a Common Application member institution. Prospective students are also required to complete a Villanova Preliminary Application for Undergraduate Admission and to submit an official high school transcript and Common Application School Report. Applicants must have their standardized test scores (SAT or ACT) reported directly to Villanova by the College Board or ACT.

High school performance is also an important selectivity factor. Each student's high school record, GPA, and class rank, along with each student's demonstration of character and personal abilities, are carefully considered. Extracurricular and volunteer activities, in addition to outstanding academic work, are helpful to applicants in this regard. Another important factor in the Villanova admissions process is the personal essay. Since Villanova doesn't interview applicants, the essay is a vehicle through which prospective students can explain to Villanova who they are and why they should be selected to become Villanovans. Recommendations are also carefully considered.

Applicants from non-English speaking countries must take the Test of English as a Foreign Language (TOEFL) or the International English Language Testing Systems (IELTS) test and have scores reported directly to the Villanova from the College Board.

Transferring to Villanova is possible, but selective.

Application and Information

The regular-decision deadline for receipt of the application by the Office of University Admission is January 7. The deadline for early action and Health Affiliation programs is November 1.

Villanova Office of University Admission
800 Lancaster Avenue
Villanova, Pennsylvania 19085-1672
Phone: 610-519-4000
Fax: 610-519-6450
E-mail: gotovu@villanova.edu
Web site: http://www.villanova.edu

St. Thomas of Villanova Church.

VIRGINIA MILITARY INSTITUTE

LEXINGTON, VIRGINIA

The Institute

The Virginia Military Institute (VMI) is the nation's oldest state-supported military college, founded in 1839 in Lexington, Virginia, and located at the southern end of the Shenandoah Valley. VMI offers qualified young men and women a demanding combination of academic study and rigorous military training that exists nowhere else, and grants B.A. and B.S. degrees in fourteen disciplines within the general fields of engineering, science, and liberal arts. The Institute's emphasis on qualities of honor, integrity, and responsibility contributes to its unique educational philosophy. Professional leadership training is provided to all cadets through the Reserve Officers' Training Corps (ROTC) programs, maintained at VMI by the Department of Defense. Cadets may pursue commissions in the U.S. Army, Air Force, Navy, or Marine Corps.

In every field of endeavor, whether it is leadership in business, industry, public service, education, the professions, or careers in the military, success comes early to a high number of VMI graduates. In an independent survey of college graduates seeking employment, armed forces commission, or admission to graduate or professional school following graduation, 95 percent of VMI graduates met their goal by the following October.

VMI's breadth is diverse. The curricula for the selected major begin in the first year. More than 20 percent of cadets major in civil, electrical, or mechanical engineering, and more than 50 percent of cadets major in liberal arts fields. The two most popular fields are economics/business and history.

The academic excellence of VMI and its stature among institutions of higher education are highlighted by the fact that *U.S. News & World Report* has named VMI among the nation's top three public liberal arts colleges for seven years in a row. Its engineering programs remain in the top tier of best undergraduate accredited programs at schools offering only bachelor's or master's degrees.

VMI's alumni support is unparalleled in many ways, especially in their financial support. The National Association of College and University Business Officers has reported that VMI has the largest endowment per student of any public institution.

VMI alumni include Nobel Peace Prize winner George C. Marshall, 11 Rhodes scholars, and 39 college presidents. VMI alumni have distinguished themselves in every American conflict since the Mexican War, and they include 7 Medal of Honor recipients and 265 general and flag officers. More than 1,000 alumni have served in war zones and in support of operations in the war on terror since 2001.

After nearly 160 years of preparing young men for distinguished leadership roles, VMI made the transition to being coeducational in 1997, successfully assimilating women in the Corps of Cadets. The Institute graduated its first women cadets in May 1999.

Today, 1,370 young men and women in the VMI Corps of Cadets represent forty-four states and nine other countries. More than 100 cadets study abroad each year, one third compete in intercollegiate athletics, and all have significant leadership opportunities.

All cadets reside in Barracks, at the centerpiece of the VMI Post. The original structure was built in 1850 and is a National Historic Landmark. An additional wing was added in 1949. A third section of the Barracks is under construction, to be followed by renovation of the existing Barracks structures. When completed, the new Barracks will also house facilities such as the bookstore, a cadet visitor's center and lounge, and other cadet-oriented functions. All cadet rooms are equipped for computer technology.

VMI cadets uphold an honor system as old as the Institute. An oath of honor is taken by each cadet, "not to lie, cheat, or steal, nor tolerate those who do," and the oath is practiced in daily life. As it is basic to cadet life, it is ingrained and builds strong character. Honor is at the cornerstone of every cadet's lifelong commitment to integrity, duty, self-discipline, and self-reliance.

One of the oldest VMI traditions is the orientation and instruction provided to new cadets by older cadets. Regardless of background or prior training, every cadet in the first year at VMI is a Rat, and each is a Brother Rat to the other. They live under the Rat System until Break Out in late winter, and their bonds formed by this experience last a lifetime.

VMI places great emphasis on physical fitness and training programs, whether cadets participate in athletics, ROTC training, or physical education programs. VMI offers fifteen intercollegiate athletics programs at the NCAA Division I level and supports numerous club sports and intramural activities. The VMI "Keydet" Club is one of the oldest and most productive athletic foundations in the country, raising more than $1 million annually for athletic scholarships and grants-in-aid to 185 cadets in all sixteen sports. Athletic grounds and facilities are within easy access to the Post.

VMI is a member of the Big South conference.

Location

Lexington is in Rockbridge County, Virginia, an area rich in history and natural beauty. VMI adjoins the campus of Washington and Lee University, the nation's ninth-oldest institution of higher learning. Both colleges are within walking distance to historic downtown Lexington, a popular tourist destination. Interstate Highways 81 and 64 intersect only minutes from VMI, north of Lexington's downtown area. U.S. Highways 11 (north-south) and 60 (east-west), the area's crossroads for two centuries, intersect in downtown Lexington. Air service to VMI is available from Roanoke Regional Airport, less than an hour's drive from Lexington.

Majors and Degrees

VMI offers the baccalaureate degree in fourteen curricula. The B.S. is awarded in chemistry, civil engineering, computer science, electrical engineering, mechanical engineering, and physics. The B.A. is conferred in economics and business, English, history, international studies, modern languages, and psychology. A B.S. or B.A. can be earned in biology and applied mathematics. A course of study leading to a B.S. or B.A. is chosen upon entering VMI, but a transfer from one major field of study to another is permitted.

Academic Programs

VMI's demanding academic program reflects established needs and emerging trends of an ever-changing, global society. A newly funded undergraduate research initiative extends through summer, affording cadets and faculty members financial incentives and continuous support for a wide range of investigative projects. The Institute's international programs include faculty and student exchanges with more than a dozen international academies and universities, seven international internships, and numerous study-abroad programs each semester and during the summer.

VMI is accredited by the Southern Association of Colleges and Schools and is a member of American Council on Education, the Association of American Colleges, the College Entrance Examination Board, and the Association of Virginia Colleges. VMI's engineering and computer science programs are ABET-accredited; the chemistry program is accredited by ACS.

Academic Facilities

The VMI Post covers 134 acres, of which 12 acres are designated a National Historic District. VMI's academic facilities, Superintendent's quarters, library, alumni hall, and other administrative buildings, along with Barracks, encircle a 12-acre parade ground used for marching drills, weekly parades, training exercises, and social gatherings. The physics department has X-ray and nuclear physics laboratories and operates both an observatory and planetarium. The George C. Marshall Research Museum and the VMI Museum are located on Post.

Costs

Charges at VMI are based on a cadet's classification as a Virginia or out-of-state resident. Total charges cover most direct expenses, including tuition, room, board (twenty-one meals per week), fees, uniforms, laundry, routine medical care, and barber services. As an example, in 2009–10 total costs were $17,982 for Virginia residents and $35,530 for non-Virginia residents. (Books and transportation are additional.) ROTC pay and allowances to qualified cadets total up to $10,000 over four years, and should be considered in net costs at VMI.

Financial Aid

Although aid is generally awarded on the basis of financial need, numerous scholarships are awarded for academic and athletic excellence and as room and board supplements to ROTC scholarship recipients. Students interested in financial assistance should write to VMI's Director of Financial Aid.

Faculty

All VMI faculty members teach in the classroom, and 97 percent of full-time faculty members hold doctoral or terminal degrees. The cadet-faculty ratio is 12:1, permitting a close, mentor relationship between a cadet and instructor. Faculty research is conducted in partnership with cadets. ROTC instructors are experienced military officers and make an outstanding contribution to cadet leadership training.

Student Government

VMI has two systems of student government. The regimental system oversees cadet accountability for conduct, appearance, military training, and all ceremonial functions. The regiment of the Corps is divided into two battalions of four companies each, plus a band company.

Although Institute regulations govern the discipline of cadets, a large measure of supervision resides in each of the four closely knit classes within the Corps. The class system administers the Corps' standards and the privileges accorded each class and governs with the regimental system to oversee cadet appearance and conduct.

Representatives to the Honor Court are elected from the Corps, by the Corps, to enforce the rules of the honor system and prosecute Honor Court cases.

Admission Requirements

Applicants must be unmarried, 16 to 22 years of age (a one-year age waiver may be granted for an applicant who has served in active duty in the armed forces or in certain other circumstances), physically fit for enrollment in ROTC, and graduated from an accredited secondary school with 16 or more academic units. Recommended course credits include 4 English, 3 social studies, 3 laboratory sciences, 3 foreign language, 3 mathematics (including 2 years of algebra and 1 of geometry), and 2 electives. The average GPA of incoming freshmen is approximately 3.3. Other qualifications include rank in the upper 50 percent of the senior class (significance of rank depends on class size and other factors), above-average scores on SAT or ACT, and satisfactory character recommendations. Extracurricular activities are viewed as favorable indicators of leadership and character traits. Transfer students are accepted, but two years of residency at VMI are required. Admissions standards are applied without regard to gender, race, nationality, or religion, and all factors are weighed in the final determination of the applicant's qualifications.

Application and Information

An application may be submitted anytime between September 1 and February 1 of the senior year in high school and should be accompanied by a nonrefundable $40 application fee, a transcript of the school record for grade 9 through the last completed semester, and SAT or ACT scores. Visits to the Institute are highly recommended. Open House visits are held throughout the academic year.

Interested students should contact:

Director of Admissions
Virginia Military Institute
Lexington, Virginia 24450
Phone: 540-464-7211
800-767-4207 (toll-free)
Fax: 540-464-7746
E-mail: admissions@vmi.edu
Web site: http://www.vmi.edu

VMI Barracks, a National Historic Landmark and home to the VMI Corps of Cadets.

WAGNER COLLEGE

STATEN ISLAND, NEW YORK

The College

Founded in 1883, Wagner College is a four-year, private residential college with a strong tradition in the liberal arts. Located in New York City's borough of Staten Island, the campus is situated atop Grymes Hill on the nineteenth-century estate of the Cunard family, founders of the famous shipping line. Wagner's 105-acre campus provides a setting that feels far away from the city; yet, Manhattan is just a free 25-minute ferry ride away. Recently, the College received attention for its nationally recognized curriculum, the Wagner Plan for the Practical Liberal Arts, which integrates courses across disciplines and directly connects course work to field experiences and internships. For the second year in a row, the College was named to *U.S. News & World Report*'s list of Up-and-Coming Schools, and it was also ranked first among master's degree-granting schools in the North. According to the magazine, the schools included in the Up-and-Coming category were singled out as those "that have recently made the most promising and innovative changes in academics, faculty, students, campus, or facilities." Only seventy-seven schools nationwide were included on this list. In a new category, Colleges with a Strong Commitment to Teaching, Wagner was again ranked first among northern master's schools. The College was also cited for its first-year experience, learning communities, and service learning in the magazine's Programs to Look For listing that recognizes "outstanding examples of academic programs that are commonly linked to student success." Wagner College is a member of the Associated New American Colleges, Project Pericles, and Colleges of Distinction.

Wagner enrolls approximately 1,950 undergraduate and 350 graduate students. About 80 percent of Wagner undergraduates live on campus in four residence halls, including a new residence hall for seniors that offers spectacular views of the New York Harbor, Manhattan, and the Atlantic Ocean. A fourth residence hall for seniors is currently being built and is expected to be ready in fall 2009. Students come from thirty-eight states and several other countries. Students choose Wagner because it offers excellent academic preparation, superb access to professional and cultural opportunities, and a traditional college campus setting. Students gain access to exceptional professional opportunities within the curriculum and through the College's large and supportive alumni base in the New York City area and beyond. Wagner strongly believes that career development is an integral part of a student's education—one that begins in a student's first year at Wagner and culminates in a senior year practicum in a specific field of study.

Student life is active on the campus with more than sixty different clubs and organizations, including both national and local fraternities and sororities. Wagner offers a full array of activities and social events, many of which are planned by the student life staff. Wagner expands students' experiences beyond the campus with trips around New York City to museums, concerts, professional sporting events, Broadway shows, and many other attractions.

The College offers outstanding athletics programs, which include NCAA Division I standing in twenty areas, many intramurals, and an excellent coaching staff. Athletic teams offered are men's baseball, basketball, football, golf, lacrosse, tennis, and track/cross-country and women's basketball, golf, lacrosse, soccer, softball, swimming, tennis, track/cross-country, and water polo; club sports are cheerleading and men's ice hockey.

In addition to undergraduate programs, Wagner offers master's degree programs in business administration (M.B.A.), education, microbiology, nursing, and physician assistant studies.

Location

Wagner's location offers students the best of both worlds. Living on a wooded campus 35 minutes from Manhattan has distinct advantages. The 105-acre campus overlooks New York Harbor and Manhattan. Students enjoy living in the beautiful Grymes Hill section of Staten Island and the proximity to the resources of Manhattan, which are easily accessible by bus, ferry, or car. Wagner has much to offer students who want the benefits of an education in New York City but who also wish to pursue their studies in a classic suburban college setting.

Majors and Degrees

Wagner College offers the Bachelor of Arts, Bachelor of Science, and Bachelor of Science in Education. Undergraduate majors and fields of concentration are in accounting (five-year program), anthropology, art, art history, arts administration, biology, biopsychology, business administration, city studies, chemistry, computer science, dance, economics, education, English, environmental studies, film/media studies, gender studies, government and politics, history, information systems, international affairs, journalism, mathematics, microbiology, modern languages, music, nursing, philosophy, physician assistant studies (five-year program), physics, psychology, public policy and administration, religious studies, sociology, and theater. Preprofessional programs are also available.

Academic Programs

Wagner's undergraduate program, the Wagner Plan, is designed to provide a broad education in the liberal arts and in-depth study in a major. Wagner also believes that students learn best by "reading, writing, and doing" and, therefore, incorporates field experiences directly into the curriculum. As part of the graduation requirements, students must complete three Learning Communities (LCs)—one in the first year, one in either sophomore or junior year, and one in the senior year in the major area of study. At Wagner, LCs consist of three courses that are linked by a single theme and share a common set of students. They are also directly connected to field experience based on the theme of the LC. Throughout the first semester, first-year students spend time at the designated site observing the organization, its practices, and its dynamics. Seniors are involved in a practicum connected to their major field of study.

Each candidate is required to complete 36 units for the baccalaureate degree. Students must elect a major as part of their studies and may select from more than sixty different majors, minors, and/or concentrations. Majors must be selected by the end of the sophomore year, with the exception of physician assistant studies and theater students, who must apply directly to the respective program. The academic year is divided into the fall semester (September–December) and spring semester (January–May). Students may also enroll in one of several summer sessions.

Off-Campus Programs

Wagner College is a member of the prestigious Institute for the International Education of Students (IES) program, which is the nation's oldest and most selective study-abroad program. Interested and qualified Wagner students may choose among semester, winter intersession (Expand Your Horizons program), summer, and vacation study-abroad programs in such diverse urban-based centers as Beijing, Berlin, Canberra, Dublin, LaPlata, London, Madrid, Paris, Tokyo, and Vienna. Classes are taught through a combination approach in which U.S. students take classes designed expressly for them by faculty members as well as classes run by universities located within the host city, thereby integrating the U.S. students with students from that nation. Wagner College also sponsors an exchange program with California Lutheran University, Universidad de Almeria in Spain, and Universite Lumiere, Lyon.

Academic Facilities

College facilities include twenty-four buildings for academic, recreational, and residential use. Wagner's recently updated science buildings house two electron microscopes and a fully functioning planetarium. Other facilities include a theater, a studio theater, an art gallery, a sports and fitness facility, an indoor pool, and a football stadium.

Computer facilities at Wagner are abundant and accessible. The Spiro Computer Technology Center features Pentium III PCs, while Novell network servers provide numerous application software programs for word processing, spreadsheet, graphics, statistical analysis, and programming languages. In addition, Wagner provides a Mac lab for graphics applications and a UNIX lab. The three residence halls are fully wired for free Internet and e-mail access in each room, along with a new voice-mail system and free cable. Students also have wireless Internet access in certain campus locations.

The Horrmann Library houses approximately 300,000 volumes as well as 1,000 titles in its periodical collection. The library is a member of the New York Metropolitan Reference and Research Agency, which provides access to more than 25 million volumes in the area.

Costs

Tuition for the 2009–10 academic year was $32,430. Room and board for the academic year were $9700.

Financial Aid

More than 70 percent of Wagner students receive some kind of financial aid. In addition to the availability of state and federal aid programs, the College itself is a source of more than $9 million in student aid each year. Counselors are available to assist in completing the Financial Aid Form.

Faculty

Because of its commitment to academic excellence, Wagner has always drawn a gifted faculty. Ninety-five percent of the 100 full-time faculty members hold a doctoral degree or the equivalent in their field. Many have published books and articles, and a large number have a combination of in-depth experience and academic qualifications. Wagner is strongly committed to keeping classes small and maintaining close relationships between faculty members and students; the student-faculty ratio is 13:1. Teaching is the first priority at Wagner, and all classes are taught by professors. Because faculty members are concerned about their students' intellectual and personal growth, they participate in all areas of College life. Faculty members regard New York City as an incomparable resource for course work and field experience.

Student Government

The Wagner College Student Government is democratically elected by the student body. The government has legislative and judicial responsibilities. Students have numerous opportunities for involvement in organizations, special interest groups, and committees. Activities and events are planned by students with the assistance of the director of cocurricular programs.

Admission Requirements

Admission to Wagner is based primarily on academic ability. The admission committee also considers personal qualities that, in the College's view, enable a student to take maximum advantage of what Wagner has to offer and to contribute to the quality of campus life.

The applicant is assessed on the basis of high school achievement, class rank, recommendations of the guidance counselor or academic teacher, standardized test scores (SAT or ACT), and an essay. In addition, the student's citizenship record (participation in extracurricular, community, or religious activities) and character record (including information derived from the recommendations) are reviewed. A personal interview is optional but recommended. Scores on the SAT or ACT are required, and SAT Subject Tests are recommended. None of these factors is considered in isolation; all are weighed together so that a clear picture of the applicant and his or her chances for success at Wagner emerge.

Students considering Wagner should have completed a minimum of 18 units in the following academic areas: English, 4; history, 3; mathematics, 3; foreign language, 2; and science, 2. Four additional units from the following list of electives are recommended: art, 1; computer science, 1; foreign language, 2–4; history, 1–3; mathematics, 1–3; music, 1–2; natural sciences, 1–3; religion, 1; and social studies, 1–2.

Application and Information

Application should be made early in the senior year of high school. In addition to the completed application form and the nonrefundable fee, students are responsible for forwarding a secondary school transcript, two letters of recommendation, their personal essay, and SAT or ACT scores to the Admissions Office. The early decision application deadline is January 1. The deadline for the theater program is December 1, and it is December 1 for physician assistant studies. The general application deadline is February 15, and there is a final application deadline of March 15.

Candidates are urged, whenever possible, to make an appointment with the Admissions Office to visit the campus and discuss their plans and goals with a member of the admission staff. They are also encouraged to talk with currently enrolled Wagner students. Arrangements can be made for candidates to meet with faculty members in departments of particular interest.

Further information may be obtained by contacting:

Admissions Office
Wagner College
1 Campus Road
Staten Island, New York 10301
Phone: 718-390-3411
800-221-1010 (toll-free outside New York)
Fax: 718-390-3105
E-mail: admissions@wagner.edu
Web site: http://www.wagner.edu

Wagner students in front of Main Hall.

COLLEGE CLOSE-UPS

WALSH UNIVERSITY

NORTH CANTON, OHIO

The University

Walsh University is a fully accredited, liberal arts and sciences Catholic university in North Canton, Ohio, offering fifty majors, five graduate programs, and an accelerated-degree program for working adults. With 2,900 students and a 15:1 student-faculty ratio, the University offers a very friendly, personable, and safe campus and a unique broad-based curriculum with close student-faculty interaction. Most residence halls and academic buildings on Walsh's 136-acre campus are new or have been renovated within the last several years, providing state-of-the-art facilities for students. Walsh also offers generous financial aid packages to 95 percent of full-time students.

Active and involved in campus and community life, more than 60 percent of Walsh students participate in extracurricular programs. Students also enjoy intramural and intercollegiate sports programs that include football, baseball, soccer, and volleyball to name a few. Walsh's Division II NAIA athletic teams have won national championships.

Walsh University welcomes students from around the world of all faiths and backgrounds. The University currently has students from numerous countries and looks forward to continued growth.

Walsh University was founded in 1960 by the Brothers of Christian Instruction and is accredited by the North Central Association/Higher Learning Commission, National League for Nursing Accrediting Commission, Ohio Department of Education, Ohio Board of Counseling and Social Work, American Physical Therapy Association, the Commission on Accreditation in Physical Therapy Education, Council for Accreditation of Counseling and Related Educational Programs, and the National Council for Accreditation of Teacher Education. Walsh is a member of the Ohio College Association, the National Association of Independent Colleges and Universities, and the Association of Catholic Colleges and Universities.

In addition to its undergraduate degree programs, Walsh offers five graduate degree programs in business (M.B.A.), counseling and human development, education (M.A.Ed.), physical therapy (D.P.T.), and theology.

Location

Walsh University has a beautiful, tree-lined campus located just 3 miles east of I-77 in North Canton, a safe, pleasant residential suburban community. Canton, which is about 5 miles south of the Walsh campus, is a city of 84,000 that offers a wide array of cultural, recreational, and athletic activities. Home of the Professional Football Hall of Fame, the President McKinley National Memorial, and the National First Ladies Library, the city also hosts a symphony orchestra, an art museum, and a civic opera, theater guild, and ballet. A number of major companies are headquartered in Stark County, including the Hoover Company, the Timken Company, and Diebold, Inc.

Majors and Degrees

Bachelor of Arts and Bachelor of Science degrees are offered in the following majors: accounting (general and specialized CPA tracks), bioinformatics, biology, chemistry, clinical laboratory science, communication, computer science, corporate communication, education (early childhood, middle childhood, adolescence to young adulthood, integrated language arts, integrated mathematics teacher licensure, integrated science teacher licensure, integrated social studies teacher, intervention specialist, life science/biology teacher licensure, life science/biology and chemistry teacher licensure, and multiage physical education), English, finance, French, general business, history, international studies, management, management information systems, marketing, mathematics, museum studies, nursing, philosophy/theology, physical education, political science, psychology, sociology, and Spanish.

Walsh offers preprofessional programs in dentistry, law, medicine, natural resources, optometry, physical therapy, podiatry, and veterinary science. Each is developed within the context of a regular academic major. Walsh's physical therapy graduates have the option to continue their studies by entering Walsh's newly accredited Doctor of Physical Therapy degree program. Students enrolled in the University's B.A./M.A. program can earn a bachelor's degree in behavioral science and a master's degree in counseling and human development in 5½ years. An affiliation with Case Western Reserve University's (CWRU) program in dentistry leads to a B.S. from Walsh and ultimately a D.D.S. from CWRU.

In addition, Walsh offers the Associate of Arts degree in accounting, finance, human services, liberal arts management, and marketing.

Academic Programs

The student's academic program comprises courses within the liberal arts, a major field of study, and elective courses. Major course work, constituting one fourth or more of a student's program of studies, is designed to help students prepare for their careers. Forty percent of a student's program of studies is within the liberal arts. Elective courses, which constitute the remaining portion of a student's program of studies, enable students to develop personal interests, take more courses within their major field, or enroll in additional core courses. The University encourages students to give careful thought to selecting a program of study and a major. While many students select double majors as a way to improve their career opportunities, the design of individual programs requires consultation with a faculty adviser and a division chair. To earn a bachelor's degree, students must successfully complete 130 semester hours.

Designed for the academically gifted, the honors program offers challenges that lead students to achieve academic excellence. Honors students take advantage of such offerings as special seminars, independent studies, internships, and research projects.

The University's School for Professional Studies Program is for working adults who have earned college credits and who wish to earn their bachelor's degree in an accelerated format. Classes are scheduled on nights and weekends to accommodate busy schedules.

Academic Facilities

The Walsh Library contains 130,000 volumes, 630 current periodical subscriptions on paper, thousands of online periodicals, a curriculum library, and an audiovisual collection.

Databases bring many full-text articles immediately for download or print, and information technology systems enable online requests for physical delivery of material, often via rapid courier. Library staff members give introductory lectures on research techniques. The library has a quiet study room, a snack lounge, and a mini-theater.

Faculty

Walsh University fosters close working relationships between faculty members and students. Beyond classroom teaching, faculty members serve as student counselors and tutors and take on roles as advisers for student organizations. The Walsh faculty is composed of full-time, part-time, and adjunct members. The student-faculty ratio is 15:1. The majority of full-time faculty members hold Ph.D.'s or terminal degrees in their respective fields.

Student Government

Walsh University Student Government provides capable, responsible student governance. Through its executive, legislative, and judicial branches, it fosters student involvement in the governance of the University, serves as a forum for student opinion, and functions as a liaison between students, faculty and staff members, and the administration. Along with the Student Affairs staff, it plans student activities and community projects.

Costs

Tuition for the 2009–10 academic year was $20,550. Tuition, fees, and room and board charges total approximately $29,350 per year and vary by residence hall. Books and personal expenses cost an estimated $700–$900 for the year. The University reserves the right to change the cost structure without notice.

Financial Aid

Walsh is dedicated to providing outstanding liberal arts education at an affordable price. The primary purpose of Walsh University's financial aid program is to assist deserving students who cannot otherwise meet the costs of a college education. Financial aid takes the form of scholarships, work-study awards, grants, or loans, depending upon the resources available. The University offers a number of scholarships in amounts from $1500 to full tuition, in addition to institutional need-based grants. The Alumni Association offers scholarships as well. State and federal grants and loans are available to students along with the University's work-study program that provides work compatible with a student's academic schedule. Financial aid is awarded for one year and is renewable in subsequent years if the student shows a continuing need and maintains an appropriate academic record.

Applicants for admission may apply for financial aid by submitting the Free Application for Federal Student Aid (FAFSA) and the University's financial aid form. To allow for timely notification of financial awards, the University recommends that the FAFSA be mailed by March 15 in order to receive full analysis by May 1. Prospective students may obtain a FAFSA from their high school guidance counselor or from the University's financial aid office. The Walsh financial aid form is available from the financial aid and admissions offices of the University.

Admission Requirements

Every student seeking admission to Walsh University is reviewed individually to assess the student's ability to meet the rigors of the University's curriculum. The composition of high school classes, grades achieved, class rank, and standardized test scores are all taken into consideration before an admission decision is rendered. Essays and interviews are highly recommended but not required.

Walsh grants credit for college-level work completed in high school and for credits earned through the College Level Examination Program. Qualified high school juniors and seniors may enroll for college credit under the University's postsecondary enrollment program. The University seeks a diverse student body.

Application and Information

Early application is recommended. Walsh University operates under a rolling admissions policy. The completed admission application, $25 application fee, ACT or SAT scores, and a high school transcript are required for a student's application to be considered for admission. Transfer students must also submit transcripts from all colleges and universities attended.

Interested students are encouraged to contact:

Brett Freshour
Dean of Enrollment Management
Walsh University
2020 East Maple Street NW
North Canton, Ohio 44720-3336
Phone: 330-492-7172
800-362-9846 (toll-free)
Fax: 330-490-7165
E-mail: admissions@walsh.edu
Web site: http://www.walsh.edu

On the campus of Walsh University.

WARNER PACIFIC COLLEGE

PORTLAND, OREGON

The College

Located in the heart of Portland, Oregon, Warner Pacific College offers an ideal home for exploring the thrilling range of cultures, places, and ideas that urban settings afford. Warner also prepares the next generation of leaders by providing educational opportunities in the liberal arts, purposefully taught with a Christian worldview. Its academic programs encourage students to explore life's most significant questions and learn to manage complex answers. The distinctive humanities core curriculum is designed to explore the paradoxes inherent in the human experience through a foundation of faith. Most importantly, Warner Pacific's liberal arts program equips students to lead and serve in a world challenged by a rapidly changing cultural landscape.

The city of Portland draws people from around the globe. It's one of the richest, most dynamic places to experience and appreciate new perspectives, art forms, foods, and cultures—and to prepare for life in today's increasingly metropolitan world. Warner Pacific College strives to develop opportunities as well as structured internships for students that reflect personal interests and career goals. The school has an extensive network of connections around Portland and a reputation for providing excellent interns. Giving students an opportunity to gain valuable hands-on experience in their chosen fields is a top priority in all of Warner Pacific's academic departments.

Warner Pacific embraces its role as a light of Christ in the city. Nationally recognized for its commitment to community service, the College was named to the 2009 President's Higher Education Community Service Honor Roll. Through various outreach projects and class projects, students engage in activities such as reading to school children, painting murals at local elementary schools, serving hot chocolate to the homeless, and doing landscaping at shelters for women and children. Beyond Portland, Warner Pacific's Missions program offers at least two major service trips a year to countries along the Pacific Rim, as well as to U.S. cities like San Francisco and New Orleans. Additionally, students can spend a semester studying abroad through the Best Semester program offered by the Coalition for Christian Colleges and Universities.

Student life at Warner Pacific is lively and dynamic. The campus is alive with activity, including residence life events aimed at building community, intramurals, drama, music, multicultural events, and ethics-bowl competition. Warner Pacific is a member of the National Association of Intercollegiate Athletics (NAIA Division II) and the Cascade Collegiate Conference. Women's sports include basketball, cross-country, golf, soccer, track and field, and volleyball. Men compete in basketball, cross-country, golf, soccer, and track and field.

Total undergraduate enrollment at Warner Pacific exceeds 1,100, with students representing eighteen states, twelve countries, and twenty-seven denominations. The College has recently opened a new dining hall, coffee shop, bookstore, and student services building. All student residences have been remodeled since 2006; options include traditional men's and women's residence halls, apartments, and houses. Residence rooms offer private phones and individual high-speed Internet connections. Wireless Internet connections are available for students throughout the campus.

Location

Warner Pacific is an urban campus adjacent to 195-acre Mount Tabor Park, just 10 minutes from downtown Portland, Oregon. Situated in the beautiful Pacific Northwest, the city of Portland was named one of the best places to live in the U.S. by CNN, *Money,* and *Outside* magazines and the greenest city in the U.S. according to SustainLane.com. It is consistently listed in the top 10 for walking, biking, and other fitness activities. In fact, Portland is known as "FitTown, USA" according to *Fit* magazine. With reliable bus and light-rail transportation available, students are able to take advantage of diverse cultural, recreational, employment, and internship opportunities. Snow-capped mountains, rugged coastlines, and the Columbia Gorge are all an hour away, where students enjoy skiing, hiking, kayaking, windsurfing, and exploring nature—and discovering why the Pacific Northwest is one of the most beautiful regions in North America.

Majors and Degrees

Warner Pacific offers Associate of Arts (A.A.) and Associate of Science (A.S.) degrees as well as Bachelor of Arts (B.A.) and Bachelor of Science (B.S.) degrees. Majors include accounting, American studies, biological science (general biology and human biology emphases), business administration, communications, early childhood education/elementary education, education, English, health and human kinetics (exercise science and health fitness management emphases), history, history and social studies, human development, human development and family studies, liberal studies, music (music performance, music studies, and music theory/composition emphases), music business, music education, music and youth ministries, physical sciences, psychology, religion and Christian ministries, social science, social work, urban studies, and worship arts leadership.

Academic Programs

In order to provide Christian excellence and an individualized education, students take courses in three categories: core studies, a major area of study, and elective credits. In general, each of these categories requires a third of a student's total program. A minor may be chosen as a part of the elective program. Unique at Warner Pacific is the humanities core curriculum, which is based on an interdisciplinary approach to learning designed to explore the ethical and pragmatic dilemmas of the human experience.

Students at the school are encouraged to think deeply about what it means to be a person of integrity and faith in a needy and increasingly urbanized world and to articulate their beliefs.

Course work to complete a bachelor's degree is available during the summer. It is also possible for students at Warner Pacific to personalize their education by designing their own major.

The College operates on a semester calendar. The core studies include a minimum of 42 semester credits divided among specific requirements in communications, humanities, religion, mathematics, laboratory science, social science, fine arts, and physical education/health. The major area of study requires completion of certain courses as specified in the College course catalog. The remainder of the credits may be earned through elective course work and/or a minor concentration, for a total of 124 semester credit hours.

Special study options include: academic remediation for entering students, accelerated degree programs, adult/continuing education programs, Advanced Placement credit, cooperative education, double majors, honors programs, independent study, internships, off-campus study, part-time degree programs, services for LD students, student-designed majors, study abroad, summer session for credit, and Air Force ROTC.

The Teacher Education program is approved by the Oregon Teacher Standards and Practices Commission. Teacher licensure may be achieved as part of a four-year bachelor degree program, or as a post-baccalaureate licensure program. Extended field-based practicums and student-teaching experiences are an integral part of the program.

Off-Campus Programs

Through the Oregon Independent Colleges Association, Warner Pacific has cooperative relationships with all of the regionally accredited private colleges and universities in the state. In addition, Warner Pacific accepts the completed Associate of Arts transfer degree from Oregon community colleges and the Associate of Arts direct transfer agreement (DTA) degree from Clark College in Vancouver, Washington, as having fulfilled the core requirements, with the exception of two religion and two upper-division humanities courses.

ROTC programs are available in cooperation with the University of Portland; study opportunities and laboratory access at the Oregon Health Sciences University in Portland are also available. The College participates in a consortium of colleges that maintains the Malheur (eastern Oregon) High Desert Study Center and is a member of the Council for Christian Colleges and Universities, which provides study opportunities in Oxford, England; Cairo, Egypt; Israel (Middle East Studies); Russia; Latin America; China; Sydney, Australia; Uganda; Los Angeles, California (Film Studies); Martha's Vineyard (Contemporary Music Studies); and Washington, D.C. (American Studies).

Academic Facilities

The Otto F. Linn Library provides study areas and housing for a collection of nearly 60,000 books and 450 periodicals. WPC World Cat is a new one-search interface for the library catalog. It allows a search not only of the WPC library's collection, but also Summit and World Cat, the catalog of the world's biggest library network.

Two biology, one physics, and two chemistry labs, and an electron microscope are available. A large performing arts auditorium features concerts and other performances and the Cellar Theatre delivers teacher- and student-led dramatic productions. There is a student computer lab as well as modem access in every student residence and wireless access in academic buildings.

Costs

Annual costs for the 2009–10 academic year were $16,974 for tuition (12 to 18 credits per semester), $630 mandatory fees, and $6980 for room and board.

Full-time tuition and fees vary according to course load, degree level, location, reciprocity agreements, and student level.

Financial Aid

Warner Pacific believes that any student who demonstrates the ability and motivation to learn should have access to Christian higher education; therefore, the staff is committed to helping parents and students find the necessary financial resources through federal and state assistance, personal and federally insured loans, private scholarships and programs, institutional assistance, and parental and student contributions. Approximately 97 percent of Warner Pacific students receive some type of aid, whether institutional or otherwise.

In 2009–10, the average Warner Pacific student received $9462 from a combination of institutional, state, and federal grants; and scholarships available at WPC. As a result, total costs at the college are 15 percent lower than the average four-year private institution, according to a U.S. Department of Education study. Students should submit a completed FAFSA to the federal processor as soon after January 1 as possible.

The College manages nearly $3 million in institutional assistance each year in the form of competitive academic merit scholarships and fellowships, talent grants in athletics, drama, music, international student awards, assistance designed to enhance ethnic diversity on campus, various types of church-related assistance (including a $1000 grant to members of the Church of God, which is headquartered in Anderson, Indiana), and awards for dependents of alumni. The scholarship priority application deadline is February 1. Students may be eligible to work on campus and are assisted in locating employment off campus.

Faculty

Warner Pacific faculty members are committed to excellence. With a 12:1 student-faculty ratio and small class sizes, students receive the individualized attention that meaningful scholarship requires. Each course is embedded with critical ethical issues relevant to the subject matter. Students are challenged to think critically and reflect deeply to find their place in an increasingly complex world. Students thrive under the leadership of dedicated professors, many of whom serve as mentors, academic advisers, and advisers to student organizations and clubs.

Student Government

Democratic self-government is essential to the development of maturity, judgment, and leadership. Student life at Warner Pacific mirrors this process. Students, administration, and faculty members enter into this process by mutual consent. The Associated Students of Warner Pacific College (ASWPC) is the executive body, composed of duly elected and appointed officers and representatives. The ASWPC, operating under its own grant of powers, creates policy that contributes to the governance of student life and activities and organizes such activities. It develops and coordinates an active social and spiritual life program to meet the needs of all students.

Admission Requirements

Warner Pacific College selects candidates for admissions who value a Christ-centered liberal arts education and provide evidence of academic achievement, aptitude, and the ability to benefit from and contribute to the opportunities at the College. Graduation from an accredited high school (or the test equivalent) is required for admission. A strong college-preparatory program is recommended. A minimum GPA of 2.5 along with a combined SAT score (critical reading and math) of at least 910 or an ACT composite score of at least 19 is required. The GPA of first-time freshmen averages 3.23. Official transcripts from each high school, college, or university attended should be sent directly from the institution to the Office of Admissions. An essay and signed community covenant is also required, along with a nonrefundable application fee of $50. A personal interview and references may be required. Students with a GPA of less than 2.5 may be considered for provisional acceptance. Transfer students with more than 20 semester credit hours are required to have a minimum 2.0 cumulative college GPA (4.0 scale).

Application and Information

Warner Pacific has a priority deadline of January 31 and a regular deadline of March 15. Applications are also accepted on a rolling basis throughout the calendar year. Applicants can expect official notification of acceptance status within 24 hours of receipt of all required materials. Requests for further information and all forms should be addressed to:

Admissions Office
Warner Pacific College
2219 Southeast 68th Avenue
Portland, Oregon 97215
Phone: 503-517-1020
800-804-1510 (toll-free)
Fax: 503-517-1352
E-mail: admissions@warnerpacific.edu
Web site: http://www.warnerpacific.edu

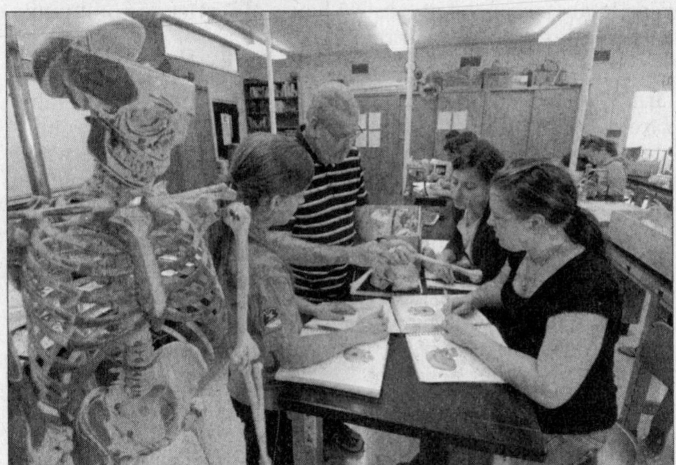

Located in Portland, Oregon, Warner Pacific is an urban, Christ-centered liberal arts college with a reduced tuition that makes it one of the most affordable private colleges in the Pacific Northwest.

WARREN WILSON COLLEGE

ASHEVILLE, NORTH CAROLINA

The College

Warren Wilson College is distinctive among American colleges and universities. Strong environmental and international emphases enhance a learning triad of academics, work, and service. The College also is recognized as a campus leader in sustainable practices and facilities. As Samuel Schuman described Warren Wilson in his book *Old Main*: "Rather like Orwell's barnyard menagerie, all small colleges are unique, but some are more unique than others. [Warren Wilson's] program, emphases, population, and atmosphere are unmistakably its own."

Since its founding in 1894, Warren Wilson College has educated students with its unique blending of a strong liberal arts program, work for the College, and service to those in need—a triad that makes Warren Wilson unlike any other college. Its 900 undergraduate students come from forty-five states and twenty countries, creating a diverse and vibrant academic community.

The academic program features a first-rate faculty that does all of the teaching and frequently participates in research with students. About 85 percent of classes have fewer than 20 students, and discussion is an important part of teaching. Twenty-one majors are offered, with a commitment to quality in each program. Art, English, creative writing, biology, outdoor leadership, and the nationally recognized environmental studies program are the most popular majors.

Students at Warren Wilson are integral to the day-to-day operation of the College. Each student works 15 hours a week at a job that is essential to running the school. This experience helps build student confidence (students learn that there is no job they cannot learn to do) and a strong sense of community at the College. Many juniors and seniors have work assignments that coincide with their majors. Students receive a work stipend in the amount of $3480 each year for the work they do.

Service is also integral to the College's way of thinking. Warren Wilson is one of only a few colleges in the country that require student participation in community service for graduation. Service is offered to a wide range of nonprofit organizations and agencies in the Asheville area and beyond. Students must engage in an average of at least 25 hours of service to community each year as a graduation requirement.

The College's 1,100-acre campus includes a 300-acre working farm, 600 acres of managed forest, a 6-acre fruit and vegetable garden and 20 miles of hiking trails. The campus and surrounding area are havens for outdoor activities such as white-water sports, hiking, camping, mountain biking, and rock climbing.

About 90 percent of students and 30 percent of faculty and staff live on campus. The College offers men's and women's intercollegiate basketball, cross-country, soccer, and swimming, and its mountain bike has finished in the top three nationally (Division II) for the past seven years. The College also offers intramural sports, a wellness program, and a wide range of outdoor programs among other activities.

Location

Warren Wilson, on the edge of the city of Asheville, North Carolina, is in the heart of the Blue Ridge Mountains. Asheville, a city of about 80,000 people, is considered one of the most livable cities in the United States and was selected by the National League of Cities as the All-America City for 1998.

Surrounded by more than 1 million acres of national forest, Asheville is located in an ideal setting, presenting views of outstanding beauty throughout all four seasons. In the spring and summer, variations in altitude together with warm southern sun favor native vegetation; dogwood, wildflowers, rhododendron, mountain laurel, and azaleas cover the mountains. The arresting beauty of the autumn colors attracts photographers, artists, and sports enthusiasts from the world over. During the winter, natural snow is enhanced by machine-made snow, producing excellent downhill skiing.

A short drive from the Warren Wilson campus are Great Smoky Mountains National Park, Pisgah National Forest, and the Blue Ridge Parkway, offering panoramic views, excellent camping facilities, and a perfect setting for class field trips.

Majors and Degrees

The bachelor's degree is awarded in art, biology, chemistry, creative writing, English, environmental studies, gender and women's studies, history and political science, global studies, integrative studies, mathematics, modern language, outdoor leadership, philosophy, psychology, religious studies, social work, and sociology/anthropology.

Academic Programs

The goal of the degree program at Warren Wilson College is the completion of three well-designed areas of study. First, students are expected to complete a core of required courses based on the theme "ways of knowing." A student earns 4 credits in each of the ten core areas. Second, students must develop a strength in one or more disciplines. A minimum of 128 semester hours is required for the baccalaureate degree, including the core plus major hours. Finally, a student must demonstrate the ability to work effectively with others by participation in the work and service programs.

There is a required freshman seminar designed to provide new students the opportunity to explore various fields. A senior seminar, designed as a capstone experience, is required, as is a senior letter to evaluate the student's college experiences.

All Warren Wilson students must demonstrate competence in writing and mathematics either through testing or by completing core courses.

Each semester in the academic calendar is broken into two 8-week terms. A student typically takes four courses per semester (3 or 4 credit hours per course).

Off-Campus Programs

In addition to academics, work, and service, all qualified students are afforded the opportunity to study abroad. The College heavily subsidizes the cost for a cross-cultural international experience taken during the junior year or summer.

Academic Facilities

The Martha Ellison Library houses a collection of 120,000 books and 450 periodicals. It provides written records in all areas of the College curriculum and contributes to the cultural enrichment of students. The library is open and served by librarians and student assistants 75 hours each week. The building provides open access to books and periodicals during these hours. Individual carrels, lounge areas, and microfilm readers and printers are available, and there are Windows and Macintosh computers that students may use as word processors or for other prescribed purposes, including access to the Internet.

Computerized literature searching is available. The Martha Ellison Library is a teaching library, providing extensive and continuing bibliographic services, including courses, for the entire student body. Any resource materials not owned by the library may be acquired through interlibrary loan.

The campus arts complex includes the modern Kittredge Theater; the Kittredge Music Wing, housing classrooms, studios, and a performance area; the Holden Arts Center, with a gallery, classrooms, studios, and a lecture hall; and an outdoor amphitheater. Instruction and performance events also take place in the chapel and the Craftshop/Ceramics Studio.

Costs

Total costs for the 2009–10 school year are $31,966. From this amount, the student's work program stipend of $3480 is deducted, leaving an actual cost of $28,486 for each student before any other aid.

Financial Aid

Warren Wilson offers a comprehensive financial aid program that seeks to enroll students from all economic backgrounds. This is accomplished through a combination of work, loans, grants, entitlements, and scholarships to students who complete their file prior to May. Students and their families should file the FAFSA and the Warren Wilson Financial Aid Application to be considered for all possible funds.

Faculty

The teaching faculty consists of 70 full-time members. Of these, 93 percent hold doctoral degrees. All classes and labs are taught by faculty members, not graduate students. Faculty members—1 for every 12 students—are available after class, during regular office hours, and in their homes.

Student Government

The student body is involved in the democratic decision-making process of the College. A wide variety of leadership positions, elected and appointed, are open to students. Campuswide elections provide opportunities for student involvement in Student Caucus, Judicial Board and other College advisory committees. Student Caucus, the representative voice of the student body, is also responsible for appointing students to positions on approximately fifteen other campus committees ranging from Admission to Library to Buildings and Grounds.

Admission Requirements

Admission to Warren Wilson College is based on both the personal and the academic qualifications of the applicant.

The selection criteria are devised to choose a student body with high standards of scholarship and personal goals and a willingness to provide community service.

Each candidate for admission must present an academic transcript from a secondary school. The transcript must show at least 12 academic units (a unit is one year's study in one subject). At least 4 years of English, 2 years of algebra, 1 year of geometry, 2 years of laboratory science, and 2 years of history are recommended for admission. Performance during high school is the best predictor of success in college. Therefore, great emphasis is placed upon the high school record. Grade trends can be very important.

Applicants must submit a recommendation from their high school counselor and scores from the SAT or ACT. Students are also required to submit a personal essay.

Transfer students must present both high school and college transcripts. Transfer applicants must be in good standing with the college last attended and should also have a minimum 2.75 cumulative grade point average. At least one school year in residence at Warren Wilson is required for a transfer student to be eligible for a degree from Warren Wilson College.

There is no fee to apply for admission to Warren Wilson College.

Application and Information

An application form and further information may be obtained by contacting:

Office of Admission
Warren Wilson College
P.O. Box 9000
Asheville, North Carolina 28815-9000
Phone: 800-934-3536 (toll-free)
E-mail: admit@warren-wilson.edu
Web site: http://www.warren-wilson.edu

Warren Wilson College's Blue Ridge Mountains home.

WASHINGTON COLLEGE

CHESTERTOWN, MARYLAND

The College

Founded in 1782, Washington College is the tenth-oldest college in the United States. George Washington, for whom the College was named, was an early benefactor and member of the College's Board of Visitors and Governors. Today, the College is one of the few nationally recognized selective liberal arts institutions with an enrollment of fewer than 1,350 students. The intimacy of a small-college environment, the tradition of a challenging liberal arts curriculum, and the relaxed informality characteristic of the Chesapeake Bay region continue to exert their influence on the College and all who come to it.

The current enrollment is 1,300 men and women. Although most students come from the Northeast, international students and students from other regions of the country are enrolled in numbers sufficient to add geographic diversity to the student body. Eighty percent of all students live in residences located on the 120-acre campus; special interest housing is available for students interested in science, foreign languages, international studies, creative arts, and Greek organizations.

The College enjoys a high participation rate in intramural sports, in the performing arts, and in student publications, community service clubs, recreational activities, and social organizations. The Division III intercollegiate program offers fifteen varsity sports, including baseball, basketball, lacrosse, rowing, soccer, swimming, and tennis for men and basketball, field hockey, lacrosse, rowing, sailing, softball, swimming, tennis, and volleyball for women.

Location

Chestertown, a community of 4,000 people, is a popular port-of-call for Chesapeake Bay boaters, outdoors enthusiasts, and tourists on day trips from nearby Philadelphia, Baltimore, and Washington, D.C. The center of this eighteenth-century river town, with its historic district, shops, and restaurants, is a 5-minute walk from campus. The "town-gown" relationship is excellent.

Majors and Degrees

The Bachelor of Arts is awarded in American studies, anthropology, art, business management, drama, economics, English, environmental studies, French, German, history, humanities, international studies, mathematics, music, philosophy, political science, psychology, sociology, and Spanish. The Bachelor of Science is awarded in biology, chemistry, physics, and psychology.

Washington College also offers certification programs in elementary and secondary education. Preprofessional programs in dentistry, medicine, or veterinary medicine may be developed within a major in the natural sciences; a preprofessional program in law is also available. A 3-2 dual-degree program in engineering with the University of Maryland, a 3-2 dual-degree program in nursing with Johns Hopkins University, and a 3-4 dual-degree program in pharmacy with the University of Maryland are also offered.

Academic Programs

The College's four-course plan is intended to broaden and deepen a student's education by providing for the intensive study of a limited number of subjects and by encouraging individual responsibility for learning. General education requirements include two freshman seminars and ten semester courses chosen from the following categories: social science, natural science, humanities, fine arts, quantitative studies, and foreign language. Candidates for a degree must satisfactorily complete thirty-two semester courses and must fulfill the senior obligation (for example, a comprehensive examination or thesis).

Washington College offers a nationally renowned creative writing program and awards the prestigious Sophie Kerr Prize every year to the graduating senior who shows the most promise for a career in literary endeavors.

Successful scores (4 or 5) on Advanced Placement examinations can provide exemption from distribution requirements. With the aid of a faculty adviser, students can construct their own major fields of study in some areas or pursue independent study for course credit.

Off-Campus Programs

At Washington College, students have multiple opportunities to become engaged in experiences designed to enhance their learning outside the classroom. The College's proximity to the major cities of Baltimore, Philadelphia, and Washington, D.C., as well as the Delmarva Peninsula, makes it possible for students to gain experience as members of premier governmental, commercial, scientific, and artistic organizations while undertaking internships, research, and participation in a variety of model programs. A study-abroad program is offered at thirty sites worldwide, including sites in England, France, Spain, Germany, Scotland, Mexico, and Japan.

Academic Facilities

The library, which has 200,000 volumes, more than 800 current periodical subscriptions, and extensive microfilm holdings, benefits from an efficient interlibrary loan system and an online card catalog. The 45,000-square-foot John S. Toll Science Center provides teaching laboratories, research laboratories, and laboratory-support space for science majors. Roy Kirby Stadium opened in 2006 and provides a state-of-the-art synthetic playing surface for men's and women's lacrosse, men's and women's soccer, and field hockey teams. The Gibson Fine Arts Center reopened in August 2009 after undergoing a $25-million renovation and expansion. The facility is home to drama and music programs and includes the Kohl Gallery. Full facilities for art majors are located in the Constance S. Larrabee Creative Art Center. Hodson Commons, a new student center and dining center, opened in November 2009.

Costs

Tuition and fees for 2009–10 were $35,350 and room and board were $7460, making a total of $42,810. Expenses, including books and transportation, usually range from $600 to $1000 annually.

Financial Aid

Washington College offers financial assistance to approximately 85 percent of its student body. Awards are based on need and academic performance. Financial aid includes scholarships, grants, loans, and jobs. The College participates in the Federal Perkins Loan Program, the Federal Stafford Student Loan

Program, and the Federal Work-Study Program. Federal Pell Grants and Federal Supplemental Educational Opportunity Grants are applicable to Washington College. In addition, financial assistance from the Maryland scholarship program and other state programs can be applied to expenses at the College.

Members of the National Honor Society and Cum Laude Society who are admitted to Washington College are awarded $50,000 academic scholarships ($12,500 annually for four years). Other academic scholarships ranging in value from $7500 to $17,500 are offered without regard to financial need.

To be eligible for financial assistance, applicants should file the FAFSA by February 15. An application for admission, with all supporting credentials, should be received by February 15 to establish eligibility. Students interested in Federal Pell Grant assistance or in-state scholarship programs must apply directly to the program concerned.

Faculty

Ninety-five percent of the more than 100 full-time faculty members hold either a doctoral degree or a terminal degree in their discipline. Faculty members engage in professional research and publication but emphasize teaching. Along with performing their classroom duties, faculty members serve as advisers to individuals and student groups. No classes are taught by graduate assistants. Faculty participation in student and College affairs reflects the strong sense of community that characterizes Washington College.

Student Government

The Student Government Association (SGA) is a significant part of the College community. In addition to coordinating social activities, the SGA plays an active role in academic affairs. Students elected by the SGA are voting members of College committees and attend faculty and board meetings.

Admission Requirements

High school students should complete a college-preparatory program, including a minimum of 4 years of English, 4 of social studies, 3 of mathematics, 3 of science, and 2 of a foreign language. SAT or ACT scores and one teacher recommendation are also required. While interviews are not usually required for admission, interested students are strongly encouraged to visit the campus. Both interviews and campus tours are available by appointment on weekdays throughout the year and on selected Saturdays during the fall semester.

Members of the College admission staff visit high schools throughout the United States, seeking above-average students with solid academic backgrounds. There are no quotas based on sex, and there are no religious, geographic, or ethnic restrictions. Indeed, the College seeks the most diverse student body possible, realizing that such diversity is an important aspect of the academic community.

Transfer students are accepted with or without the A.A. degree, and applicants with above-average records are encouraged to apply.

Application and Information

The application, a $50 fee, the high school transcript (and college transcript, for transfer applicants), scores on the SAT or ACT, and one teacher recommendation are required. Applications for early decision must be received by November 15, and candidates are notified of the admission decision by December 15. For regular admission, forms must be submitted prior to February 15. Regular decision candidates are notified of the admission decision on a rolling basis between January 15 and March 1. Applicants for financial assistance must complete the procedures outlined in the Financial Aid section.

Further information and application forms are available from:

Office of Admissions
Washington College
300 Washington Avenue
Chestertown, Maryland 21620-1197
Phone: 410-778-7700
800-422-1782 (toll-free)
E-mail: adm.off@washcoll.edu
Web site: http://www.washcoll.edu

Casey Academic Center at Washington College.

COLLEGE CLOSE-UPS

WEBBER INTERNATIONAL UNIVERSITY

BABSON PARK, FLORIDA

The University

Webber International University was founded in 1927 by Roger Babson, who was an internationally known economist in the early 1900s. The four-year independent coeducational university is located on a beautiful 110-acre campus along the shoreline of Lake Caloosa, 45 minutes from Disney World, Cypress Gardens, and many other attractions. Webber is accredited by the Southern Association of Colleges and Schools and internationally by the International Assembly for Collegiate Business Education. Built on a strong tradition that sets it apart, the University exemplifies integrity, high standards, and achievement. Webber International University provides an environment that encourages success through academic excellence and hard work. About 600 students are enrolled as undergraduates at Webber; 22 percent of the students are international and represent forty-three different countries.

Webber International University offers day, evening, weekend, and now online classes with the flexibility to fit any busy schedule. Webber's off-campus internship programs provide a real-world business environment for Webber students. Field trips also supplement students' business education.

Webber International University also offers a Master of Business Administration (M.B.A.) program with options in management, accounting, sport management, security management, and international business (online).

The University offers intercollegiate sports in baseball, basketball, beach volleyball, bowling, cross-country, football, golf, soccer, tennis, and track and field for men and basketball, beach volleyball, bowling, cheerleading, cross-country, golf, soccer, softball, tennis, track and field, and volleyball for women. For the musically talented student, the University has a marching band. Intramural athletics are also available for all students. The University's physical education complex includes two gymnasiums, a fitness room, a soccer field, a junior Olympic-size swimming pool, beach volleyball court, and tennis courts. Webber students also enjoy lakeside activities such as beach volleyball, canoeing, fishing, and kayaking. Among the wide variety of social organizations and clubs are Phi Beta Lambda, a student government association, an international club, Webber ambassadors, Eta Sigma Delta and the Society of Hosteurs, a marketing club, a tourism society, FCA, a sport management club, SIFE, and athletic boosters. These groups and others help to sponsor the various social functions at Webber.

Location

The town of Babson Park, a very small rural residential community, is located in the heart of Florida's citrus country near a chain of freshwater lakes. The area has a relaxed and friendly atmosphere. Babson Park is conveniently near many major recreational facilities and national tourist attractions in central Florida.

Majors and Degrees

Webber International University offers bachelor's and associate degrees in business administration, with ten different majors: accounting, computer information systems management, corporate communications, finance, hospitality and tourism management, management, marketing, prelaw, security management, and sport management. The University also offers a Bachelor of Science degree in general business studies.

Academic Programs

The school operates on the semester system with two 15-week semesters, a six-week Summer Term A, and a six-week Summer Term B. By fall 2010, all of Webber's courses will be available online through their e-learning program. The University requires the completion of 60 credit hours for the Associate of Science degree and 120 credit hours for the Bachelor of Science degree with a minimum grade point average of 2.0. The average course load is 15 hours per semester. Students in the Bachelor of Science degree program are required to complete approximately 30 hours in the major, 36 hours in the business core, 36 hours in the general education core, and 18 hours of tailored electives. Students in the Associate of Science degree program are required to complete 27 hours in the business core, 18 hours in the general education core, and 15 hours in the major and tailored elective.

The Bachelor of Science degree in general business studies requires the completion of 45 hours in the general business studies core, 39 hours in the general education core, and 36 hours of tailored electives.

All students must complete 30 of the last 33 hours at Webber International University to receive a degree. Credit is awarded for successful scores on Advanced Placement (AP) and College-Level Examination Program (CLEP) general tests.

Off-Campus Programs

The hospitality and marketing departments have arrangements for internship programs with major hotels and restaurants in the Orlando area and major retail stores, both in-state and out-of-state.

The finance department places student interns in various financial institutions and financial departments of local corporations.

Other off-campus experiences include elective courses in which students observe and analyze business operations and functions of local companies and present their findings in a project format comparable to a professional business consultant's.

The departmental field trip is an opportunity for students in all ten majors to travel abroad during a summer semester and to discover business techniques in an international environment.

Academic Facilities

The Roger Babson Learning Center, located in the central part of the campus, is a modern and comprehensive business library facility. The collection currently contains about 35,500 volumes, an assortment of audiovisual materials, and a CD-ROM computer program for reference materials. The library houses computers for student use. Several research databases are available for student access.

The three computer resources centers are data processing centers and teaching facilities whose microcomputers offer the latest modern technology for developing student excellence in business, communication, and creativity.

Costs

In 2010–11, the annual fee, which includes tuition, room and board, and insurance, is $27,412. For commuting students, the annual fee is $18,742. These figures are subject to change. The University estimates that $1000 is adequate for books and supplies. Laboratory fees are additional.

Financial Aid

The Student Financial Aid Department offers students its counsel and assistance in meeting their educational expenses. Aid is awarded on the basis of an applicant's need, academic performance, and promise. Approximately 90 percent of the students at Webber International University receive financial assistance. To demonstrate need, applicants are required to file the Free Application for Federal Student Aid (FAFSA). Various types of aid, such as scholarships, grants, loans, and Federal Work-Study awards, are used to meet student needs. A limited number of no-need scholarships are available; these awards are based on academic performance, on community and college service, or on athletic ability as determined by the sport's coach. Applicants for aid must reapply each year. Webber participates in the Federal Perkins Loan, Federal Supplemental Educational Opportunity Grant, and Federal Work-Study programs. All applicants are expected to apply for any entitlement grant for which they are eligible, such as the Federal Pell Grant; Florida residents must apply for a Florida Student Assistance Grant and the Florida Resident Access Grant. Federal Student Loans are also available. Webber is nationally recognized as a military-friendly school and accepts the Post-9/11 GI Bill as well as a variety of other veteran's education benefits. Financial aid applicants should submit their requests and forms before April 1 in order to be eligible for certain financial aid programs.

Faculty

More than 70 percent of Webber's full-time faculty members hold doctoral degrees. The faculty-student ratio is 1:22, and all students are assigned a faculty adviser. All faculty members have posted office hours and are available for consultation and advising. Many of Webber's faculty members have a minimum of five years' actual professional work experience in their area of specialization in addition to their years of classroom teaching. This combination of applied and classroom work experience gives them an unusual ability to relate to the needs and concerns of their students.

Student Government

The Student Government Association, the chief governing body on Webber's campus, is composed of elected student representatives and a faculty adviser and deals with nonacademic areas of student life. The association serves as an advisory and coordinating body for student organizations and involves students in campus policy and actions. Representatives from various student organizations serve on the Student Government Association, as do members elected from the University community.

Admission Requirements

Applicants must have graduated from high school with a recommended minimum of 4 years of English and 2 to 3 years of mathematics and preparation in seven other academic subjects. Most accepted candidates rank in the top 50 percent of their high school class. Scores on the SAT or ACT are required for admission. International applicants must submit scores on the Test of English as a Foreign Language (TOEFL).

Early admission is possible for promising high school juniors who have test scores near the top 15th percentile statewide or nationally, a minimum 3.0 grade point average (on a 4.0 scale), a strong recommendation from their counselor or principal, and a letter of permission from their parents or guardian. A campus interview with the Dean of Student Development is required.

Applications from transfer students are welcome, as are those from students resuming their education or adult students who have delayed their entrance to college. Transfer students must be in good standing at their former institution.

Applicants who fail to meet regular admission requirements may be considered on an individual basis for the Fresh Start program by the Fresh Start admissions committee. An interview is required for all Fresh Start applicants.

Application and Information

An application is ready for consideration by the Admissions Committee when it has been received with a $35 application fee for domestic students and $75 for international students, the required test scores and references, and transcripts from each school attended. The University uses a system of rolling admissions. It is recommended that applications be submitted as early as possible, since on-campus housing is limited. Freshmen are required to live in the dormitory unless they reside with a parent, guardian, or spouse.

For application forms, catalogs, and additional information, students should contact:

Webber International University
1201 North Scenic Highway
P.O. Box 96
Babson Park, Florida 33827-9990
Phone: 863-638-2910
E-mail: admissions@webber.edu
Web site: http://www.webber.edu

Webber's private beach and pier.

WEBB INSTITUTE

GLEN COVE, NEW YORK

The Institute

Webb Institute was founded in 1889 to provide an opportunity for worthy young students to obtain an education in the "art and science of designing ships and their propulsion systems." The Institute has followed this basic objective to the present, and its graduates are active throughout the United States in the ship design, ship construction, yacht design, and marine operations industries and in appropriate government offices.

The 26-acre campus is the former estate of Herbert L. Pratt and is located on Long Island Sound. Because of the Institute's small size and intensive academic program, varsity sports are limited. However, Webb participates in intercollegiate basketball, cross-country, sailing, soccer, tennis, and volleyball, for which ample facilities are provided. The campus has a gymnasium, tennis courts, playing fields, and a beach. Golf and swimming facilities are available nearby.

Webb Institute maintains an enrollment that ranges from 70 to 90 students, all of whom live on campus. Webb students must be U.S. citizens or permanent residents with a green card.

Location

Glen Cove is a city of more than 25,000 residents and is located on Long Island's North Shore, which is nearly an hour from New York City. Convenient train service from Glen Cove to New York brings the variety of cultural, educational, and recreational activities available in the city within easy reach of Webb students.

Majors and Degrees

Webb Institute offers an engineering program in ship design, which involves both naval architecture and marine engineering. The undergraduate degree awarded is the Bachelor of Science in naval architecture and marine engineering.

Academic Programs

The engineering program in ship design consists of fundamental foundation courses in mathematics, science, and engineering sciences, capped by extensive professional design courses. A coherent program in humanities supplements the technical program to round out undergraduate education.

In addition, students have a two-month, cooperative job experience each year in the U.S. marine and maritime industry. During this period, freshmen work as helper mechanics in shipyards, sophomores obtain seagoing experience aboard ship, and juniors and seniors work as engineering assistants in design and technical offices of various marine firms. This important part of the program provides excellent articulation of the educational and career experiences. Innovative engineering ideas are encouraged in the thesis required during the last year. The program is fully accredited. Graduates are well equipped to pursue postgraduate studies.

Semesters run from late August to mid-December and from late February to late June. January and February are winter work periods, and the period from late June to late August is designated for vacation.

Academic Facilities

Full laboratory support is provided for chemistry, physics, metallurgy, and various engineering courses. A ship-model testing tank is available for ship and boat hull studies. Computer facilities are provided on campus. The Livingston Library contains extensive holdings in naval architecture, marine engineering, and general engineering, as well as collections in literature, arts, social sciences, and music.

Costs

All students admitted to Webb are accepted on a tuition- and fee-free basis (full scholarship). Room and board costs were approximately $9500 in 2008–09. Nearly $800 per year is required for books and supplies. A $150 room deposit fee is payable on entry and refunded, less any breakage costs, on departure. The Student Organization requires a $100 deposit on entry, also refundable on departure.

Financial Aid

As stated, a full scholarship that covers tuition and fees is awarded to all accepted candidates. The winter work co-op in industry provides income for students that significantly assists in covering other expenses. Supplementary aid opportunities are available through the Federal Pell Grant, Federal Stafford Student Loans, and in-house grant programs. Students requiring financial assistance must submit the Free Application for Federal Student Aid (FAFSA) after March 31 but not later than July 1 of the year of entry.

Faculty

Webb Institute has a highly qualified faculty. Many members possess engineering licenses and engage in sponsored research programs, consult for commercial firms, and research and write technical papers. Classes are limited to 25 students, and the student-faculty ratio is 8:1. Each student is assigned a faculty adviser, and consultation with individual faculty members is encouraged.

Student Government

The Student Organization is highly active in student administrative, social, and educational affairs. It is supplemented by an Honor Council and honor system. Together, these entities provide students with a high degree of responsibility for ordering and conducting student life.

Admission Requirements

Admission to Webb is highly competitive. The qualifying requirements for admission are graduation from high school with a B+ (87) or better average in 16 credits of basic high school subjects. Admission selections are based on high school standing (generally in the upper 10 percent) and scores on the College Board's SAT and Subject Tests in Mathematics (Level 1 or 2), and Physics or Chemistry. The final selection follows a personal interview conducted at Webb or at a location convenient to the applicant. The entering class is usually restricted to 25 freshmen.

All application papers must be submitted by February 15, and all required College Board tests must be taken before that date. Advanced placement is not given in any of the course offerings. Campus visits by interested students are strongly recommended; prior appointments must be made. An early decision plan is available for qualified candidates.

Webb Institute does not discriminate in admission in the areas of gender, race, or religion. Academic qualities and career motivation are the only criteria.

Application and Information

For a catalog and application forms, students may contact:

Office of Admissions
Webb Institute
Glen Cove, New York 11542
Phone: 516-671-2213
E-mail: admissions@webb-institute.edu
Web site: http://www.webb-institute.edu

The academic facilities of Webb Institute are located on Long Island Sound in the former residence of Herbert L. Pratt.

COLLEGE CLOSE-UPS

WELLS COLLEGE

AURORA, NEW YORK

The College

Wells College is consistently ranked among the nation's top liberal arts colleges that offer high-quality education at an affordable price and has one of the most beautiful campuses in the United States. The College was established in 1868 by Henry Wells, who also founded the Wells Fargo and American Express companies.

At Wells, professors are dedicated to teaching, and because of the intimate nature of the campus community (the student body is 600), they get to know their students as individuals in and outside the classroom. Students frequently collaborate with their professors on original research and creative projects. At most other schools, these opportunities are only available to graduate students. Because faculty members at Wells know their students so well, they are especially effective advisers and mentors. Students have a competitive edge entering careers and top graduate and professional schools.

Another aspect of the Wells tradition is hands-on learning. In addition to dynamic classroom teaching, Wells students have a variety of other experiential opportunities: internships, service, study abroad, and off-campus study. Professors encourage students to apply theory in practical settings and to discover what they want to do in life through involvement.

Wells currently fields intercollegiate teams at the NCAA Division III level in men's and women's cross-country, field hockey, men's and women's lacrosse, men's and women's soccer, softball, men's and women's swimming, men's basketball, men's and women's golf, and women's tennis. A women's basketball team is planned to be added during the 2010–11 academic year. There are also a number of intramural opportunities, including basketball, soccer, swimming, skiing, tennis, and volleyball. Athletic facilities include indoor and outdoor tennis courts, a gymnasium, a newly renovated fitness center, a nine-hole golf course, and a campus boathouse and dock used in teaching sailing, canoeing, and lifeguarding.

Wells has a full range of active student organizations, including a literary magazine and newspaper, music and drama groups, environmental and political organizations, and abundant opportunities for community service, among others. A busy calendar of cultural events, symposia, and lectures enhances the academic and social life of the College.

Location

Wells is located in the village of Aurora on the eastern shore of Cayuga Lake—part of New York's scenic Finger Lakes region. The area is well known for its high concentration of prestigious colleges and universities, including Cornell University, Ithaca College, Hobart and William Smith Colleges, Colgate University, Hamilton College, and Syracuse University. Aurora is 25 miles from Ithaca and 60 miles from both Rochester and Syracuse. Students have abundant opportunities for outdoor recreation and sports, including sailing, swimming, horseback riding, skiing, and hiking.

Majors and Degrees

Wells offers majors and concentrations in African American studies, American cultures, American studies, anthropology/cross-cultural sociology, art history, biochemistry and molecular biology, biology, chemistry, computer science, creative writing, economics, English, environmental policies and values, environmental studies, ethics and philosophy, French, government and politics, historical and comparative studies, history, human nature and values, international studies, literature, management, mathematics, music, performing arts, physics, psychology, public affairs, religion, sociology, Spanish, studio art, theater and dance, visual arts, and women's studies. Students also have the option of a self-designed major. In addition, they can choose minors from a list of more than thirty programs.

The College has preprofessional programs in dentistry, education, engineering, law, medicine, teaching, and veterinary medicine. Wells has a cross-registration agreement with nearby Ithaca College, Cayuga Community College, and Cornell University and affiliations with Cornell's engineering school.

Wells awards the Bachelor of Arts degree and has a number of programs through which students can earn their bachelor's degree at Wells and a graduate or professional degree from an affiliated university. Participating schools are Clarkson University, Columbia University, Cornell University (engineering), and the University of Rochester (business, community health, and education).

Academic Programs

All Wells students benefit from an academic environment similar to honors programs available to only a small number of students at other schools. The College has a tradition of preparing students for leadership in their chosen fields, and the breadth of knowledge they gain and the range of life experiences they encounter enable them to achieve their career goals and establish a foundation for a rich and fulfilling life.

All students entering Wells to pursue a four-year course of study leading to a bachelor's degree are required to take the First-Year Experience (WLLS 101) and the New Student Experience (WLLS 111). Distribution requirements are a foreign language (two courses or exemption by exam), formal reasoning (one course), arts and humanities (three courses), natural and social sciences (three courses), and physical education (four courses). Team sports and dance technique can partially satisfy requirements.

Approximately sixteen courses must be taken in the student's major, and at least six must be taken at Wells. Eighteen credit hours must be taken at the 300 level or above. A senior project or thesis and a comprehensive evaluation are required for graduation.

A student must successfully complete 120 semester hours (60 of which must be taken at Wells and through affiliated programs, such as study abroad) to be recommended by the faculty for a degree. To learn more about the academic program and requirements for transfer students, prospective students should visit the Wells College Web site.

Off-Campus Programs

Students can spend January term, a semester, or even a year in another college or university abroad or in the United States. Typically, Wells students choose to study off campus for a semester during the junior year, but many different possibilities are available depending on a student's academic program and interests.

The College offers affiliated study-abroad experiences in Denmark, the Dominican Republic, France, Germany, Great Britain, Ireland, Italy, Japan, Mexico, Senegal, Spain, and Sweden. Currently, the three most popular programs are study abroad in Florence, Italy; Paris, France; and Seville, Spain. These off-campus study experiences are flexible as well as financially and academically accessible. After at least one semester at Wells, a student's financial aid applies to one semester of off-campus study.

Wells provides off-campus study options in the United States through its affiliations with American University, serving a wide range of academic and internship interests in Washington, D.C.; the Salt Center, offering documentary field studies in Portland, Maine; and the Public Leadership Education Network (PLEN), providing leadership development through seminars and internships in Washington, D.C. As part of the PLEN affiliation, students can spend a semester studying at the London School of Economics and Political Science and hold an internship in the British government. Through the School for Field Studies, Wells offers semester-long study-abroad experiences in Africa, Australia, the Caribbean, and other locations. The College also offers credit-bearing courses during the January term that take students to a single destination in the U.S. or abroad for intensive study that requires travel in a region or country with a faculty member.

Academic Facilities

From the contemporary elegance of Weld House to the nineteenth-century Glen Park mansion, the former home of College founder Henry Wells, the residence halls encompass enough variety to satisfy every taste. Students eat their meals together in the majestic Tudor-style dining hall in Main Building.

The Louis Jefferson Long Library has received numerous awards for its architectural design. Facilities include an online computer center, individual study carrels, seminar and group-study rooms, and an art gallery. There are department libraries in art, economics, English, mathematics, music, philosophy, and the sciences located across the campus.

The Barler Hall of Music houses a recital hall with superb acoustics, vocal and instrumental practice rooms, a music library, and a listening laboratory. Facilities for printmaking, painting, ceramics, sculpture, and photography are located in the Campbell Arts Building. The Cleveland Hall of Languages contains state-of-the-art equipment for learning foreign languages. Stratton Science Hall, completed in 2007, houses state-of-the-art laboratories for chemistry, biology, environmental science, and physics as well as a computer laboratory. Morgan Hall houses the Book Arts Center and the Wells College Press. Macmillan Hall has classrooms, faculty and administrative offices, several computer laboratories, and department libraries. The east wing of Macmillan contains the Margaret Phipps Auditorium, a theater facility used for teaching, concerts, lectures, and dramatic productions.

Costs

Wells has a long-term commitment to providing talented students with access to the best education, which requires offering excellence at an affordable price. Wells is ranked among the best liberal arts colleges in the nation, yet the cost of a Wells education is considerably less than the tuition charged by comparable schools.

The cost of a Wells education for the 2009–10 year was $28,180 for tuition, $9000 for room and board, and $1500 for fees.

Financial Aid

Approximately 90 percent of Wells students receive financial aid packaged in the form of grants, scholarships, loans, and work-study opportunities. The College works closely with students and their families to design a financial aid package that meets their needs and their budgets.

Award determinations are made on a rolling basis following acceptance. College financial aid is complex; however, Wells College's well-informed financial aid and admissions professionals are always pleased to answer questions and discuss methods of financing higher education with prospective students.

Applicants are considered for merit aid that is based largely on academic achievements and leadership abilities.

Faculty

At Wells, learning takes place in small, seminar-style classes where students are partners with faculty members in the learning process. Starting immediately in their first semester, students take classes with scholars who are recognized experts in their fields, not teaching assistants.

Nearly all Wells professors hold terminal degrees in their areas of expertise. They have been educated at the world's leading research universities, including Harvard, Yale, Columbia, Cornell, Brown, and Stanford. What students discover in Wells' classes is the importance of exploring ideas with others.

Wells is student centered, and academic programs focus on collaborative learning and teaching that meets the needs of students' different learning styles. As one would expect at a nationally recognized liberal arts college, professors are also engaged in research and a full range of scholarly activities. Their books are published by leading academic presses, their articles appear in top journals, and they are a presence at national and international conferences. Due to close faculty-student interaction, students have numerous opportunities to collaborate with faculty members on research, publications, and presentations.

Student Government

The student body is self-governing through the Collegiate Association. The three main governing bodies of the association are the Student-Faculty Administration Board, the Collegiate Council, and the Community Court. Students serve on faculty committees that make decisions concerning administrative and curricular matters.

Leadership development is an inherent part of the Wells experience, and students are encouraged to take an active role in student government and in the life of the campus community.

Admission Requirements

Wells admits students on the basis of the strength of their academic preparation. A student is expected to possess intellectual curiosity, motivation, and maturity to profit from the experience. In all cases, the College seeks students who have followed a solid college-preparatory program throughout high school.

Wells seeks students from varied backgrounds with diverse interests and talents in order to promote a stimulating learning community. Every admissions decision is made on an individual basis.

Wells students share an enthusiasm for academic pursuits and a serious intent to use their education in the future to enhance both their lives and the communities in which they choose to live.

Application and Information

Applications should be received early in the senior year of high school and not later than March 1 of the year in which entrance is desired. Applications from early decision and early action candidates must be received by December 15.

Transfer applications are reviewed on a rolling basis. Transfer students are eligible for merit scholarships and financial aid.

A campus visit is highly recommended for prospective students. For more information about Wells College or to schedule a campus visit, students should contact:

Admissions Office
Wells College
Aurora, New York 13026
Phone: 800-952-9355 (toll-free)
E-mail: admissions@wells.edu
Web site: http://www.wells.edu

The newly renovated Schwartz Athletic Center.

COLLEGE CLOSE-UPS

WENTWORTH INSTITUTE OF TECHNOLOGY

BOSTON, MASSACHUSETTS

The Institute

Wentworth Institute of Technology was founded in 1904 to provide education in the mechanical arts. Today, it is one of the nation's leading technical institutes, offering study in a variety of disciplines. Wentworth has a current undergraduate day enrollment of approximately 3,800 men and women (3,400 full-time) and graduates more engineering technicians and technologists each year than any other college in the United States. The technical education acquired at Wentworth enables graduates to assume creative and responsible careers in business and industry. Wentworth is located on a 35-acre campus on Huntington Avenue in Boston.

Wentworth provides dormitory and suite-style residence halls on campus for men and women. Students residing in the residence halls are on a full meal plan. Upperclass students have the option of living in on-campus apartments. Students residing in the apartments may prepare their own meals. A cafeteria, snack bar, and convenience store are available for those wishing to purchase their meals.

Career counseling and placement assistance are available to all alumni and to students who have completed at least one semester of study at the Institute. While many graduates of Wentworth are employed in the Boston area, alumni have secured positions throughout the United States and abroad.

Location

Boston is the educational center of New England. It is a city of charm, tradition, and elegance—a major center of art, science, music, history, medicine, and education. Wentworth is situated near the heart of Boston and is surrounded by institutions that provide the cultural advantages for which the city is famous. The Museum of Fine Arts, with its store of art treasures, is diagonally across the street, and admission is free to any student with a Wentworth ID card. Symphony Hall is just a few blocks away. The Harvard Medical School, the New England Conservatory of Music, Emmanuel College, Simmons College, Massachusetts College of Pharmacy and Allied Health Sciences, Massachusetts College of Art and Design, Roxbury Community College, and Northeastern University are among the many educational institutions within a few blocks of the campus.

Majors and Degrees

Wentworth Institute of Technology is a technical college of great diversity. Degree programs are offered in the fields of architecture, computer science, construction management, design, engineering, engineering technology, and management. Specifically, bachelor's degrees are awarded in the following majors: the Bachelor of Architecture and the Bachelor of Science in biomedical engineering (beginning in fall 2011), civil engineering technology, computer engineering technology, computer network and information systems, computer science, construction management, electromechanical engineering (optional concentration in biomedical systems engineering), electronic engineering technology, facilities planning and management, industrial design, interior design, management (optional concentrations in communication, project leadership, and technology management), and mechanical engineering technology. Baccalaureate degrees in architecture and interior design are designated as first professional degrees. Completion of a Wentworth baccalaureate degree usually requires four years (five years for the electromechanical engineering degree).

Academic Programs

At Wentworth Institute of Technology, college-level study in technological fundamentals and principles is combined with appropriate laboratory, field, and studio experience. Students apply theory to practical problems, and they acquire skills and techniques by using, operating, and controlling equipment and instruments that are particular to their area of specialization. In addition, study in the social sciences and humanities provides a balanced understanding of the world in which graduates work. Wentworth's programs of study are more practical than theoretical in approach, and the Institute's academic requirements demand extensive time and effort.

During the first two years of study in a degree program at Wentworth, students lay the foundation for more advanced study in the third and fourth (and fifth, where applicable) years. While nearly all majors allow continuous study from the freshman through the senior year, the architecture major requires a petition for acceptance to the baccalaureate program during the sophomore year.

All bachelor's degree programs are conducted as cooperative (co-op) education programs: upon entering their third year, students alternate semesters of academic study at Wentworth with semester-long periods of employment in industry. Two semesters of co-op employment are required; one additional (summer) semester of co-op is optional. Both students and the companies that hire them are enthusiastic about the co-op program and agree that it is a mutually valuable experience.

Academic Facilities

Wentworth's twenty-seven buildings house classrooms, laboratories, studios, administrative offices, and other facilities. Beatty Hall houses the Alumni Library, computer center, classrooms, dining areas, and office space. State-of-the-art laboratories, such as the Richard H. Lufkin Technology Center and the Davis Center for Advanced Graphics and Interactive Learning, are situated throughout the campus.

Costs

For 2010–11, tuition is $22,870, books and supplies are approximately $1000, and room and board are about $11,000 (this figure varies according to accommodation). Tuition includes a brand new laptop that is outfitted with the complete suite of software used in the student's academic program.

Financial Aid

Scholarships are available to students who demonstrate need and academic promise. Merit-based scholarships are also available. Wentworth also provides federal and state financial assistance, such as Federal Pell and Federal Supplemental Educational Opportunity Grants, Federal Perkins Loans, Federal Work-Study Program awards, Gilbert Matching Grants, and Massachusetts No-Interest Loans, to students with financial need in accordance with federal and state guidelines.

Wentworth participates in the Federal Direct Lending program. As a result, students are eligible to borrow under the Federal Direct Stafford Student Loan program and parents may borrow under the Federal Direct PLUS program. Individuals participating in these programs borrow money directly from the federal government rather than through lending institutions.

In addition to these need-based programs, Wentworth also participates in the MEFA loan program sponsored by the Massachusetts Educational Financing Authority. Wentworth offers several payment options through payment plans and alternative loan financing.

To apply for financial aid, new students should complete the Free Application for Federal Student Aid (FAFSA) by March 1. Applications received after this date are considered as funds allow.

Faculty

Wentworth's faculty includes 146 full-time and 123 part-time members. The primary responsibility of every faculty member is teaching. Although professors may engage in some research and related work, student development remains the central mission of Wentworth's faculty. Upon entering Wentworth, every student is assigned a faculty adviser.

Student Government

Wentworth's Student Government performs an essential function as the official representative of the student body. Its purposes are to receive and express student opinion, to advance the best interests of the student body with the administration and faculty and with other institutions and associations, to support all extracurricular activities of the student body, and to serve as a bond between the student body and the faculty to foster mutual cooperation and understanding. The Student Government is made up of elected representatives from each class section and the officers elected by the student body at large. The Student Government sponsors social functions and student organizations and serves as an advocate for student concerns.

Admission Requirements

Applicants must be graduates of secondary schools (or have passed the GED test) and must meet specific entrance requirements. All programs require four years of English, a laboratory science, and mathematics through algebra II in a college-preparatory program. Both the electromechanical engineering and the computer science programs require a background in precalculus or trigonometry. All programs require the submission of SAT or ACT scores. International students and transfers are welcome.

Application and Information

Students are admitted to Wentworth for September and January enrollment. Notification of admission is made on a rolling basis. The preferred method for applying is online at http://www.wit.edu/apply. The online application fee is $10. An application form, the application fee, transcripts from the secondary school and any colleges previously attended, SAT or ACT scores, a personal statement, and a letter of recommendation should be sent to:

Admissions Office
Wentworth Institute of Technology
550 Huntington Avenue
Boston, Massachusetts 02115
Phone: 617-989-4000
800-556-0610 (toll-free)
Fax: 617-989-4010
E-mail: admissions@wit.edu
Web site: http://www.wit.edu

Wentworth Hall.

WESLEYAN COLLEGE

MACON, GEORGIA

The College

Wesleyan College, chartered in 1836, has the distinction of being the world's first college chartered to grant degrees to women. Today, Wesleyan is still dedicated to the education of women and is regarded as one of the nation's finest liberal arts colleges. According to the seventh annual report of the National Survey of Student Engagement (NSSE), Wesleyan outperformed the top 10 percent of colleges and universities in all five categories studied: active and collaborative learning, enriching educational experiences, level of academic challenge, student-faculty interaction, and supportive campus environment.

Wesleyan is a four-year liberal arts college affiliated with the United Methodist Church. Enrollment is limited to fewer than 1,000 students, primarily to support a learner-based curriculum that limits classes to no more than 20 students and to provide opportunities for meaningful participation in the life of the College community. Wesleyan's student body has been cited as among the nation's most diverse. Students from across the U.S. and almost twenty other countries value a rigorous academic program renowned for its high quality. A student-faculty ratio of 10:1 ensures that each student is more than just a grade or a number. The acceptance rate of Wesleyan students into medical, law, business, and other graduate programs is exemplary.

Beyond the academic, Wesleyan offers a thriving residence life program, NCAA Division III athletics, a championship IHSA equestrian program, and meaningful opportunities for community involvement and leadership. The College's beautiful 200-acre wooded campus, along with thirty historically significant buildings, is listed in the National Register of Historic Places as the Wesleyan College Historic District. Beautiful, white-columned Georgian-style buildings surround a classic quadrangle that plays host to many College events. All residence halls have been recently renovated and offer single rooms and suites. On-campus apartment-style living is available. Approximately 90 percent of the students reside on campus.

A fine equestrian center and athletic complex (with fitness center, tennis courts, track, and lighted softball and soccer fields) complete the campus offerings. Other recreational facilities include a gymnasium with a heated pool and a lake with a jogging trail.

Most of the extracurricular activities of Wesleyan's students are coordinated through Activity Councils. The Campus Activities Board plans concert-dance weekends, events with nearby colleges, international fashion shows, holiday trips, and special dinners. The Student Recreation Council coordinates competitive activities in basketball, fencing, golf, soccer, softball, swimming, among others. Wesleyan is a member of the National Collegiate Athletic Association (NCAA) Division III. There are intercollegiate basketball, cross-country, soccer, softball, tennis, volleyball, and IHSA equestrian teams. The Council on Religious Concerns encourages religious life on campus and sponsors activities that involve students with community life. Students volunteer at local institutions such as the Georgia Industrial Children's Home, Macon Outreach, the Methodist Children's Home, and neighborhood schools and churches. They also participate in interest clubs, student publications, performing arts groups, honor societies, and professional fraternities. A number of College traditions are perpetuated by spirited but friendly competition among the four classes.

Location

Wesleyan is located in a suburb of the beautiful, historic city of Macon, Georgia, the third-largest city in the state. Macon is the cultural, educational, medical, and economic leader of middle Georgia and is located about an hour's drive south of Atlanta. The city of Macon offers varied entertainment and many cultural opportunities, including the Georgia Music and Sports Halls of Fame. Visits by nationally and internationally acclaimed speakers and a series of popular and classical concerts are held on the Wesleyan campus each year, as are special events associated with Macon's renowned Cherry Blossom Festival.

Majors and Degrees

Wesleyan College offers undergraduate degrees in thirty-two majors and twenty-nine minors, including self-designed majors and interdisciplinary programs as well as eight preprofessional programs, including dental, engineering, allied health services, law, medicine, pharmacy, seminary, and veterinary medicine. Master of Arts degrees in education and an accelerated Executive Master of Business Administration program enroll both men and women. Wesleyan also offers a dual-degree program in engineering with the Georgia Institute of Technology in Atlanta; Auburn University in Auburn, Alabama; and Mercer University in Macon.

The Bachelor of Arts (A.B.) is offered in accounting, advertising and marketing communication, art history, biology, business administration, chemistry, computer information systems, communication, economics, education (early childhood and middle grades), English, environmental science, French, history, human services (family services or management concentration), international business, international relations, mathematics, music (performance emphasis—piano, organ, and voice), philosophy, physics, political science, psychology, religious studies, Spanish, studio art, theater, and women's studies. In addition to these majors, the following academic concentrations are offered as minors: accounting, art history, biology, business management, chemistry, communication, computer information systems, computer science, economics, educational studies, environmental studies, English, finance, French, history, mathematics, music, neuroscience, philosophy, photography, physics, political science, psychology, religious studies, Spanish, studio art, technology in business administration, theater, and women's studies. Self-designed interdisciplinary majors are also available.

Students may elect to pursue their academic or professional interests through a double major, a major in combination with a minor program of studies, an interdisciplinary major, or an independently developed program of studies.

Wesleyan's dual-degree program in engineering is offered in cooperation with Georgia Institute of Technology, Auburn University, and Mercer University. Three years of study at Wesleyan and two years of study at Georgia Tech, Auburn, or Mercer lead to an A.B. degree from Wesleyan and a B.S. degree from the other institution. Wesleyan's traditional undergraduate programs for women are complemented by a growing number of day, evening, and weekend degree and certificate programs for nontraditional students seeking a flexible schedule.

Academic Programs

The College's goal is to prepare students for a lifetime of learning and change. Each major program contains general education requirements for breadth of learning and major field requirements for career and/or graduate school preparation. All degree programs require the completion of 120 semester hours with a cumulative average of C (2.0) or better.

Wesleyan provides a challenging academic environment coupled with individualized attention. Each student is assisted by a faculty adviser, a preprofessional or career adviser, and a peer counselor in the selection of academic and internship experiences that lead to intellectual and career fulfillment. All classes are offered in a seminar style, with an emphasis on interactive or participatory learning. Each student has a research or internship experience.

Each entering full-time student has the option to purchase a personal computer, for which the College offers special financing options. The ability to utilize information technology toward the enhancement of learning and career preparation is central to the academic program. The networked campus is connected to the Internet, which gives each student access to a world of information from her residence hall. Many common academic areas offer wireless Internet access.

Credit by examination and exemption from required courses are possible with acceptable scores on the Advanced Placement (AP), International Baccalaureate (I.B.), Cambridge International Examinations (CIE), and College-Level Examination Program (CLEP) tests or acceptable grades in high school–college joint enrollment courses. Students may also exempt courses by taking departmental examinations. Thirty semester hours of credit is the maximum a student can receive by exemption through AP, I.B., CIE, CLEP, or departmental exams.

The College operates on an early semester plan. First-semester classes begin in late August and end in early December. The second semester begins in the beginning of January and ends with graduation in early May. Wesleyan College offers an optional May term as well as two summer school sessions.

Off-Campus Programs

Through Wesleyan's International Study Abroad and Exchange Program, students can study abroad for one full year, one semester, a May term, or a summer session. Through cooperative agreements with the Institute for the International Education of Students (IES), National Student Exchange (NSE), and Business Education Initiative (BEI) students may study abroad in Argentina, Australia, Austria, China, France, Germany, Great Britain, Japan, Russia, Spain, and other countries. In addition, Wesleyan has direct exchange agreements with Sookmyung Women's University (South Korea), Osaka University (Japan), Ewha Women's University (South Korea), Ulyanovsk State University (Russia), and various schools in Northern Ireland.

Off-campus opportunities in Macon are available through the Internship Program, which places students with area businesses, community agencies, health organizations, arts groups, and the media. Summer internships can be arranged in a student's hometown and in other locations. Academic credit given for off-campus experiences varies.

Academic Facilities

Willet Memorial Library offers a variety of print and electronic resources to support student research and the College's curriculum. The core collection includes more than 143,000 volumes plus subscriptions to 615 periodicals. There are 33,438 items in microform and 4,267 tapes and records. Through the library's participation in GALILEO, students have access to more than 150 bibliographic and full-text databases. The library has informal study areas, individual carrels, seminar rooms, and two smart classrooms. The Georgia Room houses 4,500 rare volumes and treasures of Americana.

The Porter Fine Arts Building serves as a cultural center for the campus and community. It houses the music and theater departments, and, in addition to classrooms, offices, and studios, it contains two art galleries and a studio theater. Its Porter Auditorium has a seating capacity of 1,200 and contains one of the largest pipe organs in the Southeast. Tate Hall contains classrooms for the Humanities, Social Science, and Education divisions. Taylor Hall is currently under renovation but will soon house the Education division and offer new classroom spaces. The art department is located in a 10,000-square-foot building designed exclusively for teaching the studio arts.

The new Munroe Science Center, opened in 2007, is a state-of-the-art science facility that serves the increasing number of Wesleyan students enrolled and majoring in biology, chemistry, psychology, and computer science. It also addresses the great need throughout the nation for women skilled in medicine, scientific research, computer technology, and mathematics. Through its eleven teaching laboratories and nine research laboratories, the new facility encourages faculty/student collaboration on research projects, contains interactive laboratories for specific experimentation, and offers individualized instruction in an environmentally efficient and safe setting. State-of-the-art laboratories include cell biology, ecology, physiology, immunology, and instrumental analysis labs as well as general biology, physics, and chemistry labs. Although teaching laboratories serve as classrooms, a small seminar room and two technologically advanced classrooms also are used for instruction. Specialty science spaces include an astronomy observation deck, a greenhouse, a vivarium, an environmental room, and a community learning center.

Costs

Tuition for 2009–10 is $17,500. Room and board cost $8000. Students should also keep in mind the additional cost of books, supplies, travel, and personal expenses.

Financial Aid

Students seeking financial assistance are required to submit the Free Application for Federal Student Aid (FAFSA). Any student who demonstrates financial need is qualified for some type of assistance.

Wesleyan offers scholarships to incoming first-year students on the basis of academic ability, leadership, or special talents. Transfer scholarships are available based on cumulative grade point average and hours earned. Minimum requirements are a 3.0 GPA and 30 semester hours or 45 quarter hours.

Wesleyan participates in the Federal Perkins Loan, Federal Pell Grant, Federal Supplemental Educational Opportunity Grant, Federal Work-Study, and Federal Family Education Loan programs. Any resident of Georgia who wishes to attend a private college in the state and has at least a B average may apply for the Georgia Tuition Equalization Grant and HOPE Grant. Georgia Student Incentive Grants are also available, as are certain loans, other scholarships, and part-time employment. Approximately 85 percent of Wesleyan's students receive financial assistance.

Faculty

The academic program at Wesleyan is guided by an exceptionally able, dedicated, and caring faculty. There are 52 full-time faculty members; 49 have earned doctoral or terminal degrees. The student-faculty ratio is 10:1. No courses are ever taught by graduate assistants. Faculty members serve as academic advisers and help students plan their academic program. Many professors participate in extracurricular activities with students on campus.

Student Government

Wesleyan's Student Government Association (SGA) represents the Wesleyan student body. Students elect representatives to serve on Senate, which is the legislative body. SGA emphasizes responsibility and order, and supports an active liberal arts environment. SGA contributes to cocurricular life at the College, development of leadership and responsible citizenship, in conjunction with Student Affairs. In addition, the College offers more than forty student clubs and organizations.

Admission Requirements

Applicants to Wesleyan must submit a completed application with a $30 application fee, official academic transcripts, official SAT or ACT scores, an evaluation written by a teacher, a recommendation from a guidance counselor or principal, and an essay. The completion of a minimum of 16 academic course units in a secondary school is required. Wesleyan feels that a campus visit is extremely beneficial, and visitors can be full participants in campus activities. An interview is strongly recommended. Applications from transfer and international students are welcome. Credit for work below a grade of C cannot be transferred, and a minimum score of 80 (Internet-based test), 550 (paper-based), or 213 (computer-based) on the Test of English as Foreign Language (TOEFL) is required of international students. Wesleyan accepts qualified students without regard to race, religion, national or ethnic origin, age, sexual orientation, or disability.

Application and Information

Admission to Wesleyan is selective. For additional information or to request an application form, students should contact:

Wesleyan College Admission
4760 Forsyth Road
Macon, Georgia 31210
Phone: 478-757-5206
800-447-6610 (toll-free)
E-mail: admission@wesleyancollege.edu
Web site: http://www.wesleyancollege.edu

Wesleyan has the distinction of being the world's first college chartered to grant degrees to women.

WESLEY COLLEGE

DOVER, DELAWARE

The College

Wesley College, the oldest private college in Delaware, is a fully accredited, coeducational, comprehensive liberal arts institution.

Nestled in a quiet, historic residential community, Wesley College is affiliated with the United Methodist Church, with an enrollment of more than 2,100 full- and part-time students, mostly representing the mid-Atlantic region. The average class size is 17 students.

The Wesley residence community is made up of seven buildings. Each building has special characteristics that make it unique. The facilities, including two apartment-style and suite-style housing facilities, are all air conditioned, and all rooms offer Internet access. The purpose of the Residence Program is to enhance the academic mission of Wesley by providing educational and social experiences outside the classroom to help develop contributing members of society.

Each building has a Resident Director and assistant. Student staff members are selected and trained and live on each floor to provide additional resources to their peers. The living arrangement in each hall enables students to get to know one another well and to develop close-knit relationships. Students come from all over the United States and overseas, providing the opportunity to meet and live with people from diverse backgrounds.

Wesley is a member of NCAA Division III intercollegiate athletics and the Capital Athletic Conference. Men have teams in baseball, basketball, cross-country running, football, golf, lacrosse, soccer, tennis, and track and field. Women compete in basketball, cheerleading, cross-country running, field hockey, golf, lacrosse, soccer, softball, tennis, track and field, and volleyball. A well-organized intramural program offers a wide variety of athletic competitions, including, but not limited to, basketball, flag football, soccer, and volleyball. In addition, the College offers a men's club ice hockey program.

In addition to its undergraduate degrees, Wesley College awards the Master of Business Administration (M.B.A.); Master of Science (M.S.) in environmental science; Master of Education (M.Ed.) in curriculum and instruction; Master of Arts (M.A.) in curriculum and instruction; Master of Arts in Teaching (M.A.T), initial certificate; and the Master of Science in Nursing (M.S.N.) degrees.

Location

Dover is the capital of the country's first state and has approximately 35,000 residents. New York City, Baltimore, Philadelphia, and Washington, D.C., are within a 2- to 3-hour drive of the campus. The College is located within Dover's major residential community, with stores and banks within easy walking distance and malls a short commute away. Seafood is a specialty in Dover because of the city's proximity to the Delaware and Chesapeake Bays and to the Atlantic Ocean. Delaware Transit Corporation (DART) provides bus service throughout the city of Dover. Daily bus service is available to and from the campus. In addition, Delaware's famous beaches are also within easy driving distance of the campus.

Many students become involved in local activities, including volunteer work at private and public agencies. On-campus volunteer activities include a unique partnership between a state-funded elementary and secondary charter school (Campus Community Schools) and the College. Many students are employed in community businesses through the cooperative education program at Wesley. Others work in part-time jobs to earn extra money. Many local residents also attend Wesley on a part-time basis and enjoy full use of the College's facilities.

Majors and Degrees

Bachelor of Arts and Bachelor of Science degrees are awarded in accounting, American studies, biological chemistry, biology, business administration, education (K–8), English, environmental studies, history, international studies, kinesiology: exercise science, kinesiology: sports management, legal studies, liberal studies, mathematics, media arts, medical technology, nursing, physical education (K–12), political science, and psychology.

Academic Programs

The comprehensive academic calendar year consists of two semesters and a double summer session. Winter sessions are available in England and France, offering unique opportunities for travel and study.

Bachelor's degree candidates begin with the foundation core curriculum, which emphasizes an overarching theme of the individual in a global community. Interdisciplinary threads bind the core curriculum and the major programs into a purposeful design. These threads are critical thinking, communication across disciplines, technological literacy, multicultural awareness, aesthetic appreciation, and ethical sensibility. The core provides a distinctive undergraduate experience for students, establishes coherent links between the curricular and cocurricular programs, and provides community service options beyond the College campus.

Academic Facilities

The Robert H. Parker Library provides for both individual and group study in its several large reading rooms and smaller study areas. It contains a book collection and extensive video collection to support the academic program. The library houses the Office of Academic Support Services, the Writing Center, the Office of Information Systems, faculty offices, classrooms, and a computer lab. Students also have access to the Dover Public Library and Delaware State University Library.

Costs

For 2010–11, Wesley's tuition and fees are $20,050 per year. Room and board costs range from $9500 to $13,300 per year. Books and supplies cost about $2000 per year.

Financial Aid

Financial aid is available in the form of endowed scholarships, federal scholarships, grants, work-study programs, and loans. Approximately 90 percent of Wesley students receive financial aid. Wesley uses the Free Application for Federal Student Aid (FAFSA). Students and their families are urged to complete and send their FAFSA as early as possible. Financial aid awards must be confirmed by the student within fifteen days of notification.

Wesley College provides numerous academic scholarships to its top undergraduate students. Applications for these awards are not required. Interested seniors should contact the Office of Admissions.

Faculty

Wesley College emphasizes teaching. More than 80 percent of faculty members hold a doctoral or other terminal degree in their subject area and attend workshops and conferences to keep abreast of current activities in their fields. Most faculty members serve as academic advisers to students. All have regularly scheduled office hours and are available for student conferences on a regular basis.

Student Government

Student leadership develops through various aspects of College governance. Student representatives work in close cooperation with faculty members and administrators.

Admission Requirements

Many factors are considered in the selection of a Wesley student. The most important are the applicant's secondary school courses and grades, along with the required SAT or ACT scores. On-campus interviews are strongly recommended. Secondary school recommendations are also important. International students should submit their applications for admission by February 1 for the following fall semester. Admission decisions are made without regard to race, religion, color, age, gender, handicap, or national origin. Applicants should have 16 secondary school units in English, social studies, laboratory science, mathematics, and electives.

Students, parents, and counselors are welcome to contact the Office of Admissions for information and assistance.

Wesley College reserves the right to change some or all rates, policies, or courses when necessary, without prior notice.

Application and Information

Secondary school records should be attached to the Wesley College application form. Copies of official school records may also be submitted via fax.

To schedule an admissions interview and campus tour, students should call the Office of Admissions. A College prospectus, application form, and financial aid information are available by contacting:

Arthur T. Jacobs Sr.
Director of Admissions
Wesley College
120 North State Street
Dover, Delaware 19901
Phone: 302-736-2400
800-937-5398 Ext. 2400 (toll-free)
Fax: 302-736-2382
E-mail: admissions@wesley.edu
Web site: http://www.wesley.edu

A student relaxes in the beautiful surroundings of Wesley College.

WEST CHESTER UNIVERSITY OF PENNSYLVANIA

WEST CHESTER, PENNSYLVANIA

The University

West Chester University of Pennsylvania (WCU) is the second largest of the fourteen institutions in the Pennsylvania State System of Higher Education and the fourth-largest university in the Philadelphia metropolitan area. Officially founded in 1871, the University traces its heritage to the West Chester Academy, which existed from 1812 to 1869. The University's 402-acre campus has well-maintained facilities, including nine residence halls and two garden-style apartment complexes, plus a new performing arts center. In keeping with West Chester's rich heritage, the University's Quadrangle buildings, part of the original campus, are on the National Register of Historic Places.

While the University attracts the majority of its students from Pennsylvania, New Jersey, and Delaware, it also enrolls many students from other areas across the United States and from more than fifty countries. The undergraduate enrollment includes approximately 11,920 women and men.

Each year, the University community schedules an impressive series of events, including programs with well-known musicians, authors, political figures, and others. More than 210 campus groups in music, theater, athletics, and other activities, as well as clubs, fraternities, sororities, service organizations, and honor societies, provide students with the opportunity to participate in a full range of programs. The University offers twenty-four intercollegiate sports and twenty-four club sports for men and women. In addition to the facilities in the health and physical education complex, the University has a field house and a gymnasium for varsity sports.

Location

The University is located in West Chester, a community in southeastern Pennsylvania that is strategically located at the center of the mid-Atlantic corridor. The seat of Chester County government for more than two centuries, West Chester retains much of its historical charm in its buildings and unspoiled countryside, yet it offers the twenty-first-century advantages of a town in the heart of a thriving suburban area. West Chester is just 25 miles west of Philadelphia and 17 miles north of Wilmington, Delaware, putting the libraries, museums, cultural resources, entertainment, and historical sites of both cities within easy reach. It is also only 2 hours from New York City and 3 hours from Washington, D.C.

Majors and Degrees

The Bachelor of Arts is offered in American studies, anthropology, art, biology, communication studies, communicative disorders, English, French, geography–geographic analysis, geography–urban/regional planning, German, history, Latin, liberal studies, literature, mathematics, philosophy, political science, political science–international relations, political science–applied public policy, psychology, Russian, sociology, Spanish, theater arts, and women's studies.

The Bachelor of Science is offered in accounting, athletic training, biochemistry, biology, biology–cell and molecular biology, biology–ecology, biology–medical technology, biology–microbiology, business management, chemistry, chemistry–biology (premed), computer science, criminal justice, economics, exercise science, finance, forensic and toxicological chemistry, geoscience–earth systems, geoscience–environmental, geosciences–geology, health and physical education, health science–general, health science–respiratory care, liberal studies–science and mathematics, liberal studies–professional studies, marketing, mathematics, nutrition and dietetics, pharmaceutical product development, physics, physics–engineering, public health–environmental, and public health–health promotion.

The Bachelor of Science in Nursing, the Bachelor of Fine Arts (studio arts), the Bachelor of Music (music education, performance, theory and composition, studies in an outside field), and the Bachelor of Social Work degrees are also offered.

The Bachelor of Science in Education degree is offered in biology, chemistry, communication–media, communication–speech, communication–theatre emphasis, early childhood education, earth-space science–astronomy, earth-space science–geology, elementary education, English, mathematics, physics, and special education.

Paraprofessional studies are available in medicine. Also available are early admission assurance programs with Drexel School of Medicine, Pennsylvania State University College of Medicine, Temple University School of Medicine, Temple University School of Dentistry, and Arcadia University Physician Assistant Program. In cooperation with Pennsylvania State University, West Chester University offers a 3-2 dual-degree program combining liberal arts, physics, and engineering. A similar, dual degree cooperative physics/engineering program is available through affiliation with the School of Engineering and Textiles of Philadelphia University. As a member of the State System of Higher Education (PASSHE), special admission opportunities for scholarships to the Widener School of Law–Harrisburg Campus are also available.

Teacher certification programs are available in biology, chemistry, communications, early childhood education, elementary education, English, French, general science, German, health and physical education, Latin, mathematics, music education, physics, Russian, secondary education, social studies, Spanish, and special education. Certificates are also available in adapted physical education, athletic training, biology–medical technology, education for sustainability, and Russian studies.

Interdisciplinary areas of study include computer security certificate, ethnic studies, Honors College, Latin American studies, and Russian studies. Minors are available in most majors and in several interdisciplinary areas. The University also offers ROTC programs with cross-enrollment agreement with Widener University for Army ROTC and with St. Joseph's University for Air Force ROTC.

Academic Programs

West Chester University is a comprehensive institution now in its second century. The University comprises the College of Arts and Sciences, the College of Business and Public Affairs, the College of Education, the College of Health Sciences, and the College of Visual and Performing Arts. It operates on a two-semester basis; summer sessions are available.

An honors program is available to qualified students for both upper and lower division study; internships and field experiences, self-designed majors, and independent study are also offered. A variety of credit-by-examination programs are available.

Off-Campus Programs

Through the Study Abroad Program, students may spend one or more semesters in countries such as England, Italy, France, Australia, Spain, and Ireland. West Chester also sponsors a number of annual courses that include study abroad during spring, summer, and winter breaks.

West Chester University participates in the National Student Exchange Program, in which students spend up to a year at any one of more than 170 member schools across the United States, broadening their cultural and academic horizons. Automatic transfer of credit is arranged.

Academic Facilities

There are two libraries on campus: the Francis Harvey Green Library and the Presser Music Library. Library collections include more than 1,790,000 print and electronic volumes; 2,300 print journals; 934,000 microforms; 46,000 sound recordings; 9,600 films, videos, and DVDs; 3,500 maps; and Internet access to more than 150 databases; and the full-text from more than 48,000 journals. Unique digital collections include University graduate and undergraduate catalogs, 1874 to date; title pages and autographs from the Philips Autograph Library; the letters of General Anthony Wayne; and historic postcards. Services include free interlibrary loan, electronic and print reserves, more than ninety public computer workstations, twenty laptops for use in the library, and a Starbucks coffee shop.

The University's extensive computer facilities include more than 750 PC and Macintosh workstations that are available to students in more than forty computer labs. Many of the buildings and exteriors are wireless zones and Internet access is available in residence halls and computer labs. The University has Braille printers, translators, and speech synthesizers for its visually impaired students. Students can use the computing facilities 16 hours a day.

The Merion Science Center, with modern multimedia lecture halls, extensive laboratories, and study areas where students can work together, connects to the Schmucker Science Center, which houses a fully equipped observatory and planetarium. The Center's extensive laboratories have a variety of advanced instruments such as a single-side band microscope—the world's second—as well as field inversion electrophoresis equipment for DNA analysis, and equipment for RFLP, PCR and DNA sequencing. The GIS computer lab has a first-order community base station and mobile GPS units to support coursework in geography, marketing and other subjects. Undergraduates have hands-on access to this equipment, as well as automated spectrophotometers, electron analytical equipment, atomic absorption spectrometers, and a variety of chromatographs, including gas chromatograph-mass spectrometers.

The campus includes a 100-acre natural area for environmental studies; speech and hearing and reading clinics; two theaters; music facilities with practice, rehearsal, and listening rooms; a large, health and physical education complex that houses a gymnasium and a natatorium with two pool areas and a diving well; dance studios; research laboratories; physical therapy rooms; saunas; and a health resource center.

West Chester University is committed to providing barrier-free facilities for persons with impaired mobility.

Costs

West Chester University provides a high-quality education at an affordable cost. Full-time undergraduate students who are legal residents of Pennsylvania paid $5554 for annual tuition for 12 to 18 semester hours in 2009–10. For more than 18 semester hours or fewer than 12, the cost was $231 per semester hour. Out-of-state students paid $13,886 per year for 12 to 18 semester hours and $579 per semester hour for more than 18 or fewer than 12. Room and board were $7032 per year for on-campus residents in University-owned residence halls. Student fees were $1451 per year, plus a technology fee of $206 for in-state students and $310 for out-of-state students. Tuition is determined by the state.

Financial Aid

The financial aid available to students includes work-study programs, grants, loans, special awards, and scholarships. A limited number of merit scholarships are awarded based on the student's academic standing and accomplishments in high school. Students who qualify are invited to apply. About 70 percent of all full-time undergraduate students receive some form of aid.

Faculty

West Chester University has a faculty of approximately 700 members. The majority hold doctoral degrees, and many are engaged in research and serve as consultants in their field of expertise. The student-faculty ratio is 18:1.

Student Government

The Student Governmental Association represents all students on the West Chester campus. In addition, the Residence Hall Association represents resident students, and the Off Campus and Commuter Association represents commuting students.

Admission Requirements

Applicants to West Chester University are evaluated on the basis of scholarship, character, and potential for achievement. The requirements for freshman admission consideration include graduation from an approved secondary school or a General Educational Development (GED) certificate from an approved agency; satisfactory scores on either the SAT, ACT, or TOEFL (for international applicants); and completion of a personal statement. Transfer applicants must have a minimum cumulative grade point average of 2.0 for admissions consideration. Certain academic programs may require an interview or specific course prerequisites. The University does have several other admissions options such as early admission and special admissions programs, including ACT 101. Based on the scores received on Advanced Placement (AP) tests and subject examinations administered through the College-Level Examination Program (CLEP), students may receive advanced placement or credit.

Application and Information

Students are admitted for the fall or spring semester. Freshman applicants for the fall semester are urged to begin the application procedure at the start of their senior year in high school. Transfers should begin the process beginning in January for the fall semester. Applicants for the spring semester should apply by November 1. International students must apply by March 1 for the fall semester and September 1 for the spring semester. The University operates on a modified rolling admission policy; applicants with the strongest qualifications are given priority, and their applications are processed expeditiously. Students are encouraged to visit WCU's campus. To arrange a visit or to attend an information session, students may call the Office of Admissions. For updated information or directions, students should visit the University's Web site.

For additional information and required forms, students may contact:

Office of Admissions
Emil J. Messikomer Hall
West Chester University of Pennsylvania
100 West Rosedale Avenue
West Chester, Pennsylvania 19383
Phone: 610-436-3411
877-315-2165 (toll-free)
E-mail: ugadmiss@wcupa.edu
Web site: http://www.wcupa.edu

A view of the west side of the Quadrangle at West Chester University.

WESTERN CONNECTICUT STATE UNIVERSITY

DANBURY, CONNECTICUT

The University

Founded in 1903, Western Connecticut State University (WestConn) is dedicated to providing both a high-quality university education and a memorable campus experience at an affordable cost. With programs in the arts and sciences, business, and professional studies, WestConn takes pride in providing an outstanding education to more than 4,500 full-time undergraduates and nearly 2,000 graduate or part-time students.

WestConn offers excellent educational programs through five academic units: the Ancell School of Business, the School of Arts and Sciences, the School of Professional Studies, the School of Visual and Performing Arts, and the Division of Graduate Studies and External Programs. The most popular majors include communication, theater arts, education, business, justice and law administration, music, and nursing.

In addition to the University's full menu of undergraduate degrees, the Ancell School of Business offers the Master of Business Administration, Master of Health Administration, and Master of Science in justice administration. The School of Arts and Sciences offers the Master of Arts in biological and environmental sciences, earth and planetary sciences, English, history, and mathematics; the Master of Fine Arts is offered in professional writing. The School of Professional Studies offers the Master of Science in counselor education, elementary education, nursing, and secondary education; also offered is WestConn's Doctor of Education (Ed.D.) in instructional leadership. Prelaw and pre–health professions programs also are available. WestConn's newly formed School of Visual and Performing Arts offers the Master of Fine Arts in visual arts and the Master of Music Education.

The University also is rich with a number of learning and social activities beyond the classroom. Students run academic and fraternal organizations, publish an award-winning newspaper and yearbook, and run a radio station. They stage theater and musical productions, participate in cooperative education and internship programs, and administer their own campus government association.

The University provides services for learning-disabled students, study abroad, a University Scholars program, precollegiate and access initiatives, international student services, and community service learning opportunities. A variety of NCAA Division III men's and women's sports are represented on campus, and students enjoy intramural sports and a premier recreation center that includes a swimming pool, an indoor track, and weightlifting machines. The campus also features a child-care center, a counseling center, a health services office, a career development center, and campus ministries.

WestConn is accredited by the New England Association of Schools and Colleges; the Board of Governors for Higher Education, State of Connecticut; the Connecticut State Department of Education; the American Chemical Society; the Commission on Collegiate Nursing Education; the Council on Social Work Education (baccalaureate level); the Council for Accreditation of Counseling and Related Educational Programs; and the National Association of Schools of Music.

Location

WestConn offers two campuses in Danbury, in the heart of western Connecticut, as well as a satellite campus in Waterbury. Danbury is a major city in Fairfield County in the foothills of the Berkshire Mountains, just 65 miles north of Manhattan and 50 miles west of Hartford.

In Danbury, the Midtown campus is a 34-acre, fifteen-building campus with an interesting mix of old and new architecture, and it offers easy access to downtown entertainment, restaurants, and shopping. The 364-acre Westside campus is ideal for hikers and nature buffs who want to discover its woodland wonders while enjoying state-of-the-art facilities. The WestConn-at-Waterbury campus offers a convenient location closer to the center of the state, with the same level of excellent service.

Majors and Degrees

The Ancell School of Business offers the Bachelor of Business Administration in accounting, finance, management, management information systems, and marketing, as well as the Bachelor of Science in justice and law administration.

The School of Arts and Sciences offers the Associate in Science, Bachelor of Arts, and Bachelor of Science degrees. The Associate in Science is offered in liberal arts. The Bachelor of Arts is offered in American studies, anthropology/sociology, biology, chemistry, communication, computer science, earth and planetary sciences–astronomy, economics, English, English–professional writing, history, mathematics, political science, psychology, social sciences, and Spanish. The Bachelor of Science is offered in medical technology and meteorology.

The School of Professional Studies offers the Bachelor of Arts and Bachelor of Science degrees. The Bachelor of Arts is offered in social work. The Bachelor of Science is offered in elementary education, health education, health promotion studies, nursing, and secondary education.

The School of Visual and Performing Arts offers the Bachelor of Arts, Bachelor of Science, and Bachelor of Music degrees. The Bachelor of Arts is offered in art, music, and theater arts. The Bachelor of Science is offered in music education, and the Bachelor of Music is offered with options in classical: voice or instrument or in jazz studies. Auditions are required for entrance into any of the music degree options.

Academic Programs

The University has developed a diverse mix of programs that are designed to inspire students. From the enlightening category of the arts to specialized fields of education, the emphasis is on the individual student's learning experience.

Special offerings at WestConn include the nation's first program in computer information security management and the only licensed meteorology program in Connecticut.

Academic Facilities

A number of facilities contribute to academic life on campus. The newly renovated and expanded library holds more than 200,000 volumes and over 400,000 bound periodicals, microforms, government documents, music scores, electronic resources, and audiovisual items. WestConn's extraordinary Science Building opened in 2005 to great acclaim for its ecology-friendly green design and cutting-edge lab and classroom equipment. Students are also encouraged to make use of WestConn's exceptional computer laboratory facilities and are invited to hone their craft in superior theater and musical facilities. Along with the rest of the greater Danbury community, they benefit from the offerings of the WestConn International Center;

German Studies Center; Institute for Holistic Health Studies; Meteorological Studies and Weather Center; Jane Goodall Center for Excellence in Environmental Studies; Center for Collaboration; Center for Business Research; Center for Excellence in Learning and Teaching; Center for Excellence in the Study of Culture and Values; Center for Galactic Astronomy; Center for Graphics Research; Center for Professional Development; Center for Technology, Research, and Productivity; Westside Nature Preserve; and Westside Observatory and Planetarium.

Costs

As part of the Connecticut State System of Higher Education, WestConn provides a high-quality private university education at an exceptionally reasonable public school cost. It is estimated that a full-time, in-state undergraduate student who lives and has meals on campus paid $18,000 for 2009–10. This estimate of annual costs includes tuition, fees, and room and board. Books, laboratory fees, health insurance, and personal expenses are not included in the estimate.

WestConn participates in the New England Regional Student Program of the New England Board of Higher Education. This program offers residents of other New England states the opportunity to enroll at WestConn at Connecticut resident tuition rates, plus an additional fee, in programs that are not available in their home states. Details about the regional program can be obtained by contacting the Office of University Admissions.

Financial Aid

Any student who is matriculated at WestConn and registering for at least 6 credits per semester may apply for student aid, which includes federal, state, and institutional funding. Students must complete the Free Application for Federal Student Aid (FAFSA) and be sure to list WestConn's school code of 001380 in the college release section. If the student's file is selected for verification, appropriate signed copies of federal income tax returns must be submitted. Academic scholarships are available to students with superior academic credentials. Students with demonstrated financial need also have the opportunity to participate in work-study programs. For more information, students should contact the Financial Aid Office at 203-837-8580 or wcsufinancialaid@wcsu.edu.

Faculty

Nationally respected, WestConn's faculty members and administrators are continually cited for scholarly achievement. The faculty-student ratio is 1:15.6, and nearly 90 percent of the University's full-time faculty members have doctoral, terminal, or first professional degrees.

Admission Requirements

WestConn welcomes applications from all qualified individuals. Admission to the four undergraduate schools is competitive. University admissions criteria include grade point average, types of courses taken, extracurricular activities, and standardized test results. Applications are reviewed by admissions professionals. If an applicant feels that individual circumstances warrant special consideration, a personal letter explaining those circumstances may be submitted with the application.

Academic preparation is the most important factor in determining admission. Freshman candidates for admission must have a high school diploma from an accredited secondary school or an equivalency diploma. General Educational Development (GED) test scores must be converted into a State of Connecticut Equivalency Diploma.

WestConn applicants should present evidence of successful completion of the following academic units in high school with a cumulative grade average of B- (80) or higher: 4 years of English, including writing skills and literature; 3 years of mathematics, including algebra I, geometry, and algebra II; 2 years of social sciences, including U.S. history; 2 years of laboratory sciences; and 2 to 3 years of a single foreign language (3 years are recommended). Academic course work in computer science, visual arts, theater, music, or dance may be substituted for one of the areas above. Those applicants who do not meet these guidelines may be considered under the Educational Achievement and Access Program. For more information about the program, students should contact the Office of University Admissions.

For specific information about transfer student admission, early admission, freshman entrance with advanced standing, special transfer arrangements for associate degree recipients, guest student admission, readmit admission, fresh-start admission, and international student admission, students should contact the Office of University Admissions.

Interviews are not required, but candidates are encouraged to attend an information session before they enroll. These sessions provide information about the University and the admissions process and provide an important opportunity to assess how the University can help students meet their long-term educational goals. They also afford students the opportunity to meet with professors, other potential students, and current students. Student-guided tours are available. While on tour, students are able to visit the library, the residence halls, science and computer laboratories, the student center, and the recreation center. For information about appointments and campus visits, students should call the Office of University Admissions.

Application and Information

WestConn seeks to enroll students who will benefit from and contribute to the University. Rolling admissions for the fall semester begin December 1, with class spaces filled on a first-come basis. Rolling admissions for the spring semester begin October 1, with class spaces filled on a first-come basis. To apply, students should obtain an application from the Office of University Admissions or from a secondary school or community college guidance office. WestConn welcomes transfer and international student applications.

For application forms and more information, students should contact:

Office of University Admissions
Western Connecticut State University
181 White Street
Danbury, Connecticut 06810
Phone: 203-837-9000
877-837-WCSU (toll-free)
E-mail: admissions@wcsu.edu
Web site: http://www.wcsu.edu

A view of the Western Connecticut State University Midtown campus.

WESTERN MICHIGAN UNIVERSITY

KALAMAZOO, MICHIGAN

The University

Western Michigan University (WMU) is one of the country's top public universities and enjoys global recognition for its outstanding programs in aviation, fine arts, communications, and business marketing. WMU is also home to Lee Honors College, which has been in continuous operation longer than almost any other honors program in the country. More than 1,200 undergraduates are currently enrolled in Lee Honors College. With an increasing student demand for honors programs, the University plans to continue to enlarge Lee Honors College over the coming years.

Western Michigan University is focused on preparing its graduates for the competitive world of work as well as graduate and professional school. WMU is one of only 101 public universities in the United States to have a chapter of Phi Beta Kappa, the nation's premier honor society. In addition, *U.S. News & World Report* has ranked WMU among America's top 100 public universities for the past eleven years.

With 24,576 students, WMU is a large, complex university with a broad range of program offerings at both the undergraduate and graduate levels. Still, WMU maintains a comfortable student-faculty ratio, and two thirds of all undergraduate classes have 30 or fewer students. Despite its size, complexity, and variety of offerings, WMU is one of the most affordable of Michigan's fifteen public universities, ranking tenth from the top in tuition and required fees.

Founded in 1903, WMU has seven degree-granting colleges: Arts and Sciences, Aviation, the Haworth College of Business, Education and Human Development, Engineering and Applied Sciences, Fine Arts, and Health and Human Services. In addition, the Graduate College assists students pursuing advanced degrees; and the Lee Honors College challenges academically talented students. Students have 237 academic programs from which to choose, 140 of them at the undergraduate level. Because it has a vibrant graduate component that includes twenty-nine doctoral programs, the University attracts faculty members who not only enjoy teaching at the undergraduate level but have distinguished themselves internationally through their research.

WMU has focused on enhancing its out-of-class opportunities by expanding its internship opportunities and student engagement in research and service. The Haenicke Institute for Global Education provides access to study-abroad programs all over the world and supports international students coming to study at WMU.

The University is home to a diverse student body that includes students from nearly every state across the United States as well as 1,254 international students from ninety countries. Minority students also are well represented and make up 13 percent of the student population. The University's main campus enrollment of nearly 23,000 includes approximately 5,000 students who live in twenty-two campus residence halls that offer a variety of living arrangements.

There are nearly 300 registered student organizations, including a wide range of Greek, academic honorary, and professional organizations. In addition, the University has nationally recognized arts programs, a lively cultural calendar, and NCAA Division I-A Mid-American Conference and Central Collegiate Hockey Association sports teams. Its six men's and ten women's varsity sports, intramural teams, and club sports add vitality to campus life.

Location

For more than 100 years, Kalamazoo has been home to WMU. From the dedication of East Hall—the first building on campus—the community has supported Western's growth. Kalamazoo is an ideal college town, where business leaders recognize Western as their second-largest employer and where students and employees contribute more than $500 million annually to the economy of the region. Located just 40 miles from the beautiful eastern shoreline of Lake Michigan, the area embraces all four seasons with cool, sunny summers and moderate winters. Outdoor recreation abounds, from downhill skiing in winter months to every imaginable water sport available from late spring through early fall. Unlike much of eastern Michigan, southwest Michigan is composed of gently rolling hills, small recreational lakes, and dense woodlands. Fall is a particularly beautiful time to enjoy the variety of color while hiking or riding a bike on the Kal-Haven trail that connects Kalamazoo to the Lake Michigan resort town of South Haven. Nearly every weekend throughout the year Kalamazoo has something to offer its students and local residents. It is not unusual on a Saturday afternoon to find faculty members rubbing elbows with students at the annual Art Hop, Blues Festival, or Taste of Kalamazoo.

Kalamazoo, a city of more than 75,000, offers a wide array of lively entertainment including sports, such as professional baseball, hockey, and soccer; music, from jazz to heavy metal; intimate coffee houses and comedy clubs; and dining, from fast food to international cuisine. West Michigan is also home to numerous prosperous businesses, industries, and Fortune 500 companies including Haworth Inc., the Whirlpool Corporation, and the Kellogg Company. Many of these companies offer internships to WMU students.

Majors and Degrees

WMU offers a range of academic majors and programs to meet nearly everyone's needs. The College of Arts and Sciences offers undergraduate degrees in Africana studies; anthropology; biochemistry; biology; biomedical sciences; business-oriented chemistry; chemistry; communication studies; criminal justice; earth science; economics; English; film, video, and media studies; French; geochemistry; geography; geology; geophysics; German; global and international studies; history; hydrogeology; interpersonal communication; journalism; Latin; mathematics; organizational communication; philosophy; physics; political science; psychology; public history; public relations; religion; sociology; Spanish; statistics; student-planned major; telecommunications and information management; tourism and travel; preprofessional programs (dentistry, law, medicine); and coordinate majors (environmental studies, women's studies).

The College of Aviation offers programs in aviation flight science, aviation maintenance technology, and aviation science and administration.

The Haworth College of Business offers programs in accountancy, advertising and promotion, computer information systems, economics, electronic business design, finance, food and consumer package goods marketing, human resource management, integrated supply matrix management, management, marketing, personal financial planning, sales and business marketing, and telecommunications and information management.

The College of Education and Human Development offers programs in elementary education that emphasize language arts, mathematics, science, and social science. Secondary education students may major in art, biology, business, chemistry, earth science, English, family and consumer science, French, geography, German, health education, history, industrial technology, Latin, marketing, mathematics, music, physical education, physics, political science, school health education, social studies, Spanish, and technology and design. Other programs include athletic training, community health education, dietetics, exercise science, family studies, food service administration, industrial technology, interior design, recreation, special education, and textile and apparel studies.

The College of Engineering and Applied Sciences offers programs in aeronautical engineering, chemical engineering, civil engineering, computer engineering, computer science, construction engineering, electrical engineering, engineering graphics and design technology, engineering management technology, entrepreneurial engineering, manufacturing engineering, manufacturing engineering technology, mechanical engineering, paper engineering, and paper science.

The College of Fine Arts offers programs in art, art education, art history, dance, graphic design, jazz studies, music, music composition, music education, music performance, music theater performance, music therapy, theater design and technical production, theater performance, and theater stage management.

The College of Health and Human Services offers programs in interdisciplinary health services, occupational therapy, nursing, nursing (RN), social work, and speech pathology and audiology.

Academic Programs

WMU is committed to student academic success, beginning with a First-Year Experience program, which utilizes small-group seminars led by senior faculty members and upperclass student mentors. The University's college advisers help students plan their courses of study and consider program options, while advisers in University Curriculum assist undecided students in exploring academic programs and their relationships to various careers and professions. A comprehensive general education program provides the foundation for all fields of study. The Lee Honors College provides an atmosphere of small seminar classes, opportunities for research alongside faculty members, and the chance to explore new horizons through independent study. Student academic success is recognized through University, college, and department honor societies and through the prestigious Presidential Scholar Award given to outstanding graduating seniors. The Western Edge is the University's newest student-success initiative. It is a graduation compact offering students a rapid path to degree completion, a retention scholarship based on student performance, and a four-year freeze on room and board rates for students who live in campus residence halls.

Off-Campus Programs

WMU has six branch campuses and a full complement of online courses. A host of U.S. business-industry partnerships and exchange agreements with universities and other organizations around the world provide training, research, and study-abroad opportunities for graduate and undergraduate students. In addition, the University actively assists students seeking internships in their chosen fields of study.

Academic Facilities

Western Michigan University is on Intel's list of the nation's 100 most wireless college campuses. WMU's network provides access to the University libraries, the Internet, and extensive campus information services. Computer labs are available across the campus, including many residence halls. Specialized labs support the work of students in engineering, graphic arts, teacher education, business, and other fields. Western Michigan University's new chemistry building opened in January 2007, and the new James W. and Lois I. Richmond Center for Visual Arts opened in April 2007. New construction is continuously transforming the campus and increasing sustainability efforts while giving students access to acclaimed fine arts performance spaces, world-class aviation facilities, a leading-edge building for the College of Health and Human Services, and an innovative College of Engineering and Applied Sciences building that is located in a thriving business and research park.

Costs

A college education is one of the best investments a person can make, and, best of all, it never depreciates over time. Over a lifetime of work, WMU's graduates can expect to earn nearly twice that of someone with a high school diploma. WMU is committed to keeping costs as low as possible to ensure that all qualified students have access to the University. WMU's tuition and fees are among the lowest in the state. For 2009–10, resident tuition and fee costs were $8382, and room and board costs were $7591. Books and supplies and personal and travel expenses vary based on individual factors.

Financial Aid

The University annually awards more than $220 million in financial assistance to undergraduate students. Students who are qualified for need-based aid usually receive assistance through a combination of gift-aid (grants and scholarships), self-help (student loans), and employment (work-study).

A variety of academic achievement scholarships are available to students who have demonstrated academic success while in high school. A combination of awards can be sufficient to cover nearly all direct costs of attendance at WMU. Most merit awards are renewable by enrolling full-time and earning a minimum 3.0 cumulative grade point average while at WMU. The two most recognized awards are the Medallion Scholarship and the Dean's Scholarship. The Dean's Scholarship is awarded to the top academic students (based on high school grades and standardized test scores) who apply for admission in early December, compete in the Medallion competition in January, and enroll the following fall semester as new, first-time students. Medallion recipients receive $10,000 annually, and the scholarship is renewable for up to four years of full-time enrollment.

There are also scholarships for students who have earned associate degrees from state and regional community colleges and who have earned high grade point averages while completing degree requirements.

Faculty

WMU's commitment to academic excellence means that many of its 908 full-time and 527 part-time faculty members conduct research. Tenured professors teach freshman-level courses, and full-time faculty members teach the majority of all courses. Plus, hundreds of these scholars have academic or research experience outside of the United States, bringing a global perspective into the classroom.

Student Government

Governance structures include the Western Student Association and its Student Senate and the Residence Hall Association. Each provides students with a wide variety of opportunities for leadership.

Admission Requirements

Admission to the University is based primarily on a combination of high school cumulative grade point average and standardized test scores (either ACT or SAT). When admission is not conclusive or admission is sought to selective or highly competitive programs, consideration is given to academic rigor of courses taken and counselor/principal recommendations, in addition to grade point averages and test scores.

To ensure academic success at WMU, all students should have completed a minimum of 4 years of English, 3 years of mathematics (through intermediate algebra), 3 years of social sciences, 2 years of natural sciences, and 2 years of the same foreign language.

Offers of admission made to students still in high school are conditional, pending graduation from high school and the University's review of final senior-year grades.

Transfer students with a minimum of 26 transferable hours (39 quarter hours) at the time of application and a grade point average of at least 2.0 (C average) are considered for admission. The trend of the most recent grades is also taken into account. Applicants with fewer than 26 transferable hours (39 quarter hours) at the time of application also must submit a high school transcript. In such cases, admission is based on both college and high school records.

Application and Information

For an application or more information, students should contact:

Office of Admissions and Orientation
Western Michigan University
1903 West Michigan Avenue
Kalamazoo, Michigan 49008-5211
Phone: 269-387-2000
Web site: http://www.wmich.edu/admissions

The impressive high-tech home to WMU's College of Health and Human Services was the first higher education building in the nation recognized for sustainability with a LEED-EB Gold designation.

WESTERN WASHINGTON UNIVERSITY

BELLINGHAM, WASHINGTON

The University

As a public institution of higher education, Western Washington University (WWU) is committed to excellence in teaching, scholarship, and community service in a student-centered environment, with a liberal arts foundation and opportunities to develop professional skills. Since the first class of 88 students entered New Whatcom Normal School in 1899, the University has grown into the third-largest institution of higher education in the state. The Normal School became Western Washington College of Education in 1937, Western Washington State College in 1961, and then achieved university status in 1977.

For twelve consecutive years, U.S. News & World Reporttag italics has ranked WWU as the best regional public university in the Pacific Northwest and second in the western United States. In addition, Kiplinger's Personal Financetag italics magazine has ranked WWU thirty-eighth on list of 100 Best Values in Public Colleges in the United States.

Western Washington University is organized into the Graduate School and seven undergraduate units—the College of Business and Economics, the College of Fine and Performing Arts, Fairhaven College of Interdisciplinary Studies, the College of Humanities and Social Sciences, Huxley College of the Environment, the College of Sciences and Technology, and Woodring College of Education. Undergraduates take advantage of unique opportunities to engage in research and showcase their work regionally and nationally—experiences frequently reserved for graduate students at larger institutions.

The University enrolls around 14,600 students, 94 percent of whom are undergraduates; 55 percent are women. Students can choose from more than 200 student clubs in several categories, such as arts and music, cultural, departmental, political, recreational, religious, service, and special interest. The WWU Vikings compete in NCAA Division II basketball, crew, cross-country, golf, soccer, softball, track and field, and volleyball.

Students are not required to live on campus, but housing is guaranteed to newly admitted students who have paid their admissions enrollment fee, submitted a request for housing before May 1, and paid their housing deposit by June 15. All residence halls and apartments are coeducational by floor, wing, or suite. Residential communities maintain courtesy and quiet hours, which help create an academic atmosphere. The typical residence hall room is designed for occupancy by 2 people, though a limited number of single-occupancy and triple-occupancy rooms are available. Ninety percent of freshman choose to live on campus their first year.

Location

A coastal city of 75,000, Bellingham lies 90 miles north of Seattle and 55 miles south of Vancouver, British Columbia, Canada. The University's proximity to two major cities provides easy access for national and international visiting artists, scholars, and touring groups. Puget Sound and the San Juan Islands lie directly to the west; Mt. Baker and the North Cascades Mountain Range are an hour to the east. Bellingham offers a vibrant urban community with a natural setting, providing outstanding entertainment and recreation opportunities. With mountains, glaciers, rivers, saltwater, and many other natural habitats nearby, Western's location is ideal for fieldwork and outdoor research.

Majors and Degrees

Western's undergraduate programs lead to the Bachelor of Arts, Bachelor of Arts in Education, Bachelor of Fine Arts, Bachelor of Music, and Bachelor of Science. Majors are accounting; accounting/computer science; American cultural studies; anthropology*, with concentrations in archaeology, biocultural, biology, or social studies; art*; art-design; art history; art studio; behavioral neuroscience; biochemistry; biology*; biology/anthropology; cellular and molecular biology; business administration; Canadian American studies; chemistry*; communication; communication sciences and disorders; community health; computer science; dance (choreography or performance); early childhood education; East Asian studies; economics*; ecology; electronics engineering technology; elementary education; elementary education and special education (dual endorsement); English* (creative writing or literature); environmental education; environmental science; environmental studies/economics; environmental studies/journalism; environmental planning and policy; evolution and organismal biology; finance; financial economics; emergency planning and hazards mitigation; French*; general studies; geography*; geology; German*; history*; humanities*; human resource management; human services; industrial design; industrial technology (CAD/CAM or vehicle design); international business; Japanese*; journalism; kinesiology; language, literacy and cultural studies; linguistics; management; management information systems; manufacturing engineering technology; manufacturing and supply-chain management; marine biology; marketing; mathematics*; mathematics-applied; mathematics/computer science; music*; music composition; music history and literature; music performance; operations management; philosophy; physical education and health*; physics and astronomy*; plastics engineering technology; plastics engineering technology–vehicle engineering; political science; political science and social studies; politics/philosophy/economics; psychology*; recreation; secondary education; sociology*; sociology/social studies; Spanish*; special education; teaching English to speakers of other languages (TESOL); and theatre arts*. Pre-professional programs are offered in dental, engineering, law, medicine, nursing, pharmacy, and physical therapy. Fairhaven College of Interdisciplinary Studies offers students the option to work with a faculty advisor to design their own major, pulling from the resources at the college and the University at large.

*Related teaching endorsements available.

Academic Programs

Western's curriculum includes a program of broad general education; intensive studies designed to develop scholarly competence in the arts and sciences; professional programs for both public school personnel and a variety of other professionals; and graduate programs in professional education, the arts, the sciences, humanities, and business areas. The minimum number of credits required for a bachelor's degree is 180, although many majors require more. To graduate in four years, a student should plan to enroll in an average of 15 credits each quarter.

First-Year Experience (FYE) courses, which help new students with their transition to the University, are stand-alone classes offered by departments for academic credit, as either a General University Requirement (GUR) or an elective. Taught in small sections of 30 or fewer students, with registration restricted to freshmen, FYE courses provide first-year students with a small-group experience. First Year Interest Groups (FIG) is another transition program offered to freshman students where students participate in the GUR courses the same way as other students enrolled in the courses, but also get the advantage of meeting together as a small group in the seminar. The learning community environment created by a FIG cluster can help students connect more quickly to university life, and fosters a smoother transition from high school to college learning and expectations.

Off-Campus Programs

Most students enrich their education through internships, international study, fieldwork, service learning, and other hands-on experiences. WWU works closely with many community and governmental agencies and businesses that offer internship opportunities. Many academic departments require internships or make academic credit available for field experience. The Center for International Studies promotes and develops a broad array of study abroad programs, specifically those that give students a chance to broaden their global perspectives, gain foreign-language fluency, engage in service learning and volunteer opportunities, and acquire global citizenship skills. In addition to quarter- or semester-long programs, Western offers faculty-led short-term travel opportunities each quarter in a variety of disciplines and countries around the world.

Academic Facilities

The main campus and its 85 buildings occupy 215 acres along Sehome Hill, overlooking Bellingham Bay and downtown Bellingham. Two of the facilities, the state-of-the-art Wade King Recreation Center and the Academic Instructional Center, are LEED certified. Western Libraries, consisting of both the main library and a branch music library in the Performing Arts Center, house more than 1.4 million volumes of books, periodicals, government documents, sound recordings, and videos, among other items. The collection includes unique intellectual and cultural heritage materials covering the history of the University and the geographical area, as well as special collections in support of the University's curricula. Students have access to online periodical databases and other resources, many with full-text access. WWU's collection is supplemented by resources from the Orbis Cascade Alliance, a consortium of thirty-four academic libraries. In addition to the WWU network and WWU wireless network, students can use more than twenty general computer labs, numerous departmental labs with scanners and printers, residence hall computer labs, and the Student Technology Center (STC).

Costs

In 2009–10, tuition and fees for Washington residents and nonresidents were $6,150 and $17,200, respectively. Room and board averaged $8,100; books and supplies averaged $1,000.

Financial Aid

Western is committed to helping reduce the cost of attendance for students who cannot afford full tuition, on-campus housing and meals, books, and related expenses. Students who submit the Free Application for Federal Student Aid (FAFSA) are considered for need-based aid in the form of grants, tuition waivers, work-study employment, and loans. Western's financial aid priority date is February 15; no additional institutional financial aid application is required. More than 60 percent of students at WWU receive some sort of financial aid. The Scholarship Center (www.finaid.wwu.edu/scholarships) offers information on a wide variety of opportunities, such as merit-based, diversity, area high school, and academic department scholarships. About 15 percent of Western's entering freshman class is awarded scholarships based upon information provided in the application for admission.

Faculty

Distinguished faculty members teach more than 98 percent of the classes at Western. There are 623 full-time-equivalent faculty members, with 87 percent holding the highest degree in their fields. The student-faculty ratio is 23:1; 74 percent of classes have 30 or fewer students; 4 percent of classes have 75 or more students.

Student Government

The Associated Students, the official student governing body, is an association of all students, whose responsibilities include setting the policy for student activities, providing the framework for a variety of experiential learning opportunities, and serving as a vehicle for student involvement in the governance of the University. Several councils report to the board, including legislative and community affairs, activities, facilities and services, and university services (student affairs division functions). Standing subcommittees of the board deal with personnel, budget, technology, and several other topical areas.

Admission Requirements

Factors considered during the comprehensive application review include the level and difficulty of courses, grade trends, leadership, school and community involvement, special talents, multicultural experience, and strength of character; personal hardship or circumstances are additionally considered. The applicant's high school curriculum should include, at minimum, 4 years of English; 3 years of math, including geometry and 2 years of algebra beyond pre-algebra; 3 years of social studies; 2 years of science, 1 with a lab, 1 of algebra-based chemistry or physics; 2 years of a foreign language; and 1 semester or trimester in fine or performing arts. A completed application includes official high school transcripts and SAT or ACT scores, as well as the nonrefundable $50 application fee.

Application and Information

Freshman application deadlines for fall, winter, and spring quarters are March 1, October 1, and January 15, respectively. Transfer and postbaccalaureate application deadlines are the same, with the exception of the fall quarter deadline, which is April 1.

Office of Admissions
Western Washington University
516 High Street
Bellingham, Washington 98225-9009
Phone: 360-650-3440
Web site: http://admissions.wwu.edu

Western Washington University's campus is nestled between Mount Baker's peak and the waters of Bellingham Bay.

WESTMINSTER COLLEGE

SALT LAKE CITY, UTAH

The College

Westminster College offers students a unique environment for learning. A Westminster education is characterized by active and engaged learning, a vibrant community, and a record of success.

In traditional educational models, colleges focus on what is taught and measure student success by the time they spend in classes and the grades they earn. Westminster focuses on outcomes—what students actually learn and what they can do with that knowledge. Students are active participants in their own learning; faculty members are directly involved in mentoring and guiding their development through experiences that are active, experiential, collaborative, and cross-disciplinary; and learning goes beyond mastery of subject-specific skills to College-wide learning goals that integrate the skills and attributes that are critical to success in a rapidly changing world.

Westminster knows that learning takes place out of the classroom as well as within it, so it offers a full range of activities on campus: fifty clubs, health and wellness programming, plays, concerts, lectures, and the like. The College also enjoys the benefits of a diverse and vibrant city that serves as a center of state government, banking, and high technology—all of which students experience through internships, a campus concierge, and classes that expose students to the Salt Lake City's resources, challenges, and opportunities. In addition, Westminster is located near the Rocky Mountains and provides an outdoor recreation program that can get students to excellent ski resorts within 20 minutes or the solitude of forests or the wonders of national parks.

The College has been recognized by *U.S. News & World Report,* the Princeton Review, and Kaplan/*Newsweek.* Its goal is to add value to each student's experience at Westminster. After graduation, some students have gone to work at firms such as General Electric, American Express, and Hewlett-Packard; others have continued their education at schools such as Columbia, Georgetown, Berkeley, and the University of London.

Westminster is tucked into the quaint and eclectic Sugar House neighborhood of Salt Lake City and provides a welcome academic haven for learners. Distinguished by old-growth trees, a small creek, and a graceful blend of old and new architecture, the urban College campus still provides plenty of green space to enjoy in the midst of the city. The College's on-campus housing, which accommodates 500 students, includes new apartment-style suites featuring entertainment systems and cooking facilities. Off-campus rental housing is readily available in the neighborhood.

The current enrollment is approximately 2,600. Undergraduates make up 75 percent of the student body, with graduate students making up 25 percent. Students come to Westminster from thirty-seven states and twenty-four countries. The average undergraduate student age is 24, and the undergraduate ratio of men to women is 41:59.

Westminster College offers intercollegiate basketball, cross-country, golf, lacrosse, and soccer for men, and basketball, cross-country, golf, soccer, and volleyball for women, as well as men's and women's ski and snowboard teams. Most teams compete in the Frontier Conference (NAIA).

Student services include academic advising, career planning and placement, internships, personal counseling, tutoring, and testing.

Residential students are required to participate in a meal plan. Daily selections include a burger bar, a pizza station, a Mexican buffet, a fruit and salad bar, and daily specials.

Location

In 2007, *Outside* magazine gave Salt Lake plenty of kudos for its progressive thinking, and described it as "a near-perfect location for avid outdoor adventures," and in 2008 *Forbes* magazine ranked SLC first for job growth.

Downtown Salt Lake is 10 minutes away from campus by bus, car, or bicycle. The city offers internship and employment opportunities, cultural resources, clubs and restaurants, major professional sports, and great shopping. A metropolitan area of approximately 1.3 million people, Salt Lake has been rated as one of the ten most fun places to live, was home of the 2002 Winter Olympics, and offers easy access to the Sundance Film Festival.

A new campus concierge program facilitates student access to cultural events, recreational and entertainment options, student discounts, and volunteer opportunities. Salt Lake and the surrounding areas have four distinct seasons, with limited amounts of rain and snow in the valley and moderate temperatures. However, the Wasatch Mountains that border the Salt Lake Valley on the east are famous for the "greatest snow on earth." With approximately 500 inches of annual snowfall, these mountains are ideal for winter sports enthusiasts as well as for those who enjoy summer hiking, biking, and camping. Ten excellent ski and snowboard resorts lie within an hour's drive of the campus, and sixteen national parks and recreational areas are within a day's drive or less. Golf, backpacking, mountain biking, kayaking, wakeboarding, mountain climbing, canyoneering, spelunking, and rafting are all within easy reach of the campus.

Majors and Degrees

Westminster College offers more than seventy academic programs. Bachelor of Arts and Bachelor of Science degrees are awarded in accounting, art, arts administration, aviation–flight operations, aviation–management, biology, chemistry, communication, computer information systems, computer science, economics, economics prelaw, elementary education, English, environmental studies, finance, financial services, fine arts, history, international business, justice studies, management, marketing, mathematics, neuroscience, nursing, philosophy, physics, political studies, psychology, social sciences, sociology, Spanish and Latin American studies, special education, and theater. Preprofessional programs include predental, prelaw, and premedical courses. Other academic programs include Chinese, engineering 3–2, and honors. In addition to the above majors, the College offers minors in many of those program areas and minors only subjects ranging from anthropology to paleontology.

Academic Programs

By integrating a liberal arts foundation with professional education, Westminster exhibits features of both a liberal arts college and a comprehensive university. Students are challenged to experiment with ideas, raise questions, critically examine alternatives, and make informed decisions. Students are also encouraged to accept responsibility for their own learning, to discover and pursue their passions, and to act with responsibility.

Each student must complete at least 124 semester hours to receive a bachelor's degree, of which approximately 40 hours consist of liberal arts education core requirements that are common to all students regardless of major. Semester-hour requirements vary among majors, but all students are exposed to liberal arts concepts as well as practical, career-oriented experiences. Credit is awarded for successful scores on Advanced Placement and CLEP examinations.

Students can participate in the U.S. Air Force Reserve Officer Training Corps program, the U.S. Army Reserve Officers' Training Corps program, and the U.S. Naval Reserve Officers' Training Corps program through cooperative programs at the University of Utah.

The College has a 4-4-1 calendar, consisting of two 15-week semesters followed by a one-month May term, as well as a summer session. Students who attend full-time during fall and spring semesters earn free May-term tuition.

Off-Campus Programs

Westminster students may participate in travel/study trips (for credit) during May term and the summer session. Students can also make individual arrangements for international study by advisement from the College's International Studies Chair and the Career Resource Center and through a cooperative agreement with the Foreign Study Office at the University of Utah.

Students are encouraged to participate in service-learning activities through the Center for Civic Engagement, to take advantage of internships and other opportunities offered by the Career Resource

Center, and to consider integrating campus work-study opportunities with their traditional academic activities.

Westminster is also a member of the Utah Asian Studies Consortium, which promotes connections between faculty members and students in Utah and businesses and schools in Asia, offering May-term trips, internships, semester study-abroad programs, and other opportunities in several Asian countries.

Academic Facilities

Classes are never more than a 5-minute walk away on the pristine, tree-filled 27-acre campus. The Emma Eccles Jones Conservatory of Music and Theatre illustrates the careful blend of architecture. The Gore School of Business, Aviation, and Entrepreneurship, one of the most technologically advanced business education facilities in the nation, integrates innovative, new laboratories and state-of-the-art classroom facilities with the Center for Financial Analysis, offering real-time access to world market data, a behavioral simulation lab, and a flight simulation and testing center.

The Flight Operations Center, which includes a state-of-the-art hangar, flight simulators, and thirteen new aircraft, is located at Salt Lake International Airport. The Dolores Doré Eccles Health, Wellness, and Athletic Center includes a lap pool, exercise facilities, and a climbing wall and houses the School of Nursing and Health Sciences. A new Science Center is scheduled to open in fall 2010. The building, which will meet the exacting environmental standards of the United States Green Building Council, is designed to encourage interaction between various scientific disciplines and allow students to work with state-of-the-art equipment as part of their classroom activity and Westminster's undergraduate research program. Current facilities include major classroom buildings, multiple computer and presentation classrooms, a unique bi-level athletic field/parking garage structure, an award-winning library, a ceramics studio, and a nursing laboratory.

All students have Internet access and e-mail accounts, using a high-speed gigabit network. A secure student Web portal consolidates online e-mail, course, and registration services. Network connections abound in all classrooms and every residence-hall room and library seat. Eighty percent of classrooms are set up for multimedia presentations. Technical support is available to students and faculty and staff members seven days a week.

Costs

Tuition and fees for the 2009–10 academic year were $24,996 for a full-time student (12 to 16 semester hours). This figure includes costs for the fall semester, spring semester, and May term. Room and board costs were $7006 for the same period. Books and supplies were estimated at $1000 per year.

Financial Aid

For 2009–10, more than 98 percent of freshmen at Westminster received some form of financial aid, averaging approximately $20,571. Aid programs include need-based institutional grants and need-based federal aid programs, such as grants, loans, and employment (Federal Work-Study Program). The Free Application for Federal Student Aid (FAFSA) is the only form required for new students seeking financial aid. Students wishing to apply for federal aid programs should plan to submit applications by early April. Merit-based scholarships are available to incoming freshmen and transfer students as well as to continuing students through endowment and institutional aid programs. Every full-time student is automatically considered for merit-based scholarships awarded by the College, based on their GPA from previous academic course work. Scholarships are also offered for music, theater, athletics, and extracurricular achievements.

Faculty

Full-time faculty members number 130. The student-faculty ratio is 10:1. All faculty members teach; no full-time research faculty positions exist and no graduate students teach. Many full-time faculty members are actively involved as advisers and sponsors of campus-based student activities. Approximately 94 percent of the faculty members hold a Ph.D. or the highest degree available in their fields.

Student Government

The official student governing body is the Associated Students of Westminster College (ASWC), which sponsors all student activities and organizations and provides funding and authorization for them. The ASWC is made up of three branches: the executive cabinet, the legislative assembly, and the judiciary branch. The three branches function in a similar fashion to the federal government system. The president of the ASWC is considered the primary spokesperson for the student body and has access to all senior administrators of the College.

Admission Requirements

Individual applications are reviewed based on a student's potential for success at Westminster and their potential to add vibrancy to the classroom environment. Academic preparation, which includes both course work and grades, is most important. Also important to the review committee are items such as entrance exams (ACT or SAT), recommendations, and extracurricular activities. A campus visit to meet with an academic counselor is highly recommended, as it helps complete the picture for both the prospective student and the College.

Transfer students must have earned at least a 2.5 cumulative GPA in previous college work. In addition to all other admissions criteria, international students must have at least a 3.0 GPA in non-U.S. high school or college work and a Test of English as a Foreign Language (TOEFL) score of at least 550 (or equivalent).

Application and Information

To apply for admission, a student must submit an application for admission, an application fee, and official transcripts of previous high school and/or college class work. Freshman applicants must submit ACT or SAT scores. Applicants are notified of their admission status within two weeks of receipt of all required materials. Westminster operates on a rolling admissions basis, so it is best to send applications in as soon as possible. To preserve the faculty-student ratio, classes are limited. Westminster College reserves the right to close the class earlier than the dates specified if enrollment goals are met before those dates. New applicants are accepted for the start of all sessions. For application forms and additional information, students should contact:

Office of Admissions
Westminster College
1840 South 1300 East
Salt Lake City, Utah 84105
Phone: 801-832-2200
800-748-4753 (toll-free)
Web site: http://www.westminstercollege.edu

Westminster College offers high-quality education in one of the unique learning environments in the country.

WESTMONT COLLEGE

SANTA BARBARA, CALIFORNIA

The College

Westmont College is a nationally ranked Christian liberal arts college in the evangelical tradition that remains focused on undergraduate education. One of the country's most dynamic interdenominational Christian colleges, Westmont combines a world-class education with an unbeatable coastal Southern California location to prepare students for fulfilling lives of leadership and service.

Residence life, athletics, off-campus programs, and opportunities for local and international outreach contribute to balanced personal and spiritual development. Alumni enter a wide variety of professions and vocations and pursue professional-, master's-, and doctoral-level programs at the world's finest research universities, including UCLA, Stanford, Harvard, Yale, Princeton, the University of Chicago, Cambridge, and many others. Westmont's 1,200 students come to Westmont from the majority of states and many countries throughout the world, the highest percentage come from California. Approximately 60 percent are women, 25 percent are students of color, and 2 percent are international students. Approximately 80 percent of the students live in the five residence halls on campus or the apartment complex off campus.

As a member of the National Association of Intercollegiate Athletics and the Golden State Athletic Conference, Westmont provides intercollegiate sports for men and women in basketball, cross-country, soccer (NAIA champions), tennis, and track and field. Men also compete in intercollegiate baseball, club polo, club rugby, club soccer, and club volleyball, and women also compete in intercollegiate volleyball and club polo. The intramural program offers a wide variety of activities as well.

There are numerous clubs and organizations, including a student newspaper, literary magazine, yearbook, radio station, choral and music ensembles, multicultural club organizations, political organizations, theater productions, community service organizations, and Christian service, mission, and outreach programs. The Ruth Kerr Memorial Student Center (1983) houses the main campus dining facilities. An integral component of the Westmont experience is the Chapel Program, which students are required to attend three days a week. Chapel provides speakers and programs to inspire and challenge students to continue growing in their relationship with Christ.

Location

Ruth Kerr, president of the Kerr Manufacturing Company, was one of the founders of Westmont College. She was instrumental in opening the first campus in Los Angeles in 1937 and in moving the College to Santa Barbara in 1945. Westmont is located on a 111-acre campus, rich with pine, oak, and eucalyptus trees, in Montecito, an estate area of Santa Barbara between the Pacific Ocean and the Santa Ynez Mountains. Students enjoy the beach and mountain trails year-round. Santa Barbara has a wealth of history and culture, and theaters, libraries, community concerts, and other civic offerings are just minutes from the campus.

Majors and Degrees

Westmont awards Bachelor of Arts (B.A.) and Bachelor of Science (B.S.) degrees in twenty-six liberal arts majors. These include alternative major, art, biology, chemistry, communication studies, computer science, economics and business, education, engineering physics, English, English and modern languages, French, history, kinesiology and physical education, mathematics, music, philosophy, physics, political science, psychology, religious studies, social science, sociology and anthropology, Spanish, and theater arts. The College offers a teacher-preparation program, which is approved by the California Commission for Teacher Preparation and Licensing, enabling students to qualify for either the single-subject or the multiple-subject credential. Preprofessional programs include athletic training, dentistry, engineering, law, medicine, ministry and missionary studies, pharmacy, physical therapy, and veterinary studies. A 3-2 program combining liberal arts and engineering is offered in cooperation with Stanford University; the University of Southern California; the University of California, Santa Barbara; Boston University; Washington University (St. Louis); and other institutions having accredited schools of engineering.

Academic Programs

Westmont offers majors, minors, and concentrations in dozens of exciting fields and disciplines, such as dance, European studies, neuroscience, and theater arts. All majors and programs of study feature thought-provoking and inspiring ways to integrate belief, thought, and action and to come to a deeper, more accurate understanding of the world. Westmont's commitment to academic freedom is clear, not only in courses that demand students' best critical thinking, but also through a wide range of opportunities and organizations that explore the world of ideas. Students consider issues of science and religion through the Pascal Society and attend lectures in the humanities sponsored by the Erasmus Society. As an exclusively undergraduate college, Westmont has a deep understanding of the ideas and issues that absorb students. From its faculty and staff members to its alumni, Westmont is committed to helping students grow through their questions toward ever-deeper faith.

Off-Campus Programs

Off-campus programs include the Europe Semester, which is offered each fall and provides the broadest geographical scope, with extended stays in Athens, Florence, Jerusalem, London, Paris, and Rome. The England Semester, offered every other year, combines travel and residential study in the British Isles for students of literature. Semesters in France and Spain offer French and Spanish majors the opportunity to study these languages in their home countries, as does the Latin American Studies Program, which combines the study of Spanish culture and language in Belize, Chile, Costa Rica, and Honduras. Similar programs are offered at Jerusalem University College in Israel; Daystar University in Nairobi, Kenya; the Middle East Studies Program at the American University in Cairo, Egypt; and in the Russian Studies Program in Moscow, Nizhni Novgorod, and St. Petersburg (through Westmont's membership in the Council for Christian Colleges & Universities). Participants in the International Business Institute program visit the major economic and political capitals of Europe and Asia. The Westmont Economics/Business Program in Asia introduces students to the diverse economic growth in the Pacific Rim. The East Asia Program addresses contemporary world issues in China, Japan, and Taiwan. An additional summer program in Asia offers students an opportunity to study life and culture in Sri Lanka. Domestic off-campus programs include the San Francisco Urban Program, which studies modern American urban society and offers internships; the Washington Semester, highlighting national political processes and incorporating internships in national, international, and economic policy, justice, and journalism; a semester at Bethune-Cookman, a historically black college in Florida; the Consortium Visitor Program, enabling students to study at any of the Christian College Consortium's twelve other member colleges; and other programs sponsored by the Council for Christian Colleges and Universities.

Academic Facilities

New buildings currently under construction (or planned in the near future) are the Adams Center for the Visual Arts which will include a gallery, studios, offices and classrooms; Winter Hall for Science and Mathematics; Observatory; Chapel and Residence Hall. To view new facilities, visit http://www.westmont.edu/buildings. The trilevel Roger John Voskuyl Library is the academic center of Westmont. The library holds 174,246 catalogued items, 465 print periodical subscriptions, and 2,494 online periodical subscriptions as well as seven classrooms; audiovisual equipment; math, language, and computer laboratories; and three IBM RS-6000 computers, which are used for instructional purposes. Westmont's network consists of both wired and wireless components. The wired network currently extends 100 Mb/s connections to all buildings on campus, all offices, all classrooms, and all dorm rooms. Uplinks to the network's core from buildings are currently 1,000 Mb/s. In Q2 2009, the core of the network will be upgraded to 10,000 Mb/s to buildings and 1,000 Mb/s to approximately

20 percent of the network connections. Wireless coverage extends to all dorms, the dining commons, most academic buildings, and selected outdoor areas. Access to the Internet is through a 45 Mb/s connection. Although well over 90 percent of Westmont students bring their own computers, the college provides a general access computer lab consisting of thirty-five computers, as well as discipline-specified computer labs for art, biology, chemistry, computer science, economics and business, languages, music, physics, and psychology for another ninety-eight computers. Thirteen computers are available in the library for public access. Students are provided Google Apps accounts through Westmont, providing e-mail, calendaring, document sharing and 4 GB storage per student. The library features an after-hours study room, a rare book archives room, and dozens of individual carrels and lockable study cubicles for faculty members and students. It also houses the Writer's Corner and offices for the Director of First-Year Students and the Office of Life Planning department. Reynolds Art Gallery features art studios and a classroom. Students and professional artists exhibit their work year-round in the gallery. Porter Theatre contains state-of-the-art equipment for dramatic productions and concerts. The George Carroll Observatory contains a 24-inch search-grade reflector telescope, the most powerful telescope between San Francisco and Los Angeles. The Mericos H. Whittier Science Building houses the College's science program and equipment, including an ultracentrifuge, a liquid scintillation counter for measuring radioactivity, physiographic units and other equipment for advanced physiological studies, low-pressure liquid chromatography equipment, sophisticated environmental instrumentation, atomic absorption spectrophotometers, Fourier-transform NMR spectrometers, infrared and ultraviolet-visible spectrophotometers, gas and high-performance liquid chromatographs, and gamma-ray spectrometers.

Costs

Tuition and fees for 2009–10 were $33,190, and room and board for the academic year were $10,550. The cost of books, personal expenses, and transportation was estimated at $4680. Tuition for 2010–11 has not been announced.

Financial Aid

Westmont has a strong financial aid program, so no student should hesitate to apply for lack of financial resources. Eighty-five percent of Westmont's students receive some form of financial assistance; $22 million in total financial aid was awarded to students for 2009–10. Westmont offers Monroe full-tuition scholarships, which are available only to first-year applicants who apply via the early action (nonbinding) process. A select group of these applicants are invited to the campus to participate in a formal competition process. Students should contact the Office of Admission for further details. Other merit awards in the financial aid program are the President's, Provost's, and Dean's Scholarships, which range from $10,000 to $14,000. These merit scholarships are awarded to students who have demonstrated impressive academic achievement. Westmont also gives awards to students who demonstrate strength in art, computer science, music, theater arts, dance, cultural diversity, and athletics. After submitting the Free Application for Federal Student Aid (FAFSA), students may be eligible for generous state grants, aid from federal programs, institutional grants, loans, and work-study programs.

Faculty

One of the highest priorities at Westmont is the attraction and retention of outstanding Christian teachers and scholars. The College's professors are dedicated to the integration of faith and learning, while also being actively involved in the lives of students. There are 90 full-time and 52 part-time faculty members. The student-faculty ratio is 12:1; the average class size is 18. Eighty-nine percent of tenure-track faculty members hold a terminal degree. Westmont's faculty members are committed to teaching at the undergraduate level, and they have additional advising responsibilities with either incoming first-year students or students in their major. A director of first-year programs is responsible for the advising and orientation of new students. Although teaching is their primary scholarly activity, many faculty members engage in research, write books, and publish articles in leading journals and periodicals.

Student Government

The Westmont College Student Association (WCSA) is an entirely self-governing body. Students elect their own WCSA representatives, who are then responsible for organizing social, cultural, and educational activities. They actively participate in and are voting members on almost all faculty committees, while also allocating the student budget to various clubs and organizations. Westmont Student Ministries, another student-managed organization, is responsible for organizing on- and off-campus ministries and mission opportunities.

Admission Requirements

Westmont selects candidates for admission from those prospective students who produce evidence that they are prepared for the academic stimulation and spiritual vitality that are central to the character of Westmont. For example, students should place a high priority on undergraduate education, and living and learning in a classic liberal arts environment should be valued. Applicants must have a clear understanding of the Christian mission of the College as well as an explicit desire to benefit from being in this environment. In addition, applicants should possess the strong moral character, values, personal integrity, and social concern that would be in accord with the Westmont community. All applicants must submit one academic letter of recommendation, official high school or college transcripts, and official SAT or ACT scores. A pastoral/character reference is optional. An interview is strongly encouraged. For transfer students from an accredited two- or four-year college or university or a Bible college or university that is accredited by the American Association of Bible Colleges, the evaluation is based on achievement in solid, transferable course work; an assessment of the personal areas covered by the application (as stated above); and the quality of the written responses. High school records must be submitted if the applicant has completed fewer than 24 college-level credits at the time of application.

Application and Information

Entrance to Westmont is possible at the beginning of either the fall or spring semester. Westmont offers an early action plan. High school seniors interested in applying for early action must submit the application by November 1; notifications are mailed on December 20. The priority deadline for regular decision is February 20 for first-year applicants and March 1 for transfers; notifications are mailed beginning April 1. Applications should be submitted online via Westmont's Web site with an application fee of $35. The fee for Westmont's paper application and all other online versions is $50. The Office of Admission encourages applicants to complete the application process as early as possible. Visitors are welcome at any time. Campus visitors can stay overnight in the residence halls, attend classes and chapel, speak with professors or coaches, have a music audition, share a portfolio with the art department, and have meals with Westmont students. Several Preview Day events are planned each semester. Westmont desires to enroll a well-rounded and balanced first-year class. A goal of Westmont is to create a dynamic as well as culturally and traditionally diverse community of learners who bring with them a variety of attributes, accomplishments, backgrounds, and interests. For further information regarding admissions, students should contact:

Office of Admission
Westmont College
955 La Paz Road
Santa Barbara, California 93108
Phone: 800-777-9011 (toll-free)
Fax: 805-565-6234
E-mail: admissions@westmont.edu
Web site: http://www.westmont.edu/

WEST VIRGINIA UNIVERSITY INSTITUTE OF TECHNOLOGY

MONTGOMERY, WEST VIRGINIA

The University

West Virginia University Institute of Technology (WVU Tech) located in Montgomery, West Virginia, offers students programs with strong reputations that provide a high value for their investment. The institution has experienced a number of significant changes since it began as a preparatory school extension of West Virginia University in 1895.

WVU Tech provides students a family-like campus atmosphere. There are numerous social, athletic, and cultural activities on campus through which students can satisfy personal interests. Five national social fraternities and two sororities have chapters at WVU Tech.

Location

Montgomery, West Virginia, is a small town of about 2,500 residents, just 28 miles southeast of Charleston, the state capital. Interstate Highways 64, 77, and 79 all run within 30 miles of the campus, and U.S. Route 60, a major east-west artery, runs immediately adjacent to the campus. Bus services are available through Greyhound Lines as well as the Kanawha Rapid Transit (KRT) and Mountain Transit Authority (MTA). Both the KRT and the MTA run regular schedules to Montgomery with destination points in Charleston, West Virginia, and many Kanawha Valley communities.

Another major asset to WVU Tech is the Amtrak service located across from the campus. With stops such as Chicago, Cincinnati, New York City, and Washington, D.C., and the railway provides a convenient method of transportation for many students living in the continental United States. With Yeager Airport only 30 minutes away, WVU Tech is just a flight away from any destination in the world.

WVU Tech's campus is also convenient to many tourist attractions and thrill-seekers' adventures. Hawks Nest State Park, with its aerial tram to the bottom of the New River canyon, is located 30 miles from the campus. The New River, considered by many authoritative geologists to be the second-oldest river in the world, is a challenge to enthusiasts of white-water rafting, and the New River Gorge Bridge is the largest arch bridge east of the Mississippi. WVU Tech is also close to three popular skiing areas, including Snowshoe Mountain, Silver Creek, and Winter Place Ski Lodge.

Majors and Degrees

Tech offers Bachelor of Arts and Bachelor of Science degrees. The Bachelor of Arts degree is available in government and history. Bachelor of Science degrees are offered in accounting; aerospace engineering (2+2 program); athletic coaching education; biology; business management; chemical, civil, computer, electrical, and mechanical engineering; chemistry; computer science; criminal justice; electronic, industrial, and engineering technology; health-services administration; industrial relations and human resources; interdisciplinary studies; management information systems; mathematics; nursing; predental; prelaw; premedicine; prepharmacy; printing management; psychology; public service administration; sport management; and technology management. For more information on any degree programs, students should visit the WVU Tech Web site at http://www.wvutech.edu.

Academic Programs

WVU Tech, a four-year institution of higher learning, offers a variety of bachelor degree programs in areas ranging from business, science, and technology to engineering. WVU Tech has always sustained a high reputation for its accredited and nationally recognized degree programs in engineering. In addition, WVU Tech has many unique programs and newly added programs. For a full listing of available programs, students should visit the WVU Tech Web site at http://www.wvutech.edu.

To earn a bachelor's degree, students must complete a minimum of 128 semester hours. To earn an associate degree, students must complete a minimum of 64 semester hours.

Tech operates on a two-semester calendar year. The first semester begins in August and ends in December; the second begins in January and ends in May. Summer courses are also available.

Off-Campus Programs

WVU Tech offers a unique "earn while you learn" approach through the Cooperative Education Program, which combines an organized curriculum that integrated practical industrial experience. Students participate in the three-semester industry rotation that is interwoven among on-campus classroom instruction. WVU Tech also offers online courses.

Academic Facilities

The Montgomery campus consists of nineteen academic, administrative, and residential buildings situated on 200 acres. Many of the facilities are equipped for classroom instruction, auditorium lectures, and hands-on laboratories for majors such as (but not limited to) biology, chemistry, nursing, engineering, art, engineering technology, and computer science. WVU Tech also features a theater facility for seasonal productions and special performances.

Costs

For 2009–10, costs for tuition and fees per academic year ranged from $3382 to $5164 for West Virginia residents and $13,264 to $14,864 for nonresidents. Additional student fees can apply for specific majors. Room costs were approximately $2700 per semester (single occupancy—double rooms cost less); board costs ranged from $1350 to $1570 per semester. Students should expect to spend approximately $3000 each semester for books and supplies.

Financial Aid

WVU Tech offers a wide range of financial aid resources, including institutional scholarships, privately and federally funded loans, Federal Pell Grants, Federal Supplemental Educational Opportunity Grants, the National Science and Mathematics Access to Retain Talent grant (SMART), the Academic Competitiveness Grant (ACG), Federal Work-Study Program awards, privately funded scholarships for both academic and special talent, and West Virginia Higher Education Grant Program awards. The student's parents or guardians are required to submit the Free Application for Federal Student Aid (http://www.fafsa.ed.gov) for determination of eligibility. Applications for financial aid, both from incoming freshmen and from enrolled students, should be submitted to WVU Tech's Office of Student Financial Aid by April 1 in order to receive consideration for the next academic year.

Faculty

Faculty members at WVU Tech are well prepared both academically and professionally to teach the institution's career-oriented curricula. Faculty members come from all over the United States and from several other countries, and most have had considerable practical experience in their field. In the Leonard C. Nelson College of Engineering alone, nearly 90 percent of the faculty members have earned doctorates. The student-faculty ratio is 14:1. Faculty members work with students in developing academic programs, and they assist in personal counseling in addition to the professional counselors on staff.

Student Government

The Student Government Association (SGA) consists of students elected in campuswide referendums that are held each fall and spring. One of the SGA's most important functions is to develop a budget on which to base the student activity fees that fund the many diverse student activities and organizations on campus.

Admission Requirements

Applicants who are residents of West Virginia must graduate from an accredited high school or pass the GED test and must take the ACT and have test scores sent to the Institute directly from American College Testing, Inc. Out-of-state residents must graduate from an accredited high school or pass the GED test, rank in the upper three fourths of their graduating class or attain a standard composite score of at least 18 on the ACT (SAT combined score of at least 870), and have their scores sent to the Institute directly from American College Testing, Inc., or the Educational Testing Service.

Admission to the college does not necessarily admit a student to all programs. Prerequisites apply for admission to certain curricula, as follows: for engineering, 2 units of algebra, 1 unit of plane geometry, 1 unit of advanced math, a minimum 3.0 GPA, and a math ACT score of at least 19 or SAT score of at least 460. Students lacking one or more of these prerequisites are given an opportunity to enroll in pre-engineering mathematics courses. Nursing candidates must have a 3.6 GPA and ACT of 25 (or SAT of 1140) to be admitted directly into the program. They also need 2 units of algebra and 2 units of laboratory science, 1 unit of which must be in chemistry.

Application and Information

Students are encouraged to apply by January. However, applications are processed on a rolling basis.

Applications for admission and requests for further information should be addressed to:

Director of Admissions and Recruitment
West Virginia University Institute of Technology
405 Fayette Pike
Montgomery, West Virginia 25136
Phone: 888-554-TECH (toll-free)
Web site: http://www.wvutech.edu

Old Main.

COLLEGE CLOSE-UPS

WHEATON COLLEGE

WHEATON, ILLINOIS

COLLEGE CLOSE-UPS

The College

Ranked by *U.S. News & World Report* as one of the nation's top liberal arts colleges, Wheaton College attracts exceptional students from all fifty states and more than thirty countries. An interdenominational Christian liberal arts college, Wheaton takes the pursuit of faith and learning seriously. In addition to upholding an academically rigorous curriculum, Wheaton is committed to being a community that fearlessly pursues God's truth; invests in developing whole, well-rounded students; and prepares its graduates to lead lives that make a difference in the world.

Wheaton College's 150-year history demonstrates the benefits of stable leadership in private Christian higher education—it has had only 7 presidents since it was founded in 1860. Interdenominational and international in constituency, the student body consists of approximately 2,400 undergraduates (including 200 students in the Conservatory of Music). Approximately 80 percent of the undergraduate students come from outside Illinois.

Wheaton has been faithful to its original precepts, and its legacy is shown in the lives of its graduates. Many distinguished schools currently enroll Wheaton graduates in the dramatic arts, education, law, medicine, music, philosophy, science, and sociology. These include Notre Dame, Princeton, SMU, Yale, and the Universities of Chicago and Missouri–Kansas City; several of the Big Ten music schools; and the A.R.T./MXAT Institute for Advanced Theater Training at Harvard. Alumni also excel in a wealth of endeavors around the world, with many holding positions in business and finance, government and foreign service, teaching, ministry, law, medicine, and the arts. Wheaton graduates actively contribute to their communities and churches, and no matter what position they hold, they strive to make a difference in the world around them.

Wheaton offers a rich, life-changing education, with graduates trained for life, not just jobs. Students are taught to think, reason, and express themselves effectively. They should be able to attain knowledge and measure it against the truth of God's word, and understand the importance of service and the value of a faith that acts. Developing strong, life-long relationships—with classmates, professors, and Jesus Christ—is a priority. Graduates are well-positioned for whatever they want to pursue and prepared to face the challenges of life. The Wheaton experience is distinctive and living and learning at Wheaton is extraordinary.

Location

Wheaton's 80-acre campus is located in a residential suburb (population 50,000) 25 miles west of Chicago, and the educational and cultural features of the Chicago metropolitan area are easily accessible by train and regularly visited by students.

Majors and Degrees

Wheaton grants the Bachelor of Arts and Bachelor of Science degrees and, through the Wheaton Conservatory of Music, the Bachelor of Music and Bachelor of Music Education degrees.

The following majors are available in the arts and sciences: ancient languages, anthropology, applied health science, archaeology, art, biblical and theological studies, biology, business/economics, chemistry, Christian education and ministry, communication, computer science, economics, education, English, environmental studies, geology, history, interdisciplinary studies, international relations, mathematics, modern languages (French, German, and Spanish), music, philosophy, physics, political science, psychology, and sociology. Also, 3-2 programs are offered in engineering and nursing, as is a five-year cooperative engineering program with Illinois Institute of Technology and other engineering schools.

The Wheaton Conservatory of Music offers a full range of professional music majors, including composition, education, history/literature, performance, music with elective studies in an outside field, and music with an emphasis in a music-related field (such as media/film music, pedagogy, conducting, and collaborative piano). Students seeking these professional music degrees are accepted directly into the program by audition.

An on-campus program in military science leads to a commission in the U.S. Army at graduation. In addition to the majors offered, Wheaton has programs leading to teacher certification and to athletic training certification as well as programs preparing students for careers in business, health professions, law, and ministry.

Academic Programs

Wheaton is a distinctively Christian college where faculty members and students work together, both inside and outside the classroom, to apply Christian principles and values to the needs and problems of the individual and society. The vigorous search for knowledge and wisdom in any area of human activity is based on the belief that all truth is God's truth.

The academic curriculum combines with artistic, athletic, religious, service, and social activities to achieve a lively interaction of Christian faith, learning, and living. Because of the College's strong commitment to developing effective servant/leaders for the church and society worldwide, there is a particularly strong integration of faith and learning in all degree programs.

The major field is selected during the second semester of general education courses taken to meet competency and area requirements. Students must demonstrate competence (either by examination or by taking prescribed courses) in foreign language, mathematics, speech, and writing. All students must complete area requirements in applied health science, art, biblical studies, history, literature, music, natural science, philosophy, and social science. A student may be granted advanced placement or college credit on the basis of examination (SAT Subject Tests or AP). The number of credits granted and the level of placement are determined by the registrar and the chair of the department in which the course is taught.

Wheaton offers ten natural science majors—applied health science, biology, chemistry, computer science, environmental studies, geology, liberal arts engineering, liberal arts nursing, mathematics, and physics—in six academic departments. The Wheaton faculty members engage the study of science authoritatively, enthusiastically, and creatively in the classrooms and laboratories and beyond the campus. They are creative and offer more than two dozen general education courses in the natural sciences as well as the majors listed above. The programming includes the use of state-of-the-art technologies and techniques on the main Wheaton campus, cutting edge geological and biological studies in a large science station in the scientifically rich area of the Black Hills of South Dakota, and marine biology studies in Belize. In 2010, Wheaton's science departments will move into a new $80-million science and mathematics facility with expanded teaching labs and research equipment.

Off-Campus Programs

Wheaton offers a variety of off-campus opportunities to enhance students' programs of study. The Wheaton Passage program is a popular camp experience available to new students at the College's Honey Rock Camp in northern Wisconsin. Another program, Human Needs and Global Resources (HNGR), combines classroom study with a six-month, field-based, service-learning internship in the Global South. A similar program in urban studies, Wheaton in Chicago, focuses on urban issues in U.S. cities and includes a semester living in College-owned housing in urban Chicago.

Other special summer programs for credit include field study at the Wheaton College Science Station in the Black Hills of South Dakota;

working with youth at Honey Rock Camp; interdisciplinary study in East Asia; the study of English literature in England; language study in France, Germany, and Spain; the Wheaton in the Holy Lands program, involving biblical and archaeological studies; the Arts in London program, which includes course work in music, theater, and art; and an international study program based in England and the Netherlands, offering courses in economics, political science, and psychology.

Wheaton is a member of the Council of Christian Colleges and Universities, based in Washington, D.C. The council's activities increase students' learning opportunities by bringing special programs to campus and by providing off-campus study. Off-campus programs include American Studies in Washington, D.C.; the Washington Journalism Center in Washington, D.C.; the Los Angeles Film Studies Center; the Contemporary Music Center in Martha's Vineyard; Latin American Studies in Costa Rica; Middle East Studies in Cairo; the Australia Studies Center; China Studies Program; the Scholar's Semester in Oxford; Russia Studies Program; and Uganda Studies Program. Wheaton has also recently affiliated with the International Sustainable Development Studies Institute in Thailand. In addition, Wheaton's membership in the Christian College Consortium allows students a semester of study at one of the other twelve consortium colleges.

Cooperative programs in social science are available at American and Drew universities, and students may participate in a European seminar conducted by Gordon College.

Academic Facilities

A new $80-million science and mathematics facility is under construction and scheduled to open in fall 2010. The 128,000-square-feet of space will include eight teaching labs and research space designed to promote collaborative teacher-student research.

In 2009, an $11 million renovation of Adams Hall added art gallery and studio space. Edman Chapel, often the venue for concerts by world-class musicians, has undergone a $9 million renovation that added rehearsal space, including a large rehearsal room named for alum John Nelson, conductor of Ensemble Orchestral de Paris.

In 2008, Wheaton's Memorial Student Center reopened after an extensive renovation to house the J. Dennis Hastert Center for Economics, Government, and Public Policy. The facility provides classroom, research, and public discussion space geared toward the study of economics, politics, and values in business, government, and ministry. Other recent additions to campus facilities include the Todd Beamer Student Center (2004); the Wade Center (2001), which houses the books and papers of seven British authors, including C. S. Lewis and J. R. R. Tolkien; and the Sports and Recreation Complex (2000).

Costs

Tuition for the 2009–10 year was $26,520; room and board for the year were $7770.

Financial Aid

Realizing that a private college education is costly, Wheaton is committed to providing the necessary need-based financial aid so students can attend. Last year Wheaton awarded over $17 million in grants and scholarships and over $5.7 million in loans.

The average need-based aid package for freshmen is about $17,085 and some merit aid is also available. The Career Development Center helps students to secure part-time jobs, as well as future employment.

Faculty

Over 90 percent of Wheaton's 194 full-time faculty members hold earned doctorates, and more than one third graduated from the top twenty-five graduate schools as designated in *U.S. News & World Report*. The professors' primary commitment as educators and advisers is enriched by their considerable research, publishing, and artistic performance activities. In addition, the professors are active Christians who strive to show how a profound commitment to the truthfulness of God's word structures a vision of all of life, including intellectual life. They are dedicated to honoring a Christian perspective and to modeling Christ's love to their students.

All undergraduate courses are taught by faculty members.

To ensure a rich range of perspectives and expertise, every department at Wheaton has at least 3 full-time professors, and most have 5 to 10. The student-faculty ratio is 12:1.

Student Government

Student Government ensures a student voice in institutional affairs and provides a wide range of opportunities to develop leadership abilities. Student Government's 2009–10 vision is "To be excellent stewards of the influence we have been given while staying committed to each other and to the college."

Besides Student Government, there are over thirty academic, cultural, social justice, and entertainment student groups on campus. In addition, the Office of Christian Outreach provides opportunities for student ministry through student-run mission trips and ministries in urban and suburban Chicago.

Admission Requirements

Wheaton is a selective college that seeks to enroll students who evidence a vital Christian experience, high moral character, personal integrity, social concern, strong academic ability and motivation, and the desire to pursue Christian higher education as defined in the aims and objectives of the College. These qualities are evaluated by consideration of each applicant's academic record, autobiographical essays, test scores, recommendations, optional interview, and participation in extracurricular activities. For students applying to the Conservatory of Music, strong consideration is given to the evaluation of the required audition.

Applicants must have a high school diploma or the equivalent and, at the time of graduation, should have completed a college-preparatory curriculum with a minimum of 18 acceptable units.

Satisfactory scores on the SAT or on the ACT examination are required of all applicants to the freshman class. The middle 50 percent range of scores for those admitted is 27–31 (ACT) and 1220–1400 (SAT composite math and verbal scores).

Application and Information

An application packet, complete with detailed instructions and requirements, can be obtained from the Admissions Office or online. For early action (nonbinding), students seeking admission in the fall term should apply to either the College of Arts and Sciences or the Conservatory of Music by November 1. The regular action deadline is January 10; the transfer application deadline is March 1. An admissions counselor can provide more information about Wheaton in general or the application process in particular.

Further information is available from:

Admissions Office
Wheaton College
501 College Avenue
Wheaton, Illinois 60187
Phone: 630-752-5005
800-222-2419 (toll-free)
E-mail: admissions@wheaton.edu
Web site: http://www.wheaton.edu

WHEATON COLLEGE

NORTON, MASSACHUSETTS

The College

Wheaton College is an independent liberal arts college of approximately 1,600 women and men. Founded as a seminary for women in 1834, Wheaton was chartered as a college in 1912 and enrolled its first coeducational class in 1988. Students come from forty-two states and thirty-eight countries. Nearly all students live on campus in both single-sex and coed student-run dormitories.

The vitality of this classic liberal arts college grows out of each student's involvement in the social and academic life of the campus. There are many extracurricular activities and organizations, including intercollegiate and intramural sports, such as baseball, basketball, cross-country, field hockey, lacrosse, soccer, softball, synchronized swimming, tennis, and track; musical groups, such as the Whims, Wheatones, Gentleman Callers, and chamber music ensembles; the Modern Dance Group; the Black Students Association; the Student Government Association; the Christian Fellowship; Hillel; the International Students Association; the Latino Students Association; the Asian Student Association; and the newspaper, yearbook, campus radio station, and literary magazine. Wheaton also has a chapter of Phi Beta Kappa. A number of lecture series are offered, and concerts, plays, films, colloquia, art exhibits, and social events are scheduled regularly. Through the Filene Center for Academic Advising and Career Services, hundreds of students annually undertake career exploration internships and field placements in local towns as well as in Boston, Providence, and overseas. The Filene Center for Academic Advising and Career Services also provides a full range of career services, graduate and professional school counseling, alumnae networks, and databases of part-time and summer job opportunities. The new Office of Service, Spirituality, and Social Responsibility provides an inclusive place for students to participate in community service, explore spirituality, and initiate social activism.

Location

The 400-acre campus with its eighty-seven buildings is in the suburban surroundings of Norton. The newest additions to the campus include a $20-million arts complex with a state-of-the-art studio arts building; 100-bed Beard Hall; two 50-person residence halls; a multipurpose athletics facility, which includes a field house, a pool, and a gymnasium; and Sidell Baseball Stadium. Norton is located 30 minutes from Providence and 45 minutes from Boston. Public buses connect the campus to nearby commuter rail stations serving Boston, Providence, and numerous points in between. The College provides individuals with transportation for academic and internship activities as well as direct service to Boston's center and Providence, Rhode Island, on weekends. The College is also situated within an hour's drive of the beautiful beaches of Cape Cod, Massachusetts, and Newport, Rhode Island. The Comcast Center for Performing Arts is located 2½ miles away.

Majors and Degrees

Wheaton College grants the Bachelor of Arts degree with formal majors in African, African American, and diaspora studies; American studies; ancient studies; anthropology; art (history and studio); Asian studies; biochemistry; bioinformatics; biology; chemistry; classical civilization; classics (Greek and Latin); computer science; economics; economics-mathematics; English (literature, writing, and film studies); environmental science; French studies; German; German studies; Hispanic studies; history; international relations; Italian studies; Latin; mathematics; mathematics and computer science; music; philosophy; physics; physics and astronomy; political science; psychobiology; psychology; religion; religion and history; religion and philosophy; Russian; Russian studies; sociology; theater and English dramatic literature; and women's studies. Students may also create their own interdepartmental majors.

Five-year dual-degree programs are available in engineering with Thayer School of Engineering (Dartmouth) and George Washington University, in business and management with the University of Rochester, in religion with Andover-Newton Theological School, in optometry with the New England School of Optometry, in communications with Emerson College, and in fine arts with the School of the Museum of Fine Arts in Boston.

Academic Programs

Wheaton's programs reflect the traditional depth and breadth of the liberal arts while going beyond prescribed boundaries. The College's curriculum encourages students to push past one-dimensional views of the world to acquire a deeper understanding of the topics that interest them. Through a series of linked courses, Wheaton students approach the same topic from two or more academic perspectives. Thus, students who examine public policy and politics may also choose to explore environmental management. An art class in figure drawing may be paired with study of human anatomy. Or students investigating evolutionary theory may survey the literature of the Victorian society from which Darwin and his work sprung. This approach helps students discover doorways to new insights and possibilities.

Course credit is granted through the Advanced Placement and International Baccalaureate programs on an individual basis. Independent studies, research, and fieldwork are available to students for academic credit.

In addition to major department offerings, courses may be taken in education, family studies, film, geology, and linguistics.

Off-Campus Programs

Wheaton participates in the Twelve-College Exchange Program, which includes Amherst, Bowdoin, Connecticut College, Dartmouth, Mount Holyoke, Smith, Trinity, Vassar, Wellesley, Wesleyan, and Williams-Mystic Program. Locally, Wheaton students may cross-register for courses at Brown University and other colleges in the Southeastern Association for Cooperation in Higher Education in Massachusetts (SACHEM).

Wheaton students may study government or economics during a semester in Washington, D.C., sponsored by American University, explore marine ecology at the Marine Biological Laboratory at Woods Hole, or participate in a semester-long program in American maritime studies, sponsored by Williams College at Mystic Seaport. The National Theater Institute Program offers selected students the opportunity to spend a semester at the Eugene O'Neill Theater Center in Waterford, Connecticut. Students may also participate in the Salt Center for Documentary Field Studies in Portland, Maine.

Global education opportunities are coordinated through Wheaton's Center for Global Education. The Center offers study-abroad programs for first-year, sophomore, junior, and senior students during the academic year and semester, as well as short-term faculty-led programs that occur during January, spring break, or summer. Currently the center offers more than eighty academic year and semester programs in more than fifty countries, including a new semester-long program in the Kingdom of Bhutan. Wheaton has coordinated ten short-term faculty-led programs to locations such as China, Greece, South Africa, Trinidad, and Vietnam.

In addition to the traditional model of overseas study through an affiliated university or program, Wheaton students continue to pursue opportunities outside the classroom setting. Students take part in credit-bearing overseas internships in art and architecture, economics, politics, film and television, journalism, international organizations, and health and human services. They are also involved in volunteer work both coordinated directly through a study-abroad program and developed independently with advising support through the Filene Center for Academic Advising and Career Services.

The Career Exploration Internship Program assists hundreds of students in designing and securing internship positions every summer and awards domestic and international stipends to support unpaid internships, service, and structured independent research in annual amounts exceeding $300,000.

Academic Facilities

The Science Center has fully equipped laboratories for both faculty and student research and two greenhouses.

The College is in the process of undertaking its largest building project ever: a new $42-million, 77,800-square-foot science center with state-of-the-art facilities, scheduled to open in 2011.

Wheaton's library has 376,616 volumes, 15,299 current serial subscriptions, 74,078 microfilm units, 17,133 audiovisual items, and 35,154 e-books; a College Archives/Special Collections area; and the Kollett Center for Collaborative Learning. Wheaton participates in several library consortia, which provide direct access to other regional college libraries and interlibrary loan access to libraries around the country. Automated services include online searching of remote databases, full-text electronic journals, and a fully integrated system containing the Wheaton Library catalog and acquisitions and circulation information. The Library also supports the academic program through bibliographic instruction sessions, including participation in the First-Year Seminars and individual consultations.

Other facilities include a studio arts building, opened in 2007, with public exhibition space and private studio studies for students; the Balfour-Hood Student Center; the Watson Fine Arts Center with a proscenium theater, a black box theater, art studios, and a gallery; a laboratory nursery school; and the Filene Center for Advising and Career Services. The College also supports twenty-nine classrooms on campus, with permanently installed computers, digital projectors and sound systems, and sixteen computer labs with 205 computers dedicated to specific academic courses and programs, e.g., scientific imaging, geographic information systems, graphic lab design, astronomy, and languages. All academic and administrative buildings and all dormitories are part of a campuswide network, and all residence halls are wireless. Students are offered accounts for e-mail and Internet access.

Costs

The comprehensive fee for 2010–11 is $51,264, which consists of tuition, $40,790; room, $5350; board, $4830; and a student activities fee, $294.

Financial Aid

Students who demonstrate financial need normally receive a combination of grants, loans, and opportunities for employment on campus. The decision to award financial aid is made independently of the admission decision. Students applying for financial aid must complete the Free Application for Federal Student Aid (FAFSA) and the CSS PROFILE by February 1. Sixty-eight percent of Wheaton's students receive some form of financial aid.

Faculty

The student-faculty ratio is 11:1. Eighty-eight percent of the full-time faculty members hold the Ph.D. degree. Professors are very accessible to students, act as academic advisers, and often become involved with student activities.

Student Government

The Student Government Association, an active and influential organization, includes all members of the Wheaton community. Students are invited to attend faculty meetings and serve as voting members on most faculty committees. Rules are minimal, based on student self-government and an honor system stressing individual honor and responsibility.

Admission Requirements

Wheaton does not prescribe rigid entrance requirements, but most entering students have had 4 years of English, 4 years of mathematics, 4 years of one or two languages, 3 years of social studies, 3 years of science, and 2 years of history. However, these guidelines are not to be taken as requirements. Applications are reviewed on an individual basis, and the academic achievement, the challenge of the curriculum, evaluations by teachers and counselors, and the extracurricular contributions of each candidate are all taken into account.

The submission of standardized test results is optional for the purposes of admission. Those who wish their scores to be considered should arrange for official score reports to be sent from the appropriate testing agency directly to the Wheaton Office of Admission. Reports must be received no later than the application deadline for the corresponding decision plan. Unofficial test scores (i.e., those reported on high school transcripts) are not considered. A personal interview is expected for all applicants.

Transfer students are admitted to the sophomore and junior classes each year. Transfer applicants must have maintained a promising record and must be eligible for honorable dismissal from the college they are attending. A transfer student must attend Wheaton for at least two years in order to receive a degree from the College. Students who wish to enter in the spring semester must apply by November 1. The regular decision deadline for transfer students is March 1.

Application and Information

Students who consider Wheaton their first choice may apply for early decision by November 15 or early decision 2 by January 15. Decisions are mailed by December 15 and February 15, respectively. The deadline for regular decision applicants is January 15; notification for these students is made during the first week of April.

For more information, students are encouraged to contact:

Dean of Admission and Student Aid
Wheaton College
Norton, Massachusetts 02766
Phone: 508-286-8251
800-394-6003 (toll-free)
E-mail: admission@wheatoncollege.edu
Web site: http://www.wheatoncollege.edu

Park Hall, the administration building (left), and Mary Lyon Hall, a classroom building (right), are among the handsome facilities on Wheaton College's extensive 400-acre campus.

WHEELOCK COLLEGE
BOSTON, MASSACHUSETTS

The College

Wheelock College prepares students for careers that enrich the lives of children and families—and society in general. Founded in 1888, Wheelock has consistently produced progressive and highly respected professionals for such fields as elementary education, preschool and kindergarten teaching, special education, day care, social work, juvenile justice and youth advocacy, and child life work. The 800 undergraduate women and men at Wheelock come from throughout the United States and from several countries. Beginning in their freshman year, students benefit from close contact with outstanding faculty members and from direct fieldwork with children and families.

Wheelock's campus is beautifully kept, and the atmosphere is warm and friendly. Classes are small, and professors are known by their first names. Comfortable residence halls provide housing and many social activities for the two thirds of the College's students who choose to live on campus. The Student Center, with its wide-screen TV, snack bar, and often-used dance floor, is an attraction for the entire Wheelock community and for many students from neighboring schools. Wheelock students enjoy more than twenty-five clubs and organizations and actively participate in a variety of varsity and intramural sports. The College sponsors many cultural and theatrical events as well as traditional activities such as Family Weekend, the Sophomore-Senior Banquet, and Black History Month.

Location

Located in Boston and Brookline, Wheelock is ideally located across from Longwood Park and only a few blocks from the Museum of Fine Arts, several world-renowned hospitals, and many other institutions of higher learning. Students can walk to the shops and restaurants in Coolidge Corner or cheer for the Red Sox in nearby Fenway Park. They can discover the unmatched cultural and historical richness of downtown Boston, which is only a short subway ride away. They can walk the Freedom Trail, attend concerts and plays, or meet friends from other colleges for a day of fun at Faneuil Hall. The entire Boston area provides Wheelock students with exciting opportunities for extracurricular enjoyment and for their practical fieldwork with children and families.

Majors and Degrees

At Wheelock, many students pursue one of four professional directions: teaching, child life, juvenile justice and youth advocacy, or social work, while others choose to major in one of the arts and sciences. Within teaching, there are three separate areas of concentration: early childhood care and education focuses on the comprehensive care and education of children from birth to 8 years old; elementary education prepares students to become teachers of children in grades 1–6; and special education prepares professionals to work with children from prekindergarten through eighth grade with mild to moderate disabilities. The child life program is a five-year combined B.A. or B.S. and M.S. program. The child life program explores the emotional and psychological needs of hospitalized children and their families and prepares students to work as child life specialists with medical teams in hospitals or clinics. The juvenile justice and youth advocacy program prepares students to work with youth and their families in a range of settings, including preventative programs, advocacy programs, and programs for juvenile offenders. Students interested in teaching, juvenile justice and youth advocacy, or child life also major in one of six liberal arts areas: American studies, human development, the arts, communications and media literacy, the humanities, or mathematics/science. These multidisciplinary majors are designed to form a strong foundation for professional studies and for lifelong learning. Social work majors prepare to work in social service agencies, state agencies, and schools to advocate for and support children and their families. Graduates of Wheelock receive the Bachelor of Arts, Bachelor of Science, or Bachelor of Social Work degree.

Academic Programs

The focus of study at Wheelock is education and human services. Faculty members stress the importance of combining liberal arts, professional studies, and hands-on experience. Students begin work with children and families in their freshman year as part of a required course entitled Human Growth and Development. Juniors and seniors participate in supervised field experiences and student teaching in a variety of settings—elementary schools, day-care centers, nursery schools, museums, hospitals, social service agencies, and clinics—in urban and suburban locations. Professional courses provide preparation for field experience and support to students during their fieldwork. By combining the appropriate courses and field experience, Wheelock graduates are eligible for certification as early childhood, special education, or elementary school teachers and child life specialists.

Off-Campus Programs

Wheelock College is a member of the Colleges of the Fenway, a collaboration among Emmanuel College, Massachusetts College of Art, Massachusetts College of Pharmacy and Health Sciences, Simmons College, Wentworth Institute of Technology, and Wheelock College. Each college maintains its unique identity while providing students with access to academic programs and student services on all six campuses. Wheelock students can cross-register for courses and participate in social and extracurricular activities at any of the other institutions.

Academic Facilities

Wheelock's innovative Resource Center has a fully equipped workshop and holds a large collection of commercially manufactured scrap and natural materials for students to use in the creation of projects and original curriculum tools. Wheelock's library contains 92,000 volumes, providing reference and study facilities, collections in liberal arts areas, and extensive resources in children's literature and curriculum materials. The College also has extensive art studios with facilities for work in ceramics, weaving, and photography. One of the largest and best-equipped theatrical stages in Boston is found in the 700-seat Lucy Wheelock Auditorium in the Activities Building, where the Wheelock Family Theatre produces three shows each year. The Activities Building also houses science and music classrooms, the Little Theatre for theater classes and experimental theater, a music listening room, and an art gallery. All classrooms at Wheelock are equipped with data ports for Internet access and teacher workstations for integrating technology into the classroom. In addition, all students have Internet capabilities in their rooms.

Costs

In 2009–10, tuition is $27,150, room and board are $11,200, and fees are $1010, for a total of $39,360. Reasonable estimates for other expenses are $880 for books and supplies, $1400 for personal expenses, and $510 for travel to and from school.

Financial Aid

Wheelock provides financial aid for all applicants who demonstrate need. Currently, 95 percent of the student body receives financial aid, usually in a combination of grants, loans, and work. Wheelock participates in the Federal Stafford Student Loan program, Federal Perkins Loan program, Federal Supplemental Educational Opportunity Grant program, Academic Competitiveness Grant program, Federal Pell Grant program, and Federal Work-Study Program. The College uses its own funds to provide additional grants, loans, and employment. The Financial Aid Office must receive the Free Application for Federal Student Aid (FAFSA) by February 15 for students who plan to enter in September or by December 1 for midyear students.

Wheelock also offers merit scholarships for eligible first-year and transfer students. New first-year students entering in the fall semester who have earned a high school GPA of 3.0 or higher and have an SAT score of 1050 (critical reading and math combined) or higher automatically receives one of the College's Merit Scholarships ranging from $4000 to $12,000. These scholarships are renewable all four years while the student is enrolled full-time.

New transfer students entering in the fall semester who have earned a college GPA of 3.2 or higher could be eligible for one of the College's Merit Scholarships ranging from $3000 to $5000. These scholarships are renewable while the student is enrolled full-time.

Faculty

All of Wheelock's faculty members, many of whom are nationally recognized for their research and experience in the fields in which they are experts, are actively engaged in classroom teaching. Faculty members also serve as academic advisers, as fieldwork supervisors, and, often, as advisers for student organizations. A student-faculty ratio of only 10:1 allows Wheelock professors to work closely with students both in and out of the classroom.

Student Government

The student government organization is the principal undergraduate governing body on campus. Its members are elected in the spring by the student body. The board meets weekly, often with the dean of students and the president of the College, to discuss issues of concern to the student body. In addition, each residence hall has its own governing body and makes its own policies and regulations. Students sit on many of the administrative committees of the College.

Admission Requirements

Wheelock seeks and admits women and men of all ages from a variety of racial, geographic, ethnic, and economic backgrounds who have the potential for creative, effective work with children and families. Each admission decision is made after careful consideration of an applicant's academic record, SAT and/or ACT scores, graded writing sample, recommendations, and extracurricular activities. On-campus interviews are highly recommended and can be arranged by telephone or online at http://www.wheelock.edu/admissions. A telephone interview can be arranged for those students who are unable to visit the campus. The College has numerous on-campus events throughout the year for prospective students and their families. Students should visit http://www2.wheelock.edu/wheelock/Admissions/Undergraduate/Visit_Wheelock.html to register for any of the College's events.

Application and Information

Wheelock is an exclusive user of the Common Application. You will need to complete the Common Application online or print it out and send it directly to the Wheelock College Admissions Office. Please note that your application fee will be waived if you complete and submit the online version. In addition to the Common Application you need to submit one academic recommendation, one guidance counselor recommendation, your official high school transcript, and SAT and/or ACT scores. The Admissions Committee is glad to review additional information that the candidate feels would be helpful to the committee in making the admission decision. Early action applications are due by December 1, regular freshman applications on March 1, and transfer applications on April 15. Applicants can expect to hear from the Admissions Office by mid-December for early action and within one month after regular applications are completed.

For more information about Wheelock, students should contact:

Lisa Slavin
Dean of Admissions
Wheelock College
200 The Riverway
Boston, Massachusetts 02215-4176
Phone: 617-879-2206
800-734-5212 (toll-free)
E-mail: undergrad@wheelock.edu
Web site: http://www.wheelock.edu

Fieldwork in schools, hospitals, and social services settings is one of the focal points of education at Wheelock.

WILKES UNIVERSITY

WILKES-BARRE, PENNSYLVANIA

The University

Located at the foothills of the Pocono Mountains, along the shore of the Susquehanna River and within walking distance of downtown Wilkes-Barre, Pennsylvania, Wilkes University is a private, comprehensive institution with more than 2,300 undergraduate students. The University is structured into the College of Arts, Humanities, and Social Sciences; the College of Science and Engineering; the Nesbitt College of Pharmacy and Nursing; the Sidhu School of Business and Leadership; the School of Education; and University College (for undecided students). Wilkes offers a broad range of bachelor's and master's degree programs in the humanities, social and natural sciences, engineering, business administration, nursing, and education as well as the Doctor of Pharmacy degree.

The Wilkes campus features a parklike quadrangle surrounded by modern classroom buildings and historic nineteenth-century mansions that have been restored as student residences and academic buildings. Campus facilities include a sports and conference center, an outdoor athletic complex and field house, a state-of-the-art science classroom building, a modern academic classroom/office building, a performing arts center, an indoor recreation center, and a student center with a food court, café, entertainment rooms, post office, and ballroom.

Hands-on learning, small classes, and strong student-professor relationships are the hallmarks of the Wilkes experience. Programs are designed to prepare students with a well-rounded liberal arts foundation that cultivates independent thinking and gives students the credentials necessary for entrance into graduate and professional schools and professional life. Academic advising integrated with career planning is stressed, and hands-on experiences are provided in laboratory, internship, and cooperative education settings. Free tutorial services are available to all students as well.

The University is accredited by the Middle States Association of Colleges and Schools and has specialized accreditation in the sciences, engineering, nursing, education, and business. More than 99 percent of students are employed or attending graduate/professional school within six months of receiving their degrees.

First-year students enrolling prior to May 1 are guaranteed housing. Campus housing is available for all four years. Architecturally, residence halls vary from modern, multifloor buildings to mansions listed on the National Register of Historic Places. Medical and dental care, department stores, specialty shops, and other services are available within three blocks of campus. A large number of nearby houses of religious worship welcome students' participation.

At Wilkes University, student activities complement academic life. Intercollegiate athletics encompass sixteen Division III sports, and an active and varied intramural program is offered. Nearly seventy clubs and organizations recognize student achievement and provide opportunities for leadership development, professional growth, and community service. The student-run Programming Board schedules movies and performances by comedians, musicians, and other entertainers, while other organizations sponsor dinner dances, block parties, and special events. The professionally run Student Development Office organizes various activities based on leadership, adventure, or cultural themes, as well as coordinates a unique e-mentor program designed to assist freshmen with the transition to college life. Wilkes students are active community volunteers, participating in numerous local and national service projects each year.

Master's degrees are awarded in business administration, creative writing, education, electrical engineering, engineering operations and strategy, and nursing. The University also offers terminal degrees in the fields of Education (Ed.D.), Nursing (Doctor of Nursing Practice), and Pharmacy (Pharm.D.). In addition, Wilkes is the first school in Pennsylvania to offer a dual Doctor of Pharmacy and Master of Business Administration degree.

Location

The Luzerne County seat, Wilkes-Barre is a medium-sized city of 50,000 in the midst of a metropolitan area of 400,000. A wide range of recreational facilities are minutes away, including the Lackawanna County Multi-Purpose Stadium (home of the Wilkes-Barre/Scranton Yankees Triple A baseball team); the Wachovia Arena, which serves as home for the Wilkes-Barre/Scranton Penguins hockey team; the Pocono Mountain ski resorts; numerous golf courses; state parks; outdoor tennis courts; and Pocono Downs harness racing.

The University is located in the historical district, between the entertainment and residential sections of the city. The entertainment district begins at the F. M. Kirby Center of Performing Arts, featuring symphony, ballet, theatrical, and musical performances, and encompasses the Wilkes University/King's College Barnes and Noble bookstore and café, a fourteen-screen movie complex, a nightclub, and numerous shops and restaurants. Other area cultural offerings include art galleries, ethnic and community festivals, and numerous libraries and museums. The city is also approximately 2 hours from the cultural resources of both New York City and Philadelphia.

Wilkes-Barre is in proximity to the intersection of Interstates 80, 81, and 476 and within 3 to 6 hours of other major cities, such as Washington, D.C.; Baltimore; and Boston. The Wilkes-Barre/Scranton International Airport enables travelers to arrive at most domestic destinations via one-stop or nonstop flights.

Majors and Degrees

Wilkes University offers Bachelor of Arts, Bachelor of Business Administration, Bachelor of Science, and Bachelor of Fine Arts degrees. Majors include accounting; applied and engineering sciences; biochemistry; biology; business administration (concentrations in economics, finance, international business, management, and marketing); chemistry; clinical laboratory sciences; communications (concentrations in journalism, organizational communications, public relations, rhetoric and public communications, and telecommunications); computer information systems; computer science; criminology; earth and environmental sciences; electrical engineering; elementary, secondary, and special education (all with certification); engineering management; English (concentrations in literature and creative writing); entrepreneurship; environmental engineering; history; integrative media; international studies; mathematics; mechanical engineering; musical theater; nursing; philosophy; political science; psychology; sociology; and theater arts.

The premedical and prelaw preparation programs are particularly strong. In addition to the University's prepharmacy program, other preprofessional programs are available in dentistry, optometry, podiatry, and veterinary science. The University offers affiliated programs in medicine with the Philadelphia College of Osteopathic Medicine; in optometry with the Pennsylvania College of Optometry and the State University of New York (SUNY) College of Optometry; in podiatry with Temple University School of Podiatric Medicine; in occupational therapy with Temple University; in physical therapy with Drexel University, Temple University, and Widener University; in medical technology/clinical laboratory sciences with Robert Packer Hospital; and in psychology with Widener University.

Academic Programs

Through a rigorous curriculum that emphasizes hands-on experience and training, Wilkes helps students to prepare in all majors to adapt to a technologically and socially evolving world. To graduate, students are required to complete a core curriculum and must complete from 120 to 136 credits, depending upon their major field. Graduates demonstrate mastery of the fundamental intellectual skills as well as the essential concepts and techniques of their field. Wilkes also teaches students responsibility and independence by expecting and encouraging active participation in the classroom and laboratory.

The University operates on a dual-semester calendar, with optional summer sessions and a January intersession. Advanced Placement test credits, College Level Examination Program (CLEP) credits, and International Baccalaureate (I.B.) credits are accepted.

Off-Campus Programs

An extensive cooperative education program is available to all students, with credit applicable in most major fields. Many government offices and private businesses in northeastern Pennsylvania, as well as in New York City, Philadelphia, Harrisburg, and Washington, D.C., employ Wilkes students. The study-abroad adviser works with interested students, placing them in the situation best suited to their academic pursuits. Most recently, students have attended programs in Austria, England, the Dominican Republic, France, Germany, Italy, and Spain.

Academic Facilities

The Eugene S. Farley Library has more than 220,000 volumes of books and bound journals, 857 current print journal and newspaper subscriptions, hundreds of database searches, and 800,000 microforms. Complete laboratory facilities are available for biology, chemistry, earth and environmental sciences, engineering, nursing, pharmacy, and psychology. Student-produced programming is broadcast from WCLH-FM, the University's 2,000-watt radio station, and transmitted from a professional-quality television studio via a local cable provider. Technology-enhanced classrooms contain the new Intel-based Apple computers for student use. The Sordoni Art Gallery is professionally equipped and staffed and produces exhibits each year by regionally, nationally, and internationally known artists. The Dorothy Dickson Darte Center for the Performing Arts contains a fully equipped 500-seat main theater and a 45-seat black box theater presentation of plays, concerts, ballet, and other performances and lectures. Adjoining the center are studios, practice and rehearsal rooms, and faculty offices for the Department of Visual and Performing Arts. Breiseth Hall accommodates extensive computer facilities, psychology research laboratories, an integrative media lab, and modern classrooms with the latest audiovisual equipment. The University also operates a state-of-the-art distance learning facility that allows global conferencing and study using Internet and videoconferencing technology.

Costs

For the 2009–10 academic year, tuition and fees were $26,145 per year, and room and board were $10,755. Books cost approximately $900 per year.

Financial Aid

Financial aid is available to those students who demonstrate quality academic ability and/or financial need, as verified by the Free Application for Federal Student Aid (FAFSA). Merit-based and need-based aid is available from Wilkes University for qualified students. Scholarships ranging from $6000 to $13,000 per year are available to students solely on the basis of academic ability. Approximately 90 percent of the student body receive some type of financial assistance, including scholarships, grants, loans, and work-study awards.

Faculty

Wilkes University has a nationally recruited full-time faculty of 147 members, approximately 87 percent of whom have earned Ph.D.'s or terminal degrees in their chosen field. Faculty evaluation criteria emphasize teaching excellence and effective advising, while recognizing continued scholarly activities. The student-faculty ratio is 13:1.

Student Government

An active student government provides a structure for student participation in University governance and student discipline. The Inter-Residence Council and Commuter Council coordinate extracurricular activities for on-campus and commuter students.

Admission Requirements

Admission to Wilkes University is traditional. SAT or ACT scores are required. In cases where a student has taken the examination more than once, scores from the highest testing in each category are used in the evaluation process. Applicants for the freshman class should either have completed or be in the process of completing a college-preparatory course of study, including 3 to 4 years of mathematics, social studies, science, and English. Additional courses should be elected in academic subjects according to individual interests. Acceptable electives include foreign language and computing, among others. Students who have not followed this pattern may still qualify for admission if there is other strong evidence of preparation for college work. Letters of recommendation are not required but may be submitted. Students intending to pursue a major in pharmacy or pharmaceutical science or a major in the College of Science and Engineering should have completed algebra I and II, geometry, and trigonometry prior to enrollment. Students intending to major in nursing should have completed courses in biology and chemistry. An audition is required for all prospective musical theater and theater arts students. Transfer students must submit a transcript from every college previously attended. All students are admitted to the University and not to specific departments, with the exception of the professional Nesbitt College of Pharmacy and Nursing and the Department of Visual and Performing Arts. Students individually receive academic advisement at the time of registration and throughout their enrollment.

Wilkes University is an Equal Opportunity/Affirmative Action institution. No applicant shall be denied admission to the University because of race, color, gender, religion, national or ethnic origin, sexual orientation, or handicap.

Application and Information

Applications for admission should be completed early in the senior year of secondary school and sent to the Admissions Office. Applications are reviewed after all of the student's credentials have been received. The review of applications begins on September 15, and notification of the University's decision reaches the student two to four weeks after the application file is complete. The priority deadline for all applications is March 1; applications for the Guaranteed Seat Pharmacy Program must be received by February 1. Other health science programs may have additional deadlines; students should contact the Admissions Office for more information.

Admissions Office
Wilkes University
84 West South Street
Wilkes-Barre, Pennsylvania 18766
Phone: 570-408-4400
800-945-5378 Ext. 4400 (toll-free)
Web site: http://www.wilkes.edu

WILLIAM PATERSON UNIVERSITY OF NEW JERSEY

WILLIAM PATERSON UNIVERSITY

WAYNE, NEW JERSEY

The University

Since its founding in 1855, William Paterson University has grown into a comprehensive state institution whose programs reflect the area's need for challenging, affordable educational options. Ideally midsized (the total enrollment is 10,819, of whom 9,179 are degree-seeking undergraduates), William Paterson offers a wider variety of academic programs than smaller universities, yet provides students with a more personalized atmosphere than larger institutions. Once the site of the family estate of Garret Hobart, the twenty-fourth vice president of the United States, William Paterson's 370-acre spacious campus, with its wooded areas and waterfalls, offers an environment in which students may develop both intellectually and socially. Although the majority of the University's students come from the New Jersey and New York vicinity, some international and out-of-state students enroll each year. Twenty-four percent of undergraduates reside on campus in ten residence halls or apartment-style facilities, which accommodate 2,600 students. On-campus housing is offered on a first-come, first-served basis. Portions of the residence halls are dedicated to dynamic "learning communities," such as the University's Honors College, as well as substance-free living.

Social, cultural, and recreational activities complement the academic programs. Cultural events take place throughout the year, featuring both William Paterson's own talent as well as renowned professional artists. Among events are concerts presenting jazz, classical, and contemporary music; theater productions; gallery exhibits; and a distinguished-lecturer series. The recently renovated University Commons complex, including the redesigned John Victor Machuga Student Center, is the heart of the campus, where the entire University community gathers and interacts. This state-of-the-art campus center provides students with an exquisite setting for a vast array of social and extracurricular activities, dining venues, and student support services, all under one roof. The Student Activities Programming Board helps the more than seventy clubs and organizations to develop diverse activities for the entire student body. William Paterson has twenty-one social fraternities and sororities, and twenty-four honor societies. Students staff the campus radio station (WPSC) and the television station (WPC-TV), which develops a number of widely distributed television programs for local and statewide cable networks. The Recreation Center serves as the focal point for physical recreation. In addition to the main courts, which accommodate badminton, basketball, indoor tennis, and volleyball, the 4,000-seat facility has racquetball courts, an exercise room, saunas, and Jacuzzis. The University has twelve intercollegiate sports teams, five for men and seven for women, including successful NCAA teams in men's baseball and women's softball. In 2002, the Pioneers won the coed cheerleading and dance team national championship. In addition, bowling, rugby, horseback riding, and ice hockey are organized as club sports. The University has a competition-size indoor pool, outdoor tennis courts, and a lighted athletics field complex.

Guided by the University's mission to provide community outreach with opportunities for lifelong learning, the Center for Continuing and Professional Education brings the University to students and students to the University. From noncredit courses to corporate training and advanced computer skills training, the center offers today's working adults professional development as well as flexible scheduling.

Location

William Paterson University is located in northern New Jersey in the busy suburban town of Wayne. Several major recreational and cultural centers are nearby. New York City is just 20 miles to the east, the seacoast is an hour's drive south, skiing is 30 miles north, and the Meadowlands Sports Complex is a half-hour drive away.

Majors and Degrees

William Paterson University grants five undergraduate degrees—the B.A., B.S., B.F.A., B.M., and B.S.N.—and offers degree programs through its five colleges: Arts and Communication; the Cotsakos College of Business, which in 2005 became one of 15 percent of schools internationally to achieve prestigious accreditation from AACSB International (The Association to Advance Collegiate Schools of Business); Education; Humanities and Social Sciences; and Science and Health.

The Bachelor of Arts degree is awarded in African, African American, and Caribbean studies; anthropology; art; art history; Asian studies; communication; communication disorders; early childhood education; earth science; economics; elementary education; English; French and Francophone studies; geography; history; Latin American and Latino studies; liberal studies; mathematics; music; philosophy; political science; psychology; secondary education; sociology; Spanish; and women's and gender studies. The Bachelor of Science degree is conferred in accounting; applied chemistry; applied health; athletic training; biology; biotechnology; business administration; computer science; environmental science; exercise science; mathematics; physical education; professional sales; and public health. The Bachelor of Fine Arts degree, the Bachelor of Music degree, and the Bachelor of Science in Nursing are also offered. Urban studies, a cross-disciplinary minor, is part of the curriculum, as well. In addition, the Cotsakos College of Business allows students to experience several noteworthy offerings, including the Financial Learning Center, one of the few, advanced, simulated electronic trading rooms found in an academic environment, and the Russ Berrie Institute for Professional Sales, which advances professional sales for both students and business professionals.

Certification is available in early childhood, elementary, secondary, and special education. Preprofessional programs in engineering, law, medicine (dentistry, optometry, podiatry, and veterinary science), pharmacy, physical therapy, and speech-language pathology are arranged at the request of students. Students who have completed the premedical program in the College of Science and Health are consistently accepted by American medical schools.

Academic Programs

Students must complete a minimum of 128 credits to earn a baccalaureate degree (however, 120 credits for students entering as of fall 2010). Degree programs include a 53- to 54-credit general education requirement, 30–60 credits in a major, and 20–40 credits in elective courses. (In specialized degree programs, such as the B.F.A., the B.M., and the B.S.N. general education and major course requirements may differ.) Students uncertain of which career path to follow may take advantage of advisement and counseling programs. In addition, the general education requirements enable students to take up to 54 credits before declaring a major, so that they can acquire a basic understanding of all major fields of knowledge before having to choose a specific area. Diagnostic testing and career seminars, provided by the Career Development Office, also ensure that students receive the guidance necessary to make wise course selections and career decisions.

William Paterson offers a variety of special programs. Its Honors College is designed for those ambitious and well-qualified students who want to add a challenging dimension to their majors. Currently, there are ten program tracks—biopsychology, cognitive science, humanities, independent study, life science and environmental ethics, management, marketing, music, performing and literary arts, and social sciences.

Students who successfully complete Advanced Placement tests and/or College-Level Examination Program tests may receive credit for acceptable scores. Credit may also be awarded for military training and experience. William Paterson University operates on a two-semester and a one-summer-session system.

Off-Campus Programs

William Paterson offers a special opportunity for off-campus study. Semester Abroad, a 15-credit program, is open to sophomores and juniors who wish to study for a semester at selected institutions in Australia, Denmark, Great Britain, Greece, Israel, Spain, and other countries around the world.

Academic Facilities

William Paterson's facilities are easily accessible, promote interaction among students, and encourage participation by all students in the various academic, cultural, and recreational programs. The University's David and Lorraine Cheng Library contains a collection of more than 360,000 volumes, more than 17,000 audiovisual items, and access to over 23,000 electronic and print periodicals and journals. A special-collections room houses rare and out-of-print items on New Jersey and valuable editions of literary works. Media services, group studies, carrels, and computer labs provide space for a variety of student uses. An extensive collection of online journals and resources is accessible campuswide from the library Web site. Supporting William Paterson's varied cultural and artistic offerings are the Power Arts Center, a 42,600-square-foot facility accommodating an array of studio arts, such as design, photography, sculpture, ceramics, printmaking, woodworking, and painting; the Ben Shahn Center for Visual Arts, which contains art galleries, studios, and classrooms; and the Shea Center for Performing Arts, which has a 922-seat theater as well as band, choral, and orchestra practice rooms and classrooms.

Hobart Hall, a state-of-the-art communication facility, is designed to educate communication majors with the most contemporary communication technologies, including teleconferences. The facility houses two broadcast-quality TV studios, a multipurpose computer lab, a film studio, an FCC-licensed FM radio station, an uplink and four downlink satellite dishes, audio and video digital nonlinear editing systems, a cable system linking nearly all of the buildings on campus, and a computerized telephone system for voice and data transmission. In addition, William Paterson is finalizing the process of creating fiber-optic links throughout the campus. The Atrium, a two-story academic building, contains a writing center, multimedia language lab, tutorial center, and computing support facilities.

Among the other academic resources are extensive computer facilities, a filmmaking laboratory, a professionally equipped television production truck, a child-care center, a nursing instructional center, a language lab, and a speech and hearing clinic. William Paterson University has dual accreditation from the American Speech-Language-Hearing Association for its speech and hearing clinic and its undergraduate and graduate programs in communication disorders. The science research facilities contain two electron microscopes and various specialized labs.

Costs

Annual tuition (including fees) for the 2009–10 academic year was $10,838 for full-time (12 credits or more) students who are New Jersey residents and $17,592 for full-time nonresident students. Room and board cost approximately $10,280 per year. All charges are subject to change per the Board of Trustees.

Financial Aid

Financial aid is available through a number of federal and state grant, loan, scholarship, and work-study programs. To apply for need-based aid, students must file the Free Application for Federal Student Aid (FAFSA) with the United States Department of Education by the priority date of April 1.

Both the University and the Alumni Association award a number of competitive scholarships, based solely on academic merit, to entering freshmen. They are the Scholarships for Academic Excellence, Educational Enrichment Scholarships, Trustee and Presidential Scholarships, and New Jersey's Outstanding Scholars Recruitment Program. Academic Achievement Scholarships are awarded only on a competitive basis to continuing students. Each year, more than 1,000 scholarships are awarded, which total more than $23 million.

Faculty

William Paterson's 371 full-time and 555 part-time faculty members bring to the classroom a valuable blend of accomplished scholarship and practical, applied experience. Faculty members assist students with curriculum and career planning, which engenders open, personal communication between the students and faculty.

Through a formal reciprocal exchange relationship with various institutions worldwide, and through the Fulbright Scholarship Program, William Paterson University often receives visiting international scholars. Among the University faculty are more than 30 Fulbright scholars, one of the most prestigious academic distinctions in the world.

Student Government

The Student Government Association (SGA), of which all full-time and part-time students are automatically members, has become an influential voice in University decision making. Elected officers and various committees convey students' perspectives to the administration and advance their causes. The SGA is also responsible for chartering more than seventy campus organizations and allocating student activity fees among them.

Admission Requirements

Admission to William Paterson University is competitive. Admissions decisions for entering freshmen are based on a complete review of the students' academic record (course of study, grades, and rank) as well as the results of the SAT or ACT. Applicants are considered eligible if they have taken a minimum of 16 Carnegie units and have demonstrated strong academic ability. The students' secondary school record must show the following courses: English, 4 years (composition and literature); mathematics, 3 years (algebra I and II and geometry); laboratory science, 2 years (biology, chemistry, or physics); social science, 2 years (American history, world history, or political science); and additional college-preparatory subjects, 5 units (advanced mathematics, literature, foreign language, or social sciences). In addition, students selecting a major in art or music (except musical studies) must submit a portfolio for review by the Art Department or must audition for the Music Department.

Transfer students must present at least 12 college-level credits with a minimum 2.0 GPA; science and nursing majors must have a minimum 2.5 GPA; and teacher certification program applicants must have a minimum 2.75 GPA. Applicants with fewer than 12 college credits must submit a high school transcript. Application review is completed only upon receipt of official transcripts from high schools and especially colleges and universities. Unofficial transcripts or transcripts sent by students will not be used for admissions.

Application and Information

Application forms and transcripts from candidates for freshman status must be received by June 1 for fall admission and December 1 for spring admission. Transfer students, readmitted students, and students seeking a second bachelor's degree must submit their materials by June 1 and December 1 for fall and spring entry, respectively. However, the University closes the application process earlier when the number of new and continuing students strains its ability to provide effective programs and services. A $50 application fee is required. Applications are reviewed on a rolling basis. Campus tours are available during the fall and spring semesters on weekdays by appointment when classes are in session.

Office of Admissions
William Paterson University of New Jersey
Wayne, New Jersey 07470
Phone: 973-720-2125
E-mail: admissions@wpunj.edu
Web site: http://www.wpunj.edu

William Paterson University's hilltop suburban campus offers an environment where students may develop both intellectually and socially.

WITTENBERG UNIVERSITY

SPRINGFIELD, OHIO

The University

For more than 160 years, students at Wittenberg University have not only discovered their light, they have passed it on to others—on campus, in the classroom, in their communities, and around the world. Founded in 1845, Wittenberg, a four-year comprehensive liberal arts and sciences college, is affiliated with the Evangelical Lutheran Church in America (ELCA), a connection that helps the University preserve its commitment to producing graduates who have considered their own personal values and take an active interest in the health of their communities.

Wittenberg University provides a liberal arts education dedicated to intellectual inquiry and wholeness of person within a diverse residential community. Reflecting its Lutheran heritage, Wittenberg challenges students to become responsible global citizens, to discover their callings, and to lead personal, professional, and civic lives of creativity, service, compassion, and integrity. Wittenberg's primary purpose is to provide a close, supportive, caring learning environment and a superior teaching faculty committed to the liberal arts and willing to impart knowledge, inspire inquiry, and encourage independent thought.

In keeping with its motto "Having light we pass it on to others," Wittenberg also empowers students to find their light through numerous collaborative research opportunities, a strong commitment to global engagement, and a passion for service both at home and abroad.

Wittenberg is distinguished by its strong interdisciplinary programs, such as the East Asian Studies Program and the Russian Area Studies Program. Although Wittenberg's traditional strengths have been in the liberal arts, the sciences, management, communication, and education have also developed into popular majors for students. One in 4 students chooses a science major designed to emphasize collaborative problem solving among students and collaborative research among students and faculty members. Wittenberg is one of only a handful of colleges in the country to include community service as a graduation requirement. Also, Phi Beta Kappa is one of the many academic honoraries to grace the campus.

The University is accredited by the Higher Learning Commission of the North Central Association of Colleges and Schools and by the American Association of University Women.

Of Wittenberg's 2,000 students, 60 percent come from Ohio. Wittenberg hosts approximately 30 to 40 new international students each year from twenty to thirty countries. Deliberate efforts to maintain cultural, ethnic, social, and economic diversity avoid the homogeneity of many small private colleges and allow Wittenberg's student body to reflect the broader society.

Wittenberg's residential program is based on a philosophy of progressive responsibility. First- and second-year students live in the residence halls. After the second year, students have the opportunity to live in Greek housing or one of the many University-owned rental units in the University district and other theme housing. A modern, 195-bed residence hall designed for new students opened in summer 2006. The award-winning food service catered by Sodexho serves food in the Central Dining Room, a cafeteria-style eatery, and in Post 95, a café-style eatery.

Location

Wittenberg's 95-acre parklike campus is as functional as it is attractive, with beautiful rolling hills, lush green spaces, and numerous mature trees. Its twenty-seven buildings include outstanding facilities for the sciences, arts, and music, as well as comfortable residence halls and excellent recreational and athletics facilities. The school is located in Springfield, Ohio, which is a small city with a population of 65,000 that provides easy access to big-city excitement in nearby Columbus and Dayton.

While Wittenberg plays a major role in the lives of Springfield residents, the community also offers unique opportunities to the University's students. Wittenberg is a major leader in the community's cultural, academic, and athletic life, yet the University sees a great benefit to being in Springfield. The community provides an area rich in cultural opportunities and recreational activities, with lakes, public parkland, nature preserves, bike trails, and public golf courses.

Majors and Degrees

Wittenberg offers the degrees of Bachelor of Arts, Bachelor of Fine Arts, Bachelor of Music, Bachelor of Music Education, and Bachelor of Science. Many students increase the power of their education degree by double majoring or adding a minor. The Bachelor of Arts degree may be earned in American studies, art, biochemistry/molecular biology, chemistry, communication, computer science, East Asian studies, economics, education (early childhood, elementary, and middle childhood licensing), English, geography, geology, history, languages (French, Spanish, and German), management (with concentrations in accounting, finance, human resources, international business, and marketing), mathematics, music, philosophy, physics, political science, psychology, religion, Russian area studies, sociology, and theater. The Bachelor of Science degree is offered in biology, chemistry, computer science, geology, mathematics, physics, and psychology. Minors may be completed in all the above majors and the following: Africana studies, computational science, creative writing, dance, environmental studies, global studies, marine science, music composition, premodern and ancient world studies, urban studies, and women's studies.

Special areas of study include forestry and environmental studies, international education, languages (Chinese, Japanese, and Russian), and marine biology/freshwater ecology. Through one of the comprehensive preprofessional programs, Wittenberg students can prepare for law school, medical school (including dental, optometry, or veterinary school), physical therapy, theology, nursing, or another postgraduate program. Wittenberg also offers 3-2 programs in computer engineering, engineering, environmental studies, nursing, and occupational therapy. Advanced study during the two years is completed at schools such as Case Western Reserve, Columbia, Duke, Georgia Tech, Johns Hopkins, and Washington (St. Louis).

Academic Programs

Wittenberg graduates are critical thinkers who are equipped for a lifetime of success in a changing world. A Wittenberg education exposes students to a broad range of ideas and inquiries, from scientific investigations to philosophical explorations. Developing excellent communication, writing, and critical-thinking skills, as well as engaging diverse subjects, improves students as scholars and global citizens.

Wittenberg students must complete a course of study in two broad categories: comprehensive education in the liberal arts and sciences and a major program of study. Each of these categories makes up one third of the total credits required for graduation. To make up the remaining one third of the credits, students may choose either elective courses from across the curriculum or courses required for a minor within one or more particular areas. The comprehensive program is based upon general education learning goals. These goals reflect Wittenberg's emphasis on teaching and student learning.

All candidates for the Bachelor of Arts, Music, Science, and Fine Arts degrees must complete 130 semester hours of credit. Generally, a major consists of 32 to 42 semester hours of credit, and a minor consists of 20 to 22 semester hours of credit.

Off-Campus Programs

Every year, around 100 students from Wittenberg study abroad in more than twenty countries. Some programs last for only a few weeks during semester break or take place over the summer for one to two months; other programs last for a semester or an entire academic year. In addition, some students choose to study off campus with cooperative programs in such places as Washington, D.C., and Duke University.

Academic Facilities

Wittenberg's twenty-seven buildings combine the best of tradition (Myers Hall and Recitation Hall are on the National Register of Historic Places) and the best of tomorrow. Hollenbeck Hall, a state-of-the-art academic building, opened in 2000, and the Barbara Deer Kuss Science Center was dedicated in 2003. The new science center is equipped with the latest technology in its laboratories and classrooms. The Wittenberg Department of Music is housed in Krieg Hall, a spacious structure specially designed to provide the best instruction in music. The music building houses a sixteen-unit electronic keyboard laboratory that students use for advanced music composition.

All of the residence halls have computer labs open to the students around the clock. In Hollenbeck Hall, the computer lab is open 24 hours a day. Departmental labs set their own hours, and the computer lab in the Thomas Library is available during open hours. A fiber-optic network connects classroom and administration buildings, the library, and residence halls. All students are given a network account and an e-mail account. Thomas Library has 367,000 volumes and access to millions more through the statewide electronic library catalog OhioLINK.

Costs

Total annual charges for the 2009–10 academic year were $43,962. This amount included tuition ($33,890), room ($4554), and board ($4218). Estimated costs for books, travel, miscellaneous expenses, and entertainment were $2400 for in-state students. Wittenberg estimates a total of $3400 for out-of-state students to account for additional travel expenses.

Financial Aid

Two features that keep Wittenberg affordable for many families are that more than 80 percent of Wittenberg students receive nearly $25 million each year in scholarships and financial assistance and that Wittenberg's four-year graduation guarantee states that with proper planning, students should be able to graduate in four years rather than the five- to six-year average of many universities. Students are not charged additional tuition or fees if they have met minimum criteria. Financial aid packages are made up of scholarships, grants, loans, and employment on campus. In order to be considered for financial aid, students must complete the Free Application for Federal Student Aid (FAFSA). Academic and talent-based scholarships are available from $1000 per year to full tuition regardless of financial need.

Faculty

Since its founding, personal attention from Wittenberg's award-winning faculty has defined the University's innovative approach to educating young people. From providing encouraging words in one-on-one conversations or assisting with career preparation to engaging in intellectual debate or sharing some laughs after class, Wittenberg faculty members are outstanding classroom instructors and true mentors who consider students their top priority and have a genuine interest in teaching undergraduates. Many of the faculty members are also renowned experts in their fields. Robert P. Welker, an education professor, was named Ohio Professor of the Year in 2001. He is the fourth professor from Wittenberg in fifteen years to win this prestigious award. Ninety-seven percent of the faculty members have the highest degree in their field; full-time faculty members number 156, and part-time faculty members number 67. The faculty-student ratio is 1:12, which allows for the average class size of 19 students.

Student Government

The student government for the undergraduate student body is the Student Senate. The Student Senate operates primarily as a legislative body. The senate is elected/selected each spring. Through its committees this body addresses each aspect of student life.

Admission Requirements

Admission to Wittenberg is selective and is based on the following information: high school record, including the strength of the high school and its curriculum and trends in the student's academic work; cocurricular activities and community participation; recommendations; and an essay. International students and transfer students are encouraged to apply. Applicants have the option of submitting their ACT or SAT scores for review for admission and scholarships. An on-campus interview is not required but is highly recommended. Students may apply using the regular application or online at the University's Web site.

Application and Information

The deadlines for applying are as follows for incoming freshmen: early decision is November 15, early action I is December 1, early action II is January 15, and regular action is March 15. For full consideration for scholarships, a complete application for admission should be received by December 1. Transfer student application deadlines are December 1 for the spring semester and July 1 for the fall semester. The international student application deadline is March 15. More information may be obtained by contacting:

Office of Admission
Wittenberg University
Ward Street at North Wittenberg Avenue
Post Office Box 720
Springfield, Ohio 45501-0720
Phone: 937-327-6314
877-206-0332 (toll-free)
E-mail: admission@wittenberg.edu
Web site: http://www.wittenberg.edu

On the campus of Wittenberg University.

WORCESTER POLYTECHNIC INSTITUTE

WORCESTER, MASSACHUSETTS

The University

Worcester Polytechnic Institute (WPI) believes in the power of its students to make an impact. They may want to be on the first Mars mission, find alternative energy sources, or work on cancer research. To prepare them for leadership and achievement after college, students do much more than study science and technology in the classroom and lab. They complete projects on campus and around the globe where they connect what they have learned in the classroom with pressing real-life challenges, from human health and the environment to business and engineering as well as the arts and humanities. Students grow personally, professionally, and intellectually as they discover how to apply their talents and turn ideas into tangible solutions.

WPI's aim is to educate students broadly so they can achieve greatly. Though WPI has a more than a 140-year history, the curriculum, like its students, is both innovative and practical. Small classes, a flexible curriculum, and one-on-one interaction with professors at the top of their field make learning at WPI an experience unlike any other.

WPI has been widely recognized for its academic program. WPI was the only technological university out of sixteen national Leadership Institutions selected by the Association of American Colleges and Universities to serve as models of outstanding practices in liberal education. WPI is consistently ranked among the top national universities by *U.S. News & World Report.* In the National Survey of Student Engagement, WPI ranked number one for student-faculty interactions, which is a measure of the quality and quantity of time faculty members spend with undergraduates.

More than thirty-five areas of study in engineering, science, business management, and the liberal arts allow many academic options, from molecular biology to music. Exciting new interdisciplinary programs are driven by real-world demand, such as interactive media and game development, robotics engineering, and environmental studies and engineering. The school also offers preprofessional programs and a five-year B.S./M.S. program.

With so many offerings, it is not surprising that more than 40 percent of students change their major at least once. At WPI, a comprehensive academic advising program and a wide array of academic support services help students make the right choices and reach their goals.

WPI students have received some of the nation's highest academic honors: the prestigious Marshall Scholarship, the National Institute of Health Research Scholarship, the Fulbright Scholarship, the Goldwater Scholarship, the Rotary Ambassadorial Scholarship, and the Society of Women Engineers Award. In addition, 2 students were recently named to the *USA Today* All-USA College Academic Team.

WPI is a member of the Colleges of Worcester Consortium, through which WPI students may register for courses at other colleges within the consortium and may take advantage of a wide range of cultural programming offered by consortium members. A consortium shuttle provides free transportation between campuses.

WPI has twenty varsity (NCAA Division III) athletics teams and thirty-four club and intramural sports. WPI won the Worcester Cup for four of the last six years for the highest overall winning percentage in all sports in Worcester County. There are thirteen fraternities and three sororities, fifteen music or theater ensembles, and dozens of academic clubs, international organizations, religious groups, and other organizations. There are more than 200 student clubs and activities.

Location

With its beautiful architecture, grassy quad, and ivy-covered walls, WPI has a traditional New England campus. Students stop and chat with their friends and professors on tree-lined paths, play pool between classes at the Campus Center, or get a coffee with friends. They study in the sun by the fountain in Reunion Plaza, go cosmic bowling, stop and smell the roses in the formal English garden behind Higgins House, or see a student play at the Little Theatre.

Home to twelve other colleges and universities and more than 35,000 college students, Worcester is a great college town. Late-night diners, clubs, museums, concert venues, and theaters are right down the hill from WPI in Worcester's vibrant downtown. Boston is less than an hour away by commuter rail, and there are great skiing and snowboarding at nearby Wachusett Mountain. Worcester is centrally located, with easy access to Providence, New York City, the Berkshires, the White Mountains, and Cape Cod.

Majors and Degrees

WPI offers the Bachelor of Science and the Bachelor of Arts degrees. Degree programs are offered in twenty areas of engineering and science: actuarial mathematics, aerospace engineering, biochemistry, biology and biotechnology, biomedical engineering, chemical engineering, chemistry, civil engineering, computer science, electrical and computer engineering, environmental engineering, environmental science, fire protection engineering, industrial engineering, interactive media and game development, manufacturing engineering, mathematical sciences, mechanical engineering, physics, and robotics engineering.

In addition, there are seventeen areas of management and the liberal arts: business/management; economics; environmental studies; history; humanities and arts; international studies; literature; management; management engineering; management information systems; music; philosophy and religion; professional writing; psychology/psychological science; society, technology, and policy; system dynamics; and theater.

Three new interdisciplinary majors have been added to the curriculum: interactive media and game development, environmental engineering, and robotics engineering, which is the first undergraduate program in robotics in the nation. WPI offers several preprofessional programs, including dentistry, law, medicine, and veterinary medicine. Students may also design their own majors by combining courses offered in various WPI departments. Undergraduates who wish to continue their studies toward a master's degree at WPI may enroll in a combined, continuous B.S./M.S. program.

Academic Programs

Students take the equivalent of three courses (as either traditional courses or project work) during each of four 7-week terms (two in the fall and two in the spring). At WPI, learning is about more than just theories and ideas. Students learn how to put ideas into practice through the project-enriched curriculum. WPI undergraduates complete two projects before graduation: one directly related to their major and one working with a team of students to solve a problem at the intersection of society and technology—helping to bring electricity to remote villages in Thailand or studying the bioethics of cloning, for example. Students gain valuable professional skills, a talent for team work, and the confidence to dive right in no matter what the challenge.

WPI's academic program encourages collaboration, not competition. Students work closely together in project-oriented classes. Learning how to work in teams prepares students to achieve results and become leaders in life after college, no matter what path they take.

Top-tier employers seek out WPI graduates for their real-world experience and ability to work collaboratively. With a placement rate of more than 90 percent, students are recruited by leading organizations such as Pfizer, General Electric, Fidelity Investments, and IBM. Each year, WPI graduates are accepted at many prestigious graduate schools, including MIT, Yale, Princeton, Johns Hopkins, and Tufts University Medical School.

WPI graduates' starting salaries are higher than those of many other college graduates, according to the National Association of Colleges and Employers. In addition, WPI was recently recognized by the Boston Globe for having the third highest average starting salaries in New England and the twelfth highest of all universities in the nation.

Off-Campus Programs

WPI has sent more engineering and science students abroad than any other university as part of its hands-on, project-enriched curriculum. About half of WPI students complete projects outside the United States and two-thirds do projects off campus. With WPI's Global Perspective

Program, students experience the challenge of solving real-world problems with their fellow students and immerse themselves in another culture. Students complete projects on campus or at any of the more than twenty-five project centers located on five continents around the globe, including Thailand, Australia, South Africa, Costa Rica, and the U.S. Recent project sponsors include NASA Johnson Space Center, Johnson & Johnson, Morgan Stanley, Environmental Protection Agency, and UNESCO. Through their seven-week project experience, students learn valuable professional skills, including communication, teamwork, and problem solving.

Academic Facilities

Among the many teaching, research, and project facilities available to undergraduates at WPI are a 71,000-square-foot campus center and a new Life Sciences and Bioengineering Center at Gateway Park, which is a state-of-the-art 130,000-square-foot facility at the life sciences-based campus that houses research in regenerative medicine, molecular nanotechnology, biosensors, plant systems, tissue engineering, and untethered health care. An $11-million renovation created the new undergraduate Life Sciences Laboratory Center, which opened in 2009. The center has become WPI's main facility for undergraduate teaching and research in biology and biotechnology, biomedical engineering, chemistry and biochemistry, and chemical engineering. WPI's other state-of-the-art research facilities include two atomic-force microscopes, medical imaging laboratories, a fire science laboratory, a new team-based chemistry lab, a laser holography lab, a computer music lab, a satellite navigation lab, thirty multimedia classrooms and lecture halls, and a research library with thousands of electronic journals, books, databases, and nearly 300,000 volumes.

The university also has an exceptional computer and networking infrastructure. The facilities include nearly 600 computers in open-access, 24/7 labs; powerful UNIX workstations; a Web-based student information system; a high-speed data network that reaches every building and residence hall; and extensive roaming wireless access.

In addition to these existing facilities, a state-of-the-art apartment-style residence hall, with over 200 beds, opened in fall 2008. The building features recreation and fitness space, technology suites on the each floor, meeting rooms on the ground floor for group projects, and wireless access.

WPI is scheduled to open a brand-new sports and recreation center in 2012. Plans include a four-court gymnasium, indoor jogging track, 14,000 square feet of fitness space, racquetball and squash courts, competition pool, workout studios, and rowing tanks.

Costs

For 2009–10, full-time tuition was $36,890. Room and board charges were $11,160.

Financial Aid

For families with established financial need, aid, including financial aid packages, on-campus jobs, and loan programs, is available. In addition, all applicants are considered for merit scholarships. More information is available from WPI's Office of Financial Aid (http://www.wpi.edu/+finaid).

Faculty

Besides being passionate about teaching, WPI's 365 full- and part-time faculty members are committed researchers and scholars with world-class credentials. They are leading contributors to the fields of nanotechnology, cryptography, fuel cells, and more. Eleven members of the current faculty are Fulbright Scholars, and more than 40 are fellows of top national and international societies. Since 1994, 17 WPI professors have won the National Science Foundation's CAREER Award, which is its most prestigious award for young faculty members. WPI has a 14:1 student-faculty ratio. According to *U.S. News & World Report,* faculty resources, which include salary, class size, and student-faculty ratio, rank thirtieth among national universities.

Student Government

Through the Student Government Association, the Interfraternity Council, the Panhellenic Association, and the International Student Council, students self-govern and develop their own social programs. WPI prides itself on being a caring community that respects the contributions of individuals, appreciates the diversity of the student body, and emphasizes the importance of cooperation and teamwork.

Admission Requirements

Applicants for admission must have completed 4 years of English, 4 years of mathematics (including precalculus), and 2 years of lab science. Admission requirements include a school transcript, SAT or ACT scores or alternative materials through WPI's Flex Path, recommendations from a science or math teacher and a counselor, and a personal essay. For international students whose first language is not English, a TOEFL or IELTS score is required.

The university has high standards for applicants but also looks for more than just outstanding academic performance. WPI takes care to admit students who will likely thrive at the university. They tend to be creative and curious; like to work in teams to get things done; are comfortable making their own decisions and setting their own courses; love math and science but feel just as passionate about literature, music, movies, and the arts; prefer to be leaders, not followers; and are ready to make a positive impact on the world around them.

Students are encouraged to visit the WPI campus to learn more about the university, see its facilities, and hear firsthand about the WPI experience from students and faculty members. WPI is open most school holidays and offers a wide range of options for tours, group information sessions, open houses, personal interviews, and Saturday visits. Details and schedules may be obtained from the Web site of the Office of Admissions.

The deadline for early action round 1 is November 10, with notification by December 20. The deadline for early action round 2 is January 1, with notification by February 10. The regular decision deadline is February 1, with notification by April 1. For transfer admissions, the priority deadline is April 15; students are notified of admission decisions on a rolling basis.

Application and Information

To schedule a visit or request more information, students should contact:

Office of Admissions
Bartlett Center
Worcester Polytechnic Institute
100 Institute Road
Worcester, Massachusetts 01609-2280
Phone: 508-831-5286
Fax: 508-831-5875
E-mail: admissions@wpi.edu
Web site: http://admissions.wpi.edu

A view of the campus at Worcester Polytechnic Institute.

YORK UNIVERSITY

TORONTO, ONTARIO, CANADA

The University

York University is the leading interdisciplinary teaching and research university in Canada. York offers a modern academic experience at the undergraduate and graduate levels in Toronto, Canada's most international city. The third-largest university in the country, York is host to a dynamic academic community of over 50,000 students and 7,000 faculty and staff members as well as more than 200,000 alumni worldwide. York's ten faculties and twenty-six research centres conduct ambitious, groundbreaking interdisciplinary research—cutting across traditional academic boundaries. This distinctive and collaborative approach prepares students for the future and brings fresh insights and solutions to real-world challenges. In addition to its undergraduate programs, York's Faculty of Graduate Studies offers more than fifty master's, doctoral, and professional programs.

Location

York University is located in Toronto, Canada's largest city and main financial centre. Known for its friendly people, beautiful spaces, and vibrant cities, Canada is recognized as one of the best places in the world to live. As one of the world's most multicultural cities, Toronto has theatre, music, and restaurants from all around the globe. From art galleries and museums to restaurants and major-league sports, Toronto has all the elements of a world-class city. Toronto is a 1-hour flight from New York City, Boston, Chicago, or Detroit and a 90-minute drive from the U.S. border at Buffalo, New York.

Students can choose between two unique campuses. The Keele campus, in north Toronto, is home to eight of the nine undergraduate faculties and offers extensive modern facilities, including more than forty restaurants, a shopping mall, banks, a medical/dental clinic, five libraries, art galleries, theatres, an athletic complex, the Rexall™ Tennis Centre, on-campus housing, an executive learning centre, and a wide variety of events and cultural activities. The Glendon campus, a picturesque, parklike campus minutes from the boutiques, restaurants, and nightlife of midtown Toronto, is a close-knit, bilingual liberal arts community of 2,500 students.

Majors and Degrees

York University offers more than 5,000 courses through ten faculties: Education, Environmental Studies, Fine Arts, Glendon, Graduate Studies, Health, Liberal Arts and Professional Studies, Osgoode Hall Law School, Schulich School of Business, and Science and Engineering.

The Faculty of Liberal Arts and Professional Studies offers Bachelor of Arts (daytime studies, Keele campus) degrees in African studies; anthropology; business and society; business economics; Canadian studies; children's studies; classical studies/classics; cognitive science; communication studies; creative writing; criminology; culture and expression; East Asian studies; economics; English; English and professional writing; European studies; financial and business economics; French studies; geography; German studies; global political studies; health and society; Hellenic studies; history; human rights and equity studies; humanities; individualized studies; information technology; international B.A. (various topics); international development studies; Italian studies; Jewish studies; labour studies; Latin American and Caribbean studies; law and society; linguistics; philosophy; political science; Portuguese studies; professional writing; race, ethnicity, and indigeneity; religious studies; science and technology studies; sexuality studies; social and political thought; social science; sociology; South Asian studies; Spanish; undecided major; urban studies; and women's studies. Also offered are the Bachelor of Administrative Studies (accounting, business research, finance, human resources management, information technology, management, management science, marketing), Bachelor of Disaster and Emergency Management, Bachelor of Human Resources Management, Bachelor of Public Administration, and Bachelor of Social Work programs. Joint programs with some Ontario community colleges are available in communication arts and rehabilitation services. Certificates are available in accounting, antiracist research and practice, athletic therapy, biblical studies, coaching, emergency management, fitness assessment and exercise counselling, geographic information systems and remote sensing, health administration, health informatics, human resources management, logistics, management, marketing, nurse practitioner studies, professional ethics, public sector management, real estate, refugee and migration studies, sexuality studies, sport administration, teaching English to speakers of other languages, and women's studies: theory and practice.

The Faculty of Education's Bachelor of Education offers both concurrent and consecutive education programs, which are offered in primary/junior (K–6), junior/intermediate (4–10), and intermediate/senior (7–12) levels. There are no specialization subjects in the primary/junior program. Subjects of specialization in the junior/intermediate program include dance, drama, English, French as a second language, geography, history, mathematics, music, physical and health education, religious studies, science (general), and visual arts. The intermediate/senior program asks for specialization in two of the following subjects: accounting, biology, chemistry, computer science, dance, drama, economics, English, family studies, French as a second language, geography, German, history, individual and society, information management, Italian, law, marketing and merchandising, mathematics, music, physical and health education, physics, political science, religious studies, science (general), Spanish, and visual arts. Students may also pursue the Jewish Teacher Education Program or Indigenous Teacher Education Program within concurrent Education.

The Faculty of Environmental Studies provides Bachelor of Environmental Studies degrees in environmental management, environmental politics, environment and culture, and urban and regional environments. Certificates are offered in community arts practice, environmental landscape design, and geographic information systems and remote sensing. Joint college programs also offer ecosystem management, international project management, and urban sustainability.

The Faculty of Fine Arts offers Bachelor of Design, Bachelor of Fine Arts, and Bachelor of Arts degrees in the following programs: dance, design, digital media, film, fine arts cultural studies, music, theater, and visual arts (includes art history, drawing, media arts, painting, photography, printmaking, and sculpture). Certificates are available in law and social thought, public administration and public policy, rédaction professionelle, refugee and migration studies, Spanish/English translation/Traducción ingles-español, teaching English as an international language, and technical and professional writing.

The Faculty of Health offers programs in health studies (health studies, health informatics, health management, and health policy), kinesiology and health science, nursing, and psychology.

York's Osgoode Hall Law School offers a Bachelor of Laws. The Schulich School of Business offers a Bachelor of Business Administration degree in accounting, economics, entrepreneurship and family business, finance, international business, marketing, operations management and information systems, and organizational behaviour/industrial relations. An International Bachelor of Business Administration degree is also offered.

The Faculty of Science and Engineering offers a Bachelor of Science in applied math, biochemistry, biology, biomedical science, biophysics, biotechnology, chemistry, computational mathematics, computer science, computer security, earth and atmospheric science, environmental science, geography, international B.Sc., mathematics, mathematics for education, physics and astronomy, science and technology studies, and space science. A Bachelor of Arts is available in digital media. A joint program with Seneca College is available in rehabilitation services. Certificates are available in athletic therapy, coaching, fitness assessment and exercise counselling, geographic information systems and remote sensing, meteorology, and sport administration. The Bachelor of Applied Science is offered in computer engineering, geomatics engineering, and space engineering.

The Faculty of Glendon, York's bilingual campus. offers Bachelor of Arts degrees in business economics, Canadian studies, drama studies, economics, English, environmental and health studies, French studies, history, individualized/multidisciplinary studies, international B.A. (various subjects), international studies, linguistics and language studies, mathematics, mathematics for commerce, philosophy, political science, psychology, sociology, Spanish (Hispanic studies), translation, undecided major, and women's studies.

Academic Programs

Students can begin their studies at York in September (all programs) or, in a limited number of programs, in May or January, and study on a full- or part-time basis during the day or evening. All degree requirements must be completed prior to graduating. The University calendar is organized on a semester system, with two 6-week summer sessions. Detailed information about program requirements can be found in the Calendars at http://www.registrar.yorku.ca.

Off-Campus Programs

York has more than 100 partnership agreements with universities throughout the world to offer exchange and study-abroad opportunities. The University-wide Exchange Program has partnerships with universities in Australia, Barbados, Brazil, China, Denmark, England, Finland, France, Germany, Greece, Guyana, Italy, Jamaica, Japan, Korea, Latvia, Lithuania, Mexico, Mongolia, the Netherlands, Poland, Russia, Singapore, Spain, Sweden, Thailand, Trinidad and Tobago, Turkey, the United States, Venezuela, and Wales. Qualifying students must be in an honors program, have completed two years of study, have maintained at least an overall B average, and, in some cases, have proficiency in the host country's language.

Academic Facilities

York's five libraries contain more than 6.5 million books, print periodicals, e-journals, theses, archival materials, microforms, maps, films, and music CDs. The Osgoode Hall Law Library, the largest in the Commonwealth, houses a collection of approximately 450,000 volumes (including microform). With twenty-four research centres, York is one of the most highly valued and sought-after research institutions. Students have access to a wide range of computer facilities, including forty-two computer labs, more than 2,500 workstations, free e-mail, and Internet access. There are academic tutors, advisers to help with course selection, and an extensive learning disabilities program. Students whose first language is not English can get extra help at the English as a Second Language Open Learning Centre and take ESL courses that count toward their degrees. At York, facilities include visual arts studios, three theatres, three art galleries (excluding college-based student galleries), state-of-the-art science laboratories, an astronomical observatory with two telescopes, two stadiums, four gymnasiums, five sport playing fields, four softball fields, nine outdoor tennis courts, the Rexall™ Tennis Centre, seven squash courts, three dance/aerobic studios, five NHL-sized ice rinks and one international-sized rink, two swimming pools, and a newly renovated, 11,000-square-foot fitness centre. The Accolade Project houses outstanding Faculty of Fine Arts facilities, including a 325-seat proscenium theatre, a 325-seat recital hall equipped with a recording studio, a state-of-the-art screening facility, studios, and teaching spaces.

Costs

For the 2009–10 academic year, full-time tuition was a minimum of Can$5761 for Canadian citizens and permanent residents or Can$15,761 for international students. Room and board (double room) start at Can$4250, and a meal plan ranges from Can$2500 to Can$3500. Students living in residence must purchase a meal plan. Course materials, books, health insurance, and supplies range from Can$1500 to Can$3000. Further details are available at http://www.yorku.ca/osfs.

Financial Aid

International candidates can compete for the prestigious Global Leader of Tomorrow Award, worth Can$15,000 per year and renewable for up to four years, pending excellent grades; applications are necessary. Once at York, international students are eligible for continuing scholarships worth up to Can$3000 based on their academic performance. U.S. citizens may be eligible to receive FAFSA funding (FAFSA code: 07679). Full-time international students may work part-time on or off campus. Students may work for up to two years in Canada after completing their degree. Full scholarship details are available at http://www.yorku.ca/web/futurestudents/scholarships.

Faculty

York employs 2,448 professors, spread over two campuses. York's professors are mentors, known internationally for excellence and innovation in teaching and research. Excellence in research is central to York's mission and is fundamental to the University's ability to contribute to the economic, scientific, cultural, and social health of society. Research takes place in every discipline and spans the full spectrum of programs. In addition, York has renowned research strength in areas such as space science, vision science, aboriginal and indigenous studies, history, and psychology. A complete list of prestigious award recipients can be found at http://research.yorku.ca.

Student Government

Nine student governments are located within the residential colleges and Faculties. A central government, the York Federation of Students, represents all students. York students have representation on the Board of Governors, Senate, Faculty Councils, Council of Masters, and other advisory committees.

Admission Requirements

York is a selective university; therefore, only those candidates who show potential for academic success are considered. Meeting minimum requirements does not guarantee admission. Some programs may require specific preparation in certain subject areas. York's TOEFL code is 0894. Academically outstanding students with a minimum SAT score of 1300 may receive early admission.

Application and Information

Applications are available at http://www.ouac.on.ca. The deadline for international applicants interested in September admission is February 1. Students should submit their applications and materials well ahead of the deadline. Some programs require supplemental application forms. Additional information about admissions, academic requirements, programs, courses, or University events and tours is available at http://futurestudents.yorku.ca.

Office of Admissions
York University
4700 Keele Street
Toronto, Ontario M3J 1P3
Canada
Phone: 416-736-5825
Fax: 416-650-8195
Web site: http://www.yorku.ca

Vari Hall, the focal point of the Keele campus.

Indexes

Majors

ACCOUNTING

Abilene Christian U (TX)
Adams State Coll (CO)
Adelphi U (NY)
AIB Coll of Business (IA)
Alabama Ag and Mech U (AL)
Alabama State U (AL)
Albany State U (GA)
Albertus Magnus Coll (CT)
Albright Coll (PA)
Alcorn State U (MS)
Alderson-Broaddus Coll (WV)
Alfred U (NY)
Alma Coll (MI)
Alvernia U (PA)
Amberton U (TX)
American Intl Coll (MA)
American U (DC)
Anderson U (IN)
Andrews U (MI)
Angelo State U (TX)
Appalachian State U (NC)
Aquinas Coll (MI)
Arcadia U (PA)
Argosy U, Atlanta (GA)
Argosy U, Chicago (IL)
Argosy U, Dallas (TX)
Argosy U, Denver (CO)
Argosy U, Hawai'i (HI)
Argosy U, Inland Empire (CA)
Argosy U, Los Angeles (CA)
Argosy U, Phoenix (AZ)
Argosy U, Salt Lake City (UT)
Argosy U, San Diego (CA)
Argosy U, San Francisco Bay Area (CA)
Argosy U, Sarasota (FL)
Argosy U, Schaumburg (IL)
Argosy U, Tampa (FL)
Argosy U, Twin Cities (MN)
Argosy U, Washington DC (VA)
Arizona State U (AZ)
Arkansas State U—Jonesboro (AR)
Arkansas Tech U (AR)
Asbury U (KY)
Ashland U (OH)
Assumption Coll (MA)
Athabasca U (AB, Canada)
Atlantic Union Coll (MA)
Auburn U (AL)
Auburn U Montgomery (AL)
Augsburg Coll (MN)
Augustana Coll (IL)
Augustana Coll (SD)
Aurora U (IL)
Averett U (VA)
Avila U (MO)
Azusa Pacific U (CA)
Babson Coll (MA)
Baker Coll of Auburn Hills (MI)
Baker Coll of Owosso (MI)
Baker U (KS)
Baldwin-Wallace Coll (OH)
Ball State U (IN)
Barry U (FL)
Barton Coll (NC)
Baylor U (TX)
Bay Path Coll (MA)
Belhaven U (MS)
Bellarmine U (KY)
Belmont Abbey Coll (NC)
Belmont U (TN)
Bemidji State U (MN)
Benedictine Coll (KS)
Benedictine U (IL)
Bennett Coll for Women (NC)
Bentley U (MA)
Bernard M. Baruch Coll of the City U of New York (NY)
Berry Coll (GA)
Bethany Coll (KS)
Bethany Coll (WV)
Bethel Coll (IN)
Bethune-Cookman U (FL)
Birmingham-Southern Coll (AL)
Bishop's U (QC, Canada)
Blackburn Coll (IL)
Black Hills State U (SD)
Bloomfield Coll (NJ)
Bloomsburg U of Pennsylvania (PA)
Bluefield Coll (VA)
Bluefield State Coll (WV)
Bluffton U (OH)
Bob Jones U (SC)
Boise State U (ID)
Boston Coll (MA)
Boston U (MA)
Bowie State U (MD)
Bowling Green State U (OH)
Bradley U (IL)
Brenau U (GA)
Brescia U (KY)
Brewton-Parker Coll (GA)
Briar Cliff U (IA)
Bridgewater State Coll (MA)
Brigham Young U–Hawaii (HI)
Brock U (ON, Canada)
Brooklyn Coll of the City U of New York (NY)
Brown Mackie Coll–Tucson (AZ)
Bryant U (RI)
Bucknell U (PA)
Buena Vista U (IA)
Butler U (IN)
Cabrini Coll (PA)
California Baptist U (CA)
California Lutheran U (CA)
California State U, Chico (CA)
California State U, Dominguez Hills (CA)
California State U, East Bay (CA)
California State U, Fresno (CA)
California State U, Fullerton (CA)
California State U, Long Beach (CA)
California State U, Northridge (CA)
California State U, San Bernardino (CA)
California State U, San Marcos (CA)
Calumet Coll of Saint Joseph (IN)
Calvin Coll (MI)
Cameron U (OK)
Campbellsville U (KY)
Canisius Coll (NY)
Cape Breton U (NS, Canada)
Capella U (MN)
Capital U (OH)
Carlow U (PA)
Carroll U (WI)
Carson-Newman Coll (TN)
Case Western Reserve U (OH)
Castleton State Coll (VT)
The Catholic U of America (DC)
Cazenovia Coll (NY)
Cedar Crest Coll (PA)
Cedarville U (OH)
Centenary Coll (NJ)
Central Baptist Coll (AR)
Central Christian Coll of Kansas (KS)
Central Coll (IA)
Central Connecticut State U (CT)
Central Michigan U (MI)
Central Pennsylvania Coll (PA)
Central State U (OH)
Chaminade U of Honolulu (HI)
Champlain Coll (VT)
Chapman U (CA)
Chatham U (PA)
Chowan U (NC)
Christopher Newport U (VA)
City U of Seattle (WA)
Claremont McKenna Coll (CA)
Clarion U of Pennsylvania (PA)
Clark Atlanta U (GA)
Clarke Coll (IA)
Clayton State U (GA)
Clearwater Christian Coll (FL)
Cleary U (MI)
Clemson U (SC)
Cleveland State U (OH)
Coastal Carolina U (SC)
The Coll at Brockport, State U of New York (NY)
Coll of Charleston (SC)
The Coll of Idaho (ID)
Coll of Mount St. Joseph (OH)
The Coll of New Jersey (NJ)
Coll of Saint Benedict (MN)
Coll of St. Joseph (VT)
The Coll of Saint Rose (NY)
The Coll of St. Scholastica (MN)
Coll of Staten Island of the City U of New York (NY)
Coll of the Holy Cross (MA)
Coll of the Ozarks (MO)
The Coll of William and Mary (VA)
Colorado State U (CO)
Colorado State U–Pueblo (CO)
Columbia Coll (MO)
Columbia Coll (SC)
Columbus State U (GA)
Concordia Coll (MN)
Concordia U (QC, Canada)
Concordia U Chicago (IL)
Concordia U, St. Paul (MN)
Concordia U Wisconsin (WI)
Concord U (WV)
Converse Coll (SC)
Corban U (OR)
Cornerstone U (MI)
Creighton U (NE)
Culver-Stockton Coll (MO)
Cumberland U (TN)
Daemen Coll (NY)
Dakota State U (SD)
Dakota Wesleyan U (SD)
Dallas Baptist U (TX)
Dana Coll (NE)
Davenport U, Grand Rapids (MI)
Defiance Coll (OH)
Delaware State U (DE)
Delaware Valley Coll (PA)
Delta State U (MS)
DePaul U (IL)
DeSales U (PA)
Dickinson State U (ND)
Dillard U (LA)
Dixie State Coll of Utah (UT)
Doane Coll (NE)
Dominican Coll (NY)
Dominican U (IL)
Dordt Coll (IA)
Dowling Coll (NY)
Drake U (IA)
Drexel U (PA)
Drury U (MO)
Duquesne U (PA)
D'Youville Coll (NY)
East Carolina U (NC)
East Central U (OK)
Eastern Connecticut State U (CT)
Eastern Illinois U (IL)
Eastern Mennonite U (VA)
Eastern Michigan U (MI)
Eastern Nazarene Coll (MA)
Eastern New Mexico U (NM)
Eastern Washington U (WA)
East Tennessee State U (TN)
Edgewood Coll (WI)
Elizabeth City State U (NC)
Elizabethtown Coll (PA)
Elmhurst Coll (IL)
Elmira Coll (NY)
Elon U (NC)
Emory & Henry Coll (VA)
Emory U (GA)
Emporia State U (KS)
Endicott Coll (MA)
Excelsior Coll (NY)
Fairfield U (CT)
Fairleigh Dickinson U, Coll at Florham (NJ)
Fairleigh Dickinson U, Metropolitan Campus (NJ)
Fairmont State U (WV)
Faulkner U (AL)
Fayetteville State U (NC)
Felician Coll (NJ)
Ferris State U (MI)
Ferrum Coll (VA)
Fitchburg State Coll (MA)
Flagler Coll (FL)
Florida Ag and Mech U (FL)
Florida Atlantic U (FL)
Florida Gulf Coast U (FL)
Florida Inst of Technology (FL)
Florida Intl U (FL)
Florida Southern Coll (FL)
Florida State U (FL)
Fordham U (NY)
Fort Hays State U (KS)
Fort Lewis Coll (CO)
Fort Valley State U (GA)
Franciscan U of Steubenville (OH)
Francis Marion U (SC)
Franklin Coll (IN)
Franklin Pierce U (NH)
Franklin U (OH)
Freed-Hardeman U (TN)
Friends U (KS)
Frostburg State U (MD)
Furman U (SC)
Gallaudet U (DC)
Gannon U (PA)
Gardner-Webb U (NC)
Geneva Coll (PA)
George Fox U (OR)
George Mason U (VA)
Georgetown Coll (KY)
Georgetown U (DC)
The George Washington U (DC)
Georgia Coll & State U (GA)
Georgian Court U (NJ)
Georgia Southern U (GA)
Georgia State U (GA)
Gettysburg Coll (PA)
Globe Inst of Technology (NY)
Goldey-Beacom Coll (DE)
Gonzaga U (WA)
Gordon Coll (MA)
Goshen Coll (IN)
Governors State U (IL)
Grace Bible Coll (MI)
Grace Coll (IN)
Graceland U (IA)
Grambling State U (LA)
Grand Valley State U (MI)
Grand View U (IA)
Greensboro Coll (NC)
Greenville Coll (IL)
Grove City Coll (PA)
Guilford Coll (NC)
Gustavus Adolphus Coll (MN)
Gwynedd-Mercy Coll (PA)
Hamline U (MN)
Hampton U (VA)
Hannibal-LaGrange Coll (MO)
Harding U (AR)
Hardin-Simmons U (TX)
Harrison Coll, Evansville (IN)
Harrison Coll, Indianapolis (IN)
Harrison Coll, Lafayette (IN)
Harrison Coll, Muncie (IN)
Harrison Coll, Terre Haute (IN)
Harris-Stowe State U (MO)
Hartwick Coll (NY)
Hawai'i Pacific U (HI)
HEC Montreal (QC, Canada)
Heidelberg U (OH)
Henderson State U (AR)
Hendrix Coll (AR)
High Point U (NC)
Hilbert Coll (NY)
Hillsdale Coll (MI)
Hofstra U (NY)
Holy Family U (PA)
Hope Coll (MI)
Houston Baptist U (TX)
Howard Payne U (TX)
Hunter Coll of the City U of New York (NY)
Huntingdon Coll (AL)
Huntington U (IN)
Husson U (ME)
Huston-Tillotson U (TX)
Idaho State U (ID)
Illinois Coll (IL)
Illinois State U (IL)
Illinois Wesleyan U (IL)
Immaculata U (PA)
Indiana State U (IN)
Indiana Tech (IN)
Indiana U of Pennsylvania (PA)
Indiana U–Purdue U Fort Wayne (IN)
Indiana Wesleyan U (IN)
Inter American U of Puerto Rico, Aguadilla Campus (PR)
Inter American U of Puerto Rico, Arecibo Campus (PR)
Inter American U of Puerto Rico, Bayamón Campus (PR)
Inter American U of Puerto Rico, Fajardo Campus (PR)
Inter American U of Puerto Rico, Guayama Campus (PR)
Inter American U of Puerto Rico, Ponce Campus (PR)
Inter American U of Puerto Rico, San Germán Campus (PR)
Iona Coll (NY)
Iowa State U of Science and Technology (IA)
Iowa Wesleyan Coll (IA)
Ithaca Coll (NY)
Jackson State U (MS)
Jacksonville State U (AL)
Jacksonville U (FL)
James Madison U (VA)
Jamestown Coll (ND)
Jarvis Christian Coll (TX)
John Brown U (AR)
John Carroll U (OH)
Johnson & Wales U (CO)
Johnson & Wales U (FL)
Johnson & Wales U (RI)
Johnson & Wales U—Charlotte Campus (NC)
Johnson State Coll (VT)
Jones Intl U (CO)
Judson U (IL)
Juniata Coll (PA)
Kansas State U (KS)
Kaplan U, Cedar Rapids (IA)
Kaplan U, Omaha (NE)
Kean U (NJ)
Keiser U, Fort Lauderdale (FL)
Kennesaw State U (GA)
Kent State U (OH)
Kentucky Wesleyan Coll (KY)
Keuka Coll (NY)
Keystone Coll (PA)
King Coll (TN)
King's Coll (PA)
Kutztown U of Pennsylvania (PA)
Kuyper Coll (MI)
Kwantlen Polytechnic U (BC, Canada)
LaGrange Coll (GA)
Lake Erie Coll (OH)
Lakehead U (ON, Canada)
Lakeland Coll (WI)
Lake Superior State U (MI)
Lamar U (TX)
La Roche Coll (PA)
La Salle U (PA)
Lasell Coll (MA)
La Sierra U (CA)
Lebanon Valley Coll (PA)
Lee U (TN)
Lehigh U (PA)
Lehman Coll of the City U of New York (NY)
Le Moyne Coll (NY)
LeTourneau U (TX)
Lewis U (IL)
Liberty U (VA)
Limestone Coll (SC)
Lincoln Memorial U (TN)
Lincoln U (MO)
Lincoln U (PA)
Lindenwood U (MO)
Linfield Coll (OR)
Lipscomb U (TN)
Lock Haven U of Pennsylvania (PA)
Long Island U, Brooklyn Campus (NY)
Long Island U, C.W. Post Campus (NY)
Longwood U (VA)
Loras Coll (IA)
Louisiana Coll (LA)
Louisiana State U and Ag and Mech Coll (LA)
Louisiana State U in Shreveport (LA)
Louisiana Tech U (LA)
Lourdes Coll (OH)

INDEXES

U of Hawaii–West Oahu (HI)
U of Houston (TX)
U of Houston–Clear Lake (TX)
U of Houston–Downtown (TX)
U of Houston–Victoria (TX)
U of Idaho (ID)
U of Illinois at Chicago (IL)
U of Illinois at Springfield (IL)
U of Illinois at Urbana–Champaign (IL)
U of Indianapolis (IN)
The U of Iowa (IA)
The U of Kansas (KS)
U of Kentucky (KY)
U of La Verne (CA)
U of Lethbridge (AB, Canada)
U of Louisiana at Monroe (LA)
U of Louisville (KY)
U of Maine at Augusta (ME)
U of Maine at Machias (ME)
U of Maine at Presque Isle (ME)
U of Manitoba (MB, Canada)
U of Mary (ND)
U of Mary Hardin-Baylor (TX)
U of Maryland, Coll Park (MD)
U of Maryland Eastern Shore (MD)
U of Maryland U Coll (MD)
U of Massachusetts Amherst (MA)
U of Massachusetts Dartmouth (MA)
U of Memphis (TN)
U of Miami (FL)
U of Michigan–Dearborn (MI)
U of Michigan–Flint (MI)
U of Minnesota, Crookston (MN)
U of Minnesota, Duluth (MN)
U of Minnesota, Twin Cities Campus (MN)
U of Mississippi (MS)
U of Missouri (MO)
U of Missouri–Kansas City (MO)
U of Missouri–St. Louis (MO)
U of Mobile (AL)
U of Montevallo (AL)
U of Mount Union (OH)
U of Nebraska at Omaha (NE)
U of Nebraska–Lincoln (NE)
U of Nevada, Las Vegas (NV)
U of Nevada, Reno (NV)
U of New Brunswick Fredericton (NB, Canada)
U of New Haven (CT)
U of New Orleans (LA)
U of North Alabama (AL)
The U of North Carolina at Asheville (NC)
The U of North Carolina at Charlotte (NC)
The U of North Carolina at Greensboro (NC)
The U of North Carolina at Pembroke (NC)
The U of North Carolina Wilmington (NC)
U of North Dakota (ND)
U of Northern Iowa (IA)
U of North Florida (FL)
U of North Texas (TX)
U of Notre Dame (IN)
U of Oklahoma (OK)
U of Oregon (OR)
U of Ottawa (ON, Canada)
U of Pennsylvania (PA)
U of Pittsburgh (PA)
U of Pittsburgh at Bradford (PA)
U of Pittsburgh at Greensburg (PA)
U of Pittsburgh at Johnstown (PA)
U of Portland (OR)
U of Puerto Rico at Bayamón (PR)
U of Puerto Rico at Humacao (PR)
U of Puerto Rico at Utuado (PR)
U of Puerto Rico, Cayey U Coll (PR)
U of Puerto Rico, Río Piedras (PR)
U of Redlands (CA)
U of Regina (SK, Canada)
U of Rhode Island (RI)
U of Richmond (VA)
U of Rio Grande (OH)
U of St. Francis (IL)
U of Saint Mary (KS)
U of St. Thomas (MN)
U of St. Thomas (TX)
U of San Diego (CA)
U of San Francisco (CA)
U of Saskatchewan (SK, Canada)
The U of Scranton (PA)
U of South Alabama (AL)
U of South Carolina (SC)
The U of South Dakota (SD)
U of Southern California (CA)
U of Southern Indiana (IN)
U of Southern Maine (ME)
U of Southern Mississippi (MS)
U of South Florida (FL)
The U of Tampa (FL)
The U of Tennessee (TN)
The U of Tennessee at Martin (TN)
The U of Texas at Arlington (TX)
The U of Texas at Austin (TX)
The U of Texas at Brownsville (TX)
The U of Texas at Dallas (TX)
The U of Texas at El Paso (TX)
The U of Texas at San Antonio (TX)
The U of Texas at Tyler (TX)
The U of Texas of the Permian Basin (TX)
The U of Texas–Pan American (TX)
U of the Cumberlands (KY)
U of the Incarnate Word (TX)
U of the Ozarks (AR)
U of the Southwest (NM)
U of the Virgin Islands (VI)
The U of Toledo (OH)
U of Toronto (ON, Canada)
U of Tulsa (OK)
U of Utah (UT)
The U of Virginia's Coll at Wise (VA)
U of Washington (WA)
U of Washington, Bothell (WA)
U of Washington, Tacoma (WA)
U of Waterloo (ON, Canada)
The U of West Alabama (AL)
The U of Western Ontario (ON, Canada)
U of West Florida (FL)
U of West Georgia (GA)
U of Windsor (ON, Canada)
U of Wisconsin–Eau Claire (WI)
U of Wisconsin–Green Bay (WI)
U of Wisconsin–La Crosse (WI)
U of Wisconsin–Madison (WI)
U of Wisconsin–Milwaukee (WI)
U of Wisconsin–Oshkosh (WI)
U of Wisconsin–Parkside (WI)
U of Wisconsin–Platteville (WI)
U of Wisconsin–River Falls (WI)
U of Wisconsin–Stevens Point (WI)
U of Wisconsin–Superior (WI)
U of Wisconsin–Whitewater (WI)
U of Wyoming (WY)
Upper Iowa U (IA)
Ursuline Coll (OH)
Utah State U (UT)
Utah Valley U (UT)
Utica Coll (NY)
Valdosta State U (GA)
Valparaiso U (IN)
Vanguard U of Southern California (CA)
Villanova U (PA)
Virginia Commonwealth U (VA)
Virginia Polytechnic Inst and State U (VA)
Virginia State U (VA)
Virginia Union U (VA)
Viterbo U (WI)
Voorhees Coll (SC)
Wagner Coll (NY)
Wake Forest U (NC)
Walden U (MN)
Walsh U (OH)
Wartburg Coll (IA)
Washburn U (KS)
Washington & Jefferson Coll (PA)
Washington and Lee U (VA)
Washington State U (WA)
Washington U in St. Louis (MO)
Waynesburg U (PA)
Wayne State U (MI)
Webber Intl U (FL)
Weber State U (UT)
Webster U (MO)
West Chester U of Pennsylvania (PA)
Western Carolina U (NC)
Western Connecticut State U (CT)
Western Illinois U (IL)
Western Intl U (AZ)
Western Kentucky U (KY)
Western Michigan U (MI)
Western New England Coll (MA)
Western State Coll of Colorado (CO)
West Liberty U (WV)
Westminster Coll (MO)
Westminster Coll (UT)
West Virginia State U (WV)
West Virginia U (WV)
West Virginia Wesleyan Coll (WV)
Westwood Coll–Online Campus (CO)
Wheeling Jesuit U (WV)
Wichita State U (KS)
Widener U (PA)
Wilberforce U (OH)
Wilkes U (PA)
William Jewell Coll (MO)
William Paterson U of New Jersey (NJ)
William Penn U (IA)
Wilmington Coll (OH)
Wilmington U (DE)
Wilson Coll (PA)
Wingate U (NC)
Winona State U (MN)
Winston-Salem State U (NC)
Wofford Coll (SC)
Woodbury U (CA)
Wright State U (OH)
Xavier U (OH)
Xavier U of Louisiana (LA)
Yeshiva U (NY)
York Coll (NE)
York Coll of Pennsylvania (PA)
York Coll of the City U of New York (NY)
York U (ON, Canada)
Youngstown State U (OH)

ACCOUNTING AND BUSINESS/MANAGEMENT

Alaska Pacific U (AK)
Babson Coll (MA)
Bethel U (TN)
East Carolina U (NC)
Eastern Nazarene Coll (MA)
EDP Coll of Puerto Rico, Inc. (PR)
EDP Coll of Puerto Rico–San Sebastian (PR)
Florida Ag and Mech U (FL)
Florida Inst of Technology (FL)
Illinois State U (IL)
Keystone Coll (PA)
Maranatha Baptist Bible Coll (WI)
Menlo Coll (CA)
Mercy Coll (NY)
Mitchell Coll (CT)
Presbyterian Coll (SC)
Rocky Mountain Coll (MT)
Santa Clara U (CA)
Tabor Coll (KS)
U of Illinois at Urbana–Champaign (IL)
The U of Western Ontario (ON, Canada)
Western State Coll of Colorado (CO)
Westwood Coll–Annandale Campus (VA)
Westwood Coll–Arlington Ballston Campus (VA)
Westwood Coll–Atlanta Midtown (GA)
Westwood Coll–Atlanta Northlake (GA)
Westwood Coll–Chicago Du Page (IL)
Westwood Coll–Chicago Loop Campus (IL)
Westwood Coll–Chicago O'Hare Airport (IL)
Westwood Coll–Chicago River Oaks (IL)
Westwood Coll–Dallas (TX)
Westwood Coll–Denver South (CO)
Westwood Coll–Fort Worth (TX)
Westwood Coll–Los Angeles (CA)
Westwood Coll–Online Campus (CO)
Westwood Coll–South Bay Campus (CA)

ACCOUNTING AND COMPUTER SCIENCE

California State U, Chico (CA)
Fordham U (NY)
Goldey-Beacom Coll (DE)
Husson U (ME)
San Jose State U (CA)
Southern New Hampshire U (NH)

ACCOUNTING AND FINANCE

Babson Coll (MA)
Bethel U (MN)
Central Christian Coll of Kansas (KS)
Clarkson U (NY)
Drake U (IA)
Eastern Nazarene Coll (MA)
Ferris State U (MI)
Hiram Coll (OH)
Jones Intl U (CO)
Lourdes Coll (OH)
Northern Michigan U (MI)
Saint Francis U (PA)
Salem State Coll (MA)
Southern New Hampshire U (NH)
Universidad de las Américas–Puebla (Mexico)
U of North Dakota (ND)
U of Waterloo (ON, Canada)
The U of Western Ontario (ON, Canada)
U of Windsor (ON, Canada)
Western State Coll of Colorado (CO)

ACCOUNTING RELATED

Bentley U (MA)
Brigham Young U (UT)
Central Michigan U (MI)
Dana Coll (NE)
Duquesne U (PA)
Eastern Nazarene Coll (MA)
Franklin U (OH)
Keystone Coll (PA)
Maryville U of Saint Louis (MO)
North Dakota State U (ND)
Northern Michigan U (MI)
Rocky Mountain Coll (MT)
Saint Mary-of-the-Woods Coll (IN)
Saint Mary's Coll of California (CA)
State U of New York at Oswego (NY)
Trevecca Nazarene U (TN)

ACCOUNTING TECHNOLOGY AND BOOKKEEPING

Bryant U (RI)
Canisius Coll (NY)
Ferris State U (MI)
ITT Tech Inst, Miami (FL)
ITT Tech Inst, Indianapolis (IN)
ITT Tech Inst, Cordova (TN)
ITT Tech Inst, Nashville (TN)
Lewis-Clark State Coll (ID)
Nevada State Coll at Henderson (NV)
Rowan U (NJ)
St. Edward's U (TX)
U of Hawaii at Manoa (HI)

ACOUSTICS

American U (DC)

ACTING

Arcadia U (PA)
Bard Coll (NY)
Barry U (FL)
Baylor U (TX)
Bennington Coll (VT)
Boston U (MA)
Bradley U (IL)
Brigham Young U (UT)
California Baptist U (CA)
California State U, Long Beach (CA)
Central Christian Coll of Kansas (KS)
Central Michigan U (MI)
Chapman U (CA)
Coker Coll (SC)
The Coll at Brockport, State U of New York (NY)
Coll of Santa Fe (NM)
Columbia Coll Chicago (IL)
Cornish Coll of the Arts (WA)
DePaul U (IL)
Drake U (IA)
Emerson Coll (MA)
Florida State U (FL)
Greensboro Coll (NC)
Hofstra U (NY)
Illinois Wesleyan U (IL)
Ithaca Coll (NY)
Johnson State Coll (VT)
Kean U (NJ)
Keene State Coll (NH)
Kent State U (OH)
Long Island U, C.W. Post Campus (NY)
Marymount Manhattan Coll (NY)
Memorial U of Newfoundland (NL, Canada)
Michigan State U (MI)
Northwest Missouri State U (MO)
Oakland U (MI)
Ohio U (OH)
Old Dominion U (VA)
Oral Roberts U (OK)
Pace U (NY)
Penn State Abington (PA)
Penn State Altoona (PA)
Penn State Beaver (PA)
Penn State Berks (PA)
Penn State Brandywine (PA)
Penn State DuBois (PA)
Penn State Erie, The Behrend Coll (PA)
Penn State Fayette, The Eberly Campus (PA)
Penn State Greater Allegheny (PA)
Penn State Hazleton (PA)
Penn State Lehigh Valley (PA)
Penn State Mont Alto (PA)
Penn State New Kensington (PA)
Penn State Schuylkill (PA)
Penn State Shenango (PA)
Penn State U Park (PA)
Penn State Wilkes-Barre (PA)
Penn State Worthington Scranton (PA)
Penn State York (PA)
Point Park U (PA)
Roosevelt U (IL)
St. Cloud State U (MN)
Salem State Coll (MA)
Sarah Lawrence Coll (NY)
Seton Hill U (PA)
Shenandoah U (VA)
Slippery Rock U of Pennsylvania (PA)
Temple U (PA)
Texas Tech U (TX)
Trinity U (TX)
U of Connecticut (CT)
U of Hartford (CT)
U of Maryland, Baltimore County (MD)
U of Miami (FL)
U of Northern Iowa (IA)
U of Regina (SK, Canada)
U of Southern California (CA)
U of Windsor (ON, Canada)
York U (ON, Canada)

ACTUARIAL SCIENCE

Appalachian State U (NC)
Arcadia U (PA)
Aurora U (IL)
Ball State U (IN)
Bellarmine U (KY)
Bernard M. Baruch Coll of the City U of New York (NY)
Bob Jones U (SC)
Bowling Green State U (OH)
Bradley U (IL)
Brigham Young U (UT)
Bryant U (RI)
Butler U (IN)
Carroll U (WI)
Central Coll (IA)
Central Michigan U (MI)
Concordia U (QC, Canada)
Drake U (IA)
Eastern Michigan U (MI)
Elmhurst Coll (IL)
Florida Ag and Mech U (FL)
Georgia State U (GA)
Indiana U Northwest (IN)
Indiana U South Bend (IN)
Lebanon Valley Coll (PA)
Lincoln U (PA)
Maryville U of Saint Louis (MO)
The Master's Coll and Sem (CA)
Michigan Technological U (MI)
New Jersey Inst of Technology (NJ)
North Central Coll (IL)
Northwestern Coll (IA)
The Ohio State U (OH)
Ohio U (OH)
Penn State Abington (PA)
Penn State Altoona (PA)
Penn State Beaver (PA)
Penn State Berks (PA)
Penn State Brandywine (PA)
Penn State DuBois (PA)
Penn State Erie, The Behrend Coll (PA)
Penn State Fayette, The Eberly Campus (PA)
Penn State Greater Allegheny (PA)
Penn State Hazleton (PA)
Penn State Lehigh Valley (PA)
Penn State Mont Alto (PA)
Penn State New Kensington (PA)
Penn State Schuylkill (PA)
Penn State Shenango (PA)
Penn State U Park (PA)
Penn State Wilkes-Barre (PA)
Penn State Worthington Scranton (PA)
Penn State York (PA)
Pittsburg State U (KS)
Queens Coll of the City U of New York (NY)
Quinnipiac U (CT)
Rider U (NJ)
Robert Morris U (PA)
Roosevelt U (IL)
St. John's U (NY)
Saint Joseph's U (PA)
Seton Hill U (PA)
Siena Coll (NY)
Simon Fraser U (BC, Canada)
Slippery Rock U of Pennsylvania (PA)
Spring Arbor U (MI)
Tabor Coll (KS)
Temple U (PA)
Texas Christian U (TX)
Thiel Coll (PA)
Universidad de las Américas–Puebla (Mexico)
U at Albany, State U of New York (NY)
U of Central Oklahoma (OK)
U of Connecticut (CT)
U of Illinois at Urbana–Champaign (IL)
The U of Iowa (IA)
U of Manitoba (MB, Canada)
U of Michigan–Flint (MI)
U of Minnesota, Duluth (MN)

INDEXES

U of Minnesota, Twin Cities Campus (MN)
U of Nebraska–Lincoln (NE)
U of Northern Iowa (IA)
U of Pennsylvania (PA)
U of Regina (SK, Canada)
U of St. Thomas (MN)
The U of Texas at Dallas (TX)
The U of Texas at San Antonio (TX)
U of Toronto (ON, Canada)
U of Waterloo (ON, Canada)
The U of Western Ontario (ON, Canada)
U of Wisconsin–Madison (WI)
U of Wisconsin–Stevens Point (WI)
Valparaiso U (IN)
Worcester Polytechnic Inst (MA)
York U (ON, Canada)

ADMINISTRATIVE ASSISTANT AND SECRETARIAL SCIENCE

Alabama State U (AL)
Baker Coll of Muskegon (MI)
Baker Coll of Owosso (MI)
Campbellsville U (KY)
EDP Coll of Puerto Rico, Inc. (PR)
EDP Coll of Puerto Rico–San Sebastian (PR)
Florida Ag and Mech U (FL)
Fort Valley State U (GA)
Inter American U of Puerto Rico, Bayamón Campus (PR)
Lamar U (TX)
Lewis-Clark State Coll (ID)
Lincoln Christian U (IL)
Maranatha Baptist Bible Coll (WI)
Northwest Missouri State U (MO)
Oakwood U (AL)
Pontifical Catholic U of Puerto Rico (PR)
Southeast Missouri State U (MO)
Sul Ross State U (TX)
Tabor Coll (KS)
Universidad Adventista de las Antillas (PR)
U of Puerto Rico, Cayey U Coll (PR)
Valdosta State U (GA)

ADULT AND CONTINUING EDUCATION

Atlantic Union Coll (MA)
Auburn U (AL)
Brock U (ON, Canada)
Concordia U (QC, Canada)
Dakota Wesleyan U (SD)
Fisher Coll (MA)
Franklin Pierce U (NH)
Free Will Baptist Bible Coll (TN)
Iowa Wesleyan Coll (IA)
Laurentian U (ON, Canada)
Louisiana Coll (LA)
Louisiana State U and Ag and Mech Coll (LA)
Mars Hill Coll (NC)
Memorial U of Newfoundland (NL, Canada)
Midwestern State U (TX)
Prescott Coll (AZ)
San Diego Christian Coll (CA)
Tabor Coll (KS)
U of Alberta (AB, Canada)
U of Central Oklahoma (OK)
U of Nevada, Las Vegas (NV)
U of New Brunswick Fredericton (NB, Canada)
U of Regina (SK, Canada)
U of San Francisco (CA)
The U of Toledo (OH)
Western Kentucky U (KY)

ADULT AND CONTINUING EDUCATION ADMINISTRATION

Marshall U (WV)
Penn State Abington (PA)
Penn State Altoona (PA)
Penn State Beaver (PA)
Penn State Berks (PA)
Penn State Brandywine (PA)
Penn State DuBois (PA)
Penn State Erie, The Behrend Coll (PA)
Penn State Fayette, The Eberly Campus (PA)
Penn State Greater Allegheny (PA)
Penn State Hazleton (PA)
Penn State Lehigh Valley (PA)
Penn State Mont Alto (PA)
Penn State New Kensington (PA)
Penn State Schuylkill (PA)
Penn State Shenango (PA)
Penn State U Park (PA)
Penn State Wilkes-Barre (PA)
Penn State Worthington Scranton (PA)
Penn State York (PA)

ADULT DEVELOPMENT AND AGING

Arizona State U (AZ)
Bowling Green State U (OH)
Madonna U (MI)
St. Thomas U (NB, Canada)
U of Northern Colorado (CO)
York Coll of the City U of New York (NY)

ADULT HEALTH NURSING

Humboldt State U (CA)
Pennsylvania Coll of Technology (PA)
Worcester State Coll (MA)
Wright State U (OH)

ADVERTISING

Acad of Art U (CA)
Adams State Coll (CO)
Appalachian State U (NC)
Art Center Coll of Design (CA)
The Art Inst of Atlanta (GA)
The Art Inst of Atlanta–Decatur (GA)
The Art Inst of California–Orange County (CA)
The Art Inst of California–San Diego (CA)
The Art Inst of California–San Francisco (CA)
The Art Inst of Fort Lauderdale (FL)
The Art Inst of Fort Worth (TX)
The Art Inst of Michigan (MI)
The Art Inst of Ohio–Cincinnati (OH)
The Art Inst of Philadelphia (PA)
The Art Inst of Phoenix (AZ)
The Art Inst of Pittsburgh (PA)
The Art Inst of Portland (OR)
The Art Inst of Tampa (FL)
The Art Inst of Tucson (AZ)
The Art Inst of Virginia Beach (VA)
The Art Inst of Washington (VA)
The Art Inst of Washington–Northern Virginia (VA)
The Art Insts Intl–Kansas City (KS)
The Art Insts Intl Minnesota (MN)
Barry U (FL)
Belmont U (TN)
Bernard M. Baruch Coll of the City U of New York (NY)
Boise State U (ID)
Bowling Green State U (OH)
Bradley U (IL)
Brigham Young U (UT)
California State U, East Bay (CA)
California State U, Fullerton (CA)
Central Michigan U (MI)
Chapman U (CA)
Columbia Coll Chicago (IL)
Concordia Coll (MN)
Drake U (IA)
Drury U (MO)
East Central U (OK)
Eastern Nazarene Coll (MA)
Emerson Coll (MA)
Fashion Inst of Technology (NY)
Ferris State U (MI)
Florida Southern Coll (FL)
Fontbonne U (MO)
Franklin Pierce U (NH)
Gannon U (PA)
Grand Valley State U (MI)
Hampton U (VA)
Harding U (AR)
Hawai'i Pacific U (HI)
The Illinois Inst of Art–Chicago (IL)
The Illinois Inst of Art–Schaumburg (IL)
Iona Coll (NY)
Iowa State U of Science and Technology (IA)
Johnson & Wales U (RI)
Kent State U (OH)
Louisiana Coll (LA)
Loyola U Chicago (IL)
Marist Coll (NY)
Marquette U (WI)
Miami Intl U of Art & Design (FL)
Michigan State U (MI)
Minneapolis Coll of Art and Design (MN)
Minnesota State U Moorhead (MN)
Morningside Coll (IA)
The New England Inst of Art (MA)
New England School of Communications (ME)
New York Inst of Technology (NY)
Northeastern State U (OK)
Northern Arizona U (AZ)
Northwest Missouri State U (MO)
Oklahoma Christian U (OK)
Oklahoma City U (OK)
Pace U (NY)
Penn State Abington (PA)
Penn State Altoona (PA)
Penn State Beaver (PA)
Penn State Berks (PA)
Penn State Brandywine (PA)
Penn State DuBois (PA)
Penn State Erie, The Behrend Coll (PA)
Penn State Fayette, The Eberly Campus (PA)
Penn State Greater Allegheny (PA)
Penn State Hazleton (PA)
Penn State Lehigh Valley (PA)
Penn State Mont Alto (PA)
Penn State New Kensington (PA)
Penn State Schuylkill (PA)
Penn State Shenango (PA)
Penn State U Park (PA)
Penn State Wilkes-Barre (PA)
Penn State Worthington Scranton (PA)
Penn State York (PA)
Pepperdine U, Malibu (CA)
Pittsburg State U (KS)
Point Park U (PA)
Pontifical Catholic U of Puerto Rico (PR)
Portland State U (OR)
Quinnipiac U (CT)
Rider U (NJ)
Rochester Inst of Technology (NY)
Rowan U (NJ)
St. Ambrose U (IA)
St. Cloud State U (MN)
St. John's U (NY)
Salem State Coll (MA)
San Diego State U (CA)
San Jose State U (CA)
Southern Adventist U (TN)
Southern Methodist U (TX)
Southern New Hampshire U (NH)
Spring Arbor U (MI)
Stephens Coll (MO)
Syracuse U (NY)
Temple U (PA)
Texas Christian U (TX)
Texas State U–San Marcos (TX)
Texas Tech U (TX)
Texas Wesleyan U (TX)
Union U (TN)
The U of Alabama (AL)
U of Arkansas at Little Rock (AR)
U of Central Florida (FL)
U of Central Oklahoma (OK)
U of Colorado at Boulder (CO)
U of Florida (FL)
U of Georgia (GA)
U of Houston (TX)
U of Idaho (ID)
U of Illinois at Urbana–Champaign (IL)
U of Kentucky (KY)
U of Miami (FL)
U of Mississippi (MS)
U of Missouri (MO)
U of Nebraska–Lincoln (NE)
U of Nevada, Reno (NV)
U of Oklahoma (OK)
U of Oregon (OR)
U of South Carolina (SC)
U of Southern Indiana (IN)
U of Southern Mississippi (MS)
The U of Tennessee (TN)
The U of Texas at Arlington (TX)
The U of Texas at Austin (TX)
U of Wisconsin–Madison (WI)
Washington State U (WA)
Washington U in St. Louis (MO)
Waynesburg U (PA)
Webster U (MO)
Wesleyan Coll (GA)
Western Kentucky U (KY)
Western Michigan U (MI)
Western New England Coll (MA)
West Virginia U (WV)
Widener U (PA)
Winona State U (MN)
Xavier U (OH)
Youngstown State U (OH)

AERONAUTICAL/AEROSPACE ENGINEERING TECHNOLOGY

American Public U System (WV)
Bowling Green State U (OH)
New York Inst of Technology (NY)
Northeastern U (MA)
Spartan Coll of Aeronautics and Technology (OK)
Utah State U (UT)

AERONAUTICS/AVIATION/AEROSPACE SCIENCE AND TECHNOLOGY

American Public U System (WV)
Arizona State U (AZ)
Augsburg Coll (MN)
Dallas Baptist U (TX)
Delaware State U (DE)
Delta State U (MS)
Dowling Coll (NY)
Elizabeth City State U (NC)
Embry-Riddle Aeronautical U (AZ)
Embry-Riddle Aeronautical U (FL)
Embry-Riddle Aeronautical U Worldwide (FL)
Florida Inst of Technology (FL)
Henderson State U (AR)
Inter American U of Puerto Rico, Bayamón Campus (PR)
Kent State U (OH)
Liberty U (VA)
Louisiana Tech U (LA)
Metropolitan State Coll of Denver (CO)
Middle Tennessee State U (TN)
Ohio U (OH)
Oklahoma State U (OK)
Pacific Union Coll (CA)
Piedmont Baptist Coll and Graduate School (NC)
Purdue U (IN)
San Jose State U (CA)
South Dakota State U (SD)
Texas Southern U (TX)
U of Minnesota, Crookston (MN)
U of Oklahoma (OK)
U of the District of Columbia (DC)
Utah Valley U (UT)
Vaughn Coll of Aeronautics and Technology (NY)
York U (ON, Canada)

AEROSPACE, AERONAUTICAL AND ASTRONAUTICAL ENGINEERING

American Public U System (WV)
Arizona State U (AZ)
Auburn U (AL)
Boston U (MA)
California Polytechnic State U, San Luis Obispo (CA)
California State Polytechnic U, Pomona (CA)
California State U, Long Beach (CA)
Case Western Reserve U (OH)
Clarkson U (NY)
Eastern Nazarene Coll (MA)
Embry-Riddle Aeronautical U (AZ)
Embry-Riddle Aeronautical U (FL)
Florida Inst of Technology (FL)
Georgia Inst of Technology (GA)
Illinois Inst of Technology (IL)
Inter American U of Puerto Rico, Bayamón Campus (PR)
Iowa State U of Science and Technology (IA)
Massachusetts Inst of Technology (MA)
Mississippi State U (MS)
Missouri U of Science and Technology (MO)
New Mexico State U (NM)
North Carolina State U (NC)
The Ohio State U (OH)
Oklahoma State U (OK)
Penn State Abington (PA)
Penn State Altoona (PA)
Penn State Beaver (PA)
Penn State Berks (PA)
Penn State Brandywine (PA)
Penn State DuBois (PA)
Penn State Erie, The Behrend Coll (PA)
Penn State Fayette, The Eberly Campus (PA)
Penn State Greater Allegheny (PA)
Penn State Hazleton (PA)
Penn State Lehigh Valley (PA)
Penn State Mont Alto (PA)
Penn State New Kensington (PA)
Penn State Schuylkill (PA)
Penn State Shenango (PA)
Penn State U Park (PA)
Penn State Wilkes-Barre (PA)
Penn State Worthington Scranton (PA)
Penn State York (PA)
Purdue U (IN)
Rensselaer Polytechnic Inst (NY)
Rochester Inst of Technology (NY)
Saint Louis U (MO)
San Diego State U (CA)
San Jose State U (CA)
Stanford U (CA)
Syracuse U (NY)
Texas A&M U (TX)
Tuskegee U (AL)
United States Air Force Acad (CO)
United States Naval Acad (MD)
U at Buffalo, the State U of New York (NY)
The U of Alabama (AL)
The U of Arizona (AZ)
U of California, Davis (CA)
U of California, Irvine (CA)
U of California, Los Angeles (CA)
U of California, San Diego (CA)
U of Central Florida (FL)
U of Cincinnati (OH)
U of Colorado at Boulder (CO)
U of Florida (FL)
U of Illinois at Urbana–Champaign (IL)
The U of Kansas (KS)
U of Maryland, Coll Park (MD)
U of Miami (FL)
U of Michigan (MI)
U of Minnesota, Twin Cities Campus (MN)
U of Notre Dame (IN)
U of Oklahoma (OK)
U of Southern California (CA)
The U of Tennessee (TN)
The U of Texas at Arlington (TX)
The U of Texas at Austin (TX)
U of Toronto (ON, Canada)
U of Virginia (VA)
U of Washington (WA)
Utah State U (UT)
Virginia Polytechnic Inst and State U (VA)
Weber State U (UT)
Western Michigan U (MI)
West Virginia U (WV)
Wichita State U (KS)
Worcester Polytechnic Inst (MA)
York U (ON, Canada)

AFRICAN AMERICAN/BLACK STUDIES

Amherst Coll (MA)
Arizona State U (AZ)
Bard Coll at Simon's Rock (MA)
Bates Coll (ME)
Berea Coll (KY)
Bowling Green State U (OH)
Brandeis U (MA)
California State U, Dominguez Hills (CA)
California State U, East Bay (CA)
California State U, Fresno (CA)
California State U, Fullerton (CA)
California State U, Long Beach (CA)
California State U, Los Angeles (CA)
California State U, Northridge (CA)
City Coll of the City U of New York (NY)
Claflin U (SC)
Claremont McKenna Coll (CA)
Colby Coll (ME)
Colgate U (NY)
The Coll at Brockport, State U of New York (NY)
Coll of Staten Island of the City U of New York (NY)
The Coll of William and Mary (VA)
The Coll of Wooster (OH)
Columbia U (NY)
Columbia U, School of General Studies (NY)
Cornell U (NY)
Dartmouth Coll (NH)
Denison U (OH)
DePaul U (IL)
DePauw U (IN)
Dillard U (LA)
Duke U (NC)
Earlham Coll (IN)
East Carolina U (NC)
Eastern Illinois U (IL)
Eastern Michigan U (MI)
Emory U (GA)
Florida Ag and Mech U (FL)
Fordham U (NY)
Georgia State U (GA)
Gettysburg Coll (PA)
Guilford Coll (NC)
Hamilton Coll (NY)
Hampshire Coll (MA)
Harvard U (MA)
Hunter Coll of the City U of New York (NY)
Indiana State U (IN)
Indiana U Bloomington (IN)
Indiana U Northwest (IN)
Indiana U–Purdue U Indianapolis (IN)
Kent State U (OH)
Knox Coll (IL)
Lehigh U (PA)

Lehman Coll of the City U of New York (NY)
Loyola Marymount U (CA)
Loyola U Chicago (IL)
Luther Coll (IA)
Mercer U (GA)
Metropolitan State Coll of Denver (CO)
Miami U (OH)
Michigan State U (MI)
Morehouse Coll (GA)
Mount Holyoke Coll (MA)
New York U (NY)
Northeastern U (MA)
Oberlin Coll (OH)
The Ohio State U (OH)
Ohio U (OH)
Ohio Wesleyan U (OH)
Old Dominion U (VA)
Penn State Abington (PA)
Penn State Altoona (PA)
Penn State Beaver (PA)
Penn State Berks (PA)
Penn State Brandywine (PA)
Penn State DuBois (PA)
Penn State Erie, The Behrend Coll (PA)
Penn State Fayette, The Eberly Campus (PA)
Penn State Greater Allegheny (PA)
Penn State Hazleton (PA)
Penn State Lehigh Valley (PA)
Penn State Mont Alto (PA)
Penn State New Kensington (PA)
Penn State Schuylkill (PA)
Penn State Shenango (PA)
Penn State U Park (PA)
Penn State Wilkes-Barre (PA)
Penn State Worthington Scranton (PA)
Penn State York (PA)
Pitzer Coll (CA)
Pomona Coll (CA)
Purdue U (IN)
Rhode Island Coll (RI)
Roosevelt U (IL)
Rutgers, The State U of New Jersey, Camden (NJ)
Rutgers, The State U of New Jersey, Newark (NJ)
San Diego State U (CA)
San Francisco State U (CA)
San Jose State U (CA)
Sarah Lawrence Coll (NY)
Savannah State U (GA)
Scripps Coll (CA)
Seton Hall U (NJ)
Smith Coll (MA)
Sonoma State U (CA)
Southern Methodist U (TX)
Stanford U (CA)
State U of New York at Binghamton (NY)
State U of New York at New Paltz (NY)
State U of New York Coll at Cortland (NY)
State U of New York Coll at Geneseo (NY)
Stony Brook U, State U of New York (NY)
Suffolk U (MA)
Syracuse U (NY)
Talladega Coll (AL)
Temple U (PA)
Tufts U (MA)
U at Albany, State U of New York (NY)
U at Buffalo, the State U of New York (NY)
The U of Alabama (AL)
The U of Alabama at Birmingham (AL)
U of California, Berkeley (CA)
U of California, Davis (CA)
U of California, Irvine (CA)
U of California, Los Angeles (CA)
U of California, Riverside (CA)
U of California, Santa Barbara (CA)
U of Chicago (IL)
U of Cincinnati (OH)
U of Georgia (GA)
U of Illinois at Chicago (IL)
The U of Iowa (IA)
The U of Kansas (KS)
U of Louisville (KY)
U of Maryland, Baltimore County (MD)
U of Maryland, Coll Park (MD)
U of Massachusetts Amherst (MA)
U of Massachusetts Boston (MA)
U of Memphis (TN)
U of Miami (FL)
U of Michigan (MI)
U of Michigan–Flint (MI)
U of Minnesota, Twin Cities Campus (MN)
U of Nebraska at Omaha (NE)
U of Nevada, Las Vegas (NV)
U of New Mexico (NM)
The U of North Carolina at Chapel Hill (NC)
The U of North Carolina at Charlotte (NC)
The U of North Carolina at Greensboro (NC)
U of Northern Colorado (CO)
U of Notre Dame (IN)
U of Oklahoma (OK)
U of Pennsylvania (PA)
U of Pittsburgh (PA)
U of Rhode Island (RI)
U of Rochester (NY)
U of South Carolina (SC)
U of Southern California (CA)
U of South Florida (FL)
The U of Toledo (OH)
U of Virginia (VA)
U of Washington (WA)
U of Wisconsin–Madison (WI)
U of Wisconsin–Milwaukee (WI)
Vanderbilt U (TN)
Virginia Commonwealth U (VA)
Washington U in St. Louis (MO)
Wayne State U (MI)
Wellesley Coll (MA)
Wells Coll (NY)
Wesleyan U (CT)
Western Illinois U (IL)
Western Michigan U (MI)
Wheaton Coll (MA)
William Paterson U of New Jersey (NJ)
Winston-Salem State U (NC)
Wright State U (OH)
Yale U (CT)
York Coll of the City U of New York (NY)
Youngstown State U (OH)

AFRICAN LANGUAGES
U of California, Los Angeles (CA)
U of Wisconsin–Madison (WI)

AFRICAN STUDIES
Agnes Scott Coll (GA)
American Public U System (WV)
Bard Coll (NY)
Barnard Coll (NY)
Bowdoin Coll (ME)
Bowling Green State U (OH)
Brooklyn Coll of the City U of New York (NY)
Carleton Coll (MN)
Colgate U (NY)
The Coll at Brockport, State U of New York (NY)
Columbia U, School of General Studies (NY)
Connecticut Coll (CT)
Dartmouth Coll (NH)
Dickinson Coll (PA)
Drew U (NJ)
Emory U (GA)
Fordham U (NY)
Fort Valley State U (GA)
Franklin & Marshall Coll (PA)
Hampshire Coll (MA)
Haverford Coll (PA)
Hofstra U (NY)
Illinois Wesleyan U (IL)
Kennesaw State U (GA)
Marlboro Coll (VT)
Oakland U (MI)
The Ohio State U (OH)
Ohio U (OH)
Portland State U (OR)
Queens Coll of the City U of New York (NY)
Rowan U (NJ)
Rutgers, The State U of New Jersey, New Brunswick (NJ)
St. Lawrence U (NY)
Sarah Lawrence Coll (NY)
Simmons Coll (MA)
Stanford U (CA)
Tulane U (LA)
United States Military Acad (NY)
U of Chicago (IL)
The U of Iowa (IA)
The U of Kansas (KS)
U of Minnesota, Twin Cities Campus (MN)
U of Pennsylvania (PA)
U of Richmond (VA)
U of Toronto (ON, Canada)
Vassar Coll (NY)
Washington U in St. Louis (MO)
Wellesley Coll (MA)
Wheaton Coll (MA)
William Paterson U of New Jersey (NJ)
Yale U (CT)
York U (ON, Canada)

AGRIBUSINESS
Abilene Christian U (TX)
Adams State Coll (CO)
American U of Beirut (Lebanon)
Andrews U (MI)
Arkansas State U—Jonesboro (AR)
Arkansas Tech U (AR)
Brigham Young U (UT)
California Polytechnic State U, San Luis Obispo (CA)
Colorado State U (CO)
Cornell U (NY)
Delaware Valley Coll (PA)
Eastern New Mexico U (NM)
Florida Ag and Mech U (FL)
Illinois State U (IL)
Middle Tennessee State U (TN)
Mississippi State U (MS)
Missouri State U (MO)
New Mexico State U (NM)
North Carolina State U (NC)
North Dakota State U (ND)
Northwest Missouri State U (MO)
Penn State Abington (PA)
Penn State Altoona (PA)
Penn State Beaver (PA)
Penn State Berks (PA)
Penn State Brandywine (PA)
Penn State DuBois (PA)
Penn State Erie, The Behrend Coll (PA)
Penn State Fayette, The Eberly Campus (PA)
Penn State Greater Allegheny (PA)
Penn State Hazleton (PA)
Penn State Lehigh Valley (PA)
Penn State Mont Alto (PA)
Penn State New Kensington (PA)
Penn State Schuylkill (PA)
Penn State Shenango (PA)
Penn State U Park (PA)
Penn State Wilkes-Barre (PA)
Penn State Worthington Scranton (PA)
Penn State York (PA)
South Dakota State U (SD)
Southeast Missouri State U (MO)
Southwest Minnesota State U (MN)
Stephen F. Austin State U (TX)
Texas A&M U (TX)
Texas State U–San Marcos (TX)
U of Arkansas (AR)
U of Central Missouri (MO)
U of Delaware (DE)
U of Georgia (GA)
U of Maine (ME)
U of Minnesota, Crookston (MN)
U of Saskatchewan (SK, Canada)
U of Wisconsin–River Falls (WI)
U of Wyoming (WY)

AGRICULTURAL AND DOMESTIC ANIMALS SERVICES RELATED
Sterling Coll (VT)
Tarleton State U (TX)

AGRICULTURAL AND EXTENSION EDUCATION
North Carolina State U (NC)
Northwestern Oklahoma State U (OK)
Penn State Abington (PA)
Penn State Altoona (PA)
Penn State Beaver (PA)
Penn State Berks (PA)
Penn State Brandywine (PA)
Penn State DuBois (PA)
Penn State Erie, The Behrend Coll (PA)
Penn State Fayette, The Eberly Campus (PA)
Penn State Greater Allegheny (PA)
Penn State Hazleton (PA)
Penn State Lehigh Valley (PA)
Penn State Mont Alto (PA)
Penn State New Kensington (PA)
Penn State Schuylkill (PA)
Penn State Shenango (PA)
Penn State U Park (PA)
Penn State Wilkes-Barre (PA)
Penn State Worthington Scranton (PA)
Penn State York (PA)
U of Illinois at Urbana–Champaign (IL)

AGRICULTURAL AND FOOD PRODUCTS PROCESSING
Kansas State U (KS)
Texas A&M U (TX)
The U of British Columbia (BC, Canada)
U of Florida (FL)
U of Nebraska–Lincoln (NE)

AGRICULTURAL AND HORTICULTURAL PLANT BREEDING
Cornell U (NY)
Delaware State U (DE)
Sterling Coll (VT)

AGRICULTURAL ANIMAL BREEDING
U of Nevada, Reno (NV)

AGRICULTURAL/ BIOLOGICAL ENGINEERING AND BIOENGINEERING
Auburn U (AL)
California Lutheran U (CA)
California Polytechnic State U, San Luis Obispo (CA)
Clemson U (SC)
Cornell U (NY)
Dordt Coll (IA)
Florida Ag and Mech U (FL)
Fort Valley State U (GA)
Iowa State U of Science and Technology (IA)
Kansas State U (KS)
Michigan State U (MI)
Mississippi State U (MS)
Missouri U of Science and Technology (MO)
New Mexico State U (NM)
North Carolina State U (NC)
North Dakota State U (ND)
The Ohio State U (OH)
Oklahoma State U (OK)
Penn State Abington (PA)
Penn State Beaver (PA)
Penn State Brandywine (PA)
Penn State DuBois (PA)
Penn State Erie, The Behrend Coll (PA)
Penn State Fayette, The Eberly Campus (PA)
Penn State Greater Allegheny (PA)
Penn State Hazleton (PA)
Penn State Lehigh Valley (PA)
Penn State Mont Alto (PA)
Penn State New Kensington (PA)
Penn State Schuylkill (PA)
Penn State Shenango (PA)
Penn State Wilkes-Barre (PA)
Penn State Worthington Scranton (PA)
Penn State York (PA)
Polytechnic Inst of NYU (NY)
Purdue U (IN)
Rutgers, The State U of New Jersey, New Brunswick (NJ)
Santa Clara U (CA)
South Dakota State U (SD)
State U of New York Coll of Environmental Science and Forestry (NY)
Tennessee Technological U (TN)
Texas A&M U (TX)
U of Alberta (AB, Canada)
The U of Arizona (AZ)
U of Arkansas (AR)
U of California, Los Angeles (CA)
U of California, Santa Cruz (CA)
U of Delaware (DE)
U of Florida (FL)
U of Georgia (GA)
U of Hawaii at Manoa (HI)
U of Idaho (ID)
U of Illinois at Urbana–Champaign (IL)
U of Kentucky (KY)
U of Maine (ME)
U of Manitoba (MB, Canada)
U of Maryland, Coll Park (MD)
U of Minnesota, Twin Cities Campus (MN)
U of Nebraska–Lincoln (NE)
U of Saskatchewan (SK, Canada)
The U of Tennessee (TN)
U of Wisconsin–Madison (WI)
U of Wisconsin–River Falls (WI)
Utah State U (UT)

AGRICULTURAL BUSINESS AND MANAGEMENT
Alcorn State U (MS)
Arizona State U (AZ)
Brigham Young U (UT)
California State Polytechnic U, Pomona (CA)
California State U, Chico (CA)
California State U, Fresno (CA)
Clemson U (SC)
Cornell U (NY)
Delaware State U (DE)
Dickinson State U (ND)
Eastern New Mexico U (NM)
Florida Ag and Mech U (FL)
Florida Southern Coll (FL)
Fort Hays State U (KS)
Fort Lewis Coll (CO)
Freed-Hardeman U (TN)
Hardin-Simmons U (TX)
Iowa State U of Science and Technology (IA)
Kansas State U (KS)
Lincoln U (MO)
Louisiana State U and Ag and Mech Coll (LA)
Louisiana Tech U (LA)
Lubbock Christian U (TX)
Michigan State U (MI)
Montana State U (MT)
Murray State U (KY)
Northwestern Oklahoma State U (OK)
Nova Scotia Ag Coll (NS, Canada)
The Ohio State U (OH)
Oklahoma Panhandle State U (OK)
Oklahoma State U (OK)
Oregon State U (OR)
Rocky Mountain Coll (MT)
San Diego State U (CA)
South Carolina State U (SC)
Southern Arkansas U–Magnolia (AR)
Southwest Minnesota State U (MN)
Sul Ross State U (TX)
Tabor Coll (KS)
Tennessee Technological U (TN)
Texas A&M U (TX)
Texas A&M U–Commerce (TX)
Texas A&M U–Kingsville (TX)
Texas Tech U (TX)
Truman State U (MO)
Tuskegee U (AL)
U of Alberta (AB, Canada)
U of Central Missouri (MO)
U of Delaware (DE)
U of Guelph (ON, Canada)
U of Hawaii at Hilo (HI)
U of Idaho (ID)
U of Illinois at Urbana–Champaign (IL)
U of Louisiana at Monroe (LA)
U of Maryland Eastern Shore (MD)
U of Minnesota, Crookston (MN)
U of Minnesota, Twin Cities Campus (MN)
U of Missouri (MO)
U of Nebraska at Kearney (NE)
U of Nebraska–Lincoln (NE)
The U of Tennessee at Martin (TN)
U of Wisconsin–Platteville (WI)
U of Wisconsin–River Falls (WI)
Upper Iowa U (IA)
Utah State U (UT)
Washington State U (WA)
Wilmington Coll (OH)

AGRICULTURAL BUSINESS AND MANAGEMENT RELATED
Penn State New Kensington (PA)
Purdue U (IN)
U of California, Davis (CA)
The U of Tennessee (TN)
Utah State U (UT)

AGRICULTURAL BUSINESS TECHNOLOGY
Washington State U (WA)

AGRICULTURAL COMMUNICATION/ JOURNALISM
Auburn U (AL)
Kansas State U (KS)
North Dakota State U (ND)
The Ohio State U (OH)
Oklahoma State U (OK)
Texas A&M U (TX)
Texas Tech U (TX)
U of Georgia (GA)
U of Idaho (ID)
U of Illinois at Urbana–Champaign (IL)
U of Nebraska–Lincoln (NE)
U of Wyoming (WY)
Washington State U (WA)

AGRICULTURAL ECONOMICS
Alabama Ag and Mech U (AL)
Alcorn State U (MS)
Auburn U (AL)
Brigham Young U (UT)
Clemson U (SC)
Colorado State U (CO)
Cornell U (NY)
Fort Valley State U (GA)
Kansas State U (KS)
Michigan State U (MI)

Mississippi State U (MS)
New Mexico State U (NM)
North Carolina State U (NC)
North Dakota State U (ND)
Northwest Missouri State U (MO)
Nova Scotia Ag Coll (NS, Canada)
The Ohio State U (OH)
Oklahoma State U (OK)
Oregon State U (OR)
Purdue U (IN)
South Dakota State U (SD)
Southern Illinois U Carbondale (IL)
Southern U and Ag and Mech Coll (LA)
Tarleton State U (TX)
Texas A&M U (TX)
Texas A&M U–Commerce (TX)
Texas Tech U (TX)
U of Alberta (AB, Canada)
The U of Arizona (AZ)
U of Arkansas at Pine Bluff (AR)
U of Central Missouri (MO)
U of Connecticut (CT)
U of Delaware (DE)
U of Florida (FL)
U of Georgia (GA)
U of Guelph (ON, Canada)
U of Idaho (ID)
U of Illinois at Urbana–Champaign (IL)
U of Kentucky (KY)
U of Maine (ME)
U of Manitoba (MB, Canada)
U of Maryland, Coll Park (MD)
U of Massachusetts Amherst (MA)
U of Missouri (MO)
U of Nebraska–Lincoln (NE)
U of Nevada, Reno (NV)
U of Saskatchewan (SK, Canada)
The U of Tennessee (TN)
U of Wisconsin–River Falls (WI)
Utah State U (UT)
Virginia Polytechnic Inst and State U (VA)
Washington State U (WA)
West Virginia U (WV)

AGRICULTURAL/FARM SUPPLIES RETAILING AND WHOLESALING
Texas A&M U (TX)

AGRICULTURAL MECHANIZATION
California Polytechnic State U, San Luis Obispo (CA)
Clemson U (SC)
Coll of the Ozarks (MO)
Iowa State U of Science and Technology (IA)
Kansas State U (KS)
Montana State U (MT)
North Dakota State U (ND)
Penn State Abington (PA)
Penn State Altoona (PA)
Penn State Beaver (PA)
Penn State Berks (PA)
Penn State Brandywine (PA)
Penn State DuBois (PA)
Penn State Erie, The Behrend Coll (PA)
Penn State Fayette, The Eberly Campus (PA)
Penn State Greater Allegheny (PA)
Penn State Hazleton (PA)
Penn State Lehigh Valley (PA)
Penn State Mont Alto (PA)
Penn State New Kensington (PA)
Penn State Schuylkill (PA)
Penn State Shenango (PA)
Penn State U Park (PA)
Penn State Wilkes-Barre (PA)
Penn State Worthington Scranton (PA)
Penn State York (PA)
Purdue U (IN)
South Dakota State U (SD)
Stephen F. Austin State U (TX)
U of Idaho (ID)
U of Illinois at Urbana–Champaign (IL)
U of Missouri (MO)
U of Nebraska–Lincoln (NE)
U of Wisconsin–River Falls (WI)
Washington State U (WA)

AGRICULTURAL PRODUCTION
Stephen F. Austin State U (TX)
Texas A&M U (TX)

AGRICULTURAL PRODUCTION RELATED
Tarleton State U (TX)

AGRICULTURAL PUBLIC SERVICES RELATED
Oklahoma State U (OK)
U of Illinois at Urbana–Champaign (IL)

AGRICULTURAL TEACHER EDUCATION
Arkansas State U—Jonesboro (AR)
Auburn U (AL)
California Polytechnic State U, San Luis Obispo (CA)
California State Polytechnic U, Pomona (CA)
California State U, Chico (CA)
California State U, Fresno (CA)
Clemson U (SC)
Coll of the Ozarks (MO)
Colorado State U (CO)
Cornell U (NY)
Dordt Coll (IA)
Eastern New Mexico U (NM)
Iowa State U of Science and Technology (IA)
Kansas State U (KS)
Louisiana State U and Ag and Mech Coll (LA)
Louisiana Tech U (LA)
McNeese State U (LA)
Mississippi State U (MS)
Missouri State U (MO)
Montana State U (MT)
Murray State U (KY)
New Mexico State U (NM)
North Carolina State U (NC)
North Dakota State U (ND)
Northwest Missouri State U (MO)
The Ohio State U (OH)
Oklahoma Panhandle State U (OK)
Oklahoma State U (OK)
Purdue U (IN)
South Dakota State U (SD)
Southern Arkansas U–Magnolia (AR)
Southern U and Ag and Mech Coll (LA)
State U of New York at Oswego (NY)
Tarleton State U (TX)
Tennessee Technological U (TN)
Texas A&M U–Commerce (TX)
The U of Arizona (AZ)
U of Arkansas (AR)
U of Arkansas at Pine Bluff (AR)
U of Connecticut (CT)
U of Delaware (DE)
U of Florida (FL)
U of Georgia (GA)
U of Idaho (ID)
U of Illinois at Urbana–Champaign (IL)
U of Maryland Eastern Shore (MD)
U of Minnesota, Crookston (MN)
U of Minnesota, Twin Cities Campus (MN)
U of Missouri (MO)
U of Nebraska–Lincoln (NE)
U of Nevada, Reno (NV)
U of New Hampshire (NH)
The U of Tennessee (TN)
The U of Tennessee at Martin (TN)
U of Wisconsin–Platteville (WI)
U of Wisconsin–River Falls (WI)
U of Wyoming (WY)
Utah State U (UT)
Washington State U (WA)
West Virginia U (WV)
Wilmington Coll (OH)

AGRICULTURE
Alcorn State U (MS)
American U of Beirut (Lebanon)
Auburn U (AL)
Austin Peay State U (TN)
Berea Coll (KY)
California State U, Stanislaus (CA)
Cameron U (OK)
Cornell U (NY)
Delaware State U (DE)
Dordt Coll (IA)
Ferrum Coll (VA)
Florida Ag and Mech U (FL)
Fort Hays State U (KS)
Hampshire Coll (MA)
Illinois State U (IL)
Indiana U Kokomo (IN)
Iowa State U of Science and Technology (IA)
Lincoln U (MO)
Lubbock Christian U (TX)
McNeese State U (LA)
Mississippi State U (MS)
Montana State U (MT)
Morehead State U (KY)
New Mexico State U (NM)
North Dakota State U (ND)
Northwestern Oklahoma State U (OK)
Northwest Missouri State U (MO)
Nova Scotia Ag Coll (NS, Canada)
Oregon State U (OR)
Penn State Abington (PA)
Penn State Altoona (PA)
Penn State Beaver (PA)
Penn State Berks (PA)
Penn State Brandywine (PA)
Penn State DuBois (PA)
Penn State Erie, The Behrend Coll (PA)
Penn State Fayette, The Eberly Campus (PA)
Penn State Greater Allegheny (PA)
Penn State Hazleton (PA)
Penn State Lehigh Valley (PA)
Penn State Mont Alto (PA)
Penn State New Kensington (PA)
Penn State Schuylkill (PA)
Penn State Shenango (PA)
Penn State U Park (PA)
Penn State Wilkes-Barre (PA)
Penn State Worthington Scranton (PA)
Penn State York (PA)
Prairie View A&M U (TX)
Purdue U (IN)
Rutgers, The State U of New Jersey, New Brunswick (NJ)
Sam Houston State U (TX)
South Dakota State U (SD)
Southeast Missouri State U (MO)
Southern Arkansas U–Magnolia (AR)
Southern Illinois U Carbondale (IL)
Stephen F. Austin State U (TX)
Sterling Coll (VT)
Texas A&M U (TX)
Texas A&M U–Commerce (TX)
Texas A&M U–Kingsville (TX)
Texas State U–San Marcos (TX)
Texas Tech U (TX)
Thomas Edison State Coll (NJ)
Truman State U (MO)
Tuskegee U (AL)
U of Alberta (AB, Canada)
U of Arkansas at Monticello (AR)
U of Arkansas at Pine Bluff (AR)
The U of British Columbia (BC, Canada)
U of Connecticut (CT)
U of Delaware (DE)
U of Georgia (GA)
U of Guam (GU)
U of Guelph (ON, Canada)
U of Hawaii at Hilo (HI)
U of Lethbridge (AB, Canada)
U of Manitoba (MB, Canada)
U of Maryland, Coll Park (MD)
U of Maryland Eastern Shore (MD)
U of Minnesota, Twin Cities Campus (MN)
U of Missouri (MO)
U of Nebraska–Lincoln (NE)
The U of Tennessee at Martin (TN)
U of Vermont (VT)
U of Wisconsin–River Falls (WI)
Utah State U (UT)
Virginia State U (VA)
Washington State U (WA)
Western Illinois U (IL)
Western Kentucky U (KY)
Wilmington Coll (OH)

AGRICULTURE AND AGRICULTURE OPERATIONS RELATED
Coll of the Atlantic (ME)
The Evergreen State Coll (WA)
Michigan State U (MI)
Prescott Coll (AZ)
Tarleton State U (TX)
U of California, Davis (CA)
U of Kentucky (KY)

AGRONOMY AND CROP SCIENCE
Auburn U (AL)
California Polytechnic State U, San Luis Obispo (CA)
California State U, Chico (CA)
California State U, Fresno (CA)
Coll of the Ozarks (MO)
Colorado State U (CO)
Cornell U (NY)
Delaware State U (DE)
Delaware Valley Coll (PA)
Fort Hays State U (KS)
Fort Valley State U (GA)
Hardin-Simmons U (TX)
Iowa State U of Science and Technology (IA)
Kansas State U (KS)
Mississippi State U (MS)
Missouri State U (MO)
New Mexico State U (NM)
Northwest Missouri State U (MO)
The Ohio State U (OH)
Oklahoma Panhandle State U (OK)
Oregon State U (OR)
Penn State Abington (PA)
Penn State Altoona (PA)
Penn State Beaver (PA)
Penn State Berks (PA)
Penn State Brandywine (PA)
Penn State DuBois (PA)
Penn State Erie, The Behrend Coll (PA)
Penn State Fayette, The Eberly Campus (PA)
Penn State Greater Allegheny (PA)
Penn State Hazleton (PA)
Penn State Mont Alto (PA)
Penn State New Kensington (PA)
Penn State Shenango (PA)
Penn State U Park (PA)
Penn State Wilkes-Barre (PA)
Penn State Worthington Scranton (PA)
Penn State York (PA)
Purdue U (IN)
South Dakota State U (SD)
Tarleton State U (TX)
Tennessee Technological U (TN)
Texas A&M U (TX)
Texas A&M U–Commerce (TX)
Texas A&M U–Kingsville (TX)
Texas Tech U (TX)
Truman State U (MO)
Tuskegee U (AL)
U of Alberta (AB, Canada)
U of Arkansas (AR)
U of Connecticut (CT)
U of Delaware (DE)
U of Florida (FL)
U of Guelph (ON, Canada)
U of Idaho (ID)
U of Illinois at Urbana–Champaign (IL)
U of Kentucky (KY)
U of Manitoba (MB, Canada)
U of Minnesota, Crookston (MN)
U of Minnesota, Twin Cities Campus (MN)
U of Nebraska–Lincoln (NE)
The U of Tennessee at Martin (TN)
U of Vermont (VT)
U of Wisconsin–Platteville (WI)
U of Wisconsin–River Falls (WI)
Utah State U (UT)
Virginia Polytechnic Inst and State U (VA)
Washington State U (WA)

AIRCRAFT POWERPLANT TECHNOLOGY
Embry-Riddle Aeronautical U (FL)
Embry-Riddle Aeronautical U Worldwide (FL)

AIR FORCE ROTC/AIR SCIENCE
La Salle U (PA)
The U of Iowa (IA)
U of Washington (WA)
Weber State U (UT)

AIRFRAME MECHANICS AND AIRCRAFT MAINTENANCE TECHNOLOGY
Kansas State U (KS)
LeTourneau U (TX)
Lewis U (IL)
Southeastern Oklahoma State U (OK)
Thomas Edison State Coll (NJ)
Vaughn Coll of Aeronautics and Technology (NY)
Wilmington U (DE)

AIRLINE PILOT AND FLIGHT CREW
Auburn U (AL)
Baylor U (TX)
Bridgewater State Coll (MA)
Delaware State U (DE)
Delta State U (MS)
Eastern Michigan U (MI)
Embry-Riddle Aeronautical U (AZ)
Embry-Riddle Aeronautical U (FL)
Farmingdale State Coll (NY)
Indiana State U (IN)
Inter American U of Puerto Rico, Bayamón Campus (PR)
Jacksonville U (FL)
Kansas State U (KS)
LeTourneau U (TX)
Quincy U (IL)
Rocky Mountain Coll (MT)
St. Cloud State U (MN)
Saint Louis U (MO)
Southeastern Oklahoma State U (OK)
Spartan Coll of Aeronautics and Technology (OK)
U of Dubuque (IA)
U of Illinois at Urbana–Champaign (IL)
U of Louisiana at Monroe (LA)
U of North Dakota (ND)
Utah Valley U (UT)
Western Michigan U (MI)
Westminster Coll (UT)

AIR TRAFFIC CONTROL
Arizona State U (AZ)
Embry-Riddle Aeronautical U (FL)
Hampton U (VA)
Inter American U of Puerto Rico, Bayamón Campus (PR)
LeTourneau U (TX)
Lewis U (IL)
Middle Georgia Coll (GA)
St. Cloud State U (MN)
Thomas Edison State Coll (NJ)
U of Maryland Eastern Shore (MD)
U of North Dakota (ND)

AIR TRANSPORTATION RELATED
Embry-Riddle Aeronautical U (AZ)
Florida Inst of Technology (FL)
Thomas Edison State Coll (NJ)
U of North Dakota (ND)

ALLIED HEALTH AND MEDICAL ASSISTING SERVICES RELATED
Coll of Saint Elizabeth (NJ)
Jones Coll, Jacksonville (FL)
Ramapo Coll of New Jersey (NJ)
Widener U (PA)

ALLIED HEALTH DIAGNOSTIC, INTERVENTION, AND TREATMENT PROFESSIONS RELATED
Fairleigh Dickinson U, Coll at Florham (NJ)
Fairleigh Dickinson U, Metropolitan Campus (NJ)
Georgian Court U (NJ)
Gwynedd-Mercy Coll (PA)
Hofstra U (NY)
Indiana U–Purdue U Indianapolis (IN)
Lewis U (IL)
Millersville U of Pennsylvania (PA)
Rutgers, The State U of New Jersey, Newark (NJ)
Tennessee Wesleyan Coll (TN)
Thomas Edison State Coll (NJ)
U of Connecticut (CT)
The U of Toledo (OH)

ALTERNATIVE AND COMPLEMENTARY MEDICINE RELATED
Johnson State Coll (VT)

AMERICAN GOVERNMENT AND POLITICS
Bard Coll (NY)
Bennington Coll (VT)
Bridgewater State Coll (MA)
Claremont McKenna Coll (CA)
Gallaudet U (DC)
The Master's Coll and Sem (CA)
North Carolina State U (NC)
Oklahoma Christian U (OK)
Rivier Coll (NH)
United States Military Acad (NY)
The U of Akron (OH)
Wayland Baptist U (TX)

AMERICAN HISTORY
Bard Coll (NY)
Bennington Coll (VT)
Chapman U (CA)
The Coll of Saint Rose (NY)
Gettysburg Coll (PA)
Howard Payne U (TX)
Keene State Coll (NH)
Morningside Coll (IA)
Salem State Coll (MA)
Sarah Lawrence Coll (NY)
United States Military Acad (NY)
U of Puerto Rico, Río Piedras (PR)
U of Regina (SK, Canada)

The U of Western Ontario (ON, Canada)

AMERICAN INDIAN/NATIVE AMERICAN STUDIES

Arizona State U (AZ)
Bemidji State U (MN)
Black Hills State U (SD)
California State U, East Bay (CA)
Colgate U (NY)
Creighton U (NE)
Dartmouth Coll (NH)
The Evergreen State Coll (WA)
Fort Lewis Coll (CO)
Hampshire Coll (MA)
Humboldt State U (CA)
Laurentian U (ON, Canada)
Michigan State U (MI)
Northeastern State U (OK)
Northland Coll (WI)
Portland State U (OR)
St. Thomas U (NB, Canada)
San Diego State U (CA)
San Francisco State U (CA)
Sonoma State U (CA)
Stanford U (CA)
Trent U (ON, Canada)
U of Alaska Fairbanks (AK)
U of Alberta (AB, Canada)
U of California, Berkeley (CA)
U of California, Davis (CA)
U of California, Los Angeles (CA)
U of California, Riverside (CA)
U of Hawaii at Manoa (HI)
The U of Iowa (IA)
U of Lethbridge (AB, Canada)
U of Minnesota, Duluth (MN)
U of Minnesota, Twin Cities Campus (MN)
U of New Mexico (NM)
The U of North Carolina at Pembroke (NC)
U of North Dakota (ND)
U of Oklahoma (OK)
U of Ottawa (ON, Canada)
U of Regina (SK, Canada)
U of Saskatchewan (SK, Canada)
U of Science and Arts of Oklahoma (OK)
The U of South Dakota (SD)
U of Toronto (ON, Canada)
U of Washington (WA)
The U of Western Ontario (ON, Canada)
U of Wisconsin–Eau Claire (WI)
U of Wisconsin–Green Bay (WI)
U of Wisconsin–Milwaukee (WI)

AMERICAN LITERATURE

Bard Coll (NY)
Bennington Coll (VT)
Castleton State Coll (VT)
The Coll at Brockport, State U of New York (NY)
Middlebury Coll (VT)
Queens U of Charlotte (NC)
St. Lawrence U (NY)
Sarah Lawrence Coll (NY)
U of California, Los Angeles (CA)
Washington U in St. Louis (MO)

AMERICAN NATIVE/NATIVE AMERICAN EDUCATION

The Coll of St. Scholastica (MN)
Concordia U (QC, Canada)
Northeastern State U (OK)
Queen's U at Kingston (ON, Canada)
U of Lethbridge (AB, Canada)
U of Regina (SK, Canada)

AMERICAN NATIVE/NATIVE AMERICAN LANGUAGES

Bemidji State U (MN)
U of Hawaii at Manoa (HI)
U of Regina (SK, Canada)

AMERICAN SIGN LANGUAGE (ASL)

Augustana Coll (SD)
Bethel Coll (IN)
California State U, Sacramento (CA)
Gardner-Webb U (NC)
Madonna U (MI)
Maryville Coll (TN)
Northeastern U (MA)
Rochester Inst of Technology (NY)
St. Catherine U (MN)
U of Houston (TX)
U of Rochester (NY)
Utah Valley U (UT)

AMERICAN STUDIES

Albion Coll (MI)
Albright Coll (PA)
American Public U System (WV)
American U (DC)
Amherst Coll (MA)
Arizona State U (AZ)
Ashland U (OH)
Atlantic Union Coll (MA)
Bard Coll (NY)
Bard Coll at Simon's Rock (MA)
Barnard Coll (NY)
Bates Coll (ME)
Baylor U (TX)
Bennington Coll (VT)
Boston U (MA)
Bowling Green State U (OH)
Brandeis U (MA)
Brooklyn Coll of the City U of New York (NY)
Cabrini Coll (PA)
California State Polytechnic U, Pomona (CA)
California State U, Chico (CA)
California State U, Fullerton (CA)
California State U, Long Beach (CA)
California State U, San Bernardino (CA)
Carleton Coll (MN)
Case Western Reserve U (OH)
Cedarville U (OH)
Chowan U (NC)
Christopher Newport U (VA)
Claflin U (SC)
Claremont McKenna Coll (CA)
Clarkson U (NY)
Colby Coll (ME)
Coll of Saint Elizabeth (NJ)
The Coll of Saint Rose (NY)
Coll of Staten Island of the City U of New York (NY)
The Coll of William and Mary (VA)
Columbia Coll (MO)
Columbia U (NY)
Columbia U, School of General Studies (NY)
Connecticut Coll (CT)
Cornell U (NY)
Creighton U (NE)
Cumberland U (TN)
DePaul U (IL)
Dickinson Coll (PA)
Dominican Coll (NY)
Dominican U (IL)
Eckerd Coll (FL)
Elmhurst Coll (IL)
Elmira Coll (NY)
Emmanuel Coll (MA)
Emory U (GA)
Erskine Coll (SC)
Fairfield U (CT)
Fordham U (NY)
Franklin & Marshall Coll (PA)
Franklin Coll (IN)
Franklin Pierce U (NH)
Georgetown Coll (KY)
Georgetown U (DC)
The George Washington U (DC)
Gettysburg Coll (PA)
Goucher Coll (MD)
Hamilton Coll (NY)
Hampshire Coll (MA)
Hawai'i Pacific U (HI)
Hendrix Coll (AR)
High Point U (NC)
Hillsdale Coll (MI)
Hofstra U (NY)
Idaho State U (ID)
Illinois Wesleyan U (IL)
Indiana U Bloomington (IN)
Kansas State U (KS)
Keene State Coll (NH)
Kent State U (OH)
Kenyon Coll (OH)
King Coll (TN)
Knox Coll (IL)
Lafayette Coll (PA)
Lake Forest Coll (IL)
Lebanon Valley Coll (PA)
Lehigh U (PA)
Lehman Coll of the City U of New York (NY)
Lesley U (MA)
Lewis U (IL)
Lindsey Wilson Coll (KY)
Lipscomb U (TN)
Long Island U, C.W. Post Campus (NY)
Lycoming Coll (PA)
Manhattanville Coll (NY)
Marist Coll (NY)
Marlboro Coll (VT)
Miami U (OH)
Miami U Hamilton (OH)
Michigan State U (MI)
Middlebury Coll (VT)
Mills Coll (CA)
Minnesota State U Moorhead (MN)
Montana State U (MT)
Mount Allison U (NB, Canada)
Mount Holyoke Coll (MA)
Mount Ida Coll (MA)
Mount St. Mary's Coll (CA)
Muhlenberg Coll (PA)
Nazareth Coll of Rochester (NY)
Nova Southeastern U (FL)
Occidental Coll (CA)
Oglethorpe U (GA)
Oklahoma City U (OK)
Oklahoma State U (OK)
Oregon State U (OR)
Our Lady of the Lake U of San Antonio (TX)
Pace U (NY)
Penn State Abington (PA)
Penn State Berks (PA)
Penn State Brandywine (PA)
Penn State Erie, The Behrend Coll (PA)
Penn State Harrisburg (PA)
Penn State Lehigh Valley (PA)
Penn State Schuylkill (PA)
Penn State Worthington Scranton (PA)
Penn State York (PA)
Pitzer Coll (CA)
Pomona Coll (CA)
Providence Coll (RI)
Queens Coll of the City U of New York (NY)
Ramapo Coll of New Jersey (NJ)
Reed Coll (OR)
Rider U (NJ)
Rutgers, The State U of New Jersey, Newark (NJ)
Rutgers, The State U of New Jersey, New Brunswick (NJ)
St. Cloud State U (MN)
Saint Francis U (PA)
St. John Fisher Coll (NY)
Saint Joseph Coll (CT)
Saint Louis U (MO)
Saint Mary's Coll of California (CA)
Saint Michael's Coll (VT)
St. Olaf Coll (MN)
Salve Regina U (RI)
San Diego State U (CA)
San Francisco State U (CA)
San Jose State U (CA)
Sarah Lawrence Coll (NY)
Scripps Coll (CA)
Sewanee: The U of the South (TN)
Shenandoah U (VA)
Siena Coll (NY)
Skidmore Coll (NY)
Smith Coll (MA)
Sonoma State U (CA)
Southwestern U (TX)
Stanford U (CA)
State U of New York at Fredonia (NY)
State U of New York at Oswego (NY)
State U of New York Coll at Geneseo (NY)
State U of New York Coll at Old Westbury (NY)
Stetson U (FL)
Stonehill Coll (MA)
Stony Brook U, State U of New York (NY)
Syracuse U (NY)
Temple U (PA)
Tennessee Wesleyan Coll (TN)
Texas A&M U (TX)
Texas State U–San Marcos (TX)
Towson U (MD)
Trinity Coll (CT)
Tufts U (MA)
Tulane U (LA)
Union Coll (NY)
U at Buffalo, the State U of New York (NY)
The U of Alabama (AL)
U of Arkansas (AR)
U of California, Berkeley (CA)
U of California, Davis (CA)
U of California, Santa Cruz (CA)
U of Chicago (IL)
U of Connecticut (CT)
U of Dayton (OH)
U of Florida (FL)
U of Hawaii at Manoa (HI)
U of Idaho (ID)
The U of Iowa (IA)
The U of Kansas (KS)
U of Mary Hardin-Baylor (TX)
U of Maryland, Baltimore County (MD)
U of Maryland, Coll Park (MD)
U of Mary Washington (VA)
U of Massachusetts Boston (MA)
U of Massachusetts Lowell (MA)
U of Miami (FL)
U of Michigan (MI)
U of Michigan–Dearborn (MI)
U of Minnesota, Twin Cities Campus (MN)
U of Mississippi (MS)
U of Missouri–Kansas City (MO)
U of Mount Union (OH)
U of New England (ME)
U of New Mexico (NM)
The U of North Carolina at Chapel Hill (NC)
The U of North Carolina at Pembroke (NC)
U of Notre Dame (IN)
U of Pennsylvania (PA)
U of Pittsburgh at Greensburg (PA)
U of Richmond (VA)
U of Rio Grande (OH)
U of Saskatchewan (SK, Canada)
U of Southern California (CA)
U of Southern Mississippi (MS)
U of South Florida (FL)
The U of Texas at Austin (TX)
The U of Texas at Dallas (TX)
The U of Texas at San Antonio (TX)
The U of Texas–Pan American (TX)
The U of Toledo (OH)
U of Toronto (ON, Canada)
U of Washington, Bothell (WA)
U of Washington, Tacoma (WA)
The U of Western Ontario (ON, Canada)
U of Wyoming (WY)
Ursinus Coll (PA)
Utah State U (UT)
Valparaiso U (IN)
Vanderbilt U (TN)
Vassar Coll (NY)
Virginia Wesleyan Coll (VA)
Warner Pacific Coll (OR)
Washington Coll (MD)
Washington State U (WA)
Washington U in St. Louis (MO)
Wayne State U (MI)
Wellesley Coll (MA)
Wells Coll (NY)
Wesleyan Coll (GA)
Wesleyan U (CT)
West Chester U of Pennsylvania (PA)
Western Connecticut State U (CT)
Western Washington U (WA)
Wheaton Coll (MA)
Wheelock Coll (MA)
Wilfrid Laurier U (ON, Canada)
Willamette U (OR)
Williams Coll (MA)
Wittenberg U (OH)
Yale U (CT)
Youngstown State U (OH)

ANALYTICAL CHEMISTRY

Florida Inst of Technology (FL)
The U of Western Ontario (ON, Canada)
West Chester U of Pennsylvania (PA)

ANATOMY

Andrews U (MI)
Duke U (NC)
Minnesota State U Mankato (MN)
Tulane U (LA)
U of Saskatchewan (SK, Canada)
The U of Western Ontario (ON, Canada)
Wright State U (OH)

ANCIENT/CLASSICAL GREEK

Amherst Coll (MA)
Bard Coll (NY)
Barnard Coll (NY)
Baylor U (TX)
Boston Coll (MA)
Boston U (MA)
Brigham Young U (UT)
Brock U (ON, Canada)
Bryn Mawr Coll (PA)
California State U, Long Beach (CA)
Carleton Coll (MN)
Columbia U (NY)
Creighton U (NE)
Dartmouth Coll (NH)
DePauw U (IN)
Duke U (NC)
Duquesne U (PA)
Franklin & Marshall Coll (PA)
Gettysburg Coll (PA)
Hampden-Sydney Coll (VA)
Hunter Coll of the City U of New York (NY)
Indiana U Bloomington (IN)
Kenyon Coll (OH)
Lawrence U (WI)
Loyola U Chicago (IL)
Loyola U New Orleans (LA)
Monmouth Coll (IL)
Mount Allison U (NB, Canada)
Mount Holyoke Coll (MA)
Multnomah U (OR)
Ohio U (OH)
Queens Coll of the City U of New York (NY)
Randolph Coll (VA)
Randolph-Macon Coll (VA)
Rice U (TX)
Rockford Coll (IL)
Rutgers, The State U of New Jersey, New Brunswick (NJ)
St. Olaf Coll (MN)
Samford U (AL)
Santa Clara U (CA)
Smith Coll (MA)
Southwestern U (TX)
Stanford U (CA)
Swarthmore Coll (PA)
U of California, Berkeley (CA)
U of California, Los Angeles (CA)
U of Chicago (IL)
U of Georgia (GA)
U of Miami (FL)
U of Michigan (MI)
U of Nebraska–Lincoln (NE)
U of New Hampshire (NH)
U of Notre Dame (IN)
U of Oregon (OR)
U of Richmond (VA)
U of St. Thomas (MN)
The U of Scranton (PA)
U of Vermont (VT)
U of Washington (WA)
The U of Western Ontario (ON, Canada)
Vassar Coll (NY)
Wake Forest U (NC)
Washington U in St. Louis (MO)
Wellesley Coll (MA)
Wheaton Coll (MA)
Yale U (CT)

ANCIENT NEAR EASTERN AND BIBLICAL LANGUAGES

Baylor U (TX)
Belmont U (TN)
Bethany U (CA)
Carson-Newman Coll (TN)
Columbia Intl U (SC)
Concordia U (CA)
Concordia U Chicago (IL)
Concordia U Wisconsin (WI)
Howard Payne U (TX)
Indiana Wesleyan U (IN)
Lipscomb U (TN)
Luther Coll (IA)
The Master's Coll and Sem (CA)
Mid-Continent U (KY)
Northwest Nazarene U (ID)
Northwest U (WA)
Oklahoma Baptist U (OK)
Union U (TN)
U of Chicago (IL)
U of Toronto (ON, Canada)

ANCIENT STUDIES

Bates Coll (ME)
Bowdoin Coll (ME)
Columbia U (NY)
Columbia U, School of General Studies (NY)
Concordia U (QC, Canada)
Hampshire Coll (MA)
Missouri State U (MO)
Mount Holyoke Coll (MA)
Ohio Wesleyan U (OH)
Rockford Coll (IL)
St. Olaf Coll (MN)
Santa Clara U (CA)
Stanford U (CA)
Swarthmore Coll (PA)
U at Albany, State U of New York (NY)
U of California, Riverside (CA)
The U of Kansas (KS)
U of Maryland, Baltimore County (MD)
U of Miami (FL)
U of Michigan (MI)
U of Nebraska–Lincoln (NE)
U of Oregon (OR)
U of Richmond (VA)
The U of Texas at Austin (TX)
Washington U in St. Louis (MO)
Wheaton Coll (MA)

ANIMAL BEHAVIOR AND ETHOLOGY

Bucknell U (PA)
Carroll U (WI)
Franklin & Marshall Coll (PA)
Hampshire Coll (MA)
Northern Arizona U (AZ)
Southwestern U (TX)

INDEXES

U of Toronto (ON, Canada)

ANIMAL GENETICS
Cornell U (NY)
Dartmouth Coll (NH)
Jacksonville State U (AL)
Ohio Wesleyan U (OH)
Rutgers, The State U of New Jersey, New Brunswick (NJ)
Sarah Lawrence Coll (NY)
U of Alberta (AB, Canada)
The U of British Columbia (BC, Canada)
U of Manitoba (MB, Canada)
U of Minnesota, Twin Cities Campus (MN)
U of Toronto (ON, Canada)
The U of Western Ontario (ON, Canada)
U of Wisconsin–Madison (WI)
Worcester Polytechnic Inst (MA)

ANIMAL HEALTH
Sul Ross State U (TX)

ANIMAL/LIVESTOCK HUSBANDRY AND PRODUCTION
Angelo State U (TX)
Dordt Coll (IA)
Rutgers, The State U of New Jersey, New Brunswick (NJ)
Tarleton State U (TX)
Texas A&M U (TX)
The U of British Columbia (BC, Canada)
U of Illinois at Urbana–Champaign (IL)

ANIMAL PHYSIOLOGY
Boston U (MA)
California State U, Fresno (CA)
Cornell U (NY)
Minnesota State U Mankato (MN)
Rutgers, The State U of New Jersey, New Brunswick (NJ)
Sonoma State U (CA)
Texas State U–San Marcos (TX)
The U of Akron (OH)
U of Alberta (AB, Canada)
U of Connecticut (CT)
U of Minnesota, Twin Cities Campus (MN)
U of New Brunswick Fredericton (NB, Canada)
U of Saskatchewan (SK, Canada)
U of Toronto (ON, Canada)
The U of Western Ontario (ON, Canada)
Utah State U (UT)

ANIMAL SCIENCES
Abilene Christian U (TX)
Alabama Ag and Mech U (AL)
Angelo State U (TX)
Arkansas State U—Jonesboro (AR)
Auburn U (AL)
Berry Coll (GA)
California Polytechnic State U, San Luis Obispo (CA)
California State Polytechnic U, Pomona (CA)
California State U, Chico (CA)
California State U, Fresno (CA)
Clemson U (SC)
Coll of the Ozarks (MO)
Colorado State U (CO)
Cornell U (NY)
Delaware State U (DE)
Delaware Valley Coll (PA)
Dordt Coll (IA)
Florida Ag and Mech U (FL)
Fort Hays State U (KS)
Fort Valley State U (GA)
Hardin-Simmons U (TX)
Iowa State U of Science and Technology (IA)
Kansas State U (KS)
Louisiana State U and Ag and Mech Coll (LA)
Louisiana Tech U (LA)
Lubbock Christian U (TX)
Mercy Coll (NY)
Michigan State U (MI)
Middle Tennessee State U (TN)
Mississippi State U (MS)
Missouri State U (MO)
Montana State U (MT)
New Mexico State U (NM)
North Carolina State U (NC)
North Dakota State U (ND)
Northwest Missouri State U (MO)
Nova Scotia Ag Coll (NS, Canada)
The Ohio State U (OH)
Oklahoma Panhandle State U (OK)
Oklahoma State U (OK)
Oregon State U (OR)
Penn State Abington (PA)
Penn State Altoona (PA)
Penn State Beaver (PA)
Penn State Berks (PA)
Penn State Brandywine (PA)
Penn State DuBois (PA)
Penn State Erie, The Behrend Coll (PA)
Penn State Fayette, The Eberly Campus (PA)
Penn State Greater Allegheny (PA)
Penn State Hazleton (PA)
Penn State Lehigh Valley (PA)
Penn State Mont Alto (PA)
Penn State New Kensington (PA)
Penn State Schuylkill (PA)
Penn State Shenango (PA)
Penn State U Park (PA)
Penn State Wilkes-Barre (PA)
Penn State Worthington Scranton (PA)
Penn State York (PA)
Rutgers, The State U of New Jersey, New Brunswick (NJ)
South Dakota State U (SD)
Southeast Missouri State U (MO)
Southern Illinois U Carbondale (IL)
Stephen F. Austin State U (TX)
Sul Ross State U (TX)
Tarleton State U (TX)
Tennessee Technological U (TN)
Texas A&M U (TX)
Texas A&M U–Commerce (TX)
Texas A&M U–Kingsville (TX)
Texas State U–San Marcos (TX)
Texas Tech U (TX)
Thompson Rivers U (BC, Canada)
Truman State U (MO)
Tuskegee U (AL)
U of Alberta (AB, Canada)
U of Arkansas (AR)
The U of British Columbia (BC, Canada)
U of California, Davis (CA)
U of Connecticut (CT)
U of Delaware (DE)
U of Denver (CO)
The U of Findlay (OH)
U of Florida (FL)
U of Georgia (GA)
U of Guelph (ON, Canada)
U of Hawaii at Hilo (HI)
U of Hawaii at Manoa (HI)
U of Idaho (ID)
U of Illinois at Urbana–Champaign (IL)
U of Kentucky (KY)
U of Maine (ME)
U of Manitoba (MB, Canada)
U of Maryland, Coll Park (MD)
U of Massachusetts Amherst (MA)
U of Minnesota, Crookston (MN)
U of Minnesota, Twin Cities Campus (MN)
U of Missouri (MO)
U of Nebraska–Lincoln (NE)
U of Nevada, Reno (NV)
U of New Hampshire (NH)
U of Rhode Island (RI)
U of Saskatchewan (SK, Canada)
The U of Tennessee (TN)
The U of Tennessee at Martin (TN)
U of Vermont (VT)
U of Wisconsin–Platteville (WI)
U of Wisconsin–River Falls (WI)
U of Wyoming (WY)
Utah State U (UT)
Virginia Polytechnic Inst and State U (VA)
Washington State U (WA)
West Virginia U (WV)

ANIMAL SCIENCES RELATED
Delaware Valley Coll (PA)
Penn State Abington (PA)
Penn State Beaver (PA)
Penn State Brandywine (PA)
Penn State DuBois (PA)
Penn State Erie, The Behrend Coll (PA)
Penn State Fayette, The Eberly Campus (PA)
Penn State Greater Allegheny (PA)
Penn State Hazleton (PA)
Penn State Lehigh Valley (PA)
Penn State Mont Alto (PA)
Penn State New Kensington (PA)
Penn State Schuylkill (PA)
Penn State Shenango (PA)
Penn State Wilkes-Barre (PA)
Penn State Worthington Scranton (PA)
Penn State York (PA)
Southern U and Ag and Mech Coll (LA)
U of California, Davis (CA)
U of Illinois at Urbana–Champaign (IL)
U of Minnesota, Crookston (MN)

ANIMATION, INTERACTIVE TECHNOLOGY, VIDEO GRAPHICS AND SPECIAL EFFECTS
Acad of Art U (CA)
American U (DC)
Art Center Coll of Design (CA)
The Art Center Design Coll, Tucson (AZ)
The Art Inst of Atlanta (GA)
The Art Inst of Atlanta–Decatur (GA)
The Art Inst of Austin (TX)
The Art Inst of California–Hollywood (CA)
The Art Inst of California–Inland Empire (CA)
The Art Inst of California–Los Angeles (CA)
The Art Inst of California–Orange County (CA)
The Art Inst of California–Sacramento (CA)
The Art Inst of California–San Diego (CA)
The Art Inst of California–San Francisco (CA)
The Art Inst of California–Sunnyvale (CA)
The Art Inst of Colorado (CO)
The Art Inst of Dallas (TX)
The Art Inst of Fort Lauderdale (FL)
The Art Inst of Houston (TX)
The Art Inst of Houston—North (TX)
The Art Inst of Indianapolis (IN)
The Art Inst of Jacksonville (FL)
The Art Inst of Las Vegas (NV)
The Art Inst of Ohio–Cincinnati (OH)
The Art Inst of Philadelphia (PA)
The Art Inst of Phoenix (AZ)
The Art Inst of Pittsburgh (PA)
The Art Inst of Portland (OR)
The Art Inst of Salt Lake City (UT)
The Art Inst of Seattle (WA)
The Art Inst of Tampa (FL)
The Art Inst of Tennessee–Nashville (TN)
The Art Inst of Tucson (AZ)
The Art Inst of Vriginia Beach (VA)
The Art Inst of Washington (VA)
The Art Inst of Washington–Northern Virginia (VA)
The Art Inst of York–Pennsylvania (PA)
The Art Insts Intl Minnesota (MN)
Bennington Coll (VT)
Bradley U (IL)
Brigham Young U (UT)
Champlain Coll (VT)
Cogswell Polytechnical Coll (CA)
Coll for Creative Studies (MI)
Coll of the Atlantic (ME)
Concordia U (QC, Canada)
Davenport U, Grand Rapids (MI)
DigiPen Inst of Technology (WA)
East Tennessee State U (TN)
Fashion Inst of Technology (NY)
Ferris State U (MI)
Full Sail U (FL)
George Mason U (VA)
The Illinois Inst of Art–Chicago (IL)
The Illinois Inst of Art–Schaumburg (IL)
ITT Tech Inst, Bessemer (AL)
ITT Tech Inst, Tempe (AZ)
ITT Tech Inst, Tucson (AZ)
ITT Tech Inst (AR)
ITT Tech Inst, Anaheim (CA)
ITT Tech Inst, Lathrop (CA)
ITT Tech Inst, Oxnard (CA)
ITT Tech Inst, Rancho Cordova (CA)
ITT Tech Inst, San Bernardino (CA)
ITT Tech Inst, San Diego (CA)
ITT Tech Inst, San Dimas (CA)
ITT Tech Inst, Sylmar (CA)
ITT Tech Inst, Torrance (CA)
ITT Tech Inst, Fort Lauderdale (FL)
ITT Tech Inst, Lake Mary (FL)
ITT Tech Inst, Tampa (FL)
ITT Tech Inst, Duluth (GA)
ITT Tech Inst, Kennesaw (GA)
ITT Tech Inst (ID)
ITT Tech Inst, Mount Prospect (IL)
ITT Tech Inst, Fort Wayne (IN)
ITT Tech Inst, Indianapolis (IN)
ITT Tech Inst, Newburgh (IN)
ITT Tech Inst, Louisville (KY)
ITT Tech Inst, St. Rose (LA)
ITT Tech Inst (MD)
ITT Tech Inst, Norwood (MA)
ITT Tech Inst, Woburn (MA)
ITT Tech Inst, Canton (MI)
ITT Tech Inst, Troy (MI)
ITT Tech Inst, Wyoming (MI)
ITT Tech Inst (MN)
ITT Tech Inst, Arnold (MO)
ITT Tech Inst, Earth City (MO)
ITT Tech Inst (NE)
ITT Tech Inst (NV)
ITT Tech Inst (OR)
ITT Tech Inst, Greenville (SC)
ITT Tech Inst, Cordova (TN)
ITT Tech Inst, Knoxville (TN)
ITT Tech Inst, Nashville (TN)
ITT Tech Inst (UT)
ITT Tech Inst, Norfolk (VA)
ITT Tech Inst, Richmond (VA)
ITT Tech Inst, Springfield (VA)
ITT Tech Inst, Everett (WA)
ITT Tech Inst, Seattle (WA)
ITT Tech Inst, Spokane Valley (WA)
ITT Tech Inst, Green Bay (WI)
ITT Tech Inst, Greenfield (WI)
Kent State U at Tuscarawas (OH)
Loyola Marymount U (CA)
Massachusetts Coll of Art and Design (MA)
Miami Intl U of Art & Design (FL)
Montclair State U (NJ)
Mount Ida Coll (MA)
Nevada State Coll at Henderson (NV)
The New England Inst of Art (MA)
New England School of Communications (ME)
New Jersey Inst of Technology (NJ)
New Mexico State U (NM)
Northeastern U (MA)
Northwestern Coll (MN)
Platt Coll San Diego (CA)
Regent U (VA)
Ringling Coll of Art and Design (FL)
Rochester Inst of Technology (NY)
Rocky Mountain Coll of Art + Design (CO)
Sam Houston State U (TX)
Savannah Coll of Art and Design (GA)
School of the Art Inst of Chicago (IL)
State U of New York Coll of Technology at Alfred (NY)
U of Dubuque (IA)
U of Idaho (ID)
U of Lethbridge (AB, Canada)
U of the Incarnate Word (TX)
Villa Maria Coll of Buffalo (NY)
Westwood Coll–Annandale Campus (VA)
Westwood Coll–Arlington Ballston Campus (VA)
Westwood Coll–Atlanta Midtown (GA)
Westwood Coll–Atlanta Northlake (GA)
Westwood Coll–Chicago Du Page (IL)
Westwood Coll–Chicago Loop Campus (IL)
Westwood Coll–Chicago O'Hare Airport (IL)
Westwood Coll–Chicago River Oaks (IL)
Westwood Coll–Inland Empire (CA)
Westwood Coll–Los Angeles (CA)
Westwood Coll–Online Campus (CO)

ANTHROPOLOGY
Adelphi U (NY)
Agnes Scott Coll (GA)
Albion Coll (MI)
Alma Coll (MI)
American U (DC)
Amherst Coll (MA)
Appalachian State U (NC)
Arizona State U (AZ)
Athabasca U (AB, Canada)
Auburn U (AL)
Augustana Coll (IL)
Augustana Coll (SD)
Ball State U (IN)
Bard Coll (NY)
Barnard Coll (NY)
Bates Coll (ME)
Baylor U (TX)
Beloit Coll (WI)
Bennington Coll (VT)
Bloomsburg U of Pennsylvania (PA)
Boise State U (ID)
Boston U (MA)
Bowdoin Coll (ME)
Brandeis U (MA)
Brigham Young U–Hawaii (HI)
Brooklyn Coll of the City U of New York (NY)
Bryn Mawr Coll (PA)
Bucknell U (PA)
Buffalo State Coll, State U of New York (NY)
Butler U (IN)
California State Polytechnic U, Pomona (CA)
California State U, Bakersfield (CA)
California State U, Chico (CA)
California State U, Dominguez Hills (CA)
California State U, East Bay (CA)
California State U, Fresno (CA)
California State U, Fullerton (CA)
California State U, Long Beach (CA)
California State U, Los Angeles (CA)
California State U, Northridge (CA)
California State U, Sacramento (CA)
California State U, San Bernardino (CA)
California State U, Stanislaus (CA)
Canisius Coll (NY)
Cape Breton U (NS, Canada)
Carleton Coll (MN)
Case Western Reserve U (OH)
The Catholic U of America (DC)
Central Connecticut State U (CT)
Central Michigan U (MI)
City Coll of the City U of New York (NY)
Claremont McKenna Coll (CA)
Clarion U of Pennsylvania (PA)
Cleveland State U (OH)
Colby Coll (ME)
Colgate U (NY)
Coll of Charleston (SC)
The Coll of Idaho (ID)
Coll of the Holy Cross (MA)
The Coll of William and Mary (VA)
The Colorado Coll (CO)
Colorado State U (CO)
Columbia U (NY)
Columbia U, School of General Studies (NY)
Concordia U (QC, Canada)
Connecticut Coll (CT)
Cornell Coll (IA)
Cornell U (NY)
Creighton U (NE)
Dartmouth Coll (NH)
Davidson Coll (NC)
Denison U (OH)
DePaul U (IL)
DePauw U (IN)
Dickinson Coll (PA)
Dowling Coll (NY)
Drake U (IA)
Drew U (NJ)
Duke U (NC)
Earlham Coll (IN)
East Carolina U (NC)
Eastern Michigan U (MI)
Eastern New Mexico U (NM)
Eastern Washington U (WA)
East Tennessee State U (TN)
Eckerd Coll (FL)
Edinboro U of Pennsylvania (PA)
Elmira Coll (NY)
Elon U (NC)
Emory U (GA)
Florida Atlantic U (FL)
Florida Gulf Coast U (FL)
Florida State U (FL)
Fordham U (NY)
Fort Lewis Coll (CO)
Franciscan U of Steubenville (OH)
Franklin & Marshall Coll (PA)
Franklin Pierce U (NH)
George Mason U (VA)
Georgetown U (DC)
The George Washington U (DC)
Georgia Southern U (GA)
Georgia State U (GA)
Gettysburg Coll (PA)
Grand Valley State U (MI)
Green Mountain Coll (VT)
Grinnell Coll (IA)
Gustavus Adolphus Coll (MN)
Hamilton Coll (NY)
Hamline U (MN)
Hampshire Coll (MA)
Hanover Coll (IN)
Hartwick Coll (NY)
Harvard U (MA)
Haverford Coll (PA)
Hawai'i Pacific U (HI)
Heidelberg U (OH)
Hendrix Coll (AR)
Hofstra U (NY)
Humboldt State U (CA)
Hunter Coll of the City U of New York (NY)
Idaho State U (ID)
Illinois State U (IL)
Illinois Wesleyan U (IL)
Indiana State U (IN)
Indiana U Bloomington (IN)
Indiana U of Pennsylvania (PA)

INDEXES

Indiana U–Purdue U Fort Wayne (IN)
Indiana U–Purdue U Indianapolis (IN)
Iowa State U of Science and Technology (IA)
Ithaca Coll (NY)
Jacksonville State U (AL)
James Madison U (VA)
The Johns Hopkins U (MD)
Johnson State Coll (VT)
Juniata Coll (PA)
Kalamazoo Coll (MI)
Kansas State U (KS)
Kennesaw State U (GA)
Kent State U (OH)
Kenyon Coll (OH)
Knox Coll (IL)
Kutztown U of Pennsylvania (PA)
Lafayette Coll (PA)
Lake Forest Coll (IL)
Lakehead U (ON, Canada)
Laurentian U (ON, Canada)
Lawrence U (WI)
Lee U (TN)
Lehigh U (PA)
Lehman Coll of the City U of New York (NY)
Lewis & Clark Coll (OR)
Lincoln U (PA)
Linfield Coll (OR)
Long Island U, C.W. Post Campus (NY)
Longwood U (VA)
Louisiana State U and Ag and Mech Coll (LA)
Loyola U Chicago (IL)
Luther Coll (IA)
Macalester Coll (MN)
Mansfield U of Pennsylvania (PA)
Marlboro Coll (VT)
Marquette U (WI)
Marylhurst U (OR)
Massachusetts Inst of Technology (MA)
Memorial U of Newfoundland (NL, Canada)
Mercyhurst Coll (PA)
Metropolitan State Coll of Denver (CO)
Miami U (OH)
Miami U Hamilton (OH)
Michigan State U (MI)
Middle Tennessee State U (TN)
Millersville U of Pennsylvania (PA)
Millsaps Coll (MS)
Mills Coll (CA)
Minnesota State U Mankato (MN)
Minnesota State U Moorhead (MN)
Mississippi State U (MS)
Missouri State U (MO)
Monmouth Coll (IL)
Monmouth U (NJ)
Montana State U (MT)
Montclair State U (NJ)
Mount Allison U (NB, Canada)
Mount Holyoke Coll (MA)
Muhlenberg Coll (PA)
Nazareth Coll of Rochester (NY)
New Coll of Florida (FL)
New Mexico State U (NM)
New York U (NY)
North Carolina State U (NC)
North Dakota State U (ND)
Northeastern Illinois U (IL)
Northern Arizona U (AZ)
Northern Kentucky U (KY)
Oakland U (MI)
Oberlin Coll (OH)
The Ohio State U (OH)
Ohio U (OH)
Ohio Wesleyan U (OH)
Oklahoma Baptist U (OK)
Oregon State U (OR)
Pacific Lutheran U (WA)
Peace Coll (NC)
Penn State Abington (PA)
Penn State Altoona (PA)
Penn State Beaver (PA)
Penn State Berks (PA)
Penn State Brandywine (PA)
Penn State DuBois (PA)
Penn State Erie, The Behrend Coll (PA)
Penn State Fayette, The Eberly Campus (PA)
Penn State Greater Allegheny (PA)
Penn State Hazleton (PA)
Penn State Lehigh Valley (PA)
Penn State Mont Alto (PA)
Penn State New Kensington (PA)
Penn State Schuylkill (PA)
Penn State Shenango (PA)
Penn State U Park (PA)
Penn State Wilkes-Barre (PA)
Penn State Worthington Scranton (PA)
Penn State York (PA)
Pitzer Coll (CA)
Plymouth State U (NH)
Pomona Coll (CA)
Portland State U (OR)
Prescott Coll (AZ)
Princeton U (NJ)
Principia Coll (IL)
Purchase Coll, State U of New York (NY)
Queens Coll of the City U of New York (NY)
Radford U (VA)
Reed Coll (OR)
Rhode Island Coll (RI)
Rhodes Coll (TN)
Rice U (TX)
Ripon Coll (WI)
Rockford Coll (IL)
Rollins Coll (FL)
Rutgers, The State U of New Jersey, Newark (NJ)
Rutgers, The State U of New Jersey, New Brunswick (NJ)
St. Cloud State U (MN)
Saint Francis U (PA)
St. Francis Xavier U (NS, Canada)
St. John Fisher Coll (NY)
St. John's U (NY)
St. Lawrence U (NY)
Saint Mary's Coll of California (CA)
St. Mary's Coll of Maryland (MD)
St. Thomas U (NB, Canada)
Saint Vincent Coll (PA)
San Diego State U (CA)
San Francisco State U (CA)
San Jose State U (CA)
Santa Clara U (CA)
Sarah Lawrence Coll (NY)
Scripps Coll (CA)
Seton Hall U (NJ)
Sewanee: The U of the South (TN)
Skidmore Coll (NY)
Smith Coll (MA)
Sonoma State U (CA)
Southeast Missouri State U (MO)
Southern Connecticut State U (CT)
Southern Illinois U Carbondale (IL)
Southern Illinois U Edwardsville (IL)
Southern Methodist U (TX)
Southern Oregon U (OR)
Southwestern U (TX)
Spelman Coll (GA)
Stanford U (CA)
State U of New York at Binghamton (NY)
State U of New York at New Paltz (NY)
State U of New York at Oswego (NY)
State U of New York at Plattsburgh (NY)
State U of New York Coll at Cortland (NY)
State U of New York Coll at Geneseo (NY)
State U of New York Coll at Oneonta (NY)
State U of New York Coll at Potsdam (NY)
Stony Brook U, State U of New York (NY)
Swarthmore Coll (PA)
Sweet Briar Coll (VA)
Syracuse U (NY)
Temple U (PA)
Texas A&M U (TX)
Texas Christian U (TX)
Texas State U–San Marcos (TX)
Texas Tech U (TX)
Thomas Edison State Coll (NJ)
Transylvania U (KY)
Trent U (ON, Canada)
Trinity Coll (CT)
Trinity U (TX)
Tufts U (MA)
Tulane U (LA)
Union Coll (NY)
Universidad de las Américas–Puebla (Mexico)
U at Albany, State U of New York (NY)
U at Buffalo, the State U of New York (NY)
The U of Alabama (AL)
The U of Alabama at Birmingham (AL)
U of Alaska Anchorage (AK)
U of Alaska Fairbanks (AK)
U of Alberta (AB, Canada)
The U of Arizona (AZ)
U of Arkansas (AR)
U of Arkansas at Little Rock (AR)
The U of British Columbia (BC, Canada)
The U of British Columbia–Okanagan (BC, Canada)
U of California, Berkeley (CA)
U of California, Davis (CA)
U of California, Irvine (CA)
U of California, Los Angeles (CA)
U of California, Merced (CA)
U of California, Riverside (CA)
U of California, San Diego (CA)
U of California, Santa Barbara (CA)
U of California, Santa Cruz (CA)
U of Central Florida (FL)
U of Chicago (IL)
U of Cincinnati (OH)
U of Colorado at Boulder (CO)
U of Colorado at Colorado Springs (CO)
U of Colorado Denver (CO)
U of Connecticut (CT)
U of Delaware (DE)
U of Denver (CO)
U of Florida (FL)
U of Georgia (GA)
U of Guam (GU)
U of Guelph (ON, Canada)
U of Hawaii at Hilo (HI)
U of Hawaii at Manoa (HI)
U of Hawaii–West Oahu (HI)
U of Houston (TX)
U of Houston–Clear Lake (TX)
U of Idaho (ID)
U of Illinois at Chicago (IL)
U of Illinois at Urbana–Champaign (IL)
U of Indianapolis (IN)
The U of Iowa (IA)
The U of Kansas (KS)
U of Kentucky (KY)
U of King's Coll (NS, Canada)
U of La Verne (CA)
U of Lethbridge (AB, Canada)
U of Louisville (KY)
U of Maine (ME)
U of Maine at Farmington (ME)
U of Manitoba (MB, Canada)
U of Maryland, Baltimore County (MD)
U of Maryland, Coll Park (MD)
U of Mary Washington (VA)
U of Massachusetts Amherst (MA)
U of Massachusetts Boston (MA)
U of Memphis (TN)
U of Miami (FL)
U of Michigan (MI)
U of Michigan–Dearborn (MI)
U of Michigan–Flint (MI)
U of Minnesota, Duluth (MN)
U of Minnesota, Twin Cities Campus (MN)
U of Mississippi (MS)
U of Missouri (MO)
U of Missouri–St. Louis (MO)
U of Nebraska–Lincoln (NE)
U of Nevada, Las Vegas (NV)
U of Nevada, Reno (NV)
U of New Brunswick Fredericton (NB, Canada)
U of New Hampshire (NH)
U of New Mexico (NM)
U of New Orleans (LA)
The U of North Carolina at Chapel Hill (NC)
The U of North Carolina at Charlotte (NC)
The U of North Carolina at Greensboro (NC)
The U of North Carolina Wilmington (NC)
U of North Dakota (ND)
U of Northern Iowa (IA)
U of North Florida (FL)
U of North Texas (TX)
U of Notre Dame (IN)
U of Oklahoma (OK)
U of Oregon (OR)
U of Ottawa (ON, Canada)
U of Pennsylvania (PA)
U of Pittsburgh (PA)
U of Pittsburgh at Greensburg (PA)
U of Puerto Rico, Río Piedras (PR)
U of Redlands (CA)
U of Regina (SK, Canada)
U of Rhode Island (RI)
U of Richmond (VA)
U of Rochester (NY)
U of San Diego (CA)
U of Saskatchewan (SK, Canada)
U of South Alabama (AL)
U of South Carolina (SC)
The U of South Dakota (SD)
U of Southern California (CA)
U of Southern Maine (ME)
U of Southern Mississippi (MS)
U of South Florida (FL)
The U of Tennessee (TN)
The U of Texas at Arlington (TX)
The U of Texas at Austin (TX)
The U of Texas at El Paso (TX)
The U of Texas at San Antonio (TX)
The U of Texas–Pan American (TX)
U of the District of Columbia (DC)
The U of Toledo (OH)
U of Toronto (ON, Canada)
U of Tulsa (OK)
U of Utah (UT)
U of Vermont (VT)
U of Virginia (VA)
U of Washington (WA)
U of Waterloo (ON, Canada)
The U of Western Ontario (ON, Canada)
U of West Florida (FL)
U of West Georgia (GA)
U of Windsor (ON, Canada)
U of Wisconsin–Madison (WI)
U of Wisconsin–Milwaukee (WI)
U of Wisconsin–Oshkosh (WI)
U of Wyoming (WY)
Ursinus Coll (PA)
Utah State U (UT)
Vanderbilt U (TN)
Vanguard U of Southern California (CA)
Vassar Coll (NY)
Virginia Commonwealth U (VA)
Wagner Coll (NY)
Wake Forest U (NC)
Washburn U (KS)
Washington and Lee U (VA)
Washington Coll (MD)
Washington State U (WA)
Washington U in St. Louis (MO)
Wayne State U (MI)
Webster U (MO)
Wellesley Coll (MA)
Wells Coll (NY)
Wesleyan U (CT)
West Chester U of Pennsylvania (PA)
Western Carolina U (NC)
Western Connecticut State U (CT)
Western Kentucky U (KY)
Western Michigan U (MI)
Western Oregon U (OR)
Western State Coll of Colorado (CO)
Western Washington U (WA)
Westminster Coll (MO)
Westmont Coll (CA)
West Virginia U (WV)
Wheaton Coll (IL)
Wheaton Coll (MA)
Whitman Coll (WA)
Wichita State U (KS)
Widener U (PA)
Wilfrid Laurier U (ON, Canada)
Willamette U (OR)
William Paterson U of New Jersey (NJ)
Williams Coll (MA)
Wright State U (OH)
Yale U (CT)
York Coll of the City U of New York (NY)
York U (ON, Canada)
Youngstown State U (OH)

ANTHROPOLOGY RELATED

Augustana Coll (IL)
Bridgewater State Coll (MA)
Howard Payne U (TX)
U of Michigan (MI)
U of Southern California (CA)
The U of Western Ontario (ON, Canada)
Western Washington U (WA)

APPAREL AND ACCESSORIES MARKETING

Bluffton U (OH)
Michigan State U (MI)
Philadelphia U (PA)
U of Rhode Island (RI)

APPAREL AND TEXTILE MANUFACTURING

Fashion Inst of Technology (NY)
Michigan State U (MI)
North Carolina State U (NC)

APPAREL AND TEXTILE MARKETING MANAGEMENT

The Art Inst of Fort Worth (TX)
The Art Inst of Philadelphia (PA)
The Art Inst of San Antonio (TX)
The Art Inst of Vrigina Beach (VA)
The Art Inst of Washington–Northern Virginia (VA)
Colorado State U (CO)
Michigan State U (MI)
North Carolina State U (NC)
Northwest Missouri State U (MO)
South Dakota State U (SD)
Stephens Coll (MO)
U of the Incarnate Word (TX)
Wayne State U (MI)

APPAREL AND TEXTILES

Appalachian State U (NC)
Auburn U (AL)
Bluffton U (OH)
Bob Jones U (SC)
Bowling Green State U (OH)
California State Polytechnic U, Pomona (CA)
California State U, Long Beach (CA)
Cheyney U of Pennsylvania (PA)
Delaware State U (DE)
East Carolina U (NC)
Fashion Inst of Technology (NY)
Framingham State Coll (MA)
Freed-Hardeman U (TN)
Gallaudet U (DC)
Georgia Southern U (GA)
Indiana State U (IN)
Indiana U Bloomington (IN)
Iowa State U of Science and Technology (IA)
Jacksonville State U (AL)
Kansas State U (KS)
Liberty U (VA)
Lipscomb U (TN)
Michigan State U (MI)
Middle Tennessee State U (TN)
Minnesota State U Mankato (MN)
Missouri State U (MO)
Murray State U (KY)
New Mexico State U (NM)
North Dakota State U (ND)
The Ohio State U (OH)
Ohio U (OH)
Oregon State U (OR)
Philadelphia U (PA)
Purdue U (IN)
Seattle Pacific U (WA)
Southern Illinois U Carbondale (IL)
Tennessee Technological U (TN)
Texas A&M U–Kingsville (TX)
Texas Tech U (TX)
The U of Akron (OH)
The U of Alabama (AL)
U of Alberta (AB, Canada)
U of Arkansas (AR)
U of California, Davis (CA)
U of Central Missouri (MO)
U of Central Oklahoma (OK)
U of Hawaii at Manoa (HI)
U of Idaho (ID)
U of Kentucky (KY)
U of Manitoba (MB, Canada)
U of Minnesota, Twin Cities Campus (MN)
U of Missouri (MO)
U of Nebraska–Lincoln (NE)
The U of North Carolina at Greensboro (NC)
U of Northern Iowa (IA)
U of Rhode Island (RI)
U of Southern Mississippi (MS)
U of the District of Columbia (DC)
U of Wisconsin–Madison (WI)
U of Wisconsin–Stout (WI)
Virginia Polytechnic Inst and State U (VA)
Washington State U (WA)
Western Kentucky U (KY)
Western Michigan U (MI)

APPLIED ART

Athabasca U (AB, Canada)
Azusa Pacific U (CA)
Bemidji State U (MN)
Buffalo State Coll, State U of New York (NY)
California Coll of the Arts (CA)
Columbia Coll (SC)
Columbia U, School of General Studies (NY)
Converse Coll (SC)
Daemen Coll (NY)
Franklin Pierce U (NH)
Inter American U of Puerto Rico, San Germán Campus (PR)
Lamar U (TX)
Mansfield U of Pennsylvania (PA)
Midwestern State U (TX)
Minnesota State U Mankato (MN)
Minnesota State U Moorhead (MN)
Otis Coll of Art and Design (CA)
Peru State Coll (NE)
Portland State U (OR)
Pratt Inst (NY)
St. Cloud State U (MN)
School of the Museum of Fine Arts, Boston (MA)
Sewanee: The U of the South (TN)
State U of New York at Fredonia (NY)
Truman State U (MO)
U of Dayton (OH)
The U of Toledo (OH)
U of Wisconsin–Madison (WI)
Washington U in St. Louis (MO)

Lehigh U (PA)
Louisiana State U and Ag and Mech Coll (LA)
Louisiana Tech U (LA)
Marywood U (PA)
Massachusetts Coll of Art and Design (MA)
Massachusetts Inst of Technology (MA)
Miami U (OH)
Miami U Hamilton (OH)
Mississippi State U (MS)
New Jersey Inst of Technology (NJ)
Northeastern U (MA)
The Ohio State U (OH)
Oklahoma State U (OK)
Parsons The New School for Design (NY)
Penn State U Park (PA)
Philadelphia U (PA)
Polytechnic U of Puerto Rico (PR)
Portland State U (OR)
Prairie View A&M U (TX)
Pratt Inst (NY)
Princeton U (NJ)
Rensselaer Polytechnic Inst (NY)
Rice U (TX)
Savannah Coll of Art and Design (GA)
Smith Coll (MA)
South Dakota State U (SD)
Southern California Inst of Architecture (CA)
Southern Illinois U Carbondale (IL)
Southern Polytechnic State U (GA)
Southern U and Ag and Mech Coll (LA)
Syracuse U (NY)
Temple U (PA)
Texas A&M U (TX)
Texas Tech U (TX)
Tulane U (LA)
Tuskegee U (AL)
Universidad de las Américas–Puebla (Mexico)
U at Buffalo, the State U of New York (NY)
The U of Arizona (AZ)
U of Arkansas (AR)
U of California, Berkeley (CA)
U of California, Los Angeles (CA)
U of Central Florida (FL)
U of Cincinnati (OH)
U of Florida (FL)
U of Houston (TX)
U of Idaho (ID)
U of Illinois at Urbana–Champaign (IL)
The U of Kansas (KS)
U of Kentucky (KY)
U of Manitoba (MB, Canada)
U of Maryland, Coll Park (MD)
U of Memphis (TN)
U of Miami (FL)
U of Michigan (MI)
U of Minnesota, Twin Cities Campus (MN)
U of Missouri–Kansas City (MO)
U of Nebraska–Lincoln (NE)
U of Nevada, Las Vegas (NV)
U of New Mexico (NM)
The U of North Carolina at Charlotte (NC)
U of Notre Dame (IN)
U of Oklahoma (OK)
U of Oregon (OR)
U of Pennsylvania (PA)
U of San Francisco (CA)
U of Southern California (CA)
The U of Tennessee (TN)
The U of Texas at Arlington (TX)
The U of Texas at Austin (TX)
The U of Texas at San Antonio (TX)
U of the District of Columbia (DC)
U of Toronto (ON, Canada)
U of Utah (UT)
U of Virginia (VA)
U of Washington (WA)
U of Waterloo (ON, Canada)
U of Wisconsin–Milwaukee (WI)
Virginia Polytechnic Inst and State U (VA)
Washington State U (WA)
Washington U in St. Louis (MO)
Wellesley Coll (MA)
Wentworth Inst of Technology (MA)
Woodbury U (CA)
Yale U (CT)

ARCHITECTURE RELATED

Carnegie Mellon U (PA)
Coll of the Holy Cross (MA)
Columbia U (NY)
Georgia Inst of Technology (GA)
Lipscomb U (TN)
Mount Holyoke Coll (MA)
New York Inst of Technology (NY)
Northern Michigan U (MI)
School of the Art Inst of Chicago (IL)
U of Illinois at Chicago (IL)
U of Illinois at Urbana–Champaign (IL)
U of Utah (UT)
Washington U in St. Louis (MO)

AREA, ETHNIC, CULTURAL, AND GENDER STUDIES RELATED

Bard Coll at Simon's Rock (MA)
Bennington Coll (VT)
Bethel U (MN)
Brigham Young U–Hawaii (HI)
Chatham U (PA)
Claremont McKenna Coll (CA)
The Coll of Wooster (OH)
Colorado State U (CO)
Columbia Coll Chicago (IL)
Connecticut Coll (CT)
D'Youville Coll (NY)
The Evergreen State Coll (WA)
Fontbonne U (MO)
Gettysburg Coll (PA)
Kent State U (OH)
Linfield Coll (OR)
Mount Holyoke Coll (MA)
New York U (NY)
Northwest Christian U (OR)
Point Park U (PA)
Prescott Coll (AZ)
Queens Coll of the City U of New York (NY)
Saint Mary's Coll of California (CA)
Skidmore Coll (NY)
Sterling Coll (VT)
Syracuse U (NY)
U of California, Los Angeles (CA)
U of Chicago (IL)
U of Denver (CO)
U of Michigan (MI)
The U of North Carolina at Chapel Hill (NC)
The U of North Carolina at Charlotte (NC)
U of Oregon (OR)
U of Richmond (VA)
The U of Tennessee (TN)
The U of Western Ontario (ON, Canada)
Washington U in St. Louis (MO)

AREA STUDIES RELATED

Appalachian State U (NC)
Boston U (MA)
Bridgewater State Coll (MA)
Claremont McKenna Coll (CA)
Drexel U (PA)
Eastern Michigan U (MI)
Gannon U (PA)
Gettysburg Coll (PA)
Hofstra U (NY)
Illinois Wesleyan U (IL)
Kent State U (OH)
Lake Forest Coll (IL)
Lewis U (IL)
Lycoming Coll (PA)
Nevada State Coll at Henderson (NV)
Prescott Coll (AZ)
Ramapo Coll of New Jersey (NJ)
St. Francis Coll (NY)
U of Alaska Fairbanks (AK)
U of California, Los Angeles (CA)
U of California, Santa Barbara (CA)
U of Illinois at Urbana–Champaign (IL)
U of Michigan–Dearborn (MI)
U of Pittsburgh (PA)
U of Virginia (VA)
Utah State U (UT)
Virginia Commonwealth U (VA)
Washington U in St. Louis (MO)
Wright State U (OH)

ARMY ROTC/MILITARY SCIENCE

Dallas Baptist U (TX)
Hampton U (VA)
Jacksonville State U (AL)
La Salle U (PA)
Longwood U (VA)
Minnesota State U Mankato (MN)
The U of Iowa (IA)
U of Washington (WA)

ART

Agnes Scott Coll (GA)
Alabama State U (AL)
Albany State U (GA)
Alberta Coll of Art & Design (AB, Canada)
Albertus Magnus Coll (CT)
Albion Coll (MI)
Albright Coll (PA)
Alfred U (NY)
Allegheny Coll (PA)
Alma Coll (MI)
Alverno Coll (WI)
American U (DC)
Amherst Coll (MA)
Andrews U (MI)
Angelo State U (TX)
Appalachian State U (NC)
Aquinas Coll (MI)
Arcadia U (PA)
Arizona State U (AZ)
Arkansas State U—Jonesboro (AR)
Arkansas Tech U (AR)
Armstrong Atlantic State U (GA)
Art Center Coll of Design (CA)
Atlantic Union Coll (MA)
Auburn U Montgomery (AL)
Augsburg Coll (MN)
Augustana Coll (IL)
Augustana Coll (SD)
Aurora U (IL)
Austin Coll (TX)
Austin Peay State U (TN)
Averett U (VA)
Avila U (MO)
Baldwin-Wallace Coll (OH)
Ball State U (IN)
Bard Coll (NY)
Bates Coll (ME)
Baylor U (TX)
Belhaven U (MS)
Belmont U (TN)
Bemidji State U (MN)
Benedictine Coll (KS)
Bennett Coll for Women (NC)
Berea Coll (KY)
Berry Coll (GA)
Bethany Coll (KS)
Bethany Coll (WV)
Bethany Lutheran Coll (MN)
Bethel Coll (IN)
Bethel U (MN)
Birmingham-Southern Coll (AL)
Bishop's U (QC, Canada)
Blackburn Coll (IL)
Black Hills State U (SD)
Bluefield Coll (VA)
Bluffton U (OH)
Bob Jones U (SC)
Boise State U (ID)
Bowdoin Coll (ME)
Bowie State U (MD)
Bowling Green State U (OH)
Bradley U (IL)
Brescia U (KY)
Briar Cliff U (IA)
Brigham Young U–Hawaii (HI)
Brock U (ON, Canada)
Brooklyn Coll of the City U of New York (NY)
Bryn Mawr Coll (PA)
Bucknell U (PA)
Buena Vista U (IA)
Buffalo State Coll, State U of New York (NY)
California Coll of the Arts (CA)
California Lutheran U (CA)
California State Polytechnic U, Pomona (CA)
California State U, Bakersfield (CA)
California State U, Chico (CA)
California State U, Dominguez Hills (CA)
California State U, Fresno (CA)
California State U, Fullerton (CA)
California State U, Long Beach (CA)
California State U, Los Angeles (CA)
California State U, Monterey Bay (CA)
California State U, Northridge (CA)
California State U, Sacramento (CA)
California State U, San Bernardino (CA)
California State U, Stanislaus (CA)
Calvin Coll (MI)
Cameron U (OK)
Campbellsville U (KY)
Capital U (OH)
Carnegie Mellon U (PA)
Carroll U (WI)
Carson-Newman Coll (TN)
Castleton State Coll (VT)
The Catholic U of America (DC)
Cedar Crest Coll (PA)
Centenary Coll of Louisiana (LA)
Central Christian Coll of Kansas (KS)
Central Coll (IA)
Central Connecticut State U (CT)
Central Michigan U (MI)
Central State U (OH)
Chapman U (CA)
Cheyney U of Pennsylvania (PA)
City Coll of the City U of New York (NY)
Claflin U (SC)
Claremont McKenna Coll (CA)
Clarion U of Pennsylvania (PA)
Clark Atlanta U (GA)
Clarke Coll (IA)
Cleveland State U (OH)
Colby Coll (ME)
Colgate U (NY)
The Coll at Brockport, State U of New York (NY)
The Coll of Idaho (ID)
Coll of Mount St. Joseph (OH)
The Coll of New Jersey (NJ)
Coll of Notre Dame of Maryland (MD)
Coll of Saint Benedict (MN)
Coll of Saint Elizabeth (NJ)
Coll of Saint Mary (NE)
The Coll of St. Scholastica (MN)
Coll of the Atlantic (ME)
Coll of the Ozarks (MO)
The Coll of William and Mary (VA)
Columbia Coll (MO)
Columbia Coll Chicago (IL)
Concordia Coll (MN)
Concordia U (CA)
Concordia U Chicago (IL)
Concordia U Wisconsin (WI)
Connecticut Coll (CT)
Converse Coll (SC)
Corcoran Coll of Art and Design (DC)
Cornell Coll (IA)
Cornish Coll of the Arts (WA)
Creighton U (NE)
Culver-Stockton Coll (MO)
Daemen Coll (NY)
Dakota Wesleyan U (SD)
Dallas Baptist U (TX)
Dana Coll (NE)
Davidson Coll (NC)
Delaware State U (DE)
Denison U (OH)
DePaul U (IL)
Dickinson State U (ND)
Dillard U (LA)
Doane Coll (NE)
Dominican U of California (CA)
Drake U (IA)
Drew U (NJ)
Duke U (NC)
Earlham Coll (IN)
East Carolina U (NC)
East Central U (OK)
Eastern Connecticut State U (CT)
Eastern Illinois U (IL)
Eastern Mennonite U (VA)
Eastern Michigan U (MI)
Eastern New Mexico U (NM)
East Tennessee State U (TN)
Edgewood Coll (WI)
Edinboro U of Pennsylvania (PA)
Elmhurst Coll (IL)
Elmira Coll (NY)
Elon U (NC)
Emmanuel Coll (MA)
Emory & Henry Coll (VA)
Emporia State U (KS)
Erskine Coll (SC)
Evangel U (MO)
The Evergreen State Coll (WA)
Fairfield U (CT)
Fayetteville State U (NC)
Felician Coll (NJ)
Ferrum Coll (VA)
Fisk U (TN)
Florida Ag and Mech U (FL)
Florida Atlantic U (FL)
Florida Gulf Coast U (FL)
Florida Intl U (FL)
Florida Southern Coll (FL)
Fontbonne U (MO)
Fordham U (NY)
Fort Hays State U (KS)
Fort Lewis Coll (CO)
Framingham State Coll (MA)
Francis Marion U (SC)
Franklin Pierce U (NH)
Freed-Hardeman U (TN)
Friends U (KS)
Furman U (SC)
Gallaudet U (DC)
Gardner-Webb U (NC)
George Fox U (OR)
George Mason U (VA)
The George Washington U (DC)
Georgia Coll & State U (GA)
Georgian Court U (NJ)
Georgia Southern U (GA)
Georgia State U (GA)
Gettysburg Coll (PA)
Gonzaga U (WA)
Gordon Coll (MA)
Goshen Coll (IN)
Goucher Coll (MD)
Governors State U (IL)
Graceland U (IA)
Grambling State U (LA)
Grand View U (IA)
Green Mountain Coll (VT)
Greensboro Coll (NC)
Greenville Coll (IL)
Grinnell Coll (IA)
Guilford Coll (NC)
Gustavus Adolphus Coll (MN)
Hamline U (MN)
Hampton U (VA)
Hannibal-LaGrange Coll (MO)
Hanover Coll (IN)
Hartwick Coll (NY)
Haverford Coll (PA)
Henderson State U (AR)
Hendrix Coll (AR)
Hillsdale Coll (MI)
Hiram Coll (OH)
Hollins U (VA)
Holy Family U (PA)
Houghton Coll (NY)
Howard Payne U (TX)
Humboldt State U (CA)
Hunter Coll of the City U of New York (NY)
Huntington U (IN)
Idaho State U (ID)
Illinois Coll (IL)
Illinois State U (IL)
Illinois Wesleyan U (IL)
Indiana State U (IN)
Indiana U Bloomington (IN)
Indiana U East (IN)
Indiana U Northwest (IN)
Indiana U of Pennsylvania (PA)
Indiana U South Bend (IN)
Indiana U Southeast (IN)
Indiana Wesleyan U (IN)
Inter American U of Puerto Rico, San Germán Campus (PR)
Iowa State U of Science and Technology (IA)
Iowa Wesleyan Coll (IA)
Ithaca Coll (NY)
Jacksonville State U (AL)
Jacksonville U (FL)
James Madison U (VA)
Jamestown Coll (ND)
Johnson State Coll (VT)
Judson Coll (AL)
Judson U (IL)
Kalamazoo Coll (MI)
Kansas State U (KS)
Kean U (NJ)
Kennesaw State U (GA)
Kenyon Coll (OH)
Keystone Coll (PA)
Knox Coll (IL)
Kutztown U of Pennsylvania (PA)
Lafayette Coll (PA)
Lake Erie Coll (OH)
Lakehead U (ON, Canada)
Lakeland Coll (WI)
Lamar U (TX)
La Sierra U (CA)
Lebanon Valley Coll (PA)
Lehigh U (PA)
Lehman Coll of the City U of New York (NY)
Lesley U (MA)
Lewis & Clark Coll (OR)
Lincoln Memorial U (TN)
Lindenwood U (MO)
Linfield Coll (OR)
Lock Haven U of Pennsylvania (PA)
Long Island U, Brooklyn Campus (NY)
Longwood U (VA)
Louisiana Coll (LA)
Louisiana State U in Shreveport (LA)
Louisiana Tech U (LA)
Lourdes Coll (OH)
Loyola U Maryland (MD)
Loyola U New Orleans (LA)
Lubbock Christian U (TX)
Luther Coll (IA)
Lycoming Coll (PA)
Lynchburg Coll (VA)
Lyon Coll (AR)
Macalester Coll (MN)
Manchester Coll (IN)
Mansfield U of Pennsylvania (PA)
Marietta Coll (OH)
Marist Coll (NY)
Marlboro Coll (VT)
Marshall U (WV)
Mars Hill Coll (NC)
Mary Baldwin Coll (VA)
Maryland Inst Coll of Art (MD)
Marylhurst U (OR)
Marymount Manhattan Coll (NY)
Massachusetts Coll of Liberal Arts (MA)
McDaniel Coll (MD)
McKendree U (IL)
McNeese State U (LA)
McPherson Coll (KS)
Memorial U of Newfoundland (NL, Canada)

Mercer U (GA)
Mercyhurst Coll (PA)
Methodist U (NC)
Metropolitan State Coll of Denver (CO)
Miami U (OH)
Miami U Hamilton (OH)
Michigan State U (MI)
Middle Tennessee State U (TN)
Midwestern State U (TX)
Millersville U of Pennsylvania (PA)
Mills Coll (CA)
Minnesota State U Mankato (MN)
Minnesota State U Moorhead (MN)
Minot State U (ND)
Mississippi Coll (MS)
Mississippi Valley State U (MS)
Missouri Southern State U (MO)
Missouri State U (MO)
Missouri Western State U (MO)
Molloy Coll (NY)
Monmouth Coll (IL)
Monmouth U (NJ)
Montana State U (MT)
Montana State U Billings (MT)
Moore Coll of Art & Design (PA)
Moravian Coll (PA)
Morehouse Coll (GA)
Mount Mary Coll (WI)
Mount Mercy Coll (IA)
Mount Olive Coll (NC)
Mount St. Mary's Coll (CA)
Mount St. Mary's U (MD)
Mount Vernon Nazarene U (OH)
Muhlenberg Coll (PA)
Nazareth Coll of Rochester (NY)
Nebraska Wesleyan U (NE)
Newberry Coll (SC)
New England Coll (NH)
New Jersey City U (NJ)
Newman U (KS)
New Mexico Highlands U (NM)
Nicholls State U (LA)
Norfolk State U (VA)
North Carolina Central U (NC)
North Central Coll (IL)
North Dakota State U (ND)
Northeastern Illinois U (IL)
Northeastern State U (OK)
Northeastern U (MA)
Northern Arizona U (AZ)
Northern Michigan U (MI)
Northern State U (SD)
North Georgia Coll & State U (GA)
Northland Coll (WI)
Northwestern Coll (IA)
Northwest Nazarene U (ID)
Notre Dame de Namur U (CA)
Oakland City U (IN)
Oberlin Coll (OH)
Oglethorpe U (GA)
The Ohio State U (OH)
Ohio U (OH)
Oklahoma Baptist U (OK)
Oklahoma Christian U (OK)
Oklahoma Panhandle State U (OK)
Oklahoma State U (OK)
Old Dominion U (VA)
Oregon State U (OR)
Oregon State U–Cascades (OR)
Otis Coll of Art and Design (CA)
Ottawa U (KS)
Our Lady of the Lake U of San Antonio (TX)
Pace U (NY)
Pacific Lutheran U (WA)
Pacific Union Coll (CA)
Parsons The New School for Design (NY)
Penn State Abington (PA)
Penn State Altoona (PA)
Penn State Beaver (PA)
Penn State Berks (PA)
Penn State Brandywine (PA)
Penn State DuBois (PA)
Penn State Erie, The Behrend Coll (PA)
Penn State Fayette, The Eberly Campus (PA)
Penn State Greater Allegheny (PA)
Penn State Hazleton (PA)
Penn State Lehigh Valley (PA)
Penn State Mont Alto (PA)
Penn State New Kensington (PA)
Penn State Schuylkill (PA)
Penn State Shenango (PA)
Penn State U Park (PA)
Penn State Wilkes-Barre (PA)
Penn State Worthington Scranton (PA)
Penn State York (PA)
Pepperdine U, Malibu (CA)
Peru State Coll (NE)
Piedmont Coll (GA)
Pikeville Coll (KY)
Pittsburg State U (KS)
Pitzer Coll (CA)
Plymouth State U (NH)
Pomona Coll (CA)
Portland State U (OR)
Pratt Inst (NY)
Presbyterian Coll (SC)
Prescott Coll (AZ)
Purchase Coll, State U of New York (NY)
Purdue U (IN)
Queens U of Charlotte (NC)
Radford U (VA)
Randolph Coll (VA)
Redeemer U Coll (ON, Canada)
Reed Coll (OR)
Reinhardt Coll (GA)
Rhodes Coll (TN)
Rice U (TX)
Rider U (NJ)
Ripon Coll (WI)
Rivier Coll (NH)
Roanoke Coll (VA)
Roberts Wesleyan Coll (NY)
Rocky Mountain Coll (MT)
Rowan U (NJ)
Rutgers, The State U of New Jersey, Camden (NJ)
Rutgers, The State U of New Jersey, Newark (NJ)
Rutgers, The State U of New Jersey, New Brunswick (NJ)
Saginaw Valley State U (MI)
St. Ambrose U (IA)
St. Andrews Presbyterian Coll (NC)
Saint Anselm Coll (NH)
St. Catherine U (MN)
St. Cloud State U (MN)
St. Edward's U (TX)
Saint John's U (MN)
St. Lawrence U (NY)
Saint Mary-of-the-Woods Coll (IN)
Saint Mary's Coll (IN)
Saint Mary's Coll of California (CA)
St. Mary's Coll of Maryland (MD)
Saint Michael's Coll (VT)
St. Norbert Coll (WI)
St. Olaf Coll (MN)
St. Thomas Aquinas Coll (NY)
Saint Xavier U (IL)
Salem State Coll (MA)
Salisbury U (MD)
Samford U (AL)
Sam Houston State U (TX)
San Francisco State U (CA)
San Jose State U (CA)
Sarah Lawrence Coll (NY)
School of the Art Inst of Chicago (IL)
School of the Museum of Fine Arts, Boston (MA)
Scripps Coll (CA)
Seattle Pacific U (WA)
Seattle U (WA)
Sewanee: The U of the South (TN)
Shawnee State U (OH)
Shepherd U (WV)
Shippensburg U of Pennsylvania (PA)
Shorter U (GA)
Siena Heights U (MI)
Silver Lake Coll (WI)
Simmons Coll (MA)
Simon Fraser U (BC, Canada)
Simpson Coll (IA)
Skidmore Coll (NY)
Slippery Rock U of Pennsylvania (PA)
Smith Coll (MA)
Sonoma State U (CA)
Southeastern Louisiana U (LA)
Southeastern Oklahoma State U (OK)
Southeast Missouri State U (MO)
Southern Adventist U (TN)
Southern Arkansas U–Magnolia (AR)
Southern Illinois U Carbondale (IL)
Southern Illinois U Edwardsville (IL)
Southern Oregon U (OR)
Southern Utah U (UT)
Southwest Baptist U (MO)
Southwestern U (TX)
Southwest Minnesota State U (MN)
Spelman Coll (GA)
Spring Arbor U (MI)
Stanford U (CA)
State U of New York at Binghamton (NY)
State U of New York at Fredonia (NY)
State U of New York at New Paltz (NY)
State U of New York at Oswego (NY)
State U of New York at Plattsburgh (NY)
State U of New York Coll at Geneseo (NY)
State U of New York Coll at Old Westbury (NY)
State U of New York Coll at Oneonta (NY)
State U of New York Coll at Potsdam (NY)
State U of New York Empire State Coll (NY)
Stephen F. Austin State U (TX)
Sterling Coll (KS)
Stetson U (FL)
Stillman Coll (AL)
Sul Ross State U (TX)
Tarleton State U (TX)
Taylor U (IN)
Temple U (PA)
Tennessee Technological U (TN)
Texas A&M U–Commerce (TX)
Texas A&M U–Corpus Christi (TX)
Texas Coll (TX)
Texas Lutheran U (TX)
Texas Southern U (TX)
Texas State U–San Marcos (TX)
Texas Tech U (TX)
Texas Wesleyan U (TX)
Texas Woman's U (TX)
Thiel Coll (PA)
Thomas Edison State Coll (NJ)
Towson U (MD)
Transylvania U (KY)
Trinity Christian Coll (IL)
Trinity Coll (CT)
Trinity U (TX)
Troy U (AL)
Truman State U (MO)
Tulane U (LA)
Union U (TN)
Université du Québec en Outaouais (QC, Canada)
U at Albany, State U of New York (NY)
U at Buffalo, the State U of New York (NY)
The U of Alabama at Birmingham (AL)
The U of Alabama in Huntsville (AL)
U of Alaska Anchorage (AK)
U of Alaska Fairbanks (AK)
U of Alberta (AB, Canada)
U of Arkansas (AR)
U of Arkansas at Fort Smith (AR)
U of Arkansas at Little Rock (AR)
U of Arkansas at Monticello (AR)
U of Arkansas at Pine Bluff (AR)
U of California, Berkeley (CA)
U of California, Los Angeles (CA)
U of California, Riverside (CA)
U of California, San Diego (CA)
U of California, Santa Cruz (CA)
U of Central Florida (FL)
U of Central Oklahoma (OK)
U of Charleston (WV)
U of Chicago (IL)
U of Cincinnati (OH)
U of Colorado at Colorado Springs (CO)
U of Dallas (TX)
U of Delaware (DE)
U of Denver (CO)
U of Evansville (IN)
The U of Findlay (OH)
U of Georgia (GA)
U of Guam (GU)
U of Hawaii at Hilo (HI)
U of Hawaii at Manoa (HI)
U of Houston (TX)
U of Houston–Clear Lake (TX)
U of Idaho (ID)
U of Indianapolis (IN)
The U of Iowa (IA)
U of La Verne (CA)
U of Lethbridge (AB, Canada)
U of Maine (ME)
U of Maine at Farmington (ME)
U of Maine at Machias (ME)
U of Maine at Presque Isle (ME)
U of Manitoba (MB, Canada)
U of Mary Hardin-Baylor (TX)
U of Massachusetts Boston (MA)
U of Memphis (TN)
U of Miami (FL)
U of Michigan (MI)
U of Minnesota, Duluth (MN)
U of Minnesota, Twin Cities Campus (MN)
U of Mississippi (MS)
U of Missouri (MO)
U of Missouri–Kansas City (MO)
U of Mobile (AL)
U of Montevallo (AL)
U of Nebraska at Kearney (NE)
U of Nebraska at Omaha (NE)
U of Nevada, Las Vegas (NV)
U of Nevada, Reno (NV)
U of New Hampshire (NH)
U of New Mexico (NM)
The U of North Carolina at Asheville (NC)
The U of North Carolina at Charlotte (NC)
The U of North Carolina at Greensboro (NC)
U of North Dakota (ND)
U of Northern Iowa (IA)
U of North Florida (FL)
U of North Texas (TX)
U of Oklahoma (OK)
U of Oregon (OR)
U of Puerto Rico, Río Piedras (PR)
U of Puget Sound (WA)
U of Rhode Island (RI)
U of Rio Grande (OH)
U of Saint Mary (KS)
U of San Francisco (CA)
U of Science and Arts of Oklahoma (OK)
U of South Alabama (AL)
U of Southern Indiana (IN)
U of Southern Maine (ME)
U of South Florida (FL)
The U of Tampa (FL)
The U of Tennessee at Chattanooga (TN)
The U of Texas at Arlington (TX)
The U of Texas at Austin (TX)
The U of Texas at Brownsville (TX)
The U of Texas at Dallas (TX)
The U of Texas at San Antonio (TX)
The U of Texas at Tyler (TX)
The U of Texas of the Permian Basin (TX)
The U of Texas–Pan American (TX)
U of the District of Columbia (DC)
U of the Incarnate Word (TX)
U of the Pacific (CA)
The U of Toledo (OH)
U of Utah (UT)
U of Virginia (VA)
The U of Virginia's Coll at Wise (VA)
U of Washington (WA)
U of Washington, Bothell (WA)
The U of Western Ontario (ON, Canada)
U of West Florida (FL)
U of West Georgia (GA)
U of Windsor (ON, Canada)
U of Wisconsin–Eau Claire (WI)
U of Wisconsin–Green Bay (WI)
U of Wisconsin–La Crosse (WI)
U of Wisconsin–Madison (WI)
U of Wisconsin–Milwaukee (WI)
U of Wisconsin–Oshkosh (WI)
U of Wisconsin–Parkside (WI)
U of Wisconsin–Platteville (WI)
U of Wisconsin–River Falls (WI)
U of Wisconsin–Whitewater (WI)
U of Wyoming (WY)
Upper Iowa U (IA)
Ursinus Coll (PA)
Utah State U (UT)
Valdosta State U (GA)
Valley City State U (ND)
Valparaiso U (IN)
Virginia Intermont Coll (VA)
Virginia Polytechnic Inst and State U (VA)
Virginia Wesleyan Coll (VA)
Viterbo U (WI)
Wabash Coll (IN)
Wagner Coll (NY)
Wartburg Coll (IA)
Washburn U (KS)
Washington & Jefferson Coll (PA)
Washington Coll (MD)
Washington U in St. Louis (MO)
Watkins Coll of Art, Design, & Film (TN)
Wayland Baptist U (TX)
Waynesburg U (PA)
Wayne State Coll (NE)
Wayne State U (MI)
Weber State U (UT)
Webster U (MO)
Wells Coll (NY)
Wesleyan U (CT)
West Chester U of Pennsylvania (PA)
Western Carolina U (NC)
Western Connecticut State U (CT)
Western Illinois U (IL)
Western Michigan U (MI)
Western Oregon U (OR)
Western State Coll of Colorado (CO)
Western Washington U (WA)
Westfield State Coll (MA)
Westminster Coll (UT)
Westmont Coll (CA)
West Virginia State U (WV)
West Virginia U (WV)
West Virginia Wesleyan Coll (WV)
Wheaton Coll (IL)
Whitman Coll (WA)
Whittier Coll (CA)
Wichita State U (KS)
Willamette U (OR)
William Jewell Coll (MO)
William Paterson U of New Jersey (NJ)
Wilson Coll (PA)
Wingate U (NC)
Winona State U (MN)
Winston-Salem State U (NC)
Winthrop U (SC)
Wittenberg U (OH)
Wright State U (OH)
Xavier U (OH)
Xavier U of Louisiana (LA)
Yale U (CT)
York Coll of the City U of New York (NY)
York U (ON, Canada)
Youngstown State U (OH)

ART HISTORY, CRITICISM AND CONSERVATION

Adams State Coll (CO)
Adelphi U (NY)
Albertus Magnus Coll (CT)
Allegheny Coll (PA)
American U (DC)
American U of Beirut (Lebanon)
The American U of Paris (France)
Aquinas Coll (MI)
Arcadia U (PA)
Augsburg Coll (MN)
Augustana Coll (IL)
Baker U (KS)
Baldwin-Wallace Coll (OH)
Bard Coll (NY)
Bard Coll at Simon's Rock (MA)
Barnard Coll (NY)
Baylor U (TX)
Beloit Coll (WI)
Bennington Coll (VT)
Bethel U (MN)
Birmingham-Southern Coll (AL)
Bloomsburg U of Pennsylvania (PA)
Boise State U (ID)
Boston Coll (MA)
Boston U (MA)
Bowdoin Coll (ME)
Bowling Green State U (OH)
Bradley U (IL)
Brandeis U (MA)
Bridgewater State Coll (MA)
Brooklyn Coll of the City U of New York (NY)
Bryn Mawr Coll (PA)
Bucknell U (PA)
Buffalo State Coll, State U of New York (NY)
California State U, Chico (CA)
California State U, Dominguez Hills (CA)
California State U, East Bay (CA)
California State U, Fullerton (CA)
California State U, Long Beach (CA)
California State U, San Bernardino (CA)
Calvin Coll (MI)
Canisius Coll (NY)
Carleton Coll (MN)
Case Western Reserve U (OH)
The Catholic U of America (DC)
Chapman U (CA)
Chatham U (PA)
City Coll of the City U of New York (NY)
Claremont McKenna Coll (CA)
Clarke Coll (IA)
Clark U (MA)
Colby Coll (ME)
Colgate U (NY)
Coll of Charleston (SC)
The Coll of New Rochelle (NY)
Coll of Santa Fe (NM)
Coll of the Holy Cross (MA)
The Coll of William and Mary (VA)
The Coll of Wooster (OH)
The Colorado Coll (CO)
Colorado State U (CO)
Columbia U (NY)
Columbia U, School of General Studies (NY)
Concordia Coll (MN)
Concordia U (QC, Canada)
Connecticut Coll (CT)
Converse Coll (SC)
Cornell Coll (IA)
Cornell U (NY)
Dartmouth Coll (NH)
Denison U (OH)
DePaul U (IL)
DePauw U (IN)
Dominican U (IL)
Dominican U of California (CA)
Drake U (IA)
Drew U (NJ)
Drury U (MO)
Duke U (NC)
Duquesne U (PA)
East Carolina U (NC)
Eastern Michigan U (MI)
Eastern Washington U (WA)

Elon U (NC)
Emory U (GA)
Eugene Lang Coll The New School for Liberal Arts (NY)
Fairfield U (CT)
Fashion Inst of Technology (NY)
Ferris State U (MI)
Florida Intl U (FL)
Florida Southern Coll (FL)
Florida State U (FL)
Fordham U (NY)
Fort Hays State U (KS)
Franklin & Marshall Coll (PA)
Franklin Coll Switzerland (Switzerland)
Furman U (SC)
Gallaudet U (DC)
Georgetown U (DC)
The George Washington U (DC)
Gettysburg Coll (PA)
Governors State U (IL)
Grand Valley State U (MI)
Gustavus Adolphus Coll (MN)
Hamilton Coll (NY)
Hamline U (MN)
Hampshire Coll (MA)
Hanover Coll (IN)
Hartwick Coll (NY)
Harvard U (MA)
Haverford Coll (PA)
Hiram Coll (OH)
Hofstra U (NY)
Hollins U (VA)
Hope Coll (MI)
Humboldt State U (CA)
Hunter Coll of the City U of New York (NY)
Indiana U Bloomington (IN)
Indiana U–Purdue U Indianapolis (IN)
Inter American U of Puerto Rico, San Germán Campus (PR)
Ithaca Coll (NY)
Jacksonville U (FL)
James Madison U (VA)
John Cabot U (Italy)
John Carroll U (OH)
The Johns Hopkins U (MD)
Juniata Coll (PA)
Kalamazoo Coll (MI)
Kean U (NJ)
Kent State U (OH)
Kenyon Coll (OH)
Knox Coll (IL)
Lafayette Coll (PA)
Lake Forest Coll (IL)
La Salle U (PA)
Lawrence U (WI)
Lehigh U (PA)
Lehman Coll of the City U of New York (NY)
Lindenwood U (MO)
Long Island U, C.W. Post Campus (NY)
Longwood U (VA)
Lourdes Coll (OH)
Loyola Marymount U (CA)
Loyola U Chicago (IL)
Lycoming Coll (PA)
Madonna U (MI)
Manhattanville Coll (NY)
Marian U (IN)
Marist Coll (NY)
Marlboro Coll (VT)
Mars Hill Coll (NC)
Maryland Inst Coll of Art (MD)
Marymount Manhattan Coll (NY)
Maryville Coll (TN)
Massachusetts Coll of Art and Design (MA)
McDaniel Coll (MD)
Memorial U of Newfoundland (NL, Canada)
Messiah Coll (PA)
Miami U (OH)
Michigan State U (MI)
Middlebury Coll (VT)
Millsaps Coll (MS)
Mills Coll (CA)
Minnesota State U Mankato (MN)
Minnesota State U Moorhead (MN)
Missouri State U (MO)
Moore Coll of Art & Design (PA)
Moravian Coll (PA)
Mount Allison U (NB, Canada)
Mount Holyoke Coll (MA)
Nazareth Coll of Rochester (NY)
New Coll of Florida (FL)
New England Coll (NH)
North Central Coll (IL)
Northern Arizona U (AZ)
Northern Michigan U (MI)
Oakland U (MI)
Oberlin Coll (OH)
Occidental Coll (CA)
Oglethorpe U (GA)
The Ohio State U (OH)
Ohio U (OH)
Ohio Wesleyan U (OH)
Oklahoma City U (OK)
Old Dominion U (VA)
Pace U (NY)
Penn State Abington (PA)
Penn State Altoona (PA)
Penn State Beaver (PA)
Penn State Berks (PA)
Penn State Brandywine (PA)
Penn State DuBois (PA)
Penn State Erie, The Behrend Coll (PA)
Penn State Fayette, The Eberly Campus (PA)
Penn State Greater Allegheny (PA)
Penn State Hazleton (PA)
Penn State Lehigh Valley (PA)
Penn State Mont Alto (PA)
Penn State New Kensington (PA)
Penn State Schuylkill (PA)
Penn State Shenango (PA)
Penn State U Park (PA)
Penn State Wilkes-Barre (PA)
Penn State Worthington Scranton (PA)
Penn State York (PA)
Pepperdine U, Malibu (CA)
Pitzer Coll (CA)
Pomona Coll (CA)
Portland State U (OR)
Pratt Inst (NY)
Presbyterian Coll (SC)
Princeton U (NJ)
Principia Coll (IL)
Providence Coll (RI)
Purchase Coll, State U of New York (NY)
Queens Coll of the City U of New York (NY)
Queen's U at Kingston (ON, Canada)
Randolph Coll (VA)
Randolph-Macon Coll (VA)
Redeemer U Coll (ON, Canada)
Rhode Island Coll (RI)
Rhodes Coll (TN)
Rice U (TX)
Roanoke Coll (VA)
Rockford Coll (IL)
Rollins Coll (FL)
Rosemont Coll (PA)
Rutgers, The State U of New Jersey, New Brunswick (NJ)
St. Catherine U (MN)
St. Cloud State U (MN)
Saint Joseph Coll (CT)
St. Lawrence U (NY)
Saint Louis U (MO)
Saint Mary's Coll of California (CA)
St. Olaf Coll (MN)
Saint Vincent Coll (PA)
Salem Coll (NC)
Salem State Coll (MA)
Salve Regina U (RI)
San Diego State U (CA)
San Jose State U (CA)
Santa Clara U (CA)
Sarah Lawrence Coll (NY)
Savannah Coll of Art and Design (GA)
School of the Art Inst of Chicago (IL)
Scripps Coll (CA)
Seattle U (WA)
Seton Hall U (NJ)
Seton Hill U (PA)
Sewanee: The U of the South (TN)
Siena Heights U (MI)
Skidmore Coll (NY)
Smith Coll (MA)
Sonoma State U (CA)
Southern Connecticut State U (CT)
Southern Methodist U (TX)
Southwestern U (TX)
Stanford U (CA)
State U of New York at Binghamton (NY)
State U of New York at Fredonia (NY)
State U of New York at New Paltz (NY)
State U of New York at Plattsburgh (NY)
State U of New York Coll at Cortland (NY)
State U of New York Coll at Geneseo (NY)
State U of New York Coll at Oneonta (NY)
State U of New York Coll at Potsdam (NY)
Stephen F. Austin State U (TX)
Stonehill Coll (MA)
Stony Brook U, State U of New York (NY)
Susquehanna U (PA)
Swarthmore Coll (PA)
Sweet Briar Coll (VA)
Syracuse U (NY)
Temple U (PA)
Texas Christian U (TX)
Texas Tech U (TX)
Towson U (MD)
Transylvania U (KY)
Trinity Coll (CT)
Trinity U (TX)
Truman State U (MO)
Tufts U (MA)
Tulane U (LA)
Universidad de las Américas–Puebla (Mexico)
U at Albany, State U of New York (NY)
U at Buffalo, the State U of New York (NY)
The U of Akron (OH)
The U of Alabama (AL)
U of Alberta (AB, Canada)
The U of Arizona (AZ)
U of Arkansas at Little Rock (AR)
The U of British Columbia (BC, Canada)
The U of British Columbia–Okanagan (BC, Canada)
U of California, Berkeley (CA)
U of California, Davis (CA)
U of California, Irvine (CA)
U of California, Los Angeles (CA)
U of California, Riverside (CA)
U of California, San Diego (CA)
U of California, Santa Barbara (CA)
U of California, Santa Cruz (CA)
U of Chicago (IL)
U of Cincinnati (OH)
U of Colorado at Boulder (CO)
U of Connecticut (CT)
U of Dallas (TX)
U of Dayton (OH)
U of Delaware (DE)
U of Denver (CO)
U of Evansville (IN)
U of Florida (FL)
U of Georgia (GA)
U of Guelph (ON, Canada)
U of Hartford (CT)
U of Houston (TX)
U of Illinois at Chicago (IL)
U of Illinois at Urbana–Champaign (IL)
The U of Iowa (IA)
The U of Kansas (KS)
U of Kentucky (KY)
U of La Verne (CA)
U of Lethbridge (AB, Canada)
U of Louisville (KY)
U of Maine (ME)
U of Manitoba (MB, Canada)
U of Maryland, Coll Park (MD)
U of Mary Washington (VA)
U of Massachusetts Amherst (MA)
U of Massachusetts Dartmouth (MA)
U of Memphis (TN)
U of Miami (FL)
U of Michigan (MI)
U of Michigan–Dearborn (MI)
U of Minnesota, Duluth (MN)
U of Minnesota, Twin Cities Campus (MN)
U of Mississippi (MS)
U of Missouri (MO)
U of Missouri–Kansas City (MO)
U of Missouri–St. Louis (MO)
U of Nebraska at Omaha (NE)
U of Nebraska–Lincoln (NE)
U of Nevada, Las Vegas (NV)
U of Nevada, Reno (NV)
U of New Mexico (NM)
U of New Orleans (LA)
The U of North Carolina at Chapel Hill (NC)
The U of North Carolina Wilmington (NC)
U of Northern Iowa (IA)
U of North Texas (TX)
U of Notre Dame (IN)
U of Oklahoma (OK)
U of Oregon (OR)
U of Ottawa (ON, Canada)
U of Pennsylvania (PA)
U of Pittsburgh (PA)
U of Puerto Rico, Río Piedras (PR)
U of Redlands (CA)
U of Regina (SK, Canada)
U of Rhode Island (RI)
U of Richmond (VA)
U of Rochester (NY)
U of St. Thomas (MN)
U of San Diego (CA)
U of San Francisco (CA)
U of Saskatchewan (SK, Canada)
U of South Carolina (SC)
U of Southern California (CA)
U of South Florida (FL)
The U of Tennessee (TN)
The U of Texas at Arlington (TX)
The U of Texas at Austin (TX)
The U of Texas at San Antonio (TX)
U of the Incarnate Word (TX)
U of the Pacific (CA)
The U of Toledo (OH)
U of Tulsa (OK)
U of Utah (UT)
U of Vermont (VT)
U of Washington (WA)
U of Waterloo (ON, Canada)
The U of Western Ontario (ON, Canada)
U of Windsor (ON, Canada)
U of Wisconsin–Madison (WI)
U of Wisconsin–Milwaukee (WI)
U of Wisconsin–Superior (WI)
U of Wisconsin–Whitewater (WI)
Ursuline Coll (OH)
Vanderbilt U (TN)
Vassar Coll (NY)
Villanova U (PA)
Virginia Commonwealth U (VA)
Wake Forest U (NC)
Washburn U (KS)
Washington and Lee U (VA)
Washington U in St. Louis (MO)
Wayne State U (MI)
Webster U (MO)
Wellesley Coll (MA)
Wells Coll (NY)
Wesleyan Coll (GA)
Wesleyan U (CT)
Western Michigan U (MI)
Western Washington U (WA)
West Virginia U (WV)
West Virginia Wesleyan Coll (WV)
Wheaton Coll (MA)
Whitman Coll (WA)
Wichita State U (KS)
Willamette U (OR)
William Paterson U of New Jersey (NJ)
Williams Coll (MA)
Winthrop U (SC)
Wofford Coll (SC)
Wright State U (OH)
Yale U (CT)
York Coll of the City U of New York (NY)
York U (ON, Canada)
Youngstown State U (OH)

ARTIFICIAL INTELLIGENCE AND ROBOTICS

U of Windsor (ON, Canada)
Worcester Polytechnic Inst (MA)

ARTS MANAGEMENT

Appalachian State U (NC)
Aquinas Coll (MI)
Belhaven U (MS)
Benedictine Coll (KS)
Bennett Coll for Women (NC)
Bernard M. Baruch Coll of the City U of New York (NY)
Bethany Coll (KS)
Bishop's U (QC, Canada)
Brenau U (GA)
Buena Vista U (IA)
Butler U (IN)
California State U, East Bay (CA)
Chatham U (PA)
Coll of Charleston (SC)
The Coll of Idaho (ID)
Columbia Coll Chicago (IL)
Culver-Stockton Coll (MO)
Daemen Coll (NY)
Delaware State U (DE)
DePaul U (IL)
Drury U (MO)
Eastern Michigan U (MI)
Fashion Inst of Technology (NY)
Fontbonne U (MO)
Fort Lewis Coll (CO)
Indiana U Bloomington (IN)
Ithaca Coll (NY)
Long Island U, C.W. Post Campus (NY)
Marian U (IN)
Mary Baldwin Coll (VA)
Marywood U (PA)
Massachusetts Coll of Liberal Arts (MA)
Mercyhurst Coll (PA)
Messiah Coll (PA)
Nichols Coll (MA)
North Carolina State U (NC)
Northern Arizona U (AZ)
Oklahoma City U (OK)
Parsons The New School for Design (NY)
Purchase Coll, State U of New York (NY)
Randolph-Macon Coll (VA)
Rider U (NJ)
Ringling Coll of Art and Design (FL)
Saint Vincent Coll (PA)
Salem Coll (NC)
Savannah Coll of Art and Design (GA)
Seton Hill U (PA)
Shenandoah U (VA)
Simmons Coll (MA)
Southeastern Louisiana U (LA)
Spring Hill Coll (AL)
State U of New York at Fredonia (NY)
Tiffin U (OH)
The U of Iowa (IA)
U of Kentucky (KY)
U of San Francisco (CA)
U of Tulsa (OK)
U of Waterloo (ON, Canada)
The U of Western Ontario (ON, Canada)
U of Wisconsin–Stevens Point (WI)
Upper Iowa U (IA)
Viterbo U (WI)
Wagner Coll (NY)
Wartburg Coll (IA)
Waynesburg U (PA)
Westminster Coll (UT)
Wright State U (OH)

ART TEACHER EDUCATION

Abilene Christian U (TX)
Acad of Art U (CA)
Adams State Coll (CO)
Adelphi U (NY)
Alabama State U (AL)
Albright Coll (PA)
Alfred U (NY)
Alma Coll (MI)
Alverno Coll (WI)
Andrews U (MI)
Appalachian State U (NC)
Aquinas Coll (MI)
Arcadia U (PA)
Arkansas Tech U (AR)
Armstrong Atlantic State U (GA)
Asbury U (KY)
Ashland U (OH)
Assumption Coll (MA)
Augsburg Coll (MN)
Augustana Coll (IL)
Augustana Coll (SD)
Averett U (VA)
Baker U (KS)
Barton Coll (NC)
Baylor U (TX)
Belmont U (TN)
Beloit Coll (WI)
Bemidji State U (MN)
Berea Coll (KY)
Bethany Coll (KS)
Bethel U (MN)
Birmingham-Southern Coll (AL)
Bishop's U (QC, Canada)
Bob Jones U (SC)
Boise State U (ID)
Boston U (MA)
Bowling Green State U (OH)
Bradley U (IL)
Brenau U (GA)
Brescia U (KY)
Bridgewater Coll (VA)
Bridgewater State Coll (MA)
Brigham Young U–Hawaii (HI)
Brooklyn Coll of the City U of New York (NY)
Buena Vista U (IA)
Buffalo State Coll, State U of New York (NY)
California Lutheran U (CA)
California State U, Chico (CA)
California State U, Long Beach (CA)
Calumet Coll of Saint Joseph (IN)
Calvin Coll (MI)
Campbellsville U (KY)
Capital U (OH)
Carlow U (PA)
Carroll U (WI)
Carson-Newman Coll (TN)
Case Western Reserve U (OH)
Central Christian Coll of Kansas (KS)
Central Connecticut State U (CT)
Central Michigan U (MI)
City Coll of the City U of New York (NY)
Claflin U (SC)
Clarke Coll (IA)
Coker Coll (SC)
Coll for Creative Studies (MI)
Coll of Mount St. Joseph (OH)
The Coll of New Jersey (NJ)
The Coll of New Rochelle (NY)
Coll of Notre Dame of Maryland (MD)
The Coll of Saint Rose (NY)
Coll of the Ozarks (MO)
Colorado State U (CO)
Columbus State U (GA)
Concordia Coll (MN)
Concordia U (QC, Canada)
Concordia U Chicago (IL)
Concordia U, St. Paul (MN)
Concordia U Wisconsin (WI)

INDEXES

Concord U (WV)
Converse Coll (SC)
Corcoran Coll of Art and Design (DC)
Culver-Stockton Coll (MO)
Daemen Coll (NY)
Dakota Wesleyan U (SD)
Dana Coll (NE)
Defiance Coll (OH)
Delaware State U (DE)
DePaul U (IL)
Dickinson State U (ND)
Dowling Coll (NY)
East Carolina U (NC)
East Central U (OK)
Eastern Mennonite U (VA)
Eastern Michigan U (MI)
Eastern Washington U (WA)
Edgewood Coll (WI)
Elizabeth City State U (NC)
Elmhurst Coll (IL)
Elmira Coll (NY)
Escuela de Artes Plasticas de Puerto Rico (PR)
Evangel U (MO)
Fairmont State U (WV)
Fayetteville State U (NC)
Ferris State U (MI)
Flagler Coll (FL)
Florida Ag and Mech U (FL)
Florida Intl U (FL)
Florida Southern Coll (FL)
Fontbonne U (MO)
Fort Hays State U (KS)
Francis Marion U (SC)
Franklin Pierce U (NH)
Freed-Hardeman U (TN)
Friends U (KS)
Gallaudet U (DC)
Georgia State U (GA)
Goddard Coll (VT)
Grace Coll (IN)
Graceland U (IA)
Grambling State U (LA)
Grand Valley State U (MI)
Greensboro Coll (NC)
Gustavus Adolphus Coll (MN)
Hamline U (MN)
Hampton U (VA)
Hannibal-LaGrange Coll (MO)
Harding U (AR)
Hardin-Simmons U (TX)
Henderson State U (AR)
High Point U (NC)
Hofstra U (NY)
Hope Coll (MI)
Houston Baptist U (TX)
Howard Payne U (TX)
Humboldt State U (CA)
Huntington U (IN)
Indiana State U (IN)
Indiana U Bloomington (IN)
Indiana U–Purdue U Fort Wayne (IN)
Indiana U–Purdue U Indianapolis (IN)
Indiana Wesleyan U (IN)
Inter American U of Puerto Rico, San Germán Campus (PR)
Iowa Wesleyan Coll (IA)
Ithaca Coll (NY)
Johnson State Coll (VT)
Kennesaw State U (GA)
Kent State U (OH)
Kentucky Wesleyan Coll (KY)
Keystone Coll (PA)
Lamar U (TX)
Lawrence U (WI)
Lehman Coll of the City U of New York (NY)
Lincoln Memorial U (TN)
Lincoln U (MO)
Lincoln U (PA)
Lindenwood U (MO)
Lindsey Wilson Coll (KY)
Lipscomb U (TN)
Long Island U, Brooklyn Campus (NY)
Long Island U, C.W. Post Campus (NY)
Longwood U (VA)
Loras Coll (IA)
Louisiana Coll (LA)
Louisiana State U in Shreveport (LA)
Louisiana Tech U (LA)
Lubbock Christian U (TX)
Malone U (OH)
Manchester Coll (IN)
Manhattanville Coll (NY)
Mansfield U of Pennsylvania (PA)
Marian U (IN)
Marian U (WI)
Mars Hill Coll (NC)
Maryland Inst Coll of Art (MD)
Maryville U of Saint Louis (MO)
Marywood U (PA)
Massachusetts Coll of Art and Design (MA)
McKendree U (IL)
McMurry U (TX)
McNeese State U (LA)
Mercyhurst Coll (PA)
Meredith Coll (NC)
Messiah Coll (PA)
Methodist U (NC)
Miami U (OH)
Miami U Hamilton (OH)
Michigan State U (MI)
Middle Tennessee State U (TN)
Millersville U of Pennsylvania (PA)
Millikin U (IL)
Minnesota State U Mankato (MN)
Minnesota State U Moorhead (MN)
Minot State U (ND)
Mississippi Coll (MS)
Mississippi U for Women (MS)
Missouri State U (MO)
Missouri Western State U (MO)
Montana State U Billings (MT)
Moore Coll of Art & Design (PA)
Moravian Coll (PA)
Morningside Coll (IA)
Mount Mary Coll (WI)
Mount Mercy Coll (IA)
Mount Vernon Nazarene U (OH)
Murray State U (KY)
Nazareth Coll of Rochester (NY)
New Jersey City U (NJ)
New York Inst of Technology (NY)
Nicholls State U (LA)
North Carolina Central U (NC)
North Central Coll (IL)
Northeastern State U (OK)
Northern Arizona U (AZ)
Northern Michigan U (MI)
Northern State U (SD)
North Georgia Coll & State U (GA)
Northwestern Coll (IA)
Northwestern Coll (MN)
Northwest Missouri State U (MO)
Northwest Nazarene U (ID)
Nova Southeastern U (FL)
Oakland City U (IN)
Ohio Dominican U (OH)
Ohio Northern U (OH)
The Ohio State U (OH)
Ohio U (OH)
Ohio Wesleyan U (OH)
Oklahoma Baptist U (OK)
Oklahoma City U (OK)
Old Dominion U (VA)
Oral Roberts U (OK)
Ouachita Baptist U (AR)
Penn State Abington (PA)
Penn State Altoona (PA)
Penn State Beaver (PA)
Penn State Berks (PA)
Penn State Brandywine (PA)
Penn State DuBois (PA)
Penn State Erie, The Behrend Coll (PA)
Penn State Fayette, The Eberly Campus (PA)
Penn State Greater Allegheny (PA)
Penn State Hazleton (PA)
Penn State Lehigh Valley (PA)
Penn State Mont Alto (PA)
Penn State New Kensington (PA)
Penn State Schuylkill (PA)
Penn State Shenango (PA)
Penn State U Park (PA)
Penn State Wilkes-Barre (PA)
Penn State Worthington Scranton (PA)
Penn State York (PA)
Peru State Coll (NE)
Pittsburg State U (KS)
Plymouth State U (NH)
Pontifical Catholic U of Puerto Rico (PR)
Pratt Inst (NY)
Prescott Coll (AZ)
Queens Coll of the City U of New York (NY)
Rhode Island Coll (RI)
Roberts Wesleyan Coll (NY)
Rocky Mountain Coll (MT)
Rocky Mountain Coll of Art + Design (CO)
Saginaw Valley State U (MI)
St. Ambrose U (IA)
St. Catherine U (MN)
St. Cloud State U (MN)
St. Edward's U (TX)
Saint Joseph's U (PA)
Saint Mary-of-the-Woods Coll (IN)
Saint Mary's Coll (IN)
Saint Michael's Coll (VT)
Saint Vincent Coll (PA)
Saint Xavier U (IL)
Salem State Coll (MA)
School of the Art Inst of Chicago (IL)
School of the Museum of Fine Arts, Boston (MA)
Seattle Pacific U (WA)
Seton Hall U (NJ)
Seton Hill U (PA)
Shawnee State U (OH)
Shorter U (GA)
Siena Heights U (MI)
Silver Lake Coll (WI)
Slippery Rock U of Pennsylvania (PA)
South Carolina State U (SC)
Southeastern Louisiana U (LA)
Southeastern Oklahoma State U (OK)
Southeast Missouri State U (MO)
Southern Adventist U (TN)
Southern Arkansas U–Magnolia (AR)
Southern Connecticut State U (CT)
Southern U and Ag and Mech Coll (LA)
Southern Utah U (UT)
Southwest Baptist U (MO)
Southwestern Oklahoma State U (OK)
Southwest Minnesota State U (MN)
Spring Arbor U (MI)
State U of New York at New Paltz (NY)
Syracuse U (NY)
Tabor Coll (KS)
Taylor U (IN)
Temple U (PA)
Tennessee Technological U (TN)
Texas A&M U–Commerce (TX)
Texas A&M U–Corpus Christi (TX)
Texas Christian U (TX)
Texas Lutheran U (TX)
Texas Wesleyan U (TX)
Thomas More Coll (KY)
Towson U (MD)
Transylvania U (KY)
Trinity Christian Coll (IL)
Tusculum Coll (TN)
Union Coll (NE)
Union U (TN)
The U of Akron (OH)
U of Alberta (AB, Canada)
The U of Arizona (AZ)
The U of British Columbia (BC, Canada)
U of Central Florida (FL)
U of Central Missouri (MO)
U of Central Oklahoma (OK)
U of Dayton (OH)
U of Denver (CO)
U of Evansville (IN)
The U of Findlay (OH)
U of Florida (FL)
U of Guam (GU)
U of Idaho (ID)
U of Illinois at Chicago (IL)
U of Illinois at Urbana–Champaign (IL)
U of Indianapolis (IN)
The U of Iowa (IA)
The U of Kansas (KS)
U of Kentucky (KY)
U of Lethbridge (AB, Canada)
U of Louisiana at Monroe (LA)
U of Maine (ME)
U of Maine at Presque Isle (ME)
U of Maryland, Coll Park (MD)
U of Maryland Eastern Shore (MD)
U of Massachusetts Dartmouth (MA)
U of Michigan–Flint (MI)
U of Minnesota, Duluth (MN)
U of Minnesota, Twin Cities Campus (MN)
U of Missouri (MO)
The U of Montana Western (MT)
U of Nebraska–Lincoln (NE)
U of Nevada, Reno (NV)
U of New Brunswick Fredericton (NB, Canada)
U of New Mexico (NM)
The U of North Carolina at Charlotte (NC)
The U of North Carolina at Greensboro (NC)
The U of North Carolina at Pembroke (NC)
U of Northern Iowa (IA)
U of North Florida (FL)
U of Regina (SK, Canada)
U of Rio Grande (OH)
U of St. Francis (IL)
U of South Carolina (SC)
U of South Carolina Upstate (SC)
The U of South Dakota (SD)
U of Southern Maine (ME)
U of South Florida (FL)
The U of Tennessee (TN)
The U of Tennessee at Chattanooga (TN)
The U of Texas at El Paso (TX)
U of the Cumberlands (KY)
U of the District of Columbia (DC)
The U of Toledo (OH)
U of Vermont (VT)
The U of Western Ontario (ON, Canada)
U of Windsor (ON, Canada)
U of Wisconsin–La Crosse (WI)
U of Wisconsin–Madison (WI)
U of Wisconsin–Milwaukee (WI)
U of Wisconsin–Oshkosh (WI)
U of Wisconsin–River Falls (WI)
U of Wisconsin–Stout (WI)
U of Wisconsin–Superior (WI)
U of Wisconsin–Whitewater (WI)
Upper Iowa U (IA)
Ursuline Coll (OH)
Valdosta State U (GA)
Valley City State U (ND)
Valparaiso U (IN)
Virginia Commonwealth U (VA)
Virginia Intermont Coll (VA)
Virginia Wesleyan Coll (VA)
Viterbo U (WI)
Wartburg Coll (IA)
Washburn U (KS)
Washington & Jefferson Coll (PA)
Washington U in St. Louis (MO)
Wayne State Coll (NE)
Wayne State U (MI)
Weber State U (UT)
Western Carolina U (NC)
Western Michigan U (MI)
Western State Coll of Colorado (CO)
Western Washington U (WA)
West Liberty U (WV)
Westmont Coll (CA)
West Virginia State U (WV)
West Virginia Wesleyan Coll (WV)
Wichita State U (KS)
William Jewell Coll (MO)
William Paterson U of New Jersey (NJ)
Wilmington Coll (OH)
Wingate U (NC)
Winona State U (MN)
Winston-Salem State U (NC)
Wright State U (OH)
Xavier U of Louisiana (LA)
York Coll (NE)
York U (ON, Canada)
Youngstown State U (OH)

ART THERAPY

Albertus Magnus Coll (CT)
Alverno Coll (WI)
Arcadia U (PA)
Bowling Green State U (OH)
Capital U (OH)
Carlow U (PA)
Chowan U (NC)
The Coll of New Rochelle (NY)
Converse Coll (SC)
DePaul U (IL)
Edgewood Coll (WI)
Emmanuel Coll (MA)
Harding U (AR)
Lesley U (MA)
Long Island U, C.W. Post Campus (NY)
Marywood U (PA)
Mercyhurst Coll (PA)
Millikin U (IL)
Mount Mary Coll (WI)
Nazareth Coll of Rochester (NY)
Ohio Wesleyan U (OH)
Prescott Coll (AZ)
Russell Sage Coll (NY)
St. Thomas Aquinas Coll (NY)
Seton Hill U (PA)
Southern Adventist U (TN)
U of Indianapolis (IN)
U of Wisconsin–Superior (WI)
Webster U (MO)
Wright State U (OH)

ASIAN AMERICAN STUDIES

California State U, East Bay (CA)
California State U, Fullerton (CA)
California State U, Long Beach (CA)
California State U, Los Angeles (CA)
California State U, Northridge (CA)
Claremont McKenna Coll (CA)
Columbia U (NY)
Columbia U, School of General Studies (NY)
Emory U (GA)
Pitzer Coll (CA)
Pomona Coll (CA)
San Francisco State U (CA)
Scripps Coll (CA)
Stony Brook U, State U of New York (NY)
U of California, Berkeley (CA)
U of California, Davis (CA)
U of California, Irvine (CA)
U of California, Los Angeles (CA)
U of California, Riverside (CA)
U of California, Santa Barbara (CA)
U of Denver (CO)
U of Southern California (CA)

ASIAN HISTORY

Bard Coll (NY)
Gettysburg Coll (PA)
Sarah Lawrence Coll (NY)
U of Regina (SK, Canada)
U of the West (CA)

ASIAN STUDIES

American Public U System (WV)
Amherst Coll (MA)
Augustana Coll (IL)
Bard Coll (NY)
Bard Coll at Simon's Rock (MA)
Barnard Coll (NY)
Baylor U (TX)
Beloit Coll (WI)
Bennington Coll (VT)
Berea Coll (KY)
Birmingham-Southern Coll (AL)
Bowdoin Coll (ME)
Bowling Green State U (OH)
California State U, Chico (CA)
California State U, Long Beach (CA)
California State U, Los Angeles (CA)
California State U, Sacramento (CA)
Calvin Coll (MI)
Carleton Coll (MN)
Case Western Reserve U (OH)
City Coll of the City U of New York (NY)
Claremont McKenna Coll (CA)
Clark U (MA)
Colgate U (NY)
The Coll at Brockport, State U of New York (NY)
Coll of the Holy Cross (MA)
The Colorado Coll (CO)
Cornell U (NY)
Dartmouth Coll (NH)
Duke U (NC)
Emory U (GA)
Florida Intl U (FL)
Fort Lewis Coll (CO)
Furman U (SC)
The George Washington U (DC)
Gonzaga U (WA)
Hamilton Coll (NY)
Hawai'i Pacific U (HI)
Hofstra U (NY)
Illinois Wesleyan U (IL)
Indiana U of Pennsylvania (PA)
John Carroll U (OH)
Knox Coll (IL)
Lake Forest Coll (IL)
Lehigh U (PA)
Loyola Marymount U (CA)
Macalester Coll (MN)
Manhattanville Coll (NY)
Marlboro Coll (VT)
Mary Baldwin Coll (VA)
Michigan State U (MI)
Mount Holyoke Coll (MA)
Northeastern U (MA)
Occidental Coll (CA)
Ohio U (OH)
Old Dominion U (VA)
Pitzer Coll (CA)
Pomona Coll (CA)
Rice U (TX)
St. John's U (NY)
St. Lawrence U (NY)
St. Mary's Coll of Maryland (MD)
St. Olaf Coll (MN)
Samford U (AL)
San Diego State U (CA)
Sarah Lawrence Coll (NY)
Scripps Coll (CA)
Seton Hall U (NJ)
Sewanee: The U of the South (TN)
Skidmore Coll (NY)
Stanford U (CA)
State U of New York at Binghamton (NY)
State U of New York at New Paltz (NY)
Swarthmore Coll (PA)
Temple U (PA)
Texas State U–San Marcos (TX)
Trinity U (TX)
Tufts U (MA)
Tulane U (LA)
U at Albany, State U of New York (NY)
U at Buffalo, the State U of New York (NY)
The U of British Columbia (BC, Canada)
U of California, Berkeley (CA)
U of California, Los Angeles (CA)
U of California, Riverside (CA)
U of California, Santa Barbara (CA)
U of Chicago (IL)

Southern Arkansas U–Magnolia (AR)
Southern Connecticut State U (CT)
Southern Illinois U Carbondale (IL)
Southwest Baptist U (MO)
Southwestern Coll (KS)
State U of New York Coll at Cortland (NY)
Sterling Coll (KS)
Stony Brook U, State U of New York (NY)
Tabor Coll (KS)
Texas A&M U–Commerce (TX)
Texas A&M U–Corpus Christi (TX)
Texas Christian U (TX)
Texas Lutheran U (TX)
Texas State U–San Marcos (TX)
Texas Wesleyan U (TX)
Towson U (MD)
Troy U (AL)
Truman State U (MO)
Tusculum Coll (TN)
Union U (TN)
The U of Akron (OH)
The U of Alabama (AL)
U of Alberta (AB, Canada)
U of Central Florida (FL)
U of Charleston (WV)
U of Delaware (DE)
U of Evansville (IN)
U of Florida (FL)
U of Idaho (ID)
U of Illinois at Urbana–Champaign (IL)
U of Indianapolis (IN)
The U of Iowa (IA)
The U of Kansas (KS)
U of La Verne (CA)
U of Maine at Presque Isle (ME)
U of Mary (ND)
U of Mary Hardin-Baylor (TX)
U of Miami (FL)
U of Michigan (MI)
U of Minnesota, Duluth (MN)
U of Mobile (AL)
U of Mount Union (OH)
U of Nebraska–Lincoln (NE)
U of Nevada, Las Vegas (NV)
U of New England (ME)
U of New Hampshire (NH)
The U of North Carolina at Charlotte (NC)
The U of North Carolina at Pembroke (NC)
The U of North Carolina Wilmington (NC)
U of North Dakota (ND)
U of Northern Iowa (IA)
U of North Florida (FL)
U of Pittsburgh at Bradford (PA)
U of Southern Maine (ME)
U of Southern Mississippi (MS)
U of South Florida (FL)
The U of Tampa (FL)
The U of Tennessee at Martin (TN)
The U of Texas at Arlington (TX)
The U of Texas at Austin (TX)
The U of Texas of the Permian Basin (TX)
U of the Incarnate Word (TX)
U of Tulsa (OK)
U of Utah (UT)
U of Vermont (VT)
The U of West Alabama (AL)
U of Wisconsin–Eau Claire (WI)
U of Wisconsin–La Crosse (WI)
U of Wisconsin–Stevens Point (WI)
Upper Iowa U (IA)
Valdosta State U (GA)
Vanguard U of Southern California (CA)
Washburn U (KS)
Washington State U (WA)
Waynesburg U (PA)
Wayne State Coll (NE)
Weber State U (UT)
West Chester U of Pennsylvania (PA)
Western Carolina U (NC)
Western Illinois U (IL)
Western Michigan U (MI)
West Virginia Wesleyan Coll (WV)
Wheeling Jesuit U (WV)
Wichita State U (KS)
Wilmington Coll (OH)
Wingate U (NC)
Winona State U (MN)
Xavier U (OH)
Youngstown State U (OH)

ATMOSPHERIC SCIENCES AND METEOROLOGY

The Coll at Brockport, State U of New York (NY)
Cornell U (NY)
Creighton U (NE)
Embry-Riddle Aeronautical U (AZ)
Embry-Riddle Aeronautical U (FL)
Florida State U (FL)
Iowa State U of Science and Technology (IA)
Jackson State U (MS)
Millersville U of Pennsylvania (PA)
Ohio U (OH)
Penn State Abington (PA)
Penn State Altoona (PA)
Penn State Beaver (PA)
Penn State Berks (PA)
Penn State Brandywine (PA)
Penn State DuBois (PA)
Penn State Erie, The Behrend Coll (PA)
Penn State Fayette, The Eberly Campus (PA)
Penn State Greater Allegheny (PA)
Penn State Hazleton (PA)
Penn State Lehigh Valley (PA)
Penn State Mont Alto (PA)
Penn State New Kensington (PA)
Penn State Schuylkill (PA)
Penn State Shenango (PA)
Penn State U Park (PA)
Penn State Wilkes-Barre (PA)
Penn State Worthington Scranton (PA)
Penn State York (PA)
Plymouth State U (NH)
Rutgers, The State U of New Jersey, New Brunswick (NJ)
St. Cloud State U (MN)
Saint Louis U (MO)
San Francisco State U (CA)
San Jose State U (CA)
State U of New York at Oswego (NY)
State U of New York Coll at Oneonta (NY)
State U of New York Maritime Coll (NY)
Stony Brook U, State U of New York (NY)
Texas A&M U (TX)
United States Air Force Acad (CO)
U at Albany, State U of New York (NY)
U of Alberta (AB, Canada)
The U of Arizona (AZ)
The U of British Columbia (BC, Canada)
U of California, Berkeley (CA)
U of California, Davis (CA)
U of Guelph (ON, Canada)
U of Illinois at Urbana–Champaign (IL)
The U of Kansas (KS)
U of Louisiana at Monroe (LA)
U of Louisville (KY)
U of Miami (FL)
U of Michigan (MI)
U of Missouri (MO)
U of Nebraska–Lincoln (NE)
The U of North Carolina at Asheville (NC)
U of North Dakota (ND)
U of South Alabama (AL)
U of Washington (WA)
U of Waterloo (ON, Canada)
U of Wisconsin–Milwaukee (WI)
Valparaiso U (IN)
Western Connecticut State U (CT)
York U (ON, Canada)

ATMOSPHERIC SCIENCES AND METEOROLOGY RELATED

U of California, Los Angeles (CA)
U of the Incarnate Word (TX)

ATOMIC/MOLECULAR PHYSICS

Columbia U (NY)
Harvard U (MA)
Maryville Coll (TN)
San Diego State U (CA)
U of Waterloo (ON, Canada)

AUDIO ENGINEERING

Berklee Coll of Music (MA)
Cogswell Polytechnical Coll (CA)
Five Towns Coll (NY)
Michigan Technological U (MI)
New England School of Communications (ME)
Peabody Conservatory of The Johns Hopkins U (MD)
State U of New York at Fredonia (NY)
U of Hartford (CT)

AUDIOLOGY AND HEARING SCIENCES

California State U, Long Beach (CA)
Cleveland State U (OH)
Indiana U–Purdue U Fort Wayne (IN)
Stephen F. Austin State U (TX)
U of Colorado at Boulder (CO)
U of Illinois at Urbana–Champaign (IL)
U of Montevallo (AL)
U of Northern Colorado (CO)
U of Oklahoma Health Sciences Center (OK)
The U of Tennessee (TN)
The U of Western Ontario (ON, Canada)

AUDIOLOGY AND SPEECH-LANGUAGE PATHOLOGY

Adelphi U (NY)
Andrews U (MI)
Arkansas State U—Jonesboro (AR)
Auburn U (AL)
Augustana Coll (SD)
Ball State U (IN)
Bloomsburg U of Pennsylvania (PA)
Bowling Green State U (OH)
Brescia U (KY)
Brooklyn Coll of the City U of New York (NY)
Buffalo State Coll, State U of New York (NY)
California State U, East Bay (CA)
California State U, Fresno (CA)
California State U, Long Beach (CA)
California State U, Sacramento (CA)
Calvin Coll (MI)
Clarion U of Pennsylvania (PA)
The Coll of Idaho (ID)
The Coll of Saint Rose (NY)
Delta State U (MS)
East Carolina U (NC)
Eastern New Mexico U (NM)
East Stroudsburg U of Pennsylvania (PA)
Elmhurst Coll (IL)
Elmira Coll (NY)
Emerson Coll (MA)
Fontbonne U (MO)
Fort Hays State U (KS)
Geneva Coll (PA)
The George Washington U (DC)
Governors State U (IL)
Hampton U (VA)
Hardin-Simmons U (TX)
Hofstra U (NY)
Hunter Coll of the City U of New York (NY)
Idaho State U (ID)
Illinois State U (IL)
Indiana State U (IN)
Indiana U Bloomington (IN)
Indiana U of Pennsylvania (PA)
Iona Coll (NY)
Ithaca Coll (NY)
Kent State U (OH)
Lamar U (TX)
La Salle U (PA)
Lehman Coll of the City U of New York (NY)
Louisiana State U and Ag and Mech Coll (LA)
Louisiana State U in Shreveport (LA)
Louisiana Tech U (LA)
Marquette U (WI)
Marywood U (PA)
Mercy Coll (NY)
Miami U Hamilton (OH)
Michigan State U (MI)
Minnesota State U Mankato (MN)
Minnesota State U Moorhead (MN)
Missouri State U (MO)
Molloy Coll (NY)
Murray State U (KY)
Nazareth Coll of Rochester (NY)
New York U (NY)
Nicholls State U (LA)
Northeastern State U (OK)
Northeastern U (MA)
Northern State U (SD)
The Ohio State U (OH)
Ohio U (OH)
Old Dominion U (VA)
Our Lady of the Lake U of San Antonio (TX)
Purdue U (IN)
Queens Coll of the City U of New York (NY)
The Richard Stockton Coll of New Jersey (NJ)
St. Cloud State U (MN)
St. John's U (NY)
Saint Louis U (MO)
Shaw U (NC)
South Carolina State U (SC)
Southeastern Louisiana U (LA)
Southern Connecticut State U (CT)
Southern Illinois U Edwardsville (IL)
Southern U and Ag and Mech Coll (LA)
State U of New York at Fredonia (NY)
State U of New York Coll at Cortland (NY)
Stephen F. Austin State U (TX)
Syracuse U (NY)
Temple U (PA)
Texas A&M U–Kingsville (TX)
Texas State U–San Marcos (TX)
Texas Woman's U (TX)
Thiel Coll (PA)
U at Buffalo, the State U of New York (NY)
The U of Alabama (AL)
U of Arkansas (AR)
U of Arkansas at Little Rock (AR)
U of Central Florida (FL)
U of Central Oklahoma (OK)
U of Cincinnati (OH)
U of Florida (FL)
U of Hawaii at Manoa (HI)
U of Illinois at Urbana–Champaign (IL)
The U of Iowa (IA)
U of Kentucky (KY)
U of Louisiana at Monroe (LA)
U of Minnesota, Twin Cities Campus (MN)
U of Mississippi (MS)
U of New Mexico (NM)
The U of North Carolina at Greensboro (NC)
U of North Texas (TX)
U of Oklahoma Health Sciences Center (OK)
U of Pittsburgh (PA)
U of Redlands (CA)
U of South Alabama (AL)
U of Southern Mississippi (MS)
U of South Florida (FL)
The U of Texas at Dallas (TX)
The U of Texas at El Paso (TX)
The U of Texas–Pan American (TX)
U of the District of Columbia (DC)
U of the Pacific (CA)
The U of Toledo (OH)
U of Tulsa (OK)
U of Utah (UT)
U of Virginia (VA)
U of Washington (WA)
The U of Western Ontario (ON, Canada)
U of Wisconsin–Milwaukee (WI)
U of Wisconsin–Oshkosh (WI)
U of Wisconsin–Stevens Point (WI)
U of Wyoming (WY)
Utah State U (UT)
Washington State U (WA)
West Chester U of Pennsylvania (PA)
Western Michigan U (MI)
Western Washington U (WA)
West Virginia U (WV)
Wichita State U (KS)
Yeshiva U (NY)

AUDIOVISUAL COMMUNICATIONS TECHNOLOGIES RELATED

Full Sail U (FL)
Greenville Coll (IL)
Nevada State Coll at Henderson (NV)
Prescott Coll (AZ)

AUDITING

Babson Coll (MA)
Carlow U (PA)
Pontifical Catholic U of Puerto Rico (PR)
U of Illinois at Urbana–Champaign (IL)

AUSTRALIAN/OCEANIC/PACIFIC LANGUAGES

U of Hawaii–West Oahu (HI)

AUTOBODY/COLLISION AND REPAIR TECHNOLOGY

Lewis-Clark State Coll (ID)
Pittsburg State U (KS)

AUTOMOBILE/AUTOMOTIVE MECHANICS TECHNOLOGY

Lewis-Clark State Coll (ID)
McPherson Coll (KS)
Pittsburg State U (KS)

AUTOMOTIVE ENGINEERING TECHNOLOGY

Central Michigan U (MI)
Colorado State U–Pueblo (CO)
Ferris State U (MI)
Indiana State U (IN)
Minnesota State U Mankato (MN)
Pennsylvania Coll of Technology (PA)
Southern Illinois U Carbondale (IL)
Weber State U (UT)
Western Washington U (WA)

AVIATION/AIRWAY MANAGEMENT

Auburn U (AL)
Averett U (VA)
Baker Coll of Muskegon (MI)
Bob Jones U (SC)
Bridgewater State Coll (MA)
California State U, Los Angeles (CA)
Delaware State U (DE)
Dixie State Coll of Utah (UT)
Dowling Coll (NY)
Eastern Michigan U (MI)
Eastern New Mexico U (NM)
Embry-Riddle Aeronautical U Worldwide (FL)
Fairmont State U (WV)
Farmingdale State Coll (NY)
Florida Inst of Technology (FL)
Hampton U (VA)
Indiana State U (IN)
Inter American U of Puerto Rico, Bayamón Campus (PR)
Jacksonville U (FL)
Kent State U (OH)
Lewis U (IL)
Louisiana Tech U (LA)
Marywood U (PA)
Metropolitan State Coll of Denver (CO)
Middle Georgia Coll (GA)
Minnesota State U Mankato (MN)
Mountain State U (WV)
The Ohio State U (OH)
Ohio U (OH)
Quincy U (IL)
Rocky Mountain Coll (MT)
St. Cloud State U (MN)
Saint Louis U (MO)
Salem State Coll (MA)
South Dakota State U (SD)
Southeastern Oklahoma State U (OK)
Southern Illinois U Carbondale (IL)
Tarleton State U (TX)
Texas Southern U (TX)
U of Dubuque (IA)
U of Illinois at Urbana–Champaign (IL)
U of Nebraska at Kearney (NE)
U of Nebraska at Omaha (NE)
U of North Dakota (ND)
The U of Western Ontario (ON, Canada)
Vaughn Coll of Aeronautics and Technology (NY)
Western Michigan U (MI)
Westminster Coll (UT)
Wilmington U (DE)
Winona State U (MN)

AVIONICS MAINTENANCE TECHNOLOGY

Averett U (VA)
Fairmont State U (WV)
LeTourneau U (TX)
Southern Illinois U Carbondale (IL)
Vaughn Coll of Aeronautics and Technology (NY)
Western Michigan U (MI)
Wilmington U (DE)

AYURVEDIC MEDICINE

Maharishi U of Management (IA)

BAKING AND PASTRY ARTS

Johnson & Wales U (RI)
The Restaurant School at Walnut Hill Coll (PA)

BALLET

Brigham Young U (UT)
Friends U (KS)
Indiana U Bloomington (IN)
Texas Christian U (TX)
U of Utah (UT)

BANKING AND FINANCIAL SUPPORT SERVICES

Brescia U (KY)
Buena Vista U (IA)
Delaware State U (DE)
Emory U (GA)
Husson U (ME)
National U (CA)
Providence Coll (RI)
Sam Houston State U (TX)
Texas Southern U (TX)
Universidad de las Américas–Puebla (Mexico)
U of Illinois at Urbana–Champaign (IL)
U of Nebraska at Omaha (NE)
U of North Florida (FL)
U of North Texas (TX)
The U of Texas at Arlington (TX)
U of the Incarnate Word (TX)
West Liberty U (WV)

BEHAVIORAL SCIENCES

Andrews U (MI)
Augsburg Coll (MN)
Bemidji State U (MN)
California Baptist U (CA)
California State Polytechnic U, Pomona (CA)
California State U, Dominguez Hills (CA)
Carnegie Mellon U (PA)
Chaminade U of Honolulu (HI)
Coll of St. Joseph (VT)
Columbia Coll (SC)
Concordia U (CA)
Dakota Wesleyan U (SD)
Drew U (NJ)
East-West U (IL)
Evangel U (MO)
Felician Coll (NJ)
Freed-Hardeman U (TN)
George Fox U (OR)
Glenville State Coll (WV)
Granite State Coll (NH)
Indiana U Kokomo (IN)
Inter American U of Puerto Rico, San Germán Campus (PR)
The Johns Hopkins U (MD)
Laurentian U (ON, Canada)
Loyola U Chicago (IL)
Marlboro Coll (VT)
Mars Hill Coll (NC)
Methodist U (NC)
Metropolitan State Coll of Denver (CO)
Minnesota State U Mankato (MN)
Missouri Baptist U (MO)
Mount Mary Coll (WI)
National U (CA)
Northeastern U (MA)
Northern Michigan U (MI)
Oklahoma Wesleyan U (OK)
Point Park U (PA)
Purdue U North Central (IN)
Rochester Coll (MI)
Saint Augustine's Coll (NC)
St. Cloud State U (MN)
San Jose State U (CA)
Savannah State U (GA)
Sterling Coll (KS)
Tennessee Wesleyan Coll (TN)
Texas Wesleyan U (TX)
Trevecca Nazarene U (TN)
Tufts U (MA)
United States Air Force Acad (CO)
U of Chicago (IL)
U of Houston–Clear Lake (TX)
The U of Kansas (KS)
U of La Verne (CA)
U of Maine at Fort Kent (ME)
U of Maine at Machias (ME)
U of Maine at Presque Isle (ME)
U of Missouri (MO)
U of North Texas (TX)
Utah Valley U (UT)
Walsh U (OH)
Western Intl U (AZ)
Widener U (PA)
William Paterson U of New Jersey (NJ)
Wilmington U (DE)
York Coll of Pennsylvania (PA)

BENGALI

U of Chicago (IL)

BIBLICAL STUDIES

Abilene Christian U (TX)
Amridge U (AL)
Anderson U (IN)
Andrews U (MI)
Appalachian Bible Coll (WV)
Asbury U (KY)
Atlanta Christian Coll (GA)
Austin Graduate School of Theology (TX)
Azusa Pacific U (CA)
Baptist Bible Coll of Pennsylvania (PA)
The Baptist Coll of Florida (FL)
Barclay Coll (KS)
Belhaven U (MS)
Belmont U (TN)
Bethany Bible Coll (NB, Canada)
Bethany U (CA)
Bethel Coll (IN)
Bethel U (MN)
Beulah Heights U (GA)
Bluefield Coll (VA)
Blue Mountain Coll (MS)
Bob Jones U (SC)
Boston Baptist Coll (MA)
Bryan Coll (TN)
California Baptist U (CA)
Calvary Bible Coll and Theological Sem (MO)
Calvin Coll (MI)
Campbellsville U (KY)
Carolina Christian Coll (NC)
Carson-Newman Coll (TN)
Cedarville U (OH)
Central Baptist Coll (AR)
Central Christian Coll of Kansas (KS)
Cincinnati Christian U (OH)
Clear Creek Baptist Bible Coll (KY)
Clearwater Christian Coll (FL)
Coll of Biblical Studies–Houston (TX)
Columbia Intl U (SC)
Corban U (OR)
Cornerstone U (MI)
Covenant Coll (GA)
Crandall U (NB, Canada)
Crichton Coll (TN)
Crossroads Bible Coll (IN)
Davis Coll (NY)
Eastern Mennonite U (VA)
East Texas Baptist U (TX)
Ecclesia Coll (AR)
Emmanuel Bible Coll (ON, Canada)
Eugene Bible Coll (OR)
Evangel U (MO)
Faith Baptist Bible Coll and Theological Sem (IA)
Faulkner U (AL)
Florida Coll (FL)
Freed-Hardeman U (TN)
Free Will Baptist Bible Coll (TN)
Gardner-Webb U (NC)
Geneva Coll (PA)
George Fox U (OR)
Global U (MO)
Goshen Coll (IN)
Grace Bible Coll (MI)
Grace Coll (IN)
Great Lakes Christian Coll (MI)
Hannibal-LaGrange Coll (MO)
Harding U (AR)
Hardin-Simmons U (TX)
Heritage Baptist Coll and Heritage Theological Sem (ON, Canada)
Heritage Christian U (AL)
Houghton Coll (NY)
Houston Baptist U (TX)
Howard Payne U (TX)
Huntington U (IN)
Indiana Wesleyan U (IN)
John Brown U (AR)
Johnson Bible Coll (TN)
John Wesley Coll (NC)
Judson U (IL)
King Coll (TN)
Kuyper Coll (MI)
Laura and Alvin Siegal Coll of Judaic Studies (OH)
Lee U (TN)
LeTourneau U (TX)
Lincoln Christian U (IL)
Lipscomb U (TN)
Lubbock Christian U (TX)
Malone U (OH)
Maple Springs Baptist Bible Coll and Sem (MD)
Maranatha Baptist Bible Coll (WI)
Marlboro Coll (VT)
The Master's Coll and Sem (CA)
Master's Coll and Sem (ON, Canada)
Messiah Coll (PA)
Methodist U (NC)
MidAmerica Nazarene U (KS)
Mid-Atlantic Christian U (NC)
Mid-Continent U (KY)
Milligan Coll (TN)
Moody Bible Inst (IL)
Mount Vernon Nazarene U (OH)
Multnomah U (OR)
Nazarene Bible Coll (CO)
North Greenville U (SC)
Northwest Christian U (OR)
Northwestern Coll (MN)
Northwest Nazarene U (ID)
Northwest U (WA)
Nyack Coll (NY)
Oakland City U (IN)
Ohio Valley U (WV)
Oklahoma Baptist U (OK)
Oklahoma Christian U (OK)
Oral Roberts U (OK)
Ouachita Baptist U (AR)
Patten U (CA)
Philadelphia Biblical U (PA)
Piedmont Baptist Coll and Graduate School (NC)
Redeemer U Coll (ON, Canada)
Roberts Wesleyan Coll (NY)
Rochester Coll (MI)
St. Louis Christian Coll (MO)
San Diego Christian Coll (CA)
School of Urban Missions (CA)
Shasta Bible Coll (CA)
Simpson U (CA)
Somerset Christian Coll (NJ)
Southeastern Bible Coll (AL)
Southwest Baptist U (MO)
Southwestern Assemblies of God U (TX)
Spring Arbor U (MI)
Tabor Coll (KS)
Taylor U (IN)
Tri-State Bible Coll (OH)
Union U (TN)
Universidad Teológica del Caribe (PR)
U of Evansville (IN)
U of Mary Hardin-Baylor (TX)
The U of Western Ontario (ON, Canada)
Valley Forge Christian Coll (PA)
Vanguard U of Southern California (CA)
Wheaton Coll (IL)
York Coll (NE)

BILINGUAL AND MULTILINGUAL EDUCATION

Belmont U (TN)
Boise State U (ID)
Boston U (MA)
Brooklyn Coll of the City U of New York (NY)
Calvin Coll (MI)
DePaul U (IL)
Fordham U (NY)
Goddard Coll (VT)
Goshen Coll (IN)
Houston Baptist U (TX)
Long Island U, Brooklyn Campus (NY)
Loyola U Chicago (IL)
Midwestern State U (TX)
Mount Mary Coll (WI)
Nevada State Coll at Henderson (NV)
Northeastern Illinois U (IL)
Prescott Coll (AZ)
Southwestern Assemblies of God U (TX)
State U of New York Coll at Old Westbury (NY)
Texas A&M Intl U (TX)
Texas A&M U–Corpus Christi (TX)
Texas Christian U (TX)
Texas Wesleyan U (TX)
U of Alberta (AB, Canada)
U of Delaware (DE)
The U of Findlay (OH)
U of Maine at Fort Kent (ME)
U of Nebraska at Omaha (NE)
U of Regina (SK, Canada)
U of San Francisco (CA)
U of the Southwest (NM)
U of Washington (WA)
U of Wisconsin–Milwaukee (WI)
Washington State U (WA)
Weber State U (UT)
Western Illinois U (IL)
York Coll of the City U of New York (NY)
York U (ON, Canada)

BILINGUAL, MULTILINGUAL, AND MULTICULTURAL EDUCATION RELATED

The Coll at Brockport, State U of New York (NY)

BIOCHEMISTRY

Abilene Christian U (TX)
Adams State Coll (CO)
Adelphi U (NY)
Agnes Scott Coll (GA)
Albright Coll (PA)
Allegheny Coll (PA)
Alma Coll (MI)
Alvernia U (PA)
American Intl Coll (MA)
American U (DC)
Anderson U (IN)
Andrews U (MI)
Angelo State U (TX)
Arizona State U (AZ)
Asbury U (KY)
Auburn U (AL)
Augustana Coll (IL)
Augustana Coll (SD)
Austin Coll (TX)
Azusa Pacific U (CA)
Barnard Coll (NY)
Bates Coll (ME)
Baylor U (TX)
Belmont U (TN)
Beloit Coll (WI)
Benedictine Coll (KS)
Benedictine U (IL)
Bishop's U (QC, Canada)
Boston Coll (MA)
Boston U (MA)
Bowdoin Coll (ME)
Bowling Green State U (OH)
Bradley U (IL)
Brandeis U (MA)
Bridgewater State Coll (MA)
Brigham Young U–Hawaii (HI)
Brock U (ON, Canada)
Bucknell U (PA)
California Lutheran U (CA)
California Polytechnic State U, San Luis Obispo (CA)
California State U, Chico (CA)
California State U, Dominguez Hills (CA)
California State U, East Bay (CA)
California State U, Fullerton (CA)
California State U, Long Beach (CA)
California State U, Los Angeles (CA)
California State U, Northridge (CA)
California State U, San Bernardino (CA)
California State U, San Marcos (CA)
Calvin Coll (MI)
Canisius Coll (NY)
Capital U (OH)
Carroll U (WI)
Case Western Reserve U (OH)
The Catholic U of America (DC)
Cedar Crest Coll (PA)
Central Connecticut State U (CT)
Central Michigan U (MI)
Chapman U (CA)
Chatham U (PA)
Christian Brothers U (TN)
City Coll of the City U of New York (NY)
Claflin U (SC)
Claremont McKenna Coll (CA)
Clarke Coll (IA)
Clark U (MA)
Clemson U (SC)
Colby Coll (ME)
Colgate U (NY)
The Coll at Brockport, State U of New York (NY)
Coll of Charleston (SC)
Coll of Mount St. Joseph (OH)
Coll of Mount Saint Vincent (NY)
Coll of Saint Benedict (MN)
Coll of Saint Elizabeth (NJ)
The Coll of Saint Rose (NY)
The Coll of St. Scholastica (MN)
Coll of Staten Island of the City U of New York (NY)
The Coll of Wooster (OH)
The Colorado Coll (CO)
Colorado State U (CO)
Columbia U (NY)
Columbia U, School of General Studies (NY)
Connecticut Coll (CT)
Converse Coll (SC)
Cornell Coll (IA)
Cornell U (NY)
Daemen Coll (NY)
Dakota Wesleyan U (SD)
Dartmouth Coll (NH)
Denison U (OH)
DePauw U (IN)
DeSales U (PA)
Dickinson Coll (PA)
Doane Coll (NE)
Dominican U (IL)
Drake U (IA)
Drew U (NJ)
Duquesne U (PA)
Earlham Coll (IN)
East Carolina U (NC)
Eastern Connecticut State U (CT)
Eastern Mennonite U (VA)
Eastern Michigan U (MI)
Eastern Nazarene Coll (MA)
Eastern New Mexico U (NM)
East Stroudsburg U of Pennsylvania (PA)
Eckerd Coll (FL)
Elizabethtown Coll (PA)
Elmira Coll (NY)
Emmanuel Coll (MA)
Fairfield U (CT)
Fairleigh Dickinson U, Coll at Florham (NJ)
Fairleigh Dickinson U, Metropolitan Campus (NJ)
Felician Coll (NJ)
Ferris State U (MI)
Florida Inst of Technology (FL)
Florida State U (FL)
Fort Lewis Coll (CO)
Franklin & Marshall Coll (PA)
Freed-Hardeman U (TN)
Furman U (SC)
Georgetown U (DC)
Georgia Inst of Technology (GA)
Georgian Court U (NJ)
Gettysburg Coll (PA)
Gonzaga U (WA)
Grinnell Coll (IA)
Grove City Coll (PA)
Gustavus Adolphus Coll (MN)
Hamilton Coll (NY)
Hamline U (MN)
Hampden-Sydney Coll (VA)
Harding U (AR)
Hartwick Coll (NY)
Harvard U (MA)
Haverford Coll (PA)
Hiram Coll (OH)
Hofstra U (NY)
Holy Family U (PA)
Hood Coll (MD)
Houghton Coll (NY)
Humboldt State U (CA)
Huntingdon Coll (AL)
Idaho State U (ID)
Illinois Inst of Technology (IL)
Illinois State U (IL)
Immaculata U (PA)
Indiana U Bloomington (IN)
Indiana U of Pennsylvania (PA)
Indiana U South Bend (IN)
Inter American U of Puerto Rico, Bayamón Campus (PR)
Iona Coll (NY)
Iowa State U of Science and Technology (IA)
Ithaca Coll (NY)
Jamestown Coll (ND)
John Brown U (AR)
Juniata Coll (PA)
Kansas State U (KS)
Kennesaw State U (GA)
Kenyon Coll (OH)
Kettering U (MI)
Keuka Coll (NY)
King Coll (TN)
Knox Coll (IL)
Kutztown U of Pennsylvania (PA)
Lafayette Coll (PA)
LaGrange Coll (GA)
Lakeland Coll (WI)
La Salle U (PA)
La Sierra U (CA)
Laurentian U (ON, Canada)
Lawrence Technological U (MI)
Lawrence U (WI)
Lee U (TN)
Lehigh U (PA)
Lehman Coll of the City U of New York (NY)
Le Moyne Coll (NY)
Lewis U (IL)
Lipscomb U (TN)
Loras Coll (IA)
Louisiana State U and Ag and Mech Coll (LA)
Loyola Marymount U (CA)
Loyola U Chicago (IL)
Lyon Coll (AR)
Madonna U (MI)
Manhattan Coll (NY)
Manhattanville Coll (NY)
Mansfield U of Pennsylvania (PA)
Marietta Coll (OH)
Marist Coll (NY)
Marlboro Coll (VT)
Marquette U (WI)
Maryville Coll (TN)
Maryville U of Saint Louis (MO)
McDaniel Coll (MD)
McMurry U (TX)
McPherson Coll (KS)
Memorial U of Newfoundland (NL, Canada)
Mercer U (GA)
Mercyhurst Coll (PA)
Merrimack Coll (MA)
Messiah Coll (PA)
Miami U (OH)
Miami U Hamilton (OH)
Michigan State U (MI)
Michigan Technological U (MI)
Middlebury Coll (VT)
Millsaps Coll (MS)
Mills Coll (CA)
Minnesota State U Mankato (MN)

Misericordia U (PA)
Mississippi Coll (MS)
Mississippi State U (MS)
Missouri Southern State U (MO)
Missouri Western State U (MO)
Monmouth Coll (IL)
Montclair State U (NJ)
Moravian Coll (PA)
Mount Allison U (NB, Canada)
Mount Holyoke Coll (MA)
Mount St. Mary's Coll (CA)
Mount St. Mary's U (MD)
Muhlenberg Coll (PA)
Nazareth Coll of Rochester (NY)
Nebraska Wesleyan U (NE)
New Coll of Florida (FL)
Newman U (KS)
New Mexico State U (NM)
New York U (NY)
Niagara U (NY)
North Carolina State U (NC)
North Central Coll (IL)
Northeastern U (MA)
Northern Michigan U (MI)
Northwestern Coll (MN)
Northwest Nazarene U (ID)
Notre Dame de Namur U (CA)
Oakland U (MI)
Oakwood U (AL)
Oberlin Coll (OH)
Occidental Coll (CA)
Ohio Northern U (OH)
The Ohio State U (OH)
Oklahoma Baptist U (OK)
Oklahoma Christian U (OK)
Oklahoma City U (OK)
Oklahoma State U (OK)
Old Dominion U (VA)
Pace U (NY)
Pacific Union Coll (CA)
Penn State Abington (PA)
Penn State Altoona (PA)
Penn State Beaver (PA)
Penn State Berks (PA)
Penn State Brandywine (PA)
Penn State DuBois (PA)
Penn State Erie, The Behrend Coll (PA)
Penn State Fayette, The Eberly Campus (PA)
Penn State Greater Allegheny (PA)
Penn State Hazleton (PA)
Penn State Lehigh Valley (PA)
Penn State Mont Alto (PA)
Penn State New Kensington (PA)
Penn State Schuylkill (PA)
Penn State Shenango (PA)
Penn State U Park (PA)
Penn State Wilkes-Barre (PA)
Penn State Worthington Scranton (PA)
Penn State York (PA)
Philadelphia U (PA)
Pittsburg State U (KS)
Pitzer Coll (CA)
Pomona Coll (CA)
Portland State U (OR)
Providence Coll (RI)
Purchase Coll, State U of New York (NY)
Purdue U (IN)
Queen's U at Kingston (ON, Canada)
Queens U of Charlotte (NC)
Quinnipiac U (CT)
Ramapo Coll of New Jersey (NJ)
Reed Coll (OR)
Regis Coll (MA)
Rhodes Coll (TN)
Rice U (TX)
The Richard Stockton Coll of New Jersey (NJ)
Rider U (NJ)
Ripon Coll (WI)
Roanoke Coll (VA)
Roberts Wesleyan Coll (NY)
Rochester Inst of Technology (NY)
Rockford Coll (IL)
Rockhurst U (MO)
Rollins Coll (FL)
Rose-Hulman Inst of Technology (IN)
Rosemont Coll (PA)
Rowan U (NJ)
Russell Sage Coll (NY)
Rutgers, The State U of New Jersey, New Brunswick (NJ)
Sacred Heart U (CT)
Saginaw Valley State U (MI)
Saint Anselm Coll (NH)
St. Bonaventure U (NY)
St. Catherine U (MN)
St. Edward's U (TX)
St. John Fisher Coll (NY)
Saint John's U (MN)
Saint Joseph Coll (CT)
Saint Joseph's U (PA)
St. Lawrence U (NY)
Saint Louis U (MO)
Saint Mary's Coll of California (CA)
St. Mary's Coll of Maryland (MD)
St. Mary's U (TX)
Saint Mary's U of Minnesota (MN)
Saint Michael's Coll (VT)
Saint Vincent Coll (PA)
Salem State Coll (MA)
Samford U (AL)
San Francisco State U (CA)
San Jose State U (CA)
Santa Clara U (CA)
Schreiner U (TX)
Scripps Coll (CA)
Seattle Pacific U (WA)
Seattle U (WA)
Seton Hall U (NJ)
Seton Hill U (PA)
Siena Coll (NY)
Simon Fraser U (BC, Canada)
Simpson Coll (IA)
Slippery Rock U of Pennsylvania (PA)
Smith Coll (MA)
South Dakota State U (SD)
Southern Adventist U (TN)
Southern Methodist U (TX)
Southern Oregon U (OR)
Southwestern Coll (KS)
Southwestern U (TX)
Spelman Coll (GA)
Spring Arbor U (MI)
Spring Hill Coll (AL)
State U of New York at Binghamton (NY)
State U of New York at Fredonia (NY)
State U of New York at Plattsburgh (NY)
State U of New York Coll at Geneseo (NY)
State U of New York Coll at Old Westbury (NY)
State U of New York Coll at Oneonta (NY)
State U of New York Coll at Potsdam (NY)
State U of New York Coll of Environmental Science and Forestry (NY)
Stephen F. Austin State U (TX)
Stetson U (FL)
Stevens Inst of Technology (NJ)
Stonehill Coll (MA)
Stony Brook U, State U of New York (NY)
Suffolk U (MA)
Susquehanna U (PA)
Swarthmore Coll (PA)
Syracuse U (NY)
Tabor Coll (KS)
Temple U (PA)
Tennessee Technological U (TN)
Texas A&M U (TX)
Texas Christian U (TX)
Texas State U–San Marcos (TX)
Texas Tech U (TX)
Texas Wesleyan U (TX)
Texas Woman's U (TX)
Thompson Rivers U (BC, Canada)
Trent U (ON, Canada)
Trinity Coll (CT)
Trinity U (TX)
Tulane U (LA)
Union Coll (NE)
Union Coll (NY)
United States Air Force Acad (CO)
Universidad de las Américas–Puebla (Mexico)
U at Albany, State U of New York (NY)
U at Buffalo, the State U of New York (NY)
The U of Akron (OH)
U of Alberta (AB, Canada)
The U of Arizona (AZ)
The U of British Columbia (BC, Canada)
The U of British Columbia–Okanagan (BC, Canada)
U of California, Los Angeles (CA)
U of California, Riverside (CA)
U of California, San Diego (CA)
U of California, Santa Barbara (CA)
U of California, Santa Cruz (CA)
U of Chicago (IL)
U of Cincinnati (OH)
U of Colorado at Boulder (CO)
U of Dallas (TX)
U of Dayton (OH)
U of Delaware (DE)
U of Denver (CO)
U of Evansville (IN)
U of Georgia (GA)
U of Guelph (ON, Canada)
U of Houston (TX)
U of Idaho (ID)
U of Illinois at Chicago (IL)
U of Illinois at Urbana–Champaign (IL)
The U of Iowa (IA)
The U of Kansas (KS)
U of King's Coll (NS, Canada)
U of Lethbridge (AB, Canada)
U of Maine (ME)
U of Maryland, Coll Park (MD)
U of Massachusetts Boston (MA)
U of Miami (FL)
U of Michigan (MI)
U of Michigan–Dearborn (MI)
U of Minnesota, Duluth (MN)
U of Minnesota, Twin Cities Campus (MN)
U of Missouri (MO)
U of Missouri–St. Louis (MO)
U of Mount Union (OH)
U of Nebraska–Lincoln (NE)
U of Nevada, Las Vegas (NV)
U of Nevada, Reno (NV)
U of New Brunswick Fredericton (NB, Canada)
U of New England (ME)
U of New Hampshire (NH)
U of New Mexico (NM)
The U of North Carolina at Greensboro (NC)
U of Northern Iowa (IA)
U of North Texas (TX)
U of Notre Dame (IN)
U of Oklahoma (OK)
U of Oregon (OR)
U of Ottawa (ON, Canada)
U of Pennsylvania (PA)
U of Puget Sound (WA)
U of Regina (SK, Canada)
U of Rochester (NY)
U of St. Thomas (MN)
U of St. Thomas (TX)
U of San Diego (CA)
U of Saskatchewan (SK, Canada)
U of Southern California (CA)
The U of Tampa (FL)
The U of Tennessee (TN)
The U of Texas at Arlington (TX)
The U of Texas at Austin (TX)
The U of Texas at Dallas (TX)
U of the Incarnate Word (TX)
U of the Pacific (CA)
U of the Sciences in Philadelphia (PA)
U of Toronto (ON, Canada)
U of Tulsa (OK)
U of Vermont (VT)
U of Washington (WA)
U of Waterloo (ON, Canada)
The U of Western Ontario (ON, Canada)
U of Windsor (ON, Canada)
U of Wisconsin–La Crosse (WI)
U of Wisconsin–Madison (WI)
U of Wisconsin–Milwaukee (WI)
U of Wisconsin–River Falls (WI)
Valparaiso U (IN)
Vanguard U of Southern California (CA)
Vassar Coll (NY)
Villanova U (PA)
Virginia Polytechnic Inst and State U (VA)
Viterbo U (WI)
Wartburg Coll (IA)
Washburn U (KS)
Washington Adventist U (MD)
Washington & Jefferson Coll (PA)
Washington and Lee U (VA)
Washington State U (WA)
Washington U in St. Louis (MO)
Wellesley Coll (MA)
Wells Coll (NY)
Wesleyan U (CT)
West Chester U of Pennsylvania (PA)
Western Kentucky U (KY)
Western Michigan U (MI)
Western State Coll of Colorado (CO)
Western Washington U (WA)
Westminster Coll (MO)
Wheaton Coll (MA)
Whitman Coll (WA)
Whittier Coll (CA)
Widener U (PA)
Wilkes U (PA)
William Jewell Coll (MO)
Worcester Polytechnic Inst (MA)
Wright State U (OH)
Xavier U of Louisiana (LA)

BIOCHEMISTRY/ BIOPHYSICS AND MOLECULAR BIOLOGY

Bellarmine U (KY)
California State U, Long Beach (CA)
Florida Southern Coll (FL)
Harding U (AR)
Hardin-Simmons U (TX)
Harvard U (MA)
Hendrix Coll (AR)
Illinois Inst of Technology (IL)
Indiana U Bloomington (IN)
Lebanon Valley Coll (PA)
Lewis & Clark Coll (OR)
Liberty U (VA)
Michigan State U (MI)
Nebraska Wesleyan U (NE)
North Dakota State U (ND)
Oregon State U (OR)
Simmons Coll (MA)
The U of British Columbia (BC, Canada)
U of California, Irvine (CA)
U of Maryland, Baltimore County (MD)
U of Massachusetts Amherst (MA)
U of Michigan–Flint (MI)
U of Regina (SK, Canada)
U of Waterloo (ON, Canada)
The U of Western Ontario (ON, Canada)
Whitman Coll (WA)
Wilson Coll (PA)
Wittenberg U (OH)

BIOCHEMISTRY, BIOPHYSICS AND MOLECULAR BIOLOGY RELATED

Rensselaer Polytechnic Inst (NY)
Sweet Briar Coll (VA)
Towson U (MD)
U of California, Santa Barbara (CA)
U of Waterloo (ON, Canada)

BIOETHICS/MEDICAL ETHICS

Cleveland State U (OH)
William Jewell Coll (MO)

BIOINFORMATICS

Baylor U (TX)
Chatham U (PA)
Claflin U (SC)
Davenport U, Grand Rapids (MI)
Gannon U (PA)
Indiana U Bloomington (IN)
Indiana U–Purdue U Indianapolis (IN)
Indiana U South Bend (IN)
Iowa State U of Science and Technology (IA)
Loyola U Chicago (IL)
Michigan Technological U (MI)
New Jersey Inst of Technology (NJ)
Polytechnic Inst of NYU (NY)
Ramapo Coll of New Jersey (NJ)
Rensselaer Polytechnic Inst (NY)
Rochester Inst of Technology (NY)
Rockhurst U (MO)
St. Bonaventure U (NY)
St. Edward's U (TX)
Saint Vincent Coll (PA)
San Diego State U (CA)
Stevens Inst of Technology (NJ)
U at Buffalo, the State U of New York (NY)
U of Alberta (AB, Canada)
U of California, Irvine (CA)
U of California, Santa Cruz (CA)
U of Denver (CO)
U of Maryland, Baltimore County (MD)
U of Nebraska at Omaha (NE)
U of Northern Iowa (IA)
U of Pennsylvania (PA)
U of Pittsburgh (PA)
U of St. Thomas (TX)
U of Saskatchewan (SK, Canada)
U of the Sciences in Philadelphia (PA)
U of Waterloo (ON, Canada)
The U of Western Ontario (ON, Canada)
U of Windsor (ON, Canada)
Virginia Commonwealth U (VA)
Wheaton Coll (MA)

BIOLOGICAL AND BIOMEDICAL SCIENCES RELATED

Alderson-Broaddus Coll (WV)
American Jewish U (CA)
Arizona State U (AZ)
Bethel U (MN)
Boston U (MA)
Bowling Green State U (OH)
Central Michigan U (MI)
The Coll of Saint Rose (NY)
Cornell U (NY)
Dakota State U (SD)
The Evergreen State Coll (WA)
Farmingdale State Coll (NY)
Frostburg State U (MD)
Grand Valley State U (MI)
Guilford Coll (NC)
Hiram Coll (OH)
Holy Names U (CA)
Indiana U Bloomington (IN)
Inter American U of Puerto Rico, Bayamón Campus (PR)
Kent State U (OH)
King Coll (TN)
Lehigh U (PA)
Logan U–Coll of Chiropractic (MO)
Louisiana State U in Shreveport (LA)
Lynchburg Coll (VA)
Messiah Coll (PA)
Nevada State Coll at Henderson (NV)
Our Lady of the Lake Coll (LA)
Park U (MO)
Penn State Abington (PA)
Penn State Altoona (PA)
Penn State Beaver (PA)
Penn State Berks (PA)
Penn State Brandywine (PA)
Penn State DuBois (PA)
Penn State Erie, The Behrend Coll (PA)
Penn State Fayette, The Eberly Campus (PA)
Penn State Greater Allegheny (PA)
Penn State Hazleton (PA)
Penn State Lehigh Valley (PA)
Penn State Mont Alto (PA)
Penn State New Kensington (PA)
Penn State Schuylkill (PA)
Penn State Shenango (PA)
Penn State U Park (PA)
Penn State Wilkes-Barre (PA)
Penn State Worthington Scranton (PA)
Penn State York (PA)
Ramapo Coll of New Jersey (NJ)
Rochester Inst of Technology (NY)
Rutgers, The State U of New Jersey, Newark (NJ)
Sage Coll of Albany (NY)
Saint Mary's Coll of California (CA)
San Jose State U (CA)
Syracuse U (NY)
Texas Wesleyan U (TX)
Trevecca Nazarene U (TN)
Union Coll (NY)
U of Illinois at Urbana–Champaign (IL)
The U of Kansas (KS)
U of Michigan (MI)
U of New Hampshire (NH)
U of North Alabama (AL)
U of North Dakota (ND)
U of Ottawa (ON, Canada)
U of Puerto Rico at Bayamón (PR)
U of Puerto Rico at Utuado (PR)
U of Rochester (NY)
U of Wisconsin–Parkside (WI)
Ursuline Coll (OH)
Utah State U (UT)
Washington U in St. Louis (MO)
Western State Coll of Colorado (CO)

BIOLOGICAL AND PHYSICAL SCIENCES

Alfred U (NY)
Alma Coll (MI)
Alvernia U (PA)
American U (DC)
Angelo State U (TX)
Athabasca U (AB, Canada)
Augsburg Coll (MN)
Averett U (VA)
Baldwin-Wallace Coll (OH)
Belmont U (TN)
Bemidji State U (MN)
Bennington Coll (VT)
Bishop's U (QC, Canada)
Bluefield State Coll (WV)
Brevard Coll (NC)
Brock U (ON, Canada)
Buena Vista U (IA)
California State U, Fresno (CA)
Calvin Coll (MI)
Castleton State Coll (VT)
Cheyney U of Pennsylvania (PA)
Clarion U of Pennsylvania (PA)
Coll of Saint Benedict (MN)
Coll of the Atlantic (ME)
Concordia U Chicago (IL)
Covenant Coll (GA)
DePaul U (IL)
Dowling Coll (NY)
Drexel U (PA)
Eastern Michigan U (MI)
Eastern Nazarene Coll (MA)
East Stroudsburg U of Pennsylvania (PA)
The Evergreen State Coll (WA)
Fairleigh Dickinson U, Metropolitan Campus (NJ)

Florida Inst of Technology (FL)
Fordham U (NY)
Fort Hays State U (KS)
Freed-Hardeman U (TN)
Gettysburg Coll (PA)
Grand Valley State U (MI)
Houghton Coll (NY)
Huntington U (IN)
Indiana U East (IN)
Indiana U Kokomo (IN)
Indiana U of Pennsylvania (PA)
Indiana U–Purdue U Indianapolis (IN)
Iowa Wesleyan Coll (IA)
John Brown U (AR)
John Carroll U (OH)
The Johns Hopkins U (MD)
Keene State Coll (NH)
Keystone Coll (PA)
King Coll (TN)
King's Coll (PA)
Kutztown U of Pennsylvania (PA)
Lakehead U (ON, Canada)
Lees-McRae Coll (NC)
Lee U (TN)
Lehigh U (PA)
Le Moyne Coll (NY)
Lock Haven U of Pennsylvania (PA)
Louisiana State U in Shreveport (LA)
Mansfield U of Pennsylvania (PA)
Mars Hill Coll (NC)
Maryville U of Saint Louis (MO)
The Master's Coll and Sem (CA)
Memorial U of Newfoundland (NL, Canada)
Methodist U (NC)
Michigan State U (MI)
Middle Tennessee State U (TN)
Minnesota State U Mankato (MN)
Mississippi State U (MS)
Mount Allison U (NB, Canada)
Mount Vernon Nazarene U (OH)
North Central Coll (IL)
Northern State U (SD)
Northwest Missouri State U (MO)
Oakland City U (IN)
Oklahoma City U (OK)
Oklahoma Panhandle State U (OK)
Oklahoma Wesleyan U (OK)
Oregon State U–Cascades (OR)
Palmer Coll of Chiropractic (IA)
Penn State Abington (PA)
Penn State Altoona (PA)
Penn State Beaver (PA)
Penn State Berks (PA)
Penn State Brandywine (PA)
Penn State DuBois (PA)
Penn State Erie, The Behrend Coll (PA)
Penn State Fayette, The Eberly Campus (PA)
Penn State Greater Allegheny (PA)
Penn State Hazleton (PA)
Penn State Lehigh Valley (PA)
Penn State Mont Alto (PA)
Penn State New Kensington (PA)
Penn State Schuylkill (PA)
Penn State Shenango (PA)
Penn State U Park (PA)
Penn State Wilkes-Barre (PA)
Penn State Worthington Scranton (PA)
Penn State York (PA)
Peru State Coll (NE)
Pontifical Catholic U of Puerto Rico (PR)
Portland State U (OR)
Purdue U (IN)
Quinnipiac U (CT)
Ramapo Coll of New Jersey (NJ)
Redeemer U Coll (ON, Canada)
Roberts Wesleyan Coll (NY)
Rochester Coll (MI)
Rockford Coll (IL)
Saint Anselm Coll (NH)
St. Francis Xavier U (NS, Canada)
Saint John's U (MN)
St. Mary's Coll of Maryland (MD)
St. Norbert Coll (WI)
Saint Xavier U (IL)
Sam Houston State U (TX)
San Francisco State U (CA)
Sarah Lawrence Coll (NY)
Seattle U (WA)
Shawnee State U (OH)
Simon Fraser U (BC, Canada)
Southern Arkansas U–Magnolia (AR)
Spalding U (KY)
State U of New York at Fredonia (NY)
State U of New York Coll at Potsdam (NY)
State U of New York Coll of Environmental Science and Forestry (NY)
State U of New York Empire State Coll (NY)
Tabor Coll (KS)
Texas A&M U at Galveston (TX)
Texas Tech U (TX)
Trent U (ON, Canada)
Union Coll (NY)
Union U (TN)
United States Air Force Acad (CO)
The U of Alabama at Birmingham (AL)
U of Alaska Anchorage (AK)
U of Alaska Fairbanks (AK)
U of Alberta (AB, Canada)
U of Arkansas at Monticello (AR)
U of Denver (CO)
U of Dubuque (IA)
The U of Findlay (OH)
U of Georgia (GA)
U of Guam (GU)
U of Houston (TX)
U of Houston–Downtown (TX)
U of Massachusetts Amherst (MA)
U of New Brunswick Fredericton (NB, Canada)
U of Northern Iowa (IA)
U of Notre Dame (IN)
U of Oregon (OR)
U of Pittsburgh (PA)
U of Regina (SK, Canada)
U of Rochester (NY)
U of Southern Indiana (IN)
U of Southern Mississippi (MS)
U of South Florida (FL)
The U of Texas at San Antonio (TX)
The U of Toledo (OH)
U of Waterloo (ON, Canada)
The U of Western Ontario (ON, Canada)
U of West Florida (FL)
U of Windsor (ON, Canada)
U of Wisconsin–Platteville (WI)
U of Wisconsin–River Falls (WI)
U of Wisconsin–Superior (WI)
U of Wisconsin–Whitewater (WI)
Upper Iowa U (IA)
Ursinus Coll (PA)
Vanguard U of Southern California (CA)
Virginia Commonwealth U (VA)
Walsh U (OH)
Warner Pacific Coll (OR)
Washington State U (WA)
Washington U in St. Louis (MO)
Western Washington U (WA)
Wilmington Coll (OH)
Winona State U (MN)
Wright State U (OH)
Xavier U (OH)
York Coll (NE)
York U (ON, Canada)

BIOLOGY/BIOLOGICAL SCIENCES

Abilene Christian U (TX)
Acadia U (NS, Canada)
Adams State Coll (CO)
Adelphi U (NY)
Agnes Scott Coll (GA)
Alabama Ag and Mech U (AL)
Alabama State U (AL)
Albany State U (GA)
Albertus Magnus Coll (CT)
Albion Coll (MI)
Albright Coll (PA)
Alcorn State U (MS)
Alderson-Broaddus Coll (WV)
Alfred U (NY)
Allegheny Coll (PA)
Allen U (SC)
Alma Coll (MI)
Alvernia U (PA)
Alverno Coll (WI)
American Intl Coll (MA)
American U (DC)
American U of Beirut (Lebanon)
Amherst Coll (MA)
Anderson U (IN)
Andrews U (MI)
Angelo State U (TX)
Appalachian State U (NC)
Aquinas Coll (MI)
Arcadia U (PA)
Arizona State U (AZ)
Arkansas State U—Jonesboro (AR)
Arkansas Tech U (AR)
Armstrong Atlantic State U (GA)
Asbury U (KY)
Ashland U (OH)
Assumption Coll (MA)
Atlantic Union Coll (MA)
Auburn U (AL)
Auburn U Montgomery (AL)
Augsburg Coll (MN)
Augustana Coll (IL)
Augustana Coll (SD)
Aurora U (IL)
Austin Coll (TX)
Austin Peay State U (TN)
Averett U (VA)
Avila U (MO)
Azusa Pacific U (CA)
Baker U (KS)
Baldwin-Wallace Coll (OH)
Ball State U (IN)
Bard Coll (NY)
Bard Coll at Simon's Rock (MA)
Barnard Coll (NY)
Barry U (FL)
Barton Coll (NC)
Bates Coll (ME)
Baylor U (TX)
Bay Path Coll (MA)
Belhaven U (MS)
Bellarmine U (KY)
Belmont Abbey Coll (NC)
Belmont U (TN)
Beloit Coll (WI)
Bemidji State U (MN)
Benedictine Coll (KS)
Benedictine U (IL)
Bennett Coll for Women (NC)
Bennington Coll (VT)
Berea Coll (KY)
Berry Coll (GA)
Bethany Coll (KS)
Bethany Coll (WV)
Bethany Lutheran Coll (MN)
Bethel Coll (IN)
Bethel Coll (KS)
Bethel U (MN)
Bethel U (TN)
Bethune-Cookman U (FL)
Birmingham-Southern Coll (AL)
Bishop's U (QC, Canada)
Blackburn Coll (IL)
Black Hills State U (SD)
Bloomfield Coll (NJ)
Bloomsburg U of Pennsylvania (PA)
Bluefield Coll (VA)
Blue Mountain Coll (MS)
Bluffton U (OH)
Bob Jones U (SC)
Boise State U (ID)
Boston Coll (MA)
Boston U (MA)
Bowdoin Coll (ME)
Bowie State U (MD)
Bowling Green State U (OH)
Bradley U (IL)
Brandeis U (MA)
Brenau U (GA)
Brescia U (KY)
Brewton-Parker Coll (GA)
Briar Cliff U (IA)
Bridgewater Coll (VA)
Bridgewater State Coll (MA)
Brigham Young U–Hawaii (HI)
Brock U (ON, Canada)
Brooklyn Coll of the City U of New York (NY)
Bryan Coll (TN)
Bryn Athyn Coll of the New Church (PA)
Bryn Mawr Coll (PA)
Bucknell U (PA)
Buena Vista U (IA)
Buffalo State Coll, State U of New York (NY)
Butler U (IN)
Cabrini Coll (PA)
California Baptist U (CA)
California Inst of Technology (CA)
California Lutheran U (CA)
California Polytechnic State U, San Luis Obispo (CA)
California State Polytechnic U, Pomona (CA)
California State U, Bakersfield (CA)
California State U, Chico (CA)
California State U, Dominguez Hills (CA)
California State U, East Bay (CA)
California State U, Fresno (CA)
California State U, Fullerton (CA)
California State U, Long Beach (CA)
California State U, Los Angeles (CA)
California State U, Monterey Bay (CA)
California State U, Northridge (CA)
California State U, Sacramento (CA)
California State U, San Bernardino (CA)
California State U, San Marcos (CA)
California State U, Stanislaus (CA)
Calvin Coll (MI)
Cameron U (OK)
Campbellsville U (KY)
Cape Breton U (NS, Canada)
Capital U (OH)
Carleton Coll (MN)
Carlow U (PA)
Carnegie Mellon U (PA)
Carroll U (WI)
Carson-Newman Coll (TN)
Case Western Reserve U (OH)
Castleton State Coll (VT)
Catawba Coll (NC)
The Catholic U of America (DC)
Cedar Crest Coll (PA)
Cedarville U (OH)
Centenary Coll (NJ)
Centenary Coll of Louisiana (LA)
Central Baptist Coll (AR)
Central Coll (IA)
Central Connecticut State U (CT)
Central Michigan U (MI)
Central State U (OH)
Chaminade U of Honolulu (HI)
Chapman U (CA)
Chatham U (PA)
Cheyney U of Pennsylvania (PA)
Chowan U (NC)
Christopher Newport U (VA)
The Citadel, The Military Coll of South Carolina (SC)
City Coll of the City U of New York (NY)
Claflin U (SC)
Claremont McKenna Coll (CA)
Clarion U of Pennsylvania (PA)
Clark Atlanta U (GA)
Clarke Coll (IA)
Clarkson U (NY)
Clark U (MA)
Clayton State U (GA)
Clearwater Christian Coll (FL)
Clemson U (SC)
Cleveland Chiropractic Coll–Los Angeles Campus (CA)
Cleveland State U (OH)
Coastal Carolina U (SC)
Coker Coll (SC)
Colby Coll (ME)
Colgate U (NY)
The Coll at Brockport, State U of New York (NY)
Coll of Charleston (SC)
The Coll of Idaho (ID)
Coll of Mount St. Joseph (OH)
Coll of Mount Saint Vincent (NY)
The Coll of New Jersey (NJ)
The Coll of New Rochelle (NY)
Coll of Notre Dame of Maryland (MD)
Coll of Saint Benedict (MN)
Coll of Saint Elizabeth (NJ)
Coll of Saint Mary (NE)
The Coll of Saint Rose (NY)
The Coll of St. Scholastica (MN)
Coll of Staten Island of the City U of New York (NY)
Coll of the Atlantic (ME)
Coll of the Holy Cross (MA)
Coll of the Ozarks (MO)
The Coll of William and Mary (VA)
The Coll of Wooster (OH)
The Colorado Coll (CO)
Colorado State U (CO)
Colorado State U–Pueblo (CO)
Columbia Coll (MO)
Columbia Coll (SC)
Columbia U (NY)
Columbia U, School of General Studies (NY)
Columbus State U (GA)
Concordia Coll (MN)
Concordia U (CA)
Concordia U (QC, Canada)
Concordia U Chicago (IL)
Concordia U Coll of Alberta (AB, Canada)
Concordia U, St. Paul (MN)
Concordia U Texas (TX)
Concordia U Wisconsin (WI)
Concord U (WV)
Connecticut Coll (CT)
Converse Coll (SC)
Coppin State U (MD)
Cornell Coll (IA)
Cornell U (NY)
Cornerstone U (MI)
Covenant Coll (GA)
Crandall U (NB, Canada)
Creighton U (NE)
Crichton Coll (TN)
Crown Coll (MN)
Culver-Stockton Coll (MO)
Cumberland U (TN)
Curry Coll (MA)
Daemen Coll (NY)
Dakota Wesleyan U (SD)
Dallas Baptist U (TX)
Dalton State Coll (GA)
Dana Coll (NE)
Dartmouth Coll (NH)
Davidson Coll (NC)
Defiance Coll (OH)
Delaware State U (DE)
Delaware Valley Coll (PA)
Delta State U (MS)
Denison U (OH)
DePaul U (IL)
DePauw U (IN)
DeSales U (PA)
Dickinson Coll (PA)
Dickinson State U (ND)
Dillard U (LA)
Dixie State Coll of Utah (UT)
Doane Coll (NE)
Dominican Coll (NY)
Dominican U (IL)
Dominican U of California (CA)
Dordt Coll (IA)
Dowling Coll (NY)
Drake U (IA)
Drew U (NJ)
Drexel U (PA)
Drury U (MO)
Duke U (NC)
Duquesne U (PA)
D'Youville Coll (NY)
Earlham Coll (IN)
East Carolina U (NC)
East Central U (OK)
Eastern Connecticut State U (CT)
Eastern Illinois U (IL)
Eastern Mennonite U (VA)
Eastern Michigan U (MI)
Eastern Nazarene Coll (MA)
Eastern New Mexico U (NM)
Eastern Washington U (WA)
East Stroudsburg U of Pennsylvania (PA)
East Tennessee State U (TN)
East Texas Baptist U (TX)
Eckerd Coll (FL)
Edgewood Coll (WI)
Edinboro U of Pennsylvania (PA)
Edward Waters Coll (FL)
Elizabeth City State U (NC)
Elizabethtown Coll (PA)
Elmhurst Coll (IL)
Elmira Coll (NY)
Elon U (NC)
Emmanuel Coll (GA)
Emmanuel Coll (MA)
Emory & Henry Coll (VA)
Emory U (GA)
Emporia State U (KS)
Erskine Coll (SC)
Evangel U (MO)
The Evergreen State Coll (WA)
Excelsior Coll (NY)
Fairfield U (CT)
Fairleigh Dickinson U, Coll at Florham (NJ)
Fairleigh Dickinson U, Metropolitan Campus (NJ)
Fairmont State U (WV)
Faulkner U (AL)
Fayetteville State U (NC)
Felician Coll (NJ)
Ferris State U (MI)
Ferrum Coll (VA)
Fisk U (TN)
Fitchburg State Coll (MA)
Florida Ag and Mech U (FL)
Florida Atlantic U (FL)
Florida Gulf Coast U (FL)
Florida Inst of Technology (FL)
Florida Intl U (FL)
Florida Southern Coll (FL)
Florida State U (FL)
Fontbonne U (MO)
Fordham U (NY)
Fort Hays State U (KS)
Fort Valley State U (GA)
Framingham State Coll (MA)
Franciscan U of Steubenville (OH)
Francis Marion U (SC)
Franklin & Marshall Coll (PA)
Franklin Coll (IN)
Franklin Pierce U (NH)
Freed-Hardeman U (TN)
Friends U (KS)
Frostburg State U (MD)
Furman U (SC)
Gallaudet U (DC)
Gannon U (PA)
Gardner-Webb U (NC)
Geneva Coll (PA)
George Fox U (OR)
George Mason U (VA)
Georgetown Coll (KY)
Georgetown U (DC)
The George Washington U (DC)
Georgia Coll & State U (GA)
Georgia Inst of Technology (GA)
Georgian Court U (NJ)
Georgia Southern U (GA)
Georgia State U (GA)
Gettysburg Coll (PA)
Glenville State Coll (WV)
Gonzaga U (WA)
Gordon Coll (MA)
Goshen Coll (IN)
Goucher Coll (MD)
Governors State U (IL)

INDEXES

Southern Polytechnic State U (GA)
Southern U and Ag and Mech Coll (LA)
Southern U at New Orleans (LA)
Southern Utah U (UT)
Southern Wesleyan U (SC)
Southwest Baptist U (MO)
Southwestern Adventist U (TX)
Southwestern Coll (KS)
Southwestern Oklahoma State U (OK)
Southwestern U (TX)
Southwest Minnesota State U (MN)
Spelman Coll (GA)
Spring Arbor U (MI)
Spring Hill Coll (AL)
Stanford U (CA)
State U of New York at Binghamton (NY)
State U of New York at Fredonia (NY)
State U of New York at New Paltz (NY)
State U of New York at Oswego (NY)
State U of New York at Plattsburgh (NY)
State U of New York Coll at Cortland (NY)
State U of New York Coll at Geneseo (NY)
State U of New York Coll at Old Westbury (NY)
State U of New York Coll at Oneonta (NY)
State U of New York Coll at Potsdam (NY)
State U of New York Coll of Environmental Science and Forestry (NY)
Stephen F. Austin State U (TX)
Stephens Coll (MO)
Sterling Coll (KS)
Stetson U (FL)
Stevenson U (MD)
Stillman Coll (AL)
Stonehill Coll (MA)
Stony Brook U, State U of New York (NY)
Suffolk U (MA)
Sul Ross State U (TX)
Susquehanna U (PA)
Swarthmore Coll (PA)
Sweet Briar Coll (VA)
Syracuse U (NY)
Tabor Coll (KS)
Talladega Coll (AL)
Tarleton State U (TX)
Taylor U (IN)
Temple U (PA)
Tennessee Technological U (TN)
Tennessee Wesleyan Coll (TN)
Texas A&M Intl U (TX)
Texas A&M U (TX)
Texas A&M U–Commerce (TX)
Texas A&M U–Corpus Christi (TX)
Texas A&M U–Kingsville (TX)
Texas Christian U (TX)
Texas Coll (TX)
Texas Lutheran U (TX)
Texas Southern U (TX)
Texas State U–San Marcos (TX)
Texas Tech U (TX)
Texas Wesleyan U (TX)
Texas Woman's U (TX)
Thiel Coll (PA)
Thomas Edison State Coll (NJ)
Thomas More Coll (KY)
Thomas More Coll of Liberal Arts (NH)
Thompson Rivers U (BC, Canada)
Towson U (MD)
Transylvania U (KY)
Trent U (ON, Canada)
Trevecca Nazarene U (TN)
Trine U (IN)
Trinity Christian Coll (IL)
Trinity Coll (CT)
Trinity U (TX)
Troy U (AL)
Truman State U (MO)
Tufts U (MA)
Tulane U (LA)
Tusculum Coll (TN)
Tuskegee U (AL)
Union Coll (KY)
Union Coll (NE)
Union Coll (NY)
Union U (TN)
United States Air Force Acad (CO)
United States Military Acad (NY)
Universidad Adventista de las Antillas (PR)
Universidad de las Américas–Puebla (Mexico)
U at Albany, State U of New York (NY)
U at Buffalo, the State U of New York (NY)
The U of Akron (OH)
The U of Alabama (AL)
The U of Alabama at Birmingham (AL)
The U of Alabama in Huntsville (AL)
U of Alaska Fairbanks (AK)
U of Alaska Southeast (AK)
U of Alberta (AB, Canada)
The U of Arizona (AZ)
U of Arkansas (AR)
U of Arkansas at Fort Smith (AR)
U of Arkansas at Little Rock (AR)
U of Arkansas at Monticello (AR)
U of Arkansas at Pine Bluff (AR)
U of Bridgeport (CT)
The U of British Columbia (BC, Canada)
The U of British Columbia–Okanagan (BC, Canada)
U of California, Berkeley (CA)
U of California, Davis (CA)
U of California, Irvine (CA)
U of California, Los Angeles (CA)
U of California, Merced (CA)
U of California, Riverside (CA)
U of California, San Diego (CA)
U of California, Santa Barbara (CA)
U of California, Santa Cruz (CA)
U of Central Florida (FL)
U of Central Missouri (MO)
U of Central Oklahoma (OK)
U of Charleston (WV)
U of Chicago (IL)
U of Cincinnati (OH)
U of Colorado at Colorado Springs (CO)
U of Colorado Denver (CO)
U of Connecticut (CT)
U of Dallas (TX)
U of Dayton (OH)
U of Delaware (DE)
U of Denver (CO)
U of Dubuque (IA)
U of Evansville (IN)
The U of Findlay (OH)
U of Florida (FL)
U of Georgia (GA)
U of Guam (GU)
U of Guelph (ON, Canada)
U of Hartford (CT)
U of Hawaii at Hilo (HI)
U of Hawaii at Manoa (HI)
U of Houston (TX)
U of Houston–Clear Lake (TX)
U of Houston–Downtown (TX)
U of Houston–Victoria (TX)
U of Idaho (ID)
U of Illinois at Chicago (IL)
U of Illinois at Springfield (IL)
U of Illinois at Urbana–Champaign (IL)
U of Indianapolis (IN)
The U of Iowa (IA)
The U of Kansas (KS)
U of Kentucky (KY)
U of King's Coll (NS, Canada)
U of La Verne (CA)
U of Lethbridge (AB, Canada)
U of Louisiana at Monroe (LA)
U of Louisville (KY)
U of Maine (ME)
U of Maine at Augusta (ME)
U of Maine at Farmington (ME)
U of Maine at Fort Kent (ME)
U of Maine at Machias (ME)
U of Maine at Presque Isle (ME)
U of Manitoba (MB, Canada)
U of Mary (ND)
U of Mary Hardin-Baylor (TX)
U of Maryland, Baltimore County (MD)
U of Maryland, Coll Park (MD)
U of Maryland Eastern Shore (MD)
U of Mary Washington (VA)
U of Massachusetts Amherst (MA)
U of Massachusetts Boston (MA)
U of Massachusetts Dartmouth (MA)
U of Massachusetts Lowell (MA)
U of Memphis (TN)
U of Miami (FL)
U of Michigan (MI)
U of Michigan–Dearborn (MI)
U of Michigan–Flint (MI)
U of Minnesota, Crookston (MN)
U of Minnesota, Duluth (MN)
U of Minnesota, Twin Cities Campus (MN)
U of Mississippi (MS)
U of Missouri (MO)
U of Missouri–Kansas City (MO)
U of Missouri–St. Louis (MO)
U of Mobile (AL)
U of Montevallo (AL)
U of Mount Union (OH)
U of Nebraska at Kearney (NE)
U of Nebraska at Omaha (NE)
U of Nebraska–Lincoln (NE)
U of Nevada, Las Vegas (NV)
U of Nevada, Reno (NV)
U of New Brunswick Fredericton (NB, Canada)
U of New England (ME)
U of New Hampshire (NH)
U of New Haven (CT)
U of New Mexico (NM)
U of New Orleans (LA)
U of North Alabama (AL)
The U of North Carolina at Asheville (NC)
The U of North Carolina at Chapel Hill (NC)
The U of North Carolina at Charlotte (NC)
The U of North Carolina at Greensboro (NC)
The U of North Carolina at Pembroke (NC)
The U of North Carolina Wilmington (NC)
U of North Dakota (ND)
U of Northern Colorado (CO)
U of Northern Iowa (IA)
U of North Florida (FL)
U of North Texas (TX)
U of Notre Dame (IN)
U of Oregon (OR)
U of Ottawa (ON, Canada)
U of Pennsylvania (PA)
U of Pittsburgh (PA)
U of Pittsburgh at Bradford (PA)
U of Pittsburgh at Greensburg (PA)
U of Pittsburgh at Johnstown (PA)
U of Portland (OR)
U of Puerto Rico at Bayamón (PR)
U of Puerto Rico at Humacao (PR)
U of Puerto Rico at Utuado (PR)
U of Puerto Rico, Cayey U Coll (PR)
U of Puerto Rico, Río Piedras (PR)
U of Puget Sound (WA)
U of Redlands (CA)
U of Regina (SK, Canada)
U of Rhode Island (RI)
U of Richmond (VA)
U of Rio Grande (OH)
U of Rochester (NY)
U of St. Francis (IL)
U of Saint Mary (KS)
U of St. Thomas (MN)
U of St. Thomas (TX)
U of San Diego (CA)
U of San Francisco (CA)
U of Saskatchewan (SK, Canada)
U of Science and Arts of Oklahoma (OK)
The U of Scranton (PA)
U of South Alabama (AL)
U of South Carolina (SC)
U of South Carolina Aiken (SC)
U of South Carolina Beaufort (SC)
U of South Carolina Upstate (SC)
U of Southern California (CA)
U of Southern Indiana (IN)
U of Southern Maine (ME)
U of Southern Mississippi (MS)
U of South Florida (FL)
The U of Tampa (FL)
The U of Tennessee (TN)
The U of Tennessee at Chattanooga (TN)
The U of Tennessee at Martin (TN)
The U of Texas at Arlington (TX)
The U of Texas at Austin (TX)
The U of Texas at Brownsville (TX)
The U of Texas at Dallas (TX)
The U of Texas at El Paso (TX)
The U of Texas at San Antonio (TX)
The U of Texas at Tyler (TX)
The U of Texas of the Permian Basin (TX)
The U of Texas–Pan American (TX)
U of the Cumberlands (KY)
U of the District of Columbia (DC)
U of the Incarnate Word (TX)
U of the Ozarks (AR)
U of the Pacific (CA)
U of the Sciences in Philadelphia (PA)
U of the Southwest (NM)
U of the Virgin Islands (VI)
The U of Toledo (OH)
U of Toronto (ON, Canada)
U of Tulsa (OK)
U of Utah (UT)
U of Vermont (VT)
U of Virginia (VA)
The U of Virginia's Coll at Wise (VA)
U of Washington (WA)
U of Waterloo (ON, Canada)
The U of West Alabama (AL)
The U of Western Ontario (ON, Canada)
U of West Florida (FL)
U of West Georgia (GA)
U of Windsor (ON, Canada)
U of Wisconsin–Eau Claire (WI)
U of Wisconsin–Green Bay (WI)
U of Wisconsin–La Crosse (WI)
U of Wisconsin–Madison (WI)
U of Wisconsin–Milwaukee (WI)
U of Wisconsin–Oshkosh (WI)
U of Wisconsin–Platteville (WI)
U of Wisconsin–River Falls (WI)
U of Wisconsin–Stevens Point (WI)
U of Wisconsin–Superior (WI)
U of Wisconsin–Whitewater (WI)
U of Wyoming (WY)
Upper Iowa U (IA)
Ursinus Coll (PA)
Ursuline Coll (OH)
Utah State U (UT)
Utah Valley U (UT)
Utica Coll (NY)
Valdosta State U (GA)
Valley City State U (ND)
Valparaiso U (IN)
Vanderbilt U (TN)
Vanguard U of Southern California (CA)
Vassar Coll (NY)
Villanova U (PA)
Virginia Commonwealth U (VA)
Virginia Intermont Coll (VA)
Virginia Military Inst (VA)
Virginia Polytechnic Inst and State U (VA)
Virginia State U (VA)
Virginia Union U (VA)
Virginia Wesleyan Coll (VA)
Viterbo U (WI)
Voorhees Coll (SC)
Wabash Coll (IN)
Wagner Coll (NY)
Wake Forest U (NC)
Walsh U (OH)
Warner Pacific Coll (OR)
Wartburg Coll (IA)
Washburn U (KS)
Washington Adventist U (MD)
Washington & Jefferson Coll (PA)
Washington and Lee U (VA)
Washington Coll (MD)
Washington State U (WA)
Washington U in St. Louis (MO)
Wayland Baptist U (TX)
Waynesburg U (PA)
Wayne State Coll (NE)
Wayne State U (MI)
Webster U (MO)
Wellesley Coll (MA)
Wells Coll (NY)
Wesleyan Coll (GA)
Wesleyan U (CT)
West Chester U of Pennsylvania (PA)
Western Carolina U (NC)
Western Connecticut State U (CT)
Western Illinois U (IL)
Western Kentucky U (KY)
Western Michigan U (MI)
Western New England Coll (MA)
Western Oregon U (OR)
Western State Coll of Colorado (CO)
Western Washington U (WA)
Westfield State Coll (MA)
West Liberty U (WV)
Westminster Coll (MO)
Westminster Coll (UT)
Westmont Coll (CA)
West Virginia State U (WV)
West Virginia U (WV)
West Virginia Wesleyan Coll (WV)
Wheaton Coll (IL)
Wheaton Coll (MA)
Wheeling Jesuit U (WV)
Whitman Coll (WA)
Whittier Coll (CA)
Wichita State U (KS)
Widener U (PA)
Wilberforce U (OH)
Wilfrid Laurier U (ON, Canada)
Wilkes U (PA)
Willamette U (OR)
William Jewell Coll (MO)
William Paterson U of New Jersey (NJ)
William Penn U (IA)
Williams Coll (MA)
Wilmington Coll (OH)
Wilson Coll (PA)
Wingate U (NC)
Winona State U (MN)
Winston-Salem State U (NC)
Winthrop U (SC)
Wittenberg U (OH)
Wofford Coll (SC)
Worcester Polytechnic Inst (MA)
Worcester State Coll (MA)
Wright State U (OH)
Xavier U (OH)
Xavier U of Louisiana (LA)
Yale U (CT)
Yeshiva U (NY)
York Coll (NE)
York Coll of Pennsylvania (PA)
York Coll of the City U of New York (NY)
York U (ON, Canada)
Young Harris Coll (GA)
Youngstown State U (OH)

BIOLOGY/ BIOTECHNOLOGY LABORATORY TECHNICIAN

Cleveland State U (OH)
The Coll at Brockport, State U of New York (NY)
Gannon U (PA)
Michigan Technological U (MI)
Niagara U (NY)
Penn State Abington (PA)
Penn State Altoona (PA)
Penn State Beaver (PA)
Penn State Berks (PA)
Penn State Brandywine (PA)
Penn State DuBois (PA)
Penn State Erie, The Behrend Coll (PA)
Penn State Fayette, The Eberly Campus (PA)
Penn State Greater Allegheny (PA)
Penn State Hazleton (PA)
Penn State Lehigh Valley (PA)
Penn State Mont Alto (PA)
Penn State New Kensington (PA)
Penn State Schuylkill (PA)
Penn State Shenango (PA)
Penn State U Park (PA)
Penn State Wilkes-Barre (PA)
Penn State Worthington Scranton (PA)
Penn State York (PA)
Point Park U (PA)
Purdue U Calumet (IN)
St. Cloud State U (MN)
State U of New York at Fredonia (NY)
State U of New York Coll at Oneonta (NY)
Stevenson U (MD)
Suffolk U (MA)
Tusculum Coll (TN)
U of Alberta (AB, Canada)
U of Delaware (DE)
U of New Haven (CT)
Washburn U (KS)
Worcester Polytechnic Inst (MA)
York Coll of the City U of New York (NY)

BIOLOGY TEACHER EDUCATION

Abilene Christian U (TX)
Adams State Coll (CO)
Alma Coll (MI)
Alvernia U (PA)
Anderson U (IN)
Appalachian State U (NC)
Arkansas State U—Jonesboro (AR)
Arkansas Tech U (AR)
Assumption Coll (MA)
Averett U (VA)
Bethany Coll (KS)
Bethel U (MN)
Bethune-Cookman U (FL)
Bishop's U (QC, Canada)
Bluefield Coll (VA)
Blue Mountain Coll (MS)
Bowling Green State U (OH)
Bradley U (IL)
Brewton-Parker Coll (GA)
Bridgewater Coll (VA)
Bridgewater State Coll (MA)
Brigham Young U–Hawaii (HI)
Brooklyn Coll of the City U of New York (NY)
Bryan Coll (TN)
Buena Vista U (IA)
Cabrini Coll (PA)
California State U, Chico (CA)
California State U, Long Beach (CA)
Campbellsville U (KY)
Carroll U (WI)
The Catholic U of America (DC)
Cedarville U (OH)
Central Michigan U (MI)
Christian Brothers U (TN)
City Coll of the City U of New York (NY)
Clearwater Christian Coll (FL)
Coker Coll (SC)
The Coll at Brockport, State U of New York (NY)
The Coll of New Jersey (NJ)
The Coll of Saint Rose (NY)
Coll of the Ozarks (MO)
Colorado State U (CO)
Concordia Coll (MN)

Concordia U Chicago (IL)
Concordia U, St. Paul (MN)
Corban U (OR)
Cornell U (NY)
Cornerstone U (MI)
Culver-Stockton Coll (MO)
Cumberland U (TN)
Daemen Coll (NY)
Dakota State U (SD)
Dakota Wesleyan U (SD)
Dana Coll (NE)
Daytona State Coll (FL)
Delaware State U (DE)
DePaul U (IL)
Dixie State Coll of Utah (UT)
Dominican Coll (NY)
Dordt Coll (IA)
Dowling Coll (NY)
East Central U (OK)
Eastern Mennonite U (VA)
Eastern Michigan U (MI)
Eastern Nazarene Coll (MA)
Eastern Washington U (WA)
East Texas Baptist U (TX)
Edgewood Coll (WI)
Elizabeth City State U (NC)
Elmhurst Coll (IL)
Elmira Coll (NY)
Evangel U (MO)
Fayetteville State U (NC)
Ferris State U (MI)
Fitchburg State Coll (MA)
Florida Inst of Technology (FL)
Fort Lewis Coll (CO)
Franklin Coll (IN)
Freed-Hardeman U (TN)
Free Will Baptist Bible Coll (TN)
Glenville State Coll (WV)
Grambling State U (LA)
Grand Valley State U (MI)
Greensboro Coll (NC)
Greenville Coll (IL)
Gustavus Adolphus Coll (MN)
Harding U (AR)
Hofstra U (NY)
Hope Coll (MI)
Houston Baptist U (TX)
Howard Payne U (TX)
Hunter Coll of the City U of New York (NY)
Husson U (ME)
Indiana U Bloomington (IN)
Indiana U–Purdue U Fort Wayne (IN)
Indiana U South Bend (IN)
Indiana U Southeast (IN)
Indian River State Coll (FL)
Inter American U of Puerto Rico, Aguadilla Campus (PR)
Inter American U of Puerto Rico, Arecibo Campus (PR)
Inter American U of Puerto Rico, Fajardo Campus (PR)
Inter American U of Puerto Rico, Ponce Campus (PR)
Inter American U of Puerto Rico, San Germán Campus (PR)
Iona Coll (NY)
Ithaca Coll (NY)
Jamestown Coll (ND)
Johnson State Coll (VT)
Juniata Coll (PA)
Keene State Coll (NH)
Kennesaw State U (GA)
Kentucky Wesleyan Coll (KY)
Keuka Coll (NY)
King Coll (TN)
Le Moyne Coll (NY)
Liberty U (VA)
Limestone Coll (SC)
Lincoln Memorial U (TN)
Lincoln U (MO)
Lindenwood U (MO)
Lindsey Wilson Coll (KY)
Lipscomb U (TN)
Long Island U, C.W. Post Campus (NY)
Louisiana State U in Shreveport (LA)
Louisiana Tech U (LA)
Lubbock Christian U (TX)
Manhattanville Coll (NY)
Mansfield U of Pennsylvania (PA)
Marian U (WI)
Marist Coll (NY)
Maryville Coll (TN)
Maryville U of Saint Louis (MO)
Marywood U (PA)
Mayville State U (ND)
McKendree U (IL)
McMurry U (TX)
McNeese State U (LA)
Mercyhurst Coll (PA)
Messiah Coll (PA)
Miami Dade Coll (FL)
Miami U (OH)
Michigan State U (MI)
Michigan Technological U (MI)
MidAmerica Nazarene U (KS)
Millersville U of Pennsylvania (PA)
Millikin U (IL)
Minnesota State U Moorhead (MN)
Minot State U (ND)
Misericordia U (PA)
Mississippi Coll (MS)
Missouri State U (MO)
Molloy Coll (NY)
Montana State U Billings (MT)
Moravian Coll (PA)
Morningside Coll (IA)
Morris Coll (SC)
Mount Mary Coll (WI)
Mount Vernon Nazarene U (OH)
Murray State U (KY)
Nazareth Coll of Rochester (NY)
Nevada State Coll at Henderson (NV)
New York Inst of Technology (NY)
Niagara U (NY)
North Carolina Central U (NC)
North Carolina State U (NC)
North Dakota State U (ND)
Northeastern State U (OK)
Northern Arizona U (AZ)
Northern Michigan U (MI)
North Greenville U (SC)
Northwestern Coll (IA)
Northwestern State U of Louisiana (LA)
Northwest Missouri State U (MO)
Northwest Nazarene U (ID)
Northwest U (WA)
Oakland City U (IN)
Ohio Northern U (OH)
Ohio Wesleyan U (OH)
Old Dominion U (VA)
Pace U (NY)
Paine Coll (GA)
Pittsburg State U (KS)
Point Park U (PA)
Pontifical Catholic U of Puerto Rico (PR)
Prescott Coll (AZ)
Rhode Island Coll (RI)
Rivier Coll (NH)
Roberts Wesleyan Coll (NY)
Rochester Coll (MI)
Rocky Mountain Coll (MT)
Sacred Heart U (CT)
Saginaw Valley State U (MI)
St. Ambrose U (IA)
St. Catherine U (MN)
St. Edward's U (TX)
St. Francis Coll (NY)
Saint Francis U (PA)
St. John Fisher Coll (NY)
St. John's U (NY)
Saint Mary's U of Minnesota (MN)
St. Petersburg Coll (FL)
Saint Xavier U (IL)
Salve Regina U (RI)
Schreiner U (TX)
Seton Hill U (PA)
Southeastern U (FL)
Southern U and Ag and Mech Coll (LA)
Southwest Baptist U (MO)
Southwest Minnesota State U (MN)
Spring Arbor U (MI)
State U of New York at New Paltz (NY)
State U of New York at Plattsburgh (NY)
State U of New York Coll at Cortland (NY)
State U of New York Coll at Old Westbury (NY)
State U of New York Coll at Oneonta (NY)
State U of New York Coll at Potsdam (NY)
State U of New York Coll of Environmental Science and Forestry (NY)
Tabor Coll (KS)
Talladega Coll (AL)
Texas A&M Intl U (TX)
Texas Wesleyan U (TX)
Trevecca Nazarene U (TN)
Trinity Christian Coll (IL)
Tusculum Coll (TN)
Union Coll (NE)
Universidad Adventista de las Antillas (PR)
The U of Arizona (AZ)
U of Arkansas at Fort Smith (AR)
U of Charleston (WV)
U of Delaware (DE)
U of Dubuque (IA)
U of Evansville (IN)
U of Illinois at Chicago (IL)
The U of Iowa (IA)
U of Louisiana at Monroe (LA)
U of Maine (ME)
U of Maine at Farmington (ME)
U of Maine at Machias (ME)
U of Mary (ND)
U of Michigan–Flint (MI)
U of Missouri (MO)
U of Missouri–St. Louis (MO)
The U of Montana Western (MT)
U of Nebraska–Lincoln (NE)
U of New Orleans (LA)
The U of North Carolina at Greensboro (NC)
The U of North Carolina at Pembroke (NC)
The U of North Carolina Wilmington (NC)
U of Pittsburgh at Johnstown (PA)
U of Regina (SK, Canada)
U of Rio Grande (OH)
U of St. Thomas (MN)
The U of South Dakota (SD)
The U of Tennessee at Martin (TN)
U of Washington (WA)
U of Waterloo (ON, Canada)
U of West Georgia (GA)
U of Windsor (ON, Canada)
U of Wisconsin–River Falls (WI)
U of Wisconsin–Superior (WI)
Utah State U (UT)
Utah Valley U (UT)
Utica Coll (NY)
Valley City State U (ND)
Valparaiso U (IN)
Virginia Intermont Coll (VA)
Viterbo U (WI)
Washington State U (WA)
Washington U in St. Louis (MO)
Waynesburg U (PA)
Wayne State Coll (NE)
Weber State U (UT)
Western Michigan U (MI)
Western State Coll of Colorado (CO)
Western Washington U (WA)
Wheeling Jesuit U (WV)
Widener U (PA)
Wingate U (NC)
Xavier U (OH)
Xavier U of Louisiana (LA)
York Coll (NE)
York Coll of Pennsylvania (PA)
York U (ON, Canada)

BIOMATHEMATICS AND BIOINFORMATICS RELATED

Case Western Reserve U (OH)
Florida Inst of Technology (FL)
Florida State U (FL)
Trevecca Nazarene U (TN)
U of California, Los Angeles (CA)
The U of Scranton (PA)
Walsh U (OH)
Washington U in St. Louis (MO)

BIOMEDICAL/MEDICAL ENGINEERING

Alfred U (NY)
Arizona State U (AZ)
Boston U (MA)
Bucknell U (PA)
California Lutheran U (CA)
California Polytechnic State U, San Luis Obispo (CA)
California State U, Long Beach (CA)
Carnegie Mellon U (PA)
Case Western Reserve U (OH)
The Catholic U of America (DC)
City Coll of the City U of New York (NY)
Clemson U (SC)
The Coll of New Jersey (NJ)
Colorado School of Mines (CO)
Columbia U (NY)
Drexel U (PA)
Duke U (NC)
Eastern Nazarene Coll (MA)
Florida Gulf Coast U (FL)
Florida Intl U (FL)
Georgia Inst of Technology (GA)
Hofstra U (NY)
Illinois Inst of Technology (IL)
Indiana Tech (IN)
Indiana U–Purdue U Indianapolis (IN)
The Johns Hopkins U (MD)
Lawrence Technological U (MI)
Lehigh U (PA)
LeTourneau U (TX)
Louisiana State U and Ag and Mech Coll (LA)
Louisiana Tech U (LA)
Marquette U (WI)
Massachusetts Inst of Technology (MA)
Michigan State U (MI)
Michigan Technological U (MI)
Milwaukee School of Eng (WI)
Mississippi State U (MS)
New Jersey Inst of Technology (NJ)
North Carolina State U (NC)
Oral Roberts U (OK)
Oregon State U (OR)
Penn State Abington (PA)
Penn State Altoona (PA)
Penn State Beaver (PA)
Penn State Berks (PA)
Penn State Brandywine (PA)
Penn State DuBois (PA)
Penn State Erie, The Behrend Coll (PA)
Penn State Fayette, The Eberly Campus (PA)
Penn State Greater Allegheny (PA)
Penn State Hazleton (PA)
Penn State Lehigh Valley (PA)
Penn State Mont Alto (PA)
Penn State New Kensington (PA)
Penn State Schuylkill (PA)
Penn State Shenango (PA)
Penn State U Park (PA)
Penn State Wilkes-Barre (PA)
Penn State Worthington Scranton (PA)
Penn State York (PA)
Purdue U (IN)
Rensselaer Polytechnic Inst (NY)
Rice U (TX)
Rochester Inst of Technology (NY)
Rose-Hulman Inst of Technology (IN)
Rutgers, The State U of New Jersey, New Brunswick (NJ)
Saint Louis U (MO)
Stanford U (CA)
State U of New York Coll of Environmental Science and Forestry (NY)
Stevens Inst of Technology (NJ)
Stony Brook U, State U of New York (NY)
Syracuse U (NY)
Texas A&M U (TX)
Trinity Coll (CT)
Tulane U (LA)
Union Coll (NY)
U at Buffalo, the State U of New York (NY)
The U of Akron (OH)
The U of Alabama at Birmingham (AL)
The U of British Columbia (BC, Canada)
U of California, Berkeley (CA)
U of California, Davis (CA)
U of California, Irvine (CA)
U of California, Merced (CA)
U of California, Riverside (CA)
U of California, San Diego (CA)
U of California, Santa Cruz (CA)
U of Central Oklahoma (OK)
U of Connecticut (CT)
U of Guelph (ON, Canada)
U of Houston (TX)
U of Idaho (ID)
U of Illinois at Chicago (IL)
U of Illinois at Urbana–Champaign (IL)
The U of Iowa (IA)
U of Louisville (KY)
U of Memphis (TN)
U of Miami (FL)
U of Michigan (MI)
U of Nebraska–Lincoln (NE)
U of Ottawa (ON, Canada)
U of Pennsylvania (PA)
U of Pittsburgh (PA)
U of Rhode Island (RI)
U of Rochester (NY)
U of South Carolina (SC)
U of Southern California (CA)
The U of Texas at Austin (TX)
U of the Pacific (CA)
The U of Toledo (OH)
U of Toronto (ON, Canada)
U of Utah (UT)
U of Virginia (VA)
U of Wisconsin–Madison (WI)
Vanderbilt U (TN)
Virginia Commonwealth U (VA)
Washington State U (WA)
Washington U in St. Louis (MO)
Western New England Coll (MA)
Worcester Polytechnic Inst (MA)
Wright State U (OH)
Yale U (CT)

BIOMEDICAL SCIENCES

Auburn U (AL)
Bridgewater State Coll (MA)
Brigham Young U (UT)
Brock U (ON, Canada)
Central Michigan U (MI)
Charles Drew U of Medicine and Science (CA)
Christian Brothers U (TN)
City Coll of the City U of New York (NY)
Colorado State U (CO)
Florida Inst of Technology (FL)
Inter American U of Puerto Rico, Ponce Campus (PR)
Inter American U of Puerto Rico, San Germán Campus (PR)
Jefferson Coll of Health Sciences (VA)
Keuka Coll (NY)
Marist Coll (NY)
Marquette U (WI)
Maryville U of Saint Louis (MO)
McMurry U (TX)
Mississippi Coll (MS)
North Carolina Central U (NC)
Our Lady of the Lake Coll (LA)
Rochester Inst of Technology (NY)
Rutgers, The State U of New Jersey, New Brunswick (NJ)
St. Cloud State U (MN)
St. Francis Coll (NY)
Slippery Rock U of Pennsylvania (PA)
State U of New York at Fredonia (NY)
Suffolk U (MA)
Texas A&M U (TX)
Texas A&M U–Corpus Christi (TX)
Texas A&M U–Kingsville (TX)
U at Buffalo, the State U of New York (NY)
U of California, Riverside (CA)
U of Colorado Denver (CO)
U of Guelph (ON, Canada)
U of Maine (ME)
U of Michigan–Flint (MI)
U of Minnesota, Duluth (MN)
U of Mississippi (MS)
U of New England (ME)
U of Ottawa (ON, Canada)
U of Pennsylvania (PA)
U of South Alabama (AL)
U of South Florida (FL)
U of Wisconsin–Green Bay (WI)
Washington State U (WA)
Western Michigan U (MI)
Worcester Polytechnic Inst (MA)

BIOMEDICAL TECHNOLOGY

Andrews U (MI)
California State U, East Bay (CA)
DeVry Coll of New York (NY)
DeVry U, Phoenix (AZ)
DeVry U, Fremont (CA)
DeVry U, Pomona (CA)
DeVry U, Miramar (FL)
DeVry U, Orlando (FL)
DeVry U, Decatur (GA)
DeVry U, Addison (IL)
DeVry U, Chicago (IL)
DeVry U, Tinley Park (IL)
DeVry U, Kansas City (MO)
DeVry U, North Brunswick (NJ)
DeVry U, Columbus (OH)
DeVry U, Fort Washington (PA)
DeVry U, Irving (TX)
New York Inst of Technology (NY)
Rutgers, The State U of New Jersey, Camden (NJ)
Suffolk U (MA)
Thomas Edison State Coll (NJ)
Wright State U (OH)

BIOMETRY/BIOMETRICS

Carnegie Mellon U (PA)
Cornell U (NY)
Rutgers, The State U of New Jersey, New Brunswick (NJ)
Stanford U (CA)

BIOPHYSICS

Andrews U (MI)
Bob Jones U (SC)
Brandeis U (MA)
Brigham Young U (UT)
Carnegie Mellon U (PA)
Centenary Coll of Louisiana (LA)
Claremont McKenna Coll (CA)
Columbia U (NY)
Columbia U, School of General Studies (NY)
Freed-Hardeman U (TN)
Hampden-Sydney Coll (VA)
Haverford Coll (PA)
Illinois Inst of Technology (IL)
Iowa State U of Science and Technology (IA)
The Johns Hopkins U (MD)
King Coll (TN)
La Sierra U (CA)
Laurentian U (ON, Canada)
Longwood U (VA)
Loyola U Chicago (IL)
Northeastern U (MA)
Oakland U (MI)
Oklahoma City U (OK)
Pacific Union Coll (CA)
St. Bonaventure U (NY)
St. Lawrence U (NY)
Saint Mary's U of Minnesota (MN)
Southern Adventist U (TN)

- Southwestern Oklahoma State U (OK)
- State U of New York Coll at Geneseo (NY)
- Suffolk U (MA)
- Temple U (PA)
- U at Buffalo, the State U of New York (NY)
- The U of British Columbia (BC, Canada)
- U of California, Los Angeles (CA)
- U of California, San Diego (CA)
- U of Connecticut (CT)
- U of Guelph (ON, Canada)
- U of Illinois at Urbana–Champaign (IL)
- U of Michigan (MI)
- U of New Brunswick Fredericton (NB, Canada)
- U of Pennsylvania (PA)
- The U of Scranton (PA)
- U of Southern California (CA)
- U of Southern Indiana (IN)
- U of Toronto (ON, Canada)
- The U of Western Ontario (ON, Canada)
- Washington & Jefferson Coll (PA)
- Washington U in St. Louis (MO)
- Whitman Coll (WA)

BIOPSYCHOLOGY

- Bucknell U (PA)
- Carnegie Mellon U (PA)
- Columbia U (NY)
- Grand Valley State U (MI)
- Immaculata U (PA)
- Lehigh U (PA)
- Messiah Coll (PA)
- Monmouth Coll (IL)
- Morningside Coll (IA)
- Mount Allison U (NB, Canada)
- Nebraska Wesleyan U (NE)
- Northwest Missouri State U (MO)
- Oglethorpe U (GA)
- Philadelphia U (PA)
- Rider U (NJ)
- Spring Hill Coll (AL)
- U of California, Santa Barbara (CA)
- U of Pittsburgh at Johnstown (PA)
- Viterbo U (WI)
- Wagner Coll (NY)
- Washington U in St. Louis (MO)

BIOSTATISTICS

- Emmanuel Coll (MA)
- Tulane U (LA)
- U at Buffalo, the State U of New York (NY)
- The U of North Carolina at Chapel Hill (NC)
- U of Washington (WA)

BIOTECHNOLOGY

- Bay Path Coll (MA)
- Brock U (ON, Canada)
- California State Polytechnic U, Pomona (CA)
- Calvin Coll (MI)
- Central Baptist Coll (AR)
- Claflin U (SC)
- The Coll at Brockport, State U of New York (NY)
- Delaware State U (DE)
- East Stroudsburg U of Pennsylvania (PA)
- Elizabethtown Coll (PA)
- Endicott Coll (MA)
- Fayetteville State U (NC)
- Ferris State U (MI)
- Fitchburg State Coll (MA)
- Florida Gulf Coast U (FL)
- Grand View U (IA)
- Hunter Coll of the City U of New York (NY)
- Indiana U Bloomington (IN)
- Indiana U East (IN)
- Indiana U–Purdue U Indianapolis (IN)
- Inter American U of Puerto Rico, Aguadilla Campus (PR)
- Inter American U of Puerto Rico, Arecibo Campus (PR)
- James Madison U (VA)
- Kennesaw State U (GA)
- Kent State U (OH)
- Manhattan Coll (NY)
- Marywood U (PA)
- Missouri Baptist U (MO)
- Missouri Western State U (MO)
- Montana State U (MT)
- North Dakota State U (ND)
- Oregon State U (OR)
- Plymouth State U (NH)
- Point Park U (PA)
- Rochester Inst of Technology (NY)
- Roosevelt U (IL)
- Rutgers, The State U of New Jersey, New Brunswick (NJ)
- South Dakota State U (SD)
- Southeastern Oklahoma State U (OK)
- State U of New York at New Paltz (NY)
- State U of New York Coll of Environmental Science and Forestry (NY)
- U at Buffalo, the State U of New York (NY)
- The U of British Columbia (BC, Canada)
- U of California, Davis (CA)
- U of California, San Diego (CA)
- U of Central Florida (FL)
- U of Delaware (DE)
- U of Georgia (GA)
- U of Houston (TX)
- U of Illinois at Urbana–Champaign (IL)
- U of Lethbridge (AB, Canada)
- U of Maryland U Coll (MD)
- U of Massachusetts Boston (MA)
- U of Nebraska at Omaha (NE)
- U of Nevada, Reno (NV)
- The U of North Carolina at Pembroke (NC)
- U of Northern Iowa (IA)
- U of Saskatchewan (SK, Canada)
- U of Southern Maine (ME)
- U of Waterloo (ON, Canada)
- U of Windsor (ON, Canada)
- U of Wisconsin–River Falls (WI)
- Ursuline Coll (OH)
- Utah Valley U (UT)
- Wilfrid Laurier U (ON, Canada)
- Winston-Salem State U (NC)
- Worcester State Coll (MA)
- York Coll of the City U of New York (NY)
- York U (ON, Canada)

BOTANY/PLANT BIOLOGY

- Andrews U (MI)
- Arizona State U (AZ)
- Auburn U (AL)
- Bennington Coll (VT)
- California State Polytechnic U, Pomona (CA)
- California State U, Long Beach (CA)
- Coll of the Atlantic (ME)
- Colorado State U (CO)
- Connecticut Coll (CT)
- Fort Valley State U (GA)
- Goddard Coll (VT)
- Humboldt State U (CA)
- Idaho State U (ID)
- Iowa State U of Science and Technology (IA)
- Juniata Coll (PA)
- Kent State U (OH)
- Marlboro Coll (VT)
- Miami U (OH)
- Michigan State U (MI)
- North Carolina State U (NC)
- North Dakota State U (ND)
- Northern Arizona U (AZ)
- The Ohio State U (OH)
- Ohio U (OH)
- Ohio Wesleyan U (OH)
- Oklahoma State U (OK)
- Oregon State U (OR)
- Purdue U (IN)
- Rutgers, The State U of New Jersey, Newark (NJ)
- St. Cloud State U (MN)
- Saint Xavier U (IL)
- San Francisco State U (CA)
- Sonoma State U (CA)
- Southern Illinois U Carbondale (IL)
- Southern Utah U (UT)
- State U of New York Coll of Environmental Science and Forestry (NY)
- Texas State U–San Marcos (TX)
- The U of Akron (OH)
- U of Alberta (AB, Canada)
- U of California, Berkeley (CA)
- U of California, Davis (CA)
- U of California, Irvine (CA)
- U of California, Riverside (CA)
- U of Delaware (DE)
- U of Florida (FL)
- U of Georgia (GA)
- U of Hawaii at Manoa (HI)
- U of Illinois at Urbana–Champaign (IL)
- U of Maine (ME)
- U of Manitoba (MB, Canada)
- U of Minnesota, Twin Cities Campus (MN)
- U of Nebraska–Lincoln (NE)
- U of New Brunswick Fredericton (NB, Canada)
- U of New Hampshire (NH)
- U of Oklahoma (OK)
- The U of Tennessee (TN)
- The U of Texas at El Paso (TX)
- U of Toronto (ON, Canada)
- U of Vermont (VT)
- U of Washington (WA)
- U of Wisconsin–Madison (WI)
- U of Wyoming (WY)
- Utah State U (UT)
- Weber State U (UT)

BOTANY/PLANT BIOLOGY RELATED

- Frostburg State U (MD)
- Miami U Hamilton (OH)
- Pittsburg State U (KS)
- Prescott Coll (AZ)
- U of Hawaii at Manoa (HI)

BROADCAST JOURNALISM

- Auburn U (AL)
- Barry U (FL)
- Belmont U (TN)
- Bemidji State U (MN)
- Bob Jones U (SC)
- Bowie State U (MD)
- Bowling Green State U (OH)
- Brigham Young U (UT)
- Brooklyn Coll of the City U of New York (NY)
- Buffalo State Coll, State U of New York (NY)
- California State U, East Bay (CA)
- California State U, Long Beach (CA)
- Calvary Bible Coll and Theological Sem (MO)
- Carson-Newman Coll (TN)
- Central State U (OH)
- Chapman U (CA)
- Chatham U (PA)
- The Coll at Brockport, State U of New York (NY)
- The Coll of New Rochelle (NY)
- Coll of the Ozarks (MO)
- Columbia Coll Chicago (IL)
- Delaware State U (DE)
- Drake U (IA)
- Drury U (MO)
- East Carolina U (NC)
- Edinboro U of Pennsylvania (PA)
- Elon U (NC)
- Emerson Coll (MA)
- Evangel U (MO)
- Five Towns Coll (NY)
- Florida Intl U (FL)
- Florida Southern Coll (FL)
- Fordham U (NY)
- Gettysburg Coll (PA)
- Gonzaga U (WA)
- Goshen Coll (IN)
- Hampton U (VA)
- Harding U (AR)
- Hardin-Simmons U (TX)
- Hawai'i Pacific U (HI)
- Humboldt State U (CA)
- Huntington U (IN)
- Ithaca Coll (NY)
- John Brown U (AR)
- Kuyper Coll (MI)
- Lamar U (TX)
- La Salle U (PA)
- Lewis U (IL)
- Lindenwood U (MO)
- Long Island U, C.W. Post Campus (NY)
- Louisiana Coll (LA)
- Marquette U (WI)
- Minnesota State U Moorhead (MN)
- Montclair State U (NJ)
- Mount Vernon Nazarene U (OH)
- New England School of Communications (ME)
- Northern Kentucky U (KY)
- North Greenville U (SC)
- Ohio U (OH)
- Ohio Wesleyan U (OH)
- Oklahoma Christian U (OK)
- Oklahoma City U (OK)
- Paine Coll (GA)
- Point Park U (PA)
- Quinnipiac U (CT)
- St. Cloud State U (MN)
- Southern Adventist U (TN)
- Southwestern Adventist U (TX)
- Southwestern Assemblies of God U (TX)
- State U of New York at Fredonia (NY)
- State U of New York at New Paltz (NY)
- State U of New York at Oswego (NY)
- State U of New York at Plattsburgh (NY)
- Stephens Coll (MO)
- Suffolk U (MA)
- Texas Christian U (TX)
- Troy U (AL)
- Union U (TN)
- U of Central Oklahoma (OK)
- U of Cincinnati (OH)
- U of Colorado at Boulder (CO)
- U of Dayton (OH)
- The U of Findlay (OH)
- U of Georgia (GA)
- U of Illinois at Urbana–Champaign (IL)
- U of La Verne (CA)
- U of Miami (FL)
- U of Missouri (MO)
- U of Nebraska at Omaha (NE)
- U of Nebraska–Lincoln (NE)
- U of Nevada, Reno (NV)
- U of Northern Iowa (IA)
- U of North Texas (TX)
- U of Oklahoma (OK)
- U of St. Thomas (MN)
- U of South Carolina (SC)
- U of Southern California (CA)
- The U of Texas at El Paso (TX)
- U of the Ozarks (AR)
- U of Wisconsin–Madison (WI)
- U of Wisconsin–Milwaukee (WI)
- U of Wisconsin–Oshkosh (WI)
- U of Wisconsin–Platteville (WI)
- U of Wisconsin–River Falls (WI)
- U of Wisconsin–Superior (WI)
- Waldorf Coll (IA)
- Wartburg Coll (IA)
- Washington Adventist U (MD)
- Washington State U (WA)
- Webster U (MO)
- Winona State U (MN)

BUDDHIST STUDIES

- U of the West (CA)

BUILDING/CONSTRUCTION FINISHING, MANAGEMENT, AND INSPECTION RELATED

- California State U, Long Beach (CA)
- Hampton U (VA)
- John Brown U (AR)
- Minnesota State U Mankato (MN)
- Polytechnic Inst of NYU (NY)
- Pratt Inst (NY)
- U of Cincinnati (OH)
- U of Maryland Eastern Shore (MD)
- U of Minnesota, Twin Cities Campus (MN)
- U of the District of Columbia (DC)
- U of Wisconsin–Madison (WI)
- U of Wisconsin–Platteville (WI)

BUILDING/CONSTRUCTION SITE MANAGEMENT

- Bob Jones U (SC)

BUILDING/HOME/ CONSTRUCTION INSPECTION

- Tuskegee U (AL)

BUSINESS ADMINISTRATION AND MANAGEMENT

- Abilene Christian U (TX)
- Acadia U (NS, Canada)
- Adams State Coll (CO)
- Adelphi U (NY)
- AIB Coll of Business (IA)
- Alabama Ag and Mech U (AL)
- Alabama State U (AL)
- Alaska Pacific U (AK)
- Albany State U (GA)
- Albertus Magnus Coll (CT)
- Albion Coll (MI)
- Albright Coll (PA)
- Alcorn State U (MS)
- Alderson-Broaddus Coll (WV)
- Alfred U (NY)
- Allen U (SC)
- Alliant Intl U (CA)
- Alliant Intl U–México City (Mexico)
- Alma Coll (MI)
- Alvernia U (PA)
- Alverno Coll (WI)
- Amberton U (TX)
- American Intl Coll (MA)
- American Jewish U (CA)
- American Public U System (WV)
- American U (DC)
- The American U in Dubai (United Arab Emirates)
- American U of Beirut (Lebanon)
- Amridge U (AL)
- Anderson U (IN)
- Angelo State U (TX)
- Antioch U McGregor (OH)
- Appalachian State U (NC)
- Aquinas Coll (MI)
- Arcadia U (PA)
- Argosy U, Atlanta (GA)
- Argosy U, Chicago (IL)
- Argosy U, Dallas (TX)
- Argosy U, Denver (CO)
- Argosy U, Hawai'i (HI)
- Argosy U, Inland Empire (CA)
- Argosy U, Los Angeles (CA)
- Argosy U, Nashville (TN)
- Argosy U, Orange County (CA)
- Argosy U, Phoenix (AZ)
- Argosy U, Salt Lake City (UT)
- Argosy U, San Diego (CA)
- Argosy U, San Francisco Bay Area (CA)
- Argosy U, Sarasota (FL)
- Argosy U, Schaumburg (IL)
- Argosy U, Seattle (WA)
- Argosy U, Tampa (FL)
- Argosy U, Twin Cities (MN)
- Argosy U, Washington DC (VA)
- Arizona State U (AZ)
- Arkansas State U–Jonesboro (AR)
- Arkansas Tech U (AR)
- Ashland U (OH)
- Assumption Coll (MA)
- Athabasca U (AB, Canada)
- Atlanta Christian Coll (GA)
- Atlantic Union Coll (MA)
- Auburn U (AL)
- Auburn U Montgomery (AL)
- Augsburg Coll (MN)
- Augustana Coll (IL)
- Augustana Coll (SD)
- Aurora U (IL)
- Austin Coll (TX)
- Austin Peay State U (TN)
- Avila U (MO)
- Azusa Pacific U (CA)
- Babson Coll (MA)
- Baker Coll of Auburn Hills (MI)
- Baker Coll of Owosso (MI)
- Baldwin-Wallace Coll (OH)
- Ball State U (IN)
- Baptist Bible Coll of Pennsylvania (PA)
- Barclay Coll (KS)
- Barry U (FL)
- Barton Coll (NC)
- Bauder Coll (GA)
- Baylor U (TX)
- Bay Path Coll (MA)
- Belhaven U (MS)
- Belmont Abbey Coll (NC)
- Belmont U (TN)
- Beloit Coll (WI)
- Bemidji State U (MN)
- Benedictine Coll (KS)
- Bennett Coll for Women (NC)
- Bentley U (MA)
- Berea Coll (KY)
- Bernard M. Baruch Coll of the City U of New York (NY)
- Bethany Coll (KS)
- Bethany Lutheran Coll (MN)
- Bethel Coll (IN)
- Bethel U (MN)
- Bethel U (TN)
- Bethune-Cookman U (FL)
- Birmingham-Southern Coll (AL)
- Bishop's U (QC, Canada)
- Blackburn Coll (IL)
- Black Hills State U (SD)
- Bloomfield Coll (NJ)
- Bloomsburg U of Pennsylvania (PA)
- Bluefield Coll (VA)
- Bluefield State Coll (WV)
- Blue Mountain Coll (MS)
- Bluffton U (OH)
- Bob Jones U (SC)
- Boise State U (ID)
- Boston Coll (MA)
- Boston U (MA)
- Bowie State U (MD)
- Bowling Green State U (OH)
- Bradley U (IL)
- Brevard Coll (NC)
- Brewton-Parker Coll (GA)
- Briar Cliff U (IA)
- Bridgewater Coll (VA)
- Bridgewater State Coll (MA)
- Brigham Young U–Hawaii (HI)
- Brock U (ON, Canada)
- Brookline Coll, Phoenix (AZ)
- Brookline Coll, Tempe (AZ)
- Brookline Coll, Tucson (AZ)
- Brookline Coll (NM)
- Brown Mackie Coll–Albuquerque (NM)
- Brown Mackie Coll–Boise (ID)
- Brown Mackie Coll–Fort Wayne (IN)
- Brown Mackie Coll–Greenville (SC)
- Brown Mackie Coll–Indianapolis (IN)
- Brown Mackie Coll–Louisville (KY)
- Brown Mackie Coll–Merrillville (IN)
- Brown Mackie Coll–Miami (FL)

Maryville U of Saint Louis (MO)
Marywood U (PA)
Massachusetts Coll of Liberal Arts (MA)
The Master's Coll and Sem (CA)
Mayville State U (ND)
McDaniel Coll (MD)
McKendree U (IL)
McMurry U (TX)
McNeese State U (LA)
McPherson Coll (KS)
Medaille Coll (NY)
Memorial U of Newfoundland (NL, Canada)
Menlo Coll (CA)
Mercy Coll (NY)
Meredith Coll (NC)
Meritus U (NB, Canada)
Messiah Coll (PA)
Methodist U (NC)
Metropolitan Coll of New York (NY)
Metropolitan State Coll of Denver (CO)
Miami U (OH)
Michigan State U (MI)
Michigan Technological U (MI)
MidAmerica Nazarene U (KS)
Mid-Continent U (KY)
Middle Tennessee State U (TN)
Midway Coll (KY)
Midwestern State U (TX)
Millersville U of Pennsylvania (PA)
Milligan Coll (TN)
Millsaps Coll (MS)
Milwaukee School of Eng (WI)
Minnesota State U Mankato (MN)
Minnesota State U Moorhead (MN)
Minot State U (ND)
Misericordia U (PA)
Mississippi Coll (MS)
Mississippi State U (MS)
Mississippi U for Women (MS)
Mississippi Valley State U (MS)
Missouri Baptist U (MO)
Missouri State U (MO)
Missouri U of Science and Technology (MO)
Missouri Western State U (MO)
Mitchell Coll (CT)
Molloy Coll (NY)
Monmouth Coll (IL)
Monmouth U (NJ)
Monroe Coll, Bronx (NY)
Monroe Coll, New Rochelle (NY)
Montana State U Billings (MT)
Montclair State U (NJ)
Moravian Coll (PA)
Morehead State U (KY)
Morehouse Coll (GA)
Morningside Coll (IA)
Morris Coll (SC)
Mount Allison U (NB, Canada)
Mount Aloysius Coll (PA)
Mount Ida Coll (MA)
Mount Marty Coll (SD)
Mount Mary Coll (WI)
Mount Mercy Coll (IA)
Mount Olive Coll (NC)
Mount Saint Mary Coll (NY)
Mount Vernon Nazarene U (OH)
Muhlenberg Coll (PA)
Murray State U (KY)
National U (CA)
Nazareth Coll of Rochester (NY)
Nebraska Wesleyan U (NE)
Neumann U (PA)
Nevada State Coll at Henderson (NV)
Newberry Coll (SC)
Newbury Coll (MA)
New England Coll (NH)
New Jersey City U (NJ)
New Jersey Inst of Technology (NJ)
Newman U (KS)
New Mexico Highlands U (NM)
New Mexico Inst of Mining and Technology (NM)
New Mexico State U (NM)
Niagara U (NY)
Nicholls State U (LA)
Nichols Coll (MA)
Nipissing U (ON, Canada)
North Carolina Central U (NC)
North Carolina State U (NC)
North Central Coll (IL)
Northcentral U (AZ)
North Dakota State U (ND)
Northeastern Illinois U (IL)
Northeastern State U (OK)
Northeastern U (MA)
Northern Arizona U (AZ)
Northern Kentucky U (KY)
Northern Michigan U (MI)
North Georgia Coll & State U (GA)
North Greenville U (SC)
Northland Coll (WI)
Northwestern Coll (IA)
Northwestern Coll (MN)
Northwestern Oklahoma State U (OK)
Northwestern Polytechnic U (CA)
Northwestern State U of Louisiana (LA)
Northwest Missouri State U (MO)
Northwest Nazarene U (ID)
Northwest U (WA)
Notre Dame de Namur U (CA)
Nova Southeastern U (FL)
Nyack Coll (NY)
Oak Hills Christian Coll (MN)
Oakland City U (IN)
Oakwood U (AL)
Oglethorpe U (GA)
Ohio Dominican U (OH)
Ohio Northern U (OH)
The Ohio State U (OH)
Ohio U (OH)
Ohio Valley U (WV)
Ohio Wesleyan U (OH)
Oklahoma Christian U (OK)
Oklahoma City U (OK)
Oklahoma Panhandle State U (OK)
Oklahoma State U (OK)
Oklahoma Wesleyan U (OK)
Old Dominion U (VA)
Oral Roberts U (OK)
Oregon Inst of Technology (OR)
Oregon State U (OR)
Oregon State U–Cascades (OR)
Ottawa U (KS)
Ouachita Baptist U (AR)
Our Lady of the Lake U of San Antonio (TX)
Pace U (NY)
Pacific Lutheran U (WA)
Pacific States U (CA)
Pacific Union Coll (CA)
Paine Coll (GA)
Park U (MO)
Patricia Stevens Coll (MO)
Patten U (CA)
Peace Coll (NC)
Peirce Coll (PA)
Penn State Beaver (PA)
Penn State Brandywine (PA)
Penn State DuBois (PA)
Penn State Erie, The Behrend Coll (PA)
Penn State Fayette, The Eberly Campus (PA)
Penn State Greater Allegheny (PA)
Penn State Harrisburg (PA)
Penn State Hazleton (PA)
Penn State Mont Alto (PA)
Penn State New Kensington (PA)
Penn State Shenango (PA)
Penn State Wilkes-Barre (PA)
Penn State Worthington Scranton (PA)
Penn State York (PA)
Pennsylvania Coll of Technology (PA)
Pepperdine U, Malibu (CA)
Peru State Coll (NE)
Philadelphia Biblical U (PA)
Philadelphia U (PA)
Piedmont Coll (GA)
Pikeville Coll (KY)
Pioneer Pacific Coll, Wilsonville (OR)
Pittsburg State U (KS)
Plaza Coll (NY)
Plymouth State U (NH)
Point Park U (PA)
Polytechnic U of Puerto Rico (PR)
Pontifical Catholic U of Puerto Rico (PR)
Portland State U (OR)
Post U (CT)
Potomac Coll (DC)
Potomac State Coll of West Virginia U (WV)
Prairie View A&M U (TX)
Presbyterian Coll (SC)
Prescott Coll (AZ)
Principia Coll (IL)
Providence Coll (RI)
Purdue U (IN)
Purdue U Calumet (IN)
Queens U of Charlotte (NC)
Quincy U (IL)
Quinnipiac U (CT)
Radford U (VA)
Ramapo Coll of New Jersey (NJ)
Redeemer U Coll (ON, Canada)
Regent U (VA)
Reinhardt Coll (GA)
Rensselaer Polytechnic Inst (NY)
Rhode Island Coll (RI)
Rhodes Coll (TN)
Rice U (TX)
The Richard Stockton Coll of New Jersey (NJ)
Rider U (NJ)
Ripon Coll (WI)
Rivier Coll (NH)
Roanoke Coll (VA)
Robert Morris U (PA)
Robert Morris U Illinois (IL)
Roberts Wesleyan Coll (NY)
Rochester Coll (MI)
Rochester Inst of Technology (NY)
Rockford Coll (IL)
Rockhurst U (MO)
Rocky Mountain Coll (MT)
Rogers State U (OK)
Roosevelt U (IL)
Rosemont Coll (PA)
Rowan U (NJ)
Royal Military Coll of Canada (ON, Canada)
Russell Sage Coll (NY)
Rutgers, The State U of New Jersey, Camden (NJ)
Rutgers, The State U of New Jersey, Newark (NJ)
Rutgers, The State U of New Jersey, New Brunswick (NJ)
Saginaw Valley State U (MI)
St. Ambrose U (IA)
St. Andrews Presbyterian Coll (NC)
Saint Augustine's Coll (NC)
St. Bonaventure U (NY)
St. Catherine U (MN)
St. Cloud State U (MN)
St. Edward's U (TX)
St. Francis Coll (NY)
Saint Francis U (PA)
St. Francis Xavier U (NS, Canada)
St. John Fisher Coll (NY)
Saint John's U (MN)
St. John's U (NY)
Saint Joseph Coll (CT)
St. Joseph's Coll, Long Island Campus (NY)
St. Joseph's Coll, New York (NY)
Saint Joseph's U (PA)
Saint Leo U (FL)
Saint Louis U (MO)
Saint Martin's U (WA)
Saint Mary-of-the-Woods Coll (IN)
Saint Mary's Coll (IN)
Saint Mary's Coll of California (CA)
St. Mary's U (TX)
Saint Michael's Coll (VT)
St. Norbert Coll (WI)
Saint Paul's Coll (VA)
St. Petersburg Coll (FL)
St. Thomas Aquinas Coll (NY)
St. Thomas U (FL)
Saint Vincent Coll (PA)
Salem Coll (NC)
Salem State Coll (MA)
Salisbury U (MD)
Salve Regina U (RI)
Samford U (AL)
Sam Houston State U (TX)
San Diego Christian Coll (CA)
San Francisco State U (CA)
San Jose State U (CA)
Savannah State U (GA)
Schreiner U (TX)
Seattle Pacific U (WA)
Seattle U (WA)
Seton Hall U (NJ)
Seton Hill U (PA)
Shawnee State U (OH)
Shaw U (NC)
Shenandoah U (VA)
Shepherd U (WV)
Shippensburg U of Pennsylvania (PA)
Shorter U (GA)
Siena Heights U (MI)
Silicon Valley U (CA)
Silver Lake Coll (WI)
Simmons Coll (MA)
Simon Fraser U (BC, Canada)
Simpson Coll (IA)
Simpson U (CA)
Slippery Rock U of Pennsylvania (PA)
Sonoma State U (CA)
South Carolina State U (SC)
Southeastern Louisiana U (LA)
Southeastern Oklahoma State U (OK)
Southeastern U (FL)
Southeast Missouri State U (MO)
Southern Adventist U (TN)
Southern Arkansas U–Magnolia (AR)
Southern Connecticut State U (CT)
Southern Illinois U Carbondale (IL)
Southern Illinois U Edwardsville (IL)
Southern Methodist U (TX)
Southern New Hampshire U (NH)
Southern Oregon U (OR)
Southern U and Ag and Mech Coll (LA)
Southern Utah U (UT)
Southern Vermont Coll (VT)
South U (AL)
South U, Royal Palm Beach (FL)
South U, Tampa (FL)
South U (GA)
South U, Columbia (SC)
South U, Glen Allen (VA)
South U, Virginia Beach (VA)
Southwest Baptist U (MO)
Southwestern Adventist U (TX)
Southwestern Assemblies of God U (TX)
Southwestern Coll (KS)
Southwestern Oklahoma State U (OK)
Southwest Florida Coll, Fort Myers (FL)
Southwest Minnesota State U (MN)
Spring Arbor U (MI)
Spring Hill Coll (AL)
State U of New York at Binghamton (NY)
State U of New York at Fredonia (NY)
State U of New York at New Paltz (NY)
State U of New York at Oswego (NY)
State U of New York at Plattsburgh (NY)
State U of New York Coll at Geneseo (NY)
State U of New York Coll at Old Westbury (NY)
State U of New York Coll at Potsdam (NY)
State U of New York Coll of Technology at Alfred (NY)
State U of New York Empire State Coll (NY)
Stephen F. Austin State U (TX)
Stephens Coll (MO)
Sterling Coll (KS)
Stetson U (FL)
Stevens Inst of Technology (NJ)
Stevenson U (MD)
Stillman Coll (AL)
Stonehill Coll (MA)
Stony Brook U, State U of New York (NY)
Stratford U, Woodbridge (VA)
Strayer U—Akron Campus (OH)
Strayer U—Alexandria Campus (VA)
Strayer U—Allentown Campus (PA)
Strayer U—Anne Arundel Campus (MD)
Strayer U—Arlington Campus (VA)
Strayer U—Augusta Campus (GA)
Strayer U—Baymeadows Campus (FL)
Strayer U—Birmingham Campus (AL)
Strayer U—Brickell Campus (FL)
Strayer U—Center City Campus (PA)
Strayer U—Central Austin Campus (TX)
Strayer U—Chamblee Campus (GA)
Strayer U—Charleston Campus (SC)
Strayer U—Cherry Hill Campus (NJ)
Strayer U—Chesapeake Campus (VA)
Strayer U—Chesterfield Campus (VA)
Strayer U—Christiana Campus (DE)
Strayer U—Cobb County Campus (GA)
Strayer U—Columbia Campus (SC)
Strayer U—Columbus Campus (OH)
Strayer U—Coral Springs Campus (FL)
Strayer U—Cranberry Woods Campus (PA)
Strayer U—Delaware County Campus (PA)
Strayer U—Doral Campus (FL)
Strayer U—Douglasville Campus (GA)
Strayer U—Fairview Park Campus (OH)
Strayer U—Florence Campus (KY)
Strayer U—Fort Lauderdale Campus (FL)
Strayer U—Fredericksburg Campus (VA)
Strayer U—Garner Campus (NC)
Strayer U—Greensboro Campus (NC)
Strayer U—Greenville Campus (SC)
Strayer U—Henrico Campus (VA)
Strayer U—Huntersville Campus (NC)
Strayer U—Huntsville Campus (AL)
Strayer U—King of Prussia Campus (PA)
Strayer U—Knoxville Campus (TN)
Strayer U—Lawrenceville Campus (NJ)
Strayer U—Lexington Campus (KY)
Strayer U—Lithonia Campus (GA)
Strayer U—Little Rock Campus (AR)
Strayer U—Loudoun Campus (VA)
Strayer U—Louisville Campus (KY)
Strayer U—Lower Bucks County Campus (PA)
Strayer U—Maitland Campus (FL)
Strayer U—Manassas Campus (VA)
Strayer U—Mason Campus (OH)
Strayer U—Metairie Campus (LA)
Strayer U—Miramar Campus (FL)
Strayer U—Morrow Campus (GA)
Strayer U—Nashville Campus (TN)
Strayer U—New Brunswick Campus (NJ)
Strayer U—Newport News Campus (VA)
Strayer U—North Charlotte Campus (NC)
Strayer U—North Raleigh Campus (NC)
Strayer U—Orlando East Campus (FL)
Strayer U—Owings Mills Campus (MD)
Strayer U—Palm Beach Gardens Campus (FL)
Strayer U—Penn Center West Campus (PA)
Strayer U—Prince George's Campus (MD)
Strayer U—Rockville Campus (MD)
Strayer U—Roswell Campus (GA)
Strayer U—RTP Campus (NC)
Strayer U—Salt Lake Campus (UT)
Strayer U—Sand Lake Campus (FL)
Strayer U—Savannah Campus (GA)
Strayer U—Shelby Oaks Campus (TN)
Strayer U—South Charlotte Campus (NC)
Strayer U—Takoma Park Campus (DC)
Strayer U—Tampa East Campus (FL)
Strayer U—Tampa Westshore Campus (FL)
Strayer U—Teays Valley Campus (WV)
Strayer U—Thousand Oaks Campus (TN)
Strayer U—Virginia Beach Campus (VA)
Strayer U—Washington Campus (DC)
Strayer U—White Marsh Campus (MD)
Strayer U—Willingboro Campus (NJ)
Strayer U—Woodbridge Campus (VA)
Suffolk U (MA)
Sullivan U (KY)
Sul Ross State U (TX)
Susquehanna U (PA)
Syracuse U (NY)
Tabor Coll (KS)
Talladega Coll (AL)
Tarleton State U (TX)
Taylor U (IN)
Temple U (PA)
Tennessee Technological U (TN)
Tennessee Wesleyan Coll (TN)
Texas A&M Intl U (TX)
Texas A&M U (TX)
Texas A&M U at Galveston (TX)
Texas A&M U–Commerce (TX)
Texas A&M U–Corpus Christi (TX)
Texas A&M U–Kingsville (TX)
Texas Coll (TX)
Texas Lutheran U (TX)
Texas Southern U (TX)
Texas State U–San Marcos (TX)
Texas Tech U (TX)
Texas Wesleyan U (TX)
Texas Woman's U (TX)
Thiel Coll (PA)
Thomas Edison State Coll (NJ)
Thomas More Coll (KY)
Thompson Rivers U (BC, Canada)
Tiffin U (OH)
Towson U (MD)
Transylvania U (KY)
Trent U (ON, Canada)
Trevecca Nazarene U (TN)
Trine U (IN)
Trinity Christian Coll (IL)
Trinity U (TX)
Troy U (AL)
Truett-McConnell Coll (GA)
Truman State U (MO)
Tulane U (LA)

Tusculum Coll (TN)
Tuskegee U (AL)
Union Coll (KY)
Union Coll (NE)
Union Inst & U (OH)
Union U (TN)
United States Air Force Acad (CO)
United States Military Acad (NY)
Universidad Adventista de las Antillas (PR)
Universidad de las Américas–Puebla (Mexico)
Université du Québec en Outaouais (QC, Canada)
U at Albany, State U of New York (NY)
U at Buffalo, the State U of New York (NY)
The U of Akron (OH)
The U of Alabama (AL)
The U of Alabama at Birmingham (AL)
The U of Alabama in Huntsville (AL)
U of Alaska Anchorage (AK)
U of Alaska Fairbanks (AK)
U of Alaska Southeast (AK)
U of Alberta (AB, Canada)
U of Arkansas (AR)
U of Arkansas at Fort Smith (AR)
U of Arkansas at Little Rock (AR)
U of Arkansas at Monticello (AR)
U of Arkansas at Pine Bluff (AR)
U of Atlanta (GA)
U of Baltimore (MD)
The U of British Columbia (BC, Canada)
U of California, Berkeley (CA)
U of California, Irvine (CA)
U of California, Riverside (CA)
U of Central Florida (FL)
U of Central Missouri (MO)
U of Central Oklahoma (OK)
U of Charleston (WV)
U of Cincinnati (OH)
U of Colorado at Colorado Springs (CO)
U of Colorado Denver (CO)
U of Dallas (TX)
U of Dayton (OH)
U of Delaware (DE)
U of Denver (CO)
U of Dubuque (IA)
U of Evansville (IN)
The U of Findlay (OH)
U of Florida (FL)
U of Georgia (GA)
U of Guam (GU)
U of Hartford (CT)
U of Hawaii at Hilo (HI)
U of Hawaii at Manoa (HI)
U of Hawaii–West Oahu (HI)
U of Houston–Clear Lake (TX)
U of Houston–Downtown (TX)
U of Houston–Victoria (TX)
U of Illinois at Chicago (IL)
U of Illinois at Springfield (IL)
U of Illinois at Urbana–Champaign (IL)
The U of Iowa (IA)
The U of Kansas (KS)
U of La Verne (CA)
U of Lethbridge (AB, Canada)
U of Louisiana at Monroe (LA)
U of Louisville (KY)
U of Maine (ME)
U of Maine at Augusta (ME)
U of Maine at Fort Kent (ME)
U of Maine at Machias (ME)
U of Maine at Presque Isle (ME)
U of Manitoba (MB, Canada)
U of Mary (ND)
U of Mary Hardin-Baylor (TX)
U of Maryland Eastern Shore (MD)
U of Maryland U Coll (MD)
U of Mary Washington (VA)
U of Massachusetts Amherst (MA)
U of Massachusetts Boston (MA)
U of Massachusetts Lowell (MA)
U of Memphis (TN)
U of Miami (FL)
U of Michigan (MI)
U of Michigan–Dearborn (MI)
U of Michigan–Flint (MI)
U of Minnesota, Crookston (MN)
U of Mississippi (MS)
U of Missouri (MO)
U of Missouri–Kansas City (MO)
U of Missouri–St. Louis (MO)
U of Mobile (AL)
U of Montevallo (AL)
U of Mount Union (OH)
U of Nebraska at Kearney (NE)
U of Nebraska at Omaha (NE)
U of Nebraska–Lincoln (NE)
U of Nevada, Las Vegas (NV)
U of New Brunswick Fredericton (NB, Canada)
U of New England (ME)
U of New Hampshire (NH)
U of New Hampshire at Manchester (NH)
U of New Haven (CT)
U of New Mexico (NM)
U of New Orleans (LA)
U of North Alabama (AL)
The U of North Carolina at Asheville (NC)
The U of North Carolina at Chapel Hill (NC)
The U of North Carolina at Charlotte (NC)
The U of North Carolina at Greensboro (NC)
The U of North Carolina at Pembroke (NC)
The U of North Carolina Wilmington (NC)
U of North Dakota (ND)
U of Northern Colorado (CO)
U of Northern Iowa (IA)
U of North Florida (FL)
U of Oklahoma (OK)
U of Pennsylvania (PA)
U of Pittsburgh at Bradford (PA)
U of Pittsburgh at Greensburg (PA)
U of Pittsburgh at Johnstown (PA)
U of Portland (OR)
U of Puget Sound (WA)
U of Redlands (CA)
U of Regina (SK, Canada)
U of Rhode Island (RI)
U of Richmond (VA)
U of Rio Grande (OH)
U of St. Francis (IL)
U of Saint Mary (KS)
U of St. Thomas (MN)
U of St. Thomas (TX)
U of San Diego (CA)
U of San Francisco (CA)
U of Saskatchewan (SK, Canada)
The U of Scranton (PA)
U of South Alabama (AL)
U of South Carolina (SC)
U of South Carolina Aiken (SC)
U of South Carolina Beaufort (SC)
U of South Carolina Upstate (SC)
U of Southern California (CA)
U of Southern Indiana (IN)
U of Southern Maine (ME)
U of Southern Mississippi (MS)
U of South Florida (FL)
The U of Tennessee (TN)
The U of Tennessee at Chattanooga (TN)
The U of Tennessee at Martin (TN)
The U of Texas at Arlington (TX)
The U of Texas at Brownsville (TX)
The U of Texas at El Paso (TX)
The U of Texas at San Antonio (TX)
The U of Texas at Tyler (TX)
The U of Texas of the Permian Basin (TX)
The U of Texas–Pan American (TX)
U of the District of Columbia (DC)
U of the Incarnate Word (TX)
U of the Ozarks (AR)
U of the Pacific (CA)
U of the Southwest (NM)
U of the Virgin Islands (VI)
U of the West (CA)
The U of Toledo (OH)
U of Toronto (ON, Canada)
U of Tulsa (OK)
U of Utah (UT)
U of Vermont (VT)
The U of Virginia's Coll at Wise (VA)
U of Washington (WA)
U of Washington, Bothell (WA)
U of Washington, Tacoma (WA)
U of Waterloo (ON, Canada)
The U of West Alabama (AL)
The U of Western Ontario (ON, Canada)
U of West Florida (FL)
U of West Georgia (GA)
U of Windsor (ON, Canada)
U of Wisconsin–Eau Claire (WI)
U of Wisconsin–Green Bay (WI)
U of Wisconsin–La Crosse (WI)
U of Wisconsin–Madison (WI)
U of Wisconsin–Milwaukee (WI)
U of Wisconsin–Oshkosh (WI)
U of Wisconsin–Parkside (WI)
U of Wisconsin–Platteville (WI)
U of Wisconsin–River Falls (WI)
U of Wisconsin–Stevens Point (WI)
U of Wisconsin–Stout (WI)
U of Wisconsin–Superior (WI)
U of Wisconsin–Whitewater (WI)
U of Wyoming (WY)
Upper Iowa U (IA)
Ursinus Coll (PA)
Ursuline Coll (OH)
Utah State U (UT)
Utah Valley U (UT)
Utica Coll (NY)
Valdosta State U (GA)
Valley City State U (ND)
Vanguard U of Southern California (CA)
Vermont Tech Coll (VT)
Villanova U (PA)
Virginia Commonwealth U (VA)
Virginia Intermont Coll (VA)
Virginia Polytechnic Inst and State U (VA)
Virginia State U (VA)
Virginia Union U (VA)
Virginia U of Lynchburg (VA)
Virginia Wesleyan Coll (VA)
Viterbo U (WI)
Voorhees Coll (SC)
Wagner Coll (NY)
Walden U (MN)
Waldorf Coll (IA)
Walsh U (OH)
Warner Pacific Coll (OR)
Wartburg Coll (IA)
Washburn U (KS)
Washington Adventist U (MD)
Washington and Lee U (VA)
Washington Coll (MD)
Washington State U (WA)
Washington U in St. Louis (MO)
Wayland Baptist U (TX)
Waynesburg U (PA)
Wayne State Coll (NE)
Webber Intl U (FL)
Weber State U (UT)
Webster U (MO)
Wells Coll (NY)
Wesleyan Coll (GA)
West Chester U of Pennsylvania (PA)
Western Carolina U (NC)
Western Connecticut State U (CT)
Western Illinois U (IL)
Western Intl U (AZ)
Western Kentucky U (KY)
Western New England Coll (MA)
Western State Coll of Colorado (CO)
Western Washington U (WA)
Westfield State Coll (MA)
West Liberty U (WV)
Westminster Coll (MO)
West Virginia State U (WV)
West Virginia U (WV)
West Virginia Wesleyan Coll (WV)
Wheeling Jesuit U (WV)
Whittier Coll (CA)
Wichita State U (KS)
Widener U (PA)
Wilberforce U (OH)
Wilfrid Laurier U (ON, Canada)
Wilkes U (PA)
William Jewell Coll (MO)
William Paterson U of New Jersey (NJ)
William Penn U (IA)
Wilmington Coll (OH)
Wilmington U (DE)
Wilson Coll (PA)
Wingate U (NC)
Winona State U (MN)
Winston-Salem State U (NC)
Winthrop U (SC)
Wittenberg U (OH)
Woodbury U (CA)
Worcester Polytechnic Inst (MA)
Worcester State Coll (MA)
Wright State U (OH)
Xavier U (OH)
Xavier U of Louisiana (LA)
Yeshiva U (NY)
York Coll (NE)
York Coll of Pennsylvania (PA)
York Coll of the City U of New York (NY)
York U (ON, Canada)
Young Harris Coll (GA)
Youngstown State U (OH)

BUSINESS ADMINISTRATION, MANAGEMENT AND OPERATIONS RELATED

Adams State Coll (CO)
AIB Coll of Business (IA)
Albany State U (GA)
Alverno Coll (WI)
Babson Coll (MA)
Benedictine U (IL)
Bethel U (TN)
Bowling Green State U (OH)
Bradley U (IL)
Bryant & Stratton Coll—Amherst Campus (NY)
California Polytechnic State U, San Luis Obispo (CA)
California State U, Chico (CA)
Capella U (MN)
Capital U (OH)
Carlos Albizu U, Miami Campus (FL)
Central Michigan U (MI)
Cleveland State U (OH)
Cornerstone U (MI)
Culver-Stockton Coll (MO)
Dana Coll (NE)
Davenport U, Grand Rapids (MI)
DePaul U (IL)
DeVry Coll of New York (NY)
DeVry U, Phoenix (AZ)
DeVry U, Fremont (CA)
DeVry U, Long Beach (CA)
DeVry U, Pomona (CA)
DeVry U, Sherman Oaks (CA)
DeVry U, Westminster (CO)
DeVry U, Miramar (FL)
DeVry U, Orlando (FL)
DeVry U, Alpharetta (GA)
DeVry U, Decatur (GA)
DeVry U, Addison (IL)
DeVry U, Chicago (IL)
DeVry U, Tinley Park (IL)
DeVry U, Indianapolis (IN)
DeVry U (KY)
DeVry U (MD)
DeVry U (MI)
DeVry U, Edina (MN)
DeVry U, Kansas City (MO)
DeVry U (NV)
DeVry U, North Brunswick (NJ)
DeVry U, Charlotte (NC)
DeVry U, Columbus (OH)
DeVry U (OK)
DeVry U (OR)
DeVry U, Fort Washington (PA)
DeVry U, Memphis (TN)
DeVry U, Houston (TX)
DeVry U, Irving (TX)
DeVry U (UT)
DeVry U, Arlington (VA)
DeVry U, Federal Way (WA)
DeVry U, Milwaukee (WI)
DeVry U Online (IL)
Dominican U of California (CA)
Eastern New Mexico U (NM)
ECPI Coll of Technology, Virginia Beach (VA)
EDP Coll of Puerto Rico, Inc. (PR)
Elizabethtown Coll (PA)
Embry-Riddle Aeronautical U (AZ)
Embry-Riddle Aeronautical U (FL)
Embry-Riddle Aeronautical U Worldwide (FL)
Florida Inst of Technology (FL)
Franklin U (OH)
Gettysburg Coll (PA)
Grace Coll (IN)
Hodges U (FL)
Hofstra U (NY)
Howard Payne U (TX)
Indiana Tech (IN)
John Brown U (AR)
Kettering U (MI)
La Roche Coll (PA)
Lasell Coll (MA)
Le Moyne Coll (NY)
Limestone Coll (SC)
Malone U (OH)
Mayville State U (ND)
Mercer U (GA)
Miami Dade Coll (FL)
Miami U Hamilton (OH)
Millikin U (IL)
Missouri Baptist U (MO)
Missouri State U (MO)
Morris Coll (SC)
Mountain State U (WV)
Mount Mercy Coll (IA)
North Dakota State U (ND)
Northwest Christian U (OR)
Oakland City U (IN)
Ohio Northern U (OH)
Pennsylvania Coll of Technology (PA)
Point Park U (PA)
Pontifical Catholic U of Puerto Rico (PR)
Post U (CT)
Rider U (NJ)
Saint Mary-of-the-Woods Coll (IN)
St. Petersburg Coll (FL)
Samford U (AL)
San Jose State U (CA)
Somerset Christian Coll (NJ)
Texas A&M U–Kingsville (TX)
Texas Christian U (TX)
Texas Tech U (TX)
Towson U (MD)
Trinity Christian Coll (IL)
The U of Alabama at Birmingham (AL)
U of Charleston (WV)
U of Houston–Clear Lake (TX)
U of Illinois at Springfield (IL)
U of Louisville (KY)
U of Mary (ND)
U of Maryland, Baltimore County (MD)
U of Michigan–Dearborn (MI)
U of Ottawa (ON, Canada)
U of Pennsylvania (PA)
U of Puerto Rico at Bayamón (PR)
U of Puerto Rico, Cayey U Coll (PR)
U of St. Thomas (MN)
The U of Scranton (PA)
U of the Incarnate Word (TX)
The U of Toledo (OH)
U of Waterloo (ON, Canada)
The U of Western Ontario (ON, Canada)
U of Wisconsin–River Falls (WI)
U of Wyoming (WY)
Ursuline Coll (OH)
Viterbo U (WI)
Washington U in St. Louis (MO)
Widener U (PA)
William Jessup U (CA)
Woodbury U (CA)

BUSINESS AND PERSONAL/ FINANCIAL SERVICES MARKETING

Nipissing U (ON, Canada)

BUSINESS AUTOMATION/ TECHNOLOGY/DATA ENTRY

East Carolina U (NC)
East Central U (OK)
Inter American U of Puerto Rico, Bayamón Campus (PR)
Pontifical Catholic U of Puerto Rico (PR)
Universidad de las Américas–Puebla (Mexico)

BUSINESS/COMMERCE

Adams State Coll (CO)
AIB Coll of Business (IA)
Alabama Ag and Mech U (AL)
Alvernia U (PA)
American Coll of Thessaloniki (Greece)
Andrew Jackson U (AL)
Asbury U (KY)
Auburn U Montgomery (AL)
Aurora U (IL)
Avila U (MO)
Baker Coll of Jackson (MI)
Baker U (KS)
Ball State U (IN)
Baylor U (TX)
Bellarmine U (KY)
Bethel Coll (KS)
Bloomsburg U of Pennsylvania (PA)
Bob Jones U (SC)
Bowling Green State U (OH)
Brenau U (GA)
Brescia U (KY)
Brock U (ON, Canada)
Bryant & Stratton Coll (WI)
Cambridge Coll (MA)
Canisius Coll (NY)
Capella U (MN)
The Catholic U of America (DC)
Central Christian Coll of Kansas (KS)
Central State U (OH)
Champlain Coll (VT)
Clayton State U (GA)
Coll of Staten Island of the City U of New York (NY)
Colorado State U–Pueblo (CO)
Columbia Coll (MO)
Columbia Coll, Caguas (PR)
Columbia Coll, Yauco (PR)
Columbus State U (GA)
Concordia Coll (MN)
Concordia U Texas (TX)
Covenant Coll (GA)
Cumberland U (TN)
Davenport U, Grand Rapids (MI)
Delta State U (MS)
Drake U (IA)
Drexel U (PA)
Earlham Coll (IN)
Eastern Connecticut State U (CT)
Eastern Michigan U (MI)
Eastern Nazarene Coll (MA)
East Texas Baptist U (TX)
Edgewood Coll (WI)
Florida Southern Coll (FL)
Florida State U (FL)
Framingham State Coll (MA)
Franklin Coll (IN)
Franklin U (OH)
Free Will Baptist Bible Coll (TN)
Georgia Coll & State U (GA)
Glenville State Coll (WV)
Grand Valley State U (MI)
Harris-Stowe State U (MO)
Hawai'i Pacific U (HI)
HEC Montreal (QC, Canada)
Henderson State U (AR)

INDEXES

Hillsdale Free Will Baptist Coll (OK)
Hofstra U (NY)
Hollins U (VA)
Houston Baptist U (TX)
Howard Payne U (TX)
Hult Intl Business School (United Kingdom)
Huntingdon Coll (AL)
Idaho State U (ID)
Indiana U Bloomington (IN)
Indiana U East (IN)
Indiana U Kokomo (IN)
Indiana U Northwest (IN)
Indiana U of Pennsylvania (PA)
Indiana U–Purdue U Indianapolis (IN)
Indiana U South Bend (IN)
Indiana U Southeast (IN)
Ithaca Coll (NY)
Jacksonville U (FL)
The Johns Hopkins U (MD)
Johnson State Coll (VT)
Judson Coll (AL)
Juniata Coll (PA)
Kansas State U (KS)
Kendall Coll (IL)
Kentucky State U (KY)
Keystone Coll (PA)
La Sierra U (CA)
Lehigh U (PA)
Liberty U (VA)
LIM Coll (NY)
Limestone Coll (SC)
Linfield Coll (OR)
Loras Coll (IA)
Loyola U Maryland (MD)
Manchester Coll (IN)
Marian U (WI)
Maryville Coll (TN)
Maryville U of Saint Louis (MO)
Massachusetts Inst of Technology (MA)
McMurry U (TX)
Medgar Evers Coll of the City U of New York (NY)
Mercer U (GA)
Miami U Hamilton (OH)
Midway Coll (KY)
Midwestern State U (TX)
Milwaukee School of Eng (WI)
Missouri Southern State U (MO)
Missouri State U (MO)
Montana State U (MT)
Montana State U Billings (MT)
Montana Tech of The U of Montana (MT)
Mount Allison U (NB, Canada)
Mount Mercy Coll (IA)
Mount St. Mary's U (MD)
Mount Vernon Nazarene U (OH)
Murray State U (KY)
New Mexico State U (NM)
Niagara U (NY)
Nichols Coll (MA)
Norfolk State U (VA)
Northeastern Illinois U (IL)
Northeastern U (MA)
Northern Kentucky U (KY)
Northern Michigan U (MI)
Oakland U (MI)
Ohio Northern U (OH)
The Ohio State U at Lima (OH)
The Ohio State U at Marion (OH)
The Ohio State U–Mansfield Campus (OH)
The Ohio State U–Newark Campus (OH)
Ohio Valley U (WV)
Oklahoma Christian U (OK)
Oklahoma City U (OK)
Pace U (NY)
Penn State Abington (PA)
Penn State Altoona (PA)
Penn State Berks (PA)
Penn State Lehigh Valley (PA)
Penn State Schuylkill (PA)
Plymouth State U (NH)
Pontifical Catholic U of Puerto Rico (PR)
Prescott Coll (AZ)
Queen's U at Kingston (ON, Canada)
Randolph Coll (VA)
Regis Coll (MA)
Reinhardt Coll (GA)
Rhode Island Coll (RI)
Rochester Inst of Technology (NY)
Roosevelt U (IL)
Saginaw Valley State U (MI)
St. Ambrose U (IA)
Saint Anselm Coll (NH)
Saint Leo U (FL)
Saint Mary's Coll of California (CA)
Saint Vincent Coll (PA)
Saint Xavier U (IL)
Sam Houston State U (TX)
San Diego State U (CA)
Schreiner U (TX)
Skidmore Coll (NY)
Southern Arkansas U–Magnolia (AR)
Southern Methodist U (TX)
Southern Wesleyan U (SC)
Southwestern U (TX)
Spalding U (KY)
Stephen F. Austin State U (TX)
Sweet Briar Coll (VA)
Tarleton State U (TX)
Temple U (PA)
Texas A&M U–Kingsville (TX)
Texas Tech U (TX)
Thomas More Coll (KY)
Thompson Rivers U (BC, Canada)
Transylvania U (KY)
Trinity Christian Coll (IL)
Trinity Coll of Florida (FL)
TUI U (CA)
The U of Arizona (AZ)
U of Arkansas (AR)
U of Arkansas at Little Rock (AR)
U of Bridgeport (CT)
The U of British Columbia (BC, Canada)
U of Central Florida (FL)
U of Central Oklahoma (OK)
U of Colorado Denver (CO)
U of Connecticut (CT)
U of Denver (CO)
U of Georgia (GA)
U of Hawaii at Manoa (HI)
U of Houston–Clear Lake (TX)
U of Houston–Downtown (TX)
U of Illinois at Urbana–Champaign (IL)
The U of Kansas (KS)
U of Kentucky (KY)
U of Maine (ME)
U of Mary Hardin-Baylor (TX)
U of Maryland, Coll Park (MD)
U of Massachusetts Dartmouth (MA)
U of Mississippi (MS)
U of Missouri–St. Louis (MO)
The U of Montana Western (MT)
U of Nebraska at Omaha (NE)
U of Nevada, Reno (NV)
U of North Texas (TX)
U of Notre Dame (IN)
U of Oregon (OR)
U of Pittsburgh (PA)
U of Puerto Rico at Humacao (PR)
U of Puerto Rico, Cayey U Coll (PR)
U of Puerto Rico, Río Piedras (PR)
U of Redlands (CA)
U of Regina (SK, Canada)
U of Rhode Island (RI)
U of San Francisco (CA)
U of Science and Arts of Oklahoma (OK)
U of South Alabama (AL)
The U of South Dakota (SD)
U of Southern Indiana (IN)
U of South Florida (FL)
The U of Tennessee (TN)
The U of Texas at Dallas (TX)
The U of Texas at San Antonio (TX)
U of the Cumberlands (KY)
The U of Toledo (OH)
U of Tulsa (OK)
U of Utah (UT)
U of Virginia (VA)
U of Washington (WA)
The U of Western Ontario (ON, Canada)
U of Windsor (ON, Canada)
U of Wisconsin–Whitewater (WI)
Utah State U (UT)
Valley Forge Christian Coll (PA)
Wake Forest U (NC)
Washburn U (KS)
Washington & Jefferson Coll (PA)
Washington State U (WA)
Washington U in St. Louis (MO)
Webber Intl U (FL)
Webster U (MO)
West Chester U of Pennsylvania (PA)
Western Intl U (AZ)
Western Michigan U (MI)
Western New England Coll (MA)
Western Oregon U (OR)
Western Washington U (WA)
Westminster Coll (UT)
Westmont Coll (CA)
Wright State U (OH)
York U (ON, Canada)
Youngstown State U (OH)

BUSINESS/CORPORATE COMMUNICATIONS

Amridge U (AL)
Aquinas Coll (MI)
Augustana Coll (SD)
Babson Coll (MA)
Bentley U (MA)
Brock U (ON, Canada)
Calvin Coll (MI)
Dana Coll (NE)
Duquesne U (PA)
Elon U (NC)
Fort Hays State U (KS)
Hawai'i Pacific U (HI)
Holy Names U (CA)
Jones Intl U (CO)
Lycoming Coll (PA)
Marietta Coll (OH)
MidAmerica Nazarene U (KS)
Morningside Coll (IA)
Newbury Coll (MA)
Nichols Coll (MA)
North Dakota State U (ND)
Ohio Dominican U (OH)
Penn State Abington (PA)
Point Park U (PA)
Pontifical Catholic U of Puerto Rico (PR)
Rochester Coll (MI)
Rockhurst U (MO)
Saint Leo U (FL)
Southwestern Coll (KS)
Susquehanna U (PA)
The U of Findlay (OH)
U of Houston (TX)
U of Mary (ND)
U of Rio Grande (OH)
U of St. Thomas (MN)
The U of Western Ontario (ON, Canada)
Western Intl U (AZ)

BUSINESS FAMILY AND CONSUMER SCIENCES/ HUMAN SCIENCES

Brigham Young U (UT)
The Ohio State U (OH)
U of Houston (TX)
Virginia Polytechnic Inst and State U (VA)

BUSINESS, MANAGEMENT, AND MARKETING RELATED

Adelphi U (NY)
Arizona State U (AZ)
Baylor U (TX)
Benedictine U (IL)
Bentley U (MA)
Bowling Green State U (OH)
Bridgewater State Coll (MA)
California State U, Dominguez Hills (CA)
California State U, Stanislaus (CA)
Carlow U (PA)
Central Baptist Coll (AR)
Claflin U (SC)
Clemson U (SC)
Corban U (OR)
Drexel U (PA)
Eastern Nazarene Coll (MA)
The Evergreen State Coll (WA)
Full Sail U (FL)
George Mason U (VA)
Greenville Coll (IL)
Indiana Tech (IN)
Inter American U of Puerto Rico, Bayamón Campus (PR)
Loyola U Chicago (IL)
Mercy Coll (NY)
Mercyhurst Coll (PA)
Messiah Coll (PA)
Missouri U of Science and Technology (MO)
Mount Mercy Coll (IA)
Mount Vernon Nazarene U (OH)
Nebraska Wesleyan U (NE)
New Jersey Inst of Technology (NJ)
New York U (NY)
Park U (MO)
Point Park U (PA)
Presentation Coll (SD)
Purdue U North Central (IN)
Sacred Heart U (CT)
Saint Mary's U of Minnesota (MN)
Skidmore Coll (NY)
Southeastern U (FL)
Southern California Inst of Technology (CA)
Southern New Hampshire U (NH)
State U of New York at Plattsburgh (NY)
State U of New York Coll of Technology at Canton (NY)
State U of New York Maritime Coll (NY)
Syracuse U (NY)
Texas Wesleyan U (TX)
Trevecca Nazarene U (TN)
Troy U (AL)
The U of Toledo (OH)
The U of Western Ontario (ON, Canada)
U of Wisconsin–Stout (WI)
Utica Coll (NY)
Wentworth Inst of Technology (MA)
Western State Coll of Colorado (CO)

BUSINESS/MANAGERIAL ECONOMICS

Alabama Ag and Mech U (AL)
Allegheny Coll (PA)
American Intl Coll (MA)
American Jewish U (CA)
Anderson U (IN)
Andrews U (MI)
Arcadia U (PA)
Arkansas State U—Jonesboro (AR)
Auburn U (AL)
Auburn U Montgomery (AL)
Augsburg Coll (MN)
Ball State U (IN)
Bard Coll (NY)
Baylor U (TX)
Belmont U (TN)
Beloit Coll (WI)
Benedictine U (IL)
Bentley U (MA)
Bernard M. Baruch Coll of the City U of New York (NY)
Bethany Coll (KS)
Bethany Coll (WV)
Bishop's U (QC, Canada)
Boise State U (ID)
Boston Coll (MA)
Bradley U (IL)
Brock U (ON, Canada)
Buena Vista U (IA)
California Inst of Technology (CA)
California State U, East Bay (CA)
California State U, Fullerton (CA)
California State U, Long Beach (CA)
California State U, San Bernardino (CA)
Campbellsville U (KY)
Canisius Coll (NY)
Capital U (OH)
Carnegie Mellon U (PA)
Carson-Newman Coll (TN)
Catawba Coll (NC)
Chapman U (CA)
Chatham U (PA)
Christopher Newport U (VA)
Clarion U of Pennsylvania (PA)
Clark Atlanta U (GA)
Cleveland State U (OH)
Coastal Carolina U (SC)
Coll of Mount Saint Vincent (NY)
Coll of the Ozarks (MO)
The Coll of Wooster (OH)
Colorado State U–Pueblo (CO)
Converse Coll (SC)
Dallas Baptist U (TX)
Delaware State U (DE)
DePaul U (IL)
Drexel U (PA)
Duquesne U (PA)
East Central U (OK)
Eastern Michigan U (MI)
Eastern Washington U (WA)
East Tennessee State U (TN)
Elizabethtown Coll (PA)
Elmira Coll (NY)
Emmanuel Coll (MA)
Emory U (GA)
Fairleigh Dickinson U, Coll at Florham (NJ)
Fairleigh Dickinson U, Metropolitan Campus (NJ)
Ferris State U (MI)
Florida Ag and Mech U (FL)
Fordham U (NY)
Fort Hays State U (KS)
Fort Lewis Coll (CO)
Freed-Hardeman U (TN)
The George Washington U (DC)
Georgia Coll & State U (GA)
Georgia Inst of Technology (GA)
Georgia Southern U (GA)
Georgia State U (GA)
Gonzaga U (WA)
Grambling State U (LA)
Grand Valley State U (MI)
Green Mountain Coll (VT)
Greensboro Coll (NC)
Grove City Coll (PA)
Gustavus Adolphus Coll (MN)
Hampden-Sydney Coll (VA)
HEC Montreal (QC, Canada)
Hofstra U (NY)
Hope Coll (MI)
Houston Baptist U (TX)
Huntington U (IN)
Illinois Coll (IL)
Indiana U–Purdue U Fort Wayne (IN)
Inter American U of Puerto Rico, Bayamón Campus (PR)
Inter American U of Puerto Rico, San Germán Campus (PR)
Ithaca Coll (NY)
Jackson State U (MS)
James Madison U (VA)
Jamestown Coll (ND)
Kalamazoo Coll (MI)
Kennesaw State U (GA)
Kent State U (OH)
Lafayette Coll (PA)
Lake Forest Coll (IL)
Lake Superior State U (MI)
La Salle U (PA)
Lehigh U (PA)
Lewis U (IL)
Limestone Coll (SC)
Lincoln Memorial U (TN)
Lipscomb U (TN)
Longwood U (VA)
Louisiana State U and Ag and Mech Coll (LA)
Louisiana State U in Shreveport (LA)
Louisiana Tech U (LA)
Loyola U Chicago (IL)
Loyola U New Orleans (LA)
Marquette U (WI)
Marshall U (WV)
Mars Hill Coll (NC)
Merrimack Coll (MA)
Messiah Coll (PA)
Miami U (OH)
Miami U Hamilton (OH)
Michigan Technological U (MI)
Middle Tennessee State U (TN)
Midwestern State U (TX)
Mills Coll (CA)
Mississippi State U (MS)
Montana State U Billings (MT)
Morehead State U (KY)
Mount Allison U (NB, Canada)
New York U (NY)
Niagara U (NY)
Nichols Coll (MA)
Northern Arizona U (AZ)
Northern Kentucky U (KY)
Northern State U (SD)
North Georgia Coll & State U (GA)
Northwest Missouri State U (MO)
Oakland U (MI)
Occidental Coll (CA)
Oglethorpe U (GA)
Ohio U (OH)
Ohio Wesleyan U (OH)
Oklahoma City U (OK)
Oklahoma State U (OK)
Old Dominion U (VA)
Park U (MO)
Penn State Abington (PA)
Penn State Altoona (PA)
Penn State Beaver (PA)
Penn State Berks (PA)
Penn State Brandywine (PA)
Penn State DuBois (PA)
Penn State Erie, The Behrend Coll (PA)
Penn State Fayette, The Eberly Campus (PA)
Penn State Greater Allegheny (PA)
Penn State Hazleton (PA)
Penn State Lehigh Valley (PA)
Penn State Mont Alto (PA)
Penn State New Kensington (PA)
Penn State Schuylkill (PA)
Penn State Shenango (PA)
Penn State U Park (PA)
Penn State Wilkes-Barre (PA)
Penn State Worthington Scranton (PA)
Penn State York (PA)
Pontifical Catholic U of Puerto Rico (PR)
Presbyterian Coll (SC)
Quinnipiac U (CT)
Randolph-Macon Coll (VA)
Rhode Island Coll (RI)
Rider U (NJ)
Sacred Heart U (CT)
Saginaw Valley State U (MI)
Saint Anselm Coll (NH)
Samford U (AL)
Sam Houston State U (TX)
Santa Clara U (CA)
Seattle U (WA)
Seton Hall U (NJ)
Shorter U (GA)
Sonoma State U (CA)
South Carolina State U (SC)
Southern Connecticut State U (CT)
Southern Illinois U Carbondale (IL)
Southern Illinois U Edwardsville (IL)
Southern U and Ag and Mech Coll (LA)
State U of New York at Plattsburgh (NY)
State U of New York Coll at Oneonta (NY)
State U of New York Coll at Potsdam (NY)
Stephen F. Austin State U (TX)
Stetson U (FL)
Susquehanna U (PA)

Texas A&M Intl U (TX)
Texas State U–San Marcos (TX)
Texas Wesleyan U (TX)
Union U (TN)
The U of Alabama (AL)
The U of Alabama at Birmingham (AL)
U of Alaska Anchorage (AK)
U of Arkansas (AR)
U of California, Irvine (CA)
U of California, Los Angeles (CA)
U of California, Riverside (CA)
U of California, Santa Barbara (CA)
U of California, Santa Cruz (CA)
U of Central Florida (FL)
U of Central Oklahoma (OK)
U of Dayton (OH)
U of Delaware (DE)
U of Denver (CO)
U of Evansville (IN)
U of Georgia (GA)
U of Hawaii at Manoa (HI)
U of Idaho (ID)
U of Indianapolis (IN)
The U of Iowa (IA)
U of Kentucky (KY)
U of Lethbridge (AB, Canada)
U of Louisville (KY)
U of Maine at Farmington (ME)
U of Manitoba (MB, Canada)
U of Memphis (TN)
U of Miami (FL)
U of Mississippi (MS)
U of Missouri (MO)
U of Nebraska at Omaha (NE)
U of Nebraska–Lincoln (NE)
U of Nevada, Reno (NV)
U of New Brunswick Fredericton (NB, Canada)
U of New Haven (CT)
U of New Orleans (LA)
U of North Alabama (AL)
The U of North Carolina at Charlotte (NC)
The U of North Carolina at Greensboro (NC)
The U of North Carolina Wilmington (NC)
U of North Dakota (ND)
U of North Florida (FL)
U of North Texas (TX)
U of Oklahoma (OK)
U of Pittsburgh at Johnstown (PA)
U of Puerto Rico, Río Piedras (PR)
U of Rochester (NY)
U of San Diego (CA)
U of Saskatchewan (SK, Canada)
U of South Carolina (SC)
U of Southern Mississippi (MS)
U of South Florida (FL)
The U of Tennessee (TN)
The U of Tennessee at Martin (TN)
The U of Texas at Arlington (TX)
The U of Texas at San Antonio (TX)
The U of Texas of the Permian Basin (TX)
U of the Incarnate Word (TX)
The U of Toledo (OH)
The U of Western Ontario (ON, Canada)
U of West Florida (FL)
U of West Georgia (GA)
U of Windsor (ON, Canada)
U of Wisconsin–Platteville (WI)
U of Wisconsin–Superior (WI)
U of Wisconsin–Whitewater (WI)
U of Wyoming (WY)
Utica Coll (NY)
Valdosta State U (GA)
Villanova U (PA)
Virginia Commonwealth U (VA)
Virginia Polytechnic Inst and State U (VA)
Virginia State U (VA)
Washburn U (KS)
Washington U in St. Louis (MO)
Weber State U (UT)
West Chester U of Pennsylvania (PA)
Western Illinois U (IL)
Western Kentucky U (KY)
Western State Coll of Colorado (CO)
West Liberty U (WV)
Westminster Coll (UT)
Westmont Coll (CA)
West Virginia U (WV)
West Virginia Wesleyan Coll (WV)
Wheaton Coll (IL)
Widener U (PA)
William Jewell Coll (MO)
William Paterson U of New Jersey (NJ)
Wilmington Coll (OH)
Winona State U (MN)
Wofford Coll (SC)
Wright State U (OH)
Xavier U (OH)
York U (ON, Canada)
Youngstown State U (OH)

BUSINESS OPERATIONS SUPPORT AND SECRETARIAL SERVICES RELATED

Bowling Green State U (OH)
Pontifical Catholic U of Puerto Rico (PR)
U of Georgia (GA)

BUSINESS STATISTICS

Alabama Ag and Mech U (AL)
Baylor U (TX)
Cleveland State U (OH)
HEC Montreal (QC, Canada)
Southern Oregon U (OR)
U of Central Missouri (MO)
U of Denver (CO)
U of Puerto Rico, Río Piedras (PR)
York U (ON, Canada)

BUSINESS TEACHER EDUCATION

Adams State Coll (CO)
Alabama State U (AL)
Alfred U (NY)
American Intl Coll (MA)
Appalachian State U (NC)
Arkansas State U—Jonesboro (AR)
Arkansas Tech U (AR)
Armstrong Atlantic State U (GA)
Auburn U (AL)
Ball State U (IN)
Baylor U (TX)
Belmont U (TN)
Bethany Coll (KS)
Bethel Coll (IN)
Bethel U (MN)
Bethune-Cookman U (FL)
Black Hills State U (SD)
Bluefield Coll (VA)
Bowling Green State U (OH)
Brigham Young U–Hawaii (HI)
Buena Vista U (IA)
Buffalo State Coll, State U of New York (NY)
Calumet Coll of Saint Joseph (IN)
Campbellsville U (KY)
Carson-Newman Coll (TN)
Central Michigan U (MI)
Colorado State U (CO)
Concordia Coll (MN)
Concordia U Wisconsin (WI)
Concord U (WV)
Corban U (OR)
Dakota State U (SD)
Dakota Wesleyan U (SD)
Dana Coll (NE)
Defiance Coll (OH)
Delaware State U (DE)
Dickinson State U (ND)
Doane Coll (NE)
Dordt Coll (IA)
Dowling Coll (NY)
East Carolina U (NC)
East Central U (OK)
Eastern Michigan U (MI)
Eastern Nazarene Coll (MA)
Eastern New Mexico U (NM)
Eastern Washington U (WA)
Edgewood Coll (WI)
Emmanuel Coll (GA)
Evangel U (MO)
Fairmont State U (WV)
Fayetteville State U (NC)
Ferris State U (MI)
Florida Ag and Mech U (FL)
Fort Hays State U (KS)
Friends U (KS)
Glenville State Coll (WV)
Grace Coll (IN)
Gwynedd-Mercy Coll (PA)
Hampton U (VA)
Hannibal-LaGrange Coll (MO)
Hardin-Simmons U (TX)
Henderson State U (AR)
Hofstra U (NY)
Howard Payne U (TX)
Huntington U (IN)
Illinois State U (IL)
Indiana State U (IN)
Jarvis Christian Coll (TX)
John Brown U (AR)
Johnson & Wales U (CO)
Kent State U (OH)
Lakeland Coll (WI)
La Salle U (PA)
Lee U (TN)
Lehman Coll of the City U of New York (NY)
Liberty U (VA)
Lincoln U (MO)
Lindenwood U (MO)
Louisiana Coll (LA)
Louisiana State U and Ag and Mech Coll (LA)
Louisiana Tech U (LA)
Maranatha Baptist Bible Coll (WI)
McKendree U (IL)
McNeese State U (LA)
Mercyhurst Coll (PA)
Michigan Technological U (MI)
MidAmerica Nazarene U (KS)
Middle Tennessee State U (TN)
Minot State U (ND)
Mississippi Coll (MS)
Mississippi State U (MS)
Missouri Baptist U (MO)
Missouri State U (MO)
Morehead State U (KY)
Mount Mary Coll (WI)
Mount Vernon Nazarene U (OH)
Murray State U (KY)
Nazareth Coll of Rochester (NY)
New York Inst of Technology (NY)
Niagara U (NY)
Nicholls State U (LA)
Norfolk State U (VA)
Northern Kentucky U (KY)
Northern State U (SD)
Northwestern Coll (IA)
Northwestern Oklahoma State U (OK)
Northwestern State U of Louisiana (LA)
Northwest Missouri State U (MO)
Oakland City U (IN)
Oakwood U (AL)
Ohio Wesleyan U (OH)
Oklahoma Panhandle State U (OK)
Oklahoma Wesleyan U (OK)
Oral Roberts U (OK)
Pacific Union Coll (CA)
Pontifical Catholic U of Puerto Rico (PR)
Prescott Coll (AZ)
Rider U (NJ)
Robert Morris U (PA)
St. Ambrose U (IA)
Saint Mary's Coll (IN)
St. Petersburg Coll (FL)
Saint Vincent Coll (PA)
Schreiner U (TX)
South Carolina State U (SC)
Southeast Missouri State U (MO)
Southern Arkansas U–Magnolia (AR)
Southern Utah U (UT)
Suffolk U (MA)
Tabor Coll (KS)
Temple U (PA)
Texas A&M U–Commerce (TX)
Texas Christian U (TX)
Texas Southern U (TX)
Texas Wesleyan U (TX)
Thomas More Coll (KY)
Trevecca Nazarene U (TN)
Trinity Christian Coll (IL)
Tusculum Coll (TN)
Union Coll (KY)
Union Coll (NE)
Union U (TN)
U of Alberta (AB, Canada)
U of Arkansas at Pine Bluff (AR)
The U of British Columbia (BC, Canada)
U of Central Missouri (MO)
U of Central Oklahoma (OK)
The U of Findlay (OH)
U of Illinois at Urbana–Champaign (IL)
U of Indianapolis (IN)
U of Lethbridge (AB, Canada)
U of Maine at Fort Kent (ME)
U of Maine at Machias (ME)
U of Mary (ND)
U of Maryland Eastern Shore (MD)
U of Minnesota, Twin Cities Campus (MN)
U of Missouri (MO)
U of Missouri–St. Louis (MO)
The U of Montana Western (MT)
U of Nebraska at Kearney (NE)
U of Nebraska–Lincoln (NE)
U of Nevada, Reno (NV)
U of New Brunswick Fredericton (NB, Canada)
U of North Dakota (ND)
U of Northern Iowa (IA)
U of Regina (SK, Canada)
U of Rio Grande (OH)
U of Southern Indiana (IN)
U of Southern Mississippi (MS)
U of South Florida (FL)
The U of Tennessee (TN)
The U of Tennessee at Martin (TN)
U of the Cumberlands (KY)
The U of Toledo (OH)
The U of Western Ontario (ON, Canada)
U of West Georgia (GA)
U of Wisconsin–Superior (WI)
U of Wisconsin–Whitewater (WI)
Upper Iowa U (IA)
Utah State U (UT)
Utah Valley U (UT)
Utica Coll (NY)
Valdosta State U (GA)
Valley City State U (ND)
Virginia State U (VA)
Virginia Union U (VA)
Viterbo U (WI)
Wayland Baptist U (TX)
Wayne State Coll (NE)
Weber State U (UT)
Western Kentucky U (KY)
Western Michigan U (MI)
West Virginia State U (WV)
William Penn U (IA)
Wilmington Coll (OH)
Winona State U (MN)
Winthrop U (SC)
Wright State U (OH)
York Coll (NE)
Youngstown State U (OH)

CAD/CADD DRAFTING/ DESIGN TECHNOLOGY

Cameron U (OK)
Eastern Michigan U (MI)

CANADIAN GOVERNMENT AND POLITICS

The U of British Columbia (BC, Canada)

CANADIAN HISTORY

U of Regina (SK, Canada)

CANADIAN STUDIES

Acadia U (NS, Canada)
Athabasca U (AB, Canada)
Bishop's U (QC, Canada)
Brock U (ON, Canada)
Concordia U Coll of Alberta (AB, Canada)
Duke U (NC)
Franklin Coll (IN)
Memorial U of Newfoundland (NL, Canada)
Mount Allison U (NB, Canada)
Queen's U at Kingston (ON, Canada)
St. Francis Xavier U (NS, Canada)
St. Lawrence U (NY)
Simon Fraser U (BC, Canada)
State U of New York at Plattsburgh (NY)
Thompson Rivers U (BC, Canada)
Trent U (ON, Canada)
U of Alberta (AB, Canada)
The U of British Columbia (BC, Canada)
U of Lethbridge (AB, Canada)
U of Manitoba (MB, Canada)
U of New Brunswick Fredericton (NB, Canada)
U of Ottawa (ON, Canada)
U of Regina (SK, Canada)
U of Saskatchewan (SK, Canada)
U of Toronto (ON, Canada)
U of Vermont (VT)
U of Washington (WA)
U of Waterloo (ON, Canada)
The U of Western Ontario (ON, Canada)
Western Washington U (WA)
Wilfrid Laurier U (ON, Canada)
York U (ON, Canada)

CARDIOPULMONARY TECHNOLOGY

Northeastern U (MA)

CARDIOVASCULAR TECHNOLOGY

Gwynedd-Mercy Coll (PA)
Louisiana State U Health Sciences Center (LA)
Medical U of South Carolina (SC)
Nebraska Methodist Coll (NE)
Pennsylvania Coll of Technology (PA)
Pontifical Catholic U of Puerto Rico (PR)

CARIBBEAN STUDIES

Brooklyn Coll of the City U of New York (NY)
Columbia U, School of General Studies (NY)

CARTOGRAPHY

Brigham Young U (UT)
DePaul U (IL)
East Central U (OK)
Kennesaw State U (GA)
Memorial U of Newfoundland (NL, Canada)
Missouri State U (MO)
Northern Arizona U (AZ)
Northern Michigan U (MI)
Queen's U at Kingston (ON, Canada)
Salem State Coll (MA)
State U of New York at Binghamton (NY)
State U of New York Coll at Oneonta (NY)
Stephen F. Austin State U (TX)
Texas A&M U (TX)
Texas A&M U–Corpus Christi (TX)
Texas State U–San Marcos (TX)
The U of Akron (OH)
U of Alberta (AB, Canada)
U of Lethbridge (AB, Canada)
U of Ottawa (ON, Canada)
The U of Texas at Dallas (TX)
U of Wisconsin–Madison (WI)
U of Wisconsin–Platteville (WI)
Western Kentucky U (KY)

CELL AND MOLECULAR BIOLOGY

Adams State Coll (CO)
Bennington Coll (VT)
Bradley U (IL)
Bridgewater State Coll (MA)
Bucknell U (PA)
Cedarville U (OH)
The Coll at Brockport, State U of New York (NY)
Concordia U (QC, Canada)
Connecticut Coll (CT)
Florida State U (FL)
Fort Lewis Coll (CO)
Grand Valley State U (MI)
Harvard U (MA)
Missouri State U (MO)
Northwest Nazarene U (ID)
Ohio U (OH)
Pittsburg State U (KS)
Salem State Coll (MA)
State U of New York at Binghamton (NY)
Texas A&M U (TX)
Texas Tech U (TX)
Thompson Rivers U (BC, Canada)
U of California, Berkeley (CA)
U of California, Los Angeles (CA)
U of Colorado at Boulder (CO)
U of Illinois at Urbana–Champaign (IL)
U of Michigan (MI)
U of Saskatchewan (SK, Canada)
The U of Tennessee at Martin (TN)
Western Washington U (WA)

CELL BIOLOGY AND ANATOMICAL SCIENCES RELATED

Northern Arizona U (AZ)
Rutgers, The State U of New Jersey, New Brunswick (NJ)
Tulane U (LA)
U of Connecticut (CT)
U of Kentucky (KY)
Washington & Jefferson Coll (PA)
Western Kentucky U (KY)
Yale U (CT)

CELL BIOLOGY AND ANATOMY

Huntingdon Coll (AL)
The U of Western Ontario (ON, Canada)
Western State Coll of Colorado (CO)

CELL BIOLOGY AND HISTOLOGY

Beloit Coll (WI)
California State U, Dominguez Hills (CA)
California State U, Fresno (CA)
California State U, Long Beach (CA)
California State U, San Marcos (CA)
Colby Coll (ME)
The Coll at Brockport, State U of New York (NY)
The Coll of Saint Rose (NY)
Humboldt State U (CA)
Juniata Coll (PA)
Mansfield U of Pennsylvania (PA)
Marlboro Coll (VT)
Memorial U of Newfoundland (NL, Canada)
Montana State U (MT)
Northeastern State U (OK)

Rutgers, The State U of New Jersey, New Brunswick (NJ)
San Francisco State U (CA)
Sonoma State U (CA)
Thompson Rivers U (BC, Canada)
Tulane U (LA)
U of Alberta (AB, Canada)
The U of Arizona (AZ)
The U of British Columbia (BC, Canada)
U of California, Davis (CA)
U of California, Irvine (CA)
U of California, San Diego (CA)
U of California, Santa Barbara (CA)
U of California, Santa Cruz (CA)
U of Georgia (GA)
U of Illinois at Urbana–Champaign (IL)
U of Maine (ME)
U of Minnesota, Duluth (MN)
U of Minnesota, Twin Cities Campus (MN)
U of Utah (UT)
U of Washington (WA)
The U of Western Ontario (ON, Canada)
U of Wisconsin–Madison (WI)
Western Washington U (WA)
William Jewell Coll (MO)
Worcester Polytechnic Inst (MA)

CELTIC LANGUAGES

U of California, Berkeley (CA)

CERAMIC ARTS AND CERAMICS

Adams State Coll (CO)
Alberta Coll of Art & Design (AB, Canada)
Alfred U (NY)
Aquinas Coll (MI)
Arcadia U (PA)
Bard Coll at Simon's Rock (MA)
Bennington Coll (VT)
Bethany Coll (KS)
Bowling Green State U (OH)
Bradley U (IL)
Brigham Young U (UT)
California Coll of the Arts (CA)
California State U, East Bay (CA)
California State U, Long Beach (CA)
The Cleveland Inst of Art (OH)
The Coll at Brockport, State U of New York (NY)
Coll of the Atlantic (ME)
Columbia Coll (MO)
Concordia U (QC, Canada)
Concord U (WV)
Franklin Pierce U (NH)
Hampton U (VA)
Hofstra U (NY)
Indiana Wesleyan U (IN)
Inter American U of Puerto Rico, San Germán Campus (PR)
Kent State U (OH)
Maine Coll of Art (ME)
Marlboro Coll (VT)
Maryland Inst Coll of Art (MD)
Marywood U (PA)
Massachusetts Coll of Art and Design (MA)
Minnesota State U Mankato (MN)
Minnesota State U Moorhead (MN)
Northern Arizona U (AZ)
Northern Michigan U (MI)
Northwest Nazarene U (ID)
Ohio Northern U (OH)
Ohio U (OH)
Pittsburg State U (KS)
Pratt Inst (NY)
Providence Coll (RI)
Rochester Inst of Technology (NY)
Rutgers, The State U of New Jersey, New Brunswick (NJ)
St. Cloud State U (MN)
Salve Regina U (RI)
School of the Art Inst of Chicago (IL)
School of the Museum of Fine Arts, Boston (MA)
Seton Hill U (PA)
Shawnee State U (OH)
State U of New York at New Paltz (NY)
Temple U (PA)
Texas Christian U (TX)
Trinity Christian Coll (IL)
U of Dallas (TX)
U of Hartford (CT)
The U of Iowa (IA)
The U of Kansas (KS)
U of Massachusetts Dartmouth (MA)
U of Miami (FL)
U of Michigan (MI)
U of Oregon (OR)
U of Regina (SK, Canada)
The U of Texas at El Paso (TX)
U of the District of Columbia (DC)
U of Washington (WA)
U of Wisconsin–Milwaukee (WI)
Washington U in St. Louis (MO)
Western State Coll of Colorado (CO)
Western Washington U (WA)
West Virginia Wesleyan Coll (WV)

CERAMIC SCIENCES AND ENGINEERING

Alfred U (NY)
Clemson U (SC)
Missouri U of Science and Technology (MO)
Rutgers, The State U of New Jersey, New Brunswick (NJ)
U of Illinois at Urbana–Champaign (IL)
U of Washington (WA)

CHEMICAL ENGINEERING

American U of Beirut (Lebanon)
Arizona State U (AZ)
Auburn U (AL)
Bucknell U (PA)
California Inst of Technology (CA)
California State Polytechnic U, Pomona (CA)
California State U, Long Beach (CA)
Calvin Coll (MI)
Carnegie Mellon U (PA)
Case Western Reserve U (OH)
Christian Brothers U (TN)
City Coll of the City U of New York (NY)
Clarkson U (NY)
Clemson U (SC)
Cleveland State U (OH)
Colorado School of Mines (CO)
Colorado State U (CO)
Columbia U (NY)
Cooper Union for the Advancement of Science and Art (NY)
Cornell U (NY)
Drexel U (PA)
Elon U (NC)
Florida Ag and Mech U (FL)
Florida Inst of Technology (FL)
Gallaudet U (DC)
Gannon U (PA)
Geneva Coll (PA)
Georgia Inst of Technology (GA)
Hampton U (VA)
Illinois Inst of Technology (IL)
Iowa State U of Science and Technology (IA)
The Johns Hopkins U (MD)
Kansas State U (KS)
Kettering U (MI)
Lafayette Coll (PA)
Lakehead U (ON, Canada)
Lamar U (TX)
Lehigh U (PA)
Louisiana State U and Ag and Mech Coll (LA)
Louisiana Tech U (LA)
Manhattan Coll (NY)
Massachusetts Inst of Technology (MA)
Memorial U of Newfoundland (NL, Canada)
Miami U (OH)
Michigan State U (MI)
Michigan Technological U (MI)
Mississippi State U (MS)
Missouri U of Science and Technology (MO)
Montana State U (MT)
Murray State U (KY)
New Jersey Inst of Technology (NJ)
New Mexico Inst of Mining and Technology (NM)
New Mexico State U (NM)
North Carolina State U (NC)
Northeastern U (MA)
The Ohio State U (OH)
Ohio U (OH)
Oklahoma State U (OK)
Oregon State U (OR)
Penn State Abington (PA)
Penn State Altoona (PA)
Penn State Beaver (PA)
Penn State Berks (PA)
Penn State Brandywine (PA)
Penn State DuBois (PA)
Penn State Erie, The Behrend Coll (PA)
Penn State Fayette, The Eberly Campus (PA)
Penn State Greater Allegheny (PA)
Penn State Hazleton (PA)
Penn State Lehigh Valley (PA)
Penn State Mont Alto (PA)
Penn State New Kensington (PA)
Penn State Schuylkill (PA)
Penn State Shenango (PA)
Penn State U Park (PA)
Penn State Wilkes-Barre (PA)
Penn State Worthington Scranton (PA)
Penn State York (PA)
Polytechnic U of Puerto Rico (PR)
Prairie View A&M U (TX)
Princeton U (NJ)
Purdue U (IN)
Queen's U at Kingston (ON, Canada)
Rensselaer Polytechnic Inst (NY)
Rice U (TX)
Rose-Hulman Inst of Technology (IN)
Rowan U (NJ)
Royal Military Coll of Canada (ON, Canada)
Rutgers, The State U of New Jersey, New Brunswick (NJ)
San Jose State U (CA)
Savannah State U (GA)
South Dakota School of Mines and Technology (SD)
Stanford U (CA)
State U of New York Coll of Environmental Science and Forestry (NY)
Stevens Inst of Technology (NJ)
Syracuse U (NY)
Tennessee Technological U (TN)
Texas A&M U (TX)
Texas Tech U (TX)
Thiel Coll (PA)
Trine U (IN)
Tufts U (MA)
Tulane U (LA)
Tuskegee U (AL)
United States Military Acad (NY)
Universidad de las Américas–Puebla (Mexico)
U at Buffalo, the State U of New York (NY)
The U of Akron (OH)
The U of Alabama (AL)
The U of Alabama in Huntsville (AL)
U of Alberta (AB, Canada)
The U of Arizona (AZ)
U of Arkansas (AR)
The U of British Columbia (BC, Canada)
U of California, Berkeley (CA)
U of California, Davis (CA)
U of California, Irvine (CA)
U of California, Los Angeles (CA)
U of California, Riverside (CA)
U of California, San Diego (CA)
U of California, Santa Barbara (CA)
U of Cincinnati (OH)
U of Colorado at Boulder (CO)
U of Connecticut (CT)
U of Dayton (OH)
U of Delaware (DE)
U of Florida (FL)
U of Georgia (GA)
U of Guelph (ON, Canada)
U of Houston (TX)
U of Idaho (ID)
U of Illinois at Chicago (IL)
U of Illinois at Urbana–Champaign (IL)
The U of Iowa (IA)
The U of Kansas (KS)
U of Kentucky (KY)
U of Louisville (KY)
U of Maine (ME)
U of Maryland, Baltimore County (MD)
U of Maryland, Coll Park (MD)
U of Massachusetts Amherst (MA)
U of Massachusetts Lowell (MA)
U of Michigan (MI)
U of Minnesota, Duluth (MN)
U of Minnesota, Twin Cities Campus (MN)
U of Mississippi (MS)
U of Missouri (MO)
U of Nebraska–Lincoln (NE)
U of Nevada, Reno (NV)
U of New Brunswick Fredericton (NB, Canada)
U of New Hampshire (NH)
U of New Haven (CT)
U of New Mexico (NM)
U of North Dakota (ND)
U of Notre Dame (IN)
U of Oklahoma (OK)
U of Ottawa (ON, Canada)
U of Pennsylvania (PA)
U of Pittsburgh (PA)
U of Rhode Island (RI)
U of Rochester (NY)
U of Saskatchewan (SK, Canada)
U of South Alabama (AL)
U of South Carolina (SC)
U of Southern California (CA)
U of South Florida (FL)
The U of Tennessee (TN)
The U of Texas at Austin (TX)
The U of Toledo (OH)
U of Toronto (ON, Canada)
U of Tulsa (OK)
U of Utah (UT)
U of Virginia (VA)
U of Washington (WA)
U of Waterloo (ON, Canada)
The U of Western Ontario (ON, Canada)
U of Wisconsin–Madison (WI)
U of Wyoming (WY)
Vanderbilt U (TN)
Villanova U (PA)
Virginia Commonwealth U (VA)
Virginia Polytechnic Inst and State U (VA)
Washington and Lee U (VA)
Washington State U (WA)
Washington U in St. Louis (MO)
Wayne State U (MI)
Western Michigan U (MI)
West Virginia U (WV)
Widener U (PA)
Winona State U (MN)
Worcester Polytechnic Inst (MA)
Xavier U (OH)
Yale U (CT)
Youngstown State U (OH)

CHEMICAL PHYSICS

Adams State Coll (CO)
Augustana Coll (SD)
Bowdoin Coll (ME)
Carnegie Mellon U (PA)
Hamilton Coll (NY)
Hendrix Coll (AR)
Michigan State U (MI)
Michigan Technological U (MI)
Saginaw Valley State U (MI)
Simon Fraser U (BC, Canada)
Swarthmore Coll (PA)
U of Waterloo (ON, Canada)

CHEMICAL TECHNOLOGY

Dakota State U (SD)
Inter American U of Puerto Rico, Arecibo Campus (PR)
Inter American U of Puerto Rico, Bayamón Campus (PR)
Inter American U of Puerto Rico, Guayama Campus (PR)
Murray State U (KY)
New York City Coll of Technology of the City U of New York (NY)
Universidad de las Américas–Puebla (Mexico)
U of Regina (SK, Canada)

CHEMISTRY

Abilene Christian U (TX)
Acadia U (NS, Canada)
Adams State Coll (CO)
Adelphi U (NY)
Agnes Scott Coll (GA)
Alabama Ag and Mech U (AL)
Alabama State U (AL)
Albany State U (GA)
Albertus Magnus Coll (CT)
Albion Coll (MI)
Albright Coll (PA)
Alcorn State U (MS)
Alderson-Broaddus Coll (WV)
Alfred U (NY)
Allegheny Coll (PA)
Allen U (SC)
Alma Coll (MI)
Alvernia U (PA)
Alverno Coll (WI)
American Intl Coll (MA)
American U (DC)
American U of Beirut (Lebanon)
Amherst Coll (MA)
Anderson U (IN)
Andrews U (MI)
Angelo State U (TX)
Appalachian State U (NC)
Aquinas Coll (MI)
Arcadia U (PA)
Arizona State U (AZ)
Arkansas State U—Jonesboro (AR)
Arkansas Tech U (AR)
Armstrong Atlantic State U (GA)
Asbury U (KY)
Ashland U (OH)
Assumption Coll (MA)
Auburn U (AL)
Augsburg Coll (MN)
Augustana Coll (IL)
Augustana Coll (SD)
Austin Coll (TX)
Austin Peay State U (TN)
Averett U (VA)
Azusa Pacific U (CA)
Baker U (KS)
Baldwin-Wallace Coll (OH)
Ball State U (IN)
Bard Coll (NY)
Bard Coll at Simon's Rock (MA)
Barnard Coll (NY)
Barry U (FL)
Barton Coll (NC)
Bates Coll (ME)
Baylor U (TX)
Belhaven U (MS)
Bellarmine U (KY)
Belmont U (TN)
Beloit Coll (WI)
Bemidji State U (MN)
Benedictine Coll (KS)
Benedictine U (IL)
Bennett Coll for Women (NC)
Bennington Coll (VT)
Berea Coll (KY)
Berry Coll (GA)
Bethany Coll (KS)
Bethany Coll (WV)
Bethany Lutheran Coll (MN)
Bethel Coll (IN)
Bethel Coll (KS)
Bethel U (MN)
Bethel U (TN)
Bethune-Cookman U (FL)
Birmingham-Southern Coll (AL)
Bishop's U (QC, Canada)
Blackburn Coll (IL)
Black Hills State U (SD)
Bloomfield Coll (NJ)
Bloomsburg U of Pennsylvania (PA)
Bluefield Coll (VA)
Bluffton U (OH)
Bob Jones U (SC)
Boise State U (ID)
Boston Coll (MA)
Boston U (MA)
Bowdoin Coll (ME)
Bowling Green State U (OH)
Bradley U (IL)
Brandeis U (MA)
Brescia U (KY)
Briar Cliff U (IA)
Bridgewater Coll (VA)
Bridgewater State Coll (MA)
Brigham Young U–Hawaii (HI)
Brock U (ON, Canada)
Brooklyn Coll of the City U of New York (NY)
Bryn Mawr Coll (PA)
Bucknell U (PA)
Buena Vista U (IA)
Buffalo State Coll, State U of New York (NY)
Butler U (IN)
Cabrini Coll (PA)
California Inst of Technology (CA)
California Lutheran U (CA)
California Polytechnic State U, San Luis Obispo (CA)
California State Polytechnic U, Pomona (CA)
California State U, Bakersfield (CA)
California State U, Chico (CA)
California State U, Dominguez Hills (CA)
California State U, East Bay (CA)
California State U, Fresno (CA)
California State U, Fullerton (CA)
California State U, Long Beach (CA)
California State U, Los Angeles (CA)
California State U, Northridge (CA)
California State U, Sacramento (CA)
California State U, San Bernardino (CA)
California State U, San Marcos (CA)
California State U, Stanislaus (CA)
Calvin Coll (MI)
Cameron U (OK)
Campbellsville U (KY)
Canisius Coll (NY)
Cape Breton U (NS, Canada)
Capital U (OH)
Carleton Coll (MN)
Carlow U (PA)
Carnegie Mellon U (PA)
Carroll U (WI)
Carson-Newman Coll (TN)
Case Western Reserve U (OH)
Catawba Coll (NC)
The Catholic U of America (DC)
Cedar Crest Coll (PA)
Cedarville U (OH)
Centenary Coll of Louisiana (LA)
Central Coll (IA)
Central Connecticut State U (CT)
Central Michigan U (MI)
Central State U (OH)
Chapman U (CA)
Chatham U (PA)
Cheyney U of Pennsylvania (PA)
Chowan U (NC)

INDEXES

Roosevelt U (IL)
Rose-Hulman Inst of Technology (IN)
Rosemont Coll (PA)
Rowan U (NJ)
Royal Military Coll of Canada (ON, Canada)
Russell Sage Coll (NY)
Rutgers, The State U of New Jersey, Camden (NJ)
Rutgers, The State U of New Jersey, Newark (NJ)
Rutgers, The State U of New Jersey, New Brunswick (NJ)
Saginaw Valley State U (MI)
St. Ambrose U (IA)
Saint Anselm Coll (NH)
St. Bonaventure U (NY)
St. Catherine U (MN)
St. Cloud State U (MN)
St. Edward's U (TX)
St. Francis Coll (NY)
Saint Francis U (PA)
St. Francis Xavier U (NS, Canada)
St. John Fisher Coll (NY)
Saint John's U (MN)
St. John's U (NY)
Saint Joseph Coll (CT)
St. Joseph's Coll, Long Island Campus (NY)
St. Joseph's Coll, New York (NY)
Saint Joseph's U (PA)
St. Lawrence U (NY)
Saint Louis U (MO)
Saint Martin's U (WA)
Saint Mary's Coll (IN)
Saint Mary's Coll of California (CA)
St. Mary's Coll of Maryland (MD)
St. Mary's U (TX)
Saint Mary's U of Minnesota (MN)
Saint Michael's Coll (VT)
St. Norbert Coll (WI)
St. Olaf Coll (MN)
St. Thomas U (FL)
Saint Vincent Coll (PA)
Saint Xavier U (IL)
Salem Coll (NC)
Salem State Coll (MA)
Salisbury U (MD)
Salve Regina U (RI)
Samford U (AL)
Sam Houston State U (TX)
San Diego State U (CA)
San Francisco State U (CA)
San Jose State U (CA)
Santa Clara U (CA)
Sarah Lawrence Coll (NY)
Savannah State U (GA)
Schreiner U (TX)
Scripps Coll (CA)
Seattle Pacific U (WA)
Seattle U (WA)
Seton Hall U (NJ)
Seton Hill U (PA)
Sewanee: The U of the South (TN)
Shawnee State U (OH)
Shaw U (NC)
Shenandoah U (VA)
Shepherd U (WV)
Shippensburg U of Pennsylvania (PA)
Shorter U (GA)
Siena Coll (NY)
Siena Heights U (MI)
Simmons Coll (MA)
Simon Fraser U (BC, Canada)
Simpson Coll (IA)
Skidmore Coll (NY)
Slippery Rock U of Pennsylvania (PA)
Smith Coll (MA)
Sonoma State U (CA)
South Carolina State U (SC)
South Dakota School of Mines and Technology (SD)
South Dakota State U (SD)
Southeastern Louisiana U (LA)
Southeastern Oklahoma State U (OK)
Southeast Missouri State U (MO)
Southern Adventist U (TN)
Southern Arkansas U–Magnolia (AR)
Southern Connecticut State U (CT)
Southern Illinois U Carbondale (IL)
Southern Illinois U Edwardsville (IL)
Southern Methodist U (TX)
Southern Oregon U (OR)
Southern Polytechnic State U (GA)
Southern U and Ag and Mech Coll (LA)
Southern Utah U (UT)
Southern Wesleyan U (SC)
Southwest Baptist U (MO)
Southwestern Adventist U (TX)
Southwestern Coll (KS)
Southwestern Oklahoma State U (OK)
Southwestern U (TX)
Southwest Minnesota State U (MN)
Spelman Coll (GA)
Spring Arbor U (MI)
Spring Hill Coll (AL)
Stanford U (CA)
State U of New York at Binghamton (NY)
State U of New York at Fredonia (NY)
State U of New York at New Paltz (NY)
State U of New York at Oswego (NY)
State U of New York at Plattsburgh (NY)
State U of New York Coll at Cortland (NY)
State U of New York Coll at Geneseo (NY)
State U of New York Coll at Old Westbury (NY)
State U of New York Coll at Oneonta (NY)
State U of New York Coll at Potsdam (NY)
State U of New York Coll of Environmental Science and Forestry (NY)
Stephen F. Austin State U (TX)
Stetson U (FL)
Stevens Inst of Technology (NJ)
Stevenson U (MD)
Stonehill Coll (MA)
Stony Brook U, State U of New York (NY)
Suffolk U (MA)
Sul Ross State U (TX)
Susquehanna U (PA)
Swarthmore Coll (PA)
Sweet Briar Coll (VA)
Syracuse U (NY)
Tabor Coll (KS)
Talladega Coll (AL)
Tarleton State U (TX)
Taylor U (IN)
Temple U (PA)
Tennessee Technological U (TN)
Tennessee Wesleyan Coll (TN)
Texas A&M Intl U (TX)
Texas A&M U (TX)
Texas A&M U–Commerce (TX)
Texas A&M U–Corpus Christi (TX)
Texas A&M U–Kingsville (TX)
Texas Christian U (TX)
Texas Lutheran U (TX)
Texas Southern U (TX)
Texas State U–San Marcos (TX)
Texas Tech U (TX)
Texas Wesleyan U (TX)
Texas Woman's U (TX)
Thiel Coll (PA)
Thomas More Coll (KY)
Thompson Rivers U (BC, Canada)
Towson U (MD)
Transylvania U (KY)
Trent U (ON, Canada)
Trevecca Nazarene U (TN)
Trine U (IN)
Trinity Christian Coll (IL)
Trinity Coll (CT)
Trinity U (TX)
Troy U (AL)
Truman State U (MO)
Tufts U (MA)
Tulane U (LA)
Tuskegee U (AL)
Union Coll (KY)
Union Coll (NE)
Union Coll (NY)
Union U (TN)
United States Air Force Acad (CO)
United States Military Acad (NY)
United States Naval Acad (MD)
U at Albany, State U of New York (NY)
U at Buffalo, the State U of New York (NY)
The U of Akron (OH)
The U of Alabama (AL)
The U of Alabama at Birmingham (AL)
The U of Alabama in Huntsville (AL)
U of Alaska Anchorage (AK)
U of Alaska Fairbanks (AK)
U of Alberta (AB, Canada)
The U of Arizona (AZ)
U of Arkansas (AR)
U of Arkansas at Fort Smith (AR)
U of Arkansas at Little Rock (AR)
U of Arkansas at Monticello (AR)
U of Arkansas at Pine Bluff (AR)
The U of British Columbia (BC, Canada)
The U of British Columbia–Okanagan (BC, Canada)
U of California, Berkeley (CA)
U of California, Davis (CA)
U of California, Irvine (CA)
U of California, Los Angeles (CA)
U of California, Merced (CA)
U of California, Riverside (CA)
U of California, San Diego (CA)
U of California, Santa Barbara (CA)
U of California, Santa Cruz (CA)
U of Central Florida (FL)
U of Central Missouri (MO)
U of Central Oklahoma (OK)
U of Charleston (WV)
U of Chicago (IL)
U of Cincinnati (OH)
U of Colorado at Boulder (CO)
U of Colorado at Colorado Springs (CO)
U of Colorado Denver (CO)
U of Connecticut (CT)
U of Dallas (TX)
U of Dayton (OH)
U of Delaware (DE)
U of Denver (CO)
U of Evansville (IN)
The U of Findlay (OH)
U of Florida (FL)
U of Georgia (GA)
U of Guam (GU)
U of Guelph (ON, Canada)
U of Hartford (CT)
U of Hawaii at Hilo (HI)
U of Hawaii at Manoa (HI)
U of Houston (TX)
U of Houston–Clear Lake (TX)
U of Houston–Downtown (TX)
U of Idaho (ID)
U of Illinois at Chicago (IL)
U of Illinois at Springfield (IL)
U of Illinois at Urbana–Champaign (IL)
The U of Iowa (IA)
The U of Kansas (KS)
U of Kentucky (KY)
U of King's Coll (NS, Canada)
U of La Verne (CA)
U of Lethbridge (AB, Canada)
U of Louisiana at Monroe (LA)
U of Louisville (KY)
U of Maine (ME)
U of Manitoba (MB, Canada)
U of Mary Hardin-Baylor (TX)
U of Maryland, Baltimore County (MD)
U of Maryland, Coll Park (MD)
U of Maryland Eastern Shore (MD)
U of Mary Washington (VA)
U of Massachusetts Amherst (MA)
U of Massachusetts Boston (MA)
U of Massachusetts Dartmouth (MA)
U of Massachusetts Lowell (MA)
U of Memphis (TN)
U of Miami (FL)
U of Michigan (MI)
U of Michigan–Dearborn (MI)
U of Michigan–Flint (MI)
U of Minnesota, Duluth (MN)
U of Minnesota, Twin Cities Campus (MN)
U of Mississippi (MS)
U of Missouri (MO)
U of Missouri–Kansas City (MO)
U of Missouri–St. Louis (MO)
U of Montevallo (AL)
U of Mount Union (OH)
U of Nebraska at Kearney (NE)
U of Nebraska at Omaha (NE)
U of Nebraska–Lincoln (NE)
U of Nevada, Las Vegas (NV)
U of Nevada, Reno (NV)
U of New Brunswick Fredericton (NB, Canada)
U of New England (ME)
U of New Hampshire (NH)
U of New Haven (CT)
U of New Mexico (NM)
U of New Orleans (LA)
U of North Alabama (AL)
The U of North Carolina at Asheville (NC)
The U of North Carolina at Chapel Hill (NC)
The U of North Carolina at Charlotte (NC)
The U of North Carolina at Greensboro (NC)
The U of North Carolina at Pembroke (NC)
The U of North Carolina Wilmington (NC)
U of North Dakota (ND)
U of Northern Colorado (CO)
U of Northern Iowa (IA)
U of North Florida (FL)
U of North Texas (TX)
U of Notre Dame (IN)
U of Oklahoma (OK)
U of Oregon (OR)
U of Ottawa (ON, Canada)
U of Pennsylvania (PA)
U of Pittsburgh (PA)
U of Pittsburgh at Bradford (PA)
U of Pittsburgh at Greensburg (PA)
U of Pittsburgh at Johnstown (PA)
U of Portland (OR)
U of Puerto Rico at Utuado (PR)
U of Puerto Rico, Cayey U Coll (PR)
U of Puerto Rico, Río Piedras (PR)
U of Puget Sound (WA)
U of Redlands (CA)
U of Regina (SK, Canada)
U of Rhode Island (RI)
U of Richmond (VA)
U of Rio Grande (OH)
U of Rochester (NY)
U of Saint Mary (KS)
U of St. Thomas (MN)
U of St. Thomas (TX)
U of San Diego (CA)
U of San Francisco (CA)
U of Saskatchewan (SK, Canada)
U of Science and Arts of Oklahoma (OK)
The U of Scranton (PA)
U of South Alabama (AL)
U of South Carolina (SC)
U of South Carolina Aiken (SC)
U of South Carolina Upstate (SC)
The U of South Dakota (SD)
U of Southern California (CA)
U of Southern Indiana (IN)
U of Southern Maine (ME)
U of Southern Mississippi (MS)
U of South Florida (FL)
The U of Tampa (FL)
The U of Tennessee (TN)
The U of Tennessee at Chattanooga (TN)
The U of Tennessee at Martin (TN)
The U of Texas at Arlington (TX)
The U of Texas at Austin (TX)
The U of Texas at Brownsville (TX)
The U of Texas at Dallas (TX)
The U of Texas at El Paso (TX)
The U of Texas at San Antonio (TX)
The U of Texas at Tyler (TX)
The U of Texas of the Permian Basin (TX)
The U of Texas–Pan American (TX)
U of the Cumberlands (KY)
U of the District of Columbia (DC)
U of the Incarnate Word (TX)
U of the Ozarks (AR)
U of the Pacific (CA)
U of the Sciences in Philadelphia (PA)
U of the Virgin Islands (VI)
The U of Toledo (OH)
U of Tulsa (OK)
U of Utah (UT)
U of Vermont (VT)
U of Virginia (VA)
The U of Virginia's Coll at Wise (VA)
U of Washington (WA)
U of Waterloo (ON, Canada)
The U of West Alabama (AL)
The U of Western Ontario (ON, Canada)
U of West Florida (FL)
U of West Georgia (GA)
U of Windsor (ON, Canada)
U of Wisconsin–Eau Claire (WI)
U of Wisconsin–Green Bay (WI)
U of Wisconsin–La Crosse (WI)
U of Wisconsin–Madison (WI)
U of Wisconsin–Milwaukee (WI)
U of Wisconsin–Oshkosh (WI)
U of Wisconsin–Parkside (WI)
U of Wisconsin–River Falls (WI)
U of Wisconsin–Stevens Point (WI)
U of Wisconsin–Superior (WI)
U of Wisconsin–Whitewater (WI)
U of Wyoming (WY)
Upper Iowa U (IA)
Ursinus Coll (PA)
Utah State U (UT)
Utah Valley U (UT)
Utica Coll (NY)
Valdosta State U (GA)
Valley City State U (ND)
Valparaiso U (IN)
Vanderbilt U (TN)
Vanguard U of Southern California (CA)
Vassar Coll (NY)
Villanova U (PA)
Virginia Commonwealth U (VA)
Virginia Military Inst (VA)
Virginia Polytechnic Inst and State U (VA)
Virginia State U (VA)
Virginia Union U (VA)
Virginia Wesleyan Coll (VA)
Viterbo U (WI)
Wabash Coll (IN)
Wagner Coll (NY)
Wake Forest U (NC)
Walsh U (OH)
Wartburg Coll (IA)
Washburn U (KS)
Washington Adventist U (MD)
Washington & Jefferson Coll (PA)
Washington and Lee U (VA)
Washington Coll (MD)
Washington State U (WA)
Washington U in St. Louis (MO)
Wayland Baptist U (TX)
Waynesburg U (PA)
Wayne State Coll (NE)
Wayne State U (MI)
Weber State U (UT)
Wellesley Coll (MA)
Wells Coll (NY)
Wesleyan Coll (GA)
Wesleyan U (CT)
West Chester U of Pennsylvania (PA)
Western Carolina U (NC)
Western Connecticut State U (CT)
Western Illinois U (IL)
Western Kentucky U (KY)
Western Michigan U (MI)
Western New England Coll (MA)
Western Oregon U (OR)
Western State Coll of Colorado (CO)
Western Washington U (WA)
Westfield State Coll (MA)
West Liberty U (WV)
Westminster Coll (MO)
Westminster Coll (UT)
Westmont Coll (CA)
West Virginia State U (WV)
West Virginia U (WV)
West Virginia Wesleyan Coll (WV)
Wheaton Coll (IL)
Wheaton Coll (MA)
Wheeling Jesuit U (WV)
Whitman Coll (WA)
Whittier Coll (CA)
Wichita State U (KS)
Widener U (PA)
Wilfrid Laurier U (ON, Canada)
Wilkes U (PA)
Willamette U (OR)
William Jewell Coll (MO)
Williams Coll (MA)
Wilmington Coll (OH)
Wilson Coll (PA)
Wingate U (NC)
Winona State U (MN)
Winston-Salem State U (NC)
Winthrop U (SC)
Wittenberg U (OH)
Wofford Coll (SC)
Worcester Polytechnic Inst (MA)
Worcester State Coll (MA)
Wright State U (OH)
Xavier U (OH)
Xavier U of Louisiana (LA)
Yale U (CT)
Yeshiva U (NY)
York Coll of Pennsylvania (PA)
York Coll of the City U of New York (NY)
York U (ON, Canada)
Youngstown State U (OH)

CHEMISTRY RELATED

Bridgewater State Coll (MA)
California State U, Chico (CA)
Carlow U (PA)
Carnegie Mellon U (PA)
Connecticut Coll (CT)
Dartmouth Coll (NH)
Duquesne U (PA)
Eastern Nazarene Coll (MA)
Edinboro U of Pennsylvania (PA)
Florida Inst of Technology (FL)
Florida State U (FL)
Keene State Coll (NH)
Lawrence Technological U (MI)
Lehigh U (PA)
Loyola U New Orleans (LA)
Northern Arizona U (AZ)
Northern Michigan U (MI)
Northland Coll (WI)
Ohio Northern U (OH)
Pittsburg State U (KS)
Saginaw Valley State U (MI)
Saint Anselm Coll (NH)
St. Edward's U (TX)
Saint Mary's Coll of California (CA)
Saint Vincent Coll (PA)
Sam Houston State U (TX)
Stony Brook U, State U of New York (NY)
Taylor U (IN)
Texas Wesleyan U (TX)
Towson U (MD)
U at Buffalo, the State U of New York (NY)
U of California, Berkeley (CA)
U of California, Santa Barbara (CA)
U of Denver (CO)
U of Georgia (GA)

U of Houston–Downtown (TX)
U of Massachusetts Dartmouth (MA)
U of Northern Iowa (IA)
U of Notre Dame (IN)
U of Puerto Rico at Humacao (PR)
The U of Scranton (PA)
U of Southern Mississippi (MS)
U of the Pacific (CA)
U of Wisconsin–Eau Claire (WI)
U of Wisconsin–Whitewater (WI)
Washington & Jefferson Coll (PA)
Washington U in St. Louis (MO)
Wayne State U (MI)
Western Illinois U (IL)
Western Michigan U (MI)
Western State Coll of Colorado (CO)
Whitman Coll (WA)

CHEMISTRY TEACHER EDUCATION

Adams State Coll (CO)
Alma Coll (MI)
Alvernia U (PA)
Anderson U (IN)
Appalachian State U (NC)
Arkansas State U—Jonesboro (AR)
Arkansas Tech U (AR)
Assumption Coll (MA)
Averett U (VA)
Bethany Coll (KS)
Bethel U (MN)
Bethune-Cookman U (FL)
Bishop's U (QC, Canada)
Bluefield Coll (VA)
Boston U (MA)
Bowling Green State U (OH)
Bradley U (IL)
Bridgewater Coll (VA)
Brigham Young U–Hawaii (HI)
Brooklyn Coll of the City U of New York (NY)
Buena Vista U (IA)
Cabrini Coll (PA)
California State U, Chico (CA)
Cameron U (OK)
Campbellsville U (KY)
Carroll U (WI)
The Catholic U of America (DC)
Cedarville U (OH)
Central Michigan U (MI)
Christian Brothers U (TN)
City Coll of the City U of New York (NY)
Coker Coll (SC)
The Coll at Brockport, State U of New York (NY)
The Coll of New Jersey (NJ)
The Coll of Saint Rose (NY)
Coll of the Ozarks (MO)
Colorado State U (CO)
Concordia Coll (MN)
Concordia U, St. Paul (MN)
Cornell U (NY)
Dana Coll (NE)
Delaware State U (DE)
DePaul U (IL)
Dordt Coll (IA)
Dowling Coll (NY)
East Central U (OK)
Eastern Mennonite U (VA)
Eastern Michigan U (MI)
Eastern Nazarene Coll (MA)
Eastern Washington U (WA)
East Texas Baptist U (TX)
Edgewood Coll (WI)
Elizabeth City State U (NC)
Elmhurst Coll (IL)
Elmira Coll (NY)
Evangel U (MO)
Ferris State U (MI)
Florida Inst of Technology (FL)
Fort Lewis Coll (CO)
Franklin Coll (IN)
Glenville State Coll (WV)
Grand Valley State U (MI)
Greenville Coll (IL)
Gustavus Adolphus Coll (MN)
Hofstra U (NY)
Hope Coll (MI)
Huntingdon Coll (AL)
Husson U (ME)
Indiana U Bloomington (IN)
Indiana U–Purdue U Fort Wayne (IN)
Indiana U South Bend (IN)
Inter American U of Puerto Rico, San Germán Campus (PR)
Ithaca Coll (NY)
Jamestown Coll (ND)
John Brown U (AR)
Juniata Coll (PA)
Keene State Coll (NH)
Kent State U (OH)
Kentucky Wesleyan Coll (KY)
King Coll (TN)
Le Moyne Coll (NY)
Lincoln Memorial U (TN)
Lincoln U (MO)
Lindenwood U (MO)
Lipscomb U (TN)
Long Island U, Brooklyn Campus (NY)
Long Island U, C.W. Post Campus (NY)
Louisiana State U in Shreveport (LA)
Louisiana Tech U (LA)
Lubbock Christian U (TX)
Manhattanville Coll (NY)
Mansfield U of Pennsylvania (PA)
Marian U (WI)
Marist Coll (NY)
Maryville Coll (TN)
Maryville U of Saint Louis (MO)
Mayville State U (ND)
McMurry U (TX)
McNeese State U (LA)
Mercyhurst Coll (PA)
Messiah Coll (PA)
Miami Dade Coll (FL)
Miami U (OH)
Miami U Hamilton (OH)
Michigan State U (MI)
Millersville U of Pennsylvania (PA)
Millikin U (IL)
Minnesota State U Moorhead (MN)
Minot State U (ND)
Misericordia U (PA)
Mississippi Coll (MS)
Missouri State U (MO)
Montana State U Billings (MT)
Moravian Coll (PA)
Morningside Coll (IA)
Mount Marty Coll (SD)
Mount Mary Coll (WI)
Mount Vernon Nazarene U (OH)
Murray State U (KY)
Nazareth Coll of Rochester (NY)
New York Inst of Technology (NY)
Niagara U (NY)
North Carolina Central U (NC)
North Carolina State U (NC)
North Dakota State U (ND)
Northeastern State U (OK)
Northern Michigan U (MI)
Northwestern State U of Louisiana (LA)
Northwest Missouri State U (MO)
Northwest Nazarene U (ID)
Ohio Dominican U (OH)
Ohio Northern U (OH)
Ohio Wesleyan U (OH)
Old Dominion U (VA)
Pace U (NY)
Pittsburg State U (KS)
Pontifical Catholic U of Puerto Rico (PR)
Rhode Island Coll (RI)
Rivier Coll (NH)
Roberts Wesleyan Coll (NY)
Sacred Heart U (CT)
Saginaw Valley State U (MI)
St. Ambrose U (IA)
St. Catherine U (MN)
St. Cloud State U (MN)
St. Edward's U (TX)
St. Francis Coll (NY)
Saint Francis U (PA)
St. John Fisher Coll (NY)
Saint Mary's U of Minnesota (MN)
Schreiner U (TX)
Seton Hill U (PA)
Southern Arkansas U–Magnolia (AR)
Southern U and Ag and Mech Coll (LA)
Southwest Baptist U (MO)
Southwest Minnesota State U (MN)
Spring Arbor U (MI)
State U of New York at New Paltz (NY)
State U of New York at Plattsburgh (NY)
State U of New York Coll at Cortland (NY)
State U of New York Coll at Old Westbury (NY)
State U of New York Coll at Oneonta (NY)
State U of New York Coll at Potsdam (NY)
State U of New York Coll of Environmental Science and Forestry (NY)
Syracuse U (NY)
Tabor Coll (KS)
Talladega Coll (AL)
Transylvania U (KY)
Trevecca Nazarene U (TN)
Trinity Christian Coll (IL)
Union Coll (NE)
The U of Arizona (AZ)
U of Arkansas at Fort Smith (AR)
U of California, San Diego (CA)
U of Delaware (DE)
U of Evansville (IN)
U of Illinois at Chicago (IL)
U of Illinois at Urbana–Champaign (IL)
The U of Iowa (IA)
U of Louisiana at Monroe (LA)
U of Maine (ME)
U of Mary Hardin-Baylor (TX)
U of Michigan–Dearborn (MI)
U of Michigan–Flint (MI)
U of Missouri (MO)
U of Missouri–St. Louis (MO)
U of Nebraska–Lincoln (NE)
U of New Orleans (LA)
The U of North Carolina at Charlotte (NC)
The U of North Carolina Wilmington (NC)
U of Pittsburgh at Johnstown (PA)
U of Regina (SK, Canada)
U of St. Thomas (MN)
The U of Tennessee at Martin (TN)
U of Waterloo (ON, Canada)
U of West Georgia (GA)
U of Windsor (ON, Canada)
U of Wisconsin–River Falls (WI)
U of Wisconsin–Superior (WI)
Utah State U (UT)
Utah Valley U (UT)
Utica Coll (NY)
Valley City State U (ND)
Valparaiso U (IN)
Viterbo U (WI)
Washington State U (WA)
Washington U in St. Louis (MO)
Waynesburg U (PA)
Wayne State Coll (NE)
Weber State U (UT)
Western Michigan U (MI)
Western State Coll of Colorado (CO)
Western Washington U (WA)
Wheeling Jesuit U (WV)
Widener U (PA)
William Jewell Coll (MO)
Xavier U (OH)
Xavier U of Louisiana (LA)
York U (ON, Canada)

CHILD-CARE AND SUPPORT SERVICES MANAGEMENT

Brigham Young U (UT)
Ferris State U (MI)
Messiah Coll (PA)
Pacific Union Coll (CA)
Saint Mary-of-the-Woods Coll (IN)
Seton Hill U (PA)
Siena Heights U (MI)
Thomas Edison State Coll (NJ)
Walden U (MN)
Wheelock Coll (MA)

CHILD-CARE PROVISION

Brigham Young U (UT)
Walden U (MN)
Wayne State Coll (NE)

CHILD DEVELOPMENT

Albertus Magnus Coll (CT)
Alcorn State U (MS)
American Public U System (WV)
Appalachian State U (NC)
Ashland U (OH)
Atlanta Christian Coll (GA)
Auburn U (AL)
Bennington Coll (VT)
Bowling Green State U (OH)
Brigham Young U (UT)
California State U, East Bay (CA)
California State U, Fresno (CA)
California State U, Long Beach (CA)
California State U, Los Angeles (CA)
California State U, Northridge (CA)
California State U, Sacramento (CA)
Carson-Newman Coll (TN)
Central Michigan U (MI)
Coll of the Ozarks (MO)
Concordia U, St. Paul (MN)
East Carolina U (NC)
Eastern Washington U (WA)
East Tennessee State U (TN)
Florida State U (FL)
Freed-Hardeman U (TN)
Gallaudet U (DC)
Hampton U (VA)
Hannibal-LaGrange Coll (MO)
Houston Baptist U (TX)
Humboldt State U (CA)
Kansas State U (KS)
Kuyper Coll (MI)
Lasell Coll (MA)
Lesley U (MA)
Lewis-Clark State Coll (ID)
Lincoln Christian U (IL)
Louisiana Tech U (LA)
Madonna U (MI)
Meredith Coll (NC)
Michigan State U (MI)
Milligan Coll (TN)
Minnesota State U Mankato (MN)
Missouri Baptist U (MO)
Mount Ida Coll (MA)
National U (CA)
Ohio U (OH)
Oklahoma Christian U (OK)
Pittsburg State U (KS)
Portland State U (OR)
Quinnipiac U (CT)
St. Cloud State U (MN)
Saint Joseph Coll (CT)
St. Joseph's Coll, Long Island Campus (NY)
St. Joseph's Coll, New York (NY)
San Diego State U (CA)
Seton Hill U (PA)
Southern New Hampshire U (NH)
State U of New York Coll at Oneonta (NY)
Tennessee Technological U (TN)
Texas Southern U (TX)
Texas Tech U (TX)
Texas Woman's U (TX)
Towson U (MD)
Tufts U (MA)
Union Inst & U (OH)
The U of Akron (OH)
U of Alaska Fairbanks (AK)
U of Alberta (AB, Canada)
U of Central Oklahoma (OK)
U of Georgia (GA)
U of Guelph (ON, Canada)
U of Illinois at Urbana–Champaign (IL)
U of La Verne (CA)
U of Maine (ME)
U of Manitoba (MB, Canada)
U of Maryland Eastern Shore (MD)
U of Nevada, Reno (NV)
The U of North Carolina at Charlotte (NC)
The U of North Carolina at Greensboro (NC)
U of Saint Mary (KS)
The U of Tennessee at Martin (TN)
The U of Texas at Arlington (TX)
U of the Incarnate Word (TX)
The U of Western Ontario (ON, Canada)
U of Wisconsin–Madison (WI)
Vanderbilt U (TN)
Walden U (MN)
Western Michigan U (MI)
West Virginia U (WV)
Wheelock Coll (MA)
Youngstown State U (OH)

CHINESE

Augustana Coll (IL)
Bard Coll (NY)
Bates Coll (ME)
Bennington Coll (VT)
Brooklyn Coll of the City U of New York (NY)
California State U, Long Beach (CA)
California State U, Los Angeles (CA)
Calvin Coll (MI)
Carnegie Mellon U (PA)
Claremont McKenna Coll (CA)
Colgate U (NY)
Concordia Coll (MN)
Concordia U (QC, Canada)
Connecticut Coll (CT)
Dartmouth Coll (NH)
DePaul U (IL)
Emory U (GA)
Georgetown U (DC)
The George Washington U (DC)
Grinnell Coll (IA)
Hamilton Coll (NY)
Hofstra U (NY)
Hunter Coll of the City U of New York (NY)
Lawrence U (WI)
Lincoln U (PA)
Michigan State U (MI)
Middlebury Coll (VT)
New Coll of Florida (FL)
The Ohio State U (OH)
Pacific Lutheran U (WA)
Pomona Coll (CA)
Portland State U (OR)
Queens Coll of the City U of New York (NY)
Reed Coll (OR)
Rutgers, The State U of New Jersey, New Brunswick (NJ)
San Francisco State U (CA)
San Jose State U (CA)
Scripps Coll (CA)
Southwestern U (TX)
Stanford U (CA)
Swarthmore Coll (PA)
Trinity Coll (CT)
Trinity U (TX)
Tufts U (MA)
United States Military Acad (NY)
U of Alberta (AB, Canada)
The U of British Columbia (BC, Canada)
U of California, Berkeley (CA)
U of California, Davis (CA)
U of California, Irvine (CA)
U of California, Los Angeles (CA)
U of California, San Diego (CA)
U of California, Santa Barbara (CA)
U of Chicago (IL)
U of Colorado at Boulder (CO)
U of Georgia (GA)
U of Hawaii at Manoa (HI)
U of Houston (TX)
The U of Iowa (IA)
U of Maryland, Coll Park (MD)
U of Massachusetts Amherst (MA)
U of Minnesota, Twin Cities Campus (MN)
U of Notre Dame (IN)
U of Oklahoma (OK)
U of Oregon (OR)
U of Pittsburgh (PA)
U of Puget Sound (WA)
U of Regina (SK, Canada)
U of Utah (UT)
U of Vermont (VT)
U of Washington (WA)
The U of Western Ontario (ON, Canada)
U of Wisconsin–Madison (WI)
Vassar Coll (NY)
Wake Forest U (NC)
Washington U in St. Louis (MO)
Wellesley Coll (MA)
Williams Coll (MA)
Wofford Coll (SC)
Yale U (CT)

CHINESE STUDIES

Claremont McKenna Coll (CA)
The Coll of William and Mary (VA)
Drew U (NJ)
Pacific Lutheran U (WA)
Sarah Lawrence Coll (NY)
U at Albany, State U of New York (NY)
U of California, Irvine (CA)
U of North Dakota (ND)
U of the West (CA)

CHIROPRACTIC ASSISTANT

Hawai'i Pacific U (HI)

CHRISTIAN STUDIES

Alderson-Broaddus Coll (WV)
Bethany Coll (KS)
Bethel Coll (IN)
Bethel U (TN)
Bryan Coll (TN)
California Baptist U (CA)
Coll of Biblical Studies–Houston (TX)
The Coll of St. Scholastica (MN)
Dallas Baptist U (TX)
Gordon Coll (MA)
Hillsdale Coll (MI)
Howard Payne U (TX)
Inter American U of Puerto Rico, Guayama Campus (PR)
Lindenwood U (MO)
Loyola U New Orleans (LA)
Marian U (IN)
McMurry U (TX)
Mercer U (GA)
Mississippi Coll (MS)
Missouri Baptist U (MO)
Ouachita Baptist U (AR)
Seton Hall U (NJ)
Simpson U (CA)
Stonehill Coll (MA)
Tennessee Wesleyan Coll (TN)
Truett-McConnell Coll (GA)
U of Mary Hardin-Baylor (TX)
Ursuline Coll (OH)
Wayland Baptist U (TX)

CINEMATOGRAPHY AND FILM/VIDEO PRODUCTION

Acad of Art U (CA)
American U (DC)
Art Center Coll of Design (CA)
The Art Inst of Atlanta (GA)
The Art Inst of Austin (TX)
The Art Inst of California–Hollywood (CA)
The Art Inst of California–Los Angeles (CA)
The Art Inst of California–Orange County (CA)

The Art Inst of California–Sacramento (CA)
The Art Inst of California–San Francisco (CA)
The Art Inst of California–Sunnyvale (CA)
The Art Inst of Charleston (SC)
The Art Inst of Charlotte (NC)
The Art Inst of Colorado (CO)
The Art Inst of Dallas (TX)
The Art Inst of Fort Lauderdale (FL)
The Art Inst of Houston (TX)
The Art Inst of Jacksonville (FL)
The Art Inst of Las Vegas (NV)
The Art Inst of Ohio–Cincinnati (OH)
The Art Inst of Philadelphia (PA)
The Art Inst of Phoenix (AZ)
The Art Inst of Pittsburgh (PA)
The Art Inst of Portland (OR)
The Art Inst of Salt Lake City (UT)
The Art Inst of Seattle (WA)
The Art Inst of Tampa (FL)
The Art Inst of Tennessee–Nashville (TN)
The Art Inst of Tucson (AZ)
The Art Inst of Washington (VA)
The Art Insts Intl–Kansas City (KS)
The Art Insts Intl Minnesota (MN)
Bard Coll (NY)
Bennington Coll (VT)
Bob Jones U (SC)
Boston U (MA)
Brigham Young U (UT)
Brooklyn Coll of the City U of New York (NY)
California Inst of the Arts (CA)
California State U, Long Beach (CA)
California State U, Northridge (CA)
Chapman U (CA)
City Coll of the City U of New York (NY)
Collins Coll: A School of Design and Technology (AZ)
Columbia Coll Chicago (IL)
Concordia U (QC, Canada)
Drexel U (PA)
Eastern New Mexico U (NM)
Eastern Washington U (WA)
Emerson Coll (MA)
The Evergreen State Coll (WA)
Fairleigh Dickinson U, Coll at Florham (NJ)
Fitchburg State Coll (MA)
Five Towns Coll (NY)
Florida State U (FL)
Full Sail U (FL)
George Fox U (OR)
George Mason U (VA)
Hawai'i Pacific U (HI)
Hunter Coll of the City U of New York (NY)
The Illinois Inst of Art–Chicago (IL)
The Illinois Inst of Art–Schaumburg (IL)
Ithaca Coll (NY)
John Brown U (AR)
Keene State Coll (NH)
Long Island U, C.W. Post Campus (NY)
Loyola Marymount U (CA)
Maharishi U of Management (IA)
Massachusetts Coll of Art and Design (MA)
Mercy Coll (NY)
Miami Dade Coll (FL)
Miami Intl U of Art & Design (FL)
Middlebury Coll (VT)
Minneapolis Coll of Art and Design (MN)
Montana State U (MT)
Montclair State U (NJ)
The New England Inst of Art (MA)
New England School of Communications (ME)
New Mexico Highlands U (NM)
New Mexico State U (NM)
New York U (NY)
Northern Michigan U (MI)
Oakland U (MI)
Ohio U (OH)
Oklahoma City U (OK)
Point Park U (PA)
Pratt Inst (NY)
Purchase Coll, State U of New York (NY)
Quinnipiac U (CT)
Regent U (VA)
Rochester Inst of Technology (NY)
Sacred Heart U (CT)
Sarah Lawrence Coll (NY)
Savannah Coll of Art and Design (GA)
School of the Art Inst of Chicago (IL)
School of the Museum of Fine Arts, Boston (MA)
School of Visual Arts (NY)
Southern Adventist U (TN)
Southern Illinois U Carbondale (IL)
State U of New York at Binghamton (NY)
Syracuse U (NY)
U of Advancing Technology (AZ)
U of Central Florida (FL)
U of Illinois at Chicago (IL)
The U of Iowa (IA)
U of Miami (FL)
U of New Mexico (NM)
U of North Carolina School of the Arts (NC)
The U of North Carolina Wilmington (NC)
U of Oklahoma (OK)
U of Regina (SK, Canada)
U of Rhode Island (RI)
U of Southern California (CA)
Vanguard U of Southern California (CA)
Virginia Commonwealth U (VA)
Waldorf Coll (IA)
Wayne State U (MI)
Webster U (MO)
York U (ON, Canada)

CITY/URBAN, COMMUNITY AND REGIONAL PLANNING

Alabama Ag and Mech U (AL)
Appalachian State U (NC)
Arizona State U (AZ)
Ball State U (IN)
Bridgewater State Coll (MA)
Buffalo State Coll, State U of New York (NY)
California Polytechnic State U, San Luis Obispo (CA)
California State Polytechnic U, Pomona (CA)
California State U, Chico (CA)
Concordia U (QC, Canada)
Cornell U (NY)
East Carolina U (NC)
Eastern Washington U (WA)
Florida Atlantic U (FL)
Frostburg State U (MD)
Indiana U of Pennsylvania (PA)
Iowa State U of Science and Technology (IA)
Mansfield U of Pennsylvania (PA)
Massachusetts Inst of Technology (MA)
Miami U (OH)
Miami U Hamilton (OH)
Michigan State U (MI)
Minnesota State U Mankato (MN)
Missouri State U (MO)
New Mexico State U (NM)
Plymouth State U (NH)
Portland State U (OR)
St. Cloud State U (MN)
Savannah Coll of Art and Design (GA)
State U of New York Coll of Environmental Science and Forestry (NY)
Temple U (PA)
Texas A&M U (TX)
Texas State U–San Marcos (TX)
The U of Akron (OH)
The U of Arizona (AZ)
U of California, Davis (CA)
U of Cincinnati (OH)
U of Illinois at Urbana–Champaign (IL)
U of Missouri–Kansas City (MO)
U of Nevada, Las Vegas (NV)
U of New Hampshire (NH)
U of San Francisco (CA)
U of Saskatchewan (SK, Canada)
U of Virginia (VA)
U of Washington (WA)
U of Waterloo (ON, Canada)
The U of Western Ontario (ON, Canada)
Westfield State Coll (MA)
Wright State U (OH)

CIVIL ENGINEERING

Alabama Ag and Mech U (AL)
American U of Beirut (Lebanon)
Arizona State U (AZ)
Arkansas State U—Jonesboro (AR)
Auburn U (AL)
Boise State U (ID)
Bradley U (IL)
Bucknell U (PA)
California Baptist U (CA)
California Polytechnic State U, San Luis Obispo (CA)
California State Polytechnic U, Pomona (CA)
California State U, Chico (CA)
California State U, Fresno (CA)
California State U, Fullerton (CA)
California State U, Long Beach (CA)
California State U, Los Angeles (CA)
California State U, Sacramento (CA)
Calvin Coll (MI)
Carnegie Mellon U (PA)
Case Western Reserve U (OH)
The Catholic U of America (DC)
Central Connecticut State U (CT)
Christian Brothers U (TN)
The Citadel, The Military Coll of South Carolina (SC)
City Coll of the City U of New York (NY)
Clarkson U (NY)
Clemson U (SC)
Cleveland State U (OH)
The Coll of New Jersey (NJ)
Colorado State U (CO)
Columbia U (NY)
Concordia U (QC, Canada)
Cooper Union for the Advancement of Science and Art (NY)
Cornell U (NY)
Delaware State U (DE)
Dordt Coll (IA)
Drexel U (PA)
Duke U (NC)
Florida Ag and Mech U (FL)
Florida Atlantic U (FL)
Florida Gulf Coast U (FL)
Florida Inst of Technology (FL)
Florida Intl U (FL)
Gallaudet U (DC)
George Fox U (OR)
The George Washington U (DC)
Georgia Inst of Technology (GA)
Gonzaga U (WA)
Hofstra U (NY)
Idaho State U (ID)
Illinois Inst of Technology (IL)
Indiana U–Purdue U Fort Wayne (IN)
Iowa State U of Science and Technology (IA)
Jackson State U (MS)
The Johns Hopkins U (MD)
Kansas State U (KS)
Lafayette Coll (PA)
Lakehead U (ON, Canada)
Lamar U (TX)
Lawrence Technological U (MI)
Lehigh U (PA)
Lincoln U (MO)
Louisiana State U and Ag and Mech Coll (LA)
Louisiana Tech U (LA)
Loyola Marymount U (CA)
Manhattan Coll (NY)
Marquette U (WI)
Massachusetts Inst of Technology (MA)
Memorial U of Newfoundland (NL, Canada)
Merrimack Coll (MA)
Michigan State U (MI)
Michigan Technological U (MI)
Minnesota State U Mankato (MN)
Mississippi State U (MS)
Missouri U of Science and Technology (MO)
Montana State U (MT)
New Jersey Inst of Technology (NJ)
New Mexico Inst of Mining and Technology (NM)
New Mexico State U (NM)
North Carolina State U (NC)
North Dakota State U (ND)
Northeastern U (MA)
Northern Arizona U (AZ)
Ohio Northern U (OH)
The Ohio State U (OH)
Ohio U (OH)
Oklahoma State U (OK)
Old Dominion U (VA)
Oregon Inst of Technology (OR)
Oregon State U (OR)
Penn State Abington (PA)
Penn State Altoona (PA)
Penn State Beaver (PA)
Penn State Berks (PA)
Penn State Brandywine (PA)
Penn State DuBois (PA)
Penn State Erie, The Behrend Coll (PA)
Penn State Fayette, The Eberly Campus (PA)
Penn State Greater Allegheny (PA)
Penn State Harrisburg (PA)
Penn State Hazleton (PA)
Penn State Lehigh Valley (PA)
Penn State Mont Alto (PA)
Penn State New Kensington (PA)
Penn State Schuylkill (PA)
Penn State Shenango (PA)
Penn State U Park (PA)
Penn State Wilkes-Barre (PA)
Penn State Worthington Scranton (PA)
Penn State York (PA)
Polytechnic Inst of NYU (NY)
Polytechnic U of Puerto Rico (PR)
Portland State U (OR)
Prairie View A&M U (TX)
Princeton U (NJ)
Purdue U (IN)
Purdue U Calumet (IN)
Queen's U at Kingston (ON, Canada)
Rensselaer Polytechnic Inst (NY)
Rice U (TX)
Rose-Hulman Inst of Technology (IN)
Rowan U (NJ)
Royal Military Coll of Canada (ON, Canada)
Rutgers, The State U of New Jersey, New Brunswick (NJ)
Saint Louis U (MO)
Saint Martin's U (WA)
San Diego State U (CA)
San Francisco State U (CA)
San Jose State U (CA)
Santa Clara U (CA)
Savannah State U (GA)
Seattle U (WA)
South Dakota School of Mines and Technology (SD)
South Dakota State U (SD)
Southern Illinois U Carbondale (IL)
Southern Illinois U Edwardsville (IL)
Southern Methodist U (TX)
Southern Polytechnic State U (GA)
Southern U and Ag and Mech Coll (LA)
Stanford U (CA)
Stevens Inst of Technology (NJ)
Syracuse U (NY)
Temple U (PA)
Tennessee Technological U (TN)
Texas A&M U (TX)
Texas A&M U–Kingsville (TX)
Texas Tech U (TX)
Trine U (IN)
Tufts U (MA)
United States Air Force Acad (CO)
United States Coast Guard Acad (CT)
United States Military Acad (NY)
Universidad de las Américas–Puebla (Mexico)
U at Buffalo, the State U of New York (NY)
The U of Akron (OH)
The U of Alabama (AL)
The U of Alabama at Birmingham (AL)
The U of Alabama in Huntsville (AL)
U of Alaska Anchorage (AK)
U of Alaska Fairbanks (AK)
U of Alberta (AB, Canada)
The U of Arizona (AZ)
U of Arkansas (AR)
The U of British Columbia (BC, Canada)
The U of British Columbia–Okanagan (BC, Canada)
U of California, Berkeley (CA)
U of California, Davis (CA)
U of California, Irvine (CA)
U of California, Los Angeles (CA)
U of Central Florida (FL)
U of Cincinnati (OH)
U of Colorado at Boulder (CO)
U of Colorado Denver (CO)
U of Connecticut (CT)
U of Dayton (OH)
U of Delaware (DE)
U of Evansville (IN)
U of Florida (FL)
U of Hartford (CT)
U of Hawaii at Manoa (HI)
U of Houston (TX)
U of Idaho (ID)
U of Illinois at Chicago (IL)
U of Illinois at Urbana–Champaign (IL)
The U of Iowa (IA)
The U of Kansas (KS)
U of Kentucky (KY)
U of Louisville (KY)
U of Maine (ME)
U of Manitoba (MB, Canada)
U of Maryland, Coll Park (MD)
U of Massachusetts Amherst (MA)
U of Massachusetts Dartmouth (MA)
U of Massachusetts Lowell (MA)
U of Memphis (TN)
U of Miami (FL)
U of Michigan (MI)
U of Minnesota, Duluth (MN)
U of Minnesota, Twin Cities Campus (MN)
U of Mississippi (MS)
U of Missouri (MO)
U of Missouri–Kansas City (MO)
U of Missouri–St. Louis (MO)
U of Nebraska–Lincoln (NE)
U of Nevada, Las Vegas (NV)
U of Nevada, Reno (NV)
U of New Brunswick Fredericton (NB, Canada)
U of New Hampshire (NH)
U of New Haven (CT)
U of New Mexico (NM)
U of New Orleans (LA)
The U of North Carolina at Charlotte (NC)
U of North Dakota (ND)
U of North Florida (FL)
U of Oklahoma (OK)
U of Ottawa (ON, Canada)
U of Pittsburgh (PA)
U of Portland (OR)
U of Rhode Island (RI)
U of Saskatchewan (SK, Canada)
U of South Alabama (AL)
U of South Carolina (SC)
U of Southern California (CA)
U of South Florida (FL)
The U of Tennessee (TN)
The U of Texas at Arlington (TX)
The U of Texas at Austin (TX)
The U of Texas at El Paso (TX)
The U of Texas at San Antonio (TX)
The U of Texas at Tyler (TX)
U of the District of Columbia (DC)
U of the Pacific (CA)
The U of Toledo (OH)
U of Toronto (ON, Canada)
U of Utah (UT)
U of Vermont (VT)
U of Virginia (VA)
U of Washington (WA)
U of Waterloo (ON, Canada)
The U of Western Ontario (ON, Canada)
U of Windsor (ON, Canada)
U of Wisconsin–Madison (WI)
U of Wisconsin–Milwaukee (WI)
U of Wisconsin–Platteville (WI)
U of Wyoming (WY)
Ursinus Coll (PA)
Utah State U (UT)
Valparaiso U (IN)
Vanderbilt U (TN)
Villanova U (PA)
Virginia Military Inst (VA)
Virginia Polytechnic Inst and State U (VA)
Washington State U (WA)
Wayne State U (MI)
Western Kentucky U (KY)
Western Michigan U (MI)
West Virginia U (WV)
Widener U (PA)
Worcester Polytechnic Inst (MA)
Youngstown State U (OH)

CIVIL ENGINEERING RELATED

Bradley U (IL)
California Polytechnic State U, San Luis Obispo (CA)
Carnegie Mellon U (PA)
Drexel U (PA)
Embry-Riddle Aeronautical U (FL)
George Mason U (VA)
Ohio Northern U (OH)
Oregon State U (OR)

CIVIL ENGINEERING TECHNOLOGY

Alabama Ag and Mech U (AL)
Bluefield State Coll (WV)
Central Connecticut State U (CT)
Colorado State U–Pueblo (CO)
Fairleigh Dickinson U, Metropolitan Campus (NJ)
Fairmont State U (WV)
Florida Ag and Mech U (FL)
Georgia Southern U (GA)
Lakehead U (ON, Canada)
Metropolitan State Coll of Denver (CO)
Missouri Western State U (MO)
Old Dominion U (VA)
Point Park U (PA)
Rochester Inst of Technology (NY)
Savannah State U (GA)
South Carolina State U (SC)
Southern Polytechnic State U (GA)
Temple U (PA)
Texas Southern U (TX)
Thomas Edison State Coll (NJ)
United States Military Acad (NY)
U of Cincinnati (OH)
U of Houston–Downtown (TX)
The U of North Carolina at Charlotte (NC)
U of North Texas (TX)
U of Pittsburgh at Johnstown (PA)
The U of Toledo (OH)

Wentworth Inst of Technology (MA)
Western Kentucky U (KY)
Youngstown State U (OH)

CLASSICAL, ANCIENT MEDITERRANEAN AND NEAR EASTERN STUDIES AND ARCHAEOLOGY

Bowdoin Coll (ME)
Butler U (IN)
Columbia U (NY)
Creighton U (NE)
Emory U (GA)
Lycoming Coll (PA)
Michigan State U (MI)
U of California, Berkeley (CA)
U of California, Davis (CA)
U of California, Irvine (CA)
U of California, Los Angeles (CA)
U of Illinois at Chicago (IL)
U of Michigan (MI)
U of Ottawa (ON, Canada)
U of Southern California (CA)
U of Toronto (ON, Canada)
Vanderbilt U (TN)

CLASSICS AND CLASSICAL LANGUAGES RELATED

Austin Coll (TX)
Bryn Mawr Coll (PA)
California State U, Long Beach (CA)
The Catholic U of America (DC)
Columbia U, School of General Studies (NY)
Concordia Coll (MN)
Eckerd Coll (FL)
Lawrence U (WI)
New Coll of Florida (FL)
Ohio U (OH)
Rutgers, The State U of New Jersey, Newark (NJ)
Saint Louis U (MO)
San Diego State U (CA)
Tulane U (LA)
U of California, Los Angeles (CA)
U of St. Thomas (MN)
Wheaton Coll (IL)

CLASSICS AND LANGUAGES, LITERATURES AND LINGUISTICS

Acadia U (NS, Canada)
Agnes Scott Coll (GA)
Amherst Coll (MA)
Asbury U (KY)
Assumption Coll (MA)
Augustana Coll (IL)
Augustana Coll (SD)
Austin Coll (TX)
Ball State U (IN)
Barnard Coll (NY)
Baylor U (TX)
Beloit Coll (WI)
Bishop's U (QC, Canada)
Boston Coll (MA)
Boston U (MA)
Bowdoin Coll (ME)
Bowling Green State U (OH)
Brandeis U (MA)
Brooklyn Coll of the City U of New York (NY)
Bryn Mawr Coll (PA)
Bucknell U (PA)
Calvin Coll (MI)
Carleton Coll (MN)
Case Western Reserve U (OH)
The Catholic U of America (DC)
Christendom Coll (VA)
Christopher Newport U (VA)
Claremont McKenna Coll (CA)
Clark U (MA)
Colby Coll (ME)
Colgate U (NY)
Coll of Charleston (SC)
The Coll of New Rochelle (NY)
Coll of Notre Dame of Maryland (MD)
Coll of Saint Benedict (MN)
Coll of the Holy Cross (MA)
The Coll of William and Mary (VA)
The Coll of Wooster (OH)
The Colorado Coll (CO)
Columbia U (NY)
Columbia U, School of General Studies (NY)
Concordia U (QC, Canada)
Connecticut Coll (CT)
Cornell Coll (IA)
Cornell U (NY)
Dartmouth Coll (NH)
Davidson Coll (NC)
Denison U (OH)
DePauw U (IN)
Dickinson Coll (PA)
Drew U (NJ)
Duke U (NC)
Duquesne U (PA)
Earlham Coll (IN)
Elmira Coll (NY)
Emory U (GA)
The Evergreen State Coll (WA)
Fordham U (NY)
Franciscan U of Steubenville (OH)
Franklin & Marshall Coll (PA)
Furman U (SC)
Georgetown U (DC)
The George Washington U (DC)
Gettysburg Coll (PA)
Grand Valley State U (MI)
Grinnell Coll (IA)
Gustavus Adolphus Coll (MN)
Hamilton Coll (NY)
Hampden-Sydney Coll (VA)
Hanover Coll (IN)
Harvard U (MA)
Haverford Coll (PA)
Hellenic Coll (MA)
Hendrix Coll (AR)
Hillsdale Coll (MI)
Hofstra U (NY)
Hollins U (VA)
Hope Coll (MI)
Hunter Coll of the City U of New York (NY)
Illinois Wesleyan U (IL)
Indiana U Bloomington (IN)
John Carroll U (OH)
The Johns Hopkins U (MD)
Kalamazoo Coll (MI)
Kent State U (OH)
Kenyon Coll (OH)
Knox Coll (IL)
La Salle U (PA)
Laurentian U (ON, Canada)
Lawrence U (WI)
Lehigh U (PA)
Lehman Coll of the City U of New York (NY)
Loyola U Chicago (IL)
Loyola U Maryland (MD)
Loyola U New Orleans (LA)
Macalester Coll (MN)
Manhattan Coll (NY)
Manhattanville Coll (NY)
Marlboro Coll (VT)
Marquette U (WI)
Memorial U of Newfoundland (NL, Canada)
Mercer U (GA)
Miami U (OH)
Miami U Hamilton (OH)
Middlebury Coll (VT)
Millsaps Coll (MS)
Monmouth Coll (IL)
Montclair State U (NJ)
Moravian Coll (PA)
Mount Allison U (NB, Canada)
Mount Holyoke Coll (MA)
New York U (NY)
Nipissing U (ON, Canada)
North Central Coll (IL)
North Dakota State U (ND)
Oberlin Coll (OH)
The Ohio State U (OH)
Ohio U (OH)
Ohio Wesleyan U (OH)
Pacific Lutheran U (WA)
Penn State Abington (PA)
Penn State Altoona (PA)
Penn State Beaver (PA)
Penn State Berks (PA)
Penn State Brandywine (PA)
Penn State DuBois (PA)
Penn State Erie, The Behrend Coll (PA)
Penn State Fayette, The Eberly Campus (PA)
Penn State Greater Allegheny (PA)
Penn State Hazleton (PA)
Penn State Lehigh Valley (PA)
Penn State Mont Alto (PA)
Penn State New Kensington (PA)
Penn State Schuylkill (PA)
Penn State Shenango (PA)
Penn State U Park (PA)
Penn State Wilkes-Barre (PA)
Penn State Worthington Scranton (PA)
Penn State York (PA)
Pitzer Coll (CA)
Pomona Coll (CA)
Pontifical Coll Josephinum (OH)
Princeton U (NJ)
Randolph Coll (VA)
Randolph-Macon Coll (VA)
Redeemer U Coll (ON, Canada)
Reed Coll (OR)
Rhodes Coll (TN)
Rice U (TX)
Rockford Coll (IL)
Rollins Coll (FL)
Rutgers, The State U of New Jersey, Newark (NJ)
Rutgers, The State U of New Jersey, New Brunswick (NJ)
Saint Anselm Coll (NH)
St. Bonaventure U (NY)
St. Francis Xavier U (NS, Canada)
Saint John's U (MN)
Saint Michael's Coll (VT)
St. Olaf Coll (MN)
Samford U (AL)
San Diego State U (CA)
San Francisco State U (CA)
Santa Clara U (CA)
Sarah Lawrence Coll (NY)
Scripps Coll (CA)
Seattle Pacific U (WA)
Seton Hall U (NJ)
Sewanee: The U of the South (TN)
Siena Coll (NY)
Skidmore Coll (NY)
Smith Coll (MA)
Southern Illinois U Carbondale (IL)
Southwestern U (TX)
Stanford U (CA)
State U of New York at Binghamton (NY)
Swarthmore Coll (PA)
Sweet Briar Coll (VA)
Syracuse U (NY)
Temple U (PA)
Texas A&M U (TX)
Texas Tech U (TX)
Transylvania U (KY)
Trent U (ON, Canada)
Trinity Coll (CT)
Trinity U (TX)
Truman State U (MO)
Tufts U (MA)
Tulane U (LA)
Union Coll (NY)
U at Albany, State U of New York (NY)
U at Buffalo, the State U of New York (NY)
The U of Akron (OH)
U of Alberta (AB, Canada)
U of Arkansas (AR)
The U of British Columbia (BC, Canada)
U of California, Berkeley (CA)
U of California, Irvine (CA)
U of California, Riverside (CA)
U of California, San Diego (CA)
U of California, Santa Barbara (CA)
U of California, Santa Cruz (CA)
U of Chicago (IL)
U of Cincinnati (OH)
U of Colorado at Boulder (CO)
U of Connecticut (CT)
U of Dallas (TX)
U of Evansville (IN)
U of Florida (FL)
U of Georgia (GA)
U of Guelph (ON, Canada)
U of Hawaii at Manoa (HI)
U of Houston (TX)
U of Illinois at Chicago (IL)
U of Illinois at Urbana–Champaign (IL)
The U of Iowa (IA)
The U of Kansas (KS)
U of Kentucky (KY)
U of King's Coll (NS, Canada)
U of Maine (ME)
U of Manitoba (MB, Canada)
U of Maryland, Coll Park (MD)
U of Mary Washington (VA)
U of Massachusetts Amherst (MA)
U of Massachusetts Boston (MA)
U of Miami (FL)
U of Michigan (MI)
U of Missouri (MO)
U of Nebraska–Lincoln (NE)
U of New Brunswick Fredericton (NB, Canada)
U of New Hampshire (NH)
U of New Mexico (NM)
The U of North Carolina at Asheville (NC)
The U of North Carolina at Chapel Hill (NC)
The U of North Carolina at Greensboro (NC)
U of North Dakota (ND)
U of Notre Dame (IN)
U of Oklahoma (OK)
U of Oregon (OR)
U of Ottawa (ON, Canada)
U of Pennsylvania (PA)
U of Pittsburgh (PA)
U of Puget Sound (WA)
U of Regina (SK, Canada)
U of Rhode Island (RI)
U of Rochester (NY)
U of St. Thomas (MN)
U of South Carolina (SC)
U of Southern California (CA)
U of Southern Maine (ME)
U of South Florida (FL)
The U of Tennessee (TN)
The U of Texas at Austin (TX)
The U of Texas at San Antonio (TX)
U of the Pacific (CA)
The U of Toledo (OH)
U of Toronto (ON, Canada)
U of Utah (UT)
U of Vermont (VT)
U of Virginia (VA)
U of Washington (WA)
U of Waterloo (ON, Canada)
The U of Western Ontario (ON, Canada)
U of Windsor (ON, Canada)
U of Wisconsin–Madison (WI)
U of Wisconsin–Milwaukee (WI)
Ursinus Coll (PA)
Valparaiso U (IN)
Vanderbilt U (TN)
Vassar Coll (NY)
Villanova U (PA)
Virginia Wesleyan Coll (VA)
Wabash Coll (IN)
Wake Forest U (NC)
Washington and Lee U (VA)
Washington U in St. Louis (MO)
Wayne State U (MI)
Wellesley Coll (MA)
Wesleyan U (CT)
Wheaton Coll (MA)
Whitman Coll (WA)
Wilfrid Laurier U (ON, Canada)
Willamette U (OR)
Williams Coll (MA)
Wright State U (OH)
Xavier U (OH)
Yale U (CT)
Yeshiva U (NY)
York U (ON, Canada)

CLINICAL CHILD PSYCHOLOGY

St. John's U (NY)

CLINICAL LABORATORY SCIENCE/MEDICAL TECHNOLOGY

Abilene Christian U (TX)
Albany Coll of Pharmacy and Health Sciences (NY)
American Intl Coll (MA)
American U of Beirut (Lebanon)
Anderson U (IN)
Andrews U (MI)
Angelo State U (TX)
Aquinas Coll (MI)
Arizona State U (AZ)
Arkansas State U—Jonesboro (AR)
Arkansas Tech U (AR)
Armstrong Atlantic State U (GA)
Atlantic Union Coll (MA)
Auburn U (AL)
Augustana Coll (SD)
Austin Peay State U (TN)
Averett U (VA)
Ball State U (IN)
Barry U (FL)
Baylor U (TX)
Bellarmine U (KY)
Belmont U (TN)
Bemidji State U (MN)
Benedictine U (IL)
Bethune-Cookman U (FL)
Blackburn Coll (IL)
Blue Mountain Coll (MS)
Boise State U (ID)
Boston U (MA)
Bowling Green State U (OH)
Bradley U (IL)
Brescia U (KY)
Bridgewater Coll (VA)
Brigham Young U (UT)
California State U, Chico (CA)
California State U, Dominguez Hills (CA)
Cameron U (OK)
Campbellsville U (KY)
Carroll U (WI)
Carson-Newman Coll (TN)
Catawba Coll (NC)
The Catholic U of America (DC)
Cedarville U (OH)
Central Michigan U (MI)
Cheyney U of Pennsylvania (PA)
Clarion U of Pennsylvania (PA)
Coker Coll (SC)
The Coll at Brockport, State U of New York (NY)
Coll of Saint Elizabeth (NJ)
Coll of Saint Mary (NE)
The Coll of Saint Rose (NY)
Coll of Staten Island of the City U of New York (NY)
Concordia Coll (MN)
Concord U (WV)
Defiance Coll (OH)
DePaul U (IL)
DeVry U, Phoenix (AZ)
Dordt Coll (IA)
East Carolina U (NC)
Eastern Illinois U (IL)
Eastern Mennonite U (VA)
Eastern Michigan U (MI)
Eastern New Mexico U (NM)
East Stroudsburg U of Pennsylvania (PA)
Elmhurst Coll (IL)
Elmira Coll (NY)
Elon U (NC)
Emory & Henry Coll (VA)
Evangel U (MO)
Fairleigh Dickinson U, Coll at Florham (NJ)
Fairleigh Dickinson U, Metropolitan Campus (NJ)
Felician Coll (NJ)
Ferris State U (MI)
Florida Gulf Coast U (FL)
Fort Hays State U (KS)
Gannon U (PA)
George Mason U (VA)
The George Washington U (DC)
Georgian Court U (NJ)
Graceland U (IA)
Grand Valley State U (MI)
Greensboro Coll (NC)
Gwynedd-Mercy Coll (PA)
Harding U (AR)
Hartwick Coll (NY)
Henderson State U (AR)
High Point U (NC)
Holy Family U (PA)
Houghton Coll (NY)
Idaho State U (ID)
Illinois Coll (IL)
Illinois State U (IL)
Indiana State U (IN)
Indiana U Bloomington (IN)
Indiana U East (IN)
Indiana U of Pennsylvania (PA)
Indiana U–Purdue U Fort Wayne (IN)
Indiana U–Purdue U Indianapolis (IN)
Indiana U Southeast (IN)
Indiana Wesleyan U (IN)
Inter American U of Puerto Rico, San Germán Campus (PR)
Iona Coll (NY)
Jamestown Coll (ND)
Kansas State U (KS)
Kean U (NJ)
Kent State U (OH)
Kentucky Wesleyan Coll (KY)
Keuka Coll (NY)
King Coll (TN)
King's Coll (PA)
Kutztown U of Pennsylvania (PA)
Lake Superior State U (MI)
Lamar U (TX)
Lebanon Valley Coll (PA)
Lee U (TN)
Lincoln Memorial U (TN)
Lincoln U (MO)
Long Island U, Brooklyn Campus (NY)
Long Island U, C.W. Post Campus (NY)
Longwood U (VA)
Loras Coll (IA)
Louisiana Coll (LA)
Louisiana State U Health Sciences Center (LA)
Louisiana Tech U (LA)
Loyola U Chicago (IL)
Madonna U (MI)
Malone U (OH)
Manchester Coll (IN)
Mansfield U of Pennsylvania (PA)
Marist Coll (NY)
Marshall U (WV)
Mary Baldwin Coll (VA)
Maryville U of Saint Louis (MO)
Marywood U (PA)
Mayville State U (ND)
McKendree U (IL)
McNeese State U (LA)
Medical Coll of Georgia (GA)
Mercy Coll (NY)
Miami U (OH)
Miami U Hamilton (OH)
Michigan State U (MI)
Michigan Technological U (MI)
Midwestern State U (TX)
Minnesota State U Mankato (MN)
Minnesota State U Moorhead (MN)
Minot State U (ND)
Misericordia U (PA)
Mississippi State U (MS)
Missouri Southern State U (MO)
Missouri State U (MO)
Missouri Western State U (MO)
Monmouth U (NJ)
Moravian Coll (PA)

INDEXES

Morningside Coll (IA)
Mount Marty Coll (SD)
Mount Mercy Coll (IA)
Mount Saint Mary Coll (NY)
Mount Vernon Nazarene U (OH)
Murray State U (KY)
New Mexico State U (NM)
Norfolk State U (VA)
North Dakota State U (ND)
Northeastern State U (OK)
Northern State U (SD)
Northwestern Coll (IA)
Northwest Missouri State U (MO)
Oakland U (MI)
Oakwood U (AL)
Ohio Northern U (OH)
Oklahoma Christian U (OK)
Oklahoma Panhandle State U (OK)
Old Dominion U (VA)
Oral Roberts U (OK)
Oregon State U (OR)
Our Lady of the Lake Coll (LA)
Pace U (NY)
Peru State Coll (NE)
Pontifical Catholic U of Puerto Rico (PR)
Prairie View A&M U (TX)
Purdue U (IN)
Purdue U Calumet (IN)
Quincy U (IL)
Ramapo Coll of New Jersey (NJ)
Rhode Island Coll (RI)
Roanoke Coll (VA)
Rochester Inst of Technology (NY)
Rockhurst U (MO)
Rutgers, The State U of New Jersey, Camden (NJ)
Rutgers, The State U of New Jersey, Newark (NJ)
Rutgers, The State U of New Jersey, New Brunswick (NJ)
Sage Coll of Albany (NY)
Saginaw Valley State U (MI)
St. Catherine U (MN)
St. Cloud State U (MN)
St. Francis Coll (NY)
Saint Francis U (PA)
St. John's U (NY)
Saint Leo U (FL)
Saint Louis U (MO)
Saint Mary-of-the-Woods Coll (IN)
Saint Mary's Coll (IN)
Saint Mary's U of Minnesota (MN)
St. Thomas Aquinas Coll (NY)
Salem Coll (NC)
Salem State Coll (MA)
Salisbury U (MD)
San Francisco State U (CA)
Santa Fe Comm Coll (FL)
Seattle U (WA)
Seton Hill U (PA)
Slippery Rock U of Pennsylvania (PA)
South Dakota State U (SD)
Southeast Missouri State U (MO)
Southern Adventist U (TN)
Southern Arkansas U–Magnolia (AR)
Southern Wesleyan U (SC)
Southwest Baptist U (MO)
Southwestern Adventist U (TX)
Southwestern Oklahoma State U (OK)
State U of New York at Fredonia (NY)
State U of New York at Plattsburgh (NY)
State U of New York Upstate Medical U (NY)
Stony Brook U, State U of New York (NY)
Suffolk U (MA)
Tabor Coll (KS)
Tarleton State U (TX)
Texas A&M U–Corpus Christi (TX)
Texas Southern U (TX)
Texas State U–San Marcos (TX)
Texas Woman's U (TX)
Thiel Coll (PA)
Thomas Edison State Coll (NJ)
Thomas More Coll (KY)
Trevecca Nazarene U (TN)
Tuskegee U (AL)
Union Coll (NE)
Union U (TN)
U at Buffalo, the State U of New York (NY)
The U of Alabama at Birmingham (AL)
The U of Arizona (AZ)
U of Bridgeport (CT)
U of Central Florida (FL)
U of Central Missouri (MO)
U of Central Oklahoma (OK)
U of Cincinnati (OH)
U of Connecticut (CT)
U of Delaware (DE)
U of Evansville (IN)
The U of Findlay (OH)
U of Hartford (CT)
U of Hawaii at Manoa (HI)
U of Houston (TX)
U of Illinois at Springfield (IL)
U of Indianapolis (IN)
The U of Iowa (IA)
The U of Kansas (KS)
U of Kentucky (KY)
U of Louisiana at Monroe (LA)
U of Maine (ME)
U of Mary (ND)
U of Mary Hardin-Baylor (TX)
U of Maryland Eastern Shore (MD)
U of Massachusetts Dartmouth (MA)
U of Massachusetts Lowell (MA)
U of Michigan–Flint (MI)
U of Minnesota, Twin Cities Campus (MN)
U of Mississippi (MS)
U of Mount Union (OH)
U of Nebraska Medical Center (NE)
U of Nevada, Las Vegas (NV)
U of New England (ME)
U of New Hampshire (NH)
The U of North Carolina at Chapel Hill (NC)
The U of North Carolina at Charlotte (NC)
The U of North Carolina at Greensboro (NC)
U of North Dakota (ND)
U of North Texas (TX)
U of Oklahoma (OK)
U of Rhode Island (RI)
U of Rio Grande (OH)
U of St. Francis (IL)
The U of Scranton (PA)
U of South Alabama (AL)
U of Southern Mississippi (MS)
U of South Florida (FL)
The U of Tennessee (TN)
The U of Texas at Arlington (TX)
The U of Texas at Austin (TX)
The U of Texas at El Paso (TX)
The U of Texas at San Antonio (TX)
The U of Texas at Tyler (TX)
The U of Texas Medical Branch (TX)
The U of Texas–Pan American (TX)
The U of Texas Southwestern Medical Center at Dallas (TX)
U of the District of Columbia (DC)
U of the Sciences in Philadelphia (PA)
The U of Toledo (OH)
U of Utah (UT)
U of Vermont (VT)
The U of Virginia's Coll at Wise (VA)
U of Washington (WA)
U of West Florida (FL)
U of Wisconsin–La Crosse (WI)
U of Wisconsin–Milwaukee (WI)
U of Wisconsin–Oshkosh (WI)
U of Wisconsin–Stevens Point (WI)
Utah State U (UT)
Virginia Commonwealth U (VA)
Wake Forest U (NC)
Wartburg Coll (IA)
Wayne State U (MI)
Western Carolina U (NC)
Western Connecticut State U (CT)
Western Illinois U (IL)
Western Kentucky U (KY)
West Liberty U (WV)
West Virginia U (WV)
Wichita State U (KS)
Wilkes U (PA)
William Jewell Coll (MO)
Winona State U (MN)
Winston-Salem State U (NC)
Winthrop U (SC)
Wright State U (OH)
Xavier U (OH)
York Coll of Pennsylvania (PA)
York Coll of the City U of New York (NY)
Youngstown State U (OH)

CLINICAL/MEDICAL LABORATORY ASSISTANT

Edinboro U of Pennsylvania (PA)

CLINICAL/MEDICAL LABORATORY SCIENCE AND ALLIED PROFESSIONS RELATED

Allen Coll (IA)
Auburn U (AL)
Bloomfield Coll (NJ)
The Coll of Idaho (ID)
Hunter Coll of the City U of New York (NY)
Northeastern U (MA)
Roosevelt U (IL)
Saint Louis U (MO)

CLINICAL/MEDICAL LABORATORY TECHNOLOGY

Alabama State U (AL)
Argosy U, Twin Cities (MN)
Auburn U (AL)
Barry U (FL)
California State U, East Bay (CA)
Cameron U (OK)
East Central U (OK)
Edinboro U of Pennsylvania (PA)
Farmingdale State Coll (NY)
Holy Family U (PA)
Indiana U–Purdue U Fort Wayne (IN)
Long Island U, C.W. Post Campus (NY)
Longwood U (VA)
Marquette U (WI)
Northern State U (SD)
Our Lady of the Lake Coll (LA)
Penn State DuBois (PA)
Pittsburg State U (KS)
St. Thomas Aquinas Coll (NY)
Slippery Rock U of Pennsylvania (PA)
Sonoma State U (CA)
Tabor Coll (KS)
U of Alberta (AB, Canada)
The U of British Columbia (BC, Canada)
U of Maryland Eastern Shore (MD)
U of Missouri–Kansas City (MO)
U of New Mexico (NM)
U of Science and Arts of Oklahoma (OK)
Viterbo U (WI)
Washburn U (KS)
Winona State U (MN)
York Coll of the City U of New York (NY)

CLINICAL/MEDICAL SOCIAL WORK

New Mexico Highlands U (NM)
U of St. Thomas (MN)
The U of Western Ontario (ON, Canada)

CLINICAL NUTRITION

Loyola U Chicago (IL)
Messiah Coll (PA)
U of North Dakota (ND)

CLINICAL PASTORAL COUNSELING/PATIENT COUNSELING

Somerset Christian Coll (NJ)
The U of Western Ontario (ON, Canada)

CLINICAL PSYCHOLOGY

Averett U (VA)
Eastern Nazarene Coll (MA)
Franklin Pierce U (NH)
Husson U (ME)
Keene State Coll (NH)
Lakehead U (ON, Canada)
Lamar U (TX)
Mansfield U of Pennsylvania (PA)
Moravian Coll (PA)
Redeemer U Coll (ON, Canada)
Simon Fraser U (BC, Canada)
U of Alberta (AB, Canada)
The U of British Columbia (BC, Canada)
U of Michigan–Flint (MI)
U of New Brunswick Fredericton (NB, Canada)
U of Windsor (ON, Canada)
Western State Coll of Colorado (CO)

COGNITIVE PSYCHOLOGY AND PSYCHOLINGUISTICS

Averett U (VA)
California State U, Stanislaus (CA)
Dartmouth Coll (NH)
Free Will Baptist Bible Coll (TN)
The Johns Hopkins U (MD)
Lawrence U (WI)
Occidental Coll (CA)
Prescott Coll (AZ)
State U of New York at Oswego (NY)
Tulane U (LA)
U of California, San Diego (CA)
U of California, Santa Cruz (CA)
The U of Kansas (KS)
Vassar Coll (NY)
Washington U in St. Louis (MO)
Wellesley Coll (MA)
Wilfrid Laurier U (ON, Canada)
Yale U (CT)

COGNITIVE SCIENCE

California State U, Fresno (CA)
Carnegie Mellon U (PA)
Case Western Reserve U (OH)
Central Michigan U (MI)
George Fox U (OR)
Hampshire Coll (MA)
Indiana U Bloomington (IN)
Lawrence U (WI)
Lehigh U (PA)
Massachusetts Inst of Technology (MA)
Occidental Coll (CA)
Pomona Coll (CA)
Queen's U at Kingston (ON, Canada)
Rensselaer Polytechnic Inst (NY)
Simon Fraser U (BC, Canada)
State U of New York at Oswego (NY)
United States Military Acad (NY)
The U of British Columbia (BC, Canada)
U of California, Berkeley (CA)
U of California, Los Angeles (CA)
U of California, Merced (CA)
U of Connecticut (CT)
U of Evansville (IN)
U of Georgia (GA)
U of Pennsylvania (PA)
U of Richmond (VA)
U of Rochester (NY)
The U of Texas at Dallas (TX)
Vanderbilt U (TN)

COLLEGE STUDENT COUNSELING AND PERSONNEL SERVICES

Bob Jones U (SC)
Bowling Green State U (OH)
Kutztown U of Pennsylvania (PA)
Prescott Coll (AZ)
The U of North Carolina at Pembroke (NC)

COMMERCIAL AND ADVERTISING ART

Alberta Coll of Art & Design (AB, Canada)
Arcadia U (PA)
Arkansas State U—Jonesboro (AR)
Art Center Coll of Design (CA)
The Art Inst of Dallas (TX)
Ashland U (OH)
Auburn U (AL)
Baker Coll of Owosso (MI)
Bemidji State U (MN)
Black Hills State U (SD)
Bob Jones U (SC)
Boise State U (ID)
Boston U (MA)
Bowling Green State U (OH)
Buena Vista U (IA)
Buffalo State Coll, State U of New York (NY)
California Coll of the Arts (CA)
California State U, East Bay (CA)
California State U, Fresno (CA)
California State U, Long Beach (CA)
Carroll U (WI)
Carson-Newman Coll (TN)
Centenary Coll (NJ)
Champlain Coll (VT)
Clark U (MA)
The Cleveland Inst of Art (OH)
Coll for Creative Studies (MI)
The Coll of New Jersey (NJ)
The Coll of Saint Rose (NY)
Columbia Coll Chicago (IL)
Columbus Coll of Art & Design (OH)
Concordia U Chicago (IL)
Concordia U Wisconsin (WI)
Concord U (WV)
Curry Coll (MA)
Dominican U (IL)
Dordt Coll (IA)
Drake U (IA)
Drexel U (PA)
Emmanuel Coll (MA)
Fairmont State U (WV)
Fashion Inst of Technology (NY)
Felician Coll (NJ)
Ferris State U (MI)
Florida Ag and Mech U (FL)
Fontbonne U (MO)
Fordham U (NY)
Franklin Pierce U (NH)
Freed-Hardeman U (TN)
Gallaudet U (DC)
Graceland U (IA)
Hampton U (VA)
Huntington U (IN)
Indiana U–Purdue U Fort Wayne (IN)
Intl Acad of Design & Technology (IL)
Iowa State U of Science and Technology (IA)
Keene State Coll (NH)
Kent State U (OH)
Kutztown U of Pennsylvania (PA)
Lamar U (TX)
Lipscomb U (TN)
Longwood U (VA)
Louisiana Coll (LA)
Louisiana Tech U (LA)
Loyola U New Orleans (LA)
Lycoming Coll (PA)
Marian U (IN)
Marietta Coll (OH)
Marymount Manhattan Coll (NY)
Massachusetts Coll of Art and Design (MA)
Mercy Coll (NY)
Miami U (OH)
Millikin U (IL)
Minneapolis Coll of Art and Design (MN)
Minnesota State U Mankato (MN)
Minnesota State U Moorhead (MN)
Mitchell Coll (CT)
Mount Mary Coll (WI)
Mount Olive Coll (NC)
New York Inst of Technology (NY)
Northeastern State U (OK)
Northeastern U (MA)
Northern Kentucky U (KY)
Northwest Nazarene U (ID)
Ohio Northern U (OH)
Oklahoma Christian U (OK)
Oklahoma City U (OK)
O'More Coll of Design (TN)
Oral Roberts U (OK)
Otis Coll of Art and Design (CA)
Peru State Coll (NE)
Philadelphia U (PA)
Pittsburg State U (KS)
Portland State U (OR)
Pratt Inst (NY)
Purchase Coll, State U of New York (NY)
Ringling Coll of Art and Design (FL)
Rivier Coll (NH)
Rochester Inst of Technology (NY)
Rutgers, The State U of New Jersey, New Brunswick (NJ)
St. Norbert Coll (WI)
St. Thomas Aquinas Coll (NY)
Salem State Coll (MA)
Savannah Coll of Art and Design (GA)
School of Visual Arts (NY)
Seton Hall U (NJ)
Seton Hill U (PA)
Southwest Baptist U (MO)
Southwestern Oklahoma State U (OK)
State U of New York at Fredonia (NY)
State U of New York at New Paltz (NY)
State U of New York at Oswego (NY)
Suffolk U (MA)
Syracuse U (NY)
Tabor Coll (KS)
Texas A&M U–Commerce (TX)
Trinity Christian Coll (IL)
Truman State U (MO)
Union Coll (NE)
U of Advancing Technology (AZ)
U of Central Missouri (MO)
U of Central Oklahoma (OK)
U of Cincinnati (OH)
U of Dayton (OH)
U of Delaware (DE)
U of Denver (CO)
U of Indianapolis (IN)
U of Massachusetts Dartmouth (MA)
U of Minnesota, Duluth (MN)
U of Minnesota, Twin Cities Campus (MN)
U of New Haven (CT)
U of North Texas (TX)
The U of Tennessee (TN)
The U of Texas at El Paso (TX)
U of the Pacific (CA)
U of Washington (WA)
U of Wisconsin–Platteville (WI)
U of Wisconsin–Stevens Point (WI)
Upper Iowa U (IA)
Villa Maria Coll of Buffalo (NY)
Wartburg Coll (IA)
Washington U in St. Louis (MO)
Waynesburg U (PA)
Weber State U (UT)
West Liberty U (WV)
West Virginia Wesleyan Coll (WV)
Wichita State U (KS)

William Paterson U of New Jersey (NJ)
Winona State U (MN)
Woodbury U (CA)
York U (ON, Canada)

COMMERCIAL PHOTOGRAPHY

The Art Inst of Atlanta (GA)
The Art Inst of Charleston (SC)
The Art Inst of Tennessee–Nashville (TN)
The Art Inst of Washington (VA)
Fashion Inst of Technology (NY)
Minnesota State U Moorhead (MN)
Rochester Inst of Technology (NY)
Savannah Coll of Art and Design (GA)
School of Visual Arts (NY)

COMMUNICATION AND JOURNALISM RELATED

Arizona State U (AZ)
Arkansas State U—Jonesboro (AR)
Auburn U (AL)
Benedictine U (IL)
Berry Coll (GA)
Bowling Green State U (OH)
Brigham Young U (UT)
Brigham Young U–Hawaii (HI)
California Baptist U (CA)
California Lutheran U (CA)
California State U, Chico (CA)
Carlow U (PA)
Cedarville U (OH)
Centenary Coll of Louisiana (LA)
Champlain Coll (VT)
Clarke Coll (IA)
Clemson U (SC)
The Coll at Brockport, State U of New York (NY)
Columbia Coll (SC)
Concordia U (CA)
Concordia U (QC, Canada)
Culver-Stockton Coll (MO)
DeSales U (PA)
Drexel U (PA)
Eastern Nazarene Coll (MA)
The Evergreen State Coll (WA)
Flagler Coll (FL)
Franklin U (OH)
Friends U (KS)
Hannibal-LaGrange Coll (MO)
Hawai'i Pacific U (HI)
Hope Coll (MI)
Illinois Inst of Technology (IL)
Indiana U Bloomington (IN)
Indiana U Kokomo (IN)
Ithaca Coll (NY)
Lehigh U (PA)
Lehman Coll of the City U of New York (NY)
Madonna U (MI)
Malone U (OH)
Mary Baldwin Coll (VA)
Mercer U (GA)
Mercy Coll (NY)
Milwaukee School of Eng (WI)
Mississippi Coll (MS)
Mount Mercy Coll (IA)
Newbury Coll (MA)
New England School of Communications (ME)
New York U (NY)
Norfolk State U (VA)
Northern Arizona U (AZ)
Northwest Christian U (OR)
Notre Dame de Namur U (CA)
Ohio Northern U (OH)
Oklahoma Christian U (OK)
Old Dominion U (VA)
Penn State Abington (PA)
Penn State Altoona (PA)
Penn State Beaver (PA)
Penn State Berks (PA)
Penn State Brandywine (PA)
Penn State DuBois (PA)
Penn State Erie, The Behrend Coll (PA)
Penn State Fayette, The Eberly Campus (PA)
Penn State Greater Allegheny (PA)
Penn State Hazleton (PA)
Penn State Lehigh Valley (PA)
Penn State Mont Alto (PA)
Penn State New Kensington (PA)
Penn State Schuylkill (PA)
Penn State Shenango (PA)
Penn State U Park (PA)
Penn State Wilkes-Barre (PA)
Penn State Worthington Scranton (PA)
Penn State York (PA)
Point Park U (PA)
Quincy U (IL)
Quinnipiac U (CT)
Reinhardt Coll (GA)
St. John Fisher Coll (NY)
Saint Mary's Coll of California (CA)
San Diego State U (CA)
Siena Heights U (MI)
Southeastern Oklahoma State U (OK)
Sterling Coll (KS)
Tiffin U (OH)
Trevecca Nazarene U (TN)
U of Evansville (IN)
U of Illinois at Urbana–Champaign (IL)
U of Wisconsin–Green Bay (WI)
Valparaiso U (IN)
Walden U (MN)
Washington U in St. Louis (MO)
Webster U (MO)
West Virginia U (WV)
Wheeling Jesuit U (WV)

COMMUNICATION AND MEDIA RELATED

Adelphi U (NY)
Alma Coll (MI)
American Jewish U (CA)
Athabasca U (AB, Canada)
Bennington Coll (VT)
Calumet Coll of Saint Joseph (IN)
Carnegie Mellon U (PA)
Champlain Coll (VT)
The Coll at Brockport, State U of New York (NY)
Concordia U (QC, Canada)
Crown Coll (MN)
DePaul U (IL)
East Texas Baptist U (TX)
Elizabethtown Coll (PA)
Elon U (NC)
Eugene Lang Coll The New School for Liberal Arts (NY)
Fairleigh Dickinson U, Metropolitan Campus (NJ)
Florida State U (FL)
Franklin Coll Switzerland (Switzerland)
Full Sail U (FL)
Gardner-Webb U (NC)
Georgetown Coll (KY)
Green Mountain Coll (VT)
Greenville Coll (IL)
Hood Coll (MD)
Houston Baptist U (TX)
Hult Intl Business School (United Kingdom)
King's Coll (PA)
Lane Coll (TN)
La Roche Coll (PA)
Loyola U Chicago (IL)
Lycoming Coll (PA)
Lynn U (FL)
Milligan Coll (TN)
New Jersey Inst of Technology (NJ)
New York U (NY)
Penn State Erie, The Behrend Coll (PA)
Point Park U (PA)
Reinhardt Coll (GA)
Rochester Inst of Technology (NY)
Rollins Coll (FL)
St. Edward's U (TX)
Southern New Hampshire U (NH)
Southern Polytechnic State U (GA)
Southwestern Coll (KS)
Spring Arbor U (MI)
U of Central Missouri (MO)
U of Colorado at Boulder (CO)
U of Evansville (IN)
U of Illinois at Springfield (IL)
U of Mobile (AL)
U of the Cumberlands (KY)
The U of Western Ontario (ON, Canada)
Virginia Wesleyan Coll (VA)
Walden U (MN)
Walsh U (OH)
Wheelock Coll (MA)
Wilmington U (DE)

COMMUNICATION DISORDERS

Appalachian State U (NC)
Arizona State U (AZ)
Auburn U (AL)
Augustana Coll (IL)
Baldwin-Wallace Coll (OH)
Baylor U (TX)
Bob Jones U (SC)
Boston U (MA)
Bowling Green State U (OH)
Bridgewater State Coll (MA)
Brock U (ON, Canada)
Butler U (IN)
California State U, Chico (CA)
California State U, Fresno (CA)
California State U, Fullerton (CA)
California State U, Long Beach (CA)
California State U, Los Angeles (CA)
California State U, Northridge (CA)
Carlos Albizu U (PR)
Case Western Reserve U (OH)
Central Michigan U (MI)
Eastern Illinois U (IL)
Edinboro U of Pennsylvania (PA)
Emerson Coll (MA)
Fontbonne U (MO)
Hampton U (VA)
Harding U (AR)
Kansas State U (KS)
Lamar U (TX)
Longwood U (VA)
Michigan State U (MI)
Minnesota State U Mankato (MN)
Minot State U (ND)
Murray State U (KY)
Pace U (NY)
Penn State Abington (PA)
Penn State Altoona (PA)
Penn State Beaver (PA)
Penn State Berks (PA)
Penn State Brandywine (PA)
Penn State DuBois (PA)
Penn State Erie, The Behrend Coll (PA)
Penn State Fayette, The Eberly Campus (PA)
Penn State Greater Allegheny (PA)
Penn State Hazleton (PA)
Penn State Lehigh Valley (PA)
Penn State Mont Alto (PA)
Penn State New Kensington (PA)
Penn State Schuylkill (PA)
Penn State Shenango (PA)
Penn State U Park (PA)
Penn State Wilkes-Barre (PA)
Penn State Worthington Scranton (PA)
Penn State York (PA)
Queens Coll of the City U of New York (NY)
Radford U (VA)
St. Cloud State U (MN)
Saint Mary's Coll (IN)
San Diego State U (CA)
San Francisco State U (CA)
San Jose State U (CA)
Southeast Missouri State U (MO)
Southern Illinois U Carbondale (IL)
State U of New York at Fredonia (NY)
State U of New York at New Paltz (NY)
State U of New York at Plattsburgh (NY)
State U of New York Coll at Geneseo (NY)
Texas Southern U (TX)
Truman State U (MO)
The U of Arizona (AZ)
The U of British Columbia (BC, Canada)
U of Georgia (GA)
U of Houston (TX)
The U of Kansas (KS)
U of Maine (ME)
U of Massachusetts Amherst (MA)
U of Nebraska at Kearney (NE)
U of North Dakota (ND)
U of Oklahoma Health Sciences Center (OK)
U of Oregon (OR)
U of Redlands (CA)
U of Rhode Island (RI)
The U of South Dakota (SD)
The U of Texas at Austin (TX)
The U of Toledo (OH)
U of Vermont (VT)
The U of Western Ontario (ON, Canada)
U of Wisconsin–Eau Claire (WI)
U of Wisconsin–Madison (WI)
U of Wisconsin–River Falls (WI)
Wayne State U (MI)
Western Carolina U (NC)
Western Illinois U (IL)
Winthrop U (SC)
Worcester State Coll (MA)
Xavier U of Louisiana (LA)

COMMUNICATION DISORDERS SCIENCES AND SERVICES RELATED

Long Island U, Brooklyn Campus (NY)
Ouachita Baptist U (AR)
St. Cloud State U (MN)
U of Minnesota, Duluth (MN)
U of Missouri (MO)
U of New Hampshire (NH)
U of Oklahoma Health Sciences Center (OK)
The U of Western Ontario (ON, Canada)

COMMUNICATION/SPEECH COMMUNICATION AND RHETORIC

Abilene Christian U (TX)
Albertus Magnus Coll (CT)
Albright Coll (PA)
Alderson-Broaddus Coll (WV)
Alfred U (NY)
Allegheny Coll (PA)
Alliant Intl U (CA)
Alvernia U (PA)
Alverno Coll (WI)
Andrew Jackson U (AL)
Angelo State U (TX)
Aquinas Coll (MI)
Arcadia U (PA)
Arizona State U (AZ)
Arkansas Tech U (AR)
Auburn U Montgomery (AL)
Augustana Coll (SD)
Aurora U (IL)
Austin Coll (TX)
Avila U (MO)
Azusa Pacific U (CA)
Baker U (KS)
Baldwin-Wallace Coll (OH)
Baptist Bible Coll of Pennsylvania (PA)
Barry U (FL)
Baylor U (TX)
Belhaven U (MS)
Bellarmine U (KY)
Benedictine U (IL)
Bethany Coll (KS)
Bethany Coll (WV)
Bethany Lutheran Coll (MN)
Bethel Coll (IN)
Bethel U (MN)
Blackburn Coll (IL)
Bluffton U (OH)
Bob Jones U (SC)
Boston Coll (MA)
Boston U (MA)
Bowling Green State U (OH)
Bradley U (IL)
Brewton-Parker Coll (GA)
Bridgewater State Coll (MA)
Brigham Young U–Hawaii (HI)
Brock U (ON, Canada)
Brooklyn Coll of the City U of New York (NY)
Bryan Coll (TN)
Bryant U (RI)
Buena Vista U (IA)
Buffalo State Coll, State U of New York (NY)
Butler U (IN)
Cabrini Coll (PA)
California Baptist U (CA)
California State Polytechnic U, Pomona (CA)
California State U, Chico (CA)
California State U, Dominguez Hills (CA)
California State U, Fresno (CA)
California State U, Fullerton (CA)
California State U, Los Angeles (CA)
California State U, Monterey Bay (CA)
California State U, Sacramento (CA)
California State U, San Marcos (CA)
California State U, Stanislaus (CA)
Calumet Coll of Saint Joseph (IN)
Calvin Coll (MI)
Cameron U (OK)
Canisius Coll (NY)
Cape Breton U (NS, Canada)
Capital U (OH)
Carroll U (WI)
The Catholic U of America (DC)
Cedar Crest Coll (PA)
Cedarville U (OH)
Central Coll (IA)
Central Connecticut State U (CT)
Central Michigan U (MI)
Chapman U (CA)
Chatham U (PA)
Chowan U (NC)
Christopher Newport U (VA)
Clarion U of Pennsylvania (PA)
Clarkson U (NY)
Clayton State U (GA)
Clearwater Christian Coll (FL)
Cleveland State U (OH)
Coastal Carolina U (SC)
Coker Coll (SC)
The Coll at Brockport, State U of New York (NY)
Coll of Charleston (SC)
Coll of Mount St. Joseph (OH)
Coll of Notre Dame of Maryland (MD)
Coll of Saint Elizabeth (NJ)
The Coll of Saint Rose (NY)
The Coll of St. Scholastica (MN)
Coll of Staten Island of the City U of New York (NY)
Coll of the Ozarks (MO)
The Coll of Wooster (OH)
Colorado State U (CO)
Columbia Coll (MO)
Columbia Coll (SC)
Columbia Intl U (SC)
Concordia Coll (MN)
Concordia U (CA)
Concordia U (QC, Canada)
Concordia U Chicago (IL)
Corban U (OR)
Cornell U (NY)
Creighton U (NE)
Dakota Wesleyan U (SD)
Dallas Baptist U (TX)
Delta State U (MS)
DePaul U (IL)
Dixie State Coll of Utah (UT)
Dominican U (IL)
Dominican U of California (CA)
Drury U (MO)
Duquesne U (PA)
East Carolina U (NC)
Eastern Connecticut State U (CT)
Eastern Mennonite U (VA)
Eastern Michigan U (MI)
Eastern New Mexico U (NM)
Eastern Washington U (WA)
East Stroudsburg U of Pennsylvania (PA)
Eckerd Coll (FL)
Edgewood Coll (WI)
Edinboro U of Pennsylvania (PA)
Elizabeth City State U (NC)
Elmhurst Coll (IL)
Elon U (NC)
Embry-Riddle Aeronautical U (FL)
Emerson Coll (MA)
Emmanuel Coll (MA)
Emporia State U (KS)
The Evergreen State Coll (WA)
Fairfield U (CT)
Fairleigh Dickinson U, Coll at Florham (NJ)
Fayetteville State U (NC)
Ferris State U (MI)
Fitchburg State Coll (MA)
Florida Atlantic U (FL)
Florida Inst of Technology (FL)
Florida Southern Coll (FL)
Fontbonne U (MO)
Franciscan U of Steubenville (OH)
Frostburg State U (MD)
Furman U (SC)
Gallaudet U (DC)
Geneva Coll (PA)
George Fox U (OR)
Georgian Court U (NJ)
Georgia Southern U (GA)
Gordon Coll (MA)
Governors State U (IL)
Grace Coll (IN)
Grand Valley State U (MI)
Great Lakes Christian Coll (MI)
Greensboro Coll (NC)
Hamilton Coll (NY)
Hamline U (MN)
Hampshire Coll (MA)
Hannibal-LaGrange Coll (MO)
Harding U (AR)
Hardin-Simmons U (TX)
Hawai'i Pacific U (HI)
Hillsdale Coll (MI)
Hillsdale Free Will Baptist Coll (OK)
Hofstra U (NY)
Holy Family U (PA)
Hope Coll (MI)
Houston Baptist U (TX)
Howard Payne U (TX)
Huntingdon Coll (AL)
Huntington U (IN)
Idaho State U (ID)
Illinois State U (IL)
Immaculata U (PA)
Indiana State U (IN)
Indiana Tech (IN)
Indiana U Bloomington (IN)
Indiana U East (IN)
Indiana U Kokomo (IN)
Indiana U Northwest (IN)
Indiana U of Pennsylvania (PA)
Indiana U–Purdue U Fort Wayne (IN)
Indiana U–Purdue U Indianapolis (IN)
Indiana U South Bend (IN)
Indiana U Southeast (IN)
Indiana Wesleyan U (IN)
Inter American U of Puerto Rico, Bayamón Campus (PR)
Iona Coll (NY)
Jacksonville State U (AL)
Jacksonville U (FL)
James Madison U (VA)
Jamestown Coll (ND)
Juniata Coll (PA)
Kansas State U (KS)

INDEXES

Kaplan U, Davenport Campus (IA)
Kean U (NJ)
Keene State Coll (NH)
Kennesaw State U (GA)
Kent State U at Trumbull (OH)
Kentucky Wesleyan Coll (KY)
Keuka Coll (NY)
Keystone Coll (PA)
Kuyper Coll (MI)
Lake Forest Coll (IL)
La Sierra U (CA)
Lawrence Technological U (MI)
Le Moyne Coll (NY)
Lewis & Clark Coll (OR)
Lewis-Clark State Coll (ID)
Liberty U (VA)
Lincoln U (PA)
Linfield Coll (OR)
Long Island U, Brooklyn Campus (NY)
Long Island U, C.W. Post Campus (NY)
Longwood U (VA)
Loyola Marymount U (CA)
Loyola U Chicago (IL)
Loyola U Maryland (MD)
Loyola U New Orleans (LA)
Lubbock Christian U (TX)
Luther Coll (IA)
Lynchburg Coll (VA)
Madonna U (MI)
Marian U (IN)
Marian U (WI)
Marietta Coll (OH)
Marquette U (WI)
Mary Baldwin Coll (VA)
Marylhurst U (OR)
Marymount Manhattan Coll (NY)
Marymount U (VA)
Massachusetts Coll of Liberal Arts (MA)
Mayville State U (ND)
McDaniel Coll (MD)
McPherson Coll (KS)
Mercyhurst Coll (PA)
Meredith Coll (NC)
Merrimack Coll (MA)
Messiah Coll (PA)
Miami U Hamilton (OH)
Michigan State U (MI)
Michigan Technological U (MI)
Millersville U of Pennsylvania (PA)
Millikin U (IL)
Millsaps Coll (MS)
Misericordia U (PA)
Mississippi Coll (MS)
Mississippi State U (MS)
Mississippi U for Women (MS)
Missouri Baptist U (MO)
Missouri Southern State U (MO)
Missouri State U (MO)
Molloy Coll (NY)
Monmouth Coll (IL)
Monmouth U (NJ)
Montclair State U (NJ)
Moody Bible Inst (IL)
Morehead State U (KY)
Mount Mary Coll (WI)
Mount Mercy Coll (IA)
Mount St. Mary's U (MD)
Mount Vernon Nazarene U (OH)
Multnomah U (OR)
Nazareth Coll of Rochester (NY)
Nebraska Wesleyan U (NE)
Neumann U (PA)
New Jersey City U (NJ)
New Mexico Highlands U (NM)
New York U (NY)
Northeastern U (MA)
Northern Michigan U (MI)
North Greenville U (SC)
Northwest Christian U (OR)
Northwestern Coll (MN)
Northwest Nazarene U (ID)
Notre Dame de Namur U (CA)
Nova Southeastern U (FL)
Nyack Coll (NY)
Oakland U (MI)
Oglethorpe U (GA)
Ohio Dominican U (OH)
Ohio Northern U (OH)
The Ohio State U (OH)
Ohio U (OH)
Oklahoma Baptist U (OK)
Oral Roberts U (OK)
Oregon Inst of Technology (OR)
Ottawa U (KS)
Ouachita Baptist U (AR)
Our Lady of the Lake U of San Antonio (TX)
Pace U (NY)
Park U (MO)
Peace Coll (NC)
Penn State Abington (PA)
Penn State Altoona (PA)
Penn State Beaver (PA)
Penn State Berks (PA)
Penn State Brandywine (PA)
Penn State DuBois (PA)
Penn State Erie, The Behrend Coll (PA)
Penn State Fayette, The Eberly Campus (PA)
Penn State Greater Allegheny (PA)
Penn State Harrisburg (PA)
Penn State Hazleton (PA)
Penn State Lehigh Valley (PA)
Penn State Mont Alto (PA)
Penn State New Kensington (PA)
Penn State Schuylkill (PA)
Penn State Shenango (PA)
Penn State U Park (PA)
Penn State Wilkes-Barre (PA)
Penn State Worthington Scranton (PA)
Penn State York (PA)
Pepperdine U, Malibu (CA)
Pikeville Coll (KY)
Pittsburg State U (KS)
Plymouth State U (NH)
Prairie View A&M U (TX)
Prescott Coll (AZ)
Purchase Coll, State U of New York (NY)
Purdue U (IN)
Purdue U Calumet (IN)
Purdue U North Central (IN)
Radford U (VA)
Ramapo Coll of New Jersey (NJ)
Randolph Coll (VA)
Regent U (VA)
Regis Coll (MA)
Rensselaer Polytechnic Inst (NY)
Rhode Island Coll (RI)
The Richard Stockton Coll of New Jersey (NJ)
Ripon Coll (WI)
Rivier Coll (NH)
Roberts Wesleyan Coll (NY)
Rochester Coll (MI)
Rochester Inst of Technology (NY)
Rockhurst U (MO)
Rocky Mountain Coll (MT)
Roosevelt U (IL)
Rosemont Coll (PA)
Rowan U (NJ)
Rutgers, The State U of New Jersey, New Brunswick (NJ)
Saginaw Valley State U (MI)
Saint Anselm Coll (NH)
St. Francis Coll (NY)
St. John's U (NY)
Saint Joseph's U (PA)
Saint Louis U (MO)
Saint Mary's Coll (IN)
Saint Mary's Coll of California (CA)
St. Mary's U (TX)
St. Norbert Coll (WI)
Saint Vincent Coll (PA)
Saint Xavier U (IL)
Salem State Coll (MA)
Salisbury U (MD)
Samford U (AL)
Sam Houston State U (TX)
San Diego Christian Coll (CA)
San Francisco State U (CA)
Santa Clara U (CA)
Seattle Pacific U (WA)
Seton Hall U (NJ)
Seton Hill U (PA)
Shenandoah U (VA)
Shepherd U (WV)
Simmons Coll (MA)
Simon Fraser U (BC, Canada)
Simpson U (CA)
Slippery Rock U of Pennsylvania (PA)
Sonoma State U (CA)
Southeastern Louisiana U (LA)
Southeastern Oklahoma State U (OK)
Southeast Missouri State U (MO)
Southern Connecticut State U (CT)
Southern Oregon U (OR)
Southern U and Ag and Mech Coll (LA)
Southern Vermont Coll (VT)
Southern Wesleyan U (SC)
Southwest Baptist U (MO)
Southwestern Assemblies of God U (TX)
Southwestern Coll (KS)
Southwestern U (TX)
Southwest Minnesota State U (MN)
Spalding U (KY)
Spring Arbor U (MI)
Stanford U (CA)
State U of New York at New Paltz (NY)
State U of New York Coll at Cortland (NY)
State U of New York Coll at Geneseo (NY)
State U of New York Coll at Old Westbury (NY)
Stetson U (FL)
Stonehill Coll (MA)
Susquehanna U (PA)
Syracuse U (NY)
Tabor Coll (KS)
Taylor U (IN)
Texas A&M Intl U (TX)
Texas A&M U–Commerce (TX)
Texas A&M U–Corpus Christi (TX)
Texas A&M U–Kingsville (TX)
Texas Christian U (TX)
Texas Lutheran U (TX)
Texas Southern U (TX)
Thiel Coll (PA)
Thomas Edison State Coll (NJ)
Thomas More Coll (KY)
Tiffin U (OH)
Towson U (MD)
Trevecca Nazarene U (TN)
Trine U (IN)
Trinity Christian Coll (IL)
Trinity U (TX)
Truman State U (MO)
Union Coll (KY)
U at Buffalo, the State U of New York (NY)
The U of Akron (OH)
The U of Alabama (AL)
The U of Alabama at Birmingham (AL)
U of Alaska Fairbanks (AK)
The U of Arizona (AZ)
U of Arkansas (AR)
U of California, Davis (CA)
U of California, Santa Barbara (CA)
U of Central Florida (FL)
U of Central Oklahoma (OK)
U of Colorado at Boulder (CO)
U of Colorado at Colorado Springs (CO)
U of Colorado Denver (CO)
U of Connecticut (CT)
U of Delaware (DE)
U of Denver (CO)
U of Hartford (CT)
U of Hawaii at Manoa (HI)
U of Houston (TX)
U of Houston–Clear Lake (TX)
U of Illinois at Chicago (IL)
U of Illinois at Urbana–Champaign (IL)
U of Indianapolis (IN)
The U of Iowa (IA)
U of Kentucky (KY)
U of La Verne (CA)
U of Louisville (KY)
U of Maine (ME)
U of Mary Hardin-Baylor (TX)
U of Maryland, Coll Park (MD)
U of Maryland U Coll (MD)
U of Massachusetts Amherst (MA)
U of Memphis (TN)
U of Miami (FL)
U of Michigan (MI)
U of Michigan–Dearborn (MI)
U of Minnesota, Crookston (MN)
U of Missouri (MO)
U of Missouri–Kansas City (MO)
U of Missouri–St. Louis (MO)
U of Mobile (AL)
U of Nebraska–Lincoln (NE)
U of Nevada, Las Vegas (NV)
U of Nevada, Reno (NV)
U of New Hampshire (NH)
U of New Haven (CT)
U of New Mexico (NM)
U of New Orleans (LA)
The U of North Carolina at Chapel Hill (NC)
The U of North Carolina at Charlotte (NC)
The U of North Carolina Wilmington (NC)
U of North Dakota (ND)
U of Northern Colorado (CO)
U of Northern Iowa (IA)
U of Oklahoma (OK)
U of Ottawa (ON, Canada)
U of Pennsylvania (PA)
U of Puget Sound (WA)
U of Rhode Island (RI)
U of Rio Grande (OH)
U of St. Thomas (MN)
U of St. Thomas (TX)
U of San Diego (CA)
U of San Francisco (CA)
U of Science and Arts of Oklahoma (OK)
The U of Scranton (PA)
U of South Alabama (AL)
U of South Carolina Aiken (SC)
U of South Carolina Upstate (SC)
U of Southern California (CA)
U of Southern Indiana (IN)
U of Southern Maine (ME)
U of Southern Mississippi (MS)
The U of Tampa (FL)
The U of Tennessee at Chattanooga (TN)
The U of Texas at Austin (TX)
The U of Texas at Brownsville (TX)
The U of Texas at San Antonio (TX)
The U of Texas of the Permian Basin (TX)
The U of Texas–Pan American (TX)
U of the Cumberlands (KY)
U of the Incarnate Word (TX)
U of the Pacific (CA)
The U of Toledo (OH)
U of Tulsa (OK)
U of Utah (UT)
The U of Virginia's Coll at Wise (VA)
U of Washington (WA)
U of Washington, Tacoma (WA)
U of Waterloo (ON, Canada)
U of West Florida (FL)
U of Wisconsin–Eau Claire (WI)
U of Wisconsin–La Crosse (WI)
U of Wisconsin–Parkside (WI)
U of Wisconsin–River Falls (WI)
U of Wisconsin–Stevens Point (WI)
U of Wisconsin–Whitewater (WI)
U of Wyoming (WY)
Utica Coll (NY)
Valdosta State U (GA)
Vanderbilt U (TN)
Vanguard U of Southern California (CA)
Virginia Polytechnic Inst and State U (VA)
Wake Forest U (NC)
Walden U (MN)
Wartburg Coll (IA)
Washburn U (KS)
Washington U in St. Louis (MO)
Wayland Baptist U (TX)
Waynesburg U (PA)
Wayne State Coll (NE)
Wayne State U (MI)
Webber Intl U (FL)
Webster U (MO)
Wesleyan Coll (GA)
Western Carolina U (NC)
Western Connecticut State U (CT)
Western Illinois U (IL)
Western Kentucky U (KY)
Western Michigan U (MI)
Western New England Coll (MA)
Western Washington U (WA)
Westfield State Coll (MA)
Westminster Coll (UT)
Westmont Coll (CA)
West Virginia State U (WV)
West Virginia Wesleyan Coll (WV)
Wheaton Coll (IL)
Whitman Coll (WA)
Wichita State U (KS)
Wilkes U (PA)
William Jewell Coll (MO)
William Penn U (IA)
Wingate U (NC)
Wittenberg U (OH)
Woodbury U (CA)
Worcester State Coll (MA)
Wright State U (OH)
York Coll of Pennsylvania (PA)
York U (ON, Canada)

COMMUNICATIONS TECHNOLOGIES AND SUPPORT SERVICES RELATED

Alverno Coll (WI)
Framingham State Coll (MA)
Indiana U Bloomington (IN)
Lesley U (MA)
New England School of Communications (ME)
Saint Mary-of-the-Woods Coll (IN)
The U of Scranton (PA)
U of Windsor (ON, Canada)

COMMUNICATIONS TECHNOLOGY

Cedarville U (OH)
Eastern Michigan U (MI)
East Stroudsburg U of Pennsylvania (PA)
ECPI Coll of Technology, Virginia Beach (VA)
Inter American U of Puerto Rico, Bayamón Campus (PR)
Lawrence Technological U (MI)
Lewis U (IL)
Michigan State U (MI)
Sacred Heart U (CT)
Saint Mary-of-the-Woods Coll (IN)
Salve Regina U (RI)
Southern Adventist U (TN)
U of Puerto Rico at Humacao (PR)
York Coll of the City U of New York (NY)

COMMUNITY HEALTH AND PREVENTIVE MEDICINE

Florida Gulf Coast U (FL)
George Mason U (VA)
Governors State U (IL)
Hofstra U (NY)
Indiana U Bloomington (IN)
Slippery Rock U of Pennsylvania (PA)
Texas A&M U–Kingsville (TX)
Tufts U (MA)
U of Florida (FL)
U of Illinois at Urbana–Champaign (IL)
U of Massachusetts Lowell (MA)
U of Wisconsin–La Crosse (WI)
Western Kentucky U (KY)

COMMUNITY HEALTH SERVICES COUNSELING

Bethel U (MN)
Cleveland State U (OH)
Delaware State U (DE)
Eastern Washington U (WA)
Indiana State U (IN)
Indiana U–Purdue U Fort Wayne (IN)
James Madison U (VA)
Johnson C. Smith U (NC)
Longwood U (VA)
Michigan State U (MI)
Minnesota State U Moorhead (MN)
Morris Coll (SC)
Northeastern Illinois U (IL)
Northern Michigan U (MI)
Ohio U (OH)
Prairie View A&M U (TX)
Texas A&M U (TX)
The U of Kansas (KS)
U of Nebraska at Omaha (NE)
U of Northern Iowa (IA)
U of Pennsylvania (PA)
The U of Tampa (FL)
U of the Cumberlands (KY)
The U of Western Ontario (ON, Canada)
U of West Florida (FL)
Western Connecticut State U (CT)
Western Washington U (WA)
Worcester State Coll (MA)
Youngstown State U (OH)

COMMUNITY ORGANIZATION AND ADVOCACY

Alverno Coll (WI)
Bemidji State U (MN)
Bryant U (RI)
Cape Breton U (NS, Canada)
Central Michigan U (MI)
Cleveland State U (OH)
Coll of Notre Dame of Maryland (MD)
Corban U (OR)
Cornell U (NY)
DePaul U (IL)
Eastern Michigan U (MI)
Emory & Henry Coll (VA)
High Point U (NC)
Indiana U South Bend (IN)
Mercer U (GA)
New Mexico State U (NM)
New York U (NY)
Northern State U (SD)
Northland Coll (WI)
Pace U (NY)
Prescott Coll (AZ)
Providence Coll (RI)
Rockhurst U (MO)
Roosevelt U (IL)
Saint Martin's U (WA)
Siena Heights U (MI)
Southern Arkansas U–Magnolia (AR)
State U of New York Empire State Coll (NY)
Thomas Edison State Coll (NJ)
U of Alaska Fairbanks (AK)
U of Baltimore (MD)
U of Delaware (DE)
U of Hartford (CT)
U of Massachusetts Boston (MA)
U of Saint Mary (KS)
The U of Texas at El Paso (TX)
The U of Toledo (OH)

COMMUNITY PSYCHOLOGY

Cambridge Coll (MA)
Clayton State U (GA)
Kwantlen Polytechnic U (BC, Canada)
Montana State U Billings (MT)
New York Inst of Technology (NY)
Rogers State U (OK)
U of Miami (FL)
U of Saint Mary (KS)

U of Washington, Bothell (WA)
Wilfrid Laurier U (ON, Canada)
Wright State U (OH)

COMPARATIVE LITERATURE

Agnes Scott Coll (GA)
American Jewish U (CA)
The American U of Paris (France)
Arcadia U (PA)
Augustana Coll (IL)
Bard Coll (NY)
Barnard Coll (NY)
Barry U (FL)
Beloit Coll (WI)
Bernard M. Baruch Coll of the City U of New York (NY)
Bishop's U (QC, Canada)
Blackburn Coll (IL)
Brandeis U (MA)
Brock U (ON, Canada)
Brooklyn Coll of the City U of New York (NY)
Bryn Mawr Coll (PA)
California State U, Fullerton (CA)
California State U, Long Beach (CA)
Carson-Newman Coll (TN)
Case Western Reserve U (OH)
Castleton State Coll (VT)
Cazenovia Coll (NY)
Chowan U (NC)
Christendom Coll (VA)
Christopher Newport U (VA)
City Coll of the City U of New York (NY)
Claremont McKenna Coll (CA)
Clark U (MA)
The Coll at Brockport, State U of New York (NY)
Coll of the Atlantic (ME)
Coll of the Holy Cross (MA)
Coll of the Humanities and Sciences, Harrison Middleton U (AZ)
The Coll of Wooster (OH)
The Colorado Coll (CO)
Columbia U (NY)
Columbia U, School of General Studies (NY)
Cornell U (NY)
Dartmouth Coll (NH)
Duke U (NC)
Earlham Coll (IN)
East Central U (OK)
Eckerd Coll (FL)
Emory U (GA)
Eugene Lang Coll The New School for Liberal Arts (NY)
Florida State U (FL)
Fordham U (NY)
Franklin Coll Switzerland (Switzerland)
Franklin Pierce U (NH)
Georgetown U (DC)
Gettysburg Coll (PA)
Gonzaga U (WA)
Graceland U (IA)
Grove City Coll (PA)
Hamilton Coll (NY)
Harvard U (MA)
Haverford Coll (PA)
High Point U (NC)
Hillsdale Coll (MI)
Hofstra U (NY)
Houghton Coll (NY)
Hunter Coll of the City U of New York (NY)
Indiana U Bloomington (IN)
Inter American U of Puerto Rico, San Germán Campus (PR)
John Cabot U (Italy)
John Carroll U (OH)
The Johns Hopkins U (MD)
Johnson State Coll (VT)
Lake Superior State U (MI)
Lycoming Coll (PA)
Marlboro Coll (VT)
Memorial U of Newfoundland (NL, Canada)
Mills Coll (CA)
Minnesota State U Mankato (MN)
Mount Allison U (NB, Canada)
New Coll of Florida (FL)
New England Coll (NH)
New York U (NY)
Northwest U (WA)
Oberlin Coll (OH)
Occidental Coll (CA)
The Ohio State U (OH)
Ohio Wesleyan U (OH)
Penn State Abington (PA)
Penn State Altoona (PA)
Penn State Beaver (PA)
Penn State Berks (PA)
Penn State Brandywine (PA)
Penn State DuBois (PA)
Penn State Erie, The Behrend Coll (PA)
Penn State Fayette, The Eberly Campus (PA)
Penn State Greater Allegheny (PA)
Penn State Hazleton (PA)
Penn State Lehigh Valley (PA)
Penn State Mont Alto (PA)
Penn State New Kensington (PA)
Penn State Schuylkill (PA)
Penn State Shenango (PA)
Penn State U Park (PA)
Penn State Wilkes-Barre (PA)
Penn State Worthington Scranton (PA)
Penn State York (PA)
Pitzer Coll (CA)
Prescott Coll (AZ)
Princeton U (NJ)
Purchase Coll, State U of New York (NY)
Queens Coll of the City U of New York (NY)
Quinnipiac U (CT)
Ramapo Coll of New Jersey (NJ)
Reed Coll (OR)
Rochester Coll (MI)
Rockford Coll (IL)
Rutgers, The State U of New Jersey, New Brunswick (NJ)
St. Catherine U (MN)
St. Cloud State U (MN)
Saint Francis U (PA)
Saint Mary's Coll of California (CA)
San Diego State U (CA)
San Francisco State U (CA)
Sarah Lawrence Coll (NY)
Sewanee: The U of the South (TN)
Smith Coll (MA)
Sonoma State U (CA)
Stanford U (CA)
State U of New York at Binghamton (NY)
State U of New York Coll at Geneseo (NY)
State U of New York Coll at Old Westbury (NY)
Stony Brook U, State U of New York (NY)
Swarthmore Coll (PA)
Thomas More Coll of Liberal Arts (NH)
Trent U (ON, Canada)
Trinity Coll (CT)
United States Military Acad (NY)
Universidad de las Américas–Puebla (Mexico)
U of Alberta (AB, Canada)
U of Baltimore (MD)
U of California, Berkeley (CA)
U of California, Davis (CA)
U of California, Irvine (CA)
U of California, Los Angeles (CA)
U of California, Merced (CA)
U of California, Riverside (CA)
U of California, San Diego (CA)
U of California, Santa Barbara (CA)
U of California, Santa Cruz (CA)
U of Chicago (IL)
U of Cincinnati (OH)
U of Delaware (DE)
U of Georgia (GA)
U of Illinois at Urbana–Champaign (IL)
The U of Iowa (IA)
U of La Verne (CA)
U of Massachusetts Amherst (MA)
U of Michigan (MI)
U of Minnesota, Twin Cities Campus (MN)
The U of Montana Western (MT)
U of Nevada, Las Vegas (NV)
U of New Brunswick Fredericton (NB, Canada)
U of New Mexico (NM)
The U of North Carolina at Chapel Hill (NC)
U of Oregon (OR)
U of Pennsylvania (PA)
U of Pittsburgh at Greensburg (PA)
U of Pittsburgh at Johnstown (PA)
U of Puerto Rico, Río Piedras (PR)
U of Redlands (CA)
U of Rhode Island (RI)
U of Rochester (NY)
U of Saskatchewan (SK, Canada)
U of Southern California (CA)
The U of Texas at Dallas (TX)
The U of Toledo (OH)
U of Toronto (ON, Canada)
U of Utah (UT)
U of Virginia (VA)
U of Washington (WA)
The U of Western Ontario (ON, Canada)
U of Wisconsin–Madison (WI)
U of Wisconsin–Milwaukee (WI)
Washington U in St. Louis (MO)
Webster U (MO)
Wellesley Coll (MA)
West Virginia Wesleyan Coll (WV)
Wilberforce U (OH)
Willamette U (OR)
William Paterson U of New Jersey (NJ)
Williams Coll (MA)
Yale U (CT)

COMPUTATIONAL MATHEMATICS

Arizona State U (AZ)
Asbury U (KY)
Brooklyn Coll of the City U of New York (NY)
California Inst of Technology (CA)
Carnegie Mellon U (PA)
Coll of Saint Benedict (MN)
Embry-Riddle Aeronautical U (FL)
Indiana U–Purdue U Fort Wayne (IN)
Marist Coll (NY)
Marquette U (WI)
Michigan State U (MI)
Michigan Technological U (MI)
Rochester Inst of Technology (NY)
Saint John's U (MN)
Siena Coll (NY)
Southwestern U (TX)
Stevens Inst of Technology (NJ)
U of California, Davis (CA)
U of California, Los Angeles (CA)
U of Illinois at Urbana–Champaign (IL)
U of Puerto Rico at Humacao (PR)
U of Puerto Rico at Utuado (PR)
U of Southern California (CA)
U of Waterloo (ON, Canada)

COMPUTER AND INFORMATION SCIENCES

Adelphi U (NY)
Alabama Ag and Mech U (AL)
Albany State U (GA)
Alcorn State U (MS)
Alvernia U (PA)
Alverno Coll (WI)
Amberton U (TX)
American Public U System (WV)
American U (DC)
Andrews U (MI)
Angelo State U (TX)
Aquinas Coll (MI)
Arcadia U (PA)
Arizona State U (AZ)
Arkansas State U—Jonesboro (AR)
Arkansas Tech U (AR)
Assumption Coll (MA)
Athabasca U (AB, Canada)
Auburn U (AL)
Austin Peay State U (TN)
Avila U (MO)
Baker Coll of Muskegon (MI)
Ball State U (IN)
Barnard Coll (NY)
Barton Coll (NC)
Bellarmine U (KY)
Bennington Coll (VT)
Bentley U (MA)
Berea Coll (KY)
Bernard M. Baruch Coll of the City U of New York (NY)
Bethel Coll (IN)
Bethel U (MN)
Bethune-Cookman U (FL)
Bishop's U (QC, Canada)
Bloomfield Coll (NJ)
Bloomsburg U of Pennsylvania (PA)
Bluefield State Coll (WV)
Bob Jones U (SC)
Boise State U (ID)
Boston Coll (MA)
Bowie State U (MD)
Bowling Green State U (OH)
Brewton-Parker Coll (GA)
Brooklyn Coll of the City U of New York (NY)
Bryant U (RI)
Bucknell U (PA)
Butler U (IN)
California Lutheran U (CA)
California State U, Fresno (CA)
California State U, Los Angeles (CA)
California State U, San Bernardino (CA)
California State U, Stanislaus (CA)
Cameron U (OK)
Cape Breton U (NS, Canada)
Carroll U (WI)
Castleton State Coll (VT)
Cedar Crest Coll (PA)
Central Connecticut State U (CT)
Central State U (OH)
Chaminade U of Honolulu (HI)
Champlain Coll (VT)
Chapman U (CA)
Chatham U (PA)
Chowan U (NC)
Christopher Newport U (VA)
The Citadel, The Military Coll of South Carolina (SC)
Claremont McKenna Coll (CA)
Clarion U of Pennsylvania (PA)
Clark Atlanta U (GA)
Clarke Coll (IA)
Clayton State U (GA)
Clemson U (SC)
Cleveland State U (OH)
Coastal Carolina U (SC)
Coll of Charleston (SC)
Coll of Mount St. Joseph (OH)
The Coll of New Jersey (NJ)
Coll of Saint Elizabeth (NJ)
Coll of Saint Mary (NE)
The Coll of Saint Rose (NY)
The Coll of St. Scholastica (MN)
Coll of the Ozarks (MO)
The Coll of William and Mary (VA)
Colorado State U (CO)
Columbia Coll (MO)
Columbus State U (GA)
Covenant Coll (GA)
Dakota State U (SD)
Dallas Baptist U (TX)
Davenport U, Grand Rapids (MI)
Delaware State U (DE)
Dickinson Coll (PA)
Dixie State Coll of Utah (UT)
Doane Coll (NE)
Dominican Coll (NY)
Dowling Coll (NY)
Drury U (MO)
Eastern Connecticut State U (CT)
Eastern Michigan U (MI)
Eastern New Mexico U (NM)
Eastern Washington U (WA)
East Stroudsburg U of Pennsylvania (PA)
East Tennessee State U (TN)
ECPI Coll of Technology, Virginia Beach (VA)
ECPI Tech Coll, Roanoke (VA)
Edgewood Coll (WI)
Edinboro U of Pennsylvania (PA)
EDP Coll of Puerto Rico, Inc. (PR)
Elizabethtown Coll (PA)
Elon U (NC)
Emmanuel Coll (GA)
Emporia State U (KS)
The Evergreen State Coll (WA)
Excelsior Coll (NY)
Fairfield U (CT)
Fairleigh Dickinson U, Coll at Florham (NJ)
Fisher Coll (MA)
Fitchburg State Coll (MA)
Florida Ag and Mech U (FL)
Florida Atlantic U (FL)
Florida Gulf Coast U (FL)
Florida Intl U (FL)
Fordham U (NY)
Fort Lewis Coll (CO)
Framingham State Coll (MA)
Franciscan U of Steubenville (OH)
Francis Marion U (SC)
Franklin Coll (IN)
Franklin U (OH)
Freed-Hardeman U (TN)
Friends U (KS)
Frostburg State U (MD)
Gallaudet U (DC)
Gannon U (PA)
Gardner-Webb U (NC)
George Fox U (OR)
George Mason U (VA)
Georgetown Coll (KY)
The George Washington U (DC)
Georgia Coll & State U (GA)
Georgia Inst of Technology (GA)
Georgia Southern U (GA)
Georgia State U (GA)
Globe Inst of Technology (NY)
Goldey-Beacom Coll (DE)
Grace Bible Coll (MI)
Grand Valley State U (MI)
Greenville Coll (IL)
Grove City Coll (PA)
Guilford Coll (NC)
Gwynedd-Mercy Coll (PA)
Hamilton Coll (NY)
Hannibal-LaGrange Coll (MO)
Harrisburg U of Science and Technology (PA)
Hartwick Coll (NY)
Hawai'i Pacific U (HI)
Henderson State U (AR)
Herzing U (GA)
Herzing U (WI)
High Point U (NC)
Holy Family U (PA)
Hope Coll (MI)
Houston Baptist U (TX)
Huston-Tillotson U (TX)
Idaho State U (ID)
Illinois Inst of Technology (IL)
Indiana State U (IN)
Indiana U Bloomington (IN)
Indiana U Kokomo (IN)
Indiana U Northwest (IN)
Indiana U of Pennsylvania (PA)
Indiana U–Purdue U Indianapolis (IN)
Indiana U South Bend (IN)
Indiana U Southeast (IN)
Indiana Wesleyan U (IN)
Inter American U of Puerto Rico, Fajardo Campus (PR)
Ithaca Coll (NY)
Jackson State U (MS)
Jacksonville State U (AL)
Jacksonville U (FL)
James Madison U (VA)
John Jay Coll of Criminal Justice of the City U of New York (NY)
The Johns Hopkins U (MD)
Johnson & Wales U (RI)
Johnson C. Smith U (NC)
Jones Coll, Jacksonville (FL)
Juniata Coll (PA)
Kansas State U (KS)
Kean U (NJ)
Keene State Coll (NH)
Kennesaw State U (GA)
Kentucky State U (KY)
Kentucky Wesleyan Coll (KY)
King's Coll (PA)
Knox Coll (IL)
Kuyper Coll (MI)
LaGrange Coll (GA)
Lane Coll (TN)
La Roche Coll (PA)
La Salle U (PA)
Lehman Coll of the City U of New York (NY)
Le Moyne Coll (NY)
Lewis-Clark State Coll (ID)
Lewis U (IL)
Liberty U (VA)
Lincoln Memorial U (TN)
Lincoln U (PA)
Lock Haven U of Pennsylvania (PA)
Long Island U, Brooklyn Campus (NY)
Long Island U, C.W. Post Campus (NY)
Loyola Marymount U (CA)
Loyola U Chicago (IL)
Loyola U Maryland (MD)
Lubbock Christian U (TX)
Mansfield U of Pennsylvania (PA)
Marshall U (WV)
Mars Hill Coll (NC)
Maryville Coll (TN)
Massachusetts Coll of Liberal Arts (MA)
The Master's Coll and Sem (CA)
Mayville State U (ND)
McDaniel Coll (MD)
McMurry U (TX)
Mercy Coll (NY)
Mercyhurst Coll (PA)
Meredith Coll (NC)
Metropolitan State Coll of Denver (CO)
Miami U (OH)
Michigan State U (MI)
Midway Coll (KY)
Midwestern State U (TX)
Millersville U of Pennsylvania (PA)
Milligan Coll (TN)
Minnesota State U Moorhead (MN)
Misericordia U (PA)
Mississippi Coll (MS)
Mississippi State U (MS)
Missouri Baptist U (MO)
Missouri Southern State U (MO)
Missouri Western State U (MO)
Monmouth U (NJ)
Morehead State U (KY)
Morehouse Coll (GA)
Mount Mercy Coll (IA)
Mount St. Mary's U (MD)
Mount Vernon Nazarene U (OH)
Murray State U (KY)
Neumann U (PA)
Neumont U (UT)
New Jersey City U (NJ)
New Jersey Inst of Technology (NJ)
New Mexico Highlands U (NM)
New Mexico State U (NM)
New York Inst of Technology (NY)
New York U (NY)
Norfolk State U (VA)
Northeastern Illinois U (IL)
Northeastern U (MA)
Northern Arizona U (AZ)
Northern Kentucky U (KY)
Northern Michigan U (MI)
North Georgia Coll & State U (GA)
Northwest Missouri State U (MO)
Notre Dame de Namur U (CA)
Nova Southeastern U (FL)
Oakland U (MI)

The Ohio State U (OH)
Ohio U (OH)
Oklahoma Baptist U (OK)
Oklahoma Panhandle State U (OK)
Oklahoma State U (OK)
Old Dominion U (VA)
Oral Roberts U (OK)
Oregon Inst of Technology (OR)
Oregon State U (OR)
Pace U (NY)
Park U (MO)
Penn State Abington (PA)
Penn State Altoona (PA)
Penn State Beaver (PA)
Penn State Berks (PA)
Penn State Brandywine (PA)
Penn State DuBois (PA)
Penn State Erie, The Behrend Coll (PA)
Penn State Fayette, The Eberly Campus (PA)
Penn State Greater Allegheny (PA)
Penn State Harrisburg (PA)
Penn State Hazleton (PA)
Penn State Lehigh Valley (PA)
Penn State Mont Alto (PA)
Penn State New Kensington (PA)
Penn State Schuylkill (PA)
Penn State Shenango (PA)
Penn State U Park (PA)
Penn State Wilkes-Barre (PA)
Penn State Worthington Scranton (PA)
Penn State York (PA)
Philadelphia U (PA)
Pikeville Coll (KY)
Portland State U (OR)
Prairie View A&M U (TX)
Prescott Coll (AZ)
Principia Coll (IL)
Purdue U (IN)
Purdue U Calumet (IN)
Quincy U (IL)
Ramapo Coll of New Jersey (NJ)
Rhode Island Coll (RI)
Rice U (TX)
The Richard Stockton Coll of New Jersey (NJ)
Rider U (NJ)
Rochester Inst of Technology (NY)
Rowan U (NJ)
Rutgers, The State U of New Jersey, Camden (NJ)
Rutgers, The State U of New Jersey, Newark (NJ)
Saginaw Valley State U (MI)
St. Bonaventure U (NY)
St. Catherine U (MN)
St. Edward's U (TX)
St. Francis Xavier U (NS, Canada)
St. John Fisher Coll (NY)
St. John's U (NY)
Saint Joseph's U (PA)
Saint Leo U (FL)
Saint Louis U (MO)
Saint Mary-of-the-Woods Coll (IN)
St. Mary's Coll of Maryland (MD)
St. Norbert Coll (WI)
Saint Vincent Coll (PA)
Saint Xavier U (IL)
Salem State Coll (MA)
Salisbury U (MD)
Sam Houston State U (TX)
Seton Hall U (NJ)
Shaw U (NC)
Shepherd U (WV)
Shippensburg U of Pennsylvania (PA)
Shorter U (GA)
Siena Coll (NY)
Siena Heights U (MI)
Simmons Coll (MA)
Simpson Coll (IA)
Skidmore Coll (NY)
South Carolina State U (SC)
South Dakota State U (SD)
Southeastern Oklahoma State U (OK)
Southeast Missouri State U (MO)
Southern Arkansas U–Magnolia (AR)
Southern New Hampshire U (NH)
Southern Wesleyan U (SC)
Southwest Baptist U (MO)
Southwestern Oklahoma State U (OK)
Southwestern U (TX)
Spring Hill Coll (AL)
State U of New York at New Paltz (NY)
State U of New York at Plattsburgh (NY)
State U of New York Coll at Old Westbury (NY)
State U of New York Coll at Potsdam (NY)
Stephen F. Austin State U (TX)
Sterling Coll (KS)
Stetson U (FL)
Stevenson U (MD)
Stillman Coll (AL)
Suffolk U (MA)
Swarthmore Coll (PA)
Syracuse U (NY)
Tarleton State U (TX)
Taylor U (IN)
Temple U (PA)
Tennessee Wesleyan Coll (TN)
Texas A&M U–Kingsville (TX)
Texas Christian U (TX)
Texas Southern U (TX)
Texas State U–San Marcos (TX)
Texas Tech U (TX)
Texas Wesleyan U (TX)
Texas Woman's U (TX)
Thompson Rivers U (BC, Canada)
Tiffin U (OH)
Towson U (MD)
Transylvania U (KY)
Trinity U (TX)
Troy U (AL)
Truman State U (MO)
Tulane U (LA)
Union Coll (NY)
United States Military Acad (NY)
United States Naval Acad (MD)
U at Albany, State U of New York (NY)
The U of Alabama at Birmingham (AL)
The U of Alabama in Huntsville (AL)
U of Alaska Fairbanks (AK)
The U of Arizona (AZ)
U of Arkansas (AR)
U of Arkansas at Fort Smith (AR)
U of Atlanta (GA)
U of Baltimore (MD)
U of California, Irvine (CA)
U of California, Los Angeles (CA)
U of Central Florida (FL)
U of Central Missouri (MO)
U of Cincinnati (OH)
U of Colorado at Colorado Springs (CO)
U of Colorado Denver (CO)
U of Delaware (DE)
U of Dubuque (IA)
U of Evansville (IN)
U of Florida (FL)
U of Guelph (ON, Canada)
U of Hartford (CT)
U of Hawaii at Manoa (HI)
U of Houston (TX)
U of Houston–Clear Lake (TX)
U of Houston–Downtown (TX)
U of Illinois at Urbana–Champaign (IL)
The U of Kansas (KS)
U of Kentucky (KY)
U of Maine at Augusta (ME)
U of Mary (ND)
U of Mary Hardin-Baylor (TX)
U of Maryland, Coll Park (MD)
U of Maryland U Coll (MD)
U of Mary Washington (VA)
U of Massachusetts Boston (MA)
U of Massachusetts Dartmouth (MA)
U of Michigan (MI)
U of Michigan–Dearborn (MI)
U of Michigan–Flint (MI)
U of Minnesota, Duluth (MN)
U of Mississippi (MS)
U of Missouri (MO)
U of Missouri–St. Louis (MO)
U of Mobile (AL)
U of Nebraska at Kearney (NE)
U of Nebraska–Lincoln (NE)
U of Nevada, Reno (NV)
U of New Hampshire (NH)
U of New Haven (CT)
U of New Mexico (NM)
U of North Alabama (AL)
U of North Dakota (ND)
U of North Florida (FL)
U of North Texas (TX)
U of Notre Dame (IN)
U of Oregon (OR)
U of Ottawa (ON, Canada)
U of Pittsburgh at Greensburg (PA)
U of Puerto Rico at Bayamón (PR)
U of Rhode Island (RI)
U of Richmond (VA)
U of Saint Mary (KS)
U of St. Thomas (MN)
U of San Francisco (CA)
U of Science and Arts of Oklahoma (OK)
U of South Alabama (AL)
U of South Carolina (SC)
U of South Carolina Upstate (SC)
The U of South Dakota (SD)
U of Southern California (CA)
U of Southern Indiana (IN)
U of Southern Mississippi (MS)
U of South Florida (FL)
The U of Texas at Austin (TX)
The U of Texas at Brownsville (TX)
The U of Texas at Dallas (TX)
The U of Texas at Tyler (TX)
The U of Texas of the Permian Basin (TX)
The U of Texas–Pan American (TX)
U of Vermont (VT)
U of Virginia (VA)
The U of Virginia's Coll at Wise (VA)
U of Washington (WA)
U of Washington, Bothell (WA)
U of Washington, Tacoma (WA)
The U of Western Ontario (ON, Canada)
U of West Florida (FL)
U of West Georgia (GA)
U of Windsor (ON, Canada)
U of Wisconsin–Eau Claire (WI)
U of Wisconsin–La Crosse (WI)
U of Wisconsin–River Falls (WI)
U of Wisconsin–Stevens Point (WI)
U of Wisconsin–Superior (WI)
U of Wisconsin–Whitewater (WI)
Utah State U (UT)
Utica Coll (NY)
Valdosta State U (GA)
Valley City State U (ND)
Vassar Coll (NY)
Virginia Commonwealth U (VA)
Virginia Intermont Coll (VA)
Virginia Polytechnic Inst and State U (VA)
Viterbo U (WI)
Wake Forest U (NC)
Walden U (MN)
Wartburg Coll (IA)
Washburn U (KS)
Washington and Lee U (VA)
Washington State U (WA)
Washington U in St. Louis (MO)
Waynesburg U (PA)
Wayne State Coll (NE)
Wayne State U (MI)
Webber Intl U (FL)
Wentworth Inst of Technology (MA)
Wesleyan Coll (GA)
West Chester U of Pennsylvania (PA)
Western Illinois U (IL)
Western Kentucky U (KY)
Western Michigan U (MI)
Western Washington U (WA)
Westminster Coll (UT)
West Virginia Wesleyan Coll (WV)
Wichita State U (KS)
Widener U (PA)
Wilkes U (PA)
Winona State U (MN)
Worcester Polytechnic Inst (MA)
Worcester State Coll (MA)
Wright State U (OH)
Xavier U of Louisiana (LA)
Yale U (CT)
York U (ON, Canada)

COMPUTER AND INFORMATION SCIENCES AND SUPPORT SERVICES RELATED

Arizona State U (AZ)
Bloomsburg U of Pennsylvania (PA)
Cabrini Coll (PA)
California State U, Chico (CA)
California State U, Los Angeles (CA)
Capella U (MN)
City U of Seattle (WA)
Coll of Staten Island of the City U of New York (NY)
Columbia Coll (SC)
Columbia Coll Chicago (IL)
Delaware Valley Coll (PA)
DePaul U (IL)
The Evergreen State Coll (WA)
Ferris State U (MI)
Hofstra U (NY)
Indiana U East (IN)
Indiana U–Purdue U Indianapolis (IN)
Inter American U of Puerto Rico, Bayamón Campus (PR)
Inter American U of Puerto Rico, Guayama Campus (PR)
Intl Acad of Design & Technology (IL)
John Jay Coll of Criminal Justice of the City U of New York (NY)
Keene State Coll (NH)
Lehigh U (PA)
Limestone Coll (SC)
Lindenwood U (MO)
Long Island U, C.W. Post Campus (NY)
Mayville State U (ND)
Missouri U of Science and Technology (MO)
Mountain State U (WV)
New Jersey Inst of Technology (NJ)
New York U (NY)
Park U (MO)
Purdue U (IN)
Purdue U Calumet (IN)
Purdue U North Central (IN)
Roberts Wesleyan Coll (NY)
Southern Adventist U (TN)
Tiffin U (OH)
U of Evansville (IN)
U of Michigan (MI)
U of Michigan–Flint (MI)
U of Mount Union (OH)
U of Northern Iowa (IA)
U of Notre Dame (IN)
U of Pittsburgh (PA)
The U of Scranton (PA)
U of Washington, Bothell (WA)
Utah State U (UT)
Valley City State U (ND)
Walden U (MN)
Washington U in St. Louis (MO)
West Virginia U (WV)

COMPUTER AND INFORMATION SCIENCES RELATED

American Public U System (WV)
California State U, Dominguez Hills (CA)
California State U, Monterey Bay (CA)
Carnegie Mellon U (PA)
Coll of Charleston (SC)
The Colorado Coll (CO)
Columbia U, School of General Studies (NY)
Eastern Illinois U (IL)
ECPI Tech Coll, Roanoke (VA)
George Mason U (VA)
Limestone Coll (SC)
Maryville Coll (TN)
Miami U Hamilton (OH)
Missouri State U (MO)
Neumont U (UT)
New Jersey Inst of Technology (NJ)
Sacred Heart U (CT)
Taylor U (IN)
U of California, Irvine (CA)
U of Windsor (ON, Canada)
U of Wisconsin–Stout (WI)
Wagner Coll (NY)
Walden U (MN)
West Virginia U (WV)
Wilfrid Laurier U (ON, Canada)

COMPUTER AND INFORMATION SYSTEMS SECURITY

American Public U System (WV)
Capella U (MN)
Champlain Coll (VT)
Dakota State U (SD)
Davenport U, Grand Rapids (MI)
DePaul U (IL)
East Stroudsburg U of Pennsylvania (PA)
ECPI Tech Coll, Roanoke (VA)
Emporia State U (KS)
Goldey-Beacom Coll (DE)
Indiana Tech (IN)
ITT Tech Inst, Bessemer (AL)
ITT Tech Inst, Madison (AL)
ITT Tech Inst, Mobile (AL)
ITT Tech Inst, Phoenix (AZ)
ITT Tech Inst, Tempe (AZ)
ITT Tech Inst, Tucson (AZ)
ITT Tech Inst (AR)
ITT Tech Inst, Clovis (CA)
ITT Tech Inst, Concord (CA)
ITT Tech Inst, Corona (CA)
ITT Tech Inst, Lathrop (CA)
ITT Tech Inst, Oxnard (CA)
ITT Tech Inst, Rancho Cordova (CA)
ITT Tech Inst, San Bernardino (CA)
ITT Tech Inst, San Diego (CA)
ITT Tech Inst, San Dimas (CA)
ITT Tech Inst, Sylmar (CA)
ITT Tech Inst, Torrance (CA)
ITT Tech Inst, Aurora (CO)
ITT Tech Inst, Thornton (CO)
ITT Tech Inst, Fort Lauderdale (FL)
ITT Tech Inst, Fort Myers (FL)
ITT Tech Inst, Jacksonville (FL)
ITT Tech Inst, Lake Mary (FL)
ITT Tech Inst, Miami (FL)
ITT Tech Inst, Pinellas Park (FL)
ITT Tech Inst, Tallahassee (FL)
ITT Tech Inst, Tampa (FL)
ITT Tech Inst, Atlanta (GA)
ITT Tech Inst, Duluth (GA)
ITT Tech Inst, Kennesaw (GA)
ITT Tech Inst (ID)
ITT Tech Inst, Burr Ridge (IL)
ITT Tech Inst, Mount Prospect (IL)
ITT Tech Inst, Fort Wayne (IN)
ITT Tech Inst, Indianapolis (IN)
ITT Tech Inst, Merrillville (IN)
ITT Tech Inst, Newburgh (IN)
ITT Tech Inst, South Bend (IN)
ITT Tech Inst, Cedar Rapids (IA)
ITT Tech Inst, Clive (IA)
ITT Tech Inst (KS)
ITT Tech Inst, Lexington (KY)
ITT Tech Inst, Louisville (KY)
ITT Tech Inst, St. Rose (LA)
ITT Tech Inst (MD)
ITT Tech Inst, Norwood (MA)
ITT Tech Inst, Woburn (MA)
ITT Tech Inst, Canton (MI)
ITT Tech Inst, Troy (MI)
ITT Tech Inst, Wyoming (MI)
ITT Tech Inst (MN)
ITT Tech Inst (MS)
ITT Tech Inst, Arnold (MO)
ITT Tech Inst, Earth City (MO)
ITT Tech Inst, Kansas City (MO)
ITT Tech Inst, Springfield (MO)
ITT Tech Inst (NE)
ITT Tech Inst (NV)
ITT Tech Inst (NM)
ITT Tech Inst, Charlotte (NC)
ITT Tech Inst, Charlotte (NC)
ITT Tech Inst, High Point (NC)
ITT Tech Inst, Morrisville (NC)
ITT Tech Inst, Oklahoma City (OK)
ITT Tech Inst, Tulsa (OK)
ITT Tech Inst (OR)
ITT Tech Inst, Columbia (SC)
ITT Tech Inst, Greenville (SC)
ITT Tech Inst, Chattanooga (TN)
ITT Tech Inst, Cordova (TN)
ITT Tech Inst, Johnson City (TN)
ITT Tech Inst, Knoxville (TN)
ITT Tech Inst, Nashville (TN)
ITT Tech Inst, Arlington (TX)
ITT Tech Inst, Austin (TX)
ITT Tech Inst, DeSoto (TX)
ITT Tech Inst, Houston (TX)
ITT Tech Inst, Houston (TX)
ITT Tech Inst, Webster (TX)
ITT Tech Inst (UT)
ITT Tech Inst, Chantilly (VA)
ITT Tech Inst, Norfolk (VA)
ITT Tech Inst, Richmond (VA)
ITT Tech Inst, Salem (VA)
ITT Tech Inst, Springfield (VA)
ITT Tech Inst, Everett (WA)
ITT Tech Inst, Seattle (WA)
ITT Tech Inst, Spokane Valley (WA)
ITT Tech Inst, Green Bay (WI)
ITT Tech Inst, Greenfield (WI)
ITT Tech Inst, Madison (WI)
Kennesaw State U (GA)
Limestone Coll (SC)
Loyola U Chicago (IL)
Mercy Coll (NY)
Pennsylvania Coll of Technology (PA)
Pittsburg State U (KS)
Rochester Inst of Technology (NY)
St. John's U (NY)
Stratford U, Woodbridge (VA)
U of Colorado at Colorado Springs (CO)
U of Illinois at Urbana–Champaign (IL)
U of Miami (FL)
U of Washington, Tacoma (WA)
Walden U (MN)
Westwood Coll–Anaheim (CA)
Westwood Coll–Annandale Campus (VA)
Westwood Coll–Arlington Ballston Campus (VA)
Westwood Coll–Atlanta Midtown (GA)
Westwood Coll–Atlanta Northlake (GA)
Westwood Coll–Chicago Du Page (IL)
Westwood Coll–Chicago Loop Campus (IL)
Westwood Coll–Chicago O'Hare Airport (IL)
Westwood Coll–Chicago River Oaks (IL)
Westwood Coll–Dallas (TX)
Westwood Coll–Denver North (CO)
Westwood Coll–Denver South (CO)
Westwood Coll–Fort Worth (TX)
Westwood Coll–Inland Empire (CA)
Westwood Coll–Los Angeles (CA)
Westwood Coll–Online Campus (CO)
Westwood Coll–South Bay Campus (CA)

COMPUTER ENGINEERING

American U of Beirut (Lebanon)
Arizona State U (AZ)
Auburn U (AL)
Bellarmine U (KY)
Bethune-Cookman U (FL)

Bob Jones U (SC)
Boston U (MA)
Bradley U (IL)
Bucknell U (PA)
California Inst of Technology (CA)
California Polytechnic State U, San Luis Obispo (CA)
California State Polytechnic U, Pomona (CA)
California State U, Chico (CA)
California State U, Fresno (CA)
California State U, Fullerton (CA)
California State U, Long Beach (CA)
California State U, Sacramento (CA)
Capital U (OH)
Carnegie Mellon U (PA)
Case Western Reserve U (OH)
Cedarville U (OH)
Christopher Newport U (VA)
Claflin U (SC)
Clarkson U (NY)
Clemson U (SC)
Cleveland State U (OH)
The Coll of New Jersey (NJ)
Colorado State U (CO)
Columbia U (NY)
Concordia U (QC, Canada)
DigiPen Inst of Technology (WA)
Dominican U (IL)
Dordt Coll (IA)
Drexel U (PA)
Eastern Nazarene Coll (MA)
Elizabethtown Coll (PA)
Embry-Riddle Aeronautical U (AZ)
Embry-Riddle Aeronautical U (FL)
Fairfield U (CT)
Florida Ag and Mech U (FL)
Florida Atlantic U (FL)
Florida Inst of Technology (FL)
Florida Intl U (FL)
Franklin W. Olin Coll of Eng (MA)
Gallaudet U (DC)
George Fox U (OR)
George Mason U (VA)
The George Washington U (DC)
Georgia Inst of Technology (GA)
Gonzaga U (WA)
Harding U (AR)
Hofstra U (NY)
Illinois Inst of Technology (IL)
Indiana U–Purdue U Fort Wayne (IN)
Indiana U–Purdue U Indianapolis (IN)
Iowa State U of Science and Technology (IA)
Jackson State U (MS)
The Johns Hopkins U (MD)
Johnson & Wales U (RI)
Johnson C. Smith U (NC)
Kansas State U (KS)
Kettering U (MI)
Lakehead U (ON, Canada)
Lawrence Technological U (MI)
Lehigh U (PA)
LeTourneau U (TX)
Liberty U (VA)
Lipscomb U (TN)
Louisiana State U and Ag and Mech Coll (LA)
Manhattan Coll (NY)
Marquette U (WI)
Merrimack Coll (MA)
Miami U (OH)
Miami U Hamilton (OH)
Michigan State U (MI)
Michigan Technological U (MI)
Midwestern State U (TX)
Milwaukee School of Eng (WI)
Minnesota State U Mankato (MN)
Mississippi State U (MS)
Missouri U of Science and Technology (MO)
Missouri Western State U (MO)
Montana State U (MT)
Montana Tech of The U of Montana (MT)
New Jersey Inst of Technology (NJ)
North Carolina State U (NC)
North Dakota State U (ND)
Northeastern U (MA)
Northwestern Polytechnic U (CA)
Oakland U (MI)
Ohio Northern U (OH)
The Ohio State U (OH)
Oklahoma Christian U (OK)
Oklahoma State U (OK)
Old Dominion U (VA)
Oral Roberts U (OK)
Oregon State U (OR)
Penn State Abington (PA)
Penn State Altoona (PA)
Penn State Beaver (PA)
Penn State Berks (PA)
Penn State Brandywine (PA)
Penn State DuBois (PA)
Penn State Erie, The Behrend Coll (PA)
Penn State Fayette, The Eberly Campus (PA)
Penn State Greater Allegheny (PA)
Penn State Hazleton (PA)
Penn State Lehigh Valley (PA)
Penn State Mont Alto (PA)
Penn State New Kensington (PA)
Penn State Schuylkill (PA)
Penn State Shenango (PA)
Penn State U Park (PA)
Penn State Wilkes-Barre (PA)
Penn State Worthington Scranton (PA)
Penn State York (PA)
Polytechnic Inst of NYU (NY)
Polytechnic U of Puerto Rico (PR)
Portland State U (OR)
Princeton U (NJ)
Purdue U (IN)
Purdue U Calumet (IN)
Queen's U at Kingston (ON, Canada)
Rice U (TX)
Rochester Inst of Technology (NY)
Rose-Hulman Inst of Technology (IN)
Royal Military Coll of Canada (ON, Canada)
Rutgers, The State U of New Jersey, New Brunswick (NJ)
St. Cloud State U (MN)
Saint Louis U (MO)
St. Mary's U (TX)
Saint Mary's U of Minnesota (MN)
San Diego State U (CA)
San Francisco State U (CA)
San Jose State U (CA)
Santa Clara U (CA)
Savannah State U (GA)
Seattle Pacific U (WA)
Shepherd U (WV)
Silicon Valley U (CA)
South Dakota School of Mines and Technology (SD)
Southern Illinois U Carbondale (IL)
Southern Illinois U Edwardsville (IL)
Southern Methodist U (TX)
Stanford U (CA)
State U of New York at Binghamton (NY)
State U of New York at New Paltz (NY)
Stevens Inst of Technology (NJ)
Syracuse U (NY)
Taylor U (IN)
Temple U (PA)
Tennessee Technological U (TN)
Texas A&M U (TX)
Texas Tech U (TX)
Trine U (IN)
Trinity Coll (CT)
Tufts U (MA)
Université du Québec en Outaouais (QC, Canada)
U at Buffalo, the State U of New York (NY)
The U of Akron (OH)
The U of Alabama in Huntsville (AL)
U of Alaska Fairbanks (AK)
U of Alberta (AB, Canada)
The U of Arizona (AZ)
U of Arkansas (AR)
U of Bridgeport (CT)
The U of British Columbia (BC, Canada)
U of California, Irvine (CA)
U of California, Los Angeles (CA)
U of California, Merced (CA)
U of California, Riverside (CA)
U of California, San Diego (CA)
U of California, Santa Barbara (CA)
U of California, Santa Cruz (CA)
U of Central Florida (FL)
U of Cincinnati (OH)
U of Colorado at Boulder (CO)
U of Colorado at Colorado Springs (CO)
U of Connecticut (CT)
U of Dayton (OH)
U of Delaware (DE)
U of Denver (CO)
U of Evansville (IN)
U of Florida (FL)
U of Georgia (GA)
U of Hartford (CT)
U of Houston (TX)
U of Houston–Clear Lake (TX)
U of Idaho (ID)
U of Illinois at Chicago (IL)
U of Illinois at Urbana–Champaign (IL)
U of Indianapolis (IN)
The U of Kansas (KS)
U of La Verne (CA)
U of Louisville (KY)
U of Maine (ME)
U of Manitoba (MB, Canada)
U of Maryland, Baltimore County (MD)
U of Maryland, Coll Park (MD)
U of Massachusetts Amherst (MA)
U of Massachusetts Dartmouth (MA)
U of Massachusetts Lowell (MA)
U of Memphis (TN)
U of Miami (FL)
U of Michigan (MI)
U of Minnesota, Duluth (MN)
U of Missouri (MO)
U of Nebraska–Lincoln (NE)
U of Nevada, Las Vegas (NV)
U of Nevada, Reno (NV)
U of New Brunswick Fredericton (NB, Canada)
U of New Hampshire (NH)
U of New Haven (CT)
U of New Mexico (NM)
The U of North Carolina at Charlotte (NC)
U of North Texas (TX)
U of Notre Dame (IN)
U of Oklahoma (OK)
U of Ottawa (ON, Canada)
U of Pennsylvania (PA)
U of Pittsburgh (PA)
U of Portland (OR)
U of Rhode Island (RI)
U of Saskatchewan (SK, Canada)
The U of Scranton (PA)
U of South Alabama (AL)
U of South Carolina (SC)
U of Southern California (CA)
U of South Florida (FL)
The U of Tennessee (TN)
The U of Texas at Arlington (TX)
The U of Texas at Dallas (TX)
The U of Texas at San Antonio (TX)
The U of Texas–Pan American (TX)
U of the Pacific (CA)
The U of Toledo (OH)
U of Toronto (ON, Canada)
U of Utah (UT)
U of Virginia (VA)
U of Washington (WA)
U of Waterloo (ON, Canada)
The U of Western Ontario (ON, Canada)
U of West Florida (FL)
U of Wisconsin–Madison (WI)
U of Wisconsin–Stout (WI)
U of Wyoming (WY)
Utah State U (UT)
Valparaiso U (IN)
Vanderbilt U (TN)
Villanova U (PA)
Virginia Commonwealth U (VA)
Virginia Polytechnic Inst and State U (VA)
Virginia State U (VA)
Washington State U (WA)
Washington U in St. Louis (MO)
Western Michigan U (MI)
West Virginia U (WV)
Wichita State U (KS)
Wilberforce U (OH)
Worcester Polytechnic Inst (MA)
Wright State U (OH)
Xavier U of Louisiana (LA)
York Coll of Pennsylvania (PA)
York U (ON, Canada)

COMPUTER ENGINEERING RELATED

Auburn U (AL)
Ohio Northern U (OH)
U of Southern California (CA)

COMPUTER ENGINEERING TECHNOLOGIES RELATED

Old Dominion U (VA)
Thomas Edison State Coll (NJ)

COMPUTER ENGINEERING TECHNOLOGY

Arizona State U (AZ)
Brock U (ON, Canada)
California State U, Long Beach (CA)
Central Connecticut State U (CT)
DeVry Coll of New York (NY)
DeVry U, Phoenix (AZ)
DeVry U, Fremont (CA)
DeVry U, Long Beach (CA)
DeVry U, Pomona (CA)
DeVry U, Sherman Oaks (CA)
DeVry U, Westminster (CO)
DeVry U, Miramar (FL)
DeVry U, Orlando (FL)
DeVry U, Alpharetta (GA)
DeVry U, Decatur (GA)
DeVry U, Addison (IL)
DeVry U, Chicago (IL)
DeVry U, Tinley Park (IL)
DeVry U, Kansas City (MO)
DeVry U, Columbus (OH)
DeVry U, Fort Washington (PA)
DeVry U, Houston (TX)
DeVry U, Irving (TX)
DeVry U, Arlington (VA)
DeVry U, Federal Way (WA)
DeVry U Online (IL)
Eastern Michigan U (MI)
Eastern Washington U (WA)
ECPI Coll of Technology, Virginia Beach (VA)
Farmingdale State Coll (NY)
Grantham U (MO)
Indiana State U (IN)
Indiana U–Purdue U Fort Wayne (IN)
Indiana U–Purdue U Indianapolis (IN)
Lake Superior State U (MI)
LeTourneau U (TX)
Minnesota State U Mankato (MN)
Murray State U (KY)
New York City Coll of Technology of the City U of New York (NY)
Norfolk State U (VA)
Northeastern U (MA)
Oregon Inst of Technology (OR)
Rochester Inst of Technology (NY)
Savannah State U (GA)
Shawnee State U (OH)
Southern Polytechnic State U (GA)
U of Arkansas at Little Rock (AR)
U of Dayton (OH)
U of Houston (TX)
U of Houston–Downtown (TX)
U of Memphis (TN)
U of Southern Mississippi (MS)
Utah State U (UT)
Vermont Tech Coll (VT)
Wentworth Inst of Technology (MA)

COMPUTER GRAPHICS

Acad of Art U (CA)
Alberta Coll of Art & Design (AB, Canada)
American U (DC)
The Art Inst of Atlanta–Decatur (GA)
Baker Coll of Flint (MI)
Bowie State U (MD)
Brooklyn Coll of the City U of New York (NY)
California State U, Chico (CA)
California State U, East Bay (CA)
Capella U (MN)
Champlain Coll (VT)
Cogswell Polytechnical Coll (CA)
Coll of the Atlantic (ME)
Creative Center (NE)
Dakota State U (SD)
DePaul U (IL)
Dominican U of California (CA)
Full Sail U (FL)
Hampshire Coll (MA)
Harrington Coll of Design (IL)
Indiana Wesleyan U (IN)
John Brown U (AR)
Johnson & Wales U (RI)
Lewis U (IL)
Memphis Coll of Art (TN)
New England School of Communications (ME)
Oakland City U (IN)
Platt Coll San Diego (CA)
Pratt Inst (NY)
Rochester Inst of Technology (NY)
Rocky Mountain Coll of Art + Design (CO)
Rogers State U (OK)
Savannah Coll of Art and Design (GA)
School of the Art Inst of Chicago (IL)
School of the Museum of Fine Arts, Boston (MA)
State U of New York at Fredonia (NY)
State U of New York Coll at Oneonta (NY)
Sullivan Coll of Technology and Design (KY)
Texas A&M U (TX)
U of Advancing Technology (AZ)
U of California, Santa Cruz (CA)
U of Colorado at Colorado Springs (CO)
U of Dubuque (IA)
U of Houston (TX)
U of Mary Hardin-Baylor (TX)
U of Miami (FL)
U of Pennsylvania (PA)
The U of Tampa (FL)

COMPUTER HARDWARE ENGINEERING

Auburn U (AL)
DigiPen Inst of Technology (WA)
State U of New York Coll of Technology at Alfred (NY)
Stony Brook U, State U of New York (NY)
United States Naval Acad (MD)
York U (ON, Canada)

COMPUTER HARDWARE TECHNOLOGY

Temple U (PA)

COMPUTER/INFORMATION TECHNOLOGY SERVICES ADMINISTRATION RELATED

Capella U (MN)
Champlain Coll (VT)
Concordia U, St. Paul (MN)
Dordt Coll (IA)
Endicott Coll (MA)
Frostburg State U (MD)
Hodges U (FL)
Holy Names U (CA)
Johnson & Wales U (RI)
Kent State U at Trumbull (OH)
Limestone Coll (SC)
Lindenwood U (MO)
Marywood U (PA)
Point Park U (PA)
Queens U of Charlotte (NC)
Robert Morris U (PA)
St. Francis Coll (NY)
Saint Mary's U of Minnesota (MN)
St. Petersburg Coll (FL)
State U of New York Coll of Technology at Alfred (NY)
U of Maryland, Baltimore County (MD)
Washington U in St. Louis (MO)

COMPUTER INSTALLATION AND REPAIR TECHNOLOGY

Inter American U of Puerto Rico, Bayamón Campus (PR)

COMPUTER PROGRAMMING

Andrews U (MI)
Arcadia U (PA)
Baker Coll of Owosso (MI)
Belmont U (TN)
Bishop's U (QC, Canada)
Bloomfield Coll (NJ)
Brigham Young U–Hawaii (HI)
Brock U (ON, Canada)
City U of Seattle (WA)
Clayton State U (GA)
Clemson U (SC)
The Coll of Saint Rose (NY)
DePaul U (IL)
Dordt Coll (IA)
ECPI Coll of Technology, Virginia Beach (VA)
EDP Coll of Puerto Rico, Inc. (PR)
EDP Coll of Puerto Rico–San Sebastian (PR)
Farmingdale State Coll (NY)
Florida State U (FL)
Franklin Pierce U (NH)
Friends U (KS)
Gannon U (PA)
Globe Inst of Technology (NY)
Hardin-Simmons U (TX)
Husson U (ME)
Inter American U of Puerto Rico, Bayamón Campus (PR)
Inter American U of Puerto Rico, San Germán Campus (PR)
Iowa Wesleyan Coll (IA)
Kent State U (OH)
Lamar U (TX)
La Salle U (PA)
Limestone Coll (SC)
Marist Coll (NY)
Memorial U of Newfoundland (NL, Canada)
Michigan Technological U (MI)
Minnesota State U Mankato (MN)
Morningside Coll (IA)
Neumont U (UT)
Nevada State Coll at Henderson (NV)
Oregon Inst of Technology (OR)
Saint Francis U (PA)
Southwestern Coll (KS)
Thompson Rivers U (BC, Canada)
U of Advancing Technology (AZ)
U of Cincinnati (OH)
U of Illinois at Urbana–Champaign (IL)
U of Michigan–Dearborn (MI)
U of Mount Union (OH)

The U of Toledo (OH)
The U of Western Ontario (ON, Canada)
Wheeling Jesuit U (WV)
Winona State U (MN)
Youngstown State U (OH)

COMPUTER PROGRAMMING RELATED

DigiPen Inst of Technology (WA)
Farmingdale State Coll (NY)
Neumont U (UT)

COMPUTER PROGRAMMING (SPECIFIC APPLICATIONS)

DePaul U (IL)
DigiPen Inst of Technology (WA)
Full Sail U (FL)
Husson U (ME)
Indiana U Southeast (IN)
Kent State U (OH)
Neumont U (UT)
Southern Polytechnic State U (GA)
U of Washington, Bothell (WA)
U of Windsor (ON, Canada)

COMPUTER PROGRAMMING (VENDOR/ PRODUCT CERTIFICATION)

Marist Coll (NY)
Neumont U (UT)

COMPUTER SCIENCE

Abilene Christian U (TX)
Acadia U (NS, Canada)
Adams State Coll (CO)
Alabama State U (AL)
Albion Coll (MI)
Albright Coll (PA)
Alderson-Broaddus Coll (WV)
Allegheny Coll (PA)
Alma Coll (MI)
American Coll of Thessaloniki (Greece)
American U (DC)
American U of Beirut (Lebanon)
Amherst Coll (MA)
Anderson U (IN)
Andrews U (MI)
Appalachian State U (NC)
Aquinas Coll (MI)
Arcadia U (PA)
Arizona State U (AZ)
Armstrong Atlantic State U (GA)
Ashland U (OH)
Augsburg Coll (MN)
Augustana Coll (IL)
Augustana Coll (SD)
Aurora U (IL)
Austin Coll (TX)
Azusa Pacific U (CA)
Baker Coll of Muskegon (MI)
Baker Coll of Owosso (MI)
Baker U (KS)
Baldwin-Wallace Coll (OH)
Bard Coll (NY)
Bard Coll at Simon's Rock (MA)
Barry U (FL)
Baylor U (TX)
Belmont U (TN)
Beloit Coll (WI)
Bemidji State U (MN)
Benedictine Coll (KS)
Benedictine U (IL)
Bennett Coll for Women (NC)
Bennington Coll (VT)
Berry Coll (GA)
Bethany Coll (WV)
Bethel Coll (IN)
Bethune-Cookman U (FL)
Birmingham-Southern Coll (AL)
Bishop's U (QC, Canada)
Blackburn Coll (IL)
Bloomsburg U of Pennsylvania (PA)
Bluefield Coll (VA)
Bluffton U (OH)
Bob Jones U (SC)
Boise State U (ID)
Boston Coll (MA)
Boston U (MA)
Bowdoin Coll (ME)
Bradley U (IL)
Brandeis U (MA)
Bridgewater Coll (VA)
Bridgewater State Coll (MA)
Brigham Young U–Hawaii (HI)
Brock U (ON, Canada)
Bryan Coll (TN)
Buena Vista U (IA)
California Inst of Technology (CA)
California Lutheran U (CA)
California Polytechnic State U, San Luis Obispo (CA)
California State Polytechnic U, Pomona (CA)
California State U, Bakersfield (CA)
California State U, Chico (CA)
California State U, Dominguez Hills (CA)
California State U, East Bay (CA)
California State U, Fresno (CA)
California State U, Fullerton (CA)
California State U, Long Beach (CA)
California State U, Los Angeles (CA)
California State U, Northridge (CA)
California State U, Sacramento (CA)
California State U, San Bernardino (CA)
California State U, San Marcos (CA)
California State U, Stanislaus (CA)
Calumet Coll of Saint Joseph (IN)
Calvin Coll (MI)
Cameron U (OK)
Canisius Coll (NY)
Capital U (OH)
Carleton Coll (MN)
Carnegie Mellon U (PA)
Carson-Newman Coll (TN)
Case Western Reserve U (OH)
Catawba Coll (NC)
The Catholic U of America (DC)
Cedarville U (OH)
Central Coll (IA)
Central Michigan U (MI)
Central Pennsylvania Coll (PA)
Chaminade U of Honolulu (HI)
Chapman U (CA)
Cheyney U of Pennsylvania (PA)
Christian Brothers U (TN)
Christopher Newport U (VA)
City Coll of the City U of New York (NY)
Claflin U (SC)
Claremont McKenna Coll (CA)
Clark Atlanta U (GA)
Clarkson U (NY)
Clark U (MA)
Clemson U (SC)
Cleveland State U (OH)
Coker Coll (SC)
Colby Coll (ME)
The Coll at Brockport, State U of New York (NY)
Coll of Notre Dame of Maryland (MD)
Coll of Saint Benedict (MN)
Coll of Saint Elizabeth (NJ)
Coll of the Holy Cross (MA)
Coll of the Ozarks (MO)
The Coll of Wooster (OH)
Columbia Coll (MO)
Columbia U (NY)
Columbia U, School of General Studies (NY)
Concordia Coll (MN)
Concordia U (QC, Canada)
Concordia U Chicago (IL)
Concordia U Texas (TX)
Concordia U Wisconsin (WI)
Concord U (WV)
Connecticut Coll (CT)
Coppin State U (MD)
Cornell Coll (IA)
Cornell U (NY)
Creighton U (NE)
Dallas Baptist U (TX)
Dartmouth Coll (NH)
Delaware State U (DE)
Denison U (OH)
DePaul U (IL)
DePauw U (IN)
DeSales U (PA)
Dickinson State U (ND)
Dillard U (LA)
Doane Coll (NE)
Dominican U (IL)
Dordt Coll (IA)
Dowling Coll (NY)
Drake U (IA)
Drew U (NJ)
Drexel U (PA)
Drury U (MO)
Duke U (NC)
Duquesne U (PA)
Earlham Coll (IN)
East Carolina U (NC)
East Central U (OK)
Eastern Mennonite U (VA)
Eastern Michigan U (MI)
Eastern Nazarene Coll (MA)
East-West U (IL)
Eckerd Coll (FL)
ECPI Coll of Technology, Virginia Beach (VA)
ECPI Tech Coll, Roanoke (VA)
Elizabeth City State U (NC)
Elmhurst Coll (IL)
Elon U (NC)
Embry-Riddle Aeronautical U (AZ)
Embry-Riddle Aeronautical U (FL)
Emory & Henry Coll (VA)
Emory U (GA)
Endicott Coll (MA)
Evangel U (MO)
Fairleigh Dickinson U, Metropolitan Campus (NJ)
Fairmont State U (WV)
Fayetteville State U (NC)
Felician Coll (NJ)
Fisk U (TN)
Fitchburg State Coll (MA)
Florida Inst of Technology (FL)
Florida Southern Coll (FL)
Fontbonne U (MO)
Fordham U (NY)
Fort Hays State U (KS)
Fort Lewis Coll (CO)
Fort Valley State U (GA)
Franciscan U of Steubenville (OH)
Franklin Coll (IN)
Franklin Pierce U (NH)
Freed-Hardeman U (TN)
Frostburg State U (MD)
Furman U (SC)
Gallaudet U (DC)
Gardner-Webb U (NC)
Geneva Coll (PA)
Georgetown Coll (KY)
Georgetown U (DC)
The George Washington U (DC)
Georgia State U (GA)
Gettysburg Coll (PA)
Glenville State Coll (WV)
Gonzaga U (WA)
Gordon Coll (MA)
Goshen Coll (IN)
Goucher Coll (MD)
Governors State U (IL)
Graceland U (IA)
Grambling State U (LA)
Grand View U (IA)
Grantham U (MO)
Grinnell Coll (IA)
Gustavus Adolphus Coll (MN)
Hampden-Sydney Coll (VA)
Hampshire Coll (MA)
Hampton U (VA)
Hanover Coll (IN)
Harding U (AR)
Hartwick Coll (NY)
Harvard U (MA)
Harvey Mudd Coll (CA)
Haverford Coll (PA)
Hawai'i Pacific U (HI)
Heidelberg U (OH)
Hendrix Coll (AR)
High Point U (NC)
Hillsdale Coll (MI)
Hiram Coll (OH)
Hofstra U (NY)
Hood Coll (MD)
Houghton Coll (NY)
Houston Baptist U (TX)
Howard Payne U (TX)
Humboldt State U (CA)
Hunter Coll of the City U of New York (NY)
Huntington U (IN)
Huston-Tillotson U (TX)
Illinois Coll (IL)
Illinois Inst of Technology (IL)
Illinois State U (IL)
Illinois Wesleyan U (IL)
Immaculata U (PA)
Indiana Tech (IN)
Indiana U–Purdue U Fort Wayne (IN)
Inter American U of Puerto Rico, Aguadilla Campus (PR)
Inter American U of Puerto Rico, Bayamón Campus (PR)
Inter American U of Puerto Rico, Ponce Campus (PR)
Inter American U of Puerto Rico, San Germán Campus (PR)
Iona Coll (NY)
Iowa Wesleyan Coll (IA)
Ithaca Coll (NY)
Jamestown Coll (ND)
John Brown U (AR)
John Carroll U (OH)
Kalamazoo Coll (MI)
Kennesaw State U (GA)
Kent State U (OH)
Kentucky Wesleyan Coll (KY)
Kettering U (MI)
King Coll (TN)
King's Coll (PA)
The King's U Coll (AB, Canada)
Lafayette Coll (PA)
Lake Forest Coll (IL)
Lakehead U (ON, Canada)
Lakeland Coll (WI)
Lake Superior State U (MI)
Lamar U (TX)
La Roche Coll (PA)
La Salle U (PA)
La Sierra U (CA)
Laurentian U (ON, Canada)
Lawrence Technological U (MI)
Lawrence U (WI)
Lebanon Valley Coll (PA)
Lehigh U (PA)
Lehman Coll of the City U of New York (NY)
LeTourneau U (TX)
Lewis & Clark Coll (OR)
Lewis-Clark State Coll (ID)
Lewis U (IL)
Limestone Coll (SC)
Lindenwood U (MO)
Linfield Coll (OR)
Lipscomb U (TN)
Lock Haven U of Pennsylvania (PA)
Long Island U, Brooklyn Campus (NY)
Long Island U, C.W. Post Campus (NY)
Longwood U (VA)
Loras Coll (IA)
Louisiana State U and Ag and Mech Coll (LA)
Louisiana State U in Shreveport (LA)
Louisiana Tech U (LA)
Luther Coll (IA)
Lynchburg Coll (VA)
Lyon Coll (AR)
Macalester Coll (MN)
Madonna U (MI)
Maharishi U of Management (IA)
Malone U (OH)
Manchester Coll (IN)
Manhattan Coll (NY)
Manhattanville Coll (NY)
Mansfield U of Pennsylvania (PA)
Marietta Coll (OH)
Marist Coll (NY)
Marlboro Coll (VT)
Marquette U (WI)
Mars Hill Coll (NC)
Maryville Coll (TN)
Massachusetts Coll of Liberal Arts (MA)
Massachusetts Inst of Technology (MA)
McKendree U (IL)
McNeese State U (LA)
Memorial U of Newfoundland (NL, Canada)
Mercer U (GA)
Mercyhurst Coll (PA)
Meredith Coll (NC)
Messiah Coll (PA)
Methodist U (NC)
Metropolitan State Coll of Denver (CO)
Miami U Hamilton (OH)
Michigan Technological U (MI)
MidAmerica Nazarene U (KS)
Middlebury Coll (VT)
Middle Tennessee State U (TN)
Milligan Coll (TN)
Millsaps Coll (MS)
Mills Coll (CA)
Minnesota State U Mankato (MN)
Minnesota State U Moorhead (MN)
Minot State U (ND)
Mississippi Coll (MS)
Mississippi Valley State U (MS)
Missouri State U (MO)
Missouri U of Science and Technology (MO)
Molloy Coll (NY)
Monmouth Coll (IL)
Monroe Coll, Bronx (NY)
Monroe Coll, New Rochelle (NY)
Montana State U (MT)
Montana Tech of The U of Montana (MT)
Montclair State U (NJ)
Moravian Coll (PA)
Mountain State U (WV)
Mount Allison U (NB, Canada)
Mount Holyoke Coll (MA)
Mount Marty Coll (SD)
Mount Mercy Coll (IA)
Mount Vernon Nazarene U (OH)
National U (CA)
Nebraska Wesleyan U (NE)
Neumont U (UT)
Newberry Coll (SC)
Newbury Coll (MA)
New Mexico Inst of Mining and Technology (NM)
Niagara U (NY)
Nipissing U (ON, Canada)
North Carolina Central U (NC)
North Dakota State U (ND)
Northeastern Illinois U (IL)
Northeastern State U (OK)
Northeastern U (MA)
Northern Arizona U (AZ)
North Georgia Coll & State U (GA)
Northwestern Coll (IA)
Northwestern Oklahoma State U (OK)
Northwestern Polytechnic U (CA)
Northwest Nazarene U (ID)
Nova Southeastern U (FL)
Nyack Coll (NY)
Oakwood U (AL)
Oberlin Coll (OH)
Ohio Northern U (OH)
The Ohio State U (OH)
Ohio U (OH)
Ohio Wesleyan U (OH)
Oklahoma Baptist U (OK)
Oklahoma Christian U (OK)
Oklahoma City U (OK)
Oral Roberts U (OK)
Ouachita Baptist U (AR)
Pace U (NY)
Pacific Lutheran U (WA)
Pacific States U (CA)
Pacific Union Coll (CA)
Park U (MO)
Penn State Erie, The Behrend Coll (PA)
Pepperdine U, Malibu (CA)
Philadelphia U (PA)
Piedmont Coll (GA)
Plymouth State U (NH)
Polytechnic Inst of NYU (NY)
Polytechnic U of Puerto Rico (PR)
Pomona Coll (CA)
Portland State U (OR)
Prairie View A&M U (TX)
Presbyterian Coll (SC)
Providence Coll (RI)
Queens Coll of the City U of New York (NY)
Queen's U at Kingston (ON, Canada)
Quincy U (IL)
Quinnipiac U (CT)
Radford U (VA)
Randolph-Macon Coll (VA)
Redeemer U Coll (ON, Canada)
Rensselaer Polytechnic Inst (NY)
Rhode Island Coll (RI)
Rhodes Coll (TN)
The Richard Stockton Coll of New Jersey (NJ)
Ripon Coll (WI)
Rivier Coll (NH)
Roanoke Coll (VA)
Roberts Wesleyan Coll (NY)
Rochester Inst of Technology (NY)
Rockford Coll (IL)
Rocky Mountain Coll (MT)
Rollins Coll (FL)
Roosevelt U (IL)
Rose-Hulman Inst of Technology (IN)
Royal Military Coll of Canada (ON, Canada)
Rutgers, The State U of New Jersey, New Brunswick (NJ)
Sage Coll of Albany (NY)
Saginaw Valley State U (MI)
St. Ambrose U (IA)
Saint Anselm Coll (NH)
Saint Augustine's Coll (NC)
St. Bonaventure U (NY)
St. Cloud State U (MN)
St. Edward's U (TX)
Saint Francis U (PA)
Saint John's U (MN)
St. Lawrence U (NY)
Saint Martin's U (WA)
St. Mary's U (TX)
Saint Mary's U of Minnesota (MN)
Saint Michael's Coll (VT)
St. Olaf Coll (MN)
Saint Paul's Coll (VA)
St. Thomas U (FL)
Saint Xavier U (IL)
Samford U (AL)
San Diego State U (CA)
San Francisco State U (CA)
San Jose State U (CA)
Sarah Lawrence Coll (NY)
Scripps Coll (CA)
Seattle U (WA)
Seton Hill U (PA)
Sewanee: The U of the South (TN)
Shaw U (NC)
Silicon Valley U (CA)
Silver Lake Coll (WI)
Simon Fraser U (BC, Canada)
Simpson Coll (IA)
Slippery Rock U of Pennsylvania (PA)
Smith Coll (MA)
Sonoma State U (CA)
South Carolina State U (SC)
South Dakota School of Mines and Technology (SD)
Southeastern Louisiana U (LA)
Southern Adventist U (TN)
Southern California Inst of Technology (CA)
Southern Connecticut State U (CT)

INDEXES

Southern Illinois U Carbondale (IL)
Southern Illinois U Edwardsville (IL)
Southern Methodist U (TX)
Southern Oregon U (OR)
Southern Polytechnic State U (GA)
Southern U and Ag and Mech Coll (LA)
Southern Utah U (UT)
Southwest Baptist U (MO)
Southwestern Adventist U (TX)
Southwestern Coll (KS)
Southwestern Oklahoma State U (OK)
Southwest Minnesota State U (MN)
Spelman Coll (GA)
Spring Arbor U (MI)
Stanford U (CA)
State U of New York at Binghamton (NY)
State U of New York at Fredonia (NY)
State U of New York at Oswego (NY)
State U of New York at Plattsburgh (NY)
State U of New York Coll at Geneseo (NY)
State U of New York Coll at Old Westbury (NY)
State U of New York Coll at Oneonta (NY)
Stetson U (FL)
Stevens Inst of Technology (NJ)
Stonehill Coll (MA)
Stony Brook U, State U of New York (NY)
Suffolk U (MA)
Susquehanna U (PA)
Sweet Briar Coll (VA)
Tabor Coll (KS)
Talladega Coll (AL)
Taylor U (IN)
Tennessee Technological U (TN)
Texas A&M U (TX)
Texas A&M U–Commerce (TX)
Texas A&M U–Corpus Christi (TX)
Texas Coll (TX)
Texas Lutheran U (TX)
Thiel Coll (PA)
Thomas Edison State Coll (NJ)
Thompson Rivers U (BC, Canada)
Transylvania U (KY)
Trent U (ON, Canada)
Trine U (IN)
Trinity Christian Coll (IL)
Trinity Coll (CT)
Tufts U (MA)
Tulane U (LA)
Tuskegee U (AL)
Union Coll (NE)
Union U (TN)
United States Air Force Acad (CO)
United States Naval Acad (MD)
Universidad Adventista de las Antillas (PR)
Université du Québec en Outaouais (QC, Canada)
U at Albany, State U of New York (NY)
U at Buffalo, the State U of New York (NY)
The U of Akron (OH)
The U of Alabama (AL)
U of Alaska Anchorage (AK)
U of Alaska Fairbanks (AK)
U of Alberta (AB, Canada)
U of Arkansas at Little Rock (AR)
U of Arkansas at Pine Bluff (AR)
U of Atlanta (GA)
U of Bridgeport (CT)
The U of British Columbia (BC, Canada)
The U of British Columbia–Okanagan (BC, Canada)
U of California, Berkeley (CA)
U of California, Irvine (CA)
U of California, Riverside (CA)
U of California, San Diego (CA)
U of California, Santa Barbara (CA)
U of California, Santa Cruz (CA)
U of Central Oklahoma (OK)
U of Chicago (IL)
U of Cincinnati (OH)
U of Colorado at Boulder (CO)
U of Colorado at Colorado Springs (CO)
U of Connecticut (CT)
U of Dayton (OH)
U of Delaware (DE)
U of Denver (CO)
U of Dubuque (IA)
The U of Findlay (OH)
U of Georgia (GA)
U of Guam (GU)
U of Guelph (ON, Canada)
U of Hawaii at Hilo (HI)
U of Hawaii at Manoa (HI)
U of Houston–Victoria (TX)
U of Idaho (ID)
U of Illinois at Chicago (IL)
U of Illinois at Springfield (IL)
U of Illinois at Urbana–Champaign (IL)
U of Indianapolis (IN)
The U of Iowa (IA)
U of King's Coll (NS, Canada)
U of La Verne (CA)
U of Lethbridge (AB, Canada)
U of Louisiana at Monroe (LA)
U of Maine (ME)
U of Maine at Farmington (ME)
U of Maine at Fort Kent (ME)
U of Manitoba (MB, Canada)
U of Mary Hardin-Baylor (TX)
U of Maryland, Baltimore County (MD)
U of Maryland Eastern Shore (MD)
U of Maryland U Coll (MD)
U of Massachusetts Amherst (MA)
U of Massachusetts Lowell (MA)
U of Memphis (TN)
U of Miami (FL)
U of Michigan–Flint (MI)
U of Minnesota, Duluth (MN)
U of Minnesota, Twin Cities Campus (MN)
U of Missouri (MO)
U of Missouri–Kansas City (MO)
U of Nevada, Las Vegas (NV)
U of Nevada, Reno (NV)
U of New Brunswick Fredericton (NB, Canada)
U of New Haven (CT)
U of New Orleans (LA)
The U of North Carolina at Asheville (NC)
The U of North Carolina at Chapel Hill (NC)
The U of North Carolina at Charlotte (NC)
The U of North Carolina at Greensboro (NC)
The U of North Carolina at Pembroke (NC)
The U of North Carolina Wilmington (NC)
U of Northern Iowa (IA)
U of Oklahoma (OK)
U of Pittsburgh (PA)
U of Pittsburgh at Bradford (PA)
U of Pittsburgh at Johnstown (PA)
U of Portland (OR)
U of Puerto Rico, Río Piedras (PR)
U of Puget Sound (WA)
U of Redlands (CA)
U of Regina (SK, Canada)
U of Richmond (VA)
U of Rio Grande (OH)
U of Rochester (NY)
U of St. Francis (IL)
U of San Diego (CA)
U of San Francisco (CA)
U of Saskatchewan (SK, Canada)
The U of Scranton (PA)
U of South Carolina Aiken (SC)
U of Southern California (CA)
U of Southern Maine (ME)
The U of Tennessee (TN)
The U of Tennessee at Chattanooga (TN)
The U of Tennessee at Martin (TN)
The U of Texas at Arlington (TX)
The U of Texas at El Paso (TX)
The U of Texas at Tyler (TX)
The U of Texas of the Permian Basin (TX)
The U of Texas–Pan American (TX)
U of the District of Columbia (DC)
U of the Pacific (CA)
U of the Sciences in Philadelphia (PA)
The U of Toledo (OH)
U of Toronto (ON, Canada)
U of Tulsa (OK)
U of Utah (UT)
U of Vermont (VT)
U of Washington (WA)
U of Waterloo (ON, Canada)
The U of Western Ontario (ON, Canada)
U of Windsor (ON, Canada)
U of Wisconsin–Green Bay (WI)
U of Wisconsin–Madison (WI)
U of Wisconsin–Milwaukee (WI)
U of Wisconsin–Oshkosh (WI)
U of Wisconsin–Parkside (WI)
U of Wisconsin–Platteville (WI)
U of Wisconsin–River Falls (WI)
U of Wisconsin–Superior (WI)
U of Wyoming (WY)
Ursinus Coll (PA)
Utah Valley U (UT)
Valdosta State U (GA)
Valparaiso U (IN)
Vanderbilt U (TN)
Villanova U (PA)
Virginia Military Inst (VA)
Virginia Polytechnic Inst and State U (VA)
Virginia State U (VA)
Virginia Wesleyan Coll (VA)
Voorhees Coll (SC)
Wagner Coll (NY)
Walsh U (OH)
Wartburg Coll (IA)
Washington and Lee U (VA)
Washington Coll (MD)
Washington State U (WA)
Washington U in St. Louis (MO)
Waynesburg U (PA)
Webster U (MO)
Wellesley Coll (MA)
Wells Coll (NY)
Wesleyan U (CT)
Western Carolina U (NC)
Western Connecticut State U (CT)
Western Michigan U (MI)
Western New England Coll (MA)
Western Oregon U (OR)
Western State Coll of Colorado (CO)
Westfield State Coll (MA)
Westminster Coll (MO)
Westminster Coll (UT)
Westmont Coll (CA)
West Virginia U (WV)
West Virginia Wesleyan Coll (WV)
Wheaton Coll (IL)
Wheaton Coll (MA)
Wheeling Jesuit U (WV)
Widener U (PA)
Wilberforce U (OH)
Wilfrid Laurier U (ON, Canada)
Willamette U (OR)
William Paterson U of New Jersey (NJ)
William Penn U (IA)
Williams Coll (MA)
Wilmington Coll (OH)
Winona State U (MN)
Winston-Salem State U (NC)
Winthrop U (SC)
Wittenberg U (OH)
Wofford Coll (SC)
Worcester Polytechnic Inst (MA)
Wright State U (OH)
Xavier U (OH)
Xavier U of Louisiana (LA)
Yeshiva U (NY)
York Coll of Pennsylvania (PA)
York Coll of the City U of New York (NY)
York U (ON, Canada)
Youngstown State U (OH)

COMPUTER SOFTWARE AND MEDIA APPLICATIONS RELATED

Acad of Art U (CA)
California State U, Monterey Bay (CA)
Champlain Coll (VT)
Dakota State U (SD)
Dakota Wesleyan U (SD)
DePaul U (IL)
DeVry U, Addison (IL)
DeVry U, Tinley Park (IL)
DeVry U Online (IL)
Florida State U (FL)
Holy Names U (CA)
Loyola U Chicago (IL)
Neumont U (UT)
New England School of Communications (ME)
Platt Coll San Diego (CA)
U of Denver (CO)
U of Massachusetts Boston (MA)
U of Southern California (CA)
The U of Western Ontario (ON, Canada)
U of Wisconsin–Stout (WI)

COMPUTER SOFTWARE ENGINEERING

Allegheny Coll (PA)
Auburn U (AL)
Brock U (ON, Canada)
Carroll U (WI)
Champlain Coll (VT)
Clarkson U (NY)
Cogswell Polytechnical Coll (CA)
Concordia U (QC, Canada)
DeVry U, Phoenix (AZ)
DeVry U, Fremont (CA)
DeVry U, Long Beach (CA)
DeVry U, Pomona (CA)
DeVry U, Sherman Oaks (CA)
DeVry U, Westminster (CO)
DeVry U, Orlando (FL)
DeVry U, Alpharetta (GA)
DeVry U, Decatur (GA)
DeVry U, Edina (MN)
DeVry U, Fort Washington (PA)
DeVry U, Irving (TX)
DeVry U, Arlington (VA)
DeVry U, Federal Way (WA)
Embry-Riddle Aeronautical U (FL)
Fairfield U (CT)
Florida Inst of Technology (FL)
Indiana Tech (IN)
ITT Tech Inst, Bessemer (AL)
ITT Tech Inst, Madison (AL)
ITT Tech Inst, Mobile (AL)
ITT Tech Inst, Phoenix (AZ)
ITT Tech Inst, Tempe (AZ)
ITT Tech Inst, Tucson (AZ)
ITT Tech Inst (AR)
ITT Tech Inst, Clovis (CA)
ITT Tech Inst, Concord (CA)
ITT Tech Inst, San Diego (CA)
ITT Tech Inst, Torrance (CA)
ITT Tech Inst, Thornton (CO)
ITT Tech Inst, Fort Lauderdale (FL)
ITT Tech Inst, Jacksonville (FL)
ITT Tech Inst, Lake Mary (FL)
ITT Tech Inst, Miami (FL)
ITT Tech Inst, Pinellas Park (FL)
ITT Tech Inst, Tampa (FL)
ITT Tech Inst (ID)
ITT Tech Inst, Fort Wayne (IN)
ITT Tech Inst, Indianapolis (IN)
ITT Tech Inst, Newburgh (IN)
ITT Tech Inst, South Bend (IN)
ITT Tech Inst (KS)
ITT Tech Inst, Lexington (KY)
ITT Tech Inst, Louisville (KY)
ITT Tech Inst, St. Rose (LA)
ITT Tech Inst, Canton (MI)
ITT Tech Inst, Troy (MI)
ITT Tech Inst, Wyoming (MI)
ITT Tech Inst (MN)
ITT Tech Inst (MS)
ITT Tech Inst, Arnold (MO)
ITT Tech Inst, Earth City (MO)
ITT Tech Inst, Kansas City (MO)
ITT Tech Inst, Springfield (MO)
ITT Tech Inst (NV)
ITT Tech Inst (NM)
ITT Tech Inst, Oklahoma City (OK)
ITT Tech Inst, Tulsa (OK)
ITT Tech Inst (OR)
ITT Tech Inst, Chattanooga (TN)
ITT Tech Inst, Cordova (TN)
ITT Tech Inst, Knoxville (TN)
ITT Tech Inst, Nashville (TN)
ITT Tech Inst (UT)
ITT Tech Inst, Chantilly (VA)
ITT Tech Inst, Norfolk (VA)
ITT Tech Inst, Richmond (VA)
ITT Tech Inst, Springfield (VA)
ITT Tech Inst, Everett (WA)
ITT Tech Inst, Seattle (WA)
ITT Tech Inst, Spokane Valley (WA)
ITT Tech Inst, Green Bay (WI)
ITT Tech Inst, Greenfield (WI)
ITT Tech Inst, Madison (WI)
Johnson & Wales U (RI)
Liberty U (VA)
Michigan Technological U (MI)
Milwaukee School of Eng (WI)
Monmouth U (NJ)
Montana Tech of The U of Montana (MT)
National U (CA)
Ouachita Baptist U (AR)
Penn State Erie, The Behrend Coll (PA)
Robert Morris U (PA)
Rochester Inst of Technology (NY)
Rose-Hulman Inst of Technology (IN)
South Dakota State U (SD)
Southern Polytechnic State U (GA)
State U of New York at Oswego (NY)
Stratford U, Woodbridge (VA)
U of Illinois at Urbana–Champaign (IL)
U of Minnesota, Crookston (MN)
U of Ottawa (ON, Canada)
U of Regina (SK, Canada)
The U of Texas at Arlington (TX)
The U of Texas at Dallas (TX)
U of Toronto (ON, Canada)
U of Waterloo (ON, Canada)
The U of Western Ontario (ON, Canada)
U of Wisconsin–Platteville (WI)
Utah Valley U (UT)
Vermont Tech Coll (VT)
York U (ON, Canada)

COMPUTER SOFTWARE TECHNOLOGY

Grantham U (MO)
U of Regina (SK, Canada)

COMPUTER SYSTEMS ANALYSIS

Arizona State U (AZ)
Arkansas Tech U (AR)
Baldwin-Wallace Coll (OH)
California Polytechnic State U, San Luis Obispo (CA)
Clayton State U (GA)
Concordia U (QC, Canada)
DeVry Coll of New York (NY)
DeVry U, Phoenix (AZ)
DeVry U, Fremont (CA)
DeVry U, Long Beach (CA)
DeVry U, Pomona (CA)
DeVry U, Sherman Oaks (CA)
DeVry U, Westminster (CO)
DeVry U, Miramar (FL)
DeVry U, Orlando (FL)
DeVry U, Alpharetta (GA)
DeVry U, Decatur (GA)
DeVry U, Addison (IL)
DeVry U, Chicago (IL)
DeVry U, Tinley Park (IL)
DeVry U, Indianapolis (IN)
DeVry U (KY)
DeVry U (MD)
DeVry U, Edina (MN)
DeVry U, Kansas City (MO)
DeVry U (NV)
DeVry U, North Brunswick (NJ)
DeVry U, Charlotte (NC)
DeVry U, Columbus (OH)
DeVry U (OK)
DeVry U (OR)
DeVry U, Fort Washington (PA)
DeVry U, Houston (TX)
DeVry U, Irving (TX)
DeVry U (UT)
DeVry U, Arlington (VA)
DeVry U, Federal Way (WA)
DeVry U, Milwaukee (WI)
DeVry U Online (IL)
HEC Montreal (QC, Canada)
Inter American U of Puerto Rico, Bayamón Campus (PR)
Kent State U (OH)
Miami U (OH)
Miami U Hamilton (OH)
Northern Arizona U (AZ)
Northwest Missouri State U (MO)
Pace U (NY)
Pennsylvania Coll of Technology (PA)
Rochester Inst of Technology (NY)
St. Ambrose U (IA)
Seattle Pacific U (WA)
Shippensburg U of Pennsylvania (PA)
Thompson Rivers U (BC, Canada)
U of Advancing Technology (AZ)
U of Denver (CO)
U of Houston (TX)
U of North Dakota (ND)
U of Vermont (VT)
U of Washington, Bothell (WA)
U of Washington, Tacoma (WA)

COMPUTER SYSTEMS NETWORKING AND TELECOMMUNICATIONS

Baldwin-Wallace Coll (OH)
Bloomfield Coll (NJ)
Boise State U (ID)
California State U, East Bay (CA)
Cape Breton U (NS, Canada)
Capella U (MN)
Champlain Coll (VT)
Chowan U (NC)
Davenport U, Grand Rapids (MI)
DePaul U (IL)
DeVry Coll of New York (NY)
DeVry U, Phoenix (AZ)
DeVry U, Fremont (CA)
DeVry U, Long Beach (CA)
DeVry U, Pomona (CA)
DeVry U, Sherman Oaks (CA)
DeVry U, Westminster (CO)
DeVry U, Miramar (FL)
DeVry U, Orlando (FL)
DeVry U, Alpharetta (GA)
DeVry U, Decatur (GA)
DeVry U, Addison (IL)
DeVry U, Chicago (IL)
DeVry U, Tinley Park (IL)
DeVry U, Indianapolis (IN)
DeVry U (KY)
DeVry U, Edina (MN)
DeVry U, Kansas City (MO)
DeVry U (NV)
DeVry U, North Brunswick (NJ)
DeVry U, Columbus (OH)
DeVry U (OK)
DeVry U (OR)
DeVry U, Fort Washington (PA)
DeVry U, Houston (TX)
DeVry U, Irving (TX)
DeVry U (UT)
DeVry U, Arlington (VA)
DeVry U, Federal Way (WA)
DeVry U Online (IL)
Illinois State U (IL)
Indiana Tech (IN)

Inter American U of Puerto Rico, Aguadilla Campus (PR)
Inter American U of Puerto Rico, Ponce Campus (PR)
Iona Coll (NY)
ITT Tech Inst, Tempe (AZ)
ITT Tech Inst, Anaheim (CA)
ITT Tech Inst, Lathrop (CA)
ITT Tech Inst, Rancho Cordova (CA)
ITT Tech Inst, Torrance (CA)
ITT Tech Inst, Lake Mary (FL)
ITT Tech Inst, Fort Wayne (IN)
ITT Tech Inst (MD)
ITT Tech Inst (NE)
ITT Tech Inst (OR)
ITT Tech Inst, Cordova (TN)
ITT Tech Inst, Knoxville (TN)
ITT Tech Inst, Nashville (TN)
Kansas State U (KS)
Kean U (NJ)
Michigan Technological U (MI)
Montana Tech of The U of Montana (MT)
Northern Michigan U (MI)
Northwestern Oklahoma State U (OK)
Ohio U (OH)
Our Lady of the Lake U of San Antonio (TX)
Rochester Inst of Technology (NY)
Roosevelt U (IL)
St. Ambrose U (IA)
State U of New York Coll of Technology at Alfred (NY)
The U of Akron (OH)
The U of Findlay (OH)
The U of North Carolina at Greensboro (NC)
U of Pennsylvania (PA)
U of the Incarnate Word (TX)
U of Toronto (ON, Canada)
U of Wisconsin–Stout (WI)
Weber State U (UT)
Western Illinois U (IL)
Western State Coll of Colorado (CO)

COMPUTER TEACHER EDUCATION
Alma Coll (MI)
Baylor U (TX)
Bishop's U (QC, Canada)
Bowling Green State U (OH)
Bridgewater Coll (VA)
Bryan Coll (TN)
Buena Vista U (IA)
Concordia U Chicago (IL)
Dakota State U (SD)
DePaul U (IL)
Dordt Coll (IA)
Eastern Michigan U (MI)
Edgewood Coll (WI)
Florida Inst of Technology (FL)
Full Sail U (FL)
Hardin-Simmons U (TX)
Howard Payne U (TX)
Immaculata U (PA)
Keene State Coll (NH)
Liberty U (VA)
Long Island U, Brooklyn Campus (NY)
Lubbock Christian U (TX)
McMurry U (TX)
Michigan State U (MI)
Michigan Technological U (MI)
Mississippi Coll (MS)
Pace U (NY)
Southeastern Louisiana U (LA)
Southern U and Ag and Mech Coll (LA)
Texas A&M U–Corpus Christi (TX)
Texas Christian U (TX)
Union Coll (NE)
U of Nebraska–Lincoln (NE)
U of the Cumberlands (KY)
U of Wisconsin–River Falls (WI)
Utica Coll (NY)
Western Washington U (WA)
Wright State U (OH)

COMPUTER TECHNOLOGY/ COMPUTER SYSTEMS TECHNOLOGY
Bob Jones U (SC)
Central Michigan U (MI)
Colorado State U (CO)
Florida Atlantic U (FL)
Prairie View A&M U (TX)
Rensselaer Polytechnic Inst (NY)
Southwestern Coll (KS)
Universidad de las Américas–Puebla (Mexico)
Wayne State U (MI)

CONDUCTING
Bard Coll (NY)
Calvin Coll (MI)
Chapman U (CA)
Mannes Coll The New School for Music (NY)

CONSERVATION BIOLOGY
Arizona State U (AZ)
Philadelphia U (PA)
Prescott Coll (AZ)
Sterling Coll (VT)
U of Idaho (ID)
U of Maine at Machias (ME)
The U of Western Ontario (ON, Canada)

CONSTRUCTION ENGINEERING
American U of Beirut (Lebanon)
Bradley U (IL)
California State U, Long Beach (CA)
Concordia U (QC, Canada)
John Brown U (AR)
Marquette U (WI)
Michigan Technological U (MI)
National U (CA)
North Carolina State U (NC)
North Dakota State U (ND)
Oregon State U (OR)
Purdue U (IN)
Southern Polytechnic State U (GA)
State U of New York Coll of Environmental Science and Forestry (NY)
Texas A&M U–Commerce (TX)
The U of Alabama (AL)
U of Alberta (AB, Canada)
U of Cincinnati (OH)
U of Illinois at Urbana–Champaign (IL)
U of Nebraska–Lincoln (NE)
U of Nevada, Las Vegas (NV)
U of New Brunswick Fredericton (NB, Canada)
U of Southern California (CA)

CONSTRUCTION ENGINEERING TECHNOLOGY
Bemidji State U (MN)
Bowling Green State U (OH)
California State Polytechnic U, Pomona (CA)
California State U, Chico (CA)
California State U, Fresno (CA)
California State U, Long Beach (CA)
California State U, Sacramento (CA)
Central Michigan U (MI)
Colorado State U (CO)
Eastern Michigan U (MI)
Fairleigh Dickinson U, Metropolitan Campus (NJ)
Farmingdale State Coll (NY)
Fitchburg State Coll (MA)
Florida Ag and Mech U (FL)
Florida Inst of Technology (FL)
Florida Intl U (FL)
Georgia Southern U (GA)
Hampton U (VA)
Indiana U–Purdue U Fort Wayne (IN)
John Brown U (AR)
Kansas State U (KS)
Louisiana Tech U (LA)
Michigan State U (MI)
Minnesota State U Moorhead (MN)
Montana State U (MT)
Norfolk State U (VA)
Northern Michigan U (MI)
Oklahoma State U (OK)
Pittsburg State U (KS)
Prairie View A&M U (TX)
San Diego State U (CA)
South Dakota State U (SD)
Southern Illinois U Edwardsville (IL)
Southern Utah U (UT)
State U of New York Coll of Technology at Alfred (NY)
Temple U (PA)
Texas A&M U (TX)
Texas State U–San Marcos (TX)
Thomas Edison State Coll (NJ)
Tuskegee U (AL)
The U of Akron (OH)
U of Arkansas at Little Rock (AR)
U of Cincinnati (OH)
U of Florida (FL)
U of Houston (TX)
U of Louisiana at Monroe (LA)
U of Maine (ME)
U of Maryland Eastern Shore (MD)
U of Nebraska–Lincoln (NE)
U of Nevada, Reno (NV)
U of North Florida (FL)
U of North Texas (TX)
The U of Toledo (OH)
U of Wisconsin–Stout (WI)
Wayne State U (MI)
Western Carolina U (NC)
Western Kentucky U (KY)

CONSTRUCTION MANAGEMENT
Appalachian State U (NC)
Arizona State U (AZ)
California State U, Fresno (CA)
Central Connecticut State U (CT)
Clemson U (SC)
Colorado State U (CO)
Eastern Michigan U (MI)
Ferris State U (MI)
Illinois State U (IL)
ITT Tech Inst, Bessemer (AL)
ITT Tech Inst, Madison (AL)
ITT Tech Inst, Mobile (AL)
ITT Tech Inst, Phoenix (AZ)
ITT Tech Inst, Tempe (AZ)
ITT Tech Inst, Tucson (AZ)
ITT Tech Inst (AR)
ITT Tech Inst, Anaheim (CA)
ITT Tech Inst, Clovis (CA)
ITT Tech Inst, Concord (CA)
ITT Tech Inst, Corona (CA)
ITT Tech Inst, Lathrop (CA)
ITT Tech Inst, Oxnard (CA)
ITT Tech Inst, Rancho Cordova (CA)
ITT Tech Inst, San Bernardino (CA)
ITT Tech Inst, San Diego (CA)
ITT Tech Inst, San Dimas (CA)
ITT Tech Inst, Sylmar (CA)
ITT Tech Inst, Torrance (CA)
ITT Tech Inst, Thornton (CO)
ITT Tech Inst, Fort Lauderdale (FL)
ITT Tech Inst, Fort Myers (FL)
ITT Tech Inst, Jacksonville (FL)
ITT Tech Inst, Lake Mary (FL)
ITT Tech Inst, Miami (FL)
ITT Tech Inst, Pinellas Park (FL)
ITT Tech Inst, Tallahassee (FL)
ITT Tech Inst, Tampa (FL)
ITT Tech Inst, Duluth (GA)
ITT Tech Inst, Kennesaw (GA)
ITT Tech Inst (ID)
ITT Tech Inst, Burr Ridge (IL)
ITT Tech Inst, Mount Prospect (IL)
ITT Tech Inst, Orland Park (IL)
ITT Tech Inst, Fort Wayne (IN)
ITT Tech Inst, Indianapolis (IN)
ITT Tech Inst, Merrillville (IN)
ITT Tech Inst, Newburgh (IN)
ITT Tech Inst, South Bend (IN)
ITT Tech Inst, Cedar Rapids (IA)
ITT Tech Inst, Clive (IA)
ITT Tech Inst, Lexington (KY)
ITT Tech Inst, Louisville (KY)
ITT Tech Inst, St. Rose (LA)
ITT Tech Inst (MD)
ITT Tech Inst, Canton (MI)
ITT Tech Inst, Troy (MI)
ITT Tech Inst, Wyoming (MI)
ITT Tech Inst (MS)
ITT Tech Inst, Arnold (MO)
ITT Tech Inst, Earth City (MO)
ITT Tech Inst, Kansas City (MO)
ITT Tech Inst, Springfield (MO)
ITT Tech Inst (NE)
ITT Tech Inst (NV)
ITT Tech Inst (NM)
ITT Tech Inst, Charlotte (NC)
ITT Tech Inst, Charlotte (NC)
ITT Tech Inst, High Point (NC)
ITT Tech Inst, Morrisville (NC)
ITT Tech Inst, Oklahoma City (OK)
ITT Tech Inst, Tulsa (OK)
ITT Tech Inst (OR)
ITT Tech Inst, Columbia (SC)
ITT Tech Inst, Greenville (SC)
ITT Tech Inst, Chattanooga (TN)
ITT Tech Inst, Cordova (TN)
ITT Tech Inst, Johnson City (TN)
ITT Tech Inst, Knoxville (TN)
ITT Tech Inst, Nashville (TN)
ITT Tech Inst, Arlington (TX)
ITT Tech Inst, Austin (TX)
ITT Tech Inst, DeSoto (TX)
ITT Tech Inst, Houston (TX)
ITT Tech Inst, Houston (TX)
ITT Tech Inst, Webster (TX)
ITT Tech Inst (UT)
ITT Tech Inst, Chantilly (VA)
ITT Tech Inst, Norfolk (VA)
ITT Tech Inst, Richmond (VA)
ITT Tech Inst, Salem (VA)
ITT Tech Inst, Springfield (VA)
ITT Tech Inst, Everett (WA)
ITT Tech Inst, Seattle (WA)
ITT Tech Inst, Spokane Valley (WA)
ITT Tech Inst, Green Bay (WI)
ITT Tech Inst, Greenfield (WI)
ITT Tech Inst, Madison (WI)
John Brown U (AR)
Lawrence Technological U (MI)
Louisiana State U and Ag and Mech Coll (LA)
Michigan State U (MI)
Milwaukee School of Eng (WI)
Mississippi State U (MS)
Missouri State U (MO)
North Carolina State U (NC)
North Dakota State U (ND)
Northern Kentucky U (KY)
Ohio Northern U (OH)
The Ohio State U (OH)
Pennsylvania Coll of Technology (PA)
Pittsburg State U (KS)
Prescott Coll (AZ)
Southern Polytechnic State U (GA)
State U of New York Coll of Environmental Science and Forestry (NY)
U of Denver (CO)
U of Northern Iowa (IA)
U of Oklahoma (OK)
The U of Texas at Tyler (TX)
U of Washington (WA)
Vermont Tech Coll (VT)
Virginia Polytechnic Inst and State U (VA)
Washington State U (WA)
Wentworth Inst of Technology (MA)
Western Carolina U (NC)
Western Illinois U (IL)
Westwood Coll–Anaheim (CA)
Westwood Coll–Annandale Campus (VA)
Westwood Coll–Arlington Ballston Campus (VA)
Westwood Coll–Atlanta Midtown (GA)
Westwood Coll–Atlanta Northlake (GA)
Westwood Coll–Chicago Du Page (IL)
Westwood Coll–Chicago Loop Campus (IL)
Westwood Coll–Chicago O'Hare Airport (IL)
Westwood Coll–Chicago River Oaks (IL)
Westwood Coll–Dallas (TX)
Westwood Coll–Denver North (CO)
Westwood Coll–Denver South (CO)
Westwood Coll–Fort Worth (TX)
Westwood Coll–Houston South Campus (TX)
Westwood Coll–Inland Empire (CA)
Westwood Coll–Los Angeles (CA)
Westwood Coll–South Bay Campus (CA)

CONSTRUCTION TRADES RELATED
John Brown U (AR)

CONSUMER ECONOMICS
Cornell U (NY)
Louisiana Tech U (LA)
South Dakota State U (SD)
The U of Arizona (AZ)
U of Delaware (DE)
U of Georgia (GA)
U of Illinois at Urbana–Champaign (IL)
The U of Tennessee (TN)
U of Utah (UT)

CONSUMER MERCHANDISING/ RETAILING MANAGEMENT
The Art Inst of Atlanta (GA)
The Art Inst of Atlanta–Decatur (GA)
The Art Inst of Austin (TX)
The Art Inst of California–Inland Empire (CA)
The Art Inst of Charleston (SC)
The Art Inst of Colorado (CO)
The Art Inst of Dallas (TX)
The Art Inst of Houston (TX)
The Art Inst of Houston—North (TX)
The Art Inst of Indianapolis (IN)
The Art Inst of Jacksonville (FL)
The Art Inst of Las Vegas (NV)
The Art Inst of Pittsburgh (PA)
The Art Inst of Tampa (FL)
The Art Inst of Tennessee–Nashville (TN)
The Art Inst of Washington (VA)
The Art Inst of York–Pennsylvania (PA)
The Art Insts Intl Minnesota (MN)
Belmont U (TN)
Bradley U (IL)
East Central U (OK)
Fontbonne U (MO)
Governors State U (IL)
HEC Montreal (QC, Canada)
Johnson & Wales U (RI)
Lasell Coll (MA)
Lindenwood U (MO)
Madonna U (MI)
The New England Inst of Art (MA)
Oregon State U (OR)
San Francisco State U (CA)
Simmons Coll (MA)
U of Central Oklahoma (OK)
U of Memphis (TN)
U of Nebraska–Lincoln (NE)
Winona State U (MN)

CONSUMER SERVICES AND ADVOCACY
Carson-Newman Coll (TN)
State U of New York Coll at Oneonta (NY)
U of Wisconsin–Madison (WI)

COOKING AND RELATED CULINARY ARTS
Kendall Coll (IL)

CORRECTIONS
Adams State Coll (CO)
Bowling Green State U (OH)
California State U, East Bay (CA)
Coker Coll (SC)
The Coll at Brockport, State U of New York (NY)
Coll of the Ozarks (MO)
East Central U (OK)
Excelsior Coll (NY)
Jacksonville State U (AL)
Lake Superior State U (MI)
Lamar U (TX)
Lewis-Clark State Coll (ID)
Lincoln Coll–Normal (IL)
Mercyhurst Coll (PA)
Minnesota State U Mankato (MN)
Oklahoma City U (OK)
Saint Louis U (MO)
Saint Mary's U of Minnesota (MN)
Southeast Missouri State U (MO)
Spring Arbor U (MI)
Stephen F. Austin State U (TX)
Texas State U–San Marcos (TX)
Tiffin U (OH)
Tulane U (LA)
U of Arkansas at Pine Bluff (AR)
U of New Mexico (NM)
U of Pittsburgh (PA)
The U of Texas at Brownsville (TX)
Washburn U (KS)
Western Oregon U (OR)
Winona State U (MN)

CORRECTIONS ADMINISTRATION
American Public U System (WV)
Inter American U of Puerto Rico, Fajardo Campus (PR)

CORRECTIONS AND CRIMINAL JUSTICE RELATED
Albany State U (GA)
American Public U System (WV)
Averett U (VA)
Bethune-Cookman U (FL)
Bob Jones U (SC)
Coker Coll (SC)
The Coll at Brockport, State U of New York (NY)
Emporia State U (KS)
Florida Inst of Technology (FL)
Harding U (AR)
La Roche Coll (PA)
Limestone Coll (SC)
Mount Mary Coll (WI)
Russell Sage Coll (NY)
Sam Houston State U (TX)
Southern New Hampshire U (NH)
The U of Alabama at Birmingham (AL)
U of Alaska Fairbanks (AK)
U of Michigan–Flint (MI)

COUNSELING PSYCHOLOGY
Atlanta Christian Coll (GA)
Bob Jones U (SC)
Coker Coll (SC)
Delaware Valley Coll (PA)
Eastern Nazarene Coll (MA)
Eastern New Mexico U (NM)
Emmanuel Coll (MA)
Fort Lewis Coll (CO)
Grace Coll (IN)
Great Lakes Christian Coll (MI)

Jamestown Coll (ND)
Kutztown U of Pennsylvania (PA)
Lesley U (MA)
Mid-Continent U (KY)
Midwestern State U (TX)
Morningside Coll (IA)
Newman U (KS)
Oak Hills Christian Coll (MN)
Oregon Inst of Technology (OR)
Paine Coll (GA)
Pittsburg State U (KS)
Prescott Coll (AZ)
Rochester Coll (MI)
Saint Xavier U (IL)
San Diego Christian Coll (CA)
Santa Clara U (CA)
Southwestern Assemblies of God U (TX)
Texas Wesleyan U (TX)
Trinity Coll of Florida (FL)
U of North Alabama (AL)
U of the Cumberlands (KY)
Washington Adventist U (MD)
Wayne State Coll (NE)

COUNSELOR EDUCATION/ SCHOOL COUNSELING AND GUIDANCE

Amberton U (TX)
Belmont U (TN)
Bowling Green State U (OH)
Buena Vista U (IA)
Clemson U (SC)
East Central U (OK)
Eastern New Mexico U (NM)
Edinboro U of Pennsylvania (PA)
Florida Gulf Coast U (FL)
Franklin Pierce U (NH)
Goddard Coll (VT)
Houston Baptist U (TX)
John Brown U (AR)
Kutztown U of Pennsylvania (PA)
Lamar U (TX)
Marshall U (WV)
Memorial U of Newfoundland (NL, Canada)
Midwestern State U (TX)
St. Cloud State U (MN)
Southeastern Oklahoma State U (OK)
Southern Arkansas U–Magnolia (AR)
Tarleton State U (TX)
Texas A&M U–Commerce (TX)
Texas A&M U–Corpus Christi (TX)
The U of British Columbia (BC, Canada)
U of Central Oklahoma (OK)
U of Hawaii at Manoa (HI)
U of Houston–Clear Lake (TX)
U of New Brunswick Fredericton (NB, Canada)
The U of North Carolina at Pembroke (NC)
The U of South Dakota (SD)
U of Windsor (ON, Canada)
U of Wisconsin–River Falls (WI)
Wright State U (OH)

COURT REPORTING

AIB Coll of Business (IA)
U of Mississippi (MS)

CRAFTS, FOLK ART AND ARTISANRY

Bowling Green State U (OH)
Bridgewater State Coll (MA)
Brigham Young U (UT)
The Cleveland Inst of Art (OH)
Coll for Creative Studies (MI)
Indiana U–Purdue U Fort Wayne (IN)
Kent State U (OH)
Kutztown U of Pennsylvania (PA)
North Georgia Coll & State U (GA)
Oregon Coll of Art & Craft (OR)
Rochester Inst of Technology (NY)
U of Illinois at Urbana–Champaign (IL)
Virginia Commonwealth U (VA)

CREATIVE WRITING

Adams State Coll (CO)
Agnes Scott Coll (GA)
Alderson-Broaddus Coll (WV)
Allegheny Coll (PA)
Arcadia U (PA)
Arkansas Tech U (AR)
Asbury U (KY)
Ashland U (OH)
Augustana Coll (IL)
Baldwin-Wallace Coll (OH)
Bard Coll (NY)
Bard Coll at Simon's Rock (MA)
Belhaven U (MS)
Beloit Coll (WI)
Bennington Coll (VT)
Bernard M. Baruch Coll of the City U of New York (NY)
Bluffton U (OH)
Bob Jones U (SC)
Bowie State U (MD)
Bowling Green State U (OH)
Brandeis U (MA)
Briar Cliff U (IA)
Bridgewater State Coll (MA)
Brooklyn Coll of the City U of New York (NY)
Bucknell U (PA)
Butler U (IN)
California Coll of the Arts (CA)
California State U, East Bay (CA)
California State U, Long Beach (CA)
California State U, San Bernardino (CA)
Capital U (OH)
Carlow U (PA)
Carnegie Mellon U (PA)
Carroll U (WI)
Carson-Newman Coll (TN)
Central Michigan U (MI)
Champlain Coll (VT)
Chapman U (CA)
Chatham U (PA)
City Coll of the City U of New York (NY)
Colby Coll (ME)
The Coll at Brockport, State U of New York (NY)
The Coll of Idaho (ID)
Coll of Santa Fe (NM)
Coll of the Atlantic (ME)
The Colorado Coll (CO)
Colorado State U (CO)
Columbia Coll Chicago (IL)
Columbia U (NY)
Columbia U, School of General Studies (NY)
Concordia U (QC, Canada)
Converse Coll (SC)
Cornell Coll (IA)
Dartmouth Coll (NH)
Denison U (OH)
Dominican U of California (CA)
D'Youville Coll (NY)
Eastern Michigan U (MI)
Eastern Nazarene Coll (MA)
Eckerd Coll (FL)
Emerson Coll (MA)
Emory & Henry Coll (VA)
Emory U (GA)
Fairleigh Dickinson U, Coll at Florham (NJ)
Fitchburg State Coll (MA)
Florida State U (FL)
Fordham U (NY)
Franklin & Marshall Coll (PA)
Franklin Coll Switzerland (Switzerland)
Franklin Pierce U (NH)
Full Sail U (FL)
Geneva Coll (PA)
Gettysburg Coll (PA)
Goddard Coll (VT)
Green Mountain Coll (VT)
Hamilton Coll (NY)
Hamline U (MN)
Hampshire Coll (MA)
High Point U (NC)
Hiram Coll (OH)
Hofstra U (NY)
Hollins U (VA)
Houghton Coll (NY)
Indiana Wesleyan U (IN)
Ithaca Coll (NY)
The Johns Hopkins U (MD)
Johnson State Coll (VT)
Knox Coll (IL)
Lehman Coll of the City U of New York (NY)
Lewis-Clark State Coll (ID)
Linfield Coll (OR)
Loras Coll (IA)
Loyola U Maryland (MD)
Lycoming Coll (PA)
Marlboro Coll (VT)
Massachusetts Inst of Technology (MA)
McMurry U (TX)
Methodist U (NC)
Miami U Hamilton (OH)
Mills Coll (CA)
Minnesota State U Mankato (MN)
Moravian Coll (PA)
New England Coll (NH)
North Carolina State U (NC)
North Central Coll (IL)
Northern Michigan U (MI)
Northland Coll (WI)
Oberlin Coll (OH)
Ohio Northern U (OH)
Ohio U (OH)
Ohio Wesleyan U (OH)
Oklahoma Christian U (OK)
Old Dominion U (VA)
Pittsburg State U (KS)
Pitzer Coll (CA)
Pratt Inst (NY)
Prescott Coll (AZ)
Purchase Coll, State U of New York (NY)
Randolph Coll (VA)
Redeemer U Coll (ON, Canada)
Rocky Mountain Coll (MT)
St. Catherine U (MN)
St. Cloud State U (MN)
St. Lawrence U (NY)
Saint Leo U (FL)
Saint Mary's Coll (IN)
Salem Coll (NC)
San Diego State U (CA)
San Francisco State U (CA)
Sarah Lawrence Coll (NY)
Savannah Coll of Art and Design (GA)
School of the Art Inst of Chicago (IL)
Seattle U (WA)
Seton Hill U (PA)
Siena Heights U (MI)
Slippery Rock U of Pennsylvania (PA)
Southern Methodist U (TX)
Southern New Hampshire U (NH)
Southern Vermont Coll (VT)
Southwest Minnesota State U (MN)
Spalding U (KY)
State U of New York at Binghamton (NY)
State U of New York at Oswego (NY)
Stephen F. Austin State U (TX)
Stephens Coll (MO)
Susquehanna U (PA)
Sweet Briar Coll (VA)
Syracuse U (NY)
Texas Christian U (TX)
Trinity Coll (CT)
Truman State U (MO)
The U of Arizona (AZ)
The U of British Columbia (BC, Canada)
The U of British Columbia–Okanagan (BC, Canada)
U of California, Riverside (CA)
U of California, San Diego (CA)
U of Chicago (IL)
U of Denver (CO)
U of Evansville (IN)
The U of Findlay (OH)
U of Houston (TX)
U of Idaho (ID)
U of Maine at Farmington (ME)
U of Maine at Machias (ME)
U of Miami (FL)
U of Michigan (MI)
U of Mount Union (OH)
U of Nebraska at Omaha (NE)
The U of North Carolina Wilmington (NC)
U of Pittsburgh (PA)
U of Pittsburgh at Bradford (PA)
U of Pittsburgh at Greensburg (PA)
U of Pittsburgh at Johnstown (PA)
U of Redlands (CA)
U of St. Thomas (MN)
U of Southern California (CA)
The U of Tampa (FL)
The U of Texas at El Paso (TX)
U of Washington (WA)
U of Windsor (ON, Canada)
Valparaiso U (IN)
Waldorf Coll (IA)
Washington U in St. Louis (MO)
Waynesburg U (PA)
Wells Coll (NY)
Western New England Coll (MA)
Western State Coll of Colorado (CO)
Western Washington U (WA)
West Virginia Wesleyan Coll (WV)
Wofford Coll (SC)
York U (ON, Canada)

CRIMINALISTICS AND CRIMINAL SCIENCE

Florida Gulf Coast U (FL)
Inter American U of Puerto Rico, Aguadilla Campus (PR)
Inter American U of Puerto Rico, Ponce Campus (PR)
Saint Leo U (FL)
Slippery Rock U of Pennsylvania (PA)
Southern Wesleyan U (SC)
West Virginia U (WV)

CRIMINAL JUSTICE/LAW ENFORCEMENT ADMINISTRATION

Abilene Christian U (TX)
Adams State Coll (CO)
Adelphi U (NY)
Alabama State U (AL)
Albertus Magnus Coll (CT)
Alfred U (NY)
Alliant Intl U (CA)
Alvernia U (PA)
American Intl Coll (MA)
American Public U System (WV)
Anderson U (IN)
Arcadia U (PA)
Argosy U, Atlanta (GA)
Argosy U, Chicago (IL)
Argosy U, Dallas (TX)
Argosy U, Denver (CO)
Argosy U, Hawai'i (HI)
Argosy U, Inland Empire (CA)
Argosy U, Los Angeles (CA)
Argosy U, Nashville (TN)
Argosy U, Orange County (CA)
Argosy U, Phoenix (AZ)
Argosy U, Salt Lake City (UT)
Argosy U, San Diego (CA)
Argosy U, San Francisco Bay Area (CA)
Argosy U, Sarasota (FL)
Argosy U, Schaumburg (IL)
Argosy U, Seattle (WA)
Argosy U, Tampa (FL)
Argosy U, Twin Cities (MN)
Argosy U, Washington DC (VA)
Arizona State U (AZ)
Austin Peay State U (TN)
Averett U (VA)
Barton Coll (NC)
Bay Path Coll (MA)
Bemidji State U (MN)
Bethel U (TN)
Blackburn Coll (IL)
Bluefield Coll (VA)
Bob Jones U (SC)
Bowie State U (MD)
Bowling Green State U (OH)
Bradley U (IL)
Brevard Coll (NC)
Briar Cliff U (IA)
Brown Mackie Coll–Albuquerque (NM)
Brown Mackie Coll–Boise (ID)
Brown Mackie Coll–Fort Wayne (IN)
Brown Mackie Coll–Greenville (SC)
Brown Mackie Coll–Indianapolis (IN)
Brown Mackie Coll–Louisville (KY)
Brown Mackie Coll–Merrillville (IN)
Brown Mackie Coll–Miami (FL)
Brown Mackie Coll–Michigan City (IN)
Brown Mackie Coll–Phoenix (AZ)
Brown Mackie Coll–St. Louis (MO)
Brown Mackie Coll–South Bend (IN)
Brown Mackie Coll–Tucson (AZ)
Brown Mackie Coll–Tulsa (OK)
Bryant & Stratton Coll (WI)
Bryant & Stratton Coll—Virginia Beach (VA)
Bryant & Stratton Coll—Wauwatosa Campus (WI)
Buffalo State Coll, State U of New York (NY)
California Baptist U (CA)
California Lutheran U (CA)
California State U, Bakersfield (CA)
California State U, East Bay (CA)
California State U, Long Beach (CA)
California State U, Sacramento (CA)
California State U, San Bernardino (CA)
California State U, Stanislaus (CA)
Calumet Coll of Saint Joseph (IN)
Campbellsville U (KY)
Canisius Coll (NY)
Castleton State Coll (VT)
Cedarville U (OH)
Champlain Coll (VT)
The Citadel, The Military Coll of South Carolina (SC)
Claflin U (SC)
Coker Coll (SC)
The Coll at Brockport, State U of New York (NY)
The Coll of New Jersey (NJ)
Coll of St. Joseph (VT)
The Coll of Saint Rose (NY)
Columbia Coll (MO)
Concordia U Texas (TX)
Concordia U Wisconsin (WI)
Coppin State U (MD)
Culver-Stockton Coll (MO)
Cumberland U (TN)
Curry Coll (MA)
Dakota Wesleyan U (SD)
Dallas Baptist U (TX)
Dalton State Coll (GA)
Dana Coll (NE)
Delaware State U (DE)
Delaware Valley Coll (PA)
Dordt Coll (IA)
Drury U (MO)
East Central U (OK)
Eastern Nazarene Coll (MA)
East Tennessee State U (TN)
East Texas Baptist U (TX)
ECPI Coll of Technology, Virginia Beach (VA)
Edward Waters Coll (FL)
Elmira Coll (NY)
Evangel U (MO)
Excelsior Coll (NY)
Fairleigh Dickinson U, Metropolitan Campus (NJ)
Farmingdale State Coll (NY)
Faulkner U (AL)
Fayetteville State U (NC)
Ferris State U (MI)
Florida Ag and Mech U (FL)
Fordham U (NY)
Fort Valley State U (GA)
Franklin Pierce U (NH)
Frostburg State U (MD)
The George Washington U (DC)
Georgia Coll & State U (GA)
Gonzaga U (WA)
Governors State U (IL)
Grace Coll (IN)
Graceland U (IA)
Grand Valley State U (MI)
Grand View U (IA)
Granite State Coll (NH)
Grantham U (MO)
Greenville Coll (IL)
Gustavus Adolphus Coll (MN)
Hamline U (MN)
Hampton U (VA)
Hannibal-LaGrange Coll (MO)
Harris-Stowe State U (MO)
Hawai'i Pacific U (HI)
Hesser Coll, Manchester (NH)
Holy Family U (PA)
Indiana Tech (IN)
Indiana U–Purdue U Fort Wayne (IN)
Inter American U of Puerto Rico, Guayama Campus (PR)
Iona Coll (NY)
Iowa Wesleyan Coll (IA)
ITT Tech Inst, Bessemer (AL)
ITT Tech Inst, Madison (AL)
ITT Tech Inst, Mobile (AL)
ITT Tech Inst, Phoenix (AZ)
ITT Tech Inst, Tempe (AZ)
ITT Tech Inst, Tucson (AZ)
ITT Tech Inst (AR)
ITT Tech Inst, Anaheim (CA)
ITT Tech Inst, Clovis (CA)
ITT Tech Inst, Concord (CA)
ITT Tech Inst, Lathrop (CA)
ITT Tech Inst, Oxnard (CA)
ITT Tech Inst, Rancho Cordova (CA)
ITT Tech Inst, San Bernardino (CA)
ITT Tech Inst, San Diego (CA)
ITT Tech Inst, San Dimas (CA)
ITT Tech Inst, Sylmar (CA)
ITT Tech Inst, Torrance (CA)
ITT Tech Inst, Thornton (CO)
ITT Tech Inst, Fort Lauderdale (FL)
ITT Tech Inst, Fort Myers (FL)
ITT Tech Inst, Jacksonville (FL)
ITT Tech Inst, Lake Mary (FL)
ITT Tech Inst, Miami (FL)
ITT Tech Inst, Tallahassee (FL)
ITT Tech Inst, Tampa (FL)
ITT Tech Inst, Atlanta (GA)
ITT Tech Inst, Duluth (GA)
ITT Tech Inst, Kennesaw (GA)
ITT Tech Inst (ID)
ITT Tech Inst, Burr Ridge (IL)
ITT Tech Inst, Mount Prospect (IL)
ITT Tech Inst, Orland Park (IL)
ITT Tech Inst, Fort Wayne (IN)
ITT Tech Inst, Indianapolis (IN)
ITT Tech Inst, Merrillville (IN)
ITT Tech Inst, Newburgh (IN)
ITT Tech Inst, South Bend (IN)
ITT Tech Inst, Clive (IA)
ITT Tech Inst, Lexington (KY)
ITT Tech Inst, Louisville (KY)
ITT Tech Inst, St. Rose (LA)
ITT Tech Inst, Canton (MI)
ITT Tech Inst, Troy (MI)
ITT Tech Inst, Wyoming (MI)
ITT Tech Inst (MN)
ITT Tech Inst (MS)
ITT Tech Inst, Arnold (MO)
ITT Tech Inst, Earth City (MO)
ITT Tech Inst, Kansas City (MO)
ITT Tech Inst, Springfield (MO)
ITT Tech Inst (NV)
ITT Tech Inst (NM)

ITT Tech Inst, Charlotte (NC)
ITT Tech Inst, Charlotte (NC)
ITT Tech Inst, High Point (NC)
ITT Tech Inst, Morrisville (NC)
ITT Tech Inst, Oklahoma City (OK)
ITT Tech Inst, Tulsa (OK)
ITT Tech Inst (OR)
ITT Tech Inst, Columbia (SC)
ITT Tech Inst, Greenville (SC)
ITT Tech Inst, Chattanooga (TN)
ITT Tech Inst, Cordova (TN)
ITT Tech Inst, Knoxville (TN)
ITT Tech Inst, Nashville (TN)
ITT Tech Inst (UT)
ITT Tech Inst, Chantilly (VA)
ITT Tech Inst, Norfolk (VA)
ITT Tech Inst, Richmond (VA)
ITT Tech Inst, Salem (VA)
ITT Tech Inst, Springfield (VA)
ITT Tech Inst, Everett (WA)
ITT Tech Inst, Seattle (WA)
ITT Tech Inst, Spokane Valley (WA)
ITT Tech Inst, Green Bay (WI)
ITT Tech Inst, Greenfield (WI)
ITT Tech Inst, Madison (WI)
Jacksonville State U (AL)
John Jay Coll of Criminal Justice of the City U of New York (NY)
Johnson & Wales U (FL)
Johnson & Wales U (RI)
Judson Coll (AL)
Kaplan U, Cedar Rapids (IA)
Kaplan U, Lincoln (NE)
Kaplan U, Omaha (NE)
Kean U (NJ)
Keiser U, Fort Lauderdale (FL)
Keuka Coll (NY)
Keystone Coll (PA)
Lake Superior State U (MI)
Lamar U (TX)
Lees-McRae Coll (NC)
Lewis U (IL)
Liberty U (VA)
Limestone Coll (SC)
Lincoln Coll–Normal (IL)
Lincoln Coll of New England, Southington (CT)
Lincoln Memorial U (TN)
Lincoln U (MO)
Lindenwood U (MO)
Lindsey Wilson Coll (KY)
Lock Haven U of Pennsylvania (PA)
Longwood U (VA)
Lubbock Christian U (TX)
Mansfield U of Pennsylvania (PA)
Marian U (WI)
Marist Coll (NY)
Mars Hill Coll (NC)
McKendree U (IL)
Mercy Coll (NY)
Methodist U (NC)
Michigan State U (MI)
MidAmerica Nazarene U (KS)
Middle Tennessee State U (TN)
Midwestern State U (TX)
Mississippi Coll (MS)
Mississippi Valley State U (MS)
Missouri Southern State U (MO)
Mitchell Coll (CT)
Monroe Coll, Bronx (NY)
Moravian Coll (PA)
Morris Coll (SC)
Mount Aloysius Coll (PA)
Mount Ida Coll (MA)
Mount Mercy Coll (IA)
Mount Olive Coll (NC)
Mount Vernon Nazarene U (OH)
National U (CA)
Nevada State Coll at Henderson (NV)
New England Coll (NH)
Newman U (KS)
New York Inst of Technology (NY)
Niagara U (NY)
Northeastern State U (OK)
North Georgia Coll & State U (GA)
Northwest Nazarene U (ID)
Oakland City U (IN)
Ohio Dominican U (OH)
Ohio Northern U (OH)
Ohio U–Zanesville (OH)
Oklahoma City U (OK)
Pace U (NY)
Penn State Abington (PA)
Penn State Altoona (PA)
Penn State Beaver (PA)
Penn State Berks (PA)
Penn State Brandywine (PA)
Penn State DuBois (PA)
Penn State Erie, The Behrend Coll (PA)
Penn State Fayette, The Eberly Campus (PA)
Penn State Greater Allegheny (PA)
Penn State Hazleton (PA)
Penn State Lehigh Valley (PA)
Penn State Mont Alto (PA)
Penn State New Kensington (PA)
Penn State Schuylkill (PA)
Penn State Shenango (PA)
Penn State U Park (PA)
Penn State Wilkes-Barre (PA)
Penn State Worthington Scranton (PA)
Penn State York (PA)
Peru State Coll (NE)
Piedmont Coll (GA)
Point Park U (PA)
Portland State U (OR)
Post U (CT)
Radford U (VA)
Regent U (VA)
Roberts Wesleyan Coll (NY)
Rochester Inst of Technology (NY)
Rogers State U (OK)
Rutgers, The State U of New Jersey, New Brunswick (NJ)
Sacred Heart U (CT)
Saint Augustine's Coll (NC)
St. Cloud State U (MN)
Saint Francis U (PA)
St. John's U (NY)
Saint Louis U (MO)
Saint Martin's U (WA)
St. Mary's U (TX)
Saint Mary's U of Minnesota (MN)
Saint Paul's Coll (VA)
St. Thomas Aquinas Coll (NY)
St. Thomas U (FL)
Salem State Coll (MA)
Salve Regina U (RI)
San Diego State U (CA)
San Francisco State U (CA)
Savannah State U (GA)
Seattle U (WA)
Seton Hill U (PA)
Shenandoah U (VA)
Simpson Coll (IA)
Sonoma State U (CA)
South Carolina State U (SC)
Southeastern U (FL)
Southern Illinois U Carbondale (IL)
Southern Vermont Coll (VT)
South U (AL)
South U, Royal Palm Beach (FL)
South U (GA)
South U, Columbia (SC)
South U, Glen Allen (VA)
South U, Virginia Beach (VA)
Southwest Baptist U (MO)
Southwestern Coll (KS)
Southwestern Oklahoma State U (OK)
Southwest Minnesota State U (MN)
State U of New York at Fredonia (NY)
State U of New York at Oswego (NY)
State U of New York Coll at Potsdam (NY)
State U of New York Coll of Technology at Canton (NY)
Strayer U—Alexandria Campus (VA)
Strayer U—Allentown Campus (PA)
Strayer U—Arlington Campus (VA)
Strayer U—Augusta Campus (GA)
Strayer U—Baymeadows Campus (FL)
Strayer U—Birmingham Campus (AL)
Strayer U—Brickell Campus (FL)
Strayer U—Center City Campus (PA)
Strayer U—Central Austin Campus (TX)
Strayer U—Chamblee Campus (GA)
Strayer U—Charleston Campus (SC)
Strayer U—Chesapeake Campus (VA)
Strayer U—Chesterfield Campus (VA)
Strayer U—Christiana Campus (DE)
Strayer U—Cobb County Campus (GA)
Strayer U—Columbia Campus (SC)
Strayer U—Coral Springs Campus (FL)
Strayer U—Cranberry Woods Campus (PA)
Strayer U—Delaware County Campus (PA)
Strayer U—Doral Campus (FL)
Strayer U—Douglasville Campus (GA)
Strayer U—Florence Campus (KY)
Strayer U—Fort Lauderdale Campus (FL)
Strayer U—Fredericksburg Campus (VA)
Strayer U—Garner Campus (NC)
Strayer U—Greensboro Campus (NC)
Strayer U—Greenville Campus (SC)
Strayer U—Henrico Campus (VA)
Strayer U—Huntersville Campus (NC)
Strayer U—Huntsville Campus (AL)
Strayer U—King of Prussia Campus (PA)
Strayer U—Knoxville Campus (TN)
Strayer U—Lexington Campus (KY)
Strayer U—Lithonia Campus (GA)
Strayer U—Little Rock Campus (AR)
Strayer U—Loudoun Campus (VA)
Strayer U—Louisville Campus (KY)
Strayer U—Lower Bucks County Campus (PA)
Strayer U—Maitland Campus (FL)
Strayer U—Manassas Campus (VA)
Strayer U—Metairie Campus (LA)
Strayer U—Miramar Campus (FL)
Strayer U—Morrow Campus (GA)
Strayer U—Nashville Campus (TN)
Strayer U—Newport News Campus (VA)
Strayer U—North Charlotte Campus (NC)
Strayer U—North Raleigh Campus (NC)
Strayer U—Orlando East Campus (FL)
Strayer U—Palm Beach Gardens Campus (FL)
Strayer U—Penn Center West Campus (PA)
Strayer U—Roswell Campus (GA)
Strayer U—RTP Campus (NC)
Strayer U—Salt Lake Campus (UT)
Strayer U—Sand Lake Campus (FL)
Strayer U—Savannah Campus (GA)
Strayer U—Shelby Oaks Campus (TN)
Strayer U—South Charlotte Campus (NC)
Strayer U—Takoma Park Campus (DC)
Strayer U—Tampa East Campus (FL)
Strayer U—Tampa Westshore Campus (FL)
Strayer U—Teays Valley Campus (WV)
Strayer U—Thousand Oaks Campus (TN)
Strayer U—Virginia Beach Campus (VA)
Strayer U—Washington Campus (DC)
Strayer U—Woodbridge Campus (VA)
Suffolk U (MA)
Sul Ross State U (TX)
Texas A&M U–Commerce (TX)
Texas A&M U–Corpus Christi (TX)
Texas Southern U (TX)
Thomas Edison State Coll (NJ)
Tiffin U (OH)
Trevecca Nazarene U (TN)
Trine U (IN)
Trinity Christian Coll (IL)
Union Coll (KY)
Union Inst & U (OH)
U at Albany, State U of New York (NY)
U of Alaska Anchorage (AK)
U of Alberta (AB, Canada)
The U of Arizona (AZ)
U of Arkansas at Fort Smith (AR)
U of Arkansas at Little Rock (AR)
U of Atlanta (GA)
U of Baltimore (MD)
U of Central Missouri (MO)
U of Central Oklahoma (OK)
U of Cincinnati (OH)
U of Colorado at Colorado Springs (CO)
U of Colorado Denver (CO)
U of Dayton (OH)
U of Delaware (DE)
U of Dubuque (IA)
The U of Findlay (OH)
U of Guam (GU)
U of Guelph (ON, Canada)
U of Hawaii–West Oahu (HI)
U of Louisville (KY)
U of Maine at Augusta (ME)
U of Maine at Presque Isle (ME)
U of Mary Hardin-Baylor (TX)
U of Maryland Eastern Shore (MD)
U of Massachusetts Lowell (MA)
U of Memphis (TN)
U of Minnesota, Crookston (MN)
U of Missouri–Kansas City (MO)
U of Nevada, Las Vegas (NV)
U of New Haven (CT)
U of North Alabama (AL)
U of Oklahoma (OK)
U of Pittsburgh at Bradford (PA)
U of Pittsburgh at Greensburg (PA)
U of Regina (SK, Canada)
U of South Alabama (AL)
U of South Carolina (SC)
U of South Carolina Upstate (SC)
The U of South Dakota (SD)
The U of Tennessee at Chattanooga (TN)
The U of Tennessee at Martin (TN)
The U of Texas at Brownsville (TX)
The U of Texas at El Paso (TX)
The U of Texas–Pan American (TX)
U of Washington (WA)
U of Wisconsin–Milwaukee (WI)
U of Wisconsin–Oshkosh (WI)
U of Wisconsin–Parkside (WI)
U of Wisconsin–Platteville (WI)
Utah Valley U (UT)
Utica Coll (NY)
Villanova U (PA)
Virginia Commonwealth U (VA)
Virginia Intermont Coll (VA)
Voorhees Coll (SC)
Walden U (MN)
Washburn U (KS)
Washington State U (WA)
Wayland Baptist U (TX)
Waynesburg U (PA)
Western Illinois U (IL)
Western Intl U (AZ)
Western Oregon U (OR)
West Liberty U (WV)
West Virginia State U (WV)
West Virginia Wesleyan Coll (WV)
Westwood Coll–Anaheim (CA)
Westwood Coll–Annandale Campus (VA)
Westwood Coll–Arlington Ballston Campus (VA)
Westwood Coll–Atlanta Midtown (GA)
Westwood Coll–Atlanta Northlake (GA)
Westwood Coll–Chicago Du Page (IL)
Westwood Coll–Chicago Loop Campus (IL)
Westwood Coll–Chicago River Oaks (IL)
Westwood Coll–Denver North (CO)
Westwood Coll–Denver South (CO)
Westwood Coll–Inland Empire (CA)
Westwood Coll–Los Angeles (CA)
Westwood Coll–Online Campus (CO)
Westwood Coll–South Bay Campus (CA)
Wheeling Jesuit U (WV)
Widener U (PA)
Wilmington Coll (OH)
Wilmington U (DE)
Winona State U (MN)
York Coll (NE)
York Coll of Pennsylvania (PA)

CRIMINAL JUSTICE/POLICE SCIENCE

American Intl Coll (MA)
American U (DC)
Athabasca U (AB, Canada)
Bemidji State U (MN)
Bowling Green State U (OH)
California State U, East Bay (CA)
Cameron U (OK)
Coll of the Ozarks (MO)
Drury U (MO)
East Central U (OK)
Eastern Nazarene Coll (MA)
Fairmont State U (WV)
Ferris State U (MI)
Frostburg State U (MD)
George Mason U (VA)
Grambling State U (LA)
Heidelberg U (OH)
Hilbert Coll (NY)
Husson U (ME)
Jacksonville State U (AL)
Kent State U at Tuscarawas (OH)
Lake Superior State U (MI)
Lamar U (TX)
Louisiana Coll (LA)
Marian U (WI)
Memorial U of Newfoundland (NL, Canada)
Middle Tennessee State U (TN)
Minnesota State U Mankato (MN)
Monroe Coll, Bronx (NY)
Monroe Coll, New Rochelle (NY)
Newbury Coll (MA)
Northern State U (SD)
Northwestern Oklahoma State U (OK)
Ohio Northern U (OH)
Oklahoma City U (OK)
Pioneer Pacific Coll, Wilsonville (OR)
Prescott Coll (AZ)
Rowan U (NJ)
Stephen F. Austin State U (TX)
Texas A&M U–Commerce (TX)
Texas State U–San Marcos (TX)
Truman State U (MO)
U of Cincinnati (OH)
U of Guam (GU)
U of Hartford (CT)
U of Pittsburgh at Greensburg (PA)
U of Regina (SK, Canada)
U of Toronto (ON, Canada)
U of Wisconsin–Milwaukee (WI)
U of Wisconsin–Superior (WI)
Walden U (MN)
Washburn U (KS)
Western Connecticut State U (CT)
Western Oregon U (OR)
Winona State U (MN)
Wright State U (OH)

CRIMINAL JUSTICE/SAFETY

Albany State U (GA)
Alcorn State U (MS)
American U (DC)
Amridge U (AL)
Andrew Jackson U (AL)
Angelo State U (TX)
Appalachian State U (NC)
Arizona State U (AZ)
Auburn U Montgomery (AL)
Augsburg Coll (MN)
Aurora U (IL)
Baldwin-Wallace Coll (OH)
Ball State U (IN)
Bauder Coll (GA)
Bellarmine U (KY)
Bethany Coll (KS)
Bethel Coll (IN)
Bloomsburg U of Pennsylvania (PA)
Bluefield State Coll (WV)
Bluffton U (OH)
Bowling Green State U (OH)
Bowling Green State U–Firelands Coll (OH)
Bridgewater State Coll (MA)
Buena Vista U (IA)
California State U, Chico (CA)
California State U, Dominguez Hills (CA)
California State U, Fresno (CA)
California State U, Fullerton (CA)
California State U, Los Angeles (CA)
Capella U (MN)
Cazenovia Coll (NY)
Central Pennsylvania Coll (PA)
Central State U (OH)
Champlain Coll (VT)
Chowan U (NC)
Clark Atlanta U (GA)
Clayton State U (GA)
Columbia Southern U (AL)
Columbus State U (GA)
Concordia U, St. Paul (MN)
Dakota Wesleyan U (SD)
Dana Coll (NE)
Delta State U (MS)
DeSales U (PA)
Dominican Coll (NY)
East Carolina U (NC)
Eastern Nazarene Coll (MA)
Eastern New Mexico U (NM)
Edgewood Coll (WI)
Edinboro U of Pennsylvania (PA)
Elizabeth City State U (NC)
Endicott Coll (MA)
Excelsior Coll (NY)
Ferrum Coll (VA)
Fitchburg State Coll (MA)
Florida Ag and Mech U (FL)
Florida Atlantic U (FL)
Florida Gulf Coast U (FL)
Florida Intl U (FL)
Florida Southern Coll (FL)
Florida State U (FL)
Fort Hays State U (KS)
Friends U (KS)
Frostburg State U (MD)
Gannon U (PA)
Georgian Court U (NJ)
Georgia Southern U (GA)
Georgia State U (GA)
Grace Coll (IN)
Granite State Coll (NH)
Grantham U (MO)
Guilford Coll (NC)
Hamline U (MN)
Harding U (AR)
Hardin-Simmons U (TX)
Harrison Coll, Fort Wayne (IN)
Harrison Coll, Indianapolis (IN)
Harrison Coll, Muncie (IN)
High Point U (NC)
Holy Family U (PA)
Howard Payne U (TX)
Husson U (ME)
Huston-Tillotson U (TX)

Illinois State U (IL)
Indiana Tech (IN)
Indiana U Bloomington (IN)
Indiana U East (IN)
Indiana U Kokomo (IN)
Indiana U Northwest (IN)
Indiana U–Purdue U Indianapolis (IN)
Indiana U South Bend (IN)
Indiana U Southeast (IN)
Indiana Wesleyan U (IN)
Indian River State Coll (FL)
Inter American U of Puerto Rico, Aguadilla Campus (PR)
Inter American U of Puerto Rico, Arecibo Campus (PR)
Inter American U of Puerto Rico, Fajardo Campus (PR)
Inter American U of Puerto Rico, Ponce Campus (PR)
Jackson State U (MS)
Jamestown Coll (ND)
Judson U (IL)
Kaplan U, Davenport Campus (IA)
Kennesaw State U (GA)
Kent State U at Trumbull (OH)
Kentucky State U (KY)
Kentucky Wesleyan Coll (KY)
King's Coll (PA)
Kutztown U of Pennsylvania (PA)
Lakeland Coll (WI)
Lane Coll (TN)
La Roche Coll (PA)
La Salle U (PA)
Lasell Coll (MA)
Lewis U (IL)
Limestone Coll (SC)
Lincoln U (PA)
Long Island U, C.W. Post Campus (NY)
Loras Coll (IA)
Louisiana State U in Shreveport (LA)
Lourdes Coll (OH)
Loyola U Chicago (IL)
Lubbock Christian U (TX)
Lynn U (FL)
Madonna U (MI)
Marshall U (WV)
Marymount U (VA)
Marywood U (PA)
McNeese State U (LA)
Medaille Coll (NY)
Mercer U (GA)
Mercyhurst Coll (PA)
Messiah Coll (PA)
Metropolitan State Coll of Denver (CO)
Michigan State U (MI)
Minnesota State U Moorhead (MN)
Minot State U (ND)
Missouri Baptist U (MO)
Missouri Western State U (MO)
Mitchell Coll (CT)
Molloy Coll (NY)
Monmouth U (NJ)
Montana State U Billings (MT)
Mountain State U (WV)
Mount Marty Coll (SD)
Mount St. Mary's U (MD)
Mount Vernon Nazarene U (OH)
Neumann U (PA)
New Jersey City U (NJ)
New Mexico Highlands U (NM)
New Mexico State U (NM)
Nichols Coll (MA)
North Carolina Central U (NC)
North Dakota State U (ND)
Northeastern Illinois U (IL)
Northeastern U (MA)
Northern Kentucky U (KY)
Northern Michigan U (MI)
North Georgia Coll & State U (GA)
Northwestern Coll (MN)
Northwestern State U of Louisiana (LA)
Nova Southeastern U (FL)
Ohio Northern U (OH)
Penn State Abington (PA)
Penn State Altoona (PA)
Penn State Erie, The Behrend Coll (PA)
Penn State Fayette, The Eberly Campus (PA)
Penn State Harrisburg (PA)
Penn State Schuylkill (PA)
Penn State U Park (PA)
Penn State Wilkes-Barre (PA)
Pikeville Coll (KY)
Plymouth State U (NH)
Point Park U (PA)
Potomac State Coll of West Virginia U (WV)
Prairie View A&M U (TX)
Prescott Coll (AZ)
Quincy U (IL)
Quinnipiac U (CT)
Rhode Island Coll (RI)
Roanoke Coll (VA)
Rochester Inst of Technology (NY)
Roosevelt U (IL)
Rosemont Coll (PA)
Royal Roads U (BC, Canada)
Rutgers, The State U of New Jersey, Camden (NJ)
Rutgers, The State U of New Jersey, Newark (NJ)
Saginaw Valley State U (MI)
St. Ambrose U (IA)
Saint Anselm Coll (NH)
St. Edward's U (TX)
St. Francis Coll (NY)
Saint Leo U (FL)
Saint Xavier U (IL)
Sam Houston State U (TX)
San Jose State U (CA)
Seton Hall U (NJ)
Seton Hill U (PA)
Shaw U (NC)
Shippensburg U of Pennsylvania (PA)
Siena Heights U (MI)
Southeastern Louisiana U (LA)
Southeastern Oklahoma State U (OK)
Southern Arkansas U–Magnolia (AR)
Southern Illinois U Edwardsville (IL)
Southern U and Ag and Mech Coll (LA)
Southern U at New Orleans (LA)
Southwestern Assemblies of God U (TX)
Southwestern Coll (KS)
Southwest Florida Coll, Fort Myers (FL)
Southwest Minnesota State U (MN)
State U of New York at Plattsburgh (NY)
State U of New York Coll at Oneonta (NY)
State U of New York Coll at Potsdam (NY)
Sullivan U (KY)
Tarleton State U (TX)
Temple U (PA)
Texas A&M Intl U (TX)
Texas Christian U (TX)
Texas Coll (TX)
Texas State U–San Marcos (TX)
Texas Wesleyan U (TX)
Texas Woman's U (TX)
Thiel Coll (PA)
Thomas Edison State Coll (NJ)
Thomas More Coll (KY)
Troy U (AL)
Truman State U (MO)
The U of Akron (OH)
The U of Alabama (AL)
U of Arkansas (AR)
U of Arkansas at Monticello (AR)
U of Atlanta (GA)
U of Bridgeport (CT)
U of Central Florida (FL)
U of Central Oklahoma (OK)
U of Georgia (GA)
U of Houston–Downtown (TX)
U of Houston–Victoria (TX)
U of Illinois at Chicago (IL)
U of Illinois at Springfield (IL)
U of Louisiana at Monroe (LA)
U of Mary (ND)
U of Maryland U Coll (MD)
U of Massachusetts Boston (MA)
U of Michigan–Dearborn (MI)
U of Mount Union (OH)
U of Nebraska at Kearney (NE)
U of Nebraska at Omaha (NE)
The U of North Carolina at Charlotte (NC)
The U of North Carolina at Pembroke (NC)
The U of North Carolina Wilmington (NC)
U of North Dakota (ND)
U of Northern Colorado (CO)
U of North Florida (FL)
U of North Texas (TX)
U of Portland (OR)
U of Regina (SK, Canada)
U of Richmond (VA)
The U of Scranton (PA)
U of Southern Indiana (IN)
U of Southern Mississippi (MS)
The U of Texas at Arlington (TX)
The U of Texas at Brownsville (TX)
The U of Texas at San Antonio (TX)
The U of Texas at Tyler (TX)
The U of Texas of the Permian Basin (TX)
U of the Cumberlands (KY)
U of the Southwest (NM)
The U of Toledo (OH)
The U of Virginia's Coll at Wise (VA)
U of West Florida (FL)
U of Wisconsin–Eau Claire (WI)
U of Wisconsin–Superior (WI)
U of Wyoming (WY)
Valdosta State U (GA)
Virginia State U (VA)
Virginia Wesleyan Coll (VA)
Viterbo U (WI)
Walden U (MN)
Washburn U (KS)
Wayland Baptist U (TX)
Wayne State Coll (NE)
Wayne State U (MI)
West Chester U of Pennsylvania (PA)
Western Carolina U (NC)
Western Michigan U (MI)
Western New England Coll (MA)
Westfield State Coll (MA)
Westminster Coll (UT)
Wichita State U (KS)
Wilfrid Laurier U (ON, Canada)
Wilkes U (PA)
Winston-Salem State U (NC)
Worcester State Coll (MA)
Xavier U (OH)
Youngstown State U (OH)

CRIMINOLOGY
Adams State Coll (CO)
Albright Coll (PA)
Alderson-Broaddus Coll (WV)
Arcadia U (PA)
Arkansas State U—Jonesboro (AR)
Auburn U (AL)
Barry U (FL)
Butler U (IN)
Cabrini Coll (PA)
California State U, Fresno (CA)
Capital U (OH)
Castleton State Coll (VT)
Cedar Crest Coll (PA)
Centenary Coll (NJ)
Central Connecticut State U (CT)
Chaminade U of Honolulu (HI)
Coker Coll (SC)
Coll of Mount St. Joseph (OH)
Coll of Notre Dame of Maryland (MD)
Dominican U (IL)
Drury U (MO)
Eastern Michigan U (MI)
Eastern Washington U (WA)
Elizabethtown Coll (PA)
Elmhurst Coll (IL)
Emmanuel Coll (MA)
Florida State U (FL)
Gallaudet U (DC)
Husson U (ME)
Immaculata U (PA)
Indiana State U (IN)
Indiana U of Pennsylvania (PA)
John Jay Coll of Criminal Justice of the City U of New York (NY)
Johnson C. Smith U (NC)
Kwantlen Polytechnic U (BC, Canada)
Lebanon Valley Coll (PA)
Le Moyne Coll (NY)
Lindenwood U (MO)
Loyola U New Orleans (LA)
Lycoming Coll (PA)
Lynchburg Coll (VA)
Marquette U (WI)
Marymount U (VA)
Maryville U of Saint Louis (MO)
Memorial U of Newfoundland (NL, Canada)
Missouri State U (MO)
Niagara U (NY)
North Carolina State U (NC)
Northern Arizona U (AZ)
The Ohio State U (OH)
Ohio U (OH)
Old Dominion U (VA)
Paine Coll (GA)
Pittsburg State U (KS)
Pontifical Catholic U of Puerto Rico (PR)
The Richard Stockton Coll of New Jersey (NJ)
Rivier Coll (NH)
Sage Coll of Albany (NY)
Saint Anselm Coll (NH)
St. Cloud State U (MN)
St. Edward's U (TX)
Saint Francis U (PA)
St. John's U (NY)
Saint Joseph's U (PA)
St. Mary's U (TX)
St. Thomas U (NB, Canada)
San Diego State U (CA)
Simon Fraser U (BC, Canada)
Slippery Rock U of Pennsylvania (PA)
Southern Oregon U (OR)
Southern Wesleyan U (SC)
State U of New York Coll at Cortland (NY)
State U of New York Coll at Old Westbury (NY)
Stonehill Coll (MA)
Texas A&M U–Commerce (TX)
Texas A&M U–Kingsville (TX)
U of Alberta (AB, Canada)
U of California, Irvine (CA)
U of Denver (CO)
U of Florida (FL)
U of Houston–Clear Lake (TX)
U of La Verne (CA)
U of Maryland, Coll Park (MD)
U of Massachusetts Dartmouth (MA)
U of Memphis (TN)
U of Miami (FL)
U of Minnesota, Duluth (MN)
U of Missouri–Kansas City (MO)
U of Missouri–St. Louis (MO)
U of Mount Union (OH)
U of Nevada, Reno (NV)
U of New Hampshire (NH)
U of Northern Iowa (IA)
U of Ottawa (ON, Canada)
U of Saint Mary (KS)
U of St. Thomas (MN)
U of Southern Maine (ME)
The U of Tampa (FL)
The U of Texas at Dallas (TX)
The U of Texas of the Permian Basin (TX)
U of Toronto (ON, Canada)
The U of Western Ontario (ON, Canada)
U of West Georgia (GA)
U of Windsor (ON, Canada)
Upper Iowa U (IA)
Valparaiso U (IN)
Virginia Union U (VA)
Virginia Wesleyan Coll (VA)
Walden U (MN)
Western State Coll of Colorado (CO)
William Penn U (IA)
Wright State U (OH)

CROP PRODUCTION
Delaware Valley Coll (PA)
North Dakota State U (ND)
U of Minnesota, Crookston (MN)
Washington State U (WA)

CULINARY ARTS
The Art Inst of Tucson (AZ)
The Art Insts Intl–Kansas City (KS)
Coll of the Ozarks (MO)
Drexel U (PA)
Johnson & Wales U (CO)
Johnson & Wales U (FL)
Johnson & Wales U (RI)
Kendall Coll (IL)
Mountain State U (WV)
Newbury Coll (MA)
Nicholls State U (LA)
The Restaurant School at Walnut Hill Coll (PA)
Universidad de las Américas–Puebla (Mexico)
U of Nevada, Las Vegas (NV)

CULINARY ARTS RELATED
Mississippi U for Women (MS)
Newbury Coll (MA)
U of Nevada, Las Vegas (NV)

CULTURAL RESOURCE MANAGEMENT AND POLICY ANALYSIS
California State U, Dominguez Hills (CA)
Northwestern State U of Louisiana (LA)
U of Waterloo (ON, Canada)

CURRICULUM AND INSTRUCTION
Albertus Magnus Coll (CT)
Free Will Baptist Bible Coll (TN)
Midwestern State U (TX)
Northwest Missouri State U (MO)
Pittsburg State U (KS)
Prescott Coll (AZ)
Tarleton State U (TX)
U of Regina (SK, Canada)
The U of South Dakota (SD)
Utah State U (UT)
Walden U (MN)
Wright State U (OH)

CUSTOMER SERVICE MANAGEMENT
Jones Intl U (CO)
Southwest Baptist U (MO)
U of Wisconsin–Stout (WI)

CYTOGENETICS/GENETICS/CLINICAL GENETICS TECHNOLOGY
Northern Michigan U (MI)
Saint Mary's U of Minnesota (MN)

CYTOTECHNOLOGY
Albany Coll of Pharmacy and Health Sciences (NY)
Barry U (FL)
The Coll of Saint Rose (NY)
Edgewood Coll (WI)
Elmhurst Coll (IL)
Felician Coll (NJ)
Illinois Coll (IL)
Indiana U Bloomington (IN)
Indiana U East (IN)
Indiana U Kokomo (IN)
Indiana U–Purdue U Indianapolis (IN)
Indiana U Southeast (IN)
Long Island U, Brooklyn Campus (NY)
Long Island U, C.W. Post Campus (NY)
Marian U (WI)
Marshall U (WV)
Michigan Technological U (MI)
Minnesota State U Moorhead (MN)
Oakland U (MI)
Old Dominion U (VA)
Saint Louis U (MO)
Saint Mary's U of Minnesota (MN)
Slippery Rock U of Pennsylvania (PA)
State U of New York at Plattsburgh (NY)
Stony Brook U, State U of New York (NY)
Thiel Coll (PA)
Thomas Edison State Coll (NJ)
The U of Alabama at Birmingham (AL)
U of Connecticut (CT)
The U of Kansas (KS)
U of North Dakota (ND)
U of North Texas (TX)
Winona State U (MN)

CZECH
The U of Texas at Austin (TX)

DAIRY HUSBANDRY AND PRODUCTION
U of Vermont (VT)

DAIRY SCIENCE
California Polytechnic State U, San Luis Obispo (CA)
Delaware Valley Coll (PA)
Eastern New Mexico U (NM)
Iowa State U of Science and Technology (IA)
South Dakota State U (SD)
Texas A&M U (TX)
U of Alberta (AB, Canada)
U of Florida (FL)
U of Georgia (GA)
U of New Hampshire (NH)
U of Wisconsin–River Falls (WI)
Utah State U (UT)
Virginia Polytechnic Inst and State U (VA)

DANCE
Adelphi U (NY)
Agnes Scott Coll (GA)
Alma Coll (MI)
Amherst Coll (MA)
Anderson U (IN)
Appalachian State U (NC)
Arizona State U (AZ)
Ball State U (IN)
Bard Coll (NY)
Bard Coll at Simon's Rock (MA)
Barnard Coll (NY)
Belhaven U (MS)
Bennington Coll (VT)
Birmingham-Southern Coll (AL)
The Boston Conservatory (MA)
Brenau U (GA)
Butler U (IN)
California Inst of the Arts (CA)
California State U, East Bay (CA)
California State U, Fresno (CA)
California State U, Fullerton (CA)
California State U, Long Beach (CA)
California State U, Los Angeles (CA)
California State U, Sacramento (CA)
Cedar Crest Coll (PA)
Chapman U (CA)
Claremont McKenna Coll (CA)

Cleveland State U (OH)
The Coll at Brockport, State U of New York (NY)
The Colorado Coll (CO)
Colorado State U (CO)
Columbia Coll (SC)
Columbia Coll Chicago (IL)
Columbia U (NY)
Columbia U, School of General Studies (NY)
Concordia U (QC, Canada)
Connecticut Coll (CT)
Cornell U (NY)
Cornish Coll of the Arts (WA)
Denison U (OH)
DeSales U (PA)
Dominican U of California (CA)
East Carolina U (NC)
Eastern Michigan U (MI)
Elon U (NC)
Emory U (GA)
Eugene Lang Coll The New School for Liberal Arts (NY)
Florida State U (FL)
Fordham U (NY)
Franklin & Marshall Coll (PA)
George Mason U (VA)
The George Washington U (DC)
Georgian Court U (NJ)
Goucher Coll (MD)
Grand Valley State U (MI)
Gustavus Adolphus Coll (MN)
Hamilton Coll (NY)
Hampshire Coll (MA)
Hofstra U (NY)
Hollins U (VA)
Hope Coll (MI)
Hunter Coll of the City U of New York (NY)
Indiana U Bloomington (IN)
Ithaca Coll (NY)
Jacksonville U (FL)
Johnson State Coll (VT)
The Juilliard School (NY)
Keene State Coll (NH)
Kennesaw State U (GA)
Kent State U (OH)
Kenyon Coll (OH)
Lake Erie Coll (OH)
Lamar U (TX)
La Roche Coll (PA)
Lehman Coll of the City U of New York (NY)
Lindenwood U (MO)
Long Island U, Brooklyn Campus (NY)
Long Island U, C.W. Post Campus (NY)
Loyola Marymount U (CA)
Manhattanville Coll (NY)
Marlboro Coll (VT)
Marymount Manhattan Coll (NY)
Mercyhurst Coll (PA)
Meredith Coll (NC)
Middlebury Coll (VT)
Mills Coll (CA)
Missouri State U (MO)
Montclair State U (NJ)
Mount Holyoke Coll (MA)
Muhlenberg Coll (PA)
New Mexico State U (NM)
New York U (NY)
Nova Southeastern U (FL)
Oakland U (MI)
Oberlin Coll (OH)
The Ohio State U (OH)
Ohio U (OH)
Oklahoma City U (OK)
Old Dominion U (VA)
Oral Roberts U (OK)
Pitzer Coll (CA)
Point Park U (PA)
Pomona Coll (CA)
Prescott Coll (AZ)
Purchase Coll, State U of New York (NY)
Radford U (VA)
Randolph Coll (VA)
Reed Coll (OR)
Rhode Island Coll (RI)
Rutgers, The State U of New Jersey, New Brunswick (NJ)
Saint Mary's Coll of California (CA)
St. Olaf Coll (MN)
Sam Houston State U (TX)
San Diego State U (CA)
San Francisco State U (CA)
San Jose State U (CA)
Sarah Lawrence Coll (NY)
Scripps Coll (CA)
Shenandoah U (VA)
Simon Fraser U (BC, Canada)
Skidmore Coll (NY)
Slippery Rock U of Pennsylvania (PA)
Smith Coll (MA)
Southern Methodist U (TX)
Southern Utah U (UT)
State U of New York at Fredonia (NY)
State U of New York Coll at Potsdam (NY)
Stephen F. Austin State U (TX)
Stephens Coll (MO)
Swarthmore Coll (PA)
Sweet Briar Coll (VA)
Temple U (PA)
Texas State U–San Marcos (TX)
Texas Tech U (TX)
Texas Woman's U (TX)
Towson U (MD)
Trinity Coll (CT)
Tulane U (LA)
Universidad de las Américas–Puebla (Mexico)
U at Buffalo, the State U of New York (NY)
The U of Akron (OH)
The U of Alabama (AL)
U of Alberta (AB, Canada)
The U of Arizona (AZ)
U of Arkansas at Little Rock (AR)
U of California, Berkeley (CA)
U of California, Irvine (CA)
U of California, San Diego (CA)
U of California, Santa Barbara (CA)
U of Central Oklahoma (OK)
U of Cincinnati (OH)
U of Colorado at Boulder (CO)
U of Florida (FL)
U of Georgia (GA)
U of Hartford (CT)
U of Hawaii at Manoa (HI)
U of Houston (TX)
U of Idaho (ID)
U of Illinois at Urbana–Champaign (IL)
The U of Iowa (IA)
The U of Kansas (KS)
U of Maryland, Baltimore County (MD)
U of Maryland, Coll Park (MD)
U of Massachusetts Amherst (MA)
U of Michigan (MI)
U of Minnesota, Twin Cities Campus (MN)
U of Missouri–Kansas City (MO)
U of Nebraska–Lincoln (NE)
U of Nevada, Las Vegas (NV)
U of New Mexico (NM)
The U of North Carolina at Charlotte (NC)
The U of North Carolina at Greensboro (NC)
U of North Carolina School of the Arts (NC)
U of North Texas (TX)
U of Oklahoma (OK)
U of Oregon (OR)
U of Richmond (VA)
U of South Carolina (SC)
U of Southern Mississippi (MS)
U of South Florida (FL)
The U of Texas at Austin (TX)
The U of Texas–Pan American (TX)
U of Utah (UT)
U of Washington (WA)
U of Wisconsin–Milwaukee (WI)
U of Wisconsin–Stevens Point (WI)
Utah State U (UT)
Utah Valley U (UT)
Valdosta State U (GA)
Virginia Commonwealth U (VA)
Virginia Intermont Coll (VA)
Washington U in St. Louis (MO)
Wayne State U (MI)
Weber State U (UT)
Webster U (MO)
Wells Coll (NY)
Wesleyan U (CT)
West Chester U of Pennsylvania (PA)
Western Kentucky U (KY)
Western Michigan U (MI)
Western Oregon U (OR)
Western Washington U (WA)
Westmont Coll (CA)
Wheaton Coll (MA)
Winthrop U (SC)
Wright State U (OH)
York U (ON, Canada)

DANCE RELATED

Brigham Young U (UT)
California State U, Long Beach (CA)
Coker Coll (SC)
Sarah Lawrence Coll (NY)
Utah Valley U (UT)
Western Michigan U (MI)

DANCE THERAPY

Columbia Coll Chicago (IL)
Prescott Coll (AZ)

DATA MODELING/ WAREHOUSING AND DATABASE ADMINISTRATION

National U (CA)
Neumont U (UT)
Rochester Inst of Technology (NY)

DATA PROCESSING AND DATA PROCESSING TECHNOLOGY

Arkansas State U—Jonesboro (AR)
Bemidji State U (MN)
Central Baptist Coll (AR)
Clayton State U (GA)
The Coll of Saint Rose (NY)
Farmingdale State Coll (NY)
Indiana U Kokomo (IN)
Midway Coll (KY)
Pace U (NY)
Stephen F. Austin State U (TX)
U of Advancing Technology (AZ)
U of Arkansas (AR)
U of Miami (FL)
U of New Brunswick Fredericton (NB, Canada)
U of Southern Indiana (IN)
U of Southern Mississippi (MS)
U of Washington (WA)
Utah Valley U (UT)

DEMOGRAPHY AND POPULATION

The U of Western Ontario (ON, Canada)

DENTAL ASSISTING

Clayton State U (GA)

DENTAL HYGIENE

Armstrong Atlantic State U (GA)
Clayton State U (GA)
Dixie State Coll of Utah (UT)
Eastern Washington U (WA)
East Tennessee State U (TN)
Farmingdale State Coll (NY)
Ferris State U (MI)
Idaho State U (ID)
Indiana U Bloomington (IN)
Indiana U East (IN)
Indiana U Kokomo (IN)
Indiana U Northwest (IN)
Indiana U–Purdue U Indianapolis (IN)
Indiana U South Bend (IN)
Louisiana State U Health Sciences Center (LA)
Massachusetts Coll of Pharmacy and Health Sciences (MA)
Medical Coll of Georgia (GA)
Midwestern State U (TX)
Minnesota State U Mankato (MN)
New York U (NY)
Northern Arizona U (AZ)
The Ohio State U (OH)
The Ohio State U at Lima (OH)
Old Dominion U (VA)
Oregon Inst of Technology (OR)
St. Petersburg Coll (FL)
Southern Illinois U Carbondale (IL)
State U of New York Coll of Technology at Canton (NY)
Texas A&M Health Science Center (TX)
Texas Woman's U (TX)
Thomas Edison State Coll (NJ)
U of Alberta (AB, Canada)
U of Bridgeport (CT)
The U of British Columbia (BC, Canada)
U of Colorado Denver (CO)
U of Hawaii at Manoa (HI)
U of Louisiana at Monroe (LA)
U of Louisville (KY)
U of Maine at Augusta (ME)
U of Manitoba (MB, Canada)
U of Michigan (MI)
U of Minnesota, Twin Cities Campus (MN)
U of Missouri–Kansas City (MO)
U of Nebraska Medical Center (NE)
U of New England (ME)
U of New Haven (CT)
The U of North Carolina at Chapel Hill (NC)
U of Oklahoma Health Sciences Center (OK)
U of Pittsburgh (PA)
The U of South Dakota (SD)
U of Southern California (CA)
U of Southern Indiana (IN)
The U of Texas Health Science Center at Houston (TX)
U of Washington (WA)
U of Wyoming (WY)
Utah Valley U (UT)
Vermont Tech Coll (VT)
Virginia Commonwealth U (VA)
Western Kentucky U (KY)
West Liberty U (WV)
West Virginia U (WV)
Wichita State U (KS)

DENTAL LABORATORY TECHNOLOGY

Boston U (MA)

DENTAL SERVICES AND ALLIED PROFESSIONS RELATED

Indiana U–Purdue U Indianapolis (IN)

DESIGN AND APPLIED ARTS RELATED

Alverno Coll (WI)
Arizona State U (AZ)
Art Center Coll of Design (CA)
The Art Inst of Colorado (CO)
The Art Inst of Portland (OR)
The Art Insts Intl Minnesota (MN)
Drexel U (PA)
Ferris State U (MI)
Florida Ag and Mech U (FL)
Full Sail U (FL)
Harding U (AR)
Hofstra U (NY)
Lehigh U (PA)
Maryland Inst Coll of Art (MD)
McMurry U (TX)
New York Inst of Technology (NY)
North Carolina State U (NC)
Parsons The New School for Design (NY)
Penn State Altoona (PA)
Penn State Berks (PA)
Penn State U Park (PA)
Point Park U (PA)
Pratt Inst (NY)
Reinhardt Coll (GA)
Robert Morris U Illinois (IL)
Roberts Wesleyan Coll (NY)
St. Cloud State U (MN)
Salem State Coll (MA)
Savannah Coll of Art and Design (GA)
School of the Art Inst of Chicago (IL)
School of Visual Arts (NY)
Schreiner U (TX)
Taylor U (IN)
U of California, Los Angeles (CA)
U of Illinois at Chicago (IL)
U of Massachusetts Dartmouth (MA)
U of Oregon (OR)
U of Wisconsin–Stout (WI)
Washburn U (KS)
Western Washington U (WA)

DESIGN AND VISUAL COMMUNICATIONS

Acad of Art U (CA)
Alberta Coll of Art & Design (AB, Canada)
Albright Coll (PA)
Alma Coll (MI)
The American U in Dubai (United Arab Emirates)
Anderson U (IN)
The Art Inst of Michigan (MI)
The Art Inst of Ohio–Cincinnati (OH)
The Art Inst of Portland (OR)
Auburn U (AL)
Bennington Coll (VT)
Bethel Coll (IN)
Bowling Green State U (OH)
Bowling Green State U–Firelands Coll (OH)
Buffalo State Coll, State U of New York (NY)
California Inst of the Arts (CA)
California State U, Chico (CA)
Cazenovia Coll (NY)
Central Connecticut State U (CT)
Champlain Coll (VT)
Coll of Mount St. Joseph (OH)
Collins Coll: A School of Design and Technology (AZ)
Columbia Coll Chicago (IL)
Creative Center (NE)
DigiPen Inst of Technology (WA)
Drury U (MO)
Duke U (NC)
Endicott Coll (MA)
Escuela de Artes Plasticas de Puerto Rico (PR)
Farmingdale State Coll (NY)
Ferris State U (MI)
Franklin Coll Switzerland (Switzerland)
Full Sail U (FL)
Hampshire Coll (MA)
The Illinois Inst of Art–Chicago (IL)
Intl Acad of Design & Technology (IL)
Iowa State U of Science and Technology (IA)
Jacksonville U (FL)
Kean U (NJ)
La Roche Coll (PA)
Lawrence Technological U (MI)
Lehigh U (PA)
Liberty U (VA)
LIM Coll (NY)
Linfield Coll (OR)
Loyola U Chicago (IL)
Lubbock Christian U (TX)
Madonna U (MI)
Memphis Coll of Art (TN)
Missouri State U (MO)
New Mexico Highlands U (NM)
New York City Coll of Technology of the City U of New York (NY)
North Carolina State U (NC)
Northeastern State U (OK)
Northern Arizona U (AZ)
Ohio Northern U (OH)
The Ohio State U (OH)
Oral Roberts U (OK)
Parsons The New School for Design (NY)
Peace Coll (NC)
Purdue U (IN)
Radford U (VA)
Rensselaer Polytechnic Inst (NY)
Robert Morris U (PA)
Rochester Inst of Technology (NY)
Saginaw Valley State U (MI)
St. Ambrose U (IA)
Saint Mary-of-the-Woods Coll (IN)
San Diego State U (CA)
Savannah Coll of Art and Design (GA)
School of the Art Inst of Chicago (IL)
Seattle Pacific U (WA)
Southern Illinois U Carbondale (IL)
Spring Arbor U (MI)
Stevenson U (MD)
Texas A&M U–Commerce (TX)
Truman State U (MO)
Universidad de las Américas–Puebla (Mexico)
Université du Québec en Outaouais (QC, Canada)
U of Advancing Technology (AZ)
U of Evansville (IN)
U of Hartford (CT)
The U of Kansas (KS)
U of Massachusetts Dartmouth (MA)
U of Miami (FL)
U of Michigan–Flint (MI)
U of Notre Dame (IN)
The U of Tennessee at Martin (TN)
The U of Texas at Austin (TX)
Utah Valley U (UT)
Viterbo U (WI)
Washington U in St. Louis (MO)
Watkins Coll of Art, Design, & Film (TN)
Weber State U (UT)
Western Washington U (WA)
Westwood Coll–Anaheim (CA)
Westwood Coll–Annandale Campus (VA)
Westwood Coll–Arlington Ballston Campus (VA)
Westwood Coll–Atlanta Midtown (GA)
Westwood Coll–Atlanta Northlake (GA)
Westwood Coll–Chicago Du Page (IL)
Westwood Coll–Chicago Loop Campus (IL)
Westwood Coll–Chicago O'Hare Airport (IL)
Westwood Coll–Chicago River Oaks (IL)
Westwood Coll–Fort Worth (TX)
Westwood Coll–Houston South Campus (TX)
Westwood Coll–Inland Empire (CA)
Westwood Coll–Los Angeles (CA)
Westwood Coll–Online Campus (CO)
Westwood Coll–South Bay Campus (CA)
York U (ON, Canada)

DESKTOP PUBLISHING AND DIGITAL IMAGING DESIGN

Acad of Art U (CA)
Chowan U (NC)
EDP Coll of Puerto Rico, Inc. (PR)

Rochester Inst of Technology (NY)
Texas State U–San Marcos (TX)

DEVELOPMENTAL AND CHILD PSYCHOLOGY
Antioch U McGregor (OH)
Bay Path Coll (MA)
Belmont U (TN)
Bridgewater State Coll (MA)
Brooklyn Coll of the City U of New York (NY)
California State U, Bakersfield (CA)
California State U, East Bay (CA)
California State U, San Bernardino (CA)
Carson-Newman Coll (TN)
Castleton State Coll (VT)
Eastern Connecticut State U (CT)
Eastern Nazarene Coll (MA)
Eastern Washington U (WA)
Emmanuel Coll (MA)
Fitchburg State Coll (MA)
Fort Valley State U (GA)
Hampton U (VA)
Houston Baptist U (TX)
Humboldt State U (CA)
Keene State Coll (NH)
Liberty U (VA)
Longwood U (VA)
Marlboro Coll (VT)
Maryville Coll (TN)
Mills Coll (CA)
Minnesota State U Mankato (MN)
Mount St. Mary's Coll (CA)
Northeastern State U (OK)
Northern Michigan U (MI)
Prescott Coll (AZ)
Quinnipiac U (CT)
St. Joseph's Coll, Long Island Campus (NY)
St. Joseph's Coll, New York (NY)
Sarah Lawrence Coll (NY)
Sonoma State U (CA)
Spelman Coll (GA)
Suffolk U (MA)
Texas Christian U (TX)
Tufts U (MA)
U of Alberta (AB, Canada)
The U of British Columbia (BC, Canada)
U of California, Santa Cruz (CA)
U of Delaware (DE)
The U of Kansas (KS)
U of Minnesota, Twin Cities Campus (MN)
U of New Brunswick Fredericton (NB, Canada)
The U of Texas at Dallas (TX)
U of the District of Columbia (DC)
The U of Toledo (OH)
U of Windsor (ON, Canada)
U of Wisconsin–Green Bay (WI)
U of Wisconsin–Madison (WI)
Utica Coll (NY)
Vanderbilt U (TN)
Western Washington U (WA)
Whittier Coll (CA)
Wilfrid Laurier U (ON, Canada)

DEVELOPMENT ECONOMICS AND INTERNATIONAL DEVELOPMENT
Calvin Coll (MI)
Clark U (MA)
Georgia Southern U (GA)
John Brown U (AR)
Penn State Altoona (PA)
Penn State Berks (PA)
Penn State U Park (PA)
Prescott Coll (AZ)
Taylor U (IN)
U of California, Los Angeles (CA)
U of King's Coll (NS, Canada)
U of Ottawa (ON, Canada)
U of Vermont (VT)
York U (ON, Canada)

DIAGNOSTIC MEDICAL SONOGRAPHY AND ULTRASOUND TECHNOLOGY
Baptist Coll of Health Sciences (TN)
Benedictine U (IL)
Charles Drew U of Medicine and Science (CA)
The George Washington U (DC)
Lewis U (IL)
Medical Coll of Georgia (GA)
Misericordia U (PA)
Mountain State U (WV)
Nebraska Methodist Coll (NE)
Newman U (KS)
Rochester Inst of Technology (NY)
Seattle U (WA)
State U of New York Downstate Medical Center (NY)
U of Missouri (MO)
U of Nebraska Medical Center (NE)
Washburn U (KS)
Weber State U (UT)

DIESEL MECHANICS TECHNOLOGY
Lewis-Clark State Coll (ID)
Pittsburg State U (KS)

DIETETICS
Abilene Christian U (TX)
Acadia U (NS, Canada)
Andrews U (MI)
Ashland U (OH)
Ball State U (IN)
Bastyr U (WA)
Bowling Green State U (OH)
Bradley U (IL)
Buffalo State Coll, State U of New York (NY)
California Polytechnic State U, San Luis Obispo (CA)
California State Polytechnic U, Pomona (CA)
California State U, Chico (CA)
California State U, Fresno (CA)
California State U, Long Beach (CA)
California State U, Los Angeles (CA)
California State U, San Bernardino (CA)
Carson-Newman Coll (TN)
Case Western Reserve U (OH)
Central Michigan U (MI)
Coll of Saint Elizabeth (NJ)
Coll of the Ozarks (MO)
Concordia Coll (MN)
Delaware State U (DE)
Dominican U (IL)
D'Youville Coll (NY)
East Carolina U (NC)
Eastern Michigan U (MI)
Florida Intl U (FL)
Florida State U (FL)
Fontbonne U (MO)
Harding U (AR)
Idaho State U (ID)
Immaculata U (PA)
Iowa State U of Science and Technology (IA)
Jacksonville State U (AL)
Kansas State U (KS)
Keene State Coll (NH)
Lamar U (TX)
Lehman Coll of the City U of New York (NY)
Life U (GA)
Lipscomb U (TN)
Louisiana State U and Ag and Mech Coll (LA)
Louisiana Tech U (LA)
Mansfield U of Pennsylvania (PA)
Marshall U (WV)
Marywood U (PA)
Memorial U of Newfoundland (NL, Canada)
Meredith Coll (NC)
Miami U (OH)
Miami U Hamilton (OH)
Michigan State U (MI)
Minnesota State U Mankato (MN)
Missouri State U (MO)
Mount Mary Coll (WI)
Nicholls State U (LA)
North Dakota State U (ND)
Northwest Missouri State U (MO)
Oakwood U (AL)
The Ohio State U (OH)
Ohio U (OH)
Ouachita Baptist U (AR)
St. Catherine U (MN)
San Diego State U (CA)
San Francisco State U (CA)
San Jose State U (CA)
Seton Hill U (PA)
Simmons Coll (MA)
State U of New York Coll at Oneonta (NY)
Tennessee Technological U (TN)
Texas Christian U (TX)
Texas Southern U (TX)
Texas Tech U (TX)
Texas Woman's U (TX)
Tuskegee U (AL)
The U of Alabama (AL)
The U of British Columbia (BC, Canada)
U of Central Missouri (MO)
U of Central Oklahoma (OK)
U of Connecticut (CT)
U of Dayton (OH)
U of Delaware (DE)
U of Georgia (GA)
U of Illinois at Chicago (IL)
U of Illinois at Urbana–Champaign (IL)
U of Maryland, Coll Park (MD)
U of Maryland Eastern Shore (MD)
U of Missouri (MO)
U of Nebraska at Kearney (NE)
U of New Haven (CT)
U of North Dakota (ND)
U of Northern Colorado (CO)
U of Oklahoma Health Sciences Center (OK)
U of Pittsburgh (PA)
U of Rhode Island (RI)
U of Southern Mississippi (MS)
The U of Tennessee at Martin (TN)
The U of Texas–Pan American (TX)
The U of Texas Southwestern Medical Center at Dallas (TX)
U of Vermont (VT)
The U of Western Ontario (ON, Canada)
U of Wisconsin–Madison (WI)
U of Wisconsin–Stevens Point (WI)
U of Wisconsin–Stout (WI)
Viterbo U (WI)
Wayne State U (MI)
West Chester U of Pennsylvania (PA)
Western Carolina U (NC)
Youngstown State U (OH)

DIETETICS AND CLINICAL NUTRITION SERVICES RELATED
American U of Beirut (Lebanon)
Coll of Saint Benedict (MN)
Madonna U (MI)
Saint John's U (MN)
Texas Christian U (TX)
Western Michigan U (MI)

DIGITAL COMMUNICATION AND MEDIA/MULTIMEDIA
Abilene Christian U (TX)
Acad of Art U (CA)
The Art Inst of Atlanta (GA)
Baylor U (TX)
Butler U (IN)
California Baptist U (CA)
California Lutheran U (CA)
California State U, Dominguez Hills (CA)
Calvin Coll (MI)
Champlain Coll (VT)
Clarkson U (NY)
Cogswell Polytechnical Coll (CA)
Coll of Notre Dame of Maryland (MD)
Corcoran Coll of Art and Design (DC)
Dordt Coll (IA)
Eastern Mennonite U (VA)
Fitchburg State Coll (MA)
Florida Atlantic U (FL)
Georgia Inst of Technology (GA)
Georgia Southern U (GA)
Harding U (AR)
Hilbert Coll (NY)
Howard Payne U (TX)
Huntington U (IN)
Indiana U–Purdue U Indianapolis (IN)
John Brown U (AR)
Juniata Coll (PA)
Kent State U (OH)
Kutztown U of Pennsylvania (PA)
Lebanon Valley Coll (PA)
Lindenwood U (MO)
Lycoming Coll (PA)
Marist Coll (NY)
Marywood U (PA)
Miami U (OH)
Michigan Technological U (MI)
Minot State U (ND)
Mount Marty Coll (SD)
Mount Mercy Coll (IA)
Northern Michigan U (MI)
Ohio U (OH)
Platt Coll San Diego (CA)
Rensselaer Polytechnic Inst (NY)
Rochester Inst of Technology (NY)
St. Edward's U (TX)
Savannah Coll of Art and Design (GA)
School of the Art Inst of Chicago (IL)
Slippery Rock U of Pennsylvania (PA)
Southern New Hampshire U (NH)
Texas A&M U (TX)
Tiffin U (OH)
U of Baltimore (MD)
U of Denver (CO)
U of Idaho (ID)
U of Miami (FL)
U of Northern Iowa (IA)
U of Puerto Rico, Río Piedras (PR)
The U of Texas at Arlington (TX)
The U of Texas at Dallas (TX)
U of Toronto (ON, Canada)
U of Waterloo (ON, Canada)
The U of Western Ontario (ON, Canada)
Valley Forge Christian Coll (PA)
Washington State U (WA)
Wellesley Coll (MA)
Wheeling Jesuit U (WV)
Wilkes U (PA)

DIRECT ENTRY MIDWIFERY
Midwives Coll of Utah (UT)

DIRECTING AND THEATRICAL PRODUCTION
Bard Coll (NY)
Bennington Coll (VT)
Bradley U (IL)
Brigham Young U (UT)
California Inst of the Arts (CA)
California State U, Long Beach (CA)
Cornish Coll of the Arts (WA)
Drake U (IA)
Hofstra U (NY)
Keene State Coll (NH)
Lindenwood U (MO)
Lubbock Christian U (TX)
Sarah Lawrence Coll (NY)
State U of New York at Binghamton (NY)
U of Illinois at Urbana–Champaign (IL)

DIVINITY/MINISTRY
Amridge U (AL)
Atlantic Union Coll (MA)
Azusa Pacific U (CA)
Baptist Bible Coll of Pennsylvania (PA)
Barclay Coll (KS)
Belmont U (TN)
Bethany Bible Coll (NB, Canada)
Bethany U (CA)
Bethel Coll (IN)
Bluefield Coll (VA)
Campbellsville U (KY)
Central Christian Coll of Kansas (KS)
Christian Life Coll (IL)
Cincinnati Christian U (OH)
Clear Creek Baptist Bible Coll (KY)
Corban U (OR)
Crichton Coll (TN)
Dallas Baptist U (TX)
Davis Coll (NY)
Eastern Nazarene Coll (MA)
Ecclesia Coll (AR)
Emmanuel Bible Coll (ON, Canada)
Eugene Bible Coll (OR)
Faith Baptist Bible Coll and Theological Sem (IA)
Faulkner U (AL)
Global U (MO)
Great Lakes Christian Coll (MI)
Grove City Coll (PA)
Huntington U (IN)
John Brown U (AR)
John Wesley Coll (NC)
Kuyper Coll (MI)
Lincoln Christian U (IL)
The Master's Coll and Sem (CA)
Master's Coll and Sem (ON, Canada)
Moody Bible Inst (IL)
Mount Olive Coll (NC)
Northwest Nazarene U (ID)
Northwest U (WA)
Oak Hills Christian Coll (MN)
Oakland City U (IN)
Oklahoma Baptist U (OK)
Oklahoma Wesleyan U (OK)
Patten U (CA)
Providence Coll (RI)
Regent U (VA)
Roberts Wesleyan Coll (NY)
San Diego Christian Coll (CA)
Shorter U (GA)
Southwestern Assemblies of God U (TX)
Tabor Coll (KS)
Tri-State Bible Coll (OH)
The U of Western Ontario (ON, Canada)
Valley Forge Christian Coll (PA)
Viterbo U (WI)

DRAFTING AND DESIGN TECHNOLOGY
Baker Coll of Owosso (MI)
Cameron U (OK)
East Carolina U (NC)
East Central U (OK)
Grambling State U (LA)
Herzing U (WI)
Lewis-Clark State Coll (ID)
Pacific Union Coll (CA)
Prairie View A&M U (TX)
Trine U (IN)
U of Maine (ME)
U of Rio Grande (OH)

DRAFTING/DESIGN ENGINEERING TECHNOLOGIES RELATED
Lincoln U (MO)
National U (CA)
Thomas Edison State Coll (NJ)

DRAMA AND DANCE TEACHER EDUCATION
Adams State Coll (CO)
Appalachian State U (NC)
Bishop's U (QC, Canada)
Boston U (MA)
Bowling Green State U (OH)
Bradley U (IL)
Brenau U (GA)
Bridgewater State Coll (MA)
The Catholic U of America (DC)
Columbia Coll (SC)
Columbus State U (GA)
Dordt Coll (IA)
East Carolina U (NC)
East Texas Baptist U (TX)
Edgewood Coll (WI)
Emerson Coll (MA)
Greensboro Coll (NC)
Hardin-Simmons U (TX)
Hope Coll (MI)
Howard Payne U (TX)
Huntington U (IN)
Jacksonville U (FL)
Johnson State Coll (VT)
Lipscomb U (TN)
Maryville Coll (TN)
Meredith Coll (NC)
Minnesota State U Moorhead (MN)
Montclair State U (NJ)
North Carolina Central U (NC)
Northern Arizona U (AZ)
Ohio Wesleyan U (OH)
Old Dominion U (VA)
Point Park U (PA)
St. Catherine U (MN)
St. Edward's U (TX)
Shenandoah U (VA)
Texas Christian U (TX)
Texas Wesleyan U (TX)
Trevecca Nazarene U (TN)
The U of Akron (OH)
The U of Arizona (AZ)
U of Evansville (IN)
The U of Iowa (IA)
U of Lethbridge (AB, Canada)
The U of North Carolina at Charlotte (NC)
The U of North Carolina at Greensboro (NC)
U of Regina (SK, Canada)
U of St. Thomas (MN)
The U of South Dakota (SD)
U of South Florida (FL)
U of Windsor (ON, Canada)
Utah Valley U (UT)
Valparaiso U (IN)
Viterbo U (WI)
Waldorf Coll (IA)
Washington U in St. Louis (MO)
Wayne State Coll (NE)
Weber State U (UT)
Western Washington U (WA)
William Jewell Coll (MO)
York U (ON, Canada)
Youngstown State U (OH)

DRAMA THERAPY
Virginia Union U (VA)

DRAMATIC/THEATER ARTS
Abilene Christian U (TX)
Acadia U (NS, Canada)
Adelphi U (NY)
Agnes Scott Coll (GA)
Alabama State U (AL)
Albertus Magnus Coll (CT)
Albion Coll (MI)
Albright Coll (PA)
Alfred U (NY)
Allegheny Coll (PA)
Alma Coll (MI)
American U (DC)
Amherst Coll (MA)
Anderson U (IN)
Angelo State U (TX)
Appalachian State U (NC)
Aquinas Coll (MI)
Arcadia U (PA)
Arizona State U (AZ)

Dramatic/Theater Arts

Arkansas State U—Jonesboro (AR)
Armstrong Atlantic State U (GA)
Asbury U (KY)
Ashland U (OH)
Auburn U (AL)
Augsburg Coll (MN)
Augustana Coll (IL)
Augustana Coll (SD)
Aurora U (IL)
Averett U (VA)
Avila U (MO)
Baker U (KS)
Ball State U (IN)
Bard Coll (NY)
Bard Coll at Simon's Rock (MA)
Barnard Coll (NY)
Barry U (FL)
Barton Coll (NC)
Bates Coll (ME)
Baylor U (TX)
Belhaven U (MS)
Belmont U (TN)
Beloit Coll (WI)
Bemidji State U (MN)
Benedictine Coll (KS)
Bennington Coll (VT)
Berea Coll (KY)
Bethany Coll (WV)
Bethany Lutheran Coll (MN)
Bethel Coll (IN)
Bethel U (MN)
Bethel U (TN)
Birmingham-Southern Coll (AL)
Bishop's U (QC, Canada)
Bloomsburg U of Pennsylvania (PA)
Bluefield Coll (VA)
Bob Jones U (SC)
Boise State U (ID)
Boston Coll (MA)
The Boston Conservatory (MA)
Bowling Green State U (OH)
Bradley U (IL)
Brandeis U (MA)
Brenau U (GA)
Brevard Coll (NC)
Briar Cliff U (IA)
Bridgewater State Coll (MA)
Brock U (ON, Canada)
Bryan Coll (TN)
Bucknell U (PA)
Buffalo State Coll, State U of New York (NY)
Butler U (IN)
California Baptist U (CA)
California Lutheran U (CA)
California Polytechnic State U, San Luis Obispo (CA)
California State Polytechnic U, Pomona (CA)
California State U, Bakersfield (CA)
California State U, Chico (CA)
California State U, Dominguez Hills (CA)
California State U, East Bay (CA)
California State U, Fresno (CA)
California State U, Fullerton (CA)
California State U, Long Beach (CA)
California State U, Los Angeles (CA)
California State U, Northridge (CA)
California State U, Sacramento (CA)
California State U, San Bernardino (CA)
California State U, Stanislaus (CA)
Calvin Coll (MI)
Capital U (OH)
Carleton Coll (MN)
Carnegie Mellon U (PA)
Carroll U (WI)
Carson-Newman Coll (TN)
Case Western Reserve U (OH)
Castleton State Coll (VT)
Catawba Coll (NC)
The Catholic U of America (DC)
Cedar Crest Coll (PA)
Cedarville U (OH)
Centenary Coll of Louisiana (LA)
Central Coll (IA)
Central Michigan U (MI)
Chapman U (CA)
Chatham U (PA)
Cheyney U of Pennsylvania (PA)
Chowan U (NC)
Christopher Newport U (VA)
City Coll of the City U of New York (NY)
Claremont McKenna Coll (CA)
Clarion U of Pennsylvania (PA)
Clarke Coll (IA)
Clark U (MA)
Clayton State U (GA)
Cleveland State U (OH)
Coastal Carolina U (SC)
Coker Coll (SC)
Colby Coll (ME)
Colgate U (NY)
The Coll at Brockport, State U of New York (NY)
Coll of Charleston (SC)
The Coll of Idaho (ID)
Coll of Notre Dame of Maryland (MD)
Coll of Saint Benedict (MN)
Coll of Santa Fe (NM)
Coll of Staten Island of the City U of New York (NY)
Coll of the Holy Cross (MA)
Coll of the Ozarks (MO)
The Coll of William and Mary (VA)
The Coll of Wooster (OH)
The Colorado Coll (CO)
Colorado State U (CO)
Columbia Coll Chicago (IL)
Columbia U (NY)
Columbia U, School of General Studies (NY)
Columbus State U (GA)
Concordia Coll (MN)
Concordia U (CA)
Concordia U (QC, Canada)
Concordia U Chicago (IL)
Concordia U, St. Paul (MN)
Connecticut Coll (CT)
Converse Coll (SC)
Cornell Coll (IA)
Cornell U (NY)
Cornish Coll of the Arts (WA)
Covenant Coll (GA)
Creighton U (NE)
Culver-Stockton Coll (MO)
Cumberland U (TN)
Dakota Wesleyan U (SD)
Dartmouth Coll (NH)
Davidson Coll (NC)
Denison U (OH)
DePaul U (IL)
DePauw U (IN)
DeSales U (PA)
Dickinson Coll (PA)
Dickinson State U (ND)
Dillard U (LA)
Doane Coll (NE)
Dominican U (IL)
Dordt Coll (IA)
Drake U (IA)
Drew U (NJ)
Drury U (MO)
Duke U (NC)
Duquesne U (PA)
Earlham Coll (IN)
East Carolina U (NC)
Eastern Illinois U (IL)
Eastern Mennonite U (VA)
Eastern Michigan U (MI)
Eastern Nazarene Coll (MA)
Eastern New Mexico U (NM)
Eastern Washington U (WA)
East Stroudsburg U of Pennsylvania (PA)
East Tennessee State U (TN)
East Texas Baptist U (TX)
Eckerd Coll (FL)
Edinboro U of Pennsylvania (PA)
Elizabethtown Coll (PA)
Elmhurst Coll (IL)
Elmira Coll (NY)
Elon U (NC)
Emerson Coll (MA)
Emory & Henry Coll (VA)
Emory U (GA)
Emporia State U (KS)
Eugene Lang Coll The New School for Liberal Arts (NY)
The Evergreen State Coll (WA)
Fairfield U (CT)
Fairleigh Dickinson U, Coll at Florham (NJ)
Fairmont State U (WV)
Faulkner U (AL)
Ferrum Coll (VA)
Fisk U (TN)
Fitchburg State Coll (MA)
Five Towns Coll (NY)
Flagler Coll (FL)
Florida Ag and Mech U (FL)
Florida Atlantic U (FL)
Florida Gulf Coast U (FL)
Florida Intl U (FL)
Florida Southern Coll (FL)
Florida State U (FL)
Fontbonne U (MO)
Fordham U (NY)
Fort Hays State U (KS)
Fort Lewis Coll (CO)
Franciscan U of Steubenville (OH)
Francis Marion U (SC)
Franklin & Marshall Coll (PA)
Franklin Coll (IN)
Franklin Pierce U (NH)
Freed-Hardeman U (TN)
Friends U (KS)
Frostburg State U (MD)
Furman U (SC)
Gallaudet U (DC)
Gannon U (PA)
Gardner-Webb U (NC)
George Fox U (OR)
George Mason U (VA)
Georgetown Coll (KY)
The George Washington U (DC)
Georgia Coll & State U (GA)
Georgia Southern U (GA)
Gettysburg Coll (PA)
Gonzaga U (WA)
Goshen Coll (IN)
Goucher Coll (MD)
Grace Coll (IN)
Graceland U (IA)
Grambling State U (LA)
Grand Valley State U (MI)
Grand View U (IA)
Greensboro Coll (NC)
Greenville Coll (IL)
Grinnell Coll (IA)
Guilford Coll (NC)
Gustavus Adolphus Coll (MN)
Hamilton Coll (NY)
Hamline U (MN)
Hampshire Coll (MA)
Hampton U (VA)
Hannibal-LaGrange Coll (MO)
Hanover Coll (IN)
Harding U (AR)
Hardin-Simmons U (TX)
Hartwick Coll (NY)
Heidelberg U (OH)
Henderson State U (AR)
Hendrix Coll (AR)
High Point U (NC)
Hillsdale Coll (MI)
Hiram Coll (OH)
Hofstra U (NY)
Hollins U (VA)
Hope Coll (MI)
Howard Payne U (TX)
Humboldt State U (CA)
Hunter Coll of the City U of New York (NY)
Huntington U (IN)
Idaho State U (ID)
Illinois Coll (IL)
Illinois State U (IL)
Illinois Wesleyan U (IL)
Indiana State U (IN)
Indiana U Bloomington (IN)
Indiana U Northwest (IN)
Indiana U of Pennsylvania (PA)
Indiana U–Purdue U Fort Wayne (IN)
Indiana U South Bend (IN)
Iona Coll (NY)
Iowa State U of Science and Technology (IA)
Ithaca Coll (NY)
Jacksonville State U (AL)
Jacksonville U (FL)
James Madison U (VA)
Jamestown Coll (ND)
Johnson State Coll (VT)
The Juilliard School (NY)
Juniata Coll (PA)
Kalamazoo Coll (MI)
Kansas State U (KS)
Kean U (NJ)
Kennesaw State U (GA)
Kent State U (OH)
Kenyon Coll (OH)
King's Coll (PA)
Knox Coll (IL)
Kutztown U of Pennsylvania (PA)
Kuyper Coll (MI)
LaGrange Coll (GA)
Lake Erie Coll (OH)
Lake Forest Coll (IL)
Lamar U (TX)
Laurentian U (ON, Canada)
Lawrence U (WI)
Lees-McRae Coll (NC)
Lehigh U (PA)
Lehman Coll of the City U of New York (NY)
Le Moyne Coll (NY)
Lewis & Clark Coll (OR)
Lewis U (IL)
Limestone Coll (SC)
Lindenwood U (MO)
Linfield Coll (OR)
Lipscomb U (TN)
Lock Haven U of Pennsylvania (PA)
Long Island U, C.W. Post Campus (NY)
Longwood U (VA)
Louisiana Coll (LA)
Louisiana State U and Ag and Mech Coll (LA)
Loyola Marymount U (CA)
Loyola U Chicago (IL)
Loyola U New Orleans (LA)
Lubbock Christian U (TX)
Luther Coll (IA)
Lycoming Coll (PA)
Lynchburg Coll (VA)
Lyon Coll (AR)
Macalester Coll (MN)
Manchester Coll (IN)
Marietta Coll (OH)
Marist Coll (NY)
Marlboro Coll (VT)
Marquette U (WI)
Mars Hill Coll (NC)
Mary Baldwin Coll (VA)
Marymount Manhattan Coll (NY)
Maryville Coll (TN)
Marywood U (PA)
McDaniel Coll (MD)
McMurry U (TX)
McNeese State U (LA)
McPherson Coll (KS)
Memorial U of Newfoundland (NL, Canada)
Mercer U (GA)
Meredith Coll (NC)
Messiah Coll (PA)
Methodist U (NC)
Metropolitan State Coll of Denver (CO)
Miami U (OH)
Michigan State U (MI)
MidAmerica Nazarene U (KS)
Middlebury Coll (VT)
Middle Tennessee State U (TN)
Midwestern State U (TX)
Millikin U (IL)
Millsaps Coll (MS)
Minnesota State U Mankato (MN)
Minnesota State U Moorhead (MN)
Missouri Southern State U (MO)
Missouri State U (MO)
Monmouth Coll (IL)
Monmouth U (NJ)
Montana State U Billings (MT)
Montclair State U (NJ)
Moravian Coll (PA)
Morehead State U (KY)
Morehouse Coll (GA)
Morningside Coll (IA)
Mount Allison U (NB, Canada)
Mount Holyoke Coll (MA)
Mount Marty Coll (SD)
Mount Vernon Nazarene U (OH)
Muhlenberg Coll (PA)
Murray State U (KY)
Naropa U (CO)
Nazareth Coll of Rochester (NY)
Nebraska Wesleyan U (NE)
Newberry Coll (SC)
New England Coll (NH)
New Mexico State U (NM)
The New School for General Studies (NY)
New York U (NY)
Niagara U (NY)
North Carolina Central U (NC)
North Central Coll (IL)
North Dakota State U (ND)
Northeastern State U (OK)
Northeastern U (MA)
Northern Arizona U (AZ)
Northern Kentucky U (KY)
Northern Michigan U (MI)
Northern State U (SD)
North Greenville U (SC)
Northwestern Coll (IA)
Northwestern Coll (MN)
Northwestern State U of Louisiana (LA)
Northwest Missouri State U (MO)
Northwest U (WA)
Notre Dame de Namur U (CA)
Nova Southeastern U (FL)
Oakland U (MI)
Oberlin Coll (OH)
Occidental Coll (CA)
Ohio Northern U (OH)
The Ohio State U (OH)
Ohio U (OH)
Ohio Wesleyan U (OH)
Oklahoma Baptist U (OK)
Oklahoma Christian U (OK)
Oklahoma City U (OK)
Oklahoma State U (OK)
Old Dominion U (VA)
Oral Roberts U (OK)
Ottawa U (KS)
Ouachita Baptist U (AR)
Our Lady of the Lake U of San Antonio (TX)
Pace U (NY)
Paine Coll (GA)
Park U (MO)
Pepperdine U, Malibu (CA)
Piedmont Coll (GA)
Pitzer Coll (CA)
Plymouth State U (NH)
Point Park U (PA)
Pomona Coll (CA)
Portland State U (OR)
Prairie View A&M U (TX)
Presbyterian Coll (SC)
Prescott Coll (AZ)
Principia Coll (IL)
Purchase Coll, State U of New York (NY)
Purdue U (IN)
Queens Coll of the City U of New York (NY)
Queen's U at Kingston (ON, Canada)
Queens U of Charlotte (NC)
Quinnipiac U (CT)
Radford U (VA)
Ramapo Coll of New Jersey (NJ)
Randolph Coll (VA)
Randolph-Macon Coll (VA)
Redeemer U Coll (ON, Canada)
Reed Coll (OR)
Rhode Island Coll (RI)
Rhodes Coll (TN)
Ripon Coll (WI)
Roanoke Coll (VA)
Rockford Coll (IL)
Rocky Mountain Coll (MT)
Rollins Coll (FL)
Roosevelt U (IL)
Rowan U (NJ)
Russell Sage Coll (NY)
Rutgers, The State U of New Jersey, Camden (NJ)
Rutgers, The State U of New Jersey, Newark (NJ)
Rutgers, The State U of New Jersey, New Brunswick (NJ)
Sacred Heart U (CT)
Saginaw Valley State U (MI)
St. Ambrose U (IA)
St. Catherine U (MN)
St. Cloud State U (MN)
St. Edward's U (TX)
Saint John's U (MN)
St. Lawrence U (NY)
Saint Louis U (MO)
Saint Martin's U (WA)
Saint Mary-of-the-Woods Coll (IN)
Saint Mary's Coll (IN)
Saint Mary's Coll of California (CA)
St. Mary's Coll of Maryland (MD)
Saint Mary's U of Minnesota (MN)
Saint Michael's Coll (VT)
St. Norbert Coll (WI)
St. Olaf Coll (MN)
Saint Vincent Coll (PA)
Salem State Coll (MA)
Salisbury U (MD)
Salve Regina U (RI)
Samford U (AL)
Sam Houston State U (TX)
San Diego State U (CA)
San Francisco State U (CA)
San Jose State U (CA)
Santa Clara U (CA)
Sarah Lawrence Coll (NY)
Savannah Coll of Art and Design (GA)
Schreiner U (TX)
Scripps Coll (CA)
Seattle Pacific U (WA)
Seattle U (WA)
Seton Hill U (PA)
Sewanee: The U of the South (TN)
Shawnee State U (OH)
Shaw U (NC)
Shenandoah U (VA)
Shorter U (GA)
Siena Heights U (MI)
Simon Fraser U (BC, Canada)
Simpson Coll (IA)
Skidmore Coll (NY)
Slippery Rock U of Pennsylvania (PA)
Smith Coll (MA)
Sonoma State U (CA)
South Carolina State U (SC)
Southeastern Oklahoma State U (OK)
Southeastern U (FL)
Southeast Missouri State U (MO)
Southern Arkansas U–Magnolia (AR)
Southern Connecticut State U (CT)
Southern Illinois U Carbondale (IL)
Southern Illinois U Edwardsville (IL)
Southern Methodist U (TX)
Southern Oregon U (OR)
Southern U and Ag and Mech Coll (LA)
Southern Utah U (UT)
Southwest Baptist U (MO)
Southwestern Assemblies of God U (TX)
Southwestern Coll (KS)
Southwestern U (TX)
Southwest Minnesota State U (MN)
Spelman Coll (GA)
Spring Arbor U (MI)
Spring Hill Coll (AL)
Stanford U (CA)
State U of New York at Binghamton (NY)
State U of New York at Fredonia (NY)

State U of New York at New Paltz (NY)
State U of New York at Oswego (NY)
State U of New York at Plattsburgh (NY)
State U of New York Coll at Geneseo (NY)
State U of New York Coll at Oneonta (NY)
State U of New York Coll at Potsdam (NY)
Stephen F. Austin State U (TX)
Stephens Coll (MO)
Sterling Coll (KS)
Stetson U (FL)
Stevenson U (MD)
Stony Brook U, State U of New York (NY)
Suffolk U (MA)
Sul Ross State U (TX)
Susquehanna U (PA)
Swarthmore Coll (PA)
Sweet Briar Coll (VA)
Syracuse U (NY)
Tarleton State U (TX)
Taylor U (IN)
Temple U (PA)
Tennessee Wesleyan Coll (TN)
Texas A&M U (TX)
Texas A&M U–Commerce (TX)
Texas A&M U–Corpus Christi (TX)
Texas A&M U–Kingsville (TX)
Texas Christian U (TX)
Texas Lutheran U (TX)
Texas Southern U (TX)
Texas State U–San Marcos (TX)
Texas Tech U (TX)
Texas Wesleyan U (TX)
Texas Woman's U (TX)
Thomas Edison State Coll (NJ)
Thomas More Coll (KY)
Thompson Rivers U (BC, Canada)
Towson U (MD)
Transylvania U (KY)
Trevecca Nazarene U (TN)
Trinity Coll (CT)
Trinity U (TX)
Truman State U (MO)
Tufts U (MA)
Tulane U (LA)
Union U (TN)
Universidad de las Américas–Puebla (Mexico)
U at Albany, State U of New York (NY)
U at Buffalo, the State U of New York (NY)
The U of Akron (OH)
The U of Alabama (AL)
The U of Alabama at Birmingham (AL)
U of Alaska Anchorage (AK)
U of Alberta (AB, Canada)
The U of Arizona (AZ)
U of Arkansas (AR)
U of Arkansas at Fort Smith (AR)
U of Arkansas at Little Rock (AR)
The U of British Columbia (BC, Canada)
The U of British Columbia–Okanagan (BC, Canada)
U of California, Berkeley (CA)
U of California, Irvine (CA)
U of California, Los Angeles (CA)
U of California, Riverside (CA)
U of California, San Diego (CA)
U of California, Santa Barbara (CA)
U of California, Santa Cruz (CA)
U of Central Florida (FL)
U of Central Missouri (MO)
U of Central Oklahoma (OK)
U of Cincinnati (OH)
U of Colorado at Boulder (CO)
U of Colorado Denver (CO)
U of Connecticut (CT)
U of Dallas (TX)
U of Dayton (OH)
U of Denver (CO)
U of Evansville (IN)
The U of Findlay (OH)
U of Florida (FL)
U of Georgia (GA)
U of Guelph (ON, Canada)
U of Hawaii at Manoa (HI)
U of Houston (TX)
U of Idaho (ID)
U of Illinois at Chicago (IL)
U of Illinois at Urbana–Champaign (IL)
U of Indianapolis (IN)
The U of Iowa (IA)
The U of Kansas (KS)
U of Kentucky (KY)
U of King's Coll (NS, Canada)
U of La Verne (CA)
U of Lethbridge (AB, Canada)
U of Louisville (KY)
U of Maine (ME)
U of Maine at Farmington (ME)
U of Maine at Machias (ME)
U of Manitoba (MB, Canada)
U of Mary Hardin-Baylor (TX)
U of Maryland, Baltimore County (MD)
U of Maryland, Coll Park (MD)
U of Massachusetts Amherst (MA)
U of Massachusetts Boston (MA)
U of Memphis (TN)
U of Miami (FL)
U of Michigan (MI)
U of Michigan–Flint (MI)
U of Minnesota, Twin Cities Campus (MN)
U of Mississippi (MS)
U of Missouri (MO)
U of Missouri–Kansas City (MO)
U of Missouri–St. Louis (MO)
U of Mobile (AL)
The U of Montana Western (MT)
U of Montevallo (AL)
U of Mount Union (OH)
U of Nebraska at Kearney (NE)
U of Nebraska at Omaha (NE)
U of Nebraska–Lincoln (NE)
U of Nevada, Las Vegas (NV)
U of Nevada, Reno (NV)
U of New Brunswick Fredericton (NB, Canada)
U of New Hampshire (NH)
U of New Mexico (NM)
The U of North Carolina at Asheville (NC)
The U of North Carolina at Chapel Hill (NC)
The U of North Carolina at Charlotte (NC)
The U of North Carolina at Greensboro (NC)
The U of North Carolina at Pembroke (NC)
U of North Carolina School of the Arts (NC)
The U of North Carolina Wilmington (NC)
U of North Dakota (ND)
U of Northern Colorado (CO)
U of Northern Iowa (IA)
U of North Texas (TX)
U of Notre Dame (IN)
U of Oklahoma (OK)
U of Oregon (OR)
U of Ottawa (ON, Canada)
U of Pennsylvania (PA)
U of Pittsburgh (PA)
U of Pittsburgh at Johnstown (PA)
U of Portland (OR)
U of Puerto Rico, Río Piedras (PR)
U of Puget Sound (WA)
U of Regina (SK, Canada)
U of Rhode Island (RI)
U of Richmond (VA)
U of Saint Mary (KS)
U of St. Thomas (MN)
U of St. Thomas (TX)
U of San Diego (CA)
U of Saskatchewan (SK, Canada)
U of Science and Arts of Oklahoma (OK)
The U of Scranton (PA)
U of South Alabama (AL)
U of South Carolina (SC)
The U of South Dakota (SD)
U of Southern California (CA)
U of Southern Indiana (IN)
U of Southern Maine (ME)
U of Southern Mississippi (MS)
U of South Florida (FL)
The U of Tampa (FL)
The U of Tennessee (TN)
The U of Tennessee at Chattanooga (TN)
The U of Tennessee at Martin (TN)
The U of Texas at Arlington (TX)
The U of Texas at El Paso (TX)
The U of Texas–Pan American (TX)
U of the Cumberlands (KY)
U of the District of Columbia (DC)
U of the Incarnate Word (TX)
U of the Ozarks (AR)
U of the Pacific (CA)
U of the Virgin Islands (VI)
The U of Toledo (OH)
U of Tulsa (OK)
U of Utah (UT)
U of Vermont (VT)
U of Virginia (VA)
The U of Virginia's Coll at Wise (VA)
U of Washington (WA)
U of Waterloo (ON, Canada)
U of West Florida (FL)
U of West Georgia (GA)
U of Windsor (ON, Canada)
U of Wisconsin–Eau Claire (WI)
U of Wisconsin–Green Bay (WI)
U of Wisconsin–La Crosse (WI)
U of Wisconsin–Madison (WI)
U of Wisconsin–Milwaukee (WI)
U of Wisconsin–Oshkosh (WI)
U of Wisconsin–Parkside (WI)
U of Wisconsin–River Falls (WI)
U of Wisconsin–Stevens Point (WI)
U of Wisconsin–Superior (WI)
U of Wisconsin–Whitewater (WI)
U of Wyoming (WY)
Utah State U (UT)
Utah Valley U (UT)
Valdosta State U (GA)
Valparaiso U (IN)
Vanderbilt U (TN)
Vanguard U of Southern California (CA)
Vassar Coll (NY)
Virginia Commonwealth U (VA)
Virginia Intermont Coll (VA)
Virginia Polytechnic Inst and State U (VA)
Virginia Wesleyan Coll (VA)
Viterbo U (WI)
Wabash Coll (IN)
Wagner Coll (NY)
Wake Forest U (NC)
Waldorf Coll (IA)
Wartburg Coll (IA)
Washburn U (KS)
Washington and Lee U (VA)
Washington Coll (MD)
Washington U in St. Louis (MO)
Wayland Baptist U (TX)
Wayne State Coll (NE)
Wayne State U (MI)
Weber State U (UT)
Webster U (MO)
Wellesley Coll (MA)
Wells Coll (NY)
Wesleyan U (CT)
West Chester U of Pennsylvania (PA)
Western Carolina U (NC)
Western Connecticut State U (CT)
Western Illinois U (IL)
Western Kentucky U (KY)
Western Oregon U (OR)
Western State Coll of Colorado (CO)
Western Washington U (WA)
Westfield State Coll (MA)
Westmont Coll (CA)
West Virginia U (WV)
West Virginia Wesleyan Coll (WV)
Wheaton Coll (MA)
Whitman Coll (WA)
Whittier Coll (CA)
Wichita State U (KS)
Wilkes U (PA)
Willamette U (OR)
William Jewell Coll (MO)
William Paterson U of New Jersey (NJ)
Williams Coll (MA)
Wilmington Coll (OH)
Winona State U (MN)
Winthrop U (SC)
Wittenberg U (OH)
Wofford Coll (SC)
Wright State U (OH)
Yale U (CT)
York Coll of Pennsylvania (PA)
York Coll of the City U of New York (NY)
York U (ON, Canada)

DRAMATIC/THEATER ARTS AND STAGECRAFT RELATED

Adams State Coll (CO)
Baldwin-Wallace Coll (OH)
Brigham Young U (UT)
California State U, Chico (CA)
Clarke Coll (IA)
Coastal Carolina U (SC)
Coll of Santa Fe (NM)
DePaul U (IL)
Drake U (IA)
Fayetteville State U (NC)
Indiana U South Bend (IN)
Lehigh U (PA)
Lindenwood U (MO)
Meredith Coll (NC)
Nebraska Wesleyan U (NE)
North Central Coll (IL)
North Greenville U (SC)
Oakland U (MI)
Pepperdine U, Malibu (CA)
Purdue U (IN)
St. Cloud State U (MN)
Seton Hill U (PA)
Shenandoah U (VA)
Southern Illinois U Carbondale (IL)
Southwest Minnesota State U (MN)
Thompson Rivers U (BC, Canada)
U at Buffalo, the State U of New York (NY)
U of Connecticut (CT)
U of Lethbridge (AB, Canada)
U of Miami (FL)
U of Michigan–Flint (MI)
U of Nevada, Las Vegas (NV)
U of Northern Colorado (CO)
U of Regina (SK, Canada)
Webster U (MO)

DRAWING

Adams State Coll (CO)
Alberta Coll of Art & Design (AB, Canada)
Aquinas Coll (MI)
Arcadia U (PA)
Bard Coll at Simon's Rock (MA)
Bennington Coll (VT)
Bethany Coll (KS)
Birmingham-Southern Coll (AL)
Boise State U (ID)
Boston U (MA)
Bowling Green State U (OH)
Bradley U (IL)
Brigham Young U (UT)
Buffalo State Coll, State U of New York (NY)
California Coll of the Arts (CA)
California State U, East Bay (CA)
California State U, Long Beach (CA)
Carson-Newman Coll (TN)
The Cleveland Inst of Art (OH)
The Coll at Brockport, State U of New York (NY)
Coll of the Atlantic (ME)
Coll of Visual Arts (MN)
Columbus State U (GA)
Drake U (IA)
Georgia State U (GA)
Governors State U (IL)
Grace Coll (IN)
Hampton U (VA)
Indiana U–Purdue U Fort Wayne (IN)
Inter American U of Puerto Rico, San Germán Campus (PR)
Lewis U (IL)
Lindenwood U (MO)
Longwood U (VA)
Lyme Acad Coll of Fine Arts (CT)
Marlboro Coll (VT)
Maryland Inst Coll of Art (MD)
Memorial U of Newfoundland (NL, Canada)
Minneapolis Coll of Art and Design (MN)
Minnesota State U Mankato (MN)
Mount Allison U (NB, Canada)
New England Coll (NH)
Northern Michigan U (MI)
North Georgia Coll & State U (GA)
Oakland U (MI)
Otis Coll of Art and Design (CA)
Portland State U (OR)
Pratt Inst (NY)
Providence Coll (RI)
Rivier Coll (NH)
Rutgers, The State U of New Jersey, New Brunswick (NJ)
St. Cloud State U (MN)
Sarah Lawrence Coll (NY)
Savannah Coll of Art and Design (GA)
School of the Art Inst of Chicago (IL)
School of the Museum of Fine Arts, Boston (MA)
School of Visual Arts (NY)
Seton Hill U (PA)
Sewanee: The U of the South (TN)
Shawnee State U (OH)
Sonoma State U (CA)
State U of New York at Fredonia (NY)
Trinity Christian Coll (IL)
U of Alberta (AB, Canada)
U of Hartford (CT)
The U of Iowa (IA)
U of Michigan (MI)
U of Missouri–St. Louis (MO)
U of Puerto Rico, Río Piedras (PR)
U of Regina (SK, Canada)
U of San Francisco (CA)
The U of Texas at El Paso (TX)
The U of Toledo (OH)
U of Windsor (ON, Canada)
Washington U in St. Louis (MO)
Western Washington U (WA)
West Virginia Wesleyan Coll (WV)
Winona State U (MN)
Wright State U (OH)

DRIVER AND SAFETY TEACHER EDUCATION

William Penn U (IA)

DUTCH/FLEMISH

U of California, Berkeley (CA)

EARLY CHILDHOOD EDUCATION

Adams State Coll (CO)
Albany State U (GA)
Alma Coll (MI)
Arcadia U (PA)
Arizona State U (AZ)
Arkansas State U—Jonesboro (AR)
Arkansas Tech U (AR)
Atlanta Christian Coll (GA)
Auburn U (AL)
Baldwin-Wallace Coll (OH)
Baylor U (TX)
Bennington Coll (VT)
Berry Coll (GA)
Bethel Coll (IN)
Bloomsburg U of Pennsylvania (PA)
Bob Jones U (SC)
Bradley U (IL)
Brewton-Parker Coll (GA)
Bridgewater State Coll (MA)
Brigham Young U (UT)
Brooklyn Coll of the City U of New York (NY)
Bucknell U (PA)
Butler U (IN)
California Baptist U (CA)
California State U, Chico (CA)
California State U, Dominguez Hills (CA)
California State U, Fullerton (CA)
California State U, Los Angeles (CA)
California State U, Stanislaus (CA)
Capital U (OH)
Carlow U (PA)
Carroll U (WI)
The Catholic U of America (DC)
Cazenovia Coll (NY)
Cedarville U (OH)
Central Michigan U (MI)
Chaminade U of Honolulu (HI)
Champlain Coll (VT)
Chatham U (PA)
Christian Brothers U (TN)
City Coll of the City U of New York (NY)
Claflin U (SC)
Clark Atlanta U (GA)
Clemson U (SC)
Cleveland State U (OH)
Coastal Carolina U (SC)
Coker Coll (SC)
The Coll at Brockport, State U of New York (NY)
Coll of Charleston (SC)
Coll of Mount St. Joseph (OH)
The Coll of New Jersey (NJ)
Coll of Saint Mary (NE)
Coll of the Ozarks (MO)
Colorado State U (CO)
Columbia Coll Chicago (IL)
Columbus State U (GA)
Concordia U (CA)
Concordia U, St. Paul (MN)
Coppin State U (MD)
Cornerstone U (MI)
Daemen Coll (NY)
Delaware State U (DE)
DePaul U (IL)
Dowling Coll (NY)
Duquesne U (PA)
East Central U (OK)
Eastern Connecticut State U (CT)
Eastern Mennonite U (VA)
Eastern Nazarene Coll (MA)
Eastern New Mexico U (NM)
Eastern Washington U (WA)
East Stroudsburg U of Pennsylvania (PA)
Elizabethtown Coll (PA)
Endicott Coll (MA)
Evangel U (MO)
Fayetteville State U (NC)
Fitchburg State Coll (MA)
Florida Ag and Mech U (FL)
Florida Atlantic U (FL)
Florida Gulf Coast U (FL)
Florida Intl U (FL)
Florida State U (FL)
Fort Lewis Coll (CO)
Francis Marion U (SC)
Free Will Baptist Bible Coll (TN)
Frostburg State U (MD)
Gainesville State Coll (GA)
Gannon U (PA)
Georgia Coll & State U (GA)
Georgia State U (GA)
Governors State U (IL)
Grace Bible Coll (MI)
Granite State Coll (NH)
Greensboro Coll (NC)
Greenville Coll (IL)
Hannibal-LaGrange Coll (MO)
Harding U (AR)
Hardin-Simmons U (TX)
Harris-Stowe State U (MO)
Henderson State U (AR)

Hillsdale Coll (MI)
Hofstra U (NY)
Holy Family U (PA)
Hood Coll (MD)
Houston Baptist U (TX)
Idaho State U (ID)
Illinois Coll (IL)
Illinois State U (IL)
Indiana U Bloomington (IN)
Indiana U Kokomo (IN)
Indiana U of Pennsylvania (PA)
Indiana U–Purdue U Indianapolis (IN)
Indiana U South Bend (IN)
Inter American U of Puerto Rico, Aguadilla Campus (PR)
Inter American U of Puerto Rico, San Germán Campus (PR)
Iona Coll (NY)
John Brown U (AR)
Juniata Coll (PA)
Keene State Coll (NH)
Kendall Coll (IL)
Kent State U at Tuscarawas (OH)
Keystone Coll (PA)
King's Coll (PA)
LaGrange Coll (GA)
Lake Superior State U (MI)
Lebanon Valley Coll (PA)
Lincoln U (MO)
Louisiana State U and Ag and Mech Coll (LA)
Louisiana Tech U (LA)
Lourdes Coll (OH)
Loyola U Chicago (IL)
Lubbock Christian U (TX)
Lyon Coll (AR)
Madonna U (MI)
Malone U (OH)
Maranatha Baptist Bible Coll (WI)
Marian U (WI)
Marywood U (PA)
Mayville State U (ND)
McMurry U (TX)
McNeese State U (LA)
Messiah Coll (PA)
Miami U (OH)
Miami U Hamilton (OH)
Michigan State U (MI)
Midwestern State U (TX)
Millersville U of Pennsylvania (PA)
Milligan Coll (TN)
Millikin U (IL)
Missouri State U (MO)
Missouri Western State U (MO)
Mitchell Coll (CT)
Morris Coll (SC)
Mount Aloysius Coll (PA)
Mount Ida Coll (MA)
Mount Saint Mary Coll (NY)
Mount Vernon Nazarene U (OH)
Murray State U (KY)
Naropa U (CO)
New Mexico State U (NM)
New York U (NY)
Nicholls State U (LA)
Northeastern Illinois U (IL)
Northeastern State U (OK)
Northern Arizona U (AZ)
North Greenville U (SC)
Northwestern Coll (MN)
Northwestern Oklahoma State U (OK)
Northwestern State U of Louisiana (LA)
Ohio Dominican U (OH)
Ohio Northern U (OH)
The Ohio State U at Lima (OH)
The Ohio State U at Marion (OH)
The Ohio State U–Mansfield Campus (OH)
The Ohio State U–Newark Campus (OH)
Ohio U (OH)
Ohio Wesleyan U (OH)
Oklahoma Baptist U (OK)
Oklahoma Christian U (OK)
Oral Roberts U (OK)
Ouachita Baptist U (AR)
Pace U (NY)
Park U (MO)
Pittsburg State U (KS)
Plymouth State U (NH)
Point Park U (PA)
Presbyterian Coll (SC)
Prescott Coll (AZ)
Purdue U (IN)
Purdue U North Central (IN)
Reinhardt Coll (GA)
Rhode Island Coll (RI)
Ripon Coll (WI)
Roberts Wesleyan Coll (NY)
Rochester Coll (MI)
Roosevelt U (IL)
St. Ambrose U (IA)
Salem State Coll (MA)
Salisbury U (MD)
Salve Regina U (RI)
San Diego State U (CA)
San Francisco State U (CA)
San Jose State U (CA)
Sarah Lawrence Coll (NY)
Schreiner U (TX)
Shawnee State U (OH)
Shippensburg U of Pennsylvania (PA)
Silver Lake Coll (WI)
Simmons Coll (MA)
South Carolina State U (SC)
South Dakota State U (SD)
Southeastern Louisiana U (LA)
Southeast Missouri State U (MO)
Southern Arkansas U–Magnolia (AR)
Southern Connecticut State U (CT)
Southern Illinois U Carbondale (IL)
Southern Illinois U Edwardsville (IL)
Southern New Hampshire U (NH)
Southern U and Ag and Mech Coll (LA)
Southern U at New Orleans (LA)
Southern Wesleyan U (SC)
Southwest Baptist U (MO)
Southwestern Coll (KS)
Southwest Florida Coll, Fort Myers (FL)
Spring Hill Coll (AL)
State U of New York Coll at Geneseo (NY)
State U of New York Coll at Old Westbury (NY)
Stephens Coll (MO)
Stonehill Coll (MA)
Tennessee Wesleyan Coll (TN)
Texas A&M U–Commerce (TX)
Texas Christian U (TX)
Towson U (MD)
Troy U (AL)
Truett-McConnell Coll (GA)
Tusculum Coll (TN)
The U of Alabama (AL)
The U of Alabama at Birmingham (AL)
U of Arkansas (AR)
U of Arkansas at Fort Smith (AR)
U of Central Florida (FL)
U of Cincinnati (OH)
U of Hartford (CT)
U of Hawaii–West Oahu (HI)
U of Illinois at Urbana–Champaign (IL)
The U of Kansas (KS)
U of Maine at Farmington (ME)
U of Mary (ND)
U of Michigan–Dearborn (MI)
U of Michigan–Flint (MI)
U of Minnesota, Crookston (MN)
U of Missouri (MO)
U of Missouri–Kansas City (MO)
U of Missouri–St. Louis (MO)
U of Mobile (AL)
U of Mount Union (OH)
U of New Mexico (NM)
U of New Orleans (LA)
The U of North Carolina at Chapel Hill (NC)
The U of North Carolina at Greensboro (NC)
U of North Dakota (ND)
U of North Florida (FL)
U of Oklahoma (OK)
U of Regina (SK, Canada)
U of Science and Arts of Oklahoma (OK)
The U of Scranton (PA)
U of South Alabama (AL)
U of South Carolina Aiken (SC)
U of South Carolina Beaufort (SC)
U of Southern Indiana (IN)
U of South Florida (FL)
The U of Tennessee at Chattanooga (TN)
U of Tulsa (OK)
U of Vermont (VT)
The U of West Alabama (AL)
U of West Florida (FL)
U of Wisconsin–Stout (WI)
U of Wisconsin–Whitewater (WI)
Ursuline Coll (OH)
Utah Valley U (UT)
Valdosta State U (GA)
Valley Forge Christian Coll (PA)
Vanderbilt U (TN)
Waldorf Coll (IA)
Walsh U (OH)
Warner Pacific Coll (OR)
Washington State U (WA)
Wayne State Coll (NE)
Wesleyan Coll (GA)
West Chester U of Pennsylvania (PA)
Western Michigan U (MI)
Western Washington U (WA)
Westminster Coll (UT)
Wheelock Coll (MA)
Widener U (PA)
Wilmington U (DE)
Worcester State Coll (MA)
Xavier U of Louisiana (LA)
Youngstown State U (OH)

EAST ASIAN LANGUAGES

Arizona State U (AZ)
Columbia U (NY)
Eckerd Coll (FL)
Grinnell Coll (IA)
Indiana U Bloomington (IN)
Michigan State U (MI)
Northeastern U (MA)
Smith Coll (MA)
U of Illinois at Urbana–Champaign (IL)
The U of Kansas (KS)
U of Pennsylvania (PA)
U of Puget Sound (WA)
U of Southern California (CA)
The U of Western Ontario (ON, Canada)

EAST ASIAN LANGUAGES RELATED

Claremont McKenna Coll (CA)
Columbia U, School of General Studies (NY)
Dartmouth Coll (NH)
Indiana U Bloomington (IN)
Michigan State U (MI)
U of Florida (FL)
U of Southern California (CA)
Washington U in St. Louis (MO)

ECOLOGY

Appalachian State U (NC)
Averett U (VA)
Bard Coll at Simon's Rock (MA)
Barry U (FL)
Bemidji State U (MN)
Bennington Coll (VT)
Boston U (MA)
California State U, Chico (CA)
California State U, Dominguez Hills (CA)
California State U, East Bay (CA)
California State U, Fresno (CA)
California State U, Long Beach (CA)
California State U, San Marcos (CA)
Clark U (MA)
The Coll of Saint Rose (NY)
Columbia U, School of General Studies (NY)
Concordia U (QC, Canada)
Cornell U (NY)
Dartmouth Coll (NH)
Defiance Coll (OH)
East Central U (OK)
Florida Inst of Technology (FL)
Fort Lewis Coll (CO)
Franklin Pierce U (NH)
Georgetown Coll (KY)
Idaho State U (ID)
Iowa State U of Science and Technology (IA)
Jacksonville State U (AL)
Juniata Coll (PA)
Kent State U (OH)
Lawrence U (WI)
Lehigh U (PA)
Le Moyne Coll (NY)
Manchester Coll (IN)
Marlboro Coll (VT)
Mars Hill Coll (NC)
Medgar Evers Coll of the City U of New York (NY)
Memorial U of Newfoundland (NL, Canada)
Michigan Technological U (MI)
Minnesota State U Mankato (MN)
Morehead State U (KY)
New Mexico State U (NM)
New York U (NY)
North Carolina State U (NC)
Northern Arizona U (AZ)
Northern Michigan U (MI)
Oberlin Coll (OH)
Pitzer Coll (CA)
Pomona Coll (CA)
Prescott Coll (AZ)
Princeton U (NJ)
Rice U (TX)
Rocky Mountain Coll (MT)
Rutgers, The State U of New Jersey, New Brunswick (NJ)
St. Cloud State U (MN)
San Francisco State U (CA)
Sarah Lawrence Coll (NY)
Sonoma State U (CA)
State U of New York at Plattsburgh (NY)
State U of New York Coll of Environmental Science and Forestry (NY)
Sterling Coll (VT)
Susquehanna U (PA)
Thompson Rivers U (BC, Canada)
Towson U (MD)
Tufts U (MA)
Tulane U (LA)
U at Buffalo, the State U of New York (NY)
The U of Akron (OH)
U of California, Irvine (CA)
U of California, Los Angeles (CA)
U of California, San Diego (CA)
U of California, Santa Cruz (CA)
U of Colorado at Colorado Springs (CO)
U of Connecticut (CT)
U of Delaware (DE)
U of Denver (CO)
U of Georgia (GA)
U of Guelph (ON, Canada)
U of Illinois at Urbana–Champaign (IL)
U of Maine (ME)
U of Maine at Machias (ME)
U of Manitoba (MB, Canada)
U of Maryland, Coll Park (MD)
U of Maryland Eastern Shore (MD)
U of Michigan (MI)
U of Michigan–Flint (MI)
U of Minnesota, Twin Cities Campus (MN)
U of New Brunswick Fredericton (NB, Canada)
U of New Haven (CT)
U of Northern Iowa (IA)
U of Pittsburgh (PA)
U of Pittsburgh at Johnstown (PA)
U of Rio Grande (OH)
The U of Tennessee (TN)
U of Waterloo (ON, Canada)
The U of Western Ontario (ON, Canada)
U of Wisconsin–Milwaukee (WI)
Utah State U (UT)
Washington Coll (MD)
Washington U in St. Louis (MO)
William Paterson U of New Jersey (NJ)
Winona State U (MN)
Yale U (CT)
York U (ON, Canada)

ECOLOGY, EVOLUTION, SYSTEMATICS AND POPULATION BIOLOGY RELATED

Angelo State U (TX)
Hofstra U (NY)
The Ohio State U (OH)
Prescott Coll (AZ)
The U of British Columbia–Okanagan (BC, Canada)
U of California, Davis (CA)
U of California, Irvine (CA)
U of California, Santa Barbara (CA)
U of Colorado at Boulder (CO)
Vanderbilt U (TN)

E-COMMERCE

Bloomfield Coll (NJ)
Champlain Coll (VT)
Delaware State U (DE)
DePaul U (IL)
Florida Inst of Technology (FL)
Friends U (KS)
Full Sail U (FL)
Harrisburg U of Science and Technology (PA)
King Coll (TN)
Maryville U of Saint Louis (MO)
National U (CA)
Northwestern Oklahoma State U (OK)
Philadelphia U (PA)
Southern U and Ag and Mech Coll (LA)
Texas Christian U (TX)
Thiel Coll (PA)
Trevecca Nazarene U (TN)
U of La Verne (CA)
U of North Texas (TX)
U of Ottawa (ON, Canada)
U of Pennsylvania (PA)
U of South Alabama (AL)
U of Toronto (ON, Canada)
Western Michigan U (MI)
Winthrop U (SC)

ECONOMETRICS AND QUANTITATIVE ECONOMICS

Baldwin-Wallace Coll (OH)
Bowdoin Coll (ME)
Bucknell U (PA)
The Colorado Coll (CO)
Hampden-Sydney Coll (VA)
Haverford Coll (PA)
Hofstra U (NY)
Miami U Hamilton (OH)
Southern Methodist U (TX)
State U of New York at Oswego (NY)
United States Naval Acad (MD)
U of California, Irvine (CA)
U of California, Santa Barbara (CA)
U of Guelph (ON, Canada)
U of Rhode Island (RI)
U of St. Thomas (MN)
Wake Forest U (NC)

ECONOMICS

Acadia U (NS, Canada)
Adams State Coll (CO)
Adelphi U (NY)
Agnes Scott Coll (GA)
Alabama Ag and Mech U (AL)
Alabama State U (AL)
Albion Coll (MI)
Albright Coll (PA)
Alcorn State U (MS)
Alfred U (NY)
Allegheny Coll (PA)
Alma Coll (MI)
American Intl Coll (MA)
American U (DC)
American U of Beirut (Lebanon)
The American U of Paris (France)
Amherst Coll (MA)
Andrews U (MI)
Appalachian State U (NC)
Aquinas Coll (MI)
Arizona State U (AZ)
Arkansas State U—Jonesboro (AR)
Arkansas Tech U (AR)
Armstrong Atlantic State U (GA)
Ashland U (OH)
Assumption Coll (MA)
Auburn U (AL)
Augsburg Coll (MN)
Augustana Coll (IL)
Augustana Coll (SD)
Austin Coll (TX)
Babson Coll (MA)
Baker U (KS)
Baldwin-Wallace Coll (OH)
Ball State U (IN)
Bard Coll (NY)
Barnard Coll (NY)
Barry U (FL)
Barton Coll (NC)
Bates Coll (ME)
Baylor U (TX)
Bellarmine U (KY)
Belmont Abbey Coll (NC)
Belmont U (TN)
Beloit Coll (WI)
Bemidji State U (MN)
Benedictine Coll (KS)
Benedictine U (IL)
Berea Coll (KY)
Bernard M. Baruch Coll of the City U of New York (NY)
Berry Coll (GA)
Bethany Coll (WV)
Bethel U (MN)
Birmingham-Southern Coll (AL)
Bishop's U (QC, Canada)
Bloomsburg U of Pennsylvania (PA)
Bluffton U (OH)
Boise State U (ID)
Boston Coll (MA)
Boston U (MA)
Bowdoin Coll (ME)
Bowie State U (MD)
Bowling Green State U (OH)
Bradley U (IL)
Brandeis U (MA)
Bridgewater Coll (VA)
Bridgewater State Coll (MA)
Brock U (ON, Canada)
Brooklyn Coll of the City U of New York (NY)
Bryant U (RI)
Bryn Mawr Coll (PA)
Bucknell U (PA)
Buffalo State Coll, State U of New York (NY)
Butler U (IN)
California Inst of Technology (CA)
California Lutheran U (CA)
California Polytechnic State U, San Luis Obispo (CA)
California State Polytechnic U, Pomona (CA)
California State U, Bakersfield (CA)
California State U, Chico (CA)
California State U, East Bay (CA)
California State U, Fresno (CA)
California State U, Fullerton (CA)
California State U, Long Beach (CA)
California State U, Los Angeles (CA)
California State U, Northridge (CA)
California State U, Sacramento (CA)

INDEXES

ECONOMICS RELATED

EDUCATION

Freed-Hardeman U (TN)
Free Will Baptist Bible Coll (TN)
Furman U (SC)
Gallaudet U (DC)
Gardner-Webb U (NC)
Georgia Southern U (GA)
Gettysburg Coll (PA)
Glenville State Coll (WV)
Goddard Coll (VT)
Graceland U (IA)
Greensboro Coll (NC)
Gustavus Adolphus Coll (MN)
Hamline U (MN)
Hampshire Coll (MA)
Hampton U (VA)
Hannibal-LaGrange Coll (MO)
Hardin-Simmons U (TX)
Haverford Coll (PA)
Hebrew Coll (MA)
Heidelberg U (OH)
High Point U (NC)
Hillsdale Coll (MI)
Hiram Coll (OH)
Holy Family U (PA)
Houston Baptist U (TX)
Humboldt State U (CA)
Huntington U (IN)
Huston-Tillotson U (TX)
Illinois Coll (IL)
Illinois Wesleyan U (IL)
Indiana U–Purdue U Fort Wayne (IN)
Indiana U–Purdue U Indianapolis (IN)
Indiana U South Bend (IN)
Indiana Wesleyan U (IN)
Inter American U of Puerto Rico, San Germán Campus (PR)
Iona Coll (NY)
Iowa State U of Science and Technology (IA)
Iowa Wesleyan Coll (IA)
Jacksonville State U (AL)
John Brown U (AR)
John Carroll U (OH)
Johnson State Coll (VT)
Juniata Coll (PA)
Kendall Coll (IL)
Kent State U (OH)
King Coll (TN)
Knox Coll (IL)
Lake Forest Coll (IL)
Lakehead U (ON, Canada)
Lake Superior State U (MI)
Lamar U (TX)
La Salle U (PA)
Lasell Coll (MA)
Laurentian U (ON, Canada)
Lees-McRae Coll (NC)
Lee U (TN)
Lehigh U (PA)
Lesley U (MA)
Limestone Coll (SC)
Lincoln Memorial U (TN)
Lincoln U (PA)
Lindenwood U (MO)
Lindsey Wilson Coll (KY)
Lipscomb U (TN)
Long Island U, Brooklyn Campus (NY)
Long Island U, C.W. Post Campus (NY)
Longwood U (VA)
Loras Coll (IA)
Loyola U Maryland (MD)
Macalester Coll (MN)
Manchester Coll (IN)
Manhattan Coll (NY)
Manhattanville Coll (NY)
Mansfield U of Pennsylvania (PA)
Maranatha Baptist Bible Coll (WI)
Marian U (IN)
Marietta Coll (OH)
Marquette U (WI)
Mars Hill Coll (NC)
Maryville Coll (TN)
Massachusetts Coll of Liberal Arts (MA)
The Master's Coll and Sem (CA)
Mayville State U (ND)
Memorial U of Newfoundland (NL, Canada)
Mercyhurst Coll (PA)
Methodist U (NC)
Michigan State U (MI)
Midway Coll (KY)
Milligan Coll (TN)
Millsaps Coll (MS)
Minnesota State U Mankato (MN)
Mississippi Valley State U (MS)
Missouri Southern State U (MO)
Molloy Coll (NY)
Monmouth U (NJ)
Montana State U Billings (MT)
Moravian Coll (PA)
Morehouse Coll (GA)
Morningside Coll (IA)
Mount Marty Coll (SD)
Mount Mary Coll (WI)
Mount St. Mary's Coll (CA)
Mount Vernon Nazarene U (OH)
Nazareth Coll of Rochester (NY)
Nevada State Coll at Henderson (NV)
Newberry Coll (SC)
New England Coll (NH)
Newman U (KS)
New York Inst of Technology (NY)
Niagara U (NY)
Nipissing U (ON, Canada)
North Carolina State U (NC)
North Central Coll (IL)
Northeastern State U (OK)
Northern State U (SD)
North Georgia Coll & State U (GA)
Northwest U (WA)
Notre Dame de Namur U (CA)
Oakland City U (IN)
Ohio Northern U (OH)
Ohio Wesleyan U (OH)
Oklahoma Baptist U (OK)
Oklahoma City U (OK)
Oklahoma State U (OK)
Oklahoma Wesleyan U (OK)
Oral Roberts U (OK)
Oregon State U (OR)
Ouachita Baptist U (AR)
Pacific Lutheran U (WA)
Pacific Union Coll (CA)
Peace Coll (NC)
Pepperdine U, Malibu (CA)
Peru State Coll (NE)
Point Park U (PA)
Pontifical Catholic U of Puerto Rico (PR)
Presbyterian Coll (SC)
Prescott Coll (AZ)
Purdue U (IN)
Purdue U Calumet (IN)
Queen's U at Kingston (ON, Canada)
Queens U of Charlotte (NC)
Quinnipiac U (CT)
Redeemer U Coll (ON, Canada)
Regent U (VA)
Reinhardt Coll (GA)
Ripon Coll (WI)
Rivier Coll (NH)
Rockford Coll (IL)
Rockhurst U (MO)
Rollins Coll (FL)
Sacred Heart U (CT)
St. Ambrose U (IA)
St. Catherine U (MN)
St. Cloud State U (MN)
Saint Francis U (PA)
St. Francis Xavier U (NS, Canada)
St. Joseph's Coll, Long Island Campus (NY)
St. Joseph's Coll, New York (NY)
Saint Martin's U (WA)
Saint Mary-of-the-Woods Coll (IN)
Saint Mary's Coll (IN)
St. Mary's U (TX)
Saint Michael's Coll (VT)
St. Thomas Aquinas Coll (NY)
St. Thomas U (NB, Canada)
Salem Coll (NC)
Salem State Coll (MA)
San Diego Christian Coll (CA)
Sarah Lawrence Coll (NY)
Schreiner U (TX)
Shasta Bible Coll (CA)
Shawnee State U (OH)
Simon Fraser U (BC, Canada)
Smith Coll (MA)
Southeastern Oklahoma State U (OK)
Southeast Missouri State U (MO)
Southern New Hampshire U (NH)
Southern Utah U (UT)
Southern Wesleyan U (SC)
Southwestern Assemblies of God U (TX)
Southwestern Oklahoma State U (OK)
Southwestern U (TX)
Southwest Minnesota State U (MN)
Spalding U (KY)
State U of New York at Fredonia (NY)
State U of New York at New Paltz (NY)
State U of New York at Oswego (NY)
State U of New York at Plattsburgh (NY)
State U of New York Coll at Geneseo (NY)
State U of New York Coll at Oneonta (NY)
State U of New York Empire State Coll (NY)
Stetson U (FL)
Suffolk U (MA)
Tabor Coll (KS)
Talladega Coll (AL)
Tarleton State U (TX)
Tennessee Technological U (TN)
Tennessee Wesleyan Coll (TN)
Texas A&M U–Commerce (TX)
Texas Lutheran U (TX)
Texas Wesleyan U (TX)
Trent U (ON, Canada)
Trine U (IN)
Trinity Christian Coll (IL)
Trinity Coll (CT)
Union Coll (KY)
Union Coll (NE)
Union Inst & U (OH)
Union U (TN)
Universidad de las Américas–Puebla (Mexico)
Université du Québec en Outaouais (QC, Canada)
U of Alaska Anchorage (AK)
U of Alaska Fairbanks (AK)
U of Alaska Southeast (AK)
U of Alberta (AB, Canada)
U of Arkansas at Little Rock (AR)
U of Arkansas at Monticello (AR)
The U of British Columbia (BC, Canada)
The U of British Columbia–Okanagan (BC, Canada)
U of California, Santa Cruz (CA)
U of Central Missouri (MO)
U of Charleston (WV)
U of Cincinnati (OH)
U of Dallas (TX)
U of Dayton (OH)
U of Delaware (DE)
U of Evansville (IN)
The U of Findlay (OH)
U of Guam (GU)
U of Hawaii at Manoa (HI)
U of Houston–Victoria (TX)
U of Indianapolis (IN)
U of Lethbridge (AB, Canada)
U of Maine (ME)
U of Maine at Fort Kent (ME)
U of Maine at Machias (ME)
U of Maine at Presque Isle (ME)
U of Manitoba (MB, Canada)
U of Mary Hardin-Baylor (TX)
U of Maryland Eastern Shore (MD)
U of Mary Washington (VA)
U of Michigan–Dearborn (MI)
U of Minnesota, Duluth (MN)
U of Minnesota, Twin Cities Campus (MN)
U of Missouri (MO)
U of Missouri–St. Louis (MO)
The U of Montana Western (MT)
U of Nevada, Las Vegas (NV)
U of New Brunswick Fredericton (NB, Canada)
The U of North Carolina at Greensboro (NC)
U of Oregon (OR)
U of Pittsburgh at Greensburg (PA)
U of Pittsburgh at Johnstown (PA)
U of Portland (OR)
U of Redlands (CA)
U of Regina (SK, Canada)
U of Rio Grande (OH)
U of Saint Mary (KS)
U of St. Thomas (TX)
U of San Francisco (CA)
U of Saskatchewan (SK, Canada)
The U of South Dakota (SD)
U of the Pacific (CA)
U of the Southwest (NM)
The U of Toledo (OH)
U of Toronto (ON, Canada)
U of Tulsa (OK)
U of Utah (UT)
U of Vermont (VT)
U of Washington (WA)
U of Washington, Bothell (WA)
The U of Western Ontario (ON, Canada)
U of Windsor (ON, Canada)
U of Wisconsin–Green Bay (WI)
U of Wisconsin–Milwaukee (WI)
U of Wisconsin–Oshkosh (WI)
U of Wisconsin–Platteville (WI)
U of Wisconsin–River Falls (WI)
U of Wisconsin–Stevens Point (WI)
U of Wisconsin–Superior (WI)
U of Wisconsin–Whitewater (WI)
Upper Iowa U (IA)
Valley City State U (ND)
Vanderbilt U (TN)
Vanguard U of Southern California (CA)
Villanova U (PA)
Virginia Intermont Coll (VA)
Viterbo U (WI)
Wagner Coll (NY)
Waldorf Coll (IA)
Walsh U (OH)
Washburn U (KS)
Washington & Jefferson Coll (PA)
Washington State U (WA)
Washington U in St. Louis (MO)
Webster U (MO)
Wells Coll (NY)
Westfield State Coll (MA)
West Liberty U (WV)
Westminster Coll (UT)
Westmont Coll (CA)
West Virginia State U (WV)
West Virginia Wesleyan Coll (WV)
Wheeling Jesuit U (WV)
Wilfrid Laurier U (ON, Canada)
Wilkes U (PA)
William Jessup U (CA)
William Paterson U of New Jersey (NJ)
William Penn U (IA)
Wilmington Coll (OH)
Winona State U (MN)
Winston-Salem State U (NC)
Wittenberg U (OH)
Wright State U (OH)
Xavier U (OH)
Xavier U of Louisiana (LA)
York Coll (NE)
York U (ON, Canada)
Youngstown State U (OH)

EDUCATIONAL ADMINISTRATION AND SUPERVISION RELATED

Cazenovia Coll (NY)
Kendall Coll (IL)

EDUCATIONAL ASSESSMENT, EVALUATION, AND RESEARCH RELATED

Penn State Altoona (PA)
Penn State Berks (PA)
Penn State U Park (PA)

EDUCATIONAL, INSTRUCTIONAL, AND CURRICULUM SUPERVISION

Kutztown U of Pennsylvania (PA)
Prescott Coll (AZ)
Texas A&M U–Commerce (TX)
U of Wisconsin–River Falls (WI)
Wright State U (OH)

EDUCATIONAL/ INSTRUCTIONAL MEDIA DESIGN

Bowling Green State U (OH)
California State U, Chico (CA)
Ithaca Coll (NY)
Jackson State U (MS)
Jacksonville State U (AL)
Kutztown U of Pennsylvania (PA)
Midwestern State U (TX)
St. Cloud State U (MN)
Southern Arkansas U–Magnolia (AR)
U of Central Oklahoma (OK)
U of Maine (ME)
The U of Toledo (OH)
Western Illinois U (IL)
Western Oregon U (OR)
Widener U (PA)

EDUCATIONAL LEADERSHIP AND ADMINISTRATION

Cleveland State U (OH)
Edinboro U of Pennsylvania (PA)
Free Will Baptist Bible Coll (TN)
Kendall Coll (IL)
Lamar U (TX)
Midwestern State U (TX)
North Georgia Coll & State U (GA)
Oral Roberts U (OK)
Prescott Coll (AZ)
Rocky Mountain Coll (MT)
St. Cloud State U (MN)
Southern Arkansas U–Magnolia (AR)
Tarleton State U (TX)
Texas A&M U–Commerce (TX)
The U of British Columbia (BC, Canada)
U of Central Oklahoma (OK)
U of Regina (SK, Canada)
U of San Francisco (CA)
U of the Incarnate Word (TX)
U of Wisconsin–Superior (WI)
Wright State U (OH)

EDUCATIONAL PSYCHOLOGY

Alcorn State U (MS)
Cornell U (NY)
DePaul U (IL)
Edinboro U of Pennsylvania (PA)
Jacksonville State U (AL)
Mississippi State U (MS)
Prescott Coll (AZ)
Saint Vincent Coll (PA)
Shenandoah U (VA)
Texas A&M U–Commerce (TX)
U of Georgia (GA)
U of Pittsburgh (PA)
U of Regina (SK, Canada)

EDUCATIONAL STATISTICS AND RESEARCH METHODS

Bucknell U (PA)

EDUCATIONAL SYSTEM ADMINISTRATION AND SUPERINTENDENCY

Dordt Coll (IA)

EDUCATION (MULTIPLE LEVELS)

Adams State Coll (CO)
Augustana Coll (SD)
Averett U (VA)
Baptist Bible Coll of Pennsylvania (PA)
Birmingham-Southern Coll (AL)
Bowling Green State U (OH)
Canisius Coll (NY)
Central State U (OH)
Coll of Coastal Georgia (GA)
Coll of Saint Elizabeth (NJ)
Coll of Saint Mary (NE)
The Coll of St. Scholastica (MN)
Columbia Intl U (SC)
Columbia U (NY)
Concordia U Wisconsin (WI)
Connecticut Coll (CT)
Crandall U (NB, Canada)
Dakota Wesleyan U (SD)
Dickinson State U (ND)
Dominican U (IL)
Dordt Coll (IA)
Dowling Coll (NY)
Eastern Nazarene Coll (MA)
Edinboro U of Pennsylvania (PA)
Felician Coll (NJ)
Gannon U (PA)
Gardner-Webb U (NC)
Goddard Coll (VT)
Hamline U (MN)
Harding U (AR)
Hillsdale Coll (MI)
Hofstra U (NY)
Illinois Coll (IL)
Indiana U Bloomington (IN)
Indiana Wesleyan U (IN)
Iona Coll (NY)
Ithaca Coll (NY)
John Carroll U (OH)
Juniata Coll (PA)
Keystone Coll (PA)
Lake Erie Coll (OH)
Lake Superior State U (MI)
Liberty U (VA)
Lindenwood U (MO)
Lubbock Christian U (TX)
Manhattan Coll (NY)
Martin Luther Coll (MN)
Maryville U of Saint Louis (MO)
McKendree U (IL)
Methodist U (NC)
Miami U Hamilton (OH)
Mount Saint Mary Coll (NY)
New England Coll (NH)
Northland Coll (WI)
Northwest Christian U (OR)
Northwestern Coll (IA)
Ohio Dominican U (OH)
Ohio Northern U (OH)
Ohio Wesleyan U (OH)
Pacific Union Coll (CA)
Queen's U at Kingston (ON, Canada)
Quincy U (IL)
Redeemer U Coll (ON, Canada)
Rhode Island Coll (RI)
The Richard Stockton Coll of New Jersey (NJ)
St. Ambrose U (IA)
Saint Augustine's Coll (NC)
St. Cloud State U (MN)
Saint Louis U (MO)
Saint Mary-of-the-Woods Coll (IN)
Samford U (AL)
San Diego Christian Coll (CA)
Shawnee State U (OH)
Tabor Coll (KS)
Tarleton State U (TX)
Tennessee Wesleyan Coll (TN)
Texas Lutheran U (TX)
Troy U (AL)
U of Illinois at Urbana–Champaign (IL)
U of Louisville (KY)
U of Maine (ME)

U of Maine at Fort Kent (ME)
U of Memphis (TN)
The U of Montana Western (MT)
U of Nebraska–Lincoln (NE)
U of North Alabama (AL)
U of Puerto Rico at Bayamón (PR)
U of Rio Grande (OH)
U of St. Thomas (MN)
U of South Florida (FL)
The U of Tennessee at Martin (TN)
U of Washington (WA)
U of Windsor (ON, Canada)
Utah State U (UT)
Virginia Wesleyan Coll (VA)
Wake Forest U (NC)
Waldorf Coll (IA)
Washington State U (WA)
Washington U in St. Louis (MO)
Wayland Baptist U (TX)
West Virginia Wesleyan Coll (WV)
William Jewell Coll (MO)
Wright State U (OH)
York Coll (NE)
York U (ON, Canada)

EDUCATION RELATED

Albany State U (GA)
Alliant Intl U (CA)
Arizona State U (AZ)
Bowling Green State U (OH)
Brigham Young U (UT)
Cedarville U (OH)
Central State U (OH)
Cleveland State U (OH)
Concordia U, St. Paul (MN)
DePaul U (IL)
Edgewood Coll (WI)
The Evergreen State Coll (WA)
Ferris State U (MI)
Gannon U (PA)
Grace Coll (IN)
Grambling State U (LA)
Indiana U Bloomington (IN)
Jackson State U (MS)
Kendall Coll (IL)
Lindsey Wilson Coll (KY)
Madonna U (MI)
Mercer U (GA)
Midwestern State U (TX)
Mitchell Coll (CT)
Mount Holyoke Coll (MA)
Northland Coll (WI)
Northwest Missouri State U (MO)
Northwest Nazarene U (ID)
Ohio Northern U (OH)
Park U (MO)
Point Park U (PA)
Prescott Coll (AZ)
Saginaw Valley State U (MI)
St. Petersburg Coll (FL)
Southern Adventist U (TN)
State U of New York Coll at Potsdam (NY)
Sterling Coll (VT)
Swarthmore Coll (PA)
Syracuse U (NY)
Towson U (MD)
U of Lethbridge (AB, Canada)
U of Puerto Rico at Utuado (PR)
U of Waterloo (ON, Canada)
Vanderbilt U (TN)
Wayland Baptist U (TX)
Wayne State U (MI)
Wright State U (OH)

EDUCATION (SPECIFIC LEVELS AND METHODS) RELATED

Boston U (MA)
Brigham Young U (UT)
Colorado State U (CO)
Columbia Coll Chicago (IL)
Eastern Nazarene Coll (MA)
John Brown U (AR)
Kendall Coll (IL)
Marian U (WI)
Prescott Coll (AZ)
Rowan U (NJ)
St. Cloud State U (MN)
Southern Arkansas U–Magnolia (AR)
The U of North Carolina at Pembroke (NC)
The U of Toledo (OH)
Washington U in St. Louis (MO)
Western Washington U (WA)
Wright State U (OH)
Xavier U (OH)

EDUCATION (SPECIFIC SUBJECT AREAS) RELATED

Appalachian State U (NC)
Averett U (VA)
Avila U (MO)
Baylor U (TX)
Bowling Green State U (OH)
Brigham Young U (UT)
Central Michigan U (MI)
The Coll of Saint Rose (NY)
Columbia Coll Chicago (IL)
DePaul U (IL)
Drexel U (PA)
Eastern Michigan U (MI)
Eastern Nazarene Coll (MA)
Gardner-Webb U (NC)
Graceland U (IA)
Henderson State U (AR)
Hope Coll (MI)
Indiana U Bloomington (IN)
Juniata Coll (PA)
Louisiana Tech U (LA)
Madonna U (MI)
Marywood U (PA)
McNeese State U (LA)
Minot State U (ND)
Missouri State U (MO)
Northern Arizona U (AZ)
Old Dominion U (VA)
Plymouth State U (NH)
Point Park U (PA)
Prescott Coll (AZ)
Regent U (VA)
St. Edward's U (TX)
State U of New York Coll at Potsdam (NY)
Syracuse U (NY)
Thomas More Coll (KY)
Tusculum Coll (TN)
The U of Akron (OH)
The U of Arizona (AZ)
U of Central Oklahoma (OK)
U of Kentucky (KY)
U of Lethbridge (AB, Canada)
U of Louisiana at Monroe (LA)
U of Michigan–Flint (MI)
U of Nebraska–Lincoln (NE)
U of Nevada, Reno (NV)
U of New Hampshire (NH)
U of New Orleans (LA)
The U of North Carolina Wilmington (NC)
U of Ottawa (ON, Canada)
U of Regina (SK, Canada)
U of St. Thomas (MN)
The U of Toledo (OH)
U of Wisconsin–Eau Claire (WI)
U of Wisconsin–Stout (WI)
Utah State U (UT)
Wayne State Coll (NE)
Western Washington U (WA)
Wright State U (OH)

ELECTRICAL AND ELECTRONIC ENGINEERING TECHNOLOGIES RELATED

Bryant & Stratton Coll, Eastlake (OH)
Embry-Riddle Aeronautical U (FL)
Grove City Coll (PA)
Inter American U of Puerto Rico, Aguadilla Campus (PR)
Northern Michigan U (MI)
Old Dominion U (VA)
Penn State Berks (PA)
Penn State U Park (PA)
Pennsylvania Coll of Technology (PA)
Point Park U (PA)
Rochester Inst of Technology (NY)
Southern Illinois U Carbondale (IL)
Vaughn Coll of Aeronautics and Technology (NY)
Virginia State U (VA)

ELECTRICAL, ELECTRONIC AND COMMUNICATIONS ENGINEERING TECHNOLOGY

Arizona State U (AZ)
Baker Coll of Owosso (MI)
Bluefield State Coll (WV)
Bowling Green State U (OH)
Bryant & Stratton Coll, Cleveland (OH)
Buffalo State Coll, State U of New York (NY)
California State Polytechnic U, Pomona (CA)
California State U, Long Beach (CA)
Cameron U (OK)
Central Michigan U (MI)
Cleveland State U (OH)
Delaware State U (DE)
DeVry Coll of New York (NY)
DeVry U, Phoenix (AZ)
DeVry U, Fremont (CA)
DeVry U, Long Beach (CA)
DeVry U, Pomona (CA)
DeVry U, Sherman Oaks (CA)
DeVry U, Westminster (CO)
DeVry U, Miramar (FL)
DeVry U, Orlando (FL)
DeVry U, Alpharetta (GA)
DeVry U, Decatur (GA)
DeVry U, Addison (IL)
DeVry U, Chicago (IL)
DeVry U, Tinley Park (IL)
DeVry U, Kansas City (MO)
DeVry U, North Brunswick (NJ)
DeVry U, Columbus (OH)
DeVry U, Fort Washington (PA)
DeVry U, Houston (TX)
DeVry U, Irving (TX)
DeVry U, Arlington (VA)
DeVry U, Federal Way (WA)
DeVry U Online (IL)
East Central U (OK)
Eastern Michigan U (MI)
ECPI Coll of Technology, Virginia Beach (VA)
Fairleigh Dickinson U, Metropolitan Campus (NJ)
Fairmont State U (WV)
Farmingdale State Coll (NY)
Ferris State U (MI)
Fitchburg State Coll (MA)
Florida Ag and Mech U (FL)
Fort Valley State U (GA)
Georgia Southern U (GA)
Grambling State U (LA)
Grantham U (MO)
Hamilton Tech Coll (IA)
Hampton U (VA)
Herzing U (GA)
Herzing U (WI)
Indiana State U (IN)
Indiana U–Purdue U Fort Wayne (IN)
Indiana U–Purdue U Indianapolis (IN)
Inter American U of Puerto Rico, Bayamón Campus (PR)
Inter American U of Puerto Rico, San Germán Campus (PR)
ITT Tech Inst, Bessemer (AL)
ITT Tech Inst, Madison (AL)
ITT Tech Inst, Mobile (AL)
ITT Tech Inst, Phoenix (AZ)
ITT Tech Inst, Tempe (AZ)
ITT Tech Inst, Tucson (AZ)
ITT Tech Inst (AR)
ITT Tech Inst, Anaheim (CA)
ITT Tech Inst, Clovis (CA)
ITT Tech Inst, Concord (CA)
ITT Tech Inst, Corona (CA)
ITT Tech Inst, Lathrop (CA)
ITT Tech Inst, Oxnard (CA)
ITT Tech Inst, Rancho Cordova (CA)
ITT Tech Inst, San Bernardino (CA)
ITT Tech Inst, San Diego (CA)
ITT Tech Inst, San Dimas (CA)
ITT Tech Inst, Sylmar (CA)
ITT Tech Inst, Torrance (CA)
ITT Tech Inst, Aurora (CO)
ITT Tech Inst, Thornton (CO)
ITT Tech Inst, Fort Lauderdale (FL)
ITT Tech Inst, Fort Myers (FL)
ITT Tech Inst, Jacksonville (FL)
ITT Tech Inst, Lake Mary (FL)
ITT Tech Inst, Miami (FL)
ITT Tech Inst, Tallahassee (FL)
ITT Tech Inst, Tampa (FL)
ITT Tech Inst, Atlanta (GA)
ITT Tech Inst, Duluth (GA)
ITT Tech Inst, Kennesaw (GA)
ITT Tech Inst (ID)
ITT Tech Inst, Burr Ridge (IL)
ITT Tech Inst, Mount Prospect (IL)
ITT Tech Inst, Orland Park (IL)
ITT Tech Inst, Fort Wayne (IN)
ITT Tech Inst, Indianapolis (IN)
ITT Tech Inst, Merrillville (IN)
ITT Tech Inst, South Bend (IN)
ITT Tech Inst, Cedar Rapids (IA)
ITT Tech Inst, Clive (IA)
ITT Tech Inst, Lexington (KY)
ITT Tech Inst, Louisville (KY)
ITT Tech Inst, St. Rose (LA)
ITT Tech Inst (MD)
ITT Tech Inst, Norwood (MA)
ITT Tech Inst, Woburn (MA)
ITT Tech Inst, Canton (MI)
ITT Tech Inst, Troy (MI)
ITT Tech Inst, Wyoming (MI)
ITT Tech Inst (MN)
ITT Tech Inst (MS)
ITT Tech Inst, Arnold (MO)
ITT Tech Inst, Earth City (MO)
ITT Tech Inst, Kansas City (MO)
ITT Tech Inst, Springfield (MO)
ITT Tech Inst (NE)
ITT Tech Inst (NV)
ITT Tech Inst (NM)
ITT Tech Inst, Charlotte (NC)
ITT Tech Inst, Charlotte (NC)
ITT Tech Inst, High Point (NC)
ITT Tech Inst, Morrisville (NC)
ITT Tech Inst, Oklahoma City (OK)
ITT Tech Inst, Tulsa (OK)
ITT Tech Inst (OR)
ITT Tech Inst, Greenville (SC)
ITT Tech Inst, Chattanooga (TN)
ITT Tech Inst, Cordova (TN)
ITT Tech Inst, Johnson City (TN)
ITT Tech Inst, Knoxville (TN)
ITT Tech Inst, Nashville (TN)
ITT Tech Inst, Arlington (TX)
ITT Tech Inst, Austin (TX)
ITT Tech Inst, DeSoto (TX)
ITT Tech Inst, Houston (TX)
ITT Tech Inst, Houston (TX)
ITT Tech Inst, Webster (TX)
ITT Tech Inst (UT)
ITT Tech Inst, Chantilly (VA)
ITT Tech Inst, Norfolk (VA)
ITT Tech Inst, Richmond (VA)
ITT Tech Inst, Salem (VA)
ITT Tech Inst, Springfield (VA)
ITT Tech Inst, Everett (WA)
ITT Tech Inst, Seattle (WA)
ITT Tech Inst, Spokane Valley (WA)
ITT Tech Inst, Green Bay (WI)
ITT Tech Inst, Greenfield (WI)
ITT Tech Inst, Madison (WI)
Jacksonville State U (AL)
Johnson & Wales U (RI)
Kansas State U (KS)
Kean U (NJ)
Kent State U at Tuscarawas (OH)
Lakehead U (ON, Canada)
Lake Superior State U (MI)
LeTourneau U (TX)
Louisiana Tech U (LA)
Metropolitan State Coll of Denver (CO)
Miami Dade Coll (FL)
Michigan Technological U (MI)
Milwaukee School of Eng (WI)
Minnesota State U Mankato (MN)
Missouri Western State U (MO)
New York Inst of Technology (NY)
Norfolk State U (VA)
Northern Kentucky U (KY)
Northwestern State U of Louisiana (LA)
Oklahoma State U (OK)
Oregon Inst of Technology (OR)
Penn State Erie, The Behrend Coll (PA)
Pittsburg State U (KS)
Point Park U (PA)
Prairie View A&M U (TX)
Purdue U (IN)
Purdue U Calumet (IN)
St. Cloud State U (MN)
Savannah State U (GA)
South Carolina State U (SC)
South Dakota State U (SD)
Southern Polytechnic State U (GA)
Southern U and Ag and Mech Coll (LA)
Southern Utah U (UT)
Texas A&M U (TX)
Texas A&M U–Corpus Christi (TX)
Texas Tech U (TX)
Thomas Edison State Coll (NJ)
Troy U (AL)
The U of Akron (OH)
U of Arkansas at Little Rock (AR)
U of Central Missouri (MO)
U of Cincinnati (OH)
U of Dayton (OH)
U of Hartford (CT)
U of Houston (TX)
U of Maine (ME)
U of Maryland Eastern Shore (MD)
U of Memphis (TN)
U of New Hampshire (NH)
U of New Hampshire at Manchester (NH)
U of North Texas (TX)
U of Pittsburgh at Johnstown (PA)
U of Puerto Rico at Bayamón (PR)
U of Regina (SK, Canada)
U of Southern Mississippi (MS)
The U of Texas at Brownsville (TX)
The U of Toledo (OH)
Vaughn Coll of Aeronautics and Technology (NY)
Wayne State U (MI)
Wentworth Inst of Technology (MA)
Western Carolina U (NC)
Western Washington U (WA)
Youngstown State U (OH)

ELECTRICAL, ELECTRONICS AND COMMUNICATIONS ENGINEERING

Alabama Ag and Mech U (AL)
Alfred U (NY)
American U of Beirut (Lebanon)
Arizona State U (AZ)
Arkansas State U—Jonesboro (AR)
Auburn U (AL)
Baylor U (TX)
Bloomsburg U of Pennsylvania (PA)
Bob Jones U (SC)
Boise State U (ID)
Boston U (MA)
Bradley U (IL)
Bucknell U (PA)
California Baptist U (CA)
California Inst of Technology (CA)
California Polytechnic State U, San Luis Obispo (CA)
California State Polytechnic U, Pomona (CA)
California State U, Chico (CA)
California State U, Fresno (CA)
California State U, Fullerton (CA)
California State U, Long Beach (CA)
California State U, Los Angeles (CA)
California State U, Sacramento (CA)
Calvin Coll (MI)
Carnegie Mellon U (PA)
Case Western Reserve U (OH)
The Catholic U of America (DC)
Cedarville U (OH)
Central Connecticut State U (CT)
Central Michigan U (MI)
Christian Brothers U (TN)
The Citadel, The Military Coll of South Carolina (SC)
City Coll of the City U of New York (NY)
Clarkson U (NY)
Clemson U (SC)
Cleveland State U (OH)
The Coll of New Jersey (NJ)
Colorado State U (CO)
Columbia U (NY)
Concordia U (QC, Canada)
Cooper Union for the Advancement of Science and Art (NY)
Cornell U (NY)
Dominican U (IL)
Dordt Coll (IA)
Drexel U (PA)
Duke U (NC)
Eastern Nazarene Coll (MA)
Eastern Washington U (WA)
Embry-Riddle Aeronautical U (AZ)
Embry-Riddle Aeronautical U (FL)
Fairfield U (CT)
Fairleigh Dickinson U, Metropolitan Campus (NJ)
Florida Ag and Mech U (FL)
Florida Atlantic U (FL)
Florida Inst of Technology (FL)
Florida Intl U (FL)
Franklin W. Olin Coll of Eng (MA)
Gallaudet U (DC)
Gannon U (PA)
George Fox U (OR)
George Mason U (VA)
The George Washington U (DC)
Georgia Inst of Technology (GA)
Gonzaga U (WA)
Grove City Coll (PA)
Hampton U (VA)
Harding U (AR)
Hofstra U (NY)
Idaho State U (ID)
Illinois Inst of Technology (IL)
Indiana Tech (IN)
Indiana U–Purdue U Fort Wayne (IN)
Indiana U–Purdue U Indianapolis (IN)
Inter American U of Puerto Rico, Bayamón Campus (PR)
Inter American U of Puerto Rico, Ponce Campus (PR)
Iowa State U of Science and Technology (IA)
Jackson State U (MS)
Jacksonville U (FL)
John Brown U (AR)
The Johns Hopkins U (MD)
Johnson & Wales U (RI)
Kansas State U (KS)
Kettering U (MI)
Lafayette Coll (PA)
Lakehead U (ON, Canada)
Lake Superior State U (MI)
Lamar U (TX)
Lawrence Technological U (MI)
Lehigh U (PA)
LeTourneau U (TX)
Louisiana State U and Ag and Mech Coll (LA)
Louisiana Tech U (LA)
Loyola Marymount U (CA)
Loyola U Maryland (MD)
Manhattan Coll (NY)
Marquette U (WI)
Massachusetts Inst of Technology (MA)
Memorial U of Newfoundland (NL, Canada)

INDEXES

Merrimack Coll (MA)
Miami U (OH)
Michigan State U (MI)
Michigan Technological U (MI)
Milwaukee School of Eng (WI)
Minnesota State U Mankato (MN)
Mississippi State U (MS)
Missouri U of Science and Technology (MO)
Montana State U (MT)
Montana Tech of The U of Montana (MT)
New Jersey Inst of Technology (NJ)
New Mexico Highlands U (NM)
New Mexico Inst of Mining and Technology (NM)
New Mexico State U (NM)
New York Inst of Technology (NY)
Norfolk State U (VA)
North Carolina State U (NC)
North Dakota State U (ND)
Northeastern U (MA)
Northern Arizona U (AZ)
Northwestern Polytechnic U (CA)
Oakland U (MI)
Ohio Northern U (OH)
The Ohio State U (OH)
Ohio U (OH)
Oklahoma Christian U (OK)
Oklahoma State U (OK)
Old Dominion U (VA)
Oral Roberts U (OK)
Oregon State U (OR)
Penn State Abington (PA)
Penn State Altoona (PA)
Penn State Beaver (PA)
Penn State Berks (PA)
Penn State Brandywine (PA)
Penn State DuBois (PA)
Penn State Erie, The Behrend Coll (PA)
Penn State Fayette, The Eberly Campus (PA)
Penn State Greater Allegheny (PA)
Penn State Harrisburg (PA)
Penn State Hazleton (PA)
Penn State Lehigh Valley (PA)
Penn State Mont Alto (PA)
Penn State New Kensington (PA)
Penn State Schuylkill (PA)
Penn State Shenango (PA)
Penn State U Park (PA)
Penn State Wilkes-Barre (PA)
Penn State Worthington Scranton (PA)
Penn State York (PA)
Polytechnic Inst of NYU (NY)
Polytechnic U of Puerto Rico (PR)
Portland State U (OR)
Prairie View A&M U (TX)
Princeton U (NJ)
Purdue U (IN)
Purdue U Calumet (IN)
Queen's U at Kingston (ON, Canada)
Rensselaer Polytechnic Inst (NY)
Rice U (TX)
Rochester Inst of Technology (NY)
Rose-Hulman Inst of Technology (IN)
Rowan U (NJ)
Royal Military Coll of Canada (ON, Canada)
Rutgers, The State U of New Jersey, New Brunswick (NJ)
Saginaw Valley State U (MI)
St. Cloud State U (MN)
Saint Louis U (MO)
St. Mary's U (TX)
San Diego State U (CA)
San Francisco State U (CA)
San Jose State U (CA)
Santa Clara U (CA)
Seattle Pacific U (WA)
Seattle U (WA)
South Dakota School of Mines and Technology (SD)
South Dakota State U (SD)
Southern California Inst of Technology (CA)
Southern Illinois U Carbondale (IL)
Southern Illinois U Edwardsville (IL)
Southern Methodist U (TX)
Southern Polytechnic State U (GA)
Southern U and Ag and Mech Coll (LA)
Stanford U (CA)
State U of New York at Binghamton (NY)
State U of New York at New Paltz (NY)
State U of New York Coll of Technology at Alfred (NY)
State U of New York Maritime Coll (NY)
Stevens Inst of Technology (NJ)
Stony Brook U, State U of New York (NY)
Suffolk U (MA)
Syracuse U (NY)
Temple U (PA)
Tennessee Technological U (TN)
Texas A&M U (TX)
Texas A&M U–Kingsville (TX)
Texas Christian U (TX)
Texas State U–San Marcos (TX)
Texas Tech U (TX)
Trine U (IN)
Trinity Coll (CT)
Tufts U (MA)
Tulane U (LA)
Tuskegee U (AL)
Union Coll (NY)
United States Air Force Acad (CO)
United States Coast Guard Acad (CT)
United States Military Acad (NY)
United States Naval Acad (MD)
Universidad de las Américas–Puebla (Mexico)
U at Buffalo, the State U of New York (NY)
The U of Akron (OH)
The U of Alabama (AL)
The U of Alabama at Birmingham (AL)
The U of Alabama in Huntsville (AL)
U of Alaska Fairbanks (AK)
U of Alberta (AB, Canada)
The U of Arizona (AZ)
U of Arkansas (AR)
The U of British Columbia (BC, Canada)
The U of British Columbia–Okanagan (BC, Canada)
U of California, Berkeley (CA)
U of California, Davis (CA)
U of California, Irvine (CA)
U of California, Los Angeles (CA)
U of California, Riverside (CA)
U of California, San Diego (CA)
U of California, Santa Barbara (CA)
U of California, Santa Cruz (CA)
U of Central Florida (FL)
U of Colorado at Boulder (CO)
U of Colorado at Colorado Springs (CO)
U of Colorado Denver (CO)
U of Connecticut (CT)
U of Dayton (OH)
U of Delaware (DE)
U of Denver (CO)
U of Evansville (IN)
U of Florida (FL)
U of Hartford (CT)
U of Hawaii at Manoa (HI)
U of Houston (TX)
U of Idaho (ID)
U of Illinois at Chicago (IL)
U of Illinois at Urbana–Champaign (IL)
The U of Iowa (IA)
The U of Kansas (KS)
U of Kentucky (KY)
U of Louisville (KY)
U of Maine (ME)
U of Manitoba (MB, Canada)
U of Maryland, Coll Park (MD)
U of Massachusetts Amherst (MA)
U of Massachusetts Dartmouth (MA)
U of Massachusetts Lowell (MA)
U of Memphis (TN)
U of Miami (FL)
U of Michigan (MI)
U of Michigan–Dearborn (MI)
U of Minnesota, Duluth (MN)
U of Minnesota, Twin Cities Campus (MN)
U of Mississippi (MS)
U of Missouri (MO)
U of Missouri–Kansas City (MO)
U of Missouri–St. Louis (MO)
U of Nebraska–Lincoln (NE)
U of Nevada, Las Vegas (NV)
U of Nevada, Reno (NV)
U of New Brunswick Fredericton (NB, Canada)
U of New Hampshire (NH)
U of New Haven (CT)
U of New Mexico (NM)
U of New Orleans (LA)
The U of North Carolina at Charlotte (NC)
U of North Dakota (ND)
U of North Florida (FL)
U of North Texas (TX)
U of Notre Dame (IN)
U of Oklahoma (OK)
U of Ottawa (ON, Canada)
U of Pennsylvania (PA)
U of Pittsburgh (PA)
U of Portland (OR)
U of Regina (SK, Canada)
U of Rhode Island (RI)
U of Rochester (NY)
U of St. Thomas (MN)
U of San Diego (CA)
U of Saskatchewan (SK, Canada)
The U of Scranton (PA)
U of South Alabama (AL)
U of South Carolina (SC)
U of Southern California (CA)
U of Southern Maine (ME)
U of South Florida (FL)
The U of Tennessee (TN)
The U of Tennessee at Chattanooga (TN)
The U of Texas at Arlington (TX)
The U of Texas at Austin (TX)
The U of Texas at Dallas (TX)
The U of Texas at El Paso (TX)
The U of Texas at San Antonio (TX)
The U of Texas at Tyler (TX)
The U of Texas–Pan American (TX)
U of the District of Columbia (DC)
U of the Pacific (CA)
The U of Toledo (OH)
U of Toronto (ON, Canada)
U of Tulsa (OK)
U of Utah (UT)
U of Vermont (VT)
U of Virginia (VA)
U of Washington (WA)
U of Washington, Bothell (WA)
U of Waterloo (ON, Canada)
The U of Western Ontario (ON, Canada)
U of West Florida (FL)
U of Windsor (ON, Canada)
U of Wisconsin–Madison (WI)
U of Wisconsin–Milwaukee (WI)
U of Wisconsin–Platteville (WI)
U of Wyoming (WY)
Ursinus Coll (PA)
Utah State U (UT)
Valparaiso U (IN)
Vanderbilt U (TN)
Villanova U (PA)
Virginia Commonwealth U (VA)
Virginia Military Inst (VA)
Virginia Polytechnic Inst and State U (VA)
Washington State U (WA)
Washington U in St. Louis (MO)
Wayne State U (MI)
Western Carolina U (NC)
Western Kentucky U (KY)
Western Michigan U (MI)
Western New England Coll (MA)
West Virginia U (WV)
Wichita State U (KS)
Widener U (PA)
Wilberforce U (OH)
Wilkes U (PA)
Worcester Polytechnic Inst (MA)
Wright State U (OH)
Yale U (CT)
York Coll of Pennsylvania (PA)
Youngstown State U (OH)

ELECTRICAL/ ELECTRONICS EQUIPMENT INSTALLATION AND REPAIR

Cape Breton U (NS, Canada)
Lewis-Clark State Coll (ID)

ELECTRICAL/ ELECTRONICS MAINTENANCE AND REPAIR TECHNOLOGY RELATED

Pennsylvania Coll of Technology (PA)

ELECTROMECHANICAL TECHNOLOGY

Bowling Green State U (OH)
Buffalo State Coll, State U of New York (NY)
Excelsior Coll (NY)
John Brown U (AR)
Miami U Hamilton (OH)
Murray State U (KY)
Purdue U Calumet (IN)
Rochester Inst of Technology (NY)
State U of New York Coll of Technology at Alfred (NY)
Temple U (PA)
U of Northern Iowa (IA)
The U of Toledo (OH)
Vermont Tech Coll (VT)
Wayne State U (MI)

ELECTRONEURO-DIAGNOSTIC/ELECTRO-ENCEPHALOGRAPHIC TECHNOLOGY

The Johns Hopkins U (MD)

ELEMENTARY AND MIDDLE SCHOOL ADMINISTRATION/ PRINCIPALSHIP

Berea Coll (KY)
Piedmont Coll (GA)

ELEMENTARY EDUCATION

Abilene Christian U (TX)
Acadia U (NS, Canada)
Alabama Ag and Mech U (AL)
Alabama State U (AL)
Alaska Pacific U (AK)
Albion Coll (MI)
Albright Coll (PA)
Alcorn State U (MS)
Alderson-Broaddus Coll (WV)
Alfred U (NY)
Alma Coll (MI)
Alvernia U (PA)
Alverno Coll (WI)
American Intl Coll (MA)
American U (DC)
American U of Beirut (Lebanon)
Anderson U (IN)
Andrews U (MI)
Appalachian State U (NC)
Aquinas Coll (MI)
Aquinas Coll (TN)
Arcadia U (PA)
Arizona State U (AZ)
Asbury U (KY)
Ashland U (OH)
Assumption Coll (MA)
Atlantic Union Coll (MA)
Auburn U (AL)
Auburn U Montgomery (AL)
Augsburg Coll (MN)
Augustana Coll (IL)
Augustana Coll (SD)
Aurora U (IL)
Avila U (MO)
Baker U (KS)
Ball State U (IN)
Baptist Bible Coll of Pennsylvania (PA)
The Baptist Coll of Florida (FL)
Barclay Coll (KS)
Barry U (FL)
Barton Coll (NC)
Baylor U (TX)
Bay Path Coll (MA)
Belhaven U (MS)
Bellarmine U (KY)
Belmont Abbey Coll (NC)
Belmont U (TN)
Beloit Coll (WI)
Bemidji State U (MN)
Benedictine Coll (KS)
Benedictine U (IL)
Bennett Coll for Women (NC)
Bennington Coll (VT)
Bethany Bible Coll (NB, Canada)
Bethany Coll (KS)
Bethany Lutheran Coll (MN)
Bethany U (CA)
Bethel Coll (IN)
Bethel Coll (KS)
Bethel U (MN)
Bethel U (TN)
Bethune-Cookman U (FL)
Birmingham-Southern Coll (AL)
Bishop's U (QC, Canada)
Blackburn Coll (IL)
Black Hills State U (SD)
Bluefield Coll (VA)
Bluefield State Coll (WV)
Blue Mountain Coll (MS)
Bluffton U (OH)
Bob Jones U (SC)
Boise State U (ID)
Boston Coll (MA)
Boston U (MA)
Bowie State U (MD)
Bowling Green State U (OH)
Bradley U (IL)
Brenau U (GA)
Brescia U (KY)
Brevard Coll (NC)
Briar Cliff U (IA)
Bridgewater Coll (VA)
Bridgewater State Coll (MA)
Brigham Young U–Hawaii (HI)
Brock U (ON, Canada)
Brooklyn Coll of the City U of New York (NY)
Bryan Coll (TN)
Bryn Athyn Coll of the New Church (PA)
Bucknell U (PA)
Buena Vista U (IA)
Buffalo State Coll, State U of New York (NY)
Butler U (IN)
Cabrini Coll (PA)
Calumet Coll of Saint Joseph (IN)
Calvary Bible Coll and Theological Sem (MO)
Calvin Coll (MI)
Cameron U (OK)
Campbellsville U (KY)
Canisius Coll (NY)
Carlos Albizu U, Miami Campus (FL)
Carlow U (PA)
Carroll U (WI)
Carson-Newman Coll (TN)
Catawba Coll (NC)
The Catholic U of America (DC)
Cedar Crest Coll (PA)
Centenary Coll (NJ)
Central Christian Coll of Kansas (KS)
Central Coll (IA)
Central Connecticut State U (CT)
Central Michigan U (MI)
Chaminade U of Honolulu (HI)
Champlain Coll (VT)
Chatham U (PA)
Cheyney U of Pennsylvania (PA)
Chowan U (NC)
Christian Brothers U (TN)
City Coll of the City U of New York (NY)
City U of Seattle (WA)
Claflin U (SC)
Clarion U of Pennsylvania (PA)
Clarke Coll (IA)
Clark U (MA)
Clearwater Christian Coll (FL)
Clemson U (SC)
Cleveland State U (OH)
Coastal Carolina U (SC)
Coker Coll (SC)
The Coll at Brockport, State U of New York (NY)
Coll of Charleston (SC)
Coll of Mount Saint Vincent (NY)
The Coll of New Jersey (NJ)
The Coll of New Rochelle (NY)
Coll of Notre Dame of Maryland (MD)
Coll of Saint Benedict (MN)
Coll of St. Joseph (VT)
Coll of Saint Mary (NE)
The Coll of Saint Rose (NY)
The Coll of St. Scholastica (MN)
Coll of the Atlantic (ME)
Coll of the Ozarks (MO)
Columbia Coll (SC)
Concordia Coll (MN)
Concordia U (CA)
Concordia U (QC, Canada)
Concordia U Chicago (IL)
Concordia U Coll of Alberta (AB, Canada)
Concordia U, St. Paul (MN)
Concordia U Texas (TX)
Concordia U Wisconsin (WI)
Concord U (WV)
Converse Coll (SC)
Coppin State U (MD)
Corban U (OR)
Cornell Coll (IA)
Cornerstone U (MI)
Covenant Coll (GA)
Creighton U (NE)
Crichton Coll (TN)
Crown Coll (MN)
Culver-Stockton Coll (MO)
Cumberland U (TN)
Curry Coll (MA)
Daemen Coll (NY)
Dakota State U (SD)
Dakota Wesleyan U (SD)
Dallas Baptist U (TX)
Dalton State Coll (GA)
Dana Coll (NE)
Daytona State Coll (FL)
Defiance Coll (OH)
Delaware State U (DE)
Delta State U (MS)
DePaul U (IL)
DePauw U (IN)
DeSales U (PA)
Dickinson State U (ND)
Dixie State Coll of Utah (UT)
Doane Coll (NE)
Dominican Coll (NY)
Dominican U (IL)
Dordt Coll (IA)
Dowling Coll (NY)
Drake U (IA)
Drury U (MO)
D'Youville Coll (NY)
East Carolina U (NC)
East Central U (OK)
Eastern Connecticut State U (CT)
Eastern Illinois U (IL)
Eastern Mennonite U (VA)
Eastern Michigan U (MI)
Eastern Nazarene Coll (MA)
Eastern New Mexico U (NM)
East Stroudsburg U of Pennsylvania (PA)
East Texas Baptist U (TX)
Edgewood Coll (WI)
Edinboro U of Pennsylvania (PA)

Edward Waters Coll (FL)
Elizabeth City State U (NC)
Elizabethtown Coll (PA)
Elmhurst Coll (IL)
Elmira Coll (NY)
Elon U (NC)
Emmanuel Coll (GA)
Emmanuel Coll (MA)
Emporia State U (KS)
Endicott Coll (MA)
Erskine Coll (SC)
Evangel U (MO)
Fairmont State U (WV)
Faith Baptist Bible Coll and Theological Sem (IA)
Faulkner U (AL)
Fayetteville State U (NC)
Felician Coll (NJ)
Ferris State U (MI)
Fitchburg State Coll (MA)
Five Towns Coll (NY)
Flagler Coll (FL)
Florida Ag and Mech U (FL)
Florida Atlantic U (FL)
Florida Coll (FL)
Florida Gulf Coast U (FL)
Florida Intl U (FL)
Florida Southern Coll (FL)
Fontbonne U (MO)
Fordham U (NY)
Fort Hays State U (KS)
Fort Lewis Coll (CO)
Franciscan U of Steubenville (OH)
Francis Marion U (SC)
Franklin Coll (IN)
Franklin Pierce U (NH)
Freed-Hardeman U (TN)
Free Will Baptist Bible Coll (TN)
Friends U (KS)
Frostburg State U (MD)
Furman U (SC)
Gainesville State Coll (GA)
Gallaudet U (DC)
Gannon U (PA)
Gardner-Webb U (NC)
Geneva Coll (PA)
George Fox U (OR)
Georgetown Coll (KY)
Georgian Court U (NJ)
Georgia Southern U (GA)
Georgia State U (GA)
Gettysburg Coll (PA)
Glenville State Coll (WV)
Goddard Coll (VT)
Gonzaga U (WA)
Gordon Coll (MA)
Goshen Coll (IN)
Goucher Coll (MD)
Governors State U (IL)
Grace Bible Coll (MI)
Grace Coll (IN)
Graceland U (IA)
Graceland U (MO)
Grambling State U (LA)
Grand Valley State U (MI)
Grand View U (IA)
Green Mountain Coll (VT)
Greensboro Coll (NC)
Greenville Coll (IL)
Grove City Coll (PA)
Guilford Coll (NC)
Gustavus Adolphus Coll (MN)
Gwynedd-Mercy Coll (PA)
Hamline U (MN)
Hampton U (VA)
Hannibal-LaGrange Coll (MO)
Hanover Coll (IN)
Harding U (AR)
Harris-Stowe State U (MO)
Heidelberg U (OH)
Hellenic Coll (MA)
High Point U (NC)
Hillsdale Coll (MI)
Hofstra U (NY)
Holy Family U (PA)
Houghton Coll (NY)
Houston Baptist U (TX)
Howard Payne U (TX)
Humboldt State U (CA)
Hunter Coll of the City U of New York (NY)
Huntingdon Coll (AL)
Huntington U (IN)
Husson U (ME)
Huston-Tillotson U (TX)
Idaho State U (ID)
Illinois Coll (IL)
Illinois State U (IL)
Illinois Wesleyan U (IL)
Immaculata U (PA)
Indiana State U (IN)
Indiana U Bloomington (IN)
Indiana U East (IN)
Indiana U Kokomo (IN)
Indiana U Northwest (IN)
Indiana U of Pennsylvania (PA)
Indiana U–Purdue U Fort Wayne (IN)
Indiana U–Purdue U Indianapolis (IN)
Indiana U South Bend (IN)
Indiana U Southeast (IN)
Indiana Wesleyan U (IN)
Inter American U of Puerto Rico, Aguadilla Campus (PR)
Inter American U of Puerto Rico, Arecibo Campus (PR)
Inter American U of Puerto Rico, Fajardo Campus (PR)
Inter American U of Puerto Rico, Guayama Campus (PR)
Inter American U of Puerto Rico, Ponce Campus (PR)
Inter American U of Puerto Rico, San Germán Campus (PR)
Iona Coll (NY)
Iowa State U of Science and Technology (IA)
Iowa Wesleyan Coll (IA)
Jackson State U (MS)
Jacksonville State U (AL)
Jacksonville U (FL)
Jamestown Coll (ND)
Jarvis Christian Coll (TX)
John Brown U (AR)
John Carroll U (OH)
Johnson Bible Coll (TN)
Johnson C. Smith U (NC)
Johnson State Coll (VT)
John Wesley Coll (NC)
Jones Coll, Jacksonville (FL)
Judson Coll (AL)
Judson U (IL)
Juniata Coll (PA)
Kansas State U (KS)
Kean U (NJ)
Keene State Coll (NH)
Keiser U, Fort Lauderdale (FL)
Kendall Coll (IL)
Kennesaw State U (GA)
Kentucky State U (KY)
Kentucky Wesleyan Coll (KY)
Keuka Coll (NY)
Keystone Coll (PA)
King's Coll (PA)
The King's U Coll (AB, Canada)
Kutztown U of Pennsylvania (PA)
Kuyper Coll (MI)
LaGrange Coll (GA)
Lake Erie Coll (OH)
Lake Forest Coll (IL)
Lakehead U (ON, Canada)
Lakeland Coll (WI)
Lake Superior State U (MI)
Lamar U (TX)
La Roche Coll (PA)
La Salle U (PA)
Lasell Coll (MA)
Lebanon Valley Coll (PA)
Lees-McRae Coll (NC)
Lee U (TN)
Le Moyne Coll (NY)
Lesley U (MA)
LeTourneau U (TX)
Lewis-Clark State Coll (ID)
Lewis U (IL)
Liberty U (VA)
Limestone Coll (SC)
Lincoln Christian U (IL)
Lincoln Memorial U (TN)
Lincoln U (MO)
Lincoln U (PA)
Lindenwood U (MO)
Lindsey Wilson Coll (KY)
Linfield Coll (OR)
Lipscomb U (TN)
Lock Haven U of Pennsylvania (PA)
Long Island U, Brooklyn Campus (NY)
Long Island U, C.W. Post Campus (NY)
Longwood U (VA)
Loras Coll (IA)
Louisiana Coll (LA)
Louisiana State U and Ag and Mech Coll (LA)
Louisiana State U in Shreveport (LA)
Louisiana Tech U (LA)
Loyola U Chicago (IL)
Loyola U Maryland (MD)
Lubbock Christian U (TX)
Luther Coll (IA)
Lynchburg Coll (VA)
Lynn U (FL)
Maharishi U of Management (IA)
Manchester Coll (IN)
Manhattan Coll (NY)
Manhattanville Coll (NY)
Mansfield U of Pennsylvania (PA)
Maranatha Baptist Bible Coll (WI)
Marian U (IN)
Marian U (WI)
Marietta Coll (OH)
Marquette U (WI)
Marshall U (WV)
Mars Hill Coll (NC)
Martin Luther Coll (MN)
Maryville U of Saint Louis (MO)
Marywood U (PA)
The Master's Coll and Sem (CA)
Mayville State U (ND)
McKendree U (IL)
McNeese State U (LA)
Medaille Coll (NY)
Medgar Evers Coll of the City U of New York (NY)
Memorial U of Newfoundland (NL, Canada)
Mercer U (GA)
Mercyhurst Coll (PA)
Merrimack Coll (MA)
Messiah Coll (PA)
Methodist U (NC)
Michigan State U (MI)
MidAmerica Nazarene U (KS)
Mid-Continent U (KY)
Midway Coll (KY)
Millersville U of Pennsylvania (PA)
Millikin U (IL)
Minnesota State U Mankato (MN)
Minnesota State U Moorhead (MN)
Minot State U (ND)
Misericordia U (PA)
Mississippi Coll (MS)
Mississippi State U (MS)
Mississippi U for Women (MS)
Mississippi Valley State U (MS)
Missouri Baptist U (MO)
Missouri Southern State U (MO)
Missouri State U (MO)
Missouri Western State U (MO)
Molloy Coll (NY)
Monmouth Coll (IL)
Montana State U (MT)
Montana State U Billings (MT)
Moravian Coll (PA)
Morehead State U (KY)
Morningside Coll (IA)
Morris Coll (SC)
Mount Marty Coll (SD)
Mount Mary Coll (WI)
Mount Mercy Coll (IA)
Mount St. Mary's Coll (CA)
Mount St. Mary's U (MD)
Mount Vernon Nazarene U (OH)
Multnomah U (OR)
Murray State U (KY)
Nazareth Coll of Rochester (NY)
Nebraska Wesleyan U (NE)
Neumann U (PA)
Nevada State Coll at Henderson (NV)
Newberry Coll (SC)
New England Coll (NH)
New Jersey City U (NJ)
Newman U (KS)
New Mexico Highlands U (NM)
New Mexico State U (NM)
New York Inst of Technology (NY)
New York U (NY)
Niagara U (NY)
Nicholls State U (LA)
North Carolina Central U (NC)
North Central Coll (IL)
Northeastern Illinois U (IL)
Northeastern State U (OK)
Northern Arizona U (AZ)
Northern Kentucky U (KY)
Northern Michigan U (MI)
Northern State U (SD)
North Georgia Coll & State U (GA)
North Greenville U (SC)
Northwestern Coll (IA)
Northwestern Coll (MN)
Northwestern Oklahoma State U (OK)
Northwestern State U of Louisiana (LA)
Northwest Missouri State U (MO)
Northwest Nazarene U (ID)
Northwest U (WA)
Notre Dame de Namur U (CA)
Nova Southeastern U (FL)
Nyack Coll (NY)
Oakland City U (IN)
Oakland U (MI)
Oakwood U (AL)
Ohio U–Zanesville (OH)
Ohio Valley U (WV)
Ohio Wesleyan U (OH)
Oklahoma Baptist U (OK)
Oklahoma Christian U (OK)
Oklahoma City U (OK)
Oklahoma Panhandle State U (OK)
Oklahoma State U (OK)
Oklahoma Wesleyan U (OK)
Oral Roberts U (OK)
Ottawa U (KS)
Pace U (NY)
Pacific Union Coll (CA)
Paine Coll (GA)
Park U (MO)
Penn State Abington (PA)
Penn State Altoona (PA)
Penn State Beaver (PA)
Penn State Berks (PA)
Penn State Brandywine (PA)
Penn State DuBois (PA)
Penn State Erie, The Behrend Coll (PA)
Penn State Fayette, The Eberly Campus (PA)
Penn State Greater Allegheny (PA)
Penn State Harrisburg (PA)
Penn State Hazleton (PA)
Penn State Lehigh Valley (PA)
Penn State Mont Alto (PA)
Penn State New Kensington (PA)
Penn State Schuylkill (PA)
Penn State Shenango (PA)
Penn State U Park (PA)
Penn State Wilkes-Barre (PA)
Penn State Worthington Scranton (PA)
Penn State York (PA)
Pepperdine U, Malibu (CA)
Peru State Coll (NE)
Philadelphia Biblical U (PA)
Piedmont Baptist Coll and Graduate School (NC)
Pikeville Coll (KY)
Pittsburg State U (KS)
Plymouth State U (NH)
Point Park U (PA)
Pontifical Catholic U of Puerto Rico (PR)
Prescott Coll (AZ)
Principia Coll (IL)
Purdue U (IN)
Purdue U Calumet (IN)
Purdue U North Central (IN)
Queens Coll of the City U of New York (NY)
Queen's U at Kingston (ON, Canada)
Queens U of Charlotte (NC)
Quincy U (IL)
Randolph Coll (VA)
Redeemer U Coll (ON, Canada)
Rhode Island Coll (RI)
Rider U (NJ)
Ripon Coll (WI)
Rivier Coll (NH)
Robert Morris U (PA)
Roberts Wesleyan Coll (NY)
Rochester Coll (MI)
Rockford Coll (IL)
Rockhurst U (MO)
Rocky Mountain Coll (MT)
Roosevelt U (IL)
Rosemont Coll (PA)
Rowan U (NJ)
Russell Sage Coll (NY)
Sacred Heart U (CT)
Saginaw Valley State U (MI)
St. Ambrose U (IA)
St. Andrews Presbyterian Coll (NC)
St. Bonaventure U (NY)
St. Catherine U (MN)
St. Cloud State U (MN)
Saint Francis U (PA)
St. Francis Xavier U (NS, Canada)
St. John Fisher Coll (NY)
Saint John's U (MN)
St. John's U (NY)
Saint Joseph's U (PA)
Saint Leo U (FL)
Saint Martin's U (WA)
Saint Mary-of-the-Woods Coll (IN)
Saint Mary's Coll (IN)
Saint Mary's U of Minnesota (MN)
Saint Michael's Coll (VT)
St. Norbert Coll (WI)
Saint Paul's Coll (VA)
St. Petersburg Coll (FL)
St. Thomas Aquinas Coll (NY)
St. Thomas U (FL)
Saint Vincent Coll (PA)
Saint Xavier U (IL)
Salem State Coll (MA)
Salisbury U (MD)
Salve Regina U (RI)
San Diego Christian Coll (CA)
Sarah Lawrence Coll (NY)
Schreiner U (TX)
Seton Hall U (NJ)
Seton Hill U (PA)
Shawnee State U (OH)
Shaw U (NC)
Shepherd U (WV)
Shorter U (GA)
Siena Heights U (MI)
Silver Lake Coll (WI)
Simmons Coll (MA)
Simpson Coll (IA)
Skidmore Coll (NY)
Slippery Rock U of Pennsylvania (PA)
South Carolina State U (SC)
Southeastern Louisiana U (LA)
Southeastern Oklahoma State U (OK)
Southeastern U (FL)
Southeast Missouri State U (MO)
Southern Adventist U (TN)
Southern Arkansas U–Magnolia (AR)
Southern Connecticut State U (CT)
Southern Illinois U Carbondale (IL)
Southern Illinois U Edwardsville (IL)
Southern New Hampshire U (NH)
Southern U and Ag and Mech Coll (LA)
Southern U at New Orleans (LA)
Southern Utah U (UT)
Southern Wesleyan U (SC)
Southwest Baptist U (MO)
Southwestern Adventist U (TX)
Southwestern Assemblies of God U (TX)
Southwestern Coll (KS)
Southwestern Oklahoma State U (OK)
Southwestern U (TX)
Southwest Florida Coll, Fort Myers (FL)
Southwest Minnesota State U (MN)
Spalding U (KY)
Spring Arbor U (MI)
Spring Hill Coll (AL)
State U of New York at Fredonia (NY)
State U of New York at New Paltz (NY)
State U of New York at Oswego (NY)
State U of New York at Plattsburgh (NY)
State U of New York Coll at Cortland (NY)
State U of New York Coll at Geneseo (NY)
State U of New York Coll at Old Westbury (NY)
State U of New York Coll at Oneonta (NY)
State U of New York Coll at Potsdam (NY)
Stephens Coll (MO)
Sterling Coll (KS)
Stetson U (FL)
Stevenson U (MD)
Stillman Coll (AL)
Stonehill Coll (MA)
Suffolk U (MA)
Sul Ross State U (TX)
Susquehanna U (PA)
Tabor Coll (KS)
Tarleton State U (TX)
Taylor U (IN)
Temple U (PA)
Tennessee Technological U (TN)
Tennessee Wesleyan Coll (TN)
Texas A&M U–Commerce (TX)
Texas Christian U (TX)
Texas Coll (TX)
Texas Lutheran U (TX)
Texas Wesleyan U (TX)
Thiel Coll (PA)
Thomas More Coll (KY)
Thompson Rivers U (BC, Canada)
Towson U (MD)
Transylvania U (KY)
Trent U (ON, Canada)
Trevecca Nazarene U (TN)
Trine U (IN)
Trinity Christian Coll (IL)
Trinity Coll of Florida (FL)
Troy U (AL)
Tufts U (MA)
Tusculum Coll (TN)
Tuskegee U (AL)
Union Coll (KY)
Union Coll (NE)
Union Inst & U (OH)
Union U (TN)
Universidad Adventista de las Antillas (PR)
Université du Québec en Outaouais (QC, Canada)
The U of Alabama (AL)
The U of Alabama at Birmingham (AL)
The U of Alabama in Huntsville (AL)
U of Alaska Anchorage (AK)
U of Alaska Anchorage, Kenai Peninsula Coll (AK)
U of Alaska Fairbanks (AK)
U of Alberta (AB, Canada)
The U of Arizona (AZ)
U of Arkansas at Little Rock (AR)
U of Arkansas at Monticello (AR)
The U of British Columbia (BC, Canada)
U of Central Florida (FL)
U of Central Missouri (MO)
U of Central Oklahoma (OK)
U of Charleston (WV)
U of Cincinnati (OH)
U of Connecticut (CT)
U of Dallas (TX)

U of Dayton (OH)
U of Delaware (DE)
U of Dubuque (IA)
U of Evansville (IN)
The U of Findlay (OH)
U of Florida (FL)
U of Guam (GU)
U of Hartford (CT)
U of Hawaii at Hilo (HI)
U of Hawaii at Manoa (HI)
U of Hawaii–West Oahu (HI)
U of Idaho (ID)
U of Illinois at Chicago (IL)
U of Illinois at Urbana–Champaign (IL)
U of Indianapolis (IN)
The U of Iowa (IA)
The U of Kansas (KS)
U of Kentucky (KY)
U of Louisiana at Monroe (LA)
U of Louisville (KY)
U of Maine (ME)
U of Maine at Farmington (ME)
U of Maine at Fort Kent (ME)
U of Maine at Machias (ME)
U of Maine at Presque Isle (ME)
U of Manitoba (MB, Canada)
U of Mary (ND)
U of Mary Hardin-Baylor (TX)
U of Maryland, Coll Park (MD)
U of Maryland Eastern Shore (MD)
U of Mary Washington (VA)
U of Miami (FL)
U of Michigan (MI)
U of Michigan–Dearborn (MI)
U of Michigan–Flint (MI)
U of Minnesota, Duluth (MN)
U of Minnesota, Twin Cities Campus (MN)
U of Mississippi (MS)
U of Missouri (MO)
U of Missouri–Kansas City (MO)
U of Missouri–St. Louis (MO)
U of Mobile (AL)
The U of Montana Western (MT)
U of Montevallo (AL)
U of Nebraska at Kearney (NE)
U of Nebraska–Lincoln (NE)
U of Nevada, Las Vegas (NV)
U of Nevada, Reno (NV)
U of New Brunswick Fredericton (NB, Canada)
U of New England (ME)
U of New Mexico (NM)
U of New Orleans (LA)
U of North Alabama (AL)
The U of North Carolina at Chapel Hill (NC)
The U of North Carolina at Charlotte (NC)
The U of North Carolina at Greensboro (NC)
The U of North Carolina at Pembroke (NC)
The U of North Carolina Wilmington (NC)
U of North Dakota (ND)
U of Northern Iowa (IA)
U of North Florida (FL)
U of Oklahoma (OK)
U of Pennsylvania (PA)
U of Pittsburgh at Bradford (PA)
U of Pittsburgh at Johnstown (PA)
U of Portland (OR)
U of Puerto Rico at Humacao (PR)
U of Puerto Rico at Utuado (PR)
U of Puerto Rico, Río Piedras (PR)
U of Redlands (CA)
U of Regina (SK, Canada)
U of Rhode Island (RI)
U of Rio Grande (OH)
U of St. Francis (IL)
U of Saint Mary (KS)
U of St. Thomas (MN)
U of St. Thomas (TX)
U of San Francisco (CA)
U of Saskatchewan (SK, Canada)
U of Science and Arts of Oklahoma (OK)
The U of Scranton (PA)
U of South Alabama (AL)
U of South Carolina Aiken (SC)
U of South Carolina Upstate (SC)
The U of South Dakota (SD)
U of Southern Indiana (IN)
U of Southern Mississippi (MS)
U of South Florida (FL)
The U of Tampa (FL)
The U of Tennessee at Martin (TN)
U of the Cumberlands (KY)
U of the District of Columbia (DC)
U of the Incarnate Word (TX)
U of the Ozarks (AR)
U of the Southwest (NM)
U of the Virgin Islands (VI)
The U of Toledo (OH)
U of Tulsa (OK)
U of Utah (UT)
U of Vermont (VT)
U of Washington (WA)
The U of West Alabama (AL)
The U of Western Ontario (ON, Canada)
U of West Florida (FL)
U of West Georgia (GA)
U of Windsor (ON, Canada)
U of Wisconsin–Eau Claire (WI)
U of Wisconsin–La Crosse (WI)
U of Wisconsin–Madison (WI)
U of Wisconsin–Milwaukee (WI)
U of Wisconsin–Oshkosh (WI)
U of Wisconsin–Platteville (WI)
U of Wisconsin–River Falls (WI)
U of Wisconsin–Stevens Point (WI)
U of Wisconsin–Superior (WI)
U of Wisconsin–Whitewater (WI)
U of Wyoming (WY)
Upper Iowa U (IA)
Utah State U (UT)
Utah Valley U (UT)
Utica Coll (NY)
Valley City State U (ND)
Valley Forge Christian Coll (PA)
Valparaiso U (IN)
Vanderbilt U (TN)
Vanguard U of Southern California (CA)
Virginia Intermont Coll (VA)
Virginia Union U (VA)
Virginia Wesleyan Coll (VA)
Viterbo U (WI)
Wagner Coll (NY)
Waldorf Coll (IA)
Warner Pacific Coll (OR)
Wartburg Coll (IA)
Washburn U (KS)
Washington Adventist U (MD)
Washington State U (WA)
Washington U in St. Louis (MO)
Wayland Baptist U (TX)
Waynesburg U (PA)
Wayne State Coll (NE)
Wayne State U (MI)
Weber State U (UT)
Webster U (MO)
Wells Coll (NY)
West Chester U of Pennsylvania (PA)
Western Carolina U (NC)
Western Connecticut State U (CT)
Western Illinois U (IL)
Western Kentucky U (KY)
Western Michigan U (MI)
Western New England Coll (MA)
Western Washington U (WA)
Westfield State Coll (MA)
West Liberty U (WV)
Westminster Coll (MO)
Westminster Coll (UT)
Westmont Coll (CA)
West Virginia State U (WV)
West Virginia U (WV)
West Virginia Wesleyan Coll (WV)
Wheaton Coll (IL)
Wheeling Jesuit U (WV)
Wheelock Coll (MA)
Wichita State U (KS)
Widener U (PA)
Wilkes U (PA)
William Jewell Coll (MO)
William Paterson U of New Jersey (NJ)
William Penn U (IA)
Wilmington Coll (OH)
Wilson Coll (PA)
Wingate U (NC)
Winona State U (MN)
Winston-Salem State U (NC)
Winthrop U (SC)
Worcester State Coll (MA)
Wright State U (OH)
Xavier U (OH)
Xavier U of Louisiana (LA)
Yeshiva U (NY)
York Coll (NE)
York Coll of Pennsylvania (PA)
York Coll of the City U of New York (NY)
York U (ON, Canada)
Youngstown State U (OH)

EMERGENCY MEDICAL TECHNOLOGY (EMT PARAMEDIC)

Creighton U (NE)
The George Washington U (DC)
Indiana U Bloomington (IN)
Indiana U East (IN)
Indiana U Kokomo (IN)
U of Maryland, Baltimore County (MD)
U of Minnesota, Twin Cities Campus (MN)
Western Carolina U (NC)

ENERGY MANAGEMENT AND SYSTEMS TECHNOLOGY

Ferris State U (MI)
Illinois State U (IL)
Lamar U (TX)
Pennsylvania Coll of Technology (PA)
State U of New York Coll of Technology at Canton (NY)

ENGINEERING

The American U in Dubai (United Arab Emirates)
Arizona State U (AZ)
Arkansas State U—Jonesboro (AR)
Auburn U (AL)
Ball State U (IN)
Barry U (FL)
Bates Coll (ME)
Baylor U (TX)
Beloit Coll (WI)
Bethany Lutheran Coll (MN)
Bethel Coll (IN)
Boston U (MA)
Buffalo State Coll, State U of New York (NY)
California Baptist U (CA)
California State Polytechnic U, Pomona (CA)
California State U, Fullerton (CA)
California State U, Long Beach (CA)
California State U, Los Angeles (CA)
California State U, Northridge (CA)
Calvin Coll (MI)
Cape Breton U (NS, Canada)
Case Western Reserve U (OH)
Claremont McKenna Coll (CA)
Clarkson U (NY)
Clark U (MA)
Cleveland State U (OH)
Coll of Staten Island of the City U of New York (NY)
Colorado School of Mines (CO)
Colorado State U–Pueblo (CO)
Cooper Union for the Advancement of Science and Art (NY)
Cornell U (NY)
Dartmouth Coll (NH)
Dordt Coll (IA)
Drexel U (PA)
East Carolina U (NC)
Eastern Nazarene Coll (MA)
Elizabethtown Coll (PA)
Elon U (NC)
Florida Inst of Technology (FL)
Franklin W. Olin Coll of Eng (MA)
Frostburg State U (MD)
Gallaudet U (DC)
Geneva Coll (PA)
George Fox U (OR)
The George Washington U (DC)
Gonzaga U (WA)
Grand Valley State U (MI)
Harvard U (MA)
Harvey Mudd Coll (CA)
Hiram Coll (OH)
Hope Coll (MI)
Indiana U–Purdue U Indianapolis (IN)
Indiana U South Bend (IN)
Inter American U of Puerto Rico, Bayamón Campus (PR)
Inter American U of Puerto Rico, San Germán Campus (PR)
Iowa State U of Science and Technology (IA)
James Madison U (VA)
John Brown U (AR)
The Johns Hopkins U (MD)
Juniata Coll (PA)
King Coll (TN)
Lafayette Coll (PA)
Lakehead U (ON, Canada)
LeTourneau U (TX)
Liberty U (VA)
Loyola U Maryland (MD)
Lubbock Christian U (TX)
Manhattan Coll (NY)
Marshall U (WV)
Maryville Coll (TN)
Massachusetts Maritime Acad (MA)
McNeese State U (LA)
Memorial U of Newfoundland (NL, Canada)
Mercer U (GA)
Messiah Coll (PA)
Miami U (OH)
Michigan State U (MI)
Michigan Technological U (MI)
Mills Coll (CA)
Milwaukee School of Eng (WI)
Missouri U of Science and Technology (MO)
Montana State U (MT)
Montana Tech of The U of Montana (MT)
Morehouse Coll (GA)
Mount Holyoke Coll (MA)
New Mexico Highlands U (NM)
North Carolina State U (NC)
Northeastern U (MA)
Northern Arizona U (AZ)
Northland Coll (WI)
Northwestern Coll (MN)
Nova Scotia Ag Coll (NS, Canada)
Oakwood U (AL)
Oglethorpe U (GA)
Ohio Northern U (OH)
The Ohio State U (OH)
Oklahoma Christian U (OK)
Oral Roberts U (OK)
Pacific Lutheran U (WA)
Pitzer Coll (CA)
Purdue U (IN)
Purdue U Calumet (IN)
Queen's U at Kingston (ON, Canada)
Rensselaer Polytechnic Inst (NY)
Robert Morris U (PA)
Rochester Inst of Technology (NY)
Russell Sage Coll (NY)
Rutgers, The State U of New Jersey, Camden (NJ)
Rutgers, The State U of New Jersey, Newark (NJ)
Saint Anselm Coll (NH)
St. Cloud State U (MN)
Saint Francis U (PA)
Saint Mary's Coll of California (CA)
Saint Vincent Coll (PA)
San Diego State U (CA)
San Jose State U (CA)
Santa Clara U (CA)
Schreiner U (TX)
Seattle Pacific U (WA)
Seton Hill U (PA)
Spelman Coll (GA)
Stanford U (CA)
State U of New York at Binghamton (NY)
Stony Brook U, State U of New York (NY)
Swarthmore Coll (PA)
Texas Christian U (TX)
Texas Tech U (TX)
Trinity Coll (CT)
Tufts U (MA)
United States Air Force Acad (CO)
United States Naval Acad (MD)
U at Buffalo, the State U of New York (NY)
The U of Akron (OH)
U of Alberta (AB, Canada)
The U of Arizona (AZ)
U of California, Irvine (CA)
U of California, San Diego (CA)
U of Cincinnati (OH)
U of Delaware (DE)
U of Denver (CO)
U of Georgia (GA)
U of Hartford (CT)
U of Illinois at Urbana–Champaign (IL)
The U of Iowa (IA)
U of Louisville (KY)
U of Mary (ND)
U of Maryland, Baltimore County (MD)
U of Maryland, Coll Park (MD)
U of Massachusetts Amherst (MA)
U of Michigan (MI)
U of Mississippi (MS)
U of Missouri–Kansas City (MO)
U of Nebraska–Lincoln (NE)
U of New Brunswick Fredericton (NB, Canada)
U of New Haven (CT)
The U of North Carolina at Asheville (NC)
U of Oklahoma (OK)
U of Pittsburgh (PA)
U of Portland (OR)
U of Regina (SK, Canada)
U of Southern Indiana (IN)
U of South Florida (FL)
The U of Tennessee at Chattanooga (TN)
The U of Tennessee at Martin (TN)
The U of Toledo (OH)
U of Toronto (ON, Canada)
U of Utah (UT)
U of Virginia (VA)
U of Washington (WA)
U of Windsor (ON, Canada)
U of Wisconsin–Madison (WI)
U of Wisconsin–Milwaukee (WI)
Vaughn Coll of Aeronautics and Technology (NY)
Wake Forest U (NC)
Wartburg Coll (IA)
Washington U in St. Louis (MO)
Wells Coll (NY)
Widener U (PA)
Wilkes U (PA)
Winona State U (MN)
Wright State U (OH)
York U (ON, Canada)
Youngstown State U (OH)

ENGINEERING/INDUSTRIAL MANAGEMENT

California State U, Chico (CA)
California State U, Long Beach (CA)
Claremont McKenna Coll (CA)
Clarkson U (NY)
Clemson U (SC)
Columbia U (NY)
Eastern Michigan U (MI)
Farmingdale State Coll (NY)
Fort Lewis Coll (CO)
Illinois Inst of Technology (IL)
John Brown U (AR)
Lake Superior State U (MI)
Lawrence Technological U (MI)
Massachusetts Maritime Acad (MA)
Miami U (OH)
Miami U Hamilton (OH)
Middle Tennessee State U (TN)
Missouri State U (MO)
Missouri U of Science and Technology (MO)
Saginaw Valley State U (MI)
Saint Louis U (MO)
South Dakota School of Mines and Technology (SD)
South Dakota State U (SD)
State U of New York Coll of Technology at Canton (NY)
Stevens Inst of Technology (NJ)
Sweet Briar Coll (VA)
United States Military Acad (NY)
U of Illinois at Chicago (IL)
U of Massachusetts Lowell (MA)
U of Minnesota, Crookston (MN)
U of Portland (OR)
The U of Tennessee at Chattanooga (TN)
U of the Incarnate Word (TX)
U of the Pacific (CA)
U of Vermont (VT)
Western Michigan U (MI)
Widener U (PA)
Wilkes U (PA)
Worcester Polytechnic Inst (MA)

ENGINEERING MECHANICS

Clemson U (SC)
Cleveland State U (OH)
Columbia U (NY)
Dordt Coll (IA)
Fairfield U (CT)
The Johns Hopkins U (MD)
Lehigh U (PA)
Lipscomb U (TN)
Michigan Technological U (MI)
United States Air Force Acad (CO)
U of Cincinnati (OH)
U of Illinois at Urbana–Champaign (IL)
U of Michigan–Flint (MI)
U of Windsor (ON, Canada)
U of Wisconsin–Madison (WI)
Virginia Polytechnic Inst and State U (VA)
Western Illinois U (IL)
Worcester Polytechnic Inst (MA)

ENGINEERING PHYSICS

Adams State Coll (CO)
Arkansas Tech U (AR)
Augustana Coll (IL)
Augustana Coll (SD)
Bemidji State U (MN)
Bradley U (IL)
Butler U (IN)
Carroll U (WI)
Case Western Reserve U (OH)
Christian Brothers U (TN)
Colorado School of Mines (CO)
Colorado State U (CO)
Columbia U (NY)
Cornell U (NY)
Dartmouth Coll (NH)
Delaware State U (DE)
Eastern Michigan U (MI)
Eastern Nazarene Coll (MA)
Embry-Riddle Aeronautical U (FL)
Fairfield U (CT)
Fordham U (NY)
Fort Lewis Coll (CO)
Jacksonville U (FL)
John Carroll U (OH)
Juniata Coll (PA)
Kettering U (MI)
Lehigh U (PA)
Loras Coll (IA)
Miami U (OH)
Miami U Hamilton (OH)
Michigan Technological U (MI)

INDEXES

ENGINEERING RELATED

ENGINEERING-RELATED TECHNOLOGIES

ENGINEERING SCIENCE

ENGINEERING TECHNOLOGIES RELATED

ENGINEERING TECHNOLOGY

ENGLISH

The Colorado Coll (CO)
Colorado State U (CO)
Colorado State U–Pueblo (CO)
Columbia Coll (MO)
Columbia Coll (SC)
Columbia U (NY)
Columbia U, School of General Studies (NY)
Columbus State U (GA)
Concordia Coll (MN)
Concordia U (CA)
Concordia U (QC, Canada)
Concordia U Chicago (IL)
Concordia U Coll of Alberta (AB, Canada)
Concordia U, St. Paul (MN)
Concordia U Texas (TX)
Concordia U Wisconsin (WI)
Concord U (WV)
Connecticut Coll (CT)
Converse Coll (SC)
Coppin State U (MD)
Corban U (OR)
Cornell Coll (IA)
Cornell U (NY)
Cornerstone U (MI)
Covenant Coll (GA)
Crandall U (NB, Canada)
Creighton U (NE)
Crichton Coll (TN)
Crown Coll (MN)
Culver-Stockton Coll (MO)
Cumberland U (TN)
Curry Coll (MA)
Daemen Coll (NY)
Dakota Wesleyan U (SD)
Dallas Baptist U (TX)
Dalton State Coll (GA)
Dana Coll (NE)
Dartmouth Coll (NH)
Davidson Coll (NC)
Defiance Coll (OH)
Delaware State U (DE)
Delaware Valley Coll (PA)
Delta State U (MS)
Denison U (OH)
DePaul U (IL)
DePauw U (IN)
DeSales U (PA)
Dickinson Coll (PA)
Dickinson State U (ND)
Dillard U (LA)
Dixie State Coll of Utah (UT)
Doane Coll (NE)
Dominican Coll (NY)
Dominican U (IL)
Dominican U of California (CA)
Dordt Coll (IA)
Dowling Coll (NY)
Drake U (IA)
Drew U (NJ)
Drury U (MO)
Duke U (NC)
Duquesne U (PA)
D'Youville Coll (NY)
Earlham Coll (IN)
East Carolina U (NC)
East Central U (OK)
Eastern Connecticut State U (CT)
Eastern Illinois U (IL)
Eastern Mennonite U (VA)
Eastern Michigan U (MI)
Eastern Nazarene Coll (MA)
Eastern New Mexico U (NM)
Eastern Washington U (WA)
East Stroudsburg U of Pennsylvania (PA)
East Tennessee State U (TN)
East Texas Baptist U (TX)
East-West U (IL)
Eckerd Coll (FL)
Edgewood Coll (WI)
Edinboro U of Pennsylvania (PA)
Edward Waters Coll (FL)
Elizabeth City State U (NC)
Elizabethtown Coll (PA)
Elmhurst Coll (IL)
Elmira Coll (NY)
Elon U (NC)
Emmanuel Coll (GA)
Emmanuel Coll (MA)
Emory & Henry Coll (VA)
Emory U (GA)
Emporia State U (KS)
Endicott Coll (MA)
Erskine Coll (SC)
Eugene Lang Coll The New School for Liberal Arts (NY)
Evangel U (MO)
The Evergreen State Coll (WA)
Fairfield U (CT)
Fairleigh Dickinson U, Coll at Florham (NJ)
Fairleigh Dickinson U, Metropolitan Campus (NJ)
Fairmont State U (WV)
Faulkner U (AL)
Fayetteville State U (NC)
Felician Coll (NJ)
Ferrum Coll (VA)
Fisk U (TN)
Fitchburg State Coll (MA)
Flagler Coll (FL)
Florida Ag and Mech U (FL)
Florida Atlantic U (FL)
Florida Gulf Coast U (FL)
Florida Intl U (FL)
Florida Southern Coll (FL)
Florida State U (FL)
Fontbonne U (MO)
Fordham U (NY)
Fort Hays State U (KS)
Fort Lewis Coll (CO)
Framingham State Coll (MA)
Franciscan U of Steubenville (OH)
Francis Marion U (SC)
Franklin & Marshall Coll (PA)
Franklin Coll (IN)
Franklin Pierce U (NH)
Freed-Hardeman U (TN)
Free Will Baptist Bible Coll (TN)
Friends U (KS)
Frostburg State U (MD)
Furman U (SC)
Gallaudet U (DC)
Gardner-Webb U (NC)
Geneva Coll (PA)
George Fox U (OR)
George Mason U (VA)
Georgetown Coll (KY)
Georgetown U (DC)
The George Washington U (DC)
Georgia Coll & State U (GA)
Georgian Court U (NJ)
Georgia Southern U (GA)
Georgia State U (GA)
Gettysburg Coll (PA)
Glenville State Coll (WV)
Gonzaga U (WA)
Gordon Coll (MA)
Goshen Coll (IN)
Goucher Coll (MD)
Governors State U (IL)
Grace Coll (IN)
Graceland U (IA)
Grambling State U (LA)
Grand Valley State U (MI)
Grand View U (IA)
Green Mountain Coll (VT)
Greensboro Coll (NC)
Greenville Coll (IL)
Grinnell Coll (IA)
Grove City Coll (PA)
Guilford Coll (NC)
Gustavus Adolphus Coll (MN)
Gwynedd-Mercy Coll (PA)
Hamilton Coll (NY)
Hamline U (MN)
Hampden-Sydney Coll (VA)
Hampshire Coll (MA)
Hampton U (VA)
Hannibal-LaGrange Coll (MO)
Hanover Coll (IN)
Harding U (AR)
Hardin-Simmons U (TX)
Hartwick Coll (NY)
Harvard U (MA)
Haverford Coll (PA)
Hawai'i Pacific U (HI)
Heidelberg U (OH)
Henderson State U (AR)
Hendrix Coll (AR)
High Point U (NC)
Hilbert Coll (NY)
Hillsdale Coll (MI)
Hiram Coll (OH)
Hofstra U (NY)
Hollins U (VA)
Holy Family U (PA)
Holy Names U (CA)
Hood Coll (MD)
Hope Coll (MI)
Houghton Coll (NY)
Houston Baptist U (TX)
Howard Payne U (TX)
Humboldt State U (CA)
Hunter Coll of the City U of New York (NY)
Huntingdon Coll (AL)
Huntington U (IN)
Huston-Tillotson U (TX)
Idaho State U (ID)
Illinois Coll (IL)
Illinois State U (IL)
Immaculata U (PA)
Indiana State U (IN)
Indiana U Bloomington (IN)
Indiana U East (IN)
Indiana U Kokomo (IN)
Indiana U Northwest (IN)
Indiana U of Pennsylvania (PA)
Indiana U–Purdue U Fort Wayne (IN)
Indiana U–Purdue U Indianapolis (IN)
Indiana U South Bend (IN)
Indiana U Southeast (IN)
Indiana Wesleyan U (IN)
Inter American U of Puerto Rico, San Germán Campus (PR)
Iona Coll (NY)
Iowa State U of Science and Technology (IA)
Iowa Wesleyan Coll (IA)
Ithaca Coll (NY)
Jackson State U (MS)
Jacksonville State U (AL)
Jacksonville U (FL)
James Madison U (VA)
Jamestown Coll (ND)
Jarvis Christian Coll (TX)
John Brown U (AR)
John Carroll U (OH)
John Jay Coll of Criminal Justice of the City U of New York (NY)
The Johns Hopkins U (MD)
Johnson C. Smith U (NC)
Johnson State Coll (VT)
Judson Coll (AL)
Judson U (IL)
Juniata Coll (PA)
Kalamazoo Coll (MI)
Kansas State U (KS)
Kean U (NJ)
Keene State Coll (NH)
Kennesaw State U (GA)
Kent State U (OH)
Kent State U at Stark (OH)
Kent State U at Trumbull (OH)
Kentucky State U (KY)
Kentucky Wesleyan Coll (KY)
Kenyon Coll (OH)
Keuka Coll (NY)
King Coll (TN)
King's Coll (PA)
The King's U Coll (AB, Canada)
Knox Coll (IL)
Kutztown U of Pennsylvania (PA)
Lafayette Coll (PA)
LaGrange Coll (GA)
Lake Erie Coll (OH)
Lake Forest Coll (IL)
Lakehead U (ON, Canada)
Lakeland Coll (WI)
Lake Superior State U (MI)
Lamar U (TX)
Lane Coll (TN)
La Roche Coll (PA)
La Salle U (PA)
Lasell Coll (MA)
La Sierra U (CA)
Laurentian U (ON, Canada)
Lawrence Technological U (MI)
Lawrence U (WI)
Lebanon Valley Coll (PA)
Lees-McRae Coll (NC)
Lee U (TN)
Lehigh U (PA)
Lehman Coll of the City U of New York (NY)
Le Moyne Coll (NY)
Lesley U (MA)
LeTourneau U (TX)
Lewis & Clark Coll (OR)
Lewis-Clark State Coll (ID)
Lewis U (IL)
Liberty U (VA)
Limestone Coll (SC)
Lincoln Memorial U (TN)
Lincoln U (MO)
Lincoln U (PA)
Lindenwood U (MO)
Lindsey Wilson Coll (KY)
Linfield Coll (OR)
Lipscomb U (TN)
Lock Haven U of Pennsylvania (PA)
Long Island U, Brooklyn Campus (NY)
Long Island U, C.W. Post Campus (NY)
Longwood U (VA)
Loras Coll (IA)
Louisiana Coll (LA)
Louisiana State U and Ag and Mech Coll (LA)
Louisiana State U in Shreveport (LA)
Louisiana Tech U (LA)
Lourdes Coll (OH)
Loyola Marymount U (CA)
Loyola U Chicago (IL)
Loyola U Maryland (MD)
Loyola U New Orleans (LA)
Lubbock Christian U (TX)
Luther Coll (IA)
Lycoming Coll (PA)
Lynchburg Coll (VA)
Lynn U (FL)
Lyon Coll (AR)
Macalester Coll (MN)
Madonna U (MI)
Maharishi U of Management (IA)
Malone U (OH)
Manchester Coll (IN)
Manhattan Coll (NY)
Manhattanville Coll (NY)
Mansfield U of Pennsylvania (PA)
Maranatha Baptist Bible Coll (WI)
Marian U (IN)
Marian U (WI)
Marietta Coll (OH)
Marist Coll (NY)
Marlboro Coll (VT)
Marquette U (WI)
Marshall U (WV)
Mars Hill Coll (NC)
Mary Baldwin Coll (VA)
Marylhurst U (OR)
Marymount Manhattan Coll (NY)
Marymount U (VA)
Maryville Coll (TN)
Maryville U of Saint Louis (MO)
Marywood U (PA)
Massachusetts Coll of Liberal Arts (MA)
Massachusetts Inst of Technology (MA)
The Master's Coll and Sem (CA)
Mayville State U (ND)
McDaniel Coll (MD)
McKendree U (IL)
McMurry U (TX)
McNeese State U (LA)
McPherson Coll (KS)
Medaille Coll (NY)
Memorial U of Newfoundland (NL, Canada)
Mercer U (GA)
Mercy Coll (NY)
Mercyhurst Coll (PA)
Meredith Coll (NC)
Merrimack Coll (MA)
Messiah Coll (PA)
Methodist U (NC)
Metropolitan State Coll of Denver (CO)
Miami U (OH)
Miami U Hamilton (OH)
Michigan State U (MI)
Michigan Technological U (MI)
MidAmerica Nazarene U (KS)
Mid-Continent U (KY)
Middlebury Coll (VT)
Middle Tennessee State U (TN)
Midway Coll (KY)
Midwestern State U (TX)
Millersville U of Pennsylvania (PA)
Milligan Coll (TN)
Millikin U (IL)
Millsaps Coll (MS)
Mills Coll (CA)
Minnesota State U Mankato (MN)
Minnesota State U Moorhead (MN)
Minot State U (ND)
Misericordia U (PA)
Mississippi Coll (MS)
Mississippi State U (MS)
Mississippi U for Women (MS)
Mississippi Valley State U (MS)
Missouri Baptist U (MO)
Missouri Southern State U (MO)
Missouri State U (MO)
Missouri U of Science and Technology (MO)
Missouri Western State U (MO)
Molloy Coll (NY)
Monmouth Coll (IL)
Monmouth U (NJ)
Montana State U (MT)
Montana State U Billings (MT)
Montclair State U (NJ)
Moravian Coll (PA)
Morehead State U (KY)
Morehouse Coll (GA)
Morningside Coll (IA)
Morris Coll (SC)
Mount Allison U (NB, Canada)
Mount Aloysius Coll (PA)
Mount Holyoke Coll (MA)
Mount Ida Coll (MA)
Mount Marty Coll (SD)
Mount Mary Coll (WI)
Mount Mercy Coll (IA)
Mount Olive Coll (NC)
Mount Saint Mary Coll (NY)
Mount St. Mary's Coll (CA)
Mount St. Mary's U (MD)
Mount Vernon Nazarene U (OH)
Muhlenberg Coll (PA)
Murray State U (KY)
Naropa U (CO)
National U (CA)
Nazareth Coll of Rochester (NY)
Nebraska Wesleyan U (NE)
Neumann U (PA)
Nevada State Coll at Henderson (NV)
Newberry Coll (SC)
New Coll of Florida (FL)
New England Coll (NH)
New Jersey City U (NJ)
Newman U (KS)
New Mexico Highlands U (NM)
New Mexico State U (NM)
New York U (NY)
Niagara U (NY)
Nicholls State U (LA)
Nichols Coll (MA)
Nipissing U (ON, Canada)
Norfolk State U (VA)
North Carolina Central U (NC)
North Carolina State U (NC)
North Central Coll (IL)
North Dakota State U (ND)
Northeastern Illinois U (IL)
Northeastern State U (OK)
Northeastern U (MA)
Northern Arizona U (AZ)
Northern Kentucky U (KY)
Northern Michigan U (MI)
Northern State U (SD)
North Georgia Coll & State U (GA)
North Greenville U (SC)
Northwest Christian U (OR)
Northwestern Coll (IA)
Northwestern Coll (MN)
Northwestern Oklahoma State U (OK)
Northwestern State U of Louisiana (LA)
Northwest Missouri State U (MO)
Northwest Nazarene U (ID)
Northwest U (WA)
Notre Dame de Namur U (CA)
Nova Southeastern U (FL)
Nyack Coll (NY)
Oakland U (MI)
Oakwood U (AL)
Oberlin Coll (OH)
Occidental Coll (CA)
Oglethorpe U (GA)
Ohio Dominican U (OH)
The Ohio State U (OH)
The Ohio State U at Lima (OH)
The Ohio State U at Marion (OH)
The Ohio State U–Mansfield Campus (OH)
The Ohio State U–Newark Campus (OH)
Ohio U (OH)
Ohio Wesleyan U (OH)
Oklahoma Christian U (OK)
Oklahoma City U (OK)
Oklahoma Panhandle State U (OK)
Oklahoma State U (OK)
Oklahoma Wesleyan U (OK)
Old Dominion U (VA)
Oregon State U (OR)
Ottawa U (KS)
Ouachita Baptist U (AR)
Our Lady of the Lake U of San Antonio (TX)
Pace U (NY)
Pacific Lutheran U (WA)
Pacific Union Coll (CA)
Paine Coll (GA)
Park U (MO)
Peace Coll (NC)
Penn State Abington (PA)
Penn State Altoona (PA)
Penn State Beaver (PA)
Penn State Berks (PA)
Penn State Brandywine (PA)
Penn State DuBois (PA)
Penn State Erie, The Behrend Coll (PA)
Penn State Fayette, The Eberly Campus (PA)
Penn State Greater Allegheny (PA)
Penn State Harrisburg (PA)
Penn State Hazleton (PA)
Penn State Lehigh Valley (PA)
Penn State Mont Alto (PA)
Penn State New Kensington (PA)
Penn State Schuylkill (PA)
Penn State Shenango (PA)
Penn State U Park (PA)
Penn State Wilkes-Barre (PA)
Penn State Worthington Scranton (PA)
Penn State York (PA)
Pepperdine U, Malibu (CA)
Peru State Coll (NE)
Piedmont Coll (GA)
Pikeville Coll (KY)
Pittsburg State U (KS)
Pitzer Coll (CA)
Plymouth State U (NH)
Point Park U (PA)
Pomona Coll (CA)
Pontifical Catholic U of Puerto Rico (PR)
Pontifical Coll Josephinum (OH)
Portland State U (OR)
Post U (CT)
Prairie View A&M U (TX)
Presbyterian Coll (SC)
Prescott Coll (AZ)
Princeton U (NJ)
Principia Coll (IL)
Providence Coll (RI)
Purdue U (IN)
Purdue U Calumet (IN)
Purdue U North Central (IN)

Queens Coll of the City U of New York (NY)
Queen's U at Kingston (ON, Canada)
Queens U of Charlotte (NC)
Quincy U (IL)
Quinnipiac U (CT)
Radford U (VA)
Randolph Coll (VA)
Randolph-Macon Coll (VA)
Redeemer U Coll (ON, Canada)
Reed Coll (OR)
Regent U (VA)
Regis Coll (MA)
Reinhardt Coll (GA)
Rhode Island Coll (RI)
Rhodes Coll (TN)
Rice U (TX)
The Richard Stockton Coll of New Jersey (NJ)
Rider U (NJ)
Ripon Coll (WI)
Rivier Coll (NH)
Roanoke Coll (VA)
Robert Morris U (PA)
Roberts Wesleyan Coll (NY)
Rochester Coll (MI)
Rockford Coll (IL)
Rockhurst U (MO)
Rocky Mountain Coll (MT)
Rollins Coll (FL)
Roosevelt U (IL)
Rosemont Coll (PA)
Rowan U (NJ)
Royal Military Coll of Canada (ON, Canada)
Russell Sage Coll (NY)
Rutgers, The State U of New Jersey, Camden (NJ)
Rutgers, The State U of New Jersey, Newark (NJ)
Rutgers, The State U of New Jersey, New Brunswick (NJ)
Sacred Heart U (CT)
Saginaw Valley State U (MI)
St. Ambrose U (IA)
St. Andrews Presbyterian Coll (NC)
Saint Anselm Coll (NH)
Saint Augustine's Coll (NC)
St. Bonaventure U (NY)
St. Catherine U (MN)
St. Cloud State U (MN)
St. Edward's U (TX)
St. Francis Coll (NY)
Saint Francis U (PA)
St. Francis Xavier U (NS, Canada)
St. John Fisher Coll (NY)
Saint John's U (MN)
St. John's U (NY)
Saint Joseph Coll (CT)
St. Joseph's Coll, Long Island Campus (NY)
St. Joseph's Coll, New York (NY)
Saint Joseph's U (PA)
St. Lawrence U (NY)
Saint Leo U (FL)
Saint Louis U (MO)
Saint Martin's U (WA)
Saint Mary-of-the-Woods Coll (IN)
Saint Mary's Coll of California (CA)
St. Mary's Coll of Maryland (MD)
St. Mary's U (TX)
Saint Mary's U of Minnesota (MN)
Saint Michael's Coll (VT)
St. Norbert Coll (WI)
St. Olaf Coll (MN)
Saint Paul's Coll (VA)
St. Thomas Aquinas Coll (NY)
St. Thomas U (FL)
St. Thomas U (NB, Canada)
Saint Vincent Coll (PA)
Saint Xavier U (IL)
Salem Coll (NC)
Salem State Coll (MA)
Salisbury U (MD)
Salve Regina U (RI)
Samford U (AL)
Sam Houston State U (TX)
San Diego Christian Coll (CA)
San Diego State U (CA)
San Francisco State U (CA)
San Jose State U (CA)
Santa Clara U (CA)
Sarah Lawrence Coll (NY)
Savannah State U (GA)
Schreiner U (TX)
Scripps Coll (CA)
Seattle Pacific U (WA)
Seattle U (WA)
Seton Hall U (NJ)
Seton Hill U (PA)
Sewanee: The U of the South (TN)
Shawnee State U (OH)
Shaw U (NC)
Shenandoah U (VA)
Shepherd U (WV)
Shippensburg U of Pennsylvania (PA)
Shorter U (GA)
Siena Coll (NY)
Siena Heights U (MI)
Silver Lake Coll (WI)
Simmons Coll (MA)
Simon Fraser U (BC, Canada)
Simpson Coll (IA)
Simpson U (CA)
Skidmore Coll (NY)
Slippery Rock U of Pennsylvania (PA)
Smith Coll (MA)
Sonoma State U (CA)
South Carolina State U (SC)
South Dakota State U (SD)
Southeastern Baptist Theological Sem (NC)
Southeastern Louisiana U (LA)
Southeastern Oklahoma State U (OK)
Southeastern U (FL)
Southeast Missouri State U (MO)
Southern Adventist U (TN)
Southern Arkansas U–Magnolia (AR)
Southern Connecticut State U (CT)
Southern Illinois U Carbondale (IL)
Southern Illinois U Edwardsville (IL)
Southern Methodist U (TX)
Southern New Hampshire U (NH)
Southern Oregon U (OR)
Southern U and Ag and Mech Coll (LA)
Southern U at New Orleans (LA)
Southern Utah U (UT)
Southern Vermont Coll (VT)
Southern Wesleyan U (SC)
Southwest Baptist U (MO)
Southwestern Adventist U (TX)
Southwestern Assemblies of God U (TX)
Southwestern Coll (KS)
Southwestern Oklahoma State U (OK)
Southwestern U (TX)
Southwest Minnesota State U (MN)
Spelman Coll (GA)
Spring Arbor U (MI)
Spring Hill Coll (AL)
Stanford U (CA)
State U of New York at Binghamton (NY)
State U of New York at Fredonia (NY)
State U of New York at New Paltz (NY)
State U of New York at Oswego (NY)
State U of New York at Plattsburgh (NY)
State U of New York Coll at Cortland (NY)
State U of New York Coll at Geneseo (NY)
State U of New York Coll at Oneonta (NY)
State U of New York Coll at Potsdam (NY)
Stephen F. Austin State U (TX)
Stephens Coll (MO)
Sterling Coll (KS)
Stetson U (FL)
Stevens Inst of Technology (NJ)
Stevenson U (MD)
Stillman Coll (AL)
Stonehill Coll (MA)
Stony Brook U, State U of New York (NY)
Suffolk U (MA)
Sul Ross State U (TX)
Susquehanna U (PA)
Swarthmore Coll (PA)
Sweet Briar Coll (VA)
Syracuse U (NY)
Tabor Coll (KS)
Talladega Coll (AL)
Tarleton State U (TX)
Taylor U (IN)
Temple U (PA)
Tennessee Technological U (TN)
Tennessee Wesleyan Coll (TN)
Texas A&M Intl U (TX)
Texas A&M U (TX)
Texas A&M U–Commerce (TX)
Texas A&M U–Corpus Christi (TX)
Texas A&M U–Kingsville (TX)
Texas Christian U (TX)
Texas Coll (TX)
Texas Lutheran U (TX)
Texas Southern U (TX)
Texas State U–San Marcos (TX)
Texas Tech U (TX)
Texas Wesleyan U (TX)
Texas Woman's U (TX)
Thiel Coll (PA)
Thomas Edison State Coll (NJ)
Thomas More Coll (KY)
Thompson Rivers U (BC, Canada)
Tiffin U (OH)
Towson U (MD)
Transylvania U (KY)
Trent U (ON, Canada)
Trevecca Nazarene U (TN)
Trinity Christian Coll (IL)
Trinity Coll (CT)
Trinity U (TX)
Troy U (AL)
Truett-McConnell Coll (GA)
Truman State U (MO)
Tufts U (MA)
Tulane U (LA)
Tusculum Coll (TN)
Tuskegee U (AL)
Union Coll (NE)
Union Coll (NY)
Union U (TN)
United States Air Force Acad (CO)
United States Naval Acad (MD)
U at Albany, State U of New York (NY)
U at Buffalo, the State U of New York (NY)
The U of Akron (OH)
The U of Alabama (AL)
The U of Alabama at Birmingham (AL)
The U of Alabama in Huntsville (AL)
U of Alaska Anchorage (AK)
U of Alaska Fairbanks (AK)
U of Alberta (AB, Canada)
The U of Arizona (AZ)
U of Arkansas (AR)
U of Arkansas at Fort Smith (AR)
U of Arkansas at Little Rock (AR)
U of Arkansas at Monticello (AR)
U of Arkansas at Pine Bluff (AR)
U of Baltimore (MD)
U of Bridgeport (CT)
The U of British Columbia (BC, Canada)
The U of British Columbia–Okanagan (BC, Canada)
U of California, Berkeley (CA)
U of California, Davis (CA)
U of California, Irvine (CA)
U of California, Los Angeles (CA)
U of California, Riverside (CA)
U of California, San Diego (CA)
U of California, Santa Barbara (CA)
U of Central Florida (FL)
U of Central Missouri (MO)
U of Central Oklahoma (OK)
U of Charleston (WV)
U of Chicago (IL)
U of Cincinnati (OH)
U of Colorado at Boulder (CO)
U of Colorado at Colorado Springs (CO)
U of Colorado Denver (CO)
U of Connecticut (CT)
U of Dallas (TX)
U of Dayton (OH)
U of Delaware (DE)
U of Denver (CO)
U of Dubuque (IA)
U of Evansville (IN)
The U of Findlay (OH)
U of Florida (FL)
U of Georgia (GA)
U of Guam (GU)
U of Guelph (ON, Canada)
U of Hartford (CT)
U of Hawaii at Hilo (HI)
U of Hawaii at Manoa (HI)
U of Hawaii–West Oahu (HI)
U of Houston (TX)
U of Houston–Clear Lake (TX)
U of Houston–Downtown (TX)
U of Idaho (ID)
U of Illinois at Chicago (IL)
U of Illinois at Springfield (IL)
U of Illinois at Urbana–Champaign (IL)
U of Indianapolis (IN)
The U of Iowa (IA)
The U of Kansas (KS)
U of Kentucky (KY)
U of King's Coll (NS, Canada)
U of La Verne (CA)
U of Lethbridge (AB, Canada)
U of Louisiana at Monroe (LA)
U of Louisville (KY)
U of Maine (ME)
U of Maine at Farmington (ME)
U of Maine at Fort Kent (ME)
U of Maine at Machias (ME)
U of Maine at Presque Isle (ME)
U of Manitoba (MB, Canada)
U of Mary (ND)
U of Mary Hardin-Baylor (TX)
U of Maryland, Baltimore County (MD)
U of Maryland, Coll Park (MD)
U of Maryland Eastern Shore (MD)
U of Maryland U Coll (MD)
U of Mary Washington (VA)
U of Massachusetts Amherst (MA)
U of Massachusetts Boston (MA)
U of Massachusetts Dartmouth (MA)
U of Massachusetts Lowell (MA)
U of Memphis (TN)
U of Miami (FL)
U of Michigan–Dearborn (MI)
U of Michigan–Flint (MI)
U of Minnesota, Duluth (MN)
U of Minnesota, Twin Cities Campus (MN)
U of Mississippi (MS)
U of Missouri (MO)
U of Missouri–Kansas City (MO)
U of Missouri–St. Louis (MO)
U of Mobile (AL)
The U of Montana Western (MT)
U of Montevallo (AL)
U of Mount Union (OH)
U of Nebraska at Kearney (NE)
U of Nebraska at Omaha (NE)
U of Nebraska–Lincoln (NE)
U of Nevada, Las Vegas (NV)
U of Nevada, Reno (NV)
U of New Brunswick Fredericton (NB, Canada)
U of New England (ME)
U of New Hampshire (NH)
U of New Hampshire at Manchester (NH)
U of New Haven (CT)
U of New Mexico (NM)
U of New Orleans (LA)
U of North Alabama (AL)
The U of North Carolina at Asheville (NC)
The U of North Carolina at Chapel Hill (NC)
The U of North Carolina at Charlotte (NC)
The U of North Carolina at Greensboro (NC)
The U of North Carolina at Pembroke (NC)
The U of North Carolina Wilmington (NC)
U of North Dakota (ND)
U of Northern Colorado (CO)
U of Northern Iowa (IA)
U of North Florida (FL)
U of North Texas (TX)
U of Notre Dame (IN)
U of Oklahoma (OK)
U of Oregon (OR)
U of Ottawa (ON, Canada)
U of Pennsylvania (PA)
U of Pittsburgh (PA)
U of Pittsburgh at Bradford (PA)
U of Pittsburgh at Greensburg (PA)
U of Pittsburgh at Johnstown (PA)
U of Portland (OR)
U of Puerto Rico, Cayey U Coll (PR)
U of Puerto Rico, Río Piedras (PR)
U of Puget Sound (WA)
U of Redlands (CA)
U of Regina (SK, Canada)
U of Rhode Island (RI)
U of Richmond (VA)
U of Rio Grande (OH)
U of Rochester (NY)
U of St. Francis (IL)
U of Saint Mary (KS)
U of St. Thomas (MN)
U of St. Thomas (TX)
U of San Diego (CA)
U of San Francisco (CA)
U of Saskatchewan (SK, Canada)
U of Science and Arts of Oklahoma (OK)
The U of Scranton (PA)
U of South Alabama (AL)
U of South Carolina (SC)
U of South Carolina Aiken (SC)
U of South Carolina Beaufort (SC)
U of South Carolina Upstate (SC)
The U of South Dakota (SD)
U of Southern California (CA)
U of Southern Indiana (IN)
U of Southern Maine (ME)
U of Southern Mississippi (MS)
U of South Florida (FL)
U of Tampa (FL)
The U of Tennessee (TN)
The U of Tennessee at Chattanooga (TN)
The U of Tennessee at Martin (TN)
The U of Texas at Arlington (TX)
The U of Texas at Austin (TX)
The U of Texas at Brownsville (TX)
The U of Texas at El Paso (TX)
The U of Texas at San Antonio (TX)
The U of Texas at Tyler (TX)
The U of Texas of the Permian Basin (TX)
The U of Texas–Pan American (TX)
U of the Cumberlands (KY)
U of the Incarnate Word (TX)
U of the Ozarks (AR)
U of the Pacific (CA)
U of the Southwest (NM)
U of the Virgin Islands (VI)
U of the West (CA)
The U of Toledo (OH)
U of Toronto (ON, Canada)
U of Tulsa (OK)
U of Utah (UT)
U of Vermont (VT)
U of Virginia (VA)
The U of Virginia's Coll at Wise (VA)
U of Washington (WA)
U of Waterloo (ON, Canada)
The U of West Alabama (AL)
The U of Western Ontario (ON, Canada)
U of West Florida (FL)
U of West Georgia (GA)
U of Windsor (ON, Canada)
U of Wisconsin–Eau Claire (WI)
U of Wisconsin–Green Bay (WI)
U of Wisconsin–La Crosse (WI)
U of Wisconsin–Madison (WI)
U of Wisconsin–Milwaukee (WI)
U of Wisconsin–Oshkosh (WI)
U of Wisconsin–Parkside (WI)
U of Wisconsin–Platteville (WI)
U of Wisconsin–River Falls (WI)
U of Wisconsin–Stevens Point (WI)
U of Wisconsin–Superior (WI)
U of Wisconsin–Whitewater (WI)
U of Wyoming (WY)
Upper Iowa U (IA)
Ursinus Coll (PA)
Ursuline Coll (OH)
Utah State U (UT)
Utah Valley U (UT)
Utica Coll (NY)
Valdosta State U (GA)
Valley City State U (ND)
Valparaiso U (IN)
Vanderbilt U (TN)
Vanguard U of Southern California (CA)
Vassar Coll (NY)
Villanova U (PA)
Virginia Commonwealth U (VA)
Virginia Intermont Coll (VA)
Virginia Military Inst (VA)
Virginia Polytechnic Inst and State U (VA)
Virginia State U (VA)
Virginia Union U (VA)
Virginia Wesleyan Coll (VA)
Viterbo U (WI)
Voorhees Coll (SC)
Wabash Coll (IN)
Wagner Coll (NY)
Wake Forest U (NC)
Waldorf Coll (IA)
Walsh U (OH)
Warner Pacific Coll (OR)
Wartburg Coll (IA)
Washburn U (KS)
Washington Adventist U (MD)
Washington & Jefferson Coll (PA)
Washington and Lee U (VA)
Washington Coll (MD)
Washington State U (WA)
Washington U in St. Louis (MO)
Wayland Baptist U (TX)
Waynesburg U (PA)
Wayne State Coll (NE)
Wayne State U (MI)
Weber State U (UT)
Webster U (MO)
Wellesley Coll (MA)
Wells Coll (NY)
Wesleyan Coll (GA)
Wesleyan U (CT)
West Chester U of Pennsylvania (PA)
Western Carolina U (NC)
Western Connecticut State U (CT)
Western Illinois U (IL)
Western Kentucky U (KY)
Western Michigan U (MI)
Western New England Coll (MA)
Western Oregon U (OR)
Western State Coll of Colorado (CO)
Western Washington U (WA)
Westfield State Coll (MA)
West Liberty U (WV)
Westminster Coll (MO)
Westminster Coll (UT)
Westmont Coll (CA)
West Virginia State U (WV)
West Virginia U (WV)
West Virginia Wesleyan Coll (WV)
Wheaton Coll (IL)
Wheaton Coll (MA)
Wheeling Jesuit U (WV)
Whitman Coll (WA)
Whittier Coll (CA)
Wichita State U (KS)
Widener U (PA)
Wilfrid Laurier U (ON, Canada)

Wilkes U (PA)
Willamette U (OR)
William Jessup U (CA)
William Jewell Coll (MO)
William Paterson U of New Jersey (NJ)
Williams Coll (MA)
Wilmington Coll (OH)
Wilson Coll (PA)
Wingate U (NC)
Winona State U (MN)
Winston-Salem State U (NC)
Winthrop U (SC)
Wittenberg U (OH)
Wofford Coll (SC)
Worcester State Coll (MA)
Wright State U (OH)
Xavier U (OH)
Xavier U of Louisiana (LA)
Yale U (CT)
Yeshiva U (NY)
York Coll (NE)
York Coll of Pennsylvania (PA)
York Coll of the City U of New York (NY)
York U (ON, Canada)
Young Harris Coll (GA)
Youngstown State U (OH)

ENGLISH AS A SECOND/ FOREIGN LANGUAGE (TEACHING)

Aquinas Coll (MI)
Bethel U (MN)
Bridgewater Coll (VA)
Brigham Young U (UT)
Brigham Young U–Hawaii (HI)
Brock U (ON, Canada)
Calvin Coll (MI)
Concordia U (QC, Canada)
Concordia U, St. Paul (MN)
Concordia U Wisconsin (WI)
Crown Coll (MN)
Davis Coll (NY)
Doane Coll (NE)
Eastern Mennonite U (VA)
Gardner-Webb U (NC)
Goshen Coll (IN)
Hamline U (MN)
Hawai'i Pacific U (HI)
Houghton Coll (NY)
Howard Payne U (TX)
Inter American U of Puerto Rico, Aguadilla Campus (PR)
Inter American U of Puerto Rico, Arecibo Campus (PR)
Inter American U of Puerto Rico, Fajardo Campus (PR)
Inter American U of Puerto Rico, Guayama Campus (PR)
Inter American U of Puerto Rico, Ponce Campus (PR)
Inter American U of Puerto Rico, San Germán Campus (PR)
Le Moyne Coll (NY)
Liberty U (VA)
Lipscomb U (TN)
Maryville Coll (TN)
Multnomah U (OR)
Murray State U (KY)
Niagara U (NY)
Northwestern Coll (MN)
Northwest U (WA)
Nyack Coll (NY)
Oklahoma Christian U (OK)
Oklahoma Wesleyan U (OK)
Queens Coll of the City U of New York (NY)
Salisbury U (MD)
Stony Brook U, State U of New York (NY)
Tarleton State U (TX)
Texas Wesleyan U (TX)
Union U (TN)
U of Alberta (AB, Canada)
The U of British Columbia (BC, Canada)
U of Delaware (DE)
The U of Findlay (OH)
U of Nebraska–Lincoln (NE)
U of New Brunswick Fredericton (NB, Canada)
U of Northern Iowa (IA)
U of Puerto Rico at Humacao (PR)
U of Saskatchewan (SK, Canada)
U of Washington (WA)
U of Wisconsin–Oshkosh (WI)
U of Wisconsin–River Falls (WI)
Washington State U (WA)
William Penn U (IA)
Wright State U (OH)
York U (ON, Canada)

ENGLISH COMPOSITION

Aurora U (IL)
Baylor U (TX)
Bennington Coll (VT)
Brigham Young U (UT)
Columbia U, School of General Studies (NY)
DePauw U (IN)
Drury U (MO)
Eastern Michigan U (MI)
Florida Southern Coll (FL)
Gallaudet U (DC)
Georgia Southern U (GA)
Gettysburg Coll (PA)
Graceland U (IA)
Grand Valley State U (MI)
Indiana U–Purdue U Fort Wayne (IN)
Jamestown Coll (ND)
Lakeland Coll (WI)
La Roche Coll (PA)
Marian U (WI)
Marquette U (WI)
Miami U Hamilton (OH)
Northwest U (WA)
Oral Roberts U (OK)
St. Edward's U (TX)
Salem State Coll (MA)
U of Colorado Denver (CO)
U of Evansville (IN)
U of Illinois at Urbana–Champaign (IL)
U of Michigan–Flint (MI)
U of Nevada, Reno (NV)
Wartburg Coll (IA)
Wilberforce U (OH)

ENGLISH/FRENCH AS A SECOND/FOREIGN LANGUAGE (TEACHING) RELATED

U of Ottawa (ON, Canada)

ENGLISH LANGUAGE AND LITERATURE RELATED

Burlington Coll (VT)
Columbia Coll (SC)
Columbia U, School of General Studies (NY)
Dakota State U (SD)
Doane Coll (NE)
Drexel U (PA)
Duquesne U (PA)
Eastern Nazarene Coll (MA)
Emmanuel Coll (MA)
Ferris State U (MI)
Fort Lewis Coll (CO)
Harvard U (MA)
Hofstra U (NY)
Milligan Coll (TN)
Moravian Coll (PA)
Old Dominion U (VA)
Patrick Henry Coll (VA)
Pittsburg State U (KS)
Pontifical Catholic U of Puerto Rico (PR)
Rowan U (NJ)
Saint Leo U (FL)
Saint Mary-of-the-Woods Coll (IN)
Saint Mary's Coll of California (CA)
Sarah Lawrence Coll (NY)
Skidmore Coll (NY)
Spring Hill Coll (AL)
State U of New York at Binghamton (NY)
U of Alaska Southeast (AK)
U of Chicago (IL)
U of Maine at Augusta (ME)
U of Michigan (MI)
U of Nevada, Reno (NV)
U of Pennsylvania (PA)
The U of Western Ontario (ON, Canada)
Viterbo U (WI)
Washington U in St. Louis (MO)
Webster U (MO)
Western Kentucky U (KY)

ENGLISH/LANGUAGE ARTS TEACHER EDUCATION

Abilene Christian U (TX)
Adams State Coll (CO)
Alma Coll (MI)
Alvernia U (PA)
Alverno Coll (WI)
Anderson U (IN)
Appalachian State U (NC)
Aquinas Coll (MI)
Arkansas State U—Jonesboro (AR)
Arkansas Tech U (AR)
Assumption Coll (MA)
Auburn U (AL)
Averett U (VA)
The Baptist Coll of Florida (FL)
Barry U (FL)
Baylor U (TX)
Bethany Coll (KS)
Bethel Coll (IN)
Bethel U (MN)
Bethune-Cookman U (FL)
Bishop's U (QC, Canada)
Bluefield Coll (VA)
Blue Mountain Coll (MS)
Bob Jones U (SC)
Boston U (MA)
Bowling Green State U (OH)
Bradley U (IL)
Brewton-Parker Coll (GA)
Bridgewater Coll (VA)
Bridgewater State Coll (MA)
Brigham Young U–Hawaii (HI)
Brooklyn Coll of the City U of New York (NY)
Bryan Coll (TN)
Buena Vista U (IA)
Buffalo State Coll, State U of New York (NY)
Cabrini Coll (PA)
California State U, Chico (CA)
California State U, Long Beach (CA)
Calumet Coll of Saint Joseph (IN)
Campbellsville U (KY)
Capital U (OH)
Carroll U (WI)
The Catholic U of America (DC)
Cedarville U (OH)
Central Michigan U (MI)
Christian Brothers U (TN)
Claflin U (SC)
Clearwater Christian Coll (FL)
Coker Coll (SC)
The Coll at Brockport, State U of New York (NY)
The Coll of New Jersey (NJ)
The Coll of Saint Rose (NY)
Coll of the Ozarks (MO)
Colorado State U (CO)
Columbus State U (GA)
Concordia Coll (MN)
Concordia U Chicago (IL)
Corban U (OR)
Cornerstone U (MI)
Covenant Coll (GA)
Crichton Coll (TN)
Crown Coll (MN)
Culver-Stockton Coll (MO)
Daemen Coll (NY)
Dakota State U (SD)
Dakota Wesleyan U (SD)
Dana Coll (NE)
Delaware State U (DE)
Delta State U (MS)
DePaul U (IL)
Dixie State Coll of Utah (UT)
Dominican Coll (NY)
Dowling Coll (NY)
Duquesne U (PA)
East Carolina U (NC)
East Central U (OK)
Eastern Mennonite U (VA)
Eastern Michigan U (MI)
Eastern Washington U (WA)
East Texas Baptist U (TX)
Edgewood Coll (WI)
Elizabeth City State U (NC)
Elmhurst Coll (IL)
Elmira Coll (NY)
Emmanuel Coll (GA)
Faith Baptist Bible Coll and Theological Sem (IA)
Fayetteville State U (NC)
Ferris State U (MI)
Fitchburg State Coll (MA)
Florida Ag and Mech U (FL)
Florida Atlantic U (FL)
Fort Lewis Coll (CO)
Franklin Coll (IN)
Freed-Hardeman U (TN)
Free Will Baptist Bible Coll (TN)
Friends U (KS)
Gallaudet U (DC)
Gardner-Webb U (NC)
Glenville State Coll (WV)
Goddard Coll (VT)
Grace Coll (IN)
Grambling State U (LA)
Grand Valley State U (MI)
Greensboro Coll (NC)
Greenville Coll (IL)
Hannibal-LaGrange Coll (MO)
Harding U (AR)
Hardin-Simmons U (TX)
Hofstra U (NY)
Hope Coll (MI)
Houston Baptist U (TX)
Howard Payne U (TX)
Huntingdon Coll (AL)
Indiana U Bloomington (IN)
Indiana U Northwest (IN)
Indiana U–Purdue U Fort Wayne (IN)
Indiana U–Purdue U Indianapolis (IN)
Indiana U South Bend (IN)
Indiana U Southeast (IN)
Indiana Wesleyan U (IN)
Iona Coll (NY)
Ithaca Coll (NY)
Jamestown Coll (ND)
Johnson State Coll (VT)
Judson Coll (AL)
Juniata Coll (PA)
Keene State Coll (NH)
Kennesaw State U (GA)
Kent State U (OH)
Kentucky Wesleyan Coll (KY)
Keuka Coll (NY)
King Coll (TN)
La Roche Coll (PA)
Le Moyne Coll (NY)
Lewis-Clark State Coll (ID)
Liberty U (VA)
Limestone Coll (SC)
Lincoln U (MO)
Lincoln U (PA)
Lipscomb U (TN)
Long Island U, Brooklyn Campus (NY)
Long Island U, C.W. Post Campus (NY)
Louisiana State U in Shreveport (LA)
Louisiana Tech U (LA)
Malone U (OH)
Manhattanville Coll (NY)
Mansfield U of Pennsylvania (PA)
Maranatha Baptist Bible Coll (WI)
Marian U (WI)
Marist Coll (NY)
Marquette U (WI)
Maryville Coll (TN)
Maryville U of Saint Louis (MO)
Marywood U (PA)
Mayville State U (ND)
McKendree U (IL)
McMurry U (TX)
McNeese State U (LA)
Medaille Coll (NY)
Mercyhurst Coll (PA)
Messiah Coll (PA)
Miami U (OH)
Miami U Hamilton (OH)
Michigan Technological U (MI)
MidAmerica Nazarene U (KS)
Midwestern State U (TX)
Millersville U of Pennsylvania (PA)
Millikin U (IL)
Minnesota State U Moorhead (MN)
Minot State U (ND)
Misericordia U (PA)
Mississippi Coll (MS)
Mississippi Valley State U (MS)
Missouri State U (MO)
Missouri Western State U (MO)
Molloy Coll (NY)
Montana State U Billings (MT)
Morningside Coll (IA)
Morris Coll (SC)
Mount Marty Coll (SD)
Mount Mary Coll (WI)
Mount Vernon Nazarene U (OH)
Murray State U (KY)
Nazareth Coll of Rochester (NY)
Nebraska Wesleyan U (NE)
Nevada State Coll at Henderson (NV)
Nicholls State U (LA)
North Carolina Central U (NC)
North Carolina State U (NC)
North Dakota State U (ND)
Northeastern State U (OK)
Northern Arizona U (AZ)
Northern Michigan U (MI)
North Georgia Coll & State U (GA)
North Greenville U (SC)
Northwestern Coll (MN)
Northwestern Oklahoma State U (OK)
Northwestern State U of Louisiana (LA)
Northwest Missouri State U (MO)
Northwest Nazarene U (ID)
Northwest U (WA)
Ohio Northern U (OH)
Oklahoma Baptist U (OK)
Oklahoma Christian U (OK)
Old Dominion U (VA)
Oral Roberts U (OK)
Pace U (NY)
Paine Coll (GA)
Philadelphia Biblical U (PA)
Piedmont Baptist Coll and Graduate School (NC)
Pittsburg State U (KS)
Point Park U (PA)
Pontifical Catholic U of Puerto Rico (PR)
Prescott Coll (AZ)
Queens U of Charlotte (NC)
Redeemer U Coll (ON, Canada)
Reinhardt Coll (GA)
Rhode Island Coll (RI)
Rivier Coll (NH)
Roberts Wesleyan Coll (NY)
Rochester Coll (MI)
Rocky Mountain Coll (MT)
Sacred Heart U (CT)
Saginaw Valley State U (MI)
St. Ambrose U (IA)
St. Bonaventure U (NY)
St. Catherine U (MN)
St. Francis Coll (NY)
Saint Francis U (PA)
St. John Fisher Coll (NY)
St. John's U (NY)
Saint Joseph's U (PA)
Saint Mary's U of Minnesota (MN)
Saint Xavier U (IL)
Salve Regina U (RI)
Samford U (AL)
Schreiner U (TX)
Seattle Pacific U (WA)
Seton Hill U (PA)
Shawnee State U (OH)
Shaw U (NC)
Simpson U (CA)
Southeastern Louisiana U (LA)
Southeastern Oklahoma State U (OK)
Southeastern U (FL)
Southeast Missouri State U (MO)
Southern Adventist U (TN)
Southern Arkansas U–Magnolia (AR)
Southern New Hampshire U (NH)
Southern U and Ag and Mech Coll (LA)
Southern Wesleyan U (SC)
Southwest Baptist U (MO)
Southwestern Assemblies of God U (TX)
Southwestern Oklahoma State U (OK)
Southwest Minnesota State U (MN)
Spring Arbor U (MI)
State U of New York at New Paltz (NY)
State U of New York at Plattsburgh (NY)
State U of New York Coll at Oneonta (NY)
Syracuse U (NY)
Tabor Coll (KS)
Talladega Coll (AL)
Taylor U (IN)
Temple U (PA)
Texas A&M Intl U (TX)
Texas Christian U (TX)
Texas Wesleyan U (TX)
Tiffin U (OH)
Trevecca Nazarene U (TN)
Trinity Christian Coll (IL)
Tusculum Coll (TN)
Union Coll (NE)
The U of Akron (OH)
The U of Arizona (AZ)
U of Arkansas at Fort Smith (AR)
U of Central Florida (FL)
U of Central Oklahoma (OK)
U of Delaware (DE)
U of Dubuque (IA)
U of Evansville (IN)
U of Georgia (GA)
U of Idaho (ID)
U of Illinois at Chicago (IL)
U of Illinois at Urbana–Champaign (IL)
U of Indianapolis (IN)
U of Lethbridge (AB, Canada)
U of Louisiana at Monroe (LA)
U of Maine (ME)
U of Maine at Farmington (ME)
U of Maine at Fort Kent (ME)
U of Maine at Machias (ME)
U of Mary (ND)
U of Mary Hardin-Baylor (TX)
U of Maryland, Coll Park (MD)
U of Michigan–Flint (MI)
U of Minnesota, Twin Cities Campus (MN)
U of Mississippi (MS)
U of Missouri–St. Louis (MO)
The U of Montana Western (MT)
U of Nebraska–Lincoln (NE)
U of Nevada, Reno (NV)
U of New Orleans (LA)
The U of North Carolina at Charlotte (NC)
The U of North Carolina at Greensboro (NC)
The U of North Carolina at Pembroke (NC)
The U of North Carolina Wilmington (NC)
U of Oklahoma (OK)
U of Pittsburgh at Johnstown (PA)
U of Puerto Rico at Utuado (PR)
U of Puerto Rico, Cayey U Coll (PR)
U of Regina (SK, Canada)
U of Rio Grande (OH)
U of St. Francis (IL)
U of St. Thomas (MN)
The U of South Dakota (SD)
U of South Florida (FL)
The U of Tennessee at Chattanooga (TN)

INDEXES

The U of Tennessee at Martin (TN)
The U of Toledo (OH)
U of Vermont (VT)
The U of Western Ontario (ON, Canada)
U of Windsor (ON, Canada)
U of Wisconsin–River Falls (WI)
U of Wisconsin–Superior (WI)
Ursuline Coll (OH)
Utah Valley U (UT)
Utica Coll (NY)
Valley City State U (ND)
Valparaiso U (IN)
Virginia Intermont Coll (VA)
Viterbo U (WI)
Waldorf Coll (IA)
Washington Adventist U (MD)
Washington State U (WA)
Washington U in St. Louis (MO)
Wayland Baptist U (TX)
Waynesburg U (PA)
Wayne State Coll (NE)
Wayne State U (MI)
Weber State U (UT)
Western Carolina U (NC)
Western Michigan U (MI)
Western State Coll of Colorado (CO)
Western Washington U (WA)
Westmont Coll (CA)
West Virginia Wesleyan Coll (WV)
Wheeling Jesuit U (WV)
Widener U (PA)
William Jewell Coll (MO)
William Penn U (IA)
Wingate U (NC)
Winston-Salem State U (NC)
Wright State U (OH)
York Coll (NE)
York Coll of Pennsylvania (PA)
York U (ON, Canada)
Youngstown State U (OH)

ENGLISH LITERATURE (BRITISH AND COMMONWEALTH)

American U of Beirut (Lebanon)
Bard Coll (NY)
Bennington Coll (VT)
Concordia U (QC, Canada)
Gannon U (PA)
Hofstra U (NY)
Hunter Coll of the City U of New York (NY)
Indiana U–Purdue U Fort Wayne (IN)
Marian U (WI)
New York U (NY)
St. Lawrence U (NY)
Saint Mary's Coll (IN)
Sarah Lawrence Coll (NY)
Syracuse U (NY)
U of Michigan (MI)
U of Pittsburgh (PA)
Washington U in St. Louis (MO)

ENTOMOLOGY

Cornell U (NY)
Florida Ag and Mech U (FL)
Iowa State U of Science and Technology (IA)
Memorial U of Newfoundland (NL, Canada)
Michigan State U (MI)
The Ohio State U (OH)
Oklahoma State U (OK)
Purdue U (IN)
State U of New York Coll of Environmental Science and Forestry (NY)
Texas A&M U (TX)
U of Alberta (AB, Canada)
U of California, Davis (CA)
U of California, Riverside (CA)
U of Delaware (DE)
U of Florida (FL)
U of Georgia (GA)
U of Illinois at Urbana–Champaign (IL)
U of Manitoba (MB, Canada)
U of Nebraska–Lincoln (NE)
U of New Brunswick Fredericton (NB, Canada)
U of New Hampshire (NH)
U of Wisconsin–Madison (WI)
Utah State U (UT)

ENTREPRENEURIAL AND SMALL BUSINESS RELATED

Babson Coll (MA)
Crown Coll (MN)
Fairleigh Dickinson U, Coll at Florham (NJ)
Fairleigh Dickinson U, Metropolitan Campus (NJ)
Florida State U (FL)
Kendall Coll (IL)
Loyola U Chicago (IL)
Pennsylvania Coll of Technology (PA)
Stetson U (FL)
U of Alberta (AB, Canada)

ENTREPRENEURSHIP

Anderson U (IN)
Avila U (MO)
Babson Coll (MA)
Ball State U (IN)
Baylor U (TX)
Belmont U (TN)
Brigham Young U (UT)
Bryant U (RI)
Buena Vista U (IA)
California State U, Dominguez Hills (CA)
California State U, Fullerton (CA)
Canisius Coll (NY)
Cape Breton U (NS, Canada)
Central Michigan U (MI)
Clarkson U (NY)
Coll of the Atlantic (ME)
Duquesne U (PA)
East Central U (OK)
Eastern Michigan U (MI)
Ferris State U (MI)
Fordham U (NY)
Gannon U (PA)
Grove City Coll (PA)
Hampshire Coll (MA)
Hawai'i Pacific U (HI)
HEC Montreal (QC, Canada)
Hofstra U (NY)
Houston Baptist U (TX)
Inter American U of Puerto Rico, Aguadilla Campus (PR)
Inter American U of Puerto Rico, Bayamón Campus (PR)
Iowa State U of Science and Technology (IA)
Jackson State U (MS)
Johnson & Wales U (CO)
Juniata Coll (PA)
Kendall Coll (IL)
Kwantlen Polytechnic U (BC, Canada)
Lasell Coll (MA)
Lees-McRae Coll (NC)
Lindenwood U (MO)
Mars Hill Coll (NC)
Messiah Coll (PA)
Millikin U (IL)
Missouri State U (MO)
National U (CA)
Northeastern State U (OK)
Northeastern U (MA)
Northern Kentucky U (KY)
Northern Michigan U (MI)
Ohio Northern U (OH)
Oklahoma State U (OK)
Pace U (NY)
Pontifical Catholic U of Puerto Rico (PR)
Quinnipiac U (CT)
Redeemer U Coll (ON, Canada)
Reinhardt Coll (GA)
Rider U (NJ)
Rowan U (NJ)
Royal Roads U (BC, Canada)
St. Edward's U (TX)
Saint Louis U (MO)
St. Mary's U (TX)
Saint Mary's U of Minnesota (MN)
Salem State Coll (MA)
Samford U (AL)
Seton Hill U (PA)
Shaw U (NC)
South Dakota State U (SD)
Southern Polytechnic State U (GA)
Southern U at New Orleans (LA)
State U of New York at Binghamton (NY)
State U of New York at Plattsburgh (NY)
Susquehanna U (PA)
Syracuse U (NY)
Temple U (PA)
Thomas Edison State Coll (NJ)
Trine U (IN)
Union Coll (NE)
The U of British Columbia–Okanagan (BC, Canada)
U of Hartford (CT)
U of Illinois at Chicago (IL)
U of Illinois at Urbana–Champaign (IL)
U of Indianapolis (IN)
U of Maine at Machias (ME)
U of Mary (ND)
U of Miami (FL)
U of Nevada, Las Vegas (NV)
U of Nevada, Reno (NV)
U of New Orleans (LA)
The U of North Carolina at Pembroke (NC)
U of North Dakota (ND)
U of Ottawa (ON, Canada)
U of Pittsburgh at Bradford (PA)
U of St. Thomas (MN)
The U of Scranton (PA)
U of Southern Indiana (IN)
The U of Tampa (FL)
The U of Texas at San Antonio (TX)
The U of Toledo (OH)
U of Utah (UT)
U of Vermont (VT)
The U of Western Ontario (ON, Canada)
Washington State U (WA)
Washington U in St. Louis (MO)
Western Carolina U (NC)
Western Kentucky U (KY)
Western State Coll of Colorado (CO)
Wichita State U (KS)
Wilkes U (PA)
Xavier U (OH)
York Coll of Pennsylvania (PA)
York U (ON, Canada)

ENVIRONMENTAL BIOLOGY

American U (DC)
Arcadia U (PA)
Averett U (VA)
Barnard Coll (NY)
Beloit Coll (WI)
Bennington Coll (VT)
Bethel Coll (IN)
Bridgewater State Coll (MA)
California State Polytechnic U, Pomona (CA)
Carlow U (PA)
Cedar Crest Coll (PA)
Cedarville U (OH)
Chowan U (NC)
Colgate U (NY)
The Coll at Brockport, State U of New York (NY)
Coll of the Atlantic (ME)
Columbia U (NY)
Columbia U, School of General Studies (NY)
Cornerstone U (MI)
East Stroudsburg U of Pennsylvania (PA)
Elizabethtown Coll (PA)
Ferris State U (MI)
Fitchburg State Coll (MA)
Fort Lewis Coll (CO)
Franklin Pierce U (NH)
Friends U (KS)
Grace Coll (IN)
Greenville Coll (IL)
Heidelberg U (OH)
Houghton Coll (NY)
Humboldt State U (CA)
Inter American U of Puerto Rico, Bayamón Campus (PR)
Iona Coll (NY)
Iowa Wesleyan Coll (IA)
Jacksonville State U (AL)
Keystone Coll (PA)
Lakehead U (ON, Canada)
Marlboro Coll (VT)
The Master's Coll and Sem (CA)
McDaniel Coll (MD)
Memorial U of Newfoundland (NL, Canada)
Michigan State U (MI)
Midway Coll (KY)
Minnesota State U Mankato (MN)
Monmouth U (NJ)
Nipissing U (ON, Canada)
Northwestern Coll (IA)
Philadelphia U (PA)
Pittsburg State U (KS)
Plymouth State U (NH)
Prescott Coll (AZ)
Sacred Heart U (CT)
St. Cloud State U (MN)
St. Lawrence U (NY)
Saint Mary's U of Minnesota (MN)
Salem State Coll (MA)
State U of New York Coll at Cortland (NY)
State U of New York Coll of Environmental Science and Forestry (NY)
Sterling Coll (VT)
Suffolk U (MA)
Tabor Coll (KS)
Taylor U (IN)
Texas A&M U (TX)
Thompson Rivers U (BC, Canada)
Tulane U (LA)
U of Alberta (AB, Canada)
The U of British Columbia (BC, Canada)
U of Charleston (WV)
U of Dayton (OH)
U of Dubuque (IA)
U of Guelph (ON, Canada)
U of La Verne (CA)
U of Mount Union (OH)
U of Pittsburgh at Johnstown (PA)
U of Regina (SK, Canada)
The U of Tennessee at Martin (TN)
U of Windsor (ON, Canada)
Western State Coll of Colorado (CO)
Westfield State Coll (MA)
William Penn U (IA)
Wingate U (NC)
Winona State U (MN)
York U (ON, Canada)

ENVIRONMENTAL CONTROL TECHNOLOGIES RELATED

Inter American U of Puerto Rico, Bayamón Campus (PR)
New York Inst of Technology (NY)
Thomas Edison State Coll (NJ)
U of Puerto Rico at Utuado (PR)

ENVIRONMENTAL DESIGN/ ARCHITECTURE

Art Center Coll of Design (CA)
Auburn U (AL)
Ball State U (IN)
Boston Architectural Coll (MA)
Bowling Green State U (OH)
Coll of the Atlantic (ME)
Cornell U (NY)
Gainesville State Coll (GA)
Kent State U (OH)
Lawrence Technological U (MI)
Montana State U (MT)
North Carolina State U (NC)
North Dakota State U (ND)
Otis Coll of Art and Design (CA)
Prescott Coll (AZ)
Rutgers, The State U of New Jersey, New Brunswick (NJ)
State U of New York Coll of Environmental Science and Forestry (NY)
Texas A&M U (TX)
U at Buffalo, the State U of New York (NY)
U of Colorado at Boulder (CO)
U of Manitoba (MB, Canada)
U of Massachusetts Amherst (MA)
U of Memphis (TN)
U of Minnesota, Twin Cities Campus (MN)
U of New Mexico (NM)
U of Oklahoma (OK)
U of Pennsylvania (PA)
U of Puerto Rico, Río Piedras (PR)

ENVIRONMENTAL EDUCATION

Coll of the Atlantic (ME)
Johnson State Coll (VT)
Prescott Coll (AZ)
Sonoma State U (CA)
State U of New York Coll of Environmental Science and Forestry (NY)
U of Maine at Machias (ME)
York U (ON, Canada)

ENVIRONMENTAL ENGINEERING TECHNOLOGY

Bowling Green State U (OH)
California State U, Long Beach (CA)
City Coll of the City U of New York (NY)
Ferris State U (MI)
Lake Superior State U (MI)
Middle Tennessee State U (TN)
Murray State U (KY)
Shawnee State U (OH)
Temple U (PA)
United States Military Acad (NY)
The U of British Columbia (BC, Canada)
U of Delaware (DE)
U of Guelph (ON, Canada)
U of Wisconsin–Whitewater (WI)
Wright State U (OH)

ENVIRONMENTAL/ ENVIRONMENTAL HEALTH ENGINEERING

Arizona State U (AZ)
California Inst of Technology (CA)
California Polytechnic State U, San Luis Obispo (CA)
Carnegie Mellon U (PA)
Central State U (OH)
Christian Brothers U (TN)
Clarkson U (NY)
Colorado School of Mines (CO)
Colorado State U (CO)
Columbia U (NY)
Cornell U (NY)
Drexel U (PA)
Florida Gulf Coast U (FL)
Florida Intl U (FL)
Gannon U (PA)
The George Washington U (DC)
Georgia Inst of Technology (GA)
Hofstra U (NY)
Humboldt State U (CA)
The Johns Hopkins U (MD)
Lafayette Coll (PA)
Lehigh U (PA)
Louisiana State U and Ag and Mech Coll (LA)
Manhattan Coll (NY)
Marquette U (WI)
Massachusetts Inst of Technology (MA)
Massachusetts Maritime Acad (MA)
Michigan Technological U (MI)
Missouri U of Science and Technology (MO)
Montana Tech of The U of Montana (MT)
New Jersey Inst of Technology (NJ)
New Mexico Inst of Mining and Technology (NM)
North Carolina State U (NC)
Northeastern State U (OK)
Northern Arizona U (AZ)
Oregon State U (OR)
Penn State Abington (PA)
Penn State Altoona (PA)
Penn State Beaver (PA)
Penn State Berks (PA)
Penn State Brandywine (PA)
Penn State DuBois (PA)
Penn State Erie, The Behrend Coll (PA)
Penn State Fayette, The Eberly Campus (PA)
Penn State Greater Allegheny (PA)
Penn State Harrisburg (PA)
Penn State Hazleton (PA)
Penn State Lehigh Valley (PA)
Penn State Mont Alto (PA)
Penn State New Kensington (PA)
Penn State Schuylkill (PA)
Penn State Shenango (PA)
Penn State U Park (PA)
Penn State Wilkes-Barre (PA)
Penn State Worthington Scranton (PA)
Penn State York (PA)
Polytechnic U of Puerto Rico (PR)
Rensselaer Polytechnic Inst (NY)
Rice U (TX)
San Diego State U (CA)
Seattle U (WA)
South Dakota School of Mines and Technology (SD)
Southern Methodist U (TX)
Stanford U (CA)
State U of New York Coll of Environmental Science and Forestry (NY)
Stevens Inst of Technology (NJ)
Syracuse U (NY)
Taylor U (IN)
Texas Tech U (TX)
Tufts U (MA)
Tulane U (LA)
United States Air Force Acad (CO)
United States Military Acad (NY)
U at Buffalo, the State U of New York (NY)
U of Alberta (AB, Canada)
U of California, Berkeley (CA)
U of California, Irvine (CA)
U of California, Merced (CA)
U of California, Riverside (CA)
U of Central Florida (FL)
U of Colorado at Boulder (CO)
U of Connecticut (CT)
U of Delaware (DE)
U of Florida (FL)
U of Georgia (GA)
U of Idaho (ID)
U of Illinois at Urbana–Champaign (IL)
U of Miami (FL)
U of Nevada, Reno (NV)
U of New Hampshire (NH)
U of North Dakota (ND)
U of Notre Dame (IN)
U of Oklahoma (OK)
U of Pennsylvania (PA)
U of Regina (SK, Canada)
U of Saskatchewan (SK, Canada)
U of Southern California (CA)
U of Vermont (VT)
U of Waterloo (ON, Canada)
The U of Western Ontario (ON, Canada)
U of Windsor (ON, Canada)
U of Wisconsin–Madison (WI)
U of Wisconsin–Platteville (WI)

ENVIRONMENTAL HEALTH

ENVIRONMENTAL PSYCHOLOGY

ENVIRONMENTAL SCIENCE

ENVIRONMENTAL STUDIES

INDEXES

ENVIRONMENTAL TOXICOLOGY

EPIDEMIOLOGY

EQUESTRIAN STUDIES

ETHICS

ETHNIC, CULTURAL MINORITY, AND GENDER STUDIES RELATED

EUROPEAN HISTORY

EUROPEAN STUDIES

EUROPEAN STUDIES (CENTRAL AND EASTERN)

EUROPEAN STUDIES (WESTERN)

EVOLUTIONARY BIOLOGY

EXECUTIVE ASSISTANT/ EXECUTIVE SECRETARY

EXERCISE PHYSIOLOGY
Baldwin-Wallace Coll (OH)
Baylor U (TX)
Brooklyn Coll of the City U of New York (NY)
The Coll at Brockport, State U of New York (NY)
The Coll of St. Scholastica (MN)
Concordia U Wisconsin (WI)
East Carolina U (NC)
Fitchburg State Coll (MA)
Lynchburg Coll (VA)
Miami U Hamilton (OH)
Ohio Northern U (OH)
Saint Francis U (PA)
Simpson Coll (IA)
Truman State U (MO)
U at Buffalo, the State U of New York (NY)
U of California, Davis (CA)
U of Florida (FL)
U of Massachusetts Amherst (MA)
West Virginia U (WV)

EXPERIMENTAL PSYCHOLOGY
Keene State Coll (NH)
Longwood U (VA)
Marlboro Coll (VT)
Moravian Coll (PA)
Northern Michigan U (MI)
Paine Coll (GA)
Redeemer U Coll (ON, Canada)
Tiffin U (OH)
Tufts U (MA)
U of Alberta (AB, Canada)
The U of British Columbia (BC, Canada)
U of South Carolina (SC)
The U of Toledo (OH)
U of Wisconsin–Madison (WI)
Wilfrid Laurier U (ON, Canada)

FACILITIES PLANNING AND MANAGEMENT
Eastern Michigan U (MI)
Fitchburg State Coll (MA)
New York City Coll of Technology of the City U of New York (NY)

FAMILY AND COMMUNITY SERVICES
Alderson-Broaddus Coll (WV)
Andrews U (MI)
Bowling Green State U (OH)
Curry Coll (MA)
East Carolina U (NC)
Iowa State U of Science and Technology (IA)
John Brown U (AR)
Keystone Coll (PA)
Lubbock Christian U (TX)
Messiah Coll (PA)
Michigan State U (MI)
Oklahoma Baptist U (OK)
Oklahoma Christian U (OK)
Our Lady of the Lake U of San Antonio (TX)
Prairie View A&M U (TX)
Prescott Coll (AZ)
Southern U at New Orleans (LA)
Southern Utah U (UT)
Stevenson U (MD)
Texas Tech U (TX)
Union U (TN)
U of California, Santa Cruz (CA)
U of Delaware (DE)
U of Florida (FL)
U of Maine at Machias (ME)
U of Maryland, Coll Park (MD)
U of Miami (FL)
U of Minnesota, Twin Cities Campus (MN)
U of Northern Iowa (IA)
Youngstown State U (OH)

FAMILY AND CONSUMER ECONOMICS RELATED
Alabama Ag and Mech U (AL)
Andrews U (MI)
Ashland U (OH)
Bob Jones U (SC)
Bowling Green State U (OH)
Brigham Young U (UT)
California State U, Fresno (CA)
California State U, Sacramento (CA)
Carson-Newman Coll (TN)
Fairmont State U (WV)
Iowa State U of Science and Technology (IA)
Louisiana Coll (LA)
Minnesota State U Mankato (MN)
Murray State U (KY)
The U of Akron (OH)
U of Alberta (AB, Canada)
U of Delaware (DE)
U of Hawaii at Manoa (HI)
U of Maryland Eastern Shore (MD)
U of Missouri (MO)
U of Nebraska at Kearney (NE)
U of Nebraska–Lincoln (NE)
U of Northern Iowa (IA)
U of Wisconsin–Madison (WI)
U of Wisconsin–Stevens Point (WI)
Utah State U (UT)
Virginia State U (VA)

FAMILY AND CONSUMER SCIENCES/HOME ECONOMICS TEACHER EDUCATION
Appalachian State U (NC)
Ashland U (OH)
Bluffton U (OH)
Bowling Green State U (OH)
Bradley U (IL)
Bridgewater Coll (VA)
Carson-Newman Coll (TN)
Central Michigan U (MI)
Cheyney U of Pennsylvania (PA)
Coll of the Ozarks (MO)
Colorado State U (CO)
Cornell U (NY)
East Carolina U (NC)
East Central U (OK)
Fairmont State U (WV)
Ferris State U (MI)
Fontbonne U (MO)
Fort Valley State U (GA)
Georgia Southern U (GA)
Hampton U (VA)
Harding U (AR)
Immaculata U (PA)
Iowa State U of Science and Technology (IA)
Jacksonville State U (AL)
Johnson & Wales U (CO)
Kent State U (OH)
Lamar U (TX)
Liberty U (VA)
Louisiana State U and Ag and Mech Coll (LA)
Louisiana Tech U (LA)
Marywood U (PA)
McNeese State U (LA)
Mercyhurst Coll (PA)
Messiah Coll (PA)
Michigan State U (MI)
Minnesota State U Mankato (MN)
Missouri State U (MO)
Mount Vernon Nazarene U (OH)
Murray State U (KY)
New Mexico State U (NM)
North Dakota State U (ND)
Northwestern State U of Louisiana (LA)
Northwest Missouri State U (MO)
Oakwood U (AL)
The Ohio State U (OH)
Ohio U (OH)
Pittsburg State U (KS)
Pontifical Catholic U of Puerto Rico (PR)
Queens Coll of the City U of New York (NY)
St. Catherine U (MN)
Seton Hill U (PA)
South Carolina State U (SC)
Southeastern Louisiana U (LA)
Southeast Missouri State U (MO)
Southern Utah U (UT)
State U of New York Coll at Oneonta (NY)
Tennessee Technological U (TN)
The U of Akron (OH)
U of Alberta (AB, Canada)
The U of Arizona (AZ)
U of Arkansas at Pine Bluff (AR)
The U of British Columbia (BC, Canada)
U of Central Oklahoma (OK)
U of Georgia (GA)
U of Guam (GU)
U of Louisiana at Monroe (LA)
U of Maryland Eastern Shore (MD)
U of Minnesota, Twin Cities Campus (MN)
U of Nevada, Reno (NV)
U of New Brunswick Fredericton (NB, Canada)
U of Saskatchewan (SK, Canada)
The U of Tennessee (TN)
The U of Tennessee at Martin (TN)
U of the District of Columbia (DC)
U of Wisconsin–Madison (WI)
U of Wisconsin–Stevens Point (WI)
U of Wisconsin–Stout (WI)
Utah State U (UT)
Virginia Polytechnic Inst and State U (VA)
Washington State U (WA)
Wayne State Coll (NE)
Western Kentucky U (KY)
Western Michigan U (MI)
Winthrop U (SC)
Youngstown State U (OH)

FAMILY AND CONSUMER SCIENCES/HUMAN SCIENCES
Ashland U (OH)
Auburn U (AL)
Ball State U (IN)
Baylor U (TX)
Berea Coll (KY)
Bluffton U (OH)
Bowling Green State U (OH)
Bradley U (IL)
Bridgewater Coll (VA)
Brigham Young U (UT)
California State U, East Bay (CA)
California State U, Long Beach (CA)
California State U, Northridge (CA)
Cameron U (OK)
Carson-Newman Coll (TN)
Coll of the Atlantic (ME)
Coll of the Ozarks (MO)
Colorado State U (CO)
Cornell U (NY)
Delaware State U (DE)
Delta State U (MS)
East Central U (OK)
Eastern Illinois U (IL)
Eastern New Mexico U (NM)
East Tennessee State U (TN)
Fairmont State U (WV)
Fontbonne U (MO)
Framingham State Coll (MA)
Freed-Hardeman U (TN)
George Fox U (OR)
Great Lakes Christian Coll (MI)
Harding U (AR)
Henderson State U (AR)
Idaho State U (ID)
Illinois State U (IL)
Indiana State U (IN)
Indiana U of Pennsylvania (PA)
Iowa State U of Science and Technology (IA)
Jacksonville State U (AL)
Kent State U (OH)
Lamar U (TX)
Liberty U (VA)
Lipscomb U (TN)
Louisiana State U and Ag and Mech Coll (LA)
Madonna U (MI)
Marshall U (WV)
The Master's Coll and Sem (CA)
McNeese State U (LA)
Meredith Coll (NC)
Michigan State U (MI)
Minnesota State U Mankato (MN)
Mississippi State U (MS)
Montana State U (MT)
Montclair State U (NJ)
New Mexico Highlands U (NM)
Nicholls State U (LA)
North Carolina Central U (NC)
Northeastern State U (OK)
Northwestern State U of Louisiana (LA)
Oakwood U (AL)
Oregon State U (OR)
Pittsburg State U (KS)
Pontifical Catholic U of Puerto Rico (PR)
Prairie View A&M U (TX)
Prescott Coll (AZ)
Purdue U (IN)
Queens Coll of the City U of New York (NY)
Rutgers, The State U of New Jersey, New Brunswick (NJ)
St. Catherine U (MN)
Saint Joseph Coll (CT)
Sam Houston State U (TX)
San Francisco State U (CA)
Seattle Pacific U (WA)
Seton Hill U (PA)
Shepherd U (WV)
South Carolina State U (SC)
Southeastern Louisiana U (LA)
Southeast Missouri State U (MO)
Southern U and Ag and Mech Coll (LA)
Southern Utah U (UT)
State U of New York Coll at Oneonta (NY)
Stephen F. Austin State U (TX)
Tarleton State U (TX)
Tennessee Technological U (TN)
Texas A&M U–Kingsville (TX)
Texas Southern U (TX)
Texas State U–San Marcos (TX)
Texas Tech U (TX)
Texas Woman's U (TX)
The U of Alabama (AL)
U of Alberta (AB, Canada)
U of Arkansas (AR)
U of Arkansas at Pine Bluff (AR)
The U of British Columbia (BC, Canada)
U of California, San Diego (CA)
U of Central Missouri (MO)
U of Central Oklahoma (OK)
U of Kentucky (KY)
U of Manitoba (MB, Canada)
U of Maryland Eastern Shore (MD)
U of Mississippi (MS)
U of Montevallo (AL)
U of New Mexico (NM)
U of North Alabama (AL)
U of Puerto Rico, Río Piedras (PR)
The U of Tennessee at Martin (TN)
U of the District of Columbia (DC)
The U of Western Ontario (ON, Canada)
U of Wisconsin–Madison (WI)
U of Wyoming (WY)
Washington State U (WA)
Wayne State Coll (NE)
Western Illinois U (IL)
West Virginia U (WV)
Youngstown State U (OH)

FAMILY AND CONSUMER SCIENCES/HUMAN SCIENCES BUSINESS SERVICES RELATED
Brigham Young U (UT)
U of Illinois at Urbana–Champaign (IL)

FAMILY AND CONSUMER SCIENCES/HUMAN SCIENCES COMMUNICATION
U of Georgia (GA)

FAMILY AND CONSUMER SCIENCES/HUMAN SCIENCES RELATED
California State U, Long Beach (CA)
Norfolk State U (VA)
The U of Western Ontario (ON, Canada)

FAMILY PRACTICE NURSING/NURSE PRACTITIONER
D'Youville Coll (NY)
Edinboro U of Pennsylvania (PA)
Grand Valley State U (MI)
Medical Coll of Georgia (GA)
Michigan State U (MI)
North Georgia Coll & State U (GA)
The U of Virginia's Coll at Wise (VA)
The U of Western Ontario (ON, Canada)
U of Windsor (ON, Canada)

FAMILY PSYCHOLOGY
Corban U (OR)

FAMILY RESOURCE MANAGEMENT
Arizona State U (AZ)
Brigham Young U (UT)
Iowa State U of Science and Technology (IA)
Middle Tennessee State U (TN)
The Ohio State U (OH)
Ohio U (OH)
Pittsburg State U (KS)
South Dakota State U (SD)
Texas Tech U (TX)
The U of Alabama (AL)
U of Georgia (GA)

FAMILY SYSTEMS
Alderson-Broaddus Coll (WV)
Anderson U (IN)
Bowling Green State U (OH)
Central Michigan U (MI)
Gallaudet U (DC)
John Brown U (AR)
Lipscomb U (TN)
Lubbock Christian U (TX)
Mississippi U for Women (MS)
Southern Adventist U (TN)
Spring Arbor U (MI)
Texas Tech U (TX)
Towson U (MD)
The U of Akron (OH)
U of Southern Mississippi (MS)
The U of Tennessee (TN)
Weber State U (UT)
Western Michigan U (MI)

FARM AND RANCH MANAGEMENT
Iowa State U of Science and Technology (IA)
Johnson & Wales U (RI)
Tarleton State U (TX)
Texas A&M U (TX)
Texas Christian U (TX)
U of Alberta (AB, Canada)
The U of Findlay (OH)
U of Illinois at Urbana–Champaign (IL)

FASHION/APPAREL DESIGN
Acad of Art U (CA)
The Art Inst of California–Hollywood (CA)
The Art Inst of California–Inland Empire (CA)
The Art Inst of California–Los Angeles (CA)
The Art Inst of California–Orange County (CA)
The Art Inst of California–San Diego (CA)
The Art Inst of California–San Francisco (CA)
The Art Inst of Colorado (CO)
The Art Inst of Dallas (TX)
The Art Inst of Fort Lauderdale (FL)
The Art Inst of Indianapolis (IN)
The Art Inst of Philadelphia (PA)
The Art Inst of Pittsburgh (PA)
The Art Inst of Portland (OR)
The Art Inst of Seattle (WA)
The Art Inst of Tucson (AZ)
Ball State U (IN)
Baylor U (TX)
Bowling Green State U (OH)
Brenau U (GA)
Buffalo State Coll, State U of New York (NY)
California Coll of the Arts (CA)
Cazenovia Coll (NY)
Centenary Coll (NJ)
Clark Atlanta U (GA)
Columbia Coll Chicago (IL)
Columbus Coll of Art & Design (OH)
Dominican U (IL)
Drexel U (PA)
Escuela de Artes Plasticas de Puerto Rico (PR)
Fashion Inst of Technology (NY)
Hampton U (VA)
The Illinois Inst of Art–Chicago (IL)
The Illinois Inst of Art–Schaumburg (IL)
Intl Acad of Design & Technology (IL)
Iowa State U of Science and Technology (IA)
Kent State U (OH)
Kwantlen Polytechnic U (BC, Canada)
Lamar U (TX)
Lasell Coll (MA)
Lindenwood U (MO)
Marist Coll (NY)
Marymount U (VA)
Massachusetts Coll of Art and Design (MA)
Meredith Coll (NC)
Miami Intl U of Art & Design (FL)
Michigan State U (MI)
Montclair State U (NJ)
Moore Coll of Art & Design (PA)
Mount Ida Coll (MA)
Mount Mary Coll (WI)
O'More Coll of Design (TN)
Otis Coll of Art and Design (CA)
Parsons The New School for Design (NY)
Philadelphia U (PA)
Pratt Inst (NY)
St. Catherine U (MN)
Savannah Coll of Art and Design (GA)
School of the Art Inst of Chicago (IL)
Stephens Coll (MO)
Texas Southern U (TX)
Texas Tech U (TX)
Texas Woman's U (TX)
U of Cincinnati (OH)
U of Delaware (DE)
U of Maryland Eastern Shore (MD)
U of Minnesota, Twin Cities Campus (MN)
U of North Texas (TX)
U of the Incarnate Word (TX)
Ursuline Coll (OH)
Villa Maria Coll of Buffalo (NY)
Virginia Commonwealth U (VA)
Washington U in St. Louis (MO)
Woodbury U (CA)

FASHION MERCHANDISING
The Art Inst of Atlanta (GA)
The Art Inst of California–Hollywood (CA)
The Art Inst of California–Los Angeles (CA)
The Art Inst of California–Orange County (CA)
The Art Inst of California–San Diego (CA)
The Art Inst of California–San Francisco (CA)
The Art Inst of California–Sunnyvale (CA)
The Art Inst of Charlotte (NC)
The Art Inst of Colorado (CO)
The Art Inst of Fort Lauderdale (FL)
The Art Inst of Houston (TX)
The Art Inst of Michigan (MI)
The Art Inst of Ohio–Cincinnati (OH)
The Art Inst of Phoenix (AZ)
The Art Inst of Pittsburgh (PA)
The Art Inst of Portland (OR)
The Art Inst of Raleigh-Durham (NC)
The Art Inst of Seattle (WA)
The Art Inst of Tucson (AZ)
The Art Insts Intl–Kansas City (KS)
Ashland U (OH)
Baylor U (TX)
Bowling Green State U (OH)
Brenau U (GA)
Buffalo State Coll, State U of New York (NY)
California State U, Long Beach (CA)
Carson-Newman Coll (TN)
Central Michigan U (MI)
Delaware State U (DE)
Dominican U (IL)
East Central U (OK)
Fashion Inst of Technology (NY)
Fisher Coll (MA)
Fontbonne U (MO)
Freed-Hardeman U (TN)
Hampton U (VA)
Harding U (AR)
The Illinois Inst of Art–Chicago (IL)
The Illinois Inst of Art–Schaumburg (IL)
Immaculata U (PA)
Indiana U of Pennsylvania (PA)
Intl Acad of Design & Technology (IL)
Kent State U (OH)
Lamar U (TX)
Lasell Coll (MA)
Liberty U (VA)
LIM Coll (NY)
Lindenwood U (MO)
Lipscomb U (TN)
Louisiana State U and Ag and Mech Coll (LA)
Marist Coll (NY)
Mars Hill Coll (NC)
Marymount U (VA)
Mercyhurst Coll (PA)
Meredith Coll (NC)
Miami Intl U of Art & Design (FL)
Michigan State U (MI)
Mount Ida Coll (MA)
Mount Mary Coll (WI)
Newbury Coll (MA)
Northern Arizona U (AZ)
Old Dominion U (VA)
O'More Coll of Design (TN)
Our Lady of the Lake U of San Antonio (TX)
Parsons The New School for Design (NY)
Patricia Stevens Coll (MO)
Philadelphia U (PA)
Pittsburg State U (KS)
Sacred Heart U (CT)
St. Catherine U (MN)
State U of New York Coll at Oneonta (NY)
Stephen F. Austin State U (TX)
Stephens Coll (MO)
Tennessee Technological U (TN)
Texas Christian U (TX)
Texas State U–San Marcos (TX)
Texas Tech U (TX)
Texas Woman's U (TX)
U of Central Oklahoma (OK)
U of Delaware (DE)
U of Georgia (GA)
U of Illinois at Urbana–Champaign (IL)
U of Maryland Eastern Shore (MD)
U of Minnesota, Twin Cities Campus (MN)
U of North Texas (TX)
The U of Tennessee at Martin (TN)
U of Wisconsin–Madison (WI)
Ursuline Coll (OH)
Utah State U (UT)
Westwood Coll–Denver North (CO)
Westwood Coll–Online Campus (CO)
Woodbury U (CA)
Youngstown State U (OH)

FIBER, TEXTILE AND WEAVING ARTS
Adams State Coll (CO)
Alberta Coll of Art & Design (AB, Canada)
Bowling Green State U (OH)
California Coll of the Arts (CA)
California State U, Long Beach (CA)
The Cleveland Inst of Art (OH)
Cornell U (NY)
Maryland Inst Coll of Art (MD)
Massachusetts Coll of Art and Design (MA)
Mercyhurst Coll (PA)
Philadelphia U (PA)
Savannah Coll of Art and Design (GA)
School of the Art Inst of Chicago (IL)
Temple U (PA)
The U of Kansas (KS)
U of Massachusetts Dartmouth (MA)
U of Michigan (MI)
U of Oregon (OR)
U of Washington (WA)
U of Wisconsin–Milwaukee (WI)
Western Washington U (WA)

FILIPINO/TAGALOG
U of Hawaii at Manoa (HI)

FILM/CINEMA STUDIES
American U (DC)
The American U of Paris (France)
Baldwin-Wallace Coll (OH)
Bard Coll (NY)
Barnard Coll (NY)
Bennington Coll (VT)
Bishop's U (QC, Canada)
Boston Coll (MA)
Bowling Green State U (OH)
Brandeis U (MA)
Brigham Young U (UT)
Brock U (ON, Canada)
Brooklyn Coll of the City U of New York (NY)
Burlington Coll (VT)
California Coll of the Arts (CA)
California State U, Long Beach (CA)
California State U, Northridge (CA)
California State U, Sacramento (CA)
Calvin Coll (MI)
Carleton Coll (MN)
Carson-Newman Coll (TN)
Centenary Coll of Louisiana (LA)
Chapman U (CA)
Claremont McKenna Coll (CA)
Clark U (MA)
Coll of Santa Fe (NM)
Coll of Staten Island of the City U of New York (NY)
The Colorado Coll (CO)
Columbia Coll Chicago (IL)
Columbia U (NY)
Columbia U, School of General Studies (NY)
Concordia U (CA)
Concordia U (QC, Canada)
Connecticut Coll (CT)
Cornell U (NY)
Curry Coll (MA)
Dartmouth Coll (NH)
Denison U (OH)
Eastern Michigan U (MI)
Emerson Coll (MA)
Emory U (GA)
The Evergreen State Coll (WA)
Florida State U (FL)
Fordham U (NY)
Full Sail U (FL)
Georgia State U (GA)
Grace Coll (IN)
Grand Valley State U (MI)
Hampshire Coll (MA)
Hunter Coll of the City U of New York (NY)
Huntington U (IN)
Ithaca Coll (NY)
John Brown U (AR)
The Johns Hopkins U (MD)
Kean U (NJ)
Keene State Coll (NH)
La Salle U (PA)
Laurentian U (ON, Canada)
Long Island U, C.W. Post Campus (NY)
Marlboro Coll (VT)
Memphis Coll of Art (TN)
Missouri Western State U (MO)
Mount Holyoke Coll (MA)
North Carolina State U (NC)
Northeastern U (MA)
Northwest U (WA)
The Ohio State U (OH)
Pace U (NY)
Penn State Abington (PA)
Penn State Altoona (PA)
Penn State Beaver (PA)
Penn State Berks (PA)
Penn State Brandywine (PA)
Penn State DuBois (PA)
Penn State Erie, The Behrend Coll (PA)
Penn State Fayette, The Eberly Campus (PA)
Penn State Greater Allegheny (PA)
Penn State Hazleton (PA)
Penn State Lehigh Valley (PA)
Penn State Mont Alto (PA)
Penn State New Kensington (PA)
Penn State Schuylkill (PA)
Penn State Shenango (PA)
Penn State U Park (PA)
Penn State Wilkes-Barre (PA)
Penn State Worthington Scranton (PA)
Penn State York (PA)
Pitzer Coll (CA)
Pomona Coll (CA)
Prescott Coll (AZ)
Purchase Coll, State U of New York (NY)
Queens Coll of the City U of New York (NY)
Queen's U at Kingston (ON, Canada)
Quinnipiac U (CT)
Rhode Island Coll (RI)
Rutgers, The State U of New Jersey, New Brunswick (NJ)
Sacred Heart U (CT)
Saint Augustine's Coll (NC)
St. Cloud State U (MN)
San Francisco State U (CA)
Sarah Lawrence Coll (NY)
Savannah Coll of Art and Design (GA)
School of the Art Inst of Chicago (IL)
School of the Museum of Fine Arts, Boston (MA)
School of Visual Arts (NY)
Simon Fraser U (BC, Canada)
Southeastern U (FL)
Southern Methodist U (TX)
Stanford U (CA)
State U of New York at Fredonia (NY)
Stephens Coll (MO)
Temple U (PA)
U at Buffalo, the State U of New York (NY)
U of Alberta (AB, Canada)
The U of British Columbia (BC, Canada)
U of California, Berkeley (CA)
U of California, Davis (CA)
U of California, Irvine (CA)
U of California, Los Angeles (CA)
U of California, San Diego (CA)
U of California, Santa Barbara (CA)
U of California, Santa Cruz (CA)
U of Chicago (IL)
U of Colorado at Boulder (CO)
U of Georgia (GA)
U of Hartford (CT)
U of Illinois at Urbana–Champaign (IL)
The U of Iowa (IA)
The U of Kansas (KS)
U of Manitoba (MB, Canada)
U of Michigan (MI)
U of Minnesota, Twin Cities Campus (MN)
U of Nebraska–Lincoln (NE)
U of Nevada, Las Vegas (NV)
U of New Mexico (NM)
U of North Carolina School of the Arts (NC)
U of Oklahoma (OK)
U of Pennsylvania (PA)
U of Pittsburgh (PA)
U of Regina (SK, Canada)
U of Richmond (VA)
U of Rochester (NY)
U of Southern California (CA)
The U of Tampa (FL)
The U of Toledo (OH)
U of Tulsa (OK)
U of Utah (UT)
U of Vermont (VT)
U of Waterloo (ON, Canada)
The U of Western Ontario (ON, Canada)
U of Windsor (ON, Canada)
U of Wisconsin–Milwaukee (WI)
Vanderbilt U (TN)
Vassar Coll (NY)
Washington U in St. Louis (MO)
Watkins Coll of Art, Design, & Film (TN)
Wayne State U (MI)
Webster U (MO)
Wellesley Coll (MA)
Wesleyan U (CT)
Whitman Coll (WA)
Wilfrid Laurier U (ON, Canada)
Wright State U (OH)
Yale U (CT)
York U (ON, Canada)

FILM/VIDEO AND PHOTOGRAPHIC ARTS RELATED
Arizona State U (AZ)
Art Center Coll of Design (CA)
Birmingham-Southern Coll (AL)
Brigham Young U (UT)
Burlington Coll (VT)
Chatham U (PA)
Coll of the Atlantic (ME)
Columbus Coll of Art & Design (OH)
DeSales U (PA)
Fairfield U (CT)
Five Towns Coll (NY)
Full Sail U (FL)
Hollins U (VA)
La Roche Coll (PA)
Maryland Inst Coll of Art (MD)
New England School of Communications (ME)
Northern Michigan U (MI)
Old Dominion U (VA)
Pratt Inst (NY)
Ringling Coll of Art and Design (FL)
Rocky Mountain Coll of Art + Design (CO)
School of the Art Inst of Chicago (IL)
School of the Museum of Fine Arts, Boston (MA)
School of Visual Arts (NY)
Scripps Coll (CA)
Spring Arbor U (MI)
Stevenson U (MD)
Swarthmore Coll (PA)
U of Illinois at Chicago (IL)
U of Regina (SK, Canada)
U of Southern California (CA)
Wellesley Coll (MA)
Western Michigan U (MI)
Woodbury U (CA)

FINANCE
Abilene Christian U (TX)
Adams State Coll (CO)
Adelphi U (NY)
Alabama Ag and Mech U (AL)
Alabama State U (AL)
Albertus Magnus Coll (CT)
Albright Coll (PA)
Alfred U (NY)
American Intl Coll (MA)
American U (DC)
The American U of Paris (France)
Anderson U (IN)
Angelo State U (TX)
Appalachian State U (NC)
Aquinas Coll (TN)
Arcadia U (PA)
Argosy U, Atlanta (GA)
Argosy U, Chicago (IL)
Argosy U, Dallas (TX)
Argosy U, Denver (CO)
Argosy U, Hawai'i (HI)
Argosy U, Inland Empire (CA)
Argosy U, Los Angeles (CA)
Argosy U, Nashville (TN)
Argosy U, Orange County (CA)
Argosy U, Phoenix (AZ)
Argosy U, Salt Lake City (UT)
Argosy U, San Diego (CA)
Argosy U, San Francisco Bay Area (CA)
Argosy U, Sarasota (FL)
Argosy U, Schaumburg (IL)
Argosy U, Seattle (WA)
Argosy U, Tampa (FL)
Argosy U, Twin Cities (MN)
Argosy U, Washington DC (VA)
Arizona State U (AZ)
Arkansas State U—Jonesboro (AR)
Ashland U (OH)
Auburn U (AL)
Auburn U Montgomery (AL)
Augsburg Coll (MN)
Augustana Coll (IL)
Aurora U (IL)
Averett U (VA)
Avila U (MO)
Babson Coll (MA)
Baldwin-Wallace Coll (OH)
Ball State U (IN)
Barry U (FL)
Baylor U (TX)
Belmont U (TN)
Benedictine U (IL)
Bentley U (MA)
Bernard M. Baruch Coll of the City U of New York (NY)
Berry Coll (GA)
Bishop's U (QC, Canada)
Bob Jones U (SC)
Boise State U (ID)
Boston Coll (MA)
Boston U (MA)
Bowling Green State U (OH)
Bradley U (IL)
Brescia U (KY)
Bridgewater State Coll (MA)
Brock U (ON, Canada)
Bryant U (RI)
Butler U (IN)
Cabrini Coll (PA)
California State U, Bakersfield (CA)
California State U, Chico (CA)
California State U, Dominguez Hills (CA)
California State U, East Bay (CA)
California State U, Fresno (CA)
California State U, Fullerton (CA)
California State U, Long Beach (CA)
California State U, San Bernardino (CA)
Canisius Coll (NY)
Cape Breton U (NS, Canada)
Capella U (MN)
Carroll U (WI)
Castleton State Coll (VT)
The Catholic U of America (DC)
Cedarville U (OH)
Centenary Coll (NJ)
Central Connecticut State U (CT)
Central Michigan U (MI)
Christopher Newport U (VA)
Clarion U of Pennsylvania (PA)
Cleary U (MI)
Clemson U (SC)
Cleveland State U (OH)
Coastal Carolina U (SC)
The Coll at Brockport, State U of New York (NY)
The Coll of St. Scholastica (MN)
The Coll of William and Mary (VA)
Colorado State U (CO)
Columbia Coll (MO)
Columbus State U (GA)
Concordia U (QC, Canada)
Concordia U, St. Paul (MN)
Converse Coll (SC)
Corban U (OR)
Creighton U (NE)
Culver-Stockton Coll (MO)
Dakota State U (SD)
Dakota Wesleyan U (SD)
Dallas Baptist U (TX)
Davenport U, Grand Rapids (MI)
Delaware State U (DE)
Delta State U (MS)
DePaul U (IL)
DeSales U (PA)
Dickinson State U (ND)
Dominican Coll (NY)
Dowling Coll (NY)
Drake U (IA)
Drexel U (PA)
Drury U (MO)
Duquesne U (PA)
East Carolina U (NC)
East Central U (OK)
Eastern Illinois U (IL)
Eastern Michigan U (MI)
Eastern Washington U (WA)
East Tennessee State U (TN)
Elmhurst Coll (IL)
Emory U (GA)
Excelsior Coll (NY)
Fairfield U (CT)
Fairmont State U (WV)
Fayetteville State U (NC)
Ferris State U (MI)
Ferrum Coll (VA)
Fitchburg State Coll (MA)
Florida Ag and Mech U (FL)
Florida Atlantic U (FL)
Florida Gulf Coast U (FL)
Florida Intl U (FL)
Florida Southern Coll (FL)
Florida State U (FL)
Fordham U (NY)
Fort Hays State U (KS)
Fort Lewis Coll (CO)
Francis Marion U (SC)
Franklin Pierce U (NH)
Franklin U (OH)
Freed-Hardeman U (TN)
Friends U (KS)
Gannon U (PA)
Gardner-Webb U (NC)
George Mason U (VA)
Georgetown U (DC)
The George Washington U (DC)

INDEXES

Georgia Southern U (GA)
Georgia State U (GA)
Globe Inst of Technology (NY)
Goldey-Beacom Coll (DE)
Gonzaga U (WA)
Governors State U (IL)
Grace Coll (IN)
Grand Valley State U (MI)
Grove City Coll (PA)
Hamline U (MN)
Hampton U (VA)
Harding U (AR)
Hardin-Simmons U (TX)
Hawai'i Pacific U (HI)
HEC Montreal (QC, Canada)
Hilbert Coll (NY)
Hillsdale Coll (MI)
Hofstra U (NY)
Houston Baptist U (TX)
Howard Payne U (TX)
Husson U (ME)
Idaho State U (ID)
Illinois Coll (IL)
Illinois State U (IL)
Immaculata U (PA)
Indiana State U (IN)
Indiana U of Pennsylvania (PA)
Indiana U–Purdue U Fort Wayne (IN)
Indiana Wesleyan U (IN)
Inter American U of Puerto Rico, Bayamón Campus (PR)
Inter American U of Puerto Rico, Ponce Campus (PR)
Inter American U of Puerto Rico, San Germán Campus (PR)
Iona Coll (NY)
Iowa State U of Science and Technology (IA)
Ithaca Coll (NY)
Jackson State U (MS)
Jacksonville State U (AL)
Jacksonville U (FL)
James Madison U (VA)
John Carroll U (OH)
Johnson & Wales U (RI)
Jones Intl U (CO)
Juniata Coll (PA)
Kansas State U (KS)
Kean U (NJ)
Keiser U, Fort Lauderdale (FL)
Kennesaw State U (GA)
Kent State U (OH)
King Coll (TN)
King's Coll (PA)
Kutztown U of Pennsylvania (PA)
Lake Erie Coll (OH)
Lake Forest Coll (IL)
Lakehead U (ON, Canada)
Lake Superior State U (MI)
Lamar U (TX)
La Roche Coll (PA)
La Salle U (PA)
Lasell Coll (MA)
La Sierra U (CA)
Lehigh U (PA)
Le Moyne Coll (NY)
LeTourneau U (TX)
Lewis U (IL)
Lincoln Memorial U (TN)
Lincoln U (PA)
Lindenwood U (MO)
Linfield Coll (OR)
Long Island U, Brooklyn Campus (NY)
Long Island U, C.W. Post Campus (NY)
Longwood U (VA)
Loras Coll (IA)
Louisiana Coll (LA)
Louisiana State U and Ag and Mech Coll (LA)
Louisiana State U in Shreveport (LA)
Louisiana Tech U (LA)
Loyola U Chicago (IL)
Loyola U Maryland (MD)
Loyola U New Orleans (LA)
Lubbock Christian U (TX)
Lycoming Coll (PA)
Manchester Coll (IN)
Manhattan Coll (NY)
Manhattanville Coll (NY)
Marian U (IN)
Marian U (WI)
Marquette U (WI)
Marshall U (WV)
Mars Hill Coll (NC)
The Master's Coll and Sem (CA)
McKendree U (IL)
McMurry U (TX)
McNeese State U (LA)
McPherson Coll (KS)
Memorial U of Newfoundland (NL, Canada)
Menlo Coll (CA)
Merrimack Coll (MA)
Methodist U (NC)
Metropolitan State Coll of Denver (CO)
Miami U (OH)
Miami U Hamilton (OH)
Michigan State U (MI)
Michigan Technological U (MI)
Middle Tennessee State U (TN)
Midwestern State U (TX)
Millikin U (IL)
Minnesota State U Mankato (MN)
Minnesota State U Moorhead (MN)
Minot State U (ND)
Mississippi State U (MS)
Missouri State U (MO)
Missouri Western State U (MO)
Montana State U Billings (MT)
Morehead State U (KY)
Mount Vernon Nazarene U (OH)
Murray State U (KY)
National U (CA)
Newbury Coll (MA)
New England Coll (NH)
New Mexico Highlands U (NM)
New Mexico State U (NM)
New York Inst of Technology (NY)
New York U (NY)
Nicholls State U (LA)
Nichols Coll (MA)
North Carolina State U (NC)
North Central Coll (IL)
North Dakota State U (ND)
Northeastern Illinois U (IL)
Northeastern State U (OK)
Northeastern U (MA)
Northern Arizona U (AZ)
Northern Kentucky U (KY)
Northern Michigan U (MI)
Northern State U (SD)
North Georgia Coll & State U (GA)
Northwestern U (MN)
Northwest Missouri State U (MO)
Northwest Nazarene U (ID)
Nova Southeastern U (FL)
Oakland U (MI)
Ohio Dominican U (OH)
Ohio Northern U (OH)
The Ohio State U (OH)
Ohio U (OH)
Oklahoma Baptist U (OK)
Oklahoma Christian U (OK)
Oklahoma City U (OK)
Oklahoma State U (OK)
Old Dominion U (VA)
Oral Roberts U (OK)
Oregon State U (OR)
Pace U (NY)
Pacific Union Coll (CA)
Penn State Abington (PA)
Penn State Altoona (PA)
Penn State Beaver (PA)
Penn State Berks (PA)
Penn State Brandywine (PA)
Penn State DuBois (PA)
Penn State Erie, The Behrend Coll (PA)
Penn State Fayette, The Eberly Campus (PA)
Penn State Greater Allegheny (PA)
Penn State Harrisburg (PA)
Penn State Hazleton (PA)
Penn State Lehigh Valley (PA)
Penn State Mont Alto (PA)
Penn State New Kensington (PA)
Penn State Schuylkill (PA)
Penn State Shenango (PA)
Penn State U Park (PA)
Penn State Wilkes-Barre (PA)
Penn State Worthington Scranton (PA)
Penn State York (PA)
Philadelphia U (PA)
Pittsburg State U (KS)
Polytechnic U of Puerto Rico (PR)
Pontifical Catholic U of Puerto Rico (PR)
Portland State U (OR)
Post U (CT)
Prairie View A&M U (TX)
Providence Coll (RI)
Queens Coll of the City U of New York (NY)
Quincy U (IL)
Quinnipiac U (CT)
Radford U (VA)
Rhode Island Coll (RI)
Rider U (NJ)
Robert Morris U (PA)
Rochester Inst of Technology (NY)
Rockford Coll (IL)
Roosevelt U (IL)
Rowan U (NJ)
Rutgers, The State U of New Jersey, Camden (NJ)
Rutgers, The State U of New Jersey, Newark (NJ)
Rutgers, The State U of New Jersey, New Brunswick (NJ)
Sacred Heart U (CT)
Saginaw Valley State U (MI)
St. Ambrose U (IA)
Saint Anselm Coll (NH)
St. Bonaventure U (NY)
St. Cloud State U (MN)
St. Edward's U (TX)
Saint Francis U (PA)
St. John Fisher Coll (NY)
St. John's U (NY)
Saint Joseph's U (PA)
Saint Martin's U (WA)
St. Mary's U (TX)
St. Petersburg Coll (FL)
St. Thomas Aquinas Coll (NY)
St. Thomas U (FL)
Saint Vincent Coll (PA)
Salem State Coll (MA)
Salisbury U (MD)
Salve Regina U (RI)
Samford U (AL)
Sam Houston State U (TX)
San Diego State U (CA)
San Francisco State U (CA)
San Jose State U (CA)
Santa Clara U (CA)
Schreiner U (TX)
Seattle U (WA)
Seton Hall U (NJ)
Seton Hill U (PA)
Shippensburg U of Pennsylvania (PA)
Siena Coll (NY)
Simmons Coll (MA)
Slippery Rock U of Pennsylvania (PA)
Southeastern Louisiana U (LA)
Southeastern Oklahoma State U (OK)
Southeastern U (FL)
Southeast Missouri State U (MO)
Southern Adventist U (TN)
Southern Connecticut State U (CT)
Southern Illinois U Carbondale (IL)
Southern Methodist U (TX)
Southern U and Ag and Mech Coll (LA)
Southwest Baptist U (MO)
Southwestern Oklahoma State U (OK)
Southwest Minnesota State U (MN)
Spring Arbor U (MI)
Spring Hill Coll (AL)
State U of New York at Binghamton (NY)
State U of New York at Fredonia (NY)
State U of New York at New Paltz (NY)
State U of New York at Oswego (NY)
State U of New York at Plattsburgh (NY)
State U of New York Coll at Old Westbury (NY)
State U of New York Coll of Technology at Alfred (NY)
State U of New York Coll of Technology at Canton (NY)
Stephen F. Austin State U (TX)
Stetson U (FL)
Stonehill Coll (MA)
Suffolk U (MA)
Sullivan U (KY)
Susquehanna U (PA)
Syracuse U (NY)
Talladega Coll (AL)
Tarleton State U (TX)
Taylor U (IN)
Temple U (PA)
Tennessee Technological U (TN)
Tennessee Wesleyan Coll (TN)
Texas A&M Intl U (TX)
Texas A&M U (TX)
Texas A&M U–Commerce (TX)
Texas A&M U–Corpus Christi (TX)
Texas A&M U–Kingsville (TX)
Texas Christian U (TX)
Texas Lutheran U (TX)
Texas Southern U (TX)
Texas State U–San Marcos (TX)
Texas Tech U (TX)
Texas Woman's U (TX)
Thomas Edison State Coll (NJ)
Thompson Rivers U (BC, Canada)
Tiffin U (OH)
Trinity U (TX)
Troy U (AL)
Truman State U (MO)
Tulane U (LA)
Tuskegee U (AL)
Union U (TN)
The U of Alabama (AL)
The U of Alabama at Birmingham (AL)
The U of Alabama in Huntsville (AL)
U of Alaska Anchorage (AK)
U of Alberta (AB, Canada)
U of Arkansas (AR)
U of Arkansas at Little Rock (AR)
U of Atlanta (GA)
U of Baltimore (MD)
U of Bridgeport (CT)
The U of British Columbia (BC, Canada)
The U of British Columbia–Okanagan (BC, Canada)
U of Central Florida (FL)
U of Central Missouri (MO)
U of Central Oklahoma (OK)
U of Charleston (WV)
U of Cincinnati (OH)
U of Colorado at Boulder (CO)
U of Colorado at Colorado Springs (CO)
U of Connecticut (CT)
U of Dayton (OH)
U of Delaware (DE)
U of Denver (CO)
U of Evansville (IN)
The U of Findlay (OH)
U of Florida (FL)
U of Georgia (GA)
U of Guam (GU)
U of Hartford (CT)
U of Hawaii at Manoa (HI)
U of Houston (TX)
U of Houston–Clear Lake (TX)
U of Houston–Downtown (TX)
U of Idaho (ID)
U of Illinois at Chicago (IL)
U of Illinois at Urbana–Champaign (IL)
The U of Iowa (IA)
The U of Kansas (KS)
U of Kentucky (KY)
U of Lethbridge (AB, Canada)
U of Louisiana at Monroe (LA)
U of Louisville (KY)
U of Maine (ME)
U of Manitoba (MB, Canada)
U of Mary (ND)
U of Mary Hardin-Baylor (TX)
U of Maryland, Coll Park (MD)
U of Maryland U Coll (MD)
U of Massachusetts Amherst (MA)
U of Massachusetts Dartmouth (MA)
U of Memphis (TN)
U of Miami (FL)
U of Michigan–Dearborn (MI)
U of Michigan–Flint (MI)
U of Minnesota, Duluth (MN)
U of Minnesota, Twin Cities Campus (MN)
U of Mississippi (MS)
U of Missouri (MO)
U of Missouri–St. Louis (MO)
U of Montevallo (AL)
U of Nebraska at Omaha (NE)
U of Nebraska–Lincoln (NE)
U of Nevada, Las Vegas (NV)
U of Nevada, Reno (NV)
U of New Brunswick Fredericton (NB, Canada)
U of New Haven (CT)
U of New Orleans (LA)
U of North Alabama (AL)
The U of North Carolina at Charlotte (NC)
The U of North Carolina at Greensboro (NC)
The U of North Carolina Wilmington (NC)
U of North Dakota (ND)
U of Northern Iowa (IA)
U of North Florida (FL)
U of North Texas (TX)
U of Notre Dame (IN)
U of Oklahoma (OK)
U of Ottawa (ON, Canada)
U of Pennsylvania (PA)
U of Pittsburgh (PA)
U of Pittsburgh at Johnstown (PA)
U of Portland (OR)
U of Puerto Rico at Bayamón (PR)
U of Puerto Rico, Río Piedras (PR)
U of Regina (SK, Canada)
U of Rhode Island (RI)
U of St. Francis (IL)
U of St. Thomas (MN)
U of St. Thomas (TX)
U of San Diego (CA)
U of San Francisco (CA)
U of Saskatchewan (SK, Canada)
The U of Scranton (PA)
U of South Alabama (AL)
U of South Carolina (SC)
The U of South Dakota (SD)
U of Southern Indiana (IN)
U of Southern Mississippi (MS)
U of South Florida (FL)
The U of Tampa (FL)
The U of Tennessee (TN)
The U of Tennessee at Martin (TN)
The U of Texas at Austin (TX)
The U of Texas at Brownsville (TX)
The U of Texas at Dallas (TX)
The U of Texas at El Paso (TX)
The U of Texas at San Antonio (TX)
The U of Texas at Tyler (TX)
The U of Texas of the Permian Basin (TX)
The U of Texas–Pan American (TX)
U of the District of Columbia (DC)
The U of Toledo (OH)
U of Toronto (ON, Canada)
U of Tulsa (OK)
U of Utah (UT)
U of Washington, Tacoma (WA)
The U of Western Ontario (ON, Canada)
U of West Florida (FL)
U of West Georgia (GA)
U of Windsor (ON, Canada)
U of Wisconsin–Eau Claire (WI)
U of Wisconsin–La Crosse (WI)
U of Wisconsin–Madison (WI)
U of Wisconsin–Milwaukee (WI)
U of Wisconsin–Oshkosh (WI)
U of Wisconsin–Parkside (WI)
U of Wisconsin–River Falls (WI)
U of Wisconsin–Superior (WI)
U of Wisconsin–Whitewater (WI)
U of Wyoming (WY)
Utah State U (UT)
Valdosta State U (GA)
Valparaiso U (IN)
Vanguard U of Southern California (CA)
Villanova U (PA)
Virginia Polytechnic Inst and State U (VA)
Wagner Coll (NY)
Wake Forest U (NC)
Walden U (MN)
Waldorf Coll (IA)
Walsh U (OH)
Wartburg Coll (IA)
Washburn U (KS)
Washington State U (WA)
Washington U in St. Louis (MO)
Waynesburg U (PA)
Wayne State U (MI)
Webber Intl U (FL)
Weber State U (UT)
West Chester U of Pennsylvania (PA)
Western Carolina U (NC)
Western Connecticut State U (CT)
Western Illinois U (IL)
Western Kentucky U (KY)
Western Michigan U (MI)
Western New England Coll (MA)
Western Washington U (WA)
Westminster Coll (UT)
West Virginia U (WV)
West Virginia Wesleyan Coll (WV)
Wichita State U (KS)
Wilmington U (DE)
Wingate U (NC)
Winona State U (MN)
Wofford Coll (SC)
Wright State U (OH)
Xavier U (OH)
York Coll of Pennsylvania (PA)
York U (ON, Canada)
Youngstown State U (OH)

FINANCE AND FINANCIAL MANAGEMENT SERVICES RELATED

Babson Coll (MA)
Bryant U (RI)
Florida Ag and Mech U (FL)
Goldey-Beacom Coll (DE)
Grace Bible Coll (MI)
Hofstra U (NY)
James Madison U (VA)
Johnson & Wales U (CO)
Park U (MO)
Saint Mary's Coll of California (CA)
San Jose State U (CA)
Southern Methodist U (TX)
The U of Tampa (FL)
Virginia Commonwealth U (VA)
Westminster Coll (UT)

FINANCIAL PLANNING AND SERVICES

Baylor U (TX)
Bethany Coll (KS)
Brigham Young U (UT)
Bryant & Stratton Coll (WI)
Bryant & Stratton Coll—Virginia Beach (VA)
Bryant U (RI)
Central Michigan U (MI)
Cleary U (MI)
Jamestown Coll (ND)
Lubbock Christian U (TX)
Marywood U (PA)
Medaille Coll (NY)
Northern Michigan U (MI)
The Ohio State U at Lima (OH)

Financial Planning and Services

Southern Methodist U (TX)
Trinity Christian Coll (IL)
The U of Akron (OH)
U of Illinois at Urbana–Champaign (IL)
U of Maine at Augusta (ME)
U of North Texas (TX)
Western Michigan U (MI)
Widener U (PA)

FINE ARTS RELATED

Adelphi U (NY)
Allegheny Coll (PA)
Art Center Coll of Design (CA)
Birmingham-Southern Coll (AL)
Bowling Green State U (OH)
Burlington Coll (VT)
California State U, Long Beach (CA)
The Coll of Saint Rose (NY)
Coll of Staten Island of the City U of New York (NY)
Columbus Coll of Art & Design (OH)
Cornish Coll of the Arts (WA)
Covenant Coll (GA)
Grand Valley State U (MI)
Hood Coll (MD)
Kentucky Wesleyan Coll (KY)
Lindenwood U (MO)
Long Island U, Brooklyn Campus (NY)
Long Island U, C.W. Post Campus (NY)
Loyola U New Orleans (LA)
Maryland Inst Coll of Art (MD)
Monmouth U (NJ)
New York U (NY)
Northern Michigan U (MI)
Oakland U (MI)
Oregon Coll of Art & Craft (OR)
Our Lady of the Lake U of San Antonio (TX)
Pontifical Catholic U of Puerto Rico (PR)
Pratt Inst (NY)
Presbyterian Coll (SC)
Purchase Coll, State U of New York (NY)
Rutgers, The State U of New Jersey, Newark (NJ)
St. John's U (NY)
School of the Art Inst of Chicago (IL)
School of the Museum of Fine Arts, Boston (MA)
Skidmore Coll (NY)
State U of New York Coll at Potsdam (NY)
Syracuse U (NY)
U of California, Los Angeles (CA)
U of Denver (CO)
U of Hartford (CT)
U of Lethbridge (AB, Canada)
U of Maryland, Baltimore County (MD)
U of Mary Washington (VA)
U of Massachusetts Dartmouth (MA)
U of Michigan (MI)
U of North Alabama (AL)
U of Regina (SK, Canada)
The U of Western Ontario (ON, Canada)
Ursinus Coll (PA)
Virginia Commonwealth U (VA)
Widener U (PA)

FINE/STUDIO ARTS

Abilene Christian U (TX)
Acad of Art U (CA)
Alberta Coll of Art & Design (AB, Canada)
Albertus Magnus Coll (CT)
Alderson-Broaddus Coll (WV)
Alfred U (NY)
Allegheny Coll (PA)
Alma Coll (MI)
American U (DC)
American U of Beirut (Lebanon)
Amherst Coll (MA)
Anderson U (IN)
Angelo State U (TX)
Appalachian State U (NC)
Aquinas Coll (MI)
Arcadia U (PA)
Art Center Coll of Design (CA)
The Art Center Design Coll, Tucson (AZ)
The Art Inst of Boston at Lesley U (MA)
Asbury U (KY)
Ashland U (OH)
Auburn U (AL)
Augsburg Coll (MN)
Augustana Coll (IL)
Baker U (KS)
Baldwin-Wallace Coll (OH)
Bard Coll (NY)
Barton Coll (NC)
Baylor U (TX)
Bellarmine U (KY)
Belmont U (TN)
Beloit Coll (WI)
Bemidji State U (MN)
Benedictine U (IL)
Bennington Coll (VT)
Bethany Coll (WV)
Bethel Coll (KS)
Bethel U (MN)
Birmingham-Southern Coll (AL)
Bishop's U (QC, Canada)
Bloomsburg U of Pennsylvania (PA)
Boston Coll (MA)
Bowdoin Coll (ME)
Bowling Green State U (OH)
Bradley U (IL)
Brandeis U (MA)
Brenau U (GA)
Brevard Coll (NC)
Bridgewater Coll (VA)
Bridgewater State Coll (MA)
Brigham Young U (UT)
Brock U (ON, Canada)
Brooklyn Coll of the City U of New York (NY)
Bucknell U (PA)
Buffalo State Coll, State U of New York (NY)
Burlington Coll (VT)
California Coll of the Arts (CA)
California Inst of the Arts (CA)
California Polytechnic State U, San Luis Obispo (CA)
California State U, Chico (CA)
California State U, East Bay (CA)
California State U, Fullerton (CA)
California State U, Long Beach (CA)
California State U, Stanislaus (CA)
Calvin Coll (MI)
Carleton Coll (MN)
Carlow U (PA)
Carroll U (WI)
Cazenovia Coll (NY)
Cedarville U (OH)
Centenary Coll of Louisiana (LA)
Central Michigan U (MI)
Chapman U (CA)
Chatham U (PA)
Chowan U (NC)
Christian Brothers U (TN)
Christopher Newport U (VA)
Claflin U (SC)
Claremont McKenna Coll (CA)
Clarke Coll (IA)
Clark U (MA)
Coastal Carolina U (SC)
Coker Coll (SC)
Colby Coll (ME)
The Coll at Brockport, State U of New York (NY)
Coll for Creative Studies (MI)
Coll of Charleston (SC)
The Coll of Idaho (ID)
Coll of Mount St. Joseph (OH)
The Coll of New Jersey (NJ)
The Coll of New Rochelle (NY)
Coll of Saint Benedict (MN)
Coll of Santa Fe (NM)
Coll of the Holy Cross (MA)
Coll of the Ozarks (MO)
Coll of Visual Arts (MN)
The Coll of Wooster (OH)
The Colorado Coll (CO)
Colorado State U (CO)
Colorado State U–Pueblo (CO)
Columbia Coll (SC)
Columbia Coll Chicago (IL)
Concordia Coll (MN)
Concordia U (QC, Canada)
Concordia U, St. Paul (MN)
Converse Coll (SC)
Cooper Union for the Advancement of Science and Art (NY)
Corcoran Coll of Art and Design (DC)
Cornell U (NY)
Cornish Coll of the Arts (WA)
Cumberland U (TN)
Daemen Coll (NY)
Dakota Wesleyan U (SD)
Dartmouth Coll (NH)
Denison U (OH)
DePauw U (IN)
Dickinson Coll (PA)
Dominican U (IL)
Drake U (IA)
Drury U (MO)
East Carolina U (NC)
Eastern Washington U (WA)
Edinboro U of Pennsylvania (PA)
Elizabeth City State U (NC)
Elizabethtown Coll (PA)
Elmira Coll (NY)
Emmanuel Coll (MA)
Emory U (GA)
Endicott Coll (MA)
The Evergreen State Coll (WA)
Fairfield U (CT)
Fashion Inst of Technology (NY)
Felician Coll (NJ)
Ferris State U (MI)
Flagler Coll (FL)
Florida Ag and Mech U (FL)
Florida Intl U (FL)
Florida Southern Coll (FL)
Florida State U (FL)
Fontbonne U (MO)
Fordham U (NY)
Fort Hays State U (KS)
Franklin & Marshall Coll (PA)
Franklin Pierce U (NH)
Frostburg State U (MD)
Furman U (SC)
Gallaudet U (DC)
Gardner-Webb U (NC)
Georgetown Coll (KY)
Georgetown U (DC)
The George Washington U (DC)
Georgia State U (GA)
Gettysburg Coll (PA)
Governors State U (IL)
Graceland U (IA)
Grand View U (IA)
Green Mountain Coll (VT)
Hamilton Coll (NY)
Hamline U (MN)
Hampden-Sydney Coll (VA)
Hampshire Coll (MA)
Harding U (AR)
Hardin-Simmons U (TX)
High Point U (NC)
Hiram Coll (OH)
Hofstra U (NY)
Hope Coll (MI)
Houston Baptist U (TX)
Humboldt State U (CA)
Hunter Coll of the City U of New York (NY)
Huntingdon Coll (AL)
Illinois State U (IL)
Indiana State U (IN)
Indiana U Bloomington (IN)
Indiana U Kokomo (IN)
Indiana U of Pennsylvania (PA)
Indiana U–Purdue U Fort Wayne (IN)
Indiana U–Purdue U Indianapolis (IN)
Indiana U South Bend (IN)
Indiana U Southeast (IN)
Iowa Wesleyan Coll (IA)
Ithaca Coll (NY)
Jacksonville U (FL)
Jamestown Coll (ND)
Johnson State Coll (VT)
Judson U (IL)
Juniata Coll (PA)
Kean U (NJ)
Keene State Coll (NH)
Kent State U (OH)
Kentucky State U (KY)
Keystone Coll (PA)
Kutztown U of Pennsylvania (PA)
Lafayette Coll (PA)
Lake Erie Coll (OH)
Lake Forest Coll (IL)
Lamar U (TX)
La Sierra U (CA)
Lawrence U (WI)
Lewis U (IL)
Limestone Coll (SC)
Lincoln U (MO)
Lindenwood U (MO)
Lindsey Wilson Coll (KY)
Linfield Coll (OR)
Lipscomb U (TN)
Lock Haven U of Pennsylvania (PA)
Long Island U, C.W. Post Campus (NY)
Longwood U (VA)
Loras Coll (IA)
Louisiana Coll (LA)
Louisiana State U and Ag and Mech Coll (LA)
Loyola Marymount U (CA)
Loyola U Chicago (IL)
Lycoming Coll (PA)
Madonna U (MI)
Maharishi U of Management (IA)
Malone U (OH)
Manchester Coll (IN)
Manhattanville Coll (NY)
Marian U (IN)
Marian U (WI)
Marietta Coll (OH)
Marist Coll (NY)
Marlboro Coll (VT)
Mars Hill Coll (NC)
Maryland Inst Coll of Art (MD)
Marylhurst U (OR)
Marymount Manhattan Coll (NY)
Marymount U (VA)
Maryville Coll (TN)
Maryville U of Saint Louis (MO)
Massachusetts Coll of Art and Design (MA)
McMurry U (TX)
Memphis Coll of Art (TN)
Mercyhurst Coll (PA)
Meredith Coll (NC)
Merrimack Coll (MA)
Messiah Coll (PA)
Middlebury Coll (VT)
Milligan Coll (TN)
Millikin U (IL)
Millsaps Coll (MS)
Mills Coll (CA)
Minneapolis Coll of Art and Design (MN)
Minnesota State U Mankato (MN)
Minnesota State U Moorhead (MN)
Mississippi Coll (MS)
Montana State U (MT)
Montclair State U (NJ)
Moore Coll of Art & Design (PA)
Moravian Coll (PA)
Morehead State U (KY)
Morningside Coll (IA)
Mount Allison U (NB, Canada)
Mount Holyoke Coll (MA)
Murray State U (KY)
Naropa U (CO)
Nazareth Coll of Rochester (NY)
New Coll of Florida (FL)
New England Coll (NH)
New Hampshire Inst of Art (NH)
New Mexico State U (NM)
New York Inst of Technology (NY)
New York U (NY)
Nipissing U (ON, Canada)
Northeastern State U (OK)
Northeastern U (MA)
Northern Kentucky U (KY)
North Greenville U (SC)
Northwestern Coll (MN)
Northwestern State U of Louisiana (LA)
Northwest Missouri State U (MO)
Notre Dame de Namur U (CA)
Nova Southeastern U (FL)
Oakland U (MI)
Oberlin Coll (OH)
Occidental Coll (CA)
Ohio Dominican U (OH)
Ohio Northern U (OH)
The Ohio State U (OH)
Ohio U (OH)
Ohio Wesleyan U (OH)
Oklahoma Baptist U (OK)
Oklahoma City U (OK)
Old Dominion U (VA)
Oral Roberts U (OK)
Otis Coll of Art and Design (CA)
Ouachita Baptist U (AR)
Pace U (NY)
Pacific Lutheran U (WA)
Pacific Union Coll (CA)
Park U (MO)
Parsons The New School for Design (NY)
Pennsylvania Coll of Art & Design (PA)
Piedmont Coll (GA)
Pitzer Coll (CA)
Plymouth State U (NH)
Pomona Coll (CA)
Pratt Inst (NY)
Presbyterian Coll (SC)
Prescott Coll (AZ)
Principia Coll (IL)
Providence Coll (RI)
Queens Coll of the City U of New York (NY)
Queens U of Charlotte (NC)
Randolph Coll (VA)
Randolph-Macon Coll (VA)
Redeemer U Coll (ON, Canada)
Reed Coll (OR)
Rhode Island Coll (RI)
Rhodes Coll (TN)
Rice U (TX)
The Richard Stockton Coll of New Jersey (NJ)
Ringling Coll of Art and Design (FL)
Rivier Coll (NH)
Rochester Inst of Technology (NY)
Rollins Coll (FL)
Rosemont Coll (PA)
Rowan U (NJ)
Sage Coll of Albany (NY)
Saginaw Valley State U (MI)
St. Ambrose U (IA)
St. Catherine U (MN)
St. Cloud State U (MN)
Saint John's U (MN)
St. Lawrence U (NY)
Saint Louis U (MO)
Saint Mary-of-the-Woods Coll (IN)
Saint Mary's U of Minnesota (MN)
St. Thomas Aquinas Coll (NY)
Saint Vincent Coll (PA)
Salem Coll (NC)
Salisbury U (MD)
Salve Regina U (RI)
San Diego State U (CA)
San Jose State U (CA)
Santa Clara U (CA)
Sarah Lawrence Coll (NY)
School of the Art Inst of Chicago (IL)
School of the Museum of Fine Arts, Boston (MA)
School of Visual Arts (NY)
Scripps Coll (CA)
Seattle U (WA)
Seton Hill U (PA)
Sewanee: The U of the South (TN)
Shawnee State U (OH)
Shorter U (GA)
Siena Coll (NY)
Slippery Rock U of Pennsylvania (PA)
Smith Coll (MA)
Sonoma State U (CA)
South Carolina State U (SC)
Southern Arkansas U–Magnolia (AR)
Southern Connecticut State U (CT)
Southern Illinois U Carbondale (IL)
Southern Illinois U Edwardsville (IL)
Southern Methodist U (TX)
Southern U and Ag and Mech Coll (LA)
Spring Hill Coll (AL)
Stanford U (CA)
State U of New York at Fredonia (NY)
State U of New York at New Paltz (NY)
State U of New York at Plattsburgh (NY)
State U of New York Coll at Cortland (NY)
State U of New York Coll at Geneseo (NY)
State U of New York Coll at Oneonta (NY)
Stonehill Coll (MA)
Stony Brook U, State U of New York (NY)
Susquehanna U (PA)
Swarthmore Coll (PA)
Sweet Briar Coll (VA)
Syracuse U (NY)
Talladega Coll (AL)
Tarleton State U (TX)
Texas A&M U–Commerce (TX)
Texas A&M U–Corpus Christi (TX)
Texas A&M U–Kingsville (TX)
Texas Christian U (TX)
Texas Southern U (TX)
Texas State U–San Marcos (TX)
Texas Tech U (TX)
Thomas More Coll (KY)
Thompson Rivers U (BC, Canada)
Trinity Coll (CT)
Truman State U (MO)
Tulane U (LA)
Union Coll (NE)
Union Coll (NY)
Universidad de las Américas–Puebla (Mexico)
Université du Québec en Outaouais (QC, Canada)
U at Buffalo, the State U of New York (NY)
The U of Alabama (AL)
U of Alberta (AB, Canada)
The U of Arizona (AZ)
The U of British Columbia (BC, Canada)
U of California, Davis (CA)
U of California, Irvine (CA)
U of California, Riverside (CA)
U of California, San Diego (CA)
U of California, Santa Barbara (CA)
U of Central Florida (FL)
U of Central Missouri (MO)
U of Chicago (IL)
U of Colorado at Boulder (CO)
U of Colorado at Colorado Springs (CO)
U of Colorado Denver (CO)
U of Connecticut (CT)
U of Dallas (TX)
U of Dayton (OH)
U of Florida (FL)
U of Georgia (GA)
U of Guelph (ON, Canada)
U of Idaho (ID)
U of Illinois at Chicago (IL)
U of Illinois at Springfield (IL)
U of Indianapolis (IN)
The U of Kansas (KS)
U of Kentucky (KY)
U of Lethbridge (AB, Canada)
U of Louisiana at Monroe (LA)
U of Louisville (KY)
U of Maine (ME)
U of Maine at Augusta (ME)

U of Maine at Presque Isle (ME)
U of Mary Hardin-Baylor (TX)
U of Maryland, Coll Park (MD)
U of Massachusetts Amherst (MA)
U of Massachusetts Lowell (MA)
U of Miami (FL)
U of Michigan–Flint (MI)
U of Minnesota, Duluth (MN)
U of Missouri–Kansas City (MO)
U of Missouri–St. Louis (MO)
U of Mount Union (OH)
U of Nebraska–Lincoln (NE)
U of Nevada, Las Vegas (NV)
U of New Hampshire (NH)
U of New Haven (CT)
U of New Orleans (LA)
U of North Alabama (AL)
The U of North Carolina at Asheville (NC)
The U of North Carolina at Chapel Hill (NC)
The U of North Carolina at Charlotte (NC)
The U of North Carolina at Greensboro (NC)
The U of North Carolina at Pembroke (NC)
The U of North Carolina Wilmington (NC)
U of Northern Colorado (CO)
U of Northern Iowa (IA)
U of North Florida (FL)
U of North Texas (TX)
U of Notre Dame (IN)
U of Oklahoma (OK)
U of Oregon (OR)
U of Ottawa (ON, Canada)
U of Pennsylvania (PA)
U of Pittsburgh (PA)
U of Puerto Rico at Utuado (PR)
U of Puerto Rico, Río Piedras (PR)
U of Redlands (CA)
U of Richmond (VA)
U of Rochester (NY)
U of St. Thomas (TX)
U of San Diego (CA)
U of San Francisco (CA)
U of Saskatchewan (SK, Canada)
U of Science and Arts of Oklahoma (OK)
U of South Carolina (SC)
U of South Carolina Aiken (SC)
U of South Carolina Upstate (SC)
U of Southern California (CA)
U of South Florida (FL)
The U of Tennessee (TN)
The U of Texas at Arlington (TX)
The U of Texas at Dallas (TX)
The U of Texas at El Paso (TX)
The U of Texas–Pan American (TX)
U of the Cumberlands (KY)
U of the District of Columbia (DC)
U of the Ozarks (AR)
U of the Pacific (CA)
The U of Toledo (OH)
U of Tulsa (OK)
U of Vermont (VT)
U of Waterloo (ON, Canada)
The U of Western Ontario (ON, Canada)
U of West Florida (FL)
U of Windsor (ON, Canada)
U of Wisconsin–Milwaukee (WI)
U of Wisconsin–Oshkosh (WI)
U of Wisconsin–Stevens Point (WI)
U of Wisconsin–Superior (WI)
Ursuline Coll (OH)
Vanderbilt U (TN)
Vassar Coll (NY)
Viterbo U (WI)
Wake Forest U (NC)
Washington and Lee U (VA)
Washington State U (WA)
Washington U in St. Louis (MO)
Watkins Coll of Art, Design, & Film (TN)
Webster U (MO)
Wellesley Coll (MA)
Wells Coll (NY)
Wesleyan Coll (GA)
Wesleyan U (CT)
West Chester U of Pennsylvania (PA)
Western Carolina U (NC)
Western Illinois U (IL)
Western Kentucky U (KY)
Western Michigan U (MI)
Western State Coll of Colorado (CO)
Westminster Coll (UT)
West Virginia Wesleyan Coll (WV)
Wheaton Coll (MA)
Willamette U (OR)
William Paterson U of New Jersey (NJ)
Williams Coll (MA)
Wingate U (NC)
Winona State U (MN)
Xavier U (OH)
York Coll of Pennsylvania (PA)
York U (ON, Canada)
Youngstown State U (OH)

FIRE PROTECTION AND SAFETY TECHNOLOGY
Columbia Southern U (AL)
Oklahoma State U (OK)
Thomas Edison State Coll (NJ)
U of Cincinnati (OH)
U of New Haven (CT)

FIRE PROTECTION RELATED
American Public U System (WV)
The U of Akron (OH)
U of New Haven (CT)

FIRE SCIENCE
Cogswell Polytechnical Coll (CA)
Hampton U (VA)
Holy Family U (PA)
Idaho State U (ID)
John Jay Coll of Criminal Justice of the City U of New York (NY)
Lake Superior State U (MI)
Lewis-Clark State Coll (ID)
Madonna U (MI)
Providence Coll (RI)
U of Cincinnati (OH)
U of Florida (FL)
U of Maryland U Coll (MD)
U of New Brunswick Fredericton (NB, Canada)
Utah Valley U (UT)

FIRE SERVICES ADMINISTRATION
American Public U System (WV)
California State U, Los Angeles (CA)
Columbia Southern U (AL)
Fayetteville State U (NC)
Holy Family U (PA)
John Jay Coll of Criminal Justice of the City U of New York (NY)
Lewis U (IL)
Lindenwood U (MO)
Salem State Coll (MA)
Southern Illinois U Carbondale (IL)
The U of North Carolina at Charlotte (NC)
Utah Valley U (UT)
Western Oregon U (OR)

FISHING AND FISHERIES SCIENCES AND MANAGEMENT
Clemson U (SC)
Delaware State U (DE)
Humboldt State U (CA)
Iowa State U of Science and Technology (IA)
Lake Superior State U (MI)
Mansfield U of Pennsylvania (PA)
Michigan State U (MI)
Murray State U (KY)
North Carolina State U (NC)
The Ohio State U (OH)
State U of New York Coll of Environmental Science and Forestry (NY)
Texas A&M U at Galveston (TX)
Texas Tech U (TX)
U of Alaska Fairbanks (AK)
U of Arkansas at Pine Bluff (AR)
The U of British Columbia (BC, Canada)
U of Georgia (GA)
U of Idaho (ID)
U of Minnesota, Twin Cities Campus (MN)
U of Missouri (MO)
U of New Brunswick Fredericton (NB, Canada)
U of Rhode Island (RI)
The U of Tennessee at Martin (TN)
U of Washington (WA)
West Virginia U (WV)

FLIGHT INSTRUCTION
South Dakota State U (SD)
U of North Dakota (ND)

FLUID/THERMAL SCIENCES
Worcester Polytechnic Inst (MA)

FOODS AND NUTRITION RELATED
California State U, Long Beach (CA)
Kent State U (OH)
Samford U (AL)
The U of British Columbia (BC, Canada)
Utah State U (UT)

FOOD SCIENCE
Acadia U (NS, Canada)
Alabama Ag and Mech U (AL)
American U of Beirut (Lebanon)
Auburn U (AL)
California Polytechnic State U, San Luis Obispo (CA)
California State Polytechnic U, Pomona (CA)
Clemson U (SC)
Cornell U (NY)
Delaware Valley Coll (PA)
Dominican U (IL)
Framingham State Coll (MA)
Kansas State U (KS)
Lamar U (TX)
Louisiana State U and Ag and Mech Coll (LA)
Memorial U of Newfoundland (NL, Canada)
Michigan State U (MI)
Mississippi State U (MS)
North Carolina State U (NC)
North Dakota State U (ND)
The Ohio State U (OH)
Oklahoma State U (OK)
Oregon State U (OR)
Penn State Abington (PA)
Penn State Altoona (PA)
Penn State Beaver (PA)
Penn State Berks (PA)
Penn State Brandywine (PA)
Penn State DuBois (PA)
Penn State Erie, The Behrend Coll (PA)
Penn State Fayette, The Eberly Campus (PA)
Penn State Greater Allegheny (PA)
Penn State Hazleton (PA)
Penn State Lehigh Valley (PA)
Penn State Mont Alto (PA)
Penn State New Kensington (PA)
Penn State Schuylkill (PA)
Penn State Shenango (PA)
Penn State U Park (PA)
Penn State Wilkes-Barre (PA)
Penn State Worthington Scranton (PA)
Penn State York (PA)
Purdue U (IN)
Rutgers, The State U of New Jersey, New Brunswick (NJ)
San Jose State U (CA)
Simmons Coll (MA)
Texas A&M U (TX)
Texas Tech U (TX)
Tuskegee U (AL)
U of Alberta (AB, Canada)
U of Arkansas (AR)
The U of British Columbia (BC, Canada)
U of California, Davis (CA)
U of Delaware (DE)
U of Florida (FL)
U of Georgia (GA)
U of Guelph (ON, Canada)
U of Idaho (ID)
U of Illinois at Urbana–Champaign (IL)
U of Kentucky (KY)
U of Maine (ME)
U of Manitoba (MB, Canada)
U of Maryland, Coll Park (MD)
U of Massachusetts Amherst (MA)
U of Missouri (MO)
U of Nebraska–Lincoln (NE)
U of Saskatchewan (SK, Canada)
The U of Tennessee (TN)
U of the District of Columbia (DC)
U of Wisconsin–Madison (WI)
U of Wisconsin–River Falls (WI)
Virginia Polytechnic Inst and State U (VA)

FOOD SCIENCE AND TECHNOLOGY RELATED
North Dakota State U (ND)
The U of British Columbia (BC, Canada)
U of Illinois at Urbana–Champaign (IL)

FOOD SERVICE AND DINING ROOM MANAGEMENT
Johnson & Wales U (CO)
Johnson & Wales U (FL)
Johnson & Wales U—Charlotte Campus (NC)

FOOD SERVICE SYSTEMS ADMINISTRATION
Central Michigan U (MI)
Dominican U (IL)
Iowa State U of Science and Technology (IA)
Johnson & Wales U (RI)
Lipscomb U (TN)
Northwest Missouri State U (MO)
Ohio U (OH)
Rochester Inst of Technology (NY)
State U of New York Coll at Oneonta (NY)
Syracuse U (NY)
The U of North Carolina at Greensboro (NC)
U of Wisconsin–Stout (WI)
Western Michigan U (MI)

FOODS, NUTRITION, AND WELLNESS
Acadia U (NS, Canada)
Alcorn State U (MS)
Andrews U (MI)
Appalachian State U (NC)
Arizona State U (AZ)
Ashland U (OH)
Auburn U (AL)
Bastyr U (WA)
Bluffton U (OH)
Bob Jones U (SC)
Bowling Green State U (OH)
Bridgewater Coll (VA)
Brooklyn Coll of the City U of New York (NY)
California State U, Fresno (CA)
California State U, Los Angeles (CA)
California State U, San Bernardino (CA)
Carson-Newman Coll (TN)
Cedar Crest Coll (PA)
Coll of the Ozarks (MO)
Concordia Coll (MN)
Cornell U (NY)
Delaware State U (DE)
Dominican U (IL)
Florida State U (FL)
Fort Valley State U (GA)
Gallaudet U (DC)
Georgia Southern U (GA)
Georgia State U (GA)
Goddard Coll (VT)
Hunter Coll of the City U of New York (NY)
Immaculata U (PA)
Indiana State U (IN)
Indiana U of Pennsylvania (PA)
Iowa State U of Science and Technology (IA)
Ithaca Coll (NY)
Jacksonville State U (AL)
James Madison U (VA)
Kent State U (OH)
Lehman Coll of the City U of New York (NY)
Madonna U (MI)
The Master's Coll and Sem (CA)
Memorial U of Newfoundland (NL, Canada)
Middle Tennessee State U (TN)
Minnesota State U Mankato (MN)
Montclair State U (NJ)
Murray State U (KY)
New Mexico State U (NM)
New York U (NY)
Northeastern State U (OK)
The Ohio State U (OH)
Ohio U (OH)
Oklahoma State U (OK)
Pepperdine U, Malibu (CA)
Prairie View A&M U (TX)
Purdue U (IN)
Radford U (VA)
St. Catherine U (MN)
St. Francis Xavier U (NS, Canada)
Saint Louis U (MO)
Seattle Pacific U (WA)
South Carolina State U (SC)
South Dakota State U (SD)
Southern Illinois U Carbondale (IL)
State U of New York at Plattsburgh (NY)
Stephen F. Austin State U (TX)
Syracuse U (NY)
Tennessee Technological U (TN)
Texas A&M U (TX)
Texas State U–San Marcos (TX)
Texas Tech U (TX)
Texas Woman's U (TX)
Tuskegee U (AL)
Universidad de las Américas–Puebla (Mexico)
U of Alberta (AB, Canada)
U of Arkansas (AR)
The U of British Columbia (BC, Canada)
U of Central Oklahoma (OK)
U of Cincinnati (OH)
U of Dayton (OH)
U of Delaware (DE)
U of Georgia (GA)
U of Idaho (ID)
U of Kentucky (KY)
U of Maine (ME)
U of Manitoba (MB, Canada)
U of Maryland, Coll Park (MD)
U of Minnesota, Twin Cities Campus (MN)
U of Missouri (MO)
U of Nebraska–Lincoln (NE)
U of Nevada, Reno (NV)
U of New Mexico (NM)
The U of North Carolina at Chapel Hill (NC)
U of Northern Iowa (IA)
U of Ottawa (ON, Canada)
U of Puerto Rico, Río Piedras (PR)
U of Rhode Island (RI)
The U of Tennessee (TN)
U of Toronto (ON, Canada)
The U of Western Ontario (ON, Canada)
U of Wisconsin–Madison (WI)
Virginia Polytechnic Inst and State U (VA)
Washington State U (WA)
Wayne State U (MI)
Winthrop U (SC)
Youngstown State U (OH)

FOOD TECHNOLOGY AND PROCESSING
Brigham Young U (UT)
Iowa State U of Science and Technology (IA)
Johnson & Wales U (RI)
Universidad de las Américas–Puebla (Mexico)
U of Illinois at Urbana–Champaign (IL)

FOREIGN LANGUAGES AND LITERATURES
Arkansas State U—Jonesboro (AR)
Arkansas Tech U (AR)
Assumption Coll (MA)
Auburn U (AL)
Auburn U Montgomery (AL)
Augustana Coll (SD)
Austin Peay State U (TN)
Bennington Coll (VT)
Boston U (MA)
California Polytechnic State U, San Luis Obispo (CA)
California State U, Monterey Bay (CA)
Cameron U (OK)
Carnegie Mellon U (PA)
The Citadel, The Military Coll of South Carolina (SC)
Coll of Notre Dame of Maryland (MD)
Colorado State U (CO)
Colorado State U–Pueblo (CO)
Concordia U Coll of Alberta (AB, Canada)
Covenant Coll (GA)
Delta State U (MS)
Duquesne U (PA)
Eastern Illinois U (IL)
East Tennessee State U (TN)
Eckerd Coll (FL)
Elmira Coll (NY)
Elon U (NC)
Emporia State U (KS)
Eugene Lang Coll The New School for Liberal Arts (NY)
Excelsior Coll (NY)
Framingham State Coll (MA)
Francis Marion U (SC)
Frostburg State U (MD)
Gannon U (PA)
George Mason U (VA)
Gordon Coll (MA)
Grace Coll (IN)
Graceland U (IA)
Hamilton Coll (NY)
Jackson State U (MS)
James Madison U (VA)
Juniata Coll (PA)
Kansas State U (KS)
Knox Coll (IL)
Lewis & Clark Coll (OR)
Long Island U, Brooklyn Campus (NY)
Long Island U, C.W. Post Campus (NY)
Loyola U New Orleans (LA)
Lycoming Coll (PA)
Marshall U (WV)
Massachusetts Inst of Technology (MA)
Mercyhurst Coll (PA)
Middle Tennessee State U (TN)
Minnesota State U Moorhead (MN)

Mississippi State U (MS)
Monmouth U (NJ)
Montana State U (MT)
New Mexico State U (NM)
New York U (NY)
Northern Arizona U (AZ)
Oakland U (MI)
Old Dominion U (VA)
Pace U (NY)
Penn State Berks (PA)
Penn State Lehigh Valley (PA)
Pitzer Coll (CA)
Presbyterian Coll (SC)
Principia Coll (IL)
Purdue U (IN)
Purdue U Calumet (IN)
Queens U of Charlotte (NC)
Radford U (VA)
The Richard Stockton Coll of New Jersey (NJ)
Roosevelt U (IL)
Rutgers, The State U of New Jersey, New Brunswick (NJ)
St. Lawrence U (NY)
Saint Louis U (MO)
St. Mary's Coll of Maryland (MD)
Samford U (AL)
Sarah Lawrence Coll (NY)
Scripps Coll (CA)
Seton Hall U (NJ)
South Carolina State U (SC)
Southern Adventist U (TN)
Southern Illinois U Edwardsville (IL)
State U of New York Coll at Old Westbury (NY)
Stonehill Coll (MA)
Sweet Briar Coll (VA)
Syracuse U (NY)
Texas A&M U (TX)
Thomas Edison State Coll (NJ)
Troy U (AL)
Tulane U (LA)
Union Coll (NY)
Union U (TN)
Universidad de las Américas–Puebla (Mexico)
The U of Alabama (AL)
The U of Alabama at Birmingham (AL)
The U of Alabama in Huntsville (AL)
U of Alaska Anchorage (AK)
U of Alaska Fairbanks (AK)
U of California, Riverside (CA)
U of California, San Diego (CA)
U of California, Santa Cruz (CA)
U of Central Florida (FL)
U of Delaware (DE)
U of Hartford (CT)
U of Idaho (ID)
U of Maine (ME)
U of Maryland, Baltimore County (MD)
U of Mary Washington (VA)
U of Massachusetts Lowell (MA)
U of Memphis (TN)
U of Montevallo (AL)
U of Nebraska at Omaha (NE)
U of New Mexico (NM)
U of North Alabama (AL)
U of Northern Colorado (CO)
U of Northern Iowa (IA)
U of Ottawa (ON, Canada)
U of Puerto Rico, Río Piedras (PR)
U of Puget Sound (WA)
U of Rochester (NY)
The U of Scranton (PA)
U of South Alabama (AL)
U of South Carolina Beaufort (SC)
U of Southern Mississippi (MS)
The U of Tennessee at Chattanooga (TN)
The U of Texas at Arlington (TX)
The U of Texas at Austin (TX)
The U of Texas at Tyler (TX)
The U of Virginia's Coll at Wise (VA)
U of Wisconsin–River Falls (WI)
Utica Coll (NY)
Virginia Commonwealth U (VA)
Virginia Wesleyan Coll (VA)
Washington and Lee U (VA)
Washington Coll (MD)
Washington State U (WA)
Wayne State Coll (NE)
Wayne State U (MI)
Western Washington U (WA)
West Virginia U (WV)
Widener U (PA)
Wright State U (OH)
Youngstown State U (OH)

FOREIGN LANGUAGES RELATED
Arizona State U (AZ)
Augustana Coll (SD)
Bennington Coll (VT)
The Coll of New Rochelle (NY)
The Evergreen State Coll (WA)
Excelsior Coll (NY)
Georgia Southern U (GA)
Hood Coll (MD)
Houston Baptist U (TX)
Indiana State U (IN)
Indiana U of Pennsylvania (PA)
Kennesaw State U (GA)
New York U (NY)
Purchase Coll, State U of New York (NY)
Saint Mary's Coll of California (CA)
Southern Illinois U Carbondale (IL)
State U of New York at Binghamton (NY)
U of Alaska Fairbanks (AK)
U of California, Berkeley (CA)
U of California, Los Angeles (CA)
U of Lethbridge (AB, Canada)
U of Michigan–Flint (MI)
U of Northern Iowa (IA)
U of St. Thomas (MN)
U of West Georgia (GA)
Western Washington U (WA)
Yale U (CT)

FOREIGN LANGUAGE TEACHER EDUCATION
Arkansas State U—Jonesboro (AR)
Arkansas Tech U (AR)
Baylor U (TX)
Boston U (MA)
Bowling Green State U (OH)
Buffalo State Coll, State U of New York (NY)
Carroll U (WI)
The Coll at Brockport, State U of New York (NY)
DePaul U (IL)
Dowling Coll (NY)
Eastern Michigan U (MI)
Elmira Coll (NY)
Gannon U (PA)
Gardner-Webb U (NC)
Grand Valley State U (MI)
Greensboro Coll (NC)
Hofstra U (NY)
Kent State U (OH)
Lincoln U (PA)
Long Island U, C.W. Post Campus (NY)
Mercyhurst Coll (PA)
Miami U (OH)
Moravian Coll (PA)
Murray State U (KY)
Nazareth Coll of Rochester (NY)
New York U (NY)
North Carolina State U (NC)
Ohio Dominican U (OH)
Ohio Northern U (OH)
Ohio Wesleyan U (OH)
Old Dominion U (VA)
Oral Roberts U (OK)
Penn State Abington (PA)
Penn State Altoona (PA)
Penn State Beaver (PA)
Penn State Berks (PA)
Penn State Brandywine (PA)
Penn State DuBois (PA)
Penn State Erie, The Behrend Coll (PA)
Penn State Fayette, The Eberly Campus (PA)
Penn State Greater Allegheny (PA)
Penn State Mont Alto (PA)
Penn State Shenango (PA)
Penn State U Park (PA)
Penn State Worthington Scranton (PA)
Penn State York (PA)
Rhode Island Coll (RI)
Rivier Coll (NH)
Saint Francis U (PA)
Saint Joseph's U (PA)
Seton Hill U (PA)
Southeast Missouri State U (MO)
State U of New York at New Paltz (NY)
State U of New York Coll at Old Westbury (NY)
Temple U (PA)
Texas Wesleyan U (TX)
The U of Arizona (AZ)
U of Central Florida (FL)
U of Delaware (DE)
U of Georgia (GA)
U of Illinois at Urbana–Champaign (IL)
U of Maine (ME)
U of Maryland, Coll Park (MD)
U of Minnesota, Twin Cities Campus (MN)
U of Nebraska–Lincoln (NE)
U of Nevada, Reno (NV)
U of Northern Iowa (IA)
U of Oklahoma (OK)
U of St. Thomas (MN)
The U of South Dakota (SD)
U of South Florida (FL)
The U of Tennessee at Chattanooga (TN)
U of Vermont (VT)
U of Windsor (ON, Canada)
Valparaiso U (IN)
Virginia Wesleyan Coll (VA)
Washington State U (WA)
Wayne State Coll (NE)
Wheeling Jesuit U (WV)
William Jewell Coll (MO)
Wright State U (OH)
Youngstown State U (OH)

FORENSIC PSYCHOLOGY
Bay Path Coll (MA)
Florida Inst of Technology (FL)
Gwynedd-Mercy Coll (PA)
John Jay Coll of Criminal Justice of the City U of New York (NY)
St. Ambrose U (IA)
Tiffin U (OH)
U of Puerto Rico at Utuado (PR)
Western State Coll of Colorado (CO)

FORENSIC SCIENCE AND TECHNOLOGY
Albany State U (GA)
Alvernia U (PA)
Arkansas State U—Jonesboro (AR)
Buffalo State Coll, State U of New York (NY)
Carroll U (WI)
Cedar Crest Coll (PA)
Cedarville U (OH)
Chaminade U of Honolulu (HI)
Champlain Coll (VT)
Chatham U (PA)
The Coll of Saint Rose (NY)
Columbia Coll (MO)
Defiance Coll (OH)
Delaware State U (DE)
Eastern Nazarene Coll (MA)
Eastern New Mexico U (NM)
Emmanuel Coll (MA)
Fayetteville State U (NC)
Friends U (KS)
Heidelberg U (OH)
Hilbert Coll (NY)
Hofstra U (NY)
Indiana U–Purdue U Indianapolis (IN)
Inter American U of Puerto Rico, Bayamón Campus (PR)
Jacksonville State U (AL)
John Jay Coll of Criminal Justice of the City U of New York (NY)
Keystone Coll (PA)
King Coll (TN)
Lewis U (IL)
Long Island U, C.W. Post Campus (NY)
Loyola U Chicago (IL)
Madonna U (MI)
Marian U (WI)
Mercyhurst Coll (PA)
Mountain State U (WV)
Mount Ida Coll (MA)
Mount Marty Coll (SD)
Newman U (KS)
New Mexico Highlands U (NM)
Northwest Nazarene U (ID)
Our Lady of the Lake Coll (LA)
Pace U (NY)
Penn State Altoona (PA)
Penn State Berks (PA)
Penn State U Park (PA)
Roberts Wesleyan Coll (NY)
Russell Sage Coll (NY)
St. Edward's U (TX)
Saint Francis U (PA)
Seattle U (WA)
Seton Hill U (PA)
Simpson Coll (IA)
Slippery Rock U of Pennsylvania (PA)
Southern Wesleyan U (SC)
State U of New York Coll of Technology at Alfred (NY)
Texas A&M U (TX)
Thomas More Coll (KY)
Tiffin U (OH)
Towson U (MD)
Trine U (IN)
U of Baltimore (MD)
U of Central Florida (FL)
U of Central Oklahoma (OK)
The U of Findlay (OH)
U of Mississippi (MS)
U of Nebraska–Lincoln (NE)
U of New Haven (CT)
U of North Dakota (ND)
The U of Tampa (FL)
U of Toronto (ON, Canada)
U of Windsor (ON, Canada)
Utah Valley U (UT)
Virginia Commonwealth U (VA)
Washburn U (KS)
Waynesburg U (PA)
Western Carolina U (NC)
West Virginia U (WV)
Wichita State U (KS)
York Coll of Pennsylvania (PA)
Youngstown State U (OH)

FOREST ENGINEERING
Oregon State U (OR)
State U of New York Coll of Environmental Science and Forestry (NY)
U of Maine (ME)
U of New Brunswick Fredericton (NB, Canada)
U of Washington (WA)

FOREST/FOREST RESOURCES MANAGEMENT
Clemson U (SC)
Elizabethtown Coll (PA)
Louisiana State U and Ag and Mech Coll (LA)
Oregon State U (OR)
State U of New York Coll of Environmental Science and Forestry (NY)
Stephen F. Austin State U (TX)
Texas A&M U (TX)
U of Alberta (AB, Canada)
The U of British Columbia (BC, Canada)
U of California, Berkeley (CA)
U of Idaho (ID)
U of Minnesota, Twin Cities Campus (MN)
U of Toronto (ON, Canada)
U of Washington (WA)
West Virginia U (WV)

FORESTRY
Albright Coll (PA)
Baylor U (TX)
California Polytechnic State U, San Luis Obispo (CA)
Coll of Saint Benedict (MN)
Delaware State U (DE)
Georgia Southern U (GA)
Humboldt State U (CA)
Iowa State U of Science and Technology (IA)
Lakehead U (ON, Canada)
Louisiana Tech U (LA)
Michigan State U (MI)
Michigan Technological U (MI)
Mississippi State U (MS)
New Mexico Highlands U (NM)
The Ohio State U (OH)
Oklahoma State U (OK)
Purdue U (IN)
Saint John's U (MN)
Sewanee: The U of the South (TN)
Southern Illinois U Carbondale (IL)
State U of New York Coll of Environmental Science and Forestry (NY)
Stephen F. Austin State U (TX)
Texas A&M U (TX)
Thomas Edison State Coll (NJ)
U of Alberta (AB, Canada)
U of Arkansas at Monticello (AR)
The U of British Columbia (BC, Canada)
U of California, Berkeley (CA)
U of Florida (FL)
U of Georgia (GA)
U of Illinois at Urbana–Champaign (IL)
U of Maine (ME)
U of Minnesota, Twin Cities Campus (MN)
U of Missouri (MO)
U of Nevada, Reno (NV)
U of New Brunswick Fredericton (NB, Canada)
U of New Hampshire (NH)
The U of Tennessee (TN)
U of the District of Columbia (DC)
U of Toronto (ON, Canada)
U of Vermont (VT)
U of Washington (WA)
U of Wisconsin–Milwaukee (WI)
U of Wisconsin–Stevens Point (WI)
Utah State U (UT)
Virginia Polytechnic Inst and State U (VA)
West Virginia U (WV)

FORESTRY RELATED
Sterling Coll (VT)
Utah State U (UT)

FORESTRY TECHNOLOGY
Penn State Abington (PA)
Penn State Altoona (PA)
Penn State Beaver (PA)
Penn State Berks (PA)
Penn State Brandywine (PA)
Penn State DuBois (PA)
Penn State Erie, The Behrend Coll (PA)
Penn State Fayette, The Eberly Campus (PA)
Penn State Greater Allegheny (PA)
Penn State Hazleton (PA)
Penn State Lehigh Valley (PA)
Penn State Mont Alto (PA)
Penn State New Kensington (PA)
Penn State Schuylkill (PA)
Penn State Shenango (PA)
Penn State U Park (PA)
Penn State Wilkes-Barre (PA)
Penn State Worthington Scranton (PA)
Penn State York (PA)

FOREST SCIENCES AND BIOLOGY
Auburn U (AL)
Colorado State U (CO)
Memorial U of Newfoundland (NL, Canada)
Ohio Northern U (OH)
Penn State Abington (PA)
Penn State Altoona (PA)
Penn State Beaver (PA)
Penn State Berks (PA)
Penn State Brandywine (PA)
Penn State DuBois (PA)
Penn State Erie, The Behrend Coll (PA)
Penn State Fayette, The Eberly Campus (PA)
Penn State Greater Allegheny (PA)
Penn State Hazleton (PA)
Penn State Lehigh Valley (PA)
Penn State Mont Alto (PA)
Penn State New Kensington (PA)
Penn State Schuylkill (PA)
Penn State Shenango (PA)
Penn State U Park (PA)
Penn State Wilkes-Barre (PA)
Penn State Worthington Scranton (PA)
Penn State York (PA)
State U of New York Coll of Environmental Science and Forestry (NY)
U of Idaho (ID)
U of Illinois at Urbana–Champaign (IL)
U of Kentucky (KY)
U of Washington (WA)

FRANCHISING
St. Catherine U (MN)

FRENCH
Acadia U (NS, Canada)
Adelphi U (NY)
Agnes Scott Coll (GA)
Alabama State U (AL)
Albion Coll (MI)
Albright Coll (PA)
Alfred U (NY)
Allegheny Coll (PA)
Alma Coll (MI)
American U (DC)
The American U of Paris (France)
Amherst Coll (MA)
Anderson U (IN)
Andrews U (MI)
Angelo State U (TX)
Appalachian State U (NC)
Aquinas Coll (MI)
Arcadia U (PA)
Arizona State U (AZ)
Asbury U (KY)
Ashland U (OH)
Assumption Coll (MA)
Athabasca U (AB, Canada)
Auburn U (AL)
Augsburg Coll (MN)
Augustana Coll (IL)
Augustana Coll (SD)
Austin Coll (TX)
Baker U (KS)
Baldwin-Wallace Coll (OH)
Ball State U (IN)
Bard Coll (NY)
Bard Coll at Simon's Rock (MA)
Barnard Coll (NY)
Barry U (FL)
Bates Coll (ME)
Baylor U (TX)
Beloit Coll (WI)
Benedictine Coll (KS)
Bennington Coll (VT)
Berea Coll (KY)

Berry Coll (GA)
Bethany Coll (WV)
Bethel U (MN)
Birmingham-Southern Coll (AL)
Bishop's U (QC, Canada)
Bloomsburg U of Pennsylvania (PA)
Bob Jones U (SC)
Boise State U (ID)
Boston Coll (MA)
Boston U (MA)
Bowdoin Coll (ME)
Bowling Green State U (OH)
Bradley U (IL)
Brandeis U (MA)
Bridgewater Coll (VA)
Brock U (ON, Canada)
Brooklyn Coll of the City U of New York (NY)
Bryn Mawr Coll (PA)
Bucknell U (PA)
Buffalo State Coll, State U of New York (NY)
Butler U (IN)
Cabrini Coll (PA)
California Lutheran U (CA)
California State U, Chico (CA)
California State U, East Bay (CA)
California State U, Fresno (CA)
California State U, Fullerton (CA)
California State U, Long Beach (CA)
California State U, Los Angeles (CA)
California State U, Northridge (CA)
California State U, Sacramento (CA)
California State U, San Bernardino (CA)
California State U, Stanislaus (CA)
Calvin Coll (MI)
Canisius Coll (NY)
Cape Breton U (NS, Canada)
Capital U (OH)
Carleton Coll (MN)
Carnegie Mellon U (PA)
Carson-Newman Coll (TN)
Case Western Reserve U (OH)
Catawba Coll (NC)
The Catholic U of America (DC)
Centenary Coll of Louisiana (LA)
Central Coll (IA)
Central Connecticut State U (CT)
Central Michigan U (MI)
Chapman U (CA)
Chatham U (PA)
Cheyney U of Pennsylvania (PA)
Chowan U (NC)
Christopher Newport U (VA)
City Coll of the City U of New York (NY)
Claremont McKenna Coll (CA)
Clarion U of Pennsylvania (PA)
Clark Atlanta U (GA)
Clark U (MA)
Cleveland State U (OH)
Coker Coll (SC)
Colby Coll (ME)
Colgate U (NY)
The Coll at Brockport, State U of New York (NY)
Coll of Charleston (SC)
Coll of Mount Saint Vincent (NY)
The Coll of New Rochelle (NY)
Coll of Notre Dame of Maryland (MD)
Coll of Saint Benedict (MN)
Coll of the Holy Cross (MA)
The Coll of William and Mary (VA)
The Coll of Wooster (OH)
The Colorado Coll (CO)
Colorado State U (CO)
Columbia Coll (SC)
Columbia U (NY)
Columbia U, School of General Studies (NY)
Columbus State U (GA)
Concordia Coll (MN)
Concordia U (QC, Canada)
Concordia U Coll of Alberta (AB, Canada)
Connecticut Coll (CT)
Cornell Coll (IA)
Cornell U (NY)
Creighton U (NE)
Daemen Coll (NY)
Dartmouth Coll (NH)
Davidson Coll (NC)
Delaware State U (DE)
Denison U (OH)
DePaul U (IL)
DePauw U (IN)
Dickinson Coll (PA)
Dillard U (LA)
Doane Coll (NE)
Dominican U (IL)
Drew U (NJ)
Drury U (MO)
Duke U (NC)
Earlham Coll (IN)
East Carolina U (NC)
Eastern Michigan U (MI)
Eastern Washington U (WA)
East Stroudsburg U of Pennsylvania (PA)
Eckerd Coll (FL)
Edgewood Coll (WI)
Elizabethtown Coll (PA)
Elmhurst Coll (IL)
Elmira Coll (NY)
Elon U (NC)
Emory & Henry Coll (VA)
Emory U (GA)
Erskine Coll (SC)
Fairfield U (CT)
Fairleigh Dickinson U, Coll at Florham (NJ)
Fairleigh Dickinson U, Metropolitan Campus (NJ)
Fairmont State U (WV)
Florida Ag and Mech U (FL)
Florida Atlantic U (FL)
Florida Intl U (FL)
Fordham U (NY)
Fort Hays State U (KS)
Fort Valley State U (GA)
Franciscan U of Steubenville (OH)
Francis Marion U (SC)
Franklin & Marshall Coll (PA)
Franklin Coll (IN)
Furman U (SC)
Gallaudet U (DC)
Gardner-Webb U (NC)
Georgetown Coll (KY)
Georgetown U (DC)
The George Washington U (DC)
Georgia Coll & State U (GA)
Georgia Southern U (GA)
Georgia State U (GA)
Gettysburg Coll (PA)
Gonzaga U (WA)
Gordon Coll (MA)
Goucher Coll (MD)
Grace Coll (IN)
Grambling State U (LA)
Grand Valley State U (MI)
Greensboro Coll (NC)
Grinnell Coll (IA)
Grove City Coll (PA)
Guilford Coll (NC)
Gustavus Adolphus Coll (MN)
Hamilton Coll (NY)
Hamline U (MN)
Hampden-Sydney Coll (VA)
Hanover Coll (IN)
Harding U (AR)
Hartwick Coll (NY)
Haverford Coll (PA)
Hendrix Coll (AR)
High Point U (NC)
Hillsdale Coll (MI)
Hiram Coll (OH)
Hofstra U (NY)
Hollins U (VA)
Holy Family U (PA)
Hood Coll (MD)
Hope Coll (MI)
Houston Baptist U (TX)
Humboldt State U (CA)
Hunter Coll of the City U of New York (NY)
Idaho State U (ID)
Illinois Coll (IL)
Illinois State U (IL)
Illinois Wesleyan U (IL)
Immaculata U (PA)
Indiana U Bloomington (IN)
Indiana U Northwest (IN)
Indiana U of Pennsylvania (PA)
Indiana U–Purdue U Fort Wayne (IN)
Indiana U–Purdue U Indianapolis (IN)
Indiana U South Bend (IN)
Indiana U Southeast (IN)
Iona Coll (NY)
Iowa State U of Science and Technology (IA)
Ithaca Coll (NY)
Jacksonville State U (AL)
Jacksonville U (FL)
Jamestown Coll (ND)
John Carroll U (OH)
The Johns Hopkins U (MD)
Johnson C. Smith U (NC)
Juniata Coll (PA)
Kalamazoo Coll (MI)
Keene State Coll (NH)
Kent State U (OH)
Kenyon Coll (OH)
King Coll (TN)
King's Coll (PA)
Knox Coll (IL)
Kutztown U of Pennsylvania (PA)
Lafayette Coll (PA)
Lake Erie Coll (OH)
Lake Forest Coll (IL)
Lakehead U (ON, Canada)
Lamar U (TX)
Lane Coll (TN)
La Salle U (PA)
Laurentian U (ON, Canada)
Lawrence U (WI)
Lebanon Valley Coll (PA)
Lehigh U (PA)
Lehman Coll of the City U of New York (NY)
Le Moyne Coll (NY)
Lewis & Clark Coll (OR)
Lincoln U (PA)
Lindenwood U (MO)
Linfield Coll (OR)
Lipscomb U (TN)
Lock Haven U of Pennsylvania (PA)
Long Island U, C.W. Post Campus (NY)
Longwood U (VA)
Loras Coll (IA)
Louisiana Coll (LA)
Louisiana State U and Ag and Mech Coll (LA)
Louisiana State U in Shreveport (LA)
Louisiana Tech U (LA)
Loyola Marymount U (CA)
Loyola U Chicago (IL)
Loyola U Maryland (MD)
Loyola U New Orleans (LA)
Luther Coll (IA)
Lycoming Coll (PA)
Lynchburg Coll (VA)
Macalester Coll (MN)
Manchester Coll (IN)
Manhattan Coll (NY)
Manhattanville Coll (NY)
Mansfield U of Pennsylvania (PA)
Marian U (IN)
Marist Coll (NY)
Marlboro Coll (VT)
Mary Baldwin Coll (VA)
Marywood U (PA)
McDaniel Coll (MD)
McNeese State U (LA)
Memorial U of Newfoundland (NL, Canada)
Mercer U (GA)
Merrimack Coll (MA)
Messiah Coll (PA)
Methodist U (NC)
Miami U (OH)
Miami U Hamilton (OH)
Michigan State U (MI)
Middlebury Coll (VT)
Millersville U of Pennsylvania (PA)
Millsaps Coll (MS)
Mills Coll (CA)
Minnesota State U Mankato (MN)
Minot State U (ND)
Mississippi Coll (MS)
Missouri Southern State U (MO)
Missouri State U (MO)
Missouri Western State U (MO)
Molloy Coll (NY)
Monmouth Coll (IL)
Montclair State U (NJ)
Moravian Coll (PA)
Morehead State U (KY)
Morehouse Coll (GA)
Mount Allison U (NB, Canada)
Mount Holyoke Coll (MA)
Mount St. Mary's Coll (CA)
Mount St. Mary's U (MD)
Muhlenberg Coll (PA)
Murray State U (KY)
Nazareth Coll of Rochester (NY)
Nebraska Wesleyan U (NE)
Newberry Coll (SC)
New Coll of Florida (FL)
New York U (NY)
Niagara U (NY)
North Carolina Central U (NC)
North Carolina State U (NC)
North Central Coll (IL)
North Dakota State U (ND)
Northeastern Illinois U (IL)
Northeastern U (MA)
Northern Arizona U (AZ)
Northern Kentucky U (KY)
Northern Michigan U (MI)
Northern State U (SD)
North Georgia Coll & State U (GA)
Oakland U (MI)
Oakwood U (AL)
Oberlin Coll (OH)
Occidental Coll (CA)
Oglethorpe U (GA)
Ohio Northern U (OH)
The Ohio State U (OH)
Ohio U (OH)
Ohio Wesleyan U (OH)
Oklahoma City U (OK)
Oklahoma State U (OK)
Old Dominion U (VA)
Oral Roberts U (OK)
Oregon State U (OR)
Ouachita Baptist U (AR)
Pacific Lutheran U (WA)
Penn State Abington (PA)
Penn State Altoona (PA)
Penn State Beaver (PA)
Penn State Berks (PA)
Penn State Brandywine (PA)
Penn State DuBois (PA)
Penn State Erie, The Behrend Coll (PA)
Penn State Fayette, The Eberly Campus (PA)
Penn State Greater Allegheny (PA)
Penn State Hazleton (PA)
Penn State Lehigh Valley (PA)
Penn State Mont Alto (PA)
Penn State New Kensington (PA)
Penn State Schuylkill (PA)
Penn State Shenango (PA)
Penn State U Park (PA)
Penn State Wilkes-Barre (PA)
Penn State Worthington Scranton (PA)
Penn State York (PA)
Pepperdine U, Malibu (CA)
Pittsburg State U (KS)
Pitzer Coll (CA)
Plymouth State U (NH)
Pomona Coll (CA)
Portland State U (OR)
Presbyterian Coll (SC)
Princeton U (NJ)
Principia Coll (IL)
Providence Coll (RI)
Purchase Coll, State U of New York (NY)
Purdue U Calumet (IN)
Queens Coll of the City U of New York (NY)
Queen's U at Kingston (ON, Canada)
Randolph Coll (VA)
Randolph-Macon Coll (VA)
Redeemer U Coll (ON, Canada)
Reed Coll (OR)
Rhode Island Coll (RI)
Rhodes Coll (TN)
Rice U (TX)
Rider U (NJ)
Ripon Coll (WI)
Rivier Coll (NH)
Roanoke Coll (VA)
Rockford Coll (IL)
Rockhurst U (MO)
Rollins Coll (FL)
Rosemont Coll (PA)
Royal Military Coll of Canada (ON, Canada)
Rutgers, The State U of New Jersey, Camden (NJ)
Rutgers, The State U of New Jersey, Newark (NJ)
Rutgers, The State U of New Jersey, New Brunswick (NJ)
Saginaw Valley State U (MI)
St. Ambrose U (IA)
Saint Anselm Coll (NH)
St. Bonaventure U (NY)
St. Catherine U (MN)
St. Cloud State U (MN)
Saint Francis U (PA)
St. Francis Xavier U (NS, Canada)
St. John Fisher Coll (NY)
Saint John's U (MN)
St. John's U (NY)
Saint Joseph's U (PA)
St. Lawrence U (NY)
Saint Louis U (MO)
Saint Mary's Coll (IN)
Saint Mary's Coll of California (CA)
St. Mary's U (TX)
Saint Mary's U of Minnesota (MN)
Saint Michael's Coll (VT)
St. Norbert Coll (WI)
St. Olaf Coll (MN)
St. Thomas U (NB, Canada)
Saint Vincent Coll (PA)
Salem Coll (NC)
Salisbury U (MD)
Salve Regina U (RI)
Samford U (AL)
San Diego State U (CA)
San Francisco State U (CA)
San Jose State U (CA)
Santa Clara U (CA)
Sarah Lawrence Coll (NY)
Scripps Coll (CA)
Seattle U (WA)
Seton Hall U (NJ)
Sewanee: The U of the South (TN)
Shippensburg U of Pennsylvania (PA)
Shorter U (GA)
Siena Coll (NY)
Simmons Coll (MA)
Simon Fraser U (BC, Canada)
Simpson Coll (IA)
Skidmore Coll (NY)
Slippery Rock U of Pennsylvania (PA)
Smith Coll (MA)
Sonoma State U (CA)
South Dakota State U (SD)
Southeastern Louisiana U (LA)
Southeast Missouri State U (MO)
Southern Adventist U (TN)
Southern Connecticut State U (CT)
Southern Illinois U Carbondale (IL)
Southern Methodist U (TX)
Southern Oregon U (OR)
Southern U and Ag and Mech Coll (LA)
Southern Utah U (UT)
Southwestern U (TX)
Spelman Coll (GA)
Stanford U (CA)
State U of New York at Binghamton (NY)
State U of New York at Fredonia (NY)
State U of New York at New Paltz (NY)
State U of New York at Oswego (NY)
State U of New York at Plattsburgh (NY)
State U of New York Coll at Cortland (NY)
State U of New York Coll at Geneseo (NY)
State U of New York Coll at Oneonta (NY)
State U of New York Coll at Potsdam (NY)
Stephen F. Austin State U (TX)
Stetson U (FL)
Stonehill Coll (MA)
Stony Brook U, State U of New York (NY)
Suffolk U (MA)
Susquehanna U (PA)
Swarthmore Coll (PA)
Sweet Briar Coll (VA)
Syracuse U (NY)
Taylor U (IN)
Temple U (PA)
Tennessee Technological U (TN)
Tennessee Wesleyan Coll (TN)
Texas A&M U (TX)
Texas A&M U–Commerce (TX)
Texas Christian U (TX)
Texas Southern U (TX)
Texas State U–San Marcos (TX)
Texas Tech U (TX)
Transylvania U (KY)
Trent U (ON, Canada)
Trinity Coll (CT)
Trinity U (TX)
Truman State U (MO)
Tufts U (MA)
Tulane U (LA)
Union Coll (NE)
Union Coll (NY)
Union U (TN)
United States Military Acad (NY)
U at Albany, State U of New York (NY)
U at Buffalo, the State U of New York (NY)
The U of Akron (OH)
U of Alberta (AB, Canada)
The U of Arizona (AZ)
U of Arkansas (AR)
U of Arkansas at Little Rock (AR)
The U of British Columbia (BC, Canada)
The U of British Columbia–Okanagan (BC, Canada)
U of California, Berkeley (CA)
U of California, Davis (CA)
U of California, Irvine (CA)
U of California, Los Angeles (CA)
U of California, Riverside (CA)
U of California, San Diego (CA)
U of California, Santa Barbara (CA)
U of Central Florida (FL)
U of Central Missouri (MO)
U of Central Oklahoma (OK)
U of Chicago (IL)
U of Cincinnati (OH)
U of Colorado at Boulder (CO)
U of Colorado Denver (CO)
U of Connecticut (CT)
U of Dallas (TX)
U of Dayton (OH)
U of Delaware (DE)
U of Denver (CO)
U of Evansville (IN)
U of Florida (FL)
U of Georgia (GA)
U of Hawaii at Manoa (HI)
U of Houston (TX)
U of Illinois at Chicago (IL)
U of Illinois at Urbana–Champaign (IL)
U of Indianapolis (IN)
The U of Iowa (IA)
The U of Kansas (KS)
U of Kentucky (KY)

U of King's Coll (NS, Canada)
U of La Verne (CA)
U of Lethbridge (AB, Canada)
U of Louisiana at Monroe (LA)
U of Louisville (KY)
U of Maine (ME)
U of Maine at Fort Kent (ME)
U of Manitoba (MB, Canada)
U of Maryland, Coll Park (MD)
U of Massachusetts Amherst (MA)
U of Massachusetts Boston (MA)
U of Massachusetts Dartmouth (MA)
U of Miami (FL)
U of Michigan (MI)
U of Michigan–Dearborn (MI)
U of Michigan–Flint (MI)
U of Minnesota, Twin Cities Campus (MN)
U of Mississippi (MS)
U of Missouri (MO)
U of Missouri–Kansas City (MO)
U of Missouri–St. Louis (MO)
U of Mount Union (OH)
U of Nebraska at Kearney (NE)
U of Nebraska at Omaha (NE)
U of Nebraska–Lincoln (NE)
U of Nevada, Las Vegas (NV)
U of Nevada, Reno (NV)
U of New Brunswick Fredericton (NB, Canada)
U of New Hampshire (NH)
U of New Mexico (NM)
U of New Orleans (LA)
The U of North Carolina at Asheville (NC)
The U of North Carolina at Charlotte (NC)
The U of North Carolina at Greensboro (NC)
The U of North Carolina Wilmington (NC)
U of North Dakota (ND)
U of Northern Colorado (CO)
U of Northern Iowa (IA)
U of North Texas (TX)
U of Notre Dame (IN)
U of Oklahoma (OK)
U of Oregon (OR)
U of Ottawa (ON, Canada)
U of Pennsylvania (PA)
U of Pittsburgh (PA)
U of Puerto Rico at Utuado (PR)
U of Puerto Rico, Río Piedras (PR)
U of Puget Sound (WA)
U of Redlands (CA)
U of Regina (SK, Canada)
U of Rhode Island (RI)
U of Richmond (VA)
U of Rochester (NY)
U of St. Thomas (MN)
U of St. Thomas (TX)
U of San Diego (CA)
U of San Francisco (CA)
U of Saskatchewan (SK, Canada)
The U of Scranton (PA)
U of South Carolina (SC)
The U of South Dakota (SD)
U of Southern California (CA)
U of Southern Indiana (IN)
U of Southern Maine (ME)
U of South Florida (FL)
The U of Tennessee (TN)
The U of Tennessee at Martin (TN)
The U of Texas at Arlington (TX)
The U of Texas at Austin (TX)
The U of Texas at El Paso (TX)
The U of Texas at San Antonio (TX)
The U of Texas–Pan American (TX)
U of the District of Columbia (DC)
U of the Pacific (CA)
The U of Toledo (OH)
U of Toronto (ON, Canada)
U of Tulsa (OK)
U of Utah (UT)
U of Vermont (VT)
U of Virginia (VA)
The U of Virginia's Coll at Wise (VA)
U of Washington (WA)
U of Waterloo (ON, Canada)
The U of Western Ontario (ON, Canada)
U of West Georgia (GA)
U of Windsor (ON, Canada)
U of Wisconsin–Eau Claire (WI)
U of Wisconsin–Green Bay (WI)
U of Wisconsin–La Crosse (WI)
U of Wisconsin–Madison (WI)
U of Wisconsin–Milwaukee (WI)
U of Wisconsin–Oshkosh (WI)
U of Wisconsin–River Falls (WI)
U of Wisconsin–Stevens Point (WI)
U of Wisconsin–Whitewater (WI)
U of Wyoming (WY)
Ursinus Coll (PA)
Utah State U (UT)
Valdosta State U (GA)
Valparaiso U (IN)
Vanderbilt U (TN)
Vassar Coll (NY)
Villanova U (PA)
Virginia Polytechnic Inst and State U (VA)
Virginia Wesleyan Coll (VA)
Wabash Coll (IN)
Wake Forest U (NC)
Walsh U (OH)
Wartburg Coll (IA)
Washburn U (KS)
Washington & Jefferson Coll (PA)
Washington and Lee U (VA)
Washington Coll (MD)
Washington State U (WA)
Washington U in St. Louis (MO)
Weber State U (UT)
Webster U (MO)
Wellesley Coll (MA)
Wells Coll (NY)
Wesleyan Coll (GA)
Wesleyan U (CT)
West Chester U of Pennsylvania (PA)
Western Carolina U (NC)
Western Illinois U (IL)
Western Kentucky U (KY)
Western Michigan U (MI)
Western Washington U (WA)
Westminster Coll (MO)
Westmont Coll (CA)
Wheaton Coll (IL)
Wheeling Jesuit U (WV)
Whitman Coll (WA)
Whittier Coll (CA)
Wichita State U (KS)
Widener U (PA)
Wilfrid Laurier U (ON, Canada)
Willamette U (OR)
William Jewell Coll (MO)
Williams Coll (MA)
Wilson Coll (PA)
Wittenberg U (OH)
Wofford Coll (SC)
Wright State U (OH)
Xavier U (OH)
Xavier U of Louisiana (LA)
Yale U (CT)
York Coll of the City U of New York (NY)
York U (ON, Canada)
Youngstown State U (OH)

FRENCH AS A SECOND/ FOREIGN LANGUAGE (TEACHING)

Bishop's U (QC, Canada)
Saginaw Valley State U (MI)
U of Toronto (ON, Canada)
U of Windsor (ON, Canada)

FRENCH LANGUAGE TEACHER EDUCATION

Alma Coll (MI)
Anderson U (IN)
Appalachian State U (NC)
Assumption Coll (MA)
Auburn U (AL)
Bethel U (MN)
Bishop's U (QC, Canada)
Bradley U (IL)
Bridgewater Coll (VA)
Brooklyn Coll of the City U of New York (NY)
California Lutheran U (CA)
California State U, Chico (CA)
The Catholic U of America (DC)
Central Michigan U (MI)
The Coll at Brockport, State U of New York (NY)
Colorado State U (CO)
Concordia Coll (MN)
Daemen Coll (NY)
Delaware State U (DE)
DePaul U (IL)
East Carolina U (NC)
Eastern Michigan U (MI)
Eastern Washington U (WA)
Edgewood Coll (WI)
Elmhurst Coll (IL)
Elmira Coll (NY)
Franklin Coll (IN)
Gardner-Webb U (NC)
Grace Coll (IN)
Grambling State U (LA)
Grand Valley State U (MI)
Harding U (AR)
Hofstra U (NY)
Hope Coll (MI)
Indiana U Bloomington (IN)
Indiana U–Purdue U Fort Wayne (IN)
Indiana U–Purdue U Indianapolis (IN)
Indiana U South Bend (IN)
Iona Coll (NY)
Ithaca Coll (NY)
Juniata Coll (PA)
Keene State Coll (NH)
Kent State U (OH)
King Coll (TN)
Le Moyne Coll (NY)
Lindenwood U (MO)
Lipscomb U (TN)
Long Island U, C.W. Post Campus (NY)
Louisiana State U in Shreveport (LA)
Louisiana Tech U (LA)
Manhattanville Coll (NY)
Mansfield U of Pennsylvania (PA)
Marist Coll (NY)
Marywood U (PA)
McNeese State U (LA)
Messiah Coll (PA)
Miami U (OH)
Miami U Hamilton (OH)
Michigan State U (MI)
Millersville U of Pennsylvania (PA)
Minot State U (ND)
Mississippi Coll (MS)
Missouri State U (MO)
Missouri Western State U (MO)
Molloy Coll (NY)
Moravian Coll (PA)
Murray State U (KY)
Niagara U (NY)
North Carolina Central U (NC)
North Carolina State U (NC)
North Dakota State U (ND)
Northern Arizona U (AZ)
Northern Michigan U (MI)
Ohio Northern U (OH)
Ohio U (OH)
Ohio Wesleyan U (OH)
Old Dominion U (VA)
Pace U (NY)
Pittsburg State U (KS)
Rhode Island Coll (RI)
St. Ambrose U (IA)
St. Catherine U (MN)
Saint Francis U (PA)
St. John Fisher Coll (NY)
Saint Mary's U of Minnesota (MN)
Salve Regina U (RI)
Seton Hill U (PA)
Southeastern Louisiana U (LA)
Southern U and Ag and Mech Coll (LA)
State U of New York at New Paltz (NY)
State U of New York at Plattsburgh (NY)
State U of New York Coll at Cortland (NY)
State U of New York Coll at Oneonta (NY)
State U of New York Coll at Potsdam (NY)
Talladega Coll (AL)
Taylor U (IN)
The U of Akron (OH)
The U of Arizona (AZ)
U of Evansville (IN)
U of Illinois at Chicago (IL)
U of Illinois at Urbana–Champaign (IL)
U of Indianapolis (IN)
The U of Iowa (IA)
U of Lethbridge (AB, Canada)
U of Louisiana at Monroe (LA)
U of Maine (ME)
U of Maine at Fort Kent (ME)
U of Michigan–Flint (MI)
U of Minnesota, Duluth (MN)
U of Missouri–St. Louis (MO)
U of Nebraska–Lincoln (NE)
The U of North Carolina at Charlotte (NC)
The U of North Carolina at Greensboro (NC)
The U of North Carolina Wilmington (NC)
U of Regina (SK, Canada)
The U of South Dakota (SD)
The U of Tennessee at Martin (TN)
The U of Toledo (OH)
U of Toronto (ON, Canada)
U of Waterloo (ON, Canada)
U of Windsor (ON, Canada)
U of Wisconsin–River Falls (WI)
Valdosta State U (GA)
Valparaiso U (IN)
Washington State U (WA)
Washington U in St. Louis (MO)
Weber State U (UT)
Western Michigan U (MI)
Western Washington U (WA)
Wheeling Jesuit U (WV)
Widener U (PA)
Xavier U of Louisiana (LA)
Youngstown State U (OH)

FRENCH STUDIES

American U (DC)
Bard Coll (NY)
Bard Coll at Simon's Rock (MA)
Barnard Coll (NY)
Brock U (ON, Canada)
Carleton Coll (MN)
Case Western Reserve U (OH)
Claremont McKenna Coll (CA)
The Colorado Coll (CO)
Columbia U (NY)
Columbia U, School of General Studies (NY)
Fordham U (NY)
Lake Superior State U (MI)
Mills Coll (CA)
New Coll of Florida (FL)
Saint Joseph's U (PA)
Skidmore Coll (NY)
Smith Coll (MA)
U of Guelph (ON, Canada)
U of New Hampshire (NH)
U of North Florida (FL)
U of Waterloo (ON, Canada)
The U of Western Ontario (ON, Canada)
U of Windsor (ON, Canada)
Wagner Coll (NY)
Wellesley Coll (MA)
Wheaton Coll (MA)
York U (ON, Canada)

FUNERAL DIRECTION/ SERVICE

Wayne State U (MI)

FUNERAL SERVICE AND MORTUARY SCIENCE

Cincinnati Coll of Mortuary Science (OH)
Gannon U (PA)
Lincoln Coll of New England, Southington (CT)
Lindenwood U (MO)
Mount Ida Coll (MA)
Point Park U (PA)
St. John's U (NY)
Southern Illinois U Carbondale (IL)
Thiel Coll (PA)
U of Central Oklahoma (OK)
U of Minnesota, Twin Cities Campus (MN)
U of the District of Columbia (DC)

GAY/LESBIAN STUDIES

Bennington Coll (VT)
Cornell U (NY)
Hampshire Coll (MA)
Sarah Lawrence Coll (NY)
Trinity Coll (CT)
The U of Western Ontario (ON, Canada)

GENERAL STUDIES

Albertus Magnus Coll (CT)
Alfred U (NY)
Anderson U (IN)
Angelo State U (TX)
Antioch U McGregor (OH)
Antioch U Santa Barbara (CA)
Aquinas Coll (MI)
Arkansas State U—Jonesboro (AR)
Arkansas Tech U (AR)
Athabasca U (AB, Canada)
Austin Peay State U (TN)
Bluefield State Coll (WV)
Bob Jones U (SC)
Brewton-Parker Coll (GA)
Buffalo State Coll, State U of New York (NY)
Calumet Coll of Saint Joseph (IN)
The Catholic U of America (DC)
Central Coll (IA)
City U of Seattle (WA)
Clearwater Christian Coll (FL)
Cleveland State U (OH)
Coll of Mount St. Joseph (OH)
Columbia Coll (MO)
Columbia Intl U (SC)
Concordia U, St. Paul (MN)
Concordia U Wisconsin (WI)
Crichton Coll (TN)
Dallas Baptist U (TX)
DePaul U (IL)
Dordt Coll (IA)
Drexel U (PA)
Drury U (MO)
East Central U (OK)
Eastern Connecticut State U (CT)
Eastern Nazarene Coll (MA)
Eastern New Mexico U (NM)
East Tennessee State U (TN)
Emporia State U (KS)
Fairfield U (CT)
Fairleigh Dickinson U, Coll at Florham (NJ)
Fairleigh Dickinson U, Metropolitan Campus (NJ)
Florida Gulf Coast U (FL)
Florida Inst of Technology (FL)
Fort Hays State U (KS)
Fort Lewis Coll (CO)
Georgia Southern U (GA)
Hampton U (VA)
Harding U (AR)
Henderson State U (AR)
Howard Payne U (TX)
Idaho State U (ID)
Illinois State U (IL)
Indiana U Bloomington (IN)
Indiana U East (IN)
Indiana U Kokomo (IN)
Indiana U Northwest (IN)
Indiana U of Pennsylvania (PA)
Indiana U–Purdue U Fort Wayne (IN)
Indiana U–Purdue U Indianapolis (IN)
Indiana U South Bend (IN)
Indiana U Southeast (IN)
Indiana Wesleyan U (IN)
John Brown U (AR)
Kent State U (OH)
Kent State U at Stark (OH)
Kent State U at Trumbull (OH)
Kutztown U of Pennsylvania (PA)
LaGrange Coll (GA)
Lakehead U (ON, Canada)
La Roche Coll (PA)
La Salle U (PA)
Lindenwood U (MO)
Lipscomb U (TN)
Louisiana State U and Ag and Mech Coll (LA)
Louisiana State U in Shreveport (LA)
Louisiana Tech U (LA)
Loyola U Chicago (IL)
Loyola U New Orleans (LA)
Madonna U (MI)
Marist Coll (NY)
Marshall U (WV)
Mayville State U (ND)
McNeese State U (LA)
Michigan Technological U (MI)
Mid-Continent U (KY)
Minot State U (ND)
Misericordia U (PA)
Montana Tech of The U of Montana (MT)
Morehead State U (KY)
Morehouse Coll (GA)
Mount Marty Coll (SD)
Murray State U (KY)
National U (CA)
New Coll of Florida (FL)
New Mexico Inst of Mining and Technology (NM)
New Mexico State U (NM)
Nicholls State U (LA)
Northcentral U (AZ)
Northeastern State U (OK)
Northwestern Oklahoma State U (OK)
Northwestern State U of Louisiana (LA)
Northwest U (WA)
Nova Southeastern U (FL)
Ohio Dominican U (OH)
Ohio Northern U (OH)
Ohio Wesleyan U (OH)
Oklahoma State U (OK)
Pittsburg State U (KS)
Point Park U (PA)
Providence Coll (RI)
Rider U (NJ)
Roberts Wesleyan Coll (NY)
Saginaw Valley State U (MI)
St. Joseph's Coll, New York (NY)
Salem State Coll (MA)
Samford U (AL)
Seattle Pacific U (WA)
Seton Hill U (PA)
Shawnee State U (OH)
Shepherd U (WV)
Shippensburg U of Pennsylvania (PA)
Shorter U (GA)
Siena Heights U (MI)
Simon Fraser U (BC, Canada)
Southeastern Louisiana U (LA)
Southeastern Oklahoma State U (OK)
Southeast Missouri State U (MO)
Southern New Hampshire U (NH)
Southern U at New Orleans (LA)
Southwestern Coll (KS)
Southwest Minnesota State U (MN)
Spring Hill Coll (AL)
Temple U (PA)
Texas Christian U (TX)
Texas Southern U (TX)
Texas State U–San Marcos (TX)
Texas Tech U (TX)
Texas Woman's U (TX)

Thompson Rivers U (BC, Canada)
Tiffin U (OH)
Trinity Coll of Florida (FL)
U of Alaska Fairbanks (AK)
U of Alaska Southeast (AK)
The U of British Columbia–Okanagan (BC, Canada)
U of Central Florida (FL)
U of Charleston (WV)
U of Connecticut (CT)
U of Dayton (OH)
U of Hartford (CT)
U of Idaho (ID)
U of Illinois at Urbana–Champaign (IL)
U of Louisiana at Monroe (LA)
U of Maine at Farmington (ME)
U of Maine at Machias (ME)
U of Mary (ND)
U of Mary Hardin-Baylor (TX)
U of Massachusetts Amherst (MA)
U of Memphis (TN)
U of Miami (FL)
U of Michigan (MI)
U of Michigan–Dearborn (MI)
U of Missouri (MO)
U of Missouri–Kansas City (MO)
U of Mobile (AL)
U of Nebraska at Kearney (NE)
U of Nevada, Reno (NV)
U of New Haven (CT)
U of New Mexico (NM)
U of New Orleans (LA)
U of North Alabama (AL)
U of North Dakota (ND)
U of North Texas (TX)
U of St. Thomas (TX)
U of South Florida (FL)
U of Tennessee at Martin (TN)
The U of Texas at Arlington (TX)
The U of Texas at Tyler (TX)
The U of Texas–Pan American (TX)
U of the Cumberlands (KY)
U of the Ozarks (AR)
U of the Southwest (NM)
The U of Toledo (OH)
U of Utah (UT)
U of Washington (WA)
U of Wisconsin–Stevens Point (WI)
Valdosta State U (GA)
Western Illinois U (IL)
Western Kentucky U (KY)
Western Washington U (WA)
West Virginia U (WV)
Widener U (PA)
Winston-Salem State U (NC)
York Coll (NE)
Youngstown State U (OH)

GENETICS
Cedar Crest Coll (PA)
Clemson U (SC)
Iowa State U of Science and Technology (IA)
New Mexico State U (NM)
Ohio Wesleyan U (OH)
U of California, Davis (CA)
U of California, Irvine (CA)
U of Georgia (GA)
U of New Hampshire (NH)
The U of Western Ontario (ON, Canada)
Washington State U (WA)

GENETICS RELATED
The George Washington U (DC)

GEOCHEMISTRY
Bowdoin Coll (ME)
Bowling Green State U (OH)
Bridgewater State Coll (MA)
California Inst of Technology (CA)
The Coll of Saint Rose (NY)
Columbia U (NY)
Grand Valley State U (MI)
Northern Arizona U (AZ)
State U of New York at Fredonia (NY)
State U of New York at New Paltz (NY)
State U of New York at Oswego (NY)
State U of New York Coll at Cortland (NY)
State U of New York Coll at Geneseo (NY)
U of Maine at Farmington (ME)
U of New Brunswick Fredericton (NB, Canada)
U of Waterloo (ON, Canada)
Western Michigan U (MI)

GEOGRAPHY
Adams State Coll (CO)
Appalachian State U (NC)
Aquinas Coll (MI)
Arizona State U (AZ)
Arkansas State U—Jonesboro (AR)
Auburn U (AL)
Augustana Coll (IL)
Ball State U (IN)
Bard Coll at Simon's Rock (MA)
Bemidji State U (MN)
Bishop's U (QC, Canada)
Bloomsburg U of Pennsylvania (PA)
Boston U (MA)
Bowling Green State U (OH)
Bridgewater State Coll (MA)
Brock U (ON, Canada)
Bucknell U (PA)
Buffalo State Coll, State U of New York (NY)
California State Polytechnic U, Pomona (CA)
California State U, Chico (CA)
California State U, Dominguez Hills (CA)
California State U, East Bay (CA)
California State U, Fresno (CA)
California State U, Fullerton (CA)
California State U, Long Beach (CA)
California State U, Los Angeles (CA)
California State U, Northridge (CA)
California State U, Sacramento (CA)
California State U, San Bernardino (CA)
California State U, Stanislaus (CA)
Calvin Coll (MI)
Central Connecticut State U (CT)
Central Michigan U (MI)
Chowan U (NC)
City Coll of the City U of New York (NY)
Clarion U of Pennsylvania (PA)
Clark U (MA)
Colgate U (NY)
Concordia U (QC, Canada)
Concordia U Chicago (IL)
Concord U (WV)
Dartmouth Coll (NH)
DePaul U (IL)
Dickinson State U (ND)
East Carolina U (NC)
Eastern Illinois U (IL)
Eastern Michigan U (MI)
Eastern Washington U (WA)
East Stroudsburg U of Pennsylvania (PA)
East Tennessee State U (TN)
Edinboro U of Pennsylvania (PA)
Elmhurst Coll (IL)
Emory & Henry Coll (VA)
Excelsior Coll (NY)
Fayetteville State U (NC)
Fitchburg State Coll (MA)
Florida Ag and Mech U (FL)
Florida Atlantic U (FL)
Florida Intl U (FL)
Florida State U (FL)
Fort Hays State U (KS)
Framingham State Coll (MA)
Francis Marion U (SC)
Frostburg State U (MD)
George Mason U (VA)
The George Washington U (DC)
Georgia Southern U (GA)
Georgia State U (GA)
Grand Valley State U (MI)
Gustavus Adolphus Coll (MN)
Harrisburg U of Science and Technology (PA)
Hofstra U (NY)
Humboldt State U (CA)
Hunter Coll of the City U of New York (NY)
Illinois State U (IL)
Indiana State U (IN)
Indiana U Bloomington (IN)
Indiana U of Pennsylvania (PA)
Indiana U–Purdue U Indianapolis (IN)
Indiana U Southeast (IN)
Jacksonville State U (AL)
Jacksonville U (FL)
James Madison U (VA)
The Johns Hopkins U (MD)
Kansas State U (KS)
Keene State Coll (NH)
Kennesaw State U (GA)
Kent State U (OH)
Kutztown U of Pennsylvania (PA)
Lakehead U (ON, Canada)
Laurentian U (ON, Canada)
Lehman Coll of the City U of New York (NY)
Long Island U, C.W. Post Campus (NY)
Longwood U (VA)
Louisiana State U and Ag and Mech Coll (LA)
Louisiana State U in Shreveport (LA)
Louisiana Tech U (LA)
Macalester Coll (MN)
Mansfield U of Pennsylvania (PA)
Marshall U (WV)
Memorial U of Newfoundland (NL, Canada)
Miami U (OH)
Miami U Hamilton (OH)
Michigan State U (MI)
Middlebury Coll (VT)
Millersville U of Pennsylvania (PA)
Minnesota State U Mankato (MN)
Missouri State U (MO)
Montclair State U (NJ)
Morehead State U (KY)
Mount Allison U (NB, Canada)
Mount Holyoke Coll (MA)
Murray State U (KY)
New Mexico State U (NM)
Nipissing U (ON, Canada)
North Carolina Central U (NC)
Northeastern Illinois U (IL)
Northeastern State U (OK)
Northern Arizona U (AZ)
Northern Kentucky U (KY)
Northern Michigan U (MI)
Northwest Missouri State U (MO)
The Ohio State U (OH)
Ohio U (OH)
Ohio Wesleyan U (OH)
Oklahoma State U (OK)
Old Dominion U (VA)
Oregon State U (OR)
Park U (MO)
Penn State Abington (PA)
Penn State Altoona (PA)
Penn State Beaver (PA)
Penn State Berks (PA)
Penn State Brandywine (PA)
Penn State DuBois (PA)
Penn State Erie, The Behrend Coll (PA)
Penn State Fayette, The Eberly Campus (PA)
Penn State Greater Allegheny (PA)
Penn State Hazleton (PA)
Penn State Lehigh Valley (PA)
Penn State Mont Alto (PA)
Penn State New Kensington (PA)
Penn State Schuylkill (PA)
Penn State Shenango (PA)
Penn State U Park (PA)
Penn State Wilkes-Barre (PA)
Penn State Worthington Scranton (PA)
Penn State York (PA)
Pittsburg State U (KS)
Plymouth State U (NH)
Portland State U (OR)
Prescott Coll (AZ)
Queen's U at Kingston (ON, Canada)
Radford U (VA)
Redeemer U Coll (ON, Canada)
Rhode Island Coll (RI)
Rowan U (NJ)
Rutgers, The State U of New Jersey, New Brunswick (NJ)
St. Cloud State U (MN)
Salem State Coll (MA)
Salisbury U (MD)
Samford U (AL)
Sam Houston State U (TX)
San Diego State U (CA)
San Francisco State U (CA)
San Jose State U (CA)
Shippensburg U of Pennsylvania (PA)
Simon Fraser U (BC, Canada)
Slippery Rock U of Pennsylvania (PA)
Sonoma State U (CA)
South Dakota State U (SD)
Southern Connecticut State U (CT)
Southern Illinois U Carbondale (IL)
Southern Illinois U Edwardsville (IL)
Southern Oregon U (OR)
State U of New York at Binghamton (NY)
State U of New York at New Paltz (NY)
State U of New York at Plattsburgh (NY)
State U of New York Coll at Cortland (NY)
State U of New York Coll at Geneseo (NY)
State U of New York Coll at Oneonta (NY)
Stephen F. Austin State U (TX)
Stetson U (FL)
Syracuse U (NY)
Taylor U (IN)
Temple U (PA)
Texas A&M U (TX)
Texas A&M U–Kingsville (TX)
Texas Christian U (TX)
Texas State U–San Marcos (TX)
Texas Tech U (TX)
Thompson Rivers U (BC, Canada)
Towson U (MD)
Trent U (ON, Canada)
United States Air Force Acad (CO)
United States Military Acad (NY)
U at Albany, State U of New York (NY)
U at Buffalo, the State U of New York (NY)
The U of Akron (OH)
The U of Alabama (AL)
U of Alaska Fairbanks (AK)
U of Alberta (AB, Canada)
The U of Arizona (AZ)
U of Arkansas (AR)
The U of British Columbia (BC, Canada)
The U of British Columbia–Okanagan (BC, Canada)
U of California, Berkeley (CA)
U of California, Los Angeles (CA)
U of California, Santa Barbara (CA)
U of Central Missouri (MO)
U of Central Oklahoma (OK)
U of Chicago (IL)
U of Cincinnati (OH)
U of Colorado at Boulder (CO)
U of Colorado at Colorado Springs (CO)
U of Colorado Denver (CO)
U of Connecticut (CT)
U of Delaware (DE)
U of Denver (CO)
U of Florida (FL)
U of Georgia (GA)
U of Guelph (ON, Canada)
U of Hawaii at Hilo (HI)
U of Hawaii at Manoa (HI)
U of Houston–Clear Lake (TX)
U of Idaho (ID)
U of Illinois at Urbana–Champaign (IL)
The U of Iowa (IA)
The U of Kansas (KS)
U of Kentucky (KY)
U of Lethbridge (AB, Canada)
U of Louisville (KY)
U of Maine at Farmington (ME)
U of Manitoba (MB, Canada)
U of Maryland, Baltimore County (MD)
U of Maryland, Coll Park (MD)
U of Mary Washington (VA)
U of Massachusetts Amherst (MA)
U of Memphis (TN)
U of Miami (FL)
U of Minnesota, Duluth (MN)
U of Minnesota, Twin Cities Campus (MN)
U of Missouri (MO)
U of Missouri–Kansas City (MO)
U of Nebraska at Kearney (NE)
U of Nebraska at Omaha (NE)
U of Nebraska–Lincoln (NE)
U of Nevada, Reno (NV)
U of New Hampshire (NH)
U of New Mexico (NM)
U of New Orleans (LA)
U of North Alabama (AL)
The U of North Carolina at Chapel Hill (NC)
The U of North Carolina at Charlotte (NC)
The U of North Carolina at Greensboro (NC)
The U of North Carolina Wilmington (NC)
U of North Dakota (ND)
U of Northern Colorado (CO)
U of Northern Iowa (IA)
U of North Texas (TX)
U of Oklahoma (OK)
U of Oregon (OR)
U of Ottawa (ON, Canada)
U of Pittsburgh at Johnstown (PA)
U of Puerto Rico, Río Piedras (PR)
U of Regina (SK, Canada)
U of Richmond (VA)
U of St. Thomas (MN)
U of Saskatchewan (SK, Canada)
U of South Alabama (AL)
U of South Carolina (SC)
U of Southern California (CA)
U of Southern Maine (ME)
U of Southern Mississippi (MS)
U of South Florida (FL)
The U of Tennessee (TN)
The U of Tennessee at Martin (TN)
The U of Texas at Austin (TX)
The U of Texas at Dallas (TX)
The U of Texas at El Paso (TX)
The U of Texas at San Antonio (TX)
U of the District of Columbia (DC)
The U of Toledo (OH)
U of Toronto (ON, Canada)
U of Utah (UT)
U of Vermont (VT)
U of Washington (WA)
U of Waterloo (ON, Canada)
The U of Western Ontario (ON, Canada)
U of West Georgia (GA)
U of Wisconsin–Eau Claire (WI)
U of Wisconsin–La Crosse (WI)
U of Wisconsin–Madison (WI)
U of Wisconsin–Milwaukee (WI)
U of Wisconsin–Oshkosh (WI)
U of Wisconsin–Parkside (WI)
U of Wisconsin–River Falls (WI)
U of Wisconsin–Stevens Point (WI)
U of Wisconsin–Whitewater (WI)
U of Wyoming (WY)
Utah State U (UT)
Valparaiso U (IN)
Vassar Coll (NY)
Villanova U (PA)
Virginia Polytechnic Inst and State U (VA)
Wayne State Coll (NE)
Weber State U (UT)
West Chester U of Pennsylvania (PA)
Western Carolina U (NC)
Western Illinois U (IL)
Western Kentucky U (KY)
Western Michigan U (MI)
Western Oregon U (OR)
Western Washington U (WA)
West Virginia U (WV)
Wilfrid Laurier U (ON, Canada)
William Paterson U of New Jersey (NJ)
Wittenberg U (OH)
Worcester State Coll (MA)
Wright State U (OH)
York U (ON, Canada)
Youngstown State U (OH)

GEOGRAPHY RELATED
Bridgewater State Coll (MA)
Brigham Young U (UT)
Central Michigan U (MI)
Northern Michigan U (MI)
Ohio U (OH)
South Dakota State U (SD)
U of California, Los Angeles (CA)

GEOGRAPHY TEACHER EDUCATION
Bishop's U (QC, Canada)
Central Michigan U (MI)
Cumberland U (TN)
DePaul U (IL)
Fitchburg State Coll (MA)
Grand Valley State U (MI)
Mayville State U (ND)
Michigan State U (MI)
Millersville U of Pennsylvania (PA)
Northern Arizona U (AZ)
Northern Michigan U (MI)
Rhode Island Coll (RI)
Shawnee State U (OH)
The U of Tennessee at Martin (TN)
U of Windsor (ON, Canada)
Valparaiso U (IN)
Wayne State Coll (NE)
Western Michigan U (MI)

GEOLOGICAL AND EARTH SCIENCES/GEOSCIENCES RELATED
Allegheny Coll (PA)
Baylor U (TX)
Bridgewater State Coll (MA)
Brigham Young U (UT)
California State Polytechnic U, Pomona (CA)
California State U, Chico (CA)
The Coll at Brockport, State U of New York (NY)
Earlham Coll (IN)
Georgia Inst of Technology (GA)
Hamilton Coll (NY)
Lehigh U (PA)
Montclair State U (NJ)
Northeastern U (MA)
Northland Coll (WI)
Oregon State U (OR)
Pacific Lutheran U (WA)
Penn State Abington (PA)
Penn State Altoona (PA)
Penn State Beaver (PA)
Penn State Berks (PA)
Penn State Brandywine (PA)
Penn State DuBois (PA)
Penn State Erie, The Behrend Coll (PA)
Penn State Fayette, The Eberly Campus (PA)
Penn State Greater Allegheny (PA)
Penn State Hazleton (PA)
Penn State Lehigh Valley (PA)
Penn State Mont Alto (PA)
Penn State New Kensington (PA)
Penn State Schuylkill (PA)

Penn State Shenango (PA)
Penn State U Park (PA)
Penn State Wilkes-Barre (PA)
Penn State Worthington Scranton (PA)
Penn State York (PA)
Princeton U (NJ)
San Jose State U (CA)
Stanford U (CA)
Texas A&M U (TX)
Towson U (MD)
Union Coll (NY)
The U of Akron (OH)
U of Arkansas (AR)
U of California, Los Angeles (CA)
U of Illinois at Urbana–Champaign (IL)
U of Miami (FL)
U of Michigan (MI)
U of Nevada, Las Vegas (NV)
The U of North Carolina at Charlotte (NC)
U of Northern Iowa (IA)
U of Oklahoma (OK)
U of Pittsburgh (PA)
The U of Texas at Arlington (TX)
The U of Texas at Austin (TX)
U of Utah (UT)
U of West Georgia (GA)
U of Wyoming (WY)
Utah Valley U (UT)
Utica Coll (NY)
Valparaiso U (IN)
Washington and Lee U (VA)
Western State Coll of Colorado (CO)
Western Washington U (WA)
Whitman Coll (WA)
Wittenberg U (OH)
Yale U (CT)

GEOLOGICAL/ GEOPHYSICAL ENGINEERING

Colorado School of Mines (CO)
Laurentian U (ON, Canada)
Memorial U of Newfoundland (NL, Canada)
Michigan Technological U (MI)
Missouri U of Science and Technology (MO)
Montana Tech of The U of Montana (MT)
New Jersey Inst of Technology (NJ)
Queen's U at Kingston (ON, Canada)
Rutgers, The State U of New Jersey, Newark (NJ)
South Dakota School of Mines and Technology (SD)
Tufts U (MA)
U of Alaska Fairbanks (AK)
The U of British Columbia (BC, Canada)
U of California, Berkeley (CA)
U of California, Los Angeles (CA)
U of Manitoba (MB, Canada)
U of Michigan (MI)
U of Minnesota, Twin Cities Campus (MN)
U of Mississippi (MS)
U of Nevada, Reno (NV)
U of New Brunswick Fredericton (NB, Canada)
U of North Dakota (ND)
U of Rochester (NY)
U of Saskatchewan (SK, Canada)
U of Toronto (ON, Canada)
U of Utah (UT)
U of Waterloo (ON, Canada)

GEOLOGY/EARTH SCIENCE

Acadia U (NS, Canada)
Adams State Coll (CO)
Alaska Pacific U (AK)
Albion Coll (MI)
Alfred U (NY)
Allegheny Coll (PA)
American U of Beirut (Lebanon)
Amherst Coll (MA)
Appalachian State U (NC)
Arizona State U (AZ)
Arkansas Tech U (AR)
Ashland U (OH)
Auburn U (AL)
Augustana Coll (IL)
Austin Peay State U (TN)
Ball State U (IN)
Bates Coll (ME)
Baylor U (TX)
Beloit Coll (WI)
Bemidji State U (MN)
Bloomsburg U of Pennsylvania (PA)
Boise State U (ID)
Boston Coll (MA)
Boston U (MA)
Bowdoin Coll (ME)
Bowling Green State U (OH)
Bridgewater State Coll (MA)
Brock U (ON, Canada)
Brooklyn Coll of the City U of New York (NY)
Bryn Mawr Coll (PA)
Bucknell U (PA)
Buffalo State Coll, State U of New York (NY)
California Inst of Technology (CA)
California Lutheran U (CA)
California Polytechnic State U, San Luis Obispo (CA)
California State Polytechnic U, Pomona (CA)
California State U, Bakersfield (CA)
California State U, Chico (CA)
California State U, Dominguez Hills (CA)
California State U, East Bay (CA)
California State U, Fresno (CA)
California State U, Fullerton (CA)
California State U, Long Beach (CA)
California State U, Los Angeles (CA)
California State U, Northridge (CA)
California State U, Sacramento (CA)
California State U, San Bernardino (CA)
California State U, Stanislaus (CA)
Calvin Coll (MI)
Carleton Coll (MN)
Case Western Reserve U (OH)
Castleton State Coll (VT)
Centenary Coll of Louisiana (LA)
Central Connecticut State U (CT)
Central Michigan U (MI)
Central State U (OH)
City Coll of the City U of New York (NY)
Clarion U of Pennsylvania (PA)
Clark U (MA)
Clemson U (SC)
Cleveland State U (OH)
Colby Coll (ME)
Colgate U (NY)
The Coll at Brockport, State U of New York (NY)
Coll of Charleston (SC)
The Coll of William and Mary (VA)
The Coll of Wooster (OH)
The Colorado Coll (CO)
Colorado State U (CO)
Columbia U (NY)
Columbia U, School of General Studies (NY)
Columbus State U (GA)
Cornell Coll (IA)
Cornell U (NY)
Dartmouth Coll (NH)
Denison U (OH)
DePauw U (IN)
Dickinson Coll (PA)
Dickinson State U (ND)
Dowling Coll (NY)
Duke U (NC)
East Carolina U (NC)
Eastern Illinois U (IL)
Eastern Michigan U (MI)
Eastern New Mexico U (NM)
Eastern Washington U (WA)
East Stroudsburg U of Pennsylvania (PA)
East Tennessee State U (TN)
Edinboro U of Pennsylvania (PA)
Elizabeth City State U (NC)
Emporia State U (KS)
Excelsior Coll (NY)
Florida Atlantic U (FL)
Florida Intl U (FL)
Florida State U (FL)
Fort Hays State U (KS)
Fort Lewis Coll (CO)
Franklin & Marshall Coll (PA)
Frostburg State U (MD)
Furman U (SC)
George Mason U (VA)
The George Washington U (DC)
Georgia Inst of Technology (GA)
Georgia Southern U (GA)
Georgia State U (GA)
Grand Valley State U (MI)
Guilford Coll (NC)
Gustavus Adolphus Coll (MN)
Hamilton Coll (NY)
Hampshire Coll (MA)
Hanover Coll (IN)
Hardin-Simmons U (TX)
Hartwick Coll (NY)
Harvard U (MA)
Haverford Coll (PA)
Hofstra U (NY)
Hope Coll (MI)
Humboldt State U (CA)
Idaho State U (ID)
Illinois State U (IL)
Indiana State U (IN)
Indiana U Bloomington (IN)
Indiana U Northwest (IN)
Indiana U of Pennsylvania (PA)
Indiana U–Purdue U Fort Wayne (IN)
Indiana U–Purdue U Indianapolis (IN)
Iowa State U of Science and Technology (IA)
Jackson State U (MS)
Jacksonville State U (AL)
James Madison U (VA)
The Johns Hopkins U (MD)
Juniata Coll (PA)
Kansas State U (KS)
Kean U (NJ)
Keene State Coll (NH)
Kent State U (OH)
Kutztown U of Pennsylvania (PA)
Lafayette Coll (PA)
Lakehead U (ON, Canada)
Lake Superior State U (MI)
Lamar U (TX)
La Salle U (PA)
Laurentian U (ON, Canada)
Lawrence U (WI)
Lehigh U (PA)
Lehman Coll of the City U of New York (NY)
Lock Haven U of Pennsylvania (PA)
Long Island U, C.W. Post Campus (NY)
Longwood U (VA)
Louisiana State U and Ag and Mech Coll (LA)
Louisiana Tech U (LA)
Macalester Coll (MN)
Mansfield U of Pennsylvania (PA)
Marietta Coll (OH)
Marshall U (WV)
Massachusetts Inst of Technology (MA)
Memorial U of Newfoundland (NL, Canada)
Mercyhurst Coll (PA)
Miami U (OH)
Miami U Hamilton (OH)
Michigan State U (MI)
Michigan Technological U (MI)
Middlebury Coll (VT)
Middle Tennessee State U (TN)
Midwestern State U (TX)
Millersville U of Pennsylvania (PA)
Millsaps Coll (MS)
Minnesota State U Mankato (MN)
Minot State U (ND)
Mississippi State U (MS)
Missouri State U (MO)
Missouri U of Science and Technology (MO)
Montana State U (MT)
Montclair State U (NJ)
Moravian Coll (PA)
Morehead State U (KY)
Mount Allison U (NB, Canada)
Mount Holyoke Coll (MA)
Murray State U (KY)
National U (CA)
New Jersey City U (NJ)
New Mexico Highlands U (NM)
New Mexico Inst of Mining and Technology (NM)
New Mexico State U (NM)
North Carolina State U (NC)
North Dakota State U (ND)
Northeastern Illinois U (IL)
Northeastern U (MA)
Northern Arizona U (AZ)
Northern Kentucky U (KY)
Northern Michigan U (MI)
Northwest Missouri State U (MO)
Oberlin Coll (OH)
Occidental Coll (CA)
The Ohio State U (OH)
Ohio U (OH)
Ohio Wesleyan U (OH)
Oklahoma State U (OK)
Old Dominion U (VA)
Oregon State U (OR)
Pace U (NY)
Pacific Lutheran U (WA)
Penn State Abington (PA)
Penn State Altoona (PA)
Penn State Beaver (PA)
Penn State Berks (PA)
Penn State Brandywine (PA)
Penn State DuBois (PA)
Penn State Erie, The Behrend Coll (PA)
Penn State Fayette, The Eberly Campus (PA)
Penn State Greater Allegheny (PA)
Penn State Hazleton (PA)
Penn State Lehigh Valley (PA)
Penn State Mont Alto (PA)
Penn State New Kensington (PA)
Penn State Schuylkill (PA)
Penn State Shenango (PA)
Penn State U Park (PA)
Penn State Wilkes-Barre (PA)
Penn State Worthington Scranton (PA)
Penn State York (PA)
Piedmont Coll (GA)
Pomona Coll (CA)
Portland State U (OR)
Prescott Coll (AZ)
Purdue U (IN)
Queens Coll of the City U of New York (NY)
Queen's U at Kingston (ON, Canada)
Radford U (VA)
Rensselaer Polytechnic Inst (NY)
Rice U (TX)
The Richard Stockton Coll of New Jersey (NJ)
Rider U (NJ)
Rocky Mountain Coll (MT)
Rutgers, The State U of New Jersey, Newark (NJ)
Rutgers, The State U of New Jersey, New Brunswick (NJ)
St. Cloud State U (MN)
St. Francis Xavier U (NS, Canada)
St. Lawrence U (NY)
Saint Louis U (MO)
St. Mary's U (TX)
St. Norbert Coll (WI)
Salem State Coll (MA)
Sam Houston State U (TX)
San Diego State U (CA)
San Francisco State U (CA)
San Jose State U (CA)
Sarah Lawrence Coll (NY)
Scripps Coll (CA)
Sewanee: The U of the South (TN)
Shippensburg U of Pennsylvania (PA)
Simon Fraser U (BC, Canada)
Skidmore Coll (NY)
Slippery Rock U of Pennsylvania (PA)
Smith Coll (MA)
Sonoma State U (CA)
South Dakota School of Mines and Technology (SD)
Southern Connecticut State U (CT)
Southern Illinois U Carbondale (IL)
Southern Methodist U (TX)
Southern Oregon U (OR)
Southern Utah U (UT)
Stanford U (CA)
State U of New York at Binghamton (NY)
State U of New York at Fredonia (NY)
State U of New York at New Paltz (NY)
State U of New York at Oswego (NY)
State U of New York at Plattsburgh (NY)
State U of New York Coll at Cortland (NY)
State U of New York Coll at Geneseo (NY)
State U of New York Coll at Oneonta (NY)
State U of New York Coll at Potsdam (NY)
Stephen F. Austin State U (TX)
Stony Brook U, State U of New York (NY)
Sul Ross State U (TX)
Susquehanna U (PA)
Syracuse U (NY)
Tarleton State U (TX)
Taylor U (IN)
Temple U (PA)
Tennessee Technological U (TN)
Texas A&M U (TX)
Texas A&M U–Corpus Christi (TX)
Texas A&M U–Kingsville (TX)
Texas Christian U (TX)
Texas Tech U (TX)
Towson U (MD)
Trinity U (TX)
Tufts U (MA)
Tulane U (LA)
Union Coll (NY)
U at Buffalo, the State U of New York (NY)
The U of Akron (OH)
The U of Alabama (AL)
U of Alaska Fairbanks (AK)
U of Alberta (AB, Canada)
The U of Arizona (AZ)
U of Arkansas (AR)
U of Arkansas at Little Rock (AR)
The U of British Columbia (BC, Canada)
U of California, Berkeley (CA)
U of California, Davis (CA)
U of California, Irvine (CA)
U of California, Los Angeles (CA)
U of California, Merced (CA)
U of California, Riverside (CA)
U of California, San Diego (CA)
U of California, Santa Barbara (CA)
U of California, Santa Cruz (CA)
U of Central Missouri (MO)
U of Cincinnati (OH)
U of Colorado at Boulder (CO)
U of Connecticut (CT)
U of Dayton (OH)
U of Delaware (DE)
U of Florida (FL)
U of Georgia (GA)
U of Hawaii at Hilo (HI)
U of Hawaii at Manoa (HI)
U of Houston (TX)
U of Idaho (ID)
U of Illinois at Chicago (IL)
U of Illinois at Urbana–Champaign (IL)
U of Indianapolis (IN)
The U of Iowa (IA)
The U of Kansas (KS)
U of Kentucky (KY)
U of King's Coll (NS, Canada)
U of Maine (ME)
U of Maine at Farmington (ME)
U of Maine at Presque Isle (ME)
U of Manitoba (MB, Canada)
U of Maryland, Coll Park (MD)
U of Massachusetts Amherst (MA)
U of Massachusetts Boston (MA)
U of Memphis (TN)
U of Miami (FL)
U of Michigan (MI)
U of Michigan–Dearborn (MI)
U of Minnesota, Duluth (MN)
U of Minnesota, Twin Cities Campus (MN)
U of Mississippi (MS)
U of Missouri (MO)
U of Missouri–Kansas City (MO)
U of Mount Union (OH)
U of Nebraska at Omaha (NE)
U of Nebraska–Lincoln (NE)
U of Nevada, Las Vegas (NV)
U of Nevada, Reno (NV)
U of New Brunswick Fredericton (NB, Canada)
U of New Hampshire (NH)
U of New Mexico (NM)
U of New Orleans (LA)
U of North Alabama (AL)
The U of North Carolina at Chapel Hill (NC)
The U of North Carolina at Charlotte (NC)
The U of North Carolina Wilmington (NC)
U of North Dakota (ND)
U of Northern Colorado (CO)
U of Northern Iowa (IA)
U of Oklahoma (OK)
U of Oregon (OR)
U of Ottawa (ON, Canada)
U of Pennsylvania (PA)
U of Pittsburgh (PA)
U of Pittsburgh at Johnstown (PA)
U of Puget Sound (WA)
U of Regina (SK, Canada)
U of Rhode Island (RI)
U of Rochester (NY)
U of St. Thomas (MN)
U of Saskatchewan (SK, Canada)
U of South Alabama (AL)
U of South Carolina (SC)
The U of South Dakota (SD)
U of Southern California (CA)
U of Southern Indiana (IN)
U of Southern Maine (ME)
U of Southern Mississippi (MS)
U of South Florida (FL)
The U of Tennessee (TN)
The U of Tennessee at Chattanooga (TN)
The U of Tennessee at Martin (TN)
The U of Texas at Arlington (TX)
The U of Texas at Dallas (TX)
The U of Texas at El Paso (TX)
The U of Texas at San Antonio (TX)
The U of Texas of the Permian Basin (TX)
U of the Pacific (CA)
The U of Toledo (OH)
U of Tulsa (OK)
U of Utah (UT)
U of Vermont (VT)
U of Washington (WA)
U of Waterloo (ON, Canada)
The U of Western Ontario (ON, Canada)
U of West Georgia (GA)
U of Windsor (ON, Canada)
U of Wisconsin–Eau Claire (WI)
U of Wisconsin–Green Bay (WI)
U of Wisconsin–Madison (WI)
U of Wisconsin–Milwaukee (WI)
U of Wisconsin–Oshkosh (WI)
U of Wisconsin–Parkside (WI)

U of Wisconsin–Platteville (WI)
U of Wisconsin–River Falls (WI)
U of Wyoming (WY)
Utah State U (UT)
Utah Valley U (UT)
Valparaiso U (IN)
Vanderbilt U (TN)
Vassar Coll (NY)
Virginia Polytechnic Inst and State U (VA)
Virginia Wesleyan Coll (VA)
Washington and Lee U (VA)
Washington State U (WA)
Washington U in St. Louis (MO)
Wayland Baptist U (TX)
Wayne State U (MI)
Weber State U (UT)
Wellesley Coll (MA)
Wesleyan U (CT)
West Chester U of Pennsylvania (PA)
Western Carolina U (NC)
Western Connecticut State U (CT)
Western Illinois U (IL)
Western Kentucky U (KY)
Western Michigan U (MI)
Western State Coll of Colorado (CO)
Western Washington U (WA)
West Virginia U (WV)
Wheaton Coll (IL)
Whitman Coll (WA)
Wichita State U (KS)
Wilkes U (PA)
Williams Coll (MA)
Winona State U (MN)
Wittenberg U (OH)
Wright State U (OH)
York Coll of the City U of New York (NY)
York U (ON, Canada)
Youngstown State U (OH)

GEOPHYSICS AND SEISMOLOGY

Baylor U (TX)
Boise State U (ID)
Boston Coll (MA)
Bowdoin Coll (ME)
Bowling Green State U (OH)
California Inst of Technology (CA)
Eastern Michigan U (MI)
Memorial U of Newfoundland (NL, Canada)
Michigan State U (MI)
Michigan Technological U (MI)
Missouri U of Science and Technology (MO)
New Mexico Inst of Mining and Technology (NM)
Northern Arizona U (AZ)
Occidental Coll (CA)
Rice U (TX)
St. Lawrence U (NY)
Saint Louis U (MO)
Southern Methodist U (TX)
Stanford U (CA)
State U of New York at Fredonia (NY)
State U of New York Coll at Geneseo (NY)
Texas A&M U (TX)
Texas Tech U (TX)
The U of Akron (OH)
U of Alberta (AB, Canada)
The U of British Columbia (BC, Canada)
U of California, Los Angeles (CA)
U of California, Riverside (CA)
U of California, Santa Barbara (CA)
U of Chicago (IL)
U of Delaware (DE)
U of Houston (TX)
U of Minnesota, Twin Cities Campus (MN)
U of Nevada, Reno (NV)
U of New Brunswick Fredericton (NB, Canada)
U of Oklahoma (OK)
U of Ottawa (ON, Canada)
U of Saskatchewan (SK, Canada)
U of South Carolina (SC)
The U of Texas at Austin (TX)
The U of Texas at El Paso (TX)
U of Tulsa (OK)
U of Utah (UT)
U of Washington (WA)
U of Waterloo (ON, Canada)
The U of Western Ontario (ON, Canada)
U of Wisconsin–Madison (WI)
Western Michigan U (MI)
Western Washington U (WA)
Wright State U (OH)

GEOTECHNICAL ENGINEERING

U of Illinois at Urbana–Champaign (IL)
York U (ON, Canada)

GERMAN

Agnes Scott Coll (GA)
Albion Coll (MI)
Alfred U (NY)
Allegheny Coll (PA)
Alma Coll (MI)
American U (DC)
Amherst Coll (MA)
Angelo State U (TX)
Aquinas Coll (MI)
Arizona State U (AZ)
Auburn U (AL)
Augsburg Coll (MN)
Augustana Coll (IL)
Augustana Coll (SD)
Austin Coll (TX)
Baker U (KS)
Baldwin-Wallace Coll (OH)
Ball State U (IN)
Bard Coll (NY)
Bard Coll at Simon's Rock (MA)
Barnard Coll (NY)
Bates Coll (ME)
Baylor U (TX)
Beloit Coll (WI)
Bemidji State U (MN)
Berea Coll (KY)
Berry Coll (GA)
Bethany Coll (WV)
Birmingham-Southern Coll (AL)
Bishop's U (QC, Canada)
Bloomsburg U of Pennsylvania (PA)
Bob Jones U (SC)
Boise State U (ID)
Boston Coll (MA)
Boston U (MA)
Bowdoin Coll (ME)
Bowling Green State U (OH)
Bradley U (IL)
Brandeis U (MA)
Brock U (ON, Canada)
Brooklyn Coll of the City U of New York (NY)
Bryn Mawr Coll (PA)
Bucknell U (PA)
Butler U (IN)
California Lutheran U (CA)
California State U, Chico (CA)
California State U, Fullerton (CA)
California State U, Long Beach (CA)
California State U, Northridge (CA)
Calvin Coll (MI)
Canisius Coll (NY)
Carleton Coll (MN)
Carnegie Mellon U (PA)
Case Western Reserve U (OH)
The Catholic U of America (DC)
Central Connecticut State U (CT)
Central Michigan U (MI)
Christopher Newport U (VA)
Claremont McKenna Coll (CA)
Colby Coll (ME)
Colgate U (NY)
Coll of Charleston (SC)
Coll of Saint Benedict (MN)
Coll of the Holy Cross (MA)
The Coll of William and Mary (VA)
The Coll of Wooster (OH)
The Colorado Coll (CO)
Colorado State U (CO)
Columbia U (NY)
Columbia U, School of General Studies (NY)
Concordia Coll (MN)
Concordia U (QC, Canada)
Concordia U Wisconsin (WI)
Converse Coll (SC)
Cornell Coll (IA)
Cornell U (NY)
Creighton U (NE)
Dartmouth Coll (NH)
Davidson Coll (NC)
Denison U (OH)
DePaul U (IL)
DePauw U (IN)
Dickinson Coll (PA)
Doane Coll (NE)
Drew U (NJ)
Drury U (MO)
Duke U (NC)
Earlham Coll (IN)
East Carolina U (NC)
Eastern Michigan U (MI)
Edinboro U of Pennsylvania (PA)
Elizabethtown Coll (PA)
Elmhurst Coll (IL)
Emory U (GA)
Fairfield U (CT)
Florida Atlantic U (FL)
Fordham U (NY)
Fort Hays State U (KS)
Franciscan U of Steubenville (OH)
Franklin & Marshall Coll (PA)
Furman U (SC)
Georgetown Coll (KY)
Georgetown U (DC)
The George Washington U (DC)
Georgia Southern U (GA)
Georgia State U (GA)
Gettysburg Coll (PA)
Gonzaga U (WA)
Gordon Coll (MA)
Grinnell Coll (IA)
Guilford Coll (NC)
Gustavus Adolphus Coll (MN)
Hamline U (MN)
Hampden-Sydney Coll (VA)
Hanover Coll (IN)
Hartwick Coll (NY)
Harvard U (MA)
Haverford Coll (PA)
Heidelberg U (OH)
Hendrix Coll (AR)
Hillsdale Coll (MI)
Hofstra U (NY)
Hood Coll (MD)
Hope Coll (MI)
Hunter Coll of the City U of New York (NY)
Idaho State U (ID)
Illinois Coll (IL)
Illinois State U (IL)
Illinois Wesleyan U (IL)
Indiana U Bloomington (IN)
Indiana U–Purdue U Fort Wayne (IN)
Indiana U–Purdue U Indianapolis (IN)
Indiana U South Bend (IN)
Indiana U Southeast (IN)
Iowa State U of Science and Technology (IA)
Ithaca Coll (NY)
Jacksonville State U (AL)
Jamestown Coll (ND)
John Brown U (AR)
John Carroll U (OH)
The Johns Hopkins U (MD)
Juniata Coll (PA)
Kalamazoo Coll (MI)
Kent State U (OH)
Kenyon Coll (OH)
Knox Coll (IL)
Kutztown U of Pennsylvania (PA)
Lafayette Coll (PA)
Lake Erie Coll (OH)
Lakeland Coll (WI)
La Salle U (PA)
Lawrence U (WI)
Lebanon Valley Coll (PA)
Lehigh U (PA)
Lewis & Clark Coll (OR)
Linfield Coll (OR)
Lipscomb U (TN)
Lock Haven U of Pennsylvania (PA)
Longwood U (VA)
Louisiana State U and Ag and Mech Coll (LA)
Loyola U Maryland (MD)
Luther Coll (IA)
Lycoming Coll (PA)
Macalester Coll (MN)
Manchester Coll (IN)
Mansfield U of Pennsylvania (PA)
Marlboro Coll (VT)
McDaniel Coll (MD)
Memorial U of Newfoundland (NL, Canada)
Mercer U (GA)
Messiah Coll (PA)
Miami U (OH)
Miami U Hamilton (OH)
Michigan State U (MI)
Middlebury Coll (VT)
Millersville U of Pennsylvania (PA)
Minnesota State U Mankato (MN)
Minot State U (ND)
Missouri Southern State U (MO)
Missouri State U (MO)
Moravian Coll (PA)
Mount Allison U (NB, Canada)
Mount St. Mary's U (MD)
Muhlenberg Coll (PA)
Murray State U (KY)
Nazareth Coll of Rochester (NY)
Nebraska Wesleyan U (NE)
Newberry Coll (SC)
New Coll of Florida (FL)
New York U (NY)
North Central Coll (IL)
Northeastern U (MA)
Northern Arizona U (AZ)
Northern Kentucky U (KY)
Northern State U (SD)
Oakland U (MI)
Oberlin Coll (OH)
The Ohio State U (OH)
Ohio U (OH)
Ohio Wesleyan U (OH)
Oklahoma City U (OK)
Oklahoma State U (OK)
Old Dominion U (VA)
Oral Roberts U (OK)
Oregon State U (OR)
Pacific Lutheran U (WA)
Penn State Abington (PA)
Penn State Altoona (PA)
Penn State Beaver (PA)
Penn State Berks (PA)
Penn State Brandywine (PA)
Penn State DuBois (PA)
Penn State Erie, The Behrend Coll (PA)
Penn State Fayette, The Eberly Campus (PA)
Penn State Greater Allegheny (PA)
Penn State Hazleton (PA)
Penn State Lehigh Valley (PA)
Penn State Mont Alto (PA)
Penn State New Kensington (PA)
Penn State Schuylkill (PA)
Penn State Shenango (PA)
Penn State U Park (PA)
Penn State Wilkes-Barre (PA)
Penn State Worthington Scranton (PA)
Penn State York (PA)
Pepperdine U, Malibu (CA)
Pitzer Coll (CA)
Pomona Coll (CA)
Portland State U (OR)
Presbyterian Coll (SC)
Princeton U (NJ)
Principia Coll (IL)
Queens Coll of the City U of New York (NY)
Queen's U at Kingston (ON, Canada)
Randolph-Macon Coll (VA)
Reed Coll (OR)
Rhodes Coll (TN)
Rice U (TX)
Rider U (NJ)
Ripon Coll (WI)
Rosemont Coll (PA)
Rutgers, The State U of New Jersey, Camden (NJ)
Rutgers, The State U of New Jersey, Newark (NJ)
Rutgers, The State U of New Jersey, New Brunswick (NJ)
St. Ambrose U (IA)
St. Cloud State U (MN)
Saint John's U (MN)
Saint Joseph's U (PA)
St. Lawrence U (NY)
Saint Louis U (MO)
Saint Mary's Coll of California (CA)
St. Norbert Coll (WI)
St. Olaf Coll (MN)
Samford U (AL)
San Diego State U (CA)
San Francisco State U (CA)
San Jose State U (CA)
Santa Clara U (CA)
Sarah Lawrence Coll (NY)
Scripps Coll (CA)
Seattle U (WA)
Sewanee: The U of the South (TN)
Simpson Coll (IA)
Skidmore Coll (NY)
Smith Coll (MA)
South Dakota State U (SD)
Southeast Missouri State U (MO)
Southern Connecticut State U (CT)
Southern Illinois U Carbondale (IL)
Southern Methodist U (TX)
Southern Oregon U (OR)
Southern Utah U (UT)
Southwestern U (TX)
Stanford U (CA)
State U of New York at Binghamton (NY)
State U of New York at New Paltz (NY)
State U of New York at Oswego (NY)
State U of New York Coll at Cortland (NY)
Stetson U (FL)
Stony Brook U, State U of New York (NY)
Susquehanna U (PA)
Swarthmore Coll (PA)
Sweet Briar Coll (VA)
Syracuse U (NY)
Temple U (PA)
Tennessee Technological U (TN)
Texas A&M U (TX)
Texas Christian U (TX)
Texas State U–San Marcos (TX)
Texas Tech U (TX)
Transylvania U (KY)
Trent U (ON, Canada)
Trinity Coll (CT)
Trinity U (TX)
Truman State U (MO)
Tufts U (MA)
Tulane U (LA)
Union Coll (NE)
Union Coll (NY)
United States Military Acad (NY)
U at Buffalo, the State U of New York (NY)
U of Alberta (AB, Canada)
The U of Arizona (AZ)
U of Arkansas (AR)
The U of British Columbia (BC, Canada)
U of California, Berkeley (CA)
U of California, Davis (CA)
U of California, Los Angeles (CA)
U of California, San Diego (CA)
U of California, Santa Barbara (CA)
U of California, Santa Cruz (CA)
U of Central Missouri (MO)
U of Central Oklahoma (OK)
U of Chicago (IL)
U of Cincinnati (OH)
U of Connecticut (CT)
U of Dallas (TX)
U of Dayton (OH)
U of Delaware (DE)
U of Denver (CO)
U of Evansville (IN)
U of Florida (FL)
U of Georgia (GA)
U of Hawaii at Manoa (HI)
U of Houston (TX)
U of Illinois at Urbana–Champaign (IL)
U of Indianapolis (IN)
The U of Iowa (IA)
U of Kentucky (KY)
U of King's Coll (NS, Canada)
U of Lethbridge (AB, Canada)
U of Maine (ME)
U of Manitoba (MB, Canada)
U of Maryland, Coll Park (MD)
U of Massachusetts Amherst (MA)
U of Miami (FL)
U of Michigan (MI)
U of Minnesota, Twin Cities Campus (MN)
U of Mississippi (MS)
U of Missouri (MO)
U of Missouri–Kansas City (MO)
U of Missouri–St. Louis (MO)
U of Mount Union (OH)
U of Nebraska at Kearney (NE)
U of Nebraska at Omaha (NE)
U of Nebraska–Lincoln (NE)
U of Nevada, Las Vegas (NV)
U of Nevada, Reno (NV)
U of New Brunswick Fredericton (NB, Canada)
U of New Hampshire (NH)
U of New Mexico (NM)
The U of North Carolina at Asheville (NC)
The U of North Carolina at Chapel Hill (NC)
The U of North Carolina at Charlotte (NC)
The U of North Carolina at Greensboro (NC)
The U of North Carolina Wilmington (NC)
U of North Dakota (ND)
U of Northern Colorado (CO)
U of Northern Iowa (IA)
U of North Texas (TX)
U of Notre Dame (IN)
U of Oklahoma (OK)
U of Oregon (OR)
U of Ottawa (ON, Canada)
U of Pennsylvania (PA)
U of Pittsburgh (PA)
U of Puget Sound (WA)
U of Redlands (CA)
U of Regina (SK, Canada)
U of Rhode Island (RI)
U of Rochester (NY)
U of St. Thomas (MN)
U of Saskatchewan (SK, Canada)
The U of Scranton (PA)
U of South Carolina (SC)
The U of South Dakota (SD)
U of Southern Indiana (IN)
U of South Florida (FL)
The U of Tennessee (TN)
The U of Texas at Arlington (TX)
The U of Texas at Austin (TX)
The U of Texas at El Paso (TX)
U of the Pacific (CA)
The U of Toledo (OH)
U of Toronto (ON, Canada)
U of Tulsa (OK)
U of Utah (UT)
U of Virginia (VA)
U of Washington (WA)
U of Waterloo (ON, Canada)
The U of Western Ontario (ON, Canada)
U of West Georgia (GA)
U of Windsor (ON, Canada)

U of Wisconsin–La Crosse (WI)
U of Wisconsin–Madison (WI)
U of Wisconsin–Milwaukee (WI)
U of Wisconsin–Oshkosh (WI)
U of Wisconsin–Platteville (WI)
U of Wisconsin–River Falls (WI)
U of Wisconsin–Stevens Point (WI)
U of Wisconsin–Whitewater (WI)
U of Wyoming (WY)
Ursinus Coll (PA)
Utah State U (UT)
Valparaiso U (IN)
Vanderbilt U (TN)
Vassar Coll (NY)
Virginia Polytechnic Inst and State U (VA)
Virginia Wesleyan Coll (VA)
Wabash Coll (IN)
Wake Forest U (NC)
Wartburg Coll (IA)
Washburn U (KS)
Washington & Jefferson Coll (PA)
Washington and Lee U (VA)
Washington Coll (MD)
Washington U in St. Louis (MO)
Wayne State U (MI)
Weber State U (UT)
Webster U (MO)
Wellesley Coll (MA)
Wesleyan U (CT)
West Chester U of Pennsylvania (PA)
Western Carolina U (NC)
Western Kentucky U (KY)
Western Michigan U (MI)
Western Oregon U (OR)
Western Washington U (WA)
Wheaton Coll (IL)
Wheaton Coll (MA)
Whitman Coll (WA)
Willamette U (OR)
Williams Coll (MA)
Wittenberg U (OH)
Wofford Coll (SC)
Wright State U (OH)
Xavier U (OH)
Yale U (CT)
York U (ON, Canada)
Youngstown State U (OH)

GERMANIC LANGUAGES

Bennington Coll (VT)
Claremont McKenna Coll (CA)
Cleveland State U (OH)
Eastern Michigan U (MI)
Grand Valley State U (MI)
Indiana U Bloomington (IN)
New Coll of Florida (FL)
U of Colorado at Boulder (CO)
The U of Kansas (KS)
The U of Texas at San Antonio (TX)
U of Wisconsin–Eau Claire (WI)
U of Wisconsin–Green Bay (WI)
Washington U in St. Louis (MO)

GERMANIC LANGUAGES RELATED

Calvin Coll (MI)
Columbia U, School of General Studies (NY)
Ohio Northern U (OH)

GERMAN LANGUAGE TEACHER EDUCATION

Alma Coll (MI)
Auburn U (AL)
Bradley U (IL)
California Lutheran U (CA)
California State U, Chico (CA)
Central Michigan U (MI)
Colorado State U (CO)
Concordia Coll (MN)
Concordia U Wisconsin (WI)
DePaul U (IL)
East Carolina U (NC)
Eastern Michigan U (MI)
Elmhurst Coll (IL)
Grand Valley State U (MI)
Hofstra U (NY)
Hope Coll (MI)
Hunter Coll of the City U of New York (NY)
Indiana U Bloomington (IN)
Indiana U–Purdue U Fort Wayne (IN)
Indiana U–Purdue U Indianapolis (IN)
Indiana U South Bend (IN)
Ithaca Coll (NY)
Juniata Coll (PA)
Mansfield U of Pennsylvania (PA)
Messiah Coll (PA)
Miami U (OH)
Miami U Hamilton (OH)
Michigan State U (MI)
Millersville U of Pennsylvania (PA)
Minot State U (ND)
Missouri State U (MO)
Moravian Coll (PA)
Murray State U (KY)
Northern Arizona U (AZ)
Ohio Northern U (OH)
Ohio U (OH)
Ohio Wesleyan U (OH)
Old Dominion U (VA)
St. Ambrose U (IA)
State U of New York at New Paltz (NY)
The U of Arizona (AZ)
U of Evansville (IN)
U of Illinois at Chicago (IL)
U of Illinois at Urbana–Champaign (IL)
The U of Iowa (IA)
U of Lethbridge (AB, Canada)
U of Minnesota, Duluth (MN)
U of Missouri–St. Louis (MO)
U of Nebraska–Lincoln (NE)
The U of North Carolina at Charlotte (NC)
The U of North Carolina at Greensboro (NC)
The U of South Dakota (SD)
The U of Tennessee at Martin (TN)
The U of Toledo (OH)
U of Windsor (ON, Canada)
U of Wisconsin–River Falls (WI)
Valparaiso U (IN)
Washington State U (WA)
Washington U in St. Louis (MO)
Weber State U (UT)
Western Michigan U (MI)
Western Washington U (WA)

GERMAN STUDIES

American U (DC)
Bard Coll (NY)
Bard Coll at Simon's Rock (MA)
Barnard Coll (NY)
Brock U (ON, Canada)
Case Western Reserve U (OH)
Central Coll (IA)
Claremont McKenna Coll (CA)
Coll of the Holy Cross (MA)
The Coll of Wooster (OH)
Columbia U (NY)
Connecticut Coll (CT)
Cornell U (NY)
Fordham U (NY)
Franklin & Marshall Coll (PA)
Georgetown Coll (KY)
Hamilton Coll (NY)
Ithaca Coll (NY)
Kutztown U of Pennsylvania (PA)
Manhattanville Coll (NY)
Moravian Coll (PA)
Mount Holyoke Coll (MA)
Queen's U at Kingston (ON, Canada)
Smith Coll (MA)
Stanford U (CA)
Swarthmore Coll (PA)
Sweet Briar Coll (VA)
U of California, Irvine (CA)
U of California, Riverside (CA)
U of Houston (TX)
U of Illinois at Chicago (IL)
U of Minnesota, Duluth (MN)
U of Richmond (VA)
The U of Western Ontario (ON, Canada)
U of Windsor (ON, Canada)
Vanderbilt U (TN)
Wellesley Coll (MA)
Wheaton Coll (MA)
York U (ON, Canada)

GERONTOLOGY

Alfred U (NY)
Alma Coll (MI)
Bethune-Cookman U (FL)
Bishop's U (QC, Canada)
Bowling Green State U (OH)
California State U, Chico (CA)
California State U, East Bay (CA)
California State U, Sacramento (CA)
Case Western Reserve U (OH)
Cleveland State U (OH)
Dominican U (IL)
Dowling Coll (NY)
Felician Coll (NJ)
Gwynedd-Mercy Coll (PA)
Indiana U Kokomo (IN)
Ithaca Coll (NY)
John Carroll U (OH)
Lakehead U (ON, Canada)
Lindenwood U (MO)
Madonna U (MI)
Miami U (OH)
Miami U Hamilton (OH)
Minnesota State U Moorhead (MN)
Missouri State U (MO)
Mount St. Mary's Coll (CA)
Pontifical Catholic U of Puerto Rico (PR)
Quinnipiac U (CT)
St. Bonaventure U (NY)
St. Cloud State U (MN)
St. Thomas U (NB, Canada)
San Diego State U (CA)
State U of New York at Fredonia (NY)
State U of New York Coll at Oneonta (NY)
Thomas Edison State Coll (NJ)
Towson U (MD)
U of Arkansas at Pine Bluff (AR)
U of Guelph (ON, Canada)
U of Maryland U Coll (MD)
U of Nebraska at Omaha (NE)
U of Nevada, Las Vegas (NV)
U of Northern Iowa (IA)
U of North Texas (TX)
U of Regina (SK, Canada)
The U of Scranton (PA)
U of Southern California (CA)
U of South Florida (FL)
Weber State U (UT)
Wichita State U (KS)
Winston-Salem State U (NC)
York Coll of the City U of New York (NY)
York U (ON, Canada)
Youngstown State U (OH)

GEROPSYCHOLOGY

Prescott Coll (AZ)

GRAPHIC AND PRINTING EQUIPMENT OPERATION/ PRODUCTION

Arkansas State U—Jonesboro (AR)
Chowan U (NC)
Fairmont State U (WV)
Ferris State U (MI)
Florida Ag and Mech U (FL)
Georgia Southern U (GA)
Lewis-Clark State Coll (ID)
Murray State U (KY)
Western Illinois U (IL)

GRAPHIC COMMUNICATIONS

Arizona State U (AZ)
The Art Inst of San Antonio (TX)
California Polytechnic State U, San Luis Obispo (CA)
Carroll U (WI)
Chowan U (NC)
Clemson U (SC)
Eastern Washington U (WA)
Full Sail U (FL)
Grand View U (IA)
Illinois State U (IL)
Lynn U (FL)
Minnesota State U Moorhead (MN)
New England School of Communications (ME)
Rochester Inst of Technology (NY)
School of the Art Inst of Chicago (IL)
State U of New York Coll of Technology at Canton (NY)
U of North Dakota (ND)
U of Northern Iowa (IA)

GRAPHIC COMMUNICATIONS RELATED

U of the District of Columbia (DC)

GRAPHIC DESIGN

Abilene Christian U (TX)
Acad of Art U (CA)
Adams State Coll (CO)
Alberta Coll of Art & Design (AB, Canada)
Albertus Magnus Coll (CT)
Alma Coll (MI)
American U (DC)
American U of Beirut (Lebanon)
Appalachian State U (NC)
Arizona State U (AZ)
Art Center Coll of Design (CA)
The Art Center Design Coll, Tucson (AZ)
The Art Inst of Atlanta (GA)
The Art Inst of Atlanta–Decatur (GA)
The Art Inst of Austin (TX)
The Art Inst of Boston at Lesley U (MA)
The Art Inst of California–Hollywood (CA)
The Art Inst of California–Inland Empire (CA)
The Art Inst of California–Los Angeles (CA)
The Art Inst of California–Orange County (CA)
The Art Inst of California–Sacramento (CA)
The Art Inst of California–San Diego (CA)
The Art Inst of California–San Francisco (CA)
The Art Inst of California–Sunnyvale (CA)
The Art Inst of Charleston (SC)
The Art Inst of Charlotte (NC)
The Art Inst of Colorado (CO)
The Art Inst of Dallas (TX)
The Art Inst of Fort Lauderdale (FL)
The Art Inst of Fort Worth (TX)
The Art Inst of Houston (TX)
The Art Inst of Houston—North (TX)
The Art Inst of Indianapolis (IN)
The Art Inst of Jacksonville (FL)
The Art Inst of Las Vegas (NV)
The Art Inst of Philadelphia (PA)
The Art Inst of Phoenix (AZ)
The Art Inst of Pittsburgh (PA)
The Art Inst of Portland (OR)
The Art Inst of Raleigh-Durham (NC)
The Art Inst of Salt Lake City (UT)
The Art Inst of San Antonio (TX)
The Art Inst of Seattle (WA)
The Art Inst of Tampa (FL)
The Art Inst of Tennessee–Nashville (TN)
The Art Inst of Tucson (AZ)
The Art Inst of Vrginia Beach (VA)
The Art Inst of Washington (VA)
The Art Inst of Washington–Northern Virginia (VA)
The Art Inst of York–Pennsylvania (PA)
The Art Insts Intl–Kansas City (KS)
The Art Insts Intl Minnesota (MN)
Auburn U (AL)
Bradley U (IL)
Brescia U (KY)
Briar Cliff U (IA)
Bridgewater State Coll (MA)
Brigham Young U (UT)
Cabrini Coll (PA)
California Baptist U (CA)
California State Polytechnic U, Pomona (CA)
California State U, Chico (CA)
California State U, Dominguez Hills (CA)
California State U, Fresno (CA)
California State U, Long Beach (CA)
California State U, Sacramento (CA)
Cedarville U (OH)
Centenary Coll (NJ)
Central Michigan U (MI)
Champlain Coll (VT)
Chapman U (CA)
Chowan U (NC)
City Coll of the City U of New York (NY)
The Cleveland Inst of Art (OH)
Coastal Carolina U (SC)
Coker Coll (SC)
Coll for Creative Studies (MI)
Coll of Mount St. Joseph (OH)
Coll of Santa Fe (NM)
Coll of Visual Arts (MN)
Collins Coll: A School of Design and Technology (AZ)
Colorado State U (CO)
Columbia Coll (MO)
Concordia U Wisconsin (WI)
Corcoran Coll of Art and Design (DC)
Cornish Coll of the Arts (WA)
Creighton U (NE)
Curry Coll (MA)
Daemen Coll (NY)
Dana Coll (NE)
Dordt Coll (IA)
Dowling Coll (NY)
Drake U (IA)
Eastern Washington U (WA)
East Stroudsburg U of Pennsylvania (PA)
Edgewood Coll (WI)
Elizabeth City State U (NC)
Emmanuel Coll (MA)
Fashion Inst of Technology (NY)
Ferris State U (MI)
Fitchburg State Coll (MA)
Flagler Coll (FL)
Florida Ag and Mech U (FL)
Florida Southern Coll (FL)
Florida State U (FL)
Fort Hays State U (KS)
Full Sail U (FL)
Grace Coll (IN)
Grand View U (IA)
Harding U (AR)
Hardin-Simmons U (TX)
Huntington U (IN)
The Illinois Inst of Art–Schaumburg (IL)
Indiana U–Purdue U Fort Wayne (IN)
Iowa State U of Science and Technology (IA)
Iowa Wesleyan Coll (IA)
ITT Tech Inst (UT)
John Brown U (AR)
Keystone Coll (PA)
Kwantlen Polytechnic U (BC, Canada)
Lasell Coll (MA)
Limestone Coll (SC)
Madonna U (MI)
Maine Coll of Art (ME)
Mansfield U of Pennsylvania (PA)
Marian U (WI)
Marietta Coll (OH)
Mars Hill Coll (NC)
Maryland Inst Coll of Art (MD)
Marymount U (VA)
Maryville U of Saint Louis (MO)
Marywood U (PA)
Meredith Coll (NC)
Miami Intl U of Art & Design (FL)
Miami U Hamilton (OH)
MidAmerica Nazarene U (KS)
Mississippi Coll (MS)
Missouri Western State U (MO)
Montclair State U (NJ)
Moore Coll of Art & Design (PA)
Moravian Coll (PA)
Morningside Coll (IA)
Mountain State U (WV)
Mount Ida Coll (MA)
Mount Mary Coll (WI)
Mount Mercy Coll (IA)
Mount Vernon Nazarene U (OH)
Newbury Coll (MA)
The New England Inst of Art (MA)
North Carolina State U (NC)
North Central Coll (IL)
Northeastern U (MA)
Northern Michigan U (MI)
Northwestern Coll (IA)
Northwestern Coll (MN)
Northwest Nazarene U (ID)
Ohio Dominican U (OH)
Ohio Northern U (OH)
Ohio U (OH)
Oklahoma Baptist U (OK)
Old Dominion U (VA)
Ouachita Baptist U (AR)
Park U (MO)
Peace Coll (NC)
Penn State Abington (PA)
Penn State Altoona (PA)
Penn State Beaver (PA)
Penn State Berks (PA)
Penn State Brandywine (PA)
Penn State DuBois (PA)
Penn State Erie, The Behrend Coll (PA)
Penn State Fayette, The Eberly Campus (PA)
Penn State Greater Allegheny (PA)
Penn State Hazleton (PA)
Penn State Lehigh Valley (PA)
Penn State Mont Alto (PA)
Penn State New Kensington (PA)
Penn State Schuylkill (PA)
Penn State Shenango (PA)
Penn State U Park (PA)
Penn State Wilkes-Barre (PA)
Penn State Worthington Scranton (PA)
Penn State York (PA)
Pennsylvania Coll of Art & Design (PA)
Pennsylvania Coll of Technology (PA)
Philadelphia U (PA)
Pittsburg State U (KS)
Platt Coll San Diego (CA)
Plymouth State U (NH)
Pratt Inst (NY)
Queens Coll of the City U of New York (NY)
Quincy U (IL)
Ringling Coll of Art and Design (FL)
Robert Morris U Illinois (IL)
Rochester Inst of Technology (NY)
Rocky Mountain Coll of Art + Design (CO)
Sacred Heart U (CT)
Sage Coll of Albany (NY)
St. Ambrose U (IA)
St. Edward's U (TX)
St. John's U (NY)
Saint Mary's U of Minnesota (MN)
Saint Vincent Coll (PA)
Salve Regina U (RI)
Samford U (AL)
San Diego State U (CA)
San Jose State U (CA)

Savannah Coll of Art and Design (GA)
School of the Art Inst of Chicago (IL)
School of the Museum of Fine Arts, Boston (MA)
School of Visual Arts (NY)
Schreiner U (TX)
Shawnee State U (OH)
South Dakota State U (SD)
Southern Adventist U (TN)
Southern New Hampshire U (NH)
South U, Columbia (SC)
Spring Arbor U (MI)
Spring Hill Coll (AL)
Stephens Coll (MO)
Stonehill Coll (MA)
Susquehanna U (PA)
Temple U (PA)
Texas State U–San Marcos (TX)
Texas Tech U (TX)
Union Coll (NE)
The U of Akron (OH)
U of Arkansas at Fort Smith (AR)
U of Bridgeport (CT)
U of Denver (CO)
U of Florida (FL)
U of Hartford (CT)
U of Houston (TX)
U of Illinois at Chicago (IL)
U of Illinois at Urbana–Champaign (IL)
The U of Kansas (KS)
U of Miami (FL)
U of Michigan (MI)
U of Minnesota, Duluth (MN)
U of Minnesota, Twin Cities Campus (MN)
U of Missouri–St. Louis (MO)
U of North Dakota (ND)
U of Rio Grande (OH)
U of San Francisco (CA)
U of South Florida (FL)
The U of Tampa (FL)
The U of Tennessee at Martin (TN)
U of the Incarnate Word (TX)
Ursuline Coll (OH)
Villa Maria Coll of Buffalo (NY)
Virginia Commonwealth U (VA)
Viterbo U (WI)
Washington U in St. Louis (MO)
Waynesburg U (PA)
Wayne State Coll (NE)
Western Michigan U (MI)
Western State Coll of Colorado (CO)
Westwood Coll–Dallas (TX)
Wichita State U (KS)
York Coll of Pennsylvania (PA)
Youngstown State U (OH)

HAZARDOUS MATERIALS MANAGEMENT AND WASTE TECHNOLOGY
Rochester Inst of Technology (NY)

HEALTH AND MEDICAL ADMINISTRATIVE SERVICES RELATED
Kent State U (OH)
Missouri Southern State U (MO)
Mount Mercy Coll (IA)
Northeastern U (MA)
Pennsylvania Coll of Technology (PA)
Robert Morris U (PA)
Thomas Edison State Coll (NJ)
U of Baltimore (MD)
U of Michigan–Flint (MI)
U of Minnesota, Crookston (MN)
U of Minnesota, Duluth (MN)
Ursuline Coll (OH)

HEALTH AND PHYSICAL EDUCATION
Abilene Christian U (TX)
American U (DC)
Angelo State U (TX)
Arkansas State U—Jonesboro (AR)
Asbury U (KY)
Austin Peay State U (TN)
Averett U (VA)
Baker U (KS)
Baldwin-Wallace Coll (OH)
Baylor U (TX)
Belmont U (TN)
Berea Coll (KY)
Bethel Coll (IN)
Bethel Coll (KS)
Bethel U (MN)
Bethel U (TN)
Black Hills State U (SD)
Blue Mountain Coll (MS)
Bluffton U (OH)
Bob Jones U (SC)
Bridgewater Coll (VA)
Brigham Young U–Hawaii (HI)
Bryan Coll (TN)
California Polytechnic State U, San Luis Obispo (CA)
California State Polytechnic U, Pomona (CA)
California State U, Chico (CA)
California State U, Dominguez Hills (CA)
California State U, Fullerton (CA)
California State U, Monterey Bay (CA)
Cameron U (OK)
Canisius Coll (NY)
Capital U (OH)
Carroll U (WI)
Castleton State Coll (VT)
Cedarville U (OH)
Central Christian Coll of Kansas (KS)
Central Michigan U (MI)
Claflin U (SC)
The Coll at Brockport, State U of New York (NY)
Coll of the Ozarks (MO)
The Colorado Coll (CO)
Concordia Coll (MN)
Concordia U Wisconsin (WI)
Delaware State U (DE)
DePaul U (IL)
Doane Coll (NE)
Dordt Coll (IA)
Eastern Michigan U (MI)
Eastern Washington U (WA)
East Tennessee State U (TN)
East Texas Baptist U (TX)
Elmhurst Coll (IL)
Emory & Henry Coll (VA)
Evangel U (MO)
Ferrum Coll (VA)
Florida Ag and Mech U (FL)
Freed-Hardeman U (TN)
Free Will Baptist Bible Coll (TN)
Friends U (KS)
Gardner-Webb U (NC)
George Fox U (OR)
Georgia Southern U (GA)
Georgia State U (GA)
Grace Coll (IN)
Guilford Coll (NC)
Hamline U (MN)
Hanover Coll (IN)
Hardin-Simmons U (TX)
Houghton Coll (NY)
Houston Baptist U (TX)
Howard Payne U (TX)
Indiana U of Pennsylvania (PA)
Iowa State U of Science and Technology (IA)
Ithaca Coll (NY)
Jacksonville State U (AL)
James Madison U (VA)
Jarvis Christian Coll (TX)
John Brown U (AR)
Johnson State Coll (VT)
Keene State Coll (NH)
La Sierra U (CA)
Liberty U (VA)
Lincoln Memorial U (TN)
Lincoln U (PA)
Lindenwood U (MO)
Linfield Coll (OR)
Loras Coll (IA)
Louisiana Tech U (LA)
Lubbock Christian U (TX)
Luther Coll (IA)
Maryville Coll (TN)
Marywood U (PA)
The Master's Coll and Sem (CA)
Mayville State U (ND)
Miami U (OH)
Middle Tennessee State U (TN)
Milligan Coll (TN)
Minnesota State U Moorhead (MN)
Mississippi Coll (MS)
Mississippi U for Women (MS)
Missouri Western State U (MO)
Monmouth Coll (IL)
Monmouth U (NJ)
Montana State U Billings (MT)
Morehouse Coll (GA)
Mount Vernon Nazarene U (OH)
New England Coll (NH)
North Carolina Central U (NC)
Northern Michigan U (MI)
Northwestern Coll (MN)
Northwestern State U of Louisiana (LA)
Northwest Nazarene U (ID)
Ohio Northern U (OH)
The Ohio State U (OH)
Ohio U (OH)
Oklahoma Baptist U (OK)
Oklahoma Panhandle State U (OK)
Oral Roberts U (OK)
Oregon State U (OR)
Plymouth State U (NH)
Pontifical Catholic U of Puerto Rico (PR)
Prairie View A&M U (TX)
Queen's U at Kingston (ON, Canada)
Quincy U (IL)
Redeemer U Coll (ON, Canada)
Roanoke Coll (VA)
Rocky Mountain Coll (MT)
St. Ambrose U (IA)
St. Catherine U (MN)
Saint Mary's Coll of California (CA)
St. Mary's U (TX)
Salem State Coll (MA)
Samford U (AL)
San Diego State U (CA)
San Jose State U (CA)
Slippery Rock U of Pennsylvania (PA)
South Carolina State U (SC)
South Dakota State U (SD)
Southeast Missouri State U (MO)
Southern Arkansas U–Magnolia (AR)
Southern Illinois U Edwardsville (IL)
Southern Wesleyan U (SC)
Southwest Baptist U (MO)
Southwestern Adventist U (TX)
Southwestern Coll (KS)
Southwest Minnesota State U (MN)
Spring Arbor U (MI)
Stephen F. Austin State U (TX)
Sterling Coll (KS)
Tabor Coll (KS)
Tennessee Wesleyan Coll (TN)
Texas A&M Intl U (TX)
Texas A&M U (TX)
Texas A&M U–Commerce (TX)
Texas A&M U–Kingsville (TX)
Texas Christian U (TX)
Texas Coll (TX)
Texas Southern U (TX)
Texas State U–San Marcos (TX)
Texas Tech U (TX)
Texas Wesleyan U (TX)
Texas Woman's U (TX)
Tusculum Coll (TN)
U of Arkansas (AR)
U of Arkansas at Monticello (AR)
U of Delaware (DE)
U of Guam (GU)
U of Houston (TX)
U of Houston–Clear Lake (TX)
The U of Kansas (KS)
U of Louisville (KY)
U of Mary (ND)
U of Massachusetts Boston (MA)
U of Mobile (AL)
U of Montevallo (AL)
U of Nebraska at Omaha (NE)
The U of North Carolina at Chapel Hill (NC)
The U of North Carolina at Charlotte (NC)
The U of North Carolina at Pembroke (NC)
The U of North Carolina Wilmington (NC)
U of Northern Iowa (IA)
U of North Texas (TX)
U of Oklahoma (OK)
U of Ottawa (ON, Canada)
U of Regina (SK, Canada)
U of Rio Grande (OH)
U of St. Thomas (MN)
U of San Francisco (CA)
U of Science and Arts of Oklahoma (OK)
U of Southern Mississippi (MS)
The U of Tennessee at Martin (TN)
The U of Texas at Arlington (TX)
The U of Texas at Brownsville (TX)
The U of Texas at San Antonio (TX)
The U of Texas at Tyler (TX)
The U of Texas of the Permian Basin (TX)
The U of Texas–Pan American (TX)
U of the Cumberlands (KY)
U of Toronto (ON, Canada)
U of Utah (UT)
U of West Florida (FL)
U of Windsor (ON, Canada)
U of Wisconsin–Stevens Point (WI)
U of Wisconsin–Superior (WI)
Ursinus Coll (PA)
Utah Valley U (UT)
Valparaiso U (IN)
Vanguard U of Southern California (CA)
Virginia Intermont Coll (VA)
Walsh U (OH)
Washington Adventist U (MD)
Weber State U (UT)
Wesleyan U (CT)
West Chester U of Pennsylvania (PA)
Western Washington U (WA)
West Virginia U (WV)
West Virginia Wesleyan Coll (WV)
William Penn U (IA)
Wingate U (NC)
York U (ON, Canada)
Youngstown State U (OH)

HEALTH AND PHYSICAL EDUCATION RELATED
Adelphi U (NY)
Arizona State U (AZ)
Averett U (VA)
Avila U (MO)
Bloomsburg U of Pennsylvania (PA)
Bowling Green State U (OH)
Brewton-Parker Coll (GA)
Bridgewater State Coll (MA)
California Baptist U (CA)
California State U, Long Beach (CA)
Coker Coll (SC)
The Coll at Brockport, State U of New York (NY)
Concordia U Wisconsin (WI)
Cornell Coll (IA)
East Carolina U (NC)
East Stroudsburg U of Pennsylvania (PA)
Edinboro U of Pennsylvania (PA)
Greensboro Coll (NC)
Gustavus Adolphus Coll (MN)
Ithaca Coll (NY)
John Brown U (AR)
Limestone Coll (SC)
Lincoln U (PA)
Lock Haven U of Pennsylvania (PA)
Mayville State U (ND)
Midwestern State U (TX)
Missouri Southern State U (MO)
Naropa U (CO)
North Greenville U (SC)
Ohio Northern U (OH)
Pittsburg State U (KS)
Regis Coll (MA)
Reinhardt Coll (GA)
Rocky Mountain Coll (MT)
Saint Mary's Coll of California (CA)
South Dakota State U (SD)
Taylor U (IN)
Texas Christian U (TX)
Texas Lutheran U (TX)
Towson U (MD)
Tusculum Coll (TN)
U of Central Oklahoma (OK)
U of Minnesota, Twin Cities Campus (MN)
U of New England (ME)
U of Utah (UT)
U of Wisconsin–Superior (WI)
Wayne State Coll (NE)

HEALTH COMMUNICATION
Chapman U (CA)
Grand Valley State U (MI)
Juniata Coll (PA)
North Dakota State U (ND)
U of Houston (TX)

HEALTH/HEALTH-CARE ADMINISTRATION
Adams State Coll (CO)
Alaska Pacific U (AK)
Appalachian State U (NC)
Arcadia U (PA)
Argosy U, Atlanta (GA)
Argosy U, Chicago (IL)
Argosy U, Dallas (TX)
Argosy U, Denver (CO)
Argosy U, Hawai'i (HI)
Argosy U, Inland Empire (CA)
Argosy U, Los Angeles (CA)
Argosy U, Nashville (TN)
Argosy U, Orange County (CA)
Argosy U, Phoenix (AZ)
Argosy U, Salt Lake City (UT)
Argosy U, San Diego (CA)
Argosy U, San Francisco Bay Area (CA)
Argosy U, Sarasota (FL)
Argosy U, Schaumburg (IL)
Argosy U, Seattle (WA)
Argosy U, Tampa (FL)
Argosy U, Twin Cities (MN)
Argosy U, Washington DC (VA)
Auburn U (AL)
Augustana Coll (SD)
Baker Coll of Auburn Hills (MI)
Baker Coll of Owosso (MI)
Baker Coll of Port Huron (MI)
Baldwin-Wallace Coll (OH)
Baptist Coll of Health Sciences (TN)
Belhaven U (MS)
Belmont U (TN)
Benedictine U (IL)
Black Hills State U (SD)
Bowling Green State U (OH)
Brandeis U (MA)
Brock U (ON, Canada)
Brown Mackie Coll–Albuquerque (NM)
Brown Mackie Coll–Boise (ID)
Brown Mackie Coll–Greenville (SC)
Brown Mackie Coll–Louisville (KY)
Brown Mackie Coll–Merrillville (IN)
Brown Mackie Coll–Miami (FL)
Brown Mackie Coll–Michigan City (IN)
Brown Mackie Coll–St. Louis (MO)
Brown Mackie Coll–South Bend (IN)
Brown Mackie Coll–Tucson (AZ)
California State U, Dominguez Hills (CA)
California State U, Long Beach (CA)
California State U, San Bernardino (CA)
Calumet Coll of Saint Joseph (IN)
Capella U (MN)
Central Michigan U (MI)
Clayton State U (GA)
The Coll at Brockport, State U of New York (NY)
Columbia Southern U (AL)
Concordia Coll (MN)
Concordia U Wisconsin (WI)
Creighton U (NE)
Dallas Baptist U (TX)
Davenport U, Grand Rapids (MI)
Dillard U (LA)
Dominican Coll (NY)
Drexel U (PA)
Duquesne U (PA)
East Carolina U (NC)
Eastern Michigan U (MI)
Eastern Washington U (WA)
ECPI Coll of Technology, Virginia Beach (VA)
Ferris State U (MI)
Florida Ag and Mech U (FL)
Florida Atlantic U (FL)
Florida Inst of Technology (FL)
Florida Intl U (FL)
Franklin U (OH)
Friends U (KS)
Frostburg State U (MD)
Globe Inst of Technology (NY)
Goldey-Beacom Coll (DE)
Governors State U (IL)
Harding U (AR)
Harrison Coll, Evansville (IN)
Harrison Coll, Fort Wayne (IN)
Harrison Coll, Indianapolis (IN)
Harrison Coll, Muncie (IN)
Harrison Coll, Terre Haute (IN)
Harris-Stowe State U (MO)
Heidelberg U (OH)
Hodges U (FL)
Howard Payne U (TX)
Idaho State U (ID)
Immaculata U (PA)
Indiana Tech (IN)
Indiana U–Purdue U Fort Wayne (IN)
Indiana U–Purdue U Indianapolis (IN)
Indiana U South Bend (IN)
Indian River State Coll (FL)
Iona Coll (NY)
Ithaca Coll (NY)
Jackson State U (MS)
James Madison U (VA)
Jefferson Coll of Health Sciences (VA)
Jones Intl U (CO)
Lebanon Valley Coll (PA)
Lehman Coll of the City U of New York (NY)
Lindenwood U (MO)
Lourdes Coll (OH)
Loyola U Chicago (IL)
Madonna U (MI)
Marian U (WI)
Mary Baldwin Coll (VA)
Marywood U (PA)
Mercy Coll of Health Sciences (IA)
Mercy Coll of Northwest Ohio (OH)
Methodist U (NC)
Metropolitan State Coll of Denver (CO)
Midway Coll (KY)
Minnesota State U Moorhead (MN)
Misericordia U (PA)
Montana State U Billings (MT)
Mount Mercy Coll (IA)
Mount St. Mary's Coll (CA)
Newbury Coll (MA)
New England Coll (NH)
Norfolk State U (VA)
Northeastern State U (OK)
Northeastern U (MA)
The Ohio State U at Lima (OH)
Ohio U (OH)
Oregon State U (OR)
Our Lady of the Lake Coll (LA)
Penn State Abington (PA)

Penn State Altoona (PA)
Penn State Beaver (PA)
Penn State Berks (PA)
Penn State Brandywine (PA)
Penn State DuBois (PA)
Penn State Erie, The Behrend Coll (PA)
Penn State Fayette, The Eberly Campus (PA)
Penn State Greater Allegheny (PA)
Penn State Hazleton (PA)
Penn State Lehigh Valley (PA)
Penn State Mont Alto (PA)
Penn State New Kensington (PA)
Penn State Schuylkill (PA)
Penn State Shenango (PA)
Penn State U Park (PA)
Penn State Wilkes-Barre (PA)
Penn State Worthington Scranton (PA)
Penn State York (PA)
Pioneer Pacific Coll, Wilsonville (OR)
Providence Coll (RI)
Roberts Wesleyan Coll (NY)
St. John's U (NY)
St. Joseph's Coll, Long Island Campus (NY)
St. Joseph's Coll, New York (NY)
Saint Leo U (FL)
San Jose State U (CA)
Shippensburg U of Pennsylvania (PA)
Simpson U (CA)
Southern Adventist U (TN)
Southern Illinois U Carbondale (IL)
South U (AL)
South U, Royal Palm Beach (FL)
South U, Tampa (FL)
South U (GA)
South U, Columbia (SC)
South U, Glen Allen (VA)
South U, Virginia Beach (VA)
Southwestern Adventist U (TX)
Southwestern Oklahoma State U (OK)
Spring Arbor U (MI)
State U of New York at Fredonia (NY)
State U of New York Coll of Technology at Canton (NY)
Stonehill Coll (MA)
Texas Southern U (TX)
Texas State U–San Marcos (TX)
Towson U (MD)
TUI U (CA)
The U of Arizona (AZ)
U of Central Florida (FL)
U of Cincinnati (OH)
U of Connecticut (CT)
U of Evansville (IN)
U of Hawaii–West Oahu (HI)
U of Houston–Clear Lake (TX)
U of Kentucky (KY)
U of La Verne (CA)
U of Michigan–Dearborn (MI)
U of Michigan–Flint (MI)
U of Nevada, Las Vegas (NV)
U of New England (ME)
U of New Hampshire (NH)
The U of North Carolina at Chapel Hill (NC)
U of North Florida (FL)
U of Pennsylvania (PA)
U of Rhode Island (RI)
U of St. Francis (IL)
The U of Scranton (PA)
U of South Florida (FL)
The U of Texas at El Paso (TX)
U of Wisconsin–Eau Claire (WI)
U of Wisconsin–Milwaukee (WI)
Upper Iowa U (IA)
Ursuline Coll (OH)
Walden U (MN)
Washington Adventist U (MD)
Washington U in St. Louis (MO)
Waynesburg U (PA)
Weber State U (UT)
West Chester U of Pennsylvania (PA)
Western Carolina U (NC)
Western Illinois U (IL)
Western Kentucky U (KY)
Westwood Coll–Anaheim (CA)
Westwood Coll–Annandale Campus (VA)
Westwood Coll–Atlanta Midtown (GA)
Westwood Coll–Atlanta Northlake (GA)
Westwood Coll–Chicago Du Page (IL)
Westwood Coll–Chicago Loop Campus (IL)
Westwood Coll–Chicago O'Hare Airport (IL)
Westwood Coll–Chicago River Oaks (IL)
Westwood Coll–Dallas (TX)
Westwood Coll–Fort Worth (TX)
Westwood Coll–Inland Empire (CA)
Westwood Coll–Los Angeles (CA)
Westwood Coll–Online Campus (CO)
Westwood Coll–South Bay Campus (CA)
Wheeling Jesuit U (WV)
Wichita State U (KS)
Wilberforce U (OH)
Winston-Salem State U (NC)
Wright State U (OH)

HEALTH INFORMATION/ MEDICAL RECORDS ADMINISTRATION

Alabama State U (AL)
Arkansas Tech U (AR)
Baker Coll of Auburn Hills (MI)
Bowling Green State U (OH)
The Coll of St. Scholastica (MN)
Coppin State U (MD)
Dakota State U (SD)
Davenport U, Grand Rapids (MI)
East Carolina U (NC)
East Central U (OK)
Ferris State U (MI)
Florida Ag and Mech U (FL)
Georgian Court U (NJ)
Gwynedd-Mercy Coll (PA)
Illinois State U (IL)
Indiana U Bloomington (IN)
Indiana U East (IN)
Indiana U Kokomo (IN)
Indiana U–Purdue U Indianapolis (IN)
Indiana U South Bend (IN)
Indiana U Southeast (IN)
Kean U (NJ)
Keiser U, Fort Lauderdale (FL)
Long Island U, C.W. Post Campus (NY)
Louisiana Tech U (LA)
Medical Coll of Georgia (GA)
The Ohio State U (OH)
Saint Louis U (MO)
Southern U at New Orleans (LA)
Southwestern Oklahoma State U (OK)
Stephens Coll (MO)
Temple U (PA)
Texas Southern U (TX)
Texas State U–San Marcos (TX)
The U of Alabama at Birmingham (AL)
U of Central Florida (FL)
U of Cincinnati (OH)
U of Illinois at Chicago (IL)
The U of Kansas (KS)
U of Pittsburgh (PA)
The U of Toledo (OH)
The U of Western Ontario (ON, Canada)
U of Wisconsin–Milwaukee (WI)
Western Carolina U (NC)

HEALTH INFORMATION/ MEDICAL RECORDS TECHNOLOGY

Franklin U (OH)
Gwynedd-Mercy Coll (PA)
Plaza Coll (NY)
Walden U (MN)
West Suburban Coll of Nursing (IL)

HEALTH/MEDICAL PHYSICS

Bloomsburg U of Pennsylvania (PA)
California State U, Dominguez Hills (CA)
California State U, Northridge (CA)
Oregon State U (OR)
U of Nevada, Las Vegas (NV)

HEALTH/MEDICAL PREPARATORY PROGRAMS RELATED

Abilene Christian U (TX)
Allegheny Coll (PA)
Asbury U (KY)
Aurora U (IL)
Avila U (MO)
Baylor U (TX)
Benedictine U (IL)
Bob Jones U (SC)
Cedarville U (OH)
Charles Drew U of Medicine and Science (CA)
Cumberland U (TN)
Daemen Coll (NY)
Duquesne U (PA)
Eastern Nazarene Coll (MA)
Fordham U (NY)
Gannon U (PA)
Guilford Coll (NC)
Hodges U (FL)
Ithaca Coll (NY)
Juniata Coll (PA)
Le Moyne Coll (NY)
Lipscomb U (TN)
Lock Haven U of Pennsylvania (PA)
Lubbock Christian U (TX)
Madonna U (MI)
Maryville U of Saint Louis (MO)
Mercer U (GA)
Mercyhurst Coll (PA)
Meredith Coll (NC)
Northern Michigan U (MI)
Pittsburg State U (KS)
St. Cloud State U (MN)
State U of New York at Binghamton (NY)
Tusculum Coll (TN)
The U of Akron (OH)
U of Evansville (IN)
U of Missouri (MO)
U of Nevada, Reno (NV)
U of Regina (SK, Canada)
U of South Alabama (AL)
U of Waterloo (ON, Canada)
Utica Coll (NY)
Western Washington U (WA)
Wright State U (OH)

HEALTH/MEDICAL PSYCHOLOGY

Bridgewater State Coll (MA)
Jefferson Coll of Health Sciences (VA)
Massachusetts Coll of Pharmacy and Health Sciences (MA)
Prescott Coll (AZ)
U of the Sciences in Philadelphia (PA)

HEALTH OCCUPATIONS TEACHER EDUCATION

Baylor U (TX)
Midwestern State U (TX)
New York Inst of Technology (NY)
North Carolina State U (NC)
Northwest U (WA)
U of Central Oklahoma (OK)
U of Maine at Farmington (ME)

HEALTH PROFESSIONS RELATED

Alcorn State U (MS)
Alderson-Broaddus Coll (WV)
Alma Coll (MI)
Arizona State U (AZ)
Armstrong Atlantic State U (GA)
Azusa Pacific U (CA)
Baldwin-Wallace Coll (OH)
Bastyr U (WA)
Bloomsburg U of Pennsylvania (PA)
Boise State U (ID)
Boston U (MA)
Bowling Green State U (OH)
Bradley U (IL)
Brock U (ON, Canada)
California State U, East Bay (CA)
California State U, Fresno (CA)
California State U, Fullerton (CA)
California State U, Long Beach (CA)
California State U, Los Angeles (CA)
California State U, Northridge (CA)
California State U, Sacramento (CA)
California State U, San Bernardino (CA)
Castleton State Coll (VT)
Clemson U (SC)
Cleveland State U (OH)
The Coll at Brockport, State U of New York (NY)
Corban U (OR)
DeSales U (PA)
Eastern Nazarene Coll (MA)
East Tennessee State U (TN)
Elizabethtown Coll (PA)
The Evergreen State Coll (WA)
Excelsior Coll (NY)
Fairmont State U (WV)
Florida Atlantic U (FL)
Gannon U (PA)
George Mason U (VA)
Georgetown U (DC)
Gettysburg Coll (PA)
Gwynedd-Mercy Coll (PA)
Inter American U of Puerto Rico, San Germán Campus (PR)
Johnson State Coll (VT)
Kalamazoo Coll (MI)
Keiser U, Fort Lauderdale (FL)
King Coll (TN)
King's Coll (PA)
Lamar U (TX)
Lock Haven U of Pennsylvania (PA)
Long Island U, Brooklyn Campus (NY)
Long Island U, C.W. Post Campus (NY)
Longwood U (VA)
Manchester Coll (IN)
Maryville U of Saint Louis (MO)
Massachusetts Coll of Pharmacy and Health Sciences (MA)
Mercy Coll (NY)
Merrimack Coll (MA)
Milligan Coll (TN)
Minnesota State U Mankato (MN)
Misericordia U (PA)
Missouri Southern State U (MO)
Mount Olive Coll (NC)
New Jersey City U (NJ)
Newman U (KS)
Northeastern State U (OK)
Northeastern U (MA)
Oakland U (MI)
The Ohio State U (OH)
Pennsylvania Coll of Technology (PA)
Point Park U (PA)
Purdue U (IN)
Randolph Coll (VA)
Saint Augustine's Coll (NC)
St. Francis Coll (NY)
Saint Mary's Coll of California (CA)
San Diego State U (CA)
San Francisco State U (CA)
Sonoma State U (CA)
Southeastern Louisiana U (LA)
South U (AL)
South U, Royal Palm Beach (FL)
South U, Tampa (FL)
South U, Columbia (SC)
State U of New York Coll at Cortland (NY)
State U of New York Coll at Potsdam (NY)
Stony Brook U, State U of New York (NY)
Syracuse U (NY)
Tennessee Wesleyan Coll (TN)
Texas A&M U–Commerce (TX)
Texas A&M U–Corpus Christi (TX)
Texas Christian U (TX)
Towson U (MD)
Truman State U (MO)
The U of Alabama (AL)
The U of Alabama at Birmingham (AL)
U of Alaska Anchorage (AK)
U of Arkansas (AR)
U of Arkansas at Little Rock (AR)
The U of British Columbia–Okanagan (BC, Canada)
U of California, Santa Cruz (CA)
U of Charleston (WV)
U of Colorado at Colorado Springs (CO)
U of Hartford (CT)
U of Louisiana at Monroe (LA)
U of Maryland, Baltimore County (MD)
U of Nevada, Reno (NV)
U of New England (ME)
The U of North Carolina Wilmington (NC)
U of Northern Iowa (IA)
U of Pennsylvania (PA)
U of Pittsburgh (PA)
U of St. Thomas (MN)
U of Southern Indiana (IN)
U of Southern Maine (ME)
The U of Tennessee at Martin (TN)
The U of Texas at El Paso (TX)
The U of Texas at Tyler (TX)
U of Waterloo (ON, Canada)
The U of Western Ontario (ON, Canada)
U of Wisconsin–Milwaukee (WI)
U of Wisconsin–Parkside (WI)
Virginia Commonwealth U (VA)
Waldorf Coll (IA)
Washington U in St. Louis (MO)
Wayne State U (MI)
West Liberty U (WV)
Wilfrid Laurier U (ON, Canada)
William Paterson U of New Jersey (NJ)
Winona State U (MN)
Worcester State Coll (MA)
York U (ON, Canada)
Youngstown State U (OH)

HEALTH SERVICES ADMINISTRATION

Brown Mackie Coll–Phoenix (AZ)
Brown Mackie Coll–Tulsa (OK)
Bryant & Stratton Coll—Richmond Campus (VA)
Bryant & Stratton Coll—Virginia Beach (VA)
Chapman U (CA)
D'Youville Coll (NY)
East Stroudsburg U of Pennsylvania (PA)
Freed-Hardeman U (TN)
Indiana U Northwest (IN)
Indiana U–Purdue U Fort Wayne (IN)
Indiana U–Purdue U Indianapolis (IN)
Indiana U South Bend (IN)
Inter American U of Puerto Rico, Ponce Campus (PR)
Keiser U, Fort Lauderdale (FL)
Monroe Coll, Bronx (NY)
Prescott Coll (AZ)
Robert Morris U (PA)
St. Petersburg Coll (FL)
Santa Fe Comm Coll (FL)
Slippery Rock U of Pennsylvania (PA)
Thomas Edison State Coll (NJ)
U of Atlanta (GA)
U of Illinois at Urbana–Champaign (IL)
Ursuline Coll (OH)

HEALTH SERVICES/ALLIED HEALTH/HEALTH SCIENCES

Albany Coll of Pharmacy and Health Sciences (NY)
Alderson-Broaddus Coll (WV)
Baptist Coll of Health Sciences (TN)
Brenau U (GA)
Brevard Coll (NC)
California Baptist U (CA)
California State U, Chico (CA)
California State U, Dominguez Hills (CA)
California State U, Fullerton (CA)
Central Baptist Coll (AR)
Chowan U (NC)
The Coll of Idaho (ID)
The Coll of St. Scholastica (MN)
Coll of the Ozarks (MO)
Columbus State U (GA)
Corban U (OR)
Drury U (MO)
Ferrum Coll (VA)
Florida Ag and Mech U (FL)
Florida Atlantic U (FL)
Florida Gulf Coast U (FL)
Friends U (KS)
Graceland U (IA)
Gwynedd-Mercy Coll (PA)
Hendrix Coll (AR)
Hofstra U (NY)
Idaho State U (ID)
Kent State U (OH)
Lebanon Valley Coll (PA)
Liberty U (VA)
Marywood U (PA)
Mercy Coll (NY)
Miami Dade Coll (FL)
Monmouth U (NJ)
Monroe Coll, New Rochelle (NY)
Montclair State U (NJ)
Mountain State U (WV)
National U (CA)
Nicholls State U (LA)
Northern Kentucky U (KY)
Nova Southeastern U (FL)
Old Dominion U (VA)
Pontifical Catholic U of Puerto Rico (PR)
Prescott Coll (AZ)
Sacred Heart U (CT)
Saginaw Valley State U (MI)
St. Cloud State U (MN)
Saint Joseph's U (PA)
San Diego State U (CA)
San Jose State U (CA)
Stephen F. Austin State U (TX)
Stetson U (FL)
Texas A&M U (TX)
Texas A&M U–Kingsville (TX)
Texas State U–San Marcos (TX)
Texas Tech U (TX)
Texas Woman's U (TX)
Thomas Edison State Coll (NJ)
Thompson Rivers U (BC, Canada)
Truman State U (MO)
U of Central Florida (FL)
U of Florida (FL)
U of Hartford (CT)
U of Houston (TX)
U of Miami (FL)
U of Michigan–Flint (MI)
U of Minnesota, Crookston (MN)
U of North Florida (FL)
U of North Texas (TX)
U of Ottawa (ON, Canada)
U of Southern Mississippi (MS)
The U of Texas at Austin (TX)
The U of Texas at Brownsville (TX)

The U of Texas at San Antonio (TX)
The U of Texas–Pan American (TX)
U of the Sciences in Philadelphia (PA)
U of Utah (UT)
The U of Western Ontario (ON, Canada)
U of West Florida (FL)
U of Wyoming (WY)
Ursuline Coll (OH)
Washburn U (KS)
Western Kentucky U (KY)
Westminster Coll (UT)
Wheaton Coll (IL)
Widener U (PA)
York U (ON, Canada)

HEALTH TEACHER EDUCATION

Alma Coll (MI)
Appalachian State U (NC)
Aquinas Coll (MI)
Armstrong Atlantic State U (GA)
Ashland U (OH)
Auburn U (AL)
Augsburg Coll (MN)
Austin Peay State U (TN)
Averett U (VA)
Ball State U (IN)
Baylor U (TX)
Belmont U (TN)
Bemidji State U (MN)
Bethel U (MN)
Bluefield Coll (VA)
Bowling Green State U (OH)
Bridgewater State Coll (MA)
Brooklyn Coll of the City U of New York (NY)
California State U, Chico (CA)
California State U, San Bernardino (CA)
Campbellsville U (KY)
Capital U (OH)
Carroll U (WI)
Cedarville U (OH)
Central Christian Coll of Kansas (KS)
Central Michigan U (MI)
The Coll at Brockport, State U of New York (NY)
Concordia Coll (MN)
Concordia U, St. Paul (MN)
Concord U (WV)
Curry Coll (MA)
Defiance Coll (OH)
DePaul U (IL)
East Carolina U (NC)
East Central U (OK)
Eastern Illinois U (IL)
Eastern Mennonite U (VA)
Eastern Washington U (WA)
East Stroudsburg U of Pennsylvania (PA)
Elon U (NC)
Fayetteville State U (NC)
Ferris State U (MI)
Florida Ag and Mech U (FL)
Fort Valley State U (GA)
Freed-Hardeman U (TN)
Gardner-Webb U (NC)
George Mason U (VA)
Georgia Coll & State U (GA)
Graceland U (IA)
Grand Valley State U (MI)
Gustavus Adolphus Coll (MN)
Hamline U (MN)
Hampton U (VA)
Harding U (AR)
Heidelberg U (OH)
Hofstra U (NY)
Hunter Coll of the City U of New York (NY)
Idaho State U (ID)
Illinois State U (IL)
Indiana U Bloomington (IN)
Indiana U–Purdue U Indianapolis (IN)
Indiana U Southeast (IN)
Iowa State U of Science and Technology (IA)
Ithaca Coll (NY)
Jacksonville State U (AL)
John Brown U (AR)
Johnson C. Smith U (NC)
Kent State U (OH)
Lamar U (TX)
Lee U (TN)
Lehman Coll of the City U of New York (NY)
Liberty U (VA)
Lincoln Memorial U (TN)
Long Island U, C.W. Post Campus (NY)
Longwood U (VA)
Louisiana Coll (LA)
Lynchburg Coll (VA)
Malone U (OH)
Manchester Coll (IN)
Maryville Coll (TN)
Mayville State U (ND)
Miami U (OH)
Miami U Hamilton (OH)
Michigan State U (MI)
Middle Tennessee State U (TN)
Minnesota State U Mankato (MN)
Minnesota State U Moorhead (MN)
Missouri Baptist U (MO)
Montana State U Billings (MT)
Montclair State U (NJ)
Morehead State U (KY)
Mount Vernon Nazarene U (OH)
Murray State U (KY)
New Mexico Highlands U (NM)
North Carolina Central U (NC)
North Dakota State U (ND)
Northeastern State U (OK)
Northern Arizona U (AZ)
Northern Michigan U (MI)
Northern State U (SD)
Northwestern Oklahoma State U (OK)
Ohio Northern U (OH)
Ohio Wesleyan U (OH)
Oral Roberts U (OK)
Peru State Coll (NE)
Pontifical Catholic U of Puerto Rico (PR)
Portland State U (OR)
Rhode Island Coll (RI)
Rocky Mountain Coll (MT)
St. Ambrose U (IA)
St. Cloud State U (MN)
Salisbury U (MD)
Southeastern Oklahoma State U (OK)
Southern Illinois U Carbondale (IL)
Southern Illinois U Edwardsville (IL)
Southern Oregon U (OR)
Southwest Baptist U (MO)
Southwest Minnesota State U (MN)
State U of New York at Oswego (NY)
State U of New York Coll at Cortland (NY)
Tabor Coll (KS)
Tennessee Technological U (TN)
Texas A&M U–Commerce (TX)
Texas A&M U–Corpus Christi (TX)
Texas Southern U (TX)
TUI U (CA)
Union Coll (KY)
The U of Alabama at Birmingham (AL)
The U of Arizona (AZ)
U of Arkansas at Little Rock (AR)
U of Charleston (WV)
U of Cincinnati (OH)
U of Dayton (OH)
U of Delaware (DE)
U of Georgia (GA)
U of Kentucky (KY)
U of Maine (ME)
U of Maine at Farmington (ME)
U of Maine at Presque Isle (ME)
U of Maryland, Coll Park (MD)
U of Minnesota, Duluth (MN)
The U of Montana Western (MT)
U of Mount Union (OH)
U of Nebraska–Lincoln (NE)
U of Nevada, Las Vegas (NV)
U of Nevada, Reno (NV)
U of New Brunswick Fredericton (NB, Canada)
U of New Mexico (NM)
U of Northern Iowa (IA)
U of Regina (SK, Canada)
U of Rio Grande (OH)
U of St. Thomas (MN)
The U of South Dakota (SD)
The U of Tennessee (TN)
U of the Cumberlands (KY)
U of the District of Columbia (DC)
The U of Toledo (OH)
U of Toronto (ON, Canada)
U of Windsor (ON, Canada)
U of Wisconsin–La Crosse (WI)
Utah State U (UT)
Utah Valley U (UT)
Valley City State U (ND)
Virginia Commonwealth U (VA)
Waldorf Coll (IA)
Washington State U (WA)
Wayne State U (MI)
Western Connecticut State U (CT)
Western Illinois U (IL)
Western Michigan U (MI)
West Liberty U (WV)
West Virginia State U (WV)
West Virginia Wesleyan Coll (WV)
William Paterson U of New Jersey (NJ)
William Penn U (IA)
Wilmington Coll (OH)
Winona State U (MN)
Wright State U (OH)
Xavier U of Louisiana (LA)
York Coll of the City U of New York (NY)
Youngstown State U (OH)

HEATING, AIR CONDITIONING, VENTILATION AND REFRIGERATION MAINTENANCE TECHNOLOGY

Lewis-Clark State Coll (ID)

HEAVY EQUIPMENT MAINTENANCE TECHNOLOGY

Ferris State U (MI)
Pittsburg State U (KS)

HEBREW

Bard Coll (NY)
Bernard M. Baruch Coll of the City U of New York (NY)
Brandeis U (MA)
Brigham Young U (UT)
Brooklyn Coll of the City U of New York (NY)
Columbia U, School of General Studies (NY)
Concordia U Wisconsin (WI)
Dartmouth Coll (NH)
Hofstra U (NY)
Hunter Coll of the City U of New York (NY)
Laura and Alvin Siegal Coll of Judaic Studies (OH)
Lehman Coll of the City U of New York (NY)
Multnomah U (OR)
New York U (NY)
The Ohio State U (OH)
Queens Coll of the City U of New York (NY)
State U of New York at Binghamton (NY)
Temple U (PA)
U of Alberta (AB, Canada)
U of California, Los Angeles (CA)
U of Illinois at Urbana–Champaign (IL)
U of Minnesota, Twin Cities Campus (MN)
The U of Texas at Austin (TX)
U of Utah (UT)
The U of Western Ontario (ON, Canada)
U of Wisconsin–Madison (WI)
U of Wisconsin–Milwaukee (WI)
Washington U in St. Louis (MO)
York U (ON, Canada)

HERBALISM

Bastyr U (WA)

HIGHER EDUCATION/ HIGHER EDUCATION ADMINISTRATION

Wright State U (OH)

HINDI

U of Chicago (IL)

HISPANIC AMERICAN, PUERTO RICAN, AND MEXICAN AMERICAN/ CHICANO STUDIES

Arizona State U (AZ)
Boston Coll (MA)
Bowling Green State U (OH)
Brooklyn Coll of the City U of New York (NY)
California State U, Dominguez Hills (CA)
California State U, East Bay (CA)
California State U, Fresno (CA)
California State U, Fullerton (CA)
California State U, Long Beach (CA)
California State U, Los Angeles (CA)
California State U, Northridge (CA)
Cedar Crest Coll (PA)
Claremont McKenna Coll (CA)
The Colorado Coll (CO)
Columbia U (NY)
Columbia U, School of General Studies (NY)
Connecticut Coll (CT)
Dartmouth Coll (NH)
Fordham U (NY)
Fort Lewis Coll (CO)
Gettysburg Coll (PA)
Hofstra U (NY)
Hunter Coll of the City U of New York (NY)
Lewis & Clark Coll (OR)
Loyola Marymount U (CA)
Metropolitan State Coll of Denver (CO)
Mills Coll (CA)
Our Lady of the Lake U of San Antonio (TX)
Pitzer Coll (CA)
Pomona Coll (CA)
Rutgers, The State U of New Jersey, Newark (NJ)
Rutgers, The State U of New Jersey, New Brunswick (NJ)
San Diego State U (CA)
San Francisco State U (CA)
Scripps Coll (CA)
Sonoma State U (CA)
Southern Methodist U (TX)
Stanford U (CA)
State U of New York Coll at Oneonta (NY)
Sul Ross State U (TX)
Trent U (ON, Canada)
Tulane U (LA)
U at Albany, State U of New York (NY)
The U of Arizona (AZ)
U of California, Berkeley (CA)
U of California, Davis (CA)
U of California, Irvine (CA)
U of California, Los Angeles (CA)
U of California, Riverside (CA)
U of California, Santa Barbara (CA)
U of California, Santa Cruz (CA)
U of Michigan (MI)
U of Minnesota, Twin Cities Campus (MN)
U of Northern Colorado (CO)
U of Southern California (CA)
U of Southern Maine (ME)
The U of Texas at El Paso (TX)
The U of Texas at San Antonio (TX)
The U of Texas–Pan American (TX)
U of Washington (WA)
U of Washington, Tacoma (WA)
U of Wisconsin–Madison (WI)
Wheaton Coll (MA)

HISTOLOGIC TECHNOLOGY/ HISTOTECHNOLOGIST

Michigan Technological U (MI)
Northern Michigan U (MI)
Oakland U (MI)

HISTORIC PRESERVATION AND CONSERVATION

Coll of Charleston (SC)
Delaware State U (DE)
Saint Mary's Coll of California (CA)
Salve Regina U (RI)
Savannah Coll of Art and Design (GA)
U of Mary Washington (VA)
Ursuline Coll (OH)

HISTORY

Abilene Christian U (TX)
Acadia U (NS, Canada)
Adams State Coll (CO)
Adelphi U (NY)
Agnes Scott Coll (GA)
Alabama State U (AL)
Albany State U (GA)
Albertus Magnus Coll (CT)
Albion Coll (MI)
Albright Coll (PA)
Alcorn State U (MS)
Alderson-Broaddus Coll (WV)
Alfred U (NY)
Allegheny Coll (PA)
Alma Coll (MI)
Alvernia U (PA)
Alverno Coll (WI)
American Intl Coll (MA)
American Public U System (WV)
American U (DC)
American U of Beirut (Lebanon)
The American U of Paris (France)
Amherst Coll (MA)
Anderson U (IN)
Andrews U (MI)
Angelo State U (TX)
Appalachian State U (NC)
Aquinas Coll (MI)
Aquinas Coll (TN)
Arcadia U (PA)
Arizona State U (AZ)
Arkansas State U—Jonesboro (AR)
Arkansas Tech U (AR)
Armstrong Atlantic State U (GA)
Asbury U (KY)
Ashland U (OH)
Assumption Coll (MA)
Athabasca U (AB, Canada)
Auburn U (AL)
Auburn U Montgomery (AL)
Augsburg Coll (MN)
Augustana Coll (IL)
Augustana Coll (SD)
Aurora U (IL)
Austin Coll (TX)
Austin Peay State U (TN)
Averett U (VA)
Avila U (MO)
Azusa Pacific U (CA)
Baker U (KS)
Baldwin-Wallace Coll (OH)
Ball State U (IN)
Bard Coll (NY)
Barnard Coll (NY)
Barry U (FL)
Barton Coll (NC)
Bates Coll (ME)
Baylor U (TX)
Belhaven U (MS)
Bellarmine U (KY)
Belmont Abbey Coll (NC)
Belmont U (TN)
Beloit Coll (WI)
Bemidji State U (MN)
Benedictine Coll (KS)
Benedictine U (IL)
Bennington Coll (VT)
Bentley U (MA)
Berea Coll (KY)
Bernard M. Baruch Coll of the City U of New York (NY)
Berry Coll (GA)
Bethany Coll (KS)
Bethany Coll (WV)
Bethany Lutheran Coll (MN)
Bethel Coll (IN)
Bethel Coll (KS)
Bethel U (MN)
Bethel U (TN)
Birmingham-Southern Coll (AL)
Bishop's U (QC, Canada)
Blackburn Coll (IL)
Black Hills State U (SD)
Bloomfield Coll (NJ)
Bloomsburg U of Pennsylvania (PA)
Bluefield Coll (VA)
Blue Mountain Coll (MS)
Bluffton U (OH)
Bob Jones U (SC)
Boise State U (ID)
Boston Coll (MA)
Boston U (MA)
Bowdoin Coll (ME)
Bowie State U (MD)
Bowling Green State U (OH)
Bradley U (IL)
Brandeis U (MA)
Brenau U (GA)
Brescia U (KY)
Brevard Coll (NC)
Brewton-Parker Coll (GA)
Briar Cliff U (IA)
Bridgewater Coll (VA)
Bridgewater State Coll (MA)
Brigham Young U–Hawaii (HI)
Brock U (ON, Canada)
Brooklyn Coll of the City U of New York (NY)
Bryan Coll (TN)
Bryant U (RI)
Bryn Athyn Coll of the New Church (PA)
Bryn Mawr Coll (PA)
Bucknell U (PA)
Buena Vista U (IA)
Buffalo State Coll, State U of New York (NY)
Butler U (IN)
Cabrini Coll (PA)
California Baptist U (CA)
California Inst of Technology (CA)
California Lutheran U (CA)
California Polytechnic State U, San Luis Obispo (CA)
California State Polytechnic U, Pomona (CA)
California State U, Bakersfield (CA)
California State U, Chico (CA)
California State U, Dominguez Hills (CA)
California State U, East Bay (CA)
California State U, Fresno (CA)
California State U, Fullerton (CA)
California State U, Long Beach (CA)
California State U, Los Angeles (CA)
California State U, Northridge (CA)
California State U, Sacramento (CA)
California State U, San Bernardino (CA)
California State U, San Marcos (CA)

History

California State U, Stanislaus (CA)
Calvin Coll (MI)
Cameron U (OK)
Campbellsville U (KY)
Canisius Coll (NY)
Cape Breton U (NS, Canada)
Capital U (OH)
Carleton Coll (MN)
Carlow U (PA)
Carroll U (WI)
Carson-Newman Coll (TN)
Case Western Reserve U (OH)
Castleton State Coll (VT)
Catawba Coll (NC)
The Catholic U of America (DC)
Cedar Crest Coll (PA)
Cedarville U (OH)
Centenary Coll (NJ)
Centenary Coll of Louisiana (LA)
Central Christian Coll of Kansas (KS)
Central Coll (IA)
Central Connecticut State U (CT)
Central Michigan U (MI)
Central State U (OH)
Chaminade U of Honolulu (HI)
Chapman U (CA)
Chatham U (PA)
Chowan U (NC)
Christendom Coll (VA)
Christian Brothers U (TN)
Christopher Newport U (VA)
The Citadel, The Military Coll of South Carolina (SC)
City Coll of the City U of New York (NY)
Claflin U (SC)
Claremont McKenna Coll (CA)
Clarion U of Pennsylvania (PA)
Clark Atlanta U (GA)
Clarke Coll (IA)
Clarkson U (NY)
Clark U (MA)
Clayton State U (GA)
Clearwater Christian Coll (FL)
Clemson U (SC)
Coastal Carolina U (SC)
Coker Coll (SC)
Colby Coll (ME)
Colgate U (NY)
The Coll at Brockport, State U of New York (NY)
Coll of Charleston (SC)
The Coll of Idaho (ID)
Coll of Mount St. Joseph (OH)
Coll of Mount Saint Vincent (NY)
The Coll of New Jersey (NJ)
The Coll of New Rochelle (NY)
Coll of Notre Dame of Maryland (MD)
Coll of Saint Benedict (MN)
Coll of Saint Elizabeth (NJ)
Coll of St. Joseph (VT)
The Coll of St. Scholastica (MN)
Coll of Staten Island of the City U of New York (NY)
Coll of the Holy Cross (MA)
Coll of the Ozarks (MO)
The Coll of William and Mary (VA)
The Coll of Wooster (OH)
The Colorado Coll (CO)
Colorado State U (CO)
Colorado State U–Pueblo (CO)
Columbia Coll (MO)
Columbia Coll (SC)
Columbia U (NY)
Columbia U, School of General Studies (NY)
Columbus State U (GA)
Concordia Coll (MN)
Concordia U (CA)
Concordia U (QC, Canada)
Concordia U Chicago (IL)
Concordia U Coll of Alberta (AB, Canada)
Concordia U, St. Paul (MN)
Concordia U Texas (TX)
Concordia U Wisconsin (WI)
Concord U (WV)
Connecticut Coll (CT)
Converse Coll (SC)
Coppin State U (MD)
Cornell Coll (IA)
Cornell U (NY)
Cornerstone U (MI)
Covenant Coll (GA)
Crandall U (NB, Canada)
Creighton U (NE)
Crichton Coll (TN)
Crown Coll (MN)
Culver-Stockton Coll (MO)
Cumberland U (TN)
Curry Coll (MA)
Daemen Coll (NY)
Dakota Wesleyan U (SD)
Dallas Baptist U (TX)
Dalton State Coll (GA)
Dana Coll (NE)
Dartmouth Coll (NH)
Davidson Coll (NC)
Defiance Coll (OH)
Delaware State U (DE)
Delta State U (MS)
Denison U (OH)
DePaul U (IL)
DePauw U (IN)
DeSales U (PA)
Dickinson Coll (PA)
Dickinson State U (ND)
Dillard U (LA)
Doane Coll (NE)
Dominican Coll (NY)
Dominican U (IL)
Dominican U of California (CA)
Dordt Coll (IA)
Dowling Coll (NY)
Drake U (IA)
Drew U (NJ)
Drexel U (PA)
Drury U (MO)
Duke U (NC)
Duquesne U (PA)
D'Youville Coll (NY)
Earlham Coll (IN)
East Central U (OK)
Eastern Connecticut State U (CT)
Eastern Illinois U (IL)
Eastern Mennonite U (VA)
Eastern Michigan U (MI)
Eastern Nazarene Coll (MA)
Eastern New Mexico U (NM)
Eastern Washington U (WA)
East Stroudsburg U of Pennsylvania (PA)
East Tennessee State U (TN)
East Texas Baptist U (TX)
Eckerd Coll (FL)
Edgewood Coll (WI)
Edinboro U of Pennsylvania (PA)
Edward Waters Coll (FL)
Elizabeth City State U (NC)
Elizabethtown Coll (PA)
Elmhurst Coll (IL)
Elmira Coll (NY)
Elon U (NC)
Emmanuel Coll (MA)
Emory & Henry Coll (VA)
Emory U (GA)
Emporia State U (KS)
Erskine Coll (SC)
Eugene Lang Coll The New School for Liberal Arts (NY)
Evangel U (MO)
Excelsior Coll (NY)
Fairfield U (CT)
Fairleigh Dickinson U, Coll at Florham (NJ)
Fairleigh Dickinson U, Metropolitan Campus (NJ)
Fairmont State U (WV)
Faulkner U (AL)
Fayetteville State U (NC)
Felician Coll (NJ)
Ferris State U (MI)
Ferrum Coll (VA)
Fisk U (TN)
Fitchburg State Coll (MA)
Flagler Coll (FL)
Florida Ag and Mech U (FL)
Florida Atlantic U (FL)
Florida Gulf Coast U (FL)
Florida Intl U (FL)
Florida Southern Coll (FL)
Florida State U (FL)
Fontbonne U (MO)
Fordham U (NY)
Fort Hays State U (KS)
Fort Lewis Coll (CO)
Framingham State Coll (MA)
Franciscan U of Steubenville (OH)
Francis Marion U (SC)
Franklin & Marshall Coll (PA)
Franklin Coll (IN)
Franklin Coll Switzerland (Switzerland)
Franklin Pierce U (NH)
Freed-Hardeman U (TN)
Free Will Baptist Bible Coll (TN)
Friends U (KS)
Frostburg State U (MD)
Furman U (SC)
Gallaudet U (DC)
Gannon U (PA)
Gardner-Webb U (NC)
Geneva Coll (PA)
George Fox U (OR)
George Mason U (VA)
Georgetown Coll (KY)
Georgetown U (DC)
The George Washington U (DC)
Georgia Coll & State U (GA)
Georgian Court U (NJ)
Georgia Southern U (GA)
Georgia State U (GA)
Gettysburg Coll (PA)
Glenville State Coll (WV)
Gonzaga U (WA)
Gordon Coll (MA)
Goshen Coll (IN)
Goucher Coll (MD)
Grace Coll (IN)
Graceland U (IA)
Grambling State U (LA)
Grand Valley State U (MI)
Grand View U (IA)
Great Lakes Christian Coll (MI)
Green Mountain Coll (VT)
Greensboro Coll (NC)
Greenville Coll (IL)
Grinnell Coll (IA)
Grove City Coll (PA)
Guilford Coll (NC)
Gustavus Adolphus Coll (MN)
Gwynedd-Mercy Coll (PA)
Hamilton Coll (NY)
Hamline U (MN)
Hampden-Sydney Coll (VA)
Hampshire Coll (MA)
Hampton U (VA)
Hannibal-LaGrange Coll (MO)
Hanover Coll (IN)
Harding U (AR)
Hardin-Simmons U (TX)
Hartwick Coll (NY)
Harvard U (MA)
Haverford Coll (PA)
Hawai'i Pacific U (HI)
Heidelberg U (OH)
Henderson State U (AR)
Hendrix Coll (AR)
High Point U (NC)
Hillsdale Coll (MI)
Hiram Coll (OH)
Hofstra U (NY)
Hollins U (VA)
Holy Family U (PA)
Holy Names U (CA)
Hood Coll (MD)
Hope Coll (MI)
Houghton Coll (NY)
Houston Baptist U (TX)
Howard Payne U (TX)
Humboldt State U (CA)
Hunter Coll of the City U of New York (NY)
Huntingdon Coll (AL)
Huntington U (IN)
Huston-Tillotson U (TX)
Idaho State U (ID)
Illinois Coll (IL)
Illinois State U (IL)
Illinois Wesleyan U (IL)
Immaculata U (PA)
Indiana State U (IN)
Indiana U Bloomington (IN)
Indiana U Northwest (IN)
Indiana U of Pennsylvania (PA)
Indiana U–Purdue U Fort Wayne (IN)
Indiana U–Purdue U Indianapolis (IN)
Indiana U South Bend (IN)
Indiana U Southeast (IN)
Indiana Wesleyan U (IN)
Iona Coll (NY)
Iowa State U of Science and Technology (IA)
Iowa Wesleyan Coll (IA)
Ithaca Coll (NY)
Jackson State U (MS)
Jacksonville State U (AL)
Jacksonville U (FL)
James Madison U (VA)
Jamestown Coll (ND)
Jarvis Christian Coll (TX)
John Brown U (AR)
John Carroll U (OH)
The Johns Hopkins U (MD)
Johnson C. Smith U (NC)
Johnson State Coll (VT)
Judson Coll (AL)
Judson U (IL)
Juniata Coll (PA)
Kalamazoo Coll (MI)
Kansas State U (KS)
Kean U (NJ)
Keene State Coll (NH)
Kennesaw State U (GA)
Kent State U (OH)
Kent State U at Stark (OH)
Kentucky Wesleyan Coll (KY)
Kenyon Coll (OH)
Keuka Coll (NY)
King Coll (TN)
King's Coll (PA)
The King's U Coll (AB, Canada)
Knox Coll (IL)
Kutztown U of Pennsylvania (PA)
Lafayette Coll (PA)
LaGrange Coll (GA)
Lake Forest Coll (IL)
Lakehead U (ON, Canada)
Lakeland Coll (WI)
Lake Superior State U (MI)
Lamar U (TX)
Lane Coll (TN)
La Roche Coll (PA)
La Salle U (PA)
Lasell Coll (MA)
La Sierra U (CA)
Laurentian U (ON, Canada)
Lawrence U (WI)
Lebanon Valley Coll (PA)
Lees-McRae Coll (NC)
Lee U (TN)
Lehigh U (PA)
Lehman Coll of the City U of New York (NY)
Le Moyne Coll (NY)
LeTourneau U (TX)
Lewis & Clark Coll (OR)
Lewis U (IL)
Liberty U (VA)
Limestone Coll (SC)
Lincoln Memorial U (TN)
Lincoln U (MO)
Lincoln U (PA)
Lindenwood U (MO)
Lindsey Wilson Coll (KY)
Linfield Coll (OR)
Lipscomb U (TN)
Lock Haven U of Pennsylvania (PA)
Long Island U, Brooklyn Campus (NY)
Long Island U, C.W. Post Campus (NY)
Longwood U (VA)
Loras Coll (IA)
Louisiana Coll (LA)
Louisiana State U and Ag and Mech Coll (LA)
Louisiana State U in Shreveport (LA)
Louisiana Tech U (LA)
Lourdes Coll (OH)
Loyola Marymount U (CA)
Loyola U Chicago (IL)
Loyola U Maryland (MD)
Loyola U New Orleans (LA)
Lubbock Christian U (TX)
Luther Coll (IA)
Lycoming Coll (PA)
Lynchburg Coll (VA)
Lyon Coll (AR)
Macalester Coll (MN)
Madonna U (MI)
Malone U (OH)
Manchester Coll (IN)
Manhattan Coll (NY)
Manhattanville Coll (NY)
Mansfield U of Pennsylvania (PA)
Marian U (IN)
Marian U (WI)
Marietta Coll (OH)
Marist Coll (NY)
Marlboro Coll (VT)
Marquette U (WI)
Marshall U (WV)
Mars Hill Coll (NC)
Mary Baldwin Coll (VA)
Marymount Manhattan Coll (NY)
Marymount U (VA)
Maryville Coll (TN)
Maryville U of Saint Louis (MO)
Marywood U (PA)
Massachusetts Coll of Liberal Arts (MA)
Massachusetts Inst of Technology (MA)
The Master's Coll and Sem (CA)
McDaniel Coll (MD)
McKendree U (IL)
McMurry U (TX)
McNeese State U (LA)
McPherson Coll (KS)
Memorial U of Newfoundland (NL, Canada)
Mercer U (GA)
Mercy Coll (NY)
Mercyhurst Coll (PA)
Meredith Coll (NC)
Merrimack Coll (MA)
Messiah Coll (PA)
Methodist U (NC)
Metropolitan State Coll of Denver (CO)
Miami U (OH)
Miami U Hamilton (OH)
Michigan State U (MI)
Michigan Technological U (MI)
MidAmerica Nazarene U (KS)
Middlebury Coll (VT)
Middle Tennessee State U (TN)
Midwestern State U (TX)
Millersville U of Pennsylvania (PA)
Milligan Coll (TN)
Millikin U (IL)
Millsaps Coll (MS)
Mills Coll (CA)
Minnesota State U Mankato (MN)
Minnesota State U Moorhead (MN)
Minot State U (ND)
Misericordia U (PA)
Mississippi Coll (MS)
Mississippi State U (MS)
Mississippi U for Women (MS)
Mississippi Valley State U (MS)
Missouri Baptist U (MO)
Missouri Southern State U (MO)
Missouri State U (MO)
Missouri U of Science and Technology (MO)
Missouri Western State U (MO)
Molloy Coll (NY)
Monmouth Coll (IL)
Monmouth U (NJ)
Montana State U (MT)
Montana State U Billings (MT)
Montclair State U (NJ)
Moravian Coll (PA)
Morehead State U (KY)
Morehouse Coll (GA)
Morningside Coll (IA)
Morris Coll (SC)
Mount Allison U (NB, Canada)
Mount Holyoke Coll (MA)
Mount Marty Coll (SD)
Mount Mary Coll (WI)
Mount Mercy Coll (IA)
Mount Olive Coll (NC)
Mount Saint Mary Coll (NY)
Mount St. Mary's Coll (CA)
Mount St. Mary's U (MD)
Mount Vernon Nazarene U (OH)
Muhlenberg Coll (PA)
Multnomah U (OR)
Murray State U (KY)
National U (CA)
Nazareth Coll of Rochester (NY)
Nebraska Wesleyan U (NE)
Nevada State Coll at Henderson (NV)
Newberry Coll (SC)
New Coll of Florida (FL)
New England Coll (NH)
New Jersey City U (NJ)
New Jersey Inst of Technology (NJ)
Newman U (KS)
New Mexico Highlands U (NM)
New Mexico State U (NM)
New York U (NY)
Niagara U (NY)
Nicholls State U (LA)
Nipissing U (ON, Canada)
Norfolk State U (VA)
North Carolina Central U (NC)
North Carolina State U (NC)
North Central Coll (IL)
North Dakota State U (ND)
Northeastern Illinois U (IL)
Northeastern State U (OK)
Northeastern U (MA)
Northern Arizona U (AZ)
Northern Kentucky U (KY)
Northern Michigan U (MI)
Northern State U (SD)
North Georgia Coll & State U (GA)
North Greenville U (SC)
Northwest Christian U (OR)
Northwestern Coll (IA)
Northwestern Coll (MN)
Northwestern Oklahoma State U (OK)
Northwestern State U of Louisiana (LA)
Northwest Missouri State U (MO)
Northwest Nazarene U (ID)
Northwest U (WA)
Notre Dame de Namur U (CA)
Nova Southeastern U (FL)
Nyack Coll (NY)
Oakland U (MI)
Oakwood U (AL)
Oberlin Coll (OH)
Occidental Coll (CA)
Oglethorpe U (GA)
Ohio Dominican U (OH)
Ohio Northern U (OH)
The Ohio State U (OH)
The Ohio State U at Lima (OH)
The Ohio State U at Marion (OH)
The Ohio State U–Mansfield Campus (OH)
The Ohio State U–Newark Campus (OH)
Ohio U (OH)
Ohio Valley U (WV)
Ohio Wesleyan U (OH)
Oklahoma Baptist U (OK)
Oklahoma Christian U (OK)
Oklahoma City U (OK)
Oklahoma Panhandle State U (OK)
Oklahoma State U (OK)
Oklahoma Wesleyan U (OK)
Old Dominion U (VA)
Oral Roberts U (OK)
Ottawa U (KS)
Ouachita Baptist U (AR)
Our Lady of the Lake U of San Antonio (TX)
Pace U (NY)
Pacific Lutheran U (WA)
Pacific Union Coll (CA)
Paine Coll (GA)

Park U (MO)
Patrick Henry Coll (VA)
Peace Coll (NC)
Penn State Abington (PA)
Penn State Altoona (PA)
Penn State Beaver (PA)
Penn State Berks (PA)
Penn State Brandywine (PA)
Penn State DuBois (PA)
Penn State Erie, The Behrend Coll (PA)
Penn State Fayette, The Eberly Campus (PA)
Penn State Greater Allegheny (PA)
Penn State Hazleton (PA)
Penn State Lehigh Valley (PA)
Penn State Mont Alto (PA)
Penn State New Kensington (PA)
Penn State Schuylkill (PA)
Penn State Shenango (PA)
Penn State U Park (PA)
Penn State Wilkes-Barre (PA)
Penn State Worthington Scranton (PA)
Penn State York (PA)
Pepperdine U, Malibu (CA)
Peru State Coll (NE)
Piedmont Coll (GA)
Pikeville Coll (KY)
Pittsburg State U (KS)
Pitzer Coll (CA)
Plymouth State U (NH)
Point Park U (PA)
Pomona Coll (CA)
Pontifical Catholic U of Puerto Rico (PR)
Pontifical Coll Josephinum (OH)
Portland State U (OR)
Post U (CT)
Prairie View A&M U (TX)
Presbyterian Coll (SC)
Prescott Coll (AZ)
Princeton U (NJ)
Principia Coll (IL)
Providence Coll (RI)
Purchase Coll, State U of New York (NY)
Purdue U (IN)
Purdue U Calumet (IN)
Queens Coll of the City U of New York (NY)
Queen's U at Kingston (ON, Canada)
Queens U of Charlotte (NC)
Quincy U (IL)
Quinnipiac U (CT)
Radford U (VA)
Ramapo Coll of New Jersey (NJ)
Randolph Coll (VA)
Randolph-Macon Coll (VA)
Redeemer U Coll (ON, Canada)
Reed Coll (OR)
Regent U (VA)
Regis Coll (MA)
Reinhardt Coll (GA)
Rhode Island Coll (RI)
Rhodes Coll (TN)
Rice U (TX)
The Richard Stockton Coll of New Jersey (NJ)
Rider U (NJ)
Ripon Coll (WI)
Rivier Coll (NH)
Roanoke Coll (VA)
Roberts Wesleyan Coll (NY)
Rochester Coll (MI)
Rockford Coll (IL)
Rockhurst U (MO)
Rocky Mountain Coll (MT)
Rollins Coll (FL)
Roosevelt U (IL)
Rosemont Coll (PA)
Rowan U (NJ)
Royal Military Coll of Canada (ON, Canada)
Russell Sage Coll (NY)
Rutgers, The State U of New Jersey, Camden (NJ)
Rutgers, The State U of New Jersey, Newark (NJ)
Rutgers, The State U of New Jersey, New Brunswick (NJ)
Sacred Heart U (CT)
Saginaw Valley State U (MI)
St. Ambrose U (IA)
Saint Anselm Coll (NH)
Saint Augustine's Coll (NC)
St. Bonaventure U (NY)
St. Catherine U (MN)
St. Cloud State U (MN)
St. Edward's U (TX)
St. Francis Coll (NY)
Saint Francis U (PA)
St. Francis Xavier U (NS, Canada)
St. John Fisher Coll (NY)
Saint John's U (MN)
St. John's U (NY)
Saint Joseph Coll (CT)
St. Joseph's Coll, Long Island Campus (NY)
St. Joseph's Coll, New York (NY)
Saint Joseph's U (PA)
St. Lawrence U (NY)
Saint Leo U (FL)
Saint Louis U (MO)
Saint Martin's U (WA)
Saint Mary's Coll (IN)
Saint Mary's Coll of California (CA)
St. Mary's Coll of Maryland (MD)
St. Mary's U (TX)
Saint Mary's U of Minnesota (MN)
Saint Michael's Coll (VT)
St. Norbert Coll (WI)
St. Olaf Coll (MN)
St. Thomas Aquinas Coll (NY)
St. Thomas U (FL)
St. Thomas U (NB, Canada)
Saint Vincent Coll (PA)
Saint Xavier U (IL)
Salem Coll (NC)
Salem State Coll (MA)
Salisbury U (MD)
Salve Regina U (RI)
Samford U (AL)
Sam Houston State U (TX)
San Diego Christian Coll (CA)
San Diego State U (CA)
San Francisco State U (CA)
San Jose State U (CA)
Santa Clara U (CA)
Sarah Lawrence Coll (NY)
Savannah State U (GA)
Schreiner U (TX)
Scripps Coll (CA)
Seattle Pacific U (WA)
Seattle U (WA)
Seton Hall U (NJ)
Seton Hill U (PA)
Sewanee: The U of the South (TN)
Shawnee State U (OH)
Shenandoah U (VA)
Shepherd U (WV)
Shippensburg U of Pennsylvania (PA)
Shorter U (GA)
Siena Coll (NY)
Siena Heights U (MI)
Silver Lake Coll (WI)
Simmons Coll (MA)
Simon Fraser U (BC, Canada)
Simpson Coll (IA)
Simpson U (CA)
Skidmore Coll (NY)
Slippery Rock U of Pennsylvania (PA)
Smith Coll (MA)
Sonoma State U (CA)
South Carolina State U (SC)
South Dakota State U (SD)
Southeastern Baptist Theological Sem (NC)
Southeastern Louisiana U (LA)
Southeastern Oklahoma State U (OK)
Southeastern U (FL)
Southeast Missouri State U (MO)
Southern Adventist U (TN)
Southern Arkansas U–Magnolia (AR)
Southern Connecticut State U (CT)
Southern Illinois U Carbondale (IL)
Southern Illinois U Edwardsville (IL)
Southern Methodist U (TX)
Southern New Hampshire U (NH)
Southern Oregon U (OR)
Southern U and Ag and Mech Coll (LA)
Southern U at New Orleans (LA)
Southern Utah U (UT)
Southern Vermont Coll (VT)
Southern Wesleyan U (SC)
Southwest Baptist U (MO)
Southwestern Adventist U (TX)
Southwestern Assemblies of God U (TX)
Southwestern Coll (KS)
Southwestern Oklahoma State U (OK)
Southwestern U (TX)
Southwest Minnesota State U (MN)
Spelman Coll (GA)
Spring Arbor U (MI)
Spring Hill Coll (AL)
Stanford U (CA)
State U of New York at Binghamton (NY)
State U of New York at Fredonia (NY)
State U of New York at New Paltz (NY)
State U of New York at Oswego (NY)
State U of New York at Plattsburgh (NY)
State U of New York Coll at Cortland (NY)
State U of New York Coll at Geneseo (NY)
State U of New York Coll at Oneonta (NY)
State U of New York Coll at Potsdam (NY)
State U of New York Empire State Coll (NY)
Stephen F. Austin State U (TX)
Sterling Coll (KS)
Stetson U (FL)
Stevens Inst of Technology (NJ)
Stillman Coll (AL)
Stonehill Coll (MA)
Stony Brook U, State U of New York (NY)
Suffolk U (MA)
Sul Ross State U (TX)
Susquehanna U (PA)
Swarthmore Coll (PA)
Sweet Briar Coll (VA)
Syracuse U (NY)
Tabor Coll (KS)
Talladega Coll (AL)
Tarleton State U (TX)
Taylor U (IN)
Temple U (PA)
Tennessee Technological U (TN)
Tennessee Wesleyan Coll (TN)
Texas A&M Intl U (TX)
Texas A&M U (TX)
Texas A&M U–Commerce (TX)
Texas A&M U–Corpus Christi (TX)
Texas A&M U–Kingsville (TX)
Texas Christian U (TX)
Texas Coll (TX)
Texas Lutheran U (TX)
Texas Southern U (TX)
Texas State U–San Marcos (TX)
Texas Tech U (TX)
Texas Wesleyan U (TX)
Texas Woman's U (TX)
Thiel Coll (PA)
Thomas Edison State Coll (NJ)
Thomas More Coll (KY)
Thompson Rivers U (BC, Canada)
Tiffin U (OH)
Towson U (MD)
Transylvania U (KY)
Trent U (ON, Canada)
Trevecca Nazarene U (TN)
Trinity Christian Coll (IL)
Trinity Coll (CT)
Trinity U (TX)
Troy U (AL)
Truett-McConnell Coll (GA)
Truman State U (MO)
Tufts U (MA)
Tulane U (LA)
Tusculum Coll (TN)
Tuskegee U (AL)
Union Coll (KY)
Union Coll (NE)
Union Coll (NY)
Union U (TN)
United States Air Force Acad (CO)
United States Naval Acad (MD)
Universidad Adventista de las Antillas (PR)
U at Albany, State U of New York (NY)
U at Buffalo, the State U of New York (NY)
The U of Alabama (AL)
The U of Alabama at Birmingham (AL)
The U of Alabama in Huntsville (AL)
U of Alaska Anchorage (AK)
U of Alaska Fairbanks (AK)
U of Alaska Southeast (AK)
U of Alberta (AB, Canada)
U of Arkansas (AR)
U of Arkansas at Fort Smith (AR)
U of Arkansas at Little Rock (AR)
U of Arkansas at Monticello (AR)
U of Arkansas at Pine Bluff (AR)
U of Baltimore (MD)
The U of British Columbia (BC, Canada)
The U of British Columbia–Okanagan (BC, Canada)
U of California, Berkeley (CA)
U of California, Davis (CA)
U of California, Irvine (CA)
U of California, Los Angeles (CA)
U of California, Merced (CA)
U of California, Riverside (CA)
U of California, San Diego (CA)
U of California, Santa Barbara (CA)
U of California, Santa Cruz (CA)
U of Central Florida (FL)
U of Central Missouri (MO)
U of Central Oklahoma (OK)
U of Charleston (WV)
U of Chicago (IL)
U of Cincinnati (OH)
U of Colorado at Boulder (CO)
U of Colorado at Colorado Springs (CO)
U of Colorado Denver (CO)
U of Connecticut (CT)
U of Dallas (TX)
U of Dayton (OH)
U of Delaware (DE)
U of Denver (CO)
U of Evansville (IN)
The U of Findlay (OH)
U of Florida (FL)
U of Georgia (GA)
U of Guam (GU)
U of Guelph (ON, Canada)
U of Hartford (CT)
U of Hawaii at Hilo (HI)
U of Hawaii at Manoa (HI)
U of Hawaii–West Oahu (HI)
U of Houston (TX)
U of Houston–Clear Lake (TX)
U of Houston–Downtown (TX)
U of Houston–Victoria (TX)
U of Idaho (ID)
U of Illinois at Chicago (IL)
U of Illinois at Springfield (IL)
U of Illinois at Urbana–Champaign (IL)
U of Indianapolis (IN)
The U of Iowa (IA)
The U of Kansas (KS)
U of Kentucky (KY)
U of King's Coll (NS, Canada)
U of La Verne (CA)
U of Lethbridge (AB, Canada)
U of Louisiana at Monroe (LA)
U of Louisville (KY)
U of Maine (ME)
U of Maine at Farmington (ME)
U of Maine at Machias (ME)
U of Manitoba (MB, Canada)
U of Mary Hardin-Baylor (TX)
U of Maryland, Baltimore County (MD)
U of Maryland, Coll Park (MD)
U of Maryland Eastern Shore (MD)
U of Maryland U Coll (MD)
U of Mary Washington (VA)
U of Massachusetts Amherst (MA)
U of Massachusetts Boston (MA)
U of Massachusetts Dartmouth (MA)
U of Massachusetts Lowell (MA)
U of Memphis (TN)
U of Miami (FL)
U of Michigan (MI)
U of Michigan–Dearborn (MI)
U of Michigan–Flint (MI)
U of Minnesota, Duluth (MN)
U of Minnesota, Twin Cities Campus (MN)
U of Mississippi (MS)
U of Missouri (MO)
U of Missouri–Kansas City (MO)
U of Missouri–St. Louis (MO)
U of Mobile (AL)
U of Montevallo (AL)
U of Mount Union (OH)
U of Nebraska at Kearney (NE)
U of Nebraska at Omaha (NE)
U of Nebraska–Lincoln (NE)
U of Nevada, Las Vegas (NV)
U of Nevada, Reno (NV)
U of New Brunswick Fredericton (NB, Canada)
U of New England (ME)
U of New Hampshire (NH)
U of New Hampshire at Manchester (NH)
U of New Haven (CT)
U of New Mexico (NM)
U of New Orleans (LA)
U of North Alabama (AL)
The U of North Carolina at Asheville (NC)
The U of North Carolina at Chapel Hill (NC)
The U of North Carolina at Charlotte (NC)
The U of North Carolina at Greensboro (NC)
The U of North Carolina at Pembroke (NC)
The U of North Carolina Wilmington (NC)
U of North Dakota (ND)
U of Northern Colorado (CO)
U of Northern Iowa (IA)
U of North Florida (FL)
U of North Texas (TX)
U of Notre Dame (IN)
U of Oklahoma (OK)
U of Oregon (OR)
U of Ottawa (ON, Canada)
U of Pennsylvania (PA)
U of Pittsburgh (PA)
U of Pittsburgh at Bradford (PA)
U of Pittsburgh at Johnstown (PA)
U of Portland (OR)
U of Puerto Rico at Utuado (PR)
U of Puerto Rico, Cayey U Coll (PR)
U of Puget Sound (WA)
U of Redlands (CA)
U of Regina (SK, Canada)
U of Rhode Island (RI)
U of Richmond (VA)
U of Rio Grande (OH)
U of Rochester (NY)
U of St. Francis (IL)
U of Saint Mary (KS)
U of St. Thomas (MN)
U of St. Thomas (TX)
U of San Diego (CA)
U of San Francisco (CA)
U of Saskatchewan (SK, Canada)
U of Science and Arts of Oklahoma (OK)
The U of Scranton (PA)
U of South Alabama (AL)
U of South Carolina (SC)
U of South Carolina Aiken (SC)
U of South Carolina Beaufort (SC)
U of South Carolina Upstate (SC)
The U of South Dakota (SD)
U of Southern California (CA)
U of Southern Indiana (IN)
U of Southern Maine (ME)
U of Southern Mississippi (MS)
U of South Florida (FL)
The U of Tampa (FL)
The U of Tennessee (TN)
The U of Tennessee at Chattanooga (TN)
The U of Tennessee at Martin (TN)
The U of Texas at Arlington (TX)
The U of Texas at Austin (TX)
The U of Texas at Brownsville (TX)
The U of Texas at Dallas (TX)
The U of Texas at El Paso (TX)
The U of Texas at San Antonio (TX)
The U of Texas at Tyler (TX)
The U of Texas of the Permian Basin (TX)
The U of Texas–Pan American (TX)
U of the Cumberlands (KY)
U of the Incarnate Word (TX)
U of the Ozarks (AR)
U of the Pacific (CA)
U of the Southwest (NM)
U of the West (CA)
The U of Toledo (OH)
U of Toronto (ON, Canada)
U of Tulsa (OK)
U of Utah (UT)
U of Vermont (VT)
U of Virginia (VA)
The U of Virginia's Coll at Wise (VA)
U of Washington (WA)
U of Waterloo (ON, Canada)
The U of West Alabama (AL)
The U of Western Ontario (ON, Canada)
U of West Florida (FL)
U of West Georgia (GA)
U of Windsor (ON, Canada)
U of Wisconsin–Eau Claire (WI)
U of Wisconsin–Green Bay (WI)
U of Wisconsin–La Crosse (WI)
U of Wisconsin–Madison (WI)
U of Wisconsin–Milwaukee (WI)
U of Wisconsin–Oshkosh (WI)
U of Wisconsin–Parkside (WI)
U of Wisconsin–Platteville (WI)
U of Wisconsin–River Falls (WI)
U of Wisconsin–Stevens Point (WI)
U of Wisconsin–Superior (WI)
U of Wisconsin–Whitewater (WI)
U of Wyoming (WY)
Ursinus Coll (PA)
Ursuline Coll (OH)
Utah State U (UT)
Utah Valley U (UT)
Utica Coll (NY)
Valdosta State U (GA)
Valley City State U (ND)
Valparaiso U (IN)
Vanderbilt U (TN)
Vanguard U of Southern California (CA)
Vassar Coll (NY)
Villanova U (PA)
Virginia Commonwealth U (VA)
Virginia Intermont Coll (VA)
Virginia Military Inst (VA)
Virginia Polytechnic Inst and State U (VA)
Virginia State U (VA)
Virginia Union U (VA)
Virginia Wesleyan Coll (VA)
Wabash Coll (IN)
Wagner Coll (NY)
Wake Forest U (NC)
Waldorf Coll (IA)
Walsh U (OH)
Warner Pacific Coll (OR)
Wartburg Coll (IA)

Washburn U (KS)
Washington Adventist U (MD)
Washington & Jefferson Coll (PA)
Washington and Lee U (VA)
Washington Coll (MD)
Washington State U (WA)
Washington U in St. Louis (MO)
Wayland Baptist U (TX)
Waynesburg U (PA)
Wayne State Coll (NE)
Wayne State U (MI)
Weber State U (UT)
Webster U (MO)
Wellesley Coll (MA)
Wells Coll (NY)
Wesleyan Coll (GA)
Wesleyan U (CT)
West Chester U of Pennsylvania (PA)
Western Carolina U (NC)
Western Connecticut State U (CT)
Western Illinois U (IL)
Western Kentucky U (KY)
Western Michigan U (MI)
Western New England Coll (MA)
Western Oregon U (OR)
Western State Coll of Colorado (CO)
Western Washington U (WA)
Westfield State Coll (MA)
West Liberty U (WV)
Westminster Coll (MO)
Westminster Coll (UT)
Westmont Coll (CA)
West Virginia State U (WV)
West Virginia U (WV)
West Virginia Wesleyan Coll (WV)
Wheaton Coll (IL)
Wheaton Coll (MA)
Wheeling Jesuit U (WV)
Whitman Coll (WA)
Whittier Coll (CA)
Wichita State U (KS)
Widener U (PA)
Wilfrid Laurier U (ON, Canada)
Wilkes U (PA)
Willamette U (OR)
William Jewell Coll (MO)
William Paterson U of New Jersey (NJ)
William Penn U (IA)
Williams Coll (MA)
Wilmington Coll (OH)
Wingate U (NC)
Winona State U (MN)
Winston-Salem State U (NC)
Winthrop U (SC)
Wittenberg U (OH)
Wofford Coll (SC)
Woodbury U (CA)
Worcester Polytechnic Inst (MA)
Worcester State Coll (MA)
Wright State U (OH)
Xavier U (OH)
Xavier U of Louisiana (LA)
Yale U (CT)
Yeshiva U (NY)
York Coll (NE)
York Coll of Pennsylvania (PA)
York Coll of the City U of New York (NY)
York U (ON, Canada)
Youngstown State U (OH)

HISTORY AND PHILOSOPHY OF SCIENCE AND TECHNOLOGY

Bard Coll (NY)
California Inst of Technology (CA)
Case Western Reserve U (OH)
Farmingdale State Coll (NY)
Georgia Inst of Technology (GA)
Harvard U (MA)
The Johns Hopkins U (MD)
Sarah Lawrence Coll (NY)
Stevens Inst of Technology (NJ)
U of Pennsylvania (PA)
U of Pittsburgh (PA)
U of Toronto (ON, Canada)
U of Washington (WA)
U of Wisconsin–Madison (WI)
Worcester Polytechnic Inst (MA)

HISTORY RELATED

American Public U System (WV)
Arizona State U (AZ)
Bridgewater Coll (VA)
Bridgewater State Coll (MA)
Carnegie Mellon U (PA)
Cedarville U (OH)
Delaware State U (DE)
Harvard U (MA)
Indiana U Kokomo (IN)
Marquette U (WI)
Mercyhurst Coll (PA)
Mount Aloysius Coll (PA)
Saint Mary's U of Minnesota (MN)
Sarah Lawrence Coll (NY)
Trevecca Nazarene U (TN)
United States Military Acad (NY)
U of Regina (SK, Canada)
Vanderbilt U (TN)

HISTORY TEACHER EDUCATION

Abilene Christian U (TX)
Alma Coll (MI)
Appalachian State U (NC)
Assumption Coll (MA)
Auburn U (AL)
Averett U (VA)
Bishop's U (QC, Canada)
Bluefield Coll (VA)
Bowling Green State U (OH)
Bradley U (IL)
Brewton-Parker Coll (GA)
Bridgewater Coll (VA)
Bryan Coll (TN)
Buena Vista U (IA)
Campbellsville U (KY)
Carroll U (WI)
The Catholic U of America (DC)
Central Christian Coll of Kansas (KS)
Central Michigan U (MI)
Christian Brothers U (TN)
Coker Coll (SC)
The Coll at Brockport, State U of New York (NY)
The Coll of New Jersey (NJ)
Coll of the Ozarks (MO)
Concordia U Chicago (IL)
Concordia U Wisconsin (WI)
Cornerstone U (MI)
Covenant Coll (GA)
Culver-Stockton Coll (MO)
Cumberland U (TN)
Dakota Wesleyan U (SD)
Dana Coll (NE)
DePaul U (IL)
Dominican Coll (NY)
Dordt Coll (IA)
East Central U (OK)
Eastern Michigan U (MI)
Eastern Nazarene Coll (MA)
East Texas Baptist U (TX)
Elizabeth City State U (NC)
Elmhurst Coll (IL)
Elmira Coll (NY)
Evangel U (MO)
Ferris State U (MI)
Fitchburg State Coll (MA)
Free Will Baptist Bible Coll (TN)
Friends U (KS)
Gardner-Webb U (NC)
Grand Valley State U (MI)
Greenville Coll (IL)
Gwynedd-Mercy Coll (PA)
Hannibal-LaGrange Coll (MO)
Hardin-Simmons U (TX)
Hope Coll (MI)
Howard Payne U (TX)
Huntingdon Coll (AL)
Indiana U–Purdue U Fort Wayne (IN)
Ithaca Coll (NY)
Jamestown Coll (ND)
Johnson State Coll (VT)
Keene State Coll (NH)
King Coll (TN)
Liberty U (VA)
Lincoln Memorial U (TN)
Lindenwood U (MO)
Lipscomb U (TN)
Lubbock Christian U (TX)
Maranatha Baptist Bible Coll (WI)
Maryville Coll (TN)
Maryville U of Saint Louis (MO)
Mayville State U (ND)
McKendree U (IL)
McMurry U (TX)
Michigan State U (MI)
MidAmerica Nazarene U (KS)
Millersville U of Pennsylvania (PA)
Minot State U (ND)
Misericordia U (PA)
Missouri State U (MO)
Montana State U Billings (MT)
Moravian Coll (PA)
Morningside Coll (IA)
Mount Marty Coll (SD)
Mount Mary Coll (WI)
Mount Vernon Nazarene U (OH)
Murray State U (KY)
Nazareth Coll of Rochester (NY)
Nevada State Coll at Henderson (NV)
North Carolina Central U (NC)
North Carolina State U (NC)
North Dakota State U (ND)
Northern Arizona U (AZ)
Northern Michigan U (MI)
Northwest Nazarene U (ID)
Ohio Northern U (OH)
Ohio Wesleyan U (OH)
Old Dominion U (VA)
Pace U (NY)
Paine Coll (GA)
Pontifical Catholic U of Puerto Rico (PR)
Prescott Coll (AZ)
Rhode Island Coll (RI)
Rochester Coll (MI)
Rocky Mountain Coll (MT)
Sacred Heart U (CT)
Saginaw Valley State U (MI)
St. Ambrose U (IA)
St. Edward's U (TX)
Saint Francis U (PA)
St. John Fisher Coll (NY)
Saint Xavier U (IL)
Salve Regina U (RI)
Samford U (AL)
Schreiner U (TX)
Shawnee State U (OH)
Southwestern Oklahoma State U (OK)
Spring Arbor U (MI)
State U of New York at New Paltz (NY)
Tabor Coll (KS)
Talladega Coll (AL)
Texas A&M Intl U (TX)
Texas A&M U–Corpus Christi (TX)
Texas Christian U (TX)
Texas Lutheran U (TX)
Texas Wesleyan U (TX)
Tiffin U (OH)
Trevecca Nazarene U (TN)
Trinity Christian Coll (IL)
Tusculum Coll (TN)
Union Coll (NE)
Universidad Adventista de las Antillas (PR)
The U of Arizona (AZ)
U of Arkansas at Fort Smith (AR)
U of Central Oklahoma (OK)
U of Delaware (DE)
U of Illinois at Chicago (IL)
U of Illinois at Urbana–Champaign (IL)
The U of Iowa (IA)
U of Maine (ME)
U of Maine at Machias (ME)
U of Mary (ND)
U of Michigan–Flint (MI)
The U of Montana Western (MT)
U of Nebraska–Lincoln (NE)
The U of North Carolina at Charlotte (NC)
U of Pittsburgh at Johnstown (PA)
U of Puerto Rico at Utuado (PR)
U of Puerto Rico, Cayey U Coll (PR)
U of Rio Grande (OH)
The U of South Dakota (SD)
The U of Tennessee at Martin (TN)
U of Windsor (ON, Canada)
U of Wisconsin–River Falls (WI)
U of Wisconsin–Superior (WI)
Utica Coll (NY)
Valley City State U (ND)
Valparaiso U (IN)
Wartburg Coll (IA)
Washington State U (WA)
Washington U in St. Louis (MO)
Wayne State Coll (NE)
Weber State U (UT)
Western Michigan U (MI)
Western State Coll of Colorado (CO)
Western Washington U (WA)
Wheeling Jesuit U (WV)
Widener U (PA)
Xavier U of Louisiana (LA)
York Coll (NE)
York U (ON, Canada)

HOLOCAUST AND RELATED STUDIES

Keene State Coll (NH)

HOME FURNISHINGS AND EQUIPMENT INSTALLATION

Brigham Young U (UT)

HORSE HUSBANDRY/ EQUINE SCIENCE AND MANAGEMENT

Bethany Coll (WV)
Midway Coll (KY)
Oklahoma Panhandle State U (OK)
Stephens Coll (MO)
Tiffin U (OH)
U of Minnesota, Crookston (MN)
Vermont Tech Coll (VT)

HORTICULTURAL SCIENCE

Auburn U (AL)
California Polytechnic State U, San Luis Obispo (CA)
California State U, Fresno (CA)
Clemson U (SC)
Coll of the Ozarks (MO)
Colorado State U (CO)
Cornell U (NY)
Delaware Valley Coll (PA)
Ferrum Coll (VA)
Florida Ag and Mech U (FL)
Florida Southern Coll (FL)
Indiana U–Purdue U Indianapolis (IN)
Iowa State U of Science and Technology (IA)
Kansas State U (KS)
Michigan State U (MI)
Mississippi State U (MS)
Missouri State U (MO)
Montana State U (MT)
New Mexico State U (NM)
North Dakota State U (ND)
Northwest Missouri State U (MO)
Oklahoma State U (OK)
Oregon State U (OR)
Penn State Abington (PA)
Penn State Altoona (PA)
Penn State Beaver (PA)
Penn State Berks (PA)
Penn State Brandywine (PA)
Penn State DuBois (PA)
Penn State Erie, The Behrend Coll (PA)
Penn State Fayette, The Eberly Campus (PA)
Penn State Greater Allegheny (PA)
Penn State Hazleton (PA)
Penn State Lehigh Valley (PA)
Penn State Mont Alto (PA)
Penn State New Kensington (PA)
Penn State Schuylkill (PA)
Penn State Shenango (PA)
Penn State U Park (PA)
Penn State Wilkes-Barre (PA)
Penn State Worthington Scranton (PA)
Penn State York (PA)
Purdue U (IN)
Redeemer U Coll (ON, Canada)
Southeast Missouri State U (MO)
Stephen F. Austin State U (TX)
Tarleton State U (TX)
Temple U (PA)
Tennessee Technological U (TN)
Texas A&M U (TX)
Truman State U (MO)
The U of British Columbia (BC, Canada)
U of Connecticut (CT)
U of Delaware (DE)
U of Florida (FL)
U of Guelph (ON, Canada)
U of Hawaii at Hilo (HI)
U of Idaho (ID)
U of Illinois at Urbana–Champaign (IL)
U of Minnesota, Crookston (MN)
U of Nebraska–Lincoln (NE)
U of New Hampshire (NH)
U of Saskatchewan (SK, Canada)
U of Vermont (VT)
U of Wisconsin–River Falls (WI)
Utah State U (UT)
Virginia Polytechnic Inst and State U (VA)
Washington State U (WA)

HOSPITAL AND HEALTH-CARE FACILITIES ADMINISTRATION

Avila U (MO)
Black Hills State U (SD)
Carson-Newman Coll (TN)
Clayton State U (GA)
Gwynedd-Mercy Coll (PA)
Ithaca Coll (NY)
Long Island U, C.W. Post Campus (NY)
Newman U (KS)
New York City Coll of Technology of the City U of New York (NY)
Saint Joseph's U (PA)
State U of New York Coll of Technology at Canton (NY)
Thomas Edison State Coll (NJ)
The U of Alabama (AL)
The U of South Dakota (SD)
The U of Toledo (OH)
Ursuline Coll (OH)
York U (ON, Canada)
Youngstown State U (OH)

HOSPITALITY ADMINISTRATION

American Public U System (WV)
Appalachian State U (NC)
Arkansas Tech U (AR)
The Art Insts Intl Minnesota (MN)
Boston U (MA)
Bowling Green State U (OH)
Buffalo State Coll, State U of New York (NY)
California State Polytechnic U, Pomona (CA)
Cape Breton U (NS, Canada)
Central Michigan U (MI)
Champlain Coll (VT)
Coll of Charleston (SC)
Coll of the Ozarks (MO)
Concord U (WV)
Delaware State U (DE)
Delta State U (MS)
East Carolina U (NC)
Eastern Michigan U (MI)
East Stroudsburg U of Pennsylvania (PA)
Endicott Coll (MA)
Fairleigh Dickinson U, Coll at Florham (NJ)
Fairleigh Dickinson U, Metropolitan Campus (NJ)
Ferris State U (MI)
Fisher Coll (MA)
Florida Atlantic U (FL)
Florida Intl U (FL)
Florida State U (FL)
Georgian Court U (NJ)
Globe Inst of Technology (NY)
Grand Valley State U (MI)
Husson U (ME)
The Illinois Inst of Art–Chicago (IL)
Indiana U of Pennsylvania (PA)
Indiana U–Purdue U Fort Wayne (IN)
James Madison U (VA)
Johnson & Wales U (FL)
Johnson & Wales U (RI)
Johnson State Coll (VT)
Kendall Coll (IL)
Lasell Coll (MA)
Lewis-Clark State Coll (ID)
Lexington Coll (IL)
Madonna U (MI)
Marywood U (PA)
Mercyhurst Coll (PA)
Metropolitan State Coll of Denver (CO)
Michigan State U (MI)
Missouri State U (MO)
Monroe Coll, Bronx (NY)
Monroe Coll, New Rochelle (NY)
National U (CA)
New Mexico State U (NM)
New York City Coll of Technology of the City U of New York (NY)
North Carolina Central U (NC)
North Dakota State U (ND)
Northern Arizona U (AZ)
Northern Michigan U (MI)
Northwestern State U of Louisiana (LA)
The Ohio State U (OH)
The Ohio State U at Lima (OH)
Oklahoma State U (OK)
The Richard Stockton Coll of New Jersey (NJ)
Robert Morris U (PA)
Rochester Inst of Technology (NY)
Roosevelt U (IL)
Rutgers, The State U of New Jersey, Camden (NJ)
St. John's U (NY)
Saint Leo U (FL)
Salem State Coll (MA)
San Diego State U (CA)
San Francisco State U (CA)
San Jose State U (CA)
Seton Hill U (PA)
Southern New Hampshire U (NH)
Stephen F. Austin State U (TX)
Stratford U, Woodbridge (VA)
Temple U (PA)
Thomas Edison State Coll (NJ)
Thompson Rivers U (BC, Canada)
Tiffin U (OH)
Trine U (IN)
TUI U (CA)
Tuskegee U (AL)
U of Central Florida (FL)
U of Denver (CO)
U of Illinois at Urbana–Champaign (IL)
U of Kentucky (KY)
U of Massachusetts Amherst (MA)
U of Memphis (TN)
U of Minnesota, Crookston (MN)
U of Nebraska–Lincoln (NE)
U of Nevada, Las Vegas (NV)
U of Nevada, Reno (NV)
U of New Hampshire (NH)
U of New Haven (CT)
U of New Orleans (LA)
The U of North Carolina at Greensboro (NC)
U of North Texas (TX)
U of Pittsburgh at Bradford (PA)
U of South Carolina (SC)
U of South Carolina Beaufort (SC)
U of South Florida (FL)

U of West Florida (FL)
U of Wisconsin–Stout (WI)
Utah Valley U (UT)
Virginia State U (VA)
Washington State U (WA)
Webber Intl U (FL)
Western Carolina U (NC)
Western Kentucky U (KY)
Youngstown State U (OH)

HOSPITALITY ADMINISTRATION RELATED

Auburn U (AL)
California State U, Dominguez Hills (CA)
California State U, Fullerton (CA)
Champlain Coll (VT)
Drexel U (PA)
Florida State U (FL)
Indiana U–Purdue U Indianapolis (IN)
Kendall Coll (IL)
Kent State U (OH)
Lasell Coll (MA)
Lynn U (FL)
Mitchell Coll (CT)
Niagara U (NY)
Penn State Abington (PA)
Penn State Altoona (PA)
Penn State Beaver (PA)
Penn State Berks (PA)
Penn State Brandywine (PA)
Penn State DuBois (PA)
Penn State Erie, The Behrend Coll (PA)
Penn State Fayette, The Eberly Campus (PA)
Penn State Greater Allegheny (PA)
Penn State Hazleton (PA)
Penn State Lehigh Valley (PA)
Penn State Mont Alto (PA)
Penn State New Kensington (PA)
Penn State Schuylkill (PA)
Penn State Shenango (PA)
Penn State U Park (PA)
Penn State Wilkes-Barre (PA)
Penn State Worthington Scranton (PA)
Penn State York (PA)
Southern Illinois U Carbondale (IL)
Thompson Rivers U (BC, Canada)
U of Central Florida (FL)
U of Nevada, Las Vegas (NV)
U of Southern Mississippi (MS)
U of the District of Columbia (DC)
Widener U (PA)

HOSPITALITY AND RECREATION MARKETING

Cape Breton U (NS, Canada)
Champlain Coll (VT)
Ferris State U (MI)
Johnson & Wales U (RI)
Kendall Coll (IL)
Methodist U (NC)
Rochester Inst of Technology (NY)
Tuskegee U (AL)
U of Delaware (DE)

HOTEL/MOTEL ADMINISTRATION

Alliant Intl U (CA)
The Art Inst of Pittsburgh (PA)
Ashland U (OH)
Auburn U (AL)
Bethune-Cookman U (FL)
Boston U (MA)
Brigham Young U–Hawaii (HI)
Buffalo State Coll, State U of New York (NY)
California State U, Long Beach (CA)
Central Michigan U (MI)
Champlain Coll (VT)
Cheyney U of Pennsylvania (PA)
Concord U (WV)
Cornell U (NY)
Ferris State U (MI)
Georgia Southern U (GA)
Georgia State U (GA)
Grambling State U (LA)
Grand Valley State U (MI)
Hampton U (VA)
Harrison Coll, Indianapolis (IN)
Inter American U of Puerto Rico, Aguadilla Campus (PR)
Inter American U of Puerto Rico, Fajardo Campus (PR)
Inter American U of Puerto Rico, Ponce Campus (PR)
Iowa State U of Science and Technology (IA)
Johnson & Wales U (CO)
Johnson & Wales U (FL)
Johnson & Wales U (RI)
Johnson & Wales U—Charlotte Campus (NC)
Kansas State U (KS)
Kendall Coll (IL)
Keuka Coll (NY)
Mount Ida Coll (MA)
Newbury Coll (MA)
New York Inst of Technology (NY)
New York U (NY)
Niagara U (NY)
Pace U (NY)
Purdue U (IN)
Purdue U Calumet (IN)
The Restaurant School at Walnut Hill Coll (PA)
Rochester Inst of Technology (NY)
Royal Roads U (BC, Canada)
St. Thomas U (FL)
South Dakota State U (SD)
Southern Oregon U (OR)
Southwest Minnesota State U (MN)
State U of New York at Plattsburgh (NY)
Texas Tech U (TX)
Universidad de las Américas–Puebla (Mexico)
The U of Akron (OH)
U of Arkansas at Pine Bluff (AR)
U of Central Missouri (MO)
U of Central Oklahoma (OK)
U of Delaware (DE)
U of Denver (CO)
The U of Findlay (OH)
U of Guelph (ON, Canada)
U of Houston (TX)
U of Maine at Machias (ME)
U of Maryland Eastern Shore (MD)
U of Memphis (TN)
U of Missouri (MO)
U of Nevada, Las Vegas (NV)
U of New Haven (CT)
U of San Francisco (CA)
U of Southern Mississippi (MS)
The U of Tennessee (TN)
Virginia Polytechnic Inst and State U (VA)
Widener U (PA)

HOUSING AND HUMAN ENVIRONMENTS

Harding U (AR)
Missouri State U (MO)
Ohio U (OH)
Oklahoma State U (OK)
Oregon State U (OR)
The U of Akron (OH)
U of Arkansas (AR)
U of Georgia (GA)
U of Minnesota, Twin Cities Campus (MN)
U of Missouri (MO)
U of Northern Iowa (IA)
Utah State U (UT)

HOUSING AND HUMAN ENVIRONMENTS RELATED

Bob Jones U (SC)
U of Nevada, Reno (NV)

HUMAN DEVELOPMENT AND FAMILY STUDIES

Abilene Christian U (TX)
Amberton U (TX)
American Public U System (WV)
Amridge U (AL)
Antioch U McGregor (OH)
Ashland U (OH)
Auburn U (AL)
Baylor U (TX)
Boston Coll (MA)
Bowling Green State U (OH)
Brigham Young U (UT)
California State U, East Bay (CA)
California State U, Long Beach (CA)
California State U, San Bernardino (CA)
Colorado State U (CO)
Concordia U, St. Paul (MN)
Connecticut Coll (CT)
Cornell U (NY)
Eckerd Coll (FL)
Florida State U (FL)
Georgia Southern U (GA)
Hellenic Coll (MA)
Howard Payne U (TX)
Indiana State U (IN)
Indiana U of Pennsylvania (PA)
Kansas State U (KS)
Kent State U (OH)
Kentucky State U (KY)
Lee U (TN)
Lesley U (MA)
Liberty U (VA)
Lubbock Christian U (TX)
Miami U (OH)
Missouri State U (MO)
Mitchell Coll (CT)
Murray State U (KY)
New Mexico State U (NM)
North Dakota State U (ND)
Northwest Missouri State U (MO)
The Ohio State U (OH)
Ohio U (OH)
Oklahoma State U (OK)
Oregon State U (OR)
Oregon State U–Cascades (OR)
Penn State Abington (PA)
Penn State Altoona (PA)
Penn State Beaver (PA)
Penn State Berks (PA)
Penn State Brandywine (PA)
Penn State DuBois (PA)
Penn State Erie, The Behrend Coll (PA)
Penn State Fayette, The Eberly Campus (PA)
Penn State Greater Allegheny (PA)
Penn State Harrisburg (PA)
Penn State Hazleton (PA)
Penn State Lehigh Valley (PA)
Penn State Mont Alto (PA)
Penn State New Kensington (PA)
Penn State Schuylkill (PA)
Penn State Shenango (PA)
Penn State U Park (PA)
Penn State Wilkes-Barre (PA)
Penn State Worthington Scranton (PA)
Penn State York (PA)
Prescott Coll (AZ)
Purdue U (IN)
Samford U (AL)
San Diego Christian Coll (CA)
Sarah Lawrence Coll (NY)
Seattle Pacific U (WA)
South Dakota State U (SD)
State U of New York at Oswego (NY)
State U of New York at Plattsburgh (NY)
State U of New York Empire State Coll (NY)
Stephen F. Austin State U (TX)
Stephens Coll (MO)
Syracuse U (NY)
Texas State U–San Marcos (TX)
Texas Tech U (TX)
Texas Woman's U (TX)
The U of Alabama (AL)
The U of Arizona (AZ)
U of Arkansas (AR)
U of California, Davis (CA)
U of Chicago (IL)
U of Connecticut (CT)
U of Delaware (DE)
U of Houston (TX)
U of Idaho (ID)
U of Illinois at Urbana–Champaign (IL)
U of Maine (ME)
U of Memphis (TN)
U of Missouri (MO)
U of Nevada, Reno (NV)
U of New Hampshire (NH)
U of New Mexico (NM)
The U of North Carolina at Charlotte (NC)
The U of North Carolina at Greensboro (NC)
U of North Texas (TX)
U of Rhode Island (RI)
The U of Tennessee (TN)
The U of Texas at Austin (TX)
The U of Texas of the Permian Basin (TX)
U of Utah (UT)
U of Vermont (VT)
U of Waterloo (ON, Canada)
U of Wisconsin–Stout (WI)
Utah State U (UT)
Vanguard U of Southern California (CA)
Virginia Polytechnic Inst and State U (VA)
Warner Pacific Coll (OR)
Washington State U (WA)
Wheelock Coll (MA)
Youngstown State U (OH)

HUMAN DEVELOPMENT AND FAMILY STUDIES RELATED

American Public U System (WV)
Ball State U (IN)
Bowling Green State U (OH)
Columbia Coll (SC)
Harding U (AR)
Kent State U (OH)
Park U (MO)
State U of New York at Binghamton (NY)
The U of Alabama (AL)

HUMANITIES

Adelphi U (NY)
Albertus Magnus Coll (CT)
Alma Coll (MI)
Antioch U McGregor (OH)
Arizona State U (AZ)
Atlanta Christian Coll (GA)
Augsburg Coll (MN)
Baylor U (TX)
Belhaven U (MS)
Bemidji State U (MN)
Benedictine U (IL)
Bennington Coll (VT)
Bishop's U (QC, Canada)
Bluefield State Coll (WV)
Bob Jones U (SC)
Bradley U (IL)
Brigham Young U–Hawaii (HI)
Brock U (ON, Canada)
Bucknell U (PA)
Buffalo State Coll, State U of New York (NY)
California State Polytechnic U, Pomona (CA)
California State U, Chico (CA)
California State U, Dominguez Hills (CA)
California State U, Monterey Bay (CA)
California State U, Northridge (CA)
California State U, Sacramento (CA)
California State U, San Bernardino (CA)
Catawba Coll (NC)
Chaminade U of Honolulu (HI)
Chowan U (NC)
Clarion U of Pennsylvania (PA)
Clarkson U (NY)
Clearwater Christian Coll (FL)
Colgate U (NY)
Coll of Saint Benedict (MN)
Coll of Saint Mary (NE)
The Coll of St. Scholastica (MN)
Coll of the Humanities and Sciences, Harrison Middleton U (AZ)
Columbia Intl U (SC)
Concordia Coll (MN)
Concordia U (CA)
Concordia U (QC, Canada)
Concordia U Wisconsin (WI)
Corban U (OR)
DePaul U (IL)
Dominican Coll (NY)
Dominican U of California (CA)
Dowling Coll (NY)
Drexel U (PA)
Eastern Washington U (WA)
East Stroudsburg U of Pennsylvania (PA)
Eckerd Coll (FL)
Edinboro U of Pennsylvania (PA)
Elmira Coll (NY)
The Evergreen State Coll (WA)
Fairleigh Dickinson U, Coll at Florham (NJ)
Fairleigh Dickinson U, Metropolitan Campus (NJ)
Faulkner U (AL)
Felician Coll (NJ)
Florida Inst of Technology (FL)
Florida Southern Coll (FL)
Florida State U (FL)
Fort Lewis Coll (CO)
Franciscan U of Steubenville (OH)
Freed-Hardeman U (TN)
Free Will Baptist Bible Coll (TN)
The George Washington U (DC)
Georgian Court U (NJ)
Hampden-Sydney Coll (VA)
Harding U (AR)
Hofstra U (NY)
Holy Apostles Coll and Sem (CT)
Holy Family U (PA)
Holy Names U (CA)
Houghton Coll (NY)
Howard Payne U (TX)
Hunter Coll of the City U of New York (NY)
Indiana U East (IN)
Indiana U Kokomo (IN)
Jacksonville U (FL)
John Cabot U (Italy)
John Carroll U (OH)
Johnson State Coll (VT)
Juniata Coll (PA)
Kansas State U (KS)
Lasell Coll (MA)
Lawrence Technological U (MI)
Lees-McRae Coll (NC)
Lesley U (MA)
Lincoln Memorial U (TN)
Long Island U, Brooklyn Campus (NY)
Loyola Marymount U (CA)
Lubbock Christian U (TX)
Macalester Coll (MN)
Maranatha Baptist Bible Coll (WI)
Marlboro Coll (VT)
Marshall U (WV)
Marylhurst U (OR)
Memorial U of Newfoundland (NL, Canada)
Messiah Coll (PA)
Michigan State U (MI)
Midwestern State U (TX)
Milligan Coll (TN)
Minnesota State U Mankato (MN)
Minot State U (ND)
Montclair State U (NJ)
Mount Allison U (NB, Canada)
New Coll of Florida (FL)
New York U (NY)
North Central Coll (IL)
North Dakota State U (ND)
Northern Arizona U (AZ)
Northland Coll (WI)
Northwestern Coll (IA)
Northwest Missouri State U (MO)
Northwest Nazarene U (ID)
Nova Southeastern U (FL)
Oakland City U (IN)
The Ohio State U (OH)
Ohio Wesleyan U (OH)
Oklahoma Baptist U (OK)
Oklahoma City U (OK)
Our Lady of the Lake Coll (LA)
Penn State Harrisburg (PA)
Pepperdine U, Malibu (CA)
Plymouth State U (NH)
Pomona Coll (CA)
Pontifical Coll Josephinum (OH)
Portland State U (OR)
Prescott Coll (AZ)
Principia Coll (IL)
Providence Coll (RI)
Purchase Coll, State U of New York (NY)
Purdue U (IN)
Quincy U (IL)
Redeemer U Coll (ON, Canada)
Roberts Wesleyan Coll (NY)
Rockford Coll (IL)
Rosemont Coll (PA)
Sage Coll of Albany (NY)
Saint John's U (MN)
Saint Louis U (MO)
Saint Martin's U (WA)
Saint Mary-of-the-Woods Coll (IN)
Saint Mary's Coll (IN)
St. Norbert Coll (WI)
St. Thomas Aquinas Coll (NY)
San Diego State U (CA)
San Francisco State U (CA)
San Jose State U (CA)
Sarah Lawrence Coll (NY)
Schreiner U (TX)
Seattle U (WA)
Seton Hall U (NJ)
Siena Heights U (MI)
Simon Fraser U (BC, Canada)
Southeastern Baptist Theological Sem (NC)
Southeast Missouri State U (MO)
Southern Methodist U (TX)
Spring Hill Coll (AL)
State U of New York Coll at Old Westbury (NY)
State U of New York Coll at Potsdam (NY)
State U of New York Empire State Coll (NY)
Stetson U (FL)
Stevens Inst of Technology (NJ)
Stevenson U (MD)
Stony Brook U, State U of New York (NY)
Suffolk U (MA)
Syracuse U (NY)
Tabor Coll (KS)
Texas Wesleyan U (TX)
Thomas Edison State Coll (NJ)
Thomas More Coll (KY)
Trent U (ON, Canada)
Trinity U (TX)
Truett-McConnell Coll (GA)
Union Coll (NY)
United States Air Force Acad (CO)
United States Military Acad (NY)
Universidad de las Américas–Puebla (Mexico)
The U of Akron (OH)
U of Alaska Southeast (AK)
U of Alberta (AB, Canada)
U of Bridgeport (CT)
U of California, Riverside (CA)
U of Central Florida (FL)
U of Chicago (IL)
U of Cincinnati (OH)
U of Colorado at Boulder (CO)
U of Hawaii–West Oahu (HI)
U of Houston–Clear Lake (TX)
U of Houston–Downtown (TX)
U of Houston–Victoria (TX)
U of Illinois at Urbana–Champaign (IL)
The U of Kansas (KS)
U of Lethbridge (AB, Canada)
U of Maryland U Coll (MD)
U of Massachusetts Amherst (MA)

U of Michigan (MI)
U of Michigan–Dearborn (MI)
U of Mobile (AL)
U of New Hampshire (NH)
U of New Hampshire at Manchester (NH)
U of New Mexico (NM)
U of Northern Iowa (IA)
U of Oklahoma (OK)
U of Oregon (OR)
U of Ottawa (ON, Canada)
U of Pennsylvania (PA)
U of Pittsburgh (PA)
U of Pittsburgh at Bradford (PA)
U of Pittsburgh at Greensburg (PA)
U of Pittsburgh at Johnstown (PA)
U of Puerto Rico at Utuado (PR)
U of Puerto Rico, Cayey U Coll (PR)
U of Regina (SK, Canada)
U of Richmond (VA)
U of Rio Grande (OH)
U of San Diego (CA)
U of South Florida (FL)
The U of Tennessee at Chattanooga (TN)
The U of Texas at Austin (TX)
The U of Texas at Dallas (TX)
The U of Texas at San Antonio (TX)
The U of Texas of the Permian Basin (TX)
U of the Ozarks (AR)
U of the Southwest (NM)
U of the Virgin Islands (VI)
The U of Toledo (OH)
U of Toronto (ON, Canada)
U of Utah (UT)
U of Washington (WA)
U of Washington, Bothell (WA)
U of West Florida (FL)
U of Wisconsin–Green Bay (WI)
U of Wisconsin–Parkside (WI)
U of Wyoming (WY)
Ursuline Coll (OH)
Valparaiso U (IN)
Villanova U (PA)
Virginia Wesleyan Coll (VA)
Waldorf Coll (IA)
Washington Coll (MD)
Washington State U (WA)
Washington U in St. Louis (MO)
Wesleyan Coll (GA)
Wesleyan U (CT)
Western Oregon U (OR)
Western Washington U (WA)
Wheelock Coll (MA)
Widener U (PA)
Willamette U (OR)
William Paterson U of New Jersey (NJ)
Wofford Coll (SC)
Worcester Polytechnic Inst (MA)
Wright State U (OH)
Yale U (CT)
York U (ON, Canada)

HUMAN/MEDICAL GENETICS

Sarah Lawrence Coll (NY)
U of Pittsburgh (PA)

HUMAN NUTRITION

Baylor U (TX)
Cape Breton U (NS, Canada)
Case Western Reserve U (OH)
Colorado State U (CO)
Kansas State U (KS)
Kent State U (OH)
Life U (GA)
Metropolitan State Coll of Denver (CO)
The Ohio State U (OH)
Penn State Abington (PA)
Penn State Altoona (PA)
Penn State Beaver (PA)
Penn State Berks (PA)
Penn State Brandywine (PA)
Penn State DuBois (PA)
Penn State Erie, The Behrend Coll (PA)
Penn State Fayette, The Eberly Campus (PA)
Penn State Greater Allegheny (PA)
Penn State Hazleton (PA)
Penn State Lehigh Valley (PA)
Penn State Mont Alto (PA)
Penn State New Kensington (PA)
Penn State Schuylkill (PA)
Penn State Shenango (PA)
Penn State U Park (PA)
Penn State Wilkes-Barre (PA)
Penn State Worthington Scranton (PA)
Penn State York (PA)
Rochester Inst of Technology (NY)
Tarleton State U (TX)
The U of British Columbia (BC, Canada)
U of Guelph (ON, Canada)
U of Houston (TX)
U of Illinois at Urbana–Champaign (IL)
U of Massachusetts Amherst (MA)
Washington State U (WA)

HUMAN RESOURCES DEVELOPMENT

Clemson U (SC)
Concordia U Texas (TX)
Georgia State U (GA)
Hawai'i Pacific U (HI)
Limestone Coll (SC)
Midwestern State U (TX)
Nichols Coll (MA)
Oakland U (MI)
The Ohio State U (OH)
Park U (MO)
Pittsburg State U (KS)
Texas A&M U (TX)
U of Arkansas (AR)
U of Houston (TX)
U of Regina (SK, Canada)
The U of Texas at Tyler (TX)
Walden U (MN)

HUMAN RESOURCES MANAGEMENT

Alderson-Broaddus Coll (WV)
Alvernia U (PA)
Amberton U (TX)
American Intl Coll (MA)
Amridge U (AL)
Antioch U McGregor (OH)
Arcadia U (PA)
Argosy U, Atlanta (GA)
Argosy U, Chicago (IL)
Argosy U, Dallas (TX)
Argosy U, Denver (CO)
Argosy U, Hawai'i (HI)
Argosy U, Inland Empire (CA)
Argosy U, Los Angeles (CA)
Argosy U, Orange County (CA)
Argosy U, Phoenix (AZ)
Argosy U, Salt Lake City (UT)
Argosy U, San Diego (CA)
Argosy U, San Francisco Bay Area (CA)
Argosy U, Sarasota (FL)
Argosy U, Schaumburg (IL)
Argosy U, Tampa (FL)
Argosy U, Twin Cities (MN)
Argosy U, Washington DC (VA)
Athabasca U (AB, Canada)
Auburn U (AL)
Auburn U Montgomery (AL)
Avila U (MO)
Baker Coll of Owosso (MI)
Baldwin-Wallace Coll (OH)
Ball State U (IN)
Barton Coll (NC)
Baylor U (TX)
Bernard M. Baruch Coll of the City U of New York (NY)
Bishop's U (QC, Canada)
Black Hills State U (SD)
Bob Jones U (SC)
Boise State U (ID)
Boston Coll (MA)
Bowling Green State U (OH)
Bradley U (IL)
Brescia U (KY)
Briar Cliff U (IA)
Brigham Young U (UT)
Brock U (ON, Canada)
Buena Vista U (IA)
Cabrini Coll (PA)
California State U, Chico (CA)
California State U, East Bay (CA)
California State U, Fresno (CA)
California State U, Long Beach (CA)
Cape Breton U (NS, Canada)
Capella U (MN)
Carroll U (WI)
The Catholic U of America (DC)
Central Christian Coll of Kansas (KS)
Central Michigan U (MI)
Cleary U (MI)
Coll of Saint Elizabeth (NJ)
Columbia Coll (MO)
Concordia U (QC, Canada)
Concordia U, St. Paul (MN)
Converse Coll (SC)
Davenport U, Grand Rapids (MI)
Delaware State U (DE)
DePaul U (IL)
DeSales U (PA)
Dominican Coll (NY)
Drexel U (PA)
East Central U (OK)
Excelsior Coll (NY)
Faulkner U (AL)
Ferris State U (MI)
Florida Atlantic U (FL)
Florida Intl U (FL)
Fordham U (NY)
Fort Hays State U (KS)
Franklin U (OH)
Freed-Hardeman U (TN)
Friends U (KS)
The George Washington U (DC)
Goldey-Beacom Coll (DE)
Governors State U (IL)
Harding U (AR)
Hawai'i Pacific U (HI)
HEC Montreal (QC, Canada)
Holy Names U (CA)
Idaho State U (ID)
Immaculata U (PA)
Indiana State U (IN)
Indiana Tech (IN)
Indiana U of Pennsylvania (PA)
Inter American U of Puerto Rico, Arecibo Campus (PR)
Inter American U of Puerto Rico, Bayamón Campus (PR)
Inter American U of Puerto Rico, Fajardo Campus (PR)
Inter American U of Puerto Rico, Guayama Campus (PR)
Inter American U of Puerto Rico, Ponce Campus (PR)
Inter American U of Puerto Rico, San Germán Campus (PR)
Judson U (IL)
Juniata Coll (PA)
Keiser U, Fort Lauderdale (FL)
King's Coll (PA)
Kutztown U of Pennsylvania (PA)
Lakehead U (ON, Canada)
La Salle U (PA)
La Sierra U (CA)
Lewis U (IL)
Lindenwood U (MO)
Lipscomb U (TN)
Loras Coll (IA)
Louisiana Tech U (LA)
Lourdes Coll (OH)
Loyola U Chicago (IL)
Madonna U (MI)
Mansfield U of Pennsylvania (PA)
Marian U (IN)
Marian U (WI)
Marietta Coll (OH)
Marquette U (WI)
Mercyhurst Coll (PA)
Messiah Coll (PA)
Michigan State U (MI)
MidAmerica Nazarene U (KS)
Midway Coll (KY)
Mount Mercy Coll (IA)
National U (CA)
Nazareth Coll of Rochester (NY)
Newbury Coll (MA)
New York Inst of Technology (NY)
Niagara U (NY)
Nichols Coll (MA)
North Carolina State U (NC)
North Central Coll (IL)
Northeastern Illinois U (IL)
Northeastern State U (OK)
Northeastern U (MA)
Oakland City U (IN)
Oakland U (MI)
The Ohio State U (OH)
Ohio U (OH)
Ohio Valley U (WV)
Our Lady of the Lake U of San Antonio (TX)
Pace U (NY)
Peace Coll (NC)
Pennsylvania Coll of Technology (PA)
Point Park U (PA)
Pontifical Catholic U of Puerto Rico (PR)
Portland State U (OR)
Prescott Coll (AZ)
Purdue U North Central (IN)
Quinnipiac U (CT)
Redeemer U Coll (ON, Canada)
Roberts Wesleyan Coll (NY)
Roosevelt U (IL)
Rowan U (NJ)
St. Cloud State U (MN)
Saint Francis U (PA)
St. Joseph's Coll, Long Island Campus (NY)
St. Joseph's Coll, New York (NY)
Saint Leo U (FL)
Saint Louis U (MO)
Saint Mary-of-the-Woods Coll (IN)
St. Mary's U (TX)
Saint Mary's U of Minnesota (MN)
Salem State Coll (MA)
Sam Houston State U (TX)
San Diego State U (CA)
San Jose State U (CA)
Seton Hill U (PA)
Silver Lake Coll (WI)
Simpson U (CA)
Southern Adventist U (TN)
Southwestern Coll (KS)
Spring Arbor U (MI)
State U of New York at Oswego (NY)
Sullivan U (KY)
Susquehanna U (PA)
Tarleton State U (TX)
Tennessee Wesleyan Coll (TN)
Texas A&M U–Commerce (TX)
Texas Woman's U (TX)
Thomas Edison State Coll (NJ)
Thompson Rivers U (BC, Canada)
Tiffin U (OH)
Trinity Christian Coll (IL)
U of Alberta (AB, Canada)
U of Atlanta (GA)
U of Baltimore (MD)
The U of British Columbia–Okanagan (BC, Canada)
U of Central Oklahoma (OK)
The U of Findlay (OH)
U of Guelph (ON, Canada)
U of Hawaii at Manoa (HI)
U of Idaho (ID)
U of Illinois at Urbana–Champaign (IL)
The U of Iowa (IA)
U of Lethbridge (AB, Canada)
U of Maryland U Coll (MD)
U of Massachusetts Dartmouth (MA)
U of Miami (FL)
U of Michigan–Dearborn (MI)
U of Michigan–Flint (MI)
U of Minnesota, Duluth (MN)
U of Nebraska at Omaha (NE)
U of Nevada, Las Vegas (NV)
U of Nevada, Reno (NV)
U of New Brunswick Fredericton (NB, Canada)
The U of North Carolina at Chapel Hill (NC)
U of North Dakota (ND)
U of Ottawa (ON, Canada)
U of Pennsylvania (PA)
U of Puerto Rico at Humacao (PR)
U of Puerto Rico, Río Piedras (PR)
U of Regina (SK, Canada)
U of St. Francis (IL)
U of St. Thomas (MN)
U of Saskatchewan (SK, Canada)
The U of Scranton (PA)
U of Southern Mississippi (MS)
The U of Tennessee (TN)
The U of Tennessee at Martin (TN)
The U of Texas at San Antonio (TX)
U of the Incarnate Word (TX)
The U of Toledo (OH)
U of Waterloo (ON, Canada)
The U of Western Ontario (ON, Canada)
U of Windsor (ON, Canada)
U of Wisconsin–Milwaukee (WI)
U of Wisconsin–Parkside (WI)
U of Wisconsin–Whitewater (WI)
Ursuline Coll (OH)
Utah State U (UT)
Valley City State U (ND)
Walden U (MN)
Washington U in St. Louis (MO)
Weber State U (UT)
Western Illinois U (IL)
Western Intl U (AZ)
Western Washington U (WA)
Wichita State U (KS)
Wilmington U (DE)
Winona State U (MN)
Wright State U (OH)
Xavier U (OH)
York U (ON, Canada)
Youngstown State U (OH)

HUMAN RESOURCES MANAGEMENT AND SERVICES RELATED

Albertus Magnus Coll (CT)
Capella U (MN)
Carlow U (PA)
Columbia Southern U (AL)
Concordia U Coll of Alberta (AB, Canada)
Grand Valley State U (MI)
Miami U Hamilton (OH)
Mountain State U (WV)
Niagara U (NY)
Northern Kentucky U (KY)
Park U (MO)
Simpson U (CA)
Thompson Rivers U (BC, Canada)
Université du Québec en Outaouais (QC, Canada)
The U of British Columbia (BC, Canada)
U of Oklahoma (OK)
U of the District of Columbia (DC)
Western Michigan U (MI)
Widener U (PA)

HUMAN SERVICES

Alaska Pacific U (AK)
Albertus Magnus Coll (CT)
Albion Coll (MI)
American Intl Coll (MA)
Antioch U McGregor (OH)
Arcadia U (PA)
Beacon Coll (FL)
Bethel Coll (IN)
Bethel U (TN)
Black Hills State U (SD)
Burlington Coll (VT)
California State U, Dominguez Hills (CA)
California State U, Fullerton (CA)
California State U, Monterey Bay (CA)
California State U, San Bernardino (CA)
Calumet Coll of Saint Joseph (IN)
Cambridge Coll (MA)
Carson-Newman Coll (TN)
Cazenovia Coll (NY)
Champlain Coll (VT)
Coll of St. Joseph (VT)
Columbia Coll (MO)
Concordia U, St. Paul (MN)
Cornell U (NY)
Dakota Wesleyan U (SD)
Doane Coll (NE)
Drury U (MO)
East Central U (OK)
East Tennessee State U (TN)
Elizabethtown Coll (PA)
Elmira Coll (NY)
Elon U (NC)
Endicott Coll (MA)
Fairmont State U (WV)
Fisher Coll (MA)
Fitchburg State Coll (MA)
Florida Gulf Coast U (FL)
Fontbonne U (MO)
Geneva Coll (PA)
The George Washington U (DC)
Grace Bible Coll (MI)
Graceland U (IA)
Grand View U (IA)
Gwynedd-Mercy Coll (PA)
Hannibal-LaGrange Coll (MO)
Hawai'i Pacific U (HI)
High Point U (NC)
Holy Names U (CA)
Indiana Tech (IN)
Indiana U–Purdue U Fort Wayne (IN)
Inter American U of Puerto Rico, Aguadilla Campus (PR)
Kendall Coll (IL)
Kennesaw State U (GA)
Kentucky Wesleyan Coll (KY)
Lake Superior State U (MI)
La Roche Coll (PA)
Lasell Coll (MA)
Lesley U (MA)
Lincoln U (PA)
Lindenwood U (MO)
Lindsey Wilson Coll (KY)
Loyola U Chicago (IL)
Lynn U (FL)
Mercer U (GA)
Merrimack Coll (MA)
Metropolitan State Coll of Denver (CO)
Missouri Baptist U (MO)
Mount Ida Coll (MA)
Mount Marty Coll (SD)
Mount Olive Coll (NC)
Mount Saint Mary Coll (NY)
New York City Coll of Technology of the City U of New York (NY)
Northeastern U (MA)
Notre Dame de Namur U (CA)
Ottawa U (KS)
Park U (MO)
Post U (CT)
Prescott Coll (AZ)
Quincy U (IL)
Quinnipiac U (CT)
St. John's U (NY)
St. Joseph's Coll, Long Island Campus (NY)
St. Joseph's Coll, New York (NY)
Saint Leo U (FL)
Saint Mary-of-the-Woods Coll (IN)
Saint Mary's U of Minnesota (MN)
Samford U (AL)
Seton Hill U (PA)
Siena Heights U (MI)
Southeastern U (FL)
Southern Wesleyan U (SC)
Southwest Baptist U (MO)
Southwestern Assemblies of God U (TX)
State U of New York Coll at Cortland (NY)
State U of New York Empire State Coll (NY)
Suffolk U (MA)
Tennessee Wesleyan Coll (TN)

Texas A&M U–Kingsville (TX)
Thomas Edison State Coll (NJ)
Tiffin U (OH)
Union Inst & U (OH)
U of Baltimore (MD)
U of Bridgeport (CT)
U of Hartford (CT)
U of Maine at Machias (ME)
U of Nevada, Las Vegas (NV)
U of Northern Colorado (CO)
U of North Texas (TX)
U of Oregon (OR)
The U of Scranton (PA)
U of the Cumberlands (KY)
U of Wisconsin–Oshkosh (WI)
Upper Iowa U (IA)
Villanova U (PA)
Virginia Wesleyan Coll (VA)
Wayland Baptist U (TX)
Western Washington U (WA)
William Penn U (IA)
Wingate U (NC)

HYDROLOGY AND WATER RESOURCES SCIENCE
California State U, Chico (CA)
The Coll at Brockport, State U of New York (NY)
East Central U (OK)
Heidelberg U (OH)
Humboldt State U (CA)
Lakehead U (ON, Canada)
North Carolina State U (NC)
Northern Arizona U (AZ)
Rensselaer Polytechnic Inst (NY)
St. Francis Xavier U (NS, Canada)
State U of New York Coll at Oneonta (NY)
State U of New York Coll of Environmental Science and Forestry (NY)
Tarleton State U (TX)
U of California, Davis (CA)
U of California, Santa Barbara (CA)
U of New Hampshire (NH)
U of Toronto (ON, Canada)
U of Wisconsin–Madison (WI)
U of Wisconsin–Stevens Point (WI)
Western Michigan U (MI)
Wright State U (OH)

ILLUSTRATION
Acad of Art U (CA)
Alberta Coll of Art & Design (AB, Canada)
Arcadia U (PA)
Art Center Coll of Design (CA)
The Art Center Design Coll, Tucson (AZ)
The Art Inst of Atlanta (GA)
The Art Inst of Boston at Lesley U (MA)
The Art Inst of Fort Lauderdale (FL)
Brigham Young U (UT)
California State U, Long Beach (CA)
The Cleveland Inst of Art (OH)
Coll for Creative Studies (MI)
Columbus Coll of Art & Design (OH)
Cornish Coll of the Arts (WA)
Fashion Inst of Technology (NY)
Grace Coll (IN)
John Brown U (AR)
Lawrence Technological U (MI)
Lewis U (IL)
Lyme Acad Coll of Fine Arts (CT)
Maryland Inst Coll of Art (MD)
Marywood U (PA)
Moore Coll of Art & Design (PA)
Parsons The New School for Design (NY)
Pennsylvania Coll of Art & Design (PA)
Pratt Inst (NY)
Ringling Coll of Art and Design (FL)
Rochester Inst of Technology (NY)
Rocky Mountain Coll of Art + Design (CO)
St. John's U (NY)
Savannah Coll of Art and Design (GA)
School of the Art Inst of Chicago (IL)
School of the Museum of Fine Arts, Boston (MA)
School of Visual Arts (NY)
U of Bridgeport (CT)
U of Hartford (CT)
The U of Kansas (KS)
U of Michigan (MI)
U of San Francisco (CA)
Virginia Commonwealth U (VA)
Washington U in St. Louis (MO)

IMMUNOLOGY
U of Alberta (AB, Canada)
The U of Western Ontario (ON, Canada)

INDUSTRIAL AND ORGANIZATIONAL PSYCHOLOGY
Albright Coll (PA)
Averett U (VA)
Bernard M. Baruch Coll of the City U of New York (NY)
Bridgewater State Coll (MA)
Brooklyn Coll of the City U of New York (NY)
California State U, East Bay (CA)
Corban U (OR)
Eastern Connecticut State U (CT)
Farmingdale State Coll (NY)
Fitchburg State Coll (MA)
Fort Lewis Coll (CO)
Georgia Inst of Technology (GA)
Goldey-Beacom Coll (DE)
Holy Family U (PA)
Ithaca Coll (NY)
Lincoln U (PA)
Madonna U (MI)
Maryville U of Saint Louis (MO)
Marywood U (PA)
Middle Tennessee State U (TN)
Moravian Coll (PA)
Morningside Coll (IA)
Nebraska Wesleyan U (NE)
Northwest Missouri State U (MO)
Prescott Coll (AZ)
Saint Mary's Coll of California (CA)
Saint Xavier U (IL)
Southern Adventist U (TN)
Texas Wesleyan U (TX)
U of Illinois at Urbana–Champaign (IL)
U of Minnesota, Crookston (MN)
The U of Tennessee at Martin (TN)
Washington U in St. Louis (MO)
Wright State U (OH)

INDUSTRIAL ARTS
Alcorn State U (MS)
Bemidji State U (MN)
Buffalo State Coll, State U of New York (NY)
California State U, Fresno (CA)
Fairmont State U (WV)
Florida Ag and Mech U (FL)
Fort Hays State U (KS)
Humboldt State U (CA)
Northern State U (SD)
St. Cloud State U (MN)
San Francisco State U (CA)
Southern Utah U (UT)
Southwestern Oklahoma State U (OK)
Sul Ross State U (TX)
Tarleton State U (TX)
Texas A&M U–Commerce (TX)
U of Alberta (AB, Canada)
U of Arkansas at Pine Bluff (AR)
U of Maryland Eastern Shore (MD)
The U of Montana Western (MT)
U of Southern Maine (ME)
U of the District of Columbia (DC)
U of Wisconsin–Platteville (WI)
William Penn U (IA)

INDUSTRIAL DESIGN
Acad of Art U (CA)
Appalachian State U (NC)
Arizona State U (AZ)
Art Center Coll of Design (CA)
The Art Inst of California–Hollywood (CA)
The Art Inst of California–Orange County (CA)
The Art Inst of Colorado (CO)
The Art Inst of Fort Lauderdale (FL)
The Art Inst of Philadelphia (PA)
The Art Inst of Pittsburgh (PA)
The Art Inst of Portland (OR)
The Art Inst of Seattle (WA)
Auburn U (AL)
California Coll of the Arts (CA)
California State U, Long Beach (CA)
Carnegie Mellon U (PA)
Clemson U (SC)
The Cleveland Inst of Art (OH)
Coll for Creative Studies (MI)
Columbia Coll Chicago (IL)
Columbus Coll of Art & Design (OH)
Escuela de Artes Plasticas de Puerto Rico (PR)
Fashion Inst of Technology (NY)
Ferris State U (MI)
Georgia Inst of Technology (GA)
Kean U (NJ)
Massachusetts Coll of Art and Design (MA)
Metropolitan State Coll of Denver (CO)
New Jersey Inst of Technology (NJ)
North Carolina State U (NC)
The Ohio State U (OH)
Parsons The New School for Design (NY)
Philadelphia U (PA)
Pratt Inst (NY)
Rochester Inst of Technology (NY)
San Francisco State U (CA)
San Jose State U (CA)
Savannah Coll of Art and Design (GA)
Stanford U (CA)
U of Alberta (AB, Canada)
U of Bridgeport (CT)
U of Cincinnati (OH)
U of Houston (TX)
U of Illinois at Chicago (IL)
U of Illinois at Urbana–Champaign (IL)
The U of Kansas (KS)
U of Michigan (MI)
U of Washington (WA)
U of Wisconsin–Platteville (WI)
Virginia Polytechnic Inst and State U (VA)
Wentworth Inst of Technology (MA)
Western Washington U (WA)

INDUSTRIAL ELECTRONICS TECHNOLOGY
Lewis-Clark State Coll (ID)

INDUSTRIAL ENGINEERING
Arizona State U (AZ)
Auburn U (AL)
Boston U (MA)
Bradley U (IL)
California Polytechnic State U, San Luis Obispo (CA)
California State Polytechnic U, Pomona (CA)
California State U, East Bay (CA)
California State U, Long Beach (CA)
Clemson U (SC)
Cleveland State U (OH)
Columbia U (NY)
Concordia U (QC, Canada)
Drexel U (PA)
Eastern Nazarene Coll (MA)
Elizabethtown Coll (PA)
Florida Ag and Mech U (FL)
Georgia Inst of Technology (GA)
Hofstra U (NY)
Indiana Tech (IN)
Inter American U of Puerto Rico, Bayamón Campus (PR)
Iowa State U of Science and Technology (IA)
The Johns Hopkins U (MD)
Kansas State U (KS)
Kent State U (OH)
Kettering U (MI)
Lamar U (TX)
Lawrence Technological U (MI)
Lehigh U (PA)
Liberty U (VA)
Louisiana State U and Ag and Mech Coll (LA)
Louisiana Tech U (LA)
Memorial U of Newfoundland (NL, Canada)
Michigan Technological U (MI)
Milwaukee School of Eng (WI)
Mississippi State U (MS)
Missouri Southern State U (MO)
Missouri U of Science and Technology (MO)
Montana State U (MT)
New Jersey Inst of Technology (NJ)
New Mexico State U (NM)
New York Inst of Technology (NY)
North Carolina State U (NC)
North Dakota State U (ND)
Northeastern U (MA)
Oakland U (MI)
The Ohio State U (OH)
Ohio U (OH)
Oklahoma State U (OK)
Oregon State U (OR)
Penn State Abington (PA)
Penn State Altoona (PA)
Penn State Beaver (PA)
Penn State Berks (PA)
Penn State Brandywine (PA)
Penn State DuBois (PA)
Penn State Erie, The Behrend Coll (PA)
Penn State Fayette, The Eberly Campus (PA)
Penn State Greater Allegheny (PA)
Penn State Hazleton (PA)
Penn State Lehigh Valley (PA)
Penn State Mont Alto (PA)
Penn State New Kensington (PA)
Penn State Schuylkill (PA)
Penn State Shenango (PA)
Penn State U Park (PA)
Penn State Wilkes-Barre (PA)
Penn State Worthington Scranton (PA)
Penn State York (PA)
Polytechnic U of Puerto Rico (PR)
Purdue U (IN)
Rensselaer Polytechnic Inst (NY)
Rochester Inst of Technology (NY)
Rutgers, The State U of New Jersey, New Brunswick (NJ)
St. Ambrose U (IA)
St. Cloud State U (MN)
St. Mary's U (TX)
San Jose State U (CA)
Seattle U (WA)
South Dakota School of Mines and Technology (SD)
Southern Illinois U Edwardsville (IL)
State U of New York at Binghamton (NY)
State U of New York Maritime Coll (NY)
Tennessee Technological U (TN)
Texas A&M U (TX)
Texas A&M U–Commerce (TX)
Texas A&M U–Kingsville (TX)
Texas State U–San Marcos (TX)
Texas Tech U (TX)
Tufts U (MA)
Universidad de las Américas–Puebla (Mexico)
U at Buffalo, the State U of New York (NY)
The U of Alabama in Huntsville (AL)
U of Arkansas (AR)
U of Central Florida (FL)
U of Cincinnati (OH)
U of Connecticut (CT)
U of Houston (TX)
U of Illinois at Chicago (IL)
U of Illinois at Urbana–Champaign (IL)
The U of Iowa (IA)
U of Louisville (KY)
U of Manitoba (MB, Canada)
U of Massachusetts Amherst (MA)
U of Miami (FL)
U of Michigan (MI)
U of Michigan–Dearborn (MI)
U of Minnesota, Duluth (MN)
U of Minnesota, Twin Cities Campus (MN)
U of Missouri (MO)
U of Nebraska–Lincoln (NE)
U of Oklahoma (OK)
U of Pittsburgh (PA)
U of Regina (SK, Canada)
U of Rhode Island (RI)
U of San Diego (CA)
U of Southern California (CA)
U of South Florida (FL)
The U of Tennessee (TN)
The U of Texas at Arlington (TX)
The U of Texas at El Paso (TX)
The U of Toledo (OH)
U of Toronto (ON, Canada)
U of Vermont (VT)
U of Washington (WA)
U of Windsor (ON, Canada)
U of Wisconsin–Madison (WI)
U of Wisconsin–Milwaukee (WI)
U of Wisconsin–Platteville (WI)
Virginia Polytechnic Inst and State U (VA)
Wayne State U (MI)
Western Michigan U (MI)
Western New England Coll (MA)
West Virginia U (WV)
Wichita State U (KS)
Worcester Polytechnic Inst (MA)
Youngstown State U (OH)

INDUSTRIAL PRODUCTION TECHNOLOGIES RELATED
Bowling Green State U (OH)
Central Michigan U (MI)
Ferris State U (MI)
McPherson Coll (KS)
Millersville U of Pennsylvania (PA)
Missouri State U (MO)
Southern Polytechnic State U (GA)
Southwestern Coll (KS)
Tarleton State U (TX)
U of Puerto Rico at Utuado (PR)
U of Wisconsin–Stout (WI)
Utah State U (UT)
Valdosta State U (GA)
Wayne State Coll (NE)
Wayne State U (MI)

INDUSTRIAL RADIOLOGIC TECHNOLOGY
Baker Coll of Owosso (MI)
Briar Cliff U (IA)
Concordia U Wisconsin (WI)
Oregon Inst of Technology (OR)
U of Maryland Eastern Shore (MD)

INDUSTRIAL SAFETY TECHNOLOGY
Northeastern State U (OK)
Rochester Inst of Technology (NY)
South Dakota State U (SD)
Southeastern Oklahoma State U (OK)
U of Houston–Downtown (TX)

INDUSTRIAL TECHNOLOGY
Appalachian State U (NC)
Arizona State U (AZ)
Baker Coll of Flint (MI)
Ball State U (IN)
Bemidji State U (MN)
Black Hills State U (SD)
Boise State U (ID)
Bowling Green State U (OH)
Buffalo State Coll, State U of New York (NY)
California State U, Fresno (CA)
California State U, Long Beach (CA)
California State U, Los Angeles (CA)
Central Connecticut State U (CT)
Central State U (OH)
Cleveland State U (OH)
East Carolina U (NC)
Eastern Illinois U (IL)
Eastern Michigan U (MI)
Elizabeth City State U (NC)
Fairmont State U (WV)
Ferris State U (MI)
Fitchburg State Coll (MA)
Fort Hays State U (KS)
Illinois State U (IL)
Indiana State U (IN)
Indiana U–Purdue U Fort Wayne (IN)
ITT Tech Inst, San Dimas (CA)
ITT Tech Inst, Fort Wayne (IN)
ITT Tech Inst, Indianapolis (IN)
ITT Tech Inst, Newburgh (IN)
ITT Tech Inst (OR)
Jackson State U (MS)
Jacksonville State U (AL)
Kent State U (OH)
Kent State U at Tuscarawas (OH)
Lake Superior State U (MI)
Lamar U (TX)
Lawrence Technological U (MI)
Middle Tennessee State U (TN)
Millersville U of Pennsylvania (PA)
Minnesota State U Moorhead (MN)
Mississippi State U (MS)
Mississippi Valley State U (MS)
Morehead State U (KY)
Northern Kentucky U (KY)
Northern Michigan U (MI)
Northwestern State U of Louisiana (LA)
Ohio U (OH)
Oklahoma Panhandle State U (OK)
Prairie View A&M U (TX)
Sam Houston State U (TX)
South Carolina State U (SC)
Southeastern Louisiana U (LA)
Southeast Missouri State U (MO)
Southern Arkansas U–Magnolia (AR)
Southern Illinois U Carbondale (IL)
Southwestern Oklahoma State U (OK)
Tennessee Technological U (TN)
Texas A&M U–Commerce (TX)
Texas A&M U–Kingsville (TX)
Texas Southern U (TX)
Texas State U–San Marcos (TX)
U of Arkansas at Pine Bluff (AR)
U of Dayton (OH)
U of Massachusetts Lowell (MA)
The U of North Carolina at Charlotte (NC)
U of North Dakota (ND)
U of Northern Iowa (IA)
U of Rio Grande (OH)
U of Southern Mississippi (MS)
The U of Texas at Tyler (TX)
The U of Texas of the Permian Basin (TX)
The U of Toledo (OH)
The U of West Alabama (AL)
U of Wisconsin–Platteville (WI)
Wayne State U (MI)
Western Kentucky U (KY)
Western Washington U (WA)
William Penn U (IA)

INFORMATION RESOURCES MANAGEMENT
Abilene Christian U (TX)
Florida Inst of Technology (FL)

Juniata Coll (PA)
Lubbock Christian U (TX)
Michigan State U (MI)
Mount St. Mary's U (MD)
Southern Wesleyan U (SC)
U of Wisconsin–Eau Claire (WI)
Western Michigan U (MI)

INFORMATION SCIENCE/ STUDIES

Adelphi U (NY)
Alabama State U (AL)
Albertus Magnus Coll (CT)
Albright Coll (PA)
The American U in Dubai (United Arab Emirates)
Anderson U (IN)
Andrews U (MI)
Armstrong Atlantic State U (GA)
Ashland U (OH)
Athabasca U (AB, Canada)
Averett U (VA)
Baker Coll of Owosso (MI)
Baker U (KS)
Barry U (FL)
Beacon Coll (FL)
Belmont Abbey Coll (NC)
Belmont U (TN)
Bemidji State U (MN)
Benedictine U (IL)
Bernard M. Baruch Coll of the City U of New York (NY)
Bethune-Cookman U (FL)
Bluffton U (OH)
Boise State U (ID)
Boston U (MA)
Bradley U (IL)
Brewton-Parker Coll (GA)
Brigham Young U–Hawaii (HI)
Brock U (ON, Canada)
Brooklyn Coll of the City U of New York (NY)
Buffalo State Coll, State U of New York (NY)
California Lutheran U (CA)
California State U, East Bay (CA)
California State U, Fullerton (CA)
California State U, Northridge (CA)
California State U, Stanislaus (CA)
Calumet Coll of Saint Joseph (IN)
Campbellsville U (KY)
Cape Breton U (NS, Canada)
Carnegie Mellon U (PA)
Carroll U (WI)
Carson-Newman Coll (TN)
Catawba Coll (NC)
Central Coll (IA)
Champlain Coll (VT)
Chowan U (NC)
Christopher Newport U (VA)
Clarion U of Pennsylvania (PA)
Clayton State U (GA)
Cleary U (MI)
Clemson U (SC)
Cleveland State U (OH)
Coastal Carolina U (SC)
Coll of Charleston (SC)
Coll of Notre Dame of Maryland (MD)
Coll of Staten Island of the City U of New York (NY)
Colorado State U–Pueblo (CO)
Columbia U, School of General Studies (NY)
Concordia U Chicago (IL)
Concord U (WV)
Dakota State U (SD)
Delaware State U (DE)
DePaul U (IL)
Doane Coll (NE)
Dominican U (IL)
Drexel U (PA)
Eastern Michigan U (MI)
ECPI Coll of Technology, Virginia Beach (VA)
ECPI Tech Coll, Roanoke (VA)
Edward Waters Coll (FL)
Elizabethtown Coll (PA)
Emporia State U (KS)
Excelsior Coll (NY)
Faulkner U (AL)
Ferrum Coll (VA)
Florida Ag and Mech U (FL)
Florida Inst of Technology (FL)
Florida State U (FL)
Fordham U (NY)
Fort Hays State U (KS)
Fort Lewis Coll (CO)
Freed-Hardeman U (TN)
Friends U (KS)
Frostburg State U (MD)
Gallaudet U (DC)
George Fox U (OR)
Georgia Southern U (GA)
Glenville State Coll (WV)
Goldey-Beacom Coll (DE)
Gonzaga U (WA)
Grambling State U (LA)
Grand Valley State U (MI)
Grand View U (IA)
Grantham U (MO)
Guilford Coll (NC)
Hampton U (VA)
Harris-Stowe State U (MO)
HEC Montreal (QC, Canada)
Heidelberg U (OH)
Herzing U (GA)
High Point U (NC)
Houston Baptist U (TX)
Husson U (ME)
Idaho State U (ID)
Illinois Coll (IL)
Illinois State U (IL)
Immaculata U (PA)
Indiana U–Purdue U Fort Wayne (IN)
Inter American U of Puerto Rico, San Germán Campus (PR)
Iowa Wesleyan Coll (IA)
James Madison U (VA)
Johnson & Wales U (RI)
Johnson State Coll (VT)
Kansas State U (KS)
Kennesaw State U (GA)
King Coll (TN)
Lakehead U (ON, Canada)
Lamar U (TX)
La Salle U (PA)
Lasell Coll (MA)
La Sierra U (CA)
Lees-McRae Coll (NC)
Lee U (TN)
Lehigh U (PA)
LeTourneau U (TX)
Limestone Coll (SC)
Lincoln U (MO)
Lipscomb U (TN)
Long Island U, C.W. Post Campus (NY)
Louisiana State U in Shreveport (LA)
Mansfield U of Pennsylvania (PA)
Marietta Coll (OH)
Marist Coll (NY)
Marymount U (VA)
McKendree U (IL)
Medgar Evers Coll of the City U of New York (NY)
Memorial U of Newfoundland (NL, Canada)
Mercer U (GA)
Mercy Coll (NY)
Mercyhurst Coll (PA)
Messiah Coll (PA)
Michigan State U (MI)
Michigan Technological U (MI)
Midwestern State U (TX)
Minnesota State U Mankato (MN)
Missouri U of Science and Technology (MO)
Missouri Western State U (MO)
Monroe Coll, Bronx (NY)
Mount Olive Coll (NC)
National U (CA)
Nebraska Wesleyan U (NE)
New Jersey Inst of Technology (NJ)
Newman U (KS)
New Mexico Highlands U (NM)
New Mexico State U (NM)
New York City Coll of Technology of the City U of New York (NY)
New York Inst of Technology (NY)
New York U (NY)
Niagara U (NY)
North Carolina Central U (NC)
Northeastern U (MA)
Northern Kentucky U (KY)
North Georgia Coll & State U (GA)
Northwestern Oklahoma State U (OK)
Northwestern State U of Louisiana (LA)
Oakland City U (IN)
Oakwood U (AL)
Ohio Dominican U (OH)
The Ohio State U (OH)
Oklahoma Baptist U (OK)
Oklahoma Christian U (OK)
Oklahoma Wesleyan U (OK)
Old Dominion U (VA)
Ottawa U (KS)
Pace U (NY)
Peirce Coll (PA)
Penn State Abington (PA)
Penn State Altoona (PA)
Penn State Beaver (PA)
Penn State Berks (PA)
Penn State Brandywine (PA)
Penn State DuBois (PA)
Penn State Erie, The Behrend Coll (PA)
Penn State Fayette, The Eberly Campus (PA)
Penn State Greater Allegheny (PA)
Penn State Harrisburg (PA)
Penn State Lehigh Valley (PA)
Penn State Mont Alto (PA)
Penn State New Kensington (PA)
Penn State Schuylkill (PA)
Penn State Shenango (PA)
Penn State U Park (PA)
Penn State Wilkes-Barre (PA)
Penn State Worthington Scranton (PA)
Penn State York (PA)
Philadelphia U (PA)
Post U (CT)
Queens U of Charlotte (NC)
Quinnipiac U (CT)
Radford U (VA)
Ramapo Coll of New Jersey (NJ)
Reinhardt Coll (GA)
The Richard Stockton Coll of New Jersey (NJ)
Rivier Coll (NH)
Roanoke Coll (VA)
Robert Morris U (PA)
Rutgers, The State U of New Jersey, Newark (NJ)
Rutgers, The State U of New Jersey, New Brunswick (NJ)
Sage Coll of Albany (NY)
St. Ambrose U (IA)
St. Cloud State U (MN)
St. Francis Xavier U (NS, Canada)
Saint Joseph's U (PA)
Saint Martin's U (WA)
Saint Mary-of-the-Woods Coll (IN)
St. Mary's U (TX)
Saint Michael's Coll (VT)
St. Thomas Aquinas Coll (NY)
St. Thomas U (FL)
Salisbury U (MD)
Salve Regina U (RI)
San Diego State U (CA)
San Francisco State U (CA)
Silver Lake Coll (WI)
Slippery Rock U of Pennsylvania (PA)
Southeastern Oklahoma State U (OK)
Southern Illinois U Carbondale (IL)
Southern Methodist U (TX)
Southwestern Adventist U (TX)
State U of New York at Fredonia (NY)
State U of New York at Oswego (NY)
State U of New York Coll at Old Westbury (NY)
Stevenson U (MD)
Stony Brook U, State U of New York (NY)
Stratford U, Woodbridge (VA)
Suffolk U (MA)
Susquehanna U (PA)
Syracuse U (NY)
Tennessee Technological U (TN)
Texas A&M Intl U (TX)
Texas A&M U–Commerce (TX)
Texas A&M U–Corpus Christi (TX)
Texas Lutheran U (TX)
Thiel Coll (PA)
Towson U (MD)
Tulane U (LA)
Union Coll (NE)
Union U (TN)
United States Military Acad (NY)
Universidad de las Américas–Puebla (Mexico)
U at Albany, State U of New York (NY)
U at Buffalo, the State U of New York (NY)
U of Alberta (AB, Canada)
U of Arkansas at Little Rock (AR)
U of Baltimore (MD)
U of Bridgeport (CT)
U of California, Irvine (CA)
U of California, Santa Cruz (CA)
U of Cincinnati (OH)
U of Dayton (OH)
U of Guelph (ON, Canada)
U of Hartford (CT)
U of Houston (TX)
U of Houston–Clear Lake (TX)
U of Illinois at Chicago (IL)
The U of Iowa (IA)
U of Mary (ND)
U of Mary Hardin-Baylor (TX)
U of Maryland, Baltimore County (MD)
U of Maryland, Coll Park (MD)
U of Maryland U Coll (MD)
U of Miami (FL)
U of Michigan–Flint (MI)
U of Nebraska at Omaha (NE)
U of New Brunswick Fredericton (NB, Canada)
U of New Haven (CT)
The U of North Carolina at Chapel Hill (NC)
U of North Texas (TX)
U of Oklahoma (OK)
U of Pittsburgh (PA)
U of San Francisco (CA)
The U of Scranton (PA)
U of South Carolina Upstate (SC)
U of South Florida (FL)
The U of Texas at Brownsville (TX)
The U of Texas at El Paso (TX)
The U of Texas of the Permian Basin (TX)
U of the District of Columbia (DC)
U of the Pacific (CA)
The U of Toledo (OH)
U of Tulsa (OK)
U of Vermont (VT)
U of Washington (WA)
U of Washington, Bothell (WA)
The U of Western Ontario (ON, Canada)
U of Wisconsin–River Falls (WI)
U of Wisconsin–Superior (WI)
Utah State U (UT)
Utah Valley U (UT)
Valdosta State U (GA)
Virginia Commonwealth U (VA)
Virginia Polytechnic Inst and State U (VA)
Washington Adventist U (MD)
Washington U in St. Louis (MO)
Wayne State Coll (NE)
Wayne State U (MI)
Westfield State Coll (MA)
West Liberty U (WV)
West Virginia Wesleyan Coll (WV)
Widener U (PA)
Wilberforce U (OH)
Wilkes U (PA)
Winona State U (MN)
Winston-Salem State U (NC)
Woodbury U (CA)
Worcester Polytechnic Inst (MA)
Wright State U (OH)
York Coll of the City U of New York (NY)

INFORMATION TECHNOLOGY

American Public U System (WV)
Arkansas Tech U (AR)
Armstrong Atlantic State U (GA)
Baylor U (TX)
Bluefield Coll (VA)
Bluffton U (OH)
Bob Jones U (SC)
Brigham Young U (UT)
Bryant U (RI)
Cabrini Coll (PA)
California State U, Chico (CA)
California State U, Dominguez Hills (CA)
California State U, Los Angeles (CA)
Cameron U (OK)
Capella U (MN)
Carnegie Mellon U (PA)
Central Michigan U (MI)
Clayton State U (GA)
Collins Coll: A School of Design and Technology (AZ)
Columbia Southern U (AL)
Concordia U (CA)
Cornell U (NY)
Curry Coll (MA)
DePaul U (IL)
D'Youville Coll (NY)
East Carolina U (NC)
Fairleigh Dickinson U, Metropolitan Campus (NJ)
Ferris State U (MI)
Florida Intl U (FL)
Franklin U (OH)
Frostburg State U (MD)
Furman U (SC)
Gainesville State Coll (GA)
Grace Coll (IN)
Harding U (AR)
Houghton Coll (NY)
Humboldt State U (CA)
Illinois Inst of Technology (IL)
Illinois State U (IL)
Indiana State U (IN)
Indiana Tech (IN)
Indiana U Bloomington (IN)
Indiana U–Purdue U Indianapolis (IN)
Indiana U South Bend (IN)
Johnson C. Smith U (NC)
Juniata Coll (PA)
Kaplan U, Cedar Rapids (IA)
Kaplan U, Davenport Campus (IA)
Kaplan U, Lincoln (NE)
Kaplan U, Omaha (NE)
Kentucky State U (KY)
Keystone Coll (PA)
Kutztown U of Pennsylvania (PA)
Kwantlen Polytechnic U (BC, Canada)
La Roche Coll (PA)
Lawrence Technological U (MI)
Lipscomb U (TN)
Long Island U, C.W. Post Campus (NY)
Loyola U Chicago (IL)
Marian U (WI)
Marist Coll (NY)
Marquette U (WI)
Meritus U (NB, Canada)
Misericordia U (PA)
Montclair State U (NJ)
Mount Aloysius Coll (PA)
Mount Marty Coll (SD)
Mount Saint Mary Coll (NY)
National U (CA)
Nazareth Coll of Rochester (NY)
Neumont U (UT)
Newbury Coll (MA)
New Jersey Inst of Technology (NJ)
New Mexico Inst of Mining and Technology (NM)
New Mexico State U (NM)
North Carolina State U (NC)
Northern Kentucky U (KY)
Oakland U (MI)
Ohio U (OH)
Ottawa U (KS)
Pioneer Pacific Coll, Wilsonville (OR)
Plymouth State U (NH)
Point Park U (PA)
Regent U (VA)
Rensselaer Polytechnic Inst (NY)
Robert Morris U Illinois (IL)
Rochester Inst of Technology (NY)
Sacred Heart U (CT)
St. John Fisher Coll (NY)
San Diego State U (CA)
San Jose State U (CA)
Slippery Rock U of Pennsylvania (PA)
Southern Polytechnic State U (GA)
South U (AL)
South U, Royal Palm Beach (FL)
South U (GA)
South U, Columbia (SC)
Southwest Minnesota State U (MN)
State U of New York Coll of Technology at Alfred (NY)
State U of New York Coll of Technology at Canton (NY)
Stephen F. Austin State U (TX)
Sullivan U (KY)
Temple U (PA)
Texas Christian U (TX)
Thomas More Coll (KY)
Tiffin U (OH)
Trevecca Nazarene U (TN)
United States Military Acad (NY)
The U of British Columbia–Okanagan (BC, Canada)
U of Central Florida (FL)
U of Denver (CO)
U of Massachusetts Boston (MA)
U of Missouri–Kansas City (MO)
U of New Hampshire (NH)
The U of North Carolina at Pembroke (NC)
U of Rio Grande (OH)
U of St. Francis (IL)
U of Saint Mary (KS)
U of South Florida (FL)
U of Tulsa (OK)
The U of Western Ontario (ON, Canada)
U of Wisconsin–Whitewater (WI)
Vanguard U of Southern California (CA)
Vermont Tech Coll (VT)
Virginia State U (VA)
Walden U (MN)
Washington & Jefferson Coll (PA)
Western Kentucky U (KY)
Wilmington U (DE)
Winston-Salem State U (NC)
York U (ON, Canada)
Youngstown State U (OH)

INORGANIC CHEMISTRY

The U of Western Ontario (ON, Canada)

INSTITUTIONAL FOOD WORKERS

Kendall Coll (IL)

INSTRUMENTATION TECHNOLOGY

Spartan Coll of Aeronautics and Technology (OK)

INSURANCE

Appalachian State U (NC)
Baylor U (TX)
Bowling Green State U (OH)
Bradley U (IL)
Delta State U (MS)
Excelsior Coll (NY)

Gannon U (PA)
Georgia State U (GA)
Idaho State U (ID)
Illinois State U (IL)
Illinois Wesleyan U (IL)
Indiana State U (IN)
Mississippi State U (MS)
Missouri State U (MO)
The Ohio State U (OH)
St. Cloud State U (MN)
St. John's U (NY)
Seattle U (WA)
Temple U (PA)
U of Cincinnati (OH)
U of Connecticut (CT)
U of Florida (FL)
U of Georgia (GA)
U of Hartford (CT)
U of Houston–Downtown (TX)
U of Illinois at Urbana–Champaign (IL)
U of Louisiana at Monroe (LA)
U of Minnesota, Twin Cities Campus (MN)
U of Mississippi (MS)
U of North Texas (TX)
U of Pennsylvania (PA)
U of South Carolina (SC)
U of Wisconsin–Madison (WI)

INTERCULTURAL/ MULTICULTURAL AND DIVERSITY STUDIES

California Baptist U (CA)
Columbia Intl U (SC)
Concordia U (QC, Canada)
Evangel U (MO)
The Evergreen State Coll (WA)
Macalester Coll (MN)
Northwest U (WA)
St. Catherine U (MN)
U of Puerto Rico, Río Piedras (PR)
U of San Diego (CA)
U of the Incarnate Word (TX)
U of Washington, Tacoma (WA)
Vanguard U of Southern California (CA)
Western Oregon U (OR)
Wilfrid Laurier U (ON, Canada)
William Jessup U (CA)

INTERDISCIPLINARY STUDIES

Agnes Scott Coll (GA)
Albright Coll (PA)
Alfred U (NY)
Amberton U (TX)
American Jewish U (CA)
Amherst Coll (MA)
Angelo State U (TX)
Augsburg Coll (MN)
Austin Peay State U (TN)
Bard Coll (NY)
Bard Coll at Simon's Rock (MA)
Barnard Coll (NY)
Beloit Coll (WI)
Bennett Coll for Women (NC)
Bentley U (MA)
Bernard M. Baruch Coll of the City U of New York (NY)
Bethany Coll (WV)
Bethany U (CA)
Birmingham-Southern Coll (AL)
Blackburn Coll (IL)
Bluefield Coll (VA)
Boise State U (ID)
Boston Coll (MA)
Boston U (MA)
Bowdoin Coll (ME)
Brigham Young U–Hawaii (HI)
Brock U (ON, Canada)
Bryn Athyn Coll of the New Church (PA)
Bucknell U (PA)
California Baptist U (CA)
California Lutheran U (CA)
California State U, Bakersfield (CA)
California State U, East Bay (CA)
California State U, Long Beach (CA)
California State U, Los Angeles (CA)
California State U, San Bernardino (CA)
Calvin Coll (MI)
Carleton Coll (MN)
Carson-Newman Coll (TN)
Catawba Coll (NC)
Cedarville U (OH)
Centenary Coll of Louisiana (LA)
Central Coll (IA)
Chowan U (NC)
Christopher Newport U (VA)
Clark U (MA)
Cleveland State U (OH)
Colby Coll (ME)
The Coll at Brockport, State U of New York (NY)
Coll of Notre Dame of Maryland (MD)
Coll of the Atlantic (ME)
The Coll of William and Mary (VA)
The Coll of Wooster (OH)
Columbia Coll Chicago (IL)
Connecticut Coll (CT)
Corban U (OR)
Cornell Coll (IA)
Cornell U (NY)
Cornerstone U (MI)
Crandall U (NB, Canada)
Dallas Baptist U (TX)
Dana Coll (NE)
Delta State U (MS)
DePauw U (IN)
Earlham Coll (IN)
Eckerd Coll (FL)
Elmhurst Coll (IL)
Elmira Coll (NY)
Emerson Coll (MA)
Emmanuel Coll (MA)
Emory & Henry Coll (VA)
Emory U (GA)
Eugene Lang Coll The New School for Liberal Arts (NY)
Felician Coll (NJ)
Florida Inst of Technology (FL)
Fordham U (NY)
Franklin U (OH)
Freed-Hardeman U (TN)
George Fox U (OR)
Georgetown U (DC)
The George Washington U (DC)
Gettysburg Coll (PA)
Goddard Coll (VT)
Goucher Coll (MD)
Greensboro Coll (NC)
Grinnell Coll (IA)
Guilford Coll (NC)
Gustavus Adolphus Coll (MN)
Harrisburg U of Science and Technology (PA)
Harris-Stowe State U (MO)
Hendrix Coll (AR)
Hillsdale Coll (MI)
Hillsdale Free Will Baptist Coll (OK)
Hollins U (VA)
Houston Baptist U (TX)
Huston-Tillotson U (TX)
Illinois Coll (IL)
Illinois State U (IL)
Iona Coll (NY)
Iowa State U of Science and Technology (IA)
Ithaca Coll (NY)
Jacksonville U (FL)
John Brown U (AR)
John Carroll U (OH)
The Johns Hopkins U (MD)
Jones Coll, Jacksonville (FL)
Judson Coll (AL)
Kalamazoo Coll (MI)
Keiser U, Fort Lauderdale (FL)
Kentucky Wesleyan Coll (KY)
Keuka Coll (NY)
King Coll (TN)
The King's Coll (NY)
Kuyper Coll (MI)
Lake Superior State U (MI)
Lamar U (TX)
Lane Coll (TN)
Lasell Coll (MA)
Lees-McRae Coll (NC)
Lee U (TN)
Lehman Coll of the City U of New York (NY)
LeTourneau U (TX)
Lewis-Clark State Coll (ID)
Liberty U (VA)
Long Island U, Brooklyn Campus (NY)
Long Island U, C.W. Post Campus (NY)
Louisiana Coll (LA)
Loyola U Maryland (MD)
Luther Coll (IA)
Manchester Coll (IN)
Marlboro Coll (VT)
Mars Hill Coll (NC)
Martin Luther Coll (MN)
Massachusetts Coll of Liberal Arts (MA)
McPherson Coll (KS)
Merrimack Coll (MA)
Middle Tennessee State U (TN)
Midwestern State U (TX)
Mills Coll (CA)
Minneapolis Coll of Art and Design (MN)
Minnesota State U Moorhead (MN)
Molloy Coll (NY)
Mount Allison U (NB, Canada)
Mount Saint Mary Coll (NY)
National U (CA)
Nebraska Wesleyan U (NE)
Newbury Coll (MA)
New Mexico State U (NM)
North Dakota State U (ND)
North Greenville U (SC)
Northwest U (WA)
Nyack Coll (NY)
Oakland City U (IN)
Oakwood U (AL)
Oberlin Coll (OH)
Oglethorpe U (GA)
Oklahoma Baptist U (OK)
Pacific Union Coll (CA)
Peace Coll (NC)
Pepperdine U, Malibu (CA)
Piedmont Coll (GA)
Pittsburg State U (KS)
Pitzer Coll (CA)
Pomona Coll (CA)
Prairie View A&M U (TX)
Prescott Coll (AZ)
Rhodes Coll (TN)
Ripon Coll (WI)
Rochester Coll (MI)
Rochester Inst of Technology (NY)
Rocky Mountain Coll (MT)
Russell Sage Coll (NY)
Rutgers, The State U of New Jersey, New Brunswick (NJ)
St. Andrews Presbyterian Coll (NC)
St. Cloud State U (MN)
St. John's Coll (MD)
Saint Mary's Coll (IN)
Saint Mary's Coll of California (CA)
St. Thomas U (NB, Canada)
Salem Coll (NC)
San Diego Christian Coll (CA)
Santa Clara U (CA)
Sarah Lawrence Coll (NY)
Smith Coll (MA)
Sonoma State U (CA)
South Dakota School of Mines and Technology (SD)
Southern Oregon U (OR)
Stanford U (CA)
State U of New York at Fredonia (NY)
State U of New York Coll at Oneonta (NY)
State U of New York Empire State Coll (NY)
Stephens Coll (MO)
Sterling Coll (KS)
Stevenson U (MD)
Suffolk U (MA)
Sweet Briar Coll (VA)
Tabor Coll (KS)
Tarleton State U (TX)
Tennessee Technological U (TN)
Tennessee Wesleyan Coll (TN)
Texas A&M U–Commerce (TX)
Texas A&M U–Corpus Christi (TX)
Texas Southern U (TX)
Texas Tech U (TX)
Texas Woman's U (TX)
Towson U (MD)
Trent U (ON, Canada)
Trinity Coll (CT)
United States Air Force Acad (CO)
U at Albany, State U of New York (NY)
The U of Alabama (AL)
U of Alaska Anchorage (AK)
U of Alberta (AB, Canada)
U of Baltimore (MD)
U of Bridgeport (CT)
The U of British Columbia (BC, Canada)
U of California, San Diego (CA)
U of California, Santa Barbara (CA)
U of Chicago (IL)
U of Hartford (CT)
U of Hawaii at Hilo (HI)
U of Houston (TX)
The U of Iowa (IA)
U of Kentucky (KY)
U of Maine at Farmington (ME)
U of Massachusetts Dartmouth (MA)
U of Memphis (TN)
U of Minnesota, Duluth (MN)
U of Missouri (MO)
U of Missouri–Kansas City (MO)
U of Nevada, Las Vegas (NV)
U of Northern Colorado (CO)
U of North Texas (TX)
U of Pittsburgh (PA)
U of Portland (OR)
U of Puerto Rico, Río Piedras (PR)
U of Puget Sound (WA)
U of Redlands (CA)
U of Rhode Island (RI)
U of Saint Mary (KS)
U of St. Thomas (MN)
U of San Francisco (CA)
U of South Carolina Upstate (SC)
The U of Tennessee at Martin (TN)
The U of Texas at Dallas (TX)
The U of Texas at El Paso (TX)
The U of Texas at Tyler (TX)
The U of Texas of the Permian Basin (TX)
The U of Texas–Pan American (TX)
U of the Pacific (CA)
U of Vermont (VT)
The U of Virginia's Coll at Wise (VA)
U of Washington (WA)
U of Waterloo (ON, Canada)
The U of Western Ontario (ON, Canada)
U of Wisconsin–Green Bay (WI)
U of Wisconsin–Milwaukee (WI)
U of Wisconsin–Parkside (WI)
Vanguard U of Southern California (CA)
Vassar Coll (NY)
Virginia Intermont Coll (VA)
Virginia Polytechnic Inst and State U (VA)
Virginia State U (VA)
Virginia Wesleyan Coll (VA)
Wayne State Coll (NE)
Webster U (MO)
Wesleyan Coll (GA)
Wesleyan U (CT)
Western Oregon U (OR)
Western State Coll of Colorado (CO)
West Liberty U (WV)
West Virginia U (WV)
Woodbury U (CA)
Worcester Polytechnic Inst (MA)
Yeshiva U (NY)
York U (ON, Canada)

INTERIOR ARCHITECTURE

Arizona State U (AZ)
Auburn U (AL)
Boston Architectural Coll (MA)
Bowling Green State U (OH)
California Coll of the Arts (CA)
Central Michigan U (MI)
Chatham U (PA)
Ferris State U (MI)
Indiana State U (IN)
La Roche Coll (PA)
Lawrence Technological U (MI)
Louisiana State U and Ag and Mech Coll (LA)
Louisiana Tech U (LA)
Miami U (OH)
Philadelphia U (PA)
School of the Art Inst of Chicago (IL)
Stephen F. Austin State U (TX)
Syracuse U (NY)
Texas Tech U (TX)
Universidad de las Américas–Puebla (Mexico)
U of Missouri (MO)
U of Nebraska–Lincoln (NE)
U of Nevada, Las Vegas (NV)
U of New Haven (CT)
U of Oregon (OR)
U of Southern Mississippi (MS)
The U of Texas at Arlington (TX)
The U of Texas at San Antonio (TX)
U of Washington (WA)
Woodbury U (CA)

INTERIOR DESIGN

Abilene Christian U (TX)
Acad of Art U (CA)
The American U in Dubai (United Arab Emirates)
Appalachian State U (NC)
Arcadia U (PA)
Art Center Coll of Design (CA)
The Art Center Design Coll, Tucson (AZ)
The Art Inst of Atlanta (GA)
The Art Inst of Atlanta–Decatur (GA)
The Art Inst of Austin (TX)
The Art Inst of California–Hollywood (CA)
The Art Inst of California–Inland Empire (CA)
The Art Inst of California–Los Angeles (CA)
The Art Inst of California–Orange County (CA)
The Art Inst of California–Sacramento (CA)
The Art Inst of California–San Diego (CA)
The Art Inst of California–San Francisco (CA)
The Art Inst of California–Sunnyvale (CA)
The Art Inst of Charleston (SC)
The Art Inst of Charlotte (NC)
The Art Inst of Colorado (CO)
The Art Inst of Dallas (TX)
The Art Inst of Fort Lauderdale (FL)
The Art Inst of Fort Worth (TX)
The Art Inst of Houston (TX)
The Art Inst of Houston—North (TX)
The Art Inst of Indianapolis (IN)
The Art Inst of Jacksonville (FL)
The Art Inst of Las Vegas (NV)
The Art Inst of Michigan (MI)
The Art Inst of Ohio–Cincinnati (OH)
The Art Inst of Philadelphia (PA)
The Art Inst of Phoenix (AZ)
The Art Inst of Pittsburgh (PA)
The Art Inst of Portland (OR)
The Art Inst of Raleigh-Durham (NC)
The Art Inst of Salt Lake City (UT)
The Art Inst of San Antonio (TX)
The Art Inst of Seattle (WA)
The Art Inst of Tampa (FL)
The Art Inst of Tennessee–Nashville (TN)
The Art Inst of Tucson (AZ)
The Art Inst of Vrigina Beach (VA)
The Art Inst of Washington (VA)
The Art Inst of Washington–Northern Virginia (VA)
The Art Inst of York–Pennsylvania (PA)
The Art Insts Intl–Kansas City (KS)
The Art Insts Intl Minnesota (MN)
Auburn U (AL)
Baylor U (TX)
Brenau U (GA)
California State U, Chico (CA)
California State U, Fresno (CA)
California State U, Long Beach (CA)
California State U, Sacramento (CA)
Carson-Newman Coll (TN)
Cazenovia Coll (NY)
Chaminade U of Honolulu (HI)
The Cleveland Inst of Art (OH)
Coll for Creative Studies (MI)
Coll of Mount St. Joseph (OH)
Collins Coll: A School of Design and Technology (AZ)
Colorado State U (CO)
Columbia Coll Chicago (IL)
Columbus Coll of Art & Design (OH)
Concordia U Wisconsin (WI)
Converse Coll (SC)
Corcoran Coll of Art and Design (DC)
Cornish Coll of the Arts (WA)
Drexel U (PA)
East Carolina U (NC)
Eastern Michigan U (MI)
East Tennessee State U (TN)
Endicott Coll (MA)
Fashion Inst of Technology (NY)
Florida Intl U (FL)
Florida State U (FL)
Fort Hays State U (KS)
Georgia Southern U (GA)
Hampton U (VA)
Harding U (AR)
Harrington Coll of Design (IL)
High Point U (NC)
The Illinois Inst of Art–Chicago (IL)
The Illinois Inst of Art–Schaumburg (IL)
Indiana U Bloomington (IN)
Indiana U of Pennsylvania (PA)
Indiana U–Purdue U Fort Wayne (IN)
Indiana U–Purdue U Indianapolis (IN)
Interior Designers Inst (CA)
Intl Acad of Design & Technology (IL)
Iowa State U of Science and Technology (IA)
Kansas State U (KS)
Kean U (NJ)
Kent State U (OH)
Kwantlen Polytechnic U (BC, Canada)
Lamar U (TX)
Longwood U (VA)
Maryland Inst Coll of Art (MD)
Marylhurst U (OR)
Marymount U (VA)
Maryville U of Saint Louis (MO)
Marywood U (PA)
McPherson Coll (KS)
Mercyhurst Coll (PA)
Meredith Coll (NC)
Miami Intl U of Art & Design (FL)
Miami U Hamilton (OH)
Michigan State U (MI)
Middle Tennessee State U (TN)
Mississippi Coll (MS)
Moore Coll of Art & Design (PA)
Mount Ida Coll (MA)
Mount Mary Coll (WI)
Newbury Coll (MA)
The New England Inst of Art (MA)

New Jersey Inst of Technology (NJ)
New York Inst of Technology (NY)
New York School of Interior Design (NY)
North Dakota State U (ND)
Northern Arizona U (AZ)
The Ohio State U (OH)
Oklahoma Christian U (OK)
O'More Coll of Design (TN)
Oregon State U (OR)
Otis Coll of Art and Design (CA)
Park U (MO)
Parsons The New School for Design (NY)
Patricia Stevens Coll (MO)
Philadelphia U (PA)
Pittsburg State U (KS)
Pratt Inst (NY)
Ringling Coll of Art and Design (FL)
Rochester Inst of Technology (NY)
Rocky Mountain Coll of Art + Design (CO)
Salem Coll (NC)
Samford U (AL)
San Diego State U (CA)
San Francisco State U (CA)
San Jose State U (CA)
Savannah Coll of Art and Design (GA)
School of Visual Arts (NY)
Seattle Pacific U (WA)
South Dakota State U (SD)
Southern Illinois U Carbondale (IL)
Southwest Florida Coll, Fort Myers (FL)
Stephens Coll (MO)
Suffolk U (MA)
Sullivan Coll of Technology and Design (KY)
Texas Christian U (TX)
Texas State U–San Marcos (TX)
The U of Alabama (AL)
U of Bridgeport (CT)
U of Central Missouri (MO)
U of Central Oklahoma (OK)
U of Cincinnati (OH)
U of Florida (FL)
U of Idaho (ID)
The U of Kansas (KS)
U of Kentucky (KY)
U of Manitoba (MB, Canada)
U of Massachusetts Amherst (MA)
U of Minnesota, Twin Cities Campus (MN)
The U of North Carolina at Greensboro (NC)
U of Northern Iowa (IA)
U of North Texas (TX)
U of Oklahoma (OK)
The U of Tennessee (TN)
The U of Tennessee at Chattanooga (TN)
The U of Tennessee at Martin (TN)
The U of Texas at Austin (TX)
The U of Texas at San Antonio (TX)
U of the Incarnate Word (TX)
U of Wisconsin–Madison (WI)
U of Wisconsin–Stevens Point (WI)
Ursuline Coll (OH)
Utah State U (UT)
Valdosta State U (GA)
Virginia Commonwealth U (VA)
Virginia Polytechnic Inst and State U (VA)
Washington State U (WA)
Watkins Coll of Art, Design, & Film (TN)
Wentworth Inst of Technology (MA)
Western Carolina U (NC)
Western Michigan U (MI)
Westwood Coll–Anaheim (CA)
Westwood Coll–Annandale Campus (VA)
Westwood Coll–Arlington Ballston Campus (VA)
Westwood Coll–Chicago Loop Campus (IL)
Westwood Coll–Chicago O'Hare Airport (IL)
Westwood Coll–Denver North (CO)
Westwood Coll–Denver South (CO)
Westwood Coll–Inland Empire (CA)
Westwood Coll–Los Angeles (CA)
Westwood Coll–Online Campus (CO)
Westwood Coll–South Bay Campus (CA)

INTERMEDIA/MULTIMEDIA

Alberta Coll of Art & Design (AB, Canada)
Art Center Coll of Design (CA)
Bard Coll at Simon's Rock (MA)
Bennington Coll (VT)
Calumet Coll of Saint Joseph (IN)
Champlain Coll (VT)
City Coll of the City U of New York (NY)
The Cleveland Inst of Art (OH)
The Coll of New Jersey (NJ)
Coll of Santa Fe (NM)
Columbia Coll Chicago (IL)
Concordia U (QC, Canada)
DigiPen Inst of Technology (WA)
Emerson Coll (MA)
The Evergreen State Coll (WA)
Hawai'i Pacific U (HI)
Indiana U of Pennsylvania (PA)
Lewis U (IL)
Long Island U, C.W. Post Campus (NY)
Maine Coll of Art (ME)
Maryland Inst Coll of Art (MD)
Massachusetts Coll of Art and Design (MA)
Mills Coll (CA)
Minneapolis Coll of Art and Design (MN)
Missouri State U (MO)
National U (CA)
New England School of Communications (ME)
Northeastern U (MA)
Platt Coll San Diego (CA)
Purchase Coll, State U of New York (NY)
Ramapo Coll of New Jersey (NJ)
Rochester Inst of Technology (NY)
School of the Art Inst of Chicago (IL)
School of the Museum of Fine Arts, Boston (MA)
State U of New York at Fredonia (NY)
U of Central Florida (FL)
U of Florida (FL)
U of Hartford (CT)
U of Massachusetts Dartmouth (MA)
U of Oregon (OR)
U of Puerto Rico, Río Piedras (PR)
U of Regina (SK, Canada)
Western Washington U (WA)
Westwood Coll–Anaheim (CA)
Westwood Coll–Annandale Campus (VA)
Westwood Coll–Arlington Ballston Campus (VA)
Westwood Coll–Chicago Du Page (IL)
Westwood Coll–Chicago Loop Campus (IL)
Westwood Coll–Chicago O'Hare Airport (IL)
Westwood Coll–Chicago River Oaks (IL)
Westwood Coll–Denver North (CO)
Westwood Coll–Denver South (CO)
Westwood Coll–Inland Empire (CA)
Westwood Coll–Los Angeles (CA)
Westwood Coll–Online Campus (CO)
Westwood Coll–South Bay Campus (CA)
Worcester Polytechnic Inst (MA)

INTERNATIONAL AGRICULTURE

Cornell U (NY)
Florida Ag and Mech U (FL)
Iowa State U of Science and Technology (IA)
Tarleton State U (TX)
U of California, Davis (CA)
U of Illinois at Urbana–Champaign (IL)
U of Missouri (MO)
Utah State U (UT)

INTERNATIONAL BUSINESS/TRADE/COMMERCE

Adams State Coll (CO)
Albertus Magnus Coll (CT)
Albright Coll (PA)
Alliant Intl U (CA)
Alliant Intl U–México City (Mexico)
Alma Coll (MI)
Alverno Coll (WI)
American Intl Coll (MA)
The American U of Paris (France)
Anderson U (IN)
Angelo State U (TX)
Appalachian State U (NC)
Aquinas Coll (MI)
Arcadia U (PA)
Argosy U, Atlanta (GA)
Argosy U, Chicago (IL)
Argosy U, Dallas (TX)
Argosy U, Denver (CO)
Argosy U, Hawai'i (HI)
Argosy U, Inland Empire (CA)
Argosy U, Los Angeles (CA)
Argosy U, Nashville (TN)
Argosy U, Orange County (CA)
Argosy U, Phoenix (AZ)
Argosy U, Salt Lake City (UT)
Argosy U, San Diego (CA)
Argosy U, San Francisco Bay Area (CA)
Argosy U, Sarasota (FL)
Argosy U, Schaumburg (IL)
Argosy U, Seattle (WA)
Argosy U, Tampa (FL)
Argosy U, Twin Cities (MN)
Argosy U, Washington DC (VA)
Arizona State U (AZ)
Arkansas State U—Jonesboro (AR)
Assumption Coll (MA)
Auburn U (AL)
Augsburg Coll (MN)
Avila U (MO)
Babson Coll (MA)
Baker U (KS)
Baldwin-Wallace Coll (OH)
Barry U (FL)
Baylor U (TX)
Belmont U (TN)
Benedictine U (IL)
Bernard M. Baruch Coll of the City U of New York (NY)
Bethany Coll (KS)
Bethel Coll (IN)
Bethune-Cookman U (FL)
Birmingham-Southern Coll (AL)
Bishop's U (QC, Canada)
Bob Jones U (SC)
Boise State U (ID)
Boston U (MA)
Bowling Green State U (OH)
Bradley U (IL)
Bridgewater State Coll (MA)
Brigham Young U–Hawaii (HI)
Brock U (ON, Canada)
Brooklyn Coll of the City U of New York (NY)
Bryant U (RI)
Buena Vista U (IA)
Butler U (IN)
California State U, Dominguez Hills (CA)
California State U, Fresno (CA)
California State U, Fullerton (CA)
California State U, Long Beach (CA)
Canisius Coll (NY)
Cedarville U (OH)
Central Coll (IA)
Central Connecticut State U (CT)
Central Michigan U (MI)
Champlain Coll (VT)
Chatham U (PA)
City U of Seattle (WA)
Claremont McKenna Coll (CA)
Clarion U of Pennsylvania (PA)
Clemson U (SC)
The Coll at Brockport, State U of New York (NY)
Coll of Charleston (SC)
The Coll of Idaho (ID)
The Coll of St. Scholastica (MN)
Coll of the Ozarks (MO)
Columbia Coll (MO)
Columbia Southern U (AL)
Concordia Coll (MN)
Concordia U (QC, Canada)
Converse Coll (SC)
Cornell Coll (IA)
Creighton U (NE)
Davenport U, Grand Rapids (MI)
DeSales U (PA)
Dickinson Coll (PA)
Dickinson State U (ND)
Dillard U (LA)
Dominican Coll (NY)
Dominican U (IL)
Dominican U of California (CA)
Drake U (IA)
Drexel U (PA)
Drury U (MO)
Dunlap-Stone U, Phoenix (AZ)
Duquesne U (PA)
D'Youville Coll (NY)
Eastern Mennonite U (VA)
Eastern Michigan U (MI)
Eckerd Coll (FL)
Elizabethtown Coll (PA)
Elmhurst Coll (IL)
Elmira Coll (NY)
Excelsior Coll (NY)
Fairfield U (CT)
Ferris State U (MI)
Fitchburg State Coll (MA)
Florida Atlantic U (FL)
Florida Inst of Technology (FL)
Florida Intl U (FL)
Florida Southern Coll (FL)
Fordham U (NY)
Fort Lewis Coll (CO)
Franklin Coll Switzerland (Switzerland)
Franklin U (OH)
Friends U (KS)
Gannon U (PA)
Gardner-Webb U (NC)
Georgetown U (DC)
The George Washington U (DC)
Georgia Southern U (GA)
Georgia State U (GA)
Gettysburg Coll (PA)
Goldey-Beacom Coll (DE)
Gonzaga U (WA)
Grace Coll (IN)
Graceland U (IA)
Grand Valley State U (MI)
Grove City Coll (PA)
Gustavus Adolphus Coll (MN)
Hamline U (MN)
Harding U (AR)
Hawai'i Pacific U (HI)
HEC Montreal (QC, Canada)
High Point U (NC)
Hofstra U (NY)
Holy Family U (PA)
Houston Baptist U (TX)
Husson U (ME)
Illinois State U (IL)
Illinois Wesleyan U (IL)
Immaculata U (PA)
Indiana U of Pennsylvania (PA)
Inter American U of Puerto Rico, Ponce Campus (PR)
Iona Coll (NY)
Iowa State U of Science and Technology (IA)
Ithaca Coll (NY)
Jacksonville U (FL)
James Madison U (VA)
Jamestown Coll (ND)
John Brown U (AR)
Johnson & Wales U (CO)
Juniata Coll (PA)
Keiser U, Fort Lauderdale (FL)
Kennesaw State U (GA)
King Coll (TN)
King's Coll (PA)
Kutztown U of Pennsylvania (PA)
Kuyper Coll (MI)
Lake Erie Coll (OH)
Lakeland Coll (WI)
La Roche Coll (PA)
La Salle U (PA)
Lasell Coll (MA)
Lawrence Technological U (MI)
LeTourneau U (TX)
Lewis U (IL)
Lincoln U (CA)
Lindenwood U (MO)
Linfield Coll (OR)
Lipscomb U (TN)
Loras Coll (IA)
Louisiana State U and Ag and Mech Coll (LA)
Loyola U Chicago (IL)
Loyola U Maryland (MD)
Loyola U New Orleans (LA)
Madonna U (MI)
Mansfield U of Pennsylvania (PA)
Marietta Coll (OH)
Marquette U (WI)
Marshall U (WV)
Mars Hill Coll (NC)
Maryville Coll (TN)
Maryville U of Saint Louis (MO)
Marywood U (PA)
Massachusetts Maritime Acad (MA)
McPherson Coll (KS)
Menlo Coll (CA)
Merrimack Coll (MA)
Messiah Coll (PA)
Midwestern State U (TX)
Millikin U (IL)
Milwaukee School of Eng (WI)
Minnesota State U Mankato (MN)
Minnesota State U Moorhead (MN)
Minot State U (ND)
Monmouth Coll (IL)
Monmouth U (NJ)
Moravian Coll (PA)
Mount Allison U (NB, Canada)
Mount Mercy Coll (IA)
Mount St. Mary's Coll (CA)
Mount Vernon Nazarene U (OH)
Murray State U (KY)
Nazareth Coll of Rochester (NY)
Nebraska Wesleyan U (NE)
Neumann U (PA)
Newbury Coll (MA)
New Jersey Inst of Technology (NJ)
New Mexico State U (NM)
New York Inst of Technology (NY)
New York U (NY)
Niagara U (NY)
Nichols Coll (MA)
North Central Coll (IL)
Northeastern State U (OK)
Northeastern U (MA)
Northern State U (SD)
North Greenville U (SC)
Northwestern Coll (MN)
Northwest Missouri State U (MO)
Northwest Nazarene U (ID)
Ohio Dominican U (OH)
Ohio Northern U (OH)
The Ohio State U (OH)
Ohio U (OH)
Ohio Wesleyan U (OH)
Oklahoma Baptist U (OK)
Oklahoma City U (OK)
Oklahoma State U (OK)
Old Dominion U (VA)
Oral Roberts U (OK)
Pace U (NY)
Pacific Union Coll (CA)
Paine Coll (GA)
Penn State DuBois (PA)
Penn State Erie, The Behrend Coll (PA)
Penn State Harrisburg (PA)
Penn State Lehigh Valley (PA)
Penn State Schuylkill (PA)
Pepperdine U, Malibu (CA)
Philadelphia U (PA)
Pittsburg State U (KS)
Pontifical Catholic U of Puerto Rico (PR)
Post U (CT)
Potomac Coll (DC)
Queens Coll of the City U of New York (NY)
Quinnipiac U (CT)
Ramapo Coll of New Jersey (NJ)
Rhodes Coll (TN)
Rider U (NJ)
Rochester Inst of Technology (NY)
Rollins Coll (FL)
Roosevelt U (IL)
Saginaw Valley State U (MI)
St. Ambrose U (IA)
Saint Anselm Coll (NH)
St. Catherine U (MN)
St. Cloud State U (MN)
St. Edward's U (TX)
Saint Francis U (PA)
Saint Joseph's U (PA)
Saint Leo U (FL)
Saint Mary's Coll of California (CA)
St. Mary's U (TX)
Saint Mary's U of Minnesota (MN)
St. Norbert Coll (WI)
St. Petersburg Coll (FL)
St. Thomas U (FL)
Saint Vincent Coll (PA)
Saint Xavier U (IL)
Salem Coll (NC)
Salem State Coll (MA)
Samford U (AL)
Sam Houston State U (TX)
San Diego State U (CA)
San Francisco State U (CA)
San Jose State U (CA)
Savannah State U (GA)
Schreiner U (TX)
Seattle U (WA)
Seton Hill U (PA)
Shaw U (NC)
Simpson Coll (IA)
Slippery Rock U of Pennsylvania (PA)
Southeastern U (FL)
Southern Adventist U (TN)
Southern New Hampshire U (NH)
Southwestern Adventist U (TX)
Spring Hill Coll (AL)
State U of New York at Binghamton (NY)
State U of New York at New Paltz (NY)
State U of New York at Plattsburgh (NY)
Stephen F. Austin State U (TX)
Stetson U (FL)
Stonehill Coll (MA)
Strayer U—Akron Campus (OH)
Strayer U—Alexandria Campus (VA)
Strayer U—Allentown Campus (PA)
Strayer U—Anne Arundel Campus (MD)
Strayer U—Arlington Campus (VA)
Strayer U—Augusta Campus (GA)
Strayer U—Baymeadows Campus (FL)
Strayer U—Birmingham Campus (AL)
Strayer U—Brickell Campus (FL)
Strayer U—Center City Campus (PA)
Strayer U—Central Austin Campus (TX)
Strayer U—Chamblee Campus (GA)
Strayer U—Charleston Campus (SC)
Strayer U—Chesapeake Campus (VA)
Strayer U—Chesterfield Campus (VA)
Strayer U—Christiana Campus (DE)
Strayer U—Cobb County Campus (GA)

INTERNATIONAL ECONOMICS

INTERNATIONAL FINANCE

INTERNATIONAL/GLOBAL STUDIES

INTERNATIONAL MARKETING

INTERNATIONAL PUBLIC HEALTH

INTERNATIONAL RELATIONS AND AFFAIRS

INDEXES

Guilford Coll (NC)
Hamilton Coll (NY)
Hamline U (MN)
Hampden-Sydney Coll (VA)
Hampshire Coll (MA)
Hawai'i Pacific U (HI)
Heidelberg U (OH)
Hendrix Coll (AR)
High Point U (NC)
Hillsdale Coll (MI)
Hollins U (VA)
Holy Names U (CA)
Houghton Coll (NY)
Hult Intl Business School (United Kingdom)
Idaho State U (ID)
Illinois Coll (IL)
Illinois Wesleyan U (IL)
Immaculata U (PA)
Indiana U Bloomington (IN)
Indiana U of Pennsylvania (PA)
Indiana U–Purdue U Indianapolis (IN)
Indiana U Southeast (IN)
Iowa State U of Science and Technology (IA)
Jacksonville U (FL)
James Madison U (VA)
John Brown U (AR)
John Cabot U (Italy)
John Carroll U (OH)
The Johns Hopkins U (MD)
Juniata Coll (PA)
Kennesaw State U (GA)
Kent State U (OH)
Kenyon Coll (OH)
Knox Coll (IL)
Lafayette Coll (PA)
Lake Forest Coll (IL)
La Roche Coll (PA)
Lawrence U (WI)
Lees-McRae Coll (NC)
Lee U (TN)
Lehigh U (PA)
Lewis & Clark Coll (OR)
Lincoln U (PA)
Lindenwood U (MO)
Lock Haven U of Pennsylvania (PA)
Long Island U, C.W. Post Campus (NY)
Longwood U (VA)
Loras Coll (IA)
Loyola U Chicago (IL)
Lynchburg Coll (VA)
Lynn U (FL)
Manhattan Coll (NY)
Manhattanville Coll (NY)
Mansfield U of Pennsylvania (PA)
Marlboro Coll (VT)
Marshall U (WV)
Mars Hill Coll (NC)
Mary Baldwin Coll (VA)
Marymount Manhattan Coll (NY)
Maryville Coll (TN)
McKendree U (IL)
Mercer U (GA)
Meredith Coll (NC)
Methodist U (NC)
Miami U (OH)
Michigan State U (MI)
Middlebury Coll (VT)
Middle Tennessee State U (TN)
Millikin U (IL)
Mills Coll (CA)
Minnesota State U Mankato (MN)
Missouri Southern State U (MO)
Morehouse Coll (GA)
Morningside Coll (IA)
Mount Allison U (NB, Canada)
Mount Holyoke Coll (MA)
Mount Mary Coll (WI)
Mount Mercy Coll (IA)
Mount St. Mary's U (MD)
Muhlenberg Coll (PA)
Murray State U (KY)
Nazareth Coll of Rochester (NY)
New York U (NY)
Niagara U (NY)
Northeastern U (MA)
Northern Arizona U (AZ)
Northern Kentucky U (KY)
Northern Michigan U (MI)
Northwest Nazarene U (ID)
Nova Southeastern U (FL)
Oakland U (MI)
Occidental Coll (CA)
Oglethorpe U (GA)
Ohio Northern U (OH)
The Ohio State U (OH)
Ohio U (OH)
Ohio Wesleyan U (OH)
Oklahoma Baptist U (OK)
Old Dominion U (VA)
Oral Roberts U (OK)
Oregon State U (OR)
Penn State Abington (PA)
Penn State Altoona (PA)
Penn State Beaver (PA)
Penn State Berks (PA)
Penn State Brandywine (PA)
Penn State DuBois (PA)
Penn State Erie, The Behrend Coll (PA)
Penn State Fayette, The Eberly Campus (PA)
Penn State Greater Allegheny (PA)
Penn State Hazleton (PA)
Penn State Lehigh Valley (PA)
Penn State Mont Alto (PA)
Penn State New Kensington (PA)
Penn State Schuylkill (PA)
Penn State Shenango (PA)
Penn State U Park (PA)
Penn State Wilkes-Barre (PA)
Penn State Worthington Scranton (PA)
Penn State York (PA)
Pepperdine U, Malibu (CA)
Pitzer Coll (CA)
Pomona Coll (CA)
Portland State U (OR)
Queens U of Charlotte (NC)
Quinnipiac U (CT)
Randolph Coll (VA)
Redeemer U Coll (ON, Canada)
Reed Coll (OR)
Regis Coll (MA)
Rhodes Coll (TN)
Rider U (NJ)
Roanoke Coll (VA)
Rochester Inst of Technology (NY)
Rockhurst U (MO)
Rollins Coll (FL)
Roosevelt U (IL)
Saginaw Valley State U (MI)
Saint Anselm Coll (NH)
St. Catherine U (MN)
St. Cloud State U (MN)
Saint Francis U (PA)
St. John Fisher Coll (NY)
Saint Joseph's U (PA)
Saint Leo U (FL)
Saint Louis U (MO)
Saint Mary's Coll of California (CA)
St. Mary's U (TX)
St. Norbert Coll (WI)
Saint Xavier U (IL)
Salem Coll (NC)
Samford U (AL)
San Diego State U (CA)
San Francisco State U (CA)
Sarah Lawrence Coll (NY)
Scripps Coll (CA)
Seattle U (WA)
Seton Hall U (NJ)
Seton Hill U (PA)
Sewanee: The U of the South (TN)
Shawnee State U (OH)
Shaw U (NC)
Simmons Coll (MA)
Simpson Coll (IA)
Skidmore Coll (NY)
Sonoma State U (CA)
Southern Methodist U (TX)
Southern Oregon U (OR)
Southern Polytechnic State U (GA)
Southwestern Adventist U (TX)
Southwestern U (TX)
Spring Hill Coll (AL)
Stanford U (CA)
State U of New York at Binghamton (NY)
State U of New York at New Paltz (NY)
State U of New York at Oswego (NY)
State U of New York Coll at Cortland (NY)
State U of New York Coll at Geneseo (NY)
State U of New York Coll at Oneonta (NY)
Stetson U (FL)
Stonehill Coll (MA)
Susquehanna U (PA)
Sweet Briar Coll (VA)
Syracuse U (NY)
Tabor Coll (KS)
Taylor U (IN)
Texas Christian U (TX)
Texas Lutheran U (TX)
Texas State U–San Marcos (TX)
Texas Wesleyan U (TX)
Tiffin U (OH)
Towson U (MD)
Trent U (ON, Canada)
Trinity Coll (CT)
Tufts U (MA)
Tulane U (LA)
Union Coll (NE)
United States Military Acad (NY)
Universidad de las Américas–Puebla (Mexico)
The U of Akron (OH)
The U of Alabama (AL)
U of Alberta (AB, Canada)
U of Arkansas (AR)
U of Arkansas at Little Rock (AR)
U of Bridgeport (CT)
The U of British Columbia (BC, Canada)
The U of British Columbia–Okanagan (BC, Canada)
U of California, Davis (CA)
U of Cincinnati (OH)
U of Dayton (OH)
U of Delaware (DE)
U of Denver (CO)
U of Evansville (IN)
U of Georgia (GA)
U of Hartford (CT)
U of Idaho (ID)
U of Indianapolis (IN)
U of La Verne (CA)
U of Maine (ME)
U of Maine at Presque Isle (ME)
U of Mary Washington (VA)
U of Memphis (TN)
U of Miami (FL)
U of Minnesota, Duluth (MN)
U of Minnesota, Twin Cities Campus (MN)
U of Mississippi (MS)
U of Mount Union (OH)
U of Nebraska at Kearney (NE)
U of Nebraska–Lincoln (NE)
U of Nevada, Reno (NV)
U of New Brunswick Fredericton (NB, Canada)
U of Ottawa (ON, Canada)
U of Pennsylvania (PA)
U of Redlands (CA)
U of Richmond (VA)
U of Rochester (NY)
U of St. Thomas (MN)
U of St. Thomas (TX)
U of San Diego (CA)
U of Saskatchewan (SK, Canada)
The U of Scranton (PA)
U of South Carolina (SC)
U of Southern California (CA)
U of Southern Indiana (IN)
U of Southern Maine (ME)
U of Southern Mississippi (MS)
U of South Florida (FL)
The U of Tennessee at Martin (TN)
U of the Incarnate Word (TX)
U of the Pacific (CA)
The U of Toledo (OH)
U of Toronto (ON, Canada)
U of Virginia (VA)
U of Washington (WA)
U of Washington, Tacoma (WA)
U of Waterloo (ON, Canada)
The U of Western Ontario (ON, Canada)
U of West Florida (FL)
U of West Georgia (GA)
U of Windsor (ON, Canada)
U of Wisconsin–Madison (WI)
U of Wisconsin–Milwaukee (WI)
U of Wisconsin–Oshkosh (WI)
U of Wisconsin–Parkside (WI)
U of Wisconsin–Platteville (WI)
U of Wisconsin–Stevens Point (WI)
U of Wisconsin–Superior (WI)
U of Wisconsin–Whitewater (WI)
U of Wyoming (WY)
Ursinus Coll (PA)
Utica Coll (NY)
Valparaiso U (IN)
Vassar Coll (NY)
Virginia Military Inst (VA)
Virginia Polytechnic Inst and State U (VA)
Virginia Wesleyan Coll (VA)
Wagner Coll (NY)
Walsh U (OH)
Wartburg Coll (IA)
Washington Coll (MD)
Washington U in St. Louis (MO)
Webster U (MO)
Wellesley Coll (MA)
Wells Coll (NY)
Wesleyan Coll (GA)
Western Oregon U (OR)
Westminster Coll (MO)
West Virginia U (WV)
West Virginia Wesleyan Coll (WV)
Wheaton Coll (IL)
Wheaton Coll (MA)
Wheeling Jesuit U (WV)
Whittier Coll (CA)
Widener U (PA)
Wilkes U (PA)
William Jewell Coll (MO)
Wilson Coll (PA)
Wittenberg U (OH)
Wofford Coll (SC)
Wright State U (OH)
Xavier U (OH)
York Coll of Pennsylvania (PA)
York U (ON, Canada)

INVESTMENTS AND SECURITIES

Babson Coll (MA)
Bernard M. Baruch Coll of the City U of New York (NY)
Duquesne U (PA)
U of Nebraska at Omaha (NE)

IRANIAN/PERSIAN LANGUAGES

U of Maryland, Coll Park (MD)
U of Utah (UT)

ISLAMIC STUDIES

DePaul U (IL)
The Ohio State U (OH)
Swarthmore Coll (PA)
The U of Texas at Austin (TX)
The U of Western Ontario (ON, Canada)
Washington U in St. Louis (MO)
Wellesley Coll (MA)

ITALIAN

Arizona State U (AZ)
Assumption Coll (MA)
Bard Coll (NY)
Barnard Coll (NY)
Bennington Coll (VT)
Bishop's U (QC, Canada)
Boston Coll (MA)
Boston U (MA)
Brock U (ON, Canada)
Brooklyn Coll of the City U of New York (NY)
Bryn Mawr Coll (PA)
California State U, Long Beach (CA)
Central Connecticut State U (CT)
Claremont McKenna Coll (CA)
Coll of the Holy Cross (MA)
The Colorado Coll (CO)
Columbia U (NY)
Columbia U, School of General Studies (NY)
Concordia U (QC, Canada)
Connecticut Coll (CT)
Cornell U (NY)
Dartmouth Coll (NH)
DePaul U (IL)
Dominican U (IL)
Duke U (NC)
Emory U (GA)
Fairfield U (CT)
Florida Intl U (FL)
Fordham U (NY)
Georgetown U (DC)
Gettysburg Coll (PA)
Gonzaga U (WA)
Haverford Coll (PA)
Hofstra U (NY)
Hunter Coll of the City U of New York (NY)
Indiana U Bloomington (IN)
Iona Coll (NY)
Ithaca Coll (NY)
The Johns Hopkins U (MD)
Lake Erie Coll (OH)
La Salle U (PA)
Laurentian U (ON, Canada)
Lehman Coll of the City U of New York (NY)
Long Island U, C.W. Post Campus (NY)
Loyola U Chicago (IL)
Marlboro Coll (VT)
Middlebury Coll (VT)
Montclair State U (NJ)
Mount Holyoke Coll (MA)
Nazareth Coll of Rochester (NY)
New York U (NY)
Northeastern U (MA)
The Ohio State U (OH)
Penn State Abington (PA)
Penn State Altoona (PA)
Penn State Beaver (PA)
Penn State Berks (PA)
Penn State Brandywine (PA)
Penn State DuBois (PA)
Penn State Erie, The Behrend Coll (PA)
Penn State Fayette, The Eberly Campus (PA)
Penn State Greater Allegheny (PA)
Penn State Hazleton (PA)
Penn State Lehigh Valley (PA)
Penn State Mont Alto (PA)
Penn State New Kensington (PA)
Penn State Schuylkill (PA)
Penn State Shenango (PA)
Penn State U Park (PA)
Penn State Wilkes-Barre (PA)
Penn State Worthington Scranton (PA)
Penn State York (PA)
Providence Coll (RI)
Queens Coll of the City U of New York (NY)
Rosemont Coll (PA)
Rutgers, The State U of New Jersey, Newark (NJ)
Rutgers, The State U of New Jersey, New Brunswick (NJ)
St. John's U (NY)
Saint Joseph's U (PA)
Saint Louis U (MO)
Saint Mary's Coll (IN)
Saint Mary's Coll of California (CA)
San Francisco State U (CA)
Santa Clara U (CA)
Sarah Lawrence Coll (NY)
Scripps Coll (CA)
Seton Hall U (NJ)
Smith Coll (MA)
Southern Connecticut State U (CT)
Southern Methodist U (TX)
Stanford U (CA)
State U of New York at Binghamton (NY)
Stony Brook U, State U of New York (NY)
Syracuse U (NY)
Temple U (PA)
Trinity Coll (CT)
Tulane U (LA)
U at Albany, State U of New York (NY)
U at Buffalo, the State U of New York (NY)
U of Alberta (AB, Canada)
The U of Arizona (AZ)
The U of British Columbia (BC, Canada)
U of California, Berkeley (CA)
U of California, Davis (CA)
U of California, Los Angeles (CA)
U of California, San Diego (CA)
U of California, Santa Barbara (CA)
U of Chicago (IL)
U of Colorado at Boulder (CO)
U of Connecticut (CT)
U of Delaware (DE)
U of Denver (CO)
U of Georgia (GA)
U of Houston (TX)
U of Illinois at Chicago (IL)
U of Illinois at Urbana–Champaign (IL)
The U of Iowa (IA)
U of Maryland, Coll Park (MD)
U of Massachusetts Amherst (MA)
U of Massachusetts Boston (MA)
U of Michigan (MI)
U of Minnesota, Twin Cities Campus (MN)
U of Notre Dame (IN)
U of Oklahoma (OK)
U of Oregon (OR)
U of Ottawa (ON, Canada)
U of Pennsylvania (PA)
U of Pittsburgh (PA)
U of Rhode Island (RI)
The U of Scranton (PA)
U of South Carolina (SC)
U of Southern California (CA)
U of South Florida (FL)
The U of Tennessee (TN)
The U of Texas at Austin (TX)
U of Toronto (ON, Canada)
U of Virginia (VA)
U of Washington (WA)
The U of Western Ontario (ON, Canada)
U of Windsor (ON, Canada)
U of Wisconsin–Madison (WI)
U of Wisconsin–Milwaukee (WI)
Vassar Coll (NY)
Villanova U (PA)
Washington U in St. Louis (MO)
Wellesley Coll (MA)
Wesleyan U (CT)
Yale U (CT)
York Coll of the City U of New York (NY)
York U (ON, Canada)
Youngstown State U (OH)

ITALIAN STUDIES

Arcadia U (PA)
Assumption Coll (MA)
Brock U (ON, Canada)
Coll of the Holy Cross (MA)
The Colorado Coll (CO)
Columbia U (NY)
Columbia U, School of General Studies (NY)
Dickinson Coll (PA)
Fordham U (NY)
John Cabot U (Italy)
Miami U (OH)
Sweet Briar Coll (VA)
Tulane U (LA)
U of California, Santa Cruz (CA)
U of Richmond (VA)
U of Vermont (VT)

U of Windsor (ON, Canada)
Vanderbilt U (TN)
Wellesley Coll (MA)
Wheaton Coll (MA)
York U (ON, Canada)

JAPANESE
Aquinas Coll (MI)
Augustana Coll (IL)
Ball State U (IN)
Bates Coll (ME)
Bennington Coll (VT)
California State U, Fullerton (CA)
California State U, Long Beach (CA)
California State U, Los Angeles (CA)
Calvin Coll (MI)
Carnegie Mellon U (PA)
Claremont McKenna Coll (CA)
Colgate U (NY)
Connecticut Coll (CT)
Dartmouth Coll (NH)
Eastern Michigan U (MI)
Elizabethtown Coll (PA)
Emory U (GA)
Georgetown U (DC)
Gettysburg Coll (PA)
Gustavus Adolphus Coll (MN)
Lawrence U (WI)
Lincoln U (PA)
Linfield Coll (OR)
Macalester Coll (MN)
Michigan State U (MI)
Middlebury Coll (VT)
North Central Coll (IL)
Oakland U (MI)
The Ohio State U (OH)
Penn State Abington (PA)
Penn State Altoona (PA)
Penn State Beaver (PA)
Penn State Berks (PA)
Penn State Brandywine (PA)
Penn State DuBois (PA)
Penn State Erie, The Behrend Coll (PA)
Penn State Fayette, The Eberly Campus (PA)
Penn State Greater Allegheny (PA)
Penn State Hazleton (PA)
Penn State Lehigh Valley (PA)
Penn State Mont Alto (PA)
Penn State New Kensington (PA)
Penn State Schuylkill (PA)
Penn State Shenango (PA)
Penn State U Park (PA)
Penn State Wilkes-Barre (PA)
Penn State Worthington Scranton (PA)
Penn State York (PA)
Pomona Coll (CA)
Portland State U (OR)
San Diego State U (CA)
San Francisco State U (CA)
San Jose State U (CA)
Sarah Lawrence Coll (NY)
Scripps Coll (CA)
Stanford U (CA)
Swarthmore Coll (PA)
Trinity Coll (CT)
U of Alaska Fairbanks (AK)
U of Alberta (AB, Canada)
U of California, Berkeley (CA)
U of California, Davis (CA)
U of California, Irvine (CA)
U of California, Los Angeles (CA)
U of California, San Diego (CA)
U of California, Santa Barbara (CA)
U of Chicago (IL)
U of Colorado at Boulder (CO)
The U of Findlay (OH)
U of Georgia (GA)
U of Hawaii at Hilo (HI)
U of Hawaii at Manoa (HI)
The U of Iowa (IA)
U of Maryland, Coll Park (MD)
U of Massachusetts Amherst (MA)
U of Minnesota, Twin Cities Campus (MN)
U of Mount Union (OH)
U of Notre Dame (IN)
U of Oregon (OR)
U of Pittsburgh (PA)
U of Puget Sound (WA)
U of Regina (SK, Canada)
U of Rochester (NY)
U of St. Thomas (MN)
U of the Pacific (CA)
U of Utah (UT)
U of Vermont (VT)
U of Washington (WA)
The U of Western Ontario (ON, Canada)
U of Wisconsin–Madison (WI)
Vassar Coll (NY)
Wake Forest U (NC)
Washington U in St. Louis (MO)
Wellesley Coll (MA)
Western Washington U (WA)
Williams Coll (MA)
Yale U (CT)
York U (ON, Canada)

JAPANESE STUDIES
Case Western Reserve U (OH)
Claremont McKenna Coll (CA)
Earlham Coll (IN)
Gettysburg Coll (PA)
Gustavus Adolphus Coll (MN)
Hope Coll (MI)
U at Albany, State U of New York (NY)
U of San Francisco (CA)
Willamette U (OR)

JAZZ/JAZZ STUDIES
Augustana Coll (IL)
Bard Coll (NY)
Bennington Coll (VT)
Berklee Coll of Music (MA)
Bowling Green State U (OH)
Brigham Young U (UT)
Capital U (OH)
Central State U (OH)
City Coll of the City U of New York (NY)
Concordia U (QC, Canada)
Cornish Coll of the Arts (WA)
DePaul U (IL)
Drake U (IA)
Five Towns Coll (NY)
Florida Ag and Mech U (FL)
Florida State U (FL)
Hampton U (VA)
Hofstra U (NY)
Hope Coll (MI)
Ithaca Coll (NY)
Johnson State Coll (VT).
Lamar U (TX)
Limestone Coll (SC)
Long Island U, Brooklyn Campus (NY)
Loyola U New Orleans (LA)
Manhattan School of Music (NY)
Michigan State U (MI)
New England Conservatory of Music (MA)
The New School for Jazz and Contemporary Music (NY)
North Carolina Central U (NC)
North Central Coll (IL)
Oberlin Coll (OH)
The Ohio State U (OH)
Peabody Conservatory of The Johns Hopkins U (MD)
Roosevelt U (IL)
Rutgers, The State U of New Jersey, New Brunswick (NJ)
St. Cloud State U (MN)
St. Francis Xavier U (NS, Canada)
Sarah Lawrence Coll (NY)
Temple U (PA)
Texas State U–San Marcos (TX)
The U of Akron (OH)
U of Cincinnati (OH)
U of Hartford (CT)
U of Illinois at Urbana–Champaign (IL)
The U of Iowa (IA)
U of Miami (FL)
U of Michigan (MI)
U of Minnesota, Duluth (MN)
U of Nevada, Las Vegas (NV)
The U of North Carolina at Greensboro (NC)
U of North Florida (FL)
U of North Texas (TX)
U of Oregon (OR)
U of Rochester (NY)
U of Southern California (CA)
The U of Texas at Austin (TX)
Virginia Union U (VA)
Western Michigan U (MI)
William Paterson U of New Jersey (NJ)

JEWISH/JUDAIC STUDIES
American Jewish U (CA)
American U (DC)
Bard Coll (NY)
Barnard Coll (NY)
Bennington Coll (VT)
Brooklyn Coll of the City U of New York (NY)
California State U, Chico (CA)
City Coll of the City U of New York (NY)
Clark U (MA)
Concordia U (QC, Canada)
DePaul U (IL)
Dickinson Coll (PA)
Emory U (GA)
Eugene Lang Coll The New School for Liberal Arts (NY)
Florida Atlantic U (FL)
The George Washington U (DC)
Hebrew Coll (MA)
Hofstra U (NY)
Hunter Coll of the City U of New York (NY)
Indiana U Bloomington (IN)
Laura and Alvin Siegal Coll of Judaic Studies (OH)
Lehman Coll of the City U of New York (NY)
Northeastern U (MA)
Oberlin Coll (OH)
The Ohio State U (OH)
Penn State Abington (PA)
Penn State Altoona (PA)
Penn State Beaver (PA)
Penn State Berks (PA)
Penn State Brandywine (PA)
Penn State DuBois (PA)
Penn State Erie, The Behrend Coll (PA)
Penn State Fayette, The Eberly Campus (PA)
Penn State Greater Allegheny (PA)
Penn State Hazleton (PA)
Penn State Lehigh Valley (PA)
Penn State Mont Alto (PA)
Penn State New Kensington (PA)
Penn State Schuylkill (PA)
Penn State Shenango (PA)
Penn State U Park (PA)
Penn State Wilkes-Barre (PA)
Penn State Worthington Scranton (PA)
Penn State York (PA)
Piedmont Baptist Coll and Graduate School (NC)
Queens Coll of the City U of New York (NY)
Rutgers, The State U of New Jersey, New Brunswick (NJ)
San Diego State U (CA)
San Francisco State U (CA)
Scripps Coll (CA)
State U of New York at Binghamton (NY)
Temple U (PA)
Trinity Coll (CT)
Tufts U (MA)
Tulane U (LA)
U at Albany, State U of New York (NY)
The U of Arizona (AZ)
U of California, Los Angeles (CA)
U of California, San Diego (CA)
U of Chicago (IL)
U of Cincinnati (OH)
U of Florida (FL)
U of Hartford (CT)
U of Manitoba (MB, Canada)
U of Maryland, Coll Park (MD)
U of Massachusetts Amherst (MA)
U of Miami (FL)
U of Michigan (MI)
U of Minnesota, Twin Cities Campus (MN)
U of Oklahoma (OK)
U of Oregon (OR)
U of Pennsylvania (PA)
U of Southern California (CA)
The U of Texas at Austin (TX)
U of Washington (WA)
The U of Western Ontario (ON, Canada)
Vanderbilt U (TN)
Vassar Coll (NY)
Washington U in St. Louis (MO)
Wellesley Coll (MA)
Yale U (CT)
Yeshiva U (NY)
York U (ON, Canada)

JOURNALISM
Abilene Christian U (TX)
Alabama State U (AL)
Allegheny Coll (PA)
American U (DC)
Andrews U (MI)
Angelo State U (TX)
Appalachian State U (NC)
Arkansas State U—Jonesboro (AR)
Arkansas Tech U (AR)
Asbury U (KY)
Ashland U (OH)
Auburn U (AL)
Augustana Coll (SD)
Averett U (VA)
Ball State U (IN)
Barry U (FL)
Baylor U (TX)
Belmont U (TN)
Bemidji State U (MN)
Bennington Coll (VT)
Bernard M. Baruch Coll of the City U of New York (NY)
Bethel U (MN)
Boston U (MA)
Bowling Green State U (OH)
Bradley U (IL)
Brigham Young U (UT)
Brooklyn Coll of the City U of New York (NY)
Buffalo State Coll, State U of New York (NY)
Butler U (IN)
California Baptist U (CA)
California Lutheran U (CA)
California Polytechnic State U, San Luis Obispo (CA)
California State U, Chico (CA)
California State U, Dominguez Hills (CA)
California State U, East Bay (CA)
California State U, Fresno (CA)
California State U, Fullerton (CA)
California State U, Long Beach (CA)
California State U, Northridge (CA)
California State U, Sacramento (CA)
Campbellsville U (KY)
Carroll U (WI)
Carson-Newman Coll (TN)
Castleton State Coll (VT)
Cedarville U (OH)
Central Connecticut State U (CT)
Central Michigan U (MI)
Central State U (OH)
Chatham U (PA)
Cincinnati Christian U (OH)
The Coll at Brockport, State U of New York (NY)
The Coll of St. Scholastica (MN)
Coll of the Ozarks (MO)
Colorado State U (CO)
Columbia Coll (SC)
Columbia Coll Chicago (IL)
Concordia Coll (MN)
Concordia U (QC, Canada)
Corban U (OR)
Creighton U (NE)
Curry Coll (MA)
Dana Coll (NE)
Delaware State U (DE)
Delta State U (MS)
DePaul U (IL)
Doane Coll (NE)
Dominican U (IL)
Dordt Coll (IA)
Drake U (IA)
Duquesne U (PA)
Eastern Illinois U (IL)
Eastern Nazarene Coll (MA)
Eastern Washington U (WA)
Edinboro U of Pennsylvania (PA)
Edward Waters Coll (FL)
Elon U (NC)
Emerson Coll (MA)
Emory U (GA)
Florida Ag and Mech U (FL)
Florida Southern Coll (FL)
Fordham U (NY)
Fort Hays State U (KS)
Franklin Coll (IN)
Franklin Pierce U (NH)
Gannon U (PA)
Gardner-Webb U (NC)
George Fox U (OR)
The George Washington U (DC)
Georgia Coll & State U (GA)
Georgia Southern U (GA)
Georgia State U (GA)
Gettysburg Coll (PA)
Gonzaga U (WA)
Goshen Coll (IN)
Grace Coll (IN)
Grand Valley State U (MI)
Grand View U (IA)
Hampton U (VA)
Hawai'i Pacific U (HI)
Henderson State U (AR)
Hofstra U (NY)
Humboldt State U (CA)
Huntington U (IN)
Illinois Inst of Technology (IL)
Illinois State U (IL)
Indiana U Bloomington (IN)
Indiana U of Pennsylvania (PA)
Indiana U–Purdue U Indianapolis (IN)
Indiana U Southeast (IN)
Inter American U of Puerto Rico, Ponce Campus (PR)
Iona Coll (NY)
Iowa State U of Science and Technology (IA)
Ithaca Coll (NY)
John Brown U (AR)
Johnson State Coll (VT)
Kansas State U (KS)
Keene State Coll (NH)
Kent State U (OH)
Keystone Coll (PA)
Kwantlen Polytechnic U (BC, Canada)
Lamar U (TX)
La Salle U (PA)
Lasell Coll (MA)
Lehigh U (PA)
Lewis U (IL)
Liberty U (VA)
Lincoln U (MO)
Lincoln U (PA)
Lindenwood U (MO)
Lipscomb U (TN)
Lock Haven U of Pennsylvania (PA)
Long Island U, Brooklyn Campus (NY)
Long Island U, C.W. Post Campus (NY)
Longwood U (VA)
Loras Coll (IA)
Louisiana Coll (LA)
Louisiana Tech U (LA)
Loyola U Chicago (IL)
Madonna U (MI)
Mansfield U of Pennsylvania (PA)
Marietta Coll (OH)
Marist Coll (NY)
Marquette U (WI)
Marshall U (WV)
Mercer U (GA)
Messiah Coll (PA)
Metropolitan State Coll of Denver (CO)
Miami U (OH)
Miami U Hamilton (OH)
Michigan State U (MI)
Minnesota State U Mankato (MN)
Minnesota State U Moorhead (MN)
Mississippi Coll (MS)
Missouri State U (MO)
Mount Mercy Coll (IA)
Mount Vernon Nazarene U (OH)
Multnomah U (OR)
Murray State U (KY)
New England Coll (NH)
New Mexico State U (NM)
New York U (NY)
Norfolk State U (VA)
North Central Coll (IL)
Northeastern State U (OK)
Northeastern U (MA)
Northern Arizona U (AZ)
Northern Kentucky U (KY)
North Greenville U (SC)
Northwestern Coll (IA)
Northwestern Coll (MN)
Northwestern State U of Louisiana (LA)
Northwest Missouri State U (MO)
Northwest Nazarene U (ID)
Oakland U (MI)
Ohio Northern U (OH)
The Ohio State U (OH)
Ohio U (OH)
Ohio Wesleyan U (OH)
Oklahoma Baptist U (OK)
Oklahoma Christian U (OK)
Oklahoma City U (OK)
Oklahoma State U (OK)
Old Dominion U (VA)
Pacific Union Coll (CA)
Paine Coll (GA)
Patrick Henry Coll (VA)
Penn State Abington (PA)
Penn State Altoona (PA)
Penn State Beaver (PA)
Penn State Berks (PA)
Penn State Brandywine (PA)
Penn State DuBois (PA)
Penn State Erie, The Behrend Coll (PA)
Penn State Fayette, The Eberly Campus (PA)
Penn State Greater Allegheny (PA)
Penn State Hazleton (PA)
Penn State Lehigh Valley (PA)
Penn State Mont Alto (PA)
Penn State New Kensington (PA)
Penn State Schuylkill (PA)
Penn State Shenango (PA)
Penn State U Park (PA)
Penn State Wilkes-Barre (PA)
Penn State Worthington Scranton (PA)
Penn State York (PA)
Pepperdine U, Malibu (CA)
Pittsburg State U (KS)
Point Park U (PA)
Prescott Coll (AZ)
Purchase Coll, State U of New York (NY)
Queens U of Charlotte (NC)
Quinnipiac U (CT)
Radford U (VA)
Regent U (VA)
Rider U (NJ)
Rochester Inst of Technology (NY)
Roosevelt U (IL)
Rowan U (NJ)
Rutgers, The State U of New Jersey, Newark (NJ)
Rutgers, The State U of New Jersey, New Brunswick (NJ)
St. Ambrose U (IA)
Saint Augustine's Coll (NC)

St. Bonaventure U (NY)
St. Catherine U (MN)
St. Cloud State U (MN)
Saint Francis U (PA)
St. John's U (NY)
Saint Mary-of-the-Woods Coll (IN)
Saint Mary's U of Minnesota (MN)
Saint Michael's Coll (VT)
St. Thomas Aquinas Coll (NY)
St. Thomas U (NB, Canada)
Salem State Coll (MA)
Samford U (AL)
San Diego State U (CA)
San Francisco State U (CA)
San Jose State U (CA)
Seattle U (WA)
Seton Hill U (PA)
Shippensburg U of Pennsylvania (PA)
Slippery Rock U of Pennsylvania (PA)
South Dakota State U (SD)
Southeastern U (FL)
Southern Adventist U (TN)
Southern Arkansas U–Magnolia (AR)
Southern Connecticut State U (CT)
Southern Illinois U Carbondale (IL)
Southern Methodist U (TX)
Southwestern Adventist U (TX)
Spring Hill Coll (AL)
State U of New York at New Paltz (NY)
State U of New York at Oswego (NY)
State U of New York at Plattsburgh (NY)
Stephen F. Austin State U (TX)
Stillman Coll (AL)
Stony Brook U, State U of New York (NY)
Suffolk U (MA)
Susquehanna U (PA)
Syracuse U (NY)
Tabor Coll (KS)
Talladega Coll (AL)
Temple U (PA)
Tennessee Technological U (TN)
Texas A&M U–Commerce (TX)
Texas Christian U (TX)
Texas Southern U (TX)
Texas State U–San Marcos (TX)
Texas Tech U (TX)
Texas Wesleyan U (TX)
Thomas Edison State Coll (NJ)
Thompson Rivers U (BC, Canada)
Tiffin U (OH)
Troy U (AL)
Truman State U (MO)
Union Coll (NE)
Union U (TN)
U at Albany, State U of New York (NY)
The U of Alabama (AL)
U of Alaska Anchorage (AK)
U of Alaska Fairbanks (AK)
The U of Arizona (AZ)
U of Arkansas (AR)
U of Arkansas at Little Rock (AR)
U of Baltimore (MD)
U of Bridgeport (CT)
U of California, Irvine (CA)
U of Central Florida (FL)
U of Central Missouri (MO)
U of Central Oklahoma (OK)
U of Colorado at Boulder (CO)
U of Connecticut (CT)
U of Dayton (OH)
U of Delaware (DE)
U of Denver (CO)
The U of Findlay (OH)
U of Florida (FL)
U of Georgia (GA)
U of Hawaii at Manoa (HI)
U of Houston (TX)
U of Idaho (ID)
U of Illinois at Urbana–Champaign (IL)
The U of Iowa (IA)
The U of Kansas (KS)
U of Kentucky (KY)
U of King's Coll (NS, Canada)
U of La Verne (CA)
U of Maine (ME)
U of Maryland, Coll Park (MD)
U of Massachusetts Amherst (MA)
U of Memphis (TN)
U of Miami (FL)
U of Michigan–Flint (MI)
U of Minnesota, Twin Cities Campus (MN)
U of Mississippi (MS)
U of Missouri (MO)
U of Nebraska at Kearney (NE)
U of Nebraska at Omaha (NE)
U of Nevada, Reno (NV)
U of New Mexico (NM)
U of Northern Colorado (CO)
U of North Texas (TX)
U of Oklahoma (OK)
U of Oregon (OR)
U of Ottawa (ON, Canada)
U of Pittsburgh at Greensburg (PA)
U of Pittsburgh at Johnstown (PA)
U of Portland (OR)
U of Puerto Rico, Río Piedras (PR)
U of Regina (SK, Canada)
U of Rhode Island (RI)
U of Richmond (VA)
U of St. Thomas (MN)
U of South Carolina (SC)
U of Southern California (CA)
U of Southern Indiana (IN)
U of Southern Mississippi (MS)
The U of Tennessee (TN)
The U of Texas at Arlington (TX)
The U of Texas at Austin (TX)
The U of Texas at El Paso (TX)
The U of Texas at Tyler (TX)
The U of Texas–Pan American (TX)
U of the Incarnate Word (TX)
The U of Toledo (OH)
U of West Georgia (GA)
U of Wisconsin–Eau Claire (WI)
U of Wisconsin–Madison (WI)
U of Wisconsin–Milwaukee (WI)
U of Wisconsin–Oshkosh (WI)
U of Wisconsin–River Falls (WI)
U of Wisconsin–Superior (WI)
U of Wisconsin–Whitewater (WI)
U of Wyoming (WY)
Utah State U (UT)
Utica Coll (NY)
Valparaiso U (IN)
Virginia Union U (VA)
Waldorf Coll (IA)
Wartburg Coll (IA)
Washington Adventist U (MD)
Washington and Lee U (VA)
Washington State U (WA)
Waynesburg U (PA)
Wayne State U (MI)
Weber State U (UT)
Webster U (MO)
Western Illinois U (IL)
Western Kentucky U (KY)
Western Michigan U (MI)
Western New England Coll (MA)
Western Washington U (WA)
West Virginia U (WV)
Wheeling Jesuit U (WV)
Wilfrid Laurier U (ON, Canada)
William Penn U (IA)
Winona State U (MN)
Youngstown State U (OH)

JOURNALISM RELATED

Arizona State U (AZ)
Benedictine U (IL)
Bob Jones U (SC)
Boston U (MA)
Bowling Green State U (OH)
California State U, Long Beach (CA)
Central Michigan U (MI)
Champlain Coll (VT)
Columbia Coll (SC)
Dana Coll (NE)
Kent State U (OH)
Kentucky State U (KY)
Roosevelt U (IL)
Southern Adventist U (TN)
The U of Akron (OH)
U of Nebraska–Lincoln (NE)
U of Oregon (OR)
U of St. Thomas (MN)
The U of Western Ontario (ON, Canada)
Western Washington U (WA)
Wilson Coll (PA)

JUVENILE CORRECTIONS

East Central U (OK)
Harris-Stowe State U (MO)

KINDERGARTEN/ PRESCHOOL EDUCATION

Alabama Ag and Mech U (AL)
Alabama State U (AL)
Albright Coll (PA)
Alma Coll (MI)
Alvernia U (PA)
American Intl Coll (MA)
Appalachian State U (NC)
Arcadia U (PA)
Armstrong Atlantic State U (GA)
Ashland U (OH)
Atlantic Union Coll (MA)
Augsburg Coll (MN)
Ball State U (IN)
Barry U (FL)
Baylor U (TX)
Bay Path Coll (MA)
Bethany U (CA)
Black Hills State U (SD)
Bluefield Coll (VA)
Bluffton U (OH)
Boise State U (ID)
Boston Coll (MA)
Boston U (MA)
Bowie State U (MD)
Bowling Green State U (OH)
Bowling Green State U–Firelands Coll (OH)
Bucknell U (PA)
Buffalo State Coll, State U of New York (NY)
Butler U (IN)
Cabrini Coll (PA)
California Polytechnic State U, San Luis Obispo (CA)
Carson-Newman Coll (TN)
Central Christian Coll of Kansas (KS)
Champlain Coll (VT)
Cheyney U of Pennsylvania (PA)
Cincinnati Christian U (OH)
Clarion U of Pennsylvania (PA)
The Coll of Saint Rose (NY)
Columbia Coll (SC)
Columbia Coll Chicago (IL)
Concordia U (QC, Canada)
Concordia U Chicago (IL)
Concordia U Wisconsin (WI)
Concord U (WV)
Converse Coll (SC)
Curry Coll (MA)
Dallas Baptist U (TX)
Dana Coll (NE)
Delaware State U (DE)
East Carolina U (NC)
East Central U (OK)
Eastern Connecticut State U (CT)
Eastern Illinois U (IL)
Eastern Mennonite U (VA)
Eastern Nazarene Coll (MA)
Eastern New Mexico U (NM)
Edinboro U of Pennsylvania (PA)
Edward Waters Coll (FL)
Elizabeth City State U (NC)
Elmhurst Coll (IL)
Erskine Coll (SC)
Evangel U (MO)
Faulkner U (AL)
Florida Ag and Mech U (FL)
Fontbonne U (MO)
Fort Hays State U (KS)
Fort Valley State U (GA)
Franklin Pierce U (NH)
Furman U (SC)
Gallaudet U (DC)
Glenville State Coll (WV)
Governors State U (IL)
Greensboro Coll (NC)
Grove City Coll (PA)
Hampton U (VA)
Harris-Stowe State U (MO)
High Point U (NC)
Hillsdale Coll (MI)
Holy Family U (PA)
Houston Baptist U (TX)
Humboldt State U (CA)
Hunter Coll of the City U of New York (NY)
Indiana U–Purdue U Indianapolis (IN)
Inter American U of Puerto Rico, Aguadilla Campus (PR)
Inter American U of Puerto Rico, Arecibo Campus (PR)
Inter American U of Puerto Rico, Guayama Campus (PR)
Inter American U of Puerto Rico, Ponce Campus (PR)
Inter American U of Puerto Rico, San Germán Campus (PR)
Iowa Wesleyan Coll (IA)
Jacksonville State U (AL)
Jarvis Christian Coll (TX)
John Brown U (AR)
John Carroll U (OH)
Kean U (NJ)
Kendall Coll (IL)
Kent State U (OH)
King Coll (TN)
Kutztown U of Pennsylvania (PA)
Lakeland Coll (WI)
Lamar U (TX)
Lasell Coll (MA)
Lesley U (MA)
Lincoln Christian U (IL)
Lincoln Memorial U (TN)
Lincoln U (PA)
Lindenwood U (MO)
Lock Haven U of Pennsylvania (PA)
Long Island U, C.W. Post Campus (NY)
Longwood U (VA)
Loras Coll (IA)
Louisiana Coll (LA)
Louisiana Tech U (LA)
Mansfield U of Pennsylvania (PA)
Maranatha Baptist Bible Coll (WI)
Marshall U (WV)
Mars Hill Coll (NC)
Martin Luther Coll (MN)
McPherson Coll (KS)
Methodist U (NC)
Michigan State U (MI)
Middle Tennessee State U (TN)
Minnesota State U Mankato (MN)
Minnesota State U Moorhead (MN)
Mississippi Valley State U (MS)
Missouri Baptist U (MO)
Morehead State U (KY)
Mount Mary Coll (WI)
Mount Vernon Nazarene U (OH)
Neumann U (PA)
Newberry Coll (SC)
New Jersey City U (NJ)
New Mexico Highlands U (NM)
Norfolk State U (VA)
North Carolina Central U (NC)
Northeastern Illinois U (IL)
Northern Kentucky U (KY)
North Georgia Coll & State U (GA)
Northwestern Oklahoma State U (OK)
Ohio Dominican U (OH)
Ohio Northern U (OH)
Ohio Wesleyan U (OH)
Oklahoma Baptist U (OK)
Oklahoma Christian U (OK)
Oklahoma City U (OK)
Our Lady of the Lake U of San Antonio (TX)
Pacific Union Coll (CA)
Peru State Coll (NE)
Philadelphia Biblical U (PA)
Piedmont Coll (GA)
Post U (CT)
Prescott Coll (AZ)
Rivier Coll (NH)
St. Catherine U (MN)
St. Cloud State U (MN)
Saint Mary-of-the-Woods Coll (IN)
St. Thomas Aquinas Coll (NY)
Saint Xavier U (IL)
Sarah Lawrence Coll (NY)
Seton Hill U (PA)
Shawnee State U (OH)
Shaw U (NC)
Siena Heights U (MI)
Silver Lake Coll (WI)
Southeastern Oklahoma State U (OK)
Southeast Missouri State U (MO)
Southern Arkansas U–Magnolia (AR)
Southern Wesleyan U (SC)
Southwest Minnesota State U (MN)
State U of New York at Fredonia (NY)
State U of New York Coll at Cortland (NY)
State U of New York Coll at Oneonta (NY)
Stephens Coll (MO)
Susquehanna U (PA)
Tabor Coll (KS)
Tennessee Technological U (TN)
Texas A&M Intl U (TX)
Texas A&M U–Commerce (TX)
Texas A&M U–Corpus Christi (TX)
Tufts U (MA)
Union U (TN)
Université du Québec en Outaouais (QC, Canada)
U of Alaska Anchorage (AK)
U of Alberta (AB, Canada)
The U of Arizona (AZ)
U of Arkansas (AR)
U of Arkansas at Little Rock (AR)
U of Arkansas at Pine Bluff (AR)
The U of British Columbia (BC, Canada)
U of Central Oklahoma (OK)
U of Cincinnati (OH)
U of Dayton (OH)
U of Delaware (DE)
U of Georgia (GA)
U of Guam (GU)
U of Illinois at Urbana–Champaign (IL)
U of Kentucky (KY)
U of Manitoba (MB, Canada)
U of Mary Hardin-Baylor (TX)
U of Maryland, Coll Park (MD)
U of Maryland Eastern Shore (MD)
U of Minnesota, Duluth (MN)
U of Minnesota, Twin Cities Campus (MN)
U of Missouri (MO)
The U of Montana Western (MT)
U of Nevada, Las Vegas (NV)
U of New Brunswick Fredericton (NB, Canada)
U of North Alabama (AL)
The U of North Carolina at Charlotte (NC)
The U of North Carolina at Pembroke (NC)
The U of North Carolina Wilmington (NC)
U of Northern Iowa (IA)
U of Regina (SK, Canada)
The U of Scranton (PA)
U of South Carolina Upstate (SC)
The U of Tennessee at Martin (TN)
U of the District of Columbia (DC)
The U of Toledo (OH)
U of Vermont (VT)
The U of Western Ontario (ON, Canada)
U of West Georgia (GA)
U of Windsor (ON, Canada)
U of Wisconsin–Madison (WI)
U of Wisconsin–Milwaukee (WI)
U of Wisconsin–Oshkosh (WI)
U of Wisconsin–Platteville (WI)
U of Wisconsin–Stevens Point (WI)
Utah State U (UT)
Utah Valley U (UT)
Virginia Union U (VA)
Wagner Coll (NY)
Waldorf Coll (IA)
Walsh U (OH)
Wartburg Coll (IA)
Washington State U (WA)
Weber State U (UT)
Western Carolina U (NC)
Westfield State Coll (MA)
West Liberty U (WV)
West Virginia State U (WV)
West Virginia Wesleyan Coll (WV)
Wheelock Coll (MA)
Whittier Coll (CA)
Widener U (PA)
Winona State U (MN)
Winston-Salem State U (NC)
Winthrop U (SC)
Wright State U (OH)
York U (ON, Canada)

KINESIOLOGY AND EXERCISE SCIENCE

Acadia U (NS, Canada)
Adams State Coll (CO)
Alma Coll (MI)
Appalachian State U (NC)
Arizona State U (AZ)
Arkansas State U–Jonesboro (AR)
Augustana Coll (SD)
Baker U (KS)
Barry U (FL)
Bastyr U (WA)
Belhaven U (MS)
Bellarmine U (KY)
Berea Coll (KY)
Berry Coll (GA)
Bethany Lutheran Coll (MN)
Bethel Coll (IN)
Bethel U (MN)
Bluefield Coll (VA)
Boise State U (ID)
Boston U (MA)
Brevard Coll (NC)
Bridgewater State Coll (MA)
Brigham Young U (UT)
Brigham Young U–Hawaii (HI)
Brock U (ON, Canada)
Buffalo State Coll, State U of New York (NY)
Cabrini Coll (PA)
California Baptist U (CA)
California Lutheran U (CA)
California State U, Chico (CA)
California State U, East Bay (CA)
California State U, Long Beach (CA)
California State U, Los Angeles (CA)
California State U, Northridge (CA)
California State U, Sacramento (CA)
Calvin Coll (MI)
Capital U (OH)
Carroll U (WI)
Carson-Newman Coll (TN)
Castleton State Coll (VT)
Cedarville U (OH)
Central Christian Coll of Kansas (KS)
Central Coll (IA)
Central Michigan U (MI)
Chatham U (PA)
Chowan U (NC)
Clearwater Christian Coll (FL)
Cleveland State U (OH)
Coastal Carolina U (SC)
Coker Coll (SC)
The Coll at Brockport, State U of New York (NY)
The Coll of Idaho (ID)
Colorado State U (CO)
Colorado State U–Pueblo (CO)
Columbus State U (GA)
Concordia Coll (MN)
Concordia U (CA)
Concordia U (QC, Canada)

Concordia U Chicago (IL)
Concordia U, St. Paul (MN)
Concordia U Texas (TX)
Cornell Coll (IA)
Cornerstone U (MI)
Creighton U (NE)
Dakota State U (SD)
Defiance Coll (OH)
DePauw U (IN)
DeSales U (PA)
Dordt Coll (IA)
Drury U (MO)
Eastern Illinois U (IL)
Eastern Washington U (WA)
East Stroudsburg U of Pennsylvania (PA)
Elmhurst Coll (IL)
Emmanuel Coll (GA)
Fitchburg State Coll (MA)
Florida Atlantic U (FL)
Florida Gulf Coast U (FL)
Florida Southern Coll (FL)
Florida State U (FL)
Frostburg State U (MD)
Furman U (SC)
Gannon U (PA)
Georgetown Coll (KY)
The George Washington U (DC)
Georgian Court U (NJ)
Georgia Southern U (GA)
Georgia State U (GA)
Gonzaga U (WA)
Gordon Coll (MA)
Greensboro Coll (NC)
Greenville Coll (IL)
Hamline U (MN)
Hanover Coll (IN)
Harding U (AR)
Hardin-Simmons U (TX)
Hendrix Coll (AR)
High Point U (NC)
Hope Coll (MI)
Houston Baptist U (TX)
Humboldt State U (CA)
Huntingdon Coll (AL)
Huntington U (IN)
Illinois State U (IL)
Immaculata U (PA)
Indiana Wesleyan U (IN)
Iowa Wesleyan Coll (IA)
Ithaca Coll (NY)
Jacksonville State U (AL)
Jacksonville U (FL)
Jefferson Coll of Health Sciences (VA)
John Brown U (AR)
Johnson State Coll (VT)
Kansas State U (KS)
Keene State Coll (NH)
Kennesaw State U (GA)
Kent State U (OH)
Kuyper Coll (MI)
Lake Superior State U (MI)
Lasell Coll (MA)
La Sierra U (CA)
Laurentian U (ON, Canada)
Lewis-Clark State Coll (ID)
Liberty U (VA)
Lincoln Memorial U (TN)
Lindenwood U (MO)
Linfield Coll (OR)
Lipscomb U (TN)
Longwood U (VA)
Loras Coll (IA)
Louisiana Coll (LA)
Lubbock Christian U (TX)
Lynchburg Coll (VA)
Malone U (OH)
Marquette U (WI)
Marshall U (WV)
Mars Hill Coll (NC)
Marymount U (VA)
The Master's Coll and Sem (CA)
McDaniel Coll (MD)
McMurry U (TX)
Memorial U of Newfoundland (NL, Canada)
Meredith Coll (NC)
Messiah Coll (PA)
Miami U (OH)
Michigan State U (MI)
MidAmerica Nazarene U (KS)
Midwestern State U (TX)
Minnesota State U Moorhead (MN)
Mississippi Coll (MS)
Morehead State U (KY)
Mount Vernon Nazarene U (OH)
Murray State U (KY)
Nebraska Wesleyan U (NE)
Norfolk State U (VA)
North Central Coll (IL)
Northeastern State U (OK)
Northern Arizona U (AZ)
Northern Michigan U (MI)
Northwestern Coll (IA)
Northwestern Coll (MN)
Northwest Nazarene U (ID)
Notre Dame de Namur U (CA)
Nova Southeastern U (FL)
Occidental Coll (CA)
Ohio Northern U (OH)
Ohio U (OH)
Oklahoma Baptist U (OK)
Oklahoma City U (OK)
Oklahoma Wesleyan U (OK)
Old Dominion U (VA)
Oral Roberts U (OK)
Ottawa U (KS)
Ouachita Baptist U (AR)
Pacific Union Coll (CA)
Penn State Abington (PA)
Penn State Altoona (PA)
Penn State Beaver (PA)
Penn State Berks (PA)
Penn State Brandywine (PA)
Penn State DuBois (PA)
Penn State Erie, The Behrend Coll (PA)
Penn State Fayette, The Eberly Campus (PA)
Penn State Greater Allegheny (PA)
Penn State Hazleton (PA)
Penn State Lehigh Valley (PA)
Penn State Mont Alto (PA)
Penn State New Kensington (PA)
Penn State Schuylkill (PA)
Penn State Shenango (PA)
Penn State U Park (PA)
Penn State Wilkes-Barre (PA)
Penn State Worthington Scranton (PA)
Penn State York (PA)
Pennsylvania Coll of Technology (PA)
Pepperdine U, Malibu (CA)
Queens Coll of the City U of New York (NY)
Redeemer U Coll (ON, Canada)
Rice U (TX)
Roanoke Coll (VA)
Rocky Mountain Coll (MT)
Rutgers, The State U of New Jersey, New Brunswick (NJ)
Sacred Heart U (CT)
Saginaw Valley State U (MI)
St. Cloud State U (MN)
St. Edward's U (TX)
St. Francis Xavier U (NS, Canada)
Saint Louis U (MO)
Saint Mary's Coll of California (CA)
St. Mary's U (TX)
St. Olaf Coll (MN)
Salem Coll (NC)
Salem State Coll (MA)
Salisbury U (MD)
Samford U (AL)
Sam Houston State U (TX)
San Diego Christian Coll (CA)
San Francisco State U (CA)
Schreiner U (TX)
Seattle Pacific U (WA)
Shaw U (NC)
Shenandoah U (VA)
Shippensburg U of Pennsylvania (PA)
Simon Fraser U (BC, Canada)
Skidmore Coll (NY)
Slippery Rock U of Pennsylvania (PA)
Sonoma State U (CA)
Southern Adventist U (TN)
Southern Arkansas U–Magnolia (AR)
Southern Illinois U Carbondale (IL)
Southwestern Adventist U (TX)
Southwestern U (TX)
Spring Arbor U (MI)
State U of New York at Plattsburgh (NY)
State U of New York Coll at Cortland (NY)
Syracuse U (NY)
Tarleton State U (TX)
Taylor U (IN)
Temple U (PA)
Tennessee Wesleyan Coll (TN)
Texas A&M U–Commerce (TX)
Texas A&M U–Corpus Christi (TX)
Texas Lutheran U (TX)
Towson U (MD)
Transylvania U (KY)
Trevecca Nazarene U (TN)
Trinity Christian Coll (IL)
Truman State U (MO)
Tusculum Coll (TN)
Union Coll (NE)
Union U (TN)
United States Military Acad (NY)
The U of Akron (OH)
U of Alberta (AB, Canada)
The U of British Columbia (BC, Canada)
The U of British Columbia–Okanagan (BC, Canada)
U of Dayton (OH)
U of Delaware (DE)
U of Evansville (IN)
U of Hawaii at Manoa (HI)
U of Houston (TX)
U of Idaho (ID)
U of Illinois at Chicago (IL)
U of Illinois at Urbana–Champaign (IL)
U of Indianapolis (IN)
The U of Iowa (IA)
U of La Verne (CA)
U of Lethbridge (AB, Canada)
U of Louisiana at Monroe (LA)
U of Mary (ND)
U of Maryland, Coll Park (MD)
U of Massachusetts Lowell (MA)
U of Memphis (TN)
U of Miami (FL)
U of Michigan (MI)
U of Minnesota, Duluth (MN)
U of Mississippi (MS)
U of Mount Union (OH)
U of Nebraska at Omaha (NE)
U of Nevada, Las Vegas (NV)
U of New Brunswick Fredericton (NB, Canada)
U of New England (ME)
U of New Hampshire (NH)
The U of North Carolina at Greensboro (NC)
U of Northern Colorado (CO)
U of Oklahoma (OK)
U of Ottawa (ON, Canada)
U of Puget Sound (WA)
U of Regina (SK, Canada)
U of Rhode Island (RI)
U of Saskatchewan (SK, Canada)
The U of Scranton (PA)
U of South Carolina (SC)
U of South Carolina Aiken (SC)
U of Southern California (CA)
U of Southern Indiana (IN)
The U of Tampa (FL)
The U of Tennessee (TN)
The U of Tennessee at Chattanooga (TN)
The U of Texas at Tyler (TX)
The U of Texas of the Permian Basin (TX)
U of the Incarnate Word (TX)
U of the Pacific (CA)
The U of Toledo (OH)
U of Tulsa (OK)
U of Utah (UT)
U of Vermont (VT)
U of Virginia (VA)
U of Waterloo (ON, Canada)
The U of Western Ontario (ON, Canada)
U of Windsor (ON, Canada)
U of Wisconsin–Eau Claire (WI)
U of Wisconsin–La Crosse (WI)
U of Wisconsin–Superior (WI)
U of Wyoming (WY)
Upper Iowa U (IA)
Valdosta State U (GA)
Valparaiso U (IN)
Vanguard U of Southern California (CA)
Viterbo U (WI)
Wake Forest U (NC)
Warner Pacific Coll (OR)
Washington State U (WA)
Waynesburg U (PA)
Weber State U (UT)
Western Illinois U (IL)
Western Kentucky U (KY)
Western Michigan U (MI)
Western Oregon U (OR)
Western State Coll of Colorado (CO)
West Liberty U (WV)
Westmont Coll (CA)
West Virginia U (WV)
West Virginia Wesleyan Coll (WV)
Wilfrid Laurier U (ON, Canada)
Willamette U (OR)
William Paterson U of New Jersey (NJ)
Wilson Coll (PA)
Winona State U (MN)
Winston-Salem State U (NC)
Youngstown State U (OH)

KINESIOTHERAPY

Bridgewater State Coll (MA)
California State U, Long Beach (CA)
Loyola Marymount U (CA)
U of Regina (SK, Canada)

KNOWLEDGE MANAGEMENT

Framingham State Coll (MA)
Walden U (MN)

KOREAN

Brigham Young U (UT)
The Ohio State U (OH)
U of California, Irvine (CA)
U of California, Los Angeles (CA)
U of Hawaii at Manoa (HI)

KOREAN STUDIES

Claremont McKenna Coll (CA)

LABOR AND INDUSTRIAL RELATIONS

Athabasca U (AB, Canada)
Bowling Green State U (OH)
Brock U (ON, Canada)
Clarion U of Pennsylvania (PA)
Cleveland State U (OH)
Cornell U (NY)
Governors State U (IL)
Indiana U Bloomington (IN)
Indiana U Kokomo (IN)
Indiana U–Purdue U Indianapolis (IN)
Indiana U Southeast (IN)
Ithaca Coll (NY)
Lakehead U (ON, Canada)
Memorial U of Newfoundland (NL, Canada)
New York U (NY)
Penn State Abington (PA)
Penn State Altoona (PA)
Penn State Beaver (PA)
Penn State Berks (PA)
Penn State Brandywine (PA)
Penn State DuBois (PA)
Penn State Erie, The Behrend Coll (PA)
Penn State Fayette, The Eberly Campus (PA)
Penn State Greater Allegheny (PA)
Penn State Hazleton (PA)
Penn State Lehigh Valley (PA)
Penn State Mont Alto (PA)
Penn State New Kensington (PA)
Penn State Schuylkill (PA)
Penn State Shenango (PA)
Penn State U Park (PA)
Penn State Wilkes-Barre (PA)
Penn State Worthington Scranton (PA)
Penn State York (PA)
Rider U (NJ)
Rutgers, The State U of New Jersey, New Brunswick (NJ)
Saint Francis U (PA)
San Francisco State U (CA)
Seton Hall U (NJ)
State U of New York at Fredonia (NY)
State U of New York Coll at Old Westbury (NY)
State U of New York Empire State Coll (NY)
Temple U (PA)
Tennessee Technological U (TN)
Texas A&M U–Commerce (TX)
Université du Québec en Outaouais (QC, Canada)
U of Alberta (AB, Canada)
The U of British Columbia (BC, Canada)
The U of Iowa (IA)
U of Maine (ME)
U of Manitoba (MB, Canada)
U of Puerto Rico, Río Piedras (PR)
U of Toronto (ON, Canada)
U of Wisconsin–Madison (WI)
U of Wisconsin–Milwaukee (WI)
York U (ON, Canada)

LABOR STUDIES

California State U, Dominguez Hills (CA)
Eastern Michigan U (MI)
Hofstra U (NY)
Indiana U Bloomington (IN)
Indiana U Kokomo (IN)
Indiana U Northwest (IN)
Indiana U–Purdue U Fort Wayne (IN)
Indiana U–Purdue U Indianapolis (IN)
Indiana U South Bend (IN)
Le Moyne Coll (NY)
Queens Coll of the City U of New York (NY)
Rhode Island Coll (RI)
U of Windsor (ON, Canada)
Wayne State U (MI)

LANDSCAPE ARCHITECTURE

American U of Beirut (Lebanon)
Arizona State U (AZ)
Ball State U (IN)
Boston Architectural Coll (MA)
California Polytechnic State U, San Luis Obispo (CA)
California State Polytechnic U, Pomona (CA)
Clemson U (SC)
Coll of the Atlantic (ME)
Colorado State U (CO)
Cornell U (NY)
Florida Ag and Mech U (FL)
Florida Intl U (FL)
Iowa State U of Science and Technology (IA)
Louisiana State U and Ag and Mech Coll (LA)
Michigan State U (MI)
Mississippi State U (MS)
North Dakota State U (ND)
The Ohio State U (OH)
Oklahoma State U (OK)
Penn State Brandywine (PA)
Penn State Lehigh Valley (PA)
Penn State Schuylkill (PA)
Penn State U Park (PA)
Penn State Wilkes-Barre (PA)
Philadelphia U (PA)
Purdue U (IN)
State U of New York Coll of Environmental Science and Forestry (NY)
Temple U (PA)
Texas A&M U (TX)
Texas Tech U (TX)
The U of Arizona (AZ)
U of Arkansas (AR)
The U of British Columbia (BC, Canada)
U of California, Berkeley (CA)
U of California, Davis (CA)
U of Connecticut (CT)
U of Florida (FL)
U of Georgia (GA)
U of Guelph (ON, Canada)
U of Idaho (ID)
U of Illinois at Urbana–Champaign (IL)
U of Kentucky (KY)
U of Maryland, Coll Park (MD)
U of Massachusetts Amherst (MA)
U of Minnesota, Twin Cities Campus (MN)
U of Nebraska–Lincoln (NE)
U of Nevada, Las Vegas (NV)
U of Oregon (OR)
U of Rhode Island (RI)
U of Washington (WA)
Utah State U (UT)
Virginia Polytechnic Inst and State U (VA)
Washington State U (WA)
West Virginia U (WV)

LANDSCAPING AND GROUNDSKEEPING

Andrews U (MI)
Florida Ag and Mech U (FL)
Mississippi State U (MS)
Oklahoma State U (OK)
Penn State Abington (PA)
Penn State Altoona (PA)
Penn State Beaver (PA)
Penn State Berks (PA)
Penn State Brandywine (PA)
Penn State DuBois (PA)
Penn State Erie, The Behrend Coll (PA)
Penn State Fayette, The Eberly Campus (PA)
Penn State Greater Allegheny (PA)
Penn State Hazleton (PA)
Penn State Lehigh Valley (PA)
Penn State Mont Alto (PA)
Penn State New Kensington (PA)
Penn State Schuylkill (PA)
Penn State Shenango (PA)
Penn State U Park (PA)
Penn State Wilkes-Barre (PA)
Penn State Worthington Scranton (PA)
Penn State York (PA)
South Dakota State U (SD)
Tennessee Technological U (TN)
U of Maine (ME)
U of Nebraska–Lincoln (NE)

LAND USE PLANNING AND MANAGEMENT

California State U, Bakersfield (CA)
Metropolitan State Coll of Denver (CO)
Montana State U (MT)
State U of New York Coll of Environmental Science and Forestry (NY)
U of Alberta (AB, Canada)
U of Saskatchewan (SK, Canada)
The U of Western Ontario (ON, Canada)
U of Wisconsin–Platteville (WI)
U of Wisconsin–River Falls (WI)

LANGUAGE INTERPRETATION AND TRANSLATION

Bard Coll (NY)
Brigham Young U (UT)
Concordia U (QC, Canada)
Laurentian U (ON, Canada)
Mississippi Coll (MS)
Université du Québec en Outaouais (QC, Canada)
U of Ottawa (ON, Canada)
York U (ON, Canada)

LASER AND OPTICAL TECHNOLOGY

Oregon Inst of Technology (OR)

LATIN

Acadia U (NS, Canada)
Amherst Coll (MA)
Augustana Coll (IL)
Austin Coll (TX)
Ball State U (IN)
Bard Coll (NY)
Barnard Coll (NY)
Baylor U (TX)
Boston Coll (MA)
Boston U (MA)
Bowling Green State U (OH)
Bryn Mawr Coll (PA)
Butler U (IN)
Calvin Coll (MI)
Carleton Coll (MN)
The Catholic U of America (DC)
Claremont McKenna Coll (CA)
Colgate U (NY)
The Coll of New Rochelle (NY)
Coll of Notre Dame of Maryland (MD)
The Coll of Wooster (OH)
Concordia Coll (MN)
Cornell Coll (IA)
Creighton U (NE)
Dartmouth Coll (NH)
DePauw U (IN)
Duke U (NC)
Duquesne U (PA)
Emory U (GA)
Fordham U (NY)
Franklin & Marshall Coll (PA)
Furman U (SC)
Gettysburg Coll (PA)
Hampden-Sydney Coll (VA)
Haverford Coll (PA)
Hofstra U (NY)
Hunter Coll of the City U of New York (NY)
John Carroll U (OH)
Kent State U (OH)
Kenyon Coll (OH)
Lawrence U (WI)
Lehman Coll of the City U of New York (NY)
Louisiana State U and Ag and Mech Coll (LA)
Loyola U Chicago (IL)
Marlboro Coll (VT)
Memorial U of Newfoundland (NL, Canada)
Mercer U (GA)
Miami U Hamilton (OH)
Missouri State U (MO)
Monmouth Coll (IL)
Montclair State U (NJ)
Mount Allison U (NB, Canada)
Mount Holyoke Coll (MA)
Oberlin Coll (OH)
Ohio U (OH)
Queens Coll of the City U of New York (NY)
Randolph Coll (VA)
Randolph-Macon Coll (VA)
Rhodes Coll (TN)
Rice U (TX)
Rockford Coll (IL)
Rutgers, The State U of New Jersey, New Brunswick (NJ)
Saint Joseph's U (PA)
Saint Mary's Coll of California (CA)
St. Olaf Coll (MN)
Samford U (AL)
Santa Clara U (CA)
Sarah Lawrence Coll (NY)
Scripps Coll (CA)
Sewanee: The U of the South (TN)
Smith Coll (MA)
Southwestern U (TX)
Stanford U (CA)
State U of New York at Binghamton (NY)
Swarthmore Coll (PA)
Tufts U (MA)
Tulane U (LA)
U of Alberta (AB, Canada)
The U of British Columbia (BC, Canada)
U of California, Berkeley (CA)
U of California, Irvine (CA)
U of Chicago (IL)
U of Delaware (DE)
U of Georgia (GA)
The U of Iowa (IA)
U of Maine (ME)
U of Manitoba (MB, Canada)
U of Miami (FL)
U of Michigan (MI)
U of Minnesota, Twin Cities Campus (MN)
U of Missouri (MO)
U of Nebraska–Lincoln (NE)
U of New Brunswick Fredericton (NB, Canada)
U of New Hampshire (NH)
U of Oregon (OR)
U of Ottawa (ON, Canada)
U of Richmond (VA)
U of St. Thomas (MN)
The U of Scranton (PA)
The U of Texas at Austin (TX)
U of Toronto (ON, Canada)
U of Vermont (VT)
U of Washington (WA)
The U of Western Ontario (ON, Canada)
U of Windsor (ON, Canada)
U of Wisconsin–Milwaukee (WI)
Vassar Coll (NY)
Virginia Wesleyan Coll (VA)
Wabash Coll (IN)
Wake Forest U (NC)
Washington U in St. Louis (MO)
Wellesley Coll (MA)
West Chester U of Pennsylvania (PA)
Western Michigan U (MI)
Wheaton Coll (MA)
Wichita State U (KS)
Yale U (CT)
York U (ON, Canada)

LATIN AMERICAN STUDIES

Adelphi U (NY)
Albright Coll (PA)
American Public U System (WV)
American U (DC)
Assumption Coll (MA)
Ball State U (IN)
Bard Coll (NY)
Bard Coll at Simon's Rock (MA)
Barnard Coll (NY)
Baylor U (TX)
Beloit Coll (WI)
Bennington Coll (VT)
Boston U (MA)
Bowdoin Coll (ME)
Bowling Green State U (OH)
Brandeis U (MA)
Bucknell U (PA)
Burlington Coll (VT)
California State U, Chico (CA)
California State U, East Bay (CA)
California State U, Fullerton (CA)
California State U, Los Angeles (CA)
Carleton Coll (MN)
Carnegie Mellon U (PA)
City Coll of the City U of New York (NY)
Claremont McKenna Coll (CA)
Colby Coll (ME)
Colgate U (NY)
The Coll at Brockport, State U of New York (NY)
Coll of Charleston (SC)
The Coll of William and Mary (VA)
Columbia U (NY)
Columbia U, School of General Studies (NY)
Connecticut Coll (CT)
Cornell Coll (IA)
Dartmouth Coll (NH)
Denison U (OH)
DePaul U (IL)
Dickinson Coll (PA)
Earlham Coll (IN)
Edinboro U of Pennsylvania (PA)
Emory U (GA)
Flagler Coll (FL)
Fordham U (NY)
Fort Lewis Coll (CO)
George Mason U (VA)
The George Washington U (DC)
Gettysburg Coll (PA)
Gustavus Adolphus Coll (MN)
Hamline U (MN)
Hampshire Coll (MA)
Haverford Coll (PA)
Hood Coll (MD)
Hunter Coll of the City U of New York (NY)
Illinois Wesleyan U (IL)
The Johns Hopkins U (MD)
Kent State U (OH)
Lake Forest Coll (IL)
Lehman Coll of the City U of New York (NY)
Macalester Coll (MN)
Marlboro Coll (VT)
Miami U (OH)
Middlebury Coll (VT)
Millsaps Coll (MS)
Mount Holyoke Coll (MA)
New Coll of Florida (FL)
New York U (NY)
Oakland U (MI)
Oberlin Coll (OH)
Ohio U (OH)
Ohio Wesleyan U (OH)
Pace U (NY)
Penn State Abington (PA)
Penn State Altoona (PA)
Penn State Beaver (PA)
Penn State Berks (PA)
Penn State Brandywine (PA)
Penn State DuBois (PA)
Penn State Erie, The Behrend Coll (PA)
Penn State Fayette, The Eberly Campus (PA)
Penn State Greater Allegheny (PA)
Penn State Hazleton (PA)
Penn State Lehigh Valley (PA)
Penn State Mont Alto (PA)
Penn State New Kensington (PA)
Penn State Schuylkill (PA)
Penn State Shenango (PA)
Penn State U Park (PA)
Penn State Wilkes-Barre (PA)
Penn State Worthington Scranton (PA)
Penn State York (PA)
Pitzer Coll (CA)
Pomona Coll (CA)
Pontifical Coll Josephinum (OH)
Portland State U (OR)
Prescott Coll (AZ)
Queens Coll of the City U of New York (NY)
Rhode Island Coll (RI)
Rice U (TX)
Ripon Coll (WI)
Rollins Coll (FL)
Rutgers, The State U of New Jersey, New Brunswick (NJ)
St. Cloud State U (MN)
St. Edward's U (TX)
Saint Mary's Coll of California (CA)
St. Olaf Coll (MN)
Samford U (AL)
San Diego State U (CA)
Sarah Lawrence Coll (NY)
Scripps Coll (CA)
Seattle Pacific U (WA)
Skidmore Coll (NY)
Smith Coll (MA)
Southern Methodist U (TX)
Southwestern U (TX)
State U of New York at Binghamton (NY)
State U of New York at New Paltz (NY)
State U of New York at Plattsburgh (NY)
Stetson U (FL)
Syracuse U (NY)
Temple U (PA)
Texas Tech U (TX)
Trinity U (TX)
Tulane U (LA)
United States Military Acad (NY)
U at Albany, State U of New York (NY)
The U of Alabama (AL)
U of Alberta (AB, Canada)
The U of Arizona (AZ)
The U of British Columbia (BC, Canada)
U of California, Berkeley (CA)
U of California, Los Angeles (CA)
U of California, Riverside (CA)
U of California, San Diego (CA)
U of California, Santa Cruz (CA)
U of Chicago (IL)
U of Cincinnati (OH)
U of Connecticut (CT)
U of Delaware (DE)
U of Denver (CO)
U of Georgia (GA)
U of Idaho (ID)
U of Illinois at Chicago (IL)
U of Illinois at Urbana–Champaign (IL)
The U of Iowa (IA)
The U of Kansas (KS)
U of Kentucky (KY)
U of Miami (FL)
U of Michigan (MI)
U of Minnesota, Twin Cities Campus (MN)
U of Missouri (MO)
U of Nebraska at Omaha (NE)
U of Nebraska–Lincoln (NE)
U of New Mexico (NM)
The U of North Carolina at Chapel Hill (NC)
The U of North Carolina at Charlotte (NC)
U of Oregon (OR)
U of Pennsylvania (PA)
U of Rhode Island (RI)
U of Richmond (VA)
U of San Francisco (CA)
U of South Carolina (SC)
The U of Texas at Austin (TX)
The U of Texas at El Paso (TX)
The U of Toledo (OH)
U of Toronto (ON, Canada)
U of Vermont (VT)
U of Washington (WA)
The U of Western Ontario (ON, Canada)
U of Wisconsin–Eau Claire (WI)
U of Wisconsin–Milwaukee (WI)
Vanderbilt U (TN)
Vassar Coll (NY)
Washington Coll (MD)
Washington U in St. Louis (MO)
Wellesley Coll (MA)
Wesleyan U (CT)
Westminster Coll (UT)
Willamette U (OR)
Yale U (CT)
York U (ON, Canada)

LATIN TEACHER EDUCATION

Assumption Coll (MA)
Brigham Young U (UT)
Concordia Coll (MN)
Duquesne U (PA)
Indiana U Bloomington (IN)
Kent State U (OH)
McNeese State U (LA)
Miami U (OH)
Miami U Hamilton (OH)
Missouri State U (MO)
Ohio Wesleyan U (OH)
U of Illinois at Urbana–Champaign (IL)
Western Michigan U (MI)

LEGAL ADMINISTRATIVE ASSISTANT/SECRETARY

Lewis-Clark State Coll (ID)
Tabor Coll (KS)
Texas A&M U–Commerce (TX)

LEGAL ASSISTANT/ PARALEGAL

Boston U (MA)
California State U, Chico (CA)
Calumet Coll of Saint Joseph (IN)
Champlain Coll (VT)
Coll of Mount St. Joseph (OH)
Coll of Saint Mary (NE)
Concordia U Wisconsin (WI)
Davenport U, Grand Rapids (MI)
Eastern Michigan U (MI)
Faulkner U (AL)
Florida Gulf Coast U (FL)
Gannon U (PA)
Grambling State U (LA)
Grand Valley State U (MI)
Hamline U (MN)
Hampton U (VA)
Husson U (ME)
Johnson & Wales U (RI)
Jones Coll, Jacksonville (FL)
Kaplan U, Davenport Campus (IA)
Lake Erie Coll (OH)
Lake Superior State U (MI)
Lewis-Clark State Coll (ID)
Madonna U (MI)
Marymount U (VA)
Maryville U of Saint Louis (MO)
Minnesota State U Moorhead (MN)
Mississippi Coll (MS)
Mississippi U for Women (MS)
Morehead State U (KY)
Newbury Coll (MA)
New York City Coll of Technology of the City U of New York (NY)
Nova Southeastern U (FL)
Patricia Stevens Coll (MO)
Peirce Coll (PA)
Post U (CT)
Quinnipiac U (CT)
Roosevelt U (IL)
Saint Mary-of-the-Woods Coll (IN)
St. Petersburg Coll (FL)
Southern Illinois U Carbondale (IL)
State U of New York Coll of Technology at Canton (NY)
Stephen F. Austin State U (TX)
Stevenson U (MD)
Suffolk U (MA)
Sullivan U (KY)
Texas Woman's U (TX)
Thomas Edison State Coll (NJ)
U of Central Florida (FL)
U of Hartford (CT)
U of Houston–Clear Lake (TX)
U of La Verne (CA)
U of Southern Mississippi (MS)
The U of Tennessee at Chattanooga (TN)
U of West Florida (FL)
Ursuline Coll (OH)
Valdosta State U (GA)
Virginia Intermont Coll (VA)
Winona State U (MN)

LEGAL PROFESSIONS AND STUDIES RELATED

Ball State U (IN)
Bethany Coll (KS)
Central Pennsylvania Coll (PA)
Hamline U (MN)
Hodges U (FL)
Loyola U Chicago (IL)
Missouri Southern State U (MO)
Montclair State U (NJ)
New Jersey Inst of Technology (NJ)
Pennsylvania Coll of Technology (PA)
Ramapo Coll of New Jersey (NJ)
Skidmore Coll (NY)
Texas Wesleyan U (TX)
Tulane U (LA)
U of Evansville (IN)
U of Illinois at Springfield (IL)
U of Nebraska–Lincoln (NE)
U of Pennsylvania (PA)
U of Tulsa (OK)

LEGAL STUDIES

Adams State Coll (CO)
American Public U System (WV)
American U (DC)
Amherst Coll (MA)
Bay Path Coll (MA)
Brenau U (GA)
Bridgewater State Coll (MA)
Brown Mackie Coll–Albuquerque (NM)
Brown Mackie Coll–Boise (ID)
Brown Mackie Coll–Fort Wayne (IN)
Brown Mackie Coll–Greenville (SC)
Brown Mackie Coll–Indianapolis (IN)
Brown Mackie Coll–Louisville (KY)
Brown Mackie Coll–Merrillville (IN)
Brown Mackie Coll–Michigan City (IN)
Brown Mackie Coll–Phoenix (AZ)
Brown Mackie Coll–St. Louis (MO)
Brown Mackie Coll–South Bend (IN)
Brown Mackie Coll–Tucson (AZ)
Brown Mackie Coll–Tulsa (OK)
Burlington Coll (VT)
California State U, Chico (CA)
Cape Breton U (NS, Canada)
Central Michigan U (MI)
Christopher Newport U (VA)
Claremont McKenna Coll (CA)
Coll of the Atlantic (ME)
Concordia U Chicago (IL)
DeSales U (PA)
Dickinson Coll (PA)
East Central U (OK)
Florida National Coll (FL)
Franciscan U of Steubenville (OH)
Goldey-Beacom Coll (DE)
Hamline U (MN)
Hampshire Coll (MA)
Harding U (AR)
Hood Coll (MD)
James Madison U (VA)
John Jay Coll of Criminal Justice of the City U of New York (NY)
Kaplan U, Davenport Campus (IA)
Keiser U, Fort Lauderdale (FL)
Lake Superior State U (MI)
Lasell Coll (MA)
Laurentian U (ON, Canada)
Lipscomb U (TN)
Manhattanville Coll (NY)
Methodist U (NC)
Minnesota State U Moorhead (MN)
Montclair State U (NJ)
Mountain State U (WV)
National U (CA)
Newbury Coll (MA)
Nichols Coll (MA)
Northwest U (WA)
Oberlin Coll (OH)
Park U (MO)
Pennsylvania Coll of Technology (PA)
Point Park U (PA)
Pontifical Catholic U of Puerto Rico (PR)
Post U (CT)
Quinnipiac U (CT)
Rivier Coll (NH)
Sage Coll of Albany (NY)
St. John's U (NY)
Saint Joseph's U (PA)

Scripps Coll (CA)
South U (AL)
South U, Royal Palm Beach (FL)
South U (GA)
South U, Columbia (SC)
South U, Virginia Beach (VA)
State U of New York at Fredonia (NY)
Stevenson U (MD)
Suffolk U (MA)
United States Air Force Acad (CO)
U of Alberta (AB, Canada)
U of Baltimore (MD)
U of California, Berkeley (CA)
U of California, Santa Barbara (CA)
U of California, Santa Cruz (CA)
U of Hartford (CT)
U of Maryland U Coll (MD)
U of Massachusetts Amherst (MA)
U of Miami (FL)
U of New Brunswick Fredericton (NB, Canada)
U of New Haven (CT)
U of Pittsburgh (PA)
The U of Western Ontario (ON, Canada)
U of Windsor (ON, Canada)
U of Wisconsin–Superior (WI)
Virginia Intermont Coll (VA)
Washburn U (KS)
Webster U (MO)
Western Intl U (AZ)
Western New England Coll (MA)
Wilmington U (DE)
Winona State U (MN)
York U (ON, Canada)

LIBERAL ARTS AND SCIENCES AND HUMANITIES RELATED

Barton Coll (NC)
Belhaven U (MS)
Bennington Coll (VT)
Bishop's U (QC, Canada)
Brigham Young U (UT)
Bryan Coll (TN)
California Polytechnic State U, San Luis Obispo (CA)
California State U, Dominguez Hills (CA)
Carnegie Mellon U (PA)
Central Christian Coll of Kansas (KS)
Clarkson U (NY)
The Colorado Coll (CO)
Crown Coll (MN)
Dominican U of California (CA)
Duquesne U (PA)
Fairfield U (CT)
Florida Atlantic U (FL)
Geneva Coll (PA)
George Mason U (VA)
Georgia Coll & State U (GA)
Goddard Coll (VT)
Hofstra U (NY)
Howard Payne U (TX)
The Johns Hopkins U (MD)
Loyola U New Orleans (LA)
Malone U (OH)
Marshall U (WV)
Mitchell Coll (CT)
Mount Aloysius Coll (PA)
Ohio U (OH)
Purdue U (IN)
Sacred Heart U (CT)
Saint Anselm Coll (NH)
Saint Mary's Coll of California (CA)
Salem State Coll (MA)
Sarah Lawrence Coll (NY)
Southern Methodist U (TX)
Southwestern Coll (KS)
Southwestern U (TX)
State U of New York Maritime Coll (NY)
Tulane U (LA)
The U of Akron (OH)
U of California, Los Angeles (CA)
U of California, Santa Barbara (CA)
U of Illinois at Urbana–Champaign (IL)
U of Louisville (KY)
U of Mary Washington (VA)
U of Massachusetts Amherst (MA)
U of Oklahoma (OK)
U of South Alabama (AL)
U of Wisconsin–La Crosse (WI)
U of Wisconsin–River Falls (WI)
U of Wisconsin–Whitewater (WI)
Valdosta State U (GA)
Vassar Coll (NY)
Walsh U (OH)
Western Illinois U (IL)
Wright State U (OH)

LIBERAL ARTS AND SCIENCES/LIBERAL STUDIES

Abilene Christian U (TX)
Adams State Coll (CO)
Alabama State U (AL)
Alaska Pacific U (AK)
Alcorn State U (MS)
Alderson-Broaddus Coll (WV)
Alliant Intl U (CA)
Alliant Intl U–México City (Mexico)
Alma Coll (MI)
Alvernia U (PA)
Alverno Coll (WI)
American Intl Coll (MA)
American Jewish U (CA)
American U (DC)
Amridge U (AL)
Angelo State U (TX)
Antioch U McGregor (OH)
Antioch U Seattle (WA)
Appalachian State U (NC)
Aquinas Coll (MI)
Aquinas Coll (TN)
Arcadia U (PA)
Argosy U, Atlanta (GA)
Argosy U, Chicago (IL)
Argosy U, Dallas (TX)
Argosy U, Denver (CO)
Argosy U, Hawai'i (HI)
Argosy U, Inland Empire (CA)
Argosy U, Los Angeles (CA)
Argosy U, Nashville (TN)
Argosy U, Orange County (CA)
Argosy U, Phoenix (AZ)
Argosy U, Salt Lake City (UT)
Argosy U, San Diego (CA)
Argosy U, San Francisco Bay Area (CA)
Argosy U, Sarasota (FL)
Argosy U, Schaumburg (IL)
Argosy U, Seattle (WA)
Argosy U, Tampa (FL)
Argosy U, Twin Cities (MN)
Argosy U, Washington DC (VA)
Arizona State U (AZ)
Armstrong Atlantic State U (GA)
Ashland U (OH)
Athabasca U (AB, Canada)
Auburn U Montgomery (AL)
Augsburg Coll (MN)
Augustana Coll (IL)
Augustana Coll (SD)
Azusa Pacific U (CA)
Ball State U (IN)
Barry U (FL)
Bay Path Coll (MA)
Beacon Coll (FL)
Bellarmine U (KY)
Bemidji State U (MN)
Benedictine Coll (KS)
Bennington Coll (VT)
Bentley U (MA)
Bernard M. Baruch Coll of the City U of New York (NY)
Bethany Lutheran Coll (MN)
Bethany U (CA)
Bethel Coll (IN)
Bethune-Cookman U (FL)
Bishop's U (QC, Canada)
Bluefield Coll (VA)
Boise State U (ID)
Bowling Green State U (OH)
Bowling Green State U–Firelands Coll (OH)
Bradley U (IL)
Brenau U (GA)
Brescia U (KY)
Bridgewater Coll (VA)
Brigham Young U (UT)
Brock U (ON, Canada)
Bryan Coll (TN)
Buffalo State Coll, State U of New York (NY)
Butler U (IN)
Cabrini Coll (PA)
California Baptist U (CA)
California Lutheran U (CA)
California Polytechnic State U, San Luis Obispo (CA)
California State Polytechnic U, Pomona (CA)
California State U, Bakersfield (CA)
California State U, Chico (CA)
California State U, Dominguez Hills (CA)
California State U, East Bay (CA)
California State U, Fresno (CA)
California State U, Fullerton (CA)
California State U, Long Beach (CA)
California State U, Los Angeles (CA)
California State U, Monterey Bay (CA)
California State U, Northridge (CA)
California State U, Sacramento (CA)
California State U, San Bernardino (CA)
California State U, San Marcos (CA)
California State U, Stanislaus (CA)
Calumet Coll of Saint Joseph (IN)
Cambridge Coll (MA)
Carlow U (PA)
Carnegie Mellon U (PA)
Carson-Newman Coll (TN)
Cazenovia Coll (NY)
Cedar Crest Coll (PA)
Central Christian Coll of Kansas (KS)
Central Michigan U (MI)
Chapman U (CA)
Charter Oak State Coll (CT)
Christian Brothers U (TN)
Clarion U of Pennsylvania (PA)
Clayton State U (GA)
Cleveland State U (OH)
Coastal Carolina U (SC)
Coll of Mount St. Joseph (OH)
Coll of Mount Saint Vincent (NY)
The Coll of New Rochelle (NY)
Coll of Notre Dame of Maryland (MD)
Coll of Saint Benedict (MN)
Coll of St. Joseph (VT)
The Coll of St. Scholastica (MN)
Coll of Staten Island of the City U of New York (NY)
Coll of the Atlantic (ME)
Colorado State U (CO)
Colorado State U–Pueblo (CO)
Columbia Coll (SC)
Columbia Coll Chicago (IL)
Columbus State U (GA)
Concordia U (CA)
Concordia U Texas (TX)
Concordia U Wisconsin (WI)
Coppin State U (MD)
Corban U (OR)
Cornell Coll (IA)
Cornell U (NY)
Crichton Coll (TN)
Culver-Stockton Coll (MO)
Cumberland U (TN)
Dallas Baptist U (TX)
Dana Coll (NE)
Defiance Coll (OH)
DeSales U (PA)
Dickinson State U (ND)
Dominican U of California (CA)
Dowling Coll (NY)
East Carolina U (NC)
Eastern Illinois U (IL)
Eastern Mennonite U (VA)
Eastern Nazarene Coll (MA)
Eastern New Mexico U (NM)
East Stroudsburg U of Pennsylvania (PA)
East Tennessee State U (TN)
East Texas Baptist U (TX)
Elmira Coll (NY)
Emmanuel Coll (MA)
Emory U (GA)
Endicott Coll (MA)
Eugene Lang Coll The New School for Liberal Arts (NY)
The Evergreen State Coll (WA)
Excelsior Coll (NY)
Faulkner U (AL)
Ferrum Coll (VA)
Fitchburg State Coll (MA)
Flagler Coll (FL)
Florida Atlantic U (FL)
Florida Coll (FL)
Florida Gulf Coast U (FL)
Florida Intl U (FL)
Fontbonne U (MO)
Fordham U (NY)
Fort Hays State U (KS)
Fort Lewis Coll (CO)
Fort Valley State U (GA)
Framingham State Coll (MA)
Francis Marion U (SC)
Franklin Pierce U (NH)
Freed-Hardeman U (TN)
Friends U (KS)
Frostburg State U (MD)
Gannon U (PA)
George Mason U (VA)
Georgetown Coll (KY)
Georgetown U (DC)
The George Washington U (DC)
Gettysburg Coll (PA)
Gonzaga U (WA)
Governors State U (IL)
Graceland U (IA)
Grand Valley State U (MI)
Grand View U (IA)
Granite State Coll (NH)
Green Mountain Coll (VT)
Greenville Coll (IL)
Hannibal-LaGrange Coll (MO)
Harvard U (MA)
Hillsdale Free Will Baptist Coll (OK)
Hofstra U (NY)
Holy Family U (PA)
Holy Names U (CA)
Houghton Coll (NY)
Houston Baptist U (TX)
Howard Payne U (TX)
Humboldt State U (CA)
Husson U (ME)
Illinois Coll (IL)
Illinois Inst of Technology (IL)
Illinois Wesleyan U (IL)
Indiana State U (IN)
Indiana U Bloomington (IN)
Indiana U Northwest (IN)
Indiana U South Bend (IN)
Iona Coll (NY)
Iowa State U of Science and Technology (IA)
Iowa Wesleyan Coll (IA)
Ithaca Coll (NY)
Jacksonville U (FL)
James Madison U (VA)
The Johns Hopkins U (MD)
Johnson C. Smith U (NC)
Johnson State Coll (VT)
Juniata Coll (PA)
Kent State U (OH)
Kent State U at Tuscarawas (OH)
Kentucky State U (KY)
Keuka Coll (NY)
Lakehead U (ON, Canada)
Lamar U (TX)
La Roche Coll (PA)
Lasell Coll (MA)
La Sierra U (CA)
Laurentian U (ON, Canada)
Lees-McRae Coll (NC)
Lesley U (MA)
Lewis U (IL)
Limestone Coll (SC)
Lincoln Coll–Normal (IL)
Lincoln Memorial U (TN)
Lindenwood U (MO)
Lock Haven U of Pennsylvania (PA)
Long Island U, Brooklyn Campus (NY)
Long Island U, C.W. Post Campus (NY)
Longwood U (VA)
Louisiana Coll (LA)
Louisiana State U and Ag and Mech Coll (LA)
Loyola Marymount U (CA)
Lubbock Christian U (TX)
Lynn U (FL)
Manhattan Coll (NY)
Mansfield U of Pennsylvania (PA)
Marian U (WI)
Marietta Coll (OH)
Mars Hill Coll (NC)
Marymount Coll, Palos Verdes, California (CA)
Marymount Manhattan Coll (NY)
Marymount U (VA)
Maryville U of Saint Louis (MO)
Massachusetts Coll of Liberal Arts (MA)
Massachusetts Inst of Technology (MA)
The Master's Coll and Sem (CA)
McNeese State U (LA)
Medaille Coll (NY)
Mercer U (GA)
Mercy Coll (NY)
Methodist U (NC)
Miami U (OH)
Michigan Technological U (MI)
Middlebury Coll (VT)
Middle Tennessee State U (TN)
Midway Coll (KY)
Midwestern State U (TX)
Misericordia U (PA)
Mississippi Coll (MS)
Mississippi State U (MS)
Mississippi U for Women (MS)
Mitchell Coll (CT)
Monmouth Coll (IL)
Montana State U (MT)
Montana State U Billings (MT)
Montana Tech of The U of Montana (MT)
Morris Coll (SC)
Mount Allison U (NB, Canada)
Mount Aloysius Coll (PA)
Mount Ida Coll (MA)
Mount Marty Coll (SD)
Mount Mary Coll (WI)
Mount Olive Coll (NC)
Mount St. Mary's Coll (CA)
Neumann U (PA)
Nevada State Coll at Henderson (NV)
New Coll of Florida (FL)
Newman U (KS)
New Mexico Highlands U (NM)
New Saint Andrews Coll (ID)
The New School for General Studies (NY)
New York U (NY)
Niagara U (NY)
Nipissing U (ON, Canada)
North Carolina State U (NC)
North Central Coll (IL)
Northeastern Illinois U (IL)
Northeastern U (MA)
Northern Arizona U (AZ)
Northern Kentucky U (KY)
North Greenville U (SC)
Northwestern State U of Louisiana (LA)
Northwest Nazarene U (ID)
Notre Dame de Namur U (CA)
Nyack Coll (NY)
Oakland U (MI)
Ohio Dominican U (OH)
Ohio Valley U (WV)
Oklahoma Christian U (OK)
Oklahoma City U (OK)
Oklahoma State U (OK)
Oral Roberts U (OK)
Oregon State U (OR)
Oregon State U–Cascades (OR)
Our Lady of the Lake U of San Antonio (TX)
Pace U (NY)
Park U (MO)
Patrick Henry Coll (VA)
Patten U (CA)
Peace Coll (NC)
Penn State Abington (PA)
Penn State Altoona (PA)
Penn State Beaver (PA)
Penn State Berks (PA)
Penn State Brandywine (PA)
Penn State DuBois (PA)
Penn State Erie, The Behrend Coll (PA)
Penn State Fayette, The Eberly Campus (PA)
Penn State Greater Allegheny (PA)
Penn State Lehigh Valley (PA)
Penn State Mont Alto (PA)
Penn State New Kensington (PA)
Penn State Schuylkill (PA)
Penn State Shenango (PA)
Penn State U Park (PA)
Penn State Wilkes-Barre (PA)
Penn State Worthington Scranton (PA)
Penn State York (PA)
Pepperdine U, Malibu (CA)
Polytechnic Inst of NYU (NY)
Pomona Coll (CA)
Pontifical Catholic U of Puerto Rico (PR)
Portland State U (OR)
Post U (CT)
Prescott Coll (AZ)
Providence Coll (RI)
Purchase Coll, State U of New York (NY)
Purdue U North Central (IN)
Queens Coll of the City U of New York (NY)
Quinnipiac U (CT)
Ramapo Coll of New Jersey (NJ)
Randolph Coll (VA)
Redeemer U Coll (ON, Canada)
Regis Coll (MA)
Reinhardt Coll (GA)
Rhode Island Coll (RI)
The Richard Stockton Coll of New Jersey (NJ)
Rider U (NJ)
Rivier Coll (NH)
Roberts Wesleyan Coll (NY)
Rogers State U (OK)
Roosevelt U (IL)
Rowan U (NJ)
Rutgers, The State U of New Jersey, Camden (NJ)
Rutgers, The State U of New Jersey, New Brunswick (NJ)
Sacred Heart Major Sem (MI)
St. Andrews Presbyterian Coll (NC)
St. Cloud State U (MN)
St. Edward's U (TX)
St. Francis Coll (NY)
St. Francis Xavier U (NS, Canada)
St. John Fisher Coll (NY)
St. John's Coll (MD)
Saint John's U (MN)
St. John's U (NY)
Saint Joseph Coll (CT)
St. Joseph's Coll, Long Island Campus (NY)
Saint Joseph Sem Coll (LA)
Saint Joseph's U (PA)
Saint Leo U (FL)
Saint Mary-of-the-Woods Coll (IN)
Saint Mary's Coll of California (CA)
St. Olaf Coll (MN)
Saint Paul's Coll (VA)
St. Thomas U (FL)
Saint Vincent Coll (PA)
Saint Xavier U (IL)
Salisbury U (MD)
Salve Regina U (RI)

INDEXES

San Diego Christian Coll (CA)
San Diego State U (CA)
San Francisco State U (CA)
San Jose State U (CA)
Santa Clara U (CA)
Sarah Lawrence Coll (NY)
Schreiner U (TX)
Seattle Pacific U (WA)
Seattle U (WA)
Seton Hall U (NJ)
Shaw U (NC)
Shenandoah U (VA)
Shorter U (GA)
Simon Fraser U (BC, Canada)
Simpson U (CA)
Skidmore Coll (NY)
Soka U of America (CA)
Sonoma State U (CA)
South Dakota State U (SD)
Southeastern Louisiana U (LA)
Southern Connecticut State U (CT)
Southern Illinois U Carbondale (IL)
Southern Illinois U Edwardsville (IL)
Southern Oregon U (OR)
Southern Vermont Coll (VT)
Southwestern Coll (KS)
Spalding U (KY)
State U of New York at Fredonia (NY)
State U of New York at New Paltz (NY)
State U of New York at Plattsburgh (NY)
State U of New York Coll at Oneonta (NY)
Stephen F. Austin State U (TX)
Stephens Coll (MO)
Sterling Coll (VT)
Suffolk U (MA)
Sweet Briar Coll (VA)
Tarleton State U (TX)
Temple U (PA)
Texas A&M U–Commerce (TX)
Texas Christian U (TX)
Texas Coll (TX)
Texas Tech U (TX)
Thomas Aquinas Coll (CA)
Thomas Edison State Coll (NJ)
Thomas More Coll (KY)
Thompson Rivers U (BC, Canada)
Trent U (ON, Canada)
Trine U (IN)
Troy U (AL)
Tulane U (LA)
Union Coll (NY)
Union Inst & U (OH)
U at Buffalo, the State U of New York (NY)
The U of Akron (OH)
U of Alaska Anchorage, Kenai Peninsula Coll (AK)
U of Alaska Fairbanks (AK)
U of Alaska Southeast (AK)
U of Alberta (AB, Canada)
The U of Arizona (AZ)
U of Arkansas at Fort Smith (AR)
U of Arkansas at Little Rock (AR)
U of Baltimore (MD)
The U of British Columbia (BC, Canada)
U of California, Riverside (CA)
U of California, Santa Barbara (CA)
U of Central Florida (FL)
U of Central Oklahoma (OK)
U of Chicago (IL)
U of Cincinnati (OH)
U of Delaware (DE)
U of Evansville (IN)
U of Georgia (GA)
U of Hawaii at Manoa (HI)
U of Houston (TX)
U of Houston–Downtown (TX)
U of Illinois at Springfield (IL)
U of Illinois at Urbana–Champaign (IL)
The U of Iowa (IA)
The U of Kansas (KS)
U of La Verne (CA)
U of Lethbridge (AB, Canada)
U of Louisville (KY)
U of Maine (ME)
U of Maine at Farmington (ME)
U of Maine at Fort Kent (ME)
U of Maine at Presque Isle (ME)
U of Maryland Eastern Shore (MD)
U of Mary Washington (VA)
U of Massachusetts Dartmouth (MA)
U of Massachusetts Lowell (MA)
U of Memphis (TN)
U of Michigan–Dearborn (MI)
U of Michigan–Flint (MI)
U of Mississippi (MS)
U of Missouri–Kansas City (MO)
U of Missouri–St. Louis (MO)
The U of Montana Western (MT)
U of Nebraska–Lincoln (NE)
U of New Brunswick Fredericton (NB, Canada)
U of New England (ME)
U of New Haven (CT)
U of New Mexico (NM)
The U of North Carolina at Asheville (NC)
The U of North Carolina at Chapel Hill (NC)
The U of North Carolina at Greensboro (NC)
U of Northern Iowa (IA)
U of North Florida (FL)
U of Notre Dame (IN)
U of Oklahoma (OK)
U of Pennsylvania (PA)
U of Pittsburgh (PA)
U of Puerto Rico, Río Piedras (PR)
U of Redlands (CA)
U of Regina (SK, Canada)
U of Rhode Island (RI)
U of St. Francis (IL)
U of St. Thomas (TX)
U of San Diego (CA)
U of San Francisco (CA)
U of South Carolina (SC)
The U of South Dakota (SD)
U of Southern Indiana (IN)
U of South Florida (FL)
U of Tampa (FL)
The U of Texas at Tyler (TX)
U of the Incarnate Word (TX)
The U of Toledo (OH)
U of Tulsa (OK)
U of Vermont (VT)
U of Virginia (VA)
The U of Virginia's Coll at Wise (VA)
U of Washington (WA)
U of Washington, Tacoma (WA)
U of Waterloo (ON, Canada)
The U of Western Ontario (ON, Canada)
U of Wisconsin–Eau Claire (WI)
U of Wisconsin–Green Bay (WI)
U of Wisconsin–Oshkosh (WI)
U of Wisconsin–Platteville (WI)
U of Wisconsin–River Falls (WI)
U of Wisconsin–Whitewater (WI)
Utah State U (UT)
Utica Coll (NY)
Villanova U (PA)
Virginia State U (VA)
Virginia Wesleyan Coll (VA)
Viterbo U (WI)
Walsh U (OH)
Warner Pacific Coll (OR)
Washburn U (KS)
Washington Adventist U (MD)
Washington Coll (MD)
Washington State U (WA)
Washington U in St. Louis (MO)
Webster U (MO)
West Chester U of Pennsylvania (PA)
Western Carolina U (NC)
Western Connecticut State U (CT)
Western Illinois U (IL)
Western New England Coll (MA)
Western Washington U (WA)
Westfield State Coll (MA)
Westmont Coll (CA)
West Virginia U (WV)
Wheeling Jesuit U (WV)
Wheelock Coll (MA)
Whittier Coll (CA)
Wichita State U (KS)
Wilkes U (PA)
Wilmington Coll (OH)
Wingate U (NC)
Winona State U (MN)
Wittenberg U (OH)
Wright State U (OH)
Xavier U (OH)
York Coll of the City U of New York (NY)
York U (ON, Canada)
Youngstown State U (OH)

LIBRARY SCIENCE

Ball State U (IN)
Clarion U of Pennsylvania (PA)
Concord U (WV)
Kutztown U of Pennsylvania (PA)
Longwood U (VA)
Murray State U (KY)
St. Cloud State U (MN)
Southern Connecticut State U (CT)
Texas A&M U–Commerce (TX)
U of Maine at Augusta (ME)
U of Nebraska at Omaha (NE)
U of Southern Mississippi (MS)

LINGUISTIC AND COMPARATIVE LANGUAGE STUDIES RELATED

Brigham Young U (UT)
Iowa State U of Science and Technology (IA)
U of California, Los Angeles (CA)

LINGUISTICS

Baylor U (TX)
Boston U (MA)
Brandeis U (MA)
Brock U (ON, Canada)
Brooklyn Coll of the City U of New York (NY)
California State U, Chico (CA)
California State U, Dominguez Hills (CA)
California State U, Fresno (CA)
California State U, Fullerton (CA)
California State U, Northridge (CA)
Carnegie Mellon U (PA)
Central Coll (IA)
City Coll of the City U of New York (NY)
Cleveland State U (OH)
The Coll of William and Mary (VA)
Columbia U (NY)
Concordia U (QC, Canada)
Cornell U (NY)
Crown Coll (MN)
Dartmouth Coll (NH)
Duke U (NC)
Eastern Michigan U (MI)
Emory U (GA)
Florida Atlantic U (FL)
Georgetown U (DC)
Hampshire Coll (MA)
Harvard U (MA)
Hofstra U (NY)
Indiana U Bloomington (IN)
Inter American U of Puerto Rico, San Germán Campus (PR)
Iowa State U of Science and Technology (IA)
Lawrence U (WI)
Lehman Coll of the City U of New York (NY)
Liberty U (VA)
Macalester Coll (MN)
Marlboro Coll (VT)
Massachusetts Inst of Technology (MA)
Memorial U of Newfoundland (NL, Canada)
Miami U (OH)
Miami U Hamilton (OH)
Michigan State U (MI)
Mid-Atlantic Christian U (NC)
Montclair State U (NJ)
New York U (NY)
Northeastern Illinois U (IL)
Northeastern U (MA)
Oakland U (MI)
The Ohio State U (OH)
Ohio U (OH)
Oklahoma Wesleyan U (OK)
Old Dominion U (VA)
Pitzer Coll (CA)
Pomona Coll (CA)
Portland State U (OR)
Purdue U (IN)
Queens Coll of the City U of New York (NY)
Queen's U at Kingston (ON, Canada)
Reed Coll (OR)
Rice U (TX)
Rutgers, The State U of New Jersey, New Brunswick (NJ)
St. Cloud State U (MN)
San Diego State U (CA)
San Jose State U (CA)
Scripps Coll (CA)
Seattle Pacific U (WA)
Simon Fraser U (BC, Canada)
Southern Illinois U Carbondale (IL)
Stanford U (CA)
State U of New York at Binghamton (NY)
State U of New York at Oswego (NY)
Stony Brook U, State U of New York (NY)
Swarthmore Coll (PA)
Syracuse U (NY)
Temple U (PA)
Truman State U (MO)
Tulane U (LA)
U at Albany, State U of New York (NY)
U at Buffalo, the State U of New York (NY)
U of Alaska Fairbanks (AK)
U of Alberta (AB, Canada)
The U of Arizona (AZ)
The U of British Columbia (BC, Canada)
U of California, Berkeley (CA)
U of California, Davis (CA)
U of California, Los Angeles (CA)
U of California, Riverside (CA)
U of California, San Diego (CA)
U of California, Santa Barbara (CA)
U of California, Santa Cruz (CA)
U of Chicago (IL)
U of Cincinnati (OH)
U of Colorado at Boulder (CO)
U of Connecticut (CT)
U of Delaware (DE)
U of Florida (FL)
U of Georgia (GA)
U of Hawaii at Hilo (HI)
U of Houston (TX)
U of Illinois at Urbana–Champaign (IL)
The U of Iowa (IA)
The U of Kansas (KS)
U of Kentucky (KY)
U of King's Coll (NS, Canada)
U of Maryland, Coll Park (MD)
U of Massachusetts Amherst (MA)
U of Michigan (MI)
U of Minnesota, Twin Cities Campus (MN)
U of Mississippi (MS)
U of Missouri (MO)
U of New Brunswick Fredericton (NB, Canada)
U of New Hampshire (NH)
U of New Mexico (NM)
The U of North Carolina at Chapel Hill (NC)
U of Oklahoma (OK)
U of Oregon (OR)
U of Ottawa (ON, Canada)
U of Pennsylvania (PA)
U of Pittsburgh (PA)
U of Regina (SK, Canada)
U of Rochester (NY)
U of Saskatchewan (SK, Canada)
U of Southern California (CA)
U of Southern Maine (ME)
The U of Texas at Austin (TX)
The U of Texas at El Paso (TX)
The U of Toledo (OH)
U of Toronto (ON, Canada)
U of Utah (UT)
U of Washington (WA)
The U of Western Ontario (ON, Canada)
U of Wisconsin–Madison (WI)
U of Wisconsin–Milwaukee (WI)
Washington State U (WA)
Washington U in St. Louis (MO)
Wayne State U (MI)
Wellesley Coll (MA)
Western Washington U (WA)
Wright State U (OH)
Yale U (CT)
York U (ON, Canada)

LINGUISTICS OF ASL AND OTHER SIGN LANGUAGES

Kent State U (OH)

LIVESTOCK MANAGEMENT

Fort Hays State U (KS)

LOGIC

Carnegie Mellon U (PA)
U of Pennsylvania (PA)

LOGISTICS AND MATERIALS MANAGEMENT

Albany State U (GA)
Auburn U (AL)
Baylor U (TX)
Bowling Green State U (OH)
Brigham Young U (UT)
California State U, Dominguez Hills (CA)
Central Michigan U (MI)
Clarkson U (NY)
Duquesne U (PA)
Elmhurst Coll (IL)
Georgia Southern U (GA)
Iowa State U of Science and Technology (IA)
Lehigh U (PA)
Michigan State U (MI)
Middle Georgia Coll (GA)
Missouri State U (MO)
Niagara U (NY)
Northeastern State U (OK)
Northeastern U (MA)
The Ohio State U (OH)
Park U (MO)
Penn State Beaver (PA)
Penn State Brandywine (PA)
Penn State Fayette, The Eberly Campus (PA)
Penn State Greater Allegheny (PA)
Penn State Hazleton (PA)
Penn State Lehigh Valley (PA)
Penn State New Kensington (PA)
Penn State Schuylkill (PA)
Penn State Shenango (PA)
Penn State York (PA)
Portland State U (OR)
Shippensburg U of Pennsylvania (PA)
Southeastern Louisiana U (LA)
State U of New York at Binghamton (NY)
State U of New York at New Paltz (NY)
Sullivan U (KY)
U of Arkansas (AR)
The U of Findlay (OH)
U of Illinois at Urbana–Champaign (IL)
The U of Kansas (KS)
U of Maryland, Coll Park (MD)
U of Memphis (TN)
U of Nevada, Reno (NV)
U of North Texas (TX)
U of Puerto Rico at Bayamón (PR)
The U of Tennessee (TN)
The U of Toledo (OH)
U of Wisconsin–Stout (WI)
Weber State U (UT)
Western Illinois U (IL)
Wright State U (OH)

MANAGEMENT INFORMATION SYSTEMS

Adams State Coll (CO)
Albany State U (GA)
Amberton U (TX)
American Intl Coll (MA)
American U (DC)
Amridge U (AL)
Angelo State U (TX)
Appalachian State U (NC)
Aquinas Coll (TN)
Arcadia U (PA)
Arizona State U (AZ)
Auburn U (AL)
Auburn U Montgomery (AL)
Augsburg Coll (MN)
Augustana Coll (SD)
Aurora U (IL)
Avila U (MO)
Azusa Pacific U (CA)
Babson Coll (MA)
Baker Coll of Flint (MI)
Ball State U (IN)
Barry U (FL)
Baylor U (TX)
Bernard M. Baruch Coll of the City U of New York (NY)
Bethel U (TN)
Bishop's U (QC, Canada)
Boston Coll (MA)
Boston U (MA)
Bowling Green State U (OH)
Bradley U (IL)
Briar Cliff U (IA)
Bridgewater Coll (VA)
Bridgewater State Coll (MA)
Buena Vista U (IA)
Butler U (IN)
California State U, Chico (CA)
California State U, East Bay (CA)
California State U, Fresno (CA)
California State U, Long Beach (CA)
California State U, San Bernardino (CA)
Calvin Coll (MI)
Canisius Coll (NY)
Carroll U (WI)
Carson-Newman Coll (TN)
Cedarville U (OH)
Central Connecticut State U (CT)
Central Michigan U (MI)
Claflin U (SC)
Clarkson U (NY)
Cleary U (MI)
Clemson U (SC)
Colorado State U (CO)
Columbus State U (GA)
Concordia U (QC, Canada)
Corban U (OR)
Cornerstone U (MI)
Creighton U (NE)
Dallas Baptist U (TX)
Dalton State Coll (GA)
Dana Coll (NE)
Delaware Valley Coll (PA)
Delta State U (MS)
DePaul U (IL)
DeSales U (PA)
Dominican Coll (NY)
Dordt Coll (IA)
Drexel U (PA)
Duquesne U (PA)
East Carolina U (NC)
East Central U (OK)
Eastern Connecticut State U (CT)
Eastern Michigan U (MI)
Eastern New Mexico U (NM)
Eastern Washington U (WA)
Edgewood Coll (WI)
Elizabethtown Coll (PA)
Elmhurst Coll (IL)
Excelsior Coll (NY)
Fairfield U (CT)
Fayetteville State U (NC)
Ferrum Coll (VA)

INDEXES

Florida Ag and Mech U (FL)
Florida Atlantic U (FL)
Florida Gulf Coast U (FL)
Florida Inst of Technology (FL)
Florida Intl U (FL)
Fordham U (NY)
Fort Hays State U (KS)
Francis Marion U (SC)
Franklin U (OH)
Friends U (KS)
Gannon U (PA)
Gardner-Webb U (NC)
George Fox U (OR)
Georgia Southern U (GA)
Goldey-Beacom Coll (DE)
Governors State U (IL)
Grace Coll (IN)
Graceland U (IA)
Grand View U (IA)
Greenville Coll (IL)
Hardin-Simmons U (TX)
HEC Montreal (QC, Canada)
Henderson State U (AR)
Hofstra U (NY)
Holy Family U (PA)
Husson U (ME)
Illinois Coll (IL)
Indiana State U (IN)
Indiana Tech (IN)
Indiana U of Pennsylvania (PA)
Inter American U of Puerto Rico, Aguadilla Campus (PR)
Inter American U of Puerto Rico, Bayamón Campus (PR)
Inter American U of Puerto Rico, Fajardo Campus (PR)
Inter American U of Puerto Rico, Ponce Campus (PR)
Iona Coll (NY)
Iowa State U of Science and Technology (IA)
Jacksonville U (FL)
Jamestown Coll (ND)
John Brown U (AR)
Johnson State Coll (VT)
Jones Intl U (CO)
Judson U (IL)
Keiser U, Fort Lauderdale (FL)
King Coll (TN)
Lakehead U (ON, Canada)
La Salle U (PA)
Lehigh U (PA)
Le Moyne Coll (NY)
LeTourneau U (TX)
Liberty U (VA)
Lincoln U (CA)
Lindenwood U (MO)
Lipscomb U (TN)
Longwood U (VA)
Loras Coll (IA)
Louisiana Tech U (LA)
Loyola U Chicago (IL)
Lubbock Christian U (TX)
Luther Coll (IA)
Madonna U (MI)
Maranatha Baptist Bible Coll (WI)
Marshall U (WV)
Maryville U of Saint Louis (MO)
The Master's Coll and Sem (CA)
McMurry U (TX)
Menlo Coll (CA)
Miami U (OH)
Michigan State U (MI)
Michigan Technological U (MI)
Middle Tennessee State U (TN)
Milwaukee School of Eng (WI)
Minot State U (ND)
Misericordia U (PA)
Mississippi State U (MS)
Missouri State U (MO)
Monmouth Coll (IL)
Morehead State U (KY)
Mount Mercy Coll (IA)
Mount Vernon Nazarene U (OH)
Murray State U (KY)
National U (CA)
Newman U (KS)
New Mexico Highlands U (NM)
New York Inst of Technology (NY)
Nicholls State U (LA)
Nichols Coll (MA)
North Central Coll (IL)
North Dakota State U (ND)
Northeastern State U (OK)
Northeastern U (MA)
Northern Arizona U (AZ)
Northern Kentucky U (KY)
Northern Michigan U (MI)
Northern State U (SD)
Northwestern Coll (MN)
Northwest Missouri State U (MO)
Oakland U (MI)
Ohio Northern U (OH)
The Ohio State U (OH)
Ohio U (OH)
Oklahoma Baptist U (OK)
Oklahoma City U (OK)
Oklahoma State U (OK)
Old Dominion U (VA)
Oral Roberts U (OK)
Oregon Inst of Technology (OR)
Pacific Union Coll (CA)
Paine Coll (GA)
Park U (MO)
Penn State Abington (PA)
Penn State Altoona (PA)
Penn State Beaver (PA)
Penn State Berks (PA)
Penn State Brandywine (PA)
Penn State DuBois (PA)
Penn State Erie, The Behrend Coll (PA)
Penn State Fayette, The Eberly Campus (PA)
Penn State Greater Allegheny (PA)
Penn State Harrisburg (PA)
Penn State Hazleton (PA)
Penn State Lehigh Valley (PA)
Penn State Mont Alto (PA)
Penn State New Kensington (PA)
Penn State Schuylkill (PA)
Penn State Shenango (PA)
Penn State U Park (PA)
Penn State Wilkes-Barre (PA)
Penn State Worthington Scranton (PA)
Penn State York (PA)
Pennsylvania Coll of Technology (PA)
Peru State Coll (NE)
Philadelphia U (PA)
Pittsburg State U (KS)
Polytechnic Inst of NYU (NY)
Pontifical Catholic U of Puerto Rico (PR)
Post U (CT)
Prairie View A&M U (TX)
Rhode Island Coll (RI)
Robert Morris U (PA)
Rochester Inst of Technology (NY)
Rockford Coll (IL)
Rocky Mountain Coll (MT)
St. Catherine U (MN)
Saint Francis U (PA)
St. Francis Xavier U (NS, Canada)
St. John's U (NY)
Saint Joseph's U (PA)
Saint Louis U (MO)
Saint Martin's U (WA)
Saint Mary's Coll (IN)
Salem State Coll (MA)
Santa Clara U (CA)
Savannah State U (GA)
Schreiner U (TX)
Seattle U (WA)
Seton Hall U (NJ)
Seton Hill U (PA)
Shawnee State U (OH)
Simon Fraser U (BC, Canada)
Simpson U (CA)
Slippery Rock U of Pennsylvania (PA)
Southeastern U (FL)
Southern Adventist U (TN)
Southern Illinois U Edwardsville (IL)
Southern U at New Orleans (LA)
Southwestern Coll (KS)
Spring Arbor U (MI)
State U of New York at Binghamton (NY)
State U of New York at Plattsburgh (NY)
State U of New York Coll at Old Westbury (NY)
State U of New York Coll of Technology at Canton (NY)
Stetson U (FL)
Stevenson U (MD)
Strayer U—Akron Campus (OH)
Strayer U—Alexandria Campus (VA)
Strayer U—Allentown Campus (PA)
Strayer U—Anne Arundel Campus (MD)
Strayer U—Arlington Campus (VA)
Strayer U—Augusta Campus (GA)
Strayer U—Baymeadows Campus (FL)
Strayer U—Birmingham Campus (AL)
Strayer U—Brickell Campus (FL)
Strayer U—Center City Campus (PA)
Strayer U—Central Austin Campus (TX)
Strayer U—Chamblee Campus (GA)
Strayer U—Charleston Campus (SC)
Strayer U—Cherry Hill Campus (NJ)
Strayer U—Chesapeake Campus (VA)
Strayer U—Chesterfield Campus (VA)
Strayer U—Christiana Campus (DE)
Strayer U—Cobb County Campus (GA)
Strayer U—Columbia Campus (SC)
Strayer U—Columbus Campus (OH)
Strayer U—Coral Springs Campus (FL)
Strayer U—Cranberry Woods Campus (PA)
Strayer U—Delaware County Campus (PA)
Strayer U—Doral Campus (FL)
Strayer U—Douglasville Campus (GA)
Strayer U—Fairview Park Campus (OH)
Strayer U—Florence Campus (KY)
Strayer U—Fort Lauderdale Campus (FL)
Strayer U—Fredericksburg Campus (VA)
Strayer U—Garner Campus (NC)
Strayer U—Greensboro Campus (NC)
Strayer U—Greenville Campus (SC)
Strayer U—Henrico Campus (VA)
Strayer U—Huntersville Campus (NC)
Strayer U—Huntsville Campus (AL)
Strayer U—King of Prussia Campus (PA)
Strayer U—Knoxville Campus (TN)
Strayer U—Lawrenceville Campus (NJ)
Strayer U—Lexington Campus (KY)
Strayer U—Lithonia Campus (GA)
Strayer U—Little Rock Campus (AR)
Strayer U—Loudoun Campus (VA)
Strayer U—Louisville Campus (KY)
Strayer U—Lower Bucks County Campus (PA)
Strayer U—Maitland Campus (FL)
Strayer U—Manassas Campus (VA)
Strayer U—Mason Campus (OH)
Strayer U—Metairie Campus (LA)
Strayer U—Miramar Campus (FL)
Strayer U—Morrow Campus (GA)
Strayer U—Nashville Campus (TN)
Strayer U—New Brunswick Campus (NJ)
Strayer U—Newport News Campus (VA)
Strayer U—North Charlotte Campus (NC)
Strayer U—North Raleigh Campus (NC)
Strayer U—Orlando East Campus (FL)
Strayer U—Owings Mills Campus (MD)
Strayer U—Palm Beach Gardens Campus (FL)
Strayer U—Penn Center West Campus (PA)
Strayer U—Prince George's Campus (MD)
Strayer U—Rockville Campus (MD)
Strayer U—Roswell Campus (GA)
Strayer U—RTP Campus (NC)
Strayer U—Salt Lake Campus (UT)
Strayer U—Sand Lake Campus (FL)
Strayer U—Savannah Campus (GA)
Strayer U—Shelby Oaks Campus (TN)
Strayer U—South Charlotte Campus (NC)
Strayer U—Takoma Park Campus (DC)
Strayer U—Tampa East Campus (FL)
Strayer U—Tampa Westshore Campus (FL)
Strayer U—Teays Valley Campus (WV)
Strayer U—Thousand Oaks Campus (TN)
Strayer U—Virginia Beach Campus (VA)
Strayer U—Washington Campus (DC)
Strayer U—White Marsh Campus (MD)
Strayer U—Willingboro Campus (NJ)
Strayer U—Woodbridge Campus (VA)
Suffolk U (MA)
Tarleton State U (TX)
Temple U (PA)
Texas A&M U–Commerce (TX)
Texas A&M U–Corpus Christi (TX)
Texas A&M U–Kingsville (TX)
Texas State U–San Marcos (TX)
Texas Tech U (TX)
Texas Wesleyan U (TX)
Thiel Coll (PA)
Trevecca Nazarene U (TN)
Troy U (AL)
Truman State U (MO)
TUI U (CA)
Université du Québec en Outaouais (QC, Canada)
The U of Alabama (AL)
The U of Alabama at Birmingham (AL)
The U of Alabama in Huntsville (AL)
U of Alaska Anchorage (AK)
U of Alberta (AB, Canada)
U of Arkansas at Monticello (AR)
U of Atlanta (GA)
U of Baltimore (MD)
The U of British Columbia (BC, Canada)
U of Central Missouri (MO)
U of Cincinnati (OH)
U of Colorado at Boulder (CO)
U of Connecticut (CT)
U of Dayton (OH)
U of Delaware (DE)
U of Denver (CO)
U of Evansville (IN)
U of Georgia (GA)
U of Hawaii at Manoa (HI)
U of Houston (TX)
U of Houston–Clear Lake (TX)
U of Houston–Downtown (TX)
U of Idaho (ID)
U of Illinois at Urbana–Champaign (IL)
The U of Iowa (IA)
The U of Kansas (KS)
U of Lethbridge (AB, Canada)
U of Louisiana at Monroe (LA)
U of Louisville (KY)
U of Maine (ME)
U of Mary (ND)
U of Mary Hardin-Baylor (TX)
U of Massachusetts Dartmouth (MA)
U of Memphis (TN)
U of Michigan–Dearborn (MI)
U of Minnesota, Crookston (MN)
U of Minnesota, Twin Cities Campus (MN)
U of Mississippi (MS)
U of Missouri (MO)
U of Missouri–St. Louis (MO)
U of Nevada, Las Vegas (NV)
U of New Orleans (LA)
U of North Alabama (AL)
The U of North Carolina at Charlotte (NC)
The U of North Carolina Wilmington (NC)
U of Northern Iowa (IA)
U of North Texas (TX)
U of Notre Dame (IN)
U of Oklahoma (OK)
U of Ottawa (ON, Canada)
U of Pennsylvania (PA)
U of Puerto Rico, Río Piedras (PR)
U of Redlands (CA)
U of Rhode Island (RI)
U of San Francisco (CA)
U of Southern Mississippi (MS)
U of South Florida (FL)
The U of Tennessee at Martin (TN)
The U of Texas at Arlington (TX)
The U of Texas at Austin (TX)
The U of Texas at San Antonio (TX)
The U of Texas–Pan American (TX)
U of the Cumberlands (KY)
U of the Incarnate Word (TX)
The U of Toledo (OH)
U of Tulsa (OK)
U of Utah (UT)
U of Washington (WA)
The U of West Alabama (AL)
The U of Western Ontario (ON, Canada)
U of West Florida (FL)
U of West Georgia (GA)
U of Wisconsin–Green Bay (WI)
U of Wisconsin–La Crosse (WI)
U of Wisconsin–Milwaukee (WI)
U of Wisconsin–Oshkosh (WI)
U of Wisconsin–River Falls (WI)
U of Wisconsin–Whitewater (WI)
Upper Iowa U (IA)
Ursuline Coll (OH)
Villanova U (PA)
Virginia Union U (VA)
Viterbo U (WI)
Wake Forest U (NC)
Walden U (MN)
Walsh U (OH)
Washington State U (WA)
Wayne State U (MI)
Western Carolina U (NC)
Western Connecticut State U (CT)
Western Illinois U (IL)
Western Kentucky U (KY)
Western New England Coll (MA)
Western State Coll of Colorado (CO)
Western Washington U (WA)
Westminster Coll (MO)
West Virginia U (WV)
Wichita State U (KS)
Winona State U (MN)
Winston-Salem State U (NC)
Worcester Polytechnic Inst (MA)
Wright State U (OH)
Xavier U (OH)
York Coll of Pennsylvania (PA)
York Coll of the City U of New York (NY)
York U (ON, Canada)
Youngstown State U (OH)

MANAGEMENT INFORMATION SYSTEMS AND SERVICES RELATED

Buena Vista U (IA)
California State U, Chico (CA)
Columbia Southern U (AL)
Florida Ag and Mech U (FL)
Fordham U (NY)
Midwestern State U (TX)
Montana Tech of The U of Montana (MT)
Northern Michigan U (MI)
Rogers State U (OK)
St. Bonaventure U (NY)
Thomas Edison State Coll (NJ)
Westminster Coll (UT)
Widener U (PA)

MANAGEMENT SCIENCE

Aurora U (IL)
Averett U (VA)
Cambridge Coll (MA)
Capella U (MN)
Centenary Coll (NJ)
Clarion U of Pennsylvania (PA)
Coppin State U (MD)
DePaul U (IL)
Duquesne U (PA)
Eastern Illinois U (IL)
Fitchburg State Coll (MA)
Friends U (KS)
Grace Bible Coll (MI)
Grand Valley State U (MI)
Granite State Coll (NH)
Hardin-Simmons U (TX)
Hawai'i Pacific U (HI)
HEC Montreal (QC, Canada)
Inter American U of Puerto Rico, Bayamón Campus (PR)
John Brown U (AR)
Keiser U, Fort Lauderdale (FL)
La Roche Coll (PA)
Lehigh U (PA)
Louisiana State U and Ag and Mech Coll (LA)
Louisiana Tech U (LA)
Lourdes Coll (OH)
Madonna U (MI)
Manhattan Coll (NY)
Minnesota State U Mankato (MN)
Nevada State Coll at Henderson (NV)
Northeastern U (MA)
Oakland City U (IN)
Ohio Northern U (OH)
Oklahoma Baptist U (OK)
Oral Roberts U (OK)
Pace U (NY)
Pennsylvania Coll of Technology (PA)
Prescott Coll (AZ)
Quincy U (IL)
Rider U (NJ)
Rocky Mountain Coll (MT)
Roosevelt U (IL)
Rutgers, The State U of New Jersey, New Brunswick (NJ)
St. Ambrose U (IA)
Saint Louis U (MO)
Salve Regina U (RI)
Shippensburg U of Pennsylvania (PA)
Siena Coll (NY)
Simon Fraser U (BC, Canada)
Southeastern Oklahoma State U (OK)
Southern Adventist U (TN)
Southern Illinois U Carbondale (IL)
Southern Methodist U (TX)
Southern Vermont Coll (VT)
Southwestern Assemblies of God U (TX)
Southwestern Coll (KS)
State U of New York at Oswego (NY)
Stetson U (FL)
Texas A&M U (TX)
Texas Christian U (TX)
Trinity U (TX)

MANAGEMENT SCIENCES AND QUANTITATIVE METHODS RELATED

MANUFACTURING ENGINEERING

MANUFACTURING TECHNOLOGY

MARINE BIOLOGY AND BIOLOGICAL OCEANOGRAPHY

MARINE SCIENCE/ MERCHANT MARINE OFFICER

MARINE TECHNOLOGY

MARITIME SCIENCE

MARKETING/MARKETING MANAGEMENT

Kansas State U (KS)
Kean U (NJ)
Keiser U, Fort Lauderdale (FL)
Kendall Coll (IL)
Kennesaw State U (GA)
Kent State U (OH)
Keuka Coll (NY)
King's Coll (PA)
Kutztown U of Pennsylvania (PA)
Lakehead U (ON, Canada)
Lakeland Coll (WI)
Lamar U (TX)
La Roche Coll (PA)
La Salle U (PA)
Lasell Coll (MA)
La Sierra U (CA)
Lehigh U (PA)
Le Moyne Coll (NY)
LeTourneau U (TX)
Lewis U (IL)
LIM Coll (NY)
Limestone Coll (SC)
Lincoln Memorial U (TN)
Lincoln U (MO)
Lindenwood U (MO)
Lipscomb U (TN)
Long Island U, Brooklyn Campus (NY)
Long Island U, C.W. Post Campus (NY)
Longwood U (VA)
Loras Coll (IA)
Louisiana Coll (LA)
Louisiana State U and Ag and Mech Coll (LA)
Louisiana State U in Shreveport (LA)
Louisiana Tech U (LA)
Loyola U Chicago (IL)
Loyola U New Orleans (LA)
Lubbock Christian U (TX)
Lynchburg Coll (VA)
Madonna U (MI)
Manchester Coll (IN)
Manhattan Coll (NY)
Mansfield U of Pennsylvania (PA)
Maranatha Baptist Bible Coll (WI)
Marian U (IN)
Marian U (WI)
Marietta Coll (OH)
Marquette U (WI)
Marshall U (WV)
Mars Hill Coll (NC)
Maryville U of Saint Louis (MO)
Marywood U (PA)
McKendree U (IL)
McMurry U (TX)
McNeese State U (LA)
Memorial U of Newfoundland (NL, Canada)
Menlo Coll (CA)
Merrimack Coll (MA)
Messiah Coll (PA)
Metropolitan State Coll of Denver (CO)
Miami U (OH)
Michigan State U (MI)
Michigan Technological U (MI)
MidAmerica Nazarene U (KS)
Middle Tennessee State U (TN)
Midwestern State U (TX)
Millikin U (IL)
Minnesota State U Mankato (MN)
Minnesota State U Moorhead (MN)
Minot State U (ND)
Misericordia U (PA)
Mississippi Coll (MS)
Mississippi State U (MS)
Missouri Baptist U (MO)
Missouri State U (MO)
Missouri Western State U (MO)
Mitchell Coll (CT)
Montana State U (MT)
Montana State U Billings (MT)
Morehead State U (KY)
Morningside Coll (IA)
Mount Mary Coll (WI)
Mount Mercy Coll (IA)
Mount St. Mary's Coll (CA)
Mount Vernon Nazarene U (OH)
Murray State U (KY)
National U (CA)
Nazareth Coll of Rochester (NY)
Neumann U (PA)
New England Coll (NH)
New England School of Communications (ME)
New Mexico Highlands U (NM)
New Mexico State U (NM)
New York Inst of Technology (NY)
Niagara U (NY)
Nicholls State U (LA)
Nichols Coll (MA)
North Carolina State U (NC)
North Central Coll (IL)
North Dakota State U (ND)
Northeastern Illinois U (IL)
Northeastern State U (OK)
Northeastern U (MA)
Northern Kentucky U (KY)
Northern Michigan U (MI)
Northern State U (SD)
North Georgia Coll & State U (GA)
North Greenville U (SC)
Northwestern Coll (MN)
Northwest Missouri State U (MO)
Northwest Nazarene U (ID)
Northwest U (WA)
Nova Southeastern U (FL)
Oakland U (MI)
The Ohio State U (OH)
Ohio U (OH)
Ohio Valley U (WV)
Oklahoma Baptist U (OK)
Oklahoma Christian U (OK)
Oklahoma City U (OK)
Oklahoma State U (OK)
Old Dominion U (VA)
Oral Roberts U (OK)
Our Lady of the Lake U of San Antonio (TX)
Pace U (NY)
Pacific Union Coll (CA)
Paine Coll (GA)
Park U (MO)
Penn State Abington (PA)
Penn State Altoona (PA)
Penn State Beaver (PA)
Penn State Berks (PA)
Penn State Brandywine (PA)
Penn State DuBois (PA)
Penn State Erie, The Behrend Coll (PA)
Penn State Fayette, The Eberly Campus (PA)
Penn State Greater Allegheny (PA)
Penn State Harrisburg (PA)
Penn State Hazleton (PA)
Penn State Lehigh Valley (PA)
Penn State Mont Alto (PA)
Penn State New Kensington (PA)
Penn State Schuylkill (PA)
Penn State Shenango (PA)
Penn State U Park (PA)
Penn State Wilkes-Barre (PA)
Penn State Worthington Scranton (PA)
Penn State York (PA)
Pennsylvania Coll of Technology (PA)
Peru State Coll (NE)
Philadelphia U (PA)
Pittsburg State U (KS)
Plymouth State U (NH)
Polytechnic U of Puerto Rico (PR)
Pontifical Catholic U of Puerto Rico (PR)
Portland State U (OR)
Post U (CT)
Prairie View A&M U (TX)
Providence Coll (RI)
Quincy U (IL)
Quinnipiac U (CT)
Radford U (VA)
Redeemer U Coll (ON, Canada)
Rhode Island Coll (RI)
Rider U (NJ)
Robert Morris U (PA)
Roberts Wesleyan Coll (NY)
Rochester Coll (MI)
Rochester Inst of Technology (NY)
Rockford Coll (IL)
Roosevelt U (IL)
Rutgers, The State U of New Jersey, Camden (NJ)
Rutgers, The State U of New Jersey, Newark (NJ)
Rutgers, The State U of New Jersey, New Brunswick (NJ)
Sacred Heart U (CT)
Sage Coll of Albany (NY)
Saginaw Valley State U (MI)
St. Ambrose U (IA)
St. Bonaventure U (NY)
St. Catherine U (MN)
St. Cloud State U (MN)
St. Edward's U (TX)
Saint Francis U (PA)
St. John's U (NY)
Saint Joseph's U (PA)
Saint Leo U (FL)
Saint Louis U (MO)
Saint Martin's U (WA)
Saint Mary-of-the-Woods Coll (IN)
Saint Mary's Coll (IN)
St. Mary's U (TX)
Saint Mary's U of Minnesota (MN)
St. Thomas Aquinas Coll (NY)
St. Thomas U (FL)
Saint Vincent Coll (PA)
Salem State Coll (MA)
Salisbury U (MD)
Samford U (AL)
Sam Houston State U (TX)
San Diego State U (CA)
San Francisco State U (CA)
San Jose State U (CA)
Santa Clara U (CA)
Savannah State U (GA)
Schreiner U (TX)
Seattle U (WA)
Seton Hall U (NJ)
Seton Hill U (PA)
Shippensburg U of Pennsylvania (PA)
Siena Coll (NY)
Simmons Coll (MA)
Simpson Coll (IA)
Slippery Rock U of Pennsylvania (PA)
South Carolina State U (SC)
Southeastern Louisiana U (LA)
Southeastern Oklahoma State U (OK)
Southeastern U (FL)
Southeast Missouri State U (MO)
Southern Adventist U (TN)
Southern Connecticut State U (CT)
Southern Illinois U Carbondale (IL)
Southern Methodist U (TX)
Southern New Hampshire U (NH)
Southern Oregon U (OR)
Southern U and Ag and Mech Coll (LA)
Southwest Baptist U (MO)
Southwestern Assemblies of God U (TX)
Southwestern Oklahoma State U (OK)
Southwest Minnesota State U (MN)
Spring Hill Coll (AL)
State U of New York at Binghamton (NY)
State U of New York at Fredonia (NY)
State U of New York at Oswego (NY)
State U of New York at Plattsburgh (NY)
State U of New York Coll at Old Westbury (NY)
Stephen F. Austin State U (TX)
Stephens Coll (MO)
Stetson U (FL)
Stonehill Coll (MA)
Suffolk U (MA)
Sullivan U (KY)
Susquehanna U (PA)
Syracuse U (NY)
Tabor Coll (KS)
Talladega Coll (AL)
Taylor U (IN)
Temple U (PA)
Tennessee Technological U (TN)
Texas A&M Intl U (TX)
Texas A&M U (TX)
Texas A&M U–Commerce (TX)
Texas A&M U–Corpus Christi (TX)
Texas A&M U–Kingsville (TX)
Texas Christian U (TX)
Texas Southern U (TX)
Texas State U–San Marcos (TX)
Texas Tech U (TX)
Texas Wesleyan U (TX)
Texas Woman's U (TX)
Thomas Edison State Coll (NJ)
Thompson Rivers U (BC, Canada)
Tiffin U (OH)
Trevecca Nazarene U (TN)
Trine U (IN)
Trinity Christian Coll (IL)
Trinity U (TX)
Truman State U (MO)
Tulane U (LA)
Tuskegee U (AL)
Union U (TN)
Universidad de las Américas–Puebla (Mexico)
The U of Akron (OH)
The U of Alabama (AL)
The U of Alabama at Birmingham (AL)
The U of Alabama in Huntsville (AL)
U of Alaska Anchorage (AK)
U of Alberta (AB, Canada)
The U of Arizona (AZ)
U of Arkansas (AR)
U of Arkansas at Little Rock (AR)
U of Atlanta (GA)
U of Baltimore (MD)
The U of British Columbia (BC, Canada)
The U of British Columbia–Okanagan (BC, Canada)
U of Central Florida (FL)
U of Central Missouri (MO)
U of Central Oklahoma (OK)
U of Charleston (WV)
U of Cincinnati (OH)
U of Colorado at Boulder (CO)
U of Colorado at Colorado Springs (CO)
U of Connecticut (CT)
U of Dayton (OH)
U of Delaware (DE)
U of Denver (CO)
U of Evansville (IN)
The U of Findlay (OH)
U of Florida (FL)
U of Georgia (GA)
U of Guam (GU)
U of Guelph (ON, Canada)
U of Hartford (CT)
U of Hawaii at Manoa (HI)
U of Houston (TX)
U of Houston–Clear Lake (TX)
U of Houston–Downtown (TX)
U of Houston–Victoria (TX)
U of Idaho (ID)
U of Illinois at Chicago (IL)
U of Illinois at Urbana–Champaign (IL)
U of Indianapolis (IN)
The U of Iowa (IA)
The U of Kansas (KS)
U of Kentucky (KY)
U of La Verne (CA)
U of Lethbridge (AB, Canada)
U of Louisiana at Monroe (LA)
U of Louisville (KY)
U of Maine at Machias (ME)
U of Mary (ND)
U of Mary Hardin-Baylor (TX)
U of Maryland, Coll Park (MD)
U of Maryland U Coll (MD)
U of Massachusetts Amherst (MA)
U of Massachusetts Dartmouth (MA)
U of Memphis (TN)
U of Miami (FL)
U of Michigan–Dearborn (MI)
U of Michigan–Flint (MI)
U of Minnesota, Crookston (MN)
U of Minnesota, Duluth (MN)
U of Minnesota, Twin Cities Campus (MN)
U of Mississippi (MS)
U of Missouri (MO)
U of Missouri–St. Louis (MO)
U of Montevallo (AL)
U of Nebraska at Omaha (NE)
U of Nebraska–Lincoln (NE)
U of Nevada, Las Vegas (NV)
U of Nevada, Reno (NV)
U of New Brunswick Fredericton (NB, Canada)
U of New Haven (CT)
U of New Orleans (LA)
U of North Alabama (AL)
The U of North Carolina Wilmington (NC)
U of North Dakota (ND)
U of Northern Iowa (IA)
U of North Florida (FL)
U of North Texas (TX)
U of Notre Dame (IN)
U of Oklahoma (OK)
U of Ottawa (ON, Canada)
U of Pennsylvania (PA)
U of Pittsburgh (PA)
U of Portland (OR)
U of Puerto Rico at Bayamón (PR)
U of Puerto Rico, Río Piedras (PR)
U of Regina (SK, Canada)
U of Rhode Island (RI)
U of Rio Grande (OH)
U of St. Francis (IL)
U of St. Thomas (MN)
U of St. Thomas (TX)
U of San Diego (CA)
U of San Francisco (CA)
U of Saskatchewan (SK, Canada)
The U of Scranton (PA)
U of South Alabama (AL)
U of South Carolina (SC)
The U of South Dakota (SD)
U of Southern Indiana (IN)
U of Southern Mississippi (MS)
U of South Florida (FL)
The U of Tampa (FL)
The U of Tennessee (TN)
The U of Tennessee at Martin (TN)
The U of Texas at Arlington (TX)
The U of Texas at Brownsville (TX)
The U of Texas at El Paso (TX)
The U of Texas at San Antonio (TX)
The U of Texas at Tyler (TX)
The U of Texas of the Permian Basin (TX)
The U of Texas–Pan American (TX)
U of the Incarnate Word (TX)
U of the Ozarks (AR)
U of the Sciences in Philadelphia (PA)
The U of Toledo (OH)
U of Tulsa (OK)
U of Utah (UT)
U of Washington, Tacoma (WA)
The U of Western Ontario (ON, Canada)
U of West Florida (FL)
U of West Georgia (GA)
U of Windsor (ON, Canada)
U of Wisconsin–Eau Claire (WI)
U of Wisconsin–La Crosse (WI)
U of Wisconsin–Milwaukee (WI)
U of Wisconsin–Oshkosh (WI)
U of Wisconsin–Parkside (WI)
U of Wisconsin–River Falls (WI)
U of Wisconsin–Superior (WI)
U of Wisconsin–Whitewater (WI)
U of Wyoming (WY)
Upper Iowa U (IA)
Ursuline Coll (OH)
Utah State U (UT)
Valdosta State U (GA)
Valparaiso U (IN)
Vanguard U of Southern California (CA)
Villanova U (PA)
Virginia Commonwealth U (VA)
Virginia Intermont Coll (VA)
Virginia Polytechnic Inst and State U (VA)
Virginia State U (VA)
Virginia Union U (VA)
Viterbo U (WI)
Walden U (MN)
Waldorf Coll (IA)
Wartburg Coll (IA)
Washburn U (KS)
Washington State U (WA)
Washington U in St. Louis (MO)
Waynesburg U (PA)
Wayne State U (MI)
Webber Intl U (FL)
Webster U (MO)
Western Carolina U (NC)
Western Connecticut State U (CT)
Western Illinois U (IL)
Western Intl U (AZ)
Western Kentucky U (KY)
Western Michigan U (MI)
Western New England Coll (MA)
Western State Coll of Colorado (CO)
Western Washington U (WA)
West Liberty U (WV)
Westminster Coll (UT)
West Virginia U (WV)
West Virginia Wesleyan Coll (WV)
Westwood Coll–Anaheim (CA)
Westwood Coll–Annandale Campus (VA)
Westwood Coll–Arlington Ballston Campus (VA)
Westwood Coll–Atlanta Midtown (GA)
Westwood Coll–Atlanta Northlake (GA)
Westwood Coll–Chicago Du Page (IL)
Westwood Coll–Chicago Loop Campus (IL)
Westwood Coll–Chicago O'Hare Airport (IL)
Westwood Coll–Chicago River Oaks (IL)
Westwood Coll–Dallas (TX)
Westwood Coll–Denver North (CO)
Westwood Coll–Denver South (CO)
Westwood Coll–Fort Worth (TX)
Westwood Coll–Inland Empire (CA)
Westwood Coll–Los Angeles (CA)
Westwood Coll–Online Campus (CO)
Westwood Coll–South Bay Campus (CA)
Wheeling Jesuit U (WV)
Wichita State U (KS)
Widener U (PA)
Wilberforce U (OH)
Wilmington Coll (OH)
Wilmington U (DE)
Wingate U (NC)
Winona State U (MN)
Woodbury U (CA)
Wright State U (OH)
Xavier U (OH)
Xavier U of Louisiana (LA)
York Coll of Pennsylvania (PA)
York Coll of the City U of New York (NY)
York U (ON, Canada)
Youngstown State U (OH)

MARKETING RELATED

Babson Coll (MA)
Bowling Green State U (OH)
Capella U (MN)
Carlow U (PA)
Duquesne U (PA)
Eastern Nazarene Coll (MA)
Franklin U (OH)
Inter American U of Puerto Rico, San Germán Campus (PR)
Lourdes Coll (OH)
Menlo Coll (CA)
Miami U Hamilton (OH)
Newbury Coll (MA)
Troy U (AL)
The U of Akron (OH)
The U of Iowa (IA)

U of St. Thomas (TX)
Washington U in St. Louis (MO)
Western Carolina U (NC)
Western Michigan U (MI)
Western New England Coll (MA)

MARKETING RESEARCH

Ashland U (OH)
Baker Coll of Jackson (MI)
Boston U (MA)
Bowling Green State U (OH)
Fashion Inst of Technology (NY)
Inter American U of Puerto Rico, Bayamón Campus (PR)
Ithaca Coll (NY)
Methodist U (NC)
Newbury Coll (MA)
Ohio Northern U (OH)
Salve Regina U (RI)
U of Illinois at Urbana–Champaign (IL)
The U of Toledo (OH)

MARRIAGE AND FAMILY THERAPY/COUNSELING

Amridge U (AL)
Harding U (AR)
John Brown U (AR)
Michigan State U (MI)
Northcentral U (AZ)
Oklahoma Baptist U (OK)
Piedmont Baptist Coll and Graduate School (NC)
U of Nevada, Las Vegas (NV)
The U of Western Ontario (ON, Canada)

MASS COMMUNICATION/ MEDIA

Acad of Art U (CA)
Adams State Coll (CO)
Alabama State U (AL)
Albany State U (GA)
Albion Coll (MI)
Alcorn State U (MS)
Allegheny Coll (PA)
American Intl Coll (MA)
American U (DC)
The American U of Paris (France)
Anderson U (IN)
Andrews U (MI)
Arcadia U (PA)
Ashland U (OH)
Auburn U (AL)
Augsburg Coll (MN)
Augustana Coll (IL)
Austin Peay State U (TN)
Baker U (KS)
Baldwin-Wallace Coll (OH)
Barry U (FL)
Barton Coll (NC)
Belmont U (TN)
Beloit Coll (WI)
Bemidji State U (MN)
Benedictine Coll (KS)
Bennett Coll for Women (NC)
Bentley U (MA)
Berea Coll (KY)
Bethel Coll (KS)
Bethel U (MN)
Bethune-Cookman U (FL)
Black Hills State U (SD)
Bloomsburg U of Pennsylvania (PA)
Bluefield Coll (VA)
Boise State U (ID)
Boston U (MA)
Bowie State U (MD)
Brenau U (GA)
Briar Cliff U (IA)
Bridgewater Coll (VA)
Brock U (ON, Canada)
Buena Vista U (IA)
Buffalo State Coll, State U of New York (NY)
California Lutheran U (CA)
California State U, Bakersfield (CA)
California State U, Chico (CA)
California State U, East Bay (CA)
California State U, Fresno (CA)
California State U, Long Beach (CA)
California State U, Sacramento (CA)
Calvary Bible Coll and Theological Sem (MO)
Calvin Coll (MI)
Campbellsville U (KY)
Carlow U (PA)
Carson-Newman Coll (TN)
Catawba Coll (NC)
Cedarville U (OH)
Centenary Coll (NJ)
Central Pennsylvania Coll (PA)
Chaminade U of Honolulu (HI)
Champlain Coll (VT)
Cheyney U of Pennsylvania (PA)
City Coll of the City U of New York (NY)
City U of Seattle (WA)
Claflin U (SC)
Clark U (MA)
Clemson U (SC)
The Coll at Brockport, State U of New York (NY)
Coll of Mount Saint Vincent (NY)
The Coll of New Rochelle (NY)
The Coll of Wooster (OH)
Colorado State U–Pueblo (CO)
Concordia Coll (MN)
Concordia U (QC, Canada)
Concordia U, St. Paul (MN)
Concordia U Texas (TX)
Concordia U Wisconsin (WI)
Concord U (WV)
Cornerstone U (MI)
Crandall U (NB, Canada)
Curry Coll (MA)
Defiance Coll (OH)
Denison U (OH)
DePaul U (IL)
DePauw U (IN)
Dillard U (LA)
Dominican U (IL)
Dordt Coll (IA)
Drake U (IA)
East Central U (OK)
Eastern Nazarene Coll (MA)
East Tennessee State U (TN)
Emerson Coll (MA)
Emmanuel Coll (GA)
Emmanuel Coll (MA)
Emory & Henry Coll (VA)
Endicott Coll (MA)
Excelsior Coll (NY)
Felician Coll (NJ)
Fisher Coll (MA)
Five Towns Coll (NY)
Florida Ag and Mech U (FL)
Florida Gulf Coast U (FL)
Florida Intl U (FL)
Fordham U (NY)
Fort Valley State U (GA)
Francis Marion U (SC)
Franklin Pierce U (NH)
Frostburg State U (MD)
Gallaudet U (DC)
Gardner-Webb U (NC)
The George Washington U (DC)
Gonzaga U (WA)
Goshen Coll (IN)
Goucher Coll (MD)
Governors State U (IL)
Grambling State U (LA)
Grand View U (IA)
Greenville Coll (IL)
Grove City Coll (PA)
Gustavus Adolphus Coll (MN)
Hamline U (MN)
Hampton U (VA)
Hanover Coll (IN)
Hardin-Simmons U (TX)
Hawai'i Pacific U (HI)
Heidelberg U (OH)
High Point U (NC)
Hiram Coll (OH)
Hofstra U (NY)
Hollins U (VA)
Houston Baptist U (TX)
Howard Payne U (TX)
Hunter Coll of the City U of New York (NY)
Huntington U (IN)
Idaho State U (ID)
Illinois Coll (IL)
Illinois State U (IL)
Indiana U–Purdue U Fort Wayne (IN)
Indiana U South Bend (IN)
Inter American U of Puerto Rico, Bayamón Campus (PR)
Iona Coll (NY)
Iowa State U of Science and Technology (IA)
Iowa Wesleyan Coll (IA)
Ithaca Coll (NY)
Jackson State U (MS)
John Brown U (AR)
John Cabot U (Italy)
John Carroll U (OH)
Johnson & Wales U (RI)
Johnson Bible Coll (TN)
Johnson C. Smith U (NC)
Kent State U (OH)
Kuyper Coll (MI)
Lamar U (TX)
La Salle U (PA)
Lees-McRae Coll (NC)
Lee U (TN)
Lehman Coll of the City U of New York (NY)
Lewis U (IL)
Lincoln Memorial U (TN)
Lindenwood U (MO)
Lindsey Wilson Coll (KY)
Linfield Coll (OR)
Lipscomb U (TN)
Loras Coll (IA)
Louisiana Coll (LA)
Louisiana State U and Ag and Mech Coll (LA)
Louisiana State U in Shreveport (LA)
Lubbock Christian U (TX)
Lynn U (FL)
Manchester Coll (IN)
Mansfield U of Pennsylvania (PA)
Marian U (IN)
Mars Hill Coll (NC)
Marylhurst U (OR)
Marymount Coll, Palos Verdes, California (CA)
Maryville U of Saint Louis (MO)
Massachusetts Inst of Technology (MA)
The Master's Coll and Sem (CA)
McKendree U (IL)
McNeese State U (LA)
Medaille Coll (NY)
Mercer U (GA)
Mercy Coll (NY)
Meredith Coll (NC)
Methodist U (NC)
Miami U (OH)
Miami U Hamilton (OH)
MidAmerica Nazarene U (KS)
Middle Tennessee State U (TN)
Midwestern State U (TX)
Minnesota State U Mankato (MN)
Minnesota State U Moorhead (MN)
Mississippi Coll (MS)
Mississippi Valley State U (MS)
Missouri State U (MO)
Mitchell Coll (CT)
Morris Coll (SC)
Mount Saint Mary Coll (NY)
Murray State U (KY)
Newberry Coll (SC)
New England Coll (NH)
Newman U (KS)
Niagara U (NY)
Nicholls State U (LA)
North Carolina Central U (NC)
North Carolina State U (NC)
Northeastern U (MA)
North Greenville U (SC)
Northwestern Oklahoma State U (OK)
Northwest Nazarene U (ID)
Oakwood U (AL)
Oklahoma Baptist U (OK)
Oklahoma Christian U (OK)
Oklahoma City U (OK)
Oklahoma Wesleyan U (OK)
Ottawa U (KS)
Ouachita Baptist U (AR)
Pace U (NY)
Pacific Union Coll (CA)
Piedmont Coll (GA)
Point Park U (PA)
Pontifical Catholic U of Puerto Rico (PR)
Prescott Coll (AZ)
Principia Coll (IL)
Queens Coll of the City U of New York (NY)
Queens U of Charlotte (NC)
Quinnipiac U (CT)
Robert Morris U (PA)
Rochester Coll (MI)
Russell Sage Coll (NY)
Rutgers, The State U of New Jersey, New Brunswick (NJ)
Sacred Heart U (CT)
Sage Coll of Albany (NY)
St. Ambrose U (IA)
St. Catherine U (MN)
St. Cloud State U (MN)
Saint Francis U (PA)
Saint Mary-of-the-Woods Coll (IN)
St. Mary's U (TX)
St. Thomas Aquinas Coll (NY)
St. Thomas U (FL)
St. Thomas U (NB, Canada)
Salem Coll (NC)
Sam Houston State U (TX)
San Diego State U (CA)
Savannah State U (GA)
Scripps Coll (CA)
Seattle U (WA)
Shaw U (NC)
Simpson Coll (IA)
Sonoma State U (CA)
South Carolina State U (SC)
Southern Arkansas U–Magnolia (AR)
Southern Illinois U Edwardsville (IL)
Southern U and Ag and Mech Coll (LA)
Southern Utah U (UT)
Southern Vermont Coll (VT)
Southwestern Adventist U (TX)
Southwestern Oklahoma State U (OK)
State U of New York at Fredonia (NY)
State U of New York at Oswego (NY)
State U of New York at Plattsburgh (NY)
State U of New York Coll at Oneonta (NY)
Stephens Coll (MO)
Suffolk U (MA)
Sul Ross State U (TX)
Susquehanna U (PA)
Tabor Coll (KS)
Talladega Coll (AL)
Taylor U (IN)
Texas Christian U (TX)
Texas State U–San Marcos (TX)
Texas Wesleyan U (TX)
Thiel Coll (PA)
Tiffin U (OH)
Towson U (MD)
Trevecca Nazarene U (TN)
Truman State U (MO)
Tulane U (LA)
Union U (TN)
Universidad de las Américas–Puebla (Mexico)
U at Albany, State U of New York (NY)
U at Buffalo, the State U of New York (NY)
U of Alaska Anchorage (AK)
U of Baltimore (MD)
U of Bridgeport (CT)
U of California, Berkeley (CA)
U of California, San Diego (CA)
U of Charleston (WV)
U of Cincinnati (OH)
U of Dayton (OH)
U of Delaware (DE)
U of Dubuque (IA)
U of Guam (GU)
U of Hawaii at Manoa (HI)
U of Illinois at Urbana–Champaign (IL)
The U of Iowa (IA)
U of Louisiana at Monroe (LA)
U of Maine (ME)
U of Mary (ND)
U of Mary Hardin-Baylor (TX)
U of Maryland, Baltimore County (MD)
U of Maryland Eastern Shore (MD)
U of Memphis (TN)
U of Miami (FL)
U of Minnesota, Twin Cities Campus (MN)
U of Missouri (MO)
U of Missouri–Kansas City (MO)
U of Missouri–St. Louis (MO)
U of Nebraska at Kearney (NE)
U of Nevada, Las Vegas (NV)
U of New Hampshire at Manchester (NH)
U of New Mexico (NM)
The U of North Carolina at Asheville (NC)
The U of North Carolina at Chapel Hill (NC)
The U of North Carolina at Greensboro (NC)
The U of North Carolina at Pembroke (NC)
U of North Florida (FL)
U of Oregon (OR)
U of Pittsburgh (PA)
U of Pittsburgh at Greensburg (PA)
U of Pittsburgh at Johnstown (PA)
U of Portland (OR)
U of Puerto Rico, Río Piedras (PR)
U of Rio Grande (OH)
U of St. Francis (IL)
U of San Francisco (CA)
U of Southern Indiana (IN)
U of Southern Maine (ME)
The U of Tampa (FL)
The U of Tennessee at Chattanooga (TN)
The U of Texas at El Paso (TX)
The U of Texas at San Antonio (TX)
The U of Texas of the Permian Basin (TX)
U of the District of Columbia (DC)
U of the Incarnate Word (TX)
U of the Ozarks (AR)
The U of Toledo (OH)
U of Toronto (ON, Canada)
U of Utah (UT)
U of Washington, Bothell (WA)
The U of Western Ontario (ON, Canada)
U of Wisconsin–Eau Claire (WI)
U of Wisconsin–Madison (WI)
U of Wisconsin–Milwaukee (WI)
U of Wisconsin–Oshkosh (WI)
U of Wisconsin–Platteville (WI)
U of Wisconsin–Superior (WI)
Upper Iowa U (IA)
Ursinus Coll (PA)
Valdosta State U (GA)
Valley City State U (ND)
Valparaiso U (IN)
Vassar Coll (NY)
Villanova U (PA)
Virginia Commonwealth U (VA)
Virginia State U (VA)
Virginia Wesleyan Coll (VA)
Voorhees Coll (SC)
Walden U (MN)
Waldorf Coll (IA)
Wartburg Coll (IA)
Washburn U (KS)
Washington Adventist U (MD)
Washington State U (WA)
Wayland Baptist U (TX)
Wayne State Coll (NE)
Western New England Coll (MA)
West Liberty U (WV)
West Virginia U (WV)
Widener U (PA)
Wilberforce U (OH)
Wilfrid Laurier U (ON, Canada)
William Paterson U of New Jersey (NJ)
William Penn U (IA)
Wilmington Coll (OH)
Wilson Coll (PA)
Winona State U (MN)
Winston-Salem State U (NC)
Winthrop U (SC)
Worcester State Coll (MA)
Wright State U (OH)
Xavier U of Louisiana (LA)
York Coll of Pennsylvania (PA)
York U (ON, Canada)

MATERIALS ENGINEERING

Alfred U (NY)
Arizona State U (AZ)
Auburn U (AL)
California Polytechnic State U, San Luis Obispo (CA)
California State U, Long Beach (CA)
Case Western Reserve U (OH)
Clemson U (SC)
Cornell U (NY)
Drexel U (PA)
Georgia Inst of Technology (GA)
Illinois Inst of Technology (IL)
Iowa State U of Science and Technology (IA)
The Johns Hopkins U (MD)
Lehigh U (PA)
Massachusetts Inst of Technology (MA)
Michigan State U (MI)
Michigan Technological U (MI)
New Mexico Inst of Mining and Technology (NM)
North Carolina State U (NC)
The Ohio State U (OH)
Purdue U (IN)
Rensselaer Polytechnic Inst (NY)
Rice U (TX)
San Jose State U (CA)
U at Albany, State U of New York (NY)
The U of Alabama at Birmingham (AL)
The U of British Columbia (BC, Canada)
U of California, Davis (CA)
U of California, Irvine (CA)
U of California, Los Angeles (CA)
U of California, Merced (CA)
U of Connecticut (CT)
U of Florida (FL)
U of Idaho (ID)
U of Illinois at Urbana–Champaign (IL)
U of Kentucky (KY)
U of Maryland, Coll Park (MD)
U of Minnesota, Twin Cities Campus (MN)
U of Pennsylvania (PA)
U of Pittsburgh (PA)
The U of Tennessee (TN)
U of Toronto (ON, Canada)
U of Utah (UT)
U of Washington (WA)
The U of Western Ontario (ON, Canada)
U of Windsor (ON, Canada)
U of Wisconsin–Milwaukee (WI)
Virginia Polytechnic Inst and State U (VA)
Washington State U (WA)
Winona State U (MN)
Worcester Polytechnic Inst (MA)
Wright State U (OH)

MATERIALS SCIENCE

California Inst of Technology (CA)
Carnegie Mellon U (PA)
Case Western Reserve U (OH)

Columbia U (NY)
Duke U (NC)
The Johns Hopkins U (MD)
Michigan State U (MI)
North Carolina State U (NC)
The Ohio State U (OH)
Penn State Abington (PA)
Penn State Altoona (PA)
Penn State Beaver (PA)
Penn State Berks (PA)
Penn State Brandywine (PA)
Penn State DuBois (PA)
Penn State Erie, The Behrend Coll (PA)
Penn State Fayette, The Eberly Campus (PA)
Penn State Greater Allegheny (PA)
Penn State Hazleton (PA)
Penn State Lehigh Valley (PA)
Penn State Mont Alto (PA)
Penn State New Kensington (PA)
Penn State Schuylkill (PA)
Penn State Shenango (PA)
Penn State U Park (PA)
Penn State Wilkes-Barre (PA)
Penn State Worthington Scranton (PA)
Penn State York (PA)
Rice U (TX)
Stanford U (CA)
United States Air Force Acad (CO)
The U of Arizona (AZ)
U of California, Berkeley (CA)
U of California, Los Angeles (CA)
U of California, Riverside (CA)
U of Illinois at Urbana–Champaign (IL)
U of Michigan (MI)
U of Minnesota, Twin Cities Campus (MN)
U of North Texas (TX)
U of Pennsylvania (PA)
U of Toronto (ON, Canada)
Worcester Polytechnic Inst (MA)

MATERNAL AND CHILD HEALTH
Union Inst & U (OH)

MATERNAL/CHILD HEALTH AND NEONATAL NURSING
U of Washington (WA)

MATHEMATICAL STATISTICS AND PROBABILITY
Carnegie Mellon U (PA)
Concordia U (QC, Canada)
U of Alaska Fairbanks (AK)
U of Miami (FL)
The U of Western Ontario (ON, Canada)

MATHEMATICS
Abilene Christian U (TX)
Acadia U (NS, Canada)
Adams State Coll (CO)
Adelphi U (NY)
Agnes Scott Coll (GA)
Alabama Ag and Mech U (AL)
Alabama State U (AL)
Albany State U (GA)
Albertus Magnus Coll (CT)
Albion Coll (MI)
Albright Coll (PA)
Alcorn State U (MS)
Alfred U (NY)
Allegheny Coll (PA)
Allen U (SC)
Alma Coll (MI)
Alvernia U (PA)
Alverno Coll (WI)
American Intl Coll (MA)
American U (DC)
American U of Beirut (Lebanon)
Amherst Coll (MA)
Anderson U (IN)
Andrews U (MI)
Angelo State U (TX)
Antioch U McGregor (OH)
Appalachian State U (NC)
Aquinas Coll (MI)
Arcadia U (PA)
Arizona State U (AZ)
Arkansas State U—Jonesboro (AR)
Arkansas Tech U (AR)
Armstrong Atlantic State U (GA)
Asbury U (KY)
Ashland U (OH)
Assumption Coll (MA)
Auburn U (AL)
Auburn U Montgomery (AL)
Augsburg Coll (MN)
Augustana Coll (IL)
Augustana Coll (SD)
Aurora U (IL)
Austin Coll (TX)
Austin Peay State U (TN)
Averett U (VA)
Avila U (MO)
Azusa Pacific U (CA)
Baker U (KS)
Baldwin-Wallace Coll (OH)
Ball State U (IN)
Bard Coll (NY)
Bard Coll at Simon's Rock (MA)
Barnard Coll (NY)
Barry U (FL)
Barton Coll (NC)
Bates Coll (ME)
Baylor U (TX)
Belhaven U (MS)
Bellarmine U (KY)
Belmont Abbey Coll (NC)
Belmont U (TN)
Beloit Coll (WI)
Bemidji State U (MN)
Benedictine Coll (KS)
Benedictine U (IL)
Bennett Coll for Women (NC)
Bennington Coll (VT)
Bentley U (MA)
Berea Coll (KY)
Bernard M. Baruch Coll of the City U of New York (NY)
Berry Coll (GA)
Bethany Coll (KS)
Bethany Coll (WV)
Bethany Lutheran Coll (MN)
Bethel Coll (IN)
Bethel Coll (KS)
Bethel U (MN)
Bethel U (TN)
Bethune-Cookman U (FL)
Birmingham-Southern Coll (AL)
Bishop's U (QC, Canada)
Blackburn Coll (IL)
Black Hills State U (SD)
Bloomfield Coll (NJ)
Bloomsburg U of Pennsylvania (PA)
Bluefield Coll (VA)
Blue Mountain Coll (MS)
Bluffton U (OH)
Bob Jones U (SC)
Boise State U (ID)
Boston Coll (MA)
Boston U (MA)
Bowdoin Coll (ME)
Bowie State U (MD)
Bowling Green State U (OH)
Bradley U (IL)
Brandeis U (MA)
Brevard Coll (NC)
Brewton-Parker Coll (GA)
Briar Cliff U (IA)
Bridgewater Coll (VA)
Bridgewater State Coll (MA)
Brigham Young U–Hawaii (HI)
Brock U (ON, Canada)
Brooklyn Coll of the City U of New York (NY)
Bryan Coll (TN)
Bryn Mawr Coll (PA)
Bucknell U (PA)
Buena Vista U (IA)
Buffalo State Coll, State U of New York (NY)
Butler U (IN)
Cabrini Coll (PA)
California Baptist U (CA)
California Inst of Technology (CA)
California Lutheran U (CA)
California Polytechnic State U, San Luis Obispo (CA)
California State Polytechnic U, Pomona (CA)
California State U, Bakersfield (CA)
California State U, Chico (CA)
California State U, Dominguez Hills (CA)
California State U, East Bay (CA)
California State U, Fresno (CA)
California State U, Fullerton (CA)
California State U, Long Beach (CA)
California State U, Los Angeles (CA)
California State U, Monterey Bay (CA)
California State U, Northridge (CA)
California State U, Sacramento (CA)
California State U, San Bernardino (CA)
California State U, San Marcos (CA)
California State U, Stanislaus (CA)
Calvin Coll (MI)
Cameron U (OK)
Campbellsville U (KY)
Canisius Coll (NY)
Cape Breton U (NS, Canada)
Capital U (OH)
Carleton Coll (MN)
Carlow U (PA)
Carnegie Mellon U (PA)
Carroll U (WI)
Carson-Newman Coll (TN)
Case Western Reserve U (OH)
Castleton State Coll (VT)
Catawba Coll (NC)
The Catholic U of America (DC)
Cedar Crest Coll (PA)
Cedarville U (OH)
Centenary Coll (NJ)
Centenary Coll of Louisiana (LA)
Central Christian Coll of Kansas (KS)
Central Coll (IA)
Central Connecticut State U (CT)
Central Michigan U (MI)
Central State U (OH)
Chapman U (CA)
Chatham U (PA)
Cheyney U of Pennsylvania (PA)
Chowan U (NC)
Christian Brothers U (TN)
Christopher Newport U (VA)
The Citadel, The Military Coll of South Carolina (SC)
City Coll of the City U of New York (NY)
Claflin U (SC)
Claremont McKenna Coll (CA)
Clarion U of Pennsylvania (PA)
Clark Atlanta U (GA)
Clarke Coll (IA)
Clarkson U (NY)
Clark U (MA)
Clayton State U (GA)
Clearwater Christian Coll (FL)
Clemson U (SC)
Cleveland State U (OH)
Coker Coll (SC)
Colby Coll (ME)
Colgate U (NY)
The Coll at Brockport, State U of New York (NY)
Coll of Charleston (SC)
The Coll of Idaho (ID)
Coll of Mount St. Joseph (OH)
Coll of Mount Saint Vincent (NY)
The Coll of New Jersey (NJ)
The Coll of New Rochelle (NY)
Coll of Notre Dame of Maryland (MD)
Coll of Saint Benedict (MN)
Coll of Saint Elizabeth (NJ)
Coll of Saint Mary (NE)
The Coll of Saint Rose (NY)
The Coll of St. Scholastica (MN)
Coll of Staten Island of the City U of New York (NY)
Coll of the Holy Cross (MA)
Coll of the Ozarks (MO)
The Coll of William and Mary (VA)
The Coll of Wooster (OH)
The Colorado Coll (CO)
Colorado School of Mines (CO)
Colorado State U (CO)
Colorado State U–Pueblo (CO)
Columbia Coll (MO)
Columbia Coll (SC)
Columbia U (NY)
Columbia U, School of General Studies (NY)
Columbus State U (GA)
Concordia Coll (MN)
Concordia U (CA)
Concordia U (QC, Canada)
Concordia U Chicago (IL)
Concordia U Coll of Alberta (AB, Canada)
Concordia U, St. Paul (MN)
Concordia U Texas (TX)
Concordia U Wisconsin (WI)
Concord U (WV)
Connecticut Coll (CT)
Converse Coll (SC)
Coppin State U (MD)
Corban U (OR)
Cornell Coll (IA)
Cornell U (NY)
Covenant Coll (GA)
Creighton U (NE)
Culver-Stockton Coll (MO)
Cumberland U (TN)
Daemen Coll (NY)
Dakota Wesleyan U (SD)
Dallas Baptist U (TX)
Dalton State Coll (GA)
Dana Coll (NE)
Dartmouth Coll (NH)
Davidson Coll (NC)
Defiance Coll (OH)
Delaware State U (DE)
Delaware Valley Coll (PA)
Delta State U (MS)
Denison U (OH)
DePaul U (IL)
DePauw U (IN)
DeSales U (PA)
Dickinson Coll (PA)
Dickinson State U (ND)
Dillard U (LA)
Doane Coll (NE)
Dominican Coll (NY)
Dominican U (IL)
Dordt Coll (IA)
Dowling Coll (NY)
Drake U (IA)
Drew U (NJ)
Drexel U (PA)
Drury U (MO)
Duke U (NC)
Duquesne U (PA)
D'Youville Coll (NY)
Earlham Coll (IN)
East Carolina U (NC)
East Central U (OK)
Eastern Connecticut State U (CT)
Eastern Illinois U (IL)
Eastern Mennonite U (VA)
Eastern Michigan U (MI)
Eastern Nazarene Coll (MA)
Eastern New Mexico U (NM)
Eastern Washington U (WA)
East Stroudsburg U of Pennsylvania (PA)
East Tennessee State U (TN)
East Texas Baptist U (TX)
East-West U (IL)
Eckerd Coll (FL)
Edgewood Coll (WI)
Edinboro U of Pennsylvania (PA)
Edward Waters Coll (FL)
Elizabeth City State U (NC)
Elizabethtown Coll (PA)
Elmhurst Coll (IL)
Elmira Coll (NY)
Elon U (NC)
Emmanuel Coll (GA)
Emmanuel Coll (MA)
Emory & Henry Coll (VA)
Emory U (GA)
Emporia State U (KS)
Erskine Coll (SC)
Evangel U (MO)
Excelsior Coll (NY)
Fairfield U (CT)
Fairleigh Dickinson U, Coll at Florham (NJ)
Fairleigh Dickinson U, Metropolitan Campus (NJ)
Fairmont State U (WV)
Fayetteville State U (NC)
Felician Coll (NJ)
Ferris State U (MI)
Ferrum Coll (VA)
Fisk U (TN)
Fitchburg State Coll (MA)
Florida Ag and Mech U (FL)
Florida Atlantic U (FL)
Florida Gulf Coast U (FL)
Florida Inst of Technology (FL)
Florida Intl U (FL)
Florida Southern Coll (FL)
Florida State U (FL)
Fontbonne U (MO)
Fordham U (NY)
Fort Hays State U (KS)
Fort Lewis Coll (CO)
Fort Valley State U (GA)
Framingham State Coll (MA)
Franciscan U of Steubenville (OH)
Francis Marion U (SC)
Franklin & Marshall Coll (PA)
Franklin Coll (IN)
Franklin Pierce U (NH)
Freed-Hardeman U (TN)
Friends U (KS)
Frostburg State U (MD)
Furman U (SC)
Gallaudet U (DC)
Gannon U (PA)
Gardner-Webb U (NC)
George Fox U (OR)
George Mason U (VA)
Georgetown Coll (KY)
Georgetown U (DC)
The George Washington U (DC)
Georgia Coll & State U (GA)
Georgian Court U (NJ)
Georgia Southern U (GA)
Georgia State U (GA)
Gettysburg Coll (PA)
Gonzaga U (WA)
Gordon Coll (MA)
Goshen Coll (IN)
Goucher Coll (MD)
Governors State U (IL)
Grace Coll (IN)
Graceland U (IA)
Grambling State U (LA)
Grand Valley State U (MI)
Greensboro Coll (NC)
Greenville Coll (IL)
Grinnell Coll (IA)
Grove City Coll (PA)
Guilford Coll (NC)
Gustavus Adolphus Coll (MN)
Gwynedd-Mercy Coll (PA)
Hamilton Coll (NY)
Hamline U (MN)
Hampden-Sydney Coll (VA)
Hampshire Coll (MA)
Hampton U (VA)
Hannibal-LaGrange Coll (MO)
Hanover Coll (IN)
Harding U (AR)
Hardin-Simmons U (TX)
Hartwick Coll (NY)
Harvard U (MA)
Harvey Mudd Coll (CA)
Haverford Coll (PA)
Heidelberg U (OH)
Henderson State U (AR)
Hendrix Coll (AR)
High Point U (NC)
Hillsdale Coll (MI)
Hiram Coll (OH)
Hofstra U (NY)
Hollins U (VA)
Holy Family U (PA)
Hood Coll (MD)
Hope Coll (MI)
Houghton Coll (NY)
Houston Baptist U (TX)
Howard Payne U (TX)
Humboldt State U (CA)
Hunter Coll of the City U of New York (NY)
Huntingdon Coll (AL)
Huntington U (IN)
Huston-Tillotson U (TX)
Idaho State U (ID)
Illinois Coll (IL)
Illinois State U (IL)
Illinois Wesleyan U (IL)
Immaculata U (PA)
Indiana State U (IN)
Indiana U Bloomington (IN)
Indiana U Kokomo (IN)
Indiana U Northwest (IN)
Indiana U of Pennsylvania (PA)
Indiana U–Purdue U Fort Wayne (IN)
Indiana U–Purdue U Indianapolis (IN)
Indiana U South Bend (IN)
Indiana U Southeast (IN)
Indiana Wesleyan U (IN)
Inter American U of Puerto Rico, Bayamón Campus (PR)
Inter American U of Puerto Rico, San Germán Campus (PR)
Iona Coll (NY)
Iowa State U of Science and Technology (IA)
Iowa Wesleyan Coll (IA)
Ithaca Coll (NY)
Jackson State U (MS)
Jacksonville State U (AL)
Jacksonville U (FL)
James Madison U (VA)
Jamestown Coll (ND)
Jarvis Christian Coll (TX)
John Brown U (AR)
John Carroll U (OH)
The Johns Hopkins U (MD)
Johnson C. Smith U (NC)
Johnson State Coll (VT)
Judson Coll (AL)
Judson U (IL)
Juniata Coll (PA)
Kalamazoo Coll (MI)
Kansas State U (KS)
Kean U (NJ)
Keene State Coll (NH)
Kennesaw State U (GA)
Kent State U (OH)
Kentucky State U (KY)
Kentucky Wesleyan Coll (KY)
Kenyon Coll (OH)
Keuka Coll (NY)
King Coll (TN)
King's Coll (PA)
Knox Coll (IL)
Kutztown U of Pennsylvania (PA)
Lafayette Coll (PA)
LaGrange Coll (GA)
Lake Erie Coll (OH)
Lake Forest Coll (IL)
Lakehead U (ON, Canada)
Lakeland Coll (WI)
Lake Superior State U (MI)
Lamar U (TX)
Lane Coll (TN)
La Roche Coll (PA)
La Salle U (PA)
Lasell Coll (MA)
La Sierra U (CA)
Laurentian U (ON, Canada)
Lawrence Technological U (MI)
Lawrence U (WI)
Lebanon Valley Coll (PA)
Lees-McRae Coll (NC)
Lee U (TN)
Lehigh U (PA)
Lehman Coll of the City U of New York (NY)

Le Moyne Coll (NY)
LeTourneau U (TX)
Lewis & Clark Coll (OR)
Lewis-Clark State Coll (ID)
Lewis U (IL)
Liberty U (VA)
Limestone Coll (SC)
Lincoln Memorial U (TN)
Lincoln U (MO)
Lincoln U (PA)
Lindenwood U (MO)
Linfield Coll (OR)
Lipscomb U (TN)
Lock Haven U of Pennsylvania (PA)
Long Island U, Brooklyn Campus (NY)
Long Island U, C.W. Post Campus (NY)
Longwood U (VA)
Loras Coll (IA)
Louisiana Coll (LA)
Louisiana State U and Ag and Mech Coll (LA)
Louisiana State U in Shreveport (LA)
Louisiana Tech U (LA)
Loyola Marymount U (CA)
Loyola U Chicago (IL)
Loyola U Maryland (MD)
Loyola U New Orleans (LA)
Lubbock Christian U (TX)
Luther Coll (IA)
Lycoming Coll (PA)
Lynchburg Coll (VA)
Lyon Coll (AR)
Macalester Coll (MN)
Madonna U (MI)
Maharishi U of Management (IA)
Malone U (OH)
Manchester Coll (IN)
Manhattan Coll (NY)
Manhattanville Coll (NY)
Mansfield U of Pennsylvania (PA)
Marian U (IN)
Marian U (WI)
Marietta Coll (OH)
Marist Coll (NY)
Marlboro Coll (VT)
Marquette U (WI)
Marshall U (WV)
Mars Hill Coll (NC)
Mary Baldwin Coll (VA)
Marymount U (VA)
Maryville Coll (TN)
Maryville U of Saint Louis (MO)
Marywood U (PA)
Massachusetts Coll of Liberal Arts (MA)
Massachusetts Inst of Technology (MA)
The Master's Coll and Sem (CA)
Mayville State U (ND)
McDaniel Coll (MD)
McKendree U (IL)
McMurry U (TX)
McNeese State U (LA)
McPherson Coll (KS)
Memorial U of Newfoundland (NL, Canada)
Mercer U (GA)
Mercy Coll (NY)
Mercyhurst Coll (PA)
Meredith Coll (NC)
Merrimack Coll (MA)
Messiah Coll (PA)
Methodist U (NC)
Metropolitan State Coll of Denver (CO)
Miami U (OH)
Miami U Hamilton (OH)
Michigan State U (MI)
Michigan Technological U (MI)
MidAmerica Nazarene U (KS)
Mid-Continent U (KY)
Middlebury Coll (VT)
Middle Tennessee State U (TN)
Midway Coll (KY)
Midwestern State U (TX)
Millersville U of Pennsylvania (PA)
Milligan Coll (TN)
Millsaps Coll (MS)
Mills Coll (CA)
Minnesota State U Mankato (MN)
Minnesota State U Moorhead (MN)
Minot State U (ND)
Misericordia U (PA)
Mississippi Coll (MS)
Mississippi State U (MS)
Mississippi U for Women (MS)
Mississippi Valley State U (MS)
Missouri Baptist U (MO)
Missouri Southern State U (MO)
Missouri State U (MO)
Missouri Western State U (MO)
Molloy Coll (NY)
Monmouth Coll (IL)
Monmouth U (NJ)
Montana State U (MT)
Montana State U Billings (MT)
Montana Tech of The U of Montana (MT)
Montclair State U (NJ)
Moravian Coll (PA)
Morehead State U (KY)
Morehouse Coll (GA)
Morningside Coll (IA)
Morris Coll (SC)
Mount Allison U (NB, Canada)
Mount Holyoke Coll (MA)
Mount Marty Coll (SD)
Mount Mary Coll (WI)
Mount Mercy Coll (IA)
Mount Olive Coll (NC)
Mount Saint Mary Coll (NY)
Mount St. Mary's Coll (CA)
Mount St. Mary's U (MD)
Mount Vernon Nazarene U (OH)
Muhlenberg Coll (PA)
Murray State U (KY)
National U (CA)
Nazareth Coll of Rochester (NY)
Nebraska Wesleyan U (NE)
Newberry Coll (SC)
New Coll of Florida (FL)
New Jersey City U (NJ)
New Jersey Inst of Technology (NJ)
Newman U (KS)
New Mexico Highlands U (NM)
New Mexico Inst of Mining and Technology (NM)
New Mexico State U (NM)
New York U (NY)
Niagara U (NY)
Nicholls State U (LA)
Nichols Coll (MA)
Nipissing U (ON, Canada)
Norfolk State U (VA)
North Carolina Central U (NC)
North Carolina State U (NC)
North Central Coll (IL)
North Dakota State U (ND)
Northeastern Illinois U (IL)
Northeastern State U (OK)
Northeastern U (MA)
Northern Arizona U (AZ)
Northern Kentucky U (KY)
Northern Michigan U (MI)
Northern State U (SD)
North Georgia Coll & State U (GA)
North Greenville U (SC)
Northland Coll (WI)
Northwest Christian U (OR)
Northwestern Coll (IA)
Northwestern Coll (MN)
Northwestern Oklahoma State U (OK)
Northwestern State U of Louisiana (LA)
Northwest Missouri State U (MO)
Northwest Nazarene U (ID)
Northwest U (WA)
Nyack Coll (NY)
Oakland City U (IN)
Oakland U (MI)
Oakwood U (AL)
Oberlin Coll (OH)
Occidental Coll (CA)
Oglethorpe U (GA)
Ohio Dominican U (OH)
Ohio Northern U (OH)
The Ohio State U (OH)
Ohio U (OH)
Ohio Wesleyan U (OH)
Oklahoma Baptist U (OK)
Oklahoma Christian U (OK)
Oklahoma City U (OK)
Oklahoma Panhandle State U (OK)
Oklahoma State U (OK)
Oklahoma Wesleyan U (OK)
Old Dominion U (VA)
Oral Roberts U (OK)
Oregon State U (OR)
Oregon State U–Cascades (OR)
Ottawa U (KS)
Ouachita Baptist U (AR)
Our Lady of the Lake U of San Antonio (TX)
Pace U (NY)
Pacific Lutheran U (WA)
Pacific Union Coll (CA)
Paine Coll (GA)
Park U (MO)
Penn State Abington (PA)
Penn State Altoona (PA)
Penn State Beaver (PA)
Penn State Berks (PA)
Penn State Brandywine (PA)
Penn State DuBois (PA)
Penn State Erie, The Behrend Coll (PA)
Penn State Fayette, The Eberly Campus (PA)
Penn State Greater Allegheny (PA)
Penn State Hazleton (PA)
Penn State Lehigh Valley (PA)
Penn State Mont Alto (PA)
Penn State New Kensington (PA)
Penn State Schuylkill (PA)
Penn State Shenango (PA)
Penn State U Park (PA)
Penn State Wilkes-Barre (PA)
Penn State Worthington Scranton (PA)
Penn State York (PA)
Pepperdine U, Malibu (CA)
Peru State Coll (NE)
Piedmont Coll (GA)
Pikeville Coll (KY)
Pittsburg State U (KS)
Pitzer Coll (CA)
Plymouth State U (NH)
Polytechnic Inst of NYU (NY)
Pomona Coll (CA)
Pontifical Catholic U of Puerto Rico (PR)
Portland State U (OR)
Prairie View A&M U (TX)
Presbyterian Coll (SC)
Princeton U (NJ)
Principia Coll (IL)
Providence Coll (RI)
Purchase Coll, State U of New York (NY)
Purdue U (IN)
Purdue U Calumet (IN)
Queens Coll of the City U of New York (NY)
Queen's U at Kingston (ON, Canada)
Queens U of Charlotte (NC)
Quincy U (IL)
Quinnipiac U (CT)
Radford U (VA)
Ramapo Coll of New Jersey (NJ)
Randolph Coll (VA)
Randolph-Macon Coll (VA)
Redeemer U Coll (ON, Canada)
Reed Coll (OR)
Regent U (VA)
Reinhardt Coll (GA)
Rensselaer Polytechnic Inst (NY)
Rhode Island Coll (RI)
Rhodes Coll (TN)
Rice U (TX)
The Richard Stockton Coll of New Jersey (NJ)
Rider U (NJ)
Ripon Coll (WI)
Rivier Coll (NH)
Roanoke Coll (VA)
Roberts Wesleyan Coll (NY)
Rochester Inst of Technology (NY)
Rockford Coll (IL)
Rockhurst U (MO)
Rocky Mountain Coll (MT)
Rollins Coll (FL)
Roosevelt U (IL)
Rose-Hulman Inst of Technology (IN)
Rosemont Coll (PA)
Rowan U (NJ)
Russell Sage Coll (NY)
Rutgers, The State U of New Jersey, Camden (NJ)
Rutgers, The State U of New Jersey, Newark (NJ)
Rutgers, The State U of New Jersey, New Brunswick (NJ)
Saginaw Valley State U (MI)
St. Ambrose U (IA)
Saint Anselm Coll (NH)
Saint Augustine's Coll (NC)
St. Bonaventure U (NY)
St. Catherine U (MN)
St. Cloud State U (MN)
St. Edward's U (TX)
St. Francis Coll (NY)
Saint Francis U (PA)
St. Francis Xavier U (NS, Canada)
St. John Fisher Coll (NY)
Saint John's U (MN)
St. John's U (NY)
Saint Joseph Coll (CT)
St. Joseph's Coll, Long Island Campus (NY)
St. Joseph's Coll, New York (NY)
Saint Joseph's U (PA)
St. Lawrence U (NY)
Saint Leo U (FL)
Saint Louis U (MO)
Saint Martin's U (WA)
Saint Mary-of-the-Woods Coll (IN)
Saint Mary's Coll (IN)
Saint Mary's Coll of California (CA)
St. Mary's Coll of Maryland (MD)
St. Mary's U (TX)
Saint Mary's U of Minnesota (MN)
Saint Michael's Coll (VT)
St. Norbert Coll (WI)
St. Olaf Coll (MN)
Saint Paul's Coll (VA)
St. Thomas Aquinas Coll (NY)
St. Thomas U (NB, Canada)
Saint Vincent Coll (PA)
Saint Xavier U (IL)
Salem Coll (NC)
Salem State Coll (MA)
Salisbury U (MD)
Salve Regina U (RI)
Samford U (AL)
Sam Houston State U (TX)
San Diego Christian Coll (CA)
San Diego State U (CA)
San Francisco State U (CA)
San Jose State U (CA)
Santa Clara U (CA)
Sarah Lawrence Coll (NY)
Savannah State U (GA)
Schreiner U (TX)
Scripps Coll (CA)
Seattle Pacific U (WA)
Seattle U (WA)
Seton Hall U (NJ)
Seton Hill U (PA)
Sewanee: The U of the South (TN)
Shawnee State U (OH)
Shaw U (NC)
Shenandoah U (VA)
Shepherd U (WV)
Shippensburg U of Pennsylvania (PA)
Shorter U (GA)
Siena Coll (NY)
Siena Heights U (MI)
Silver Lake Coll (WI)
Simmons Coll (MA)
Simon Fraser U (BC, Canada)
Simpson Coll (IA)
Simpson U (CA)
Skidmore Coll (NY)
Slippery Rock U of Pennsylvania (PA)
Smith Coll (MA)
Sonoma State U (CA)
South Carolina State U (SC)
South Dakota School of Mines and Technology (SD)
South Dakota State U (SD)
Southeastern Louisiana U (LA)
Southeastern Oklahoma State U (OK)
Southeastern U (FL)
Southeast Missouri State U (MO)
Southern Adventist U (TN)
Southern Arkansas U–Magnolia (AR)
Southern Connecticut State U (CT)
Southern Illinois U Carbondale (IL)
Southern Illinois U Edwardsville (IL)
Southern Methodist U (TX)
Southern Oregon U (OR)
Southern Polytechnic State U (GA)
Southern U and Ag and Mech Coll (LA)
Southern U at New Orleans (LA)
Southern Utah U (UT)
Southern Wesleyan U (SC)
Southwest Baptist U (MO)
Southwestern Adventist U (TX)
Southwestern Coll (KS)
Southwestern Oklahoma State U (OK)
Southwestern U (TX)
Southwest Minnesota State U (MN)
Spelman Coll (GA)
Spring Arbor U (MI)
Spring Hill Coll (AL)
Stanford U (CA)
State U of New York at Binghamton (NY)
State U of New York at Fredonia (NY)
State U of New York at New Paltz (NY)
State U of New York at Oswego (NY)
State U of New York at Plattsburgh (NY)
State U of New York Coll at Cortland (NY)
State U of New York Coll at Geneseo (NY)
State U of New York Coll at Old Westbury (NY)
State U of New York Coll at Oneonta (NY)
State U of New York Coll at Potsdam (NY)
State U of New York Empire State Coll (NY)
Stephen F. Austin State U (TX)
Sterling Coll (KS)
Stetson U (FL)
Stevens Inst of Technology (NJ)
Stillman Coll (AL)
Stonehill Coll (MA)
Stony Brook U, State U of New York (NY)
Suffolk U (MA)
Sul Ross State U (TX)
Susquehanna U (PA)
Swarthmore Coll (PA)
Sweet Briar Coll (VA)
Syracuse U (NY)
Tabor Coll (KS)
Talladega Coll (AL)
Tarleton State U (TX)
Taylor U (IN)
Temple U (PA)
Tennessee Technological U (TN)
Tennessee Wesleyan Coll (TN)
Texas A&M Intl U (TX)
Texas A&M U (TX)
Texas A&M U–Commerce (TX)
Texas A&M U–Corpus Christi (TX)
Texas A&M U–Kingsville (TX)
Texas Christian U (TX)
Texas Coll (TX)
Texas Lutheran U (TX)
Texas Southern U (TX)
Texas State U–San Marcos (TX)
Texas Tech U (TX)
Texas Wesleyan U (TX)
Texas Woman's U (TX)
Thiel Coll (PA)
Thomas Edison State Coll (NJ)
Thomas More Coll (KY)
Thompson Rivers U (BC, Canada)
Towson U (MD)
Transylvania U (KY)
Trent U (ON, Canada)
Trevecca Nazarene U (TN)
Trine U (IN)
Trinity Christian Coll (IL)
Trinity Coll (CT)
Trinity U (TX)
Troy U (AL)
Truman State U (MO)
Tufts U (MA)
Tulane U (LA)
Tusculum Coll (TN)
Tuskegee U (AL)
Union Coll (KY)
Union Coll (NE)
Union Coll (NY)
Union U (TN)
United States Air Force Acad (CO)
United States Military Acad (NY)
United States Naval Acad (MD)
Universidad de las Américas–Puebla (Mexico)
U at Albany, State U of New York (NY)
U at Buffalo, the State U of New York (NY)
The U of Akron (OH)
The U of Alabama (AL)
The U of Alabama at Birmingham (AL)
The U of Alabama in Huntsville (AL)
U of Alaska Anchorage (AK)
U of Alaska Fairbanks (AK)
U of Alaska Southeast (AK)
U of Alberta (AB, Canada)
The U of Arizona (AZ)
U of Arkansas (AR)
U of Arkansas at Fort Smith (AR)
U of Arkansas at Little Rock (AR)
U of Arkansas at Monticello (AR)
U of Arkansas at Pine Bluff (AR)
U of Bridgeport (CT)
The U of British Columbia (BC, Canada)
The U of British Columbia–Okanagan (BC, Canada)
U of California, Berkeley (CA)
U of California, Davis (CA)
U of California, Irvine (CA)
U of California, Los Angeles (CA)
U of California, Riverside (CA)
U of California, San Diego (CA)
U of California, Santa Barbara (CA)
U of California, Santa Cruz (CA)
U of Central Florida (FL)
U of Central Missouri (MO)
U of Central Oklahoma (OK)
U of Chicago (IL)
U of Cincinnati (OH)
U of Colorado at Boulder (CO)
U of Colorado at Colorado Springs (CO)
U of Colorado Denver (CO)
U of Connecticut (CT)
U of Dallas (TX)
U of Dayton (OH)
U of Delaware (DE)
U of Denver (CO)
U of Evansville (IN)
The U of Findlay (OH)
U of Florida (FL)
U of Georgia (GA)
U of Guam (GU)
U of Guelph (ON, Canada)
U of Hartford (CT)
U of Hawaii at Hilo (HI)
U of Hawaii at Manoa (HI)
U of Houston (TX)
U of Houston–Clear Lake (TX)
U of Houston–Downtown (TX)
U of Houston–Victoria (TX)
U of Idaho (ID)
U of Illinois at Chicago (IL)
U of Illinois at Springfield (IL)

U of Illinois at Urbana–Champaign (IL)
U of Indianapolis (IN)
The U of Iowa (IA)
The U of Kansas (KS)
U of Kentucky (KY)
U of King's Coll (NS, Canada)
U of La Verne (CA)
U of Lethbridge (AB, Canada)
U of Louisiana at Monroe (LA)
U of Louisville (KY)
U of Maine (ME)
U of Maine at Farmington (ME)
U of Manitoba (MB, Canada)
U of Mary (ND)
U of Mary Hardin-Baylor (TX)
U of Maryland, Baltimore County (MD)
U of Maryland, Coll Park (MD)
U of Maryland Eastern Shore (MD)
U of Mary Washington (VA)
U of Massachusetts Amherst (MA)
U of Massachusetts Boston (MA)
U of Massachusetts Dartmouth (MA)
U of Massachusetts Lowell (MA)
U of Memphis (TN)
U of Miami (FL)
U of Michigan (MI)
U of Michigan–Dearborn (MI)
U of Michigan–Flint (MI)
U of Minnesota, Duluth (MN)
U of Minnesota, Twin Cities Campus (MN)
U of Mississippi (MS)
U of Missouri (MO)
U of Missouri–Kansas City (MO)
U of Missouri–St. Louis (MO)
U of Mobile (AL)
U of Montevallo (AL)
U of Mount Union (OH)
U of Nebraska at Kearney (NE)
U of Nebraska at Omaha (NE)
U of Nebraska–Lincoln (NE)
U of Nevada, Las Vegas (NV)
U of Nevada, Reno (NV)
U of New Brunswick Fredericton (NB, Canada)
U of New England (ME)
U of New Hampshire (NH)
U of New Haven (CT)
U of New Mexico (NM)
U of New Orleans (LA)
U of North Alabama (AL)
The U of North Carolina at Asheville (NC)
The U of North Carolina at Chapel Hill (NC)
The U of North Carolina at Charlotte (NC)
The U of North Carolina at Greensboro (NC)
The U of North Carolina at Pembroke (NC)
The U of North Carolina Wilmington (NC)
U of North Dakota (ND)
U of Northern Colorado (CO)
U of Northern Iowa (IA)
U of North Florida (FL)
U of North Texas (TX)
U of Notre Dame (IN)
U of Oklahoma (OK)
U of Oregon (OR)
U of Ottawa (ON, Canada)
U of Pennsylvania (PA)
U of Pittsburgh (PA)
U of Pittsburgh at Johnstown (PA)
U of Portland (OR)
U of Puerto Rico, Cayey U Coll (PR)
U of Puerto Rico, Río Piedras (PR)
U of Puget Sound (WA)
U of Redlands (CA)
U of Regina (SK, Canada)
U of Rhode Island (RI)
U of Richmond (VA)
U of Rio Grande (OH)
U of Rochester (NY)
U of St. Francis (IL)
U of Saint Mary (KS)
U of St. Thomas (MN)
U of St. Thomas (TX)
U of San Diego (CA)
U of San Francisco (CA)
U of Saskatchewan (SK, Canada)
U of Science and Arts of Oklahoma (OK)
The U of Scranton (PA)
U of South Carolina (SC)
U of South Carolina Upstate (SC)
The U of South Dakota (SD)
U of Southern California (CA)
U of Southern Indiana (IN)
U of Southern Maine (ME)
U of Southern Mississippi (MS)
U of South Florida (FL)
The U of Tampa (FL)
The U of Tennessee (TN)
The U of Tennessee at Chattanooga (TN)
The U of Tennessee at Martin (TN)
The U of Texas at Arlington (TX)
The U of Texas at Austin (TX)
The U of Texas at Brownsville (TX)
The U of Texas at Dallas (TX)
The U of Texas at El Paso (TX)
The U of Texas at San Antonio (TX)
The U of Texas at Tyler (TX)
The U of Texas of the Permian Basin (TX)
The U of Texas–Pan American (TX)
U of the Cumberlands (KY)
U of the District of Columbia (DC)
U of the Incarnate Word (TX)
U of the Ozarks (AR)
U of the Pacific (CA)
U of the Virgin Islands (VI)
The U of Toledo (OH)
U of Tulsa (OK)
U of Utah (UT)
U of Vermont (VT)
U of Virginia (VA)
The U of Virginia's Coll at Wise (VA)
U of Washington (WA)
U of Waterloo (ON, Canada)
The U of West Alabama (AL)
The U of Western Ontario (ON, Canada)
U of West Florida (FL)
U of West Georgia (GA)
U of Windsor (ON, Canada)
U of Wisconsin–Eau Claire (WI)
U of Wisconsin–Green Bay (WI)
U of Wisconsin–La Crosse (WI)
U of Wisconsin–Madison (WI)
U of Wisconsin–Milwaukee (WI)
U of Wisconsin–Oshkosh (WI)
U of Wisconsin–Parkside (WI)
U of Wisconsin–Platteville (WI)
U of Wisconsin–River Falls (WI)
U of Wisconsin–Stevens Point (WI)
U of Wisconsin–Superior (WI)
U of Wisconsin–Whitewater (WI)
U of Wyoming (WY)
Upper Iowa U (IA)
Ursinus Coll (PA)
Ursuline Coll (OH)
Utah State U (UT)
Utah Valley U (UT)
Utica Coll (NY)
Valdosta State U (GA)
Valley City State U (ND)
Valparaiso U (IN)
Vanderbilt U (TN)
Vanguard U of Southern California (CA)
Vassar Coll (NY)
Villanova U (PA)
Virginia Commonwealth U (VA)
Virginia Military Inst (VA)
Virginia Polytechnic Inst and State U (VA)
Virginia State U (VA)
Virginia Union U (VA)
Virginia Wesleyan Coll (VA)
Viterbo U (WI)
Voorhees Coll (SC)
Wabash Coll (IN)
Wagner Coll (NY)
Wake Forest U (NC)
Walsh U (OH)
Wartburg Coll (IA)
Washburn U (KS)
Washington Adventist U (MD)
Washington & Jefferson Coll (PA)
Washington and Lee U (VA)
Washington Coll (MD)
Washington State U (WA)
Washington U in St. Louis (MO)
Wayland Baptist U (TX)
Waynesburg U (PA)
Wayne State Coll (NE)
Wayne State U (MI)
Weber State U (UT)
Webster U (MO)
Wellesley Coll (MA)
Wells Coll (NY)
Wesleyan Coll (GA)
Wesleyan U (CT)
West Chester U of Pennsylvania (PA)
Western Carolina U (NC)
Western Connecticut State U (CT)
Western Illinois U (IL)
Western Kentucky U (KY)
Western Michigan U (MI)
Western New England Coll (MA)
Western Oregon U (OR)
Western State Coll of Colorado (CO)
Western Washington U (WA)
Westfield State Coll (MA)
West Liberty U (WV)
Westminster Coll (MO)
Westminster Coll (UT)
Westmont Coll (CA)
West Virginia State U (WV)
West Virginia U (WV)
West Virginia Wesleyan Coll (WV)
Wheaton Coll (IL)
Wheaton Coll (MA)
Wheeling Jesuit U (WV)
Whitman Coll (WA)
Whittier Coll (CA)
Wichita State U (KS)
Widener U (PA)
Wilfrid Laurier U (ON, Canada)
Wilkes U (PA)
Willamette U (OR)
William Jewell Coll (MO)
William Paterson U of New Jersey (NJ)
Williams Coll (MA)
Wilmington Coll (OH)
Wilson Coll (PA)
Wingate U (NC)
Winona State U (MN)
Winston-Salem State U (NC)
Winthrop U (SC)
Wittenberg U (OH)
Wofford Coll (SC)
Worcester Polytechnic Inst (MA)
Worcester State Coll (MA)
Wright State U (OH)
Xavier U (OH)
Xavier U of Louisiana (LA)
Yale U (CT)
Yeshiva U (NY)
York Coll of Pennsylvania (PA)
York Coll of the City U of New York (NY)
York U (ON, Canada)
Youngstown State U (OH)

MATHEMATICS AND COMPUTER SCIENCE

Anderson U (IN)
Augustana Coll (IL)
Bennington Coll (VT)
Boston U (MA)
Bowdoin Coll (ME)
Brescia U (KY)
Bryan Coll (TN)
Central Coll (IA)
Central Michigan U (MI)
The Colorado Coll (CO)
Delaware State U (DE)
DePaul U (IL)
Drew U (NJ)
Eastern Illinois U (IL)
Friends U (KS)
George Mason U (VA)
Hampden-Sydney Coll (VA)
Hofstra U (NY)
Immaculata U (PA)
Indiana U–Purdue U Fort Wayne (IN)
Ithaca Coll (NY)
Lake Superior State U (MI)
Lawrence Technological U (MI)
Lawrence U (WI)
Long Island U, C.W. Post Campus (NY)
Loyola U Chicago (IL)
Massachusetts Inst of Technology (MA)
Mount Allison U (NB, Canada)
Paine Coll (GA)
Piedmont Coll (GA)
Redeemer U Coll (ON, Canada)
Rochester Inst of Technology (NY)
Sacred Heart U (CT)
Saint Francis U (PA)
St. Joseph's Coll, Long Island Campus (NY)
St. Joseph's Coll, New York (NY)
St. Lawrence U (NY)
Saint Mary's Coll (IN)
Saint Mary's Coll of California (CA)
Saint Mary's U of Minnesota (MN)
Salem State Coll (MA)
Santa Clara U (CA)
Southern Oregon U (OR)
Stanford U (CA)
Tabor Coll (KS)
Temple U (PA)
Tusculum Coll (TN)
U at Albany, State U of New York (NY)
U of Illinois at Chicago (IL)
U of Illinois at Urbana–Champaign (IL)
U of Oregon (OR)
U of Regina (SK, Canada)
U of St. Francis (IL)
The U of Tampa (FL)
U of Waterloo (ON, Canada)
U of Windsor (ON, Canada)
Washington U in St. Louis (MO)
Western Washington U (WA)
Whitman Coll (WA)
Yale U (CT)
York U (ON, Canada)

MATHEMATICS AND STATISTICS RELATED

The American U of Paris (France)
Anderson U (IN)
Asbury U (KY)
Bernard M. Baruch Coll of the City U of New York (NY)
Carnegie Mellon U (PA)
Columbia U, School of General Studies (NY)
Dakota State U (SD)
The Evergreen State Coll (WA)
Hofstra U (NY)
Indiana U of Pennsylvania (PA)
Lycoming Coll (PA)
Miami U Hamilton (OH)
New York U (NY)
Ohio U (OH)
Oregon State U (OR)
Purchase Coll, State U of New York (NY)
Sacred Heart U (CT)
Saint Mary's Coll of California (CA)
Seattle Pacific U (WA)
Taylor U (IN)
Trevecca Nazarene U (TN)
Tulane U (LA)
The U of British Columbia–Okanagan (BC, Canada)
U of New Hampshire (NH)
U of Pittsburgh (PA)
U of Regina (SK, Canada)
U of Rochester (NY)
The U of Scranton (PA)
U of South Alabama (AL)
Western State Coll of Colorado (CO)

MATHEMATICS RELATED

California State U, Monterey Bay (CA)
Carlow U (PA)
Eastern Nazarene Coll (MA)
Hillsdale Coll (MI)
Ohio Northern U (OH)
Reinhardt Coll (GA)
Sacred Heart U (CT)
Seton Hill U (PA)
Sweet Briar Coll (VA)
United States Military Acad (NY)
U of California, Los Angeles (CA)
U of Miami (FL)
U of Pittsburgh (PA)
U of Waterloo (ON, Canada)
Wheelock Coll (MA)

MATHEMATICS TEACHER EDUCATION

Abilene Christian U (TX)
Adams State Coll (CO)
Alma Coll (MI)
Alvernia U (PA)
Anderson U (IN)
Appalachian State U (NC)
Arkansas State U—Jonesboro (AR)
Arkansas Tech U (AR)
Assumption Coll (MA)
Auburn U (AL)
Averett U (VA)
Baptist Bible Coll of Pennsylvania (PA)
Baylor U (TX)
Berry Coll (GA)
Bethany Coll (KS)
Bethel Coll (IN)
Bethel U (MN)
Bishop's U (QC, Canada)
Black Hills State U (SD)
Bluefield Coll (VA)
Blue Mountain Coll (MS)
Bob Jones U (SC)
Boston U (MA)
Bowie State U (MD)
Bowling Green State U (OH)
Bradley U (IL)
Brewton-Parker Coll (GA)
Bridgewater Coll (VA)
Brigham Young U–Hawaii (HI)
Brock U (ON, Canada)
Brooklyn Coll of the City U of New York (NY)
Bryan Coll (TN)
Buena Vista U (IA)
Buffalo State Coll, State U of New York (NY)
Cabrini Coll (PA)
California Lutheran U (CA)
California State U, Chico (CA)
California State U, Long Beach (CA)
Campbellsville U (KY)
Capital U (OH)
Carroll U (WI)
Castleton State Coll (VT)
The Catholic U of America (DC)
Cedarville U (OH)
Central Michigan U (MI)
Chipola Coll (FL)
Christian Brothers U (TN)
City Coll of the City U of New York (NY)
Claflin U (SC)
Clearwater Christian Coll (FL)
Clemson U (SC)
Coker Coll (SC)
The Coll at Brockport, State U of New York (NY)
The Coll of New Jersey (NJ)
Coll of Notre Dame of Maryland (MD)
The Coll of Saint Rose (NY)
Coll of the Ozarks (MO)
Colorado State U (CO)
Columbus State U (GA)
Concordia Coll (MN)
Concordia U Chicago (IL)
Concordia U, St. Paul (MN)
Corban U (OR)
Cornell U (NY)
Cornerstone U (MI)
Covenant Coll (GA)
Culver-Stockton Coll (MO)
Cumberland U (TN)
Daemen Coll (NY)
Dakota State U (SD)
Dakota Wesleyan U (SD)
Dana Coll (NE)
Daytona State Coll (FL)
Delaware State U (DE)
Delta State U (MS)
DePaul U (IL)
Dominican Coll (NY)
Dowling Coll (NY)
Duquesne U (PA)
East Carolina U (NC)
East Central U (OK)
Eastern Mennonite U (VA)
Eastern Michigan U (MI)
Eastern Washington U (WA)
East Texas Baptist U (TX)
Edgewood Coll (WI)
Elizabeth City State U (NC)
Elmhurst Coll (IL)
Elmira Coll (NY)
Emmanuel Coll (GA)
Fayetteville State U (NC)
Felician Coll (NJ)
Ferris State U (MI)
Fitchburg State Coll (MA)
Florida Ag and Mech U (FL)
Florida Atlantic U (FL)
Florida Inst of Technology (FL)
Franklin Coll (IN)
Freed-Hardeman U (TN)
Friends U (KS)
Gardner-Webb U (NC)
Geneva Coll (PA)
Glenville State Coll (WV)
Grace Coll (IN)
Grambling State U (LA)
Grand Valley State U (MI)
Greensboro Coll (NC)
Greenville Coll (IL)
Gustavus Adolphus Coll (MN)
Gwynedd-Mercy Coll (PA)
Hannibal-LaGrange Coll (MO)
Harding U (AR)
Hardin-Simmons U (TX)
Hawai'i Pacific U (HI)
Hofstra U (NY)
Hope Coll (MI)
Houston Baptist U (TX)
Howard Payne U (TX)
Hunter Coll of the City U of New York (NY)
Huntingdon Coll (AL)
Huntington U (IN)
Indiana U Bloomington (IN)
Indiana U Northwest (IN)
Indiana U–Purdue U Fort Wayne (IN)
Indiana U South Bend (IN)
Indiana U Southeast (IN)
Indiana Wesleyan U (IN)
Indian River State Coll (FL)
Inter American U of Puerto Rico, Arecibo Campus (PR)
Inter American U of Puerto Rico, San Germán Campus (PR)
Iona Coll (NY)
Ithaca Coll (NY)
Jackson State U (MS)
Jamestown Coll (ND)
John Brown U (AR)
Johnson C. Smith U (NC)
Johnson State Coll (VT)
Judson Coll (AL)
Juniata Coll (PA)
Keene State Coll (NH)
Kennesaw State U (GA)
Kentucky Wesleyan Coll (KY)
Keuka Coll (NY)
Keystone Coll (PA)
King Coll (TN)
Lake Forest Coll (IL)
Le Moyne Coll (NY)

Lewis-Clark State Coll (ID)
Liberty U (VA)
Limestone Coll (SC)
Lincoln Memorial U (TN)
Lincoln U (MO)
Lincoln U (PA)
Lindenwood U (MO)
Lindsey Wilson Coll (KY)
Lipscomb U (TN)
Long Island U, Brooklyn Campus (NY)
Long Island U, C.W. Post Campus (NY)
Louisiana State U in Shreveport (LA)
Louisiana Tech U (LA)
Loyola U Chicago (IL)
Madonna U (MI)
Manhattanville Coll (NY)
Mansfield U of Pennsylvania (PA)
Maranatha Baptist Bible Coll (WI)
Marian U (WI)
Marist Coll (NY)
Marquette U (WI)
Maryville Coll (TN)
Maryville U of Saint Louis (MO)
Marywood U (PA)
Mayville State U (ND)
McKendree U (IL)
McMurry U (TX)
McNeese State U (LA)
Medaille Coll (NY)
Mercyhurst Coll (PA)
Messiah Coll (PA)
Miami Dade Coll (FL)
Miami U (OH)
Miami U Hamilton (OH)
Michigan State U (MI)
Michigan Technological U (MI)
MidAmerica Nazarene U (KS)
Midwestern State U (TX)
Millersville U of Pennsylvania (PA)
Millikin U (IL)
Minnesota State U Moorhead (MN)
Minot State U (ND)
Misericordia U (PA)
Mississippi Coll (MS)
Mississippi Valley State U (MS)
Missouri State U (MO)
Molloy Coll (NY)
Montana State U Billings (MT)
Moravian Coll (PA)
Morningside Coll (IA)
Morris Coll (SC)
Mount Marty Coll (SD)
Mount Mary Coll (WI)
Mount Vernon Nazarene U (OH)
Murray State U (KY)
Nazareth Coll of Rochester (NY)
Nevada State Coll at Henderson (NV)
New York Inst of Technology (NY)
New York U (NY)
Niagara U (NY)
Nicholls State U (LA)
North Carolina Central U (NC)
North Carolina State U (NC)
North Dakota State U (ND)
Northeastern State U (OK)
Northern Arizona U (AZ)
Northern Michigan U (MI)
North Georgia Coll & State U (GA)
North Greenville U (SC)
Northland Coll (WI)
Northwestern Coll (MN)
Northwestern Oklahoma State U (OK)
Northwestern State U of Louisiana (LA)
Northwest Missouri State U (MO)
Northwest Nazarene U (ID)
Northwest U (WA)
Oakland City U (IN)
Ohio Dominican U (OH)
Ohio Northern U (OH)
Ohio Valley U (WV)
Ohio Wesleyan U (OH)
Oklahoma Baptist U (OK)
Oklahoma Christian U (OK)
Old Dominion U (VA)
Oral Roberts U (OK)
Pace U (NY)
Paine Coll (GA)
Pepperdine U, Malibu (CA)
Philadelphia Biblical U (PA)
Pittsburg State U (KS)
Point Park U (PA)
Pontifical Catholic U of Puerto Rico (PR)
Prescott Coll (AZ)
Queens U of Charlotte (NC)
Regis Coll (MA)
Rhode Island Coll (RI)
Rivier Coll (NH)
Roberts Wesleyan Coll (NY)
Rochester Coll (MI)
Rocky Mountain Coll (MT)
Sacred Heart U (CT)
Saginaw Valley State U (MI)
St. Ambrose U (IA)
St. Catherine U (MN)
St. Edward's U (TX)
St. Francis Coll (NY)
Saint Francis U (PA)
St. John Fisher Coll (NY)
St. John's U (NY)
Saint Joseph's U (PA)
Saint Mary's U of Minnesota (MN)
St. Petersburg Coll (FL)
Saint Xavier U (IL)
Salve Regina U (RI)
Schreiner U (TX)
Seattle Pacific U (WA)
Seton Hill U (PA)
Shawnee State U (OH)
Shaw U (NC)
Shorter U (GA)
Simpson U (CA)
Southeastern Louisiana U (LA)
Southeastern Oklahoma State U (OK)
Southeastern U (FL)
Southeast Missouri State U (MO)
Southern Arkansas U–Magnolia (AR)
Southern U and Ag and Mech Coll (LA)
Southern Wesleyan U (SC)
Southwest Baptist U (MO)
Southwestern Coll (KS)
Southwest Minnesota State U (MN)
Spring Arbor U (MI)
State U of New York at New Paltz (NY)
State U of New York Coll at Cortland (NY)
State U of New York Coll at Old Westbury (NY)
State U of New York Coll at Oneonta (NY)
State U of New York Coll at Potsdam (NY)
Syracuse U (NY)
Tabor Coll (KS)
Talladega Coll (AL)
Taylor U (IN)
Temple U (PA)
Texas A&M Intl U (TX)
Texas A&M U–Corpus Christi (TX)
Texas Christian U (TX)
Texas Lutheran U (TX)
Texas Wesleyan U (TX)
Trevecca Nazarene U (TN)
Trine U (IN)
Trinity Christian Coll (IL)
Tusculum Coll (TN)
Union Coll (NE)
Universidad Adventista de las Antillas (PR)
The U of Akron (OH)
The U of Arizona (AZ)
U of Arkansas at Fort Smith (AR)
U of California, San Diego (CA)
U of Central Florida (FL)
U of Central Oklahoma (OK)
U of Delaware (DE)
U of Evansville (IN)
U of Georgia (GA)
U of Illinois at Chicago (IL)
U of Illinois at Urbana–Champaign (IL)
U of Indianapolis (IN)
The U of Iowa (IA)
U of Lethbridge (AB, Canada)
U of Louisiana at Monroe (LA)
U of Maine (ME)
U of Maine at Farmington (ME)
U of Maine at Fort Kent (ME)
U of Maine at Machias (ME)
U of Mary (ND)
U of Mary Hardin-Baylor (TX)
U of Maryland, Coll Park (MD)
U of Michigan–Dearborn (MI)
U of Michigan–Flint (MI)
U of Minnesota, Duluth (MN)
U of Minnesota, Twin Cities Campus (MN)
U of Mississippi (MS)
U of Missouri (MO)
U of Missouri–St. Louis (MO)
The U of Montana Western (MT)
U of Nebraska–Lincoln (NE)
U of Nevada, Reno (NV)
U of New Hampshire (NH)
U of New Orleans (LA)
The U of North Carolina at Charlotte (NC)
The U of North Carolina at Greensboro (NC)
The U of North Carolina at Pembroke (NC)
The U of North Carolina Wilmington (NC)
U of North Dakota (ND)
U of Northern Iowa (IA)
U of North Florida (FL)
U of Oklahoma (OK)
U of Pittsburgh at Johnstown (PA)
U of Puerto Rico at Utuado (PR)
U of Puerto Rico, Cayey U Coll (PR)
U of Regina (SK, Canada)
U of Rio Grande (OH)
U of St. Francis (IL)
U of St. Thomas (MN)
The U of South Dakota (SD)
U of South Florida (FL)
The U of Tennessee at Chattanooga (TN)
The U of Tennessee at Martin (TN)
The U of Toledo (OH)
U of Tulsa (OK)
U of Vermont (VT)
U of Waterloo (ON, Canada)
The U of Western Ontario (ON, Canada)
U of Windsor (ON, Canada)
U of Wisconsin–River Falls (WI)
U of Wisconsin–Superior (WI)
Ursuline Coll (OH)
Utah State U (UT)
Utah Valley U (UT)
Utica Coll (NY)
Valley City State U (ND)
Valparaiso U (IN)
Viterbo U (WI)
Walsh U (OH)
Wartburg Coll (IA)
Washington Adventist U (MD)
Washington State U (WA)
Washington U in St. Louis (MO)
Waynesburg U (PA)
Wayne State Coll (NE)
Wayne State U (MI)
Western Carolina U (NC)
Western Michigan U (MI)
Western State Coll of Colorado (CO)
Western Washington U (WA)
Westmont Coll (CA)
West Virginia Wesleyan Coll (WV)
Wheeling Jesuit U (WV)
Widener U (PA)
William Penn U (IA)
Wingate U (NC)
Winston-Salem State U (NC)
Wright State U (OH)
York Coll (NE)
York Coll of Pennsylvania (PA)
York U (ON, Canada)
Youngstown State U (OH)

MECHANICAL DRAFTING AND CAD/CADD

Eastern Michigan U (MI)
Indiana U South Bend (IN)
Murray State U (KY)
Purdue U (IN)
Purdue U Calumet (IN)

MECHANICAL ENGINEERING

Alabama Ag and Mech U (AL)
Alfred U (NY)
American U of Beirut (Lebanon)
Andrews U (MI)
Arizona State U (AZ)
Arkansas State U—Jonesboro (AR)
Arkansas Tech U (AR)
Auburn U (AL)
Baker Coll of Flint (MI)
Baylor U (TX)
Boston U (MA)
Bradley U (IL)
Bucknell U (PA)
California Baptist U (CA)
California Inst of Technology (CA)
California Maritime Acad (CA)
California Polytechnic State U, San Luis Obispo (CA)
California State Polytechnic U, Pomona (CA)
California State U, Chico (CA)
California State U, Fresno (CA)
California State U, Fullerton (CA)
California State U, Long Beach (CA)
California State U, Los Angeles (CA)
California State U, Sacramento (CA)
Calvin Coll (MI)
Carnegie Mellon U (PA)
Case Western Reserve U (OH)
The Catholic U of America (DC)
Cedarville U (OH)
Central Michigan U (MI)
Christian Brothers U (TN)
City Coll of the City U of New York (NY)
Clarkson U (NY)
Clemson U (SC)
Cleveland State U (OH)
The Coll of New Jersey (NJ)
Colorado State U (CO)
Columbia U (NY)
Concordia U (QC, Canada)
Cooper Union for the Advancement of Science and Art (NY)
Cornell U (NY)
Delaware State U (DE)
Dordt Coll (IA)
Drexel U (PA)
Duke U (NC)
Eastern Nazarene Coll (MA)
Embry-Riddle Aeronautical U (AZ)
Embry-Riddle Aeronautical U (FL)
Fairfield U (CT)
Florida Ag and Mech U (FL)
Florida Atlantic U (FL)
Florida Inst of Technology (FL)
Florida Intl U (FL)
Franklin W. Olin Coll of Eng (MA)
Gallaudet U (DC)
Gannon U (PA)
George Fox U (OR)
The George Washington U (DC)
Georgia Inst of Technology (GA)
Gonzaga U (WA)
Grove City Coll (PA)
Harding U (AR)
Hofstra U (NY)
Idaho State U (ID)
Illinois Inst of Technology (IL)
Indiana Tech (IN)
Indiana U–Purdue U Fort Wayne (IN)
Indiana U–Purdue U Indianapolis (IN)
Inter American U of Puerto Rico, Bayamón Campus (PR)
Iowa State U of Science and Technology (IA)
Jacksonville U (FL)
John Brown U (AR)
The Johns Hopkins U (MD)
Kansas State U (KS)
Kettering U (MI)
Lafayette Coll (PA)
Lakehead U (ON, Canada)
Lake Superior State U (MI)
Lamar U (TX)
Lawrence Technological U (MI)
Lehigh U (PA)
LeTourneau U (TX)
Lipscomb U (TN)
Louisiana State U and Ag and Mech Coll (LA)
Louisiana Tech U (LA)
Loyola Marymount U (CA)
Manhattan Coll (NY)
Marquette U (WI)
Massachusetts Inst of Technology (MA)
Memorial U of Newfoundland (NL, Canada)
Miami U (OH)
Michigan State U (MI)
Michigan Technological U (MI)
Milwaukee School of Eng (WI)
Minnesota State U Mankato (MN)
Mississippi State U (MS)
Missouri U of Science and Technology (MO)
Montana State U (MT)
Murray State U (KY)
New Jersey Inst of Technology (NJ)
New Mexico Inst of Mining and Technology (NM)
New Mexico State U (NM)
New York Inst of Technology (NY)
North Carolina State U (NC)
North Dakota State U (ND)
Northeastern U (MA)
Northern Arizona U (AZ)
Oakland U (MI)
Ohio Northern U (OH)
The Ohio State U (OH)
Ohio U (OH)
Oklahoma Christian U (OK)
Oklahoma State U (OK)
Old Dominion U (VA)
Oral Roberts U (OK)
Oregon State U (OR)
Penn State Abington (PA)
Penn State Altoona (PA)
Penn State Beaver (PA)
Penn State Berks (PA)
Penn State Brandywine (PA)
Penn State DuBois (PA)
Penn State Erie, The Behrend Coll (PA)
Penn State Fayette, The Eberly Campus (PA)
Penn State Greater Allegheny (PA)
Penn State Harrisburg (PA)
Penn State Hazleton (PA)
Penn State Lehigh Valley (PA)
Penn State Mont Alto (PA)
Penn State New Kensington (PA)
Penn State Schuylkill (PA)
Penn State Shenango (PA)
Penn State U Park (PA)
Penn State Wilkes-Barre (PA)
Penn State Worthington Scranton (PA)
Penn State York (PA)
Polytechnic Inst of NYU (NY)
Polytechnic U of Puerto Rico (PR)
Portland State U (OR)
Prairie View A&M U (TX)
Princeton U (NJ)
Purdue U (IN)
Purdue U Calumet (IN)
Purdue U North Central (IN)
Queen's U at Kingston (ON, Canada)
Rensselaer Polytechnic Inst (NY)
Rice U (TX)
Rochester Inst of Technology (NY)
Rose-Hulman Inst of Technology (IN)
Rowan U (NJ)
Royal Military Coll of Canada (ON, Canada)
Rutgers, The State U of New Jersey, New Brunswick (NJ)
Saginaw Valley State U (MI)
St. Cloud State U (MN)
Saint Louis U (MO)
Saint Martin's U (WA)
San Diego State U (CA)
San Francisco State U (CA)
San Jose State U (CA)
Santa Clara U (CA)
Seattle U (WA)
South Dakota School of Mines and Technology (SD)
South Dakota State U (SD)
Southern Illinois U Carbondale (IL)
Southern Illinois U Edwardsville (IL)
Southern Methodist U (TX)
Southern Polytechnic State U (GA)
Southern U and Ag and Mech Coll (LA)
Stanford U (CA)
State U of New York at Binghamton (NY)
State U of New York Maritime Coll (NY)
Stevens Inst of Technology (NJ)
Stony Brook U, State U of New York (NY)
Syracuse U (NY)
Temple U (PA)
Tennessee Technological U (TN)
Texas A&M U (TX)
Texas A&M U–Corpus Christi (TX)
Texas A&M U–Kingsville (TX)
Texas Christian U (TX)
Texas Tech U (TX)
Trine U (IN)
Trinity Coll (CT)
Tufts U (MA)
Tulane U (LA)
Tuskegee U (AL)
Union Coll (NY)
United States Air Force Acad (CO)
United States Coast Guard Acad (CT)
United States Military Acad (NY)
United States Naval Acad (MD)
Universidad de las Américas–Puebla (Mexico)
U at Buffalo, the State U of New York (NY)
The U of Akron (OH)
The U of Alabama (AL)
The U of Alabama at Birmingham (AL)
The U of Alabama in Huntsville (AL)
U of Alaska Fairbanks (AK)
U of Alberta (AB, Canada)
The U of Arizona (AZ)
U of Arkansas (AR)
The U of British Columbia (BC, Canada)
The U of British Columbia–Okanagan (BC, Canada)
U of California, Berkeley (CA)
U of California, Davis (CA)
U of California, Irvine (CA)
U of California, Los Angeles (CA)
U of California, Merced (CA)
U of California, Riverside (CA)
U of California, San Diego (CA)
U of California, Santa Barbara (CA)
U of Central Florida (FL)
U of Cincinnati (OH)
U of Colorado at Boulder (CO)
U of Colorado at Colorado Springs (CO)
U of Colorado Denver (CO)
U of Connecticut (CT)
U of Dayton (OH)
U of Delaware (DE)
U of Denver (CO)
U of Evansville (IN)
U of Florida (FL)
U of Hartford (CT)
U of Hawaii at Manoa (HI)
U of Houston (TX)

U of Idaho (ID)
U of Illinois at Chicago (IL)
U of Illinois at Urbana–Champaign (IL)
U of Indianapolis (IN)
The U of Iowa (IA)
The U of Kansas (KS)
U of Kentucky (KY)
U of Louisville (KY)
U of Maine (ME)
U of Manitoba (MB, Canada)
U of Maryland, Baltimore County (MD)
U of Maryland, Coll Park (MD)
U of Massachusetts Amherst (MA)
U of Massachusetts Dartmouth (MA)
U of Massachusetts Lowell (MA)
U of Memphis (TN)
U of Miami (FL)
U of Michigan (MI)
U of Michigan–Dearborn (MI)
U of Minnesota, Twin Cities Campus (MN)
U of Mississippi (MS)
U of Missouri (MO)
U of Missouri–Kansas City (MO)
U of Missouri–St. Louis (MO)
U of Nebraska–Lincoln (NE)
U of Nevada, Las Vegas (NV)
U of Nevada, Reno (NV)
U of New Brunswick Fredericton (NB, Canada)
U of New Hampshire (NH)
U of New Haven (CT)
U of New Mexico (NM)
U of New Orleans (LA)
The U of North Carolina at Charlotte (NC)
U of North Dakota (ND)
U of North Florida (FL)
U of North Texas (TX)
U of Notre Dame (IN)
U of Oklahoma (OK)
U of Ottawa (ON, Canada)
U of Pennsylvania (PA)
U of Pittsburgh (PA)
U of Portland (OR)
U of Rhode Island (RI)
U of Rochester (NY)
U of St. Thomas (MN)
U of San Diego (CA)
U of Saskatchewan (SK, Canada)
U of South Alabama (AL)
U of South Carolina (SC)
U of Southern California (CA)
U of South Florida (FL)
The U of Tennessee (TN)
The U of Tennessee at Chattanooga (TN)
The U of Texas at Arlington (TX)
The U of Texas at Austin (TX)
The U of Texas at Dallas (TX)
The U of Texas at El Paso (TX)
The U of Texas at San Antonio (TX)
The U of Texas at Tyler (TX)
The U of Texas of the Permian Basin (TX)
The U of Texas–Pan American (TX)
U of the District of Columbia (DC)
U of the Pacific (CA)
The U of Toledo (OH)
U of Toronto (ON, Canada)
U of Tulsa (OK)
U of Utah (UT)
U of Vermont (VT)
U of Virginia (VA)
U of Washington (WA)
U of Waterloo (ON, Canada)
The U of Western Ontario (ON, Canada)
U of Windsor (ON, Canada)
U of Wisconsin–Madison (WI)
U of Wisconsin–Milwaukee (WI)
U of Wisconsin–Platteville (WI)
U of Wyoming (WY)
Ursinus Coll (PA)
Utah State U (UT)
Valparaiso U (IN)
Vanderbilt U (TN)
Villanova U (PA)
Virginia Commonwealth U (VA)
Virginia Military Inst (VA)
Virginia Polytechnic Inst and State U (VA)
Washington State U (WA)
Washington U in St. Louis (MO)
Wayne State U (MI)
Western Kentucky U (KY)
Western Michigan U (MI)
Western New England Coll (MA)
West Virginia U (WV)
Wichita State U (KS)
Widener U (PA)
Wilkes U (PA)
William Penn U (IA)
Winona State U (MN)
Worcester Polytechnic Inst (MA)
Wright State U (OH)
Yale U (CT)
York Coll of Pennsylvania (PA)
Youngstown State U (OH)

MECHANICAL ENGINEERING/ MECHANICAL TECHNOLOGY

Alabama Ag and Mech U (AL)
Arizona State U (AZ)
Bluefield State Coll (WV)
Boise State U (ID)
Bowling Green State U (OH)
Buffalo State Coll, State U of New York (NY)
California State U, Long Beach (CA)
California State U, Sacramento (CA)
Central Connecticut State U (CT)
Central Michigan U (MI)
Delaware State U (DE)
Eastern Michigan U (MI)
Eastern Washington U (WA)
Fairleigh Dickinson U, Metropolitan Campus (NJ)
Fairmont State U (WV)
Farmingdale State Coll (NY)
Ferris State U (MI)
Georgia Southern U (GA)
Indiana U–Purdue U Fort Wayne (IN)
Kent State U at Tuscarawas (OH)
Lakehead U (ON, Canada)
Lake Superior State U (MI)
LeTourneau U (TX)
Metropolitan State Coll of Denver (CO)
Miami U Hamilton (OH)
Michigan Technological U (MI)
Midwestern State U (TX)
Milwaukee School of Eng (WI)
Montana State U (MT)
Nicholls State U (LA)
Northeastern U (MA)
Northern Michigan U (MI)
Oklahoma State U (OK)
Oregon Inst of Technology (OR)
Penn State Erie, The Behrend Coll (PA)
Pennsylvania Coll of Technology (PA)
Pittsburg State U (KS)
Point Park U (PA)
Savannah State U (GA)
South Carolina State U (SC)
Southern Polytechnic State U (GA)
State U of New York Coll of Technology at Alfred (NY)
Texas A&M U–Corpus Christi (TX)
Texas Tech U (TX)
Thomas Edison State Coll (NJ)
United States Military Acad (NY)
The U of Akron (OH)
U of Arkansas at Little Rock (AR)
The U of British Columbia (BC, Canada)
U of Cincinnati (OH)
U of Dayton (OH)
U of Hartford (CT)
U of Houston (TX)
U of Houston–Downtown (TX)
U of Maine (ME)
U of New Hampshire (NH)
U of New Hampshire at Manchester (NH)
The U of North Carolina at Charlotte (NC)
U of North Texas (TX)
U of Pittsburgh at Johnstown (PA)
U of Rio Grande (OH)
The U of Texas at Brownsville (TX)
The U of Toledo (OH)
Virginia State U (VA)
Wayne State U (MI)
Wentworth Inst of Technology (MA)
Youngstown State U (OH)

MECHANICAL ENGINEERING TECHNOLOGIES RELATED

Cleveland State U (OH)
Grove City Coll (PA)
Indiana State U (IN)
Indiana U–Purdue U Indianapolis (IN)
New York Inst of Technology (NY)
Old Dominion U (VA)
Purdue U (IN)
Purdue U North Central (IN)
Thomas Edison State Coll (NJ)
U of Hartford (CT)
Vaughn Coll of Aeronautics and Technology (NY)

MECHANICS AND REPAIR

Lewis-Clark State Coll (ID)

MEDICAL ADMINISTRATIVE ASSISTANT AND MEDICAL SECRETARY

Baker Coll of Auburn Hills (MI)
Mercyhurst Coll (PA)
Tabor Coll (KS)
U of Cincinnati (OH)

MEDICAL/CLINICAL ASSISTANT

California State U, Dominguez Hills (CA)
Pennsylvania Coll of Technology (PA)

MEDICAL/HEALTH MANAGEMENT AND CLINICAL ASSISTANT

Davenport U, Grand Rapids (MI)
Lewis-Clark State Coll (ID)
Stratford U, Woodbridge (VA)

MEDICAL ILLUSTRATION

Alma Coll (MI)
Arcadia U (PA)
The Cleveland Inst of Art (OH)
Iowa State U of Science and Technology (IA)
Rochester Inst of Technology (NY)

MEDICAL ILLUSTRATION AND INFORMATICS RELATED

Florida Ag and Mech U (FL)

MEDICAL INFORMATICS

Capella U (MN)
Montana Tech of The U of Montana (MT)
Montclair State U (NJ)
U of Waterloo (ON, Canada)
Walden U (MN)

MEDICAL MICROBIOLOGY AND BACTERIOLOGY

Adams State Coll (CO)
Auburn U (AL)
Bowling Green State U (OH)
California Polytechnic State U, San Luis Obispo (CA)
Humboldt State U (CA)
Indiana U Bloomington (IN)
Inter American U of Puerto Rico, Bayamón Campus (PR)
Inter American U of Puerto Rico, San Germán Campus (PR)
Memorial U of Newfoundland (NL, Canada)
Michigan Technological U (MI)
Minnesota State U Mankato (MN)
Mississippi State U (MS)
Mississippi U for Women (MS)
Montana State U (MT)
New Mexico State U (NM)
Ohio Wesleyan U (OH)
Penn State Abington (PA)
Penn State Altoona (PA)
Penn State Beaver (PA)
Penn State Berks (PA)
Penn State Brandywine (PA)
Penn State DuBois (PA)
Penn State Erie, The Behrend Coll (PA)
Penn State Fayette, The Eberly Campus (PA)
Penn State Greater Allegheny (PA)
Penn State Hazleton (PA)
Penn State Lehigh Valley (PA)
Penn State Mont Alto (PA)
Penn State New Kensington (PA)
Penn State Schuylkill (PA)
Penn State Shenango (PA)
Penn State U Park (PA)
Penn State Wilkes-Barre (PA)
Penn State Worthington Scranton (PA)
Penn State York (PA)
Pomona Coll (CA)
Quinnipiac U (CT)
Rutgers, The State U of New Jersey, New Brunswick (NJ)
St. Cloud State U (MN)
San Francisco State U (CA)
Sonoma State U (CA)
U of Alberta (AB, Canada)
The U of British Columbia (BC, Canada)
U of California, Los Angeles (CA)
U of California, San Diego (CA)
U of California, Santa Barbara (CA)
U of Central Florida (FL)
U of Cincinnati (OH)
U of Florida (FL)
U of King's Coll (NS, Canada)
U of Maine (ME)
U of Manitoba (MB, Canada)
U of Miami (FL)
U of Minnesota, Twin Cities Campus (MN)
U of New Brunswick Fredericton (NB, Canada)
U of Rochester (NY)
U of Saskatchewan (SK, Canada)
U of South Florida (FL)
The U of Tennessee (TN)
The U of Texas at El Paso (TX)
U of Toronto (ON, Canada)
U of Vermont (VT)
U of Washington (WA)
The U of Western Ontario (ON, Canada)
U of Wisconsin–La Crosse (WI)
U of Wisconsin–Madison (WI)
U of Wisconsin–Oshkosh (WI)
Utah State U (UT)
Wagner Coll (NY)
Weber State U (UT)
Worcester Polytechnic Inst (MA)
Xavier U of Louisiana (LA)

MEDICAL OFFICE ASSISTANT

Concordia U Wisconsin (WI)
Lewis-Clark State Coll (ID)

MEDICAL PHARMACOLOGY AND PHARMACEUTICAL SCIENCES

The Ohio State U (OH)
South Dakota State U (SD)
Universidad de las Américas–Puebla (Mexico)
U of Michigan (MI)
U of the Sciences in Philadelphia (PA)
West Chester U of Pennsylvania (PA)

MEDICAL RADIOLOGIC TECHNOLOGY

Alderson-Broaddus Coll (WV)
Arkansas State U—Jonesboro (AR)
Avila U (MO)
Baptist Coll of Health Sciences (TN)
Bloomsburg U of Pennsylvania (PA)
California State U, Long Beach (CA)
Carroll U (WI)
Charles Drew U of Medicine and Science (CA)
Coll of Notre Dame of Maryland (MD)
Fairleigh Dickinson U, Coll at Florham (NJ)
Grand Valley State U (MI)
Idaho State U (ID)
Indiana U East (IN)
Indiana U Kokomo (IN)
Indiana U–Purdue U Indianapolis (IN)
Indiana U South Bend (IN)
Indiana U Southeast (IN)
Kent State U at Salem (OH)
La Roche Coll (PA)
Long Island U, C.W. Post Campus (NY)
Massachusetts Coll of Pharmacy and Health Sciences (MA)
Minot State U (ND)
Misericordia U (PA)
Missouri Southern State U (MO)
Morehead State U (KY)
Mount Aloysius Coll (PA)
Mount Marty Coll (SD)
North Central Coll (IL)
Oakland U (MI)
Oregon Health & Science U (OR)
Roosevelt U (IL)
St. Francis Coll (NY)
Saint Louis U (MO)
Southern Illinois U Carbondale (IL)
Southern Vermont Coll (VT)
State U of New York Upstate Medical U (NY)
Texas State U–San Marcos (TX)
Thomas Edison State Coll (NJ)
U of Hartford (CT)
U of Michigan–Flint (MI)
U of Missouri (MO)
U of Nebraska Medical Center (NE)
U of Nevada, Las Vegas (NV)
U of New Mexico (NM)
The U of North Carolina at Chapel Hill (NC)
U of St. Francis (IL)
U of Southern Indiana (IN)
The U of Texas Southwestern Medical Center at Dallas (TX)
U of Vermont (VT)
U of Wisconsin–La Crosse (WI)
Wayne State U (MI)

MEDICAL STAFF SERVICES TECHNOLOGY

Converse Coll (SC)
East Central U (OK)

MEDICINAL AND PHARMACEUTICAL CHEMISTRY

King Coll (TN)
Michigan Technological U (MI)
Ohio Northern U (OH)
Pittsburg State U (KS)
U of California, San Diego (CA)
U of Michigan (MI)
U of the Sciences in Philadelphia (PA)
Worcester Polytechnic Inst (MA)

MEDIEVAL AND RENAISSANCE STUDIES

Bard Coll (NY)
Barnard Coll (NY)
The Catholic U of America (DC)
Coll of the Holy Cross (MA)
The Coll of William and Mary (VA)
Columbia U (NY)
Cornell Coll (IA)
Dickinson Coll (PA)
Duke U (NC)
Emory U (GA)
Fordham U (NY)
Georgetown U (DC)
Hanover Coll (IN)
Marlboro Coll (VT)
Memorial U of Newfoundland (NL, Canada)
Mount Allison U (NB, Canada)
Mount Holyoke Coll (MA)
New Coll of Florida (FL)
The Ohio State U (OH)
Ohio Wesleyan U (OH)
Penn State Abington (PA)
Penn State Altoona (PA)
Penn State Beaver (PA)
Penn State Berks (PA)
Penn State Brandywine (PA)
Penn State DuBois (PA)
Penn State Erie, The Behrend Coll (PA)
Penn State Fayette, The Eberly Campus (PA)
Penn State Greater Allegheny (PA)
Penn State Hazleton (PA)
Penn State Lehigh Valley (PA)
Penn State Mont Alto (PA)
Penn State New Kensington (PA)
Penn State Schuylkill (PA)
Penn State Shenango (PA)
Penn State U Park (PA)
Penn State Wilkes-Barre (PA)
Penn State Worthington Scranton (PA)
Penn State York (PA)
Rutgers, The State U of New Jersey, New Brunswick (NJ)
Sewanee: The U of the South (TN)
Smith Coll (MA)
Southern Methodist U (TX)
State U of New York at Binghamton (NY)
Swarthmore Coll (PA)
Tulane U (LA)
U at Albany, State U of New York (NY)
U of California, Santa Barbara (CA)
U of Chicago (IL)
The U of Iowa (IA)
U of Manitoba (MB, Canada)
U of Michigan (MI)
U of Nebraska–Lincoln (NE)
U of Notre Dame (IN)
U of Oregon (OR)
U of Ottawa (ON, Canada)
U of Regina (SK, Canada)
U of Saskatchewan (SK, Canada)
The U of Toledo (OH)
U of Waterloo (ON, Canada)
Vassar Coll (NY)
Washington and Lee U (VA)
Washington U in St. Louis (MO)
Wellesley Coll (MA)
Wesleyan U (CT)
Wilfrid Laurier U (ON, Canada)

MENTAL AND SOCIAL HEALTH SERVICES AND ALLIED PROFESSIONS RELATED
Edinboro U of Pennsylvania (PA)
Franklin U (OH)
Old Dominion U (VA)
Pennsylvania Coll of Technology (PA)
Thomas Edison State Coll (NJ)
U of Maine at Augusta (ME)
The U of Toledo (OH)
Wright State U (OH)

MENTAL HEALTH/ REHABILITATION
Governors State U (IL)
Prescott Coll (AZ)
St. Cloud State U (MN)
Tufts U (MA)
U of Maine at Farmington (ME)

MERCHANDISING
U of Minnesota, Twin Cities Campus (MN)

MERCHANDISING, SALES, AND MARKETING OPERATIONS RELATED (GENERAL)
Eastern Michigan U (MI)
U of Hartford (CT)
Washington U in St. Louis (MO)

MERCHANDISING, SALES, AND MARKETING OPERATIONS RELATED (SPECIALIZED)
Baylor U (TX)
Eastern Michigan U (MI)
Fashion Inst of Technology (NY)
Gannon U (PA)
Saint Joseph's U (PA)

METAL AND JEWELRY ARTS
Adams State Coll (CO)
Alberta Coll of Art & Design (AB, Canada)
Arcadia U (PA)
Bowling Green State U (OH)
California Coll of the Arts (CA)
California State U, Long Beach (CA)
The Cleveland Inst of Art (OH)
The Coll at Brockport, State U of New York (NY)
Edinboro U of Pennsylvania (PA)
Ferris State U (MI)
Hofstra U (NY)
Kent State U (OH)
Maine Coll of Art (ME)
Massachusetts Coll of Art and Design (MA)
Northern Arizona U (AZ)
Northern Michigan U (MI)
Pittsburg State U (KS)
Pratt Inst (NY)
Rochester Inst of Technology (NY)
Savannah Coll of Art and Design (GA)
School of the Art Inst of Chicago (IL)
School of the Museum of Fine Arts, Boston (MA)
Seton Hill U (PA)
State U of New York at New Paltz (NY)
Temple U (PA)
The U of Iowa (IA)
The U of Kansas (KS)
U of Massachusetts Dartmouth (MA)
U of Michigan (MI)
U of Oregon (OR)
U of Washington (WA)
U of Wisconsin–Milwaukee (WI)
Western State Coll of Colorado (CO)

METALLURGICAL ENGINEERING
Cleveland State U (OH)
Colorado School of Mines (CO)
Laurentian U (ON, Canada)
Michigan Technological U (MI)
Missouri U of Science and Technology (MO)
Montana Tech of The U of Montana (MT)
South Dakota School of Mines and Technology (SD)
The U of Alabama (AL)
U of Alberta (AB, Canada)
The U of British Columbia (BC, Canada)
U of Cincinnati (OH)
U of Illinois at Urbana–Champaign (IL)
U of Nevada, Reno (NV)
U of Pittsburgh (PA)
The U of Texas at El Paso (TX)
U of Toronto (ON, Canada)
U of Utah (UT)
U of Washington (WA)
U of Wisconsin–Madison (WI)
Ursinus Coll (PA)

METALLURGICAL TECHNOLOGY
U of Cincinnati (OH)

METEOROLOGY
Central Michigan U (MI)
The Coll at Brockport, State U of New York (NY)
Florida Inst of Technology (FL)
Florida State U (FL)
Metropolitan State Coll of Denver (CO)
North Carolina State U (NC)
U of Hawaii at Manoa (HI)
U of Miami (FL)
The U of North Carolina at Charlotte (NC)
U of Oklahoma (OK)
U of the Incarnate Word (TX)
U of Utah (UT)
Western Illinois U (IL)
Western Kentucky U (KY)

MICROBIOLOGICAL SCIENCES AND IMMUNOLOGY RELATED
U of California, Irvine (CA)
The U of Western Ontario (ON, Canada)
Wright State U (OH)

MICROBIOLOGY
Arizona State U (AZ)
Auburn U (AL)
Brigham Young U (UT)
California State Polytechnic U, Pomona (CA)
California State U, Chico (CA)
California State U, Dominguez Hills (CA)
California State U, Long Beach (CA)
California State U, Los Angeles (CA)
Clemson U (SC)
Colorado State U (CO)
Cornell U (NY)
Idaho State U (ID)
Indiana U Bloomington (IN)
Inter American U of Puerto Rico, Aguadilla Campus (PR)
Inter American U of Puerto Rico, Ponce Campus (PR)
Iowa State U of Science and Technology (IA)
Juniata Coll (PA)
Kansas State U (KS)
Louisiana State U and Ag and Mech Coll (LA)
Miami U (OH)
Miami U Hamilton (OH)
Michigan State U (MI)
Michigan Technological U (MI)
North Carolina State U (NC)
North Dakota State U (ND)
Northern Arizona U (AZ)
Northern Michigan U (MI)
The Ohio State U (OH)
Ohio U (OH)
Oklahoma State U (OK)
Oregon State U (OR)
San Diego State U (CA)
South Dakota State U (SD)
Southern Illinois U Carbondale (IL)
Texas A&M U (TX)
Texas State U–San Marcos (TX)
Texas Tech U (TX)
The U of Akron (OH)
The U of Alabama (AL)
The U of British Columbia–Okanagan (BC, Canada)
U of California, Berkeley (CA)
U of California, Davis (CA)
U of California, Santa Barbara (CA)
U of Georgia (GA)
U of Guelph (ON, Canada)
U of Hawaii at Manoa (HI)
U of Houston–Downtown (TX)
U of Idaho (ID)
U of Illinois at Urbana–Champaign (IL)
The U of Kansas (KS)
U of Maryland, Coll Park (MD)
U of Massachusetts Amherst (MA)
U of Michigan (MI)
U of Michigan–Dearborn (MI)
U of Northern Iowa (IA)
U of Oklahoma (OK)
U of Pittsburgh (PA)
U of Puerto Rico at Humacao (PR)
U of Rhode Island (RI)
U of Saskatchewan (SK, Canada)
The U of Texas at Arlington (TX)
U of the Sciences in Philadelphia (PA)
U of Toronto (ON, Canada)
U of Vermont (VT)
The U of Western Ontario (ON, Canada)
U of Wisconsin–La Crosse (WI)
U of Wyoming (WY)
Washington State U (WA)

MIDDLE/NEAR EASTERN AND SEMITIC LANGUAGES RELATED
Bryn Mawr Coll (PA)
Columbia U, School of General Studies (NY)
Indiana U Bloomington (IN)
Sarah Lawrence Coll (NY)
U of Michigan (MI)
Wayne State U (MI)

MIDDLE SCHOOL EDUCATION
Abilene Christian U (TX)
Alaska Pacific U (AK)
Albany State U (GA)
Albertus Magnus Coll (CT)
Alverno Coll (WI)
American Intl Coll (MA)
Appalachian State U (NC)
Arkansas State U—Jonesboro (AR)
Arkansas Tech U (AR)
Armstrong Atlantic State U (GA)
Asbury U (KY)
Ashland U (OH)
Assumption Coll (MA)
Avila U (MO)
Baker U (KS)
Baldwin-Wallace Coll (OH)
Barton Coll (NC)
Bellarmine U (KY)
Bennett Coll for Women (NC)
Bennington Coll (VT)
Berea Coll (KY)
Berry Coll (GA)
Bethel Coll (IN)
Black Hills State U (SD)
Bloomsburg U of Pennsylvania (PA)
Bluefield Coll (VA)
Bluffton U (OH)
Bob Jones U (SC)
Bowling Green State U (OH)
Brenau U (GA)
Brescia U (KY)
Brewton-Parker Coll (GA)
Butler U (IN)
Capital U (OH)
Carlow U (PA)
Carroll U (WI)
Catawba Coll (NC)
Cedarville U (OH)
Central State U (OH)
Champlain Coll (VT)
Christopher Newport U (VA)
Claflin U (SC)
Clark U (MA)
Clayton State U (GA)
Cleveland State U (OH)
Coastal Carolina U (SC)
The Coll at Brockport, State U of New York (NY)
Coll of Charleston (SC)
Coll of Mount St. Joseph (OH)
Coll of the Atlantic (ME)
Coll of the Ozarks (MO)
Columbia Coll (SC)
Columbus State U (GA)
Concordia U, St. Paul (MN)
Concordia U Texas (TX)
Concordia U Wisconsin (WI)
Dakota Wesleyan U (SD)
Delaware State U (DE)
Dowling Coll (NY)
Duquesne U (PA)
East Carolina U (NC)
Eastern Mennonite U (VA)
Eastern Nazarene Coll (MA)
Elizabeth City State U (NC)
Elizabethtown Coll (PA)
Elmira Coll (NY)
Elon U (NC)
Emmanuel Coll (GA)
Evangel U (MO)
Fayetteville State U (NC)
Fitchburg State Coll (MA)
Florida Inst of Technology (FL)
Florida State U (FL)
Fontbonne U (MO)
Gardner-Webb U (NC)
Georgetown Coll (KY)
Georgia Coll & State U (GA)
Georgia Southern U (GA)
Georgia State U (GA)
Gettysburg Coll (PA)
Gordon Coll (MA)
Governors State U (IL)
Grambling State U (LA)
Grand Valley State U (MI)
Greensboro Coll (NC)
Hampton U (VA)
Harding U (AR)
Harris-Stowe State U (MO)
Henderson State U (AR)
High Point U (NC)
Houston Baptist U (TX)
Howard Payne U (TX)
Huntington U (IN)
Indiana Wesleyan U (IN)
Ithaca Coll (NY)
Jacksonville State U (AL)
John Brown U (AR)
Johnson Bible Coll (TN)
Johnson State Coll (VT)
Kennesaw State U (GA)
Kent State U (OH)
Kent State U at Stark (OH)
Kentucky Wesleyan Coll (KY)
Keystone Coll (PA)
King Coll (TN)
LaGrange Coll (GA)
Lakeland Coll (WI)
Lake Superior State U (MI)
Le Moyne Coll (NY)
Lesley U (MA)
Lincoln U (MO)
Lindenwood U (MO)
Lindsey Wilson Coll (KY)
Louisiana Tech U (LA)
Lourdes Coll (OH)
Lubbock Christian U (TX)
Malone U (OH)
Manhattan Coll (NY)
Marian U (WI)
Marquette U (WI)
Mars Hill Coll (NC)
Maryville U of Saint Louis (MO)
The Master's Coll and Sem (CA)
McKendree U (IL)
McMurry U (TX)
Medaille Coll (NY)
Memorial U of Newfoundland (NL, Canada)
Mercer U (GA)
Merrimack Coll (MA)
Miami U (OH)
Michigan State U (MI)
MidAmerica Nazarene U (KS)
Midway Coll (KY)
Millersville U of Pennsylvania (PA)
Minnesota State U Moorhead (MN)
Missouri Baptist U (MO)
Missouri State U (MO)
Morehead State U (KY)
Mount Mercy Coll (IA)
Mount Olive Coll (NC)
Mount Vernon Nazarene U (OH)
Murray State U (KY)
Nebraska Wesleyan U (NE)
Nicholls State U (LA)
North Carolina Central U (NC)
North Carolina State U (NC)
Northern Kentucky U (KY)
North Georgia Coll & State U (GA)
Northwestern State U of Louisiana (LA)
Northwest Missouri State U (MO)
Oakland City U (IN)
Ohio Dominican U (OH)
Ohio Northern U (OH)
The Ohio State U (OH)
The Ohio State U at Lima (OH)
The Ohio State U at Marion (OH)
The Ohio State U–Mansfield Campus (OH)
The Ohio State U–Newark Campus (OH)
Ohio Wesleyan U (OH)
Ouachita Baptist U (AR)
Paine Coll (GA)
Peru State Coll (NE)
Piedmont Coll (GA)
Pikeville Coll (KY)
Presbyterian Coll (SC)
Prescott Coll (AZ)
Reinhardt Coll (GA)
Sacred Heart U (CT)
St. Cloud State U (MN)
Saint Leo U (FL)
Salem State Coll (MA)
Schreiner U (TX)
Shawnee State U (OH)
Shippensburg U of Pennsylvania (PA)
Shorter U (GA)
South Carolina State U (SC)
Southeastern Louisiana U (LA)
Southeast Missouri State U (MO)
Southern Arkansas U–Magnolia (AR)
Southern U and Ag and Mech Coll (LA)
Southwest Baptist U (MO)
State U of New York Coll at Cortland (NY)
State U of New York Coll at Old Westbury (NY)
State U of New York Coll at Oneonta (NY)
Stevenson U (MD)
Tabor Coll (KS)
Tarleton State U (TX)
Texas Lutheran U (TX)
Thomas More Coll (KY)
Transylvania U (KY)
Trinity Christian Coll (IL)
Tusculum Coll (TN)
Union Coll (KY)
The U of Akron (OH)
U of Arkansas at Fort Smith (AR)
U of Central Missouri (MO)
U of Florida (FL)
U of Georgia (GA)
The U of Kansas (KS)
U of Kentucky (KY)
U of Mary Hardin-Baylor (TX)
U of Minnesota, Duluth (MN)
U of Missouri (MO)
U of Missouri–Kansas City (MO)
U of Mount Union (OH)
U of Nebraska–Lincoln (NE)
The U of North Carolina at Chapel Hill (NC)
The U of North Carolina at Charlotte (NC)
The U of North Carolina at Greensboro (NC)
The U of North Carolina at Pembroke (NC)
The U of North Carolina Wilmington (NC)
U of North Dakota (ND)
U of Northern Iowa (IA)
U of North Florida (FL)
U of Regina (SK, Canada)
U of St. Thomas (MN)
U of South Carolina Aiken (SC)
U of South Carolina Upstate (SC)
The U of Tennessee at Chattanooga (TN)
U of the Cumberlands (KY)
U of the Ozarks (AR)
U of Vermont (VT)
The U of Western Ontario (ON, Canada)
U of West Florida (FL)
U of West Georgia (GA)
U of Wisconsin–Platteville (WI)
Ursuline Coll (OH)
Valdosta State U (GA)
Valparaiso U (IN)
Virginia Wesleyan Coll (VA)
Waldorf Coll (IA)
Walsh U (OH)
Warner Pacific Coll (OR)
Washington U in St. Louis (MO)
Wayland Baptist U (TX)
Wayne State Coll (NE)
West Chester U of Pennsylvania (PA)
Western Carolina U (NC)
Western Kentucky U (KY)
Westminster Coll (MO)
West Virginia Wesleyan Coll (WV)
Wheeling Jesuit U (WV)
William Jewell Coll (MO)
Wilmington U (DE)
Wingate U (NC)
Winona State U (MN)
Winston-Salem State U (NC)
Wright State U (OH)
Xavier U (OH)
Xavier U of Louisiana (LA)
York Coll (NE)
York U (ON, Canada)
Youngstown State U (OH)

MILITARY STUDIES
Hawai'i Pacific U (HI)
Pacific Lutheran U (WA)
United States Air Force Acad (CO)

MILITARY TECHNOLOGIES
American Public U System (WV)
Eastern Washington U (WA)
Royal Military Coll of Canada (ON, Canada)
United States Military Acad (NY)
Wright State U (OH)

MINING AND MINERAL ENGINEERING

Colorado School of Mines (CO)
Laurentian U (ON, Canada)
Missouri U of Science and Technology (MO)
Montana Tech of The U of Montana (MT)
New Mexico Inst of Mining and Technology (NM)
Penn State Abington (PA)
Penn State Altoona (PA)
Penn State Beaver (PA)
Penn State Berks (PA)
Penn State Brandywine (PA)
Penn State DuBois (PA)
Penn State Erie, The Behrend Coll (PA)
Penn State Fayette, The Eberly Campus (PA)
Penn State Greater Allegheny (PA)
Penn State Hazleton (PA)
Penn State Lehigh Valley (PA)
Penn State Mont Alto (PA)
Penn State New Kensington (PA)
Penn State Schuylkill (PA)
Penn State Shenango (PA)
Penn State U Park (PA)
Penn State Wilkes-Barre (PA)
Penn State Worthington Scranton (PA)
Penn State York (PA)
Queen's U at Kingston (ON, Canada)
South Dakota School of Mines and Technology (SD)
Southern Illinois U Carbondale (IL)
U of Alaska Fairbanks (AK)
U of Alberta (AB, Canada)
The U of Arizona (AZ)
The U of British Columbia (BC, Canada)
U of Kentucky (KY)
U of Nevada, Reno (NV)
U of Toronto (ON, Canada)
U of Utah (UT)
U of Wisconsin–Madison (WI)
Virginia Polytechnic Inst and State U (VA)
West Virginia U (WV)

MINING TECHNOLOGY

Bluefield State Coll (WV)

MISSIONARY STUDIES AND MISSIOLOGY

Abilene Christian U (TX)
Asbury U (KY)
Baptist Bible Coll of Pennsylvania (PA)
Bethel Coll (IN)
Bob Jones U (SC)
California Baptist U (CA)
Calvary Bible Coll and Theological Sem (MO)
Cedarville U (OH)
Central Baptist Coll (AR)
Central Christian Coll of Kansas (KS)
Concordia U, St. Paul (MN)
Concordia U Wisconsin (WI)
Corban U (OR)
Crown Coll (MN)
Dordt Coll (IA)
East Texas Baptist U (TX)
Emmanuel Bible Coll (ON, Canada)
Eugene Bible Coll (OR)
Faith Baptist Bible Coll and Theological Sem (IA)
Freed-Hardeman U (TN)
Free Will Baptist Bible Coll (TN)
Gardner-Webb U (NC)
Global U (MO)
Grace Bible Coll (MI)
Grace Coll (IN)
Hannibal-LaGrange Coll (MO)
Harding U (AR)
Hardin-Simmons U (TX)
Hillsdale Free Will Baptist Coll (OK)
Howard Payne U (TX)
Huntington U (IN)
John Brown U (AR)
Kuyper Coll (MI)
LeTourneau U (TX)
Lipscomb U (TN)
Lubbock Christian U (TX)
Maranatha Baptist Bible Coll (WI)
Master's Coll and Sem (ON, Canada)
MidAmerica Nazarene U (KS)
Mid-Atlantic Christian U (NC)
Mid-Continent U (KY)
Moody Bible Inst (IL)
Mount Vernon Nazarene U (OH)
Multnomah U (OR)
North Greenville U (SC)
Northwestern Coll (MN)
Northwest Nazarene U (ID)
Northwest U (WA)
Nyack Coll (NY)
Oklahoma Christian U (OK)
Oral Roberts U (OK)
Ouachita Baptist U (AR)
Piedmont Baptist Coll and Graduate School (NC)
Redeemer U Coll (ON, Canada)
Rochester Coll (MI)
Simpson U (CA)
Southeastern Baptist Theological Sem (NC)
Southeastern U (FL)
Southwest Baptist U (MO)
Spring Arbor U (MI)
Trinity Coll of Florida (FL)
Valley Forge Christian Coll (PA)
Vanguard U of Southern California (CA)

MODERN GREEK

Belmont U (TN)
Boston U (MA)
Butler U (IN)
Calvin Coll (MI)
Claremont McKenna Coll (CA)
Colgate U (NY)
Columbia U (NY)
Concordia U Wisconsin (WI)
Cornell Coll (IA)
Emory U (GA)
Florida State U (FL)
Fordham U (NY)
Furman U (SC)
Haverford Coll (PA)
John Carroll U (OH)
Lehman Coll of the City U of New York (NY)
Marlboro Coll (VT)
Memorial U of Newfoundland (NL, Canada)
Oberlin Coll (OH)
The Ohio State U (OH)
Rhodes Coll (TN)
Saint Louis U (MO)
Saint Mary's Coll of California (CA)
Sewanee: The U of the South (TN)
Trent U (ON, Canada)
Tufts U (MA)
Tulane U (LA)
U of Alberta (AB, Canada)
U of Manitoba (MB, Canada)
U of Michigan (MI)
U of Minnesota, Twin Cities Campus (MN)
U of New Brunswick Fredericton (NB, Canada)
U of Toronto (ON, Canada)
U of Wisconsin–Madison (WI)
U of Wisconsin–Milwaukee (WI)
Wabash Coll (IN)
Wright State U (OH)
York U (ON, Canada)

MODERN LANGUAGES

Albion Coll (MI)
Alma Coll (MI)
Beloit Coll (WI)
Bemidji State U (MN)
Bishop's U (QC, Canada)
Claremont McKenna Coll (CA)
Clark U (MA)
Clemson U (SC)
Coll of Mount Saint Vincent (NY)
The Coll of William and Mary (VA)
Cornell Coll (IA)
Dallas Baptist U (TX)
Dillard U (LA)
Eckerd Coll (FL)
Fordham U (NY)
Franklin Coll Switzerland (Switzerland)
Gettysburg Coll (PA)
Grove City Coll (PA)
Hampton U (VA)
Immaculata U (PA)
Judson Coll (AL)
Kenyon Coll (OH)
King Coll (TN)
Lake Erie Coll (OH)
La Salle U (PA)
Laurentian U (ON, Canada)
Lee U (TN)
Long Island U, Brooklyn Campus (NY)
Longwood U (VA)
Louisiana Coll (LA)
Marlboro Coll (VT)
Metropolitan State Coll of Denver (CO)
Middlebury Coll (VT)
Minnesota State U Mankato (MN)
Mount Allison U (NB, Canada)
Nazareth Coll of Rochester (NY)
Northeastern U (MA)
Pomona Coll (CA)
Presbyterian Coll (SC)
Purchase Coll, State U of New York (NY)
Rivier Coll (NH)
St. Bonaventure U (NY)
Saint Francis U (PA)
St. Francis Xavier U (NS, Canada)
St. Lawrence U (NY)
Saint Mary's Coll of California (CA)
Saint Michael's Coll (VT)
St. Thomas Aquinas Coll (NY)
Sarah Lawrence Coll (NY)
Scripps Coll (CA)
Suffolk U (MA)
Trent U (ON, Canada)
Trinity Coll (CT)
U of Alberta (AB, Canada)
U of Chicago (IL)
U of Maine (ME)
U of New Brunswick Fredericton (NB, Canada)
U of Ottawa (ON, Canada)
U of Southern Maine (ME)
U of Toronto (ON, Canada)
The U of Western Ontario (ON, Canada)
U of Windsor (ON, Canada)
Virginia Military Inst (VA)
Walsh U (OH)
Washington U in St. Louis (MO)
Westmont Coll (CA)
Widener U (PA)
Wilmington Coll (OH)
Winthrop U (SC)
Wright State U (OH)
York U (ON, Canada)

MOLECULAR BIOCHEMISTRY

Clarkson U (NY)
Michigan Technological U (MI)
Polytechnic Inst of NYU (NY)
Simon Fraser U (BC, Canada)
U of California, Davis (CA)
U of Richmond (VA)

MOLECULAR BIOLOGY

Alverno Coll (WI)
Arizona State U (AZ)
Assumption Coll (MA)
Auburn U (AL)
Baker U (KS)
Beloit Coll (WI)
Benedictine U (IL)
Blackburn Coll (IL)
Boston U (MA)
California Lutheran U (CA)
California State U, Fresno (CA)
California State U, San Marcos (CA)
Central Connecticut State U (CT)
Clarion U of Pennsylvania (PA)
Clark U (MA)
Colby Coll (ME)
Colgate U (NY)
The Coll at Brockport, State U of New York (NY)
The Coll of Wooster (OH)
Connecticut Coll (CT)
Dartmouth Coll (NH)
Florida Ag and Mech U (FL)
Florida Inst of Technology (FL)
Gettysburg Coll (PA)
Grove City Coll (PA)
Hamilton Coll (NY)
Hampton U (VA)
Houston Baptist U (TX)
Humboldt State U (CA)
Juniata Coll (PA)
Kenyon Coll (OH)
Lakehead U (ON, Canada)
Lawrence Technological U (MI)
Lehigh U (PA)
Marlboro Coll (VT)
Marquette U (WI)
Meredith Coll (NC)
Messiah Coll (PA)
Michigan State U (MI)
Middlebury Coll (VT)
Millikin U (IL)
Montclair State U (NJ)
Ohio Northern U (OH)
Pitzer Coll (CA)
Pomona Coll (CA)
Princeton U (NJ)
Rutgers, The State U of New Jersey, New Brunswick (NJ)
San Francisco State U (CA)
San Jose State U (CA)
Sarah Lawrence Coll (NY)
Scripps Coll (CA)
Simon Fraser U (BC, Canada)
Stetson U (FL)
Texas Lutheran U (TX)
Thompson Rivers U (BC, Canada)
Tulane U (LA)
Universidad de las Américas–Puebla (Mexico)
U at Albany, State U of New York (NY)
U of Alberta (AB, Canada)
The U of British Columbia–Okanagan (BC, Canada)
U of California, San Diego (CA)
U of California, Santa Barbara (CA)
U of California, Santa Cruz (CA)
U of Denver (CO)
U of Guelph (ON, Canada)
U of Idaho (ID)
The U of Kansas (KS)
U of Maine (ME)
U of Michigan–Flint (MI)
U of Minnesota, Duluth (MN)
U of New Brunswick Fredericton (NB, Canada)
U of Pittsburgh (PA)
U of Puget Sound (WA)
The U of Texas at Dallas (TX)
U of Toronto (ON, Canada)
U of Vermont (VT)
U of Washington (WA)
U of Wisconsin–Eau Claire (WI)
U of Wisconsin–Madison (WI)
U of Wisconsin–Parkside (WI)
U of Wyoming (WY)
Vanderbilt U (TN)
Wayland Baptist U (TX)
Wells Coll (NY)
Wesleyan U (CT)
Western New England Coll (MA)
Whitman Coll (WA)
William Jewell Coll (MO)
Winston-Salem State U (NC)
Worcester Polytechnic Inst (MA)
Yale U (CT)
York U (ON, Canada)

MOLECULAR GENETICS

Michigan State U (MI)
The Ohio State U (OH)
Texas A&M U (TX)
U of Guelph (ON, Canada)
U of Rochester (NY)
U of Vermont (VT)
Washington State U (WA)

MONTESSORI TEACHER EDUCATION

Oklahoma City U (OK)
Siena Heights U (MI)
Xavier U (OH)

MOVEMENT THERAPY AND MOVEMENT EDUCATION

Brock U (ON, Canada)
Eastern Nazarene Coll (MA)
Pacific Lutheran U (WA)
Texas Christian U (TX)
U of Vermont (VT)

MULTICULTURAL EDUCATION

Carnegie Mellon U (PA)
Florida State U (FL)
Fort Lewis Coll (CO)
Goddard Coll (VT)

MULTI/INTERDISCIPLINARY STUDIES RELATED

Abilene Christian U (TX)
Adams State Coll (CO)
Adelphi U (NY)
Agnes Scott Coll (GA)
Albright Coll (PA)
Allegheny Coll (PA)
American Public U System (WV)
Anderson U (IN)
Angelo State U (TX)
Arcadia U (PA)
Arizona State U (AZ)
Arkansas State U—Jonesboro (AR)
Austin Coll (TX)
Baldwin-Wallace Coll (OH)
Bates Coll (ME)
Baylor U (TX)
Bellarmine U (KY)
Bentley U (MA)
Berea Coll (KY)
Berry Coll (GA)
Bethel U (MN)
Bethel U (TN)
Bluffton U (OH)
Bowling Green State U (OH)
Brandeis U (MA)
Brevard Coll (NC)
Brigham Young U–Hawaii (HI)
Bucknell U (PA)
Buena Vista U (IA)
Buffalo State Coll, State U of New York (NY)
Burlington Coll (VT)
California Lutheran U (CA)
California Polytechnic State U, San Luis Obispo (CA)
California State U, Chico (CA)
California State U, Dominguez Hills (CA)
California State U, Long Beach (CA)
California State U, Los Angeles (CA)
California State U, Monterey Bay (CA)
California State U, Stanislaus (CA)
Cambridge Coll (MA)
Cameron U (OK)
Capital U (OH)
Central Connecticut State U (CT)
Clarkson U (NY)
Cleveland State U (OH)
The Coll of Idaho (ID)
The Coll of New Jersey (NJ)
The Coll of New Rochelle (NY)
Coll of Saint Benedict (MN)
Coll of Saint Elizabeth (NJ)
The Coll of Saint Rose (NY)
Coll of Santa Fe (NM)
The Coll of William and Mary (VA)
The Coll of Wooster (OH)
The Colorado Coll (CO)
Columbia Coll Chicago (IL)
Connecticut Coll (CT)
Cornell Coll (IA)
Cornell U (NY)
Cornerstone U (MI)
Covenant Coll (GA)
Dallas Baptist U (TX)
Dartmouth Coll (NH)
Davidson Coll (NC)
DePauw U (IN)
Dixie State Coll of Utah (UT)
D'Youville Coll (NY)
Earlham Coll (IN)
Eastern Illinois U (IL)
Eastern Mennonite U (VA)
Eastern Michigan U (MI)
Eastern New Mexico U (NM)
Eastern Washington U (WA)
East Tennessee State U (TN)
East Texas Baptist U (TX)
Edgewood Coll (WI)
Embry-Riddle Aeronautical U (AZ)
Embry-Riddle Aeronautical U (FL)
Emporia State U (KS)
The Evergreen State Coll (WA)
Fairleigh Dickinson U, Metropolitan Campus (NJ)
Florida Inst of Technology (FL)
Florida Southern Coll (FL)
Franklin & Marshall Coll (PA)
Frostburg State U (MD)
Gannon U (PA)
Georgetown Coll (KY)
Georgetown U (DC)
Georgia Inst of Technology (GA)
Georgian Court U (NJ)
Georgia State U (GA)
Glenville State Coll (WV)
Grace Bible Coll (MI)
Granite State Coll (NH)
Grantham U (MO)
Greenville Coll (IL)
Hamilton Coll (NY)
Hamline U (MN)
Hampshire Coll (MA)
Hood Coll (MD)
Hope Coll (MI)
Humboldt State U (CA)
Illinois Wesleyan U (IL)
Indiana U Bloomington (IN)
Indiana U–Purdue U Indianapolis (IN)
Indiana U Southeast (IN)
Iowa State U of Science and Technology (IA)
Ithaca Coll (NY)
Jackson State U (MS)
John Brown U (AR)
Juniata Coll (PA)
Keene State Coll (NH)
Kennesaw State U (GA)
Kent State U (OH)
Kentucky Wesleyan Coll (KY)
Knox Coll (IL)
Lane Coll (TN)
Lebanon Valley Coll (PA)
Lewis-Clark State Coll (ID)
Liberty U (VA)
Long Island U, Brooklyn Campus (NY)
Lourdes Coll (OH)
Loyola Marymount U (CA)
Lycoming Coll (PA)
Marian U (WI)
Marquette U (WI)
Marylhurst U (OR)
Maryville Coll (TN)
Marywood U (PA)
McDaniel Coll (MD)
McMurry U (TX)
Mercer U (GA)

Mercyhurst Coll (PA)
Meredith Coll (NC)
Messiah Coll (PA)
Miami U Hamilton (OH)
Mid-Continent U (KY)
Middle Tennessee State U (TN)
Midway Coll (KY)
Midwestern State U (TX)
Millikin U (IL)
Millsaps Coll (MS)
Mississippi State U (MS)
Mississippi U for Women (MS)
Missouri Baptist U (MO)
Missouri Western State U (MO)
Monmouth U (NJ)
Montana State U Billings (MT)
Montclair State U (NJ)
Morningside Coll (IA)
Mountain State U (WV)
Mount Holyoke Coll (MA)
Mount Mercy Coll (IA)
Mount St. Mary's U (MD)
Naropa U (CO)
Nevada State Coll at Henderson (NV)
Newman U (KS)
New York Inst of Technology (NY)
Norfolk State U (VA)
North Central Coll (IL)
Northeastern State U (OK)
Northern Arizona U (AZ)
Northland Coll (WI)
Northwest Christian U (OR)
Northwestern Coll (MN)
Northwestern Oklahoma State U (OK)
Northwestern State U of Louisiana (LA)
Northwest Missouri State U (MO)
Ohio Wesleyan U (OH)
Old Dominion U (VA)
Pace U (NY)
Park U (MO)
Penn State Erie, The Behrend Coll (PA)
Penn State Harrisburg (PA)
Pikeville Coll (KY)
Plymouth State U (NH)
Prairie View A&M U (TX)
Prescott Coll (AZ)
Princeton U (NJ)
Queens Coll of the City U of New York (NY)
Radford U (VA)
Regis Coll (MA)
Rice U (TX)
The Richard Stockton Coll of New Jersey (NJ)
Robert Morris U (PA)
Robert Morris U Illinois (IL)
Rochester Coll (MI)
Rocky Mountain Coll (MT)
Rogers State U (OK)
Rowan U (NJ)
Rutgers, The State U of New Jersey, Camden (NJ)
Rutgers, The State U of New Jersey, Newark (NJ)
Sage Coll of Albany (NY)
St. Ambrose U (IA)
St. Cloud State U (MN)
Saint John's U (MN)
Saint Mary's Coll of California (CA)
St. Mary's Coll of Maryland (MD)
St. Olaf Coll (MN)
Sam Houston State U (TX)
San Diego Christian Coll (CA)
San Diego State U (CA)
San Francisco State U (CA)
San Jose State U (CA)
Scripps Coll (CA)
Shippensburg U of Pennsylvania (PA)
Simmons Coll (MA)
Sonoma State U (CA)
Southeastern Oklahoma State U (OK)
Southeast Missouri State U (MO)
Southern Arkansas U–Magnolia (AR)
Southern Illinois U Carbondale (IL)
Southern Methodist U (TX)
Southwestern Coll (KS)
State U of New York at Binghamton (NY)
State U of New York Coll at Potsdam (NY)
Stephen F. Austin State U (TX)
Sterling Coll (VT)
Stonehill Coll (MA)
Stony Brook U, State U of New York (NY)
Tarleton State U (TX)
Tennessee Wesleyan Coll (TN)
Texas A&M U (TX)
Texas A&M U at Galveston (TX)
Texas A&M U–Kingsville (TX)
Texas Southern U (TX)
Texas State U–San Marcos (TX)
Texas Tech U (TX)
Texas Wesleyan U (TX)
Thomas Edison State Coll (NJ)
Thomas More Coll (KY)
Trevecca Nazarene U (TN)
Truett-McConnell Coll (GA)
Truman State U (MO)
Tulane U (LA)
Tusculum Coll (TN)
U at Albany, State U of New York (NY)
U at Buffalo, the State U of New York (NY)
The U of Akron (OH)
The U of Alabama (AL)
U of Alaska Fairbanks (AK)
The U of Arizona (AZ)
U of Arkansas at Fort Smith (AR)
U of Arkansas at Monticello (AR)
U of California, Berkeley (CA)
U of California, Davis (CA)
U of California, Irvine (CA)
U of California, Los Angeles (CA)
U of California, Santa Barbara (CA)
U of Colorado at Colorado Springs (CO)
U of Colorado Denver (CO)
U of Connecticut (CT)
U of Denver (CO)
U of Evansville (IN)
U of Florida (FL)
U of Houston–Clear Lake (TX)
U of Houston–Downtown (TX)
U of Idaho (ID)
U of Kentucky (KY)
U of King's Coll (NS, Canada)
U of Lethbridge (AB, Canada)
U of Maryland, Baltimore County (MD)
U of Maryland, Coll Park (MD)
U of Maryland U Coll (MD)
U of Mary Washington (VA)
U of Massachusetts Amherst (MA)
U of Massachusetts Boston (MA)
U of Memphis (TN)
U of Michigan (MI)
U of Michigan–Dearborn (MI)
U of Michigan–Flint (MI)
U of Minnesota, Crookston (MN)
U of Mobile (AL)
U of Nebraska at Omaha (NE)
U of New Hampshire (NH)
The U of North Carolina at Pembroke (NC)
U of North Dakota (ND)
U of Northern Colorado (CO)
U of North Texas (TX)
U of Oklahoma (OK)
U of Oregon (OR)
U of Pittsburgh (PA)
U of Richmond (VA)
U of St. Francis (IL)
U of Saint Mary (KS)
U of St. Thomas (MN)
U of South Alabama (AL)
The U of South Dakota (SD)
U of Southern California (CA)
U of South Florida (FL)
The U of Tennessee (TN)
The U of Texas at Arlington (TX)
The U of Texas at Brownsville (TX)
The U of Texas at Tyler (TX)
The U of Texas of the Permian Basin (TX)
The U of Texas–Pan American (TX)
The U of Toledo (OH)
U of Virginia (VA)
U of Washington, Bothell (WA)
U of Washington, Tacoma (WA)
U of Waterloo (ON, Canada)
The U of Western Ontario (ON, Canada)
U of Wisconsin–River Falls (WI)
U of Wisconsin–Stout (WI)
U of Wisconsin–Superior (WI)
U of Wyoming (WY)
Ursinus Coll (PA)
Utah State U (UT)
Utah Valley U (UT)
Valparaiso U (IN)
Vanderbilt U (TN)
Vassar Coll (NY)
Virginia Commonwealth U (VA)
Virginia Wesleyan Coll (VA)
Viterbo U (WI)
Walden U (MN)
Washington & Jefferson Coll (PA)
Washington and Lee U (VA)
Washington Coll (MD)
Washington State U (WA)
Washington U in St. Louis (MO)
Wayne State U (MI)
Western Washington U (WA)
Wheaton Coll (IL)
Wilkes U (PA)
Wilson Coll (PA)
Wright State U (OH)
Yale U (CT)

MUSEUM STUDIES

Beloit Coll (WI)
Centenary Coll of Louisiana (LA)
Coll of the Atlantic (ME)
Juniata Coll (PA)
Randolph Coll (VA)
Tusculum Coll (TN)
U of Idaho (ID)
The U of Iowa (IA)
Walsh U (OH)

MUSIC

Abilene Christian U (TX)
Acadia U (NS, Canada)
Adams State Coll (CO)
Adelphi U (NY)
Agnes Scott Coll (GA)
Alabama State U (AL)
Albany State U (GA)
Albion Coll (MI)
Albright Coll (PA)
Alderson-Broaddus Coll (WV)
Allegheny Coll (PA)
Allen U (SC)
Alma Coll (MI)
Alverno Coll (WI)
American U (DC)
Amherst Coll (MA)
Andrews U (MI)
Angelo State U (TX)
Aquinas Coll (MI)
Arizona State U (AZ)
Arkansas State U—Jonesboro (AR)
Arkansas Tech U (AR)
Armstrong Atlantic State U (GA)
Asbury U (KY)
Ashland U (OH)
Assumption Coll (MA)
Atlanta Christian Coll (GA)
Auburn U (AL)
Augsburg Coll (MN)
Augustana Coll (IL)
Augustana Coll (SD)
Austin Coll (TX)
Austin Peay State U (TN)
Averett U (VA)
Avila U (MO)
Azusa Pacific U (CA)
Baker U (KS)
Baldwin-Wallace Coll (OH)
Ball State U (IN)
Baptist Bible Coll of Pennsylvania (PA)
Bard Coll (NY)
Bard Coll at Simon's Rock (MA)
Barnard Coll (NY)
Bates Coll (ME)
Baylor U (TX)
Belhaven U (MS)
Bellarmine U (KY)
Belmont U (TN)
Beloit Coll (WI)
Bemidji State U (MN)
Benedictine Coll (KS)
Benedictine U (IL)
Bennett Coll for Women (NC)
Bennington Coll (VT)
Berea Coll (KY)
Berklee Coll of Music (MA)
Bernard M. Baruch Coll of the City U of New York (NY)
Berry Coll (GA)
Bethany Bible Coll (NB, Canada)
Bethany Coll (KS)
Bethany Coll (WV)
Bethany Lutheran Coll (MN)
Bethel Coll (IN)
Bethel U (MN)
Bethel U (TN)
Birmingham-Southern Coll (AL)
Bishop's U (QC, Canada)
Blackburn Coll (IL)
Black Hills State U (SD)
Bloomsburg U of Pennsylvania (PA)
Bluefield Coll (VA)
Blue Mountain Coll (MS)
Bluffton U (OH)
Boise State U (ID)
Boston Coll (MA)
The Boston Conservatory (MA)
Bowdoin Coll (ME)
Bowling Green State U (OH)
Bradley U (IL)
Brandeis U (MA)
Brenau U (GA)
Brevard Coll (NC)
Brewton-Parker Coll (GA)
Briar Cliff U (IA)
Bridgewater State Coll (MA)
Brigham Young U–Hawaii (HI)
Brock U (ON, Canada)
Brooklyn Coll of the City U of New York (NY)
Bryan Coll (TN)
Bryn Mawr Coll (PA)
Bucknell U (PA)
Buffalo State Coll, State U of New York (NY)
Butler U (IN)
California Baptist U (CA)
California Lutheran U (CA)
California Polytechnic State U, San Luis Obispo (CA)
California State Polytechnic U, Pomona (CA)
California State U, Bakersfield (CA)
California State U, Chico (CA)
California State U, Dominguez Hills (CA)
California State U, East Bay (CA)
California State U, Fresno (CA)
California State U, Fullerton (CA)
California State U, Long Beach (CA)
California State U, Los Angeles (CA)
California State U, Monterey Bay (CA)
California State U, Northridge (CA)
California State U, Sacramento (CA)
California State U, San Bernardino (CA)
California State U, Stanislaus (CA)
Calvin Coll (MI)
Cameron U (OK)
Campbellsville U (KY)
Canisius Coll (NY)
Capital U (OH)
Carleton Coll (MN)
Carroll U (WI)
Carson-Newman Coll (TN)
Case Western Reserve U (OH)
Castleton State Coll (VT)
Catawba Coll (NC)
The Catholic U of America (DC)
Cedar Crest Coll (PA)
Cedarville U (OH)
Centenary Coll of Louisiana (LA)
Central Baptist Coll (AR)
Central Christian Coll of Kansas (KS)
Central Coll (IA)
Central Connecticut State U (CT)
Central Michigan U (MI)
Chapman U (CA)
Chatham U (PA)
Cheyney U of Pennsylvania (PA)
Chowan U (NC)
Christopher Newport U (VA)
City Coll of the City U of New York (NY)
Claflin U (SC)
Claremont McKenna Coll (CA)
Clark Atlanta U (GA)
Clarke Coll (IA)
Clark U (MA)
Clayton State U (GA)
Clearwater Christian Coll (FL)
Cleveland State U (OH)
Coastal Carolina U (SC)
Colby Coll (ME)
Colgate U (NY)
Coll of Charleston (SC)
The Coll of Idaho (ID)
Coll of Mount St. Joseph (OH)
The Coll of New Jersey (NJ)
Coll of Notre Dame of Maryland (MD)
Coll of Saint Benedict (MN)
Coll of Saint Elizabeth (NJ)
The Coll of Saint Rose (NY)
Coll of Santa Fe (NM)
Coll of Staten Island of the City U of New York (NY)
Coll of the Atlantic (ME)
Coll of the Holy Cross (MA)
Coll of the Ozarks (MO)
The Coll of William and Mary (VA)
The Coll of Wooster (OH)
The Colorado Coll (CO)
Colorado State U (CO)
Colorado State U–Pueblo (CO)
Columbia Coll (SC)
Columbia Coll Chicago (IL)
Columbia U (NY)
Columbia U, School of General Studies (NY)
Columbus State U (GA)
Concordia Coll (MN)
Concordia U (CA)
Concordia U (QC, Canada)
Concordia U Chicago (IL)
Concordia U Coll of Alberta (AB, Canada)
Concordia U, St. Paul (MN)
Concordia U Wisconsin (WI)
Connecticut Coll (CT)
Converse Coll (SC)
Corban U (OR)
Cornell Coll (IA)
Cornell U (NY)
Cornerstone U (MI)
Cornish Coll of the Arts (WA)
Covenant Coll (GA)
Creighton U (NE)
Crown Coll (MN)
Culver-Stockton Coll (MO)
Cumberland U (TN)
Dakota Wesleyan U (SD)
Dallas Baptist U (TX)
Dana Coll (NE)
Dartmouth Coll (NH)
Davidson Coll (NC)
Delaware State U (DE)
Delta State U (MS)
Denison U (OH)
DePauw U (IN)
Dickinson Coll (PA)
Dickinson State U (ND)
Dillard U (LA)
Dixie State Coll of Utah (UT)
Doane Coll (NE)
Dominican U of California (CA)
Dordt Coll (IA)
Dowling Coll (NY)
Drake U (IA)
Drew U (NJ)
Drexel U (PA)
Drury U (MO)
Duke U (NC)
Earlham Coll (IN)
East Central U (OK)
Eastern Illinois U (IL)
Eastern Mennonite U (VA)
Eastern Michigan U (MI)
Eastern Nazarene Coll (MA)
Eastern Washington U (WA)
East Tennessee State U (TN)
East Texas Baptist U (TX)
Eckerd Coll (FL)
Edgewood Coll (WI)
Edinboro U of Pennsylvania (PA)
Elizabeth City State U (NC)
Elizabethtown Coll (PA)
Elmhurst Coll (IL)
Elmira Coll (NY)
Elon U (NC)
Emmanuel Coll (GA)
Emory & Henry Coll (VA)
Emory U (GA)
Emporia State U (KS)
Erskine Coll (SC)
Evangel U (MO)
Excelsior Coll (NY)
Fairfield U (CT)
Fayetteville State U (NC)
Fisk U (TN)
Five Towns Coll (NY)
Florida Ag and Mech U (FL)
Florida Atlantic U (FL)
Florida Coll (FL)
Florida Intl U (FL)
Florida Southern Coll (FL)
Florida State U (FL)
Fordham U (NY)
Fort Hays State U (KS)
Fort Lewis Coll (CO)
Francis Marion U (SC)
Franklin & Marshall Coll (PA)
Franklin Pierce U (NH)
Freed-Hardeman U (TN)
Free Will Baptist Bible Coll (TN)
Friends U (KS)
Frostburg State U (MD)
Furman U (SC)
Gardner-Webb U (NC)
Geneva Coll (PA)
George Fox U (OR)
Georgetown Coll (KY)
The George Washington U (DC)
Georgia Coll & State U (GA)
Georgian Court U (NJ)
Georgia Southern U (GA)
Gettysburg Coll (PA)
Gonzaga U (WA)
Gordon Coll (MA)
Goucher Coll (MD)
Grace Bible Coll (MI)
Graceland U (IA)
Grand Valley State U (MI)
Grand View U (IA)
Greensboro Coll (NC)
Greenville Coll (IL)
Grinnell Coll (IA)
Grove City Coll (PA)
Guilford Coll (NC)
Gustavus Adolphus Coll (MN)
Hamilton Coll (NY)
Hamline U (MN)
Hampshire Coll (MA)
Hampton U (VA)
Hannibal-LaGrange Coll (MO)
Hanover Coll (IN)
Harding U (AR)
Hardin-Simmons U (TX)
Hartwick Coll (NY)
Harvard U (MA)
Haverford Coll (PA)
Hebrew Coll (MA)
Heidelberg U (OH)
Henderson State U (AR)
Hendrix Coll (AR)
Hillsdale Coll (MI)

MUSICAL INSTRUMENT FABRICATION AND REPAIR

MUSIC HISTORY, LITERATURE, AND THEORY

MUSIC MANAGEMENT AND MERCHANDISING

MUSICOLOGY AND ETHNOMUSICOLOGY

MUSIC PEDAGOGY

MUSIC PERFORMANCE

Moravian Coll (PA)
Morningside Coll (IA)
Mount Allison U (NB, Canada)
Mount Vernon Nazarene U (OH)
Naropa U (CO)
Nazareth Coll of Rochester (NY)
Nebraska Wesleyan U (NE)
New England Conservatory of Music (MA)
New Mexico State U (NM)
The New School for Jazz and Contemporary Music (NY)
New York U (NY)
Northern Arizona U (AZ)
North Greenville U (SC)
Northwestern Coll (MN)
Northwestern State U of Louisiana (LA)
Northwest Nazarene U (ID)
Notre Dame de Namur U (CA)
Oakland City U (IN)
Oakland U (MI)
Ohio Northern U (OH)
The Ohio State U (OH)
Ohio U (OH)
Ohio Wesleyan U (OH)
Oklahoma Baptist U (OK)
Oklahoma Wesleyan U (OK)
Old Dominion U (VA)
Oral Roberts U (OK)
Ouachita Baptist U (AR)
Peace Coll (NC)
Penn State U Park (PA)
Piedmont Coll (GA)
Pittsburg State U (KS)
Presbyterian Coll (SC)
Queens Coll of the City U of New York (NY)
Randolph Coll (VA)
Redeemer U Coll (ON, Canada)
Rhode Island Coll (RI)
Rice U (TX)
Rockford Coll (IL)
Rocky Mountain Coll (MT)
Roosevelt U (IL)
Rowan U (NJ)
St. Cloud State U (MN)
Saint Mary-of-the-Woods Coll (IN)
Saint Mary's U of Minnesota (MN)
St. Olaf Coll (MN)
Saint Vincent Coll (PA)
Saint Xavier U (IL)
Salem Coll (NC)
Samford U (AL)
Sam Houston State U (TX)
San Francisco Conservatory of Music (CA)
San Francisco State U (CA)
San Jose State U (CA)
Sarah Lawrence Coll (NY)
Seton Hall U (NJ)
Seton Hill U (PA)
Shenandoah U (VA)
Simpson Coll (IA)
Slippery Rock U of Pennsylvania (PA)
Southeastern Louisiana U (LA)
Southeastern Oklahoma State U (OK)
Southeastern U (FL)
Southern Adventist U (TN)
Southern Methodist U (TX)
Southern U and Ag and Mech Coll (LA)
Southwestern Assemblies of God U (TX)
Southwestern Coll (KS)
State U of New York at Binghamton (NY)
State U of New York Coll at Potsdam (NY)
Stetson U (FL)
Susquehanna U (PA)
Syracuse U (NY)
Talladega Coll (AL)
Temple U (PA)
Texas A&M U–Commerce (TX)
Texas A&M U–Kingsville (TX)
Texas Christian U (TX)
Texas State U–San Marcos (TX)
Texas Tech U (TX)
Transylvania U (KY)
Trinity Christian Coll (IL)
Trinity U (TX)
Truman State U (MO)
Tulane U (LA)
Union Coll (NE)
Union U (TN)
U at Buffalo, the State U of New York (NY)
U of Alaska Anchorage (AK)
The U of Arizona (AZ)
U of Arkansas (AR)
U of California, Irvine (CA)
U of Central Florida (FL)
U of Colorado at Boulder (CO)
U of Denver (CO)
U of Evansville (IN)
U of Georgia (GA)
U of Hartford (CT)
U of Houston (TX)
U of Idaho (ID)
U of Illinois at Urbana–Champaign (IL)
U of Indianapolis (IN)
The U of Kansas (KS)
U of Kentucky (KY)
U of Louisiana at Monroe (LA)
U of Mary (ND)
U of Mary Hardin-Baylor (TX)
U of Maryland, Coll Park (MD)
U of Massachusetts Amherst (MA)
U of Massachusetts Lowell (MA)
U of Miami (FL)
U of Michigan (MI)
U of Michigan–Flint (MI)
U of Missouri–Kansas City (MO)
U of Missouri–St. Louis (MO)
U of Mount Union (OH)
U of Nebraska at Omaha (NE)
U of Nevada, Reno (NV)
U of New Mexico (NM)
The U of North Carolina at Chapel Hill (NC)
The U of North Carolina at Charlotte (NC)
The U of North Carolina at Greensboro (NC)
The U of North Carolina at Pembroke (NC)
U of North Carolina School of the Arts (NC)
The U of North Carolina Wilmington (NC)
U of North Dakota (ND)
U of Northern Iowa (IA)
U of North Florida (FL)
U of North Texas (TX)
U of Oregon (OR)
U of Puget Sound (WA)
U of Redlands (CA)
U of Rhode Island (RI)
U of St. Francis (IL)
The U of South Dakota (SD)
U of Southern California (CA)
U of Southern Maine (ME)
U of South Florida (FL)
The U of Tampa (FL)
The U of Tennessee at Martin (TN)
The U of Texas at Austin (TX)
The U of Texas at San Antonio (TX)
U of Tulsa (OK)
U of Vermont (VT)
U of Washington (WA)
The U of Western Ontario (ON, Canada)
U of West Florida (FL)
U of West Georgia (GA)
U of Windsor (ON, Canada)
U of Wisconsin–Superior (WI)
U of Wyoming (WY)
Valdosta State U (GA)
Valley Forge Christian Coll (PA)
Valparaiso U (IN)
Vanderbilt U (TN)
Vanguard U of Southern California (CA)
Virginia Commonwealth U (VA)
Viterbo U (WI)
Waldorf Coll (IA)
Wartburg Coll (IA)
Washburn U (KS)
Washington Adventist U (MD)
Washington State U (WA)
Wayland Baptist U (TX)
Weber State U (UT)
Webster U (MO)
West Chester U of Pennsylvania (PA)
Western Carolina U (NC)
Western Connecticut State U (CT)
Western Illinois U (IL)
Western Michigan U (MI)
Western Washington U (WA)
Wheaton Coll (IL)
Whitman Coll (WA)
Willamette U (OR)
William Jewell Coll (MO)
Wright State U (OH)
Xavier U of Louisiana (LA)
York U (ON, Canada)
Youngstown State U (OH)

MUSIC RELATED

Acad of Art U (CA)
Bellarmine U (KY)
Bethel Coll (KS)
Bob Jones U (SC)
Bowling Green State U (OH)
Brigham Young U (UT)
California State U, Chico (CA)
Calvary Bible Coll and Theological Sem (MO)
Capital U (OH)
Central Michigan U (MI)
Claremont McKenna Coll (CA)
Coker Coll (SC)
Coll of Santa Fe (NM)
Connecticut Coll (CT)
DePaul U (IL)
Dickinson Coll (PA)
Duquesne U (PA)
Eastern Nazarene Coll (MA)
Greenville Coll (IL)
Hampton U (VA)
Illinois Wesleyan U (IL)
Indiana U Bloomington (IN)
Indiana U South Bend (IN)
Keene State Coll (NH)
Long Island U, Brooklyn Campus (NY)
Loyola U New Orleans (LA)
Marylhurst U (OR)
Mercer U (GA)
Messiah Coll (PA)
Milligan Coll (TN)
Ohio Northern U (OH)
Roosevelt U (IL)
Saint Mary's U of Minnesota (MN)
St. Olaf Coll (MN)
San Diego State U (CA)
School of the Art Inst of Chicago (IL)
Shenandoah U (VA)
Transylvania U (KY)
The U of Akron (OH)
The U of Arizona (AZ)
U of Denver (CO)
U of Hartford (CT)
U of Lethbridge (AB, Canada)
U of Memphis (TN)
U of Miami (FL)
U of Michigan (MI)
The U of North Carolina at Asheville (NC)
U of Tulsa (OK)
The U of Western Ontario (ON, Canada)
Vanderbilt U (TN)
Western Illinois U (IL)
Western Kentucky U (KY)
Western Michigan U (MI)
West Virginia U (WV)
Wheaton Coll (IL)

MUSIC TEACHER EDUCATION

Abilene Christian U (TX)
Acadia U (NS, Canada)
Adams State Coll (CO)
Alabama Ag and Mech U (AL)
Alabama State U (AL)
Albany State U (GA)
Alderson-Broaddus Coll (WV)
Alma Coll (MI)
Alverno Coll (WI)
Anderson U (IN)
Andrews U (MI)
Appalachian State U (NC)
Aquinas Coll (MI)
Arizona State U (AZ)
Arkansas State U—Jonesboro (AR)
Arkansas Tech U (AR)
Armstrong Atlantic State U (GA)
Asbury U (KY)
Ashland U (OH)
Auburn U (AL)
Augsburg Coll (MN)
Augustana Coll (IL)
Augustana Coll (SD)
Baker U (KS)
Baldwin-Wallace Coll (OH)
Baptist Bible Coll of Pennsylvania (PA)
The Baptist Coll of Florida (FL)
Baylor U (TX)
Belmont U (TN)
Beloit Coll (WI)
Bemidji State U (MN)
Benedictine Coll (KS)
Bennett Coll for Women (NC)
Berea Coll (KY)
Berklee Coll of Music (MA)
Berry Coll (GA)
Bethany Coll (KS)
Bethany U (CA)
Bethel Coll (IN)
Bethel U (MN)
Bethel U (TN)
Bethune-Cookman U (FL)
Birmingham-Southern Coll (AL)
Bishop's U (QC, Canada)
Bluefield Coll (VA)
Blue Mountain Coll (MS)
Bluffton U (OH)
Bob Jones U (SC)
Boise State U (ID)
The Boston Conservatory (MA)
Boston U (MA)
Bowling Green State U (OH)
Bradley U (IL)
Brenau U (GA)
Brevard Coll (NC)
Brewton-Parker Coll (GA)
Bridgewater Coll (VA)
Bridgewater State Coll (MA)
Brigham Young U–Hawaii (HI)
Brock U (ON, Canada)
Brooklyn Coll of the City U of New York (NY)
Bryan Coll (TN)
Bucknell U (PA)
Buena Vista U (IA)
Buffalo State Coll, State U of New York (NY)
Butler U (IN)
California Lutheran U (CA)
California State U, Chico (CA)
California State U, Fresno (CA)
California State U, Fullerton (CA)
Calvary Bible Coll and Theological Sem (MO)
Calvin Coll (MI)
Campbellsville U (KY)
Capital U (OH)
Carroll U (WI)
Carson-Newman Coll (TN)
Case Western Reserve U (OH)
Castleton State Coll (VT)
Catawba Coll (NC)
The Catholic U of America (DC)
Cedarville U (OH)
Central Christian Coll of Kansas (KS)
Central Coll (IA)
Central Connecticut State U (CT)
Central Michigan U (MI)
Chapman U (CA)
Chowan U (NC)
City Coll of the City U of New York (NY)
Claflin U (SC)
Clarion U of Pennsylvania (PA)
Clarke Coll (IA)
Clearwater Christian Coll (FL)
Coker Coll (SC)
The Coll of New Jersey (NJ)
Coll of Notre Dame of Maryland (MD)
The Coll of Saint Rose (NY)
Coll of the Ozarks (MO)
The Coll of Wooster (OH)
Colorado State U (CO)
Columbia Coll (SC)
Columbus State U (GA)
Concordia Coll (MN)
Concordia U Chicago (IL)
Concordia U, St. Paul (MN)
Concordia U Wisconsin (WI)
Concord U (WV)
Converse Coll (SC)
Corban U (OR)
Cornell Coll (IA)
Cornerstone U (MI)
Crown Coll (MN)
Culver-Stockton Coll (MO)
Cumberland U (TN)
Dakota Wesleyan U (SD)
Dallas Baptist U (TX)
Dana Coll (NE)
Delaware State U (DE)
Delta State U (MS)
DePaul U (IL)
DePauw U (IN)
Dickinson State U (ND)
Dordt Coll (IA)
Dowling Coll (NY)
Drake U (IA)
Drury U (MO)
Duquesne U (PA)
East Carolina U (NC)
East Central U (OK)
Eastern Mennonite U (VA)
Eastern Michigan U (MI)
Eastern Nazarene Coll (MA)
Eastern Washington U (WA)
East Texas Baptist U (TX)
Edgewood Coll (WI)
Elmhurst Coll (IL)
Elon U (NC)
Emmanuel Coll (GA)
Emporia State U (KS)
Evangel U (MO)
Fairfield U (CT)
Fairmont State U (WV)
Faith Baptist Bible Coll and Theological Sem (IA)
Fayetteville State U (NC)
Fisk U (TN)
Five Towns Coll (NY)
Florida Ag and Mech U (FL)
Florida Atlantic U (FL)
Florida Southern Coll (FL)
Florida State U (FL)
Fort Hays State U (KS)
Fort Lewis Coll (CO)
Freed-Hardeman U (TN)
Free Will Baptist Bible Coll (TN)
Friends U (KS)
Furman U (SC)
Gardner-Webb U (NC)
Geneva Coll (PA)
George Fox U (OR)
Georgetown Coll (KY)
Georgia Coll & State U (GA)
Georgia Southern U (GA)
Gettysburg Coll (PA)
Glenville State Coll (WV)
Gonzaga U (WA)
Gordon Coll (MA)
Grace Coll (IN)
Graceland U (IA)
Grambling State U (LA)
Grand Valley State U (MI)
Greensboro Coll (NC)
Greenville Coll (IL)
Grove City Coll (PA)
Gustavus Adolphus Coll (MN)
Hamline U (MN)
Hampton U (VA)
Hannibal-LaGrange Coll (MO)
Harding U (AR)
Hardin-Simmons U (TX)
Hartwick Coll (NY)
Heidelberg U (OH)
Henderson State U (AR)
Hofstra U (NY)
Hope Coll (MI)
Houghton Coll (NY)
Houston Baptist U (TX)
Howard Payne U (TX)
Humboldt State U (CA)
Huntingdon Coll (AL)
Huntington U (IN)
Idaho State U (ID)
Illinois State U (IL)
Illinois Wesleyan U (IL)
Immaculata U (PA)
Indiana U Bloomington (IN)
Indiana U–Purdue U Fort Wayne (IN)
Indiana U South Bend (IN)
Indiana Wesleyan U (IN)
Inter American U of Puerto Rico, San Germán Campus (PR)
Iowa State U of Science and Technology (IA)
Iowa Wesleyan Coll (IA)
Ithaca Coll (NY)
Jackson State U (MS)
Jacksonville State U (AL)
Jacksonville U (FL)
Jamestown Coll (ND)
Jarvis Christian Coll (TX)
John Brown U (AR)
Johnson State Coll (VT)
Judson Coll (AL)
Judson U (IL)
Kansas State U (KS)
Kean U (NJ)
Keene State Coll (NH)
Kennesaw State U (GA)
Kent State U (OH)
Lakeland Coll (WI)
Lamar U (TX)
La Sierra U (CA)
Lawrence U (WI)
Lebanon Valley Coll (PA)
Lee U (TN)
Liberty U (VA)
Limestone Coll (SC)
Lincoln U (MO)
Lincoln U (PA)
Lindenwood U (MO)
Lipscomb U (TN)
Long Island U, Brooklyn Campus (NY)
Long Island U, C.W. Post Campus (NY)
Longwood U (VA)
Louisiana Coll (LA)
Louisiana State U and Ag and Mech Coll (LA)
Louisiana Tech U (LA)
Loyola U New Orleans (LA)
Lubbock Christian U (TX)
Malone U (OH)
Manchester Coll (IN)
Manhattanville Coll (NY)
Mansfield U of Pennsylvania (PA)
Maranatha Baptist Bible Coll (WI)
Marian U (IN)
Marian U (WI)
Marietta Coll (OH)
Mars Hill Coll (NC)
Maryville Coll (TN)
Marywood U (PA)
The Master's Coll and Sem (CA)
McKendree U (IL)
McMurry U (TX)
McNeese State U (LA)
Memorial U of Newfoundland (NL, Canada)
Mercer U (GA)
Mercyhurst Coll (PA)
Meredith Coll (NC)
Messiah Coll (PA)
Methodist U (NC)
Metropolitan State Coll of Denver (CO)
Miami U (OH)
Miami U Hamilton (OH)
Michigan State U (MI)

MidAmerica Nazarene U (KS)
Midwestern State U (TX)
Millersville U of Pennsylvania (PA)
Milligan Coll (TN)
Millikin U (IL)
Minnesota State U Mankato (MN)
Minnesota State U Moorhead (MN)
Minot State U (ND)
Mississippi Coll (MS)
Mississippi State U (MS)
Mississippi Valley State U (MS)
Missouri Baptist U (MO)
Missouri State U (MO)
Missouri Western State U (MO)
Montana State U (MT)
Montana State U Billings (MT)
Moravian Coll (PA)
Morningside Coll (IA)
Mount Marty Coll (SD)
Mount Mercy Coll (IA)
Mount Vernon Nazarene U (OH)
Murray State U (KY)
Nazareth Coll of Rochester (NY)
Nebraska Wesleyan U (NE)
Newberry Coll (SC)
New Jersey City U (NJ)
New Mexico State U (NM)
New York U (NY)
Nicholls State U (LA)
North Carolina Central U (NC)
North Central Coll (IL)
North Dakota State U (ND)
Northeastern State U (OK)
Northern Arizona U (AZ)
Northern Michigan U (MI)
Northern State U (SD)
North Georgia Coll & State U (GA)
North Greenville U (SC)
Northwestern Coll (IA)
Northwestern Coll (MN)
Northwestern Oklahoma State U (OK)
Northwestern State U of Louisiana (LA)
Northwest Missouri State U (MO)
Northwest Nazarene U (ID)
Northwest U (WA)
Nyack Coll (NY)
Oakland City U (IN)
Oakland U (MI)
Oakwood U (AL)
Oberlin Coll (OH)
Ohio Northern U (OH)
The Ohio State U (OH)
Ohio Wesleyan U (OH)
Oklahoma Baptist U (OK)
Oklahoma Christian U (OK)
Oklahoma City U (OK)
Oklahoma State U (OK)
Old Dominion U (VA)
Oral Roberts U (OK)
Ouachita Baptist U (AR)
Pacific Lutheran U (WA)
Pacific Union Coll (CA)
Peabody Conservatory of The Johns Hopkins U (MD)
Penn State U Park (PA)
Pepperdine U, Malibu (CA)
Peru State Coll (NE)
Piedmont Baptist Coll and Graduate School (NC)
Pittsburg State U (KS)
Plymouth State U (NH)
Pontifical Catholic U of Puerto Rico (PR)
Presbyterian Coll (SC)
Prescott Coll (AZ)
Providence Coll (RI)
Queens Coll of the City U of New York (NY)
Quincy U (IL)
Rhode Island Coll (RI)
Rider U (NJ)
Ripon Coll (WI)
Roberts Wesleyan Coll (NY)
Rocky Mountain Coll (MT)
Roosevelt U (IL)
Rutgers, The State U of New Jersey, New Brunswick (NJ)
Saginaw Valley State U (MI)
St. Ambrose U (IA)
St. Catherine U (MN)
St. Cloud State U (MN)
Saint Mary-of-the-Woods Coll (IN)
Saint Mary's Coll (IN)
Saint Mary's U of Minnesota (MN)
St. Norbert Coll (WI)
St. Olaf Coll (MN)
Saint Xavier U (IL)
Salem Coll (NC)
Salve Regina U (RI)
San Diego Christian Coll (CA)
San Diego State U (CA)
Schreiner U (TX)
Seton Hill U (PA)
Shenandoah U (VA)
Shorter U (GA)
Silver Lake Coll (WI)
Simpson Coll (IA)
Simpson U (CA)
Sonoma State U (CA)
South Carolina State U (SC)
South Dakota State U (SD)
Southeastern Louisiana U (LA)
Southeastern Oklahoma State U (OK)
Southeastern U (FL)
Southeast Missouri State U (MO)
Southern Adventist U (TN)
Southern Arkansas U–Magnolia (AR)
Southern Methodist U (TX)
Southern U and Ag and Mech Coll (LA)
Southern Utah U (UT)
Southern Wesleyan U (SC)
Southwest Baptist U (MO)
Southwestern Assemblies of God U (TX)
Southwestern Coll (KS)
Southwestern Oklahoma State U (OK)
Southwestern U (TX)
Southwest Minnesota State U (MN)
Spring Arbor U (MI)
State U of New York at Fredonia (NY)
State U of New York Coll at Potsdam (NY)
Sterling Coll (KS)
Stetson U (FL)
Susquehanna U (PA)
Syracuse U (NY)
Tabor Coll (KS)
Talladega Coll (AL)
Tarleton State U (TX)
Taylor U (IN)
Temple U (PA)
Tennessee Technological U (TN)
Texas A&M U–Commerce (TX)
Texas A&M U–Corpus Christi (TX)
Texas Christian U (TX)
Texas Lutheran U (TX)
Texas Wesleyan U (TX)
Towson U (MD)
Transylvania U (KY)
Trevecca Nazarene U (TN)
Trinity Christian Coll (IL)
Union Coll (NE)
Union U (TN)
Universidad Adventista de las Antillas (PR)
The U of Akron (OH)
The U of Alabama (AL)
U of Alaska Anchorage (AK)
U of Alberta (AB, Canada)
The U of Arizona (AZ)
U of Arkansas at Fort Smith (AR)
U of Arkansas at Monticello (AR)
The U of British Columbia (BC, Canada)
U of Central Florida (FL)
U of Central Missouri (MO)
U of Central Oklahoma (OK)
U of Charleston (WV)
U of Cincinnati (OH)
U of Colorado at Boulder (CO)
U of Connecticut (CT)
U of Dayton (OH)
U of Delaware (DE)
U of Evansville (IN)
U of Florida (FL)
U of Georgia (GA)
U of Guam (GU)
U of Hartford (CT)
U of Idaho (ID)
U of Illinois at Urbana–Champaign (IL)
U of Indianapolis (IN)
The U of Iowa (IA)
The U of Kansas (KS)
U of Kentucky (KY)
U of Lethbridge (AB, Canada)
U of Louisiana at Monroe (LA)
U of Louisville (KY)
U of Maine (ME)
U of Mary (ND)
U of Mary Hardin-Baylor (TX)
U of Maryland, Coll Park (MD)
U of Maryland Eastern Shore (MD)
U of Miami (FL)
U of Michigan (MI)
U of Michigan–Flint (MI)
U of Minnesota, Duluth (MN)
U of Minnesota, Twin Cities Campus (MN)
U of Missouri (MO)
U of Missouri–Kansas City (MO)
U of Missouri–St. Louis (MO)
The U of Montana Western (MT)
U of Mount Union (OH)
U of Nebraska at Omaha (NE)
U of Nebraska–Lincoln (NE)
U of Nevada, Reno (NV)
U of New Brunswick Fredericton (NB, Canada)
U of New Mexico (NM)
U of New Orleans (LA)
The U of North Carolina at Charlotte (NC)
The U of North Carolina at Greensboro (NC)
The U of North Carolina at Pembroke (NC)
The U of North Carolina Wilmington (NC)
U of North Dakota (ND)
U of Northern Colorado (CO)
U of Northern Iowa (IA)
U of North Florida (FL)
U of Oklahoma (OK)
U of Oregon (OR)
U of Portland (OR)
U of Puget Sound (WA)
U of Redlands (CA)
U of Regina (SK, Canada)
U of Rhode Island (RI)
U of Rio Grande (OH)
U of Rochester (NY)
U of St. Francis (IL)
U of St. Thomas (MN)
U of St. Thomas (TX)
U of Saskatchewan (SK, Canada)
U of South Carolina (SC)
U of South Carolina Aiken (SC)
The U of South Dakota (SD)
U of Southern California (CA)
U of Southern Maine (ME)
U of Southern Mississippi (MS)
U of South Florida (FL)
The U of Tampa (FL)
The U of Tennessee (TN)
The U of Tennessee at Chattanooga (TN)
The U of Tennessee at Martin (TN)
U of the Cumberlands (KY)
U of the District of Columbia (DC)
U of the Incarnate Word (TX)
U of the Pacific (CA)
U of the Virgin Islands (VI)
The U of Toledo (OH)
U of Toronto (ON, Canada)
U of Tulsa (OK)
U of Vermont (VT)
U of Washington (WA)
The U of Western Ontario (ON, Canada)
U of West Georgia (GA)
U of Windsor (ON, Canada)
U of Wisconsin–Madison (WI)
U of Wisconsin–Milwaukee (WI)
U of Wisconsin–Oshkosh (WI)
U of Wisconsin–River Falls (WI)
U of Wisconsin–Stevens Point (WI)
U of Wisconsin–Superior (WI)
U of Wisconsin–Whitewater (WI)
U of Wyoming (WY)
Utah State U (UT)
Utah Valley U (UT)
Valdosta State U (GA)
Valley City State U (ND)
Valley Forge Christian Coll (PA)
Valparaiso U (IN)
Vanderbilt U (TN)
VanderCook Coll of Music (IL)
Vanguard U of Southern California (CA)
Viterbo U (WI)
Waldorf Coll (IA)
Warner Pacific Coll (OR)
Wartburg Coll (IA)
Washburn U (KS)
Washington Adventist U (MD)
Washington State U (WA)
Wayland Baptist U (TX)
Wayne State Coll (NE)
Weber State U (UT)
Webster U (MO)
Western Carolina U (NC)
Western Connecticut State U (CT)
Western Michigan U (MI)
Western State Coll of Colorado (CO)
Western Washington U (WA)
West Liberty U (WV)
West Virginia State U (WV)
West Virginia Wesleyan Coll (WV)
Wheaton Coll (IL)
Wichita State U (KS)
William Jewell Coll (MO)
William Paterson U of New Jersey (NJ)
Wilmington Coll (OH)
Wingate U (NC)
Winona State U (MN)
Winston-Salem State U (NC)
Winthrop U (SC)
Wright State U (OH)
Xavier U (OH)
Xavier U of Louisiana (LA)
York Coll (NE)
York Coll of Pennsylvania (PA)
York U (ON, Canada)
Youngstown State U (OH)

MUSIC THEORY AND COMPOSITION

Adams State Coll (CO)
American U (DC)
Arizona State U (AZ)
Baldwin-Wallace Coll (OH)
Bard Coll (NY)
Bard Coll at Simon's Rock (MA)
Baylor U (TX)
Bennington Coll (VT)
Berklee Coll of Music (MA)
Birmingham-Southern Coll (AL)
The Boston Conservatory (MA)
Boston U (MA)
Bowling Green State U (OH)
Bradley U (IL)
Brooklyn Coll of the City U of New York (NY)
Bucknell U (PA)
Butler U (IN)
California Baptist U (CA)
California Inst of the Arts (CA)
California State U, Chico (CA)
California State U, Long Beach (CA)
Calvin Coll (MI)
Capital U (OH)
Carnegie Mellon U (PA)
Carson-Newman Coll (TN)
The Catholic U of America (DC)
Cedarville U (OH)
Central Michigan U (MI)
Chapman U (CA)
Christopher Newport U (VA)
City Coll of the City U of New York (NY)
Clayton State U (GA)
The Coll of Wooster (OH)
Colorado State U (CO)
Concordia Coll (MN)
Concordia U (QC, Canada)
Dallas Baptist U (TX)
DePaul U (IL)
DePauw U (IN)
Drury U (MO)
East Carolina U (NC)
Eastern Nazarene Coll (MA)
Florida State U (FL)
Full Sail U (FL)
Gardner-Webb U (NC)
Georgia Southern U (GA)
Hardin-Simmons U (TX)
Hofstra U (NY)
Hope Coll (MI)
Houghton Coll (NY)
Houston Baptist U (TX)
Illinois Wesleyan U (IL)
Indiana Wesleyan U (IN)
Ithaca Coll (NY)
Jacksonville U (FL)
Keene State Coll (NH)
Lawrence U (WI)
Lehigh U (PA)
Linfield Coll (OR)
Lipscomb U (TN)
Long Island U, Brooklyn Campus (NY)
Loyola U New Orleans (LA)
Mannes Coll The New School for Music (NY)
Marylhurst U (OR)
McNally Smith Coll of Music (MN)
Memorial U of Newfoundland (NL, Canada)
Meredith Coll (NC)
Michigan State U (MI)
Minnesota State U Moorhead (MN)
Mississippi Coll (MS)
Moravian Coll (PA)
New England Conservatory of Music (MA)
The New School for Jazz and Contemporary Music (NY)
Northwestern Coll (MN)
Northwest Nazarene U (ID)
Nyack Coll (NY)
Oberlin Coll (OH)
Ohio Northern U (OH)
The Ohio State U (OH)
Ohio U (OH)
Oklahoma Baptist U (OK)
Oklahoma City U (OK)
Old Dominion U (VA)
Oral Roberts U (OK)
Ouachita Baptist U (AR)
Randolph Coll (VA)
Rice U (TX)
Rider U (NJ)
Roosevelt U (IL)
Rowan U (NJ)
St. Cloud State U (MN)
St. Olaf Coll (MN)
Samford U (AL)
San Francisco Conservatory of Music (CA)
Sarah Lawrence Coll (NY)
Seton Hill U (PA)
Shenandoah U (VA)
Southern Adventist U (TN)
Southern Methodist U (TX)
Southwestern U (TX)
State U of New York Coll at Potsdam (NY)
Stetson U (FL)
Syracuse U (NY)
Temple U (PA)
Texas Christian U (TX)
Texas Tech U (TX)
Trinity U (TX)
Tulane U (LA)
The U of British Columbia (BC, Canada)
U of Central Missouri (MO)
U of Delaware (DE)
U of Georgia (GA)
U of Houston (TX)
U of Idaho (ID)
U of Illinois at Urbana–Champaign (IL)
The U of Kansas (KS)
U of Mary Hardin-Baylor (TX)
U of Miami (FL)
U of Michigan (MI)
U of Missouri–Kansas City (MO)
U of Nebraska at Omaha (NE)
U of Nevada, Las Vegas (NV)
The U of North Carolina at Greensboro (NC)
U of Northern Iowa (IA)
U of North Texas (TX)
U of Oregon (OR)
U of Redlands (CA)
U of Regina (SK, Canada)
U of Rhode Island (RI)
U of Rochester (NY)
U of Southern California (CA)
The U of Texas at San Antonio (TX)
U of the Pacific (CA)
U of Tulsa (OK)
U of Washington (WA)
The U of Western Ontario (ON, Canada)
U of West Georgia (GA)
U of Windsor (ON, Canada)
Valparaiso U (IN)
Vanderbilt U (TN)
Wartburg Coll (IA)
Washington State U (WA)
Washington U in St. Louis (MO)
Webster U (MO)
Western Connecticut State U (CT)
Western Michigan U (MI)
Western Washington U (WA)
Wheaton Coll (IL)
Whitman Coll (WA)
Willamette U (OR)
William Jewell Coll (MO)
Wright State U (OH)
York U (ON, Canada)
Youngstown State U (OH)

MUSIC THERAPY

Alverno Coll (WI)
Appalachian State U (NC)
Arizona State U (AZ)
Augsburg Coll (MN)
Baldwin-Wallace Coll (OH)
Berklee Coll of Music (MA)
The Coll of Wooster (OH)
Colorado State U (CO)
Converse Coll (SC)
Duquesne U (PA)
East Carolina U (NC)
Eastern Michigan U (MI)
Elizabethtown Coll (PA)
Florida State U (FL)
Georgia Coll & State U (GA)
Immaculata U (PA)
Indiana U–Purdue U Fort Wayne (IN)
Loyola U New Orleans (LA)
Lubbock Christian U (TX)
Marylhurst U (OR)
Maryville U of Saint Louis (MO)
Marywood U (PA)
Molloy Coll (NY)
Montclair State U (NJ)
Nazareth Coll of Rochester (NY)
Queens U of Charlotte (NC)
Saint Mary-of-the-Woods Coll (IN)
Sam Houston State U (TX)
Seton Hill U (PA)
Shenandoah U (VA)
Slippery Rock U of Pennsylvania (PA)
Southern Methodist U (TX)
Southwestern Oklahoma State U (OK)
State U of New York at Fredonia (NY)
State U of New York at New Paltz (NY)
Temple U (PA)
Texas Woman's U (TX)
U of Dayton (OH)
U of Evansville (IN)
U of Georgia (GA)

The U of Iowa (IA)
The U of Kansas (KS)
U of Louisville (KY)
U of Miami (FL)
U of Minnesota, Twin Cities Campus (MN)
U of Missouri–Kansas City (MO)
U of North Dakota (ND)
U of the Incarnate Word (TX)
U of the Pacific (CA)
U of Windsor (ON, Canada)
U of Wisconsin–Milwaukee (WI)
U of Wisconsin–Oshkosh (WI)
Utah State U (UT)
Wartburg Coll (IA)
Western Michigan U (MI)
Wilfrid Laurier U (ON, Canada)

NATURAL RESOURCE ECONOMICS

Baldwin-Wallace Coll (OH)
Colorado State U (CO)
Cornell U (NY)
Michigan State U (MI)
U of New Hampshire (NH)

NATURAL RESOURCES AND CONSERVATION RELATED

Bowling Green State U (OH)
California Polytechnic State U, San Luis Obispo (CA)
Mount Mercy Coll (IA)
Northwest Missouri State U (MO)
Penn State Abington (PA)
Penn State Altoona (PA)
Penn State Beaver (PA)
Penn State Berks (PA)
Penn State Brandywine (PA)
Penn State DuBois (PA)
Penn State Erie, The Behrend Coll (PA)
Penn State Fayette, The Eberly Campus (PA)
Penn State Greater Allegheny (PA)
Penn State Hazleton (PA)
Penn State Lehigh Valley (PA)
Penn State Mont Alto (PA)
Penn State New Kensington (PA)
Penn State Schuylkill (PA)
Penn State Shenango (PA)
Penn State U Park (PA)
Penn State Wilkes-Barre (PA)
Penn State Worthington Scranton (PA)
Penn State York (PA)
Sterling Coll (VT)
Texas A&M U–Kingsville (TX)
U of Alaska Fairbanks (AK)
The U of British Columbia (BC, Canada)
U of California, Davis (CA)
U of New Hampshire (NH)
Utah State U (UT)

NATURAL RESOURCES/ CONSERVATION

Ball State U (IN)
Carroll U (WI)
Central Michigan U (MI)
Clemson U (SC)
Colorado State U (CO)
Cornell U (NY)
The Evergreen State Coll (WA)
Frostburg State U (MD)
Grand Valley State U (MI)
Gustavus Adolphus Coll (MN)
Humboldt State U (CA)
Indiana U–Purdue U Indianapolis (IN)
Kent State U (OH)
Louisiana Tech U (LA)
Marlboro Coll (VT)
Montana State U (MT)
Mount Vernon Nazarene U (OH)
New Jersey Inst of Technology (NJ)
Northern Michigan U (MI)
Northland Coll (WI)
Oregon State U (OR)
Penn State Abington (PA)
Penn State Altoona (PA)
Penn State Beaver (PA)
Penn State Berks (PA)
Penn State Brandywine (PA)
Penn State DuBois (PA)
Penn State Erie, The Behrend Coll (PA)
Penn State Fayette, The Eberly Campus (PA)
Penn State Greater Allegheny (PA)
Penn State Hazleton (PA)
Penn State Lehigh Valley (PA)
Penn State Mont Alto (PA)
Penn State New Kensington (PA)
Penn State Schuylkill (PA)
Penn State Shenango (PA)
Penn State U Park (PA)
Penn State Wilkes-Barre (PA)
Penn State Worthington Scranton (PA)
Penn State York (PA)
Peru State Coll (NE)
Prescott Coll (AZ)
Purdue U (IN)
Rutgers, The State U of New Jersey, New Brunswick (NJ)
Southeastern Oklahoma State U (OK)
State U of New York Coll of Environmental Science and Forestry (NY)
Sterling Coll (VT)
Texas A&M U (TX)
Texas A&M U at Galveston (TX)
Texas A&M U–Commerce (TX)
Texas Tech U (TX)
Thompson Rivers U (BC, Canada)
Tusculum Coll (TN)
U of Alaska Southeast (AK)
U of Alberta (AB, Canada)
The U of British Columbia (BC, Canada)
U of California, Berkeley (CA)
U of California, Davis (CA)
U of Connecticut (CT)
U of Georgia (GA)
U of Illinois at Urbana–Champaign (IL)
U of Kentucky (KY)
U of Maryland, Coll Park (MD)
U of Michigan–Flint (MI)
U of Minnesota, Crookston (MN)
U of Missouri (MO)
U of Nebraska–Lincoln (NE)
U of Nevada, Reno (NV)
U of New Hampshire (NH)
U of Vermont (VT)
U of Wisconsin–Milwaukee (WI)
U of Wisconsin–River Falls (WI)
U of Wisconsin–Stevens Point (WI)
Upper Iowa U (IA)
Washington State U (WA)
Washington U in St. Louis (MO)
Winona State U (MN)

NATURAL RESOURCES/ CONSERVATION RELATED

Arizona State U (AZ)
Prescott Coll (AZ)
Sterling Coll (VT)
U of Illinois at Urbana–Champaign (IL)

NATURAL RESOURCES MANAGEMENT

Delaware State U (DE)
Glenville State Coll (WV)
Green Mountain Coll (VT)
Humboldt State U (CA)
Keystone Coll (PA)
Massachusetts Maritime Acad (MA)
Moravian Coll (PA)
Oregon State U–Cascades (OR)
Prescott Coll (AZ)
Rutgers, The State U of New Jersey, New Brunswick (NJ)
St. Petersburg Coll (FL)
Sterling Coll (VT)
The U of British Columbia (BC, Canada)
U of Illinois at Urbana–Champaign (IL)
U of Saskatchewan (SK, Canada)
The U of Tennessee at Martin (TN)

NATURAL RESOURCES MANAGEMENT AND POLICY

Alaska Pacific U (AK)
Albright Coll (PA)
Angelo State U (TX)
Bowling Green State U (OH)
California State U, Chico (CA)
Carnegie Mellon U (PA)
Clark U (MA)
Colorado State U (CO)
Delaware State U (DE)
Dominican U of California (CA)
Fort Hays State U (KS)
Humboldt State U (CA)
Iowa State U of Science and Technology (IA)
Johnson State Coll (VT)
Louisiana State U and Ag and Mech Coll (LA)
New Mexico Highlands U (NM)
North Dakota State U (ND)
Oregon State U (OR)
Oregon State U–Cascades (OR)
Prescott Coll (AZ)
Roanoke Coll (VA)
Rochester Inst of Technology (NY)
Royal Roads U (BC, Canada)
Sewanee: The U of the South (TN)
South Dakota State U (SD)
State U of New York Coll of Environmental Science and Forestry (NY)
Sterling Coll (VT)
Texas A&M U (TX)
Tuskegee U (AL)
U of Alberta (AB, Canada)
The U of British Columbia (BC, Canada)
U of California, Berkeley (CA)
U of Delaware (DE)
U of Guelph (ON, Canada)
U of Hawaii at Manoa (HI)
U of Idaho (ID)
U of Illinois at Urbana–Champaign (IL)
U of La Verne (CA)
U of Maine (ME)
U of Massachusetts Amherst (MA)
U of Miami (FL)
U of Minnesota, Twin Cities Campus (MN)
U of Nebraska–Lincoln (NE)
U of Nevada, Reno (NV)
U of Rhode Island (RI)
The U of Tennessee at Martin (TN)
U of Washington (WA)
The U of Western Ontario (ON, Canada)
U of Wisconsin–Stevens Point (WI)
Western Carolina U (NC)
West Virginia U (WV)

NATURAL SCIENCES

Alderson-Broaddus Coll (WV)
Arcadia U (PA)
Atlantic Union Coll (MA)
Augsburg Coll (MN)
Azusa Pacific U (CA)
Bemidji State U (MN)
Benedictine Coll (KS)
Bernard M. Baruch Coll of the City U of New York (NY)
Bethel Coll (KS)
Bishop's U (QC, Canada)
Blue Mountain Coll (MS)
California State U, Dominguez Hills (CA)
California State U, Fresno (CA)
California State U, Los Angeles (CA)
California State U, San Bernardino (CA)
Calvin Coll (MI)
Cameron U (OK)
Case Western Reserve U (OH)
Castleton State Coll (VT)
Central Christian Coll of Kansas (KS)
Central Coll (IA)
Christian Brothers U (TN)
Colgate U (NY)
Coll of Mount St. Joseph (OH)
Coll of Saint Benedict (MN)
Coll of Saint Mary (NE)
The Coll of St. Scholastica (MN)
Coll of the Atlantic (ME)
Coll of the Humanities and Sciences, Harrison Middleton U (AZ)
Colorado State U (CO)
Concordia U Chicago (IL)
Daemen Coll (NY)
Dallas Baptist U (TX)
Defiance Coll (OH)
Doane Coll (NE)
Dordt Coll (IA)
Edgewood Coll (WI)
The Evergreen State Coll (WA)
Felician Coll (NJ)
Fordham U (NY)
Georgian Court U (NJ)
Hofstra U (NY)
Houghton Coll (NY)
Humboldt State U (CA)
Indiana U East (IN)
Inter American U of Puerto Rico, San Germán Campus (PR)
Iowa Wesleyan Coll (IA)
The Johns Hopkins U (MD)
Johnson C. Smith U (NC)
Juniata Coll (PA)
Kansas State U (KS)
Lakehead U (ON, Canada)
Lees-McRae Coll (NC)
Lee U (TN)
Lesley U (MA)
LeTourneau U (TX)
Lewis-Clark State Coll (ID)
Longwood U (VA)
Loyola Marymount U (CA)
Madonna U (MI)
Marlboro Coll (VT)
The Master's Coll and Sem (CA)
McPherson Coll (KS)
Minnesota State U Mankato (MN)
Missouri Western State U (MO)
Mount Allison U (NB, Canada)
Mount Saint Mary Coll (NY)
Muhlenberg Coll (PA)
New Coll of Florida (FL)
Oakwood U (AL)
Oklahoma Baptist U (OK)
Oklahoma Wesleyan U (OK)
Oregon State U (OR)
Our Lady of the Lake U of San Antonio (TX)
Park U (MO)
Pepperdine U, Malibu (CA)
Peru State Coll (NE)
Redeemer U Coll (ON, Canada)
St. Cloud State U (MN)
Saint John's U (MN)
St. Thomas Aquinas Coll (NY)
San Jose State U (CA)
Sarah Lawrence Coll (NY)
Shawnee State U (OH)
Shorter U (GA)
Siena Heights U (MI)
Spelman Coll (GA)
State U of New York Coll at Geneseo (NY)
Tabor Coll (KS)
Taylor U (IN)
Thomas Edison State Coll (NJ)
Trent U (ON, Canada)
U of Alaska Anchorage (AK)
U of Alaska Fairbanks (AK)
U of Cincinnati (OH)
U of Hawaii at Hilo (HI)
U of La Verne (CA)
U of Maine (ME)
U of Nebraska at Omaha (NE)
U of Pennsylvania (PA)
U of Pittsburgh at Greensburg (PA)
U of Pittsburgh at Johnstown (PA)
U of Puerto Rico at Utuado (PR)
U of Puerto Rico, Cayey U Coll (PR)
U of Puerto Rico, Río Piedras (PR)
U of Puget Sound (WA)
U of Science and Arts of Oklahoma (OK)
The U of Toledo (OH)
U of Wisconsin–River Falls (WI)
U of Wisconsin–Stevens Point (WI)
Virginia Wesleyan Coll (VA)
Viterbo U (WI)
Washington U in St. Louis (MO)
Western Oregon U (OR)
Winona State U (MN)
Xavier U (OH)
York Coll (NE)
York U (ON, Canada)

NAVAL ARCHITECTURE AND MARINE ENGINEERING

Massachusetts Maritime Acad (MA)
Memorial U of Newfoundland (NL, Canada)
State U of New York Maritime Coll (NY)
Stevens Inst of Technology (NJ)
Texas A&M U at Galveston (TX)
United States Coast Guard Acad (CT)
United States Naval Acad (MD)
U of Michigan (MI)
U of New Orleans (LA)
Webb Inst (NY)

NAVY/MARINE CORPS ROTC/NAVAL SCIENCE

Hampton U (VA)
State U of New York Maritime Coll (NY)
U of Idaho (ID)
U of Washington (WA)

NEAR AND MIDDLE EASTERN STUDIES

American Public U System (WV)
Bard Coll (NY)
Brandeis U (MA)
Claremont McKenna Coll (CA)
Columbia Intl U (SC)
Columbia U (NY)
Columbia U, School of General Studies (NY)
Cornell U (NY)
Dartmouth Coll (NH)
Dickinson Coll (PA)
Emory & Henry Coll (VA)
Emory U (GA)
Fordham U (NY)
The George Washington U (DC)
Hampshire Coll (MA)
Harvard U (MA)
The Johns Hopkins U (MD)
New York U (NY)
Northeastern U (MA)
Oberlin Coll (OH)
Portland State U (OR)
Princeton U (NJ)
Rutgers, The State U of New Jersey, New Brunswick (NJ)
Sarah Lawrence Coll (NY)
Smith Coll (MA)
Syracuse U (NY)
Texas State U–San Marcos (TX)
United States Military Acad (NY)
The U of Arizona (AZ)
U of California, Berkeley (CA)
U of California, Santa Barbara (CA)
U of Chicago (IL)
U of Massachusetts Amherst (MA)
U of Michigan (MI)
U of Minnesota, Twin Cities Campus (MN)
The U of Toledo (OH)
U of Toronto (ON, Canada)
U of Utah (UT)
U of Washington (WA)
Washington U in St. Louis (MO)
Wellesley Coll (MA)

NEUROBIOLOGY AND NEUROPHYSIOLOGY

Andrews U (MI)
Georgetown U (DC)
Harvard U (MA)
New Coll of Florida (FL)
St. Lawrence U (NY)
U of California, Davis (CA)

NEUROSCIENCE

Agnes Scott Coll (GA)
Allegheny Coll (PA)
Amherst Coll (MA)
Baldwin-Wallace Coll (OH)
Bard Coll (NY)
Barnard Coll (NY)
Bates Coll (ME)
Baylor U (TX)
Bishop's U (QC, Canada)
Boston U (MA)
Bowdoin Coll (ME)
Bowling Green State U (OH)
Brandeis U (MA)
Brock U (ON, Canada)
Bucknell U (PA)
Carnegie Mellon U (PA)
Cedar Crest Coll (PA)
Centenary Coll of Louisiana (LA)
Central Michigan U (MI)
Clark U (MA)
Colby Coll (ME)
Colgate U (NY)
The Coll of William and Mary (VA)
The Coll of Wooster (OH)
The Colorado Coll (CO)
Columbia U, School of General Studies (NY)
Concordia U (QC, Canada)
Connecticut Coll (CT)
Dickinson Coll (PA)
Dominican U (IL)
Drake U (IA)
Drew U (NJ)
Emmanuel Coll (MA)
Emory U (GA)
Franklin & Marshall Coll (PA)
Furman U (SC)
George Mason U (VA)
Hamilton Coll (NY)
Hampshire Coll (MA)
Haverford Coll (PA)
Hiram Coll (OH)
Indiana U Bloomington (IN)
John Carroll U (OH)
The Johns Hopkins U (MD)
Kenyon Coll (OH)
King Coll (TN)
King's Coll (PA)
Knox Coll (IL)
Lake Forest Coll (IL)
Lawrence U (WI)
Lehigh U (PA)
Macalester Coll (MN)
Massachusetts Inst of Technology (MA)
Memorial U of Newfoundland (NL, Canada)
Middlebury Coll (VT)
Mount Holyoke Coll (MA)
Muhlenberg Coll (PA)
New York U (NY)
Northeastern U (MA)
Northwest Nazarene U (ID)
Oberlin Coll (OH)
Ohio U (OH)
Ohio Wesleyan U (OH)
Pitzer Coll (CA)
Pomona Coll (CA)
Rice U (TX)
St. Lawrence U (NY)
Scripps Coll (CA)
Skidmore Coll (NY)
Smith Coll (MA)
Stonehill Coll (MA)
Texas Christian U (TX)
Thiel Coll (PA)

Trinity Coll (CT)
Trinity U (TX)
Tulane U (LA)
Union Coll (NY)
The U of Alabama at Birmingham (AL)
U of California, Irvine (CA)
U of California, Los Angeles (CA)
U of California, Riverside (CA)
U of California, Santa Cruz (CA)
U of Delaware (DE)
U of Evansville (IN)
U of Illinois at Chicago (IL)
U of King's Coll (NS, Canada)
U of Lethbridge (AB, Canada)
U of Miami (FL)
U of Michigan (MI)
U of Minnesota, Twin Cities Campus (MN)
U of Mount Union (OH)
U of Pennsylvania (PA)
U of Pittsburgh (PA)
U of Rochester (NY)
The U of Scranton (PA)
U of Southern California (CA)
The U of Texas at Dallas (TX)
U of Windsor (ON, Canada)
Ursinus Coll (PA)
Vanderbilt U (TN)
Washington and Lee U (VA)
Washington State U (WA)
Washington U in St. Louis (MO)
Wellesley Coll (MA)
Western Washington U (WA)
Westminster Coll (UT)
Westmont Coll (CA)

NONPROFIT MANAGEMENT

Alaska Pacific U (AK)
Arizona State U (AZ)
Austin Peay State U (TN)
Duquesne U (PA)
Franklin U (OH)
Friends U (KS)
Gettysburg Coll (PA)
Grace Coll (IN)
Hawai'i Pacific U (HI)
Indiana Tech (IN)
Lakeland Coll (WI)
Manchester Coll (IN)
Pace U (NY)
Salem Coll (NC)
Southern Adventist U (TN)
Southern Vermont Coll (VT)
Southwest Minnesota State U (MN)
Tiffin U (OH)
U of Baltimore (MD)
U of Guelph (ON, Canada)
U of South Carolina Upstate (SC)
Washburn U (KS)

NORWEGIAN

Brigham Young U (UT)
Pacific Lutheran U (WA)
St. Olaf Coll (MN)

NUCLEAR AND INDUSTRIAL RADIOLOGIC TECHNOLOGIES RELATED

Mount Mary Coll (WI)

NUCLEAR ENGINEERING

Georgia Inst of Technology (GA)
Idaho State U (ID)
Kansas State U (KS)
Massachusetts Inst of Technology (MA)
Missouri U of Science and Technology (MO)
North Carolina State U (NC)
Oregon State U (OR)
Penn State Abington (PA)
Penn State Altoona (PA)
Penn State Beaver (PA)
Penn State Berks (PA)
Penn State Brandywine (PA)
Penn State DuBois (PA)
Penn State Erie, The Behrend Coll (PA)
Penn State Fayette, The Eberly Campus (PA)
Penn State Greater Allegheny (PA)
Penn State Hazleton (PA)
Penn State Lehigh Valley (PA)
Penn State Mont Alto (PA)
Penn State New Kensington (PA)
Penn State Schuylkill (PA)
Penn State Shenango (PA)
Penn State U Park (PA)
Penn State Wilkes-Barre (PA)
Penn State Worthington Scranton (PA)
Penn State York (PA)
Purdue U (IN)
Rensselaer Polytechnic Inst (NY)
South Carolina State U (SC)
Texas A&M U (TX)
United States Military Acad (NY)
The U of Arizona (AZ)
U of California, Berkeley (CA)
U of Cincinnati (OH)
U of Florida (FL)
U of Illinois at Urbana–Champaign (IL)
U of Michigan (MI)
U of New Mexico (NM)
The U of Tennessee (TN)
U of Wisconsin–Madison (WI)
Worcester Polytechnic Inst (MA)

NUCLEAR ENGINEERING TECHNOLOGY

Old Dominion U (VA)
Thomas Edison State Coll (NJ)
United States Military Acad (NY)

NUCLEAR MEDICAL TECHNOLOGY

Allen Coll (IA)
Baptist Coll of Health Sciences (TN)
Barry U (FL)
Benedictine U (IL)
Cedar Crest Coll (PA)
Charles Drew U of Medicine and Science (CA)
Ferris State U (MI)
Indiana U Bloomington (IN)
Indiana U East (IN)
Indiana U Kokomo (IN)
Indiana U of Pennsylvania (PA)
Indiana U–Purdue U Indianapolis (IN)
Indiana U South Bend (IN)
Lewis U (IL)
Long Island U, Brooklyn Campus (NY)
Long Island U, C.W. Post Campus (NY)
Loras Coll (IA)
Manhattan Coll (NY)
Massachusetts Coll of Pharmacy and Health Sciences (MA)
Medical Coll of Georgia (GA)
North Central Coll (IL)
Oakland U (MI)
Old Dominion U (VA)
Peru State Coll (NE)
Robert Morris U (PA)
Roosevelt U (IL)
St. Cloud State U (MN)
Saint Louis U (MO)
Saint Mary's U of Minnesota (MN)
Salem State Coll (MA)
Thomas Edison State Coll (NJ)
U at Buffalo, the State U of New York (NY)
The U of Alabama at Birmingham (AL)
U of Cincinnati (OH)
The U of Findlay (OH)
The U of Iowa (IA)
U of Missouri (MO)
U of Nebraska Medical Center (NE)
U of Nevada, Las Vegas (NV)
U of Oklahoma Health Sciences Center (OK)
U of St. Francis (IL)
U of the Incarnate Word (TX)
U of Vermont (VT)
U of Wisconsin–La Crosse (WI)
Weber State U (UT)
Wheeling Jesuit U (WV)
York Coll of Pennsylvania (PA)

NUCLEAR/NUCLEAR POWER TECHNOLOGY

U of North Texas (TX)

NURSE ANESTHETIST

Texas Wesleyan U (TX)

NURSING ADMINISTRATION

Clarkson Coll (NE)
Clayton State U (GA)
Huntington U (IN)
Midwestern State U (TX)
Nebraska Wesleyan U (NE)
Ohio Northern U (OH)
U of San Francisco (CA)
U of Saskatchewan (SK, Canada)
U of Washington, Tacoma (WA)
The U of Western Ontario (ON, Canada)
Wheeling Jesuit U (WV)

NURSING (LICENSED PRACTICAL/VOCATIONAL NURSE TRAINING)

The U of Akron (OH)
The U of Western Ontario (ON, Canada)
York Coll of Pennsylvania (PA)

NURSING MIDWIFERY

U of Toronto (ON, Canada)

NURSING (REGISTERED NURSE TRAINING)

Abilene Christian U (TX)
Adams State Coll (CO)
Adelphi U (NY)
Albany State U (GA)
Alcorn State U (MS)
Alderson-Broaddus Coll (WV)
Allen Coll (IA)
Alvernia U (PA)
Alverno Coll (WI)
American Intl Coll (MA)
American U of Beirut (Lebanon)
Anderson U (IN)
Andrews U (MI)
Angelo State U (TX)
Appalachian State U (NC)
Aquinas Coll (TN)
Arizona State U (AZ)
Arkansas State U—Jonesboro (AR)
Arkansas Tech U (AR)
Armstrong Atlantic State U (GA)
Athabasca U (AB, Canada)
Atlantic Union Coll (MA)
Auburn U (AL)
Auburn U Montgomery (AL)
Augsburg Coll (MN)
Augustana Coll (SD)
Aurora U (IL)
Austin Peay State U (TN)
Azusa Pacific U (CA)
Baker U (KS)
Ball State U (IN)
Baptist Coll of Health Sciences (TN)
Barry U (FL)
Barton Coll (NC)
Baylor U (TX)
Bellarmine U (KY)
Belmont U (TN)
Bemidji State U (MN)
Benedictine U (IL)
Berea Coll (KY)
Berry Coll (GA)
Bethel Coll (IN)
Bethel Coll (KS)
Bethel U (MN)
Bethel U (TN)
Bethune-Cookman U (FL)
Blessing-Rieman Coll of Nursing (IL)
Bloomfield Coll (NJ)
Bloomsburg U of Pennsylvania (PA)
Bob Jones U (SC)
Boise State U (ID)
Boston Coll (MA)
Bowie State U (MD)
Bowling Green State U (OH)
Bradley U (IL)
Brenau U (GA)
Briar Cliff U (IA)
California Baptist U (CA)
California State U, Bakersfield (CA)
California State U, Chico (CA)
California State U, Dominguez Hills (CA)
California State U, East Bay (CA)
California State U, Fresno (CA)
California State U, Fullerton (CA)
California State U, Long Beach (CA)
California State U, Los Angeles (CA)
California State U, Northridge (CA)
California State U, Sacramento (CA)
California State U, San Bernardino (CA)
California State U, Stanislaus (CA)
Calvin Coll (MI)
Cape Breton U (NS, Canada)
Capella U (MN)
Capital U (OH)
Carlow U (PA)
Carroll U (WI)
Carson-Newman Coll (TN)
Case Western Reserve U (OH)
Castleton State Coll (VT)
The Catholic U of America (DC)
Cedarville U (OH)
Central Connecticut State U (CT)
Chatham U (PA)
Clarion U of Pennsylvania (PA)
Clarke Coll (IA)
Clarkson Coll (NE)
Clayton State U (GA)
Clemson U (SC)
Cleveland State U (OH)
The Coll at Brockport, State U of New York (NY)
Coll of Coastal Georgia (GA)
Coll of Mount St. Joseph (OH)
Coll of Mount Saint Vincent (NY)
The Coll of New Jersey (NJ)
The Coll of New Rochelle (NY)
Coll of Notre Dame of Maryland (MD)
Coll of Saint Benedict (MN)
Coll of Saint Mary (NE)
The Coll of St. Scholastica (MN)
Coll of Staten Island of the City U of New York (NY)
Coll of the Ozarks (MO)
Colorado State U–Pueblo (CO)
Columbia Coll, Yauco (PR)
Columbia Intl U (SC)
Columbus State U (GA)
Concordia Coll (MN)
Concordia U Chicago (IL)
Concordia U Wisconsin (WI)
Coppin State U (MD)
Creighton U (NE)
Crown Coll (MN)
Culver-Stockton Coll (MO)
Cumberland U (TN)
Curry Coll (MA)
Daemen Coll (NY)
Dakota Wesleyan U (SD)
Davenport U, Grand Rapids (MI)
Defiance Coll (OH)
Delaware State U (DE)
Delta State U (MS)
DePaul U (IL)
DeSales U (PA)
Dickinson State U (ND)
Dillard U (LA)
Dixie State Coll of Utah (UT)
Dominican Coll (NY)
Dominican U of California (CA)
Dordt Coll (IA)
Duquesne U (PA)
D'Youville Coll (NY)
East Carolina U (NC)
East Central U (OK)
Eastern Illinois U (IL)
Eastern Mennonite U (VA)
Eastern Michigan U (MI)
Eastern New Mexico U (NM)
Eastern Washington U (WA)
East Stroudsburg U of Pennsylvania (PA)
East Tennessee State U (TN)
East Texas Baptist U (TX)
ECPI Coll of Technology, Virginia Beach (VA)
Edgewood Coll (WI)
Edinboro U of Pennsylvania (PA)
Elmhurst Coll (IL)
Elmira Coll (NY)
Emory U (GA)
Emporia State U (KS)
Endicott Coll (MA)
Fairfield U (CT)
Fairleigh Dickinson U, Metropolitan Campus (NJ)
Fairmont State U (WV)
Farmingdale State Coll (NY)
Fayetteville State U (NC)
Felician Coll (NJ)
Ferris State U (MI)
Fisk U (TN)
Fitchburg State Coll (MA)
Florida Atlantic U (FL)
Florida Gulf Coast U (FL)
Florida Intl U (FL)
Florida Southern Coll (FL)
Florida State U (FL)
Fort Hays State U (KS)
Framingham State Coll (MA)
Franciscan U of Steubenville (OH)
Francis Marion U (SC)
Frostburg State U (MD)
Gannon U (PA)
Gardner-Webb U (NC)
George Fox U (OR)
George Mason U (VA)
Georgetown U (DC)
Georgia Coll & State U (GA)
Georgian Court U (NJ)
Georgia Southern U (GA)
Georgia State U (GA)
Glenville State Coll (WV)
Goldfarb School of Nursing at Barnes-Jewish Coll (MO)
Gonzaga U (WA)
Goshen Coll (IN)
Governors State U (IL)
Graceland U (IA)
Graceland U (MO)
Grambling State U (LA)
Grand Valley State U (MI)
Grand View U (IA)
Gustavus Adolphus Coll (MN)
Gwynedd-Mercy Coll (PA)
Hampton U (VA)
Hannibal-LaGrange Coll (MO)
Harding U (AR)
Hardin-Simmons U (TX)
Hartwick Coll (NY)
Hawai'i Pacific U (HI)
Henderson State U (AR)
Hiram Coll (OH)
Holy Names U (CA)
Hope Coll (MI)
Houston Baptist U (TX)
Humboldt State U (CA)
Hunter Coll of the City U of New York (NY)
Husson U (ME)
Idaho State U (ID)
Illinois State U (IL)
Illinois Wesleyan U (IL)
Indiana State U (IN)
Indiana U Bloomington (IN)
Indiana U East (IN)
Indiana U Kokomo (IN)
Indiana U Northwest (IN)
Indiana U of Pennsylvania (PA)
Indiana U–Purdue U Fort Wayne (IN)
Indiana U–Purdue U Indianapolis (IN)
Indiana U South Bend (IN)
Indiana U Southeast (IN)
Indiana Wesleyan U (IN)
Indian River State Coll (FL)
Inter American U of Puerto Rico, Aguadilla Campus (PR)
Inter American U of Puerto Rico, Arecibo Campus (PR)
Inter American U of Puerto Rico, Guayama Campus (PR)
Inter American U of Puerto Rico, San Germán Campus (PR)
Iowa Wesleyan Coll (IA)
Jacksonville State U (AL)
Jacksonville U (FL)
James Madison U (VA)
Jamestown Coll (ND)
Jefferson Coll of Health Sciences (VA)
The Johns Hopkins U (MD)
Keiser U, Fort Lauderdale (FL)
Kennesaw State U (GA)
Kent State U (OH)
Kent State U at Stark (OH)
Kent State U at Tuscarawas (OH)
Kentucky State U (KY)
Keuka Coll (NY)
King Coll (TN)
Kutztown U of Pennsylvania (PA)
Kuyper Coll (MI)
Kwantlen Polytechnic U (BC, Canada)
LaGrange Coll (GA)
Lakehead U (ON, Canada)
Lake Superior State U (MI)
Lakeview Coll of Nursing (IL)
Lamar U (TX)
La Roche Coll (PA)
La Salle U (PA)
Laurentian U (ON, Canada)
Lehman Coll of the City U of New York (NY)
Le Moyne Coll (NY)
Lewis-Clark State Coll (ID)
Lewis U (IL)
Liberty U (VA)
Lincoln Memorial U (TN)
Lincoln U (MO)
Lindsey Wilson Coll (KY)
Linfield Coll (OR)
Lipscomb U (TN)
Lock Haven U of Pennsylvania (PA)
Long Island U, Brooklyn Campus (NY)
Long Island U, C.W. Post Campus (NY)
Longwood U (VA)
Louisiana Coll (LA)
Lourdes Coll (OH)
Loyola U Chicago (IL)
Lubbock Christian U (TX)
Luther Coll (IA)
Lynchburg Coll (VA)
Madonna U (MI)
Malone U (OH)
Mansfield U of Pennsylvania (PA)
Maranatha Baptist Bible Coll (WI)
Maria Coll (NY)
Marian U (IN)
Marian U (WI)
Marquette U (WI)
Marshall U (WV)
Marymount U (VA)
Maryville Coll (TN)
Maryville U of Saint Louis (MO)
Marywood U (PA)
Massachusetts Coll of Pharmacy and Health Sciences (MA)
McKendree U (IL)
McMurry U (TX)
McNeese State U (LA)
Medcenter One Coll of Nursing (ND)
Medgar Evers Coll of the City U of New York (NY)

INDEXES

Medical Coll of Georgia (GA)
Medical U of South Carolina (SC)
Memorial U of Newfoundland (NL, Canada)
Mercer U (GA)
Mercy Coll (NY)
Mercy Coll of Health Sciences (IA)
Mercy Coll of Northwest Ohio (OH)
Messiah Coll (PA)
Methodist U (NC)
Metropolitan State Coll of Denver (CO)
Miami Dade Coll (FL)
Miami U (OH)
Michigan State U (MI)
MidAmerica Nazarene U (KS)
Middle Tennessee State U (TN)
Midway Coll (KY)
Midwestern State U (TX)
Milligan Coll (TN)
Millikin U (IL)
Milwaukee School of Eng (WI)
Minnesota State U Mankato (MN)
Minnesota State U Moorhead (MN)
Minot State U (ND)
Misericordia U (PA)
Mississippi Coll (MS)
Mississippi U for Women (MS)
Missouri Southern State U (MO)
Missouri State U (MO)
Missouri Western State U (MO)
Molloy Coll (NY)
Montana State U (MT)
Montana Tech of The U of Montana (MT)
Moravian Coll (PA)
Morehead State U (KY)
Morningside Coll (IA)
Mountain State U (WV)
Mount Carmel Coll of Nursing (OH)
Mount Marty Coll (SD)
Mount Mary Coll (WI)
Mount Mercy Coll (IA)
Mount Saint Mary Coll (NY)
Mount St. Mary's Coll (CA)
Mount Vernon Nazarene U (OH)
Murray State U (KY)
Nazareth Coll of Rochester (NY)
Nebraska Methodist Coll (NE)
Neumann U (PA)
Nevada State Coll at Henderson (NV)
Newman U (KS)
New Mexico Highlands U (NM)
New Mexico State U (NM)
New York Inst of Technology (NY)
New York U (NY)
Niagara U (NY)
Nicholls State U (LA)
Nipissing U (ON, Canada)
Norfolk State U (VA)
North Carolina Central U (NC)
North Dakota State U (ND)
Northeastern State U (OK)
Northeastern U (MA)
Northern Arizona U (AZ)
Northern Kentucky U (KY)
Northern Michigan U (MI)
North Georgia Coll & State U (GA)
Northwestern Coll (IA)
Northwestern Oklahoma State U (OK)
Northwestern State U of Louisiana (LA)
Northwest Florida State Coll (FL)
Northwest Missouri State U (MO)
Northwest Nazarene U (ID)
Northwest U (WA)
Nova Southeastern U (FL)
Nyack Coll (NY)
Oakland U (MI)
Oakwood U (AL)
The Ohio State U (OH)
The Ohio State U at Lima (OH)
The Ohio State U at Marion (OH)
Ohio U (OH)
Oklahoma Baptist U (OK)
Oklahoma Christian U (OK)
Oklahoma City U (OK)
Oklahoma Wesleyan U (OK)
Old Dominion U (VA)
Oral Roberts U (OK)
Oregon Health & Science U (OR)
Our Lady of the Lake Coll (LA)
Pace U (NY)
Pacific Lutheran U (WA)
Pacific Union Coll (CA)
Penn State Abington (PA)
Penn State Altoona (PA)
Penn State Beaver (PA)
Penn State Berks (PA)
Penn State Brandywine (PA)
Penn State DuBois (PA)
Penn State Erie, The Behrend Coll (PA)
Penn State Fayette, The Eberly Campus (PA)
Penn State Greater Allegheny (PA)
Penn State Harrisburg (PA)
Penn State Hazleton (PA)
Penn State Lehigh Valley (PA)
Penn State Mont Alto (PA)
Penn State New Kensington (PA)
Penn State Schuylkill (PA)
Penn State Shenango (PA)
Penn State U Park (PA)
Penn State Wilkes-Barre (PA)
Penn State Worthington Scranton (PA)
Penn State York (PA)
Piedmont Coll (GA)
Pittsburg State U (KS)
Pontifical Catholic U of Puerto Rico (PR)
Prairie View A&M U (TX)
Presentation Coll (SD)
Purdue U (IN)
Purdue U North Central (IN)
Queen's U at Kingston (ON, Canada)
Quincy U (IL)
Quinnipiac U (CT)
Radford U (VA)
Ramapo Coll of New Jersey (NJ)
Regis Coll (MA)
Rhode Island Coll (RI)
The Richard Stockton Coll of New Jersey (NJ)
Rivier Coll (NH)
Robert Morris U (PA)
Roberts Wesleyan Coll (NY)
Rockford Coll (IL)
Rockhurst U (MO)
Rogers State U (OK)
Rowan U (NJ)
Russell Sage Coll (NY)
Rutgers, The State U of New Jersey, Camden (NJ)
Rutgers, The State U of New Jersey, Newark (NJ)
Rutgers, The State U of New Jersey, New Brunswick (NJ)
Sacred Heart U (CT)
Saginaw Valley State U (MI)
St. Ambrose U (IA)
St. Catherine U (MN)
St. Cloud State U (MN)
Saint Francis Medical Center Coll of Nursing (IL)
Saint Francis U (PA)
St. Francis Xavier U (NS, Canada)
St. John Fisher Coll (NY)
Saint John's U (MN)
Saint Joseph Coll (CT)
St. Joseph's Coll, Long Island Campus (NY)
St. Joseph's Coll, New York (NY)
Saint Louis U (MO)
Saint Mary's Coll (IN)
Saint Mary's Coll of California (CA)
St. Olaf Coll (MN)
St. Petersburg Coll (FL)
Saint Xavier U (IL)
Salem State Coll (MA)
Salisbury U (MD)
Salve Regina U (RI)
Samford U (AL)
Samuel Merritt U (CA)
San Diego State U (CA)
San Francisco State U (CA)
San Jose State U (CA)
Seattle Pacific U (WA)
Seattle U (WA)
Seton Hall U (NJ)
Shawnee State U (OH)
Shenandoah U (VA)
Shepherd U (WV)
Shorter U (GA)
Silver Lake Coll (WI)
Simmons Coll (MA)
Slippery Rock U of Pennsylvania (PA)
Sonoma State U (CA)
South Carolina State U (SC)
South Dakota State U (SD)
Southeastern Louisiana U (LA)
Southeast Missouri State U (MO)
Southern Arkansas U–Magnolia (AR)
Southern Connecticut State U (CT)
Southern Illinois U Edwardsville (IL)
Southern Oregon U (OR)
Southern U and Ag and Mech Coll (LA)
Southern Vermont Coll (VT)
South U (AL)
South U, Royal Palm Beach (FL)
South U, Tampa (FL)
South U, Columbia (SC)
South U, Glen Allen (VA)
South U, Virginia Beach (VA)
Southwest Baptist U (MO)
Southwestern Adventist U (TX)
Southwestern Assemblies of God U (TX)
Southwestern Coll (KS)
Southwestern Oklahoma State U (OK)
Spalding U (KY)
Spring Hill Coll (AL)
State Coll of Florida Manatee-Sarasota (FL)
State U of New York at Binghamton (NY)
State U of New York at New Paltz (NY)
State U of New York at Plattsburgh (NY)
State U of New York Coll of Technology at Canton (NY)
State U of New York Downstate Medical Center (NY)
State U of New York Empire State Coll (NY)
Stephen F. Austin State U (TX)
Stevenson U (MD)
Stillman Coll (AL)
Stony Brook U, State U of New York (NY)
Stratford U, Woodbridge (VA)
Tarleton State U (TX)
Temple U (PA)
Tennessee Technological U (TN)
Tennessee Wesleyan Coll (TN)
Texas A&M Intl U (TX)
Texas A&M U–Corpus Christi (TX)
Texas Christian U (TX)
Texas Southern U (TX)
Texas State U–San Marcos (TX)
Texas Woman's U (TX)
Thomas Edison State Coll (NJ)
Thomas More Coll (KY)
Thompson Rivers U (BC, Canada)
Towson U (MD)
Trent U (ON, Canada)
Trevecca Nazarene U (TN)
Trinity Christian Coll (IL)
Troy U (AL)
Truman State U (MO)
Tuskegee U (AL)
Union Coll (NE)
Union U (TN)
Universidad Adventista de las Antillas (PR)
Université du Québec en Outaouais (QC, Canada)
U at Buffalo, the State U of New York (NY)
The U of Alabama (AL)
The U of Alabama at Birmingham (AL)
The U of Alabama in Huntsville (AL)
U of Alaska Anchorage (AK)
U of Alberta (AB, Canada)
U of Arkansas (AR)
U of Arkansas at Fort Smith (AR)
U of Arkansas at Little Rock (AR)
U of Arkansas at Monticello (AR)
U of Arkansas at Pine Bluff (AR)
The U of British Columbia (BC, Canada)
The U of British Columbia–Okanagan (BC, Canada)
U of Central Florida (FL)
U of Central Missouri (MO)
U of Central Oklahoma (OK)
U of Charleston (WV)
U of Cincinnati (OH)
U of Colorado at Colorado Springs (CO)
U of Colorado Denver (CO)
U of Connecticut (CT)
U of Delaware (DE)
U of Dubuque (IA)
U of Evansville (IN)
U of Florida (FL)
U of Guam (GU)
U of Hartford (CT)
U of Hawaii at Hilo (HI)
U of Hawaii at Manoa (HI)
U of Houston–Victoria (TX)
U of Illinois at Chicago (IL)
The U of Iowa (IA)
U of Kentucky (KY)
U of Lethbridge (AB, Canada)
U of Louisiana at Monroe (LA)
U of Louisville (KY)
U of Maine (ME)
U of Maine at Augusta (ME)
U of Maine at Fort Kent (ME)
U of Manitoba (MB, Canada)
U of Mary (ND)
U of Mary Hardin-Baylor (TX)
U of Massachusetts Amherst (MA)
U of Massachusetts Boston (MA)
U of Massachusetts Dartmouth (MA)
U of Massachusetts Lowell (MA)
U of Memphis (TN)
U of Miami (FL)
U of Michigan (MI)
U of Michigan–Flint (MI)
U of Minnesota, Twin Cities Campus (MN)
U of Missouri (MO)
U of Missouri–Kansas City (MO)
U of Missouri–St. Louis (MO)
U of Mobile (AL)
U of Nebraska Medical Center (NE)
U of Nevada, Las Vegas (NV)
U of Nevada, Reno (NV)
U of New Brunswick Fredericton (NB, Canada)
U of New England (ME)
U of New Hampshire (NH)
U of New Mexico (NM)
U of North Alabama (AL)
The U of North Carolina at Chapel Hill (NC)
The U of North Carolina at Charlotte (NC)
The U of North Carolina at Greensboro (NC)
The U of North Carolina at Pembroke (NC)
The U of North Carolina Wilmington (NC)
U of North Dakota (ND)
U of Northern Colorado (CO)
U of North Florida (FL)
U of Oklahoma Health Sciences Center (OK)
U of Ottawa (ON, Canada)
U of Pennsylvania (PA)
U of Pittsburgh (PA)
U of Pittsburgh at Bradford (PA)
U of Portland (OR)
U of Puerto Rico at Humacao (PR)
U of Puerto Rico at Utuado (PR)
U of Rhode Island (RI)
U of Rochester (NY)
U of St. Francis (IL)
U of Saint Mary (KS)
U of San Diego (CA)
U of San Francisco (CA)
U of Saskatchewan (SK, Canada)
The U of Scranton (PA)
U of South Alabama (AL)
U of South Carolina (SC)
U of South Carolina Aiken (SC)
U of South Carolina Beaufort (SC)
U of South Carolina Upstate (SC)
U of Southern Indiana (IN)
U of Southern Maine (ME)
U of Southern Mississippi (MS)
U of South Florida (FL)
The U of Tampa (FL)
The U of Tennessee (TN)
The U of Tennessee at Chattanooga (TN)
The U of Tennessee at Martin (TN)
The U of Texas at Arlington (TX)
The U of Texas at Austin (TX)
The U of Texas at Brownsville (TX)
The U of Texas at El Paso (TX)
The U of Texas at Tyler (TX)
The U of Texas Health Science Center at Houston (TX)
The U of Texas Medical Branch (TX)
The U of Texas–Pan American (TX)
U of the Incarnate Word (TX)
U of the Virgin Islands (VI)
The U of Toledo (OH)
U of Toronto (ON, Canada)
U of Tulsa (OK)
U of Utah (UT)
U of Vermont (VT)
U of Virginia (VA)
U of Washington (WA)
U of Washington, Bothell (WA)
U of Washington, Tacoma (WA)
The U of Western Ontario (ON, Canada)
U of West Florida (FL)
U of West Georgia (GA)
U of Windsor (ON, Canada)
U of Wisconsin–Eau Claire (WI)
U of Wisconsin–Green Bay (WI)
U of Wisconsin–Madison (WI)
U of Wisconsin–Milwaukee (WI)
U of Wisconsin–Oshkosh (WI)
U of Wisconsin–Parkside (WI)
U of Wyoming (WY)
Ursuline Coll (OH)
Utah Valley U (UT)
Utica Coll (NY)
Valdosta State U (GA)
Valparaiso U (IN)
Vanguard U of Southern California (CA)
Villanova U (PA)
Virginia Commonwealth U (VA)
Viterbo U (WI)
Wagner Coll (NY)
Walden U (MN)
Walsh U (OH)
Washburn U (KS)
Washington Adventist U (MD)
Washington State U (WA)
Waynesburg U (PA)
Webster U (MO)
West Chester U of Pennsylvania (PA)
Western Carolina U (NC)
Western Connecticut State U (CT)
Western Illinois U (IL)
Western Kentucky U (KY)
Western Michigan U (MI)
West Liberty U (WV)
Westminster Coll (UT)
West Suburban Coll of Nursing (IL)
West Virginia U (WV)
West Virginia Wesleyan Coll (WV)
Wheeling Jesuit U (WV)
Widener U (PA)
Wilkes U (PA)
William Jewell Coll (MO)
William Paterson U of New Jersey (NJ)
Wilmington U (DE)
Winona State U (MN)
Winston-Salem State U (NC)
Worcester State Coll (MA)
Wright State U (OH)
York Coll of Pennsylvania (PA)
York Coll of the City U of New York (NY)
York U (ON, Canada)
Youngstown State U (OH)

NURSING RELATED

Adelphi U (NY)
Agnes Scott Coll (GA)
Alverno Coll (WI)
Avila U (MO)
Bluefield State Coll (WV)
Edinboro U of Pennsylvania (PA)
EDP Coll of Puerto Rico–San Sebastian (PR)
Kutztown U of Pennsylvania (PA)
Long Island U, Brooklyn Campus (NY)
Long Island U, C.W. Post Campus (NY)
Loyola U New Orleans (LA)
Lubbock Christian U (TX)
Madonna U (MI)
Mercy Coll (NY)
Minot State U (ND)
New York Inst of Technology (NY)
New York U (NY)
Northeastern U (MA)
Ohio Northern U (OH)
Roberts Wesleyan Coll (NY)
Saint Anselm Coll (NH)
St. Francis Coll (NY)
San Diego State U (CA)
Thomas More Coll (KY)
U of California, Irvine (CA)
U of California, Los Angeles (CA)
U of Kentucky (KY)
U of Massachusetts Dartmouth (MA)
U of Pennsylvania (PA)
The U of Toledo (OH)
Wheaton Coll (IL)
Wright State U (OH)

NURSING SCIENCE

Brock U (ON, Canada)
Cedar Crest Coll (PA)
Clarkson Coll (NE)
Coll of Saint Elizabeth (NJ)
Columbia Coll, Caguas (PR)
Holy Family U (PA)
Holy Names U (CA)
Immaculata U (PA)
Kean U (NJ)
Kent State U at Trumbull (OH)
Midway Coll (KY)
Millersville U of Pennsylvania (PA)
Missouri Baptist U (MO)
Monmouth U (NJ)
National U (CA)
New Jersey City U (NJ)
New Jersey Inst of Technology (NJ)
The Ohio State U (OH)
Queens U of Charlotte (NC)
St. Francis Xavier U (NS, Canada)
Southern Adventist U (TN)
South U (AL)
South U, Royal Palm Beach (FL)
South U, Tampa (FL)
South U, Columbia (SC)
State U of New York Upstate Medical U (NY)
Thompson Rivers U (BC, Canada)
U of Delaware (DE)
The U of Kansas (KS)
U of New Hampshire at Manchester (NH)
Wayne State U (MI)
Wichita State U (KS)
Xavier U (OH)
York U (ON, Canada)

NUTRITION SCIENCES

Auburn U (AL)
Benedictine U (IL)
Boston U (MA)

California State U, Los Angeles (CA)
Case Western Reserve U (OH)
Coll of Saint Benedict (MN)
Concordia Coll (MN)
Cornell U (NY)
Drexel U (PA)
Elmhurst Coll (IL)
Florida State U (FL)
Goddard Coll (VT)
Huntington Coll of Health Sciences (TN)
La Salle U (PA)
Messiah Coll (PA)
Michigan State U (MI)
New York Inst of Technology (NY)
Russell Sage Coll (NY)
Rutgers, The State U of New Jersey, New Brunswick (NJ)
Saint John's U (MN)
Saint Joseph Coll (CT)
Southern Illinois U Carbondale (IL)
Texas Woman's U (TX)
The U of Arizona (AZ)
U of California, Berkeley (CA)
U of California, Davis (CA)
U of Connecticut (CT)
U of Delaware (DE)
U of Guelph (ON, Canada)
U of Hawaii at Manoa (HI)
U of Nevada, Las Vegas (NV)
U of New Hampshire (NH)
The U of North Carolina at Greensboro (NC)
U of Southern Indiana (IN)
U of the District of Columbia (DC)
U of the Incarnate Word (TX)
U of Vermont (VT)

OCCUPATIONAL HEALTH AND INDUSTRIAL HYGIENE

California State U, Fresno (CA)
Grand Valley State U (MI)
Montana Tech of The U of Montana (MT)
Oakland U (MI)
Ohio U (OH)

OCCUPATIONAL SAFETY AND HEALTH TECHNOLOGY

California State U, Fresno (CA)
Columbia Southern U (AL)
Embry-Riddle Aeronautical U (FL)
Fairmont State U (WV)
Grand Valley State U (MI)
Indiana State U (IN)
Indiana U of Pennsylvania (PA)
Indiana U Southeast (IN)
Jacksonville State U (AL)
Keene State Coll (NH)
Marshall U (WV)
Millersville U of Pennsylvania (PA)
Murray State U (KY)
National U (CA)
Rochester Inst of Technology (NY)
Slippery Rock U of Pennsylvania (PA)
Southeastern Louisiana U (LA)
Southeastern Oklahoma State U (OK)
Southwest Baptist U (MO)
U of Central Missouri (MO)
U of Central Oklahoma (OK)
U of Houston–Downtown (TX)
U of New Haven (CT)
U of North Dakota (ND)
U of Regina (SK, Canada)
U of Wisconsin–Whitewater (WI)
Utah State U (UT)

OCCUPATIONAL THERAPY

Alabama State U (AL)
American Intl Coll (MA)
Augustana Coll (IL)
Baker Coll of Flint (MI)
Bay Path Coll (MA)
Boston U (MA)
Brenau U (GA)
Calvin Coll (MI)
Cleveland State U (OH)
Coll of Saint Benedict (MN)
Concordia U Wisconsin (WI)
Dominican Coll (NY)
Dominican U of California (CA)
Drury U (MO)
Duquesne U (PA)
D'Youville Coll (NY)
Eastern Michigan U (MI)
Elizabethtown Coll (PA)
Elmhurst Coll (IL)
Grand Valley State U (MI)
Hawai'i Pacific U (HI)
Husson U (ME)
Illinois Coll (IL)
Indiana U–Purdue U Indianapolis (IN)
Ithaca Coll (NY)
Keuka Coll (NY)
Long Island U, Brooklyn Campus (NY)
Maryville U of Saint Louis (MO)
McKendree U (IL)
Mount Mary Coll (WI)
Nevada State Coll at Henderson (NV)
New York Inst of Technology (NY)
Penn State Mont Alto (PA)
Queen's U at Kingston (ON, Canada)
Quinnipiac U (CT)
Sacred Heart U (CT)
St. Catherine U (MN)
Saint Francis U (PA)
Saint John's U (MN)
Saint Louis U (MO)
Saint Vincent Coll (PA)
San Jose State U (CA)
Spalding U (KY)
State U of New York Downstate Medical Center (NY)
Stephens Coll (MO)
Stony Brook U, State U of New York (NY)
Texas Woman's U (TX)
Towson U (MD)
Tuskegee U (AL)
U at Buffalo, the State U of New York (NY)
U of Alberta (AB, Canada)
The U of Findlay (OH)
U of Manitoba (MB, Canada)
U of Minnesota, Twin Cities Campus (MN)
U of Missouri (MO)
U of New England (ME)
U of New Hampshire (NH)
U of Ottawa (ON, Canada)
U of Pittsburgh (PA)
The U of South Dakota (SD)
U of Southern California (CA)
U of Southern Indiana (IN)
U of the Sciences in Philadelphia (PA)
U of Utah (UT)
U of Washington (WA)
The U of Western Ontario (ON, Canada)
U of Wisconsin–Madison (WI)
U of Wisconsin–Milwaukee (WI)
Wartburg Coll (IA)
Western Michigan U (MI)
West Virginia U (WV)
Winston-Salem State U (NC)
Worcester State Coll (MA)
York Coll of the City U of New York (NY)

OCEAN ENGINEERING

California State U, Long Beach (CA)
Florida Atlantic U (FL)
Florida Inst of Technology (FL)
Memorial U of Newfoundland (NL, Canada)
Texas A&M U (TX)
Texas A&M U at Galveston (TX)
United States Naval Acad (MD)
U of Rhode Island (RI)
Virginia Polytechnic Inst and State U (VA)

OCEANOGRAPHY (CHEMICAL AND PHYSICAL)

Central Michigan U (MI)
Coll of the Atlantic (ME)
Elizabeth City State U (NC)
Florida Inst of Technology (FL)
Hawai'i Pacific U (HI)
Humboldt State U (CA)
Kutztown U of Pennsylvania (PA)
Lamar U (TX)
Louisiana State U and Ag and Mech Coll (LA)
Memorial U of Newfoundland (NL, Canada)
Millersville U of Pennsylvania (PA)
North Carolina State U (NC)
Old Dominion U (VA)
Rider U (NJ)
Texas A&M U at Galveston (TX)
United States Coast Guard Acad (CT)
United States Naval Acad (MD)
The U of British Columbia (BC, Canada)
U of Miami (FL)
U of Michigan (MI)
U of Rhode Island (RI)
U of South Carolina (SC)
U of Washington (WA)
U of West Florida (FL)

OFFICE MANAGEMENT

Adams State Coll (CO)
Babson Coll (MA)
Ball State U (IN)
Bob Jones U (SC)
Bowling Green State U (OH)
Clayton State U (GA)
Eastern Michigan U (MI)
Globe Inst of Technology (NY)
Indiana State U (IN)
Indiana U of Pennsylvania (PA)
Inter American U of Puerto Rico, Aguadilla Campus (PR)
Inter American U of Puerto Rico, Arecibo Campus (PR)
Inter American U of Puerto Rico, Fajardo Campus (PR)
Inter American U of Puerto Rico, Guayama Campus (PR)
Inter American U of Puerto Rico, Ponce Campus (PR)
Loyola U Chicago (IL)
Maranatha Baptist Bible Coll (WI)
Miami U Hamilton (OH)
Middle Tennessee State U (TN)
Mississippi Valley State U (MS)
Mount Vernon Nazarene U (OH)
Murray State U (KY)
Pontifical Catholic U of Puerto Rico (PR)
Prescott Coll (AZ)
Rider U (NJ)
Southeast Missouri State U (MO)
Southwest Baptist U (MO)
Tabor Coll (KS)
Tarleton State U (TX)
U of Central Missouri (MO)
U of North Dakota (ND)
U of Puerto Rico at Utuado (PR)
U of South Carolina (SC)
U of Southern Indiana (IN)
Valley City State U (ND)
Weber State U (UT)
Wright State U (OH)

OPERATIONS MANAGEMENT

Arizona State U (AZ)
Auburn U (AL)
Babson Coll (MA)
Ball State U (IN)
Boise State U (ID)
Boston Coll (MA)
Boston U (MA)
Bowling Green State U (OH)
California State U, Chico (CA)
California State U, Dominguez Hills (CA)
California State U, Long Beach (CA)
Central Michigan U (MI)
Clayton State U (GA)
Concordia U (QC, Canada)
Dalton State Coll (GA)
Edinboro U of Pennsylvania (PA)
Excelsior Coll (NY)
Farmingdale State Coll (NY)
Ferris State U (MI)
Fort Lewis Coll (CO)
Franklin U (OH)
Friends U (KS)
Indiana U–Purdue U Fort Wayne (IN)
Indiana U–Purdue U Indianapolis (IN)
Iowa State U of Science and Technology (IA)
Kent State U (OH)
Le Moyne Coll (NY)
Louisiana Tech U (LA)
Loyola U Chicago (IL)
Marian U (WI)
Miami U (OH)
Michigan Technological U (MI)
Missouri Baptist U (MO)
National U (CA)
Northeastern State U (OK)
Oakland U (MI)
The Ohio State U (OH)
Purdue U (IN)
Purdue U North Central (IN)
Saginaw Valley State U (MI)
San Diego State U (CA)
Seattle U (WA)
State U of New York Coll of Technology at Canton (NY)
Tennessee Technological U (TN)
Texas A&M U–Commerce (TX)
Texas Southern U (TX)
Thomas Edison State Coll (NJ)
Trine U (IN)
The U of Akron (OH)
U of Atlanta (GA)
U of Delaware (DE)
U of Houston (TX)
U of Idaho (ID)
U of Illinois at Urbana–Champaign (IL)
U of Indianapolis (IN)
U of Massachusetts Dartmouth (MA)
U of Michigan–Flint (MI)
U of Nebraska at Kearney (NE)
The U of North Carolina at Asheville (NC)
The U of North Carolina at Charlotte (NC)
U of North Dakota (ND)
U of North Texas (TX)
U of Pennsylvania (PA)
U of Puerto Rico, Río Piedras (PR)
U of St. Thomas (MN)
U of Saskatchewan (SK, Canada)
The U of Scranton (PA)
U of Southern Indiana (IN)
The U of Texas at San Antonio (TX)
The U of Toledo (OH)
U of Wisconsin–Stout (WI)
U of Wisconsin–Whitewater (WI)
Utah State U (UT)
Utah Valley U (UT)
Washington State U (WA)
Washington U in St. Louis (MO)
Wentworth Inst of Technology (MA)
Western Washington U (WA)
Widener U (PA)
Wright State U (OH)

OPERATIONS RESEARCH

Babson Coll (MA)
Bernard M. Baruch Coll of the City U of New York (NY)
Bob Jones U (SC)
Bowling Green State U (OH)
California State U, Fullerton (CA)
Carnegie Mellon U (PA)
Columbia U (NY)
Cornell U (NY)
Long Island U, Brooklyn Campus (NY)
New York U (NY)
Princeton U (NJ)
United States Air Force Acad (CO)
United States Coast Guard Acad (CT)
United States Military Acad (NY)
U of California, Berkeley (CA)
U of Cincinnati (OH)
U of Illinois at Urbana–Champaign (IL)
U of New Brunswick Fredericton (NB, Canada)
U of Toronto (ON, Canada)
U of Waterloo (ON, Canada)
York U (ON, Canada)

OPHTHALMIC AND OPTOMETRIC SUPPORT SERVICES AND ALLIED PROFESSIONS RELATED

Tennessee Wesleyan Coll (TN)

OPHTHALMIC LABORATORY TECHNOLOGY

Abilene Christian U (TX)
U of Ottawa (ON, Canada)

OPHTHALMIC TECHNOLOGY

Old Dominion U (VA)

OPTICAL SCIENCES

Saginaw Valley State U (MI)
The U of Arizona (AZ)
U of Rochester (NY)
Western Washington U (WA)

OPTOMETRIC TECHNICIAN

Indiana U Bloomington (IN)
Texas A&M U–Corpus Christi (TX)

ORGANIC CHEMISTRY

Sarah Lawrence Coll (NY)
The U of Western Ontario (ON, Canada)

ORGANIZATIONAL BEHAVIOR

Anderson U (IN)
Argosy U, Atlanta (GA)
Argosy U, Chicago (IL)
Argosy U, Dallas (TX)
Argosy U, Denver (CO)
Argosy U, Hawai'i (HI)
Argosy U, Los Angeles (CA)
Argosy U, Orange County (CA)
Argosy U, Phoenix (AZ)
Argosy U, Salt Lake City (UT)
Argosy U, San Diego (CA)
Argosy U, San Francisco Bay Area (CA)
Argosy U, Sarasota (FL)
Argosy U, Schaumburg (IL)
Argosy U, Seattle (WA)
Argosy U, Tampa (FL)
Argosy U, Twin Cities (MN)
Argosy U, Washington DC (VA)
Athabasca U (AB, Canada)
Benedictine U (IL)
Bluffton U (OH)
Boston U (MA)
Bowling Green State U (OH)
Brenau U (GA)
Calvary Bible Coll and Theological Sem (MO)
Carroll U (WI)
Central Baptist Coll (AR)
Claflin U (SC)
Coll of Mount St. Joseph (OH)
The Coll of St. Scholastica (MN)
Denison U (OH)
DePaul U (IL)
Eastern Mennonite U (VA)
Greenville Coll (IL)
Indian River State Coll (FL)
John Brown U (AR)
LaGrange Coll (GA)
Loyola U Chicago (IL)
Manhattan Coll (NY)
Memorial U of Newfoundland (NL, Canada)
Miami U (OH)
Mid-Atlantic Christian U (NC)
Mid-Continent U (KY)
Midway Coll (KY)
National U (CA)
Northern Kentucky U (KY)
Oakland City U (IN)
Oral Roberts U (OK)
Penn State Abington (PA)
Penn State Altoona (PA)
Penn State Beaver (PA)
Penn State Berks (PA)
Penn State Brandywine (PA)
Penn State DuBois (PA)
Penn State Erie, The Behrend Coll (PA)
Penn State Fayette, The Eberly Campus (PA)
Penn State Greater Allegheny (PA)
Penn State Harrisburg (PA)
Penn State Hazleton (PA)
Penn State Lehigh Valley (PA)
Penn State Mont Alto (PA)
Penn State New Kensington (PA)
Penn State Schuylkill (PA)
Penn State Shenango (PA)
Penn State U Park (PA)
Penn State Wilkes-Barre (PA)
Penn State Worthington Scranton (PA)
Penn State York (PA)
Pitzer Coll (CA)
Regent U (VA)
Rider U (NJ)
Robert Morris U (PA)
Roosevelt U (IL)
St. Ambrose U (IA)
Saint Louis U (MO)
Santa Clara U (CA)
Scripps Coll (CA)
Simpson U (CA)
United States Military Acad (NY)
U of Houston (TX)
U of Illinois at Urbana–Champaign (IL)
U of Michigan (MI)
U of Michigan–Flint (MI)
U of Mobile (AL)
U of North Texas (TX)
U of Richmond (VA)
U of St. Francis (IL)
U of San Francisco (CA)
U of the Cumberlands (KY)
U of the Incarnate Word (TX)
The U of Toledo (OH)
U of Tulsa (OK)
The U of Western Ontario (ON, Canada)
Valley Forge Christian Coll (PA)
Wayne State U (MI)
Woodbury U (CA)
York U (ON, Canada)

ORGANIZATIONAL COMMUNICATION

Aquinas Coll (MI)
Assumption Coll (MA)
Bradley U (IL)
Brigham Young U (UT)
Buena Vista U (IA)
California State U, Chico (CA)
Capital U (OH)
Carroll U (WI)
Cedarville U (OH)
Central Michigan U (MI)

The Coll at Brockport, State U of New York (NY)
Dana Coll (NE)
Emmanuel Coll (GA)
Franklin U (OH)
George Fox U (OR)
Indiana U–Purdue U Fort Wayne (IN)
Iona Coll (NY)
Lindenwood U (MO)
Lipscomb U (TN)
Lubbock Christian U (TX)
Marian U (WI)
Marist Coll (NY)
Marylhurst U (OR)
McKendree U (IL)
Missouri State U (MO)
Montana State U Billings (MT)
North Central Coll (IL)
Northwest Missouri State U (MO)
Northwest U (WA)
Ohio Northern U (OH)
Pace U (NY)
Rockhurst U (MO)
Roosevelt U (IL)
St. Francis Coll (NY)
Shorter U (GA)
Southeastern U (FL)
Tabor Coll (KS)
Temple U (PA)
Trevecca Nazarene U (TN)
The U of Akron (OH)
U of Idaho (ID)
U of Illinois at Urbana–Champaign (IL)
U of Michigan–Flint (MI)
U of Mount Union (OH)
U of Northern Iowa (IA)
Valparaiso U (IN)
Viterbo U (WI)
Washington State U (WA)
Western Kentucky U (KY)
Western Michigan U (MI)
Wright State U (OH)

ORNAMENTAL HORTICULTURE

California Polytechnic State U, San Luis Obispo (CA)
California State U, Fresno (CA)
Cornell U (NY)
Delaware Valley Coll (PA)
Fort Valley State U (GA)
Iowa State U of Science and Technology (IA)
Tarleton State U (TX)
Texas A&M U (TX)
U of Delaware (DE)
U of Florida (FL)
U of Illinois at Urbana–Champaign (IL)
The U of Tennessee (TN)
U of the District of Columbia (DC)
U of Wisconsin–Platteville (WI)

ORTHOTICS/PROSTHETICS

St. Petersburg Coll (FL)
The U of Texas Southwestern Medical Center at Dallas (TX)
U of Washington (WA)

PACIFIC AREA/PACIFIC RIM STUDIES

Brigham Young U–Hawaii (HI)
Claremont McKenna Coll (CA)
Hawai'i Pacific U (HI)
U of Hawaii–West Oahu (HI)

PAINTING

Adams State Coll (CO)
Alberta Coll of Art & Design (AB, Canada)
Aquinas Coll (MI)
Arcadia U (PA)
Art Center Coll of Design (CA)
Bennington Coll (VT)
Bethany Coll (KS)
Birmingham-Southern Coll (AL)
Boston U (MA)
Bowling Green State U (OH)
Bradley U (IL)
Brigham Young U (UT)
Buffalo State Coll, State U of New York (NY)
California Coll of the Arts (CA)
California State U, East Bay (CA)
California State U, Long Beach (CA)
The Cleveland Inst of Art (OH)
The Coll at Brockport, State U of New York (NY)
Coll of Santa Fe (NM)
Columbia Coll (MO)
Concordia U (QC, Canada)
Drake U (IA)
Escuela de Artes Plasticas de Puerto Rico (PR)
Ferris State U (MI)
Grace Coll (IN)
Harding U (AR)
Hofstra U (NY)
Indiana U–Purdue U Fort Wayne (IN)
Indiana Wesleyan U (IN)
Keystone Coll (PA)
Lewis U (IL)
Lyme Acad Coll of Fine Arts (CT)
Maine Coll of Art (ME)
Maryland Inst Coll of Art (MD)
Marywood U (PA)
Massachusetts Coll of Art and Design (MA)
Memorial U of Newfoundland (NL, Canada)
Minneapolis Coll of Art and Design (MN)
Minnesota State U Moorhead (MN)
Northern Arizona U (AZ)
Northern Michigan U (MI)
Northwest Nazarene U (ID)
Oakland U (MI)
Ohio Northern U (OH)
Ohio U (OH)
Pittsburg State U (KS)
Pratt Inst (NY)
Prescott Coll (AZ)
Providence Coll (RI)
Ringling Coll of Art and Design (FL)
Rivier Coll (NH)
Rochester Inst of Technology (NY)
Rocky Mountain Coll of Art + Design (CO)
Rutgers, The State U of New Jersey, New Brunswick (NJ)
St. Cloud State U (MN)
Salem State Coll (MA)
Salve Regina U (RI)
Sarah Lawrence Coll (NY)
Savannah Coll of Art and Design (GA)
School of the Art Inst of Chicago (IL)
School of the Museum of Fine Arts, Boston (MA)
School of Visual Arts (NY)
Seton Hill U (PA)
Shawnee State U (OH)
State U of New York at New Paltz (NY)
Temple U (PA)
Texas Christian U (TX)
Trinity Christian Coll (IL)
U of Dallas (TX)
U of Hartford (CT)
U of Houston (TX)
U of Illinois at Urbana–Champaign (IL)
The U of Iowa (IA)
The U of Kansas (KS)
U of Massachusetts Dartmouth (MA)
U of Miami (FL)
U of Missouri–St. Louis (MO)
U of Oregon (OR)
U of Puerto Rico, Río Piedras (PR)
U of Regina (SK, Canada)
U of San Francisco (CA)
U of Washington (WA)
U of Windsor (ON, Canada)
Virginia Commonwealth U (VA)
Washington U in St. Louis (MO)
Western State Coll of Colorado (CO)
Western Washington U (WA)
West Virginia Wesleyan Coll (WV)
York U (ON, Canada)

PALEONTOLOGY

Bowling Green State U (OH)
Mercyhurst Coll (PA)
North Carolina State U (NC)
Northern Arizona U (AZ)
U of Alberta (AB, Canada)
U of Saskatchewan (SK, Canada)

PARASITOLOGY

Bowling Green State U (OH)

PARKS, RECREATION AND LEISURE

Alabama State U (AL)
Alaska Pacific U (AK)
Alcorn State U (MS)
Arizona State U (AZ)
Ashland U (OH)
Aurora U (IL)
Belmont U (TN)
Bemidji State U (MN)
Bethany Coll (KS)
Black Hills State U (SD)
Bluffton U (OH)
Boston U (MA)
Bowling Green State U (OH)
Brevard Coll (NC)
Bridgewater State Coll (MA)
Brock U (ON, Canada)
California Polytechnic State U, San Luis Obispo (CA)
California State U, Chico (CA)
California State U, Dominguez Hills (CA)
California State U, East Bay (CA)
California State U, Fresno (CA)
California State U, Long Beach (CA)
California State U, Northridge (CA)
California State U, Sacramento (CA)
Calvin Coll (MI)
Campbellsville U (KY)
Carson-Newman Coll (TN)
Catawba Coll (NC)
Central Michigan U (MI)
Central State U (OH)
Cheyney U of Pennsylvania (PA)
The Coll at Brockport, State U of New York (NY)
Concordia U (QC, Canada)
Cumberland U (TN)
Dordt Coll (IA)
Eastern Washington U (WA)
Elon U (NC)
Emporia State U (KS)
Evangel U (MO)
Ferrum Coll (VA)
Fort Lewis Coll (CO)
Frostburg State U (MD)
Georgia Coll & State U (GA)
Georgia Southern U (GA)
Gordon Coll (MA)
Graceland U (IA)
Grambling State U (LA)
Green Mountain Coll (VT)
Greenville Coll (IL)
High Point U (NC)
Houghton Coll (NY)
Humboldt State U (CA)
Huntington U (IN)
Indiana U Bloomington (IN)
Ithaca Coll (NY)
Jacksonville State U (AL)
Johnson & Wales U (RI)
Johnson & Wales U—Charlotte Campus (NC)
Johnson State Coll (VT)
Kutztown U of Pennsylvania (PA)
Lakehead U (ON, Canada)
Lake Superior State U (MI)
Lindenwood U (MO)
Lindsey Wilson Coll (KY)
Lock Haven U of Pennsylvania (PA)
Mars Hill Coll (NC)
Maryville Coll (TN)
Memorial U of Newfoundland (NL, Canada)
Messiah Coll (PA)
Metropolitan State Coll of Denver (CO)
Michigan State U (MI)
Minnesota State U Mankato (MN)
Missouri State U (MO)
Montclair State U (NJ)
Morris Coll (SC)
Mount Olive Coll (NC)
New England Coll (NH)
New Mexico Highlands U (NM)
North Dakota State U (ND)
Northern Arizona U (AZ)
Northern Michigan U (MI)
North Greenville U (SC)
Northwest Nazarene U (ID)
The Ohio State U (OH)
Ohio U (OH)
Oklahoma Baptist U (OK)
Oklahoma State U (OK)
Oregon State U (OR)
Oregon State U–Cascades (OR)
Pacific Union Coll (CA)
Prescott Coll (AZ)
Presentation Coll (SD)
Radford U (VA)
Redeemer U Coll (ON, Canada)
St. Andrews Presbyterian Coll (NC)
St. Thomas Aquinas Coll (NY)
Salem State Coll (MA)
San Diego State U (CA)
San Francisco State U (CA)
San Jose State U (CA)
Shaw U (NC)
Shepherd U (WV)
Shorter U (GA)
Simpson U (CA)
Slippery Rock U of Pennsylvania (PA)
Southeastern Oklahoma State U (OK)
Southeast Missouri State U (MO)
Southern Connecticut State U (CT)
Southern Illinois U Carbondale (IL)
Southwest Baptist U (MO)
Southwestern Oklahoma State U (OK)
Spring Arbor U (MI)
State U of New York at Plattsburgh (NY)
State U of New York Coll at Cortland (NY)
State U of New York Coll of Environmental Science and Forestry (NY)
Sterling Coll (VT)
Tabor Coll (KS)
Temple U (PA)
Texas A&M U (TX)
Thomas Edison State Coll (NJ)
U of Alberta (AB, Canada)
U of Arkansas (AR)
U of Arkansas at Pine Bluff (AR)
U of Central Missouri (MO)
U of Dubuque (IA)
U of Illinois at Urbana–Champaign (IL)
The U of Iowa (IA)
U of Maine at Machias (ME)
U of Maine at Presque Isle (ME)
U of Mary Hardin-Baylor (TX)
U of Mississippi (MS)
U of Missouri (MO)
U of Nebraska at Kearney (NE)
U of Nebraska at Omaha (NE)
U of Nevada, Las Vegas (NV)
U of Nevada, Reno (NV)
U of New Brunswick Fredericton (NB, Canada)
U of New Mexico (NM)
The U of North Carolina at Greensboro (NC)
U of Northern Iowa (IA)
U of Ottawa (ON, Canada)
U of South Alabama (AL)
The U of South Dakota (SD)
U of Southern Mississippi (MS)
The U of Toledo (OH)
U of Utah (UT)
U of Waterloo (ON, Canada)
U of Wisconsin–Madison (WI)
U of Wisconsin–Milwaukee (WI)
Upper Iowa U (IA)
Utah State U (UT)
Virginia Commonwealth U (VA)
Virginia Wesleyan Coll (VA)
Western Michigan U (MI)
Western State Coll of Colorado (CO)
Western Washington U (WA)
Westfield State Coll (MA)
West Virginia State U (WV)
West Virginia U (WV)
William Jewell Coll (MO)
William Paterson U of New Jersey (NJ)
William Penn U (IA)
Wingate U (NC)
Winona State U (MN)
York Coll of Pennsylvania (PA)

PARKS, RECREATION AND LEISURE FACILITIES MANAGEMENT

Alderson-Broaddus Coll (WV)
Appalachian State U (NC)
Arkansas Tech U (AR)
Asbury U (KY)
California State U, Chico (CA)
California State U, Fresno (CA)
California State U, Sacramento (CA)
Carroll U (WI)
Central Michigan U (MI)
Clemson U (SC)
Coll of the Ozarks (MO)
Colorado State U (CO)
Concord U (WV)
Delaware State U (DE)
East Carolina U (NC)
Eastern Illinois U (IL)
Eastern Michigan U (MI)
Eastern Washington U (WA)
East Stroudsburg U of Pennsylvania (PA)
Ferris State U (MI)
Florida Intl U (FL)
Florida State U (FL)
Franklin Pierce U (NH)
Hannibal-LaGrange Coll (MO)
Henderson State U (AR)
High Point U (NC)
Humboldt State U (CA)
Illinois State U (IL)
Indiana State U (IN)
Indiana Tech (IN)
Indiana Wesleyan U (IN)
John Brown U (AR)
Johnson & Wales U (CO)
Johnson & Wales U (FL)
Johnson & Wales U (RI)
Johnson & Wales U—Charlotte Campus (NC)
Kansas State U (KS)
Kean U (NJ)
Kent State U (OH)
Keystone Coll (PA)
Lake Superior State U (MI)
Marshall U (WV)
Methodist U (NC)
Middle Tennessee State U (TN)
Minnesota State U Mankato (MN)
Missouri Western State U (MO)
Mount Marty Coll (SD)
Murray State U (KY)
New England Coll (NH)
New Mexico Highlands U (NM)
New Mexico State U (NM)
New York U (NY)
North Carolina Central U (NC)
North Carolina State U (NC)
Northwest Missouri State U (MO)
Old Dominion U (VA)
Oral Roberts U (OK)
Penn State Abington (PA)
Penn State Altoona (PA)
Penn State Beaver (PA)
Penn State Berks (PA)
Penn State Brandywine (PA)
Penn State DuBois (PA)
Penn State Erie, The Behrend Coll (PA)
Penn State Fayette, The Eberly Campus (PA)
Penn State Greater Allegheny (PA)
Penn State Hazleton (PA)
Penn State Lehigh Valley (PA)
Penn State Mont Alto (PA)
Penn State New Kensington (PA)
Penn State Schuylkill (PA)
Penn State Shenango (PA)
Penn State U Park (PA)
Penn State Wilkes-Barre (PA)
Penn State Worthington Scranton (PA)
Penn State York (PA)
Pittsburg State U (KS)
Prescott Coll (AZ)
Savannah State U (GA)
Slippery Rock U of Pennsylvania (PA)
South Dakota State U (SD)
State U of New York Coll at Cortland (NY)
Stephen F. Austin State U (TX)
Sterling Coll (VT)
Texas A&M U (TX)
Texas State U–San Marcos (TX)
Trine U (IN)
Union Coll (KY)
Union U (TN)
U of Alberta (AB, Canada)
The U of British Columbia (BC, Canada)
U of Connecticut (CT)
U of Florida (FL)
U of Houston–Clear Lake (TX)
U of Idaho (ID)
U of Maine (ME)
U of Maine at Machias (ME)
U of Minnesota, Twin Cities Campus (MN)
U of New Hampshire (NH)
The U of North Carolina at Chapel Hill (NC)
The U of North Carolina at Pembroke (NC)
The U of North Carolina Wilmington (NC)
U of North Dakota (ND)
U of Northern Colorado (CO)
U of North Texas (TX)
U of St. Francis (IL)
The U of Tennessee (TN)
U of Vermont (VT)
U of Waterloo (ON, Canada)
U of West Georgia (GA)
U of Wisconsin–La Crosse (WI)
Wayland Baptist U (TX)
Webber Intl U (FL)
Western Carolina U (NC)
Western Illinois U (IL)
Western Kentucky U (KY)
Western State Coll of Colorado (CO)
West Virginia U (WV)
Winona State U (MN)
Winston-Salem State U (NC)

PARKS, RECREATION, AND LEISURE RELATED

Belhaven U (MS)
Brigham Young U (UT)
Coker Coll (SC)
The Coll at Brockport, State U of New York (NY)
Franklin Coll (IN)
Hawai'i Pacific U (HI)
New England Coll (NH)
North Carolina State U (NC)
Ottawa U (KS)

Plymouth State U (NH)
St. Edward's U (TX)
Southern Wesleyan U (SC)
Trinity Christian Coll (IL)
U of North Alabama (AL)
The U of Toledo (OH)
U of Waterloo (ON, Canada)
Utah State U (UT)
Western State Coll of Colorado (CO)

PASTORAL COUNSELING AND SPECIALIZED MINISTRIES RELATED

Abilene Christian U (TX)
Brescia U (KY)
Calvary Bible Coll and Theological Sem (MO)
Davis Coll (NY)
George Fox U (OR)
Greenville Coll (IL)
John Brown U (AR)
Lipscomb U (TN)
Madonna U (MI)
Malone U (OH)
Multnomah U (OR)
Northwestern Coll (MN)
Oak Hills Christian Coll (MN)
Ouachita Baptist U (AR)

PASTORAL STUDIES/ COUNSELING

Amridge U (AL)
Baptist Bible Coll of Pennsylvania (PA)
The Baptist Coll of Florida (FL)
Barclay Coll (KS)
Belmont U (TN)
Bethany U (CA)
Bethel Coll (IN)
Calvary Bible Coll and Theological Sem (MO)
Campbellsville U (KY)
Cedarville U (OH)
Central Christian Coll of Kansas (KS)
Clearwater Christian Coll (FL)
Collège Dominicain de Philosophie et de Théologie (ON, Canada)
Coll of Mount St. Joseph (OH)
Columbia Intl U (SC)
Concordia U Chicago (IL)
Concordia U Wisconsin (WI)
Corban U (OR)
Cornerstone U (MI)
Crown Coll (MN)
Dallas Baptist U (TX)
Davis Coll (NY)
Eastern Nazarene Coll (MA)
East Texas Baptist U (TX)
Ecclesia Coll (AR)
Emmanuel Bible Coll (ON, Canada)
Emmanuel Coll (GA)
Eugene Bible Coll (OR)
Faith Baptist Bible Coll and Theological Sem (IA)
Faulkner U (AL)
Free Will Baptist Bible Coll (TN)
Gardner-Webb U (NC)
Grace Bible Coll (MI)
Greenville Coll (IL)
Hillsdale Free Will Baptist Coll (OK)
Houghton Coll (NY)
Indiana Wesleyan U (IN)
John Brown U (AR)
John Wesley Coll (NC)
Kuyper Coll (MI)
Lee U (TN)
Lindenwood U (MO)
Maple Springs Baptist Bible Coll and Sem (MD)
Maranatha Baptist Bible Coll (WI)
Marian U (IN)
The Master's Coll and Sem (CA)
Milligan Coll (TN)
Moody Bible Inst (IL)
Mount Vernon Nazarene U (OH)
Multnomah U (OR)
Nazarene Bible Coll (CO)
Newman U (KS)
North Greenville U (SC)
Northwest Nazarene U (ID)
Northwest U (WA)
Nyack Coll (NY)
Oak Hills Christian Coll (MN)
Oral Roberts U (OK)
Ouachita Baptist U (AR)
Pacific Union Coll (CA)
Patten U (CA)
Saint Francis U (PA)
St. Thomas U (FL)
San Diego Christian Coll (CA)
Simpson U (CA)
Southeastern Baptist Theological Sem (NC)
Southwest Baptist U (MO)
Southwestern Assemblies of God U (TX)
Southwestern Coll (KS)
Spring Arbor U (MI)
Tabor Coll (KS)
Trinity Coll of Florida (FL)
Union Coll (NE)
Universidad Adventista de las Antillas (PR)
Universidad Teológica del Caribe (PR)
U of Mary Hardin-Baylor (TX)
U of Saint Mary (KS)
U of St. Thomas (TX)
Valley Forge Christian Coll (PA)
Vanguard U of Southern California (CA)
Walsh U (OH)
Warner Pacific Coll (OR)

PATHOLOGIST ASSISTANT

St. John's U (NY)
Wayne State U (MI)

PATHOLOGY/ EXPERIMENTAL PATHOLOGY

Penn State Berks (PA)
Penn State U Park (PA)
U of Connecticut (CT)
The U of North Carolina at Chapel Hill (NC)

PEACE STUDIES AND CONFLICT RESOLUTION

American Public U System (WV)
Bennington Coll (VT)
Bethel U (MN)
California State U, Dominguez Hills (CA)
Chapman U (CA)
Clark U (MA)
Colgate U (NY)
Coll of Saint Benedict (MN)
DePauw U (IN)
Earlham Coll (IN)
Eastern Mennonite U (VA)
Fordham U (NY)
George Mason U (VA)
Gettysburg Coll (PA)
Goshen Coll (IN)
Goucher Coll (MD)
Guilford Coll (NC)
Hamline U (MN)
Hampshire Coll (MA)
Haverford Coll (PA)
Juniata Coll (PA)
Kent State U (OH)
Le Moyne Coll (NY)
Manchester Coll (IN)
Molloy Coll (NY)
Naropa U (CO)
Nazareth Coll of Rochester (NY)
Ohio Dominican U (OH)
Saint John's U (MN)
U of California, Berkeley (CA)
U of Missouri (MO)
The U of North Carolina at Chapel Hill (NC)
U of Ottawa (ON, Canada)
U of St. Thomas (MN)
U of Toronto (ON, Canada)
The U of Western Ontario (ON, Canada)
U of Wisconsin–Milwaukee (WI)
U of Wisconsin–Superior (WI)
Wellesley Coll (MA)

PERFUSION TECHNOLOGY

State U of New York Upstate Medical U (NY)
Thomas Edison State Coll (NJ)

PERIOPERATIVE/ OPERATING ROOM AND SURGICAL NURSING

Murray State U (KY)
Tabor Coll (KS)
Texas A&M Intl U (TX)

PETROLEUM ENGINEERING

Colorado School of Mines (CO)
Louisiana State U and Ag and Mech Coll (LA)
Marietta Coll (OH)
Missouri U of Science and Technology (MO)
Montana Tech of The U of Montana (MT)
New Mexico Inst of Mining and Technology (NM)
Penn State Abington (PA)
Penn State Altoona (PA)
Penn State Beaver (PA)
Penn State Berks (PA)
Penn State Brandywine (PA)
Penn State DuBois (PA)
Penn State Erie, The Behrend Coll (PA)
Penn State Fayette, The Eberly Campus (PA)
Penn State Greater Allegheny (PA)
Penn State Hazleton (PA)
Penn State Lehigh Valley (PA)
Penn State Mont Alto (PA)
Penn State New Kensington (PA)
Penn State Schuylkill (PA)
Penn State Shenango (PA)
Penn State U Park (PA)
Penn State Wilkes-Barre (PA)
Penn State Worthington Scranton (PA)
Penn State York (PA)
Texas A&M U (TX)
Texas A&M U–Kingsville (TX)
Texas Tech U (TX)
U of Alaska Fairbanks (AK)
U of Alberta (AB, Canada)
U of Houston (TX)
The U of Kansas (KS)
U of Oklahoma (OK)
U of Regina (SK, Canada)
U of Southern California (CA)
The U of Texas at Austin (TX)
U of Toronto (ON, Canada)
U of Tulsa (OK)
U of Wyoming (WY)
West Virginia U (WV)

PETROLEUM PRODUCTS RETAILING OPERATIONS

Cape Breton U (NS, Canada)

PETROLEUM TECHNOLOGY

American U of Beirut (Lebanon)
Cape Breton U (NS, Canada)
Mercyhurst Coll (PA)
Nicholls State U (LA)
U of Pittsburgh at Bradford (PA)

PHARMACOLOGY

Georgia Southern U (GA)
Stony Brook U, State U of New York (NY)
U of Alberta (AB, Canada)
The U of British Columbia (BC, Canada)
U of California, Santa Barbara (CA)
U of Cincinnati (OH)
U of Ottawa (ON, Canada)
The U of Western Ontario (ON, Canada)
U of Wisconsin–Madison (WI)

PHARMACOLOGY AND TOXICOLOGY

U at Buffalo, the State U of New York (NY)
U of the Sciences in Philadelphia (PA)
The U of Western Ontario (ON, Canada)
Wright State U (OH)

PHARMACOLOGY AND TOXICOLOGY RELATED

The George Washington U (DC)
Massachusetts Coll of Pharmacy and Health Sciences (MA)

PHARMACY

Butler U (IN)
The Coll of Idaho (ID)
Drake U (IA)
Eastern Nazarene Coll (MA)
Illinois Inst of Technology (IL)
Lipscomb U (TN)
Long Island U, Brooklyn Campus (NY)
Massachusetts Coll of Pharmacy and Health Sciences (MA)
Memorial U of Newfoundland (NL, Canada)
Northeastern U (MA)
The Ohio State U (OH)
Purdue U (IN)
Rutgers, The State U of New Jersey, New Brunswick (NJ)
St. John's U (NY)
St. Louis Coll of Pharmacy (MO)
Saint Vincent Coll (PA)
South Dakota State U (SD)
Southwestern Oklahoma State U (OK)
U of Alberta (AB, Canada)
The U of British Columbia (BC, Canada)
U of Cincinnati (OH)
U of Connecticut (CT)
The U of Iowa (IA)
The U of Kansas (KS)
U of Louisiana at Monroe (LA)
U of Manitoba (MB, Canada)
U of Mississippi (MS)
U of Missouri–Kansas City (MO)
U of New Mexico (NM)
U of Pittsburgh (PA)
U of Rhode Island (RI)
U of Saskatchewan (SK, Canada)
U of the Pacific (CA)
U of the Sciences in Philadelphia (PA)
The U of Toledo (OH)
U of Toronto (ON, Canada)
U of Utah (UT)
U of Washington (WA)
U of Wisconsin–Madison (WI)

PHARMACY ADMINISTRATION/ PHARMACEUTICS

DeSales U (PA)
Drake U (IA)
U of Michigan (MI)

PHARMACY, PHARMACEUTICAL SCIENCES, AND ADMINISTRATION RELATED

Albany Coll of Pharmacy and Health Sciences (NY)
Duquesne U (PA)
Massachusetts Coll of Pharmacy and Health Sciences (MA)
North Dakota State U (ND)
Ohio Northern U (OH)
U at Buffalo, the State U of New York (NY)
U of California, Irvine (CA)
U of Connecticut (CT)
U of Houston (TX)
The U of North Carolina at Chapel Hill (NC)
U of the Sciences in Philadelphia (PA)
The U of Toledo (OH)
Wilkes U (PA)

PHILOSOPHY

Acadia U (NS, Canada)
Adelphi U (NY)
Agnes Scott Coll (GA)
Albertus Magnus Coll (CT)
Albion Coll (MI)
Albright Coll (PA)
Alfred U (NY)
Allegheny Coll (PA)
Alma Coll (MI)
Alvernia U (PA)
Alverno Coll (WI)
American Intl Coll (MA)
American Public U System (WV)
American U (DC)
American U of Beirut (Lebanon)
Amherst Coll (MA)
Anderson U (IN)
Appalachian State U (NC)
Aquinas Coll (MI)
Arcadia U (PA)
Arizona State U (AZ)
Arkansas State U—Jonesboro (AR)
Asbury U (KY)
Ashland U (OH)
Assumption Coll (MA)
Auburn U (AL)
Augsburg Coll (MN)
Augustana Coll (IL)
Augustana Coll (SD)
Austin Coll (TX)
Austin Peay State U (TN)
Azusa Pacific U (CA)
Baker U (KS)
Baldwin-Wallace Coll (OH)
Ball State U (IN)
Bard Coll (NY)
Bard Coll at Simon's Rock (MA)
Barnard Coll (NY)
Barry U (FL)
Bates Coll (ME)
Baylor U (TX)
Belhaven U (MS)
Bellarmine U (KY)
Belmont Abbey Coll (NC)
Belmont U (TN)
Beloit Coll (WI)
Bemidji State U (MN)
Benedictine Coll (KS)
Benedictine U (IL)
Bennington Coll (VT)
Bentley U (MA)
Berea Coll (KY)
Bernard M. Baruch Coll of the City U of New York (NY)
Bethany Coll (KS)
Bethel Coll (IN)
Bethel U (MN)
Birmingham-Southern Coll (AL)
Bishop's U (QC, Canada)
Bloomfield Coll (NJ)
Bloomsburg U of Pennsylvania (PA)
Boise State U (ID)
Boston Coll (MA)
Boston U (MA)
Bowdoin Coll (ME)
Bowling Green State U (OH)
Bradley U (IL)
Brandeis U (MA)
Bridgewater State Coll (MA)
Brock U (ON, Canada)
Brooklyn Coll of the City U of New York (NY)
Bryn Mawr Coll (PA)
Bucknell U (PA)
Buffalo State Coll, State U of New York (NY)
Butler U (IN)
Cabrini Coll (PA)
California Baptist U (CA)
California Inst of Technology (CA)
California Lutheran U (CA)
California Polytechnic State U, San Luis Obispo (CA)
California State Polytechnic U, Pomona (CA)
California State U, Bakersfield (CA)
California State U, Chico (CA)
California State U, Dominguez Hills (CA)
California State U, East Bay (CA)
California State U, Fresno (CA)
California State U, Fullerton (CA)
California State U, Long Beach (CA)
California State U, Los Angeles (CA)
California State U, Northridge (CA)
California State U, Sacramento (CA)
California State U, San Bernardino (CA)
California State U, Stanislaus (CA)
Calvin Coll (MI)
Canisius Coll (NY)
Cape Breton U (NS, Canada)
Capital U (OH)
Carleton Coll (MN)
Carlow U (PA)
Carnegie Mellon U (PA)
Carson-Newman Coll (TN)
Case Western Reserve U (OH)
Castleton State Coll (VT)
Catawba Coll (NC)
The Catholic U of America (DC)
Cedarville U (OH)
Centenary Coll of Louisiana (LA)
Central Coll (IA)
Central Connecticut State U (CT)
Central Michigan U (MI)
Chapman U (CA)
Chowan U (NC)
Christendom Coll (VA)
Christian Brothers U (TN)
Christopher Newport U (VA)
City Coll of the City U of New York (NY)
Claremont McKenna Coll (CA)
Clarion U of Pennsylvania (PA)
Clark Atlanta U (GA)
Clarke Coll (IA)
Clark U (MA)
Clemson U (SC)
Cleveland State U (OH)
Coastal Carolina U (SC)
Colby Coll (ME)
Colgate U (NY)
The Coll at Brockport, State U of New York (NY)
Collège Dominicain de Philosophie et de Théologie (ON, Canada)
Coll of Charleston (SC)
The Coll of Idaho (ID)
Coll of Mount Saint Vincent (NY)
The Coll of New Jersey (NJ)
The Coll of New Rochelle (NY)
Coll of Notre Dame of Maryland (MD)
Coll of Saint Benedict (MN)
Coll of Saint Elizabeth (NJ)
The Coll of Saint Rose (NY)
Coll of Staten Island of the City U of New York (NY)
Coll of the Atlantic (ME)
Coll of the Holy Cross (MA)
Coll of the Ozarks (MO)
The Coll of William and Mary (VA)
The Coll of Wooster (OH)
The Colorado Coll (CO)
Colorado State U (CO)
Columbia U (NY)
Columbia U, School of General Studies (NY)
Concordia Coll (MN)

U of Idaho (ID)
U of Illinois at Chicago (IL)
U of Illinois at Springfield (IL)
U of Illinois at Urbana–Champaign (IL)
U of Indianapolis (IN)
The U of Iowa (IA)
The U of Kansas (KS)
U of Kentucky (KY)
U of King's Coll (NS, Canada)
U of La Verne (CA)
U of Lethbridge (AB, Canada)
U of Louisville (KY)
U of Maine (ME)
U of Manitoba (MB, Canada)
U of Maryland, Baltimore County (MD)
U of Maryland, Coll Park (MD)
U of Mary Washington (VA)
U of Massachusetts Amherst (MA)
U of Massachusetts Boston (MA)
U of Massachusetts Dartmouth (MA)
U of Massachusetts Lowell (MA)
U of Memphis (TN)
U of Miami (FL)
U of Michigan (MI)
U of Michigan–Dearborn (MI)
U of Michigan–Flint (MI)
U of Minnesota, Duluth (MN)
U of Minnesota, Twin Cities Campus (MN)
U of Mississippi (MS)
U of Missouri (MO)
U of Missouri–Kansas City (MO)
U of Missouri–St. Louis (MO)
U of Mount Union (OH)
U of Nebraska at Omaha (NE)
U of Nebraska–Lincoln (NE)
U of Nevada, Las Vegas (NV)
U of Nevada, Reno (NV)
U of New Brunswick Fredericton (NB, Canada)
U of New Hampshire (NH)
U of New Mexico (NM)
U of New Orleans (LA)
The U of North Carolina at Asheville (NC)
The U of North Carolina at Chapel Hill (NC)
The U of North Carolina at Charlotte (NC)
The U of North Carolina at Greensboro (NC)
U of North Dakota (ND)
U of Northern Colorado (CO)
U of Northern Iowa (IA)
U of North Florida (FL)
U of North Texas (TX)
U of Notre Dame (IN)
U of Oklahoma (OK)
U of Oregon (OR)
U of Ottawa (ON, Canada)
U of Pennsylvania (PA)
U of Pittsburgh (PA)
U of Portland (OR)
U of Puerto Rico, Río Piedras (PR)
U of Puget Sound (WA)
U of Redlands (CA)
U of Regina (SK, Canada)
U of Rhode Island (RI)
U of Richmond (VA)
U of Rochester (NY)
U of St. Thomas (MN)
U of St. Thomas (TX)
U of San Diego (CA)
U of San Francisco (CA)
U of Saskatchewan (SK, Canada)
The U of Scranton (PA)
U of South Alabama (AL)
U of South Carolina (SC)
The U of South Dakota (SD)
U of Southern California (CA)
U of Southern Indiana (IN)
U of Southern Maine (ME)
U of Southern Mississippi (MS)
U of South Florida (FL)
The U of Tampa (FL)
The U of Tennessee (TN)
The U of Tennessee at Martin (TN)
The U of Texas at Arlington (TX)
The U of Texas at Austin (TX)
The U of Texas at El Paso (TX)
The U of Texas at San Antonio (TX)
The U of Texas–Pan American (TX)
U of the Incarnate Word (TX)
U of the Ozarks (AR)
U of the Pacific (CA)
U of the West (CA)
The U of Toledo (OH)
U of Tulsa (OK)
U of Utah (UT)
U of Vermont (VT)
U of Virginia (VA)
U of Washington (WA)
U of Waterloo (ON, Canada)
The U of Western Ontario (ON, Canada)
U of West Florida (FL)
U of West Georgia (GA)
U of Windsor (ON, Canada)
U of Wisconsin–Eau Claire (WI)
U of Wisconsin–Green Bay (WI)
U of Wisconsin–La Crosse (WI)
U of Wisconsin–Madison (WI)
U of Wisconsin–Milwaukee (WI)
U of Wisconsin–Oshkosh (WI)
U of Wisconsin–Parkside (WI)
U of Wisconsin–Platteville (WI)
U of Wisconsin–Stevens Point (WI)
U of Wyoming (WY)
Ursinus Coll (PA)
Ursuline Coll (OH)
Utah State U (UT)
Utah Valley U (UT)
Utica Coll (NY)
Valdosta State U (GA)
Valparaiso U (IN)
Vanderbilt U (TN)
Vassar Coll (NY)
Villanova U (PA)
Virginia Commonwealth U (VA)
Virginia Polytechnic Inst and State U (VA)
Virginia Wesleyan Coll (VA)
Wabash Coll (IN)
Wagner Coll (NY)
Wake Forest U (NC)
Walsh U (OH)
Wartburg Coll (IA)
Washburn U (KS)
Washington & Jefferson Coll (PA)
Washington and Lee U (VA)
Washington Coll (MD)
Washington State U (WA)
Washington U in St. Louis (MO)
Wayne State U (MI)
Webster U (MO)
Wellesley Coll (MA)
Wells Coll (NY)
Wesleyan Coll (GA)
Wesleyan U (CT)
West Chester U of Pennsylvania (PA)
Western Carolina U (NC)
Western Illinois U (IL)
Western Kentucky U (KY)
Western Michigan U (MI)
Western New England Coll (MA)
Western Oregon U (OR)
Western Washington U (WA)
Westminster Coll (MO)
Westminster Coll (UT)
Westmont Coll (CA)
West Virginia U (WV)
West Virginia Wesleyan Coll (WV)
Wheaton Coll (IL)
Wheaton Coll (MA)
Wheeling Jesuit U (WV)
Whitman Coll (WA)
Whittier Coll (CA)
Wichita State U (KS)
Wilfrid Laurier U (ON, Canada)
Wilkes U (PA)
Willamette U (OR)
William Jewell Coll (MO)
William Paterson U of New Jersey (NJ)
Williams Coll (MA)
Wilmington Coll (OH)
Wilson Coll (PA)
Wingate U (NC)
Winthrop U (SC)
Wittenberg U (OH)
Wofford Coll (SC)
Worcester Polytechnic Inst (MA)
Wright State U (OH)
Xavier U (OH)
Xavier U of Louisiana (LA)
Yale U (CT)
Yeshiva U (NY)
York Coll of Pennsylvania (PA)
York Coll of the City U of New York (NY)
York U (ON, Canada)
Youngstown State U (OH)

PHILOSOPHY AND RELIGIOUS STUDIES RELATED

Alderson-Broaddus Coll (WV)
Arizona State U (AZ)
Barton Coll (NC)
Berry Coll (GA)
Bethune-Cookman U (FL)
Bridgewater Coll (VA)
Buena Vista U (IA)
Butler U (IN)
Claflin U (SC)
Claremont McKenna Coll (CA)
Coll of the Humanities and Sciences, Harrison Middleton U (AZ)
Columbia Coll (MO)
Covenant Coll (GA)
Eastern Mennonite U (VA)
Eastern Nazarene Coll (MA)
The Evergreen State Coll (WA)
Fisk U (TN)
Florida Ag and Mech U (FL)
Friends U (KS)
Graceland U (IA)
Hendrix Coll (AR)
Holy Names U (CA)
Iowa Wesleyan Coll (IA)
James Madison U (VA)
John Brown U (AR)
Juniata Coll (PA)
Kean U (NJ)
Lyon Coll (AR)
Mary Baldwin Coll (VA)
Marymount Manhattan Coll (NY)
Millsaps Coll (MS)
Ouachita Baptist U (AR)
Pace U (NY)
Quincy U (IL)
Radford U (VA)
The Richard Stockton Coll of New Jersey (NJ)
Roberts Wesleyan Coll (NY)
Rocky Mountain Coll (MT)
Rowan U (NJ)
Samford U (AL)
San Francisco State U (CA)
Sarah Lawrence Coll (NY)
Southwestern Coll (KS)
State U of New York at Oswego (NY)
Sterling Coll (KS)
Stillman Coll (AL)
Syracuse U (NY)
Union U (TN)
U of Maine at Farmington (ME)
U of Mary Washington (VA)
The U of North Carolina at Pembroke (NC)
The U of North Carolina Wilmington (NC)
U of Notre Dame (IN)
The U of Tennessee at Chattanooga (TN)
U of the Cumberlands (KY)
U of the Ozarks (AR)
Viterbo U (WI)
Washington U in St. Louis (MO)
West Virginia Wesleyan Coll (WV)
Wheaton Coll (MA)

PHILOSOPHY RELATED

Claremont McKenna Coll (CA)
Lewis U (IL)
Marlboro Coll (VT)
Ohio Northern U (OH)
U of Massachusetts Boston (MA)
U of Pennsylvania (PA)
U of Regina (SK, Canada)
U of Richmond (VA)

PHOTOGRAPHIC AND FILM/ VIDEO TECHNOLOGY

Kent State U (OH)
New England School of Communications (ME)
Rochester Inst of Technology (NY)
St. John's U (NY)
Towson U (MD)
Villa Maria Coll of Buffalo (NY)

PHOTOGRAPHY

Acad of Art U (CA)
Adams State Coll (CO)
Alberta Coll of Art & Design (AB, Canada)
Albertus Magnus Coll (CT)
Aquinas Coll (MI)
Arcadia U (PA)
Art Center Coll of Design (CA)
The Art Center Design Coll, Tucson (AZ)
The Art Inst of Austin (TX)
The Art Inst of Boston at Lesley U (MA)
The Art Inst of California–Hollywood (CA)
The Art Inst of Charlotte (NC)
The Art Inst of Colorado (CO)
The Art Inst of Dallas (TX)
The Art Inst of Fort Lauderdale (FL)
The Art Inst of Fort Worth (TX)
The Art Inst of Houston (TX)
The Art Inst of Houston—North (TX)
The Art Inst of Indianapolis (IN)
The Art Inst of Jacksonville (FL)
The Art Inst of Las Vegas (NV)
The Art Inst of Michigan (MI)
The Art Inst of Philadelphia (PA)
The Art Inst of Phoenix (AZ)
The Art Inst of Pittsburgh (PA)
The Art Inst of Portland (OR)
The Art Inst of Salt Lake City (UT)
The Art Inst of San Antonio (TX)
The Art Inst of Seattle (WA)
The Art Inst of Tampa (FL)
The Art Inst of Tucson (AZ)
The Art Inst of Vrginia Beach (VA)
The Art Inst of Washington–Northern Virginia (VA)
The Art Insts Intl–Kansas City (KS)
The Art Insts Intl Minnesota (MN)
Bard Coll (NY)
Bard Coll at Simon's Rock (MA)
Barry U (FL)
Bennington Coll (VT)
Bowling Green State U (OH)
Bradley U (IL)
Bridgewater State Coll (MA)
Buffalo State Coll, State U of New York (NY)
Burlington Coll (VT)
California Coll of the Arts (CA)
California Inst of the Arts (CA)
California State U, East Bay (CA)
California State U, Long Beach (CA)
California State U, Sacramento (CA)
Carroll U (WI)
Carson-Newman Coll (TN)
Cazenovia Coll (NY)
Chatham U (PA)
The Cleveland Inst of Art (OH)
Coker Coll (SC)
Coll for Creative Studies (MI)
Coll of Santa Fe (NM)
Coll of Visual Arts (MN)
Columbia Coll (MO)
Columbia Coll Chicago (IL)
Concordia U (QC, Canada)
Corcoran Coll of Art and Design (DC)
Dominican U (IL)
Drexel U (PA)
Eastern Mennonite U (VA)
Ferris State U (MI)
Fitchburg State Coll (MA)
Fordham U (NY)
Gallaudet U (DC)
Governors State U (IL)
Grand Valley State U (MI)
Hampton U (VA)
Hofstra U (NY)
The Illinois Inst of Art–Chicago (IL)
The Illinois Inst of Art–Schaumburg (IL)
Indiana U–Purdue U Fort Wayne (IN)
Indiana Wesleyan U (IN)
Inter American U of Puerto Rico, San Germán Campus (PR)
Ithaca Coll (NY)
John Brown U (AR)
Long Island U, C.W. Post Campus (NY)
Louisiana Tech U (LA)
Maine Coll of Art (ME)
Marlboro Coll (VT)
Maryland Inst Coll of Art (MD)
Marymount Manhattan Coll (NY)
Marywood U (PA)
Massachusetts Coll of Art and Design (MA)
Memorial U of Newfoundland (NL, Canada)
Memphis Coll of Art (TN)
Miami Intl U of Art & Design (FL)
Minneapolis Coll of Art and Design (MN)
Moore Coll of Art & Design (PA)
Morningside Coll (IA)
Mount Allison U (NB, Canada)
New England Coll (NH)
The New England Inst of Art (MA)
New York U (NY)
Northern Arizona U (AZ)
Northern Michigan U (MI)
Oakland U (MI)
Ohio U (OH)
Otis Coll of Art and Design (CA)
Pacific Union Coll (CA)
Parsons The New School for Design (NY)
Pennsylvania Coll of Art & Design (PA)
Point Park U (PA)
Pratt Inst (NY)
Prescott Coll (AZ)
Purchase Coll, State U of New York (NY)
Ringling Coll of Art and Design (FL)
Rivier Coll (NH)
Rutgers, The State U of New Jersey, New Brunswick (NJ)
Sage Coll of Albany (NY)
St. Edward's U (TX)
St. John's U (NY)
Salem State Coll (MA)
Salve Regina U (RI)
Sam Houston State U (TX)
Sarah Lawrence Coll (NY)
Savannah Coll of Art and Design (GA)
School of the Art Inst of Chicago (IL)
School of the Museum of Fine Arts, Boston (MA)
School of Visual Arts (NY)
Seattle U (WA)
Shawnee State U (OH)
Southern Adventist U (TN)
State U of New York at New Paltz (NY)
Syracuse U (NY)
Temple U (PA)
Texas A&M U–Commerce (TX)
Texas Christian U (TX)
Texas State U–San Marcos (TX)
Thomas Edison State Coll (NJ)
Trinity Christian Coll (IL)
The U of Akron (OH)
U of Central Florida (FL)
U of Central Missouri (MO)
U of Central Oklahoma (OK)
U of Dayton (OH)
U of Hartford (CT)
U of Houston (TX)
U of Illinois at Chicago (IL)
U of Illinois at Urbana–Champaign (IL)
The U of Iowa (IA)
U of Massachusetts Dartmouth (MA)
U of Miami (FL)
U of Missouri–St. Louis (MO)
U of Oregon (OR)
U of Puerto Rico, Río Piedras (PR)
U of Washington (WA)
Virginia Commonwealth U (VA)
Virginia Intermont Coll (VA)
Washington U in St. Louis (MO)
Watkins Coll of Art, Design, & Film (TN)
Weber State U (UT)
Webster U (MO)
Western State Coll of Colorado (CO)
Western Washington U (WA)
Wright State U (OH)
York U (ON, Canada)
Youngstown State U (OH)

PHOTOJOURNALISM

Bradley U (IL)
Central Michigan U (MI)
Corcoran Coll of Art and Design (DC)
Harding U (AR)
Hawai'i Pacific U (HI)
Ohio U (OH)
Pittsburg State U (KS)
Point Park U (PA)
Prescott Coll (AZ)
Rochester Inst of Technology (NY)
Texas Tech U (TX)
U of Miami (FL)
U of Missouri (MO)
Western Kentucky U (KY)

PHYSICAL AND THEORETICAL CHEMISTRY

Lehigh U (PA)
Rice U (TX)
The U of Western Ontario (ON, Canada)

PHYSICAL ANTHROPOLOGY

The U of Western Ontario (ON, Canada)

PHYSICAL EDUCATION TEACHING AND COACHING

Abilene Christian U (TX)
Adams State Coll (CO)
Adelphi U (NY)
Alabama Ag and Mech U (AL)
Alabama State U (AL)
Albany State U (GA)
Albion Coll (MI)
Alderson-Broaddus Coll (WV)
Alma Coll (MI)
Anderson U (IN)
Appalachian State U (NC)
Aquinas Coll (MI)
Arkansas State U—Jonesboro (AR)
Arkansas Tech U (AR)
Armstrong Atlantic State U (GA)
Asbury U (KY)
Ashland U (OH)
Auburn U (AL)
Augsburg Coll (MN)
Augustana Coll (IL)
Augustana Coll (SD)
Aurora U (IL)
Averett U (VA)
Azusa Pacific U (CA)
Ball State U (IN)

Baptist Bible Coll of Pennsylvania (PA)
Barry U (FL)
Barton Coll (NC)
Baylor U (TX)
Belmont U (TN)
Bemidji State U (MN)
Benedictine Coll (KS)
Berry Coll (GA)
Bethany Coll (KS)
Bethany Coll (WV)
Bethel Coll (IN)
Bethel U (MN)
Bethune-Cookman U (FL)
Blackburn Coll (IL)
Bluefield Coll (VA)
Blue Mountain Coll (MS)
Boise State U (ID)
Boston U (MA)
Bowling Green State U (OH)
Brewton-Parker Coll (GA)
Briar Cliff U (IA)
Bridgewater Coll (VA)
Bridgewater State Coll (MA)
Brigham Young U–Hawaii (HI)
Brock U (ON, Canada)
Brooklyn Coll of the City U of New York (NY)
Bryan Coll (TN)
Buena Vista U (IA)
California Baptist U (CA)
California Lutheran U (CA)
California State U, Bakersfield (CA)
California State U, Chico (CA)
California State U, East Bay (CA)
California State U, Fresno (CA)
California State U, Long Beach (CA)
California State U, San Bernardino (CA)
California State U, Stanislaus (CA)
Calvin Coll (MI)
Cameron U (OK)
Campbellsville U (KY)
Canisius Coll (NY)
Capital U (OH)
Carroll U (WI)
Carson-Newman Coll (TN)
Castleton State Coll (VT)
Catawba Coll (NC)
Cedarville U (OH)
Central Christian Coll of Kansas (KS)
Central Connecticut State U (CT)
Central Michigan U (MI)
Chowan U (NC)
The Citadel, The Military Coll of South Carolina (SC)
Clarke Coll (IA)
Clearwater Christian Coll (FL)
Cleveland State U (OH)
Coastal Carolina U (SC)
Coker Coll (SC)
The Coll at Brockport, State U of New York (NY)
Coll of Charleston (SC)
The Coll of Idaho (ID)
The Coll of New Jersey (NJ)
Coll of the Ozarks (MO)
Columbus State U (GA)
Concordia Coll (MN)
Concordia U Chicago (IL)
Concordia U, St. Paul (MN)
Concordia U Wisconsin (WI)
Concord U (WV)
Corban U (OR)
Cornell Coll (IA)
Cornerstone U (MI)
Crown Coll (MN)
Culver-Stockton Coll (MO)
Cumberland U (TN)
Dakota State U (SD)
Dakota Wesleyan U (SD)
Dallas Baptist U (TX)
Defiance Coll (OH)
Delaware State U (DE)
Delta State U (MS)
Denison U (OH)
DePaul U (IL)
DePauw U (IN)
Dickinson State U (ND)
Doane Coll (NE)
Dordt Coll (IA)
Dowling Coll (NY)
Drury U (MO)
East Carolina U (NC)
East Central U (OK)
Eastern Connecticut State U (CT)
Eastern Mennonite U (VA)
Eastern Michigan U (MI)
Eastern Nazarene Coll (MA)
Eastern New Mexico U (NM)
East Stroudsburg U of Pennsylvania (PA)
East Texas Baptist U (TX)
Edward Waters Coll (FL)
Elizabeth City State U (NC)
Elmhurst Coll (IL)
Elon U (NC)
Endicott Coll (MA)
Erskine Coll (SC)
Evangel U (MO)
Fairmont State U (WV)
Faulkner U (AL)
Fayetteville State U (NC)
Florida Intl U (FL)
Florida Southern Coll (FL)
Florida State U (FL)
Fort Hays State U (KS)
Fort Lewis Coll (CO)
Fort Valley State U (GA)
Franklin Coll (IN)
Freed-Hardeman U (TN)
Free Will Baptist Bible Coll (TN)
Friends U (KS)
Frostburg State U (MD)
Gallaudet U (DC)
Gardner-Webb U (NC)
George Mason U (VA)
Georgia Coll & State U (GA)
Georgia Southern U (GA)
Georgia State U (GA)
Gettysburg Coll (PA)
Glenville State Coll (WV)
Gonzaga U (WA)
Goshen Coll (IN)
Grace Coll (IN)
Graceland U (IA)
Grambling State U (LA)
Grand Valley State U (MI)
Grand View U (IA)
Greensboro Coll (NC)
Greenville Coll (IL)
Gustavus Adolphus Coll (MN)
Hamline U (MN)
Hampton U (VA)
Hannibal-LaGrange Coll (MO)
Hardin-Simmons U (TX)
Heidelberg U (OH)
Henderson State U (AR)
High Point U (NC)
Hillsdale Coll (MI)
Hofstra U (NY)
Hope Coll (MI)
Houghton Coll (NY)
Houston Baptist U (TX)
Howard Payne U (TX)
Humboldt State U (CA)
Hunter Coll of the City U of New York (NY)
Huntingdon Coll (AL)
Huntington U (IN)
Husson U (ME)
Huston-Tillotson U (TX)
Idaho State U (ID)
Illinois Coll (IL)
Illinois State U (IL)
Indiana State U (IN)
Indiana Tech (IN)
Indiana U Bloomington (IN)
Indiana U–Purdue U Indianapolis (IN)
Indiana Wesleyan U (IN)
Inter American U of Puerto Rico, Aguadilla Campus (PR)
Inter American U of Puerto Rico, Arecibo Campus (PR)
Inter American U of Puerto Rico, Guayama Campus (PR)
Inter American U of Puerto Rico, San Germán Campus (PR)
Iowa Wesleyan Coll (IA)
Ithaca Coll (NY)
Jackson State U (MS)
Jacksonville State U (AL)
Jacksonville U (FL)
Jamestown Coll (ND)
Jarvis Christian Coll (TX)
John Carroll U (OH)
Johnson C. Smith U (NC)
Johnson State Coll (VT)
Judson U (IL)
Kean U (NJ)
Keene State Coll (NH)
Kennesaw State U (GA)
Kent State U (OH)
Kentucky State U (KY)
Kentucky Wesleyan Coll (KY)
Lakehead U (ON, Canada)
Lamar U (TX)
Lane Coll (TN)
Laurentian U (ON, Canada)
Lees-McRae Coll (NC)
Lee U (TN)
LeTourneau U (TX)
Lewis-Clark State Coll (ID)
Liberty U (VA)
Limestone Coll (SC)
Lincoln Memorial U (TN)
Lincoln U (MO)
Lindenwood U (MO)
Lindsey Wilson Coll (KY)
Lipscomb U (TN)
Lock Haven U of Pennsylvania (PA)
Long Island U, Brooklyn Campus (NY)
Long Island U, C.W. Post Campus (NY)
Longwood U (VA)
Loras Coll (IA)
Louisiana Coll (LA)
Louisiana State U and Ag and Mech Coll (LA)
Louisiana State U in Shreveport (LA)
Louisiana Tech U (LA)
Lubbock Christian U (TX)
Luther Coll (IA)
Lynchburg Coll (VA)
Malone U (OH)
Manchester Coll (IN)
Manhattan Coll (NY)
Maranatha Baptist Bible Coll (WI)
Marian U (IN)
Marshall U (WV)
Mars Hill Coll (NC)
Maryville Coll (TN)
The Master's Coll and Sem (CA)
Mayville State U (ND)
McKendree U (IL)
McMurry U (TX)
McNeese State U (LA)
McPherson Coll (KS)
Memorial U of Newfoundland (NL, Canada)
Meredith Coll (NC)
Messiah Coll (PA)
Methodist U (NC)
Miami U (OH)
Miami U Hamilton (OH)
Michigan State U (MI)
MidAmerica Nazarene U (KS)
Millikin U (IL)
Minnesota State U Mankato (MN)
Minnesota State U Moorhead (MN)
Minot State U (ND)
Mississippi Coll (MS)
Mississippi State U (MS)
Mississippi Valley State U (MS)
Missouri Baptist U (MO)
Missouri State U (MO)
Monmouth Coll (IL)
Montana State U Billings (MT)
Montclair State U (NJ)
Morehead State U (KY)
Mount Vernon Nazarene U (OH)
Murray State U (KY)
Nebraska Wesleyan U (NE)
Newberry Coll (SC)
New England Coll (NH)
New Mexico Highlands U (NM)
New Mexico State U (NM)
Nicholls State U (LA)
Nipissing U (ON, Canada)
North Carolina Central U (NC)
North Central Coll (IL)
North Dakota State U (ND)
Northeastern Illinois U (IL)
Northeastern State U (OK)
Northern Kentucky U (KY)
Northern Michigan U (MI)
Northern State U (SD)
North Georgia Coll & State U (GA)
Northwestern Coll (IA)
Northwestern Coll (MN)
Northwestern Oklahoma State U (OK)
Northwestern State U of Louisiana (LA)
Northwest Missouri State U (MO)
Northwest Nazarene U (ID)
Oakland City U (IN)
Oakwood U (AL)
Ohio Northern U (OH)
The Ohio State U (OH)
Ohio U (OH)
Ohio Valley U (WV)
Ohio Wesleyan U (OH)
Oklahoma Baptist U (OK)
Oklahoma Christian U (OK)
Oklahoma City U (OK)
Oklahoma State U (OK)
Oklahoma Wesleyan U (OK)
Old Dominion U (VA)
Oral Roberts U (OK)
Ouachita Baptist U (AR)
Pacific Union Coll (CA)
Pepperdine U, Malibu (CA)
Peru State Coll (NE)
Philadelphia Biblical U (PA)
Piedmont Baptist Coll and Graduate School (NC)
Pittsburg State U (KS)
Pontifical Catholic U of Puerto Rico (PR)
Prescott Coll (AZ)
Purdue U (IN)
Queens Coll of the City U of New York (NY)
Queen's U at Kingston (ON, Canada)
Quincy U (IL)
Radford U (VA)
Redeemer U Coll (ON, Canada)
Reinhardt Coll (GA)
Rhode Island Coll (RI)
Ripon Coll (WI)
Roberts Wesleyan Coll (NY)
Rockford Coll (IL)
Rocky Mountain Coll (MT)
Rowan U (NJ)
Sage Coll of Albany (NY)
Saginaw Valley State U (MI)
St. Ambrose U (IA)
St. Andrews Presbyterian Coll (NC)
St. Bonaventure U (NY)
St. Catherine U (MN)
St. Cloud State U (MN)
St. Edward's U (TX)
St. Francis Coll (NY)
St. Francis Xavier U (NS, Canada)
Salem State Coll (MA)
Salisbury U (MD)
Samford U (AL)
San Diego Christian Coll (CA)
San Francisco State U (CA)
Schreiner U (TX)
Seattle Pacific U (WA)
Shenandoah U (VA)
Simpson Coll (IA)
Slippery Rock U of Pennsylvania (PA)
Sonoma State U (CA)
South Carolina State U (SC)
Southeastern Louisiana U (LA)
Southeastern Oklahoma State U (OK)
Southeast Missouri State U (MO)
Southern Adventist U (TN)
Southern Arkansas U–Magnolia (AR)
Southern Illinois U Carbondale (IL)
Southern Oregon U (OR)
Southern U and Ag and Mech Coll (LA)
Southern Utah U (UT)
Southern Wesleyan U (SC)
Southwest Baptist U (MO)
Southwestern Oklahoma State U (OK)
Southwestern U (TX)
Southwest Minnesota State U (MN)
Spring Arbor U (MI)
State U of New York at Plattsburgh (NY)
State U of New York Coll at Cortland (NY)
Sterling Coll (KS)
Stillman Coll (AL)
Sul Ross State U (TX)
Syracuse U (NY)
Tabor Coll (KS)
Tarleton State U (TX)
Taylor U (IN)
Temple U (PA)
Tennessee Technological U (TN)
Texas A&M Intl U (TX)
Texas A&M U–Commerce (TX)
Texas A&M U–Corpus Christi (TX)
Texas Christian U (TX)
Texas Lutheran U (TX)
Texas Southern U (TX)
Texas Wesleyan U (TX)
Towson U (MD)
Transylvania U (KY)
Trevecca Nazarene U (TN)
Trine U (IN)
Trinity Christian Coll (IL)
Tusculum Coll (TN)
Union Coll (KY)
Union Coll (NE)
Union Inst & U (OH)
Union U (TN)
United States Sports Acad (AL)
The U of Akron (OH)
The U of Alabama (AL)
The U of Alabama at Birmingham (AL)
U of Alaska Anchorage (AK)
U of Alberta (AB, Canada)
The U of Arizona (AZ)
U of Arkansas at Monticello (AR)
U of Arkansas at Pine Bluff (AR)
U of Central Florida (FL)
U of Central Missouri (MO)
U of Central Oklahoma (OK)
U of Cincinnati (OH)
U of Connecticut (CT)
U of Delaware (DE)
U of Dubuque (IA)
U of Evansville (IN)
The U of Findlay (OH)
U of Georgia (GA)
U of Guam (GU)
U of Idaho (ID)
U of Illinois at Urbana–Champaign (IL)
U of Indianapolis (IN)
The U of Kansas (KS)
U of Kentucky (KY)
U of Lethbridge (AB, Canada)
U of Louisiana at Monroe (LA)
U of Maine (ME)
U of Maine at Presque Isle (ME)
U of Manitoba (MB, Canada)
U of Mary (ND)
U of Mary Hardin-Baylor (TX)
U of Maryland, Coll Park (MD)
U of Maryland Eastern Shore (MD)
U of Memphis (TN)
U of Michigan (MI)
U of Minnesota, Duluth (MN)
U of Minnesota, Twin Cities Campus (MN)
U of Missouri–St. Louis (MO)
The U of Montana Western (MT)
U of Mount Union (OH)
U of Nebraska at Kearney (NE)
U of Nebraska–Lincoln (NE)
U of Nevada, Las Vegas (NV)
U of Nevada, Reno (NV)
U of New Brunswick Fredericton (NB, Canada)
U of New Mexico (NM)
The U of North Carolina at Greensboro (NC)
The U of North Carolina at Pembroke (NC)
The U of North Carolina Wilmington (NC)
U of North Dakota (ND)
U of Northern Iowa (IA)
U of North Florida (FL)
U of Pittsburgh (PA)
U of Pittsburgh at Bradford (PA)
U of Puerto Rico at Utuado (PR)
U of Puerto Rico, Cayey U Coll (PR)
U of Regina (SK, Canada)
U of Rhode Island (RI)
U of Rio Grande (OH)
U of St. Thomas (MN)
U of San Francisco (CA)
U of Saskatchewan (SK, Canada)
U of South Alabama (AL)
U of South Carolina (SC)
U of South Carolina Upstate (SC)
The U of South Dakota (SD)
U of Southern Indiana (IN)
U of Southern Mississippi (MS)
U of South Florida (FL)
U of the Cumberlands (KY)
U of the District of Columbia (DC)
U of the Incarnate Word (TX)
U of the Ozarks (AR)
U of the Southwest (NM)
The U of Toledo (OH)
U of Vermont (VT)
The U of West Alabama (AL)
The U of Western Ontario (ON, Canada)
U of West Georgia (GA)
U of Windsor (ON, Canada)
U of Wisconsin–Madison (WI)
U of Wisconsin–Oshkosh (WI)
U of Wisconsin–River Falls (WI)
U of Wisconsin–Stevens Point (WI)
U of Wisconsin–Superior (WI)
U of Wisconsin–Whitewater (WI)
U of Wyoming (WY)
Upper Iowa U (IA)
Utah State U (UT)
Utah Valley U (UT)
Valdosta State U (GA)
Valley City State U (ND)
Valparaiso U (IN)
Vanguard U of Southern California (CA)
Virginia Intermont Coll (VA)
Virginia State U (VA)
Voorhees Coll (SC)
Waldorf Coll (IA)
Walsh U (OH)
Warner Pacific Coll (OR)
Wartburg Coll (IA)
Washburn U (KS)
Washington State U (WA)
Wayland Baptist U (TX)
Wayne State Coll (NE)
Wayne State U (MI)
Weber State U (UT)
Western Carolina U (NC)
Western Illinois U (IL)
Western Kentucky U (KY)
Western Michigan U (MI)
Western State Coll of Colorado (CO)
Western Washington U (WA)
West Liberty U (WV)
Westminster Coll (MO)
Westmont Coll (CA)
West Virginia State U (WV)
West Virginia U (WV)
West Virginia Wesleyan Coll (WV)
Whittier Coll (CA)
Wichita State U (KS)
Wilfrid Laurier U (ON, Canada)
William Jewell Coll (MO)
William Paterson U of New Jersey (NJ)
William Penn U (IA)
Wilmington Coll (OH)
Winona State U (MN)

Winston-Salem State U (NC)
Winthrop U (SC)
Wright State U (OH)
Xavier U of Louisiana (LA)
York Coll (NE)
York Coll of the City U of New York (NY)
York U (ON, Canada)
Youngstown State U (OH)

PHYSICAL SCIENCES

Arkansas Tech U (AR)
Asbury U (KY)
Auburn U Montgomery (AL)
Bemidji State U (MN)
Bennington Coll (VT)
Black Hills State U (SD)
Brigham Young U–Hawaii (HI)
Brock U (ON, Canada)
California State U, East Bay (CA)
California State U, Sacramento (CA)
California State U, Stanislaus (CA)
Calvin Coll (MI)
Chowan U (NC)
Colgate U (NY)
Colorado State U (CO)
Concordia U Chicago (IL)
Dakota State U (SD)
Defiance Coll (OH)
Doane Coll (NE)
East Stroudsburg U of Pennsylvania (PA)
Emporia State U (KS)
The Evergreen State Coll (WA)
Florida State U (FL)
Fordham U (NY)
Fort Hays State U (KS)
Freed-Hardeman U (TN)
Grace Coll (IN)
Graceland U (IA)
Hampton U (VA)
Juniata Coll (PA)
Kansas State U (KS)
Keene State Coll (NH)
La Sierra U (CA)
Lincoln U (PA)
Linfield Coll (OR)
Long Island U, Brooklyn Campus (NY)
Loras Coll (IA)
The Master's Coll and Sem (CA)
Michigan State U (MI)
Michigan Technological U (MI)
Midwestern State U (TX)
Minnesota State U Mankato (MN)
Minot State U (ND)
Mississippi U for Women (MS)
Montana Tech of The U of Montana (MT)
Mount Vernon Nazarene U (OH)
Muhlenberg Coll (PA)
New Mexico Inst of Mining and Technology (NM)
Northern Arizona U (AZ)
Pacific Union Coll (CA)
Penn State Erie, The Behrend Coll (PA)
Ripon Coll (WI)
Rowan U (NJ)
St. Cloud State U (MN)
St. Francis Xavier U (NS, Canada)
St. John's U (NY)
Saint Michael's Coll (VT)
Saint Vincent Coll (PA)
San Diego State U (CA)
San Francisco State U (CA)
Shawnee State U (OH)
Southern Utah U (UT)
Southwestern U (TX)
Texas A&M Intl U (TX)
Trent U (ON, Canada)
Trine U (IN)
Troy U (AL)
United States Military Acad (NY)
United States Naval Acad (MD)
U of Alberta (AB, Canada)
U of Arkansas at Monticello (AR)
U of California, Berkeley (CA)
U of California, Riverside (CA)
U of Dayton (OH)
U of Guam (GU)
U of Guelph (ON, Canada)
U of Houston–Clear Lake (TX)
U of Maryland, Coll Park (MD)
U of North Alabama (AL)
U of North Dakota (ND)
U of Ottawa (ON, Canada)
U of Pittsburgh (PA)
U of Pittsburgh at Bradford (PA)
U of Rio Grande (OH)
U of Southern California (CA)
U of the Pacific (CA)
The U of Toledo (OH)
U of Utah (UT)
U of Wisconsin–River Falls (WI)
U of Wisconsin–Superior (WI)
U of Wyoming (WY)
Warner Pacific Coll (OR)
Washington State U (WA)
Wayland Baptist U (TX)
Wesleyan Coll (GA)
Westfield State Coll (MA)
William Paterson U of New Jersey (NJ)
Winona State U (MN)
Worcester State Coll (MA)
Yeshiva U (NY)
York U (ON, Canada)

PHYSICAL SCIENCES RELATED

Baldwin-Wallace Coll (OH)
Bowling Green State U (OH)
Cedar Crest Coll (PA)
Central Connecticut State U (CT)
The Coll of St. Scholastica (MN)
Covenant Coll (GA)
Eastern Michigan U (MI)
Florida Inst of Technology (FL)
Florida State U (FL)
Frostburg State U (MD)
George Mason U (VA)
John Brown U (AR)
New Mexico Inst of Mining and Technology (NM)
Northern Arizona U (AZ)
Redeemer U Coll (ON, Canada)
Rochester Inst of Technology (NY)
Stony Brook U, State U of New York (NY)
Union Coll (NY)
The U of Alabama in Huntsville (AL)
U of California, Davis (CA)
U of Mary Washington (VA)
The U of North Carolina at Chapel Hill (NC)
U of the Ozarks (AR)
U of Utah (UT)
U of Wisconsin–Eau Claire (WI)
Wayne State U (MI)
Worcester Polytechnic Inst (MA)

PHYSICAL SCIENCE TECHNOLOGIES RELATED

Missouri State U (MO)

PHYSICAL THERAPY

American Intl Coll (MA)
Andrews U (MI)
Armstrong Atlantic State U (GA)
Boston U (MA)
Bowling Green State U (OH)
California State U, Fresno (CA)
Clarke Coll (IA)
Cleveland State U (OH)
Coll of Saint Benedict (MN)
Concordia U Wisconsin (WI)
Duquesne U (PA)
D'Youville Coll (NY)
Eastern Nazarene Coll (MA)
Elmhurst Coll (IL)
Grand Valley State U (MI)
Gustavus Adolphus Coll (MN)
Hampton U (VA)
Hawai'i Pacific U (HI)
Husson U (ME)
Indiana U East (IN)
Indiana U–Purdue U Indianapolis (IN)
Ithaca Coll (NY)
Keystone Coll (PA)
Long Island U, Brooklyn Campus (NY)
Loyola U Chicago (IL)
Marquette U (WI)
Maryville U of Saint Louis (MO)
Merrimack Coll (MA)
Midwestern State U (TX)
Mount Saint Mary Coll (NY)
Mount Vernon Nazarene U (OH)
Nazareth Coll of Rochester (NY)
New York Inst of Technology (NY)
Northeastern U (MA)
Northwest Nazarene U (ID)
Oklahoma Wesleyan U (OK)
Queen's U at Kingston (ON, Canada)
Quinnipiac U (CT)
Sacred Heart U (CT)
St. Cloud State U (MN)
Saint Francis U (PA)
Saint John's U (MN)
Saint Louis U (MO)
Saint Mary's U of Minnesota (MN)
Saint Vincent Coll (PA)
Simmons Coll (MA)
State U of New York Coll of Environmental Science and Forestry (NY)
State U of New York Downstate Medical Center (NY)
Stony Brook U, State U of New York (NY)
Tarleton State U (TX)
U of Alberta (AB, Canada)
U of Connecticut (CT)
The U of Findlay (OH)
U of Hartford (CT)
U of Kentucky (KY)
U of Manitoba (MB, Canada)
U of Maryland Eastern Shore (MD)
U of Minnesota, Twin Cities Campus (MN)
U of New England (ME)
U of North Dakota (ND)
U of Ottawa (ON, Canada)
U of St. Francis (IL)
U of Saskatchewan (SK, Canada)
The U of South Dakota (SD)
The U of Tennessee at Chattanooga (TN)
U of the Sciences in Philadelphia (PA)
The U of Toledo (OH)
U of Utah (UT)
U of Washington (WA)
The U of Western Ontario (ON, Canada)
U of Wisconsin–Milwaukee (WI)
Vanguard U of Southern California (CA)
West Virginia U (WV)
Wheeling Jesuit U (WV)
Wichita State U (KS)
Winona State U (MN)

PHYSICIAN ASSISTANT

Augsburg Coll (MN)
Bethel U (TN)
Brenau U (GA)
Butler U (IN)
Catawba Coll (NC)
Charles Drew U of Medicine and Science (CA)
City Coll of the City U of New York (NY)
Duquesne U (PA)
D'Youville Coll (NY)
Elmhurst Coll (IL)
Gannon U (PA)
The George Washington U (DC)
Grand Valley State U (MI)
High Point U (NC)
Hofstra U (NY)
Long Island U, Brooklyn Campus (NY)
Marquette U (WI)
Methodist U (NC)
New York Inst of Technology (NY)
Peru State Coll (NE)
Philadelphia U (PA)
Quinnipiac U (CT)
Rochester Inst of Technology (NY)
Rocky Mountain Coll (MT)
St. Francis Coll (NY)
Saint Francis U (PA)
St. John's U (NY)
Saint Vincent Coll (PA)
Salem Coll (NC)
Seton Hill U (PA)
Southern Illinois U Carbondale (IL)
State U of New York Downstate Medical Center (NY)
Union Coll (NE)
U of New England (ME)
U of New Mexico (NM)
U of St. Francis (IL)
The U of South Dakota (SD)
The U of Texas–Pan American (TX)
U of Washington (WA)
U of Wisconsin–Madison (WI)
U of Wisconsin–Parkside (WI)
Wagner Coll (NY)
Wake Forest U (NC)
Wichita State U (KS)

PHYSICS

Abilene Christian U (TX)
Acadia U (NS, Canada)
Adams State Coll (CO)
Adelphi U (NY)
Agnes Scott Coll (GA)
Alabama Ag and Mech U (AL)
Albion Coll (MI)
Albright Coll (PA)
Alfred U (NY)
Allegheny Coll (PA)
Alma Coll (MI)
American U (DC)
American U of Beirut (Lebanon)
Amherst Coll (MA)
Anderson U (IN)
Andrews U (MI)
Angelo State U (TX)
Appalachian State U (NC)
Aquinas Coll (MI)
Arizona State U (AZ)
Arkansas State U—Jonesboro (AR)
Armstrong Atlantic State U (GA)
Ashland U (OH)
Auburn U (AL)
Augsburg Coll (MN)
Augustana Coll (IL)
Augustana Coll (SD)
Austin Coll (TX)
Austin Peay State U (TN)
Azusa Pacific U (CA)
Baker U (KS)
Baldwin-Wallace Coll (OH)
Ball State U (IN)
Bard Coll (NY)
Bard Coll at Simon's Rock (MA)
Barnard Coll (NY)
Bates Coll (ME)
Baylor U (TX)
Belmont U (TN)
Beloit Coll (WI)
Bemidji State U (MN)
Benedictine Coll (KS)
Benedictine U (IL)
Bennington Coll (VT)
Berea Coll (KY)
Berry Coll (GA)
Bethany Coll (WV)
Bethel U (MN)
Birmingham-Southern Coll (AL)
Bishop's U (QC, Canada)
Bloomsburg U of Pennsylvania (PA)
Bluffton U (OH)
Bob Jones U (SC)
Boise State U (ID)
Boston Coll (MA)
Boston U (MA)
Bowdoin Coll (ME)
Bowling Green State U (OH)
Bradley U (IL)
Brandeis U (MA)
Bridgewater Coll (VA)
Bridgewater State Coll (MA)
Brock U (ON, Canada)
Brooklyn Coll of the City U of New York (NY)
Bryn Mawr Coll (PA)
Bucknell U (PA)
Buena Vista U (IA)
Buffalo State Coll, State U of New York (NY)
Butler U (IN)
California Inst of Technology (CA)
California Lutheran U (CA)
California Polytechnic State U, San Luis Obispo (CA)
California State Polytechnic U, Pomona (CA)
California State U, Bakersfield (CA)
California State U, Chico (CA)
California State U, Dominguez Hills (CA)
California State U, East Bay (CA)
California State U, Fresno (CA)
California State U, Fullerton (CA)
California State U, Long Beach (CA)
California State U, Los Angeles (CA)
California State U, Northridge (CA)
California State U, Sacramento (CA)
California State U, San Bernardino (CA)
California State U, Stanislaus (CA)
Calvin Coll (MI)
Cameron U (OK)
Canisius Coll (NY)
Carleton Coll (MN)
Carnegie Mellon U (PA)
Carroll U (WI)
Carson-Newman Coll (TN)
The Catholic U of America (DC)
Cedarville U (OH)
Central Coll (IA)
Central Connecticut State U (CT)
Central Michigan U (MI)
Chatham U (PA)
Christian Brothers U (TN)
Christopher Newport U (VA)
The Citadel, The Military Coll of South Carolina (SC)
City Coll of the City U of New York (NY)
Claremont McKenna Coll (CA)
Clarion U of Pennsylvania (PA)
Clark Atlanta U (GA)
Clarkson U (NY)
Clark U (MA)
Clemson U (SC)
Cleveland State U (OH)
Coastal Carolina U (SC)
Colby Coll (ME)
Colgate U (NY)
The Coll at Brockport, State U of New York (NY)
Coll of Charleston (SC)
The Coll of Idaho (ID)
The Coll of New Jersey (NJ)
The Coll of New Rochelle (NY)
Coll of Notre Dame of Maryland (MD)
Coll of Saint Benedict (MN)
Coll of Staten Island of the City U of New York (NY)
Coll of the Holy Cross (MA)
The Coll of William and Mary (VA)
The Coll of Wooster (OH)
The Colorado Coll (CO)
Colorado State U (CO)
Colorado State U–Pueblo (CO)
Columbia U (NY)
Columbia U, School of General Studies (NY)
Concordia Coll (MN)
Concordia U (QC, Canada)
Cornell Coll (IA)
Cornell U (NY)
Covenant Coll (GA)
Creighton U (NE)
Curry Coll (MA)
Dartmouth Coll (NH)
Davidson Coll (NC)
Delaware State U (DE)
Denison U (OH)
DePaul U (IL)
DePauw U (IN)
Dickinson Coll (PA)
Dillard U (LA)
Doane Coll (NE)
Dordt Coll (IA)
Drake U (IA)
Drew U (NJ)
Drury U (MO)
Duke U (NC)
Duquesne U (PA)
Earlham Coll (IN)
East Carolina U (NC)
East Central U (OK)
Eastern Illinois U (IL)
Eastern Michigan U (MI)
Eastern Nazarene Coll (MA)
Eastern Washington U (WA)
East Stroudsburg U of Pennsylvania (PA)
East Tennessee State U (TN)
Eckerd Coll (FL)
Edinboro U of Pennsylvania (PA)
Elizabeth City State U (NC)
Elizabethtown Coll (PA)
Elmhurst Coll (IL)
Elon U (NC)
Emory & Henry Coll (VA)
Emory U (GA)
Emporia State U (KS)
Erskine Coll (SC)
Excelsior Coll (NY)
Fairfield U (CT)
Fairleigh Dickinson U, Metropolitan Campus (NJ)
Fisk U (TN)
Florida Atlantic U (FL)
Florida Inst of Technology (FL)
Florida Intl U (FL)
Florida State U (FL)
Fordham U (NY)
Fort Hays State U (KS)
Francis Marion U (SC)
Franklin & Marshall Coll (PA)
Frostburg State U (MD)
Furman U (SC)
Gallaudet U (DC)
Geneva Coll (PA)
George Mason U (VA)
Georgetown Coll (KY)
Georgetown U (DC)
The George Washington U (DC)
Georgia Coll & State U (GA)
Georgia Inst of Technology (GA)
Georgian Court U (NJ)
Georgia Southern U (GA)
Georgia State U (GA)
Gettysburg Coll (PA)
Gonzaga U (WA)
Gordon Coll (MA)
Goshen Coll (IN)
Goucher Coll (MD)
Grambling State U (LA)
Grand Valley State U (MI)
Greenville Coll (IL)
Grinnell Coll (IA)
Grove City Coll (PA)
Guilford Coll (NC)
Gustavus Adolphus Coll (MN)
Hamilton Coll (NY)
Hamline U (MN)
Hampden-Sydney Coll (VA)
Hampshire Coll (MA)
Hampton U (VA)
Hanover Coll (IN)
Harding U (AR)
Hardin-Simmons U (TX)
Hartwick Coll (NY)
Harvard U (MA)
Harvey Mudd Coll (CA)
Haverford Coll (PA)
Heidelberg U (OH)
Henderson State U (AR)
Hendrix Coll (AR)
Hillsdale Coll (MI)
Hiram Coll (OH)
Hofstra U (NY)

Hollins U (VA)
Hope Coll (MI)
Houghton Coll (NY)
Houston Baptist U (TX)
Humboldt State U (CA)
Hunter Coll of the City U of New York (NY)
Huntington U (IN)
Idaho State U (ID)
Illinois Coll (IL)
Illinois Inst of Technology (IL)
Illinois State U (IL)
Illinois Wesleyan U (IL)
Indiana U Bloomington (IN)
Indiana U of Pennsylvania (PA)
Indiana U–Purdue U Fort Wayne (IN)
Indiana U–Purdue U Indianapolis (IN)
Indiana U South Bend (IN)
Iona Coll (NY)
Iowa State U of Science and Technology (IA)
Ithaca Coll (NY)
Jackson State U (MS)
Jacksonville State U (AL)
Jacksonville U (FL)
James Madison U (VA)
John Carroll U (OH)
The Johns Hopkins U (MD)
Juniata Coll (PA)
Kalamazoo Coll (MI)
Kansas State U (KS)
Kent State U (OH)
Kentucky Wesleyan Coll (KY)
Kenyon Coll (OH)
Kettering U (MI)
King Coll (TN)
Knox Coll (IL)
Kutztown U of Pennsylvania (PA)
Lafayette Coll (PA)
Lake Forest Coll (IL)
Lakehead U (ON, Canada)
Lamar U (TX)
Lane Coll (TN)
Laurentian U (ON, Canada)
Lawrence Technological U (MI)
Lawrence U (WI)
Lebanon Valley Coll (PA)
Lehigh U (PA)
Lehman Coll of the City U of New York (NY)
Le Moyne Coll (NY)
Lewis & Clark Coll (OR)
Lewis U (IL)
Lincoln U (MO)
Lincoln U (PA)
Linfield Coll (OR)
Lipscomb U (TN)
Lock Haven U of Pennsylvania (PA)
Long Island U, Brooklyn Campus (NY)
Long Island U, C.W. Post Campus (NY)
Longwood U (VA)
Loras Coll (IA)
Louisiana Coll (LA)
Louisiana State U and Ag and Mech Coll (LA)
Louisiana State U in Shreveport (LA)
Louisiana Tech U (LA)
Loyola Marymount U (CA)
Loyola U Chicago (IL)
Loyola U Maryland (MD)
Loyola U New Orleans (LA)
Luther Coll (IA)
Lycoming Coll (PA)
Lynchburg Coll (VA)
Macalester Coll (MN)
Manchester Coll (IN)
Manhattan Coll (NY)
Manhattanville Coll (NY)
Mansfield U of Pennsylvania (PA)
Marietta Coll (OH)
Marlboro Coll (VT)
Marquette U (WI)
Marshall U (WV)
Mary Baldwin Coll (VA)
Massachusetts Coll of Liberal Arts (MA)
Massachusetts Inst of Technology (MA)
McDaniel Coll (MD)
McMurry U (TX)
McNeese State U (LA)
Memorial U of Newfoundland (NL, Canada)
Mercer U (GA)
Messiah Coll (PA)
Metropolitan State Coll of Denver (CO)
Miami U (OH)
Miami U Hamilton (OH)
Michigan State U (MI)
Michigan Technological U (MI)
Middlebury Coll (VT)
Middle Tennessee State U (TN)
Midwestern State U (TX)
Millersville U of Pennsylvania (PA)
Millikin U (IL)
Millsaps Coll (MS)
Minnesota State U Mankato (MN)
Minnesota State U Moorhead (MN)
Minot State U (ND)
Mississippi Coll (MS)
Mississippi State U (MS)
Missouri Southern State U (MO)
Missouri State U (MO)
Missouri U of Science and Technology (MO)
Monmouth Coll (IL)
Montana State U (MT)
Montclair State U (NJ)
Moravian Coll (PA)
Morehead State U (KY)
Morehouse Coll (GA)
Morningside Coll (IA)
Mount Allison U (NB, Canada)
Mount Holyoke Coll (MA)
Mount Vernon Nazarene U (OH)
Muhlenberg Coll (PA)
Murray State U (KY)
Nebraska Wesleyan U (NE)
New Coll of Florida (FL)
New Jersey City U (NJ)
New Jersey Inst of Technology (NJ)
New Mexico Highlands U (NM)
New Mexico Inst of Mining and Technology (NM)
New Mexico State U (NM)
New York Inst of Technology (NY)
New York U (NY)
Norfolk State U (VA)
North Carolina Central U (NC)
North Carolina State U (NC)
North Central Coll (IL)
North Dakota State U (ND)
Northeastern Illinois U (IL)
Northeastern U (MA)
Northern Arizona U (AZ)
Northern Kentucky U (KY)
Northern Michigan U (MI)
North Georgia Coll & State U (GA)
Northwestern Oklahoma State U (OK)
Northwestern State U of Louisiana (LA)
Northwest Missouri State U (MO)
Northwest Nazarene U (ID)
Oakland U (MI)
Oberlin Coll (OH)
Occidental Coll (CA)
Oglethorpe U (GA)
Ohio Northern U (OH)
The Ohio State U (OH)
Ohio U (OH)
Ohio Wesleyan U (OH)
Oklahoma Baptist U (OK)
Oklahoma City U (OK)
Oklahoma State U (OK)
Old Dominion U (VA)
Oral Roberts U (OK)
Oregon State U (OR)
Ouachita Baptist U (AR)
Pacific Lutheran U (WA)
Pacific Union Coll (CA)
Penn State Abington (PA)
Penn State Altoona (PA)
Penn State Beaver (PA)
Penn State Berks (PA)
Penn State Brandywine (PA)
Penn State DuBois (PA)
Penn State Erie, The Behrend Coll (PA)
Penn State Fayette, The Eberly Campus (PA)
Penn State Greater Allegheny (PA)
Penn State Hazleton (PA)
Penn State Lehigh Valley (PA)
Penn State Mont Alto (PA)
Penn State New Kensington (PA)
Penn State Schuylkill (PA)
Penn State Shenango (PA)
Penn State U Park (PA)
Penn State Wilkes-Barre (PA)
Penn State Worthington Scranton (PA)
Penn State York (PA)
Piedmont Coll (GA)
Pittsburg State U (KS)
Pitzer Coll (CA)
Polytechnic Inst of NYU (NY)
Pomona Coll (CA)
Pontifical Catholic U of Puerto Rico (PR)
Portland State U (OR)
Prairie View A&M U (TX)
Presbyterian Coll (SC)
Princeton U (NJ)
Principia Coll (IL)
Purchase Coll, State U of New York (NY)
Purdue U (IN)
Purdue U Calumet (IN)
Queens Coll of the City U of New York (NY)
Queen's U at Kingston (ON, Canada)
Radford U (VA)
Ramapo Coll of New Jersey (NJ)
Randolph Coll (VA)
Randolph-Macon Coll (VA)
Redeemer U Coll (ON, Canada)
Reed Coll (OR)
Rensselaer Polytechnic Inst (NY)
Rhode Island Coll (RI)
Rhodes Coll (TN)
Rice U (TX)
The Richard Stockton Coll of New Jersey (NJ)
Rider U (NJ)
Roanoke Coll (VA)
Roberts Wesleyan Coll (NY)
Rockhurst U (MO)
Rollins Coll (FL)
Rose-Hulman Inst of Technology (IN)
Rowan U (NJ)
Royal Military Coll of Canada (ON, Canada)
Rutgers, The State U of New Jersey, Camden (NJ)
Rutgers, The State U of New Jersey, Newark (NJ)
Rutgers, The State U of New Jersey, New Brunswick (NJ)
Saginaw Valley State U (MI)
St. Ambrose U (IA)
Saint Anselm Coll (NH)
St. Bonaventure U (NY)
St. Catherine U (MN)
St. Cloud State U (MN)
St. Francis Xavier U (NS, Canada)
St. John Fisher Coll (NY)
Saint John's U (MN)
St. John's U (NY)
Saint Joseph's U (PA)
St. Lawrence U (NY)
Saint Louis U (MO)
Saint Mary's Coll of California (CA)
St. Mary's Coll of Maryland (MD)
St. Mary's U (TX)
Saint Michael's Coll (VT)
St. Norbert Coll (WI)
St. Olaf Coll (MN)
Saint Vincent Coll (PA)
Salisbury U (MD)
Samford U (AL)
Sam Houston State U (TX)
San Diego State U (CA)
San Francisco State U (CA)
San Jose State U (CA)
Santa Clara U (CA)
Sarah Lawrence Coll (NY)
Scripps Coll (CA)
Seattle Pacific U (WA)
Seattle U (WA)
Seton Hall U (NJ)
Sewanee: The U of the South (TN)
Shaw U (NC)
Shippensburg U of Pennsylvania (PA)
Siena Coll (NY)
Simmons Coll (MA)
Simon Fraser U (BC, Canada)
Simpson Coll (IA)
Skidmore Coll (NY)
Slippery Rock U of Pennsylvania (PA)
Smith Coll (MA)
Sonoma State U (CA)
South Carolina State U (SC)
South Dakota School of Mines and Technology (SD)
South Dakota State U (SD)
Southeastern Louisiana U (LA)
Southeast Missouri State U (MO)
Southern Adventist U (TN)
Southern Connecticut State U (CT)
Southern Illinois U Carbondale (IL)
Southern Illinois U Edwardsville (IL)
Southern Methodist U (TX)
Southern Oregon U (OR)
Southern Polytechnic State U (GA)
Southern U and Ag and Mech Coll (LA)
Southwestern Coll (KS)
Southwestern Oklahoma State U (OK)
Southwestern U (TX)
Spelman Coll (GA)
Spring Arbor U (MI)
Stanford U (CA)
State U of New York at Binghamton (NY)
State U of New York at Fredonia (NY)
State U of New York at New Paltz (NY)
State U of New York at Oswego (NY)
State U of New York at Plattsburgh (NY)
State U of New York Coll at Cortland (NY)
State U of New York Coll at Geneseo (NY)
State U of New York Coll at Oneonta (NY)
State U of New York Coll at Potsdam (NY)
Stephen F. Austin State U (TX)
Stetson U (FL)
Stevens Inst of Technology (NJ)
Stonehill Coll (MA)
Stony Brook U, State U of New York (NY)
Suffolk U (MA)
Susquehanna U (PA)
Swarthmore Coll (PA)
Sweet Briar Coll (VA)
Syracuse U (NY)
Tarleton State U (TX)
Taylor U (IN)
Temple U (PA)
Tennessee Technological U (TN)
Texas A&M U (TX)
Texas A&M U–Commerce (TX)
Texas A&M U–Kingsville (TX)
Texas Christian U (TX)
Texas Lutheran U (TX)
Texas Southern U (TX)
Texas State U–San Marcos (TX)
Texas Tech U (TX)
Thiel Coll (PA)
Thomas More Coll (KY)
Thompson Rivers U (BC, Canada)
Towson U (MD)
Transylvania U (KY)
Trent U (ON, Canada)
Trevecca Nazarene U (TN)
Trinity Coll (CT)
Trinity U (TX)
Truman State U (MO)
Tufts U (MA)
Tulane U (LA)
Tuskegee U (AL)
Union Coll (NE)
Union Coll (NY)
Union U (TN)
United States Air Force Acad (CO)
United States Military Acad (NY)
United States Naval Acad (MD)
Universidad de las Américas–Puebla (Mexico)
U at Albany, State U of New York (NY)
U at Buffalo, the State U of New York (NY)
The U of Akron (OH)
The U of Alabama (AL)
The U of Alabama at Birmingham (AL)
The U of Alabama in Huntsville (AL)
U of Alaska Fairbanks (AK)
U of Alberta (AB, Canada)
The U of Arizona (AZ)
U of Arkansas (AR)
U of Arkansas at Little Rock (AR)
U of Arkansas at Pine Bluff (AR)
The U of British Columbia (BC, Canada)
The U of British Columbia–Okanagan (BC, Canada)
U of California, Berkeley (CA)
U of California, Davis (CA)
U of California, Irvine (CA)
U of California, Los Angeles (CA)
U of California, Merced (CA)
U of California, Riverside (CA)
U of California, San Diego (CA)
U of California, Santa Barbara (CA)
U of California, Santa Cruz (CA)
U of Central Florida (FL)
U of Central Missouri (MO)
U of Central Oklahoma (OK)
U of Chicago (IL)
U of Cincinnati (OH)
U of Colorado at Boulder (CO)
U of Colorado at Colorado Springs (CO)
U of Colorado Denver (CO)
U of Connecticut (CT)
U of Dallas (TX)
U of Dayton (OH)
U of Delaware (DE)
U of Denver (CO)
U of Evansville (IN)
U of Florida (FL)
U of Georgia (GA)
U of Guelph (ON, Canada)
U of Hartford (CT)
U of Hawaii at Hilo (HI)
U of Hawaii at Manoa (HI)
U of Houston (TX)
U of Idaho (ID)
U of Illinois at Chicago (IL)
U of Illinois at Urbana–Champaign (IL)
U of Indianapolis (IN)
The U of Iowa (IA)
The U of Kansas (KS)
U of Kentucky (KY)
U of King's Coll (NS, Canada)
U of La Verne (CA)
U of Lethbridge (AB, Canada)
U of Louisville (KY)
U of Maine (ME)
U of Manitoba (MB, Canada)
U of Maryland, Baltimore County (MD)
U of Maryland, Coll Park (MD)
U of Mary Washington (VA)
U of Massachusetts Amherst (MA)
U of Massachusetts Boston (MA)
U of Massachusetts Dartmouth (MA)
U of Massachusetts Lowell (MA)
U of Memphis (TN)
U of Miami (FL)
U of Michigan (MI)
U of Michigan–Dearborn (MI)
U of Michigan–Flint (MI)
U of Minnesota, Duluth (MN)
U of Minnesota, Twin Cities Campus (MN)
U of Mississippi (MS)
U of Missouri (MO)
U of Missouri–Kansas City (MO)
U of Missouri–St. Louis (MO)
U of Mount Union (OH)
U of Nebraska at Kearney (NE)
U of Nebraska at Omaha (NE)
U of Nebraska–Lincoln (NE)
U of Nevada, Las Vegas (NV)
U of Nevada, Reno (NV)
U of New Brunswick Fredericton (NB, Canada)
U of New Hampshire (NH)
U of New Mexico (NM)
U of New Orleans (LA)
U of North Alabama (AL)
The U of North Carolina at Asheville (NC)
The U of North Carolina at Chapel Hill (NC)
The U of North Carolina at Charlotte (NC)
The U of North Carolina at Greensboro (NC)
The U of North Carolina at Pembroke (NC)
The U of North Carolina Wilmington (NC)
U of North Dakota (ND)
U of Northern Colorado (CO)
U of North Florida (FL)
U of North Texas (TX)
U of Notre Dame (IN)
U of Oklahoma (OK)
U of Oregon (OR)
U of Ottawa (ON, Canada)
U of Pennsylvania (PA)
U of Pittsburgh (PA)
U of Portland (OR)
U of Puerto Rico, Río Piedras (PR)
U of Puget Sound (WA)
U of Redlands (CA)
U of Regina (SK, Canada)
U of Rhode Island (RI)
U of Richmond (VA)
U of Rochester (NY)
U of St. Thomas (MN)
U of San Diego (CA)
U of San Francisco (CA)
U of Saskatchewan (SK, Canada)
U of Science and Arts of Oklahoma (OK)
The U of Scranton (PA)
U of South Alabama (AL)
U of South Carolina (SC)
The U of South Dakota (SD)
U of Southern California (CA)
U of Southern Maine (ME)
U of Southern Mississippi (MS)
U of South Florida (FL)
The U of Tennessee (TN)
The U of Tennessee at Chattanooga (TN)
The U of Texas at Arlington (TX)
The U of Texas at Austin (TX)
The U of Texas at Brownsville (TX)
The U of Texas at Dallas (TX)
The U of Texas at El Paso (TX)
The U of Texas at San Antonio (TX)
The U of Texas–Pan American (TX)
U of the Cumberlands (KY)
U of the District of Columbia (DC)
U of the Pacific (CA)
U of the Sciences in Philadelphia (PA)
The U of Toledo (OH)
U of Tulsa (OK)
U of Utah (UT)
U of Vermont (VT)
U of Virginia (VA)
U of Washington (WA)
U of Waterloo (ON, Canada)
The U of Western Ontario (ON, Canada)
U of West Florida (FL)

INDEXES

U of West Georgia (GA)
U of Windsor (ON, Canada)
U of Wisconsin–Eau Claire (WI)
U of Wisconsin–La Crosse (WI)
U of Wisconsin–Milwaukee (WI)
U of Wisconsin–Oshkosh (WI)
U of Wisconsin–Parkside (WI)
U of Wisconsin–River Falls (WI)
U of Wisconsin–Stevens Point (WI)
U of Wisconsin–Whitewater (WI)
U of Wyoming (WY)
Ursinus Coll (PA)
Utah State U (UT)
Utah Valley U (UT)
Utica Coll (NY)
Valdosta State U (GA)
Valparaiso U (IN)
Vanderbilt U (TN)
Vassar Coll (NY)
Villanova U (PA)
Virginia Commonwealth U (VA)
Virginia Military Inst (VA)
Virginia Polytechnic Inst and State U (VA)
Virginia State U (VA)
Wabash Coll (IN)
Wagner Coll (NY)
Wake Forest U (NC)
Wartburg Coll (IA)
Washburn U (KS)
Washington & Jefferson Coll (PA)
Washington and Lee U (VA)
Washington Coll (MD)
Washington State U (WA)
Washington U in St. Louis (MO)
Wayne State U (MI)
Weber State U (UT)
Wellesley Coll (MA)
Wells Coll (NY)
Wesleyan Coll (GA)
Wesleyan U (CT)
West Chester U of Pennsylvania (PA)
Western Illinois U (IL)
Western Kentucky U (KY)
Western Michigan U (MI)
Western State Coll of Colorado (CO)
Western Washington U (WA)
Westminster Coll (MO)
Westminster Coll (UT)
Westmont Coll (CA)
West Virginia U (WV)
West Virginia Wesleyan Coll (WV)
Wheaton Coll (IL)
Wheaton Coll (MA)
Wheeling Jesuit U (WV)
Whitman Coll (WA)
Whittier Coll (CA)
Wichita State U (KS)
Widener U (PA)
Wilfrid Laurier U (ON, Canada)
Willamette U (OR)
William Jewell Coll (MO)
Williams Coll (MA)
Winona State U (MN)
Wittenberg U (OH)
Wofford Coll (SC)
Worcester Polytechnic Inst (MA)
Xavier U (OH)
Xavier U of Louisiana (LA)
Yale U (CT)
Yeshiva U (NY)
York Coll of the City U of New York (NY)
York U (ON, Canada)
Youngstown State U (OH)

PHYSICS RELATED

Angelo State U (TX)
Arcadia U (PA)
Bridgewater Coll (VA)
Bridgewater State Coll (MA)
Brigham Young U (UT)
California State U, Chico (CA)
Carson-Newman Coll (TN)
The Coll at Brockport, State U of New York (NY)
Coll of Saint Benedict (MN)
The Coll of Wooster (OH)
Drexel U (PA)
Embry-Riddle Aeronautical U (AZ)
Embry-Riddle Aeronautical U (FL)
Florida Inst of Technology (FL)
Fort Lewis Coll (CO)
Hampden-Sydney Coll (VA)
Indiana U of Pennsylvania (PA)
Lawrence Technological U (MI)
Linfield Coll (OR)
New Jersey Inst of Technology (NJ)
North Carolina State U (NC)
Ohio Northern U (OH)
Pittsburg State U (KS)
Presbyterian Coll (SC)
Rensselaer Polytechnic Inst (NY)
Rutgers, The State U of New Jersey, Newark (NJ)
St. Bonaventure U (NY)
Saint John's U (MN)
Southern Arkansas U–Magnolia (AR)
Spring Arbor U (MI)
U of Alaska Fairbanks (AK)
U of California, Davis (CA)
U of Nevada, Las Vegas (NV)
U of Northern Iowa (IA)
U of North Texas (TX)
U of Notre Dame (IN)
U of Puerto Rico at Humacao (PR)
U of Puerto Rico at Utuado (PR)
U of Regina (SK, Canada)
U of Rochester (NY)
The U of Western Ontario (ON, Canada)
Whitman Coll (WA)
Wright State U (OH)

PHYSICS TEACHER EDUCATION

Alma Coll (MI)
Anderson U (IN)
Appalachian State U (NC)
Arkansas State U—Jonesboro (AR)
Auburn U (AL)
Bethel U (MN)
Bethune-Cookman U (FL)
Bishop's U (QC, Canada)
Bowling Green State U (OH)
Bradley U (IL)
Bridgewater Coll (VA)
Brigham Young U–Hawaii (HI)
Brooklyn Coll of the City U of New York (NY)
Buena Vista U (IA)
Cedarville U (OH)
Central Michigan U (MI)
Christian Brothers U (TN)
City Coll of the City U of New York (NY)
The Coll at Brockport, State U of New York (NY)
The Coll of New Jersey (NJ)
Colorado State U (CO)
Concordia Coll (MN)
Cornell U (NY)
Delaware State U (DE)
DePaul U (IL)
East Central U (OK)
Eastern Michigan U (MI)
Eastern Nazarene Coll (MA)
Eastern Washington U (WA)
Elmhurst Coll (IL)
Florida Inst of Technology (FL)
Grambling State U (LA)
Grand Valley State U (MI)
Greenville Coll (IL)
Gustavus Adolphus Coll (MN)
Hofstra U (NY)
Hope Coll (MI)
Husson U (ME)
Indiana U Bloomington (IN)
Indiana U–Purdue U Fort Wayne (IN)
Indiana U South Bend (IN)
Ithaca Coll (NY)
Juniata Coll (PA)
King Coll (TN)
Le Moyne Coll (NY)
Lincoln U (MO)
Lipscomb U (TN)
Louisiana State U in Shreveport (LA)
Louisiana Tech U (LA)
Mansfield U of Pennsylvania (PA)
Maryville Coll (TN)
Miami Dade Coll (FL)
Miami U (OH)
Miami U Hamilton (OH)
Michigan State U (MI)
Millersville U of Pennsylvania (PA)
Minnesota State U Moorhead (MN)
Minot State U (ND)
Missouri State U (MO)
Moravian Coll (PA)
Morningside Coll (IA)
Mount Vernon Nazarene U (OH)
Murray State U (KY)
New York Inst of Technology (NY)
North Carolina Central U (NC)
North Carolina State U (NC)
North Dakota State U (ND)
Northeastern State U (OK)
Northern Arizona U (AZ)
Northern Michigan U (MI)
Northwestern State U of Louisiana (LA)
Northwest Missouri State U (MO)
Ohio Dominican U (OH)
Ohio Northern U (OH)
Ohio Wesleyan U (OH)
Old Dominion U (VA)
Pittsburg State U (KS)
Queens Coll of the City U of New York (NY)
Rhode Island Coll (RI)
Roberts Wesleyan Coll (NY)
Saginaw Valley State U (MI)
St. Ambrose U (IA)
St. John Fisher Coll (NY)
St. John's U (NY)
Saint Mary's U of Minnesota (MN)
Saint Vincent Coll (PA)
Shawnee State U (OH)
Southern U and Ag and Mech Coll (LA)
State U of New York at New Paltz (NY)
State U of New York Coll at Cortland (NY)
State U of New York Coll at Oneonta (NY)
State U of New York Coll at Potsdam (NY)
Syracuse U (NY)
Trevecca Nazarene U (TN)
Union Coll (NE)
The U of Arizona (AZ)
U of California, San Diego (CA)
U of Central Missouri (MO)
U of Delaware (DE)
U of Evansville (IN)
U of Illinois at Chicago (IL)
U of Illinois at Urbana–Champaign (IL)
U of Maryland, Baltimore County (MD)
U of Michigan–Flint (MI)
U of Missouri (MO)
U of Missouri–St. Louis (MO)
U of Nebraska–Lincoln (NE)
U of Regina (SK, Canada)
U of Rio Grande (OH)
U of St. Thomas (MN)
The U of South Dakota (SD)
U of Waterloo (ON, Canada)
U of West Georgia (GA)
U of Windsor (ON, Canada)
U of Wisconsin–River Falls (WI)
Utah State U (UT)
Utica Coll (NY)
Valparaiso U (IN)
Washington State U (WA)
Washington U in St. Louis (MO)
Weber State U (UT)
Western Michigan U (MI)
Wheeling Jesuit U (WV)
William Jewell Coll (MO)
Xavier U (OH)
York U (ON, Canada)

PHYSIOLOGICAL PSYCHOLOGY/ PSYCHOBIOLOGY

Albright Coll (PA)
Arcadia U (PA)
Averett U (VA)
Carnegie Mellon U (PA)
Claremont McKenna Coll (CA)
Earlham Coll (IN)
Florida Atlantic U (FL)
Holy Family U (PA)
Holy Names U (CA)
The Johns Hopkins U (MD)
La Sierra U (CA)
Lebanon Valley Coll (PA)
Lincoln U (PA)
Mills Coll (CA)
Mount Allison U (NB, Canada)
Northwest Missouri State U (MO)
Oberlin Coll (OH)
Occidental Coll (CA)
Quinnipiac U (CT)
Ripon Coll (WI)
Saint Mary's Coll of California (CA)
Scripps Coll (CA)
Simmons Coll (MA)
Southern Adventist U (TN)
State U of New York at Binghamton (NY)
Swarthmore Coll (PA)
U of California, Los Angeles (CA)
U of Colorado Denver (CO)
U of Michigan (MI)
U of New Brunswick Fredericton (NB, Canada)
U of New England (ME)
U of St. Thomas (TX)
The U of Western Ontario (ON, Canada)
Vassar Coll (NY)
Washington Coll (MD)
Wheaton Coll (MA)
Wilson Coll (PA)
York Coll (NE)

PHYSIOLOGY

Brigham Young U (UT)
California State U, Long Beach (CA)
Michigan State U (MI)
Northern Arizona U (AZ)
Northern Michigan U (MI)
Oklahoma Baptist U (OK)
Oklahoma State U (OK)
San Jose State U (CA)
Southern Illinois U Carbondale (IL)
U of Alberta (AB, Canada)
The U of British Columbia (BC, Canada)
U of California, Los Angeles (CA)
U of California, Santa Barbara (CA)
U of Colorado at Boulder (CO)
U of Illinois at Urbana–Champaign (IL)
U of Oregon (OR)
U of Ottawa (ON, Canada)
U of Saskatchewan (SK, Canada)
The U of Western Ontario (ON, Canada)
U of Wyoming (WY)

PIANO AND ORGAN

Abilene Christian U (TX)
Acadia U (NS, Canada)
Andrews U (MI)
Augustana Coll (IL)
Baldwin-Wallace Coll (OH)
Baptist Bible Coll of Pennsylvania (PA)
Bard Coll (NY)
Barry U (FL)
Belmont U (TN)
Bennington Coll (VT)
Berklee Coll of Music (MA)
Birmingham-Southern Coll (AL)
Bob Jones U (SC)
The Boston Conservatory (MA)
Boston U (MA)
Bowling Green State U (OH)
Brigham Young U (UT)
Brigham Young U–Hawaii (HI)
Butler U (IN)
California State U, Chico (CA)
Calvary Bible Coll and Theological Sem (MO)
Calvin Coll (MI)
Campbellsville U (KY)
Capital U (OH)
Carnegie Mellon U (PA)
Carson-Newman Coll (TN)
Catawba Coll (NC)
The Catholic U of America (DC)
Cincinnati Christian U (OH)
Coker Coll (SC)
The Colburn School Conservatory of Music (CA)
Columbia Coll (SC)
Concordia U Chicago (IL)
Converse Coll (SC)
Cornish Coll of the Arts (WA)
Dallas Baptist U (TX)
Dordt Coll (IA)
Drake U (IA)
East Central U (OK)
Eastern Nazarene Coll (MA)
East Texas Baptist U (TX)
Florida State U (FL)
Furman U (SC)
Grace Coll (IN)
Hannibal-LaGrange Coll (MO)
Hardin-Simmons U (TX)
Heidelberg U (OH)
Hillsdale Free Will Baptist Coll (OK)
Hope Coll (MI)
Houghton Coll (NY)
Illinois Wesleyan U (IL)
Indiana U–Purdue U Fort Wayne (IN)
Inter American U of Puerto Rico, San Germán Campus (PR)
Ithaca Coll (NY)
Kent State U (OH)
Lamar U (TX)
Lawrence U (WI)
Lee U (TN)
Lincoln Christian U (IL)
Lipscomb U (TN)
Louisiana Coll (LA)
Manhattan School of Music (NY)
Mannes Coll The New School for Music (NY)
Maranatha Baptist Bible Coll (WI)
Maryville Coll (TN)
The Master's Coll and Sem (CA)
Memorial U of Newfoundland (NL, Canada)
Millikin U (IL)
Minnesota State U Mankato (MN)
Minnesota State U Moorhead (MN)
Mississippi Coll (MS)
Mount Allison U (NB, Canada)
Newberry Coll (SC)
New England Conservatory of Music (MA)
The New School for Jazz and Contemporary Music (NY)
Northwestern Coll (MN)
Notre Dame de Namur U (CA)
Nyack Coll (NY)
Oakland U (MI)
Oberlin Coll (OH)
The Ohio State U (OH)
Ohio U (OH)
Oklahoma City U (OK)
Oral Roberts U (OK)
Ouachita Baptist U (AR)
Pacific Union Coll (CA)
Peabody Conservatory of The Johns Hopkins U (MD)
Queens U of Charlotte (NC)
Rider U (NJ)
Roberts Wesleyan Coll (NY)
Roosevelt U (IL)
St. Cloud State U (MN)
Samford U (AL)
San Francisco Conservatory of Music (CA)
Sarah Lawrence Coll (NY)
Seton Hill U (PA)
Shenandoah U (VA)
Shorter U (GA)
Southeastern U (FL)
Southern Methodist U (TX)
Southwestern Oklahoma State U (OK)
Spring Arbor U (MI)
State U of New York at Fredonia (NY)
State U of New York at New Paltz (NY)
Stetson U (FL)
Tabor Coll (KS)
Texas A&M U–Commerce (TX)
Texas Christian U (TX)
Trinity Christian Coll (IL)
Truman State U (MO)
Union U (TN)
U of Alberta (AB, Canada)
The U of British Columbia (BC, Canada)
U of Central Oklahoma (OK)
U of Cincinnati (OH)
U of Delaware (DE)
The U of Iowa (IA)
The U of Kansas (KS)
U of Miami (FL)
U of Nebraska at Omaha (NE)
U of Redlands (CA)
U of Southern California (CA)
The U of Tennessee at Martin (TN)
U of the Pacific (CA)
U of Tulsa (OK)
U of Washington (WA)
The U of Western Ontario (ON, Canada)
Valparaiso U (IN)
Vanderbilt U (TN)
Weber State U (UT)
Willamette U (OR)
Xavier U of Louisiana (LA)
York U (ON, Canada)

PLANETARY ASTRONOMY AND SCIENCE

California Inst of Technology (CA)
Florida Inst of Technology (FL)
U of Waterloo (ON, Canada)
The U of Western Ontario (ON, Canada)

PLANT MOLECULAR BIOLOGY

Pittsburg State U (KS)
U of Illinois at Urbana–Champaign (IL)

PLANT NURSERY MANAGEMENT

Colorado State U (CO)

PLANT PATHOLOGY/ PHYTOPATHOLOGY

Cornell U (NY)
Michigan State U (MI)
New Mexico State U (NM)
State U of New York Coll of Environmental Science and Forestry (NY)
U of Florida (FL)

PLANT PHYSIOLOGY

Pittsburg State U (KS)
State U of New York Coll of Environmental Science and Forestry (NY)

PLANT PROTECTION AND INTEGRATED PEST MANAGEMENT

California State Polytechnic U, Pomona (CA)
Iowa State U of Science and Technology (IA)
Mississippi State U (MS)
State U of New York Coll of Environmental Science and Forestry (NY)
U of Delaware (DE)

U of Hawaii at Manoa (HI)
U of Illinois at Urbana–Champaign (IL)
U of Nebraska–Lincoln (NE)
The U of Tennessee (TN)
Washington State U (WA)

PLANT SCIENCES

Arkansas State U—Jonesboro (AR)
Auburn U (AL)
California State U, Fresno (CA)
Cornell U (NY)
Lakehead U (ON, Canada)
Louisiana State U and Ag and Mech Coll (LA)
Louisiana Tech U (LA)
Lubbock Christian U (TX)
Middle Tennessee State U (TN)
Montana State U (MT)
Nova Scotia Ag Coll (NS, Canada)
The Ohio State U (OH)
Rutgers, The State U of New Jersey, New Brunswick (NJ)
Southeast Missouri State U (MO)
Southern Illinois U Carbondale (IL)
State U of New York Coll of Environmental Science and Forestry (NY)
Tuskegee U (AL)
U of California, Santa Cruz (CA)
U of Florida (FL)
U of Maine (ME)
U of Maryland, Coll Park (MD)
U of Massachusetts Amherst (MA)
U of Minnesota, Twin Cities Campus (MN)
U of Missouri (MO)
U of New Hampshire (NH)
The U of Tennessee (TN)
U of Vermont (VT)
The U of Western Ontario (ON, Canada)
Utah State U (UT)
Washington State U (WA)

PLANT SCIENCES RELATED

Auburn U (AL)
Sterling Coll (VT)
U of Hawaii at Manoa (HI)
U of Wyoming (WY)
Utah State U (UT)
West Virginia U (WV)

PLASTICS ENGINEERING TECHNOLOGY

Eastern Michigan U (MI)
Ferris State U (MI)
Pittsburg State U (KS)
Shawnee State U (OH)
Western Washington U (WA)

PLAYWRITING AND SCREENWRITING

Bard Coll (NY)
Bennington Coll (VT)
Brigham Young U (UT)
Chapman U (CA)
Columbia Coll Chicago (IL)
Concordia U (QC, Canada)
DePaul U (IL)
Drexel U (PA)
Emerson Coll (MA)
Fordham U (NY)
Loyola Marymount U (CA)
Ohio U (OH)
Purchase Coll, State U of New York (NY)
Sarah Lawrence Coll (NY)
Slippery Rock U of Pennsylvania (PA)
U of Southern California (CA)
York U (ON, Canada)

POLISH

U of Illinois at Chicago (IL)
U of Michigan (MI)
U of Pittsburgh (PA)

POLITICAL COMMUNICATION

Cedarville U (OH)
Emerson Coll (MA)
Nebraska Wesleyan U (NE)

POLITICAL SCIENCE AND GOVERNMENT

Abilene Christian U (TX)
Acadia U (NS, Canada)
Adelphi U (NY)
Agnes Scott Coll (GA)
Alabama Ag and Mech U (AL)
Alabama State U (AL)
Albany State U (GA)
Albertus Magnus Coll (CT)
Albion Coll (MI)
Albright Coll (PA)
Alcorn State U (MS)
Alderson-Broaddus Coll (WV)
Alfred U (NY)
Allegheny Coll (PA)
Alma Coll (MI)
Alvernia U (PA)
Alverno Coll (WI)
American Intl Coll (MA)
American Jewish U (CA)
American Public U System (WV)
American U (DC)
American U of Beirut (Lebanon)
Amherst Coll (MA)
Anderson U (IN)
Andrews U (MI)
Angelo State U (TX)
Appalachian State U (NC)
Aquinas Coll (MI)
Arcadia U (PA)
Arizona State U (AZ)
Arkansas State U—Jonesboro (AR)
Arkansas Tech U (AR)
Armstrong Atlantic State U (GA)
Asbury U (KY)
Ashland U (OH)
Assumption Coll (MA)
Athabasca U (AB, Canada)
Auburn U (AL)
Auburn U Montgomery (AL)
Augsburg Coll (MN)
Augustana Coll (IL)
Augustana Coll (SD)
Aurora U (IL)
Austin Coll (TX)
Austin Peay State U (TN)
Averett U (VA)
Avila U (MO)
Azusa Pacific U (CA)
Baker U (KS)
Baldwin-Wallace Coll (OH)
Ball State U (IN)
Bard Coll (NY)
Bard Coll at Simon's Rock (MA)
Barnard Coll (NY)
Barry U (FL)
Barton Coll (NC)
Bates Coll (ME)
Baylor U (TX)
Belhaven U (MS)
Bellarmine U (KY)
Belmont U (TN)
Beloit Coll (WI)
Bemidji State U (MN)
Benedictine Coll (KS)
Benedictine U (IL)
Bennett Coll for Women (NC)
Bennington Coll (VT)
Berea Coll (KY)
Bernard M. Baruch Coll of the City U of New York (NY)
Berry Coll (GA)
Bethany Coll (KS)
Bethany Coll (WV)
Bethel U (MN)
Bethune-Cookman U (FL)
Birmingham-Southern Coll (AL)
Bishop's U (QC, Canada)
Blackburn Coll (IL)
Black Hills State U (SD)
Bloomfield Coll (NJ)
Bloomsburg U of Pennsylvania (PA)
Bob Jones U (SC)
Boise State U (ID)
Boston Coll (MA)
Boston U (MA)
Bowdoin Coll (ME)
Bowie State U (MD)
Bowling Green State U (OH)
Bradley U (IL)
Brescia U (KY)
Brewton-Parker Coll (GA)
Briar Cliff U (IA)
Bridgewater Coll (VA)
Bridgewater State Coll (MA)
Brigham Young U–Hawaii (HI)
Brock U (ON, Canada)
Brooklyn Coll of the City U of New York (NY)
Bryant U (RI)
Bryn Mawr Coll (PA)
Bucknell U (PA)
Buena Vista U (IA)
Buffalo State Coll, State U of New York (NY)
Butler U (IN)
Cabrini Coll (PA)
California Baptist U (CA)
California Inst of Technology (CA)
California Lutheran U (CA)
California Polytechnic State U, San Luis Obispo (CA)
California State Polytechnic U, Pomona (CA)
California State U, Bakersfield (CA)
California State U, Chico (CA)
California State U, Dominguez Hills (CA)
California State U, East Bay (CA)
California State U, Fresno (CA)
California State U, Fullerton (CA)
California State U, Long Beach (CA)
California State U, Los Angeles (CA)
California State U, Northridge (CA)
California State U, Sacramento (CA)
California State U, San Bernardino (CA)
California State U, San Marcos (CA)
California State U, Stanislaus (CA)
Calumet Coll of Saint Joseph (IN)
Calvin Coll (MI)
Cameron U (OK)
Campbellsville U (KY)
Canisius Coll (NY)
Cape Breton U (NS, Canada)
Capital U (OH)
Carleton Coll (MN)
Carlow U (PA)
Carroll U (WI)
Carson-Newman Coll (TN)
Case Western Reserve U (OH)
Catawba Coll (NC)
The Catholic U of America (DC)
Cedar Crest Coll (PA)
Cedarville U (OH)
Centenary Coll (NJ)
Centenary Coll of Louisiana (LA)
Central Coll (IA)
Central Connecticut State U (CT)
Central Michigan U (MI)
Central State U (OH)
Chapman U (CA)
Chatham U (PA)
Cheyney U of Pennsylvania (PA)
Chowan U (NC)
Christendom Coll (VA)
Christopher Newport U (VA)
The Citadel, The Military Coll of South Carolina (SC)
City Coll of the City U of New York (NY)
Claremont McKenna Coll (CA)
Clarion U of Pennsylvania (PA)
Clark Atlanta U (GA)
Clarkson U (NY)
Clark U (MA)
Clayton State U (GA)
Clemson U (SC)
Cleveland State U (OH)
Coastal Carolina U (SC)
Coker Coll (SC)
Colby Coll (ME)
Colgate U (NY)
The Coll at Brockport, State U of New York (NY)
Coll of Charleston (SC)
The Coll of Idaho (ID)
The Coll of New Jersey (NJ)
The Coll of New Rochelle (NY)
Coll of Notre Dame of Maryland (MD)
Coll of Saint Benedict (MN)
The Coll of Saint Rose (NY)
Coll of Staten Island of the City U of New York (NY)
Coll of the Holy Cross (MA)
The Coll of William and Mary (VA)
The Coll of Wooster (OH)
The Colorado Coll (CO)
Colorado State U (CO)
Colorado State U–Pueblo (CO)
Columbia Coll (MO)
Columbia Coll (SC)
Columbia U (NY)
Columbia U, School of General Studies (NY)
Columbus State U (GA)
Concordia Coll (MN)
Concordia U (CA)
Concordia U (QC, Canada)
Concordia U Chicago (IL)
Concordia U Coll of Alberta (AB, Canada)
Concord U (WV)
Connecticut Coll (CT)
Converse Coll (SC)
Cornell Coll (IA)
Cornell U (NY)
Creighton U (NE)
Culver-Stockton Coll (MO)
Cumberland U (TN)
Curry Coll (MA)
Daemen Coll (NY)
Dallas Baptist U (TX)
Dartmouth Coll (NH)
Davidson Coll (NC)
Delaware State U (DE)
Delta State U (MS)
Denison U (OH)
DePaul U (IL)
DePauw U (IN)
DeSales U (PA)
Dickinson Coll (PA)
Dickinson State U (ND)
Dillard U (LA)
Doane Coll (NE)
Dominican U (IL)
Dominican U of California (CA)
Dordt Coll (IA)
Dowling Coll (NY)
Drake U (IA)
Drew U (NJ)
Drury U (MO)
Duke U (NC)
Duquesne U (PA)
Earlham Coll (IN)
East Carolina U (NC)
East Central U (OK)
Eastern Connecticut State U (CT)
Eastern Illinois U (IL)
Eastern Michigan U (MI)
Eastern New Mexico U (NM)
Eastern Washington U (WA)
East Stroudsburg U of Pennsylvania (PA)
East Tennessee State U (TN)
East Texas Baptist U (TX)
Eckerd Coll (FL)
Edgewood Coll (WI)
Edinboro U of Pennsylvania (PA)
Elizabeth City State U (NC)
Elizabethtown Coll (PA)
Elmhurst Coll (IL)
Elmira Coll (NY)
Elon U (NC)
Emmanuel Coll (MA)
Emory & Henry Coll (VA)
Emory U (GA)
Emporia State U (KS)
Erskine Coll (SC)
Evangel U (MO)
The Evergreen State Coll (WA)
Excelsior Coll (NY)
Fairfield U (CT)
Fairleigh Dickinson U, Coll at Florham (NJ)
Fairleigh Dickinson U, Metropolitan Campus (NJ)
Fairmont State U (WV)
Faulkner U (AL)
Fayetteville State U (NC)
Felician Coll (NJ)
Ferris State U (MI)
Ferrum Coll (VA)
Fisk U (TN)
Fitchburg State Coll (MA)
Flagler Coll (FL)
Florida Atlantic U (FL)
Florida Gulf Coast U (FL)
Florida Intl U (FL)
Florida Southern Coll (FL)
Florida State U (FL)
Fordham U (NY)
Fort Hays State U (KS)
Fort Lewis Coll (CO)
Fort Valley State U (GA)
Framingham State Coll (MA)
Franciscan U of Steubenville (OH)
Francis Marion U (SC)
Franklin & Marshall Coll (PA)
Franklin Coll (IN)
Franklin Pierce U (NH)
Friends U (KS)
Frostburg State U (MD)
Furman U (SC)
Gannon U (PA)
Gardner-Webb U (NC)
Geneva Coll (PA)
George Fox U (OR)
Georgetown Coll (KY)
Georgetown U (DC)
The George Washington U (DC)
Georgia Coll & State U (GA)
Georgia Southern U (GA)
Georgia State U (GA)
Gettysburg Coll (PA)
Gonzaga U (WA)
Gordon Coll (MA)
Goucher Coll (MD)
Grambling State U (LA)
Grand Valley State U (MI)
Grand View U (IA)
Greensboro Coll (NC)
Greenville Coll (IL)
Grinnell Coll (IA)
Grove City Coll (PA)
Guilford Coll (NC)
Gustavus Adolphus Coll (MN)
Hamilton Coll (NY)
Hamline U (MN)
Hampden-Sydney Coll (VA)
Hampshire Coll (MA)
Hampton U (VA)
Hanover Coll (IN)
Harding U (AR)
Hardin-Simmons U (TX)
Hartwick Coll (NY)
Harvard U (MA)
Haverford Coll (PA)
Hawai'i Pacific U (HI)
Heidelberg U (OH)
Henderson State U (AR)
Hendrix Coll (AR)
High Point U (NC)
Hillsdale Coll (MI)
Hiram Coll (OH)
Hofstra U (NY)
Hollins U (VA)
Hood Coll (MD)
Hope Coll (MI)
Houghton Coll (NY)
Houston Baptist U (TX)
Howard Payne U (TX)
Humboldt State U (CA)
Hunter Coll of the City U of New York (NY)
Huntingdon Coll (AL)
Huntington U (IN)
Huston-Tillotson U (TX)
Idaho State U (ID)
Illinois Coll (IL)
Illinois Inst of Technology (IL)
Illinois State U (IL)
Illinois Wesleyan U (IL)
Indiana State U (IN)
Indiana U Bloomington (IN)
Indiana U East (IN)
Indiana U Northwest (IN)
Indiana U of Pennsylvania (PA)
Indiana U–Purdue U Fort Wayne (IN)
Indiana U–Purdue U Indianapolis (IN)
Indiana U South Bend (IN)
Indiana U Southeast (IN)
Indiana Wesleyan U (IN)
Inter American U of Puerto Rico, San Germán Campus (PR)
Iona Coll (NY)
Iowa State U of Science and Technology (IA)
Ithaca Coll (NY)
Jackson State U (MS)
Jacksonville State U (AL)
Jacksonville U (FL)
James Madison U (VA)
John Brown U (AR)
John Cabot U (Italy)
John Carroll U (OH)
John Jay Coll of Criminal Justice of the City U of New York (NY)
The Johns Hopkins U (MD)
Johnson C. Smith U (NC)
Johnson State Coll (VT)
Juniata Coll (PA)
Kalamazoo Coll (MI)
Kansas State U (KS)
Kean U (NJ)
Keene State Coll (NH)
Kennesaw State U (GA)
Kent State U (OH)
Kentucky State U (KY)
Kentucky Wesleyan Coll (KY)
Kenyon Coll (OH)
King Coll (TN)
King's Coll (PA)
Knox Coll (IL)
Kutztown U of Pennsylvania (PA)
Lafayette Coll (PA)
LaGrange Coll (GA)
Lake Erie Coll (OH)
Lake Forest Coll (IL)
Lakehead U (ON, Canada)
Lake Superior State U (MI)
Lamar U (TX)
La Roche Coll (PA)
La Salle U (PA)
Laurentian U (ON, Canada)
Lawrence U (WI)
Lebanon Valley Coll (PA)
Lehigh U (PA)
Lehman Coll of the City U of New York (NY)
Le Moyne Coll (NY)
Lewis & Clark Coll (OR)
Lewis U (IL)
Liberty U (VA)
Lincoln U (MO)
Lincoln U (PA)
Lindenwood U (MO)
Linfield Coll (OR)
Lipscomb U (TN)
Lock Haven U of Pennsylvania (PA)
Long Island U, Brooklyn Campus (NY)
Long Island U, C.W. Post Campus (NY)
Longwood U (VA)
Loras Coll (IA)
Louisiana State U and Ag and Mech Coll (LA)
Louisiana State U in Shreveport (LA)
Louisiana Tech U (LA)
Loyola Marymount U (CA)
Loyola U Chicago (IL)
Loyola U Maryland (MD)
Loyola U New Orleans (LA)

INDEXES

Luther Coll (IA)
Lycoming Coll (PA)
Lynchburg Coll (VA)
Lyon Coll (AR)
Macalester Coll (MN)
Malone U (OH)
Manchester Coll (IN)
Manhattan Coll (NY)
Manhattanville Coll (NY)
Mansfield U of Pennsylvania (PA)
Marian U (IN)
Marian U (WI)
Marietta Coll (OH)
Marist Coll (NY)
Marlboro Coll (VT)
Marquette U (WI)
Marshall U (WV)
Mars Hill Coll (NC)
Mary Baldwin Coll (VA)
Marymount Manhattan Coll (NY)
Marymount U (VA)
Maryville Coll (TN)
Massachusetts Coll of Liberal Arts (MA)
Massachusetts Inst of Technology (MA)
The Master's Coll and Sem (CA)
McDaniel Coll (MD)
McKendree U (IL)
McMurry U (TX)
McNeese State U (LA)
Memorial U of Newfoundland (NL, Canada)
Mercer U (GA)
Mercy Coll (NY)
Mercyhurst Coll (PA)
Meredith Coll (NC)
Merrimack Coll (MA)
Messiah Coll (PA)
Methodist U (NC)
Metropolitan State Coll of Denver (CO)
Miami U (OH)
Miami U Hamilton (OH)
Michigan State U (MI)
Middlebury Coll (VT)
Middle Tennessee State U (TN)
Midwestern State U (TX)
Millersville U of Pennsylvania (PA)
Millikin U (IL)
Millsaps Coll (MS)
Mills Coll (CA)
Minnesota State U Mankato (MN)
Minnesota State U Moorhead (MN)
Mississippi Coll (MS)
Mississippi State U (MS)
Mississippi U for Women (MS)
Mississippi Valley State U (MS)
Missouri Southern State U (MO)
Missouri State U (MO)
Missouri Western State U (MO)
Molloy Coll (NY)
Monmouth Coll (IL)
Monmouth U (NJ)
Montana State U (MT)
Montclair State U (NJ)
Moravian Coll (PA)
Morehead State U (KY)
Morehouse Coll (GA)
Morningside Coll (IA)
Morris Coll (SC)
Mount Allison U (NB, Canada)
Mount Holyoke Coll (MA)
Mount Mercy Coll (IA)
Mount Saint Mary Coll (NY)
Mount St. Mary's Coll (CA)
Mount St. Mary's U (MD)
Muhlenberg Coll (PA)
Murray State U (KY)
Nazareth Coll of Rochester (NY)
Nebraska Wesleyan U (NE)
Neumann U (PA)
Newberry Coll (SC)
New Coll of Florida (FL)
New England Coll (NH)
New Jersey City U (NJ)
New Mexico Highlands U (NM)
New Mexico State U (NM)
New York Inst of Technology (NY)
New York U (NY)
Niagara U (NY)
Nicholls State U (LA)
Norfolk State U (VA)
North Carolina Central U (NC)
North Carolina State U (NC)
North Central Coll (IL)
North Dakota State U (ND)
Northeastern Illinois U (IL)
Northeastern State U (OK)
Northeastern U (MA)
Northern Arizona U (AZ)
Northern Kentucky U (KY)
Northern Michigan U (MI)
Northern State U (SD)
North Georgia Coll & State U (GA)
Northwestern Coll (IA)
Northwestern Oklahoma State U (OK)
Northwestern State U of Louisiana (LA)
Northwest Missouri State U (MO)
Northwest Nazarene U (ID)
Northwest U (WA)
Notre Dame de Namur U (CA)
Oakland U (MI)
Oberlin Coll (OH)
Occidental Coll (CA)
Oglethorpe U (GA)
Ohio Dominican U (OH)
Ohio Northern U (OH)
The Ohio State U (OH)
Ohio U (OH)
Ohio Wesleyan U (OH)
Oklahoma Baptist U (OK)
Oklahoma City U (OK)
Oklahoma State U (OK)
Oklahoma Wesleyan U (OK)
Old Dominion U (VA)
Oral Roberts U (OK)
Oregon State U (OR)
Ouachita Baptist U (AR)
Our Lady of the Lake U of San Antonio (TX)
Pace U (NY)
Pacific Lutheran U (WA)
Pacific Union Coll (CA)
Park U (MO)
Patrick Henry Coll (VA)
Penn State Abington (PA)
Penn State Altoona (PA)
Penn State Beaver (PA)
Penn State Berks (PA)
Penn State Brandywine (PA)
Penn State DuBois (PA)
Penn State Erie, The Behrend Coll (PA)
Penn State Fayette, The Eberly Campus (PA)
Penn State Greater Allegheny (PA)
Penn State Hazleton (PA)
Penn State Lehigh Valley (PA)
Penn State Mont Alto (PA)
Penn State New Kensington (PA)
Penn State Schuylkill (PA)
Penn State Shenango (PA)
Penn State U Park (PA)
Penn State Wilkes-Barre (PA)
Penn State Worthington Scranton (PA)
Penn State York (PA)
Pepperdine U, Malibu (CA)
Piedmont Coll (GA)
Pittsburg State U (KS)
Pitzer Coll (CA)
Plymouth State U (NH)
Point Park U (PA)
Pomona Coll (CA)
Pontifical Catholic U of Puerto Rico (PR)
Portland State U (OR)
Prairie View A&M U (TX)
Presbyterian Coll (SC)
Prescott Coll (AZ)
Princeton U (NJ)
Principia Coll (IL)
Providence Coll (RI)
Purchase Coll, State U of New York (NY)
Purdue U (IN)
Purdue U Calumet (IN)
Queens Coll of the City U of New York (NY)
Queen's U at Kingston (ON, Canada)
Queens U of Charlotte (NC)
Quincy U (IL)
Quinnipiac U (CT)
Radford U (VA)
Ramapo Coll of New Jersey (NJ)
Randolph Coll (VA)
Randolph-Macon Coll (VA)
Redeemer U Coll (ON, Canada)
Reed Coll (OR)
Regis Coll (MA)
Rhode Island Coll (RI)
Rhodes Coll (TN)
Rice U (TX)
The Richard Stockton Coll of New Jersey (NJ)
Rider U (NJ)
Ripon Coll (WI)
Rivier Coll (NH)
Roanoke Coll (VA)
Rochester Inst of Technology (NY)
Rockford Coll (IL)
Rockhurst U (MO)
Rocky Mountain Coll (MT)
Rollins Coll (FL)
Roosevelt U (IL)
Rosemont Coll (PA)
Rowan U (NJ)
Russell Sage Coll (NY)
Rutgers, The State U of New Jersey, Camden (NJ)
Rutgers, The State U of New Jersey, Newark (NJ)
Rutgers, The State U of New Jersey, New Brunswick (NJ)
Saginaw Valley State U (MI)
St. Ambrose U (IA)
Saint Anselm Coll (NH)
Saint Augustine's Coll (NC)
St. Bonaventure U (NY)
St. Catherine U (MN)
St. Cloud State U (MN)
St. Edward's U (TX)
St. Francis Coll (NY)
Saint Francis U (PA)
St. Francis Xavier U (NS, Canada)
St. John Fisher Coll (NY)
Saint John's U (MN)
St. John's U (NY)
Saint Joseph's U (PA)
St. Lawrence U (NY)
Saint Leo U (FL)
Saint Louis U (MO)
Saint Martin's U (WA)
Saint Mary's Coll (IN)
Saint Mary's Coll of California (CA)
St. Mary's Coll of Maryland (MD)
St. Mary's U (TX)
Saint Michael's Coll (VT)
St. Norbert Coll (WI)
St. Olaf Coll (MN)
Saint Paul's Coll (VA)
St. Thomas U (FL)
St. Thomas U (NB, Canada)
Saint Vincent Coll (PA)
Saint Xavier U (IL)
Salem State Coll (MA)
Salisbury U (MD)
Salve Regina U (RI)
Samford U (AL)
Sam Houston State U (TX)
San Diego State U (CA)
San Francisco State U (CA)
San Jose State U (CA)
Santa Clara U (CA)
Sarah Lawrence Coll (NY)
Savannah State U (GA)
Schreiner U (TX)
Scripps Coll (CA)
Seattle Pacific U (WA)
Seattle U (WA)
Seton Hall U (NJ)
Seton Hill U (PA)
Sewanee: The U of the South (TN)
Shaw U (NC)
Shenandoah U (VA)
Shepherd U (WV)
Shippensburg U of Pennsylvania (PA)
Siena Coll (NY)
Simmons Coll (MA)
Simon Fraser U (BC, Canada)
Simpson Coll (IA)
Skidmore Coll (NY)
Slippery Rock U of Pennsylvania (PA)
Smith Coll (MA)
Sonoma State U (CA)
South Carolina State U (SC)
South Dakota State U (SD)
Southeastern Louisiana U (LA)
Southeastern Oklahoma State U (OK)
Southeast Missouri State U (MO)
Southern Arkansas U–Magnolia (AR)
Southern Connecticut State U (CT)
Southern Illinois U Carbondale (IL)
Southern Illinois U Edwardsville (IL)
Southern Methodist U (TX)
Southern New Hampshire U (NH)
Southern Oregon U (OR)
Southern Polytechnic State U (GA)
Southern U and Ag and Mech Coll (LA)
Southern Utah U (UT)
Southwest Baptist U (MO)
Southwestern Oklahoma State U (OK)
Southwestern U (TX)
Southwest Minnesota State U (MN)
Spelman Coll (GA)
Spring Arbor U (MI)
Spring Hill Coll (AL)
Stanford U (CA)
State U of New York at Binghamton (NY)
State U of New York at Fredonia (NY)
State U of New York at New Paltz (NY)
State U of New York at Oswego (NY)
State U of New York at Plattsburgh (NY)
State U of New York Coll at Cortland (NY)
State U of New York Coll at Geneseo (NY)
State U of New York Coll at Oneonta (NY)
State U of New York Coll at Potsdam (NY)
Stephen F. Austin State U (TX)
Stetson U (FL)
Stonehill Coll (MA)
Stony Brook U, State U of New York (NY)
Suffolk U (MA)
Sul Ross State U (TX)
Susquehanna U (PA)
Swarthmore Coll (PA)
Sweet Briar Coll (VA)
Syracuse U (NY)
Tarleton State U (TX)
Taylor U (IN)
Temple U (PA)
Tennessee Technological U (TN)
Texas A&M Intl U (TX)
Texas A&M U (TX)
Texas A&M U–Commerce (TX)
Texas A&M U–Corpus Christi (TX)
Texas A&M U–Kingsville (TX)
Texas Christian U (TX)
Texas Coll (TX)
Texas Lutheran U (TX)
Texas Southern U (TX)
Texas State U–San Marcos (TX)
Texas Tech U (TX)
Texas Wesleyan U (TX)
Texas Woman's U (TX)
Thiel Coll (PA)
Thomas Edison State Coll (NJ)
Thomas More Coll (KY)
Thomas More Coll of Liberal Arts (NH)
Thompson Rivers U (BC, Canada)
Towson U (MD)
Transylvania U (KY)
Trent U (ON, Canada)
Trinity Coll (CT)
Trinity U (TX)
Troy U (AL)
Truman State U (MO)
Tufts U (MA)
Tulane U (LA)
Tuskegee U (AL)
Union Coll (NY)
Union U (TN)
United States Air Force Acad (CO)
United States Coast Guard Acad (CT)
United States Military Acad (NY)
United States Naval Acad (MD)
Universidad de las Américas–Puebla (Mexico)
U at Albany, State U of New York (NY)
U at Buffalo, the State U of New York (NY)
The U of Alabama (AL)
The U of Alabama at Birmingham (AL)
The U of Alabama in Huntsville (AL)
U of Alaska Anchorage (AK)
U of Alaska Fairbanks (AK)
U of Alberta (AB, Canada)
The U of Arizona (AZ)
U of Arkansas (AR)
U of Arkansas at Little Rock (AR)
U of Arkansas at Monticello (AR)
U of Arkansas at Pine Bluff (AR)
U of Baltimore (MD)
The U of British Columbia (BC, Canada)
The U of British Columbia–Okanagan (BC, Canada)
U of California, Berkeley (CA)
U of California, Davis (CA)
U of California, Irvine (CA)
U of California, Los Angeles (CA)
U of California, Merced (CA)
U of California, Riverside (CA)
U of California, San Diego (CA)
U of California, Santa Barbara (CA)
U of California, Santa Cruz (CA)
U of Central Florida (FL)
U of Central Missouri (MO)
U of Central Oklahoma (OK)
U of Charleston (WV)
U of Chicago (IL)
U of Cincinnati (OH)
U of Colorado at Boulder (CO)
U of Colorado at Colorado Springs (CO)
U of Colorado Denver (CO)
U of Connecticut (CT)
U of Dallas (TX)
U of Dayton (OH)
U of Delaware (DE)
U of Denver (CO)
U of Evansville (IN)
The U of Findlay (OH)
U of Florida (FL)
U of Georgia (GA)
U of Guam (GU)
U of Guelph (ON, Canada)
U of Hartford (CT)
U of Hawaii at Hilo (HI)
U of Hawaii at Manoa (HI)
U of Hawaii–West Oahu (HI)
U of Houston (TX)
U of Houston–Clear Lake (TX)
U of Houston–Downtown (TX)
U of Idaho (ID)
U of Illinois at Chicago (IL)
U of Illinois at Springfield (IL)
U of Illinois at Urbana–Champaign (IL)
U of Indianapolis (IN)
The U of Iowa (IA)
The U of Kansas (KS)
U of Kentucky (KY)
U of King's Coll (NS, Canada)
U of La Verne (CA)
U of Lethbridge (AB, Canada)
U of Louisiana at Monroe (LA)
U of Louisville (KY)
U of Maine (ME)
U of Maine at Farmington (ME)
U of Maine at Presque Isle (ME)
U of Manitoba (MB, Canada)
U of Mary Hardin-Baylor (TX)
U of Maryland, Baltimore County (MD)
U of Maryland, Coll Park (MD)
U of Maryland U Coll (MD)
U of Mary Washington (VA)
U of Massachusetts Amherst (MA)
U of Massachusetts Boston (MA)
U of Massachusetts Dartmouth (MA)
U of Massachusetts Lowell (MA)
U of Memphis (TN)
U of Miami (FL)
U of Michigan (MI)
U of Michigan–Dearborn (MI)
U of Michigan–Flint (MI)
U of Minnesota, Duluth (MN)
U of Minnesota, Twin Cities Campus (MN)
U of Mississippi (MS)
U of Missouri (MO)
U of Missouri–Kansas City (MO)
U of Missouri–St. Louis (MO)
U of Mobile (AL)
U of Montevallo (AL)
U of Mount Union (OH)
U of Nebraska at Kearney (NE)
U of Nebraska at Omaha (NE)
U of Nebraska–Lincoln (NE)
U of Nevada, Las Vegas (NV)
U of Nevada, Reno (NV)
U of New Brunswick Fredericton (NB, Canada)
U of New England (ME)
U of New Hampshire (NH)
U of New Haven (CT)
U of New Mexico (NM)
U of New Orleans (LA)
U of North Alabama (AL)
The U of North Carolina at Asheville (NC)
The U of North Carolina at Chapel Hill (NC)
The U of North Carolina at Charlotte (NC)
The U of North Carolina at Greensboro (NC)
The U of North Carolina at Pembroke (NC)
The U of North Carolina Wilmington (NC)
U of North Dakota (ND)
U of Northern Colorado (CO)
U of Northern Iowa (IA)
U of North Florida (FL)
U of North Texas (TX)
U of Notre Dame (IN)
U of Oklahoma (OK)
U of Oregon (OR)
U of Ottawa (ON, Canada)
U of Pennsylvania (PA)
U of Pittsburgh (PA)
U of Pittsburgh at Bradford (PA)
U of Pittsburgh at Greensburg (PA)
U of Pittsburgh at Johnstown (PA)
U of Portland (OR)
U of Puerto Rico at Utuado (PR)
U of Puerto Rico, Río Piedras (PR)
U of Puget Sound (WA)
U of Redlands (CA)
U of Regina (SK, Canada)
U of Rhode Island (RI)
U of Richmond (VA)
U of Rio Grande (OH)
U of Rochester (NY)
U of St. Francis (IL)
U of Saint Mary (KS)
U of St. Thomas (MN)
U of St. Thomas (TX)
U of San Diego (CA)
U of San Francisco (CA)
U of Saskatchewan (SK, Canada)
U of Science and Arts of Oklahoma (OK)
The U of Scranton (PA)
U of South Alabama (AL)

U of South Carolina (SC)
U of South Carolina Aiken (SC)
U of South Carolina Upstate (SC)
The U of South Dakota (SD)
U of Southern California (CA)
U of Southern Indiana (IN)
U of Southern Maine (ME)
U of Southern Mississippi (MS)
U of South Florida (FL)
The U of Tampa (FL)
The U of Tennessee (TN)
The U of Tennessee at Chattanooga (TN)
The U of Tennessee at Martin (TN)
The U of Texas at Arlington (TX)
The U of Texas at Brownsville (TX)
The U of Texas at Dallas (TX)
The U of Texas at El Paso (TX)
The U of Texas at San Antonio (TX)
The U of Texas at Tyler (TX)
The U of Texas of the Permian Basin (TX)
The U of Texas–Pan American (TX)
U of the Cumberlands (KY)
U of the District of Columbia (DC)
U of the Incarnate Word (TX)
U of the Ozarks (AR)
U of the Pacific (CA)
The U of Toledo (OH)
U of Toronto (ON, Canada)
U of Tulsa (OK)
U of Utah (UT)
U of Vermont (VT)
U of Virginia (VA)
The U of Virginia's Coll at Wise (VA)
U of Washington (WA)
U of Washington, Tacoma (WA)
U of Waterloo (ON, Canada)
The U of Western Ontario (ON, Canada)
U of West Florida (FL)
U of West Georgia (GA)
U of Windsor (ON, Canada)
U of Wisconsin–Eau Claire (WI)
U of Wisconsin–Green Bay (WI)
U of Wisconsin–La Crosse (WI)
U of Wisconsin–Madison (WI)
U of Wisconsin–Milwaukee (WI)
U of Wisconsin–Oshkosh (WI)
U of Wisconsin–Parkside (WI)
U of Wisconsin–Platteville (WI)
U of Wisconsin–River Falls (WI)
U of Wisconsin–Stevens Point (WI)
U of Wisconsin–Superior (WI)
U of Wisconsin–Whitewater (WI)
U of Wyoming (WY)
Ursinus Coll (PA)
Utah State U (UT)
Utah Valley U (UT)
Utica Coll (NY)
Valdosta State U (GA)
Valparaiso U (IN)
Vanderbilt U (TN)
Vanguard U of Southern California (CA)
Vassar Coll (NY)
Villanova U (PA)
Virginia Commonwealth U (VA)
Virginia Intermont Coll (VA)
Virginia Polytechnic Inst and State U (VA)
Virginia State U (VA)
Virginia Union U (VA)
Virginia Wesleyan Coll (VA)
Wabash Coll (IN)
Wagner Coll (NY)
Wake Forest U (NC)
Walsh U (OH)
Wartburg Coll (IA)
Washburn U (KS)
Washington Adventist U (MD)
Washington & Jefferson Coll (PA)
Washington and Lee U (VA)
Washington Coll (MD)
Washington State U (WA)
Washington U in St. Louis (MO)
Wayland Baptist U (TX)
Wayne State Coll (NE)
Wayne State U (MI)
Weber State U (UT)
Webster U (MO)
Wellesley Coll (MA)
Wells Coll (NY)
Wesleyan Coll (GA)
Wesleyan U (CT)
West Chester U of Pennsylvania (PA)
Western Carolina U (NC)
Western Connecticut State U (CT)
Western Illinois U (IL)
Western Kentucky U (KY)
Western Michigan U (MI)
Western New England Coll (MA)
Western Oregon U (OR)
Western State Coll of Colorado (CO)
Western Washington U (WA)
Westfield State Coll (MA)
West Liberty U (WV)
Westminster Coll (MO)
Westminster Coll (UT)
Westmont Coll (CA)
West Virginia State U (WV)
West Virginia U (WV)
West Virginia Wesleyan Coll (WV)
Wheaton Coll (IL)
Wheaton Coll (MA)
Wheeling Jesuit U (WV)
Whitman Coll (WA)
Whittier Coll (CA)
Wichita State U (KS)
Widener U (PA)
Wilberforce U (OH)
Wilfrid Laurier U (ON, Canada)
Wilkes U (PA)
Willamette U (OR)
William Jessup U (CA)
William Jewell Coll (MO)
William Paterson U of New Jersey (NJ)
William Penn U (IA)
Williams Coll (MA)
Wilmington Coll (OH)
Winona State U (MN)
Winston-Salem State U (NC)
Winthrop U (SC)
Wittenberg U (OH)
Wofford Coll (SC)
Woodbury U (CA)
Wright State U (OH)
Xavier U (OH)
Xavier U of Louisiana (LA)
Yale U (CT)
Yeshiva U (NY)
York Coll of Pennsylvania (PA)
York Coll of the City U of New York (NY)
York U (ON, Canada)
Youngstown State U (OH)

POLITICAL SCIENCE AND GOVERNMENT RELATED

Brandeis U (MA)
Buena Vista U (IA)
Capital U (OH)
Claflin U (SC)
Claremont McKenna Coll (CA)
Columbia U, School of General Studies (NY)
Delaware State U (DE)
George Mason U (VA)
Georgetown Coll (KY)
Muhlenberg Coll (PA)
North Carolina State U (NC)
Peace Coll (NC)
Prescott Coll (AZ)
Regis Coll (MA)
Sacred Heart U (CT)
Saint Mary's Coll of California (CA)
Saint Mary's U of Minnesota (MN)
Southern Vermont Coll (VT)
U of California, Davis (CA)
U of Hartford (CT)
U of Northern Iowa (IA)
Whitman Coll (WA)

POLYMER CHEMISTRY

Clemson U (SC)
Georgia Inst of Technology (GA)
Pittsburg State U (KS)
State U of New York Coll of Environmental Science and Forestry (NY)
The U of Akron (OH)
U of Wisconsin–Stevens Point (WI)
Winona State U (MN)

POLYMER/PLASTICS ENGINEERING

Case Western Reserve U (OH)
Penn State Erie, The Behrend Coll (PA)
The U of Akron (OH)
U of Illinois at Urbana–Champaign (IL)
U of Massachusetts Lowell (MA)
U of Southern California (CA)
U of Wisconsin–Stout (WI)
Winona State U (MN)

PORTUGUESE

Brooklyn Coll of the City U of New York (NY)
Florida Intl U (FL)
Georgetown U (DC)
Indiana U Bloomington (IN)
Marlboro Coll (VT)
The Ohio State U (OH)
Rutgers, The State U of New Jersey, New Brunswick (NJ)
Smith Coll (MA)
Tulane U (LA)
United States Military Acad (NY)
U of California, Los Angeles (CA)
U of California, Santa Barbara (CA)
U of Florida (FL)
U of Illinois at Urbana–Champaign (IL)
The U of Iowa (IA)
U of Massachusetts Amherst (MA)
U of Massachusetts Dartmouth (MA)
U of Minnesota, Twin Cities Campus (MN)
U of New Mexico (NM)
The U of Texas at Austin (TX)
U of Toronto (ON, Canada)
U of Wisconsin–Madison (WI)
Yale U (CT)

POULTRY SCIENCE

Auburn U (AL)
Delaware State U (DE)
Mississippi State U (MS)
Stephen F. Austin State U (TX)
Texas A&M U (TX)
Tuskegee U (AL)
U of Arkansas (AR)
U of Florida (FL)
U of Georgia (GA)
U of Maryland Eastern Shore (MD)
Virginia Polytechnic Inst and State U (VA)

PRE-DENTISTRY STUDIES

Abilene Christian U (TX)
Acadia U (NS, Canada)
Albertus Magnus Coll (CT)
Allegheny Coll (PA)
Alma Coll (MI)
American Intl Coll (MA)
American U (DC)
Anderson U (IN)
Arcadia U (PA)
Ashland U (OH)
Atlantic Union Coll (MA)
Auburn U (AL)
Augsburg Coll (MN)
Augustana Coll (IL)
Augustana Coll (SD)
Baldwin-Wallace Coll (OH)
Ball State U (IN)
Barry U (FL)
Baylor U (TX)
Belmont Abbey Coll (NC)
Beloit Coll (WI)
Bethany Coll (WV)
Birmingham-Southern Coll (AL)
Blackburn Coll (IL)
Boise State U (ID)
Boston U (MA)
Buffalo State Coll, State U of New York (NY)
California State U, Chico (CA)
California State U, East Bay (CA)
Calvin Coll (MI)
Campbellsville U (KY)
Carroll U (WI)
Catawba Coll (NC)
Cedar Crest Coll (PA)
Cedarville U (OH)
Centenary Coll of Louisiana (LA)
Central Christian Coll of Kansas (KS)
Chapman U (CA)
City Coll of the City U of New York (NY)
Claremont McKenna Coll (CA)
Clark U (MA)
The Coll at Brockport, State U of New York (NY)
Coll of Mount Saint Vincent (NY)
Coll of Saint Benedict (MN)
Coll of Saint Mary (NE)
Concordia Coll (MN)
Concordia U Chicago (IL)
Cornerstone U (MI)
Cumberland U (TN)
Defiance Coll (OH)
Dickinson State U (ND)
Dominican U (IL)
Dordt Coll (IA)
Drake U (IA)
Drury U (MO)
East Central U (OK)
Eastern Mennonite U (VA)
Eastern Nazarene Coll (MA)
Elizabethtown Coll (PA)
Elmhurst Coll (IL)
Elmira Coll (NY)
Elon U (NC)
Emory & Henry Coll (VA)
Evangel U (MO)
Florida Southern Coll (FL)
Florida State U (FL)
Fordham U (NY)
Franklin Pierce U (NH)
Furman U (SC)
Gardner-Webb U (NC)
The George Washington U (DC)
Georgia Southern U (GA)
Gettysburg Coll (PA)
Graceland U (IA)
Grand Valley State U (MI)
Grove City Coll (PA)
Gustavus Adolphus Coll (MN)
Hamline U (MN)
Hampton U (VA)
Harding U (AR)
Heidelberg U (OH)
High Point U (NC)
Hillsdale Coll (MI)
Hofstra U (NY)
Houghton Coll (NY)
Illinois Coll (IL)
Immaculata U (PA)
Indiana U–Purdue U Fort Wayne (IN)
Indiana Wesleyan U (IN)
Iowa State U of Science and Technology (IA)
Iowa Wesleyan Coll (IA)
Jacksonville U (FL)
John Carroll U (OH)
Juniata Coll (PA)
Kent State U (OH)
Kentucky Wesleyan Coll (KY)
Keuka Coll (NY)
King's Coll (PA)
LaGrange Coll (GA)
Lake Erie Coll (OH)
Lake Superior State U (MI)
Lamar U (TX)
La Salle U (PA)
Lawrence U (WI)
Lehigh U (PA)
Le Moyne Coll (NY)
LeTourneau U (TX)
Lewis U (IL)
Limestone Coll (SC)
Lindenwood U (MO)
Lindsey Wilson Coll (KY)
Lipscomb U (TN)
Lock Haven U of Pennsylvania (PA)
Longwood U (VA)
Loyola U New Orleans (LA)
Manchester Coll (IN)
Marian U (IN)
Marquette U (WI)
Maryville U of Saint Louis (MO)
Mayville State U (ND)
McKendree U (IL)
Mercer U (GA)
Mercyhurst Coll (PA)
Methodist U (NC)
Michigan Technological U (MI)
Midwestern State U (TX)
Millikin U (IL)
Minnesota State U Mankato (MN)
Minnesota State U Moorhead (MN)
Mississippi Coll (MS)
Molloy Coll (NY)
Mount Allison U (NB, Canada)
Mount Mary Coll (WI)
Mount Mercy Coll (IA)
Mount Vernon Nazarene U (OH)
Nazareth Coll of Rochester (NY)
Newberry Coll (SC)
Newman U (KS)
Niagara U (NY)
North Central Coll (IL)
Northern Michigan U (MI)
Northern State U (SD)
North Georgia Coll & State U (GA)
Northwestern Oklahoma State U (OK)
Northwest Nazarene U (ID)
Notre Dame de Namur U (CA)
Oglethorpe U (GA)
Ohio Northern U (OH)
The Ohio State U (OH)
Ohio Wesleyan U (OH)
Oklahoma City U (OK)
Oklahoma Wesleyan U (OK)
Ouachita Baptist U (AR)
Pacific Union Coll (CA)
Pepperdine U, Malibu (CA)
Peru State Coll (NE)
Pittsburg State U (KS)
Purdue U Calumet (IN)
Queens U of Charlotte (NC)
Quinnipiac U (CT)
Redeemer U Coll (ON, Canada)
Rhode Island Coll (RI)
Ripon Coll (WI)
Rivier Coll (NH)
Roberts Wesleyan Coll (NY)
Rochester Inst of Technology (NY)
Rockford Coll (IL)
Rutgers, The State U of New Jersey, New Brunswick (NJ)
Sacred Heart U (CT)
Saint Anselm Coll (NH)
St. Catherine U (MN)
St. Cloud State U (MN)
Saint Francis U (PA)
St. Francis Xavier U (NS, Canada)
Saint John's U (MN)
Saint Martin's U (WA)
Saint Mary-of-the-Woods Coll (IN)
Saint Michael's Coll (VT)
St. Thomas U (FL)
Sarah Lawrence Coll (NY)
Seton Hill U (PA)
Simpson Coll (IA)
Sonoma State U (CA)
Southwestern Oklahoma State U (OK)
Southwest Minnesota State U (MN)
Spring Hill Coll (AL)
State U of New York at Oswego (NY)
State U of New York Coll at Cortland (NY)
State U of New York Coll at Geneseo (NY)
State U of New York Coll at Oneonta (NY)
State U of New York Coll of Environmental Science and Forestry (NY)
Stetson U (FL)
Stevens Inst of Technology (NJ)
Sul Ross State U (TX)
Susquehanna U (PA)
Tabor Coll (KS)
Tarleton State U (TX)
Tennessee Technological U (TN)
Texas A&M U–Corpus Christi (TX)
Texas Lutheran U (TX)
Texas Wesleyan U (TX)
Thiel Coll (PA)
Thompson Rivers U (BC, Canada)
Trinity Christian Coll (IL)
Trinity U (TX)
Truman State U (MO)
Union U (TN)
U of Alberta (AB, Canada)
U of Bridgeport (CT)
U of Central Missouri (MO)
U of Colorado at Colorado Springs (CO)
U of Dallas (TX)
U of Dayton (OH)
U of Evansville (IN)
U of Hartford (CT)
U of Illinois at Chicago (IL)
U of Indianapolis (IN)
The U of Iowa (IA)
U of Manitoba (MB, Canada)
U of Maryland, Coll Park (MD)
U of Maryland Eastern Shore (MD)
U of Massachusetts Amherst (MA)
U of Minnesota, Duluth (MN)
U of Minnesota, Twin Cities Campus (MN)
U of Missouri–Kansas City (MO)
U of Missouri–St. Louis (MO)
U of Nebraska–Lincoln (NE)
U of New Brunswick Fredericton (NB, Canada)
U of New England (ME)
U of Pittsburgh at Johnstown (PA)
U of Portland (OR)
U of Regina (SK, Canada)
U of Rio Grande (OH)
U of St. Francis (IL)
U of St. Thomas (TX)
U of San Francisco (CA)
U of Saskatchewan (SK, Canada)
The U of Tennessee (TN)
The U of Tennessee at Martin (TN)
The U of Toledo (OH)
U of Windsor (ON, Canada)
U of Wisconsin–Milwaukee (WI)
U of Wisconsin–Oshkosh (WI)
U of Wisconsin–Parkside (WI)
U of Wisconsin–River Falls (WI)
Upper Iowa U (IA)
Utah State U (UT)
Utica Coll (NY)
Valley City State U (ND)
Virginia Wesleyan Coll (VA)
Wagner Coll (NY)
Walsh U (OH)
Washburn U (KS)
Washington Adventist U (MD)
Washington Coll (MD)
Washington U in St. Louis (MO)
Waynesburg U (PA)
Wells Coll (NY)
West Liberty U (WV)
Westmont Coll (CA)
West Virginia State U (WV)
West Virginia Wesleyan Coll (WV)
Wheeling Jesuit U (WV)
Widener U (PA)
William Paterson U of New Jersey (NJ)
William Penn U (IA)
Wilmington Coll (OH)
Winona State U (MN)
Wofford Coll (SC)
Wright State U (OH)
Xavier U of Louisiana (LA)
York U (ON, Canada)
Youngstown State U (OH)

PRE-ENGINEERING
Azusa Pacific U (CA)
Bethel U (TN)
Delaware State U (DE)
Drake U (IA)
Eastern Mennonite U (VA)
Eastern Nazarene Coll (MA)
Faulkner U (AL)
Lewis U (IL)
Midwestern State U (TX)
Northwest Nazarene U (ID)
Ouachita Baptist U (AR)
Pittsburg State U (KS)
Redeemer U Coll (ON, Canada)
Roberts Wesleyan Coll (NY)
Scripps Coll (CA)
Simpson Coll (IA)
Slippery Rock U of Pennsylvania (PA)
Valley City State U (ND)
Wagner Coll (NY)
Waynesburg U (PA)

PRE-LAW STUDIES
Abilene Christian U (TX)
Acadia U (NS, Canada)
Albertus Magnus Coll (CT)
Albion Coll (MI)
Albright Coll (PA)
Allegheny Coll (PA)
Alma Coll (MI)
Alvernia U (PA)
American Intl Coll (MA)
American U (DC)
Anderson U (IN)
Andrews U (MI)
Aquinas Coll (MI)
Arcadia U (PA)
Ashland U (OH)
Atlantic Union Coll (MA)
Auburn U (AL)
Augsburg Coll (MN)
Augustana Coll (IL)
Augustana Coll (SD)
Azusa Pacific U (CA)
Babson Coll (MA)
Bard Coll (NY)
Barry U (FL)
Baylor U (TX)
Bay Path Coll (MA)
Belmont Abbey Coll (NC)
Beloit Coll (WI)
Bemidji State U (MN)
Bennington Coll (VT)
Bethany Coll (WV)
Bethel Coll (IN)
Birmingham-Southern Coll (AL)
Blackburn Coll (IL)
Bowling Green State U (OH)
Brewton-Parker Coll (GA)
Buffalo State Coll, State U of New York (NY)
California State U, Dominguez Hills (CA)
California State U, Fresno (CA)
Calumet Coll of Saint Joseph (IN)
Calvin Coll (MI)
Campbellsville U (KY)
Catawba Coll (NC)
Cedar Crest Coll (PA)
Cedarville U (OH)
Centenary Coll of Louisiana (LA)
Central Christian Coll of Kansas (KS)
Champlain Coll (VT)
Chowan U (NC)
Christopher Newport U (VA)
City Coll of the City U of New York (NY)
Claremont McKenna Coll (CA)
Clark U (MA)
Clearwater Christian Coll (FL)
The Coll at Brockport, State U of New York (NY)
Coll of Mount Saint Vincent (NY)
The Coll of New Rochelle (NY)
Coll of Saint Benedict (MN)
Coll of Saint Mary (NE)
Concordia Coll (MN)
Concordia U Chicago (IL)
Concordia U Wisconsin (WI)
Corban U (OR)
Creighton U (NE)
Crichton Coll (TN)
Crown Coll (MN)
Cumberland U (TN)
Curry Coll (MA)
Defiance Coll (OH)
Dickinson State U (ND)
Dominican Coll (NY)
Dominican U (IL)
Dordt Coll (IA)
Drake U (IA)
Drury U (MO)
East Central U (OK)
Eastern Mennonite U (VA)
Eastern Nazarene Coll (MA)
Elmhurst Coll (IL)
Elmira Coll (NY)
Elon U (NC)
Emmanuel Coll (GA)
Emory & Henry Coll (VA)
Evangel U (MO)
Faulkner U (AL)
Felician Coll (NJ)
Florida State U (FL)
Fontbonne U (MO)
Fordham U (NY)
Fort Hays State U (KS)
Francis Marion U (SC)
Franklin Pierce U (NH)
Furman U (SC)
Gannon U (PA)
Gardner-Webb U (NC)
The George Washington U (DC)
Gettysburg Coll (PA)
Graceland U (IA)
Grambling State U (LA)
Grand View U (IA)
Grove City Coll (PA)
Gustavus Adolphus Coll (MN)
Hamline U (MN)
Hampton U (VA)
Hannibal-LaGrange Coll (MO)
Hartwick Coll (NY)
Haverford Coll (PA)
Hawai'i Pacific U (HI)
Heidelberg U (OH)
High Point U (NC)
Hiram Coll (OH)
Hofstra U (NY)
Houghton Coll (NY)
Houston Baptist U (TX)
Huntington U (IN)
Illinois Coll (IL)
Indiana Wesleyan U (IN)
Iowa State U of Science and Technology (IA)
Iowa Wesleyan Coll (IA)
Ithaca Coll (NY)
Jacksonville U (FL)
John Carroll U (OH)
Juniata Coll (PA)
Kentucky Wesleyan Coll (KY)
Keuka Coll (NY)
Keystone Coll (PA)
King Coll (TN)
King's Coll (PA)
LaGrange Coll (GA)
Lake Erie Coll (OH)
Lake Superior State U (MI)
Lasell Coll (MA)
Lawrence U (WI)
Lees-McRae Coll (NC)
Le Moyne Coll (NY)
LeTourneau U (TX)
Lewis U (IL)
Limestone Coll (SC)
Lincoln Memorial U (TN)
Lindenwood U (MO)
Lindsey Wilson Coll (KY)
Lipscomb U (TN)
Longwood U (VA)
Louisiana Coll (LA)
Lubbock Christian U (TX)
Manchester Coll (IN)
Mansfield U of Pennsylvania (PA)
Marian U (IN)
Marlboro Coll (VT)
Marquette U (WI)
Mars Hill Coll (NC)
Maryville U of Saint Louis (MO)
The Master's Coll and Sem (CA)
Mayville State U (ND)
McKendree U (IL)
Medaille Coll (NY)
Methodist U (NC)
Michigan State U (MI)
Michigan Technological U (MI)
Midwestern State U (TX)
Millikin U (IL)
Minnesota State U Mankato (MN)
Minnesota State U Moorhead (MN)
Mississippi Coll (MS)
Molloy Coll (NY)
Mount Allison U (NB, Canada)
Mount Mary Coll (WI)
Mount Mercy Coll (IA)
Mount Vernon Nazarene U (OH)
National U (CA)
Nazareth Coll of Rochester (NY)
Newberry Coll (SC)
Newbury Coll (MA)
New England Coll (NH)
Newman U (KS)
Niagara U (NY)
North Central Coll (IL)
Northern Michigan U (MI)
Northern State U (SD)
Northwestern Oklahoma State U (OK)
Northwest Nazarene U (ID)
Notre Dame de Namur U (CA)
Nova Southeastern U (FL)
Oakland City U (IN)
Oglethorpe U (GA)
Ohio Northern U (OH)
Ohio Wesleyan U (OH)
Oklahoma Christian U (OK)
Oklahoma City U (OK)
Oklahoma Wesleyan U (OK)
Ouachita Baptist U (AR)
Pacific Lutheran U (WA)
Pacific Union Coll (CA)
Pepperdine U, Malibu (CA)
Peru State Coll (NE)
Pittsburg State U (KS)
Pontifical Catholic U of Puerto Rico (PR)
Purdue U Calumet (IN)
Queens U of Charlotte (NC)
Quinnipiac U (CT)
Redeemer U Coll (ON, Canada)
Rensselaer Polytechnic Inst (NY)
Rhode Island Coll (RI)
Ripon Coll (WI)
Rivier Coll (NH)
Roberts Wesleyan Coll (NY)
Rochester Inst of Technology (NY)
Rockford Coll (IL)
Rutgers, The State U of New Jersey, New Brunswick (NJ)
St. Andrews Presbyterian Coll (NC)
Saint Anselm Coll (NH)
St. Catherine U (MN)
St. Cloud State U (MN)
Saint Francis U (PA)
St. Francis Xavier U (NS, Canada)
Saint John's U (MN)
St. Joseph's Coll, Long Island Campus (NY)
St. Joseph's Coll, New York (NY)
Saint Martin's U (WA)
Saint Mary-of-the-Woods Coll (IN)
Saint Michael's Coll (VT)
St. Thomas U (FL)
Sarah Lawrence Coll (NY)
Seton Hill U (PA)
Shawnee State U (OH)
Siena Heights U (MI)
Simpson Coll (IA)
Smith Coll (MA)
Sonoma State U (CA)
Southern Oregon U (OR)
Southern Vermont Coll (VT)
Southwestern Oklahoma State U (OK)
Southwest Minnesota State U (MN)
State U of New York at Binghamton (NY)
State U of New York at Fredonia (NY)
State U of New York at New Paltz (NY)
State U of New York at Oswego (NY)
State U of New York Coll at Cortland (NY)
State U of New York Coll at Geneseo (NY)
State U of New York Coll at Oneonta (NY)
State U of New York Coll of Environmental Science and Forestry (NY)
Stephens Coll (MO)
Stetson U (FL)
Stevens Inst of Technology (NJ)
Suffolk U (MA)
Sul Ross State U (TX)
Susquehanna U (PA)
Tabor Coll (KS)
Talladega Coll (AL)
Tennessee Technological U (TN)
Texas A&M U–Corpus Christi (TX)
Texas Lutheran U (TX)
Texas Wesleyan U (TX)
Thiel Coll (PA)
Trine U (IN)
Trinity U (TX)
Truman State U (MO)
Tusculum Coll (TN)
Union U (TN)
United States Military Acad (NY)
Universidad de las Américas–Puebla (Mexico)
U of Alberta (AB, Canada)
U of Bridgeport (CT)
U of California, Santa Barbara (CA)
U of California, Santa Cruz (CA)
U of Cincinnati (OH)
U of Colorado at Colorado Springs (CO)
U of Dallas (TX)
U of Dayton (OH)
The U of Findlay (OH)
U of Illinois at Urbana–Champaign (IL)
U of Indianapolis (IN)
The U of Iowa (IA)
U of Manitoba (MB, Canada)
U of Maryland, Coll Park (MD)
U of Maryland Eastern Shore (MD)
U of Minnesota, Twin Cities Campus (MN)
U of Missouri–Kansas City (MO)
U of Missouri–St. Louis (MO)
The U of Montana Western (MT)
U of New Brunswick Fredericton (NB, Canada)
U of Pittsburgh at Greensburg (PA)
U of Pittsburgh at Johnstown (PA)
U of Portland (OR)
U of Regina (SK, Canada)
U of Rio Grande (OH)
U of St. Francis (IL)
U of St. Thomas (TX)
U of Saskatchewan (SK, Canada)
The U of Toledo (OH)
U of Windsor (ON, Canada)
U of Wisconsin–Milwaukee (WI)
U of Wisconsin–Oshkosh (WI)
U of Wisconsin–River Falls (WI)
U of Wisconsin–Superior (WI)
Utah State U (UT)
Utica Coll (NY)
Valley City State U (ND)
Vanguard U of Southern California (CA)
Virginia Intermont Coll (VA)
Wabash Coll (IN)
Wagner Coll (NY)
Warner Pacific Coll (OR)
Washburn U (KS)
Washington Adventist U (MD)
Washington Coll (MD)
Waynesburg U (PA)
Webber Intl U (FL)
Wells Coll (NY)
Western State Coll of Colorado (CO)
West Liberty U (WV)
Westminster Coll (MO)
Westmont Coll (CA)
West Virginia Wesleyan Coll (WV)
Wheeling Jesuit U (WV)
William Paterson U of New Jersey (NJ)
William Penn U (IA)
Wilmington Coll (OH)
Wingate U (NC)
Winona State U (MN)
Wofford Coll (SC)
Wright State U (OH)
Xavier U of Louisiana (LA)
York U (ON, Canada)
Youngstown State U (OH)

PREMEDICAL STUDIES
Abilene Christian U (TX)
Acadia U (NS, Canada)
Alabama State U (AL)
Albertus Magnus Coll (CT)
Albion Coll (MI)
Allegheny Coll (PA)
Alma Coll (MI)
Alvernia U (PA)
American Intl Coll (MA)
American Jewish U (CA)
American U (DC)
Anderson U (IN)
Andrews U (MI)
Arcadia U (PA)
Ashland U (OH)
Atlantic Union Coll (MA)
Auburn U (AL)
Augsburg Coll (MN)
Augustana Coll (IL)
Augustana Coll (SD)
Averett U (VA)
Baldwin-Wallace Coll (OH)
Ball State U (IN)
Bard Coll (NY)
Bard Coll at Simon's Rock (MA)
Barry U (FL)
Baylor U (TX)
Belmont Abbey Coll (NC)
Beloit Coll (WI)
Bemidji State U (MN)
Bennington Coll (VT)
Bethany Coll (WV)
Bethel Coll (IN)
Birmingham-Southern Coll (AL)
Blackburn Coll (IL)
Bluffton U (OH)
Bob Jones U (SC)
Boise State U (ID)
Bowling Green State U (OH)
Buffalo State Coll, State U of New York (NY)
California State U, Chico (CA)
California State U, East Bay (CA)
Calvin Coll (MI)
Campbellsville U (KY)
Carroll U (WI)
Catawba Coll (NC)
Cedar Crest Coll (PA)
Cedarville U (OH)
Centenary Coll of Louisiana (LA)
Central Christian Coll of Kansas (KS)
Chapman U (CA)
Chowan U (NC)
City Coll of the City U of New York (NY)
Claremont McKenna Coll (CA)
Clark U (MA)
Clearwater Christian Coll (FL)
The Coll at Brockport, State U of New York (NY)
Coll of Mount Saint Vincent (NY)
The Coll of New Rochelle (NY)
Coll of Saint Benedict (MN)
Coll of Saint Mary (NE)
Coll of the Holy Cross (MA)
Concordia Coll (MN)
Concordia U Chicago (IL)
Concord U (WV)
Cornell U (NY)
Cornerstone U (MI)
Cumberland U (TN)
Defiance Coll (OH)
Dickinson State U (ND)
Dominican U (IL)
Dordt Coll (IA)
Drake U (IA)
Drury U (MO)
Duquesne U (PA)
Earlham Coll (IN)
East Central U (OK)
Eastern Mennonite U (VA)
Eastern Nazarene Coll (MA)
Elmhurst Coll (IL)
Elmira Coll (NY)
Elon U (NC)
Emory & Henry Coll (VA)
Evangel U (MO)
Felician Coll (NJ)
Florida Southern Coll (FL)
Florida State U (FL)
Fordham U (NY)
Franklin Pierce U (NH)
Furman U (SC)
Gannon U (PA)
Gardner-Webb U (NC)
The George Washington U (DC)
Georgia Southern U (GA)
Gettysburg Coll (PA)
Graceland U (IA)
Grand Valley State U (MI)
Grove City Coll (PA)
Gustavus Adolphus Coll (MN)
Hamline U (MN)
Hampton U (VA)
Harding U (AR)
Hartwick Coll (NY)
Haverford Coll (PA)
Hawai'i Pacific U (HI)
Heidelberg U (OH)
High Point U (NC)
Hillsdale Coll (MI)
Hofstra U (NY)
Houghton Coll (NY)
Huntington U (IN)
Illinois Coll (IL)
Indiana U–Purdue U Fort Wayne (IN)
Indiana Wesleyan U (IN)
Inter American U of Puerto Rico, Bayamón Campus (PR)
Iowa State U of Science and Technology (IA)
Iowa Wesleyan Coll (IA)
Ithaca Coll (NY)
Jacksonville U (FL)
John Carroll U (OH)
Johnson State Coll (VT)
Juniata Coll (PA)
Kent State U (OH)
Kentucky Wesleyan Coll (KY)
Keuka Coll (NY)
Keystone Coll (PA)
King Coll (TN)
King's Coll (PA)
LaGrange Coll (GA)
Lake Erie Coll (OH)
La Salle U (PA)
Lawrence U (WI)
Lees-McRae Coll (NC)
Lehigh U (PA)
Le Moyne Coll (NY)
LeTourneau U (TX)
Lewis U (IL)
Limestone Coll (SC)
Lincoln Memorial U (TN)
Lindenwood U (MO)
Lindsey Wilson Coll (KY)
Lipscomb U (TN)
Lock Haven U of Pennsylvania (PA)
Longwood U (VA)
Loyola U New Orleans (LA)
Manchester Coll (IN)
Manhattanville Coll (NY)
Marian U (IN)
Marlboro Coll (VT)
Marquette U (WI)
Mars Hill Coll (NC)
Maryville U of Saint Louis (MO)
Massachusetts Coll of Pharmacy and Health Sciences (MA)
The Master's Coll and Sem (CA)
Mayville State U (ND)
McKendree U (IL)

Memorial U of Newfoundland (NL, Canada)
Mercer U (GA)
Mercy Coll of Health Sciences (IA)
Methodist U (NC)
Michigan State U (MI)
Michigan Technological U (MI)
Midwestern State U (TX)
Millikin U (IL)
Minnesota State U Mankato (MN)
Minnesota State U Moorhead (MN)
Mississippi Coll (MS)
Molloy Coll (NY)
Mount Allison U (NB, Canada)
Mount Mary Coll (WI)
Mount Mercy Coll (IA)
Mount Vernon Nazarene U (OH)
Nazareth Coll of Rochester (NY)
Newberry Coll (SC)
Newman U (KS)
New York Inst of Technology (NY)
Niagara U (NY)
North Central Coll (IL)
Northern Michigan U (MI)
Northern State U (SD)
North Georgia Coll & State U (GA)
Northwestern Oklahoma State U (OK)
Northwest Nazarene U (ID)
Notre Dame de Namur U (CA)
Nova Southeastern U (FL)
Oakland City U (IN)
Oglethorpe U (GA)
Ohio Northern U (OH)
Ohio Wesleyan U (OH)
Oklahoma City U (OK)
Oklahoma Wesleyan U (OK)
Oregon Inst of Technology (OR)
Ouachita Baptist U (AR)
Pacific Lutheran U (WA)
Pacific Union Coll (CA)
Penn State Abington (PA)
Penn State Altoona (PA)
Penn State Beaver (PA)
Penn State Berks (PA)
Penn State Brandywine (PA)
Penn State DuBois (PA)
Penn State Erie, The Behrend Coll (PA)
Penn State Fayette, The Eberly Campus (PA)
Penn State Greater Allegheny (PA)
Penn State Hazleton (PA)
Penn State Lehigh Valley (PA)
Penn State Mont Alto (PA)
Penn State New Kensington (PA)
Penn State Schuylkill (PA)
Penn State Shenango (PA)
Penn State U Park (PA)
Penn State Wilkes-Barre (PA)
Penn State Worthington Scranton (PA)
Penn State York (PA)
Pepperdine U, Malibu (CA)
Peru State Coll (NE)
Philadelphia U (PA)
Pittsburg State U (KS)
Pitzer Coll (CA)
Pomona Coll (CA)
Pontifical Catholic U of Puerto Rico (PR)
Purdue U Calumet (IN)
Queens U of Charlotte (NC)
Quinnipiac U (CT)
Redeemer U Coll (ON, Canada)
Rensselaer Polytechnic Inst (NY)
Rhode Island Coll (RI)
Ripon Coll (WI)
Rivier Coll (NH)
Roberts Wesleyan Coll (NY)
Rochester Inst of Technology (NY)
Rockford Coll (IL)
Rutgers, The State U of New Jersey, New Brunswick (NJ)
Sacred Heart U (CT)
St. Andrews Presbyterian Coll (NC)
Saint Anselm Coll (NH)
St. Catherine U (MN)
St. Cloud State U (MN)
Saint Francis U (PA)
St. Francis Xavier U (NS, Canada)
Saint John's U (MN)
Saint Martin's U (WA)
Saint Mary-of-the-Woods Coll (IN)
Saint Michael's Coll (VT)
St. Thomas Aquinas Coll (NY)
St. Thomas U (FL)
Samford U (AL)
Sarah Lawrence Coll (NY)
Scripps Coll (CA)
Seton Hill U (PA)
Shawnee State U (OH)
Simpson Coll (IA)
Slippery Rock U of Pennsylvania (PA)
Smith Coll (MA)
Sonoma State U (CA)
Southeastern U (FL)
Southern Oregon U (OR)
Southern Wesleyan U (SC)
Southwestern Oklahoma State U (OK)
Southwest Minnesota State U (MN)
Spring Hill Coll (AL)
State U of New York at Binghamton (NY)
State U of New York at Fredonia (NY)
State U of New York at Oswego (NY)
State U of New York Coll at Cortland (NY)
State U of New York Coll at Geneseo (NY)
State U of New York Coll at Oneonta (NY)
State U of New York Coll of Environmental Science and Forestry (NY)
Stetson U (FL)
Stevens Inst of Technology (NJ)
Sul Ross State U (TX)
Susquehanna U (PA)
Tabor Coll (KS)
Tarleton State U (TX)
Tennessee Technological U (TN)
Texas A&M U–Corpus Christi (TX)
Texas Lutheran U (TX)
Texas Wesleyan U (TX)
Thiel Coll (PA)
Thompson Rivers U (BC, Canada)
Trine U (IN)
Trinity Christian Coll (IL)
Trinity U (TX)
Truman State U (MO)
Tusculum Coll (TN)
Union U (TN)
Universidad de las Américas–Puebla (Mexico)
U of Alberta (AB, Canada)
U of Arkansas (AR)
U of Bridgeport (CT)
U of California, Santa Cruz (CA)
U of Central Missouri (MO)
U of Cincinnati (OH)
U of Colorado at Colorado Springs (CO)
U of Dallas (TX)
U of Dayton (OH)
U of Evansville (IN)
The U of Findlay (OH)
U of Hartford (CT)
U of Indianapolis (IN)
The U of Iowa (IA)
U of Maine (ME)
U of Maine at Machias (ME)
U of Manitoba (MB, Canada)
U of Maryland Eastern Shore (MD)
U of Massachusetts Amherst (MA)
U of Minnesota, Duluth (MN)
U of Minnesota, Twin Cities Campus (MN)
U of Missouri–Kansas City (MO)
U of Missouri–St. Louis (MO)
The U of Montana Western (MT)
U of Nebraska–Lincoln (NE)
U of Nevada, Reno (NV)
U of New Brunswick Fredericton (NB, Canada)
U of New England (ME)
U of Notre Dame (IN)
U of Pittsburgh at Johnstown (PA)
U of Portland (OR)
U of Regina (SK, Canada)
U of Rio Grande (OH)
U of St. Francis (IL)
U of St. Thomas (TX)
U of San Francisco (CA)
U of Saskatchewan (SK, Canada)
The U of Tennessee (TN)
The U of Tennessee at Martin (TN)
The U of Toledo (OH)
U of Windsor (ON, Canada)
U of Wisconsin–Milwaukee (WI)
U of Wisconsin–Oshkosh (WI)
U of Wisconsin–Parkside (WI)
U of Wisconsin–River Falls (WI)
Upper Iowa U (IA)
Utah State U (UT)
Utica Coll (NY)
Valley City State U (ND)
Vanguard U of Southern California (CA)
Virginia Intermont Coll (VA)
Virginia Wesleyan Coll (VA)
Wabash Coll (IN)
Wagner Coll (NY)
Walsh U (OH)
Warner Pacific Coll (OR)
Washburn U (KS)
Washington Adventist U (MD)
Washington Coll (MD)
Washington State U (WA)
Washington U in St. Louis (MO)
Waynesburg U (PA)
Wells Coll (NY)
West Chester U of Pennsylvania (PA)
West Liberty U (WV)
Westmont Coll (CA)
West Virginia State U (WV)
West Virginia Wesleyan Coll (WV)
Wheeling Jesuit U (WV)
Widener U (PA)
William Paterson U of New Jersey (NJ)
William Penn U (IA)
Wilmington Coll (OH)
Wingate U (NC)
Winona State U (MN)
Wofford Coll (SC)
Wright State U (OH)
Xavier U of Louisiana (LA)
York U (ON, Canada)
Youngstown State U (OH)

PRENURSING STUDIES

Allegheny Coll (PA)
Baylor U (TX)
Brigham Young U (UT)
California State U, Fullerton (CA)
Cleveland State U (OH)
The Coll of Idaho (ID)
Delaware State U (DE)
Dordt Coll (IA)
Eastern Mennonite U (VA)
Eastern Nazarene Coll (MA)
Gettysburg Coll (PA)
Humboldt State U (CA)
Juniata Coll (PA)
Limestone Coll (SC)
Lindenwood U (MO)
Lipscomb U (TN)
McMurry U (TX)
Nevada State Coll at Henderson (NV)
Oklahoma City U (OK)
Ouachita Baptist U (AR)
Redeemer U Coll (ON, Canada)
State U of New York Coll at Geneseo (NY)
Tennessee Wesleyan Coll (TN)
U of Missouri–Kansas City (MO)

PRE-PHARMACY STUDIES

Abilene Christian U (TX)
Allegheny Coll (PA)
Ashland U (OH)
Auburn U (AL)
Baldwin-Wallace Coll (OH)
Barry U (FL)
Belmont Abbey Coll (NC)
Benedictine U (IL)
Bethel U (TN)
Carroll U (WI)
Central Christian Coll of Kansas (KS)
Coll of Saint Benedict (MN)
Cumberland U (TN)
Dordt Coll (IA)
Drury U (MO)
East Central U (OK)
Eastern Nazarene Coll (MA)
Elmhurst Coll (IL)
Florida State U (FL)
Fordham U (NY)
Gardner-Webb U (NC)
Georgia Southern U (GA)
Gettysburg Coll (PA)
Iowa Wesleyan Coll (IA)
Juniata Coll (PA)
King Coll (TN)
King's Coll (PA)
Le Moyne Coll (NY)
Lewis U (IL)
Limestone Coll (SC)
Lindsey Wilson Coll (KY)
Lipscomb U (TN)
Long Island U, C.W. Post Campus (NY)
Longwood U (VA)
Mayville State U (ND)
Michigan Technological U (MI)
Midwestern State U (TX)
Millikin U (IL)
Mississippi Coll (MS)
Mount Allison U (NB, Canada)
Mount Vernon Nazarene U (OH)
Northern Michigan U (MI)
Northwest Nazarene U (ID)
Oklahoma City U (OK)
Ouachita Baptist U (AR)
Pittsburg State U (KS)
Roberts Wesleyan Coll (NY)
St. Cloud State U (MN)
Saint John's U (MN)
Saint Martin's U (WA)
Saint Mary-of-the-Woods Coll (IN)
Simpson Coll (IA)
Slippery Rock U of Pennsylvania (PA)
Tabor Coll (KS)
Tarleton State U (TX)
Texas Southern U (TX)
Truman State U (MO)
Tusculum Coll (TN)
Union U (TN)
U of Central Missouri (MO)
U of Charleston (WV)
U of Connecticut (CT)
The U of Iowa (IA)
U of Minnesota, Duluth (MN)
U of Missouri–Kansas City (MO)
U of Missouri–St. Louis (MO)
U of Nebraska–Lincoln (NE)
U of Regina (SK, Canada)
U of St. Francis (IL)
U of St. Thomas (TX)
U of Saskatchewan (SK, Canada)
The U of Tennessee (TN)
The U of Tennessee at Martin (TN)
U of Windsor (ON, Canada)
U of Wisconsin–Parkside (WI)
U of Wisconsin–River Falls (WI)
Valley City State U (ND)
Washburn U (KS)
Washington U in St. Louis (MO)
Western New England Coll (MA)
Westmont Coll (CA)
West Virginia Wesleyan Coll (WV)
Wingate U (NC)
Wright State U (OH)
York U (ON, Canada)
Youngstown State U (OH)

PRE-THEOLOGY/PRE-MINISTERIAL STUDIES

Alma Coll (MI)
Ashland U (OH)
Atlanta Christian Coll (GA)
Baptist Bible Coll of Pennsylvania (PA)
California Baptist U (CA)
Central Christian Coll of Kansas (KS)
Coll of Saint Benedict (MN)
Columbia Intl U (SC)
Concordia Coll (MN)
Concordia U Chicago (IL)
Concordia U Coll of Alberta (AB, Canada)
Corban U (OR)
Cornerstone U (MI)
Eastern Nazarene Coll (MA)
John Brown U (AR)
Kuyper Coll (MI)
Loras Coll (IA)
Martin Luther Coll (MN)
Mid-Atlantic Christian U (NC)
Mount Allison U (NB, Canada)
Northwestern Coll (MN)
Ohio Northern U (OH)
Ohio Wesleyan U (OH)
Redeemer U Coll (ON, Canada)
Saint John's U (MN)
Shorter U (GA)
Simpson Coll (IA)
Southeastern U (FL)
Tennessee Wesleyan Coll (TN)
Trinity Christian Coll (IL)
Trinity Coll of Florida (FL)
U of Dallas (TX)
U of Indianapolis (IN)
U of Rio Grande (OH)
Washburn U (KS)
Waynesburg U (PA)
Westmont Coll (CA)

PRE-VETERINARY STUDIES

Abilene Christian U (TX)
Acadia U (NS, Canada)
Albertus Magnus Coll (CT)
Albion Coll (MI)
Allegheny Coll (PA)
Alma Coll (MI)
American Intl Coll (MA)
Anderson U (IN)
Andrews U (MI)
Arcadia U (PA)
Ashland U (OH)
Atlantic Union Coll (MA)
Auburn U (AL)
Augsburg Coll (MN)
Augustana Coll (IL)
Augustana Coll (SD)
Baldwin-Wallace Coll (OH)
Barry U (FL)
Belmont Abbey Coll (NC)
Bemidji State U (MN)
Bethany Coll (WV)
Blackburn Coll (IL)
Bob Jones U (SC)
Boise State U (ID)
Buffalo State Coll, State U of New York (NY)
California State U, Chico (CA)
California State U, East Bay (CA)
Calvin Coll (MI)
Campbellsville U (KY)
Carroll U (WI)
Catawba Coll (NC)
Cedar Crest Coll (PA)
Cedarville U (OH)
Centenary Coll of Louisiana (LA)
Central Christian Coll of Kansas (KS)
Chapman U (CA)
City Coll of the City U of New York (NY)
Clark U (MA)
The Coll at Brockport, State U of New York (NY)
Coll of Saint Benedict (MN)
Coll of Saint Mary (NE)
Coll of the Atlantic (ME)
Concordia Coll (MN)
Concord U (WV)
Cornerstone U (MI)
Cumberland U (TN)
Defiance Coll (OH)
Delaware State U (DE)
Dickinson State U (ND)
Dominican U (IL)
Dordt Coll (IA)
Drake U (IA)
Drury U (MO)
East Central U (OK)
Eastern Mennonite U (VA)
Eastern Nazarene Coll (MA)
Elmhurst Coll (IL)
Elmira Coll (NY)
Elon U (NC)
Emory & Henry Coll (VA)
Evangel U (MO)
Florida Southern Coll (FL)
Florida State U (FL)
Fordham U (NY)
Franklin Pierce U (NH)
Furman U (SC)
Gardner-Webb U (NC)
Georgia Southern U (GA)
Gettysburg Coll (PA)
Grand Valley State U (MI)
Grove City Coll (PA)
Gustavus Adolphus Coll (MN)
Hamline U (MN)
Hampton U (VA)
Harding U (AR)
Hartwick Coll (NY)
Haverford Coll (PA)
Heidelberg U (OH)
High Point U (NC)
Hillsdale Coll (MI)
Hofstra U (NY)
Houghton Coll (NY)
Illinois Coll (IL)
Immaculata U (PA)
Indiana U–Purdue U Fort Wayne (IN)
Indiana Wesleyan U (IN)
Iowa State U of Science and Technology (IA)
Iowa Wesleyan Coll (IA)
Jacksonville U (FL)
John Carroll U (OH)
Juniata Coll (PA)
Kentucky Wesleyan Coll (KY)
Keuka Coll (NY)
King Coll (TN)
King's Coll (PA)
LaGrange Coll (GA)
Lake Erie Coll (OH)
La Salle U (PA)
Lawrence U (WI)
Lees-McRae Coll (NC)
Le Moyne Coll (NY)
LeTourneau U (TX)
Lewis U (IL)
Limestone Coll (SC)
Lincoln Memorial U (TN)
Lindenwood U (MO)
Lindsey Wilson Coll (KY)
Lipscomb U (TN)
Lock Haven U of Pennsylvania (PA)
Longwood U (VA)
Loyola U New Orleans (LA)
Manchester Coll (IN)
Marian U (IN)
Marlboro Coll (VT)
Mars Hill Coll (NC)
Mayville State U (ND)
McKendree U (IL)
Mercyhurst Coll (PA)
Methodist U (NC)
Michigan Technological U (MI)
Midwestern State U (TX)
Millikin U (IL)
Minnesota State U Mankato (MN)
Minnesota State U Moorhead (MN)
Mississippi Coll (MS)
Molloy Coll (NY)
Montana State U (MT)
Mount Allison U (NB, Canada)
Mount Mary Coll (WI)
Mount Mercy Coll (IA)
Mount Vernon Nazarene U (OH)
Nazareth Coll of Rochester (NY)
Newberry Coll (SC)
Newman U (KS)
Niagara U (NY)
North Central Coll (IL)
Northern Michigan U (MI)

INDEXES

North Georgia Coll & State U (GA)
Northwest Missouri State U (MO)
Northwest Nazarene U (ID)
Nova Scotia Ag Coll (NS, Canada)
Oakland City U (IN)
Oglethorpe U (GA)
Ohio Northern U (OH)
Ohio Wesleyan U (OH)
Oklahoma City U (OK)
Oklahoma Wesleyan U (OK)
Ouachita Baptist U (AR)
Pacific Union Coll (CA)
Peru State Coll (NE)
Pittsburg State U (KS)
Purdue U (IN)
Purdue U Calumet (IN)
Queens U of Charlotte (NC)
Quinnipiac U (CT)
Redeemer U Coll (ON, Canada)
Rhode Island Coll (RI)
Ripon Coll (WI)
Rivier Coll (NH)
Roberts Wesleyan Coll (NY)
Rochester Inst of Technology (NY)
Rockford Coll (IL)
Sacred Heart U (CT)
St. Andrews Presbyterian Coll (NC)
St. Catherine U (MN)
St. Cloud State U (MN)
Saint Francis U (PA)
St. Francis Xavier U (NS, Canada)
Saint John's U (MN)
Saint Martin's U (WA)
Saint Mary-of-the-Woods Coll (IN)
Saint Michael's Coll (VT)
Sarah Lawrence Coll (NY)
Seton Hill U (PA)
Simpson Coll (IA)
Sonoma State U (CA)
Southwestern Oklahoma State U (OK)
Southwest Minnesota State U (MN)
Spring Hill Coll (AL)
State U of New York at Binghamton (NY)
State U of New York at Fredonia (NY)
State U of New York at Oswego (NY)
State U of New York Coll at Geneseo (NY)
State U of New York Coll at Oneonta (NY)
State U of New York Coll of Environmental Science and Forestry (NY)
Stetson U (FL)
Sul Ross State U (TX)
Susquehanna U (PA)
Tabor Coll (KS)
Tarleton State U (TX)
Tennessee Technological U (TN)
Texas A&M U (TX)
Texas A&M U–Corpus Christi (TX)
Texas Lutheran U (TX)
Thiel Coll (PA)
Thompson Rivers U (BC, Canada)
Trinity Christian Coll (IL)
Trinity U (TX)
Truman State U (MO)
Tusculum Coll (TN)
U of Alberta (AB, Canada)
The U of Arizona (AZ)
U of Bridgeport (CT)
The U of British Columbia (BC, Canada)
U of Central Missouri (MO)
U of Cincinnati (OH)
U of Colorado at Colorado Springs (CO)
U of Evansville (IN)
The U of Findlay (OH)
U of Illinois at Urbana–Champaign (IL)
U of Indianapolis (IN)
The U of Iowa (IA)
U of Maine (ME)
U of Manitoba (MB, Canada)
U of Maryland, Coll Park (MD)
U of Massachusetts Amherst (MA)
U of Minnesota, Crookston (MN)
U of Minnesota, Duluth (MN)
U of Minnesota, Twin Cities Campus (MN)
U of Missouri–Kansas City (MO)
U of Missouri–St. Louis (MO)
The U of Montana Western (MT)
U of Nebraska–Lincoln (NE)
U of Nevada, Reno (NV)
U of New Brunswick Fredericton (NB, Canada)
U of Pittsburgh at Johnstown (PA)
U of Regina (SK, Canada)
U of Rio Grande (OH)
U of St. Francis (IL)
U of St. Thomas (TX)
U of San Francisco (CA)
U of Saskatchewan (SK, Canada)
The U of Tennessee at Martin (TN)
The U of Toledo (OH)
U of Wisconsin–Oshkosh (WI)
U of Wisconsin–Parkside (WI)
U of Wisconsin–River Falls (WI)
Upper Iowa U (IA)
Utah State U (UT)
Utica Coll (NY)
Valley City State U (ND)
Virginia Intermont Coll (VA)
Virginia Wesleyan Coll (VA)
Wabash Coll (IN)
Walsh U (OH)
Warner Pacific Coll (OR)
Washburn U (KS)
Washington Adventist U (MD)
Washington Coll (MD)
Washington U in St. Louis (MO)
Waynesburg U (PA)
Wells Coll (NY)
Westmont Coll (CA)
West Virginia State U (WV)
West Virginia Wesleyan Coll (WV)
Wheeling Jesuit U (WV)
Widener U (PA)
Wilmington Coll (OH)
Wingate U (NC)
Winona State U (MN)
Wofford Coll (SC)
Wright State U (OH)
Xavier U of Louisiana (LA)
York U (ON, Canada)
Youngstown State U (OH)

PRINTING MANAGEMENT
Carroll U (WI)
Ferris State U (MI)
Kean U (NJ)
Pittsburg State U (KS)
Rochester Inst of Technology (NY)
U of Wisconsin–Stout (WI)

PRINTMAKING
Adams State Coll (CO)
Alberta Coll of Art & Design (AB, Canada)
Aquinas Coll (MI)
Bennington Coll (VT)
Birmingham-Southern Coll (AL)
Bowling Green State U (OH)
Bradley U (IL)
Brigham Young U (UT)
Buffalo State Coll, State U of New York (NY)
California Coll of the Arts (CA)
California State U, East Bay (CA)
California State U, Long Beach (CA)
The Cleveland Inst of Art (OH)
Coll of Visual Arts (MN)
Columbia Coll (MO)
Concordia U (QC, Canada)
Drake U (IA)
Escuela de Artes Plasticas de Puerto Rico (PR)
Indiana U–Purdue U Fort Wayne (IN)
Indiana Wesleyan U (IN)
Kent State U (OH)
Keystone Coll (PA)
Longwood U (VA)
Maine Coll of Art (ME)
Maryland Inst Coll of Art (MD)
Massachusetts Coll of Art and Design (MA)
Memorial U of Newfoundland (NL, Canada)
Minneapolis Coll of Art and Design (MN)
Minnesota State U Moorhead (MN)
Mount Allison U (NB, Canada)
Northern Michigan U (MI)
Northwest Nazarene U (ID)
Ohio Northern U (OH)
Ohio U (OH)
Pratt Inst (NY)
Purchase Coll, State U of New York (NY)
Ringling Coll of Art and Design (FL)
Rutgers, The State U of New Jersey, New Brunswick (NJ)
St. Cloud State U (MN)
Salem State Coll (MA)
Sarah Lawrence Coll (NY)
Savannah Coll of Art and Design (GA)
School of the Art Inst of Chicago (IL)
School of the Museum of Fine Arts, Boston (MA)
School of Visual Arts (NY)
Seton Hill U (PA)
Sonoma State U (CA)
State U of New York at New Paltz (NY)
Temple U (PA)
Texas Christian U (TX)
Trinity Christian Coll (IL)
U of Alberta (AB, Canada)
U of Dallas (TX)
U of Hartford (CT)
The U of Iowa (IA)
The U of Kansas (KS)
U of Miami (FL)
U of Michigan (MI)
U of Missouri–St. Louis (MO)
U of Oregon (OR)
U of Regina (SK, Canada)
U of San Francisco (CA)
The U of Texas at El Paso (TX)
U of Washington (WA)
U of Windsor (ON, Canada)
Washington U in St. Louis (MO)
Western State Coll of Colorado (CO)
Western Washington U (WA)
York U (ON, Canada)

PROFESSIONAL STUDIES
Bemidji State U (MN)
Briar Cliff U (IA)
Champlain Coll (VT)
Coll of St. Joseph (VT)
Kent State U (OH)
Saint Mary-of-the-Woods Coll (IN)
Slippery Rock U of Pennsylvania (PA)
Southern Vermont Coll (VT)
U of Dubuque (IA)
U of Memphis (TN)

PSYCHIATRIC/MENTAL HEALTH SERVICES TECHNOLOGY
Franciscan U of Steubenville (OH)
Indiana U–Purdue U Fort Wayne (IN)
Northern Kentucky U (KY)

PSYCHOLOGY
Abilene Christian U (TX)
Acadia U (NS, Canada)
Adams State Coll (CO)
Adelphi U (NY)
Agnes Scott Coll (GA)
Alabama Ag and Mech U (AL)
Alabama State U (AL)
Alaska Pacific U (AK)
Albany State U (GA)
Albertus Magnus Coll (CT)
Albion Coll (MI)
Albright Coll (PA)
Alcorn State U (MS)
Alderson-Broaddus Coll (WV)
Alfred U (NY)
Allegheny Coll (PA)
Alliant Intl U (CA)
Alliant Intl U–México City (Mexico)
Alma Coll (MI)
Alvernia U (PA)
Alverno Coll (WI)
American Intl Coll (MA)
American Jewish U (CA)
American Public U System (WV)
American U (DC)
The American U of Beirut (Lebanon)
The American U of Paris (France)
Amherst Coll (MA)
Anderson U (IN)
Andrews U (MI)
Angelo State U (TX)
Appalachian State U (NC)
Aquinas Coll (MI)
Arcadia U (PA)
Argosy U, Atlanta (GA)
Argosy U, Chicago (IL)
Argosy U, Dallas (TX)
Argosy U, Denver (CO)
Argosy U, Hawai'i (HI)
Argosy U, Inland Empire (CA)
Argosy U, Los Angeles (CA)
Argosy U, Nashville (TN)
Argosy U, Orange County (CA)
Argosy U, Phoenix (AZ)
Argosy U, Salt Lake City (UT)
Argosy U, San Diego (CA)
Argosy U, San Francisco Bay Area (CA)
Argosy U, Sarasota (FL)
Argosy U, Schaumburg (IL)
Argosy U, Seattle (WA)
Argosy U, Tampa (FL)
Argosy U, Twin Cities (MN)
Argosy U, Washington DC (VA)
Arizona State U (AZ)
Arkansas State U—Jonesboro (AR)
Arkansas Tech U (AR)
Armstrong Atlantic State U (GA)
Asbury U (KY)
Ashland U (OH)
Assumption Coll (MA)
Athabasca U (AB, Canada)
Atlantic Union Coll (MA)
Auburn U (AL)
Auburn U Montgomery (AL)
Augsburg Coll (MN)
Augustana Coll (IL)
Augustana Coll (SD)
Aurora U (IL)
Austin Coll (TX)
Austin Peay State U (TN)
Averett U (VA)
Avila U (MO)
Azusa Pacific U (CA)
Baker U (KS)
Baldwin-Wallace Coll (OH)
Ball State U (IN)
Baptist Bible Coll of Pennsylvania (PA)
Barclay Coll (KS)
Bard Coll (NY)
Bard Coll at Simon's Rock (MA)
Barnard Coll (NY)
Barry U (FL)
Barton Coll (NC)
Bastyr U (WA)
Bates Coll (ME)
Baylor U (TX)
Bay Path Coll (MA)
Belhaven U (MS)
Bellarmine U (KY)
Belmont Abbey Coll (NC)
Belmont U (TN)
Beloit Coll (WI)
Bemidji State U (MN)
Benedictine Coll (KS)
Benedictine U (IL)
Bennett Coll for Women (NC)
Bennington Coll (VT)
Berea Coll (KY)
Bernard M. Baruch Coll of the City U of New York (NY)
Berry Coll (GA)
Bethany Coll (KS)
Bethany Coll (WV)
Bethany Lutheran Coll (MN)
Bethany U (CA)
Bethel Coll (IN)
Bethel Coll (KS)
Bethel U (MN)
Bethel U (TN)
Bethune-Cookman U (FL)
Birmingham-Southern Coll (AL)
Bishop's U (QC, Canada)
Blackburn Coll (IL)
Black Hills State U (SD)
Bloomfield Coll (NJ)
Bloomsburg U of Pennsylvania (PA)
Bluefield Coll (VA)
Blue Mountain Coll (MS)
Bluffton U (OH)
Boise State U (ID)
Boston Coll (MA)
Boston U (MA)
Bowdoin Coll (ME)
Bowie State U (MD)
Bowling Green State U (OH)
Brandeis U (MA)
Brenau U (GA)
Brescia U (KY)
Brevard Coll (NC)
Brewton-Parker Coll (GA)
Briar Cliff U (IA)
Bridgewater Coll (VA)
Bridgewater State Coll (MA)
Brigham Young U–Hawaii (HI)
Brock U (ON, Canada)
Brooklyn Coll of the City U of New York (NY)
Bryan Coll (TN)
Bryant U (RI)
Bryn Mawr Coll (PA)
Bucknell U (PA)
Buena Vista U (IA)
Buffalo State Coll, State U of New York (NY)
Burlington Coll (VT)
Butler U (IN)
Cabrini Coll (PA)
California Baptist U (CA)
California Lutheran U (CA)
California Polytechnic State U, San Luis Obispo (CA)
California State Polytechnic U, Pomona (CA)
California State U, Bakersfield (CA)
California State U, Chico (CA)
California State U, Dominguez Hills (CA)
California State U, East Bay (CA)
California State U, Fresno (CA)
California State U, Fullerton (CA)
California State U, Long Beach (CA)
California State U, Los Angeles (CA)
California State U, Monterey Bay (CA)
California State U, Northridge (CA)
California State U, Sacramento (CA)
California State U, San Bernardino (CA)
California State U, San Marcos (CA)
California State U, Stanislaus (CA)
Calumet Coll of Saint Joseph (IN)
Calvin Coll (MI)
Cambridge Coll (MA)
Cameron U (OK)
Campbellsville U (KY)
Canisius Coll (NY)
Cape Breton U (NS, Canada)
Capella U (MN)
Capital U (OH)
Carleton Coll (MN)
Carlos Albizu U (PR)
Carlos Albizu U, Miami Campus (FL)
Carlow U (PA)
Carnegie Mellon U (PA)
Carroll U (WI)
Carson-Newman Coll (TN)
Case Western Reserve U (OH)
Castleton State Coll (VT)
Catawba Coll (NC)
The Catholic U of America (DC)
Cazenovia Coll (NY)
Cedar Crest Coll (PA)
Cedarville U (OH)
Centenary Coll (NJ)
Centenary Coll of Louisiana (LA)
Central Baptist Coll (AR)
Central Christian Coll of Kansas (KS)
Central Coll (IA)
Central Connecticut State U (CT)
Central Michigan U (MI)
Central State U (OH)
Chaminade U of Honolulu (HI)
Chapman U (CA)
Chatham U (PA)
Cheyney U of Pennsylvania (PA)
Chowan U (NC)
Christian Brothers U (TN)
Christopher Newport U (VA)
Cincinnati Christian U (OH)
The Citadel, The Military Coll of South Carolina (SC)
City Coll of the City U of New York (NY)
City U of Seattle (WA)
Claremont McKenna Coll (CA)
Clarion U of Pennsylvania (PA)
Clark Atlanta U (GA)
Clarke Coll (IA)
Clarkson U (NY)
Clark U (MA)
Clearwater Christian Coll (FL)
Clemson U (SC)
Cleveland State U (OH)
Coastal Carolina U (SC)
Coker Coll (SC)
Colby Coll (ME)
Colgate U (NY)
Coll of Charleston (SC)
The Coll of Idaho (ID)
Coll of Mount St. Joseph (OH)
Coll of Mount Saint Vincent (NY)
The Coll of New Jersey (NJ)
The Coll of New Rochelle (NY)
Coll of Notre Dame of Maryland (MD)
Coll of Saint Benedict (MN)
Coll of Saint Elizabeth (NJ)
Coll of St. Joseph (VT)
Coll of Saint Mary (NE)
The Coll of Saint Rose (NY)
The Coll of St. Scholastica (MN)
Coll of Staten Island of the City U of New York (NY)
Coll of the Atlantic (ME)
Coll of the Holy Cross (MA)
Coll of the Ozarks (MO)
The Coll of William and Mary (VA)
The Coll of Wooster (OH)
The Colorado Coll (CO)
Colorado State U (CO)
Colorado State U–Pueblo (CO)
Columbia Coll (MO)
Columbia Coll (SC)
Columbia Intl U (SC)
Columbia Southern U (AL)
Columbia U (NY)
Columbia U, School of General Studies (NY)
Columbus State U (GA)
Concordia Coll (MN)
Concordia U (CA)
Concordia U (QC, Canada)
Concordia U Chicago (IL)
Concordia U Coll of Alberta (AB, Canada)
Concordia U, St. Paul (MN)
Concordia U Wisconsin (WI)
Concord U (WV)
Connecticut Coll (CT)
Converse Coll (SC)
Coppin State U (MD)
Corban U (OR)
Cornell Coll (IA)
Cornell U (NY)

INDEXES

Cornerstone U (MI)
Covenant Coll (GA)
Crandall U (NB, Canada)
Creighton U (NE)
Crichton Coll (TN)
Crown Coll (MN)
Culver-Stockton Coll (MO)
Cumberland U (TN)
Curry Coll (MA)
Daemen Coll (NY)
Dakota Wesleyan U (SD)
Dallas Baptist U (TX)
Dana Coll (NE)
Dartmouth Coll (NH)
Davidson Coll (NC)
Defiance Coll (OH)
Delaware State U (DE)
Delta State U (MS)
Denison U (OH)
DePaul U (IL)
DePauw U (IN)
DeSales U (PA)
Dickinson Coll (PA)
Dickinson State U (ND)
Dillard U (LA)
Doane Coll (NE)
Dominican Coll (NY)
Dominican U (IL)
Dominican U of California (CA)
Dordt Coll (IA)
Dowling Coll (NY)
Drake U (IA)
Drew U (NJ)
Drexel U (PA)
Drury U (MO)
Duke U (NC)
Duquesne U (PA)
D'Youville Coll (NY)
Earlham Coll (IN)
East Carolina U (NC)
East Central U (OK)
Eastern Connecticut State U (CT)
Eastern Illinois U (IL)
Eastern Mennonite U (VA)
Eastern Michigan U (MI)
Eastern Nazarene Coll (MA)
Eastern New Mexico U (NM)
Eastern Washington U (WA)
East Stroudsburg U of Pennsylvania (PA)
East Tennessee State U (TN)
East Texas Baptist U (TX)
Eckerd Coll (FL)
Edgewood Coll (WI)
Edinboro U of Pennsylvania (PA)
Edward Waters Coll (FL)
Elizabeth City State U (NC)
Elizabethtown Coll (PA)
Elmhurst Coll (IL)
Elmira Coll (NY)
Elon U (NC)
Emmanuel Coll (GA)
Emmanuel Coll (MA)
Emory & Henry Coll (VA)
Emory U (GA)
Emporia State U (KS)
Endicott Coll (MA)
Erskine Coll (SC)
Eugene Lang Coll The New School for Liberal Arts (NY)
Evangel U (MO)
Excelsior Coll (NY)
Fairfield U (CT)
Fairleigh Dickinson U, Coll at Florham (NJ)
Fairleigh Dickinson U, Metropolitan Campus (NJ)
Fairmont State U (WV)
Faulkner U (AL)
Fayetteville State U (NC)
Felician Coll (NJ)
Ferris State U (MI)
Ferrum Coll (VA)
Fisk U (TN)
Fitchburg State Coll (MA)
Flagler Coll (FL)
Florida Atlantic U (FL)
Florida Gulf Coast U (FL)
Florida Inst of Technology (FL)
Florida Intl U (FL)
Florida Southern Coll (FL)
Florida State U (FL)
Fontbonne U (MO)
Fordham U (NY)
Fort Hays State U (KS)
Fort Lewis Coll (CO)
Fort Valley State U (GA)
Framingham State Coll (MA)
Franciscan U of Steubenville (OH)
Francis Marion U (SC)
Franklin & Marshall Coll (PA)
Franklin Coll (IN)
Franklin Pierce U (NH)
Freed-Hardeman U (TN)
Friends U (KS)
Frostburg State U (MD)
Furman U (SC)
Gallaudet U (DC)
Gannon U (PA)
Gardner-Webb U (NC)
Geneva Coll (PA)
George Fox U (OR)
George Mason U (VA)
Georgetown Coll (KY)
Georgetown U (DC)
The George Washington U (DC)
Georgia Coll & State U (GA)
Georgian Court U (NJ)
Georgia Southern U (GA)
Georgia State U (GA)
Gettysburg Coll (PA)
Goldey-Beacom Coll (DE)
Gonzaga U (WA)
Gordon Coll (MA)
Goshen Coll (IN)
Goucher Coll (MD)
Governors State U (IL)
Grace Coll (IN)
Graceland U (IA)
Grambling State U (LA)
Grand Valley State U (MI)
Grand View U (IA)
Green Mountain Coll (VT)
Greensboro Coll (NC)
Greenville Coll (IL)
Grinnell Coll (IA)
Grove City Coll (PA)
Guilford Coll (NC)
Gustavus Adolphus Coll (MN)
Gwynedd-Mercy Coll (PA)
Hamilton Coll (NY)
Hamline U (MN)
Hampden-Sydney Coll (VA)
Hampshire Coll (MA)
Hampton U (VA)
Hannibal-LaGrange Coll (MO)
Hanover Coll (IN)
Harding U (AR)
Hardin-Simmons U (TX)
Hartwick Coll (NY)
Harvard U (MA)
Haverford Coll (PA)
Hawai'i Pacific U (HI)
Heidelberg U (OH)
Henderson State U (AR)
Hendrix Coll (AR)
Hesser Coll, Manchester (NH)
High Point U (NC)
Hilbert Coll (NY)
Hillsdale Coll (MI)
Hillsdale Free Will Baptist Coll (OK)
Hiram Coll (OH)
Hofstra U (NY)
Hollins U (VA)
Holy Family U (PA)
Holy Names U (CA)
Hood Coll (MD)
Hope Coll (MI)
Houghton Coll (NY)
Houston Baptist U (TX)
Howard Payne U (TX)
Humboldt State U (CA)
Hunter Coll of the City U of New York (NY)
Huntingdon Coll (AL)
Huntington U (IN)
Huston-Tillotson U (TX)
Idaho State U (ID)
Illinois Coll (IL)
Illinois Inst of Technology (IL)
Illinois State U (IL)
Illinois Wesleyan U (IL)
Immaculata U (PA)
Indiana State U (IN)
Indiana Tech (IN)
Indiana U Bloomington (IN)
Indiana U East (IN)
Indiana U Kokomo (IN)
Indiana U Northwest (IN)
Indiana U of Pennsylvania (PA)
Indiana U–Purdue U Fort Wayne (IN)
Indiana U–Purdue U Indianapolis (IN)
Indiana U South Bend (IN)
Indiana U Southeast (IN)
Indiana Wesleyan U (IN)
Inter American U of Puerto Rico, San Germán Campus (PR)
Iona Coll (NY)
Iowa State U of Science and Technology (IA)
Iowa Wesleyan Coll (IA)
Ithaca Coll (NY)
Jackson State U (MS)
Jacksonville State U (AL)
Jacksonville U (FL)
James Madison U (VA)
Jamestown Coll (ND)
John Brown U (AR)
John Carroll U (OH)
The Johns Hopkins U (MD)
Johnson C. Smith U (NC)
Johnson State Coll (VT)
John Wesley Coll (NC)
Judson Coll (AL)
Judson U (IL)
Juniata Coll (PA)
Kalamazoo Coll (MI)
Kansas State U (KS)
Kean U (NJ)
Keene State Coll (NH)
Kennesaw State U (GA)
Kent State U (OH)
Kent State U at Stark (OH)
Kentucky State U (KY)
Kentucky Wesleyan Coll (KY)
Kenyon Coll (OH)
Keuka Coll (NY)
Keystone Coll (PA)
King Coll (TN)
King's Coll (PA)
The King's U Coll (AB, Canada)
Knox Coll (IL)
Kutztown U of Pennsylvania (PA)
Lafayette Coll (PA)
LaGrange Coll (GA)
Lake Erie Coll (OH)
Lake Forest Coll (IL)
Lakehead U (ON, Canada)
Lakeland Coll (WI)
Lake Superior State U (MI)
Lamar U (TX)
La Roche Coll (PA)
La Salle U (PA)
Lasell Coll (MA)
La Sierra U (CA)
Laurentian U (ON, Canada)
Lawrence Technological U (MI)
Lawrence U (WI)
Lebanon Valley Coll (PA)
Lees-McRae Coll (NC)
Lee U (TN)
Lehigh U (PA)
Lehman Coll of the City U of New York (NY)
Le Moyne Coll (NY)
LeTourneau U (TX)
Lewis & Clark Coll (OR)
Lewis-Clark State Coll (ID)
Lewis U (IL)
Liberty U (VA)
Life U (GA)
Limestone Coll (SC)
Lincoln Memorial U (TN)
Lincoln U (MO)
Lincoln U (PA)
Lindenwood U (MO)
Lindsey Wilson Coll (KY)
Linfield Coll (OR)
Lipscomb U (TN)
Lock Haven U of Pennsylvania (PA)
Long Island U, Brooklyn Campus (NY)
Long Island U, C.W. Post Campus (NY)
Longwood U (VA)
Loras Coll (IA)
Louisiana Coll (LA)
Louisiana State U and Ag and Mech Coll (LA)
Louisiana State U in Shreveport (LA)
Louisiana Tech U (LA)
Lourdes Coll (OH)
Loyola Marymount U (CA)
Loyola U Chicago (IL)
Loyola U Maryland (MD)
Loyola U New Orleans (LA)
Lubbock Christian U (TX)
Luther Coll (IA)
Lycoming Coll (PA)
Lynchburg Coll (VA)
Lynn U (FL)
Lyon Coll (AR)
Macalester Coll (MN)
Madonna U (MI)
Malone U (OH)
Manchester Coll (IN)
Manhattan Coll (NY)
Manhattanville Coll (NY)
Mansfield U of Pennsylvania (PA)
Marian U (IN)
Marian U (WI)
Marietta Coll (OH)
Marist Coll (NY)
Marlboro Coll (VT)
Marquette U (WI)
Marshall U (WV)
Mars Hill Coll (NC)
Mary Baldwin Coll (VA)
Marylhurst U (OR)
Marymount Manhattan Coll (NY)
Marymount U (VA)
Maryville Coll (TN)
Maryville U of Saint Louis (MO)
Marywood U (PA)
Massachusetts Coll of Liberal Arts (MA)
McDaniel Coll (MD)
McKendree U (IL)
McMurry U (TX)
McNeese State U (LA)
McPherson Coll (KS)
Medaille Coll (NY)
Medgar Evers Coll of the City U of New York (NY)
Memorial U of Newfoundland (NL, Canada)
Menlo Coll (CA)
Mercer U (GA)
Mercy Coll (NY)
Mercyhurst Coll (PA)
Meredith Coll (NC)
Merrimack Coll (MA)
Messiah Coll (PA)
Methodist U (NC)
Metropolitan State Coll of Denver (CO)
Miami U (OH)
Miami U Hamilton (OH)
Michigan State U (MI)
Michigan Technological U (MI)
MidAmerica Nazarene U (KS)
Mid-Continent U (KY)
Middlebury Coll (VT)
Middle Tennessee State U (TN)
Midway Coll (KY)
Midwestern State U (TX)
Millersville U of Pennsylvania (PA)
Milligan Coll (TN)
Millikin U (IL)
Millsaps Coll (MS)
Mills Coll (CA)
Minnesota State U Mankato (MN)
Minnesota State U Moorhead (MN)
Minot State U (ND)
Misericordia U (PA)
Mississippi Coll (MS)
Mississippi State U (MS)
Mississippi U for Women (MS)
Missouri Baptist U (MO)
Missouri State U (MO)
Missouri U of Science and Technology (MO)
Missouri Western State U (MO)
Mitchell Coll (CT)
Molloy Coll (NY)
Monmouth Coll (IL)
Monmouth U (NJ)
Montana State U (MT)
Montana State U Billings (MT)
Montclair State U (NJ)
Moravian Coll (PA)
Morehead State U (KY)
Morehouse Coll (GA)
Morningside Coll (IA)
Mountain State U (WV)
Mount Allison U (NB, Canada)
Mount Aloysius Coll (PA)
Mount Holyoke Coll (MA)
Mount Ida Coll (MA)
Mount Marty Coll (SD)
Mount Mary Coll (WI)
Mount Mercy Coll (IA)
Mount Olive Coll (NC)
Mount Saint Mary Coll (NY)
Mount St. Mary's Coll (CA)
Mount St. Mary's U (MD)
Mount Vernon Nazarene U (OH)
Muhlenberg Coll (PA)
Multnomah U (OR)
Murray State U (KY)
Naropa U (CO)
National U (CA)
Nazareth Coll of Rochester (NY)
Nebraska Wesleyan U (NE)
Neumann U (PA)
Nevada State Coll at Henderson (NV)
Newberry Coll (SC)
Newbury Coll (MA)
New Coll of Florida (FL)
New England Coll (NH)
New Jersey City U (NJ)
Newman U (KS)
New Mexico Highlands U (NM)
New Mexico Inst of Mining and Technology (NM)
New Mexico State U (NM)
New York Inst of Technology (NY)
New York U (NY)
Niagara U (NY)
Nicholls State U (LA)
Nichols Coll (MA)
Nipissing U (ON, Canada)
Norfolk State U (VA)
North Carolina Central U (NC)
North Carolina State U (NC)
North Central Coll (IL)
Northcentral U (AZ)
North Dakota State U (ND)
Northeastern Illinois U (IL)
Northeastern State U (OK)
Northeastern U (MA)
Northern Arizona U (AZ)
Northern Kentucky U (KY)
Northern Michigan U (MI)
Northern State U (SD)
North Georgia Coll & State U (GA)
North Greenville U (SC)
Northwestern Coll (IA)
Northwestern Coll (MN)
Northwestern Oklahoma State U (OK)
Northwestern State U of Louisiana (LA)
Northwest Missouri State U (MO)
Northwest Nazarene U (ID)
Northwest U (WA)
Notre Dame de Namur U (CA)
Nova Southeastern U (FL)
Nyack Coll (NY)
Oakland U (MI)
Oakwood U (AL)
Oberlin Coll (OH)
Occidental Coll (CA)
Oglethorpe U (GA)
Ohio Dominican U (OH)
Ohio Northern U (OH)
The Ohio State U (OH)
The Ohio State U at Lima (OH)
The Ohio State U at Marion (OH)
The Ohio State U–Mansfield Campus (OH)
The Ohio State U–Newark Campus (OH)
Ohio U (OH)
Ohio Valley U (WV)
Ohio Wesleyan U (OH)
Oklahoma Baptist U (OK)
Oklahoma Christian U (OK)
Oklahoma City U (OK)
Oklahoma Panhandle State U (OK)
Oklahoma State U (OK)
Old Dominion U (VA)
Oral Roberts U (OK)
Oregon State U (OR)
Oregon State U–Cascades (OR)
Ottawa U (KS)
Ouachita Baptist U (AR)
Our Lady of the Lake U of San Antonio (TX)
Pace U (NY)
Pacific Lutheran U (WA)
Pacific Union Coll (CA)
Paine Coll (GA)
Park U (MO)
Peace Coll (NC)
Penn State Abington (PA)
Penn State Altoona (PA)
Penn State Beaver (PA)
Penn State Berks (PA)
Penn State Brandywine (PA)
Penn State DuBois (PA)
Penn State Erie, The Behrend Coll (PA)
Penn State Fayette, The Eberly Campus (PA)
Penn State Greater Allegheny (PA)
Penn State Harrisburg (PA)
Penn State Hazleton (PA)
Penn State Lehigh Valley (PA)
Penn State Mont Alto (PA)
Penn State New Kensington (PA)
Penn State Schuylkill (PA)
Penn State Shenango (PA)
Penn State U Park (PA)
Penn State Wilkes-Barre (PA)
Penn State Worthington Scranton (PA)
Penn State York (PA)
Pepperdine U, Malibu (CA)
Peru State Coll (NE)
Philadelphia U (PA)
Piedmont Coll (GA)
Pikeville Coll (KY)
Pittsburg State U (KS)
Pitzer Coll (CA)
Plymouth State U (NH)
Point Park U (PA)
Pomona Coll (CA)
Pontifical Catholic U of Puerto Rico (PR)
Portland State U (OR)
Post U (CT)
Prairie View A&M U (TX)
Presbyterian Coll (SC)
Prescott Coll (AZ)
Presentation Coll (SD)
Princeton U (NJ)
Providence Coll (RI)
Purchase Coll, State U of New York (NY)
Purdue U (IN)
Purdue U Calumet (IN)
Queens Coll of the City U of New York (NY)
Queen's U at Kingston (ON, Canada)
Queens U of Charlotte (NC)
Quincy U (IL)
Quinnipiac U (CT)
Radford U (VA)
Ramapo Coll of New Jersey (NJ)
Randolph Coll (VA)
Randolph-Macon Coll (VA)
Redeemer U Coll (ON, Canada)
Reed Coll (OR)
Regent U (VA)
Regis Coll (MA)
Reinhardt Coll (GA)

Rensselaer Polytechnic Inst (NY)
Rhode Island Coll (RI)
Rhodes Coll (TN)
Rice U (TX)
The Richard Stockton Coll of New Jersey (NJ)
Rider U (NJ)
Ripon Coll (WI)
Rivier Coll (NH)
Roanoke Coll (VA)
Robert Morris U (PA)
Roberts Wesleyan Coll (NY)
Rochester Coll (MI)
Rochester Inst of Technology (NY)
Rockford Coll (IL)
Rockhurst U (MO)
Rocky Mountain Coll (MT)
Rollins Coll (FL)
Roosevelt U (IL)
Rosemont Coll (PA)
Rowan U (NJ)
Royal Military Coll of Canada (ON, Canada)
Russell Sage Coll (NY)
Rutgers, The State U of New Jersey, Camden (NJ)
Rutgers, The State U of New Jersey, Newark (NJ)
Rutgers, The State U of New Jersey, New Brunswick (NJ)
Sacred Heart U (CT)
Sage Coll of Albany (NY)
Saginaw Valley State U (MI)
St. Ambrose U (IA)
St. Andrews Presbyterian Coll (NC)
Saint Anselm Coll (NH)
Saint Augustine's Coll (NC)
St. Bonaventure U (NY)
St. Catherine U (MN)
St. Cloud State U (MN)
St. Edward's U (TX)
St. Francis Coll (NY)
Saint Francis U (PA)
St. Francis Xavier U (NS, Canada)
St. John Fisher Coll (NY)
Saint John's U (MN)
St. John's U (NY)
Saint Joseph Coll (CT)
St. Joseph's Coll, Long Island Campus (NY)
St. Joseph's Coll, New York (NY)
Saint Joseph's U (PA)
St. Lawrence U (NY)
Saint Leo U (FL)
Saint Louis U (MO)
Saint Martin's U (WA)
Saint Mary-of-the-Woods Coll (IN)
Saint Mary's Coll (IN)
Saint Mary's Coll of California (CA)
St. Mary's Coll of Maryland (MD)
St. Mary's U (TX)
Saint Mary's U of Minnesota (MN)
Saint Michael's Coll (VT)
St. Norbert Coll (WI)
St. Olaf Coll (MN)
St. Thomas Aquinas Coll (NY)
St. Thomas U (FL)
St. Thomas U (NB, Canada)
Saint Vincent Coll (PA)
Saint Xavier U (IL)
Salem Coll (NC)
Salem State Coll (MA)
Salisbury U (MD)
Salve Regina U (RI)
Samford U (AL)
Sam Houston State U (TX)
San Diego Christian Coll (CA)
San Diego State U (CA)
San Francisco State U (CA)
San Jose State U (CA)
Santa Clara U (CA)
Sarah Lawrence Coll (NY)
Schreiner U (TX)
Scripps Coll (CA)
Seattle Pacific U (WA)
Seattle U (WA)
Seton Hall U (NJ)
Seton Hill U (PA)
Sewanee: The U of the South (TN)
Shawnee State U (OH)
Shaw U (NC)
Shenandoah U (VA)
Shepherd U (WV)
Shippensburg U of Pennsylvania (PA)
Shorter U (GA)
Siena Coll (NY)
Siena Heights U (MI)
Silver Lake Coll (WI)
Simmons Coll (MA)
Simon Fraser U (BC, Canada)
Simpson Coll (IA)
Simpson U (CA)
Skidmore Coll (NY)
Slippery Rock U of Pennsylvania (PA)
Smith Coll (MA)
Sonoma State U (CA)
South Carolina State U (SC)
South Dakota State U (SD)
Southeastern Louisiana U (LA)
Southeastern Oklahoma State U (OK)
Southeastern U (FL)
Southeast Missouri State U (MO)
Southern Adventist U (TN)
Southern Arkansas U–Magnolia (AR)
Southern Connecticut State U (CT)
Southern Illinois U Carbondale (IL)
Southern Illinois U Edwardsville (IL)
Southern Methodist U (TX)
Southern New Hampshire U (NH)
Southern Oregon U (OR)
Southern Polytechnic State U (GA)
Southern U and Ag and Mech Coll (LA)
Southern U at New Orleans (LA)
Southern Utah U (UT)
Southern Vermont Coll (VT)
Southern Wesleyan U (SC)
South U (AL)
South U, Royal Palm Beach (FL)
South U, Tampa (FL)
South U (GA)
South U, Columbia (SC)
South U, Glen Allen (VA)
South U, Virginia Beach (VA)
Southwest Baptist U (MO)
Southwestern Adventist U (TX)
Southwestern Coll (KS)
Southwestern Oklahoma State U (OK)
Southwestern U (TX)
Southwest Minnesota State U (MN)
Spalding U (KY)
Spelman Coll (GA)
Spring Arbor U (MI)
Spring Hill Coll (AL)
Stanford U (CA)
State U of New York at Binghamton (NY)
State U of New York at Fredonia (NY)
State U of New York at New Paltz (NY)
State U of New York at Oswego (NY)
State U of New York at Plattsburgh (NY)
State U of New York Coll at Cortland (NY)
State U of New York Coll at Geneseo (NY)
State U of New York Coll at Old Westbury (NY)
State U of New York Coll at Oneonta (NY)
State U of New York Coll at Potsdam (NY)
Stephen F. Austin State U (TX)
Stephens Coll (MO)
Stetson U (FL)
Stevenson U (MD)
Stillman Coll (AL)
Stonehill Coll (MA)
Stony Brook U, State U of New York (NY)
Suffolk U (MA)
Sul Ross State U (TX)
Susquehanna U (PA)
Swarthmore Coll (PA)
Sweet Briar Coll (VA)
Syracuse U (NY)
Tabor Coll (KS)
Talladega Coll (AL)
Tarleton State U (TX)
Taylor U (IN)
Temple U (PA)
Tennessee Technological U (TN)
Tennessee Wesleyan Coll (TN)
Texas A&M Intl U (TX)
Texas A&M U (TX)
Texas A&M U–Commerce (TX)
Texas A&M U–Corpus Christi (TX)
Texas A&M U–Kingsville (TX)
Texas Christian U (TX)
Texas Lutheran U (TX)
Texas Southern U (TX)
Texas State U–San Marcos (TX)
Texas Tech U (TX)
Texas Wesleyan U (TX)
Texas Woman's U (TX)
Thiel Coll (PA)
Thomas Edison State Coll (NJ)
Thomas More Coll (KY)
Thompson Rivers U (BC, Canada)
Tiffin U (OH)
Towson U (MD)
Transylvania U (KY)
Trent U (ON, Canada)
Trevecca Nazarene U (TN)
Trine U (IN)
Trinity Christian Coll (IL)
Trinity Coll (CT)
Trinity U (TX)
Troy U (AL)
Truman State U (MO)
Tufts U (MA)
Tulane U (LA)
Tusculum Coll (TN)
Tuskegee U (AL)
Union Coll (KY)
Union Coll (NE)
Union Coll (NY)
Union Inst & U (OH)
Union U (TN)
United States Military Acad (NY)
Universidad de las Américas–Puebla (Mexico)
Université du Québec en Outaouais (QC, Canada)
U at Albany, State U of New York (NY)
U at Buffalo, the State U of New York (NY)
The U of Akron (OH)
The U of Alabama (AL)
The U of Alabama at Birmingham (AL)
The U of Alabama in Huntsville (AL)
U of Alaska Anchorage (AK)
U of Alaska Anchorage, Kenai Peninsula Coll (AK)
U of Alaska Fairbanks (AK)
U of Alberta (AB, Canada)
The U of Arizona (AZ)
U of Arkansas (AR)
U of Arkansas at Fort Smith (AR)
U of Arkansas at Little Rock (AR)
U of Arkansas at Monticello (AR)
U of Arkansas at Pine Bluff (AR)
U of Baltimore (MD)
U of Bridgeport (CT)
The U of British Columbia (BC, Canada)
The U of British Columbia–Okanagan (BC, Canada)
U of California, Berkeley (CA)
U of California, Davis (CA)
U of California, Irvine (CA)
U of California, Los Angeles (CA)
U of California, Merced (CA)
U of California, Riverside (CA)
U of California, San Diego (CA)
U of California, Santa Barbara (CA)
U of California, Santa Cruz (CA)
U of Central Florida (FL)
U of Central Missouri (MO)
U of Central Oklahoma (OK)
U of Charleston (WV)
U of Chicago (IL)
U of Cincinnati (OH)
U of Colorado at Boulder (CO)
U of Colorado at Colorado Springs (CO)
U of Colorado Denver (CO)
U of Connecticut (CT)
U of Dallas (TX)
U of Dayton (OH)
U of Delaware (DE)
U of Denver (CO)
U of Dubuque (IA)
U of Evansville (IN)
The U of Findlay (OH)
U of Florida (FL)
U of Georgia (GA)
U of Guam (GU)
U of Guelph (ON, Canada)
U of Hartford (CT)
U of Hawaii at Hilo (HI)
U of Hawaii at Manoa (HI)
U of Hawaii–West Oahu (HI)
U of Houston (TX)
U of Houston–Clear Lake (TX)
U of Houston–Downtown (TX)
U of Houston–Victoria (TX)
U of Idaho (ID)
U of Illinois at Chicago (IL)
U of Illinois at Springfield (IL)
U of Illinois at Urbana–Champaign (IL)
U of Indianapolis (IN)
The U of Iowa (IA)
The U of Kansas (KS)
U of Kentucky (KY)
U of King's Coll (NS, Canada)
U of La Verne (CA)
U of Lethbridge (AB, Canada)
U of Louisiana at Monroe (LA)
U of Louisville (KY)
U of Maine (ME)
U of Maine at Farmington (ME)
U of Maine at Machias (ME)
U of Manitoba (MB, Canada)
U of Mary (ND)
U of Mary Hardin-Baylor (TX)
U of Maryland, Baltimore County (MD)
U of Maryland, Coll Park (MD)
U of Maryland U Coll (MD)
U of Mary Washington (VA)
U of Massachusetts Amherst (MA)
U of Massachusetts Boston (MA)
U of Massachusetts Dartmouth (MA)
U of Massachusetts Lowell (MA)
U of Memphis (TN)
U of Miami (FL)
U of Michigan (MI)
U of Michigan–Dearborn (MI)
U of Michigan–Flint (MI)
U of Minnesota, Duluth (MN)
U of Minnesota, Twin Cities Campus (MN)
U of Mississippi (MS)
U of Missouri (MO)
U of Missouri–Kansas City (MO)
U of Missouri–St. Louis (MO)
U of Mobile (AL)
U of Montevallo (AL)
U of Mount Union (OH)
U of Nebraska at Kearney (NE)
U of Nebraska at Omaha (NE)
U of Nebraska–Lincoln (NE)
U of Nevada, Las Vegas (NV)
U of Nevada, Reno (NV)
U of New Brunswick Fredericton (NB, Canada)
U of New England (ME)
U of New Hampshire (NH)
U of New Hampshire at Manchester (NH)
U of New Haven (CT)
U of New Mexico (NM)
U of New Orleans (LA)
U of North Alabama (AL)
The U of North Carolina at Asheville (NC)
The U of North Carolina at Chapel Hill (NC)
The U of North Carolina at Charlotte (NC)
The U of North Carolina at Greensboro (NC)
The U of North Carolina at Pembroke (NC)
The U of North Carolina Wilmington (NC)
U of North Dakota (ND)
U of Northern Colorado (CO)
U of Northern Iowa (IA)
U of North Florida (FL)
U of North Texas (TX)
U of Notre Dame (IN)
U of Oklahoma (OK)
U of Oregon (OR)
U of Ottawa (ON, Canada)
U of Pennsylvania (PA)
U of Pittsburgh (PA)
U of Pittsburgh at Bradford (PA)
U of Pittsburgh at Greensburg (PA)
U of Pittsburgh at Johnstown (PA)
U of Portland (OR)
U of Puerto Rico, Cayey U Coll (PR)
U of Puerto Rico, Río Piedras (PR)
U of Puget Sound (WA)
U of Redlands (CA)
U of Regina (SK, Canada)
U of Rhode Island (RI)
U of Richmond (VA)
U of Rochester (NY)
U of St. Francis (IL)
U of Saint Mary (KS)
U of St. Thomas (MN)
U of St. Thomas (TX)
U of San Diego (CA)
U of San Francisco (CA)
U of Saskatchewan (SK, Canada)
U of Science and Arts of Oklahoma (OK)
The U of Scranton (PA)
U of South Alabama (AL)
U of South Carolina Aiken (SC)
U of South Carolina Beaufort (SC)
U of South Carolina Upstate (SC)
The U of South Dakota (SD)
U of Southern California (CA)
U of Southern Indiana (IN)
U of Southern Maine (ME)
U of Southern Mississippi (MS)
U of South Florida (FL)
The U of Tampa (FL)
The U of Tennessee (TN)
The U of Tennessee at Chattanooga (TN)
The U of Tennessee at Martin (TN)
The U of Texas at Arlington (TX)
The U of Texas at Austin (TX)
The U of Texas at Brownsville (TX)
The U of Texas at Dallas (TX)
The U of Texas at El Paso (TX)
The U of Texas at San Antonio (TX)
The U of Texas at Tyler (TX)
The U of Texas of the Permian Basin (TX)
The U of Texas–Pan American (TX)
U of the Cumberlands (KY)
U of the District of Columbia (DC)
U of the Incarnate Word (TX)
U of the Ozarks (AR)
U of the Pacific (CA)
U of the Sciences in Philadelphia (PA)
U of the Virgin Islands (VI)
U of the West (CA)
The U of Toledo (OH)
U of Tulsa (OK)
U of Utah (UT)
U of Vermont (VT)
U of Virginia (VA)
The U of Virginia's Coll at Wise (VA)
U of Washington (WA)
U of Washington, Tacoma (WA)
U of Waterloo (ON, Canada)
The U of West Alabama (AL)
The U of Western Ontario (ON, Canada)
U of West Florida (FL)
U of West Georgia (GA)
U of Windsor (ON, Canada)
U of Wisconsin–Eau Claire (WI)
U of Wisconsin–Green Bay (WI)
U of Wisconsin–La Crosse (WI)
U of Wisconsin–Madison (WI)
U of Wisconsin–Milwaukee (WI)
U of Wisconsin–Oshkosh (WI)
U of Wisconsin–Parkside (WI)
U of Wisconsin–Platteville (WI)
U of Wisconsin–River Falls (WI)
U of Wisconsin–Stevens Point (WI)
U of Wisconsin–Stout (WI)
U of Wisconsin–Superior (WI)
U of Wisconsin–Whitewater (WI)
U of Wyoming (WY)
Upper Iowa U (IA)
Ursinus Coll (PA)
Ursuline Coll (OH)
Utah State U (UT)
Utah Valley U (UT)
Utica Coll (NY)
Valdosta State U (GA)
Valley City State U (ND)
Valley Forge Christian Coll (PA)
Valparaiso U (IN)
Vanderbilt U (TN)
Vanguard U of Southern California (CA)
Vassar Coll (NY)
Villanova U (PA)
Virginia Commonwealth U (VA)
Virginia Intermont Coll (VA)
Virginia Military Inst (VA)
Virginia Polytechnic Inst and State U (VA)
Virginia State U (VA)
Virginia Union U (VA)
Virginia Wesleyan Coll (VA)
Viterbo U (WI)
Wabash Coll (IN)
Wagner Coll (NY)
Wake Forest U (NC)
Walden U (MN)
Waldorf Coll (IA)
Walsh U (OH)
Warner Pacific Coll (OR)
Wartburg Coll (IA)
Washburn U (KS)
Washington Adventist U (MD)
Washington & Jefferson Coll (PA)
Washington and Lee U (VA)
Washington Coll (MD)
Washington State U (WA)
Washington U in St. Louis (MO)
Wayland Baptist U (TX)
Waynesburg U (PA)
Wayne State Coll (NE)
Wayne State U (MI)
Weber State U (UT)
Webster U (MO)
Wellesley Coll (MA)
Wells Coll (NY)
Wesleyan Coll (GA)
Wesleyan U (CT)
West Chester U of Pennsylvania (PA)
Western Carolina U (NC)
Western Connecticut State U (CT)
Western Illinois U (IL)
Western Kentucky U (KY)
Western Michigan U (MI)
Western New England Coll (MA)
Western Oregon U (OR)
Western State Coll of Colorado (CO)
Western Washington U (WA)
Westfield State Coll (MA)
West Liberty U (WV)
Westminster Coll (MO)
Westminster Coll (UT)
Westmont Coll (CA)
West Virginia State U (WV)
West Virginia U (WV)
West Virginia Wesleyan Coll (WV)
Wheaton Coll (IL)
Wheaton Coll (MA)
Wheeling Jesuit U (WV)
Whitman Coll (WA)
Whittier Coll (CA)
Wichita State U (KS)

PSYCHOLOGY RELATED

PSYCHOLOGY TEACHER EDUCATION

PSYCHOMETRICS AND QUANTITATIVE PSYCHOLOGY

PUBLIC ADMINISTRATION

PUBLIC ADMINISTRATION AND SOCIAL SERVICE PROFESSIONS RELATED

PUBLIC/APPLIED HISTORY AND ARCHIVAL ADMINISTRATION

PUBLIC HEALTH

PUBLIC HEALTH/ COMMUNITY NURSING

PUBLIC HEALTH EDUCATION AND PROMOTION

PUBLIC HEALTH RELATED

PUBLIC POLICY ANALYSIS

PUBLIC RELATIONS, ADVERTISING, AND APPLIED COMMUNICATION RELATED

Champlain Coll (VT)
The Coll at Brockport, State U of New York (NY)
The Coll of St. Scholastica (MN)
Columbia Coll (MO)
DePaul U (IL)
Duquesne U (PA)
East Central U (OK)
Grace Coll (IN)
Hardin-Simmons U (TX)
Howard Payne U (TX)
John Brown U (AR)
Keystone Coll (PA)
Loyola U Chicago (IL)
Marietta Coll (OH)
Marywood U (PA)
Metropolitan State Coll of Denver (CO)
Murray State U (KY)
Northern Michigan U (MI)
Ohio Northern U (OH)
Pittsburg State U (KS)
Rochester Inst of Technology (NY)
Royal Roads U (BC, Canada)
Saint Mary's U of Minnesota (MN)
Shorter U (GA)
Southern New Hampshire U (NH)
Spring Arbor U (MI)
Spring Hill Coll (AL)
Syracuse U (NY)
Thompson Rivers U (BC, Canada)
The U of Tampa (FL)
U of Vermont (VT)
U of Wisconsin–River Falls (WI)
Virginia State U (VA)
Washington State U (WA)
Western Michigan U (MI)

PUBLIC RELATIONS/IMAGE MANAGEMENT

Alabama State U (AL)
American U (DC)
Andrews U (MI)
Appalachian State U (NC)
Auburn U (AL)
Avila U (MO)
Baldwin-Wallace Coll (OH)
Barry U (FL)
Bob Jones U (SC)
Boston U (MA)
Bowie State U (MD)
Bowling Green State U (OH)
Bradley U (IL)
Buffalo State Coll, State U of New York (NY)
California Lutheran U (CA)
California State U, Chico (CA)
California State U, Dominguez Hills (CA)
California State U, East Bay (CA)
California State U, Fresno (CA)
California State U, Fullerton (CA)
California State U, Long Beach (CA)
Capital U (OH)
Carroll U (WI)
Castleton State Coll (VT)
Central Michigan U (MI)
Champlain Coll (VT)
Chapman U (CA)
Christian Brothers U (TN)
Cleveland State U (OH)
The Coll at Brockport, State U of New York (NY)
Coll of the Ozarks (MO)
Colorado State U (CO)
Columbia Coll (SC)
Columbia Coll Chicago (IL)
Concordia Coll (MN)
Curry Coll (MA)
Delaware State U (DE)
Drake U (IA)
Drury U (MO)
Duquesne U (PA)
East Central U (OK)
Eastern Michigan U (MI)
Emerson Coll (MA)
Ferris State U (MI)
Florida Southern Coll (FL)
Fort Hays State U (KS)
Freed-Hardeman U (TN)
Georgia Southern U (GA)
Gonzaga U (WA)
Goshen Coll (IN)
Greenville Coll (IL)
Hampton U (VA)
Harding U (AR)
Hawai'i Pacific U (HI)
Heidelberg U (OH)
Hofstra U (NY)
Huntington U (IN)
Illinois State U (IL)
Inter American U of Puerto Rico, Ponce Campus (PR)
Iona Coll (NY)
Ithaca Coll (NY)
John Brown U (AR)
Johnson & Wales U (CO)
Johnson & Wales U (FL)
Johnson & Wales U (RI)
Johnson & Wales U—Charlotte Campus (NC)
Kent State U (OH)
La Salle U (PA)
Lasell Coll (MA)
Lewis U (IL)
Lindenwood U (MO)
Lipscomb U (TN)
Long Island U, C.W. Post Campus (NY)
Loras Coll (IA)
Mansfield U of Pennsylvania (PA)
Marist Coll (NY)
Marquette U (WI)
The Master's Coll and Sem (CA)
McKendree U (IL)
McPherson Coll (KS)
Miami U (OH)
Michigan State U (MI)
MidAmerica Nazarene U (KS)
Middle Tennessee State U (TN)
Minnesota State U Mankato (MN)
Minnesota State U Moorhead (MN)
Mississippi Coll (MS)
Monmouth Coll (IL)
Montana State U Billings (MT)
Mount Mary Coll (WI)
Mount Mercy Coll (IA)
Mount Saint Mary Coll (NY)
Mount Vernon Nazarene U (OH)
Murray State U (KY)
New England Coll (NH)
New England School of Communications (ME)
North Carolina State U (NC)
North Dakota State U (ND)
Northeastern State U (OK)
Northern Arizona U (AZ)
Northern Kentucky U (KY)
Northern Michigan U (MI)
Northwestern Coll (IA)
Northwestern Coll (MN)
Northwest Missouri State U (MO)
Northwest Nazarene U (ID)
Ohio Dominican U (OH)
Ohio U–Zanesville (OH)
Oklahoma Christian U (OK)
Oklahoma City U (OK)
Pacific Union Coll (CA)
Paine Coll (GA)
Pepperdine U, Malibu (CA)
Pontifical Catholic U of Puerto Rico (PR)
Purdue U Calumet (IN)
Quinnipiac U (CT)
Regis Coll (MA)
Rochester Inst of Technology (NY)
Roosevelt U (IL)
Rowan U (NJ)
St. Ambrose U (IA)
St. Cloud State U (MN)
Saint Francis U (PA)
St. John's U (NY)
Salem State Coll (MA)
San Diego State U (CA)
San Jose State U (CA)
Seattle U (WA)
Simmons Coll (MA)
Slippery Rock U of Pennsylvania (PA)
Southern Adventist U (TN)
Southern Methodist U (TX)
State U of New York at New Paltz (NY)
State U of New York at Oswego (NY)
Stephens Coll (MO)
Suffolk U (MA)
Susquehanna U (PA)
Tabor Coll (KS)
Temple U (PA)
Texas State U–San Marcos (TX)
Texas Tech U (TX)
Tiffin U (OH)
Union Coll (NE)
Union U (TN)
The U of Akron (OH)
The U of Alabama (AL)
U of Central Missouri (MO)
U of Central Oklahoma (OK)
U of Dayton (OH)
U of Delaware (DE)
The U of Findlay (OH)
U of Florida (FL)
U of Georgia (GA)
U of Houston (TX)
U of Idaho (ID)
U of Miami (FL)
U of Northern Iowa (IA)
U of Oregon (OR)
U of Ottawa (ON, Canada)
U of Pittsburgh at Bradford (PA)
U of Puerto Rico, Río Piedras (PR)
U of Rhode Island (RI)
U of Rio Grande (OH)
U of South Carolina (SC)
U of Southern California (CA)
The U of Texas at Arlington (TX)
The U of Texas at Austin (TX)
U of Toronto (ON, Canada)
U of Wisconsin–Madison (WI)
U of Wisconsin–River Falls (WI)
Ursuline Coll (OH)
Utica Coll (NY)
Valparaiso U (IN)
Walden U (MN)
Wartburg Coll (IA)
Washington State U (WA)
Wayne State U (MI)
Weber State U (UT)
Webster U (MO)
Western Kentucky U (KY)
Western New England Coll (MA)
West Virginia Wesleyan Coll (WV)
Wheeling Jesuit U (WV)
William Penn U (IA)
Winona State U (MN)
Xavier U (OH)
York Coll of Pennsylvania (PA)

PUBLISHING

California State U, Chico (CA)
Emerson Coll (MA)
Graceland U (IA)
Rochester Inst of Technology (NY)
Saint Mary's U of Minnesota (MN)
U of Missouri (MO)

PURCHASING, PROCUREMENT/ ACQUISITIONS AND CONTRACTS MANAGEMENT

Arizona State U (AZ)
California State U, East Bay (CA)
Central Michigan U (MI)
North Georgia Coll & State U (GA)
Northwest Florida State Coll (FL)
Potomac Coll (DC)
Saint Joseph's U (PA)
Saint Louis U (MO)
Southwestern Coll (KS)
U of Houston–Downtown (TX)
U of Illinois at Urbana–Champaign (IL)
U of the District of Columbia (DC)
Wright State U (OH)

QUALITY CONTROL AND SAFETY TECHNOLOGIES RELATED

Madonna U (MI)
Rochester Inst of Technology (NY)
U of Central Oklahoma (OK)

QUALITY CONTROL TECHNOLOGY

Bowling Green State U (OH)
California State U, Dominguez Hills (CA)
California State U, Long Beach (CA)
Ferris State U (MI)
San Jose State U (CA)
Southern Polytechnic State U (GA)
Spartan Coll of Aeronautics and Technology (OK)
U of Puerto Rico at Utuado (PR)
Winona State U (MN)

RABBINICAL STUDIES

Ohr Somayach/Joseph Tanenbaum Educational Center (NY)

RADIATION PROTECTION/ HEALTH PHYSICS TECHNOLOGY

Indiana U Bloomington (IN)
Indiana U East (IN)
Indiana U Kokomo (IN)
Indiana U–Purdue U Indianapolis (IN)
Indiana U South Bend (IN)
Indiana U Southeast (IN)
Lewis U (IL)
Thomas Edison State Coll (NJ)

RADIO AND TELEVISION

Alabama State U (AL)
American U (DC)
Appalachian State U (NC)
Arkansas State U—Jonesboro (AR)
Auburn U (AL)
Ball State U (IN)
Barry U (FL)
Belmont U (TN)
Bemidji State U (MN)
Bob Jones U (SC)
Boston U (MA)
Bowling Green State U (OH)
Bradley U (IL)
Brooklyn Coll of the City U of New York (NY)
Buffalo State Coll, State U of New York (NY)
Butler U (IN)
California State U, Fresno (CA)
California State U, Fullerton (CA)
California State U, Long Beach (CA)
California State U, Los Angeles (CA)
California State U, Monterey Bay (CA)
Castleton State Coll (VT)
Cedarville U (OH)
The Coll at Brockport, State U of New York (NY)
Colorado State U (CO)
Columbia Coll Chicago (IL)
Concordia Coll (MN)
Curry Coll (MA)
Delaware State U (DE)
Drake U (IA)
East Central U (OK)
Eastern Nazarene Coll (MA)
Emerson Coll (MA)
Evangel U (MO)
Fordham U (NY)
Franklin Pierce U (NH)
Freed-Hardeman U (TN)
Gallaudet U (DC)
The George Washington U (DC)
Georgia Southern U (GA)
Grand Valley State U (MI)
Grand View U (IA)
Hardin-Simmons U (TX)
Hofstra U (NY)
Indiana U–Purdue U Indianapolis (IN)
Iona Coll (NY)
Ithaca Coll (NY)
John Brown U (AR)
Kent State U (OH)
Lamar U (TX)
La Salle U (PA)
Lasell Coll (MA)
Loyola Marymount U (CA)
Marietta Coll (OH)
Marist Coll (NY)
The Master's Coll and Sem (CA)
Messiah Coll (PA)
Michigan State U (MI)
Minot State U (ND)
Murray State U (KY)
New England School of Communications (ME)
New York Inst of Technology (NY)
North Central Coll (IL)
Northern Arizona U (AZ)
Northwestern Coll (MN)
Northwest Missouri State U (MO)
Ohio Northern U (OH)
Ohio U (OH)
Oklahoma Christian U (OK)
Oklahoma City U (OK)
Pittsburg State U (KS)
Point Park U (PA)
Pontifical Catholic U of Puerto Rico (PR)
Sacred Heart U (CT)
St. Ambrose U (IA)
St. Cloud State U (MN)
St. Francis Coll (NY)
San Diego State U (CA)
San Francisco State U (CA)
San Jose State U (CA)
Southeastern U (FL)
Southern Illinois U Carbondale (IL)
Southwest Minnesota State U (MN)
State U of New York at Fredonia (NY)
State U of New York at Plattsburgh (NY)
Stephen F. Austin State U (TX)
Stephens Coll (MO)
Susquehanna U (PA)
Syracuse U (NY)
Temple U (PA)
Texas A&M U–Commerce (TX)
Texas Christian U (TX)
Texas Southern U (TX)
Texas State U–San Marcos (TX)
Texas Tech U (TX)
Texas Wesleyan U (TX)
Troy U (AL)
Union U (TN)
The U of Akron (OH)
The U of Alabama (AL)
The U of Arizona (AZ)
U of Arkansas at Little Rock (AR)
U of Central Florida (FL)
U of Central Missouri (MO)
U of Central Oklahoma (OK)
U of Cincinnati (OH)
U of Dayton (OH)
U of Florida (FL)
U of Houston (TX)
U of Kentucky (KY)
U of Miami (FL)
U of Mississippi (MS)
U of Missouri (MO)
U of Montevallo (AL)
U of Northern Iowa (IA)
U of North Texas (TX)
U of Pittsburgh at Bradford (PA)
U of Southern California (CA)
U of Southern Indiana (IN)
U of Southern Mississippi (MS)
The U of Tennessee (TN)
The U of Texas at Arlington (TX)
The U of Texas at Austin (TX)
U of the Incarnate Word (TX)
The U of Western Ontario (ON, Canada)
U of Wisconsin–Madison (WI)
U of Wisconsin–Oshkosh (WI)
U of Wisconsin–River Falls (WI)
U of Wisconsin–Superior (WI)
Valparaiso U (IN)
Vanguard U of Southern California (CA)
Wartburg Coll (IA)
Waynesburg U (PA)
Wayne State U (MI)
Weber State U (UT)
Webster U (MO)
Western Illinois U (IL)
Western Kentucky U (KY)
Winona State U (MN)
Xavier U (OH)
Youngstown State U (OH)

RADIO AND TELEVISION BROADCASTING TECHNOLOGY

Alabama Ag and Mech U (AL)
Asbury U (KY)
The Coll of Saint Rose (NY)
Eastern Michigan U (MI)
Emerson Coll (MA)
Ferris State U (MI)
Gannon U (PA)
Gardner-Webb U (NC)
Iona Coll (NY)
Lewis U (IL)
New England School of Communications (ME)
New York U (NY)
Northwest Nazarene U (ID)
Rowan U (NJ)
U of Georgia (GA)
U of Puerto Rico at Utuado (PR)
Worcester State Coll (MA)

RADIOLOGIC TECHNOLOGY/SCIENCE

Alderson-Broaddus Coll (WV)
Austin Peay State U (TN)
Averett U (VA)
Baptist Coll of Health Sciences (TN)
Bluefield State Coll (WV)
Champlain Coll (VT)
Clarion U of Pennsylvania (PA)
Coll of St. Joseph (VT)
Fort Hays State U (KS)
Friends U (KS)
The George Washington U (DC)
Holy Family U (PA)
Indiana U Bloomington (IN)
Indiana U East (IN)
Indiana U Kokomo (IN)
Indiana U Northwest (IN)
Indiana U–Purdue U Indianapolis (IN)
Indiana U South Bend (IN)
Indiana U Southeast (IN)
Inter American U of Puerto Rico, Ponce Campus (PR)
Jamestown Coll (ND)
Kent State U (OH)
Manhattan Coll (NY)
Marian U (WI)
Marshall U (WV)
Massachusetts Coll of Pharmacy and Health Sciences (MA)
McNeese State U (LA)
Midwestern State U (TX)
Missouri State U (MO)
North Dakota State U (ND)
Northern Arizona U (AZ)
Northwestern State U of Louisiana (LA)
Oakland U (MI)
The Ohio State U (OH)
Oregon Inst of Technology (OR)
Presentation Coll (SD)
Quinnipiac U (CT)
State U of New York Upstate Medical U (NY)
Suffolk U (MA)
U of Arkansas at Fort Smith (AR)
U of Charleston (WV)
U of Louisiana at Monroe (LA)

U of Mary (ND)
U of Missouri (MO)
U of Nebraska Medical Center (NE)
U of Oklahoma Health Sciences Center (OK)
U of Pittsburgh at Bradford (PA)
U of St. Francis (IL)
U of South Alabama (AL)
U of Toronto (ON, Canada)
Virginia Commonwealth U (VA)
Widener U (PA)

RADIO, TELEVISION, AND DIGITAL COMMUNICATION RELATED

Brigham Young U (UT)
Central Michigan U (MI)
Clark Atlanta U (GA)
The Coll at Brockport, State U of New York (NY)
Drake U (IA)
Drury U (MO)
Emerson Coll (MA)
Florida State U (FL)
Hofstra U (NY)
Howard Payne U (TX)
John Brown U (AR)
Keystone Coll (PA)
Madonna U (MI)
Mitchell Coll (CT)
Neumann U (PA)
North Dakota State U (ND)
Rogers State U (OK)
Sacred Heart U (CT)
Spring Hill Coll (AL)
The U of Akron (OH)
Washington State U (WA)
Western Carolina U (NC)

RANGE SCIENCE AND MANAGEMENT

Colorado State U (CO)
Fort Hays State U (KS)
Humboldt State U (CA)
Montana State U (MT)
New Mexico State U (NM)
North Dakota State U (ND)
Oregon State U (OR)
South Dakota State U (SD)
Sul Ross State U (TX)
Tarleton State U (TX)
Texas A&M U (TX)
Texas Tech U (TX)
U of Alberta (AB, Canada)
U of Idaho (ID)
U of Nebraska–Lincoln (NE)
U of Wyoming (WY)
Utah State U (UT)

READING TEACHER EDUCATION

Aquinas Coll (MI)
Baylor U (TX)
Boise State U (ID)
Catawba Coll (NC)
Clarion U of Pennsylvania (PA)
Dordt Coll (IA)
Eastern Michigan U (MI)
Eastern Washington U (WA)
Edinboro U of Pennsylvania (PA)
Grand Valley State U (MI)
Harding U (AR)
Hardin-Simmons U (TX)
Kutztown U of Pennsylvania (PA)
Longwood U (VA)
Michigan State U (MI)
Midwestern State U (TX)
Murray State U (KY)
North Georgia Coll & State U (GA)
St. Cloud State U (MN)
State U of New York Coll at Cortland (NY)
State U of New York Coll at Oneonta (NY)
Texas A&M Intl U (TX)
Texas A&M U–Commerce (TX)
Texas A&M U–Corpus Christi (TX)
Texas Wesleyan U (TX)
U of Alberta (AB, Canada)
The U of British Columbia (BC, Canada)
U of Central Missouri (MO)
U of Central Oklahoma (OK)
U of Nebraska–Lincoln (NE)
The U of North Carolina at Pembroke (NC)
U of Northern Iowa (IA)
U of Wisconsin–River Falls (WI)
U of Wisconsin–Superior (WI)
Upper Iowa U (IA)
Washington State U (WA)
Wheelock Coll (MA)
William Penn U (IA)
Wingate U (NC)
Winona State U (MN)
Wright State U (OH)
York Coll (NE)

REAL ESTATE

Angelo State U (TX)
Arizona State U (AZ)
Baylor U (TX)
Bernard M. Baruch Coll of the City U of New York (NY)
Bowling Green State U (OH)
California State U, Dominguez Hills (CA)
California State U, East Bay (CA)
California State U, Fresno (CA)
Central Michigan U (MI)
Clarion U of Pennsylvania (PA)
Colorado State U (CO)
DePaul U (IL)
Florida Atlantic U (FL)
Florida Intl U (FL)
Georgia State U (GA)
La Roche Coll (PA)
Marylhurst U (OR)
Menlo Coll (CA)
Minnesota State U Mankato (MN)
Mississippi State U (MS)
Morehead State U (KY)
New Mexico State U (NM)
New York U (NY)
The Ohio State U (OH)
St. Cloud State U (MN)
San Diego State U (CA)
Syracuse U (NY)
Temple U (PA)
Texas Christian U (TX)
Thomas Edison State Coll (NJ)
The U of British Columbia (BC, Canada)
U of Central Florida (FL)
U of Central Oklahoma (OK)
U of Cincinnati (OH)
U of Connecticut (CT)
U of Denver (CO)
U of Florida (FL)
U of Georgia (GA)
U of Guelph (ON, Canada)
U of Illinois at Urbana–Champaign (IL)
U of Miami (FL)
U of Mississippi (MS)
U of Missouri (MO)
U of Nebraska at Omaha (NE)
U of Nevada, Las Vegas (NV)
U of Northern Iowa (IA)
U of North Texas (TX)
U of Pennsylvania (PA)
U of St. Thomas (MN)
U of San Diego (CA)
U of South Carolina (SC)
The U of Texas at Arlington (TX)
The U of Texas at El Paso (TX)
U of West Georgia (GA)
U of Wisconsin–Madison (WI)
U of Wisconsin–Milwaukee (WI)
U of Wisconsin–Stout (WI)
Washington State U (WA)

RECORDING ARTS TECHNOLOGY

American U (DC)
The Art Inst of Atlanta (GA)
The Art Inst of Austin (TX)
The Art Inst of California–Inland Empire (CA)
The Art Inst of California–Los Angeles (CA)
The Art Inst of California–San Diego (CA)
The Art Inst of California–San Francisco (CA)
The Art Inst of Houston (TX)
The Art Inst of Las Vegas (NV)
The Art Inst of Philadelphia (PA)
The Art Inst of Phoenix (AZ)
The Art Inst of Seattle (WA)
The Art Inst of Tennessee–Nashville (TN)
The Art Inst of Washington (VA)
Butler U (IN)
Columbia Coll Chicago (IL)
Full Sail U (FL)
Greenville Coll (IL)
The Illinois Inst of Art–Chicago (IL)
The Illinois Inst of Art–Schaumburg (IL)
Indiana U Bloomington (IN)
Ithaca Coll (NY)
Lebanon Valley Coll (PA)
Loyola Marymount U (CA)
Malone U (OH)
Miami Intl U of Art & Design (FL)
Mississippi Valley State U (MS)
The New England Inst of Art (MA)
New England School of Communications (ME)
Savannah Coll of Art and Design (GA)
Texas Southern U (TX)
Texas State U–San Marcos (TX)
The U of Texas at Austin (TX)
York Coll of Pennsylvania (PA)

REGIONAL STUDIES

The Colorado Coll (CO)
Columbia U, School of General Studies (NY)
Mercer U (GA)
Pitzer Coll (CA)
Prescott Coll (AZ)
United States Military Acad (NY)
Washington U in St. Louis (MO)

REHABILITATION AND THERAPEUTIC PROFESSIONS RELATED

Assumption Coll (MA)
East Stroudsburg U of Pennsylvania (PA)
Hilbert Coll (NY)
Indiana U of Pennsylvania (PA)
Montana State U Billings (MT)
Penn State Abington (PA)
Penn State Altoona (PA)
Penn State Beaver (PA)
Penn State Berks (PA)
Penn State Brandywine (PA)
Penn State DuBois (PA)
Penn State Erie, The Behrend Coll (PA)
Penn State Fayette, The Eberly Campus (PA)
Penn State Greater Allegheny (PA)
Penn State Hazleton (PA)
Penn State Lehigh Valley (PA)
Penn State Mont Alto (PA)
Penn State New Kensington (PA)
Penn State Schuylkill (PA)
Penn State Shenango (PA)
Penn State U Park (PA)
Penn State Wilkes-Barre (PA)
Penn State Worthington Scranton (PA)
Penn State York (PA)
Prescott Coll (AZ)
Southern Illinois U Carbondale (IL)
Southern U and Ag and Mech Coll (LA)
Stephen F. Austin State U (TX)
Troy U (AL)
U of Maine at Farmington (ME)
U of North Texas (TX)
U of Pittsburgh (PA)
The U of Texas–Pan American (TX)
U of Waterloo (ON, Canada)
The U of Western Ontario (ON, Canada)
Wilson Coll (PA)

REHABILITATION THERAPY

Baker Coll of Muskegon (MI)
Boston U (MA)
California State U, Los Angeles (CA)
East Stroudsburg U of Pennsylvania (PA)
Ithaca Coll (NY)
Montana State U Billings (MT)
Southern U and Ag and Mech Coll (LA)
U of Maine at Farmington (ME)
U of Manitoba (MB, Canada)
U of Maryland Eastern Shore (MD)
Wilberforce U (OH)
York U (ON, Canada)

RELIGIOUS EDUCATION

Andrews U (MI)
Aquinas Coll (MI)
Asbury U (KY)
Ashland U (OH)
Baptist Bible Coll of Pennsylvania (PA)
Barclay Coll (KS)
Bethany Bible Coll (NB, Canada)
Bob Jones U (SC)
Bryan Coll (TN)
Calvary Bible Coll and Theological Sem (MO)
Campbellsville U (KY)
Cedarville U (OH)
Cincinnati Christian U (OH)
Coll of Mount St. Joseph (OH)
Coll of Saint Benedict (MN)
Columbia Coll (SC)
Columbia Intl U (SC)
Concordia U (CA)
Concordia U Chicago (IL)
Concordia U, St. Paul (MN)
Concordia U Texas (TX)
Corban U (OR)
Crown Coll (MN)
Dallas Baptist U (TX)
Defiance Coll (OH)
Eastern Nazarene Coll (MA)
East Texas Baptist U (TX)
Edgewood Coll (WI)
Emmanuel Bible Coll (ON, Canada)
Eugene Bible Coll (OR)
Faith Baptist Bible Coll and Theological Sem (IA)
Florida Southern Coll (FL)
Franciscan U of Steubenville (OH)
Free Will Baptist Bible Coll (TN)
Gardner-Webb U (NC)
Global U (MO)
Great Lakes Christian Coll (MI)
Griggs U (MD)
Hannibal-LaGrange Coll (MO)
Harding U (AR)
Hebrew Coll (MA)
Heritage Baptist Coll and Heritage Theological Sem (ON, Canada)
Heritage Bible Coll (NC)
Hillsdale Free Will Baptist Coll (OK)
Holy Family U (PA)
Houghton Coll (NY)
Howard Payne U (TX)
Huntingdon Coll (AL)
Indiana Wesleyan U (IN)
John Brown U (AR)
John Carroll U (OH)
John Wesley Coll (NC)
Kuyper Coll (MI)
LaGrange Coll (GA)
La Roche Coll (PA)
La Salle U (PA)
Lee U (TN)
Lincoln Christian U (IL)
Lindsey Wilson Coll (KY)
Louisiana Coll (LA)
Loyola U Chicago (IL)
Loyola U New Orleans (LA)
Malone U (OH)
Maranatha Baptist Bible Coll (WI)
Marian U (IN)
The Master's Coll and Sem (CA)
Master's Coll and Sem (ON, Canada)
Messiah Coll (PA)
Mid-Continent U (KY)
Missouri Baptist U (MO)
Moody Bible Inst (IL)
Morris Coll (SC)
Mount Mary Coll (WI)
Mount Vernon Nazarene U (OH)
Multnomah U (OR)
Nazarene Bible Coll (CO)
North Greenville U (SC)
Northwestern Coll (IA)
Northwest Nazarene U (ID)
Northwest U (WA)
Nyack Coll (NY)
Oak Hills Christian Coll (MN)
Oakland City U (IN)
Oakwood U (AL)
Oklahoma Christian U (OK)
Oklahoma City U (OK)
Oral Roberts U (OK)
Pepperdine U, Malibu (CA)
Piedmont Baptist Coll and Graduate School (NC)
St. Edward's U (TX)
Saint John's U (MN)
St. Louis Christian Coll (MO)
Saint Mary's U of Minnesota (MN)
Saint Vincent Coll (PA)
Seton Hall U (NJ)
Simpson U (CA)
Southern Adventist U (TN)
Southwest Baptist U (MO)
Sterling Coll (KS)
Texas Wesleyan U (TX)
Thiel Coll (PA)
Trinity Christian Coll (IL)
Tri-State Bible Coll (OH)
Union Coll (NE)
Universidad Adventista de las Antillas (PR)
Universidad Teológica del Caribe (PR)
U of Dayton (OH)
U of the Cumberlands (KY)
The U of Western Ontario (ON, Canada)
Valley Forge Christian Coll (PA)
Vanguard U of Southern California (CA)
Washington Adventist U (MD)
Wayland Baptist U (TX)
West Virginia Wesleyan Coll (WV)
Wheaton Coll (IL)
York Coll (NE)

RELIGIOUS/SACRED MUSIC

Anderson U (IN)
Aquinas Coll (MI)
Asbury U (KY)
Augustana Coll (IL)
Baptist Bible Coll of Pennsylvania (PA)
Barclay Coll (KS)
Baylor U (TX)
Belmont U (TN)
Bethany Lutheran Coll (MN)
Bethany U (CA)
Bethel U (MN)
Bethel U (TN)
Bluefield Coll (VA)
Blue Mountain Coll (MS)
Bowling Green State U (OH)
Calvary Bible Coll and Theological Sem (MO)
Calvin Coll (MI)
Campbellsville U (KY)
Cedarville U (OH)
Central Baptist Coll (AR)
Central Christian Coll of Kansas (KS)
Cincinnati Christian U (OH)
Clarke Coll (IA)
Clearwater Christian Coll (FL)
Coll of the Ozarks (MO)
Columbia Intl U (SC)
Concordia U Chicago (IL)
Concordia U, St. Paul (MN)
Concordia U Texas (TX)
Corban U (OR)
Crown Coll (MN)
Dallas Baptist U (TX)
Drake U (IA)
Eastern Nazarene Coll (MA)
East Texas Baptist U (TX)
Emmanuel Bible Coll (ON, Canada)
Emmanuel Coll (GA)
Eugene Bible Coll (OR)
Evangel U (MO)
Faith Baptist Bible Coll and Theological Sem (IA)
Franciscan U of Steubenville (OH)
Free Will Baptist Bible Coll (TN)
Furman U (SC)
Gardner-Webb U (NC)
Great Lakes Christian Coll (MI)
Gustavus Adolphus Coll (MN)
Hannibal-LaGrange Coll (MO)
Hardin-Simmons U (TX)
Hebrew Coll (MA)
Heritage Baptist Coll and Heritage Theological Sem (ON, Canada)
Hillsdale Free Will Baptist Coll (OK)
Houston Baptist U (TX)
Howard Payne U (TX)
Huntington U (IN)
Indiana Wesleyan U (IN)
John Brown U (AR)
Johnson Bible Coll (TN)
Kuyper Coll (MI)
Liberty U (VA)
Lincoln Christian U (IL)
Louisiana Coll (LA)
Madonna U (MI)
Malone U (OH)
Maranatha Baptist Bible Coll (WI)
The Master's Coll and Sem (CA)
Mississippi Coll (MS)
Missouri Baptist U (MO)
Moody Bible Inst (IL)
Moravian Coll (PA)
Mount Vernon Nazarene U (OH)
Multnomah U (OR)
Nazarene Bible Coll (CO)
Newberry Coll (SC)
North Carolina Central U (NC)
North Greenville U (SC)
Northwest Nazarene U (ID)
Northwest U (WA)
Nyack Coll (NY)
Oklahoma Baptist U (OK)
Oklahoma City U (OK)
Oral Roberts U (OK)
Ouachita Baptist U (AR)
Patten U (CA)
Piedmont Baptist Coll and Graduate School (NC)
Presbyterian Coll (SC)
Rider U (NJ)
St. Louis Christian Coll (MO)
Saint Mary's U of Minnesota (MN)
Samford U (AL)
San Diego Christian Coll (CA)
Seton Hill U (PA)
Shorter U (GA)
Southeastern U (FL)
Southern Wesleyan U (SC)
Southwestern Assemblies of God U (TX)
Southwestern Oklahoma State U (OK)
Texas Christian U (TX)
Union U (TN)
U of Hartford (CT)
U of Mary (ND)
U of Mary Hardin-Baylor (TX)
U of Mobile (AL)
Valley Forge Christian Coll (PA)
Valparaiso U (IN)
Wartburg Coll (IA)
Wayland Baptist U (TX)
William Jewell Coll (MO)

RELIGIOUS STUDIES

Agnes Scott Coll (GA)
Albertus Magnus Coll (CT)

Religious Studies

Albion Coll (MI)
Albright Coll (PA)
Allegheny Coll (PA)
Allen U (SC)
Alma Coll (MI)
Alvernia U (PA)
Alverno Coll (WI)
American Public U System (WV)
Amherst Coll (MA)
Anderson U (IN)
Andrews U (MI)
Appalachian State U (NC)
Aquinas Coll (MI)
Arizona State U (AZ)
Ashland U (OH)
Atlantic Union Coll (MA)
Augsburg Coll (MN)
Augustana Coll (IL)
Augustana Coll (SD)
Austin Coll (TX)
Averett U (VA)
Avila U (MO)
Azusa Pacific U (CA)
Baker U (KS)
Baldwin-Wallace Coll (OH)
Ball State U (IN)
Bard Coll (NY)
Barnard Coll (NY)
Bates Coll (ME)
Baylor U (TX)
Beloit Coll (WI)
Bemidji State U (MN)
Benedictine Coll (KS)
Berea Coll (KY)
Bernard M. Baruch Coll of the City U of New York (NY)
Bethany Bible Coll (NB, Canada)
Bethany Coll (KS)
Bethany Coll (WV)
Bethany Lutheran Coll (MN)
Bethel Coll (KS)
Birmingham-Southern Coll (AL)
Bishop's U (QC, Canada)
Bloomfield Coll (NJ)
Bluefield Coll (VA)
Bluffton U (OH)
Boston U (MA)
Bowdoin Coll (ME)
Bradley U (IL)
Brevard Coll (NC)
Brewton-Parker Coll (GA)
Brooklyn Coll of the City U of New York (NY)
Bryn Mawr Coll (PA)
Bucknell U (PA)
Butler U (IN)
Cabrini Coll (PA)
California Lutheran U (CA)
California State U, Bakersfield (CA)
California State U, Dominguez Hills (CA)
California State U, East Bay (CA)
California State U, Fresno (CA)
California State U, Fullerton (CA)
California State U, Long Beach (CA)
California State U, Northridge (CA)
California State U, Sacramento (CA)
Calumet Coll of Saint Joseph (IN)
Calvin Coll (MI)
Campbellsville U (KY)
Canisius Coll (NY)
Cape Breton U (NS, Canada)
Capital U (OH)
Carleton Coll (MN)
Carroll U (WI)
Carson-Newman Coll (TN)
Case Western Reserve U (OH)
Catawba Coll (NC)
The Catholic U of America (DC)
Centenary Coll of Louisiana (LA)
Central Christian Coll of Kansas (KS)
Central Coll (IA)
Central Michigan U (MI)
Chaminade U of Honolulu (HI)
Chapman U (CA)
Chowan U (NC)
Christian Brothers U (TN)
Claremont McKenna Coll (CA)
Clark Atlanta U (GA)
Clarke Coll (IA)
Cleveland State U (OH)
Colby Coll (ME)
Colgate U (NY)
Coll of Charleston (SC)
The Coll of Idaho (ID)
Coll of Mount St. Joseph (OH)
Coll of Mount Saint Vincent (NY)
The Coll of New Rochelle (NY)
Coll of Notre Dame of Maryland (MD)
The Coll of Saint Rose (NY)
The Coll of St. Scholastica (MN)
Coll of the Holy Cross (MA)
Coll of the Ozarks (MO)
The Coll of William and Mary (VA)
The Coll of Wooster (OH)
The Colorado Coll (CO)
Columbia Coll (SC)
Columbia U (NY)
Columbia U, School of General Studies (NY)
Concordia Coll (MN)
Concordia U (QC, Canada)
Concordia U Coll of Alberta (AB, Canada)
Concordia U Texas (TX)
Concordia U Wisconsin (WI)
Connecticut Coll (CT)
Converse Coll (SC)
Corban U (OR)
Cornell Coll (IA)
Cornell U (NY)
Crandall U (NB, Canada)
Culver-Stockton Coll (MO)
Daemen Coll (NY)
Dakota Wesleyan U (SD)
Dana Coll (NE)
Dartmouth Coll (NH)
Davidson Coll (NC)
Defiance Coll (OH)
Denison U (OH)
DePaul U (IL)
DePauw U (IN)
Dickinson Coll (PA)
Dillard U (LA)
Doane Coll (NE)
Dominican U of California (CA)
Dordt Coll (IA)
Drake U (IA)
Drew U (NJ)
Drury U (MO)
Duke U (NC)
Earlham Coll (IN)
Eastern Nazarene Coll (MA)
Eastern New Mexico U (NM)
East Texas Baptist U (TX)
Eckerd Coll (FL)
Edgewood Coll (WI)
Elizabethtown Coll (PA)
Elmira Coll (NY)
Elon U (NC)
Emmanuel Coll (MA)
Emory & Henry Coll (VA)
Emory U (GA)
Erskine Coll (SC)
Eugene Lang Coll The New School for Liberal Arts (NY)
Fairfield U (CT)
Faulkner U (AL)
Felician Coll (NJ)
Ferrum Coll (VA)
Florida Intl U (FL)
Florida Southern Coll (FL)
Florida State U (FL)
Fontbonne U (MO)
Fordham U (NY)
Franklin & Marshall Coll (PA)
Franklin Coll (IN)
Furman U (SC)
Gardner-Webb U (NC)
George Fox U (OR)
George Mason U (VA)
Georgetown Coll (KY)
The George Washington U (DC)
Georgian Court U (NJ)
Georgia State U (GA)
Gettysburg Coll (PA)
Gonzaga U (WA)
Goucher Coll (MD)
Graceland U (IA)
Grand View U (IA)
Greensboro Coll (NC)
Greenville Coll (IL)
Griggs U (MD)
Grinnell Coll (IA)
Grove City Coll (PA)
Guilford Coll (NC)
Gustavus Adolphus Coll (MN)
Hamilton Coll (NY)
Hamline U (MN)
Hampden-Sydney Coll (VA)
Hampshire Coll (MA)
Hampton U (VA)
Hartwick Coll (NY)
Harvard U (MA)
Haverford Coll (PA)
Heidelberg U (OH)
Hellenic Coll (MA)
Hendrix Coll (AR)
High Point U (NC)
Hillsdale Coll (MI)
Hiram Coll (OH)
Hofstra U (NY)
Hollins U (VA)
Holy Apostles Coll and Sem (CT)
Holy Family U (PA)
Holy Names U (CA)
Hood Coll (MD)
Hope Coll (MI)
Houghton Coll (NY)
Houston Baptist U (TX)
Humboldt State U (CA)
Hunter Coll of the City U of New York (NY)
Huntingdon Coll (AL)
Huntington U (IN)
Illinois Coll (IL)
Illinois Wesleyan U (IL)
Indiana U Bloomington (IN)
Indiana U East (IN)
Indiana U of Pennsylvania (PA)
Indiana U–Purdue U Indianapolis (IN)
Iona Coll (NY)
Iowa State U of Science and Technology (IA)
Jamestown Coll (ND)
Jarvis Christian Coll (TX)
John Brown U (AR)
John Carroll U (OH)
John Wesley Coll (NC)
Judson Coll (AL)
Juniata Coll (PA)
Kalamazoo Coll (MI)
Kentucky Mountain Bible Coll (KY)
Kenyon Coll (OH)
King Coll (TN)
Lafayette Coll (PA)
LaGrange Coll (GA)
Lake Forest Coll (IL)
Lakeland Coll (WI)
Lane Coll (TN)
La Roche Coll (PA)
La Salle U (PA)
La Sierra U (CA)
Laura and Alvin Siegal Coll of Judaic Studies (OH)
Laurentian U (ON, Canada)
Lawrence U (WI)
Lebanon Valley Coll (PA)
Lees-McRae Coll (NC)
Lehigh U (PA)
Le Moyne Coll (NY)
LeTourneau U (TX)
Lewis & Clark Coll (OR)
Lewis U (IL)
Liberty U (VA)
Lincoln U (PA)
Lindenwood U (MO)
Linfield Coll (OR)
Loras Coll (IA)
Louisiana Coll (LA)
Lourdes Coll (OH)
Loyola U Maryland (MD)
Loyola U New Orleans (LA)
Luther Coll (IA)
Lycoming Coll (PA)
Lynchburg Coll (VA)
Macalester Coll (MN)
Madonna U (MI)
Manchester Coll (IN)
Manhattan Coll (NY)
Manhattanville Coll (NY)
Maranatha Baptist Bible Coll (WI)
Marian U (WI)
Marlboro Coll (VT)
Mars Hill Coll (NC)
Mary Baldwin Coll (VA)
Marylhurst U (OR)
Marymount U (VA)
Maryville Coll (TN)
Marywood U (PA)
The Master's Coll and Sem (CA)
McDaniel Coll (MD)
McKendree U (IL)
Medgar Evers Coll of the City U of New York (NY)
Memorial U of Newfoundland (NL, Canada)
Mercyhurst Coll (PA)
Meredith Coll (NC)
Merrimack Coll (MA)
Methodist U (NC)
Miami U (OH)
Michigan State U (MI)
MidAmerica Nazarene U (KS)
Middlebury Coll (VT)
Millsaps Coll (MS)
Missouri Baptist U (MO)
Missouri State U (MO)
Molloy Coll (NY)
Monmouth Coll (IL)
Montclair State U (NJ)
Moravian Coll (PA)
Morehouse Coll (GA)
Morningside Coll (IA)
Mountain State U (WV)
Mount Allison U (NB, Canada)
Mount Holyoke Coll (MA)
Mount Marty Coll (SD)
Mount Mary Coll (WI)
Mount Mercy Coll (IA)
Mount Olive Coll (NC)
Mount St. Mary's Coll (CA)
Mount Vernon Nazarene U (OH)
Muhlenberg Coll (PA)
Naropa U (CO)
Nazareth Coll of Rochester (NY)
Nebraska Wesleyan U (NE)
Newberry Coll (SC)
New Coll of Florida (FL)
New York U (NY)
Niagara U (NY)
North Carolina State U (NC)
North Central Coll (IL)
Northeastern U (MA)
Northern Arizona U (AZ)
North Greenville U (SC)
Northwestern Coll (IA)
Northwest Nazarene U (ID)
Northwest U (WA)
Notre Dame de Namur U (CA)
Nyack Coll (NY)
Oakland City U (IN)
Oberlin Coll (OH)
Occidental Coll (CA)
Ohio Northern U (OH)
Ohio U (OH)
Ohio Valley U (WV)
Ohio Wesleyan U (OH)
Oklahoma Baptist U (OK)
Oklahoma Christian U (OK)
Oklahoma City U (OK)
Oklahoma Wesleyan U (OK)
Ottawa U (KS)
Our Lady of the Lake U of San Antonio (TX)
Pacific Lutheran U (WA)
Pacific Union Coll (CA)
Paine Coll (GA)
Penn State Abington (PA)
Penn State Altoona (PA)
Penn State Beaver (PA)
Penn State Berks (PA)
Penn State Brandywine (PA)
Penn State DuBois (PA)
Penn State Erie, The Behrend Coll (PA)
Penn State Fayette, The Eberly Campus (PA)
Penn State Greater Allegheny (PA)
Penn State Hazleton (PA)
Penn State Lehigh Valley (PA)
Penn State Mont Alto (PA)
Penn State New Kensington (PA)
Penn State Schuylkill (PA)
Penn State Shenango (PA)
Penn State U Park (PA)
Penn State Wilkes-Barre (PA)
Penn State Worthington Scranton (PA)
Penn State York (PA)
Pepperdine U, Malibu (CA)
Philadelphia Biblical U (PA)
Piedmont Coll (GA)
Pikeville Coll (KY)
Pitzer Coll (CA)
Pomona Coll (CA)
Presbyterian Coll (SC)
Prescott Coll (AZ)
Princeton U (NJ)
Principia Coll (IL)
Queens Coll of the City U of New York (NY)
Queen's U at Kingston (ON, Canada)
Queens U of Charlotte (NC)
Randolph Coll (VA)
Randolph-Macon Coll (VA)
Redeemer U Coll (ON, Canada)
Reed Coll (OR)
Reinhardt Coll (GA)
Rhodes Coll (TN)
Rice U (TX)
Ripon Coll (WI)
Roanoke Coll (VA)
Roberts Wesleyan Coll (NY)
Rocky Mountain Coll (MT)
Rollins Coll (FL)
Rosemont Coll (PA)
Rutgers, The State U of New Jersey, New Brunswick (NJ)
Sacred Heart U (CT)
St. Francis Coll (NY)
Saint Francis U (PA)
St. Francis Xavier U (NS, Canada)
St. John Fisher Coll (NY)
Saint Joseph Coll (CT)
Saint Joseph's U (PA)
St. Lawrence U (NY)
Saint Leo U (FL)
Saint Martin's U (WA)
Saint Mary-of-the-Woods Coll (IN)
Saint Mary's Coll (IN)
Saint Mary's Coll of California (CA)
St. Mary's Coll of Maryland (MD)
Saint Michael's Coll (VT)
St. Norbert Coll (WI)
St. Olaf Coll (MN)
St. Thomas Aquinas Coll (NY)
St. Thomas U (FL)
St. Thomas U (NB, Canada)
Saint Xavier U (IL)
Salem Coll (NC)
Salve Regina U (RI)
Samford U (AL)
San Diego State U (CA)
San Jose State U (CA)
Santa Clara U (CA)
Sarah Lawrence Coll (NY)
Schreiner U (TX)
Scripps Coll (CA)
Seattle U (WA)
Seton Hall U (NJ)
Seton Hill U (PA)
Sewanee: The U of the South (TN)
Shaw U (NC)
Shenandoah U (VA)
Shorter U (GA)
Siena Coll (NY)
Siena Heights U (MI)
Simpson Coll (IA)
Skidmore Coll (NY)
Smith Coll (MA)
Southern Adventist U (TN)
Southern Methodist U (TX)
Southern Wesleyan U (SC)
Southwest Baptist U (MO)
Southwestern Adventist U (TX)
Southwestern U (TX)
Spelman Coll (GA)
Spring Arbor U (MI)
Stanford U (CA)
State U of New York Coll at Old Westbury (NY)
Stetson U (FL)
Stonehill Coll (MA)
Stony Brook U, State U of New York (NY)
Susquehanna U (PA)
Swarthmore Coll (PA)
Sweet Briar Coll (VA)
Syracuse U (NY)
Tabor Coll (KS)
Temple U (PA)
Tennessee Wesleyan Coll (TN)
Texas Christian U (TX)
Texas Coll (TX)
Texas Wesleyan U (TX)
Thiel Coll (PA)
Thomas Edison State Coll (NJ)
Thomas More Coll (KY)
Towson U (MD)
Transylvania U (KY)
Trevecca Nazarene U (TN)
Trinity Christian Coll (IL)
Trinity Coll (CT)
Trinity U (TX)
Truman State U (MO)
Tulane U (LA)
Union Coll (KY)
Union Coll (NE)
Union Coll (NY)
Union U (TN)
U at Albany, State U of New York (NY)
The U of Alabama (AL)
U of Alberta (AB, Canada)
The U of Arizona (AZ)
U of Bridgeport (CT)
The U of British Columbia (BC, Canada)
U of California, Berkeley (CA)
U of California, Davis (CA)
U of California, Irvine (CA)
U of California, Los Angeles (CA)
U of California, Riverside (CA)
U of California, San Diego (CA)
U of California, Santa Barbara (CA)
U of Central Florida (FL)
U of Chicago (IL)
U of Colorado at Boulder (CO)
U of Dayton (OH)
U of Denver (CO)
U of Dubuque (IA)
The U of Findlay (OH)
U of Florida (FL)
U of Georgia (GA)
U of Hawaii at Manoa (HI)
U of Illinois at Urbana–Champaign (IL)
U of Indianapolis (IN)
The U of Iowa (IA)
The U of Kansas (KS)
U of King's Coll (NS, Canada)
U of La Verne (CA)
U of Lethbridge (AB, Canada)
U of Manitoba (MB, Canada)
U of Mary (ND)
U of Mary Hardin-Baylor (TX)
U of Mary Washington (VA)
U of Miami (FL)
U of Michigan (MI)
U of Minnesota, Twin Cities Campus (MN)
U of Missouri (MO)
U of Mobile (AL)
U of Mount Union (OH)
U of Nebraska at Omaha (NE)
U of New Mexico (NM)
The U of North Carolina at Asheville (NC)
The U of North Carolina at Chapel Hill (NC)
The U of North Carolina at Charlotte (NC)
The U of North Carolina at Greensboro (NC)
U of North Dakota (ND)
U of Northern Iowa (IA)
U of Oklahoma (OK)
U of Oregon (OR)

U of Ottawa (ON, Canada)
U of Pennsylvania (PA)
U of Pittsburgh (PA)
U of Puget Sound (WA)
U of Redlands (CA)
U of Regina (SK, Canada)
U of Richmond (VA)
U of Rochester (NY)
U of St. Thomas (MN)
U of San Diego (CA)
U of San Francisco (CA)
U of Saskatchewan (SK, Canada)
The U of Scranton (PA)
U of South Carolina (SC)
U of Southern California (CA)
U of Southern Mississippi (MS)
U of South Florida (FL)
The U of Tennessee (TN)
The U of Texas at Austin (TX)
U of the Incarnate Word (TX)
U of the Ozarks (AR)
U of the Pacific (CA)
U of the Southwest (NM)
The U of Toledo (OH)
U of Tulsa (OK)
U of Vermont (VT)
U of Virginia (VA)
U of Washington (WA)
U of Waterloo (ON, Canada)
The U of Western Ontario (ON, Canada)
U of Wisconsin–Eau Claire (WI)
U of Wisconsin–Milwaukee (WI)
U of Wisconsin–Oshkosh (WI)
U of Wyoming (WY)
Vanderbilt U (TN)
Vanguard U of Southern California (CA)
Vassar Coll (NY)
Villanova U (PA)
Virginia Commonwealth U (VA)
Virginia Intermont Coll (VA)
Virginia U of Lynchburg (VA)
Virginia Wesleyan Coll (VA)
Viterbo U (WI)
Wabash Coll (IN)
Wake Forest U (NC)
Warner Pacific Coll (OR)
Wartburg Coll (IA)
Washburn U (KS)
Washington & Jefferson Coll (PA)
Washington and Lee U (VA)
Washington U in St. Louis (MO)
Webster U (MO)
Wellesley Coll (MA)
Wells Coll (NY)
Wesleyan Coll (GA)
Wesleyan U (CT)
Western Illinois U (IL)
Western Kentucky U (KY)
Western Michigan U (MI)
Westminster Coll (MO)
Westmont Coll (CA)
West Virginia Wesleyan Coll (WV)
Wheaton Coll (MA)
Wheeling Jesuit U (WV)
Whitman Coll (WA)
Whittier Coll (CA)
Wilfrid Laurier U (ON, Canada)
Willamette U (OR)
William Jewell Coll (MO)
Williams Coll (MA)
Wilmington Coll (OH)
Wilson Coll (PA)
Wingate U (NC)
Winthrop U (SC)
Wittenberg U (OH)
Wofford Coll (SC)
Wright State U (OH)
Yale U (CT)
York Coll (NE)
York U (ON, Canada)
Youngstown State U (OH)

RELIGIOUS STUDIES RELATED
Bryn Athyn Coll of the New Church (PA)
Claremont McKenna Coll (CA)
Ohio Northern U (OH)
Saint Louis U (MO)
Sarah Lawrence Coll (NY)
U of Regina (SK, Canada)
U of the West (CA)
The U of Western Ontario (ON, Canada)
Ursuline Coll (OH)

REPRODUCTIVE BIOLOGY
Bradley U (IL)

RESORT MANAGEMENT
California State U, Chico (CA)
Coastal Carolina U (SC)
Florida Gulf Coast U (FL)
Green Mountain Coll (VT)
Lakeland Coll (WI)
Mitchell Coll (CT)
Rochester Inst of Technology (NY)

RESPIRATORY CARE THERAPY
Armstrong Atlantic State U (GA)
Ball State U (IN)
Baptist Coll of Health Sciences (TN)
Bellarmine U (KY)
Boise State U (ID)
Dakota State U (SD)
Fairleigh Dickinson U, Coll at Florham (NJ)
Gannon U (PA)
Georgia State U (GA)
Gwynedd-Mercy Coll (PA)
Indiana U Bloomington (IN)
Indiana U East (IN)
Indiana U Kokomo (IN)
Indiana U of Pennsylvania (PA)
Indiana U–Purdue U Indianapolis (IN)
Indiana U South Bend (IN)
Indiana U Southeast (IN)
La Roche Coll (PA)
Long Island U, Brooklyn Campus (NY)
Marshall U (WV)
Medical Coll of Georgia (GA)
Midwestern State U (TX)
Missouri State U (MO)
Nebraska Methodist Coll (NE)
North Dakota State U (ND)
Northern Michigan U (MI)
The Ohio State U (OH)
St. Catherine U (MN)
Salisbury U (MD)
Shenandoah U (VA)
State U of New York Upstate Medical U (NY)
Stony Brook U, State U of New York (NY)
Texas Southern U (TX)
Texas State U–San Marcos (TX)
Thomas Edison State Coll (NJ)
Thompson Rivers U (BC, Canada)
Universidad Adventista de las Antillas (PR)
The U of Akron (OH)
The U of Alabama at Birmingham (AL)
U of Hartford (CT)
U of Indianapolis (IN)
The U of Kansas (KS)
U of Mary (ND)
U of Missouri (MO)
U of South Alabama (AL)
The U of Texas Medical Branch (TX)
U of Waterloo (ON, Canada)
Wheeling Jesuit U (WV)
York Coll of Pennsylvania (PA)
Youngstown State U (OH)

RESTAURANT, CULINARY, AND CATERING MANAGEMENT
The Art Inst of Atlanta (GA)
The Art Inst of Austin (TX)
The Art Inst of California–Hollywood (CA)
The Art Inst of California–Inland Empire (CA)
The Art Inst of California–Los Angeles (CA)
The Art Inst of California–Orange County (CA)
The Art Inst of California–Sacramento (CA)
The Art Inst of California–San Diego (CA)
The Art Inst of California–San Francisco (CA)
The Art Inst of California–Sunnyvale (CA)
The Art Inst of Charleston (SC)
The Art Inst of Charlotte (NC)
The Art Inst of Colorado (CO)
The Art Inst of Dallas (TX)
The Art Inst of Fort Lauderdale (FL)
The Art Inst of Houston (TX)
The Art Inst of Indianapolis (IN)
The Art Inst of Jacksonville (FL)
The Art Inst of Las Vegas (NV)
The Art Inst of Michigan (MI)
The Art Inst of Ohio–Cincinnati (OH)
The Art Inst of Philadelphia (PA)
The Art Inst of Phoenix (AZ)
The Art Inst of Pittsburgh (PA)
The Art Inst of Portland (OR)
The Art Inst of Raleigh-Durham (NC)
The Art Inst of Salt Lake City (UT)
The Art Inst of San Antonio (TX)
The Art Inst of Seattle (WA)
The Art Inst of Tampa (FL)
The Art Inst of Tennessee–Nashville (TN)
The Art Inst of Virginia Beach (VA)
The Art Inst of Washington (VA)
The Art Insts Intl Minnesota (MN)
Bowling Green State U (OH)
Coll of the Ozarks (MO)
The Illinois Inst of Art–Chicago (IL)
Johnson & Wales U (RI)
Kendall Coll (IL)
U of Hawaii–West Oahu (HI)
U of Illinois at Urbana–Champaign (IL)

RESTAURANT/FOOD SERVICES MANAGEMENT
Coll of the Ozarks (MO)
Colorado State U (CO)
Cornell U (NY)
The Culinary Inst of America (NY)
Culinary Inst of Virginia (VA)
Johnson & Wales U (CO)
Kendall Coll (IL)
Niagara U (NY)
The Ohio State U (OH)
The Restaurant School at Walnut Hill Coll (PA)
Rochester Inst of Technology (NY)
Southwest Minnesota State U (MN)
The U of Alabama (AL)
U of Central Florida (FL)
U of Missouri (MO)
U of San Francisco (CA)

RETAILING
Bowling Green State U (OH)
Capella U (MN)
Central Michigan U (MI)
Johnson & Wales U (RI)
Patricia Stevens Coll (MO)
Southern New Hampshire U (NH)
U of Central Oklahoma (OK)
U of South Carolina (SC)
Westwood Coll–Anaheim (CA)
Westwood Coll–Denver North (CO)
Westwood Coll–Denver South (CO)
Westwood Coll–Inland Empire (CA)
Westwood Coll–Los Angeles (CA)
Westwood Coll–South Bay Campus (CA)

ROBOTICS TECHNOLOGY
Alcorn State U (MS)
Indiana State U (IN)
Indiana U–Purdue U Indianapolis (IN)
Lake Superior State U (MI)
Purdue U (IN)
U of Rio Grande (OH)

ROMANCE LANGUAGES
Bard Coll (NY)
Beloit Coll (WI)
Bernard M. Baruch Coll of the City U of New York (NY)
Bowdoin Coll (ME)
Bryn Mawr Coll (PA)
Cameron U (OK)
Carleton Coll (MN)
The Catholic U of America (DC)
City Coll of the City U of New York (NY)
Colgate U (NY)
Dartmouth Coll (NH)
DePauw U (IN)
Elmira Coll (NY)
Fordham U (NY)
Franklin Coll Switzerland (Switzerland)
Gettysburg Coll (PA)
Harvard U (MA)
Haverford Coll (PA)
Hunter Coll of the City U of New York (NY)
Marlboro Coll (VT)
Merrimack Coll (MA)
Mount Allison U (NB, Canada)
Mount Holyoke Coll (MA)
Oberlin Coll (OH)
Pitzer Coll (CA)
Pomona Coll (CA)
Ripon Coll (WI)
Rockford Coll (IL)
St. Thomas Aquinas Coll (NY)
Sarah Lawrence Coll (NY)
Truman State U (MO)
Tufts U (MA)
U at Albany, State U of New York (NY)
U of Alberta (AB, Canada)
The U of British Columbia (BC, Canada)
U of Chicago (IL)
U of Cincinnati (OH)
U of Georgia (GA)
U of Hawaii at Manoa (HI)
U of Illinois at Chicago (IL)
U of Maine (ME)
U of Maryland, Coll Park (MD)
U of Michigan (MI)
U of Nevada, Las Vegas (NV)
U of New Brunswick Fredericton (NB, Canada)
U of Notre Dame (IN)
U of Oregon (OR)
U of Toronto (ON, Canada)
U of Washington (WA)
Vanderbilt U (TN)
Washington U in St. Louis (MO)
Wesleyan U (CT)
York U (ON, Canada)

ROMANCE LANGUAGES RELATED
Hood Coll (MD)
Houston Baptist U (TX)
Merrimack Coll (MA)
U of Lethbridge (AB, Canada)
U of Michigan–Flint (MI)
The U of North Carolina at Chapel Hill (NC)
U of Pennsylvania (PA)

RUSSIAN
American U (DC)
Amherst Coll (MA)
Arizona State U (AZ)
Bard Coll (NY)
Barnard Coll (NY)
Bates Coll (ME)
Baylor U (TX)
Beloit Coll (WI)
Boston Coll (MA)
Boston U (MA)
Bowdoin Coll (ME)
Bowling Green State U (OH)
Brandeis U (MA)
Brooklyn Coll of the City U of New York (NY)
Bryn Mawr Coll (PA)
Bucknell U (PA)
Carleton Coll (MN)
Claremont McKenna Coll (CA)
Colgate U (NY)
Coll of the Holy Cross (MA)
The Colorado Coll (CO)
Columbia U (NY)
Columbia U, School of General Studies (NY)
Cornell Coll (IA)
Cornell U (NY)
Dartmouth Coll (NH)
Dickinson Coll (PA)
Drew U (NJ)
Duke U (NC)
Emory U (GA)
Ferrum Coll (VA)
Fordham U (NY)
Georgetown U (DC)
The George Washington U (DC)
Goucher Coll (MD)
Grinnell Coll (IA)
Gustavus Adolphus Coll (MN)
Haverford Coll (PA)
Hofstra U (NY)
Hunter Coll of the City U of New York (NY)
Juniata Coll (PA)
Kent State U (OH)
La Salle U (PA)
Lawrence U (WI)
Lehman Coll of the City U of New York (NY)
Macalester Coll (MN)
Memorial U of Newfoundland (NL, Canada)
Miami U Hamilton (OH)
Michigan State U (MI)
Middlebury Coll (VT)
New Coll of Florida (FL)
New York U (NY)
Oberlin Coll (OH)
The Ohio State U (OH)
Ohio U (OH)
Oklahoma State U (OK)
Ouachita Baptist U (AR)
Penn State Abington (PA)
Penn State Altoona (PA)
Penn State Beaver (PA)
Penn State Berks (PA)
Penn State Brandywine (PA)
Penn State DuBois (PA)
Penn State Erie, The Behrend Coll (PA)
Penn State Fayette, The Eberly Campus (PA)
Penn State Greater Allegheny (PA)
Penn State Hazleton (PA)
Penn State Lehigh Valley (PA)
Penn State Mont Alto (PA)
Penn State New Kensington (PA)
Penn State Schuylkill (PA)
Penn State Shenango (PA)
Penn State U Park (PA)
Penn State Wilkes-Barre (PA)
Penn State Worthington Scranton (PA)
Penn State York (PA)
Pitzer Coll (CA)
Pomona Coll (CA)
Portland State U (OR)
Queens Coll of the City U of New York (NY)
Reed Coll (OR)
Rider U (NJ)
Rutgers, The State U of New Jersey, New Brunswick (NJ)
Saint Louis U (MO)
St. Olaf Coll (MN)
San Diego State U (CA)
Sarah Lawrence Coll (NY)
Scripps Coll (CA)
Sewanee: The U of the South (TN)
Smith Coll (MA)
Stony Brook U, State U of New York (NY)
Swarthmore Coll (PA)
Syracuse U (NY)
Temple U (PA)
Texas A&M U (TX)
Trinity Coll (CT)
Trinity U (TX)
Truman State U (MO)
Tufts U (MA)
Tulane U (LA)
United States Military Acad (NY)
U at Albany, State U of New York (NY)
U of Alberta (AB, Canada)
The U of Arizona (AZ)
The U of British Columbia (BC, Canada)
U of California, Davis (CA)
U of California, Los Angeles (CA)
U of California, San Diego (CA)
U of Chicago (IL)
U of Denver (CO)
U of Florida (FL)
U of Georgia (GA)
U of Hawaii at Manoa (HI)
U of Illinois at Chicago (IL)
U of Illinois at Urbana–Champaign (IL)
The U of Iowa (IA)
U of Kentucky (KY)
U of King's Coll (NS, Canada)
U of Manitoba (MB, Canada)
U of Maryland, Coll Park (MD)
U of Michigan (MI)
U of Minnesota, Twin Cities Campus (MN)
U of Missouri (MO)
U of Nebraska–Lincoln (NE)
U of New Brunswick Fredericton (NB, Canada)
U of New Hampshire (NH)
U of New Mexico (NM)
U of Northern Iowa (IA)
U of Notre Dame (IN)
U of Oklahoma (OK)
U of Ottawa (ON, Canada)
U of Pennsylvania (PA)
U of Pittsburgh (PA)
U of Rochester (NY)
U of St. Thomas (MN)
U of Saskatchewan (SK, Canada)
U of South Carolina (SC)
U of Southern California (CA)
U of South Florida (FL)
The U of Tennessee (TN)
The U of Texas at Arlington (TX)
The U of Texas at Austin (TX)
U of Toronto (ON, Canada)
U of Utah (UT)
U of Vermont (VT)
U of Washington (WA)
U of Waterloo (ON, Canada)
U of Wisconsin–Madison (WI)
U of Wisconsin–Milwaukee (WI)
U of Wyoming (WY)
Vanderbilt U (TN)
Vassar Coll (NY)
Wake Forest U (NC)
Washington U in St. Louis (MO)
Wellesley Coll (MA)
Wesleyan U (CT)
West Chester U of Pennsylvania (PA)
Wheaton Coll (MA)
Williams Coll (MA)
Yale U (CT)
York U (ON, Canada)

RUSSIAN STUDIES
American U (DC)
Bard Coll (NY)
Beloit Coll (WI)
Boston Coll (MA)
Boston U (MA)
Bowling Green State U (OH)
California State U, Fullerton (CA)
Carleton Coll (MN)

Russian Studies

Carnegie Mellon U (PA)
Claremont McKenna Coll (CA)
Colby Coll (ME)
Colgate U (NY)
Coll of the Holy Cross (MA)
The Coll of Wooster (OH)
The Colorado Coll (CO)
Columbia U (NY)
Columbia U, School of General Studies (NY)
Concordia Coll (MN)
Cornell Coll (IA)
Cornell U (NY)
Dartmouth Coll (NH)
DePauw U (IN)
Fordham U (NY)
George Mason U (VA)
The George Washington U (DC)
Grand Valley State U (MI)
Gustavus Adolphus Coll (MN)
Hamilton Coll (NY)
Iowa State U of Science and Technology (IA)
Kent State U (OH)
Lafayette Coll (PA)
La Salle U (PA)
Lawrence U (WI)
Luther Coll (IA)
Marlboro Coll (VT)
Michigan State U (MI)
Middlebury Coll (VT)
Mount Holyoke Coll (MA)
Muhlenberg Coll (PA)
Oberlin Coll (OH)
Rhodes Coll (TN)
Rutgers, The State U of New Jersey, New Brunswick (NJ)
St. Olaf Coll (MN)
San Diego State U (CA)
Sewanee: The U of the South (TN)
Smith Coll (MA)
Stetson U (FL)
Syracuse U (NY)
Texas State U–San Marcos (TX)
Texas Tech U (TX)
Tufts U (MA)
Tulane U (LA)
United States Military Acad (NY)
U at Albany, State U of New York (NY)
U of Alaska Fairbanks (AK)
U of Alberta (AB, Canada)
The U of British Columbia (BC, Canada)
U of California, Los Angeles (CA)
U of California, Riverside (CA)
U of California, San Diego (CA)
U of California, Santa Cruz (CA)
U of Chicago (IL)
U of Colorado at Boulder (CO)
U of Houston (TX)
U of Illinois at Urbana–Champaign (IL)
The U of Kansas (KS)
U of Manitoba (MB, Canada)
U of Maryland, Coll Park (MD)
U of Massachusetts Amherst (MA)
U of Michigan (MI)
U of Minnesota, Twin Cities Campus (MN)
U of Missouri (MO)
U of New Mexico (NM)
U of Northern Iowa (IA)
U of Oregon (OR)
U of Richmond (VA)
U of Rochester (NY)
U of St. Thomas (MN)
U of Southern Maine (ME)
The U of Texas at Austin (TX)
U of Toronto (ON, Canada)
U of Tulsa (OK)
U of Vermont (VT)
U of Washington (WA)
U of Waterloo (ON, Canada)
U of Wisconsin–Milwaukee (WI)
Washington and Lee U (VA)
Washington U in St. Louis (MO)
Wellesley Coll (MA)
Wesleyan U (CT)
Wheaton Coll (MA)
Wittenberg U (OH)
Yale U (CT)
York U (ON, Canada)

SALES AND MARKETING/ MARKETING AND DISTRIBUTION TEACHER EDUCATION

Bowling Green State U (OH)
Colorado State U (CO)
East Carolina U (NC)
Eastern New Mexico U (NM)
Fayetteville State U (NC)
Kent State U (OH)
Louisiana State U and Ag and Mech Coll (LA)
Middle Tennessee State U (TN)
New York Inst of Technology (NY)
North Carolina State U (NC)
Old Dominion U (VA)
Rider U (NJ)
State U of New York at Oswego (NY)
U of Nebraska–Lincoln (NE)
U of Wisconsin–Stout (WI)
Utah State U (UT)
Wright State U (OH)

SALES, DISTRIBUTION AND MARKETING

Babson Coll (MA)
Baylor U (TX)
Black Hills State U (SD)
Bowling Green State U (OH)
Brock U (ON, Canada)
Champlain Coll (VT)
Dalton State Coll (GA)
Hampton U (VA)
Harding U (AR)
HEC Montreal (QC, Canada)
Husson U (ME)
Johnson & Wales U (RI)
Johnson & Wales U—Charlotte Campus (NC)
Jones Intl U (CO)
Kennesaw State U (GA)
McKendree U (IL)
Middle Tennessee State U (TN)
New York U (NY)
Quinnipiac U (CT)
Seton Hill U (PA)
Texas A&M U (TX)
Trinity Christian Coll (IL)
Tuskegee U (AL)
The U of Akron (OH)
U of Baltimore (MD)
U of Central Oklahoma (OK)
The U of Findlay (OH)
U of Houston (TX)
U of Illinois at Urbana–Champaign (IL)
U of Memphis (TN)
U of North Texas (TX)
U of Pennsylvania (PA)
U of the Incarnate Word (TX)
U of Wisconsin–Stout (WI)
U of Wisconsin–Superior (WI)
West Chester U of Pennsylvania (PA)
Wichita State U (KS)
York U (ON, Canada)

SANSKRIT AND CLASSICAL INDIAN LANGUAGES

Bard Coll (NY)
Harvard U (MA)
U of Chicago (IL)

SCANDINAVIAN LANGUAGES

Augsburg Coll (MN)
Augustana Coll (IL)
Concordia Coll (MN)
Gustavus Adolphus Coll (MN)
U of Alberta (AB, Canada)
U of California, Berkeley (CA)
U of California, Los Angeles (CA)
U of Minnesota, Twin Cities Campus (MN)
U of North Dakota (ND)
The U of Texas at Austin (TX)
U of Washington (WA)
U of Wisconsin–Madison (WI)

SCANDINAVIAN STUDIES

Gustavus Adolphus Coll (MN)
Luther Coll (IA)
Pacific Lutheran U (WA)
U of Washington (WA)

SCHOOL LIBRARIAN/ SCHOOL LIBRARY MEDIA

The Coll of St. Scholastica (MN)

SCHOOL PSYCHOLOGY

Fort Hays State U (KS)
Iona Coll (NY)
Texas Wesleyan U (TX)
U of Wisconsin–River Falls (WI)

SCIENCE TEACHER EDUCATION

Abilene Christian U (TX)
Adams State Coll (CO)
Alabama State U (AL)
Alfred U (NY)
Alma Coll (MI)
Alvernia U (PA)
Alverno Coll (WI)
Andrews U (MI)
Aquinas Coll (MI)
Arcadia U (PA)
Arkansas Tech U (AR)
Ashland U (OH)
Assumption Coll (MA)
Auburn U (AL)
Augustana Coll (IL)
Ball State U (IN)
Baptist Bible Coll of Pennsylvania (PA)
Baylor U (TX)
Beloit Coll (WI)
Bemidji State U (MN)
Bethel Coll (IN)
Bishop's U (QC, Canada)
Black Hills State U (SD)
Bluefield Coll (VA)
Bob Jones U (SC)
Boise State U (ID)
Boston U (MA)
Bowie State U (MD)
Bowling Green State U (OH)
Bradley U (IL)
Brewton-Parker Coll (GA)
Brigham Young U (UT)
Brigham Young U–Hawaii (HI)
Brock U (ON, Canada)
Buena Vista U (IA)
Buffalo State Coll, State U of New York (NY)
California Lutheran U (CA)
California State U, San Marcos (CA)
Calumet Coll of Saint Joseph (IN)
Calvin Coll (MI)
Campbellsville U (KY)
Capital U (OH)
Carroll U (WI)
Castleton State Coll (VT)
Cedarville U (OH)
Central Michigan U (MI)
Chipola Coll (FL)
City Coll of the City U of New York (NY)
Clarion U of Pennsylvania (PA)
Clemson U (SC)
The Coll at Brockport, State U of New York (NY)
Coll of Notre Dame of Maryland (MD)
Coll of Saint Mary (NE)
Coll of the Atlantic (ME)
Coll of the Ozarks (MO)
Colorado State U (CO)
Columbus State U (GA)
Concordia Coll (MN)
Concordia U Chicago (IL)
Concordia U Wisconsin (WI)
Cornell U (NY)
Cornerstone U (MI)
Covenant Coll (GA)
Dallas Baptist U (TX)
Dana Coll (NE)
Defiance Coll (OH)
Delaware State U (DE)
DePaul U (IL)
Dickinson State U (ND)
Dixie State Coll of Utah (UT)
Doane Coll (NE)
Dordt Coll (IA)
Dowling Coll (NY)
East Carolina U (NC)
East Central U (OK)
Eastern Illinois U (IL)
Eastern Michigan U (MI)
Eastern Nazarene Coll (MA)
Eastern Washington U (WA)
Edgewood Coll (WI)
Elizabethtown Coll (PA)
Elmira Coll (NY)
Elon U (NC)
Evangel U (MO)
Fairmont State U (WV)
Florida Ag and Mech U (FL)
Florida Atlantic U (FL)
Florida Inst of Technology (FL)
Florida State U (FL)
Fort Hays State U (KS)
Freed-Hardeman U (TN)
Gettysburg Coll (PA)
Glenville State Coll (WV)
Governors State U (IL)
Grace Coll (IN)
Graceland U (IA)
Grand Valley State U (MI)
Greensboro Coll (NC)
Grove City Coll (PA)
Hamline U (MN)
Hannibal-LaGrange Coll (MO)
Harding U (AR)
Hardin-Simmons U (TX)
Heidelberg U (OH)
Henderson State U (AR)
Hofstra U (NY)
Hope Coll (MI)
Houston Baptist U (TX)
Hunter Coll of the City U of New York (NY)
Huntington U (IN)
Indiana State U (IN)
Indiana U Bloomington (IN)
Indiana U–Purdue U Fort Wayne (IN)
Indiana U South Bend (IN)
Indiana U Southeast (IN)
Indiana Wesleyan U (IN)
Indian River State Coll (FL)
Inter American U of Puerto Rico, San Germán Campus (PR)
Iona Coll (NY)
Ithaca Coll (NY)
Judson Coll (AL)
Juniata Coll (PA)
Keene State Coll (NH)
Kent State U (OH)
Lakehead U (ON, Canada)
Lakeland Coll (WI)
La Salle U (PA)
Le Moyne Coll (NY)
Lewis-Clark State Coll (ID)
Lincoln Memorial U (TN)
Lindenwood U (MO)
Longwood U (VA)
Louisiana Coll (LA)
Loyola U Chicago (IL)
Lubbock Christian U (TX)
Madonna U (MI)
Malone U (OH)
Manchester Coll (IN)
Mansfield U of Pennsylvania (PA)
Maranatha Baptist Bible Coll (WI)
Marian U (WI)
Marquette U (WI)
Mars Hill Coll (NC)
Marywood U (PA)
The Master's Coll and Sem (CA)
Memorial U of Newfoundland (NL, Canada)
Mercyhurst Coll (PA)
Methodist U (NC)
Miami U (OH)
Miami U Hamilton (OH)
Michigan State U (MI)
Michigan Technological U (MI)
Midwestern State U (TX)
Millersville U of Pennsylvania (PA)
Minnesota State U Mankato (MN)
Minnesota State U Moorhead (MN)
Minot State U (ND)
Mississippi Coll (MS)
Mississippi Valley State U (MS)
Missouri Baptist U (MO)
Missouri State U (MO)
Montana State U (MT)
Montana State U Billings (MT)
Moravian Coll (PA)
Morningside Coll (IA)
Mount Mercy Coll (IA)
Mount Vernon Nazarene U (OH)
Murray State U (KY)
Nebraska Wesleyan U (NE)
Nevada State Coll at Henderson (NV)
New Mexico Highlands U (NM)
New York U (NY)
Niagara U (NY)
Nicholls State U (LA)
North Carolina State U (NC)
North Dakota State U (ND)
Northeastern State U (OK)
Northern Arizona U (AZ)
Northern Michigan U (MI)
North Georgia Coll & State U (GA)
Northland Coll (WI)
Northwestern Oklahoma State U (OK)
Northwest Missouri State U (MO)
Oakland City U (IN)
Oakwood U (AL)
Ohio Dominican U (OH)
Ohio Northern U (OH)
Oklahoma Baptist U (OK)
Oklahoma Christian U (OK)
Oklahoma City U (OK)
Oklahoma Wesleyan U (OK)
Oral Roberts U (OK)
Ouachita Baptist U (AR)
Pace U (NY)
Peru State Coll (NE)
Pontifical Catholic U of Puerto Rico (PR)
Prescott Coll (AZ)
Queen's U at Kingston (ON, Canada)
Rhode Island Coll (RI)
Rider U (NJ)
Rochester Coll (MI)
Sacred Heart U (CT)
St. Ambrose U (IA)
St. Cloud State U (MN)
Saint Francis U (PA)
Saint Joseph's U (PA)
St. Petersburg Coll (FL)
Seattle Pacific U (WA)
Shawnee State U (OH)
Southeastern Louisiana U (LA)
Southeastern Oklahoma State U (OK)
Southeastern U (FL)
Southeast Missouri State U (MO)
Southern Arkansas U–Magnolia (AR)
Southern Illinois U Edwardsville (IL)
Southern U and Ag and Mech Coll (LA)
Southern Wesleyan U (SC)
Southwest Baptist U (MO)
Southwestern Oklahoma State U (OK)
State U of New York at Fredonia (NY)
State U of New York at New Paltz (NY)
State U of New York at Oswego (NY)
State U of New York Coll at Cortland (NY)
State U of New York Coll at Old Westbury (NY)
State U of New York Coll at Oneonta (NY)
State U of New York Coll of Environmental Science and Forestry (NY)
Tabor Coll (KS)
Talladega Coll (AL)
Tarleton State U (TX)
Taylor U (IN)
Temple U (PA)
Texas A&M Intl U (TX)
Texas A&M U–Corpus Christi (TX)
Texas Christian U (TX)
Texas Wesleyan U (TX)
Trine U (IN)
Trinity Christian Coll (IL)
Union U (TN)
The U of Akron (OH)
U of Alberta (AB, Canada)
The U of Arizona (AZ)
The U of British Columbia (BC, Canada)
U of Central Florida (FL)
U of Central Oklahoma (OK)
U of Charleston (WV)
U of Dayton (OH)
U of Evansville (IN)
The U of Findlay (OH)
U of Georgia (GA)
U of Illinois at Urbana–Champaign (IL)
U of Indianapolis (IN)
The U of Iowa (IA)
U of Kentucky (KY)
U of Lethbridge (AB, Canada)
U of Maine (ME)
U of Maine at Farmington (ME)
U of Maine at Machias (ME)
U of Maine at Presque Isle (ME)
U of Manitoba (MB, Canada)
U of Mary Hardin-Baylor (TX)
U of Maryland, Coll Park (MD)
U of Michigan–Dearborn (MI)
U of Michigan–Flint (MI)
U of Minnesota, Duluth (MN)
U of Minnesota, Twin Cities Campus (MN)
U of Mississippi (MS)
U of Missouri (MO)
The U of Montana Western (MT)
U of Nebraska–Lincoln (NE)
U of Nevada, Reno (NV)
U of New Brunswick Fredericton (NB, Canada)
The U of North Carolina at Pembroke (NC)
U of North Dakota (ND)
U of Northern Iowa (IA)
U of North Florida (FL)
U of Notre Dame (IN)
U of Oklahoma (OK)
U of Pittsburgh at Johnstown (PA)
U of Puerto Rico at Utuado (PR)
U of Puerto Rico, Cayey U Coll (PR)
U of Regina (SK, Canada)
U of Rio Grande (OH)
U of St. Francis (IL)
U of St. Thomas (MN)
The U of South Dakota (SD)
U of South Florida (FL)
The U of Tennessee at Chattanooga (TN)
The U of Tennessee at Martin (TN)
The U of Toledo (OH)
U of Toronto (ON, Canada)
U of Vermont (VT)
U of Washington (WA)
U of Windsor (ON, Canada)
U of Wisconsin–Eau Claire (WI)
U of Wisconsin–La Crosse (WI)
U of Wisconsin–Madison (WI)
U of Wisconsin–Platteville (WI)
U of Wisconsin–River Falls (WI)
U of Wisconsin–Stout (WI)
U of Wisconsin–Superior (WI)
U of Wisconsin–Whitewater (WI)
Upper Iowa U (IA)
Ursuline Coll (OH)

Utah State U (UT)
Utah Valley U (UT)
Valley City State U (ND)
Valparaiso U (IN)
Viterbo U (WI)
Walsh U (OH)
Warner Pacific Coll (OR)
Washington State U (WA)
Washington U in St. Louis (MO)
Wayland Baptist U (TX)
Waynesburg U (PA)
Wayne State Coll (NE)
Wayne State U (MI)
Weber State U (UT)
Western Carolina U (NC)
Western Michigan U (MI)
Western State Coll of Colorado (CO)
Western Washington U (WA)
West Virginia State U (WV)
Wheeling Jesuit U (WV)
Wichita State U (KS)
Widener U (PA)
William Penn U (IA)
Wilmington Coll (OH)
Wilmington U (DE)
Winona State U (MN)
Wright State U (OH)
Xavier U (OH)
Xavier U of Louisiana (LA)
York Coll (NE)
York Coll of Pennsylvania (PA)
York U (ON, Canada)
Youngstown State U (OH)

SCIENCE TECHNOLOGIES RELATED

Arizona State U (AZ)
Bridgewater State Coll (MA)
Clemson U (SC)
Kean U (NJ)
Lehigh U (PA)
Madonna U (MI)
Northern Arizona U (AZ)
U of Wisconsin–Stout (WI)
Willamette U (OR)

SCIENCE, TECHNOLOGY AND SOCIETY

Arizona State U (AZ)
Butler U (IN)
Cleveland State U (OH)
Colby Coll (ME)
Cornell U (NY)
Georgetown U (DC)
Georgia Inst of Technology (GA)
James Madison U (VA)
Lehigh U (PA)
Massachusetts Inst of Technology (MA)
Michigan State U (MI)
New Jersey Inst of Technology (NJ)
North Carolina State U (NC)
Pitzer Coll (CA)
Rensselaer Polytechnic Inst (NY)
Rutgers, The State U of New Jersey, Newark (NJ)
Scripps Coll (CA)
Slippery Rock U of Pennsylvania (PA)
Stanford U (CA)
U of Alaska Anchorage (AK)
U of King's Coll (NS, Canada)
U of Nevada, Reno (NV)
U of Puget Sound (WA)
U of Washington, Bothell (WA)
U of Windsor (ON, Canada)
Vanderbilt U (TN)
Vassar Coll (NY)
Washington U in St. Louis (MO)
Wesleyan U (CT)
Worcester Polytechnic Inst (MA)
York U (ON, Canada)

SCULPTURE

Alberta Coll of Art & Design (AB, Canada)
Aquinas Coll (MI)
Bard Coll at Simon's Rock (MA)
Bennington Coll (VT)
Bethany Coll (KS)
Birmingham-Southern Coll (AL)
Boston U (MA)
Bowling Green State U (OH)
Bradley U (IL)
Brigham Young U (UT)
Buffalo State Coll, State U of New York (NY)
California Coll of the Arts (CA)
California State U, East Bay (CA)
California State U, Long Beach (CA)
The Cleveland Inst of Art (OH)
The Coll at Brockport, State U of New York (NY)
Coll of Santa Fe (NM)
Coll of Visual Arts (MN)
Concordia U (QC, Canada)
Drake U (IA)
Escuela de Artes Plasticas de Puerto Rico (PR)
Ferris State U (MI)
Indiana U–Purdue U Fort Wayne (IN)
Inter American U of Puerto Rico, San Germán Campus (PR)
Kent State U (OH)
Keystone Coll (PA)
Longwood U (VA)
Lyme Acad Coll of Fine Arts (CT)
Maine Coll of Art (ME)
Marlboro Coll (VT)
Maryland Inst Coll of Art (MD)
Marywood U (PA)
Massachusetts Coll of Art and Design (MA)
Memorial U of Newfoundland (NL, Canada)
Minneapolis Coll of Art and Design (MN)
Minnesota State U Mankato (MN)
Minnesota State U Moorhead (MN)
Mount Allison U (NB, Canada)
Northern Arizona U (AZ)
Northern Michigan U (MI)
Northwest Nazarene U (ID)
Notre Dame de Namur U (CA)
Ohio Northern U (OH)
Ohio U (OH)
Otis Coll of Art and Design (CA)
Portland State U (OR)
Pratt Inst (NY)
Ringling Coll of Art and Design (FL)
Rochester Inst of Technology (NY)
Rocky Mountain Coll of Art + Design (CO)
Rutgers, The State U of New Jersey, New Brunswick (NJ)
St. Cloud State U (MN)
Salem State Coll (MA)
Sarah Lawrence Coll (NY)
Savannah Coll of Art and Design (GA)
School of the Art Inst of Chicago (IL)
School of the Museum of Fine Arts, Boston (MA)
School of Visual Arts (NY)
Seton Hill U (PA)
Sonoma State U (CA)
State U of New York at New Paltz (NY)
Temple U (PA)
Texas Christian U (TX)
Trinity Christian Coll (IL)
U of Alberta (AB, Canada)
U of Dallas (TX)
U of Hartford (CT)
U of Houston (TX)
U of Illinois at Urbana–Champaign (IL)
The U of Iowa (IA)
The U of Kansas (KS)
U of Massachusetts Dartmouth (MA)
U of Miami (FL)
U of Michigan (MI)
U of Oregon (OR)
U of Puerto Rico, Río Piedras (PR)
U of Regina (SK, Canada)
The U of Texas at El Paso (TX)
U of Washington (WA)
U of Windsor (ON, Canada)
U of Wisconsin–Milwaukee (WI)
Virginia Commonwealth U (VA)
Washington U in St. Louis (MO)
Western State Coll of Colorado (CO)
Western Washington U (WA)
York U (ON, Canada)

SECONDARY EDUCATION

Abilene Christian U (TX)
Acadia U (NS, Canada)
Alabama Ag and Mech U (AL)
Alabama State U (AL)
Albertus Magnus Coll (CT)
Albion Coll (MI)
Albright Coll (PA)
Alderson-Broaddus Coll (WV)
Alfred U (NY)
Alma Coll (MI)
American Intl Coll (MA)
American U (DC)
Andrews U (MI)
Aquinas Coll (MI)
Arcadia U (PA)
Arizona State U (AZ)
Ashland U (OH)
Assumption Coll (MA)
Atlantic Union Coll (MA)
Auburn U (AL)
Auburn U Montgomery (AL)
Augsburg Coll (MN)
Augustana Coll (IL)
Augustana Coll (SD)
Baker U (KS)
Baptist Bible Coll of Pennsylvania (PA)
Baylor U (TX)
Beloit Coll (WI)
Bemidji State U (MN)
Benedictine Coll (KS)
Benedictine U (IL)
Bennington Coll (VT)
Bethel Coll (IN)
Birmingham-Southern Coll (AL)
Bishop's U (QC, Canada)
Blackburn Coll (IL)
Black Hills State U (SD)
Bluefield Coll (VA)
Boise State U (ID)
Boston Coll (MA)
Bowie State U (MD)
Brewton-Parker Coll (GA)
Briar Cliff U (IA)
Brigham Young U–Hawaii (HI)
Brock U (ON, Canada)
Bucknell U (PA)
Buffalo State Coll, State U of New York (NY)
Butler U (IN)
Calumet Coll of Saint Joseph (IN)
Calvary Bible Coll and Theological Sem (MO)
Calvin Coll (MI)
Cameron U (OK)
Campbellsville U (KY)
Canisius Coll (NY)
Carson-Newman Coll (TN)
Catawba Coll (NC)
The Catholic U of America (DC)
Cedar Crest Coll (PA)
Centenary Coll (NJ)
Central Christian Coll of Kansas (KS)
Central State U (OH)
Champlain Coll (VT)
Cheyney U of Pennsylvania (PA)
Chipola Coll (FL)
The Citadel, The Military Coll of South Carolina (SC)
City Coll of the City U of New York (NY)
Clarke Coll (IA)
Clark U (MA)
Clemson U (SC)
The Coll at Brockport, State U of New York (NY)
Coll of Charleston (SC)
The Coll of New Jersey (NJ)
Coll of Notre Dame of Maryland (MD)
Coll of Saint Benedict (MN)
Coll of St. Joseph (VT)
Coll of Saint Mary (NE)
Coll of the Atlantic (ME)
Coll of the Ozarks (MO)
Concordia Coll (MN)
Concordia U Chicago (IL)
Concordia U, St. Paul (MN)
Concordia U Texas (TX)
Concordia U Wisconsin (WI)
Concord U (WV)
Converse Coll (SC)
Corban U (OR)
Cornell Coll (IA)
Cornerstone U (MI)
Crichton Coll (TN)
Cumberland U (TN)
Dakota Wesleyan U (SD)
Dallas Baptist U (TX)
Dana Coll (NE)
Daytona State Coll (FL)
Defiance Coll (OH)
Delaware State U (DE)
Delaware Valley Coll (PA)
DePaul U (IL)
Dickinson State U (ND)
Dominican Coll (NY)
Dordt Coll (IA)
Drake U (IA)
Drury U (MO)
Duquesne U (PA)
D'Youville Coll (NY)
East Central U (OK)
Eastern Connecticut State U (CT)
Eastern Mennonite U (VA)
Eastern Nazarene Coll (MA)
East Stroudsburg U of Pennsylvania (PA)
Edward Waters Coll (FL)
Elmhurst Coll (IL)
Elmira Coll (NY)
Elon U (NC)
Emmanuel Coll (MA)
Emporia State U (KS)
Evangel U (MO)
Fairmont State U (WV)
Faulkner U (AL)
Fitchburg State Coll (MA)
Flagler Coll (FL)
Florida Gulf Coast U (FL)
Florida Southern Coll (FL)
Fontbonne U (MO)
Fordham U (NY)
Fort Lewis Coll (CO)
Franklin Pierce U (NH)
Freed-Hardeman U (TN)
Free Will Baptist Bible Coll (TN)
Frostburg State U (MD)
Furman U (SC)
Gallaudet U (DC)
Gannon U (PA)
Gardner-Webb U (NC)
Gettysburg Coll (PA)
Glenville State Coll (WV)
Gonzaga U (WA)
Grace Bible Coll (MI)
Graceland U (IA)
Grand Valley State U (MI)
Green Mountain Coll (VT)
Greensboro Coll (NC)
Grove City Coll (PA)
Guilford Coll (NC)
Gustavus Adolphus Coll (MN)
Gwynedd-Mercy Coll (PA)
Hamline U (MN)
Hampton U (VA)
Hannibal-LaGrange Coll (MO)
Harding U (AR)
Harris-Stowe State U (MO)
Heidelberg U (OH)
High Point U (NC)
Hillsdale Coll (MI)
Hillsdale Free Will Baptist Coll (OK)
Hofstra U (NY)
Holy Family U (PA)
Houghton Coll (NY)
Houston Baptist U (TX)
Humboldt State U (CA)
Hunter Coll of the City U of New York (NY)
Huntington U (IN)
Huston-Tillotson U (TX)
Idaho State U (ID)
Illinois Coll (IL)
Indiana U Bloomington (IN)
Indiana U East (IN)
Indiana U Kokomo (IN)
Indiana U Northwest (IN)
Indiana U–Purdue U Fort Wayne (IN)
Indiana U–Purdue U Indianapolis (IN)
Indiana U South Bend (IN)
Indiana U Southeast (IN)
Indiana Wesleyan U (IN)
Inter American U of Puerto Rico, San Germán Campus (PR)
Iona Coll (NY)
Iowa State U of Science and Technology (IA)
Iowa Wesleyan Coll (IA)
Ithaca Coll (NY)
Jacksonville State U (AL)
Jacksonville U (FL)
Jarvis Christian Coll (TX)
John Brown U (AR)
John Carroll U (OH)
Johnson State Coll (VT)
Judson U (IL)
Juniata Coll (PA)
Kansas State U (KS)
Keene State Coll (NH)
Kentucky Wesleyan Coll (KY)
Keuka Coll (NY)
King's Coll (PA)
The King's U Coll (AB, Canada)
Kutztown U of Pennsylvania (PA)
Kuyper Coll (MI)
Lake Forest Coll (IL)
Lakehead U (ON, Canada)
Lakeland Coll (WI)
Lake Superior State U (MI)
Lamar U (TX)
La Salle U (PA)
Lasell Coll (MA)
Lawrence U (WI)
Lee U (TN)
Le Moyne Coll (NY)
Lesley U (MA)
LeTourneau U (TX)
Lincoln Christian U (IL)
Lincoln Memorial U (TN)
Lincoln U (PA)
Lindenwood U (MO)
Lindsey Wilson Coll (KY)
Lock Haven U of Pennsylvania (PA)
Long Island U, Brooklyn Campus (NY)
Long Island U, C.W. Post Campus (NY)
Longwood U (VA)
Loras Coll (IA)
Louisiana Coll (LA)
Louisiana State U and Ag and Mech Coll (LA)
Lourdes Coll (OH)
Loyola U Chicago (IL)
Lubbock Christian U (TX)
Madonna U (MI)
Maharishi U of Management (IA)
Manchester Coll (IN)
Manhattanville Coll (NY)
Mansfield U of Pennsylvania (PA)
Maranatha Baptist Bible Coll (WI)
Marian U (IN)
Marian U (WI)
Marietta Coll (OH)
Marist Coll (NY)
Marquette U (WI)
Marshall U (WV)
Mars Hill Coll (NC)
The Master's Coll and Sem (CA)
McKendree U (IL)
McMurry U (TX)
Medaille Coll (NY)
Memorial U of Newfoundland (NL, Canada)
Mercyhurst Coll (PA)
Merrimack Coll (MA)
Methodist U (NC)
Miami U (OH)
Michigan State U (MI)
Michigan Technological U (MI)
MidAmerica Nazarene U (KS)
Midway Coll (KY)
Midwestern State U (TX)
Minnesota State U Mankato (MN)
Minnesota State U Moorhead (MN)
Mississippi Coll (MS)
Mississippi State U (MS)
Missouri Southern State U (MO)
Missouri State U (MO)
Missouri U of Science and Technology (MO)
Molloy Coll (NY)
Monmouth U (NJ)
Montana State U Billings (MT)
Moravian Coll (PA)
Mount Aloysius Coll (PA)
Mount Marty Coll (SD)
Mount Mary Coll (WI)
Mount Mercy Coll (IA)
Mount Saint Mary Coll (NY)
Mount Vernon Nazarene U (OH)
Murray State U (KY)
Nazareth Coll of Rochester (NY)
Nevada State Coll at Henderson (NV)
Newberry Coll (SC)
New England Coll (NH)
Newman U (KS)
New Mexico State U (NM)
Niagara U (NY)
Nichols Coll (MA)
North Carolina State U (NC)
North Central Coll (IL)
Northeastern State U (OK)
Northern Michigan U (MI)
Northern State U (SD)
North Georgia Coll & State U (GA)
Northwestern Coll (IA)
Northwestern Oklahoma State U (OK)
Northwest Nazarene U (ID)
Northwest U (WA)
Nova Southeastern U (FL)
Nyack Coll (NY)
Oakland City U (IN)
Ohio Dominican U (OH)
Ohio U (OH)
Ohio Valley U (WV)
Ohio Wesleyan U (OH)
Oklahoma Christian U (OK)
Oklahoma City U (OK)
Oklahoma State U (OK)
Oklahoma Wesleyan U (OK)
Ouachita Baptist U (AR)
Penn State Abington (PA)
Penn State Altoona (PA)
Penn State Beaver (PA)
Penn State Berks (PA)
Penn State Brandywine (PA)
Penn State DuBois (PA)
Penn State Erie, The Behrend Coll (PA)
Penn State Fayette, The Eberly Campus (PA)
Penn State Greater Allegheny (PA)
Penn State Hazleton (PA)
Penn State Lehigh Valley (PA)
Penn State Mont Alto (PA)
Penn State New Kensington (PA)
Penn State Schuylkill (PA)
Penn State Shenango (PA)
Penn State U Park (PA)
Penn State Wilkes-Barre (PA)
Penn State Worthington Scranton (PA)
Penn State York (PA)
Pepperdine U, Malibu (CA)
Peru State Coll (NE)
Point Park U (PA)
Prescott Coll (AZ)
Presentation Coll (SD)
Providence Coll (RI)
Purdue U Calumet (IN)
Purdue U North Central (IN)
Queens U of Charlotte (NC)
Rhode Island Coll (RI)

Rider U (NJ)
Ripon Coll (WI)
Rivier Coll (NH)
Rochester Coll (MI)
Rockford Coll (IL)
Rockhurst U (MO)
Rocky Mountain Coll (MT)
Sacred Heart U (CT)
St. Ambrose U (IA)
Saint Anselm Coll (NH)
St. Catherine U (MN)
St. Cloud State U (MN)
Saint Francis U (PA)
St. Francis Xavier U (NS, Canada)
Saint John's U (MN)
St. John's U (NY)
Saint Joseph's U (PA)
Saint Martin's U (WA)
Saint Mary-of-the-Woods Coll (IN)
Saint Michael's Coll (VT)
St. Thomas Aquinas Coll (NY)
St. Thomas U (FL)
Salem State Coll (MA)
Salve Regina U (RI)
San Diego Christian Coll (CA)
Seton Hall U (NJ)
Shawnee State U (OH)
Shepherd U (WV)
Siena Coll (NY)
Siena Heights U (MI)
Simmons Coll (MA)
Simpson Coll (IA)
Slippery Rock U of Pennsylvania (PA)
Southeastern Oklahoma State U (OK)
Southeast Missouri State U (MO)
Southern Arkansas U–Magnolia (AR)
Southern Connecticut State U (CT)
Southern U and Ag and Mech Coll (LA)
Southern Utah U (UT)
Southwestern Assemblies of God U (TX)
Southwestern Oklahoma State U (OK)
Spring Arbor U (MI)
Spring Hill Coll (AL)
State U of New York at Fredonia (NY)
State U of New York at New Paltz (NY)
State U of New York at Oswego (NY)
State U of New York Coll at Cortland (NY)
State U of New York Coll at Old Westbury (NY)
State U of New York Coll at Oneonta (NY)
Stetson U (FL)
Suffolk U (MA)
Susquehanna U (PA)
Tabor Coll (KS)
Tarleton State U (TX)
Tennessee Technological U (TN)
Tennessee Wesleyan Coll (TN)
Texas A&M U–Commerce (TX)
Texas Christian U (TX)
Thiel Coll (PA)
Thomas More Coll (KY)
Trent U (ON, Canada)
Trine U (IN)
Trinity Christian Coll (IL)
Troy U (AL)
Tufts U (MA)
Tusculum Coll (TN)
Union Coll (KY)
Union Coll (NE)
Union Inst & U (OH)
Union U (TN)
Universidad Adventista de las Antillas (PR)
Université du Québec en Outaouais (QC, Canada)
The U of Alabama (AL)
The U of Alabama at Birmingham (AL)
U of Alaska Anchorage (AK)
U of Alberta (AB, Canada)
The U of Arizona (AZ)
U of Arkansas at Pine Bluff (AR)
The U of British Columbia (BC, Canada)
U of Central Missouri (MO)
U of Central Oklahoma (OK)
U of Cincinnati (OH)
U of Dallas (TX)
U of Dayton (OH)
U of Dubuque (IA)
The U of Findlay (OH)
U of Guam (GU)
U of Hartford (CT)
U of Hawaii at Hilo (HI)
U of Hawaii at Manoa (HI)
U of Idaho (ID)
U of Illinois at Urbana–Champaign (IL)
U of Indianapolis (IN)
The U of Iowa (IA)
The U of Kansas (KS)
U of Maine (ME)
U of Maine at Farmington (ME)
U of Maine at Presque Isle (ME)
U of Manitoba (MB, Canada)
U of Maryland, Coll Park (MD)
U of Michigan (MI)
U of Michigan–Dearborn (MI)
U of Mississippi (MS)
U of Missouri (MO)
U of Missouri–Kansas City (MO)
U of Missouri–St. Louis (MO)
The U of Montana Western (MT)
U of Nebraska at Omaha (NE)
U of Nevada, Las Vegas (NV)
U of New Brunswick Fredericton (NB, Canada)
U of New Mexico (NM)
U of New Orleans (LA)
U of North Alabama (AL)
U of North Florida (FL)
U of Pittsburgh at Bradford (PA)
U of Pittsburgh at Johnstown (PA)
U of Portland (OR)
U of Puerto Rico, Río Piedras (PR)
U of Redlands (CA)
U of Regina (SK, Canada)
U of Rhode Island (RI)
U of Rio Grande (OH)
U of St. Thomas (TX)
U of San Francisco (CA)
U of Saskatchewan (SK, Canada)
The U of Scranton (PA)
U of South Alabama (AL)
U of South Carolina Aiken (SC)
U of South Carolina Upstate (SC)
The U of South Dakota (SD)
The U of Tampa (FL)
The U of Tennessee at Chattanooga (TN)
U of the Ozarks (AR)
U of the Southwest (NM)
The U of Toledo (OH)
U of Vermont (VT)
U of Washington (WA)
The U of Western Ontario (ON, Canada)
U of West Georgia (GA)
U of Windsor (ON, Canada)
U of Wisconsin–Madison (WI)
U of Wisconsin–Milwaukee (WI)
U of Wisconsin–Oshkosh (WI)
U of Wisconsin–Platteville (WI)
U of Wisconsin–River Falls (WI)
U of Wisconsin–Stevens Point (WI)
U of Wisconsin–Whitewater (WI)
U of Wyoming (WY)
Utah State U (UT)
Utica Coll (NY)
Valdosta State U (GA)
Valley City State U (ND)
Valparaiso U (IN)
Vanderbilt U (TN)
Vanguard U of Southern California (CA)
Villanova U (PA)
Virginia Intermont Coll (VA)
Virginia Polytechnic Inst and State U (VA)
Virginia Wesleyan Coll (VA)
Wagner Coll (NY)
Walsh U (OH)
Warner Pacific Coll (OR)
Wartburg Coll (IA)
Washburn U (KS)
Washington State U (WA)
Washington U in St. Louis (MO)
Waynesburg U (PA)
Weber State U (UT)
Wells Coll (NY)
Western Connecticut State U (CT)
Western New England Coll (MA)
Western Oregon U (OR)
West Liberty U (WV)
Westminster Coll (MO)
Westmont Coll (CA)
West Virginia State U (WV)
West Virginia U (WV)
West Virginia Wesleyan Coll (WV)
Wheaton Coll (IL)
Wheeling Jesuit U (WV)
Wichita State U (KS)
William Jewell Coll (MO)
William Paterson U of New Jersey (NJ)
William Penn U (IA)
Wilmington Coll (OH)
Winona State U (MN)
Wright State U (OH)
Xavier U of Louisiana (LA)
York Coll (NE)
York Coll of the City U of New York (NY)
York U (ON, Canada)
Youngstown State U (OH)

SECONDARY SCHOOL ADMINISTRATION/ PRINCIPALSHIP
The U of North Carolina at Pembroke (NC)

SECURITIES SERVICES ADMINISTRATION
American Public U System (WV)
Central Pennsylvania Coll (PA)
The Coll at Brockport, State U of New York (NY)
Davenport U, Grand Rapids (MI)
Herzing U (GA)
St. John's U (NY)
Southwestern Coll (KS)
Webber Intl U (FL)

SECURITY AND LOSS PREVENTION
Farmingdale State Coll (NY)
Northern Michigan U (MI)

SECURITY AND PROTECTIVE SERVICES RELATED
American Public U System (WV)
Capella U (MN)
Eastern Michigan U (MI)
Embry-Riddle Aeronautical U (FL)
Keiser U, Fort Lauderdale (FL)
Lewis U (IL)
Madonna U (MI)
Massachusetts Maritime Acad (MA)
Miami Dade Coll (FL)
Midway Coll (KY)
North Dakota State U (ND)
Northwestern Oklahoma State U (OK)
Penn State Altoona (PA)
Penn State Berks (PA)
Penn State U Park (PA)
Point Park U (PA)
Roberts Wesleyan Coll (NY)
St. Ambrose U (IA)
St. Petersburg Coll (FL)
Savannah State U (GA)
Thomas Edison State Coll (NJ)
Tiffin U (OH)
Virginia Commonwealth U (VA)
Washburn U (KS)
Western Illinois U (IL)

SELLING SKILLS AND SALES
Bradley U (IL)
Jones Intl U (CO)
U of Memphis (TN)

SEMITIC LANGUAGES
U of Pennsylvania (PA)

SIGN LANGUAGE INTERPRETATION AND TRANSLATION
Augustana Coll (SD)
Bethel Coll (IN)
Bloomsburg U of Pennsylvania (PA)
Columbia Coll Chicago (IL)
Gallaudet U (DC)
Goshen Coll (IN)
Idaho State U (ID)
Indiana U–Purdue U Indianapolis (IN)
Maryville Coll (TN)
Mount Aloysius Coll (PA)
Quincy U (IL)
Rochester Inst of Technology (NY)
Troy U (AL)
U of Arkansas at Little Rock (AR)
U of Louisville (KY)
U of New Hampshire at Manchester (NH)
U of New Mexico (NM)
U of Northern Colorado (CO)
U of North Florida (FL)
Valdosta State U (GA)
Western Oregon U (OR)
York U (ON, Canada)

SLAVIC, BALTIC, AND ALBANIAN LANGUAGES RELATED
Rutgers, The State U of New Jersey, Newark (NJ)
The U of North Carolina at Chapel Hill (NC)

SLAVIC LANGUAGES
Boston Coll (MA)
Columbia U (NY)
Columbia U, School of General Studies (NY)
Duke U (NC)
Harvard U (MA)
Indiana U Bloomington (IN)
Princeton U (NJ)
Stanford U (CA)
U of Alberta (AB, Canada)
The U of British Columbia (BC, Canada)
U of California, Berkeley (CA)
U of California, Los Angeles (CA)
U of California, Santa Barbara (CA)
U of Chicago (IL)
U of Illinois at Chicago (IL)
U of Illinois at Urbana–Champaign (IL)
The U of Kansas (KS)
U of Manitoba (MB, Canada)
U of Pittsburgh (PA)
U of Toronto (ON, Canada)
U of Virginia (VA)
U of Washington (WA)
U of Wisconsin–Madison (WI)
U of Wisconsin–Milwaukee (WI)
Wayne State U (MI)

SLAVIC STUDIES
Barnard Coll (NY)
Baylor U (TX)
Columbia U, School of General Studies (NY)
Connecticut Coll (CT)
Lawrence U (WI)
Oakland U (MI)
U of Ottawa (ON, Canada)
U of Waterloo (ON, Canada)

SMALL BUSINESS ADMINISTRATION
Adams State Coll (CO)
Arcadia U (PA)
Avila U (MO)
Babson Coll (MA)
Bradley U (IL)
Carroll U (WI)
Carson-Newman Coll (TN)
Chowan U (NC)
Husson U (ME)
Kendall Coll (IL)
Lewis-Clark State Coll (ID)
Lincoln U (CA)
North Central Coll (IL)
Northern Michigan U (MI)
Pontifical Catholic U of Puerto Rico (PR)
Redeemer U Coll (ON, Canada)
U of Nebraska at Omaha (NE)

SOCIAL AND PHILOSOPHICAL FOUNDATIONS OF EDUCATION
Washington U in St. Louis (MO)

SOCIAL PSYCHOLOGY
Bennington Coll (VT)
Brigham Young U (UT)
Clarion U of Pennsylvania (PA)
Eastern Nazarene Coll (MA)
Florida Atlantic U (FL)
Grand Valley State U (MI)
Kwantlen Polytechnic U (BC, Canada)
Lawrence U (WI)
Maryville U of Saint Louis (MO)
Moravian Coll (PA)
Northwest Missouri State U (MO)
Paine Coll (GA)
Penn State Abington (PA)
Prescott Coll (AZ)
U of California, Irvine (CA)
U of Nevada, Reno (NV)
U of New England (ME)
U of Wisconsin–Superior (WI)

SOCIAL SCIENCES
Adelphi U (NY)
Alabama State U (AL)
Albertus Magnus Coll (CT)
Allen U (SC)
Alma Coll (MI)
Alvernia U (PA)
Alverno Coll (WI)
American Intl Coll (MA)
American Public U System (WV)
Andrews U (MI)
Aquinas Coll (MI)
Arizona State U (AZ)
Asbury U (KY)
Ashland U (OH)
Atlanta Christian Coll (GA)
Augsburg Coll (MN)
Azusa Pacific U (CA)
Ball State U (IN)
Belhaven U (MS)
Bemidji State U (MN)
Benedictine Coll (KS)
Benedictine U (IL)
Bennington Coll (VT)
Berry Coll (GA)
Bethany Lutheran Coll (MN)
Bethany U (CA)
Bethel Coll (IN)
Bethel U (MN)
Bishop's U (QC, Canada)
Black Hills State U (SD)
Bluefield Coll (VA)
Bluefield State Coll (WV)
Blue Mountain Coll (MS)
Bluffton U (OH)
Boise State U (ID)
Bowling Green State U (OH)
Brescia U (KY)
Brewton-Parker Coll (GA)
Brock U (ON, Canada)
Buena Vista U (IA)
California Baptist U (CA)
California Lutheran U (CA)
California Polytechnic State U, San Luis Obispo (CA)
California State Polytechnic U, Pomona (CA)
California State U, Los Angeles (CA)
California State U, Monterey Bay (CA)
California State U, Sacramento (CA)
California State U, San Bernardino (CA)
California State U, San Marcos (CA)
California State U, Stanislaus (CA)
Calvin Coll (MI)
Campbellsville U (KY)
Castleton State Coll (VT)
Cazenovia Coll (NY)
Central Christian Coll of Kansas (KS)
Central Coll (IA)
Central Connecticut State U (CT)
Central Michigan U (MI)
Chaminade U of Honolulu (HI)
Cheyney U of Pennsylvania (PA)
Clarion U of Pennsylvania (PA)
Clarkson U (NY)
Cleveland State U (OH)
Colgate U (NY)
Coll of Mount Saint Vincent (NY)
Coll of Saint Benedict (MN)
Coll of Saint Mary (NE)
The Coll of St. Scholastica (MN)
Coll of the Humanities and Sciences, Harrison Middleton U (AZ)
Colorado State U (CO)
Colorado State U–Pueblo (CO)
Columbia Coll (SC)
Concordia U Coll of Alberta (AB, Canada)
Coppin State U (MD)
Corban U (OR)
Cornell U (NY)
Cumberland U (TN)
Dana Coll (NE)
Defiance Coll (OH)
Delta State U (MS)
DePaul U (IL)
Dickinson State U (ND)
Doane Coll (NE)
Dominican Coll (NY)
Dominican U (IL)
Dordt Coll (IA)
Dowling Coll (NY)
Drexel U (PA)
Eastern Mennonite U (VA)
Eastern Michigan U (MI)
Eastern New Mexico U (NM)
East Stroudsburg U of Pennsylvania (PA)
Edgewood Coll (WI)
Edinboro U of Pennsylvania (PA)
Edward Waters Coll (FL)
Elizabethtown Coll (PA)
Elmira Coll (NY)
Embry-Riddle Aeronautical U (AZ)
Emporia State U (KS)
Eugene Lang Coll The New School for Liberal Arts (NY)
The Evergreen State Coll (WA)
Faulkner U (AL)
Felician Coll (NJ)
Ferrum Coll (VA)
Florida Atlantic U (FL)
Florida Southern Coll (FL)
Florida State U (FL)
Fontbonne U (MO)
Fordham U (NY)
Fort Valley State U (GA)
Freed-Hardeman U (TN)

INDEXES

SOCIAL SCIENCES RELATED

SOCIAL SCIENCE TEACHER EDUCATION

SOCIAL STUDIES TEACHER EDUCATION

Central Christian Coll of Kansas (KS)
Central Michigan U (MI)
City Coll of the City U of New York (NY)
Clarion U of Pennsylvania (PA)
Clearwater Christian Coll (FL)
The Coll at Brockport, State U of New York (NY)
The Coll of Saint Rose (NY)
Coll of the Ozarks (MO)
Colorado State U (CO)
Columbus State U (GA)
Concordia Coll (MN)
Concordia U, St. Paul (MN)
Corban U (OR)
Cornerstone U (MI)
Crown Coll (MN)
Daemen Coll (NY)
Dordt Coll (IA)
Dowling Coll (NY)
Duquesne U (PA)
East Carolina U (NC)
Eastern Michigan U (MI)
Eastern Washington U (WA)
East Texas Baptist U (TX)
Elmira Coll (NY)
Erskine Coll (SC)
Ferris State U (MI)
Franklin Coll (IN)
Gannon U (PA)
Glenville State Coll (WV)
Grace Coll (IN)
Grambling State U (LA)
Grand Valley State U (MI)
Greensboro Coll (NC)
Gustavus Adolphus Coll (MN)
Harding U (AR)
Hardin-Simmons U (TX)
Hofstra U (NY)
Holy Family U (PA)
Hope Coll (MI)
Houston Baptist U (TX)
Howard Payne U (TX)
Huston-Tillotson U (TX)
Illinois State U (IL)
Indiana State U (IN)
Indiana U Bloomington (IN)
Indiana U Northwest (IN)
Indiana U–Purdue U Fort Wayne (IN)
Indiana U–Purdue U Indianapolis (IN)
Indiana U South Bend (IN)
Indiana U Southeast (IN)
Indiana Wesleyan U (IN)
Inter American U of Puerto Rico, Fajardo Campus (PR)
Inter American U of Puerto Rico, San Germán Campus (PR)
Iona Coll (NY)
Ithaca Coll (NY)
John Brown U (AR)
Johnson State Coll (VT)
Juniata Coll (PA)
Keene State Coll (NH)
Kennesaw State U (GA)
Kent State U (OH)
Kentucky Wesleyan Coll (KY)
Keuka Coll (NY)
Keystone Coll (PA)
Le Moyne Coll (NY)
Limestone Coll (SC)
Long Island U, Brooklyn Campus (NY)
Long Island U, C.W. Post Campus (NY)
Louisiana State U in Shreveport (LA)
Louisiana Tech U (LA)
Lubbock Christian U (TX)
Madonna U (MI)
Malone U (OH)
Manhattanville Coll (NY)
Mansfield U of Pennsylvania (PA)
Maranatha Baptist Bible Coll (WI)
Marian U (WI)
Marist Coll (NY)
Maryville Coll (TN)
McNeese State U (LA)
Messiah Coll (PA)
Miami U (OH)
Miami U Hamilton (OH)
Michigan State U (MI)
MidAmerica Nazarene U (KS)
Midwestern State U (TX)
Millersville U of Pennsylvania (PA)
Minnesota State U Mankato (MN)
Minnesota State U Moorhead (MN)
Mississippi Coll (MS)
Molloy Coll (NY)
Moravian Coll (PA)
Morris Coll (SC)
Mount Vernon Nazarene U (OH)
Murray State U (KY)
Nazareth Coll of Rochester (NY)
New York Inst of Technology (NY)
New York U (NY)
Niagara U (NY)
Nicholls State U (LA)
North Carolina State U (NC)
North Dakota State U (ND)
Northeastern State U (OK)
Northern Michigan U (MI)
North Greenville U (SC)
Northland Coll (WI)
Northwestern Coll (MN)
Northwestern State U of Louisiana (LA)
Northwest U (WA)
Oakland City U (IN)
Ohio Dominican U (OH)
Ohio Northern U (OH)
Ohio Wesleyan U (OH)
Oklahoma Baptist U (OK)
Oklahoma Christian U (OK)
Oral Roberts U (OK)
Ouachita Baptist U (AR)
Pace U (NY)
Penn State Harrisburg (PA)
Philadelphia Biblical U (PA)
Pittsburg State U (KS)
Pontifical Catholic U of Puerto Rico (PR)
Prescott Coll (AZ)
Queens Coll of the City U of New York (NY)
Redeemer U Coll (ON, Canada)
Rhode Island Coll (RI)
Roberts Wesleyan Coll (NY)
Rochester Coll (MI)
Rocky Mountain Coll (MT)
St. Catherine U (MN)
St. Edward's U (TX)
St. Francis Coll (NY)
Saint Francis U (PA)
St. John Fisher Coll (NY)
St. John's U (NY)
Saint Joseph's U (PA)
St. Mary's U (TX)
St. Olaf Coll (MN)
Seton Hill U (PA)
Shawnee State U (OH)
Siena Heights U (MI)
Southeastern Louisiana U (LA)
Southeastern Oklahoma State U (OK)
Southeast Missouri State U (MO)
Southern Arkansas U–Magnolia (AR)
Southern New Hampshire U (NH)
Southern U and Ag and Mech Coll (LA)
Southwestern Assemblies of God U (TX)
Spring Arbor U (MI)
State U of New York at New Paltz (NY)
State U of New York Coll at Cortland (NY)
State U of New York Coll at Old Westbury (NY)
State U of New York Coll at Potsdam (NY)
Syracuse U (NY)
Tabor Coll (KS)
Taylor U (IN)
Temple U (PA)
Texas A&M Intl U (TX)
Texas A&M U–Corpus Christi (TX)
Texas Christian U (TX)
Texas Lutheran U (TX)
Texas Wesleyan U (TX)
Trine U (IN)
Universidad Adventista de las Antillas (PR)
The U of Akron (OH)
The U of Arizona (AZ)
U of Central Oklahoma (OK)
U of Charleston (WV)
U of Evansville (IN)
U of Georgia (GA)
U of Illinois at Urbana–Champaign (IL)
U of Indianapolis (IN)
The U of Iowa (IA)
U of Lethbridge (AB, Canada)
U of Louisiana at Monroe (LA)
U of Maine (ME)
U of Mary Hardin-Baylor (TX)
U of Maryland, Coll Park (MD)
U of Michigan–Dearborn (MI)
U of Michigan–Flint (MI)
U of Minnesota, Duluth (MN)
U of Mississippi (MS)
U of Missouri (MO)
U of Missouri–St. Louis (MO)
U of Nevada, Reno (NV)
U of New Orleans (LA)
The U of North Carolina at Greensboro (NC)
The U of North Carolina at Pembroke (NC)
U of Northern Iowa (IA)
U of Oklahoma (OK)
U of Pittsburgh at Johnstown (PA)
U of Puerto Rico, Cayey U Coll (PR)
U of Regina (SK, Canada)
U of St. Francis (IL)
U of St. Thomas (MN)
The U of Tennessee at Chattanooga (TN)
U of the Cumberlands (KY)
The U of Toledo (OH)
U of Vermont (VT)
U of Wisconsin–Eau Claire (WI)
U of Wisconsin–La Crosse (WI)
U of Wisconsin–River Falls (WI)
U of Wisconsin–Superior (WI)
Ursuline Coll (OH)
Utah State U (UT)
Utica Coll (NY)
Virginia Intermont Coll (VA)
Virginia Wesleyan Coll (VA)
Viterbo U (WI)
Waldorf Coll (IA)
Warner Pacific Coll (OR)
Washington State U (WA)
Washington U in St. Louis (MO)
Waynesburg U (PA)
Wayne State U (MI)
Weber State U (UT)
Western Carolina U (NC)
Western Michigan U (MI)
Western Washington U (WA)
Wheaton Coll (IL)
Wheeling Jesuit U (WV)
Widener U (PA)
Wingate U (NC)
Winston-Salem State U (NC)
Wright State U (OH)
Xavier U of Louisiana (LA)
York Coll (NE)
York Coll of Pennsylvania (PA)
York U (ON, Canada)
Youngstown State U (OH)

SOCIAL WORK

Abilene Christian U (TX)
Adams State Coll (CO)
Adelphi U (NY)
Alabama Ag and Mech U (AL)
Alabama State U (AL)
Albany State U (GA)
Albertus Magnus Coll (CT)
Alvernia U (PA)
Anderson U (IN)
Andrews U (MI)
Appalachian State U (NC)
Arizona State U (AZ)
Arkansas State U—Jonesboro (AR)
Asbury U (KY)
Ashland U (OH)
Auburn U (AL)
Augsburg Coll (MN)
Augustana Coll (SD)
Aurora U (IL)
Austin Peay State U (TN)
Avila U (MO)
Azusa Pacific U (CA)
Ball State U (IN)
Barton Coll (NC)
Baylor U (TX)
Belmont U (TN)
Bemidji State U (MN)
Bennett Coll for Women (NC)
Bethany Coll (KS)
Bethany Coll (WV)
Bethel Coll (KS)
Bethel U (MN)
Bloomsburg U of Pennsylvania (PA)
Bluffton U (OH)
Boise State U (ID)
Bowie State U (MD)
Bowling Green State U (OH)
Bradley U (IL)
Brescia U (KY)
Briar Cliff U (IA)
Bridgewater State Coll (MA)
Brigham Young U–Hawaii (HI)
Buena Vista U (IA)
Buffalo State Coll, State U of New York (NY)
Cabrini Coll (PA)
California State U, East Bay (CA)
California State U, Fresno (CA)
California State U, Long Beach (CA)
California State U, Los Angeles (CA)
California State U, Sacramento (CA)
California State U, San Bernardino (CA)
Calvin Coll (MI)
Campbellsville U (KY)
Capital U (OH)
Carlow U (PA)
Castleton State Coll (VT)
The Catholic U of America (DC)
Cedar Crest Coll (PA)
Cedarville U (OH)
Centenary Coll (NJ)
Central Baptist Coll (AR)
Central Connecticut State U (CT)
Central Michigan U (MI)
Central State U (OH)
Champlain Coll (VT)
Chapman U (CA)
Chatham U (PA)
Christopher Newport U (VA)
Clark Atlanta U (GA)
Clarke Coll (IA)
Cleveland State U (OH)
Coker Coll (SC)
Coll of Mount St. Joseph (OH)
The Coll of New Rochelle (NY)
The Coll of Saint Rose (NY)
The Coll of St. Scholastica (MN)
Coll of Staten Island of the City U of New York (NY)
Coll of the Ozarks (MO)
Colorado State U (CO)
Colorado State U–Pueblo (CO)
Columbia Coll (SC)
Concordia Coll (MN)
Concordia U Chicago (IL)
Concordia U Wisconsin (WI)
Concord U (WV)
Coppin State U (MD)
Cornerstone U (MI)
Creighton U (NE)
Daemen Coll (NY)
Dalton State Coll (GA)
Dana Coll (NE)
Defiance Coll (OH)
Delaware State U (DE)
Delta State U (MS)
Dickinson State U (ND)
Dominican Coll (NY)
Dordt Coll (IA)
East Carolina U (NC)
East Central U (OK)
Eastern Connecticut State U (CT)
Eastern Mennonite U (VA)
Eastern Michigan U (MI)
Eastern Nazarene Coll (MA)
Eastern New Mexico U (NM)
Eastern Washington U (WA)
East Tennessee State U (TN)
Edinboro U of Pennsylvania (PA)
Edward Waters Coll (FL)
Elizabeth City State U (NC)
Elizabethtown Coll (PA)
Elmira Coll (NY)
Evangel U (MO)
Ferris State U (MI)
Ferrum Coll (VA)
Florida Atlantic U (FL)
Florida Gulf Coast U (FL)
Florida Intl U (FL)
Florida State U (FL)
Fontbonne U (MO)
Fordham U (NY)
Fort Hays State U (KS)
Fort Valley State U (GA)
Franciscan U of Steubenville (OH)
Franklin Pierce U (NH)
Freed-Hardeman U (TN)
Frostburg State U (MD)
Gallaudet U (DC)
Gannon U (PA)
George Fox U (OR)
George Mason U (VA)
Georgian Court U (NJ)
Georgia State U (GA)
Gordon Coll (MA)
Goshen Coll (IN)
Governors State U (IL)
Grace Coll (IN)
Graceland U (IA)
Grambling State U (LA)
Grand Valley State U (MI)
Greenville Coll (IL)
Gwynedd-Mercy Coll (PA)
Hampton U (VA)
Harding U (AR)
Hardin-Simmons U (TX)
Hawai'i Pacific U (HI)
Henderson State U (AR)
Holy Family U (PA)
Hood Coll (MD)
Hope Coll (MI)
Howard Payne U (TX)
Humboldt State U (CA)
Huntington U (IN)
Idaho State U (ID)
Illinois State U (IL)
Immaculata U (PA)
Indiana State U (IN)
Indiana U Bloomington (IN)
Indiana U East (IN)
Indiana U Kokomo (IN)
Indiana U–Purdue U Indianapolis (IN)
Indiana Wesleyan U (IN)
Inter American U of Puerto Rico, Arecibo Campus (PR)
Inter American U of Puerto Rico, Fajardo Campus (PR)
Iona Coll (NY)
Jackson State U (MS)
Jacksonville State U (AL)
James Madison U (VA)
Johnson C. Smith U (NC)
Juniata Coll (PA)
Kansas State U (KS)
Kean U (NJ)
Kent State U (OH)
Kentucky State U (KY)
Keuka Coll (NY)
Kutztown U of Pennsylvania (PA)
Kuyper Coll (MI)
LaGrange Coll (GA)
Lakehead U (ON, Canada)
Lamar U (TX)
La Salle U (PA)
La Sierra U (CA)
Laurentian U (ON, Canada)
Lehman Coll of the City U of New York (NY)
Lewis-Clark State Coll (ID)
Lewis U (IL)
Limestone Coll (SC)
Lincoln Memorial U (TN)
Lindenwood U (MO)
Lipscomb U (TN)
Lock Haven U of Pennsylvania (PA)
Long Island U, Brooklyn Campus (NY)
Long Island U, C.W. Post Campus (NY)
Longwood U (VA)
Loras Coll (IA)
Louisiana Coll (LA)
Lourdes Coll (OH)
Loyola U Chicago (IL)
Lubbock Christian U (TX)
Luther Coll (IA)
Madonna U (MI)
Malone U (OH)
Manchester Coll (IN)
Mansfield U of Pennsylvania (PA)
Marian U (WI)
Marist Coll (NY)
Marquette U (WI)
Marshall U (WV)
Mars Hill Coll (NC)
Mary Baldwin Coll (VA)
Marywood U (PA)
McDaniel Coll (MD)
McKendree U (IL)
Medgar Evers Coll of the City U of New York (NY)
Memorial U of Newfoundland (NL, Canada)
Mercy Coll (NY)
Mercyhurst Coll (PA)
Meredith Coll (NC)
Messiah Coll (PA)
Methodist U (NC)
Metropolitan State Coll of Denver (CO)
Miami U (OH)
Michigan State U (MI)
Middle Tennessee State U (TN)
Midwestern State U (TX)
Millersville U of Pennsylvania (PA)
Millikin U (IL)
Minnesota State U Mankato (MN)
Minnesota State U Moorhead (MN)
Minot State U (ND)
Misericordia U (PA)
Mississippi Coll (MS)
Mississippi State U (MS)
Mississippi Valley State U (MS)
Missouri State U (MO)
Missouri Western State U (MO)
Molloy Coll (NY)
Monmouth U (NJ)
Montclair State U (NJ)
Morehead State U (KY)
Mountain State U (WV)
Mount Mary Coll (WI)
Mount Mercy Coll (IA)
Mount Saint Mary Coll (NY)
Mount St. Mary's Coll (CA)
Mount Vernon Nazarene U (OH)
Murray State U (KY)
Nazareth Coll of Rochester (NY)
Nebraska Wesleyan U (NE)
New Mexico State U (NM)
New York U (NY)
Niagara U (NY)
Norfolk State U (VA)
North Carolina Central U (NC)
North Carolina State U (NC)
Northeastern Illinois U (IL)
Northeastern State U (OK)
Northern Arizona U (AZ)
Northern Kentucky U (KY)
Northern Michigan U (MI)
Northwestern Coll (IA)
Northwestern Oklahoma State U (OK)
Northwestern State U of Louisiana (LA)
Northwest Nazarene U (ID)
Nyack Coll (NY)
Oakland U (MI)
Oakwood U (AL)
Oglethorpe U (GA)

Ohio Dominican U (OH)
The Ohio State U (OH)
Ohio U (OH)
Oral Roberts U (OK)
Our Lady of the Lake U of San Antonio (TX)
Pacific Lutheran U (WA)
Pacific Union Coll (CA)
Philadelphia Biblical U (PA)
Pikeville Coll (KY)
Pittsburg State U (KS)
Plymouth State U (NH)
Pontifical Catholic U of Puerto Rico (PR)
Prairie View A&M U (TX)
Presentation Coll (SD)
Providence Coll (RI)
Purdue U North Central (IN)
Radford U (VA)
Ramapo Coll of New Jersey (NJ)
Redeemer U Coll (ON, Canada)
Regis Coll (MA)
Rhode Island Coll (RI)
The Richard Stockton Coll of New Jersey (NJ)
Roberts Wesleyan Coll (NY)
Rockford Coll (IL)
Rutgers, The State U of New Jersey, Camden (NJ)
Rutgers, The State U of New Jersey, Newark (NJ)
Rutgers, The State U of New Jersey, New Brunswick (NJ)
Sacred Heart U (CT)
Saginaw Valley State U (MI)
St. Augustine Coll (IL)
St. Catherine U (MN)
St. Cloud State U (MN)
St. Edward's U (TX)
Saint Francis U (PA)
Saint Joseph Coll (CT)
Saint Leo U (FL)
Saint Louis U (MO)
Saint Mary's Coll (IN)
St. Olaf Coll (MN)
St. Thomas U (NB, Canada)
Salem State Coll (MA)
Salisbury U (MD)
Salve Regina U (RI)
San Diego State U (CA)
San Francisco State U (CA)
San Jose State U (CA)
Savannah State U (GA)
Seattle U (WA)
Seton Hall U (NJ)
Seton Hill U (PA)
Shaw U (NC)
Shepherd U (WV)
Shippensburg U of Pennsylvania (PA)
Siena Coll (NY)
Siena Heights U (MI)
Skidmore Coll (NY)
Slippery Rock U of Pennsylvania (PA)
South Carolina State U (SC)
Southeastern Louisiana U (LA)
Southeastern U (FL)
Southeast Missouri State U (MO)
Southern Adventist U (TN)
Southern Arkansas U–Magnolia (AR)
Southern Connecticut State U (CT)
Southern Illinois U Carbondale (IL)
Southern Illinois U Edwardsville (IL)
Southern U and Ag and Mech Coll (LA)
Southern U at New Orleans (LA)
Southwestern Adventist U (TX)
Southwestern Assemblies of God U (TX)
Southwestern Oklahoma State U (OK)
Southwest Minnesota State U (MN)
Spalding U (KY)
Spring Arbor U (MI)
State U of New York at Fredonia (NY)
State U of New York at New Paltz (NY)
State U of New York at Plattsburgh (NY)
State U of New York Coll at Cortland (NY)
Stephen F. Austin State U (TX)
Stony Brook U, State U of New York (NY)
Suffolk U (MA)
Syracuse U (NY)
Talladega Coll (AL)
Tarleton State U (TX)
Taylor U (IN)
Temple U (PA)
Tennessee Technological U (TN)
Texas A&M U–Commerce (TX)
Texas A&M U–Kingsville (TX)
Texas Christian U (TX)
Texas Coll (TX)
Texas Southern U (TX)
Texas State U–San Marcos (TX)
Texas Tech U (TX)
Texas Woman's U (TX)
Thompson Rivers U (BC, Canada)
Trevecca Nazarene U (TN)
Trinity Christian Coll (IL)
Troy U (AL)
Tuskegee U (AL)
Union Coll (NE)
Union Inst & U (OH)
Union U (TN)
Université du Québec en Outaouais (QC, Canada)
U at Albany, State U of New York (NY)
The U of Akron (OH)
The U of Alabama (AL)
The U of Alabama at Birmingham (AL)
U of Alaska Anchorage (AK)
U of Alaska Fairbanks (AK)
U of Arkansas (AR)
U of Arkansas at Little Rock (AR)
U of Arkansas at Monticello (AR)
U of Arkansas at Pine Bluff (AR)
The U of British Columbia (BC, Canada)
The U of British Columbia–Okanagan (BC, Canada)
U of California, Berkeley (CA)
U of Central Florida (FL)
U of Central Missouri (MO)
U of Cincinnati (OH)
The U of Findlay (OH)
U of Georgia (GA)
U of Guam (GU)
U of Hawaii at Manoa (HI)
U of Houston–Clear Lake (TX)
U of Houston–Downtown (TX)
U of Illinois at Chicago (IL)
U of Illinois at Springfield (IL)
U of Indianapolis (IN)
The U of Iowa (IA)
The U of Kansas (KS)
U of Kentucky (KY)
U of Louisiana at Monroe (LA)
U of Louisville (KY)
U of Maine (ME)
U of Maine at Presque Isle (ME)
U of Manitoba (MB, Canada)
U of Mary (ND)
U of Mary Hardin-Baylor (TX)
U of Maryland, Baltimore County (MD)
U of Maryland Eastern Shore (MD)
U of Massachusetts Boston (MA)
U of Memphis (TN)
U of Michigan–Flint (MI)
U of Mississippi (MS)
U of Missouri (MO)
U of Missouri–St. Louis (MO)
U of Montevallo (AL)
U of Nebraska at Kearney (NE)
U of Nevada, Las Vegas (NV)
U of Nevada, Reno (NV)
U of New Hampshire (NH)
U of North Alabama (AL)
The U of North Carolina at Charlotte (NC)
The U of North Carolina at Greensboro (NC)
The U of North Carolina at Pembroke (NC)
The U of North Carolina Wilmington (NC)
U of North Dakota (ND)
U of Northern Iowa (IA)
U of North Texas (TX)
U of Oklahoma (OK)
U of Ottawa (ON, Canada)
U of Pittsburgh (PA)
U of Portland (OR)
U of Puerto Rico at Humacao (PR)
U of Puerto Rico at Utuado (PR)
U of Puerto Rico, Río Piedras (PR)
U of Regina (SK, Canada)
U of Rio Grande (OH)
U of St. Francis (IL)
U of St. Thomas (MN)
The U of South Dakota (SD)
U of Southern Indiana (IN)
U of Southern Maine (ME)
U of Southern Mississippi (MS)
U of South Florida (FL)
The U of Tennessee (TN)
The U of Tennessee at Chattanooga (TN)
The U of Tennessee at Martin (TN)
The U of Texas at Arlington (TX)
The U of Texas at Austin (TX)
The U of Texas at El Paso (TX)
The U of Texas of the Permian Basin (TX)
The U of Texas–Pan American (TX)
U of the Cumberlands (KY)
U of the District of Columbia (DC)
U of the Virgin Islands (VI)
The U of Toledo (OH)
U of Utah (UT)
U of Vermont (VT)
U of Washington (WA)
U of Washington, Tacoma (WA)
U of Waterloo (ON, Canada)
The U of Western Ontario (ON, Canada)
U of West Florida (FL)
U of Windsor (ON, Canada)
U of Wisconsin–Eau Claire (WI)
U of Wisconsin–Green Bay (WI)
U of Wisconsin–Madison (WI)
U of Wisconsin–Milwaukee (WI)
U of Wisconsin–Oshkosh (WI)
U of Wisconsin–River Falls (WI)
U of Wisconsin–Superior (WI)
U of Wisconsin–Whitewater (WI)
U of Wyoming (WY)
Ursuline Coll (OH)
Utah State U (UT)
Valley Forge Christian Coll (PA)
Valparaiso U (IN)
Virginia Commonwealth U (VA)
Virginia Intermont Coll (VA)
Virginia State U (VA)
Virginia Union U (VA)
Virginia Wesleyan Coll (VA)
Viterbo U (WI)
Warner Pacific Coll (OR)
Wartburg Coll (IA)
Washburn U (KS)
Wayne State U (MI)
Weber State U (UT)
West Chester U of Pennsylvania (PA)
Western Carolina U (NC)
Western Connecticut State U (CT)
Western Illinois U (IL)
Western Kentucky U (KY)
Western Michigan U (MI)
Western New England Coll (MA)
Westfield State Coll (MA)
West Virginia State U (WV)
West Virginia U (WV)
Wheelock Coll (MA)
Whittier Coll (CA)
Wichita State U (KS)
Widener U (PA)
Wilberforce U (OH)
Wilmington Coll (OH)
Winona State U (MN)
Winthrop U (SC)
Wright State U (OH)
Xavier U (OH)
York Coll (NE)
York Coll of the City U of New York (NY)
York U (ON, Canada)
Youngstown State U (OH)

SOCIAL WORK RELATED

Miami U Hamilton (OH)
The U of Western Ontario (ON, Canada)

SOCIOBIOLOGY

Beloit Coll (WI)
Tufts U (MA)

SOCIOLOGY

Abilene Christian U (TX)
Acadia U (NS, Canada)
Adelphi U (NY)
Agnes Scott Coll (GA)
Alabama Ag and Mech U (AL)
Alabama State U (AL)
Albany State U (GA)
Albertus Magnus Coll (CT)
Albion Coll (MI)
Albright Coll (PA)
Alcorn State U (MS)
Alfred U (NY)
Alma Coll (MI)
Alverno Coll (WI)
American Intl Coll (MA)
American Public U System (WV)
American U (DC)
American U of Beirut (Lebanon)
Amherst Coll (MA)
Anderson U (IN)
Andrews U (MI)
Angelo State U (TX)
Appalachian State U (NC)
Aquinas Coll (MI)
Arcadia U (PA)
Arizona State U (AZ)
Arkansas State U—Jonesboro (AR)
Arkansas Tech U (AR)
Asbury U (KY)
Ashland U (OH)
Assumption Coll (MA)
Athabasca U (AB, Canada)
Auburn U (AL)
Auburn U Montgomery (AL)
Augsburg Coll (MN)
Augustana Coll (IL)
Augustana Coll (SD)
Aurora U (IL)
Austin Coll (TX)
Austin Peay State U (TN)
Averett U (VA)
Avila U (MO)
Azusa Pacific U (CA)
Baker U (KS)
Baldwin-Wallace Coll (OH)
Ball State U (IN)
Bard Coll (NY)
Bard Coll at Simon's Rock (MA)
Barnard Coll (NY)
Barry U (FL)
Bates Coll (ME)
Baylor U (TX)
Bellarmine U (KY)
Belmont Abbey Coll (NC)
Belmont U (TN)
Beloit Coll (WI)
Bemidji State U (MN)
Benedictine Coll (KS)
Benedictine U (IL)
Bennington Coll (VT)
Berea Coll (KY)
Bernard M. Baruch Coll of the City U of New York (NY)
Bethany Coll (KS)
Bethany Lutheran Coll (MN)
Bethel Coll (IN)
Bethel U (TN)
Bethune-Cookman U (FL)
Birmingham-Southern Coll (AL)
Bishop's U (QC, Canada)
Black Hills State U (SD)
Bloomfield Coll (NJ)
Bloomsburg U of Pennsylvania (PA)
Bluffton U (OH)
Boise State U (ID)
Boston Coll (MA)
Boston U (MA)
Bowdoin Coll (ME)
Bowie State U (MD)
Bowling Green State U (OH)
Bradley U (IL)
Brandeis U (MA)
Brewton-Parker Coll (GA)
Bridgewater Coll (VA)
Bridgewater State Coll (MA)
Brock U (ON, Canada)
Brooklyn Coll of the City U of New York (NY)
Bryant U (RI)
Bryn Mawr Coll (PA)
Bucknell U (PA)
Buena Vista U (IA)
Buffalo State Coll, State U of New York (NY)
Butler U (IN)
Cabrini Coll (PA)
California Baptist U (CA)
California Lutheran U (CA)
California Polytechnic State U, San Luis Obispo (CA)
California State Polytechnic U, Pomona (CA)
California State U, Bakersfield (CA)
California State U, Dominguez Hills (CA)
California State U, East Bay (CA)
California State U, Fresno (CA)
California State U, Fullerton (CA)
California State U, Long Beach (CA)
California State U, Los Angeles (CA)
California State U, Northridge (CA)
California State U, Sacramento (CA)
California State U, San Bernardino (CA)
California State U, San Marcos (CA)
California State U, Stanislaus (CA)
Calvin Coll (MI)
Cameron U (OK)
Campbellsville U (KY)
Canisius Coll (NY)
Cape Breton U (NS, Canada)
Capital U (OH)
Carleton Coll (MN)
Carlow U (PA)
Carroll U (WI)
Carson-Newman Coll (TN)
Case Western Reserve U (OH)
Castleton State Coll (VT)
Catawba Coll (NC)
The Catholic U of America (DC)
Cedarville U (OH)
Centenary Coll (NJ)
Centenary Coll of Louisiana (LA)
Central Christian Coll of Kansas (KS)
Central Coll (IA)
Central Connecticut State U (CT)
Central Michigan U (MI)
Central State U (OH)
Chapman U (CA)
Cheyney U of Pennsylvania (PA)
Chowan U (NC)
Christopher Newport U (VA)
City Coll of the City U of New York (NY)
Claflin U (SC)
Claremont McKenna Coll (CA)
Clarion U of Pennsylvania (PA)
Clark Atlanta U (GA)
Clarkson U (NY)
Clark U (MA)
Clemson U (SC)
Cleveland State U (OH)
Coastal Carolina U (SC)
Coker Coll (SC)
Colby Coll (ME)
Colgate U (NY)
The Coll at Brockport, State U of New York (NY)
Coll of Charleston (SC)
Coll of Mount St. Joseph (OH)
Coll of Mount Saint Vincent (NY)
The Coll of New Jersey (NJ)
The Coll of New Rochelle (NY)
Coll of Saint Benedict (MN)
Coll of Saint Elizabeth (NJ)
The Coll of Saint Rose (NY)
Coll of the Holy Cross (MA)
Coll of the Ozarks (MO)
The Coll of William and Mary (VA)
The Coll of Wooster (OH)
The Colorado Coll (CO)
Colorado State U (CO)
Colorado State U–Pueblo (CO)
Columbia Coll (MO)
Columbia U (NY)
Columbia U, School of General Studies (NY)
Columbus State U (GA)
Concordia Coll (MN)
Concordia U (QC, Canada)
Concordia U Chicago (IL)
Concordia U Coll of Alberta (AB, Canada)
Concordia U, St. Paul (MN)
Concord U (WV)
Connecticut Coll (CT)
Converse Coll (SC)
Cornell Coll (IA)
Cornell U (NY)
Covenant Coll (GA)
Crandall U (NB, Canada)
Creighton U (NE)
Cumberland U (TN)
Curry Coll (MA)
Dallas Baptist U (TX)
Dartmouth Coll (NH)
Davidson Coll (NC)
Delaware State U (DE)
Denison U (OH)
DePaul U (IL)
DePauw U (IN)
Dickinson Coll (PA)
Dillard U (LA)
Doane Coll (NE)
Dominican U (IL)
Dordt Coll (IA)
Dowling Coll (NY)
Drake U (IA)
Drew U (NJ)
Drexel U (PA)
Drury U (MO)
Duke U (NC)
Duquesne U (PA)
D'Youville Coll (NY)
Earlham Coll (IN)
East Carolina U (NC)
East Central U (OK)
Eastern Connecticut State U (CT)
Eastern Illinois U (IL)
Eastern Mennonite U (VA)
Eastern Michigan U (MI)
Eastern Nazarene Coll (MA)
Eastern New Mexico U (NM)
Eastern Washington U (WA)
East Stroudsburg U of Pennsylvania (PA)
East Tennessee State U (TN)
East Texas Baptist U (TX)
Eckerd Coll (FL)
Edgewood Coll (WI)
Edinboro U of Pennsylvania (PA)
Edward Waters Coll (FL)
Elizabeth City State U (NC)
Elmhurst Coll (IL)
Elmira Coll (NY)
Elon U (NC)
Emmanuel Coll (MA)
Emory & Henry Coll (VA)
Emory U (GA)
Emporia State U (KS)
Evangel U (MO)
The Evergreen State Coll (WA)
Excelsior Coll (NY)
Fairfield U (CT)
Fairleigh Dickinson U, Coll at Florham (NJ)
Fairleigh Dickinson U, Metropolitan Campus (NJ)
Fairmont State U (WV)
Fayetteville State U (NC)

INDEXES

Sociology

Felician Coll (NJ)
Ferris State U (MI)
Fisk U (TN)
Fitchburg State Coll (MA)
Flagler Coll (FL)
Florida Atlantic U (FL)
Florida Gulf Coast U (FL)
Florida Intl U (FL)
Florida Southern Coll (FL)
Florida State U (FL)
Fontbonne U (MO)
Fordham U (NY)
Fort Hays State U (KS)
Fort Lewis Coll (CO)
Fort Valley State U (GA)
Framingham State Coll (MA)
Franciscan U of Steubenville (OH)
Francis Marion U (SC)
Franklin & Marshall Coll (PA)
Franklin Coll (IN)
Franklin Pierce U (NH)
Friends U (KS)
Frostburg State U (MD)
Furman U (SC)
Gallaudet U (DC)
Gardner-Webb U (NC)
Geneva Coll (PA)
George Fox U (OR)
George Mason U (VA)
Georgetown Coll (KY)
Georgetown U (DC)
The George Washington U (DC)
Georgia Coll & State U (GA)
Georgian Court U (NJ)
Georgia Southern U (GA)
Georgia State U (GA)
Gettysburg Coll (PA)
Gonzaga U (WA)
Gordon Coll (MA)
Goshen Coll (IN)
Goucher Coll (MD)
Grace Coll (IN)
Graceland U (IA)
Grambling State U (LA)
Grand Valley State U (MI)
Green Mountain Coll (VT)
Greensboro Coll (NC)
Greenville Coll (IL)
Grinnell Coll (IA)
Grove City Coll (PA)
Guilford Coll (NC)
Gustavus Adolphus Coll (MN)
Gwynedd-Mercy Coll (PA)
Hamilton Coll (NY)
Hamline U (MN)
Hampshire Coll (MA)
Hampton U (VA)
Hannibal-LaGrange Coll (MO)
Hanover Coll (IN)
Hardin-Simmons U (TX)
Hartwick Coll (NY)
Harvard U (MA)
Haverford Coll (PA)
Hawai'i Pacific U (HI)
Henderson State U (AR)
Hendrix Coll (AR)
High Point U (NC)
Hillsdale Coll (MI)
Hiram Coll (OH)
Hofstra U (NY)
Hollins U (VA)
Holy Family U (PA)
Holy Names U (CA)
Hood Coll (MD)
Hope Coll (MI)
Houghton Coll (NY)
Houston Baptist U (TX)
Howard Payne U (TX)
Humboldt State U (CA)
Hunter Coll of the City U of New York (NY)
Huntington U (IN)
Huston-Tillotson U (TX)
Idaho State U (ID)
Illinois Coll (IL)
Illinois State U (IL)
Illinois Wesleyan U (IL)
Immaculata U (PA)
Indiana U Bloomington (IN)
Indiana U East (IN)
Indiana U Kokomo (IN)
Indiana U Northwest (IN)
Indiana U of Pennsylvania (PA)
Indiana U–Purdue U Fort Wayne (IN)
Indiana U–Purdue U Indianapolis (IN)
Indiana U South Bend (IN)
Indiana U Southeast (IN)
Indiana Wesleyan U (IN)
Inter American U of Puerto Rico, San Germán Campus (PR)
Iona Coll (NY)
Iowa State U of Science and Technology (IA)
Ithaca Coll (NY)
Jackson State U (MS)
Jacksonville State U (AL)
Jacksonville U (FL)
James Madison U (VA)
Jarvis Christian Coll (TX)
John Carroll U (OH)
The Johns Hopkins U (MD)
Johnson State Coll (VT)
Judson U (IL)
Juniata Coll (PA)
Kalamazoo Coll (MI)
Kansas State U (KS)
Kean U (NJ)
Keene State Coll (NH)
Kennesaw State U (GA)
Kent State U (OH)
Kentucky Wesleyan Coll (KY)
Kenyon Coll (OH)
Keuka Coll (NY)
King's Coll (PA)
The King's U Coll (AB, Canada)
Knox Coll (IL)
Kutztown U of Pennsylvania (PA)
Lafayette Coll (PA)
LaGrange Coll (GA)
Lake Erie Coll (OH)
Lake Forest Coll (IL)
Lakehead U (ON, Canada)
Lakeland Coll (WI)
Lake Superior State U (MI)
Lamar U (TX)
Lane Coll (TN)
La Roche Coll (PA)
La Salle U (PA)
Lasell Coll (MA)
La Sierra U (CA)
Laurentian U (ON, Canada)
Lebanon Valley Coll (PA)
Lees-McRae Coll (NC)
Lee U (TN)
Lehigh U (PA)
Lehman Coll of the City U of New York (NY)
Le Moyne Coll (NY)
Lewis & Clark Coll (OR)
Lewis U (IL)
Lincoln U (MO)
Lincoln U (PA)
Lindenwood U (MO)
Linfield Coll (OR)
Lock Haven U of Pennsylvania (PA)
Long Island U, Brooklyn Campus (NY)
Long Island U, C.W. Post Campus (NY)
Longwood U (VA)
Loras Coll (IA)
Louisiana Coll (LA)
Louisiana State U and Ag and Mech Coll (LA)
Louisiana State U in Shreveport (LA)
Louisiana Tech U (LA)
Lourdes Coll (OH)
Loyola Marymount U (CA)
Loyola U Chicago (IL)
Loyola U Maryland (MD)
Loyola U New Orleans (LA)
Luther Coll (IA)
Lycoming Coll (PA)
Lynchburg Coll (VA)
Macalester Coll (MN)
Madonna U (MI)
Manchester Coll (IN)
Manhattan Coll (NY)
Manhattanville Coll (NY)
Mansfield U of Pennsylvania (PA)
Marian U (IN)
Marlboro Coll (VT)
Marquette U (WI)
Marshall U (WV)
Mars Hill Coll (NC)
Mary Baldwin Coll (VA)
Marylhurst U (OR)
Marymount Manhattan Coll (NY)
Marymount U (VA)
Maryville Coll (TN)
Maryville U of Saint Louis (MO)
Massachusetts Coll of Liberal Arts (MA)
McDaniel Coll (MD)
McKendree U (IL)
McMurry U (TX)
McNeese State U (LA)
McPherson Coll (KS)
Memorial U of Newfoundland (NL, Canada)
Mercer U (GA)
Mercy Coll (NY)
Mercyhurst Coll (PA)
Meredith Coll (NC)
Merrimack Coll (MA)
Messiah Coll (PA)
Methodist U (NC)
Metropolitan State Coll of Denver (CO)
Miami U (OH)
Miami U Hamilton (OH)
Michigan State U (MI)
MidAmerica Nazarene U (KS)
Middlebury Coll (VT)
Middle Tennessee State U (TN)
Midwestern State U (TX)
Millersville U of Pennsylvania (PA)
Milligan Coll (TN)
Millikin U (IL)
Millsaps Coll (MS)
Mills Coll (CA)
Minnesota State U Mankato (MN)
Minnesota State U Moorhead (MN)
Minot State U (ND)
Mississippi Coll (MS)
Mississippi State U (MS)
Mississippi Valley State U (MS)
Missouri Southern State U (MO)
Missouri State U (MO)
Molloy Coll (NY)
Monmouth Coll (IL)
Monmouth U (NJ)
Montana State U (MT)
Montana State U Billings (MT)
Montclair State U (NJ)
Moravian Coll (PA)
Morehead State U (KY)
Morehouse Coll (GA)
Morris Coll (SC)
Mount Allison U (NB, Canada)
Mount Holyoke Coll (MA)
Mount Mercy Coll (IA)
Mount Saint Mary Coll (NY)
Mount St. Mary's Coll (CA)
Mount St. Mary's U (MD)
Mount Vernon Nazarene U (OH)
Muhlenberg Coll (PA)
Murray State U (KY)
National U (CA)
Nazareth Coll of Rochester (NY)
Nebraska Wesleyan U (NE)
Newberry Coll (SC)
New Coll of Florida (FL)
New England Coll (NH)
New Jersey City U (NJ)
Newman U (KS)
New Mexico State U (NM)
New York Inst of Technology (NY)
New York U (NY)
Niagara U (NY)
Nicholls State U (LA)
Nipissing U (ON, Canada)
Norfolk State U (VA)
North Carolina Central U (NC)
North Carolina State U (NC)
North Central Coll (IL)
North Dakota State U (ND)
Northeastern Illinois U (IL)
Northeastern State U (OK)
Northeastern U (MA)
Northern Arizona U (AZ)
Northern Kentucky U (KY)
Northern Michigan U (MI)
Northern State U (SD)
North Georgia Coll & State U (GA)
Northland Coll (WI)
Northwestern Coll (IA)
Northwestern Oklahoma State U (OK)
Northwestern State U of Louisiana (LA)
Northwest Missouri State U (MO)
Notre Dame de Namur U (CA)
Nova Southeastern U (FL)
Oakland U (MI)
Oberlin Coll (OH)
Occidental Coll (CA)
Oglethorpe U (GA)
Ohio Dominican U (OH)
Ohio Northern U (OH)
The Ohio State U (OH)
Ohio U (OH)
Ohio Wesleyan U (OH)
Oklahoma Baptist U (OK)
Oklahoma City U (OK)
Oklahoma State U (OK)
Old Dominion U (VA)
Oregon State U (OR)
Ottawa U (KS)
Ouachita Baptist U (AR)
Our Lady of the Lake U of San Antonio (TX)
Pacific Lutheran U (WA)
Pacific Union Coll (CA)
Paine Coll (GA)
Park U (MO)
Penn State Abington (PA)
Penn State Altoona (PA)
Penn State Beaver (PA)
Penn State Berks (PA)
Penn State Brandywine (PA)
Penn State DuBois (PA)
Penn State Erie, The Behrend Coll (PA)
Penn State Fayette, The Eberly Campus (PA)
Penn State Greater Allegheny (PA)
Penn State Harrisburg (PA)
Penn State Hazleton (PA)
Penn State Lehigh Valley (PA)
Penn State Mont Alto (PA)
Penn State New Kensington (PA)
Penn State Schuylkill (PA)
Penn State Shenango (PA)
Penn State U Park (PA)
Penn State Wilkes-Barre (PA)
Penn State Worthington Scranton (PA)
Penn State York (PA)
Pepperdine U, Malibu (CA)
Piedmont Coll (GA)
Pikeville Coll (KY)
Pittsburg State U (KS)
Pitzer Coll (CA)
Plymouth State U (NH)
Pomona Coll (CA)
Pontifical Catholic U of Puerto Rico (PR)
Portland State U (OR)
Post U (CT)
Prairie View A&M U (TX)
Presbyterian Coll (SC)
Prescott Coll (AZ)
Princeton U (NJ)
Principia Coll (IL)
Providence Coll (RI)
Purchase Coll, State U of New York (NY)
Purdue U (IN)
Purdue U Calumet (IN)
Queens Coll of the City U of New York (NY)
Queen's U at Kingston (ON, Canada)
Quinnipiac U (CT)
Radford U (VA)
Ramapo Coll of New Jersey (NJ)
Randolph Coll (VA)
Randolph-Macon Coll (VA)
Redeemer U Coll (ON, Canada)
Reed Coll (OR)
Regis Coll (MA)
Reinhardt Coll (GA)
Rhode Island Coll (RI)
Rhodes Coll (TN)
Rice U (TX)
The Richard Stockton Coll of New Jersey (NJ)
Rider U (NJ)
Ripon Coll (WI)
Rivier Coll (NH)
Roanoke Coll (VA)
Rockford Coll (IL)
Rocky Mountain Coll (MT)
Rollins Coll (FL)
Roosevelt U (IL)
Rosemont Coll (PA)
Rowan U (NJ)
Russell Sage Coll (NY)
Rutgers, The State U of New Jersey, Camden (NJ)
Rutgers, The State U of New Jersey, Newark (NJ)
Rutgers, The State U of New Jersey, New Brunswick (NJ)
Sacred Heart U (CT)
Saginaw Valley State U (MI)
St. Ambrose U (IA)
Saint Anselm Coll (NH)
Saint Augustine's Coll (NC)
St. Bonaventure U (NY)
St. Catherine U (MN)
St. Cloud State U (MN)
St. Edward's U (TX)
St. Francis Coll (NY)
Saint Francis U (PA)
St. Francis Xavier U (NS, Canada)
St. John Fisher Coll (NY)
Saint John's U (MN)
St. John's U (NY)
Saint Joseph's U (PA)
St. Lawrence U (NY)
Saint Leo U (FL)
Saint Louis U (MO)
Saint Mary's Coll (IN)
Saint Mary's Coll of California (CA)
St. Mary's Coll of Maryland (MD)
St. Mary's U (TX)
Saint Mary's U of Minnesota (MN)
Saint Michael's Coll (VT)
St. Norbert Coll (WI)
St. Olaf Coll (MN)
Saint Paul's Coll (VA)
St. Thomas U (FL)
St. Thomas U (NB, Canada)
Saint Vincent Coll (PA)
Saint Xavier U (IL)
Salem Coll (NC)
Salem State Coll (MA)
Salisbury U (MD)
Salve Regina U (RI)
Samford U (AL)
Sam Houston State U (TX)
San Diego State U (CA)
San Francisco State U (CA)
San Jose State U (CA)
Santa Clara U (CA)
Sarah Lawrence Coll (NY)
Savannah State U (GA)
Scripps Coll (CA)
Seattle Pacific U (WA)
Seattle U (WA)
Seton Hall U (NJ)
Seton Hill U (PA)
Shawnee State U (OH)
Shaw U (NC)
Shenandoah U (VA)
Shepherd U (WV)
Shippensburg U of Pennsylvania (PA)
Shorter U (GA)
Siena Coll (NY)
Simmons Coll (MA)
Simon Fraser U (BC, Canada)
Simpson Coll (IA)
Skidmore Coll (NY)
Smith Coll (MA)
Sonoma State U (CA)
South Carolina State U (SC)
South Dakota State U (SD)
Southeastern Louisiana U (LA)
Southeastern Oklahoma State U (OK)
Southern Arkansas U–Magnolia (AR)
Southern Connecticut State U (CT)
Southern Illinois U Carbondale (IL)
Southern Illinois U Edwardsville (IL)
Southern Methodist U (TX)
Southern Oregon U (OR)
Southern U and Ag and Mech Coll (LA)
Southern U at New Orleans (LA)
Southern Utah U (UT)
Southwest Baptist U (MO)
Southwestern U (TX)
Southwest Minnesota State U (MN)
Spelman Coll (GA)
Spring Arbor U (MI)
Stanford U (CA)
State U of New York at Binghamton (NY)
State U of New York at Fredonia (NY)
State U of New York at New Paltz (NY)
State U of New York at Oswego (NY)
State U of New York at Plattsburgh (NY)
State U of New York Coll at Cortland (NY)
State U of New York Coll at Geneseo (NY)
State U of New York Coll at Old Westbury (NY)
State U of New York Coll at Oneonta (NY)
State U of New York Coll at Potsdam (NY)
Stephen F. Austin State U (TX)
Stetson U (FL)
Stonehill Coll (MA)
Stony Brook U, State U of New York (NY)
Suffolk U (MA)
Susquehanna U (PA)
Sweet Briar Coll (VA)
Syracuse U (NY)
Tabor Coll (KS)
Talladega Coll (AL)
Tarleton State U (TX)
Taylor U (IN)
Temple U (PA)
Tennessee Technological U (TN)
Texas A&M Intl U (TX)
Texas A&M U (TX)
Texas A&M U–Commerce (TX)
Texas A&M U–Corpus Christi (TX)
Texas A&M U–Kingsville (TX)
Texas Christian U (TX)
Texas Coll (TX)
Texas Lutheran U (TX)
Texas Southern U (TX)
Texas State U–San Marcos (TX)
Texas Tech U (TX)
Texas Wesleyan U (TX)
Texas Woman's U (TX)
Thiel Coll (PA)
Thomas Edison State Coll (NJ)
Thomas More Coll (KY)
Thompson Rivers U (BC, Canada)
Transylvania U (KY)
Trent U (ON, Canada)
Trevecca Nazarene U (TN)
Trinity Christian Coll (IL)
Trinity Coll (CT)
Trinity U (TX)
Troy U (AL)
Truman State U (MO)
Tufts U (MA)
Tulane U (LA)
Tuskegee U (AL)
Union Coll (NY)
Union U (TN)
Université du Québec en Outaouais (QC, Canada)
U at Albany, State U of New York (NY)
U at Buffalo, the State U of New York (NY)

www.facebook.com/find.colleges

The U of Akron (OH)
The U of Alabama (AL)
The U of Alabama at Birmingham (AL)
The U of Alabama in Huntsville (AL)
U of Alaska Anchorage (AK)
U of Alaska Fairbanks (AK)
U of Alberta (AB, Canada)
The U of Arizona (AZ)
U of Arkansas (AR)
U of Arkansas at Little Rock (AR)
U of Arkansas at Pine Bluff (AR)
The U of British Columbia (BC, Canada)
The U of British Columbia–Okanagan (BC, Canada)
U of California, Berkeley (CA)
U of California, Davis (CA)
U of California, Irvine (CA)
U of California, Los Angeles (CA)
U of California, Riverside (CA)
U of California, San Diego (CA)
U of California, Santa Barbara (CA)
U of California, Santa Cruz (CA)
U of Central Florida (FL)
U of Central Missouri (MO)
U of Central Oklahoma (OK)
U of Chicago (IL)
U of Cincinnati (OH)
U of Colorado at Boulder (CO)
U of Colorado at Colorado Springs (CO)
U of Colorado Denver (CO)
U of Connecticut (CT)
U of Dayton (OH)
U of Delaware (DE)
U of Denver (CO)
U of Dubuque (IA)
U of Evansville (IN)
The U of Findlay (OH)
U of Florida (FL)
U of Georgia (GA)
U of Guam (GU)
U of Guelph (ON, Canada)
U of Hartford (CT)
U of Hawaii at Hilo (HI)
U of Hawaii at Manoa (HI)
U of Hawaii–West Oahu (HI)
U of Houston (TX)
U of Houston–Clear Lake (TX)
U of Houston–Downtown (TX)
U of Idaho (ID)
U of Illinois at Chicago (IL)
U of Illinois at Urbana–Champaign (IL)
U of Indianapolis (IN)
The U of Iowa (IA)
The U of Kansas (KS)
U of Kentucky (KY)
U of King's Coll (NS, Canada)
U of La Verne (CA)
U of Lethbridge (AB, Canada)
U of Louisiana at Monroe (LA)
U of Louisville (KY)
U of Maine (ME)
U of Maine at Farmington (ME)
U of Maine at Presque Isle (ME)
U of Manitoba (MB, Canada)
U of Mary Hardin-Baylor (TX)
U of Maryland, Baltimore County (MD)
U of Maryland, Coll Park (MD)
U of Maryland Eastern Shore (MD)
U of Mary Washington (VA)
U of Massachusetts Amherst (MA)
U of Massachusetts Boston (MA)
U of Massachusetts Dartmouth (MA)
U of Massachusetts Lowell (MA)
U of Memphis (TN)
U of Miami (FL)
U of Michigan (MI)
U of Michigan–Dearborn (MI)
U of Michigan–Flint (MI)
U of Minnesota, Duluth (MN)
U of Minnesota, Twin Cities Campus (MN)
U of Mississippi (MS)
U of Missouri (MO)
U of Missouri–Kansas City (MO)
U of Missouri–St. Louis (MO)
U of Mobile (AL)
U of Montevallo (AL)
U of Mount Union (OH)
U of Nebraska at Kearney (NE)
U of Nebraska at Omaha (NE)
U of Nebraska–Lincoln (NE)
U of Nevada, Las Vegas (NV)
U of Nevada, Reno (NV)
U of New Brunswick Fredericton (NB, Canada)
U of New England (ME)
U of New Hampshire (NH)
U of New Mexico (NM)
U of New Orleans (LA)
U of North Alabama (AL)
The U of North Carolina at Asheville (NC)
The U of North Carolina at Chapel Hill (NC)
The U of North Carolina at Charlotte (NC)
The U of North Carolina at Greensboro (NC)
The U of North Carolina at Pembroke (NC)
The U of North Carolina Wilmington (NC)
U of North Dakota (ND)
U of Northern Colorado (CO)
U of Northern Iowa (IA)
U of North Florida (FL)
U of North Texas (TX)
U of Notre Dame (IN)
U of Oklahoma (OK)
U of Oregon (OR)
U of Ottawa (ON, Canada)
U of Pennsylvania (PA)
U of Pittsburgh (PA)
U of Pittsburgh at Bradford (PA)
U of Pittsburgh at Johnstown (PA)
U of Portland (OR)
U of Puerto Rico at Utuado (PR)
U of Puerto Rico, Cayey U Coll (PR)
U of Puerto Rico, Río Piedras (PR)
U of Puget Sound (WA)
U of Redlands (CA)
U of Regina (SK, Canada)
U of Rhode Island (RI)
U of Richmond (VA)
U of Rio Grande (OH)
U of Saint Mary (KS)
U of St. Thomas (MN)
U of San Diego (CA)
U of San Francisco (CA)
U of Saskatchewan (SK, Canada)
U of Science and Arts of Oklahoma (OK)
The U of Scranton (PA)
U of South Alabama (AL)
U of South Carolina (SC)
U of South Carolina Aiken (SC)
U of South Carolina Upstate (SC)
The U of South Dakota (SD)
U of Southern California (CA)
U of Southern Indiana (IN)
U of Southern Maine (ME)
U of Southern Mississippi (MS)
U of South Florida (FL)
The U of Tampa (FL)
The U of Tennessee (TN)
The U of Tennessee at Martin (TN)
The U of Texas at Arlington (TX)
The U of Texas at Austin (TX)
The U of Texas at Brownsville (TX)
The U of Texas at Dallas (TX)
The U of Texas at El Paso (TX)
The U of Texas at San Antonio (TX)
The U of Texas at Tyler (TX)
The U of Texas of the Permian Basin (TX)
The U of Texas–Pan American (TX)
U of the District of Columbia (DC)
U of the Incarnate Word (TX)
U of the Ozarks (AR)
U of the Pacific (CA)
The U of Toledo (OH)
U of Toronto (ON, Canada)
U of Tulsa (OK)
U of Utah (UT)
U of Vermont (VT)
U of Virginia (VA)
The U of Virginia's Coll at Wise (VA)
U of Washington (WA)
U of Waterloo (ON, Canada)
The U of West Alabama (AL)
The U of Western Ontario (ON, Canada)
U of West Georgia (GA)
U of Windsor (ON, Canada)
U of Wisconsin–Eau Claire (WI)
U of Wisconsin–La Crosse (WI)
U of Wisconsin–Madison (WI)
U of Wisconsin–Milwaukee (WI)
U of Wisconsin–Oshkosh (WI)
U of Wisconsin–Parkside (WI)
U of Wisconsin–River Falls (WI)
U of Wisconsin–Stevens Point (WI)
U of Wisconsin–Superior (WI)
U of Wisconsin–Whitewater (WI)
U of Wyoming (WY)
Upper Iowa U (IA)
Ursinus Coll (PA)
Ursuline Coll (OH)
Utah State U (UT)
Utica Coll (NY)
Valdosta State U (GA)
Valparaiso U (IN)
Vanderbilt U (TN)
Vanguard U of Southern California (CA)
Vassar Coll (NY)
Villanova U (PA)
Virginia Commonwealth U (VA)
Virginia Polytechnic Inst and State U (VA)
Virginia State U (VA)
Virginia Union U (VA)
Virginia U of Lynchburg (VA)
Virginia Wesleyan Coll (VA)
Viterbo U (WI)
Voorhees Coll (SC)
Wagner Coll (NY)
Wake Forest U (NC)
Walsh U (OH)
Wartburg Coll (IA)
Washburn U (KS)
Washington & Jefferson Coll (PA)
Washington and Lee U (VA)
Washington Coll (MD)
Washington State U (WA)
Wayland Baptist U (TX)
Waynesburg U (PA)
Wayne State Coll (NE)
Wayne State U (MI)
Weber State U (UT)
Wellesley Coll (MA)
Wells Coll (NY)
Wesleyan U (CT)
West Chester U of Pennsylvania (PA)
Western Carolina U (NC)
Western Connecticut State U (CT)
Western Illinois U (IL)
Western Kentucky U (KY)
Western Michigan U (MI)
Western New England Coll (MA)
Western Oregon U (OR)
Western State Coll of Colorado (CO)
Western Washington U (WA)
Westfield State Coll (MA)
West Liberty U (WV)
Westminster Coll (MO)
Westminster Coll (UT)
Westmont Coll (CA)
West Virginia State U (WV)
West Virginia U (WV)
West Virginia Wesleyan Coll (WV)
Wheaton Coll (IL)
Wheaton Coll (MA)
Whitman Coll (WA)
Whittier Coll (CA)
Wichita State U (KS)
Widener U (PA)
Wilberforce U (OH)
Wilfrid Laurier U (ON, Canada)
Wilkes U (PA)
Willamette U (OR)
William Paterson U of New Jersey (NJ)
William Penn U (IA)
Williams Coll (MA)
Wilson Coll (PA)
Wingate U (NC)
Winona State U (MN)
Winston-Salem State U (NC)
Winthrop U (SC)
Wittenberg U (OH)
Wofford Coll (SC)
Worcester State Coll (MA)
Wright State U (OH)
Xavier U (OH)
Xavier U of Louisiana (LA)
Yale U (CT)
Yeshiva U (NY)
York Coll of Pennsylvania (PA)
York Coll of the City U of New York (NY)
York U (ON, Canada)
Youngstown State U (OH)

SOIL SCIENCE AND AGRONOMY

California Polytechnic State U, San Luis Obispo (CA)
Colorado State U (CO)
Michigan State U (MI)
New Mexico State U (NM)
North Carolina State U (NC)
North Dakota State U (ND)
Oklahoma State U (OK)
Penn State Abington (PA)
Penn State Altoona (PA)
Penn State Beaver (PA)
Penn State Berks (PA)
Penn State Brandywine (PA)
Penn State DuBois (PA)
Penn State Erie, The Behrend Coll (PA)
Penn State Fayette, The Eberly Campus (PA)
Penn State Greater Allegheny (PA)
Penn State Hazleton (PA)
Penn State Lehigh Valley (PA)
Penn State Mont Alto (PA)
Penn State New Kensington (PA)
Penn State Schuylkill (PA)
Penn State Shenango (PA)
Penn State U Park (PA)
Penn State Wilkes-Barre (PA)
Penn State Worthington Scranton (PA)
Penn State York (PA)
The U of British Columbia (BC, Canada)
U of California, Davis (CA)
U of Delaware (DE)
U of Florida (FL)
U of Maine (ME)
U of Minnesota, Twin Cities Campus (MN)
U of Nebraska–Lincoln (NE)
U of New Hampshire (NH)
U of Saskatchewan (SK, Canada)
The U of Tennessee at Martin (TN)
U of Wisconsin–River Falls (WI)
U of Wisconsin–Stevens Point (WI)
Utah State U (UT)
Washington State U (WA)

SOIL SCIENCES RELATED

Brigham Young U (UT)
U of Hawaii at Manoa (HI)

SOLAR ENERGY TECHNOLOGY

Appalachian State U (NC)

SOUTH ASIAN LANGUAGES

Claremont McKenna Coll (CA)
The U of British Columbia (BC, Canada)
U of Chicago (IL)
Yale U (CT)

SPANISH

Abilene Christian U (TX)
Adams State Coll (CO)
Adelphi U (NY)
Agnes Scott Coll (GA)
Alabama State U (AL)
Albany State U (GA)
Albertus Magnus Coll (CT)
Albion Coll (MI)
Albright Coll (PA)
Alfred U (NY)
Allegheny Coll (PA)
Alma Coll (MI)
American U (DC)
Amherst Coll (MA)
Anderson U (IN)
Andrews U (MI)
Angelo State U (TX)
Appalachian State U (NC)
Aquinas Coll (MI)
Arcadia U (PA)
Arizona State U (AZ)
Armstrong Atlantic State U (GA)
Asbury U (KY)
Ashland U (OH)
Assumption Coll (MA)
Auburn U (AL)
Augsburg Coll (MN)
Augustana Coll (IL)
Augustana Coll (SD)
Aurora U (IL)
Austin Coll (TX)
Austin Peay State U (TN)
Azusa Pacific U (CA)
Baker U (KS)
Baldwin-Wallace Coll (OH)
Ball State U (IN)
Bard Coll (NY)
Bard Coll at Simon's Rock (MA)
Barnard Coll (NY)
Barry U (FL)
Barton Coll (NC)
Bates Coll (ME)
Baylor U (TX)
Belmont U (TN)
Beloit Coll (WI)
Bemidji State U (MN)
Benedictine Coll (KS)
Benedictine U (IL)
Bennington Coll (VT)
Berea Coll (KY)
Bernard M. Baruch Coll of the City U of New York (NY)
Berry Coll (GA)
Bethany Coll (WV)
Bethel Coll (IN)
Bethel U (MN)
Birmingham-Southern Coll (AL)
Bishop's U (QC, Canada)
Blackburn Coll (IL)
Black Hills State U (SD)
Bloomsburg U of Pennsylvania (PA)
Blue Mountain Coll (MS)
Bluffton U (OH)
Bob Jones U (SC)
Boise State U (ID)
Boston Coll (MA)
Boston U (MA)
Bowdoin Coll (ME)
Bowling Green State U (OH)
Bradley U (IL)
Brandeis U (MA)
Brescia U (KY)
Briar Cliff U (IA)
Bridgewater Coll (VA)
Bridgewater State Coll (MA)
Brock U (ON, Canada)
Brooklyn Coll of the City U of New York (NY)
Bryan Coll (TN)
Bryn Mawr Coll (PA)
Bucknell U (PA)
Buena Vista U (IA)
Buffalo State Coll, State U of New York (NY)
Butler U (IN)
Cabrini Coll (PA)
California Baptist U (CA)
California Lutheran U (CA)
California State Polytechnic U, Pomona (CA)
California State U, Bakersfield (CA)
California State U, Dominguez Hills (CA)
California State U, East Bay (CA)
California State U, Fresno (CA)
California State U, Fullerton (CA)
California State U, Long Beach (CA)
California State U, Los Angeles (CA)
California State U, Northridge (CA)
California State U, Sacramento (CA)
California State U, San Bernardino (CA)
California State U, San Marcos (CA)
California State U, Stanislaus (CA)
Calvin Coll (MI)
Canisius Coll (NY)
Capital U (OH)
Carleton Coll (MN)
Carlow U (PA)
Carnegie Mellon U (PA)
Carroll U (WI)
Carson-Newman Coll (TN)
Case Western Reserve U (OH)
Castleton State Coll (VT)
Catawba Coll (NC)
The Catholic U of America (DC)
Cedarville U (OH)
Central Coll (IA)
Central Connecticut State U (CT)
Central Michigan U (MI)
Chapman U (CA)
Chatham U (PA)
Cheyney U of Pennsylvania (PA)
Chowan U (NC)
Christopher Newport U (VA)
City Coll of the City U of New York (NY)
Claremont McKenna Coll (CA)
Clarion U of Pennsylvania (PA)
Clark Atlanta U (GA)
Clarke Coll (IA)
Clark U (MA)
Cleveland State U (OH)
Coastal Carolina U (SC)
Colby Coll (ME)
Colgate U (NY)
The Coll at Brockport, State U of New York (NY)
Coll of Charleston (SC)
The Coll of Idaho (ID)
Coll of Mount Saint Vincent (NY)
The Coll of New Jersey (NJ)
The Coll of New Rochelle (NY)
Coll of Notre Dame of Maryland (MD)
Coll of Saint Benedict (MN)
Coll of Saint Elizabeth (NJ)
The Coll of Saint Rose (NY)
The Coll of St. Scholastica (MN)
Coll of Staten Island of the City U of New York (NY)
Coll of the Holy Cross (MA)
Coll of the Ozarks (MO)
The Coll of Wooster (OH)
The Colorado Coll (CO)
Colorado State U (CO)
Columbia Coll (SC)
Columbia U (NY)
Columbia U, School of General Studies (NY)
Columbus State U (GA)
Concordia Coll (MN)
Concordia U (QC, Canada)
Concordia U Wisconsin (WI)
Connecticut Coll (CT)
Converse Coll (SC)
Cornell Coll (IA)
Cornell U (NY)
Cornerstone U (MI)
Creighton U (NE)
Daemen Coll (NY)
Dana Coll (NE)
Dartmouth Coll (NH)
Davidson Coll (NC)

INDEXES

Delaware State U (DE)
Denison U (OH)
DePaul U (IL)
DePauw U (IN)
DeSales U (PA)
Dickinson Coll (PA)
Dickinson State U (ND)
Dillard U (LA)
Doane Coll (NE)
Dominican Coll (NY)
Dominican U (IL)
Dordt Coll (IA)
Drew U (NJ)
Drury U (MO)
Duke U (NC)
Duquesne U (PA)
Earlham Coll (IN)
East Carolina U (NC)
Eastern Connecticut State U (CT)
Eastern Mennonite U (VA)
Eastern Michigan U (MI)
Eastern New Mexico U (NM)
Eastern Washington U (WA)
East Stroudsburg U of Pennsylvania (PA)
East Texas Baptist U (TX)
Eckerd Coll (FL)
Edgewood Coll (WI)
Edinboro U of Pennsylvania (PA)
Elizabethtown Coll (PA)
Elmhurst Coll (IL)
Elmira Coll (NY)
Elon U (NC)
Emmanuel Coll (MA)
Emory & Henry Coll (VA)
Emory U (GA)
Endicott Coll (MA)
Erskine Coll (SC)
Evangel U (MO)
Fairfield U (CT)
Fairleigh Dickinson U, Coll at Florham (NJ)
Fairleigh Dickinson U, Metropolitan Campus (NJ)
Fayetteville State U (NC)
Ferrum Coll (VA)
Fisk U (TN)
Flagler Coll (FL)
Florida Atlantic U (FL)
Florida Gulf Coast U (FL)
Florida Intl U (FL)
Florida Southern Coll (FL)
Fordham U (NY)
Fort Hays State U (KS)
Fort Lewis Coll (CO)
Franciscan U of Steubenville (OH)
Francis Marion U (SC)
Franklin & Marshall Coll (PA)
Franklin Coll (IN)
Friends U (KS)
Furman U (SC)
Gallaudet U (DC)
Gardner-Webb U (NC)
George Fox U (OR)
Georgetown Coll (KY)
Georgetown U (DC)
The George Washington U (DC)
Georgia Coll & State U (GA)
Georgian Court U (NJ)
Georgia State U (GA)
Gettysburg Coll (PA)
Gonzaga U (WA)
Gordon Coll (MA)
Goshen Coll (IN)
Goucher Coll (MD)
Grace Coll (IN)
Graceland U (IA)
Grambling State U (LA)
Grand Valley State U (MI)
Greensboro Coll (NC)
Greenville Coll (IL)
Grinnell Coll (IA)
Grove City Coll (PA)
Guilford Coll (NC)
Gustavus Adolphus Coll (MN)
Hamilton Coll (NY)
Hamline U (MN)
Hampden-Sydney Coll (VA)
Hanover Coll (IN)
Harding U (AR)
Hardin-Simmons U (TX)
Hartwick Coll (NY)
Haverford Coll (PA)
Heidelberg U (OH)
Henderson State U (AR)
Hendrix Coll (AR)
High Point U (NC)
Hillsdale Coll (MI)
Hiram Coll (OH)
Hofstra U (NY)
Hollins U (VA)
Holy Family U (PA)
Holy Names U (CA)
Hood Coll (MD)
Hope Coll (MI)
Houghton Coll (NY)
Houston Baptist U (TX)
Howard Payne U (TX)
Humboldt State U (CA)
Hunter Coll of the City U of New York (NY)
Idaho State U (ID)
Illinois Coll (IL)
Illinois State U (IL)
Illinois Wesleyan U (IL)
Immaculata U (PA)
Indiana U Bloomington (IN)
Indiana U Northwest (IN)
Indiana U of Pennsylvania (PA)
Indiana U–Purdue U Fort Wayne (IN)
Indiana U–Purdue U Indianapolis (IN)
Indiana U South Bend (IN)
Indiana U Southeast (IN)
Indiana Wesleyan U (IN)
Inter American U of Puerto Rico, San Germán Campus (PR)
Iona Coll (NY)
Iowa State U of Science and Technology (IA)
Ithaca Coll (NY)
Jacksonville State U (AL)
Jacksonville U (FL)
Jamestown Coll (ND)
John Brown U (AR)
John Carroll U (OH)
The Johns Hopkins U (MD)
Johnson C. Smith U (NC)
Juniata Coll (PA)
Kalamazoo Coll (MI)
Kean U (NJ)
Keene State Coll (NH)
Kent State U (OH)
Kentucky Wesleyan Coll (KY)
Kenyon Coll (OH)
King Coll (TN)
King's Coll (PA)
Knox Coll (IL)
Kutztown U of Pennsylvania (PA)
Lafayette Coll (PA)
LaGrange Coll (GA)
Lake Erie Coll (OH)
Lake Forest Coll (IL)
Lakeland Coll (WI)
Lamar U (TX)
La Roche Coll (PA)
La Salle U (PA)
La Sierra U (CA)
Laurentian U (ON, Canada)
Lawrence U (WI)
Lebanon Valley Coll (PA)
Lehigh U (PA)
Lehman Coll of the City U of New York (NY)
Le Moyne Coll (NY)
Lewis & Clark Coll (OR)
Liberty U (VA)
Lincoln U (MO)
Lincoln U (PA)
Lindenwood U (MO)
Linfield Coll (OR)
Lipscomb U (TN)
Lock Haven U of Pennsylvania (PA)
Long Island U, C.W. Post Campus (NY)
Longwood U (VA)
Loras Coll (IA)
Louisiana Coll (LA)
Louisiana State U and Ag and Mech Coll (LA)
Louisiana State U in Shreveport (LA)
Louisiana Tech U (LA)
Loyola Marymount U (CA)
Loyola U Chicago (IL)
Loyola U Maryland (MD)
Loyola U New Orleans (LA)
Luther Coll (IA)
Lycoming Coll (PA)
Lynchburg Coll (VA)
Lyon Coll (AR)
Macalester Coll (MN)
Madonna U (MI)
Malone U (OH)
Manchester Coll (IN)
Manhattan Coll (NY)
Manhattanville Coll (NY)
Mansfield U of Pennsylvania (PA)
Marian U (IN)
Marian U (WI)
Marietta Coll (OH)
Marist Coll (NY)
Marlboro Coll (VT)
Marquette U (WI)
Mars Hill Coll (NC)
Mary Baldwin Coll (VA)
Maryville Coll (TN)
Marywood U (PA)
McDaniel Coll (MD)
McMurry U (TX)
McNeese State U (LA)
McPherson Coll (KS)
Memorial U of Newfoundland (NL, Canada)
Mercer U (GA)
Mercy Coll (NY)
Meredith Coll (NC)
Merrimack Coll (MA)
Messiah Coll (PA)
Methodist U (NC)
Miami U (OH)
Miami U Hamilton (OH)
Michigan State U (MI)
MidAmerica Nazarene U (KS)
Middlebury Coll (VT)
Midwestern State U (TX)
Millersville U of Pennsylvania (PA)
Millikin U (IL)
Millsaps Coll (MS)
Mills Coll (CA)
Minnesota State U Mankato (MN)
Minnesota State U Moorhead (MN)
Minot State U (ND)
Mississippi Coll (MS)
Mississippi U for Women (MS)
Missouri Southern State U (MO)
Missouri State U (MO)
Missouri Western State U (MO)
Molloy Coll (NY)
Monmouth Coll (IL)
Montana State U Billings (MT)
Montclair State U (NJ)
Moravian Coll (PA)
Morehead State U (KY)
Morehouse Coll (GA)
Morningside Coll (IA)
Mount Allison U (NB, Canada)
Mount Holyoke Coll (MA)
Mount Mary Coll (WI)
Mount Saint Mary Coll (NY)
Mount St. Mary's Coll (CA)
Mount St. Mary's U (MD)
Mount Vernon Nazarene U (OH)
Muhlenberg Coll (PA)
Murray State U (KY)
Nazareth Coll of Rochester (NY)
Nebraska Wesleyan U (NE)
Newberry Coll (SC)
New Coll of Florida (FL)
New Jersey City U (NJ)
New Mexico Highlands U (NM)
New York U (NY)
Niagara U (NY)
North Carolina Central U (NC)
North Carolina State U (NC)
North Central Coll (IL)
North Dakota State U (ND)
Northeastern Illinois U (IL)
Northeastern State U (OK)
Northeastern U (MA)
Northern Arizona U (AZ)
Northern Kentucky U (KY)
Northern Michigan U (MI)
Northern State U (SD)
North Georgia Coll & State U (GA)
Northwestern Coll (IA)
Northwestern Coll (MN)
Northwestern Oklahoma State U (OK)
Northwest Missouri State U (MO)
Northwest Nazarene U (ID)
Oakland U (MI)
Oakwood U (AL)
Oberlin Coll (OH)
Occidental Coll (CA)
Oglethorpe U (GA)
Ohio Northern U (OH)
The Ohio State U (OH)
Ohio U (OH)
Ohio Wesleyan U (OH)
Oklahoma Baptist U (OK)
Oklahoma Christian U (OK)
Oklahoma City U (OK)
Oklahoma State U (OK)
Old Dominion U (VA)
Oral Roberts U (OK)
Oregon State U (OR)
Ouachita Baptist U (AR)
Our Lady of the Lake U of San Antonio (TX)
Pace U (NY)
Pacific Lutheran U (WA)
Pacific Union Coll (CA)
Park U (MO)
Peace Coll (NC)
Penn State Abington (PA)
Penn State Altoona (PA)
Penn State Beaver (PA)
Penn State Berks (PA)
Penn State Brandywine (PA)
Penn State DuBois (PA)
Penn State Erie, The Behrend Coll (PA)
Penn State Fayette, The Eberly Campus (PA)
Penn State Greater Allegheny (PA)
Penn State Hazleton (PA)
Penn State Lehigh Valley (PA)
Penn State Mont Alto (PA)
Penn State New Kensington (PA)
Penn State Schuylkill (PA)
Penn State Shenango (PA)
Penn State U Park (PA)
Penn State Wilkes-Barre (PA)
Penn State Worthington Scranton (PA)
Penn State York (PA)
Pepperdine U, Malibu (CA)
Piedmont Coll (GA)
Pittsburg State U (KS)
Pitzer Coll (CA)
Plymouth State U (NH)
Pomona Coll (CA)
Pontifical Catholic U of Puerto Rico (PR)
Portland State U (OR)
Prairie View A&M U (TX)
Presbyterian Coll (SC)
Prescott Coll (AZ)
Princeton U (NJ)
Principia Coll (IL)
Providence Coll (RI)
Purchase Coll, State U of New York (NY)
Queens Coll of the City U of New York (NY)
Queen's U at Kingston (ON, Canada)
Quinnipiac U (CT)
Ramapo Coll of New Jersey (NJ)
Randolph Coll (VA)
Randolph-Macon Coll (VA)
Reed Coll (OR)
Regis Coll (MA)
Rhode Island Coll (RI)
Rhodes Coll (TN)
Rice U (TX)
Rider U (NJ)
Ripon Coll (WI)
Rivier Coll (NH)
Roanoke Coll (VA)
Roberts Wesleyan Coll (NY)
Rockford Coll (IL)
Rockhurst U (MO)
Rollins Coll (FL)
Roosevelt U (IL)
Rosemont Coll (PA)
Rowan U (NJ)
Russell Sage Coll (NY)
Rutgers, The State U of New Jersey, Camden (NJ)
Rutgers, The State U of New Jersey, Newark (NJ)
Rutgers, The State U of New Jersey, New Brunswick (NJ)
Sacred Heart U (CT)
Saginaw Valley State U (MI)
St. Ambrose U (IA)
Saint Anselm Coll (NH)
St. Bonaventure U (NY)
St. Catherine U (MN)
St. Cloud State U (MN)
St. Edward's U (TX)
St. Francis Coll (NY)
Saint Francis U (PA)
St. John Fisher Coll (NY)
Saint John's U (MN)
St. John's U (NY)
Saint Joseph Coll (CT)
St. Joseph's Coll, Long Island Campus (NY)
St. Joseph's Coll, New York (NY)
Saint Joseph's U (PA)
St. Lawrence U (NY)
Saint Louis U (MO)
Saint Mary's Coll (IN)
Saint Mary's Coll of California (CA)
St. Mary's U (TX)
Saint Mary's U of Minnesota (MN)
Saint Michael's Coll (VT)
St. Norbert Coll (WI)
St. Olaf Coll (MN)
St. Thomas Aquinas Coll (NY)
St. Thomas U (NB, Canada)
Saint Vincent Coll (PA)
Saint Xavier U (IL)
Salem Coll (NC)
Salem State Coll (MA)
Salisbury U (MD)
Salve Regina U (RI)
Samford U (AL)
Sam Houston State U (TX)
San Diego State U (CA)
San Francisco State U (CA)
San Jose State U (CA)
Santa Clara U (CA)
Sarah Lawrence Coll (NY)
Scripps Coll (CA)
Seattle U (WA)
Seton Hall U (NJ)
Seton Hill U (PA)
Sewanee: The U of the South (TN)
Shaw U (NC)
Shenandoah U (VA)
Shepherd U (WV)
Shippensburg U of Pennsylvania (PA)
Shorter U (GA)
Siena Coll (NY)
Siena Heights U (MI)
Simmons Coll (MA)
Simpson Coll (IA)
Skidmore Coll (NY)
Slippery Rock U of Pennsylvania (PA)
Smith Coll (MA)
Sonoma State U (CA)
South Dakota State U (SD)
Southeastern Louisiana U (LA)
Southeastern Oklahoma State U (OK)
Southeast Missouri State U (MO)
Southern Adventist U (TN)
Southern Arkansas U–Magnolia (AR)
Southern Connecticut State U (CT)
Southern Illinois U Carbondale (IL)
Southern Methodist U (TX)
Southern Oregon U (OR)
Southern U and Ag and Mech Coll (LA)
Southern Utah U (UT)
Southwest Baptist U (MO)
Southwestern U (TX)
Southwest Minnesota State U (MN)
Spelman Coll (GA)
Spring Arbor U (MI)
Stanford U (CA)
State U of New York at Binghamton (NY)
State U of New York at Fredonia (NY)
State U of New York at New Paltz (NY)
State U of New York at Oswego (NY)
State U of New York at Plattsburgh (NY)
State U of New York Coll at Cortland (NY)
State U of New York Coll at Geneseo (NY)
State U of New York Coll at Old Westbury (NY)
State U of New York Coll at Oneonta (NY)
State U of New York Coll at Potsdam (NY)
Stephen F. Austin State U (TX)
Stetson U (FL)
Stonehill Coll (MA)
Stony Brook U, State U of New York (NY)
Suffolk U (MA)
Sul Ross State U (TX)
Susquehanna U (PA)
Swarthmore Coll (PA)
Sweet Briar Coll (VA)
Syracuse U (NY)
Tarleton State U (TX)
Taylor U (IN)
Temple U (PA)
Tennessee Technological U (TN)
Tennessee Wesleyan Coll (TN)
Texas A&M Intl U (TX)
Texas A&M U (TX)
Texas A&M U–Commerce (TX)
Texas A&M U–Corpus Christi (TX)
Texas A&M U–Kingsville (TX)
Texas Christian U (TX)
Texas Lutheran U (TX)
Texas Southern U (TX)
Texas State U–San Marcos (TX)
Texas Tech U (TX)
Texas Wesleyan U (TX)
Thomas More Coll (KY)
Transylvania U (KY)
Trinity Christian Coll (IL)
Trinity Coll (CT)
Trinity U (TX)
Truman State U (MO)
Tufts U (MA)
Tulane U (LA)
Union Coll (NE)
Union Coll (NY)
Union U (TN)
United States Military Acad (NY)
Universidad Adventista de las Antillas (PR)
U at Albany, State U of New York (NY)
U at Buffalo, the State U of New York (NY)
The U of Akron (OH)
The U of Alabama (AL)
U of Alberta (AB, Canada)
The U of Arizona (AZ)
U of Arkansas (AR)
U of Arkansas at Fort Smith (AR)
U of Arkansas at Little Rock (AR)
The U of British Columbia (BC, Canada)
The U of British Columbia–Okanagan (BC, Canada)
U of California, Berkeley (CA)
U of California, Davis (CA)
U of California, Irvine (CA)
U of California, Los Angeles (CA)
U of California, Riverside (CA)
U of California, San Diego (CA)
U of California, Santa Barbara (CA)
U of Central Florida (FL)

U of Central Missouri (MO)
U of Central Oklahoma (OK)
U of Chicago (IL)
U of Cincinnati (OH)
U of Colorado at Boulder (CO)
U of Colorado at Colorado Springs (CO)
U of Colorado Denver (CO)
U of Connecticut (CT)
U of Dallas (TX)
U of Dayton (OH)
U of Delaware (DE)
U of Denver (CO)
U of Evansville (IN)
The U of Findlay (OH)
U of Florida (FL)
U of Georgia (GA)
U of Guelph (ON, Canada)
U of Hawaii at Manoa (HI)
U of Houston (TX)
U of Houston–Downtown (TX)
U of Illinois at Chicago (IL)
U of Illinois at Urbana–Champaign (IL)
U of Indianapolis (IN)
The U of Iowa (IA)
The U of Kansas (KS)
U of Kentucky (KY)
U of King's Coll (NS, Canada)
U of La Verne (CA)
U of Louisiana at Monroe (LA)
U of Louisville (KY)
U of Maine (ME)
U of Manitoba (MB, Canada)
U of Mary Hardin-Baylor (TX)
U of Maryland, Coll Park (MD)
U of Massachusetts Amherst (MA)
U of Massachusetts Boston (MA)
U of Massachusetts Dartmouth (MA)
U of Miami (FL)
U of Michigan (MI)
U of Michigan–Dearborn (MI)
U of Michigan–Flint (MI)
U of Minnesota, Duluth (MN)
U of Minnesota, Twin Cities Campus (MN)
U of Mississippi (MS)
U of Missouri (MO)
U of Missouri–Kansas City (MO)
U of Missouri–St. Louis (MO)
U of Mount Union (OH)
U of Nebraska at Kearney (NE)
U of Nebraska at Omaha (NE)
U of Nebraska–Lincoln (NE)
U of Nevada, Las Vegas (NV)
U of Nevada, Reno (NV)
U of New Brunswick Fredericton (NB, Canada)
U of New Hampshire (NH)
U of New Mexico (NM)
U of New Orleans (LA)
The U of North Carolina at Asheville (NC)
The U of North Carolina at Charlotte (NC)
The U of North Carolina at Greensboro (NC)
The U of North Carolina at Pembroke (NC)
The U of North Carolina Wilmington (NC)
U of North Dakota (ND)
U of Northern Colorado (CO)
U of Northern Iowa (IA)
U of North Florida (FL)
U of North Texas (TX)
U of Notre Dame (IN)
U of Oklahoma (OK)
U of Oregon (OR)
U of Ottawa (ON, Canada)
U of Pennsylvania (PA)
U of Pittsburgh (PA)
U of Pittsburgh at Greensburg (PA)
U of Portland (OR)
U of Puerto Rico at Utuado (PR)
U of Puerto Rico, Cayey U Coll (PR)
U of Puerto Rico, Río Piedras (PR)
U of Puget Sound (WA)
U of Redlands (CA)
U of Regina (SK, Canada)
U of Rhode Island (RI)
U of Richmond (VA)
U of Rochester (NY)
U of St. Thomas (MN)
U of St. Thomas (TX)
U of San Diego (CA)
U of San Francisco (CA)
U of Saskatchewan (SK, Canada)
The U of Scranton (PA)
U of South Carolina (SC)
U of South Carolina Upstate (SC)
The U of South Dakota (SD)
U of Southern California (CA)
U of Southern Indiana (IN)
U of South Florida (FL)
The U of Tennessee (TN)
The U of Tennessee at Martin (TN)
The U of Texas at Arlington (TX)
The U of Texas at Austin (TX)
The U of Texas at Brownsville (TX)
The U of Texas at El Paso (TX)
The U of Texas at San Antonio (TX)
The U of Texas at Tyler (TX)
The U of Texas of the Permian Basin (TX)
The U of Texas–Pan American (TX)
U of the Cumberlands (KY)
U of the District of Columbia (DC)
U of the Incarnate Word (TX)
U of the Ozarks (AR)
U of the Pacific (CA)
The U of Toledo (OH)
U of Toronto (ON, Canada)
U of Tulsa (OK)
U of Utah (UT)
U of Vermont (VT)
U of Virginia (VA)
The U of Virginia's Coll at Wise (VA)
U of Washington (WA)
U of Waterloo (ON, Canada)
The U of Western Ontario (ON, Canada)
U of West Georgia (GA)
U of Windsor (ON, Canada)
U of Wisconsin–Eau Claire (WI)
U of Wisconsin–Green Bay (WI)
U of Wisconsin–La Crosse (WI)
U of Wisconsin–Madison (WI)
U of Wisconsin–Milwaukee (WI)
U of Wisconsin–Oshkosh (WI)
U of Wisconsin–Parkside (WI)
U of Wisconsin–Platteville (WI)
U of Wisconsin–River Falls (WI)
U of Wisconsin–Stevens Point (WI)
U of Wisconsin–Whitewater (WI)
U of Wyoming (WY)
Ursinus Coll (PA)
Utah State U (UT)
Utah Valley U (UT)
Valdosta State U (GA)
Valley City State U (ND)
Valparaiso U (IN)
Vanderbilt U (TN)
Vassar Coll (NY)
Villanova U (PA)
Virginia Polytechnic Inst and State U (VA)
Virginia Wesleyan Coll (VA)
Viterbo U (WI)
Wabash Coll (IN)
Wagner Coll (NY)
Wake Forest U (NC)
Walsh U (OH)
Wartburg Coll (IA)
Washburn U (KS)
Washington & Jefferson Coll (PA)
Washington and Lee U (VA)
Washington Coll (MD)
Washington State U (WA)
Washington U in St. Louis (MO)
Wayland Baptist U (TX)
Wayne State Coll (NE)
Weber State U (UT)
Webster U (MO)
Wellesley Coll (MA)
Wells Coll (NY)
Wesleyan Coll (GA)
Wesleyan U (CT)
West Chester U of Pennsylvania (PA)
Western Carolina U (NC)
Western Connecticut State U (CT)
Western Illinois U (IL)
Western Kentucky U (KY)
Western Michigan U (MI)
Western Oregon U (OR)
Western State Coll of Colorado (CO)
Western Washington U (WA)
Westminster Coll (MO)
Westmont Coll (CA)
Wheaton Coll (IL)
Wheeling Jesuit U (WV)
Whitman Coll (WA)
Whittier Coll (CA)
Wichita State U (KS)
Widener U (PA)
Wilfrid Laurier U (ON, Canada)
Wilkes U (PA)
Willamette U (OR)
William Jewell Coll (MO)
William Paterson U of New Jersey (NJ)
Williams Coll (MA)
Wilmington Coll (OH)
Wilson Coll (PA)
Winona State U (MN)
Winston-Salem State U (NC)
Wittenberg U (OH)
Wofford Coll (SC)
Worcester State Coll (MA)
Wright State U (OH)
Xavier U (OH)
Xavier U of Louisiana (LA)
Yale U (CT)
York Coll of Pennsylvania (PA)
York Coll of the City U of New York (NY)
York U (ON, Canada)
Youngstown State U (OH)

SPANISH AND IBERIAN STUDIES

Bard Coll (NY)
Bard Coll at Simon's Rock (MA)
Fordham U (NY)
The U of Western Ontario (ON, Canada)
Vanderbilt U (TN)
York U (ON, Canada)

SPANISH LANGUAGE TEACHER EDUCATION

Abilene Christian U (TX)
Adams State Coll (CO)
Alma Coll (MI)
Anderson U (IN)
Appalachian State U (NC)
Assumption Coll (MA)
Auburn U (AL)
Baylor U (TX)
Bethel Coll (IN)
Bethel U (MN)
Bishop's U (QC, Canada)
Blue Mountain Coll (MS)
Bob Jones U (SC)
Bradley U (IL)
Bridgewater Coll (VA)
Brooklyn Coll of the City U of New York (NY)
Bryan Coll (TN)
Buena Vista U (IA)
California Lutheran U (CA)
Carroll U (WI)
The Catholic U of America (DC)
Cedarville U (OH)
Central Michigan U (MI)
The Coll at Brockport, State U of New York (NY)
Coll of Saint Mary (NE)
The Coll of Saint Rose (NY)
Colorado State U (CO)
Concordia Coll (MN)
Concordia U Wisconsin (WI)
Daemen Coll (NY)
Dana Coll (NE)
Delaware State U (DE)
DePaul U (IL)
Dordt Coll (IA)
Dowling Coll (NY)
Duquesne U (PA)
East Carolina U (NC)
Eastern Mennonite U (VA)
Eastern Washington U (WA)
East Texas Baptist U (TX)
Edgewood Coll (WI)
Elmhurst Coll (IL)
Elmira Coll (NY)
Evangel U (MO)
Fayetteville State U (NC)
Franklin Coll (IN)
Friends U (KS)
Gardner-Webb U (NC)
Georgia Southern U (GA)
Grace Coll (IN)
Grand Valley State U (MI)
Greensboro Coll (NC)
Greenville Coll (IL)
Harding U (AR)
Hardin-Simmons U (TX)
Hofstra U (NY)
Hope Coll (MI)
Howard Payne U (TX)
Indiana U Bloomington (IN)
Indiana U Northwest (IN)
Indiana U–Purdue U Fort Wayne (IN)
Indiana U–Purdue U Indianapolis (IN)
Indiana U South Bend (IN)
Inter American U of Puerto Rico, Aguadilla Campus (PR)
Inter American U of Puerto Rico, Arecibo Campus (PR)
Inter American U of Puerto Rico, Fajardo Campus (PR)
Iona Coll (NY)
Ithaca Coll (NY)
Juniata Coll (PA)
Keene State Coll (NH)
Kent State U (OH)
Kentucky Wesleyan Coll (KY)
King Coll (TN)
Le Moyne Coll (NY)
Liberty U (VA)
Lindenwood U (MO)
Lipscomb U (TN)
Long Island U, Brooklyn Campus (NY)
Long Island U, C.W. Post Campus (NY)
Lubbock Christian U (TX)
Malone U (OH)
Manhattanville Coll (NY)
Mansfield U of Pennsylvania (PA)
Marian U (WI)
Marist Coll (NY)
Maryville Coll (TN)
Marywood U (PA)
McMurry U (TX)
McNeese State U (LA)
Messiah Coll (PA)
Miami U (OH)
Miami U Hamilton (OH)
Michigan State U (MI)
MidAmerica Nazarene U (KS)
Millersville U of Pennsylvania (PA)
Minnesota State U Moorhead (MN)
Minot State U (ND)
Mississippi Coll (MS)
Missouri State U (MO)
Missouri Western State U (MO)
Molloy Coll (NY)
Montana State U Billings (MT)
Moravian Coll (PA)
Morningside Coll (IA)
Mount Mary Coll (WI)
Mount Vernon Nazarene U (OH)
Murray State U (KY)
Niagara U (NY)
North Carolina Central U (NC)
North Carolina State U (NC)
North Dakota State U (ND)
Northeastern State U (OK)
Northern Arizona U (AZ)
Northern Michigan U (MI)
Northwest Missouri State U (MO)
Northwest Nazarene U (ID)
Ohio Northern U (OH)
Ohio U (OH)
Ohio Wesleyan U (OH)
Oklahoma Baptist U (OK)
Old Dominion U (VA)
Oral Roberts U (OK)
Pace U (NY)
Pittsburg State U (KS)
Pontifical Catholic U of Puerto Rico (PR)
Rhode Island Coll (RI)
Roberts Wesleyan Coll (NY)
Sacred Heart U (CT)
Saginaw Valley State U (MI)
St. Ambrose U (IA)
St. Catherine U (MN)
St. Edward's U (TX)
St. John Fisher Coll (NY)
St. John's U (NY)
Saint Mary's U of Minnesota (MN)
Saint Xavier U (IL)
Salem State Coll (MA)
Salve Regina U (RI)
Seton Hill U (PA)
Southeastern Louisiana U (LA)
Southeastern Oklahoma State U (OK)
Southern Arkansas U–Magnolia (AR)
Southern U and Ag and Mech Coll (LA)
Southwest Minnesota State U (MN)
State U of New York at New Paltz (NY)
State U of New York at Plattsburgh (NY)
State U of New York Coll at Cortland (NY)
State U of New York Coll at Old Westbury (NY)
State U of New York Coll at Oneonta (NY)
State U of New York Coll at Potsdam (NY)
Taylor U (IN)
Texas A&M Intl U (TX)
Texas A&M U–Corpus Christi (TX)
Texas Christian U (TX)
The U of Akron (OH)
The U of Arizona (AZ)
U of Arkansas at Fort Smith (AR)
U of Evansville (IN)
U of Illinois at Chicago (IL)
U of Illinois at Urbana–Champaign (IL)
U of Indianapolis (IN)
The U of Iowa (IA)
U of Louisiana at Monroe (LA)
U of Maine (ME)
U of Michigan–Flint (MI)
U of Minnesota, Duluth (MN)
U of Missouri–St. Louis (MO)
U of Nebraska–Lincoln (NE)
The U of North Carolina at Charlotte (NC)
The U of North Carolina at Greensboro (NC)
The U of North Carolina Wilmington (NC)
U of Puerto Rico at Utuado (PR)
U of Puerto Rico, Cayey U Coll (PR)
The U of South Dakota (SD)
The U of Tennessee at Martin (TN)
U of the Cumberlands (KY)
The U of Toledo (OH)
U of Wisconsin–River Falls (WI)
Utah Valley U (UT)
Valdosta State U (GA)
Valley City State U (ND)
Valparaiso U (IN)
Viterbo U (WI)
Washington State U (WA)
Washington U in St. Louis (MO)
Weber State U (UT)
Western Carolina U (NC)
Western Michigan U (MI)
Western State Coll of Colorado (CO)
Western Washington U (WA)
Wheeling Jesuit U (WV)
Widener U (PA)
William Jewell Coll (MO)
Winston-Salem State U (NC)
Xavier U of Louisiana (LA)
Youngstown State U (OH)

SPECIAL EDUCATION

Abilene Christian U (TX)
Adams State Coll (CO)
Alabama Ag and Mech U (AL)
Alabama State U (AL)
Albany State U (GA)
Albright Coll (PA)
Alcorn State U (MS)
American Intl Coll (MA)
Arizona State U (AZ)
Armstrong Atlantic State U (GA)
Ashland U (OH)
Auburn U (AL)
Augustana Coll (SD)
Aurora U (IL)
Austin Peay State U (TN)
Avila U (MO)
Barry U (FL)
Barton Coll (NC)
Baylor U (TX)
Bellarmine U (KY)
Belmont U (TN)
Benedictine Coll (KS)
Benedictine U (IL)
Bennett Coll for Women (NC)
Bethel U (TN)
Black Hills State U (SD)
Bloomsburg U of Pennsylvania (PA)
Bob Jones U (SC)
Boise State U (ID)
Boston U (MA)
Bowie State U (MD)
Bowling Green State U (OH)
Brescia U (KY)
Bridgewater State Coll (MA)
Brigham Young U (UT)
Brigham Young U–Hawaii (HI)
Buena Vista U (IA)
Buffalo State Coll, State U of New York (NY)
Cabrini Coll (PA)
Calvin Coll (MI)
Canisius Coll (NY)
Capital U (OH)
Carlow U (PA)
Carson-Newman Coll (TN)
Cedarville U (OH)
Centenary Coll (NJ)
Central State U (OH)
Cheyney U of Pennsylvania (PA)
Christian Brothers U (TN)
City U of Seattle (WA)
Clarion U of Pennsylvania (PA)
Clemson U (SC)
Cleveland State U (OH)
Coastal Carolina U (SC)
Coll of Charleston (SC)
Coll of Mount St. Joseph (OH)
The Coll of New Jersey (NJ)
The Coll of New Rochelle (NY)
Coll of Saint Mary (NE)
The Coll of Saint Rose (NY)
Columbia Coll (SC)
Concord U (WV)
Converse Coll (SC)
Coppin State U (MD)
Cumberland U (TN)
Curry Coll (MA)
Daemen Coll (NY)
Dakota Wesleyan U (SD)
Dana Coll (NE)
Delaware State U (DE)
DePaul U (IL)
Doane Coll (NE)
Dominican Coll (NY)
Dowling Coll (NY)
East Carolina U (NC)
East Central U (OK)
Eastern Illinois U (IL)
Eastern Michigan U (MI)
Eastern Nazarene Coll (MA)
Eastern New Mexico U (NM)
Eastern Washington U (WA)

East Stroudsburg U of Pennsylvania (PA)
East Tennessee State U (TN)
Edinboro U of Pennsylvania (PA)
Elizabeth City State U (NC)
Elmhurst Coll (IL)
Elon U (NC)
Erskine Coll (SC)
Evangel U (MO)
Fairmont State U (WV)
Felician Coll (NJ)
Fisk U (TN)
Fitchburg State Coll (MA)
Florida Atlantic U (FL)
Florida Gulf Coast U (FL)
Florida Intl U (FL)
Fontbonne U (MO)
Freed-Hardeman U (TN)
Furman U (SC)
Gannon U (PA)
Geneva Coll (PA)
Georgia Coll & State U (GA)
Georgia Southern U (GA)
Glenville State Coll (WV)
Gonzaga U (WA)
Gordon Coll (MA)
Goshen Coll (IN)
Goucher Coll (MD)
Grace Coll (IN)
Grambling State U (LA)
Grand Valley State U (MI)
Green Mountain Coll (VT)
Greensboro Coll (NC)
Greenville Coll (IL)
Gwynedd-Mercy Coll (PA)
Hampton U (VA)
Heidelberg U (OH)
High Point U (NC)
Holy Family U (PA)
Houghton Coll (NY)
Houston Baptist U (TX)
Huntington U (IN)
Idaho State U (ID)
Illinois State U (IL)
Indiana State U (IN)
Indiana U Bloomington (IN)
Indiana U of Pennsylvania (PA)
Indiana U South Bend (IN)
Indiana U Southeast (IN)
Indiana Wesleyan U (IN)
Indian River State Coll (FL)
Inter American U of Puerto Rico, Aguadilla Campus (PR)
Inter American U of Puerto Rico, Arecibo Campus (PR)
Inter American U of Puerto Rico, Fajardo Campus (PR)
Inter American U of Puerto Rico, Ponce Campus (PR)
Iowa Wesleyan Coll (IA)
Jackson State U (MS)
Jacksonville State U (AL)
Jacksonville U (FL)
John Brown U (AR)
John Carroll U (OH)
Kean U (NJ)
Kent State U (OH)
Keuka Coll (NY)
King's Coll (PA)
Kutztown U of Pennsylvania (PA)
Lamar U (TX)
La Salle U (PA)
Lebanon Valley Coll (PA)
Lee U (TN)
Le Moyne Coll (NY)
Lesley U (MA)
Lewis U (IL)
Liberty U (VA)
Lincoln U (MO)
Lincoln U (PA)
Lindenwood U (MO)
Lock Haven U of Pennsylvania (PA)
Longwood U (VA)
Louisiana Coll (LA)
Louisiana State U in Shreveport (LA)
Louisiana Tech U (LA)
Loyola U Chicago (IL)
Loyola U Maryland (MD)
Lubbock Christian U (TX)
Manchester Coll (IN)
Manhattan Coll (NY)
Mansfield U of Pennsylvania (PA)
Marian U (IN)
Marist Coll (NY)
Mars Hill Coll (NC)
Marywood U (PA)
McNeese State U (LA)
McPherson Coll (KS)
Medaille Coll (NY)
Medgar Evers Coll of the City U of New York (NY)
Memorial U of Newfoundland (NL, Canada)
Mercyhurst Coll (PA)
Methodist U (NC)
Metropolitan State Coll of Denver (CO)
Miami Dade Coll (FL)
Miami U (OH)
Miami U Hamilton (OH)
Michigan State U (MI)
Middle Tennessee State U (TN)
Midway Coll (KY)
Midwestern State U (TX)
Millersville U of Pennsylvania (PA)
Minnesota State U Moorhead (MN)
Misericordia U (PA)
Mississippi Coll (MS)
Mississippi State U (MS)
Missouri State U (MO)
Molloy Coll (NY)
Monmouth U (NJ)
Montana State U Billings (MT)
Morehead State U (KY)
Morningside Coll (IA)
Mount Marty Coll (SD)
Mount Vernon Nazarene U (OH)
Murray State U (KY)
Nazareth Coll of Rochester (NY)
Nebraska Wesleyan U (NE)
Nevada State Coll at Henderson (NV)
Newberry Coll (SC)
New England Coll (NH)
New Jersey City U (NJ)
New Mexico Highlands U (NM)
Niagara U (NY)
Northeastern Illinois U (IL)
Northeastern State U (OK)
Northern Arizona U (AZ)
Northern Michigan U (MI)
Northern State U (SD)
North Georgia Coll & State U (GA)
Northwestern Oklahoma State U (OK)
Nova Southeastern U (FL)
Ohio Dominican U (OH)
The Ohio State U (OH)
Ohio U (OH)
Oklahoma Baptist U (OK)
Oral Roberts U (OK)
Our Lady of the Lake U of San Antonio (TX)
Penn State Abington (PA)
Penn State Altoona (PA)
Penn State Beaver (PA)
Penn State Berks (PA)
Penn State Brandywine (PA)
Penn State DuBois (PA)
Penn State Erie, The Behrend Coll (PA)
Penn State Fayette, The Eberly Campus (PA)
Penn State Greater Allegheny (PA)
Penn State Hazleton (PA)
Penn State Lehigh Valley (PA)
Penn State Mont Alto (PA)
Penn State New Kensington (PA)
Penn State Schuylkill (PA)
Penn State Shenango (PA)
Penn State U Park (PA)
Penn State Wilkes-Barre (PA)
Penn State Worthington Scranton (PA)
Penn State York (PA)
Peru State Coll (NE)
Piedmont Coll (GA)
Pontifical Catholic U of Puerto Rico (PR)
Presbyterian Coll (SC)
Prescott Coll (AZ)
Providence Coll (RI)
Quincy U (IL)
Rhode Island Coll (RI)
Rivier Coll (NH)
Roberts Wesleyan Coll (NY)
Rockford Coll (IL)
Roosevelt U (IL)
Saginaw Valley State U (MI)
St. Bonaventure U (NY)
St. Cloud State U (MN)
Saint Francis U (PA)
St. John Fisher Coll (NY)
St. John's U (NY)
Saint Joseph Coll (CT)
Saint Joseph's U (PA)
Saint Martin's U (WA)
Saint Mary-of-the-Woods Coll (IN)
St. Petersburg Coll (FL)
St. Thomas Aquinas Coll (NY)
Salve Regina U (RI)
Seattle Pacific U (WA)
Seton Hall U (NJ)
Seton Hill U (PA)
Shawnee State U (OH)
Simmons Coll (MA)
Slippery Rock U of Pennsylvania (PA)
South Carolina State U (SC)
Southeastern Louisiana U (LA)
Southeastern U (FL)
Southeast Missouri State U (MO)
Southern Connecticut State U (CT)
Southern Illinois U Carbondale (IL)
Southern Illinois U Edwardsville (IL)
Southern U and Ag and Mech Coll (LA)
Southern Utah U (UT)
Southern Wesleyan U (SC)
Southwestern Oklahoma State U (OK)
Southwestern U (TX)
Southwest Minnesota State U (MN)
Spalding U (KY)
Spring Arbor U (MI)
State U of New York at New Paltz (NY)
State U of New York at Plattsburgh (NY)
State U of New York Coll at Geneseo (NY)
State U of New York Coll at Old Westbury (NY)
Syracuse U (NY)
Tabor Coll (KS)
Tennessee Technological U (TN)
Texas A&M Intl U (TX)
Texas A&M U–Commerce (TX)
Texas A&M U–Corpus Christi (TX)
Texas Christian U (TX)
Towson U (MD)
Trevecca Nazarene U (TN)
Trinity Christian Coll (IL)
Tufts U (MA)
Tusculum Coll (TN)
Union Coll (KY)
Union U (TN)
Université du Québec en Outaouais (QC, Canada)
The U of Akron (OH)
The U of Alabama (AL)
The U of Alabama at Birmingham (AL)
U of Alberta (AB, Canada)
The U of Arizona (AZ)
U of Arkansas at Pine Bluff (AR)
The U of British Columbia (BC, Canada)
U of Central Florida (FL)
U of Central Missouri (MO)
U of Central Oklahoma (OK)
U of Cincinnati (OH)
U of Connecticut (CT)
U of Dayton (OH)
U of Evansville (IN)
The U of Findlay (OH)
U of Florida (FL)
U of Georgia (GA)
U of Guam (GU)
U of Idaho (ID)
U of Illinois at Urbana–Champaign (IL)
U of Kentucky (KY)
U of Lethbridge (AB, Canada)
U of Maine at Farmington (ME)
U of Mary Hardin-Baylor (TX)
U of Maryland, Coll Park (MD)
U of Maryland Eastern Shore (MD)
U of Memphis (TN)
U of Mississippi (MS)
U of Missouri–St. Louis (MO)
U of Mount Union (OH)
U of Nebraska at Kearney (NE)
U of Nebraska at Omaha (NE)
U of Nevada, Las Vegas (NV)
U of Nevada, Reno (NV)
U of New Brunswick Fredericton (NB, Canada)
U of New Mexico (NM)
U of North Alabama (AL)
The U of North Carolina at Greensboro (NC)
The U of North Carolina at Pembroke (NC)
The U of North Carolina Wilmington (NC)
U of Northern Colorado (CO)
U of Northern Iowa (IA)
U of North Florida (FL)
U of Oklahoma (OK)
U of Puerto Rico, Cayey U Coll (PR)
U of St. Francis (IL)
The U of Scranton (PA)
U of South Alabama (AL)
U of South Carolina Aiken (SC)
The U of South Dakota (SD)
U of Southern Mississippi (MS)
U of South Florida (FL)
The U of Tennessee (TN)
The U of Tennessee at Chattanooga (TN)
The U of Tennessee at Martin (TN)
U of the Cumberlands (KY)
U of the District of Columbia (DC)
U of the Pacific (CA)
U of the Southwest (NM)
The U of Toledo (OH)
U of Utah (UT)
The U of West Alabama (AL)
The U of Western Ontario (ON, Canada)
U of West Florida (FL)
U of West Georgia (GA)
U of Windsor (ON, Canada)
U of Wisconsin–Eau Claire (WI)
U of Wisconsin–Madison (WI)
U of Wisconsin–Milwaukee (WI)
U of Wisconsin–Oshkosh (WI)
U of Wisconsin–Stout (WI)
U of Wisconsin–Superior (WI)
U of Wisconsin–Whitewater (WI)
U of Wyoming (WY)
Ursuline Coll (OH)
Utah State U (UT)
Valdosta State U (GA)
Vanderbilt U (TN)
Virginia Union U (VA)
Virginia Wesleyan Coll (VA)
Walsh U (OH)
Washington Adventist U (MD)
Washington State U (WA)
Waynesburg U (PA)
Wayne State Coll (NE)
Wayne State U (MI)
West Chester U of Pennsylvania (PA)
Western Carolina U (NC)
Western Illinois U (IL)
Western Kentucky U (KY)
Western Washington U (WA)
Westfield State Coll (MA)
Westminster Coll (UT)
West Virginia Wesleyan Coll (WV)
Wheelock Coll (MA)
Widener U (PA)
William Paterson U of New Jersey (NJ)
William Penn U (IA)
Winona State U (MN)
Winston-Salem State U (NC)
Winthrop U (SC)
Xavier U (OH)
Xavier U of Louisiana (LA)
York Coll (NE)
York U (ON, Canada)
Youngstown State U (OH)

SPECIAL EDUCATION (ADMINISTRATION)

Wright State U (OH)

SPECIAL EDUCATION (DEVELOPMENTALLY DELAYED)

Tabor Coll (KS)

SPECIAL EDUCATION (EARLY CHILDHOOD)

Canisius Coll (NY)
Cazenovia Coll (NY)
Daytona State Coll (FL)
Delaware State U (DE)
Eastern Washington U (WA)
Edgewood Coll (WI)
Harding U (AR)
Inter American U of Puerto Rico, Aguadilla Campus (PR)
Inter American U of Puerto Rico, Ponce Campus (PR)
Juniata Coll (PA)
Keuka Coll (NY)
Millersville U of Pennsylvania (PA)
Prescott Coll (AZ)
Roberts Wesleyan Coll (NY)
Silver Lake Coll (WI)
State U of New York Coll at Geneseo (NY)
U of Illinois at Urbana–Champaign (IL)
U of Northern Iowa (IA)
U of Vermont (VT)

SPECIAL EDUCATION (EMOTIONALLY DISTURBED)

Augsburg Coll (MN)
Central Michigan U (MI)
Eastern Mennonite U (VA)
Eastern Michigan U (MI)
Grand Valley State U (MI)
Greensboro Coll (NC)
Hope Coll (MI)
Loras Coll (IA)
Marywood U (PA)
Minnesota State U Moorhead (MN)
Northern Michigan U (MI)
Tabor Coll (KS)
Trinity Christian Coll (IL)
U of Maine at Farmington (ME)
U of South Florida (FL)
The U of Toledo (OH)
Western Michigan U (MI)
Wright State U (OH)

SPECIAL EDUCATION (GIFTED AND TALENTED)

Flagler Coll (FL)
Grand Valley State U (MI)
Texas Christian U (TX)
Wright State U (OH)

SPECIAL EDUCATION (HEARING IMPAIRED)

Augustana Coll (SD)
Barton Coll (NC)
Boston U (MA)
Bowling Green State U (OH)
The Coll of New Jersey (NJ)
Converse Coll (SC)
Eastern Michigan U (MI)
Flagler Coll (FL)
Grand Valley State U (MI)
Indiana U of Pennsylvania (PA)
Michigan State U (MI)
Minot State U (ND)
Texas Christian U (TX)
U of Arkansas at Little Rock (AR)
U of Nebraska–Lincoln (NE)
The U of North Carolina at Greensboro (NC)
U of Science and Arts of Oklahoma (OK)
U of Southern Mississippi (MS)
The U of Toledo (OH)
U of Tulsa (OK)
Utah Valley U (UT)
Valdosta State U (GA)

SPECIAL EDUCATION (MENTALLY RETARDED)

Bowling Green State U (OH)
Brenau U (GA)
Central Michigan U (MI)
Columbus State U (GA)
Eastern Mennonite U (VA)
Eastern Michigan U (MI)
Elizabeth City State U (NC)
Grand Valley State U (MI)
Greensboro Coll (NC)
Loras Coll (IA)
Minnesota State U Moorhead (MN)
Minot State U (ND)
Northern Michigan U (MI)
Oakland City U (IN)
Prescott Coll (AZ)
Shaw U (NC)
Silver Lake Coll (WI)
Tabor Coll (KS)
Trinity Christian Coll (IL)
U of Maine at Farmington (ME)
U of Mary (ND)
The U of North Carolina at Charlotte (NC)
U of Northern Iowa (IA)
U of Rio Grande (OH)
U of South Florida (FL)
U of Wisconsin–Stout (WI)
Western Michigan U (MI)
Wright State U (OH)

SPECIAL EDUCATION (MULTIPLY DISABLED)

Ball State U (IN)
Bowling Green State U (OH)
Bradley U (IL)
Dominican Coll (NY)
Grand Valley State U (MI)
Northwest Missouri State U (MO)
Tabor Coll (KS)
U of Illinois at Urbana–Champaign (IL)
The U of North Carolina Wilmington (NC)
U of Northern Iowa (IA)
The U of Toledo (OH)
Wright State U (OH)

SPECIAL EDUCATION (ORTHOPEDIC AND OTHER PHYSICAL HEALTH IMPAIRMENTS)

Eastern Michigan U (MI)
Grand Valley State U (MI)
U of Puerto Rico at Bayamón (PR)
Wright State U (OH)

SPECIAL EDUCATION RELATED

Auburn U (AL)
Bowling Green State U (OH)
Dakota State U (SD)
East Carolina U (NC)
Eastern Nazarene Coll (MA)
Harding U (AR)
Hood Coll (MD)
Juniata Coll (PA)
Kean U (NJ)
Keene State Coll (NH)

Lock Haven U of Pennsylvania (PA)
Minot State U (ND)
Nevada State Coll at Henderson (NV)
Southeastern Oklahoma State U (OK)
U of Hartford (CT)
U of Missouri (MO)
U of Nebraska–Lincoln (NE)
U of Southern Indiana (IN)
The U of Toledo (OH)
U of Wyoming (WY)
Valdosta State U (GA)
Wright State U (OH)
Xavier U of Louisiana (LA)
York Coll of Pennsylvania (PA)

SPECIAL EDUCATION (SPECIFIC LEARNING DISABILITIES)

Appalachian State U (NC)
Aquinas Coll (MI)
Baldwin-Wallace Coll (OH)
Bethune-Cookman U (FL)
Bowling Green State U (OH)
Bradley U (IL)
Eastern Mennonite U (VA)
Eastern Michigan U (MI)
Elizabeth City State U (NC)
Flagler Coll (FL)
Greensboro Coll (NC)
Harding U (AR)
Hope Coll (MI)
Malone U (OH)
Michigan State U (MI)
Minnesota State U Moorhead (MN)
Northeastern State U (OK)
Prescott Coll (AZ)
Silver Lake Coll (WI)
State U of New York at New Paltz (NY)
Tabor Coll (KS)
Trinity Christian Coll (IL)
U of Maine at Farmington (ME)
U of Rio Grande (OH)
U of South Carolina Upstate (SC)
U of South Florida (FL)
The U of Toledo (OH)
West Virginia Wesleyan Coll (WV)
Wheeling Jesuit U (WV)
Winston-Salem State U (NC)
Wright State U (OH)

SPECIAL EDUCATION (SPEECH OR LANGUAGE IMPAIRED)

Alabama Ag and Mech U (AL)
Baylor U (TX)
Brooklyn Coll of the City U of New York (NY)
Buffalo State Coll, State U of New York (NY)
Eastern Michigan U (MI)
Emerson Coll (MA)
Ithaca Coll (NY)
Kutztown U of Pennsylvania (PA)
Long Island U, Brooklyn Campus (NY)
Louisiana Tech U (LA)
Minot State U (ND)
Pace U (NY)
State U of New York Coll at Cortland (NY)
U of Nebraska at Omaha (NE)
The U of Toledo (OH)
Wayne State U (MI)

SPECIAL EDUCATION (VISION IMPAIRED)

Eastern Michigan U (MI)
Hood Coll (MD)
Kutztown U of Pennsylvania (PA)
St. Francis Coll (NY)
The U of Toledo (OH)

SPECIAL PRODUCTS MARKETING

Buffalo State Coll, State U of New York (NY)
Concord U (WV)
Dominican U (IL)
Fashion Inst of Technology (NY)
Iowa State U of Science and Technology (IA)
Johnson & Wales U (RI)
Rochester Inst of Technology (NY)
Saint Joseph's U (PA)
Stephen F. Austin State U (TX)
U of Alberta (AB, Canada)
U of Maryland Eastern Shore (MD)
U of North Texas (TX)

SPEECH AND RHETORIC

Alabama State U (AL)
Albany State U (GA)
Arkansas State U—Jonesboro (AR)
Asbury U (KY)
Ashland U (OH)
Auburn U (AL)
Augsburg Coll (MN)
Augustana Coll (IL)
Ball State U (IN)
Bates Coll (ME)
Belmont U (TN)
Bemidji State U (MN)
Bethune-Cookman U (FL)
Black Hills State U (SD)
Bloomsburg U of Pennsylvania (PA)
Bob Jones U (SC)
Bowling Green State U (OH)
Brigham Young U (UT)
Butler U (IN)
California Polytechnic State U, San Luis Obispo (CA)
California State U, East Bay (CA)
California State U, Fresno (CA)
California State U, Fullerton (CA)
California State U, Long Beach (CA)
California State U, Los Angeles (CA)
Calvin Coll (MI)
Cape Breton U (NS, Canada)
Carson-Newman Coll (TN)
Clarion U of Pennsylvania (PA)
Clark Atlanta U (GA)
Clemson U (SC)
The Coll at Brockport, State U of New York (NY)
The Coll of New Jersey (NJ)
Coll of Saint Benedict (MN)
Concordia Coll (MN)
Cornell Coll (IA)
Cornerstone U (MI)
Creighton U (NE)
Denison U (OH)
Dickinson State U (ND)
Drake U (IA)
Duquesne U (PA)
East Central U (OK)
Eastern Illinois U (IL)
East Tennessee State U (TN)
East Texas Baptist U (TX)
Emerson Coll (MA)
Evangel U (MO)
Fairmont State U (WV)
Ferris State U (MI)
Frostburg State U (MD)
George Mason U (VA)
The George Washington U (DC)
Georgia Coll & State U (GA)
Georgia Southern U (GA)
Georgia State U (GA)
Gonzaga U (WA)
Governors State U (IL)
Graceland U (IA)
Greenville Coll (IL)
Gustavus Adolphus Coll (MN)
Hannibal-LaGrange Coll (MO)
Hardin-Simmons U (TX)
Henderson State U (AR)
Houston Baptist U (TX)
Humboldt State U (CA)
Illinois Coll (IL)
Illinois State U (IL)
Indiana U South Bend (IN)
Iowa State U of Science and Technology (IA)
Ithaca Coll (NY)
Jackson State U (MS)
Kent State U (OH)
Kutztown U of Pennsylvania (PA)
Lehman Coll of the City U of New York (NY)
Lewis U (IL)
Lipscomb U (TN)
Lock Haven U of Pennsylvania (PA)
Long Island U, Brooklyn Campus (NY)
Louisiana Coll (LA)
Louisiana State U and Ag and Mech Coll (LA)
Louisiana State U in Shreveport (LA)
Louisiana Tech U (LA)
Madonna U (MI)
Manchester Coll (IN)
Marietta Coll (OH)
Marshall U (WV)
The Master's Coll and Sem (CA)
McKendree U (IL)
McNeese State U (LA)
Metropolitan State Coll of Denver (CO)
Miami U (OH)
Minnesota State U Mankato (MN)
Minnesota State U Moorhead (MN)
Minot State U (ND)
Mississippi Valley State U (MS)
Monmouth Coll (IL)
Mount Mercy Coll (IA)
Murray State U (KY)
Nebraska Wesleyan U (NE)
Newberry Coll (SC)
North Central Coll (IL)
Northeastern Illinois U (IL)
Northeastern State U (OK)
Northern Kentucky U (KY)
Northern State U (SD)
Northwestern Coll (IA)
Northwestern Oklahoma State U (OK)
Northwestern State U of Louisiana (LA)
Northwest Missouri State U (MO)
Ohio U (OH)
Oklahoma Baptist U (OK)
Oklahoma Christian U (OK)
Oklahoma City U (OK)
Old Dominion U (VA)
Oregon State U (OR)
Ouachita Baptist U (AR)
Pace U (NY)
Pepperdine U, Malibu (CA)
Portland State U (OR)
Rider U (NJ)
St. Catherine U (MN)
St. Cloud State U (MN)
Saint John's U (MN)
St. John's U (NY)
St. Joseph's Coll, Long Island Campus (NY)
St. Joseph's Coll, New York (NY)
San Diego State U (CA)
San Jose State U (CA)
Shippensburg U of Pennsylvania (PA)
South Dakota State U (SD)
Southeast Missouri State U (MO)
Southern Illinois U Carbondale (IL)
Southern Illinois U Edwardsville (IL)
Southern U and Ag and Mech Coll (LA)
Southern Utah U (UT)
State U of New York at New Paltz (NY)
State U of New York Coll at Cortland (NY)
State U of New York Coll at Oneonta (NY)
State U of New York Coll at Potsdam (NY)
Stephen F. Austin State U (TX)
Susquehanna U (PA)
Syracuse U (NY)
Tarleton State U (TX)
Temple U (PA)
Texas A&M U (TX)
Texas Southern U (TX)
Texas State U–San Marcos (TX)
Texas Tech U (TX)
Texas Wesleyan U (TX)
Trinity U (TX)
Troy U (AL)
Truman State U (MO)
Union U (TN)
U at Albany, State U of New York (NY)
The U of Alabama in Huntsville (AL)
U of Arkansas at Little Rock (AR)
U of Arkansas at Monticello (AR)
U of Arkansas at Pine Bluff (AR)
U of California, Berkeley (CA)
U of Central Missouri (MO)
U of Dubuque (IA)
U of Georgia (GA)
U of Houston–Downtown (TX)
U of Illinois at Urbana–Champaign (IL)
The U of Iowa (IA)
The U of Kansas (KS)
U of Louisiana at Monroe (LA)
U of Montevallo (AL)
U of Nebraska at Kearney (NE)
U of Nebraska at Omaha (NE)
U of New Mexico (NM)
U of North Alabama (AL)
The U of North Carolina at Greensboro (NC)
U of Northern Iowa (IA)
U of North Texas (TX)
U of Pittsburgh (PA)
U of Richmond (VA)
The U of South Dakota (SD)
U of South Florida (FL)
The U of Tennessee (TN)
The U of Texas at Arlington (TX)
The U of Texas at El Paso (TX)
The U of Texas at Tyler (TX)
U of the Cumberlands (KY)
U of the Virgin Islands (VI)
U of Washington (WA)
U of Waterloo (ON, Canada)
U of Wisconsin–Platteville (WI)
U of Wisconsin–River Falls (WI)
U of Wisconsin–Superior (WI)
U of Wisconsin–Whitewater (WI)
Utah State U (UT)
Valdosta State U (GA)
Wabash Coll (IN)
West Chester U of Pennsylvania (PA)
West Virginia Wesleyan Coll (WV)
Willamette U (OR)
William Jewell Coll (MO)
Winona State U (MN)
Yeshiva U (NY)
York Coll of the City U of New York (NY)
Youngstown State U (OH)

SPEECH-LANGUAGE PATHOLOGY

Abilene Christian U (TX)
Augustana Coll (IL)
Ball State U (IN)
Bob Jones U (SC)
Brooklyn Coll of the City U of New York (NY)
Columbia Coll (SC)
Duquesne U (PA)
Eastern Michigan U (MI)
Eastern Washington U (WA)
Emerson Coll (MA)
Grambling State U (LA)
Harding U (AR)
Jackson State U (MS)
James Madison U (VA)
Lehman Coll of the City U of New York (NY)
Loyola U Maryland (MD)
Marshall U (WV)
Marymount Manhattan Coll (NY)
Miami U (OH)
Miami U Hamilton (OH)
Mississippi U for Women (MS)
Mount Saint Mary Coll (NY)
Nazareth Coll of Rochester (NY)
Nevada State Coll at Henderson (NV)
Northern Michigan U (MI)
Oklahoma State U (OK)
Pace U (NY)
Rockhurst U (MO)
St. Cloud State U (MN)
Saint Xavier U (IL)
Texas Christian U (TX)
Towson U (MD)
U of Central Missouri (MO)
U of Maryland, Coll Park (MD)
U of Montevallo (AL)
U of Nebraska–Lincoln (NE)
U of Nevada, Reno (NV)
U of Northern Colorado (CO)
U of Northern Iowa (IA)
U of Oklahoma Health Sciences Center (OK)
U of Science and Arts of Oklahoma (OK)
The U of Tennessee (TN)
The U of Toledo (OH)
The U of Western Ontario (ON, Canada)
U of West Georgia (GA)
U of Wisconsin–Whitewater (WI)
Valdosta State U (GA)
Xavier U of Louisiana (LA)

SPEECH TEACHER EDUCATION

Anderson U (IN)
Arkansas Tech U (AR)
Augustana Coll (SD)
Baptist Bible Coll of Pennsylvania (PA)
Bemidji State U (MN)
Boston U (MA)
Bowling Green State U (OH)
Bradley U (IL)
Brigham Young U (UT)
Brooklyn Coll of the City U of New York (NY)
Buena Vista U (IA)
Capital U (OH)
Central Michigan U (MI)
Colorado State U (CO)
Concordia U Chicago (IL)
Culver-Stockton Coll (MO)
Dickinson State U (ND)
Dordt Coll (IA)
East Central U (OK)
East Texas Baptist U (TX)
Elmira Coll (NY)
Evangel U (MO)
Harding U (AR)
Hardin-Simmons U (TX)
Howard Payne U (TX)
Indiana U Bloomington (IN)
Indiana U–Purdue U Fort Wayne (IN)
Indiana U–Purdue U Indianapolis (IN)
Kean U (NJ)
King Coll (TN)
Louisiana Tech U (LA)
Lubbock Christian U (TX)
McKendree U (IL)
McNeese State U (LA)
Minnesota State U Moorhead (MN)
Missouri Western State U (MO)
Murray State U (KY)
Northeastern State U (OK)
Northwestern Coll (IA)
Northwestern Oklahoma State U (OK)
Northwestern State U of Louisiana (LA)
Northwest U (WA)
Oklahoma City U (OK)
Saginaw Valley State U (MI)
St. Ambrose U (IA)
St. Catherine U (MN)
St. Cloud State U (MN)
Southeastern Louisiana U (LA)
Southeast Missouri State U (MO)
Southwest Baptist U (MO)
Southwestern Coll (KS)
Southwest Minnesota State U (MN)
State U of New York at New Paltz (NY)
Taylor U (IN)
Texas A&M U–Corpus Christi (TX)
Texas Wesleyan U (TX)
Trevecca Nazarene U (TN)
The U of Arizona (AZ)
U of Indianapolis (IN)
The U of Iowa (IA)
U of Louisiana at Monroe (LA)
U of Maine (ME)
U of Michigan–Flint (MI)
U of Northern Iowa (IA)
U of Rio Grande (OH)
U of St. Thomas (MN)
The U of South Dakota (SD)
U of Windsor (ON, Canada)
Wartburg Coll (IA)
Wayne State Coll (NE)
Western Washington U (WA)
William Jewell Coll (MO)
York Coll (NE)
York U (ON, Canada)

SPORT AND FITNESS ADMINISTRATION/ MANAGEMENT

Abilene Christian U (TX)
Adelphi U (NY)
Albertus Magnus Coll (CT)
Alderson-Broaddus Coll (WV)
Alvernia U (PA)
American Public U System (WV)
American U (DC)
Arkansas State U—Jonesboro (AR)
Asbury U (KY)
Augustana Coll (SD)
Averett U (VA)
Baker U (KS)
Baldwin-Wallace Coll (OH)
Barry U (FL)
Barton Coll (NC)
Belhaven U (MS)
Bemidji State U (MN)
Bethany Coll (KS)
Bethany Coll (WV)
Bethel Coll (IN)
Black Hills State U (SD)
Bluffton U (OH)
Bowling Green State U (OH)
Bridgewater State Coll (MA)
Brock U (ON, Canada)
Buena Vista U (IA)
Calvin Coll (MI)
Cape Breton U (NS, Canada)
Cazenovia Coll (NY)
Cedarville U (OH)
Centenary Coll (NJ)
Central Christian Coll of Kansas (KS)
Central Michigan U (MI)
Chowan U (NC)
Claflin U (SC)
Clarke Coll (IA)
Clayton State U (GA)
Cleveland State U (OH)
Coastal Carolina U (SC)
Coker Coll (SC)
The Coll at Brockport, State U of New York (NY)
The Coll of Idaho (ID)
Coll of Mount St. Joseph (OH)
Columbia Coll (MO)
Columbia Southern U (AL)
Concordia U Wisconsin (WI)
Coppin State U (MD)
Corban U (OR)
Crown Coll (MN)
Culver-Stockton Coll (MO)
Dakota Wesleyan U (SD)
Dana Coll (NE)
Davenport U, Grand Rapids (MI)
Defiance Coll (OH)
Delaware State U (DE)
DeSales U (PA)

INDEXES

Drury U (MO)
Eastern Connecticut State U (CT)
Eastern Mennonite U (VA)
Eastern Nazarene Coll (MA)
East Tennessee State U (TN)
Ecclesia Coll (AR)
Edinboro U of Pennsylvania (PA)
Elmhurst Coll (IL)
Elon U (NC)
Emmanuel Coll (GA)
Endicott Coll (MA)
Erskine Coll (SC)
Faulkner U (AL)
Ferrum Coll (VA)
Fitchburg State Coll (MA)
Flagler Coll (FL)
Florida Southern Coll (FL)
Florida State U (FL)
Fontbonne U (MO)
Fort Lewis Coll (CO)
Franklin Pierce U (NH)
Friends U (KS)
Frostburg State U (MD)
Gannon U (PA)
Gardner-Webb U (NC)
Georgia Southern U (GA)
Glenville State Coll (WV)
Globe Inst of Technology (NY)
Goldey-Beacom Coll (DE)
Gonzaga U (WA)
Grace Coll (IN)
Greensboro Coll (NC)
Greenville Coll (IL)
Guilford Coll (NC)
Hamline U (MN)
Hampton U (VA)
Harding U (AR)
Henderson State U (AR)
High Point U (NC)
Holy Family U (PA)
Howard Payne U (TX)
Huntingdon Coll (AL)
Husson U (ME)
Indiana Tech (IN)
Indiana Wesleyan U (IN)
Iowa Wesleyan Coll (IA)
Ithaca Coll (NY)
John Brown U (AR)
Johnson C. Smith U (NC)
Johnson State Coll (VT)
Judson U (IL)
Keiser U, Fort Lauderdale (FL)
Kennesaw State U (GA)
Kentucky Wesleyan Coll (KY)
Keystone Coll (PA)
King Coll (TN)
Lasell Coll (MA)
Laurentian U (ON, Canada)
LeTourneau U (TX)
Lewis U (IL)
Liberty U (VA)
Limestone Coll (SC)
Lincoln Coll–Normal (IL)
Lindenwood U (MO)
Lock Haven U of Pennsylvania (PA)
Longwood U (VA)
Loras Coll (IA)
Louisiana State U and Ag and Mech Coll (LA)
Lubbock Christian U (TX)
Lynchburg Coll (VA)
Madonna U (MI)
Malone U (OH)
Marian U (IN)
Marian U (WI)
Mars Hill Coll (NC)
Marymount U (VA)
Maryville U of Saint Louis (MO)
Medaille Coll (NY)
Menlo Coll (CA)
Messiah Coll (PA)
Methodist U (NC)
Miami U (OH)
MidAmerica Nazarene U (KS)
Midway Coll (KY)
Midwestern State U (TX)
Millikin U (IL)
Minnesota State U Mankato (MN)
Minnesota State U Moorhead (MN)
Minot State U (ND)
Misericordia U (PA)
Mississippi Coll (MS)
Missouri Baptist U (MO)
Mitchell Coll (CT)
Montana State U (MT)
Montana State U Billings (MT)
Morehead State U (KY)
Mount Ida Coll (MA)
Mount St. Mary's U (MD)
National U (CA)
Nebraska Wesleyan U (NE)
Neumann U (PA)
New England Coll (NH)
Niagara U (NY)
Nichols Coll (MA)
North Carolina State U (NC)
North Central Coll (IL)
North Dakota State U (ND)
Northern Kentucky U (KY)
Northern Michigan U (MI)
Northern State U (SD)
North Greenville U (SC)
Nova Southeastern U (FL)
Ohio Dominican U (OH)
Ohio Northern U (OH)
Oklahoma Baptist U (OK)
Oklahoma Christian U (OK)
Old Dominion U (VA)
Principia Coll (IL)
Quincy U (IL)
Reinhardt Coll (GA)
Rice U (TX)
Roanoke Coll (VA)
Robert Morris U (PA)
Rochester Coll (MI)
Rockhurst U (MO)
Rocky Mountain Coll (MT)
Rogers State U (OK)
Sacred Heart U (CT)
St. Ambrose U (IA)
St. Bonaventure U (NY)
St. John Fisher Coll (NY)
St. John's U (NY)
Saint Leo U (FL)
Saint Mary's Coll of California (CA)
St. Thomas U (FL)
Salem State Coll (MA)
Samford U (AL)
Schreiner U (TX)
Seattle Pacific U (WA)
Seton Hall U (NJ)
Seton Hill U (PA)
Shawnee State U (OH)
Siena Heights U (MI)
Simpson Coll (IA)
Slippery Rock U of Pennsylvania (PA)
Southeastern Louisiana U (LA)
Southeastern U (FL)
Southeast Missouri State U (MO)
Southern Adventist U (TN)
Southern Illinois U Carbondale (IL)
Southern New Hampshire U (NH)
Southwest Baptist U (MO)
Southwestern Assemblies of God U (TX)
Southwestern Coll (KS)
Spring Arbor U (MI)
State U of New York at Oswego (NY)
Stetson U (FL)
Tabor Coll (KS)
Taylor U (IN)
Tennessee Wesleyan Coll (TN)
Texas A&M U (TX)
Texas Lutheran U (TX)
Texas State U–San Marcos (TX)
Texas Wesleyan U (TX)
Thomas More Coll (KY)
Tiffin U (OH)
Towson U (MD)
Trevecca Nazarene U (TN)
Trine U (IN)
Troy U (AL)
Tusculum Coll (TN)
Union Coll (KY)
Union Coll (NE)
Union U (TN)
United States Sports Acad (AL)
The U of Akron (OH)
U of Alberta (AB, Canada)
U of Dayton (OH)
U of Delaware (DE)
U of Evansville (IN)
U of Florida (FL)
U of Georgia (GA)
U of Houston (TX)
U of Illinois at Urbana–Champaign (IL)
U of Indianapolis (IN)
The U of Iowa (IA)
U of Louisville (KY)
U of Mary (ND)
U of Mary Hardin-Baylor (TX)
U of Massachusetts Amherst (MA)
U of Memphis (TN)
U of Miami (FL)
U of Michigan (MI)
U of Minnesota, Crookston (MN)
U of Mount Union (OH)
U of Nebraska at Kearney (NE)
U of Nevada, Las Vegas (NV)
U of New England (ME)
U of North Florida (FL)
U of Pittsburgh at Bradford (PA)
U of Regina (SK, Canada)
U of Saint Mary (KS)
U of South Carolina (SC)
The U of Tampa (FL)
The U of Tennessee (TN)
The U of Texas at Austin (TX)
U of the Cumberlands (KY)
U of the Incarnate Word (TX)
U of the Sciences in Philadelphia (PA)
U of Tulsa (OK)
U of Windsor (ON, Canada)
U of Wisconsin–Parkside (WI)
Valparaiso U (IN)
Virginia Intermont Coll (VA)
Viterbo U (WI)
Wartburg Coll (IA)
Washington State U (WA)
Wayland Baptist U (TX)
Wayne State Coll (NE)
Western Carolina U (NC)
Western Kentucky U (KY)
Western New England Coll (MA)
Western State Coll of Colorado (CO)
West Virginia U (WV)
West Virginia Wesleyan Coll (WV)
Wichita State U (KS)
Widener U (PA)
William Penn U (IA)
Wilmington Coll (OH)
Wilmington U (DE)
Wilson Coll (PA)
Wingate U (NC)
Winona State U (MN)
Winston-Salem State U (NC)
Winthrop U (SC)
Xavier U (OH)
York Coll (NE)
York Coll of Pennsylvania (PA)
York U (ON, Canada)

STATISTICS

American U (DC)
American U of Beirut (Lebanon)
Appalachian State U (NC)
Barnard Coll (NY)
Baylor U (TX)
Bernard M. Baruch Coll of the City U of New York (NY)
Bowling Green State U (OH)
Brock U (ON, Canada)
California Polytechnic State U, San Luis Obispo (CA)
California State U, East Bay (CA)
California State U, Fullerton (CA)
California State U, Long Beach (CA)
Carnegie Mellon U (PA)
Case Western Reserve U (OH)
Central Michigan U (MI)
Colorado State U (CO)
Columbia U (NY)
Columbia U, School of General Studies (NY)
Concordia U (QC, Canada)
DePaul U (IL)
Eastern Michigan U (MI)
Florida Intl U (FL)
Florida State U (FL)
The George Washington U (DC)
Grace Coll (IN)
Grand Valley State U (MI)
Harvard U (MA)
Hunter Coll of the City U of New York (NY)
Idaho State U (ID)
Indiana U Bloomington (IN)
Indiana U–Purdue U Fort Wayne (IN)
Iowa State U of Science and Technology (IA)
Kansas State U (KS)
Lehigh U (PA)
Loyola U Chicago (IL)
Luther Coll (IA)
Marquette U (WI)
Memorial U of Newfoundland (NL, Canada)
Mercyhurst Coll (PA)
Miami U (OH)
Miami U Hamilton (OH)
Michigan State U (MI)
Michigan Technological U (MI)
Montana State U (MT)
Mount Holyoke Coll (MA)
North Carolina State U (NC)
North Dakota State U (ND)
Northwest Missouri State U (MO)
Oakland U (MI)
Ohio Northern U (OH)
Ohio Wesleyan U (OH)
Oklahoma State U (OK)
Old Dominion U (VA)
Penn State Abington (PA)
Penn State Altoona (PA)
Penn State Beaver (PA)
Penn State Berks (PA)
Penn State Brandywine (PA)
Penn State DuBois (PA)
Penn State Erie, The Behrend Coll (PA)
Penn State Fayette, The Eberly Campus (PA)
Penn State Greater Allegheny (PA)
Penn State Hazleton (PA)
Penn State Lehigh Valley (PA)
Penn State Mont Alto (PA)
Penn State New Kensington (PA)
Penn State Schuylkill (PA)
Penn State Shenango (PA)
Penn State U Park (PA)
Penn State Wilkes-Barre (PA)
Penn State Worthington Scranton (PA)
Penn State York (PA)
Purdue U (IN)
Queen's U at Kingston (ON, Canada)
Rice U (TX)
Rochester Inst of Technology (NY)
Rutgers, The State U of New Jersey, New Brunswick (NJ)
St. Cloud State U (MN)
St. John Fisher Coll (NY)
San Diego State U (CA)
San Francisco State U (CA)
Simon Fraser U (BC, Canada)
Slippery Rock U of Pennsylvania (PA)
Sonoma State U (CA)
Southern Methodist U (TX)
Stanford U (CA)
State U of New York Coll at Oneonta (NY)
The U of Akron (OH)
U of Alberta (AB, Canada)
The U of British Columbia (BC, Canada)
U of California, Berkeley (CA)
U of California, Davis (CA)
U of California, Los Angeles (CA)
U of California, Riverside (CA)
U of California, Santa Barbara (CA)
U of Central Florida (FL)
U of Chicago (IL)
U of Connecticut (CT)
U of Florida (FL)
U of Georgia (GA)
U of Guelph (ON, Canada)
U of Illinois at Chicago (IL)
U of Illinois at Urbana–Champaign (IL)
The U of Iowa (IA)
U of King's Coll (NS, Canada)
U of Manitoba (MB, Canada)
U of Maryland, Baltimore County (MD)
U of Michigan (MI)
U of Minnesota, Duluth (MN)
U of Missouri (MO)
U of Missouri–Kansas City (MO)
U of Nebraska at Kearney (NE)
U of Nevada, Las Vegas (NV)
U of New Brunswick Fredericton (NB, Canada)
U of New Mexico (NM)
The U of North Carolina Wilmington (NC)
U of North Florida (FL)
U of Ottawa (ON, Canada)
U of Pennsylvania (PA)
U of Pittsburgh (PA)
U of Regina (SK, Canada)
U of Rochester (NY)
U of Saskatchewan (SK, Canada)
U of South Carolina (SC)
U of South Florida (FL)
The U of Tennessee (TN)
The U of Tennessee at Martin (TN)
The U of Texas at Dallas (TX)
The U of Texas at El Paso (TX)
The U of Texas at San Antonio (TX)
U of Vermont (VT)
U of Washington (WA)
U of Waterloo (ON, Canada)
The U of Western Ontario (ON, Canada)
U of Wisconsin–Madison (WI)
U of Wisconsin–Milwaukee (WI)
U of Wyoming (WY)
Utah State U (UT)
Virginia Polytechnic Inst and State U (VA)
Washington U in St. Louis (MO)
Western Michigan U (MI)
Winona State U (MN)
Wright State U (OH)
Xavier U of Louisiana (LA)
York U (ON, Canada)

STATISTICS RELATED

Carnegie Mellon U (PA)
Ohio Northern U (OH)
United States Military Acad (NY)

STRUCTURAL BIOLOGY

U of Connecticut (CT)

STRUCTURAL ENGINEERING

Lehigh U (PA)
Penn State Harrisburg (PA)
U at Buffalo, the State U of New York (NY)
U of California, San Diego (CA)
U of Central Florida (FL)
U of Illinois at Urbana–Champaign (IL)
U of Southern California (CA)
The U of Toledo (OH)
Western Michigan U (MI)

STUDENT COUNSELING AND PERSONNEL SERVICES RELATED

Samford U (AL)
Southern Arkansas U–Magnolia (AR)

SUBSTANCE ABUSE/ ADDICTION COUNSELING

Alvernia U (PA)
Argosy U, Chicago (IL)
Argosy U, Denver (CO)
Argosy U, Nashville (TN)
Argosy U, Orange County (CA)
Argosy U, Phoenix (AZ)
Argosy U, Salt Lake City (UT)
Argosy U, Schaumburg (IL)
Argosy U, Seattle (WA)
Argosy U, Twin Cities (MN)
Argosy U, Washington DC (VA)
Bethany U (CA)
Calumet Coll of Saint Joseph (IN)
Chowan U (NC)
The Coll at Brockport, State U of New York (NY)
Coll of St. Joseph (VT)
Dominican U (IL)
Hawai'i Pacific U (HI)
Indiana U–Purdue U Fort Wayne (IN)
Indiana Wesleyan U (IN)
Minot State U (ND)
Newman U (KS)
Northwestern State U of Louisiana (LA)
Rhode Island Coll (RI)
St. Catherine U (MN)
St. Cloud State U (MN)
Tiffin U (OH)
U of Lethbridge (AB, Canada)
U of Mary (ND)
The U of South Dakota (SD)
The U of Texas–Pan American (TX)
The U of Western Ontario (ON, Canada)
Viterbo U (WI)
Washburn U (KS)

SURGICAL TECHNOLOGY

Nebraska Methodist Coll (NE)

SURVEYING ENGINEERING

Florida Atlantic U (FL)
State U of New York Coll of Technology at Alfred (NY)
U of Maine (ME)

SURVEY TECHNOLOGY

East Tennessee State U (TN)
Ferris State U (MI)
Idaho State U (ID)
Metropolitan State Coll of Denver (CO)
Michigan Technological U (MI)
New Mexico State U (NM)
Nicholls State U (LA)
Oregon Inst of Technology (OR)
Penn State Wilkes-Barre (PA)
Polytechnic U of Puerto Rico (PR)
Southern Polytechnic State U (GA)
Texas A&M U–Corpus Christi (TX)
Thomas Edison State Coll (NJ)
Troy U (AL)
The U of Akron (OH)
U of Alaska Anchorage (AK)
U of Arkansas at Little Rock (AR)
U of Arkansas at Monticello (AR)
U of Florida (FL)
U of Houston (TX)
U of Maine (ME)
U of New Brunswick Fredericton (NB, Canada)
U of Wisconsin–Madison (WI)

SWEDISH

Augustana Coll (IL)
Brigham Young U (UT)

SYSTEM ADMINISTRATION

Champlain Coll (VT)
Dordt Coll (IA)
Michigan Technological U (MI)
Rochester Inst of Technology (NY)
Simmons Coll (MA)

SYSTEM, NETWORKING, AND LAN/WAN MANAGEMENT
Alcorn State U (MS)
Capella U (MN)
Champlain Coll (VT)
Dakota State U (SD)
Herzing U (GA)
Northern Michigan U (MI)
Rochester Inst of Technology (NY)
Texas A&M U (TX)
U of Hawaii–West Oahu (HI)
U of Northern Iowa (IA)
Westwood Coll–Anaheim (CA)
Westwood Coll–Annandale Campus (VA)
Westwood Coll–Arlington Ballston Campus (VA)
Westwood Coll–Atlanta Midtown (GA)
Westwood Coll–Atlanta Northlake (GA)
Westwood Coll–Chicago Du Page (IL)
Westwood Coll–Chicago Loop Campus (IL)
Westwood Coll–Chicago O'Hare Airport (IL)
Westwood Coll–Chicago River Oaks (IL)
Westwood Coll–Dallas (TX)
Westwood Coll–Denver North (CO)
Westwood Coll–Fort Worth (TX)
Westwood Coll–Houston South Campus (TX)
Westwood Coll–Inland Empire (CA)
Westwood Coll–Los Angeles (CA)
Westwood Coll–Online Campus (CO)
Westwood Coll–South Bay Campus (CA)

SYSTEMS ENGINEERING
Case Western Reserve U (OH)
Delaware State U (DE)
Eastern Nazarene Coll (MA)
George Mason U (VA)
The George Washington U (DC)
Lehigh U (PA)
Providence Coll (RI)
Rochester Inst of Technology (NY)
Southern Polytechnic State U (GA)
Stevens Inst of Technology (NJ)
United States Military Acad (NY)
United States Naval Acad (MD)
Universidad de las Américas–Puebla (Mexico)
The U of Arizona (AZ)
U of Florida (FL)
U of Maine (ME)
U of Pennsylvania (PA)
U of Southern California (CA)
U of Virginia (VA)
U of Waterloo (ON, Canada)
U of Wyoming (WY)
Washington U in St. Louis (MO)
Wright State U (OH)

SYSTEMS SCIENCE AND THEORY
Carnegie Mellon U (PA)
Indiana U Bloomington (IN)
James Madison U (VA)
Marshall U (WV)
Stanford U (CA)
United States Military Acad (NY)
Washington U in St. Louis (MO)
Wright State U (OH)
Yale U (CT)

TAMIL
U of Chicago (IL)

TAXATION
Drexel U (PA)
Fontbonne U (MO)
Grand Valley State U (MI)

TECHNICAL AND BUSINESS WRITING
Bob Jones U (SC)
Boise State U (ID)
Bowling Green State U (OH)
Brescia U (KY)
Carlow U (PA)
Carnegie Mellon U (PA)
Cedarville U (OH)
Champlain Coll (VT)
Coker Coll (SC)
Drexel U (PA)
Eastern Michigan U (MI)
Elizabethtown Coll (PA)
Farmingdale State Coll (NY)
Ferris State U (MI)
Fitchburg State Coll (MA)
Indiana U–Purdue U Fort Wayne (IN)
Iowa State U of Science and Technology (IA)
James Madison U (VA)
Juniata Coll (PA)
King Coll (TN)
Kutztown U of Pennsylvania (PA)
Lubbock Christian U (TX)
Madonna U (MI)
Maryville Coll (TN)
Miami U Hamilton (OH)
Michigan State U (MI)
Michigan Technological U (MI)
Missouri State U (MO)
Montana Tech of The U of Montana (MT)
Mount Mary Coll (WI)
New Jersey Inst of Technology (NJ)
New Mexico Inst of Mining and Technology (NM)
New York Inst of Technology (NY)
Ohio Northern U (OH)
Penn State Berks (PA)
Penn State Lehigh Valley (PA)
Pennsylvania Coll of Technology (PA)
Pittsburg State U (KS)
Salem State Coll (MA)
San Francisco State U (CA)
Slippery Rock U of Pennsylvania (PA)
Spring Arbor U (MI)
Tarleton State U (TX)
Tennessee Technological U (TN)
Texas Tech U (TX)
U of Arkansas at Fort Smith (AR)
U of Arkansas at Little Rock (AR)
U of Baltimore (MD)
U of Hartford (CT)
U of Houston–Downtown (TX)
U of Idaho (ID)
U of Rhode Island (RI)
U of Washington (WA)
U of Wisconsin–Stout (WI)
Valparaiso U (IN)
Weber State U (UT)
Webster U (MO)
Winthrop U (SC)
Worcester Polytechnic Inst (MA)
York Coll of Pennsylvania (PA)
York U (ON, Canada)
Youngstown State U (OH)

TECHNICAL TEACHER EDUCATION
Bowling Green State U (OH)
Eastern Illinois U (IL)
Ferris State U (MI)
Mississippi State U (MS)
Montana State U (MT)
New York Inst of Technology (NY)
Northern Arizona U (AZ)
The Ohio State U (OH)
Oklahoma State U (OK)
Pittsburg State U (KS)
Queen's U at Kingston (ON, Canada)
Rhode Island Coll (RI)
South Dakota State U (SD)
The U of Akron (OH)
U of Arkansas (AR)
U of Georgia (GA)
U of Idaho (ID)
U of Illinois at Urbana–Champaign (IL)
U of Missouri (MO)
U of Nebraska at Kearney (NE)
U of Saskatchewan (SK, Canada)
The U of Tennessee (TN)
U of Wisconsin–Stout (WI)
Utah State U (UT)
Valley City State U (ND)
Wayne State U (MI)
Wright State U (OH)

TECHNOLOGY/INDUSTRIAL ARTS TEACHER EDUCATION
Appalachian State U (NC)
Ball State U (IN)
Bemidji State U (MN)
Berea Coll (KY)
Bowling Green State U (OH)
Buffalo State Coll, State U of New York (NY)
Central Connecticut State U (CT)
Central Michigan U (MI)
The Coll of New Jersey (NJ)
Coll of the Ozarks (MO)
Colorado State U (CO)
Drury U (MO)
Eastern Michigan U (MI)
Fitchburg State Coll (MA)
Georgia Southern U (GA)
Humboldt State U (CA)
Illinois State U (IL)
Jackson State U (MS)
Keene State Coll (NH)
Kent State U (OH)
Lindenwood U (MO)
Michigan Technological U (MI)
Middle Tennessee State U (TN)
Millersville U of Pennsylvania (PA)
Mississippi State U (MS)
Missouri State U (MO)
Murray State U (KY)
New Mexico Highlands U (NM)
New York City Coll of Technology of the City U of New York (NY)
North Carolina State U (NC)
Northern Arizona U (AZ)
Northern Michigan U (MI)
Ohio Northern U (OH)
The Ohio State U (OH)
Pittsburg State U (KS)
Purdue U (IN)
Rhode Island Coll (RI)
St. Cloud State U (MN)
St. Petersburg Coll (FL)
South Carolina State U (SC)
Southeast Missouri State U (MO)
Southwestern Oklahoma State U (OK)
State U of New York at Oswego (NY)
Texas A&M U–Corpus Christi (TX)
Texas Wesleyan U (TX)
U of Idaho (ID)
The U of Montana Western (MT)
U of Nevada, Reno (NV)
U of New Mexico (NM)
U of Northern Iowa (IA)
U of Southern Mississippi (MS)
U of the Ozarks (AR)
U of Wisconsin–Stout (WI)
U of Wyoming (WY)
Utah State U (UT)
Valley City State U (ND)
Viterbo U (WI)
Wayne State Coll (NE)
Western Michigan U (MI)
Western Washington U (WA)
Westfield State Coll (MA)

TELECOMMUNICATIONS TECHNOLOGY
Ball State U (IN)
California State U, East Bay (CA)
Ferris State U (MI)
Inter American U of Puerto Rico, Bayamón Campus (PR)
Ithaca Coll (NY)
Lawrence Technological U (MI)
Murray State U (KY)
National U (CA)
New York City Coll of Technology of the City U of New York (NY)
New York Inst of Technology (NY)
Pace U (NY)
Pepperdine U, Malibu (CA)
Rochester Inst of Technology (NY)
St. John's U (NY)
Southern Polytechnic State U (GA)
Spartan Coll of Aeronautics and Technology (OK)
U of Wisconsin–Platteville (WI)

TEXTILE SCIENCE
Michigan State U (MI)
North Carolina State U (NC)

TEXTILE SCIENCES AND ENGINEERING
Auburn U (AL)
Clemson U (SC)
Georgia Inst of Technology (GA)
North Carolina State U (NC)
Philadelphia U (PA)
U of Massachusetts Dartmouth (MA)

THEATER DESIGN AND TECHNOLOGY
The Art Inst of California–Hollywood (CA)
Bard Coll at Simon's Rock (MA)
Baylor U (TX)
Bennington Coll (VT)
Boston U (MA)
Brigham Young U (UT)
California Inst of the Arts (CA)
Centenary Coll (NJ)
Central Michigan U (MI)
Coker Coll (SC)
Coll of Santa Fe (NM)
Coll of the Ozarks (MO)
Columbia Coll Chicago (IL)
Cornell U (NY)
Cornish Coll of the Arts (WA)
DePaul U (IL)
Doane Coll (NE)
Elon U (NC)
Emerson Coll (MA)
Fitchburg State Coll (MA)
Five Towns Coll (NY)
Greensboro Coll (NC)
Huntington U (IN)
Illinois Wesleyan U (IL)
Ithaca Coll (NY)
Kean U (NJ)
Keene State Coll (NH)
Lindenwood U (MO)
Memorial U of Newfoundland (NL, Canada)
Michigan Technological U (MI)
Millikin U (IL)
New York City Coll of Technology of the City U of New York (NY)
Northwest Missouri State U (MO)
Oakland U (MI)
Ohio U (OH)
Oklahoma City U (OK)
Oral Roberts U (OK)
Penn State Abington (PA)
Penn State Altoona (PA)
Penn State Beaver (PA)
Penn State Berks (PA)
Penn State Brandywine (PA)
Penn State DuBois (PA)
Penn State Erie, The Behrend Coll (PA)
Penn State Fayette, The Eberly Campus (PA)
Penn State Greater Allegheny (PA)
Penn State Hazleton (PA)
Penn State Lehigh Valley (PA)
Penn State Mont Alto (PA)
Penn State New Kensington (PA)
Penn State Schuylkill (PA)
Penn State Shenango (PA)
Penn State U Park (PA)
Penn State Wilkes-Barre (PA)
Penn State Worthington Scranton (PA)
Penn State York (PA)
Purchase Coll, State U of New York (NY)
Rocky Mountain Coll (MT)
Salem State Coll (MA)
Seton Hill U (PA)
Shenandoah U (VA)
Slippery Rock U of Pennsylvania (PA)
State U of New York at Binghamton (NY)
State U of New York at New Paltz (NY)
Stephens Coll (MO)
Texas Tech U (TX)
Trinity U (TX)
U of Alaska Fairbanks (AK)
U of Alberta (AB, Canada)
The U of Arizona (AZ)
U of Connecticut (CT)
U of Delaware (DE)
The U of Kansas (KS)
U of Lethbridge (AB, Canada)
U of Miami (FL)
U of Michigan (MI)
U of Michigan–Flint (MI)
U of New Mexico (NM)
U of North Carolina School of the Arts (NC)
U of Regina (SK, Canada)
U of Southern California (CA)
Vanguard U of Southern California (CA)
Webster U (MO)
Western State Coll of Colorado (CO)
Wright State U (OH)

THEATER LITERATURE, HISTORY AND CRITICISM
Albertus Magnus Coll (CT)
Averett U (VA)
Bard Coll (NY)
Bard Coll at Simon's Rock (MA)
Bennington Coll (VT)
Boston U (MA)
Bowdoin Coll (ME)
Buena Vista U (IA)
Clark Atlanta U (GA)
DePaul U (IL)
Eugene Lang Coll The New School for Liberal Arts (NY)
Keene State Coll (NH)
Marymount Manhattan Coll (NY)
Memorial U of Newfoundland (NL, Canada)
Moravian Coll (PA)
Saint Mary's Coll of California (CA)
Salem State Coll (MA)
State U of New York at New Paltz (NY)
Texas Christian U (TX)
U of Connecticut (CT)
U of Illinois at Urbana–Champaign (IL)
U of Saskatchewan (SK, Canada)
Washington & Jefferson Coll (PA)
Washington U in St. Louis (MO)
Western Michigan U (MI)
West Virginia U (WV)

THEATER/THEATER ARTS MANAGEMENT
Berry Coll (GA)
Brooklyn Coll of the City U of New York (NY)
Cedarville U (OH)
Coll of Santa Fe (NM)
East Central U (OK)
Eastern Michigan U (MI)
Juniata Coll (PA)
Miami U Hamilton (OH)
Michigan State U (MI)
Nazareth Coll of Rochester (NY)
Oglethorpe U (GA)
Ohio Northern U (OH)
Ohio U (OH)
Peace Coll (NC)
Pittsburg State U (KS)
Regent U (VA)
Reinhardt Coll (GA)
St. Cloud State U (MN)
Seton Hill U (PA)
Slippery Rock U of Pennsylvania (PA)
Stephens Coll (MO)
The U of British Columbia (BC, Canada)
U of Evansville (IN)
U of Miami (FL)
U of Minnesota, Duluth (MN)
U of Regina (SK, Canada)
U of Southern California (CA)

THEOLOGICAL AND MINISTERIAL STUDIES RELATED
Baptist Bible Coll of Pennsylvania (PA)
California Baptist U (CA)
Concordia U (QC, Canada)
Hardin-Simmons U (TX)
Huntington U (IN)
John Brown U (AR)
Northwest Christian U (OR)
Northwestern Coll (MN)
Trevecca Nazarene U (TN)
Trinity Coll of Florida (FL)
Viterbo U (WI)

THEOLOGY
American Baptist Coll of American Baptist Theological Sem (TN)
Anderson U (IN)
Andrews U (MI)
Apex School of Theology (NC)
Appalachian Bible Coll (WV)
Aquinas Coll (TN)
Assumption Coll (MA)
Atlanta Christian Coll (GA)
Atlantic Union Coll (MA)
Augsburg Coll (MN)
Azusa Pacific U (CA)
Barry U (FL)
Bellarmine U (KY)
Belmont Abbey Coll (NC)
Benedictine U (IL)
Bethany U (CA)
Bluefield Coll (VA)
Bob Jones U (SC)
Boston Coll (MA)
Brescia U (KY)
Brewton-Parker Coll (GA)
Briar Cliff U (IA)
California Baptist U (CA)
Calumet Coll of Saint Joseph (IN)
Calvin Coll (MI)
Carlow U (PA)
Cedarville U (OH)
Christendom Coll (VA)
Collège Dominicain de Philosophie et de Théologie (ON, Canada)
Coll of Saint Benedict (MN)
Coll of Saint Elizabeth (NJ)
Coll of Saint Mary (NE)
Concordia U (CA)
Concordia U (QC, Canada)
Concordia U Chicago (IL)
Concordia U, St. Paul (MN)
Concordia U Wisconsin (WI)
Corban U (OR)
Creighton U (NE)
Crown Coll (MN)
DeSales U (PA)
Dominican U (IL)
Dordt Coll (IA)
Duquesne U (PA)
Eastern Mennonite U (VA)
Eastern Nazarene Coll (MA)
East Texas Baptist U (TX)
Elmhurst Coll (IL)
Emmanuel Bible Coll (ON, Canada)
Faulkner U (AL)

INDEXES

Fordham U (NY)
Franciscan U of Steubenville (OH)
Gannon U (PA)
Georgetown U (DC)
Global U (MO)
Grace Bible Coll (MI)
Griggs U (MD)
Hanover Coll (IN)
Hardin-Simmons U (TX)
Hellenic Coll (MA)
Heritage Baptist Coll and Heritage Theological Sem (ON, Canada)
Hillsdale Free Will Baptist Coll (OK)
Houghton Coll (NY)
Howard Payne U (TX)
Huntington U (IN)
Immaculata U (PA)
Indiana Wesleyan U (IN)
John Brown U (AR)
John Wesley Coll (NC)
King's Coll (PA)
The King's U Coll (AB, Canada)
Kuyper Coll (MI)
Lee U (TN)
Lincoln Christian U (IL)
Louisiana Coll (LA)
Loyola Marymount U (CA)
Loyola U Chicago (IL)
Lubbock Christian U (TX)
Madonna U (MI)
Marian U (IN)
Martin Luther Coll (MN)
The Master's Coll and Sem (CA)
Master's Coll and Sem (ON, Canada)
MidAmerica Nazarene U (KS)
Moody Bible Inst (IL)
Morris Coll (SC)
Mount St. Mary's U (MD)
Mount Vernon Nazarene U (OH)
Multnomah U (OR)
Newman U (KS)
North Greenville U (SC)
Northwest Nazarene U (ID)
Nyack Coll (NY)
Oakland City U (IN)
Oakwood U (AL)
Ohio Dominican U (OH)
Oklahoma Wesleyan U (OK)
Oral Roberts U (OK)
Ouachita Baptist U (AR)
Pacific Lutheran U (WA)
Pacific Union Coll (CA)
Piedmont Baptist Coll and Graduate School (NC)
Providence Coll (RI)
Queen's U at Kingston (ON, Canada)
Redeemer U Coll (ON, Canada)
Roanoke Coll (VA)
Rockhurst U (MO)
St. Ambrose U (IA)
Saint Anselm Coll (NH)
St. Bonaventure U (NY)
St. Catherine U (MN)
Saint John's U (MN)
St. John's U (NY)
St. Louis Christian Coll (MO)
Saint Louis U (MO)
Saint Mary-of-the-Woods Coll (IN)
Saint Mary's Coll of California (CA)
St. Mary's U (TX)
Saint Mary's U of Minnesota (MN)
Saint Vincent Coll (PA)
San Diego Christian Coll (CA)
Seattle Pacific U (WA)
Silver Lake Coll (WI)
Southeastern Baptist Theological Sem (NC)
Southern Adventist U (TN)
Southwest Baptist U (MO)
Southwestern Adventist U (TX)
Southwestern Assemblies of God U (TX)
Spring Arbor U (MI)
Spring Hill Coll (AL)
Tabor Coll (KS)
Texas Lutheran U (TX)
Trinity Christian Coll (IL)
Union Coll (NE)
Union U (TN)
Universidad Adventista de las Antillas (PR)
U of Dallas (TX)
U of Dubuque (IA)
U of Evansville (IN)
U of Mary (ND)
U of Mary Hardin-Baylor (TX)
U of Notre Dame (IN)
U of Portland (OR)
U of St. Francis (IL)
U of Saint Mary (KS)
U of St. Thomas (TX)
U of San Francisco (CA)
The U of Western Ontario (ON, Canada)
Valley Forge Christian Coll (PA)
Valparaiso U (IN)
Vanguard U of Southern California (CA)
Walsh U (OH)
Warner Pacific Coll (OR)
Washington Adventist U (MD)
Wheeling Jesuit U (WV)
William Jessup U (CA)
Xavier U (OH)
Xavier U of Louisiana (LA)

THEOLOGY AND RELIGIOUS VOCATIONS RELATED

Abilene Christian U (TX)
Baptist Bible Coll of Pennsylvania (PA)
Cedarville U (OH)
Concordia U Coll of Alberta (AB, Canada)
Eastern Nazarene Coll (MA)
Marquette U (WI)
Master's Coll and Sem (ON, Canada)
Missouri Baptist U (MO)
Newman U (KS)
Ouachita Baptist U (AR)
St. Edward's U (TX)
Simpson U (CA)
Southeastern U (FL)
Thiel Coll (PA)
Union U (TN)
U of St. Thomas (TX)
Valley Forge Christian Coll (PA)
Wayland Baptist U (TX)

THEORETICAL AND MATHEMATICAL PHYSICS

Oregon State U (OR)
Sweet Briar Coll (VA)
U at Buffalo, the State U of New York (NY)
U of Guelph (ON, Canada)
U of Ottawa (ON, Canada)
U of Saskatchewan (SK, Canada)
The U of Western Ontario (ON, Canada)

THERAPEUTIC RECREATION

Alderson-Broaddus Coll (WV)
Ashland U (OH)
Brigham Young U (UT)
California State U, Chico (CA)
California State U, East Bay (CA)
Calvin Coll (MI)
Catawba Coll (NC)
Central Michigan U (MI)
Coker Coll (SC)
The Coll at Brockport, State U of New York (NY)
Concordia U (QC, Canada)
East Carolina U (NC)
Eastern Michigan U (MI)
Eastern Washington U (WA)
Gallaudet U (DC)
Grand Valley State U (MI)
Hampton U (VA)
Indiana Tech (IN)
Ithaca Coll (NY)
Lincoln U (PA)
Longwood U (VA)
Minnesota State U Mankato (MN)
Pittsburg State U (KS)
Prescott Coll (AZ)
St. Andrews Presbyterian Coll (NC)
St. Cloud State U (MN)
Shaw U (NC)
Shorter U (GA)
Slippery Rock U of Pennsylvania (PA)
Southern U and Ag and Mech Coll (LA)
Southwestern Oklahoma State U (OK)
State U of New York Coll at Cortland (NY)
Temple U (PA)
The U of Akron (OH)
The U of Iowa (IA)
U of Nebraska at Kearney (NE)
The U of North Carolina Wilmington (NC)
U of Southern Maine (ME)
U of Waterloo (ON, Canada)
U of Wisconsin–La Crosse (WI)
U of Wisconsin–Milwaukee (WI)
Utica Coll (NY)
Western Carolina U (NC)
West Virginia State U (WV)
Winona State U (MN)
Winston-Salem State U (NC)

TIBETAN

U of Chicago (IL)

TOOL AND DIE TECHNOLOGY

Utah State U (UT)

TOURISM AND TRAVEL SERVICES MANAGEMENT

Arizona State U (AZ)
Black Hills State U (SD)
Bowling Green State U (OH)
Brigham Young U–Hawaii (HI)
Brock U (ON, Canada)
California State U, Chico (CA)
Cape Breton U (NS, Canada)
Champlain Coll (VT)
Concord U (WV)
Delaware State U (DE)
Fort Hays State U (KS)
Fort Lewis Coll (CO)
Hawai'i Pacific U (HI)
Indiana U–Purdue U Indianapolis (IN)
Johnson & Wales U (RI)
Johnson & Wales U—Charlotte Campus (NC)
Johnson State Coll (VT)
Mansfield U of Pennsylvania (PA)
Niagara U (NY)
North Carolina State U (NC)
Northeastern State U (OK)
Oregon State U–Cascades (OR)
Pontifical Catholic U of Puerto Rico (PR)
St. Cloud State U (MN)
St. Thomas U (FL)
Salem State Coll (MA)
Slippery Rock U of Pennsylvania (PA)
Southern New Hampshire U (NH)
State U of New York Maritime Coll (NY)
Sullivan U (KY)
Texas A&M U (TX)
U of Central Florida (FL)
U of Guelph (ON, Canada)
U of Hawaii at Manoa (HI)
U of Maine at Machias (ME)
The U of Montana Western (MT)
U of Nevada, Las Vegas (NV)
The U of Texas at San Antonio (TX)

TOURISM AND TRAVEL SERVICES MARKETING

Johnson & Wales U (RI)
Mitchell Coll (CT)
Rochester Inst of Technology (NY)
Thompson Rivers U (BC, Canada)
U of Central Missouri (MO)
Western Michigan U (MI)

TOURISM PROMOTION

Bowling Green State U (OH)
Cape Breton U (NS, Canada)

TOXICOLOGY

Ashland U (OH)
Eastern Michigan U (MI)
Felician Coll (NJ)
Northeastern U (MA)
Penn State Beaver (PA)
Penn State Berks (PA)
Penn State DuBois (PA)
Penn State Fayette, The Eberly Campus (PA)
Penn State Greater Allegheny (PA)
Penn State Hazleton (PA)
Penn State Mont Alto (PA)
Penn State New Kensington (PA)
Penn State Shenango (PA)
Penn State U Park (PA)
Penn State Wilkes-Barre (PA)
Penn State York (PA)
St. John's U (NY)
U of California, Berkeley (CA)
U of Louisiana at Monroe (LA)
U of Saskatchewan (SK, Canada)
U of Toronto (ON, Canada)
The U of Western Ontario (ON, Canada)
U of Wisconsin–Madison (WI)

TRADE AND INDUSTRIAL TEACHER EDUCATION

Auburn U (AL)
Bemidji State U (MN)
Bowling Green State U (OH)
Buffalo State Coll, State U of New York (NY)
California State U, Long Beach (CA)
California State U, San Bernardino (CA)
The Coll of Saint Rose (NY)
Colorado State U (CO)
Delaware State U (DE)
Eastern New Mexico U (NM)
Fitchburg State Coll (MA)
Indiana State U (IN)
Indiana U of Pennsylvania (PA)
Iowa State U of Science and Technology (IA)
Kent State U (OH)
Lindenwood U (MO)
Memorial U of Newfoundland (NL, Canada)
New York Inst of Technology (NY)
Norfolk State U (VA)
Northern Kentucky U (KY)
Prairie View A&M U (TX)
San Diego State U (CA)
Southern Illinois U Carbondale (IL)
State U of New York at Oswego (NY)
Temple U (PA)
Texas A&M U–Commerce (TX)
Texas A&M U–Corpus Christi (TX)
U of Alberta (AB, Canada)
U of Arkansas at Pine Bluff (AR)
U of Central Florida (FL)
U of Central Oklahoma (OK)
U of Louisville (KY)
U of Nebraska–Lincoln (NE)
U of Nevada, Reno (NV)
U of North Florida (FL)
U of Saskatchewan (SK, Canada)
U of Southern Maine (ME)
U of South Florida (FL)
U of the District of Columbia (DC)
U of the Virgin Islands (VI)
The U of Toledo (OH)
U of West Florida (FL)
U of Wyoming (WY)
Upper Iowa U (IA)
Valdosta State U (GA)
Virginia State U (VA)
Wayland Baptist U (TX)
Western Kentucky U (KY)
Wright State U (OH)

TRANSPORTATION AND HIGHWAY ENGINEERING

U of Toronto (ON, Canada)

TRANSPORTATION AND MATERIALS MOVING RELATED

Niagara U (NY)
Syracuse U (NY)
Texas A&M U at Galveston (TX)
The U of British Columbia (BC, Canada)
U of Cincinnati (OH)

TRANSPORTATION MANAGEMENT

American Public U System (WV)
Bridgewater State Coll (MA)
U of North Florida (FL)
U of Pennsylvania (PA)
U of Wisconsin–Superior (WI)

TURF AND TURFGRASS MANAGEMENT

Clemson U (SC)
Delaware Valley Coll (PA)
Florida Southern Coll (FL)
New Mexico State U (NM)
North Carolina State U (NC)
North Dakota State U (ND)
The Ohio State U (OH)
Penn State Abington (PA)
Penn State Altoona (PA)
Penn State Beaver (PA)
Penn State Berks (PA)
Penn State Brandywine (PA)
Penn State DuBois (PA)
Penn State Erie, The Behrend Coll (PA)
Penn State Fayette, The Eberly Campus (PA)
Penn State Greater Allegheny (PA)
Penn State Hazleton (PA)
Penn State Lehigh Valley (PA)
Penn State Mont Alto (PA)
Penn State New Kensington (PA)
Penn State Schuylkill (PA)
Penn State Shenango (PA)
Penn State U Park (PA)
Penn State Wilkes-Barre (PA)
Penn State Worthington Scranton (PA)
Penn State York (PA)
Rutgers, The State U of New Jersey, New Brunswick (NJ)
Tennessee Technological U (TN)
Texas A&M U (TX)
U of Georgia (GA)
U of Minnesota, Crookston (MN)
U of Nebraska–Lincoln (NE)
U of Rhode Island (RI)

TURKISH

U of Chicago (IL)
The U of Texas at Austin (TX)
U of Utah (UT)

UKRAINIAN

U of Saskatchewan (SK, Canada)

URBAN EDUCATION AND LEADERSHIP

The Coll of New Jersey (NJ)
Harris-Stowe State U (MO)
U of Missouri–Kansas City (MO)

URBAN FORESTRY

Southern U and Ag and Mech Coll (LA)
Texas A&M U (TX)
U of California, Davis (CA)
U of Illinois at Urbana–Champaign (IL)

URBAN STUDIES/AFFAIRS

Albertus Magnus Coll (CT)
Aquinas Coll (MI)
Arizona State U (AZ)
Augsburg Coll (MN)
Ball State U (IN)
Barnard Coll (NY)
Beulah Heights U (GA)
Boston U (MA)
Bryn Mawr Coll (PA)
Buffalo State Coll, State U of New York (NY)
Butler U (IN)
California State U, Dominguez Hills (CA)
California State U, Northridge (CA)
Calvary Bible Coll and Theological Sem (MO)
Canisius Coll (NY)
Cleveland State U (OH)
Coll of Charleston (SC)
Coll of Mount Saint Vincent (NY)
The Coll of Wooster (OH)
Columbia U (NY)
Columbia U, School of General Studies (NY)
Concordia U (QC, Canada)
Connecticut Coll (CT)
Coppin State U (MD)
Delaware State U (DE)
DePaul U (IL)
Dillard U (LA)
Elmhurst Coll (IL)
Eugene Lang Coll The New School for Liberal Arts (NY)
Fordham U (NY)
Furman U (SC)
Georgia State U (GA)
Hamline U (MN)
Hampshire Coll (MA)
Harris-Stowe State U (MO)
Haverford Coll (PA)
Hunter Coll of the City U of New York (NY)
Jackson State U (MS)
Lipscomb U (TN)
Loyola Marymount U (CA)
Manhattan Coll (NY)
Metropolitan Coll of New York (NY)
Minnesota State U Mankato (MN)
Morehouse Coll (GA)
Mount Mercy Coll (IA)
New Coll of Florida (FL)
New Jersey City U (NJ)
New York U (NY)
Northeastern Illinois U (IL)
Oglethorpe U (GA)
Ohio U (OH)
Ohio Wesleyan U (OH)
Portland State U (OR)
Purchase Coll, State U of New York (NY)
Queens Coll of the City U of New York (NY)
Rhodes Coll (TN)
Rutgers, The State U of New Jersey, Camden (NJ)
Rutgers, The State U of New Jersey, New Brunswick (NJ)
St. Cloud State U (MN)
Saint Louis U (MO)
San Diego State U (CA)
San Francisco State U (CA)
Sarah Lawrence Coll (NY)
Stanford U (CA)
Towson U (MD)
Trinity U (TX)
Tufts U (MA)
U at Albany, State U of New York (NY)
U of Alberta (AB, Canada)
The U of British Columbia (BC, Canada)
U of California, Berkeley (CA)

U of California, Irvine (CA)
U of California, San Diego (CA)
U of Cincinnati (OH)
U of Connecticut (CT)
U of Illinois at Chicago (IL)
U of Lethbridge (AB, Canada)
U of Minnesota, Duluth (MN)
U of Minnesota, Twin Cities Campus (MN)
U of Missouri–Kansas City (MO)
U of New Orleans (LA)
U of Pennsylvania (PA)
U of Pittsburgh (PA)
The U of Texas at Austin (TX)
The U of Toledo (OH)
U of Utah (UT)
U of Washington, Tacoma (WA)
The U of Western Ontario (ON, Canada)
U of Wisconsin–Green Bay (WI)
U of Wisconsin–Madison (WI)
U of Wisconsin–Milwaukee (WI)
U of Wisconsin–Oshkosh (WI)
Vassar Coll (NY)
Virginia Commonwealth U (VA)
Warner Pacific Coll (OR)
Washington U in St. Louis (MO)
Wayne State U (MI)
Worcester State Coll (MA)
Wright State U (OH)
York U (ON, Canada)

URDU
U of Chicago (IL)

VEHICLE MAINTENANCE AND REPAIR TECHNOLOGIES RELATED
McPherson Coll (KS)

VETERINARY/ANIMAL HEALTH TECHNOLOGY
Brigham Young U (UT)
Medaille Coll (NY)
Michigan State U (MI)
Mount Ida Coll (MA)
Murray State U (KY)
North Dakota State U (ND)
Purdue U (IN)
St. Petersburg Coll (FL)
State U of New York Coll of Technology at Canton (NY)
Thomas Edison State Coll (NJ)
U of Nebraska–Lincoln (NE)
Wilson Coll (PA)

VIOLIN, VIOLA, GUITAR AND OTHER STRINGED INSTRUMENTS
Acadia U (NS, Canada)
Augustana Coll (IL)
Bard Coll (NY)
Bennington Coll (VT)
Berklee Coll of Music (MA)
The Boston Conservatory (MA)
Brigham Young U (UT)
Butler U (IN)
Carnegie Mellon U (PA)
The Colburn School Conservatory of Music (CA)
Converse Coll (SC)
Cornish Coll of the Arts (WA)
Eastern Nazarene Coll (MA)
Five Towns Coll (NY)
Florida State U (FL)
Hardin-Simmons U (TX)
Heidelberg U (OH)
Hope Coll (MI)
Houghton Coll (NY)
Inter American U of Puerto Rico, San Germán Campus (PR)
Lamar U (TX)
Lawrence U (WI)
Manhattan School of Music (NY)
Mannes Coll The New School for Music (NY)
Memorial U of Newfoundland (NL, Canada)
Mount Allison U (NB, Canada)
New England Conservatory of Music (MA)
The New School for Jazz and Contemporary Music (NY)
Northwestern Coll (MN)
Oberlin Coll (OH)
Oklahoma City U (OK)
Peabody Conservatory of The Johns Hopkins U (MD)
Roosevelt U (IL)
St. Cloud State U (MN)
San Francisco Conservatory of Music (CA)
Sarah Lawrence Coll (NY)
Seton Hill U (PA)
State U of New York at Fredonia (NY)
Stetson U (FL)
U of Alberta (AB, Canada)
The U of British Columbia (BC, Canada)
U of Central Oklahoma (OK)
U of Cincinnati (OH)
The U of Iowa (IA)
The U of Kansas (KS)
U of Nebraska at Omaha (NE)
U of Southern California (CA)
U of Washington (WA)
The U of Western Ontario (ON, Canada)
U of Wisconsin–Milwaukee (WI)
Vanderbilt U (TN)
Willamette U (OR)
Xavier U of Louisiana (LA)

VISION SCIENCE/ PHYSIOLOGICAL OPTICS
U of the Incarnate Word (TX)

VISUAL AND PERFORMING ARTS
Alderson-Broaddus Coll (WV)
Angelo State U (TX)
Arizona State U (AZ)
Armstrong Atlantic State U (GA)
Art Center Coll of Design (CA)
Assumption Coll (MA)
Bard Coll at Simon's Rock (MA)
Barnard Coll (NY)
Bennington Coll (VT)
Bloomfield Coll (NJ)
Blue Mountain Coll (MS)
Bucknell U (PA)
California Baptist U (CA)
California State U, San Marcos (CA)
Cazenovia Coll (NY)
Centenary Coll of Louisiana (LA)
Chowan U (NC)
Claremont McKenna Coll (CA)
Clemson U (SC)
Columbia U (NY)
Columbia U, School of General Studies (NY)
Concordia U (QC, Canada)
Concordia U Coll of Alberta (AB, Canada)
Cooper Union for the Advancement of Science and Art (NY)
Delta State U (MS)
Dowling Coll (NY)
Eastern Connecticut State U (CT)
East Stroudsburg U of Pennsylvania (PA)
Eckerd Coll (FL)
Edgewood Coll (WI)
Emerson Coll (MA)
Eugene Lang Coll The New School for Liberal Arts (NY)
The Evergreen State Coll (WA)
Fairleigh Dickinson U, Coll at Florham (NJ)
Fairleigh Dickinson U, Metropolitan Campus (NJ)
Ferrum Coll (VA)
Frostburg State U (MD)
Gannon U (PA)
Gettysburg Coll (PA)
Harvard U (MA)
Indiana U of Pennsylvania (PA)
Iowa State U of Science and Technology (IA)
Ithaca Coll (NY)
Jackson State U (MS)
Jacksonville U (FL)
Johnson C. Smith U (NC)
Johnson State Coll (VT)
King Coll (TN)
LaGrange Coll (GA)
Lindenwood U (MO)
Long Island U, C.W. Post Campus (NY)
Loras Coll (IA)
Maryland Inst Coll of Art (MD)
Massachusetts Coll of Liberal Arts (MA)
Miami Intl U of Art & Design (FL)
Mississippi State U (MS)
Mississippi U for Women (MS)
Missouri State U (MO)
Naropa U (CO)
New Mexico Highlands U (NM)
New Mexico State U (NM)
Ohio Northern U (OH)
Oregon State U (OR)
Oregon State U–Cascades (OR)
Penn State Abington (PA)
Penn State Altoona (PA)
Penn State Beaver (PA)
Penn State Berks (PA)
Penn State Brandywine (PA)
Penn State DuBois (PA)
Penn State Erie, The Behrend Coll (PA)
Penn State Fayette, The Eberly Campus (PA)
Penn State Greater Allegheny (PA)
Penn State Hazleton (PA)
Penn State Lehigh Valley (PA)
Penn State Mont Alto (PA)
Penn State New Kensington (PA)
Penn State Schuylkill (PA)
Penn State Shenango (PA)
Penn State U Park (PA)
Penn State Wilkes-Barre (PA)
Penn State Worthington Scranton (PA)
Penn State York (PA)
Prescott Coll (AZ)
Providence Coll (RI)
Purchase Coll, State U of New York (NY)
Ramapo Coll of New Jersey (NJ)
Rensselaer Polytechnic Inst (NY)
The Richard Stockton Coll of New Jersey (NJ)
Rogers State U (OK)
Rutgers, The State U of New Jersey, New Brunswick (NJ)
Saint Augustine's Coll (NC)
St. Bonaventure U (NY)
Saint Joseph's U (PA)
San Jose State U (CA)
Sarah Lawrence Coll (NY)
Savannah Coll of Art and Design (GA)
Savannah State U (GA)
School of the Art Inst of Chicago (IL)
Seton Hall U (NJ)
Shenandoah U (VA)
South Dakota State U (SD)
Southeast Missouri State U (MO)
State U of New York at New Paltz (NY)
State U of New York Coll at Old Westbury (NY)
Stonehill Coll (MA)
Texas Wesleyan U (TX)
Thompson Rivers U (BC, Canada)
Truman State U (MO)
Tusculum Coll (TN)
The U of Arizona (AZ)
The U of British Columbia (BC, Canada)
The U of British Columbia–Okanagan (BC, Canada)
U of Houston–Downtown (TX)
U of Maine at Machias (ME)
U of Maryland, Baltimore County (MD)
U of Mary Washington (VA)
U of North Carolina School of the Arts (NC)
U of Oklahoma (OK)
U of Pennsylvania (PA)
U of Puerto Rico, Río Piedras (PR)
U of Regina (SK, Canada)
U of Rio Grande (OH)
U of St. Francis (IL)
U of Saint Mary (KS)
U of San Francisco (CA)
The U of South Dakota (SD)
U of Southern California (CA)
U of Southern Mississippi (MS)
The U of Tampa (FL)
The U of Tennessee at Martin (TN)
The U of Texas at Dallas (TX)
U of Toronto (ON, Canada)
U of Utah (UT)
U of Windsor (ON, Canada)
U of Wisconsin–Superior (WI)
Valdosta State U (GA)
Vassar Coll (NY)
Virginia State U (VA)
Viterbo U (WI)
Western Kentucky U (KY)
Western Washington U (WA)
Wheelock Coll (MA)
Wichita State U (KS)
William Jessup U (CA)
Worcester State Coll (MA)
York U (ON, Canada)

VISUAL AND PERFORMING ARTS RELATED
Adelphi U (NY)
Alverno Coll (WI)
Baldwin-Wallace Coll (OH)
The Baptist Coll of Florida (FL)
Bard Coll at Simon's Rock (MA)
Brigham Young U (UT)
California Inst of the Arts (CA)
Cameron U (OK)
Central Michigan U (MI)
Claremont McKenna Coll (CA)
Clemson U (SC)
Coll of Visual Arts (MN)
Columbia U, School of General Studies (NY)
Cumberland U (TN)
Dana Coll (NE)
The Evergreen State Coll (WA)
Illinois State U (IL)
Illinois Wesleyan U (IL)
Indiana U Bloomington (IN)
Indiana U–Purdue U Indianapolis (IN)
Maine Coll of Art (ME)
Marywood U (PA)
Millikin U (IL)
New York U (NY)
Ohio Northern U (OH)
Penn State Altoona (PA)
Providence Coll (RI)
Purchase Coll, State U of New York (NY)
Rice U (TX)
St. Cloud State U (MN)
Saint Mary's Coll of California (CA)
Samford U (AL)
Sarah Lawrence Coll (NY)
School of the Art Inst of Chicago (IL)
School of the Museum of Fine Arts, Boston (MA)
Scripps Coll (CA)
Simon Fraser U (BC, Canada)
Spring Arbor U (MI)
State U of New York Coll at Geneseo (NY)
State U of New York Coll at Potsdam (NY)
Stetson U (FL)
Syracuse U (NY)
Thompson Rivers U (BC, Canada)
U of California, Davis (CA)
U of Lethbridge (AB, Canada)
U of Michigan (MI)
U of New Haven (CT)
U of Puerto Rico at Utuado (PR)
U of South Florida (FL)
U of Washington, Bothell (WA)
U of Wisconsin–Green Bay (WI)
Western State Coll of Colorado (CO)

VOCATIONAL REHABILITATION COUNSELING
Bowling Green State U (OH)
East Carolina U (NC)
Emporia State U (KS)
Florida State U (FL)
Louisiana State U Health Sciences Center (LA)
Maryville U of Saint Louis (MO)
Southern U and Ag and Mech Coll (LA)
U of Illinois at Urbana–Champaign (IL)
U of North Dakota (ND)
U of Northern Colorado (CO)
U of Wisconsin–Stout (WI)
Winston-Salem State U (NC)
Wright State U (OH)

VOICE AND OPERA
Abilene Christian U (TX)
Acadia U (NS, Canada)
Andrews U (MI)
Augustana Coll (IL)
Baldwin-Wallace Coll (OH)
Bard Coll (NY)
Barry U (FL)
Belmont U (TN)
Bennington Coll (VT)
Berklee Coll of Music (MA)
Birmingham-Southern Coll (AL)
Black Hills State U (SD)
The Boston Conservatory (MA)
Boston U (MA)
Bowling Green State U (OH)
Brigham Young U (UT)
Brigham Young U–Hawaii (HI)
Butler U (IN)
California State U, Long Beach (CA)
Calvary Bible Coll and Theological Sem (MO)
Calvin Coll (MI)
Campbellsville U (KY)
Capital U (OH)
Carnegie Mellon U (PA)
Carson-Newman Coll (TN)
Catawba Coll (NC)
The Catholic U of America (DC)
Chapman U (CA)
Cincinnati Christian U (OH)
Coker Coll (SC)
Columbia Coll (SC)
Concordia Coll (MN)
Concordia U Chicago (IL)
Converse Coll (SC)
Corban U (OR)
Cornish Coll of the Arts (WA)
Delaware State U (DE)
Dordt Coll (IA)
Drake U (IA)
East Central U (OK)
Eastern Nazarene Coll (MA)
East Texas Baptist U (TX)
Five Towns Coll (NY)
Florida State U (FL)
Furman U (SC)
Grace Coll (IN)
Hannibal-LaGrange Coll (MO)
Hardin-Simmons U (TX)
Heidelberg U (OH)
Hope Coll (MI)
Houghton Coll (NY)
Illinois Wesleyan U (IL)
Indiana U–Purdue U Fort Wayne (IN)
Inter American U of Puerto Rico, San Germán Campus (PR)
Ithaca Coll (NY)
Jacksonville U (FL)
Lamar U (TX)
Lawrence U (WI)
Lee U (TN)
Lincoln Christian U (IL)
Lipscomb U (TN)
Long Island U, C.W. Post Campus (NY)
Louisiana Coll (LA)
Manhattan School of Music (NY)
Mannes Coll The New School for Music (NY)
Maryville Coll (TN)
The Master's Coll and Sem (CA)
Memorial U of Newfoundland (NL, Canada)
MidAmerica Nazarene U (KS)
Millikin U (IL)
Minnesota State U Mankato (MN)
Minnesota State U Moorhead (MN)
Mississippi Coll (MS)
Mount Allison U (NB, Canada)
Newberry Coll (SC)
New England Conservatory of Music (MA)
Northern Arizona U (AZ)
Northern State U (SD)
Northwestern Coll (MN)
Notre Dame de Namur U (CA)
Nyack Coll (NY)
Oakland U (MI)
Oberlin Coll (OH)
The Ohio State U (OH)
Ohio U (OH)
Oklahoma Baptist U (OK)
Oklahoma Christian U (OK)
Oklahoma City U (OK)
Oral Roberts U (OK)
Ouachita Baptist U (AR)
Peabody Conservatory of The Johns Hopkins U (MD)
Peru State Coll (NE)
Prairie View A&M U (TX)
Queens U of Charlotte (NC)
Rider U (NJ)
Roberts Wesleyan Coll (NY)
Roosevelt U (IL)
St. Cloud State U (MN)
Samford U (AL)
San Diego Christian Coll (CA)
San Francisco Conservatory of Music (CA)
Sarah Lawrence Coll (NY)
Seton Hill U (PA)
Shorter U (GA)
Southeastern U (FL)
Southern Methodist U (TX)
Southwestern Oklahoma State U (OK)
State U of New York at Fredonia (NY)
State U of New York at New Paltz (NY)
Stetson U (FL)
Tabor Coll (KS)
Talladega Coll (AL)
Temple U (PA)
Texas Wesleyan U (TX)
Trinity U (TX)
Truman State U (MO)
Union U (TN)
U of Alberta (AB, Canada)
The U of British Columbia (BC, Canada)
U of Central Oklahoma (OK)
U of Cincinnati (OH)
U of Idaho (ID)
U of Illinois at Urbana–Champaign (IL)
The U of Iowa (IA)
The U of Kansas (KS)
U of Miami (FL)
U of Mobile (AL)
U of Nebraska at Omaha (NE)
U of North Carolina School of the Arts (NC)
U of Redlands (CA)
U of Southern California (CA)
The U of Tennessee at Martin (TN)
U of the Pacific (CA)

U of Tulsa (OK)
U of Washington (WA)
The U of Western Ontario (ON, Canada)
U of Wisconsin–Milwaukee (WI)
Valparaiso U (IN)
Vanderbilt U (TN)
Washington U in St. Louis (MO)
Willamette U (OR)
William Paterson U of New Jersey (NJ)
York U (ON, Canada)

WALDORF/STEINER TEACHER EDUCATION
Prescott Coll (AZ)

WATER QUALITY AND WASTEWATER TREATMENT MANAGEMENT AND RECYCLING TECHNOLOGY
Mississippi Valley State U (MS)

WATER RESOURCES ENGINEERING
Central State U (OH)
State U of New York Coll of Environmental Science and Forestry (NY)
The U of Arizona (AZ)
U of Guelph (ON, Canada)
U of Illinois at Urbana–Champaign (IL)
U of Nevada, Reno (NV)

WATER, WETLANDS, AND MARINE RESOURCES MANAGEMENT
Colorado State U (CO)
Florida Gulf Coast U (FL)
Sterling Coll (VT)
Texas State U–San Marcos (TX)
U of Georgia (GA)
U of New Hampshire (NH)
U of Rhode Island (RI)
The U of Western Ontario (ON, Canada)
Western State Coll of Colorado (CO)

WEB/MULTIMEDIA MANAGEMENT AND WEBMASTER
Champlain Coll (VT)
Hawai'i Pacific U (HI)
Lewis-Clark State Coll (ID)
Limestone Coll (SC)
Mars Hill Coll (NC)
New England School of Communications (ME)
Northern Michigan U (MI)
Platt Coll San Diego (CA)
Rochester Inst of Technology (NY)
State U of New York Coll of Technology at Alfred (NY)
U of Dubuque (IA)
U of St. Francis (IL)

WEB PAGE, DIGITAL/ MULTIMEDIA AND INFORMATION RESOURCES DESIGN
Acad of Art U (CA)
The Art Inst of Atlanta (GA)
The Art Inst of Atlanta–Decatur (GA)
The Art Inst of Austin (TX)
The Art Inst of California–Hollywood (CA)
The Art Inst of California–Inland Empire (CA)
The Art Inst of California–Los Angeles (CA)
The Art Inst of California–Orange County (CA)
The Art Inst of California–Sacramento (CA)
The Art Inst of California–San Diego (CA)
The Art Inst of California–San Francisco (CA)
The Art Inst of California–Sunnyvale (CA)
The Art Inst of Charleston (SC)
The Art Inst of Charlotte (NC)
The Art Inst of Colorado (CO)
The Art Inst of Dallas (TX)
The Art Inst of Fort Lauderdale (FL)
The Art Inst of Fort Worth (TX)
The Art Inst of Houston (TX)
The Art Inst of Indianapolis (IN)
The Art Inst of Jacksonville (FL)
The Art Inst of Las Vegas (NV)
The Art Inst of Michigan (MI)
The Art Inst of Ohio–Cincinnati (OH)
The Art Inst of Philadelphia (PA)
The Art Inst of Phoenix (AZ)
The Art Inst of Pittsburgh (PA)
The Art Inst of Portland (OR)
The Art Inst of Raleigh-Durham (NC)
The Art Inst of Salt Lake City (UT)
The Art Inst of San Antonio (TX)
The Art Inst of Seattle (WA)
The Art Inst of Tampa (FL)
The Art Inst of Tennessee–Nashville (TN)
The Art Inst of Tucson (AZ)
The Art Inst of Virginia Beach (VA)
The Art Inst of Washington (VA)
The Art Inst of Washington–Northern Virginia (VA)
The Art Inst of York–Pennsylvania (PA)
The Art Insts Intl–Kansas City (KS)
The Art Insts Intl Minnesota (MN)
Azusa Pacific U (CA)
Bishop's U (QC, Canada)
Capella U (MN)
Champlain Coll (VT)
The Cleveland Inst of Art (OH)
Columbia Coll Chicago (IL)
Dakota State U (SD)
Dakota Wesleyan U (SD)
Dana Coll (NE)
DePaul U (IL)
DeVry U, Phoenix (AZ)
DeVry U, Fremont (CA)
DeVry U, Long Beach (CA)
DeVry U, Pomona (CA)
DeVry U, Sherman Oaks (CA)
DeVry U, Westminster (CO)
DeVry U, Miramar (FL)
DeVry U, Orlando (FL)
DeVry U, Alpharetta (GA)
DeVry U, Decatur (GA)
DeVry U, Addison (IL)
DeVry U, Chicago (IL)
DeVry U, Tinley Park (IL)
DeVry U, Indianapolis (IN)
DeVry U (KY)
DeVry U, Edina (MN)
DeVry U, Kansas City (MO)
DeVry U (NV)
DeVry U (OK)
DeVry U (OR)
DeVry U, Arlington (VA)
DeVry U, Federal Way (WA)
DeVry U Online (IL)
Drexel U (PA)
Duquesne U (PA)
Franklin U (OH)
Full Sail U (FL)
Harding U (AR)
The Illinois Inst of Art–Chicago (IL)
The Illinois Inst of Art–Schaumburg (IL)
Indiana Tech (IN)
Iona Coll (NY)
Lasell Coll (MA)
Liberty U (VA)
Medaille Coll (NY)
Miami Intl U of Art & Design (FL)
Neumont U (UT)
The New England Inst of Art (MA)
New England School of Communications (ME)
New Jersey Inst of Technology (NJ)
Northwest Missouri State U (MO)
Platt Coll San Diego (CA)
Quinnipiac U (CT)
Rochester Inst of Technology (NY)
Santa Clara U (CA)
School of the Art Inst of Chicago (IL)
Silver Lake Coll (WI)
Stetson U (FL)
Tennessee Technological U (TN)
Thiel Coll (PA)
Trevecca Nazarene U (TN)
U of Dubuque (IA)
U of Mount Union (OH)
The U of North Carolina at Asheville (NC)
U of Wisconsin–Stevens Point (WI)
Utah Valley U (UT)
Westwood Coll–Atlanta Midtown (GA)
Westwood Coll–Atlanta Northlake (GA)
Westwood Coll–Online Campus (CO)

WELDING TECHNOLOGY
Ferris State U (MI)
LeTourneau U (TX)
Lewis-Clark State Coll (ID)
The Ohio State U (OH)

WILDLIFE AND WILDLANDS SCIENCE AND MANAGEMENT
Arkansas State U—Jonesboro (AR)
Arkansas Tech U (AR)
Auburn U (AL)
Coll of the Ozarks (MO)
Dakota Wesleyan U (SD)
Delaware State U (DE)
Delaware Valley Coll (PA)
Eastern New Mexico U (NM)
Fort Hays State U (KS)
Frostburg State U (MD)
Humboldt State U (CA)
Juniata Coll (PA)
Lake Superior State U (MI)
Lincoln Memorial U (TN)
McNeese State U (LA)
Michigan State U (MI)
Michigan Technological U (MI)
Mississippi State U (MS)
Missouri State U (MO)
Montana State U (MT)
Murray State U (KY)
New Mexico State U (NM)
North Carolina State U (NC)
Northwest Missouri State U (MO)
The Ohio State U (OH)
Peru State Coll (NE)
Prescott Coll (AZ)
Purdue U (IN)
South Dakota State U (SD)
State U of New York Coll of Environmental Science and Forestry (NY)
Stephen F. Austin State U (TX)
Sterling Coll (VT)
Sul Ross State U (TX)
Tarleton State U (TX)
Tennessee Technological U (TN)
Texas A&M U (TX)
Texas A&M U–Kingsville (TX)
Texas Tech U (TX)
U of Alberta (AB, Canada)
The U of Arizona (AZ)
U of Arkansas at Monticello (AR)
The U of British Columbia (BC, Canada)
U of Delaware (DE)
U of Georgia (GA)
U of Idaho (ID)
U of Illinois at Urbana–Champaign (IL)
U of Maine (ME)
U of Missouri (MO)
U of Nevada, Reno (NV)
U of New Brunswick Fredericton (NB, Canada)
U of New Hampshire (NH)
U of Puerto Rico at Humacao (PR)
U of Rhode Island (RI)
The U of Tennessee (TN)
The U of Tennessee at Martin (TN)
U of Washington (WA)
U of Wisconsin–Stevens Point (WI)
Utah State U (UT)
Washington State U (WA)
West Virginia U (WV)

WILDLIFE BIOLOGY
Adams State Coll (CO)
Baker U (KS)
Clemson U (SC)
Coll of the Atlantic (ME)
Colorado State U (CO)
Friends U (KS)
Frostburg State U (MD)
Kansas State U (KS)
Lees-McRae Coll (NC)
Northeastern State U (OK)
Northern Arizona U (AZ)
Ohio U (OH)
Pittsburg State U (KS)
Prescott Coll (AZ)
St. Cloud State U (MN)
State U of New York Coll of Environmental Science and Forestry (NY)
Sterling Coll (VT)
Texas State U–San Marcos (TX)
U of Alaska Fairbanks (AK)
U of Guelph (ON, Canada)
U of Michigan–Flint (MI)
U of New Brunswick Fredericton (NB, Canada)
U of Vermont (VT)
U of Wyoming (WY)
Winona State U (MN)

WIND/PERCUSSION INSTRUMENTS
Acadia U (NS, Canada)
Augustana Coll (IL)
Berklee Coll of Music (MA)
The Boston Conservatory (MA)
Butler U (IN)
Chapman U (CA)
The Colburn School Conservatory of Music (CA)
Concordia U Chicago (IL)
Eastern Nazarene Coll (MA)
Five Towns Coll (NY)
Florida State U (FL)
Houghton Coll (NY)
Inter American U of Puerto Rico, San Germán Campus (PR)
Lawrence U (WI)
Manhattan School of Music (NY)
Maryville Coll (TN)
Memorial U of Newfoundland (NL, Canada)
Minnesota State U Mankato (MN)
Minnesota State U Moorhead (MN)
Mount Allison U (NB, Canada)
New England Conservatory of Music (MA)
Oberlin Coll (OH)
Oklahoma Christian U (OK)
Oklahoma City U (OK)
Peabody Conservatory of The Johns Hopkins U (MD)
Peru State Coll (NE)
Prairie View A&M U (TX)
San Francisco Conservatory of Music (CA)
Sarah Lawrence Coll (NY)
Seton Hill U (PA)
Southwestern Oklahoma State U (OK)
State U of New York at Fredonia (NY)
Temple U (PA)
Texas Wesleyan U (TX)
U of Alberta (AB, Canada)
U of Central Oklahoma (OK)
U of Cincinnati (OH)
The U of Iowa (IA)
The U of Kansas (KS)
U of Wisconsin–Milwaukee (WI)
Xavier U of Louisiana (LA)

WOMEN'S STUDIES
Agnes Scott Coll (GA)
Albion Coll (MI)
Albright Coll (PA)
Allegheny Coll (PA)
American Public U System (WV)
American U (DC)
Amherst Coll (MA)
Arizona State U (AZ)
Athabasca U (AB, Canada)
Augsburg Coll (MN)
Augustana Coll (IL)
Ball State U (IN)
Bard Coll at Simon's Rock (MA)
Barnard Coll (NY)
Bates Coll (ME)
Beloit Coll (WI)
Bennington Coll (VT)
Berea Coll (KY)
Bishop's U (QC, Canada)
Bowdoin Coll (ME)
Bowling Green State U (OH)
Brandeis U (MA)
Brock U (ON, Canada)
Brooklyn Coll of the City U of New York (NY)
Bucknell U (PA)
California State U, Fresno (CA)
California State U, Fullerton (CA)
California State U, Long Beach (CA)
California State U, Northridge (CA)
California State U, San Marcos (CA)
Carleton Coll (MN)
Case Western Reserve U (OH)
Central Michigan U (MI)
Chatham U (PA)
City Coll of the City U of New York (NY)
Claremont McKenna Coll (CA)
Clark U (MA)
Colby Coll (ME)
Colgate U (NY)
The Coll at Brockport, State U of New York (NY)
The Coll of New Jersey (NJ)
The Coll of New Rochelle (NY)
Coll of Saint Elizabeth (NJ)
The Coll of Saint Rose (NY)
Coll of Staten Island of the City U of New York (NY)
The Coll of William and Mary (VA)
The Coll of Wooster (OH)
The Colorado Coll (CO)
Columbia U (NY)
Columbia U, School of General Studies (NY)
Concordia U (QC, Canada)
Connecticut Coll (CT)
Cornell Coll (IA)
Cornell U (NY)
Curry Coll (MA)
Dartmouth Coll (NH)
Denison U (OH)
DePaul U (IL)
DePauw U (IN)
Dickinson Coll (PA)
Dominican U of California (CA)
Drew U (NJ)
Duke U (NC)
Duquesne U (PA)
Earlham Coll (IN)
East Carolina U (NC)
Eastern Michigan U (MI)
Eastern Washington U (WA)
East Tennessee State U (TN)
Eckerd Coll (FL)
Edinboro U of Pennsylvania (PA)
Emory U (GA)
Florida Intl U (FL)
Fordham U (NY)
Fort Lewis Coll (CO)
Georgetown U (DC)
Georgia State U (GA)
Gettysburg Coll (PA)
Goucher Coll (MD)
Grand Valley State U (MI)
Guilford Coll (NC)
Gustavus Adolphus Coll (MN)
Hamilton Coll (NY)
Hamline U (MN)
Hampshire Coll (MA)
Harvard U (MA)
Haverford Coll (PA)
Hofstra U (NY)
Hollins U (VA)
Hope Coll (MI)
Hunter Coll of the City U of New York (NY)
Illinois Wesleyan U (IL)
Indiana U Bloomington (IN)
Indiana U–Purdue U Fort Wayne (IN)
Indiana U South Bend (IN)
Iowa State U of Science and Technology (IA)
Kansas State U (KS)
Kenyon Coll (OH)
Knox Coll (IL)
Lakehead U (ON, Canada)
Laurentian U (ON, Canada)
Lehigh U (PA)
Louisiana State U and Ag and Mech Coll (LA)
Loyola Marymount U (CA)
Loyola U Chicago (IL)
Luther Coll (IA)
Macalester Coll (MN)
Marlboro Coll (VT)
Marquette U (WI)
Mars Hill Coll (NC)
Memorial U of Newfoundland (NL, Canada)
Miami U (OH)
Michigan State U (MI)
Middlebury Coll (VT)
Mills Coll (CA)
Minnesota State U Mankato (MN)
Montclair State U (NJ)
Nazareth Coll of Rochester (NY)
Nebraska Wesleyan U (NE)
New Mexico State U (NM)
Nipissing U (ON, Canada)
North Dakota State U (ND)
Northeastern Illinois U (IL)
Northeastern U (MA)
Northern Arizona U (AZ)
Oakland U (MI)
Oberlin Coll (OH)
Occidental Coll (CA)
The Ohio State U (OH)
Ohio U (OH)
Ohio Wesleyan U (OH)
Old Dominion U (VA)
Oregon State U (OR)
Pace U (NY)
Pacific Lutheran U (WA)
Penn State Abington (PA)
Penn State Altoona (PA)
Penn State Beaver (PA)
Penn State Berks (PA)
Penn State Brandywine (PA)
Penn State DuBois (PA)
Penn State Erie, The Behrend Coll (PA)
Penn State Fayette, The Eberly Campus (PA)
Penn State Greater Allegheny (PA)
Penn State Hazleton (PA)
Penn State Lehigh Valley (PA)
Penn State Mont Alto (PA)
Penn State New Kensington (PA)
Penn State Schuylkill (PA)
Penn State Shenango (PA)
Penn State U Park (PA)
Penn State Wilkes-Barre (PA)
Penn State Worthington Scranton (PA)
Penn State York (PA)
Pitzer Coll (CA)
Pomona Coll (CA)
Portland State U (OR)
Prescott Coll (AZ)

INDEXES

Purchase Coll, State U of New York (NY)
Queens Coll of the City U of New York (NY)
Queen's U at Kingston (ON, Canada)
Randolph-Macon Coll (VA)
Rhode Island Coll (RI)
Rice U (TX)
Rosemont Coll (PA)
Rutgers, The State U of New Jersey, Newark (NJ)
Rutgers, The State U of New Jersey, New Brunswick (NJ)
St. Bonaventure U (NY)
St. Catherine U (MN)
St. Francis Xavier U (NS, Canada)
Saint John's U (MN)
Saint Joseph Coll (CT)
Saint Louis U (MO)
Saint Mary's Coll of California (CA)
St. Olaf Coll (MN)
St. Thomas U (NB, Canada)
Salem Coll (NC)
San Diego State U (CA)
San Francisco State U (CA)
Santa Clara U (CA)
Sarah Lawrence Coll (NY)
Scripps Coll (CA)
Simmons Coll (MA)
Simon Fraser U (BC, Canada)
Skidmore Coll (NY)
Smith Coll (MA)
Sonoma State U (CA)
Southwestern U (TX)
Spelman Coll (GA)
Stanford U (CA)
State U of New York at Fredonia (NY)
State U of New York at New Paltz (NY)
State U of New York at Oswego (NY)
State U of New York at Plattsburgh (NY)
State U of New York Coll at Potsdam (NY)
Stony Brook U, State U of New York (NY)
Suffolk U (MA)
Swarthmore Coll (PA)
Temple U (PA)
Texas A&M U (TX)
Towson U (MD)
Trent U (ON, Canada)
Trinity Coll (CT)
Tufts U (MA)
Tulane U (LA)
U at Albany, State U of New York (NY)
U at Buffalo, the State U of New York (NY)
U of Alberta (AB, Canada)
The U of Arizona (AZ)
The U of British Columbia (BC, Canada)
U of California, Berkeley (CA)
U of California, Davis (CA)
U of California, Irvine (CA)
U of California, Los Angeles (CA)
U of California, Riverside (CA)
U of California, San Diego (CA)
U of California, Santa Barbara (CA)
U of California, Santa Cruz (CA)
U of Colorado at Boulder (CO)
U of Connecticut (CT)
U of Delaware (DE)
U of Florida (FL)
U of Georgia (GA)
U of Guelph (ON, Canada)
U of Hartford (CT)
U of Hawaii at Manoa (HI)
U of Houston–Clear Lake (TX)
U of Illinois at Urbana–Champaign (IL)
The U of Iowa (IA)
The U of Kansas (KS)
U of King's Coll (NS, Canada)
U of Lethbridge (AB, Canada)
U of Louisville (KY)
U of Maine (ME)
U of Manitoba (MB, Canada)
U of Maryland, Baltimore County (MD)
U of Maryland, Coll Park (MD)
U of Massachusetts Amherst (MA)
U of Massachusetts Boston (MA)
U of Massachusetts Dartmouth (MA)
U of Miami (FL)
U of Michigan (MI)
U of Michigan–Dearborn (MI)
U of Minnesota, Duluth (MN)
U of Minnesota, Twin Cities Campus (MN)
U of Nebraska at Omaha (NE)
U of Nebraska–Lincoln (NE)
U of Nevada, Las Vegas (NV)
U of Nevada, Reno (NV)
U of New Hampshire (NH)
U of New Mexico (NM)
U of New Orleans (LA)
The U of North Carolina at Asheville (NC)
The U of North Carolina at Chapel Hill (NC)
The U of North Carolina at Greensboro (NC)
U of Oklahoma (OK)
U of Oregon (OR)
U of Ottawa (ON, Canada)
U of Pennsylvania (PA)
U of Regina (SK, Canada)
U of Rhode Island (RI)
U of Richmond (VA)
U of Rochester (NY)
U of St. Thomas (MN)
U of Saskatchewan (SK, Canada)
U of South Carolina (SC)
U of Southern Maine (ME)
U of South Florida (FL)
The U of Texas at Austin (TX)
The U of Toledo (OH)
U of Toronto (ON, Canada)
U of Utah (UT)
U of Vermont (VT)
U of Washington (WA)
U of Waterloo (ON, Canada)
The U of Western Ontario (ON, Canada)
U of Windsor (ON, Canada)
U of Wisconsin–Eau Claire (WI)
U of Wisconsin–La Crosse (WI)
U of Wisconsin–Madison (WI)
U of Wisconsin–Milwaukee (WI)
U of Wisconsin–Whitewater (WI)
U of Wyoming (WY)
Vanderbilt U (TN)
Vassar Coll (NY)
Virginia Commonwealth U (VA)
Virginia Wesleyan Coll (VA)
Washington State U (WA)
Washington U in St. Louis (MO)
Wellesley Coll (MA)
Wells Coll (NY)
Wesleyan U (CT)
West Chester U of Pennsylvania (PA)
Western Illinois U (IL)
Western Michigan U (MI)
Wheaton Coll (MA)
Wichita State U (KS)
Wilfrid Laurier U (ON, Canada)
Willamette U (OR)
Williams Coll (MA)
Wright State U (OH)
Yale U (CT)
York U (ON, Canada)

WOOD SCIENCE AND WOOD PRODUCTS/PULP AND PAPER TECHNOLOGY

Miami U (OH)
Mississippi State U (MS)
State U of New York Coll of Environmental Science and Forestry (NY)
The U of British Columbia (BC, Canada)
U of Idaho (ID)
U of Maine (ME)
U of Massachusetts Amherst (MA)
U of Minnesota, Twin Cities Campus (MN)
U of Toronto (ON, Canada)
U of Washington (WA)
U of Wisconsin–Stevens Point (WI)
West Virginia U (WV)

WOODWORKING

Rochester Inst of Technology (NY)

WOODWORKING RELATED

Pittsburg State U (KS)

WORK AND FAMILY STUDIES

Brigham Young U (UT)
Miami U Hamilton (OH)
The U of North Carolina at Charlotte (NC)
Ursuline Coll (OH)

YOUTH MINISTRY

Abilene Christian U (TX)
Anderson U (IN)
Andrews U (MI)
Asbury U (KY)
Baptist Bible Coll of Pennsylvania (PA)
Benedictine Coll (KS)
Bethel Coll (IN)
Bethel U (MN)
Bluffton U (OH)
Calvary Bible Coll and Theological Sem (MO)
Cedarville U (OH)
Central Christian Coll of Kansas (KS)
Columbia Intl U (SC)
Concordia U Wisconsin (WI)
Corban U (OR)
Davis Coll (NY)
Dordt Coll (IA)
Eastern Mennonite U (VA)
Eastern Nazarene Coll (MA)
East Texas Baptist U (TX)
Emmanuel Bible Coll (ON, Canada)
Eugene Bible Coll (OR)
Geneva Coll (PA)
Gordon Coll (MA)
Grace Bible Coll (MI)
Grace Coll (IN)
Great Lakes Christian Coll (MI)
Greenville Coll (IL)
Harding U (AR)
Hardin-Simmons U (TX)
Hillsdale Free Will Baptist Coll (OK)
Howard Payne U (TX)
Huntingdon Coll (AL)
John Brown U (AR)
King Coll (TN)
Kuyper Coll (MI)
Lipscomb U (TN)
Lubbock Christian U (TX)
Malone U (OH)
Maranatha Baptist Bible Coll (WI)
Master's Coll and Sem (ON, Canada)
MidAmerica Nazarene U (KS)
Mid-Atlantic Christian U (NC)
Mount Vernon Nazarene U (OH)
Multnomah U (OR)
North Greenville U (SC)
Northwestern Coll (MN)
Northwest U (WA)
Oak Hills Christian Coll (MN)
Ohio Northern U (OH)
Ouachita Baptist U (AR)
Piedmont Baptist Coll and Graduate School (NC)
Redeemer U Coll (ON, Canada)
Rochester Coll (MI)
Saint Mary's U of Minnesota (MN)
Simpson U (CA)
Southwestern Assemblies of God U (TX)
Spring Arbor U (MI)
Tabor Coll (KS)
Trinity Coll of Florida (FL)
U of Indianapolis (IN)
Valley Forge Christian Coll (PA)
Vanguard U of Southern California (CA)

YOUTH SERVICES

Stony Brook U, State U of New York (NY)
U of Hawaii at Manoa (HI)
The U of Western Ontario (ON, Canada)
Wheelock Coll (MA)

ZOOLOGY/ANIMAL BIOLOGY

Andrews U (MI)
Auburn U (AL)
Bennington Coll (VT)
California State Polytechnic U, Pomona (CA)
California State U, Long Beach (CA)
Central Christian Coll of Kansas (KS)
Coll of the Atlantic (ME)
Colorado State U (CO)
Delaware Valley Coll (PA)
Fort Valley State U (GA)
Humboldt State U (CA)
Idaho State U (ID)
Juniata Coll (PA)
Kent State U (OH)
Malone U (OH)
Mars Hill Coll (NC)
Memorial U of Newfoundland (NL, Canada)
Miami U (OH)
Miami U Hamilton (OH)
Michigan State U (MI)
North Carolina State U (NC)
North Dakota State U (ND)
Northern Arizona U (AZ)
Northern Michigan U (MI)
The Ohio State U (OH)
Ohio U (OH)
Ohio Wesleyan U (OH)
Oklahoma State U (OK)
Oregon State U (OR)
Prescott Coll (AZ)
Rutgers, The State U of New Jersey, Newark (NJ)
San Francisco State U (CA)
Sonoma State U (CA)
Southeastern Oklahoma State U (OK)
Southern Illinois U Carbondale (IL)
Southern Utah U (UT)
State U of New York at Oswego (NY)
State U of New York Coll of Environmental Science and Forestry (NY)
Tarleton State U (TX)
Texas A&M U (TX)
Texas State U–San Marcos (TX)
Texas Tech U (TX)
Texas Woman's U (TX)
The U of Akron (OH)
U of Alberta (AB, Canada)
The U of British Columbia (BC, Canada)
The U of British Columbia–Okanagan (BC, Canada)
U of California, Davis (CA)
U of California, Santa Barbara (CA)
U of Florida (FL)
U of Guelph (ON, Canada)
U of Hawaii at Manoa (HI)
U of Maine (ME)
U of Manitoba (MB, Canada)
U of New Brunswick Fredericton (NB, Canada)
U of New Hampshire (NH)
U of Oklahoma (OK)
U of Rhode Island (RI)
The U of Tennessee (TN)
The U of Texas at El Paso (TX)
U of Toronto (ON, Canada)
U of Vermont (VT)
U of Washington (WA)
U of Wisconsin–Madison (WI)
U of Wisconsin–Milwaukee (WI)
U of Wyoming (WY)
Utah State U (UT)
Washington State U (WA)
Weber State U (UT)
Winona State U (MN)

ZOOLOGY/ANIMAL BIOLOGY RELATED

Thompson Rivers U (BC, Canada)

Entrance Difficulty

This index groups colleges by their own assessment of their entrance difficulty level. The colleges were asked to select the level that most closely corresponds to their entrance difficulty, according to the guidelines below. Institutions for which high school class rank and/or standardized test scores do not apply as admission criteria were asked to select the level that best indicates their entrance difficulty as compared to other institutions.

Most Difficult

More than 75 percent of the freshmen were in the top 10 percent of their high school class and scored over 1310 on the SAT (critical reading and mathematical combined) or over 29 on the ACT (composite); about 30 percent or fewer of the applicants were accepted.

Very Difficult

More than 50 percent of the freshmen were in the top 10 percent of their high school class and scored over 1230 on the SAT or over 26 on the ACT; about 60 percent or fewer applicants were accepted.

The U of Texas at Dallas (TX)
The U of Texas Medical Branch (TX)
U of Toronto (ON, Canada)
U of Tulsa (OK)
U of Virginia (VA)
The U of Western Ontario (ON, Canada)
U of Wisconsin–Madison (WI)
Ursinus Coll (PA)
Vanderbilt U (TN)
Vassar Coll (NY)
Villanova U (PA)
Wake Forest U (NC)
Washington & Jefferson Coll (PA)
Wheaton Coll (IL)
Wheaton Coll (MA)
Whitman Coll (WA)
Willamette U (OR)
Wofford Coll (SC)
Worcester Polytechnic Inst (MA)

Moderately Difficult

More than 75 percent of the freshmen were in the top half of their high school class and scored over 1010 on the SAT or over 18 on the ACT; about 85 percent or fewer of the applicants were accepted.

Abilene Christian U (TX)
Acadia U (NS, Canada)
Adams State Coll (CO)
Adelphi U (NY)
Alaska Pacific U (AK)
Alberta Coll of Art & Design (AB, Canada)
Albertus Magnus Coll (CT)
Albion Coll (MI)
Albright Coll (PA)
Alcorn State U (MS)
Alderson-Broaddus Coll (WV)
Alfred U (NY)
Allen Coll (IA)
Alliant Intl U–México City (Mexico)
Alma Coll (MI)
Alvernia U (PA)
Alverno Coll (WI)
American Intl Coll (MA)
American Jewish U (CA)
The American U of Paris (France)
Anderson U (IN)
Andrews U (MI)
Angelo State U (TX)
Appalachian State U (NC)
Aquinas Coll (MI)
Arcadia U (PA)
Arizona State U (AZ)
Arkansas Tech U (AR)
The Art Center Design Coll, Tucson (AZ)
Asbury U (KY)
Ashland U (OH)
Assumption Coll (MA)
Atlanta Christian Coll (GA)
Atlantic Union Coll (MA)
Auburn U (AL)
Auburn U Montgomery (AL)
Augsburg Coll (MN)
Augustana Coll (IL)
Augustana Coll (SD)
Aurora U (IL)
Austin Peay State U (TN)
Averett U (VA)
Azusa Pacific U (CA)
Baker U (KS)
Baldwin-Wallace Coll (OH)
Ball State U (IN)
Baptist Coll of Health Sciences (TN)
Barry U (FL)
Baylor U (TX)
Bay Path Coll (MA)
Belhaven U (MS)
Bellarmine U (KY)
Belmont Abbey Coll (NC)
Belmont U (TN)
Bemidji State U (MN)
Benedictine Coll (KS)
Benedictine U (IL)
Bennett Coll for Women (NC)
Berklee Coll of Music (MA)
Berry Coll (GA)
Bethany Bible Coll (NB, Canada)
Bethany Coll (KS)
Bethany Coll (WV)
Bethany Lutheran Coll (MN)
Bethel Coll (KS)
Bethel U (MN)
Birmingham-Southern Coll (AL)
Bishop's U (QC, Canada)
Blackburn Coll (IL)
Blessing-Rieman Coll of Nursing (IL)
Bloomfield Coll (NJ)
Bloomsburg U of Pennsylvania (PA)
Bluffton U (OH)
Boise State U (ID)
Boston Baptist Coll (MA)
The Boston Conservatory (MA)
Bowling Green State U (OH)
Brenau U (GA)
Brescia U (KY)
Briar Cliff U (IA)
Bridgewater Coll (VA)
Bridgewater State Coll (MA)
Brigham Young U (UT)
Brigham Young U–Hawaii (HI)
Brock U (ON, Canada)
Brooklyn Coll of the City U of New York (NY)
Bryan Coll (TN)
Bryant U (RI)
Buena Vista U (IA)
Buffalo State Coll, State U of New York (NY)
Burlington Coll (VT)
Butler U (IN)
Cabrini Coll (PA)
California Coll of the Arts (CA)
California Lutheran U (CA)
California Maritime Acad (CA)
California Polytechnic State U, San Luis Obispo (CA)
California State Polytechnic U, Pomona (CA)
California State U, Bakersfield (CA)
California State U, Chico (CA)
California State U, Dominguez Hills (CA)
California State U, East Bay (CA)
California State U, Fullerton (CA)
California State U, Long Beach (CA)
California State U, Los Angeles (CA)
California State U, Monterey Bay (CA)
California State U, Northridge (CA)
California State U, Sacramento (CA)
California State U, San Bernardino (CA)
California State U, San Marcos (CA)
California State U, Stanislaus (CA)
Calvin Coll (MI)
Campbellsville U (KY)
Canisius Coll (NY)
Cape Breton U (NS, Canada)
Capital U (OH)
Carlow U (PA)
Carroll U (WI)
Carson-Newman Coll (TN)
Castleton State Coll (VT)
Catawba Coll (NC)
The Catholic U of America (DC)
Cedar Crest Coll (PA)
Cedarville U (OH)
Centenary Coll (NJ)
Centenary Coll of Louisiana (LA)
Central Coll (IA)
Central Connecticut State U (CT)
Central Michigan U (MI)
Chaminade U of Honolulu (HI)
Champlain Coll (VT)
Charles Drew U of Medicine and Science (CA)
Chatham U (PA)
Christian Brothers U (TN)
Cincinnati Coll of Mortuary Science (OH)
The Citadel, The Military Coll of South Carolina (SC)
City Coll of the City U of New York (NY)
Clark Atlanta U (GA)
Clarke Coll (IA)
Clarkson Coll (NE)
Clark U (MA)
Cleary U (MI)
Clemson U (SC)
The Cleveland Inst of Art (OH)
Cleveland State U (OH)
Coastal Carolina U (SC)
Cogswell Polytechnical Coll (CA)
Coker Coll (SC)
The Coll at Brockport, State U of New York (NY)
Coll for Creative Studies (MI)
Coll of Charleston (SC)
The Coll of Idaho (ID)
Coll of Mount St. Joseph (OH)
Coll of Mount Saint Vincent (NY)
The Coll of New Rochelle (NY)
Coll of Notre Dame of Maryland (MD)
Coll of Saint Benedict (MN)
Coll of Saint Elizabeth (NJ)
The Coll of Saint Rose (NY)
The Coll of St. Scholastica (MN)
Coll of Santa Fe (NM)
Coll of Staten Island of the City U of New York (NY)
Coll of the Ozarks (MO)
Coll of Visual Arts (MN)
The Coll of Wooster (OH)
Colorado State U (CO)
Colorado State U–Pueblo (CO)
Columbia Coll (MO)
Columbia Coll (SC)
Columbia Coll Chicago (IL)
Columbus Coll of Art & Design (OH)
Concordia Coll (MN)
Concordia U (CA)
Concordia U (QC, Canada)
Concordia U Chicago (IL)
Concordia U Coll of Alberta (AB, Canada)
Concordia U Texas (TX)
Concordia U Wisconsin (WI)
Converse Coll (SC)
Coppin State U (MD)
Corban U (OR)
Corcoran Coll of Art and Design (DC)
Cornell Coll (IA)
Cornish Coll of the Arts (WA)
Covenant Coll (GA)
Creighton U (NE)
The Culinary Inst of America (NY)
Culver-Stockton Coll (MO)
Cumberland U (TN)
Curry Coll (MA)
Daemen Coll (NY)
Dakota Wesleyan U (SD)
Dallas Baptist U (TX)
Dana Coll (NE)
Defiance Coll (OH)
Delaware State U (DE)
Delaware Valley Coll (PA)
DePaul U (IL)
DePauw U (IN)
DeSales U (PA)
Dillard U (LA)
Doane Coll (NE)
Dominican U (IL)
Dominican U of California (CA)
Dordt Coll (IA)
Dowling Coll (NY)
Drake U (IA)
Drew U (NJ)
Drexel U (PA)
Drury U (MO)
Duquesne U (PA)
D'Youville Coll (NY)
East Carolina U (NC)
Eastern Connecticut State U (CT)
Eastern Illinois U (IL)
Eastern Mennonite U (VA)
Eastern Michigan U (MI)
Eastern Nazarene Coll (MA)
Eastern Washington U (WA)
East Stroudsburg U of Pennsylvania (PA)
East Tennessee State U (TN)
East Texas Baptist U (TX)
Eckerd Coll (FL)
ECPI Coll of Technology, Virginia Beach (VA)
ECPI Tech Coll, Roanoke (VA)
Edgewood Coll (WI)
Edinboro U of Pennsylvania (PA)
Elizabeth City State U (NC)
Elizabethtown Coll (PA)
Elmhurst Coll (IL)
Elmira Coll (NY)
Elon U (NC)
Embry-Riddle Aeronautical U (AZ)
Embry-Riddle Aeronautical U (FL)
Emmanuel Bible Coll (ON, Canada)
Emmanuel Coll (MA)
Emory & Henry Coll (VA)
Endicott Coll (MA)
Erskine Coll (SC)
Escuela de Artes Plasticas de Puerto Rico (PR)
Evangel U (MO)
The Evergreen State Coll (WA)
Fairfield U (CT)
Fairleigh Dickinson U, Coll at Florham (NJ)
Fairleigh Dickinson U, Metropolitan Campus (NJ)
Farmingdale State Coll (NY)
Fashion Inst of Technology (NY)
Felician Coll (NJ)
FIDM/The Fashion Inst of Design & Merchandising, Los Angeles Campus (CA)
Fisk U (TN)
Fitchburg State Coll (MA)
Five Towns Coll (NY)
Flagler Coll (FL)
Florida Ag and Mech U (FL)
Florida Atlantic U (FL)
Florida Coll (FL)

Moderately Difficult

Florida Gulf Coast U (FL)
Florida Inst of Technology (FL)
Florida Intl U (FL)
Florida Southern Coll (FL)
Fontbonne U (MO)
Fort Lewis Coll (CO)
Fort Valley State U (GA)
Framingham State Coll (MA)
Franciscan U of Steubenville (OH)
Francis Marion U (SC)
Franklin Coll (IN)
Franklin Coll Switzerland (Switzerland)
Franklin Pierce U (NH)
Freed-Hardeman U (TN)
Friends U (KS)
Frostburg State U (MD)
Gallaudet U (DC)
Gannon U (PA)
Gardner-Webb U (NC)
Geneva Coll (PA)
George Fox U (OR)
George Mason U (VA)
Georgetown Coll (KY)
Georgia Coll & State U (GA)
Georgian Court U (NJ)
Georgia Southern U (GA)
Georgia State U (GA)
Goddard Coll (VT)
Goldey-Beacom Coll (DE)
Gonzaga U (WA)
Gordon Coll (MA)
Goshen Coll (IN)
Goucher Coll (MD)
Grace Coll (IN)
Graceland U (IA)
Grand Valley State U (MI)
Great Lakes Christian Coll (MI)
Green Mountain Coll (VT)
Greensboro Coll (NC)
Greenville Coll (IL)
Guilford Coll (NC)
Gwynedd-Mercy Coll (PA)
Hamline U (MN)
Hampden-Sydney Coll (VA)
Hampshire Coll (MA)
Hampton U (VA)
Hannibal-LaGrange Coll (MO)
Hanover Coll (IN)
Harding U (AR)
Hardin-Simmons U (TX)
Harrison Coll, Elkhart (IN)
Harrison Coll, Evansville (IN)
Harrison Coll, Fort Wayne (IN)
Harrison Coll, Indianapolis (IN)
Harrison Coll, Lafayette (IN)
Harrison Coll, Muncie (IN)
Harrison Coll, Terre Haute (IN)
Hartwick Coll (NY)
Hawai'i Pacific U (HI)
HEC Montreal (QC, Canada)
Heidelberg U (OH)
Henderson State U (AR)
Herzing U (GA)
Herzing U (WI)
High Point U (NC)
Hiram Coll (OH)
Hofstra U (NY)
Hollins U (VA)
Holy Family U (PA)
Holy Names U (CA)
Hood Coll (MD)
Hope Coll (MI)
Houghton Coll (NY)
Houston Baptist U (TX)
Howard Payne U (TX)
Hult Intl Business School (United Kingdom)
Humboldt State U (CA)
Hunter Coll of the City U of New York (NY)
Huntingdon Coll (AL)
Huntington U (IN)
Husson U (ME)
Huston-Tillotson U (TX)
Illinois Coll (IL)
Illinois State U (IL)
Immaculata U (PA)
Indiana State U (IN)
Indiana Tech (IN)
Indiana U Bloomington (IN)
Indiana U East (IN)
Indiana U of Pennsylvania (PA)
Indiana U–Purdue U Indianapolis (IN)
Indiana U South Bend (IN)
Indiana Wesleyan U (IN)
Inter American U of Puerto Rico, Aguadilla Campus (PR)
Inter American U of Puerto Rico, Arecibo Campus (PR)
Inter American U of Puerto Rico, Fajardo Campus (PR)
Inter American U of Puerto Rico, Guayama Campus (PR)
Inter American U of Puerto Rico, Ponce Campus (PR)
Inter American U of Puerto Rico, San Germán Campus (PR)
Iona Coll (NY)
Iowa State U of Science and Technology (IA)
Iowa Wesleyan Coll (IA)
Ithaca Coll (NY)
Jacksonville U (FL)
Jefferson Coll of Health Sciences (VA)
John Brown U (AR)
John Cabot U (Italy)
John Carroll U (OH)
John Jay Coll of Criminal Justice of the City U of New York (NY)
Johnson Bible Coll (TN)
Johnson C. Smith U (NC)
Johnson State Coll (VT)
Judson Coll (AL)
Judson U (IL)
Juniata Coll (PA)
Kean U (NJ)
Keene State Coll (NH)
Kendall Coll (IL)
Kennesaw State U (GA)
Kent State U (OH)
Kentucky Wesleyan Coll (KY)
Keuka Coll (NY)
King Coll (TN)
King's Coll (PA)
The King's U Coll (AB, Canada)
Kutztown U of Pennsylvania (PA)
Kuyper Coll (MI)
LaGrange Coll (GA)
Lake Erie Coll (OH)
Lakehead U (ON, Canada)
Lake Superior State U (MI)
Lakeview Coll of Nursing (IL)
La Salle U (PA)
Lasell Coll (MA)
La Sierra U (CA)
Lawrence Technological U (MI)
Lebanon Valley Coll (PA)
Lehman Coll of the City U of New York (NY)
Le Moyne Coll (NY)
Lewis U (IL)
LIM Coll (NY)
Lincoln Christian U (IL)
Lincoln Memorial U (TN)
Lincoln U (PA)
Lindenwood U (MO)
Linfield Coll (OR)
Lipscomb U (TN)
Lock Haven U of Pennsylvania (PA)
Logan U–Coll of Chiropractic (MO)
Long Island U, C.W. Post Campus (NY)
Longwood U (VA)
Loras Coll (IA)
Louisiana Coll (LA)
Louisiana State U and Ag and Mech Coll (LA)
Louisiana State U in Shreveport (LA)
Louisiana Tech U (LA)
Loyola U Chicago (IL)
Loyola U Maryland (MD)
Loyola U New Orleans (LA)
Lubbock Christian U (TX)
Luther Coll (IA)
Lycoming Coll (PA)
Lyme Acad Coll of Fine Arts (CT)
Lynchburg Coll (VA)
Lynn U (FL)
Lyon Coll (AR)
Madonna U (MI)
Maharishi U of Management (IA)
Maine Coll of Art (ME)
Malone U (OH)
Manchester Coll (IN)
Manhattan Coll (NY)
Manhattanville Coll (NY)
Mansfield U of Pennsylvania (PA)
Marian U (IN)
Marian U (WI)
Marietta Coll (OH)
Marlboro Coll (VT)
Marquette U (WI)
Marshall U (WV)
Mars Hill Coll (NC)
Martin Luther Coll (MN)
Mary Baldwin Coll (VA)
Marymount Manhattan Coll (NY)
Marymount U (VA)
Maryville Coll (TN)
Maryville U of Saint Louis (MO)
Marywood U (PA)
Massachusetts Coll of Liberal Arts (MA)
Massachusetts Coll of Pharmacy and Health Sciences (MA)
Massachusetts Maritime Acad (MA)
The Master's Coll and Sem (CA)
McDaniel Coll (MD)
McKendree U (IL)
McMurry U (TX)
McNally Smith Coll of Music (MN)
McNeese State U (LA)
McPherson Coll (KS)
Medaille Coll (NY)
Medcenter One Coll of Nursing (ND)
Medical Coll of Georgia (GA)
Memorial U of Newfoundland (NL, Canada)
Memphis Coll of Art (TN)
Menlo Coll (CA)
Mercer U (GA)
Mercy Coll (NY)
Mercy Coll of Northwest Ohio (OH)
Mercyhurst Coll (PA)
Meredith Coll (NC)
Merrimack Coll (MA)
Messiah Coll (PA)
Methodist U (NC)
Metropolitan Coll of New York (NY)
Miami U (OH)
Michigan State U (MI)
Michigan Technological U (MI)
MidAmerica Nazarene U (KS)
Middle Tennessee State U (TN)
Millersville U of Pennsylvania (PA)
Milligan Coll (TN)
Millikin U (IL)
Millsaps Coll (MS)
Mills Coll (CA)
Milwaukee School of Eng (WI)
Minneapolis Coll of Art and Design (MN)
Minnesota State U Mankato (MN)
Minnesota State U Moorhead (MN)
Misericordia U (PA)
Mississippi Coll (MS)
Mississippi State U (MS)
Mississippi U for Women (MS)
Missouri Baptist U (MO)
Missouri Southern State U (MO)
Missouri State U (MO)
Mitchell Coll (CT)
Molloy Coll (NY)
Monmouth Coll (IL)
Monmouth U (NJ)
Monroe Coll, Bronx (NY)
Monroe Coll, New Rochelle (NY)
Montana State U (MT)
Montana State U Billings (MT)
Montana Tech of The U of Montana (MT)
Montclair State U (NJ)
Moody Bible Inst (IL)
Moore Coll of Art & Design (PA)
Moravian Coll (PA)
Morehouse Coll (GA)
Morningside Coll (IA)
Mount Allison U (NB, Canada)
Mount Carmel Coll of Nursing (OH)
Mount Ida Coll (MA)
Mount Mary Coll (WI)
Mount Mercy Coll (IA)
Mount Saint Mary Coll (NY)
Mount St. Mary's Coll (CA)
Mount St. Mary's U (MD)
Mount Vernon Nazarene U (OH)
Multnomah U (OR)
Murray State U (KY)
Naropa U (CO)
Nazareth Coll of Rochester (NY)
Nebraska Methodist Coll (NE)
Nebraska Wesleyan U (NE)
Neumann U (PA)
Neumont U (UT)
Newberry Coll (SC)
New Hampshire Inst of Art (NH)
New Jersey City U (NJ)
New Jersey Inst of Technology (NJ)
New Mexico Inst of Mining and Technology (NM)
New Mexico State U (NM)
New Saint Andrews Coll (ID)
The New School for General Studies (NY)
New York Inst of Technology (NY)
New York School of Interior Design (NY)
Niagara U (NY)
Nichols Coll (MA)
Nipissing U (ON, Canada)
North Central Coll (IL)
North Dakota State U (ND)

Entrance Difficulty

Moderately Difficult

U of Illinois at Chicago (IL)
U of Illinois at Springfield (IL)
U of Indianapolis (IN)
The U of Iowa (IA)
The U of Kansas (KS)
U of Kentucky (KY)
U of King's Coll (NS, Canada)
U of La Verne (CA)
U of Lethbridge (AB, Canada)
U of Louisville (KY)
U of Maine (ME)
U of Maine at Farmington (ME)
U of Maine at Machias (ME)
U of Manitoba (MB, Canada)
U of Mary Hardin-Baylor (TX)
U of Maryland, Baltimore County (MD)
U of Maryland, Coll Park (MD)
U of Maryland Eastern Shore (MD)
U of Massachusetts Amherst (MA)
U of Massachusetts Boston (MA)
U of Massachusetts Dartmouth (MA)
U of Massachusetts Lowell (MA)
U of Memphis (TN)
U of Michigan–Dearborn (MI)
U of Michigan–Flint (MI)
U of Minnesota, Crookston (MN)
U of Minnesota, Duluth (MN)
U of Minnesota, Twin Cities Campus (MN)
U of Mississippi (MS)
U of Missouri (MO)
U of Missouri–Kansas City (MO)
U of Missouri–St. Louis (MO)
U of Mobile (AL)
U of Montevallo (AL)
U of Mount Union (OH)
U of Nebraska at Kearney (NE)
U of Nebraska–Lincoln (NE)
U of Nevada, Las Vegas (NV)
U of Nevada, Reno (NV)
U of New Brunswick Fredericton (NB, Canada)
U of New England (ME)
U of New Hampshire (NH)
U of New Hampshire at Manchester (NH)
U of New Haven (CT)
U of New Mexico (NM)
U of New Orleans (LA)
The U of North Carolina at Asheville (NC)
The U of North Carolina at Charlotte (NC)
The U of North Carolina at Greensboro (NC)
The U of North Carolina at Pembroke (NC)
The U of North Carolina Wilmington (NC)
U of Northern Colorado (CO)
U of Northern Iowa (IA)
U of Oklahoma (OK)
U of Oregon (OR)
U of Ottawa (ON, Canada)
U of Pittsburgh (PA)
U of Pittsburgh at Greensburg (PA)
U of Pittsburgh at Johnstown (PA)
U of Portland (OR)
U of Puerto Rico at Humacao (PR)
U of Puerto Rico at Utuado (PR)
U of Puerto Rico, Cayey U Coll (PR)
U of Redlands (CA)
U of Rhode Island (RI)
U of St. Francis (IL)
U of Saint Mary (KS)
U of St. Thomas (MN)
U of St. Thomas (TX)
U of San Francisco (CA)
U of Saskatchewan (SK, Canada)
U of Science and Arts of Oklahoma (OK)
The U of Scranton (PA)
U of South Alabama (AL)
U of South Carolina (SC)
U of South Carolina Aiken (SC)
U of South Carolina Upstate (SC)
The U of South Dakota (SD)
U of Southern Indiana (IN)
U of Southern Maine (ME)
U of Southern Mississippi (MS)
U of South Florida (FL)
The U of Tampa (FL)
The U of Tennessee (TN)
The U of Tennessee at Chattanooga (TN)
The U of Tennessee at Martin (TN)
The U of Texas at Arlington (TX)
The U of Texas at San Antonio (TX)
The U of Texas at Tyler (TX)
The U of Texas Health Science Center at Houston (TX)
The U of Texas of the Permian Basin (TX)
The U of Texas Southwestern Medical Center at Dallas (TX)
U of the Cumberlands (KY)
U of the Incarnate Word (TX)
U of the Ozarks (AR)
U of the Pacific (CA)
U of the Sciences in Philadelphia (PA)
U of the Southwest (NM)
U of Utah (UT)
U of Vermont (VT)
The U of Virginia's Coll at Wise (VA)
U of Washington (WA)
U of Washington, Bothell (WA)
U of Waterloo (ON, Canada)
U of West Florida (FL)
U of Windsor (ON, Canada)
U of Wisconsin–Eau Claire (WI)
U of Wisconsin–Green Bay (WI)
U of Wisconsin–La Crosse (WI)
U of Wisconsin–Milwaukee (WI)
U of Wisconsin–Oshkosh (WI)
U of Wisconsin–Parkside (WI)
U of Wisconsin–Platteville (WI)
U of Wisconsin–River Falls (WI)
U of Wisconsin–Stevens Point (WI)
U of Wisconsin–Stout (WI)
U of Wisconsin–Superior (WI)
U of Wisconsin–Whitewater (WI)
U of Wyoming (WY)
Upper Iowa U (IA)
Utah State U (UT)
Utica Coll (NY)
Valdosta State U (GA)
Valparaiso U (IN)
VanderCook Coll of Music (IL)
Vanguard U of Southern California (CA)
Vermont Tech Coll (VT)
Virginia Military Inst (VA)
Virginia Polytechnic Inst and State U (VA)
Virginia Union U (VA)
Virginia Wesleyan Coll (VA)
Viterbo U (WI)
Voorhees Coll (SC)
Wabash Coll (IN)
Wagner Coll (NY)
Waldorf Coll (IA)
Walsh U (OH)
Warner Pacific Coll (OR)
Wartburg Coll (IA)
Washington Adventist U (MD)
Washington Coll (MD)
Washington State U (WA)
Watkins Coll of Art, Design, & Film (TN)
Waynesburg U (PA)
Wayne State U (MI)
Webber Intl U (FL)
Webster U (MO)
Wells Coll (NY)
Wentworth Inst of Technology (MA)
Wesleyan Coll (GA)
West Chester U of Pennsylvania (PA)
Western Carolina U (NC)
Western Connecticut State U (CT)
Western Illinois U (IL)
Western Intl U (AZ)
Western Michigan U (MI)
Western New England Coll (MA)
Western Oregon U (OR)
Western State Coll of Colorado (CO)
Western Washington U (WA)
Westfield State Coll (MA)
Westminster Coll (MO)
Westminster Coll (UT)
Westmont Coll (CA)
West Suburban Coll of Nursing (IL)
West Virginia U (WV)
West Virginia Wesleyan Coll (WV)
Wheeling Jesuit U (WV)
Whittier Coll (CA)
Widener U (PA)
Wilkes U (PA)
William Jewell Coll (MO)
William Paterson U of New Jersey (NJ)
William Penn U (IA)
Wilmington Coll (OH)
Wilson Coll (PA)
Wingate U (NC)
Winona State U (MN)
Winthrop U (SC)
Wittenberg U (OH)
Woodbury U (CA)
Worcester State Coll (MA)
Xavier U (OH)
Xavier U of Louisiana (LA)
Yeshiva U (NY)
York Coll (NE)
York Coll of Pennsylvania (PA)
York Coll of the City U of New York (NY)
York U (ON, Canada)
Young Harris Coll (GA)

Minimally Difficult

Most freshmen were not in the top half of their high school class and scored somewhat below 1010 on the SAT or below 19 on the ACT; up to 95 percent the applicants were accepted.

AIB Coll of Business (IA)
Alabama Ag and Mech U (AL)
Alabama State U (AL)
Albany State U (GA)
Allen U (SC)
Amberton U (TX)
American Coll of Thessaloniki (Greece)
Amridge U (AL)
Aquinas Coll (TN)
Arkansas State U—Jonesboro (AR)
Armstrong Atlantic State U (GA)
Austin Graduate School of Theology (TX)
Avila U (MO)
Baker Coll of Allen Park (MI)
Baker Coll of Auburn Hills (MI)
Baker Coll of Cadillac (MI)
Baker Coll of Clinton Township (MI)
Baker Coll of Flint (MI)
Baker Coll of Jackson (MI)
Baker Coll of Muskegon (MI)
Baker Coll of Owosso (MI)
Baker Coll of Port Huron (MI)
Baptist Bible Coll of Pennsylvania (PA)
Barclay Coll (KS)
Barton Coll (NC)
Beacon Coll (FL)
Bethany U (CA)
Bethel Coll (IN)
Bethel U (TN)
Bethune-Cookman U (FL)
Black Hills State U (SD)
Bluefield Coll (VA)
Blue Mountain Coll (MS)
Bob Jones U (SC)
Bowie State U (MD)
Bradley U (IL)
Brevard Coll (NC)
Brewton-Parker Coll (GA)
Bryant & Stratton Coll, Cleveland (OH)
Bryant & Stratton Coll, Eastlake (OH)
Bryant & Stratton Coll, Parma (OH)
Bryant & Stratton Coll (WI)
Bryant & Stratton Coll—Richmond Campus (VA)
Bryant & Stratton Coll—Virginia Beach (VA)
Bryn Athyn Coll of the New Church (PA)
California Baptist U (CA)
California State U, Fresno (CA)
Calvary Bible Coll and Theological Sem (MO)
Cameron U (OK)
Capella U (MN)
Cazenovia Coll (NY)
Central Baptist Coll (AR)
Central Christian Coll of Kansas (KS)
Central Pennsylvania Coll (PA)
Central State U (OH)
Cheyney U of Pennsylvania (PA)
Chowan U (NC)
Cincinnati Christian U (OH)
Claflin U (SC)
Clarion U of Pennsylvania (PA)
Clayton State U (GA)
Clearwater Christian Coll (FL)
Cleveland Chiropractic Coll–Los Angeles Campus (CA)
Coll of St. Joseph (VT)
Coll of Saint Mary (NE)
Columbia Intl U (SC)
Columbus State U (GA)
Concordia U, St. Paul (MN)
Concord U (WV)
Cornerstone U (MI)
Crandall U (NB, Canada)
Crichton Coll (TN)
Crown Coll (MN)
Culinary Inst of Virginia (VA)
Dakota State U (SD)
Davenport U, Grand Rapids (MI)
Davis Coll (NY)
DeVry Coll of New York (NY)
DeVry U, Phoenix (AZ)
DeVry U, Fremont (CA)
DeVry U, Long Beach (CA)
DeVry U, Pomona (CA)
DeVry U, Miramar (FL)
DeVry U, Orlando (FL)
DeVry U, Alpharetta (GA)

INDEXES

DeVry U, Decatur (GA)
DeVry U, Addison (IL)
DeVry U, Chicago (IL)
DeVry U, Tinley Park (IL)
DeVry U, Indianapolis (IN)
DeVry U (MD)
DeVry U, Kansas City (MO)
DeVry U (NV)
DeVry U, North Brunswick (NJ)
DeVry U, Charlotte (NC)
DeVry U, Columbus (OH)
DeVry U (OR)
DeVry U, Fort Washington (PA)
DeVry U, Irving (TX)
DeVry U, Arlington (VA)
DeVry U, Federal Way (WA)
DeVry U, Milwaukee (WI)
Dickinson State U (ND)
DigiPen Inst of Technology (WA)
East Central U (OK)
Eastern New Mexico U (NM)
East-West U (IL)
EDP Coll of Puerto Rico, Inc. (PR)
EDP Coll of Puerto Rico–San Sebastian (PR)
Embry-Riddle Aeronautical U Worldwide (FL)
Emmanuel Coll (GA)
Eugene Bible Coll (OR)
Fairmont State U (WV)
Faith Baptist Bible Coll and Theological Sem (IA)
Faulkner U (AL)
Fayetteville State U (NC)
Ferris State U (MI)
Ferrum Coll (VA)
Fisher Coll (MA)
Globe Inst of Technology (NY)
Goodwin Coll (CT)
Grace Bible Coll (MI)
Grand View U (IA)
Griggs U (MD)
Harrisburg U of Science and Technology (PA)
Hebrew Coll (MA)
Hellenic Coll (MA)
Heritage Bible Coll (NC)
Hilbert Coll (NY)
Hodges U (FL)
Idaho State U (ID)
Indiana U Kokomo (IN)
Indiana U Northwest (IN)
Indiana U–Purdue U Fort Wayne (IN)
Indiana U Southeast (IN)
Intl Acad of Design & Technology (IL)
ITT Tech Inst, Bessemer (AL)
ITT Tech Inst, Phoenix (AZ)
ITT Tech Inst, Tucson (AZ)
ITT Tech Inst (AR)
ITT Tech Inst, Anaheim (CA)
ITT Tech Inst, Lathrop (CA)
ITT Tech Inst, Oxnard (CA)
ITT Tech Inst, Rancho Cordova (CA)
ITT Tech Inst, San Bernardino (CA)
ITT Tech Inst, San Diego (CA)
ITT Tech Inst, San Dimas (CA)
ITT Tech Inst, Sylmar (CA)
ITT Tech Inst, Torrance (CA)
ITT Tech Inst, Thornton (CO)
ITT Tech Inst, Fort Lauderdale (FL)
ITT Tech Inst, Jacksonville (FL)
ITT Tech Inst, Lake Mary (FL)
ITT Tech Inst, Miami (FL)
ITT Tech Inst, Tampa (FL)
ITT Tech Inst, Duluth (GA)
ITT Tech Inst (ID)
ITT Tech Inst, Burr Ridge (IL)
ITT Tech Inst, Mount Prospect (IL)
ITT Tech Inst, Orland Park (IL)
ITT Tech Inst, Fort Wayne (IN)
ITT Tech Inst, Indianapolis (IN)
ITT Tech Inst, Newburgh (IN)
ITT Tech Inst, Louisville (KY)
ITT Tech Inst, St. Rose (LA)
ITT Tech Inst, Norwood (MA)
ITT Tech Inst, Woburn (MA)
ITT Tech Inst, Canton (MI)
ITT Tech Inst, Troy (MI)
ITT Tech Inst, Wyoming (MI)
ITT Tech Inst, Arnold (MO)
ITT Tech Inst, Earth City (MO)
ITT Tech Inst (NE)
ITT Tech Inst (NV)
ITT Tech Inst (NM)
ITT Tech Inst (OR)
ITT Tech Inst, Greenville (SC)
ITT Tech Inst, Cordova (TN)
ITT Tech Inst, Knoxville (TN)
ITT Tech Inst, Nashville (TN)
ITT Tech Inst, Arlington (TX)
ITT Tech Inst, Austin (TX)
ITT Tech Inst, Houston (TX)
ITT Tech Inst, Houston (TX)
ITT Tech Inst, Webster (TX)
ITT Tech Inst (UT)
ITT Tech Inst, Chantilly (VA)
ITT Tech Inst, Norfolk (VA)
ITT Tech Inst, Richmond (VA)
ITT Tech Inst, Springfield (VA)
ITT Tech Inst, Seattle (WA)
ITT Tech Inst, Spokane Valley (WA)
ITT Tech Inst, Green Bay (WI)
ITT Tech Inst, Greenfield (WI)
Jackson State U (MS)
Jacksonville State U (AL)
Jamestown Business Coll (NY)
Jamestown Coll (ND)
Jarvis Christian Coll (TX)
Johnson & Wales U (CO)
Johnson & Wales U (FL)
Johnson & Wales U (RI)
Johnson & Wales U—Charlotte Campus (NC)
John Wesley Coll (NC)
Kentucky State U (KY)
Keystone Coll (PA)
Lakeland Coll (WI)
Lamar U (TX)
Lane Coll (TN)
La Roche Coll (PA)
Lees-McRae Coll (NC)
Lee U (TN)
Lewis-Clark State Coll (ID)
Liberty U (VA)
Life U (GA)
Limestone Coll (SC)
Lincoln Coll–Normal (IL)
Lincoln Coll of New England, Southington (CT)
Lincoln U (CA)
Lindsey Wilson Coll (KY)
Long Island U, Brooklyn Campus (NY)
Lourdes Coll (OH)
Maple Springs Baptist Bible Coll and Sem (MD)
Maria Coll (NY)
Marymount Coll, Palos Verdes, California (CA)
Metropolitan State Coll of Denver (CO)
Mid-Atlantic Christian U (NC)
Mid-Continent U (KY)
Middle Georgia Coll (GA)
Midway Coll (KY)
Midwestern State U (TX)
Minot State U (ND)
Mississippi Valley State U (MS)
Morehead State U (KY)
Mount Aloysius Coll (PA)
Mount Marty Coll (SD)
Mount Olive Coll (NC)
National U (CA)
Nevada State Coll at Henderson (NV)
Newbury Coll (MA)
New England Coll (NH)
New England School of Communications (ME)
Newman U (KS)
New Mexico Highlands U (NM)
North Carolina Central U (NC)
Northcentral U (AZ)
Northeastern Illinois U (IL)
Northern Kentucky U (KY)
Northern Michigan U (MI)
Northern State U (SD)
North Greenville U (SC)
Notre Dame de Namur U (CA)
Nova Scotia Ag Coll (NS, Canada)
Oak Hills Christian Coll (MN)
Oakland City U (IN)
Oakwood U (AL)
Ohio Valley U (WV)
Oklahoma Wesleyan U (OK)
Oregon Coll of Art & Craft (OR)
Our Lady of the Lake Coll (LA)
Pacific States U (CA)
Paine Coll (GA)
Pittsburg State U (KS)
Polytechnic U of Puerto Rico (PR)
Pontifical Coll Josephinum (OH)
Post U (CT)
Purdue U North Central (IN)
Regent U (VA)
Robert Morris U (PA)
Robert Morris U Illinois (IL)
Rochester Coll (MI)
Sage Coll of Albany (NY)
Saint Joseph Sem Coll (LA)
St. Louis Christian Coll (MO)
Saint Paul's Coll (VA)
Salem State Coll (MA)
Savannah State U (GA)
Shaw U (NC)
Silver Lake Coll (WI)
Somerset Christian Coll (NJ)
South Carolina State U (SC)
South Dakota State U (SD)
Southeastern U (FL)
Southern Vermont Coll (VT)
Southern Wesleyan U (SC)
Southwestern Adventist U (TX)
Southwestern Oklahoma State U (OK)
Southwest Minnesota State U (MN)
State U of New York Coll of Technology at Canton (NY)
State U of New York Empire State Coll (NY)
Steinbach Bible Coll (MB, Canada)
Sterling Coll (KS)
Stillman Coll (AL)
Sullivan U (KY)
Tennessee Wesleyan Coll (TN)
Texas Woman's U (TX)
Trinity Coll of Florida (FL)
Truett-McConnell Coll (GA)
TUI U (CA)
Union Inst & U (OH)
Universidad Adventista de las Antillas (PR)
U of Alaska Fairbanks (AK)
U of Arkansas at Fort Smith (AR)
U of Arkansas at Little Rock (AR)
U of Baltimore (MD)
U of Central Oklahoma (OK)
U of Houston–Clear Lake (TX)
U of Houston–Victoria (TX)
U of Louisiana at Monroe (LA)
U of Maine at Fort Kent (ME)
U of Maine at Presque Isle (ME)
U of Mary (ND)
The U of Montana Western (MT)
U of Nebraska at Omaha (NE)
U of North Alabama (AL)
U of North Dakota (ND)
U of Pittsburgh at Bradford (PA)
U of Pittsburgh at Titusville (PA)
U of Regina (SK, Canada)
U of South Carolina Beaufort (SC)
The U of Texas at El Paso (TX)
U of the Virgin Islands (VI)
U of Washington, Tacoma (WA)
The U of West Alabama (AL)
U of West Georgia (GA)
Ursuline Coll (OH)
Valley Forge Christian Coll (PA)
Valley Forge Christian Coll Woodbridge Campus (VA)
Vaughn Coll of Aeronautics and Technology (NY)
Villa Maria Coll of Buffalo (NY)
Virginia Intermont Coll (VA)
Virginia State U (VA)
Wayland Baptist U (TX)
Western Kentucky U (KY)
West Liberty U (WV)
West Virginia State U (WV)
Wheelock Coll (MA)
Wilberforce U (OH)
Wilfrid Laurier U (ON, Canada)
Winston-Salem State U (NC)
Wright State U (OH)

Noncompetitive

Virtually all applicants were accepted regardless of high school rank or test scores.

Acad of Art U (CA)
American Baptist Coll of American Baptist Theological Sem (TN)
American Public U System (WV)
Andrew Jackson U (AL)
Antioch U McGregor (OH)
Antioch U Seattle (WA)
Appalachian Bible Coll (WV)
Athabasca U (AB, Canada)
The Baptist Coll of Florida (FL)
Beulah Heights U (GA)
Bluefield State Coll (WV)
Boston Architectural Coll (MA)
Bowling Green State U–Firelands Coll (OH)
Brookline Coll, Phoenix (AZ)
Brookline Coll, Tempe (AZ)
Brookline Coll (NM)
Calumet Coll of Saint Joseph (IN)

Entrance Difficulty

Noncompetitive

Cambridge Coll (MA)
Carlos Albizu U (PR)
Carolina Christian Coll (NC)
Charter Oak State Coll (CT)
Chipola Coll (FL)
Christian Life Coll (IL)
City U of Seattle (WA)
Clear Creek Baptist Bible Coll (KY)
Collège Dominicain de Philosophie et de Théologie (ON, Canada)
Coll of Biblical Studies–Houston (TX)
Coll of Coastal Georgia (GA)
Columbia Coll, Caguas (PR)
Columbia Southern U (AL)
Crossroads Bible Coll (IN)
Dalton State Coll (GA)
Daymar Inst, Clarksville (TN)
Daytona State Coll (FL)
Delta State U (MS)
DeVry U, Westminster (CO)
Dixie State Coll of Utah (UT)
Dominican Coll (NY)
Donnelly Coll (KS)
Ecclesia Coll (AR)
Edward Waters Coll (FL)
Emporia State U (KS)
Excelsior Coll (NY)
Florida National Coll (FL)
Fort Hays State U (KS)
Franklin U (OH)
Free Will Baptist Bible Coll (TN)
Gainesville State Coll (GA)
Glenville State Coll (WV)
Global U (MO)
Grambling State U (LA)
Granite State Coll (NH)
Grantham U (MO)
Hamilton Tech Coll (IA)
Harrington Coll of Design (IL)
Harris-Stowe State U (MO)
Heritage Baptist Coll and Heritage Theological Sem (ON, Canada)
Heritage Christian U (AL)
Hillsdale Free Will Baptist Coll (OK)
Holy Apostles Coll and Sem (CT)
Huntington Coll of Health Sciences (TN)
Indian River State Coll (FL)
Jones Coll, Jacksonville (FL)
Jones Intl U (CO)
Kansas State U (KS)
Kent State U at Ashtabula (OH)
Kent State U at Salem (OH)
Kent State U at Stark (OH)
Kent State U at Trumbull (OH)
Kent State U at Tuscarawas (OH)
Laura and Alvin Siegal Coll of Judaic Studies (OH)
Lexington Coll (IL)
Lincoln U (MO)
Maranatha Baptist Bible Coll (WI)
Marylhurst U (OR)
Master's Coll and Sem (ON, Canada)
Mayville State U (ND)
Medgar Evers Coll of the City U of New York (NY)
Miami Dade Coll (FL)
Miami U Hamilton (OH)
Midland Coll (TX)
Midwives Coll of Utah (UT)
Missouri Western State U (MO)
Morris Coll (SC)
Mountain State U (WV)
Nazarene Bible Coll (CO)
New York City Coll of Technology of the City U of New York (NY)
Nicholls State U (LA)
Northwest Florida State Coll (FL)
The Ohio State U at Lima (OH)
The Ohio State U at Marion (OH)
The Ohio State U–Mansfield Campus (OH)
The Ohio State U–Newark Campus (OH)
Ohio U–Zanesville (OH)
Oklahoma Christian U (OK)
Oklahoma Panhandle State U (OK)
Oklahoma State U, Oklahoma City (OK)
Palmer Coll of Chiropractic (IA)
Patten U (CA)
Peirce Coll (PA)
Pennsylvania Coll of Technology (PA)
Peru State Coll (NE)
Piedmont Baptist Coll and Graduate School (NC)
Pikeville Coll (KY)
Pioneer Pacific Coll, Wilsonville (OR)
Polk State Coll (FL)
Potomac Coll (DC)
Potomac State Coll of West Virginia U (WV)
Presentation Coll (SD)
Rogers State U (OK)
St. Augustine Coll (IL)
St. Petersburg Coll (FL)
Santa Fe Comm Coll (FL)
Shasta Bible Coll (CA)
Shawnee State U (OH)
Southern U at New Orleans (LA)
Southwestern Assemblies of God U (TX)
Southwest Florida Coll, Fort Myers (FL)
Spartan Coll of Aeronautics and Technology (OK)
State Coll of Florida Manatee-Sarasota (FL)
Sul Ross State U (TX)
Texas Coll (TX)
Texas Southern U (TX)
Thomas Edison State Coll (NJ)
Université du Québec en Outaouais (QC, Canada)
U of Alaska Anchorage (AK)
U of Alaska Anchorage, Kenai Peninsula Coll (AK)
U of Alaska Southeast (AK)
U of Arkansas at Monticello (AR)
U of Guam (GU)
U of Houston–Downtown (TX)
U of Maine at Augusta (ME)
U of Maryland U Coll (MD)
U of Rio Grande (OH)
The U of Texas at Brownsville (TX)
The U of Texas–Pan American (TX)
U of the District of Columbia (DC)
The U of Toledo (OH)
Utah Valley U (UT)
Valley City State U (ND)
Vincennes U Jasper Campus (IN)
Virginia U of Lynchburg (VA)
Washburn U (KS)
Wayne State Coll (NE)
Weber State U (UT)
Wichita State U (KS)
William Jessup U (CA)
Wilmington U (DE)
Youngstown State U (OH)

Cost Ranges

Less than $2000

Colleges with No Room and Board or with Room Only
Andrew Jackson U (AL)

Colleges with Room and Board
The Colburn School Conservatory of Music (CA)
United States Air Force Acad (CO)
United States Military Acad (NY)

$2000–$3999

Colleges with No Room and Board or with Room Only
Chipola Coll (FL)
Coll of Coastal Georgia (GA)
Dalton State Coll (GA)
Daytona State Coll (FL)
Gainesville State Coll (GA)
Louisiana State U in Shreveport (LA)
Metropolitan State Coll of Denver (CO)
Miami Dade Coll (FL)
Nevada State Coll at Henderson (NV)
Northwest Florida State Coll (FL)
Oklahoma State U, Oklahoma City (OK)
Polk State Coll (FL)
Santa Fe Comm Coll (FL)
Southern U at New Orleans (LA)
State Coll of Florida Manatee-Sarasota (FL)
U of Atlanta (GA)
U of Puerto Rico at Bayamón (PR)
U of Puerto Rico at Humacao (PR)

$4000–$5999

Colleges with No Room and Board or with Room Only
Amberton U (TX)
Bernard M. Baruch Coll of the City U of New York (NY)
Bluefield State Coll (WV)
Bowling Green State U–Firelands Coll (OH)
Brooklyn Coll of the City U of New York (NY)
California State U, San Bernardino (CA)
City Coll of the City U of New York (NY)
Coll of Biblical Studies–Houston (TX)
Coll of Staten Island of the City U of New York (NY)
Embry-Riddle Aeronautical U Worldwide (FL)
Indiana U East (IN)
Indiana U Kokomo (IN)
Indiana U Northwest (IN)
Inter American U of Puerto Rico, Aguadilla Campus (PR)
Inter American U of Puerto Rico, Bayamón Campus (PR)
Inter American U of Puerto Rico, Guayama Campus (PR)
Inter American U of Puerto Rico, Ponce Campus (PR)
Inter American U of Puerto Rico, San Germán Campus (PR)
John Jay Coll of Criminal Justice of the City U of New York (NY)
Kent State U at Ashtabula (OH)
Kent State U at Stark (OH)
Kent State U at Tuscarawas (OH)
Lincoln U (MO)
Logan U–Coll of Chiropractic (MO)
Medgar Evers Coll of the City U of New York (NY)
Miami U Hamilton (OH)
Montana State U (MT)
Norfolk State U (VA)
The Ohio State U at Lima (OH)
The Ohio State U at Marion (OH)
The Ohio State U–Newark Campus (OH)
Ohio U–Zanesville (OH)
Oregon State U–Cascades (OR)
State U of New York Empire State Coll (NY)
Thomas Edison State Coll (NJ)
U of Hawaii–West Oahu (HI)
U of Houston–Downtown (TX)
U of Houston–Victoria (TX)
U of Maryland U Coll (MD)
U of Oklahoma Health Sciences Center (OK)
U of the District of Columbia (DC)
York Coll of the City U of New York (NY)

Colleges with Room and Board
Coll of the Ozarks (MO)
Universidad Teológica del Caribe (PR)

$6000–$7999

Colleges with No Room and Board or with Room Only
American Public U System (WV)
Amridge U (AL)
Austin Graduate School of Theology (TX)
Baker Coll of Allen Park (MI)
Baker Coll of Auburn Hills (MI)
Baker Coll of Cadillac (MI)
Baker Coll of Clinton Township (MI)
Baker Coll of Jackson (MI)
Baker Coll of Port Huron (MI)
Carlos Albizu U (PR)
Cleveland Chiropractic Coll–Los Angeles Campus (CA)
Dunlap-Stone U, Phoenix (AZ)
EDP Coll of Puerto Rico, Inc. (PR)
EDP Coll of Puerto Rico–San Sebastian (PR)
Granite State Coll (NH)
Grantham U (MO)
Griggs U (MD)
Indiana U South Bend (IN)
Iowa State U of Science and Technology (IA)
Jones Coll, Jacksonville (FL)
Master's Coll and Sem (ON, Canada)
Medical Coll of Georgia (GA)
Montclair State U (NJ)
Northern Kentucky U (KY)
Purdue U North Central (IN)
Southern Utah U (UT) **(room only)**
Université du Québec en Outaouais (QC, Canada) **(room only)**
U of Baltimore (MD)
U of Maine at Augusta (ME)
U of Washington, Bothell (WA)
Valley Forge Christian Coll Woodbridge Campus (VA)
Wilmington U (DE)

Colleges with Room and Board
American Baptist Coll of American Baptist Theological Sem (TN)
Berea Coll (KY)
Dixie State Coll of Utah (UT)
East Central U (OK)
Midland Coll (TX)
New York City Coll of Technology of the City U of New York (NY)
Oklahoma Panhandle State U (OK)

$8000–$9999

Colleges with No Room and Board or with Room Only
Baptist Coll of Health Sciences (TN)
Clear Creek Baptist Bible Coll (KY)
Columbia Coll, Caguas (PR)
Edward Waters Coll (FL)
Holy Apostles Coll and Sem (CT)
Maria Coll (NY)
Nazarene Bible Coll (CO)
New Saint Andrews Coll (ID)
Northeastern Illinois U (IL)
Rogers State U (OK) **(room only)**
St. Augustine Coll (IL)
TUI U (CA)
U of Arkansas at Fort Smith (AR) **(room only)**
U of Michigan–Dearborn (MI)
Walden U (MN)

Colleges with Room and Board
Alcorn State U (MS)
Armstrong Atlantic State U (GA)
Brigham Young U–Hawaii (HI)
Cameron U (OK)
Dickinson State U (ND)
Eastern New Mexico U (NM)
Elizabeth City State U (NC)
Heritage Bible Coll (NC)
Memorial U of Newfoundland (NL, Canada)
Middle Georgia Coll (GA)
Minot State U (ND)
Mississippi U for Women (MS)
Missouri Southern State U (MO)
Moody Bible Inst (IL)
New Mexico Highlands U (NM)
Northeastern State U (OK)
Peru State Coll (NE)
Southeastern Oklahoma State U (OK)
Southern U and Ag and Mech Coll (LA)
Sul Ross State U (TX)
Universidad Adventista de las Antillas (PR)
U of Arkansas at Monticello (AR)
The U of North Carolina at Pembroke (NC)
U of Puerto Rico, Río Piedras (PR)
U of Science and Arts of Oklahoma (OK)
The U of Texas–Pan American (TX)
The U of West Alabama (AL)
Utah State U (UT)
Virginia U of Lynchburg (VA)

$10,000–$11,999

Colleges with No Room and Board or with Room Only
Allen U (SC)
Auburn U Montgomery (AL) **(room only)**
Baker Coll of Flint (MI) **(room only)**
Baker Coll of Muskegon (MI) **(room only)**
Baker Coll of Owosso (MI) **(room only)**
Beulah Heights U (GA) **(room only)**
Boston Architectural Coll (MA)
California State U, San Marcos (CA) **(room only)**
Cambridge Coll (MA)
Capella U (MN)
Carlos Albizu U, Miami Campus (FL)
Crichton Coll (TN)
Franklin U (OH)
Hunter Coll of the City U of New York (NY) **(room only)**
Indiana U–Purdue U Fort Wayne (IN) **(room only)**
Indiana U–Purdue U Indianapolis (IN) **(room only)**
Indiana U Southeast (IN) **(room only)**
Jamestown Business Coll (NY)
Jones Intl U (CO)
Louisiana State U Health Sciences Center (LA) **(room only)**
Medcenter One Coll of Nursing (ND)
Mercy Coll of Northwest Ohio (OH)
National U (CA)
The Ohio State U–Mansfield Campus (OH) **(room only)**
Plaza Coll (NY)
Shasta Bible Coll (CA) **(room only)**
Somerset Christian Coll (NJ)
U of Massachusetts Boston (MA)
U of New Hampshire at Manchester (NH)
The U of Texas Medical Branch (TX) **(room only)**
Western Intl U (AZ)

Colleges with Room and Board
Adams State Coll (CO)
Alabama State U (AL)

Cost Ranges

$10,000–$11,999

Albany State U (GA)
Appalachian State U (NC)
Arkansas Tech U (AR)
Austin Peay State U (TN)
Black Hills State U (SD)
Boise State U (ID)
Brigham Young U (UT)
Cape Breton U (NS, Canada)
Colorado State U–Pueblo (CO)
Concord U (WV)
Dakota State U (SD)
Delta State U (MS)
East Carolina U (NC)
East Tennessee State U (TN)
Emporia State U (KS)
Fort Hays State U (KS)
Glenville State Coll (WV)
Grambling State U (LA)
Henderson State U (AR)
Idaho State U (ID)
Jacksonville State U (AL)
Kennesaw State U (GA)
Louisiana Tech U (LA)
Mayville State U (ND)
Midwestern State U (TX)
Montana State U Billings (MT)
New Mexico Inst of Mining and Technology (NM)
New Mexico State U (NM)
Nicholls State U (LA)
Northern State U (SD)
North Georgia Coll & State U (GA)
Northwestern State U of Louisiana (LA)
Pittsburg State U (KS)
South Dakota School of Mines and Technology (SD)
South Dakota State U (SD)
Southeastern Louisiana U (LA)
Southern Arkansas U–Magnolia (AR)
Southern Polytechnic State U (GA)
Texas A&M U–Kingsville (TX)
U of Arkansas at Pine Bluff (AR)
U of Central Oklahoma (OK)
U of Florida (FL)
The U of Montana Western (MT)
U of Montevallo (AL)
U of New Orleans (LA)
U of North Alabama (AL)
The U of North Carolina at Asheville (NC)
The U of North Carolina at Charlotte (NC)
The U of North Carolina at Greensboro (NC)
U of Puerto Rico, Cayey U Coll (PR)
U of South Alabama (AL)
U of Southern Mississippi (MS)
The U of Tennessee at Martin (TN)
The U of Texas at Brownsville (TX)
The U of Texas of the Permian Basin (TX)
U of Utah (UT)
U of West Florida (FL)
U of West Georgia (GA)
U of Wisconsin–River Falls (WI)
Valdosta State U (GA)
Valley City State U (ND)
Washburn U (KS)
Wayne State Coll (NE)
Webb Inst (NY)
Western Carolina U (NC)
West Liberty U (WV)
Winston-Salem State U (NC)

$12,000–$13,999

Colleges with No Room and Board or with Room Only
Antioch U Seattle (WA)
Calumet Coll of Saint Joseph (IN)
Christian Life Coll (IL) **(room only)**
Crossroads Bible Coll (IN) **(room only)**
Florida National Coll (FL)
John Wesley Coll (NC) **(room only)**
Lakeview Coll of Nursing (IL)
Laura and Alvin Siegal Coll of Judaic Studies (OH)
Medical U of South Carolina (SC)
Mercy Coll of Health Sciences (IA)
Northwestern Polytechnic U (CA) **(room only)**
Penn State Abington (PA)
Penn State Brandywine (PA)
Penn State DuBois (PA)
Penn State Fayette, The Eberly Campus (PA)
Penn State Lehigh Valley (PA)
Penn State New Kensington (PA)
Penn State Schuylkill (PA)
Penn State Shenango (PA)
Penn State Wilkes-Barre (PA)
Penn State Worthington Scranton (PA)
Penn State York (PA)
Salem State Coll (MA) **(room only)**
Southeastern Bible Coll (AL) **(room only)**
U of Houston–Clear Lake (TX) **(room only)**
U of Wisconsin–Milwaukee (WI) **(room only)**
Western Connecticut State U (CT) **(room only)**

Colleges with Room and Board
Angelo State U (TX)
Arkansas State U—Jonesboro (AR)
The Baptist Coll of Florida (FL)
Bemidji State U (MN)
Bethany Bible Coll (NB, Canada)
Bloomsburg U of Pennsylvania (PA)
Blue Mountain Coll (MS)
Bowie State U (MD)
California State U, Fresno (CA)
California State U, Fullerton (CA)
California State U, Los Angeles (CA)
California State U, Monterey Bay (CA)
California State U, Stanislaus (CA)
Calvary Bible Coll and Theological Sem (MO)
Central State U (OH)
Columbus State U (GA)
Coppin State U (MD)
Eastern Washington U (WA)
East Stroudsburg U of Pennsylvania (PA)
Emmanuel Bible Coll (ON, Canada)
Fairmont State U (WV)
Florida Atlantic U (FL)
Florida Gulf Coast U (FL)
Florida State U (FL)
Francis Marion U (SC)
Frostburg State U (MD)
Georgia Southern U (GA)
Harris-Stowe State U (MO)
Heritage Baptist Coll and Heritage Theological Sem (ON, Canada)
Kansas State U (KS)
Kentucky State U (KY)
Lamar U (TX)
Lane Coll (TN)
Lock Haven U of Pennsylvania (PA)
Louisiana State U and Ag and Mech Coll (LA)
Marshall U (WV)
Middle Tennessee State U (TN)
Minnesota State U Mankato (MN)
Minnesota State U Moorhead (MN)
Mississippi State U (MS)
Missouri State U (MO)
Missouri Western State U (MO)
Montana Tech of The U of Montana (MT)
Morehead State U (KY)
Murray State U (KY)
New Coll of Florida (FL)
North Carolina State U (NC)
North Dakota State U (ND)
Nova Scotia Ag Coll (NS, Canada)
Oklahoma State U (OK)
Prairie View A&M U (TX)
Purdue U Calumet (IN)
Radford U (VA)
St. Cloud State U (MN)
San Jose State U (CA)
Shepherd U (WV)
Southeast Missouri State U (MO)
Tarleton State U (TX)
Tennessee Technological U (TN)
Texas A&M Intl U (TX)
Texas A&M U at Galveston (TX)
Texas A&M U–Commerce (TX)
Texas State U–San Marcos (TX)
Texas Woman's U (TX)
Troy U (AL)
Truman State U (MO)
The U of Alabama at Birmingham (AL)
The U of Alabama in Huntsville (AL)
U of Alaska Anchorage (AK)
U of Alaska Fairbanks (AK)
U of Arkansas (AR)
U of Central Florida (FL)
U of Central Missouri (MO)
U of Colorado at Colorado Springs (CO)
U of Idaho (ID)
U of Louisville (KY)
U of Maine at Fort Kent (ME)
U of Maine at Machias (ME)
U of Maryland Eastern Shore (MD)
U of Mary Washington (VA)
U of Memphis (TN)
U of Nebraska at Kearney (NE)
U of Nebraska at Omaha (NE)
U of New Mexico (NM)
U of North Carolina School of the Arts (NC)
The U of North Carolina Wilmington (NC)
U of North Dakota (ND)
U of Northern Colorado (CO)
U of North Texas (TX)
U of Oklahoma (OK)
U of South Carolina Beaufort (SC)
The U of South Dakota (SD)
U of Southern Indiana (IN)
U of South Florida (FL)
The U of Tennessee at Chattanooga (TN)
U of the Virgin Islands (VI)
U of Wisconsin–Eau Claire (WI)
U of Wisconsin–Green Bay (WI)
U of Wisconsin–La Crosse (WI)
U of Wisconsin–Parkside (WI)
U of Wisconsin–Platteville (WI)
U of Wisconsin–Stevens Point (WI)
U of Wisconsin–Stout (WI)
U of Wisconsin–Superior (WI)
U of Wisconsin–Whitewater (WI)
U of Wyoming (WY)
Utah Valley U (UT)
Western Kentucky U (KY)
Western State Coll of Colorado (CO)
West Virginia U (WV)
Wichita State U (KS)

$14,000–$15,999

Colleges with No Room and Board or with Room Only
Allen Coll (IA)
Alliant Intl U (CA)
American U of Beirut (Lebanon) **(room only)**
Antioch U Santa Barbara (CA)
Brookline Coll, Phoenix (AZ)
Brookline Coll, Tempe (AZ)
Brookline Coll, Tucson (AZ)
Brookline Coll (NM)
Bryant & Stratton Coll—Virginia Beach (VA)
City U of Seattle (WA)
Cleary U (MI)
Daymar Inst, Clarksville (TN)
DeVry Coll of New York (NY)
DeVry U, Phoenix (AZ)
DeVry U, Fremont (CA)
DeVry U, Long Beach (CA)
DeVry U, Pomona (CA)
DeVry U, Sherman Oaks (CA)
DeVry U, Westminster (CO)
DeVry U, Miramar (FL)
DeVry U, Orlando (FL)
DeVry U, Alpharetta (GA)
DeVry U, Decatur (GA)
DeVry U, Addison (IL)
DeVry U, Chicago (IL)
DeVry U, Tinley Park (IL)
DeVry U, Indianapolis (IN)
DeVry U (KY)
DeVry U (MD)
DeVry U (MI)
DeVry U, Edina (MN)
DeVry U, Kansas City (MO)
DeVry U (NV)
DeVry U, North Brunswick (NJ)
DeVry U, Charlotte (NC)
DeVry U, Columbus (OH)
DeVry U (OK)
DeVry U (OR)
DeVry U, Fort Washington (PA)
DeVry U, Memphis (TN)
DeVry U, Houston (TX)
DeVry U, Irving (TX)
DeVry U (UT)
DeVry U, Arlington (VA)
DeVry U, Federal Way (WA)
DeVry U, Milwaukee (WI)
East-West U (IL)
Ecclesia Coll (AR)
Herzing U (GA)
Intl Acad of Design & Technology (IL)
Lourdes Coll (OH)
Peirce Coll (PA)
Villa Maria Coll of Buffalo (NY)

Colleges with Room and Board
Alberta Coll of Art & Design (AB, Canada)
Appalachian Bible Coll (WV)
Arizona State U (AZ)
Auburn U (AL)
Ball State U (IN)
Buffalo State Coll, State U of New York (NY)
California Maritime Acad (CA)
California Polytechnic State U, San Luis Obispo (CA)
California State Polytechnic U, Pomona (CA)
California State U, Chico (CA)
California State U, Dominguez Hills (CA)

California State U, East Bay (CA)
California State U, Long Beach (CA)
Cheyney U of Pennsylvania (PA)
The Citadel, The Military Coll of South Carolina (SC)
Clarion U of Pennsylvania (PA)
The Coll at Brockport, State U of New York (NY)
Colorado State U (CO)
Edinboro U of Pennsylvania (PA)
The Evergreen State Coll (WA)
Fitchburg State Coll (MA)
Fort Lewis Coll (CO)
Framingham State Coll (MA)
George Mason U (VA)
Georgia Coll & State U (GA)
Georgia Inst of Technology (GA)
Goddard Coll (VT)
Hillsdale Free Will Baptist Coll (OK)
Humboldt State U (CA)
Indiana State U (IN)
Indiana U of Pennsylvania (PA)
James Madison U (VA)
Johnson Bible Coll (TN)
Kutztown U of Pennsylvania (PA)
Lincoln U (PA)
Martin Luther Coll (MN)
Massachusetts Coll of Liberal Arts (MA)
Massachusetts Maritime Acad (MA)
Millersville U of Pennsylvania (PA)
Morris Coll (SC)
Mountain State U (WV)
Northern Arizona U (AZ)
Northern Michigan U (MI)
Northwest Missouri State U (MO)
Old Dominion U (VA)
Oregon Inst of Technology (OR)
Oregon State U (OR)
Saginaw Valley State U (MI)
St. Louis Christian Coll (MO)
Salisbury U (MD)
Sam Houston State U (TX)
San Francisco State U (CA)
Shawnee State U (OH)
Shippensburg U of Pennsylvania (PA)
Slippery Rock U of Pennsylvania (PA)
Sonoma State U (CA)
Southern Illinois U Edwardsville (IL)
Southwest Minnesota State U (MN)
State U of New York at Fredonia (NY)
State U of New York at New Paltz (NY)
State U of New York at Plattsburgh (NY)
State U of New York Coll at Geneseo (NY)
State U of New York Coll at Old Westbury (NY)
State U of New York Coll at Oneonta (NY)
State U of New York Coll at Potsdam (NY)
State U of New York Coll of Technology at Alfred (NY)
State U of New York Coll of Technology at Canton (NY)
State U of New York Upstate Medical U (NY)
Stephen F. Austin State U (TX)
Texas A&M U–Corpus Christi (TX)
Texas Tech U (TX)
The U of Alabama (AL)
U of Georgia (GA)
U of Guam (GU)
U of Houston (TX)
The U of Iowa (IA)
The U of Kansas (KS)
U of Maine at Presque Isle (ME)
U of Michigan–Flint (MI)
U of Nebraska–Lincoln (NE)
U of Nevada, Las Vegas (NV)
U of Nevada, Reno (NV)
The U of North Carolina at Chapel Hill (NC)
U of Northern Iowa (IA)
U of North Florida (FL)
U of South Carolina Upstate (SC)
The U of Tennessee (TN)
The U of Texas at Arlington (TX)
The U of Texas at Tyler (TX)
U of the West (CA)
The U of Virginia's Coll at Wise (VA)
U of Washington (WA)
U of Wisconsin–Madison (WI)
Virginia Commonwealth U (VA)
Virginia State U (VA)
Wayne State U (MI)
West Chester U of Pennsylvania (PA)
Western Oregon U (OR)
Western Washington U (WA)
Westfield State Coll (MA)
Winona State U (MN)
Worcester State Coll (MA)
Wright State U (OH)
Youngstown State U (OH)

$16,000–$17,999

Colleges with No Room and Board or with Room Only

AIB Coll of Business (IA) **(room only)**
Aquinas Coll (TN)
Clarkson Coll (NE) **(room only)**
Goldfarb School of Nursing at Barnes-Jewish Coll (MO)
Goodwin Coll (CT)
Hodges U (FL)
Marylhurst U (OR)
Mercy Coll (NY)
Metropolitan Coll of New York (NY)
Oregon Health & Science U (OR)
Pennsylvania Coll of Art & Design (PA)
Saint Francis Medical Center Coll of Nursing (IL) **(room only)**
St. Joseph's Coll, Long Island Campus (NY)
St. Joseph's Coll, New York (NY)
U of Washington, Tacoma (WA) **(room only)**

Colleges with Room and Board

Bob Jones U (SC)
Bowling Green State U (OH)
Bridgewater State Coll (MA)
Castleton State Coll (VT)
Central Baptist Coll (AR)
Central Connecticut State U (CT)
Coastal Carolina U (SC)
Delaware State U (DE)
Eastern Illinois U (IL)
Eastern Michigan U (MI)
Farmingdale State Coll (NY)
Fashion Inst of Technology (NY)
Florida Intl U (FL)
Georgia State U (GA)
Grace Bible Coll (MI)
Grand Valley State U (MI)
Heritage Christian U (AL)
Indiana U Bloomington (IN)
Jarvis Christian Coll (TX)
Johnson State Coll (VT)
Keene State Coll (NH)
Kent State U (OH)
Lake Superior State U (MI)
Lee U (TN)
Lehman Coll of the City U of New York (NY)
Lincoln U (CA)
Longwood U (VA)
Louisiana Coll (LA)
Maranatha Baptist Bible Coll (WI)
Mid-Atlantic Christian U (NC)
Missouri U of Science and Technology (MO)
Oakland U (MI)
The Ohio State U (OH)
Paine Coll (GA)
Park U (MO)
Piedmont Baptist Coll and Graduate School (NC)
Plymouth State U (NH)
Portland State U (OR)
Purchase Coll, State U of New York (NY)
Purdue U (IN)
Queens Coll of the City U of New York (NY)
Rhode Island Coll (RI)
San Diego State U (CA)
South Carolina State U (SC)
State U of New York at Binghamton (NY)
State U of New York at Oswego (NY)
State U of New York Maritime Coll (NY)
Stony Brook U, State U of New York (NY)
Texas A&M U (TX)
Texas Coll (TX)
Towson U (MD)
Universidad de las Américas–Puebla (Mexico)
U at Albany, State U of New York (NY)
U at Buffalo, the State U of New York (NY)
The U of Akron (OH)
U of Hawaii at Manoa (HI)
U of Kentucky (KY)
U of Maine (ME)
U of Maine at Farmington (ME)
U of Maryland, Coll Park (MD)
U of Minnesota, Crookston (MN)
U of Minnesota, Duluth (MN)
U of Missouri (MO)
U of Missouri–St. Louis (MO)
U of Oregon (OR)
U of South Carolina (SC)
The U of Texas at San Antonio (TX)
The U of Texas Southwestern Medical Center at Dallas (TX)
The U of Toledo (OH)
U of Virginia (VA)
Virginia Military Inst (VA)
Voorhees Coll (SC)
Washington State U (WA)
Wayland Baptist U (TX)
Western Illinois U (IL)
Western Michigan U (MI)

$18,000–$19,999

Colleges with No Room and Board or with Room Only

Bastyr U (WA)
Dakota Wesleyan U (SD)
Harrington Coll of Design (IL)
Harrisburg U of Science and Technology (PA)
Mount Carmel Coll of Nursing (OH) **(room only)**
Nebraska Methodist Coll (NE) **(room only)**
Piedmont Coll (GA)
Regent U (VA) **(room only)**

Colleges with Room and Board

Bethel U (TN)
Boston Baptist Coll (MA)
Carolina Christian Coll (NC)
Central Michigan U (MI)
Cincinnati Christian U (OH)
Claflin U (SC)
Clemson U (SC)
Cleveland State U (OH)
Coll of Charleston (SC)
The Coll of William and Mary (VA)
Davis Coll (NY)
Emmanuel Coll (GA)
Eugene Bible Coll (OR)
Faith Baptist Bible Coll and Theological Sem (IA)
Florida Coll (FL)
Free Will Baptist Bible Coll (TN)
Great Lakes Christian Coll (MI)
Grove City Coll (PA)
Harding U (AR)
Huston-Tillotson U (TX)
Illinois State U (IL)
Lincoln Christian U (IL)
Madonna U (MI)
Massachusetts Coll of Art and Design (MA)
Michigan State U (MI)
Michigan Technological U (MI)
Mississippi Coll (MS)
Monroe Coll, New Rochelle (NY)
Mount Olive Coll (NC)
New England School of Communications (ME)
New Jersey City U (NJ)
North Greenville U (SC)
Oak Hills Christian Coll (MN)
Ohio U (OH)
Polytechnic U of Puerto Rico (PR)
Presentation Coll (SD)
Saint Paul's Coll (VA)
Southern Connecticut State U (CT)
Southern Illinois U Carbondale (IL)
Southwestern Assemblies of God U (TX)
State U of New York Coll of Environmental Science and Forestry (NY)
Stillman Coll (AL)
Texas Southern U (TX)
Trinity Coll of Florida (FL)
Truett-McConnell Coll (GA)
U of California, Riverside (CA)
U of Cincinnati (OH)
U of Colorado at Boulder (CO)
U of Colorado Denver (CO)
U of Delaware (DE)
U of Illinois at Springfield (IL)
U of Mary (ND)
U of Maryland, Baltimore County (MD)
U of Massachusetts Dartmouth (MA)
U of Massachusetts Lowell (MA)
U of Minnesota, Twin Cities Campus (MN)
U of Missouri–Kansas City (MO)
U of Pittsburgh at Bradford (PA)
U of Pittsburgh at Greensburg (PA)
U of Pittsburgh at Johnstown (PA)
U of Pittsburgh at Titusville (PA)
U of Rhode Island (RI)
The U of Texas at Austin (TX)
The U of Texas at Dallas (TX)
Vermont Tech Coll (VT)
Winthrop U (SC)

$20,000–$24,999

Colleges with No Room and Board or with Room Only

Antioch U McGregor (OH)
Cincinnati Coll of Mortuary Science (OH)

$20,000–$24,999

Coll of Visual Arts (MN)
DigiPen Inst of Technology (WA)
Goldey-Beacom Coll (DE) **(room only)**
Johnson & Wales U (RI)
Lexington Coll (IL)
Lincoln Coll–Normal (IL) **(room only)**
Lincoln Coll of New England, Southington (CT) **(room only)**
Lyme Acad Coll of Fine Arts (CT)
McNally Smith Coll of Music (MN)
Molloy Coll (NY)
Pacific States U (CA) **(room only)**
Saint Louis U–Madrid Campus (Spain) **(room only)**
Sullivan Coll of Technology and Design (KY) **(room only)**
Watkins Coll of Art, Design, & Film (TN) **(room only)**
West Suburban Coll of Nursing (IL)
Wheeling Jesuit U (WV)

Colleges with Room and Board
Atlanta Christian Coll (GA)
Atlantic Union Coll (MA)
Baptist Bible Coll of Pennsylvania (PA)
Barclay Coll (KS)
Belhaven U (MS)
Bethune-Cookman U (FL)
Brewton-Parker Coll (GA)
Bryan Coll (TN)
Bryn Athyn Coll of the New Church (PA)
Central Christian Coll of Kansas (KS)
Central Pennsylvania Coll (PA)
Charles Drew U of Medicine and Science (CA)
Christopher Newport U (VA)
Clark Atlanta U (GA)
Clearwater Christian Coll (FL)
The Coll of New Jersey (NJ)
Colorado School of Mines (CO)
Columbia Coll (MO)
Columbia Intl U (SC)
Dallas Baptist U (TX)
Davenport U, Grand Rapids (MI)
Dillard U (LA)
Eastern Connecticut State U (CT)
East Texas Baptist U (TX)
Evangel U (MO)
Faulkner U (AL)
Flagler Coll (FL)
Freed-Hardeman U (TN)
Gallaudet U (DC)
Hampton U (VA)
Hannibal-LaGrange Coll (MO)
Husson U (ME)
Jamestown Coll (ND)
Jefferson Coll of Health Sciences (VA)
Johnson C. Smith U (NC)
Judson Coll (AL)
Kean U (NJ)
Kentucky Wesleyan Coll (KY)
Kuyper Coll (MI)
Liberty U (VA)
Life U (GA)
Lincoln Memorial U (TN)
Lindenwood U (MO)
Lubbock Christian U (TX)
Miami U (OH)
Mid-Continent U (KY)
Midway Coll (KY)
Missouri Baptist U (MO)
Monroe Coll, Bronx (NY)
Mount Aloysius Coll (PA)
Mount Marty Coll (SD)
New Jersey Inst of Technology (NJ)
Oakland City U (IN)
Ohio Valley U (WV)
Oklahoma Baptist U (OK)
Oklahoma Christian U (OK)
Oklahoma Wesleyan U (OK)
Patten U (CA)
Penn State Altoona (PA)
Penn State Beaver (PA)
Penn State Berks (PA)
Penn State Erie, The Behrend Coll (PA)
Penn State Greater Allegheny (PA)
Penn State Harrisburg (PA)
Penn State Hazleton (PA)
Penn State Mont Alto (PA)
Penn State U Park (PA)
Pennsylvania Coll of Technology (PA)
Pikeville Coll (KY)
Ramapo Coll of New Jersey (NJ)
Reinhardt Coll (GA)
The Richard Stockton Coll of New Jersey (NJ)
Rochester Coll (MI)
Rowan U (NJ)
Rutgers, The State U of New Jersey, Camden (NJ)
Rutgers, The State U of New Jersey, Newark (NJ)
Rutgers, The State U of New Jersey, New Brunswick (NJ)
Sacred Heart Major Sem (MI)
Saint Augustine's Coll (NC)
St. Charles Borromeo Sem, Overbrook (PA)
Saint Joseph Sem Coll (LA)
St. Mary's Coll of Maryland (MD)
Southeastern U (FL)
Southern Adventist U (TN)
Southwest Baptist U (MO)
Southwestern Adventist U (TX)
Temple U (PA)
Tennessee Wesleyan Coll (TN)
Texas Wesleyan U (TX)
Tuskegee U (AL)
Union Coll (KY)
Union Coll (NE)
U of California, Davis (CA)
U of California, Irvine (CA)
U of California, Los Angeles (CA)
U of California, San Diego (CA)
U of California, Santa Barbara (CA)
U of California, Santa Cruz (CA)
U of Connecticut (CT)
U of Illinois at Chicago (IL)
U of Illinois at Urbana–Champaign (IL)
U of Massachusetts Amherst (MA)
U of Michigan (MI)
U of Mobile (AL)
U of New Hampshire (NH)
U of Pittsburgh (PA)
U of the Cumberlands (KY)
U of the Southwest (NM)
U of Vermont (VT)
Valley Forge Christian Coll (PA)
Virginia Union U (VA)
Waldorf Coll (IA)
Warner Pacific Coll (OR)
Webber Intl U (FL)
William Paterson U of New Jersey (NJ)
Xavier U of Louisiana (LA)
York Coll (NE)
York Coll of Pennsylvania (PA)

$25,000–$29,999

Colleges with No Room and Board or with Room Only
The Art Center Design Coll, Tucson (AZ)
Burlington Coll (VT) **(room only)**
Coll of the Humanities and Sciences, Harrison Middleton U (AZ)
Minneapolis Coll of Art and Design (MN)
New Hampshire Inst of Art (NH) **(room only)**
Platt Coll San Diego (CA)
Prescott Coll (AZ) **(room only)**
Rocky Mountain Coll of Art + Design (CO)
Southern California Inst of Architecture (CA)

Colleges with Room and Board
Abilene Christian U (TX)
Alderson-Broaddus Coll (WV)
Andrews U (MI)
Aquinas Coll (MI)
Asbury U (KY)
Augustana Coll (SD)
Aurora U (IL)
Averett U (VA)
Avila U (MO)
Baker U (KS)
Barton Coll (NC)
Benedictine Coll (KS)
Benedictine U (IL)
Bethany Coll (KS)
Bethany Lutheran Coll (MN)
Bethany U (CA)
Bethel Coll (IN)
Bethel Coll (KS)
Bluefield Coll (VA)
Brescia U (KY)
Brevard Coll (NC)
Briar Cliff U (IA)
Campbellsville U (KY)
Carson-Newman Coll (TN)
Cedarville U (OH)
Chaminade U of Honolulu (HI)
Chowan U (NC)
Christendom Coll (VA)
Christian Brothers U (TN)
Cogswell Polytechnical Coll (CA)
Coker Coll (SC)
The Coll of Idaho (ID)
Coll of Mount St. Joseph (OH)
Coll of St. Joseph (VT)
Coll of Saint Mary (NE)
Columbia Coll (SC)
Concordia U Texas (TX)
Concordia U Wisconsin (WI)
Cornerstone U (MI)
Crown Coll (MN)
Culver-Stockton Coll (MO)
Cumberland U (TN)
Dana Coll (NE)
Doane Coll (NE)
Dordt Coll (IA)
Drury U (MO)
D'Youville Coll (NY)
Edgewood Coll (WI)
Fisk U (TN)
Fontbonne U (MO)
Franciscan U of Steubenville (OH)
Friends U (KS)
Gardner-Webb U (NC)
Grace Coll (IN)
Graceland U (IA)
Grand View U (IA)
Greenville Coll (IL)
Hardin-Simmons U (TX)
Hawai'i Pacific U (HI)
Hilbert Coll (NY)
Hillsdale Coll (MI)
Howard Payne U (TX)
Huntingdon Coll (AL)
Huntington U (IN)
Illinois Coll (IL)
Indiana Tech (IN)
Indiana Wesleyan U (IN)
Iowa Wesleyan Coll (IA)
John Brown U (AR)
Keystone Coll (PA)
King Coll (TN)
LaGrange Coll (GA)
Lakeland Coll (WI)
Limestone Coll (SC)
Lindsey Wilson Coll (KY)
Lipscomb U (TN)
Lyon Coll (AR)
Malone U (OH)
Marian U (WI)
Mars Hill Coll (NC)
Maryville U of Saint Louis (MO)
McKendree U (IL)
McMurry U (TX)
McPherson Coll (KS)
Medaille Coll (NY)
MidAmerica Nazarene U (KS)
Milligan Coll (TN)
Mount Mary Coll (WI)
Mount Mercy Coll (IA)
Mount Vernon Nazarene U (OH)
Nebraska Wesleyan U (NE)
Newman U (KS)
Northwest Christian U (OR)
Northwestern Coll (IA)
Northwest Nazarene U (ID)
Northwest U (WA)
Nova Southeastern U (FL)
Nyack Coll (NY)
Oral Roberts U (OK)
Oregon Coll of Art & Craft (OR)
Ottawa U (KS)
Ouachita Baptist U (AR)
Our Lady of the Lake U of San Antonio (TX)
Philadelphia Biblical U (PA)
Rocky Mountain Coll (MT)
St. Andrews Presbyterian Coll (NC)
Saint Leo U (FL)
St. Thomas U (FL)
Samford U (AL)
Schreiner U (TX)
Siena Heights U (MI)
Silver Lake Coll (WI)
Simpson U (CA)
Southern Wesleyan U (SC)
Southwestern Coll (KS)
Spring Arbor U (MI)
Sterling Coll (KS)
Tabor Coll (KS)
Texas Lutheran U (TX)
Thiel Coll (PA)
Thomas Aquinas Coll (CA)
Tiffin U (OH)
Trevecca Nazarene U (TN)
Trinity Christian Coll (IL)
Tusculum Coll (TN)
Union U (TN)
U of Advancing Technology (AZ)
U of California, Berkeley (CA)
U of Dubuque (IA)
U of Indianapolis (IN)

U of Mary Hardin-Baylor (TX)
U of Rio Grande (OH)
U of Saint Mary (KS)
U of St. Thomas (TX)
U of the Ozarks (AR)
Upper Iowa U (IA)
Vaughn Coll of Aeronautics and Technology (NY)
Viterbo U (WI)
Washington Adventist U (MD)
Waynesburg U (PA)
Wesleyan Coll (GA)
Westminster Coll (MO)
William Jessup U (CA)
William Penn U (IA)
Wingate U (NC)
Young Harris Coll (GA)

$30,000 and over

Colleges with No Room and Board or with Room Only

Art Center Coll of Design (CA)
California Coll of the Arts (CA) **(room only)**
Columbia Coll Chicago (IL) **(room only)**
The King's Coll (NY) **(room only)**
Marquette U (WI)
Neumont U (UT) **(room only)**
New York School of Interior Design (NY) **(room only)**
Otis Coll of Art and Design (CA)
Samuel Merritt U (CA)
San Francisco Conservatory of Music (CA)
School of the Art Inst of Chicago (IL) **(room only)**
School of the Museum of Fine Arts, Boston (MA) **(room only)**

Colleges with Room and Board

Acad of Art U (CA)
Agnes Scott Coll (GA)
Alaska Pacific U (AK)
Albany Coll of Pharmacy and Health Sciences (NY)
Albertus Magnus Coll (CT)
Albion Coll (MI)
Albright Coll (PA)
Alfred U (NY)
Allegheny Coll (PA)
Alma Coll (MI)
Alvernia U (PA)
American Jewish U (CA)
American U (DC)
Amherst Coll (MA)
Anderson U (IN)
Arcadia U (PA)
The Art Inst of Boston at Lesley U (MA)
Ashland U (OH)
Assumption Coll (MA)
Augsburg Coll (MN)
Augustana Coll (IL)
Austin Coll (TX)
Azusa Pacific U (CA)
Babson Coll (MA)
Baldwin-Wallace Coll (OH)
Bard Coll (NY)
Bard Coll at Simon's Rock (MA)
Barnard Coll (NY)
Barry U (FL)
Bates Coll (ME)
Baylor U (TX)
Bay Path Coll (MA)
Beacon Coll (FL)
Bellarmine U (KY)
Belmont Abbey Coll (NC)
Belmont U (TN)
Beloit Coll (WI)
Bennington Coll (VT)
Bentley U (MA)
Berklee Coll of Music (MA)
Berry Coll (GA)
Bethany Coll (WV)
Bethel U (MN)
Blessing-Rieman Coll of Nursing (IL)
Bloomfield Coll (NJ)
Bluffton U (OH)
Boston Coll (MA)
The Boston Conservatory (MA)
Boston U (MA)
Bowdoin Coll (ME)
Bradley U (IL)
Brandeis U (MA)
Brenau U (GA)
Bridgewater Coll (VA)
Bryant U (RI)
Bryn Mawr Coll (PA)
Bucknell U (PA)
Buena Vista U (IA)
Butler U (IN)
Cabrini Coll (PA)
California Baptist U (CA)
California Inst of the Arts (CA)
California Lutheran U (CA)
Calvin Coll (MI)
Canisius Coll (NY)
Capital U (OH)
Carleton Coll (MN)
Carlow U (PA)
Carnegie Mellon U (PA)
Carroll U (WI)
Case Western Reserve U (OH)
Catawba Coll (NC)
The Catholic U of America (DC)
Cazenovia Coll (NY)
Cedar Crest Coll (PA)
Centenary Coll of Louisiana (LA)
Central Coll (IA)
Champlain Coll (VT)
Chapman U (CA)
Claremont McKenna Coll (CA)
Clarke Coll (IA)
Clarkson U (NY)
Clark U (MA)
The Cleveland Inst of Art (OH)
Colby Coll (ME)
Colgate U (NY)
Coll for Creative Studies (MI)
Coll of Mount Saint Vincent (NY)
The Coll of New Rochelle (NY)
Coll of Notre Dame of Maryland (MD)
Coll of Saint Benedict (MN)
Coll of Saint Elizabeth (NJ)
The Coll of Saint Rose (NY)
The Coll of St. Scholastica (MN)
Coll of Santa Fe (NM)
Coll of the Atlantic (ME)
Coll of the Holy Cross (MA)
The Coll of Wooster (OH)
The Colorado Coll (CO)
Columbia U (NY)
Columbia U, School of General Studies (NY)
Columbus Coll of Art & Design (OH)
Concordia Coll (MN)
Concordia U (CA)
Concordia U Chicago (IL)
Concordia U, St. Paul (MN)
Connecticut Coll (CT)
Converse Coll (SC)
Cooper Union for the Advancement of Science and Art (NY)
Corban U (OR)
Cornell Coll (IA)
Cornell U (NY)
Cornish Coll of the Arts (WA)
Covenant Coll (GA)
Creighton U (NE)
The Culinary Inst of America (NY)
Daemen Coll (NY)
Dartmouth Coll (NH)
Davidson Coll (NC)
Defiance Coll (OH)
Delaware Valley Coll (PA)
Denison U (OH)
DePaul U (IL)
DePauw U (IN)
DeSales U (PA)
Dickinson Coll (PA)
Dominican Coll (NY)
Dominican U (IL)
Dominican U of California (CA)
Dowling Coll (NY)
Drake U (IA)
Drew U (NJ)
Drexel U (PA)
Duke U (NC)
Duquesne U (PA)
Earlham Coll (IN)
Eastern Mennonite U (VA)
Eastern Nazarene Coll (MA)
Eckerd Coll (FL)
Elizabethtown Coll (PA)
Elmhurst Coll (IL)
Elmira Coll (NY)
Elon U (NC)
Embry-Riddle Aeronautical U (AZ)
Embry-Riddle Aeronautical U (FL)
Emerson Coll (MA)
Emmanuel Coll (MA)
Emory & Henry Coll (VA)
Emory U (GA)
Endicott Coll (MA)
Erskine Coll (SC)
Eugene Lang Coll The New School for Liberal Arts (NY)
Fairfield U (CT)
Fairleigh Dickinson U, Coll at Florham (NJ)
Fairleigh Dickinson U, Metropolitan Campus (NJ)
Felician Coll (NJ)
Ferrum Coll (VA)
Fisher Coll (MA)
Five Towns Coll (NY)
Florida Inst of Technology (FL)
Florida Southern Coll (FL)
Franklin & Marshall Coll (PA)
Franklin Coll (IN)
Franklin Coll Switzerland (Switzerland)
Franklin Pierce U (NH)
Franklin W. Olin Coll of Eng (MA)
Furman U (SC)
Gannon U (PA)
Geneva Coll (PA)
George Fox U (OR)
Georgetown Coll (KY)
The George Washington U (DC)
Georgian Court U (NJ)
Gordon Coll (MA)
Goshen Coll (IN)
Goucher Coll (MD)
Green Mountain Coll (VT)
Greensboro Coll (NC)
Grinnell Coll (IA)
Guilford Coll (NC)
Gustavus Adolphus Coll (MN)
Gwynedd-Mercy Coll (PA)
Hamilton Coll (NY)
Hamline U (MN)
Hampden-Sydney Coll (VA)
Hampshire Coll (MA)
Hanover Coll (IN)
Hartwick Coll (NY)
Harvard U (MA)
Harvey Mudd Coll (CA)
Haverford Coll (PA)
Heidelberg U (OH)
Hellenic Coll (MA)
Hendrix Coll (AR)
High Point U (NC)
Hiram Coll (OH)
Hofstra U (NY)
Hollins U (VA)
Holy Family U (PA)
Holy Names U (CA)
Hood Coll (MD)
Hope Coll (MI)
Houghton Coll (NY)
Houston Baptist U (TX)
Illinois Inst of Technology (IL)
Illinois Wesleyan U (IL)
Immaculata U (PA)
Iona Coll (NY)
Ithaca Coll (NY)
Jacksonville U (FL)
John Cabot U (Italy)
John Carroll U (OH)
The Johns Hopkins U (MD)
Johnson & Wales U (CO)
Johnson & Wales U (FL)
Johnson & Wales U—Charlotte Campus (NC)
Judson U (IL)
The Juilliard School (NY)
Juniata Coll (PA)
Kalamazoo Coll (MI)
Kenyon Coll (OH)
Kettering U (MI)
Keuka Coll (NY)
King's Coll (PA)
Knox Coll (IL)
Lafayette Coll (PA)
Lake Erie Coll (OH)
Lake Forest Coll (IL)
La Roche Coll (PA)
La Salle U (PA)
Lasell Coll (MA)
La Sierra U (CA)
Lawrence Technological U (MI)
Lawrence U (WI)
Lebanon Valley Coll (PA)
Lehigh U (PA)
Le Moyne Coll (NY)
Lesley U (MA)
LeTourneau U (TX)
Lewis & Clark Coll (OR)
Lewis U (IL)
LIM Coll (NY)
Linfield Coll (OR)
Loras Coll (IA)
Loyola Marymount U (CA)
Loyola U Chicago (IL)
Loyola U Maryland (MD)
Loyola U New Orleans (LA)

Cost Ranges

$30,000 and over

Luther Coll (IA)
Lycoming Coll (PA)
Lynchburg Coll (VA)
Lynn U (FL)
Macalester Coll (MN)
Maharishi U of Management (IA)
Maine Coll of Art (ME)
Manchester Coll (IN)
Manhattan Coll (NY)
Manhattan School of Music (NY)
Manhattanville Coll (NY)
Mannes Coll The New School for Music (NY)
Marian U (IN)
Marietta Coll (OH)
Marist Coll (NY)
Marlboro Coll (VT)
Mary Baldwin Coll (VA)
Maryland Inst Coll of Art (MD)
Marymount Coll, Palos Verdes, California (CA)
Marymount Manhattan Coll (NY)
Marymount U (VA)
Maryville Coll (TN)
Marywood U (PA)
Massachusetts Coll of Pharmacy and Health Sciences (MA)
Massachusetts Inst of Technology (MA)
The Master's Coll and Sem (CA)
McDaniel Coll (MD)
Memphis Coll of Art (TN)
Menlo Coll (CA)
Mercer U (GA)
Mercyhurst Coll (PA)
Merrimack Coll (MA)
Messiah Coll (PA)
Methodist U (NC)
Middlebury Coll (VT)
Millikin U (IL)
Millsaps Coll (MS)
Mills Coll (CA)
Milwaukee School of Eng (WI)
Misericordia U (PA)
Mitchell Coll (CT)
Monmouth Coll (IL)
Monmouth U (NJ)
Moore Coll of Art & Design (PA)
Moravian Coll (PA)
Morehouse Coll (GA)
Morningside Coll (IA)
Mount Holyoke Coll (MA)
Mount Ida Coll (MA)
Mount Saint Mary Coll (NY)
Mount St. Mary's Coll (CA)
Mount St. Mary's U (MD)
Muhlenberg Coll (PA)
Naropa U (CO)
Nazareth Coll of Rochester (NY)
Neumann U (PA)
Newberry Coll (SC)
Newbury Coll (MA)
New England Coll (NH)
New England Conservatory of Music (MA)
The New School for General Studies (NY)
The New School for Jazz and Contemporary Music (NY)
New York Inst of Technology (NY)
New York U (NY)
Niagara U (NY)
Nichols Coll (MA)
North Central Coll (IL)
Northeastern U (MA)
Northland Coll (WI)
Northwestern Coll (MN)
Notre Dame de Namur U (CA)
Oberlin Coll (OH)
Occidental Coll (CA)
Oglethorpe U (GA)
Ohio Dominican U (OH)
Ohio Northern U (OH)
Ohio Wesleyan U (OH)
Oklahoma City U (OK)
Pace U (NY)
Pacific Lutheran U (WA)
Pacific Union Coll (CA)
Palm Beach Atlantic U (FL)
Parsons The New School for Design (NY)
Patrick Henry Coll (VA)
Peabody Conservatory of The Johns Hopkins U (MD)
Peace Coll (NC)
Pepperdine U, Malibu (CA)
Philadelphia U (PA)
Pitzer Coll (CA)
Point Park U (PA)
Polytechnic Inst of NYU (NY)
Pomona Coll (CA)
Post U (CT)
Pratt Inst (NY)
Presbyterian Coll (SC)
Princeton U (NJ)
Principia Coll (IL)
Providence Coll (RI)
Queens U of Charlotte (NC)
Quincy U (IL)
Quinnipiac U (CT)
Randolph Coll (VA)
Randolph-Macon Coll (VA)
Reed Coll (OR)
Regis Coll (MA)
Rensselaer Polytechnic Inst (NY)
Rhodes Coll (TN)
Rice U (TX)
Rider U (NJ)
Ringling Coll of Art and Design (FL)
Ripon Coll (WI)
Rivier Coll (NH)
Roanoke Coll (VA)
Robert Morris U (PA)
Robert Morris U Illinois (IL)
Roberts Wesleyan Coll (NY)
Rochester Inst of Technology (NY)
Rockford Coll (IL)
Rockhurst U (MO)
Rollins Coll (FL)
Roosevelt U (IL)
Rose-Hulman Inst of Technology (IN)
Rosemont Coll (PA)
Russell Sage Coll (NY)
Sacred Heart U (CT)
Sage Coll of Albany (NY)
St. Ambrose U (IA)
Saint Anselm Coll (NH)
St. Bonaventure U (NY)
St. Catherine U (MN)
St. Edward's U (TX)
St. Francis Coll (NY)
Saint Francis U (PA)
St. John Fisher Coll (NY)
St. John's Coll (MD)
Saint John's U (MN)
St. John's U (NY)
Saint Joseph Coll (CT)
Saint Joseph's U (PA)
St. Lawrence U (NY)
St. Louis Coll of Pharmacy (MO)
Saint Louis U (MO)
Saint Martin's U (WA)
Saint Mary-of-the-Woods Coll (IN)
Saint Mary's Coll (IN)
Saint Mary's Coll of California (CA)
St. Mary's U (TX)
Saint Mary's U of Minnesota (MN)
Saint Michael's Coll (VT)
St. Norbert Coll (WI)
St. Olaf Coll (MN)
St. Thomas Aquinas Coll (NY)
Saint Vincent Coll (PA)
Saint Xavier U (IL)
Salem Coll (NC)
Salve Regina U (RI)
San Diego Christian Coll (CA)
Santa Clara U (CA)
Savannah Coll of Art and Design (GA)
Scripps Coll (CA)
Seattle Pacific U (WA)
Seattle U (WA)
Seton Hall U (NJ)
Seton Hill U (PA)
Sewanee: The U of the South (TN)
Shenandoah U (VA)
Siena Coll (NY)
Simmons Coll (MA)
Simpson Coll (IA)
Skidmore Coll (NY)
Smith Coll (MA)
Soka U of America (CA)
Southern Methodist U (TX)
Southern New Hampshire U (NH)
Southwestern U (TX)
Spelman Coll (GA)
Spring Hill Coll (AL)
Stanford U (CA)
Stephens Coll (MO)
Sterling Coll (VT)
Stetson U (FL)
Stevens Inst of Technology (NJ)
Stevenson U (MD)
Stonehill Coll (MA)
Suffolk U (MA)
Susquehanna U (PA)
Swarthmore Coll (PA)
Sweet Briar Coll (VA)
Syracuse U (NY)
Taylor U (IN)
Texas Christian U (TX)
Thomas More Coll (KY)
Transylvania U (KY)
Trine U (IN)
Trinity Coll (CT)
Trinity U (TX)
Tufts U (MA)
Tulane U (LA)
Union Coll (NY)
U of Bridgeport (CT)
U of Charleston (WV)
U of Chicago (IL)
U of Dallas (TX)
U of Dayton (OH)
U of Denver (CO)
U of Evansville (IN)
The U of Findlay (OH)
U of Hartford (CT)
U of La Verne (CA)
U of Miami (FL)
U of Mount Union (OH)
U of New England (ME)
U of New Haven (CT)
U of Notre Dame (IN)
U of Pennsylvania (PA)
U of Portland (OR)
U of Puget Sound (WA)
U of Redlands (CA)
U of Richmond (VA)
U of Rochester (NY)
U of St. Francis (IL)
U of St. Thomas (MN)
U of San Diego (CA)
U of San Francisco (CA)
The U of Scranton (PA)
U of Southern California (CA)
The U of Tampa (FL)
U of the Incarnate Word (TX)
U of the Pacific (CA)
U of the Sciences in Philadelphia (PA)
U of Tulsa (OK)
Ursinus Coll (PA)
Ursuline Coll (OH)
Utica Coll (NY)
Valparaiso U (IN)
Vanderbilt U (TN)
VanderCook Coll of Music (IL)
Vanguard U of Southern California (CA)
Vassar Coll (NY)
Villanova U (PA)
Virginia Intermont Coll (VA)
Virginia Wesleyan Coll (VA)
Wabash Coll (IN)
Wagner Coll (NY)
Wake Forest U (NC)
Walsh U (OH)
Wartburg Coll (IA)
Washington & Jefferson Coll (PA)
Washington and Lee U (VA)
Washington Coll (MD)
Washington U in St. Louis (MO)
Webster U (MO)
Wellesley Coll (MA)
Wells Coll (NY)
Wentworth Inst of Technology (MA)
Wesleyan U (CT)
Western New England Coll (MA)
Westminster Coll (UT)
Westmont Coll (CA)
West Virginia Wesleyan Coll (WV)
Wheaton Coll (IL)
Wheaton Coll (MA)
Wheelock Coll (MA)
Whitman Coll (WA)
Whittier Coll (CA)
Widener U (PA)
Wilkes U (PA)
Willamette U (OR)
William Jewell Coll (MO)
Williams Coll (MA)
Wilmington Coll (OH)
Wilson Coll (PA)
Wittenberg U (OH)
Wofford Coll (SC)
Woodbury U (CA)
Worcester Polytechnic Inst (MA)
Xavier U (OH)
Yale U (CT)
Yeshiva U (NY)

Geographical Listing of Close-Ups

U.S. AND U.S. TERRITORIES

INDEXES

Kentucky

Louisiana

Maine

Maryland

Massachusetts

Michigan

Minnesota

Missouri

Montana

Nebraska

Nevada

New Hampshire

New Jersey

New Mexico

New York

North Carolina

Alphabetical Listing of Colleges and Universities

In this index, the page locations of the profiles are printed in regular type and **College Close-Ups** in **bold type.** When there is more than one number in **bold type,** it indicates that the institution has more than one **College Close-Up;** in most such cases, the first of the series is a general **College Close-Up.**

INDEXES

INDEXES

INDEXES

INDEXES